106th Congress, 2d Session . . . . H. Doc. 106–162, Vol. II

APPENDIX

BUDGET OF THE UNITED STATES GOVERNMENT

Fiscal Year 2001

THE BUDGET DOCUMENTS

Budget of the United States Government, Fiscal Year 2001 contains the Budget Message of the President and information on the President's 2001 budget proposals. In addition, the *Budget* includes the Nation's third comprehensive Government-wide Performance Plan.

Analytical Perspectives, Budget of the United States Government, Fiscal Year 2001 contains analyses that are designed to highlight specified subject areas or provide other significant presentations of budget data that place the budget in perspective.

The *Analytical Perspectives* volume includes economic and accounting analyses; information on Federal receipts and collections; analyses of Federal spending; detailed information on Federal borrowing and debt; the Budget Enforcement Act preview report; current services estimates; and other technical presentations. It also includes information on the budget system and concepts and a listing of the Federal programs by agency and account.

Historical Tables, Budget of the United States Government, Fiscal Year 2001 provides data on budget receipts, outlays, surpluses or deficits, Federal debt, and Federal employment covering an extended time period—in most cases beginning in fiscal year 1940 or earlier and ending in fiscal year 2005. These are much longer time periods than those covered by similar tables in other budget documents. As much as possible, the data in this volume and all other historical data in the budget documents have been made consistent with the concepts and presentation used in the 2001 Budget, so the data series are comparable over time.

Budget of the United States Government, Fiscal Year 2001—Appendix contains detailed information on the various appropriations and funds that constitute the budget and is designed primarily for the use of the Appropriations Committee. The *Appendix* contains more detailed financial information on individual programs and appropriation accounts than any of the other budget documents. It includes for each agency: the proposed text of appropriations language, budget schedules for each account, new legislative proposals, explanations of the work to be performed and the funds needed, and proposed general provisions applicable to the appropriations of entire agencies or group of agencies. Information is also provided on certain activities whose outlays are not part of the budget totals.

A Citizen's Guide to the Federal Budget, Budget of the United States Government, Fiscal Year 2001 provides general information about the budget and the budget process for the general public.

Budget System and Concepts, Fiscal Year 2001 contains an explanation of the system and concepts used to formulate the President's budget proposals.

Budget Information for States, Fiscal Year 2001 is an Office of Management and Budget (OMB) publication that provides proposed State-by-State obligations for the major Federal formula grant programs to State and local governments. The allocations are based on the proposals in the President's budget. The report is released after the budget and can be obtained from the Publications Office of the Executive Office of the President, 725 17th Street NW, Washington, DC 20503; (202) 395–7332.

AUTOMATED SOURCES OF BUDGET INFORMATION

The information contained in these documents is available in electronic format from the following sources:

CD-ROM. The CD-ROM contains all of the budget documents and software to support reading, printing, and searching the documents. The CD-ROM also has many of the tables in the budget in spreadsheet format.

Internet. All budget documents, including documents that are released at a future date, will be available for downloading in several formats from the Internet. To access documents through the *World Wide Web,* use the following address:

http://www.gpo.gov/usbudget

For more information on access to the budget documents, call (202) 512–1530 in the D.C. area or toll-free (888) 293–6498.

GENERAL NOTES

1. All years referred to are fiscal years, unless otherwise noted.
2. Detail in this document may not add to the totals due to rounding.

U.S. GOVERNMENT PRINTING OFFICE
WASHINGTON 2000

For sale by the U.S. Government Printing Office
Superintendent of Documents, Mail Stop: SSOP, Washington, DC 20402-9328
ISBN 0-16-050236-5

TABLE OF CONTENTS

DETAILED BUDGET ESTIMATES

EXPLANATION OF ESTIMATES

"DETAILED BUDGET ESTIMATES" contains various tables and schedules in support of the budget. It includes explanations of the work to be performed and the money needed. It includes the language proposed for enactment by Congress on each item that requires congressional action in an appropriations bill. It also contains the language proposed for the general provisions of appropriations acts that apply to entire agencies or groups of agencies.

ARRANGEMENT

The first section of this chapter presents general provisions of law that apply to all government activities (see explanation below). Sections for the Legislative Branch and the Judiciary follow. These are followed by sections for the Executive Branch. The cabinet departments appear first in alphabetical order. They are followed by the larger nondepartmental agencies, groupings for "International Assistance Programs" and "Other Defense Civil Programs," the Executive Office of the President, and the remaining agencies, under the heading "Other Independent Agencies." If the amounts in the individual accounts for other independent agencies are below the million-dollar reporting threshold applicable to data in the *Appendix*, the data are consolidated into a single set of schedules under "Other Commissions and Boards." Appropriation language for these agencies is presented individually under the same heading.

A section for a large agency is usually organized by major subordinate organizations within the agency (usually bureaus) or by major program area.

Within each bureau or major program area, accounts usually appear in the following order:

—general fund accounts in the following order: accounts for which appropriations are requested for the budget year; accounts for which appropriations were made in the current year and not requested in the budget year; other unexpired accounts; expired accounts;

—special fund accounts in the following order: accounts for which appropriations are requested for the budget year; accounts for which appropriations were made in the current year and not requested in the budget year; other unexpired accounts; expired accounts;

—public enterprise funds;

—intragovernmental revolving funds and management funds;

—credit reform accounts, in the following order: program account, financing account, and liquidating account;

—trust funds;

—trust revolving funds.

By law, the Old-Age and Survivors Insurance and Disability Insurance trust funds (Social Security) are outside the budget totals. These accounts are presented in the Social Security Administration section. Also, by law the Postal Service Fund is outside the budget totals. A presentation for the Fund is included in the Other Independent Agencies section.

General provisions are provisions in appropriations acts that apply to more than one appropriation. In some instances, they apply only to the appropriations for one agency. In other instances, they apply to the appropriations for two or more agencies covered by the act. In one instance, they apply to all appropriations Government-wide. The proposed language for general provisions that are only applicable to one agency appears at the end of the section for that agency. The general provisions that apply to two or more agencies, appear at the end of the section for one of the agencies.

The following table indicates the location of all general provisions. The second column of the table lists the most recently enacted appropriations and the major agencies responsible for programs funded by each act. Several appropriations acts for 2000 were enacted as part of the Consolidated Apropriations Act, 2000 (Public Law 106–113). The third column provides the location of the general provisions that apply to the agencies listed in the second column. The general provisions that are Government-wide in scope (identified "Departments, Agencies, and Corporations"), normally contained in the Treasury, Postal Service, and General Government Appropriations Act, appear in a separate section following this one. Proposed changes to general provisions are presented in the manner described below for appropriations language.

	Appropriation Act	*Section in which general provisions appear*
1.	Legislative Branch Appropriations Act, 2000 (Public Law 106–57)	Legislative Branch.
2.	Foreign Operations, Export Financing, and Related Programs Appropriations Act, 2000 (Public Law 106–113, section 1000(a)(2)). Department of Defense Department of State Agency for International Development Department of Agriculture	International Assistance Programs.
3.	Agriculture, Rural Development, Food and Drug Administration, and Related Agencies Appropriations Act, 2000 (Public Law 106–78). Department of Agriculture Department of Health and Human Services	Department of Agriculture.
4.	Departments of Commerce, Justice, and State, the Judiciary, and Related Agencies Appropriations Act, 2000 (Public Law 106–113, section 1000(a)(1)). Department of Commerce Department of Justice Department of State The Judiciary Department of Transportation Small Business Administration	Department of Commerce.
5.	Department of Defense Appropriations Act, 2000 (Public Law 106–79)	Department of Defense.
6.	Military Construction Appropriations Act, 2000 (Public Law 106–52)	Department of Defense.

	Appropriation Act	*Section in which general provisions appear*
7.	Energy and Water Development Appropriations Act, 2000 (Public Law 106–60)	Department of Energy.
	Department of Energy	
	Corps of Engineers	
	Department of Interior	
8.	Departments of Veterans Affairs and Housing and Urban Development, and Independent Agencies Appropriations Act, 2000 (Public Law 106–74).	Department of Veterans Affairs.
	Housing and Urban Development	
	NASA	
	Veterans Affairs	
	Environmental Protection Agency	
	General Services Administration	
9.	Department of the Interior and Related Agencies Appropriations Act, 2000 (Public Law 106–113, section 1000(a)(3)).	Department of the Interior.
	Department of Interior	
	Department of Agriculture	
	Department of Energy	
	Department of Education	
	Department of Health and Human Services	
10.	Departments of Labor, Health and Human Services, and Education and Related Agencies Appropriations Act, 2000 (Public Law 106–113, section 1000(a)(4)).	Department of Labor.
	Department of Labor	
	Department of Health and Human Services	
	Department of Education	
11.	Department of Transportation and Related Agencies Appropriations Act, 2000 (Public Law 106–69).	Department of Transportation.
12.	Treasury, Postal Service and General Government Appropriations Act, 2000 (Public Law 106–58).	Department of Treasury.
	All departments, agencies, and corporations	Government-wide General Provisions.
13.	Miscellaneous Appropriations Act, 2000 (Public Law 106–113, section 1000(a)(5))	Government-wide General Provisions.

FORM OF DETAILED MATERIAL

APPROPRIATIONS LANGUAGE

The language proposed for inclusion in the 2001 appropriations acts appears following the account title. Language for enacted 2000 appropriations, printed in roman type, is used as a base. Brackets enclose material that is proposed for deletion; italic type indicates proposed new language. If the appropriation is being proposed for the first time, all of the language is printed in italics. The amounts in appropriations language are stated in dollars. Citations to any relevant authorizing legislation and to the specific appropriations act from which the basic text of the 2000 language is taken appear at the end of the final language paragraph, printed in italic within parentheses. An illustration of proposed appropriations language for 2001 follows:

OPERATING EXPENSES

For necessary expenses of the Office of Climate Information, [$30,290,000] *$28,870,000* of which [$150,000] *$400,000* shall remain available until expended. (*34 U.S.C. 218 et seq.; Department of Government Appropriation Act, 2000.*)

BASIS FOR SCHEDULES

Dollar amounts in *Appendix* schedules are stated in millions, unless otherwise specified.

The 1999 column of the budget presents the actual transactions and balances for that year, as recorded in agency accounts.

For 2000, the regular schedules include enacted appropriations. They also include indefinite appropriations on the basis of amounts likely to be required.

The 2001 column of the regular schedules includes proposed appropriations for all programs under existing legislation, including those that require extension or renewal of expiring laws.

Amounts for proposed new legislation are shown generally in separate schedules, following the regular schedules or in budget sequence in the respective bureau. These schedules are identified as "Legislative proposals, subject to PAYGO" or "Legislative proposals not subject to PAYGO." The term "PAYGO" refers to the "pay-as-you-go" requirements of the Budget Enforcement Act of 1990. Appropriations language is included with the regular schedules, but usually not with the separate schedules for proposed legislation. Usually the necessary appropriations language is transmitted later upon enactment of the proposed legislation. In some years, the *Appendix* includes special schedules that identify a special type of legislative proposal. For example, this budget includes schedules labeled "legislative proposal, discretionary offset," in order to identify several proposals in the budget that would offset discretionary spending under the rules of the Budget Enforcement Act.

PROGRAM AND FINANCING SCHEDULE

This schedule provides the following information:
—obligations by program activity;
—budgetary resources available for obligation;
—detailed information on new budget authority (gross);
—change in unpaid obligations;
—detailed information on outlays (gross);
—offsets to gross budget authority and outlays; and
—net budget authority and outlays.

The "Obligations by program activity" section shows obligations for specific activities or projects. The activity structure is developed for each appropriation or fund account to provide a meaningful presentation of information for the program. Where the amounts are significant, this section distinguishes between operating expenses and capital investment and between direct and reimbursable programs. The last entry, "Total obligations," indicates the amount of budgetary resources required to finance the activities of the account.

The "Budgetary resources available for obligation" section shows the budgetary resources available or estimated to be available to finance the obligations. The resources available for obligation include the start-of-year unobligated balances of a prior year that have not expired, new budget authority, and adjusting entries, such as recoveries from prior year obligations. New obligations are subtracted from these resources, resulting in the end-of-year unobligated balances.

The "New budget authority (gross), detail" section provides detailed information on the total new budget authority available to finance the program. It includes information on the type of budget authority that is available, rescissions, reductions, and amounts precluded from obligation.

The "Change in unpaid obligations" section shows the difference between obligations and outlays. New obligations are added to the obligations that were incurred in a previous year but not liquidated. Total disbursements (outlays, gross) are subtracted from these amounts. Adjusting entries, such as adjustments in expired accounts, are included, as appropriate, resulting in the end-of-year unpaid obligations. Where applicable, this section separately identifies total unpaid obligations, orders on hand from Federal sources, and obligated balances, which are the unpaid obligations less the orders on hand from Federal sources.

The "Outlays (gross), detail" section indicates whether the outlays pertain to current or permanent budget authority and to balances or new authority.

The "Offsets" and "Net budget authority and outlays" sections indicate the amounts to be deducted from gross budget authority and outlays and the resulting net budget authority and outlay amounts. Offsetting collections (cash) and the change in orders on hand from Federal sources are deducted from gross budget authority; only offsetting collections (cash) are deducted from gross outlays.

Program and Financing (in millions of dollars)

Identification code 16–1186–0–1–755		1999 actual	2000 est.	2001 est.
	Obligations by program activity:			
	Direct program:			
00.01	Policy and program development	38	39	42
00.02	Departmental management and administration	39	38	38
00.03	Facilities operations, maintenance, and repair	11	12	15
	Total direct program	88	89	95
01.01	Reimbursable program	42	44	45
10.00	Total obligations	130	133	140
	Budgetary resources available for obligation:			
22.00	New budget authority (gross)	132	133	140
22.30	Unobligated balance expiring	−2		
23.90	Total budgetary resources available for obligation	130	133	140
23.95	New obligations	−130	−133	−140
	New budget authority (gross), detail:			
	Discretionary:			
40.00	Appropriation (definite)	90	89	95
	Mandatory:			
	Spending authority from offsetting collections:			
68.00	Offetting collections (cash)	43	43	45
68.10	Change in orders on hand from Federal sources	−1	1	
68.90	Spending authority from offsetting collections (total)	42	44	45
70.00	Total new budget authority (gross)	132	133	140
	Change in unpaid obligations:			
	Unpaid obligations, start of year:			
72.90	Obligated balance: Fund balance	3	6	9
72.95	Orders on hand from Federal sources	1		1
72.99	Total unpaid obligations, start of year	4	6	10
73.10	New obligations	130	133	140
73.20	Total outlays (gross)	−127	−129	−134
73.40	Adjustments in expired accounts	−1		
	Unpaid obligations, end of year:			
74.90	Obligated balance: Fund balance	6	9	15
74.95	Orders on hand from Federal sources		1	1
74.99	Total unpaid obligations, end of year	6	10	16
	Outlays (gross), detail:			
86.90	Outlays from new discretionary authority	83	82	87
86.93	Outlays from discretionary balances	2	3	2
86.97	Outlays from new mandatory authority	42	44	45
87.00	Total outlays (gross)	127	129	134
	Offsets:			
	Against gross budget authority and outlays:			
88.00	Offsetting collections (cash) from: Federal sources	43	43	45
	Against gross budget authority only:			
88.95	Change in orders on hand from Federal sources	−1	1	
	Net budget authority and outlays:			
89.00	Budget authority	90	89	95
90.00	Outlays	84	86	89

A schedule entitled "Summary of Budget Authority and Outlays" immediately follows the first program and financing schedule for any account that has additional program and financing schedules for supplemental requests, legislative proposals, or rescission proposals.

NARRATIVE STATEMENT OF PROGRAM AND PERFORMANCE

Narrative statements present briefly the objectives of the program and the work to be financed primarily for 2001. They may include measures of expected performance and describe relationship to the financial estimates.

SCHEDULE OF OBJECT CLASSIFICATION AND PERSONNEL SUMMARY

There is shown for each account a schedule of obligations, according to the following uniform list of object classifications:

10 PERSONAL SERVICES AND BENEFITS
11.1 Full-time permanent
11.3 Other than full-time permanent
11.5 Other personnel compensation
11.7 Military personnel
11.8 Special personal services payments
11.9 Total personnel compensation
12.1 Civilian personnel benefits
12.2 Military personnel benefits
13.0 Benefits for former personnel
20 CONTRACTUAL SERVICES AND SUPPLIES
21.0 Travel and transportation of persons
22.0 Transportation of things
23.1 Rental payments to GSA
23.2 Rental payments to others
23.3 Communications, utilities, and miscellaneous charges
24.0 Printing and reproduction
25.1 Advisory and assistance services
25.2 Other services
25.3 Purchases of goods and services from Government accounts
25.4 Operation and maintenance of facilities
25.5 Research and development contracts
25.6 Medical care
25.7 Operations and maintenance of equipment
25.8 Subsistence and support of persons
26.0 Supplies and materials
30 ACQUISITION OF ASSETS
31.0 Equipment
32.0 Land and structures
33.0 Investments and loans
40 GRANTS AND FIXED CHARGES
41.0 Grants, subsidies, and contributions
42.0 Insurance claims and indemnities
43.0 Interest and dividends
44.0 Refunds
90 OTHER
91.0 Unvouchered
92.0 Undistributed
93.0 Limitation on expenses
99.0 SUBTOTAL DIRECT OBLIGATIONS
99.0 Reimbursable obligations
99.5 Below reporting threshold
99.9 TOTAL GROSS OBLIGATIONS

Object classes reflect the nature of the things or services purchased, regardless of the purpose of the program for which they are used. Object class entry 11.9, Total personnel compensation, sums the amounts in object classes 11.1 through

11.8. Except for revolving funds, reimbursable obligations are aggregated in a single line and not identified by object class. Amounts for any object class that are below the reporting threshold (i.e., amounts that are $500 thousand or less) are reported together as a single entry. Data, classified by object, are illustrated in the following schedule:

Object Classification (in millions of dollars)

Identification code 17–0643–0–1–452		1999 actual	2000 est.	2001 est.
	Direct obligations:			
	Personnel compensation:			
11.1	Full-time permanent	113	112	115
11.3	Other than full-time permanent	3	3	3
11.5	Other personnel compensation	3	3	3
11.8	Special personal services payments	1	1	1
11.9	Total personnel compensation	120	119	122
12.1	Civilian personnel benefits	24	24	25
23.1	Rental payments to GSA	23	23	24
26.0	Supplies and materials	5	5	5
31.0	Equipment	6	6	5
32.0	Land and structures	33	31	28
99.0	Subtotal, direct obligations	211	208	209
99.0	Reimbursable obligations	26	27	28
99.5	Below reporting threshold	1	2	2
99.9	Total obligations	238	237	239

When obligations for personnel compensation are shown in the object classification schedule, a personnel summary generally follows the object classification schedule, as illustrated below:

Personnel Summary

Identification code 17–0643–0–1–452		1999 actual	2000 est.	2001 est.
	Direct: Total compensable workyears:			
1001	Full-time equivalent employment	774	748	706
1005	Full-time equivalent of overtime and holiday hours	23	17	19
	Reimbursable: Total compensable workyears:			
2001	Full-time equivalent employment	8	12	12

Federal civilian employment generally is stated on a full-time equivalent (FTE) basis for the executive branch. It is the total number of hours worked (or to be worked) divided by the number of compensable hours applicable to each fiscal year.

FINANCIAL STATEMENTS

Financial statements are presented for all direct and guaranteed loan liquidating and financing accounts (balance sheets only), all Government-sponsored enterprises, and certain revolving and trust revolving funds conducting business with the public. They are occasionally presented for funds conducting business within the Government.

Statement of Operations

The statement of operations shows net income or loss for the year. This statement usually includes accrued revenue (e.g., revenue earned) and accrued expenditures (e.g., including costs incurred but not yet paid), whether funded or unfunded. The amounts in the 1998 column are audited.

Statement of Operations (in millions of dollars)

Identification code 16–4023–0–3–754		1998 actual	1999 actual	2000 est.	2001 est.
	Industrial Program:				
0111	Revenue	9	14	6	10
0112	Expense	–7	–8	–8	–8
0119	Net income of loss (–)	2	6	–2	2
	Sales program:				
0121	Revenue	25	27	18	15
0122	Expense	–15	–20	–11	–10
0129	Net Income or loss (–)	10	7	7	5
	Power program:				
0131	Revenue	39	28	34	22
0132	Expense	–13	–18	–20	–14
0139	Net income of loss (–)	26	10	14	8
0191	Total revenues	73	69	58	47
0192	Total expenses	–35	–46	–39	–32
0199	Total income or loss (–)	38	23	19	15

Balance Sheet

The balance sheets show assets, liabilities, and equity for the fund at the close of each fiscal year. In addition to this information, which is similar to commercial balance sheet data, budget needs also require additional information, such as appropriated capital, which is shown in the equity section. The amounts in the 1998 column are audited. Other amounts are unaudited and subject to change.

Balance Sheet (in millions of dollars)

Identification code 16–4023–0–3–754		1998 actual	1999 actual	2000 est.	2001 est.
	Assets:				
	Federal assets:				
	Investments in US securities				
1102	Treasury securities, net	4	4	4	4
1104	Agency securities, net	1	2	2	2
1106	Receivables, net	1	1	1	1
	Non-Federal assets:				
1201	Investments in non-Federal securities, net	1	2	2	2
1999					
	Total assets	**7**	**9**	**9**	**9**
	Liabilities:				
	Federal liabilities:				
2103	Debt	2	2	2	2
	Non-Federal liabilities:				
2203	Debt	3	3	3	3
2999	**Total liabilities**	**6**	**6**	**6**	**6**
	Net Position:				
3100	Unexpended appropriations	3	3	3	3
3999	**Total net position**	**2**	**3**	**3**	**3**
4999	**Total liabilities and net position**	**7**	**9**	**9**	**9**

FEDERAL CREDIT SCHEDULES

Federal credit programs provide benefits to the public in the form of direct loans and loan guarantees. The Federal Credit Reform Act of 1990 requires that the estimated costs arising from the direct and guaranteed loans of a program be calculated on a net present value basis, excluding administrative costs. For most programs, direct loan obligations and loan guarantee commitments cannot be made unless appropriations for the cost have been provided in advance in annual appropriations acts. In addition, annual limitations on the amount of obligations and commitments may be enacted in appropriations language.

Appropriations for costs are recorded as budget authority in credit program accounts. The administrative expenses associated with a credit program are also financed in the program account, but on a cash basis. All cash flows arising from direct loan obligations and loan guarantee commitments are recorded in separate financing accounts. The transactions of the financing accounts are not included in the budget totals. Program accounts make subsidy payments, recorded as budget outlays, to the financing accounts at the time of the disbursement of the direct or guaranteed loans.

The transactions associated with direct loan obligations and loan guarantee commitments made prior to 1992 continue to be accounted for on a cash flow basis and are recorded in liquidating accounts. In most cases, the liquidating account is the account that was used for the program prior to the enactment of the new requirements.

Program and Financing schedules (described above) are shown for program, financing, and liquidating accounts. In addition, a Summary of Loan Levels, Subsidy Budget Authority, and Outlays by Program schedule is shown for program accounts. Status of Direct Loans and Status of Guaranteed Loans schedules (as applicable) are shown for liquidating accounts and financing accounts. Examples of these schedules are shown below. Summary information on Federal credit programs is provided in the chapter entitled "Underwriting Federal Credit and Insurance" in the *Analytical Perspectives* volume.

Summary of Loan Levels, Subsidy Budget Authority and Outlays by Program (in millions of dollars)

Identification code 83–0100–0–1–155	1999 actual	2000 est.	2001 est.
Direct loan levels supportable by subsidy budget authority:			
1150 Economic opportunity loans	301	250	225
1150 Handicapped loans	199	150	150
1150 Minority enterprise loans	215	200	195
1159 Total direct loan levels	715	600	570
Direct loan subsidy rates (in percent):			
1320 Economic opportunity loans	8.00	8.00	8.00
1320 Handicapped loans	3.01	2.66	2.66
1320 Minority enterprise loans	4.20	4.00	3.59
1329 Weighted average subsidy rate	5.45	5.39	5.19
Direct loan subsidy budget authority:			
1330 Economic opportunity loans	24	20	18
1330 Handicapped loans	6	4	4
1330 Minority enterprise loans	9	8	7
1339 Total subsidy budget authority	39	32	29
Direct loan subsidy outlays:			
1340 Economic opportunity loans	12	10	9
1340 Handicapped loans	3	4	4
1340 Minority enterprise loans	4	7	8
1349 Total, subsidy outlays	19	21	21
Guaranteed loan levels supportable by subsidy budget authority:			
2150 General business loans	1,120	1,200	1,215
2150 Minority enterprise loans	8,790	9,000	9,250
2159 Total guaranteed loan levels	10,000	10,200	10,465
Guaranteed loan subsidy rates (in percent):			
2320 General business loans	2.41	2.42	2.47
2320 Minority enterprise loans	0.91	0.90	0.92
2329 Weighted average subsidy rate	1.07	1.08	1.10
Guaranteed loan subsidy budget authority:			
2330 General business loans	27	29	30
2330 Minority enterprise loans	80	81	85
2339 Total subsidy budget authority	107	110	115
Guaranteed loan subsidy outlays:			
2340 General business loans	13	25	29
2340 Minority enterprise loans	40	72	83
2349 Total subsidy outlays	53	97	112
Administrative expense data:			
3510 Budget authority	19	18	17
3590 Outlays from new authority	19	18	17

Status of Direct Loans (in millions of dollars)

Identification code 83–4200–0–3–155	1999 actual	2000 est.	2001 est.
Position with respect to appropriations act limitation on obligations:			
1111 Limitation on direct loans	715	600	570
1150 Total direct loan obligations	715	600	570
Cumulative balance of direct loans outstanding:			
1210 Outstanding, start of year	....	325	905
1231 Disbursements: Direct loan disbursements	338	586	597
1251 Repayments: Repayments and prepayments	−3	−6	−7
Write-offs for default:			
1263 Direct loans	−10	....	....
1290 Outstanding, end of year	325	905	1,495

Status of Guaranteed Loans (in millions of dollars)

Identification code 83–4100–0–3–155	1999 actual	2000 est.	2001 est.
Position with respect to appropriations act limitations on commitments:			
2111 Limitations on guaranteed loans made by private lenders	10,000	10,200	10,465
2150 Total guaranteed loan commitments	10,000	10,200	10,465
MEMORANDUM			
2199 Guaranteed amount of guaranteed loan commitments	7,500	7,650	7,849
Cumulative balance of guaranteed loans outstanding:			
2210 Disbursements: Outstanding start of year	....	5,000	13,895
2231 Repayments: Disbursements of new guaranteed loans	5,000	9,100	10,312
2251 Repayments and prepayments	....	−200	−375
Adjustments:			
2261 Terminations for default that result in a loan receivable	....	−5	−13
2290 Outstanding, end of year	5,000	13,895	23,820
MEMORANDUM			
2299 Guaranteed amount of guaranteed loans outstanding, end of year	3,750	10,421	17,865
ADDENDUM			
Cumulative balance of defaulted guaranteed loans that result in loans receivable:			
2310 Outstanding, start of year	....	....	5
2331 Disbursements for guaranteed loan claims	....	5	13
2351 Repayments of loans receivable	....	....	−3
2361 Write-off of loans receivable	....	....	−2
2390 Outstanding, start of year	....	5	13

UNAVAILABLE COLLECTIONS SCHEDULE

This schedule is printed for special fund and trust fund accounts to show the amount of receipts that are credited to them. It also shows any balances of unappropriated receipts or receipts that are precluded from obligation because of a provision of law, such as a benefit formula or limitation on obligations. The schedule also is printed for other types of accounts with offsetting collections that are unavailable for obligation because of limitations on obligations.

STATUS OF CONTRACT AUTHORITY SCHEDULE

Contract authority is a form of budget authority that permits obligations to be incurred but requires a subsequent appropriation to liquidate (pay) the obligation. Where applicable, this schedule follows the program and financing schedule and reports the amount of contract authority for which appropriations to liquidate have not been provided or requested.

BUDGET PLAN SCHEDULE

This schedule is printed only for certain accounts in the Department of Defense—Military chapter. It shows obligations incurred or estimated to be incurred from an appropriation, regardless of the timing of the obligation.

STATUS OF FUNDS SCHEDULE

This schedule reports balances, cash income, and cash outgo for major trust funds and certain other accounts. When present, it appears after the narrative statement for the fund or account.

GENERAL FUND RECEIPT ACCOUNTS SCHEDULE

This schedule shows the amount of receipts attributed to an agency that are credited to the general fund of the Treasury. It is printed at the end of the presentation for the agency, before any general provisions. (Receipts that are credited to a special fund or trust fund for which the agency is responsible are shown in an Unavailable Collections schedule presented with other schedules for the fund.)

ALLOCATIONS BETWEEN AGENCIES

In some cases, funds appropriated to the President or to an agency are allocated to one or more agencies that help to carry out a program. Obligations incurred under such allocations are included in the data for the account to which the appropriation is made in the allocating agency. The object classification schedule for such accounts identifies the amount of such obligations by performing agency. A note at the end of a bureau or equivalent grouping identifies allocations received from other agencies.

BUDGETS NOT SUBJECT TO REVIEW

In accordance with law or established practice, the presentations for the Legislative Branch, the Judiciary, the Milk Market Orders Assessment Fund of the Department of Agriculture, and the International Trade Commission have been included, without review, in the amounts submitted by the agencies.

The budgets of the privately owned Government-sponsored enterprises and the Board of Governors of the Federal Reserve System, are not subject to review; they are included for information purposes only.

GOVERNMENT-WIDE GENERAL PROVISIONS

TITLE VI—GENERAL PROVISIONS

DEPARTMENTS, AGENCIES, AND CORPORATIONS

SEC. 601. Funds appropriated in this or any other Act may be used to pay travel to the United States for the immediate family of employees serving abroad in cases of death or life threatening illness of said employee.

SEC. 602. No department, agency, or instrumentality of the United States receiving appropriated funds under this or any other Act for fiscal year [2000] *2001* shall obligate or expend any such funds, unless such department, agency, or instrumentality has in place, and will continue to administer in good faith, a written policy designed to ensure that all of its workplaces are free from the illegal use, possession, or distribution of controlled substances (as defined in the Controlled Substances Act) by the officers and employees of such department, agency, or instrumentality.

SEC. 603. Unless otherwise specifically provided, the maximum amount allowable during the current fiscal year in accordance with section 16 of the Act of August 2, 1946 (60 Stat. 810), for the purchase of any passenger motor vehicle (exclusive of buses, ambulances, law enforcement, and undercover surveillance vehicles), is hereby fixed at $8,100 except station wagons for which the maximum shall be $9,100: *Provided*, That these limits may be exceeded by not to exceed $3,700 for police-type vehicles, and by not to exceed $4,000 for special heavy-duty vehicles: *Provided further*, That the limits set forth in this section may not be exceeded by more than 5 percent for electric or hybrid vehicles purchased for demonstration under the provisions of the Electric and Hybrid Vehicle Research, Development, and Demonstration Act of 1976: *Provided further*, That the limits set forth in this section may be exceeded by the incremental cost of clean alternative fuels vehicles acquired pursuant to Public Law 101–549 over the cost of comparable conventionally fueled vehicles.

SEC. 604. Appropriations of the executive departments and independent establishments for the current fiscal year available for expenses of travel, or for the expenses of the activity concerned, are hereby made available for quarters allowances and cost-of-living allowances, in accordance with 5 U.S.C. 5922–5924.

SEC. 605. Unless otherwise specified during the current fiscal year, no part of any appropriation contained in this or any other Act shall be used to pay the compensation of any officer or employee of the Government of the United States (including any agency the majority of the stock of which is owned by the Government of the United States) whose post of duty is in the continental United States unless such person: (1) is a citizen of the United States; (2) is a person in the service of the United States on the date of the enactment of this Act who, being eligible for citizenship, has filed a declaration of intention to become a citizen of the United States prior to such date and is actually residing in the United States; (3) is a person who owes allegiance to the United States; (4) is an alien from Cuba, Poland, South Vietnam, the countries of the former Soviet Union, or the Baltic countries lawfully admitted to the United States for permanent residence; (5) is a South Vietnamese, Cambodian, or Laotian refugee paroled in the United States after January 1, 1975; or (6) is a national of the People's Republic of China who qualifies for adjustment of status pursuant to the Chinese Student Protection Act of 1992: *Provided*, That for the purpose of this section, an affidavit signed by any such person shall be considered prima facie evidence that the requirements of this section with respect to his or her status have been complied with: *Provided further*, That any person making a false affidavit shall be guilty of a felony, and, upon conviction, shall be fined no more than $4,000 or imprisoned for not more than 1 year, or both: *Provided further*, That the above penal clause shall be in addition to, and not in substitution for, any other provisions of existing law: *Provided further*, That any payment made to any officer or employee contrary to the provisions of this section shall be recoverable in action by the Federal Government. This section shall not apply to citizens of Ireland, Israel, or the Republic of the Philippines, or to nationals of those countries allied with the United States in a current defense effort, or to international broadcasters employed by the United States Information Agency, or to temporary employment of translators, or to temporary employment in the field service (not to exceed 60 days) as a result of emergencies.

SEC. 606. Appropriations available to any department or agency during the current fiscal year for necessary expenses, including maintenance or operating expenses, shall also be available for payment to the General Services Administration for charges for space and services and those expenses of renovation and alteration of buildings and facilities which constitute public improvements performed in accordance with the Public Buildings Act of 1959 (73 Stat. 749), the Public Buildings Amendments of 1972 (87 Stat. 216), or other applicable law.

SEC. 607. In addition to funds provided in this or any other Act, all Federal agencies are authorized to receive and use funds resulting from the sale of materials, including Federal records disposed of pursuant to a records schedule recovered through recycling or waste prevention programs. Such funds shall be available until expended for the following purposes:

(1) Acquisition, waste reduction and prevention, and recycling programs as described in Executive Order No. 13101 (September 14, 1998), including any such programs adopted prior to the effective date of the Executive order.

(2) Other Federal agency environmental management programs, including, but not limited to, the development and implementation of hazardous waste management and pollution prevention programs.

(3) Other employee programs as authorized by law or as deemed appropriate by the head of the Federal agency.

SEC. 608. Funds made available by this or any other Act for administrative expenses in the current fiscal year of the corporations and agencies subject to chapter 91 of title 31, United States Code, shall be available, in addition to objects for which such funds are otherwise available, for rent in the District of Columbia; services in accordance with 5 U.S.C. 3109; and the objects specified under this head, all the provisions of which shall be applicable to the expenditure of such funds unless otherwise specified in the Act by which they are made available: *Provided*, That in the event any functions budgeted as administrative expenses are subsequently transferred to or paid from other funds, the limitations on administrative expenses shall be correspondingly reduced.

[SEC. 609. No part of any appropriation for the current fiscal year contained in this or any other Act shall be paid to any person for the filling of any position for which he or she has been nominated after the Senate has voted not to approve the nomination of said person.]

[SEC. 610. No part of any appropriation contained in this or any other Act shall be available for interagency financing of boards (except Federal Executive Boards), commissions, councils, committees, or similar groups (whether or not they are interagency entities) which do not have a prior and specific statutory approval to receive financial support from more than one agency or instrumentality.]

SEC. [611] *609*. Funds made available by this or any other Act to the Postal Service Fund (39 U.S.C. 2003) shall be available for employment of guards for all buildings and areas owned or occupied by the Postal Service and under the charge and control of the Postal Service, and such guards shall have, with respect to such property, the powers of special policemen provided by the first section of the Act of June 1, 1948, as amended (62 Stat. 281; 40 U.S.C. 318), and, as to property owned or occupied by the Postal Service, the Postmaster General may take the same actions as the Administrator of General Services may take under the provisions of sections 2 and 3 of the Act of June 1, 1948, as amended (62 Stat. 281; 40 U.S.C. 318a and 318b), attaching thereto penal consequences under the authority and within the limits provided in section 4 of the Act of June 1, 1948, as amended (62 Stat. 281; 40 U.S.C. 318c).

[SEC. 612. None of the funds made available pursuant to the provisions of this Act shall be used to implement, administer, or enforce any regulation which has been disapproved pursuant to a resolution of disapproval duly adopted in accordance with the applicable law of the United States.]

DEPARTMENTS, AGENCIES, AND CORPORATIONS—Continued

SEC. [613] *610*. (a) Notwithstanding any other provision of law, and except as otherwise provided in this section, no part of any of the funds appropriated for fiscal year [2000] *2001*, by this or any other Act, may be used to pay any prevailing rate employee described in section 5342(a)(2)(A) of title 5, United States Code—

(1) during the period from the date of expiration of the limitation imposed by section [614] *613* of the Treasury and General Government Appropriations Act, [1999] *2000*, until the normal effective date of the applicable wage survey adjustment that is to take effect in fiscal year [2000] *2001*, in an amount that exceeds the rate payable for the applicable grade and step of the applicable wage schedule in accordance with such section [614] *613*; and

(2) during the period consisting of the remainder of fiscal year [2000] *2001*, in an amount that exceeds, as a result of a wage survey adjustment, the rate payable under paragraph (1) by more than the sum of—

(A) the percentage adjustment taking effect in fiscal year [2000] *2001* under section 5303 of title 5, United States Code, in the rates of pay under the General Schedule; and

(B) the difference between the overall average percentage of the locality-based comparability payments taking effect in fiscal year [2000] *2001* under section 5304 of such title (whether by adjustment or otherwise), and the overall average percentage of such payments which was effective in fiscal year [1999] *2000* under such section.

(b) Notwithstanding any other provision of law, no prevailing rate employee described in subparagraph (B) or (C) of section 5342(a)(2) of title 5, United States Code, and no employee covered by section 5348 of such title, may be paid during the periods for which subsection (a) is in effect at a rate that exceeds the rates that would be payable under subsection (a) were subsection (a) applicable to such employee.

(c) For the purposes of this section, the rates payable to an employee who is covered by this section and who is paid from a schedule not in existence on September 30, [1999] *2000*, shall be determined under regulations prescribed by the Office of Personnel Management.

(d) Notwithstanding any other provision of law, rates of premium pay for employees subject to this section may not be changed from the rates in effect on September 30, [1999] *2000*, except to the extent determined by the Office of Personnel Management to be consistent with the purpose of this section.

(e) This section shall apply with respect to pay for service performed after September 30, [1999] *2000*.

(f) For the purpose of administering any provision of law (including any rule or regulation that provides premium pay, retirement, life insurance, or any other employee benefit) that requires any deduction or contribution, or that imposes any requirement or limitation on the basis of a rate of salary or basic pay, the rate of salary or basic pay payable after the application of this section shall be treated as the rate of salary or basic pay.

(g) Nothing in this section shall be considered to permit or require the payment to any employee covered by this section at a rate in excess of the rate that would be payable were this section not in effect.

(h) The Office of Personnel Management may provide for exceptions to the limitations imposed by this section if the Office determines that such exceptions are necessary to ensure the recruitment or retention of qualified employees.

SEC. [614] *611*. During the period in which the head of any department or agency, or any other officer or civilian employee of the Government appointed by the President of the United States, holds office, no funds may be obligated or expended in excess of $5,000 to furnish or redecorate the office of such department head, agency head, officer, or employee, or to purchase furniture or make improvements for any such office, unless advance notice of such furnishing or redecoration is expressly [approved by] *transmitted to* the Committees on Appropriations. For the purposes of this section, the word "office" shall include the entire suite of offices assigned to the individual, as well as any other space used primarily by the individual or the use of which is directly controlled by the individual.

SEC. [615] *612*. Notwithstanding any other provision of law, no executive branch agency shall purchase, construct, and/or lease any additional facilities, except within or contiguous to existing locations, to be used for the purpose of conducting Federal law enforcement training without [the advance approval of] *advance notification to* the Committees on Appropriations, except that the Federal Law Enforcement Training Center is authorized to obtain the temporary use of additional facilities by lease, contract, or other agreement for training which cannot be accommodated in existing Center facilities.

SEC. [616] *613*. Notwithstanding section 1346 of title 31, United States Code, [or section 610 of this Act,] funds made available for fiscal year [2000] *2001* by this or any other Act shall be available for the interagency funding of national security and emergency preparedness telecommunications initiatives which benefit multiple Federal departments, agencies, or entities, as provided by Executive Order No. 12472 (April 3, 1984).

SEC. [617] *614*. (a) None of the funds appropriated by this or any other Act may be obligated or expended by any Federal department, agency, or other instrumentality for the salaries or expenses of any employee appointed to a position of a confidential or policy-determining character excepted from the competitive service pursuant to section 3302 of title 5, United States Code, without a certification to the Office of Personnel Management from the head of the Federal department, agency, or other instrumentality employing the Schedule C appointee that the Schedule C position was not created solely or primarily in order to detail the employee to the White House.

(b) The provisions of this section shall not apply to Federal employees or members of the armed services detailed to or from—

(1) the Central Intelligence Agency;

(2) the National Security Agency;

(3) the Defense Intelligence Agency;

(4) the offices within the Department of Defense for the collection of specialized national foreign intelligence through reconnaissance programs;

(5) the Bureau of Intelligence and Research of the Department of State;

(6) any agency, office, or unit of the Army, Navy, Air Force, and Marine Corps, the Federal Bureau of Investigation and the Drug Enforcement Administration of the Department of Justice, the Department of Transportation, the Department of the Treasury, and the Department of Energy performing intelligence functions; and

(7) the Director of Central Intelligence.

SEC. [618] *615*. No department, agency, or instrumentality of the United States receiving appropriated funds under this or any other Act for fiscal year [2000] *2001* shall obligate or expend any such funds, unless such department, agency, or instrumentality has in place, and will continue to administer in good faith, a written policy designed to ensure that all of its workplaces are free from discrimination and sexual harassment and that all of its workplaces are not in violation of title VII of the Civil Rights Act of 1964, as amended, the Age Discrimination in Employment Act of 1967, and the Rehabilitation Act of 1973.

[SEC. 619. No part of any appropriation contained in this Act may be used to pay for the expenses of travel of employees, including employees of the Executive Office of the President, not directly responsible for the discharge of official governmental tasks and duties: *Provided*, That this restriction shall not apply to the family of the President, Members of Congress or their spouses, Heads of State of a foreign country or their designees, persons providing assistance to the President for official purposes, or other individuals so designated by the President.]

SEC. [620] *616*. None of the funds appropriated in this or any other Act shall be used to acquire information technologies which do not comply with part 39.106 (Year 2000 compliance) of the Federal Acquisition Regulation, unless an agency's Chief Information Officer determines that noncompliance with part 39.106 is necessary to the function and operation of the requesting agency or the acquisition is required by a signed contract with the agency in effect before the date of the enactment of this Act. Any waiver granted by the Chief Information Officer shall be reported to the Office of Management and Budget, and copies shall be provided to Congress.

SEC. [621] *617*. None of the funds made available in this Act for the United States Customs Service may be used to allow the importation into the United States of any good, ware, article, or merchandise mined, produced, or manufactured by forced or indentured child labor, as determined pursuant to section 307 of the Tariff Act of 1930 (19 U.S.C. 1307).

SEC. [622] *618*. No part of any appropriation contained in this or any other Act shall be available for the payment of the salary of any officer or employee of the Federal Government, who—

(1) prohibits or prevents, or attempts or threatens to prohibit or prevent, any other officer or employee of the Federal Government

from having any direct oral or written communication or contact with any Member, committee, or subcommittee of the Congress in connection with any matter pertaining to the employment of such other officer or employee or pertaining to the department or agency of such other officer or employee in any way, irrespective of whether such communication or contact is at the initiative of such other officer or employee or in response to the request or inquiry of such Member, committee, or subcommittee; or

(2) removes, suspends from duty without pay, demotes, reduces in rank, seniority, status, pay, or performance of efficiency rating, denies promotion to, relocates, reassigns, transfers, disciplines, or discriminates in regard to any employment right, entitlement, or benefit, or any term or condition of employment of, any other officer or employee of the Federal Government, or attempts or threatens to commit any of the foregoing actions with respect to such other officer or employee, by reason of any communication or contact of such other officer or employee with any Member, committee, or subcommittee of the Congress as described in paragraph (1).

[SEC. 623. Section 627(b) of the Treasury and General Government Appropriations Act, 1999 (as contained in section 101(h) of division A of Public Law 105–277) is amended by striking "Notwithstanding" and inserting the following: "Effective on the date of the enactment of this Act and thereafter, and notwithstanding".]

[SEC. 624. Notwithstanding any provision of law, the President, or his designee, must certify to Congress, annually, that no person or persons with direct or indirect responsibility for administering the Executive Office of the President's Drug-Free Workplace Plan are themselves subject to a program of individual random drug testing.]

[SEC. 625. (a) None of the funds made available in this or any other Act may be obligated or expended for any employee training that—

(1) does not meet identified needs for knowledge, skills, and abilities bearing directly upon the performance of official duties;

(2) contains elements likely to induce high levels of emotional response or psychological stress in some participants;

(3) does not require prior employee notification of the content and methods to be used in the training and written end of course evaluation;

(4) contains any methods or content associated with religious or quasi-religious belief systems or "new age" belief systems as defined in Equal Employment Opportunity Commission Notice N–915.022, dated September 2, 1988; or

(5) is offensive to, or designed to change, participants' personal values or lifestyle outside the workplace.

(b) Nothing in this section shall prohibit, restrict, or otherwise preclude an agency from conducting training bearing directly upon the performance of official duties.]

[SEC. 626. No funds appropriated in this or any other Act for fiscal year 2000 may be used to implement or enforce the agreements in Standard Forms 312 and 4355 of the Government or any other nondisclosure policy, form, or agreement if such policy, form, or agreement does not contain the following provisions: "These restrictions are consistent with and do not supersede, conflict with, or otherwise alter the employee obligations, rights, or liabilities created by Executive Order No. 12958; section 7211 of title 5, United States Code (governing disclosures to Congress); section 1034 of title 10, United States Code, as amended by the Military Whistleblower Protection Act (governing disclosure to Congress by members of the military); section 2302(b)(8) of title 5, United States Code, as amended by the Whistleblower Protection Act (governing disclosures of illegality, waste, fraud, abuse or public health or safety threats); the Intelligence Identities Protection Act of 1982 (50 U.S.C. 421 et seq.) (governing disclosures that could expose confidential Government agents); and the statutes which protect against disclosure that may compromise the national security, including sections 641, 793, 794, 798, and 952 of title 18, United States Code, and section 4(b) of the Subversive Activities Act of 1950 (50 U.S.C. 783(b)). The definitions, requirements, obligations, rights, sanctions, and liabilities created by said Executive order and listed statutes are incorporated into this agreement and are controlling.": *Provided*, That notwithstanding the preceding paragraph, a nondisclosure policy form or agreement that is to be executed by a person connected with the conduct of an intelligence or intelligence-related activity, other than an employee or officer of the United States Government, may contain provisions appropriate to the particular activity for which such document is to be used. Such form or agreement shall, at a minimum, require that the person will not disclose any classified information received in the course of such activity unless specifically authorized to do so by the United States Government. Such nondisclosure forms shall also make it clear that they do not bar disclosures to Congress or to an authorized official of an executive agency or the Department of Justice that are essential to reporting a substantial violation of law.]

SEC. [627] *619*. No part of any funds appropriated in this or any other Act shall be used by an agency of the executive branch, other than for normal and recognized executive-legislative relationships, for publicity or propaganda purposes, and for the preparation, distribution or use of any kit, pamphlet, booklet, publication, radio, television or film presentation designed to support or defeat legislation pending before the Congress, except in presentation to the Congress itself.

SEC. [628] *620*. (a) IN GENERAL.—For calendar year [2001] *2002*, the Director of the Office of Management and Budget shall prepare and submit to Congress, with the budget submitted under section 1105 of title 31, United States Code, an accounting statement and associated report containing—

(1) an estimate of the total annual costs and benefits (including quantifiable and nonquantifiable effects) of Federal rules and paperwork, to the extent feasible—

(A) in the aggregate;

(B) by agency and agency program; and

(C) by major rule;

(2) an analysis of impacts of Federal regulation on State, local, and tribal government, small business, wages, and economic growth; and

(3) recommendations for reform.

(b) NOTICE.—The Director of the Office of Management and Budget shall provide public notice and an opportunity to comment on the statement and report under subsection (a) before the statement and report are submitted to Congress.

(c) GUIDELINES.—To implement this section, the Director of the Office of Management and Budget shall issue guidelines to agencies to standardize—

(1) measures of costs and benefits; and

(2) the format of accounting statements.

(d) PEER REVIEW.—The Director of the Office of Management and Budget shall provide for independent and external peer review of the guidelines and each accounting statement and associated report under this section. Such peer review shall not be subject to the Federal Advisory Committee Act (5 U.S.C. App.).

[SEC. 629. None of the funds appropriated by this Act or any other Act, may be used by an agency to provide a Federal employee's home address to any labor organization except when the employee has authorized such disclosure or when such disclosure has been ordered by a court of competent jurisdiction.]

SEC. [630] *621*. The Secretary of the Treasury is authorized to establish scientific certification standards for explosives detection canines, and shall provide, on a reimbursable basis, for the certification of explosives detection canines employed by Federal agencies, or other agencies providing explosives detection services at airports in the United States.

[SEC. 631. None of the funds made available in this Act or any other Act may be used to provide any non-public information such as mailing or telephone lists to any person or any organization outside of the Federal Government without the approval of the Committees on Appropriations.]

SEC. [632] *622*. No part of any appropriation contained in this or any other Act shall be used for publicity or propaganda purposes within the United States not heretofore authorized by the Congress.

[SEC. 633. (a) In this section the term "agency"—

(1) means an Executive agency as defined under section 105 of title 5, United States Code;

(2) includes a military department as defined under section 102 of such title, the Postal Service, and the Postal Rate Commission; and

(3) shall not include the General Accounting Office.

(b) Unless authorized in accordance with law or regulations to use such time for other purposes, an employee of an agency shall use official time in an honest effort to perform official duties. An employee not under a leave system, including a Presidential appointee exempted under section 6301(2) of title 5, United States Code, has an obligation to expend an honest effort and a reasonable proportion of such employee's time in the performance of official duties.]

SEC. [634] *623*. None of the funds made available in this or any other Act with respect to any fiscal year may be used for any system

DEPARTMENTS, AGENCIES, AND CORPORATIONS—Continued

to implement section 922(t) of title 18, United States Code, unless the system allows, in connection with a person's delivery of a firearm to a Federal firearms licensee as collateral for a loan, the background check to be performed at the time the collateral is offered for delivery to such licensee: *Provided*, That the licensee notifies local law enforcement within 48 hours of the licensee receiving a denial on the person offering the collateral: *Provided further*, That the provisions of section 922(t) shall apply at the time of the redemption of the firearm.

SEC. [635] *624*. (a) None of the funds appropriated by this Act may be used to enter into or renew a contract which includes a provision providing prescription drug coverage, except where the contract also includes a provision for contraceptive coverage.

(b) Nothing in this section shall apply to a contract with—

(1) any of the following religious plans:

[(A) Providence Health Plan;]

[(B)] *(A)* Personal Care's HMO;

[(C)] *(B)* Care Choices;

[(D)] *(C)* OSF Health Plans, Inc.;

[(E) Yellowstone Community Health Plan;] and

(2) any existing or future plan, if [the carrier for] the plan objects to such coverage on the basis of religious beliefs.

(c) In implementing this section, any plan that enters into or renews a contract under this section may not subject any individual to discrimination on the basis that the individual refuses to prescribe [or otherwise provide for] contraceptives because such activities would be contrary to the individual's religious beliefs or moral convictions.

(d) Nothing in this section shall be construed to require coverage of abortion or abortion-related services.

SEC. [636] *625*. Notwithstanding 31 U.S.C. 1346 [and section 610 of this Act], funds made available for fiscal year [2000] *2001* by this or any other Act to any department or agency, which is a member of the Joint Financial Management Improvement Program (JFMIP), shall be available to finance an appropriate share of JFMIP administrative costs, as determined by the JFMIP, but not to exceed a total of $800,000 including the salary of the Executive Director and staff support.

SEC. [637] *626*. Notwithstanding 31 U.S.C. 1346 [and section 610 of this Act], the head of each Executive department and agency is hereby authorized to transfer to the "Policy and Operations" account, General Services Administration, with the approval of the Director of the Office of Management and Budget, funds made available for fiscal year [2000] *2001* by this or any other Act, including rebates from charge card and other contracts. These funds shall be administered by the Administrator of General Services to support Government-wide financial, information technology, procurement, and other management innovations, initiatives, and activities, as approved by the Director of the Office of Management and Budget, in consultation with the appropriate interagency groups designated by the Director (including the Chief Financial Officers Council and the Joint Financial Management Improvement Program for financial management initiatives, [and] the Chief Information Officers Council for information technology initiatives*, and the Procurement Executives Council for procurement initiatives*). The total funds transferred shall not exceed [$7,000,000] *$17,000,000*. Such transfers may only be made 15 days following notification of the House and Senate Committees on Appropriations by the Director of the Office of Management and Budget.

[SEC. 638. (a) IN GENERAL.—Section 901 of title 31, United States Code, is amended by adding at the end the following:

"(c)(1) There shall be within the Executive Office of the President a Chief Financial Officer, who shall be designated or appointed by the President from among individuals meeting the standards described in subsection (a)(3). The position of Chief Financial Officer established under this paragraph may be so established in any Office (including the Office of Administration) of the Executive Office of the President.

"(2) The Chief Financial Officer designated or appointed under this subsection shall, to the extent that the President determines appropriate and in the interest of the United States, have the same authority and perform the same functions as apply in the case of a Chief Financial Officer of an agency described in subsection (b).

"(3) The President shall submit to Congress notification with respect to any provision of section 902 that the President determines shall not apply to a Chief Financial Officer designated or appointed under this subsection.

"(4) The President may designate an employee of the Executive Office of the President (other than the Chief Financial Officer), who shall be deemed 'the head of the agency' for purposes of carrying out section 902, with respect to the Executive Office of the President.".]

[(b) PLAN FOR IMPLEMENTATION.—Not later than 90 days after the effective date of this section, the President shall communicate in writing, to the Chairmen of the Committees on Appropriations, the Chairman of the Committee on Government Reform of the House of Representatives, and the Chairman of the Committee on Governmental Affairs of the Senate, a plan for implementation of the provisions of, and amendments made by, this section.]

[(c) DEADLINE FOR APPOINTMENT.—The Chief Financial Officer designated or appointed under section 901(c) of title 31, United States Code (as added by subsection (a)), shall be so designated or appointed not later than 180 days after the effective date of this section.]

[(d) PAY.—The Chief Financial Officer designated or appointed under such section shall receive basic pay at the rate payable for level IV of the Executive Schedule under section 5315 of title 5, United States Code.]

[(e) TRANSFER OF FUNCTIONS.—(1) The President may transfer such offices, functions, powers, or duties thereof, as the President determines are properly related to the functions of the Chief Financial Officer under section 901(c) of title 31, United States Code (as added by subsection (a)).

(2) The personnel, assets, liabilities, contracts, property, records, and unexpended balances of appropriations, authorizations, allocations, and other funds employed, held, used, arising from, available or to be made available, of any office the functions, powers, or duties of which are transferred under paragraph (1) shall also be so transferred.]

[(f) SEPARATE BUDGET REQUEST.—Section 1105(a) of title 31, United States Code, is amended by inserting after paragraph (30) the following new paragraph:

"(31) a separate statement of the amount of appropriations requested for the Chief Financial Officer in the Executive Office of the President.".]

[(g) TECHNICAL AND CONFORMING AMENDMENTS.—Section 503(a) of title 31, United States Code, is amended—

(1) in paragraph (7) by striking "respectively." and inserting "respectively (excluding any officer designated or appointed under section 901(c)).''; and

(2) in paragraph (8) by striking "Officers." and inserting "Officers (excluding any officer designated or appointed under section 901(c)).".]

[(h) EFFECTIVE DATE.—This section shall take effect at noon on January 20, 2001.]

[SEC. 639. (a) Section 304(a) of the Federal Election Campaign Act of 1971 (2 U.S.C. 434(a)) is amended by striking paragraph (11) and inserting the following:

"(11)(A) The Commission shall promulgate a regulation under which a person required to file a designation, statement, or report under this Act—

"(i) is required to maintain and file a designation, statement, or report for any calendar year in electronic form accessible by computers if the person has, or has reason to expect to have, aggregate contributions or expenditures in excess of a threshold amount determined by the Commission; and

"(ii) may maintain and file a designation, statement, or report in electronic form or an alternative form if not required to do so under the regulation promulgated under clause (i).

"(B) The Commission shall make a designation, statement, report, or notification that is filed electronically with the Commission accessible to the public on the Internet not later than 24 hours after the designation, statement, report, or notification is received by the Commission.

"(C) In promulgating a regulation under this paragraph, the Commission shall provide methods (other than requiring a signature on the document being filed) for verifying designations, statements, and reports covered by the regulation. Any document verified under any of the methods shall be treated for all purposes (including penalties for perjury) in the same manner as a document verified by signature.

"(D) As used in this paragraph, the term 'report' means, with respect to the Commission, a report, designation, or statement required by this Act to be filed with the Commission.".]

[(b) The amendments made by this section shall be effective for reporting periods beginning after December 31, 2000.]

[SEC. 640. (a) IN GENERAL.—Section 309(a)(4) of the Federal Election Campaign Act of 1971 (2 U.S.C. 437g(a)(4)) is amended—

(1) in subparagraph (A)(i), by striking "clause (ii)" and inserting "clauses (ii) and subparagraph (C)"; and

(2) by adding at the end the following new subparagraph:

"(C)(i) Notwithstanding subparagraph (A), in the case of a violation of any requirement of section 304(a) of the Act (2 U.S.C. 434(a)), the Commission may—

"(I) find that a person committed such a violation on the basis of information obtained pursuant to the procedures described in paragraphs (1) and (2); and

"(II) based on such finding, require the person to pay a civil money penalty in an amount determined under a schedule of penalties which is established and published by the Commission and which takes into account the amount of the violation involved, the existence of previous violations by the person, and such other factors as the Commission considers appropriate.

"(ii) The Commission may not make any determination adverse to a person under clause (i) until the person has been given written notice and an opportunity to be heard before the Commission.

"(iii) Any person against whom an adverse determination is made under this subparagraph may obtain a review of such determination in the district court of the United States for the district in which the person resides, or transacts business, by filing in such court (prior to the expiration of the 30-day period which begins on the date the person receives notification of the determination) a written petition requesting that the determination be modified or set aside.".]

[(b) CONFORMING AMENDMENT.—Section 309(a)(6)(A) of such Act (2 U.S.C. 437g(a)(6)(A)) is amended by striking "paragraph (4)(A)" and inserting "paragraph (4)".]

[(c) EFFECTIVE DATE.—The amendments made by this section shall apply with respect to violations occurring between January 1, 2000 and December 31, 2001.]

[SEC. 641. (a) Section 304(b) of the Federal Election Campaign Act (2 U.S.C. 434(b)) is amended by inserting "(or election cycle, in the case of an authorized committee of a candidate for Federal office)" after "calendar year" each place it appears in paragraphs (2), (3), (4), (6), and (7).]

[(b) The amendment made by this section shall become effective with respect to reporting periods beginning after December 31, 2000.]

[SEC. 642. (a) IN GENERAL.—Section 636 of the Treasury Postal Service, and General Government Appropriations Act, 1997 (5 U.S.C. prec. 5941 note) is amended in the first sentence by striking "may" and inserting "shall".]

[(b) EFFECTIVE DATE.—The amendment made by subsection (a) shall take effect on October 1, 1999, or the date of the enactment of this Act, whichever is later.]

SEC. [643] *627.* (a) IN GENERAL.—[Upon promulgation of the regulations required under subsection (c)] *In accordance with regulations promulgated by the Office of Personnel Management*, an Executive agency which provides or proposes to provide child care services for Federal employees may use appropriated funds (otherwise available to such agency for salaries) to provide child care, in a Federal or leased facility, or through contract, for civilian employees of such agency.

(b) AFFORDABILITY.—Amounts so provided with respect to any such facility or contractor shall be applied to improve the affordability of child care for lower income Federal employees using or seeking to use the child care services offered by such facility or contractor.

[(c) REGULATIONS.—The Office of Personnel Management shall, within 180 days after the date of the enactment of this Act, issue regulations necessary to carry out this section.]

[(d)] *(c)* DEFINITION.—For purposes of this section, the term "Executive agency" has the meaning given such term by section 105 of title 5, United States Code, but does not include the General Accounting Office.

[(e)] *(d)* NOTIFICATION.—None of the funds made available in this or any other Act may be used to implement the provisions of this section absent advance notification to the Committees on Appropriations.

[SEC. 644. (a) INCREASE IN ANNUAL COMPENSATION.—Section 102 of title 3, United States Code, is amended by striking "$200,000" and inserting "$400,000".

(b) EFFECTIVE DATE.—The amendment made by this section shall take effect at noon on January 20, 2001.]

[SEC. 645. Effective October 1, 1999, all personnel of the General Accounting Office employed or maintained to carry out functions of the Joint Financial Management Improvement Program (JFMIP) shall be transferred to the General Services Administration. The Director of the Office of Personnel Management shall provide to the General Services Administration one permanent Senior Executive Service allocation for the position of the Executive Director of the JFMIP. Personnel transferred pursuant to this section shall not be separated or reduced in classification or compensation for 1 year after any such transfer, except for cause.]

[SEC. 646. (a) The adjustment in rates of basic pay for the statutory pay systems that takes effect in fiscal year 2000 under sections 5303 and 5304 of title 5, United States Code, shall be an increase of 4.8 percent.

(b) Funds used to carry out this section shall be paid from appropriations which are made to each applicable department or agency for salaries and expenses for fiscal year 2000.]

SEC. [647] *628.* Notwithstanding any other provision of law, a woman may breastfeed her child at any location in a Federal building or on Federal property, if the woman and her child are otherwise authorized to be present at the location.

SEC. [648] *629.* FEDERAL FUNDS IDENTIFIED. Any request for proposals, solicitation, grant application, form, notification, press release, or other publications involving the distribution of Federal funds shall indicate the agency providing the funds and the amount provided. This provision shall apply to direct payments, formula funds, and grants received by a State receiving Federal funds.

SEC. 630. Nothwithstanding section 1346 of title 31, United States Code, funds made available for fiscal year 2001 by this or any other Act shall be available for the interagency funding of specific projects, workshops, studies, and similar efforts to carry out the purposes of the Natinal Science and Technology Council (authorized by Executive Order No. 12881), which benefit multiple Federal departments, agencies, or entities.

[SEC. 649. (a) Congress finds that—

(1) the Veterans of Foreign Wars of the United States (in this section referred to as the "VFW"), which was formed by veterans of the Spanish-American War and the Philippine Insurrection to help secure rights and benefits for their service, will be celebrating its 100th anniversary in 1999;

(2) members of the VFW have fought, bled, and died in every war, conflict, police action, and military intervention in which the United States has engaged during this century;

(3) over its history, the VFW has ably represented the interests of veterans in Congress and State Legislatures across the Nation and established a network of trained service officers who, at no charge, have helped millions of veterans and their dependents to secure the education, disability compensation, pension, and health care benefits they are rightfully entitled to receive as a result of the military service performed by those veterans;

(4) the VFW has also been deeply involved in national education projects, awarding nearly $2,700,000 in scholarships annually, as well as countless community projects initiated by its 10,000 posts; and

(5) the United States Postal Service has issued commemorative postage stamps honoring the VFW's 50th and 75th anniversaries, respectively.

(b) Therefore, it is the sense of the Congress that the United States Postal Service is encouraged to issue a commemorative postage stamp in honor of the 100th anniversary of the founding of the Veterans of Foreign Wars of the United States.]

[SEC. 650. ITEMIZED INCOME TAX RECEIPT. (a) IN GENERAL.—Not later than April 15, 2000, the Secretary of the Treasury shall establish an interactive program on an Internet website where any taxpayer may generate an itemized receipt showing a proportionate allocation (in money terms) of the taxpayer's total tax payments among the major expenditure categories.]

[(b) INFORMATION NECESSARY TO GENERATE RECEIPT.—For purposes of generating an itemized receipt under subsection (a), the interactive program—

(1) shall only require the input of the taxpayer's total tax payments; and

(2) shall not require any identifying information relating to the taxpayer.]

[(c) TOTAL TAX PAYMENTS.—For purposes of this section, total tax payments of an individual for any taxable year are—

(1) the tax imposed by subtitle A of the Internal Revenue Code of 1986 for such taxable year (as shown on his return); and

(2) the tax imposed by section 3101 of such Code on wages received during such taxable year.]

[(d) CONTENT OF TAX RECEIPT.—

DEPARTMENTS, AGENCIES, AND CORPORATIONS—Continued

(1) MAJOR EXPENDITURE CATEGORIES.—For purposes of subsection (a), the major expenditure categories are:

(A) National defense.
(B) International affairs.
(C) Medicaid.
(D) Medicare.
(E) Means-tested entitlements.
(F) Domestic discretionary.
(G) Social Security.
(H) Interest payments.
(I) All other.

(2) OTHER ITEMS ON RECEIPT.—

(A) IN GENERAL.—In addition, the tax receipt shall include selected examples of more specific expenditure items, including the items listed in subparagraph (B), either at the budget function, subfunction, or program, project, or activity levels, along with any other information deemed appropriate by the Secretary of the Treasury and the Director of the Office of Management and Budget to enhance taxpayer understanding of the Federal budget.

(B) LISTED ITEMS.—The expenditure items listed in this subparagraph are as follows:

(i) Public schools funding programs.
(ii) Student loans and college aid.
(iii) Low-income housing programs.
(iv) Food stamp and welfare programs.
(v) Law enforcement, including the Federal Bureau of Investigation, law enforcement grants to the States, and other Federal law enforcement personnel.
(vi) Infrastructure, including roads, bridges, and mass transit.
(vii) Farm subsidies.
(viii) Congressional Member and staff salaries.
(ix) Health research programs.
(x) Aid to the disabled.
(xi) Veterans health care and pension programs.
(xii) Space programs.
(xiii) Environmental cleanup programs.
(xiv) United States embassies.
(xv) Military salaries.
(xvi) Foreign aid.
(xvii) Contributions to the North Atlantic Treaty Organization.
(xviii) Amtrak.
(xix) United States Postal Service.]

[(e) COST.—No charge shall be imposed to cover any cost associated with the production or distribution of the tax receipt.]

[(f) REGULATIONS.—The Secretary of the Treasury may prescribe such regulations as may be necessary to carry out this section.]

[SEC. 651. (a) Section 7001 of Public Law 105–174 (112 Stat. 91) is amended by striking each place it appears "for purposes of the period beginning on the date of enactment of this Act and ending on September 30, 1999," and inserting "May 1, 1998,".

(b) Section 1109 of Public Law 105–261 (112 Stat. 2143) is repealed.]

[SEC. 652. (a) The American Battle Monuments Commission and the World War II Memorial Advisory Board (as referred to in Public Law 103–32 (40 U.S.C. 1003 note; 107 Stat. 90)) shall each be considered to qualify for the rates of postage currently in effect under former section 4452 of title 39, United States Code, for third-class mail matter mailed by a qualified nonprofit organization.]

[(b) Rates of postage afforded by subsection (a) shall be available only with respect to official mail sent for the furtherance of the purpose of section 2(c)(1) or 3 of Public Law 103–32, as applicable.

(c) This section shall apply with respect to fiscal year 2000 and each fiscal year thereafter.]

[SEC. 653. (a) ESTABLISHMENT.—There is established the National Intellectual Property Law Enforcement Coordination Council (in this section referred to as the "Council"). The Council shall consist of the following members—

(1) The Assistant Secretary of Commerce and Commissioner of Patents and Trademarks, who shall serve as co-chair of the Council.

(2) The Assistant Attorney General, Criminal Division, who shall serve as co-chair of the Council.

(3) The Under Secretary of State for Economic and Agricultural Affairs.

(4) The Ambassador, Deputy United States Trade Representative.

(5) The Commissioner of Customs.

(6) The Under Secretary of Commerce for International Trade.]

[(b) DUTIES.—The Council established in subsection (a) shall coordinate domestic and international intellectual property law enforcement among federal and foreign entities.]

[(c) CONSULTATION REQUIRED.—The Council shall consult with the Register of Copyrights on law enforcement matters relating to copyright and related rights and matters.]

[(d) NON-DEROGATION.—Nothing in this section shall derogate from the duties of the Secretary of State or from the duties of the United States Trade Representative as set forth in section 141 of the Trade Act of 1974 (19 U.S.C. 2171), or from the duties and functions of the Register of Copyrights, or otherwise alter current authorities relating to copyright matters.]

[(e) REPORT.—The Council shall report annually on its coordination activities to the President, and to the Committees on Appropriations and on the Judiciary of the Senate and the House of Representatives.]

[(f) FUNDING.—Notwithstanding section 1346 of title 31, United States Code, or section 610 of this Act, funds made available for fiscal year 2000 and hereafter by this or any other Act shall be available for interagency funding of the National Intellectual Property Law Enforcement Coordination Council.]

[SEC. 654. In addition to funds otherwise provided under the heading "National Oceanic and Atmospheric Administration" for "Operations, Research, and Facilities" in Public Law 105–277 (112 Stat. 2681–83), $5,650,000 is appropriated for necessary retired pay expenses under the Retired Serviceman's Family Protection and Survivor Benefit Plan, and for payment for medical care of retired personnel and their dependents under the Dependents Medical Care Act (10 U.S.C. ch. 55).] *(Treasury and General Government Appropriations Act, 2000).*

MISCELLANEOUS PROVISIONS—MISCELLANEOUS APPROPRIATIONS ACT, 2000

[SEC. 234. Effective on November 15, 1999, or the last day of the 1st session of the 106th Congress, whichever is later, in addition to amounts otherwise provided to address the expenses of Year 2000 conversion of Federal information technology systems, not to exceed 10 percent of any appropriation for salaries and expenses made available to an agency for fiscal year 2000 in this or any other Act may be used by the agency for implementation of agency business continuity and contingency plans in furtherance of Year 2000 compliance by Federal agencies: *Provided*, That such amounts may be transferred between agency accounts: *Provided further*, That the transfer authority provided in this section is in addition to any other transfer authority provided in this or any other Act: *Provided further*, That notice of any transfer under this section shall be transmitted to House and Senate Committees on Appropriations, the Senate Special Committee on the Year 2000 Technology Problem, the House Committee on Science, and the House Committee on Government Reform 10 days in advance of such transfer: *Provided further*, That, under circumstances reasonably requiring immediate action, such notice shall be transmitted as soon as possible but in no case more than 5 days after such transfer: *Provided further*, That the authority granted in this section shall expire on February 29, 2000.]

[SEC. 301. (a) GOVERNMENT-WIDE RESCISSIONS.—There is hereby rescinded an amount equal to 0.38 percent of the discretionary budget authority provided (or obligation limit imposed) for fiscal year 2000 in this or any other Act for each department, agency, instrumentality, or entity of the Federal Government.]

(b) [RESTRICTIONS.—In carrying out the rescissions made by subsection (a),—

(1) no program, project, or activity of any department, agency, instrumentality, or entity may be reduced by more than 15 percent (with "programs, projects, and activities" as delineated in the appropriations Act or accompanying report for the relevant account, or for accounts and items not included in appropriations Acts, as delineated in the most recently submitted President's budget),

(2) no reduction shall be taken from any military personnel account, and

(3) the reduction for the Department of Defense and Department of Energy Defense Activities shall be applied proportionately to all Defense accounts.]

[(c) REPORT.—The Director of the Office of Management and Budget shall include in the President's budget submitted for fiscal year 2001 a report specifying the reductions made to each account pursuant to this section.]

[SEC. 305. Notwithstanding section 3324 of title 31, United States Code, and section 1006(h) of title 37, United States Code, the basic pay and allowances that accrues to members of the Army, Navy, Marine Corps, and Air Force for the pay period ending on September 30, 2000, shall be paid, whether by electronic transfer of funds or otherwise, no earlier than October 1, 2000.]

[SEC. 306. The pay of any Federal officer or employee that would be payable on September 29, 2000, or September 30, 2000, for the preceding applicable pay period (if not for this section) shall be paid, whether by electronic transfer of funds or otherwise, on October 1, 2000.] *(Miscellaneous Appropriations, 2000, as enacted by section 1000(a)(5) of the Consolidated Appropriations Act, 2000 (P.L. 106–113).)*

LEGISLATIVE BRANCH

SENATE

EXPENSE ALLOWANCES

For expense allowances of the Vice President, $10,000; the President Pro Tempore of the Senate, $10,000; Majority Leader of the Senate, $10,000; Minority Leader of the Senate, $10,000; Majority Whip of the Senate, $5,000; Minority Whip of the Senate, $5,000; and Chairmen of the Majority and Minority Conference Committees, $3,000 for each Chairman; in all, $56,000.

REPRESENTATION ALLOWANCES FOR THE MAJORITY AND MINORITY LEADERS

For representation allowances of the Majority and Minority Leaders of the Senate, $15,000 for each such Leader; in all, $30,000.

SALARIES, OFFICERS AND EMPLOYEES

For compensation of officers, employees, and others as authorized by law, including agency contributions, [$89,968,000] *$93,253,000*, which shall be paid from this appropriation without regard to the below limitations, as follows:

OFFICE OF THE VICE PRESIDENT

For the Office of the Vice President, [$1,721,000] *$1,785,000*.

OFFICE OF THE PRESIDENT PRO TEMPORE

For the Office of the President Pro Tempore, [$437,000] *$453,000*.

OFFICES OF THE MAJORITY AND MINORITY LEADERS

For Offices of the Majority and Minority Leaders, [$2,644,000] *$2,742,000*.

OFFICES OF THE MAJORITY AND MINORITY WHIPS

For Offices of the Majority and Minority Whips, [$1,634,000] *$1,770,000*.

COMMITTEE ON APPROPRIATIONS

For salaries of the Committee on Appropriations, [$6,525,000] *$6,917,000*.

CONFERENCE COMMITTEES

For the Conference of the Majority and the Conference of the Minority, at rates of compensation to be fixed by the Chairman of each such committee, [$1,132,000] *$1,175,000* for each such committee; in all, [$2,264,000] *$2,350,000*.

OFFICES OF THE SECRETARIES OF THE CONFERENCE OF THE MAJORITY AND THE CONFERENCE OF THE MINORITY

For Offices of the Secretaries of the Conference of the Majority and the Conference of the Minority, [$590,000] *$732,000*.

POLICY COMMITTEES

For salaries of the Majority Policy Committee and the Minority Policy Committee, [$1,151,000] *$1,254,000* for each such committee; in all, [$2,302,000] *$2,508,000*.

OFFICE OF THE CHAPLAIN

For Office of the Chaplain, [$277,000] *$288,000*.

OFFICE OF THE SECRETARY

For Office of the Secretary, [$14,202,000] *$14,738,000*.

OFFICE OF THE SERGEANT AT ARMS AND DOORKEEPER

For Office of the Sergeant at Arms and Doorkeeper, [$34,794,000] *$35,341,000*.

OFFICES OF THE SECRETARIES FOR THE MAJORITY AND MINORITY

For Offices of the Secretary for the Majority and the Secretary for the Minority, [$1,246,000] *$1,292,000*.

AGENCY CONTRIBUTIONS AND RELATED EXPENSES

For agency contributions for employee benefits, as authorized by law, and related expenses, [$21,332,000] *$22,337,000*.

OFFICE OF THE LEGISLATIVE COUNSEL OF THE SENATE

For salaries and expenses of the Office of the Legislative Counsel of the Senate, [$3,901,000] *$4,046,000*.

OFFICE OF SENATE LEGAL COUNSEL

For salaries and expenses of the Office of Senate Legal Counsel, [$1,035,000] *$1,069,000*.

EXPENSE ALLOWANCES OF THE SECRETARY OF THE SENATE, SERGEANT AT ARMS AND DOORKEEPER OF THE SENATE, AND SECRETARIES FOR THE MAJORITY AND MINORITY OF THE SENATE

For expense allowances of the Secretary of the Senate, $3,000; Sergeant at Arms and Doorkeeper of the Senate, $3,000; Secretary for the Majority of the Senate, $3,000; Secretary for the Minority of the Senate, $3,000; in all, $12,000.

CONTINGENT EXPENSES OF THE SENATE

INQUIRIES AND INVESTIGATIONS

For expenses of inquiries and investigations ordered by the Senate, or conducted pursuant to section 134(a) of Public Law 601, Seventy-ninth Congress, as amended, section 112 of Public Law 96–304 and Senate Resolution 281, agreed to March 11, 1980, [$71,604,000] *$74,136,000*.

EXPENSES OF THE UNITED STATES SENATE CAUCUS ON INTERNATIONAL NARCOTICS CONTROL

For expenses of the United States Senate Caucus on International Narcotics Control, [$370,000] *$370,000*.

SECRETARY OF THE SENATE

For expenses of the Office of the Secretary of the Senate, $1,511,000.

SERGEANT AT ARMS AND DOORKEEPER OF THE SENATE

For expenses of the Office of the Sergeant at Arms and Doorkeeper of the Senate, [$66,261,000] *$101,228,000*.

MISCELLANEOUS ITEMS

For miscellaneous items, [$8,665,000] *$8,655,000*.

SENATORS' OFFICIAL PERSONNEL AND OFFICE EXPENSE ACCOUNT

For Senators' Official Personnel and Office Expense Account, [$245,703,000] *$273,366,000*.

OFFICIAL MAIL COSTS

For expenses necessary for official mail costs of the Senate, $300,000.

[ADMINISTRATIVE PROVISIONS]

[SECTION 1. Effective in the case of any fiscal year which begins on or after October 1, 1999, clause (iii) of paragraph (3)(A) of section 506(b) of the Supplemental Appropriations Act, 1973 (2 U.S.C. 58(b)) is amended to read as follows:

"(iii) subject to subparagraph (B)—

"(I) in case the Senator represents Alabama, $116,300, Alaska, $221,600, Arizona, $128,975, Arkansas, $118,250, California, $168,950, Colorado, $124,100, Connecticut, $105,575, Delaware, $95,825, Florida, $120,200, Georgia, $116,300, Hawaii, $245,000, Idaho, $128,000, Illinois, $138,725, Indiana, $116,300, Iowa, $119,225, Kansas, $119,225, Kentucky, $115,325, Louisiana, $120,200, Maine, $110,450, Maryland, $100,700, Massachusetts, $114,350, Michigan, $124,100, Minnesota, $120,200, Mississippi, $118,250, Missouri, $121,175, Montana, $128,000, Nebraska, $120,200, Nevada, $129,950, New Hampshire, $106,550, New Jersey, $110,450, New Mexico, $125,075, New York, $145,550, North Carolina, $112,400, North Dakota, $119,225, Ohio, $129,950, Oklahoma, $123,125, Oregon, $132,875, Pennsylvania, $128,975, Rhode Island, $104,600, South Carolina, $110,450, South Dakota, $120,200, Tennessee, $116,300, Texas, $149,450, Utah, $128,000, Vermont, $105,575, Virginia, $106,550, Washington, $135,800, West Virginia, $105,575, Wisconsin, $119,225, Wyoming, $123,125, plus

"(II) the amount that is equal to the Senator's share for the fiscal year, as determined in accordance with regulations of the Committee on Rules and Administration, of the amount made available within the Senators' Official Personnel and Office Expense Account in the contingent fund of the Senate for official mail expenses of Senators, plus".

(b) Subparagraph (B) of section 506(b)(3) of the Supplemental Appropriations Act, 1973 (2 U.S.C. 58(b)(3)) is amended—

(1) by striking "that part of the amount referred to in subparagraph (A)(iii) that is not specifically allocated for official mail expenses" and inserting "the amount referred to in subparagraph (A)(iii)(I)"; and

(2) by striking "the part of the amount referred to in subparagraph (A)(iii) that is allocated for official mail expenses" and inserting "the amount referred to in subparagraph (A)(iii)(II)".

(c) The amendments made by this section shall apply to any fiscal year which begins on or after October 1, 1999.]

[SEC. 2. Effective on and after October 1, 1999, each of the dollar amounts contained in the table under section 105(d)(1)(A) of the Legislative Branch Appropriations Act, 1968 (2 U.S.C. 61–1(d)(1)(A)) shall be deemed to be the dollar amounts in that table, as increased by section 8 of Public Law 105–275, increased by an additional $50,000 each.]

[SEC. 3. SENATE OFFICE SPACE ALLOCATIONS. Section 3 under the heading "ADMINISTRATIVE PROVISIONS" in the appropriation for the Senate in the Legislative Branch Appropriations Act, 1975 (2 U.S.C. 59; 88 Stat. 428) is amended—

(1) in subsection (b)—

(A) by striking paragraphs (1) and (2) and inserting the following:

"(1) 5,000 square feet if the population of the State of the Senator is less than 3,000,000;";

(B) by striking "8,000" in paragraph (13) and inserting "8,200"; and

(C) by redesignating paragraphs (3) through (13) as paragraphs (2) through (12), respectively; and

(2) in subsection (c)(2)—

(A) by striking "$30,000" and inserting "$40,000";

(B) by striking "4,800" and inserting "5,000";

(C) by striking "$734" and inserting "$1,000"; and

(D) by adding at the end the following: "Effective beginning with the 106th Congress, the aggregate amount in effect under this paragraph for any Congress shall be increased by the inflation adjustment factor for the calendar year in which the Congress begins. For purposes of the preceding sentence, the inflation adjustment factor for any calendar year is a fraction the numerator of which is the implicit price deflator for the gross domestic product as computed and published by the Department of Commerce for the preceding calendar year and the denominator of which is such deflator for the calendar year 1998.".]

[SEC. 4. Section 6(c) of the Legislative Branch Appropriations Act, 1999 (Public Law 105–275; 2 U.S.C. 121b–1(c)) is amended by adding at the end the following:

"(3) The provisions of section 4 of the Act of July 31, 1946 (40 U.S.C. 193d), except for the provisions relating to solicitation, shall not apply to any activity carried out pursuant to this section, subject to approval of such activities by the Committee on Rules and Administration.".]

[SEC. 5. The first section of Public Law 87–82 (40 U.S.C. 174j–1) is amended by adding at the end the following: "The provisions of section 4 of the Act of July 31, 1946 (40 U.S.C. 193d), except for the provisions relating to solicitation, shall not apply to any activity carried out pursuant to this section, subject to the approval of such activities by the Committee on Rules and Administration.".]

[SEC. 6. The Legislative Counsel may, subject to the approval of the President pro tempore of the Senate, designate one of the Senior Counsels appointed under section 102 of the Legislative Branch Appropriation Act, 1979 (2 U.S.C. 274 note; Public Law 95–391; 92 Stat. 771) as Deputy Legislative Counsel. The Deputy Legislative Counsel shall perform the functions of the Legislative Counsel during the absence or disability of the Legislative Counsel, or when the office is vacant.]

[SEC. 7. Section 814(i) of the Foreign Relations Authorization Act, Fiscal Years 1986 and 1987 (22 U.S.C. 2291 note) is amended by striking "September 30, 1999" and inserting "September 30, 2002".] *(Congressional Operations Appropriations Act, 2000.)*

[SEC. 223. For a payment to Virginia C. Chafee, widow of John H. Chafee, late a Senator from Rhode Island, $136,700.] *(Miscellaneous Appropriations, 2000, as enacted by section 1000(a)(5) of the Consolidated Appropriations Act, 2000 (P.L. 106–113).)*

HOUSE OF REPRESENTATIVES

SALARIES AND EXPENSES

For salaries and expenses of the House of Representatives, [$760,884,000] *$800,738,000*, as follows:

HOUSE LEADERSHIP OFFICES

For salaries and expenses, as authorized by law, [$14,202,000] *$14,704,000*, including: Office of the Speaker, [$1,740,000] *$1,798,000*, including $25,000 for official expenses of the Speaker; Office of the Majority Floor Leader, [$1,705,000] *$1,761,000*, including $10,000 for official expenses of the Majority Leader; Office of the Minority Floor Leader, [$2,071,000] *$2,140,000*, including $10,000 for official expenses of the Minority Leader; Office of the Majority Whip, including the Chief Deputy Majority Whip, [$1,423,000] *$1,500,000*, including $5,000 for official expenses of the Majority Whip; Office of the Minority Whip, including the Chief Deputy Minority Whip, [$1,057,000] *$1,121,000*, including $5,000 for official expenses of the Minority Whip; Speaker's Office for Legislative Floor Activities, [$406,000] *$417,000*; Republican Steering Committee, [$757,000] *$779,000*; Republican Conference, [$1,244,000] *$1,289,000*; Democratic Steering and Policy Committee, [$1,337,000] *$1,381,000*; Democratic Caucus, [$664,000] *$687,000*; nine minority employees, [$1,218,000] *$1,251,000*; training and program development—majority, $290,000; and training and program development—minority, $290,000[: *Provided*, That the amounts otherwise provided under this heading for the various leadership offices shall be reduced in a manner approved by the Committee on Appropriations such that the aggregate amount appropriated under this heading is $142,000 less than the aggregate amount otherwise provided].

MEMBERS' REPRESENTATIONAL ALLOWANCES

INCLUDING MEMBERS' CLERK HIRE, OFFICIAL EXPENSES OF MEMBERS, AND OFFICIAL MAIL

For Members' representational allowances, including Members' clerk hire, official expenses, and official mail, [$406,279,000] *$422,894,000*.

COMMITTEE EMPLOYEES

STANDING COMMITTEES, SPECIAL AND SELECT

For salaries and expenses of standing committees, special and select, authorized by House resolutions, [$93,878,000] *$99,242,000*: *Provided*, That such amount shall remain available for such salaries and expenses until December 31, [2000] *2002*.

COMMITTEE ON APPROPRIATIONS

For salaries and expenses of the Committee on Appropriations, [$21,095,000] *$22,530,000*, including studies and examinations of executive agencies and temporary personal services for such committee, to be expended in accordance with section 202(b) of the Legislative Reorganization Act of 1946 and to be available for reimbursement to agencies for services performed: *Provided,* That such amount shall remain available for such salaries and expenses until December 31, [2000] *2002*.

SALARIES, OFFICERS AND EMPLOYEES

For compensation and expenses of officers and employees, as authorized by law, [$90,150,000] *$98,546,000*, including: for salaries and expenses of the Office of the Clerk, including not more than $3,500, of which not more than $2,500 is for the Family Room, for official representation and reception expenses, [$14,881,000] *$15,862,000*; for salaries and expenses of the Office of the Sergeant at Arms, including the position of Superintendent of Garages, and including not more than $750 for official representation and reception expenses, [$3,746,000] *$3,858,000*; for salaries and expenses of the Office of the Chief Administrative Officer, [$57,289,000] *$64,180,000*, of which [$2,500,000] *$3,173,000* shall remain available until expended, including [$25,519,000] *$27,028,000* for salaries, expenses and temporary personal services of House Information Resources, of which [$24,641,000] *$26,928,000* is provided herein: *Provided,* That of the amount provided for House Information Resources, [$6,260,000] *$6,416,000* shall be for net expenses of telecommunications: *Provided further*, That House Information Resources is authorized to receive reimbursement from Members of the House of Representatives and other governmental entities for services provided and such reimbursement shall be deposited in the Treasury for credit to this account; for salaries and expenses of the Office of the Inspector General, [$3,926,000] *$4,040,000*; for salaries and expenses of the Office of General Counsel, [$840,000] *$877,000*; for the Office of the Chaplain, [$136,000] *$139,000*; for salaries and expenses of the Office of the Parliamentarian, including the Parliamentarian and $2,000 for preparing the Digest of Rules, [$1,172,000] *$1,256,000*; for salaries and expenses of the Office of the Law Revision Counsel of the House, [$2,045,000] *$2,130,000*; for salaries and expenses of the Office of the Legislative Counsel of the House, [$5,085,000] *$5,140,000*; for salaries and expenses of the Corrections Calendar Office, [$825,000] *$851,000*; and for other authorized employees, [$205,000] *$213,000*.

ALLOWANCES AND EXPENSES

For allowances and expenses as authorized by House resolution or law, [$135,422,000] *$142,822,000*, including: supplies, materials, administrative costs and Federal tort claims, [$2,741,000] *$3,381,000*; official mail for committees, leadership offices, and administrative offices of the House, $410,000; Government contributions for health, retirement, Social Security, and other applicable employee benefits, [$131,595,000] *$138,355,000*; and miscellaneous items including purchase, exchange, maintenance, repair and operation of House motor vehicles, interparliamentary receptions, and gratuities to heirs of deceased employees of the House, $676,000.

CHILD CARE CENTER

For salaries and expenses of the House of Representatives Child Care Center, such amounts as are deposited in the account established by section 312(d)(1) of the Legislative Branch Appropriations Act, 1992 (40 U.S.C. 184g(d)(1)), subject to the level specified in the budget of the Center, as submitted to the Committee on Appropriations of the House of Representatives. *(Congressional Operations Appropriations Act, 2000.)*

[ADMINISTRATIVE PROVISIONS]

[SEC. 101. (a) COMPLIANCE WITH ADMISSION REQUIREMENTS.—The General Counsel of the House of Representatives and any other counsel in the Office of the General Counsel of the House of Representatives, including any counsel specially retained by the Office of General Counsel, shall be entitled, for the purpose of performing the counsel's functions, to enter an appearance in any proceeding before any court of the United States or of any State or political subdivision thereof without compliance with any requirements for admission to practice before such court, except that the authorization conferred by this subsection shall not apply with respect to the admission of any such person to practice before the United States Supreme Court.]

[(b) NOTIFICATION BY ATTORNEY GENERAL.—The Attorney General shall notify the General Counsel of the House of Representatives with respect to any proceeding in which the United States is a party of any determination by the Attorney General or Solicitor General not to appeal any court decision affecting the constitutionality of an Act or joint resolution of Congress within such time as will enable the House to direct the General Counsel to intervene as a party in such proceeding pursuant to applicable rules of the House of Representatives.]

[(c) GENERAL COUNSEL DEFINITION.—In this section, the term "General Counsel of the House of Representatives" means—

(1) the head of the Office of General Counsel established and operating under clause 8 of rule II of the Rules of the House of Representatives;

(2) the head of any successor office to the Office of General Counsel which is established after the date of the enactment of this Act; and

(3) any other person authorized and directed in accordance with the Rules of the House of Representatives to provide legal assistance and representation to the House in connection with the matters described in this section.]

[(d) EFFECTIVE DATE.—The provisions of this section shall become effective beginning with the date of the enactment of this Act.]

[SEC. 102. Section 104(a) of the Legislative Branch Appropriations Act, 1999 (Public Law 105–275; 112 Stat. 2439) is amended by striking "(2 U.S.C. 59(e)(2))" and inserting "(2 U.S.C. 59e(e)(2))".]

[SEC. 103. (a) CLARIFICATION OF RULES REGARDING USE OF FUNDS FOR OFFICIAL MAIL.—

(1) IN GENERAL.—Section 311(e)(1) of the Legislative Branch Appropriations Act, 1991 (2 U.S.C. 59e(e)(1)) is amended—

(A) in the matter preceding subparagraph (A), by striking "There is established" and all that follows through "shall be prescribed—" and inserting the following: "The use of funds of the House of Representatives which are made available for official mail of Members, officers, and employees of the House of Representatives who are persons entitled to use the congressional frank shall be governed by regulations promulgated—"; and

(B) in subparagraph (A), by striking "the Allowance" and inserting "official mail (except as provided in subparagraph (B))".

(2) LIMITATIONS ON AVAILABILITY OF FUNDS.—Section 311(e)(2) of such Act (2 U.S.C. 59e(e)(2)), as amended by section 104(a) of the Legislative Branch Appropriations Act, 1999, is amended—

(A) in the matter preceding subparagraph (A), by striking "The Official Mail Allowance" and inserting "Funds used for official mail";

(B) by striking subparagraph (A); and

(C) by redesignating subparagraphs (B) and (C) as subparagraphs (A) and (B).

(3) REPEAL OF OBSOLETE TRANSFER AUTHORITY.—Section 311(e) of such Act (2 U.S.C. 59e(e)) is amended by striking paragraph (3).

(4) CONFORMING AMENDMENTS.—(A) Section 1(a) of House Resolution 457, Ninety-second Congress, agreed to July 21, 1971, as enacted into permanent law by chapter IV of the Supplemental Appropriations Act, 1972 (2 U.S.C. 57(a)), is amended by striking "the Official Mail Allowance" each place it appears and inserting "official mail".

(B) Section 311(a)(3) of the Legislative Branch Appropriations Act, 1991 (2 U.S.C. 59e(a)(3)) is amended by striking "costs charged against the Official Mail Allowance for" and inserting "costs incurred for official mail by".]

[(b) REPEAL OF OBSOLETE REFERENCES TO CLERK HIRE ALLOWANCE.—

(1) IN GENERAL.—Section 104(a) of the House of Representatives Administrative Reform Technical Corrections Act (2 U.S.C. 92(a)) is amended by striking "clerk hire" each place it appears.

(2) CONFORMING AMENDMENT.—The heading of section 104 of such Act (2 U.S.C. 92(a)) is amended by striking "**CLERK HIRE**".]

[(c) EFFECTIVE DATE.—The amendments made by this section shall apply with respect to the first session of the One Hundred Sixth Congress and each succeeding session of Congress.]

[SEC. 104. REQUIRING AMOUNTS REMAINING IN MEMBERS' REPRESENTATIONAL ALLOWANCES TO BE USED FOR DEFICIT REDUCTION OR TO REDUCE THE FEDERAL DEBT.—Notwithstanding any other provision of law, any amounts appropriated under this Act for "HOUSE OF REPRESENTATIVES—SALARIES AND EXPENSES—MEMBERS' REP-

[ADMINISTRATIVE PROVISIONS]—Continued

RESENTATIONAL ALLOWANCES" shall be available only for fiscal year 2000. Any amount remaining after all payments are made under such allowances for fiscal year 2000 shall be deposited in the Treasury and used for deficit reduction (or, if there is no Federal budget deficit after all such payments have been made, for reducing the Federal debt, in such manner as the Secretary of the Treasury considers appropriate).] *(Congressional Operations Appropriations Act, 2000.)*

JOINT ITEMS

For Joint Committees, as follows:

JOINT ECONOMIC COMMITTEE

For salaries and expenses of the Joint Economic Committee, [$3,200,000] *$3,315,000*, to be disbursed by the Secretary of the Senate.

JOINT COMMITTEE ON TAXATION

For salaries and expenses of the Joint Committee on Taxation, [$6,456,000] *$6,747,000*, to be disbursed by the Chief Administrative Officer of the House.

For other joint items, as follows:

OFFICE OF THE ATTENDING PHYSICIAN

For medical supplies, equipment, and contingent expenses of the emergency rooms, and for the Attending Physician and his assistants, including: (1) an allowance of $1,500 per month to the Attending Physician; (2) an allowance of $500 per month each to three medical officers while on duty in the Office of the Attending Physician; (3) an allowance of $500 per month to one assistant and $400 per month each not to exceed 11 assistants on the basis heretofore provided for such assistants; and (4) [$1,002,600] *$1,159,904* for reimbursement to the Department of the Navy for expenses incurred for staff and equipment assigned to the Office of the Attending Physician, which shall be advanced and credited to the applicable appropriation or appropriations from which such salaries, allowances, and other expenses are payable and shall be available for all the purposes thereof, [$1,898,000] *$1,835,000*, to be disbursed by the Chief Administrative Officer of the House.

CAPITOL POLICE BOARD

CAPITOL POLICE

SALARIES

For the Capitol Police Board for salaries of officers, members, and employees of the Capitol Police, including overtime, hazardous duty pay differential, clothing allowance of not more than $600 each for members required to wear civilian attire, and Government contributions for health, retirement, Social Security, and other applicable employee benefits, [$78,501,000] *$101,292,000*, of which [$37,725,000] *$49,366,000* is provided to the Sergeant at Arms of the House of Representatives, to be disbursed by the Chief Administrative Officer of the House, and [$40,776,000] *$51,926,000* is provided to the Sergeant at Arms and Doorkeeper of the Senate, to be disbursed by the Secretary of the Senate: *Provided*, That, of the amounts appropriated under this heading, such amounts as may be necessary may be transferred between the Sergeant at Arms of the House of Representatives and the Sergeant at Arms and Doorkeeper of the Senate, upon approval of the Committee on Appropriations of the House of Representatives and the Committee on Appropriations of the Senate.

GENERAL EXPENSES

For the Capitol Police Board for necessary expenses of the Capitol Police, including motor vehicles, communications and other equipment, security equipment and installation, uniforms, weapons, supplies, materials, training, medical services, forensic services, stenographic services, personal and professional services, the employee assistance program, not more than $2,000 for the awards program, postage, telephone service, travel advances, relocation of instructor and liaison personnel for the Federal Law Enforcement Training Center, and $85 per month for extra services performed for the Capitol Police Board by an employee of the Sergeant at Arms of the Senate or the House of Representatives designated by the Chairman of the Board, [$6,574,000] *$9,960,000*, to be disbursed by the Capitol Police Board or their delegee: *Provided*, That, notwithstanding any other provision of law, the cost of basic training for the Capitol Police at the Federal Law Enforcement Training Center for fiscal year [2000] *2001* shall be paid by the Secretary of the Treasury from funds available to the Department of the Treasury. *(Congressional Operations Appropriations Act, 2000.)*

ADMINISTRATIVE PROVISION

SEC. [105] *101*. Amounts appropriated for fiscal year [2000] *2001* for the Capitol Police Board for the Capitol Police may be transferred between the headings "SALARIES" and "GENERAL EXPENSES" upon the approval of—

(1) the Committee on Appropriations of the House of Representatives, in the case of amounts transferred from the appropriation provided to the Sergeant at Arms of the House of Representatives under the heading "SALARIES";

(2) the Committee on Appropriations of the Senate, in the case of amounts transferred from the appropriation provided to the Sergeant at Arms and Doorkeeper of the Senate under the heading "SALARIES"; and

(3) the Committees on Appropriations of the Senate and the House of Representatives, in the case of other transfers.

CAPITOL GUIDE SERVICE AND SPECIAL SERVICES OFFICE

For salaries and expenses of the Capitol Guide Service and Special Services Office, [$2,293,000] *$2,371,000*, to be disbursed by the Secretary of the Senate: *Provided*, That no part of such amount may be used to employ more than 43 individuals: *Provided further*, That the Capitol Guide Board is authorized, during emergencies, to employ not more than two additional individuals for not more than 120 days each, and not more than 10 additional individuals for not more than 6 months each, for the Capitol Guide Service.

STATEMENTS OF APPROPRIATIONS

For the preparation, under the direction of the Committees on Appropriations of the Senate and the House of Representatives, of the statements for the [first] *second* session of the One Hundred Sixth Congress, showing appropriations made, indefinite appropriations, and contracts authorized, together with a chronological history of the regular appropriations Acts as required by law, $30,000, to be paid to the persons designated by the chairmen of such committees to supervise the work. *(Congressional Operations Appropriations Act, 2000.)*

OFFICE OF COMPLIANCE

Federal Funds

General and special funds:

SALARIES AND EXPENSES

For salaries and expenses of the Office of Compliance, as authorized by section 305 of the Congressional Accountability Act of 1995 (2 U.S.C. 1385), [$2,000,000] *$2,095,000*. *(Congressional Operations Appropriations Act, 2000.)*

Program and Financing (in millions of dollars)

Identification code 09–1600–0–1–801	1999 actual	2000 est.	2001 est.
Obligations by program activity:			
10.00 Total new obligations	2	2	2
Budgetary resources available for obligation:			
22.00 New budget authority (gross)	2	2	2
23.95 Total new obligations	−2	−2	−2

	New budget authority (gross), detail:			
	Discretionary:			
40.00	Appropriation	2	2	2
	Change in unpaid obligations:			
73.10	Total new obligations	2	2	2
73.20	Total outlays (gross)	−2	−2	−2
	Outlays (gross), detail:			
86.90	Outlays from new discretionary authority	2	2	2
	Net budget authority and outlays:			
89.00	Budget authority	2	2	2
90.00	Outlays	2	2	2

The Congressional Accountability Act of 1995 (CAA) established an independent Office of Compliance to apply the rights and protections of the following eleven labor and employment statutes to covered employees within the legislative branch: the Fair Labor Standards Act of 1938, Title VII of the Civil Rights Act of 1964, the Americans with Disabilities Act of 1990, the Age Discrimination in Employment Act of 1967, the Family and Medical Leave Act of 1993, the Occupational Safety and Health Act of 1970, chapter 71 of title 5 of the U.S. Code (relating to Federal service labor-management relations), the Employee Polygraph Protection Act of 1988, the Worker Adjustment and Retraining Notification Act, the Rehabilitation Act of 1973, and chapter 43 of title 38 of the U.S. Code (relating to veterans' employment and reemployment).

The Office provides employees with an independent, neutral dispute resolution process, as an alternative to the court system, through which they may pursue claims under the laws applied by the CAA. The Office is headed by a five-member Board of Directors, who are appointed jointly by the House and Senate majority and minority leadership.

Object Classification (in millions of dollars)

Identification code 09–1600–0–1–801		1999 actual	2000 est.	2001 est.
11.1	Direct obligations: Personnel compensation: Full-time permanent	1	1	1
99.5	Below reporting threshold	1	1	1
99.9	Total new obligations	2	2	2

Personnel Summary

Identification code 09–1600–0–1–801		1999 actual	2000 est.	2001 est.
1011	Total compensable workyears: Exempt Full-time equivalent employment	17	17	15

CONGRESSIONAL BUDGET OFFICE

Federal Funds

General and special funds:

SALARIES AND EXPENSES

For salaries and expenses necessary to carry out the provisions of the Congressional Budget Act of 1974 (Public Law 93–344), including not more than [$2,500] *$3,000* to be expended on the certification of the Director of the Congressional Budget Office in connection with official representation and reception expenses, [$26,221,000] *$28,493,000*: *Provided,* That no part of such amount may be used for the purchase or hire of a passenger motor vehicle. *(2 U.S.C. 601 et seq.; Congressional Operations Appropriations Act, 2000.)*

Program and Financing (in millions of dollars)

Identification code 08–0100–0–1–801		1999 actual	2000 est.	2001 est.
	Obligations by program activity:			
10.00	Total new obligations	25	26	28
	Budgetary resources available for obligation:			
22.00	New budget authority (gross)	26	26	28
23.95	Total new obligations	−25	−26	−28
23.98	Unobligated balance expiring or withdrawn	−1		
	New budget authority (gross), detail:			
	Discretionary:			
40.00	Appropriation	26	26	28
	Change in unpaid obligations:			
72.40	Unpaid obligations, start of year: Obligated balance, start of year	2	4	3
73.10	Total new obligations	25	26	28
73.20	Total outlays (gross)	−24	−27	−29
74.40	Unpaid obligations, end of year: Obligated balance, end of year	4	3	2
	Outlays (gross), detail:			
86.90	Outlays from new discretionary authority	22	24	26
86.93	Outlays from discretionary balances	2	3	3
87.00	Total outlays (gross)	24	27	29
	Net budget authority and outlays:			
89.00	Budget authority	26	26	28
90.00	Outlays	24	27	29

The Congressional Budget Office was created by Title II of the Congressional Budget and Impoundment Control Act of 1974 (2 U.S.C. 601 et seq.) to provide assistance to Congress in fulfilling its responsibilities to ensure effective congressional control over the budgetary process; to determine each year the appropriate level of Federal revenues and expenditures; and to establish national budget priorities.

Object Classification (in millions of dollars)

Identification code 08–0100–0–1–801		1999 actual	2000 est.	2001 est.
	Personnel compensation:			
11.1	Full-time permanent	16	17	18
11.3	Other than full-time permanent	1	1	1
11.9	Total personnel compensation	17	18	19
12.1	Civilian personnel benefits	4	5	5
25.2	Other services	1	1	1
25.3	Purchases of goods and services from Government accounts	1	1	1
31.0	Equipment	2	1	1
99.0	Subtotal, direct obligations	25	26	27
99.5	Below reporting threshold			1
99.9	Total new obligations	25	26	28

Personnel Summary

Identification code 08–0100–0–1–801		1999 actual	2000 est.	2001 est.
1011	Total compensable workyears: Exempt Full-time equivalent employment	215	225	228

[ADMINISTRATIVE PROVISION]

[SEC. 106. (a) The Director of the Congressional Budget Office shall have the authority to make lump-sum payments to enhance staff recruitment and to reward exceptional performance by an employee or a group of employees.

(b) Subsection (a) shall apply with respect to fiscal years beginning after September 30, 1999.] *(Legislative Branch Appropriations Act, 2000.)*

[SEC. 224. Paragraph (5) of section 201(a) of the Congressional Budget Act of 1974 (2 U.S.C. 601(a)) is amended to read as follows:

"(5)(A) The Director shall receive compensation at an annual rate of pay that is equal to the lower of—

"(i) the highest annual rate of compensation of any officer of the Senate; or

"(ii) the highest annual rate of compensation of any officer of the House of Representatives.

General and special funds—Continued

[ADMINISTRATIVE PROVISION]—Continued

"(B) The Deputy Director shall receive compensation at an annual rate of pay that is $1,000 less than the annual rate of pay received by the Director, as determined under subparagraph (A).".] *(Miscellaneous Appropriations, 2000, as enacted by section 1000(a)(5) of the Consolidated Appropriations Act, 2000 (P.L. 106–113).)*

ARCHITECT OF THE CAPITOL

Federal Funds

General and special funds:

CAPITOL BUILDINGS AND GROUNDS

CAPITOL BUILDINGS

SALARIES AND EXPENSES

For salaries for the Architect of the Capitol, the Assistant Architect of the Capitol, and other personal services, at rates of pay provided by law; for surveys and studies in connection with activities under the care of the Architect of the Capitol; for all necessary expenses for the maintenance, care and operation of the Capitol and electrical substations of the Senate and House office buildings under the jurisdiction of the Architect of the Capitol, including furnishings and office equipment, including not more than $1,000 for official reception and representation expenses, to be expended as the Architect of the Capitol may approve; for purchase or exchange, maintenance and operation of a passenger motor vehicle; and not to exceed $20,000 for attendance, when specifically authorized by the Architect of the Capitol, at meetings or conventions in connection with subjects related to work under the Architect of the Capitol, [$46,836,000] *$60,038,000*, of which [$4,390,000] *$13,935,000* shall remain available until expended. *(2 U.S.C. 141; 5 U.S.C. 5304, 5306, 5318, 5341–5344, 5346, 5349; 40 U.S.C. 161, 162, 162a, 163, 163a, 166, 166a–1, 166b–2, 166b–3b, 166b–7, 166f; Congressional Operations Appropriations Act, 2000.)*

Program and Financing (in millions of dollars)

Identification code 01–0105–0–1–801	1999 actual	2000 est.	2001 est.
Obligations by program activity:			
10.00 Total new obligations	43	55	59
Budgetary resources available for obligation:			
21.40 Unobligated balance available, start of year	17	16	8
22.00 New budget authority (gross)	45	47	60
22.21 Unobligated balance transferred to other accounts	−3		
22.22 Unobligated balance transferred from other accounts	2		
23.90 Total budgetary resources available for obligation	60	63	68
23.95 Total new obligations	−43	−55	−59
23.98 Unobligated balance expiring or withdrawn	−1		
24.40 Unobligated balance available, end of year	16	8	9
New budget authority (gross), detail:			
Discretionary:			
40.00 Appropriation	44	47	60
42.00 Transferred from other accounts	1		
43.00 Appropriation (total discretionary)	45	47	60
Change in unpaid obligations:			
72.40 Unpaid obligations, start of year: Obligated balance, start of year	10	13	6
73.10 Total new obligations	43	55	59
73.20 Total outlays (gross)	−40	−62	−60
74.40 Unpaid obligations, end of year: Obligated balance, end of year	13	6	5
Outlays (gross), detail:			
86.90 Outlays from new discretionary authority	29	40	49
86.93 Outlays from discretionary balances	11	22	12
87.00 Total outlays (gross)	40	62	60
Net budget authority and outlays:			
89.00 Budget authority	45	47	60
90.00 Outlays	40	62	60

Included in this presentation are "Contingent expenses," "Alterations and improvements, buildings and grounds, to provide facilities for the physically handicapped," and "West central front of the Capitol."

Object Classification (in millions of dollars)

Identification code 01–0105–0–1–801	1999 actual	2000 est.	2001 est.
Personnel compensation:			
11.1 Full-time permanent	14	17	19
11.5 Other personnel compensation	1	1	1
11.9 Total personnel compensation	15	18	20
12.1 Civilian personnel benefits	7	7	8
13.0 Benefits for former personnel		1	1
23.2 Rental payments to others	1	1	1
25.4 Operation and maintenance of facilities	19	27	28
26.0 Supplies and materials	1	1	1
99.9 Total new obligations	43	55	59

Personnel Summary

Identification code 01–0105–0–1–801	1999 actual	2000 est.	2001 est.
1011 Total compensable workyears: Exempt Full-time equivalent employment	346	388	388

CAPITOL GROUNDS

For all necessary expenses for care and improvement of grounds surrounding the Capitol, the Senate and House office buildings, and the Capitol Power Plant, [$5,427,000] *$6,120,000*, of which [$155,000] *$355,000* shall remain available until expended. *(5 U.S.C. 5304, 5306, 5318, 5341–5344, 5346, 5349; 40 U.S.C. 162, 166a–1, 166b–3b, 166b–7, 184a, 193a, 223; Congressional Operations Appropriations Act, 2000.)*

Program and Financing (in millions of dollars)

Identification code 01–0108–0–1–801	1999 actual	2000 est.	2001 est.
Obligations by program activity:			
10.00 Total new obligations	6	14	12
Budgetary resources available for obligation:			
21.40 Unobligated balance available, start of year	20	16	7
22.00 New budget authority (gross)	6	5	6
22.21 Unobligated balance transferred to other accounts	−4		
23.90 Total budgetary resources available for obligation	22	21	13
23.95 Total new obligations	−6	−14	−12
24.40 Unobligated balance available, end of year	16	7	1
New budget authority (gross), detail:			
Discretionary:			
40.00 Appropriation	6	5	6
Change in unpaid obligations:			
72.40 Unpaid obligations, start of year: Obligated balance, start of year	1	1	1
73.10 Total new obligations	6	14	12
73.20 Total outlays (gross)	−5	−14	−12
74.40 Unpaid obligations, end of year: Obligated balance, end of year	1	1	1
Outlays (gross), detail:			
86.90 Outlays from new discretionary authority	4	5	5
86.93 Outlays from discretionary balances	1	10	8
87.00 Total outlays (gross)	5	14	12
Net budget authority and outlays:			
89.00 Budget authority	6	5	6
90.00 Outlays	5	14	12

Object Classification (in millions of dollars)

Identification code 01–0108–0–1–801	1999 actual	2000 est.	2001 est.
11.1 Personnel compensation: Full-time permanent	3	3	3

12.1	Civilian personnel benefits	1	1	1
25.2	Other services	2	10	8
99.9	Total new obligations	6	14	12

Personnel Summary

Identification code 01–0108–0–1–801		1999 actual	2000 est.	2001 est.
1011	Total compensable workyears: Exempt Full-time equivalent employment	70	75	75

CONGRESSIONAL CEMETERY

Program and Financing (in millions of dollars)

Identification code 01–0110–0–1–801		1999 actual	2000 est.	2001 est.
	Obligations by program activity:			
10.00	Total new obligations (object class 41.0)	1		
	Budgetary resources available for obligation:			
22.00	New budget authority (gross)	1		
23.95	Total new obligations	–1		
	New budget authority (gross), detail:			
	Discretionary:			
40.00	Appropriation	1		
	Change in unpaid obligations:			
73.10	Total new obligations	1		
	Outlays (gross), detail:			
86.90	Outlays from new discretionary authority	1		
	Net budget authority and outlays:			
89.00	Budget authority	1		
90.00	Outlays	1		

SENATE OFFICE BUILDINGS

For all necessary expenses for maintenance, care and operation of Senate office buildings; and furniture and furnishings to be expended under the control and supervision of the Architect of the Capitol, [$64,038,000] *$66,628,000*, of which [$22,305,000] *$22,119,000* shall remain available until expended. *(5 U.S.C. 5304, 5306, 5318, 5341–5344, 5346, 5349; 40 U.S.C. 166a–1, 166b–2, 166b–3b, 166b–7, 174b, 174b–1, 174c, 174j–1, 174j–8, 185a; Congressional Operations Appropriations Act, 2000.)*

Program and Financing (in millions of dollars)

Identification code 01–0123–0–1–801		1999 actual	2000 est.	2001 est.
	Obligations by program activity:			
10.00	Total new obligations	54	61	60
	Budgetary resources available for obligation:			
21.40	Unobligated balance available, start of year	15	12	15
22.00	New budget authority (gross)	54	64	67
22.21	Unobligated balance transferred to other accounts	–2		
23.90	Total budgetary resources available for obligation	67	76	82
23.95	Total new obligations	–54	–61	–60
23.98	Unobligated balance expiring or withdrawn	–1		
24.40	Unobligated balance available, end of year	12	15	22
	New budget authority (gross), detail:			
	Discretionary:			
40.00	Appropriation	54	64	67
	Change in unpaid obligations:			
72.40	Unpaid obligations, start of year: Obligated balance, start of year	8	11	5
73.10	Total new obligations	54	61	60
73.20	Total outlays (gross)	–51	–67	–58
74.40	Unpaid obligations, end of year: Obligated balance, end of year	11	5	6
	Outlays (gross), detail:			
86.90	Outlays from new discretionary authority	36	47	40
86.93	Outlays from discretionary balances	15	19	17
87.00	Total outlays (gross)	51	67	58
	Net budget authority and outlays:			
89.00	Budget authority	54	64	67
90.00	Outlays	52	67	58

This presentation includes the Senate restaurant fund.

Object Classification (in millions of dollars)

Identification code 01–0123–0–1–801		1999 actual	2000 est.	2001 est.
	Personnel compensation:			
11.1	Full-time permanent	15	19	21
11.5	Other personnel compensation	3	3	3
11.9	Total personnel compensation	18	22	24
12.1	Civilian personnel benefits	4	6	7
23.3	Communications, utilities, and miscellaneous charges	7	7	7
25.4	Operation and maintenance of facilities	23	24	19
26.0	Supplies and materials	1	1	1
31.0	Equipment	1	1	2
99.9	Total new obligations	54	61	60

Personnel Summary

Identification code 01–0123–0–1–801		1999 actual	2000 est.	2001 est.
1011	Total compensable workyears: Exempt Full-time equivalent employment	516	609	609

HOUSE OFFICE BUILDINGS

For all necessary expenses for the maintenance, care and operation of the House office buildings, [$37,279,000] *$53,269,000*, of which [$4,442,000] *$18,134,000* shall remain available until expended. *(5 U.S.C. 5304, 5306, 5318, 5341–5344, 5346, 5349; 40 U.S.C. 166a–1, 166b–2, 166b–3b, 166b–7, 174k, 175, 193a; 45 Stat. 1071–1072; 69 Stat. 41–42; Congressional Operations Appropriations Act, 2000.)*

Program and Financing (in millions of dollars)

Identification code 01–0127–0–1–801		1999 actual	2000 est.	2001 est.
	Obligations by program activity:			
10.00	Total new obligations	38	48	56
	Budgetary resources available for obligation:			
21.40	Unobligated balance available, start of year	11	19	8
22.00	New budget authority (gross)	48	37	53
23.90	Total budgetary resources available for obligation	58	56	61
23.95	Total new obligations	–38	–48	–56
23.98	Unobligated balance expiring or withdrawn	–1		
24.40	Unobligated balance available, end of year	19	8	5
	New budget authority (gross), detail:			
	Discretionary:			
40.00	Appropriation	42	37	53
40.15	Appropriation (emergency)	6		
43.00	Appropriation (total discretionary)	48	37	53
	Change in unpaid obligations:			
72.40	Unpaid obligations, start of year: Obligated balance, start of year	5	12	4
73.10	Total new obligations	38	48	56
73.20	Total outlays (gross)	–31	–55	–55
74.40	Unpaid obligations, end of year: Obligated balance, end of year	12	4	5
	Outlays (gross), detail:			
86.90	Outlays from new discretionary authority	26	33	43
86.93	Outlays from discretionary balances	5	22	12
87.00	Total outlays (gross)	31	55	55
	Net budget authority and outlays:			
89.00	Budget authority	48	37	53

General and special funds—Continued

CAPITOL BUILDINGS AND GROUNDS—Continued

HOUSE OFFICE BUILDINGS—Continued

Program and Financing (in millions of dollars)—Continued

Identification code 01–0127–0–1–801	1999 actual	2000 est.	2001 est.
90.00 Outlays	31	55	55

This presentation includes the House of Representatives gymnasium fund.

Object Classification (in millions of dollars)

Identification code 01–0127–0–1–801	1999 actual	2000 est.	2001 est.
Personnel compensation:			
11.1 Full-time permanent	16	19	21
11.5 Other personnel compensation	3	3	3
11.9 Total personnel compensation	19	22	24
12.1 Civilian personnel benefits	5	6	6
25.4 Operation and maintenance of facilities	13	19	25
26.0 Supplies and materials	1	1	1
99.9 Total new obligations	38	48	56

Personnel Summary

Identification code 01–0127–0–1–801	1999 actual	2000 est.	2001 est.
1011 Total compensable workyears: Exempt Full-time equivalent employment	528	649	649

CAPITOL POWER PLANT

For all necessary expenses for the maintenance, care and operation of the Capitol Power Plant; lighting, heating, power (including the purchase of electrical energy) and water and sewer services for the Capitol, Senate and House office buildings, Library of Congress buildings, and the grounds about the same, Botanic Garden, Senate garage, and air conditioning refrigeration not supplied from plants in any of such buildings; heating the Government Printing Office and Washington City Post Office, and heating and chilled water for air conditioning for the Supreme Court Building, the Union Station complex, the Thurgood Marshall Federal Judiciary Building and the Folger Shakespeare Library, expenses for which shall be advanced or reimbursed upon request of the Architect of the Capitol and amounts so received shall be deposited into the Treasury to the credit of this appropriation, [$38,054,000] *$40,872,000*, of which [$3,000,000] *$873,000* shall remain available until expended: *Provided*, That not more than [$4,000,000] *$4,400,000* of the funds credited or to be reimbursed to this appropriation as herein provided shall be available for obligation during fiscal year [2000] *2001. (5 U.S.C. 5304, 5306, 5318, 5341–5344, 5346, 5349; 40 U.S.C. 166a–1, 166b–7, 185; 33 Stat. 479; 34 Stat. 36; 42 Stat. 767–768; 44 Stat. 1262; 45 Stat. 1071–1072, 1694–1696; 46 Stat. 51, 583–584; 50 Stat. 9–10; 52 Stat. 392; 62 Stat. 1028–1029; 63 Stat. 933–934; 68 Stat. 803; 69 Stat. 41; 79 Stat. 987; 85 Stat. 637; 86 Stat. 1510; 91 Stat. 1374; 95 Stat. 1672; 102 Stat. 2170, 2331; 103 Stat. 1280–1282; 111 Stat. 2667–2668; Congressional Operations Appropriations Act, 2000.)*

Program and Financing (in millions of dollars)

Identification code 01–0133–0–1–801	1999 actual	2000 est.	2001 est.
Obligations by program activity:			
00.01 Direct Program Activity	32	42	41
09.01 Reimbursable program	4	4	4
10.00 Total new obligations	36	46	45
Budgetary resources available for obligation:			
21.40 Unobligated balance available, start of year	2	7	3
22.00 New budget authority (gross)	42	42	45
23.90 Total budgetary resources available for obligation	44	49	48
23.95 Total new obligations	–36	–46	–45
23.98 Unobligated balance expiring or withdrawn	–1		
24.40 Unobligated balance available, end of year	7	3	3
New budget authority (gross), detail:			
Discretionary:			
40.00 Appropriation	38	38	41
68.00 Spending authority from offsetting collections: Offsetting collections (cash)	4	4	4
70.00 Total new budget authority (gross)	42	42	45
Change in unpaid obligations:			
72.40 Unpaid obligations, start of year: Obligated balance, start of year	3	4	6
73.10 Total new obligations	36	46	45
73.20 Total outlays (gross)	–36	–44	–44
74.40 Unpaid obligations, end of year: Obligated balance, end of year	4	6	7
Outlays (gross), detail:			
86.90 Outlays from new discretionary authority	32	36	43
86.93 Outlays from discretionary balances	4	8	3
87.00 Total outlays (gross)	36	44	44
Offsets:			
Against gross budget authority and outlays:			
88.00 Offsetting collections (cash) from: Federal sources	–4	–4	–4
Net budget authority and outlays:			
89.00 Budget authority	38	38	41
90.00 Outlays	32	40	44

Object Classification (in millions of dollars)

Identification code 01–0133–0–1–801	1999 actual	2000 est.	2001 est.
Direct obligations:			
11.1 Personnel compensation: Full-time permanent	3	4	4
12.1 Civilian personnel benefits	1	1	1
23.3 Communications, utilities, and miscellaneous charges	25	27	31
25.4 Operation and maintenance of facilities	2	9	3
26.0 Supplies and materials	1	1	2
99.0 Subtotal, direct obligations	32	42	41
99.0 Reimbursable obligations	4	4	4
99.9 Total new obligations	36	46	45

Personnel Summary

Identification code 01–0133–0–1–801	1999 actual	2000 est.	2001 est.
Direct:			
1011 Total compensable workyears: Exempt Full-time equivalent employment	78	78	78
Reimbursable:			
2011 Total compensable workyears: Exempt Full-time equivalent employment	10	19	19

LIBRARY BUILDINGS AND GROUNDS

STRUCTURAL AND MECHANICAL CARE

For all necessary expenses for the mechanical and structural maintenance, care and operation of the Library buildings and grounds, [$16,033,000] *$20,278,000*, of which [$3,650,000] *$7,150,000* shall remain available until expended. *(2 U.S.C. 141, 167j; 5 U.S.C. 5304, 5306, 5318, 5341–5344, 5346, 5349; 40 U.S.C. 166a–1, 166b–3b, 166b–7; 46 Stat. 583–584; Legislative Branch Appropriations Act, 2000.)*

Program and Financing (in millions of dollars)

Identification code 01–0155–0–1–801	1999 actual	2000 est.	2001 est.
Obligations by program activity:			
10.00 Total new obligations	17	18	18
Budgetary resources available for obligation:			
21.40 Unobligated balance available, start of year	7	7	5
22.00 New budget authority (gross)	15	16	20
22.22 Unobligated balance transferred from other accounts	3		

		1999 actual	2000 est.	2001 est.
23.90	Total budgetary resources available for obligation	24	23	25
23.95	Total new obligations	−17	−18	−18
24.40	Unobligated balance available, end of year	7	5	6
	New budget authority (gross), detail:			
	Discretionary:			
40.00	Appropriation	13	16	20
42.00	Transferred from other accounts	2		
43.00	Appropriation (total discretionary)	15	16	20
	Change in unpaid obligations:			
72.40	Unpaid obligations, start of year: Obligated balance, start of year	5	10	3
73.10	Total new obligations	17	18	18
73.20	Total outlays (gross)	−11	−26	−19
74.40	Unpaid obligations, end of year: Obligated balance, end of year	10	3	2
	Outlays (gross), detail:			
86.90	Outlays from new discretionary authority	9	13	14
86.93	Outlays from discretionary balances	2	13	7
87.00	Total outlays (gross)	11	26	19
	Net budget authority and outlays:			
89.00	Budget authority	15	16	20
90.00	Outlays	11	26	19

Object Classification (in millions of dollars)

Identification code 01–0155–0–1–801		1999 actual	2000 est.	2001 est.
	Personnel compensation:			
11.1	Full-time permanent	5	6	6
11.5	Other personnel compensation	1	1	1
11.9	Total personnel compensation	6	7	7
12.1	Civilian personnel benefits	1	1	1
25.4	Operation and maintenance of facilities	9	9	9
26.0	Supplies and materials	1	1	1
99.9	Total new obligations	17	18	18

Personnel Summary

Identification code 01–0155–0–1–801		1999 actual	2000 est.	2001 est.
1011	Total compensable workyears: Exempt Full-time equivalent employment	134	144	144

Capitol Visitor Center

Program and Financing (in millions of dollars)

Identification code 01–0161–0–1–801		1999 actual	2000 est.	2001 est.
	Obligations by program activity:			
10.00	Total new obligations		15	85
	Budgetary resources available for obligation:			
21.40	Unobligated balance available, start of year		100	85
22.00	New budget authority (gross)	100		
23.90	Total budgetary resources available for obligation	100	100	85
23.95	Total new obligations		−15	−85
24.40	Unobligated balance available, end of year	100	85	
	New budget authority (gross), detail:			
	Discretionary:			
40.15	Appropriation (emergency)	100		
	Change in unpaid obligations:			
72.40	Unpaid obligations, start of year: Obligated balance, start of year			5
73.10	Total new obligations		15	85
73.20	Total outlays (gross)		−10	−21
74.40	Unpaid obligations, end of year: Obligated balance, end of year		5	69
	Outlays (gross), detail:			
86.93	Outlays from discretionary balances		10	21
	Net budget authority and outlays:			
89.00	Budget authority	100		
90.00	Outlays		10	21

Intragovernmental funds:

Judiciary Office Building Development and Operations Fund

(TECHNICAL ADJUSTMENT TO LEGISLATIVE BRANCH REQUEST)

Program and Financing (in millions of dollars)

Identification code 01–4518–0–4–801		1999 actual	2000 est.	2001 est.
	Obligations by program activity:			
09.01	Project management	6	6	6
09.01	Interest	15	15	15
10.00	Total new obligations	21	21	21
	Budgetary resources available for obligation:			
21.40	Unobligated balance available, start of year	474	474	474
22.00	New budget authority (gross)	21	21	21
23.90	Total budgetary resources available for obligation	495	495	495
23.95	Total new obligations	−21	−21	−21
24.40	Unobligated balance available, end of year	474	474	474
	New budget authority (gross), detail:			
	Mandatory:			
69.00	Offsetting collections (cash)	23	23	23
69.47	Portion applied to repay debt	−2	−2	−2
69.90	Spending authority from offsetting collections (total mandatory)	21	21	21
	Change in unpaid obligations:			
73.10	Total new obligations	21	21	21
73.20	Total outlays (gross)	−21	−21	−21
	Outlays (gross), detail:			
86.97	Outlays from new mandatory authority	21	21	21
	Offsets:			
	Against gross budget authority and outlays:			
	Offsetting collections (cash) from:			
	Federal sources:			
88.00	Federal sources—Lease Payment	−17	−17	−17
88.00	Federal sources—Project Management	−6	−6	−6
88.90	Total, offsetting collections (cash)	−23	−23	−23
	Net budget authority and outlays:			
89.00	Budget authority	−2	−2	−2
90.00	Outlays	−1	−2	−2

The Judiciary Office Building Development Act, Public Law 100–480, among other purposes, authorizes the Architect of the Capitol to contract for the design and construction of a building adjacent to Union Station in the District of Columbia to be leased to the Judicial Branch of the United States. This schedule reflects the costs associated with the construction of the building. Costs of construction were financed by an initial $125 million of Federal agency debt (sales price less unamortized discount) issued in 1989.

Estimates prepared by the Legislative Branch assumed the financial arrangements to be a lease-purchase, which would distribute outlays associated with acquisition of the building over a period of thirty years. However, the arrangements involve Federally guaranteed financing and other characteristics that make them substantively the same as direct Federal construction, financed by direct Federal borrowing. Because estimated expenditures of the Legislative Branch are required to be included in the budget as submitted and without change, this separate schedule is included as an adjustment to reflect direct construction costs and associated interest costs, consistent with standard budget concepts and scoring conventions.

Intragovernmental funds—Continued

JUDICIARY OFFICE BUILDING DEVELOPMENT AND OPERATIONS FUND—Continued

Estimates shown are consistent with the requirements of the Budget Enforcement Act and are presented with the agreement of the Budget and Appropriations Committees.

Object Classification (in millions of dollars)

Identification code 01–4518–0–4–801	1999 actual	2000 est.	2001 est.
25.2 Other services	6	6	6
43.0 Interest and dividends	15	15	15
99.9 Total new obligations	21	21	21

GIFTS AND DONATIONS

This account was established to reflect the transfer of a property located at Culpeper, Virginia to the Architect of the Capitol. Schedules for this account are not included because the transfer is expected to happen after 2001.

BOTANIC GARDEN

Federal Funds

General and special funds:

SALARIES AND EXPENSES

For all necessary expenses for the maintenance, care and operation of the Botanic Garden and the nurseries, buildings, grounds, and collections; and purchase and exchange, maintenance, repair, and operation of a passenger motor vehicle; all under the direction of the Joint Committee on the Library, [$3,425,000] *$4,916,000, of which $203,000 shall remain available until expended. (5 U.S.C. 5304, 5306, 5318, 5341–5344, 5346, 5349; 40 U.S.C. 166a–1, 166b–7, 216, 216b, 216c; Legislative Branch Appropriations Act, 2000.)*

Program and Financing (in millions of dollars)

Identification code 09–0200–0–1–801	1999 actual	2000 est.	2001 est.
Obligations by program activity:			
10.00 Total new obligations	5	3	8
Budgetary resources available for obligation:			
21.40 Unobligated balance available, start of year	5	4	4
22.00 New budget authority (gross)	3	3	5
23.90 Total budgetary resources available for obligation	8	7	9
23.95 Total new obligations	–5	–3	–8
24.40 Unobligated balance available, end of year	4	4	1
New budget authority (gross), detail:			
Discretionary:			
40.00 Appropriation	3	3	5
Change in unpaid obligations:			
72.40 Unpaid obligations, start of year: Obligated balance, start of year	29	26	10
73.10 Total new obligations	5	3	8
73.20 Total outlays (gross)	–8	–19	–17
74.40 Unpaid obligations, end of year: Obligated balance, end of year	26	10	1
Outlays (gross), detail:			
86.90 Outlays from new discretionary authority	3	3	4
86.93 Outlays from discretionary balances	6	16	14
87.00 Total outlays (gross)	8	19	17
Net budget authority and outlays:			
89.00 Budget authority	3	3	5
90.00 Outlays	8	19	17

Object Classification (in millions of dollars)

Identification code 09–0200–0–1–801	1999 actual	2000 est.	2001 est.
11.1 Personnel compensation: Full-time permanent	2	2	3
12.1 Civilian personnel benefits		1	1
25.2 Other services	3		4
99.9 Total new obligations	5	3	8

Personnel Summary

Identification code 09–0200–0–1–801	1999 actual	2000 est.	2001 est.
1011 Total compensable workyears: Exempt Full-time equivalent employment	40	50	50

Trust Funds

GIFTS AND DONATIONS

Unavailable Collections (in millions of dollars)

Identification code 09–8292–0–7–801	1999 actual	2000 est.	2001 est.
Balance, start of year:			
01.99 Balance, start of year			
Receipts:			
02.01 Botanic Garden		6	2
Appropriation:			
05.01 Botanic Garden: Gifts and donations		–6	–2
07.99 Total balance, end of year			

Program and Financing (in millions of dollars)

Identification code 09–8292–0–7–801	1999 actual	2000 est.	2001 est.
Obligations by program activity:			
10.00 Total new obligations (object class 25.2)		6	2
Budgetary resources available for obligation:			
22.00 New budget authority (gross)		6	2
23.95 Total new obligations		–6	–2
New budget authority (gross), detail:			
Mandatory:			
60.27 Appropriation (trust fund, indefinite)		6	2
Change in unpaid obligations:			
73.10 Total new obligations		6	2
73.20 Total outlays (gross)		–6	–2
Outlays (gross), detail:			
86.97 Outlays from new mandatory authority		6	2
Net budget authority and outlays:			
89.00 Budget authority		6	2
90.00 Outlays		6	2

Pursuant to 40 U.S.C. 216c, as amended, the Architect of the Capitol, subject to the direction of the Joint Committee on the Library, is authorized to construct a National Garden and to solicit and accept certain gifts on behalf of the United States Botanic Garden for the purpose of constructing the National Garden, or for the general benefit of the Botanic Garden and the renovation of the Botanic Garden conservatory, to deposit such gift funds in the Treasury of the United States, and, subject to approval in appropriations Acts, to obligate and expend such sums.

LIBRARY OF CONGRESS

Federal Funds

General and special funds:

SALARIES AND EXPENSES

For necessary expenses of the Library of Congress not otherwise provided for, including development and maintenance of the Union

Catalogs; custody and custodial care of the Library buildings; special clothing; cleaning, laundering and repair of uniforms; preservation of motion pictures in the custody of the Library; operation and maintenance of the American Folklife Center in the Library; preparation and distribution of catalog records and other publications of the Library; hire or purchase of one passenger motor vehicle; and expenses of the Library of Congress Trust Fund Board not properly chargeable to the income of any trust fund held by the Board, **[**$256,779,000**]** *$292,174,000*, of which not more than $6,500,000 shall be derived from collections credited to this appropriation during fiscal year **[**2000**]** *2001*, and shall remain available until expended, under the Act of June 28, 1902 (chapter 1301; 32 Stat. 480; 2 U.S.C. 150) and not more than $350,000 shall be derived from collections during fiscal year **[**2000**]** *2001* and shall remain available until expended for the development and maintenance of an international legal information database and activities related thereto: *Provided*, That the Library of Congress may not obligate or expend any funds derived from collections under the Act of June 28, 1902, in excess of the amount authorized for obligation or expenditure in appropriations Acts: *Provided further*, That the total amount available for obligation shall be reduced by the amount by which collections are less than the $6,850,000: *Provided further*, That of the total amount appropriated, **[**$10,321,380**]** *$10,654,380* is to remain available until expended for acquisition of books, periodicals, newspapers, and all other materials including subscriptions for bibliographic services for the Library, including $40,000 to be available solely for the purchase, when specifically approved by the Librarian, of special and unique materials for additions to the collections: *Provided further*, That of the total amount appropriated, **[**$2,347,000**]** *$2,506,000* is to remain available until expended for the acquisition and partial support for implementation of an Integrated Library System (ILS): *Provided further*, That of the total amount appropriated, **[**$5,579,000**]** *$5,557,800* is to remain available until expended for the purpose of teaching educators how to incorporate the Library's digital collections into school curricula, which amount shall be transferred to the educational consortium formed to conduct the "Joining Hands Across America: Local Community Initiative" project as approved by the Library**[**: *Provided further*, That of the total amount appropriated, $600,000 is to remain available until expended for the purpose of digitizing archival materials relating to ethnic groups of California, including Japanese Americans, which amount shall be transferred to an educational archive able to conduct such a project as approved by the Library**]**. *(2 U.S.C. 131–182; 5 U.S.C. 5102, 5305, 5318, 7901–7903; 17 U.S.C. 201–205; 20 U.S.C. 91, 2101–2107; 28 U.S.C. 2672; 36 U.S.C. 5701–5708; 41 U.S.C. 2531–2532, 254c; 44 U.S.C. 1718, 1719; Legislative Branch Appropriations Act, 2000.)*

Program and Financing (in millions of dollars)

Identification code 03–0101–0–1–503		1999 actual	2000 est.	2001 est.
	Obligations by program activity:			
	Direct program:			
00.01	Library services	150	152	175
00.02	Law library	6	7	8
00.03	Management support services	84	90	102
09.01	Reimbursable program—Interagency	62	86	80
09.02	Reimbursable program—Library Services	5	7	7
10.00	Total new obligations	307	342	372
	Budgetary resources available for obligation:			
21.40	Unobligated balance available, start of year	6	10	11
22.00	New budget authority (gross)	310	342	372
22.10	Resources available from recoveries of prior year obligations	2	1	1
23.90	Total budgetary resources available for obligation	318	353	384
23.95	Total new obligations	−307	−342	−372
23.98	Unobligated balance expiring or withdrawn	−1	−1	−1
24.40	Unobligated balance available, end of year	10	11	12
	New budget authority (gross), detail:			
	Discretionary:			
40.00	Appropriation	232	250	285
40.76	Reduction pursuant to P.L. 106–113		−1	
42.00	Transferred from other accounts	13		
43.00	Appropriation (total discretionary)	245	249	285
	Spending authority from offsetting collections:			
68.00	Offsetting collections (cash)	66	93	87
68.10	From Federal sources: Change in receivables and unpaid, unfilled orders	−1		
68.90	Spending authority from offsetting collections (total discretionary)	65	93	87
70.00	Total new budget authority (gross)	310	342	372
	Change in unpaid obligations:			
	Unpaid obligations, start of year:			
72.40	Obligated balance, start of year	73	75	100
72.95	From Federal sources: Receivables and unpaid, unfilled orders	5	4	4
72.99	Total unpaid obligations, start of year	78	79	104
73.10	Total new obligations	307	342	372
73.20	Total outlays (gross)	−301	−316	−356
73.40	Adjustments in expired accounts (net)	−3		
73.45	Adjustments in unexpired accounts	−2	−1	−1
	Unpaid obligations, end of year:			
74.40	Obligated balance, end of year	75	100	115
74.95	From Federal sources: Receivables and unpaid, unfilled orders	4	4	4
74.99	Total unpaid obligations, end of year	79	104	119
	Outlays (gross), detail:			
86.90	Outlays from new discretionary authority	251	271	297
86.93	Outlays from discretionary balances	50	45	58
87.00	Total outlays (gross)	301	316	356
	Offsets:			
	Against gross budget authority and outlays:			
	Offsetting collections (cash) from:			
88.40	Non-Federal sources	−6	−6	−6
88.45	Offsetting governmental collections from the public	−60	−87	−81
88.90	Total, offsetting collections (cash)	−66	−93	−87
	Against gross budget authority only:			
88.95	From Federal sources: Change in receivables and unpaid, unfilled orders	1		
	Net budget authority and outlays:			
89.00	Budget authority	245	249	285
90.00	Outlays	236	223	269

Personal services and necessary expenses to provide support for the basic operations of the Library are financed from this appropriation.

Library services.—Library Services has as its mission the acquisition of materials; the cataloging, classification, and preparation of materials for use; serving the public and maintaining and managing the Library's universal collections, which are the largest in the world; and, the preservation of materials for use now and in the future. It also develops, produces, markets, and distributes the printed catalog records, cataloging data in machine-readable form, book catalogs, technical publications and selected bibliographies made available from the automated databases. It contributes directly to the Nation's educational intellectual life through programs that interpret the Library's resources and promotes the use of its unparalleled collections. Library Services provides many basic technical services to the Library of Congress as well as the world's research and library communities. Finally, this program coordinates Federal library and information resources.

Law library.—The Law Library is responsible for the custody, development, and service of the law collection, in all formats, of the Library of Congress and functions as the foreign and international law research arm of the United States Congress.

Management support services.—This activity supports the executive staff of the Office of the Librarian: budget and finance; human resources; contracts and logistics; buildings management; automation; and other centralized services. It also includes rental of space off Capitol Hill.

General and special funds—Continued

SALARIES AND EXPENSES—Continued

Object Classification (in millions of dollars)

Identification code 03–0101–0–1–503		1999 actual	2000 est.	2001 est.
	Direct obligations:			
	Personnel compensation:			
11.1	Full-time permanent	135	144	161
11.3	Other than full-time permanent	1	1	1
11.5	Other personnel compensation	4	2	2
11.9	Total personnel compensation	140	147	164
12.1	Civilian personnel benefits	28	29	34
21.0	Travel and transportation of persons	1	1	1
23.1	Rental payments to GSA	2	3	3
23.3	Communications, utilities, and miscellaneous charges	3	5	4
24.0	Printing and reproduction	3	4	4
25.1	Advisory and assistance services	4	3	6
25.2	Other services	17	13	18
25.3	Purchases of goods and services from Government accounts	2	2	2
25.4	Operation and maintenance of facilities	4	4	4
25.7	Operation and maintenance of equipment	5	5	5
26.0	Supplies and materials	2	3	3
31.0	Equipment	27	24	30
41.0	Grants, subsidies, and contributions	2	6	6
99.0	Subtotal, direct obligations	240	249	284
99.0	Reimbursable obligations	66	92	87
99.5	Below reporting threshold	1	1	1
99.9	Total new obligations	307	342	372

Personnel Summary

Identification code 03–0101–0–1–503		1999 actual	2000 est.	2001 est.
	Direct:			
1011	Total compensable workyears: Exempt Full-time equivalent employment	2,569	2,646	2,837
	Reimbursable:			
2011	Total compensable workyears: Exempt Full-time equivalent employment	147	157	156

COPYRIGHT OFFICE

SALARIES AND EXPENSES

For necessary expenses of the Copyright Office, [$37,628,000] *$38,903,000*, of which not more than [$20,800,000] *$21,000,000*, to remain available until expended, shall be derived from collections credited to this appropriation during fiscal year [2000] *2001* under 17 U.S.C. 708(d): *Provided*, That the Copyright Office may not obligate or expend any funds derived from collections under 17 U.S.C. 708(d), in excess of the amount authorized for obligation or expenditure in appropriations Acts: *Provided further*, That not more than [$5,454,000] *$5,783,000* shall be derived from collections during fiscal year [2000] *2001* under 17 U.S.C. 111(d)(2), 119(b)(2), 802(h), and 1005: *Provided further*, That the total amount available for obligation shall be reduced by the amount by which collections are less than [$26,254,000] *$26,783,000*: *Provided further*, That not more than $100,000 of the amount appropriated is available for the maintenance of an "International Copyright Institute" in the Copyright Office of the Library of Congress for the purpose of training nationals of developing countries in intellectual property laws and policies: *Provided further*, That not more than $4,250 may be expended, on the certification of the Librarian of Congress, in connection with official representation and reception expenses for activities of the International Copyright Institute and for copyright delegations, visitors, and seminars. *(17 U.S.C. 101–710, 801–803, 901–914; 5 U.S.C. 5305; 2 U.S.C. 169; 41 U.S.C. 2531–2532, 254c; Legislative Branch Appropriations Act, 2000.)*

Program and Financing (in millions of dollars)

Identification code 03–0102–0–1–376		1999 actual	2000 est.	2001 est.
	Obligations by program activity:			
00.01	Registration, recordation, cataloging, acquisitions, and public reference	14	11	12
	Reimbursable obligations by program activity:			
09.01	Registration, recordation, cataloging, acquisitions, and public reference	15	21	21
09.02	Licensing	3	3	3
09.03	Arbitration royalty panels		2	3
10.00	Total new obligations	32	37	39
	Budgetary resources available for obligation:			
21.40	Unobligated balance available, start of year	1	2	2
22.00	New budget authority (gross)	33	37	39
23.90	Total budgetary resources available for obligation	34	39	41
23.95	Total new obligations	−32	−37	−39
24.40	Unobligated balance available, end of year	2	2	2
	New budget authority (gross), detail:			
	Discretionary:			
40.00	Appropriation	14	11	12
68.00	Spending authority from offsetting collections: Offsetting collections (cash)	19	26	27
70.00	Total new budget authority (gross)	33	37	39
	Change in unpaid obligations:			
72.40	Unpaid obligations, start of year: Obligated balance, start of year	2	3	7
73.10	Total new obligations	32	37	39
73.20	Total outlays (gross)	−31	−33	−36
74.40	Unpaid obligations, end of year: Obligated balance, end of year	3	7	10
	Outlays (gross), detail:			
86.90	Outlays from new discretionary authority	29	31	33
86.93	Outlays from discretionary balances	2	2	3
87.00	Total outlays (gross)	31	33	36
	Offsets:			
	Against gross budget authority and outlays:			
88.40	Offsetting collections (cash) from: Non-Federal sources	−19	−26	−27
	Net budget authority and outlays:			
89.00	Budget authority	14	11	12
90.00	Outlays	13	7	9

The Office is conducted for the most part on a self-sustaining basis. The amount requested is substantially counterbalanced by fees received for services rendered and the value of books and other library materials deposited in accordance with the Copyright Act and transferred to the Library of Congress. The income and obligations for 1999, and estimates for 2000 and 2001 are as follows:

	1999 actual	*2000 est.*	*2001 est.*
Income:			
Gross receipts	$19,397,524	$26,254,000	$26,783,000
Estimated value of materials deposited and transferred to the Library of Congress	36,435,429	44,000,000	52,000,000
Total income	$55,832,953	$70,254,000	$78,783,000
Obligations	$31,704,693	$37,485,000	$38,854,000

Registration, recordation, cataloging, acquisitions, and public reference.—The Copyright Office is responsible for registering and recording copyright claims, assignments, and renewals, for supplying copyright information to the public, for collecting and accounting for copyright fees, and for publishing complete and indexed catalogs for each class of copyright entries. These activities are predicated on an estimated 615,000 copyright registrations during 2001, an estimated 605,000 during 2000, and registrations of 594,501 during 1999.

Licensing Division.—The Licensing Division performs the responsibilities connected with the licensing activities of cable television stations and satellite carriers and the licensing of digital audio recording devices and media.

Copyright Arbitration Royalty Panels (CARP).—The CARP unit is responsible for administering procedures which are necessary for rate-making and distribution of royalties that are paid under cable, satellite and other compulsory licenses in the copyright law. These duties were formerly the responsibility of the Copyright Royalty Tribunal; unless the interested parties can come to agreement, distribution and rate-making are now established by arbitration panels whose work is reviewed by the Register of Copyrights and the Librarian of Congress.

Object Classification (in millions of dollars)

Identification code 03–0102–0–1–376		1999 actual	2000 est.	2001 est.
	Direct obligations:			
11.1	Personnel compensation: Full-time permanent	9	8	9
12.1	Civilian personnel benefits	2	2	2
25.5	Research and development contracts	1		
31.0	Equipment	1		
99.0	Subtotal, direct obligations	13	10	11
99.0	Reimbursable obligations	16	24	25
99.5	Below reporting threshold	3	3	3
99.9	Total new obligations	32	37	39

Personnel Summary

Identification code 03–0102–0–1–376		1999 actual	2000 est.	2001 est.
	Direct:			
1011	Total compensable workyears: Exempt Full-time equivalent employment	211	169	177
	Reimbursable:			
2011	Total compensable workyears: Exempt Full-time equivalent employment	277	347	340

Congressional Research Service

SALARIES AND EXPENSES

For necessary expenses to carry out the provisions of section 203 of the Legislative Reorganization Act of 1946 (2 U.S.C. 166) and to revise and extend the Annotated Constitution of the United States of America, [$71,244,000] *$75,640,000*: *Provided,* That no part of such amount may be used to pay any salary or expense in connection with any publication, or preparation of material therefor (except the Digest of Public General Bills), to be issued by the Library of Congress unless such publication has obtained prior approval of either the Committee on House Administration of the House of Representatives or the Committee on Rules and Administration of the Senate. *(2 U.S.C. 166, 168–168d, 169; 5 U.S.C. 5305, 5318; 41 U.S.C. 2531–2532, 254c; Congressional Operations Appropriations Act, 2000.)*

Program and Financing (in millions of dollars)

Identification code 03–0127–0–1–801		1999 actual	2000 est.	2001 est.
	Obligations by program activity:			
00.01	Policy analysis and research	47	50	54
00.02	Information and legislative documentation	10	11	11
00.03	Executive direction and support	10	10	11
10.00	Total new obligations	67	71	76
	Budgetary resources available for obligation:			
22.00	New budget authority (gross)	67	71	76
23.95	Total new obligations	−67	−71	−76
	New budget authority (gross), detail:			
	Discretionary:			
40.00	Appropriation	67	71	76
	Change in unpaid obligations:			
72.40	Unpaid obligations, start of year: Obligated balance, start of year	6	6	7
73.10	Total new obligations	67	71	76
73.20	Total outlays (gross)	−67	−70	−75
74.40	Unpaid obligations, end of year: Obligated balance, end of year	6	7	8
	Outlays (gross), detail:			
86.90	Outlays from new discretionary authority	61	65	69
86.93	Outlays from discretionary balances	6	5	6
87.00	Total outlays (gross)	67	70	75
	Net budget authority and outlays:			
89.00	Budget authority	67	71	76
90.00	Outlays	67	70	75

The Congressional Research Service (CRS) works exclusively and directly for all Members and committees of the Congress in support of their legislative, oversight, and representative functions. The Service provides research, analysis, and informational services that are timely, objective, nonpartisan, and confidential. The CRS staff responds to and anticipates congressional needs and addresses policy issues in an interdisciplinary, integrative manner. The Service maintains close ties with the Congress and, consistent with its broad congressional mandate, provides a wide variety of services with the goal of contributing to an informed national legislature.

Object Classification (in millions of dollars)

Identification code 03–0127–0–1–801		1999 actual	2000 est.	2001 est.
11.1	Personnel compensation: Full-time permanent	50	53	56
12.1	Civilian personnel benefits	9	10	11
23.3	Communications, utilities, and miscellaneous charges	1	1	1
25.1	Advisory and assistance services	1	1	1
25.2	Other services	2	2	2
26.0	Supplies and materials	2	2	2
31.0	Equipment	1	1	1
99.0	Subtotal, direct obligations	66	70	74
99.5	Below reporting threshold	1	1	2
99.9	Total new obligations	67	71	76

Personnel Summary

Identification code 03–0127–0–1–801		1999 actual	2000 est.	2001 est.
1011	Total compensable workyears: Exempt Full-time equivalent employment	703	747	747

Books for the Blind and Physically Handicapped

SALARIES AND EXPENSES

For salaries and expenses to carry out the Act of March 3, 1931 (chapter 400; 46 Stat. 1487; 2 U.S.C. 135a), [$47,984,000] *$48,983,000*, of which [$14,019,000] *$14,299,000* shall remain available until expended. *(2 U.S.C. 135a, 135a–1, 135b, 169; 5 U.S.C. 5305; 41 U.S.C. 2531–2532, 254c; Legislative Branch Appropriations Act, 2000.)*

Program and Financing (in millions of dollars)

Identification code 03–0141–0–1–503		1999 actual	2000 est.	2001 est.
	Obligations by program activity:			
00.01	Direct service to users	38	39	40
00.02	Support services	9	9	9
10.00	Total new obligations	47	48	49
	Budgetary resources available for obligation:			
22.00	New budget authority (gross)	47	48	49
23.95	Total new obligations	−47	−48	−49
	New budget authority (gross), detail:			
	Discretionary:			
40.00	Appropriation	47	48	49
	Change in unpaid obligations:			
72.40	Unpaid obligations, start of year: Obligated balance, start of year	28	29	32
73.10	Total new obligations	47	48	49
73.20	Total outlays (gross)	−45	−45	−47
74.40	Unpaid obligations, end of year: Obligated balance, end of year	29	32	34

General and special funds—Continued

BOOKS FOR THE BLIND AND PHYSICALLY HANDICAPPED—Continued

SALARIES AND EXPENSES—Continued

Program and Financing (in millions of dollars)—Continued

Identification code 03–0141–0–1–503	1999 actual	2000 est.	2001 est.
Outlays (gross), detail:			
86.90 Outlays from new discretionary authority	21	22	22
86.93 Outlays from discretionary balances	24	23	25
87.00 Total outlays (gross)	45	45	47
Net budget authority and outlays:			
89.00 Budget authority	47	48	49
90.00 Outlays	45	45	47

The National Library Service for the Blind and Physically Handicapped (NLS) is responsible for administering a national program to provide reading material for blind and physically handicapped residents of the United States, its outlying areas, and for U.S. citizens residing abroad.

Direct service to users.—During the past five-year period, 1995–1999, the blind and physically handicapped readership throughout the country ranged from 764,600 to 772,100 and circulation ranged from approximately 22,665,000 units (volumes and containers) to almost 22,900,000.

Support services.—A variety of professional, technical, and clerical functions are performed by the NLS staff. A combined total of 15,400 interlibrary loan searches and requests for information concerning library and related services available to the blind and to other physically handicapped persons were received in 1999.

Object Classification (in millions of dollars)

Identification code 03–0141–0–1–503	1999 actual	2000 est.	2001 est.
11.1 Personnel compensation: Full-time permanent	6	6	6
12.1 Civilian personnel benefits	1	1	1
23.1 Rental payments to GSA	1	1	1
24.0 Printing and reproduction	1	1	1
25.2 Other services	2	3	3
25.5 Research and development contracts	1		
25.7 Operation and maintenance of equipment		1	1
26.0 Supplies and materials	2	2	2
31.0 Equipment	32	32	33
99.0 Subtotal, direct obligations	46	47	48
99.5 Below reporting threshold	1	1	1
99.9 Total new obligations	47	48	49

Personnel Summary

Identification code 03–0141–0–1–503	1999 actual	2000 est.	2001 est.
1011 Total compensable workyears: Exempt Full-time equivalent employment	123	121	121

FURNITURE AND FURNISHINGS

For necessary expenses for the purchase, installation, maintenance, and repair of furniture, furnishings, office and library equipment, [$5,415,000] *$6,020,000. (2 U.S.C. 141, 169; 41 U.S.C. 2531–2532, 254c; Legislative Branch Appropriations Act, 2000.)*

Program and Financing (in millions of dollars)

Identification code 03–0146–0–1–503	1999 actual	2000 est.	2001 est.
Obligations by program activity:			
00.01 Replacement furniture and furnishings	4	5	6
00.02 Jefferson and Adams Buildings, furniture and furnishings	1	1	1
10.00 Total new obligations	5	6	7
Budgetary resources available for obligation:			
21.40 Unobligated balance available, start of year	3	2	1
22.00 New budget authority (gross)	4	5	6
23.90 Total budgetary resources available for obligation	7	7	7
23.95 Total new obligations	−5	−6	−7
24.40 Unobligated balance available, end of year	2	1	
New budget authority (gross), detail:			
Discretionary:			
40.00 Appropriation	4	5	6
Change in unpaid obligations:			
72.40 Unpaid obligations, start of year: Obligated balance, start of year	3	4	6
73.10 Total new obligations	5	6	7
73.20 Total outlays (gross)	−4	−4	−5
74.40 Unpaid obligations, end of year: Obligated balance, end of year	4	6	8
Outlays (gross), detail:			
86.90 Outlays from new discretionary authority	2	2	3
86.93 Outlays from discretionary balances	2	2	2
87.00 Total outlays (gross)	4	4	5
Net budget authority and outlays:			
89.00 Budget authority	4	5	6
90.00 Outlays	4	4	5

This activity provides for the purchase, installation, maintenance, and repair of furniture, furnishings, and office and library equipment to support Library operations.

Object Classification (in millions of dollars)

Identification code 03–0146–0–1–503	1999 actual	2000 est.	2001 est.
Equipment:			
31.0 Annual furniture and equipment	4	5	6
31.0 Furnishings in Jefferson and Adams Buildings	1	1	1
99.9 Total new obligations	5	6	7

PAYMENTS TO COPYRIGHT OWNERS

Unavailable Collections (in millions of dollars)

Identification code 03–5175–0–2–376	1999 actual	2000 est.	2001 est.
Balance, start of year:			
01.99 Balance, start of year			
Receipts:			
02.01 Fees from cable television, satellite, and DART, Copyright Office	215	159	174
02.02 Interest on investments in public debt securities, Copyright Office	28	21	38
02.99 Total receipts	243	180	212
Appropriation:			
05.01 Payments to copyright owners	−243	−180	−212
07.99 Total balance, end of year			

Program and Financing (in millions of dollars)

Identification code 03–5175–0–2–376	1999 actual	2000 est.	2001 est.
Obligations by program activity:			
00.01 Licensing costs	3	3	3
00.02 Arbitration royalty panels	2	2	3
00.03 Payments to copyright owners	169	450	83
10.00 Total new obligations	174	455	89
Budgetary resources available for obligation:			
21.40 Unobligated balance available, start of year	703	772	497
22.00 New budget authority (gross)	243	180	212
23.90 Total budgetary resources available for obligation	946	952	709
23.95 Total new obligations	−174	−455	−89
24.40 Unobligated balance available, end of year	772	497	620

		1999 actual	2000 est.	2001 est.
	New budget authority (gross), detail:			
	Mandatory:			
60.25	Appropriation (special fund, indefinite)	243	180	212
	Change in unpaid obligations:			
73.10	Total new obligations	174	455	89
73.20	Total outlays (gross)	−174	−455	−89
	Outlays (gross), detail:			
86.97	Outlays from new mandatory authority	5	5	6
86.98	Outlays from mandatory balances	169	450	83
87.00	Total outlays (gross)	174	455	89
	Net budget authority and outlays:			
89.00	Budget authority	243	180	212
90.00	Outlays	174	455	89
	Memorandum (non-add) entries:			
92.01	Total investments, start of year: U.S. securities: Par value	705	776	501
92.02	Total investments, end of year: U.S. securities: Par value	776	501	624

The receipts from cable systems, satellite carriers, and digital audio devices are disbursed to the copyright owners through this appropriation after deduction of administrative costs for the Copyright Office Licensing Division. Disbursements are made in accordance with the schedule established in Public Law 94–553, as amended, Public Law 100–617, and Public Law 102–563.

Object Classification (in millions of dollars)

Identification code 03–5175–0–2–376		1999 actual	2000 est.	2001 est.
25.2	Other services	5	5	6
41.0	Grants, subsidies, and contributions	169	450	83
99.9	Total new obligations	174	455	89

Cooperative Acquisitions Program Revolving Fund

Program and Financing (in millions of dollars)

Identification code 03–4325–0–3–503		1999 actual	2000 est.	2001 est.
	Obligations by program activity:			
09.00	Reimbursable program	2	2	3
10.00	Total new obligations	2	2	3
	Budgetary resources available for obligation:			
21.40	Unobligated balance available, start of year	2	2	2
22.00	New budget authority (gross)	2	2	3
23.90	Total budgetary resources available for obligation	4	4	5
23.95	Total new obligations	−2	−2	−3
24.40	Unobligated balance available, end of year	2	2	2
	New budget authority (gross), detail:			
	Discretionary:			
68.00	Spending authority from offsetting collections (gross): Offsetting collections (cash)	2	2	3
	Change in unpaid obligations:			
72.40	Unpaid obligations, start of year: Obligated balance, start of year		1	1
73.10	Total new obligations	2	2	3
73.20	Total outlays (gross)	−2	−2	−3
74.40	Unpaid obligations, end of year: Obligated balance, end of year	1	1	1
	Outlays (gross), detail:			
86.90	Outlays from new discretionary authority	2	2	3
	Offsets:			
	Against gross budget authority and outlays:			
88.40	Offsetting collections (cash) from: Non-Federal sources	−2	−2	−3
	Net budget authority and outlays:			
89.00	Budget authority			
90.00	Outlays			

Under the authority of 2 U.S.C. 182; P.L. 105–55, the Library of Congress operates a revolving fund for the acquisition of foreign research materials for participating institutions through the Library's overseas offices.

Object Classification (in millions of dollars)

Identification code 03–4325–0–3–503		1999 actual	2000 est.	2001 est.
31.0	Reimbursable obligations: Equipment	1	1	2
99.5	Below reporting threshold	1	1	1
99.9	Total new obligations	2	2	3

Trust Funds

Gift and Trust Fund Accounts

Unavailable Collections (in millions of dollars)

Identification code 03–9971–0–7–503		1999 actual	2000 est.	2001 est.
	Balance, start of year:			
01.99	Balance, start of year			
	Receipts:			
02.02	Contributions to Library of Congress gift fund	6	23	29
02.03	Contributions, Library of Congress permanent loan account	13	19	11
02.04	Interest, Library of Congress permanent loan account	2	2	2
02.05	Income from donated securities, Library of Congress	2		
02.06	Deposits, service fees, Library of Congress	8	8	8
02.99	Total receipts	31	52	50
	Appropriation:			
05.01	Gift and trust fund accounts	−31	−52	−50
07.99	Total balance, end of year			

Program and Financing (in millions of dollars)

Identification code 03–9971–0–7–503		1999 actual	2000 est.	2001 est.
	Obligations by program activity:			
00.01	Library Services	18	32	33
00.02	Congressional Research Service	1	1	1
00.03	Gift Revolving	8	12	12
10.00	Total new obligations	27	45	46
	Budgetary resources available for obligation:			
21.40	Unobligated balance available, start of year	41	46	53
22.00	New budget authority (gross)	31	52	50
23.90	Total budgetary resources available for obligation	72	98	103
23.95	Total new obligations	−27	−45	−46
24.40	Unobligated balance available, end of year	46	53	58
	New budget authority (gross), detail:			
	Mandatory:			
60.27	Appropriation (trust fund, indefinite)	31	52	50
	Change in unpaid obligations:			
72.40	Unpaid obligations, start of year: Obligated balance, start of year	6	6	4
73.10	Total new obligations	27	45	46
73.20	Total outlays (gross)	−26	−47	−50
74.40	Unpaid obligations, end of year: Obligated balance, end of year	6	4	
	Outlays (gross), detail:			
86.97	Outlays from new mandatory authority	23	41	42
86.98	Outlays from mandatory balances	3	6	8
87.00	Total outlays (gross)	26	47	50
	Net budget authority and outlays:			
89.00	Budget authority	31	52	50

GIFT AND TRUST FUND ACCOUNTS—Continued

Program and Financing (in millions of dollars)—Continued

Identification code 03–9971–0–7–503		1999 actual	2000 est.	2001 est.
90.00	Outlays	26	47	50
	Memorandum (non-add) entries:			
92.01	Total investments, start of year: U.S. securities: Par value	28	33	38
92.02	Total investments, end of year: U.S. securities: Par value	33	38	39

This schedule covers: (1) funds received as gifts for immediate expenditure, funds received as trust funds for expenditure, and receipts from the sale of recordings, publications, photoduplication, and other materials financed from capital originally received as gifts; (2) income from investments held by or for the Library of Congress Trust Fund Board; and (3) interest paid by the Treasury on the principal funds deposited therewith as described under "Library of Congress Trust Fund, Principal Accounts".

The Library has six program areas related to Gift and Trust funds:

Library Services.—This includes traditional library activities of acquisitions, cataloging, research and reference, and preservation.

Law Library.—The Law Library of Congress supplies legal research covering more than 200 foreign jurisdictions to the Congress, the Judiciary, Federal agencies, and the public—serving 100,000 users annually.

Copyright Office.—The Copyright Office administers the U.S. copyright laws, provides copyright expertise to the Congress and executive branch agencies, and promotes international protection for intellectual property.

Congressional Research Service.—The Congressional Research Service provides non-partisan analytical research and information to all Members and committees of the Congress.

National Library Service for the Blind and Physically Handicapped.—The National Library Service for the Blind and Physically Handicapped manages a free national reading program for blind and physically handicapped people—circulating at no cost to users approximately 22.5 million items a year.

Revolving Gift Funds.—Under the authority of 2 U.S.C. 160, the Library of Congress operates ten gift revolving activities to provide, in various formats, duplication and preservation services; exhibits and other special programs; and retail marketing, to other Government agencies, libraries, other institutions, and the general public.

Object Classification (in millions of dollars)

Identification code 03–9971–0–7–503		1999 actual	2000 est.	2001 est.
11.1	Personnel compensation: Full-time permanent	7	8	8
12.1	Civilian personnel benefits	2	2	2
23.3	Communications, utilities, and miscellaneous charges	1	1	1
24.0	Printing and reproduction	1	1	1
25.1	Advisory and assistance services	2	2	2
25.2	Other services	5	5	5
26.0	Supplies and materials	2	2	2
31.0	Equipment	1	18	19
33.0	Investments and loans	3	3	3
41.0	Grants, subsidies, and contributions	1	1	1
44.0	Refunds	1	1	1
99.0	Subtotal, direct obligations	26	44	45
99.5	Below reporting threshold	1	1	1
99.9	Total new obligations	27	45	46

Personnel Summary

Identification code 03–9971–0–7–503		1999 actual	2000 est.	2001 est.
1011	Total compensable workyears: Exempt Full-time equivalent employment	194	195	195

ADMINISTRATIVE PROVISIONS

SEC. 201. Appropriations in this Act available to the Library of Congress shall be available, in an amount of not more than [$198,390] *$202,300*, of which [$59,300] *$60,500* is for the Congressional Research Service, when specifically authorized by the Librarian of Congress, for attendance at meetings concerned with the function or activity for which the appropriation is made.

[SEC. 202. (a) No part of the funds appropriated in this Act shall be used by the Library of Congress to administer any flexible or compressed work schedule which—

(1) applies to any manager or supervisor in a position the grade or level of which is equal to or higher than GS–15; and

(2) grants such manager or supervisor the right to not be at work for all or a portion of a workday because of time worked by the manager or supervisor on another workday.

(b) For purposes of this section, the term "manager or supervisor" means any management official or supervisor, as such terms are defined in section 7103(a)(10) and (11) of title 5, United States Code.]

SEC. [203] *202.* Appropriated funds received by the Library of Congress from other Federal agencies to cover general and administrative overhead costs generated by performing reimbursable work for other agencies under the authority of 31 U.S.C. 1535 and 1536 shall not be used to employ more than 65 employees and may be expended or obligated—

(1) in the case of a reimbursement, only to such extent or in such amounts as are provided in appropriations Acts; or

(2) in the case of an advance payment, only—

(A) to pay for such general or administrative overhead costs as are attributable to the work performed for such agency; or

(B) to such extent or in such amounts as are provided in appropriations Acts, with respect to any purpose not allowable under subparagraph (A).

SEC. [204] *203.* Of the amounts appropriated to the Library of Congress in this Act, not more than $5,000 may be expended, on the certification of the Librarian of Congress, in connection with official representation and reception expenses for the incentive awards program.

SEC. [205] *204.* Of the amount appropriated to the Library of Congress in this Act, not more than $12,000 may be expended, on the certification of the Librarian of Congress, in connection with official representation and reception expenses for the Overseas Field Offices.

SEC. [206] *205.* (a) For fiscal year [2000] *2001*, the obligational authority of the Library of Congress for the activities described in subsection (b) may not exceed [$98,788,000] *$92,845,000*.

(b) The activities referred to in subsection (a) are reimbursable and revolving fund activities that are funded from sources other than appropriations to the Library in appropriations Acts for the legislative branch.

[SEC. 207. The Library of Congress may use available funds, now and hereafter, to enter into contracts for the lease or acquisition of severable services for a period that begins in one fiscal year and ends in the next fiscal year and to enter into multi-year contracts for the acquisition of property and services pursuant to sections 303L and 304B, respectively, of the Federal Property and Administrative Services Act (41 U.S.C. 253l and 254c).]

[SEC. 208. (a) Notwithstanding any other provision of law regarding the qualifications and method of appointment of employees of the Library of Congress, the Librarian of Congress, using such method of appointment as the Librarian may select, may appoint not more than three individuals who meet such qualifications as the Librarian may impose to serve as management specialists for a term not to exceed 3 years.

(b) No individual appointed as a management specialist under subsection (a) may serve in such position after December 31, 2004.]

[SEC. 209. (a) Section 904 of the Supplemental Appropriations Act, 1983 (2 U.S.C. 136a–2) is amended to read as follows:

"SEC. 904. Notwithstanding any other provision of law—

"(1) the Librarian of Congress shall be compensated at an annual rate of pay which is equal to the annual rate of basic pay payable for positions at level II of the Executive Schedule under section 5313 of title 5, United States Code; and

"(2) the Deputy Librarian of Congress shall be compensated at an annual rate of pay which is equal to the annual rate of basic pay payable for positions at level III of the Executive Schedule under section 5314 of title 5, United States Code.".

(b) Section 203(c)(1) of the Legislative Reorganization Act of 1946 (2 U.S.C. 166(c)(1)) is amended by striking the second sentence and inserting the following: "The basic pay of the Director shall be at a per annum rate equal to the rate of basic pay provided for level III of the Executive Schedule under section 5314 of title 5, United States Code.".

(c) The amendments made by this section shall apply with respect to the first pay period which begins on or after the date of the enactment of this Act and each subsequent pay period.] *(Legislative Branch Appropriations Act, 2000.)*

GOVERNMENT PRINTING OFFICE

Federal Funds

General and special funds:

CONGRESSIONAL PRINTING AND BINDING

For authorized printing and binding for the Congress and the distribution of Congressional information in any format; printing and binding for the Architect of the Capitol; expenses necessary for preparing the semimonthly and session index to the Congressional Record, as authorized by law (44 U.S.C. 902); printing and binding of Government publications authorized by law to be distributed to Members of Congress; and printing, binding, and distribution of Government publications authorized by law to be distributed without charge to the recipient, [$73,577,000] *$80,800,000*: *Provided*, That this appropriation shall not be available for paper copies of the permanent edition of the Congressional Record for individual Representatives, Resident Commissioners or Delegates authorized under 44 U.S.C. 906: *Provided further*, That this appropriation shall be available for the payment of obligations incurred under the appropriations for similar purposes for preceding fiscal years: *Provided further*, That notwithstanding the 2-year limitation under section 718 of title 44, United States Code, none of the funds appropriated or made available under this Act or any other Act for printing and binding and related services provided to Congress under chapter 7 of title 44, United States Code, may be expended to print a document, report, or publication after the 27-month period beginning on the date that such document, report, or publication is authorized by Congress to be printed, unless Congress reauthorizes such printing in accordance with section 718 of title 44, United States Code. *(1 U.S.C. 205, 208, 211, 212; 44 U.S.C. 501, 701–704, 706, 708, 709, 711–13, 715–17, 719–21, 723, 724, 727–28, 733–35, 737, 901, 902, 906, 907, 1107, 1301, 1713, 1714, 1717, 1718, 1908; Congressional Operations Appropriations Act, 2000.)*

Program and Financing (in millions of dollars)

Identification code 04–0203–0–1–801	1999 actual	2000 est.	2001 est.
Obligations by program activity:			
10.00 Total new obligations (object class 24.0)	74	73	81
Budgetary resources available for obligation:			
22.00 New budget authority (gross)	74	73	81
23.95 Total new obligations	–74	–73	–81
New budget authority (gross), detail:			
Discretionary:			
40.00 Appropriation	74	73	81
Change in unpaid obligations:			
72.40 Unpaid obligations, start of year: Obligated balance, start of year	37	34	30
73.10 Total new obligations	74	73	81
73.20 Total outlays (gross)	–77	–77	–80
74.40 Unpaid obligations, end of year: Obligated balance, end of year	34	30	31
Outlays (gross), detail:			
86.90 Outlays from new discretionary authority	59	53	58
86.93 Outlays from discretionary balances	18	24	22
87.00 Total outlays (gross)	77	77	80
Net budget authority and outlays:			
89.00 Budget authority	74	73	81
90.00 Outlays	77	77	80

This appropriation covers authorized printing and binding for the Congress and the Architect of the Capitol, and for printing and binding of Government publications authorized by law to be distributed to Members of Congress. Also, this appropriation includes funding for printing, binding, and distribution of Government publications authorized by law to be distributed without charge to the recipients.

OFFICE OF SUPERINTENDENT OF DOCUMENTS

SALARIES AND EXPENSES

For expenses of the Office of Superintendent of Documents necessary to provide for the cataloging and indexing of Government publications and their distribution to the public, Members of Congress, other Government agencies, and designated depository and international exchange libraries as authorized by law, [$29,986,000] *$34,451,000*: *Provided*, That travel expenses, including travel expenses of the Depository Library Council to the Public Printer, shall not exceed $175,000: *Provided further*, That amounts of not more than $2,000,000 from current year appropriations are authorized for producing and disseminating Congressional serial sets and other related publications for [1998 and] 1999 *and 2000* to depository and other designated libraries. *(44 U.S.C. 305, 1702–04, 1710, 1711, 1719, 1902, 1903, 1909; Legislative Branch Appropriations Act, 2000.)*

Program and Financing (in millions of dollars)

Identification code 04–0201–0–1–808	1999 actual	2000 est.	2001 est.
Obligations by program activity:			
00.01 Depository library distribution	25	26	30
00.02 Cataloging and indexing	3	3	3
00.03 International exchange	1	1	1
10.00 Total new obligations	29	30	34
Budgetary resources available for obligation:			
22.00 New budget authority (gross)	29	30	34
23.95 Total new obligations	–29	–30	–34
New budget authority (gross), detail:			
Discretionary:			
40.00 Appropriation	29	30	34
Change in unpaid obligations:			
72.40 Unpaid obligations, start of year: Obligated balance, start of year	21	20	20
73.10 Total new obligations	29	30	34
73.20 Total outlays (gross)	–31	–31	–31
74.40 Unpaid obligations, end of year: Obligated balance, end of year	20	20	23
Outlays (gross), detail:			
86.90 Outlays from new discretionary authority	21	21	24
86.93 Outlays from discretionary balances	10	10	7
87.00 Total outlays (gross)	31	31	31
Net budget authority and outlays:			
89.00 Budget authority	29	30	34
90.00 Outlays	31	31	31

The Office of the Superintendent of Documents operates under a separate appropriation that provides funds for: (1) the mailing for Members of Congress and other Government agencies of certain Government publications, as authorized by law; (2) the distribution of Government publications to designated depository libraries, including tangible Government information products, online access, and locator services provided via the Internet from GPO Access; (3) the compila-

General and special funds—Continued

OFFICE OF SUPERINTENDENT OF DOCUMENTS—Continued

SALARIES AND EXPENSES—Continued

tion of catalogs and indexes of Government publications; and (4) the distribution of Government publications in the International Exchange Program. These four functions are related to the publication activity of other agencies and to the demands of the public, Members of Congress, and depository libraries. Consequently, the Office of the Superintendent of Documents can exercise little control over the volume of work which it may be called upon to perform. Following is a description of these four functions.

Distribution for other Government agencies and Members of Congress.—The Office of Superintendent of Documents maintains mailing lists and mails, at the request of Government agencies and Members of Congress, certain publications specified by public law.

Depository library distribution.—As required, Government publications are supplied to libraries which are designated as depositories for Government publications. This includes tangible information products, online access, and locator services provided via the internet from GPO Access.

Cataloging and indexing.—The Office of Superintendent of Documents is charged with preparing catalogs and indexes of all publications issued by the Federal Government. The principal publication is the "Monthly Catalog of U.S. Government Publications."

International exchange.—The Office of Superintendent of Documents distributes Government publications to foreign governments which agree, as indicated by the Library of Congress, to send to the United States similar publications of their governments for delivery to the Library of Congress.

Object Classification (in millions of dollars)

Identification code 04–0201–0–1–808	1999 actual	2000 est.	2001 est.
11.1 Personnel compensation: Full-time permanent	6	6	7
12.1 Civilian personnel benefits	1	1	1
22.0 Transportation of things	2	2	2
23.3 Communications, utilities, and miscellaneous charges		1	1
24.0 Printing and reproduction	13	14	15
25.2 Other services	6	5	7
26.0 Supplies and materials	1	1	1
99.9 Total new obligations	29	30	34

Personnel Summary

Identification code 04–0201–0–1–808	1999 actual	2000 est.	2001 est.
1011 Total compensable workyears: Exempt Full-time equivalent employment	134	138	147

Intragovernmental funds:

GOVERNMENT PRINTING OFFICE REVOLVING FUND

For payment to the "Government Printing Office revolving fund", $6,000,000, to remain available until expended, for air-conditioning systems.

The Government Printing Office is hereby authorized to make such expenditures, within the limits of funds available and in accord with the law, and to make such contracts and commitments without regard to fiscal year limitations as provided by section 9104 of title 31, United States Code, as may be necessary in carrying out the programs and purposes set forth in the budget for the current fiscal year for the Government Printing Office revolving fund: *Provided,* That not more than $2,500 may be expended on the certification of the Public Printer in connection with official representation and reception expenses: *Provided further,* That the revolving fund shall be available for the hire or purchase of not more than 12 passenger motor vehicles: *Provided further,* That expenditures in connection with travel expenses of the advisory councils to the Public Printer shall be deemed necessary to carry out the provisions of title 44, United States Code: *Provided further,* That the revolving fund shall be available for temporary or intermittent services under section 3109(b) of title 5, United States Code, but at rates for individuals not more than the daily equivalent of the annual rate of basic pay for level V of the Executive Schedule under section 5316 of such title: *Provided further,* That the revolving fund and the funds provided under the headings "OFFICE OF SUPERINTENDENT OF DOCUMENTS" and "SALARIES AND EXPENSES" together may not be available for the full-time equivalent employment of more than [3,313] *3,285* workyears: (or such other number of workyears as the Public Printer may request, subject to the approval of the Committees on Appropriations of the Senate and the House of Representatives): *Provided further,* That activities financed through the revolving fund may provide information in any format: *Provided further,* That the revolving fund shall not be used to administer any flexible or compressed work schedule which applies to any manager or supervisor in a position the grade or level of which is equal to or higher than GS–15: *Provided further,* That expenses for attendance at meetings shall not exceed $75,000. *(31 U.S.C. 1343(b), 9104; 44 U.S.C. 301, 309, 1502, 1504, 1509, 1510; Legislative Branch Appropriations Act, 2000.)*

Program and Financing (in millions of dollars)

Identification code 04–4505–0–4–808	1999 actual	2000 est.	2001 est.
Obligations by program activity:			
09.01 Printing and binding	694	745	714
09.02 Sales of publications	58	58	58
09.03 Agency distribution	5	6	6
09.11 Capital investment	9	16	9
10.00 Total new obligations	766	825	787
Budgetary resources available for obligation:			
21.40 Unobligated balance available, start of year	11	54	42
22.00 New budget authority (gross)	809	813	782
23.90 Total budgetary resources available for obligation	820	867	824
23.95 Total new obligations	−766	−825	−787
24.40 Unobligated balance available, end of year	54	42	37
New budget authority (gross), detail:			
Discretionary:			
40.00 Appropriation			6
42.00 Transferred from other accounts	3		
43.00 Appropriation (total discretionary)	3		6
68.10 Spending authority from offsetting collections: From Federal sources: Change in receivables and unpaid, unfilled orders			
Mandatory:			
69.00 Offsetting collections (cash)	770	793	761
69.10 From Federal sources: Change in receivables and unpaid, unfilled orders	36	20	15
69.90 Spending authority from offsetting collections (total mandatory)	806	813	776
70.00 Total new budget authority (gross)	809	813	782
Change in unpaid obligations:			
Unpaid obligations, start of year:			
72.40 Obligated balance, start of year	359	330	313
72.95 From Federal sources: Receivables and unpaid, unfilled orders	226	262	282
72.99 Total unpaid obligations, start of year	585	592	595
73.10 Total new obligations	766	825	787
73.20 Total outlays (gross)	−759	−822	−776
Unpaid obligations, end of year:			
74.40 Obligated balance, end of year	330	313	310
74.95 From Federal sources: Receivables and unpaid, unfilled orders	262	282	297
74.99 Total unpaid obligations, end of year	592	595	607
Outlays (gross), detail:			
86.90 Outlays from new discretionary authority			1
86.97 Outlays from new mandatory authority	647	699	681
86.98 Outlays from mandatory balances	112	123	94
87.00 Total outlays (gross)	759	822	776

		1999 actual	2000 est.	2001 est.
	Offsets:			
	Against gross budget authority and outlays:			
	Offsetting collections (cash) from:			
88.00	Federal sources	−691	−725	−683
88.40	Non-Federal sources	−79	−68	−78
88.90	Total, offsetting collections (cash)	−770	−793	−761
	Against gross budget authority only:			
88.95	From Federal sources: Change in receivables and unpaid, unfilled orders	−36	−20	−15
	Net budget authority and outlays:			
89.00	Budget authority	3		6
90.00	Outlays	−13	29	15

The Government Printing Office executes orders for printing, binding, and blankbook work, CD–ROMs and electronic formats, placed by Congress and the various agencies of the Federal Government, and furnishes on order blank paper, inks, and similar supplies. The Government Printing Office also sells publications to the public through its sales of publications program, and distributes publications to the public for other Government agencies.

Such work is financed through the Government Printing Office revolving fund (44 U.S.C. 309). The fund is reimbursed by the customer agencies and receipts from sales of publications to the general public.

Object Classification (in millions of dollars)

Identification code 04–4505–0–4–808		1999 actual	2000 est.	2001 est.
	Personnel compensation:			
11.1	Full-time permanent	145	152	156
11.5	Other personnel compensation	15	16	17
11.9	Total personnel compensation	160	168	173
12.1	Civilian personnel benefits	39	39	40
21.0	Travel and transportation of persons	1	1	1
22.0	Transportation of things	6	7	7
23.1	Rental payments to GSA	2	2	2
23.2	Rental payments to others	4	4	4
23.3	Communications, utilities, and miscellaneous charges	15	19	18
24.0	Printing and reproduction	473	510	473
25.2	Other services	20	21	22
26.0	Supplies and materials	37	38	38
31.0	Equipment	9	16	9
99.9	Total new obligations	766	825	787

Personnel Summary

Identification code 04–4505–0–4–808		1999 actual	2000 est.	2001 est.
2011	Total compensable workyears: Exempt Full-time equivalent employment	3,126	3,175	3,138

ADMINISTRATIVE [PROVISION] *PROVISIONS*

[SEC. 210. (a) Section 311 of title 44, United States Code, is amended by adding at the end the following new subsection:

"(c) Notwithstanding any other provision of law, section 3709 of the Revised Statutes (41 U.S.C. 5) shall apply with respect to purchases and contracts for the Government Printing Office as if the reference to '$25,000' in clause (1) of such section were a reference to '$100,000'.".

(b) The heading of section 311 of title 44, United States Code, is amended by striking "**AUTHORITY**" and inserting "**AUTHORITY; SMALL PURCHASE THRESHOLD**".

(c) The table of sections for chapter 3 of title 44, United States Code, is amended by striking the item relating to section 311 and inserting the following:

"311. Purchases exempt from the Federal Property and Administrative Services Act; contract negotiation authority; small purchase threshold.".] *(Legislative Branch Appropriations Act, 2000.)*

SEC. *206. Section 303 of title 44, U.S.C., is amended to read as follows:*

"The annual rate of pay for the Public Printer shall be a rate which is equal to the rate for level II of the Executive Schedule of subchapter II of chapter 53 of Title 5. The annual rate of pay for the Deputy Public Printer shall be a rate which is equal to the rate for level III of such Executive Schedule.".

SEC. *207. Section 1708 of title 44, U.S.C., is amended to read as follows:*

Section 1708. Prices for sales copies of Government information products; resale by dealers; sales agents

"(a) Sales prices for Government information products will be established by the Public Printer to cover the costs of production, dissemination, and other appropriate costs associated with this service, including the offering of sales discounts and any other costs associated with the Sales Program.".

"(b) The Superintendent of Documents may prescribe terms and conditions under which he authorizes the resale of Government information products by book dealers, and he may designate any Government officer his agent for the sale of Government information products under regulations agreed upon by the Superintendent of Documents and the head of the respective department or establishment of the Government.".

GENERAL ACCOUNTING OFFICE

Federal Funds

General and special funds:

SALARIES AND EXPENSES

For necessary expenses of the General Accounting Office, including not more than [$7,000] *$10,000* to be expended on the certification of the Comptroller General of the United States in connection with official representation and reception expenses; temporary or intermittent services under section 3109(b) of title 5, United States Code, but at rates for individuals not more than the daily equivalent of the annual rate of basic pay for level IV of the Executive Schedule under section 5315 of such title; hire of one passenger motor vehicle; advance payments in foreign countries in accordance with 31 U.S.C. 3324; benefits comparable to those payable under sections 901(5), 901(6), and 901(8) of the Foreign Service Act of 1980 (22 U.S.C. 4081(5), 4081(6), and 4081(8)); and under regulations prescribed by the Comptroller General of the United States, rental of living quarters in foreign countries, [$379,000,000] *$399,918,000: Provided, That not more than $1,900,000 of reimbursements received incident to the operation of the General Accounting Office building shall be available for use in fiscal year 2001: Provided further,* That notwithstanding 31 U.S.C. 9105 hereafter amounts reimbursed to the Comptroller General pursuant to that section shall be deposited to the appropriation of the General Accounting Office then available and remain available until expended, and not more than [$1,400,000] *$1,100,000* of such funds shall be available for use in fiscal year [2000] *2001: Provided further,* That this appropriation and appropriations for administrative expenses of any other department or agency which is a member of the National Intergovernmental Audit Forum or a Regional Intergovernmental Audit Forum shall be available to finance an appropriate share of either Forum's costs as determined by the respective Forum, including necessary travel expenses of non-Federal participants. Payments hereunder to the Forum may be credited as reimbursements to any appropriation from which costs involved are initially financed: *Provided further*, That this appropriation and appropriations for administrative expenses of any other department or agency which is a member of the American Consortium on International Public Administration (ACIPA) shall be available to finance an appropriate share of ACIPA costs as determined by the ACIPA, including any expenses attributable to membership of ACIPA in the International Institute of Administrative Sciences. *(Legislative Branch Appropriations Act, 2000.)*

Unavailable Collections (in millions of dollars)

Identification code 05–0107–0–1–801		1999 actual	2000 est.	2001 est.
	Balance, start of year:			
01.99	Balance, start of year	2		
	Appropriation:			
05.01	Salaries and expenses	−2		
07.99	Total balance, end of year			

General and special funds—Continued

Salaries and Expenses—Continued

Program and Financing (in millions of dollars)

Identification code 05–0107–0–1–801	1999 actual	2000 est.	2001 est.
Obligations by program activity:			
Direct program:			
00.01 Top Management	1	1	1
00.02 Accounting and Information Management Division	40	43	45
00.03 General Government Division	27	30	31
00.04 Health, Education and Human Services Division	26	30	32
00.05 National Security and International Affairs Division	36	38	40
00.06 Resources, Community and Economic Development Division	32	35	36
00.07 Office of the Chief Economist	1	1	1
00.08 Office of the General Counsel	17	19	20
00.09 Office of Special Investigations	4	4	4
00.10 Field Offices	81	83	87
00.11 Mission Support—Personnel Related	37	36	38
00.12 Mission Support—Non-Personnel Related	52	58	65
09.01 Reimbursable program	11	1	3
09.99 Total reimbursable program	11	1	3
10.00 Total new obligations	365	379	403
Budgetary resources available for obligation:			
21.40 Unobligated balance available, start of year	1	2	1
22.00 New budget authority (gross)	368	380	403
23.90 Total budgetary resources available for obligation	369	382	404
23.95 Total new obligations	−365	−379	−403
24.40 Unobligated balance available, end of year	2	1	1
New budget authority (gross), detail:			
Discretionary:			
40.00 Appropriation	354	379	400
40.76 Reduction pursuant to P.L. 106–113		−1	
42.00 Transferred from other accounts	2		
43.00 Appropriation (total discretionary)	356	378	400
Spending authority from offsetting collections:			
68.00 Offsetting collections (cash)	9	1	3
68.10 From Federal sources: Change in receivables and unpaid, unfilled orders	1	1	
68.26 Offsetting collections (unavailable balances)	2		
68.90 Spending authority from offsetting collections (total discretionary)	12	2	3
70.00 Total new budget authority (gross)	368	380	403
Change in unpaid obligations:			
Unpaid obligations, start of year:			
72.40 Obligated balance, start of year	58	52	54
72.95 From Federal sources: Receivables and unpaid, unfilled orders	−2	−1	
72.99 Total unpaid obligations, start of year	56	51	54
73.10 Total new obligations	365	379	403
73.20 Total outlays (gross)	−369	−376	−427
Unpaid obligations, end of year:			
74.40 Obligated balance, end of year	52	54	30
74.95 From Federal sources: Receivables and unpaid, unfilled orders	−1		
74.99 Total unpaid obligations, end of year	51	54	30
Outlays (gross), detail:			
86.90 Outlays from new discretionary authority	328	359	381
86.93 Outlays from discretionary balances	41	18	46
87.00 Total outlays (gross)	369	376	427
Offsets:			
Against gross budget authority and outlays:			
88.00 Offsetting collections (cash) from: Federal sources	−9	−1	−3
Against gross budget authority only:			
88.95 From Federal sources: Change in receivables and unpaid, unfilled orders	−1	−1	
Net budget authority and outlays:			
89.00 Budget authority	358	378	400
90.00 Outlays	360	375	424

The General Accounting Office's mission is to improve government operations by providing timely and reliable information and advice to Congress, determining the legality of public expenditures, and providing guidance on financial management matters.

Object Classification (in millions of dollars)

Identification code 05–0107–0–1–801	1999 actual	2000 est.	2001 est.
Direct obligations:			
11.1 Personnel compensation: Full-time permanent	246	258	273
12.1 Civilian personnel benefits	48	52	54
21.0 Travel and transportation of persons	10	10	10
23.1 Rental payments to GSA	7	7	7
23.3 Communications, utilities, and miscellaneous charges	8	9	9
24.0 Printing and reproduction	1	1	1
25.1 Advisory and assistance services	4	10	13
25.2 Other services	6	10	10
25.3 Purchases of goods and services from Government accounts	11	3	3
25.4 Operation and maintenance of facilities	2	8	8
25.7 Operation and maintenance of equipment	6	6	6
26.0 Supplies and materials	2	2	2
31.0 Equipment	3	2	4
99.0 Subtotal, direct obligations	354	378	400
99.0 Reimbursable obligations	11	1	3
99.9 Total new obligations	365	379	403

Personnel Summary

Identification code 05–0107–0–1–801	1999 actual	2000 est.	2001 est.
1011 Total compensable workyears: Exempt Full-time equivalent employment	3,275	3,275	3,275

Information Technology Systems and Related Expenses

Program and Financing (in millions of dollars)

Identification code 05–0109–0–1–808	1999 actual	2000 est.	2001 est.
Obligations by program activity:			
00.01 Information technology expenses	1		
10.00 Total new obligations (object class 25.2)	1		
Budgetary resources available for obligation:			
23.95 Total new obligations	−1		
New budget authority (gross), detail:			
Discretionary:			
41.00 Transferred to other accounts	−5		
42.00 Transferred from other accounts	5		
43.00 Appropriation (total discretionary)			
Change in unpaid obligations:			
72.40 Unpaid obligations, start of year: Obligated balance, start of year		1	
73.10 Total new obligations	1		
74.40 Unpaid obligations, end of year: Obligated balance, end of year	1		
Net budget authority and outlays:			
89.00 Budget authority			
90.00 Outlays			

As required by Public Law 105–277, upon approval of the House and Senate Appropriations Committees, the Comptroller General of the United States transferred funds to Legislative Branch entities other than the U.S. Senate and the U.S. House of Representatives for expenses related to Year 2000 conversion of information technology systems.

UNITED STATES TAX COURT

Federal Funds

General and special funds:

SALARIES AND EXPENSES

For necessary expenses, including contract reporting and other services as authorized by 5 U.S.C. 3109, [$35,179,000] *$37,439,000*: *Provided*, That travel expenses of the judges shall be paid upon the written certificate of the judge. *(Independent Agencies Appropriations Act, 2000.)*

Program and Financing (in millions of dollars)

Identification code 23–0100–0–1–752	1999 actual	2000 est.	2001 est.
Obligations by program activity:			
10.00 Total new obligations	33	35	37
Budgetary resources available for obligation:			
22.00 New budget authority (gross)	33	35	37
23.95 Total new obligations	−33	−35	−37
23.98 Unobligated balance expiring or withdrawn			
New budget authority (gross), detail:			
Discretionary:			
40.00 Appropriation	33	35	37
Change in unpaid obligations:			
72.40 Unpaid obligations, start of year: Obligated balance, start of year	4	4	8
73.10 Total new obligations	33	35	37
73.20 Total outlays (gross)	−33	−31	−37
74.40 Unpaid obligations, end of year: Obligated balance, end of year	4	8	8
Outlays (gross), detail:			
86.90 Outlays from new discretionary authority	31	31	33
86.93 Outlays from discretionary balances	2		4
87.00 Total outlays (gross)	33	31	37
Net budget authority and outlays:			
89.00 Budget authority	33	35	37
90.00 Outlays	33	31	37

The United States Tax Court is a Court of record established under Article I of the Constitution of the United States. The Court is composed of a Chief Judge and eighteen judges. Judges of the Tax Court are appointed by the President, by and with the advice and consent of the Senate, for 15 year terms. Decisions by the Court are reviewable by the United States Courts of Appeals and, if certiorari is granted, by the Supreme Court.

In their judicial duties, the judges are assisted by Senior Judges, who participate in the adjudication of regular cases, and by Special Trial Judges, who hear small tax cases and certain regular cases assigned to them by the Chief Judge.

The Court conducts trial sessions throughout the United States, including Hawaii and Alaska.

The matters over which the Court has jurisdiction are set forth in various sections of Title 26 of the U.S. Code.

For 2001, the Court proposes a trial program of 600 weeks consisting of 264 weeks of trial sessions assigned to Presidentially appointed Judges, 236 weeks of trial sessions assigned to Special Trial Judges, and 100 weeks of lengthy special sessions. Trials are held in approximately 80 cities throughout the United States.

Statistics on the actual and estimated number of cases before the court are presented in the following tabulation:

	1999 actual	*2000 est.*	*2001 est.*
Pending, beginning year	23,138	20,131	70,131
Docketed during year	20,302	105,000	105,000
Adjustments during year	260	—	—
Disposed of during year	23,569	55,000	55,000
Pending, end of year	20,131	70,131	120,131

This presentation includes the "Tax Court independent counsel" fund. This fund is established pursuant to 26 U.S.C. 7475. The fund is used by the Tax Court to employ independent counsel to pursue disciplinary matters involving practitioners admitted to practice before the Court.

Object Classification (in millions of dollars)

Identification code 23–0100–0–1–752	1999 actual	2000 est.	2001 est.
11.1 Personnel compensation: Full-time permanent	16	17	18
12.1 Civilian personnel benefits	3	3	4
13.0 Benefits for former personnel	1	1	1
21.0 Travel and transportation of persons	1	1	1
23.1 Rental payments to GSA	8	8	8
25.2 Other services	3	3	3
26.0 Supplies and materials	1	1	1
31.0 Equipment		1	1
99.9 Total new obligations	33	35	37

Personnel Summary

Identification code 23–0100–0–1–752	1999 actual	2000 est.	2001 est.
1011 Total compensable workyears: Exempt Full-time equivalent employment	335	335	335

Trust Funds

TAX COURT JUDGES SURVIVORS ANNUITY FUND

Program and Financing (in millions of dollars)

Identification code 23–8115–0–7–602	1999 actual	2000 est.	2001 est.
Budgetary resources available for obligation:			
21.40 Unobligated balance available, start of year	6	7	7
23.95 Total new obligations			
24.40 Unobligated balance available, end of year	7	7	7
Net budget authority and outlays:			
89.00 Budget authority			
90.00 Outlays			
Memorandum (non-add) entries:			
92.01 Total investments, start of year: U.S. securities: Par value	6	7	7
92.02 Total investments, end of year: U.S. securities: Par value	7	7	7

This fund, established pursuant to 26 U.S.C. 7448, is used to pay survivorship benefits to eligible surviving spouses and dependent children of deceased judges of the U.S. Tax Court. Participating judges pay 3.5 percent of their salaries or retired pay into the fund to cover creditable service for which payment is required. Additional funds, as are needed, are provided through the annual appropriation to the U.S. Tax Court.

On September 30, 1999, 23 judges of the court were participating in the fund, and 1 eligible dependent and 8 eligible widows were receiving survivorship annuity payments.

OTHER LEGISLATIVE BRANCH AGENCIES

Federal Funds

General and special funds:

NATIONAL BIPARTISAN COMMISSION ON THE FUTURE OF MEDICARE

Program and Financing (in millions of dollars)

Identification code 48–1750–0–1–571	1999 actual	2000 est.	2001 est.
Obligations by program activity:			
10.00 Total new obligations (object class 99.5)	1		
Budgetary resources available for obligation:			
22.00 New budget authority (gross)	1		

General and special funds—Continued

NATIONAL BIPARTISAN COMMISSION ON THE FUTURE OF MEDICARE—Continued

Program and Financing (in millions of dollars)—Continued

Identification code 48–1750–0–1–571	1999 actual	2000 est.	2001 est.
23.95 Total new obligations	−1		
New budget authority (gross), detail:			
Discretionary:			
68.00 Spending authority from offsetting collections (gross): Offsetting collections (cash)	1		
Change in unpaid obligations:			
73.10 Total new obligations	1		
73.20 Total outlays (gross)	−1		
Outlays (gross), detail:			
86.90 Outlays from new discretionary authority	1		
Offsets:			
Against gross budget authority and outlays:			
88.00 Offsetting collections (cash) from: Federal sources	−1		
Net budget authority and outlays:			
89.00 Budget authority			
90.00 Outlays			

The Balanced Budget Act of 1997 provided for the establishment of the National Bipartisan Commission on the Future of Medicare to review and analyze the long-term financial condition of the Medicare program.

MEDICARE PAYMENT ADVISORY COMMISSION

SALARIES AND EXPENSES

For expenses necessary to carry out section 1805 of the Social Security Act, [$7,015,000] *$8,000,000*, to be transferred to this appropriation from the Federal Hospital Insurance and the Federal Supplementary Medical Insurance Trust Funds. *(Departments of Labor, Health and Human Services, and Education, and Related Agencies Appropriations Act, 2000, as enacted by section 1000(a)(4) of the Consolidated Appropriations Act, 2000 (P.L. 106–113).)*

Program and Financing (in millions of dollars)

Identification code 48–1550–0–1–999	1999 actual	2000 est.	2001 est.
Obligations by program activity:			
10.00 Total new obligations	6	7	8
Budgetary resources available for obligation:			
22.00 New budget authority (gross)	7	7	8
23.95 Total new obligations	−6	−7	−8
23.98 Unobligated balance expiring or withdrawn	−1		
New budget authority (gross), detail:			
Discretionary:			
68.00 Spending authority from offsetting collections (gross): Offsetting collections (cash)	7	7	8
Change in unpaid obligations:			
72.40 Unpaid obligations, start of year: Obligated balance, start of year	3	2	
73.10 Total new obligations	6	7	8
73.20 Total outlays (gross)	−6	−9	−8
74.40 Unpaid obligations, end of year: Obligated balance, end of year	2		
Outlays (gross), detail:			
86.90 Outlays from new discretionary authority	3	7	8
86.93 Outlays from discretionary balances	3		
87.00 Total outlays (gross)	6	9	8
Offsets:			
Against gross budget authority and outlays:			
88.00 Offsetting collections (cash) from: Federal sources	−7	−7	−8
Net budget authority and outlays:			
89.00 Budget authority			
90.00 Outlays	−1	2	

The Medicare Payment Advisory Commission, established under section 1805 of the Social Security Act (42 U.S.C. 1395 b–6) as added by section 4022 of the Balanced Budget Act of 1997 (P.L. 105–33), is an independent legislative agency charged with advising the Congress on payment and other policy issues affecting the Medicare program, as well as on the implications of changes in health care delivery in the United States and in the market for health care services on the Medicare program.

The Commission's 17 members represent diverse points of view including providers, payers, consumers, employers, and individuals with expertise in biomedical, health services, and health economics research. It maintains a full time staff of 35 in Washington, D.C.

The Commission is required by law to report to the Congress on March 1 and June 1 of each year, and to comment on actions of the Secretary of Health and Human Services relevant to its mandate.

Object Classification (in millions of dollars)

Identification code 48–1550–0–1–999	1999 actual	2000 est.	2001 est.
11.1 Personnel compensation: Full-time permanent	2	3	3
12.1 Civilian personnel benefits	1	1	1
23.3 Communications, utilities, and miscellaneous charges	1	1	1
25.1 Advisory and assistance services	1	1	2
99.0 Subtotal, direct obligations	5	6	7
99.5 Below reporting threshold	1	1	1
99.9 Total new obligations	6	7	8

Personnel Summary

Identification code 48–1550–0–1–999	1999 actual	2000 est.	2001 est.
1011 Total compensable workyears: Exempt Full-time equivalent employment	32	38	40

CENSUS MONITORING BOARD

For necessary expenses of the Census Monitoring Board, as authorized by section 210 of Public Law 105–119, $4,000,000, to remain available until expended.

Program and Financing (in millions of dollars)

Identification code 48–2050–0–1–376	1999 actual	2000 est.	2001 est.
Obligations by program activity:			
00.01 Pay	2	2	2
00.02 Non-Pay	2	3	3
10.00 Total new obligations	4	5	5
Budgetary resources available for obligation:			
21.40 Unobligated balance available, start of year	3	3	1
22.00 New budget authority (gross)	4	4	4
23.90 Total budgetary resources available for obligation	7	7	5
23.95 Total new obligations	−4	−5	−5
24.40 Unobligated balance available, end of year	3	1	
New budget authority (gross), detail:			
Discretionary:			
40.00 Appropriation			4
42.00 Transferred from other accounts	4	4	
43.00 Appropriation (total discretionary)	4	4	4
Change in unpaid obligations:			
72.40 Unpaid obligations, start of year: Obligated balance, start of year	1	1	1

73.10	Total new obligations	4	5	5
73.20	Total outlays (gross)	–4	–5	–6
74.40	Unpaid obligations, end of year: Obligated balance, end of year	1	1	
	Outlays (gross), detail:			
86.90	Outlays from new discretionary authority		4	4
86.93	Outlays from discretionary balances	4		1
87.00	Total outlays (gross)	4	5	6
	Net budget authority and outlays:			
89.00	Budget authority	4	4	4
90.00	Outlays	4	5	6

The Census Monitoring Board is an eight-member bipartisan oversight board charged with observing and monitoring all aspects of the preparation and implementation of the 2000 decennial census. The Board submits periodic reports to both Congress and the President detailing the Census Bureau's preparedness to conduct a successful census. Census data are used to determine Congressional apportionment and the allocation of billions of Federal dollars.

Object Classification (in millions of dollars)

Identification code 48–2050–0–1–376		1999 actual	2000 est.	2001 est.
11.1	Direct obligations: Personnel compensation: Full-time permanent	2	2	2
99.5	Below reporting threshold	2	3	3
99.9	Total new obligations	4	5	5

Personnel Summary

Identification code 48–2050–0–1–376		1999 actual	2000 est.	2001 est.
1011	Total compensable workyears: Exempt Full-time equivalent employment	25	30	29

United States Commission on International Religious Freedom

For necessary expenses for the United States Commission on International Religious Freedom, as authorized by title II of the International Religious Freedom Act of 1998 (Public Law 105–292), $3,000,000, to remain available until expended.

Program and Financing (in millions of dollars)

Identification code 48–2975–0–1–801		1999 actual	2000 est.	2001 est.
	Obligations by program activity:			
10.00	Total new obligations		3	3
	Budgetary resources available for obligation:			
21.40	Unobligated balance available, start of year		3	
22.00	New budget authority (gross)	3		3
23.90	Total budgetary resources available for obligation	3	3	3
23.95	Total new obligations		–3	–3
24.40	Unobligated balance available, end of year	3		
	New budget authority (gross), detail:			
	Discretionary:			
40.00	Appropriation	3		3
	Change in unpaid obligations:			
73.10	Total new obligations		3	3
73.20	Total outlays (gross)		–3	–3
	Outlays (gross), detail:			
86.90	Outlays from new discretionary authority			3
86.93	Outlays from discretionary balances		3	
87.00	Total outlays (gross)		3	3
	Net budget authority and outlays:			
89.00	Budget authority	3		3
90.00	Outlays		3	3

The Commission on International Religious Freedom, established in Public Law 105–292, is an independent agency charged with the annual and ongoing review and reporting of the facts and circumstances of violations of religious freedom. The Commission shall consider and recommend options for United States policies with respect to foreign countries which engage in or tolerate violations of religious freedom. Not later than May 1 of each year, the Commission shall submit a report to the President, the Secretary of State, and Congress.

Object Classification (in millions of dollars)

Identification code 48–2975–0–1–801		1999 actual	2000 est.	2001 est.
11.1	Direct obligations: Personnel compensation: Full-time permanent		1	1
99.5	Below reporting threshold		2	2
99.9	Total new obligations		3	3

Personnel Summary

Identification code 48–2975–0–1–801		1999 actual	2000 est.	2001 est.
1011	Total compensable workyears: Exempt Full-time equivalent employment		20	20

Gambling Impact Study Commission

salaries and expenses

Program and Financing (in millions of dollars)

Identification code 48–2101–0–1–801		1999 actual	2000 est.	2001 est.
	Obligations by program activity:			
10.00	Total new obligations (object class 99.5)	1		
	Budgetary resources available for obligation:			
21.40	Unobligated balance available, start of year	1		
23.95	Total new obligations	–1		
	New budget authority (gross), detail:			
	Discretionary:			
40.00	Appropriation			
	Change in unpaid obligations:			
72.40	Unpaid obligations, start of year: Obligated balance, start of year	2		
73.10	Total new obligations	1		
73.20	Total outlays (gross)	–3		
	Outlays (gross), detail:			
86.93	Outlays from discretionary balances	3		
	Net budget authority and outlays:			
89.00	Budget authority			
90.00	Outlays	3		

The National Gambling Impact Study Commission was established by Public Law 104–169 to conduct a comprehensive legal and factual study of the social and economic impacts of gambling in the United States. The Commission submitted its report in June 1999, and terminated in August 1999.

Personnel Summary

Identification code 48–2101–0–1–801		1999 actual	2000 est.	2001 est.
1011	Total compensable workyears: Exempt Full-time equivalent employment	10		

OTHER LEGISLATIVE BRANCH BOARDS AND COMMISSIONS

COMMISSION ON SECURITY AND COOPERATION IN EUROPE

SALARIES AND EXPENSES

For necessary expenses of the Commission on Security and Cooperation in Europe, as authorized by Public Law 94–304, [$1,182,000] *$1,370,000*, to remain available until expended as authorized by section 3 of Public Law 99–7. *(Departments of Commerce, Justice, and State, the Judiciary, and Related Agencies Appropriations Act, 2000, as enacted by section 1000(a)(1) of the Consolidated Appropriations Act, 2000 (P.L. 106–113).)*

[ADVISORY COMMISSION ON ELECTRONIC COMMERCE]

[For the necessary expenses of the Advisory Commission on Electronic Commerce, as authorized by Public Law 105–77, $1,400,000.] *(Departments of Commerce, Justice, and State, the Judiciary, and Related Agencies Appropriations Act, 2000, as enacted by section 1000(a)(1) of the Consolidated Appropriations Act, 2000 (P.L. 106–113).)*

Program and Financing (in millions of dollars)

Identification code 09–9911–0–1–999	1999 actual	2000 est.	2001 est.
Obligations by program activity:			
10.00 Total new obligations	4	2	1
Budgetary resources available for obligation:			
21.40 Unobligated balance available, start of year	3	3	3
22.00 New budget authority (gross)	4	2	1
23.90 Total budgetary resources available for obligation	7	5	4
23.95 Total new obligations	−4	−2	−1
24.40 Unobligated balance available, end of year	3	3	3
New budget authority (gross), detail:			
Discretionary:			
40.00 Appropriation	4	2	1
Change in unpaid obligations:			
72.40 Unpaid obligations, start of year: Obligated balance, start of year	1	1	1
73.10 Total new obligations	4	2	1
73.20 Total outlays (gross)	−3	−2	−2
74.40 Unpaid obligations, end of year: Obligated balance, end of year	1	1	1
Outlays (gross), detail:			
86.90 Outlays from new discretionary authority	3	2	1
86.93 Outlays from discretionary balances			1
87.00 Total outlays (gross)	3	2	2
Net budget authority and outlays:			
89.00 Budget authority	4	2	1
90.00 Outlays	3	2	2

This presentation includes a number of accounts including Competitiveness Policy Council; Commission on Immigration Reform; National Commission on Cost of Higher Education; National Commission on Restructuring the Internal Revenue Service and the following:

Oliver Wendell Holmes Devise Fund.—The Oliver Wendell Holmes Devise Fund and, the permanent committee for the Oliver Wendell Holmes devise to administer it, were created by an act of Congress, approved August 5, 1955 (69 Stat. 533).

The current program is devoted primarily to the preparation of a History of the Supreme Court of the United States, of which the first two volumes were published by the Macmillan Co. in 1972. The third, fourth and fifth volumes were published in August 1974, September 1981, and August 1985, respectively. The sixth and seventh volumes were published in 1988. The eighth volume was published in 1993. Additional volumes are nearing completion.

Commission on Security and Cooperation in Europe.—The Commission on Security and Cooperation in Europe is authorized and directed to monitor the acts of the signatories which reflect compliance with or violation of the articles of the Final Act of the Conference on Security and Cooperation in Europe, with particular regard to the provisions relating to Cooperation in Humanitarian Fields. The law establishing the Commission on Security and Cooperation in Europe also mandated it to monitor and encourage U.S. Government and private activities designed to expand East-West trade and the exchange of people and ideas. The Commission will receive semiannual reports from the President on the signatories' compliance with the Final Act and on U.S. activities in trade and cultural/humanitarian exchange and it will itself make advisory reports to the Congress on the progress of implementation.

The Commission is made up of nine Senators, nine Members of the House of Representatives and one Commissioner each from the Departments of State, Defense, and Commerce.

Advisory Commission on Electronic Commerce.—In 1998, the Congress of the United States passed the Internet Tax Freedom Act ("ITFA") which created the Advisory Commission on Electronic Commerce ("Commission"). The Commission is comprised of 19 members: three federal officials (the U.S. Trade Representative, and the Secretaries of Commerce and Treasury); eight state and local representatives, and eight business and consumer representatives. The mission of this Commission is to "conduct a thorough study of Federal, state and local, and international taxation and tariff treatment of transactions using the Internet and Internet access and other comparable intrastate, interstate or international sales activities." The Commission must then report its findings to Congress together with "such legislative recommendations as required to address the findings."

The Commission may include within the study, the following:

(1) An examination of: (a) barriers imposed in foreign markets on United States providers of property, goods, services, or information engaged in electronic commerce and on United States providers of telecommiunication services; and, (b) how the imposition of such barriers will affect United States consumers, the competitiveness of United States citizens providing property, goods, services or information in foreign markets and the growth and maturing of the Internet.

(2) An examination of the collection and administration of consumption taxes on electronic commerce and the impact of those activities on the global economy.

(3) An examination of the impact of the Internet and Internet access (particularly voice transmission) on the revenue base for the Federal communications excise tax.

(4) An examination of model state legislation that: a) would provide uniform definitions of categories of property, goods, services or information subject to or exempt from sales or use taxes; and b) would ensure that Internet access services, online services and communications and transactions using the Internet, Internet access services or online services would be treated in a tax and technologically neutral manner relative to other forms of remote sales.

(5) An examination of the effects of taxation (including the absence of taxation) on all interstate saies transactions (including transactions using the Internet), retail businesses, and state and local governments. This examination may include a review of the efforts of state and local governments to collect sales and use taxes owed on in-state purchases from out-of-state sellers.

(6) An examination of ways to simplify Federal and state and local taxation of the telecommunications services.

National Commission on Terrorism.—The Commission was created in Public Law 105–277 to review counter-terrorism policies regarding the prevention and punishment of international acts of terrorism directed at the United States. The Commission is composed of ten members, all appointed by the Congress. Funding to enable the Commission's work was appropriated in Public Law 106–31. The Commission's final report is expected to be submitted in May, 2000.

Dwight D. Eisenhower Memorial Commission.—The Commission was created in Public Law 106–79, the Defense Appropriations Act, to consider and formulate plans for a permanent memorial to Dwight D. Eisenhower.

Trade Deficit Review Commission.—The Commission was created in Public Law 105–277 to study the nature, causes, and consequences of the United States merchandise trade and current account deficits.

International Conferences and Contingencies.—The International Conferences and Contingencies account provides funds to cover the expenses of House and Senate participants in international meetings.

Copyright Royalty Tribunal.—Under Public Law 94–553, the general revision of the copyright law, an independent Copyright Royalty Tribunal was created in the Legislative Branch. The Tribunal is composed of three commissioners appointed by the President with the advice and consent of the Senate for staggered terms of 7 years each.

The Tribunal's statutory responsibilities are: (a) to make determinations concerning copyright royalty rates (1) in the area of cable television (17 U.S.C. 111), (2) for phonorecords (17 U.S.C. 115), (3) for coin-operated phonorecord players (jukeboxes) (17 U.S.C. 116), (4) for non-commercial broadcasting (17 U.S.C. 118), and (5) for digital audio devices (17 U.S.C. 1004); and (b) to distribute cable television, satellite carrier, jukebox, and digital audio devices and media royalties deposited with the Register of Copyrights (17 U.S.C. 111, 116, 119, 1005, and 1007).

Public Law 103–198 abolished the Copyright Royalty Tribunal and created a Copyright Arbitration Royalty Panel System administered by the Library of Congress Copyright Office.

Commission on the Advancement of Federal Law Enforcement.—The Commission was authorized in 1996 (P.L. 104–132) to review, ascertain, evaluate, and recommend action to Congress on a range of issues related to Federal law enforcement. The Commission is composed of five members, serving for its life, of whom: one is appointed by the President of the Senate; one is appointed by the Senate Minority Leader; one is appointed by the Speaker of the House; one is appointed by the House Minority Leader; and one, the Chairperson, is appointed by the Chief Justice of the Supreme Court. The Commission will issue a report on its findings in January, 2000.

Object Classification (in millions of dollars)

Identification code 09–9911–0–1–999	1999 actual	2000 est.	2001 est.
11.1 Direct obligations: Personnel compensation: Full-time permanent	1	1	1
99.5 Below reporting threshold	3	1	
99.9 Total new obligations	4	2	1

Personnel Summary

Identification code 09–9911–0–1–999	1999 actual	2000 est.	2001 est.
1011 Total compensable workyears: Exempt Full-time equivalent employment	19	15	15

Trust Funds

U.S. Capitol Preservation Commission

Unavailable Collections (in millions of dollars)

Identification code 09–8300–0–7–801	1999 actual	2000 est.	2001 est.
Balance, start of year:			
01.99 Balance, start of year			
Receipts:			
02.02 Interest on investments, U.S. Capitol Preservation Commission	1	1	8
Appropriation:			
05.01 Capitol Preservation Commission trust fund	−1	−1	−8
07.99 Total balance, end of year			

Program and Financing (in millions of dollars)

Identification code 09–8300–0–7–801	1999 actual	2000 est.	2001 est.
Budgetary resources available for obligation:			
21.40 Unobligated balance available, start of year	27	28	29
22.00 New budget authority (gross)	1	1	8
23.90 Total budgetary resources available for obligation	28	29	37
23.95 Total new obligations			
24.40 Unobligated balance available, end of year	28	29	37
New budget authority (gross), detail:			
Mandatory:			
60.27 Appropriation (trust fund, indefinite)	1	1	8
Net budget authority and outlays:			
89.00 Budget authority	1	1	8
90.00 Outlays			
Memorandum (non-add) entries:			
92.01 Total investments, start of year: U.S. securities: Par value	27	28	29
92.02 Total investments, end of year: U.S. securities: Par value	28	29	37

John C. Stennis Center for Public Service Training and Development

Unavailable Collections (in millions of dollars)

Identification code 09–8275–0–7–801	1999 actual	2000 est.	2001 est.
Balance, start of year:			
01.99 Balance, start of year			
Receipts:			
02.01 Interest	1	1	1
Appropriation:			
05.01 John C. Stennis Center for Public Service Development trust fund	−1	−1	−1
07.99 Total balance, end of year			

Program and Financing (in millions of dollars)

Identification code 09–8275–0–7–801	1999 actual	2000 est.	2001 est.
Obligations by program activity:			
10.00 Total new obligations (object class 99.5)	1	1	1
Budgetary resources available for obligation:			
21.40 Unobligated balance available, start of year	9	9	9
22.00 New budget authority (gross)	1	1	1
23.90 Total budgetary resources available for obligation	10	10	10
23.95 Total new obligations	−1	−1	−1
24.40 Unobligated balance available, end of year	9	9	9
New budget authority (gross), detail:			
Mandatory:			
60.27 Appropriation (trust fund, indefinite)	1	1	1
Change in unpaid obligations:			
73.10 Total new obligations	1	1	1
73.20 Total outlays (gross)	−1	−1	−1
Outlays (gross), detail:			
86.97 Outlays from new mandatory authority	1	1	1
Net budget authority and outlays:			
89.00 Budget authority	1	1	1
90.00 Outlays	1	1	1

JOHN C. STENNIS CENTER FOR PUBLIC SERVICE TRAINING AND DEVELOPMENT—Continued

Program and Financing (in millions of dollars)—Continued

Identification code 09–8275–0–7–801	1999 actual	2000 est.	2001 est.
Memorandum (non-add) entries:			
92.01 Total investments, start of year: U.S. securities: Par value	9	9	9
92.02 Total investments, end of year: U.S. securities: Par value	9	9	9

The principal for this fund was established by the transfer of $7,500,000 from the appropriation "Payment to the John C. Stennis Center".

Personnel Summary

Identification code 09–8275–0–7–801	1999 actual	2000 est.	2001 est.
1011 Total compensable workyears: Exempt Full-time equivalent employment	5	5	5

TITLE III—GENERAL PROVISIONS

SEC. 301. No part of the funds appropriated in this Act shall be used for the maintenance or care of private vehicles, except for emergency assistance and cleaning as may be provided under regulations relating to parking facilities for the House of Representatives issued by the Committee on House Administration and for the Senate issued by the Committee on Rules and Administration.

SEC. 302. No part of the funds appropriated in this Act shall remain available for obligation beyond fiscal year [2000] *2001* unless expressly so provided in this Act.

SEC. 303. Whenever in this Act any office or position not specifically established by the Legislative Pay Act of 1929 is appropriated for or the rate of compensation or designation of any office or position appropriated for is different from that specifically established by such Act, the rate of compensation and the designation in this Act shall be the permanent law with respect thereto: *Provided,* That the provisions in this Act for the various items of official expenses of Members, officers, and committees of the Senate and House of Representatives, and clerk hire for Senators and Members of the House of Representatives shall be the permanent law with respect thereto.

SEC. 304. The expenditure of any appropriation under this Act for any consulting service through procurement contract, pursuant to 5 U.S.C. 3109, shall be limited to those contracts where such expenditures are a matter of public record and available for public inspection, except where otherwise provided under existing law, or under existing Executive order issued pursuant to existing law.

SEC. 305. (a) It is the sense of the Congress that, to the greatest extent practicable, all equipment and products purchased with funds made available in this Act should be American-made.

(b) In providing financial assistance to, or entering into any contract with, any entity using funds made available in this Act, the head of each Federal agency, to the greatest extent practicable, shall provide to such entity a notice describing the statement made in subsection (a) by the Congress.

(c) If it has been finally determined by a court or Federal agency that any person intentionally affixed a label bearing a "Made in America" inscription, or any inscription with the same meaning, to any product sold in or shipped to the United States that is not made in the United States, such person shall be ineligible to receive any contract or subcontract made with funds provided pursuant to this Act, pursuant to the debarment, suspension, and ineligibility procedures described in section 9.400 through 9.409 of title 48, Code of Federal Regulations.

SEC. 306. Such sums as may be necessary are appropriated to the account described in subsection (a) of section 415 of Public Law 104–1 to pay awards and settlements as authorized under such subsection.

SEC. 307. Amounts available for administrative expenses of any legislative branch entity which participates in the Legislative Branch Financial Managers Council (LBFMC) established by charter on March 26, 1996, shall be available to finance an appropriate share of LBFMC costs as determined by the LBFMC, except that the total LBFMC costs to be shared among all participating legislative branch entities (in such allocations among the entities as the entities may determine) may not exceed [$1,500] *$252,000*.

[SEC. 308. Section 308 of the Legislative Branch Appropriations Act, 1999 (Public Law 105–275; 112 Stat. 2452) is amended—

(1) in subsection (b), by striking "(40 U.S.C. 174j–1(b)(1))" and inserting "(40 U.S.C. 174j–1 note)";

(2) in subsection (c), by striking "(40 U.S.C. 174j–1(c))" and inserting "(40 U.S.C. 174j–1 note)"; and

(3) in subsection (d), by striking "(40 U.S.C. 174j–1(e))" and inserting "(40 U.S.C. 174j–1 note)".]

SEC. [309] *308*. Section 316 of Public Law 101–302 is amended in the first sentence of subsection (a) by striking ["1999"] *"2000"* and inserting ["2000"] *"2001"*.

[SEC. 310. Chapter 5 of title II of division B of the Omnibus Consolidated and Emergency Supplemental Appropriations Act, 1999 (Public Law 105–277; 112 Stat. 2681–569) is amended in the matter under the subheading "CAPITOL VISITOR CENTER" under the heading "ARCHITECT OF THE CAPITOL" by striking "the Committee on Rules and Administration of the Senate, the Committee on House Oversight of the House of Representatives, the Committees on Appropriations of the House of Representatives and of the Senate, and other appropriate committees of the House of Representatives and of the Senate" and inserting "the United States Capitol Preservation Commission established under section 801 of the Arizona-Idaho Conservation Act of 1988 (40 U.S.C. 188a)".]

[SEC. 311. TRADE DEFICIT REVIEW COMMISSION. (a) APPROPRIATIONS.—Section 127(i) of the Trade Deficit Review Commission Act (19 U.S.C. 2213 note) is amended by adding at the end the following new sentence:

"Amounts appropriated pursuant to this subsection shall remain available until the date which is 90 days after the date on which the Commission submits the final report described in subsection (e).".

(b) APPLICABILITY OF CERTAIN PAY AUTHORITIES TO MEMBERS OF THE COMMISSION.—Section 127(g) of the Trade Deficit Review Commission Act is amended by adding at the end the following new paragraph:

"(6) APPLICABILITY OF CERTAIN PAY AUTHORITIES.—

"(A) IN GENERAL.—An individual who is a member of the Commission and is an annuitant or otherwise covered by section 8344 or 8468 of title 5, United States Code, by reason of membership on the Commission is not subject to the provisions of section 8344 or 8468 (whichever is applicable) with respect to such membership.

"(B) UNIFORMED SERVICE.—An individual who is a member of the Commission and is a member or former member of a uniformed service is not subject to the provisions of subsections (b) and (c) of section 5532, United States Code, with respect to membership on the Commission.".

(c) TERMINATION OF COMMISSION AND OTHER MATTERS.—Section 127 of the Trade Deficit Review Commission Act is amended by adding at the end the following new subsections:

"(j) FEDERAL ADVISORY COMMITTEE ACT.—The provisions of the Federal Advisory Committee Act (Public Law 92–463; 5 U.S.C. App.) shall not apply to the Commission.

"(k) TERMINATION.—The Commission shall terminate 90 days after the date on which the Commission submits the final report under subsection (e).".]

[SEC. 312. CREDITABLE SERVICE WITH CONGRESSIONAL CAMPAIGN COMMITTEES. Section 8332(m)(1)(A) of title 5, United States Code, is amended to read as follows:

"(A) such employee has at least 4 years and 6 months of service on such committees as of December 12, 1980; and".

SEC. 313. Section 507 of Public Law 104–1 (109 Stat. 43; 2 U.S.C. 1436) is repealed.] *(Legislative Branch Appropriations Act, 2000.)*

JUDICIAL BRANCH

SUPREME COURT OF THE UNITED STATES

Federal Funds

General and special funds:

SALARIES AND EXPENSES

For expenses necessary for the operation of the Supreme Court, as required by law, excluding care of the building and grounds, including purchase or hire, driving, maintenance, and operation of an automobile for the Chief Justice, not to exceed $10,000 for the purpose of transporting Associate Justices, and hire of passenger motor vehicles as authorized by 31 U.S.C. 1343 and 1344; not to exceed $10,000 for official reception and representation expenses; and for miscellaneous expenses, to be expended as the Chief Justice may approve; [$35,492,000] *$37,745,000*. *(The Judiciary Appropriations Act, 2000, as enacted by section 1000(a)(1) of the Consolidated Appropriations Act, 2000 (P.L. 106–113).)*

Program and Financing (in millions of dollars)

Identification code 10–0100–0–1–752		1999 actual	2000 est.	2001 est.
	Obligations by program activity:			
10.00	Total new obligations	31	36	38
	Budgetary resources available for obligation:			
21.40	Unobligated balance available, start of year	....	1	....
22.00	New budget authority (gross)	32	35	38
23.90	Total budgetary resources available for obligation	32	36	38
23.95	Total new obligations	−31	−36	−38
24.40	Unobligated balance available, end of year	1	....	....
	New budget authority (gross), detail:			
	Discretionary:			
40.00	Appropriation	29	34	36
	Mandatory:			
60.00	Appropriation	2	2	2
70.00	Total new budget authority (gross)	31	36	38
	Change in unpaid obligations:			
72.40	Unpaid obligations, start of year: Obligated balance, start of year	10	10	11
73.10	Total new obligations	31	36	38
73.20	Total outlays (gross)	−29	−35	−36
73.40	Adjustments in expired accounts (net)	−2	....	....
74.40	Unpaid obligations, end of year: Obligated balance, end of year	10	11	15
	Outlays (gross), detail:			
86.90	Outlays from new discretionary authority	24	28	30
86.93	Outlays from discretionary balances	3	5	4
86.97	Outlays from new mandatory authority	2	2	2
87.00	Total outlays (gross)	29	35	36
	Net budget authority and outlays:			
89.00	Budget authority	32	36	38
90.00	Outlays	29	35	36

The Supreme Court of the United States is the highest court of our country and stands at the apex of the judicial branch of our constitutional form of government. The U.S. Supreme Court is the only constitutionally indispensable court in the Federal court system of the United States. The jurisdiction of the Supreme Court is spelled out in the Constitution and allotted by Congress. The funds herein requested are required to enable the U.S. Supreme Court to carry out its constitutional and congressionally allotted responsibilities.

Object Classification (in millions of dollars)

Identification code 10–0100–0–1–752		1999 actual	2000 est.	2001 est.
	Personnel compensation:			
11.1	Full-time permanent	18	20	21
11.3	Other than full-time permanent	1	2	2
11.9	Total personnel compensation	19	22	23
12.1	Civilian personnel benefits	4	5	6
24.0	Printing and reproduction	1	1	1
25.2	Other services	3	4	4
26.0	Supplies and materials	1	1	1
31.0	Equipment	3	3	3
99.9	Total new obligations	31	36	38

Personnel Summary

Identification code 10–0100–0–1–752		1999 actual	2000 est.	2001 est.
1011	Total compensable workyears: Exempt Full-time equivalent employment	371	411	414

CARE OF THE [BUILDINGS] *BUILDING* AND GROUNDS

For such expenditures as may be necessary to enable the Architect of the Capitol to carry out the duties imposed upon the Architect by the Act approved May 7, 1934 (40 U.S.C. 13a–13b), [$8,002,000] *$7,530,000*, of which [$5,101,000] *$4,460,000* shall remain available until expended. *(The Judiciary Appropriations Act, 2000, as enacted by section 1000(a)(1) of the Consolidated Appropriations Act, 2000 (P.L. 106–113).)*

Program and Financing (in millions of dollars)

Identification code 10–0103–0–1–752		1999 actual	2000 est.	2001 est.
	Obligations by program activity:			
10.00	Total new obligations	4	7	6
	Budgetary resources available for obligation:			
21.40	Unobligated balance available, start of year	1	2	3
22.00	New budget authority (gross)	5	8	8
23.90	Total budgetary resources available for obligation	6	10	10
23.95	Total new obligations	−4	−7	−6
24.40	Unobligated balance available, end of year	2	3	4
	New budget authority (gross), detail:			
	Discretionary:			
40.00	Appropriation	5	8	8
	Change in unpaid obligations:			
72.40	Unpaid obligations, start of year: Obligated balance, start of year	1	1	1
73.10	Total new obligations	4	7	6
73.20	Total outlays (gross)	−4	−7	−6
74.40	Unpaid obligations, end of year: Obligated balance, end of year	1	1	1
	Outlays (gross), detail:			
86.90	Outlays from new discretionary authority	3	5	4
86.93	Outlays from discretionary balances	1	2	3
87.00	Total outlays (gross)	4	7	6
	Net budget authority and outlays:			
89.00	Budget authority	5	8	8
90.00	Outlays	4	7	6

General and special funds—Continued

CARE OF THE [BUILDINGS] *BUILDING* AND GROUNDS—Continued

Object Classification (in millions of dollars)

Identification code 10–0103–0–1–752	1999 actual	2000 est.	2001 est.
11.1 Personnel compensation: Full-time permanent	1	1	2
23.3 Communications, utilities, and miscellaneous charges	1	1	1
25.2 Other services	2	5	3
99.9 Total new obligations	4	7	6

Personnel Summary

Identification code 10–0103–0–1–752	1999 actual	2000 est.	2001 est.
1011 Total compensable workyears: Exempt Full-time equivalent employment	21	26	26

UNITED STATES COURT OF APPEALS FOR THE FEDERAL CIRCUIT

Federal Funds

General and special funds:

SALARIES AND EXPENSES

For salaries of the chief judge, judges, and other officers and employees, and for necessary expenses of the court, as authorized by law, [$16,797,000] *$19,533,000. (The Judiciary Appropriations Act, 2000, as enacted by section 1000(a)(1) of the Consolidated Appropriations Act, 2000 (P.L. 106–113).)*

Program and Financing (in millions of dollars)

Identification code 10–0510–0–1–752	1999 actual	2000 est.	2001 est.
Obligations by program activity:			
10.00 Total new obligations	16	17	20
Budgetary resources available for obligation:			
22.00 New budget authority (gross)	16	17	20
23.95 Total new obligations	−16	−17	−20
New budget authority (gross), detail:			
Discretionary:			
40.00 Appropriation	14	15	17
Mandatory:			
60.00 Appropriation	2	2	3
70.00 Total new budget authority (gross)	16	17	20
Change in unpaid obligations:			
72.40 Unpaid obligations, start of year: Obligated balance, start of year	7	3	4
73.10 Total new obligations	16	17	20
73.20 Total outlays (gross)	−16	−16	−18
73.40 Adjustments in expired accounts (net)	−4		
74.40 Unpaid obligations, end of year: Obligated balance, end of year	3	4	6
Outlays (gross), detail:			
86.90 Outlays from new discretionary authority	11	11	12
86.93 Outlays from discretionary balances	3	3	4
86.97 Outlays from new mandatory authority	2	2	2
87.00 Total outlays (gross)	16	16	18
Net budget authority and outlays:			
89.00 Budget authority	16	17	20
90.00 Outlays	16	16	18

The United States Court of Appeals for the Federal Circuit has exclusive nationwide jurisdiction over a large number of diverse subject areas, such as appeals in all patent cases, all government contract cases, all cases involving monetary claims against the United States under the Tucker Acts, veterans cases, and many others. Additional subject areas have been added to this Court's jurisdiction almost yearly. To keep abreast of its varied and growing jurisdiction, the court is requesting necessary increases in its funding as detailed below.

The following is a more complete listing of the Federal Circuit's exclusive jurisdiction. It hears appeals from: (A) final decisions of all Federal district courts in cases arising under 28 U.S.C. §1338(a), relating to patent laws generally, 35 U.S.C. §§145–146, relating to review of decisions of the Patent and Trademark Office, Board of Patent Appeals and Interferences, 28 U.S.C. §1346(a)(2), relating to Little Tucker Act claims against the United States, and section 211 of the Economic Stabilization Act of 1970, section 5 of the Emergency Petroleum Allocation Act of 1973, section 506(c) of the Natural Gas Policy Act of 1978, and section 523 of the Energy Policy and Conservation Act, relating to all statutes formerly under the jurisdiction of the Temporary Emergency Court of Appeals; (B) final decisions of the United States Court of International Trade, 28 U.S.C. §2645(c); (C) final decisions of the United States Court of Veterans Appeals, 38 U.S.C. §7292; (D) final decisions of the United States Court of Federal Claims, 28 U.S.C. §2522 and 42 U.S.C. §§300aa–12(f); (E) final decisions of the High Court of the Trust Territory of the Pacific Islands, 48 U.S.C. §1681 note (1988) (Compact of Free Association; Federated States of Micronesia, Republic of Marshall Islands, TITLE II, Title One, Article VII, §174(c)); (F) final determinations of the United States International Trade Commission relating to unfair practices in import trade made under 19 U.S.C. §1337; (G) findings of the Secretary of Commerce under U.S. note 6 to subchapter X of chapter 98 of the Harmonized Tariff Schedule of the United States relating to importation of educational or scientific instruments and apparatus; (H) final orders or decisions of the Merit Systems Protection Board and certain arbitrators, 5 U.S.C. §7703; (I) final decisions of the General Accounting Office Personnel Appeals Board, 31 U.S.C. §755; (J) final decisions of all agency Boards of Contract Appeals, 41 U.S.C. §607(g); (K) final decisions of the Patent and Trademark Office tribunals on patent applications and interferences, trademark applications and interferences, cancellations, concurrent use proceedings, and oppositions, 35 U.S.C. §142, 15 U.S.C. §1071, 37 CFR §§1.304, 2.145; (L) appeals under section 71 of the Plant Variety Protection Act of 1970, 7 U.S.C. §2461; (M) certain actions of the Secretary of Veterans Affairs, 38 U.S.C. §502; (N) certain final orders of the Equal Employment Opportunity Commission relating to certain Presidential appointees, 2 U.S.C. §1219(a)(3) and 28 U.S.C. §2344; (O) final decisions of the Office of Personnel Management under 5 U.S.C. §8902a(g)(2); (P) certain actions of the Board of Directors of the Office of Compliance of the U.S. Congress under 2 U.S.C. §1407(a); and (Q) final decisions of certain agencies pursuant to 28 U.S.C. §1296. (This is a new section of T.28 established by the Presidential and Executive Office Accountability Act of 1996, P.L. 104–331.)

The Federal Circuit also has exclusive jurisdiction pursuant to 28 U.S.C. §1292(c) of: (1) appealable interlocutory orders or decrees in cases where the court would otherwise have jurisdiction over an appeal; and (2) appeals from judgments in civil actions for patent infringement otherwise appealable to the court and final except for accounting. Under the provisions of 28 U.S.C. §1292(d), the court has: (1) exclusive jurisdiction of appeals from interlocutory orders granting or denying, in whole or in part, a motion to transfer an action to the Court of Federal Claims; and (2) may, in its discretion, permit an appeal from an interlocutory order of a judge who certifies that there is a controlling question of law and a substantial ground for difference of opinion thereon, and that an immediate appeal may materially advance the ultimate termination of the litigation. Pursuant to 38 U.S.C. §7292(b)(1), the court has exclusive jurisdiction of certain interlocutory orders of the Court of Veterans Appeals.

New legislation having an impact on the Federal Circuit is contained in P.L. 105–339 (51021) October 31, 1998, Veterans Opportunities Act of 1998.

Object Classification (in millions of dollars)

Identification code 10–0510–0–1–752		1999 actual	2000 est.	2001 est.
11.1	Personnel compensation: Full-time permanent	8	9	10
12.1	Civilian personnel benefits	1	1	2
23.1	Rental payments to GSA	4	4	4
25.2	Other services	2	1	2
31.0	Equipment	1	1	1
99.0	Subtotal, direct obligations	16	16	19
99.5	Below reporting threshold		1	1
99.9	Total new obligations	16	17	20

Personnel Summary

Identification code 10–0510–0–1–752		1999 actual	2000 est.	2001 est.
1011	Total compensable workyears: Exempt Full-time equivalent employment	113	116	123

UNITED STATES COURT OF INTERNATIONAL TRADE

Federal Funds

General and special funds:

SALARIES AND EXPENSES

For salaries of the chief judge and eight judges, salaries of the officers and employees of the court, services as authorized by 5 U.S.C. 3109, and necessary expenses of the court, as authorized by law, [$11,957,000] *$12,506,000*. *(The Judiciary Appropriations Act, 2000, as enacted by section 1000(a)(1) of the Consolidated Appropriations Act, 2000 (P.L. 106–113).)*

Program and Financing (in millions of dollars)

Identification code 10–0400–0–1–752		1999 actual	2000 est.	2001 est.
	Obligations by program activity:			
10.00	Total new obligations	12	12	13
	Budgetary resources available for obligation:			
22.00	New budget authority (gross)	12	12	13
23.95	Total new obligations	−12	−12	−13
	New budget authority (gross), detail:			
	Discretionary:			
40.00	Appropriation	11	10	11
41.00	Transferred to other accounts	−1		
43.00	Appropriation (total discretionary)	10	10	11
	Mandatory:			
60.00	Appropriation	2	2	2
70.00	Total new budget authority (gross)	12	12	13
	Change in unpaid obligations:			
72.40	Unpaid obligations, start of year: Obligated balance, start of year	1	1	1
73.10	Total new obligations	12	12	13
73.20	Total outlays (gross)	−12	−12	−13
74.40	Unpaid obligations, end of year: Obligated balance, end of year	1	1	1
	Outlays (gross), detail:			
86.90	Outlays from new discretionary authority	9	10	10
86.93	Outlays from discretionary balances	1		1
86.97	Outlays from new mandatory authority	2	2	2
87.00	Total outlays (gross)	12	12	13
	Net budget authority and outlays:			
89.00	Budget authority	12	12	13
90.00	Outlays	12	12	13

The United States Court of International Trade, established under Article III of the Constitution of the United States, was created by the Act of October 10, 1980 (94 Stat. 1727), effective November 1, 1980, as successor to the former United States Customs Court. The court has original and exclusive jurisdiction of civil actions against the United States, its agencies and officers, and certain civil actions brought by the United States, arising out of import transactions and Federal statutes affecting international trade. The court possesses all the powers in law and equity of, or as conferred by statute upon, a district court of the United States, and is authorized to conduct jury trials. The geographical jurisdiction of the court is nationwide and trials before the court or hearings may be held at any place within the jurisdiction of the United States. The court also is authorized to hold hearings in foreign countries. The principal statutory provisions pertaining to the court are contained in the following sections of title 28 of the United States Code: Organization, sections 251 to 258; Jurisdiction, sections 1581 to 1585; and Procedures, sections 2631–2646.

Object Classification (in millions of dollars)

Identification code 10–0400–0–1–752		1999 actual	2000 est.	2001 est.
11.1	Personnel compensation: Full-time permanent	4	5	5
12.1	Civilian personnel benefits	1	1	1
23.1	Rental payments to GSA	5	5	5
25.2	Other services		1	1
31.0	Equipment	1		
99.0	Subtotal, direct obligations	11	12	12
99.5	Below reporting threshold	1		1
99.9	Total new obligations	12	12	13

Personnel Summary

Identification code 10–0400–0–1–752		1999 actual	2000 est.	2001 est.
1011	Total compensable workyears: Exempt Full-time equivalent employment	73	80	80

COURTS OF APPEALS, DISTRICT COURTS, AND OTHER JUDICIAL SERVICES

Federal Funds

General and special funds:

SALARIES AND EXPENSES

(INCLUDING TRANSFER OF FUNDS)

For the salaries of circuit and district judges (including judges of the territorial courts of the United States), justices and judges retired from office or from regular active service, judges of the United States Court of Federal Claims, bankruptcy judges, magistrate judges, and all other officers and employees of the Federal Judiciary not otherwise specifically provided for, and necessary expenses of the courts, as authorized by law, [$2,958,138,000] *$3,498,694,000* (including the purchase of firearms and ammunition); of which not to exceed [$13,454,000] *$17,817,000* shall remain available until expended for space alteration projects; and of which not to exceed $10,000,000 shall remain available until expended for furniture and furnishings related to new space alteration and construction projects.

[In addition, for activities of the Federal Judiciary as authorized by law, $156,539,000, to remain available until expended, which shall be derived from the Violent Crime Reduction Trust Fund, as authorized by section 190001(a) of Public Law 103–322, and sections 818 and 823 of Public Law 104–132.]

In addition, for expenses of the United States Court of Federal Claims associated with processing cases under the National Childhood Vaccine Injury Act of 1986, not to exceed [$2,515,000] *$2,602,000*, to be appropriated from the Vaccine Injury Compensation Trust Fund. *(The Judiciary Appropriations Act, 2000, as enacted by section 1000(a)(1) of the Consolidated Appropriations Act, 2000 (P.L. 106–113).)*

General and special funds—Continued

SALARIES AND EXPENSES—Continued

(INCLUDING TRANSFER OF FUNDS)—Continued

Program and Financing (in millions of dollars)

Identification code 10–0920–0–1–752		1999 actual	2000 est.	2001 est.
	Obligations by program activity:			
	Direct program:			
00.01	Courts of appeals	324	354	408
00.02	District courts	1,380	1,441	1,656
00.03	Bankruptcy courts	553	575	671
00.04	Probation/Pretrial	587	618	764
09.01	Reimbursable program	280	418	213
10.00	Total new obligations	3,124	3,406	3,712
	Budgetary resources available for obligation:			
21.40	Unobligated balance available, start of year	37	16	
22.00	New budget authority (gross)	3,103	3,390	3,712
23.90	Total budgetary resources available for obligation	3,140	3,406	3,712
23.95	Total new obligations	−3,124	−3,406	−3,712
24.40	Unobligated balance available, end of year	16		
	New budget authority (gross), detail:			
	Discretionary:			
40.00	Appropriation	2,599	2,732	3,251
42.00	Transferred from other accounts	1	4	
43.00	Appropriation (total discretionary)	2,600	2,736	3,251
	Mandatory:			
60.00	Appropriation	223	236	248
	Discretionary:			
68.00	Spending authority from offsetting collections: Offsetting collections (cash)	280	418	213
70.00	Total new budget authority (gross)	3,103	3,390	3,712
	Change in unpaid obligations:			
72.40	Unpaid obligations, start of year: Obligated balance, start of year	144	102	111
73.10	Total new obligations	3,124	3,406	3,712
73.20	Total outlays (gross)	−3,171	−3,397	−3,702
73.40	Adjustments in expired accounts (net)	5		
74.40	Unpaid obligations, end of year: Obligated balance, end of year	102	111	121
	Outlays (gross), detail:			
86.90	Outlays from new discretionary authority	2,804	3,059	3,344
86.93	Outlays from discretionary balances	144	102	111
86.97	Outlays from new mandatory authority	223	236	248
87.00	Total outlays (gross)	3,171	3,397	3,702
	Offsets:			
	Against gross budget authority and outlays:			
	Offsetting collections (cash) from:			
88.00	Federal sources	−239	−377	−171
88.40	Non-Federal sources—User Fee	−41	−41	−42
88.90	Total, offsetting collections (cash)	−280	−418	−213
	Net budget authority and outlays:			
89.00	Budget authority	2,823	2,972	3,499
90.00	Outlays	2,891	2,979	3,489

Funds appropriated under this heading are for the salaries and benefits of judges and supporting personnel and all operating expenses of the United States courts of appeals, district courts, bankruptcy courts, and United States Court of Federal Claims and are shown by activity:

Courts of Appeals.—This activity includes the salaries and benefits of all active United States circuit judges, and all such judges who have retired from office or from regular active service in pursuance of law. In addition, it provides for the salaries and expenses of the Courts of Appeals supporting personnel such as the administrative and legal aides required to assist the judges in the hearing and decision of appeals, and other judicial functions including all expenses of operation and maintenance such as travel expenses incurred by judges and supporting personnel in attending sessions of court or transacting other official business, and for relocation expenses, communications, printing, contractual services, supplies, equipment, and lawbooks and for rental of space, alterations, and related services for United States court facilities.

District Courts.—This activity includes the salaries and benefits of all active United States district judges, magistrate judges and all such judges who have retired from office or from regular active service in pursuance of law. In addition, it provides for the salaries and expenses of the District Court supporting personnel such as the administrative and legal aides required to assist the judges in conduct of hearings, trials, and other judicial functions including all expenses of operation and maintenance such as travel expenses incurred by judges and supporting personnel in attending sessions of court or transacting other official business, and for relocation expenses, communications, printing, contractual services, supplies, equipment, and lawbooks and for rental of space, alterations, and related services for United States court facilities.

Bankruptcy Courts.—This activity includes the salaries and benefits of all active United States bankruptcy judges. In addition, it provides for the salaries and expenses of the Bankruptcy Court supporting personnel including all expenses of operation and maintenance such as travel expenses incurred by judges and supporting personnel in attending sessions of court or transacting other official business, and for relocation expenses, communications, printing, contractual services, supplies, equipment, and lawbooks and for rental of space, alterations, and related services for United States court facilities.

Probation/Pretrial.—This activity includes the salaries and benefits of all probation and pretrial services officers and supporting personnel. It provides for all expenses of operation and maintenance such as travel expenses incurred by probation officers and supporting personnel in attending sessions of court or transacting other official business, and for relocation expenses, communications, printing, contractual services, supplies, equipment, and lawbooks and for rental of space, alterations, and related services for Federal Probation Service facilities.

Object Classification (in millions of dollars)

Identification code 10–0920–0–1–752		1999 actual	2000 est.	2001 est.
	Direct obligations:			
	Personnel compensation:			
11.1	Full-time permanent	1,403	1,588	1,762
11.3	Other than full-time permanent	159	159	159
11.9	Total personnel compensation	1,562	1,747	1,921
12.1	Civilian personnel benefits	361	414	461
13.0	Benefits for former personnel	1	2	2
21.0	Travel and transportation of persons	28	20	27
22.0	Transportation of things	4	3	3
23.1	Rental payments to GSA	491	487	669
23.2	Rental payments to others	18	15	20
23.3	Communications, utilities, and miscellaneous charges	59	51	66
24.0	Printing and reproduction	15	15	18
25.2	Other services	141	94	129
26.0	Supplies and materials	18	15	21
31.0	Equipment	146	125	162
99.0	Subtotal, direct obligations	2,844	2,988	3,499
99.0	Reimbursable obligations	280	418	213
99.9	Total new obligations	3,124	3,406	3,712

Personnel Summary

Identification code 10–0920–0–1–752		1999 actual	2000 est.	2001 est.
	Direct:			
1011	Total compensable workyears: Exempt Full-time equivalent employment	27,780	28,714	30,322

	Reimbursable:			
2011	Total compensable workyears: Exempt Full-time equivalent employment	21	21	21

Defender Services

For the operation of Federal Public Defender and Community Defender organizations; the compensation and reimbursement of expenses of attorneys appointed to represent persons under the Criminal Justice Act of 1964, as amended; the compensation and reimbursement of expenses of persons furnishing investigative, expert and other services under the Criminal Justice Act of 1964 (18 U.S.C. 3006A(e)); the compensation (in accordance with Criminal Justice Act maximums) and reimbursement of expenses of attorneys appointed to assist the court in criminal cases where the defendant has waived representation by counsel; the compensation and reimbursement of travel expenses of guardians ad litem acting on behalf of financially eligible minor or incompetent offenders in connection with transfers from the United States to foreign countries with which the United States has a treaty for the execution of penal sentences; and the compensation of attorneys appointed to represent jurors in civil actions for the protection of their employment, as authorized by 28 U.S.C. 1875(d), [$358,848,000] *$440,351,000*, to remain available until expended as authorized by 18 U.S.C. 3006A(i).

[In addition, for activities of the Federal Judiciary as authorized by law, $26,247,000, to remain available until expended, which shall be derived from the Violent Crime Reduction Trust Fund, as authorized by section 19001(a) of Public Law 103–322, and sections 818 and 823 of Public Law 104–132.] *(The Judiciary Appropriations Act, 2000, as enacted by section 1000(a)(1) of the Consolidated Appropriations Act, 2000 (P.L. 106–113).)*

Program and Financing (in millions of dollars)

Identification code 10–0923–0–1–752		1999 actual	2000 est.	2001 est.
	Direct program:			
	Direct program:			
00.01	Federal Defender Organizations	211	245	267
00.02	Panel attorneys	121	132	173
00.04	General administrative expenses	2	4	4
09.10	VCRTF—Reimbursable Panel Attorneys	31	26	....
10.00	Total new obligations	365	407	444
	Budgetary resources available for obligation:			
21.40	Unobligated balance available, start of year	7	36	4
22.00	New budget authority (gross)	392	375	440
22.10	Resources available from recoveries of prior year obligations	2	....	....
23.90	Total budgetary resources available for obligation	401	411	444
23.95	Total new obligations	−365	−407	−444
24.40	Unobligated balance available, end of year	36	4	....
	New budget authority (gross), detail:			
	Discretionary:			
40.00	Appropriation	361	359	440
40.76	Reduction pursuant to P.L. 106–113	....	−6	....
41.00	Transferred to other accounts	....	−4	....
43.00	Appropriation (total discretionary)	361	349	440
68.00	Spending authority from offsetting collections: Offsetting collections (VCRTF)	31	26	....
70.00	Total new budget authority (gross)	392	375	440
	Change in unpaid obligations:			
72.40	Unpaid obligations, start of year: Obligated balance, start of year	12	15	16
73.10	Total new obligations	365	407	444
73.20	Total outlays (gross)	−361	−405	−443
73.45	Adjustments in unexpired accounts	−2	....	....
74.40	Unpaid obligations, end of year: Obligated balance, end of year	15	16	18
	Outlays (gross), detail:			
86.90	Outlays from new discretionary authority	349	355	422
86.93	Outlays from discretionary balances	12	51	20
87.00	Total outlays (gross)	361	405	443
	Offsets:			
	Against gross budget authority and outlays:			
88.00	Offsetting collections (cash) from: Federal sources VCRTF	−31	−26	....
	Net budget authority and outlays:			
89.00	Budget authority	361	349	440
90.00	Outlays	330	379	443

Funds appropriated under this heading provide for the administration and operation of the Criminal Justice Act of 1964 (18 U.S.C. 3006A), as amended, which provides for furnishing representation for any person financially unable to obtain adequate representation who: (1) is charged with a felony or Class A, B, and C misdemeanor or infraction for which a sentence to confinement is authorized, or with committing an act of juvenile delinquency, or with a violation of probation; (2) is under arrest, when such representation is required by law; (3) is entitled to appointment of counsel in parole proceedings (18 U.S.C. 311); (4) is charged with a violation of supervised release or faces modification, reduction, or enlargement of condition, or extension or revocation of a term of supervised release; (5) is subject to a mental condition hearing (18 U.S.C. 311); (6) is in custody as a material witness; (7) is entitled to appointment of counsel under the sixth amendment to the Constitution; (8) faces loss of liberty in a case, and Federal law requires the appointment of counsel; (9) is entitled to the appointment of counsel under 18 U.S.C. 4109; or (10) is seeking relief under 28 U.S.C. 2241, 2254, or 2255. Representation includes counsel and investigative, expert, and other necessary services. The appropriation includes funding for the compensation and expenses of court-appointed counsel and persons providing investigative, expert and other services under the Act, for the operation of the Federal Defender organizations, and for the continuing education and training of persons providing representational services under the Act. In addition, this appropriation is available for the compensation of counsel: (1) appointed pursuant to 5 U.S.C. 3109 to assist the court in criminal cases where the defendant has waived representation by counsel; and (2) appointed pursuant to 28 U.S.C. 1875 to represent jurors in civil actions for the protection of their employment.

Object Classification (in millions of dollars)

Identification code 10–0923–0–1–752		1999 actual	2000 est.	2001 est.
	Direct obligations:			
11.1	Personnel compensation: Full-time permanent	103	121	134
12.1	Civilian personnel benefits	27	31	34
21.0	Travel and transportation of persons	4	5	5
23.1	Rental payments to GSA	16	18	19
23.3	Communications, utilities, and miscellaneous charges	4	4	4
	Other services:			
25.2	Compensation and out-of-pocket expenses of court-appointed counsel	100	112	154
25.2	Transcripts	7	8	8
25.2	Investigators, interpreters, psychiatrists, and other experts	18	19	20
25.2	Other services	3	3	3
26.0	Supplies and materials	1	1	1
31.0	Equipment	5	6	6
41.0	Grants, subsidies, and contributions	46	53	56
99.0	Subtotal, direct obligations	334	381	444
99.0	Reimbursable obligations	31	26	....
99.9	Total new obligations	365	407	444

Personnel Summary

Identification code 10–0923–0–1–752		1999 actual	2000 est.	2001 est.
1011	Total compensable workyears: Exempt Full-time equivalent employment	1,589	1,751	1,830

General and special funds—Continued

FEES OF JURORS AND COMMISSIONERS

For fees and expenses of jurors as authorized by 28 U.S.C. 1871 and 1876; compensation of jury commissioners as authorized by 28 U.S.C. 1863; and compensation of commissioners appointed in condemnation cases pursuant to rule 71A(h) of the Federal Rules of Civil Procedure (28 U.S.C. Appendix Rule 71A(h)), [$60,918,000] *$60,821,000*, to remain available until expended: *Provided*, That the compensation of land commissioners shall not exceed the daily equivalent of the highest rate payable under section 5332 of title 5, United States Code. *(The Judiciary Appropriations Act, 2000, as enacted by section 1000(a)(1) of the Consolidated Appropriations Act, 2000 (P.L. 106–113).)*

Program and Financing (in millions of dollars)

Identification code 10–0925–0–1–752	1999 actual	2000 est.	2001 est.
Obligations by program activity:			
00.03 Grand jurors	16	17	17
00.04 Petit jurors	47	46	44
10.00 Total new obligations	63	63	61
Budgetary resources available for obligation:			
21.40 Unobligated balance available, start of year	5	9	
22.00 New budget authority (gross)	67	54	61
23.90 Total budgetary resources available for obligation	72	63	61
23.95 Total new obligations	−63	−63	−61
24.40 Unobligated balance available, end of year	9		
New budget authority (gross), detail:			
Discretionary:			
40.00 Appropriation	67	61	61
40.76 Reduction pursuant to P.L. 106–113		−7	
43.00 Appropriation (total discretionary)	67	54	61
Change in unpaid obligations:			
72.40 Unpaid obligations, start of year: Obligated balance, start of year	3	5	5
73.10 Total new obligations	63	63	61
73.20 Total outlays (gross)	−61	−63	−61
74.40 Unpaid obligations, end of year: Obligated balance, end of year	5	5	5
Outlays (gross), detail:			
86.90 Outlays from new discretionary authority	58	49	56
86.93 Outlays from discretionary balances	3	14	5
87.00 Total outlays (gross)	61	63	61
Net budget authority and outlays:			
89.00 Budget authority	67	54	61
90.00 Outlays	61	63	61

This appropriation provides for the statutory fees and allowances of jurors, refreshments of jurors, and compensation of land commissioners appointed in condemnation cases pursuant to Rule 71A(h) of the Federal Rules of Civil Procedure. Budgetary requirements depend largely on the volume and length of jury trials demanded by the parties to both civil and criminal actions and the number of grand juries being convened by the courts at the request of United States attorneys.

Object Classification (in millions of dollars)

Identification code 10–0925–0–1–752	1999 actual	2000 est.	2001 est.
11.8 Personnel compensation: Special personal services payments	38	38	37
21.0 Travel and transportation of persons (jurors)	22	23	22
23.3 Communications, utilities, and miscellaneous charges	1	1	1
25.2 Other services (meals and lodging furnished sequestered juror	1	1	1
26.0 Supplies and materials	1		
99.9 Total new obligations	63	63	61

COURT SECURITY

For necessary expenses, not otherwise provided for, incident to *providing protective guard services and* the procurement, installation, and maintenance of security equipment [and protective services] for [the] United States [Courts in courtrooms and adjacent areas] *Courthouses and other facilities housing federal court operations*, including building ingress-egress control, inspection of *mail and* packages, directed security patrols, and other similar activities as authorized by section 1010 of the Judicial Improvement and Access to Justice Act (Public Law 100–702), [$193,028,000] *$215,353,000*, of which not to exceed $10,000,000 shall remain available until expended [for security systems], to be expended directly or transferred to the United States Marshals Service, which shall be responsible for administering [elements of] the Judicial Facility Security Program consistent with standards or guidelines agreed to by the Director of the Administrative Office of the United States Courts and the Attorney General. *(The Judiciary Appropriations Act, 2000, as enacted by section 1000(a)(1) of the Consolidated Appropriations Act, 2000 (P.L. 106–113).)*

Program and Financing (in millions of dollars)

Identification code 10–0930–0–1–752	1999 actual	2000 est.	2001 est.
Obligations by program activity:			
00.01 Direct program	174	201	215
09.10 Reimbursable program	3		
10.00 Total new obligations	177	201	215
Budgetary resources available for obligation:			
21.40 Unobligated balance available, start of year	7	8	
22.00 New budget authority (gross)	178	193	215
22.10 Resources available from recoveries of prior year obligations	1		
23.90 Total budgetary resources available for obligation	186	201	215
23.95 Total new obligations	−177	−201	−215
23.98 Unobligated balance expiring or withdrawn	−1		
24.40 Unobligated balance available, end of year	8		
New budget authority (gross), detail:			
Discretionary:			
40.00 Appropriation	175	193	215
42.00 Transferred from other accounts			
43.00 Appropriation (total discretionary)	175	193	215
68.00 Spending authority from offsetting collections: Offsetting collections (cash)	3		
70.00 Total new budget authority (gross)	178	193	215
Change in unpaid obligations:			
72.40 Unpaid obligations, start of year: Obligated balance, start of year	50	47	59
73.10 Total new obligations	177	201	215
73.20 Total outlays (gross)	−177	−189	−209
73.45 Adjustments in unexpired accounts	−1		
74.40 Unpaid obligations, end of year: Obligated balance, end of year	47	59	65
Outlays (gross), detail:			
86.90 Outlays from new discretionary authority	143	148	164
86.93 Outlays from discretionary balances	34	41	45
87.00 Total outlays (gross)	177	189	209
Offsets:			
Against gross budget authority and outlays:			
88.00 Offsetting collections (cash) from: Federal sources	−3		
Net budget authority and outlays:			
89.00 Budget authority	175	193	215
90.00 Outlays	174	189	209

This appropriation provides for the necessary expenses of security and protective services for the United States Courts in courtrooms and adjacent areas, including building ingress-egress control, inspection of packages, directed security patrols, and other similar activities, to be expended directly or transferred to the United States Marshals Service which shall be responsible for administering elements of the judicial facility security program.

Object Classification (in millions of dollars)

Identification code 10–0930–0–1–752		1999 actual	2000 est.	2001 est.
	Direct obligations:			
11.1	Personnel compensation: Full-time permanent	3	3	3
12.1	Civilian personnel benefits	1	1	1
21.0	Travel and transportation of persons	1	1	1
23.1	Rental payments to GSA	2	2	2
25.2	Other services	152	173	181
31.0	Equipment	15	21	27
99.0	Subtotal, direct obligations	174	201	215
99.0	Reimbursable obligations	3		
99.9	Total new obligations	177	201	215

Personnel Summary

Identification code 10–0930–0–1–752		1999 actual	2000 est.	2001 est.
1011	Total compensable workyears: Exempt Full-time equivalent employment	35	35	35

JUDICIARY FILING FEES

Unavailable Collections (in millions of dollars)

Identification code 10–5100–0–2–752		1999 actual	2000 est.	2001 est.
	Balance, start of year:			
01.99	Balance, start of year			
	Receipts:			
02.01	Filing Fees, U.S. Courts, Judiciary	107	109	114
	Appropriation:			
05.01	Judiciary filing fees	−107	−109	−114
07.99	Total balance, end of year			

Program and Financing (in millions of dollars)

Identification code 10–5100–0–2–752		1999 actual	2000 est.	2001 est.
	Obligations by program activity:			
10.00	Total new obligations (object class 25.2)	211	154	145
	Budgetary resources available for obligation:			
21.40	Unobligated balance available, start of year	180	76	31
22.00	New budget authority (gross)	107	109	114
23.90	Total budgetary resources available for obligation	287	185	145
23.95	Total new obligations	−211	−154	−145
24.40	Unobligated balance available, end of year	76	31	
	New budget authority (gross), detail:			
	Mandatory:			
60.25	Appropriation (special fund, indefinite)	107	109	114
	Change in unpaid obligations:			
72.40	Unpaid obligations, start of year: Obligated balance, start of year	114	210	
73.10	Total new obligations	211	154	145
73.20	Total outlays (gross)	−115	−364	−145
74.40	Unpaid obligations, end of year: Obligated balance, end of year	210		
	Outlays (gross), detail:			
86.97	Outlays from new mandatory authority	1	78	114
86.98	Outlays from mandatory balances	114	286	31
87.00	Total outlays (gross)	115	364	145
	Net budget authority and outlays:			
89.00	Budget authority	107	109	114
90.00	Outlays	115	364	145

REGISTRY ADMINISTRATION

Unavailable Collections (in millions of dollars)

Identification code 10–5101–0–2–752		1999 actual	2000 est.	2001 est.
	Balance, start of year:			
01.99	Balance, start of year			
	Receipts:			
02.01	Fees, Registry administration, Judiciary	3	3	3
	Appropriation:			
05.01	Registry administration	−3	−3	−3
07.99	Total balance, end of year			

Program and Financing (in millions of dollars)

Identification code 10–5101–0–2–752		1999 actual	2000 est.	2001 est.
	Obligations by program activity:			
10.00	Total new obligations (object class 25.2)	3	3	3
	Budgetary resources available for obligation:			
22.00	New budget authority (gross)	3	3	3
23.95	Total new obligations	−3	−3	−3
	New budget authority (gross), detail:			
	Mandatory:			
60.25	Appropriation (special fund, indefinite)	3	3	3
	Change in unpaid obligations:			
73.10	Total new obligations	3	3	3
73.20	Total outlays (gross)	−3	−3	−3
	Outlays (gross), detail:			
86.97	Outlays from new mandatory authority	3	3	3
	Net budget authority and outlays:			
89.00	Budget authority	3	3	3
90.00	Outlays	3	3	3

This schedule reflects funds available to the Federal Judiciary, pursuant to Public Law 100–459, which provides that any funds collected by the Judiciary as a charge for services rendered in administering accounts kept in a court's registry shall be deposited into this account.

JUDICIARY INFORMATION TECHNOLOGY FUND

Unavailable Collections (in millions of dollars)

Identification code 10–5114–0–2–752		1999 actual	2000 est.	2001 est.
	Balance, start of year:			
01.99	Balance, start of year			
	Receipts:			
02.01	Advances and reimbursements	214	164	205
02.02	Proceeds from sale of property	14	12	12
02.99	Total receipts	228	176	217
	Appropriation:			
05.01	Judiciary information technology fund	−228	−176	−217
07.99	Total balance, end of year			

Program and Financing (in millions of dollars)

Identification code 10–5114–0–2–752		1999 actual	2000 est.	2001 est.
	Obligations by program activity:			
00.01	Information Technology	231	226	237
10.00	Total new obligations	231	226	237
	Budgetary resources available for obligation:			
21.40	Unobligated balance available, start of year	60	70	20
22.00	New budget authority (gross)	241	176	217
23.90	Total budgetary resources available for obligation	301	246	237
23.95	Total new obligations	−231	−226	−237
24.40	Unobligated balance available, end of year	70	20	

General and special funds—Continued

JUDICIARY INFORMATION TECHNOLOGY FUND—Continued

Program and Financing (in millions of dollars)—Continued

Identification code 10–5114–0–2–752		1999 actual	2000 est.	2001 est.
	New budget authority (gross), detail:			
	Discretionary:			
42.00	Transferred from other accounts	13		
	Mandatory:			
60.25	Appropriation (special fund, indefinite)	228	176	217
70.00	Total new budget authority (gross)	241	176	217
	Change in unpaid obligations:			
72.40	Unpaid obligations, start of year: Obligated balance, start of year	108	106	118
73.10	Total new obligations	231	226	237
73.20	Total outlays (gross)	−233	−214	−227
74.40	Unpaid obligations, end of year: Obligated balance, end of year	106	118	128
	Outlays (gross), detail:			
86.90	Outlays from new discretionary authority	10		
86.97	Outlays from new mandatory authority	115	108	119
86.98	Outlays from mandatory balances	108	106	108
87.00	Total outlays (gross)	233	214	227
	Net budget authority and outlays:			
89.00	Budget authority	241	176	217
90.00	Outlays	233	214	227

The Judiciary Information Technology Fund is a stable and flexible funding vehicle for the expansion, management, and use of information technology throughout the Judiciary in accordance with the Long Range Plan for Information Technology in the Federal Judiciary. Funds are available without fiscal year limitation. The Fund consists of deposits and transfers from appropriations, reimbursements, user fees, and sale of surplus equipment. Appropriate information technology costs are paid directly out of the Fund.

Object Classification (in millions of dollars)

Identification code 10–5114–0–2–752		1999 actual	2000 est.	2001 est.
11.1	Personnel compensation: Full-time permanent	16	17	18
12.1	Civilian personnel benefits	3	3	4
21.0	Travel and transportation of persons	6	6	6
23.3	Communications, utilities, and miscellaneous charges	43	43	46
24.0	Printing and reproduction	14	15	16
25.2	Other services	62	54	57
26.0	Supplies and materials	3	3	3
31.0	Equipment	84	85	87
99.9	Total new obligations	231	226	237

Personnel Summary

Identification code 10–5114–0–2–752		1999 actual	2000 est.	2001 est.
1011	Total compensable workyears: Exempt Full-time equivalent employment	13	13	13

NATIONAL FINE CENTER

Program and Financing (in millions of dollars)

Identification code 10–5115–0–2–752		1999 actual	2000 est.	2001 est.
	Budgetary resources available for obligation:			
21.40	Unobligated balance available, start of year	1		
22.21	Unobligated balance transferred to other accounts	−1		
23.90	Total budgetary resources available for obligation			
	Net budget authority and outlays:			
89.00	Budget authority			
90.00	Outlays			

The National Fine Center was established in accordance with the Criminal Fine Improvements Act of 1987, P.L. 100–185, effective December 11, 1987, which provided authority (18 U.S.C. 3611 and 3612) for the Director of the Administrative Office of the U.S. Courts to specify that payments of fines be made to the clerk of the court or as provided by his authority to "establish procedures and mechanisms within the judicial branch for processing fines, restitution, forfeitures of bail bonds or collateral, and assessments" (28 U.S.C. 604(a)(18)).

The National Fine Center closed on December 31, 1996, after an independent assessment determined that a national approach to fine collection was not viable. Nearly all unobligated balances were transferred back to the Crime Victims Fund in 1997, with the remaining balances transferred in 1999.

ADMINISTRATIVE OFFICE OF THE UNITED STATES COURTS

Federal Funds

General and special funds:

SALARIES AND EXPENSES

For necessary expenses of the Administrative Office of the United States Courts as authorized by law, including travel as authorized by 31 U.S.C. 1345, hire of a passenger motor vehicle as authorized by 31 U.S.C. 1343(b), advertising and rent in the District of Columbia and elsewhere, [$55,000,000] *$61,215,000*, of which not to exceed [$8,500] *$10,000* is authorized for official reception and representation expenses. *(The Judiciary Appropriations Act, 2000, as enacted by section 1000(a)(1) of the Consolidated Appropriations Act, 2000 (P.L. 106–113).)*

Program and Financing (in millions of dollars)

Identification code 10–0927–0–1–752		1999 actual	2000 est.	2001 est.
	Obligations by program activity:			
	Direct program:			
00.01	Executive direction	1	1	1
00.02	Program direction and policy formulation	7	7	8
00.03	Court programs	8	9	9
00.04	Facilities, Security and Administrative Services	20	22	23
00.05	Finance and Budget	7	7	8
00.06	Human resources and statistics	12	11	12
00.07	Information technology	3	3	4
00.08	Judges programs	5	6	6
09.10	Reimbursable program	28	31	34
10.00	Total new obligations	91	97	105
	Budgetary resources available for obligation:			
22.00	New budget authority (gross)	93	97	105
23.95	Total new obligations	−91	−97	−105
	New budget authority (gross), detail:			
	Discretionary:			
40.00	Appropriation	55	55	61
68.00	Spending authority from offsetting collections: Offsetting collections (cash)	38	42	44
70.00	Total new budget authority (gross)	93	97	105
	Change in unpaid obligations:			
72.40	Unpaid obligations, start of year: Obligated balance, start of year	7	5	5
73.10	Total new obligations	91	97	105
73.20	Total outlays (gross)	−93	−97	−105
74.40	Unpaid obligations, end of year: Obligated balance, end of year	5	5	5
	Outlays (gross), detail:			
86.90	Outlays from new discretionary authority	93	97	105

	Offsets:			
	Against gross budget authority and outlays:			
88.00	Offsetting collections (cash) from: Federal sources	−38	−42	−44
	Net budget authority and outlays:			
89.00	Budget authority	55	55	61
90.00	Outlays	57	55	61

The Office, pursuant to section 604 of title 28, United States Code, under the supervision and direction of the Judicial Conference of the United States, is responsible for the administration of the U.S. courts, including the probation and bankruptcy systems. The principal functions consist of providing staff and services for the courts; conducting a continuous study of the rules of practice and procedure in the Federal courts; examining the state of dockets of the various courts; compiling and publishing statistical data concerning the business transacted by the courts; and administering the Judicial Survivors' Annuities Fund under title 28, United States Code, section 376. The Office also is responsible for: the preparation and submission of the annual budget estimates as well as supplemental and deficiency estimates; the disbursement of and accounting for moneys appropriated for the operation of the courts, and the Federal Judicial Center; the audit and examination of accounts; the purchase and distribution of supplies and equipment; providing automated data processing services; securing adequate space for occupancy by the courts; and such other matters as may be assigned by the Supreme Court and Judicial Conference of the United States.

Object Classification (in millions of dollars)

Identification code 10–0927–0–1–752		1999 actual	2000 est.	2001 est.
	Direct obligations:			
	Personnel compensation:			
11.1	Full-time permanent	46	49	53
11.3	Other than full-time permanent	1	1	1
11.9	Total personnel compensation	47	50	54
12.1	Civilian personnel benefits	9	10	11
21.0	Travel and transportation of persons	1	1	1
23.3	Communications, utilities, and miscellaneous charges	1	1	1
25.2	Other services	4	3	3
31.0	Equipment	1	1	1
99.0	Subtotal, direct obligations	63	66	71
99.0	Reimbursable obligations	28	31	34
99.9	Total new obligations	91	97	105

Personnel Summary

Identification code 10–0927–0–1–752		1999 actual	2000 est.	2001 est.
	Direct:			
1011	Total compensable workyears: Exempt Full-time equivalent employment	659	659	663
	Reimbursable:			
2011	Total compensable workyears: Exempt Full-time equivalent employment	270	278	278

FEDERAL JUDICIAL CENTER

Federal Funds

General and special funds:

SALARIES AND EXPENSES

For necessary expenses of the Federal Judicial Center, as authorized by Public Law 90–219, [$18,000,000] *$19,337,000*; of which $1,800,000 shall remain available through September 30, [2001] *2002*, to provide education and training to Federal court personnel; and of which not to exceed $1,000 is authorized for official reception and representation expenses. *(The Judiciary Appropriations Act, 2000, as enacted by section 1000(a)(1) of the Consolidated Appropriations Act, 2000 (P.L. 106–113).)*

Program and Financing (in millions of dollars)

Identification code 10–0928–0–1–752		1999 actual	2000 est.	2001 est.
	Obligations by program activity:			
00.01	Education and training	11	12	13
00.02	Research	3	3	3
00.03	Program support	4	3	3
10.00	Total new obligations	18	18	19
	Budgetary resources available for obligation:			
22.00	New budget authority (gross)	18	18	19
23.95	Total new obligations	−18	−18	−19
	New budget authority (gross), detail:			
	Discretionary:			
40.00	Appropriation	18	18	19
	Change in unpaid obligations:			
72.40	Unpaid obligations, start of year: Obligated balance, start of year	4	3	4
73.10	Total new obligations	18	18	19
73.20	Total outlays (gross)	−19	−17	−19
74.40	Unpaid obligations, end of year: Obligated balance, end of year	3	4	4
	Outlays (gross), detail:			
86.90	Outlays from new discretionary authority	15	14	15
86.93	Outlays from discretionary balances	4	3	4
87.00	Total outlays (gross)	19	17	19
	Net budget authority and outlays:			
89.00	Budget authority	18	18	19
90.00	Outlays	19	17	19

This appropriation provides for the operation of the Federal Judicial Center pursuant to 28 U.S.C. § 620 et. seq. The Center is charged with the responsibility for furthering the development and adoption of improved judicial administration in the courts of the United States.

Object Classification (in millions of dollars)

Identification code 10–0928–0–1–752		1999 actual	2000 est.	2001 est.
11.1	Personnel compensation: Full-time permanent	9	10	11
12.1	Civilian personnel benefits	2	2	2
21.0	Travel and transportation of persons	3	3	3
23.3	Communications, utilities, and miscellaneous charges	1	1	1
25.2	Other services	1	1	1
26.0	Supplies and materials	1	1	1
99.0	Subtotal, direct obligations	17	18	19
99.5	Below reporting threshold	1		
99.9	Total new obligations	18	18	19

Personnel Summary

Identification code 10–0928–0–1–752		1999 actual	2000 est.	2001 est.
1011	Total compensable workyears: Exempt Full-time equivalent employment	142	146	154

Trust Funds

GIFTS AND DONATIONS, FEDERAL JUDICIAL CENTER FOUNDATION

Unavailable Collections (in millions of dollars)

Identification code 10–8123–0–7–752		1999 actual	2000 est.	2001 est.
	Balance, start of year:			
01.99	Balance, start of year	....	....	....
	Receipts:			
02.01	Gifts and donations, Federal Judicial Center Foundation	....	1	1

GIFTS AND DONATIONS, FEDERAL JUDICIAL CENTER FOUNDATION—Continued

Unavailable Collections (in millions of dollars)—Continued

Identification code 10–8123–0–7–752	1999 actual	2000 est.	2001 est.
Appropriation:			
05.01 Gifts and donations, Federal Judicial Center Foundation	....	−1	−1
07.99 Total balance, end of year	....	....	....

Program and Financing (in millions of dollars)

Identification code 10–8123–0–7–752	1999 actual	2000 est.	2001 est.
Obligations by program activity:			
10.00 Total new obligations (object class 99.5)	....	1	1
Budgetary resources available for obligation:			
21.40 Unobligated balance available, start of year	1	1	....
22.00 New budget authority (gross)	....	....	1
23.90 Total budgetary resources available for obligation	1	1	1
23.95 Total new obligations	....	−1	−1
24.40 Unobligated balance available, end of year	1	....	1
New budget authority (gross), detail:			
Mandatory:			
60.27 Appropriation (trust fund, indefinite)	....	1	1
Change in unpaid obligations:			
72.40 Unpaid obligations, start of year: Obligated balance, start of year	....	....	....
73.10 Total new obligations	....	1	1
73.20 Total outlays (gross)	−1	−1	−1
74.40 Unpaid obligations, end of year: Obligated balance, end of year	....	....	....
Outlays (gross), detail:			
86.97 Outlays from new mandatory authority	....	1	1
86.98 Outlays from mandatory balances	1	....	....
87.00 Total outlays (gross)	1	1	1
Net budget authority and outlays:			
89.00 Budget authority	....	1	1
90.00 Outlays	1	1	1

This schedule reflects funds available to the Federal Judicial Center pursuant to 28 U.S.C. §629, which provides that the purpose of the Federal Judicial Center Foundation shall be to have sole authority to accept and receive gifts of real and personal property and services made for the purpose of aiding or facilitating the work of the Federal Judicial Center and that, gifts of money and proceeds from sales of other property received as gifts shall be deposited in a separate fund in the Treasury of the United States and disbursed on the order of the Director of the Center.

JUDICIAL RETIREMENT FUNDS

PAYMENT TO JUDICIARY TRUST FUNDS

For payment to the Judicial Officers' Retirement Fund, as authorized by 28 U.S.C. 377(o), [$29,500,000] *$25,700,000*; to the Judicial Survivors' Annuities Fund, as authorized by 28 U.S.C. 376(c), [$8,000,000] *$8,100,000*; and to the United States Court of Federal Claims Judges' Retirement Fund, as authorized by 28 U.S.C. 178(l), [$2,200,000] *$1,900,000*. *(The Judiciary Appropriations Act, 2000, as enacted by section 1000(a)(1) of the Consolidated Appropriations Act, 2000 (P.L. 106–113).)*

Program and Financing (in millions of dollars)

Identification code 10–0941–0–1–752	1999 actual	2000 est.	2001 est.
Obligations by program activity:			
00.01 Payment to Judicial Officers' Retirement Fund	28	30	26
00.02 Payment to Court of Federal Claims Judges Retirement Fund	2	2	2
00.03 Payment to Judicial Survivors' Annuities Fund	8	8	8
10.00 Total new obligations (object class 12.1)	38	40	36
Budgetary resources available for obligation:			
22.00 New budget authority (gross)	38	40	36
23.95 Total new obligations	−38	−40	−36
New budget authority (gross), detail:			
Mandatory:			
60.00 Appropriation	38	40	36
Change in unpaid obligations:			
73.10 Total new obligations	38	40	36
73.20 Total outlays (gross)	−38	−40	−36
Outlays (gross), detail:			
86.97 Outlays from new mandatory authority	38	40	36
Net budget authority and outlays:			
89.00 Budget authority	38	40	36
90.00 Outlays	37	40	36

This appropriation request would provide funds necessary to pay the retirement annuities of bankruptcy judges and magistrate judges, pursuant to 28 U.S.C. sec. 377, the retirement annuities of the United States Court of Federal Claims judges, pursuant to 28 U.S.C. sec. 178, and annuities to participants' surviving widows and dependent children, pursuant to 28 U.S.C. sec. 376.

Trust Funds

JUDICIAL OFFICERS' RETIREMENT FUND

Unavailable Collections (in millions of dollars)

Identification code 10–8122–0–7–602	1999 actual	2000 est.	2001 est.
Balance, start of year:			
01.99 Balance, start of year	....	....	....
Receipts:			
02.02 Interest and profits on investments, judicial officers retirement annuity	5	9	10
02.04 Federal payment to judicial officers retirement fund, BRD	28	30	26
02.99 Total receipts	33	39	36
Appropriation:			
05.01 Judicial officers' retirement fund	−33	−39	−36
05.99 Subtotal appropriation	−33	−39	−36
07.99 Total balance, end of year	....	....	....

Program and Financing (in millions of dollars)

Identification code 10–8122–0–7–602	1999 actual	2000 est.	2001 est.
Obligations by program activity:			
00.10 Judicial Officers Retirement Fund	14	15	16
10.00 Total new obligations (object class 42.0)	14	15	16
Budgetary resources available for obligation:			
21.40 Unobligated balance available, start of year	102	120	144
22.00 New budget authority (gross)	33	39	36
23.90 Total budgetary resources available for obligation	135	159	180
23.95 Total new obligations	−14	−15	−16
24.40 Unobligated balance available, end of year	120	144	164
New budget authority (gross), detail:			
Mandatory:			
60.26 Appropriation (trust fund, definite)	28	30	26
60.27 Appropriation (trust fund, indefinite)	5	9	10
62.50 Appropriation (total mandatory)	33	39	36
Change in unpaid obligations:			
73.10 Total new obligations	14	15	16

73.20 Total outlays (gross)	−14	−15	−16
Outlays (gross), detail:			
86.97 Outlays from new mandatory authority	14	15	16
Net budget authority and outlays:			
89.00 Budget authority	33	39	36
90.00 Outlays	14	15	16
Memorandum (non-add) entries:			
92.01 Total investments, start of year: U.S. securities: Par value	101	119	145
92.02 Total investments, end of year: U.S. securities: Par value	119	145	166

This fund provides the retirement annuities of bankruptcy judges and magistrate judges pursuant to 28 U.S.C. section 377.

JUDICIAL SURVIVORS' ANNUITIES FUND

Unavailable Collections (in millions of dollars)

Identification code 10–8110–0–7–602	1999 actual	2000 est.	2001 est.
Balance, start of year:			
01.99 Balance, start of year			
Receipts:			
02.01 Judicial survivors annuity fund, deductions from employees salaries	4	4	4
02.02 Judicial survivors annuity, interest and profits on investments	25	22	24
02.03 Federal payment to judicial survivors annuities fund	8	8	8
02.99 Total receipts	37	34	36
Appropriation:			
05.01 Judicial survivors' annuities fund	−37	−34	−36
05.99 Subtotal appropriation	−37	−34	−36
07.99 Total balance, end of year			

Program and Financing (in millions of dollars)

Identification code 10–8110–0–7–602	1999 actual	2000 est.	2001 est.
Obligations by program activity:			
00.10 Judicial Survivor's Annuity Fund	11	12	12
10.00 Total new obligations (object class 42.0)	11	12	12
Budgetary resources available for obligation:			
21.40 Unobligated balance available, start of year	292	318	340
22.00 New budget authority (gross)	37	34	36
23.90 Total budgetary resources available for obligation	329	352	376
23.95 Total new obligations	−11	−12	−12
24.40 Unobligated balance available, end of year	318	340	364
New budget authority (gross), detail:			
Mandatory:			
60.26 Appropriation (trust fund, definite)	8	8	8
60.27 Appropriation (trust fund, indefinite)	29	26	28
62.50 Appropriation (total mandatory)	37	34	36
Change in unpaid obligations:			
73.10 Total new obligations	11	12	12
73.20 Total outlays (gross)	−11	−12	−12
Outlays (gross), detail:			
86.97 Outlays from new mandatory authority	11	12	12
Net budget authority and outlays:			
89.00 Budget authority	37	34	36
90.00 Outlays	11	12	12
Memorandum (non-add) entries:			
92.01 Total investments, start of year: U.S. securities: Par value	292	318	344
92.02 Total investments, end of year: U.S. securities: Par value	318	344	368

The Judicial Survivors' Annuities Fund (section 376 of title 28, United States Code) was established to receive sums deducted and withheld from salaries of justices, judges, the Director of the Federal Judicial Center, the Director of the Administrative Office of the U.S. Courts, and the Administrative Assistant to the Chief Justice who have elected to bring themselves within the purview of the above section as well as amounts received from said judicial officers covering Federal civilian service prior to date of election.

This fund provides an annuity for participants' surviving widows and dependent children.

UNITED STATES COURT OF FEDERAL CLAIMS JUDGES' RETIREMENT FUND

Unavailable Collections (in millions of dollars)

Identification code 10–8124–0–7–602	1999 actual	2000 est.	2001 est.
Balance, start of year:			
01.99 Balance, start of year			
Receipts:			
02.01 Federal payment to Court of Federal Claims Judges' Retirement Fund	2	2	2
Appropriation:			
05.01 Court of Federal Claims judges' retirement fund	−2	−2	−2
07.99 Total balance, end of year			

Program and Financing (in millions of dollars)

Identification code 10–8124–0–7–602	1999 actual	2000 est.	2001 est.
Obligations by program activity:			
00.01 Court of Federal Claims Judges Retirement Fund	1	1	1
10.00 Total new obligations (object class 42.0)	1	1	1
Budgetary resources available for obligation:			
21.40 Unobligated balance available, start of year	6	7	8
22.00 New budget authority (gross)	2	2	2
23.90 Total budgetary resources available for obligation	8	9	10
23.95 Total new obligations	−1	−1	−1
24.40 Unobligated balance available, end of year	7	8	9
New budget authority (gross), detail:			
Mandatory:			
60.26 Appropriation (trust fund, definite)	2	2	2
Change in unpaid obligations:			
73.10 Total new obligations	1	1	1
Outlays (gross), detail:			
86.97 Outlays from new mandatory authority	1	1	1
Net budget authority and outlays:			
89.00 Budget authority	2	2	2
90.00 Outlays	1	1	1
Memorandum (non-add) entries:			
92.01 Total investments, start of year: U.S. securities: Par value	6	7	8
92.02 Total investments, end of year: U.S. securities: Par value	7	8	9

This fund provides the retirement annuities of United States Court of Federal Claims judges pursuant to 28 U.S.C. section 178.

UNITED STATES SENTENCING COMMISSION

Federal Funds

General and special funds:

SALARIES AND EXPENSES

For the salaries and expenses necessary to carry out the provisions of chapter 58 of title 28, United States Code, [$8,500,000]

General and special funds—Continued

SALARIES AND EXPENSES—Continued

$10,600,000, of which not to exceed $1,000 is authorized for official reception and representation expenses. *(The Judiciary Appropriations Act, 2000, as enacted by section 1000(a)(1) of the Consolidated Appropriations Act, 2000 (P.L. 106–113).)*

Program and Financing (in millions of dollars)

Identification code 10–0938–0–1–752	1999 actual	2000 est.	2001 est.
Obligations by program activity:			
10.00 Total new obligations	9	9	11
Budgetary resources available for obligation:			
21.40 Unobligated balance available, start of year	1	1	
22.00 New budget authority (gross)	9	8	11
23.90 Total budgetary resources available for obligation	10	9	11
23.95 Total new obligations	−9	−9	−11
24.40 Unobligated balance available, end of year	1		
New budget authority (gross), detail:			
Discretionary:			
40.00 Appropriation	9	8	11
Change in unpaid obligations:			
72.40 Unpaid obligations, start of year: Obligated balance, start of year	3	3	4
73.10 Total new obligations	9	9	11
73.20 Total outlays (gross)	−8	−8	−11
73.40 Adjustments in expired accounts (net)	−1		
74.40 Unpaid obligations, end of year: Obligated balance, end of year	3	4	4
Outlays (gross), detail:			
86.90 Outlays from new discretionary authority	7	5	8
86.93 Outlays from discretionary balances	1	3	3
87.00 Total outlays (gross)	8	8	11
Net budget authority and outlays:			
89.00 Budget authority	9	8	11
90.00 Outlays	8	8	11

The United States Sentencing Commission, an independent agency within the judicial branch, was established pursuant to provisions of the Comprehensive Crime Control Act of 1984 (Public Law 98–473, Title II), as amended. The Commission's principal purposes are: (1) to establish sentencing policies and practices for the federal courts, including guidelines prescribing the appropriate form and severity of punishment for offenders convicted of federal crimes; (2) to advise and assist Congress and the executive branch in the development of effective and efficient crime policy; and (3) to collect, analyze, and distribute a broad array of information on federal crime and sentencing issues, serving as an information resource for Congress, the executive branch, the courts, criminal justice practitioners, the academic community, and the public.

Object Classification (in millions of dollars)

Identification code 10–0938–0–1–752	1999 actual	2000 est.	2001 est.
11.1 Personnel compensation: Full-time permanent	5	6	7
12.1 Civilian personnel benefits	1	1	2
25.2 Other services	1	1	1
99.0 Subtotal, direct obligations	7	8	10
99.5 Below reporting threshold	2	1	1
99.9 Total new obligations	9	9	11

Personnel Summary

Identification code 10–0938–0–1–752	1999 actual	2000 est.	2001 est.
1011 Total compensable workyears: Exempt Full-time equivalent employment	86	84	104

VIOLENT CRIME REDUCTION PROGRAMS

VIOLENT CRIME REDUCTION PROGRAMS

Program and Financing (in millions of dollars)

Identification code 10–8516–0–1–752	1999 actual	2000 est.	2001 est.
Obligations by program activity:			
10.00 Total new obligations (object class 25.3)	41	183	
Budgetary resources available for obligation:			
22.00 New budget authority (gross)	41	183	
23.95 Total new obligations	−41	−183	
New budget authority (gross), detail:			
Discretionary:			
42.00 Transferred from other accounts	41	183	
Change in unpaid obligations:			
73.10 Total new obligations	41	183	
73.20 Total outlays (gross)	−41	−183	
Outlays (gross), detail:			
86.90 Outlays from new discretionary authority	41	183	
Net budget authority and outlays:			
89.00 Budget authority	41	183	
90.00 Outlays	41	183	

The Violent Crime Control and Law Enforcement Act of 1994 created the Violent Crime Reduction Trust Fund (VCRTF). Funds are authorized to be appropriated to the Judiciary to help meet the increased demands for judicial activities resulting from the act, including drug testing of Federal offenders on post-conviction release, as well as provisions of the Antiterrorism and Effective Death Penalty Act of 1996. Beginning in 2001, the Judiciary's requirements under these acts will be included in the requests for the Courts of Appeals, District courts, and Other Judicial Services, Salaries and Expenses, and Defender Services Appropriations.

GENERAL PROVISIONS—THE JUDICIARY

SEC. 301. Appropriations and authorizations made in this title which are available for salaries and expenses shall be available for services as authorized by 5 U.S.C. 3109.

SEC. 302. Not to exceed 5 percent of any appropriation made available for the current fiscal year for the Judiciary in this Act may be transferred between such appropriations, but no such appropriation, except "Courts of Appeals, District Courts, and Other Judicial Services, Defender Services" and "Courts of Appeals, District Courts, and Other Judicial Services, Fees of Jurors and Commissioners", shall be increased by more than 10 percent by any such transfers: *Provided*, That any transfer pursuant to this section shall be treated as a reprogramming of funds under section 605 of this Act and shall not be available for obligation or expenditure except in compliance with the procedures set forth in that section.

SEC. 303. Notwithstanding any other provision of law, the salaries and expenses appropriation for district courts, courts of appeals, and other judicial services shall be available for official reception and representation expenses of the Judicial Conference of the United States: *Provided*, That such available funds shall not exceed [$11,000] *$12,000* and shall be administered by the Director of the Administrative Office of the United States Courts in the capacity as Secretary of the Judicial Conference.

SEC. 304. Pursuant to section 140 of Public Law 97–92, Justices and judges of the United States are authorized during fiscal year [2000] *2001*, to receive a salary adjustment in accordance with 28 U.S.C. 461[: *Provided*, That $9,611,000 is appropriated for salary adjustments pursuant to this section and such funds shall be transferred to and merged with appropriations in title III of this Act.]

[SEC. 305. Section 604(a)(5) of title 28, United States Code, is amended by adding before the semicolon at the end thereof the following: ", and, notwithstanding any other provision of law, pay on behalf of Justices and judges of the United States appointed to hold office during good behavior, aged 65 or over, any increases in the cost of Federal Employees' Group Life Insurance imposed after April 24, 1999, including any expenses generated by such payments, as authorized by the Judicial Conference of the United States".]

[SEC. 306. The second paragraph of section 112(c) of title 28, United States Code, is amended to read "Court for the Eastern District shall be held at Brooklyn, Hauppauge, Hempstead (including the village of Uniondale), and Central Islip.".]

[SEC. 307. Pursuant to the requirements of section 156(d) of title 28, United States Code, Congress hereby approves the consolidation of the Office of the Bankruptcy Clerk with the Office of the District Clerk of Court in the Southern District of West Virginia.]

[SEC. 308. (a) IN GENERAL.—Section 3006A(d)(4)(D)(vi) of title 18, United States Code, is amended by adding after the word "require" the following: ", except that the amount of the fees shall not be considered a reason justifying any limited disclosure under section 3006A(d)(4) of title 18, United States Code".]

[(b) EFFECTIVE DATE.—This section shall apply to all disclosures made under section 3006A(d) of title 18, United States Code, related to any criminal trial or appeal involving a sentence of death where the underlying alleged criminal conduct took place on or after April 19, 1995.]

[SEC. 309. (a) The President shall appoint, by and with the advice and consent of the Senate—

(1) three additional district judges for the district of Arizona;

(2) four additional district judges for the middle district of Florida; and

(3) two additional district judges for the district of Nevada.

(b) In order that the table contained in section 133 of title 28, United States Code, will reflect the changes in the total number of permanent district judgeships authorized as a result of subsection (a) of this section—

(1) the item relating to Arizona in such table is amended to read as follows:

"Arizona .... 11";

(2) the item relating to Florida in such table is amended to read as follows:

"Florida:
Northern 14
Middle 15
Southern .... 16";

and

(3) the item relating to Nevada in such table is amended to read as follows:

"Nevada .... 6".

(c) There are authorized to be appropriated such sums as may be necessary to carry out the provisions of this section, including such sums as may be necessary to provide appropriate space and facilities for the judicial positions created by this section.]

SEC. 305. Any unexpended balances transferred to the Commission on Structural Alternative in Federal Appellate Courts may be expended on court operations under the "Courts of Appeals, District Courts and Other Judicial Services, Salaries and Expenses.

SEC. 306. (a) The Director of the Administrative Office of the United States Courts (the Director) may designate in writing officers and employees of the judicial branch of the United States Government, including the courts as defined in section 610 of title 28, United States Code, but excluding the Supreme Court, to be disbursing officers in such numbers and locations as the Director considers necessary. These disbursing officers will (1) disburse moneys appropriated to the judicial branch and other funds only in strict accordance with payment requests certified by the Director or in accordance with subsection (b) of this section, (2) examine payment requests as necessary to ascertain whether they are in proper form, certified, and approved, and (3) be held accountable as provided by law. However, a disbursing officer will not be held accountable or responsible for any illegal, improper, or incorrect payment resulting from any false, inaccurate, or misleading certificate for which a certifying officer is responsible under subsection (b) of this section.

(b)(1) The Director may designate in writing officers and employees of the judicial branch of the United States Government, including the courts as defined in section 610 of title 28, United States Code, but excluding the Supreme Court, to certify payment requests payable from appropriations and funds. These certifying officers will be responsible and accountable for (A) the existence and correctness of the facts recited in the certificate of other request for payment or its supporting papers, (B) the legality of the proposed payment under the appropriation or fund involved, and (C) the correctness of the computations of certified payment requests.

(2) The liability of a certifying officer will be enforced in the same manner and to the same extent as provided by law with respect to the enforcement of the liability of disbursing and other accountable officers. A certifying officer shall be required to make restitution to the United States for the amount of any illegal, improper, or incorrect payment resulting from any false, inaccurate, or misleading certificates made by the certifying officer, as well as for any payment prohibited by law or which did not represent a legal obligation under the appropriation or fund involved.

(c) A certifying or disbursing officer (1) has the right to apply for and obtain a decision by the Comptroller General or any question of law involved in a payment request presented for certification, and (2) is entitled to relief from liability arising under this section as provided by law.

(d) The Director shall disburse, directly or through officials designated pursuant to this section, appropriations and other funds for the maintenance and operation of the courts.

(e) Nothing in this section affects the authority of the courts to receive or disburse moneys in accordance with chapter 129 of title 28, United States Code.

(f) This section shall be effective for fiscal year 2000 and hereafter. (The Judiciary Appropriations Act, 2000, as enacted by section 1000(a)(1) of the Consolidated Appropriations Act, 2000 (P.L. 106–113).)

DEPARTMENT OF AGRICULTURE

OFFICE OF THE SECRETARY

Federal Funds

General and special funds:

OFFICE OF THE SECRETARY

(INCLUDING TRANSFERS OF FUNDS)

For necessary expenses of the Office of the Secretary of Agriculture, and not to exceed $75,000 for employment under 5 U.S.C. 3109, [$15,436,000, of which, $12,600,000, to remain available until expended, shall be available only for the development and implementation of a common computing environment] *$3,314,000*: *Provided*, That not to exceed $11,000 of this amount, along with any unobligated balances of representation funds in the Foreign Agricultural Service, shall be available for official reception and representation expenses, not otherwise provided for, as determined by the Secretary: [*Provided further*, That the funds made available for the development and implementation of a common computing environment shall only be available upon approval of the Committees on Appropriations and Agriculture of the House of Representatives and the Senate of a plan for the development and implementation of a common computing environment:] *Provided further*, That none of the funds appropriated or otherwise made available by this Act may be used to pay the salaries and expenses of personnel of the Department of Agriculture to carry out section 793(c)(1)(C) of Public Law 104–127: *Provided further*, That none of the funds made available by this Act may be used to enforce section 793(d) of Public Law 104–127.

OFFICE OF THE ASSISTANT SECRETARY FOR ADMINISTRATION

For necessary salaries and expenses of the Office of the Assistant Secretary for Administration to carry out the programs funded by this Act, [$613,000] *$629,000*.

OFFICE OF THE ASSISTANT SECRETARY FOR CONGRESSIONAL RELATIONS

(INCLUDING TRANSFERS OF FUNDS)

For necessary salaries and expenses of the Office of the Assistant Secretary for Congressional Relations to carry out the programs funded by this Act, including programs involving intergovernmental affairs and liaison within the executive branch, [$3,568,000] *$3,778,000*: *Provided*, That no other funds appropriated to the Department by this Act shall be available to the Department for support of activities of congressional relations: *Provided further*, That not less than [$2,241,000] *$2,312,000* shall be transferred to agencies funded by this Act to maintain personnel at the agency level.

OFFICE OF THE UNDER SECRETARY FOR RESEARCH, EDUCATION AND ECONOMICS

For necessary salaries and expenses of the Office of the Under Secretary for Research, Education and Economics to administer the laws enacted by the Congress for the Economic Research Service, the National Agricultural Statistics Service, the Agricultural Research Service, and the Cooperative State Research, Education, and Extension Service, [$540,000] *$1,356,000*.

OFFICE OF THE UNDER SECRETARY FOR MARKETING AND REGULATORY PROGRAMS

For necessary salaries and expenses of the Office of the Under Secretary for Marketing and Regulatory Programs to administer programs under the laws enacted by the Congress for the Animal and Plant Health Inspection Service, the Agricultural Marketing Service, and the Grain Inspection, Packers and Stockyards Administration, [$618,000] *$635,000*.

OFFICE OF THE UNDER SECRETARY FOR FOOD SAFETY

For necessary salaries and expenses of the Office of the Under Secretary for Food Safety to administer the laws enacted by the Congress for the Food Safety and Inspection Service, [$446,000] *$560,000*.

OFFICE OF THE UNDER SECRETARY FOR FARM AND FOREIGN AGRICULTURAL SERVICES

For necessary salaries and expenses of the Office of the Under Secretary for Farm and Foreign Agricultural Services to administer the laws enacted by Congress for the Farm Service Agency, the Foreign Agricultural Service, the Risk Management Agency, and the Commodity Credit Corporation, [$572,000] *$589,000*.

OFFICE OF THE UNDER SECRETARY FOR NATURAL RESOURCES AND ENVIRONMENT

For necessary salaries and expenses of the Office of the Under Secretary for Natural Resources and Environment to administer the laws enacted by the Congress for the Forest Service and the Natural Resources Conservation Service, [$693,000] *$711,000*.

OFFICE OF THE UNDER SECRETARY FOR RURAL DEVELOPMENT

For necessary salaries and expenses of the Office of the Under Secretary for Rural Development to administer programs under the laws enacted by the Congress for the Rural Housing Service, the Rural Business-Cooperative Service, and the Rural Utilities Service of the Department of Agriculture, [$588,000] *$605,000*.

OFFICE OF THE UNDER SECRETARY FOR FOOD, NUTRITION AND CONSUMER SERVICES

For necessary salaries and expenses of the Office of the Under Secretary for Food, Nutrition and Consumer Services to administer the laws enacted by the Congress for the Food and Nutrition Service, [$554,000] *$570,000. (7 U.S.C. 2201–2202; Agriculture, Rural Development, Food and Drug Administration, and Related Agencies Appropriations Act, 2000.)*

Program and Financing (in millions of dollars)

Identification code 12–9913–0–1–352	1999 actual	2000 est.	2001 est.
Obligations by program activity:			
00.01 Office of the Secretary	23	3	3
00.02 Under/Assistant Secretaries	5	6	7
00.03 Service center implementation/common computing environment	3	13	
10.00 Total new obligations	31	22	10
Budgetary resources available for obligation:			
21.40 Unobligated balance available, start of year	1	2	2
22.00 New budget authority (gross)	31	24	12
23.90 Total budgetary resources available for obligation	32	26	14
23.95 Total new obligations	−31	−22	−10
24.40 Unobligated balance available, end of year	2	2	5
New budget authority (gross), detail:			
Discretionary:			
40.00 Appropriation	31	24	12
41.00 Transferred to other accounts			−30
43.00 Appropriation (total discretionary)	31	24	−18
55.00 Advance appropriation			30
70.00 Total new budget authority (gross)	31	24	12
Change in unpaid obligations:			
72.40 Unpaid obligations, start of year: Obligated balance, start of year	2	24	9
73.10 Total new obligations	31	22	10
73.20 Total outlays (gross)	−9	−37	−18
74.40 Unpaid obligations, end of year: Obligated balance, end of year	24	9	1
Outlays (gross), detail:			
86.90 Outlays from new discretionary authority	8	16	9
86.93 Outlays from discretionary balances	1	23	8
87.00 Total outlays (gross)	9	37	18

General and special funds—Continued

Office of the Under Secretary for Food, Nutrition and Consumer Services—Continued

Program and Financing (in millions of dollars)—Continued

Identification code 12–9913–0–1–352	1999 actual	2000 est.	2001 est.
Net budget authority and outlays:			
89.00 Budget authority	31	24	12
90.00 Outlays	9	37	18

The Office of the Secretary covers the overall planning, coordination, and administration of the Department's programs. This includes the Secretary, Deputy Secretary, Under Secretaries, Assistant Secretaries, and their immediate staffs, who provide top policy guidance for the Department; maintain relationships with agricultural organizations and others in the development of farm programs; and provide liaison with the Executive Office of the President and Members of Congress on all matters pertaining to agricultural policy.

Object Classification (in millions of dollars)

Identification code 12–9913–0–1–352	1999 actual	2000 est.	2001 est.
11.1 Personnel compensation: Full-time permanent	6	6	6
12.1 Civilian personnel benefits	1	1	2
25.2 Other services	4	14	2
41.0 Grants, subsidies, and contributions	20		
99.0 Subtotal, direct obligations	31	21	10
99.5 Below reporting threshold		1	
99.9 Total new obligations	31	22	10

Personnel Summary

Identification code 12–9913–0–1–352	1999 actual	2000 est.	2001 est.
1001 Total compensable workyears: Full-time equivalent employment	63	82	82

Fund for Rural America

Program and Financing (in millions of dollars)

Identification code 12–0012–0–1–999	1999 actual	2000 est.	2001 est.
Obligations by program activity:			
00.01 Rural development activities		40	30
00.02 Research, extension and education grants	2	20	30
10.00 Total new obligations (object class 41.0)	2	60	60
Budgetary resources available for obligation:			
21.40 Unobligated balance available, start of year	12		
22.00 New budget authority (gross)		60	60
23.90 Total budgetary resources available for obligation	12	60	60
23.95 Total new obligations	−2	−60	−60
23.98 Unobligated balance expiring or withdrawn	−10		
New budget authority (gross), detail:			
Discretionary:			
40.35 Appropriation deferred			−60
Mandatory:			
60.00 Appropriation	60	120	120
60.35 Appropriation deferred	−60	−60	
62.50 Appropriation (total mandatory)		60	120
70.00 Total new budget authority (gross)		60	60
Change in unpaid obligations:			
72.40 Unpaid obligations, start of year: Obligated balance, start of year	28	20	60
73.10 Total new obligations	2	60	60
73.20 Total outlays (gross)	−10	−20	−60
74.40 Unpaid obligations, end of year: Obligated balance, end of year	20	60	60
Outlays (gross), detail:			
86.90 Outlays from new discretionary authority			−31
86.97 Outlays from new mandatory authority		9	63
86.98 Outlays from mandatory balances	10	11	28
87.00 Total outlays (gross)	10	20	60
Net budget authority and outlays:			
89.00 Budget authority		60	60
90.00 Outlays	10	20	60

Summary of Loan Levels, Subsidy Budget Authority and Outlays by Program (in millions of dollars)

Identification code 12–0012–0–1–999	1999 actual	2000 est.	2001 est.
Guaranteed loan levels supportable by subsidy budget authority:			
2150 Guaranteed Business and Industry Loans		42	
2159 Total loan guarantee levels		42	
Guaranteed loan subsidy (in percent):			
2320 Guaranteed Business and Industry Loans		3.11	
2329 Weighted average subsidy rate		3.11	
Guaranteed loan subsidy budget authority:			
2330 Guaranteed Business and Industry Loans		1	
2339 Total subsidy budget authority		1	
Guaranteed loan subsidy outlays:			
2340 Guaranteed Business and Industry Loans		1	
2349 Total subsidy outlays		1	

The Federal Agriculture Improvement and Reform Act of 1996 (1996 Act) established the Fund for Rural America to provide support to rural communities across the United States. The 1996 Act provided that $100 million be made available on January 1, 1997 for use by the Fund. The 1997 Emergency Supplemental Appropriations Act for Recovery from Natural Disasters (P.L. 105–18) limited the available funding for the Fund to $80 million. As authorized by the 1996 Act, the Secretary of Agriculture allocated the available funding between rural development and research activities. The Act specifies that at least one-third of the funds be allocated to rural development activities and one-third to research activities. No more than two-thirds of the available funds may be made available for rural development activities.

In 1997, the Secretary allocated $44 million of the available funding to support ongoing rural development activities. Another $36 million was provided for research, extension, and education grants.

The 1996 Farm Bill authorized $100 million for the Fund in each of 1997, 1999, and 2000. The Department's 1998 budget included a proposal to shift the $100 million available in 2000 to 1998 in order to facilitate more consistent and efficient program delivery. Since this proposal was not accepted, no funding was authorized for the Fund in 1998.

The Agricultural Research, Extension, and Education Reform Act of 1998, P.L. 105–185 extended authorization for the Fund for Rural America through October 1, 2002, but reduced the amount to be available annually for the Fund to $60 million beginning in 1999. These funds are available for two years. The 1999 appropriations language blocked the use of 1999 funds in 1999. However, these carryover funds are available for use in 2000. The Secretary allocated $40 million of the available $60 million funding in 2000 to support outreach for socially disadvantaged producers, water and waste grants and loans, farm labor housing grants, and other ongoing rural development activities. Another $20 million was provided for center grants for research focused on minority land and community security, food entrepreneurship, manure and animal waste management, site-specific resource management, and people in forest communities. The 2000 appropriations language blocks the use of the 2000 appropriation in 2000. The 2001 budget allows the use of the second year's availability of the 2000 funds, but disallows the expenditure of the authorized $60 million for 2001.

Trust Funds

GIFTS AND BEQUESTS

Unavailable Collections (in millions of dollars)

Identification code 12–8203–0–7–352	1999 actual	2000 est.	2001 est.
Balance, start of year:			
01.99 Balance, start of year			
Receipts:			
02.01 Gifts and bequests	1	1	1
Appropriation:			
05.01 Gifts and bequests	−1	−1	−1
07.99 Total balance, end of year			

Program and Financing (in millions of dollars)

Identification code 12–8203–0–7–352	1999 actual	2000 est.	2001 est.
Obligations by program activity:			
10.00 Total new obligations (object class 99.5)	1	1	1
Budgetary resources available for obligation:			
21.40 Unobligated balance available, start of year	2	2	2
22.00 New budget authority (gross)	1	1	1
23.90 Total budgetary resources available for obligation	3	3	3
23.95 Total new obligations	−1	−1	−1
24.40 Unobligated balance available, end of year	2	2	2
New budget authority (gross), detail:			
Mandatory:			
60.27 Appropriation (trust fund, indefinite)	1	1	1
Change in unpaid obligations:			
73.10 Total new obligations	1	1	1
73.20 Total outlays (gross)	−1	−1	−1
Outlays (gross), detail:			
86.97 Outlays from new mandatory authority	1	1	1
Net budget authority and outlays:			
89.00 Budget authority	1	1	1
90.00 Outlays	1	1	1

The Secretary is authorized to accept and administer gifts and bequests of real and personal property to facilitate the work of the Department. Property and the proceeds thereof are used in accordance with the terms of the gift or bequest (7 U.S.C. 2269).

EXECUTIVE OPERATIONS

Federal Funds

General and special funds:

EXECUTIVE OPERATIONS

CHIEF ECONOMIST

For necessary expenses of the Chief Economist, including economic analysis, risk assessment, cost-benefit analysis, energy and new uses, and the functions of the World Agricultural Outlook Board, as authorized by the Agricultural Marketing Act of 1946 (7 U.S.C. 1622g), and including employment pursuant to the second sentence of section 706(a) of the Organic Act of 1944 (7 U.S.C. 2225), of which not to exceed $5,000 is for employment under 5 U.S.C. 3109, [$6,411,000] *$8,612,000*.

NATIONAL APPEALS DIVISION

For necessary expenses of the National Appeals Division, including employment pursuant to the second sentence of section 706(a) of the Organic Act of 1944 (7 U.S.C. 2225), of which not to exceed $25,000 is for employment under 5 U.S.C. 3109, [$11,718,000] *$12,610,000*.

OFFICE OF BUDGET AND PROGRAM ANALYSIS

For necessary expenses of the Office of Budget and Program Analysis, including employment pursuant to the second sentence of section 706(a) of the Organic Act of 1944 (7 U.S.C. 2225), of which not to exceed $5,000 is for employment under 5 U.S.C. 3109, [$6,583,000] *$6,765,000. (7 U.S.C. 2201, 2202; 42 U.S.C. 2000d; Agriculture, Rural Development, Food and Drug Administration, and Related Agencies Appropriations Act, 2000.)*

Program and Financing (in millions of dollars)

Identification code 12–0705–0–1–352	1999 actual	2000 est.	2001 est.
Obligations by program activity:			
00.01 Chief Economist	6	6	9
00.03 National Appeals Division	12	12	12
00.04 Budget and program analysis	6	7	7
09.01 Reimbursable program	1	1	1
10.00 Total new obligations	25	26	29
Budgetary resources available for obligation:			
22.00 New budget authority (gross)	25	26	29
23.95 Total new obligations	−25	−26	−29
New budget authority (gross), detail:			
Discretionary:			
40.00 Appropriation	23	25	28
42.00 Transferred from other accounts	1		
43.00 Appropriation (total discretionary)	24	25	28
68.00 Spending authority from offsetting collections: Offsetting collections (cash)	1	1	1
70.00 Total new budget authority (gross)	25	26	29
Change in unpaid obligations:			
72.40 Unpaid obligations, start of year: Obligated balance, start of year	4	4	4
73.10 Total new obligations	25	26	29
73.20 Total outlays (gross)	−24	−24	−28
74.40 Unpaid obligations, end of year: Obligated balance, end of year	4	4	4
Outlays (gross), detail:			
86.90 Outlays from new discretionary authority	22	23	26
86.93 Outlays from discretionary balances	2		3
87.00 Total outlays (gross)	24	24	28
Offsets:			
Against gross budget authority and outlays:			
88.00 Offsetting collections (cash) from: Federal sources	−1	−1	−1
Net budget authority and outlays:			
89.00 Budget authority	24	25	28
90.00 Outlays	23	24	27

Executive Operations provides support for USDA policy officials and selected Departmentwide services.

The Office of the Chief Economist advises the Secretary of Agriculture on the economic implications of Department policies and programs and proposed legislation. The Office serves as the single focal point for the Nation's economic intelligence and analysis, risk assessment, and cost-benefit analysis related to domestic and international food and agriculture, provides policy direction for biofuels and new uses, and is responsible for coordination and clearance review of all commodity and aggregate agricultural and food-related data used to develop outlook and situation material within the Department.

WORKLOAD INDICATORS

	1999 actual	*2000 est.*	*2001 est.*
World Agricultural Supply and Demand Estimates Reports issued	12	12	12
Weekly Weather and Crop Bulletin issued	52	52	52

General and special funds—Continued

OFFICE OF BUDGET AND PROGRAM ANALYSIS—Continued

The Federal Agriculture Improvement and Reform (FAIR) Act of 1996 authorized the Commission on the 21st Century Production Agriculture to (1) conduct comprehensive review and assessment of the success of production flexibility contracts in supporting the viability of U.S. farming, and (2) review the future of production agriculture and the appropriate role of the Federal government in it.

The National Appeals Division conducts administrative hearings and reviews of adverse program decisions made by the Farm Service Agency, the Risk Management Agency, the Natural Resources Conservation Service, and the Rural Development mission area.

WORKLOAD INDICATORS

	1999 actual	2000 est.	2001 est.
Regional or National Training	3	1	3
Percent of Hearing Officer determinations upheld on review	76.3	78.3	78.3

The Office of Budget and Program Analysis provides overall direction and administration of the Department's budgetary functions including: development, presentation, and execution of the budget; review of program and legislative proposals for programs and budget implications; and analysis of program issues and alternatives and preparation of summaries of pertinent data to aid Departmental policy officials and agency program managers in the decisionmaking process.

Object Classification (in millions of dollars)

Identification code 12–0705–0–1–352		1999 actual	2000 est.	2001 est.
	Direct obligations:			
11.1	Personnel compensation: Full-time permanent	16	17	18
12.1	Civilian personnel benefits	4	4	6
21.0	Travel and transportation of persons	1	1	1
23.3	Communications, utilities, and miscellaneous charges	1	1	1
25.2	Other services	1	1	1
31.0	Equipment	1	1	1
99.0	Subtotal, direct obligations	24	25	28
99.0	Reimbursable obligations	1	1	1
99.9	Total new obligations	25	26	29

Personnel Summary

Identification code 12–0705–0–1–352		1999 actual	2000 est.	2001 est.
1001	Total compensable workyears: Full-time equivalent employment	239	260	266

OFFICE OF THE CHIEF FINANCIAL OFFICER

For necessary expenses of the Office of the Chief Financial Officer, including employment pursuant to the second sentence of section 706(a) of the Organic Act of 1944 (7 U.S.C. 2225), of which not to exceed $10,000 is for employment under 5 U.S.C. 3109, [$4,783,000] *$6,465,000*. *(Agriculture, Rural Development, Food and Drug Administration, and Related Agencies Appropriations Act, 2000.)*

Program and Financing (in millions of dollars)

Identification code 12–0014–0–1–352		1999 actual	2000 est.	2001 est.
	Obligations by program activity:			
00.01	Direct program	4	5	6
09.01	Reimbursable program	2	2	2
10.00	Total new obligations	6	7	8
	Budgetary resources available for obligation:			
22.00	New budget authority (gross)	6	7	8
23.95	Total new obligations	−6	−7	−8
	New budget authority (gross), detail:			
	Discretionary:			
40.00	Appropriation	4	5	6
	Spending authority from offsetting collections:			
68.00	Offsetting collections (cash)	1	2	2
68.10	From Federal sources: Change in receivables and unpaid, unfilled orders	1		
68.90	Spending authority from offsetting collections (total discretionary)	2	2	2
70.00	Total new budget authority (gross)	6	7	8
	Change in unpaid obligations:			
72.95	Unpaid obligations, start of year: From Federal sources: Receivables and unpaid, unfilled orders		1	1
73.10	Total new obligations	6	7	8
73.20	Total outlays (gross)	−6	−7	−8
74.95	Unpaid obligations, end of year: From Federal sources: Receivables and unpaid, unfilled orders	1	1	1
	Outlays (gross), detail:			
86.90	Outlays from new discretionary authority	6	7	8
	Offsets:			
	Against gross budget authority and outlays:			
88.00	Offsetting collections (cash) from: Federal sources	−1	−2	−2
	Against gross budget authority only:			
88.95	From Federal sources: Change in receivables and unpaid, unfilled orders	−1		
	Net budget authority and outlays:			
89.00	Budget authority	4	5	6
90.00	Outlays	4	5	6

The Office of the Chief Financial Officer (OCFO) supports the Chief Financial Officer in carrying out the dual roles of chief financial management policy officer and chief financial management advisor to the Secretary and mission area heads. OCFO provides leadership for all financial management, accounting, travel, Federal assistance, and performance measurement activities within the Department. It is responsible for the management and operation of the National Finance Center and the Departmental Working Capital Fund, and provides budget, accounting, and fiscal services to the Office of the Secretary, Departmental Staff Offices, Office of Communications, Office of the Chief Information Officer and Executive Operations.

PERFORMANCE MEASURES

	1999 actual	2000 est.	2001 est.
Percent of audits where corrective action is proceeding as scheduled	60%	70%	75%
Percent of material FMFIA internal control deficiencies where corrective action is proceeding as scheduled	70%	90%	90%
Decrease the percentage of collectible delinquencies to the total receivables	1.5%	1.0%	1.0%
Issue management accountability report by March 31, 2000	Project planning	Performance report on time	Accountability report issued

Object Classification (in millions of dollars)

Identification code 12–0014–0–1–352		1999 actual	2000 est.	2001 est.
	Direct obligations:			
11.1	Personnel compensation: Full-time permanent	3	4	5
12.1	Civilian personnel benefits	1	1	1
99.0	Subtotal, direct obligations	4	5	6
99.0	Reimbursable obligations	2	2	2
99.9	Total new obligations	6	7	8

Personnel Summary

Identification code 12–0014–0–1–352		1999 actual	2000 est.	2001 est.
	Direct:			
1001	Total compensable workyears: Full-time equivalent employment	48	69	69

		1999 actual	2000 est.	2001 est.
	Reimbursable:			
2001	Total compensable workyears: Full-time equivalent employment	15	19	19

Office of the Chief Information Officer

For necessary expenses of the Office of the Chief Information Officer, including employment pursuant to the second sentence of section 706(a) of the Organic Act of 1944 (7 U.S.C. 2225), of which not to exceed $10,000 is for employment under 5 U.S.C. 3109, **[**$6,051,000**]** *$14,680,000. (Agriculture, Rural Development, Food and Drug Administration, and Related Agencies Appropriations Act, 2000.)*

Program and Financing (in millions of dollars)

Identification code 12–0013–0–1–352		1999 actual	2000 est.	2001 est.
	Obligations by program activity:			
00.01	Office of the Chief Information Officer	6	6	15
00.02	Year 2000 remediation	46	4	....
09.01	Reimbursable program	1	1	1
10.00	Total new obligations	53	11	16
	Budgetary resources available for obligation:			
21.40	Unobligated balance available, start of year	....	7	7
22.00	New budget authority (gross)	60	11	16
23.90	Total budgetary resources available for obligation	60	18	23
23.95	Total new obligations	–53	–11	–16
24.40	Unobligated balance available, end of year	7	7	7
	New budget authority (gross), detail:			
	Discretionary:			
40.00	Appropriation	6	6	15
42.00	Transferred from other accounts	53	4	....
43.00	Appropriation (total discretionary)	59	10	15
68.00	Spending authority from offsetting collections: Offsetting collections (cash)	1	1	1
70.00	Total new budget authority (gross)	60	11	16
	Change in unpaid obligations:			
	Unpaid obligations, start of year:			
72.40	Obligated balance, start of year	1	34	....
72.95	From Federal sources: Receivables and unpaid, unfilled orders	6	6	6
72.99	Total unpaid obligations, start of year	7	40	6
73.10	Total new obligations	53	11	16
73.20	Total outlays (gross)	–20	–45	–16
	Unpaid obligations, end of year:			
74.40	Obligated balance, end of year	34	....	....
74.95	From Federal sources: Receivables and unpaid, unfilled orders	6	6	6
74.99	Total unpaid obligations, end of year	40	6	6
	Outlays (gross), detail:			
86.90	Outlays from new discretionary authority	17	11	16
86.93	Outlays from discretionary balances	3	34	....
87.00	Total outlays (gross)	20	45	16
	Offsets:			
	Against gross budget authority and outlays:			
88.00	Offsetting collections (cash) from: Federal sources	–1	–1	–1
	Net budget authority and outlays:			
89.00	Budget authority	59	10	15
90.00	Outlays	19	44	15

The Clinger-Cohen Act of 1996 required the establishment of a Chief Information Officer (CIO) for major Federal agencies. To meet the intent of the law and to provide a Departmental focus for information resources management issues, Secretary's Memorandum 1030–30, dated August 8, 1996, established the Office of the Chief Information Officer (OCIO). OCIO provides Departmentwide policy guidance, leadership, coordination and direction to the Department's information management and information technology investment activities in support of USDA program delivery. The Office provides information security for long-range planning guidance, implements measures to ensure that technology investments are economical and effective, and implements standards and oversight to promote information exchange and technical interoperability.

This office also provides telecommunications and ADP services to USDA agencies throughout the National Information Technology Center with locations in Ft. Collins, Colorado, and Kansas City, Missouri. Direct ADP operational services are also provided to the Office of the Secretary, Office of the General Counsel, Office of Communications, the Office of Chief Financial Officer, and Executive Operations.

Public Law 105–277 appropriated funds to be available beginning in fiscal year 1999 through 2001, for Year 2000 remediation activities. The Year 2000 Program office provides oversight and guidance to ensure the uninterrupted delivery of USDA programs and services. 2000 reflects a transfer of $4.4 million of these funds to USDA for a total of $57 million.

Performance Measures for 1998–2000

	1999 actual	2000 est.	2001 est.
Number of USDA agencies using CPIC in the selection, evaluation, and control of their IT investment portfolio	27	27	27
Number of agency IT management reviews performed	2	6	6
Number of Service Center Oversight Implementation Independent Validations and Verifications conducted	9	3	3
Ensure all USDA agency critical information systems are Year 2000 compliant and operational (%)	100	N.A.	N.A.
Percent of agencies identifying critical assets and assessing them for vulnerability	10	26	30
Percent of agencies using information system technology architecture	25	35	50

Object Classification (in millions of dollars)

Identification code 12–0013–0–1–352		1999 actual	2000 est.	2001 est.
	Direct obligations:			
11.1	Personnel compensation: Full-time permanent	4	4	5
12.1	Civilian personnel benefits	1	1	1
25.2	Other services	21	2	5
25.3	Purchases of goods and services from Government accounts	2	2	3
26.0	Supplies and materials	3	....	....
31.0	Equipment	20	1	....
41.0	Grants, subsidies, and contributions	1	....	....
99.0	Subtotal, direct obligations	52	10	14
99.0	Reimbursable obligations	1	1	1
99.5	Below reporting threshold	....	....	1
99.9	Total new obligations	53	11	16

Personnel Summary

Identification code 12–0013–0–1–352		1999 actual	2000 est.	2001 est.
	Direct:			
1001	Total compensable workyears: Full-time equivalent employment	50	69	81
	Reimbursable:			
2001	Total compensable workyears: Full-time equivalent employment	5	7	7

Common Computing Environment

For necessary expenses to acquire a Common Computing Environment for the Natural Resources Conservation Service, and the Farm and Foreign Agricultural Service and Rural Development Mission Areas, $75,000,000, to remain available until expended, for the capital asset acquisition of shared information technology systems, including services as authorized by 7 U.S.C. 6915–16 and 40 U.S.C. 1421–28: Provided, That obligation of these funds shall be consistent with the Department of Agriculture Service Center Modernization Plan of the county-based Agencies, and shall be with the concurrence of the Department's Chief Information Officer.

General and special funds—Continued

COMMON COMPUTING ENVIRONMENT—Continued

Program and Financing (in millions of dollars)

Identification code 12–3900–0–4–352	1999 actual	2000 est.	2001 est.
Obligations by program activity:			
10.00 Total new obligations (object class 31.0)			75
Budgetary resources available for obligation:			
22.00 New budget authority (gross)			75
23.95 Total new obligations			–75
New budget authority (gross), detail:			
Discretionary:			
40.00 Appropriation			75
Change in unpaid obligations:			
73.10 Total new obligations			75
73.20 Total outlays (gross)			–63
74.40 Unpaid obligations, end of year: Obligated balance, end of year			12
Outlays (gross), detail:			
86.90 Outlays from new discretionary authority			63
Net budget authority and outlays:			
89.00 Budget authority			75
90.00 Outlays			63

The Department of Agriculture Reorganization Act of 1994 requires the Secretary of Agriculture to procure and use computer systems in a manner that enhances efficiency, productivity, and client services, and that promotes computer information sharing among agencies of the Department. In addition, the Clinger Cohen Act of 1996 requires USDA to maximize the value of information technology acquisitions to improve the efficiency and effectiveness of USDA programs. Congress has also expressed a strong desire for and is considering additional legislation, that would require these county-based agencies to make more services available to the public electronically. Since its beginning in 1996, the USDA Service Center modernization initiative has been working to restructure county field offices, modernize and integrate business approaches and replace the current stove-pipe and aging information systems with a modern Common Computing Environment (CCE) that optimizes information sharing, customer service, and staff efficiencies. The funds requested under this account would fund essential capital investments needed to achieve the goal of a fully operational CCE in 2002 as set forth in the modernization plan. Economies of scale in the procurement and management of information technology systems present compelling arguments for coordinating information technology investments. Without these investments, the Department's ability to provide timely and efficient services will continue to erode and the costs of maintaining the separate, aging systems will increase. Additional funds in the individual agency budgets will support the reengineering of business processes and data acquisition needed to maximize the benefits of this technology.

Intragovernmental funds:

WORKING CAPITAL FUND

Program and Financing (in millions of dollars)

Identification code 12–4609–0–4–352	1999 actual	2000 est.	2001 est.
Obligations by program activity:			
Operating expenses:			
09.01 Administration	22	23	23
09.02 Communications	5	5	5
09.03 Finance and management	162	180	196
09.04 Information technology	58	57	57
09.05 Executive secretariat	1	1	1
09.09 Subtotal, operating expenses	248	266	282
Purchase of equipment:			
09.11 Administration	1		1
09.12 Finance and management	10	15	9
09.13 Information technology	11	10	8
09.19 Subtotal, purchase of equipment	22	25	18
10.00 Total new obligations	270	291	300
Budgetary resources available for obligation:			
21.40 Unobligated balance available, start of year	25	23	23
22.00 New budget authority (gross)	267	291	300
22.10 Resources available from recoveries of prior year obligations	3		
23.90 Total budgetary resources available for obligation	295	314	323
23.95 Total new obligations	–270	–291	–300
24.40 Unobligated balance available, end of year	23	23	23
New budget authority (gross), detail:			
Discretionary:			
68.00 Spending authority from offsetting collections (gross): Offsetting collections (cash)	267	291	300
Change in unpaid obligations:			
72.40 Unpaid obligations, start of year: Obligated balance, start of year	12	18	18
73.10 Total new obligations	270	291	300
73.20 Total outlays (gross)	–263	–291	–300
73.45 Adjustments in unexpired accounts	–3		
74.40 Unpaid obligations, end of year: Obligated balance, end of year	18	18	18
Outlays (gross), detail:			
86.90 Outlays from new discretionary authority	263	291	300
Offsets:			
Against gross budget authority and outlays:			
88.00 Offsetting collections (cash) from: Federal sources	–267	–291	–300
Net budget authority and outlays:			
89.00 Budget authority			
90.00 Outlays	–4		

This fund finances by advances or reimbursements certain central services in the Department of Agriculture, including duplicating and other visual information services, art and graphics, video services, supply, centralized accounting systems, centralized automated data processing systems for payroll, personnel, and related services, voucher payments services, and ADP systems. The National Finance Center's expenses are also funded through this fund. The capital consists of $400 thousand appropriated (7 U.S.C. 2235), and subsequent appropriations of $32 million as of September 30, 1999. Earnings are kept at a low level through adjustments in rates charged for services to maintain as nearly as possible the nonprofit nature of the fund.

Object Classification (in millions of dollars)

Identification code 12–4609–0–4–352	1999 actual	2000 est.	2001 est.
Personnel compensation:			
11.1 Full-time permanent	86	101	107
11.3 Other than full-time permanent	2	2	2
11.5 Other personnel compensation	5	4	4
11.9 Total personnel compensation	93	107	113
12.1 Civilian personnel benefits	17	20	21
21.0 Travel and transportation of persons	2	2	2
22.0 Transportation of things	1	1	1
23.1 Rental payments to GSA	5	5	5
23.2 Rental payments to others	2	2	2
23.3 Communications, utilities, and miscellaneous charges	26	21	22
24.0 Printing and reproduction	2	2	2
25.2 Other services	90	97	106
26.0 Supplies and materials	7	6	6
31.0 Equipment	25	28	20
99.9 Total new obligations	270	291	300

Personnel Summary

Identification code 12–4609–0–4–352	1999 actual	2000 est.	2001 est.
2001 Total compensable workyears: Full-time equivalent employment	2,052	2,089	2,089

DEPARTMENTAL ADMINISTRATION

Federal Funds

General and special funds:

DEPARTMENTAL ADMINISTRATION

(INCLUDING TRANSFERS OF FUNDS)

For Departmental Administration, **[**$34,738,000**]** *$40,740,000*, to provide for necessary expenses for management support services to offices of the Department and for general administration and disaster management of the Department, repairs and alterations, and other miscellaneous supplies and expenses not otherwise provided for and necessary for the practical and efficient work of the Department, including employment pursuant to the second sentence of section 706(a) of the Organic Act of 1944 (7 U.S.C. 2225), of which not to exceed $10,000 is for employment under 5 U.S.C. 3109: *Provided*, That this appropriation shall be reimbursed from applicable appropriations in this Act for travel expenses incident to the holding of hearings as required by 5 U.S.C. 551–558. *(Agriculture, Rural Development, Food and Drug Administration, and Related Agencies Appropriations Act, 2000.)*

Program and Financing (in millions of dollars)

Identification code 12–0120–0–1–352	1999 actual	2000 est.	2001 est.
Obligations by program activity:			
00.08 Direct program	32	35	41
09.01 Reimbursable program	29	13	14
10.00 Total new obligations	61	48	55
Budgetary resources available for obligation:			
22.00 New budget authority (gross)	36	48	55
23.95 Total new obligations	–61	–48	–55
New budget authority (gross), detail:			
Discretionary:			
40.00 Appropriation	32	35	41
Spending authority from offsetting collections:			
68.00 Offsetting collections (cash)	21	13	14
68.10 From Federal sources: Change in receivables and unpaid, unfilled orders	–8	–32	
68.15 From Federal sources: Adjustments to receivables and unpaid, unfilled orders	–9	32	
68.90 Spending authority from offsetting collections (total discretionary)	4	13	14
70.00 Total new budget authority (gross)	36	48	55
Change in unpaid obligations:			
Unpaid obligations, start of year:			
72.40 Obligated balance, start of year	–28	–6	28
72.95 From Federal sources: Receivables and unpaid, unfilled orders	40	32	
72.99 Total unpaid obligations, start of year	12	26	28
73.10 Total new obligations	61	48	55
73.20 Total outlays (gross)	–42	–46	–53
Unpaid obligations, end of year:			
74.40 Obligated balance, end of year	–6	28	30
74.95 From Federal sources: Receivables and unpaid, unfilled orders	32		
74.99 Total unpaid obligations, end of year	26	28	30
Outlays (gross), detail:			
86.90 Outlays from new discretionary authority	34	46	51
86.93 Outlays from discretionary balances	13		2
87.00 Total outlays (gross)	42	46	53
Offsets:			
Against gross budget authority and outlays:			
88.00 Offsetting collections (cash) from: Federal sources	–21	–13	–14
Against gross budget authority only:			
88.95 From Federal sources: Change in receivables and unpaid, unfilled orders	8	32	
88.96 From Federal sources: Adjustment to receivables and unpaid, unfilled orders	9	–32	
Net budget authority and outlays:			
89.00 Budget authority	32	35	41
90.00 Outlays	26	33	39

Departmental Administration is comprised of activities that provide staff support to top policy officials and overall direction and coordination of the Department. These activities include Department-wide programs for human resource management, ethics, management improvement, occupational safety and health management, real and personal property management, procurement, contracting, motor vehicle and aircraft management, supply management, civil rights and equal opportunity, participation of small and disadvantaged businesses, and socially disadvantaged farmers and ranchers in the Department's program activities, emergency preparedness, and the regulatory hearing and administrative proceedings conducted by the Administrative Law Judges, Judicial Officer, and Board of Contract Appeals.

Departmental Administration is also responsible for representing USDA in the development of government-wide policies and initiatives; analyzing the impact of government-wide trends and developing appropriate USDA principles, policies, and standards. In addition, Departmental Administration engages in strategic planning and evaluating programs to ensure USDA-wide compliance with applicable laws, rules, and regulations pertaining to administrative matters for the Secretary and general officers of the Department.

DEPARTMENTAL ADMINISTRATION WORKLOAD INDICATORS

	1999 actual	2000 est.	2001 est.
Subcontracting plans reviewed	46	40	40
Small businesses counseled	6,800	6,800	6,800
Small business procurement conferences conducted or sponsored by USDA/OSDBU	8	6	6
Number of outreach conferences attended by OSDBU staff	18	15	15
Procurement assistance reviews conducted	0	1	1
Training conferences conducted	4	4	4

Object Classification (in millions of dollars)

Identification code 12–0120–0–1–352	1999 actual	2000 est.	2001 est.
Direct obligations:			
11.1 Personnel compensation: Full-time permanent	19	25	28
12.1 Civilian personnel benefits	4	5	6
23.3 Communications, utilities, and miscellaneous charges	1	1	
25.2 Other services	3	1	3
25.3 Purchases of goods and services from Government accounts	3	2	2
31.0 Equipment	2	1	1
99.0 Subtotal, direct obligations	32	35	40
99.0 Reimbursable obligations	29	13	14
99.5 Below reporting threshold			1
99.9 Total new obligations	61	48	55

Personnel Summary

Identification code 12–0120–0–1–352	1999 actual	2000 est.	2001 est.
Direct:			
1001 Total compensable workyears: Full-time equivalent employment	312	374	392
Reimbursable:			
2001 Total compensable workyears: Full-time equivalent employment	62	77	75

General and special funds—Continued

HAZARDOUS [WASTE] *MATERIALS* MANAGEMENT

(INCLUDING TRANSFERS OF FUNDS)

For necessary expenses of the Department of Agriculture, to comply with [the requirement of section 107(g) of] the Comprehensive Environmental Response, Compensation, and Liability Act, 42 U.S.C. [9607(g)] *9601, et seq.*, and [section 6001 of] the Resource Conservation and Recovery Act, 42 U.S.C. [6961] *9601, et seq.*, [$15,700,000] *$30,073,000*, to remain available until expended: *Provided*, That appropriations and funds available herein to the Department for Hazardous [Waste] *Materials* Management may be transferred to any agency of the Department for its use in meeting all requirements pursuant to the above Acts on Federal and non-Federal lands. *(42 U.S.C. 6961, et seq., 42 U.S.C. 9601, et seq.; Agriculture, Rural Development, Food and Drug Administration, and Related Agencies Appropriations Act, 2000.)*

Program and Financing (in millions of dollars)

Identification code 12–0500–0–1–304	1999 actual	2000 est.	2001 est.
Obligations by program activity:			
00.01 Direct program	15	16	30
09.00 Reimbursable program	1		
10.00 Total new obligations	16	16	30
Budgetary resources available for obligation:			
21.40 Unobligated balance available, start of year	1	1	1
22.00 New budget authority (gross)	16	16	30
23.90 Total budgetary resources available for obligation	17	17	31
23.95 Total new obligations	–16	–16	–30
24.40 Unobligated balance available, end of year	1	1	1
New budget authority (gross), detail:			
Discretionary:			
40.00 Appropriation	16	16	30
68.00 Spending authority from offsetting collections: Offsetting collections (cash)	1		
70.00 Total new budget authority (gross)	17	16	30
Change in unpaid obligations:			
72.40 Unpaid obligations, start of year: Obligated balance, start of year	21	18	19
73.10 Total new obligations	16	16	30
73.20 Total outlays (gross)	–19	–15	–30
74.40 Unpaid obligations, end of year: Obligated balance, end of year	18	19	19
Outlays (gross), detail:			
86.90 Outlays from new discretionary authority	9	14	27
86.93 Outlays from discretionary balances	10	1	3
87.00 Total outlays (gross)	19	15	30
Offsets:			
Against gross budget authority and outlays:			
88.40 Offsetting collections (cash) from: Non-Federal sources	–1		
Net budget authority and outlays:			
89.00 Budget authority	15	16	30
90.00 Outlays	18	15	30

Under the Comprehensive Environmental Response, Compensation, and Liability Act and the Resource Conservation and Recovery Act, the Department has the responsibility to meet the same standards for storage and disposition of hazardous wastes as private businesses. Since the Department has substantial commitments under these Acts, a central fund has been established so that resources may be allocated to the Department's agencies. Allocations are made according to objective criteria.

PERFORMANCE INDICATORS

	1999 actual	*2000 est.*	*2001 est.*
Number of sites assessed/characterized on need for cleanup	53	78	27
Number of removal and remediation plans completed [1]	9	17	12
Number of removal and remedial actions completed [2]	42	61	22
Number of mine cleanups completed [3]	6	12	7
Number of cleanup/restoration agreements with potentially responsible parties (PRP's) [4]	7	10	10
Estimated value of cleanup/restoration work performed by PRP's ($ millions) [4]	$34	$35	$35
Number of UST cleanups completed	6	N.A.	N.A.

[1] Until 1999, site assessment and cleanup planning were combined.
[2] Includes response actions under CERCLA, RCRA corrective action, and UST removals and cleanups.
[3] New performance indicator for priority activities under the Clean Water Initiative.
[4] Prior to 1998, PRP and USDA cleanups were combined. The number of agreements and estimated value of cleanup work performed by PRPs will vary from year to year. Enforceable agreements are always executed when the PRP agrees to perform cleanup work.

Object Classification (in millions of dollars)

Identification code 12–0500–0–1–304	1999 actual	2000 est.	2001 est.
25.2 Direct obligations: Other services	14	15	29
99.0 Reimbursable obligations: Subtotal, reimbursable obligations	1		
99.5 Below reporting threshold	1	1	1
99.9 Total new obligations	16	16	30

Personnel Summary

Identification code 12–0500–0–1–304	1999 actual	2000 est.	2001 est.
1001 Total compensable workyears: Full-time equivalent employment	4	6	6

AGRICULTURE BUILDINGS AND FACILITIES AND RENTAL PAYMENTS

(INCLUDING TRANSFERS OF FUNDS)

For payment of space rental and related costs pursuant to Public Law 92–313, including authorities pursuant to the 1984 delegation of authority from the Administrator of General Services to the Department of Agriculture under 40 U.S.C. 486, for programs and activities of the Department which are included in this Act, and for the operation, maintenance, *improvement*, and repair of Agriculture buildings, [$140,364,000] *$182,747,000, to remain available until expended*: *Provided*, That in the event an agency within the Department should require modification of space needs, the Secretary of Agriculture may transfer a share of that agency's appropriation made available by this Act to this appropriation, or may transfer a share of this appropriation to that agency's appropriation, but such transfers shall not exceed 5 percent of the funds made available for space rental and related costs to or from this account. *(7 U.S.C. 2201, 2202, 2208; Agriculture, Rural Development, Food and Drug Administration, and Related Agencies Appropriations Act, 2000.)*

Program and Financing (in millions of dollars)

Identification code 12–0117–0–1–352	1999 actual	2000 est.	2001 est.
Obligations by program activity:			
Direct program:			
00.01 Rental payments to GSA: Non-recurring repairs	106	118	126
00.02 Building operations and maintenance	24	32	31
00.04 Strategic space plan	7	1	26
09.02 Reimbursable program	7	6	1
10.00 Total new obligations	144	157	184
Budgetary resources available for obligation:			
21.40 Unobligated balance available, start of year	11	7	
22.00 New budget authority (gross)	141	150	184
23.90 Total budgetary resources available for obligation	152	157	184
23.95 Total new obligations	–144	–157	–184
24.40 Unobligated balance available, end of year	7		
New budget authority (gross), detail:			
Discretionary:			
40.00 Appropriation	137	140	183
68.00 Spending authority from offsetting collections: Offsetting collections (cash)	4	10	1
70.00 Total new budget authority (gross)	141	150	184

	Change in unpaid obligations:			
72.40	Unpaid obligations, start of year: Obligated balance, start of year	33	21	10
73.10	Total new obligations	144	157	184
73.20	Total outlays (gross)	−157	−169	−184
74.40	Unpaid obligations, end of year: Obligated balance, end of year	21	10	10
	Outlays (gross), detail:			
86.90	Outlays from new discretionary authority	124	148	182
86.93	Outlays from discretionary balances	33	21	2
87.00	Total outlays (gross)	157	169	184
	Offsets:			
	Against gross budget authority and outlays:			
88.00	Offsetting collections (cash) from: Federal sources	−4	−10	−1
	Net budget authority and outlays:			
89.00	Budget authority	137	140	183
90.00	Outlays	153	159	183

This account finances the General Services Administration's fees for rental of space and related services. The appropriation covers all fees for all regular appropriated accounts within the Department of Agriculture with the exception of the Forest Service. This account also finances the operation and maintenance of four buildings in the Headquarters area.

Beginning in 1995, the account included funds for USDA's strategic space plan. Since then, funds were made available for the construction and occupancy of an office facility at the Beltsville Agricultural Research Center and the design and implementation of a long-term program to renovate and modernize the South Building.

WORKLOAD INDICATORS

	1999 actual	2000 est.	2001 est.
Maintenance and Repairs:			
Minor repairs (number)	389	350	350
Maintenance (thousands of hours)	13	13	13
Service calls (thousands)	11	11	11

Object Classification (in millions of dollars)

Identification code 12–0117–0–1–352		1999 actual	2000 est.	2001 est.
	Direct obligations:			
11.1	Personnel compensation: Full-time permanent	5	5	5
12.1	Civilian personnel benefits	1	1	1
23.1	Rental payments to GSA	106	118	126
23.3	Communications, utilities, and miscellaneous charges	5	5	5
25.2	Other services	20	22	46
99.0	Subtotal, direct obligations	137	151	183
99.0	Reimbursable obligations	7	6	1
99.9	Total new obligations	144	157	184

Personnel Summary

Identification code 12–0117–0–1–352		1999 actual	2000 est.	2001 est.
1001	Total compensable workyears: Full-time equivalent employment	77	86	88

Outreach for Socially Disadvantaged Farmers

For grants and contracts pursuant to section 2501 of the Food, Agriculture, Conservation, and Trade Act of 1990 (7 U.S.C. 2279), [$3,000,000] *$10,000,000*, to remain available until expended. *(Agriculture, Rural Development, Food and Drug Administration, and Related Agencies Appropriations Act, 2000.)*

Program and Financing (in millions of dollars)

Identification code 12–0601–0–1–351		1999 actual	2000 est.	2001 est.
	Obligations by program activity:			
00.01	Direct program	3	3	10
09.00	Reimbursable program	1	1	
10.00	Total new obligations	4	4	10
	Budgetary resources available for obligation:			
22.00	New budget authority (gross)	4	4	10
23.95	Total new obligations	−4	−4	−10
	New budget authority (gross), detail:			
	Discretionary:			
40.00	Appropriation	3	3	10
	Spending authority from offsetting collections:			
68.00	Offsetting collections (cash)	2		
68.10	From Federal sources: Change in receivables and unpaid, unfilled orders	−1		
68.90	Spending authority from offsetting collections (total discretionary)	1		
70.00	Total new budget authority (gross)	4	3	10
	Change in unpaid obligations:			
	Unpaid obligations, start of year:			
72.40	Obligated balance, start of year	3	2	
72.95	From Federal sources: Receivables and unpaid, unfilled orders	3	2	2
72.99	Total unpaid obligations, start of year	6	4	2
73.10	Total new obligations	4	4	10
73.20	Total outlays (gross)	−6	−6	−10
	Unpaid obligations, end of year:			
74.40	Obligated balance, end of year	2		
74.95	From Federal sources: Receivables and unpaid, unfilled orders	2	2	2
74.99	Total unpaid obligations, end of year	4	2	2
	Outlays (gross), detail:			
86.90	Outlays from new discretionary authority	1	3	10
86.93	Outlays from discretionary balances	5	2	
87.00	Total outlays (gross)	6	6	10
	Offsets:			
	Against gross budget authority and outlays:			
88.00	Offsetting collections (cash) from: Federal sources	−2		
	Against gross budget authority only:			
88.95	From Federal sources: Change in receivables and unpaid, unfilled orders	1		
	Net budget authority and outlays:			
89.00	Budget authority	3	3	10
90.00	Outlays	4	3	10

Farm Outreach and Assistance Grants.—This program is authorized under section 2501 of Title XXV of the Food, Agriculture, Conservation, and Trade Act of 1990. Section 2501 requires the Secretary of Agriculture to provide outreach and technical assistance to encourage and assist socially disadvantaged farmers and ranchers to own and operate farms and ranches and to participate in agricultural programs.

The Secretary may make grants to and enter into contracts and other agreements with eligible community-based organizations, 1890/1862/1994 Land-Grant Institutions, Tuskegee University, Native American Community Colleges and Hispanic Servicing Institutions with demonstrated experience in providing education or other agriculture-related services to socially disadvantaged farmers and ranchers.

The USDA through partnership agreements will provide outreach, training, technical assistance, and sound farm management and production to small farmers and ranchers by providing assistance in custom farm plans, production, crop diversification, marketing practices, farm accounting, and recordkeeping. The overall objective of the program is to enhance the ability of small and minority producers to operate a farming or ranching enterprise independently and produce income to service an adequate standard of living. Services are provided by non-federal employees who are employed by the entities.

General and special funds—Continued

OUTREACH FOR SOCIALLY DISADVANTAGED FARMERS—Continued

GRANT OBLIGATIONS

	1999 actual	2000 est.	2001 est.
Number of grants	26	26	26
Amount of grants (in millions of dollars)	3	3	10

Object Classification (in millions of dollars)

Identification code 12–0601–0–1–351		1999 actual	2000 est.	2001 est.
41.0	Direct obligations: Grants, subsidies, and contributions	3	3	10
99.0	Reimbursable obligations: Subtotal, reimbursable obligations	1	1	
99.9	Total new obligations	4	4	10

OFFICE OF COMMUNICATIONS

Federal Funds

General and special funds:

OFFICE OF COMMUNICATIONS

For necessary expenses to carry on services relating to the coordination of programs involving public affairs, for the dissemination of agricultural information, and the coordination of information, work, and programs authorized by Congress in the Department, [$8,138,000] *$9,031,000*, including employment pursuant to the second sentence of section 706(a) of the Organic Act of 1944 (7 U.S.C. 2225), of which not to exceed $10,000 shall be available for employment under 5 U.S.C. 3109, and not to exceed $2,000,000 may be used for farmers' bulletins. *(Agriculture, Rural Development, Food and Drug Administration, and Related Agencies Appropriations Act, 2000.)*

Program and Financing (in millions of dollars)

Identification code 12–0150–0–1–352		1999 actual	2000 est.	2001 est.
	Obligations by program activity:			
00.01	Public affairs	8	8	9
09.01	Reimbursable program	1	1	1
10.00	Total new obligations	9	9	10
	Budgetary resources available for obligation:			
22.00	New budget authority (gross)	9	10	11
23.95	Total new obligations	−9	−9	−10
	New budget authority (gross), detail:			
	Discretionary:			
40.00	Appropriation	8	8	9
	Spending authority from offsetting collections:			
68.00	Offsetting collections (cash)	1	1	1
68.10	From Federal sources: Change in receivables and unpaid, unfilled orders		1	1
68.90	Spending authority from offsetting collections (total discretionary)	1	2	2
70.00	Total new budget authority (gross)	9	10	11
	Change in unpaid obligations:			
72.95	Unpaid obligations, start of year: From Federal sources: Receivables and unpaid, unfilled orders			1
73.10	Total new obligations	9	9	10
73.20	Total outlays (gross)	−9	−8	−11
74.95	Unpaid obligations, end of year: From Federal sources: Receivables and unpaid, unfilled orders		1	2
	Outlays (gross), detail:			
86.90	Outlays from new discretionary authority	9	9	10
86.93	Outlays from discretionary balances			1
87.00	Total outlays (gross)	9	8	11
	Offsets:			
	Against gross budget authority and outlays:			
88.00	Offsetting collections (cash) from: Federal sources	−1	−1	−1
	Against gross budget authority only:			
88.95	From Federal sources: Change in receivables and unpaid, unfilled orders		−1	−1
	Net budget authority and outlays:			
89.00	Budget authority	8	8	9
90.00	Outlays	8	7	9

Public affairs.—This office provides general direction, leadership, and coordination of the Department's information program. The major objective is to provide a balanced and useful information program that reports on USDA's research, administrative action, and regulatory activities using all communications media in order to enable the general public and the agricultural industry to have a better understanding of agriculture's services to farmers and to society.

PERFORMANCE MEASURES

	1999 actual	2000 est.	2001 est.
Random surveys of selected communications initiatives reveal that intended audience received the material or information distributed	90%	95%	98%

Object Classification (in millions of dollars)

Identification code 12–0150–0–1–352		1999 actual	2000 est.	2001 est.
	Direct obligations:			
11.1	Personnel compensation: Full-time permanent	6	6	7
12.1	Civilian personnel benefits	1	1	1
25.2	Other services	1	1	1
99.0	Subtotal, direct obligations	8	8	9
99.0	Reimbursable obligations	1	1	1
99.9	Total new obligations	9	9	10

Personnel Summary

Identification code 12–0150–0–1–352		1999 actual	2000 est.	2001 est.
1001	Total compensable workyears: Full-time equivalent employment	89	95	95

OFFICE OF THE INSPECTOR GENERAL

Federal Funds

General and special funds:

OFFICE OF THE INSPECTOR GENERAL

(INCLUDING TRANSFERS OF FUNDS)

For necessary expenses of the Office of the Inspector General, including employment pursuant to the second sentence of section 706(a) of the Organic Act of 1944 (7 U.S.C. 2225), and the Inspector General Act of 1978, [$65,128,000] *$70,214,000*, including such sums as may be necessary for contracting and other arrangements with public agencies and private persons pursuant to section 6(a)(9) of the Inspector General Act of 1978, including not to exceed $50,000 for employment under 5 U.S.C. 3109; and including not to exceed $125,000 for certain confidential operational expenses, including the payment of informants, to be expended under the direction of the Inspector General pursuant to Public Law 95–452 and section 1337 of Public Law 97–98. *(7 U.S.C. 450b, 2201, 2202, 2220, 2270; Public Law 100–504; Agriculture, Rural Development, Food and Drug Administration, and Related Agencies Appropriations Act, 2000.)*

Program and Financing (in millions of dollars)

Identification code 12–0900–0–1–352		1999 actual	2000 est.	2001 est.
	Obligations by program activity:			
00.01	Direct program	65	65	70
09.01	Reimbursable program	3	3	3
10.00	Total new obligations	68	68	73
	Budgetary resources available for obligation:			
22.00	New budget authority (gross)	68	68	73

		1999 actual	2000 est.	2001 est.
23.95	Total new obligations	−68	−68	−73
	New budget authority (gross), detail:			
	Discretionary:			
40.00	Appropriation	65	65	70
68.00	Spending authority from offsetting collections: Offsetting collections (cash)	3	3	3
70.00	Total new budget authority (gross)	68	68	73
	Change in unpaid obligations:			
72.40	Unpaid obligations, start of year: Obligated balance, start of year	3	6	6
73.10	Total new obligations	68	68	73
73.20	Total outlays (gross)	−65	−68	−73
74.40	Unpaid obligations, end of year: Obligated balance, end of year	6	6	6
	Outlays (gross), detail:			
86.90	Outlays from new discretionary authority	62	62	67
86.93	Outlays from discretionary balances	3	6	6
87.00	Total outlays (gross)	65	68	73
	Offsets:			
	Against gross budget authority and outlays:			
88.00	Offsetting collections (cash) from: Federal sources	−3	−3	−3
	Net budget authority and outlays:			
89.00	Budget authority	65	65	70
90.00	Outlays	62	65	70

The Office keeps the Secretary and Congress informed about fraud, other serious problems, mismanagement, and deficiencies in Department programs and operations, recommends corrective action, and reports on the progress made in correcting the problems. It reviews existing and proposed legislation and regulations and makes recommendations to the Secretary and Congress regarding the impact these laws have on the Department's programs and the prevention and detection of fraud and mismanagement in such programs. The Office provides policy direction and conducts, supervises, and coordinates all audits and investigations. The office supervises and coordinates other activities in the Department and between the Department and other Federal, State and local government agencies whose purposes are to: (a) promote economy and efficiency; (b) prevent and detect fraud and mismanagement; and (c) identify and prosecute people involved in fraud or mismanagement.

Object Classification (in millions of dollars)

Identification code 12–0900–0–1–352		1999 actual	2000 est.	2001 est.
	Direct obligations:			
	Personnel compensation:			
11.1	Full-time permanent	38	40	42
11.5	Other personnel compensation	4	4	4
11.9	Total personnel compensation	42	44	46
12.1	Civilian personnel benefits	12	12	13
21.0	Travel and transportation of persons	4	5	5
23.3	Communications, utilities, and miscellaneous charges	1	1	1
25.2	Other services	1	1	1
25.3	Purchases of goods and services from Government accounts	1	1	1
31.0	Equipment	1	....	1
99.0	Subtotal, direct obligations	62	64	68
99.0	Reimbursable obligations	3	3	3
99.5	Below reporting threshold	3	1	2
99.9	Total new obligations	68	68	73

Personnel Summary

Identification code 12–0900–0–1–352		1999 actual	2000 est.	2001 est.
1001	Total compensable workyears: Full-time equivalent employment	701	753	760

OFFICE OF THE GENERAL COUNSEL

Federal Funds

General and special funds:

OFFICE OF THE GENERAL COUNSEL

For necessary expenses of the Office of the General Counsel, [$29,194,000] *$32,881,000. (7 U.S.C. 2201; 2202, 2214a; Agriculture, Rural Development, Food and Drug Administration, and Related Agencies Appropriations Act, 2000.)*

Program and Financing (in millions of dollars)

Identification code 12–2300–0–1–352		1999 actual	2000 est.	2001 est.
	Obligations by program activity:			
00.01	Direct program	29	29	33
09.00	Reimbursable program	1	2	2
10.00	Total new obligations	30	31	35
	Budgetary resources available for obligation:			
22.00	New budget authority (gross)	30	31	35
23.95	Total new obligations	−30	−31	−35
	New budget authority (gross), detail:			
	Discretionary:			
40.00	Appropriation	29	29	33
68.00	Spending authority from offsetting collections: Offsetting collections (cash)	1	2	2
70.00	Total new budget authority (gross)	30	31	35
	Change in unpaid obligations:			
72.40	Unpaid obligations, start of year: Obligated balance, start of year		1	2
73.10	Total new obligations	30	31	35
73.20	Total outlays (gross)	−30	−31	−35
74.40	Unpaid obligations, end of year: Obligated balance, end of year	1	2	2
	Outlays (gross), detail:			
86.90	Outlays from new discretionary authority	29	29	33
86.93	Outlays from discretionary balances			2
87.00	Total outlays (gross)	30	31	35
	Offsets:			
	Against gross budget authority and outlays:			
88.00	Offsetting collections (cash) from: Federal sources	−1	−2	−2
	Net budget authority and outlays:			
89.00	Budget authority	29	29	33
90.00	Outlays	28	29	33

The Office of the General Counsel of the Department of Agriculture provides all legal advice, counsel, and services to the Secretary and to all agencies, offices, and corporations of the Department on all aspects of their operations. It represents the Department in administrative proceedings; nonlitigation debt collection proceedings; state water rights adjudications; proceedings before the Environmental Protection Agency, Interstate Commerce Commission, Federal Maritime Administration and International Trade Commission; and, in conjunction with the Department of Justice, in judicial proceedings and litigation. All attorneys and related support personnel of the Department are under the supervision of the General Counsel.

Object Classification (in millions of dollars)

Identification code 12–2300–0–1–352		1999 actual	2000 est.	2001 est.
	Direct obligations:			
11.1	Personnel compensation: Full-time permanent	23	24	26
12.1	Civilian personnel benefits	5	5	6
23.3	Communications, utilities, and miscellaneous charges	1	....	1
99.0	Subtotal, direct obligations	29	29	33
99.0	Reimbursable obligations	1	2	2

General and special funds—Continued

OFFICE OF THE GENERAL COUNSEL—Continued

Object Classification (in millions of dollars)—Continued

Identification code 12–2300–0–1–352	1999 actual	2000 est.	2001 est.
99.9 Total new obligations	30	31	35

Personnel Summary

Identification code 12–2300–0–1–352	1999 actual	2000 est.	2001 est.
Direct:			
1001 Total compensable workyears: Full-time equivalent employment	333	343	363
Reimbursable:			
2001 Total compensable workyears: Full-time equivalent employment	6	7	7

ECONOMIC RESEARCH SERVICE

Federal Funds

General and special funds:

ECONOMIC RESEARCH SERVICE

For necessary expenses of the Economic Research Service in conducting economic research and analysis, as authorized by the Agricultural Marketing Act of 1946 (7 U.S.C. 1621–1627) and other laws, [$65,419,000] *$55,424,000*: *Provided*, [That $1,000,000 shall be transferred to and merged with the appropriation for "Food and Nutrition Service, Food Program Administration" for studies and evaluations: *Provided further*,] That this appropriation shall be available for employment pursuant to the second sentence of section 706(a) of the Organic Act of 1944 (7 U.S.C. 2225). *(7 U.S.C. 292, 411, 427, 1441a, 1704, 1761–68, 2201, 2202, 3103, 3291, 3311, 3504; 22 U.S.C. 3101; 42 U.S.C. 1891–93; 44 U.S.C. 3501–11; 50 U.S.C. 2061 et seq., 2251 et seq.; Agriculture, Rural Development, Food and Drug Administration, and Related Agencies Appropriations Act, 2000.)*

Program and Financing (in millions of dollars)

Identification code 12–1701–0–1–352	1999 actual	2000 est.	2001 est.
Obligations by program activity:			
00.01 Direct program	62	64	55
09.00 Reimbursable program	3	4	4
10.00 Total new obligations	65	68	59
Budgetary resources available for obligation:			
22.00 New budget authority (gross)	66	68	59
23.95 Total new obligations	–65	–68	–59
New budget authority (gross), detail:			
Discretionary:			
40.00 Appropriation	66	65	55
41.00 Transferred to other accounts	–3	–1	
43.00 Appropriation (total discretionary)	63	64	55
68.00 Spending authority from offsetting collections: Offsetting collections (cash)	3	4	4
70.00 Total new budget authority (gross)	66	68	59
Change in unpaid obligations:			
72.40 Unpaid obligations, start of year: Obligated balance, start of year	24	28	38
73.10 Total new obligations	65	68	59
73.20 Total outlays (gross)	–61	–60	–60
74.40 Unpaid obligations, end of year: Obligated balance, end of year	28	38	35
Outlays (gross), detail:			
86.90 Outlays from new discretionary authority	45	60	52
86.93 Outlays from discretionary balances	16		8
87.00 Total outlays (gross)	61	60	60
Offsets:			
Against gross budget authority and outlays:			
88.00 Offsetting collections (cash) from: Federal sources	–3	–4	–4
Net budget authority and outlays:			
89.00 Budget authority	63	64	55
90.00 Outlays	58	56	56

The Economic Research Service provides economic and other social science research and analysis for public and private decisions on agriculture, food, natural resources, and rural America.

Miscellaneous funds received from States, local organizations, and others are available for support of economic research and analysis (7 U.S.C. 450b, 450h, 3318b).

The 2001 request includes funding for three new initiatives: an initiative on structural change, coordination and concentration in food and agriculture; an initiative on global research, statistics, and outreach; and an initiative, concerning the economic incentives for carbon sequestration and trace gas emissions control in agriculture. The 2000 appropriation included funds for certain evaluation activities of the USDA Food and Nutrition Service, which are proposed to be funded through that account in 2001.

Object Classification (in millions of dollars)

Identification code 12–1701–0–1–352	1999 actual	2000 est.	2001 est.
Direct obligations:			
Personnel compensation:			
11.1 Full-time permanent	32	32	32
11.3 Other than full-time permanent	2	2	2
11.9 Total personnel compensation	34	34	34
12.1 Civilian personnel benefits	6	6	6
21.0 Travel and transportation of persons	1	1	1
23.3 Communications, utilities, and miscellaneous charges	1	1	1
25.2 Other services	4	2	2
25.3 Purchases of goods and services from Government accounts	4	6	5
25.5 Research and development contracts	8	10	4
26.0 Supplies and materials	1	1	1
31.0 Equipment	1	1	1
41.0 Grants, subsidies, and contributions	2	2	
99.0 Subtotal, direct obligations	62	64	55
99.0 Reimbursable obligations	3	4	4
99.9 Total new obligations	65	68	59

Personnel Summary

Identification code 12–1701–0–1–352	1999 actual	2000 est.	2001 est.
Direct:			
1001 Total compensable workyears: Full-time equivalent employment	506	506	517
Reimbursable:			
2001 Total compensable workyears: Full-time equivalent employment	5	5	5

NATIONAL AGRICULTURAL STATISTICS SERVICE

Federal Funds

General and special funds:

NATIONAL AGRICULTURAL STATISTICS SERVICE

For necessary expenses of the National Agricultural Statistics Service in conducting statistical reporting and service work, including crop and livestock estimates, statistical coordination and improvements, marketing surveys, and the Census of Agriculture, as authorized by 7 U.S.C. 1621–1627, Public Law 105–113, and other laws, [$99,405,000] *$100,615,000*, of which up to [$16,490,000] *$15,000,000* shall be available until expended for the Census of Agriculture: *Provided*, That this appropriation shall be available for employment pursuant to the second sentence of section 706(a) of the Organic Act of 1944 (7 U.S.C. 2225), and not to exceed $40,000 shall be available for employment under 5 U.S.C. 3109. *(7 U.S.C. 411, 411a, 411b, 427, 471, 475, 476, 501, 951, 953, 955–57, 1621–27, 2201, 2202, 2204, 2225, 2248, 3103, 3311, 3504; 18 U.S.C. 1902, 1905, 2072; 42 U.S.C. 1891–93; 44 U.S.C. 3501–11; 50 U.S.C. 2061 et seq., 2251 et seq.; Agriculture, Rural Development, Food and Drug Administration, and Related Agencies Appropriations Act, 2000.)*

Program and Financing (in millions of dollars)

Identification code 12–1801–0–1–352		1999 actual	2000 est.	2001 est.
	Obligations by program activity:			
	Direct program:			
00.01	Agricultural estimates	76	79	82
00.02	Statistical research and service	4	4	4
00.03	Census of Agriculture	23	16	15
09.01	Reimbursable program	10	10	10
10.00	Total new obligations	113	109	111
	Budgetary resources available for obligation:			
22.00	New budget authority (gross)	114	109	111
23.95	Total new obligations	−113	−109	−111
	New budget authority (gross), detail:			
	Discretionary:			
40.00	Appropriation	104	99	101
68.00	Spending authority from offsetting collections: Offsetting collections (cash)	10	10	10
70.00	Total new budget authority (gross)	114	109	111
	Change in unpaid obligations:			
72.40	Unpaid obligations, start of year: Obligated balance, start of year	9	13	11
73.10	Total new obligations	113	109	111
73.20	Total outlays (gross)	−116	−110	−110
73.40	Adjustments in expired accounts (net)	7		
74.40	Unpaid obligations, end of year: Obligated balance, end of year	13	11	11
	Outlays (gross), detail:			
86.90	Outlays from new discretionary authority	114	98	100
86.93	Outlays from discretionary balances	1	12	11
87.00	Total outlays (gross)	116	110	110
	Offsets:			
	Against gross budget authority and outlays:			
	Offsetting collections (cash) from:			
88.00	Federal sources	−8	−8	−8
88.40	Non-Federal sources	−2	−2	−2
88.90	Total, offsetting collections (cash)	−10	−10	−10
	Net budget authority and outlays:			
89.00	Budget authority	104	99	101
90.00	Outlays	106	100	100

Agricultural estimates.—The Service provides the official National and State estimates of acreage, yield, and production of crops, stocks, and value of farm commodities, and numbers of inventory values of livestock items. Data on approximately 120 crops and 45 livestock products are covered in nearly 400 reports issued each year. Detailed data are also collected on agricultural chemical use, labor, and expenditures. In addition, the Census of Agriculture is conducted every five years which provides comprehensive data on the Nation's agricultural industry down to the county level.

The work under this activity is conducted through 45 State offices serving the 50 States; most of these offices are operated as joint State and Federal services. Cooperative arrangements with State agencies provide additional State and county data. The 2001 program includes increases for development of NASS Computer Security Architecture, implementation of a hog survey, expansion of the environmental statistics program, and a reduction in lower priority programs.

Statistical research and service.—This activity is designed to improve the statistical methods and related technologies by improving sample survey designs and procedures and by testing new forecasting and estimating techniques, such as the use of remote sensing and geographic information systems.

Census of Agriculture.—The Census of Agriculture is conducted every five years. In 2001, a decrease reflects removal of the Agricultural Economics and Land Ownership Survey. An increase is requested to fund cyclical activities associated with preparations for the 2002 Census of Agriculture.

Miscellaneous funds received from local organizations, commodity groups, and others are available for dissemination of reports and for survey work conducted under cooperative agreements (7 U.S.C. 450b, 450h, 3318b).

PERFORMANCE MEASURES AND INDICATORS

Performance Measures	Indicators 1999 actual	2000 est.	2001 est.
Percentage of total national agricultural production included in the NASS program	94	95	95
Percentage of reports issued that meet scheduled release date and contain no data errors	96	99	99

Object Classification (in millions of dollars)

Identification code 12–1801–0–1–352		1999 actual	2000 est.	2001 est.
	Direct obligations:			
	Personnel compensation:			
11.1	Full-time permanent	50	52	54
11.3	Other than full-time permanent	1	1	1
11.5	Other personnel compensation	1	1	1
11.9	Total personnel compensation	52	54	56
12.1	Civilian personnel benefits	12	12	13
21.0	Travel and transportation of persons	2	2	2
23.3	Communications, utilities, and miscellaneous charges	3	4	3
24.0	Printing and reproduction	1	1	1
25.2	Other services	21	15	15
25.3	Purchases of goods and services from Government accounts	7	6	6
25.7	Operation and maintenance of equipment	1	1	1
26.0	Supplies and materials	1	1	1
31.0	Equipment	3	3	3
99.0	Subtotal, direct obligations	103	99	101
99.0	Reimbursable obligations	9	9	9
99.5	Below reporting threshold	1	1	1
99.9	Total new obligations	113	109	111

Personnel Summary

Identification code 12–1801–0–1–352		1999 actual	2000 est.	2001 est.
	Direct:			
1001	Total compensable workyears: Full-time equivalent employment	1,030	1,030	1,028
	Reimbursable:			
2001	Total compensable workyears: Full-time equivalent employment	107	107	107

AGRICULTURAL RESEARCH SERVICE

Federal Funds

General and special funds:

Agricultural Research Service

For necessary expenses to enable the Agricultural Research Service to perform agricultural research and demonstration relating to production, utilization, marketing, and distribution (not otherwise provided for); home economics or nutrition and consumer use including the acquisition, preservation, and dissemination of agricultural information; and for acquisition of lands by donation, exchange, or purchase at a nominal cost not to exceed $100, and for land exchanges where the lands exchanged shall be of equal value or shall be equalized by a payment of money to the grantor which shall not exceed 25 percent of the total value of the land or interests transferred out of Federal ownership, [$834,322,000] *$894,258,000: Provided,*

General and special funds—Continued

AGRICULTURAL RESEARCH SERVICE—Continued

That appropriations hereunder shall be available for temporary employment pursuant to the second sentence of section 706(a) of the Organic Act of 1944 (7 U.S.C. 2225), and not to exceed $115,000 shall be available for employment under 5 U.S.C. 3109: *Provided further*, That appropriations hereunder shall be available for the operation and maintenance of aircraft and the purchase of not to exceed one for replacement only: *Provided further*, That appropriations hereunder shall be available pursuant to 7 U.S.C. 2250 for the construction, alteration, and repair of buildings and improvements, but unless otherwise provided, the cost of constructing any one building shall not exceed [$250,000] *$375,000*, except for headhouses or greenhouses which shall each be limited to [$1,000,000] *$1,200,000*, and except for 10 buildings to be constructed or improved at a cost not to exceed [$500,000] *$750,000* each, and the cost of altering any one building during the fiscal year shall not exceed 10 percent of the current replacement value of the building or [$250,000] *$375,000*, whichever is greater: *Provided further*, That the limitations on alterations contained in this Act shall not apply to modernization or replacement of existing facilities at Beltsville, Maryland: *Provided further*, That appropriations hereunder shall be available for granting easements at the Beltsville Agricultural Research Center, including an easement to the University of Maryland to construct the Transgenic Animal Facility which upon completion shall be accepted by the Secretary as a gift: *Provided further*, That the foregoing limitations shall not apply to replacement of buildings needed to carry out the Act of April 24, 1948 (21 U.S.C. 113a): *Provided further, That the foregoing limitations on purchase of land shall not apply to the purchase of land at Corvallis, Oregon; Parlier, California and Florence, South Carolina: Provided further*, That funds may be received from any State, other political subdivision, organization, or individual for the purpose of establishing or operating any research facility or research project of the Agricultural Research Service, as authorized by law.

None of the funds in the foregoing paragraph shall be available to carry out research related to the production, processing or marketing of tobacco or tobacco products.

In fiscal year [2000] *2001*, the agency is authorized to charge fees, commensurate with the fair market value, for any permit, easement, lease, or other special use authorization for the occupancy or use of land and facilities (including land and facilities at the Beltsville Agricultural Research Center) issued by the agency, as authorized by law, and such fees shall be credited to this account and shall remain available until expended for authorized purposes. *(7 U.S.C. 328, 427, 427i, 1281 note, 1621, 2201, 2204, 2225, 2250, 3101 note; 10 U.S.C. 2306; 16 U.S.C. 590(a)–590(b), 590(k); 18 U.S.C. 1114; 19 U.S.C. 1306(a), 1306(c); 20 U.S.C. 191–194; 21 U.S.C. 113a, 114c, 114e–131; 42 U.S.C. 1476(e), 1483; Agriculture, Rural Development, Food and Drug Administration, and Related Agencies Appropriations Act, 2000.)*

Program and Financing (in millions of dollars)

Identification code 12–1400–0–1–352		1999 actual	2000 est.	2001 est.
	Obligations by program activity:			
	Direct program:			
00.01	Research on soil, water and air science	82	89	110
00.02	Research on plant science	295	296	301
00.03	Research on animal science	119	133	141
00.04	Research on commodity conversion and delivery	156	172	184
00.05	Human nutrition research	67	72	89
00.06	Integration of agricultural systems	29	31	30
00.07	Repair and maintenance of facilities	18	18	18
00.08	Contingencies	1		
00.09	Collaborative research program	2		
00.10	Agricultural information and library science	20	19	21
09.00	Reimbursable program	48	60	60
10.00	Total new obligations	837	890	954
	Budgetary resources available for obligation:			
21.40	Unobligated balance available, start of year	1	1	
22.00	New budget authority (gross)	842	890	954
23.90	Total budgetary resources available for obligation	843	891	954
23.95	Total new obligations	−837	−890	−954
23.98	Unobligated balance expiring or withdrawn	−3		
24.40	Unobligated balance available, end of year	1		
	New budget authority (gross), detail:			
	Discretionary:			
40.00	Appropriation	786	834	894
40.15	Appropriation (emergency)	23		
40.35	Appropriation rescinded	−22		
40.76	Reduction pursuant to P.L. 106–113		−4	
42.00	Transferred from other accounts	7		
43.00	Appropriation (total discretionary)	794	830	894
68.00	Spending authority from offsetting collections: Offsetting collections (cash)	48	60	60
70.00	Total new budget authority (gross)	842	890	954
	Change in unpaid obligations:			
72.40	Unpaid obligations, start of year: Obligated balance, start of year	205	234	241
73.10	Total new obligations	837	890	954
73.20	Total outlays (gross)	−809	−885	−942
73.40	Adjustments in expired accounts (net)	1		
74.40	Unpaid obligations, end of year: Obligated balance, end of year	234	241	253
	Outlays (gross), detail:			
86.90	Outlays from new discretionary authority	655	724	775
86.93	Outlays from discretionary balances	154	160	166
87.00	Total outlays (gross)	809	885	942
	Offsets:			
	Against gross budget authority and outlays:			
	Offsetting collections (cash) from:			
88.00	Federal sources	−44	−55	−55
88.40	Non-Federal sources	−4	−5	−5
88.90	Total, offsetting collections (cash)	−48	−60	−60
	Net budget authority and outlays:			
89.00	Budget authority	794	830	894
90.00	Outlays	761	825	882

Funding for the Agricultural Research Service is proposed as part of the Research Fund for America. This proposal highlights the Administration's priority to providing needed and sustained investments in important Federal research programs on a deficit neutral basis. A discussion of the Research Fund for America, and two other funds for the environment and transportation, can be found in Section II of the *Budget* volume.

The Agricultural Research Service conducts research to provide the means for a safer, more economical supply of agricultural products for the Nation and to provide producers with technologies to competitively supply these products. Technology needs of regulatory, technical assistance and education agencies of USDA and other Federal agencies are supported through ARS research. The Service uses coordinated, interdisciplinary approaches to perform basic and applied research on soil and water conservation, plant and animal sciences, commodity conversion and delivery, human nutrition, and integrated agricultural systems. In 2001, the Service proposes increased emphases for critical research needs in agriculture, such as: Emerging and exotic diseases, Invasive species, biobased products and new uses, the President's Food Safety Initiative, Human Nutrition, Agricultural genomics and genetics, Pest Management requirements of the Food Quality Protection Act, Integrated sciences for ecological challenges, Air quality, Global climate change, and Agricultural information and library services. The Service expects to submit 70 new patent applications, participate in 90 new Cooperative research and development agreements (CRADAs), license 30 new products, and develop 70 new plant varieties to release to industry for further development and marketing in 2000.

Research on soil, water, and air sciences.—Research is conducted to improve soil and water management, irrigation, and conservation practices; to protect natural resources from harmful effects of soil, air, and water pollutants and to minimize certain agricultural pollution problems; and to determine the relation of soil types and water to plant, animal, and human nutrition.

Research on plant science.—Research is conducted to increase plant productivity by improving plant varieties, developing new crop resources, and improving crop production practices, including methods to control plant diseases, nematodes, insects, and weeds.

Research on animal science.—Research is conducted to increase livestock productivity (including poultry) through improved breeding, feeding, and management practices, and to develop methods for controlling diseases, parasites, and insect pests affecting these animals.

Research on commodity conversion and delivery.—Research is conducted to develop new and improved foods, feeds, products, and processes for agricultural commodities and to improve the processing, transportation, storage, wholesaling, and retailing of products. Research is also conducted on means to ensure the safety of food and feed supplies, control insect pests of man and his belongings, and reduce the hazards to human life resulting from pesticide residues and other causes.

Human nutrition research.—Research is conducted on subjects such as human nutritional requirements and the composition and nutritive value of foods, to promote optimum human health through improved nutrition.

Integration of agricultural systems.—Research is conducted to develop integrated systems for efficiently producing, processing, and marketing agricultural products, and to develop alternative agricultural systems that are less dependent upon nonrenewable resources and that are productive, efficient, and sustainable in the long term.

Agricultural information and library services.—The National Agricultural Library provides a variety of information products and services through: (1) the administration of a unique collection of books, journals, and other information materials about food and agriculture to ensure accessibility to their contents; (2) the development and maintenance of cooperative efforts in the library and related information areas, with other Federal agencies and with educational institutions in each State; and (3) an active program of information dissemination.

Repair and maintenance of facilities.—Funds are used to restore, upgrade, and maintain Federal facilities to meet OSHA and EPA requirements, provide suitable workspace for in-house research programs, and to retrofit existing structures for better energy utilization.

Contingencies.—Funds available to meet urgent needs that develop unexpectedly during the year when such needs cannot be met by redirection of resources from other projects.

Collaborative Research Program.—Funds from the U.S. Agency for International Development (AID), allows USDA to provide short-term scientific exchanges to the New Independent States of the former Soviet Union (NIS), in developing a market-based agricultural system necessary to meet the food needs of their populations and to develop and strengthen trade linkages between their countries and related agribusiness and agricultural enterprise in the U.S.

Reimbursements.—Agricultural Research Service performs program research activities and services for other USDA, Federal, and non-Federal agencies. These activities and services are paid for on a reimbursable basis.

Object Classification (in millions of dollars)

Identification code 12–1400–0–1–352		1999 actual	2000 est.	2001 est.
	Direct obligations:			
	Personnel compensation:			
11.1	Full-time permanent	315	337	355
11.3	Other than full-time permanent	21	23	24
11.5	Other personnel compensation	15	15	15
11.9	Total personnel compensation	351	375	394
12.1	Civilian personnel benefits	81	88	92
21.0	Travel and transportation of persons	16	17	18
22.0	Transportation of things	2	2	2
23.2	Rental payments to others	1	2	2
23.3	Communications, utilities, and miscellaneous charges	31	31	35
24.0	Printing and reproduction	1	1	2
25.2	Other services	3	9	12
25.3	Purchases of goods and services from Government accounts	5	4	5
25.4	Operation and maintenance of facilities	26	27	30
25.5	Research and development contracts	119	125	141
25.7	Operation and maintenance of equipment	6	6	7
25.8	Subsistence and support of persons	1	1	1
26.0	Supplies and materials	71	72	75
31.0	Equipment	45	47	51
32.0	Land and structures	6	6	6
41.0	Grants, subsidies, and contributions	24	17	21
99.0	Subtotal, direct obligations	789	830	894
99.0	Reimbursable obligations	48	60	60
99.9	Total new obligations	837	890	954

Personnel Summary

Identification code 12–1400–0–1–352		1999 actual	2000 est.	2001 est.
	Direct:			
1001	Total compensable workyears: Full-time equivalent employment	7,301	7,518	7,518
	Reimbursable:			
2001	Total compensable workyears: Full-time equivalent employment	138	138	138

BUILDINGS AND FACILITIES

For acquisition of land, construction, repair, improvement, extension, alteration, and purchase of fixed equipment or facilities as necessary to carry out the agricultural research programs of the Department of Agriculture, where not otherwise provided, **[**$52,500,000**]** *$39,300,000*, to remain available until expended (7 U.S.C. 2209b): *Provided*, That funds may be received from any State, other political subdivision, organization, or individual for the purpose of establishing any research facility of the Agricultural Research Service, as authorized by law. *(Agriculture, Rural Development, Food and Drug Administration, and Related Agencies Appropriations Act, 2000.)*

Program and Financing (in millions of dollars)

Identification code 12–1401–0–1–352		1999 actual	2000 est.	2001 est.
	Obligations by program activity:			
10.00	Total new obligations	73	65	59
	Budgetary resources available for obligation:			
21.40	Unobligated balance available, start of year	102	86	73
22.00	New budget authority (gross)	56	53	39
23.90	Total budgetary resources available for obligation	158	139	112
23.95	Total new obligations	−73	−65	−59
24.40	Unobligated balance available, end of year	86	73	53
	New budget authority (gross), detail:			
	Discretionary:			
40.00	Appropriation	56	53	39
	Change in unpaid obligations:			
72.40	Unpaid obligations, start of year: Obligated balance, start of year	68	72	72
73.10	Total new obligations	73	65	59
73.20	Total outlays (gross)	−68	−65	−65
73.40	Adjustments in expired accounts (net)	−1		
74.40	Unpaid obligations, end of year: Obligated balance, end of year	72	72	66
	Outlays (gross), detail:			
86.90	Outlays from new discretionary authority	3	6	5
86.93	Outlays from discretionary balances	65	59	60
87.00	Total outlays (gross)	68	65	65
	Net budget authority and outlays:			
89.00	Budget authority	56	53	39

General and special funds—Continued

BUILDINGS AND FACILITIES—Continued

Program and Financing (in millions of dollars)—Continued

Identification code 12–1401–0–1–352	1999 actual	2000 est.	2001 est.
90.00 Outlays	68	65	65

This account provides funds for acquisition of land, construction, repair, improvement, extension, alterations, and purchases of fixed equipment or facilities of or used by the Agricultural Research Service. The 2001 request provides the continuing modernization of the Beltsville Agricultural Research Center, Beltsville, MD; the modernizing of ARS and APHIS facilities at the National Animal Disease Center (NADC) at Ames, IA; ongoing upgrades to existing facilities at Plum Island; and Albany, CA; and other high priority projects.

Object Classification (in millions of dollars)

Identification code 12–1401–0–1–352	1999 actual	2000 est.	2001 est.
25.2 Other services	53	25	22
32.0 Land and structures	19	40	37
41.0 Grants, subsidies, and contributions	1		
99.9 Total new obligations	73	65	59

Trust Funds

MISCELLANEOUS CONTRIBUTED FUNDS

Unavailable Collections (in millions of dollars)

Identification code 12–8214–0–7–352	1999 actual	2000 est.	2001 est.
Balance, start of year:			
01.99 Balance, start of year			
Receipts:			
02.01 Science and education contributed funds	22	23	23
Appropriation:			
05.01 Miscellaneous contributed funds	−22	−23	−23
07.99 Total balance, end of year			

Program and Financing (in millions of dollars)

Identification code 12–8214–0–7–352	1999 actual	2000 est.	2001 est.
Obligations by program activity:			
10.00 Total new obligations	20	23	23
Budgetary resources available for obligation:			
21.40 Unobligated balance available, start of year	12	14	13
22.00 New budget authority (gross)	22	23	23
23.90 Total budgetary resources available for obligation	34	37	36
23.95 Total new obligations	−20	−23	−23
24.40 Unobligated balance available, end of year	14	13	13
New budget authority (gross), detail:			
Mandatory:			
60.27 Appropriation (trust fund, indefinite)	22	23	23
Change in unpaid obligations:			
72.40 Unpaid obligations, start of year: Obligated balance, start of year	5	8	6
73.10 Total new obligations	20	23	23
73.20 Total outlays (gross)	−18	−23	−23
74.40 Unpaid obligations, end of year: Obligated balance, end of year	8	6	6
Outlays (gross), detail:			
86.97 Outlays from new mandatory authority	6	7	7
86.98 Outlays from mandatory balances	12	16	16
87.00 Total outlays (gross)	18	23	23
Net budget authority and outlays:			
89.00 Budget authority	22	23	23
90.00 Outlays	18	23	23

Miscellaneous contributed funds received from States, local organizations, individuals, and others are available for work under cooperative agreements on research activities.

Object Classification (in millions of dollars)

Identification code 12–8214–0–7–352	1999 actual	2000 est.	2001 est.
11.1 Personnel compensation: Full-time permanent	5	5	5
12.1 Civilian personnel benefits	1	1	1
25.2 Other services	10	13	13
26.0 Supplies and materials	3	3	3
31.0 Equipment	1	1	1
99.9 Total new obligations	20	23	23

Personnel Summary

Identification code 12–8214–0–7–352	1999 actual	2000 est.	2001 est.
1001 Total compensable workyears: Full-time equivalent employment	106	106	106

COOPERATIVE STATE RESEARCH, EDUCATION, AND EXTENSION SERVICE

Federal Funds

General and special funds:

INTEGRATED ACTIVITIES

[For the integrated research, education, and extension competitive grants programs, including necessary administrative expenses, $89,541,000 as follows: payments for the water quality program, $18,000,000; payments for the food safety program, $15,000,000; payments for the national agriculture pesticide impact assessment program, $4,541,000; payments for the Food Quality Protection Act risk mitigation program for major food crop systems, $4,000,000; payments for crops affected by the Food Quality Protection Act implementation, $1,000,000; and payments for the methyl bromide transition program, $2,000,000, as authorized under section 406 of the Agricultural Research, Extension, and Education Reform Act of 1998 (7 U.S.C. 7626).]

For the integrated research, education, and extension competitive grants programs, including necessary administrative expenses, $76,194,000: (1) for payments as authorized under section 406 of the Agricultural Research, Extension and Education Reform Act of 1998 (7 U.S.C. 7626), for the small farms initiative, $4,000,000; for the water quality program, $16,204,000; for the food safety program, $15,000,000; for the national agriculture pesticide impact assessment program, $4,640,000; for the Food Quality Protection Act risk mitigation program for major food crop systems, $10,000,000; for the crops affected by FQPA implementation, $3,000,000; for the methyl bromide transition program, $5,000,000; for the invasive species program, $1,500,000; for the biobased products program, $9,600,000; for the organic transition program, $1,000,000; (2) payments for the international research, extension, and teaching activities for grants under section 1459A of the National Agricultural Research, Extension, and Teaching Policy Act of 1977 (7 U.S.C. 3291), as amended, to remain available until expended, $1,000,000; and (3) payments for anti-hunger and food security grants program under the same terms and conditions as those found in subsections (c), (d), (f), and (g) of section 25 of the Food Stamp Act of 1977, $5,250,000.

Program and Financing (in millions of dollars)

Identification code 12–1502–0–1–352	1999 actual	2000 est.	2001 est.
Obligations by program activity:			
Direct program:			
00.10 Small farms initiative			4
00.20 Water quality		13	16
00.30 Food safety		15	15
00.40 Pesticide impact assessment		5	5
00.50 Crops at risk		1	3

Identification code		1999 actual	2000 est.	2001 est.
00.60	Food Quality Protection Act risk mitigation program		4	10
00.70	Methyl bromide transition program		2	5
00.80	Anti-hunger and food security grants			5
00.85	International science and education grants			1
00.86	Biobased products program			10
00.87	Invasive species			1
00.88	Organic transition-risk assessment			1
10.00	Total new obligations		40	76
	Budgetary resources available for obligation:			
22.00	New budget authority (gross)		40	76
23.95	Total new obligations		−40	−76
	New budget authority (gross), detail:			
	Discretionary:			
40.00	Appropriation		40	76
	Change in unpaid obligations:			
72.40	Unpaid obligations, start of year: Obligated balance, start of year			38
73.10	Total new obligations		40	76
73.20	Total outlays (gross)		−2	−17
74.40	Unpaid obligations, end of year: Obligated balance, end of year		38	97
	Outlays (gross), detail:			
86.90	Outlays from new discretionary authority		2	4
86.93	Outlays from discretionary balances			14
87.00	Total outlays (gross)		2	17
	Net budget authority and outlays:			
89.00	Budget authority		40	76
90.00	Outlays		2	17

Note.—2000 and 2001 estimates includes water quality grants, food safety and pesticide impact assessments, activities previously financed from the USDA Cooperative State Research, Education, and Extension Service Research and Education Activities and Extension Activities accounts.

Section 406 of the Agricultural Research, Extension, and Education Reform Act of 1998 authorized integrated research, education, and extension competitive grants to provide funding for integrated, multifunctional agricultural research, extension, and education activities. A 100% non-Federal match is required for commodity or location-specific activities. Programs proposed for funding under this account are:

Small farms initiative.—In 2001, a small farms initiative, to be implemented through the Department's Land-Grant partners, is proposed in support of the Secretary's Civil Rights Initiative to strengthen USDA's research and educational assistance to the socially disadvantaged.

Water quality.—This funding will enable CSREES and the State Agricultural Experiment Stations and the Cooperative Extension system to become viable partners with other state and federal agencies in addressing water quality issues of national importance. Funds will be awarded based upon peer review of competitive proposals for projects that have components for research and extension.

Food safety.—Funding will support research, education and extension programs to improve safety of food products and create a more informed public about food safety issues.

National agricultural pesticide impact assessment.—Funding will provide management and coordination for USDA and State activities that support informed regulatory decisions concerning pesticides that significantly benefit U.S. food production without causing adverse effects on the environment.

Crops at risk from FQPA implementation.—Funding will support the development of new multi-tactic IPM strategies. Grant opportunities will be available to state Land-Grant and federal scientists, non-Land-Grant institutions, and grower commodity group partnerships with these groups.

FQPA Risk mitigation program for major food crop systems.—Funds are proposed to support a program to address risk mitigation that will have a food production system focus, integrating food safety and water quality considerations as impacted by FQPA. Emphasis will be placed on development and implementation of new innovative pest management systems designed to maintain crop productivity and profitability while meeting or exceeding environmental quality and human health standards.

Methyl bromide transition program.—This is a competitive grants program designed to support the discovery and implementation of practical pest management alternatives for commodities affected by the methyl bromide phase-out in 2005.

Anti-Hunger and Food Security grants program.—Funds are proposed to establish an anti-hunger and food security program which will support competitively-awarded projects. This program will provide funds to non-profit entities for projects that reduce hunger, improve nutrition, bolster community food security, and help families move from poverty to self-sufficiency.

Invasive species program.—This program will support a new competitive grant program that supports integrated research, extension, and education activities in collaboration with representative individuals, groups and agencies at a local level to address invasive species issues on an ecoregional basis.

Biobased products program.—This funding will enable CSREES to work with other agencies to increase economic opportunities for U.S. farmers by developing and expanding markets through research, development, and commercialization of new, economically competitive and environmentally preferable products from biobased resources.

Organic transition program.—This program supports the development and implementation of biologically based pest management practices that mitigate the ecological, agronomic, and economic risks associated with the transition from conventional to organic agricultural production systems.

International science and education grants.—This program supports the globalization of colleges and universities to strengthen U.S. economic competitiveness and to promote international market development for U.S. agriculture.

Object Classification (in millions of dollars)

Identification code 12–1502–0–1–352		1999 actual	2000 est.	2001 est.
11.1	Personnel compensation: Full-time permanent		1	1
25.2	Other services			1
25.3	Purchases of goods and services from Government accounts		1	1
41.0	Grants, subsidies, and contributions		38	73
99.9	Total new obligations		40	76

Personnel Summary

Identification code 12–1502–0–1–352		1999 actual	2000 est.	2001 est.
1001	Total compensable workyears: Full-time equivalent employment		8	10

Initiative for Future Agriculture and Food Systems

Program and Financing (in millions of dollars)

Identification code 12–1503–0–1–352		1999 actual	2000 est.	2001 est.
	Obligations by program activity:			
10.00	Total new obligations		120	120
	Budgetary resources available for obligation:			
22.00	New budget authority (gross)		120	120
23.95	Total new obligations		−120	−120
	New budget authority (gross), detail:			
	Discretionary:			
40.35	Appropriation deferred			−120
	Mandatory:			
60.00	Appropriation	120	240	240
60.35	Appropriation deferred	−120	−120	
62.50	Appropriation (total mandatory)		120	240

General and special funds—Continued

INITIATIVE FOR FUTURE AGRICULTURE AND FOOD SYSTEMS—Continued

Program and Financing (in millions of dollars)—Continued

Identification code 12–1503–0–1–352	1999 actual	2000 est.	2001 est.
70.00 Total new budget authority (gross)		120	120
Change in unpaid obligations:			
72.40 Unpaid obligations, start of year: Obligated balance, start of year			114
73.10 Total new obligations		120	120
73.20 Total outlays (gross)		−6	−48
74.40 Unpaid obligations, end of year: Obligated balance, end of year		114	186
Outlays (gross), detail:			
86.90 Outlays from new discretionary authority			−6
86.97 Outlays from new mandatory authority		6	12
86.98 Outlays from mandatory balances			42
87.00 Total outlays (gross)		6	48
Net budget authority and outlays:			
89.00 Budget authority		120	120
90.00 Outlays		6	48

1998 Research Act.—The Agricultural Research, Extension, and Education Reform Act of 1998 authorized the annual appropriation of $120 million for high priority research, extension, and education. These funds are available for two years. The 1999 appropriations language blocked the use of 1999 funds in 1999. However, these funds are available in 2000. The 2000 appropriations language blocked the use of 2000 funds in 2000. The 2001 budget allows the use of the second year's availability of the 2000 funds, but disallows the expenditure of the authorized $120 million for 2001.

Object Classification (in millions of dollars)

Identification code 12–1503–0–1–352	1999 actual	2000 est.	2001 est.
11.3 Personnel compensation: Other than full-time permanent		1	1
25.2 Other services		1	1
41.0 Grants, subsidies, and contributions		118	118
99.9 Total new obligations		120	120

Personnel Summary

Identification code 12–1503–0–1–352	1999 actual	2000 est.	2001 est.
1001 Total compensable workyears: Full-time equivalent employment		10	20

RESEARCH AND EDUCATION ACTIVITIES

For payments to agricultural experiment stations, for cooperative forestry and other research, for facilities, and for other expenses, including $180,545,000 to carry into effect the provisions of the Hatch Act (7 U.S.C. 361a–i); $21,932,000 for grants for cooperative forestry research (16 U.S.C. 582a–a7); $30,676,000 for payments to the 1890 land-grant colleges, including Tuskegee University (7 U.S.C. 3222), of which $1,000,000 shall be made available to West Virginia State College in Institute, West Virginia, which for fiscal year [2000] *2001* and thereafter shall be designated as an eligible institution under section 1445 of the National Agricultural Research, Extension, and Teaching Policy Act of 1977 (7 U.S.C. 3222); [$63,238,000] *$6,394,000* for special grants for agricultural research (7 U.S.C. 450i(c)); [$13,721,000] *$18,369,000* for special grants for agricultural research on improved pest control (7 U.S.C. 450i(c)); [$119,300,000] *$150,000,000* for competitive research grants (7 U.S.C. 450i(b)); $5,109,000 for the support of animal health and disease programs (7 U.S.C. 3195); [$750,000 for supplemental and alternative crops and products (7 U.S.C. 3319d); $650,000 for grants for research pursuant to the Critical Agricultural Materials Act of 1984 (7 U.S.C. 178) and section 1472 of the Food and Agriculture Act of 1977 (7 U.S.C. 3318), to remain available until expended; $500,000] *$1,000,000* for the 1994 research program (7 U.S.C. 301 note), *to remain available until expended;* [$3,000,000] *$5,000,000* for higher education graduate fellowship grants (7 U.S.C. 3152(b)(6)), to remain available until expended (7 U.S.C. 2209b); [$4,350,000] *$6,000,000* for higher education challenge grants (7 U.S.C. 3152(b)(1)); [$1,000,000] *$2,000,000* for a higher education multicultural scholars program (7 U.S.C. 3152(b)(5)), to remain available until expended (7 U.S.C. 2209b); [$2,850,000] *$3,500,000* for an education grants program for Hispanic-serving Institutions (7 U.S.C. 3241); $500,000 for a secondary agriculture education program and 2-year post-secondary education (7 U.S.C. 3152(h)); $4,000,000 for aquaculture grants (7 U.S.C. 3322); [$8,000,000] *$10,500,000* for sustainable agriculture research and education (7 U.S.C. 5811); [$9,200,000] *$9,500,000* for a program of capacity building grants (7 U.S.C. 3152(b)(4)) to colleges eligible to receive funds under the Act of August 30, 1890 (7 U.S.C. 321–326 and 328), including Tuskegee University, to remain available until expended (7 U.S.C. 2209b); $1,552,000 for payments to the 1994 Institutions pursuant to section 534(a)(1) of Public Law 103–382; and [$14,825,000] *$4,288,000* for necessary expenses of Research and Education Activities, of which not to exceed $100,000 shall be for employment under 5 U.S.C. 3109; in all, [$485,698,000] *$460,865,000*.

None of the funds in the foregoing paragraph shall be available to carry out research related to the production, processing or marketing of tobacco or tobacco products.

NATIVE AMERICAN INSTITUTIONS ENDOWMENT FUND

For establishment of a Native American institutions endowment fund, as authorized by Public Law 103–382 (7 U.S.C. 301 note), [$4,600,000] *$7,100,000: Provided, That hereafter, any distribution of the adjusted income from the Native American institutions endowment fund is authorized to be used for facility renovation, repair, construction, and maintenance, in addition to other authorized purposes. (Agriculture, Rural Development, Food and Drug Administration, and Related Agencies Appropriations Act, 2000.)*

Unavailable Collections (in millions of dollars)

Identification code 12–1500–0–1–352	1999 actual	2000 est.	2001 est.
Balance, start of year:			
01.99 Balance, start of year	14	19	24
Receipts:			
02.01 Federal payment, Native American Institutions Endowment Fund	5	5	7
02.02 Earnings on investments		1	2
02.99 Total receipts	5	6	9
04.00 Total: Balances and collections	19	25	33
Appropriation:			
05.01 Cooperative state research activities		−1	−1
07.99 Total balance, end of year	19	24	32

Program and Financing (in millions of dollars)

Identification code 12–1500–0–1–352	1999 actual	2000 est.	2001 est.
Obligations by program activity:			
Direct program:			
00.01 Payments under the Hatch Act	181	181	181
00.02 Cooperative forestry research	22	22	22
00.03 Payments to 1890 colleges and Tuskegee University	30	31	31
00.04 Special research grants	92	91	40
00.05 National research initiative competitive grants	118	163	150
00.06 Animal health and disease research	5	5	5
00.07 Federal administration	10	15	4
00.08 Higher education	20	25	28
00.09 Native American Institutions Endowment Fund	6	6	8
09.00 Reimbursable program	17	16	16
10.00 Total new obligations	501	555	485
Budgetary resources available for obligation:			
21.40 Unobligated balance available, start of year	63	66	15
22.00 New budget authority (gross)	504	504	485
23.90 Total budgetary resources available for obligation	567	570	500
23.95 Total new obligations	−501	−555	−485

24.40	Unobligated balance available, end of year	66	15	15
	New budget authority (gross), detail:			
	Discretionary:			
40.00	Appropriation	486	490	468
40.25	Appropriation (special fund, indefinite)		1	1
40.76	Reduction pursuant to P.L. 106–113		−4	
43.00	Appropriation (total discretionary)	486	487	469
68.00	Spending authority from offsetting collections: Offsetting collections (cash)	17	16	16
70.00	Total new budget authority (gross)	503	503	485
	Change in unpaid obligations:			
72.40	Unpaid obligations, start of year: Obligated balance, start of year	373	428	497
73.10	Total new obligations	501	555	485
73.20	Total outlays (gross)	−446	−486	−497
74.40	Unpaid obligations, end of year: Obligated balance, end of year	428	497	485
	Outlays (gross), detail:			
86.90	Outlays from new discretionary authority	234	256	256
86.93	Outlays from discretionary balances	212	230	240
87.00	Total outlays (gross)	446	486	497
	Offsets:			
	Against gross budget authority and outlays:			
88.00	Offsetting collections (cash) from: Federal sources	−17	−16	−16
	Net budget authority and outlays:			
89.00	Budget authority	487	488	469
90.00	Outlays	429	470	481
	Memorandum (non-add) entries:			
92.01	Total investments, start of year: U.S. securities: Par value	14	18	23
92.02	Total investments, end of year: U.S. securities: Par value	18	23	30

Note.—In 2000 and 2001 funding for water quality grants, food safety and pesticide impact assessments is included in the account for integrated activities.

Cooperative State Research, Education, and Extension Service participates in a nationwide system of agricultural research and education program planning and coordination between State institutions and the U.S. Department of Agriculture. It assists in maintaining cooperation among the State institutions, and between the State institutions and their Federal research partners. The Agency administers grants and payments to State institutions to supplement State and local funding for agricultural research and higher education.

Payments under the Hatch Act.—Funds under the Hatch Act are allocated on a formula basis to agricultural experiment stations of the land-grant colleges in the 50 States, the District of Columbia, Puerto Rico, Guam, the Virgin Islands, American Samoa, Micronesia, and Northern Mariana Islands.

Cooperative forestry research.—These funds are allocated by formula to land-grant colleges or agricultural experiment stations in the 50 States, Puerto Rico, Guam, the Virgin Islands, and other State-supported colleges and universities having a forestry school and offering graduate training in forestry sciences.

Payments to 1890 colleges and Tuskegee University.—Funds allocated on a formula basis support agricultural research and broaden the curricula at the seventeen 1890 land-grant colleges, including Tuskegee University.

Special research grants.—This program addresses research areas of national interest. Increased funding is proposed for grant programs in IR–4 minor crop pest management, pest management alternatives, and sustainable agriculture. Funding is also proposed for integrated pest management. Advances in these areas will provide producers with safe, alternative pest control methods resulting in more farmers increasing the number of acres on which Integrated Pest Management (IPM) methods are used. The program goal is the implementation of IPM methods on 75 percent of crop acreage by the year 2000, with an outcome of creating an agricultural system that is highly competitive in the global economy. Funding proposed for IR–4 minor crop pest management and minor use animal drugs will address the growing need for registration of safe pesticides and drugs for minor crops and animals and lead to reduced levels of chemical and drug residues in food products by half. These pest management programs will be coordinated to address Food Quality and Protection Act issues. A $2 million grant program for global change is proposed for research at universities as part of a coordinated Federal initiative. Funding is also proposed for the National Biological Impact Assessment Program, rural development centers, and aquaculture centers.

National research initiative competitive grants.—Increased funding is being proposed for the National Research Initiative (NRI). Research scientists throughout the U.S. scientific community compete for funding under this program. The performance goal has been to attract the widest possible involvement of U.S. scientists in agricultural research to increase the knowledge base related to U.S. agriculture, food, and the environment and maintain world leadership in agricultural science and engineering. NRI funding has resulted in increased participation by universities which are not traditionally considered agricultural schools and of highly skilled researchers in projects addressing agricultural issues. The outcomes include the efficient communication of research results to scientific, engineering, and community user groups. These grants support research in plants and animals; natural resources and the environment; nutrition, food safety, and health; markets, trade, and rural development; and processing for adding value or developing new products. This initiative includes funding for a plant genome mapping program for which the Agricultural Research Service serves as the lead agency. Global change research being carried out through the NRI is part of a government-wide program. In 2001 the proposed increase to $150 million will provide resources needed for the program to enhance and develop scientific areas that are critical such as: agricultural genomics, food safety, environment and natural resource management and competitiveness and profitability of agriculture.

Animal health and disease research.—Funds, distributed by formula, support livestock and poultry disease research in sixty-seven colleges of veterinary medicine and in eligible agricultural experiment stations.

1994 Institutions Research.—Funding is proposed to continue the competitive research grants program to build the research capacity at the thirty 1994 institutions by supporting agricultural research activities that address tribal, national and multistate priorities.

Federal administration.—A coordinating and review staff assists in maintaining cooperation within and among the States, and between the States and their Federal research partners. This staff also administers research and education grants and payments to States. Federal administration is funded from a combination of program set-asides from formula and grant programs and from direct appropriation for administration.

Higher education.—Increased funding is proposed for graduate fellowships grants, competitive challenge grants, Hispanic-serving institutions education grants program, and a multicultural scholars program. Funding is also proposed for a Native American institutions program. Proposed funding for these higher education programs would support approximately 150 grants. These programs will enable universities to broaden their curricula; increase faculty development; student research projects; and the number of new scholars recruited in the food and agricultural sciences. In addition, an increased number of graduate students, including minority graduate students, will be enrolled in the agricultural

General and special funds—Continued

NATIVE AMERICAN INSTITUTIONS ENDOWMENT FUND—Continued

sciences. Funding is also proposed for a capacity building program at the 1890 institutions as part of the USDA initiative to strengthen these institutions through a broadening of curricula, increased faculty development and student research projects. Proposed funding would support approximately 49 teaching and research grants.

Reimbursable program.—Funds support basic and applied agriculture research and activities performed for other USDA, Federal, and non-Federal agencies.

Native American Institutions Endowment Fund.—This program provides for an endowment for the 1994 land-grant institutions (30 Tribally controlled colleges) to strengthen the infrastructure of these institutions and develop Indian expertise for the food and agricultural sciences and businesses and their own communities. At the termination of each fiscal year, the Secretary shall withdraw the income from the endowment fund for the fiscal year, and after making adjustments for the cost of administering the fund, distribute the adjusted income on a formula basis to the 1994 land-grant institutions.

Object Classification (in millions of dollars)

Identification code 12–1500–0–1–352		1999 actual	2000 est.	2001 est.
	Direct obligations:			
11.1	Personnel compensation: Full-time permanent	11	12	13
12.1	Civilian personnel benefits	2	2	2
21.0	Travel and transportation of persons	1	1	1
24.0	Printing and reproduction	1	1	1
25.1	Advisory and assistance services	1	1	1
25.2	Other services	2	3	1
25.3	Purchases of goods and services from Government accounts	1	2	1
41.0	Grants, subsidies, and contributions	465	517	449
99.0	Subtotal, direct obligations	484	539	469
99.0	Reimbursable obligations	17	16	16
99.9	Total new obligations	501	555	485

Personnel Summary

Identification code 12–1500–0–1–352		1999 actual	2000 est.	2001 est.
	Direct:			
1001	Total compensable workyears: Full-time equivalent employment	187	202	207
	Reimbursable:			
2001	Total compensable workyears: Full-time equivalent employment	9	9	9

BUILDINGS AND FACILITIES

Program and Financing (in millions of dollars)

Identification code 12–1501–0–1–352		1999 actual	2000 est.	2001 est.
	Obligations by program activity:			
10.00	Total new obligations (object class 41.0)	1	3	
	Budgetary resources available for obligation:			
21.40	Unobligated balance available, start of year	4	3	
23.95	Total new obligations	–1	–3	
24.40	Unobligated balance available, end of year	3		
	Change in unpaid obligations:			
72.40	Unpaid obligations, start of year: Obligated balance, start of year	139	99	77
73.10	Total new obligations	1	3	
73.20	Total outlays (gross)	–41	–25	–33
74.40	Unpaid obligations, end of year: Obligated balance, end of year	99	77	44
	Outlays (gross), detail:			
86.93	Outlays from discretionary balances	41	25	33
	Net budget authority and outlays:			
89.00	Budget authority			
90.00	Outlays	41	25	33

Funds provide grants to States and other eligible recipients for the acquisition of land, construction, repair, improvement, extension, alteration and purchase of fixed equipment or facilities to carry out agricultural research, extension, and teaching programs. No funding is proposed in 2001.

Personnel Summary

Identification code 12–1501–0–1–352		1999 actual	2000 est.	2001 est.
1001	Total compensable workyears: Full-time equivalent employment	1	1	

EXTENSION ACTIVITIES

Payments to States, the District of Columbia, Puerto Rico, Guam, the Virgin Islands, Micronesia, Northern Marianas, and American Samoa: For payments for cooperative extension work under the Smith-Lever Act, to be distributed under sections 3(b) and 3(c) of said Act, and under section 208(c) of Public Law 93–471, for retirement and employees' compensation costs for extension agents and for costs of penalty mail for cooperative extension agents and State extension directors, $276,548,000; payments for extension work at the 1994 Institutions under the Smith-Lever Act (7 U.S.C. 343(b)(3)), [$3,060,000] *$3,500,000*; payments for the nutrition and family education program for low-income areas under section 3[(a)] *(d)* of the Act, [$58,695,000] *$61,043,000*; payments for the pest management program under section 3(d) of the Act, [$10,783,000; payments for the farm safety program under section 3(d) of the Act, $4,000,000] *$12,269,000; payments for pesticide applicator training under section 3(d) of the Act, $1,500,000*; payments to upgrade research, extension, and teaching facilities at the 1890 land-grant colleges, including Tuskegee University, as authorized by section 1447 of Public Law 95–113 (7 U.S.C. 3222b), $12,000,000, to remain available until expended; payments for the rural development centers under section 3(d) of the Act, $908,000; payments for youth-at-risk programs under section 3(d) of the Act, [$9,000,000] *$10,000,000; for youth farm safety education and certification extension grants, to be awarded competitively under section 3(d) of the Act, $5,000,000;* payments for carrying out the provisions of the Renewable Resources Extension Act of 1978, $3,192,000; payments for Indian reservation agents under section 3(d) of the Act, [$1,714,000] *$5,000,000*; payments for sustainable agriculture programs under section 3(d) of the Act, [$3,309,000; payments for rural health and safety education as authorized by section 2390 of Public Law 101–624 (7 U.S.C. 2661 note, 2662), $2,628,000] *$4,500,000*; payments for cooperative extension work by the colleges receiving the benefits of the second Morrill Act (7 U.S.C. 321–326 and 328) and Tuskegee University, $26,843,000, of which $1,000,000 shall be made available to West Virginia State College in Institute, West Virginia, which for fiscal year [2000] *2001* and thereafter shall be designated as an eligible institution under section 1444 of the National Agricultural Research, Extension, and Teaching Policy Act of 1977 (7 U.S.C. 3221); and for Federal administration and coordination including administration of the Smith-Lever Act, and the Act of September 29, 1977 (7 U.S.C. 341–349), and section 1361(c) of the Act of October 3, 1980 (7 U.S.C. 301 note), and to coordinate and provide program leadership for the extension work of the Department and the several States and insular possessions, [$12,242,000] *$5,933,000*; in all, [$424,922,000] *$428,236,000*: *Provided*, That funds hereby appropriated pursuant to section 3(c) of the Act of June 26, 1953, and section 506 of the Act of June 23, 1972, shall not be paid to any State, the District of Columbia, Puerto Rico, Guam, or the Virgin Islands, Micronesia, Northern Marianas, and American Samoa prior to availability of an equal sum from non-Federal sources for expenditure during the current fiscal year. *(Agriculture, Rural Development, Food and Drug Administration, and Related Agencies Appropriations Act, 2000.)*

Program and Financing (in millions of dollars)

Identification code 12–0502–0–1–352	1999 actual	2000 est.	2001 est.
Obligations by program activity:			
Direct program:			
00.01 Smith-Lever Act, 3(b) and 3(c)	276	276	276
00.02 Youth at risk	9	9	10
00.03 Water quality	10		
00.04 Expanded food and nutrition education program (EFNEP)	59	59	61
00.05 Pest management	11	11	12
00.06 Farm safety	3	4	
00.07 Pesticide impact assessment	3		
00.08 Pesticide applicator training			2
00.09 Indian reservation extension agents	2	2	5
00.11 Food safety	7		
00.12 Rural development	1	1	1
00.13 Payments to 1890 colleges and Tuskegee University	26	27	27
00.15 Renewable resources extension act	3	3	3
00.16 Federal administration	12	12	6
00.18 Rural health and safety education	3	3	
00.19 1890 facilities (section 1447)	7	14	12
00.21 Sustainable agriculture	3	3	4
00.22 1994 institutions activities	2	3	4
00.23 Youth farm safety pilot program			5
09.00 Reimbursable program	18	25	25
10.00 Total new obligations	455	452	453
Budgetary resources available for obligation:			
21.40 Unobligated balance available, start of year	4	2	
22.00 New budget authority (gross)	455	449	453
23.90 Total budgetary resources available for obligation	459	451	453
23.95 Total new obligations	–455	–452	–453
24.40 Unobligated balance available, end of year	2		
New budget authority (gross), detail:			
Discretionary:			
40.00 Appropriation	437	425	428
40.76 Reduction pursuant to P.L. 106–113		–1	
43.00 Appropriation (total discretionary)	437	424	428
68.00 Spending authority from offsetting collections: Offsetting collections (cash)	18	25	25
70.00 Total new budget authority (gross)	455	449	453
Change in unpaid obligations:			
72.40 Unpaid obligations, start of year: Obligated balance, start of year	221	251	226
73.10 Total new obligations	455	452	453
73.20 Total outlays (gross)	–425	–477	–446
74.40 Unpaid obligations, end of year: Obligated balance, end of year	251	226	233
Outlays (gross), detail:			
86.90 Outlays from new discretionary authority	265	279	281
86.93 Outlays from discretionary balances	160	197	164
87.00 Total outlays (gross)	425	477	446
Offsets:			
Against gross budget authority and outlays:			
88.00 Offsetting collections (cash) from: Federal sources	–18	–25	–25
Net budget authority and outlays:			
89.00 Budget authority	437	424	428
90.00 Outlays	407	452	421

Note.—In 2000 and 2001 funding for water quality grants, food safety and pesticide impact assessments is included in the account for integrated activities.

The Cooperative Extension System, a national educational network, is a dynamic organization pledged to meeting the country's needs for research-based educational programs that will enable people to make practical decisions to improve their lives. To accomplish its mission, the Cooperative Extension System adjusts programs to meet the shifting needs and priorities of the people it serves.

The nonformal educational network combines the expertise and resources of federal, state, and local partners. The partners in this unique System are: (a) The Cooperative State Research, Education, and Extension Service at the U.S. Department of Agriculture; (b) Extension professionals at land-grant universities throughout the United States and its territories; and (c) Extension professionals in nearly all of the Nation's 3,150 counties. Thousands of paraprofessionals and nearly 3 million volunteers support this partnership and magnify its impact. Strong linkages with both public and private external groups are also crucial to the Cooperative Extension System's strength and vitality.

Base programs, funded by the Smith-Lever 3(b) and (c) legislated formula funds, are the major educational efforts central to the mission of the System and common to most Extension units. They are the ongoing priority efforts of the System, involving many discipline-based and multi-disciplinary programs. The System's base programs are the foundation of the Extension organization and partnership that are intended to increase the number of community-based projects, families, and individuals reached to disseminate research findings as widely and quickly as possible. The use of electronic mail, satellite transmission of courses, and computer-assisted instruction are encouraged to communicate ideas.

Extension resources are provided to the States by these formula funds and competitively-awarded programs such as sustainable agriculture. Smith-Lever 3(b) and (c) funds and payments to the 1890 colleges and Tuskegee University provide funds to support the Extension infrastructure.

Funds for designated programs, funded by Smith-Lever 3(d) such as youth-at-risk and expanded food and nutrition education program (EFNEP), provide support for the Cooperative Extension System to address identified priority issues.

National initiatives funded by legislative formulas, administratively determined distribution, Congressional and Executive intent, and competitively-awarded projects, are the System's commitment to respond to important problems of broad national concern with additional resources and significantly increased effort to achieve a major impact on national priorities. They are the most current significant and complex issues on which the Extension System has the potential to make a difference—usually in cooperation with other agencies, groups, and units of government. The goal is to inform and educate these extension agriculture professionals and volunteers who, in turn, educate the professional farmers and end-users regarding these critical initiatives and concerns.

In 2001 increases have been requested for: the Expanded Food and Nutrition Education Program, pest management, children, youth and families at risk, a youth farm safety education and certification pilot project, extension services on Indian reservations, sustainable agriculture, pesticide applicator training, and 1994 (Native American) institutions.

Object Classification (in millions of dollars)

Identification code 12–0502–0–1–352	1999 actual	2000 est.	2001 est.
Direct obligations:			
11.1 Personnel compensation: Full-time permanent	9	10	10
12.1 Civilian personnel benefits	2	2	2
21.0 Travel and transportation of persons	1	2	2
23.3 Communications, utilities, and miscellaneous charges	1		1
24.0 Printing and reproduction	1		1
25.2 Other services	2	1	1
25.3 Purchases of goods and services from Government accounts	2	1	
41.0 Grants, subsidies, and contributions	419	411	411
99.0 Subtotal, direct obligations	437	427	428
99.0 Reimbursable obligations	18	25	25
99.9 Total new obligations	455	452	453

General and special funds—Continued

EXTENSION ACTIVITIES—Continued

Personnel Summary

Identification code 12–0502–0–1–352	1999 actual	2000 est.	2001 est.
1001 Total compensable workyears: Full-time equivalent employment	193	210	205

ANIMAL AND PLANT HEALTH INSPECTION SERVICE

Federal Funds

General and special funds:

SALARIES AND EXPENSES

(INCLUDING TRANSFERS OF FUNDS)

For expenses, not otherwise provided for, including those pursuant to the Act of February 28, 1947 (21 U.S.C. 114b–c), necessary to prevent, control, and eradicate pests and plant and animal diseases; to carry out inspection, quarantine, and regulatory activities; to discharge the authorities of the Secretary of Agriculture under the Act of March 2, 1931 (46 Stat. 1468; 7 U.S.C. 426–426b); and to protect the environment, as authorized by law, [$441,263,000] *$512,044,000*, of which $4,105,000 shall be available for the control of outbreaks of insects, plant diseases, animal diseases and for control of pest animals and birds to the extent necessary to meet emergency conditions: *Provided*, That no funds shall be used to formulate or administer a brucellosis eradication program for the current fiscal year that does not require minimum matching by the States of at least 40 percent: *Provided further*, That this appropriation shall be available for field employment pursuant to the second sentence of section 706(a) of the Organic Act of 1944 (7 U.S.C. 2225), and not to exceed $40,000 shall be available for employment under 5 U.S.C. 3109: *Provided further*, That this appropriation shall be available for the operation and maintenance of aircraft and the purchase of not to exceed four, of which two shall be for replacement only: *Provided further*, That, in addition, in emergencies which threaten any segment of the agricultural production industry of this country, the Secretary may transfer from other appropriations or funds available to the agencies or corporations of the Department such sums as may be deemed necessary, to be available only in such emergencies for the arrest and eradication of contagious or infectious disease or pests of animals, poultry, or plants, and for expenses in accordance with the Act of February 28, 1947, and section 102 of the Act of September 21, 1944, and any unexpended balances of funds transferred for such emergency purposes in the [next] preceding fiscal year shall be merged with such transferred amounts: *Provided further*, That appropriations hereunder shall be available pursuant to law (7 U.S.C. 2250) for the repair and alteration of leased buildings and improvements, but unless otherwise provided the cost of altering any one building during the fiscal year shall not exceed 10 percent of the current replacement value of the building.

In fiscal year [2000] *2001*, the agency is authorized to collect fees to cover the total costs of providing technical assistance, goods, or services requested by States, other political subdivisions, domestic and international organizations, foreign governments, or individuals, provided that such fees are structured such that any entity's liability for such fees is reasonably based on the technical assistance, goods, or services provided to the entity by the agency, and such fees shall be credited to this account, to remain available until expended, without further appropriation, for providing such assistance, goods, or services.

Of the total amount available under this heading in fiscal year [2000] *2001*, $87,000,000 shall be derived from user fees deposited in the Agricultural Quarantine Inspection User Fee Account. *(10 U.S.C. 2306; 15 U.S.C. 69e, 1821–31; 16 U.S.C. 1531–43; 18 U.S.C. 1114; 19 U.S.C. 1306, 21 U.S.C. 101–105, 111–114, 114a–114c; 114d–1, 114e–131, 134–135b, 151–158; 26 U.S.C. 4491–94; 45 U.S.C. 71–74; 46 U.S.C. 466a–466(b); 49 U.S.C. 1471(a)–1509(d), 1741; 46 Stat. 67; 78 Stat. 939–940; 99 Stat. 1645–1650, 1654–1656, 1658–1659; Agriculture, Rural Development, Food and Drug Administration, and Related Agencies Appropriations Act, 2000.)*

Unavailable Collections (in millions of dollars)

Identification code 12–1600–0–1–352	1999 actual	2000 est.	2001 est.
Balance, start of year:			
01.99 Balance, start of year	105	117	130
Receipts:			
02.01 Agricultural quarantine inspection fees	172	188	215
04.00 Total: Balances and collections	277	305	345
Appropriation:			
05.01 Salaries and expenses	–160	–175	–202
05.99 Subtotal appropriation	–160	–175	–202
07.99 Total balance, end of year	117	130	143

Program and Financing (in millions of dollars)

Identification code 12–1600–0–1–352	1999 actual	2000 est.	2001 est.
Obligations by program activity:			
Direct program:			
00.01 Pest and disease exclusion	264	288	352
00.02 Plant and animal health monitoring	74	79	88
00.03 Pest and disease management programs	90	91	104
00.04 Animal care	10	11	16
00.05 Scientific and technical services	54	53	54
00.06 Contingencies	5	4	4
00.07 Emergency program funding	118	84	
00.08 Invasive species			9
01.00 Total direct program	615	610	627
09.01 Reimbursable program	64	64	75
10.00 Total new obligations	679	674	702
Budgetary resources available for obligation:			
21.40 Unobligated balance available, start of year	12	35	31
22.00 New budget authority (gross)	557	586	687
22.22 Unobligated balance transferred from other accounts	146	84	
23.90 Total budgetary resources available for obligation	715	705	718
23.95 Total new obligations	–679	–674	–702
24.40 Unobligated balance available, end of year	35	31	16
New budget authority (gross), detail:			
Discretionary:			
40.00 Appropriation	338	354	425
40.20 Appropriation (special fund, definite)	88	87	87
40.76 Reduction pursuant to P.L. 106–113		–3	
41.00 Transferred to other accounts	–1		
43.00 Appropriation (total discretionary)	425	438	512
Mandatory:			
60.25 Appropriation (special fund, indefinite)	72	88	115
Discretionary:			
68.00 Spending authority from offsetting collections: Offsetting collections (cash)	60	60	60
70.00 Total new budget authority (gross)	557	586	687
Change in unpaid obligations:			
72.40 Unpaid obligations, start of year: Obligated balance, start of year	68	98	75
73.10 Total new obligations	679	674	702
73.20 Total outlays (gross)	–649	–697	–683
74.40 Unpaid obligations, end of year: Obligated balance, end of year	98	75	94
Outlays (gross), detail:			
86.90 Outlays from new discretionary authority	404	476	546
86.93 Outlays from discretionary balances	173	133	22
86.97 Outlays from new mandatory authority	71	88	115
86.98 Outlays from mandatory balances	1		
87.00 Total outlays (gross)	649	697	683
Offsets:			
Against gross budget authority and outlays:			
Offsetting collections (cash) from:			
88.00 Federal sources	–10	–10	–10
88.40 Non-Federal sources	–50	–50	–50
88.90 Total, offsetting collections (cash)	–60	–60	–60

		1999 actual	2000 est.	2001 est.
	Net budget authority and outlays:			
89.00	Budget authority	497	526	627
90.00	Outlays	589	637	623

Summary of Budget Authority and Outlays

(in millions of dollars)

Enacted/requested:	1999 actual	2000 est.	2001 est.
Budget Authority	497	526	627
Outlays	589	637	623
Legislative proposal, not subject to PAYGO:			
Budget Authority			–11
Outlays			–11
Total:			
Budget Authority	497	526	616
Outlays	589	637	612

The major objectives of the Animal and Plant Health Inspection Service (APHIS) are to protect the animal and plant resources of the Nation from destructive pests and diseases. This mission is carried out under the five major areas of activity, as follows:

Pest and disease exclusion.—The agency conducts inspection and quarantine activities at U.S. ports-of-entry to prevent the introduction of exotic animal and plant diseases and pests. APHIS develops and conducts preclearance programs to ensure that agricultural products destined for U.S. ports-of-entry do not present a risk to U.S. agriculture. APHIS engages in cooperative programs in foreign countries to control pests of imminent concern to the United States. APHIS also certifies plants and plant products for export and regulates imports and exports of designated endangered plant species. User fees have been implemented to recover the cost of certain agricultural quarantine inspection services.

Plant and animal health monitoring.—The Agency conducts programs to assess animal and plant health and to detect endemic and exotic diseases and pests. The plant and animal health monitoring programs are primarily cooperative efforts of the Federal and State governments, and industry. The Agency also carries out surveys in cooperation with the States to detect harmful plant and animal pests and diseases and to determine if there is a need for pest eradication programs.

Pest and disease management programs.—The Agency carries out programs to control and eradicate infestations and animal diseases that threaten the United States; to reduce agricultural losses caused by predatory animals, birds, and rodents; to provide technical assistance to States, counties, farmer or rancher groups, and foundations; and to ensure compliance with interstate movement and disease control regulations. Interstate shipments of plants, livestock, and related materials are monitored and regulated to prevent the spread of disease. APHIS protects agriculture from detrimental animal predators through identification, demonstration, and application of the most appropriate methods of control.

Animal care.—The Agency conducts regulatory activities which ensure the humane care and handling of animals used in research, exhibition, or the wholesale pet trade. The Agency is also responsible for administering the Horse Protection Act, which prohibits the showing, selling, or exhibition of sore horses.

Scientific and technical services.—APHIS develops methods to control animals and pests that are detrimental to agriculture, other wildlife, and public safety. The agency regulates genetic research to guard against the release of potentially harmful organisms into the environment. APHIS also conducts veterinary diagnostic laboratory activities and biologic regulatory enforcement to ensure that the products developed for combatting disease are potent, safe, and pure. It also provides and directs technology development in coordination with other groups in APHIS and Plant Protection and Quarantine (PPQ) officials to support PPQ programs of the Agency and its cooperators at the State, national, and international levels.

Object Classification (in millions of dollars)

Identification code 12–1600–0–1–352		1999 actual	2000 est.	2001 est.
	Direct obligations:			
	Personnel compensation:			
11.1	Full-time permanent	204	235	273
11.3	Other than full-time permanent	15	16	17
11.5	Other personnel compensation	34	36	41
11.9	Total personnel compensation	253	287	331
12.1	Civilian personnel benefits	61	71	80
13.0	Benefits for former personnel			1
21.0	Travel and transportation of persons	20	20	22
22.0	Transportation of things	8	7	5
23.2	Rental payments to others	5	6	6
23.3	Communications, utilities, and miscellaneous charges	13	15	14
24.0	Printing and reproduction	1	1	2
25.2	Other services	104	102	83
26.0	Supplies and materials	44	28	34
31.0	Equipment	22	17	16
	Grants, subsidies, and contributions:			
41.0	United States-Colombia Commission to Prevent Foot-and-Mouth Disease	1	2	2
41.0	Joint Screwworm eradication programs	19	5	5
41.0	Joint Commission on the Mediterranean fruit fly	4	5	5
41.0	Other grants, subsidies, and contributions	2	11	17
	Insurance claims and indemnities:			
42.0	Brucellosis	4	2	2
42.0	Pseudorabies	52	30	
42.0	Other insurance claims and indemnities	2	1	3
99.0	Subtotal, direct obligations	615	610	628
99.0	Reimbursable obligations	64	64	74
99.9	Total new obligations	679	674	702

Personnel Summary

Identification code 12–1600–0–1–352		1999 actual	2000 est.	2001 est.
	Direct:			
	Total compensable workyears:			
1001	Full-time equivalent employment	3,499	5,825	5,953
1011	Exempt Full-time equivalent employment	2,025		
	Reimbursable:			
2001	Total compensable workyears: Full-time equivalent employment	696	715	834

Salaries and Expenses

(Legislative proposal, not subject to PAYGO)

Program and Financing (in millions of dollars)

Identification code 12–1600–2–1–352		1999 actual	2000 est.	2001 est.
	Obligations by program activity:			
	Direct program:			
00.01	Animal welfare			–5
00.02	Biotechnology			–6
01.00	Total direct program			–11
09.01	Reimbursable program			11
10.00	Total new obligations			
	New budget authority (gross), detail:			
	Discretionary:			
40.00	Appropriation			–11
68.00	Spending authority from offsetting collections: Offsetting collections (cash)			11
	Offsets:			
	Against gross budget authority and outlays:			
88.40	Offsetting collections (cash) from: Non-Federal sources			–11
	Net budget authority and outlays:			
89.00	Budget authority			–11

General and special funds—Continued

SALARIES AND EXPENSES—Continued

Program and Financing (in millions of dollars)—Continued

Identification code 12–1600–2–1–352	1999 actual	2000 est.	2001 est.
90.00 Outlays			–11

Legislation will be proposed to establish user fees for APHIS' costs for animal welfare inspections, such as for animal research centers, humane societies, and kennels, and for activities associated with the issuance of biotechnology certificates.

This is one of several proposals in the budget to charge fees to users directly availing themselves of, or subject to, a government service, program, or activity, in order to cover the government's costs. Legislation will be proposed to authorize the fees.

Object Classification (in millions of dollars)

Identification code 12–1600–2–1–352	1999 actual	2000 est.	2001 est.
Direct obligations:			
11.1 Personnel compensation: Full-time permanent			–6
12.1 Civilian personnel benefits			–2
25.2 Other services			–1
26.0 Supplies and materials			–1
31.0 Equipment			–1
99.0 Subtotal, direct obligations			–11
99.0 Reimbursable obligations			11
99.9 Total new obligations			

Personnel Summary

Identification code 12–1600–2–1–352	1999 actual	2000 est.	2001 est.
Direct:			
1001 Total compensable workyears: Full-time equivalent employment			–123
Reimbursable:			
2001 Total compensable workyears: Full-time equivalent employment			123

BUILDINGS AND FACILITIES

For plans, construction, repair, preventive maintenance, environmental support, improvement, extension, alteration, and purchase of fixed equipment or facilities, as authorized by 7 U.S.C. 2250, and acquisition of land as authorized by 7 U.S.C. 428a, $5,200,000, to remain available until expended. *(Agriculture, Rural Development, Food and Drug Administration, and Related Agencies Appropriations Act, 2000.)*

Program and Financing (in millions of dollars)

Identification code 12–1601–0–1–352	1999 actual	2000 est.	2001 est.
Obligations by program activity:			
10.00 Total new obligations (object class 25.2)	8	6	7
Budgetary resources available for obligation:			
21.40 Unobligated balance available, start of year	5	5	5
22.00 New budget authority (gross)	8	5	5
23.90 Total budgetary resources available for obligation	13	10	10
23.95 Total new obligations	–8	–6	–7
24.40 Unobligated balance available, end of year	5	5	3
New budget authority (gross), detail:			
Discretionary:			
40.00 Appropriation	8	5	5
Change in unpaid obligations:			
72.40 Unpaid obligations, start of year: Obligated balance, start of year	17	15	14
73.10 Total new obligations	8	6	7
73.20 Total outlays (gross)	–10	–7	–9
74.40 Unpaid obligations, end of year: Obligated balance, end of year	15	14	12
Outlays (gross), detail:			
86.90 Outlays from new discretionary authority	1	1	1
86.93 Outlays from discretionary balances	9	7	8
87.00 Total outlays (gross)	10	7	9
Net budget authority and outlays:			
89.00 Budget authority	8	5	5
90.00 Outlays	10	7	9

The buildings and facilities fund provides for construction, repairs, preventive maintenance, and alterations, as needed, for APHIS operated facilities, which include animal quarantine stations, border inspection stations, sterile insect rearing facilities, and laboratories.

The 2001 budget proposes $5 million for this program, which consists of $2 million for repairs, alterations, preventive maintenance, and renovations for currently owned APHIS facilities, and $3 million for the modernization of the Plum Island, New York, Animal Disease Center.

Trust Funds

MISCELLANEOUS TRUST FUNDS

Unavailable Collections (in millions of dollars)

Identification code 12–9971–0–7–352	1999 actual	2000 est.	2001 est.
Balance, start of year:			
01.99 Balance, start of year			
Receipts:			
02.02 Miscellaneous contributed funds	13	13	13
Appropriation:			
05.01 Miscellaneous trust funds	–13	–13	–13
07.99 Total balance, end of year			

Program and Financing (in millions of dollars)

Identification code 12–9971–0–7–352	1999 actual	2000 est.	2001 est.
Obligations by program activity:			
10.00 Total new obligations	12	11	11
Budgetary resources available for obligation:			
21.40 Unobligated balance available, start of year	5	6	6
22.00 New budget authority (gross)	13	13	13
23.90 Total budgetary resources available for obligation	18	19	19
23.95 Total new obligations	–12	–11	–11
24.40 Unobligated balance available, end of year	6	6	6
New budget authority (gross), detail:			
Mandatory:			
60.27 Appropriation (trust fund, indefinite)	13	13	13
Change in unpaid obligations:			
73.10 Total new obligations	12	11	11
73.20 Total outlays (gross)	–13	–13	–13
Outlays (gross), detail:			
86.97 Outlays from new mandatory authority	8	8	8
86.98 Outlays from mandatory balances	5	5	5
87.00 Total outlays (gross)	13	13	13
Net budget authority and outlays:			
89.00 Budget authority	13	13	13
90.00 Outlays	13	13	13

The following services are financed by fees and miscellaneous contributions advanced by importers, manufacturers, States, organizations, individuals, and others:

Miscellaneous contributed funds.—Funds are received from States, local organizations, individuals, and others and are available for plant and animal quarantine inspection and cooperative plant and animal disease and pest control activities (7 U.S.C. 450b, 2220). Commencing in 1979, fees were collected for the importation of commercial birds.

Object Classification (in millions of dollars)

Identification code 12–9971–0–7–352		1999 actual	2000 est.	2001 est.
	Personnel compensation:			
11.1	Full-time permanent	3	3	3
11.3	Other than full-time permanent	2	2	2
11.5	Other personnel compensation	1	1	1
11.9	Total personnel compensation	6	6	6
12.1	Civilian personnel benefits	1	1	1
21.0	Travel and transportation of persons	2	2	2
25.2	Other services	2	1	1
26.0	Supplies and materials	1	1	1
99.9	Total new obligations	12	11	11

Personnel Summary

Identification code 12–9971–0–7–352		1999 actual	2000 est.	2001 est.
1001	Total compensable workyears: Full-time equivalent employment	101	101	101

FOOD SAFETY AND INSPECTION SERVICE

The following table depicts the total funding for the Food Safety and Inspection Service, which includes appropriated funds and proceeds from proposed user fees:

[In millions of dollars]

	1999 actual	2000 est.	2001 est.
Appropriations:			
Enacted/requested:			
Budget authority	617	649	688
Outlays	616	648	688
User Fee:			
Budget authority			–534
Outlays			–534
Total:			
Budget authority	617	649	154
Outlays	616	648	154

Federal Funds

General and special funds:

SALARIES AND EXPENSES

For necessary expenses to carry out services authorized by the Federal Meat Inspection Act, the Poultry Products Inspection Act, and the Egg Products Inspection Act, [$649,411,000, of which no less than $544,902,000 shall be available for Federal food inspection] *$687,904,000*, and in addition, $1,000,000 may be credited to this account from fees collected for the cost of laboratory accreditation as authorized by section 1017 of Public Law 102–237: *Provided*, [That this appropriation shall not be available for shell egg surveillance under section 5(d) of the Egg Products Inspection Act (21 U.S.C. 1034(d)): *Provided further*,] That this appropriation shall be available for field employment pursuant to the second sentence of section 706(a) of the Organic Act of 1944 (7 U.S.C. 2225), and not to exceed $75,000 shall be available for employment under 5 U.S.C. 3109: *Provided further That in addition, the Secretary may transfer from other appropriations or funds available to the agencies or corporations of the Department such sums as may be necessary to address food safety emergencies, including outbreaks of foodborne illness, recall of adulterated products in commerce, or bioterrorist events; that these funds are available only in such emergency situations, and that any unobligated balances of funds transferred for such emergency purposes in excess of amounts needed shall be returned to the providing account: Provided further*, That this appropriation shall be available pursuant to law (7 U.S.C. 2250) for the alteration and repair of buildings and improvements, but the cost of altering any one building during the fiscal year shall not exceed 10 percent of the current replacement value of the building. *(7 U.S.C. 450, 1901–06; 10 U.S.C. 2306; 18 U.S.C. 1114; 21 U.S.C. 451–470, 601–624, 641–645, 661, 671–680, 691–692; 694–695; Public Law 99–641; Agriculture, Rural Development, Food and Drug Administration, and Related Agencies Appropriations Act, 2000.)*

Program and Financing (in millions of dollars)

Identification code 12–3700–0–1–554		1999 actual	2000 est.	2001 est.
	Obligations by program activity:			
00.01	Direct program	616	650	688
09.01	Reimbursable program	93	99	80
10.00	Total new obligations	709	749	768
	Budgetary resources available for obligation:			
21.40	Unobligated balance available, start of year	1	2	
22.00	New budget authority (gross)	712	748	768
23.90	Total budgetary resources available for obligation	713	750	768
23.95	Total new obligations	–709	–749	–768
23.98	Unobligated balance expiring or withdrawn	–1		
24.40	Unobligated balance available, end of year	2		
	New budget authority (gross), detail:			
	Discretionary:			
40.00	Appropriation	617	649	688
68.00	Spending authority from offsetting collections: Offsetting collections (cash)	95	99	80
70.00	Total new budget authority (gross)	712	748	768
	Change in unpaid obligations:			
72.40	Unpaid obligations, start of year: Obligated balance, start of year	33	53	53
73.10	Total new obligations	709	749	768
73.20	Total outlays (gross)	–695	–748	–768
73.40	Adjustments in expired accounts (net)	6		
74.40	Unpaid obligations, end of year: Obligated balance, end of year	53	53	53
	Outlays (gross), detail:			
86.90	Outlays from new discretionary authority	661	717	737
86.93	Outlays from discretionary balances	34	31	31
87.00	Total outlays (gross)	695	748	768
	Offsets:			
	Against gross budget authority and outlays:			
88.40	Offsetting collections (cash) from: Non-Federal sources	–95	–99	–80
	Net budget authority and outlays:			
89.00	Budget authority	617	649	688
90.00	Outlays	600	649	688

Summary of Budget Authority and Outlays

(in millions of dollars)

	1999 actual	2000 est.	2001 est.
Enacted/requested:			
Budget Authority	617	649	688
Outlays	600	649	688
Legislative proposal, not subject to PAYGO:			
Budget Authority			–534
Outlays			–534
Total:			
Budget Authority	617	649	154
Outlays	600	649	154

The primary objectives of the Food Safety and Inspection Service are to ensure that meat, poultry, shell egg, and egg products are wholesome, unadulterated, and properly labeled and packaged, as required by the Federal Meat Inspection Act, the Poultry Products Inspection Act, and the Egg Products Inspection Act. Providing adequate resources for Federal food safety agencies continues to be a priority of the Administration, and the 2001 budget proposes a $38 million increase for inspection of meat, poultry, shell egg and egg products. This increase will cover pay cost increases for Federal and

General and special funds—Continued

SALARIES AND EXPENSES—Continued

State inspection programs, and initiatives for: redeployment and enhanced capabilities of the inspection workforce; improved risk assessment and collaborative programs with States; verification of foreign and domestic inspection systems for HACCP compliance; and expanded support of Codex Alimentarius.

The meat, poultry, shell egg and egg products inspection program of the Food Safety and Inspection Service provides in-plant inspection of all domestic plants preparing meat, poultry, shell eggs, or egg products for sale or distribution; reviews foreign inspection systems and establishments that prepare meat, poultry, or egg products for export to the United States; and provides technical and financial assistance to States which maintain meat and poultry inspection programs.

In 2001, the Administration is proposing a new user fee to offset the cost of Federal meat, poultry, shell egg and egg products inspection. The proposal would require industry to reimburse the government for all Federal services. This proposal would ensure that sufficient resources are available to provide the level of in-plant inspection necessary to meet the demands of the industry.

On January 25, 1997, the President announced the 1998 President's National Food Safety Initiative. The initiatives for 1998 through 2000 have laid the foundation for building a strong, scientific base for a farm-to-table food safety system that protects public health by monitoring and addressing a broad range of food safety hazards. The 2001 Food Safety Initiative builds on this foundation and will increase funding department-wide by $28 million over the 2000 level of $136 million. Resources are targeted to: (1) further develop a nationally integrated food safety system by expanding and strengthening the partnership between Federal, State, and local agencies; (2) continue enhancing surveillance of foodborne diseases and increasing the speed and efficiency of responses to outbreaks of foodborne illness; and (3) put greater emphasis on the control of foodborne hazards in the pre-harvest phase of the farm-to-table continuum. Continued investment is required to realize the President's goal of establishing a seamless, science-based food safety system.

In 1998 the President's Council on Food Safety was established to develop a comprehensive strategy for food safety activities, including coordinating research efforts and budget submissions among the food safety agencies.

FEDERALLY FUNDED INSPECTION ACTIVITIES

	1999 actual	2000 est.	2001 est.
Federally inspected establishments:			
Slaughter plants	262	258	255
Processing plants	4,343	4,325	4,315
Combination slaughter and processing plants	968	960	954
Talmadge-Aiken plants	254	248	245
Import establishments	129	125	120
Egg plants	75	73	71
Federally inspected and passed production (millions of pounds):			
Meat slaughter	53,114	53,000	53,000
Poultry slaughter	46,882	46,000	46,000
Egg products	3,383	3,400	3,400
Product inspected and passed under HACCP system: [a]	95,516	95,000	95,000
Import/export activity (millions of pounds):			
Meat and poultry imported	3,190	3,200	3,200
Meat and poultry exported	8,655	8,700	8,700
States and territories with cooperative programs: [b]			
Intrastate inspection	26	25	27
Talmadge-Aiken inspection	9	9	9
Number of slaughter and/or processing plants (excludes exempt plants)	2,370	2,370	2,420
Pounds inspected slaughter (millions)	552	552	600
Compliance activities:			
Marketplace reviews [c]	5,600	30,000	30,000
Corrective action reviews	43,976	46,000	46,000
Corrective actions completed	941	1,200	1,400
Product Testing (samples analyzed):			
Food chemistry	12,251	8,000	5,000
Food microbiology	88,347	90,000	90,000
Chemical residues	55,285	40,000	40,000
Antibiotic residues	180,939	182,000	185,000
Pathology samples	3,997	4,000	4,000
Egg Products:			
Food microbiology	1,928	2,000	2,000
Chemical residues	1,083	1,000	1,000
Consumer Education and public outreach:			
Meat and Poultry Hotline Calls received	110,805	115,000	115,000
Epidemiological Investigations:			
Cooperative efforts with State and public health offices	30	30	30
Illnesses reported and treated [d]	7,392	8,000	8,000
Field Automation and Information Management Project:			
Number of computers to be provided to federal field inspection staff	3,539	800	900
Number of computers to be provided to state field inspection staff	565	607	203

[a] Production data on meat and poultry slaughter operations reflect estimated output of establishments required to produce under HACCP systems.
[b] States with cooperative agreements which are operating programs.
[c] Includes marketplace sampling, testing, reviewing and evaluation.
[d] Data must be collected over a number of years to chart national trends and estimate the incidence of foodborne illness and treatment.

Object Classification (in millions of dollars)

Identification code 12–3700–0–1–554		1999 actual	2000 est.	2001 est.
	Direct obligations:			
	Personnel compensation:			
11.1	Full-time permanent	348	363	377
11.3	Other than full-time permanent	16	23	23
11.5	Other personnel compensation	16	17	18
11.9	Total personnel compensation	380	403	418
12.1	Civilian personnel benefits	110	116	126
13.0	Benefits for former personnel	1	1	1
21.0	Travel and transportation of persons	23	23	26
22.0	Transportation of things	2	3	3
23.2	Rental payments to others	2	2	2
23.3	Communications, utilities, and miscellaneous charges	6	7	7
24.0	Printing and reproduction	1	1	1
25.1	Advisory and assistance services	9	10	11
25.2	Other services	4	4	9
25.3	Purchases of goods and services from Government accounts	13	13	13
25.4	Operation and maintenance of facilities	2	2	2
25.8	Subsistence and support of persons	....	1	1
26.0	Supplies and materials	9	10	10
31.0	Equipment	8	8	9
41.0	Grants, subsidies, and contributions	45	45	46
99.0	Subtotal, direct obligations	615	649	685
99.0	Reimbursable obligations	92	97	81
99.5	Below reporting threshold	2	3	2
99.9	Total new obligations	709	749	768

Personnel Summary

Identification code 12–3700–0–1–554		1999 actual	2000 est.	2001 est.
	Direct:			
1001	Total compensable workyears: Full-time equivalent employment	9,325	9,649	9,547
	Reimbursable:			
2001	Total compensable workyears: Full-time equivalent employment	231	231	171

SALARIES AND EXPENSES

(Legislative proposal, not subject to PAYGO)

Program and Financing (in millions of dollars)

Identification code 12–3700–2–1–554		1999 actual	2000 est.	2001 est.
	Obligations by program activity:			
00.01	Direct program	....	....	–534
09.01	Reimbursable program	....	....	534
10.00	Total new obligations	....	....	....

	1999 actual	2000 est.	2001 est.
New budget authority (gross), detail:			
Discretionary:			
40.00 Appropriation			−534
68.00 Spending authority from offsetting collections: Offsetting collections (cash)			534
Offsets:			
Against gross budget authority and outlays:			
88.40 Offsetting collections (cash) from: Non-Federal sources			−534
Net budget authority and outlays:			
89.00 Budget authority			−534
90.00 Outlays			−534

Legislation will be proposed to charge fees for the cost of all Federal inspection of meat, poultry, shell egg and egg products at all establishments inspected by the Food Safety and Inspection Service (FSIS). Currently, fees to reimburse the cost of overtime inspection are required at some FSIS-inspected establishments, but not at others. Requiring the payment of user fees for inspection services would not only result in savings to the taxpayer, but would also ensure that sufficient resources are available to provide the mandatory inspection services needed to meet increasing industry demand. These fees would result in a cost of less than one cent per pound of product to consumers, but would allow the government to maintain its level of inspection effort to ensure a safe supply of meat, poultry and egg products. The implementation of the user fee authority would be designed to be fair and equitable; promote accountability and efficiency; and minimize any impact on the competitive balance among affected industries.

This is one of several proposals in the budget to charge fees to users directly availing themselves of, or subject to, a government service, program, or activity, in order to cover the government's costs.

Object Classification (in millions of dollars)

Identification code 12–3700–2–1–554	1999 actual	2000 est.	2001 est.
Direct obligations:			
Personnel compensation:			
11.1 Full-time permanent			−314
11.3 Other than full-time permanent			−19
11.5 Other personnel compensation			−15
11.9 Total personnel compensation			−348
12.1 Civilian personnel benefits			−105
13.0 Benefits for former personnel			−1
21.0 Travel and transportation of persons			−22
22.0 Transportation of things			−3
23.2 Rental payments to others			−2
23.3 Communications, utilities, and miscellaneous charges			−5
24.0 Printing and reproduction			−1
25.1 Advisory and assistance services			−9
25.2 Other services			−8
25.3 Purchases of goods and services from Government accounts			−11
25.4 Operation and maintenance of facilities			−2
25.8 Subsistence and support of persons			−1
26.0 Supplies and materials			−9
31.0 Equipment			−7
99.0 Subtotal, direct obligations			−534
99.0 Reimbursable obligations			534
99.9 Total new obligations			

Personnel Summary

Identification code 12–3700–2–1–554	1999 actual	2000 est.	2001 est.
Direct:			
1001 Total compensable workyears: Full-time equivalent employment			−7,410
Reimbursable:			
2001 Total compensable workyears: Full-time equivalent employment			7,410

Trust Funds

Expenses and Refunds, Inspection and Grading of Farm Products

Unavailable Collections (in millions of dollars)

Identification code 12–8137–0–7–352	1999 actual	2000 est.	2001 est.
Balance, start of year:			
01.99 Balance, start of year			
Receipts:			
02.01 Fees for inspection and grading of farm products	4	4	4
Appropriation:			
05.01 Expenses and refunds, inspection and grading of farm products	−4	−4	−4
07.99 Total balance, end of year			

Program and Financing (in millions of dollars)

Identification code 12–8137–0–7–352	1999 actual	2000 est.	2001 est.
Obligations by program activity:			
10.00 Total new obligations	3	4	4
Budgetary resources available for obligation:			
22.00 New budget authority (gross)	4	4	4
23.95 Total new obligations	−3	−4	−4
New budget authority (gross), detail:			
Mandatory:			
60.27 Appropriation (trust fund, indefinite)	4	4	4
Change in unpaid obligations:			
73.10 Total new obligations	3	4	4
73.20 Total outlays (gross)	−4	−4	−4
Outlays (gross), detail:			
86.97 Outlays from new mandatory authority	4	4	4
Net budget authority and outlays:			
89.00 Budget authority	4	4	4
90.00 Outlays	4	4	4

Under authority of the Agricultural Marketing Act of 1946, Federal meat and poultry inspection services are provided upon request and for a fee in cases where inspection is not mandated by statute. This service includes: certifying products for export beyond the requirements of export certificates; inspecting certain animals and poultry intended for human food where inspection is not required by statute, such as buffalo, rabbit, and quail; and inspecting products intended for animal consumption.

Object Classification (in millions of dollars)

Identification code 12–8137–0–7–352	1999 actual	2000 est.	2001 est.
Personnel compensation:			
11.1 Full-time permanent	1	2	2
11.5 Other personnel compensation	1	1	1
11.9 Total personnel compensation	2	3	3
12.1 Civilian personnel benefits		1	1
99.0 Subtotal, direct obligations	2	4	4
99.5 Below reporting threshold	1		
99.9 Total new obligations	3	4	4

Personnel Summary

Identification code 12–8137–0–7–352	1999 actual	2000 est.	2001 est.
1001 Total compensable workyears: Full-time equivalent employment	34	34	34

GRAIN INSPECTION, PACKERS AND STOCKYARDS ADMINISTRATION

Federal Funds

General and special funds:

SALARIES AND EXPENSES

For necessary expenses to carry out the provisions of the United States Grain Standards Act, for the administration of the Packers and Stockyards Act, for certifying procedures used to protect purchasers of farm products, and the standardization activities related to grain under the Agricultural Marketing Act of 1946, including field employment pursuant to the second sentence of section 706(a) of the Organic Act of 1944 (7 U.S.C. 2225), and not to exceed $25,000 for employment under 5 U.S.C. 3109, **[**$26,448,000**]** *$33,549,000*: *Provided*, That this appropriation shall be available pursuant to law (7 U.S.C. 2250) for the alteration and repair of buildings and improvements, but the cost of altering any one building during the fiscal year shall not exceed 10 percent of the current replacement value of the building. *(7 U.S.C. 71, 74–79, 84–87, 181–229, 1621–27; Agriculture, Rural Development, Food and Drug Administration, and Related Agencies Appropriations Act, 2000.)*

Program and Financing (in millions of dollars)

Identification code 12–2400–0–1–352	1999 actual	2000 est.	2001 est.
Obligations by program activity:			
00.01 Standardization	3	4	4
00.02 Compliance	5	4	5
00.03 Methods development	3	3	6
00.04 Packers and stockyards program	16	15	19
10.00 Total new obligations	27	26	34
Budgetary resources available for obligation:			
22.00 New budget authority (gross)	27	26	34
23.95 Total new obligations	−27	−26	−34
New budget authority (gross), detail:			
Discretionary:			
40.00 Appropriation	27	26	34
Change in unpaid obligations:			
72.40 Unpaid obligations, start of year: Obligated balance, start of year	4	4	4
73.10 Total new obligations	27	26	34
73.20 Total outlays (gross)	−26	−26	−34
74.40 Unpaid obligations, end of year: Obligated balance, end of year	4	4	4
Outlays (gross), detail:			
86.90 Outlays from new discretionary authority	24	23	30
86.93 Outlays from discretionary balances	2	3	3
87.00 Total outlays (gross)	26	26	34
Net budget authority and outlays:			
89.00 Budget authority	27	26	34
90.00 Outlays	26	26	34

Summary of Budget Authority and Outlays

(in millions of dollars)

Enacted/requested:	*1999 actual*	*2000 est.*	*2001 est.*
Budget Authority	27	26	34
Outlays	26	26	33
Legislative proposal, not subject to PAYGO:			
Budget Authority			−19
Outlays			−19
Total:			
Budget Authority	27	26	15
Outlays	26	26	14

The Grain Inspection, Packers and Stockyards Administration (GIPSA) establishes official United States standards for grain, promotes the uniform application thereof by official inspection personnel, provides for an official inspection system for grain, and regulates the weighing and certification of the weight of grain shipped in interstate or foreign commerce as authorized by the U.S. Grain Standards Act (USGSA), as amended, and the regulations thereof, and the Agricultural Marketing Act of 1946 (AMA).

Standardization activities include establishing and updating U.S. grain standards, research, and developing and improving methods to ensure the accurate and uniform application of the standards.

The compliance activities ensure the accurate and uniform application of the USGSA and applicable provisions of the AMA. The compliance program functions include: (1) evaluating alleged violations and initiating preliminary investigations; (2) initiating the implementation of corrective actions; (3) conducting management and technical reviews; (4) administering the designations and delegations of State and private agencies to perform official functions and monitoring the performance of the agencies; (5) identifying and, where appropriate, waiving and monitoring conflicts of interest; (6) licensing personnel of delegated States and designated agencies; (7) registering persons/firms engaged in the business of buying grain for sale in foreign commerce, and in the business of handling, weighing, or transporting of grain for sale in foreign commerce; (8) responding to audits of Grain Inspection programs; and (9) reviewing and, when appropriate, approving official agencies' fee schedules.

The International Monitoring Staff briefs foreign buyers, assesses foreign inspection and weighing techniques, and responds to foreign quality and quantity complaints.

An advisory committee consisting of members from the grain industry exists to advise the Agency regarding efficient and economical implementation of the USGSA.

The Grain Quality Improvement Act of 1986 was enacted on November 10, 1986, to improve the quality of U.S. grain by prohibiting the introduction and reintroduction of dockage and foreign material to grain.

For 2001, authorizing legislation will be submitted to permit, subject to appropriations, the collection and use of fees to cover the cost of standardization activities.

The goal of the Packers and Stockyards program is to ensure the integrity of the livestock, meat, and poultry markets and the marketplace in order to protect producers against unfair, deceptive, or discriminatory practices as well as those that are predatory or monopolistic in nature. Consumers and members of the livestock, poultry, and meat industries are also protected against unfair business practices in the marketing of livestock, meat and poultry, and from restrictions on competition which could unduly affect prices. The Agency also carries out the Secretary's responsibilities under Section 1324 of the Food Security Act of 1985 covering "central filing systems" established by States for pre-notification of security interests against farm products.

Authorizing legislation will be submitted that would establish a license fee that, subject to appropriations, would allow the collection and expenditure of funds for all costs associated with administering the Packers and Stockyards Act.

MAIN WORKLOAD FACTORS

	1999 actual	*2000 est.*	*2001 est.*
U.S. standards in effect at end of year	19	19	19
Standards reviews in progress	3	3	3
Standards reviews completed		3	3
Inspection techniques developed	28	2	2
On-site investigations	5	7	8
Designations renewed	17	21	21
Registration certificates issued	78	81	81
Investigations	1,218	1,800	1,800
Market agencies/dealers registered	6,434	6,350	6,300
Stockyards posted	1,287	1,285	1,280
Slaughtering and processing packers subject to the Act (estimated)	6,000	6,000	6,000
Distributors, brokers, and dealers subject to the Act (estimated)	6,800	6,800	6,800
Poultry operations subject to the Act	205	205	205

Object Classification (in millions of dollars)

Identification code 12–2400–0–1–352	1999 actual	2000 est.	2001 est.
11.1 Personnel compensation: Full-time permanent	16	16	19
12.1 Civilian personnel benefits	4	4	5
21.0 Travel and transportation of persons	2	2	2
23.3 Communications, utilities, and miscellaneous charges	1	1	1
25.2 Other services	2	2	4
26.0 Supplies and materials			1
31.0 Equipment	2	1	2
99.9 Total new obligations	27	26	34

Personnel Summary

Identification code 12–2400–0–1–352	1999 actual	2000 est.	2001 est.
1001 Total compensable workyears: Full-time equivalent employment	291	312	361

SALARIES AND EXPENSES

(Legislative proposal, not subject to PAYGO)

Program and Financing (in millions of dollars)

Identification code 12–2400–2–1–352	1999 actual	2000 est.	2001 est.
Obligations by program activity:			
00.01 Standardization			−4
00.04 Packers and stockyards program			−19
00.05 Start-up costs			4
09.01 Reimbursable program			23
10.00 Total new obligations			4
Budgetary resources available for obligation:			
22.00 New budget authority (gross)			4
23.95 Total new obligations			−4
New budget authority (gross), detail:			
Discretionary:			
40.00 Appropriation			−19
68.00 Spending authority from offsetting collections: Offsetting collections (cash)			23
70.00 Total new budget authority (gross)			4
Change in unpaid obligations:			
73.10 Total new obligations			4
73.20 Total outlays (gross)			−4
Outlays (gross), detail:			
86.90 Outlays from new discretionary authority			4
Offsets:			
Against gross budget authority and outlays:			
88.40 Offsetting collections (cash) from: Non-Federal sources			−23
Net budget authority and outlays:			
89.00 Budget authority			−19
90.00 Outlays			−19

Legislation will be proposed to establish a fee for the standardization activities of the Grain Inspection, Packers and Stockyards Administration, and a licensing fee to cover the costs of administering meat packing and stockyard activities.

This is one of several proposals in the budget to charge fees to users directly availing themselves of, or subject to, a government service, program, or activity, in order to cover the government's costs. Legislation will be proposed to authorize the fees.

Object Classification (in millions of dollars)

Identification code 12–2400–2–1–352	1999 actual	2000 est.	2001 est.
Direct obligations:			
11.1 Personnel compensation: Full-time permanent			−10
12.1 Civilian personnel benefits			−2
21.0 Travel and transportation of persons			−2
23.3 Communications, utilities, and miscellaneous charges			−1
25.2 Other services			−2
26.0 Supplies and materials			−1
31.0 Equipment			−1
99.0 Subtotal, direct obligations			−19
99.0 Reimbursable obligations			23
99.9 Total new obligations			4

Personnel Summary

Identification code 12–2400–2–1–352	1999 actual	2000 est.	2001 est.
Direct:			
1001 Total compensable workyears: Full-time equivalent employment			−222
Reimbursable:			
2001 Total compensable workyears: Full-time equivalent employment			222

Public enterprise funds:

INSPECTION AND WEIGHING SERVICES

LIMITATION ON INSPECTION AND WEIGHING SERVICE EXPENSES

Not to exceed $42,557,000 (from fees collected) shall be obligated during the current fiscal year for inspection and weighing services: *Provided*, That if grain export activities require additional supervision and oversight, or other uncontrollable factors occur, this limitation may be exceeded by up to 10 percent with notification to the Appropriations Committees. *(7 U.S.C. 71, 74–79, 84–87, 1621–27; Agriculture, Rural Development, Food and Drug Administration, and Related Agencies Appropriations Act, 2000.)*

Program and Financing (in millions of dollars)

Identification code 12–4050–0–3–352	1999 actual	2000 est.	2001 est.
Obligations by program activity:			
10.00 Total new obligations	35	43	43
Budgetary resources available for obligation:			
21.40 Unobligated balance available, start of year	4	6	6
22.00 New budget authority (gross)	37	43	43
23.90 Total budgetary resources available for obligation	41	49	49
23.95 Total new obligations	−35	−43	−43
24.40 Unobligated balance available, end of year	6	6	6
New budget authority (gross), detail:			
Mandatory:			
69.00 Offsetting collections (cash)	37	43	43
Change in unpaid obligations:			
72.40 Unpaid obligations, start of year: Obligated balance, start of year	2	2	2
73.10 Total new obligations	35	43	43
73.20 Total outlays (gross)	−35	−43	−43
74.40 Unpaid obligations, end of year: Obligated balance, end of year	2	2	2
Outlays (gross), detail:			
86.97 Outlays from new mandatory authority	35	43	43
Offsets:			
Against gross budget authority and outlays:			
88.40 Offsetting collections (cash) from: Non-Federal sources	−37	−43	−43
Net budget authority and outlays:			
89.00 Budget authority			
90.00 Outlays	−4		

The Grain Inspection, Packers and Stockyards Administration (GIPSA) provides a uniform system for the inspection and weighing of grain. Services provided under this system are financed through a fee supported revolving fund. This authority has been extended through September 2000.

Public enterprise funds—Continued

INSPECTION AND WEIGHING SERVICES—Continued

LIMITATION ON INSPECTION AND WEIGHING SERVICE EXPENSES—Continued

Fee supported programs include direct services, supervision activities and administrative functions. Direct services include official grain inspection and weighing by GIPSA employees at certain export ports as well as the inspection of U.S. grain shipped through Canada. The Agency supervises the inspection and weighing activities performed by its own employees. The Agency also oversees the inspection and weighing of grain performed by employees of 8 delegated States and 51 designated State and private agencies. The Agency provides an appeal service of original grain inspections and a registration system for grain exporting firms. Through support from the Association of American Railroads and user fees, GIPSA conducts a railroad track scale testing program. In addition, the agency provides grading services, on request, for rice and grain related products under the authority of the Agricultural Marketing Act of 1946 (AMA).

	1999 actual	*2000 est.*	*2001 est.*
Export grain inspected and/or weighed (million metric tons):			
By Federal personnel	85.3	80.3	89.4
By delegated States	26.1	24.5	27.3
Quantity of grain inspected (all official inspections) domestically million metric tons	127.3	129.1	123.6
Number of inspections and reinspections:			
By Federal personnel	126,753	125,000	127,000
By delegated state/official agency licenses	1,852,031	1,800,000	1,800,000
Number of appeals	3,103	3,000	3,000
Number of appeals carried to the Board of Appeals and Review	373	300	300
Quantity of rice inspected (million metric tons)	3.5	3.5	3.5
Quantity of rice exports (million metric tons)	3.1	3.1	3.1

Object Classification (in millions of dollars)

Identification code 12–4050–0–3–352		1999 actual	2000 est.	2001 est.
	Personnel compensation:			
11.1	Full-time permanent	17	22	22
11.3	Other than full-time permanent	1	1	1
11.5	Other personnel compensation	5	5	5
11.9	Total personnel compensation	23	28	28
12.1	Civilian personnel benefits	5	5	5
21.0	Travel and transportation of persons	1	1	1
23.1	Rental payments to GSA	1	1	1
23.3	Communications, utilities, and miscellaneous charges	1	1	1
25.2	Other services	3	6	6
26.0	Supplies and materials	1	1	1
99.9	Total new obligations	35	43	43

Personnel Summary

Identification code 12–4050–0–3–352		1999 actual	2000 est.	2001 est.
2001	Total compensable workyears: Full-time equivalent employment	449	453	453

AGRICULTURAL MARKETING SERVICE

Federal Funds

General and special funds:

MARKETING SERVICES

For necessary expenses to carry on services related to consumer protection, agricultural marketing and distribution, transportation, and regulatory programs, as authorized by law, and for administration and coordination of payments to States, including field employment pursuant to the second sentence of section 706(a) of the Organic Act of 1944 (7 U.S.C. 2225) and not to exceed $90,000 for employment under 5 U.S.C. 3109, [$51,625,000] *$66,572,000*, including funds for the wholesale market development program for the design and development of wholesale and farmer market facilities for the major metropolitan areas of the country: *Provided*, That this appropriation shall be available pursuant to law (7 U.S.C. 2250) for the alteration and repair of buildings and improvements, but the cost of altering any one building during the fiscal year shall not exceed 10 percent of the current replacement value of the building.

Fees may be collected for the cost of standardization activities, as established by regulation pursuant to law (31 U.S.C. 9701). *(7 U.S.C. 1291, 1621–27: 15 U.S.C. 714–714p: 21 U.S.C. 1031–56: 26 U.S.C. 6804, 7701.)*

LIMITATION ON ADMINISTRATIVE EXPENSES LEVEL

Not to exceed $60,730,000 (from fees collected) shall be obligated during the current fiscal year for administrative expenses: *Provided*, That if crop size is understated and/or other uncontrollable events occur, the agency may exceed this limitation by up to 10 percent with notification to the Appropriations Committees.*(Agriculture, Rural Development, Food and Drug Administration, and Related Agencies Appropriations Act, 2000.)*

Program and Financing (in millions of dollars)

Identification code 12–2500–0–1–352		1999 actual	2000 est.	2001 est.
	Obligations by program activity:			
	Direct program:			
00.01	Market news service	22	22	29
00.02	Inspection and standardization	6	6	6
00.03	Market protection and promotion	16	18	26
00.04	Wholesale market development	2	3	3
00.05	Transportation services	3	3	3
09.01	Reimbursable program	45	64	64
10.00	Total new obligations	94	116	131
	Budgetary resources available for obligation:			
21.40	Unobligated balance available, start of year	40	40	40
22.00	New budget authority (gross)	94	116	131
23.90	Total budgetary resources available for obligation	134	156	171
23.95	Total new obligations	−94	−116	−131
24.40	Unobligated balance available, end of year	40	40	40
	New budget authority (gross), detail:			
	Discretionary:			
40.00	Appropriation	49	52	67
68.00	Spending authority from offsetting collections: Offsetting collections (cash)	45	64	64
70.00	Total new budget authority (gross)	94	116	131
	Change in unpaid obligations:			
72.40	Unpaid obligations, start of year: Obligated balance, start of year	−27	−19	−15
73.10	Total new obligations	94	116	131
73.20	Total outlays (gross)	−86	−112	−129
74.40	Unpaid obligations, end of year: Obligated balance, end of year	−19	−15	−13
	Outlays (gross), detail:			
86.90	Outlays from new discretionary authority	86	110	123
86.93	Outlays from discretionary balances	....	....	6
87.00	Total outlays (gross)	86	112	129
	Offsets:			
	Against gross budget authority and outlays:			
88.40	Offsetting collections (cash) from: Non-Federal sources	−45	−64	−64
	Net budget authority and outlays:			
89.00	Budget authority	49	52	67
90.00	Outlays	42	48	65

Agricultural Marketing Service activities assist producers and handlers of agricultural commodities by providing a variety of marketing services. These services continue to become more complex as the volume of agricultural commodities increases, as a greater number of new processed commodities are developed, and as the agricultural market structure undergoes extensive changes. Marketing changes include increased concentration in food retailing, direct buying, decentralization of processing, growth of interregional competition, vertical integration, and contract farming.

In 2001, $6 million has been included as part of the Administration's Food Safety Initiative. This represents an increase of $3 million from the $3 million provided in 2000. These funds will be used to monitor microbiological pathogens and establish a baseline for the level of these on fruits and vegetables. In addition $6 million is included to implement to provision of the mandatory livestock price reporting legislation enacted in 2000.

The individual Marketing Services activities include:

Market news service.—The market news program provides the agricultural community with information pertaining to the movement of agricultural products. This nationwide service provides daily reports on the supply, demand, and price of over 700 commodities on domestic and foreign markets. The 2001 request includes almost $6 million to fund the mandatory livestock reporting program enacted in 2000.

Inspection, grading and standardization.—Nationally uniform standards of quality for agricultural products are established and applied to specific lots of products to: promote confidence between buyers and sellers; reduce hazards in marketing due to misunderstandings and disputes arising from the use of nonstandard descriptions; and encourage better preparation of uniform quality products for market. Grading services are provided for cotton and domestic and imported tobacco.

Quarterly inspection of egg handlers and hatcheries is conducted to ensure the proper disposition of shell eggs unfit for human consumption.

MARKET NEWS PROGRAM

	1999 actual	2000 est.	2001 est.
Percentage of reports released on time	90	93	93

COTTON AND TOBACCO USER FEE PROGRAM

	1999 actual	2000 est.	2001 est.
Cotton classed (samples in millions)	14.5	16.8	16.8
Tobacco graded at auction markets (million pounds)	1,417	1,848	1,848
Imported tobacco inspected at markets and ports of entry (million pounds)	233	186	186

FEDERALLY FUNDED INSPECTION AND PROCUREMENT ACTIVITIES

	1999 actual	2000 est.	2001 est.
States and Commonwealths with cooperative agreements	40	40	38
Percentage of noncomplying shell egg lots that are reprocessed or diverted	100	100	100

STANDARDIZATION ACTIVITIES

	1999 actual	2000 est.	2001 est.
International and U.S. standards in effect, end of fiscal year	538	533	521
Number of commodities covered	172	214	214

Market protection and promotion.—This program consists of: (1) the research and promotion programs which are designed to improve the competitive position and expand markets for cotton, eggs and egg products, honey, pork, beef, dairy products, potatoes, watermelons, mushrooms, soybeans, fluid milk and popcorn; (2) the Federal Seed Act; and (3) the administration of the Capper-Volstead Act and the Agricultural Fair Practices Act. The 2001 request includes an increase of over $6 million as part of the President's Food safety initiative to initiate a scientifically-sound microbiological data program.

The pesticide recordkeeping program monitors compliance of private certified applicators with Federal regulations requiring them to keep records of restricted pesticides used in agricultural production.

The pesticide data program develops comprehensive, statistically defensible information on pesticide residues in food to improve government dietary risk procedures.

Federal seed inspectors conduct tests on seed samples to help ensure truthful labeling of agricultural and vegetable seeds sold in interstate commerce.

The Capper-Volstead Act and the Agricultural Fair Practices Act protect producers against discriminatory practices by handlers, permit producers to engage in cooperative efforts, and ensure that such cooperatives do not engage in practices that monopolize or restrain trade.

The national organic program is being established to certify that organically produced food products meet national standards.

MARKET PROTECTION AND PROMOTION ACTIVITIES

	1999 actual	2000 est.	2001 est.
Pesticide Data Program:			
Number of analyses performed	46,000	55,000	52,000
Percentage of sampling and analysis goal	100	100	100
Pesticide Recordkeeping:			
Number of State/Federal Inspections conducted	4,704	4,600	4,600
Percentage of sampling goal attained	100	98	98
Seed Act:			
Interstate investigations:			
Completed	381	500	500
Pending	560	500	500
Seed samples tested	2,135	2,200	2,200
Percentage of cases submitted that are completed	90	92	92
Plant Variety Protection Act:			
Percentage of application processing goal completed	100	100	100
Number of applications received	430	400	400
Certificates of protection issued	219	240	240
Research and promotion collections (dollars in millions)	619	631	636
Percentage of board budgets and marketing plans approved within time frame goal	91	91	93

[1] Partially funded by EPA.

[2] Decrease in number of samples due to change in type of chemical analysis and type of product (fresh vs. processed).

Wholesale market development.—This program is designed to enhance the marketing of agricultural commodities in the United States by conducting research into more efficient marketing methods for agricultural commodities and by providing technical assistance to urban areas interested in improving their food distribution facilities.

Transportation Services.—The activities are designed to ensure that the Nation's transportation systems will adequately serve the needs of agriculture and rural areas of the United States.

WHOLESALE MARKET DEVELOPMENT ACTIVITIES

	1999 actual	2000 est.	2001 est.
Number of projects completed	7	8	8

TRANSPORTATION SERVICES ACTIVITIES

	1999 actual	2000 est.	2001 est.
Number of projects completed	5	6	7

Object Classification (in millions of dollars)

Identification code 12–2500–0–1–352		1999 actual	2000 est.	2001 est.
	Direct obligations:			
	Personnel compensation:			
11.1	Full-time permanent	21	22	25
11.3	Other than full-time permanent	1	1	1
11.9	Total personnel compensation	22	23	26
12.1	Civilian personnel benefits	5	5	6
21.0	Travel and transportation of persons	1	1	2
23.2	Rental payments to others	1	1	1
23.3	Communications, utilities, and miscellaneous charges	2	2	3
25.2	Other services	13	15	23
25.3	Purchases of goods and services from Government accounts	2	2	2
25.7	Operation and maintenance of equipment	1	1	2
26.0	Supplies and materials	1	1	1
31.0	Equipment	1	1	1
99.0	Subtotal, direct obligations	49	52	67
99.0	Reimbursable obligations	45	64	64

General and special funds—Continued

MARKETING SERVICES—Continued

LIMITATION ON ADMINISTRATIVE EXPENSES LEVEL—Continued

Object Classification (in millions of dollars)—Continued

Identification code 12–2500–0–1–352	1999 actual	2000 est.	2001 est.
99.9 Total new obligations	94	116	131

Personnel Summary

Identification code 12–2500–0–1–352	1999 actual	2000 est.	2001 est.
Direct:			
1001 Total compensable workyears: Full-time equivalent employment	464	474	551
Reimbursable:			
2001 Total compensable workyears: Full-time equivalent employment	624	631	631

PAYMENTS TO STATES AND POSSESSIONS

For payments to departments of agriculture, bureaus and departments of markets, and similar agencies for marketing activities under section 204(b) of the Agricultural Marketing Act of 1946 (7 U.S.C. 1623(b)), **[**$1,200,000**]** *$1,500,000. (Agriculture, Rural Development, Food and Drug Administration, and Related Agencies Appropriations Act, 2000.)*

Program and Financing (in millions of dollars)

Identification code 12–2501–0–1–352	1999 actual	2000 est.	2001 est.
Obligations by program activity:			
10.00 Total new obligations (object class 41.0)	1	1	2
Budgetary resources available for obligation:			
22.00 New budget authority (gross)	1	1	2
23.95 Total new obligations	−1	−1	−2
New budget authority (gross), detail:			
Discretionary:			
40.00 Appropriation	1	1	2
Change in unpaid obligations:			
72.40 Unpaid obligations, start of year: Obligated balance, start of year	2	2	1
73.10 Total new obligations	1	1	2
73.20 Total outlays (gross)	−1	−1	−2
74.40 Unpaid obligations, end of year: Obligated balance, end of year	2	1	1
Outlays (gross), detail:			
86.90 Outlays from new discretionary authority	....	....	1
86.93 Outlays from discretionary balances	1	....	1
87.00 Total outlays (gross)	1	1	2
Net budget authority and outlays:			
89.00 Budget authority	1	1	2
90.00 Outlays	1	1	2

Grants are made on a matching fund basis to State departments of agriculture to carry out specifically approved programs designed to enhance marketing efficiency. Under this activity, specialists work with farmers, marketing firms, and other agencies in solving marketing problems and in using research results. The 2001 budget requests an increase of $0.3 million for this program.

PERISHABLE AGRICULTURAL COMMODITIES ACT FUND

Unavailable Collections (in millions of dollars)

Identification code 12–5070–0–2–352	1999 actual	2000 est.	2001 est.
Balance, start of year:			
01.99 Balance, start of year	....	....	....
Receipts:			
02.01 Deposits of Perishable Agricultural Commodities Act fees	8	7	7
Appropriation:			
05.01 Perishable Agricultural Commodities Act fund	−8	−7	−7
07.99 Total balance, end of year	....	....	....

Program and Financing (in millions of dollars)

Identification code 12–5070–0–2–352	1999 actual	2000 est.	2001 est.
Obligations by program activity:			
10.00 Total new obligations	8	9	9
Budgetary resources available for obligation:			
21.40 Unobligated balance available, start of year	6	6	4
22.00 New budget authority (gross)	8	7	7
23.90 Total budgetary resources available for obligation	14	13	11
23.95 Total new obligations	−8	−9	−9
24.40 Unobligated balance available, end of year	6	4	2
New budget authority (gross), detail:			
Mandatory:			
60.25 Appropriation (special fund, indefinite)	8	7	7
Change in unpaid obligations:			
72.40 Unpaid obligations, start of year: Obligated balance, start of year	5	4	4
73.10 Total new obligations	8	9	9
73.20 Total outlays (gross)	−7	−9	−9
74.40 Unpaid obligations, end of year: Obligated balance, end of year	4	4	4
Outlays (gross), detail:			
86.97 Outlays from new mandatory authority	8	7	7
86.98 Outlays from mandatory balances	1	1	1
87.00 Total outlays (gross)	7	9	9
Net budget authority and outlays:			
89.00 Budget authority	8	7	7
90.00 Outlays	7	9	9

License fees are deposited in this special fund and are used to meet the costs of administering the Perishable Agricultural Commodities and the Produce Agency Acts (7 U.S.C. 491–497, 499a–499s).

The Acts are intended to ensure equitable treatment to farmers and others in the marketing of fresh and frozen fruits and vegetables. Commission merchants, dealers, and brokers handling these products in interstate and foreign commerce are licensed. Complaints of violations are investigated and violations dealt with by (a) informal agreements between the two parties, (b) formal decisions involving payment of reparation awards, and/or (c) suspension or revocation of license and/or publication of the facts. Beginning October 1, 1994, an additional fee was instituted for the filing of formal and informal complaints of violations of the Act. The November 1995 amendments to the Perishable Agricultural Commodities Act: (1) increase the license fee and phase out fees for wholesale grocers and retailers by 1999; (2) provide permanent authority to the Secretary of Agriculture to set license and reparation complaint filing fees; and repeal the 25 percent maximum funding reserve cap.

A 1984 amendment to the Perishable Agricultural Commodities Act requires traders to have trust assets on hand to meet their obligations to fruit and vegetable suppliers. To preserve their trust and establish their rights ahead of other creditors, unpaid suppliers file notice with both the Department and their debtors that payment is due.

PERISHABLE AGRICULTURAL COMMODITIES ACT ACTIVITIES

	1999 actual	*2000 est.*	*2001 est.*
Percentage of informal reparation complaints completed within time frame goal	82	85	85

Object Classification (in millions of dollars)

Identification code 12–5070–0–2–352	1999 actual	2000 est.	2001 est.
11.1 Personnel compensation: Full-time permanent	4	5	5
12.1 Civilian personnel benefits	1	1	1
23.3 Communications, utilities, and miscellaneous charges	1	1	1
25.3 Purchases of goods and services from Government accounts	2	2	2
99.9 Total new obligations	8	9	9

Personnel Summary

Identification code 12–5070–0–2–352	1999 actual	2000 est.	2001 est.
1001 Total compensable workyears: Full-time equivalent employment	90	95	95

Funds for Strengthening Markets, Income, and Supply (Section 32)

(INCLUDING TRANSFERS OF FUNDS)

Funds available under section 32 of the Act of August 24, 1935 (7 U.S.C. 612c) shall be used only for commodity program expenses as authorized therein, and other related operating expenses, except for: (1) transfers to the Department of Commerce as authorized by the Fish and Wildlife Act of August 8, 1956; (2) transfers otherwise provided in this Act; and (3) not more than [$12,443,000] *$13,438,000* for formulation and administration of marketing agreements and orders pursuant to the Agricultural Marketing Agreement Act of 1937 and the Agricultural Act of 1961. *(Agriculture, Rural Development, Food and Drug Administration, and Related Agencies Appropriations Act, 2000.)*

Unavailable Collections (in millions of dollars)

Identification code 12–5209–0–2–605	1999 actual	2000 est.	2001 est.
Balance, start of year:			
01.99 Balance, start of year	372	358	895
Receipts:			
02.01 30% of customs duties, funds for strengthening markets, income and supply (section 32)	5,680	6,266	6,661
04.00 Total: Balances and collections	6,052	6,624	7,556
Appropriation:			
05.01 Funds for strengthening markets, income, and supply (section 32)	–5,702	–5,736	–5,576
06.10 Unobligated balance returned to receipts		7	
06.20 Reduction pursuant to Public Law 106–51	8		
07.99 Total balance, end of year	358	895	1,980

Program and Financing (in millions of dollars)

Identification code 12–5209–0–2–605	1999 actual	2000 est.	2001 est.
Obligations by program activity:			
Direct program:			
Commodity program payments:			
00.01 Child nutrition program purchases	400	400	400
00.02 Emergency surplus removal	144	115	115
00.03 Disaster relief	7		
00.04 Diversion payments	178		
00.91 Subtotal, Commodity program payments	729	515	515
01.01 Administrative expenses	17	21	23
01.92 Total direct program	746	536	538
09.11 Reimbursable program	1	1	1
10.00 Total new obligations	747	537	539
Budgetary resources available for obligation:			
21.40 Unobligated balance available, start of year	132	113	300
22.00 New budget authority (gross)	726	732	539
22.10 Resources available from recoveries of prior year obligations	4		
23.90 Total budgetary resources available for obligation	862	845	839
23.95 Total new obligations	–747	–537	–539
23.98 Unobligated balance expiring or withdrawn		–7	
24.40 Unobligated balance available, end of year	113	300	300
New budget authority (gross), detail:			
Discretionary:			
40.00 Appropriation			
40.75 Reduction pursuant to P.L. 106–51	–8		
43.00 Appropriation (total discretionary)	–8		
Mandatory:			
60.05 Appropriation (indefinite)	145		
60.25 Appropriation (special fund, indefinite)	5,702	5,736	5,576
61.00 Transferred to other accounts	–5,114	–5,005	–5,038
62.50 Appropriation (total mandatory)	733	730	538
69.00 Offsetting collections (cash)	1	1	1
70.00 Total new budget authority (gross)	726	732	539
Change in unpaid obligations:			
72.40 Unpaid obligations, start of year: Obligated balance, start of year	105	15	15
73.10 Total new obligations	747	537	539
73.20 Total outlays (gross)	–833	–536	–538
73.45 Adjustments in unexpired accounts	–4		
74.40 Unpaid obligations, end of year: Obligated balance, end of year	15	15	15
Outlays (gross), detail:			
86.97 Outlays from new mandatory authority	596	408	410
86.98 Outlays from mandatory balances	237	128	128
87.00 Total outlays (gross)	833	536	538
Offsets:			
Against gross budget authority and outlays:			
88.40 Offsetting collections (cash) from: Non-Federal sources	–1	–1	–1
Net budget authority and outlays:			
89.00 Budget authority	725	731	538
90.00 Outlays	833	535	537

Under section 32 of the act of August 24, 1935, as amended (7 U.S.C. 612c), an amount equal to 30 percent of customs receipts collected during each calendar year is automatically appropriated for expanding outlets for nonbasic commodities. An amount equal to 30 percent of receipts collected on fishery products is transferred to the Department of Commerce. Most of the funds are transferred to the Food and Nutrition Service and are used to purchase commodities under section 6 of the National School Lunch Act and other authorities specified in the child nutrition appropriation. If unforeseen commodity surpluses should develop, unobligated reserve balances are available for surplus removal.

Object Classification (in millions of dollars)

Identification code 12–5209–0–2–605	1999 actual	2000 est.	2001 est.
Direct obligations:			
11.1 Personnel compensation: Full-time permanent	9	10	11
12.1 Civilian personnel benefits	2	2	3
21.0 Travel and transportation of persons		1	1
22.0 Transportation of things	4	4	4
25.2 Other services	16	9	9
25.3 Purchases of goods and services from Government accounts	2	3	3
25.7 Operation and maintenance of equipment	1	1	1
26.0 Supplies and materials: Grants of commodities to States	711	505	505
31.0 Equipment	1	1	1
99.0 Subtotal, direct obligations	746	536	538
99.0 Reimbursable obligations	1	1	1
99.9 Total new obligations	747	537	539

Personnel Summary

Identification code 12–5209–0–2–605	1999 actual	2000 est.	2001 est.
Direct:			
1001 Total compensable workyears: Full-time equivalent employment	154	162	168

General and special funds—Continued

FUNDS FOR STRENGTHENING MARKETS, INCOME, AND SUPPLY (SECTION 32)—Continued

(INCLUDING TRANSFERS OF FUNDS)—Continued

Personnel Summary—Continued

Identification code 12–5209–0–2–605	1999 actual	2000 est.	2001 est.
Reimbursable:			
2001 Total compensable workyears: Full-time equivalent employment	13	13	13

Trust Funds

EXPENSES AND REFUNDS, INSPECTION AND GRADING OF FARM PRODUCTS

Program and Financing (in millions of dollars)

Identification code 12–8015–0–7–352	1999 actual	2000 est.	2001 est.
Obligations by program activity:			
00.01 Dairy products	5	5	5
00.02 Fruits and vegetables	54	53	53
00.03 Meat grading	22	22	22
00.04 Poultry products	23	23	23
00.05 Miscellaneous agricultural commodities	8	7	7
10.00 Total new obligations	112	110	110
Budgetary resources available for obligation:			
21.40 Unobligated balance available, start of year	21	25	25
22.00 New budget authority (gross)	116	110	110
23.90 Total budgetary resources available for obligation	137	135	135
23.95 Total new obligations	–112	–110	–110
24.40 Unobligated balance available, end of year	25	25	25
New budget authority (gross), detail:			
Mandatory:			
60.27 Appropriation (trust fund, indefinite)	116	110	110
Change in unpaid obligations:			
72.40 Unpaid obligations, start of year: Obligated balance, start of year	–16	–10	–10
73.10 Total new obligations	112	110	110
73.20 Total outlays (gross)	–106	–110	–110
74.40 Unpaid obligations, end of year: Obligated balance, end of year	–10	–10	–10
Outlays (gross), detail:			
86.97 Outlays from new mandatory authority	100	104	104
86.98 Outlays from mandatory balances	5	6	6
87.00 Total outlays (gross)	106	110	110
Net budget authority and outlays:			
89.00 Budget authority	116	110	110
90.00 Outlays	106	110	110

Expenses and refunds, inspection and grading of farm products.—The commodity grading programs provide grading, examination, and certification services for a wide variety of fresh and processed food commodities using federally approved grade standards and purchase specifications. Commodities graded include poultry, livestock, meat, dairy products, and fresh and processed fruits and vegetables. These programs use official grade standards which reflect the relative quality of a particular food commodity based on laboratory testing and characteristics such as taste, color, weight, and physical condition. Producers voluntarily request grading and certification services which are provided on a fee for service basis.

WORKLOAD INDICATORS

	1999 actual	*2000 est.*	*2001 est.*
Weighted average cost per cwt. (1990 index)	$0.08	$0.08	$0.08

Object Classification (in millions of dollars)

Identification code 12–8015–0–7–352	1999 actual	2000 est.	2001 est.
Personnel compensation:			
11.1 Full-time permanent	57	56	56
11.3 Other than full-time permanent	5	5	5
11.5 Other personnel compensation	9	9	9
11.9 Total personnel compensation	71	70	70
12.1 Civilian personnel benefits	17	17	17
13.0 Benefits for former personnel	1	1	1
21.0 Travel and transportation of persons	6	6	6
23.1 Rental payments to GSA	1	1	1
23.2 Rental payments to others	1	1	1
23.3 Communications, utilities, and miscellaneous charges	2	2	2
24.0 Printing and reproduction	1	1	1
25.2 Other services	6	6	6
25.3 Purchases of goods and services from Government accounts	3	2	2
26.0 Supplies and materials	2	2	2
31.0 Equipment	1	1	1
99.9 Total new obligations	112	110	110

Personnel Summary

Identification code 12–8015–0–7–352	1999 actual	2000 est.	2001 est.
1001 Total compensable workyears: Full-time equivalent employment	1,612	1,575	1,492

MILK MARKET ORDERS ASSESSMENT FUND

Program and Financing (in millions of dollars)

Identification code 12–8412–0–8–351	1999 actual	2000 est.	2001 est.
Obligations by program activity:			
09.01 Administration	39	35	38
09.02 Marketing service	6	6	6
10.00 Total new obligations	45	41	44
Budgetary resources available for obligation:			
21.40 Unobligated balance available, start of year	28	19	19
22.00 New budget authority (gross)	36	41	42
23.90 Total budgetary resources available for obligation	64	60	61
23.95 Total new obligations	–45	–41	–44
24.40 Unobligated balance available, end of year	19	19	17
New budget authority (gross), detail:			
Mandatory:			
69.00 Offsetting collections (cash)	36	41	42
Change in unpaid obligations:			
72.40 Unpaid obligations, start of year: Obligated balance, start of year	–2	–19	–19
73.10 Total new obligations	45	41	44
73.20 Total outlays (gross)	–62	–41	–42
74.40 Unpaid obligations, end of year: Obligated balance, end of year	–19	–19	–17
Outlays (gross), detail:			
86.97 Outlays from new mandatory authority	36	41	42
86.98 Outlays from mandatory balances	26		
87.00 Total outlays (gross)	62	41	42
Offsets:			
Against gross budget authority and outlays:			
88.40 Offsetting collections (cash) from: Non-Federal sources	–36	–41	–42
Net budget authority and outlays:			
89.00 Budget authority			
90.00 Outlays	26		
Memorandum (non-add) entries:			
92.01 Total investments, start of year: U.S. securities: Par value	6		

Note.—The administration fund totals are comprised of 31 separate independent order accounts in 1998.

The Secretary of Agriculture is authorized by the Agricultural Marketing Agreement Act of 1937, as amended—under certain conditions—to issue Federal milk marketing orders establishing minimum prices which handlers are required to pay for milk purchased from producers. The Secretary has reduced the number of milk marketing orders from 31 to 11, consistent with the 1996 Farm Bill authorities.

Market administrators are appointed by the Secretary and are responsible for carrying out the terms of specific marketing orders. Their operating expenses, partly financed by assessments on regulated handlers and partly by deductions from producers, are reported in these schedules. These funds are collected locally, deposited in local banks, and disbursed directly by the market administrator.

Expenses of local offices are met from an administrative fund and a marketing service fund, which are prescribed in each order. The administrative fund is derived from prorated handler assessments. The marketing service fund of the individual order disseminates market information to producers who are not members of a qualified cooperative. It also provides for the verification of the weights, sampling, and testing of milk from these producers. The cost of these services is borne by such producers.

The maximum rates for administrative assessment and for marketing services are set forth in each order and adjustments below these rates are made from time to time upon recommendations by the market administrator and upon approval of the Agricultural Marketing Service to provide reserves at about a 6-month operating level. Upon termination of any order, the statute provides for distributing the proceeds from net assets pro rata to contributing handlers or producers, as the case may be.

WORKLOAD INDICATORS

	1999 actual	2000 est.	2001 est.
Percentage of formal and informal rulemaking completed within internal timeframes	94	85	85

Object Classification (in millions of dollars)

Identification code 12–8412–0–8–351	1999 actual	2000 est.	2001 est.
11.1 Personnel compensation: Full-time permanent	28	27	28
12.1 Civilian personnel benefits	6	5	6
21.0 Travel and transportation of persons	2	2	2
23.2 Rental payments to others	3	3	3
23.3 Communications, utilities, and miscellaneous charges	1	1	1
25.2 Other services	2	1	1
26.0 Supplies and materials	2	1	2
31.0 Equipment	1	1	1
99.9 Total new obligations	45	41	44

Personnel Summary

Identification code 12–8412–0–8–351	1999 actual	2000 est.	2001 est.
2001 Total compensable workyears: Full-time equivalent employment	432	442	442

RISK MANAGEMENT AGENCY

Federal Funds

General and special funds:

Administrative and Operating Expenses

For administrative and operating expenses, as authorized by the Federal Agriculture Improvement and Reform Act of 1996 (7 U.S.C. 6933), **[**$64,000,000**]** *$67,700,000*: *Provided*, That not to exceed $700 shall be available for official reception and representation expenses, as authorized by 7 U.S.C. 1506(i). *(Agriculture, Rural Development, Food and Drug Administration, and Related Agencies Appropriations Act, 2000.)*

Program and Financing (in millions of dollars)

Identification code 12–2707–0–1–351	1999 actual	2000 est.	2001 est.
Obligations by program activity:			
10.00 Total new obligations	64	64	68
Budgetary resources available for obligation:			
22.00 New budget authority (gross)	64	64	68
23.95 Total new obligations	−64	−64	−68
23.98 Unobligated balance expiring or withdrawn	−1		
New budget authority (gross), detail:			
Discretionary:			
40.00 Appropriation	64	64	68
Change in unpaid obligations:			
72.40 Unpaid obligations, start of year: Obligated balance, start of year	21	31	31
73.10 Total new obligations	64	64	68
73.20 Total outlays (gross)	−54	−64	−67
74.40 Unpaid obligations, end of year: Obligated balance, end of year	31	31	32
Outlays (gross), detail:			
86.90 Outlays from new discretionary authority	48	58	61
86.93 Outlays from discretionary balances	6	6	6
87.00 Total outlays (gross)	54	64	67
Net budget authority and outlays:			
89.00 Budget authority	64	64	68
90.00 Outlays	54	64	67

This appropriation finances the administrative and operating expenses of the Risk Management Agency (RMA), which provides crop insurance to farmers. The 2001 budget includes an additional $1 million to support the President's Bioproducts Initiative. This funding will allow RMA to begin the process of research, analysis, and the development of biobased crop insurance policies, such as switch grass.

The Federal government reimburses private insurance companies for certain administrative expenses incurred while delivering the crop insurance program. In 1998, discretionary funding was provided for the reimbursement of agents' sales commissions in accordance with the Federal Crop Insurance Reform Act of 1994. The Agricultural Research, Extension and Education Reform Act of 1998 (P.L. 105–185), provides mandatory funding for the reimbursement of administrative expenses to private insurance companies for delivering crop insurance for the 1999 and subsequent crop years.

Object Classification (in millions of dollars)

Identification code 12–2707–0–1–351	1999 actual	2000 est.	2001 est.
Personnel compensation:			
11.1 Full-time permanent	27	30	31
11.3 Other than full-time permanent	3	3	3
11.9 Total personnel compensation	30	33	34
12.1 Civilian personnel benefits	7	7	8
21.0 Travel and transportation of persons	2	2	2
23.2 Rental payments to others	1	1	1
23.3 Communications, utilities, and miscellaneous charges	1	1	1
25.2 Other services	19	18	20
26.0 Supplies and materials	1	1	1
31.0 Equipment	3	1	1
99.9 Total new obligations	64	64	68

Personnel Summary

Identification code 12–2707–0–1–351	1999 actual	2000 est.	2001 est.
1001 Total compensable workyears: Full-time equivalent employment	528	568	568

General and special funds—Continued

CORPORATIONS

The following corporations and agencies are hereby authorized to make expenditures, within the limits of funds and borrowing authority available to each such corporation or agency and in accord with law, and to make contracts and commitments without regard to fiscal year limitations as provided by section 104 of the Government Corporation Control Act as may be necessary in carrying out the programs set forth in the budget for the current fiscal year for such corporation or agency, except as hereinafter provided. *(Agriculture, Rural Development, Food and Drug Administration, and Related Agencies Appropriations Act, 2000.)*

Public enterprise funds:

FEDERAL CROP INSURANCE CORPORATION FUND

For payments as authorized by section 516 of the Federal Crop Insurance Act, such sums as may be necessary, to remain available until expended (7 U.S.C. 2209b). *(Agriculture, Rural Development, Food and Drug Administration, and Related Agencies Appropriations Act, 2000.)*

Program and Financing (in millions of dollars)

Identification code 12–4085–0–3–351	1999 actual	2000 est.	2001 est.
Obligations by program activity:			
00.02 Delivery and other expenses	500	490	511
01.01 Indemnities	1,988	2,417	2,461
10.00 Total new obligations	2,488	2,907	2,972
Budgetary resources available for obligation:			
21.40 Unobligated balance available, start of year	1,449	1,124	600
22.00 New budget authority (gross)	2,172	1,553	2,972
22.21 Unobligated balance transferred to other accounts	–9		
22.22 Unobligated balance transferred from other accounts		830	
23.90 Total budgetary resources available for obligation	3,612	3,507	3,572
23.95 Total new obligations	–2,488	–2,907	–2,972
24.40 Unobligated balance available, end of year	1,124	600	600
New budget authority (gross), detail:			
Mandatory:			
60.00 Appropriation	1,550	711	1,728
69.00 Offsetting collections (cash)	622	842	1,244
70.00 Total new budget authority (gross)	2,172	1,553	2,972
Change in unpaid obligations:			
72.40 Unpaid obligations, start of year: Obligated balance, start of year	949	1,138	1,267
73.10 Total new obligations	2,488	2,907	2,972
73.20 Total outlays (gross)	–2,299	–2,778	–3,228
74.40 Unpaid obligations, end of year: Obligated balance, end of year	1,138	1,267	1,011
Outlays (gross), detail:			
86.97 Outlays from new mandatory authority	1,209	1,520	1,938
86.98 Outlays from mandatory balances	1,090	1,258	1,290
87.00 Total outlays (gross)	2,299	2,778	3,228
Offsets:			
Against gross budget authority and outlays:			
88.40 Offsetting collections (cash) from: Non-Federal sources	–622	–842	–1,244
Net budget authority and outlays:			
89.00 Budget authority	1,550	711	1,728
90.00 Outlays	1,677	1,936	1,984

Summary of Budget Authority and Outlays

(in millions of dollars)

Enacted/requested:	*1999 actual*	*2000 est.*	*2001 est.*
Budget Authority	1,550	711	1,728
Outlays	1,677	1,936	1,984
Legislative proposal, subject to PAYGO:			
Budget Authority			910
Outlays			545
Total:			
Budget Authority	1,550	711	2,638
Outlays	1,677	1,936	2,529

The Federal Crop Insurance Corporation (FCIC), a wholly-owned government corporation, provides multi-peril and catastrophic crop insurance protection against losses from unavoidable natural events. The Federal Crop Insurance Reform Act of 1994 (Reform Act) and the Federal Agriculture Improvement and Reform Act of 1996 (1996 Act) brought many changes to the program. With the reduced price support activities promulgated by the 1996 Act, the crop insurance program is an integral part of the broad-based safety net and includes programs involving revenue insurance, and education in the use of futures markets to manage risks.

Under the 1996 Act, farmers are no longer required to obtain Catastrophic Crop insurance (CAT), as previously mandated by the Reform Act. Producers can instead agree in writing to waive eligibility for emergency crop loss assistance in connection with the crop. However, the 2000 Appropriation Act required uninsured producers who elected to receive the emergency crop loss payments provided by the Act to enroll in crop insurance for the subsequent two crop years. For producers who continue to obtain CAT, which compensates the farmer for losses up to 50 percent of the individual's average yield at 55 percent of the expected market price, premium is entirely subsidized. The cost to the producer for this type of coverage is an annual administrative fee of $60 per crop per county. Commercial insurance companies deliver the product to the producer in all states.

Additional coverage is available to producers who wish to insure crops above the 50 percent coverage level/55 percent price level. Policyholders can elect to be paid up to 100 percent of the market price established by FCIC for each unit of production their actual yield is less than the individual yield guarantee. Premium rates for additional coverage depend on the level of coverage of protection selected and vary from crop to crop and county to county. Producers are assessed a fee of $20 per crop (may be $60 in some cases of limited coverage), in addition to a share of premium. The additional levels of insurance coverage are more attractive to farmers due to availability of optional units, other policy provisions not available with CAT coverage, and the ability to obtain a level of protection that permits them to use crop insurance as loan collateral and to achieve greater financial security.

As mandated by the 1996 Act, revenue insurance programs are available under which producers of wheat, certain feed grains, soybeans, rice, and cotton are protected against loss of revenue stemming from low prices, poor yields, or a combination of both. Two of the revenue insurance plans were privately developed and submitted to FCIC: Crop Revenue Coverage (CRC) and Revenue Assurance (RA). The Income Protection (IP) plan was developed by FCIC. These three plans have many similar features and some very distinctive features. All provide a guaranteed revenue by combining coverage on both yield and price variability. CRC and RA also provide protection against price increases at the time of harvest from an initial price guarantee established near the time of planting. Indemnities are due when any combination of yield and price result in revenue that is less than the revenue guarantee. Revenue protection for all products is provided by extending traditional multi-peril crop insurance protection, based on actual production history, to include price variability. The price component common to CRC, RA, and IP uses the commodity futures market for price discovery. These programs all seek to help ensure a certain level of annual income and are offered through private insurance companies. For 1999, a Group Risk Income Protection plan was developed by the private sector to provide protection against decline in county revenue, based on futures market prices and NASS county average yields, as adjusted by FCIC. FCIC is also piloting an Adjusted Gross Revenue (AGR) program, which is designed to insure a portion of a producers gross revenue based on their Schedule F Farm and Income Tax reports.

RMA plans to roll out Round II of the Dairy Options Pilot Program (DOPP) during 2000 which includes reaching producers in 61 counties in 32 states. RMA's partners in the program are registered commodities brokers who are authorized by the Commodity Futures Trading Commission to buy put options on behalf of DOPP participants on the Chicago Mercantile Exchange and the New York Board of Trade.

RMA also continues to improve and update the terms and conditions of all crop insurance policies, which better clarifies and defines the insurance protection provided by the insurance policies and the duties and responsibilities of the policyholder and insurance provider.

In crop year 1999, 196.2 million acres were insured, with an estimated $2,322 million in total premium income, including $952 million in premium subsidy.

The Corporation's budget is presented in accordance with generally accepted accounting principles, the Financial Accounting Standards Board (FASB) Statement No. 60, "Accounting and Reporting by Insurance Enterprises," and Statement No. 5, "Accounting for Contingencies."

The following table compares the scope of the insurance operations planned for 2001. Amounts in the 1999 column are as of September 30, 1999, and pertain to the 1999 crop year.

	1999 crop year estimate	2000 crop year estimate	2001 crop year estimate
Number of States	50	50	50
Number of counties	3,022	3,022	3,022
Insurance in force (millions)	30,826	28,754	30,841
Insured acreage (millions)	196	194	191
Producer premium (millions)[1]	1,370	1,357	1,370
Premium subsidy (millions)[1]	952	879	970
Total premium (millions)[1]	2,322	2,236	2,340
Indemnities (million)[1]	2,170	2,403	2,515
Loss ratio	0.93	1.075	1.075

[1] Includes amounts that will appear on the books of the reinsured companies. The Corporation records will only reflect the net reinsurance income and net reinsurance loss.

Financing.—The Corporation is authorized under the Federal Crop Insurance Act, as amended, to use funds from the issuance of capital stock which provides working capital for the Corporation.

Receipts, which are for deposit to this fund, come mainly from premiums paid by farmers. The principal payments from this fund are for indemnities to insured farmers, and administrative expenses for approved insurance providers.

Premium subsidies are authorized by section 508(b) of the Federal Crop Insurance Act, as amended, and are received through appropriations.

PREMIUM AND SUBSIDY

[In millions of dollars]

	1999 fiscal year actual	2000 fiscal year estimate	2001 fiscal year estimate
Premiums:			
Producer premium	811	960	1,368
Amount of subsidies	938	890	956
Additional coverage	637	642	657
Catastrophic coverage—Reinsurance	301	248	299
Total premiums	1,749	1,850	2,324
Indemnities	1,988	2,417	2,461
Additional coverage	1,990	2,151	2,178
Catastrophic coverage—Reinsurance		266	283
Noninsured Assistance Program	–2		

For crop years 1948 through 1998, indemnities ($18,478 million) exceeded premium income ($16,401 million) by $2,077 million; the loss ratio for the period was 1.13.

The following table summarizes the insurance operations for 1999, 2000 and 2001:

NET INCOME OR LOSS (–) ON INSURANCE OPERATIONS

[In millions of dollars]

	1999 crop year est.	2000 crop year est.	2001 crop year est.
Premium less indemnities	–1,177	–1,457	–1,093
Interest expense, net	2		
Delivery expenses[1]	–495	–486	–508
Other income or expense, net	9	23	5
Research and development expenses	–4	–4	–4
Reinsurance underwriting gain (+) or loss (–)	–325	–157	–163
Net income or loss (–)	–1,990	–2,081	–1,773

[1] Figures reflect delivery expenses borne by the Fund in accordance with the Agricultural Research, Extension and Education Reform Act of 1998, P.L. 105–185.

Statement of Operations (in millions of dollars)

Identification code 12–4085–0–3–351	1998 actual	1999 actual	2000 est.	2001 est.
0101 Revenue	527	622	842	1,244
0102 Expense	–1,643	–2,488	–2,907	–2,972
0105 Net income or loss (–)	–1,116	–1,866	–2,065	–1,728
0199 Total comprehensive income	–1,116	–1,866	–2,065	–1,728

Balance Sheet (in millions of dollars)

Identification code 12–4085–0–3–351	1998 actual	1999 actual	2000 est.	2001 est.
ASSETS:				
1101 Federal assets: Fund balances with Treasury	2,544	2,794	2,300	2,300
1206 Non-Federal assets: Receivables, net	760	827	850	850
1803 Other Federal assets: Property, plant and equipment, net	1	1	1	1
1999 Total assets	3,305	3,622	3,151	3,151
LIABILITIES:				
Federal liabilities:				
2101 Accounts payable	9	12	1	1
2105 Other	175	249	175	175
Non-Federal liabilities:				
2201 Accounts payable	70	80	70	70
2207 Other	1,749	1,797	1,750	1,750
2999 Total liabilities	2,003	2,138	1,996	1,996
NET POSITION:				
3100 Appropriated capital	680	864	534	534
3300 Cumulative results of operations	621	621	621	621
3999 Total net position	1,301	1,485	1,155	1,155
4999 Total liabilities and net position	3,304	3,623	3,151	3,151

Object Classification (in millions of dollars)

Identification code 12–4085–0–3–351	1999 actual	2000 est.	2001 est.
25.2 Other services	500	490	511
Insurance claims and indemnities:			
42.0 Insurance claims and indemnities (reinsured buyup)	1,990	2,417	2,461
42.0 Insurance claims and indemnities (NAP Operations)	–2		
99.9 Total new obligations	2,488	2,907	2,972

Federal Crop Insurance Fund

(Legislative proposal, subject to PAYGO)

Program and Financing (in millions of dollars)

Identification code 12–4085–4–3–351	1999 actual	2000 est.	2001 est.
Obligations by program activity:			
00.02 Delivery and other expenses			58

Public enterprise funds—Continued

FEDERAL CROP INSURANCE FUND—Continued

Program and Financing (in millions of dollars)—Continued

Identification code 12–4085–4–3–351	1999 actual	2000 est.	2001 est.
00.03 Crop insurance reform			673
01.01 Indemnities			179
10.00 Total new obligations			910
Budgetary resources available for obligation:			
22.00 New budget authority (gross)			979
23.95 Total new obligations			–910
24.40 Unobligated balance available, end of year			69
New budget authority (gross), detail:			
Mandatory:			
60.00 Appropriation			910
69.00 Offsetting collections (cash)			69
70.00 Total new budget authority (gross)			979
Change in unpaid obligations:			
73.10 Total new obligations			910
73.20 Total outlays (gross)			–614
74.40 Unpaid obligations, end of year: Obligated balance, end of year			296
Outlays (gross), detail:			
86.97 Outlays from new mandatory authority			614
Offsets:			
Against gross budget authority and outlays:			
88.40 Offsetting collections (cash) from: Non-Federal sources			–69
Net budget authority and outlays:			
89.00 Budget authority			910
90.00 Outlays			545

As part of a comprehensive package to strengthen the farm safety net, the Administration is proposing crop insurance reform in 2001. The proposal would continue, for the 2001 crop year, the crop insurance premium discounts which were offered for the 1999 and 2000 crop years. In addition, the proposal calls for the establishment of multi-year loss coverage which would provide an insurance plan to protect producers in cases of consecutive crop years' losses. The Administration's reform proposal will also include provisions to provide risk management education, conduct more research and development, conduct a pilot program for insuring livestock, and remove the area-wide trigger requirement for non-insured payment assistance.

Object Classification (in millions of dollars)

Identification code 12–4085–4–3–351	1999 actual	2000 est.	2001 est.
25.2 Other services			270
42.0 Insurance claims and indemnities (reinsured buyup)			640
99.9 Total new obligations			910

FARM SERVICE AGENCY

SALARIES AND EXPENSES

(INCLUDING TRANSFERS OF FUNDS)

For necessary expenses for carrying out the administration and implementation of programs administered by the Farm Service Agency, **[**$794,839,000**]** *$828,385,000*: *Provided*, That the Secretary is authorized to use the services, facilities, and authorities (but not the funds) of the Commodity Credit Corporation to make program payments for all programs administered by the Agency: *Provided further*, That other funds made available to the Agency for authorized activities may be advanced to and merged with this account: *Provided further*, That these funds shall be available for employment pursuant to the second sentence of section 706(a) of the Organic Act of 1944 (7 U.S.C. 2225), and not to exceed $1,000,000 shall be available for employment under 5 U.S.C. 3109. *(Agriculture, Rural Development, Food and Drug Administration, and Related Agencies Appropriations Act, 2000.)*

Program and Financing (in millions of dollars)

Identification code 12–0600–0–1–351	1999 actual	2000 est.	2001 est.
Obligations by program activity:			
Direct program:			
00.01 Farm programs	619	611	641
00.02 Conservation and environment	157	163	162
00.04 Commodity operations	21	21	25
03.00 Subtotal, direct program	797	795	828
Reimbursable program:			
09.01 Farm loans	210	210	265
09.02 Other programs	94	145	87
09.99 Subtotal, reimbursable program	304	355	352
10.00 Total new obligations	1,101	1,150	1,180
Budgetary resources available for obligation:			
22.00 New budget authority (gross)	1,101	1,150	1,180
23.95 Total new obligations	–1,101	–1,150	–1,180
New budget authority (gross), detail:			
Discretionary:			
40.00 Appropriation	797	795	828
68.00 Spending authority from offsetting collections: Offsetting collections (cash)	304	355	352
70.00 Total new budget authority (gross)	1,101	1,150	1,180
Change in unpaid obligations:			
72.40 Unpaid obligations, start of year: Obligated balance, start of year	108	135	189
73.10 Total new obligations	1,101	1,150	1,180
73.20 Total outlays (gross)	–1,072	–1,085	–1,177
73.40 Adjustments in expired accounts (net)	–2	–11	–3
74.40 Unpaid obligations, end of year: Obligated balance, end of year	135	189	189
Outlays (gross), detail:			
86.90 Outlays from new discretionary authority	1,003	1,068	1,095
86.93 Outlays from discretionary balances	69	17	82
87.00 Total outlays (gross)	1,072	1,085	1,177
Offsets:			
Against gross budget authority and outlays:			
Offsetting collections (cash) from:			
88.00 Federal sources	–277	–331	–328
88.40 Non-Federal sources	–27	–24	–24
88.90 Total, offsetting collections (cash)	–304	–355	–352
Net budget authority and outlays:			
89.00 Budget authority	797	795	828
90.00 Outlays	768	730	825

The Farm Service Agency (FSA) was established October 3, 1994, pursuant to the Federal Crop Insurance Reform and Department of Agriculture Reorganization Act of 1994, P.L. 103–354. The Department of Agriculture Reorganization Act of 1994 was amended on April 4, 1996, by the Federal Agriculture Improvement and Reform Act of 1996 (1996 Act), P.L. 104–127. The FSA administers a variety of activities, such as farm income support programs through various loans and payments; the Conservation Reserve Program (CRP); the Emergency Conservation Program; the Hazardous Waste Management Program; the Commodity Operation Programs including the warehouse examination function; farm ownership, farm operating, emergency disaster, and other loan programs; price support and production control programs for tobacco and peanuts; and the Noninsured Crop Disaster Assistance Program (NAP), which provides crop loss protection for growers of many crops for which crop insurance is not available. The Agency also assists in the administration of several conservation cost-share programs financed by the Commodity Credit Corporation (CCC), including the Environmental Quality Incentives Program (EQIP). In addition, FSA currently provides certain administrative support services to the Foreign Agricultural Service (FAS) and to the Risk Management Agency (RMA).

This consolidated administrative expenses account includes funds to cover expenses of programs administered by, and functions assigned to, the Agency. The funds consist of a direct appropriation, transfers from program loan accounts under credit reform procedures, user fees, and advances and reimbursements from other sources. This is a consolidated account for administrative expenses of national, regional, State, and county offices. Currently, the majority of FSA county office employees are not Federal employees, although their salaries and benefits are fully paid through Federal funds appropriated to this account. The Administration is proposing legislation to make all FSA employees Federal employees.

Farm Programs.—These programs provide an economic safety net through farm income support to eligible producers, cooperatives, and associations to help improve the economic stability and viability of the agricultural sector and to ensure the production of an adequate and reasonably priced supply of food and fiber. Objectives of the Agency include maintaining a high Agricultural Market Transition Act (AMTA) participation rate for eligible acreage, providing marketing assistance loans and loan deficiency payments enabling recipients to continue farming operations without marketing their product immediately after harvest, stabilizing the price and production of tobacco and peanuts, and providing a financial assistance safety net to eligible producers when natural disasters result in a catastrophic loss of production or prevents planting of noninsured crops, and timely designating eligible Noninsured Crop Disaster Assistance Program (NAP) areas and approving crop prices, average yields, and payment factors.

Farm program activities include the following functions dealing with the administration of programs carried out through the farmer committee system of the FSA: (a) developing program regulations and procedures; (b) collecting and compiling basic data for individual farms; (c) establishing individual farm allotments for tobacco and peanuts and farm planting history; (d) notifying producers of established allotments and farm planting histories; (e) determining farm marketing quotas for tobacco and peanuts; (f) conducting referendums and certifying results; (g) accepting farmer certifications and checking compliance for specific purposes; (h) issuing marketing cards so that production from the allotted acreage can be marketed without penalty; (i) processing commodity loan documents and issuing checks; (j) processing production flexibility contract payments and market loss assistance payments and issuing checks; (k) certifying payment eligibility and monitoring payment limitations; and (l) processing farm storage facility loans and issuing checks.

Conservation and Environment.—These programs assist agricultural producers and landowners in achieving a high level of stewardship of soil, water, air, and wildlife resources on America's farmland and ranches while protecting the human and natural environment. Objectives of the Agency include improving environmental quality, protecting natural resources, and enhancing habitat for fish and wildlife, including threatened and endangered species, providing Emergency Conservation Program funding for farmers and ranchers to rehabilitate damaged farmland and for carrying out emergency conservation measures during periods of severe drought or flooding protecting the public health of communities through implementation of the Hazardous Waste Management Program, assisting NRCS with EQIP program policy and procedure development, and implementing administrative processes and procedures for contracting, financial reporting, and other financial operations. This activity includes: (a) processing producer requests for conservation cost-sharing and issuing conservation reserve rental payments; and (b) issuing checks for other conservation programs.

Commodity Operations.—This activity includes: (a) overall management of CCC-owned commodities; (b) purchasing commodities; (c) donating commodities; (d) selling commodities; (e) accounting for loans and commodities; and (f) commercial warehouse activities, which include improving the effectiveness and efficiency of FSA's commodity acquisition, procurement, storage, and distribution activities to support domestic and international food assistance programs and administering the U.S. Warehouse Act (USWA). The Agency provides for the examination of warehouses licensed under the U.S. Warehouse Act and non-licensed warehouses storing CCC-owned or pledged commodities. Examiners perform periodic examinations of the facilities and the warehouse records to ensure protection of depositors against potential losses of the stored commodities and to ensure compliance with the U.S. Warehouse Act and any CCC storage agreements.

Farm Loans (Reimbursable).—Provides for administering the direct and guaranteed loan programs covered under the Agricultural Credit Insurance Fund (ACIF). Objectives of the Agency include improving the economic viability of farmers and ranchers, reducing losses in direct loan programs, responding to loan making and servicing requests, and maximizing financial and technical assistance to under-served groups. Activities include reviewing applications, servicing the loan portfolio, and providing technical assistance and guidance to borrowers. These administrative expenses are transferred to this consolidated account from the ACIF. Appropriations representing subsidy amounts necessary to support the individual program loan levels under Federal Credit Reform are made to the ACIF account.

Other Reimbursable Activities.—FSA collects a fee or is reimbursed for performing a variety of services for other Federal agencies, CCC, industry, and others, including certain administrative support services for the Risk Management Agency and the Foreign Agricultural Service, and for county office services provided to Federal and non-Federal entities, including a variety of services to producers.

Object Classification (in millions of dollars)

Identification code 12–0600–0–1–351		1999 actual	2000 est.	2001 est.
	Direct obligations:			
	Personnel compensation:			
11.1	Full-time permanent	118	139	143
11.3	Other than full-time permanent	8	8	8
11.5	Other personnel compensation	3	5	6
11.9	Total personnel compensation	129	152	157
12.1	Civilian personnel benefits	28	34	35
21.0	Travel and transportation of persons	9	13	11
22.0	Transportation of things	2	3	2
23.2	Rental payments to others	8	9	10
23.3	Communications, utilities, and miscellaneous charges	8	11	14
24.0	Printing and reproduction	1	1	1
25.2	Other services	37	41	35
26.0	Supplies and materials	8	8	6
31.0	Equipment	11	4	3
41.0	Grants, subsidies, and contributions	556	518	553
42.0	Insurance claims and indemnities	....	1	1
99.0	Subtotal, direct obligations	797	795	828
99.0	Reimbursable obligations	304	355	352
99.9	Total new obligations	1,101	1,150	1,180

SALARIES AND EXPENSES—Continued

(INCLUDING TRANSFERS OF FUNDS)—Continued

Personnel Summary

Identification code 12–0600–0–1–351	1999 actual	2000 est.	2001 est.
Direct:			
1001 Total compensable workyears: Full-time equivalent employment	2,445	2,644	2,560
Reimbursable:			
2001 Total compensable workyears: Full-time equivalent employment	3,264	3,257	3,341

STATE MEDIATION GRANTS

For grants pursuant to section 502(b) of the Agricultural Credit Act of 1987, *as amended* (7 U.S.C. 5101–5106), [$3,000,000] *$4,000,000. (Agriculture, Rural Development, Food and Drug Administration, and Related Agencies Appropriations Act, 2000.)*

Program and Financing (in millions of dollars)

Identification code 12–0170–0–1–351	1999 actual	2000 est.	2001 est.
Obligations by program activity:			
10.00 Total new obligations (object class 41.0)	2	3	4
Budgetary resources available for obligation:			
22.00 New budget authority (gross)	2	3	4
23.95 Total new obligations	−2	−3	−4
New budget authority (gross), detail:			
Discretionary:			
40.00 Appropriation	2	3	4
Change in unpaid obligations:			
72.40 Unpaid obligations, start of year: Obligated balance, start of year	1	1	2
73.10 Total new obligations	2	3	4
73.20 Total outlays (gross)	−2	−3	−3
74.40 Unpaid obligations, end of year: Obligated balance, end of year	1	2	2
Outlays (gross), detail:			
86.90 Outlays from new discretionary authority	1	1	2
86.93 Outlays from discretionary balances	1		1
87.00 Total outlays (gross)	2	3	3
Net budget authority and outlays:			
89.00 Budget authority	2	3	4
90.00 Outlays	2	3	3

This grant program is authorized by Title V of the Agricultural Credit Act of 1987, P.L. 100–233, as amended. Originally designed to address agricultural credit disputes, the program was expanded by the Federal Crop Insurance Reform and Department of Agriculture Reorganization Act of 1994 (P.L. 103–354) to include other agricultural issues such as wetland determinations, conservation compliance, rural water loan programs, grazing on National Forest System lands, and pesticide use. Grants are made to States whose agricultural mediation programs have been certified by the Farm Service Agency. A grant will not exceed 70 percent of the total fiscal year funds that a qualifying State requires to operate and administer its agricultural loan mediation program. In no case will the total amount of a grant exceed $500,000 annually.

GRANT OBLIGATIONS

	1999 actual	*2000 est.*	*2001 est.*
Number of States receiving grants	22	21	22
Amount of grants (in millions of dollars)	2	3	4

TREE ASSISTANCE PROGRAM

Program and Financing (in millions of dollars)

Identification code 12–2701–0–1–351	1999 actual	2000 est.	2001 est.
Obligations by program activity:			
10.00 Total new obligations (object class 41.0)	2		
Budgetary resources available for obligation:			
22.00 New budget authority (gross)	3		
23.95 Total new obligations	−2		
23.98 Unobligated balance expiring or withdrawn	−1		
New budget authority (gross), detail:			
Discretionary:			
50.05 Reappropriation (indefinite)	3		
Change in unpaid obligations:			
72.40 Unpaid obligations, start of year: Obligated balance, start of year	13	8	2
73.10 Total new obligations	2		
73.20 Total outlays (gross)	−7	−6	−2
74.40 Unpaid obligations, end of year: Obligated balance, end of year	8	2	
Outlays (gross), detail:			
86.93 Outlays from discretionary balances	7	6	2
Net budget authority and outlays:			
89.00 Budget authority	3		
90.00 Outlays	7	6	2

Funding for the Tree Assistance Program (TAP) was provided by the 1998 Emergency Supplemental Appropriations Act, P.L. 105–174, enacted May 1, 1998. The $14 million appropriation was made available for obligation through September 30, 1998, with any unobligated funding expiring. However, the 1999 Appropriations Act, P.L. 105–277, Section 757 of the General Provisions, authorized the use of unobligated 1998 TAP funds for losses due to disasters that occurred between May 1 and August 1, 1998. Eligibility for these funds was also extended to producers whose trees were lost or destroyed by May 31, 1999, as a direct result of fire blight infestation (a destructive disease caused by bacteria) that was caused by a natural disaster. This funding was available for obligation through September 30, 1999, with any unobligated balance expiring.

TAP provided cost-share payments of up to 100 percent to orchard and vineyard growers who replanted or rehabilitated orchard trees and vineyards lost to damaging weather, including freezes, excessive rainfalls, floods, droughts, tornadoes, and earthquakes. Eligible owners may not receive more than $25,000 per person.

During 1999, $2 million was obligated in Michigan, and the remaining unobligated balance of $1 million expired.

CONSERVATION RESERVE PROGRAM

Program and Financing (in millions of dollars)

Identification code 12–3319–0–1–302	1999 actual	2000 est.	2001 est.
Obligations by program activity:			
00.01 Technical assistance	21	1	
10.00 Total new obligations (object class 25.2)	21	1	
Budgetary resources available for obligation:			
21.40 Unobligated balance available, start of year	21	1	
22.10 Resources available from recoveries of prior year obligations	1		
23.90 Total budgetary resources available for obligation	22	1	
23.95 Total new obligations	−21	−1	
24.40 Unobligated balance available, end of year	1		

Change in unpaid obligations:			
72.40 Unpaid obligations, start of year: Obligated balance, start of year	52	20	
73.10 Total new obligations	21	1	
73.20 Total outlays (gross)	−52	−21	
73.45 Adjustments in unexpired accounts	−1		
74.40 Unpaid obligations, end of year: Obligated balance, end of year	20		
Outlays (gross), detail:			
86.98 Outlays from mandatory balances	52	21	
Net budget authority and outlays:			
89.00 Budget authority			
90.00 Outlays	52	21	

The Conservation Reserve Program (CRP) was originally mandated by the Food Security Act of 1985. The Federal Agriculture Improvement and Reform Act of 1996 (the 1996 Act), enacted April 4, 1996, retains the CRP as part of the Environmental Conservation Acreage Reserve Program (ECARP) but changed the funding source from direct appropriation to the Commodity Credit Corporation. Only very minimal CCC funds were used for program operations in 1996 since annual rental payments had been made very early in the fiscal year using CRP appropriated funds.

In 1999, annual rental and cost-share payments for acres enrolled in the program were paid through the Commodity Credit Corporation. Remaining unobligated funds from the fiscal year 1996 appropriated account have been used for CRP technical assistance and were nearly exhausted in 1999. Less than $1 million remained at year end. In providing technical assistance, the Natural Resources Conservation Service (NRCS) determines eligibility, develops conservation plans, and helps install approved practices. The Forest Service (FS) and cooperating State forestry agencies develop plans for tree planting and assist in carrying them out. The Cooperative State Research, Education, and Extension Service provides information and educational assistance to inform landowners and operators about the program. Local soil and water conservation districts approve conservation plans. To ensure maximum program benefits, USDA consults with land grant universities, State soil and water agencies, State fish and wildlife agencies, the U.S. Fish and Wildlife Services, and others. In fiscal year 1999, $21 million was obligated for the technical assistance services of NRCS and FS and outlays of $53 million in CRP appropriated funds were made to NRCS and FS.

CRP program payments are included under the Commodity Credit Corporation account.

Agricultural Conservation Program

Program and Financing (in millions of dollars)

Identification code 12–3315–0–1–302	1999 actual	2000 est.	2001 est.
Budgetary resources available for obligation:			
21.40 Unobligated balance available, start of year	33	40	40
22.10 Resources available from recoveries of prior year obligations	7		
23.90 Total budgetary resources available for obligation	40	40	40
24.40 Unobligated balance available, end of year	40	40	40
Change in unpaid obligations:			
72.40 Unpaid obligations, start of year: Obligated balance, start of year	43	25	17
73.20 Total outlays (gross)	−11	−8	−8
73.45 Adjustments in unexpired accounts	−7		
74.40 Unpaid obligations, end of year: Obligated balance, end of year	25	17	9
Outlays (gross), detail:			
86.93 Outlays from discretionary balances	11	8	8
Net budget authority and outlays:			
89.00 Budget authority			
90.00 Outlays	11	8	8

This program was terminated at the beginning of 1997 in accordance with the Federal Agriculture Improvement and Reform Act of 1996. The objectives of the Agricultural Conservation Program (ACP) were incorporated into the Environmental Quality Incentives Program which is funded by the Commodity Credit Corporation and administered under the lead of the Natural Resources Conservation Service.

The primary objectives of the program were to conserve soil and water resources. Along with annual agreements, cost sharing was authorized for long-term agreements of 3–10 years. At the end of 1999, there were $25 million in unliquidated obligations for ACP agreements.

Emergency Conservation Program

[For an additional amount for the "Emergency Conservation Program" for expenses resulting from natural disasters, $50,000,000, to remain available until expended.] *(Miscellaneous Appropriations, 2000, as enacted by section 1000(a)(5) of the Consolidated Appropriations Act, 2000 (P.L. 106–113).)*

Program and Financing (in millions of dollars)

Identification code 12–3316–0–1–453	1999 actual	2000 est.	2001 est.
Obligations by program activity:			
10.00 Total new obligations (object class 41.0)	39	91	32
Budgetary resources available for obligation:			
21.40 Unobligated balance available, start of year	84	73	32
22.00 New budget authority (gross)	28	50	
23.90 Total budgetary resources available for obligation	112	123	32
23.95 Total new obligations	−39	−91	−32
24.40 Unobligated balance available, end of year	73	32	
New budget authority (gross), detail:			
Discretionary:			
40.00 Appropriation	28	50	
Change in unpaid obligations:			
72.40 Unpaid obligations, start of year: Obligated balance, start of year	26	25	48
73.10 Total new obligations	39	91	32
73.20 Total outlays (gross)	−40	−68	−41
74.40 Unpaid obligations, end of year: Obligated balance, end of year	25	48	39
Outlays (gross), detail:			
86.93 Outlays from discretionary balances	40	68	41
Net budget authority and outlays:			
89.00 Budget authority	28	50	
90.00 Outlays	40	68	41

This program was authorized by the Agricultural Credit Act of 1978 (16 U.S.C. 2201–05). It provides funds for sharing the cost of emergency measures to deal with cases of severe damage to farmlands and rangelands resulting from natural disasters.

For 1999, pursuant to P.L. 106–31, enacted May 21, 1999, $28 million in supplemental funding was provided to the Emergency Conservation Program, to remain available until expended. Under the 1999 program, cost-sharing and technical assistance were provided in 42 States as well as the Virgin Islands to treat farmlands damaged by floods, hurricanes, drought, ice storms, tornadoes, and other natural disasters. The 1999 program rehabilitated approximately 4,889,922 acres of farmland damaged by these natural disasters.

No funding was provided in the 2000 Agriculture Appropriations Act for this program. However, $50 million in supplemental funding was provided by title I of the 2000 Consoli-

EMERGENCY CONSERVATION PROGRAM—Continued

dated Appropriations Act, P.L. 106–113, enacted November 29, 1999. The 2001 budget proposes no funding.

Credit accounts:

AGRICULTURAL CREDIT INSURANCE FUND PROGRAM ACCOUNT

(INCLUDING TRANSFERS OF FUNDS)

For gross obligations for the principal amount of direct and guaranteed loans as authorized by 7 U.S.C. 1928–1929, to be available from funds in the Agricultural Credit Insurance Fund, as follows: farm ownership loans, [$559,422,000] *$1,128,000,000*, of which [$431,373,000] *$1,000,000,000* shall be for guaranteed loans; operating loans, [$2,397,842,000] *$3,177,868,000*, of which [$1,697,842,000] *$2,000,000,000* shall be for unsubsidized guaranteed loans and [$200,000,000] *$477,868,000* shall be for subsidized guaranteed loans; Indian tribe land acquisition loans as authorized by 25 U.S.C. 488, [$1,028,000] *$2,006,000*; for emergency insured loans, [$25,000,000] *$150,064,000* to meet the needs resulting from natural disasters; and for boll weevil eradication program loans as authorized by 7 U.S.C. 1989, $100,000,000.

For the cost of direct and guaranteed loans, including the cost of modifying loans as defined in section 502 of the Congressional Budget Act of 1974, as follows: farm ownership loans, [$7,243,000] *$18,886,000*, of which [$2,416,000] *$5,100,000*, shall be for guaranteed loans; operating loans, [$70,860,000] *$129,534,000*, of which [$23,940,000] *$27,400,000* shall be for unsubsidized guaranteed loans and [$17,620,000] *$38,994,000* shall be for subsidized guaranteed loans; Indian tribe land acquisition loans as authorized by 25 U.S.C. 488, [$21,000] *$323,000*; and for emergency insured loans, [$3,882,000] *$36,811,000* to meet the needs resulting from natural disasters.

In addition, for administrative expenses necessary to carry out the direct and guaranteed loan programs, [$214,161,000] *$269,454,000*, of which [$209,861,000] *$265,315,000* shall be transferred to and merged with the appropriation for "Farm Service Agency, Salaries and Expenses".

Funds appropriated by this Act to the Agricultural Credit Insurance Program Account for farm ownership and operating direct loans and guaranteed loans may be transferred among these programs with [the prior approval of] *advance notice to* the House and Senate Committees on Appropriations.

DAIRY INDEMNITY PROGRAM

(INCLUDING TRANSFERS OF FUNDS)

For necessary expenses involved in making indemnity payments to dairy farmers for milk or cows producing such milk and manufacturers of dairy products who have been directed to remove their milk or dairy products from commercial markets because it contained residues of chemicals registered and approved for use by the Federal Government, and in making indemnity payments for milk, or cows producing such milk, at a fair market value to any dairy farmer who is directed to remove his milk from commercial markets because of: (1) the presence of products of nuclear radiation or fallout if such contamination is not due to the fault of the farmer; or (2) residues of chemicals or toxic substances not included under the first sentence of the Act of August 13, 1968 (7 U.S.C. 450j), if such chemicals or toxic substances were not used in a manner contrary to applicable regulations or labeling instructions provided at the time of use and the contamination is not due to the fault of the farmer, $450,000, to remain available until expended (7 U.S.C. 2209b): *Provided*, That none of the funds contained in this Act shall be used to make indemnity payments to any farmer whose milk was removed from commercial markets as a result of the farmer's willful failure to follow procedures prescribed by the Federal Government: *Provided further*, That this amount shall be transferred to the Commodity Credit Corporation: *Provided further*, That the Secretary is authorized to utilize the services, facilities, and authorities of the Commodity Credit Corporation for the purpose of making dairy indemnity disbursements. *(Agriculture, Rural Development, Food and Drug Administration, and Related Agencies Appropriations Act, 2000.)*

[AGRICULTURAL CREDIT INSURANCE FUND PROGRAM ACCOUNT]

[For additional gross obligations for the principal amount of direct and guaranteed loans as authorized by 7 U.S.C. 1928–1929, to be available from funds in the Agricultural Credit Insurance Fund to meet the needs resulting from natural disasters, as follows: farm ownership loans, $590,578,000, of which $568,627,000 shall be for guaranteed loans; operating loans, $1,404,716,000, of which $302,158,000 shall be for unsubsidized guaranteed loans and $702,558,000 shall be for subsidized guaranteed loans; and for emergency loans, $547,000,000.]

[For the additional cost of direct and guaranteed loans to meet the needs resulting from natural disasters, including the cost of modifying loans as defined in section 502 of the Congressional Budget Act of 1974, to remain available until expended, as follows: farm ownership loans, $4,012,000, of which $3,184,000 shall be for guaranteed loans; operating loans, $89,596,000, of which $4,260,000 shall be for unsubsidized guaranteed loans and $61,895,000 shall be for subsidized guaranteed loans; and for emergency loans, $84,949,000.] *(Miscellaneous Appropriations, 2000, as enacted by section 1000(a)(5) of the Consolidated Appropriations Act, 2000 (P.L. 106–113).)*

General Fund Credit Receipt Accounts (in millions of dollars)

Identification code 12–1140–0–1–351		1999 actual	2000 est.	2001 est.
0101	Agriculture credit insurance, downward reestimates of subsidies		417	

Program and Financing (in millions of dollars)

Identification code 12–1140–0–1–351		1999 actual	2000 est.	2001 est.
	Obligations by program activity:			
00.01	Direct loan subsidy	158	152	114
00.02	Guaranteed loan subsidy	73	116	72
00.05	Reestimates of direct loan subsidy		484	
00.06	Interest on reestimates of direct loan subsidy		84	
00.07	Reestimates of guaranteed loan subsidy		124	
00.08	Interest on reestimates of guaranteed loan subsidy		34	
	Administrative expenses:			
00.09	Administrative expenses—salaries and expenses	210	210	265
00.10	Administrative expenses—non-recoverable costs	10	8	4
10.00	Total new obligations	451	1,212	455
	Budgetary resources available for obligation:			
21.40	Unobligated balance available, start of year	15	14	14
22.00	New budget authority (gross)	451	1,212	455
23.90	Total budgetary resources available for obligation	466	1,226	469
23.95	Total new obligations	−451	−1,212	−455
23.98	Unobligated balance expiring or withdrawn	−1		
24.40	Unobligated balance available, end of year	14	14	14
	New budget authority (gross), detail:			
	Discretionary:			
40.00	Appropriation	345	486	455
40.15	Appropriation (emergency)	106		
43.00	Appropriation (total discretionary)	451	486	455
	Mandatory:			
60.05	Appropriation (indefinite)		726	
70.00	Total new budget authority (gross)	451	1,212	455
	Change in unpaid obligations:			
72.40	Unpaid obligations, start of year: Obligated balance, start of year	16	32	50
73.10	Total new obligations	451	1,212	455
73.20	Total outlays (gross)	−433	−1,194	−479
74.40	Unpaid obligations, end of year: Obligated balance, end of year	32	50	26
	Outlays (gross), detail:			
86.90	Outlays from new discretionary authority	417	455	439
86.93	Outlays from discretionary balances	16	13	40
86.97	Outlays from new mandatory authority		726	
87.00	Total outlays (gross)	433	1,194	479
	Net budget authority and outlays:			
89.00	Budget authority	451	1,212	455
90.00	Outlays	433	1,194	479

Summary of Loan Levels, Subsidy Budget Authority and Outlays by Program (in millions of dollars)

Identification code 12–1140–0–1–351	1999 actual	2000 est.	2001 est.
Direct loan levels supportable by subsidy budget authority:			
1150 Farm ownership	171	150	128
1150 Farm operating	789	900	700
1150 Emergency disaster	276	572	150
1150 Indian tribe land acquisition	....	1	2
1150 Boll weevil eradication	100	100	100
1159 Total direct loan levels	1,336	1,723	1,080
Direct loan subsidy (in percent):			
1320 Farm ownership	14.97	3.77	10.77
1320 Farm operating	6.83	5.86	9.02
1320 Emergency disaster	23.60	15.53	24.53
1320 Indian tribe land acquisition	15.25	2.04	16.10
1320 Boll weevil eradication	1.44	−4.38	−3.23
1329 Weighted average subsidy rate	8.33	5.42	10.26
Direct loan subsidy budget authority:			
1330 Farm ownership	26	6	14
1330 Farm operating	54	53	63
1330 Emergency disaster	65	89	37
1330 Boll weevil eradication	1	....	....
1339 Total subsidy budget authority	146	148	114
Direct loan subsidy outlays:			
1340 Farm ownership	24	7	13
1340 Farm operating	52	55	63
1340 Emergency disaster	63	82	39
1340 Boll weevil eradication	1	....	....
1349 Total subsidy outlays	140	144	115
Guaranteed loan levels supportable by subsidy budget authority:			
2150 Farm ownership, unsubsidized	774	1,000	1,000
2150 Farm operating, unsubsidized	1,251	2,000	2,000
2150 Farm operating, subsidized	526	903	478
2159 Total loan guarantee levels	2,551	3,903	3,478
Guaranteed loan subsidy (in percent):			
2320 Farm ownership, unsubsidized	1.59	0.56	0.51
2320 Farm operating, unsubsidized	1.16	1.41	1.37
2320 Farm operating, subsidized	8.74	8.81	8.16
2329 Weighted average subsidy rate	2.70	1.57	2.06
Guaranteed loan subsidy budget authority:			
2330 Farmer ownership, unsubsidized	12	6	5
2330 Farm operating, unsubsidized	15	28	27
2330 Farm operating, subsidized	46	80	39
2339 Total subsidy budget authority	73	114	71
Guaranteed loan subsidy outlays:			
2340 Farmer ownership, unsubsidized	14	3	5
2340 Farm operating, unsubsidized	14	22	28
2340 Farm operating, subsidized	45	55	60
2349 Total subsidy outlays	73	80	93
Administrative expense data:			
3510 Budget authority	220	219	269
3580 Outlays from balances	....	....	....
3590 Outlays	220	219	269

The Agricultural Credit Insurance Fund Program Account's loans are authorized by title III of the Consolidated Farm and Rural Development Act, as amended.

This program account includes subsidies to provide direct and guaranteed loans for farm ownership, farm operating, and emergency loans to individuals. Indian tribes and tribal corporations are eligible for Indian land acquisition loans.

Additional funding was provided by a 1999 supplemental appropriation, P.L. 106–31, for direct and guaranteed farm ownership, direct and guaranteed operating, and emergency disaster loans. Funding is available until September 30, 2000.

Additional funding was also provided by a 2000 supplemental appropriation, P.L. 106–113, for direct and guaranteed farm ownership, direct and guaranteed operating, and emergency disaster loans. Funding is available until expended.

For 2001, legislation will be proposed to expand eligibility for emergency disaster loans to agricultural-related enterprises that are currently ineligible for either USDA or Small Business Administration disaster loans. Interest rates on these loans will be above those charged for family-sized farms.

As required by the Federal Credit Reform Act of 1990, this account records, for this program, the subsidy costs associated with the direct loans obligated and loan guarantees committed in 1992 and beyond (including credit sales of acquired property), as well as administrative expenses of this program. The subsidy amounts are estimated on a present value basis; the administrative expenses are estimated on a cash basis.

Under the Dairy Indemnity Program (DIP), payments are made to farmers and manufacturers of dairy products who are directed to remove their milk or milk products from commercial markets because they contain residues of chemicals that have been registered and approved by the Federal Government, other chemicals, nuclear radiation, or nuclear fallout. Indemnification may also be paid for cows producing such milk.

In 2000, an estimated $650 thousand will be paid to producers and manufacturers who file claims under the program. The 2001 budget requests $450 thousand for this program.

Object Classification (in millions of dollars)

Identification code 12–1140–0–1–351	1999 actual	2000 est.	2001 est.
25.3 Purchases of goods and services from Government accounts	220	218	269
41.0 Grants, subsidies, and contributions	231	994	186
99.9 Total new obligations	451	1,212	455

Agricultural Credit Insurance Fund Direct Loan Financing Account

Program and Financing (in millions of dollars)

Identification code 12–4212–0–3–351	1999 actual	2000 est.	2001 est.
Obligations by program activity:			
Operating program:			
00.01 Direct loans	1,393	1,723	1,080
00.02 Advances on behalf of borrowers	3	3	3
00.04 Interest on Treasury borrowing	217	174	108
00.91 Subtotal, Operating program	1,613	1,900	1,191
Reestimates:			
08.02 Downward reestimate of subsidy	....	163	....
08.04 Downward reestimate of subsidy—interest	....	56	....
08.91 Subtotal, reestimates	....	219	....
10.00 Total new obligations	1,613	2,119	1,191
Budgetary resources available for obligation:			
21.40 Unobligated balance available, start of year	208	95	....
22.00 New financing authority (gross)	2,217	2,024	1,191
22.10 Resources available from recoveries of prior year obligations	12	....	....
22.60 Portion applied to repay debt	−723	....	....
22.70 Balance of authority to borrow withdrawn	−7	....	....
23.90 Total budgetary resources available for obligation	1,707	2,119	1,191
23.95 Total new obligations	−1,613	−2,119	−1,191
24.40 Unobligated balance available, end of year	95	....	....
New financing authority (gross), detail:			
Mandatory:			
67.15 Authority to borrow (indefinite)	1,368	784	328
Spending authority from offsetting collections:			
Discretionary:			
68.00 Offsetting collections (cash)	834	1,227	891
68.10 From Federal sources: Change in receivables and unpaid, unfilled orders	15	13	−28

Credit accounts—Continued

AGRICULTURAL CREDIT INSURANCE FUND DIRECT LOAN FINANCING ACCOUNT—Continued

Program and Financing (in millions of dollars)—Continued

Identification code 12–4212–0–3–351		1999 actual	2000 est.	2001 est.
68.90	Spending authority from offsetting collections (total discretionary)	849	1,240	863
70.00	Total new financing authority (gross)	2,217	2,024	1,191
	Change in unpaid obligations:			
	Unpaid obligations, start of year:			
72.40	Obligated balance, start of year	70	178	271
72.95	Receivables from program account	9	24	37
72.99	Total unpaid obligations, start of year	79	202	308
73.10	Total new obligations	1,613	2,119	1,191
73.20	Total financing disbursements (gross)	−1,477	−2,013	−1,425
73.45	Adjustments in unexpired accounts	−12		
	Unpaid obligations, end of year:			
74.40	Obligated balance, end of year	178	271	65
74.95	Receivables from program account	24	37	9
74.99	Total unpaid obligations, end of year	202	308	74
87.00	Total financing disbursements (gross)	1,477	2,013	1,425
	Offsets:			
	Against gross financing authority and financing disbursements:			
	Offsetting collections (cash) from:			
88.00	Federal sources: Payments from program account	−142	−363	−114
88.25	Interest on uninvested funds	−76	−196	−62
	Non-Federal sources:			
88.40	Repayments of principal	−503	−538	−565
88.40	Non-Federal sources	−113	−130	−150
88.90	Total, offsetting collections (cash)	−834	−1,227	−891
	Against gross financing authority only:			
88.95	Change in receivables from program accounts	−15	−13	28
	Net financing authority and financing disbursements:			
89.00	Financing authority	1,368	784	328
90.00	Financing disbursements	643	786	534

Status of Direct Loans (in millions of dollars)

Identification code 12–4212–0–3–351		1999 actual	2000 est.	2001 est.
	Position with respect to appropriations act limitation on obligations:			
1111	Limitation on direct loans	872	1,797	1,080
1112	Unobligated direct loan limitation	74		
1113	Unobligated limitation carried forward	53	−74	
1150	Total direct loan obligations	999	1,723	1,080
	Cumulative balance of direct loans outstanding:			
1210	Outstanding, start of year	2,715	3,443	4,392
1231	Disbursements: Direct loan disbursements	1,278	1,637	1,026
1251	Repayments: Repayments and prepayments	−513	−654	−715
1263	Write-offs for default: Direct loans	−37	−34	−44
1290	Outstanding, end of year	3,443	4,392	4,659

As required by the Federal Credit Reform Act of 1990, this non-budgetary account records all cash flows to and from the Government resulting from direct loans obligated in 1992 and beyond (including credit sales of acquired property that resulted from obligations in any year). The amounts in this account are a means of financing and are not included in the budget totals.

This account finances direct loans for farm ownership, farm operating, emergency disaster, and credit sales of acquired property.

Balance Sheet (in millions of dollars)

Identification code 12–4212–0–3–351		1998 actual	1999 actual	2000 est.	2001 est.
	ASSETS:				
	Investments in US securities:				
1106	Federal assets: Receivables, net	278	275	351	363
	Net value of assets related to post–1991 direct loans receivable:				
1401	Direct loans receivable, gross	2,715	3,004	3,821	3,952
1402	Interest receivable	42	40	44	45
1403	Accounts receivable from foreclosed property	13	15	18	18
1405	Allowance for subsidy cost (–)	–697	–760	–966	–999
1499	Net present value of assets related to direct loans	2,073	2,299	2,917	3,016
1999	Total assets	2,351	2,574	3,268	3,379
	LIABILITIES:				
2103	Federal liabilities: Debt	2,344	2,562	3,253	3,364
2207	Non-Federal liabilities: Other	9	12	15	15
2999	Total liabilities	2,353	2,574	3,268	3,379
	NET POSITION:				
3100	Appropriated capital				
3999	Total net position				
4999	Total liabilities and net position	2,353	2,574	3,268	3,379

AGRICULTURAL CREDIT INSURANCE FUND GUARANTEED LOAN FINANCING ACCOUNT

Program and Financing (in millions of dollars)

Identification code 12–4213–0–3–351		1999 actual	2000 est.	2001 est.
	Obligations by program activity:			
	Operating program:			
00.01	Default claims	59	64	69
00.02	Interest assistance on guaranteed loans	125	100	167
00.04	Interest payments to Treasury	5	7	8
00.05	Capital investments	6	8	9
00.91	Subtotal, Operating program	195	179	253
	Reestimates:			
08.02	Downward reestimate of subsidy		155	
08.04	Downward reestimate of subsidy—interest		43	
08.91	Subtotal, reestimates		198	
10.00	Total new obligations	195	377	253
	Budgetary resources available for obligation:			
21.40	Unobligated balance available, start of year	132	104	
22.00	New financing authority (gross)	141	273	253
22.10	Resources available from recoveries of prior year obligations	25		
23.90	Total budgetary resources available for obligation	298	377	253
23.95	Total new obligations	−195	−377	−253
24.40	Unobligated balance available, end of year	104		
	New financing authority (gross), detail:			
	Mandatory:			
67.15	Authority to borrow (indefinite)	30	94	143
	Discretionary:			
68.00	Spending authority from offsetting collections: Offsetting collections (cash)	111	179	110
70.00	Total new financing authority (gross)	141	273	253
	Change in unpaid obligations:			
72.40	Unpaid obligations, start of year: Obligated balance, start of year	184	261	180
73.10	Total new obligations	195	377	253
73.20	Total financing disbursements (gross)	−93	−458	−92
73.45	Adjustments in unexpired accounts	−25		
74.40	Unpaid obligations, end of year: Obligated balance, end of year	261	180	341
87.00	Total financing disbursements (gross)	93	458	92

		1999 actual	2000 est.	2001 est.
	Offsets:			
	Against gross financing authority and financing disbursements:			
	Offsetting collections (cash) from:			
88.00	Payments from program account	−72	−116	−71
88.25	Interest on uninvested funds	−20	−32	−20
88.40	Fees and premiums	−19	−31	−19
88.90	Total, offsetting collections (cash)	−111	−179	−110
	Net financing authority and financing disbursements:			
89.00	Financing authority	30	94	143
90.00	Financing disbursements	−19	279	−18

Status of Guaranteed Loans (in millions of dollars)

Identification code 12–4213–0–3–351		1999 actual	2000 est.	2001 est.
	Position with respect to appropriations act limitation on commitments:			
2111	Limitation on guaranteed loans made by private lenders	2,551	4,042	3,478
2150	Total guaranteed loan commitments	2,551	4,042	3,478
	Cumulative balance of guaranteed loans outstanding:			
2210	Outstanding, start of year	6,292	7,023	7,982
2231	Disbursements of new guaranteed loans	2,349	3,083	3,130
2251	Repayments and prepayments	−1,558	−2,035	−2,314
2263	Adjustments: Terminations for default that result in claim payments	−60	−89	−92
2290	Outstanding, end of year	7,023	7,982	8,706
	Memorandum:			
2299	Guaranteed amount of guaranteed loans outstanding, end of year	6,476	7,343	8,010

As required by the Federal Credit Reform Act of 1990, this non-budgetary account records all cash flows to and from the Government resulting from loan guarantees committed in 1992 and beyond. The amounts in this account are a means of financing and are not included in the budget totals.

This account finances commitments made for farm ownership and operating guaranteed loan programs.

Balance Sheet (in millions of dollars)

Identification code 12–4213–0–3–351		1998 actual	1999 actual	2000 est.	2001 est.
	ASSETS:				
	Federal assets:				
1101	Fund balances with Treasury	316	365	399	357
	Investments in US securities:				
1106	Receivables, net		158		
1206	Non-Federal assets: Receivables, net		1		
1999	Total assets	316	524	399	357
	LIABILITIES:				
	Non-Federal liabilities:				
2201	Accounts payable	184	459	231	207
2203	Debt	60	90	76	68
2204	Liabilities for loan guarantees	73	−25	92	82
2999	Total liabilities	317	524	399	357
4999	Total liabilities and net position	317	524	399	357

Agricultural Credit Insurance Fund Liquidating Account

Program and Financing (in millions of dollars)

Identification code 12–4140–0–3–351		1999 actual	2000 est.	2001 est.
	Obligations by program activity:			
	Capital investment:			
00.02	Repurchase of public certificates of beneficial ownership	2		
00.04	Purchase of guaranteed loans from investors	1		
00.08	Loan recoverable costs	13	13	13
00.91	Total capital investment	16	13	13
	Operating expenses:			
01.07	Loss settlement expenses on guaranteed loans	5	5	4
01.08	Admininstrative expenses—Department of Justice fees	1	1	1
01.09	Costs incident to acquisition of property	2	3	3
01.10	Undistributed charges	2	1	1
01.13	Interest assistance—guaranteed loans	1	1	
01.17	Unclassified costs	3	5	5
01.91	Total operating expenses	14	16	14
10.00	Total new obligations	30	29	27
	Budgetary resources available for obligation:			
21.40	Unobligated balance available, start of year	2		
22.00	New budget authority (gross)	18	29	27
22.10	Resources available from recoveries of prior year obligations	10		
23.90	Total budgetary resources available for obligation	30	29	27
23.95	Total new obligations	−30	−29	−27
	New budget authority (gross), detail:			
	Mandatory:			
69.00	Offsetting collections (cash)	1,060	1,130	1,135
69.27	Capital transfer to general fund	−1,042	−1,101	−1,108
69.90	Spending authority from offsetting collections (total mandatory)	18	29	27
	Change in unpaid obligations:			
72.40	Unpaid obligations, start of year: Obligated balance, start of year	72	61	61
73.10	Total new obligations	30	29	27
73.20	Total outlays (gross)	−32	−29	−27
73.45	Adjustments in unexpired accounts	−10		
74.40	Unpaid obligations, end of year: Obligated balance, end of year	61	61	61
	Outlays (gross), detail:			
86.97	Outlays from new mandatory authority	18	29	27
86.98	Outlays from mandatory balances	12		
87.00	Total outlays (gross)	32	29	27
	Offsets:			
	Against gross budget authority and outlays:			
	Offsetting collections (cash) from:			
	Non-Federal sources:			
88.40	Rent on acquired property	−2	−3	−3
88.40	Guaranteed ibsurance purchased from holders—principal	−2	−1	−1
88.40	Interest on loans	−340	−360	−350
88.40	Guaranteed loss recoveries		−1	−1
88.40	Loan repayments received on behalf of investors	−1	−1	−1
88.40	Interest on judgments	−2	−1	−1
88.40	Repayments on loans—principal	−642	−690	−680
88.40	Judgments—principal	−13	−12	−12
88.40	Shared appreciation recapture	−18	−13	−13
88.40	Sale of acquired property/chattels	−45	−50	−70
88.40	Miscellaneous income	−1	−1	−1
88.40	Undistributed receipts	6	3	−2
88.90	Total, offsetting collections (cash)	−1,060	−1,130	−1,135
	Net budget authority and outlays:			
89.00	Budget authority	−1,042	−1,101	−1,108
90.00	Outlays	−1,028	−1,101	−1,108

Status of Direct Loans (in millions of dollars)

Identification code 12–4140–0–3–351		1999 actual	2000 est.	2001 est.
	Cumulative balance of direct loans outstanding:			
1210	Outstanding, start of year	6,699	5,817	4,850
1232	Disbursements: Purchase of loans assets from the public	1	2	2
1251	Repayments: Repayments and prepayments	−640	−696	−686
1261	Adjustments: Capitalized interest	32	30	48
	Write-offs for default:			
1263	Direct loans	−241	−250	−300
1264	Other adjustments, net[1]	−34	−53	−49
1290	Outstanding, end of year	5,817	4,850	3,865

[1] Amounts shown are based on payment of delinquent installments, advances on behalf of borrowers, acquired property and chattels, loans in kind, and judgments.

Credit accounts—Continued

AGRICULTURAL CREDIT INSURANCE FUND LIQUIDATING ACCOUNT—Continued

Status of Guaranteed Loans (in millions of dollars)

Identification code 12–4140–0–3–351	1999 actual	2000 est.	2001 est.
Cumulative balance of guaranteed loans outstanding:			
2210 Outstanding, start of year	776	594	389
2251 Repayments and prepayments	–181	–200	–100
2263 Adjustments: Terminations for default that result in claim payments	–1	–5	–12
2290 Outstanding, end of year	594	389	277
Memorandum:			
2299 Guaranteed amount of guaranteed loans outstanding, end of year	535	350	217

As required by the Federal Credit Reform Act of 1990, this account records for the farm loan programs all cash flows to and from the Government resulting from direct loans obligated, loan guarantees committed, and grants made prior to 1992. New loan activity in 1992 and beyond (including credit sales of acquired property that resulted from obligations or commitments in any year) is recorded in corresponding program and financing accounts. Payments to settle certain discrimination claims against USDA may also be made from this account.

Statement of Operations (in millions of dollars)

Identification code 12–4140–0–3–351	1998 actual	1999 actual	2000 est.	2001 est.
0101 Revenue	440	386	377	534
0102 Expense	–309	856	125	–175
0105 Net income or loss (–)	131	1,242	502	359

Balance Sheet (in millions of dollars)

Identification code 12–4140–0–3–351	1998 actual	1999 actual	2000 est.	2001 est.
ASSETS:				
1101 Federal assets: Fund balances with Treasury	74	61	5	50
Net value of assets related to pre–1992 direct loans receivable and acquired defaulted guaranteed loans receivable:				
1601 Direct loans, gross	6,699	5,817	4,850	3,865
1602 Interest receivable	374	354	389	395
1603 Allowance for estimated uncollectible loans and interest (–)	–1,574	–904	–1,000	–1,000
1604 Direct loans and interest receivable, net	5,499	5,267	4,239	3,260
1606 Foreclosed property	125	95	94	95
1699 Value of assets related to direct loans	5,624	5,362	4,333	3,355
1999 Total assets	5,698	5,423	4,338	3,405
LIABILITIES:				
2104 Federal liabilities: Resources payable to Treasury	5,597	4,687	4,500	3,800
Non-Federal liabilities:				
2201 Accounts payable	182	112	108	31
2202 Interest payable	....	....	....	1
2207 Other	35	10	25	25
2999 Total liabilities	5,814	4,809	4,633	3,857
NET POSITION:				
3300 Cumulative results of operations	–118	614	–295	–452
3999 Total net position	–118	614	–295	–452
4999 Total liabilities and net position	5,696	5,423	4,338	3,405

Object Classification (in millions of dollars)

Identification code 12–4140–0–3–351	1999 actual	2000 est.	2001 est.
25.2 Other services	9	10	9
33.0 Investments and loans	20	18	17
43.0 Interest and dividends	1	1	1
99.9 Total new obligations	30	29	27

COMMODITY CREDIT CORPORATION

CORPORATIONS

The following corporations and agencies are hereby authorized to make expenditures, within the limits of funds and borrowing authority available to each such corporation or agency and in accord with law, and to make contracts and commitments without regard to fiscal year limitations as provided by section 104 of the Government Corporation Control Act as may be necessary in carrying out the programs set forth in the budget for the current fiscal year for such corporation or agency, except as hereinafter provided. *(Agriculture, Rural Development, Food and Drug Administration, and Related Agencies Appropriations Act, 2000.)*

Public enterprise funds:

COMMODITY CREDIT CORPORATION FUND

REIMBURSEMENT FOR NET REALIZED LOSSES

For fiscal year [2000] *2001*, such sums as may be necessary to reimburse the Commodity Credit Corporation for net realized losses sustained, but not previously reimbursed, pursuant to section 2 of the Act of August 17, 1961 (15 U.S.C. 713a–11).

OPERATIONS AND MAINTENANCE FOR HAZARDOUS WASTE MANAGEMENT

For fiscal year [2000] *2001*, the Commodity Credit Corporation shall not expend more than $5,000,000 for *site investigation and cleanup expenses, and operations and maintenance* expenses to comply with the requirement of section 107(g) of the Comprehensive Environmental Response, Compensation, and Liability Act, *as amended*, 42 U.S.C. 9607(g), and section 6001 of the Resource Conservation and Recovery Act, *as amended*, 42 U.S.C. 6961[: *Provided*, That expenses shall be for operations and maintenance costs only and that other hazardous waste management costs shall be paid for by the USDA Hazardous Waste Management appropriation in this Act]. *(Agriculture, Rural Development, Food and Drug Administration, and Related Agencies Appropriations Act, 2000.)*

[CROP LOSS ASSISTANCE]

[For an additional amount for crop loss assistance authorized by section 801 of Public Law 106–78, $186,000,000: *Provided*, That this assistance shall be under the same terms and conditions as in section 801 of Public Law 106–78.]

[SPECIALTY CROP ASSISTANCE]

[For an additional amount for specialty crop assistance authorized by section 803(c)(1) of Public Law 106–78, $2,800,000: *Provided*, That the definition of eligible persons in section 803(c)(2) of Public Law 106–78 shall include producers who have suffered quality or quantity losses due to natural disasters on crops harvested and placed in a warehouse and not sold.]

[LIVESTOCK ASSISTANCE]

[For an additional amount for livestock assistance authorized by section 805 of Public Law 106–78, $10,000,000: *Provided*, That the Secretary of Agriculture may use this additional amount to provide assistance to persons who raise livestock owned by other persons for income losses sustained with respect to livestock during 1999 if the Secretary finds that such losses are the result of natural disasters.] *(Miscellaneous Appropriations, 2000, as enacted by section 1000(a)(5) of the Consolidated Appropriations Act, 2000 (P.L. 106–113).)*

Unavailable Collections (in millions of dollars)

Identification code 12–4336–0–3–999	1999 actual	2000 est.	2001 est.
Balance, start of year:			
01.99 Balance, start of year	....	39	....
Appropriation:			
05.01 Commodity credit corporation fund	....	–39	....

06.20	Reduction pursuant to Public Law 106–51	39		
07.99	Total balance, end of year	39		

Program and Financing (in millions of dollars)

Identification code 12–4336–0–3–999		1999 actual	2000 est.	2001 est.
	Obligations by program activity:			
	Support and related programs:			
	Operating expenses:			
00.01	Commodity purchases and related inventory transactions	1,427	1,072	633
00.02	Storage, transportation, and other obligations not included above	164	207	180
00.03	Export enhancement program	1	579	478
00.04	Market access program	114	132	96
00.05	Dairy export incentive program	69	188	66
00.06	Section 416/Food for progress ocean transportation	323	291	161
00.07	Foreign market development cooperative		27	27
00.08	Quality samples program		3	3
00.09	Tobacco quota payments to states/warehouse payment		331	
	Direct producer payments:			
00.10	Feed grains	5,646	8,907	4,034
00.11	Wheat	3,127	3,766	1,464
00.12	Rice	811	1,027	447
00.13	Cotton	1,543	2,187	1,145
00.14	Dairy—Marketing loss assistance	200	123	
00.15	Dairy option pilot program	1	9	9
00.16	Noninsured assistance program	54	75	85
00.17	Oilseeds loan deficency	1,041	2,038	3,058
00.18	Oilseeds payments program		463	
00.19	Peanut marketing assistance program		49	
00.20	Marketing loan writeoffs	988	1,465	1,054
00.21	Crop disaster	1,913	1,342	
00.22	Livestock assistance	269	188	
00.23	Livestock indemnity	4	12	
00.24	Disaster reserve assistance/American indian livestock feed	13	7	2
00.25	Disaster reserve flood compensation	41		
00.26	Conservation reserve program	1,435	1,574	1,690
00.27	Environmental quality incentives program (EQIP)	133	137	156
00.28	Wetlands reserve program	113	165	46
00.30	Conservation farm option program			46
00.31	Reimbursement agreement and transfers to State and Federal agencies	35	36	36
00.32	Biofuels program			87
	Interest:			
00.33	Treasury	630	789	596
00.34	Other	23	22	18
00.35	EQIP technical assistance	33	33	38
00.36	EQIP educational assistance	4	4	6
00.91	Total operating expenses	20,155	27,248	15,661
	Capital investment:			
	Direct loans:			
01.02	Purchase of ADP equipment	11		
01.92	Total support and related programs	20,166	27,248	15,661
	Reimbursable program:			
09.01	Commodity loans	8,358	9,399	9,057
09.02	Dairy recourse commodity loans			200
09.03	Commodities procured—PL 480 Titles II and III commodity costs	503	549	500
09.04	PL 480 ocean transportation	464	392	357
09.09	Subtotal, reimbursable programs	9,325	10,340	10,114
10.00	Total new obligations	29,491	37,588	25,775
	Budgetary resources available for obligation:			
21.40	Unobligated balance available, start of year	9,804	559	619
22.00	New budget authority (gross)	30,331	38,558	27,371
22.21	Unobligated balance transferred to other accounts	−892	−914	
22.22	Unobligated balance transferred from other accounts	9	4	
22.60	Portion applied to repay debt	−9,202		
23.90	Total budgetary resources available for obligation	30,050	38,207	27,990
23.95	Total new obligations	−29,491	−37,588	−25,775
24.40	Unobligated balance available, end of year	559	619	2,216
	New budget authority (gross), detail:			
	Discretionary:			
40.00	Appropriation	8,432	30,037	27,771
40.47	Portion applied to repay debt	−8,400	−30,037	−27,771
40.76	Reduction pursuant to P.L. 106–113		−28	
41.00	Transferred to other accounts	−32		
43.00	Appropriation (total discretionary)		−28	
	Mandatory:			
67.15	Authority to borrow (indefinite)	20,488	27,745	14,877
69.00	Offsetting collections (cash)	9,882	10,802	12,494
69.26	Offsetting collections (unavailable balances)		39	
69.75	Reduction pursuant to P.L. 104–208	−39		
69.90	Spending authority from offsetting collections (total mandatory)	9,843	10,841	12,494
70.00	Total new budget authority (gross)	30,331	38,558	27,371
	Change in unpaid obligations:			
72.40	Unpaid obligations, start of year: Obligated balance, start of year	1,956	804	379
73.10	Total new obligations	29,491	37,588	25,775
73.20	Total outlays (gross)	−29,182	−38,013	−27,830
73.40	Adjustments in expired accounts (net)	−1,461		
74.40	Unpaid obligations, end of year: Obligated balance, end of year	804	379	−1,676
	Outlays (gross), detail:			
86.97	Outlays from new mandatory authority	20,291	27,597	9,078
86.98	Outlays from mandatory balances	8,891	10,416	18,752
87.00	Total outlays (gross)	29,182	38,013	27,830
	Offsets:			
	Against gross budget authority and outlays:			
	Offsetting collections (cash) from:			
	Federal sources:			
	Federal sources:			
88.00	Sales to special activities	−503	−549	−500
88.00	Interest revenue	−2		
88.00	Advance from foreign assistance programs (P.L. 480)	−1,116	−821	−857
	Non-Federal sources (62 stat.1070): Support and related programs:			
	Non-Federal sources:			
88.40	Sales and other proceeds	−241	−171	−235
88.40	Assessments	−58		
88.40	Interest revenue	−17	−32	−35
88.40	Other revenue	−4		
88.40	Loans repaid	−7,902	−9,191	−10,801
88.40	Export credit sales program repayments	−9	−10	−10
88.40	Interest revenue	−30	−28	−28
88.90	Total, offsetting collections (cash)	−9,882	−10,802	−12,466
	Net budget authority and outlays:			
89.00	Budget authority	20,449	27,756	14,905
90.00	Outlays	19,300	27,211	15,364

Summary of Budget Authority and Outlays

(in millions of dollars)

	1999 actual	2000 est.	2001 est.
Enacted/requested:			
Budget Authority	20,449	27,756	14,905
Outlays	19,300	27,211	15,364
Legislative proposal, not subject to PAYGO:			
Budget Authority			−50
Outlays			−4
Legislative proposal, subject to PAYGO:			
Budget Authority		710	3,917
Outlays		710	3,615
Total:			
Budget Authority	20,449	28,466	18,772
Outlays	19,300	27,921	18,975

NOTES

Contingent liabilities, commitments, and other obligations do not become charges against the statutory borrowing authority until they result in borrowing from Treasury.

Excludes amounts for activities currently funded in the CCC Export Guarantee Loan Programs account.

Status of Direct Loans (in millions of dollars)

Identification code 12–4336–0–3–999		1999 actual	2000 est.	2001 est.
	SHORT TERM CREDIT LOANS			
	Cumulative balance of direct loans outstanding:			
1210	Outstanding, start of year	384	375	366

Public enterprise funds—Continued

COMMODITY CREDIT CORPORATION FUND—Continued

[LIVESTOCK ASSISTANCE]—Continued

Status of Direct Loans (in millions of dollars)—Continued

Identification code 12–4336–0–3–999		1999 actual	2000 est.	2001 est.
1251	Repayments: Repayments and prepayments	−9	−9	−10
1290	Outstanding, end of year	375	366	356
	COMMODITY LOANS			
	Position with respect to appropriations act limitation on obligations:			
1111	Limitation on direct loans	....	....	....
1131	Direct loan obligations exempt from limitation	8,358	9,399	9,257
1150	Total direct loan obligations	8,358	9,399	9,257
	Cumulative balance of direct loans outstanding:			
1210	Outstanding, start of year	2,219	2,441	2,371
1231	Disbursements: Direct loan disbursements	8,358	9,399	9,257
1251	Repayments: Repayments and prepayments	−7,902	−9,191	−9,233
1264	Write-offs for default: Other adjustments, net	−234	−278	−326
1290	Outstanding, end of year	2,441	2,371	2,069
	SALE OF INVENTORY ON CREDIT TERMS			
	Cumulative balance of direct loans outstanding:			
1210	Outstanding, start of year	30	30	30
1290	Outstanding, end of year	30	30	30

The Commodity Credit Corporation (CCC) was created to: stabilize, support, and protect farm income and prices; help maintain balanced and adequate supplies of agricultural commodities, their products, foods, feeds, and fibers; and help in their orderly distribution.

The Corporation's capital stock of $100 million is held by the U.S. Treasury. Under present law, up to $30 billion may be borrowed from the U.S. Treasury to finance operations.

Current, indefinite appropriation authority is requested to cover all net realized losses. Appropriations to the Corporation for net realized losses have no effect on budget authority, as they are used to repay debt directly with the Treasury.

Budget assumptions.—The following general assumptions form the basis for the Corporation's 2000 and 2001 budget estimates: (a) national income will rise both in 2000 and 2001 from the present level; (b) 2000 crop production will decrease from 1999 crop levels for some commodities; (c) generally, exports of agricultural commodities in 2001 are expected to be higher than 2000 levels; (d) yields for the 2000 crops are based on recent averages adjusted for trend; (e) acreage allotments and marketing quotas will be in effect for the 2000 crops of certain kinds of tobacco; and (f) poundage quotas will be in effect for the 2000 crop of peanuts. Marketing loan rates for the 2000 crop are assumed to equal rates for the 1999 crop.

It is difficult to accurately forecast requirements for the year ending September 30, 2001, since the projections are subject to complex and unpredictable factors such as weather, other factors which affect the volume of production of crops not yet planted, feed and food needs here and overseas, and available dollar exchange.

The Federal Agriculture Improvement and Reform Act of 1996 (the 1996 Act) enacted April 4, 1996, retains the CRP as part of the Environmental Conservation Acreage Reserve Program (ECARP) but changed the funding source from direct appropriation to the Commodity Credit Corporation. The CRP is assumed to be gradually increased to 36.4 million acres by 2002. CRP is USDA's largest conservation/environmental program. The purpose of CRP, administered by FSA, is to cost-effectively assist farm owners and operators in conserving and improving soil, water, air, and wildlife resources by converting highly erodible and other environmentally sensitive acreage normally devoted to the production of agricultural commodities to a long-term resource-conserving cover. CRP participants enroll contracts for periods from 10 to 15 years in exchange for annual rental payments and cost-share and technical assistance for installing approved conservation practices.

A general CRP signup was held (signup 18) October 26 through December 11, 1998. Of the 7.1 million acres offered, a total of 5 million acres were approved for enrollment beginning in fiscal year 2000. The national average annual rental payment for this acreage is estimated to be about $46 per acre. Technical assistance for this signup was funded with unobligated and appropriated funds. Rental payments for signup 18 begin in fiscal year 2001.

The general CRP signup, signup 20, will be held from January 18 through February 11, 2000. It is assumed for budgeting purposes that approximately 1.8 million acres, of the 5 million acres offered, will be accepted in the program beginning with the 2001 program year. Conservation Reserve Program acreage also contributes to the USDA Conservation Buffer Initiative and the Conservation Reserve Enhancement Program and to other purposes which are estimated to enroll 4.2 million acres through 2002.

As part of the Administration's farm safety net proposal, the Budget proposes to increase the CRP enrollment cap by almost $4 million acres to 40 million. Also, the Administration will offer bonuses totaling up to $100 million in FY 2000 and up to $125 million annually in FY 2001–2002 to producers who enroll land in CRP through the continuous sign up.

These assumptions have been developed for budget purposes as the best estimate of acreage bid into the program that will be both eligible and of high environmental quality. As such, the estimate may not reflect the actual acreage selected for Signup 20. USDA's goal is that lands selected for the CRP will only be those lands where the benefits to the Nation of retirement are greater than the benefits of continued production.

Appropriations are made to reimburse the Corporation for net realized losses sustained in carrying out its operations:

2001 ESTIMATE

[In millions of dollars]

Program	Gross obligations	Net outlays	Net realized loss for year
Farm income, marketing assistance loans, and price support:			
Commodity loans	9,057	1,079	....
Dairy recourse loan program	200	....	....
Feed grain payments	4,545	4,545	4,545
Wheat payments	1,464	1,569	1,464
Rice payments	447	458	447
Cotton payments	1,145	1,145	1,145
Export enhancement program	478	478	478
Other support and related	5,371	3,614	5,145
Other items not distributed by program:			
Interest	614	704	550
All other	114	378	113
Total, farm income, marketing assistance loans, and price-support programs	23,435	13,970	13,887
Conservation programs:			
Conservation reserve program	1,690	1,690	1,836
Environmental quality incentives program	200	165	165
Wetlands reserve program	53	132	132
Farmland protection program	....	4	4
Conservation farm option program	50	4	4
Total, conservation programs	1,993	1,995	2,141
Total, Commodity Credit Corporation	25,428	15,965	16,028

PROGRAMS OF THE CORPORATION

Price support, marketing assistance loans, and related stabilization programs.—The Corporation conducts programs to support farm income and prices and stabilize the market for agricultural commodities. Price support is provided to producers of agricultural commodities through loans, purchases, payments, and other means. This is done mainly under the Commodity Credit Corporation Charter Act, as amended, the Agricultural Act of 1949 (the 1949 Act), as amended, and the Federal Agriculture Improvement and Reform Act of 1996 (the 1996 Act).

Price support is mandatory for tobacco, peanuts, and dairy products. Marketing assistance loans are mandatory for wheat, feed grains, oilseeds, upland cotton, and rice. Loans are also required to be made for sugar and extra long staple cotton.

One method of providing support is loans to and purchases from producers. With limited exceptions, loans made on commodities are nonrecourse. The commodities serve as collateral for the loan and on maturity the producer may deliver or forfeit such collateral to satisfy the loan obligation without further payment.

Direct purchases may be made from processors as well as producers, depending on the commodity involved. Also, special purchases are made under various laws for the removal of surpluses; for example, the Act of August 19, 1958, as amended, and section 416 of the Agricultural Act of 1949, as amended.

Production flexibility contract payments.—The 1996 Act requires that the Corporation offer eligible producers a one-time opportunity to execute 7-year production flexibility contracts. Production flexibility contract participants who comply with applicable provisions receive annual payments beginning in 1996 and ending in 2002. Participants received a 50-percent advance payment for the 1996 crop within 30 days after contract approval. The balance of the 1996 payment was issued by September 30, 1996. In subsequent years, participants will receive final payments by September 30, with an option to receive advances on December 15 or January 15. For fiscal years 2001 through 2002, producers may choose to receive fiscal year production flexibility contract payments as two 50 percent payments or one 100 percent payment at any time during the fiscal year. Depending on each contract participant's prior contract-crop acreage history and payment yield, as well as total program participation, the participant shares a portion of a statutorily specified, annual dollar amount. In return, participants must comply with certain requirements regarding land conservation, wetland protection, and agricultural use. Contract crops, for the purposes of determining eligible cropland and payments, include wheat, corn, grain sorghum, barley, oats, upland cotton, and rice. No production adjustment requirements or related provisions are included in this program, except for restrictions on the planting of fruits and vegetables and other minor requirements. The one-time enrollment took place between May 1 and August 1, 1996; however, producers with Conservation Reserve Program (CRP) contracts will have the opportunity to enroll acreage currently in the CRP that meets the eligibility requirements for a production flexibility contract. These enrollments will occur as CRP contracts expire.

Marketing assessments.—The 1949 Act mandates assessments for tobacco, and the 1996 Act requires such assessments for peanuts and sugar. Tobacco marketing assessments are authorized through crop year 1998.

Peanut price support program.—The 1996 Act and the Agricultural Adjustment Act of 1938, as amended (the 1938 Act), provide for a peanut loan and poundage quota program for the 1996 through 2002 peanut crops. The 1996 Act makes the peanut program, effectively, a no-cost program. The Secretary is required to provide a nonrefundable per-pound marketing assessment equal to 1.15 percent of the national average quota or additional peanut loan rate for the applicable 1996 crop and 1.2 percent of the national average quota or additional peanut loan rate for each of the applicable 1997 through 2002 crops. Assessments will be used to offset losses in area quota pools, and any assessments not required to cover these losses will be remitted to the Treasury. If the use of all other available authority does not produce funds sufficient to cover losses in area quota pools, the Secretary must increase the marketing assessment by an amount that will cover the losses.

Sugar Program.—The 1996 Act requires that loans be made available to eligible sugar processors for the 1996 through 2002 crops of domestically produced sugar beets and sugarcane. The announced Tariff Rate Quota (TRQ) determines the type of loan in effect. If the TRQ is not above 1,500,000 short tons, raw value, at the time of loan approval and has never been above 1,500,000 short tons, raw value, at any time during the fiscal year, recourse loans will be in effect. If the TRQ exceeds 1,500,000 short tons, raw value, at the time of loan approval or has exceeded 1,500,000 short tons, raw value, at any time during the fiscal year, nonrecourse loans will be in effect.

Options Pilot Program.—The 1996 Act authorizes the Secretary to utilize CCC, until December 31, 2002, to conduct a pilot program for one or more agricultural commodities supported under Title I of the 1996 Act to ascertain whether futures and options contracts can reasonably protect producers from the financial risks of fluctuations in price, yield, and income inherent in the production and marketing of the commodities. The pilot program is under the supervision of the Administrator of the Risk Management Agency. To the maximum extent practicable, the Secretary shall operate the pilot program in a budget neutral manner.

The Federal Crop Insurance Reform Act of 1994 expanded current crop insurance authorities to provide for catastrophic coverage at 50 percent yield protection at a flat fee for crops currently covered by insurance programs. Where crop insurance is not available, producers of crops for food and fiber and certain other crops will be covered under the Noninsured Assistance Program. The Farm Service Agency administers CCC's Noninsured Assistance Program. The program will reimburse producers at the same rates and terms as the catastrophic program where assistance is triggered by area wide disasters.

Dairy.—The 1996 Act provides for a dairy price support program that sets the minimum support price for milk at $10.35 per hundredweight for calendar year 1996, $10.20 per hundredweight for calendar year 1997, $10.05 per hundredweight for calendar year 1999, and $9.90 per hundredweight for calendar year 1999. The 2000 Act extended the price support program through calendar year 2000 at the $9.90 per hundred-weight support level. In lieu of the price support program, Section 142 of the 1996 Act establishes a recourse loan program beginning on January 1, 2000, and continuing through 2002, during which time processors will be eligible for recourse loans on dairy products at a milk equivalent rate of $9.90 per hundredweight. However, the 2000 Act postponed the start of the Dairy Recourse Loan Program until January 1, 2001. The program will assist dairy processors in managing their inventories of eligible dairy products and assure a greater degree of price stability for the dairy industry. The program is a transition between the Dairy Price Support Program that has been in effect since 1949 and the dairy industry functioning with no Governmental intervention in a global economy. Dairy processors acquire their milk from dairy farmers that manufacture these eligible dairy products. The program indirectly assists dairy farmers similar to the Dairy price Support Program. The Food Security Act of 1985, as amended (the 1985 Act), authorizes the Dairy Export Incentive Program (DEIP) through calendar year 2002. The DEIP provides subsidies to exporters of U.S. dairy products to help them compete with other subsidizing nations.

Public enterprise funds—Continued

COMMODITY CREDIT CORPORATION FUND—Continued

PROGRAMS OF THE CORPORATION—Continued

Emergency Livestock Feed Assistance.—In calendar year (CY) 1998, $200 million in CCC funds were made available for livestock feed assistance for producers affected by disasters. An additional $70 million was authorized by the FY 1999 Emergency Supplemental Act (P.L. 106–31). The FY 2000 Act allows for not less than $200 million to be provided to livestock producers.

Payment limitations.—The 1996 Act and the Food Security Act of 1985, as amended, limit the amount of production flexibility contract payments during any fiscal year to $40,000 and the sum of marketing assistance gains and loan deficiency payments during any crop year to $75,000. This limitation has been raised to $150,000 for the 1999 crop only.

Conservation programs.—The Environmental Conservation Acreage Reserve Program (ECARP) was re-established by the 1996 Act to begin in 1996 and continue through 2002. ECARP consists of the Conservation Reserve Program (CRP), the Wetlands Reserve Program (WRP), and the Environmental Quality Incentives Program (EQIP). The 1996 Act amended the 1985 Act to require the use of CCC funds for these programs.

The CRP is authorized in all 50 States, Puerto Rico, and the Virgin Islands, on all highly erodible cropland, other environmentally sensitive cropland, and certain marginal pastureland meeting the eligibility criteria. In addition to cropland in areas adjacent to lakes and streams that can be devoted to filter strips, and cropland subject to overflow and suffering from scour erosion, eligible land may include shelterbelts windbreaks cropland contributing to water quality problems, and other lands posing environmental threats. Also eligible for the CRP are water quality or wildlife habitat impaired areas that do not meet the highly erodible land (HEL) criteria, such as the Chesapeake Bay, Great Lakes, and Long Island Sound watershed regions.

The establishment and funding for Conservation Priority Areas (CPA) under both EQIP and CRP will be harmonized in a manner to ensure program availability is coordinated to best address environmental concerns, keeping in mind the varied and diverse purposes for which the CRP and EQIP are authorized.

The EQIP combines the functions of the former Agricultural Conservation Program (ACP), the Water Quality Incentives Program (WQIP), the Great Plains Conservation Program (GPCP), and the Colorado River Basin Salinity Control Program (CRSC). The 1996 Act provided that EQIP would be phased in over a 6-month interim period, ending not later than October 4, 1996. CCC funding of $130 million was provided for the interim 1996 program. Thereafter, through fiscal year 2002, $200 million in CCC funding must be made available annually for the program. The fiscal year 1999 and 2000 programs were limited to $174 million by provisions of the FY 1999 and FY 2000 Agriculture Appropriation Acts, but will return to the statutory level of $200 million in FY 2001 and 2002. As part of the Administration's farm safety net proposal, the Budget provides an additional $125 million over authorized levels, for a program total of $325 million. Beginning in FY 2001, comprehensive nutrient management plans will be required of all EQIP participants with livestock-or animal waste management-related contracts.

The Farmland Protection Program (FPP) authorizes the Secretary to assist State, local, and tribal governments in purchasing conservation easements. The Secretary was authorized to use $35 million in CCC funds to carry out the program. These funds were exhausted in 1998. The FY 2000 Appropriations Act provided $250,000 for the use in the state of New Hampshire. In support of the farm safety net proposal, $65 million is proposed for FY 2001.

The Wildlife Habitat Incentives Program (WHIP) makes available assistance to help landowners improve wildlife habitat on private lands. A total of $50 million in CRP funds were made available for fiscal years 1996 through 2002 for this program. These funds were exhausted in 1999. $50 million is provided for FY 2001 as part of the farm safety net.

The Conservation Farm Option Program (CFO) is a pilot program for producers of wheat, feed grains, upland cotton, and rice who are eligible for production flexibility contracts. Under this program, producers may consolidate their production flexibility contract, CRP, WRP, and EQIP payments into one annual payment if they enter into a 10-year contract and adopt an approved conservation farm plan. CCC must make available the following funding for the CFO: $15 million in fiscal year 1999, $25 million in fiscal year 1999, $37.5 million in fiscal year 2000, $50 million in fiscal year 2001, and $62.5 million in fiscal year 2002. Total authorized funding is $197.5 million. However, no obligations have been incurred in fiscal years 1997–1999. The 1999 and 2000 Appropriations Acts precluded operations of the CFO in 1999 and 2000. In 2001, savings in the CFO are proposed to offset other conservation program initiatives.

The primary objectives of the Wetlands Reserve Program (WRP) are to restore and protect wetlands, improve wildlife habitat, and protect mirgratory waterfowl. This program offers landowners an opportunity to establish long-term conservation and wildlife practices and protection beyond that which can be obtained through other USDA programs. The Secretary of Agriculture, through NRCS field offices, uses program funds to acquire permanent or 30-year easements or to enter into 10-year restoration cost-share agreements. For easements, participants receive compensation in an amount not to exceed the agricultural fair market value of the land being offered. In addition, they receive cost-share assistance in amounts up to 75 percent for 30-year easements and 100 percent for permanent easements for establishing required wetlands restoration and wildlife practices. CCC pays for all the overhead costs associated with recording the easement in the local land records office including recording fees, charges for abstracts, surveys, appraisal fees, and title insurance associated with acquiring an easement. For restoration cost-share agreements, participants receive up to 75 percent of the cost of establishing required practices. Other agencies and private organizations may provide additional assistance for easement payments and restoration costs as a way to leverage program funds and achieve greater program benefits.

Under current law, WRP is authorized to enroll 975,000 cumulative acres. The FY 2000 Agriculture Appropriations Act allowed WRP to enroll 150,000 acres, leaving approximately 40,000 acres remaining under the cap in FY 2001. As part of the Administration's farm safety net proposal, the Budget proposes to enroll an additional 210,000 acres, bringing total enrollment in FY 2001 to 250,000 acres.

Surplus Removal and Other CCC Activities.—Section 5 of the CCC Charter Act authorizes CCC to undertake specific actions with respect to agricultural commodities. Section 5(d) specifically authorizes CCC to remove and dispose of or aid in the removal or disposition of surplus agricultural commodities. Pursuant to this authority, CCC will purchase 5 million metric tons of wheat in the course of 1999 and 2000, which will subsequently be used for donation purposes under Section 416(b) of the Agricultural Act of 1949. A portion of this initiative is a part of the comprehensive U.S. food aid package to Russia, as announced by the President in November 1998. An estimated 1,500,000 metric tons shall be shipped to Russia during 1999 and 2000. The wheat initiative includes purchases of primarily wheat and wheat flour during 1999 and 2000.

Supply and foreign purchases.—The Corporation can procure from domestic and foreign sources food, agricultural commodities, and products and related materials to supply the needs of Federal agencies, foreign governments, and private and international relief agencies, under section 5 (b) and (c) of the Commodity Credit Corporation Charter Act, as amended.

Commodity exports.—The Corporation promotes the export of agricultural commodities and products through sales for dollars or foreign currency, payments, extension of credit, assumption of certain risks, and conduct of other operations with respect to the exportation of commodities. Such commodities and products may be those held in private trade channels as well as those acquired by the Corporation. These programs are carried out under the authority of the CCC Charter Act and other specific legislation.

Foreign donations.—The Corporation may furnish commodities under the authority of section 416(b) of the Agricultural Act of 1949 to carry out programs of assistance in developing countries and friendly countries and pay costs associated with making the commodities available. The Corporation may also use its funds to furnish commodities overseas under the authority of the Food for Progress Act of 1985; however, not more than 500,000 metric tons of commodities may be provided under this authority in each fiscal year, and not more than $30 million of the funds of the Corporation (exclusive of the costs of commodities) may be used for each fiscal year. In addition, under the Food for Progress Act of 1985, not to exceed $10 million of the Corporation's funds or commodities may be used each fiscal year to enhance the development of private sector agriculture in countries receiving commodities under the Food for Progress Act of 1985. Section 1125 of the FY 1999 Agriculture Appropriations Act increased the $30 million and $10 million limitations to $35 million and $15 million, respectively, for fiscal year 1999 only.

Loan operations.—The following table reflects commodity loan operations of the Corporation:

[In millions of dollars]

Item	1999 actual	2000 est.	2001 est.
Loans outstanding, gross, start of year:			
Commodity Credit Corporation	2,219	2,441	2,371
Additional loans made	8,357	9,398	9,257
Deduct:			
Loans repaid	−7,902	−9,191	−9,233
Acquisition of loan collateral	−203	−277	−326
Write-offs	−30		
Total loans outstanding, gross, end of year	2,441	2,371	2,069

Inventory operations.—The following table reflects the inventory operations applicable to the preceding programs:

AGRICULTURAL COMMODITIES

[In millions of dollars]

Item	1999 actual	2000 est.	2001 est.
On hand, start of year, gross	531	713	707
Acquisitions:			
Forfeiture of loan collateral	203	277	325
Excess of collateral acquired over loans canceled	6	6	6
Purchases	1,407	1,059	626
Carrying charges:			
Charges to inventory	14	7	1
Storage and handling (non-add)	(43)	(48)	(50)
Transportation (non-add)	(5)	(6)	(4)
Total acquisitions	1,630	1,349	958
Dispositions:			
Domestic donations to:			
Families	17	67	46
Institutions	11	65	47
Total domestic donations	28	132	93
Export donations	665	474	313
Sales and transfers:			
Special programs: Title II, Public Law 480	477	549	500
Title III, Public Law 480	26		
Other sales	236	177	233
Net loss or gain (−) on sales and transfers	16	23	−11
Total sales and transfers	755	749	722
Total dispositions	1,448	1,355	1,128
On hand, end of year, gross	713	707	538
Allowances for losses	−186	−185	−140
On hand, end of year, net	527	522	398

Other data.—The following table reflects other data which are applicable to price support and related programs:

DATA ON SUPPORT AND RELATED PROGRAMS

[In millions of dollars]

Item	1999 actual	2000 est.	2001 est.
Loans made	8,358	9,399	9,257
Loans repaid	7,902	9,191	9,233
Loan collateral forfeited	203	277	326
Loans outstanding, end of year	2,441	2,371	2,069
Acquisitions	1,630	1,349	958
Cost of commodities sold	755	749	722
Cost of commodities donated	693	606	406
Inventory, end of year	713	707	538
Investment in loans and inventory, end of year	3,154	3,078	2,607
Direct producer payments	16,101	22,366	12,815
Net expenditures	19,223	26,067	15,963
Realized losses	20,632	27,771	16,028

Operating expenses.—The Corporation carries out its functions through utilization of employees and facilities of other Government agencies. Administrative expenses are incurred by: the Farm Service Agency (FSA); the Foreign Agricultural Service; the Natural Resources Conservation Service; the Risk Management Agency; other agencies of the Department engaged in the Corporation's activities; and the Office of the Inspector General for audit functions. Additional expenses are incurred by FSA county offices for work related to programs of the Corporation, other FSA expenses offset by revenue, custodian, and agency expenses of the Federal Reserve banks and lending agencies, and miscellaneous costs.

Expenses are incurred for acquisition, operation, maintenance, improvement, or disposition of existing property that the Corporation owns or in which it has an interest. These expenses are treated as program expenses. Such program expenses include inspection, classing, and grading work performed on a fee basis by Federal employees or Federal- or State-licensed inspectors; and special services performed by Federal agencies within and outside this Department. Most of these general expenses, including storage and handling, transportation, inspection, classing and grading, and producer storage payments, are included in program costs. They are shown in the program and financing schedule in the entries entitled "Storage, transportation, and other obligations not included above," and "Producer storage payments."

Section 161 of the 1996 Act amended the CCC Charter Act to significantly limit the use of CCC funds. CCC no longer has authority to purchase personal property except within authorized limitations. CCC spending for equipment or services relating to automated data processing (ADP), information technologies, or related items (including telecommunications equipment and computer hardware and software, but excluding reimbursable agreements) was limited to $170 million in fiscal year 1996, and $275 million for the six-year period including fiscal years 1997 through 2002, unless additional amounts for such contracts and agreements are provided in advance in appropriation acts. The 1996 Act also requires that CCC submit an itemized report to Congress on a quarterly basis of all expenditures, excluding program payments, of over $10,000. Subsequent legislation reduced allowable ADP expenditures through 2002 to $188 million. The remain-

Public enterprise funds—Continued

COMMODITY CREDIT CORPORATION FUND—Continued

PROGRAMS OF THE CORPORATION—Continued

ing funds are expected to be exhausted during 2000, and the Budget proposes to fund $35 million per year through 2002 on these expenditures through CCC.

Section 161 of the 1996 Act also amended section 11 of the CCC Charter Act to limit the use of CCC funds for the transfer and allotment of funds to State and Federal agencies. Beginning on October 1, 1996, the total of these allotments and transfers under that section in a fiscal year, including agreements for ADP or information resource management activities, may not exceed the total of such alloments and transfers in fiscal year 1995. The obligations for these Section 11 activities in fiscal year 1995 were $46.188 million. The fiscal year 1995 cap was revised to $36.209 million effective fiscal year 1999 to exclude the Emerging Markets Program because such transfers are not made pursuant to Section 11 of the CCC Charter Act.

The Corporation receives reimbursement for grain requisitioned pursuant to Public Law 87–152 by the States from Corporation stocks to feed resident wildlife threatened with starvation through the appropriation reimbursement for net realized losses. There have been no requisitions in recent years, however.

SPECIAL ACTIVITIES

These activities are carried out under authority of section 5(g) of the Corporation's charter act and specific statutory authorizations or directives with respect thereto that are currently in effect or which may subsequently be enacted.

A summary of such current activities not included under other designated activities is as follows:

Item	2001 estimate [In millions of dollars] Gross obligations	Outlays (reimbursable)
(1) Financing sales of agricultural commodities for foreign currencies or for dollars on credit terms	159	224
(2) Commodities supplied in connection with dispositions abroad (Title II)	837	843
(3) Commodities supplied in connection with dispositions abroad (Title III)	0	3
Total	996	1,070

The Corporation receives appropriations or reimbursement for the cost of these activities as described under each.

Activities currently being carried out are as follows (see Foreign Assistance programs for details of items (1), (2) and (3)).

(1) Financing the sale and exportation of agricultural commodities for foreign currencies or for dollars (title I, of P.L. 480).

(2) Commodities supplied in connection with dispositions abroad (title II, of P.L. 480).

(3) Commodities supplied in connection with dispositions abroad (title III, of P.L. 480).

(4) Commodities supplied in connection with dispositions abroad (Food for Progress Act of 1985).

FINANCING

Borrowing authority.—The Corporation has an authorized capital stock of $100 million held by the U.S. Treasury and, effective in 1988, authority to have outstanding borrowings up to $30 billion at any one time.

Funds are borrowed from the Treasury and may also be borrowed from private lending agencies and others. The Corporation reserves a sufficient amount of its borrowing authority to purchase at any time all notes and other obligations evidencing loans made to the Corporation by such agencies and others. All bonds, notes, debentures, and similar obligations issued by the Corporation are subject to approval by the Secretary of the Treasury as required by the Act of March 8, 1938.

Interest on borrowings from the Treasury (and on capital stock) is paid at a rate based upon the average interest rate of all outstanding marketable obligations (of comparable maturity date) of the United States as of the preceding month. Interest is also paid on other notes and obligations at a rate prescribed by the Corporation and approved by the Secretary of the Treasury.

The Department of Agriculture and Related Agencies Appropriation Act, 1966, made provision for terminating interest after June 30, 1964 on the portion of the Corporation's borrowings from the Treasury equal to the unreimbursed realized losses recorded on the books of the Corporation after the end of the fiscal year in which such losses are realized.

POSITION WITH RESPECT TO BORROWING AUTHORITY, END OF YEAR

[In millions of dollars]

Item	1999 actual	2000 est.	2001 est.
Statutory borrowing authority	30,000	30,000	30,000
Deduct: Borrowings from Treasury	28,712	27,139	15,349
Net statutory borrowing authority available	1,288	2,861	14,651

Note.—Accounts payable, accrued liabilities, and other outstanding obligations not reflected on this table do not become charges against the statutory borrowing authority until they result in borrowings from the Treasury.

Contract authority.—Price support and other programs required by statute may result in the Corporation incurring obligations in excess of available funds and borrowing authority. Such obligations are liquidated from subsequent appropriations and other funds that may become available to the Corporation. Any increase in obligations in excess of available fund resources is reported as contract authority in the year involved; a decrease is reported as the application of appropriations and other funds to liquidate the authority.

Appropriations.—Under section 2 of Public Law 87–155 annual appropriations are authorized for each fiscal year to reimburse the Corporation for net realized losses incurred as of the close of each year.

The special activities are financed as indicated in the program descriptions above. In addition to certain reimbursements from other agencies, appropriations are made for foreign assistance programs.

Deficit.—The net realized losses of the Corporation have previously been reimbursed as follows:

SUPPORT AND RELATED PROGRAMS

[In millions of dollars]		1999 actual
Realized losses, 1933 to 1999, inclusive		283,358
Reimbursements by the Treasury:		
Reimbursements of realized losses:		
Appropriations (60 times)	250,163	
Note cancellations (6 times)	2,698	
Less dividends paid to Treasury (4 times)	−138	
Total reimbursements for net realized losses	252,723	
Other reimbursements:		
Appropriations (2 times)	542	
Note cancellation (1 time)	56	
Total other reimbursements	598	
Total		253,321
Realized deficit as of September 30, 1999, support and related programs		30,037

Foreign Market Development Cooperator Program (FMDCP) and Quality Samples Program. In FY 2000, funding for the FMSCP shifted from the Foreign Agricultural Service annual appropriation to CCC funding. Funding FMDCP from CCC is consistent with Section 5(f) of the CCC Charter Act which authorizes the use of CCC funds for export promotion and overseas market development activities of U.S. agricultural products. The FY 2000 program level is $27.5 million.

Beginning also in FY 2000, CCC is funding the Quality Samples Program at an authorized annual level of $2.5 million. Under this initiative, samples of U.S. agricultural products will be provided to foreign importers to promote a better understanding and appreciation for the high quality of U.S. products.

Commodity Certificates. Subtitle B of the 2000 Act allows for the use of commodity certificates. In making in-kind payments, CCC may (a) acquire and use commodities that have been pledged to the Commodity Credit Corporation as collateral for loans made by the Corporation;" (b) "use other commodities owned by the Commodity Credit Corporation;" and (c) "redeem negotiable marketing certificates for cash under terms and conditions established. Implementation regarding implementation of commodity certificates is under consideration.

Farm Storage Facility Loan Program (FSFL). The FSFL program was established by CCC in 1949 to offer low-cost financing to producers for the construction or upgrade of on-farm storage facilities. USDA will resume this program in FY 2000. Direct loans would finance about $1 billion worth of farm storage facilities from FY 2000 through 2002. The cost to the U.S. government 2002 for the FSFL program would be estimated using procedures stipulated by the Federal Credit Reform Act of 1990.

Ethanol Grain Program. As part of the Farm Safety Net proposal, the FY 2001 President's Budget assumes that CCC will make payments under a new Ethanol Grain Program to ethanol producers who increase their purchase of surplus grain for conversion into fuel ethanol. The program, which is authorized by Executive Order 13134, the Agricultural Act of 1949 as amended by the Food Security Act of 1985 (PL 99–198), and the CCC Charter Act, will remove surplus grain from the market and encourage ethanol production.

Statement of Operations (in millions of dollars)

Identification code 12–4336–0–3–999	1998 actual	1999 actual	2000 est.	2001 est.
0101 Revenue	1,078	1,022	845	1,125
0102 Expense	–10,396	–21,654	–28,616	–17,153
0105 Net income or loss (–)	–9,318	–20,632	–27,771	–16,028

Balance Sheet (in millions of dollars)

Identification code 12–4336–0–3–999	1998 actual	1999 actual	2000 est.	2001 est.
ASSETS:				
Federal assets:				
1101 Fund balances with Treasury	–1,568	–1,410	–1,410	–1,410
Investments in US securities:				
1106 Receivables, net	49	151	26	26
1107 Advances and prepayments	56	4	33	33
Non-Federal assets:				
1206 Receivables, net	44	38	35	35
1207 Advances and prepayments	5	11	5	5
Net value of assets related to pre–1992 direct loans receivable and acquired defaulted guaranteed loans receivable:				
1601 Direct loans, gross	2,632	2,846	2,766	2,455
1602 Interest receivable	209	232	210	197
1603 Allowance for estimated uncollectible loans and interest (–)	–180	–274	–180	–173
1604 Direct loans and interest receivable, net	2,661	2,804	2,796	2,479
1699 Value of assets related to direct loans	2,661	2,804	2,796	2,479
Other Federal assets:				
1801 Cash and other monetary assets	77	77	77	77
1802 Inventories and related properties	345	355	336	207
1803 Property, plant and equipment, net	87	46	67	68
1999 Total assets	1,756	2,076	1,965	1,520
LIABILITIES:				
Federal liabilities:				
2101 Accounts payable	4	430	5	5
2102 Interest payable	160	510	350	192
2103 Debt	16,692	28,712	27,139	15,349
2105 Other	370	444	398	398
Non-Federal liabilities:				
2201 Accounts payable	63	10	107	107
2206 Pension and other actuarial liabilities	30			
2207 Other	2,426	2,537	2,537	2,537
2999 Total liabilities	19,745	32,643	30,536	18,588
NET POSITION:				
3300 Cumulative results of operations	–17,990	–30,566	–28,571	–17,068
3999 Total net position	–17,990	–30,566	–28,571	–17,068
4999 Total liabilities and net position	1,755	2,077	1,965	1,520

Note.—In addition to obligations other than liabilities, the Corporation does not reflect in its accounts claims by the Corporation on which adequate proof has not been established.

Object Classification (in millions of dollars)

Identification code 12–4336–0–3–999	1999 actual	2000 est.	2001 est.
Direct obligations:			
22.0 Transportation of things	328	297	165
Other services:			
25.2 Other services	168	97	80
25.2 Other services: Storage and handling	43	48	50
26.0 Supplies and materials: Costs of commodities sold or donated-PL 480	1,427	1,071	633
31.0 ADP equipment	11		
41.0 Grants, subsidies, and contributions	17,537	24,924	14,119
43.0 Interest and dividends	652	811	614
99.0 Subtotal, direct obligations	20,166	27,248	15,661
Reimbursable obligations:			
22.0 Transportation of things:PL 480 ocean transportation	464	392	357
26.0 Supplies and materials: Cost of commodities sold or donated—PL 480	503	549	500
33.0 Investments and loans	8,358	9,399	9,257
99.0 Subtotal, reimbursable obligations	9,325	10,340	10,114
99.9 Total new obligations	29,491	37,588	25,775

Commodity Credit Corporation Fund

(Legislative proposal, not subject to PAYGO)

Program and Financing (in millions of dollars)

Identification code 12–4336–2–3–999	1999 actual	2000 est.	2001 est.
Obligations by program activity:			
Support and related programs:			
Operating expenses:			
Direct producer payments:			
00.31 Conservation farm option program			–50
10.00 Total new obligations (object class 41.0)			–50
Budgetary resources available for obligation:			
22.00 New budget authority (gross)			–50
23.95 Total new obligations			50
New budget authority (gross), detail:			
Discretionary:			
40.00 Appropriation			–50
Change in unpaid obligations:			
73.10 Total new obligations			–50
73.20 Total outlays (gross)			4
74.40 Unpaid obligations, end of year: Obligated balance, end of year			–46
Outlays (gross), detail:			
86.90 Outlays from new discretionary authority			–4
Net budget authority and outlays:			
89.00 Budget authority			–50
90.00 Outlays			–4

Public enterprise funds—Continued

COMMODITY CREDIT CORPORATION FUND—Continued

In 2001, the Budget proposes to cut the Conservation Farm Option by $50 million to offset increases for other high priority conservation initiatives.

COMMODITY CREDIT CORPORATION FUND

(Legislative proposal, subject to PAYGO)

Program and Financing (in millions of dollars)

Identification code 12–4336–4–3–999	1999 actual	2000 est.	2001 est.
Obligations by program activity:			
Support and related programs:			
Operating expenses:			
Direct producer payments:			
00.23 Supplementary income assistance payments		600	2,464
00.25 Dairy price support program			150
00.26 Noninsured assistance program (NAP)		110	110
00.27 Cooperative development			80
00.28 Environmental quality incentives program (EQIP)			125
00.29 Wetlands reserve program			213
00.30 Farmland protection program			65
00.31 Conservation farm option			−50
00.32 Technical assistance- Wetlands reserve program/Conservation reserve program			75
00.33 Conservation security program			600
00.91 Total operating expenses		710	3,832
Capital investment:			
01.02 Purchase of ADP equipment			35
01.92 Total support and related programs		710	3,867
10.00 Total new obligations		710	3,867
Budgetary resources available for obligation:			
22.00 New budget authority (gross)		710	3,917
22.21 Unobligated balance transferred to other accounts			−50
23.90 Total budgetary resources available for obligation		710	3,867
23.95 Total new obligations		−710	−3,867
24.40 Unobligated balance available, end of year			
New budget authority (gross), detail:			
Mandatory:			
67.15 Authority to borrow (indefinite)		710	3,917
Change in unpaid obligations:			
73.10 Total new obligations		710	3,867
73.20 Total outlays (gross)		−710	−3,615
74.40 Unpaid obligations, end of year: Obligated balance, end of year			252
Outlays (gross), detail:			
86.97 Outlays from new mandatory authority		710	3,615
Net budget authority and outlays:			
89.00 Budget authority		710	3,917
90.00 Outlays		710	3,615

This schedule reflects the CCC portion of the Administration's proposed Farm Safety Net reform. The proposal includes counter-cyclical farm income support to provide additional payments through the expected enactment of the next farm bill, which would provide producers 92 percent of their lost farm revenue relative to a rolling five-year average. The proposal would also: extend the dairy price-support program; provide financing to cooperatives for livestock processing and other value-added facilities; and waive certain area triggers for crop insurance provided under the Non-insured Assistance Program. (Additional crop insurance reforms that are part of the Farm Safety Net proposal can be found in the Crop Insurance schedules.)

The proposal includes a comprehensive conservation initiative. A new Conservation Security Program would be funded at $600 million to provide annual payments to farmers and ranchers who implement high-value conservation practices such as comprehensive nutrient management, low-impact grazing practices, windbreaks and grassed waterways. This program would be administered by the Natural Resources Conservation Service. The Environmental Quality Incentives Program would increase from its authorized $200 million to $325 million per year, for farmers and ranchers implementing conservation and livestock management practices. The Conservation Reserve Program's cumulative enrollment cap would be increased from its current 36.4 million acres to 40 million acres. Bonuses totaling up to $100 million in FY 2000 and $125 million in FY 2001 and 2002 would be offered under current authority to producers who enroll land in the CRP's continuous signup program for high-value acreage such as filter strips and grass waterways. Annual enrollments under the Wetlands Reserve Program would increase to 250,000 acres per year and the current cumulative enrollment cap of 975,000 acres, expected to be reached in FY 2001, would be eliminated.

In addition, funding for the Farmland Protection Program would be provided at $65 million per year. This program, which is also part of the President's Lands Legacy Initiative, provides matching funds to purchase permanent easements on farmland threatened by urban and suburban sprawl. The Wildlife Habitat Incentives Program would be funded at $50 million annually, to provide cost-share assistance to farmers and other landowners for habitat restoration. Both these programs have exhausted their authorized funding.

Associated technical assistance would also be funded through this proposal, including a $35 million increase in the cap on CCC-funded ADP obligations for FY 2001 and 2002, to compensate for prior-year appropriations reductions to the 7-year cap established by the 1996 Farm Bill.

Object Classification (in millions of dollars)

Identification code 12–4336–4–3–999	1999 actual	2000 est.	2001 est.
25.2 Other services			248
31.0 ADP equipment			35
41.0 Grants, subsidies, and contributions		710	3,584
99.9 Total new obligations		710	3,867

COMMODITY CREDIT CORPORATION EXPORT LOANS PROGRAM ACCOUNT

(INCLUDING TRANSFERS OF FUNDS)

For administrative expenses to carry out the Commodity Credit Corporation's export guarantee program, GSM 102 and GSM 103, $3,820,000; to cover common overhead expenses as permitted by section 11 of the Commodity Credit Corporation Charter Act and in conformity with the Federal Credit Reform Act of 1990, of which $3,231,000 may be transferred to and merged with the appropriation for "Foreign Agricultural Service and General Sales Manager" and $589,000 may be transferred to and merged with the appropriation for "Farm Service Agency, Salaries and Expenses". *(Agriculture, Rural Development, Food and Drug Administration, and Related Agencies Appropriations Act, 2000.)*

Program and Financing (in millions of dollars)

Identification code 12–1336–0–1–351	1999 actual	2000 est.	2001 est.
Obligations by program activity:			
00.02 Guaranteed loan subsidy	158	320	323
00.07 Reestimates of guaranteed loan subsidy		343	
00.08 Interest on reestimates of guaranteed loan subsidy		181	
00.09 Administrative expenses	4	4	4
10.00 Total new obligations	162	848	327
Budgetary resources available for obligation:			
21.40 Unobligated balance available, start of year	166	330	999

		1999 actual	2000 est.	2001 est.
22.00	New budget authority (gross)	326	1,517	327
23.90	Total budgetary resources available for obligation	492	1,847	1,326
23.95	Total new obligations	−162	−848	−327
24.40	Unobligated balance available, end of year	330	999	999
	New budget authority (gross), detail:			
	Discretionary:			
40.00	Appropriation	4	4	4
	Mandatory:			
60.05	Appropriation (indefinite)	322	734	323
69.00	Offsetting collections (cash)		779	
70.00	Total new budget authority (gross)	326	1,517	327
	Change in unpaid obligations:			
72.40	Unpaid obligations, start of year: Obligated balance, start of year	199	204	218
73.10	Total new obligations	162	848	327
73.20	Total outlays (gross)	−157	−834	−327
74.40	Unpaid obligations, end of year: Obligated balance, end of year	204	218	218
	Outlays (gross), detail:			
86.90	Outlays from new discretionary authority	4	4	4
86.97	Outlays from new mandatory authority	138	692	259
86.98	Outlays from mandatory balances	15	138	64
87.00	Total outlays (gross)	157	834	327
	Offsets:			
	Against gross budget authority and outlays:			
88.00	Offsetting collections (cash) from: Offsetting collections (cash) from: Downward Reestimates		−779	
	Net budget authority and outlays:			
89.00	Budget authority	326	738	327
90.00	Outlays	157	55	327

Summary of Loan Levels, Subsidy Budget Authority and Outlays by Program (in millions of dollars)

Identification code 12–1336–0–1–351		1999 actual	2000 est.	2001 est.
	Guaranteed loan levels supportable by subsidy budget authority:			
2150	Loan guarantee levels	3,045	3,787	3,792
2159	Total loan guarantee levels	3,045	3,787	3,792
	Guaranteed loan subsidy (in percent):			
2320	Subsidy rate	10.57	8.45	8.52
2329	Weighted average subsidy rate	10.57	8.45	8.52
	Guaranteed loan subsidy budget authority:			
2330	Subsidy budget authority	322	734	323
2339	Total subsidy budget authority	322	734	323
	Guaranteed loan subsidy outlays:			
2340	Subsidy outlays	153	51	323
2349	Total subsidy outlays	153	51	323
	Administrative expense data:			
3510	Budget authority—administrative expenses	4	4	4
3590	Outlays from new authority	4	4	4

This is the program account for the GSM–102 and GSM–103 CCC Export Credit Guarantee Programs. The Export Credit Guarantee Program (GSM–102) covers credit terms of up to 3 years. The Intermediate Export Credit Guarantee Program (GSM–103) covers longer credit terms of between 3 and 10 years. Under these programs, CCC does not provide financing, but guarantees payments due from foreign banks and buyers. Because payment is guaranteed, financial institutions in the United States can offer competitive credit terms to foreign banks, usually with interest rates based on the London Inter-Bank Offered Rate (LIBOR). If the foreign bank fails to make any payment as agreed, the exporter or assignee must submit a notice of default to the CCC. A claim for loss must be filed, and the CCC will promptly pay claims found to be in good order. CCC usually guarantees 98 percent of the principal payment due and interest based on a percentage of the one-year Treasury rate.

A portion of the guarantees made available under the GSM–102 program is provided as Supplier Credit Guarantees. Under this activity, CCC guarantees a portion of payment due from importers under short-term financing (for up to 180 days) that exporters have extended directly to the importers for the purchase of U.S. agricultural commodities and products. CCC does not provide financing, but guarantees payment due from an importer. A substantially smaller portion of the value of exports (currently 60 percent) is guaranteed under Supplier Credit Guarantees than under regular GSM–102 guarantees where CCC is guaranteeing foreign bank obligations.

A portion of the GSM–102 guarantees is also made available as Facilities Guarantees. Under this activity, CCC guarantees export financing for capital goods and services to improve handling, marketing, processing, storage, or distribution of imported agricultural commodities and products.

The subsidy estimates for the GSM–102 and GSM–103 programs are determined in large part by the obligor's sovereign or non-sovereign country risk grade. These grades are developed annually by the International Credit Risk Assessment System Committee (ICRAS). In unusual circumstances, an ICRAS grade for a country may change during the fiscal year. The default estimates for GSM guarantees are determined in large part by the risk premia assigned for each risk grade.

As required by the Federal Credit Reform Act of 1990, this account records, for this program, the subsidy costs associated with the credit guarantees committed in 1992 and beyond (including modifications of credit guarantees that resulted from obligations or commitments in any year), as well as administrative expenses of this program. The subsidy amounts are estimated on a present value basis; the administrative expenses are estimated on a cash basis. The 2001 budget displays the GSM loan guarantee volume and the subsidy level that can be justified by forecast economic conditions, the expected supply/demand conditions of countries requesting GSM loan guarantees.

Object Classification (in millions of dollars)

Identification code 12–1336–0–1–351		1999 actual	2000 est.	2001 est.
25.3	Purchases of goods and services from Government accounts	4	4	4
41.0	Grants, subsidies, and contributions	158	844	323
99.9	Total new obligations	162	848	327

Commodity Credit Corporation Export Guarantee Financing Account

Program and Financing (in millions of dollars)

Identification code 12–4337–0–3–351		1999 actual	2000 est.	2001 est.
	Obligations by program activity:			
	New loans:			
00.01	Default claims	244	425	390
00.02	Interest on debt to Treasury	62	62	62
00.91	Subtotal, new loans	306	487	452
	Reestimates:			
08.02	Reestimates of guaranteed loan subsidy		596	
08.04	Interest on reestimates of guranteed loan subsidy		184	
08.91	Subtotal, reestimates		780	
10.00	Total new obligations	306	1,267	452
	Budgetary resources available for obligation:			
21.40	Unobligated balance available, start of year	1,548	1,539	463
22.00	New financing authority (gross)	229	191	467

Public enterprise funds—Continued

COMMODITY CREDIT CORPORATION EXPORT GUARANTEE FINANCING ACCOUNT—Continued

Program and Financing (in millions of dollars)—Continued

Identification code 12–4337–0–3–351	1999 actual	2000 est.	2001 est.
22.10 Resources available from recoveries of prior year obligations	68		
23.90 Total budgetary resources available for obligation	1,845	1,730	930
23.95 Total new obligations	−306	−1,267	−452
24.40 Unobligated balance available, end of year	1,539	463	478
New financing authority (gross), detail:			
Mandatory:			
69.00 Offsetting collections (cash)	229	191	467
Change in unpaid obligations:			
72.40 Unpaid obligations, start of year: Obligated balance, start of year	−199	−204	−332
73.10 Total new obligations	306	1,267	452
73.20 Total financing disbursements (gross)	−244	−1,395	−465
73.45 Adjustments in unexpired accounts	−68		
74.40 Unpaid obligations, end of year: Obligated balance, end of year	−204	−332	−345
87.00 Total financing disbursements (gross)	244	1,395	465
Offsets:			
Against gross financing authority and financing disbursements:			
Offsetting collections (cash) from:			
88.00 Payments from program account	−157	−55	−327
88.25 Interest on uninvested funds		−36	−38
Non-Federal sources:			
88.40 Loan origination fee	−14	−28	−29
88.40 Principal collections	−4	−7	−9
88.40 Interest collections	−54	−65	−64
88.90 Total, offsetting collections (cash)	−229	−191	−467
Against gross financing authority only:			
88.95 Change in receivables from program accounts			
Net financing authority and financing disbursements:			
89.00 Financing authority			
90.00 Financing disbursements	15	1,204	−2

Status of Guaranteed Loans (in millions of dollars)

Identification code 12–4337–0–3–351	1999 actual	2000 est.	2001 est.
Position with respect to appropriations act limitation on commitments:			
2111 Limitation on guaranteed loans made by private lenders			
2131 Guaranteed loan commitments exempt from limitation	3,045	3,787	3,792
2150 Total guaranteed loan commitments	3,045	3,787	3,792
Cumulative balance of guaranteed loans outstanding:			
2210 Outstanding, start of year	6,826	6,739	5,689
2231 Disbursements of new guaranteed loans	244	3,501	3,501
2251 Repayments and prepayments	−83	−4,126	−3,701
2261 Adjustments: Terminations for default that result in loans receivable	−248	−425	−390
2290 Outstanding, end of year	6,739	5,689	5,099
Memorandum:			
2299 Guaranteed amount of guaranteed loans outstanding, end of year	6,065	5,575	4,581
Addendum:			
Cumulative balance of defaulted guaranteed loans that result in loans receivable:			
2310 Outstanding, start of year	96	336	754
2331 Disbursements for guaranteed loan claims	248	425	390
2351 Repayments of loans receivable	−8	−7	−9
2390 Outstanding, end of year	336	754	1,135

As required by the Federal Credit Reform Act of 1990, this non-budgetary account records all cash flows to and from the Government resulting from loan guarantees committed in 1992 and beyond. The amounts in this account are a means of financing and are not included in the budget totals.

Balance Sheet (in millions of dollars)

Identification code 12–4337–0–3–351	1998 actual	1999 actual	2000 est.	2001 est.
ASSETS:				
1101 Federal assets: Fund balances with Treasury	1,548	1,539	463	478
Net value of assets related to post-1991 acquired defaulted guaranteed loans receivable:				
1501 Defaulted guaranteed loans receivable, gross	1,375	336	754	1,135
1599 Net present value of assets related to defaulted guaranteed loans	1,375	336	754	1,135
1999 Total assets	2,923	1,875	1,217	1,613
LIABILITIES:				
2103 Federal liabilities: Debt	851	851	851	851
2204 Non-Federal liabilities: Liabilities for loan guarantees	2,245	1,024	366	762
2999 Total liabilities	3,096	1,875	1,217	1,613
4999 Total liabilities and net position	3,096	1,875	1,217	1,613

COMMODITY CREDIT CORPORATION GUARANTEED LOANS LIQUIDATING ACCOUNT

Program and Financing (in millions of dollars)

Identification code 12–4338–0–3–351	1999 actual	2000 est.	2001 est.
Budgetary resources available for obligation:			
21.40 Unobligated balance available, start of year	277	59	
22.00 New budget authority (gross)	234	316	328
22.40 Capital transfer to general fund	−451	−375	−328
23.90 Total budgetary resources available for obligation	60		
24.40 Unobligated balance available, end of year	59		
New budget authority (gross), detail:			
Mandatory:			
69.00 Offsetting collections (cash)	234	316	328
Offsets:			
Against gross budget authority and outlays:			
Offsetting collections (cash) from:			
Non-Federal sources:			
88.40 Repayments of principal	−83	−114	−158
88.40 Interest received on loans	−151	−202	−170
88.90 Total, offsetting collections (cash)	−234	−316	−328
Net budget authority and outlays:			
89.00 Budget authority			
90.00 Outlays	−234	−316	−328

Note.—Includes amounts for activities previously funded in the Commodity Credit Corporation Fund.

Status of Guaranteed Loans (in millions of dollars)

Identification code 12–4338–0–3–351	1999 actual	2000 est.	2001 est.
Cumulative balance of guaranteed loans outstanding:			
2210 Outstanding, start of year	214		
2251 Repayments and prepayments	−214		
2290 Outstanding, end of year			
Memorandum:			
2299 Guaranteed amount of guaranteed loans outstanding, end of year			
Addendum:			
Cumulative balance of defaulted guaranteed loans that result in loans receivable:			
2310 Outstanding, start of year	4,292	4,210	4,096
2351 Repayments of loans receivable	−82	−114	−158
2390 Outstanding, end of year	4,210	4,096	3,938

As required by the Federal Credit Reform Act of 1990, this account records, for this program, all cash flows to and from the Government resulting from loan guarantees committed prior to 1992. This account is shown on a cash basis. All new activity in this program in 1992 and beyond is recorded in corresponding program and financing accounts.

Balance Sheet (in millions of dollars)

Identification code 12–4338–0–3–351	1998 actual	1999 actual	2000 est.	2001 est.
ASSETS:				
1101 Federal assets: Fund balances with Treasury	277	277		
Net value of assets related to pre–1992 direct loans receivable and acquired defaulted guaranteed loans receivable:				
Defaulted guaranteed loans, gross:				
1701 Defaulted guaranteed loans, gross	4,292	4,210	4,096	3,938
1701 Defaulted guaranteed loans, adjustment—Debt Reduction				
1702 Interest receivable	25	167	167	167
1703 Allowance for estimated uncollectible loans and interest (–)	–1,456	–3,054	–3,031	–3,019
1799 Value of assets related to loan guarantees	2,861	1,323	1,232	1,086
1999 Total assets	3,138	1,600	1,232	1,086
LIABILITIES:				
2104 Federal liabilities: Resources payable to Treasury	3,745	2,664	2,483	2,372
2207 Non-Federal liabilities: Other	24	25		
2999 Total liabilities	3,769	2,689	2,483	2,372
4999 Total liabilities and net position	3,769	2,689	2,483	2,372

Farm Storage Facility Loans Program Account

Program and Financing (in millions of dollars)

Identification code 12–3301–0–1–351	1999 actual	2000 est.	2001 est.
Obligations by program activity:			
00.01 Direct loan subsidy		10	4
10.00 Total new obligations (object class 41.0)		10	4
Budgetary resources available for obligation:			
22.00 New budget authority (gross)		10	4
23.95 Total new obligations		–10	–4
New budget authority (gross), detail:			
Mandatory:			
60.05 Appropriation (indefinite)		10	4
Change in unpaid obligations:			
73.10 Total new obligations		10	4
73.20 Total outlays (gross)		–10	–4
Outlays (gross), detail:			
86.97 Outlays from new mandatory authority		10	4
Net budget authority and outlays:			
89.00 Budget authority		10	4
90.00 Outlays		10	4

Summary of Loan Levels, Subsidy Budget Authority and Outlays by Program (in millions of dollars)

Identification code 12–3301–0–1–351	1999 actual	2000 est.	2001 est.
Direct loan levels supportable by subsidy budget authority:			
1150 Direct loan levels		350	150
1159 Total direct loan levels		350	150
Direct loan subsidy (in percent):			
1320 Subsidy rate		2.85	2.85
1329 Weighted average subsidy rate		2.85	2.85
Direct loan subsidy budget authority:			
1330 Subsidy budget authority		10	4
1339 Total subsidy budget authority		10	4
Direct loan subsidy outlays:			
1340 Subsidy outlays		10	4
1349 Total subsidy outlays		10	4

Farm Storage Facility Loan Program. The Farm Storage Facility Loan (FSLA) program was established by CCC in 1949. The program was authorized in 1948 by the CCC Charter Act. CCC stopped making new loans under the FSLA program in 1982 based on studies that revealed that producers had sufficient storage for their crops at that time. Recent studies reflected that grain elevators currently have insufficient capacity to allow farmers to store their grain off the farm at harvest when prices are usually at their lowest. Due to this severe shortage of available storage, low-cost financing for producers to build or upgrade on-farm commodity storage and handling facilities is provided through the FSLA program. The program is being implemented in 2000 by CCC under Section 504(c) of the Federal Credit Reform Act of 1990. This program will provide producers financing with five to ten-year repayment terms and low interest rates. The program gives producers greater marketing flexibility when farm storage is limited and/or transportation difficulties cause storage problems, allows farmers to benefit from new marketing and technological advances, and maximizes their returns through identity-preserved marketing.

As required by the Federal Credit Reform Act of 1990, this account records, for this program, the subsidy costs associated with the direct loans obligated in 1992 and beyond (including modifications of direct loans or loan guarantees that resulted from obligations or commitments in any year), as well as administrative expenses of this program. The subsidy amounts are estimated on a present value basis; the administrative expenses are estimated on a cash basis.

Farm Storage Facility Direct Loan Financing Account

Program and Financing (in millions of dollars)

Identification code 12–4158–0–3–351	1999 actual	2000 est.	2001 est.
Obligations by program activity:			
00.01 Direct loans		350	150
00.03 Interest to Treasury		9	22
10.00 Total new obligations		359	172
Budgetary resources available for obligation:			
21.40 Unobligated balance available, start of year			7
22.00 New financing authority (gross)		366	175
23.90 Total budgetary resources available for obligation		366	182
23.95 Total new obligations		–359	–172
24.40 Unobligated balance available, end of year		7	10
New financing authority (gross), detail:			
Mandatory:			
67.15 Authority to borrow (indefinite)		356	171
Offsetting collections (cash):			
69.00 Payments from program account		10	4
69.00 Repayment of principal			84
69.47 Portion applied to repay debt			–84
69.90 Spending authority from offsetting collections (total mandatory)		10	4
70.00 Total new financing authority (gross)		366	175
Change in unpaid obligations:			
73.10 Total new obligations		359	172
73.20 Total financing disbursements (gross)		–359	–172
87.00 Total financing disbursements (gross)		359	172

Public enterprise funds—Continued

FARM STORAGE FACILITY DIRECT LOAN FINANCING ACCOUNT—Continued

Program and Financing (in millions of dollars)—Continued

Identification code 12–4158–0–3–351		1999 actual	2000 est.	2001 est.
	Offsets:			
	Against gross financing authority and financing disbursements:			
	Offsetting collections (cash) from:			
88.00	Federal sources		–10	–4
	Non-Federal sources:			
88.40	Principal collections			–61
88.40	Interest collections			–23
88.90	Total, offsetting collections (cash)		–10	–88
	Net financing authority and financing disbursements:			
89.00	Financing authority		356	87
90.00	Financing disbursements		349	84

Status of Direct Loans (in millions of dollars)

Identification code 12–4158–0–3–351		1999 actual	2000 est.	2001 est.
	Position with respect to appropriations act limitation on obligations:			
1111	Limitation on direct loans			
1131	Direct loan obligations exempt from limitation		350	150
1150	Total direct loan obligations		350	150
	Cumulative balance of direct loans outstanding:			
1210	Outstanding, start of year			350
1231	Disbursements: Direct loan disbursements		350	150
1251	Repayments: Repayments and prepayments			–84
1290	Outstanding, end of year		350	416

Balance Sheet (in millions of dollars)

Identification code 12–4158–0–3–351		1998 actual	1999 actual	2000 est.	2001 est.
	ASSETS:				
	Net value of assets related to post–1991 direct loans receivable:				
1401	Direct loans receivable, gross			350	416
1402	Interest receivable			72	80
1499	Net present value of assets related to direct loans			422	496
1999	Total assets			422	496
	LIABILITIES:				
2104	Federal liabilities: Resources payable to Treasury			368	479
2999	Total liabilities			368	479

As required by the Federal Credit Reform Act of 1990, this non-budgetary account records all cash flows to and from the Government resulting from direct loans obligated in 1992 and beyond (including modifications of direct loans that resulted from obligations in any year). The amounts in this account are a means of financing and are not included in the budget totals.

NATURAL RESOURCES CONSERVATION SERVICE

CONSERVATION OPERATIONS

For necessary expenses for carrying out the provisions of the Act of April 27, 1935 (16 U.S.C. 590a–f), including preparation of conservation plans and establishment of measures to conserve soil and water (including farm irrigation and land drainage and such special measures for soil and water management as may be necessary to prevent floods and the siltation of reservoirs and to control agricultural related pollutants); operation of conservation plant materials centers; classification and mapping of soil; dissemination of information; acquisition of lands, water, and interests therein for use in the plant materials program by donation, exchange, or purchase at a nominal cost not to exceed $100 pursuant to the Act of August 3, 1956 (7 U.S.C. 428a); purchase and erection or alteration or improvement of permanent and temporary buildings; and operation and maintenance of aircraft, [$661,243,000] *$747,243,000*, to remain available until expended (7 U.S.C. 2209b), of which not less than [$5,990,000] *$5,990,000* is for snow survey and water forecasting and not less than [$9,125,000] *$9,125,000* is for operation and establishment of the plant materials centers: *Provided*, That appropriations hereunder shall be available pursuant to 7 U.S.C. 2250 for construction and improvement of buildings and public improvements at plant materials centers, except that the cost of alterations and improvements to other buildings and other public improvements shall not exceed $250,000: *Provided further*, That when buildings or other structures are erected on non-Federal land, that the right to use such land is obtained as provided in 7 U.S.C. 2250a: *Provided further*, That this appropriation shall be available for technical assistance and related expenses to carry out programs authorized by section 202(c) of title II of the Colorado River Basin Salinity Control Act of 1974 (43 U.S.C. 1592(c)): *Provided further*, That this appropriation shall be available for employment pursuant to the second sentence of section 706(a) of the Organic Act of 1944 (7 U.S.C. 2225), and not to exceed $25,000 shall be available for employment under 5 U.S.C. 3109: *Provided further*, That qualified local engineers may be temporarily employed at per diem rates to perform the technical planning work of the Service (16 U.S.C. 590e–2). *(7 U.S.C. 2201–02; 16 U.S.C. 1101–5; 33 U.S.C. 7016–11; Agriculture, Rural Development, Food and Drug Administration, and Related Agencies Appropriations Act, 2000.)*

Program and Financing (in millions of dollars)

Identification code 12–1000–0–1–302		1999 actual	2000 est.	2001 est.
	Obligations by program activity:			
00.01	Technical assistance	546	581	654
00.02	Soil Surveys	78	80	78
00.03	Snow Survey and Water Forecasting	6	6	6
00.04	Plant Materials Centers	10	9	9
09.00	Reimbursable program	156	156	278
10.00	Total new obligations	796	832	1,025
	Budgetary resources available for obligation:			
21.40	Unobligated balance available, start of year	14	15	
22.00	New budget authority (gross)	797	817	1,025
23.90	Total budgetary resources available for obligation	811	832	1,025
23.95	Total new obligations	–796	–832	–1,025
24.40	Unobligated balance available, end of year	15		
	New budget authority (gross), detail:			
	Discretionary:			
40.00	Appropriation	641	661	747
68.00	Spending authority from offsetting collections: Offsetting collections (cash)	156	156	278
70.00	Total new budget authority (gross)	797	817	1,025
	Change in unpaid obligations:			
72.40	Unpaid obligations, start of year: Obligated balance, start of year	130	113	103
73.10	Total new obligations	796	832	1,025
73.20	Total outlays (gross)	–813	–842	–1,017
74.40	Unpaid obligations, end of year: Obligated balance, end of year	113	103	111
	Outlays (gross), detail:			
86.90	Outlays from new discretionary authority	697	738	935
86.93	Outlays from discretionary balances	116	104	81
87.00	Total outlays (gross)	813	842	1,017
	Offsets:			
	Against gross budget authority and outlays:			
	Offsetting collections (cash) from:			
88.00	Federal sources	–142	–140	–262
88.40	Non-Federal sources	–14	–16	–16
88.90	Total, offsetting collections (cash)	–156	–156	–278

Net budget authority and outlays:			
89.00 Budget authority	641	661	747
90.00 Outlays	657	686	739

Technical assistance.—Technical assistance is provided through 2,955 conservation districts or special districts to land users and decisionmakers, including individual landowners and operators, community groups, units of government, Indian tribes, and others for the planning of conservation programs and installation of needed conservation systems on the land, including design, layout, installation, and consultation services.

This account includes $10 million in competitive partnership grants as part of the Clean Water Action Plan, to enhance institutional capacity for locally-based institutions, including watershed councils, conservation districts, and co-operatives. In particular, funds would be directed for hiring non-federal watershed coordinators to develop watershed partnerships that include all stakeholders, to resolve differences and produce and help implement strategic plans to restore impaired watersheds. Watersheds would be selected through an inter-agency review process; however local entities may receive a preference in competing for funding if their States have prepared memoranda of understanding (MOU) for coordinating with the Federal government. Up to 10 percent of available funds may be used for developing MOUs among States and Federal agencies. In addition, $3 million is available for environmental monitoring and research work related to the Clean Water Action Plan.

In support of the Clean Water Action Plan's Animal Feeding Operations (AFOs) Strategy, conservation technical assistance funding targeted to AFOs will increase by $54 million over 2000 levels, for a total of $110 million in 2001. These funds will help livestock producers develop comprehensive nutrient management plans, a cornerstone of the strategy.

In support of the Administration's Livability Initiative, $5 million is provided for the Community/Federal Information Partnership. These funds will be used to enter into cooperative agreements with state and local governments to develop publicly available geospatial data that adheres to Federal Geographic Data Commission standards. This data will allow states and communities to make more informed land-use planning decisions, promoting "smart growth."

Of this program's $15 million in additional climate change funds, $12 million would expand soil carbon studies in support of the U.S. Global Change Research Program. These projects would provide validated soil carbon inventories and assess alternative soil management impacts on soil carbon stocks at national, regional, and field levels. In cooperation with the Agricultural Research Service, NRCS will field test soil carbon prediction and planning tools. An additional $3 million is provided as part of the Climate Change Technology Initiative. These funds would be used to carry out research pilot projects on AFO and livestock management issues and cropland management.

As part of the Administration's bioproducts initiative, $5 million is included to provide grants and technical assistance to farmers who market or produce bioenergy or biobased products. These funds would expand the economic opportunities available to farmers while promoting environmentally-friendly technologies.

MAIN WORKLOAD FACTORS

	1999 est.	2000 est.	2001 est.
Customers served	2,481,000	2,292,000	2,857,000
Onsite technical assistance	630,000	581,400	636,800
Acres receiving conservation technical assistance	42,068,000	38,872,000	48,447,000

Inventory and monitoring, resource appraisal, and program development activities are also funded through this account. Resource inventories are conducted to provide soil, water, and related resource data for evaluating land-use changes and trends; and for guidance in the development and implementation of Federal, State, and local resource conservation programs. Resource appraisal and program development provides periodic reports to the public and Congress as required by the Soil and Water Resources Conservation Act of 1977 as amended.

Soil surveys.—Soil surveys and investigations are made of the Nation's soil resources, and NRCS provides interpretations and publications that provide physical land facts needed for program development, resource conservation planning, installation of planned practices, and information for use by other Federal, State, and local agencies in making land-use decisions. National leadership is provided for digitizing soil surveys in cooperation with States, and other users of soil survey data. Legislation requires that "a substantial portion of the survey costs for NRCS are to be reimbursed by survey recipients."

MAIN WORKLOAD FACTORS

	1999 actual	2000 est.	2001 est.
Acres mapped annually (millions)	24	24	24
Soil surveys ready for publication (number)	32	32	32

Snow survey water forecasting.—Water supply forecasts prepared from snow surveys in western states are used in making efficient seasonal use of water for irrigation, flood control, fish and wildlife, recreation, power generation, municipal and industrial water supply, and water quality management.

Operation of plant materials centers.—The selection and evaluation of plant materials are made at 26 plant materials centers through field trials to determine their suitability for erosion control, conservation, and other environmental improvements. Native plant species will be preferred and exotic species introductions phased out for this program.

Object Classification (in millions of dollars)

Identification code 12–1000–0–1–302		1999 actual	2000 est.	2001 est.
	Direct obligations:			
	Personnel compensation:			
11.1	Full-time permanent	347	361	402
11.3	Other than full-time permanent	12	13	14
11.5	Other personnel compensation	5	6	6
11.9	Total personnel compensation	364	380	422
12.1	Civilian personnel benefits	85	90	101
13.0	Benefits for former personnel	1	1	1
21.0	Travel and transportation of persons	15	15	16
22.0	Transportation of things	3	3	3
23.2	Rental payments to others	11	11	12
23.3	Communications, utilities, and miscellaneous charges	24	24	26
24.0	Printing and reproduction	4	4	4
25.2	Other services	87	101	106
26.0	Supplies and materials	14	15	16
31.0	Equipment	31	32	36
41.0	Grants, subsidies, and contributions			4
99.0	Subtotal, direct obligations	639	676	747
99.0	Reimbursable obligations	156	154	278
99.5	Below reporting threshold	1	2	
99.9	Total new obligations	796	832	1,025

Personnel Summary

Identification code 12–1000–0–1–302		1999 actual	2000 est.	2001 est.
	Direct:			
1001	Total compensable workyears: Full-time equivalent employment	7,549	7,592	7,993
	Reimbursable:			
2001	Total compensable workyears: Full-time equivalent employment	2,651	2,493	4,293

WATERSHED SURVEYS AND PLANNING

For necessary expenses to conduct research, investigation, and surveys of watersheds of rivers and other waterways, and for small watershed investigations and planning, in accordance with the Watershed Protection and Flood Prevention Act approved August 4, 1954 (16 U.S.C. 1001–1009), $10,368,000: *Provided*, That this appropriation shall be available for employment pursuant to the second sentence of section 706(a) of the Organic Act of 1944 (7 U.S.C. 2225), and not to exceed $110,000 shall be available for employment under 5 U.S.C. 3109. *(7 U.S.C. 2201–02; 16 U.S.C. 1101–5; 33 U.S.C. 7016–11; Agriculture, Rural Development, Food and Drug Administration, and Related Agencies Appropriations Act, 2000.)*

Program and Financing (in millions of dollars)

Identification code 12–1066–0–1–301	1999 actual	2000 est.	2001 est.
Obligations by program activity:			
00.01 Direct program	10	10	10
09.01 Reimbursable program		1	1
10.00 Total new obligations	10	11	11
Budgetary resources available for obligation:			
22.00 New budget authority (gross)	10	11	11
23.95 Total new obligations	−10	−11	−11
New budget authority (gross), detail:			
Discretionary:			
40.00 Appropriation	10	10	10
68.00 Spending authority from offsetting collections: Offsetting collections (cash)		1	1
70.00 Total new budget authority (gross)	10	11	11
Change in unpaid obligations:			
72.40 Unpaid obligations, start of year: Obligated balance, start of year	2	1	1
73.10 Total new obligations	10	11	11
73.20 Total outlays (gross)	−11	−11	−11
74.40 Unpaid obligations, end of year: Obligated balance, end of year	1	1	1
Outlays (gross), detail:			
86.90 Outlays from new discretionary authority	9	10	10
86.93 Outlays from discretionary balances	2	1	1
87.00 Total outlays (gross)	11	11	11
Offsets:			
Against gross budget authority and outlays:			
88.40 Offsetting collections (cash) from: Non-Federal sources		−1	−1
Net budget authority and outlays:			
89.00 Budget authority	10	10	10
90.00 Outlays	11	10	10

Under the authorities of Public Law 83–566, watershed planning assistance is provided to States and communities to address specific resource problems on a watershed scale. The Watershed Surveys and Planning funds are used to cooperate with other agencies and the States in providing local decision makers with resource data, derived from Cooperative River Basin Surveys and Floodplain Management studies, for use in decision making. Leveraging program funds by cost-sharing with districts or States is strongly encouraged. Watershed plans are developed that provide alternatives to reduce the damage from floodwater, sediment, nonpoint source pollution, and erosion; conserve, develop, and use water resources; and conserve and properly use lands.

Funding provided to the Watershed Surveys and Planning program will be used to address one of the most critical strategic objectives of the USDA Government Performance and Results Act (GPRA) Strategic Plan: "Restoring healthy watersheds, providing clean and abundant water supplies for people and the environment." Program activities reflect high priority natural resource concerns such as: agriculture-induced water quality impacts, wetlands restoration, and flood damage risk reduction. All of these activities also support the Clean Water Act and the Safe Drinking Water Act.

In 2001, $2 million is proposed to provide technical assistance to communities for disaster mitigation planning.

Object Classification (in millions of dollars)

Identification code 12–1066–0–1–301	1999 actual	2000 est.	2001 est.
Direct obligations:			
11.1 Personnel compensation: Full-time permanent	6	6	6
12.1 Civilian personnel benefits	1	1	1
25.2 Other services	2	2	2
99.0 Subtotal, direct obligations	9	9	9
99.0 Reimbursable obligations		1	1
99.5 Below reporting threshold	1	1	1
99.9 Total new obligations	10	11	11

Personnel Summary

Identification code 12–1066–0–1–301	1999 actual	2000 est.	2001 est.
Direct:			
1001 Total compensable workyears: Full-time equivalent employment	113	110	105
Reimbursable:			
2001 Total compensable workyears: Full-time equivalent employment	9	13	13

WATERSHED AND FLOOD PREVENTION OPERATIONS

For necessary expenses to carry out preventive measures, including but not limited to research, engineering operations, methods of cultivation, the growing of vegetation, rehabilitation of existing works and changes in use of land, in accordance with the Watershed Protection and Flood Prevention Act approved August 4, 1954 (16 U.S.C. 1001–1005 and 1007–1009), the provisions of the Act of April 27, 1935 (16 U.S.C. 590a–f), and in accordance with the provisions of laws relating to the activities of the Department, [$99,443,000] *$83,423,000*, to remain available until expended (7 U.S.C. 2209b) (of which up to [$15,000,000] *$8,000,000* may be available for the watersheds authorized under the Flood Control Act approved June 22, 1936 (33 U.S.C. 701 and 16 U.S.C. 1006a)): *Provided*, That not to exceed [$47,000,000] *$44,423,000* of this appropriation shall be available for technical assistance: *Provided further*, That this appropriation shall be available for employment pursuant to the second sentence of section 706(a) of the Organic Act of 1944 (7 U.S.C. 2225), and not to exceed $200,000 shall be available for employment under 5 U.S.C. 3109: *Provided further*, That not to exceed $1,000,000 of this appropriation is available to carry out the purposes of the Endangered Species Act of 1973 (Public Law 93–205), including cooperative efforts as contemplated by that Act to relocate endangered or threatened species to other suitable habitats as may be necessary to expedite project construction: *Provided further*, That [of the funds available for Emergency Watershed Protection activities, $8,000,000 shall be available for Mississippi, New Mexico, Ohio, and Wisconsin for financial and technical assistance for pilot rehabilitation projects of small, upstream dams built under the Watershed and Flood Prevention Act (16 U.S.C. 1001 et seq., section 13 of the Act of December 22, 1994; Public Law 78–534; 58 Stat. 905), and the pilot watershed program authorized under the heading "FLOOD PREVENTION" of the Department of Agriculture Appropriation Act, 1954 (Public Law 83–156; 67 Stat. 214)] *up to $4,170,000 is for the costs of loans, as authorized by the Watershed Protection and Flood Prevention Act (16 U.S.C. 1006a), for rehabilitation of small, upstream dams built under the Watershed Protection and Flood Prevention Act (16 U.S.C. et seq.), section 13 of the Act of December 22, 1944 (Public Law 78–534, 58 Stat. 905), and the pilot watershed program authorized under the heading "Flood Prevention" of the Department of Agriculture Appropriations Act, 1954 (Public Law 83–156, 67 Stat. 214): Provided further, That such costs, including the cost of modifying such loans, shall be as defined in section 502 of the Congressional Budget Act of 1974: Provided further, That none of the costs for such rehabilitation activities (including any technical assistance costs such as planning, design, and engineering costs) shall be borne by the Department of Agriculture: Provided further, That the Department may provide* *technical assistance for such rehabilitation projects to the extent that the costs of such assistance shall be reimbursed by the borrower, and such reimbursements shall be deposited into the accounts that incurred such costs and shall be available until expended without further appropriation. In addition, for expenses necessary to administer the loans, such sums as may be necessary shall be transferred to and merged with the appropriation for "Rural Development, Salaries and Expenses". (7 U.S.C. 2201–02; 33 U.S.C. 701b–1, 701b–11; Agriculture, Rural Development, Food and Drug Administration, and Related Agencies Appropriations Act, 2000.)*

[For an additional amount for "Watershed and Flood Prevention Operations" to repair damages to the waterways and watersheds resulting from natural disasters, $80,000,000, to remain available until expended.] *(Miscellaneous Appropriations, 2000, as enacted by section 1000(a)(5) of the Consolidated Appropriations Act, 2000 (P.L. 106–113).)*

Program and Financing (in millions of dollars)

Identification code 12–1072–0–1–301		1999 actual	2000 est.	2001 est.
	Obligations by program activity:			
	Direct program:			
00.01	Watershed operations (P.L. 534)	15	8	8
00.02	Dam rehabilitation loans			4
00.03	Emergency watershed protection operations	153	152	
00.04	Small watershed operations (P.L. 566)	87	85	71
09.01	Reimbursable program	19	25	25
10.00	Total new obligations	274	270	108
	Budgetary resources available for obligation:			
21.40	Unobligated balance available, start of year	135	74	
22.00	New budget authority (gross)	213	196	108
23.90	Total budgetary resources available for obligation	348	270	108
23.95	Total new obligations	−274	−270	−108
24.40	Unobligated balance available, end of year	74		
	New budget authority (gross), detail:			
	Discretionary:			
40.00	Appropriation	99	99	83
40.15	Appropriation (emergency)	95	80	
40.76	Reduction pursuant to P.L. 106–113		−8	
43.00	Appropriation (total discretionary)	194	171	83
68.00	Spending authority from offsetting collections: Offsetting collections (cash)	19	25	25
70.00	Total new budget authority (gross)	213	196	108
	Change in unpaid obligations:			
72.40	Unpaid obligations, start of year: Obligated balance, start of year	185	233	228
73.10	Total new obligations	274	270	108
73.20	Total outlays (gross)	−227	−275	−222
74.40	Unpaid obligations, end of year: Obligated balance, end of year	233	228	114
	Outlays (gross), detail:			
86.90	Outlays from new discretionary authority	125	124	81
86.93	Outlays from discretionary balances	102	150	141
87.00	Total outlays (gross)	227	275	222
	Offsets:			
	Against gross budget authority and outlays:			
	Offsetting collections (cash) from:			
88.00	Federal sources	−8	−13	−11
88.40	Non-Federal sources	−11	−12	−14
88.90	Total, offsetting collections (cash)	−19	−25	−25
	Net budget authority and outlays:			
89.00	Budget authority	194	171	83
90.00	Outlays	208	250	197

Summary of Loan Levels, Subsidy Budget Authority and Outlays by Program (in millions of dollars)

Identification code 12–1072–0–1–301		1999 actual	2000 est.	2001 est.
	Direct loan levels supportable by subsidy budget authority:			
1150	Direct loan levels			60
1159	Total direct loan levels			60
	Direct loan subsidy (in percent):			
1320	Subsidy rate			6.95
1329	Weighted average subsidy rate			6.95
	Direct loan subsidy budget authority:			
1330	Subsidy budget authority			4
1339	Total subsidy budget authority			4
	Direct loan subsidy outlays:			
1340	Subsidy outlays			1
1349	Total subsidy outlays			1

These programs provide for cooperative actions between the Federal Government and States and their political subdivisions to reduce damage from floodwater, sediment, and erosion, for the conservation, development, utilization, and disposal of water, and for the conservation and proper utilization of land. Funds in Watershed and Flood Prevention Operations can be used for either flood prevention projects or flood damage rehabilitation efforts, depending upon the needs and opportunities. $3 million is proposed to provide technical and financial assistance to communities to implement disaster mitigation plans.

Watershed operations authorized by Public Law 534.—The Department cooperates with soil conservation districts and other local organizations in planning and installing flood prevention improvements in 11 watersheds authorized by the Flood Control Act of 1944. The Federal Government shares the cost of improvements for flood prevention, agricultural water management, recreation, and fish and wildlife development.

Within the 11 authorized projects, 395 subwatershed areas have been identified for planning purposes. Installation progress in these subwatersheds is as follows:

Emergency watershed protection operations.—This program authorizes the Secretary of Agriculture to undertake such emergency measures for runoff retardation and soil erosion prevention as may be needed to safeguard life and property from floods and the products of erosion on any watershed whenever natural elements or forces cause a sudden impairment of that watershed. An emergency is considered to exist when a watershed is suddenly impaired by flood, fire, wind, earthquake, or other natural causes and consequently life and property are endangered by floodwater, erosion, or sediment discharge. The emergency area need not be declared a national disaster area to be eligible for emergency watershed protection. Emergency watershed protection is applicable to small scale, localized disasters as well as large scale disasters. State environmental, natural resource, fish and game, and other agencies participate in planning and coordinating emergency work.

To improve the delivery and defensibility of the program, NRCS is currently drafting a programmatic environmental impact statement (EIS) to assess various program alternatives. Through the EIS public feedback and information gathering process, NRCS ultimately will be able to make the program more beneficial to communities and the environment.

Small watershed operations authorized by Public Law 566.—The Department provides technical and financial assistance to local organizations to install measures for watershed protection, flood prevention, agricultural water management, recreation, and fish and wildlife enhancement. Significant reforms were begun in 1997 to make this program environmentally beneficial, with higher investment returns to society.

WATERSHED AND FLOOD PREVENTION OPERATIONS—Continued

High priority P.L. 534 projects are eligible to compete for funding for P.L. 566 funding.

Watershed work plans are prepared by sponsoring local organizations with the Department's assistance or through State and local resources. After work plans are approved by the Department or Congress (projects where the estimated Federal contribution will exceed $5 million require congressional approval), financial assistance is provided for specific works of improvements. Since 1944, the Federal government has invested $8.5 billion to develop a watershed infrastructure through the Small Watershed program. This investment yields annual benefits estimated at $800 million.

Included in the funding level is $4 million in subsidy budget authority for a new $60 million loan program that will provide loans to State, local, and tribal governments to rehabilitate aging PL–534 and PL–566 watershed structures. Over the last 50 years, NRCS has constructed more than 10,000 dams through these programs. Many of these dams, which were built with a 50 year lifespan, have reached or nearly reached their life expectancy, and as they age may pose a safety risk to the communities that surround them. While NRCS bears no legal responsibility for maintaining these structures, the Administration wants to work with the communities to address this issue.

Loans through the Agricultural Credit Insurance Fund have been made in previous years to the local sponsors in order to fund the local cost of Public Law 566 or 534 projects. No funding for these loans is assumed in 2001.

The following tabulation shows the status of Public Law 566 projects:

MAIN WORKLOAD FACTORS

Status of operational projects:	1999 actual	2000 est.	2001 est.
Projects receiving land treatment	193	198	203
Structural projects	261	261	261
Land treatment and structural	62	62	62
Subtotal active projects	516	521	526
Projects continuing post-installation assistance	913	915	920
Inactive projects	18	18	18
Completed projects	36	38	40
Deauthorized projects	158	159	160
Total operational projects	1,641	1,651	1,664
New projects approved during year	11	10	13

Object Classification (in millions of dollars)

Identification code 12–1072–0–1–301	1999 actual	2000 est.	2001 est.
Direct obligations:			
Personnel compensation:			
11.1 Full-time permanent	41	40	25
11.3 Other than full-time permanent	1	1	
11.5 Other personnel compensation	1	1	1
11.9 Total personnel compensation	43	42	26
12.1 Civilian personnel benefits	10	9	6
21.0 Travel and transportation of persons	3	3	2
23.2 Rental payments to others	2	1	1
23.3 Communications, utilities, and miscellaneous charges	2	2	1
Other services:			
25.2 Other services	8	8	4
25.2 Other services	79	79	23
26.0 Supplies and materials	1	1	1
31.0 Equipment	4	4	2
32.0 Land and structures	34	26	
41.0 Grants, subsidies, and contributions	67	69	17
99.0 Subtotal, direct obligations	253	244	83
99.0 Reimbursable obligations	18	25	25
Allocation Account:			
11.1 Personnel compensation: Full-time permanent	1		
25.2 Other services	1		
99.0 Subtotal, allocation account	2		
99.5 Below reporting threshold		1	1
99.9 Total new obligations	274	270	108

Personnel Summary

Identification code 12–1072–0–1–301	1999 actual	2000 est.	2001 est.
Direct:			
1001 Total compensable workyears: Full-time equivalent employment	855	925	493
Reimbursable:			
2001 Total compensable workyears: Full-time equivalent employment	38	43	50

RESOURCE CONSERVATION AND DEVELOPMENT

For necessary expenses in planning and carrying out projects for resource conservation and development and for sound land use pursuant to the provisions of section 32(e) of title III of the Bankhead-Jones Farm Tenant Act (7 U.S.C. 1010–1011; 76 Stat. 607), the Act of April 27, 1935 (16 U.S.C. 590a–f), and the Agriculture and Food Act of 1981 (16 U.S.C. 3451–3461), [$35,265,000] *$36,265,000*, to remain available until expended (7 U.S.C. 2209b): *Provided*, That this appropriation shall be available for employment pursuant to the second sentence of section 706(a) of the Organic Act of 1944 (7 U.S.C. 2225), and not to exceed $50,000 shall be available for employment under 5 U.S.C. 3109. *(7 U.S.C. 2201–02; 33 U.S.C. 701b–11; Agriculture, Rural Development, Food and Drug Administration, and Related Agencies Appropriations Act, 2000.)*

Program and Financing (in millions of dollars)

Identification code 12–1010–0–1–302	1999 actual	2000 est.	2001 est.
Obligations by program activity:			
00.02 Technical assistance	35	35	36
09.01 Reimbursable program	1	1	1
10.00 Total new obligations	36	36	37
Budgetary resources available for obligation:			
21.40 Unobligated balance available, start of year	1	1	1
22.00 New budget authority (gross)	36	36	37
23.90 Total budgetary resources available for obligation	37	37	38
23.95 Total new obligations	−36	−36	−37
24.40 Unobligated balance available, end of year	1	1	1
New budget authority (gross), detail:			
Discretionary:			
40.00 Appropriation	35	35	36
68.00 Spending authority from offsetting collections: Offsetting collections (cash)	1	1	1
70.00 Total new budget authority (gross)	36	36	37
Change in unpaid obligations:			
72.40 Unpaid obligations, start of year: Obligated balance, start of year	9	10	11
73.10 Total new obligations	36	36	37
73.20 Total outlays (gross)	−35	−35	−37
74.40 Unpaid obligations, end of year: Obligated balance, end of year	10	11	11
Outlays (gross), detail:			
86.90 Outlays from new discretionary authority	33	33	33
86.93 Outlays from discretionary balances	4	1	3
87.00 Total outlays (gross)	35	35	37
Offsets:			
Against gross budget authority and outlays:			
88.40 Offsetting collections (cash) from: Non-Federal sources	−1	−1	−1
Net budget authority and outlays:			
89.00 Budget authority	35	35	36
90.00 Outlays	35	34	36

Under this program, the Department assists States, local units of government, groups and individuals in developing area plans for resource conservation and development (RC and D).

Designated RC and D areas are provided technical assistance to help States and local units of government prepare plans for resource development and economic improvement and to plan and install community-related conservation projects. Financial contributions, loans, and other Federal assistance may be used to help carry out projects specified in RC and D area plans. Program financial resources are focused on the RC and D coordinators who assist the local area councils. These coordinators help the area councils develop plans and proposals to compete for financial assistance from other Federal, State and private sources.

The following tabulation shows the status of RC and D areas authorized to receive technical and financial assistance.

MAIN WORKLOAD FACTORS

	1999 actual	*2000 est.*	*2001 est.*
Areas authorized at beginning of year	315	315	315
Areas authorized at end of year	315	315	315
Project plans adopted	3,100	3,100	3,100
Projects completed	2,800	2,800	2,800

Object Classification (in millions of dollars)

Identification code 12–1010–0–1–302	1999 actual	2000 est.	2001 est.
Direct obligations:			
Personnel compensation:			
11.1 Full-time permanent	19	20	21
11.3 Other than full-time permanent	1		
11.9 Total personnel compensation	20	20	21
12.1 Civilian personnel benefits	4	4	4
21.0 Travel and transportation of persons	1	1	1
23.2 Rental payments to others	1	1	1
23.3 Communications, utilities, and miscellaneous charges	1	1	1
25.2 Other services	6	6	6
26.0 Supplies and materials	1	1	1
31.0 Equipment	1	1	1
99.0 Subtotal, direct obligations	35	35	36
99.0 Reimbursable obligations	1	1	1
99.9 Total new obligations	36	36	37

Personnel Summary

Identification code 12–1010–0–1–302	1999 actual	2000 est.	2001 est.
Direct:			
1001 Total compensable workyears: Full-time equivalent employment	390	388	376
Reimbursable:			
2001 Total compensable workyears: Full-time equivalent employment	9	9	9

GREAT PLAINS CONSERVATION PROGRAM

Program and Financing (in millions of dollars)

Identification code 12–2268–0–1–302	1999 actual	2000 est.	2001 est.
Budgetary resources available for obligation:			
21.40 Unobligated balance available, start of year	2	3	3
22.10 Resources available from recoveries of prior year obligations	1		
23.90 Total budgetary resources available for obligation	3	3	3
24.40 Unobligated balance available, end of year	3	3	3
Change in unpaid obligations:			
72.40 Unpaid obligations, start of year: Obligated balance, start of year	11	9	6
73.20 Total outlays (gross)	–2	–3	–3
73.45 Adjustments in unexpired accounts	–1		
74.40 Unpaid obligations, end of year: Obligated balance, end of year	9	6	3
Outlays (gross), detail:			
86.93 Outlays from discretionary balances	2	3	3
Net budget authority and outlays:			
89.00 Budget authority			
90.00 Outlays	2	3	3

The 1996 Farm Bill combined the authority for this and several other conservation programs into the Environmental Quality Incentives Program. Prior-year account balances are maintained in this account until expended.

This program provides cost-share assistance to participating landowners or operators in the Great Plains area in the development and installation of long-term conservation plans and practices for their land under contracts entered into in prior years. It is a voluntary program in 556 designated counties of 10 Great Plains States. Contracts with individual landowners range in time from 3 to 10 years.

MAIN WORKLOAD FACTORS

	1999 actual	*2000 est.*	*2001 est.*
Program participants:			
Number of contracts serviced during year	3,970	2,294	1,600
Number of acres under contracts	7,415,989	4,285,200	2,988,800

As of October 1, 1999, there were 2,294 active contracts on hand. Co-landowners or operators finance the entire cost of installing recurring management-type practices and pay a specified part of the cost-shared practices installed on their land. Program regulations provide that cost-share rates offered in any contract shall not exceed 80 percent of the cost of installing eligible practices within the designated county. There is a cost-sharing limitation of $35 thousand for any contract.

[FORESTRY INCENTIVES PROGRAM]

[For necessary expenses, not otherwise provided for, to carry out the program of forestry incentives, as authorized by the Cooperative Forestry Assistance Act of 1978 (16 U.S.C. 2101), including technical assistance and related expenses, $6,325,000, to remain available until expended, as authorized by that Act.] *(Agriculture, Rural Development, Food and Drug Administration, and Related Agencies Appropriations Act, 2000.)*

Program and Financing (in millions of dollars)

Identification code 12–3336–0–1–302	1999 actual	2000 est.	2001 est.
Obligations by program activity:			
10.00 Total new obligations (object class 41.0)	11	11	
Budgetary resources available for obligation:			
21.40 Unobligated balance available, start of year		5	
22.00 New budget authority (gross)	16	6	
23.90 Total budgetary resources available for obligation	16	11	
23.95 Total new obligations	–11	–11	
24.40 Unobligated balance available, end of year	5		
New budget authority (gross), detail:			
Discretionary:			
40.00 Appropriation	16	6	
40.76 Reduction pursuant to P.L. 106–113		–1	
43.00 Appropriation (total discretionary)	16	5	
Change in unpaid obligations:			
72.40 Unpaid obligations, start of year: Obligated balance, start of year	12	18	16
73.10 Total new obligations	11	11	
73.20 Total outlays (gross)	–6	–12	–7
74.40 Unpaid obligations, end of year: Obligated balance, end of year	18	16	9
Outlays (gross), detail:			
86.90 Outlays from new discretionary authority	2	2	
86.93 Outlays from discretionary balances	4	9	9
87.00 Total outlays (gross)	6	12	7

[FORESTRY INCENTIVES PROGRAM]—Continued

Program and Financing (in millions of dollars)—Continued

Identification code 12–3336–0–1–302	1999 actual	2000 est.	2001 est.
Net budget authority and outlays:			
89.00 Budget authority	16	6	....
90.00 Outlays	6	12	7

No funds are proposed for the Forestry Incentives Program (FIP). The FIP was authorized by the Cooperative Forestry Assistance Act of 1978 (16 U.S.C. 2101). The objectives of the program are to bring private, nonindustrial forest land under improved management, to increase timber production, to ensure adequate supplies of timber products, and to enhance other forest resources. Activities in this program are redundant with, and more effectively served through, assistance provided by the Forest Service.

FIP shares up to 65 percent of the cost of tree planting and timber stand improvement. The percentage cost-shared depends on the rate set in a particular State and county by NRCS, after consulting with the State forester. The program is available in designated counties based on a Forest Service survey of total eligible private timberland available for production of timber products. Technical assistance is provided by Forest Service.

The 1999, program provided funding for 82,172 acres of tree planting, and 19,832 acres in timber stand improvements, and 4,505 acres targeted towards special forestry and site preparation.

WATER BANK PROGRAM

Program and Financing (in millions of dollars)

Identification code 12–3320–0–1–302	1999 actual	2000 est.	2001 est.
Budgetary resources available for obligation:			
21.40 Unobligated balance available, start of year	1	1	1
24.40 Unobligated balance available, end of year	1	1	1
Change in unpaid obligations:			
72.40 Unpaid obligations, start of year: Obligated balance, start of year	22	16	10
73.20 Total outlays (gross)	−6	−6	−6
74.40 Unpaid obligations, end of year: Obligated balance, end of year	16	10	4
Outlays (gross), detail:			
86.93 Outlays from discretionary balances	6	6	6
Net budget authority and outlays:			
89.00 Budget authority	....	....	....
90.00 Outlays	6	6	6

The objectives of the Water Bank Program are to conserve water; preserve, maintain, and improve the Nation's wetlands; increase waterfowl habitat in migratory waterfowl nesting, breeding, and feeding areas in the United States; and secure recreational and environmental benefits for the Nation. The program was authorized by the Water Bank Act of 1970, as amended by Public Law 96–182, approved January 2, 1980. The Water Bank Extension Act of 1994 extends for one year 1985 agreements entered into under the Water Bank Act of 1970, and due to expire on December 31, 1995. Funding for the expiring 1985 Water Bank agreements were transferred from the Wetlands Reserve Program 1995 appropriation to this account as authorized under the Water Bank Extension Act of 1994. Congress did not provide funding for this account in 2000. For 2001, USDA does not request program funding.

Under the Water Bank Program, the Secretary of Agriculture, through designated county offices, uses program funds to enter into 10-year agreements with landowners and operators for the conservation of specified wetlands. Provisions exist to renew agreements for additional periods, to make annual payments on agreements, and under certain conditions to increase payment rates in the fifth year of a contract or at the time of renewal. During the period of the agreement, the landowner agrees not to drain, burn, fill, or otherwise destroy the wetland character of such areas.

COLORADO RIVER BASIN SALINITY CONTROL PROGRAM

Program and Financing (in millions of dollars)

Identification code 12–3318–0–1–304	1999 actual	2000 est.	2001 est.
Budgetary resources available for obligation:			
21.40 Unobligated balance available, start of year	1	1	1
24.40 Unobligated balance available, end of year	1	1	1
Change in unpaid obligations:			
72.40 Unpaid obligations, start of year: Obligated balance, start of year	3	2	1
73.20 Total outlays (gross)	−1	−1	−1
74.40 Unpaid obligations, end of year: Obligated balance, end of year	2	1	....
Outlays (gross), detail:			
86.93 Outlays from discretionary balances	1	1	1
Net budget authority and outlays:			
89.00 Budget authority	....	....	....
90.00 Outlays	1	1	1

The Colorado River Basin Salinity Control Program (CRBSC), was authorized under section 202(c) of Title II of the Colorado River Basin Salinity Control Act, as amended by section 334, subtitle D, Title III of the Federal Agriculture Improvement Act of 1996. The FAIR Act, combined authority of the Agricultural Conservation Program (ACP), Water Quality Incentive Program (WQIP), Great Plains Conservation Program (GPCP), and the Colorado River Basin Salinity Control Program (CRBSC), into the Environmental Quality Incentive Program (EQIP). The FAIR Act also repealed CRBSC authority, while maintaining program account balances until expended.

Beginning in 1996, EQIP was implemented on an interim program level for CRBSC. Program funding in 1999 provided cost-share assistance to landowners and others in the Colorado River Basin States to include: Colorado, Utah and Wyoming. The program's main objective is to enhance the supply and quality of water in the Colorado River for delivery to downstream users in the U.S. and Mexico.

WETLANDS RESERVE PROGRAM

Program and Financing (in millions of dollars)

Identification code 12–1080–0–1–302	1999 actual	2000 est.	2001 est.
Obligations by program activity:			
00.03 Technical assistance	2	3	....
00.04 Easement overhead costs	1	....	....
10.00 Total new obligations	3	3	....
Budgetary resources available for obligation:			
21.40 Unobligated balance available, start of year	6	3	....
23.95 Total new obligations	−3	−3	....
24.40 Unobligated balance available, end of year	3	....	....
Change in unpaid obligations:			
72.40 Unpaid obligations, start of year: Obligated balance, start of year	25	14	8
73.10 Total new obligations	3	3	....
73.20 Total outlays (gross)	−14	−9	−8

74.40 Unpaid obligations, end of year: Obligated balance, end of year	14	8	
Outlays (gross), detail:			
86.98 Outlays from mandatory balances	14	9	8
Net budget authority and outlays:			
89.00 Budget authority			
90.00 Outlays	14	9	8

The Wetlands Reserve Program (WRP) is authorized by Section 1237 of the Food Security Act of 1985 (P.L. 99–198), as amended by the Food, Agriculture, Conservation and Trade Act of 1990 (P.L. 101–624), the Omnibus Budget Reconciliation Act of 1993 (P.L. 103–66), the Federal Agriculture Improvement and Reform Act of 1996 (P.L. 104–127). WRP is a mandatory Commodity Credit Corporation (CCC) program administered by the Natural Resources Conservation Service (NRCS). However, the Farm Service Agency (FSA), with CCC financial responsibility, handles program payments and financial reporting.

Information displayed in this section represents unobligated balances from the non-CCC account in which WRP was funded prior to the 1996 Farm Bill. All remaining unobligated balances are expected to be obligated in 2000. For additional information on WRP, see the Commodity Credit Corporation section.

Object Classification (in millions of dollars)

Identification code 12–1080–0–1–302	1999 actual	2000 est.	2001 est.
11.1 Personnel compensation: Full-time permanent	2	2	
12.1 Civilian personnel benefits	1	1	
99.9 Total new obligations	3	3	

Personnel Summary

Identification code 12–1080–0–1–302	1999 actual	2000 est.	2001 est.
1001 Total compensable workyears: Full-time equivalent employment	37	27	

WILDLIFE HABITAT INCENTIVES PROGRAM

Program and Financing (in millions of dollars)

Identification code 12–3322–0–1–302	1999 actual	2000 est.	2001 est.
Obligations by program activity:			
10.00 Total new obligations	22	2	
Budgetary resources available for obligation:			
21.40 Unobligated balance available, start of year	4	2	
22.22 Unobligated balance transferred from other accounts	20		
23.90 Total budgetary resources available for obligation	24	2	
23.95 Total new obligations	−22	−2	
24.40 Unobligated balance available, end of year	2		
Change in unpaid obligations:			
72.40 Unpaid obligations, start of year: Obligated balance, start of year	22	33	26
73.10 Total new obligations	22	2	
73.20 Total outlays (gross)	−11	−9	−7
74.40 Unpaid obligations, end of year: Obligated balance, end of year	33	26	19
Outlays (gross), detail:			
86.98 Outlays from mandatory balances	11	9	7
Net budget authority and outlays:			
89.00 Budget authority			
90.00 Outlays	11	10	7

The Wildlife Habitat Incentives Program (WHIP) is a voluntary program to support and encourage landowners through technical assistance and cost share payments to develop and improve fish and wildlife habitat on private lands. The 1996 Federal Agriculture Improvement and Reform Act made available a total of $50 million for WHIP from the Commodity Credit Corporation for the years 1996–2002. These funds were exhausted in 1999. The conservation initiative portion of the Budget's farm safety net proposal includes $50 million in annual direct spending for WHIP.

NRCS and the participant enter into a cost-share agreement for wildlife habitat development. This agreement generally lasts from 5 to 10 years from the date the agreement is signed. WHIP funds are distributed to states based on state wildlife habitat priorities which may include: wildlife habitat areas; targeted species and their habitats; and specific practices. Partnerships with other entities are preferred: WHIP may be implemented in cooperation with other Federal, State, or local agencies, conservation districts, or private conservation groups. State priorities are developed through a locally led process to identify wildlife resource needs and are finalized in consultation with the State Technical Committee.

Object Classification (in millions of dollars)

Identification code 12–3322–0–1–302	1999 actual	2000 est.	2001 est.
11.1 Personnel compensation: Full-time permanent	3		
12.1 Civilian personnel benefits	1		
41.0 Grants, subsidies, and contributions	18	2	
99.9 Total new obligations	22	2	

Personnel Summary

Identification code 12–3322–0–1–302	1999 actual	2000 est.	2001 est.
1001 Total compensable workyears: Full-time equivalent employment	65		

WILDLIFE HABITAT INCENTIVES PROGRAM

(Legislative proposal, subject to PAYGO)

Legislation will be proposed to transfer $50 million annually from the Commodity Credit Corporation to finance the program. This proposal is not reflected in the database due to an error. However, 2001 outlays would be $13 million, and 111 FTEs would be funded through this increase.

RURAL CLEAN WATER PROGRAM

Program and Financing (in millions of dollars)

Identification code 12–3337–0–1–304	1999 actual	2000 est.	2001 est.
Budgetary resources available for obligation:			
21.40 Unobligated balance available, start of year	3	5	5
22.10 Resources available from recoveries of prior year obligations	2		
23.90 Total budgetary resources available for obligation	5	5	5
24.40 Unobligated balance available, end of year	5	5	5
Change in unpaid obligations:			
72.40 Unpaid obligations, start of year: Obligated balance, start of year	2	2	2
73.45 Adjustments in unexpired accounts	−2		
74.40 Unpaid obligations, end of year: Obligated balance, end of year	2	2	2
Net budget authority and outlays:			
89.00 Budget authority			
90.00 Outlays			

This experimental Rural Clean Water Program, authorized by Public Law 96–108 and Public Law 96–528, was a cooperative endeavor among farmers, various USDA agencies, and

RURAL CLEAN WATER PROGRAM—Continued

other organizations to develop and test means of controlling agricultural nonpoint source water pollution in rural areas.

Recommended project areas were developed by local and State committees and approved by the Secretary of Agriculture in consultation with the Administrator of the Environmental Protection Agency. Full funding was provided in previous appropriations for all approved projects. The implementation period for all projects has ended, and no additional obligations will be incurred. The final payment is expected to be made in 2000. Similar activities will be carried out through the mandatory Environmental Quality Incentives Program.

Credit accounts:

AGRICULTURAL RESOURCE CONSERVATION DEMONSTRATION GUARANTEED LOAN FINANCING ACCOUNT

Program and Financing (in millions of dollars)

Identification code 12–4177–0–3–351	1999 actual	2000 est.	2001 est.
Obligations by program activity:			
00.01 interest assistance on guaranteed loans	1	1	1
10.00 Total new obligations	1	1	1
Budgetary resources available for obligation:			
21.40 Unobligated balance available, start of year	3	2	1
23.95 Total new obligations	−1	−1	−1
24.40 Unobligated balance available, end of year	2	1	1
Change in unpaid obligations:			
73.10 Total new obligations	1	1	1
73.20 Total financing disbursements (gross)	−1	−1	−1
87.00 Total financing disbursements (gross)	1	1	1
Net financing authority and financing disbursements:			
89.00 Financing authority	....	....	....
90.00 Financing disbursements	1	1	1

Status of Guaranteed Loans (in millions of dollars)

Identification code 12–4177–0–3–351	1999 actual	2000 est.	2001 est.
Position with respect to appropriations act limitation on commitments:			
2111 Limitation on guaranteed loans made by private lenders	....	....	....
2150 Total guaranteed loan commitments	....	....	....
Cumulative balance of guaranteed loans outstanding:			
2210 Outstanding, start of year	24	24	24
2251 Repayments and prepayments	....	....	....
2290 Outstanding, end of year	24	24	24
Memorandum:			
2299 Guaranteed amount of guaranteed loans outstanding, end of year	24	24	24

This program, also known as "Farms for the Future," provides guarantees and interest assistance on loans made to State trust funds, who in turn finance acquisitions to preserve farmland in selected states. No guarantees have been made since 1993.

As required by the Federal Credit Reform Act of 1990, this non-budgetary account records all cash flows to and from the Government resulting from guaranteed loans committed in 1992 and beyond. The amounts in this account are a means of financing and are not included in the budget totals.

Balance Sheet (in millions of dollars)

Identification code 12–4177–0–3–351	1998 actual	1999 actual	2000 est.	2001 est.
ASSETS:				
1101 Federal assets: Fund balances with Treasury	5	3	3	3
1999 Total assets	5	3	3	3

WATERSHED AND FLOOD PREVENTION OPERATIONS DIRECT LOAN FINANCING ACCOUNT

Program and Financing (in millions of dollars)

Identification code 12–4083–0–3–301	1999 actual	2000 est.	2001 est.
Obligations by program activity:			
00.01 Direct loan obligations	....	....	60
10.00 Total new obligations	....	....	60
Budgetary resources available for obligation:			
22.00 New financing authority (gross)	....	....	61
23.95 Total new obligations	....	....	−60
New financing authority (gross), detail:			
Mandatory:			
67.15 Authority to borrow (indefinite)	....	....	60
Discretionary:			
68.00 Spending authority from offsetting collections: Offsetting collections (cash)	....	....	1
70.00 Total new financing authority (gross)	....	....	61
Change in unpaid obligations:			
73.10 Total new obligations	....	....	60
73.20 Total financing disbursements (gross)	....	....	−7
74.40 Unpaid obligations, end of year: Obligated balance, end of year	....	....	53
87.00 Total financing disbursements (gross)	....	....	7
Offsets:			
Against gross financing authority and financing disbursements:			
88.00 Offsetting collections (cash) from: Payments from program account	....	....	−1
Net financing authority and financing disbursements:			
89.00 Financing authority	....	....	60
90.00 Financing disbursements	....	....	6

Status of Direct Loans (in millions of dollars)

Identification code 12–4083–0–3–301	1999 actual	2000 est.	2001 est.
Position with respect to appropriations act limitation on obligations:			
1111 Limitation on direct loans	....	....	....
1131 Direct loan obligations exempt from limitation	....	....	60
1150 Total direct loan obligations	....	....	60
Cumulative balance of direct loans outstanding:			
1210 Outstanding, start of year	....	....	....
1231 Disbursements: Direct loan disbursements	....	....	7
1290 Outstanding, end of year	....	....	7

As required by the Federal Credit Reform Act of 1990, this non-budgetary account records all cash flows to and from the Government resulting from direct loans obligated in 1992 and beyond (including modifications of direct loans that resulted from obligations in any year). The amounts in this account are a means of financing and are not included in the budget totals.

Balance Sheet (in millions of dollars)

Identification code 12–4083–0–3–301	1998 actual	1999 actual	2000 est.	2001 est.
ASSETS:				
1101 Federal assets: Fund balances with Treasury				56
Net value of assets related to post-1991 direct loans receivable:				
1401 Direct loans receivable, gross				7
1405 Allowance for subsidy cost (–)				–56
1499 Net present value of assets related to direct loans				–49
1999 Total assets				7
LIABILITIES:				
2104 Federal liabilities: Resources payable to Treasury				56
2999 Total liabilities				56
4999 Total liabilities and net position				56

Trust Funds

Miscellaneous Contributed Funds

Unavailable Collections (in millions of dollars)

Identification code 12–8210–0–7–302	1999 actual	2000 est.	2001 est.
Balance, start of year:			
01.99 Balance, start of year	2	3	4
Receipts:			
02.01 Miscellaneous contributed funds	5	1	1
04.00 Total: Balances and collections	7	4	5
Appropriation:			
05.01 Miscellaneous contributed funds, Natural Resources Conservation Service	–4		
07.99 Total balance, end of year	3	4	5

Program and Financing (in millions of dollars)

Identification code 12–8210–0–7–302	1999 actual	2000 est.	2001 est.
Obligations by program activity:			
10.00 Total new obligations (object class 25.2)	22	1	
Budgetary resources available for obligation:			
21.40 Unobligated balance available, start of year	19	1	
22.00 New budget authority (gross)	4		
23.90 Total budgetary resources available for obligation	23	1	
23.95 Total new obligations	–22	–1	
24.40 Unobligated balance available, end of year	1		
New budget authority (gross), detail:			
Mandatory:			
60.27 Appropriation (trust fund, indefinite)	4		
Change in unpaid obligations:			
72.40 Unpaid obligations, start of year: Obligated balance, start of year	1	21	18
73.10 Total new obligations	22	1	
73.20 Total outlays (gross)	–2	–4	–4
74.40 Unpaid obligations, end of year: Obligated balance, end of year	21	18	14
Outlays (gross), detail:			
86.98 Outlays from mandatory balances	2	4	4
Net budget authority and outlays:			
89.00 Budget authority	4		
90.00 Outlays	2	4	4

Funds received from State and local organizations, and others are available for work under cooperative agreements for soil survey, watershed protection, and resource conservation and development activities.

Personnel Summary

Identification code 12–8210–0–7–302	1999 actual	2000 est.	2001 est.
1001 Total compensable workyears: Full-time equivalent employment	4	1	1

RURAL DEVELOPMENT

Federal Funds

General and special funds:

[Salaries and Expenses]

[For necessary expenses of the Rural Housing Service, including administering the programs authorized by the Consolidated Farm and Rural Development Act, title V of the Housing Act of 1949, and cooperative agreements, $61,979,000: *Provided*, That this appropriation shall be available for employment pursuant to the second sentence of section 706(a) of the Organic Act of 1944 (7 U.S.C. 2225), and not to exceed $520,000 may be used for employment under 5 U.S.C. 3109: *Provided further*, That the Administrator may expend not more than $10,000 to provide modest nonmonetary awards to non-USDA employees.]

[Salaries and Expenses]

[For necessary expenses of the Rural Business-Cooperative Service, including administering the programs authorized by the Consolidated Farm and Rural Development Act; section 1323 of the Food Security Act of 1985; the Cooperative Marketing Act of 1926; for activities relating to the marketing aspects of cooperatives, including economic research findings, as authorized by the Agricultural Marketing Act of 1946; for activities with institutions concerning the development and operation of agricultural cooperatives; and for cooperative agreements, $24,612,000: *Provided*, That this appropriation shall be available for employment pursuant to the second sentence of section 706(a) of the Organic Act of 1944 (7 U.S.C. 2225), and not to exceed $260,000 may be used for employment under 5 U.S.C. 3109.]

[Salaries and Expenses]

[For necessary expenses of the Rural Utilities Service, including administering the programs authorized by the Rural Electrification Act of 1936, and the Consolidated Farm and Rural Development Act, and for cooperative agreements, $34,107,000: *Provided*, That this appropriation shall be available for employment pursuant to the second sentence of section 706(a) of the Organic Act of 1944 (7 U.S.C. 2225), and not to exceed $105,000 may be used for employment under 5 U.S.C. 3109.]

Salaries and Expenses

For necessary expenses of administering Rural Development programs authorized by the Rural Electrification Act of 1936; the Consolidated Farm and Rural Development Act; title V of the Housing Act of 1949: section 1323 of the Food Security Act of 1985; the Cooperative Marketing Act of 1926; for activities related to marketing aspects of cooperatives, including economic research findings, authorized by the Agricultural Marketing Act of 1946; for activities with institutions concerning the development and operation of agricultural cooperatives: $130,371,000: Provided. That this appropriation shall be available for employment pursuant to the second sentence of section 706(a) of the Organic Act of 1944 (7 U.S.C. 2225), and not to exceed $1,000,000 may be used for employment under 5 U.S.C. 3109: Provided further, That not more than $10,000 may be expended to provide modest nonmonetary awards to non-USDA employees: Provided further, That any balances available for the Rural Utilities Service, Rural Housing Service, and the Rural Business-Cooperative Service salaries and expenses accounts shall be transferred to and merged with this account. (Agriculture, Rural Development, Food and Drug Administration, and Related Agencies Appropriations Act, 2000.)

Program and Financing (in millions of dollars)

Identification code 12–0403–0–1–452	1999 actual	2000 est.	2001 est.
Obligations by program activity:			
00.01 Direct program	117	120	130
09.01 Reimbursable program	470	483	469
10.00 Total new obligations	587	603	599

General and special funds—Continued

SALARIES AND EXPENSES—Continued

Program and Financing (in millions of dollars)—Continued

Identification code 12–0403–0–1–452	1999 actual	2000 est.	2001 est.
Budgetary resources available for obligation:			
22.00 New budget authority (gross)	590	603	599
23.95 Total new obligations	−587	−603	−599
23.98 Unobligated balance expiring or withdrawn	−2		
New budget authority (gross), detail:			
Discretionary:			
40.00 Appropriation	120	120	130
68.00 Spending authority from offsetting collections: Offsetting collections (cash)	470	483	469
70.00 Total new budget authority (gross)	590	603	599
Change in unpaid obligations:			
72.40 Unpaid obligations, start of year: Obligated balance, start of year	110	123	121
73.10 Total new obligations	587	603	599
73.20 Total outlays (gross)	−580	−605	−599
73.40 Adjustments in expired accounts (net)	6		
74.40 Unpaid obligations, end of year: Obligated balance, end of year	123	121	121
Outlays (gross), detail:			
86.90 Outlays from new discretionary authority	494	507	503
86.93 Outlays from discretionary balances	86	98	96
87.00 Total outlays (gross)	580	605	599
Offsets:			
Against gross budget authority and outlays:			
88.00 Offsetting collections (cash) from: Federal sources	−470	−483	−469
Net budget authority and outlays:			
89.00 Budget authority	120	120	130
90.00 Outlays	109	122	130

In 2001, a new consolidated Salaries and Expenses account is being established to administer all Rural Development programs, including the Rural Utilities Service (RUS), the Rural Housing Service (RHS), and the Rural Business-Cooperative Service (RBS). This change will result in a more simplified and manageable administration of Salaries and Expenses funds and activities for the Rural Development mission area. The separate Salaries and Expenses accounts for RUS, RHS, and RBS will be deleted and any obligated and unobligated balances available from prior years will be transferred to and merged with the Rural Development account.

The program functions of the Rural Development agencies will not be affected by this administrative change. The three agencies, which were all formed as a result of the Secretary's 1995 reorganization plan, will continue to provide outreach and deliver their programs to rural customers.

RUS provides grants, direct loans and loan guarantees to suppliers of electric, telecommunications (for general purpose and for distance learning/telemedicine), and water and wastewater services in rural areas. Through the water and wastewater program, RUS also provides technical assistance. The programs are administered in Washington, DC. The Rural Development field office staff performs the services related to the water and wastewater grant and loan programs. For the electric and telecommunication loans, general field representatives visit borrowers periodically and maintain liaisons between the borrowers and headquarters.

RHS was formed from the Rural Housing section of the Farmers Home Administration and the Community Facilities Division of the Rural Development Administration. RHS delivers rural housing and community facility programs through a system of State, area, and local offices. In 1997, the Dedicated Loan Origination and Servicing System (DLOS) was implemented to centralize and streamline the servicing activities of the agency. This innovation reduced the cost of operating the individual housing loan programs.

RBS includes programs from the former Rural Development Administration, rural development programs form the former Rural Electrification Administration, and the Agricultural Cooperative Service. This agency delivers loan and grant programs, as well as technical assistance, to cooperatives and rural businesses.

Object Classification (in millions of dollars)

Identification code 12–0403–0–1–452	1999 actual	2000 est.	2001 est.
Direct obligations:			
Personnel compensation:			
11.1 Full-time permanent	68	65	76
11.3 Other than full-time permanent	3	1	2
11.5 Other personnel compensation		1	1
11.9 Total personnel compensation	71	67	79
12.1 Civilian personnel benefits	15	15	17
21.0 Travel and transportation of persons	4	3	3
23.2 Rental payments to others	4	7	5
23.3 Communications, utilities, and miscellaneous charges	5	8	6
25.2 Other services	11	7	10
25.3 Purchases of goods and services from Government accounts	4	8	6
25.7 Operation and maintenance of equipment	1	2	2
26.0 Supplies and materials	1	1	1
31.0 Equipment	1	2	1
99.0 Subtotal, direct obligations	117	120	130
99.0 Reimbursable obligations	470	483	469
99.9 Total new obligations	587	603	599

Personnel Summary

Identification code 12–0403–0–1–452	1999 actual	2000 est.	2001 est.
Direct:			
1001 Total compensable workyears: Full-time equivalent employment	1,424	1,555	1,575
Reimbursable:			
2001 Total compensable workyears: Full-time equivalent employment	5,529	5,345	5,445

RURAL COMMUNITY ADVANCEMENT PROGRAM

(INCLUDING TRANSFERS OF FUNDS)

For the cost of direct loans, loan guarantees, and grants, as authorized by 7 U.S.C. 1926, 1926a, 1926c, 1926d, and 1932, except for sections 381E[–H], *381G, 381H*, 381N, and 381O of the Consolidated Farm and Rural Development Act (7 U.S.C. 2009f), [$718,837,000] *$762,542,000*, to remain available until expended, of which [$23,150,000] *$53,225,000* shall be for rural community programs described in section 381E(d)(1) of such Act; of which [$631,088,000] *$647,618,000* shall be for the rural utilities programs described in [section] *sections* 381E(d)(2), 306C(a)(2), and 306D of such Act; and of which [$64,599,000] *$61,699,000* shall be for the rural business and cooperative development programs described in [section] *sections,* 381E(d)(3) *and 310B(f)* of such Act[;]*: Provided, that of the total amount appropriated in this account, $24,000,000 shall be for loans and grants to benefit Federally Recognized Native American Tribes*: *Provided further*, That of the amount appropriated for rural community programs, $6,000,000 shall be available for a Rural Community Development Initiative: *Provided further*, That such funds shall be used solely to develop the capacity and ability of private, nonprofit community-based housing and community development organizations, and low-income rural communities to undertake projects to improve housing, community facilities, community and economic development projects in rural areas: *Provided further*, That such funds shall be made available to qualified private and public (including tribal) intermediary organizations proposing to carry out a program of technical assistance: *Provided further*, That such intermediary organizations shall provide matching funds from other sources in an amount not less than funds provided: *Provided further, That of the amount appropriated for rural community programs not to exceed $5,000,000 shall be for hazardous weather early warning* *systems: Provided further*, That of the amount appropriated for the rural business and cooperative development programs, not to exceed $500,000 shall be made available for a grant to a qualified national organization to provide technical assistance for rural transportation in order to promote economic development; *$5,000,000 shall be for Rural partnership technical assistance grants; $2,000,000 shall be for grants to Mississippi Delta Region Counties; and not to exceed $2,000,000 may be for loans to firms that market and process bio-based products: Provided further*, That of the amount appropriated for rural utilities programs, not to exceed $20,000,000 shall be for water and waste disposal systems to benefit the Colonias along the United States/Mexico borders, including grants pursuant to section 306C of such Act; [not to exceed $12,000,000 shall be for water and waste disposal systems to benefit Federally Recognized Native American Tribes, including grants pursuant to section 306C of such Act: *Provided further*, That the Federally Recognized Native American Tribe is not eligible for any other rural utilities programs set aside under the Rural Community Advancement Program;] not to exceed $20,000,000 shall be for water and waste disposal systems for rural and native villages in Alaska pursuant to section 306D of such Act [with up to], *of which* one percent [available] *may be transferred to and merged with "Rural Development, Salaries and expenses"* to administer the program [and up to one percent available to improve interagency coordination]; not to exceed $16,215,000 shall be for technical assistance grants for rural waste systems pursuant to section 306(a)(14) of such Act; and not to exceed $7,300,000 shall be for contracting with qualified national organizations for a circuit rider program to provide technical assistance for rural water systems: *Provided further*, That of the total amount appropriated, not to exceed [$45,245,000] *$42,574,650* shall be available through June 30, [2000] *2001*, for authorized empowerment zones and enterprise communities [and communities designated by the Secretary of Agriculture as Rural Economic Area Partnership Zones]; of which [$34,704,000] *$30,000,000* shall be for the rural utilities programs described in section 381E(d)(2) of such Act; *and* of which [$8,435,000] *$9,113,400* shall be for the rural business and cooperative development programs described in section 381E(d)(3) of such Act[: *Provided further*, That any obligated and unobligated balances available from prior years for the "Rural Utilities Assistance Program" account shall be transferred to and merged with this account]. *(Agriculture, Rural Development, Food and Drug Administration, and Related Agencies Appropriations Act, 2000.)*

General Fund Credit Receipt Accounts (in millions of dollars)

Identification code 12–0400–0–1–452	1999 actual	2000 est.	2001 est.
0102 Rural business and industry, negative subsidies and downward reestimates	4		
0104 Rural water and waste disposal, downward reestimates of subsidies	18		
0105 Rural community facility, downward reestimates of subsidies	18		

Program and Financing (in millions of dollars)

Identification code 12–0400–0–1–452	1999 actual	2000 est.	2001 est.
Obligations by program activity:			
00.01 Direct loan subsidy	141	87	172
00.02 Guaranteed loan subsidy	13	28	10
00.05 Reestimate of direct loan subsidy	35		
00.06 Interest on reestimate of direct loan subsidy	3		
00.07 Reestimate of guaranteed loan subsidy	45		
00.08 Interest on reestimate of guaranteed loan subsidy	8		
00.11 Water and waste disposal systems grants	570	529	503
00.12 Solid waste management grants	3	3	5
00.13 Community facility grants	7	13	24
00.14 Rural business enterprise grants	37	40	41
00.15 Rural opportunity grants		4	8
10.00 Total new obligations (object class 41.0)	862	704	763
Budgetary resources available for obligation:			
21.40 Unobligated balance available, start of year	13	5	
22.00 New budget authority (gross)	844	699	763
22.10 Resources available from recoveries of prior year obligations	10		
23.90 Total budgetary resources available for obligation	867	704	763
23.95 Total new obligations	–862	–704	–763
24.40 Unobligated balance available, end of year	5		
New budget authority (gross), detail:			
Discretionary:			
40.00 Appropriation	753	724	763
40.76 Reduction pursuant to P.L. 106–113		–25	
43.00 Appropriation (total discretionary)	753	699	763
Mandatory:			
60.05 Appropriation (indefinite) reestimates	91		
70.00 Total new budget authority (gross)	844	699	763
Change in unpaid obligations:			
72.40 Unpaid obligations, start of year: Obligated balance, start of year	1,687	1,851	1,841
73.10 Total new obligations	862	704	763
73.20 Total outlays (gross)	–680	–714	–658
73.40 Adjustments in expired accounts (net)	–9		
73.45 Adjustments in unexpired accounts	–10		
74.40 Unpaid obligations, end of year: Obligated balance, end of year	1,851	1,841	1,946
Outlays (gross), detail:			
86.90 Outlays from new discretionary authority	45	54	45
86.93 Outlays from discretionary balances	544	660	613
86.97 Outlays from new mandatory authority	91		
87.00 Total outlays (gross)	680	714	658
Net budget authority and outlays:			
89.00 Budget authority	844	699	763
90.00 Outlays	679	714	658

Summary of Loan Levels, Subsidy Budget Authority and Outlays by Program (in millions of dollars)

Identification code 12–0400–0–1–452	1999 actual	2000 est.	2001 est.
Direct loan levels supportable by subsidy budget authority:			
1150 Direct water and waste disposal loan levels	721	679	1,032
1150 Direct community facility loan levels	163	185	250
1150 Direct business and industry loan levels	26	50	50
1159 Total direct loan levels	910	914	1,332
Direct loan subsidy (in percent):			
1320 Direct water and waste disposal loans subsidy rate	16.52	7.10	13.59
1320 Direct community facility loans subsidy rate	13.74	6.06	11.69
1320 Direct business and industry loans subsidy rate	–14.64	–14.16	5.82
1329 Weighted average subsidy rate	19.34	8.32	12.91
Direct loan subsidy budget authority:			
1330 Direct water and waste disposal loans subsidy budget authority	157	73	140
1330 Direct community facility loans subsidy budget authority	23	10	29
1330 Direct business and industry subsidy budget authority	–4	–7	3
1339 Total subsidy budget authority	176	76	172
Direct loan subsidy outlays:			
1340 Direct water and waste disposal loans subsidy outlays	116	129	94
1340 Direct community facility loans subsidy outlays	18	23	16
1349 Total subsidy outlays	134	152	110
Guaranteed loan levels supportable by subsidy budget authority:			
2150 Water and waste disposal loan guarantee levels	6	75	75
2150 Community facility loan guarantee levels	107	210	210
2150 Business and industry loan guarantee levels	1,180	869	1,250
2159 Total loan guarantee levels	1,293	1,154	1,535
Guaranteed loan subsidy (in percent):			
2320 Guaranteed water and waste disposal loan subsidy rate	–1.08	–0.83	–1.50
2320 Guranteed community facility loan subsidy rate	–0.54	–0.54	–0.54
2320 Guaranteed business and industry loan subsidy rate	1.02	3.11	0.81
2329 Weighted average subsidy rate	4.95	2.08	0.52
Guaranteed loan subsidy budget authority:			
2330 Guaranteed water and waste loans subsidy budget authority		–1	–1
2330 Guaranteed community facility loans subsidy budget authority	–1	–1	–1
2330 Guaranteed business and industry loans subsidy budget authority	65	26	10
2339 Total subsidy budget authority	64	24	8

General and special funds—Continued

RURAL COMMUNITY ADVANCEMENT PROGRAM—Continued

(INCLUDING TRANSFERS OF FUNDS)—Continued

Summary of Loan Levels, Subsidy Budget Authority and Outlays by Program (in millions of dollars)—Continued

Identification code 12–0400–0–1–452	1999 actual	2000 est.	2001 est.
Guaranteed loan subsidy outlays:			
2340 Guaranteed community facility loan subsidy outlays			
2340 Guranteed business and industry loan subsidy outlays	64	27	10
2349 Total subsidy outlays	64	27	10

This account consolidates under the Rural Community Advancement Program (RCAP) funding for the direct and guaranteed water and waste disposal loans, water and waste disposal grants, emergency community water assistance grants, solid waste management grants, direct and guaranteed community facility loans, community facility grants, direct and guaranteed business and industry loans, rural business enterprise grants, and rural business opportunity grants. This is in accordance with the provisions set forth in the Federal Agriculture Improvement and Reform Act of 1996, as amended, Public Law 104–127 (the 1996 Act). Consolidating funding for these 12 loan and grant programs under RCAP provides greater flexibility to tailor financial assistance to applicant needs.

RCAP is composed of the following three funding streams: Rural Community Facilities, Rural Utilities, and Rural Business and Cooperative Development. For 2001 the Budget proposes the full flexibility authorized in the 1996 Act for up to 25 percent of the resources in each stream to shift to other streams, in order to respond to the unique rural development needs of states and localities. Funds for Native American Communities are provided as part of the whole amount appropriated for these streams as part of the Native Americans Initiative. The funds are allocated to all three funding streams.

Water and waste disposal loans are authorized under 7 U.S.C. 1926. The program provides direct loans to municipalities, counties, special purpose districts, certain Indian Tribes, and non-profit corporations to develop water and waste disposal systems in rural areas and towns with populations of less than 10,000. The program also guarantees water and waste disposal loans made by banks and other eligible lenders.

Water and waste disposal grants are authorized under Section 306(a)(2) of the Consolidated Farm and Rural Development Act, as amended. Grants are authorized to be made to associations, including nonprofit corporations, municipalities, counties, public and quasi-public agencies, and certain Indian tribes. The grants can be used to finance development, storage, treatment, purification, or distribution of water or the collection, treatment, or disposal of waste in rural areas and cities or towns with populations of less than 10,000. The amount of any development grant may not exceed 75 percent of the eligible development cost of the project.

Emergency community water assistance grants are authorized under Section 306A of the Consolidated Farm and Rural Development Act, as amended. Grants are made to public bodies and nonprofit organizations for construction or extension of water lines, repair or maintenance of existing systems, replacement of equipment, and payment of costs to correct emergency situations.

Solid waste management grants are authorized under Section 310B(b) of the Consolidated Farm and Rural Development Act, as amended. Grants are made to non-profit organizations to provide regional technical assistance to local and regional governments and related agencies for the purpose of reducing or eliminating pollution of water resources, and for improving the planning and management of solid waste disposal facilities.

Community facility loans and grants are authorized under sections 306(a)(1) and 306(a)(19) of the Consolidated Farm and Rural Development Act, as amended. Loans are provided to local governments and nonprofit organizations for the construction and improvement of community facilities providing essential services in rural areas of not more than 50,000 population, such as hospitals and fire stations. Grants to finance early warning radar systems are also proposed, to provide communities susceptible to sudden, dangerous weather such as tornadoes and flooding, with early warning alarm transmitters.

Business and industry guaranteed and direct loans are authorized under section 310B(a)(1) of the Consolidated Farm and Rural Development, as amended. These loans are made to public, private or cooperative organizations, Indian tribes or tribal groups, corporate entities, or individuals for the purpose of improving the economic climate in rural areas.

Rural business enterprise grants are authorized under sections 310B(c) and 310B(f) of the Consolidated Farm and Rural Development Act, as amended. These grants enable public and nonprofit organizations to operate rural economic development projects. In general, these grants provide investments in the human and physical resources of rural communities. Past projects have enabled rural communities to acquire and develop land, create technical assistance programs, encourage small business growth and create new jobs.

Rural Business Opportunity Grants are authorized under section 306(a)(11)(A) of the Consolidated Farm and Rural Development Act, as amended. These grants enable public bodies and private nonprofit organizations to provide for technical assistance, training, and planning activities that improve economic conditions in rural area. Partnership Technical Assistance Grants are proposed to help rural communities develop comprehensive strategies for revitalization and to better coordinate Federal and other sources of assistance.

RURAL HOUSING SERVICE

Federal Funds

General and special funds:

SALARIES AND EXPENSES

(FARMERS HOME ADMINISTRATION)

Program and Financing (in millions of dollars)

Identification code 12–2001–0–1–452	1999 actual	2000 est.	2001 est.
Change in unpaid obligations:			
72.40 Unpaid obligations, start of year: Obligated balance, start of year	14	6	
73.20 Total outlays (gross)	−3		
73.40 Adjustments in expired accounts (net)	−5	−6	
74.40 Unpaid obligations, end of year: Obligated balance, end of year	6		
Outlays (gross), detail:			
86.93 Outlays from discretionary balances	3		
Net budget authority and outlays:			
89.00 Budget authority			
90.00 Outlays	3		

These funds were used to administer the direct loan, loan guarantee, and grant programs of the Farmers Home Administration and the Rural Development Administration.

In 1995, under the reorganization by the Secretary of Agriculture the Agency has been eliminated and activities previously administered through this account transferred to other Department accounts.

RURAL HOUSING ASSISTANCE GRANTS

For grants and contracts for [housing for domestic farm labor,] very low-income housing repair, supervisory and technical assistance, compensation for construction defects, and rural housing preservation made by the Rural Housing Service, as authorized by 42 U.S.C. 1474, 1479(c), [1486,] 1490e, and 1490m, [$45,000,000] *$39,000,000*, to remain available until expended: *Provided*, That of the total amount appropriated, [$1,200,000] *$2,000,000* shall be available through June 30, [2000] *2001*, for authorized empowerment zones and enterprise communities [and communities designated by the Secretary of Agriculture as Rural Economic Area Partnership Zones]. *(Agriculture, Rural Development, Food and Drug Administration, and Related Agencies Appropriations Act, 2000.)*

[For the additional cost of grants and contracts for domestic farm labor and very low-income housing repair made available by the Rural Housing Service, as authorized by 42 U.S.C. 1474 and 1486, to meet the needs resulting from natural disasters, $14,500,000, to remain available until expended.] *(Miscellaneous Appropriations, 2000, as enacted by section 1000(a)(5) of the Consolidated Appropriations Act, 2000 (P.L. 106–113).)*

Program and Financing (in millions of dollars)

Identification code 12–1953–0–1–604	1999 actual	2000 est.	2001 est.
Obligations by program activity:			
00.01 Domestic farm labor grants	13	14	
00.02 Domestic farm labor natural disaster grants		3	
00.03 Very low-income housing repair grants	20	26	30
00.04 Very low-income housing repair natural disaster grants	1	12	
00.05 Supervisory and technical assistance grants		2	1
00.07 Rural housing preservation grants	7	6	8
10.00 Total new obligations (object class 41.0)	42	63	39
Budgetary resources available for obligation:			
21.40 Unobligated balance available, start of year	2	4	1
22.00 New budget authority (gross)	42	60	39
22.10 Resources available from recoveries of prior year obligations	2		
23.90 Total budgetary resources available for obligation	46	63	40
23.95 Total new obligations	−42	−63	−39
24.40 Unobligated balance available, end of year	4	1	
New budget authority (gross), detail:			
Discretionary:			
40.00 Appropriation	42	60	39
Change in unpaid obligations:			
72.40 Unpaid obligations, start of year: Obligated balance, start of year	57	41	37
73.10 Total new obligations	42	63	39
73.20 Total outlays (gross)	−57	−67	−53
73.45 Adjustments in unexpired accounts	−2		
74.40 Unpaid obligations, end of year: Obligated balance, end of year	41	37	24
Outlays (gross), detail:			
86.90 Outlays from new discretionary authority	21	37	29
86.93 Outlays from discretionary balances	36	29	24
87.00 Total outlays (gross)	57	67	53
Net budget authority and outlays:			
89.00 Budget authority	42	60	39
90.00 Outlays	57	67	53

The rural housing for domestic farm labor grant program is authorized under section 516 of the Housing Act of 1949, as amended. This program is being requested in the Farm labor program account.

The very low-income housing repair grant program is authorized under section 504 of the Housing Act of 1949, as amended. This grant program enables very low-income elderly residents in rural areas to improve or modernize their dwellings, to make the dwelling safer or more sanitary, or to remove health and safety hazards.

The supervisory and technical assistance grant program is carried out under the provisions of section 509(f) and 525 of the Housing Act of 1949, as amended. Under section 509, grants are made to public and private nonprofit organizations for packaging loan applications for housing under sections 502, 504, 514/516, 515, and 533 of the Housing Act of 1949, as amended. The assistance is to be directed to underserved areas where at least 20 percent or more of the population is at or below the poverty level, and at least 10 percent or more of the population resides in substandard housing. Under section 525, grants are made to public and private nonprofit organizations and other associations for the developing, conducting, administering or coordinating of technical and supervisory assistance programs to demonstrate the benefits of Federal, State, and local housing programs for low-income families in rural areas.

The compensation for construction defects program is carried out under the provisions of section 509(c) of the Housing Act of 1949, as amended. The Secretary of Agriculture is authorized to make expenditures to correct structural defects, or to pay claims of owners arising from such defects on newly constructed dwellings purchased with RHS financial assistance. Requests for compensation for construction defects must be made within 18 months after the date financial assistance was granted.

The rural housing preservation grant program is authorized under section 533 of the Housing Act of 1949, as amended. Grants are made to eligible nonprofit groups, Indian tribes, or government agencies for rehabilitation of single family housing owned by low- and very low-income families and the rehabilitation of rental and cooperative housing for low- and very low-income families.

FARM LABOR PROGRAM ACCOUNT

For the cost of direct loans, grants, and contracts, as authorized by 42 U.S.C. 1484 and 1486, $30,777,000, to remain available until expended for direct farm labor housing loans and domestic farm labor housing grants and contracts. In addition, for grants to assist low-income migrant and seasonal farmworkers, as authorized by 42 U.S.C. 5177a, $5,000,000, to remain available until expended.

Program and Financing (in millions of dollars)

Identification code 12–1954–0–1–604	1999 actual	2000 est.	2001 est.
Obligations by program activity:			
00.01 Direct loan subsidy			16
00.02 Farm labor housing grants			15
00.03 Migrant farmworkers grants			5
10.00 Total new obligations (object class 41.0)			36
Budgetary resources available for obligation:			
22.00 New budget authority (gross)			36
23.95 Total new obligations			−36
New budget authority (gross), detail:			
Discretionary:			
40.00 Appropriation			36
Change in unpaid obligations:			
73.10 Total new obligations			36
73.20 Total outlays (gross)			−7
74.40 Unpaid obligations, end of year: Obligated balance, end of year			29
Outlays (gross), detail:			
86.90 Outlays from new discretionary authority			7
Net budget authority and outlays:			
89.00 Budget authority			36
90.00 Outlays			7

General and special funds—Continued

FARM LABOR PROGRAM ACCOUNT—Continued

Summary of Loan Levels, Subsidy Budget Authority and Outlays by Program (in millions of dollars)

Identification code 12–1954–0–1–604	1999 actual	2000 est.	2001 est.
Direct loan levels supportable by subsidy budget authority:			
1150 Direct loan levels			30
1159 Total direct loan levels			30
Direct loan subsidy (in percent):			
1320 Subsidy rate			52.59
1329 Weighted average subsidy rate			52.59
Direct loan subsidy budget authority:			
1330 Subsidy budget authority			16
1339 Total subsidy budget authority			16
Direct loan subsidy outlays:			
1340 Subsidy outlays			3
1349 Total subsidy outlays			3

This new account is being requested to consolidate three farm labor programs into one account. This consolidation will provide more flexibility for distributing rural farm labor housing assistance and allows the total assistance being provided specifically to farm laborers to be identified in one place. The account consists of direct farm labor housing loans, domestic farm labor housing grants, and low-income migrant and seasonal farm-worker grants.

The direct farm labor loan program is authorized under section 514 and the rural housing for domestic farm labor grant program is authorized under section 516 of the Housing Act of 1949, as amended. The loans, grants, and contracts are made to public and private nonprofit organizations for low-rent housing and related facilities for domestic farm labor. Grants assistance may not exceed 90 percent of the cost of a project. Loans and grants may be used for construction of new structures, site acquisition and development, rehabilitation of existing structures, and purchase of furnishings and equipment for dwellings, dining halls, community rooms, and infirmaries.

The low-income migrant and seasonal farmworkers grants are made to public agencies or private organizations with tax exempt status under section 501(c)(3) of the Internal Revenue Code of 1986, that have experience in providing services to low-income migrants and seasonal farmworkers. The types of assistance to be provided is determined by the Secretary of Agriculture. In FY 1999 $20 million in grants were made to assist low-income migrant and seasonal farmworkers in California and Florida.

RENTAL ASSISTANCE PROGRAM

For rental assistance agreements entered into or renewed pursuant to the authority under section 521(a)(2) or agreements entered into in lieu of debt forgiveness or payments for eligible households as authorized by section 502(c)(5)(D) of the Housing Act of 1949, **[**$640,000,000**]** *$680,000,000*; and, in addition, such sums as may be necessary, as authorized by section 521(c) of the Act, to liquidate debt incurred prior to fiscal year 1992 to carry out the rental assistance program under section 521(a)(2) of the Act: *Provided*, That of this amount, not more than $5,900,000 shall be available for debt forgiveness or payments for eligible households as authorized by section 502(c)(5)(D) of the Act, and not to exceed $10,000 per project for advances to nonprofit organizations or public agencies to cover direct costs (other than purchase price) incurred in purchasing projects pursuant to section 502(c)(5)(C) of the Act: *Provided further*, That agreements entered into or renewed during fiscal year **[**2000**]** *2001* shall be funded for a 5-year period, although the life of any such agreement may be extended to fully utilize amounts obligated. *(Agriculture, Rural Development, Food and Drug Administration, and Related Agencies Appropriations Act, 2000.)*

Program and Financing (in millions of dollars)

Identification code 12–0137–0–1–604	1999 actual	2000 est.	2001 est.
Obligations by program activity:			
10.00 Total new obligations (object class 41.0)	583	640	680
Budgetary resources available for obligation:			
22.00 New budget authority (gross)	583	640	680
23.95 Total new obligations	–583	–640	–680
New budget authority (gross), detail:			
Discretionary:			
40.00 Appropriation	583	640	680
40.05 Appropriation (indefinite)	67	62	60
40.47 Portion applied to repay debt	–67	–62	–60
43.00 Appropriation (total discretionary)	583	640	680
Change in unpaid obligations:			
Unpaid obligations, start of year:			
Obligated balance, start of year:			
72.40 Obligated balance, appropriation, start of year	1,742	1,837	1,941
72.40 Obligated balance, authority to borrow, start of year	811	745	683
72.99 Total unpaid obligations, start of year	2,553	2,582	2,624
73.10 Total new obligations	583	640	680
73.20 Total outlays (gross)	–555	–597	–631
Unpaid obligations, end of year:			
Obligated balance, end of year:			
74.40 Obligated balance, appropriation, end of year	1,837	1,941	2,050
74.40 Obligated balance, authority to borrow, end of year	745	683	622
74.99 Total unpaid obligations, end of year	2,582	2,624	2,672
Outlays (gross), detail:			
86.90 Outlays from new discretionary authority	21	22	24
86.93 Outlays from discretionary balances	534	575	607
87.00 Total outlays (gross)	555	597	631
Net budget authority and outlays:			
89.00 Budget authority	583	640	680
90.00 Outlays	555	597	631

The rental assistance program is authorized under section 521(a)(2) of the Housing Act of 1949, as amended, and is designed to reduce rents paid by very low-income and low-income families living in RHS-financed rural rental and farm labor housing projects. Funding under this account is provided for renewals of existing rental assistance contracts, assistance for newly constructed units financed by the section 515 rural rental and cooperative housing program or the 514/516 farm labor housing loan and grant programs, and for additional servicing assistance for existing projects. Assistance is also provided in lieu of debt forgiveness or payments for eligible households to subsidize tenant rents in projects purchased by eligible nonprofit organizations or public agencies as authorized by section 502(c)(5)(D) of the Act.

From 1978 through 1991, the rental assistance program was funded under the Rural Housing Insurance Fund. Beginning in 1992, pursuant to Credit Reform, a separate grant account was established for this program.

RURAL HOUSING VOUCHER PROGRAM

Program and Financing (in millions of dollars)

Identification code 12–2002–0–1–604	1999 actual	2000 est.	2001 est.
Change in unpaid obligations:			
72.40 Unpaid obligations, start of year: Obligated balance, start of year	3	2	2
74.40 Unpaid obligations, end of year: Obligated balance, end of year	2	2	2

	Net budget authority and outlays:			
89.00	Budget authority			
90.00	Outlays			

Prior year outlays reflect funding for rental assistance for newly constructed units provided in limited amounts in 1984 and 1985. From 1986 through 1991 rental assistance for newly constructed units, as well as existing rental assistance contract renewals and additional servicing assistance for existing projects, had been funded under the Rural Housing Insurance Fund. Beginning in 1992, pursuant to Credit Reform, a separate grant account was established for the rental assistance program.

Mutual and Self-Help Housing Grants

For grants and contracts pursuant to section 523(b)(1)(A) of the Housing Act of 1949 (42 U.S.C. 1490c), [$28,000,000] *$40,000,000*, to remain available until expended (7 U.S.C. 2209b)[: *Provided*, That of the total amount appropriated,] *of which* $1,000,000 shall be available through June 30, [2000] *2001*, for authorized empowerment zones and enterprise communities [and communities designated by the Secretary of Agriculture as Rural Economic Area Partnership Zones]. *(Agriculture, Rural Development, Food and Drug Administration, and Related Agencies Appropriations Act, 2000.)*

Program and Financing (in millions of dollars)

Identification code 12–2006–0–1–604		1999 actual	2000 est.	2001 est.
	Obligations by program activity:			
10.00	Total new obligations (object class 41.0)	26	29	40
	Budgetary resources available for obligation:			
21.40	Unobligated balance available, start of year		1	
22.00	New budget authority (gross)	25	28	40
22.10	Resources available from recoveries of prior year obligations	2		
23.90	Total budgetary resources available for obligation	27	29	40
23.95	Total new obligations	–26	–29	–40
24.40	Unobligated balance available, end of year	1		
	New budget authority (gross), detail:			
	Discretionary:			
40.00	Appropriation	26	28	40
	Change in unpaid obligations:			
72.40	Unpaid obligations, start of year: Obligated balance, start of year	34	39	42
73.10	Total new obligations	26	29	40
73.20	Total outlays (gross)	–20	–26	–32
73.45	Adjustments in unexpired accounts	–2		
74.40	Unpaid obligations, end of year: Obligated balance, end of year	39	42	51
	Outlays (gross), detail:			
86.90	Outlays from new discretionary authority	3	6	8
86.93	Outlays from discretionary balances	17	20	24
87.00	Total outlays (gross)	20	26	32
	Net budget authority and outlays:			
89.00	Budget authority	25	28	40
90.00	Outlays	20	26	32

This program is authorized under section 523 of the Housing Act of 1949, as amended. Grants and contracts are made for the purpose of providing technical and supervisory assistance to groups of families to enable them to build their own homes through the mutual exchange of labor.

Rural Community Fire Protection Grants

Program and Financing (in millions of dollars)

Identification code 12–2067–0–1–452		1999 actual	2000 est.	2001 est.
	Change in unpaid obligations:			
72.40	Unpaid obligations, start of year: Obligated balance, start of year	2		1
74.40	Unpaid obligations, end of year: Obligated balance, end of year		1	1
	Net budget authority and outlays:			
89.00	Budget authority			
90.00	Outlays	2		

This assistance was authorized by section 7 of the Cooperative Forestry Assistance Act of 1978 (16 U.S.C. 2106). Grants are made to public bodies to organize, train, and equip local firefighting forces, including those of Indian tribes or other Native American groups, to prevent, control, and suppress fires threatening human lives, crops, livestock, farmsteads or other improvements, pastures, orchards, wildlife, rangeland, woodland, and other resources in rural areas.

In 1997, funding for the Rural Community Fire Protection grant program was appropriated to the Rural Housing Assistance Program and transferred to this account for administration. In 1998, funding for these grants was appropriated to this account. Beginning in 1999, funding for this program is requested by the Forest Service.

Credit accounts:

Rural Community Facility Direct Loans Financing Account

Program and Financing (in millions of dollars)

Identification code 12–4225–0–3–452		1999 actual	2000 est.	2001 est.
	Obligations by program activity:			
	Operating program:			
00.01	Direct loans	163	185	250
00.02	Interest on Treasury borrowing	52	56	70
00.91	Subtotal, Operating program	215	241	320
	Reestimates:			
08.02	Downward reestimate paid to receipt account	12		
08.04	Interest on downward reestimate paid to receipt account	2		
08.91	Subtotal, Reestimates	14		
10.00	Total new obligations	229	241	320
	Budgetary resources available for obligation:			
21.40	Unobligated balance available, start of year	11	11	
22.00	New financing authority (gross)	226	230	320
22.10	Resources available from recoveries of prior year obligations	27		
22.70	Balance of authority to borrow withdrawn	–24		
23.90	Total budgetary resources available for obligation	240	241	320
23.95	Total new obligations	–229	–241	–320
24.40	Unobligated balance available, end of year	11		
	New financing authority (gross), detail:			
	Mandatory:			
67.15	Authority to borrow (indefinite)	167	124	176
	Spending authority from offsetting collections:			
	Discretionary:			
68.00	Offsetting collections (cash)	90	120	131
68.10	From Federal sources: Change in receivables and unpaid, unfilled orders	1	–14	13
68.47	Portion applied to repay debt	–32		
68.90	Spending authority from offsetting collections (total discretionary)	59	106	144
70.00	Total new financing authority (gross)	226	230	320

Credit accounts—Continued

RURAL COMMUNITY FACILITY DIRECT LOANS FINANCING ACCOUNT—Continued

Program and Financing (in millions of dollars)—Continued

Identification code 12–4225–0–3–452	1999 actual	2000 est.	2001 est.
Change in unpaid obligations:			
Unpaid obligations, start of year:			
72.40 Obligated balance, start of year	339	306	281
72.95 Receivables from program account	39	40	26
72.99 Total unpaid obligations, start of year	378	346	307
73.10 Total new obligations	229	241	320
73.20 Total financing disbursements (gross)	–233	–280	–249
73.45 Adjustments in unexpired accounts	–27		
Unpaid obligations, end of year:			
74.40 Obligated balance, end of year	306	281	340
74.95 Receivables from program account	40	26	39
74.99 Total unpaid obligations, end of year	346	307	379
87.00 Total financing disbursements (gross)	233	280	249
Offsets:			
Against gross financing authority and financing disbursements:			
Offsetting collections (cash) from:			
88.00 Federal sources	–18	–23	–16
88.25 Interest on uninvested funds	–14	–26	–33
Non-Federal sources:			
88.40 Repayment of principal	–27	–22	–25
88.40 Interest received on loans	–32	–49	–57
88.40 Other	1		
88.90 Total, offsetting collections (cash)	–90	–120	–131
Against gross financing authority only:			
88.95 Change in receivables from program accounts	–1	14	–13
Net financing authority and financing disbursements:			
89.00 Financing authority	135	124	176
90.00 Financing disbursements	143	160	118

Status of Direct Loans (in millions of dollars)

Identification code 12–4225–0–3–452	1999 actual	2000 est.	2001 est.
Position with respect to appropriations act limitation on obligations:			
1111 Limitation on direct loans	162	167	250
1131 Direct loan obligations exempt from limitation	1	18	
1150 Total direct loan obligations	163	185	250
Cumulative balance of direct loans outstanding:			
1210 Outstanding, start of year	606	747	951
1231 Disbursements: Direct loan disbursements	168	226	178
1251 Repayments: Repayments and prepayments	–27	–22	–25
1290 Outstanding, end of year	747	951	1,104

As required by the Federal Credit Reform Act of 1990, this non-budgetary account records all cash flows to and from the Government resulting from direct loans obligated in 1992 and beyond. The amounts in this account are a means of financing and are not included in the budget totals. Loans made prior to 1992 are recorded in the Rural Development Insurance Fund Liquidating Account.

This account provides funding to non-profit organizations and local governments for the construction and improvement of community facilities providing essential services in rural areas, such as hospitals, telecommunications applications, child care centers and fire stations.

Balance Sheet (in millions of dollars)

Identification code 12–4225–0–3–452	1998 actual	1999 actual	2000 est.	2001 est.
ASSETS:				
Federal assets:				
1101 Fund balances with Treasury	82	31	160	160
Investments in US securities:				
1106 Receivables, net	39	40	26	39
Net value of assets related to post–1991 direct loans receivable:				
1401 Direct loans receivable, gross	606	747	951	1,104
1402 Interest receivable	26	9	9	9
1405 Allowance for subsidy cost (–)	–128	–82	–211	–211
1499 Net present value of assets related to direct loans	504	674	749	902
1999 Total assets	625	745	935	1,101
LIABILITIES:				
2101 Federal liabilities: Accounts payable	606	704	908	1,061
2203 Non-Federal liabilities: Liability for deposit funds	1	1	1	1
2999 Total liabilities	607	705	909	1,062
NET POSITION:				
3100 Appropriated capital	18	40	26	39
3999 Total net position	18	40	26	39
4999 Total liabilities and net position	625	745	935	1,101

RURAL COMMUNITY FACILITY GUARANTEED LOANS FINANCING ACCOUNT

Program and Financing (in millions of dollars)

Identification code 12–4228–0–3–452	1999 actual	2000 est.	2001 est.
Obligations by program activity:			
08.01 Negative subsidy paid to receipt account	1	1	1
08.02 Downward reestimate paid to receipt account	4		
10.00 Total new obligations	5	1	1
Budgetary resources available for obligation:			
21.40 Unobligated balance available, start of year	7	3	3
22.00 New financing authority (gross)	1	1	1
23.90 Total budgetary resources available for obligation	8	4	4
23.95 Total new obligations	–5	–1	–1
24.40 Unobligated balance available, end of year	3	3	3
New financing authority (gross), detail:			
Discretionary:			
68.00 Spending authority from offsetting collections (gross): Offsetting collections (cash)	1	1	1
Change in unpaid obligations:			
73.10 Total new obligations	5	1	1
73.20 Total financing disbursements (gross)	–4	–1	–1
87.00 Total financing disbursements (gross)	4	1	1
Offsets:			
Against gross financing authority and financing disbursements:			
88.40 Offsetting collections (cash) from: Non-Federal sources	–1	–1	–1
Net financing authority and financing disbursements:			
89.00 Financing authority			
90.00 Financing disbursements	4		

Status of Guaranteed Loans (in millions of dollars)

Identification code 12–4228–0–3–452	1999 actual	2000 est.	2001 est.
Position with respect to appropriations act limitation on commitments:			
2111 Limitation on guaranteed loans made by private lenders	210	210	210
2112 Uncommitted loan guarantee limitation	–104		
2131 Guaranteed loan commitments exempt from limitation	1		
2150 Total guaranteed loan commitments	107	210	210
2199 Guaranteed amount of guaranteed loan commitments	107	168	168
Cumulative balance of guaranteed loans outstanding:			
2210 Outstanding, start of year	155	194	313
2231 Disbursements of new guaranteed loans	59	131	165
2251 Repayments and prepayments	–20	–12	–18
2290 Outstanding, end of year	194	313	460

Memorandum:			
2299 Guaranteed amount of guaranteed loans outstanding, end of year	158	279	396

As required by the Federal Credit Reform Act of 1990, this non-budgetary account records all cash flows to and from the Government resulting from guaranteed loans committed in 1992 and beyond. The amounts in this account are a means of financing and are not included in the budget totals. Loans made prior to 1992 are recorded in the Rural Development Insurance Fund Liquidating Account.

This account finances loan guarantee commitments for essential community facilities in rural areas.

Balance Sheet (in millions of dollars)

Identification code 12–4228–0–3–452	1998 actual	1999 actual	2000 est.	2001 est.
ASSETS:				
1101 Federal assets: Fund balances with Treasury	7	4	7	7
1999 Total assets	7	4	7	7
LIABILITIES:				
2204 Non-Federal liabilities: Liabilities for loan guarantees	7	4	7	7
2999 Total liabilities	7	4	7	7
4999 Total liabilities and net position	7	4	7	7

Rural Housing Insurance Fund Program Account

(including transfers of funds)

For gross obligations for the principal amount of direct and guaranteed loans as authorized by title V of the Housing Act of 1949, to be available from funds in the rural housing insurance fund, as follows: [$4,300,000,000] *$5,000,000,000* for loans to section 502 borrowers, as determined by the Secretary, of which [$3,200,000,000] *$3,700,000,000* shall be for unsubsidized guaranteed loans; [$32,396,000] *$40,000,000* for section 504 housing repair loans; [$100,000,000] *$200,000,000* for section 538 guaranteed multi-family housing loans; [$25,001,000 for section 514 farm labor housing; $114,321,000] *$120,000,000* for section 515 rental housing; [$5,152,000] *$5,000,000* for section 524 site loans; [$7,503,000] *$15,000,000* for credit sales of acquired property, of which up to [$1,250,000] *$5,000,000* may be for multi-family credit sales; and [$5,000,000] *$5,009,000* for section 523 self-help housing land development loans.

For the cost of direct and guaranteed loans, including the cost of modifying loans, as defined in section 502 of the Congressional Budget Act of 1974, as follows: section 502 loans, [$113,350,000] *$253,180,000* of which [$19,520,000] *$44,400,000* shall be for unsubsidized guaranteed loans; section 504 housing repair loans, [$9,900,000] *$14,176,000*; section 538 multi-family housing guaranteed loans, [$480,000; section 514 farm labor housing, $11,308,000] *$3,040,000*; section 515 rental housing, [$45,363,000 section 524 site loans, $4,000;] *$59,124,000; multi-family* credit sales of acquired property, [$874,000, of which up to $494,250 may be for multi-family credit sales] *$2,452,000*; and section 523 self-help housing land development loans, [$281,000] *$279,000*: *Provided*, That of the total amount appropriated in this paragraph, [$11,180,000] *$13,832,000* shall be available through June 30, [2000] *2001*, for authorized empowerment zones and enterprise communities [and communities designated by the Secretary of Agriculture as Rural Economic Area Partnership Zones].

In addition, for administrative expenses necessary to carry out the direct and guaranteed loan programs, [$375,879,000] *$409,233,000*, which shall be transferred to and merged with the appropriation for "Rural [Housing Service] *Development*, Salaries and Expenses": [*Provided*, That of this amount the Secretary of Agriculture may transfer up to $7,000,000 to the appropriation for "Outreach for Socially Disadvantaged Farmers"]. *(Agriculture, Rural Development, Food and Drug Administration, and Related Agencies Appropriations Act, 2000.)*

[For additional gross obligations for the principal amount of direct loans as authorized by title V of the Housing Act of 1949, to be available from funds in the rural housing insurance fund to meet the needs resulting from natural disasters, as follows: $50,000,000 for loans to section 502 borrowers, as determined by the Secretary; $15,000,000 for section 504 housing repair loans; and $5,000,000 for section 514 farm labor housing.]

[For the additional cost of direct loans to meet the needs resulting from natural disasters, including the cost of modifying loans, as defined in section 502 of the Congressional Budget Act of 1974, to remain available until expended, as follows: section 502 loans, $4,265,000; section 504 loans, $4,584,000; and section 514 farm labor housing, $2,250,000.] *(Miscellaneous Appropriations, 2000, as enacted by section 1000(a)(5) of the Consolidated Appropriations Act, 2000 (P.L. 106–113).)*

General Fund Credit Receipt Accounts (in millions of dollars)

Identification code 12–2081–0–1–371	1999 actual	2000 est.	2001 est.
0101 Rural housing insurance, downward reestimates of subsidies	34		

Program and Financing (in millions of dollars)

Identification code 12–2081–0–1–371	1999 actual	2000 est.	2001 est.
Obligations by program activity:			
00.01 Direct loan subsidy	192	174	285
00.02 Guaranteed loan subsidy	5	20	47
00.05 Reestimates of direct loan subsidy	96		
00.06 Interest on reestimates of direct loan subsidy	20		
00.07 Reestimates of guaranteed loan subsidy	109		
00.08 Interest on reestimates of guaranteed loan subsidy	13		
00.09 Administrative expenses	361	376	409
10.00 Total new obligations	796	570	741
Budgetary resources available for obligation:			
21.40 Unobligated balance available, start of year		1	
22.00 New budget authority (gross)	798	568	741
23.90 Total budgetary resources available for obligation	798	569	741
23.95 Total new obligations	−796	−570	−741
24.40 Unobligated balance available, end of year	1		
New budget authority (gross), detail:			
Discretionary:			
40.00 Appropriation	560	568	741
Mandatory:			
60.05 Appropriation (indefinite)	238		
70.00 Total new budget authority (gross)	798	568	741
Change in unpaid obligations:			
72.40 Unpaid obligations, start of year: Obligated balance, start of year	200	187	165
73.10 Total new obligations	796	570	741
73.20 Total outlays (gross)	−804	−592	−719
73.40 Adjustments in expired accounts (net)	−6		
74.40 Unpaid obligations, end of year: Obligated balance, end of year	187	165	187
Outlays (gross), detail:			
86.90 Outlays from new discretionary authority	459	488	623
86.93 Outlays from discretionary balances	106	104	96
86.97 Outlays from new mandatory authority	238		
87.00 Total outlays (gross)	804	592	719
Net budget authority and outlays:			
89.00 Budget authority	798	568	741
90.00 Outlays	804	592	719

Summary of Budget Authority and Outlays

(in millions of dollars)

	1999 actual	*2000 est.*	*2001 est.*
Enacted/requested:			
Budget Authority	797	568	741
Outlays	803	592	719
Legislative proposal, not subject to PAYGO:			
Budget Authority			−40
Outlays			−40
Total:			
Budget Authority	797	568	701
Outlays	803	592	679

Credit accounts—Continued

RURAL HOUSING INSURANCE FUND PROGRAM ACCOUNT—Continued

(INCLUDING TRANSFERS OF FUNDS)—Continued

Summary of Loan Levels, Subsidy Budget Authority and Outlays by Program (in millions of dollars)

Identification code 12–2081–0–1–371		1999 actual	2000 est.	2001 est.
	Direct loan levels supportable by subsidy budget authority:			
1150	Direct 502 Single family housing	967	1,161	1,300
1150	Direct 515 Multi-family housing	114	114	120
1150	Direct 504 Housing repair	25	48	40
1150	Direct 514 Farm labor housing	20	30	
1150	Direct 524 Site development	3	5	5
1150	Single family credit sales	17	6	10
1150	Multi-family credit sales	4	1	5
1150	Direct 523 Self-help housing		5	5
1159	Total direct loan levels	1,150	1,371	1,485
	Direct loan subsidy (in percent):			
1320	Direct 502 Single family housing	11.82	8.53	16.06
1320	Direct 515 Multi-family housing	48.25	39.68	49.27
1320	Direct 504 Housing repair	35.23	30.56	35.44
1320	Direct 514 Farm labor housing	52.03	45.23	0.00
1320	Direct 524 Site development	0.33	0.08	−0.12
1320	Single family credit sales	9.02	6.08	−3.23
1320	Multi-family credit sales	48.31	39.54	49.03
1320	Direct 523 Self-help housing	5.64	5.61	5.57
1329	Weighted average subsidy rate	23.80	12.68	19.15
	Direct loan subsidy budget authority:			
1330	Direct 502 Single family housing	192	98	209
1330	Direct 515 Multi-family housing	72	45	59
1330	Direct 504Housing repair		15	14
1330	Direct 514 Farm labor housing	10	14	
1330	Single family credit sales	−1		
1330	Multi-family credit sales	3	1	2
1330	Direct 523 Self-help housing			
1339	Total subsidy budget authority	276	173	284
	Direct loan subsidy outlays:			
1340	Direct 502 Single family housing	211	103	174
1340	Direct 515 Multi-family housing	86	67	63
1340	Direct 504 Housing repair	8	14	14
1340	Direct 514 Farm labor housing	6	11	9
1340	Single family credit sales	1		
1340	Multi-family credit sales	2		2
1340	Direct 523 Self-help housing			
1349	Total subsidy outlays	314	195	262
	Guaranteed loan levels supportable by subsidy budget authority:			
2150	Guaranteed 502 Single family housing—unsubsidized	2,977	3,200	3,700
2150	Guaranteed 538 Multi-family housing	75	100	200
2159	Total loan guarantee levels	3,052	3,300	3,900
	Guaranteed loan subsidy (in percent):			
2320	Guaranteed 502 Single family housing—unsubsidized	0.09	0.61	1.20
2320	Guaranteed 538 Multi-family housing	3.10	0.48	1.52
2329	Weighted average subsidy rate	4.14	0.61	1.22
	Guaranteed loan subsidy budget authority:			
2330	Guaranteed 502 Single family housing—unsubsidized	125	20	44
2330	Guaranteed 538 Multi-family housing	2		3
2339	Total subsidy budget authority	127	20	47
	Guaranteed loan subsidy outlays:			
2340	Guaranteed 502 Single family housing—unsubsidized	125	20	44
2340	Guaranteed 538 Multi-family housing	2		3
2349	Total subsidy outlays	127	20	47
	Administrative expense data:			
3510	Budget authority	361	376	409
3590	Outlays	361	376	409

Rural housing insurance fund—This fund was established in 1965 (Public Law 89–117) pursuant to section 517 of title V of the Housing Act of 1949, as amended.

The programs funded through the Rural Housing Insurance Fund Program account are: section 502 very low and low to moderate income homeownership loans and guarantees; section 504 very low-income housing repair loans; section 514 domestic farm labor housing loans; section 515 rural rental housing loans; section 524 housing site loans, single family and multi-family housing credit sales of acquired property, and section 538 multi-family housing guarantees. The section 523 self-help housing land development loan program is included under this heading beginning in 1997. Previously, this loan program was accounted for under the separate heading of "Self-Help Housing Land Development Fund Program Account." The Budget requests the section 514 domestic farm labor housing loans be funded under the new Farm Labor Program Account in order to provide flexibility between these loans and the farm labor housing grants.

Loan programs are limited to rural areas that include towns, villages, and other places which are not part of an urban area and that have a population not in excess of 2,500 inhabitants, or is in excess of 2,500 but not in excess of 10,000 if rural in character, or has a population in excess of 10,000 but not more than 20,000 and is not within a standard metropolitan statistical area and has a serious lack of mortgage credit for low- and moderate-income borrowers.

As required by the Federal Credit Reform Act of 1990, this account records, for this program, the subsidy costs associated with the direct loans obligated and loan guarantees committed in 1992 and beyond (including credit sales of acquired property), as well as administrative expenses of this program. The subsidy amounts are estimated on a present value basis; the administrative expenses are estimated on a cash basis.

Object Classification (in millions of dollars)

Identification code 12–2081–0–1–371		1999 actual	2000 est.	2001 est.
25.3	Purchases of goods and services from Government accounts	361	377	409
41.0	Grants, subsidies, and contributions	435	193	332
99.9	Total new obligations	796	570	741

RURAL HOUSING INSURANCE FUND PROGRAM ACCOUNT

(Legislative proposal, not subject to PAYGO)

Program and Financing (in millions of dollars)

Identification code 12–2081–2–1–371		1999 actual	2000 est.	2001 est.
	Obligations by program activity:			
00.02	Guaranteed loan subsidy			−40
10.00	Total new obligations (object class 41.0)			−40
	Budgetary resources available for obligation:			
22.00	New budget authority (gross)			−40
23.95	Total new obligations			40
	New budget authority (gross), detail:			
	Discretionary:			
40.00	Appropriation			−40
	Change in unpaid obligations:			
73.10	Total new obligations			−40
73.20	Total outlays (gross)			40
	Outlays (gross), detail:			
86.90	Outlays from new discretionary authority			−40
	Net budget authority and outlays:			
89.00	Budget authority			−40
90.00	Outlays			−40

Summary of Loan Levels, Subsidy Budget Authority and Outlays by Program (in millions of dollars)

Identification code 12–2081–2–1–371		1999 actual	2000 est.	2001 est.
	Guaranteed loan levels supportable by subsidy budget authority:			
2150	Single family housing—unsubsidized			
2150	Multi-family housing			
2159	Total loan guarantee levels			
	Guaranteed loan subsidy (in percent):			
2320	Single family housing—unsubsidized			–1.00
2320	Multi-family housing			–4.38
2329	Weighted average subsidy rate			–1.04
	Guaranteed loan subsidy budget authority:			
2330	Single family housing—unsubsidized			–37
2330	Multi-family housing			–3
2339	Total subsidy budget authority			–40
	Guaranteed loan subsidy outlays:			
2340	Single family housing—unsubsidized			–37
2340	Multi-family housing			–3
2349	Total subsidy outlays			–40

This proposed legislation would eliminate the provision in the Housing Act of 1949 that requires that at least 20 percent of the section 538 multi-family housing loans be subsidized through interest rate buydowns. In most cases, the tenants this program serves have incomes high enough to guarantee sufficient cash flow to borrowers to allow them to pay back the loan.

Proposed legislation would also establish for section 502 guaranteed single family housing loans a guarantee fee of 2 percent which lowers the subsidy rate of the program and allows the administration to provide more loans at less cost to the taxpayer.

Rural Housing Insurance Fund Direct Loan Financing Account

Program and Financing (in millions of dollars)

Identification code 12–4215–0–3–371		1999 actual	2000 est.	2001 est.
	Obligations by program activity:			
	Operating program:			
00.01	Direct loans	1,169	1,371	1,515
00.02	Advances on behalf of borrowers	72	85	94
00.03	Collateral acquired by default	1	5	6
00.04	Interest on Treasury borrowing	555	611	668
00.06	Other expenses	9	10	11
00.91	Subtotal, Operating program	1,806	2,082	2,294
	Reestimates:			
08.02	Downward subsidy reestimate paid to receipt account	25		
08.04	Interest on downward reestimate paid to receipt account	9		
08.91	Subtotal, Reestimates	34		
10.00	Total new obligations	1,840	2,082	2,294
	Budgetary resources available for obligation:			
21.40	Unobligated balance available, start of year	58	101	
22.00	New financing authority (gross)	1,860	1,981	2,294
22.10	Resources available from recoveries of prior year obligations	47		
22.70	Balance of authority to borrow withdrawn	–24		
23.90	Total budgetary resources available for obligation	1,942	2,082	2,294
23.95	Total new obligations	–1,840	–2,082	–2,294
24.40	Unobligated balance available, end of year	101		
	New financing authority (gross), detail:			
	Mandatory:			
67.15	Authority to borrow (indefinite)	1,066	1,227	1,356
	Spending authority from offsetting collections:			
	Discretionary:			
68.00	Offsetting collections (cash)	1,173	1,158	1,351
68.10	From Federal sources: Change in receivables and unpaid, unfilled orders	–12	–22	34
68.47	Portion applied to repay debt	–367	–383	–447
68.90	Spending authority from offsetting collections (total discretionary)	794	753	938
70.00	Total new financing authority (gross)	1,860	1,980	2,294
	Change in unpaid obligations:			
	Unpaid obligations, start of year:			
	Obligated balance, start of year:			
72.40	Obligated balance with Treasury, start of year	180	196	203
72.40	Obligated balance, authority to borrow, start of year	300	327	380
72.95	Receivables from program account	196	184	162
72.99	Total unpaid obligations, start of year	676	707	745
73.10	Total new obligations	1,840	2,082	2,294
73.20	Total financing disbursements (gross)	–1,762	–2,043	–2,227
73.45	Adjustments in unexpired accounts	–47		
	Unpaid obligations, end of year:			
	Obligated balance, end of year:			
74.40	Obligated balance with Treasury, end of year	196	203	213
74.40	Obligated balance, authority to borrow, end of year	327	380	403
74.95	Receivables from program account	184	162	196
74.99	Total unpaid obligations, end of year	707	745	812
87.00	Total financing disbursements (gross)	1,762	2,043	2,227
	Offsets:			
	Against gross financing authority and financing disbursements:			
	Offsetting collections (cash) from:			
88.00	Federal sources: payments from program account	–315	–196	–266
88.25	Interest on uninvested funds	–75	–79	–86
	Non-Federal sources:			
88.40	Non-Federal sources: Repayments of principal	–367	–431	–503
88.40	Interest received on loans	–378	–414	–455
88.40	Undistributed receipts	–2		
88.40	Proceeds on sale of acquired property	–21	–20	–21
88.40	Recaptured income	–10	–12	–14
88.40	Appraisal fees	–4	–4	–4
88.40	Miscellaneous collections	–1	–2	–2
88.90	Total, offsetting collections (cash)	–1,173	–1,158	–1,351
	Against gross financing authority only:			
88.95	Change in receivables from program accounts	12	22	–34
	Net financing authority and financing disbursements:			
89.00	Financing authority	699	845	909
90.00	Financing disbursements	590	885	876

Status of Direct Loans (in millions of dollars)

Identification code 12–4215–0–3–371		1999 actual	2000 est.	2001 est.
	Position with respect to appropriations act limitation on obligations:			
1111	Limitation on direct loans	1,167	1,360	1,515
1112	Unobligated direct loan limitation	–13		
1113	Unobligated limitation carried forward	11	11	
1131	Direct loan obligations exempt from limitation	4		
1150	Total direct loan obligations	1,169	1,371	1,515
	Cumulative balance of direct loans outstanding:			
1210	Outstanding, start of year	9,411	10,180	11,173
1231	Disbursements: Direct loan disbursements	1,137	1,332	1,448
1251	Repayments: Repayments and prepayments	–373	–431	–503
1261	Adjustments: Capitalized interest	31	34	37
	Write-offs for default:			
1263	Direct loans	–26	–27	–30
1264	Other adjustments, net		85	94
1290	Outstanding, end of year	10,180	11,173	12,219

As required by the Federal Credit Reform Act of 1990, this non-budgetary account records all cash flows to and from the Government resulting from direct loans obligated in 1992 and beyond including credit sales of acquired property. The amounts in this account are a means of financing and are not included in the budget totals.

Credit accounts—Continued

RURAL HOUSING INSURANCE FUND DIRECT LOAN FINANCING ACCOUNT—Continued

This account finances direct rural housing loans for: section 502 very low- and low-to-moderate-income home ownership loan program; section 504 very low income housing repair loan program; section 514 domestic farm labor housing loan program; section 515 rural rental housing loan program; sections 523 self-help housing loans, and 524 site development loans; and single family and multi-family housing credit sales of acquired property.

Loan programs are limited to rural areas that include towns, villages and other places which are not part of an urban area and that have a population not in excess of 2,500 inhabitants, or is in excess of 2,500 but not in excess of 10,000 if rural in character, or has a population in excess of 10,000 but not more than 20,000 and is not within a standard metropolitan statistical area and has a serious lack of mortgage credit for low and moderate-income borrowers.

Balance Sheet (in millions of dollars)

Identification code 12–4215–0–3–371		1998 actual	1999 actual	2000 est.	2001 est.
	ASSETS:				
	Federal assets:				
1101	Fund balances with Treasury	180	196	203	213
	Investments in US securities:				
1106	Receivables, net	312	184	162	196
	Net value of assets related to post-1991 direct loans receivable:				
1401	Direct loans receivable, gross	9,411	10,180	11,173	12,219
1402	Interest receivable	42	40	44	48
1404	Foreclosed property	15	12	18	27
1405	Allowance for subsidy cost (–)	–2,497	–2,584	–2,703	–2,883
1499	Net present value of assets related to direct loans	6,971	7,648	8,532	9,411
1999	Total assets	7,463	8,028	8,897	9,820
	LIABILITIES:				
	Federal liabilities:				
2101	Accounts payable	33			
2103	Debt	7,197	7,802	8,694	9,581
2104	Liability for subsidy related to undisbursed loans	196	184	162	196
2105	Other		5	5	5
2207	Non-Federal liabilities: Other	37	37	36	38
2999	Total liabilities	7,463	8,028	8,897	9,820
4999	Total liabilities and net position	7,463	8,028	8,897	9,820

RURAL HOUSING INSURANCE FUND GUARANTEED LOAN FINANCING ACCOUNT

Program and Financing (in millions of dollars)

Identification code 12–4216–0–3–371		1999 actual	2000 est.	2001 est.
	Obligations by program activity:			
00.01	Default claims	36	56	71
00.02	Interest assistance paid to lenders		1	1
10.00	Total new obligations	36	57	72
	Budgetary resources available for obligation:			
21.40	Unobligated balance available, start of year	80	210	216
22.00	New financing authority (gross)	166	63	97
23.90	Total budgetary resources available for obligation	246	273	313
23.95	Total new obligations	–36	–57	–72
24.40	Unobligated balance available, end of year	210	216	241
	New financing authority (gross), detail:			
	Discretionary:			
68.00	Spending authority from offsetting collections (gross): Offsetting collections (cash)	166	63	97
	Change in unpaid obligations:			
73.10	Total new obligations	36	57	72
73.20	Total financing disbursements (gross)	–36	–57	–72
87.00	Total financing disbursements (gross)	36	57	72
	Offsets:			
	Against gross financing authority and financing disbursements:			
	Offsetting collections (cash) from:			
88.00	Federal sources	–127	–20	–47
88.25	Interest on uninvested funds	–9	–13	–14
88.40	Non-Federal sources: guarantee fees	–30	–30	–36
88.90	Total, offsetting collections (cash)	–166	–63	–97
	Net financing authority and financing disbursements:			
89.00	Financing authority			
90.00	Financing disbursements	–130	–6	–25

Status of Guaranteed Loans (in millions of dollars)

Identification code 12–4216–0–3–371		1999 actual	2000 est.	2001 est.
	Position with respect to appropriations act limitation on commitments:			
2111	Limitation on guaranteed loans made by private lenders	3,075	3,300	3,900
2112	Uncommitted loan guarantee limitation	–23		
2150	Total guaranteed loan commitments	3,052	3,300	3,900
	Cumulative balance of guaranteed loans outstanding:			
2210	Outstanding, start of year	7,206	9,772	12,059
2231	Disbursements of new guaranteed loans	3,085	2,966	3,497
2251	Repayments and prepayments	–480	–617	–757
2263	Adjustments: Terminations for default that result in claim payments	–40	–62	–79
2290	Outstanding, end of year	9,772	12,059	14,720
	Memorandum:			
2299	Guaranteed amount of guaranteed loans outstanding, end of year	8,812	11,211	13,568

As required by the Federal Credit Reform Act of 1990, this non-budgetary account records all cash flows to and from the Government resulting from guaranteed loan commitments made in 1992 and beyond. The amounts in this account are a means of financing and are not included in the budget totals.

This account finances the nonsubsidized guaranteed section 502 low-to-moderate-income home ownership loan program and section 538 multi-family housing loan program. The guaranteed programs enable RHS to utilize private sector resources for the making and servicing of loans while the Agency provides a financial guarantee to encourage private sector activity.

Balance Sheet (in millions of dollars)

Identification code 12–4216–0–3–371		1998 actual	1999 actual	2000 est.	2001 est.
	ASSETS:				
1101	Federal assets: Fund balances with Treasury	80	210	216	241
1999	Total assets	80	210	216	241
	LIABILITIES:				
2204	Non-Federal liabilities: Liabilities for loan guarantees	80	210	216	241
2999	Total liabilities	80	210	216	241
4999	Total liabilities and net position	80	210	216	241

RURAL HOUSING INSURANCE FUND GUARANTEED LOAN FINANCING ACCOUNT

(Legislative proposal, not subject to PAYGO)

Program and Financing (in millions of dollars)

Identification code 12–4216–2–3–371		1999 actual	2000 est.	2001 est.
	Budgetary resources available for obligation:			
22.00	New financing authority (gross)			–15
23.95	Total new obligations			
24.40	Unobligated balance available, end of year			–15
	New financing authority (gross), detail:			
	Discretionary:			
68.00	Spending authority from offsetting collections (gross): Offsetting collections (cash)			–15
87.00	Total financing disbursements (gross)			
	Offsets:			
	Against gross financing authority and financing disbursements:			
	Offsetting collections (cash) from:			
88.00	Federal sources			40
88.25	Interest on uninvested funds			1
88.40	Non-Federal sources: guarantee fees			–26
88.90	Total, offsetting collections (cash)			15
	Net financing authority and financing disbursements:			
89.00	Financing authority			
90.00	Financing disbursements			15

This account reflects for section 538 multi-family housing loans the decrease in the subsidy as a result of eliminating the requirement that a certain percentage of guaranteed loans be subsidized through an interest rate buydown. Also, reflected is the decrease in the subsidy for section 502 guaranteed single family housing loans as a result of increase to the guarantee fee from one percent to one percent.

As required by the Federal Credit Reform Act of 1990, this non-budgetary account records all cash flows to and from the Government resulting from guaranteed loan commitments made in 1992 and beyond. The amounts in this account are a means of financing and are not included in the budget totals.

Balance Sheet (in millions of dollars)

Identification code 12–4216–2–3–371		1998 actual	1999 actual	2000 est.	2001 est.
	ASSETS:				
1101	Federal assets: Fund balances with Treasury				–15
1999	Total assets				–15
	LIABILITIES:				
2204	Non-Federal liabilities: Liabilities for loan guarantees				–15
2999	Total liabilities				–15
4999	Total liabilities and net position				–15

RURAL HOUSING INSURANCE FUND LIQUIDATING ACCOUNT

Program and Financing (in millions of dollars)

Identification code 12–4141–0–3–371		1999 actual	2000 est.	2001 est.
	Obligations by program activity:			
	Capital investment:			
00.02	Advances on behalf of borrowers	96	88	96
00.04	Purchases of certificates of beneficial ownership	1	7	
00.05	Collateral acquired by default	2	3	3
00.06	Judgments		1	1
00.07	Unclassified recoverable costs	13		
00.91	Total capital investment	111	99	100
	Operating expenses:			
01.02	Interest on certificates of beneficial ownership	1	1	
01.03	Interest on FFB borrowings	857	566	450
01.06	Interest credits on loans sold to investors	2	2	1
01.07	Other costs incident to loans	4	3	3
01.91	Total operating expenses	865	572	454
10.00	Total new obligations	976	671	554
	Budgetary resources available for obligation:			
22.00	New budget authority (gross)	976	671	553
22.10	Resources available from recoveries of prior year obligations	8		
22.60	Portion applied to repay debt	–8		
23.90	Total budgetary resources available for obligation	976	671	553
23.95	Total new obligations	–976	–671	–554
	New budget authority (gross), detail:			
	Mandatory:			
60.05	Appropriation (indefinite)	1,171	200	
60.47	Portion applied to repay debt	–195		
62.50	Appropriation (total mandatory)	976	200	
69.00	Offsetting collections (cash)	2,172	2,056	1,927
69.27	Capital transfer to general fund			–989
69.47	Portion applied to repay debt	–2,172	–1,585	–385
69.90	Spending authority from offsetting collections (total mandatory)		471	553
70.00	Total new budget authority (gross)	976	671	553
	Change in unpaid obligations:			
72.40	Unpaid obligations, start of year: Obligated fund balance with treasury, end of year	583	483	382
73.10	Total new obligations	976	671	554
73.20	Total outlays (gross)	–1,068	–771	–587
73.45	Adjustments in unexpired accounts	–8		
74.40	Unpaid obligations, end of year: Obligated fund balance with Treasury, end of year	483	382	349
	Outlays (gross), detail:			
86.97	Outlays from new mandatory authority	933	534	415
86.98	Outlays from mandatory balances	135	237	172
87.00	Total outlays (gross)	1,068	771	587
	Offsets:			
	Against gross budget authority and outlays:			
	Offsetting collections (cash) from:			
	Non-Federal sources:			
88.40	Repayments of loans and advances	–1,182	–1,116	–1,054
88.40	Proceeds from sale of acquired property	–32	–38	–40
88.40	Payments on judgments	–2	–3	–3
88.40	Interest payments from borrowers	–843	–778	–716
88.40	Recapture of subsidies	–116	–120	–113
88.40	Fees and other revenue	–5	–1	–1
88.40	Undistributed receipts	8		
88.90	Total, offsetting collections (cash)	–2,172	–2,056	–1,927
	Net budget authority and outlays:			
89.00	Budget authority	–1,196	–1,385	–1,374
90.00	Outlays	–1,104	–1,285	–1,340

Status of Direct Loans (in millions of dollars)

Identification code 12–4141–0–3–371		1999 actual	2000 est.	2001 est.
	Cumulative balance of direct loans outstanding:			
1210	Outstanding, start of year	19,704	18,373	17,246
1251	Repayments: Repayments and prepayments	–1,182	–1,116	–1,054
1261	Adjustments: Capitalized interest	66	56	52
	Write-offs for default:			
1263	Direct loans	–69	–65	–61
1264	Other adjustments, net	–146	–2	11
1290	Outstanding, end of year	18,373	17,246	16,194

Status of Guaranteed Loans (in millions of dollars)

Identification code 12–4141–0–3–371		1999 actual	2000 est.	2001 est.
	Cumulative balance of guaranteed loans outstanding:			
2210	Outstanding, start of year	27	23	21

Credit accounts—Continued

RURAL HOUSING INSURANCE FUND LIQUIDATING ACCOUNT—Continued

Status of Guaranteed Loans (in millions of dollars)—Continued

Identification code 12–4141–0–3–371	1999 actual	2000 est.	2001 est.
2251 Repayments and prepayments	−3	−3	−2
2290 Outstanding, end of year	23	21	18
Memorandum:			
2299 Guaranteed amount of guaranteed loans outstanding, end of year	21	19	16

As required by the Federal Credit Reform Act of 1990, this account records, for this program, all cash flows to and from the Government resulting from direct loans obligated and loan guarantees committed prior to 1992. New loan activity in 1992 and beyond (including credit sales of acquired property that resulted from obligations or commitments in any year) is recorded in corresponding program and financing accounts.

Statement of Operations (in millions of dollars)

Identification code 12–4141–0–3–371	1998 actual	1999 actual	2000 est.	2001 est.
0101 Revenue	1,275	991	908	831
0102 Expense	−1,515	−958	−672	−552
0105 Net income or loss (−)	−240	33	236	279

Balance Sheet (in millions of dollars)

Identification code 12–4141–0–3–371	1998 actual	1999 actual	2000 est.	2001 est.
ASSETS:				
1101 Federal assets: Fund balances with Treasury	583	483	382	349
Net value of assets related to pre-1992 direct loans receivable and acquired defaulted guaranteed loans receivable:				
1601 Direct loans, gross	19,704	18,373	17,246	16,194
1602 Interest receivable	279	391	374	348
1603 Allowance for estimated uncollectible loans and interest (−)	−7,517	−6,349	−5,962	−5,597
1604 Direct loans and interest receivable, net	12,466	12,415	11,658	10,945
1606 Foreclosed property	43	52	54	51
1699 Value of assets related to direct loans	12,509	12,467	11,712	10,996
1901 Other Federal assets: Other assets	21	23	21	21
1999 Total assets	13,113	12,973	12,115	11,366
LIABILITIES:				
Federal liabilities:				
2101 Accounts payable	1	1	1	1
2102 Interest payable	525	398	297	264
2103 Debt	9,500	7,125	5,540	5,155
2104 Resources payable to Treasury	2,978	5,343	6,179	5,848
2105 Liabilities for loan guarantees	4	3	2	2
Non-Federal liabilities:				
2202 Interest payable	1	1	1	1
2203 Debt	10	9	2	2
2207 Other	93	93	93	93
2999 Total liabilities	13,112	12,973	12,115	11,366
4999 Total liabilities and net position	13,112	12,973	12,115	11,366

Object Classification (in millions of dollars)

Identification code 12–4141–0–3–371	1999 actual	2000 est.	2001 est.
25.2 Other services	4	3	3
33.0 Investments and loans	111	99	100
41.0 Grants, subsidies, and contributions	2	2	1
43.0 Interest and dividends	859	567	450

99.9 Total new obligations	976	671	554

RURAL BUSINESS-COOPERATIVE SERVICE

Federal Funds

General and special funds:

[RURAL EMPOWERMENT ZONES]

[For grants for the rural empowerment zone and enterprise communities programs, as designated by the Secretary of Agriculture, $15,000,000 to the Secretary of Agriculture for grants for designated empowerment zones in rural areas and for grants for designated rural enterprise communities, to remain available until expended.] *(Departments of Veterans Affairs and Housing and Urban Development, and Independent Agencies Appropriations Act, 2000.)*

Program and Financing (in millions of dollars)

Identification code 12–0402–0–1–452	1999 actual	2000 est.	2001 est.
Obligations by program activity:			
10.00 Total new obligations (object class 41.0)	....	30	....
Budgetary resources available for obligation:			
21.40 Unobligated balance available, start of year	....	15	....
22.00 New budget authority (gross)	15	15	....
23.90 Total budgetary resources available for obligation	15	30	....
23.95 Total new obligations	....	−30	....
24.40 Unobligated balance available, end of year	15	....	....
New budget authority (gross), detail:			
Discretionary:			
40.00 Appropriation	15	15	....
Change in unpaid obligations:			
72.40 Unpaid obligations, start of year: Obligated balance, start of year	....	....	24
73.10 Total new obligations	....	30	....
73.20 Total outlays (gross)	....	−6	−12
74.40 Unpaid obligations, end of year: Obligated balance, end of year	....	24	12
Outlays (gross), detail:			
86.93 Outlays from discretionary balances	....	6	12
Net budget authority and outlays:			
89.00 Budget authority	15	15	....
90.00 Outlays	....	6	12

Summary of Budget Authority and Outlays

(in millions of dollars)

	1999 actual	*2000 est.*	*2001 est.*
Enacted/requested:			
Budget Authority	15	15	....
Outlays	....	6	12
Legislative proposal, subject to PAYGO:			
Budget Authority	....	....	15
Outlays	....	....	....
Total:			
Budget Authority	15	15	15
Outlays	....	6	12

The goal of the Empowerment Zone/Enterprise Community (EZ/EC) initiative is to revitalize rural communities in a manner that attracts private sector investment and thereby provides self-sustaining community and economic development. The first two years of the authorized ten-year for EZ/EC's designated as part of the second round of this initiative was provided through the FY 1999 and 2000 appropriation acts. Legislation will be proposed to provide the outyear follow-on funding for the five new rural empowerment zones, and 20 new entereprise communities as authorized by the Taxpayer Relief Act of 1997, to create economic opportunity in the most distressed rural communities. A similar proposal is requested for urban zones through the Department of Housing and Urban Development.

The flexible grant funding is available for a wide variety of community and economic development purposes that link human capital needs with economic development initiatives. The purposes may include revolving loan funds for business capitalization or community development, job training and job counseling, infrastructure investment, home ownership and home ownership counseling, health care and related facilities, child care and administrative costs linked to redevelopment efforts.

Similar to the first round, the second round was a multi-year effort based on a comprehensive development plan involving community residents, the private sector, the non-profit community and local, State and Federal governments. Experience from the initial round of urban and rural designations demonstrates significant successes that are stimulating billions of dollars in private sector investment, reviving communities that had given up hope for economic opportunity and creating thousands of jobs, moving people from dependency to active participation in the economy. Round two is built on the successes of the initial round.

Rural Empowerment Zones

(Proposed legislation, subject to PAYGO)

Program and Financing (in millions of dollars)

Identification code 12–0402–4–1–452	1999 actual	2000 est.	2001 est.
Obligations by program activity:			
10.00 Total new obligations (object class 41.0)			15
Budgetary resources available for obligation:			
22.00 New budget authority (gross)			15
23.95 Total new obligations			−15
New budget authority (gross), detail:			
Mandatory:			
60.00 Appropriation			15
Change in unpaid obligations:			
73.10 Total new obligations			15
74.40 Unpaid obligations, end of year: Obligated balance, end of year			15
Net budget authority and outlays:			
89.00 Budget authority			15
90.00 Outlays			

This account provides grants for 5 rural empowerment zones and 20 rural enterprise communities that are entities designated under section 1391(g) of the Internal Revenue Code of 1986, to continue a second round of the empowerment zone program in rural areas. Funds for the rural enterprise communities are not for tax treatment under the Internal Revenue Code. Second round EZ/EC recipients were designated in January 1999. Legislation will be proposed to provide mandatory funding in 2001 and the out years for these recipients.

Salaries and Expenses

(rural development administration)

Program and Financing (in millions of dollars)

Identification code 12–3400–0–1–452	1999 actual	2000 est.	2001 est.
Change in unpaid obligations:			
72.40 Unpaid obligations, start of year: Obligated balance, start of year	2	1	
73.20 Total outlays (gross)		−1	
73.40 Adjustments in expired accounts (net)	−1		
74.40 Unpaid obligations, end of year: Obligated balance, end of year	1		
Outlays (gross), detail:			
86.93 Outlays from discretionary balances		1	
Net budget authority and outlays:			
89.00 Budget authority			
90.00 Outlays		1	

Beginning in 1995, programs and services formerly provided by the Rural Development Administration are included in other Department accounts.

Rural Cooperative Development Grants

For rural cooperative development grants authorized under section 310B(e) of the Consolidated Farm and Rural Development Act (7 U.S.C. 1932), [$6,000,000, of which $1,500,000] *$11,500,000, of which $2,000,000* shall be available for cooperative agreements for the appropriate technology transfer for rural areas program, *and $2,000,000 shall be available for cooperative research agreements*: *Provided*, That [at least 25 percent] *not to exceed $1,500,000* of the total amount appropriated shall be made available to cooperatives or associations of cooperatives that assist small, minority producers: *Provided further, that $1,500,000 of the total amount appropriated shall be for grants to cooperatives that process and market bio-based products, of which $1,000,000 is for a pilot program for Rural Utilities Service electric borrowers to demonstrate the efficiency of bio-mass fuel generation. (Agriculture, Rural Development, Food and Drug Administration, and Related Agencies Appropriations Act, 2000.)*

Program and Financing (in millions of dollars)

Identification code 12–1900–0–1–452	1999 actual	2000 est.	2001 est.
Obligations by program activity:			
00.01 Rural cooperative development grants	2	3	8
00.02 Appropriate technology transfer for rural areas	1	2	2
00.03 Cooperative research agreements		1	2
10.00 Total new obligations (object class 41.0)	3	6	12
Budgetary resources available for obligation:			
22.00 New budget authority (gross)	3	6	12
23.95 Total new obligations	−3	−6	−12
New budget authority (gross), detail:			
Discretionary:			
40.00 Appropriation	3	6	12
Change in unpaid obligations:			
72.40 Unpaid obligations, start of year: Obligated balance, start of year	4	3	4
73.10 Total new obligations	3	6	12
73.20 Total outlays (gross)	−3	−6	−7
74.40 Unpaid obligations, end of year: Obligated balance, end of year	3	4	8
Outlays (gross), detail:			
86.90 Outlays from new discretionary authority	1	3	4
86.93 Outlays from discretionary balances	2	3	3
87.00 Total outlays (gross)	3	6	7
Net budget authority and outlays:			
89.00 Budget authority	3	6	12
90.00 Outlays	3	6	7

Grants for rural cooperative development were authorized under section 310B(e) of the Consolidated Farm and Rural Development Act by Public Law 104–127, April 4, 1996. These grants are made available to nonprofit corporations and institutions of higher education to fund the establishment and operation of centers for rural cooperative development. The primary purpose of the centers is the improvement of economic conditions of rural areas through the development of new cooperatives and improving operations of existing cooperatives. RBS can fund up to 75 percent of any project and associated administrative costs and requires at least a 25 percent matching share from the applicant which must be from non-Federal sources.

The Appropriate Technology Transfer to Rural Areas (ATTRA) program was first authorized by the Food Security

General and special funds—Continued

RURAL COOPERATIVE DEVELOPMENT GRANTS—Continued

Act of 1985. The program provides information and technical assistance to agricultural producers to adopt sustainable agricultural practices that are environmentally friendly and lower production costs.

Funds are requested for cooperative research agreements to help the Rural Development mission area maintain a predictable level of research on agricultural and non-agricultural cooperative issues. Also, $2 million is requested for grants for cooperatives that process and market bio-based products. Of this amount, $1 million is for a pilot program through the Rural Utilities Service to demonstrate the efficiency of bio-mass fuel generation.

RURAL ECONOMIC DEVELOPMENT GRANTS

Program and Financing (in millions of dollars)

Identification code 12–3105–0–1–452	1999 actual	2000 est.	2001 est.
Obligations by program activity:			
10.00 Total new obligations (object class 41.0)	11	4	4
Budgetary resources available for obligation:			
21.40 Unobligated balance available, start of year	17	7	4
22.00 New budget authority (gross)	2	3	3
22.10 Resources available from recoveries of prior year obligations	1		
23.90 Total budgetary resources available for obligation	20	10	7
23.95 Total new obligations	−11	−4	−4
24.40 Unobligated balance available, end of year	7	4	2
New budget authority (gross), detail:			
Mandatory:			
69.00 Offsetting collections (cash)	2	3	3
Change in unpaid obligations:			
Unpaid obligations, start of year:			
72.40 Obligated balance, start of year	14	14	8
72.95 From Federal sources: Receivables and unpaid, unfilled orders	3	3	3
72.99 Total unpaid obligations, start of year	17	17	11
73.10 Total new obligations	11	4	4
73.20 Total outlays (gross)	−11	−10	−7
73.45 Adjustments in unexpired accounts	−1		
Unpaid obligations, end of year:			
74.40 Obligated balance, end of year	14	8	5
74.95 From Federal sources: Receivables and unpaid, unfilled orders	3	3	3
74.99 Total unpaid obligations, end of year	17	11	8
Outlays (gross), detail:			
86.97 Outlays from new mandatory authority	1		
86.98 Outlays from mandatory balances	11	9	7
87.00 Total outlays (gross)	11	10	7
Offsets:			
Against gross budget authority and outlays:			
88.00 Offsetting collections (cash) from: Federal sources	−2	−3	−3
Net budget authority and outlays:			
89.00 Budget authority			
90.00 Outlays	11	7	4

This grant program is authorized under section 313 of the Rural Electrification Act, as amended, and provides funds for the purpose of promoting rural economic development and job creation projects, including funding for project feasibility studies, start-up costs, incubator projects and other expenses for the purpose of fostering rural development.

Funding for this program is provided from the interest differential on Rural Utilities Service borrowers' cushion of credit accounts.

NATIONAL SHEEP INDUSTRY IMPROVEMENT CENTER REVOLVING FUND

For National Sheep Industry Improvement Center Revolving Fund authorized under section 375 of the Consolidated Farm and Rural Development Act, as amended (7 U.S.C. 2008j), $5,000,000, to remain available until expended.

Program and Financing (in millions of dollars)

Identification code 12–1906–0–1–452	1999 actual	2000 est.	2001 est.
Obligations by program activity:			
10.00 Total new obligations (object class 41.0)		10	5
Budgetary resources available for obligation:			
21.40 Unobligated balance available, start of year	20	20	10
22.00 New budget authority (gross)			5
23.90 Total budgetary resources available for obligation	20	20	15
23.95 Total new obligations		−10	−5
24.40 Unobligated balance available, end of year	20	10	10
New budget authority (gross), detail:			
Discretionary:			
40.00 Appropriation			5
Change in unpaid obligations:			
73.10 Total new obligations		10	5
73.20 Total outlays (gross)		−10	−5
Outlays (gross), detail:			
86.90 Outlays from new discretionary authority			5
86.98 Outlays from mandatory balances		10	
87.00 Total outlays (gross)		10	5
Net budget authority and outlays:			
89.00 Budget authority			5
90.00 Outlays		10	5

The Federal Agriculture Improvement Act of 1996 established the National Sheep Industry Improvement Center to promote activities to strengthen and enhance production or marketing of sheep and goat products in the United States. The Center may provide loans or grants to eligible entities to provide assistance to the industry for infrastructure development, business development, production, resource development, and market and environmental research. The 1996 Act provided up to $20 million in mandatory funding for the establishment and operation of the Center and authorized additional discretionary funding of $30 million. In 2000, $10 million was granted to an intermediary to provide assistance to the sheep and lamb industry. An additional $5 million in discretionary funds are requested in 2001 to help the domestic lamb industry adjust to foreign competition, as part of the President's initiative supporting the domestic lamb industry.

Credit accounts:

RURAL BUSINESS AND INDUSTRY DIRECT LOANS FINANCING ACCOUNT

Program and Financing (in millions of dollars)

Identification code 12–4223–0–3–452	1999 actual	2000 est.	2001 est.
Obligations by program activity:			
Operating program:			
00.01 Direct loans	26	50	50
00.02 Interest on Treasury borrowings	3	4	6
00.03 Default claims		6	10
00.91 Subtotal, Operating program	29	60	66
Reestimates:			
08.01 Negative subsidy paid to receipt account	4	7	
08.02 Downward reestimate paid to receipt account	2		
08.91 Subtotal, Reestimates	6	7	

10.00	Total new obligations	35	67	66
	Budgetary resources available for obligation:			
21.40	Unobligated balance available, start of year		1	
22.00	New financing authority (gross)	35	66	66
22.10	Resources available from recoveries of prior year obligations	2		
22.70	Balance of authority to borrow withdrawn	−1		
23.90	Total budgetary resources available for obligation	36	67	66
23.95	Total new obligations	−35	−67	−66
24.40	Unobligated balance available, end of year	1		
	New financing authority (gross), detail:			
	Mandatory:			
67.15	Authority to borrow (indefinite)	32	58	50
	Spending authority from offsetting collections:			
	Discretionary:			
68.00	Offsetting collections (cash)	3	8	14
68.10	From Federal sources: Change in receivables and unpaid, unfilled orders			2
68.90	Spending authority from offsetting collections (total discretionary)	3	8	16
70.00	Total new financing authority (gross)	35	66	66
	Change in unpaid obligations:			
72.40	Unpaid obligations, start of year: Obligated balance, start of year	15	21	40
73.10	Total new obligations	35	67	66
73.20	Total financing disbursements (gross)	−27	−48	−66
73.40	Adjustments in expired accounts (net)	−2		
73.45	Adjustments in unexpired accounts	−2		
	Unpaid obligations, end of year:			
74.40	Obligated balance, end of year	21	40	38
74.95	Receivables from program account			2
74.99	Total unpaid obligations, end of year	21	40	40
87.00	Total financing disbursements (gross)	27	48	66
	Offsets:			
	Against gross financing authority and financing disbursements:			
	Offsetting collections (cash) from:			
88.25	Interest on uninvested funds	−1		
	Non-Federal sources:			
88.40	Repayments of principal	−1	−2	−4
88.40	Interest received on loans	−1	−6	−10
88.90	Total, offsetting collections (cash)	−3	−8	−14
	Against gross financing authority only:			
88.95	Change in receivables from program accounts			−2
	Net financing authority and financing disbursements:			
89.00	Financing authority	32	58	50
90.00	Financing disbursements	23	40	52

Status of Direct Loans (in millions of dollars)

Identification code 12–4223–0–3–452		1999 actual	2000 est.	2001 est.
	Position with respect to appropriations act limitation on obligations:			
1111	Limitation on direct loans	50	50	50
1112	Unobligated direct loan limitation	−24		
1150	Total direct loan obligations	26	50	50
	Cumulative balance of direct loans outstanding:			
1210	Outstanding, start of year	19	38	61
1231	Disbursements: Direct loan disbursements	20	31	51
1251	Repayments: Repayments and prepayments	−1	−2	−4
1263	Write-offs for default: Direct loans		−6	−10
1290	Outstanding, end of year	38	61	98

As required by the Federal Credit Reform Act of 1990, this non-budgetary account records all cash flows to and from the Government resulting from direct loans obligated in 1992 and beyond. The amounts in this account are a means of financing and are not included in the budget totals. The subsidy cost of these programs is funded through the Rural Community Advancement Program. Loans made prior to 1992 are recorded in the Rural Development Insurance Fund Liquidating Account.

Direct business and industry loans are made to public, private, or cooperative organizations, Indian tribes or tribal groups, corporate entities, or individuals for the purpose of improving the economic climate in rural areas.

Balance Sheet (in millions of dollars)

Identification code 12–4223–0–3–452		1998 actual	1999 actual	2000 est.	2001 est.
	ASSETS:				
	Federal assets:				
1101	Fund balances with Treasury	2	5	5	5
	Investments in US securities:				
1107	Advances and prepayments		7		
1206	Non-Federal assets: Receivables, net		1		
	Net value of assets related to post-1991 direct loans receivable:				
1401	Direct loans receivable, gross	19	38	61	98
1499	Net present value of assets related to direct loans	19	38	61	98
1999	Total assets	21	51	66	103
	LIABILITIES:				
	Federal liabilities:				
2101	Accounts payable	2	3	4	5
2104	Resources payable to Treasury	19	48	57	93
2999	Total liabilities	21	51	61	98
4999	Total liabilities and net position	21	51	61	98

Rural Business and Industry Guaranteed Loans Financing Account

Program and Financing (in millions of dollars)

Identification code 12–4227–0–3–452		1999 actual	2000 est.	2001 est.
	Obligations by program activity:			
00.01	Default claims	28	33	35
10.00	Total new obligations	28	33	35
	Budgetary resources available for obligation:			
21.40	Unobligated balance available, start of year	54	107	127
22.00	New financing authority (gross)	80	54	35
23.90	Total budgetary resources available for obligation	134	161	162
23.95	Total new obligations	−28	−33	−35
24.40	Unobligated balance available, end of year	107	127	127
	New financing authority (gross), detail:			
	Spending authority from offsetting collections:			
	Discretionary:			
68.00	Offsetting collections (cash)	85	54	35
68.47	Portion applied to repay debt	−5		
68.90	Spending authority from offsetting collections (total discretionary)	80	54	35
	Change in unpaid obligations:			
73.10	Total new obligations	28	33	35
73.20	Total financing disbursements (gross)	−28	−33	−35
87.00	Total financing disbursements (gross)	28	33	35
	Offsets:			
	Against gross financing authority and financing disbursements:			
	Offsetting collections (cash) from:			
88.00	Federal sources	−64	−29	−10
88.25	Interest on uninvested funds	−5	−5	−6
	Non-Federal sources:			
88.40	Interest and principal on purchased loans from secondary market		−3	−3
88.40	Guarantee fees	−16	−17	−16
88.90	Total, offsetting collections (cash)	−85	−54	−35
	Net financing authority and financing disbursements:			
89.00	Financing authority	−5		

Credit accounts—Continued

RURAL BUSINESS AND INDUSTRY GUARANTEED LOANS FINANCING ACCOUNT—Continued

Program and Financing (in millions of dollars)—Continued

Identification code 12–4227–0–3–452	1999 actual	2000 est.	2001 est.
90.00 Financing disbursements	–57	–21	

Status of Guaranteed Loans (in millions of dollars)

Identification code 12–4227–0–3–452	1999 actual	2000 est.	2001 est.
Position with respect to appropriations act limitation on commitments:			
2111 Limitation on guaranteed loans made by private lenders	1,000	850	1,250
2112 Uncommitted loan guarantee limitation	262		
2131 Guaranteed loan commitments exempt from limitation	19	19	
2150 Total guaranteed loan commitments	1,281	869	1,250
2199 Guaranteed amount of guaranteed loan commitments	866	791	791
Cumulative balance of guaranteed loans outstanding:			
2210 Outstanding, start of year	1,876	2,763	3,719
2231 Disbursements of new guaranteed loans	1,027	1,134	1,059
2251 Repayments and prepayments	–107	–145	–188
2263 Adjustments: Terminations for default that result in claim payments	–33	–33	–33
2290 Outstanding, end of year	2,763	3,719	4,557
Memorandum:			
2299 Guaranteed amount of guaranteed loans outstanding, end of year	2,228	2,807	3,434

As required by the Federal Credit Reform Act of 1990, this non-budgetary account records all cash flows to and from the Government resulting from guaranteed loans committed in 1992 and beyond. The amounts in this account are a means of financing and are not included in the budget totals. The subsidy cost of this program is funded through the Rural Community Advancement Program. Loans made prior to 1992 are recorded in the Rural Development Insurance Fund Liquidating Account.

This account finances loan guarantee commitments for industrial development in rural areas.

Balance Sheet (in millions of dollars)

Identification code 12–4227–0–3–452	1998 actual	1999 actual	2000 est.	2001 est.
ASSETS:				
1101 Federal assets: Fund balances with Treasury	54	103	86	86
1999 Total assets	54	103	86	86
LIABILITIES:				
2204 Non-Federal liabilities: Liabilities for loan guarantees	54	103	86	86
2999 Total liabilities	54	103	86	86
4999 Total liabilities and net position	54	103	86	86

RURAL DEVELOPMENT LOAN FUND PROGRAM ACCOUNT

(INCLUDING TRANSFERS OF FUNDS)

For the cost of direct loans, [$16,615,000] *$32,834,000*, as authorized by the Rural Development Loan Fund (42 U.S.C. 9812(a)), *of which, $2,036,000 shall be for Federally Recognized Native American Tribes: and $4,072,000 shall be for the Mississippi Delta Region Counties (as defined by P.L. 100–460) Provided*, That such costs, including the cost of modifying such loans, shall be as defined in section 502 of the Congressional Budget Act of 1974: *Provided further*, That these funds are available to subsidize gross obligations for the principal amount of direct loans of [$38,256,000] *$64,495,000*: *Provided further*, That of the total amount appropriated, [$3,216,000] *$5,091,000* shall be available through June 30, [2000] *2001*, for the cost of direct loans for authorized empowerment zones and enterprise communities [and communities designated by the Secretary of Agriculture as Rural Economic Area Partnership Zones].

In addition, for administrative expenses to carry out the direct loan programs, [$3,337,000] *$3,640,000* shall be transferred to and merged with the appropriation for "Rural [Business-Cooperative Service] *Development*, Salaries and Expenses". *(Agriculture, Rural Development, Food and Drug Administration, and Related Agencies Appropriations Act, 2000.)*

General Fund Credit Receipt Accounts (in millions of dollars)

Identification code 12–2069–0–1–452	1999 actual	2000 est.	2001 est.
0101 Rural development loans, downward reestimates of subsidies	8		

Program and Financing (in millions of dollars)

Identification code 12–2069–0–1–452	1999 actual	2000 est.	2001 est.
Obligations by program activity:			
00.01 Direct loan subsidy	17	17	33
00.05 Reestimates of direct loan subsidy	1		
00.09 Administrative expense	3	3	3
10.00 Total new obligations	21	20	36
Budgetary resources available for obligation:			
22.00 New budget authority (gross)	21	20	36
23.95 Total new obligations	–21	–20	–36
New budget authority (gross), detail:			
Discretionary:			
40.00 Appropriation	20	20	36
Mandatory:			
60.05 Appropriation (indefinite)	1		
70.00 Total new budget authority (gross)	21	20	36
Change in unpaid obligations:			
72.40 Unpaid obligations, start of year: Obligated balance, start of year	61	55	50
73.10 Total new obligations	21	20	36
73.20 Total outlays (gross)	–27	–25	–25
74.40 Unpaid obligations, end of year: Obligated balance, end of year	55	50	61
Outlays (gross), detail:			
86.90 Outlays from new discretionary authority	4	4	5
86.93 Outlays from discretionary balances	22	21	20
86.97 Outlays from new mandatory authority	1		
87.00 Total outlays (gross)	27	25	25
Net budget authority and outlays:			
89.00 Budget authority	21	20	36
90.00 Outlays	27	25	25

Summary of Loan Levels, Subsidy Budget Authority and Outlays by Program (in millions of dollars)

Identification code 12–2069–0–1–452	1999 actual	2000 est.	2001 est.
Direct loan levels supportable by subsidy budget authority:			
1150 Intermediary Relending Loans	33	38	64
1159 Total direct loan levels	33	38	64
Direct loan subsidy (in percent):			
1320 Subsidy rate	50.35	43.43	50.91
1329 Weighted average subsidy rate	50.35	43.43	50.91
Direct loan subsidy budget authority:			
1330 Subsidy budget authority	17	17	33
1339 Total subsidy budget authority	17	17	33
Direct loan subsidy outlays:			
1340 Subsidy outlays	24	22	21
1349 Total subsidy outlays	24	22	21
Administrative expense data:			
3510 Budget authority	3	3	3

3590	Outlays from new authority	3	3	3

This account finances loans to intermediary borrowers, who in turn relend the funds to small rural businesses, community development corporations, and other organizations for the purpose of improving economic opportunities in rural areas. Through the use of local intermediaries, this program serves small-scale enterprises and gives preference to those communities with the greatest need.

As required by the Federal Credit Reform Act of 1990, this account records, for this program, the subsidy costs associated with the direct loans obligated in 1992 and beyond, as well as administrative expenses of this program. The subsidy amounts are estimated on a present value basis; the administrative expenses are estimated on a cash basis.

Object Classification (in millions of dollars)

Identification code 12–2069–0–1–452		1999 actual	2000 est.	2001 est.
25.3	Purchases of goods and services from Government accounts	3	3	3
41.0	Grants, subsidies, and contributions	18	17	33
99.9	Total new obligations	21	20	36

Rural Development Loan Fund Direct Loan Financing Account

Program and Financing (in millions of dollars)

Identification code 12–4219–0–3–452		1999 actual	2000 est.	2001 est.
	Obligations by program activity:			
	Operating program:			
00.01	Direct loans	33	38	64
00.03	Interest on Treasury borrowing	9	11	17
00.91	Subtotal, Operating program	42	49	81
	Non-operating program:			
08.02	Downward subsidy reestimates paid to the receipt account	7		
08.04	Interest on downward reestimate paid to receipt account	1		
08.91	Subtotal, Non-operating program	8		
10.00	Total new obligations	50	49	81
	Budgetary resources available for obligation:			
22.00	New financing authority (gross)	51	49	80
22.60	Portion applied to repay debt	1		
23.90	Total budgetary resources available for obligation	52	49	80
23.95	Total new obligations	−50	−49	−81
	New financing authority (gross), detail:			
	Mandatory:			
67.15	Authority to borrow (indefinite)	24	21	35
	Spending authority from offsetting collections:			
	Discretionary:			
68.00	Offsetting collections (cash)	34	33	34
68.10	From Federal sources: Change in receivables and unpaid, unfilled orders	−6	−5	11
68.47	Portion applied to repay debt	−1		
68.90	Spending authority from offsetting collections (total discretionary)	27	28	45
70.00	Total new financing authority (gross)	51	49	80
	Change in unpaid obligations:			
	Unpaid obligations, start of year:			
72.40	Obligated balance, start of year	57	52	51
72.95	Receivables from program account	61	55	50
72.99	Total unpaid obligations, start of year	118	107	101
73.10	Total new obligations	50	49	81
73.20	Total financing disbursements (gross)	−62	−55	−61
	Unpaid obligations, end of year:			
74.40	Obligated balance, end of year	52	51	60
74.95	Receivables from program account	55	50	61
74.99	Total unpaid obligations, end of year	107	101	121
87.00	Total financing disbursements (gross)	62	55	61
	Offsets:			
	Against gross financing authority and financing disbursements:			
	Offsetting collections (cash) from:			
88.00	Payments from program account	−24	−22	−21
88.25	Interest on uninvested funds	−2	−2	−2
	Non-Federal sources:			
88.40	Non-Federal sources—repayment of principal	−6	−6	−7
88.40	Non-Federal sources—interest on loans	−2	−3	−4
88.90	Total, offsetting collections (cash)	−34	−33	−34
	Against gross financing authority only:			
88.95	Change in receivables from program accounts	6	5	−11
	Net financing authority and financing disbursements:			
89.00	Financing authority	23	21	35
90.00	Financing disbursements	28	22	27

Status of Direct Loans (in millions of dollars)

Identification code 12–4219–0–3–452		1999 actual	2000 est.	2001 est.
	Position with respect to appropriations act limitation on obligations:			
1111	Limitation on direct loans	33	38	64
1150	Total direct loan obligations	33	38	64
	Cumulative balance of direct loans outstanding:			
1210	Outstanding, start of year	209	249	285
1231	Disbursements: Direct loan disbursements	44	42	41
1251	Repayments: Repayments and prepayments	−4	−6	−8
1290	Outstanding, end of year	249	285	318

As required by the Federal Credit Reform Act of 1990, this non-budgetary account records all cash flows to and from the Government resulting from direct loans obligated in 1992 and beyond. The amounts in this account are a means of financing and are not included in the budget totals.

This account finances loans to intermediary borrowers, who in turn relend the funds to small rural businesses, community development corporations, or other organizations for the purpose of improving economic opportunities in rural areas. Through the use of local intermediaries, this program serves small-scale enterprises and gives preference to those communities with the greatest need.

Balance Sheet (in millions of dollars)

Identification code 12–4219–0–3–452		1998 actual	1999 actual	2000 est.	2001 est.
	ASSETS:				
	Federal assets:				
1101	Fund balances with Treasury	24	20	22	22
	Investments in US securities:				
1106	Receivables, net	61	55	50	69
	Net value of assets related to post-1991 direct loans receivable:				
1401	Direct loans receivable, gross	209	248	285	289
1402	Interest receivable	1	1	3	3
1405	Allowance for subsidy cost (−)	−106	−118	−135	−138
1499	Net present value of assets related to direct loans	104	131	153	154
1999	Total assets	189	206	225	245
	LIABILITIES:				
	Federal liabilities:				
2104	Resources payable to Treasury	128	151	175	180
2105	Other	61	55	50	65
2999	Total liabilities	189	206	225	245
4999	Total liabilities and net position	189	206	225	245

Credit accounts—Continued

RURAL DEVELOPMENT LOAN FUND LIQUIDATING ACCOUNT

Program and Financing (in millions of dollars)

Identification code 12–4233–0–3–452	1999 actual	2000 est.	2001 est.
Budgetary resources available for obligation:			
21.40 Unobligated balance available, start of year	1	1	
22.00 New budget authority (gross)	1		
22.40 Capital transfer to general fund		−1	−1
23.90 Total budgetary resources available for obligation	2		−1
24.40 Unobligated balance available, end of year	1		
New budget authority (gross), detail:			
Mandatory:			
69.00 Offsetting collections (cash)	4	4	4
69.27 Capital transfer to general fund	−3	−4	−4
69.90 Spending authority from offsetting collections (total mandatory)	1		
Change in unpaid obligations:			
72.40 Unpaid obligations, start of year: Obligated balance, start of year	2	1	
73.20 Total outlays (gross)	−1	−1	
74.40 Unpaid obligations, end of year: Obligated balance, end of year	1		
Outlays (gross), detail:			
86.98 Outlays from mandatory balances	1	1	
Offsets:			
Against gross budget authority and outlays:			
88.40 Offsetting collections (cash) from: Non-Federal sources	−4	−4	−4
Net budget authority and outlays:			
89.00 Budget authority	−3	−4	−4
90.00 Outlays	−3	−4	−4

Status of Direct Loans (in millions of dollars)

Identification code 12–4233–0–3–452	1999 actual	2000 est.	2001 est.
Cumulative balance of direct loans outstanding:			
1210 Outstanding, start of year	77	72	68
1231 Disbursements: Direct loan disbursements		1	1
1251 Repayments: Repayments and prepayments	−4	−4	−4
1263 Write-offs for default: Direct loans	−1	−1	−1
1290 Outstanding, end of year	72	68	64

[1] Amounts shown include advances on behalf of borrowers.

As required by the Federal Credit Reform Act of 1990, this account records, for this program, all cash flows to and from the Government resulting from direct loans obligated prior to 1992. New loan activity in 1992 and beyond is recorded in corresponding program and financing accounts.

Statement of Operations (in millions of dollars)

Identification code 12–4233–0–3–452	1998 actual	1999 actual	2000 est.	2001 est.
0101 Revenue	1	1	1	1
0102 Expense	6	5	4	4
0105 Net income or loss (−)	7	6	5	5

Balance Sheet (in millions of dollars)

Identification code 12–4233–0–3–452	1998 actual	1999 actual	2000 est.	2001 est.
ASSETS:				
1101 Federal assets: Fund balances with Treasury	3	2	2	2
1206 Non-Federal assets: Receivables, net	1	1	1	1
Net value of assets related to pre-1992 direct loans receivable and acquired defaulted guaranteed loans receivable:				
1601 Direct loans, gross	77	73	70	65
1603 Allowance for estimated uncollectible loans and interest (−)	−31	−25	−20	−16
1604 Direct loans and interest receivable, net	46	48	50	49
1699 Value of assets related to direct loans	46	48	50	49
1999 Total assets	50	51	53	52
LIABILITIES:				
2104 Federal liabilities: Resources payable to Treasury	50	51	52	52
2999 Total liabilities	50	51	52	52
4999 Total liabilities and net position	50	51	52	52

RURAL ECONOMIC DEVELOPMENT LOANS PROGRAM ACCOUNT

(INCLUDING RESCISSION OF FUNDS)

For the principal amount of direct loans, as authorized under section 313 of the Rural Electrification Act, for the purpose of promoting rural economic development and job creation projects, $15,000,000.

For the cost of direct loans, including the cost of modifying loans as defined in section 502 of the Congressional Budget Act of 1974, [$3,453,000] *$3,911,000*.

Of the funds derived from interest on the cushion of credit payments in fiscal year [2000] *2001*, as authorized by section 313 of the Rural Electrification Act of 1936, [$3,453,000] *$3,911,000* shall not be obligated and [$3,453,000] *$3,911,000* are rescinded. *(Agriculture, Rural Development, Food and Drug Administration, and Related Agencies Appropriations Act, 2000.)*

General Fund Credit Receipt Accounts (in millions of dollars)

Identification code 12–3108–0–1–452	1999 actual	2000 est.	2001 est.
0101 Rural economic development loans, downward reestimates of subsidies	2		

Program and Financing (in millions of dollars)

Identification code 12–3108–0–1–452	1999 actual	2000 est.	2001 est.
Obligations by program activity:			
00.01 Direct loan subsidy	4	3	4
10.00 Total new obligations (object class 41.0)	4	3	4
Budgetary resources available for obligation:			
22.00 New budget authority (gross)	4	3	4
23.95 Total new obligations	−4	−3	−4
New budget authority (gross), detail:			
Discretionary:			
40.00 Appropriation	4	3	4
Change in unpaid obligations:			
72.40 Unpaid obligations, start of year: Obligated balance, start of year	6	4	3
73.10 Total new obligations	4	3	4
73.20 Total outlays (gross)	−6	−4	−4
74.40 Unpaid obligations, end of year: Obligated balance, end of year	4	3	4
Outlays (gross), detail:			
86.90 Outlays from new discretionary authority	1		1
86.93 Outlays from discretionary balances	5	4	3
87.00 Total outlays (gross)	6	4	4
Net budget authority and outlays:			
89.00 Budget authority	4	3	4
90.00 Outlays	6	4	4

Summary of Loan Levels, Subsidy Budget Authority and Outlays by Program (in millions of dollars)

Identification code 12–3108–0–1–452	1999 actual	2000 est.	2001 est.
Direct loan levels supportable by subsidy budget authority:			
1150 Direct loan levels	15	15	15
1159 Total direct loan levels	15	15	15
Direct loan subsidy (in percent):			
1320 Subsidy rate	25.22	23.02	26.07
1329 Weighted average subsidy rate	25.22	23.02	26.07
Direct loan subsidy budget authority:			
1330 Subsidy budget authority	4	3	4
1339 Total subsidy budget authority	4	3	4
Direct loan subsidy outlays:			
1340 Subsidy outlays	6	4	4
1349 Total subsidy outlays	6	4	4

Rural economic development loans are made for the purpose of promoting rural economic development and job creation projects. Loans are made to electric and telecommunication borrowers, who in turn finance rural development projects in their service areas. Program costs are derived from interest earnings on borrowers' "cushion of credit" loan prepayments.

As required by the Federal Credit Reform Act of 1990, this account records, for this program, the subsidy costs associated with the direct loans obligated in 1992 and beyond. The subsidy amounts are estimated on a present value basis.

Rural Economic Development Direct Loan Financing Account

Program and Financing (in millions of dollars)

Identification code 12–4176–0–3–452	1999 actual	2000 est.	2001 est.
Obligations by program activity:			
Operating program:			
00.01 Direct loans	15	15	15
00.03 Interest expense	4	6	7
00.91 Subtotal, Operating program	19	21	22
08.04 Interest on downward re-estimate	2	1	
10.00 Total new obligations	21	22	22
Budgetary resources available for obligation:			
21.40 Unobligated balance available, start of year	9	10	9
22.00 New financing authority (gross)	22	20	21
22.10 Resources available from recoveries of prior year obligations	3		
22.70 Balance of authority to borrow withdrawn	−2		
23.90 Total budgetary resources available for obligation	32	30	30
23.95 Total new obligations	−21	−22	−22
24.40 Unobligated balance available, end of year	10	9	9
New financing authority (gross), detail:			
Mandatory:			
67.15 Authority to borrow (indefinite)	13	12	12
Spending authority from offsetting collections:			
Discretionary:			
68.00 Offsetting collections (cash)	15	15	16
68.10 From Federal sources: Change in receivables and unpaid, unfilled orders	−2		
68.47 Portion applied to repay debt	−4	−7	−7
68.90 Spending authority from offsetting collections (total discretionary)	9	8	9
70.00 Total new financing authority (gross)	22	20	21
Change in unpaid obligations:			
Unpaid obligations, start of year:			
72.40 Obligated balance, start of year	20	11	10
72.95 Receivables from program account	6	4	4
72.99 Total unpaid obligations, start of year	26	15	14
73.10 Total new obligations	21	22	22
73.20 Total financing disbursements (gross)	−30	−21	−21
73.45 Adjustments in unexpired accounts	−3		
Unpaid obligations, end of year:			
74.40 Obligated balance, end of year	11	10	11
74.95 Receivables from program account	4	4	4
74.99 Total unpaid obligations, end of year	15	14	15
87.00 Total financing disbursements (gross)	30	21	21
Offsets:			
Against gross financing authority and financing disbursements:			
Offsetting collections (cash) from:			
88.00 Federal Funds: Program Account	−6	−4	−4
88.25 Interest on uninvested funds	−1	−1	−1
88.40 Non-Federal sources: Repayment of Principal	−8	−10	−11
88.90 Total, offsetting collections (cash)	−15	−15	−16
Against gross financing authority only:			
88.95 Change in receivables from program accounts	2		
Net financing authority and financing disbursements:			
89.00 Financing authority	9	5	5
90.00 Financing disbursements	14	6	5

Status of Direct Loans (in millions of dollars)

Identification code 12–4176–0–3–452	1999 actual	2000 est.	2001 est.
Position with respect to appropriations act limitation on obligations:			
1111 Limitation on direct loans	15	15	15
1150 Total direct loan obligations	15	15	15
Cumulative balance of direct loans outstanding:			
1210 Outstanding, start of year	50	66	72
1231 Disbursements: Direct loan disbursements	23	16	15
1251 Repayments: Repayments and prepayments	−7	−10	−10
1290 Outstanding, end of year	66	72	77

As required by the Federal Credit Reform Act of 1990, this non-budgetary account records all cash flows to and from the Government resulting from direct loans obligated in 1992 and beyond. The amounts in this account are a means of financing and are not included in the budget totals.

Balance Sheet (in millions of dollars)

Identification code 12–4176–0–3–452	1998 actual	1999 actual	2000 est.	2001 est.
ASSETS:				
Federal assets:				
1101 Fund balances with Treasury	9	8	8	8
Investments in US securities:				
1106 Program Account	6	4	5	5
Net value of assets related to post-1991 direct loans receivable:				
1401 Direct loans receivable, gross	50	66	72	75
1405 Allowance for subsidy cost (−)	−11	−12	−4	−4
1499 Net present value of assets related to direct loans	39	54	68	71
1999 Total assets	54	66	81	84
LIABILITIES:				
Federal liabilities:				
2104 Resources payable to Treasury	49	62	76	76
2105 Other	6	4	5	8
2999 Total liabilities	55	66	81	84
4999 Total liabilities and net position	55	66	81	84

Rural Economic Development Loans Liquidating Account

Program and Financing (in millions of dollars)

Identification code 12–3104–0–1–271	1999 actual	2000 est.	2001 est.
Budgetary resources available for obligation:			
21.40 Unobligated balance available, start of year	8	1	

Credit accounts—Continued

RURAL ECONOMIC DEVELOPMENT LOANS LIQUIDATING ACCOUNT—Continued

Program and Financing (in millions of dollars)—Continued

Identification code 12–3104–0–1–271	1999 actual	2000 est.	2001 est.
22.00 New budget authority (gross)		1	1
22.40 Capital transfer to general fund	−7	−1	
23.90 Total budgetary resources available for obligation	1	1	1
23.95 Total new obligations			
24.40 Unobligated balance available, end of year	1		
New budget authority (gross), detail:			
Mandatory:			
69.00 Offsetting collections (cash)	1	1	1
69.27 Capital transfer to general fund	−1		
69.90 Spending authority from offsetting collections (total mandatory)		1	1
Change in unpaid obligations:			
73.20 Total outlays (gross)	1	1	1
Outlays (gross), detail:			
86.97 Outlays from new mandatory authority	−1	−1	−1
Offsets:			
Against gross budget authority and outlays:			
88.40 Offsetting collections (cash) from: Non-Federal sources: Repayment of principal	−1	−1	−1
Net budget authority and outlays:			
89.00 Budget authority	−1		
90.00 Outlays	−1	−2	−2

Status of Direct Loans (in millions of dollars)

Identification code 12–3104–0–1–271	1999 actual	2000 est.	2001 est.
Cumulative balance of direct loans outstanding:			
1210 Outstanding, start of year	3	2	1
1251 Repayments: Repayments and prepayments	−1	−1	−1
1290 Outstanding, end of year	2	1	

As required by the Federal Credit Reform Act of 1990, this account records, for this program, all cash flows to and from the Government resulting from direct loans obligated prior to 1992. All new activity in this program is recorded in corresponding program and financing accounts.

Statement of Operations (in millions of dollars)

Identification code 12–3104–0–1–271	1998 actual	1999 actual	2000 est.	2001 est.
0111 Revenue	1	1	1	1
0112 Expense	–1	–1		
0115 Net income or loss (–)			1	1
0195 Total income or loss (–)			1	1

Balance Sheet (in millions of dollars)

Identification code 12–3104–0–1–271	1998 actual	1999 actual	2000 est.	2001 est.
ASSETS:				
1101 Federal assets: Fund balances with Treasury	1	1		1
1601 Net value of assets related to pre–1992 direct loans receivable and acquired defaulted guaranteed loans receivable: Direct loans, gross	2	2	1	2
1999 Total assets	3	3	1	3
LIABILITIES:				
2104 Federal liabilities: Resources payable to Treasury	3	3	1	3
2999 Total liabilities	3	3	1	3
4999 Total liabilities and net position	3	3	1	3

Public enterprise funds:

ALTERNATIVE AGRICULTURAL RESEARCH AND COMMERCIALIZATION CORPORATION REVOLVING FUND

Program and Financing (in millions of dollars)

Identification code 12–4144–0–3–352	1999 actual	2000 est.	2001 est.
Obligations by program activity:			
00.01 Administrative expense	1	1	
00.02 Program activity	5		
10.00 Total new obligations	6	1	
Budgetary resources available for obligation:			
21.40 Unobligated balance available, start of year	2	1	
22.00 New budget authority (gross)	5		
23.90 Total budgetary resources available for obligation	7	1	
23.95 Total new obligations	−6	−1	
24.40 Unobligated balance available, end of year	1		
New budget authority (gross), detail:			
Discretionary:			
40.00 Appropriation	4		
68.00 Spending authority from offsetting collections: Offsetting collections (cash)	1		
70.00 Total new budget authority (gross)	5		
Change in unpaid obligations:			
72.40 Unpaid obligations, start of year: Obligated balance, start of year	1	2	
73.10 Total new obligations	6	1	
73.20 Total outlays (gross)	−5	−3	
74.40 Unpaid obligations, end of year: Obligated balance, end of year	2		
Outlays (gross), detail:			
86.90 Outlays from new discretionary authority	4		
86.93 Outlays from discretionary balances	1	3	
87.00 Total outlays (gross)	5	3	
Offsets:			
Against gross budget authority and outlays:			
88.40 Offsetting collections (cash) from: Non-Federal sources	−1		
Net budget authority and outlays:			
89.00 Budget authority	4		
90.00 Outlays	5	3	

These funds support programs authorized by the Alternative Agricultural Research and Commercialization Act of 1990 (7 U.S.C. 5901 et seq.). This Act authorizes the provision of assistance on a competitive basis to foster the development and commercialization of new nonfood, nonfeed products derived from agricultural and forestry material and animal byproducts. No funds were appropriated in 2000 and no funding is requested in 2001.

Object Classification (in millions of dollars)

Identification code 12–4144–0–3–352	1999 actual	2000 est.	2001 est.
11.1 Personnel compensation: Full-time permanent	1	1	
41.0 Grants, subsidies, and contributions	5		
99.9 Total new obligations	6	1	

Personnel Summary

Identification code 12–4144–0–3–352	1999 actual	2000 est.	2001 est.
1001 Total compensable workyears: Full-time equivalent employment	6	6	

RURAL UTILITIES SERVICE

Federal Funds

Credit accounts:

Rural Water and Waste Disposal Direct Loans Financing Account

Program and Financing (in millions of dollars)

Identification code 12–4226–0–3–452		1999 actual	2000 est.	2001 est.
	Obligations by program activity:			
	Operating program:			
00.01	Direct loans	721	679	1,032
00.03	Interest on Treasury borrowing	206	229	284
00.04	Restoration of prior cancellation	5		
00.91	Subtotal, Operating program	932	908	1,316
	Reestimates:			
08.02	Downward reestimate paid to receipt account	16		
08.04	Interest on downward reestimate	2		
08.91	Subtotal reestimates	18		
10.00	Total new obligations	950	908	1,316
	Budgetary resources available for obligation:			
21.40	Unobligated balance available, start of year	14	10	
22.00	New financing authority (gross)	934	898	1,316
22.10	Resources available from recoveries of prior year obligations	54		
22.70	Balance of authority to borrow withdrawn	−42		
23.90	Total budgetary resources available for obligation	960	908	1,316
23.95	Total new obligations	−950	−908	−1,316
24.40	Unobligated balance available, end of year	10		
	New financing authority (gross), detail:			
	Mandatory:			
67.15	Authority to borrow (indefinite)	620	385	788
	Spending authority from offsetting collections:			
	Discretionary:			
68.00	Offsetting collections (cash)	381	450	481
68.10	From Federal sources: Change in receivables and unpaid, unfilled orders	37	63	47
68.47	Portion applied to repay debt	−104		
68.90	Spending authority from offsetting collections (total discretionary)	314	513	528
70.00	Total new financing authority (gross)	934	898	1,316
	Change in unpaid obligations:			
	Unpaid obligations, start of year:			
72.40	Obligated balance, start of year	1,662	1,679	1,459
72.95	Receivables from program account	225	262	325
72.99	Total unpaid obligations, start of year	1,887	1,941	1,784
73.10	Total new obligations	950	908	1,316
73.20	Total financing disbursements (gross)	−842	−1,064	−1,145
73.45	Adjustments in unexpired accounts	−54		
	Unpaid obligations, end of year:			
74.40	Obligated balance, end of year	1,679	1,459	1,583
74.95	Receivables from program account	262	325	372
74.99	Total unpaid obligations, end of year	1,941	1,784	1,955
87.00	Total financing disbursements (gross)	842	1,064	1,145
	Offsets:			
	Against gross financing authority and financing disbursements:			
	Offsetting collections (cash) from:			
88.00	Federal sources	−116	−129	−94
88.25	Interest on uninvested funds	−41	−64	−83
	Non-Federal sources:			
88.40	Repayment of principal	−83	−49	−59
88.40	Interest received on loans	−141	−208	−245
88.90	Total, offsetting collections (cash)	−381	−450	−481
	Against gross financing authority only:			
88.95	Change in receivables from program accounts	−37	−63	−47
	Net financing authority and financing disbursements:			
89.00	Financing authority	516	385	788
90.00	Financing disbursements	461	614	664

Status of Direct Loans (in millions of dollars)

Identification code 12–4226–0–3–452		1999 actual	2000 est.	2001 est.
	Position with respect to appropriations act limitation on obligations:			
1111	Limitation on direct loans	707	679	1,032
1131	Direct loan obligations exempt from limitation	14		
1150	Total direct loan obligations	721	679	1,032
	Cumulative balance of direct loans outstanding:			
1210	Outstanding, start of year	2,810	3,345	4,131
1231	Disbursements: Direct loan disbursements	619	835	862
1251	Repayments: Repayments and prepayments	−84	−49	−59
1290	Outstanding, end of year	3,345	4,131	4,934

As required by the Federal Credit Reform Act of 1990, this non-budgetary account records all cash flows to and from the Government resulting from direct loans obligated in 1992 and beyond. The amounts in this account are a means of financing and are not included in the budget totals. The subsidy cost of these loans is provided through the Rural Community Advancement Program. Loans made prior to 1992 are recorded in the Rural Development Insurance Fund Liquidating Account.

The water and waste disposal program makes loans and grants to finance water and waste disposal facilities in rural areas.

Balance Sheet (in millions of dollars)

Identification code 12–4226–0–3–452		1998 actual	1999 actual	2000 est.	2001 est.
	ASSETS:				
	Federal assets:				
1101	Fund balances with Treasury	200	126	126	126
	Investments in US securities:				
1106	Receivables, net	225	262	262	262
	Net value of assets related to post-1991 direct loans receivable:				
1401	Direct loans receivable, gross	2,807	3,345	4,131	4,934
1402	Interest receivable	36	42	48	54
1405	Allowance for subsidy cost (–)	–430	–588	–899	–1,368
1499	Net present value of assets related to direct loans	2,413	2,799	3,280	3,620
1999	Total assets	2,838	3,187	3,668	4,008
	LIABILITIES:				
2103	Federal liabilities: Debt	2,760	2,917	3,335	3,628
2203	Non-Federal liabilities: Debt	1	8	8	8
2999	Total liabilities	2,761	2,925	3,343	3,636
	NET POSITION:				
3100	Appropriated capital	77	262	325	372
3999	Total net position	77	262	325	372
4999	Total liabilities and net position	2,838	3,187	3,668	4,008

Rural Water and Waste Disposal Guaranteed Loans Financing Account

Program and Financing (in millions of dollars)

Identification code 12–4218–0–3–452		1999 actual	2000 est.	2001 est.
	Budgetary resources available for obligation:			
22.00	New financing authority (gross)		1	1
22.10	Resources available from recoveries of prior year obligations	1		
22.70	Balance of authority to borrow withdrawn	−1		
23.90	Total budgetary resources available for obligation		1	1
23.95	Total new obligations			

Credit accounts—Continued

RURAL WATER AND WASTE DISPOSAL GUARANTEED LOANS FINANCING ACCOUNT—Continued

Program and Financing (in millions of dollars)—Continued

Identification code 12–4218–0–3–452	1999 actual	2000 est.	2001 est.
New financing authority (gross), detail:			
Discretionary:			
68.00 Spending authority from offsetting collections (gross): Offsetting collections (cash)		1	1
Change in unpaid obligations:			
72.40 Unpaid obligations, start of year: Obligated balance, start of year	1		
73.10 Total new obligations			
73.20 Total financing disbursements (gross)		–1	–1
73.45 Adjustments in unexpired accounts	–1		
87.00 Total financing disbursements (gross)		1	1
Offsets:			
Against gross financing authority and financing disbursements:			
88.40 Offsetting collections (cash) from: Fees		–1	–1
Net financing authority and financing disbursements:			
89.00 Financing authority			
90.00 Financing disbursements			

Status of Guaranteed Loans (in millions of dollars)

Identification code 12–4218–0–3–452	1999 actual	2000 est.	2001 est.
Position with respect to appropriations act limitation on commitments:			
2111 Limitation on guaranteed loans made by private lenders	75	75	75
2112 Uncommitted loan guarantee limitation	–69		
2150 Total guaranteed loan commitments	6	75	75
2199 Guaranteed amount of guaranteed loan commitments		60	60
Cumulative balance of guaranteed loans outstanding:			
2210 Outstanding, start of year	1	20	87
2231 Disbursements of new guaranteed loans	20	69	44
2251 Repayments and prepayments	–1	–2	–3
2290 Outstanding, end of year	20	87	128
Memorandum:			
2299 Guaranteed amount of guaranteed loans outstanding, end of year	13	78	110

As required by the Federal Credit Reform Act of 1990, this non-budgetary account records all cash flows to and from the Government resulting from guaranteed loans committed in 1992 and beyond. The amounts in this account are a means of financing and are not included in the budget totals. Loans made prior to 1992 are recorded in the Rural Development Insurance Fund Liquidating Account.

This account finances loan guarantee commitments for water systems, and waste disposal facilities in rural areas.

RURAL ELECTRIFICATION AND TELECOMMUNICATIONS LOANS PROGRAM ACCOUNT

(INCLUDING TRANSFERS OF FUNDS)

Insured loans pursuant to the authority of section 305 of the Rural Electrification Act of 1936 (7 U.S.C. 935) shall be made as follows: 5 percent rural electrification loans, [$121,500,000] *$50,000,000*; 5 percent rural telecommunications loans, $75,000,000; cost of money rural telecommunications loans, $300,000,000; municipal rate rural electric loans, [$295,000,000] *$300,000,000*; and loans made pursuant to section 306 of that Act, rural electric, [$1,700,000,000] *$1,200,000,000* and rural telecommunications, $120,000,000[, to remain available until expended].

For the cost, as defined in section 502 of the Congressional Budget Act of 1974, including the cost of modifying loans, of direct and guaranteed loans authorized by the Rural Electrification Act of 1936 (7 U.S.C. 935 and 936), as follows: cost of [direct loans, $1,935,000; cost of municipal rate loans, $10,827,000; cost of money rural telecommunications loans, $2,370,000] *rural electric loans, $25,870,000, and the cost of telecommunication loans; $7,770,000*: *Provided*, That notwithstanding section 305(d)(2) of the Rural Electrification Act of 1936, borrower interest rates may exceed 7 percent per year.

In addition, for administrative expenses necessary to carry out the direct and guaranteed loan programs, [$31,046,000], *$34,716,000*, which shall be transferred to and merged with the appropriation for "Rural [Utilities Service] *Development*, Salaries and Expenses". *(Agriculture, Rural Development, Food and Drug Administration, and Related Agencies Appropriations Act, 2000.)*

General Fund Credit Receipt Accounts (in millions of dollars)

Identification code 12–1230–0–1–271	1999 actual	2000 est.	2001 est.
0101 Rural electrification and telephone loans, negative subsidies		5	8
0102 Rural electrification and telephone loans, downward reestimates of subsidies	167		

Program and Financing (in millions of dollars)

Identification code 12–1230–0–1–271	1999 actual	2000 est.	2001 est.
Obligations by program activity:			
00.01 Direct loan subsidy	43	15	34
00.05 Reestimate of the direct loan subsidy	94		
00.06 Interest on reestimates of direct loan subsidy	6		
00.09 Administrative expenses subject to limitation	30	31	35
10.00 Total new obligations	174	46	68
Budgetary resources available for obligation:			
22.00 New budget authority (gross)	174	46	68
23.95 Total new obligations	–174	–46	–68
New budget authority (gross), detail:			
Discretionary:			
40.00 Appropriation	73	46	68
Mandatory:			
60.05 Appropriation (indefinite)	101		
70.00 Total new budget authority (gross)	174	46	68
Change in unpaid obligations:			
72.40 Unpaid obligations, start of year: Obligated balance, start of year	132	118	76
73.10 Total new obligations	174	46	68
73.20 Total outlays (gross)	–183	–88	–74
73.40 Adjustments in expired accounts (net)	–4		
74.40 Unpaid obligations, end of year: Obligated balance, end of year	118	76	71
Outlays (gross), detail:			
86.90 Outlays from new discretionary authority	40	33	39
86.93 Outlays from discretionary balances	42	55	35
86.97 Outlays from new mandatory authority	101		
87.00 Total outlays (gross)	183	88	74
Net budget authority and outlays:			
89.00 Budget authority	174	46	68
90.00 Outlays	184	88	74

Summary of Loan Levels, Subsidy Budget Authority and Outlays by Program (in millions of dollars)

Identification code 12–1230–0–1–271	1999 actual	2000 est.	2001 est.
Direct loan levels supportable by subsidy budget authority:			
1150 Direct loans, hardship electric	72	122	50
1150 Direct loans, municipal electric	295	294	300
1150 Direct loans, FFB electric	1,050	1,700	800
1150 Direct loans, hardship telephone	75	75	75
1150 Direct loans, Treasury telephone	217	300	300
1150 Direct loans, FFB telephone	55	120	120
1159 Total direct loan levels	1,763	2,610	1,645
Direct loan subsidy (in percent):			
1320 Direct loans, hardship electric	13.04	0.90	9.96

1320 Direct loans, municipal electric	8.76	3.67	6.95
1320 Direct loans, FFB electric	−0.38	−1.18	−3.09
1320 Direct loans, hardship telephone	9.79	1.12	10.36
1320 Direct loans, Treasury telephone	0.27	0.79	−1.00
1320 Direct loans, FFB telephone	−0.81	−0.46	−2.04
1329 Weighted average subsidy rate	7.88	−0.23	0.24
Direct loan subsidy budget authority:			
1330 Direct loans, hardship electric	11	1	5
1330 Direct loans, municipal electric	113	11	21
1330 Direct loans, FFB electric	−3	−20	−25
1330 Direct loans, hardship telephone	10	1	8
1330 Direct loans, Treasury telephone	6	2	−3
1330 Direct loans, FFB telephone	2	−1	−2
1339 Total subsidy budget authority	139	−6	4
Direct loan subsidy outlays:			
1340 Direct loans, hardship electric	11	12	5
1340 Direct loans, municipal electric	123	27	20
1340 Direct loans, FFB electric	2	3	1
1340 Direct loans, hardship telephone	10	14	13
1340 Direct loans, Treasury telephone	5		
1340 Direct loans, FFB telephone	2		
1349 Total subsidy outlays	153	57	39
Guaranteed loan levels supportable by subsidy budget authority:			
2150 Guaranteed loans, electric	150	500	400
2159 Total loan guarantee levels	150	500	400
Guaranteed loan subsidy (in percent):			
2320 Guaranteed loans, electric	0.00	0.01	0.01
2329 Weighted average subsidy rate	0.00	0.01	0.01
Administrative expense data:			
3510 Budget authority	30	31	35
3590 Outlays	30	31	35

The Rural Utilities Service conducts the rural electrification and the rural telecommunications loan programs. The rural electrification loan program is financed through RUS direct and guaranteed loans for the operation of generating plants, electric transmission, and distribution lines or systems. The rural telecommunications loan program is financed through RUS direct loans for construction, expansion, and operation of telecommunications lines and facilities or systems.

As required by the Federal Credit Reform Act of 1990, this account records, for rural electrification and telecommunications programs, the subsidy costs associated with the direct loans obligated in 1992 and beyond (including modifications of direct loans or loan guarantees that resulted from obligations or commitments in any year), as well as administrative expenses of this program. The subsidy amounts are estimated on a present value basis; the administrative expenses are estimated on a cash basis.

Object Classification (in millions of dollars)

Identification code 12–1230–0–1–271	1999 actual	2000 est.	2001 est.
25.3 Purchases of goods and services from Government accounts	30	31	35
41.0 Grants, subsidies, and contributions	144	15	34
99.9 Total new obligations	174	46	68

Rural Electrification and Telecommunications Direct Loan Financing Account

Program and Financing (in millions of dollars)

Identification code 12–4208–0–3–271	1999 actual	2000 est.	2001 est.
Obligations by program activity:			
Operating program:			
00.01 Direct loans	1,763	2,610	1,645
00.02 Interest on Treasury borrowing	371	459	553
00.91 Subtotal, Operating program	2,134	3,069	2,198
Non-operating program:			
08.01 Negative subsidy paid to receipt account	4	21	30
08.02 Downward reestimate paid to receipt account	133		
08.04 Interest on downward reestimate paid to receipt account	35		
08.91 Subtotal, Non-operating program	172	21	30
10.00 Total new obligations	2,306	3,090	2,228
Budgetary resources available for obligation:			
21.40 Unobligated balance available, start of year	25	29	
22.00 New financing authority (gross)	2,307	3,061	2,228
22.10 Resources available from recoveries of prior year obligations	146		
22.70 Balance of authority to borrow withdrawn	−143		
23.90 Total budgetary resources available for obligation	2,335	3,090	2,228
23.95 Total new obligations	−2,306	−3,090	−2,228
24.40 Unobligated balance available, end of year	29		
New financing authority (gross), detail:			
Mandatory:			
67.15 Authority to borrow (indefinite)	1,892	2,414	1,444
Spending authority from offsetting collections:			
Discretionary:			
68.00 Offsetting collections (cash)	831	689	789
68.10 From Federal sources: Change in receivables and unpaid, unfilled orders	−9	−42	−5
68.47 Portion applied to repay debt	−407		
68.90 Spending authority from offsetting collections (total discretionary)	414	648	784
70.00 Total new financing authority (gross)	2,307	3,061	2,228
Change in unpaid obligations:			
Unpaid obligations, start of year:			
72.40 Obligated balance, start of year	3,607	4,164	5,136
72.95 Receivables from program account	127	118	76
72.99 Total unpaid obligations, start of year	3,734	4,282	5,213
73.10 Total new obligations	2,306	3,090	2,228
73.20 Total financing disbursements (gross)	−1,612	−2,160	−2,144
73.45 Adjustments in unexpired accounts	−146		
Unpaid obligations, end of year:			
74.40 Obligated balance, end of year	4,164	5,136	5,226
74.95 Receivables from program account	118	76	71
74.99 Total unpaid obligations, end of year	4,282	5,213	5,296
87.00 Total financing disbursements (gross)	1,612	2,160	2,144
Offsets:			
Against gross financing authority and financing disbursements:			
Offsetting collections (cash) from:			
88.00 Payment from program account	−153	−57	−39
88.25 Interest on uninvested funds	−44	−57	−68
Non-Federal sources:			
88.40 Repayment of principal	−328	−142	−170
88.40 Interest received on loans	−297	−433	−512
88.40 Miscellaneous Income	−9		
88.90 Total, offsetting collections (cash)	−831	−689	−789
Against gross financing authority only:			
88.95 Change in receivables from program accounts	9	42	5
Net financing authority and financing disbursements:			
89.00 Financing authority	1,485	2,414	1,444
90.00 Financing disbursements	781	1,470	1,355

Status of Direct Loans (in millions of dollars)

Identification code 12–4208–0–3–271	1999 actual	2000 est.	2001 est.
Position with respect to appropriations act limitation on obligations:			
1111 Limitation on direct loans	1,911	2,610	1,645
1112 Unobligated direct loan limitation	−148		
1150 Total direct loan obligations	1,763	2,610	1,645
Cumulative balance of direct loans outstanding:			
1210 Outstanding, start of year	5,189	5,949	7,496
1231 Disbursements: Direct loan disbursements	1,093	1,689	1,582
1251 Repayments: Repayments and prepayments	−328	−142	−170

Credit accounts—Continued

RURAL ELECTRIFICATION AND TELECOMMUNICATIONS DIRECT LOAN FINANCING ACCOUNT—Continued

Status of Direct Loans (in millions of dollars)—Continued

Identification code 12–4208–0–3–271	1999 actual	2000 est.	2001 est.
1262 Adjustments: Discount on loan asset sales to the public or discounted	−5	....	....
1290 Outstanding, end of year	5,949	7,496	8,908

As required by the Federal Credit Reform Act of 1990, this non-budgetary account records all cash flows to and from the Government resulting from electric and telecommunication direct loans obligated in 1992 and beyond (including modifications of direct loans that resulted from obligations in any year). The amounts in this account are a means of financing and are not included in the budget totals.

Balance Sheet (in millions of dollars)

Identification code 12–4208–0–3–271	1998 actual	1999 actual	2000 est.	2001 est.
ASSETS:				
Federal assets:				
1101 Fund balances with Treasury	170	10	15	166
Investments in US securities:				
1106 Receivables, net	....	78	....	....
Net value of assets related to post-1991 direct loans receivable:				
1401 Direct loans receivable, gross	4,351	5,007	6,136	7,170
1405 Allowance for subsidy cost (-)	–433	–473	–520	–546
1499 Net present value of assets related to direct loans	3,918	4,534	5,616	6,624
1999 Total assets	4,088	4,622	5,631	6,790
LIABILITIES:				
Federal liabilities:				
2101 Accounts payable	....	9	....	....
2103 Debt	3,963	4,535	5,553	6,713
2999 Total liabilities	3,963	4,543	5,553	6,713
NET POSITION:				
3100 Appropriated capital	125	79	78	77
3999 Total net position	125	79	78	77
4999 Total liabilities and net position	4,088	4,622	5,631	6,790
ASSETS:				
Federal assets:				
1101 Fund balances with Treasury	136	1	10	42
Investments in US securities:				
1106 Receivables, net	....	43	....	....
Net value of assets related to post-1991 direct loans receivable:				
1401 Direct loans receivable, gross	755	941	1,360	1,737
1405 Allowance for subsidy cost (-)	–63	–50	–96	–98
1499 Net present value of assets related to direct loans	692	891	1,264	1,639
1999 Total assets	828	935	1,274	1,681
LIABILITIES:				
Federal liabilities:				
2101 Accounts payable	....	3	....	....
2103 Debt	770	877	1,229	1,642
2999 Total liabilities	770	881	1,229	1,642
NET POSITION:				
3100 Appropriated capital	58	54	45	39
3999 Total net position	58	54	45	39
4999 Total liabilities and net position	828	935	1,274	1,681

RURAL ELECTRIFICATION AND TELECOMMUNICATIONS GUARANTEED LOANS FINANCING ACCOUNT

(Legislative proposal, not subject to PAYGO)

Status of Guaranteed Loans (in millions of dollars)

Identification code 12–4209–0–3–271	1999 actual	2000 est.	2001 est.
Position with respect to appropriations act limitation on commitments:			
2111 Limitation on guaranteed loans made by private lenders	150	500	400
2150 Total guaranteed loan commitments	150	500	400
Cumulative balance of guaranteed loans outstanding:			
2210 Outstanding, start of year	....	16	147
2231 Disbursements of new guaranteed loans	16	133	176
2251 Repayments and prepayments	....	−2	−3
2290 Outstanding, end of year	16	147	320
Memorandum:			
2299 Guaranteed amount of guaranteed loans outstanding, end of year	16	147	320

As required by the Federal Credit Reform Act of 1990, this non-budgetary account records all cash flows to and from the Government resulting from guaranteed loans committed in 1992 and beyond. The amounts in this account are a means of financing and are not included in the budget totals.

This account finances loan guarantee commitments.

RURAL ELECTRIFICATION AND TELECOMMUNICATIONS LIQUIDATING ACCOUNT

Program and Financing (in millions of dollars)

Identification code 12–4230–0–3–271	1999 actual	2000 est.	2001 est.
Obligations by program activity:			
00.01 Interest expense on certificates of beneficial ownership	466	762	437
00.02 Interest expense, FFB direct	854	811	771
00.03 Other interest expense	251	9	9
00.05 Other	9	7	7
10.00 Total new obligations	1,580	1,589	1,224
Budgetary resources available for obligation:			
22.00 New budget authority (gross)	1,568	1,589	1,224
22.10 Resources available from recoveries of prior year obligations	24	....	....
22.70 Balance of authority to borrow withdrawn	−12	....	....
23.90 Total budgetary resources available for obligation	1,580	1,589	1,224
23.95 Total new obligations	−1,580	−1,589	−1,224
New budget authority (gross), detail:			
Discretionary:			
40.36 Unobligated balance rescinded	....	....	−4
Mandatory:			
60.36 Unobligated balance rescinded	−4	−3	....
62.00 Transferred from other accounts	26	25	24
62.50 Appropriation (total mandatory)	22	22	24
67.15 Authority to borrow (indefinite)	500	....	....
67.16 Authority to borrow (indefinite) (12 U.S.C. 2281–96)	5	....	....
67.90 Authority to borrow (total mandatory)	505	....	....
69.00 Offsetting collections (cash)	2,788	4,411	3,138
69.10 From Federal sources: Change in receivables and unpaid, unfilled orders	−1,008	....	....
69.47 Portion applied to repay debt	−739	−2,844	−1,934
69.90 Spending authority from offsetting collections (total mandatory)	1,041	1,567	1,204
70.00 Total new budget authority (gross)	1,568	1,589	1,224
Change in unpaid obligations:			
Unpaid obligations, start of year:			
72.40 Obligated balance, start of year	96	517	591

		1999 actual	2000 est.	2001 est.
72.95	From Federal sources: Receivables and unpaid, unfilled orders	1,053	45	45
72.99	Total unpaid obligations, start of year	1,149	562	636
73.10	Total new obligations	1,580	1,589	1,224
73.20	Total outlays (gross)	−2,143	−1,516	−1,370
73.45	Adjustments in unexpired accounts	−24		
	Unpaid obligations, end of year:			
74.40	Obligated balance, end of year	517	591	445
74.95	From Federal sources: Receivables and unpaid, unfilled orders	45	45	45
74.99	Total unpaid obligations, end of year	562	636	490
	Outlays (gross), detail:			
86.97	Outlays from new mandatory authority	994	954	782
86.98	Outlays from mandatory balances	1,149	562	588
87.00	Total outlays (gross)	2,143	1,516	1,370
	Offsets:			
	Against gross budget authority and outlays:			
	Offsetting collections (cash) from:			
	Non-Federal sources:			
88.40	Loans repaid	−1,432	−1,751	−1,663
88.40	Interest from loans	−1,428	−1,553	−1,475
88.40	Other	72	−1,107	
88.90	Total, offsetting collections (cash)	−2,788	−4,411	−3,138
	Against gross budget authority only:			
88.95	From Federal sources: Change in receivables and unpaid, unfilled orders	1,008		
	Net budget authority and outlays:			
89.00	Budget authority	−212	−2,822	−1,914
90.00	Outlays	−645	−2,895	−1,768

Status of Direct Loans (in millions of dollars)

Identification code 12–4230–0–3–271		1999 actual	2000 est.	2001 est.
	Cumulative balance of direct loans outstanding:			
1210	Outstanding, start of year	27,076	25,867	24,837
1231	Disbursements: Direct loan disbursements	19	8	19
1251	Repayments: Repayments and prepayments	−1,432	−1,031	−1,204
1264	Write-offs for default: Other adjustments, net	204	−7	−4
1290	Outstanding, end of year	25,867	24,837	23,648

Status of Guaranteed Loans (in millions of dollars)

Identification code 12–4230–0–3–271		1999 actual	2000 est.	2001 est.
	Cumulative balance of guaranteed loans outstanding:			
2210	Outstanding, start of year	561	409	389
2251	Repayments and prepayments	−45	−20	−20
2263	Adjustments: Terminations for default that result in claim payments	−107		
2290	Outstanding, end of year	409	389	369
	Memorandum:			
2299	Guaranteed amount of guaranteed loans outstanding, end of year	409	389	369

STATUS OF AGENCY DEBT

[In millions of dollars]

	1999 actual	*2000 est.*	*2001 est.*
Agency Debt Held by FFB:			
Outstanding FFB Direct, start of year	12,594	12,130	10,575
Outstanding Certificate of Beneficial Ownership (CBO's), start of year	4,599	4,599	4,327
Repayments and prepayments, FFB Direct	−464	−1,555	−402
Outstanding FFB Direct, end of year	12,130	10,575	10,173
Outstanding CBO's, end of year	4,599	4,327	4,270

As required by the Federal Credit Reform Act of 1990, this account records, for rural electrification and telecommunications programs, all cash flows to and from the Government resulting from direct loans obligated and loan guarantees committed prior to 1992. All new activity in RETRF in 1992 and beyond is recorded in corresponding program and financing accounts.

The Rural Utilities Service will continue to service all loans in this account providing business management and technical assistance to the borrowers on a regular basis over the life of the loans.

Rural electric.—This program is financed through RUS direct loans for the construction and operation of generating plants, electric transmission, and distribution lines or systems.

The following tables reflect statistics on loans made through the liquidating account only. Since 1992 new electric and telephone loans have been made through a separate, program account.

ELECTRIC PROGRAM STATISTICS

[dollars in millions]

	1999 actual	*2000 est.*	*2001 est.*
Cumulative RUS financed direct loans	21,857	21,857	21,857
Cumulative FFB financed direct loans	27,136	27,136	27,136
Cumulative RUS funds advanced	21,831	21,832	21,833
Unadvanced RUS funds, end of year	22	21	20
Cumulative RUS principal repaid	13,446	14,271	15,234
Cumulative RUS interest paid	11,041	12,283	13,463
Cumulative loan guarantee commitments[1]	3,967	3,967	3,967
Number of borrowers	807	728	635

[1] Represents loans financed by private lenders, including refinanced direct loans, FFB.

Rural telecommunications.—This loan program is financed through RUS direct loans for the construction, expansion, and operation of telecommunications lines and facilities or systems.

TELECOMMUNICATIONS PROGRAM STATISTICS

[dollars in millions]

	1999 actual	*2000 est.*	*2001 est.*
Cumulative RUS financed direct loans	6,053	6,053	6,053
Cumulative FFB financed direct loans	579	579	579
Cumulative RUS funds advanced	5,869	5,876	5,894
Unadvanced RUS funds, end of period	186	179	161
Cumulative RUS principal repaid	3,325	3,531	3,772
Cumulative RUS interest paid	2,646	2,957	3,252
Cumulative loan guarantee commitments[1]	3	3	3
Number of borrowers	800	735	675

[1] Other lenders—privately financed direct loans, FFB.

Statement of Operations (in millions of dollars)

Identification code 12–4230–0–3–271		1998 actual	1999 actual	2000 est.	2001 est.
	ELECTRIC PROGRAM:				
0111	Revenue	1,812	1,352	2,504	1,327
0112	Expense	–147	–596	–545	–317
0115	Net income or loss (–)	1,665	756	1,959	1,010
	TELEPHONE PROGRAM:				
0121	Revenue	188	159	155	147
0122	Expense	–178	–246	–477	–367
0125	Net income or loss (–)	10	–87	–322	–220
0191	Total revenues	2,000	1,511	2,659	1,474
0192	Total expenses	–325	–842	–1,022	–684
0195	Total income or loss (–)	1,675	669	1,637	790
0199	Net loss (–)	1,675	669	1,637	790

Balance Sheet (in millions of dollars)

Identification code 12–4230–0–3–271		1998 actual	1999 actual	2000 est.	2001 est.
	ASSETS:				
1101	Federal assets: Fund balances with Treasury		247	247	247
	Net value of assets related to pre-1992 direct loans receivable and acquired defaulted guaranteed loans receivable:				
1601	Direct loans, gross (Electric)	24,203	23,214	22,279	21,212
1602	Interest receivable	15	19	19	19
1603	Allowance for estimated uncollectible loans and interest (–)	–3,087	–2,439	–2,340	–2,228

Credit accounts—Continued

RURAL ELECTRIFICATION AND TELECOMMUNICATIONS LIQUIDATING ACCOUNT—Continued

Balance Sheet (in millions of dollars)—Continued

Identification code 12–4230–0–3–271		1998 actual	1999 actual	2000 est.	2001 est.
1604	Direct loans and interest receivable, net	21,131	20,794	19,958	19,003
1699	Value of assets related to direct loans	21,131	20,794	19,958	19,003
1901	Other Federal assets: Other assets	3,527			
1999	Total assets	24,658	21,041	20,205	19,250
	LIABILITIES:				
	Federal liabilities:				
2101	Accounts payable		659	632	603
2103	Debt	21,198	20,853	19,935	18,863
2104	Resources payable to Treasury		–608	–497	–344
2105	Other	837	3		
	Non-Federal liabilities:				
2202	Interest payable	9	11	11	11
2203	Debt	807			
2204	Liabilities for loan guarantees	142	18	18	17
2207	Other		105	106	100
2999	Total liabilities	22,993	21,041	20,205	19,250
	NET POSITION:				
3300	Cumulative results of operations	1,665			
3999	Total net position	1,665			
4999	Total liabilities and net position	24,658	21,041	20,205	19,250

	ASSETS:				
1101	Federal assets: Fund balances with Treasury		189	189	189
	Non-Federal assets:				
1201	Investments in non-Federal securities, net	528	502	527	551
1206	Receivables, net	662	660	780	359
	Net value of assets related to pre–1992 direct loans receivable and acquired defaulted guaranteed loans receivable:				
1601	Direct loans, gross (Telephone)	2,874	2,653	2,558	2,436
1602	Interest receivable	6	6	6	6
1603	Allowance for estimated uncollectible loans and interest (–)	126	–32	–30	–29
1604	Direct loans and interest receivable, net	3,006	2,627	2,534	2,413
1699	Value of assets related to direct loans	3,006	2,627	2,534	2,413
1999	Total assets	4,196	3,978	4,030	3,512
	LIABILITIES:				
	Federal liabilities:				
2103	Debt	2,163	2,061	1,947	1,815
2104	Resources payable to Treasury	2,019	1,903	2,073	1,687
2105	Other	4	4		
2999	Total liabilities	4,186	3,968	4,020	3,502
	NET POSITION:				
3300	Cumulative results of operations	10	10	10	10
3999	Total net position	10	10	10	10
4999	Total liabilities and net position	4,196	3,978	4,030	3,512

Object Classification (in millions of dollars)

Identification code 12–4230–0–3–271		1999 actual	2000 est.	2001 est.
25.2	Other services	9	7	7
33.0	Investments and loans	251	9	9
43.0	Interest and dividends	1,320	1,573	1,208
99.9	Total new obligations	1,580	1,589	1,224

RURAL TELEPHONE BANK PROGRAM ACCOUNT

(INCLUDING TRANSFERS OF FUNDS)

The Rural Telephone Bank is hereby authorized to make such expenditures, within the limits of funds available to such corporation in accord with law, and to make such contracts and commitments without regard to fiscal year limitations as provided by section 104 of the Government Corporation Control Act, as may be necessary in carrying out its authorized programs. During fiscal year [2000] *2001* and within the resources and authority available, gross obligations for the principal amount of direct loans shall be $175,000,000.

For the cost, as defined in section 502 of the Congressional Budget Act of 1974, including the cost of modifying loans, of direct loans authorized by the Rural Electrification Act of 1936 (7 U.S.C. 935), [$3,290,000] *$2,590,000, to be derived by transfer from the shareholders' equity as contained in the unobligated balances in the Rural Telephone Bank Liquidating Account*.

In addition, for administrative expenses, *including audits,* necessary to carry out the loan programs, $3,000,000, *to be derived by transfer from the shareholders' equity as contained in the unobligated balances in the Rural Telephone Bank Liquidating Account,* which shall be transferred to and merged with the appropriation for "Rural [Utilities Service] *Development*, Salaries and Expenses". *(Agriculture, Rural Development, Food and Drug Administration, and Related Agencies Appropriations Act, 2000.)*

General Fund Credit Receipt Accounts (in millions of dollars)

Identification code 12–1231–0–1–452		1999 actual	2000 est.	2001 est.
0101	Rural telephone bank loans, downward reestimate of subsidies	12	1	

Program and Financing (in millions of dollars)

Identification code 12–1231–0–1–452		1999 actual	2000 est.	2001 est.
	Obligations by program activity:			
00.01	Direct loan subsidy	3	3	3
00.05	Reestimates on direct loan subsidy		1	
00.09	Administrative expenses subject to limitation	3	3	3
10.00	Total new obligations	6	7	6
	Budgetary resources available for obligation:			
22.00	New budget authority (gross)	8	7	6
23.95	Total new obligations	–6	–7	–6
23.98	Unobligated balance expiring or withdrawn	–1		
	New budget authority (gross), detail:			
	Discretionary:			
40.00	Appropriation	7	6	
42.00	Transferred from other accounts			6
43.00	Appropriation (total discretionary)	7	6	6
	Mandatory:			
60.05	Appropriation (indefinite)		1	
70.00	Total new budget authority (gross)	8	7	6
	Change in unpaid obligations:			
72.40	Unpaid obligations, start of year: Obligated balance, start of year	10	12	14
73.10	Total new obligations	6	7	6
73.20	Total outlays (gross)	–4	–6	–5
74.40	Unpaid obligations, end of year: Obligated balance, end of year	12	14	15
	Outlays (gross), detail:			
86.90	Outlays from new discretionary authority	3	3	3
86.93	Outlays from discretionary balances	1	2	2
86.98	Outlays from mandatory balances		1	
87.00	Total outlays (gross)	4	6	5
	Net budget authority and outlays:			
89.00	Budget authority	8	7	6
90.00	Outlays	4	6	5

Summary of Loan Levels, Subsidy Budget Authority and Outlays by Program (in millions of dollars)

Identification code 12–1231–0–1–452	1999 actual	2000 est.	2001 est.
Direct loan levels supportable by subsidy budget authority:			
1150 Direct loan levels	114	175	175
1159 Total direct loan levels	114	175	175
Direct loan subsidy (in percent):			
1320 Subsidy rate	2.65	1.88	1.48
1329 Weighted average subsidy rate	2.65	1.88	1.48
Direct loan subsidy budget authority:			
1330 Subsidy budget authority	3	4	3
1339 Total subsidy budget authority	3	4	3
Direct loan subsidy outlays:			
1340 Subsidy outlays	1	3	2
1349 Total subsidy outlays	1	3	2
Administrative expense data:			
3510 Budget authority	3	3	3
3590 Outlays	3	3	3

In 2001, the Rural Telephone Bank (RTB) is proposed to become a Performance Based Organization to establish its financial and operational independence prior to its being privatized within ten years. Funding for the RTB's loan subsidies and administrative expenses will be transferred from the unobligated balances in the RTB liquidating account.

As required by the Federal Credit Reform Act of 1990, this account records, for the Rural Telephone Bank, the subsidy costs associated with the direct loans obligated in 1992 and beyond as well as administrative expenses for the program. The subsidy amounts are estimated on a present value basis; administrative expenses are estimated on a cash basis.

Object Classification (in millions of dollars)

Identification code 12–1231–0–1–452	1999 actual	2000 est.	2001 est.
25.2 Other services	3	3	3
41.0 Grants, subsidies, and contributions	3	4	3
99.9 Total new obligations	6	7	6

RURAL TELEPHONE BANK DIRECT LOAN FINANCING ACCOUNT

Program and Financing (in millions of dollars)

Identification code 12–4210–0–3–452	1999 actual	2000 est.	2001 est.
Obligations by program activity:			
Operating program:			
00.01 Direct loans	114	175	175
00.03 Interest on Treasury borrowing	16	19	27
00.91 Subtotal, Operating program	130	194	202
Reestimate:			
08.02 Downward reestimate	9	1	
08.04 Interest on downward reestimate	3		
08.91 Subtotal, reestimate	12	1	
10.00 Total new obligations	142	195	202
Budgetary resources available for obligation:			
22.00 New financing authority (gross)	143	195	202
22.10 Resources available from recoveries of prior year obligations	31		
22.70 Balance of authority to borrow withdrawn	–32		
23.90 Total budgetary resources available for obligation	142	195	202
23.95 Total new obligations	–142	–195	–202
New financing authority (gross), detail:			
Mandatory:			
67.15 Authority to borrow (indefinite)	123	153	151
Spending authority from offsetting collections:			
Discretionary:			
68.00 Offsetting collections (cash)	28	40	50
68.10 From Federal sources: Change in receivables and unpaid, unfilled orders	2	2	1
68.47 Portion applied to repay debt	–9		
68.90 Spending authority from offsetting collections (total discretionary)	21	42	51
70.00 Total new financing authority (gross)	143	195	202
Change in unpaid obligations:			
Unpaid obligations, start of year:			
72.40 Obligated balance, start of year	775	818	875
72.95 Receivables from program account	10	12	14
72.99 Total unpaid obligations, start of year	786	830	889
73.10 Total new obligations	142	195	202
73.20 Total financing disbursements (gross)	–66	–137	–172
73.45 Adjustments in unexpired accounts	–31		
Unpaid obligations, end of year:			
74.40 Obligated balance, end of year	818	875	903
74.95 Receivables from program account	12	14	15
74.99 Total unpaid obligations, end of year	830	889	918
87.00 Total financing disbursements (gross)	66	137	172
Offsets:			
Against gross financing authority and financing disbursements:			
Offsetting collections (cash) from:			
88.00 Federal sources: Payment from Program Account	–1	–3	–2
88.25 Interest on uninvested funds	–4	–3	–4
Non-Federal sources:			
88.40 Principal received on loans	–8	–10	–11
88.40 Interest received on loans	–13	–19	–26
88.40 Sale of RTB Stock	–2	–5	–7
88.90 Total, offsetting collections (cash)	–28	–40	–50
Against gross financing authority only:			
88.95 Change in receivables from program accounts	–2	–2	–1
Net financing authority and financing disbursements:			
89.00 Financing authority	113	153	151
90.00 Financing disbursements	39	97	122

Status of Direct Loans (in millions of dollars)

Identification code 12–4210–0–3–452	1999 actual	2000 est.	2001 est.
Position with respect to appropriations act limitation on obligations:			
1111 Limitation on direct loans	158	175	175
1112 Unobligated direct loan limitation	–44		
1150 Total direct loan obligations	114	175	175
Cumulative balance of direct loans outstanding:			
1210 Outstanding, start of year	197	246	353
1231 Disbursements: Direct loan disbursements	58	117	145
1251 Repayments: Repayments and prepayments	–8	–10	–11
1290 Outstanding, end of year	246	353	487

As required by the Federal Credit Reform Act of 1990, this non-budgetary account records all cash flows to and from the Government resulting from direct loans obligated in 1992 and beyond. The amounts in this account are a means of financing and are not included in the budget totals.

Balance Sheet (in millions of dollars)

Identification code 12–4210–0–3–452	1998 actual	1999 actual	2000 est.	2001 est.
ASSETS:				
Federal assets:				
1101 Fund balances with Treasury	322	423	600	702
Investments in US securities:				
1106 Program Account	11	12	14	15
Net value of assets related to post-1991 direct loans receivable:				
1401 Direct loans receivable, gross	232	246	353	487
1402 Interest receivable	11	13	19	26
1405 Allowance for subsidy cost (–)	–17	–19	–17	–15

Credit accounts—Continued

Rural Telephone Bank Direct Loan Financing Account—Continued

Balance Sheet (in millions of dollars)—Continued

Identification code 12–4210–0–3–452	1998 actual	1999 actual	2000 est.	2001 est.
1499 Net present value of assets related to direct loans	226	240	355	498
1999 Total assets	559	675	969	1,215
LIABILITIES:				
2103 Federal liabilities: Debt	544	659	952	1,197
2201 Non-Federal liabilities: Accounts payable	11	12	14	15
2999 Total liabilities	555	671	966	1,212
NET POSITION:				
3100 Appropriated capital	4	4	3	3
3999 Total net position	4	4	3	3
4999 Total liabilities and net position	559	675	969	1,215

Rural Telephone Bank Liquidating Account

Program and Financing (in millions of dollars)

Identification code 12–4231–0–3–452	1999 actual	2000 est.	2001 est.
Obligations by program activity:			
00.01 Dividends	14	15	16
10.00 Total new obligations (object class 43.0)	14	15	16
Budgetary resources available for obligation:			
21.40 Unobligated balance available, start of year	396	508	609
22.00 New budget authority (gross)	129	126	176
22.10 Resources available from recoveries of prior year obligations	8		
22.40 Capital transfer to general fund	−11	−10	−9
23.90 Total budgetary resources available for obligation	522	624	776
23.95 Total new obligations	−14	−15	−16
24.40 Unobligated balance available, end of year	508	609	760
New budget authority (gross), detail:			
Discretionary:			
41.00 Transferred to other accounts			−6
Mandatory:			
61.00 Transferred to other accounts	−26	−25	−24
69.00 Offsetting collections (cash)	318	233	226
69.47 Portion applied to repay debt	−163	−82	−20
69.90 Spending authority from offsetting collections (total mandatory)	155	151	206
70.00 Total new budget authority (gross)	129	126	176
Change in unpaid obligations:			
72.40 Unpaid obligations, start of year: Obligated balance, start of year	175	149	134
73.10 Total new obligations	14	15	16
73.20 Total outlays (gross)	−32	−30	−29
73.45 Adjustments in unexpired accounts	−8		
74.40 Unpaid obligations, end of year: Obligated balance, end of year	149	134	121
Outlays (gross), detail:			
86.97 Outlays from new mandatory authority	14	15	16
86.98 Outlays from mandatory balances	18	15	13
87.00 Total outlays (gross)	32	30	29
Offsets:			
Against gross budget authority and outlays:			
Offsetting collections (cash) from:			
88.25 Interest on uninvested funds	−36	−41	−47
Non-Federal sources:			
88.40 Loans repaid	−203	−125	−119
88.40 Interest from loans	−78	−66	−59
88.40 Sales of stock	−1	−1	−1
88.90 Total, offsetting collections (cash)	−318	−233	−226
Net budget authority and outlays:			
89.00 Budget authority	−189	−107	−50
90.00 Outlays	−286	−203	−197

Status of Direct Loans (in millions of dollars)

Identification code 12–4231–0–3–452	1999 actual	2000 est.	2001 est.
Cumulative balance of direct loans outstanding:			
1210 Outstanding, start of year	1,172	986	876
1231 Disbursements: Direct loan disbursements	17	15	13
1251 Repayments: Repayments and prepayments	−203	−125	−119
1290 Outstanding, end of year	986	876	770

As required by the Federal Credit Reform Act of 1990, this account records, for the Rural Telephone Bank (RTB), all cash flows to and from the Government resulting from direct loans obligated prior to 1992. This account is shown on a cash basis. All new activity in this program in 1992 and beyond is recorded in corresponding program and financing accounts. Funding for both subsidy budget authority and the related salaries and expenses will be transferred from the unobligated balances in the RTB liquidating account in 2001.

The RTB provides a supplemental source of financing for rural telecommunications borrowers. The Bank charges an interest rate based on the cost of money to the Bank, as prescribed by law, but not less than 5 percent per annum.

In accordance with section 406(c) of the Rural Electrification Act of 1936, as amended, the first redemption of class A stock occurred on September 30, 1996. Redemption of class A stock will continue, as allowed by law, toward the full privatization of the Rural Telephone Bank required by law. In 2001, the RTB is proposed to become a Performance Based Organization to establish its commercial viability prior to its being privatized within ten years.

Administrative support is provided for the general operations of the Bank by RUS employees and the Office of the General Counsel.

PROGRAM STATISTICS

[dollars in millions]

	1999 actual	*2000 est.*	*2001 est.*
Cumulative net loans	2,584	2,583	2,583
Cumulative loan funds, advanced	2,449	2,464	2,477
Unadvanced loan funds, end of year	134	119	106
Cumulative principal repaid	1,463	1,588	1,707
Cumulative interest paid	2,165	2,231	2,290
Number of borrowers	398	390	385

Statement of Operations (in millions of dollars)

Identification code 12–4231–0–3–452	1998 actual	1999 actual	2000 est.	2001 est.
0101 Revenue	130	126	119	118
0102 Expense	−25	−11	−5	−1
0105 Net income or loss (–)	105	115	114	117

Balance Sheet (in millions of dollars)

Identification code 12–4231–0–3–452	1998 actual	1999 actual	2000 est.	2001 est.
ASSETS:				
1101 Federal assets: Fund balances with Treasury	571	657	743	887
1206 Non-Federal assets: Receivables, net	3	3	3	3
Net value of assets related to pre-1992 direct loans receivable and acquired defaulted guaranteed loans receivable:				
1601 Direct loans, gross	1,172	986	876	770
1603 Allowance for estimated uncollectible loans and interest (–)	−8	−7	−6	−5
1604 Direct loans and interest receivable, net	1,164	979	870	765

1699	Value of assets related to direct loans	1,164	979	870	765
1999	Total assets	1,738	1,639	1,616	1,655
	LIABILITIES:				
2103	Federal liabilities: Debt	265	102	20	
2207	Non-Federal liabilities: Other	945	1,035	1,119	1,202
2999	Total liabilities	1,210	1,137	1,139	1,202
	NET POSITION:				
3100	Appropriated capital	528	502	477	453
3999	Total net position	528	502	477	453
4999	Total liabilities and net position	1,738	1,639	1,616	1,655

Distance Learning and Telemedicine Program

For the cost of direct loans and grants, as authorized by 7 U.S.C. 950aaa et seq., [$20,700,000] *$25,000,000*, to remain available until expended, to be available for loans and grants for telemedicine and distance learning services in rural areas; *in addition, for the cost of direct loans and grants, for a pilot program to finance broadband transmission and local dial-up Internet service $2,000,000, to remain available until expended: Provided, That the definition of "rural area" contained in section 203(b) of the Rural Electrification Act (7 U.S.C. 924(b)) shall be applicable in carrying out this pilot program: Provided further*, That the costs of direct loans shall be as defined in section 502 of the Congressional Budget Act of 1974. *(Agriculture, Rural Development, Food and Drug Administration, and Related Agencies Appropriations Act, 2000.)*

Program and Financing (in millions of dollars)

Identification code 12–1232–0–1–452		1999 actual	2000 est.	2001 est.
	Obligations by program activity:			
00.01	Direct loan subsidy		1	
00.02	Distance learning and telemedicine grants	13	21	27
10.00	Total new obligations (object class 41.0)	13	21	27
	Budgetary resources available for obligation:			
21.40	Unobligated balance available, start of year	1	1	
22.00	New budget authority (gross)	13	21	27
23.90	Total budgetary resources available for obligation	14	21	27
23.95	Total new obligations	−13	−21	−27
24.40	Unobligated balance available, end of year	1		
	New budget authority (gross), detail:			
	Discretionary:			
40.00	Appropriation grant budget authority	13	21	27
	Change in unpaid obligations:			
72.40	Unpaid obligations, start of year: Obligated balance, start of year	27	30	36
73.10	Total new obligations	13	21	27
73.20	Total outlays (gross)	−9	−15	−18
74.40	Unpaid obligations, end of year: Obligated balance, end of year	30	36	46
	Outlays (gross), detail:			
86.90	Outlays from new discretionary authority		1	1
86.93	Outlays from discretionary balances	9	14	17
87.00	Total outlays (gross)	9	15	18
	Net budget authority and outlays:			
89.00	Budget authority	13	21	27
90.00	Outlays	9	15	18

Summary of Loan Levels, Subsidy Budget Authority and Outlays by Program (in millions of dollars)

Identification code 12–1232–0–1–452		1999 actual	2000 est.	2001 est.
	Direct loan levels supportable by subsidy budget authority:			
1150	Direct loan levels	55	200	400
1159	Total direct loan levels	55	200	400
	Direct loan subsidy (in percent):			
1320	Subsidy rate	0.12	0.35	−0.61
1329	Weighted average subsidy rate	0.12	0.35	−0.61
	Direct loan subsidy budget authority:			
1330	Subsidy budget authority		1	−2
1339	Total subsidy budget authority		1	−2

The loan and grant program provides access to advanced telecommunications services for improved education and health care in rural areas throughout the country. The loans and grants help education and health care providers bring the most modern technology, level of care, and education to rural America so its citizens can compete regionally, nationally, and globally. Additionally, the budget proposes a pilot program for grants and loans to finance installation of broadband transmission capacity (i.e. the necessary fiber optic cable capacity needed in order to provide any enhanced services such as the Internet or high speed modems) to and through rural communities, and to provide local dial-up Internet service to under-served rural areas.

Distance Learning and Telemedicine Link Direct Loan Financing Account

Program and Financing (in millions of dollars)

Identification code 12–4146–0–3–452		1999 actual	2000 est.	2001 est.
	Obligations by program activity:			
	Operating program:			
00.01	Direct loans	55	200	400
00.02	Interest on Treasury borrowing		4	17
00.91	Subtotal, operating program	55	204	417
08.01	Negative subsidy			2
10.00	Total new obligations	55	204	419
	Budgetary resources available for obligation:			
22.00	New financing authority (gross)	55	204	418
22.10	Resources available from recoveries of prior year obligations	1		
22.70	Balance of authority to borrow withdrawn	−1		
23.90	Total budgetary resources available for obligation	55	204	418
23.95	Total new obligations	−55	−204	−419
	New financing authority (gross), detail:			
	Mandatory:			
67.15	Authority to borrow (indefinite)	55	188	370
	Spending authority from offsetting collections:			
	Discretionary:			
68.00	Offsetting collections (cash)		15	49
68.10	From Federal sources: Change in receivables and unpaid, unfilled orders		1	−1
68.90	Spending authority from offsetting collections (total discretionary)		15	48
70.00	Total new financing authority (gross)	55	204	418
	Change in unpaid obligations:			
	Unpaid obligations, start of year:			
72.40	Obligated balance, start of year	5	58	161
72.95	Receivables from program account			1
72.99	Total unpaid obligations, start of year	5	58	161
73.10	Total new obligations	55	204	419
73.20	Total financing disbursements (gross)	−1	−101	−233
73.45	Adjustments in unexpired accounts	−1		
	Unpaid obligations, end of year:			
74.40	Obligated balance, end of year	58	161	347
74.95	Receivables from program account		1	
74.99	Total unpaid obligations, end of year	58	161	347
87.00	Total financing disbursements (gross)	1	101	233
	Offsets:			
	Against gross financing authority and financing disbursements:			
	Offsetting collections (cash) from:			
88.25	Interest on uninvested funds		−1	−5

Credit accounts—Continued

DISTANCE LEARNING AND TELEMEDICINE LINK DIRECT LOAN FINANCING ACCOUNT—Continued

Program and Financing (in millions of dollars)—Continued

Identification code 12–4146–0–3–452		1999 actual	2000 est.	2001 est.
	Non-Federal sources:			
88.40	Repayment of principal	....	–8	–26
88.40	Interest received on loans	....	–6	–18
88.90	Total, offsetting collections (cash)	....	–15	–49
	Against gross financing authority only:			
88.95	Change in receivables from program accounts	....	–1	1
	Net financing authority and financing disbursements:			
89.00	Financing authority	55	188	370
90.00	Financing disbursements	1	86	184

Status of Direct Loans (in millions of dollars)

Identification code 12–4146–0–3–452		1999 actual	2000 est.	2001 est.
	Position with respect to appropriations act limitation on obligations:			
1111	Limitation on direct loans	55	200	400
1150	Total direct loan obligations	55	200	400
	Cumulative balance of direct loans outstanding:			
1210	Outstanding, start of year	....	1	94
1231	Disbursements: Direct loan disbursements	1	101	232
1251	Repayments: Repayments and prepayments	....	–8	–26
1290	Outstanding, end of year	1	94	300

As required by the Federal Credit Reform Act of 1990, this non-budgetary account records all cash flows to and from the Government resulting from direct loans obligated in 1992 and beyond. The amounts in this account are a means of financing and are not included in the budget totals.

Balance Sheet (in millions of dollars)

Identification code 12–4146–0–3–452		1998 actual	1999 actual	2000 est.	2001 est.
	ASSETS:				
	Investments in US securities:				
1106	Federal assets: Receivables, net	....	....	1	....
	Net value of assets related to post–1991 direct loans receivable:				
1401	Direct loans receivable, gross	....	1	93	299
1402	Interest receivable	....	....	6	18
1405	Allowance for subsidy cost (–)	....	....	–5	–18
1499	Net present value of assets related to direct loans	....	1	94	299
1999	Total assets	....	1	94	299
	LIABILITIES:				
2101	Federal liabilities: Accounts payable	....	1	93	299
2999	Total liabilities	....	1	93	299
	NET POSITION:				
3999	Total net position	....	....	1	....
4999	Total liabilities and net position	....	1	93	299

RURAL DEVELOPMENT INSURANCE FUND LIQUIDATING ACCOUNT

Program and Financing (in millions of dollars)

Identification code 12–4155–0–3–452		1999 actual	2000 est.	2001 est.
	Obligations by program activity:			
	Operating expenses:			
00.02	Purchase of loans from investors	....	1	1
00.03	Redemption of public certificate of beneficial ownership debt	1	1	....
00.91	Total operating expenses	1	2	1
	Capital investment:			
01.01	Interest on FFB borrowings	502	478	429
01.05	Interest on Treasury borrowings	163	95	67
01.06	Loss settlement expense on guaranteed loans	–2	5	6
01.08	Other expenses	2	....	....
01.09	Undistributed charges	2	....	....
01.91	Total capital investment	667	578	502
10.00	Total new obligations	668	580	503
	Budgetary resources available for obligation:			
21.40	Unobligated balance available, start of year	18	....	....
22.00	New budget authority (gross)	650	588	503
22.70	Balance of authority to borrow withdrawn	....	–8	....
23.90	Total budgetary resources available for obligation	668	580	503
23.95	Total new obligations	–668	–580	–503
	New budget authority (gross), detail:			
	Mandatory:			
60.05	Appropriation (indefinite)	449	210	1,304
60.47	Portion applied to repay debt	....	....	–801
62.50	Appropriation (total mandatory)	449	210	503
69.00	Offsetting collections (cash)	541	483	439
69.47	Portion applied to repay debt	–340	–105	–439
69.90	Spending authority from offsetting collections (total mandatory)	201	378	....
70.00	Total new budget authority (gross)	650	588	503
	Change in unpaid obligations:			
72.40	Unpaid obligations, start of year: Obligated balance, start of year	188	229	229
73.10	Total new obligations	668	580	503
73.20	Total outlays (gross)	–627	–580	–329
74.40	Unpaid obligations, end of year: Obligated balance, end of year	229	229	403
	Outlays (gross), detail:			
86.97	Outlays from new mandatory authority	627	580	329
	Offsets:			
	Against gross budget authority and outlays:			
	Offsetting collections (cash) from:			
	Non-Federal sources:			
88.40	Non-Federal sources	–339	–278	–255
88.40	Repayments of guaranteed loans purchased from investors	–3	–6	–2
88.40	Interest revenue	–202	–194	–177
88.40	Interest Income on Investment	....	–5	–5
88.40	Undistributed	3	....	....
88.90	Total, offsetting collections (cash)	–541	–483	–439
	Net budget authority and outlays:			
89.00	Budget authority	109	105	64
90.00	Outlays	86	97	–110

Status of Direct Loans (in millions of dollars)

Identification code 12–4155–0–3–452		1999 actual	2000 est.	2001 est.
	Cumulative balance of direct loans outstanding:			
1210	Outstanding, start of year	3,808	3,470	3,189
1231	Disbursements: Direct loan disbursements	2	....	....
1251	Repayments: Repayments and prepayments	–339	–278	–255
1261	Adjustments: Capitalized interest	1	....	....
1263	Write-offs for default: Direct loans	–2	–3	–3
1290	Outstanding, end of year	3,470	3,189	2,931

Status of Guaranteed Loans (in millions of dollars)

Identification code 12–4155–0–3–452		1999 actual	2000 est.	2001 est.
	Cumulative balance of guaranteed loans outstanding:			
2210	Outstanding, start of year	227	131	80
2251	Repayments and prepayments	–38	–33	–20
	Adjustments:			
2263	Terminations for default that result in claim payments	–1	–18	–11
2264	Other adjustments, net	–57	....	....

2290	Outstanding, end of year	131	80	49
	Memorandum:			
2299	Guaranteed amount of guaranteed loans outstanding, end of year	116	71	43

The Rural Development Insurance Fund (RDIF) was established on October 1, 1972, pursuant to section 116 of the Rural Development Act of 1972 (Public Law 92–419).

The fund is used to insure or guarantee loans for water systems and waste disposal facilities, community facilities, and industrial development in rural areas. Communities unable to afford low interest loans for water and waste disposal facilities are also able to obtain water and waste disposal grants.

As required by the Federal Credit Reform Act of 1990, this account records, for this program, all cash flows to and from the Government resulting from direct loans obligated and loan guarantees committed prior to 1992. All new activity in this program is recorded in corresponding program accounts and financing accounts.

In 1994, these loan programs were administered by the Rural Development Administration. Under reorganization of the Department of Agriculture, the water and waste direct and guaranteed loan programs are administered by the Rural Utilities Service, the community facility direct and guaranteed loan programs are adminsitered by the Rural Housing Service, and the business and industry direct and guaranteed loan programs are administered by the Rural Business-Cooperative Service.

Statement of Operations (in millions of dollars)

Identification code 12–4155–0–3–452		1998 actual	1999 actual	2000 est.	2001 est.
0101	Revenue	226	205	193	193
0102	Expense	–664	–277	–681	–681
0105	Net income or loss (–)	–438	–72	–488	–488

Balance Sheet (in millions of dollars)

Identification code 12–4155–0–3–452		1998 actual	1999 actual	2000 est.	2001 est.
	ASSETS:				
1101	Federal assets: Fund balances with Treasury	223	229	210	210
	Non-Federal assets:				
1201	Investments in non-Federal securities, net	34	34	34	34
1206	Receivables, net	56	53	45	45
	Net value of assets related to pre–1992 direct loans receivable and acquired defaulted guaranteed loans receivable:				
1601	Direct loans, gross	3,808	3,470	3,189	2,931
1603	Allowance for estimated uncollectible loans and interest (–)	–1,245	–1,058	–1,022	–1,022
1604	Direct loans and interest receivable, net	2,563	2,412	2,167	1,909
1699	Value of assets related to direct loans	2,563	2,412	2,167	1,909
1901	Other Federal assets: Other assets	29	23	4	4
1999	Total assets	2,905	2,751	2,460	2,202
	LIABILITIES:				
	Federal liabilities:				
2103	Debt	4,753	4,412	4,306	4,306
2104	Resources payable to Treasury	7	3		
2105	Other	17	7	13	13
	Non-Federal liabilities:				
2201	Public	98	56	119	119
2202	Interest payable	104	189	70	70
2999	Total liabilities	4,980	4,667	4,508	4,508
	NET POSITION:				
3300	Cumulative results of operations	–2,075	–1,916	–2,048	–2,306
3999	Total net position	–2,075	–1,916	–2,048	–2,306
4999	Total liabilities and net position	2,904	2,751	2,460	2,202

Object Classification (in millions of dollars)

Identification code 12–4155–0–3–452		1999 actual	2000 est.	2001 est.
25.2	Other services		5	6
33.0	Investments and loans		1	1
43.0	Interest and dividends	666	574	496
92.0	Undistributed	2		
99.9	Total new obligations	668	580	503

Rural Communication Development Fund Liquidating Account

Program and Financing (in millions of dollars)

Identification code 12–4142–0–3–452		1999 actual	2000 est.	2001 est.
	Obligations by program activity:			
10.00	Total new obligations (object class 43.0)	3	3	3
	Budgetary resources available for obligation:			
22.00	New budget authority (gross)	3	3	3
23.95	Total new obligations	–3	–3	–3
	New budget authority (gross), detail:			
	Mandatory:			
60.05	Appropriation (indefinite)	2	2	2
69.00	Offsetting collections (cash)	1	1	1
70.00	Total new budget authority (gross)	3	3	3
	Change in unpaid obligations:			
72.40	Unpaid obligations, start of year: Obligated balance, start of year	1	1	1
73.10	Total new obligations	3	3	3
73.20	Total outlays (gross)	–3	–3	–3
74.40	Unpaid obligations, end of year: Obligated balance, end of year	1	1	1
	Outlays (gross), detail:			
86.97	Outlays from new mandatory authority	2	3	3
86.98	Outlays from mandatory balances	1		
87.00	Total outlays (gross)	3	3	3
	Offsets:			
	Against gross budget authority and outlays:			
88.40	Offsetting collections (cash) from: Non-Federal sources	–1	–1	–1
	Net budget authority and outlays:			
89.00	Budget authority	2	2	2
90.00	Outlays	2	2	2

Status of Direct Loans (in millions of dollars)

Identification code 12–4142–0–3–452		1999 actual	2000 est.	2001 est.
	Cumulative balance of direct loans outstanding:			
1210	Outstanding, start of year	8	7	6
1251	Repayments: Repayments and prepayments	–1	–1	–1
1290	Outstanding, end of year	7	6	6

Status of Guaranteed Loans (in millions of dollars)

Identification code 12–4142–0–3–452		1999 actual	2000 est.	2001 est.
	Cumulative balance of guaranteed loans outstanding:			
2210	Outstanding, start of year	5	4	4
2290	Outstanding, end of year	4	4	4
	Memorandum:			
2299	Guaranteed amount of guaranteed loans outstanding, end of year	4	4	4

The Rural Communication Development Fund was established pursuant to the Secretary's Memorandum No. 1988,

Credit accounts—Continued

RURAL COMMUNICATION DEVELOPMENT FUND LIQUIDATING ACCOUNT—Continued

approved May 22, 1979. No loans have been made through this account since before 1992.

Statement of Operations (in millions of dollars)

Identification code 12–4142–0–3–452	1998 actual	1999 actual	2000 est.	2001 est.
0101 Revenue	1	3	1	1
0102 Expense	–3	–6	–3	–3
0105 Net income or loss (–)	–2	–3	–2	–2

Balance Sheet (in millions of dollars)

Identification code 12–4142–0–3–452	1998 actual	1999 actual	2000 est.	2001 est.
ASSETS:				
1101 Federal assets: Fund balances with Treasury	1	1	3	3
Net value of assets related to pre–1992 direct loans receivable and acquired defaulted guaranteed loans receivable:				
1601 Direct loans, gross	8	8	7	7
1603 Allowance for estimated uncollectible loans and interest (–)	–3	–2	–3	–3
1604 Direct loans and interest receivable, net	5	6	4	4
1699 Value of assets related to direct loans	5	6	4	4
1999 Total assets	6	7	7	7
LIABILITIES:				
Federal liabilities:				
2102 Interest payable	1	1	3	3
2103 Debt	24	25	23	23
2204 Non-Federal liabilities: Liabilities for loan guarantees	1	–16	1	1
2999 Total liabilities	26	10	27	27
NET POSITION:				
3100 Appropriated capital	14		18	18
3300 Cumulative results of operations	–34	–3	–38	–38
3999 Total net position	–20	–3	–20	–20
4999 Total liabilities and net position	6	7	7	7

FOREIGN AGRICULTURAL SERVICE

Federal Funds

General and special funds:

FOREIGN AGRICULTURAL SERVICE [AND GENERAL SALES MANAGER (INCLUDING TRANSFERS OF FUNDS)]

For necessary expenses of the Foreign Agricultural Service, including carrying out title VI of the Agricultural Act of 1954 (7 U.S.C. 1761–1768), market development activities abroad, and for enabling the Secretary to coordinate and integrate activities of the Department in connection with foreign agricultural work, including not to exceed $128,000 for representation allowances and for expenses pursuant to section 8 of the Act approved August 3, 1956 (7 U.S.C. 1766), [$109,203,000] *$113,587,000*: *Provided*, That the Service may utilize advances of funds, or reimburse this appropriation for expenditures made on behalf of Federal agencies, public and private organizations and institutions under agreements executed pursuant to the agricultural food production assistance programs (7 U.S.C. 1737) and the foreign assistance programs of the United States Agency for International Development.

None of the funds in the foregoing paragraph shall be available to promote the sale or export of tobacco or tobacco products. *(Agriculture, Rural Development, Food and Drug Administration and Related Agencies Appropriations Act, 2000.)*

Program and Financing (in millions of dollars)

Identification code 12–2900–0–1–352	1999 actual	2000 est.	2001 est.
Obligations by program activity:			
Direct program:			
00.01 Market access	26	26	27
00.02 Market development	60	32	34
00.03 Market intelligence	23	23	24
00.04 Financial marketing assistance	9	9	9
00.05 Long-term market and infrastructure development	18	19	20
09.00 Reimbursable program	69	60	58
10.00 Total new obligations	205	169	172
Budgetary resources available for obligation:			
21.40 Unobligated balance available, start of year	15	24	24
22.00 New budget authority (gross)	212	169	172
22.22 Unobligated balance transferred from other accounts	2		
23.90 Total budgetary resources available for obligation	229	193	196
23.95 Total new obligations	−205	−169	−172
24.40 Unobligated balance available, end of year	24	24	24
New budget authority (gross), detail:			
Discretionary:			
40.00 Appropriation	136	109	114
42.00 Transferred from other accounts	11		
43.00 Appropriation (total discretionary)	147	109	114
68.00 Spending authority from offsetting collections: Offsetting collections (cash)	65	60	58
70.00 Total new budget authority (gross)	212	169	172
Change in unpaid obligations:			
72.40 Unpaid obligations, start of year: Obligated balance, start of year	34	45	50
73.10 Total new obligations	205	169	172
73.20 Total outlays (gross)	−194	−164	−171
74.40 Unpaid obligations, end of year: Obligated balance, end of year	45	50	51
Outlays (gross), detail:			
86.90 Outlays from new discretionary authority	176	164	166
86.93 Outlays from discretionary balances	18		5
87.00 Total outlays (gross)	194	164	171
Offsets:			
Against gross budget authority and outlays:			
88.00 Offsetting collections (cash) from: Federal sources	−65	−60	−58
Net budget authority and outlays:			
89.00 Budget authority	147	109	114
90.00 Outlays	131	104	113

The mission of the Foreign Agricultural Service (FAS) is to open, expand and maintain global market opportunities through international trade, cooperation, and sustainable development activities which secure the long-term economic vitality and global competitiveness of America's rural communities and related food and agricultural enterprises.

FAS conducts a demand-driven export strategy, deploying five major policy objectives to execute the strategy, while integrating commodity and country market priorities for allocating scarce export assistance resources. These objectives include:

Market Access: FAS initiates, directs and coordinates the Department's formulation of trade policies and programs with the goal of maintaining and expanding world markets for U.S. agricultural products. It monitors international compliance with bilateral and multilateral trade agreements. It identifies restrictive tariff and trade practices which act as barriers to the import of U.S. agricultural commodities, then supports negotiations to remove them. It acts to counter and eliminate unfair trade practices of other countries that hinder U.S. agricultural exports to those markets. In virtually every foreign market, U.S. agricultural exports are subject to import duties and non-tariff trade restrictions. Trade information sent to Washington from FAS personnel overseas is used to map strategies for improving market access, pursuing U.S. rights under trade agreements, and developing programs and policies to make U.S. farm products more competitive. Staff increases to improve market access work will be achieved by shifting resources from FAS' financial marketing efforts.

Market Development, Promotion and Outreach: FAS develops foreign markets for U.S. farm products through aggressive market expansion activities. It provides services to the U.S. and foreign agricultural trade sectors that are necessary to establish, build and maintain overseas markets for U.S. agricultural products. Public Law 83–690, approved August 28, 1954, includes authority to establish up to 25 Agricultural Trade Offices. Currently 17 such offices are in operation at key foreign trading centers to assist U.S. exporters, trade groups and state export marketing officials in trade promotion. Promotional activities are carried out chiefly in cooperation with non-profit agricultural trade associations and firms on a cost-sharing basis. The largest of FAS's promotional programs is the Foreign Market Development Cooperator Program and Market Access Program. In addition, FAS sponsors U.S. participation in several major trade shows and a number of single-industry exhibitions each year. These programs are designed to create demand for U.S. agricultural products in foreign markets, introduce U.S. food and agricultural products to potential foreign customers, and show foreign customers how to use U.S. products.

FAS strategic outreach efforts focus on facilitating export readiness and help link both export-ready and new-to-export firms to market entry opportunities, and increase domestic awareness of export opportunities/global consumer quality and product safety expectations. These efforts are designed to strengthen the export knowledge/skills of producers and exporters so they can compete more effectively in the international marketplace. Outreach also includes targeting foreign buyers in educating them about the merits of U.S. products and how they can be purchased.

Market Intelligence: FAS provides U.S. farmers and traders with information on world agricultural production and trade that they can use to adjust to changes in world demand for U.S. agricultural products. This is done through a continuous program of reporting by 63 posts located throughout the world covering some 130 countries. Reporting includes information and/or data on foreign government policies, analysis of supply and demand conditions, commercial trade relationships and market opportunities. Advanced computer and telecommunications technology is used to improve and speed the flow of information between the posts and Washington. FAS analyzes agricultural information essential to the assessment of foreign supply and demand conditions in order to provide estimates of the current situation and to forecast the export potential for specific U.S. agricultural commodities.

Financial Marketing Assistance: FAS administers a number of price/credit and risk assistance programs designed to develop overseas markets and expand the levels of U.S. agricultural commodities. These programs include CCC Export Credit Guarantee Programs, export subsidy programs, including the Export Enhancement Program and Dairy Export Incentive Program, and food assistance activities such as Public Law 480, Food for Progress and the Section 416(b) program. These programs are designed to help developing nations make the transition from concessional financing to cash purchases, give U.S. producers the ability to counter export subsidies of foreign competitors and allow U.S. exporters to compete with sales terms offered by foreign competitors.

Long-term Market and Infrastructure Development: FAS helps USDA and other federal agencies, U.S. universities and others enhance the global competitiveness of U.S. agriculture and helps increase income and food availability in developing nations by mobilizing expertise for agriculturally led economic growth. Through the administration of a number of collaborative programs, FAS works to enhance U.S. agriculture's competitiveness by providing linkages to world resources and international organizations and building a spirit of cooperation. These linkages produce new technologies that are vital to improving the agricultural demand base and producing new and alternative products. Direct program activities include the administration of the Cochran Fellowship Program and management of USDA's bilateral exchange and cooperative research programs with foreign governments and institutions. Another activity is the Emerging Markets Program under which technical assistance and related activities are carried out in emerging markets aimed at enhancing their food and rural business systems and expanding U.S. agricultural exports. At the request of the Agency for International Development, international organizations and foreign governments, technical assistance and training in agriculture and rural development are provided on a reimbursable or advance of funds basis.

In 2000 and 2001, the Foreign market development cooperator program and the Quality samples program will receive mandatory funding from CCC, administered by FAS.

The new Quality samples program will provide samples of U.S. agricultural products to foreign importers to display the high quality of U.S. products.

Object Classification (in millions of dollars)

Identification code 12–2900–0–1–352		1999 actual	2000 est.	2001 est.
	Direct obligations:			
	Personnel compensation:			
11.1	Full-time permanent	41	45	47
11.3	Other than full-time permanent	2	2	2
11.5	Other personnel compensation	1	1	1
11.8	Special personal services payments	2	2	2
11.9	Total personnel compensation	46	50	52
12.1	Civilian personnel benefits	12	14	15
21.0	Travel and transportation of persons	4	4	4
22.0	Transportation of things	1	1	1
23.2	Rental payments to others	7	7	7
23.3	Communications, utilities, and miscellaneous charges	4	4	4
24.0	Printing and reproduction	1	1	1
25.2	Other services	58	26	28
26.0	Supplies and materials	2	2	2
31.0	Equipment	1		
99.0	Subtotal, direct obligations	136	109	114
99.0	Reimbursable obligations	69	60	58
99.9	Total new obligations	205	169	172

Personnel Summary

Identification code 12–2900–0–1–352		1999 actual	2000 est.	2001 est.
	Direct:			
1001	Total compensable workyears: Full-time equivalent employment	730	760	780
	Reimbursable:			
2001	Total compensable workyears: Full-time equivalent employment	193	193	193

FOREIGN AGRICULTURAL SERVICE AND GENERAL SALES MANAGER

(Legislative proposal, not subject to PAYGO)

In 2001, FAS will establish an account to manage unanticipated fluctuations in foreign currency exchange rates. Under this proposal, up to $2,000,000 in annual gains from favorable exchange rate movement will be transferred to a FAS account to be used solely for the purpose of offsetting future exchange rate losses.

General and special funds—Continued

SCIENTIFIC ACTIVITIES OVERSEAS (FOREIGN CURRENCY PROGRAM)

Program and Financing (in millions of dollars)

Identification code 12–1404–0–1–352	1999 actual	2000 est.	2001 est.
Budgetary resources available for obligation:			
21.40 Unobligated balance available, start of year	1	1	1
23.95 Total new obligations			
24.40 Unobligated balance available, end of year	1	1	1
Change in unpaid obligations:			
72.40 Unpaid obligations, start of year: Obligated balance, start of year	3	2	1
73.20 Total outlays (gross)	−1	−1	−1
74.40 Unpaid obligations, end of year: Obligated balance, end of year	2	1	1
Outlays (gross), detail:			
86.93 Outlays from discretionary balances	1	1	1
Net budget authority and outlays:			
89.00 Budget authority			
90.00 Outlays	1	1	1

As authorized by the Agricultural Trade Development and Assistance Act of 1954 (Public Law 480), as amended, USDA uses foreign currencies to support research on problems of mutual interest to the United States and participating foreign countries. After 1991 no new foreign currency programs have been or are proposed to be initiated.

FOREIGN ASSISTANCE PROGRAMS

The funds and facilities of the Commodity Credit Corporation may, by law, be used in carrying out programs to encourage the export of agricultural commodities.

Included in this category are the following activities carried out under the Agricultural Trade Development and Assistance Act of 1954, Public Law 480, 83rd Congress, as amended (P.L. 480): Financing sales of agricultural commodities to developing countries for dollars on credit terms, or for local currencies (including for local currencies on credit terms) for use under sec. 104 (title I); for dispositions abroad (titles II and III); and for furnishing commodities to carry out the Food for Progress Act of 1985, as amended. Agreements may provide for commodities to be made available on a multi-year basis.

[PUBLIC LAW 480 PROGRAM AND GRANT ACCOUNTS]

[(INCLUDING TRANSFERS OF FUNDS)]

[For expenses during the current fiscal year, not otherwise recoverable, and unrecovered prior years' costs, including interest thereon, under the Agricultural Trade Development and Assistance Act of 1954 (7 U.S.C. 1691, 1701–1704, 1721–1726a, 1727–1727e, 1731–1736g–3, and 1737), as follows: (1) $155,000,000 for Public Law 480 title I credit, including Food for Progress programs; (2) $21,000,000 is hereby appropriated for ocean freight differential costs for the shipment of agricultural commodities pursuant to title I of said Act and the Food for Progress Act of 1985; and (3) $800,000,000 is hereby appropriated for commodities supplied in connection with dispositions abroad pursuant to title II of said Act: *Provided*, That not to exceed 15 percent of the funds made available to carry out any title of said Act may be used to carry out any other title of said Act: *Provided further*, That such sums shall remain available until expended (7 U.S.C. 2209b).

For the cost, as defined in section 502 of the Congressional Budget Act of 1974, of direct credit agreements as authorized by the Agricultural Trade Development and Assistance Act of 1954, and the Food for Progress Act of 1985, including the cost of modifying credit agreements under said Act, $127,813,000.

In addition, for administrative expenses to carry out the Public Law 480 title I credit program, and the Food for Progress Act of 1985, to the extent funds appropriated for Public Law 480 are utilized, $1,850,000, of which $1,035,000 may be transferred to and merged with the appropriation for "Foreign Agricultural Service and General Sales Manager" and $815,000 may be transferred to and merged with the appropriation for "Farm Service Agency, Salaries and Expenses".] *(Agriculture, Rural Development, Food and Drug Administration, and Related Agencies Appropriations Act, 2000.)*

PUBLIC LAW 480 TITLE I OCEAN FREIGHT DIFFERENTIAL GRANTS

For expense during the current fiscal year, not otherwise recoverable, and unrecovered prior years' costs, including interest thereon, under the Agricultural Trade Development and Assistance Act of 1954, as amended, $20,322,000, to remain available until expended, for ocean freight differential costs for the shipment of agricultural commodities under title I of said Act: Provided, That funds made available for the cost of title I agreements and for title I ocean freight differential may be used interchangeably between the two accounts. (7 U.S.C. 1701b, 2209b)

Program and Financing (in millions of dollars)

Identification code 12–2271–0–1–351	1999 actual	2000 est.	2001 est.
Obligations by program activity:			
00.01 P.L. 480 Grant—Title I: Ocean freight differential (OFD)	38	114	20
10.00 Total new obligations (object class 41.0)	38	114	20
Budgetary resources available for obligation:			
21.40 Unobligated balance available, start of year	21	93	
22.00 New budget authority (gross)	16	21	20
22.10 Resources available from recoveries of prior year obligations	4		
22.22 Unobligated balance transferred from other accounts	88		
23.90 Total budgetary resources available for obligation	129	114	20
23.95 Total new obligations	−38	−114	−20
24.40 Unobligated balance available, end of year	93		
New budget authority (gross), detail:			
Discretionary:			
40.00 Appropriation	16	21	20
Change in unpaid obligations:			
72.40 Unpaid obligations, start of year: Obligated balance, start of year	46	38	46
73.10 Total new obligations	38	114	20
73.20 Total outlays (gross)	−41	−105	−34
73.45 Adjustments in unexpired accounts	−4		
74.40 Unpaid obligations, end of year: Obligated balance, end of year	38	46	33
Outlays (gross), detail:			
86.90 Outlays from new discretionary authority	16	12	11
86.93 Outlays from discretionary balances	25	93	23
87.00 Total outlays (gross)	41	105	34
Net budget authority and outlays:			
89.00 Budget authority	16	21	20
90.00 Outlays	41	105	34

This account funds the title I ocean freight differential program.

PUBLIC LAW 480 GRANTS—TITLES II AND III

For expense during the current fiscal year, not otherwise recoverable, and unrecovered prior years' costs, including interest thereon, under the Agricultural Trade Development and Assistance Act of 1954, as amended, $837,000,000, to remain available until expended, for commodities supplied in connection with dispositions abroad under title II of said Act, of which up to 15 percent may be used for commodities supplied in connection with dispositions abroad under title III of said Act. (7 U.S.C. 1691, 1721–26a. 1727–27e, 1731–36g–3, 1737, 2209b)

Program and Financing (in millions of dollars)

Identification code 12–2278–0–1–151	1999 actual	2000 est.	2001 est.
Obligations by program activity:			
00.01 Commodities supplied in connection with dispositions abroad (Title II)	949	962	837
00.02 Commodities supplied in connection with dispositions abroad (Title III)	28	5	
10.00 Total new obligations (object class 41.0)	977	967	837
Budgetary resources available for obligation:			
21.40 Unobligated balance available, start of year	23	128	
22.00 New budget authority (gross)	1,011	800	837
22.10 Resources available from recoveries of prior year obligations	71		
22.22 Unobligated balance transferred from other accounts	1	39	
23.90 Total budgetary resources available for obligation	1,106	967	837
23.95 Total new obligations	–977	–967	–837
24.40 Unobligated balance available, end of year	128		
New budget authority (gross), detail:			
Discretionary:			
40.00 Appropriation	1,011	800	837
Change in unpaid obligations:			
72.40 Unpaid obligations, start of year: Obligated balance, start of year	691	671	607
73.10 Total new obligations	977	967	837
73.20 Total outlays (gross)	–926	–1,031	–863
73.45 Adjustments in unexpired accounts	–71		
74.40 Unpaid obligations, end of year: Obligated balance, end of year	671	607	581
Outlays (gross), detail:			
86.90 Outlays from new discretionary authority	503	420	439
86.93 Outlays from discretionary balances	423	611	424
87.00 Total outlays (gross)	926	1,031	863
Net budget authority and outlays:			
89.00 Budget authority	1,011	800	837
90.00 Outlays	926	1,031	863

This account funds the non-credit components of Public Law 480, title II and title III.

Credit accounts:

PUBLIC LAW 480 PROGRAM ACCOUNT

For the cost as defined in section 502 of the Congressional Budget Act of 1974, of agreements under the Agricultural Trade Development and Assistance Act of 1954, as amended, and the Food For Progress Act of 1985, as amended, including the cost of modifying credit arrangements under said Acts, $114,186,000, to remain available until expended.

In addition, for administrative expenses to carry out the credit program of title I, Public Law 83–480, and the Food for Progress Act of 1985, as amended, to the extent funds appropriated for Public Law 83–480 are utilized, $1,850,000, of which not to exceed $1,035,000 may be transferred to and merged with "Salaries and expenses", Foreign Agricultural Service, and of which not to exceed $815,000 may be transferred to and merged with "Salaries and expenses," Farm Service Agency. (7 U.S.C. 1691, 1701–04, 1731–36g–3, 2209b).

Program and Financing (in millions of dollars)

Identification code 12–2277–0–1–351	1999 actual	2000 est.	2001 est.
Obligations by program activity:			
00.01 Direct credit subsidy	119	202	114
00.02 Direct credit subsidy: Russia food assistance	149	480	
00.05 Reestimates of direct credit subsidy		20	
00.06 Interest on reestimates of direct credit subsidy		3	
00.09 Administrative expenses	2	2	2
00.10 Monitor expenses: Russia food assistance	1	2	
10.00 Total new obligations	271	709	116
Budgetary resources available for obligation:			
21.40 Unobligated balance available, start of year	58	603	
22.00 New budget authority (gross)	178	145	116
22.21 Unobligated balance transferred to other accounts	–1	–39	
22.22 Unobligated balance transferred from other accounts	638		
23.90 Total budgetary resources available for obligation	873	709	116
23.95 Total new obligations	–271	–709	–116
24.40 Unobligated balance available, end of year	603		
New budget authority (gross), detail:			
Discretionary:			
40.00 Appropriation	178	130	116
40.76 Reduction pursuant to P.L. 106–113		–8	
43.00 Appropriation (total discretionary)	178	122	116
Mandatory:			
60.05 Appropriation (indefinite)		23	
70.00 Total new budget authority (gross)	178	145	116
Change in unpaid obligations:			
72.40 Unpaid obligations, start of year: Obligated balance, start of year	131	72	90
73.10 Total new obligations	271	709	116
73.20 Total outlays (gross)	–329	–691	–142
74.40 Unpaid obligations, end of year: Obligated balance, end of year	72	90	64
Outlays (gross), detail:			
86.90 Outlays from new current authority	121	70	67
86.93 Outlays from current balances	208	598	75
86.97 Outlays from new mandatory authority		23	
87.00 Total outlays (gross)	329	691	142
Net budget authority and outlays:			
89.00 Budget authority	178	145	116
90.00 Outlays	329	691	142

Summary of Loan Levels, Subsidy Budget Authority and Outlays by Program (in millions of dollars)

Identification code 12–2277–0–1–351	1999 actual	2000 est.	2001 est.
Direct loan levels supportable by subsidy budget authority:			
1150 Direct credit levels	203	145	160
1150 Direct credit levels: Russia food assistance	760		
1159 Total direct loan levels	963	145	160
Direct loan subsidy (in percent):			
1320 Subsidy rate	86.79	82.46	71.51
1329 Weighted average subsidy rate	86.79	82.46	71.51
Direct loan subsidy budget authority:			
1330 Subsidy budget authority	176	120	114
1330 Subsidy budget authority: Russia food assistance	635		
1339 Total subsidy budget authority	811	120	114
Direct loan subsidy outlays:			
1340 Subsidy outlays	326	667	140
1349 Total subsidy outlays	326	667	140
Administrative expense data:			
3510 Budget authority	4	2	2
3590 Outlays from new authority	3	2	2

Food Aid to Russia.—As part of a comprehensive package of U.S. assistance for Russia announced by the Secretary of Agriculture in 1998, $638 million and $88 million was transferred from CCC to the P.L. 480, Title I Program, and Title I Ocean Freight Differential, respectively, under provisions of the Secretary of Agriculture's Interchange Authority (7 U.S.C. 2257). The package of assistance announced for Russia includes a proposed concessional credit program USDA will carry out under the authority of Title I of the Agricultural Trade Development and Assistance Act of 1954 (P.L. 83–480) and a Food for Progress grant program funded under Title I.

As required by the Federal Credit Reform Act of 1990, this account records, for the P.L. 480 Program, the subsidy

Credit accounts—Continued

PUBLIC LAW 480 PROGRAM ACCOUNT—Continued

costs associated with the direct loans obligated in 1992 and beyond (including modifications of direct loans that resulted from obligation in any year), as well as administrative expenses of this program. The subsidy amounts are estimated on a present value basis; the administrative expenses are estimated on a cash basis.

Object Classification (in millions of dollars)

Identification code 12–2277–0–1–351		1999 actual	2000 est.	2001 est.
25.3	Purchases of goods and services from Government accounts	3	3	2
41.0	Grants, subsidies, and contributions	268	706	114
99.9	Total new obligations	271	709	116

P.L. 480 DIRECT CREDIT FINANCING ACCOUNT

Program and Financing (in millions of dollars)

Identification code 12–4049–0–3–351		1999 actual	2000 est.	2001 est.
	Obligations by program activity:			
00.01	Direct loans	282	907	160
00.02	Interest on Treasury borrowing	38	33	32
00.05	Reestimates of direct loan subsidy		55	
00.06	Interest on reestimates of direct loan subsidy		26	
10.00	Total new obligations	320	1,021	192
	Budgetary resources available for obligation:			
21.40	Unobligated balance available, start of year	45	188	108
22.00	New financing authority (gross)	464	941	192
23.90	Total budgetary resources available for obligation	509	1,129	300
23.95	Total new obligations	−320	−1,021	−192
24.40	Unobligated balance available, end of year	188	108	108
	New financing authority (gross), detail:			
	Mandatory:			
67.15	Authority to borrow (indefinite)	164	267	28
	Spending authority from offsetting collections:			
	Discretionary:			
68.00	Offsetting collections (cash)	392	678	164
68.10	Change in receivables from program account	−58	−4	
68.47	Portion applied to repay debt	−34		
68.90	Spending authority from offsetting collections (total discretionary)	300	674	164
70.00	Total new financing authority (gross)	464	941	192
	Change in unpaid obligations:			
	Unpaid obligations, start of year:			
72.40	Obligated balance, start of year	2	−59	108
72.95	Receivables from program account	130	72	68
72.99	Total unpaid obligations, start of year	132	13	176
73.10	Total new obligations	320	1,021	192
73.20	Total financing disbursements (gross)	−439	−858	−195
	Unpaid obligations, end of year:			
74.40	Obligated balance, end of year	−59	108	105
74.95	Receivables from program account	72	68	68
74.99	Total unpaid obligations, end of year	13	176	173
87.00	Total financing disbursements (gross)	439	858	195
	Offsets:			
	Against gross financing authority and financing disbursements:			
	Offsetting collections (cash) from:			
88.00	Payments from program account	−347	−665	−148
	Non-Federal sources:			
88.40	Interest received on loans	−34	−8	−8
88.40	Principal received on loans	−11	−5	−8
88.90	Total, offsetting collections (cash)	−392	−678	−164
	Against gross financing authority only:			
88.95	Change in receivables from program accounts	58	4	
	Net financing authority and financing disbursements:			
89.00	Financing authority	130	267	28
90.00	Financing disbursements	47	180	31

Status of Direct Loans (in millions of dollars)

Identification code 12–4049–0–3–351		1999 actual	2000 est.	2001 est.
	Position with respect to appropriations act limitation on obligations:			
1111	Limitation on direct loans	282	907	160
1150	Total direct loan obligations	282	907	160
	Cumulative balance of direct loans outstanding:			
1210	Outstanding, start of year	1,529	1,927	2,699
1231	Disbursements: Direct loan disbursements	401	777	195
1251	Repayments: Repayments and prepayments	−3	−5	−8
1290	Outstanding, end of year	1,927	2,699	2,886

As required by the Federal Credit Reform Act of 1990, this non-budgetary account records all cash flows to and from the Government resulting from direct loans obligated in 1992 and beyond (including modifications of direct loans that resulted from obligations in any year). The amounts in this account are a means of financing and are not included in the budget totals.

Balance Sheet (in millions of dollars)

Identification code 12–4049–0–3–351		1998 actual	1999 actual	2000 est.	2001 est.
	ASSETS:				
	Federal assets:				
1101	Fund balances with Treasury	45	188	188	188
	Investments in US securities:				
1106	Receivables, net	131	72	68	68
	Net value of assets related to post-1991 direct loans receivable:				
1401	Direct loans receivable, gross	1,529	1,927	2,699	2,886
1402	Interest receivable	23	34	8	8
1405	Allowance for subsidy cost (−)	−1,220	−1,566	−2,205	−2,346
1499	Net present value of assets related to direct loans	332	395	502	548
1901	Other Federal assets: Other assets	20			
1999	Total assets	528	655	758	804
	LIABILITIES:				
	Federal liabilities:				
2101	Accounts payable	4	8	8	8
2103	Debt	417	539	560	560
2105	Other	122	102	105	105
2999	Total liabilities	543	649	673	673
4999	Total liabilities and net position	543	649	673	673

DEBT REDUCTION—FINANCING ACCOUNT

Program and Financing (in millions of dollars)

Identification code 12–4143–0–3–351		1999 actual	2000 est.	2001 est.
	Obligations by program activity:			
00.01	Payment to liquidating account		24	32
00.02	Interest on debt to Treasury		4	4
00.05	Reestimates of direct loan subsidy		1	
00.06	Interest on reestimates of direct loan subsidy		1	
10.00	Total new obligations		30	36
	Budgetary resources available for obligation:			
21.40	Unobligated balance available, start of year		2	19
22.00	New financing authority (gross)	9	45	51
22.40	Capital transfer to general fund	−7		
23.90	Total budgetary resources available for obligation	2	47	70
23.95	Total new obligations		−30	−36
24.40	Unobligated balance available, end of year	2	19	34

		1999 actual	2000 est.	2001 est.
	New financing authority (gross), detail:			
	Mandatory:			
67.15	Authority to borrow (indefinite)	....	11	....
	Discretionary:			
68.00	Spending authority from offsetting collections: Offsetting collections (cash)	9	34	51
70.00	Total new financing authority (gross)	9	45	51
	Change in unpaid obligations:			
72.40	Unpaid obligations, start of year: Obligated balance, start of year	....	−1	−18
73.10	Total new obligations	....	30	36
73.20	Total financing disbursements (gross)	....	−45	−52
74.40	Unpaid obligations, end of year: Obligated balance, end of year	−1	−18	−33
87.00	Total financing disbursements (gross)	....	45	52
	Offsets:			
	Against gross financing authority and financing disbursements:			
	Offsetting collections (cash) from:			
88.00	Federal sources	−1	−32	−49
88.40	Non-Federal sources	−8	−2	−2
88.90	Total, offsetting collections (cash)	−9	−34	−51
	Net financing authority and financing disbursements:			
89.00	Financing authority	....	11	....
90.00	Financing disbursements	−9	11	1

Status of Direct Loans (in millions of dollars)

Identification code 12–4143–0–3–351		1999 actual	2000 est.	2001 est.
	Position with respect to appropriations act limitation on obligations:			
1111	Limitation on direct loans	....	....	....
1150	Total direct loan obligations	....	....	....
	Cumulative balance of direct loans outstanding:			
1210	Outstanding, start of year	63	63	61
1251	Repayments: Repayments and prepayments	....	−2	−2
1290	Outstanding, end of year	63	61	59

As required by the Federal Credit Reform Act of 1990, this non-budgetary account records all cash flows to and from the Government resulting from direct loans obligated in 1992 and beyond (including modifications of direct loans that resulted from obligations in any year). The amounts in this account are a means of financing and are not included in the budget totals.

Balance Sheet (in millions of dollars)

Identification code 12–4143–0–3–351		1998 actual	1999 actual	2000 est.	2001 est.
	ASSETS:				
	Net value of assets related to post-1991 direct loans receivable:				
1401	Direct loans receivable, gross	63	63	61	59
1405	Allowance for subsidy cost (−)	–25	–17	–18	–18
1499	Net present value of assets related to direct loans	38	46	43	41
1999	Total assets	38	46	43	41
	LIABILITIES:				
2103	Federal liabilities: Debt	38	46	36	36
2203	Non-Federal liabilities: Debt	....	....	14	14
2999	Total liabilities	38	46	50	50
	NET POSITION:				
3300	Cumulative results of operations	....	....	–7	–9
3999	Total net position	....	....	–7	–9
4999	Total liabilities and net position	38	46	43	41

P.L. 480 Title I Food for Progress Credits, Program Account

Program and Financing (in millions of dollars)

Identification code 12–2273–0–1–351		1999 actual	2000 est.	2001 est.
	Budgetary resources available for obligation:			
21.40	Unobligated balance available, start of year	4	4	....
22.21	Unobligated balance transferred to other accounts	....	−4	....
23.90	Total budgetary resources available for obligation	4	....	....
23.95	Total new obligations	....	....	....
24.40	Unobligated balance available, end of year	4	....	....
	Net budget authority and outlays:			
89.00	Budget authority	....	....	....
90.00	Outlays	....	....	....

Sales of U.S. commodities under the credit portion of the Food for Progress were made to Russia in 1993. The assistance is subject to credit reform budgeting. No credit has been issued since.

P.L. 480 Title I Food for Progress Credits, Financing Account

Program and Financing (in millions of dollars)

Identification code 12–4078–0–3–351		1999 actual	2000 est.	2001 est.
	Obligations by program activity:			
00.02	Interest to Treasury on borrowings	12	12	12
00.05	Reestimates of direct loan subsidy	....	33	....
00.06	Interest on reestimates of direct loan subsidy	....	14	....
10.00	Total new obligations	12	59	12
	Budgetary resources available for obligation:			
21.40	Unobligated balance available, start of year	28	35	....
22.00	New financing authority (gross)	15	59	12
22.40	Capital transfer to general fund	4	−35	....
23.90	Total budgetary resources available for obligation	47	59	12
23.95	Total new obligations	−12	−59	−12
24.40	Unobligated balance available, end of year	35	....	....
	New financing authority (gross), detail:			
	Mandatory:			
67.15	Authority to borrow (indefinite)	....	52	5
	Discretionary:			
68.00	Spending authority from offsetting collections: Offsetting collections (cash)	15	7	7
70.00	Total new financing authority (gross)	15	59	12
	Change in unpaid obligations:			
73.10	Total new obligations	12	59	12
73.20	Total financing disbursements (gross)	−12	−59	−12
87.00	Total financing disbursements (gross)	12	59	12
	Offsets:			
	Against gross financing authority and financing disbursements:			
88.40	Offsetting collections (cash) from: Interest collections	−15	−7	−7
	Net financing authority and financing disbursements:			
89.00	Financing authority	....	52	5
90.00	Financing disbursements	−3	52	5

Status of Direct Loans (in millions of dollars)

Identification code 12–4078–0–3–351		1999 actual	2000 est.	2001 est.
	Position with respect to appropriations act limitation on obligations:			
1111	Limitation on direct loans	....	....	....
1150	Total direct loan obligations	....	....	....
	Cumulative balance of direct loans outstanding:			
1210	Outstanding, start of year	508	508	508

Credit accounts—Continued

P.L. 480 TITLE I FOOD FOR PROGRESS CREDITS, FINANCING ACCOUNT—Continued

Status of Direct Loans (in millions of dollars)—Continued

Identification code 12–4078–0–3–351	1999 actual	2000 est.	2001 est.
1251 Repayments: Repayments and prepayments	....	....	....
1290 Outstanding, end of year	508	508	508

As required by the Federal Credit Reform Act of 1990, this non-budgetary account records all cash flows to and from the Government resulting from direct loans obligated in 1992 and beyond (including modifications of direct loans that resulted from obligations in any year). The amounts in this account are a means of financing and are not included in the budget totals.

Balance Sheet (in millions of dollars)

Identification code 12–4078–0–3–351	1998 actual	1999 actual	2000 est.	2001 est.
ASSETS:				
Net value of assets related to post-1991 direct loans receivable:				
1401 Direct loans receivable, gross	508	508	508	508
1402 Interest receivable	11	15	15	15
1405 Allowance for subsidy cost (-)	–268	–328	–328	–328
1499 Net present value of assets related to direct loans	251	195	195	195
1999 Total assets	251	195	195	195
LIABILITIES:				
Federal liabilities:				
2103 Debt	183	195	195	195
2105 Other	68	....	....	....
2999 Total liabilities	251	195	195	195
4999 Total liabilities and net position	251	195	195	195

EXPENSES, PUBLIC LAW 480, FOREIGN ASSISTANCE PROGRAMS, AGRICULTURE, LIQUIDATING ACCOUNT

Program and Financing (in millions of dollars)

Identification code 12–2274–0–1–151	1999 actual	2000 est.	2001 est.
Budgetary resources available for obligation:			
21.40 Unobligated balance available, start of year	523	75	....
22.00 New budget authority (gross)	478	1	24
22.40 Capital transfer to general fund	– 926	– 75	– 24
23.90 Total budgetary resources available for obligation	75	1	....
24.40 Unobligated balance available, end of year	75	....	....
New budget authority (gross), detail:			
Mandatory:			
Offsetting collections (cash):			
69.00 Offsetting collections (cash)	478	442	436
69.00 Offsetting collections (cash)	....	1	24
69.27 Capital transfer to general fund	....	– 442	– 436
69.90 Spending authority from offsetting collections (total mandatory)	478	1	24
Offsets:			
Against gross budget authority and outlays:			
Offsetting collections (cash) from:			
88.00 Federal sources—debt reduction	....	– 1	– 24
88.40 Principal and interest collections	– 478	– 442	– 436
88.90 Total, offsetting collections (cash)	– 478	– 443	– 460
Net budget authority and outlays:			
89.00 Budget authority	....	– 442	– 436
90.00 Outlays	– 478	– 443	– 460

Status of Direct Loans (in millions of dollars)

Identification code 12–2274–0–1–151	1999 actual	2000 est.	2001 est.
Cumulative balance of direct loans outstanding:			
1210 Outstanding, start of year	9,146	8,810	8,535
Repayments:			
Repayments and prepayments:			
1251 Repayments and prepayments	– 336	– 272	– 273
1251 Repayments and prepayments—debt reduction	....	– 1	– 24
1264 Write-offs for default: Other adjustments, net—debt reduction	....	– 2	– 242
1290 Outstanding, end of year	8,810	8,535	7,996

Program Activities

[In millions of dollars]

	1999 actual	*2000 est.*	*2001 est.*
Ocean freight differential (title I)	38	114	20
Commodities supplied in connection with dispositions abroad (title II)	949	962	837
Commodities supplied in connection with dispositions abroad (title III)	28	5	....
Total program level	1,015	1,081	857

RECONCILIATION OF PROGRAM LEVEL TO PROGRAM COSTS FUNDED BY P.L. 480

[In millions of dollars]

	1999 actual	*2000 est.*	*2001 est.*
Title I			
Commodity credits	804	255	159
Ocean freight differential and ocean transportation	38	95	20
Total program level, current year	842	350	179
Prior year obligations financed	141	266	137
Obligations financed in succeeding years	–266	–137	–94
Administrative costs	4	2	2
Total program costs, funded program level	721	481	224
Title II			
Commodity costs	492	554	480
Ocean and inland transportation	457	408	357
Total program level, current year	949	962	837
Prior year obligations financed	505	565	614
Current year obligations financed in succeeding years	–565	–613	–607
Total program costs, funded program level	889	912	844
Title III			
Commodity costs	20	3	....
Ocean and inland transportation	8	2	....
Total program level, current year	28	5	....
Prior year obligations financed	28	19	4
Current year obligations financed in succeeding years	–19	–5	....
Total program costs, funded program level	37	19	4

Financing sales of agricultural commodities to developing countries for dollars on credit terms, or for local currencies (including for local currencies on credit terms) for use under sec. 104; and for furnishing commodities to carry out the Food for Progress Act of 1985, as amended (title I).—Funds appropriated for P.L. 480 are used to finance all sales made pursuant to agreements concluded under the authority of Title I. The Corporation may serve as the purchasing or shipping agent, or both, for the importing country or may award contracts for freight agent services on behalf of the Corporation to handle shipping of commodities under P.L. 480.

Sales are made to developing countries as defined in section 402(4) of P.L. 480 and must not displace expected commercial sales (secs. 403(e) and (h)). Agreements are made with developing countries for delivery in accordance with the terms of the agreement.

When U.S.-flag vessels are required to ship commodities under this title, the Corporation will pay the difference between U.S.-flag rates and foreign-flag rates. In limited cases, full transportation costs to port-of-entry or point-of-entry abroad may be included along with the cost of the commodity in the amount financed by CCC in order to ensure that U.S. food aid can reach the most needy recipients.

Financing sales of agricultural commodities for dollars on credit terms (title I).—Payment by developing countries or private entities may be made over a period of not more than 30 years with a deferral of principal payments for up to 5 years. Interest accrues at a concessional rate as determined appropriate.

Section 411 of P.L. 480 authorizes the President to waive payments of principal and interest under dollar credit sales agreements for countries that meet certain enumerated requirements. Such debt relief may be provided only if the President notifies Congress and may not exceed the amount approved for such purpose in an Act appropriating funds to carry out P.L. 480.

Financing sales of agricultural commodities for local currency, including for local currency on credit terms.—Payment by a recipient country may be made in local currencies for use in carrying out activities under section 104 of P.L. 480.

Foreign currency received in payment for credit extended may be used for payment of U.S. obligations abroad, subject to the appropriation process. The P.L. 480 program is reimbursed for the dollar value of currencies so used.

The financing of sales of agricultural commodities for local currencies on credit terms is subject to the same terms that are applicable to dollar credit financing.

Furnishing commodities to carry out the Food for Progress Act of 1985, as amended (title I).—Funds appropriated to carry out title I may be used to furnish commodities to carry out the Food for Progress Act of 1985. Such commodities may be furnished on credit terms or on a grant basis in order to assist developing countries and countries that are emerging democracies that have made a commitment to introduce and expand free enterprise elements in their agricultural economies.

The following table reflects the composition of the combined appropriations (in millions of dollars):

SALES FOR DOLLARS ON CREDIT TERMS

[In millions of dollars]

Item:	1999 actual	2000 est.	2001 est.
Expenses of shipments (Title I):			
Commodity costs:			
Long-term credit	804	255	159
Total commodity costs	804	255	159
Ocean freight and freight differential (support of U.S. Merchant Marine):			
Long-term credit	38	21	20
Total ocean freight and freight differential	38	21	20
Total expenses of shipments	842	277	179
Appropriation—Title I loan subsidy	177	128	114
Appropriation—Ocean freight differential	16	21	20
Title I credit not subsidized through appropriation	152	27	45

Commodities supplied in connection with dispositions abroad (title II).—Under title II, agricultural commodities are furnished to meet famine or other emergency relief needs, combat malnutrition, carry out activities to alleviate the causes of hunger, mortality and morbidity, promote economic and community development, promote sound environmental practices, and carry out feeding programs. Agricultural commodities are provided through governments for emergencies only, and for non-emergencies through public and private agencies, including intergovernmental organizations.

The Corporation is authorized to pay the costs of acquisition, packaging, processing, enrichment, preservation, fortification, transportation, handling, and other incidental costs incurred up to the time of delivery at U.S. ports. The Corporation also pays ocean freight charges, and pays transportation costs to points of entry other than ports in the case of landlocked countries, where carriers to a specific country are not available, where ports cannot be used effectively, or where a substantial savings in costs or time can be effected, and pays general average contributions arising from ocean transport. In addition, transportation costs from designated points of entry or ports of entry abroad to storage and distribution sites and associated storage and distribution costs may be paid for commodities made available to meet urgent and extraordinary relief requirements. The Budget proposes to authorize the transfer of up to 15 percent of Title II funds to Title III funds. This will allow for increased flexibility in the Title II and Title III programs.

The following table reflects the composition of the appropriations (in millions of dollars):

COMMODITIES SUPPLIED IN CONNECTION WITH DISPOSITIONS ABROAD

(TITLE II)

[In millions of dollars]

Item:	1999 actual	2000 est.	2001 est.
Expenses of shipments:			
Commodity Credit Corporation stocks and other costs in connection with commodities supplied	492	554	480
Ocean transportation	457	408	357
Total program costs	949	962	837
Appropriation or estimate	949	962	837

Commodities supplied in connection with dispositions abroad (title III).—Under title III, agricultural commodities are furnished to least developed countries as defined in section 302(a). They are provided through foreign governments for direct feeding, development of emergency food reserves or may be sold with the proceeds of such sale used by the recipient country for specific economic development purposes.

The Corporation may pay, in connection with furnishing commodities under title III, the same cost items as authorized under title II. Although no funding is requested for Title III, up to 15 percent of funds from other titles under P.L. 480 may be transferred for this program.

Balance Sheet (in millions of dollars)

Identification code 12–2274–0–1–151		1998 actual	1999 actual	2000 est.	2001 est.
	ASSETS:				
1101	Federal assets: Fund balances with Treasury	523			
	Net value of assets related to pre–1992 direct loans receivable and acquired defaulted guaranteed loans receivable:				
	Direct loans, gross:				
1601	Direct loans, gross	9,146	8,810	8,538	8,265
1601	Direct loans, adjustment—Debt Reduction			–3	–269
1602	Interest receivable	116	115		
1603	Allowance, loans receivable (–)	–5,516	–5,639		
1699	Value of assets related to direct loans	3,746	3,286	8,535	7,996
1999	Total assets	4,269	3,286	8,535	7,996
	LIABILITIES:				
2104	Federal liabilities: Resources payable to Treasury	4,269	3,286	8,538	8,265
2999	Total liabilities	4,269	3,286	8,538	8,265

Credit accounts—Continued

EXPENSES, PUBLIC LAW 480, FOREIGN ASSISTANCE PROGRAMS, AGRICULTURE, LIQUIDATING ACCOUNT—Continued

Balance Sheet (in millions of dollars)—Continued

Identification code 12–2274–0–1–151	1998 actual	1999 actual	2000 est.	2001 est.
NET POSITION:				
3300 Cumulative results of operations—Debt Reduction			–3	–269
3999 Total net position			–3	–269
4999 Total liabilities and net position	4,269	3,286	8,535	7,996

Trust Funds

MISCELLANEOUS CONTRIBUTED FUNDS

Unavailable Collections (in millions of dollars)

Identification code 12–8232–0–7–352	1999 actual	2000 est.	2001 est.
Balance, start of year:			
01.99 Balance, start of year			
Receipts:			
02.01 Receipts	2	4	4
Appropriation:			
05.01 Appropriation	–2	–4	–4
07.99 Total balance, end of year			

Program and Financing (in millions of dollars)

Identification code 12–8232–0–7–352	1999 actual	2000 est.	2001 est.
Obligations by program activity:			
10.00 Total new obligations (object class 41.0)	3	3	3
Budgetary resources available for obligation:			
21.40 Unobligated balance available, start of year	4	5	6
22.00 New budget authority (gross)	2	4	4
23.90 Total budgetary resources available for obligation	6	9	10
23.95 Total new obligations	–3	–3	–3
24.40 Unobligated balance available, end of year	5	6	6
New budget authority (gross), detail:			
Mandatory:			
60.27 Appropriation (trust fund, indefinite)	2	4	4
Change in unpaid obligations:			
72.40 Unpaid obligations, start of year: Obligated balance, start of year	2	2	2
73.10 Total new obligations	3	3	3
73.20 Total outlays (gross)	–1	–4	–4
74.40 Unpaid obligations, end of year: Obligated balance, end of year	2	2	2
Outlays (gross), detail:			
86.97 Outlays from new mandatory authority	1	4	4
Net budget authority and outlays:			
89.00 Budget authority	2	4	4
90.00 Outlays	1	4	4

Miscellaneous funds are received from other Federal agencies, international organizations, and developing countries, for USDA development assistance and international research projects (22 U.S.C. 2392).

FOOD AND NUTRITION SERVICE

Federal Funds

General and special funds:

FOOD PROGRAM ADMINISTRATION

For necessary administrative expenses of the domestic food programs funded under this Act, [$111,561,000] *$128,558,000*, of which $5,000,000 shall be available only for simplifying procedures, reducing overhead costs, tightening regulations, improving food stamp [coupon handling] *benefit delivery*, and assisting in the prevention, identification, and prosecution of fraud and other violations of law and of which not less than [$3,000,000] *$8,000,000* shall be available to improve integrity in the Food Stamp and Child Nutrition programs: *Provided*, That this appropriation shall be available for employment pursuant to the second sentence of section 706(a) of the Organic Act of 1944 (7 U.S.C. 2225), and not to exceed $150,000 shall be available for employment under 5 U.S.C. 3109. *(Agriculture, Rural Development, Food and Drug Administration, and Related Agencies Appropriations Act, 2000.)*

Note.—The following schedule includes $2 million provided by section 746.

Program and Financing (in millions of dollars)

Identification code 12–3508–0–1–605	1999 actual	2000 est.	2001 est.
Obligations by program activity:			
Direct program:			
00.01 Food program administration	111	112	129
00.03 Congressional hunger center fellowships		2	
09.01 Reimbursable administrative services provided to Federal agencies	1		
10.00 Total new obligations	112	114	129
Budgetary resources available for obligation:			
22.00 New budget authority (gross)	112	114	129
23.95 Total new obligations	–112	–114	–129
New budget authority (gross), detail:			
Discretionary:			
40.00 Appropriation	109	113	129
42.00 Transferred from other accounts	2	1	
43.00 Appropriation (total discretionary)	111	114	129
68.00 Spending authority from offsetting collections: Offsetting collections (cash)	1		
70.00 Total new budget authority (gross)	112	114	129
Change in unpaid obligations:			
72.40 Unpaid obligations, start of year: Obligated balance, start of year	14	14	12
73.10 Total new obligations	112	114	129
73.20 Total outlays (gross)	–112	–116	–127
74.40 Unpaid obligations, end of year: Obligated balance, end of year	14	12	14
Outlays (gross), detail:			
86.90 Outlays from new discretionary authority	100	102	115
86.93 Outlays from discretionary balances	11	14	12
87.00 Total outlays (gross)	112	116	127
Offsets:			
Against gross budget authority and outlays:			
88.00 Offsetting collections (cash) from: Federal sources	–1		
Net budget authority and outlays:			
89.00 Budget authority	111	114	129
90.00 Outlays	110	116	127

Food program administration funds most of the Federal operating expenses of the Food and Nutrition Service.

Funds are provided for an initiative to identify and address error in the Food Stamp and Child Nutrition programs.

Funds are also provided to build partnerships that will improve the delivery of currently authorized federal programs to impoverished areas along the United States/Mexico border.

Object Classification (in millions of dollars)

Identification code 12–3508–0–1–605	1999 actual	2000 est.	2001 est.
Personnel compensation:			
11.1 Full-time permanent	75	78	85
11.3 Other than full-time permanent	2	2	2
11.5 Other personnel compensation	1	1	2
11.9 Total personnel compensation	78	81	89

12.1	Civilian personnel benefits	16	16	18
21.0	Travel and transportation of persons	3	3	4
23.3	Communications, utilities, and miscellaneous charges	2	3	3
24.0	Printing and reproduction			2
25.2	Other services	9	6	8
26.0	Supplies and materials	1	1	2
31.0	Equipment	2	2	3
41.0	Grants, subsidies, and contributions		2	
99.0	Subtotal, direct obligations	111	114	129
99.5	Below reporting threshold	1		
99.9	Total new obligations	112	114	129

Personnel Summary

Identification code 12–3508–0–1–605		1999 actual	2000 est.	2001 est.
1001	Total compensable workyears: Full-time equivalent employment	1,442	1,531	1,675

FOOD STAMP PROGRAM

For necessary expenses to carry out the Food Stamp Act (7 U.S.C. 2011 et seq.), [$21,071,751,000] *$22,131,993,000*, of which [$100,000,000] *$1,000,000,000* shall be placed in reserve for use only in such amounts and at such times as may become necessary to carry out program operations: *Provided*, [That none of the funds made available under this heading shall be used for studies and evaluations: *Provided further*,] That funds provided herein shall be expended in accordance with section 16 of the Food Stamp Act: *Provided further*, That this appropriation shall be subject to any work registration or workfare requirements as may be required by law: *Provided further*, That funds made available for Employment and Training under this heading shall remain available until expended, as authorized by section 16(h)(1) of the Food Stamp Act. *(Agriculture, Rural Development, Food and Drug Administration, and Related Agencies Appropriations Act, 2000.)*

Program and Financing (in millions of dollars)

Identification code 12–3505–0–1–605		1999 actual	2000 est.	2001 est.
	Obligations by program activity:			
	Direct program:			
00.01	Properly issued benefits	14,117	14,368	15,556
00.02	Estimated state erroneous issuances	1,604	1,509	1,576
00.03	State administration	1,716	2,026	2,046
00.04	Employment and training program	291	314	337
00.05	Other program costs	54	67	87
00.06	Puerto Rico	1,236	1,268	1,301
00.07	Food distribution program on Indian reservations (Commodities in lieu of food stamps)	54	54	54
00.08	Food distribution program on Indian reservations (Cooperator administrative expense)	21	21	23
00.09	The emergency food assistance program (commodities)	90	98	100
00.10	Modified food stamp program in American Samoa	5	5	5
00.11	Community food project	3	3	3
09.01	Reimbursable program	194	197	197
10.00	Total new obligations	19,385	19,930	21,285
	Budgetary resources available for obligation:			
21.40	Unobligated balance available, start of year	87	74	166
22.00	New budget authority (gross)	21,430	21,269	22,329
22.10	Resources available from recoveries of prior year obligations	46	76	
23.90	Total budgetary resources available for obligation	21,563	21,419	22,495
23.95	Total new obligations	−19,385	−19,930	−21,285
23.98	Unobligated balance expiring or withdrawn	−2,105	−1,323	−1,000
24.40	Unobligated balance available, end of year	74	166	210
	New budget authority (gross), detail:			
	Discretionary:			
40.00	Appropriation	4	5	28
	Mandatory:			
60.00	Appropriation	21,232	21,067	22,104
69.00	Offsetting collections (cash)	194	197	197
70.00	Total new budget authority (gross)	21,430	21,269	22,329
	Change in unpaid obligations:			
72.40	Unpaid obligations, start of year: Obligated balance, start of year	723	806	736
73.10	Total new obligations	19,385	19,930	21,285
73.20	Total outlays (gross)	−19,199	−19,924	−21,232
73.40	Adjustments in expired accounts (net)	−57		
73.45	Adjustments in unexpired accounts	−46	−76	
74.40	Unpaid obligations, end of year: Obligated balance, end of year	806	736	789
	Outlays (gross), detail:			
86.90	Outlays from new discretionary authority	2	4	20
86.93	Outlays from discretionary balances			2
86.97	Outlays from new mandatory authority	18,474	19,114	20,476
86.98	Outlays from mandatory balances	723	806	734
87.00	Total outlays (gross)	19,199	19,924	21,232
	Offsets:			
	Against gross budget authority and outlays:			
88.40	Offsetting collections (cash) from: Non-Federal sources	−194	−197	−197
	Net budget authority and outlays:			
89.00	Budget authority	21,236	21,072	22,132
90.00	Outlays	19,005	19,727	21,035

Summary of Budget Authority and Outlays

(in millions of dollars)

	1999 actual	*2000 est.*	*2001 est.*
Enacted/requested:			
Budget Authority	21,236	21,072	22,132
Outlays	19,005	19,727	21,035
Legislative proposal, subject to PAYGO:			
Budget Authority			24
Outlays			24
Total:			
Budget Authority	21,236	21,072	22,156
Outlays	19,005	19,727	21,059

The Food Stamp Program is the primary source of nutrition assistance for low-income Americans.

Some of these funds provide a grant to Puerto Rico in lieu of the food stamp program which gives the Commonwealth flexibility to continue a nutrition assistance program tailored to the needs of its low-income households.

Funds in this account are also used to carry out the Emergency Food Assistance Act of 1983 and for food distribution and administrative expenses for Native Americans under section 4(b) of the Food Stamp Act.

Object Classification (in millions of dollars)

Identification code 12–3505–0–1–605		1999 actual	2000 est.	2001 est.
	Direct obligations:			
11.1	Personnel compensation: Full-time permanent	3	4	4
12.1	Civilian personnel benefits	1	1	1
21.0	Travel and transportation of persons	1	1	1
23.3	Communications, utilities, and miscellaneous charges	3	3	3
24.0	Printing and reproduction	8	7	6
25.2	Other services	35	48	68
26.0	Supplies and materials	145	153	155
31.0	Equipment	2	2	2
41.0	Grants, subsidies, and contributions	18,993	19,514	20,848
99.0	Subtotal, direct obligations	19,191	19,733	21,088
99.0	Reimbursable obligations	194	197	197
99.9	Total new obligations	19,385	19,930	21,285

Personnel Summary

Identification code 12–3505–0–1–605		1999 actual	2000 est.	2001 est.
1001	Total compensable workyears: Full-time equivalent employment	51	56	56

General and special funds—Continued

FOOD STAMP PROGRAM

(Legislative proposal, subject to PAYGO)

Program and Financing (in millions of dollars)

Identification code 12–3505–4–1–605	1999 actual	2000 est.	2001 est.
Obligations by program activity:			
Direct program:			
00.01 Legal immigrant restoration			25
00.02 Vehicle proposal			1
00.03 Income definition conformity			5
00.04 Interaction with child support enforcement proposals			–7
10.00 Total new obligations (object class 41.0)			24
Budgetary resources available for obligation:			
22.00 New budget authority (gross)			24
23.95 Total new obligations			–24
New budget authority (gross), detail:			
Mandatory:			
60.00 Appropriation			24
Change in unpaid obligations:			
73.10 Total new obligations			24
73.20 Total outlays (gross)			–24
Outlays (gross), detail:			
86.97 Outlays from new mandatory authority			24
Net budget authority and outlays:			
89.00 Budget authority			24
90.00 Outlays			24

The Administration is proposing to restore Food Stamp benefits to certain legal immigrants made ineligible by restrictions in the Personal Responsibility and Work Opportunity Reconciliation Act of 1996.

This proposal also provides States with the option to: (1) conform their food stamp vehicle policy with their Temporary assistance for needy families vehicle policy, so long as food stamp households are held harmless; and, (2) conform food stamp and Medicaid income definitions.

The proposal is net of food stamp savings due to child support enforcement proposals.

CHILD NUTRITION PROGRAMS

(INCLUDING TRANSFERS OF FUNDS)

For necessary expenses to carry out the National School Lunch Act (42 U.S.C. 1751 et seq.), except section 21, and the Child Nutrition Act of 1966 (42 U.S.C. 1771 et seq.), except sections 17 and 21; [$9,554,028,000] *$9,546,056,000*, to remain available through September 30, [2001] *2002*, of which [$4,618,829,000] *$4,578,482,000* is hereby appropriated and [$4,935,199,000] *$4,967,574,000* shall be derived by transfer from funds available under section 32 of the Act of August 24, 1935 (7 U.S.C. 612c): *Provided*, [That, except as specifically provided under this heading, none of the funds made available under this heading shall be used for studies and evaluations: *Provided further*,] That of the funds made available under this heading, up to [$7,000,000] *$6,000,000* shall be for school breakfast pilot projects, including the evaluation required under section 18(e) of the National School Lunch Act: *Provided further*, That up to [$4,363,000] *$4,511,000* shall be available for independent verification of school food service claims[: *Provided further*, That none of the funds under this heading shall be available unless the value of bonus commodities provided under section 32 of the Act of August 24, 1935 (49 Stat. 774, chapter 641; 7 U.S.C. 612c), and section 416 of the Agricultural Act of 1949 (7 U.S.C. 1431) is included in meeting the minimum commodity assistance requirement of section 6(g) of the National School Lunch Act (42 U.S.C. 1755(g))]. *(Agriculture, Rural Development, Food and Drug Administration, and Related Agencies Appropriations Act, 2000.)*

Program and Financing (in millions of dollars)

Identification code 12–3539–0–1–605	1999 actual	2000 est.	2001 est.
Obligations by program activity:			
School lunch program:			
00.01 Above 185% of poverty	268	320	335
00.02 130–185% of poverty	596	550	574
00.03 Below 130% of poverty	4,653	4,682	4,894
00.91 Subtotal, school lunch program	5,517	5,552	5,803
School breakfast program:			
01.01 Above 185% of poverty	78	81	86
01.02 130–185% of poverty	134	140	148
01.03 Below 130% of poverty	1,143	1,188	1,262
01.91 Subtotal, school breakfast program	1,355	1,409	1,496
Child and adult care feeding program:			
02.01 Above 185% of poverty	188	194	208
02.02 130–185% of poverty	86	91	97
02.03 Below 130% of poverty	1,304	1,381	1,478
02.04 Audits	21	24	24
02.91 Subtotal, child and adult care feeding program	1,599	1,690	1,807
Other mandatory activities:			
03.01 Summer food service program	296	298	324
03.02 Special milk program	18	17	17
03.03 State administrative expenses	114	118	127
03.04 Commodity procurement	327	325	351
03.91 Subtotal, Other mandatory activities	755	758	819
Discretionary activities:			
04.01 School meals initiative	9	10	10
04.02 Coordinated review	4	4	5
04.03 Nutrition studies and surveys			3
04.04 Nutrition education and training			2
04.05 Computer support and processing	6	9	9
04.06 School breakfast demonstrations		7	6
04.07 Food safety education	2	2	2
04.91 Subtotal, discretionary activities	21	32	37
Activities with permanent appropriations:			
05.01 Homeless children nutrition program	1		
05.02 Food service management institute and information clearinghouse	3	3	3
05.03 Alternative meal count grants		2	2
05.91 Subtotal, activities with permanent appropriations	4	5	5
10.00 Total new obligations	9,251	9,446	9,967
Budgetary resources available for obligation:			
21.40 Unobligated balance available, start of year	13	56	419
22.00 New budget authority (gross)	9,184	9,559	9,551
22.10 Resources available from recoveries of prior year obligations	147	250	
23.90 Total budgetary resources available for obligation	9,344	9,865	9,970
23.95 Total new obligations	–9,251	–9,446	–9,967
23.98 Unobligated balance expiring or withdrawn	–38		
24.40 Unobligated balance available, end of year	56	419	3
New budget authority (gross), detail:			
Discretionary:			
40.00 Appropriation	5	14	18
Mandatory:			
60.00 Appropriation	4,131	4,610	4,565
62.00 Transferred from other accounts	5,048	4,935	4,968
62.50 Appropriation (total mandatory)	9,179	9,545	9,533
70.00 Total new budget authority (gross)	9,184	9,559	9,551
Change in unpaid obligations:			
72.40 Unpaid obligations, start of year: Obligated balance, start of year	1,322	1,541	1,384
73.10 Total new obligations	9,251	9,446	9,967
73.20 Total outlays (gross)	–8,878	–9,354	–9,892
73.40 Adjustments in expired accounts (net)	–6		
73.45 Adjustments in unexpired accounts	–147	–250	
74.40 Unpaid obligations, end of year: Obligated balance, end of year	1,541	1,384	1,459
Outlays (gross), detail:			
86.90 Outlays from new discretionary authority	5	7	10
86.93 Outlays from discretionary balances	8	8	7
86.97 Outlays from new mandatory authority	7,551	7,797	8,491

86.98	Outlays from mandatory balances	1,314	1,542	1,384
87.00	Total outlays (gross)	8,878	9,354	9,892
	Net budget authority and outlays:			
89.00	Budget authority	9,184	9,559	9,551
90.00	Outlays	8,878	9,354	9,892

Summary of Budget Authority and Outlays

(in millions of dollars)

	1999 actual	2000 est.	2001 est.
Enacted/requested:			
Budget Authority	9,184	9,559	9,551
Outlays	8,878	9,354	9,892
Legislative proposal, subject to PAYGO:			
Budget Authority			−1
Outlays			−3
Total:			
Budget Authority	9,184	9,559	9,550
Outlays	8,878	9,354	9,889

Payments are made for cash and commodity meal subsidies through the School Lunch, School Breakfast, Summer Food Service, and Child and Adult Care Food programs.

The Budget reflects discretionary funding for a school breakfast demonstration project.

Object Classification (in millions of dollars)

Identification code 12–3539–0–1–605		1999 actual	2000 est.	2001 est.
11.1	Personnel compensation: Full-time permanent	6	6	6
12.1	Civilian personnel benefits	1	1	1
21.0	Travel and transportation of persons	1	1	1
24.0	Printing and reproduction	2	3	3
25.2	Other services	5	8	8
26.0	Supplies and materials (Commodities)	327	325	351
41.0	Grants, subsidies, and contributions	8,909	9,102	9,597
99.9	Total new obligations	9,251	9,446	9,967

Personnel Summary

Identification code 12–3539–0–1–605		1999 actual	2000 est.	2001 est.
1001	Total compensable workyears: Full-time equivalent employment	113	130	130

Child Nutrition Programs

(Legislative proposal, subject to PAYGO)

Program and Financing (in millions of dollars)

Identification code 12–3539–4–1–605		1999 actual	2000 est.	2001 est.
	Obligations by program activity:			
	Child and adult care feeding program:			
02.01	Above 185% of poverty			−7
02.04	Audits			6
10.00	Total new obligations (object class 41.0)			−1
	Budgetary resources available for obligation:			
22.00	New budget authority (gross)			−1
23.95	Total new obligations			1
	New budget authority (gross), detail:			
	Mandatory:			
60.00	Appropriation			−1
	Change in unpaid obligations:			
73.10	Total new obligations			−1
73.20	Total outlays (gross)			3
	Outlays (gross), detail:			
86.97	Outlays from new mandatory authority			−3
	Net budget authority and outlays:			
89.00	Budget authority			−1
90.00	Outlays			−3

This legislative proposal will improve management and oversight in the Child and Adult Care Food Program.

Special Supplemental Nutrition Program for Women, Infants, and Children (WIC)

For necessary expenses to carry out the special supplemental nutrition program as authorized by section 17 of the Child Nutrition Act of 1966 (42 U.S.C. 1786), [$4,032,000,000] *$4,148,100,000*, to remain available through September 30, [2001] *2002*: *Provided*, That [none of the funds made available under this heading shall be used for studies and evaluations: *Provided further*, That of the total amount available, the Secretary shall obligate $10,000,000 for the farmers' market nutrition program within 45 days of the enactment of this Act, and an additional $5,000,000 for the farmers' market nutrition program from any funds not needed to maintain current caseload levels] *notwithstanding section 17(h)(10)(A) of such Act, up to $14,000,000 shall be available for the purposes specified in section 17(h)(10)(B), no less than $6,000,000 of which shall be used for the development of electronic benefit transfer systems*: *Provided further*, That none of the funds in this Act shall be available to pay administrative expenses of WIC clinics except those that have an announced policy of prohibiting smoking within the space used to carry out the program: *Provided further*, That none of the funds provided in this account shall be available for the purchase of infant formula except in accordance with the cost containment and competitive bidding requirements specified in section 17 of [the Child Nutrition Act of 1966] *such Act*: *Provided further*, That none of the funds provided shall be available for activities that are not fully reimbursed by other Federal Government departments or agencies unless authorized by section 17 of [the Child Nutrition Act of 1966] *such Act*. *(Agriculture, Rural Development, Food and Drug Administration, and Related Agencies Appropriations Act, 2000.)*

Program and Financing (in millions of dollars)

Identification code 12–3510–0–1–605		1999 actual	2000 est.	2001 est.
	Obligations by program activity:			
10.00	Total new obligations	4,076	4,158	4,248
	Budgetary resources available for obligation:			
21.40	Unobligated balance available, start of year		2	
22.00	New budget authority (gross)	3,924	4,032	4,148
22.10	Resources available from recoveries of prior year obligations	155	124	101
23.90	Total budgetary resources available for obligation	4,079	4,158	4,249
23.95	Total new obligations	−4,076	−4,158	−4,248
23.98	Unobligated balance expiring or withdrawn	−1		
24.40	Unobligated balance available, end of year	2		
	New budget authority (gross), detail:			
	Discretionary:			
40.00	Appropriation	3,924	4,032	4,148
	Change in unpaid obligations:			
72.40	Unpaid obligations, start of year: Obligated balance, start of year	310	283	258
73.10	Total new obligations	4,076	4,158	4,248
73.20	Total outlays (gross)	−3,942	−4,059	−4,149
73.40	Adjustments in expired accounts (net)	−6		
73.45	Adjustments in unexpired accounts	−155	−124	−101
74.40	Unpaid obligations, end of year: Obligated balance, end of year	283	258	257
	Outlays (gross), detail:			
86.90	Outlays from new discretionary authority	3,638	3,899	3,891
86.93	Outlays from discretionary balances	304	159	257
87.00	Total outlays (gross)	3,942	4,059	4,149
	Net budget authority and outlays:			
89.00	Budget authority	3,924	4,032	4,148
90.00	Outlays	3,942	4,059	4,149

The Special Supplemental Nutrition Program for Women, Infants, and Children (WIC) provides at-risk pregnant and

General and special funds—Continued

SPECIAL SUPPLEMENTAL NUTRITION PROGRAM FOR WOMEN, INFANTS, AND CHILDREN (WIC)—Continued

post-partum women, infants, and children with vouchers for nutritious supplemental food packages, nutrition education and counseling, and health and immunization referrals.

Object Classification (in millions of dollars)

Identification code 12–3510–0–1–605		1999 actual	2000 est.	2001 est.
25.1	Advisory and assistance services	....	....	3
41.0	Grants, subsidies, and contributions	4,076	4,158	4,245
99.9	Total new obligations	4,076	4,158	4,248

COMMODITY ASSISTANCE PROGRAM

For necessary expenses to carry out the commodity supplemental food program as authorized by section 4(a) of the Agriculture and Consumer Protection Act of 1973 (7 U.S.C. 612c note); *the Farmers' Market Nutrition Program as authorized by section 17(m) of the Child Nutrition Act of 1966; and* the Emergency Food Assistance Act of 1983, [$133,300,000] *$158,300,000*, to remain available through September 30, [2001] *2002*: *Provided*, That none of these funds shall be available to reimburse the Commodity Credit Corporation for commodities donated to the program. *(Agriculture, Rural Development, Food and Drug Administration, and Related Agencies Appropriations Act, 2000.)*

Program and Financing (in millions of dollars)

Identification code 12–3507–0–1–605		1999 actual	2000 est.	2001 est.
	Obligations by program activity:			
	Commodity supplemental food program:			
00.01	Commodity procurement	70	80	74
00.02	Administrative costs	20	20	19
01.92	Subtotal, commodity supplemental food program	90	100	93
	The emergency food assistance program:			
02.01	Administrative costs	45	45	45
03.01	Farmers' market nutrition program	....	....	20
10.00	Total new obligations	135	145	158
	Budgetary resources available for obligation:			
21.40	Unobligated balance available, start of year	10	8	....
22.00	New budget authority (gross)	131	133	158
22.10	Resources available from recoveries of prior year obligations	2	4	....
23.90	Total budgetary resources available for obligation	143	145	158
23.95	Total new obligations	−135	−145	−158
24.40	Unobligated balance available, end of year	8	....	....
	New budget authority (gross), detail:			
	Discretionary:			
40.00	Appropriation	131	133	158
	Change in unpaid obligations:			
72.40	Unpaid obligations, start of year: Obligated balance, start of year	18	14	23
73.10	Total new obligations	135	145	158
73.20	Total outlays (gross)	−136	−132	−168
73.40	Adjustments in expired accounts (net)	−1	....	....
73.45	Adjustments in unexpired accounts	−2	−4	....
74.40	Unpaid obligations, end of year: Obligated balance, end of year	14	23	13
	Outlays (gross), detail:			
86.90	Outlays from new discretionary authority	118	122	144
86.93	Outlays from discretionary balances	18	10	23
87.00	Total outlays (gross)	136	132	168
	Net budget authority and outlays:			
89.00	Budget authority	131	133	158
90.00	Outlays	136	132	168

The Commodity Assistance Program includes the Commodity Supplemental Food Program (CSFP), the Emergency Food Assistance Program and the Farmers' Market Nutrition Program.

The CSFP provides food packages for low-income women, infants, and children as well as low-income elderly persons. It also funds State administrative expenses.

The Emergency Food Assistance Program provides cash to support State administrative activities and maintain the storage and distribution pipeline for USDA and privately donated commodities.

The Farmers' Market Nutrition Program (previously funded under the Special Supplemental Nutrition Program for Women, Infants, and Children) provides cash to support States' administrative expenses and vouchers redeemable by participants for fresh produce at farmers' markets.

Object Classification (in millions of dollars)

Identification code 12–3507–0–1–605		1999 actual	2000 est.	2001 est.
26.0	Supplies and materials (commodities)	70	80	74
41.0	Grants, subsidies, and contributions	65	65	84
99.9	Total new obligations	135	145	158

FOOD DONATIONS PROGRAMS

For necessary expenses to carry out section 4(a) of the Agriculture and Consumer Protection Act of 1973; special assistance for the nuclear affected islands as authorized by section 103(h)(2) of the Compacts of Free Association Act of 1985, as amended; and section 311 of the Older Americans Act of 1965, [$141,081,000] *$151,081,000*, to remain available through September 30, [2001] *2002*. *(7 U.S.C. 612c note; 42 U.S.C. 3030a; 48 U.S.C. 1903 (h)(2); Agriculture, Rural Development, Food and Drug Administration, and Related Agencies Appropriations Act, 2000.)*

Program and Financing (in millions of dollars)

Identification code 12–3503–0–1–605		1999 actual	2000 est.	2001 est.
	Obligations by program activity:			
00.01	Nutrition program for the elderly	141	141	150
00.02	Pacific island assistance	1	1	1
10.00	Total new obligations	142	142	151
	Budgetary resources available for obligation:			
21.40	Unobligated balance available, start of year	....	1	....
22.00	New budget authority (gross)	141	141	151
22.10	Resources available from recoveries of prior year obligations	1	....	....
23.90	Total budgetary resources available for obligation	142	142	151
23.95	Total new obligations	−142	−142	−151
24.40	Unobligated balance available, end of year	1	....	....
	New budget authority (gross), detail:			
	Discretionary:			
40.00	Appropriation	141	141	151
	Change in unpaid obligations:			
72.40	Unpaid obligations, start of year: Obligated balance, start of year	33	29	28
73.10	Total new obligations	142	142	151
73.20	Total outlays (gross)	−144	−143	−151
73.45	Adjustments in unexpired accounts	−1	....	....
74.40	Unpaid obligations, end of year: Obligated balance, end of year	29	28	30
	Outlays (gross), detail:			
86.90	Outlays from new discretionary authority	111	114	122
86.93	Outlays from discretionary balances	33	28	27
87.00	Total outlays (gross)	144	143	151
	Net budget authority and outlays:			
89.00	Budget authority	141	141	151

90.00 Outlays	144	143	151

Food Donations Programs include the Nutrition Program for the Elderly (NPE) and disaster assistance for the Pacific islands. The NPE provides cash and commodities for per-meal reimbursement for elderly persons served in senior citizens' centers and similar settings. Assistance is also provided to residents of Nuclear Affected Islands and funds are made available for non-presidentially declared disasters.

Object Classification (in millions of dollars)

Identification code 12–3503–0–1–605	1999 actual	2000 est.	2001 est.
26.0 Supplies and materials (grants of commodities to States)	4	3	4
41.0 Grants, subsidies, and contributions	138	139	147
99.9 Total new obligations	142	142	151

FOREST SERVICE

Federal Funds

General and special funds:

NATIONAL FOREST SYSTEM

For necessary expenses of the Forest Service, not otherwise provided for, for management, protection, improvement, and utilization of the National Forest System, [and for administrative expenses associated with the management of funds provided under the headings "Forest and Rangeland Research", "State and Private Forestry", "National Forest System", "Wildland Fire Management", "Reconstruction and Maintenance", and "Land Acquisition", $1,269,504,000] *$1,286,571,000*, to remain available until expended, which shall include 50 percent of all moneys received during prior fiscal years as fees collected under the Land and Water Conservation Fund Act of 1965, as amended, in accordance with section 4 of the Act (16 U.S.C. 460l–6a(i)): *Provided*, That [unobligated balances available at the start of fiscal year 2000 shall be displayed by extended budget line item in the fiscal year 2001 budget justification] *up to $30,000,000 may be transferred to the infrastructure account to fund the construction enhancement, or maintenance of recreation facilities or trails to further tourism, rural development and recreation goals: Provided further, That up to $15,000,000 shall be available for those forests or regions that have implemented innovative practices to improve customer service, enhance coordination and reduce overhead. (Department of the Interior and Related Agencies Appropriations Act, 2000, as enacted by section 1000(a)(3) of the Consolidated Appropriations Act, 2000 (P.L. 106–113.)*

Unavailable Collections (in millions of dollars)

Identification code 12–1106–0–1–302	1999 actual	2000 est.	2001 est.
Balance, start of year:			
01.99 Balance, start of year	74	78	82
Receipts:			
02.01 Fees, operation and maintenance of recreational facilities	4	4	4
04.00 Total: Balances and collections	78	82	86
07.99 Total balance, end of year	78	82	86

Program and Financing (in millions of dollars)

Identification code 12–1106–0–1–302	1999 actual	2000 est.	2001 est.
Obligations by program activity:			
Direct program:			
00.01 National forest system	1,327	1,281	1,325
00.04 Flood supplemental	5	4	
00.05 Disaster relief	13	12	
09.01 Reimbursable program	73	71	73
10.00 Total new obligations	1,418	1,368	1,398
Budgetary resources available for obligation:			
21.40 Unobligated balance available, start of year	114	86	51
22.00 New budget authority (gross)	1,350	1,333	1,360
22.10 Resources available from recoveries of prior year obligations	43		
22.21 Unobligated balance transferred to other accounts	–5		
22.22 Unobligated balance transferred from other accounts	1	1	1
23.90 Total budgetary resources available for obligation	1,503	1,420	1,412
23.95 Total new obligations	–1,418	–1,368	–1,398
24.40 Unobligated balance available, end of year	86	51	12
New budget authority (gross), detail:			
Discretionary:			
40.00 Appropriation	1,299	1,269	1,287
40.15 Appropriation (emergency)	2		
40.76 Reduction pursuant to P.L. 106–113		–8	
41.00 Transferred to other accounts	–1		
42.00 Transferred from other accounts		1	
43.00 Appropriation (total discretionary)	1,300	1,262	1,287
68.00 Spending authority from offsetting collections: Offsetting collections (cash)	50	71	73
70.00 Total new budget authority (gross)	1,350	1,333	1,360
Change in unpaid obligations:			
72.40 Unpaid obligations, start of year: Obligated balance, start of year	122	197	226
73.10 Total new obligations	1,418	1,368	1,398
73.20 Total outlays (gross)	–1,301	–1,338	–1,356
73.45 Adjustments in unexpired accounts	–43		
74.40 Unpaid obligations, end of year: Obligated balance, end of year	197	226	268
Outlays (gross), detail:			
86.90 Outlays from new discretionary authority	1,179	1,144	1,168
86.93 Outlays from discretionary balances	122	193	189
86.98 Outlays from mandatory balances		2	
87.00 Total outlays (gross)	1,301	1,338	1,356
Offsets:			
Against gross budget authority and outlays:			
Offsetting collections (cash) from:			
88.00 Federal sources	–39	–56	–57
88.40 Non-Federal sources	–11	–15	–16
88.90 Total, offsetting collections (cash)	–50	–71	–73
Net budget authority and outlays:			
89.00 Budget authority	1,300	1,262	1,287
90.00 Outlays	1,251	1,267	1,283

The 156 National Forests, 20 National Grasslands, and nine land utilization projects located in 44 States, Puerto Rico and the Virgin Islands are managed under multiple-use and sustained-yield principles. The natural resources of timber, minerals, range, wildlife, outdoor recreation, watershed, and soil are used in a planned combination that will best meet the needs of the Nation without impairing productivity of the land or damaging the environment. These management and utilization principles are recognized in the Multiple-Use, Sustained-Yield Act of 1960 (16 U.S.C. 528–531) and use an ecological approach to managing the National Forest System.

National Forest System (NFS) operations and maintenance provide for the planning, assessment, and conservation of ecosystems while delivering multiple public services and uses. These are delivered through the principal NFS programs of land management planning, inventory, and monitoring, recreation use, wildlife and fisheries habitat management, rangeland management, forestland management, soil, water, and air management, minerals and geology management, landownership management, and law enforcement. These programs maintain the capability to manage natural resources in a manner consistent with ecological principles and responsibilities. Funds have not been included for the general administration activity programs now financed directly by the Forest and Rangeland Research, State and Private Forestry, National Forest System, Wildland Fire Management, Reconstruction and Construction, and Land Acquisition appropria-

General and special funds—Continued

NATIONAL FOREST SYSTEM—Continued

tions. In prior years, administration of these programs was funded through NFS.

The 2001 Budget includes an emphasis on sustainable forestry. The proportion of timber production resulting from a stewardship purpose rather than a commodity purpose continues to rise, more than doubling since 1994. Supporting these goals, the Administration is proposing a new $10 million pilot Forest health stewardship program that will better enable the use of underutilized and small diameter woody material to achieve sustainable forest management and watershed health and restoration. In addition, FS continues to advance in measuring forest integrity and evaluating sustainable forestry, such as through the Montreal criteria and indicators.

The Budget proposes a new $65 million Planning, Inventory and Monitoring Initiative. The initiative includes funds for forest land management planning, and wildlife and resource inventory and monitoring. These funds are needed to adequately follow through on the new Forest Planning regulations, including funds to: accelerate forest planning work that has been slowed in recent years; support the proposed community advisory groups, bio-regional and watershed planning; select species representatives; establish new protocols for focal species monitoring; enhance monitoring to better evaluate survey populations and pursue adaptive management. In addition, funds are included to pursue the Clean Water Action Plan assessment costs, called for under the Unified Federal Policy for Watershed Management on Federal Lands.

Increased funds are also included for the Survey and Manage monitoring work. $10 million in additional funding for these activities is provided in timber sale management; $10 million is provided in inventory and monitoring; and additional funds are dispersed throughout different budget line items.

The Watershed Restoration and Enhancement Agreements is proposed for use by the National Forest System when carrying out forest and watershed planning. The purpose of this funding is to enhance the forest planning process—particularly the bio-regional and watershed assessments—by providing funding to non-federal entities for work on lands surrounding or adjacent to national forests as part of the forest planning process for the betterment of the national forest. The program would emphasize corridor creations and cooperative arrangements among land owning entities, in which $5 million would be available to establish or enhance buffers around national forests for habitat protection, wildlife corridors between national forests and other federal and state land holdings, and riparian zones to protect rare aquatic species present within the national forest. (Sec. 323 of the Department of the Interior and Related Agencies Appropriations Act, 1999, as included in Public Law 105–277, section 101(e).).

$30 million in new funding is proposed for a new Tourism/Rural Development Initiative for developing tourism plans, analyzing special use permits, developing trails, restoring or constructing recreational facilities and enhancing tourism appeal on national forests. The sites chosen for this program target lower income, resource-dependent areas, adjacent to National Forests, where there are promising tourism opportunities. This initiative would target roughly 20 priority forest locations, and after discussions with local communities, would develop "destination" tourism infrastructure and opportunities, establishing new economic prospects for these gateway communities.

To support management reforms, an advance appropriation of $15 million will be available to reward those forests that adopt approved restructuring or streamlining management practices (efficiency-enhancing, cost-savings or customer service-producing) by the end of 2001. FS will publish a list of different management practices at the beginning of 2001 and management units will be evaluated for those that achieve these goals by the end of the year.

Recommendations from the Report by the National Academy of Public Administration note that the current discretionary budget structure for the Forest Service does not support adequate linkage of the agency strategic plan, forest plans, and performance measures. As a result, accountability and financial integrity have suffered. Accordingly, USDA will present the Congressional Justification for the 2001 Budget in a format that supports a performance-based budgeting approach. This budget proposal is a significant opportunity to present a budget based on performance in a manner consistent with the agency strategic plan and the Government Performance and Results Act. The new budget structure will accomplish the following:

—Focus debate on outputs and outcomes rather than budget line items;

—Reflect the nature of the real work being done by the Forest Service (ecosystem and multiple use), allowing the field staff to avoid artificially categorizing a task to match budget lines;

—Eventually link forest plans and the budget (a Committee of Scientist recommendation):

—Provide increased accountability in agency program delivery;

—Simplify the agency accounting, allowing field staff to do more natural resource related work instead of accounting work (estimated by GAO to account for tens of millions of dollars annually);

—Simplify the budget (e.g., reducing the National Forest System's budget line items and extended budget line items from 29 to 3), supporting the goal of achieving a clean opinion for the agency's financial statements.

Object Classification (in millions of dollars)

Identification code 12–1106–0–1–302		1999 actual	2000 est.	2001 est.
	Direct obligations:			
	Personnel compensation:			
11.1	Full-time permanent	504	531	560
11.3	Other than full-time permanent	54	57	60
11.5	Other personnel compensation	19	20	21
11.9	Total personnel compensation	577	608	641
12.1	Civilian personnel benefits	128	135	142
13.0	Benefits for former personnel	18	19	20
21.0	Travel and transportation of persons	55	54	54
22.0	Transportation of things	9	7	7
23.1	Rental payments to GSA	47	47	47
23.2	Rental payments to others	19	16	15
23.3	Communications, utilities, and miscellaneous charges	51	42	41
24.0	Printing and reproduction	5	4	4
25.2	Other services	292	244	237
26.0	Supplies and materials	75	62	60
31.0	Equipment	39	33	32
32.0	Land and structures	3	2	2
41.0	Grants, subsidies, and contributions	23	20	19
42.0	Insurance claims and indemnities	2	2	2
99.0	Subtotal, direct obligations	1,343	1,295	1,323
99.0	Reimbursable obligations	73	71	73
	Allocation Account:			
11.1	Personnel compensation: Full-time permanent	1	1	1
25.2	Other services	1	1	1
99.0	Subtotal, allocation account	2	2	2
99.9	Total new obligations	1,418	1,368	1,398

Personnel Summary

Identification code 12–1106–0–1–302		1999 actual	2000 est.	2001 est.
	Direct:			
1001	Total compensable workyears: Full-time equivalent employment	15,786	16,602	17,486

Reimbursable:			
2001 Total compensable workyears: Full-time equivalent employment	756	723	740
Allocation account:			
3001 Total compensable workyears: Full-time equivalent employment	10	10	10

[RECONSTRUCTION AND MAINTENANCE] *INFRASTRUCTURE*

For necessary expenses of the Forest Service, not otherwise provided for, [$398,927,000] ***$424,914,000***, to remain available until expended for construction, reconstruction, maintenance and acquisition of buildings and other facilities, and for construction, reconstruction, repair and maintenance of forest roads and trails by the Forest Service as authorized by 16 U.S.C. 532–538 and 23 U.S.C. 101 and 205: *Provided*, That up to $15,000,000 of the funds provided herein for road maintenance shall be available for the decommissioning of roads, including unauthorized roads not part of the transportation system, which are no longer needed[: *Provided further*, That no funds shall be expended to decommission any system road until notice and an opportunity for public comment has been provided on each decommissioning project: *Provided further*, That any unobligated balances of amounts previously appropriated to the Forest Service "Reconstruction and Construction" account as well as any unobligated balances remaining in the "National Forest System" account for the facility maintenance and trail maintenance extended budget line items at the end of fiscal year 1999 may be transferred to and merged with the "Reconstruction and Maintenance" account]. *(Department of the Interior and Related Agencies Appropriations Act, 2000, as enacted by section 1000(a)(3) of the Consolidated Appropriations Act, 2000 (P.L. 106–113.)*

Program and Financing (in millions of dollars)

Identification code 12–1103–0–1–302	1999 actual	2000 est.	2001 est.
Obligations by program activity:			
Direct program:			
00.01 Reconstruction and construction	284	392	436
00.03 Flood supplemental	22	13	
09.01 Reimbursable program	1	1	1
10.00 Total new obligations	307	406	437
Budgetary resources available for obligation:			
21.40 Unobligated balance available, start of year	112	119	111
22.00 New budget authority (gross)	300	398	426
22.10 Resources available from recoveries of prior year obligations	7		
22.22 Unobligated balance transferred from other accounts	5		
23.90 Total budgetary resources available for obligation	424	517	537
23.95 Total new obligations	–307	–406	–437
24.40 Unobligated balance available, end of year	119	111	100
New budget authority (gross), detail:			
Discretionary:			
40.00 Appropriation	297	399	425
40.15 Appropriation (emergency)	2		
40.76 Reduction pursuant to P.L. 106–113		–2	
43.00 Appropriation (total discretionary)	299	397	425
68.00 Spending authority from offsetting collections: Offsetting collections (cash)	1	1	1
70.00 Total new budget authority (gross)	300	398	426
Change in unpaid obligations:			
72.40 Unpaid obligations, start of year: Obligated balance, start of year	81	120	161
73.10 Total new obligations	307	406	437
73.20 Total outlays (gross)	–260	–365	–400
73.45 Adjustments in unexpired accounts	–7		
74.40 Unpaid obligations, end of year: Obligated balance, end of year	120	161	198
Outlays (gross), detail:			
86.90 Outlays from new discretionary authority	219	299	320
86.93 Outlays from discretionary balances	41	66	79
87.00 Total outlays (gross)	260	365	400
Offsets:			
Against gross budget authority and outlays:			
88.40 Offsetting collections (cash) from: Non-Federal sources	–1	–1	–1
Net budget authority and outlays:			
89.00 Budget authority	299	397	425
90.00 Outlays	259	364	399

Funding for infrastructure provides capital improvements and maintenance of facilities, roads, and trails. The program emphasizes: better resource management decisions based on the best scientific information and knowledge; an efficient and effective infrastructure that supports public and administrative uses; and quality recreation experiences with minimal impact to ecosystem stability and conditions.

Facilities.—Provides for capital improvements and maintenance of research, fire, administrative, and other (FA&O), and recreation facilities, including site components such as roads and trails and the acquisition of buildings and other facilities necessary to carry out the mission of the Forest Service. Capital Improvements include: new construction of a facility; alteration of an existing facility to change the function; and expansion of a facility to change the capacity or to serve needs that are different from what was originally intended. Maintenance is divided into four primary areas: annual maintenance, deferred maintenance, decommissioning, and operations. Deferred maintenance work includes the repair, rehabilitation, or replacement of the facility or components of the facility.

Roads.—Provides for capital improvements and maintenance of roads. The program also focuses on decommissioning unneeded roads and/or roads that are degrading the ecosystem. Capital improvements include: new road construction; alteration of an existing road to change the function; and expansion of the road to change the capacity or to serve needs that are different from what was originally intended. The agency will continue to address the growing road system maintenance backlog. Funding priorities are health and safety, resource protection, and mission critical needs. Maintenance is divided into four primary areas: annual road maintenance, deferred road maintenance, road operations, and decommissioning.

Trails.—Provides for capital improvements and maintenance of trails. Capital improvements include: new trail construction; alteration of an existing trail to change the function; and expansion of the trail to change the capacity or to serve needs that are different from what was originally intended. Maintenance funding is used to protect capital investments by keeping trails open for access and protecting vegetation, soil, and water quality. Work includes clearing the pathway of encroaching vegetation and fallen trees, and repairing or improving trail signs, treadways, drainage facilities, and bridges. Maintenance is divided into four primary areas: annual trail maintenance, deferred trail maintenance, trail operations, and trail decommissioning.

Object Classification (in millions of dollars)

Identification code 12–1103–0–1–302	1999 actual	2000 est.	2001 est.
Direct obligations:			
Personnel compensation:			
11.1 Full-time permanent	118	127	122
11.3 Other than full-time permanent	12	13	12
11.5 Other personnel compensation	5	5	5
11.9 Total personnel compensation	135	145	139
12.1 Civilian personnel benefits	31	33	32
13.0 Benefits for former personnel	2	2	2
21.0 Travel and transportation of persons	5	8	9
22.0 Transportation of things	1	1	1
23.1 Rental payments to GSA	6	6	6
23.2 Rental payments to others	2	3	3
23.3 Communications, utilities, and miscellaneous charges	4	7	8

General and special funds—Continued

[RECONSTRUCTION AND MAINTENANCE] *INFRASTRUCTURE*—Continued

Object Classification (in millions of dollars)—Continued

Identification code 12–1103–0–1–302		1999 actual	2000 est.	2001 est.
24.0	Printing and reproduction		1	1
25.2	Other services	85	142	168
26.0	Supplies and materials	10	16	19
31.0	Equipment	5	8	9
32.0	Land and structures	18	30	35
41.0	Grants, subsidies, and contributions	2	3	4
99.0	Subtotal, direct obligations	306	405	436
99.0	Reimbursable obligations	1	1	1
99.9	Total new obligations	307	406	437

Personnel Summary

Identification code 12–1103–0–1–302		1999 actual	2000 est.	2001 est.
	Direct:			
1001	Total compensable workyears: Full-time equivalent employment	3,502	3,737	3,587
	Reimbursable:			
2001	Total compensable workyears: Full-time equivalent employment	4	4	4

ROAD AND TRAIL FUND

(Legislative proposal, subject to PAYGO)

Program and Financing (in millions of dollars)

Identification code 12–1128–4–1–303		1999 actual	2000 est.	2001 est.
	Obligations by program activity:			
10.00	Total new obligations			25
	Budgetary resources available for obligation:			
22.00	New budget authority (gross)			31
23.95	Total new obligations			−25
24.40	Unobligated balance available, end of year			6
	New budget authority (gross), detail:			
	Mandatory:			
60.00	Appropriation			25
62.00	Transferred from other accounts			6
62.50	Appropriation (total mandatory)			31
	Change in unpaid obligations:			
73.10	Total new obligations			25
73.20	Total outlays (gross)			−20
73.32	Obligated balance transferred from other accounts			5
74.40	Unpaid obligations, end of year: Obligated balance, end of year			10
	Outlays (gross), detail:			
86.97	Outlays from new mandatory authority			20
	Net budget authority and outlays:			
89.00	Budget authority			31
90.00	Outlays			20

This proposal would decouple the road and trail fund from the receipts of national forests. Instead, fixed mandatory funding would be available for annual expenditures. The program would continue to focus on infrastructure needs of reconstruction and maintenance for roads and trails. In addition, the fund would be managed so as to give priority to opportunities to provide contracts to support public works contracts and other job creating programs in rural communities through Jobs in the Woods, Youth Conservation Corps, and similar special employment programs to employ displaced timber workers and residents of rural communities near national forests.

Object Classification (in millions of dollars)

Identification code 12–1128–4–1–303		1999 actual	2000 est.	2001 est.
	Personnel compensation:			
11.1	Full-time permanent			7
11.3	Other than full-time permanent			1
11.5	Other personnel compensation			1
11.9	Total personnel compensation			9
12.1	Civilian personnel benefits			2
23.1	Rental payments to GSA			1
25.2	Other services			6
26.0	Supplies and materials			3
33.0	Investments and loans			4
99.9	Total new obligations			25

Personnel Summary

Identification code 12–1128–4–1–303		1999 actual	2000 est.	2001 est.
1001	Total compensable workyears: Full-time equivalent employment			209

FOREST AND RANGELAND RESEARCH

For necessary expenses of forest and rangeland research as authorized by law, [$202,700,000] *$231,008,000*, to remain available until expended.

GIFTS, DONATIONS AND BEQUESTS FOR FOREST AND RANGELAND RESEARCH

For expenses authorized by 16 U.S.C. 1643(b), $92,000, to remain available until expended, to be derived from the fund established pursuant to the above Act. *(Department of the Interior and Related Agencies Appropriations Act, 2000, as enacted by section 1000(a)(3) of the Consolidated Appropriations Act, 2000 (P.L. 106–113.)*

Program and Financing (in millions of dollars)

Identification code 12–1104–0–1–302		1999 actual	2000 est.	2001 est.
	Obligations by program activity:			
00.06	Forest and rangeland research	197	201	229
09.01	Reimbursable program	21	22	24
10.00	Total new obligations	218	223	253
	Budgetary resources available for obligation:			
21.40	Unobligated balance available, start of year	20	13	15
22.00	New budget authority (gross)	209	225	255
22.10	Resources available from recoveries of prior year obligations	2		
23.90	Total budgetary resources available for obligation	231	238	270
23.95	Total new obligations	−218	−223	−253
24.40	Unobligated balance available, end of year	13	15	17
	New budget authority (gross), detail:			
	Discretionary:			
40.00	Appropriation	197	203	231
40.15	Appropriation (emergency)	1		
42.00	Transferred from other accounts	1		
43.00	Appropriation (total discretionary)	199	203	231
68.00	Spending authority from offsetting collections: Offsetting collections (cash)	10	22	24
70.00	Total new budget authority (gross)	209	225	255
	Change in unpaid obligations:			
72.40	Unpaid obligations, start of year: Obligated balance, start of year	56	78	77
73.10	Total new obligations	218	223	253
73.20	Total outlays (gross)	−194	−224	−247
73.45	Adjustments in unexpired accounts	−2		
74.40	Unpaid obligations, end of year: Obligated balance, end of year	78	77	83
	Outlays (gross), detail:			
86.90	Outlays from new discretionary authority	138	164	186
86.93	Outlays from discretionary balances	56	60	61

87.00	Total outlays (gross)	194	224	247
	Offsets:			
	Against gross budget authority and outlays:			
	Offsetting collections (cash) from:			
88.00	Federal sources	–9	–20	–22
88.40	Non-Federal sources	–1	–2	–2
88.90	Total, offsetting collections (cash)	–10	–22	–24
	Net budget authority and outlays:			
89.00	Budget authority	199	203	231
90.00	Outlays	184	202	223

The mission of Forest and Rangeland Research is to serve society by developing and communicating the scientific information and technology needed to protect, manage, use, and sustain the natural resources of the Nation's forests and rangelands. This information is essential for formulating policy and wisely managing and conserving both public and private forests and rangelands. Research is the key to sustaining our forest and rangeland productivity and health while providing a quality environment. Forest and Rangeland Research is conducted and disseminated through six Forest and Range Experiment Station headquarters and their laboratories, the Forest Products Laboratory, and the International Institute of Tropical Forestry.

Priority will be placed on supporting the implementation of forest planning regulations. This includes analyzing watershed integrity measurement and systems, evaluating monitoring systems and assessing results, providing information about compatible forest uses. In order to appropriately designate the new "focal" species, additional funding in this budget will emphasize priority wildlife habitat research; however, because these projects affect other agencies in addition to the FS, FS Research is enhancing existing coordination mechanisms to ensure that no overlapping and redundant work occurs. Funds are also included for global climate change research, particularly the use of small diameter trees for biomass energy uses and carbon cycle studies. Finally, work will continue on development of improved quantitative analytical tools to support forest planning goals to maximize net public benefits in a more objective and transparent manner.

Object Classification (in millions of dollars)

Identification code 12–1104–0–1–302		1999 actual	2000 est.	2001 est.
	Direct obligations:			
	Personnel compensation:			
11.1	Full-time permanent	96	101	99
11.3	Other than full-time permanent	7	8	8
11.5	Other personnel compensation	1	1	1
11.9	Total personnel compensation	104	110	108
12.1	Civilian personnel benefits	22	24	23
13.0	Benefits for former personnel	1	1	1
21.0	Travel and transportation of persons	8	7	11
22.0	Transportation of things	1	1	1
23.1	Rental payments to GSA	3	3	3
23.3	Communications, utilities, and miscellaneous charges	6	5	8
24.0	Printing and reproduction	1	1	1
25.2	Other services	10	10	14
25.5	Research and development contracts	22	21	33
26.0	Supplies and materials	8	8	11
31.0	Equipment	6	6	9
41.0	Grants, subsidies, and contributions	5	4	6
99.0	Subtotal, direct obligations	197	201	229
99.0	Reimbursable obligations	21	22	24
99.9	Total new obligations	218	223	253

Personnel Summary

Identification code 12–1104–0–1–302		1999 actual	2000 est.	2001 est.
	Direct:			
1001	Total compensable workyears: Full-time equivalent employment	2,271	2,414	2,369
	Reimbursable:			
2001	Total compensable workyears: Full-time equivalent employment	61	61	62

STATE [AND], PRIVATE *AND INTERNATIONAL* FORESTRY

For necessary expenses of cooperating with and providing technical and financial assistance to States, territories, possessions, and others, and for forest health management, cooperative forestry, and education and land conservation activities, [$202,534,000] *$261,331,000*, to remain available until expended, as authorized by law, *of which $106,000,000 is for Lands Legacy: Provided, That $6,000,000 for the costs of direct loans may be transferred to the USDA's Rural Business-Cooperative Service to carry out an intermediate relending program with State and local governments, non-profit corporations, Indian tribes and cooperatives to enable businesses, private non-profit organizations, and land trusts to support land acquisition and land uses that enhance smart growth, community green space, and community development goals, as authorized under the Development Loans Fund: Provided further, That such costs, including the cost of modifying such loans, shall be defined as in section 502 of the Congressional Budget Act of 1974: Provided further, That these funds are available to subsidize gross obligations for the principal amount of direct loans of $50,000,000: Provided further, That the loan levels provided in this Act shall be considered estimates, not limitations.* (Department of the Interior and Related Agencies Appropriations Act, 2000, as enacted by section 1000(a)(3) of the Consolidated Appropriations Act, 2000 (P.L. 106–113.)

Program and Financing (in millions of dollars)

Identification code 12–1105–0–1–302		1999 actual	2000 est.	2001 est.
	Obligations by program activity:			
	Direct program:			
00.05	Forest health management	61	62	61
00.06	Cooperative fire protection	24	28	35
00.07	Cooperative forestry	114	121	169
00.08	International forestry			10
09.01	Reimbursable program	4	5	7
10.00	Total new obligations	203	216	282
	Budgetary resources available for obligation:			
21.40	Unobligated balance available, start of year	59	27	24
22.00	New budget authority (gross)	171	212	268
23.90	Total budgetary resources available for obligation	230	239	292
23.95	Total new obligations	–203	–216	–282
24.40	Unobligated balance available, end of year	27	24	10
	New budget authority (gross), detail:			
	Discretionary:			
40.00	Appropriation	171	202	261
40.20	Appropriation (special fund, definite)		5	
43.00	Appropriation (total discretionary)	171	207	261
68.00	Spending authority from offsetting collections: Offsetting collections (cash)		5	7
70.00	Total new budget authority (gross)	171	212	268
	Change in unpaid obligations:			
72.40	Unpaid obligations, start of year: Obligated balance, start of year	160	183	196
73.10	Total new obligations	203	216	282
73.20	Total outlays (gross)	–180	–203	–254
74.40	Unpaid obligations, end of year: Obligated balance, end of year	183	196	224
	Outlays (gross), detail:			
86.90	Outlays from new discretionary authority	128	160	203
86.93	Outlays from discretionary balances	52	43	51
87.00	Total outlays (gross)	180	203	254

General and special funds—Continued

STATE [AND], PRIVATE *AND INTERNATIONAL* FORESTRY—Continued

Program and Financing (in millions of dollars)—Continued

Identification code 12–1105–0–1–302		1999 actual	2000 est.	2001 est.
	Offsets:			
	Against gross budget authority and outlays:			
88.00	Offsetting collections (cash) from: Federal sources		−5	−7
	Net budget authority and outlays:			
89.00	Budget authority	171	207	261
90.00	Outlays	180	198	247
	Distribution of budget authority by account:			
	State and private forestry			
	Distribution of outlays by account:			
	State and private forestry			
	Emergency pest suppression fund			

State, Private, and International Forestry programs provide assistance to manage, use, and protect forest resources on State, urban, and private lands to meet domestic and international demands for goods and services. Assistance is provided to a wide range of customers including all States, Puerto Rico, the Virgin Islands, Guam, the Northern Mariana Islands and the Trust Terrority of the Pacific.

Forest health management.—Includes Federal lands, and cooperative lands.

Cooperative Fire Protection.—Includes funding to enhance the capacity of States to provide coordinated fire suppression response and to promote safe and effective initial fire attack in wildland/urban interface areas by volunteer fire departments.

The new Wildland/Urban Interface Program will reduce fire damages and personal risks. Fire Management will be used to encourage greater community participation in reducing fire risk in the Wildland/Urban Interface, through competitive grants to partially support community planning and disaster prevention and hazard mitigation assistance. Community implementation of fire hazard mitigation projects will save Federal wildfire suppression costs. Insurance company participation may provide a subsequent reduction in insurance premiums for participating communities.

Cooperative Forestry.—Includes forest stewardship, the stewardship incentives program, the forest legacy program, urban and community forestry, economic action programs, and Pacific Northwest community assistance programs. Forest stewardship includes: forest resource management; and seedlings, nursery, and tree improvement programs. Economic action programs include economic recovery, rural development, and forest products conservation and recycling programs.

Funding for the Forest Legacy, Urban and Community Forestry and the Smart Growth Partnership Loans within this account is proposed as part of a new Lands Legacy discretionary spending catergory to provide dedicated and protected funding for the President's Lands Legacy Initiative. See the Environment Chapter in the Budget for a summary of the Initiative. These funds along with increases in other accounts highlight the Administration's commitment to making new tools available, and working with states, tribes, local governments and private partners to protect great places; to conserve open space for recreation and wildlife habitat; and to preserve forest, farmlands, and coastal areas.

New funding in the Economic Action Programs will be targeted to support new agreements for rural development cooperation in forest resource dependent locations. Also, the Smart Growth Partnership is a new USDA direct loan program to use subsidized loans for smart growth land acquisition, management and use through partnerships with state, local, and tribal governments. The program would allow communities to protect open spaces to help limit sprawl, enhance water quality protections, reduce greenhouse emissions and increase greenspace.

International Programs.—The 2001 Budget expands International Programs to $10 million (as a specific line item). The programs will emphasize habitat protection for migratory birds along the length of the flyway, preventing the introduction of new invasive species, and sustainable forestry techniques development for other timber exporting nations.

Object Classification (in millions of dollars)

Identification code 12–1105–0–1–302		1999 actual	2000 est.	2001 est.
	Direct obligations:			
	Personnel compensation:			
11.1	Full-time permanent	32	36	33
11.3	Other than full-time permanent	2	2	2
11.9	Total personnel compensation	34	38	35
12.1	Civilian personnel benefits	7	8	7
21.0	Travel and transportation of persons	5	5	8
23.1	Rental payments to GSA	2	2	2
23.3	Communications, utilities, and miscellaneous charges	1	1	2
25.2	Other services	27	28	39
26.0	Supplies and materials	4	4	5
31.0	Equipment	2	2	3
41.0	Grants, subsidies, and contributions	116	122	173
99.0	Subtotal, direct obligations	198	210	274
99.0	Reimbursable obligations	4	5	7
25.2	Allocation Account: Other services	1	1	1
99.9	Total new obligations	203	216	282

Personnel Summary

Identification code 12–1105–0–1–302		1999 actual	2000 est.	2001 est.
	Direct:			
1001	Total compensable workyears: Full-time equivalent employment	700	768	708
	Reimbursable:			
2001	Total compensable workyears: Full-time equivalent employment	5	5	5

HEALTHY INVESTMENTS IN RURAL ENVIRONMENTS

(Legislative proposal, subject to PAYGO)

Program and Financing (in millions of dollars)

Identification code 12–1126–4–1–302		1999 actual	2000 est.	2001 est.
	Obligations by program activity:			
10.00	Total new obligations			315
	Budgetary resources available for obligation:			
22.00	New budget authority (gross)			745
23.95	Total new obligations			−315
24.40	Unobligated balance available, end of year			430
	New budget authority (gross), detail:			
	Mandatory:			
60.00	Appropriation			315
62.00	Transferred from other accounts			430
62.50	Appropriation (total mandatory)			745
	Change in unpaid obligations:			
73.10	Total new obligations			315
73.20	Total outlays (gross)			−315
73.32	Obligated balance transferred from other accounts			63
74.40	Unpaid obligations, end of year: Obligated balance, end of year			64
	Outlays (gross), detail:			
86.97	Outlays from new mandatory authority			252
86.98	Outlays from mandatory balances			63
87.00	Total outlays (gross)			315

		1999 actual	2000 est.	2001 est.
	Net budget authority and outlays:			
89.00	Budget authority			745
90.00	Outlays			315

The Forest Service will propose legislation to decouple its mandatory spending programs from timber receipts and instead to authorize spending from the Treasury at current baseline-assumed levels (fixed, specific levels of spending) under a new, broader-purposed program.

The revised policy would improve management and increase accountability by severing the linkage between program spending and timber harvest volumes, thereby eliminating concerns that the source of funds influences decisions on the choices for management prescriptions, and increase agency reliance on the funds to finance organizational costs. The new mandatory account structure will preserve funding at known, fixed, and dependable amounts, and display budget information more visibly allowing the agency, Congress, and the public an expanded role in funding allocation decisions. To ensure greater funding visibility and improved targeting, funding decisions for the new account will be displayed in the agency's Congressional Justification for the Budget, using the annual performance measures to indicate the outcomes of the intended spending. This results in a comparable effect to putting the spending "on-line" through the discretionary budget.

The reforms to the permanent appropriations would establish the new Healthy Investments in Rural Environments (HIRE) initiative to hire thousands of skilled workers in rural communities through public works contracts and begin to reduce the backlog of priority maintenance, reconstruction, and forest health projects on National Forest System lands. The HIRE would use Jobs in the Woods, Youth Conservation Corps, and similar special employment programs to employ displaced timber workers and other rural workers. HIRE would fund a range of different projects, including reforestation, timber stand improvement, road maintenance, fuels reduction, wildlife habitat restoration, erosion control, or survey and monitoring work. In addition to the activities now carried out with these funds (e.g., reforestation), other priorities include road maintenance, and prescribed burns and other hazardous fuels reduction. Funds could be leveraged through challenge cost-share to best accomplish the program goals.

These changes would make mandatory funding more visible to the public, more transparent for the budget and accounting system, better targeted toward Forest Service priorities, removed from any unintended incentives that affect management decisions, and available for increased rural employment.

Object Classification (in millions of dollars)

Identification code 12–1126–4–1–302		1999 actual	2000 est.	2001 est.
	Personnel compensation:			
11.1	Full-time permanent			96
11.3	Other than full-time permanent			13
11.5	Other personnel compensation			5
11.9	Total personnel compensation			114
12.1	Civilian personnel benefits			25
13.0	Benefits for former personnel			1
21.0	Travel and transportation of persons			3
22.0	Transportation of things			4
23.1	Rental payments to GSA			2
23.2	Rental payments to others			8
23.3	Communications, utilities, and miscellaneous charges			4
24.0	Printing and reproduction			1
25.2	Other services			114
26.0	Supplies and materials			16
31.0	Equipment			4
32.0	Land and structures			1
41.0	Grants, subsidies, and contributions			18
99.9	Total new obligations			315

Personnel Summary

Identification code 12–1126–4–1–302		1999 actual	2000 est.	2001 est.
1001	Total compensable workyears: Full-time equivalent employment			2,675

Management of National Forest Lands for Subsistence Uses

subsistence management, forest service

For necessary expenses of the Forest Service to manage federal lands in Alaska for subsistence uses under title VIII of the Alaska National Interest Lands Conservation Act (Public Law 96–487), $5,500,000, to remain available until expended.

Program and Financing (in millions of dollars)

Identification code 12–1119–0–1–302		1999 actual	2000 est.	2001 est.
	Obligations by program activity:			
10.00	Total new obligations (object class 41.0)		3	6
	Budgetary resources available for obligation:			
21.40	Unobligated balance available, start of year		3	
22.00	New budget authority (gross)	3		6
23.90	Total budgetary resources available for obligation	3	3	6
23.95	Total new obligations		−3	−6
24.40	Unobligated balance available, end of year	3		
	New budget authority (gross), detail:			
	Discretionary:			
40.00	Appropriation	3		6
	Change in unpaid obligations:			
73.10	Total new obligations		3	6
73.20	Total outlays (gross)		−3	−6
	Outlays (gross), detail:			
86.90	Outlays from new discretionary authority			6
86.93	Outlays from discretionary balances		3	
87.00	Total outlays (gross)		3	6
	Net budget authority and outlays:			
89.00	Budget authority	3		6
90.00	Outlays		3	6

Funding under this program primarily supports fisheries and wildlife habitat management activities in the areas of population assessment, forecasting, harvest regulations, and law enforcement to ensure that the subsistence needs of qualified rural Alaskans are met under the Alaska National Interest Lands Conservation Act (Public Law 96–487).

Wildland Fire Management

For necessary expenses for forest fire presuppression activities on National Forest System lands, for emergency fire suppression on or adjacent to such lands or other lands under fire protection agreement, *for support to federal emergency response,* and for emergency rehabilitation of burned-over National Forest System lands and water, [$561,354,000] *$620,372,000,* to remain available until expended: *Provided,* That such funds are available for repayment of advances from other appropriations accounts previously transferred for such purposes: [*Provided further,* That not less than 50 percent of any unobligated balances remaining (exclusive of amounts for hazardous fuels reduction) at the end of fiscal year 1999 shall be transferred, as repayment for post advances that have not been repaid, to the fund established pursuant to section 3 of Public Law 71–319 (16 U.S.C. 576 et seq.):] *Provided further,* That notwithstanding any other provision of law, up to $4,000,000 of funds appropriated under this appropriation may be used for Fire Science Research in support of the Joint Fire Science Program: *Provided further,* That all authorities for the use of funds, including the use of contracts, grants, and cooperative agreements, available to execute the Forest Service and Rangeland Research appropriation, are also available in the utilization of these funds for Fire Science Research.

General and special funds—Continued

WILDLAND FIRE MANAGEMENT—Continued

For an additional amount to cover necessary expenses for emergency rehabilitation, presuppression due to emergencies, and wildfire suppression activities of the Forest Service, [$90,000,000] *$150,000,000*, to remain available until expended: *Provided,* That the entire amount is [designed] *designated* by Congress as an emergency requirement pursuant to section 251(b)(2)(A) of the Balanced Budget and Emergency Deficit Control Act of 1985, as amended: *Provided further,* That these funds shall be available only to the extent an official budget request for a specific dollar amount, that includes designation of the entire amount of the request as an emergency requirement as defined in the Balanced Budget and Emergency Deficit Control Act of 1985, as amended, is transmitted by the President to the Congress. *(Department of the Interior and Related Agencies Appropriations Act, 2000, as enacted by section 1000(a)(3) of the Consolidated Appropriations Act, 2000 (P.L. 106–113.)*

Program and Financing (in millions of dollars)

Identification code 12–1115–0–1–302	1999 actual	2000 est.	2001 est.
Obligations by program activity:			
00.01 Fire management	724	557	632
09.01 Reimbursable program	141	87	95
10.00 Total new obligations	865	644	727
Budgetary resources available for obligation:			
21.40 Unobligated balance available, start of year	135	113	117
22.00 New budget authority (gross)	837	648	865
22.10 Resources available from recoveries of prior year obligations	6		
23.90 Total budgetary resources available for obligation	978	761	982
23.95 Total new obligations	−865	−644	−727
24.40 Unobligated balance available, end of year	113	117	255
New budget authority (gross), detail:			
Discretionary:			
40.00 Appropriation	762	562	620
40.15 Appropriation (emergency)			150
40.76 Reduction pursuant to P.L. 106–113		−1	
43.00 Appropriation (total discretionary)	762	561	770
68.00 Spending authority from offsetting collections: Offsetting collections (cash)	75	87	95
70.00 Total new budget authority (gross)	837	648	865
Change in unpaid obligations:			
72.40 Unpaid obligations, start of year: Obligated balance, start of year	103	62	119
73.10 Total new obligations	865	644	727
73.20 Total outlays (gross)	−899	−587	−700
73.45 Adjustments in unexpired accounts	−6		
74.40 Unpaid obligations, end of year: Obligated balance, end of year	62	119	146
Outlays (gross), detail:			
86.90 Outlays from new discretionary authority	797	511	653
86.93 Outlays from discretionary balances	103	77	47
87.00 Total outlays (gross)	899	587	700
Offsets:			
Against gross budget authority and outlays:			
Offsetting collections (cash) from:			
88.00 Federal sources	−73	−84	−92
88.40 Non-Federal sources	−2	−3	−3
88.90 Total, offsetting collections (cash)	−75	−87	−95
Net budget authority and outlays:			
89.00 Budget authority	762	561	770
90.00 Outlays	824	500	605

Wildland fire management.—This appropriation provides funding for Forest Service fire management, presuppression, and suppression on National Forest System lands, adjacent State and private lands, and other lands under fire protection agreement.

Preparedness.—To protect National Forest System (NFS) lands from damage by wildfires commensurate with the threat to life, values at risk, public values, and management objectives.

Preparedness provides the basic fire organization and capability to prevent forest fires and to take prompt, effective initial attack suppression operations action on wildfires. This funding covers expenses associated with planning, prevention, detection, information and education; pre-incident training; equipment and supply purchase and replacement; and other preparedness activities, including the base salary and travel of the regular Forest Service firefighting organization. Through this program the Forest Service also assists other Federal agencies and States with training programs, planning assistance, sharing joint equipment use contracts and interagency fire coordination centers.

Fire Operations.—To efficiently suppress wildland fires on or threatening National Forest System (NFS) lands or other lands under fire protection agreement. Fire Operations provides funds for all hazardous fuel reduction program activities including planning and implementation, mechanical treatments, prescribed fire, and monitoring of fuel treatment accomplishments. Fuel treatment activities are performed to minimize the potential for large, destructive wildfires.

Fire Operations funds are used to immediately and efficiently rehabilitate severely burned NFS lands to prevent further destruction of natural resources, including soil loss and flooding. Funds are used to increase the level of fire preparedness when predicted or actual burning conditions exceed normal levels.

Contingency Funds.—This budget includes $150,000,000 in contingent funding for 2001 to be utilized for emergency wildland fire activities, if needed, beyond the amount requested in this budget.

Object Classification (in millions of dollars)

Identification code 12–1115–0–1–302	1999 actual	2000 est.	2001 est.
Direct obligations:			
Personnel compensation:			
11.1 Full-time permanent	128	135	129
11.3 Other than full-time permanent	23	25	24
11.5 Other personnel compensation	57	61	58
11.8 Special personal services payments	2	2	2
11.9 Total personnel compensation	210	223	213
12.1 Civilian personnel benefits	43	46	44
13.0 Benefits for former personnel	6	6	6
21.0 Travel and transportation of persons	28	28	28
22.0 Transportation of things	6	4	5
23.1 Rental payments to GSA	6	6	6
23.2 Rental payments to others	5	3	4
23.3 Communications, utilities, and miscellaneous charges	15	9	12
24.0 Printing and reproduction	1	1	1
25.2 Other services	342	196	265
26.0 Supplies and materials	48	27	37
31.0 Equipment	11	7	9
41.0 Grants, subsidies, and contributions	3	1	2
99.0 Subtotal, direct obligations	724	557	632
99.0 Reimbursable obligations	141	87	95
99.9 Total new obligations	865	644	727

Personnel Summary

Identification code 12–1115–0–1–302	1999 actual	2000 est.	2001 est.
Direct:			
1001 Total compensable workyears: Full-time equivalent employment	6,393	6,790	6,496
Reimbursable:			
2001 Total compensable workyears: Full-time equivalent employment	10	10	10

PAYMENTS TO STATES—NORTHERN SPOTTED OWL GUARANTEE

Program and Financing (in millions of dollars)

Identification code 12–1117–0–1–806	1999 actual	2000 est.	2001 est.
Obligations by program activity:			
10.00 Total new obligations (object class 41.0)	125	120	115
Budgetary resources available for obligation:			
22.00 New budget authority (gross)	125	120	115
23.95 Total new obligations	−125	−120	−115
New budget authority (gross), detail:			
Mandatory:			
60.05 Appropriation (indefinite)	125	120	115
Change in unpaid obligations:			
73.10 Total new obligations	125	120	115
73.20 Total outlays (gross)	−125	−120	−115
Outlays (gross), detail:			
86.97 Outlays from new mandatory authority	125	120	115
Net budget authority and outlays:			
89.00 Budget authority	125	120	115
90.00 Outlays	125	120	115

Summary of Budget Authority and Outlays

(in millions of dollars)

	1999 actual	*2000 est.*	*2001 est.*
Enacted/requested:			
Budget Authority	125	120	115
Outlays	125	120	115
Legislative proposal, subject to PAYGO:			
Budget Authority			−115
Outlays			−115
Total:			
Budget Authority	125	120	
Outlays	125	120	

Payments to States, Northern Spotted Owl Guarantee.—For payment to the States of Oregon, Washington, and California for the benefit of counties in which National Forests are situated and that are affected by decisions related to the northern spotted owl, pursuant to section 13982 of Public Law 103–66 as amended by Public Law 103–443.

PAYMENTS TO STATES—NORTHERN SPOTTED OWL GUARANTEE

(Legislative proposal subjecct to PAYGO)

Program and Financing (in millions of dollars)

Identification code 12–1117–4–1–806	1999 actual	2000 est.	2001 est.
Obligations by program activity:			
10.00 Total new obligations (object class 41.0)			−115
Budgetary resources available for obligation:			
22.00 New budget authority (gross)			−115
23.95 Total new obligations			115
New budget authority (gross), detail:			
Mandatory:			
60.05 Appropriation (indefinite)			−115
Change in unpaid obligations:			
73.10 Total new obligations			−115
73.20 Total outlays (gross)			115
Outlays (gross), detail:			
86.97 Outlays from new mandatory authority			−115
Net budget authority and outlays:			
89.00 Budget authority			−115
90.00 Outlays			−115

Proposed legislation would stabilize funding levels through payments to States nationwide, beginning in 2001, to provide predictable stable payments for county roads and schools.

PAYMENTS TO STATES STABILIZATION

(Legislative proposal, subject to PAYGO)

Program and Financing (in millions of dollars)

Identification code 12–1112–4–1–806	1999 actual	2000 est.	2001 est.
Obligations by program activity:			
10.00 Total new obligations (object class 41.0)			270
Budgetary resources available for obligation:			
22.00 New budget authority (gross)			270
23.95 Total new obligations			−270
New budget authority (gross), detail:			
Mandatory:			
60.05 Appropriation (indefinite)			270
Change in unpaid obligations:			
73.10 Total new obligations			270
73.20 Total outlays (gross)			−270
Outlays (gross), detail:			
86.97 Outlays from new mandatory authority			270
Net budget authority and outlays:			
89.00 Budget authority			270
90.00 Outlays			270

Current receipt sharing payments (25% payments) are proposed to be replaced by a stable, guaranteed level of payments based on the concept of the guaranteed payments, "Payments to States, Northern Spotted Owl Guarantee". The Administration's objective is to secure a stable and permanent source of funding for rural schools and other infrastructure needs. The Administration's proposal would significantly increase funding for these activities over current baseline levels.

Nationally, payments to States funding has declined 37% since 1989, from $361 million down to $229 million last year (the 1999 payment is based on 1998 receipts). The Administration's proposal would provide a guaranteed $270 million annually to States. The Administration fully recognizes the importance of these payments to local communities for public schools and roads as a result of Federal landownership. By virtue of this stabilization proposal, the Administration has shown its commitment to continuation of the payments and will work to ensure they are permanently provided every year in the future.

The Administration stands ready to work with Congress to produce legislation that provides increased, guaranteed, stable payments to States and communities. Any proposals, including those that would establish a portion of the funding for "special projects," should allow the counties the option to participate or to use the full funding for schools.

The Administration would consider additional special project funding if the projects are targeted to provide better management, improved community stewardship, or ecological restoration of the National Forests, and Grasslands. This could provide opportunities for the Forest Service to provide public works contracts and other job creating programs in rural communities through Jobs in the Woods, Youth Conservation Corps, and similar such special employment programs to increase employment in rural areas.

General and special funds—Continued

SOUTHEAST ALASKA ECONOMIC DISASTER *ASSISTANCE* FUND

Program and Financing (in millions of dollars)

Identification code 12–1108–0–1–451	1999 actual	2000 est.	2001 est.
Obligations by program activity:			
10.00 Total new obligations (object class 41.0)	20	10	7
Budgetary resources available for obligation:			
21.40 Unobligated balance available, start of year	20		12
22.00 New budget authority (gross)		22	
23.90 Total budgetary resources available for obligation	20	22	12
23.95 Total new obligations	–20	–10	–7
24.40 Unobligated balance available, end of year		12	5
New budget authority (gross), detail:			
Discretionary:			
40.00 Appropriation		22	
Change in unpaid obligations:			
73.10 Total new obligations	20	10	7
73.20 Total outlays (gross)	–20	–10	–7
Outlays (gross), detail:			
86.90 Outlays from new discretionary authority		10	
86.93 Outlays from discretionary balances	20		7
87.00 Total outlays (gross)	20	10	7
Net budget authority and outlays:			
89.00 Budget authority		22	
90.00 Outlays	20	10	7

Public Law 104–134 established this appropriation, for the period 1996 through 2002, to provide assistance to employ former timber workers in Wrangell and Sitka and for related community development projects in Sitka, Wrangell, Ketchican, and selected organized boroughs in Southeast Alaska. Distribution to the unorganized boroughs was based on the proportion of 1995 timber receipts from each borough.

FACILITIES ACQUISITION AND ENHANCEMENT FUND

(Legislative Proposal, subject to PAYGO)

Unavailable Collections (in millions of dollars)

Identification code 12–5353–0–2–302	1999 actual	2000 est.	2001 est.
Balance, start of year:			
01.99 Balance, start of year			
Receipts:			
02.01 Collections for facilities acquisition and enhancement fund [Legislative proposal, not subject to PAYGO]			2
Appropriation:			
05.01 Facilities acquisition and enhancement fund [Legislative proposal, not subject to PAYGO]			–2
07.99 Total balance, end of year			

Program and Financing (in millions of dollars)

Identification code 12–5353–4–2–302	1999 actual	2000 est.	2001 est.
Obligations by program activity:			
10.00 Total new obligations (object class 32.0)			2
Budgetary resources available for obligation:			
22.00 New budget authority (gross)			2
23.95 Total new obligations			–2
New budget authority (gross), detail:			
Mandatory:			
60.20 Appropriation (special fund, indefinite)			2
Change in unpaid obligations:			
73.10 Total new obligations			2
73.20 Total outlays (gross)			–2
Outlays (gross), detail:			
86.97 Outlays from new mandatory authority			2
Net budget authority and outlays:			
89.00 Budget authority			2
90.00 Outlays			2

Forest Service, in cooperation with the General Services Administration, will propose that the agency have authority to sell facilities, buildings, constructed features and any appurtenant land, excess to its needs, and to use the proceeds for acquiring or developing land and improvements. This proposal would establish a real property capital account for the management, replacement, and capital improvements for facilities.

The proposed real property capital account is a special fund, a federal fund account both for receipts that are earmarked for specific purposes and for the expenditure of these receipts. Unlike a general fund account, receipts and expenditures are linked and, the receipts are available only for a specific purpose.

[RANGE BETTERMENT FUND]

[For necessary expenses of range rehabilitation, protection, and improvement, 50 percent of all moneys received during the prior fiscal year, as fees for grazing domestic livestock on lands in National Forests in the 16 Western States, pursuant to section 401(b)(1) of Public Law 94–579, as amended, to remain available until expended, of which not to exceed 6 percent shall be available for administrative expenses associated with on-the-ground range rehabilitation, protection, and improvements.] *(Department of the Interior and Related Agencies Appropriations Act, 2000, as enacted by section 1000(a)(3) of the Consolidated Appropriations Act, 2000 (P.L. 106–113.)*

Unavailable Collections (in millions of dollars)

Identification code 12–5207–0–2–302	1999 actual	2000 est.	2001 est.
Balance, start of year:			
01.99 Balance, start of year	2	2	2
Receipts:			
02.01 Cooperative range improvements	3	3	3
02.02 Legislative proposal not subject to PAYGO			–3
02.99 Total receipts	3	3	
04.00 Total: Balances and collections	5	5	2
Appropriation:			
05.01 Range betterment fund	–3	–3	
07.99 Total balance, end of year	2	2	2

Program and Financing (in millions of dollars)

Identification code 12–5207–0–2–302	1999 actual	2000 est.	2001 est.
Obligations by program activity:			
10.00 Total new obligations	3	3	
Budgetary resources available for obligation:			
21.40 Unobligated balance available, start of year	1	1	1
22.00 New budget authority (gross)	3	3	
23.90 Total budgetary resources available for obligation	4	4	1
23.95 Total new obligations	–3	–3	
24.40 Unobligated balance available, end of year	1	1	1
New budget authority (gross), detail:			
Discretionary:			
40.25 Appropriation (special fund, indefinite)	3	3	
Change in unpaid obligations:			
72.40 Unpaid obligations, start of year: Obligated balance, start of year	1	1	1
73.10 Total new obligations	3	3	
73.20 Total outlays (gross)	–3	–3	–1

74.40 Unpaid obligations, end of year: Obligated balance, end of year	1	1	....
Outlays (gross), detail:			
86.90 Outlays from new discretionary authority	2	2	....
86.93 Outlays from discretionary balances	1	1	1
87.00 Total outlays (gross)	3	3	1
Net budget authority and outlays:			
89.00 Budget authority	3	3	....
90.00 Outlays	3	3	1

Funding for this activity will be available through the new Healthy Investments in Rural Environments established through legislative reforms to the existing permanent appropriations. Additional funds are included in the National Forest System.

Object Classification (in millions of dollars)

Identification code 12–5207–0–2–302	1999 actual	2000 est.	2001 est.
11.1 Personnel compensation: Full-time permanent	1	1	....
25.2 Other services	1	1	....
26.0 Supplies and materials	1	1	....
99.9 Total new obligations	3	3	....

Personnel Summary

Identification code 12–5207–0–2–302	1999 actual	2000 est.	2001 est.
1001 Total compensable workyears: Full-time equivalent employment	33	37	....

LAND ACQUISITION ACCOUNTS

[LAND ACQUISITION]

[For expenses necessary to carry out the provisions of the Land and Water Conservation Fund Act of 1965, as amended (16 U.S.C. 4601–4 through 11), including administrative expenses, and for acquisition of land or waters, or interest therein, in accordance with statutory authority applicable to the Forest Service, $79,575,000, to be derived from the Land and Water Conservation Fund, to remain available until expended, of which not to exceed $40,000,000 may be available for the acquisition of lands or interests within the tract known as the Baca Location No. 1 in New Mexico only upon: (1) the enactment of legislation authorizing the acquisition of lands, or interests in lands, within such tract; (2) completion of a review, not to exceed 90 days, by the Comptroller General of the United States of an appraisal conforming with the Uniform Appraisal Standards for Federal Land Acquisition of all lands and interests therein to be acquired by the United States; and (3) submission of the Comptroller General's review of such appraisal to the Committee on Resources of the House of Representatives, the Committee on Energy and Natural Resources of the Senate, and the Committees on Appropriations of the House and Senate: *Provided*, That subject to valid existing rights, all federally-owned lands and interests in lands within the New World Mining District comprising approximately 26,223 acres, more or less, which are described in a Federal Register notice dated August 19, 1997 (62 Fed. Reg. 44136–44137), are hereby withdrawn from all forms of entry, appropriation, and disposal under the public land laws, and from location, entry and patent under the mining laws, and from disposition under all mineral and geothermal leasing laws.]

[ACQUISITION OF LANDS FOR NATIONAL FORESTS SPECIAL ACTS]

[For acquisition of lands within the exterior boundaries of the Cache, Uinta, and Wasatch National Forests, Utah; the Toiyabe National Forest, Nevada; and the Angeles, San Bernardino, Sequoia, and Cleveland National Forests, California, as authorized by law, $1,069,000, to be derived from forest receipts.]

[ACQUISITION OF LANDS TO COMPLETE LAND EXCHANGES]

[For acquisition of lands, such sums, to be derived from funds deposited by State, county, or municipal governments, public school districts, or other public school authorities pursuant to the Act of December 4, 1967, as amended (16 U.S.C. 484a), to remain available until expended.] *For acquisition of lands, waters, or interests therein, as authorized by law,* [*$130,000,000,*] *$130,265,000,* for Lands Legacy, to remain available until expended, to be derived from the Land and Water Conservation Fund, as amended and funds deposited by State, county, or municipal governments, public school districts, or other public school authorities pursuant to the Act of December 4, 1967: Provided, That funds made available for the Beartooth Highway restoration under Title V, Public Law 105–83, are available until expended. *(16 U.S.C. 4601–4–11, 4601–516–617a, 555a; P.L. 96–586; P.L. 76–589, 76–591; 78–310, and 16 U.S.C. 484a; Department of the Interior and Related Agencies Appropriations Act, 2000, as enacted by section 1000(a)(3) of the Consolidated Appropriations Act, 2000 (P.L. 106–113.)*

Unavailable Collections (in millions of dollars)

Identification code 12–9923–0–2–300	1999 actual	2000 est.	2001 est.
Balance, start of year:			
01.99 Balance, start of year	....	....	....
Receipts:			
02.01 National forest lands under special acts	1	1	1
02.03 National forest lands under special acts, legislative proposal not subject to PAYGO	....	....	−1
02.99 Total receipts	1	1	....
Appropriation:			
05.01 Land acquisition accounts	−1	−1	....
07.99 Total balance, end of year	....	....	....

Program and Financing (in millions of dollars)

Identification code 12–9923–0–2–300	1999 actual	2000 est.	2001 est.
Obligations by program activity:			
10.00 Total new obligations	107	217	179
Budgetary resources available for obligation:			
21.40 Unobligated balance available, start of year	138	150	90
22.00 New budget authority (gross)	119	157	130
23.90 Total budgetary resources available for obligation	257	307	220
23.95 Total new obligations	−107	−217	−179
24.40 Unobligated balance available, end of year	150	90	41
New budget authority (gross), detail:			
Discretionary:			
Appropriation (special fund, definite):			
40.20 Appropriation (LWCF)	118	156	130
40.20 Appropriation (special act))	1	1	....
43.00 Appropriation (total discretionary)	119	157	130
Change in unpaid obligations:			
72.40 Unpaid obligations, start of year: Obligated balance, start of year	8	23	97
73.10 Total new obligations	107	217	179
73.20 Total outlays (gross)	−92	−143	−139
74.40 Unpaid obligations, end of year: Obligated balance, end of year	23	97	137
Outlays (gross), detail:			
86.90 Outlays from new discretionary authority	86	104	86
86.93 Outlays from discretionary balances	7	40	53
87.00 Total outlays (gross)	92	143	139
Net budget authority and outlays:			
89.00 Budget authority	119	157	130
90.00 Outlays	92	143	139

This appropriation consolidates land acquisition authorities for acquisition of lands, waters, or interest therein, as authorized by law.

Land and water conservation fund.—Recreation lands and interests are acquired within areas of the National Forest System, wilderness, wildlife and fisheries habitat management areas, and endangered species and other areas for public outdoor recreation purposes.

General and special funds—Continued

LAND ACQUISITION ACCOUNTS—Continued

[ACQUISITION OF LANDS TO COMPLETE LAND EXCHANGES]—Continued

Funding for this account is proposed as part of a new Lands Legacy discretionary spending category to provide dedicated and protected funding for the President's Lands Legacy Initiative. See the Environment Chapter in the Budget for a summary of the Initiative. These funds, along with increases in other accounts, highlight the Administration's commitment to making new tools available, and working with states, tribes, local governments and private partners to protect great places; to conserve open space for recreation and wildlife habitat; and to preserve forest, farmlands, and coastal areas.

The request proposes to extend the availability of title V, FY 1997 Interior and Related Agencies funds to be used for continuation of maintenance and rehabilitation work on the Beartooth Highway. Funds are due to expire on September 30, 2001. Extension of funding availability allows continuation for road maintenance while the Environmental Impact Statement (EIS) is being completed; the EIS, required by law, must be completed before rehabilitation may commence.

Acquisition of lands to complete land exchanges.—Deposits made by State, county, or municipal governments, public school districts, or other public school authorities for cash equalization of certain land exchanges are used to acquire similar lands suitable for National Forest System purposes in the same State as the National Forest lands conveyed in the land exchange.

The Forest Service will propose administrative and legislative reforms to land investments, including changes to the land exchange program and increased authority for land sales and acquisition to more efficiently acquire additional high priority lands to ensure increased environmental benefits and government value.

The Forest Service has already taken the various actions (some recommended by the Office of Inspector General) to the Land Ownership program. On-going and future actions include:

—Implemented a National Policy that requires all FS land exchanges to be reviewed and approved by the National Land Adjustments Oversight Team (that has examined over 90 proposed exchanges to date), and established national policy and guidelines (November 1998) on roles and responsibilities of third party facilators in landownership adjustments;

—Issued guidance on September 10, 1999 requiring all desired landownership configurations to be incorporated in Forest Plan revisions;

—Announced that the future new policy will include full disclosure of all appraisal information involving land exchanges;

—Determined that, along with the increased public information and involvement in exchanges, an effort will be made to seek competition in land exchanges by permitting other interested parties to enter into the bidding for a FS property;

—Will propose new legislation permitting the Forest Service to acquire new lands and dispose of unneeded existing property in order to enhance managerial efficiencies, gain high quality recreational and scenic plots, and protect and increase critical habitat for sensitive species. This increased authority to buy and sell lands—along with restrictions to protect environmentally valuable properties—will enable the agency to use the commercial real estate markets for more transactions. The new authority will rely upon full openness in land-related transactions, along with high levels of competition (no "one-on-one" transactions).

Object Classification (in millions of dollars)

Identification code 12–9923–0–2–300	1999 actual	2000 est.	2001 est.
11.1 Personnel compensation: Full-time permanent	5	5	5
12.1 Civilian personnel benefits	1	1	1
25.2 Other services	17	36	30
32.0 Land and structures	84	175	143
99.9 Total new obligations	107	217	179

Personnel Summary

Identification code 12–9923–0–2–300	1999 actual	2000 est.	2001 est.
1001 Total compensable workyears: Full-time equivalent employment	101	111	100

LAND ACQUISITION REINVESTMENT FUND

(Legislative proposal, Subject to PAYGO)

Unavailable Collections (in millions of dollars)

Identification code 12–5359–0–2–302	1999 actual	2000 est.	2001 est.
Balance, start of year:			
01.99 Balance, start of year			
Receipts:			
02.01 Proceeds of land sales, Forest Service, legislative proposal subject to PAYGO			1
Appropriation:			
05.01 Land acquisition reinvestment fund, legislative proposal subject to PAYGO			−1
07.99 Total balance, end of year			

Program and Financing (in millions of dollars)

Identification code 12–5359–4–2–302	1999 actual	2000 est.	2001 est.
Obligations by program activity:			
10.00 Total new obligations (object class 32.0)			1
Budgetary resources available for obligation:			
22.00 New budget authority (gross)			1
23.95 Total new obligations			−1
New budget authority (gross), detail:			
Mandatory:			
60.25 Appropriation (special fund, indefinite)			1
Change in unpaid obligations:			
73.10 Total new obligations			1
73.20 Total outlays (gross)			−1
Outlays (gross), detail:			
86.97 Outlays from new mandatory authority			1
Net budget authority and outlays:			
89.00 Budget authority			1
90.00 Outlays			1

Through increased authority for land sales and acquisitions, this proposed legislation would focus on acquiring high priority wetlands, riparian areas, threatened and endangered species habitat, areas of high biological diversity, wildlife corridors, and other high value conservation areas to ensure increased environmental benefits and government value. Proposed legislation would facilitate making appropriate sales and re-investment in Forest Service lands, including lands where encumbrances or community needs make them more appropriate for other public or private ownership, and where opportunities for achieving market value for a property are better through a sale than an exchange. The legislation will include sideboards or restrictions needed to avoid potential land sale abuses, and ensure only appropriate lands are available for sales (and reinvestment in new lands) at any one time.

The proposed Land Acquisition Reinvestment Fund is a special federal fund account for both receipts that are earmarked for specific purposes and for the expenditure of these receipts. Unlike a general fund account, receipts and expenditures are linked and, the receipts are available for only a specific purpose.

Forest Service Permanent Appropriations

Unavailable Collections (in millions of dollars)

Identification code 12–9921–0–2–999	1999 actual	2000 est.	2001 est.
Balance, start of year:			
01.99 Balance, start of year	340	274	282
Receipts:			
02.01 National forests fund, Agriculture	–64		
02.02 Payments to states	103	114	106
02.03 Payments to states, legislative proposal subject to PAYGO			–106
02.04 Timber roads, purchaser elections	6	6	6
02.05 Road and trails for States, National Forest Fund	27	26	25
02.06 Timber salvage sales	90	128	119
02.07 Deposits, brush disposal	21	26	26
02.08 Recreational fee demonstration program	26	25	26
02.09 Rents and charges for quarters	7	8	8
02.10 National Grasslands	–4	6	6
02.11 Miscellaneous special funds, Forest Service	4	2	2
02.12 National forests fund, Interior	8	14	10
02.13 Timber sales pipeline restoration fund	3	6	6
02.14 Midwin national tallgrass prairie rental fees	1		
02.15 Road and trails for States, legislative proposal subject to PAYGO			–25
02.16 Timber salvage sales, legislative proposal subject to PAYGO			–119
02.17 Timber sales pipeline restoration fund, legislative proposal subject to PAYGO			–6
02.18 National Grasslands, legislative proposal subject to PAYGO			–6
02.19 Miscellaneous special funds, legislative proposal subject to PAYGO			6
02.99 Total receipts	228	361	84
04.00 Total: Balances and collections	568	635	366
Appropriation:			
05.01 Forest Service permanent appropriations	–294	–353	–336
05.03 Legislative proposal subject to PAYGO			262
05.99 Subtotal appropriation	–294	–353	–74
07.99 Total balance, end of year	274	282	292

Program and Financing (in millions of dollars)

Identification code 12–9921–0–2–999	1999 actual	2000 est.	2001 est.
Obligations by program activity:			
00.01 Payments to States, National forest fund	103	113	105
00.02 Payment to Minnesota	1	1	1
00.03 Payments to counties, National grasslands	5	6	6
00.04 Recreation fee collection costs	1	1	1
00.05 Recreation demonstration pilot project	20	39	26
00.06 Timber purchaser roads constructed by Forest Service	2	6	8
00.07 Timber salvage sales	124	119	119
00.08 Roads and trails for States	33	35	32
00.09 Expenses, brush disposal	17	21	18
00.10 Restoration of forest lands and improvements	32	4	7
00.11 Operation and maintenance of quarters	7	8	8
00.13 Pipeline restoration fund	4	6	6
00.14 Land between the lakes		4	4
10.00 Total new obligations	349	363	341
Budgetary resources available for obligation:			
21.40 Unobligated balance available, start of year	291	268	263
22.00 New budget authority (gross)	317	359	342
22.10 Resources available from recoveries of prior year obligations	7		
23.90 Total budgetary resources available for obligation	615	627	605
23.95 Total new obligations	–349	–363	–341
24.40 Unobligated balance available, end of year	268	263	264
New budget authority (gross), detail:			
Mandatory:			
60.25 Appropriation (special fund, indefinite)	294	353	336
61.00 Transferred to other accounts	–4		
62.00 Transferred from other accounts	27	6	6
62.50 Appropriation (total mandatory)	317	358	342
Change in unpaid obligations:			
72.40 Unpaid obligations, start of year: Obligated balance, start of year	64	38	53
73.10 Total new obligations	349	363	341
73.20 Total outlays (gross)	–367	–348	–336
73.45 Adjustments in unexpired accounts	–7		
74.40 Unpaid obligations, end of year: Obligated balance, end of year	38	53	58
Outlays (gross), detail:			
86.97 Outlays from new mandatory authority	302	311	289
86.98 Outlays from mandatory balances	64	38	47
87.00 Total outlays (gross)	367	348	336
Net budget authority and outlays:			
89.00 Budget authority	317	359	342
90.00 Outlays	366	348	336

Summary of Budget Authority and Outlays

(in millions of dollars)

Enacted/requested:	*1999 actual*	*2000 est.*	*2001 est.*
Budget Authority	317	358	342
Outlays	366	349	336
Legislative proposal, subject to PAYGO:			
Budget Authority			–429
Outlays			–278
Total:			
Budget Authority	317	358	–87
Outlays	366	349	58

Operation and maintenance of quarters.—Quarters rental deductions are collected from employees occupying Forest Service facilities. Amounts are deposited into a special fund and are available for the maintenance and operation of employee-occupied quarters. (5 U.S.C. 5911)

Resource management, timber receipts.—Funds in this special account are available for trail maintenance, reconstruction, and construction; wildlife and fisheries habitat management; soil, water, and air management; cultural/heritage resource management; wilderness management; reforestation; and timber sale administration and management.

Recreation fee demonstration program.—Pursuant to Sec. 315 of Title III—General Provisions, Omnibus Consolidated Rescissions and Appropriations Act of 1996, Public Law 104–134 of April 26, 1996 as amended, amounts collected at fee demonstration areas, sites, or projects are available for maintenance and development of recreation facilities. A legislative proposal to authorize collection and use of all recreation receipts in fiscal year 2002 and after is included in the budget.

Midewin National Tallgrass Prairie rental fees.—Monies received under a special use authorization (issued under subsection (b) of Public Law 104–106, Title XXIX, Subtitle A, Section 2915, after distribution to the State of Illinois and affected counties pursuant to the Act of May 23, 1908) are available to cover the cost to the United States of prairie improvement work at the Midewin National Tallgrass Prairie.

Midewin National Tallgrass Prairie Restoration Fund.—Monies received from user fees and the salvage value proceeds from sale of any facilities and improvements pursuant to Section 2915(d) and (e) of Public Law 104–106, as amended by Public Law 105–83, are available to cover the costs of restoration and administrative activities.

Payment to Minnesota.—At the close of each fiscal year, the State of Minnesota is paid 0.75 percent of the appraised value of certain Superior National Forest lands in the counties of Cook Lake and St. Louis for distribution to these counties (16 U.S.C. 577g).

General and special funds—Continued

FOREST SERVICE PERMANENT APPROPRIATIONS—Continued

Payments to counties, National Grasslands.—Of the revenues received in a calendar year from the use of National Grasslands, 25 percent is paid to the counties in which such land is situated for funding local schools and roads (7 U.S.C. 1012).

Payments to States, National Forests Fund.—With minor exceptions, 25 percent of the money received from the National Forests, including all the collections under 16 U.S.C. 576b, and all amounts allowed any timber purchaser for construction of roads, is paid at the end of each fiscal year to the States for funding local schools and roads of the county in which such forests are situated (16 U.S.C. 500 and 97 Stat. 1123). Proposed legislation, to be transmitted later, would stabilize funding levels through payments to States, beginning in 2001, to provide predictable payment for county roads and schools.

Expenses, brush disposal.—Funds from payments by purchasers of National Forest timber to dispose of or treat slash and other debris that result from cutting operations (16 U.S.C. 490). Proposed legislation, to be transmitted later would pool certain receipt-based funding, including the Salvage and Knutson-Vandenberg Funds into the Healthy Investments in Rural Environments program. Funding would be available for priority multiple-use projects in the locations of greatest need, while emphasizing employment opportunities like Jobs-in-the-Woods.

Licensee programs, Forest Service.—Funds from fees for the use of characters by private enterprises are collected under regulations promulgated by the Secretary as follows:

Smokey Bear.—For furthering the nationwide forest fire prevention campaign (16 U.S.C. 580(2)).

Woodsy Owl.—For promoting wise use of the environment and programs which foster maintenance and improvement of environmental quality (16 U.S.C. 580(1)).

Restoration of northern forestlands and improvements.—Funds from claim settlements involving damage to lands or improvements and from forfeiture of deposits and bonds by permittees and timber purchasers are used for the restoration made necessary by the action which led to the settlement of forfeiture (16 U.S.C. 579c).

Timber purchaser roads constructed by Forest Service.—Funds from timber receipts for Government constructed permanent roads for purchasers of timber who qualify as small businesses and elect to have the Forest Service construct the roads designated under the timber sale contract where costs exceed $20,000 (16 U.S.C. 472a(i)).

Recreation fee collection costs.—Under authority of Section 10002(b) of the Omnibus Budget Reconciliation Act of 1993 (P.L. 103–66), which amended Section 4(i)(1) of the L&WCF Act, the Secretaries of Agriculture and Interior are authorized to withhold a portion of all recreation fees collected (not to exceed 15 percent), to be available during the current fiscal year, without further appropriation to cover fee collection costs.

Tongass timber supply fund.—Funds from sales of Alaska timber to maintain the timber supply from the Tongass National Forest at a specified level (16 U.S.C. 539d).

Timber salvage sales.—Funds are used for salvage of insect-infested, dead, damaged, or down timber, and to remove associated trees for stand improvement (16 U.S.C. 472a(h)).

Timber Sales Pipeline Restoration Fund.—As authorized under Section 327 of the Omnibus Consolidated Recissions and Appropriations Act of 1996, funds from revenues received from timber sales released under Section 2001(k) of the 1995 Supplemental Appropriations for Disaster Assistance and Recissions Act for the purpose of restoring the timber pipeline and funding the backlog of recreation projects on National Forest System lands.

Object Classification (in millions of dollars)

Identification code 12–9921–0–2–999		1999 actual	2000 est.	2001 est.
	Personnel compensation:			
11.1	Full-time permanent	86	81	73
11.3	Other than full-time permanent	11	10	9
11.5	Other personnel compensation	4	4	3
11.9	Total personnel compensation	101	95	85
12.1	Civilian personnel benefits	23	22	20
13.0	Benefits for former personnel	1	1	1
21.0	Travel and transportation of persons	2	2	2
22.0	Transportation of things	1	1	1
23.1	Rental payments to GSA	1	1	1
23.2	Rental payments to others	5	6	6
23.3	Communications, utilities, and miscellaneous charges	3	4	4
24.0	Printing and reproduction	1	1	1
25.2	Other services	49	69	67
26.0	Supplies and materials	23	31	31
31.0	Equipment	3	4	4
32.0	Land and structures	27	6	6
41.0	Grants, subsidies, and contributions	109	120	112
99.9	Total new obligations	349	363	341

Personnel Summary

Identification code 12–9921–0–2–999		1999 actual	2000 est.	2001 est.
1001	Total compensable workyears: Full-time equivalent employment	2,697	2,535	2,291

MISCELLANEOUS PERMANENT APPROPRIATIONS

(Legislative proposal, subject to PAYGO)

Program and Financing (in millions of dollars)

Identification code 12–9921–4–2–999		1999 actual	2000 est.	2001 est.
	Obligations by program activity:			
00.01	Payments to States, National forest fund			–105
00.02	Payment to Minnesota			–1
00.03	Payments to counties, National grasslands			–6
00.07	Timber salvage sales			–119
00.08	Roads and trails for States			–25
00.13	Pipeline restoration fund			–6
10.00	Total new obligations			–262
	Budgetary resources available for obligation:			
22.00	New budget authority (gross)			–429
23.95	Total new obligations			262
24.40	Unobligated balance available, end of year			–167
	New budget authority (gross), detail:			
	Mandatory:			
60.25	Appropriation (special fund, indefinite)			–262
61.00	Transferred to other accounts			–167
62.50	Appropriation (total mandatory)			–429
	Change in unpaid obligations:			
73.10	Total new obligations			–262
73.20	Total outlays (gross)			278
73.31	Obligated balance transferred to other accounts			–30
74.40	Unpaid obligations, end of year: Obligated balance, end of year			–14
	Outlays (gross), detail:			
86.97	Outlays from new mandatory authority			–248
86.98	Outlays from mandatory balances			–30
87.00	Total outlays (gross)			–278
	Net budget authority and outlays:			
89.00	Budget authority			–429
90.00	Outlays			–278

Current receipt sharing payments ("Twenty-Five Percent Fund") are proposed to be replaced by a stable, guaranteed level of payments based on the concept of the guaranteed payments "Payments to States, Northern Spotted Own Guarantee". See the legislative proposal following that account.

The Recreation Fee Demonstration Program is proposed to be permanently extended beyond 2001, and would authorize the direct expenditure of all recreation fees collected by the Forest Service and Department of Interior agencies.

This proposal would permit non-timber interests to bid on timber sales to enable recreation and conservation groups to participate in auctions of timber harvest rights from federal lands. The proposal would alter the 3-year requirement for harvesting timber from national forests. The proposal serves to increase competition as more parties could bid on timber sales. In addition, receipts would increase because environmental and recreation groups may bid greater than the market value of the timber, reflecting values different than only timber uses. A portion of the receipts would be used for community employment and stability work, such as using Jobs-in-the Woods restoration projects.

Proposed legislation would also require that the minimum bid level, including rollbacks, on timber sales for commodity purposes, should be equal to the costs of sale preparation and harvest management. The proposal would not apply to stewardship timber sales. This will better enable the agency to establish minimum appraisal levels for timber sales. In 1914, minimum bids were set at 0.5/mbf, which was intended to cover the costs of sale preparation and administration. In the 1950s, existing minimum rates were reviewed and Regional Foresters instructed to set a minimum price level of "at least $1.00/mbf, which was deemed to be the absolute minimum cost required to prepare and administer commercial timber sales."

In addition, the proposal would require a new timber contract to avoid future damages. The proposal would establish new contract cancellation procedures that would reimburse timber sale purchasers for out-of-pocket expenses, but not for the cost of replacement timber as current contracts now do. It would also require that the timber sale purchaser obtain general liability insurance to protect the government from liability; the contract would transfer title for the timber to the purchaser at the time of payment, when the timber is cut, rather than after the timber is removed from the sale site. The new contract also would establish that timber sales purchasers could not cut undesignated trees.

The proposal would also require the receipt of fair market value from ski resorts on National Forest System lands in order to ensure that the rental charges remain fair and equitable to both the United States and the ski area permittees as mandated by Congress on the 1996 Omnibus Parks bill.

A concession reform proposal would amend the Granger-Thye Act of 1950 to authorize up to 15 pilot projects to enable the private sector to reconstruct, construct, or maintain, as well as to operate federally owned facilities in a public/private pilot basis. The proposal would target resorts, campgrounds, and marinas, to improve recreation opportunities and enhance visitor experiences, while reducing the large facility maintenance backlog. The proposal would also require that the agency collect fair market value for recreation concessions other than ski areas using appraisals, a competitive bid process, or other method based on sound business management principles, as appropriate. Such fees collected would be available for spending without further appropriation for the purposes of increased concession opportunities and enhanced visitor services, including infrastructure maintenance.

Fees charged for commercial film and photography would be retained by the Forest Service for the purpose of enhancing national forest recreational opportunities, increasing watershed and habitat conservation and restoration, and administration and management of special uses on National Forest System lands. Funds are available until expended, with the authority to spend one year after funds were collected.

Legislation would require the collection of market values for special use permits for linear rights-of-way special uses, such as powerlines and pipelines. Increased fee collections, above the 2000 collections would be retained by the Forest Service for the purpose of enhancing national forest recreational opportunities, increasing watershed and habitat conservation and restoration, and administration and management of special uses on National Forest System lands. Funds are available until expended, with the authority to spend one year after funds were collected.

Proposed legislation would require all timber sales to be sold using the sealed bidding method, rather than open bids as is now the case in some places. The change would enhance the opportunities for achieving market value for timber sales on federal lands. A waiver permitting open bids would be available as determined by the Forest Service Chief where oral auction would yield higher bids.

Object Classification (in millions of dollars)

Identification code 12–9921–4–2–999		1999 actual	2000 est.	2001 est.
	Personnel compensation:			
11.1	Full-time permanent			−56
11.3	Other than full-time permanent			−7
11.5	Other personnel compensation			−3
11.9	Total personnel compensation			−66
12.1	Civilian personnel benefits			−15
13.0	Benefits for former personnel			−1
21.0	Travel and transportation of persons			−2
22.0	Transportation of things			−1
23.1	Rental payments to GSA			−1
23.2	Rental payments to others			−3
23.3	Communications, utilities, and miscellaneous charges			−2
24.0	Printing and reproduction			−1
25.2	Other services			−44
26.0	Supplies and materials			−12
31.0	Equipment			−2
41.0	Grants, subsidies, and contributions			−112
99.9	Total new obligations			−262

Personnel Summary

Identification code 12–9921–4–2–999		1999 actual	2000 est.	2001 est.
1001	Total compensable workyears: Full-time equivalent employment			−1,759

Intragovernmental funds:

WORKING CAPITAL FUND

Program and Financing (in millions of dollars)

Identification code 12–4605–0–4–302		1999 actual	2000 est.	2001 est.
	Obligations by program activity:			
09.01	Operating expenses	110	115	112
09.02	Capital investment	48	36	35
10.00	Total new obligations	158	151	147
	Budgetary resources available for obligation:			
21.40	Unobligated balance available, start of year	106	115	98
22.00	New budget authority (gross)	165	134	134
22.10	Resources available from recoveries of prior year obligations	2		
23.90	Total budgetary resources available for obligation	273	249	232
23.95	Total new obligations	−158	−151	−147
24.40	Unobligated balance available, end of year	115	98	85

Intragovernmental funds—Continued

WORKING CAPITAL FUND—Continued

Program and Financing (in millions of dollars)—Continued

Identification code 12–4605–0–4–302		1999 actual	2000 est.	2001 est.
	New budget authority (gross), detail:			
	Mandatory:			
69.00	Offsetting collections (cash)	165	134	134
	Change in unpaid obligations:			
72.40	Unpaid obligations, start of year: Obligated balance, start of year	52	57	74
73.10	Total new obligations	158	151	147
73.20	Total outlays (gross)	–151	–134	–134
73.45	Adjustments in unexpired accounts	–2		
74.40	Unpaid obligations, end of year: Obligated balance, end of year	57	74	87
	Outlays (gross), detail:			
86.97	Outlays from new mandatory authority	151	134	134
	Offsets:			
	Against gross budget authority and outlays:			
88.00	Offsetting collections (cash) from: Federal sources	–165	–134	–134
	Net budget authority and outlays:			
89.00	Budget authority			
90.00	Outlays	–14		

The Working Capital Fund is a self-sustaining revolving fund that provides services to National Forests, to Research Experiment Stations, to other Federal agencies when necessary, to State and private agencies as provided by law, and to persons who cooperate with the Forest Service in fire control and other authorized programs.

Forestry-related supply and support services include:

Equipment Services.—The fund owns, operates, maintains, replaces, and repairs common-use, motor-driven, and similar equipment. This equipment is rented to administrative units, that is, National Forests, Research Experiment Stations, and other units, and, in some cases, to other agencies, at rates which recover the cost of operation, repair and maintenance, management, and depreciation. The rates also include an increment which provides additional cash which, when added to depreciation earnings and the residual value of equipment, provides sufficient funds to replace the equipment.

Aircraft Services.—The fund operates, maintains, and repairs Forest Service owned aircraft used in fire surveillance and suppression and in other Forest Service programs. The aircraft are rented to National Forests, Research Experiment Stations, and in some cases to other agencies, at rates which recover the cost of depreciation, operation, maintenance, repair, and improvements in the airworthiness of the aircraft. Aircraft replacement costs are financed from either appropriated funds or the Forest Service Working Capital Fund, or a combination of both.

Computer Services.—The Fund provides computer hardware, software, and radio equipment.

Supply Services.—The fund operates the following common services, and provides for cost-recovery of Working Capital Fund Program Management:

Photo reproduction laboratories that store, reproduce, and supply aerial photographs, aerial maps, and other photographs of National Forest lands. Photographic reproductions are sold to National Forests, Experiment Stations, and others at cost.

Sign shops that manufacture and supply special signs for the National Forests for use in regulating traffic and as information to the public and other users of the National Forests. Signs are sold to National Forests and Experiment Stations at cost.

Seed supply services that provide tree seed for direct seeding or sowing in nurseries for the production of trees. Includes purchase or collection of cones, extraction of seeds, cleaning and testing, and storage and delivery. Operates in conjunction with tree nurseries; that is, forest tree nurseries and cold storage facilities for storage of tree seedlings. Tree seedlings are sold to National Forests, State foresters, and other cooperators at cost.

Object Classification (in millions of dollars)

Identification code 12–4605–0–4–302		1999 actual	2000 est.	2001 est.
13.0	Benefits for former personnel	2	2	2
21.0	Travel and transportation of persons	3	3	3
23.2	Rental payments to others	1	1	1
23.3	Communications, utilities, and miscellaneous charges	2	2	1
25.2	Other services	1	1	1
26.0	Supplies and materials	22	20	19
31.0	Equipment	127	122	120
99.9	Total new obligations	158	151	147

Note.—Personnel totals are included with personnel totals of all other Forest Service programs.

Trust Funds

FOREST SERVICE TRUST FUNDS

Unavailable Collections (in millions of dollars)

Identification code 12–9974–0–7–302		1999 actual	2000 est.	2001 est.
	Balance, start of year:			
01.99	Balance, start of year			
	Receipts:			
02.01	Forest Service Cooperative fund	163	166	210
02.02	Transfers from general fund of amounts equal to certain customs duties	30	30	30
02.04	Forest Service Cooperative fund, legislative proposal subject to PAYGO			–160
02.05	Transfers from general fund of amounts equal to certain customs duties, legislative proposal subject to PAYGO			–30
02.06	Transfer from TVA for land between the lakes trust fund			1
02.99	Total receipts	193	196	51
	Appropriation:			
05.01	Forest Service trust funds	–193	–196	–240
05.03	Legislative proposal subject to PAYGO			190
05.99	Subtotal appropriation	–193	–196	–50
07.99	Total balance, end of year			1

Program and Financing (in millions of dollars)

Identification code 12–9974–0–7–302		1999 actual	2000 est.	2001 est.
	Obligations by program activity:			
10.00	Total new obligations	117	239	216
	Budgetary resources available for obligation:			
21.40	Unobligated balance available, start of year	286	369	327
22.00	New budget authority (gross)	193	196	240
22.10	Resources available from recoveries of prior year obligations	7		
23.90	Total budgetary resources available for obligation	486	565	567
23.95	Total new obligations	–117	–239	–216
24.40	Unobligated balance available, end of year	369	327	352
	New budget authority (gross), detail:			
	Mandatory:			
60.27	Appropriation (trust fund, indefinite)	193	196	240
	Change in unpaid obligations:			
72.40	Unpaid obligations, start of year: Obligated balance, start of year	61	39	83
73.10	Total new obligations	117	239	216
73.20	Total outlays (gross)	–133	–195	–231
73.45	Adjustments in unexpired accounts	–7		

		1999 actual	2000 est.	2001 est.
74.40	Unpaid obligations, end of year: Obligated balance, end of year	39	83	68
	Outlays (gross), detail:			
86.97	Outlays from new mandatory authority	72	157	192
86.98	Outlays from mandatory balances	61	38	39
87.00	Total outlays (gross)	133	195	231
	Net budget authority and outlays:			
89.00	Budget authority	193	196	240
90.00	Outlays	133	195	231

Summary of Budget Authority and Outlays

(in millions of dollars)

	1999 actual	2000 est.	2001 est.
Enacted/requested:			
Budget Authority	193	196	240
Outlays	133	195	231
Legislative proposal, subject to PAYGO:			
Budget Authority			–459
Outlays			–190
Total:			
Budget Authority	193	196	–219
Outlays	133	195	41

Reforestation trust fund.—Amounts from this account are used for reforestation as authorized by 16 U.S.C. 1606a (d) and (e).

Cooperative work trust fund.—Funds including deposits from purchasers of timber, are received and used for specified work in forest investigations, protection, and improvement of the National Forest System, including protection, reforestation, and administration of private lands adjacent to National Forests (7 U.S.C. 2269; 16 U.S.C. 498, 535, 565a, 572, 572a, 576b, 1643; and 31 U.S.C. 1321).

Object Classification (in millions of dollars)

Identification code 12–9974–0–7–302		1999 actual	2000 est.	2001 est.
	Personnel compensation:			
11.1	Full-time permanent	62	55	53
11.3	Other than full-time permanent	9	8	7
11.5	Other personnel compensation	3	3	3
11.9	Total personnel compensation	74	66	63
12.1	Civilian personnel benefits	16	14	14
13.0	Benefits for former personnel	1	1	1
21.0	Travel and transportation of persons	3	3	3
23.1	Rental payments to GSA	1	1	1
23.2	Rental payments to others	4	8	6
23.3	Communications, utilities, and miscellaneous charges	1	3	2
25.2	Other services	10	130	114
26.0	Supplies and materials	4	7	6
31.0	Equipment	1	2	2
32.0	Land and structures	1	2	2
41.0	Grants, subsidies, and contributions	1	1	1
44.0	Refunds		1	1
99.9	Total new obligations	117	239	216

Personnel Summary

Identification code 12–9974–0–7–302		1999 actual	2000 est.	2001 est.
1001	Total compensable workyears: Full-time equivalent employment	2,038	1,804	1,742

FOREST SERVICE TRUST FUNDS

(Legislative proposal, subject to PAYGO)

Program and Financing (in millions of dollars)

Identification code 12–9974–4–7–302		1999 actual	2000 est.	2001 est.
	Obligations by program activity:			
10.00	Total new obligations			–190
	Budgetary resources available for obligation:			
22.00	New budget authority (gross)			–459
23.95	Total new obligations			190
24.40	Unobligated balance available, end of year			–269
	New budget authority (gross), detail:			
	Mandatory:			
60.27	Appropriation (trust fund, indefinite)			–190
61.00	Transferred to other accounts			–269
62.50	Appropriation (total mandatory)			–459
	Change in unpaid obligations:			
73.10	Total new obligations			–190
73.20	Total outlays (gross)			190
73.31	Obligated balance transferred to other accounts			–38
74.40	Unpaid obligations, end of year: Obligated balance, end of year			–38
	Outlays (gross), detail:			
86.97	Outlays from new mandatory authority			–152
86.98	Outlays from mandatory balances			–38
87.00	Total outlays (gross)			–190
	Net budget authority and outlays:			
89.00	Budget authority			–459
90.00	Outlays			–190

Proposed legislation would pool certain receipt-based funding, including the Salvage and Knutson-Vandenberg Fund into the Healthy Investments in Rural Environments Program. Funds would be available for priority multiple-use projects in locations of greatest need, while emphasizing employment opportunities, like Jobs-in-the Woods.

Object Classification (in millions of dollars)

Identification code 12–9974–4–7–302		1999 actual	2000 est.	2001 est.
	Personnel compensation:			
11.1	Full-time permanent			–40
11.3	Other than full-time permanent			–6
11.5	Other personnel compensation			–2
11.9	Total personnel compensation			–48
12.1	Civilian personnel benefits			–10
21.0	Travel and transportation of persons			–1
22.0	Transportation of things			–3
23.1	Rental payments to GSA			–1
23.2	Rental payments to others			–5
23.3	Communications, utilities, and miscellaneous charges			–2
25.2	Other services			–89
26.0	Supplies and materials			–4
31.0	Equipment			–2
32.0	Land and structures			–1
41.0	Grants, subsidies, and contributions			–24
99.9	Total new obligations			–190

Personnel Summary

Identification code 12–9974–4–7–302		1999 actual	2000 est.	2001 est.
1001	Total compensable workyears: Full-time equivalent employment			–1,005

ALLOCATIONS AND ALLOTMENTS RECEIVED FROM OTHER ACCOUNTS

Note.—Obligations incurred under allocations or allotments from other accounts are included in the schedule of the parent appropriations, as follows:

Agriculture:
- Agricultural Research Service.
- Animal and Plant Health Inspection Service.
- Natural Resources Conservation Service.
  - Watershed and flood prevention operations.
  - Resource conservation and development.
  - Watershed planning.
  - River basin surveys and investigations.
- Conservation Reserve Program.
- Department Administration:
  - Hazardous materials management.
- Rural Housing; Rural community fire protection grants.

Transportation: Federal Highway Administration, Highway Trust Fund.

Labor: Employment and Training Administration, Training and employment services.

ADMINISTRATIVE PROVISIONS, FOREST SERVICE

Appropriations to the Forest Service for the current fiscal year shall be available for: (1) purchase of not to exceed [110] *132* passenger motor vehicles of which [15] *13* will be used primarily for law enforcement purposes and of which [109] *129* shall be for replacement; acquisition of 25 passenger motor vehicles from excess sources, and hire of such vehicles; operation and maintenance of aircraft, the purchase of not to exceed [three] *six* for replacement only, and acquisition of sufficient aircraft from excess sources to maintain the operable fleet at [213] [*198*] *192* aircraft for use in Forest Service wildland fire programs and other Forest Service programs; notwithstanding other provisions of law, existing aircraft being replaced may be sold, with proceeds derived or trade-in value used to offset the purchase price for the replacement aircraft; (2) services pursuant to 7 U.S.C. 2225, and not to exceed $100,000 for employment under 5 U.S.C. 3109; (3) purchase, erection, and alteration of buildings and other public improvements (7 U.S.C. 2250); (4) acquisition of land, waters, and interests therein, pursuant to 7 U.S.C. 428a; (5) for expenses pursuant to the Volunteers in the National Forest Act of 1972 (16 U.S.C. 558a, 558d, and 558a note); (6) the cost of uniforms as authorized by 5 U.S.C. 5901–5902; and (7) for debt collection contracts in accordance with 31 U.S.C. 3718(c).

[None of the funds made available under this Act shall be obligated or expended to abolish any region, to move or close any regional office for National Forest System administration of the Forest Service, Department of Agriculture without the consent of the House and Senate Committees on Appropriations.]

Any appropriations or funds available to the Forest Service may be transferred to the Wildland Fire Management appropriation for forest firefighting, emergency rehabilitation of burned-over or damaged lands or waters under its jurisdiction, and fire preparedness due to severe burning conditions [if and only if all previously appropriated emergency contingent funds under the heading "Wildland Fire Management" have been released by the President and apportioned].

Funds appropriated to the Forest Service shall be available for assistance to or through the Agency for International Development and the Foreign Agricultural Service in connection with forest and rangeland research, technical information, and assistance in foreign countries, and shall be available to support forestry and related natural resource activities outside the United States and its territories and possessions, including technical assistance, education and training, and cooperation with United States and international organizations.

[None of the funds made available to the Forest Service under this Act shall be subject to transfer under the provisions of section 702(b) of the Department of Agriculture Organic Act of 1944 (7 U.S.C. 2257) or 7 U.S.C. 147b unless the proposed transfer is approved in advance by the House and Senate Committees on Appropriations in compliance with the reprogramming procedures contained in House Report No. 105–163.]

[None of the funds available to the Forest Service may be reprogrammed without the advance approval of the House and Senate Committees on Appropriations in accordance with the procedures contained in House Report No. 105–163.]

[No funds appropriated to the Forest Service shall be transferred to the Working Capital Fund of the Department of Agriculture without the approval of the Chief of the Forest Service.]

Funds available to the Forest Service shall be available to conduct a program of not less than [$1,000,000] *$4,000,000* for high priority projects within the scope of the approved budget which shall be carried out by the Youth Conservation Corps as authorized by the Act of August 13, 1970, as amended by Public Law 93–408.

Of the funds available to the Forest Service, [$1,500] *$2,500* is available to the Chief of the Forest Service for official reception and representation expenses.

To the greatest extent possible, and in accordance with the Final Amendment to the Shawnee National Forest Plan, none of the funds available in this Act shall be used for preparation of timber sales using clearcutting or other forms of even-aged management in hardwood stands in the Shawnee National Forest, Illinois.

Pursuant to sections 405(b) and 410(b) of Public Law 101–593, of the funds available to the Forest Service, up to $2,250,000 may be advanced in a lump sum as Federal financial assistance to the National Forest Foundation, without regard to when the Foundation incurs expenses, for administrative expenses or projects on or benefitting National Forest System lands or related to Forest Service programs: *Provided*, That of the Federal funds made available to the Foundation, no more than $400,000 shall be available for administrative expenses: *Provided further*, That the Foundation shall obtain, by the end of the period of Federal financial assistance, private contributions to match on at least one-for-one basis funds made available by the Forest Service: *Provided further*, That the Foundation may transfer Federal funds to a non-Federal recipient for a project at the same rate that the recipient has obtained the non-Federal matching funds: *Provided further*, That hereafter, the National Forest Foundation may hold Federal funds made available but not immediately disbursed and may use any interest or other investment income earned (before, on, or after the date of the enactment of this Act) on Federal funds to carry out the purposes of Public Law 101–593: *Provided further*, That such investments may be made only in interest-bearing obligations of the United States or in obligations guaranteed as to both principal and interest by the United States.

Pursuant to section 2(b)(2) of Public Law 98–244, $2,650,000 of the funds available to the Forest Service shall be available for matching funds to the National Fish and Wildlife Foundation, as authorized by 16 U.S.C. 3701–3709, and may be advanced in a lump sum as Federal financial assistance, without regard to when expenses are incurred, for projects on or benefitting National Forest System lands or related to Forest Service programs: *Provided*, That the Foundation shall obtain, by the end of the period of Federal financial assistance, private contributions to match on at least one-for-one basis funds advanced by the Forest Service: *Provided further*, That the Foundation may transfer Federal funds to a non-Federal recipient for a project at the same rate that the recipient has obtained the non-Federal matching funds.

Funds appropriated to the Forest Service shall be available for interactions with and providing technical assistance to rural communities for sustainable rural development purposes.

[Notwithstanding any other provision of law, 80 percent of the funds appropriated to the Forest Service in the "National Forest System" and "Reconstruction and Construction" accounts and planned to be allocated to activities under the "Jobs in the Woods" program for projects on National Forest land in the State of Washington may be granted directly to the Washington State Department of Fish and Wildlife for accomplishment of planned projects. Twenty percent of said funds shall be retained by the Forest Service for planning and administering projects. Project selection and prioritization shall be accomplished by the Forest Service with such consultation with the State of Washington as the Forest Service deems appropriate.] *Notwithstanding any other provision of law, up to 80 percent of the funds appropriated to the Forest Service in the "National Forest System", "Infrastructure", and "Wildland Fire Management" accounts, which are planned for support of "Jobs in the Woods," Youth Conservation Corps, and similar such special employment programs to employ displaced timber workers and other skilled rural workers, for projects on National Forest land, may be granted directly to State agencies for accomplishment of planned projects. Twenty percent of said funds may be retained by the Forest Service for planning and administering projects. The Forest Service in consultation with respective state agencies shall accomplish project selection and prioritization, as the Forest Service deems appropriate.*

Funds appropriated to the Forest Service shall be available for payments to counties within the Columbia River Gorge National Scenic Area, pursuant to sections 14(c)(1) and (2), and section 16(a)(2) of Public Law 99–663.

The Secretary of Agriculture is authorized to enter into grants, contracts, and cooperative agreements as appropriate with the Pinchot Institute for Conservation, as well as with public and other private agencies, organizations, institutions, and individuals, to provide for the development, administration, maintenance, or restoration of land, facilities, or Forest Service programs, at the Grey Towers National Historic Landmark: *Provided*, That, subject to such terms and conditions as the Secretary of Agriculture may prescribe, any such public or private agency, organization, institution, or individual may solicit, accept, and administer private gifts of money and real or personal property for the benefit of, or in connection with, the activities and services at the Grey Towers National Historic Landmark: *Provided further*, That such gifts may be accepted notwithstanding the fact that a donor conducts business with the Department of Agriculture in any capacity.

Funds appropriated to the Forest Service shall be available, as determined by the Secretary, for payments to Del Norte County,

California, pursuant to sections 13(e) and 14 of the Smith River National Recreation Area Act (Public Law 101-612).

[For purposes of the Southeast Alaska Economic Disaster Fund as set forth in section 101(c) of Public Law 104–134, the direct grants provided from the Fund shall be considered direct payments for purposes of all applicable law except that these direct grants may not be used for lobbying activities: *Provided*, That a total of $22,000,000 is hereby appropriated and shall be deposited into the Southeast Alaska Economic Disaster Fund established pursuant to Public Law 104–134, as amended, without further appropriation or fiscal year limitation of which $10,000,000 shall be distributed in fiscal year 2000, $7,000,000 shall be distributed in fiscal year 2001, and $5,000,000 shall be distributed in fiscal year 2002. The Secretary of Agriculture shall allocate the funds to local communities suffering economic hardship because of mill closures and economic dislocation in the timber industry to employ unemployed timber workers and for related community redevelopment projects as follows:

(1) in fiscal year 2000, $4,000,000 for the Ketchikan Gateway Borough, $2,000,000 for the City of Petersburg, $2,000,000 for the City and Borough of Sitka, and $2,000,000 for the Metlakatla Indian Community;

(2) in fiscal year 2001, $3,000,000 for the Ketchikan Gateway Borough, $1,000,000 for the City of Petersburg, $1,500,000 for the City and Borough of Sitka, and $1,500,000 for the Metlakatla Indian Community; and

(3) in fiscal year 2002, $3,000,000 for the Ketchikan Gateway Borough, $500,000 for the City and Borough of Sitka, and $1,500,000 for the Metlakatla Indian Community.]

Notwithstanding any other provision of law, any appropriations or funds available to the Forest Service not to exceed $500,000 may be used to reimburse the Office of the General Counsel (OGC), Department of Agriculture, for travel and related expenses incurred as a result of OGC assistance or participation requested by the Forest Service at meetings, training sessions, management reviews, land purchase negotiations and similar non-litigation related matters. [Future budget justifications for both the Forest Service and the Department of Agriculture should clearly display the sums previously transferred and the requested funding transfers.]

[No employee of the Department of Agriculture may be detailed or assigned from an agency or office funded by this Act to any other agency or office of the department for more than 30 days unless the individual's employing agency or office is fully reimbursed by the receiving agency or office for the salary and expenses of the employee for the period of assignment.]

The Forest Service shall fund overhead, national commitments, indirect expenses, and any other category for use of funds which are expended at any units, that are not directly related to the accomplishment of specific work on-the-ground (referred to as "indirect expenditures"), from funds available to the Forest Service, unless otherwise prohibited by law: *Provided*, That the Forest Service shall implement and adhere to the definitions of indirect expenditures established pursuant to Public Law 105–277 on a nationwide basis without flexibility for modification by any organizational level except the Washington Office, and when changed by the Washington Office, such changes in definition shall be reported in budget requests submitted by the Forest Service[: *Provided further*, That the Forest Service shall provide in all future budget justifications, planned indirect expenditures in accordance with the definitions, summarized and displayed to the Regional, Station, Area, and detached unit office level. The justification shall display the estimated source and amount of indirect expenditures, by expanded budget line item, of funds in the agency's annual budget justification. The display shall include appropriated funds and the Knutson-Vandenberg, Brush Disposal, Cooperative Work-Other, and Salvage Sale funds. Changes between estimated and actual indirect expenditures shall be reported in subsequent budget justifications: *Provided further*, That during fiscal year 2000 the Secretary shall limit total annual indirect obligations from the Brush Disposal, Cooperative Work-Other, Knutson-Vandenberg, Reforestation, Salvage Sale, and Roads and Trails funds to 20 percent of the total obligations from each fund].

Any appropriations or funds available to the Forest Service may be used for necessary expenses in the event of law enforcement emergencies as necessary to protect natural resources and public or employee safety[: *Provided*, That such amounts shall not exceed $500,000].

[From any unobligated balances available at the start of fiscal year 2000, the amount of $5,000,000 shall be allocated to the Alaska Region, in addition to the funds appropriated to sell timber in the Alaska Region under this Act, for expenses directly related to preparing sufficient additional timber for sale in the Alaska Region to establish a 3-year timber supply.]

[The Forest Service is authorized through the Forest Service existing budget to reimburse Harry Frey, $143,406 (1997 dollars) because his home was destroyed by arson on June 21, 1990 in retaliation for his work with the Forest Service.] *(Department of the Interior and Related Agencies Appropriations Act, 2000, as enacted by section 1000(a)(3) of the Consolidated Appropriations Act, 2000 (P.L. 106–113.)*

GENERAL FUND RECEIPT ACCOUNTS

(in millions of dollars)

	1999 actual	2000 est.	2001 est.
Offsetting receipts from the public:			
12–181100 National grasslands	18	24	24
12–222100 National forest fund	132	96	97
Legislative proposal, subject to PAYGO	....	....	8
12–223700 Collections to offset payments to states stabilization: Legislative proposal, subject to PAYGO	....	....	155
12–223800 Collections to offset healthy investments in rural environments: Legislative proposal, subject to PAYGO	....	....	285
12–270130 Agriculture credit insurance, downward reestimates of subsidies	....	417	....
12–270210 Rural electrification and telephone loans, negative subsidies	....	5	8
12–270230 Rural electrification and telephone loans, downward reestimates of subsidies	167	....	....
12–270310 Rural water and waste disposal, negative subsidies	18	....	....
12–270510 Rural community facility, negative subsidies	18	....	....
12–270630 Rural housing insurance, downward reestimates of subsidies	34	....	....
12–270710 Rural business and industry, negative subsidies	4	....	....
12–271030 Rural development loans, downward reestimates of subsidies	8	....	....
12–271130 Rural telephone bank loans, downward reestimates of subsidies	12	1	....
12–271330 Economic development loans, downward reestimates of subsidies	2	....	....
12–311000 Collections to offset road and trail fund: Legislative proposal, subject to PAYGO	....	....	25
General Fund Offsetting receipts from the public	413	543	602

OTHER CONSOLIDATED RECEIPT ACCOUNTS

(in millions of dollars)

	1999 actual	2000 est.	2001 est.
12–977210 Miscellaneous contributed funds	5	1	1

TITLE VII—GENERAL PROVISIONS

SEC. 701. Within the unit limit of cost fixed by law, appropriations and authorizations made for the Department of Agriculture for the fiscal year [2000] *2001* under this Act shall be available for the purchase, in addition to those specifically provided for, of not to exceed [365] *389* passenger motor vehicles, of which [361] *385* shall be for replacement only, and for the hire of such vehicles.

SEC. 702. Funds in this Act available to the Department of Agriculture shall be available for uniforms or allowances therefor as authorized by law (5 U.S.C. 5901–5902).

SEC. 703. Not less than $1,500,000 of the appropriations of the Department of Agriculture in this Act for research and service work authorized by the Acts of August 14, 1946, and July 28, 1954 (7 U.S.C. 427 and 1621–1629), and by chapter 63 of title 31, United States Code, shall be available for contracting in accordance with said Acts and chapter.

SEC. 704. The [cumulative total of transfers] *Secretary may transfer funds provided under this Act and other available unobligated balances of the Department of Agriculture* to the Working Capital Fund for the [purpose of accumulating growth capital for data services and National Finance Center operations shall not exceed $2,000,000: *Provided*, That no funds in this Act appropriated to an agency of the Department shall be transferred to the Working Capital Fund without the approval of the agency administrator] *acquisition of plant and capital equipment necessary for the delivery of financial, administrative, and information technology services.*

SEC. 705. New obligational authority provided for the following appropriation items in this Act shall remain available until expended: Animal and Plant Health Inspection Service, the contingency fund to meet emergency conditions, fruit fly program, integrated systems acquisition project, boll weevil program, up to 10 percent of the screwworm program, and up to $2,000,000 for costs associated with colocating regional offices; Food Safety and Inspection Service, field automation and information management project; funds appropriated for rental payments; Cooperative State Research, Education, and Extension Service, funds for competitive research grants (7 U.S.C. 450i(b)) and funds for the Native American Institutions Endowment Fund; Farm Service Agency, salaries and expenses funds made available to county committees; [and] Foreign Agricultural Service, middle-income country training program *and up to $2,000,000 of the Foreign Agricultural Service appropriation solely for the purpose of offsetting fluctuations in international currency exchange rates, subject to documentation by the Foreign Agricultural Service.*

SEC. 706. No part of any appropriation contained in this Act shall remain available for obligation beyond the current fiscal year unless expressly so provided herein.

SEC. 707. Not to exceed $50,000 of the appropriations available to the Department of Agriculture in this Act shall be available to provide appropriate orientation and language training pursuant to Public Law 94–449.

SEC. 708. No funds appropriated by this Act may be used to pay negotiated indirect cost rates on cooperative agreements or similar arrangements between the United States Department of Agriculture and nonprofit institutions in excess of 10 percent of the total direct cost of the agreement when the purpose of such cooperative arrangements is to carry out programs of mutual interest between the two parties. This does not preclude appropriate payment of indirect costs on grants and contracts with such institutions when such indirect costs are computed on a similar basis for all agencies for which appropriations are provided in this Act.

SEC. 709. Notwithstanding any other provision of this Act, commodities acquired by the Department in connection with the Commodity Credit Corporation and section 32 price support operations may be used, as authorized by law (15 U.S.C. 714c and 7 U.S.C. 612c), to provide commodities to individuals in cases of hardship as determined by the Secretary of Agriculture.

SEC. 710. None of the funds in this Act shall be available to restrict the authority of the Commodity Credit Corporation to lease space for its own use or to lease space on behalf of other agencies of the Department of Agriculture when such space will be jointly occupied.

SEC. 711. None of the funds in this Act shall be available to pay indirect costs charged against competitive agricultural research, education, or extension grant awards issued by the Cooperative State Research, Education, and Extension Service that exceed 19 percent of total Federal funds provided under each award: *Provided*, That notwithstanding section 1462 of the National Agricultural Research, Extension, and Teaching Policy Act of 1977 (7 U.S.C. 3310), funds provided by this Act for grants awarded competitively by the Cooperative State Research, Education, and Extension Service shall be available to pay full allowable indirect costs for each grant awarded under the Small Business Innovation Development Act of 1982, Public Law 97–219 (15 U.S.C. 638).

SEC. 712. Notwithstanding any other provision of this Act, all loan levels provided in this Act shall be considered estimates, not limitations.

[SEC. 713. Notwithstanding any other provision of law, effective on September 29, 1999, appropriations made available to the Rural Housing Insurance Fund Program Account for the costs of direct and guaranteed loans and to the Rural Housing Assistance Grants Account in fiscal years 1994, 1995, 1996, 1997, 1998, and 1999 shall remain available until expended to cover obligations made in each of those fiscal years respectively with regard to each account.]

SEC. [714] *713.* Appropriations to the Department of Agriculture for the cost of direct and guaranteed loans made available in fiscal year [2000] *2001* shall remain available until expended to cover obligations made in fiscal year [2000] *2001* for the following accounts: the rural development loan fund program account; the Rural Telephone Bank program account; the rural electrification and telecommunications loans program account; the Rural Housing Insurance Fund Program Account; and the rural economic development loans program account.

SEC. [715] *714.* Such sums as may be necessary for fiscal year [2000] *2001* pay raises for programs funded by this Act shall be absorbed within the levels appropriated by this Act.

SEC. [716] *715.* Notwithstanding the Federal Grant and Cooperative Agreement Act, marketing services of the Agricultural Marketing Service; Grain Inspection, Packers and Stockyards Administration; the Animal and Plant Health Inspection Service; and the food safety activities of the Food Safety and Inspection Service may use cooperative agreements to reflect a relationship between the Agricultural Marketing Service; the Grain Inspection, Packers and Stockyards Administration; the Animal and Plant Health Inspection Service; or the Food Safety and Inspection Service and a State or Cooperator to carry out agricultural marketing programs, to carry out programs to protect the Nation's animal and plant resources, or to carry out educational programs or special studies to improve the safety of the Nation's food supply.

SEC. [717] *716.* Notwithstanding any other provision of law (including provisions of law requiring competition), the Secretary may enter into cooperative agreements (which may provide for the acquisition of goods or services, including personal services) with a State, political subdivision, or agency thereof, a public or private agency, organization, or any other person, if the Secretary determines that the objectives of the agreement will: (1) serve a mutual interest of the parties to the agreement in carrying out the Wetlands Reserve Program; and (2) all parties will contribute resources to the accomplishment of these objectives: *Provided*, That Commodity Credit Corporation funds obligated for such purposes shall not exceed the level obligated by the Commodity Credit Corporation for such purposes in fiscal year 1998.

[SEC. 718. None of the funds in this Act may be used to retire more than 5 percent of the Class A stock of the Rural Telephone Bank or to maintain any account or subaccount within the accounting records of the Rural Telephone Bank the creation of which has not specifically been authorized by statute: *Provided*, That notwithstanding any other provision of law, none of the funds appropriated or otherwise made available in this Act may be used to transfer to the Treasury or to the Federal Financing Bank any unobligated balance of the Rural Telephone Bank telephone liquidating account which is in excess of current requirements and such balance shall receive interest as set forth for financial accounts in section 505(c) of the Federal Credit Reform Act of 1990.]

[SEC. 719. Of the funds made available by this Act, not more than $1,800,000 shall be used to cover necessary expenses of activities related to all advisory committees, panels, commissions, and task forces of the Department of Agriculture, except for panels used to comply with negotiated rule makings and panels used to evaluate competitively awarded grants: *Provided*, That interagency funding is authorized to carry out the purposes of the National Drought Policy Commission.]

SEC. [720] *717.* None of the funds appropriated by this Act may be used to carry out the provisions of section 918 of Public Law 104–127, the Federal Agriculture Improvement and Reform Act.

[SEC. 721. No employee of the Department of Agriculture may be detailed or assigned from an agency or office funded by this Act to any other agency or office of the Department for more than 30 days unless the individual's employing agency or office is fully reimbursed by the receiving agency or office for the salary and expenses of the employee for the period of assignment.]

[SEC. 722. None of the funds appropriated or otherwise made available to the Department of Agriculture shall be used to transmit or otherwise make available to any non-Department of Agriculture employee questions or responses to questions that are a result of information requested for the appropriations hearing process.]

SEC. [723] *718.* None of the funds made available to the Department of Agriculture by this Act may be used to acquire new information technology systems or significant upgrades, as determined by the Office of the Chief Information Officer, without the approval of the Chief Information Officer and the concurrence of the Executive Information Technology Investment Review Board[: *Provided*, That notwithstanding any other provision of law, none of the funds appropriated or otherwise made available by this Act may be transferred to the Office of the Chief Information Officer without the prior approval of the Committee on Appropriations of both Houses of Congress].

[SEC. 724. (a) None of the funds provided by this Act, or provided by previous Appropriations Acts to the agencies funded by this Act that remain available for obligation or expenditure in fiscal year 2000, or provided from any accounts in the Treasury of the United States derived by the collection of fees available to the agencies funded by this Act, shall be available for obligation or expenditure through a reprogramming of funds which: (1) creates new programs; (2) eliminates a program, project, or activity; (3) increases funds or personnel by any means for any project or activity for which funds have been denied or restricted; (4) relocates an office or employees; (5) reorganizes offices, programs, or activities; or (6) contracts out or privatizes any functions or activities presently performed by Federal employees; unless the Committee on Appropriations of both Houses of Congress are notified 15 days in advance of such reprogramming of funds.

(b) None of the funds provided by this Act, or provided by previous Appropriations Acts to the agencies funded by this Act that remain available for obligation or expenditure in fiscal year 2000, or provided from any accounts in the Treasury of the United States derived by the collection of fees available to the agencies funded by this Act, shall be available for obligation or expenditure for activities, programs, or projects through a reprogramming of funds in excess of $500,000 or 10 percent, whichever is less, that: (1) augments existing programs, projects, or activities; (2) reduces by 10 percent funding for any existing program, project, or activity, or numbers of personnel by 10 percent as approved by Congress; or (3) results from any general savings from a reduction in personnel which would result in a change in existing programs, activities, or projects as approved by Congress; unless the Committee on Appropriations of both Houses of Congress are notified 15 days in advance of such reprogramming of funds.]

SEC. [725] *719.* None of the funds appropriated or otherwise made available by this Act or any other Act may be used to pay the salaries and expenses of personnel to carry out the transfer or obligation of fiscal year [2000] *2001* funds under the provisions of section 793 of Public Law 104–127, *the Fund for Rural America.*

[SEC. 726. None of the funds appropriated or otherwise made available by this Act shall be used to pay the salaries and expenses of personnel who carry out an environmental quality incentives program authorized by sections 334–341 of Public Law 104–127 in excess of $174,000,000.]

[SEC. 727. None of the funds appropriated or otherwise available to the Department of Agriculture in fiscal year 2000 or thereafter may be used to administer the provision of contract payments to a producer under the Agricultural Market Transition Act (7 U.S.C. 7201 et seq.) for contract acreage on which wild rice is planted unless the contract payment is reduced by an acre for each contract acre planted to wild rice.]

[SEC. 728. None of the funds appropriated or otherwise made available by this Act shall be used to pay the salaries and expenses of personnel to enroll in excess of 150,000 acres in the fiscal year 2000 wetlands reserve program as authorized by 16 U.S.C. 3837.]

SEC. [729] *720.* None of the funds appropriated or otherwise made available by this or any other Act shall be used to pay the salaries and expenses of personnel to carry out the transfer or obligation of fiscal year [2000] *2001* funds under the provisions of section 401 of Public Law 105–185, the Initiative for Future Agriculture and Food Systems.

[SEC. 730. Notwithstanding section 381A of the Consolidated Farm and Rural Development Act (7 U.S.C. 2009), in fiscal year 2000 and thereafter, the definitions of rural areas for certain business programs administered by the Rural Business-Cooperative Service and the community facilities programs administered by the Rural Housing Service shall be those provided for in statute and regulations prior to the enactment of Public Law 104–127.]

[SEC. 731. None of the funds appropriated or otherwise made available by this Act shall be used to carry out any commodity purchase program that would prohibit eligibility or participation by farmer-owned cooperatives.]

SEC. [732] *721.* None of the funds appropriated or otherwise made available by this Act shall be used to pay the salaries and expenses of personnel to carry out a conservation farm option program, as authorized by section 335 of Public Law 104–127.

[SEC. 733. None of the funds made available to the Food and Drug Administration by this Act shall be used to close or relocate, or to plan to close or relocate, the Food and Drug Administration Division of Drug Analysis in St. Louis, Missouri, or the Food and Drug Administration Detroit, Michigan, District Office Laboratory; or to reduce the Detroit, Michigan, Food and Drug Administration District Office below the operating and full-time equivalent staffing level of July 31, 1999; or to change the Detroit District Office to a station, residence post or similarly modified office; or to reassign residence posts assigned to the Detroit District Office.]

[SEC. 734. None of the funds made available by this Act or any other Act for any fiscal year may be used to carry out section 302(h) of the Agricultural Marketing Act of 1946 (7 U.S.C. 1622(h)) unless the Secretary of Agriculture inspects and certifies agricultural processing equipment, and imposes a fee for the inspection and certification, in a manner that is similar to the inspection and certification of agricultural products under that section, as determined by the Secretary: *Provided*, That this provision shall not affect the authority of the Secretary to carry out the Federal Meat Inspection Act (21 U.S.C. 601 et seq.), the Poultry Products Inspection Act (21 U.S.C. 451 et seq.), or the Egg Products Inspection Act (21 U.S.C. 1031 et seq.).]

[SEC. 735. None of the funds appropriated by this Act or any other Act shall be used to pay the salaries and expenses of personnel who prepare or submit appropriations language as part of the President's Budget submission to the Congress of the United States for programs under the jurisdiction of the Appropriations Subcommittees on Agriculture, Rural Development, and Related Agencies that assumes revenues or reflects a reduction from the previous year due to user fees proposals that have not been enacted into law prior to the submission of the Budget unless such Budget submission identifies which additional spending reductions should occur in the event the users fees proposals are not enacted prior to the date of the convening of a committee of conference for the fiscal year 2001 appropriations Act.]

[SEC. 736. None of the funds appropriated or otherwise made available by this Act shall be used to establish an Office of Community Food Security or any similar office within the United States Department of Agriculture without the prior approval of the Committee on Appropriations of both Houses of Congress.]

[SEC. 737. None of the funds appropriated or otherwise made available by this or any other Act may be used to carry out provision of section 612 of Public Law 105–185.]

[SEC. 738. None of the funds appropriated or otherwise made available by this Act shall be used to pay the salaries and expenses of personnel to carry out the emergency food assistance program authorized by section 27(a) of the Food Stamp Act (7 U.S.C. 2036(a)) if such program exceeds $98,000,000.]

[SEC. 739. None of the funds appropriated by this Act shall be used to propose or issue rules, regulations, decrees, or orders for the purpose of implementation, or in preparation for implementation of the Kyoto Protocol which was adopted on December 11, 1997, in Kyoto, Japan.]

[SEC. 740. Notwithstanding any other provision of law, in fiscal year 2000 and thereafter, permanent employees of county committees employed on or after October 1, 1998, pursuant to 8(b) of the Soil Conservation and Domestic Allotment Act (16 U.S.C. 590h(b)) shall be considered as having Federal Civil Service status only for the purpose of applying for United States Department of Agriculture Civil Service vacancies.]

[SEC. 741. None of the funds appropriated or otherwise made available by this Act may be used to declare excess or surplus all or part of the lands and facilities owned by the Federal Government and administered by the Secretary of Agriculture at Fort Reno, Oklahoma, or to transfer or convey such lands or facilities, without the specific authorization of Congress.]

[SEC. 742. Notwithstanding any other provision of law, the Chief of the Natural Resources Conservation Service shall provide funds, within discretionary amounts available, for the settlement of claims associated with the Chuquatonchee Watershed Project in Mississippi to close out this project.]

[SEC. 743. (a) Not later than 180 days after the date of the enactment of this Act, the Secretary of Agriculture shall offer to enter into an agreement with the Governor of the State of Hawaii to conduct a pilot program to inspect mail entering the State of Hawaii for any plant, plant product, plant pest, or other organism that is subject to Federal quarantine laws.

(b) The agreement described in subsection (a) shall contain the same terms and conditions as are contained in the memorandum of understanding entered into between the Secretary and the State of California, dated February 1, 1999, unless the Secretary and the Governor agree to different terms or conditions.

(c) Unless the Secretary and the Governor agree otherwise, the agreement described in subsection (b) shall terminate on the later of—

(1) the date that is 1 year after the date the agreement becomes effective; or

(2) the date that the February 1, 1999 memorandum of understanding terminates.]

[SEC. 744. Notwithstanding any other provision of law, the Secretary is authorized under section 306 of the Consolidated Farm and Rural Development Act, as amended (7 U.S.C. 1926), to provide guaranteed lines of credit, including working capital loans, for health care facilities, to address Year 2000 computer conversion issues.]

[SEC. 745. After taking any action involving the seizure, quarantine, treatment, destruction, or disposal of wheat infested with karnal bunt, the Secretary of Agriculture shall compensate the producers and handlers for economic losses incurred as the result of the action not later than 45 days after receipt of a claim that includes all appropriate paperwork.]

[SEC. 746. In addition to amounts otherwise appropriated or made available by this Act, $2,000,000 is appropriated for the purpose of providing Bill Emerson and Mickey Leland Hunger Fellowships through the Congressional Hunger Center, which is an organization described in subsection (c)(3) of section 501 of the Internal Revenue Code of 1986 and is exempt from taxation under subsection (a) of such section.]

[SEC. 747. Notwithstanding any other provision of law, there are hereby appropriated $250,000 for the program authorized under section 388 of the Federal Agriculture Improvement and Reform Act of 1996, solely for use in the State of New Hampshire.]

[SEC. 748. The Immigration and Nationality Act (8 U.S.C. 1188 et seq.) is amended—

(1) in section 218(c)(1) by striking "60 days" and inserting "45 days"; and

(2) in section 218(c)(3)(A) by striking "20 days" and inserting "30 days".]

[SEC. 749. SUCCESSORSHIP PROVISIONS RELATING TO BARGAINING UNITS AND EXCLUSIVE REPRESENTATIVES. (a) VOLUNTARY AGREEMENT.—

(1) IN GENERAL.—If the exercise of the Secretary of Agriculture's authority under this section results in changes to an existing bargaining unit that has been certified under chapter 71 of title 5, United States Code, the affected parties shall attempt to reach a voluntary agreement on a new bargaining unit and an exclusive representative for such unit.

(2) CRITERIA.—In carrying out the requirements of this subsection, the affected parties shall use criteria set forth in—

(A) sections 7103(a)(4), 7111(e), 7111(f)(1), and 7120 of title 5, United States Code, relating to determining an exclusive representative; and

(B) section 7112 of title 5, United States Code (disregarding subsections (b)(5) and (d) thereof), relating to determining appropriate units.

(b) EFFECT OF AN AGREEMENT.—

(1) IN GENERAL.—If the affected parties reach agreement on the appropriate unit and the exclusive representative for such unit under subsection (a), the Federal Labor Relations Authority shall certify the terms of such agreement, subject to paragraph (2)(A). Nothing in this subsection shall be considered to require the holding of any hearing or election as a condition for certification.

(2) RESTRICTIONS.—

(A) CONDITIONS REQUIRING NONCERTIFICATION.—The Federal Labor Relations Authority may not certify the terms of an agreement under paragraph (1) if—

(i) it determines that any of the criteria referred to in subsection (a)(2) (disregarding section 7112(a) of title 5, United States Code) have not been met; or

(ii) after the Secretary's exercise of authority and before certification under this section, a valid election under section 7111(b) of title 5, United States Code, is held covering any employees who would be included in the unit proposed for certification.

(B) TEMPORARY WAIVER OF PROVISION THAT WOULD BAR AN ELECTION AFTER A COLLECTIVE BARGAINING AGREEMENT IS REACHED.—Nothing in section 7111(f)(3) of title 5, United States Code, shall prevent the holding of an election under section 7111(b) of such title that covers employees within a unit certified under paragraph (1), or giving effect to the results of such an election (including a decision not to be represented by any labor organization), if the election is held before the end of the 12-month period beginning on the date such unit is so certified.

(C) CLARIFICATION.—The certification of a unit under paragraph (1) shall not, for purposes of the last sentence of section 7111(b) of title 5, United States Code, or section 7111(f)(4) of such title, be treated as if it had occurred pursuant to an election.

(3) DELEGATION.—

(A) IN GENERAL.—The Federal Labor Relations Authority may delegate to any regional director (as referred to in section 7105(e) of title 5, United States Code) its authority under the preceding provisions of this subsection.

(B) REVIEW.—Any action taken by a regional director under subparagraph (A) shall be subject to review under the provisions of section 7105(f) of title 5, United States Code, in the same manner as if such action had been taken under section 7105(e) of such title, except that in the case of a decision not to certify, such review shall be required if application therefore is filed by an affected party within the time specified in such provisions.

(c) DEFINITION.—For purposes of this section, the term "affected party" means—

(1) with respect to an exercise of authority by the Secretary of Agriculture under this section, any labor organization affected thereby; and

(2) the Department of Agriculture.]

[SEC. 750. None of the funds appropriated or otherwise made available by this Act or any other Act shall be used for the implementation of a Support Services Bureau or similar organization.]

[SEC. 751. CONTRACTS FOR PROCUREMENT OR PROCESSING OF CERTAIN COMMODITIES. (a) DEFINITIONS.—In this section:

(1) HUBZONE SOLE SOURCE CONTRACT.—The term "HUBZone sole source contract" means a sole source contract authorized by section 31 of the Small Business Act (15 U.S.C. 657a).

(2) HUBZONE PRICE EVALUATION PREFERENCE.—The term "HUBZone price evaluation preference" means a price evaluation preference authorized by section 31 of the Small Business Act (15 U.S.C. 657a).

(3) QUALIFIED HUBZONE SMALL BUSINESS CONCERN.—The term "qualified HUBZone small business concern" has the meaning given the term in section 3(p) of the Small Business Act (15 U.S.C. 632(p)).

(4) COVERED PROCUREMENT.—The term "covered procurement" means a contract for the procurement or processing of a commodity furnished under title II or III of the Agricultural Trade Development and Assistance Act of 1954 (7 U.S.C. 1721 et seq.), section 416(b) of the Agricultural Act of 1949 (7 U.S.C. 1431(b)), the Food for Progress Act of 1985 (7 U.S.C. 1736o), or any other commodity procurement or acquisition by the Commodity Credit Corporation under any other law.

(b) PROHIBITION OF USE OF FUNDS.—None of the funds made available by this Act may be used:

(1) to award a HUBZone sole source contract or a contract awarded through full and open competition in combination with a HUBZone price evaluation preference to any qualified HUBZone small business concern in any covered procurement if performance of the contract by the business concern would exceed the production capacity of the business concern or would require the business concern to subcontract to any other company or enterprise for the purchase of the commodity being procured through the covered procurement; and

(2) in any contract awarded through full and open competition in any covered procurement—

(A) to fund a price evaluation preference greater than 5 percent if the dollar value of the contract awarded is not greater than 50 percent of the total dollar value being procured in a single tender for a commodity; or

(B) to fund any price evaluation preference at all if the dollar value of the contract awarded is greater than 50 percent of the total dollar value being procured in a single tender for a commodity.]

[SEC. 752. REDESIGNATION OF NATIONAL SCHOOL LUNCH ACT AS RICHARD B. RUSSELL NATIONAL SCHOOL LUNCH ACT. (a) IN GENERAL.—The first section of the National School Lunch Act (42 U.S.C.

1751 note) is amended by striking "National School Lunch Act" and inserting "Richard B. Russell National School Lunch Act".

(b) CONFORMING AMENDMENTS.—The following provisions of law are amended by striking "National School Lunch Act" each place it appears and inserting "Richard B. Russell National School Lunch Act":

(1) Sections 3 and 13(3)(A) of the Commodity Distribution Reform Act and WIC Amendments of 1987 (7 U.S.C. 612c note; Public Law 100–237).

(2) Section 404 of the Agricultural Act of 1949 (7 U.S.C. 1424).

(3) Section 201(a) of the Act entitled "An Act to extend the Agricultural Trade Development and Assistance Act of 1954, and for other purposes", approved September 21, 1959 (7 U.S.C. 1431c(a); 73 Stat. 610).

(4) Section 211(a) of the Agricultural Trade Suspension Adjustment Act of 1980 (7 U.S.C. 4004(a)).

(5) Section 245A(h)(4)(A) of the Immigration and Nationality Act (8 U.S.C. 1255a(h)(4)(A)).

(6) Sections 403(c)(2)(C), 422(b)(3), 423(d)(3), 741(a)(1), and 742 of the Personal Responsibility and Work Opportunity Reconciliation Act of 1996 (8 U.S.C. 1613(c)(2)(C), 1632(b)(3), 1183a note, 42 U.S.C. 1751 note, 8 U.S.C. 1615; Public Law 104–193).

(7) Section 2243(b) of title 10, United States Code.

(8) Sections 404B(g)(1)(A), 404D(c)(2), and 404F(a)(2) of the Higher Education Act of 1965 (20 U.S.C. 1070a–22(g)(1)(A), 1070a–24(c)(2), 1070a–26(a)(2); Public Law 105–244).

(9) Section 231(d)(3)(A)(i) of the Carl D. Perkins Vocational Education Act (20 U.S.C. 2341(d)(3)(A)(i)).

(10) Section 1113(a)(5) of the Elementary and Secondary Education Act of 1965 (20 U.S.C. 6313(a)(5)).

(11) Section 1397E(d)(4)(A)(iv)(II) of the Internal Revenue Code of 1986.

(12) Sections 254(b)(2)(B) and 263(a)(2)(C) of the Job Training Partnership Act (29 U.S.C. 1633(b)(2)(B), 1643(a)(2)(C)).

(13) Section 3803(c)(2)(C)(xiii) of title 31, United States Code.

(14) Section 602(d)(9)(A) of the Federal Property and Administrative Services Act of 1949 (40 U.S.C. 474(d)(9)(A)).

(15) Sections 2(4), 3(1), and 301 of the Healthy Meals for Healthy Americans Act of 1994 (42 U.S.C. 1751 note; Public Law 103–448).

(16) Sections 3, 4, 7, 10, 13, 16(b), 17, and 19(d) of the Child Nutrition Act of 1966 (42 U.S.C. 1772, 1773, 1776, 1779, 1782, 1785(b), 1786, 1788(d)).

(17) Section 658O(b)(3) of the Child Care and Development Block Grant Act of 1990 (42 U.S.C. 9858m(b)(3)).

(18) Subsection (b) of the first section of Public Law 87–688 (48 U.S.C. 1666(b)).

(19) Section 10405(a)(2)(H) of the Omnibus Budget Reconciliation Act of 1989 (Public Law 101–239; 103 Stat. 2489).]

[SEC. 753. Public Law 105–199 (112 Stat. 641) is amended in section 3(b)(1)(G) by striking "persons" and inserting "governors, who may be represented on the Commission by their respective designees,".]

[SEC. 754. Section 889 of the Federal Agriculture Improvement and Reform Act of 1996 is amended—

(1) in the heading, by inserting "HARRY K. DUPREE" before "STUTTGART";

(2) in subsection (b)(1)—

(A) in the heading, by inserting "HARRY K. DUPREE" before "STUTTGART"; and

(B) in subparagraphs (A) and (B), by inserting "Harry K. Dupree" before "Stuttgart National Aquaculture Research Center" each place it appears.]

[SEC. 755. TOBACCO LEASING AND INFORMATION. (a) CROSS-COUNTY LEASING.—Section 319(l) of the Agricultural Adjustment Act of 1938 (7 U.S.C. 1314e(l)) is amended in the second sentence by inserting ", Ohio, Indiana, Kentucky," after "Tennessee".

(b) TOBACCO PRODUCTION AND MARKETING INFORMATION.—Part I of subtitle B of title III of the Agricultural Adjustment Act of 1938 (7 U.S.C. 1311 et seq.) is amended by adding at the end the following:

"SEC. 320D. TOBACCO PRODUCTION AND MARKETING INFORMATION.

"(a) IN GENERAL.—Notwithstanding any other provision of law, the Secretary may, subject to subsection (b), release marketing information submitted by persons relating to the production and marketing of tobacco to State trusts or similar organizations engaged in the distribution of national trust funds to tobacco producers and other persons with interests associated with the production of tobacco, as determined by the Secretary.

"(b) LIMITATIONS.—

"(1) IN GENERAL.—Information may be released under subsection (a) only to the extent that—

"(A) the release is in the interest of tobacco producers, as determined by the Secretary; and

"(B) the information is released to a State trust or other organization that is created to, or charged with, distributing funds to tobacco producers or other parties with an interest in tobacco production or tobacco farms under a national or State trust or settlement.

"(2) EXEMPTION FROM RELEASE.—The Secretary shall, to the maximum extent practicable, in advance of making a release of information under subsection (a), allow, by announcement, a period of at least 15 days for persons whose consent would otherwise be required by law to effectuate the release, to elect to be exempt from the release.

"(c) ASSISTANCE.—

"(1) IN GENERAL.—In making a release under subsection (a), the Secretary may provide such other assistance with respect to information released under subsection (a) as will facilitate the interest of producers in receiving the funds that are the subject of a trust described in subsection (a).

"(2) FUNDS.—The Secretary shall use amounts made available for salaries and expenses of the Department to carry out paragraph (1).

"(d) RECORDS.—

"(1) IN GENERAL.—A person who obtains information described in subsection (a) shall maintain records that are consistent with the purposes of the release and shall not use the records for any purpose not authorized under this section.

"(2) PENALTY.—A person who knowingly violates this subsection shall be fined not more than $10,000, imprisoned not more than 1 year, or both.

"(e) APPLICATION.—This section shall not apply to—

"(1) records submitted by cigarette manufacturers with respect to the production of cigarettes;

"(2) records that were submitted as expected purchase intentions in connection with the establishment of national tobacco quotas; or

"(3) records that aggregate the purchases of particular buyers.".]

[SEC. 756. Notwithstanding section 306(a)(7) of the Consolidated Farm and Rural Development Act (7 U.S.C. 1926(a)(7)), the City of Berlin, New Hampshire, shall be eligible during fiscal year 2000 for a rural utilities grant or loan under the Rural Community Advancement Program.]

[SEC. 757. CRANBERRY MARKETING ORDERS. (a) PAID ADVERTISING FOR CRANBERRIES AND CRANBERRY PRODUCTS.—Section 8c(6)(I) of the Agricultural Adjustment Act (7 U.S.C. 608c(6)(I)), reenacted with amendments by the Agricultural Marketing Agreement Act of 1937, is amended in the first proviso—

(1) by striking "or Florida grown strawberries" and inserting ", Florida grown strawberries, or cranberries"; and

(2) by striking "and Florida Indian River grapefruit" and inserting "Florida Indian River grapefruit, and cranberries".

(b) COLLECTION OF CRANBERRY INVENTORY DATA.—Section 8d of the Agricultural Adjustment Act (7 U.S.C. 608d), reenacted with amendments by the Agricultural Marketing Agreement Act of 1937, is amended by adding at the end the following:

"(3) COLLECTION OF CRANBERRY INVENTORY DATA.—

"(A) IN GENERAL.—If an order is in effect with respect to cranberries, the Secretary of Agriculture may require persons engaged in the handling or importation of cranberries or cranberry products (including producer-handlers, second handlers, processors, brokers, and importers) to provide such information as the Secretary considers necessary to effectuate the declared policy of this title, including information on acquisitions, inventories, and dispositions of cranberries and cranberry products.

"(B) DELEGATION TO COMMITTEE.—The Secretary may delegate the authority to carry out subparagraph (A) to any committee that is responsible for administering an order covering cranberries.

"(C) CONFIDENTIALITY.—Paragraph (2) shall apply to information provided under this paragraph.

"(D) VIOLATIONS.—Any person who violates this paragraph shall be subject to the penalties provided under section 8c(14).".]

[SEC. 758. Beginning in fiscal year 2001 and thereafter, the Food Stamp Act (Public Law 95–113, section 16(a)) is amended by inserting

"SEC. 320D. TOBACCO PRODUCTION AND MARKETING INFORMATION.—Continued

after the phrase "Indian reservation under section 11(d) of this Act" the following new phrase: "or in a Native village within the State of Alaska identified in section 11(b) of Public Law 92–203, as amended.".]

[SEC. 759. EDUCATION GRANTS TO ALASKA NATIVE SERVING INSTITUTIONS AND NATIVE HAWAIIAN SERVING INSTITUTIONS. (a) EDUCATION GRANTS PROGRAM FOR ALASKA NATIVE SERVING INSTITUTIONS.—

(1) GRANT AUTHORITY.—The Secretary of Agriculture may make competitive grants (or grants without regard to any requirement for competition) to Alaska Native serving institutions for the purpose of promoting and strengthening the ability of Alaska Native serving institutions to carry out education, applied research, and related community development programs.

(2) USE OF GRANT FUNDS.—Grants made under this section shall be used—

(A) to support the activities of consortia of Alaska Native serving institutions to enhance educational equity for under represented students;

(B) to strengthen institutional educational capacities, including libraries, curriculum, faculty, scientific instrumentation, instruction delivery systems, and student recruitment and retention, in order to respond to identified State, regional, national, or international educational needs in the food and agriculture sciences;

(C) to attract and support undergraduate and graduate students from under represented groups in order to prepare them for careers related to the food, agricultural, and natural resource systems of the United States, beginning with the mentoring of students at the high school level including by village elders and continuing with the provision of financial support for students through their attainment of a doctoral degree; and

(D) to facilitate cooperative initiatives between two or more Alaska Native serving institutions, or between Alaska Native serving institutions and units of State government or the private sector, to maximize the development and use of resources, such as faculty, facilities, and equipment, to improve food and agricultural sciences teaching programs.

(3) AUTHORIZATION OF APPROPRIATIONS.—There are authorized to be appropriated to make grants under this subsection $10,000,000 in fiscal years 2001 through 2006.

(b) EDUCATION GRANTS PROGRAM FOR NATIVE HAWAIIAN SERVING INSTITUTIONS.—

(1) GRANT AUTHORITY.—The Secretary of Agriculture may make competitive grants (or grants without regard to any requirement for competition) to Native Hawaiian serving institutions for the purpose of promoting and strengthening the ability of Native Hawaiian serving institutions to carry out education, applied research, and related community development programs.

(2) USE OF GRANT FUNDS.—Grants made under this section shall be used—

(A) to support the activities of consortia of Native Hawaiian serving institutions to enhance educational equity for under represented students;

(B) to strengthen institutional educational capacities, including libraries, curriculum, faculty, scientific instrumentation, instruction delivery systems, and student recruitment and retention, in order to respond to identified State, regional, national, or international educational needs in the food and agriculture sciences;

(C) to attract and support undergraduate and graduate students from under represented groups in order to prepare them for careers related to the food, agricultural, and natural resource systems of the United States, beginning with the mentoring of students at the high school level and continuing with the provision of financial support for students through their attainment of a doctoral degree; and

(D) to facilitate cooperative initiatives between two or more Native Hawaiian serving institutions, or between Native Hawaiian serving institutions and units of State government or the private sector, to maximize the development and use of resources, such as faculty, facilities, and equipment, to improve food and agricultural sciences teaching programs.

(3) AUTHORIZATION OF APPROPRIATIONS.—There are authorized to be appropriated to make grants under this subsection $10,000,000 for each of fiscal years 2001 through 2006.]

[SEC. 760. Effective October 1, 1999, section 8c(11) of the Agricultural Adjustment Act (7 U.S.C. 608c(11)), reenacted with amendments by the Agricultural Marketing Agreement Act of 1937, is amended by adding at the end the following: "The price of milk paid by a handler at a plant operating in Clark County, Nevada shall not be subject to any order issued under this section.".]

[SEC. 761. Notwithstanding any other provision of law, the City of Olean, New York, shall be eligible for grants and loans administered by the Rural Utilities Service.]

[SEC. 762. Notwithstanding any other provision of law, the Municipality of Carolina, Puerto Rico shall be eligible for grants and loans administered by the Rural Utilities Service.]

[SEC. 763. Section 1232(a) of the Food Security Act of 1985 (16 U.S.C. 3832(a)) is amended—

(1) in paragraph (9), by adding "and" after the semicolon at the end;

(2) in paragraph (10), by striking "; and" and inserting a period; and

(3) by striking paragraph (11).]

[SEC. 764. None of the funds made available by this or any other Act shall be used to implement Notice CRP–338, issued by the Farm Service Agency on March 10, 1999, nor shall funds be used to implement any related administrative action including implementation of such procedures published in Farm Service Agency program manuals: *Provided*, That rental payments for any lands enrolled in the Conservation Reserve Program under this section shall be reduced by an amount equal to the Federal cost of any remaining value of a federally cost-shared conservation practice as determined by the Secretary.]

[SEC. 765. None of the funds made available by this or any other Act shall be used to implement Notice CRP–327, issued by the Farm Service Agency on October 26, 1998, nor shall funds be used to implement any related administrative action including implementation of such procedures published in Farm Service Agency program manuals: *Provided*, That this section shall not apply to any lands for which there is not full compliance with the conservation practices required under terms of the CRP contract.]

[SEC. 766. The Federal facility located in Riverside, California, and known as the "U.S. Salinity Laboratory", shall be known and designated as the "George E. Brown, Jr., Salinity Laboratory": *Provided*, That any reference in any law, map, regulation, document, paper, or other record of the United States to such Federal facility shall be deemed to be a reference to the "George E. Brown, Jr., Salinity Laboratory".]

[SEC. 767. Sections 657, 658, 1006, and 1014 of title 18, United States Code, are amended by—

(1) inserting "or successor agency" after "Farmers Home Administration" each place it appears; and

(2) inserting "or successor agency" after "Rural Development Administration" each place it appears.]

[SEC. 768. Notwithstanding any other provision of law, the maximum income limits established for single family housing for families and individuals in the high cost areas of Alaska shall be 150 percent of the State metropolitan income level for Alaska.]

[SEC. 769. Section 1232(a)(7) of the Food Security Act of 1985 is amended—

(1) by striking "except that the Secretary may permit harvesting" and inserting "except that the Secretary—

"(A) may permit—

"(i) harvesting";

(2) by striking "emergency, and the Secretary may permit limited" and inserting "emergency; and

"(ii) limited";

(3) by inserting "and" after the semicolon at the end; and

(4) by adding at the end the following:

"(B) shall approve not more than six projects, no more than one of which may be in any State, under which land subject to the contract may be harvested for recovery of biomass used in energy production if—

"(i) no acreage subject to the contract is harvested more than once every other year;

"(ii) not more than 25 percent of the total acreage enrolled in the program under this subchapter in any crop reporting district (as designated by the Secretary), is harvested in any 1 year;

"(iii) no portion of the crop is used for any commercial purpose other than energy production from biomass;

"(iv) no wetland, or acreage of any type enrolled in a partial field conservation practice (including riparian forest buffers, filter strips, and buffer strips), is harvested;

"(v) the owner or operator agrees to a payment reduction under this section in an amount determined by the Secretary.

"(C) the total acres for all of the projects shall not exceed 250,000 acres.".] *(Agriculture, Rural Development, Food and Drug Administration, and Related Agencies Appropriations Act, 2000.)*

GENERAL PROVISIONS—THIS CHAPTER

[SEC. 101. Notwithstanding section 196 of the Agricultural Market Transition Act (7 U.S.C. 7333), the Secretary of Agriculture shall provide up to $20,000,000 in assistance under the noninsured crop assistance program under that section, without any requirement for an area loss, to producers located in a county with respect to which a natural disaster was declared by the Secretary, or a major disaster or emergency was declared by the President under the Robert T. Stafford Disaster Relief and Emergency Assistance Act (42 U.S.C. 5121 et seq.).]

[SEC. 102. Section 814 of Public Law 106–78 is amended by inserting the following after "year": "(and 2001 crop year for citrus fruit, avocados in California, and macadamia nuts)".]

[SEC. 103. Of the funds made available under section 802 of Public Law 106–78 not otherwise needed to fully implement that section, the Secretary of Agriculture may use up to $4,700,000 to carry out title IX of Public Law 106–78.]

[SEC. 104. (a) Of the funds made available under section 802 of Public Law 106–78 (excluding any funds authorized by this Act to carry out title IX of Public Law 106–78) and under section 1111 of Public Law 105–277 not otherwise needed to fully implement those sections, the Secretary of Agriculture may provide assistance to producers or first-handlers for the 1999 crop of cottonseed.

(b) Of the funds made available under section 802 of Public Law 106–78 and section 1111 of Public Law 105–277 not otherwise needed to fully implement those sections (excluding any funds authorized by this Act to carry out title IX and to provide assistance to producers or first-handlers for the 1999 crop of cottonseed under subsection (a) of this section), the Secretary may provide funds to carry out subsection (c) of this section.

(c) The Agricultural Market Transition Act is amended by inserting after section 136 (7 U.S.C. 7236), the following new section:

"SEC. 136A. SPECIAL COMPETITIVE PROVISIONS FOR EXTRA LONG STAPLE COTTON.

"(a) COMPETITIVENESS PROGRAM.—Notwithstanding any other provision of law, during the period beginning on October 1, 1999, and ending on July 31, 2003, the Secretary shall carry out a program to maintain and expand the domestic use of extra long staple cotton produced in the United States, to increase exports of extra long staple cotton produced in the United States, and to ensure that extra long staple cotton produced in the United States remains competitive in world markets.

"(b) PAYMENTS UNDER PROGRAM; TRIGGER.—Under the program, the Secretary shall make payments available under this section whenever—

"(1) for a consecutive 4-week period, the world market price for the lowest priced competing growth of extra long staple cotton (adjusted to United States quality and location and for other factors affecting the competitiveness of such cotton), as determined by the Secretary, is below the prevailing United States price for a competing growth of extra long staple cotton; and

"(2) the lowest priced competing growth of extra long staple cotton (adjusted to United States quality and location and for other factors affecting the competitiveness of such cotton), as determined by the Secretary, is less than 134 percent of the loan rate for extra long staple cotton.

"(c) ELIGIBLE RECIPIENTS.—The Secretary shall make payments available under this section to domestic users of extra long staple cotton produced in the United States and exporters of extra long staple cotton produced in the United States who enter into an agreement with the Commodity Credit Corporation to participate in the program under this section.

"(d) PAYMENT AMOUNT.—Payments under this section shall be based on the amount of the difference in the prices referred to in subsection (b)(1) during the fourth week of the consecutive 4-week period multiplied by the amount of documented purchases by domestic users and sales for export by exporters made in the week following such a consecutive 4-week period.

"(e) FORM OF PAYMENT.—Payments under this section shall be made through the issuance of cash or marketing certificates, at the option of eligible recipients of the payments.".]

[SEC. 105. The entire amount necessary to carry out this chapter and the amendments made by this chapter shall be available only to the extent that an official budget request for the entire amount, that includes designation of the entire amount of the request as an emergency requirement as defined in the Balanced Budget and Emergency Deficit Control Act of 1985, as amended, is transmitted by the President to the Congress: *Provided*, That the entire amount is designated by the Congress as an emergency requirement pursuant to section 251(b)(2)(A) of such Act.] *(Miscellaneous Appropriations, 2000, as enacted by section 1000(a)(5) of the Consolidated Appropriations Act, 2000 (P.L. 106–113.)*

TITLE II—OTHER APPROPRIATIONS MATTERS

[SEC. 201. Section 733 of Public Law 106–78 is amended by striking after "Missouri" ", or the Food and Drug Administration Detroit, Michigan, District Office Laboratory; or to reduce the Detroit, Michigan, Food and Drug Administration District Office below the operating and full-time equivalent staffing level of July 31, 1999; or to change the Detroit District Office to a station, residence post or similarly modified office; or to reassign residence posts assigned to the Detroit District Office".]

[SEC. 202. None of the funds made available to the Food and Drug Administration by Public Law 106–78 or any other Act for fiscal year 2000 shall be used to reduce the Detroit, Michigan, Food and Drug Administration District Office below the operating and full-time equivalent staffing level of July 31, 1999; or to change the Detroit District Office to a station, residence post or similarly modified office; or to reassign residence posts assigned to the Detroit District Office: *Provided*, That this section shall not apply to Food and Drug Administration field laboratory facilities or operations currently located in Detroit, Michigan, if the full-time equivalent staffing level of laboratory personnel as of July 31, 1999, is assigned to locations in the general vicinity of Detroit, Michigan, pursuant to cooperative agreements between the Food and Drug Administration and other laboratory facilities associated with the State of Michigan.]

[SEC. 203. Notwithstanding any other provision of law, the Secretary of Agriculture may use funds provided for rural housing assistance grants in Public Law 106–78 for a pilot project to provide home ownership for farm workers and workers involved in the processing of farm products in Salinas, California, and the surrounding area.]

[SEC. 204. Notwithstanding any other provision of law (including the Federal Grants and Cooperative Agreements Act), the Secretary of Agriculture shall use not more than $9,000,000 of Commodity Credit Corporation funds for a cooperative program with the State of Florida to replace commercial trees removed to control citrus canker until the earlier of December 31, 1999, or the date crop insurance coverage is made available with respect to citrus canker; and the Secretary of Agriculture shall use not more than $7,000,000 of Commodity Credit Corporation funds to replace non-commercial trees (known as dooryard citrus trees), owned by private homeowners, and removed to control citrus canker.]

[SEC. 205. (a) CONTINUATION OF REVENUE INSURANCE PILOT.—Section 508(h)(9)(A) of the Federal Crop Insurance Act (7 U.S.C. 1508(h)(9)(A)) is amended by striking "1997, 1998, 1999, and 2000" and inserting "1997 through 2001".

(b) EXPANSION OF CROP INSURANCE PILOTS.—In the case of any pilot program offered under the Federal Crop Insurance Act that was approved by the Board of Directors of the Federal Crop Insurance Corporation on or before September 30, 1999, the pilot program may be offered on a regional, whole State, or national basis for the 2000 and 2001 crop years notwithstanding section 553 of title 5, United States Code.]

[SEC. 206. SALES CLOSING DATES FOR CROP INSURANCE.—Section 508(f)(2) of the Federal Crop Insurance Act (7 U.S.C. 1508(f)(2)) is amended—

(1) by inserting "(A) IN GENERAL.—" before the first sentence;

(2) by striking the last sentence; and

(3) by adding at the end the following:

"(B) ESTABLISHED DATES.—Except as provided in subparagraph (C), the Corporation shall establish, for an insurance policy for each insurable crop that is planted in the spring, a sales closing date that is 30 days earlier than the corresponding sales closing date that was established for the 1994 crop year.

"(C) EXCEPTION.—If compliance with subparagraph (B) results in a sales closing date for an agricultural commodity that is earlier than January 31, the sales closing date for that commodity shall be January 31 beginning with the 2000 crop year.".]

[SEC. 207. The Secretary of Agriculture may use not more than $1,090,000 of funds of the Commodity Credit Corporation to provide emergency assistance to producers on farms located in Harney County, Oregon, who suffered flood-related crop and forage losses in 1999 and several previous years and are expected to suffer continuing economic losses until the floodwaters recede. The amount made available under this section shall be available for such losses for such years as determined appropriate by the Secretary to compensate such producers for hay, grain, and pasture losses due to the floods and for related economic losses.]

[SEC. 208. TILLAMOOK RAILROAD DISASTER REPAIRS. In addition to amounts appropriated or otherwise made available for rural development programs of the United States Department of Agriculture by Public Law 106–78, there are appropriated $5,000,000 which may be made available to repair damage to the Tillamook Railroad caused by flooding and high winds (FEMA Disaster Number 1099–DR–OR) notwithstanding any other provision of law.]

[SEC. 209. At the end of section 746 of Public Law 106–78, insert the following before the period: ": *Provided*, That the Congressional Hunger Center may invest such funds and expend the income from such funds in a manner consistent with this section: *Provided further*, That notwithstanding any other provision of law, funds appropriated pursuant to this section may be paid directly to the Congressional Hunger Center.".]

[SEC. 210. The Secretary of Agriculture may reprogram funds appropriated by Public Law 106–78 for the cost of rural electrification and telecommunications loans to provide up to $100,000 for the cost of guaranteed loans authorized by section 306 of the Rural Electrification Act of 1936.]

[SEC. 211. Section 755(b) of Public Law 106–78 is hereby repealed.] *(Miscellaneous Appropriations, 2000, as enacted by section 1000(a)(5) of the Consolidated Appropriations Act, 2000 (P.L. 106–113.)*

DEPARTMENT OF COMMERCE

[GENERAL ADMINISTRATION]
DEPARTMENTAL MANAGEMENT

Federal Funds

General and special funds:

SALARIES AND EXPENSES

For expenses necessary for the general administration of the Department of Commerce provided for by law, including not to exceed $3,000 for official entertainment, [$31,500,000] *$32,340,000. (Department of Commerce and Related Agencies Appropriations Act, 2000, as enacted by section 1000(a)(1) of the Consolidated Appropriations Act, 2000 (P.L. 106–113).)*

Program and Financing (in millions of dollars)

Identification code 13–0120–0–1–376		1999 actual	2000 est.	2001 est.
	Obligations by program activity:			
	Direct program:			
00.01	Executive direction	15	14	13
00.02	Departmental staff services	20	22	19
09.01	Reimbursable program	50	348	358
10.00	Total new obligations	85	384	390
	Budgetary resources available for obligation:			
21.40	Unobligated balance available, start of year	1	5	
22.00	New budget authority (gross)	88	379	390
22.22	Unobligated balance transferred from other accounts	1		
23.90	Total budgetary resources available for obligation	90	384	390
23.95	Total new obligations	–85	–384	–390
24.40	Unobligated balance available, end of year	5		
	New budget authority (gross), detail:			
	Discretionary:			
40.00	Appropriation	30	31	32
40.76	Reduction pursuant to P.L. 106–113			
42.00	Transferred from other accounts	8		
43.00	Appropriation (total discretionary)	38	31	32
68.00	Spending authority from offsetting collections: Offsetting collections (cash)	50	348	358
70.00	Total new budget authority (gross)	88	379	390
	Change in unpaid obligations:			
	Unpaid obligations, start of year:			
72.40	Obligated balance, start of year	3	4	4
72.95	From Federal sources: Receivables and unpaid, unfilled orders	6	6	6
72.99	Total unpaid obligations, start of year	9	10	10
73.10	Total new obligations	85	384	390
73.20	Total outlays (gross)	–83	–384	–391
	Unpaid obligations, end of year:			
74.40	Obligated balance, end of year	4	4	3
74.95	From Federal sources: Receivables and unpaid, unfilled orders	6	6	6
74.99	Total unpaid obligations, end of year	10	10	9
	Outlays (gross), detail:			
86.90	Outlays from new discretionary authority	80	375	386
86.93	Outlays from discretionary balances	3	9	5
87.00	Total outlays (gross)	83	384	391
	Offsets:			
	Against gross budget authority and outlays:			
88.00	Offsetting collections (cash) from: Federal sources	–50	–348	–358
	Net budget authority and outlays:			
89.00	Budget authority	38	31	32
90.00	Outlays	33	36	33

Executive direction.—Provides for the formulation of Department of Commerce policy on National and Governmental issues affecting programs and functions assigned to the Department.

Departmental staff services.—Provides for the formulation of internal Departmental policy establishing the framework for Departmental operations.

Performance measures.—Departmental Management performs Departmental planning, establishes Departmental policies, and provides administrative guidance and performance oversight to accomplish the Department's mission.

Reimbursable program.—Provides a centralized collection source for special tasks or costs and their billing to users. The increase is due to the inclusion of Commerce Information Technology Solutions (COMMITS), an information technology Government-wide Acquisition Contract set-aside exclusively for small, small disadvantaged, 8(a) and women-owned small businesses.

Object Classification (in millions of dollars)

Identification code 13–0120–0–1–376		1999 actual	2000 est.	2001 est.
	Direct obligations:			
11.1	Personnel compensation: Full-time permanent	16	18	17
12.1	Civilian personnel benefits	3	4	3
23.1	Rental payments to GSA	4	3	3
23.3	Communications, utilities, and miscellaneous charges		1	1
25.2	Other services	6	2	2
25.3	Purchases of goods and services from Government accounts	6	7	5
31.0	Equipment		1	1
99.0	Subtotal, direct obligations	35	36	32
99.0	Reimbursable obligations	50	348	358
99.9	Total new obligations	85	384	390

Personnel Summary

Identification code 13–0120–0–1–376		1999 actual	2000 est.	2001 est.
	Direct:			
1001	Total compensable workyears: Full-time equivalent employment	207	220	213
	Reimbursable:			
2001	Total compensable workyears: Full-time equivalent employment	46	48	48

DIGITAL DEPARTMENT

In addition to funds otherwise made available by this Act, for expenses necessary to implement the Digital Department Program of the Department of Commerce, $5,800,000, to remain available until expended.

Program and Financing (in millions of dollars)

Identification code 13–0129–0–1–376		1999 actual	2000 est.	2001 est.
	Obligations by program activity:			
00.01	Chief Information Office			6
10.00	Total new obligations (object class 25.2)			6
	Budgetary resources available for obligation:			
22.00	New budget authority (gross)			6
23.95	Total new obligations			–6

General and special funds—Continued

DIGITAL DEPARTMENT—Continued

Program and Financing (in millions of dollars)—Continued

Identification code 13–0129–0–1–376	1999 actual	2000 est.	2001 est.
New budget authority (gross), detail:			
Discretionary:			
40.00 Appropriation			6
Change in unpaid obligations:			
73.10 Total new obligations			6
73.20 Total outlays (gross)			−4
74.40 Unpaid obligations, end of year: Obligated balance, end of year			2
Outlays (gross), detail:			
86.90 Outlays from new discretionary authority			4
Net budget authority and outlays:			
89.00 Budget authority			6
90.00 Outlays			4

Digital Department.—Provides standards-based interoperable office support infrastructure, develops a secure intranet and creates a telecommunications infrastructure allowing employees to have access to necessary information to perform their functions, and expands the web-based procurement and human resources systems. The Department of Commerce will move from a paper based administrative system to electronic-based digital department systems.

Performance measures.—In order to accomplish the objectives and goals of the Digital Department, affinity groups will be established to identify projects and schedule resource requirements; implementation plans will be completed; a set of standards for hardware and software purchases will be developed; and antiquated cabling and network infrastructure will be replaced.

Reimbursable program.—Provides a centralized collection source for special tasks or costs and their billing to users.

SECURITY

For necessary expenses of basic and enhanced security services of the Department of Commerce, $13,268,000, to remain available until expended.

Program and Financing (in millions of dollars)

Identification code 13–0130–0–1–376	1999 actual	2000 est.	2001 est.
Obligations by program activity:			
00.01 Dept Security Office			13
09.01 Reimbursable program			9
10.00 Total new obligations			22
Budgetary resources available for obligation:			
22.00 New budget authority (gross)			22
23.95 Total new obligations			−22
New budget authority (gross), detail:			
Discretionary:			
40.00 Appropriation			13
68.00 Spending authority from offsetting collections: Offsetting collections (cash)			9
70.00 Total new budget authority (gross)			22
Change in unpaid obligations:			
73.10 Total new obligations			22
73.20 Total outlays (gross)			−21
74.40 Unpaid obligations, end of year: Obligated balance, end of year			1
Outlays (gross), detail:			
86.90 Outlays from new discretionary authority			21
Offsets:			
Against gross budget authority and outlays:			
88.00 Offsetting collections (cash) from: Federal sources			−9
Net budget authority and outlays:			
89.00 Budget authority			13
90.00 Outlays			12

Security.—Provides for the necessary planning, development and implementation of policies and procedures and the delivery of security services for the Department of Commerce.

Performance measures.—Effectively protect the personnel, facilities, infrastructure, and information that constitute the Department of Commerce through risk management to include: promulgation of effective policies; compliance reviews conducted; multi-disciplinary security operations support to the Office of the Secretary, bureaus, and operating units; Secretarial trips supported; facility vulnerability assessments completed.

Contribution to the Department's responsibility in protecting the national security through effective Countermeasures Program to include Counterintelligence (CI) and Information Assurance. Measurements include: ongoing CI cases managed; compromises detected; compromises prevented; personnel provided security awareness briefings; liaison conducted; information technology systems accredited; communications security equipment maintained operational; personnel security actions completed.

Ensuring the continuity of the Department's mission to include: updating of the continuity of operations plan; establishment of a relocation site; conducting at least one exercise to test capabilities; effective support of Federal Response Plan and National Emergency Management Team members.

Reimbursable program.—Provides a centralized collection source for special tasks or costs and their billing to users.

Object Classification (in millions of dollars)

Identification code 13–0130–0–1–376	1999 actual	2000 est.	2001 est.
Direct obligations:			
11.1 Personnel compensation: Full-time permanent			7
12.1 Civilian personnel benefits			2
21.0 Travel and transportation of persons			1
25.2 Other services			2
31.0 Equipment			1
99.0 Subtotal, direct obligations			13
99.0 Reimbursable obligations			9
99.9 Total new obligations			22

Personnel Summary

Identification code 13–0130–0–1–376	1999 actual	2000 est.	2001 est.
1001 Total compensable workyears: Full-time equivalent employment			154

OFFICE OF INSPECTOR GENERAL

For necessary expenses of the Office of Inspector General in carrying out the provisions of the Inspector General Act of 1978, as amended (5 U.S.C. App. 1–11, as amended by Public Law 100–504), [$20,000,000] *$22,726,000*. *(Department of Commerce and Related Agencies Appropriations Act, 2000, as enacted by section 1000(a)(1) of the Consolidated Appropriations Act, 2000 (P.L. 106–113).)*

Program and Financing (in millions of dollars)

Identification code 13–0126–0–1–376	1999 actual	2000 est.	2001 est.
Obligations by program activity:			
00.01 Direct program	21	20	23
10.00 Total new obligations	21	20	23
Budgetary resources available for obligation:			
22.00 New budget authority (gross)	21	20	23
23.95 Total new obligations	−21	−20	−23

	New budget authority (gross), detail:			
	Discretionary:			
40.00	Appropriation	21	20	23
	Change in unpaid obligations:			
72.40	Unpaid obligations, start of year: Obligated balance, start of year	3	3	2
73.10	Total new obligations	21	20	23
73.20	Total outlays (gross)	−21	−21	−22
74.40	Unpaid obligations, end of year: Obligated balance, end of year	3	2	3
	Outlays (gross), detail:			
86.90	Outlays from new discretionary authority	17	18	20
86.93	Outlays from discretionary balances	3	3	2
87.00	Total outlays (gross)	21	21	22
	Net budget authority and outlays:			
89.00	Budget authority	21	20	23
90.00	Outlays	20	21	22

This appropriation provides for agency-wide audits, inspections, and investigative functions to identify and recommend corrections for management and administrative deficiencies that create conditions for existing or potential instances of fraud, waste, and mismanagement. The audit function provides for internal audits and contract audits. Contract audits provide professional advice to agency contracting officials on accounting and financial matters related to negotiation, award, administration, repricing, and settlement of contracts. Internal audits review and evaluate all facets of agency operations. Inspections services provide detailed technical evaluations of agency operations. The investigative function provides for the detection and investigation of improper and illegal activities involving programs, personnel, and operations.

Activities under the Office of Inspector General's (OIG) account support the Commerce Annual Performance Plan: U.S. competitiveness in the global marketplace; American competitiveness through science and technology and an unrivaled information base; and, effective stewardship of our Nation's resources and assets to ensure sustainable economic opportunities.

The OIG concentrates on programs and operations that have the greatest potential for identifying fraud, recovering funds, precluding unnecessary outlays, and improving management. The OIG identifies the audit, inspection, and investigative universe and determines how it will focus its work on areas that significantly affect the Department's ability to prevent and detect fraud, waste, abuse, and mismanagement.

The OIG's Semiannual Report to the Congress provides the following Statistical Highlights:

- Value of questioned costs identified in audit reports.
- Value of audit recommendations that funds be put to better use.
- Value of audit recommendations agreed to by management.
- Arrests, indictments, convictions, personnel actions, administrative actions, and fines, restitutions, judgments, and civil and administrative recoveries.

Object Classification (in millions of dollars)

Identification code 13–0126–0–1–376		1999 actual	2000 est.	2001 est.
11.1	Personnel compensation: Full-time permanent	12	12	13
12.1	Civilian personnel benefits	3	3	3
21.0	Travel and transportation of persons			1
23.1	Rental payments to GSA	2	2	2
25.2	Other services	3	2	3
25.3	Purchases of goods and services from Government accounts	1	1	1
99.9	Total new obligations	21	20	23

Personnel Summary

Identification code 13–0126–0–1–376		1999 actual	2000 est.	2001 est.
1001	Total compensable workyears: Full-time equivalent employment	177	200	200

Intragovernmental funds:

WORKING CAPITAL FUND

Program and Financing (in millions of dollars)

Identification code 13–4511–0–4–376		1999 actual	2000 est.	2001 est.
	Obligations by program activity:			
09.01	Departmental staff services	75	88	71
09.02	General counsel	21	25	26
09.03	Public affairs	2	2	2
09.99	Total reimbursable program	98	115	99
10.00	Total new obligations	98	115	99
	Budgetary resources available for obligation:			
21.40	Unobligated balance available, start of year	3	3	3
22.00	New budget authority (gross)	97	115	99
23.90	Total budgetary resources available for obligation	100	118	102
23.95	Total new obligations	−98	−115	−99
24.40	Unobligated balance available, end of year	3	3	3
	New budget authority (gross), detail:			
	Mandatory:			
69.00	Offsetting collections (cash)	92	115	99
69.10	From Federal sources: Change in receivables and unpaid, unfilled orders	5		
69.90	Spending authority from offsetting collections (total mandatory)	97	115	99
	Change in unpaid obligations:			
	Unpaid obligations, start of year:			
72.40	Obligated balance, start of year	−7	−9	−9
72.95	From Federal sources: Receivables and unpaid, unfilled orders	28	33	33
72.99	Total unpaid obligations, start of year	21	24	24
73.10	Total new obligations	98	115	99
73.20	Total outlays (gross)	−94	−115	−99
	Unpaid obligations, end of year:			
74.40	Obligated balance, end of year	−9	−9	−9
74.95	From Federal sources: Receivables and unpaid, unfilled orders	33	33	33
74.99	Total unpaid obligations, end of year	24	24	24
	Outlays (gross), detail:			
86.97	Outlays from new mandatory authority	92	115	99
86.98	Outlays from mandatory balances	2		
87.00	Total outlays (gross)	94	115	99
	Offsets:			
	Against gross budget authority and outlays:			
88.00	Offsetting collections (cash) from: Federal sources	−92	−115	−99
	Against gross budget authority only:			
88.95	From Federal sources: Change in receivables and unpaid, unfilled orders	−5		
	Net budget authority and outlays:			
89.00	Budget authority			
90.00	Outlays	2		

This fund finances, on a reimbursable basis, Department-wide administrative functions that are more efficiently and economically performed on a centralized basis.

Object Classification (in millions of dollars)

Identification code 13–4511–0–4–376		1999 actual	2000 est.	2001 est.
11.1	Personnel compensation: Full-time permanent	35	45	40

Intragovernmental funds—Continued

WORKING CAPITAL FUND—Continued

Object Classification (in millions of dollars)—Continued

Identification code 13–4511–0–4–376	1999 actual	2000 est.	2001 est.
12.1 Civilian personnel benefits	7	9	9
23.1 Rental payments to GSA	5	6	6
23.3 Communications, utilities, and miscellaneous charges	4	4	4
24.0 Printing and reproduction		1	1
25.2 Other services	35	42	32
25.3 Purchases of goods and services from Government accounts	2	3	3
26.0 Supplies and materials	3	3	3
31.0 Equipment	7	2	1
99.9 Total new obligations	98	115	99

Personnel Summary

Identification code 13–4511–0–4–376	1999 actual	2000 est.	2001 est.
2001 Total compensable workyears: Full-time equivalent employment	559	721	591

FRANCHISE FUND

Program and Financing (in millions of dollars)

Identification code 13–4564–0–4–376	1999 actual	2000 est.	2001 est.
Obligations by program activity:			
09.02 O/S Office of Computer Services	16	17	23
10.00 Total new obligations	16	17	23
Budgetary resources available for obligation:			
21.40 Unobligated balance available, start of year	1	1	1
22.00 New budget authority (gross)	16	17	23
23.90 Total budgetary resources available for obligation	17	18	24
23.95 Total new obligations	−16	−17	−23
24.40 Unobligated balance available, end of year	1	1	1
New budget authority (gross), detail:			
Mandatory:			
69.00 Offsetting collections (cash)	18	17	23
69.10 From Federal sources: Change in receivables and unpaid, unfilled orders	−2		
69.90 Spending authority from offsetting collections (total mandatory)	16	17	23
Change in unpaid obligations:			
Unpaid obligations, start of year:			
72.40 Obligated balance, start of year	−1	−3	−1
72.95 From Federal sources: Receivables and unpaid, unfilled orders	5	3	3
72.99 Total unpaid obligations, start of year	4		2
73.10 Total new obligations	16	17	23
73.20 Total outlays (gross)	−21	−17	−23
Unpaid obligations, end of year:			
74.40 Obligated balance, end of year	−3	−1	−1
74.95 From Federal sources: Receivables and unpaid, unfilled orders	3	3	3
74.99 Total unpaid obligations, end of year		2	2
Outlays (gross), detail:			
86.97 Outlays from new mandatory authority	16	17	23
86.98 Outlays from mandatory balances	5	1	
87.00 Total outlays (gross)	21	17	23
Offsets:			
Against gross budget authority and outlays:			
88.00 Offsetting collections (cash) from: Federal sources	−18	−17	−23
Against gross budget authority only:			
88.95 From Federal sources: Change in receivables and unpaid, unfilled orders	2		
Net budget authority and outlays:			
89.00 Budget authority			
90.00 Outlays	3		

This fund finances computer services and other administrative support services on a fully competitive and cost reimbursable basis to Federal customers.

Object Classification (in millions of dollars)

Identification code 13–4564–0–4–376	1999 actual	2000 est.	2001 est.
11.1 Personnel compensation: Full-time permanent	3	3	3
23.3 Communications, utilities, and miscellaneous charges	1	1	1
25.2 Other services	12	13	19
99.9 Total new obligations	16	17	23

Personnel Summary

Identification code 13–4564–0–4–376	1999 actual	2000 est.	2001 est.
2001 Total compensable workyears: Full-time equivalent employment	26	34	34

Credit accounts:

EMERGENCY OIL AND GAS GUARANTEED LOAN PROGRAM ACCOUNT

Program and Financing (in millions of dollars)

Identification code 13–0121–0–1–376	1999 actual	2000 est.	2001 est.
Guarantee loan subsidy:			
Obligations by program activity:			
00.02 Guarantee loan subsidy		123	
00.09 Administrative expenses		2	
10.00 Total new obligations		125	
Budgetary resources available for obligation:			
21.40 Unobligated balance available, start of year		125	
22.00 New budget authority (gross)	125		
23.90 Total budgetary resources available for obligation	125	125	
23.95 Total new obligations		−125	
24.40 Unobligated balance available, end of year	125		
New budget authority (gross), detail:			
Discretionary:			
40.00 Appropriation	125		
Change in unpaid obligations:			
73.10 Total new obligations		125	
73.20 Total outlays (gross)		−125	
Outlays (gross), detail:			
86.93 Outlays from discretionary balances		125	
Net budget authority and outlays:			
89.00 Budget authority	125		
90.00 Outlays		125	

As required by the Federal Credit Reform Act of 1990, this account records the administrative expenses for this program, as well as the subsidy costs associated with the loan guarantees committed in 1992 and thereafter, if any. The subsidy amounts are estimated on a present value basis; the administrative expenses are estimated on a cash basis.

Summary of Loan Levels, Subsidy Budget Authority and Outlays by Program (in millions of dollars)

Identification code 13–0121–0–1–376	1999 actual	2000 est.	2001 est.
Guaranteed loan levels supportable by subsidy budget authority:			
2150 Loan guarantee levels		500	
2159 Total loan guarantee levels		500	
Guaranteed loan subsidy (in percent):			
2320 Subsidy rate	24.50	24.50	

		1999 actual	2000 est.	2001 est.
2329	Weighted average subsidy rate	24.50	24.50	
	Guaranteed loan subsidy budget authority:			
2330	Subsidy budget authority	123		
2339	Total subsidy budget authority	123		
	Guaranteed loan subsidy outlays:			
2340	Subsidy outlays		123	
2349	Total subsidy outlays		123	
	Administrative expense data:			
3510	Budget authority	2		
3580	Outlays from balances		2	
3590	Outlays from new authority			

Object Classification (in millions of dollars)

Identification code 13–0121–0–1–376		1999 actual	2000 est.	2001 est.
25.3	Purchases of goods and services from Government accounts		2	
41.0	Grants, subsidies, and contributions		123	
99.9	Total new obligations		125	

Emergency Oil and Gas Guaranteed Loan Financing Account

Program and Financing (in millions of dollars)

Identification code 13–4327–0–3–376		1999 actual	2000 est.	2001 est.
	Budgetary resources available for obligation:			
21.40	Unobligated balance available, start of year			128
22.00	New financing authority (gross)		128	6
23.90	Total budgetary resources available for obligation		128	134
24.40	Unobligated balance available, end of year		128	134
	New financing authority (gross), detail:			
	Discretionary:			
68.00	Spending authority from offsetting collections (gross): Offsetting collections (cash)		128	6
	Offsets:			
	Against gross financing authority and financing disbursements:			
	Offsetting collections (cash) from:			
88.00	Federal sources		–123	
88.25	Interest on uninvested funds		–3	–6
88.40	Non-Federal sources—fees		–2	
88.90	Total, offsetting collections (cash)		–128	–6
	Net financing authority and financing disbursements:			
89.00	Financing authority			
90.00	Financing disbursements		–128	–6

As required by the Federal Credit Reform Act of 1990, this non-budgetary account records all cash flows to and from the Government resulting from direct loans obligated in 1992 and thereafter (including modifications of direct loans that resulted from obligations in any year). The amounts in this account are a means of financing and are not included in the budget totals.

Status of Guaranteed Loans (in millions of dollars)

Identification code 13–4327–0–3–376		1999 actual	2000 est.	2001 est.
	Position with respect to appropriations act limitation on commitments:			
2111	Limitation on guaranteed loans made by private lenders		500	
2150	Total guaranteed loan commitments		500	
	Cumulative balance of guaranteed loans outstanding:			
2210	Outstanding, start of year			500
2231	Disbursements of new guaranteed loans		500	
2251	Repayments and prepayments			–50
2290	Outstanding, end of year		500	450
	Memorandum:			
2299	Guaranteed amount of guaranteed loans outstanding, end of year		500	450

Balance Sheet (in millions of dollars)

Identification code 13–4327–0–3–376		1998 actual	1999 actual	2000 est.	2001 est.
	ASSETS:				
1101	Federal assets: Fund balances with Treasury			128	134
1999	Total assets			128	134
	LIABILITIES:				
2999	Total liabilities				
	NET POSITION:				
3100	Appropriated capital			128	134
3999	Total net position			128	134
4999	Total liabilities and net position			128	134

Emergency Steel Guaranteed Loan Program Account

Program and Financing (in millions of dollars)

Identification code 13–0122–0–1–376		1999 actual	2000 est.	2001 est.
	Obligations by program activity:			
00.02	Guarantee loan subsidy		140	
00.09	Administrative expenses		5	
10.00	Total new obligations		145	
	Budgetary resources available for obligation:			
21.40	Unobligated balance available, start of year		145	
22.00	New budget authority (gross)	145		
23.90	Total budgetary resources available for obligation	145	145	
23.95	Total new obligations		–145	
24.40	Unobligated balance available, end of year	145		
	New budget authority (gross), detail:			
	Discretionary:			
40.00	Appropriation	145		
	Change in unpaid obligations:			
73.10	Total new obligations		145	
73.20	Total outlays (gross)		–145	
	Outlays (gross), detail:			
86.93	Outlays from discretionary balances		145	
	Net budget authority and outlays:			
89.00	Budget authority	145		
90.00	Outlays		145	

As required by the Federal Credit Reform Act of 1990, this account records the administrative expenses for this program, as well as the subsidy costs associated with the loan guarantees committed in 1992 and thereafter, if any. The subsidy amounts are estimated on a present value basis; the administrative expenses are estimated on a cash basis.

Summary of Loan Levels, Subsidy Budget Authority and Outlays by Program (in millions of dollars)

Identification code 13–0122–0–1–376		1999 actual	2000 est.	2001 est.
	Guaranteed loan levels supportable by subsidy budget authority:			
2150	Loan guarantee levels		1,000	
	Guaranteed loan subsidy (in percent):			
2320	Subsidy rate	14.00	14.00	
	Guaranteed loan subsidy budget authority:			
2330	Subsidy budget authority	140		
	Guaranteed loan subsidy outlays:			
2340	Subsidy outlays		140	
	Administrative expense data:			
3510	Budget authority	5		

Credit accounts—Continued

EMERGENCY STEEL GUARANTEED LOAN PROGRAM ACCOUNT—Continued

Summary of Loan Levels, Subsidy Budget Authority and Outlays by Program (in millions of dollars)—Continued

Identification code 13–0122–0–1–376	1999 actual	2000 est.	2001 est.
3580 Outlays from balances	....	5	....
3590 Outlays from new authority	....	....	....

Object Classification (in millions of dollars)

Identification code 13–0122–0–1–376	1999 actual	2000 est.	2001 est.
25.3 Purchases of goods and services from Government accounts	....	5	....
41.0 Grants, subsidies, and contributions	....	140	....
99.9 Total new obligations	....	145	....

EMERGENCY STEEL GUARANTEED LOAN FINANCING ACCOUNT

Program and Financing (in millions of dollars)

Identification code 13–4328–0–3–376	1999 actual	2000 est.	2001 est.
Budgetary resources available for obligation:			
21.40 Unobligated balance available, start of year	....	....	149
22.00 New financing authority (gross)	....	149	7
23.90 Total budgetary resources available for obligation	....	149	156
24.40 Unobligated balance available, end of year	....	149	156
New financing authority (gross), detail:			
Discretionary:			
68.00 Spending authority from offsetting collections (gross): Offsetting collections (cash)	....	149	7
Offsets:			
Against gross financing authority and financing disbursements:			
Offsetting collections (cash) from:			
88.00 Federal sources	....	−140	....
88.25 Interest on uninvested funds	....	−4	−7
88.40 Non-Federal sources—fees	....	−5	....
88.90 Total, offsetting collections (cash)	....	−149	−7
Net financing authority and financing disbursements:			
89.00 Financing authority	....	....	....
90.00 Financing disbursements	....	−149	−7

As required by the Federal Credit Reform Act of 1990, this non-budgetary account records all cash flows to and from the Government resulting from direct loans obligated in 1992 and thereafter (including modifications of direct loans that resulted from obligations in any year). The amounts in this account are a means of financing and are not included in the budget totals.

Status of Guaranteed Loans (in millions of dollars)

Identification code 13–4328–0–3–376	1999 actual	2000 est.	2001 est.
Position with respect to appropriations act limitation on commitments:			
2111 Limitation on guaranteed loans made by private lenders	....	1,000	....
Cumulative balance of guaranteed loans outstanding:			
2210 Outstanding, start of year	....	....	1,000
2231 Disbursements of new guaranteed loans	....	1,000	....
2251 Repayments and prepayments	....	....	−100
2290 Outstanding, end of year	....	1,000	900
Memorandum:			
2299 Guaranteed amount of guaranteed loans outstanding, end of year	....	1,000	900

Balance Sheet (in millions of dollars)

Identification code 13–4328–0–3–376	1998 actual	1999 actual	2000 est.	2001 est.
ASSETS:				
1101 Federal assets: Fund balances with Treasury	....	....	149	156
1999 Total assets	....	....	149	156
LIABILITIES:				
2999 Total liabilities	....	....	....	....
NET POSITION:				
3100 Appropriated capital	....	....	149	156
3999 Total net position	....	....	149	156
4999 Total liabilities and net position	....	....	149	156

Trust Funds

GIFTS AND BEQUESTS

Unavailable Collections (in millions of dollars)

Identification code 13–8501–0–7–376	1999 actual	2000 est.	2001 est.
Balance, start of year:			
01.99 Balance, start of year	....	....	....
Receipts:			
02.01 Gifts and bequests	1	1	1
Appropriation:			
05.01 Gifts and bequests	−1	−1	−1
07.99 Total balance, end of year	....	....	....

Program and Financing (in millions of dollars)

Identification code 13–8501–0–7–376	1999 actual	2000 est.	2001 est.
Obligations by program activity:			
10.00 Total new obligations (object class 25.2)	1	1	1
Budgetary resources available for obligation:			
21.40 Unobligated balance available, start of year	....	1	1
22.00 New budget authority (gross)	1	1	1
23.90 Total budgetary resources available for obligation	1	2	2
23.95 Total new obligations	−1	−1	−1
24.40 Unobligated balance available, end of year	1	1	1
New budget authority (gross), detail:			
Mandatory:			
60.27 Appropriation (trust fund, indefinite)	1	1	1
Change in unpaid obligations:			
73.10 Total new obligations	1	1	1
73.20 Total outlays (gross)	−1	−1	−1
Outlays (gross), detail:			
86.97 Outlays from new mandatory authority	1	1	1
86.98 Outlays from mandatory balances	....	1	....
87.00 Total outlays (gross)	1	1	1
Net budget authority and outlays:			
89.00 Budget authority	1	1	1
90.00 Outlays	1	1	1

The Secretary of Commerce is authorized to accept, hold, administer, and utilize gifts and bequests of property, both real and personal, for the purpose of aiding or facilitating the work of the Department of Commerce. Property and the proceeds thereof are used as nearly as possible in accordance with the terms of the gift or bequest.

ECONOMIC DEVELOPMENT ADMINISTRATION

Federal Funds

General and special funds:

SALARIES AND EXPENSES

For necessary expenses of administering the economic development assistance programs as provided for by law, [$26,500,000] *$27,688,000*: *Provided*, That these funds may be used to monitor projects approved pursuant to title I of the Public Works Employment Act of 1976, as amended, title II of the Trade Act of 1974, as amended, and the Community Emergency Drought Relief Act of 1977. *(19 U.S.C. 2346(b); 42 U.S.C. 3218(c), 3219, 5184, and 6701; Department of Commerce and Related Agencies Appropriations Act, 2000, as enacted by section 1000(a)(1) of the Consolidated Appropriations Act, 2000 (P.L. 106–113).)*

Program and Financing (in millions of dollars)

Identification code 13–0125–0–1–452	1999 actual	2000 est.	2001 est.
Obligations by program activity:			
00.01 Direct program	27	29	28
09.01 Reimbursable program	2	2	1
10.00 Total new obligations	29	31	29
Budgetary resources available for obligation:			
21.40 Unobligated balance available, start of year	3	2	
22.00 New budget authority (gross)	28	29	29
23.90 Total budgetary resources available for obligation	31	31	29
23.95 Total new obligations	−29	−31	−29
24.40 Unobligated balance available, end of year	2		
New budget authority (gross), detail:			
Discretionary:			
40.00 Appropriation	24	27	28
42.00 Transferred from other accounts	2		
43.00 Appropriation (total discretionary)	26	27	28
68.00 Spending authority from offsetting collections: Offsetting collections (cash)	2	2	1
70.00 Total new budget authority (gross)	28	29	29
Change in unpaid obligations:			
72.40 Unpaid obligations, start of year: Obligated balance, start of year	2	3	4
73.10 Total new obligations	29	31	29
73.20 Total outlays (gross)	−28	−30	−29
74.40 Unpaid obligations, end of year: Obligated balance, end of year	3	4	4
Outlays (gross), detail:			
86.90 Outlays from new discretionary authority	26	26	26
86.93 Outlays from discretionary balances	2	4	3
87.00 Total outlays (gross)	28	30	29
Offsets:			
Against gross budget authority and outlays:			
88.00 Offsetting collections (cash) from: Federal sources	−2	−2	−1
Net budget authority and outlays:			
89.00 Budget authority	26	27	28
90.00 Outlays	26	28	28

Summary of Budget Authority and Outlays

(in millions of dollars)

	1999 actual	*2000 est.*	*2001 est.*
Enacted/requested:			
Budget Authority	26	27	28
Outlays	26	28	28
Supplemental proposal:			
Budget Authority		1	
Outlays		1	
Total:			
Budget Authority	26	28	28
Outlays	26	29	28

The administration of EDA's economic development assistance programs is carried out through a network of headquarters and regional personnel.

Direct program.—These activities include preapplication development, application processing, and project monitoring as well as general support functions such as economic development research, information dissemination, legal, civil rights, environmental compliance, budgeting and debt management.

Reimbursable program.—EDA provides grant review and processing services to other Federal agencies on a reimbursable basis. Funds received cover the cost of performing this work.

Object Classification (in millions of dollars)

Identification code 13–0125–0–1–452	1999 actual	2000 est.	2001 est.
Direct obligations:			
11.1 Personnel compensation: Full-time permanent	17	17	17
12.1 Civilian personnel benefits	3	4	4
21.0 Travel and transportation of persons	1	1	1
23.1 Rental payments to GSA	2	2	2
25.2 Other services	1	2	1
25.3 Purchases of goods and services from Government accounts	2	2	2
25.7 Operation and maintenance of equipment	1	1	1
99.0 Subtotal, direct obligations	27	29	28
99.0 Reimbursable obligations	2	2	1
99.9 Total new obligations	29	31	29

Personnel Summary

Identification code 13–0125–0–1–452	1999 actual	2000 est.	2001 est.
Direct:			
1001 Total compensable workyears: Full-time equivalent employment	249	261	262
Reimbursable:			
2001 Total compensable workyears: Full-time equivalent employment	13	7	7

ECONOMIC DEVELOPMENT ASSISTANCE PROGRAMS

For grants for economic development assistance as provided by the Public Works and Economic Development Act of 1965, as amended, and for trade adjustment assistance, [$361,879,000] *$409,250,000* to [be made] *remain* available until expended. *(19 U.S.C. 2343, 2355; 42 U.S.C. 3121, 3141, 3143, 3145, 3147, 3149, 3171, 3173, and 3231–3233; Department of Commerce and Related Agencies Appropriations Act, 2000, as enacted by section 1000(a)(1) of the Consolidated Appropriations Act, 2000 (P.L. 106–113).)*

Program and Financing (in millions of dollars)

Identification code 13–2050–0–1–452	1999 actual	2000 est.	2001 est.
Obligations by program activity:			
Direct program:			
00.01 Planning grants	24	24	26
00.02 Technical assistance grants	9	9	11
00.03 Public works grants	206	205	241
00.04 Economic adjustment grants	34	35	70
00.05 Research and evaluation	1	1	1
00.06 Defense economic conversion	85	77	50
00.07 Trade adjustment assistance	10	10	10
00.08 Hurricanes Andrew, Fran and Hortense	2	1	
00.09 Tri-State Floods (Grant) & Upper Midwest Floods	12	1	
00.10 Alaska	3	16	
00.11 Norton Sound Fisheries			10
09.01 Reimbursable program	17	1	1
10.00 Total new obligations	403	380	420
Budgetary resources available for obligation:			
21.40 Unobligated balance available, start of year	17	18	
22.00 New budget authority (gross)	404	362	420
22.10 Resources available from recoveries of prior year obligations	1		
23.90 Total budgetary resources available for obligation	422	380	420

General and special funds—Continued

ECONOMIC DEVELOPMENT ASSISTANCE PROGRAMS—Continued

Program and Financing (in millions of dollars)—Continued

Identification code 13–2050–0–1–452	1999 actual	2000 est.	2001 est.
23.95 Total new obligations	–403	–380	–420
24.40 Unobligated balance available, end of year	18		
New budget authority (gross), detail:			
Discretionary:			
40.00 Appropriation	368	362	409
40.76 Reduction pursuant to P.L. 106–113		–1	
42.00 Transferred from other accounts	19		10
43.00 Appropriation (total discretionary)	387	361	419
68.00 Spending authority from offsetting collections: Offsetting collections (cash)	17	1	1
70.00 Total new budget authority (gross)	404	362	420
Change in unpaid obligations:			
72.40 Unpaid obligations, start of year: Obligated balance, start of year	972	973	946
73.10 Total new obligations	403	380	420
73.20 Total outlays (gross)	–372	–406	–399
73.40 Adjustments in expired accounts (net)	–28		
73.45 Adjustments in unexpired accounts	–1		
74.40 Unpaid obligations, end of year: Obligated balance, end of year	973	946	967
Outlays (gross), detail:			
86.90 Outlays from new discretionary authority	72	19	22
86.93 Outlays from discretionary balances	300	387	377
87.00 Total outlays (gross)	372	406	399
Offsets:			
Against gross budget authority and outlays:			
88.00 Offsetting collections (cash) from: Federal sources	–17	–1	–1
Net budget authority and outlays:			
89.00 Budget authority	387	361	419
90.00 Outlays	355	405	398

Summary of Budget Authority and Outlays

(in millions of dollars)

	1999 actual	2000 est.	2001 est.
Enacted/requested:			
Budget Authority	387	361	419
Outlays	355	405	398
Supplemental proposal:			
Budget Authority		24	
Outlays		3	13
Total:			
Budget Authority	387	385	419
Outlays	355	408	411

The Economic Development Administration (EDA) provides grants for public works facilities, other financial assistance, and planning and coordination assistance needed to alleviate conditions of substantial and persistent unemployment and underemployment in economically distressed areas and regions. EDA assistance stimulates job creation and increases income in distressed communities, promotes greater national productivity and balanced economic growth.

In 2001, EDA's Community and Regional Economic Enhancement program will continue to serve as the catalyst for assisting distressed communities in achieving their long-term competitive economic potential through the strategic investment of resources based upon locally and regionally developed priorities. EDA will implement an e-commerce program which will create equitable access to new technologies and create the broadband networks necessary to support full access to e-commerce in all communities. EDA will strengthen its efforts to assist American Indian Tribes and Alaskan Native Villages by providing capacity building and developing finance and infrastructure projects needed to enable these communities to be more effective and competitive in their economic development efforts. EDA will also provide comprehensive support for economic development efforts in the highly distressed communities of the lower Mississippi Delta Region and will continue to help distressed communities recover from sudden and/or severe economic downturns such as those caused by increased foreign imports, international trade agreements and industry downsizing.

EDA responds to community priorities and strives to meet its objectives through the use of a broad range of program tools:

Planning grants.—Support the design and implementation of effective economic development policies and programs by local organizations.

Technical assistance grants.—Provide for local feasibility and industry studies, funding for a network of university centers that assist public bodies, nonprofit organizations, and businesses to plan and implement activities designed to generate jobs and income in distressed areas.

Public works grants.—Provide for infrastructure projects that foster the establishment or expansion of industrial and commercial businesses generating employment in communities experiencing high unemployment, low per-capita income, or out-migration.

Economic adjustment grants.—Provide a package of assistance tools, including planning, technical assistance, revolving loan funds and infrastructure development, to help communities counteract either a gradual erosion or a sudden dislocation of their local economic structure as a result of natural disasters, international trade competition, or major plant closings. Provide grants to support Brownfields redevelopment.

Research evaluation grants.—Support studies about the causes of economic distress and approaches to alleviating and preventing such problems, national demonstrations of innovative economic development techniques, and dissemination of economic development information.

Defense economic adjustment grants.—Provide communities impacted by Department of Defense and Department of Energy downsizing, as well as defense contract reductions, with tools for developing integrated plans to adjust to economic dislocations and assist in the implementation of these plans.

Trade adjustment assistance.—Provide technical assistance, through a national network of 12 Trade Adjustment Assistance Centers, to certified U.S. manufacturing firms and industries economically injured as the result of international trade competition.

Performance measures.—All EDA program activities under this account support the Department of Commerce strategic goals to expand economic growth, trade, and prosperity; to stimulate innovation for American competitiveness; and to advance sustainable economic development. For investments made in 1999, 2000, and 2001, long-term outcome results will be reported by grantees over a period of nine years following grant award and project completion. For example, 2001 grants for construction and revolving loan fund projects are expected to create or retain 61,543 jobs by 2010. Below are EDA's strategic goals and selected performance measures that demonstrate EDA's support of Commerce strategic goals:

EDA Goal 1: Creation of jobs in economically distressed areas

Performance measure	Projected outcomes		
	FY 2004	FY 2007	FY 2010
Permanent number of jobs created or retained	6,154	30,722	61,543
	FY 1999	FY 2000	FY 2001
Percent of awards invested in areas of highest distress	36	30	30

EDA Goal 2: Build local capacity to achieve and sustain economic growth

Performance measure	Projected outcomes FY 1999	FY 2000	FY 2001
Percent of awards invested in areas of highest distress	31	25	25

Note: For FY1999 actual results have been tabulated.

A more detailed presentation of goals, performance measures and targets is found in the Commerce Annual Performance Plan.

Object Classification (in millions of dollars)

Identification code 13–2050–0–1–452	1999 actual	2000 est.	2001 est.
41.0 Direct obligations: Grants, subsidies, and contributions	386	379	419
99.0 Reimbursable obligations: Subtotal, reimbursable obligations	17	1	1
99.9 Total new obligations	403	380	420

Public enterprise funds:

ECONOMIC DEVELOPMENT REVOLVING FUND LIQUIDATING ACCOUNT

Program and Financing (in millions of dollars)

Identification code 13–4406–0–3–452	1999 actual	2000 est.	2001 est.
Obligations by program activity:			
00.01 Interest expense	3	3	3
00.02 Defaults and care and protection of collateral	2	2	2
10.00 Total new obligations	5	5	5
Budgetary resources available for obligation:			
21.40 Unobligated balance available, start of year		6	
22.00 New budget authority (gross)	11	5	5
22.40 Capital transfer to general fund		−6	
23.90 Total budgetary resources available for obligation	11	5	5
23.95 Total new obligations	−5	−5	−5
24.40 Unobligated balance available, end of year	6		
New budget authority (gross), detail:			
Mandatory:			
69.00 Offsetting collections (cash)	11	5	5
Change in unpaid obligations:			
72.40 Unpaid obligations, start of year: Obligated balance, start of year	4	3	4
73.10 Total new obligations	5	5	5
73.20 Total outlays (gross)	−5	−5	−5
74.40 Unpaid obligations, end of year: Obligated balance, end of year	3	4	4
Outlays (gross), detail:			
86.97 Outlays from new mandatory authority	1	5	5
86.98 Outlays from mandatory balances	4		
87.00 Total outlays (gross)	5	5	5
Offsets:			
Against gross budget authority and outlays:			
88.40 Offsetting collections (cash) from: Non-Federal sources	−11	−5	−5
Net budget authority and outlays:			
89.00 Budget authority			
90.00 Outlays	−5		

Status of Direct Loans (in millions of dollars)

Identification code 13–4406–0–3–452	1999 actual	2000 est.	2001 est.
Cumulative balance of direct loans outstanding:			
1210 Outstanding, start of year	54	43	37
1251 Repayments: Repayments and prepayments	−7	−5	−3
Write-offs for default:			
1263 Direct loans	−3	−1	−1
1264 Other adjustments, net	−1		
1290 Outstanding, end of year	43	37	33

Status of Guaranteed Loans (in millions of dollars)

Identification code 13–4406–0–3–452	1999 actual	2000 est.	2001 est.
Cumulative balance of guaranteed loans outstanding:			
2210 Outstanding, start of year	13	3	1
2251 Repayments and prepayments	−5		
2264 Adjustments: Other adjustments, net	−5	−2	
2290 Outstanding, end of year	3	1	1
Memorandum:			
2299 Guaranteed amount of guaranteed loans outstanding, end of year	2		

As required by the Federal Credit Reform Act of 1990, this account records, for these programs, all cash flows to and from the Government resulting from direct loans obligated and loan guarantees committed prior to 1992. This includes interest loans outstanding; principal repayments from loans made under the Area Redevelopment Act, the Public Works and Economic Development Act of 1965, and the Trade Act of 1974; and proceeds from the sale of collateral are deposited in this fund.

No new loan or guarantee activity is proposed for 2001.

Statement of Operations (in millions of dollars)

Identification code 13–4406–0–3–452	1998 actual	1999 actual	2000 est.	2001 est.
0101 Revenue	2	3	3	2
0102 Expense	−2	−2	−2	−2
0105 Net income or loss (−)		1	1	

Balance Sheet (in millions of dollars)

Identification code 13–4406–0–3–452	1998 actual	1999 actual	2000 est.	2001 est.
ASSETS:				
1101 Federal assets: Fund balances with Treasury	4	9	5	5
Net value of assets related to pre–1992 direct loans receivable and acquired defaulted guaranteed loans receivable:				
1601 Direct loans, gross	52	45	37	33
1603 Allowance for estimated uncollectible loans and interest (−)	−5	−1	−1	−1
1604 Direct loans and interest receivable, net	47	44	36	32
1699 Value of assets related to direct loans	47	44	36	32
1999 Total assets	51	53	41	37
LIABILITIES:				
2102 Federal liabilities: Interest payable	3	3	3	2
2999 Total liabilities	3	3	3	2
NET POSITION:				
3100 Appropriated capital	49	50	38	35
3999 Total net position	49	50	38	35
4999 Total liabilities and net position	52	53	41	37

Object Classification (in millions of dollars)

Identification code 13–4406–0–3–452	1999 actual	2000 est.	2001 est.
25.2 Other services	2	2	2
43.0 Interest and dividends	3	3	3
99.9 Total new obligations	5	5	5

BUREAU OF THE CENSUS

Federal Funds

General and special funds:

SALARIES AND EXPENSES

For expenses necessary for collecting, compiling, analyzing, preparing, and publishing statistics, provided for by law, **[**$140,000,000**]** *$173,826,000. (13 U.S.C. 4, 6, 8(b), 12, 61–63, 181, 182, 301–307, 401; 15 U.S.C. 1516, 4901 et seq.; 19 U.S.C. 1484(e), 2354, 2393; 44 U.S.C. 1343; Department of Commerce and Related Agencies Appropriations Act, 2000, as enacted by section 1000(a)(1) of the Consolidated Appropriations Act, 2000 (P.L. 106–113).)*

Program and Financing (in millions of dollars)

Identification code 13–0401–0–1–376	1999 actual	2000 est.	2001 est.
Obligations by program activity:			
Direct program:			
Current economic statistics:			
00.01 Current economic statistics	92	89	112
00.02 Current demographic statistics	60	67	78
00.03 Survey development and data services	3	4	4
10.00 Total new obligations	155	160	194
Budgetary resources available for obligation:			
22.00 New budget authority (gross)	156	160	194
23.95 Total new obligations	–155	–160	–194
New budget authority (gross), detail:			
Discretionary:			
40.00 Appropriation	136	140	174
42.00 Transferred from other accounts	10		
43.00 Appropriation (total discretionary)	146	140	174
Mandatory:			
60.00 Appropriation	10	20	20
70.00 Total new budget authority (gross)	156	160	194
Change in unpaid obligations:			
72.40 Unpaid obligations, start of year: Obligated balance, start of year	11	2	42
73.10 Total new obligations	155	160	194
73.20 Total outlays (gross)	–165	–120	–173
74.40 Unpaid obligations, end of year: Obligated balance, end of year	2	42	63
Outlays (gross), detail:			
86.90 Outlays from new discretionary authority	146	104	129
86.93 Outlays from discretionary balances	10	1	25
86.97 Outlays from new mandatory authority	9	15	15
86.98 Outlays from mandatory balances	1		5
87.00 Total outlays (gross)	165	120	173
Net budget authority and outlays:			
89.00 Budget authority	156	160	194
90.00 Outlays	165	120	173

The activities of this appropriation provide for the collection, compilation, and publication of a broad range of current economic, demographic, and social statistics.

Current economic statistics.—The business statistics program provides current information on sales and related measures of retail and wholesale trade and selected service industries.

Construction statistics reports are provided on significant construction activity such as housing permits and starts, value of new construction, residential alterations and repairs, and quarterly price indexes for new single-family houses.

Manufacturing statistics survey key industrial commodities and manufacturing activities, providing current statistics on the quantity and value of industrial output.

General economic statistics provide a Standard Statistical Establishment List (SSEL) of all U.S. business firms and their establishments, uniform classification data based on the North American Industry Classification System (NAICS), annual county business data, and corporate financial data. The 2001 program includes initiatives to measure e-business and to conduct an annual Survey of Minority-Owned Business Enterprises (SMOBE).

Foreign trade statistics provide for publication of monthly, cumulative, and annual reports on the quantity, shipping weight, and dollar value of imports and exports, by mode of transportation, detailed commodity category, customs districts, and country of origin or destination. This program covers the Census Bureau responsibilities under the Trade Act of 1974. The 2001 program includes additional funding to improve export data.

Government statistics reports provide information on the revenue, expenditures, indebtedness and debt transactions, financial assets, employment, and payrolls of State and local governments. The Census Bureau provides quarterly information on State and local tax revenue on the national level by type of tax and governmental level, and provides information on financial assistance programs of the Federal government.

Current demographic statistics.—Household surveys provide information on the number, geographic distribution, and the social and economic characteristics of the population. In addition, the demographic statistics program includes an initiative to measure economic well-being.

The Census Bureau compiles housing statistics on the Nation's housing inventory and provides national and regional estimates of housing vacancy rates. Population and housing analyses provide current demographic reports on the geographic distribution and on the demographic, social, and economic characteristics of the population, as well as current estimates and future projections of the population of the United States, and special analyses of demographic, social and economic trends. International statistics provide estimates of population, labor force, and economic activity, including spatial distribution, and analyses concerning aspects of demographic policies, economic policies, and trends for various countries.

Survey development and data services.—The *Statistical Abstract* that the Census Bureau prepares annually summarizes Government and private statistics of the industrial, social, political, and economic activities of the United States. The Bureau conducts general research on survey methods and techniques to find ways of improving the efficiency, accuracy, and timeliness of statistical programs. Data systems development provides advanced data capture, data processing, and information retrieval technology to meet Census Bureau program requirements.

Survey of Program Dynamics.—The Personal Responsibility and Work Opportunity Act of 1996 required that the Survey of Income and Program Participation be expanded to evaluate the impact of welfare reforms made by that Act. The Survey of Program Dynamics will collect data necessary to determine the impact of these provisions. $10 million per year for 7 years (1996–2002) was made available for this study.

The Children's Health Insurance Program (CHIP) was established and funded through mandatory appropriations by the Medicare, Medicaid, and State Children's Health Insurance Program Balanced Budget Refinement Act of 1999 (P.L. 106–113). $10 million was appropriated to produce statistically reliable annual State data on the number of low-income children who do not have health insurance coverage. The CHIP will allocate funds to States based on statistics from an enhanced March Income Supplement to the Current Population Survey (CPS).

Performance measures.—Activities under the Salaries and Expenses account support the Department of Commerce's strategic goal involving promotion of economic growth. The performance goals are to provide quality data and to provide timely and relevant data.

A more detailed presentation of the goals, performance measures, and targets is found in the Commerce Annual Performance Plan.

Object Classification (in millions of dollars)

Identification code 13–0401–0–1–376		1999 actual	2000 est.	2001 est.
	Personnel compensation:			
11.1	Full-time permanent	78	75	90
11.3	Other than full-time permanent	14	15	20
11.5	Other personnel compensation	4	4	4
11.9	Total personnel compensation	96	94	114
12.1	Civilian personnel benefits	10	21	25
21.0	Travel and transportation of persons	5	5	6
22.0	Transportation of things		1	1
23.1	Rental payments to GSA	6	5	5
23.3	Communications, utilities, and miscellaneous charges	5	5	5
24.0	Printing and reproduction	1		1
25.1	Advisory and assistance services	7	5	10
25.2	Other services	5	6	8
25.3	Purchases of goods and services from Government accounts	7	5	3
25.4	Operation and maintenance of facilities	1	1	1
25.5	Research and development contracts		1	
25.7	Operation and maintenance of equipment			1
26.0	Supplies and materials	5	4	5
31.0	Equipment	7	7	9
99.9	Total new obligations	155	160	194

Personnel Summary

Identification code 13–0401–0–1–376		1999 actual	2000 est.	2001 est.
1001	Total compensable workyears: Full-time equivalent employment	1,959	2,149	2,484

PERIODIC CENSUSES AND PROGRAMS

[For necessary expenses to conduct the decennial census, $4,476,253,000 to remain available until expended: of which $20,240,000 is for Program Development and Management; of which $194,623,000 is for Data Content and Products; of which $3,449,952,000 is for Field Data Collection and Support Systems; of which $43,663,000 is for Address List Development; of which $477,379,000 is for Automated Data Processing and Telecommunications Support; of which $15,988,000 is for Testing and Evaluation; of which $71,416,000 is for activities related to Puerto Rico, the Virgin Islands and Pacific Areas; of which $199,492,000 is for Marketing, Communications and Partnerships activities; and of which $3,500,000 is for the Census Monitoring Board, as authorized by section 210 of Public Law 105–119: *Provided*, That the entire amount shall be available only to the extent that an official budget request, that includes designation of the entire amount of the request as an emergency requirement as defined in the Balanced Budget and Emergency Deficit Control Act of 1985, as amended, is transmitted by the President to the Congress: *Provided further*, That the entire amount is designated by the Congress as an emergency requirement pursuant to section 251(b)(2)(A) of the Balanced Budget and Emergency Deficit Control Act of 1985, as amended: *Provided further*, That for purposes of reprogramming among the amounts set forth in the preceding part of this paragraph, the notification requirements of section 605 shall be 3 days, and the reprogramming obligation or expenditure threshold designated in section 605(b) shall be $1,000,000 or 10 percent, whichever is less.]

[In addition, for] *For* expenses to collect and publish statistics for [other] periodic censuses and programs provided for by law, [$142,320,000] *$542,179,000*, to remain available until expended. *In addition, for space planning of renovated existing facilities at headquarters in Suitland, Maryland, $3,200,000, to remain available until expanded. (13 U.S.C. 4, 6, 12, 131, 141, 161, 181, 191; 15 U.S.C. 1516; 42 U.S.C. 1973aa–5; Department of Commerce and Related Agencies Appropriations Act, 2000, as enacted by section 1000(a)(1) of the Consolidated Appropriations Act, 2000 (P.L. 106–113).*

Program and Financing (in millions of dollars)

Identification code 13–0450–0–1–376		1999 actual	2000 est.	2001 est.
	Obligations by program activity:			
	Economic statistics programs:			
00.01	Economic censuses	54	46	43
00.02	Census of governments	4	4	3
	Demographic statistics programs:			
00.06	Intercensal demographic estimates	5	5	6
00.08	2000 Decennial census	1,084	4,510	421
00.09	Continuous measurement	20	20	25
00.10	Demographic surveys sample redesign	5	5	8
00.11	Electronic information collection	8	6	6
00.12	Geographic support	42	33	35
00.13	Data processing	25	23	23
00.14	Suitland Federal Center Office Space Renovation/Construction			3
10.00	Total new obligations	1,247	4,652	573
	Budgetary resources available for obligation:			
21.40	Unobligated balance available, start of year	10	2	
22.00	New budget authority (gross)	1,235	4,610	545
22.10	Resources available from recoveries of prior year obligations	4	40	28
23.90	Total budgetary resources available for obligation	1,249	4,652	573
23.95	Total new obligations	−1,247	−4,652	−573
24.40	Unobligated balance available, end of year	2		
	New budget authority (gross), detail:			
	Discretionary:			
40.00	Appropriation	1,232	142	545
40.15	Appropriation (emergency)		4,477	
40.75	Reduction pursuant to P.L. 106–51	−4		
40.76	Reduction pursuant to P.L. 106–113		−5	
41.00	Transferred to other accounts	−4	−4	
42.00	Transferred from other accounts	11		
43.00	Appropriation (total discretionary)	1,235	4,610	545
	Change in unpaid obligations:			
72.40	Unpaid obligations, start of year: Obligated balance, start of year	165	404	745
73.10	Total new obligations	1,247	4,652	573
73.20	Total outlays (gross)	−1,006	−4,271	−1,169
73.45	Adjustments in unexpired accounts	−4	−40	−28
74.40	Unpaid obligations, end of year: Obligated balance, end of year	404	745	121
	Outlays (gross), detail:			
86.90	Outlays from new discretionary authority	841	3,872	431
86.93	Outlays from discretionary balances	165	399	738
87.00	Total outlays (gross)	1,006	4,271	1,169
	Net budget authority and outlays:			
89.00	Budget authority	1,235	4,610	545
90.00	Outlays	1,006	4,271	1,169

This appropriation funds legislatively mandated economic and periodic demographic censuses and other authorized activities.

Economic statistics programs.—

Economic censuses.—The economic censuses provide data on manufactures, mining, retail and wholesale trade and service industries, construction, and transportation. The censuses are taken every fifth year, covering calendar years ending in two and seven. 2001 is the second year in the 2002 Economic Census cycle, and planning for that census will include initial design of forms and development of processing systems.

Census of governments.—This census collects State and local government data on taxes, tax valuations, governmental receipts, expenditures, indebtedness, and number of employees. This census is taken every fifth year for calendar years ending in two and seven. 2001 is the second year in the five-year cycle of the 2002 Census of governments. The focus for 2001 is planning for the census.

Demographic statistics programs.—

General and special funds—Continued

PERIODIC CENSUSES AND PROGRAMS—Continued

Intercensal demographic estimates.—This program develops updated population estimates in years between decennial censuses, for States, counties, metropolitan areas and urban places; and, prepares a variety of data to meet diverse legislative needs.

Decennial census.—In 2001 Decennial Census activities will focus on the final tabulation and dissemination of data collected during Census 2000. The requested funding will enable the Bureau to complete field work associated with Accuracy and Coverage Evaluation (A.C.E.) follow-up operations, to create a repository for metadata, and to closeout remaining data capture centers and field offices that were opened longer due to increased workloads. 2001 funding will also be used to compare data from the American Community Survey (ACS) with Census 2000 results, and to issue a report on census operations.

The Bureau will deliver to the President, by December 31, 2000, the data used to apportion Congressional seats. Additionally, the population counts from Census 2000 will be delivered to the states for redistricting as required by P.L. 94–171.

Continuous Measurement.—The continuous measurement program will allow the Census Bureau to collect and disseminate, on an annual basis, the types of data collected on the Decennial Census long form. The continuous measurement program will make the Census Bureau the premier source for current population and housing data needed for both near and long-term economic development. The Bureau will continue developing and testing the program in 2001.

Demographic Surveys Sample Redesign.—This program provides for revisions to all of the monthly, quarterly and annual household survey samples to conform to the redistribution of population measured in the decennial census. This is done after each decennial census to update the accuracy of the ongoing surveys. A funding increase is required to complete work for Bureau-specific surveys.

Electronic Information Collection (EIC).—EIC is the Bureau's program to transform the Bureau's business processes—the collection, processing, and dissemination of information. Making the greatest possible use of automation and telecommunications, EIC seeks to provide the tools and systems to deliver to our customers accurate information quickly and efficiently, with as little burden as possible on those who provide the data to the Bureau.

Geographic support.—The activity's goal is to determine the correct location of every business establishment, farm, and residence in the U.S. and its territories. The activity's major components include the Topologically Integrated Geographic Encoding and Referencing (TIGER) data base and the Master Address File (MAF). TIGER provides maps and other geographic information; MAF provides residential addresses for the Nation. TIGER and MAF are important because they provide essential information and products for conducting many of the Bureau's programs.

Data processing systems.—This activity provides for the purchasing or renting of hardware and software needed for the Bureau's general purpose computing facilities.

Suitland Federal Center Office Space Renovation/Construction.—Funding is requested in 2001 for the Bureau's share of space planning to correct the aging, inadequate, and failing building systems at the Bureau's headquarters in the Suitland, MD Federal Center.

Performance measures.—Activities under the Periodic Censuses and Programs account support the Department of Commerce's strategic goal involving promotion of economic growth. The goals are to provide quality data, and to provide timely and relevant data.

A selected performance goal for the Bureau is below.

Goal	Measure	Target for 2001
Conduct an accurate, timely, relevant, and cost-effective decennial census	Produce apportionment counts using traditional census taking methods	100% on time

A more detailed presentation of the goals, performance measures, and targets is found in the Commerce Annual Performance Plan.

Object Classification (in millions of dollars)

Identification code 13–0450–0–1–376		1999 actual	2000 est.	2001 est.
	Personnel compensation:			
11.1	Full-time permanent	150	165	206
11.3	Other than full-time permanent	289	2,479	102
11.5	Other personnel compensation	22	2	7
11.9	Total personnel compensation	461	2,646	315
12.1	Civilian personnel benefits	65	258	51
21.0	Travel and transportation of persons	64	281	17
22.0	Transportation of things	7	23	5
23.1	Rental payments to GSA	33	24	18
23.2	Rental payments to others	4	166	3
23.3	Communications, utilities, and miscellaneous charges	27	283	8
24.0	Printing and reproduction	95	29	2
25.1	Advisory and assistance services	132	26	71
25.2	Other services	187	620	35
25.3	Purchases of goods and services from Government accounts	33	56	8
25.4	Operation and maintenance of facilities	3	12	9
25.5	Research and development contracts	15	13	
25.7	Operation and maintenance of equipment	7	1	2
25.8	Subsistence and support of persons	2		
26.0	Supplies and materials	56	41	9
31.0	Equipment	56	173	20
99.9	Total new obligations	1,247	4,652	573

Personnel Summary

Identification code 13–0450–0–1–376		1999 actual	2000 est.	2001 est.
1001	Total compensable workyears: Full-time equivalent employment	16,060	99,843	7,412

CENSUS WORKING CAPITAL FUND

Program and Financing (in millions of dollars)

Identification code 13–4512–0–4–376		1999 actual	2000 est.	2001 est.
	Obligations by program activity:			
	Reimbursable program:			
09.01	Current economic statistics	31	29	35
09.02	Current demographic statistics	137	161	148
09.03	Other	5	5	5
10.00	Total new obligations	173	195	188
	Budgetary resources available for obligation:			
21.40	Unobligated balance available, start of year	9	9	
22.00	New budget authority (gross)	171	186	188
22.10	Resources available from recoveries of prior year obligations	2		
23.90	Total budgetary resources available for obligation	182	195	188
23.95	Total new obligations	−173	−195	−188
24.40	Unobligated balance available, end of year	9		
	New budget authority (gross), detail:			
	Mandatory:			
69.00	Offsetting collections (cash)	171	186	188

	Change in unpaid obligations:			
72.40	Unpaid obligations, start of year: Obligated balance, start of year	53	93	102
73.10	Total new obligations	173	195	188
73.20	Total outlays (gross)	−131	−186	−188
73.45	Adjustments in unexpired accounts	−2		
74.40	Unpaid obligations, end of year: Obligated balance, end of year	93	102	102
	Outlays (gross), detail:			
86.97	Outlays from new mandatory authority	131	186	188
	Offsets:			
	Against gross budget authority and outlays:			
88.00	Offsetting collections (cash) from: Federal sources	−171	−186	−188
	Net budget authority and outlays:			
89.00	Budget authority			
90.00	Outlays	−40		

The Working Capital Fund finances, on a reimbursable basis, functions within the Bureau of the Census which are more efficiently and economically performed on a centralized basis. The fund also finances reimbursable work that the Bureau performs for other public and private entities.

Object Classification (in millions of dollars)

Identification code 13–4512–0–4–376		1999 actual	2000 est.	2001 est.
	Personnel compensation:			
11.1	Full-time permanent	64	69	70
11.3	Other than full-time permanent	32	34	35
11.5	Other personnel compensation	5	5	5
11.9	Total personnel compensation	101	108	110
12.1	Civilian personnel benefits	20	22	22
21.0	Travel and transportation of persons	12	13	13
22.0	Transportation of things	1	1	1
23.1	Rental payments to GSA	5	5	5
23.3	Communications, utilities, and miscellaneous charges	6	7	7
24.0	Printing and reproduction	2	2	2
25.1	Advisory and assistance services	6	7	7
25.2	Other services	3	13	4
25.3	Purchases of goods and services from Government accounts	6	6	6
25.4	Operation and maintenance of facilities	1	1	1
25.7	Operation and maintenance of equipment	1	1	1
25.8	Subsistence and support of persons	1	1	1
26.0	Supplies and materials	3	3	3
31.0	Equipment	5	5	5
99.9	Total new obligations	173	195	188

Personnel Summary

Identification code 13–4512–0–4–376		1999 actual	2000 est.	2001 est.
2001	Total compensable workyears: Full-time equivalent employment	2,620	2,924	3,015

ECONOMIC AND INFORMATION INFRASTRUCTURE

ECONOMIC AND STATISTICAL ANALYSIS

Federal Funds

General and special funds:

SALARIES AND EXPENSES

For necessary expenses, as authorized by law, of economic and statistical analysis programs of the Department of Commerce, **[**$49,499,000**]** *$54,713,000*, to remain available until September 30, **[**2001**]** *2002. (15 U.S.C. 171 et seq., 1501 et seq.; 22 U.S.C. 286f, 3101 et seq.; Department of Commerce and Related Agencies Appropriations Act, 2000, as enacted by section 1000(a)(1) of the Consolidated Appropriations Act, 2000 (P.L. 106–113).)*

Program and Financing (in millions of dollars)

Identification code 13–1500–0–1–376		1999 actual	2000 est.	2001 est.
	Obligations by program activity:			
	Direct program:			
00.01	Bureau of Economic Analysis	43	45	49
00.02	Policy support	6	6	6
09.01	Reimbursable program	1	2	2
10.00	Total new obligations	50	53	57
	Budgetary resources available for obligation:			
21.40	Unobligated balance available, start of year	2	2	
22.00	New budget authority (gross)	50	51	57
23.90	Total budgetary resources available for obligation	52	53	57
23.95	Total new obligations	−50	−53	−57
24.40	Unobligated balance available, end of year	2		
	New budget authority (gross), detail:			
	Discretionary:			
40.00	Appropriation	48	49	55
68.00	Spending authority from offsetting collections: Offsetting collections (cash)	2	2	2
70.00	Total new budget authority (gross)	50	51	57
	Change in unpaid obligations:			
72.40	Unpaid obligations, start of year: Obligated balance, start of year	6	5	6
73.10	Total new obligations	50	53	57
73.20	Total outlays (gross)	−51	−52	−56
74.40	Unpaid obligations, end of year: Obligated balance, end of year	5	6	7
	Outlays (gross), detail:			
86.90	Outlays from new discretionary authority	44	45	50
86.93	Outlays from discretionary balances	7	7	6
87.00	Total outlays (gross)	51	52	56
	Offsets:			
	Against gross budget authority and outlays:			
88.00	Offsetting collections (cash) from: Reimbursable projects	−2	−2	−2
	Net budget authority and outlays:			
89.00	Budget authority	48	49	55
90.00	Outlays	49	50	54

Bureau of Economic Analysis.—The Bureau of Economic Analysis (BEA), a principal Federal statistical agency, provides the most comprehensive statistical picture available of U.S. economic activity. It prepares, develops, and interprets the national, international, and regional economic accounts of the United States. These accounts provide key information on economic growth, regional development, and the Nation's position in the world economy.

BEA's statistics are used in formulating and evaluating national economic policy, in planning and formulating Federal budgets, and in allocating over $115 billion in Federal funds annually. They are used by State and local governments for a variety of planning and analytical activities. Because they can have a major impact on interest rates, exchange rates, and cost-of-living adjustments, they are also of vital interest to businesses for market analysis and decisionmaking, and to households for financial planning.

To prepare the accounts, BEA assembles thousands of monthly, quarterly, and annual economic data series—ranging from national level retail sales to county level wages and salaries—and combines them into consistent and comprehensive sets of accounts.

National economic accounts.—The national accounts are a system of economic accounts that detail the relationship between production and the incomes generated in production and trace the principal economic flows among the major sectors and industries of the economy. They are best known by summary measures such as gross domestic prod-

General and special funds—Continued

SALARIES AND EXPENSES—Continued

uct (GDP), corporate profits, and personal saving. In addition, they provide information on the U.S. capital stock by type and industry; GDP-by-industry; and, through the input-output accounts, information on how industries interact—providing inputs to, and taking outputs from, each other to produce GDP. The national accounts statistics are regarded as the mainstay of macroeconomic analysis.

International economic accounts.—The international transactions accounts are a system of economic accounts that provide information on international transactions in goods, services, investment income, and government and private financial flows. They are best known by summary measures such as the balance of payments and the balance on goods and services. In addition, the accounts provide information on the U.S. international investment position, which measures the value of U.S. international assets and liabilities and changes in those values. The international transactions accounts and the international investment position are critical statistical tools used in formulating and evaluating international economic policy. BEA's data on direct investment—the most detailed data set on the operations of multinational companies available among the major industrialized nations of the world—are used to assess the vital role these companies play in the global economy.

Regional economic accounts.—The regional accounts are consistent with the national accounts and provide data on total and per capita personal income by region, State, metropolitan area, and county, and on gross State product. The regional accounts statistics are essential for State government revenue forecasting, the allocation of Federal funds to the States, and for private sector investment decisions.

Analysis and dissemination of data on economic trends.—This work consists of the analysis of BEA data on the current economic situation, the publication of the *Survey of Current Business* and other BEA publications, the electronic dissemination of data, and the provision of BEA information to customers.

Implementing BEA's Strategic Plan.—The dynamic U.S. economy, with its dramatic growth in information technology and services, has changed so rapidly that our data system has been unable to keep pace. Evidence of the serious gaps in our knowledge of how the economy is performing is the statistical discrepancy, which is the difference between GDP as measured by the final expenditures for goods and services produced by the U.S. economy and GDP as measured by the costs incurred and incomes earned in the production of those goods and services (gross domestic income). In theory, these measures should be equal, but in recent years, the divergence between them has grown significantly. In 2001, BEA will focus on improving its economic accounts by taking steps to fill gaps in coverage and reduce existing discrepancies. BEA will work toward expanding and improving the coverage of hard-to-measure services and rapidly growing and changing economic activities, such as e-business. Also, BEA will further improve its measures of the Nation's capital stock and will work toward implementing improved price indexes.

Improving information technology.—Although BEA has made progress in building its critically needed new information technology architecture, the actual re-engineering of systems is still underway. In 2001, BEA will continue to re-engineer work processes on the local area network (LAN) to take full advantage of the efficiencies of the new microcomputer environment. The new LAN and the re-engineered systems will improve the accuracy, reliability, and timeliness of BEA's data and will improve accessibility of the data to customers. In addition, BEA will work to enhance the security of its data.

Policy support.—The Economics and Statistics Administration's headquarters operation advises the Secretary of Commerce and other Government officials on matters related to economic developments and forecasts, and the development of options and positions relating to both macroeconomic and microeconomic policy.

Reimbursable.—ESA provides economic and statistical data and analyses on a reimbursable and advance payment basis to other Federal agencies, individuals, and firms requesting such information. Funds received for these services cover the cost of performing this work.

Activities under Economic and Statistical Analysis support the Commerce strategic goal involving promotion of economic growth.

Performance measures.—

Goal: Provide quality data

	1999 actual	2000 est.	2001 est.
Performance measure:			
Accuracy score (as determined by comprehensive evaluation system)	N/A	>85	>85

Goal: Provide timely and relevant data

	1999 actual	2000 est.	2001 est.
Performance measures:			
Mean customer satisfaction rating (on a scale of 1 to 5)	N/A	>4	>4
Percent of scheduled releases issued on time	100	100	100

A more detailed presentation of goals, performance measures, and targets is found in the Commerce Annual Performance Plan.

Object Classification (in millions of dollars)

Identification code 13–1500–0–1–376		1999 actual	2000 est.	2001 est.
	Direct obligations:			
	Personnel compensation:			
11.1	Full-time permanent	28	29	29
11.3	Other than full-time permanent	1	1	1
11.9	Total personnel compensation	29	30	30
12.1	Civilian personnel benefits	6	7	9
23.1	Rental payments to GSA	5	5	6
23.3	Communications, utilities, and miscellaneous charges	1	1	2
25.1	Advisory and assistance services	1	1	1
25.2	Other services	2	2	2
25.3	Purchases of goods and services from Government accounts	5	5	5
99.0	Subtotal, direct obligations	49	51	55
99.0	Reimbursable obligations		2	2
99.9	Total new obligations	50	53	57

Personnel Summary

Identification code 13–1500–0–1–376		1999 actual	2000 est.	2001 est.
	Direct:			
1001	Total compensable workyears: Full-time equivalent employment	464	484	503
	Reimbursable:			
2001	Total compensable workyears: Full-time equivalent employment	18	18	18

ECONOMICS AND STATISTICS ADMINISTRATION REVOLVING FUND

Program and Financing (in millions of dollars)

Identification code 13–4323–0–3–376		1999 actual	2000 est.	2001 est.
	Obligations by program activity:			
10.00	Total new obligations	5	3	3
	Budgetary resources available for obligation:			
21.40	Unobligated balance available, start of year	2	2	2

		1999 actual	2000 est.	2001 est.
22.00	New budget authority (gross)	5	3	3
23.90	Total budgetary resources available for obligation	7	5	5
23.95	Total new obligations	−5	−3	−3
24.40	Unobligated balance available, end of year	2	2	2
	New budget authority (gross), detail:			
	Discretionary:			
68.00	Spending authority from offsetting collections (gross): Offsetting collections (cash)	5	3	3
	Change in unpaid obligations:			
72.40	Unpaid obligations, start of year: Obligated balance, start of year	2		1
73.10	Total new obligations	5	3	3
73.20	Total outlays (gross)	−6	−3	−3
74.40	Unpaid obligations, end of year: Obligated balance, end of year		1	1
	Outlays (gross), detail:			
	outlays from balances:			
86.90	Outlays from new discretionary authority	5	3	3
86.93	Outlays from discretionary balances	1		
87.00	Total outlays (gross)	6	3	3
	Offsets:			
	Against gross budget authority and outlays:			
	Offsetting collections (cash) from:			
88.00	Federal sources	−2	−1	−1
88.40	Subscription and fee sales	−3	−2	−2
88.90	Total, offsetting collections (cash)	−5	−3	−3
	Net budget authority and outlays:			
89.00	Budget authority			
90.00	Outlays	1		

Revolving Fund.—The Economics and Statistics Administration operates this revolving fund for the payment of all expenses incurred in the electronic dissemination of data, including the acquisition and public sale of domestic, federally funded, and foreign business, trade, and economic information products.

The measures below reflect the performance goals of the Economics and Statistics Administration's revolving fund.

Goal: Increase customer base from 80,000 to 90,000.

Goal: Maintain high level of customer satisfaction, over 90%.

Goal: Increase information content.

Goal: Increase the quality of the STAT–USA/Internet customer experience.

A more detailed presentation of STAT–USA's goals, objectives and performance measures is found in the Commerce Annual Performance Plan.

Object Classification (in millions of dollars)

Identification code 13–4323–0–3–376		1999 actual	2000 est.	2001 est.
11.1	Personnel compensation: Full-time permanent	2	2	2
25.2	Other services	1	1	1
99.0	Subtotal, reimbursable obligations	3	3	3
99.5	Below reporting threshold	2		
99.9	Total new obligations	5	3	3

Personnel Summary

Identification code 13–4323–0–3–376		1999 actual	2000 est.	2001 est.
2001	Total compensable workyears: Full-time equivalent employment	19	35	35

INTERNATIONAL TRADE ADMINISTRATION

Federal Funds

General and special funds:

Operations and Administration

For necessary expenses for international trade activities of the Department of Commerce provided for by law, and engaging in trade promotional activities abroad, including expenses of grants and cooperative agreements for the purpose of promoting exports of United States firms, without regard to 44 U.S.C. 3702 and 3703; full medical coverage for dependent members of immediate families of employees stationed overseas and employees temporarily posted overseas; travel and transportation of employees of the United States and Foreign Commercial Service between two points abroad, without regard to 49 U.S.C. 1517; employment of Americans and aliens by contract for services; rental of space abroad for periods not exceeding 10 years, and expenses of alteration, repair, or improvement; purchase or construction of temporary demountable exhibition structures for use abroad; payment of tort claims, in the manner authorized in the first paragraph of 28 U.S.C. 2672 when such claims arise in foreign countries; not to exceed $327,000 for official representation expenses abroad; purchase of passenger motor vehicles for official use abroad, not to exceed $30,000 per vehicle; obtain insurance on official motor vehicles; and rent tie lines and teletype equipment, [$311,503,000] *$360,147,000*, to remain available until expended, of which $3,000,000 is to be derived from fees to be retained and used by the International Trade Administration, notwithstanding 31 U.S.C. 3302: *Provided*, That [of the $313,503,000 provided for in direct obligations (of which $308,503,000 is appropriated from the general fund, $3,000,000 is derived from fee collections, and $2,000,000 is derived from unobligated balances and deobligations from prior years), $62,376,000] *$62,395,000* shall be for Trade Development, [$19,755,000] *$28,855,000* shall be for Market Access and Compliance, *of which up to $3,000,000 may be transferred to and merged with "Diplomatic and Consular Programs," Department of State, for joint trade compliance activities,* [$32,473,000] *$46,870,000* shall be for the Import Administration, [$186,693,000] *$205,703,000* shall be for the United States and Foreign Commercial Service, and [$12,206,000] *$16,324,000* shall be for Executive Direction and Administration: *Provided further*, That the provisions of the first sentence of section 105(f) and all of section 108(c) of the Mutual Educational and Cultural Exchange Act of 1961 (22 U.S.C. 2455(f) and 2458(c)) shall apply in carrying out these activities without regard to section 5412 of the Omnibus Trade and Competitiveness Act of 1988 (15 U.S.C. 4912); and that for the purpose of this Act, contributions under the provisions of the Mutual Educational and Cultural Exchange Act shall include payment for assessments for services provided as part of these activities. *(15 U.S.C. 637(e), 649, 1501 et seq., 1871, 4001 et seq., 4011 et seq.; 19 U.S.C. 81a et seq., 1202nt., 1303, 1671 et seq., 1673 et seq., 1862, 2031, 2155, 2354, 2411 et seq.; 22 U.S.C. 801 et seq., 2451 et seq., 2651 et seq., 3101 et seq.; 40 U.S.C. 512, 42 U.S.C. 300j; 50 U.S.C. 98–98h, 401 et seq., 2061 et seq., 2401 et seq.; Public Law 99–64; Department of Commerce and Related Agencies Appropriations Act, 2000, as enacted by section 1000(a)(1) of the Consolidated Appropriations Act, 2000 (P.L. 106–113).)*

Program and Financing (in millions of dollars)

Identification code 13–1250–0–1–376		1999 actual	2000 est.	2001 est.
	Obligations by program activity:			
	Direct program:			
00.01	Trade development	60	62	62
00.02	Market access and compliance	25	28	29
00.03	Import administration	31	32	47
00.04	U.S. and foreign commercial services	188	185	203
00.05	Administration and executive direction	13	12	16
01.00	Total direct program	317	319	357
09.01	Reimbursable program	11	31	31
10.00	Total new obligations	328	350	388
	Budgetary resources available for obligation:			
21.40	Unobligated balance available, start of year	16	12	
22.00	New budget authority (gross)	315	338	388
22.10	Resources available from recoveries of prior year obligations	8		
22.22	Unobligated balance transferred from other accounts	1		

General and special funds—Continued

OPERATIONS AND ADMINISTRATION—Continued

Program and Financing (in millions of dollars)—Continued

Identification code 13–1250–0–1–376	1999 actual	2000 est.	2001 est.
23.90 Total budgetary resources available for obligation	340	350	388
23.95 Total new obligations	−328	−350	−388
24.40 Unobligated balance available, end of year	12		
New budget authority (gross), detail:			
Discretionary:			
40.00 Appropriation	285	308	357
40.75 Reduction pursuant to P.L. 106–51	−1		
40.76 Reduction pursuant to P.L. 106–113		−1	
42.00 Transferred from other accounts	17		
43.00 Appropriation (total discretionary)	301	307	357
68.00 Spending authority from offsetting collections: Offsetting collections (cash)	14	31	31
70.00 Total new budget authority (gross)	315	338	388
Change in unpaid obligations:			
72.40 Unpaid obligations, start of year: Obligated balance, start of year	83	103	124
73.10 Total new obligations	328	350	388
73.20 Total outlays (gross)	−300	−331	−371
73.45 Adjustments in unexpired accounts	−8		
74.40 Unpaid obligations, end of year: Obligated balance, end of year	103	124	141
Outlays (gross), detail:			
86.90 Outlays from new discretionary authority	227	246	281
86.93 Outlays from discretionary balances	73	85	90
87.00 Total outlays (gross)	300	331	371
Offsets:			
Against gross budget authority and outlays:			
88.40 Offsetting collections (cash) from: Non-Federal sources	−14	−31	−31
Net budget authority and outlays:			
89.00 Budget authority	301	307	357
90.00 Outlays	286	300	340

The activities of the International Trade Administration in the Department of Commerce are intended to develop the export potential of U.S. firms in a manner consistent with national security and foreign and economic policy and to promote an improved trade posture for U.S. industry.

Working as a key part of the Government-wide Trade Promotion Coordinating Committee, the International Trade Administration (ITA) will accomplish this objective by achieving program success within four Secretarial Initiatives.

Enhance the U.S. Statistical Infrastructure.—ITA will provide American businesses, governmental units and the general public with statistical information necessary to improve their ability to export. In 2001, ITA will expand its trade statistics effort by strengthening and increasing analysis of industry statistics.

Stimulating Manufacturing and Environmental Technology Exports.—ITA will increase its efforts to assist U.S. firms to become exporters, aid exporters in entering new markets or increase exports in established markets, protect U.S. firms from unfair foreign competition, and to ensure that U.S. firms reap the benefits of international trade agreements. In 2001, ITA will: further aid U.S. firms to enter key Emerging Markets such as Africa and Latin America; enforce aggressively the Nation's trade compliance agreements, enhance market access programs, with emphasis on implementing the Uruguay Round Agreements Act and defending U.S. AD/CVD decisions when challenged through the WTO dispute settlement process by foreign interests; and enhance efforts in trade education and outreach.

Accelerating the Transition to Electronic Commerce.—Efforts within this Secretarial Initiative include automation of information and services for exporters and potential exporters and expansion of electronic commerce. In 2001 ITA will greatly expand its use of electronic commerce methodologies to improve service delivery and better assist small and medium-sized firms to use electronic commerce to increase exports. Additionally, ITA will assist exporters by bringing U.S. Government's tariff/taxes and customs information services for exporters up-to-date and on par with those offered by the European Commission to European exporters.

Addressing Critical Construction and Base Needs.—ITA will continue to move forward in its efforts to attain a clean financial audit. In 2001, ITA intends to restore funding in its US&FCS unit for fees and base funding.

Native American Economic Development.—ITA will strengthen its focus on aiding Native Americans to become exporters, enter new markets, and increase exports in established markets. In 2001, ITA intends to assist Native Americans to increase cultural heritage tourism as part of their economic and community development plans.

These four initiatives will be accomplished within the five major subdivisions of ITA and through a reimbursable program as follows:

Trade Development.—The trade development program assesses the competitiveness of various U.S. industries and performs trade and investment analyses; works with manufacturing and service industry associations and firms to identify and to capitalize on trade opportunities and to pinpoint and to overcome obstacles to increased U.S. exports; articulates U.S. industries' needs, interests and concerns to American negotiators of international trade agreements and assists in the preparation and implementation of negotiating strategies; and conducts export promotion programs directed toward industry sectors. Increased emphasis will be placed on sector-specific initiatives to improve market access, ensure compliance with international trade agreements, and improve trade statistics.

Market Access and Compliance.—The Market Access and Compliance Unit (MAC) is the U.S. Government's front-line offensive team working to unlock foreign markets for American goods and services country-by-country and region-by-region. MAC concentrates on market access issues and the development of strategies to overcome market access obstacles faced by U.S. businesses. MAC maintains in-depth knowledge of the trade policies of our trading partners. It monitors foreign country compliance with numerous multilateral and bilateral trade-related agreements, identifying compliance problems and other market access obstacles. MAC's specialists work with other Government agencies to address barriers rapidly, and to ensure that U.S. firms know how to use the market opening agreements. It provides information on foreign trade and business practices to U.S. firms and works to find opportunities and to develop market strategies in traditional markets and in the emerging markets. MAC's objective is to develop and to update continuously current and long-term market access strategies, including developing the information needed to conduct trade negotiations to open markets. MAC's specialists work hand-in-hand with U.S. business, trade associations and other business organizations, Commerce's industry and technical specialists, and the U.S. Commercial Service's domestic and overseas offices. This unit will continue to provide support for the operation of the North American Free Trade Agreement.

Import Administration.—Import Administration investigates antidumping and countervailing duty cases to ensure compliance with applicable U.S. statutes and administers certain other statutory programs relating to imports and foreign trade zones.

U.S. and Foreign Commercial Service.—The U.S. and Foreign Commercial Service counsels U.S. businesses on exporting through offices in the United States and overseas countries. The program's goals are to increase the number of U.S. firms that export and the number of foreign markets to which they export; to provide export market information; to promote and facilitate participation of U.S. firms in trade shows; and to encourage and sponsor additional involvement by private, State and local organizations.

Reimbursable program.—This account includes receipts for services rendered to other Federal agencies and receipts received on a cost recovery basis from private entities for trade events and export information services. ITA proposes to raise fees to offset the costs associated with services and products provided. In 1999, ITA conducted a study of its existing products and services. In 2001, ITA will improve existing products and services to U.S. businesses.

Administration and Executive Direction.—Adminstration and Executive Direction provide policy leadership and administration services for the other ITA subdivisions. Executive Direction includes the Office of the Under Secretary for International Trade, the Deputy Under Secretary for International Trade, and subordinate offices covering Legislative and Intergovernmental Affairs, Public Affairs, and the Trade Promotion Coordinating Committee staff. Administration provides office automation and information technology support systems, human resources services, financial management services, and general administrative assistance for the other ITA subdivisions.

Activities under the ITA account support the Commerce's strategic goal relating to promotion of economic growth.

	1999 actual	2000 est.	2001 est.
Goals—Performance Measures:			
Implement the President's National Export Strategy in conjunction with the Trade Promotion Coordinating Committee (TPCC):			
New to market firms	67,835	64,914	66,187
Enforce U.S. trade laws and agreements to promote free and fair trade:			
Value of market openings	$2.3 billion	$2.0 billion	$2.4 billion
Increase the number of small business exporters:			
New to export firms	42,351	36,066	36,949
Strengthen and institutionalize trade promotion and advocacy efforts, placing special emphasis on Big Emerging Markets (BEMs):			
Dollar value of gross exports supported through advocacy efforts	$9.8 billion	$10.5 billion	$11.0 billion

A more detailed presentation of goals, performance measures and targets can be found in the Commerce Annual Performance Plan.

Object Classification (in millions of dollars)

Identification code 13–1250–0–1–376		1999 actual	2000 est.	2001 est.
	Direct obligations:			
	Personnel compensation:			
11.1	Full-time permanent	128	124	139
11.3	Other than full-time permanent	4	5	5
11.5	Other personnel compensation	3	3	3
11.8	Special personal services payments	2		
11.9	Total personnel compensation	137	132	147
12.1	Civilian personnel benefits	30	31	32
13.0	Benefits for former personnel	1	1	1
21.0	Travel and transportation of persons	12	11	12
22.0	Transportation of things	1	1	1
23.1	Rental payments to GSA	14	15	17
23.2	Rental payments to others	9	9	9
23.3	Communications, utilities, and miscellaneous charges	13	10	10
24.0	Printing and reproduction	3	2	2
25.1	Advisory and assistance services	1	1	1
25.2	Other services	37	44	65
25.3	Purchases of goods and services from Government accounts	33	35	45
26.0	Supplies and materials	5	5	5
31.0	Equipment	9	8	8
41.0	Grants, subsidies, and contributions	12	14	2
99.0	Subtotal, direct obligations	317	319	357
99.0	Reimbursable obligations	11	31	31
99.9	Total new obligations	328	350	388

Personnel Summary

Identification code 13–1250–0–1–376		1999 actual	2000 est.	2001 est.
	Direct:			
1001	Total compensable workyears: Full-time equivalent employment	2,185	2,314	2,464
	Reimbursable:			
2001	Total compensable workyears: Full-time equivalent employment	16	30	30

Foreign Service National Separation Liability Trust Fund

Program and Financing (in millions of dollars)

Identification code 13–8344–0–7–602		1999 actual	2000 est.	2001 est.
	Obligations by program activity:			
10.00	Total new obligations (object class 25.2)	11		
	Budgetary resources available for obligation:			
21.40	Unobligated balance available, start of year	11		
23.95	Total new obligations	–11		
	Change in unpaid obligations:			
73.10	Total new obligations	11		
73.20	Total outlays (gross)	–11		
	Outlays (gross), detail:			
86.93	Outlays from discretionary balances	11		
	Net budget authority and outlays:			
89.00	Budget authority			
90.00	Outlays	11		

This fund is maintained to pay separation costs for Foreign Service National employees of the Department of Commerce, in those countries in which pay is legally authorized. The fund, as authorized by section 151 of Public Law 102–138, is maintained by annual Government contributions which are appropriated in the Department's operating accounts.

EXPORT ADMINISTRATION

Federal Funds

General and special funds:

Operations and Administration

For necessary expenses for export administration and national security activities of the Department of Commerce, including costs associated with the performance of export administration field activities both domestically and abroad; full medical coverage for dependent members of immediate families of employees stationed overseas; employment of Americans and aliens by contract for services abroad; payment of tort claims, in the manner authorized in the first paragraph of 28 U.S.C. 2672 when such claims arise in foreign countries; not to exceed $15,000 for official representation expenses abroad; awards of compensation to informers under the Export Administration Act of 1979, and as authorized by 22 U.S.C. 401(b); purchase of passenger motor vehicles for official use and motor vehicles for law enforcement use with special requirement vehicles eligible for purchase without regard to any price limitation otherwise established by law, [$54,038,000] *$71,554,000*, to remain available until expended, of which [$1,877,000] *$5,138,000* shall be for inspections and other activities related to national security: *Provided*, That the provisions of the first sentence of section 105(f) and all of section 108(c) of the Mutual Educational and Cultural Exchange Act of 1961 (22 U.S.C. 2455(f) and 2458(c)) shall apply in carrying out these activities: *Provided further*, That payments and contributions col-

General and special funds—Continued

OPERATIONS AND ADMINISTRATION—Continued

lected and accepted for materials or services provided as part of such activities may be retained for use in covering the cost of such activities, and for providing information to the public with respect to the export administration and national security activities of the Department of Commerce and other export control programs of the United States and other governments[: *Provided further*, That no funds may be obligated or expended for processing licenses for the export of satellites of United States origin (including commercial satellites and satellite components) to the People's Republic of China, unless, at least 15 days in advance, the Committees on Appropriations of the House of Representatives and the Senate and other appropriate committees of the Congress are notified of such proposed action]. *(P.L. 105–85, sections 1211–1215; 10 U.S.C. 7430(e); 15 U.S.C. 1501 et seq.; 1531; 19 U.S.C. 1862; 22 U.S.C. 401(b), 2455(f), 2458(c), 3922, 6004–6005; 30 U.S.C. 185(s), 185(u), 42 U.S.C. 300j, 2139a, 5195, 6212, 43 U.S.C. 1354; 46 U.S.C. app. 466c, 50 U.S.C. 82, 98–98h, app. 468, app. 2061 et seq., app. 2401 et seq., app 2411; Department of Commerce and Related Agencies Appropriations Act, 2000, as enacted by section 1000(a)(1) of the Consolidated Appropriations Act, 2000 (P.L. 106–113).)*

Program and Financing (in millions of dollars)

Identification code 13–0300–0–1–999		1999 actual	2000 est.	2001 est.
	Obligations by program activity:			
	Direct program:			
00.01	Management and policy coordination	4	4	5
00.02	Export administration	23	24	33
00.03	Export enforcement	24	24	27
00.04	Critical infrastructure	4	4	7
01.00	Total direct program	55	56	72
09.01	Reimbursable program	5	10	5
10.00	Total new obligations	60	66	77
	Budgetary resources available for obligation:			
21.40	Unobligated balance available, start of year	4	11	
22.00	New budget authority (gross)	65	59	77
22.10	Resources available from recoveries of prior year obligations	1		
22.21	Unobligated balance transferred to other accounts		−4	
23.90	Total budgetary resources available for obligation	70	66	77
23.95	Total new obligations	−60	−66	−77
24.40	Unobligated balance available, end of year	11		
	New budget authority (gross), detail:			
	Discretionary:			
40.00	Appropriation	52	54	72
42.00	Transferred from other accounts	4		
43.00	Appropriation (total discretionary)	56	54	72
68.00	Spending authority from offsetting collections: Offsetting collections (cash)	9	5	5
70.00	Total new budget authority (gross)	65	59	77
	Change in unpaid obligations:			
	Unpaid obligations, start of year:			
72.40	Obligated balance, start of year	6	10	10
72.95	From Federal sources: Receivables and unpaid, unfilled orders	2	2	
72.99	Total unpaid obligations, start of year	8	12	10
73.10	Total new obligations	60	66	77
73.20	Total outlays (gross)	−55	−68	−75
73.45	Adjustments in unexpired accounts	−1		
	Unpaid obligations, end of year:			
74.40	Obligated balance, end of year	10	10	12
74.95	From Federal sources: Receivables and unpaid, unfilled orders	2		
74.99	Total unpaid obligations, end of year	12	10	12
	Outlays (gross), detail:			
86.90	Outlays from new discretionary authority	46	51	66
86.93	Outlays from discretionary balances	9	17	9
87.00	Total outlays (gross)	55	68	75
	Offsets:			
	Against gross budget authority and outlays:			
	Offsetting collections (cash) from:			
88.00	Federal sources	−8	−4	−4
88.40	Non-Federal sources	−1	−1	−1
88.90	Total, offsetting collections (cash)	−9	−5	−5
	Net budget authority and outlays:			
89.00	Budget authority	56	54	72
90.00	Outlays	46	63	70

The activities of the Bureau of Export Administration (BXA) are designed to enforce U.S. export trade laws consistent with national security, foreign policy, and short supply objectives. The program strives to achieve a balance between the interests of U.S. exporters, the U.S. economy and U.S. national security requirements.

Management and policy coordination.—The management and policy coordination program controls the development, analysis, coordination, and consolidation of policy initiatives and responses within the BXA. Under BXA's nonproliferation and export control cooperation mission, BXA works directly with government leaders in the Newly Independent States (NIS) to develop effective controls on their strategic commodities and data.

An increase is being requested to continue to engage Russia and other nations of the former Soviet Union and Central Europe in cooperative export control work and to engage China, India, Pakistan, and other countries thought to pose proliferation risks. In order to build a comprehensive program that taps the full range of BXA's expertise for assisting in development of export controls in countries of greatest consequence to our national security, BXA is seeking funding to institute these programs in China, India, Pakistan, and several other key states.

Export administration.—The export administration program assures that export activity is consistent with national security and foreign policy requirements.

An increase is being requested to fully administer the new and complex declaration processing functions and on-site inspection requirements imposed on commercial chemical manufacturing facilities under the Chemical Weapons Convention (CWC). This increase supports the Secretarial broadening trade initiative by insuring that our own domestic chemical industry is not adversely affected by CWC trade restrictions while denying proliferators access to both chemical weapons and their precursors.

Export enforcement.—The export enforcement program detects and prevents the illegal distribution of controlled U.S. goods and technical data in violation of the export administration provisions of the U.S. Code. Other program responsibilities include enforcement of prohibitions against participating in unsanctioned boycotts against countries friendly to the United States.

An increase is being requested to enable Export Enforcement to address key concerns regarding Weapons of Mass Destruction, Counterterrorism and the Chemical Weapons Convention. Enforcement will investigate in-bound shipments; increase counterterrorism work with the FBI, Customs, CIA, and the State Department, enforce data declaration and inspection requirements, enforce export controls on chemicals, and enforce import restrictions on scheduled chemicals.

Critical Infrastructure Program.—The Critical Infrastructure Assurance Office (CIAO) provides support to the National Coordinator's. This includes working with government agencies and the private sector in developing a national plan. The office will also coordinate a national education and awareness program.

An increase is being requested to restore the CIAO to the 1999 level and to provide funding for work with information sharing and analysis centers (ISAC). This increase will permit the CIAO to perform its coordination and facilitation role in support of Presidential Decision Directive 63.

Activities under this account support the Commerce strategic goal to promote economic growth.

Stimulate Innovation for American Competitiveness

	1999 actual	2000 est.	2001 est.
Goals and outcome measures:			
Restructure export controls:			
Number of high risk transactions deterred	504	508	512
Maintain enforcement programs:			
Number of investigations accepted for criminal/administrative remedies	68	70	70
Transition of defense industries:			
Strategic industry analyses completed	352	295	300

A more detailed presentation of goals, objectives, and performance measures is found in the Commerce Annual Performance Plan.

Object Classification (in millions of dollars)

Identification code 13–0300–0–1–999		1999 actual	2000 est.	2001 est.
	Direct obligations:			
	Personnel compensation:			
11.1	Full-time permanent	21	21	24
11.3	Other than full-time permanent	1	1	1
11.5	Other personnel compensation	2	2	2
11.9	Total personnel compensation	24	24	27
12.1	Civilian personnel benefits	6	6	7
21.0	Travel and transportation of persons	2	2	3
23.1	Rental payments to GSA	4	4	5
23.3	Communications, utilities, and miscellaneous charges	1	1	1
25.2	Other services	4	6	9
25.3	Purchases of goods and services from Government accounts	12	11	17
26.0	Supplies and materials	1	1	2
31.0	Equipment	1	1	1
99.0	Subtotal, direct obligations	55	56	72
99.0	Reimbursable obligations	5	10	5
99.9	Total new obligations	60	66	77

Personnel Summary

Identification code 13–0300–0–1–999		1999 actual	2000 est.	2001 est.
	Direct:			
1001	Total compensable workyears: Full-time equivalent employment	374	461	497
	Reimbursable:			
2001	Total compensable workyears: Full-time equivalent employment	4	4	4

MINORITY BUSINESS DEVELOPMENT AGENCY

Federal Funds

General and special funds:

MINORITY BUSINESS DEVELOPMENT

For necessary expenses of the Department of Commerce in fostering, promoting, and developing minority business enterprise, including expenses of grants, contracts, and other agreements with public or private organizations, [$27,314,000] *$28,156,000. (Department of Commerce and Related Agencies Appropriations Act, 2000, as enacted by section 1000(a)(1) of the Consolidated Appropriations Act, 2000 (P.L. 106–113).)*

Program and Financing (in millions of dollars)

Identification code 13–0201–0–1–376		1999 actual	2000 est.	2001 est.
	Obligations by program activity:			
10.00	Total new obligations	29	30	28
	Budgetary resources available for obligation:			
21.40	Unobligated balance available, start of year	1	3	
22.00	New budget authority (gross)	27	27	28
22.10	Resources available from recoveries of prior year obligations	4		
23.90	Total budgetary resources available for obligation	32	30	28
23.95	Total new obligations	–29	–30	–28
24.40	Unobligated balance available, end of year	3		
	New budget authority (gross), detail:			
	Discretionary:			
40.00	Appropriation	27	27	28
	Change in unpaid obligations:			
72.40	Unpaid obligations, start of year: Obligated balance, start of year	20	12	17
73.10	Total new obligations	29	30	28
73.20	Total outlays (gross)	–31	–26	–28
73.45	Adjustments in unexpired accounts	–4		
74.40	Unpaid obligations, end of year: Obligated balance, end of year	12	17	16
	Outlays (gross), detail:			
86.90	Outlays from new discretionary authority	12	14	14
86.93	Outlays from discretionary balances	19	12	14
87.00	Total outlays (gross)	31	26	28
	Net budget authority and outlays:			
89.00	Budget authority	27	27	28
90.00	Outlays	31	26	28

The Minority Business Development Agency (MBDA) has the lead role in the Federal Government of coordinating all minority business development programs. The mission of the Agency is to build and to expand minority-owned businesses, which is critical to the national economy. The agency was created to promote private and public sector investment in the development of competitive minority-owned businesses in this country.

Minority Business Development.—This activity provides a variety of direct and indirect business services through public/private partnerships. MBDA coordinates and leverages resources, expands domestic and international market opportunities, collects and disseminates vital business information, and provides management and technical assistance. MBDA also provides support for research, advocacy, and technology to reduce information barriers and improve the participation rate of minority-owned businesses in the U.S. as well as the global marketplace.

In 2001, MBDA will continue to develop databases from a variety of public and private sector sources. These databases will provide timely on-line market information to minority business owners concerning available business opportunities. Additionally, MBDA plans to initiate several projects with the Small Business Administration that are aimed at greater coordination of resources.

Performance measures.—MBDA activities support the Department of Commerce's strategic goal of promoting economic growth. MBDA's activities include goals on improving opportunities for minority-owned businesses in the marketplace and improving opportunities for minority-owned businesses to pursue financing. Additionally, MBDA will promote electronic-commerce as well as provide business services electronically.

	1999 actual	2000 est.	2001 est.
Goal:			
Improve opportunities for minority-owned businesses to have access to the marketplace			
Performance Measure:			
Dollar value of contracts (in millions)	616	620	650

Object Classification (in millions of dollars)

Identification code 13–0201–0–1–376		1999 actual	2000 est.	2001 est.
	Personnel compensation:			
11.1	Full-time permanent	6	6	6
11.5	Other personnel compensation	1		

General and special funds—Continued

MINORITY BUSINESS DEVELOPMENT—Continued

Object Classification (in millions of dollars)—Continued

Identification code 13–0201–0–1–376		1999 actual	2000 est.	2001 est.
11.9	Total personnel compensation	7	6	6
12.1	Civilian personnel benefits		1	1
23.1	Rental payments to GSA	2	2	2
25.2	Other services	4	7	4
25.3	Purchases of goods and services from Government accounts	2	1	2
41.0	Grants, subsidies, and contributions	12	12	13
99.0	Subtotal, direct obligations	27	29	28
99.5	Below reporting threshold	2	1	
99.9	Total new obligations	29	30	28

Personnel Summary

Identification code 13–0201–0–1–376		1999 actual	2000 est.	2001 est.
1001	Total compensable workyears: Full-time equivalent employment	96	120	120

UNITED STATES TRAVEL AND TOURISM ADMINISTRATION

Federal Funds

General and special funds:

Program and Financing (in millions of dollars)

Identification code 13–0700–0–1–376		1999 actual	2000 est.	2001 est.
	Budgetary resources available for obligation:			
21.40	Unobligated balance available, start of year	1		
22.00	New budget authority (gross)	–1		
23.90	Total budgetary resources available for obligation			
	New budget authority (gross), detail:			
	Discretionary:			
40.36	Unobligated balance rescinded	–1		
	Net budget authority and outlays:			
89.00	Budget authority	–1		
90.00	Outlays			

This program was terminated in 1996.

NATIONAL OCEANIC AND ATMOSPHERIC ADMINISTRATION

Federal Funds

General and special funds:

OPERATIONS, RESEARCH, AND FACILITIES

(INCLUDING TRANSFER OF FUNDS)

For necessary expenses of activities authorized by law for the National Oceanic and Atmospheric Administration, including maintenance, operation, and hire of aircraft; grants, contracts, or other payments to *state and local governments, and* nonprofit organizations for the purposes of conducting activities [pursuant to cooperative agreements] *consistent with NOAA programs*; and relocation of facilities as authorized by 33 U.S.C. 883i, [$1,688,189,000] *$1,882,189,000*, to remain available until expended *of which $217,700,000 is for Lands Legacy*: *Provided*, That fees and donations received by the National Ocean Service for the management of the national marine sanctuaries may be retained and used for the salaries and expenses associated with those activities, notwithstanding 31 U.S.C. 3302: *Provided further*, That in addition, $68,000,000 shall be derived by transfer from the fund entitled "Promote and Develop Fishery Products and Research Pertaining to American Fisheries": [*Provided further*, That grants to States pursuant to sections 306 and 306A of the Coastal Zone Management Act of 1972, as amended, shall not exceed $2,000,000: *Provided further*, That not to exceed $31,439,000 shall be expended for Executive Direction and Administration, which consists of the Offices of the Undersecretary, the Executive Secretariat, Policy and Strategic Planning, International Affairs, Legislative Affairs, Public Affairs, Sustainable Development, the Chief Scientist, and the General Counsel: *Provided further*, That the aforementioned offices, excluding the Office of the General Counsel, shall not be augmented by personnel details, temporary transfers of personnel on either a reimbursable or nonreimbursable basis or any other type of formal or informal transfer or reimbursement of personnel or funds on either a temporary or long-term basis above the level of 33 personnel: *Provided further*, That no general administrative charge shall be applied against any assigned activity included in this Act and, further, that any direct administrative expenses applied against assigned activities shall be limited to 5 percent of the funds provided for that assigned activity: *Provided further*, That of the amount made available under this heading for the National Marine Fisheries Services Pacific Salmon Treaty Program, $10,000,000 is appropriated for a Southern Boundary and Transboundary Rivers Restoration Fund, subject to express authorization] *Provided further, That in addition, not to exceed $3,200,000 shall be derived by transfer from the fund entitled "Coastal Zone Management".*

In addition, for necessary retired pay expenses under the Retired Serviceman's Family Protection and Survivor Benefits Plan, and for payments for medical care of retired personnel and their dependents under the Dependents Medical Care Act (10 U.S.C. ch. 55), such sums as may be necessary. *15 U.S.C. ch. 9, 9A, 40, 56; 16 U.S.C. ch. 32, 32A, 33; 33 U.S.C. ch. 17, 22, 26; 42 U.S.C. ch. 97, 103; 43 U.S.C. ch. 29; Department of Commerce and Related Agencies Appropriations Act, 2000, as enacted by section 1000(a)(1) of the Consolidated Appropriations Act, 2000 (P.L. 106–113).)*

FOREIGN FISHING OBSERVER FUND

For expenses necessary to carry out the provisions of the Atlantic Tunas Convention Act of 1975, as amended (Public Law 96–339), and the Magnuson-Stevens Fishery Conservation and Management Act of 1976, as amended (Public Law 100–627), and the American Fisheries Promotion Act (Public Law 96–561), to be derived from the fees imposed under the foreign fishery observer program authorized by these Acts, not to exceed [$189,000] *$191,000*, to remain available until expended. *(16 U.S.C. 1824(b)(10), 1827; Department of Commerce and Related Agencies Appropriations Act, 2000, as enacted by section 1000(a)(1) of the Consolidated Appropriations Act, 2000 (P.L. 106–113).)*

Program and Financing (in millions of dollars)

Identification code 13–1450–0–1–306		1999 actual	2000 est.	2001 est.
	Obligations by program activity:			
	Direct program:			
00.01	National Ocean Service	275	281	406
00.02	National Marine Fisheries Service	392	432	455
00.03	Oceanic and Atmospheric Research	293	297	303
00.04	National Weather Service	561	602	635
00.05	National Environmental Satellite, Data, and Information Service	111	110	108
00.06	Program support	70	66	82
00.07	Facilities	28	11	11
00.08	Fleet maintenance and planning	13	21	9
00.14	Foreign Fishing Observer Fund		2	
00.15	Rent Savings		–5	
00.16	Retired Pay for NOAA Corps Officers	6	14	14
00.17	Y2K Funding	3	4	
01.00	Direct funding	1,752	1,835	2,023
09.01	National Ocean Service	57	37	17
09.02	National Marine Fisheries Service	39	54	26
09.03	Oceanic and Atomospheric Research	53	49	38
09.04	National Weather Service	50	81	56
09.05	National Environmental Satellite, Data and Information Service	17	30	26
09.06	Program support	40	44	45
09.99	Total reimbursable program	256	295	208
10.00	Total new obligations	2,008	2,130	2,231

	Budgetary resources available for obligation:			
21.40	Unobligated balance available, start of year	120	98	
22.00	New budget authority (gross)	1,947	1,996	2,195
22.10	Resources available from recoveries of prior year obligations	32	36	36
22.21	Unobligated balance transferred to other accounts			
22.22	Unobligated balance transferred from other accounts	5		
23.90	Total budgetary resources available for obligation	2,104	2,130	2,231
23.95	Total new obligations	−2,008	−2,130	−2,231
24.40	Unobligated balance available, end of year	98		
	New budget authority (gross), detail:			
	Discretionary:			
40.00	Operations, research & facilities	1,586	1,688	1,882
	Appropriation (emergency):			
40.15	Appropriation (emergency)	5		
40.15	Appropriation (emergency)	2		
40.75	Reduction pursuant to P.L. 106–51	−6		
40.76	Reduction pursuant to P.L. 106–113		−15	
41.00	Transferred to other accounts			
42.00	Transferred from other accounts	77	68	91
43.00	Appropriation (total discretionary)	1,664	1,741	1,973
	Mandatory:			
60.00	Appropriation		14	14
	Spending authority from offsetting collections:			
	Discretionary:			
68.00	Offsetting collections (cash)	266	241	208
68.10	From Federal sources: Change in receivables and unpaid, unfilled orders	14		
68.90	Spending authority from offsetting collections (total discretionary)	280	241	208
	Mandatory:			
69.62	Transferred from other accounts	3		
70.00	Total new budget authority (gross)	1,947	1,996	2,195
	Change in unpaid obligations:			
	Unpaid obligations, start of year:			
72.40	Obligated balance, start of year	849	760	977
72.95	From Federal sources: Receivables and unpaid, unfilled orders	128	142	142
72.99	Total unpaid obligations, start of year	977	902	1,119
73.10	Total new obligations	2,008	2,130	2,231
73.20	Total outlays (gross)	−2,050	−1,877	−2,076
73.45	Adjustments in unexpired accounts	−32	−36	−36
	Unpaid obligations, end of year:			
74.40	Obligated balance, end of year	760	977	1,096
74.95	From Federal sources: Receivables and unpaid, unfilled orders	142	142	142
74.99	Total unpaid obligations, end of year	902	1,119	1,238
	Outlays (gross), detail:			
86.90	Outlays from new discretionary authority	1,280	1,321	1,431
86.93	Outlays from discretionary balances	767	542	629
86.97	Outlays from new mandatory authority	3	14	14
87.00	Total outlays (gross)	2,050	1,877	2,076
	Offsets:			
	Against gross budget authority and outlays:			
	Offsetting collections (cash) from:			
88.00	Federal sources	−195	−176	−148
88.40	Non-Federal sources	−71	−65	−60
88.90	Total, offsetting collections (cash)	−266	−241	−208
	Against gross budget authority only:			
88.95	From Federal sources: Change in receivables and unpaid, unfilled orders	−14		
	Net budget authority and outlays:			
89.00	Budget authority	1,667	1,755	1,987
90.00	Outlays	1,784	1,636	1,868
	Memorandum (non-add) entries:			
92.01	Total investments, start of year: U.S. securities: Par value	1	1	1
92.02	Total investments, end of year: U.S. securities: Par value	1	1	1

Summary of Budget Authority and Outlays

(in millions of dollars)

	1999 actual	2000 est.	2001 est.
Enacted/requested:			
Budget Authority	1,667	1,755	1,987
Outlays	1,784	1,636	1,866
Supplemental proposal:			
Budget Authority		26	
Outlays		16	10
Legislative proposal, not subject to PAYGO:			
Budget Authority			−34
Outlays			−34
Total:			
Budget Authority	1,667	1,781	1,953
Outlays	1,784	1,652	1,842

National Ocean Service (NOS).—Funding for the U.S. Coral Reef Task Force, the Coastal Zone Management Program, the National Estuarine Research Reserves Program, and the National Marine Sanctuaries Program within this account is proposed as part of a new Lands Legacy discretionary spending category to provide dedicated and protected funding for the President's Lands Legacy Initiative. See the Environment Chapter in the Budget for a summary of the Initiative. These programs provide scientific, technical, and management expertise to promote safe navigation; assess the health of coastal and marine resources and respond to natural and human induced threats; monitor and protect the coastal ocean and global environments; and protect and manage the Nation's coastal resources. NOS's role as leader in coastal stewardship supports many of the recommendations contained in the recently released National Ocean Report. "Turning to the Sea: America's Ocean Future." These recommendations help provide the framework for a comprehensive ocean agenda which will guide Federal efforts into the 21st Century. To meet the challenges posed in this report, NOS seeks increases under the President's Lands Legacy, National Ocean Conference, South Florida, and Clean Water Initiatives for its suite of navigation, response and restoration, and coastal science and management programs. These increases will help strengthen the understanding and protection of our valuable ocean resources, as well as our Nation's economic competitiveness by promoting safe maritime commerce through real-time physical oceanographic data and powerful new digital nautical chart products. As part of the Clean Water Initiative, increases are proposed for Coastal Zone Management grants to improve support to States and local communities to address pollution, harmful algal blooms, and other symptoms of a degraded coastal ecosystem.

National Marine Fisheries Service.—Funding for the U.S. Coral Reef Task Force program within this account is proposed as part of a new Lands Legacy discretionary spending category to provide dedicated and protected funding for the President's Lands Legacy Initiative. See the Environment Chapter in the Budget for a summary of the Initiative. These programs provide for the management and conservation of the Nation's living marine resources and their environment, including marine mammals and endangered species. Through conservation and wise use, these resources can be managed to benefit the Nation on a sustained basis. Increases are proposed to carry out the legislative mandates of the Magnuson-Stevens Fishery Conservation and Management Act, the Endangered Species Act, and the Marine Mammal Protection Act. These increases will support the NOAA Strategic Plan goals to build sustainable fisheries, recover protected species and promote healthy coastal ecosystems.

Office of Oceanic and Atmospheric Research (OAR).—These programs provide the critical environmental research and technology needed to improve NOAA services (weather warnings and forecasts, solar-terrestrial services, climate predictions, and marine services) to enable the Nation to balance a growing economy with effective management and prediction of our environment and natural resources. To accomplish

General and special funds—Continued

FOREIGN FISHING OBSERVER FUND—Continued

these goals, OAR supports a network of Federal scientists in environmental research laboratories and university/private-sector researchers through the National Sea Grant College Program, National Undersea Research Program, and Joint Cooperative Institutes. OAR provides the scientific basis for national policy formulation in key environmental areas e.g., climate change, air quality, stratospheric ozone depletion, marine biotechnology, aquaculture, and environmental observing technologies. Funding to support Presidential initiatives is also proposed for the Global Learning and Observations to Benefit the Environment program, the Climate and Global Change Program and the High Performance Computing and Communications (HPCC) Program. OAR programs are included in the 21st Century Research Fund.

National Weather Service.—These programs provide timely and accurate meteorologic, hydrologic, and oceanographic warnings, forecasts, and planning information to ensure the safety of the population, mitigate property losses, and improve the economic efficiency of the Nation. NOAA will continue the NWS operational transition necessary to assimilate the new technologies and the associated work force restructuring for future operations.

National Environmental Satellite, Data, and Information Service.—These programs provide for operation of environmental polar-orbiting and geostationary satellites; and for the collection and archiving of global environmental data and information; and services for distribution to users in commerce, industry, agriculture, science and engineering, the general public and Federal, State and local agencies.

Program Support.—These programs provide for overall NOAA management, NOAA's share of the regional Administrative Support Centers, and aircraft to support NOAA missions.

Facilities.—This program provides for repair and maintenance to existing facilities; facilities planning and design; and environmental compliance.

Fleet Maintenance and Planning.—This program provides for the repair and maintenance of vessels, including related equipment to maintain the existing fleet and for the planning of future modernization.

Foreign Fishing Observer Fund.—This fund is financed through collections from foreign vessel owners who fish within the U.S. Exclusive Economic Zone. Collections to the fund are used by the Secretary of Commerce to pay the salaries of observers and program support personnel and the costs of data management and analysis of the observer program. The observers collect scientific information on the foreign catch and monitor compliance with provisions of the Magnuson-Stevens Fishery Conservation and Management Act of 1976 as amended.

Performance measures.—Activities under this account support NOAA's seven goals and three Commerce strategic goals. Each theme and goal have key performance measures that support the theme and goal:

Theme: Build for the future and promote U.S. competitiveness in the global marketplace by strengthening and safeguarding the Nation's economic infrastructure.

Goal: Advance Short-term Warning and Forecast Services.

	1999 actual	*2000 est.*	*2001 est.*
Increased Lead-time (min) and (percent) for severe weather warnings	12	12	13
Percent	70	70	70

Goal: Promote Safe Navigation.

	1999 actual	*2000 est.*	*2001 est.*
Cumulative reduction in critical area hydrographic survey backlog (percent)	20.7	24.3	27.8

Goal: Implement Seasonal to Interannual Climate Forecasts.

	1999 actual	*2000 est.*	*2001 est.*
Accuracy of El Nino/Southern oscillation (ENSO) climate forecasts (correlation with actual conditions)	0.85	0.85	0.85

Goal: Predict and Assess Decadal to Centennial Climate Change.

	1999 actual	*2000 est.*	*2001 est.*
Results of 90 percent of research activities cited in the 2001 intergovernmental panel on climate change—third assessment of climate change	NA	NA	90%

Goal: Build Sustainable Fisheries.

	1999 actual	*2000 est.*	*2001 est.*
By 2004, ensure that 60% of stocks have sufficient essential fish habitat (percent)	NA	10%	40%

Goal: Recover Protected Species.

Protected species with population status improved (annual)	11	16	NA

Goal: Sustain Healthy Coasts.

Acres of coastal habitat area restored (cumulative)	43,000	55,000	70,000

A more detailed listing of goals, performance measures, and targets are found in the Commerce Annual Performance Plan.

Object Classification (in millions of dollars)

Identification code 13–1450–0–1–306		1999 actual	2000 est.	2001 est.
	Direct obligations:			
	Personnel compensation:			
11.1	Full-time permanent	587	617	685
11.3	Other than full-time permanent	10	10	15
11.5	Other personnel compensation	39	40	46
11.9	Total personnel compensation	636	667	746
12.1	Civilian personnel benefits	153	158	189
13.0	Benefits for former personnel	12	19	20
21.0	Travel and transportation of persons	33	35	38
22.0	Transportation of things	11	12	13
23.1	Rental payments to GSA	40	40	43
23.2	Rental payments to others	11	12	13
23.3	Communications, utilities, and miscellaneous charges	53	56	58
24.0	Printing and reproduction	5	5	6
25.1	Advisory and assistance services	65	66	68
25.2	Other services	183	184	206
25.3	Purchases of goods and services from Government accounts	68	70	73
25.5	Research and development contracts	2	3	3
26.0	Supplies and materials	73	75	91
31.0	Equipment	44	48	51
32.0	Land and structures	3	2	3
41.0	Grants, subsidies, and contributions	360	383	402
99.0	Subtotal, direct obligations	1,752	1,835	2,023
99.0	Reimbursable obligations	256	295	208
99.9	Total new obligations	2,008	2,130	2,231

Personnel Summary

Identification code 13–1450–0–1–306		1999 actual	2000 est.	2001 est.
	Direct:			
1001	Total compensable workyears: Full-time equivalent employment	11,298	11,840	11,900
	Reimbursable:			
2001	Total compensable workyears: Full-time equivalent employment	1,009	1,219	1,219

OPERATIONS, RESEARCH, AND FACILITIES

(Legislative proposal, not subject to PAYGO)

Contingent upon the enactment of authorizing legislation, the Secretary shall charge fees for any navigation services provided and for any fisheries management and enforcement services provided, and such fees shall be deposited as offsetting collections to this appropriation, to remain available until expended for the purpose of such services: Provided, That upon enactment of such legislation, the amount appropriated above from the General Fund shall be reduced by

$14,000,000 for navigation services and $20,000,000 for fisheries management and enforcement services.

Program and Financing (in millions of dollars)

Identification code 13–1450–2–1–306	1999 actual	2000 est.	2001 est.
Obligations by program activity:			
Direct program:			
00.01 National Ocean Service			–14
00.02 National Marine Fisheries Service			–20
01.00 Direct funding			–34
09.01 National Ocean Service			14
09.02 National Marine Fisheries Service			20
09.99 Total reimbursable program			34
10.00 Total new obligations			
New budget authority (gross), detail:			
Discretionary:			
40.00 Operations, research & facilities			–34
68.00 Spending authority from offsetting collections: Offsetting collections (cash)			34
Offsets:			
Against gross budget authority and outlays:			
88.40 Offsetting collections (cash) from: Non-Federal sources			–34
Net budget authority and outlays:			
89.00 Budget authority			–34
90.00 Outlays			–34

A proposal is included in conjunction with the U.S. Coast Guard for navigation services. A proposal is also included for fee collections from U.S. fishermen for fisheries management services.

Object Classification (in millions of dollars)

Identification code 13–1450–2–1–306	1999 actual	2000 est.	2001 est.
25.2 Direct obligations: Other services			–34
99.0 Reimbursable obligations: Subtotal, reimbursable obligations			34
99.9 Total new obligations			

PROCUREMENT, ACQUISITION AND CONSTRUCTION

(INCLUDING TRANSFERS OF FUNDS)

For procurement, acquisition and construction of capital assets, including alteration and modification costs, of the National Oceanic and Atmospheric Administration, [$596,067,000] *$635,222,000*, to remain available until expended, *of which $11,000,000 is for Lands Legacy*: *Provided further*, That unexpended balances of amounts previously made available in the "Operations, Research, and Facilities" account for activities funded under this heading may be transferred to and merged with this account, to remain available until expended for the purposes for which the funds were originally appropriated.

In addition, for such purposes, to become available on October 1 of the fiscal year specified and remain available until expended: fiscal year 2002, $732,499,000; fiscal year 2003, $705,499,000; fiscal year 2004, $706,499,000; fiscal year 2005, $657,499,000; fiscal year 2006, $674,499,000; fiscal year 2007, $691,000,000; fiscal year 2008, $709,000,000; fiscal year 2009, $726,000,000; fiscal year 2010, $745,000,000; fiscal year 2011, $10,000,000; fiscal year 2012, $10,000,000; fiscal year 2013, $10,000,000; fiscal year 2014, $10,000,000; fiscal year 2015, $10,000,000; fiscal year 2016, $5,000,000; fiscal year 2017, $5,000,000; fiscal year 2018, $5,000,000; and fiscal year 2019, $5,000,000: Provided, That such funds are available for the Commerce Administrative Management System; Next Generation Weather Radars; the Automated Surface Observing System Network; the Advanced Weather Interactive Processing System; Central Computer Facility Upgrades; the Radiosonde Replacement Program; the NOAA Weather Radio Expansion; the Geophysical Fluid Dynamics Laboratory Supercomputer; the Polar-Orbiting Operational Environmental Satellites (K–N'series); National Polar-Orbiting Operational Environmental Satellite System; Geostationary Operational Environmental Satellites (I–M and N–Q series); acquisition and deployment of the Evansville Doppler radar system enhancing NOAA's environmental data archive; consolidation of the Western Regional Center; construction of the National Weather Service weather forecast offices; the National Estuarine Research Reserves System; reinforcement of the La Jolla bluffs to prevent degradation of the National Marine Fisheries Service laboratory thereon; the consolidation of the Norman, Oklahoma research and weather facilities; the National Marine Sanctuaries; the Juneau, Alaska facility; procurement of three state-of-the-art Fisheries Research Vessels; construction of the Satellite Operations Center in Suitland, Maryland, and refurbishment of the NOAA Ship ADVENTUROUS. (Department of Commerce and Related Agencies Appropriations Act, 2000, as enacted by section 1000(a)(1) of the Consolidated Appropriations Act, 2000 (P.L. 106–113).)

Program and Financing (in millions of dollars)

Identification code 13–1460–0–1–306	1999 actual	2000 est.	2001 est.
Obligations by program activity:			
Systems Acquisition:			
00.01 NEXRAD	8	8	10
00.02 ASOS	4	4	5
00.03 AWIPS	71	16	17
00.04 Central Computer Upgrade	10	11	13
00.05 Polar	150	130	137
00.06 GOES	269	267	292
00.07 Polar Convergence	50	60	78
00.08 Radiosonde Replacement		7	7
00.09 GFDL Supercomputer		5	7
00.10 NOAA Weather Radio			6
Construction:			
00.11 Boulder	5		
00.12 NWS Construction	9	9	10
00.15 NERRS Construction	7	13	8
00.18 Gulf Coast Lab	6		
00.20 Pribilof Island Cleanup	2		
00.21 Marine Sanctuaries		3	3
00.22 Santa Cruz	14		
00.23 Other	3	55	8
00.25 NOAA Operations & Research Center Rehab.		3	
00.26 Fleet Modernization		51	16
00.27 Central Administration Management System			16
00.28 Evansville Doppler Radar			6
00.29 National Data Archive			4
10.00 Total new obligations	608	642	643
Budgetary resources available for obligation:			
21.40 Unobligated balance available, start of year	65	42	
22.00 New budget authority (gross)	585	593	635
22.10 Resources available from recoveries of prior year obligations		7	7
23.90 Total budgetary resources available for obligation	650	642	642
23.95 Total new obligations	–608	–642	–643
24.40 Unobligated balance available, end of year	42		
New budget authority (gross), detail:			
Discretionary:			
40.00 Appropriation	585	596	635
40.76 Reduction pursuant to P.L. 106–113		–3	
43.00 Appropriation (total discretionary)	585	593	635
Change in unpaid obligations:			
72.40 Unpaid obligations, start of year: Obligated balance, start of year	282	298	533
73.10 Total new obligations	608	642	643
73.20 Total outlays (gross)	–592	–399	–524
73.45 Adjustments in unexpired accounts		–7	–7
74.40 Unpaid obligations, end of year: Obligated balance, end of year	298	533	645
Outlays (gross), detail:			
86.90 Outlays from new discretionary authority	388	207	223
86.93 Outlays from discretionary balances	204	191	300
87.00 Total outlays (gross)	592	399	524
Net budget authority and outlays:			
89.00 Budget authority	585	593	635
90.00 Outlays	592	399	524

General and special funds—Continued

PROCUREMENT, ACQUISITION AND CONSTRUCTION—Continued

(INCLUDING TRANSFERS OF FUNDS)—Continued

The request for advance appropriations in the Procurement, acquisition and construction account responds to the requirements of the Federal Acquisition Streamlining Act of 1994 and the Information Technology Management Reform Act of 1996. This account is consistent with and supports the Administration's fixed asset policy by seeking advanced appropriations for multi-year projects. The Administration supports full funding as part of an ongoing attempt to improve cost and performance of agency procurements. The Administration's goal is to ensure that capital assets support the core/priority mission of the agency; the assets have demonstrated a projected return on investment that is clearly articulated; cost-benefits of acquisition have been evaluated; and that implementation helps ensure accountability.

Full Cost of Procurement, Acquisition and Construction

(In millions of dollars)

	2001 est.	2002 est.	2003 est.	2004 est.	2005 est.	2006–2019 est.
Commerce Administrative Management System	16	13	9	8	8	42
Next Generation Weather Radars	10	17	16	12	13	66
Automated Surface Observing System Network	5	5	5	5	5	26
Advanced Weather Interactive Processing System	17	17	10	9	9	43
Central Computer Facility Upgrades	15	18	19	19	20	100
Radiosonde Replacement Program	7	7	7	7	5	0
NOAA Weather Radio Expansion	6					
Geophysical Fluid Dynamics Laboratory Supercomputer	7	7	7	7	7	45
Polar-Orbiting Operational Environmental Satellite Systems (K–N' series)	137	137	103	86	79	73
National Polar-Orbiting Operational Environmental Satellite System	77	157	236	306	325	2,385
Geostationary Operational Environmental Satellites (I–M and N–Q series)	291	236	220	190	184	835
Acquisition and deployment of the Evansville Doppler radar system	6					
Consolidation of the Western Regional Center						
Construction of the National Weather Service weather forecast offices	10	10	10	10	10	48
National Estuarine Research Reserves System	8					
Reinforcement of the La Jolla Bluffs	5	5				
Consolidation of the Norman, OK research and weather facilities	3	22				
National Marine Sanctuaries	3					
Juneau, Alaska facility	1	20	15			
State-of-the art Fisheries Research Vessels (FRVs)	8	53	53	53		
Construction of the Satellite Operations Center in Suitland, Maryland		15	3			
National Data Archives/NEDAAS	4					
Replacement of a fisheries research vessel and refurbishment of the NOAA ship ADVENTUROUS	8					
Less financing from recoveries	−7	−8	−8	−8	−8	
Total approp estimate	635	732	705	706	657	N/A

Funding for the National Estuarine Research Reserves Systems Construction and the National Marine Sanctuaries Construction program within this account is proposed as part of a new Lands Legacy discretionary spending category to provide dedicated and protected funding for the President's Lands Legacy Initiative. See the Environment Chapter in the Budget for a summary of the Initiative.

The projects included in this account support NOAA's operational mission across all line offices. In particular, projects related to the modernized National Weather Service and on-going operations are included. Increases are proposed for the follow-on series of geostationary satellites and for the Department of Commerce's continued participation in the tri-agency converged polar satellite program. Small increases are also requested for the NEXRAD and ASOS programs. Funds are also requested to convert a surplus Navy T–AGOS vessel for fisheries research.

Object Classification (in millions of dollars)

Identification code 13–1460–0–1–306		1999 actual	2000 est.	2001 est.
11.1	Personnel compensation: Full-time permanent	19	19	19
12.1	Civilian personnel benefits	4	4	4
21.0	Travel and transportation of persons	2	2	2
23.1	Rental payments to GSA	3	3	3
23.2	Rental payments to others	1	1	1
23.3	Communications, utilities, and miscellaneous charges	1	1	1
25.1	Advisory and assistance services	18	18	18
25.2	Other services	75	66	65
25.3	Purchases of goods and services from Government accounts	424	467	469
25.5	Research and development contracts	2	2	2
26.0	Supplies and materials	5	5	5
31.0	Equipment	28	28	28
32.0	Land and structures	3	3	3
41.0	Grants, subsidies, and contributions	23	23	23
99.9	Total new obligations	608	642	643

Personnel Summary

Identification code 13–1460–0–1–306		1999 actual	2000 est.	2001 est.
1001	Total compensable workyears: Full-time equivalent employment	198	245	245

PACIFIC COASTAL SALMON RECOVERY

For necessary expenses associated with the restoration of Pacific salmon populations and the implementation of the 1999 Pacific Salmon Treaty Agreement between the United States and Canada, [$58,000,000] *$160,000,000, of which $100,000,000 is for Lands Legacy, to remain available until expended. (Department of Commerce and Related Agencies Appropriations Act, 2000, as enacted by section 1000(a)(1) of the Consolidated Appropriations Act, 2000 (P.L. 106–113).)*

Program and Financing (in millions of dollars)

Identification code 13–1451–0–1–306		1999 actual	2000 est.	2001 est.
	Obligations by program activity:			
10.00	Total new obligations (object class 41.0)		58	160
	Budgetary resources available for obligation:			
22.00	New budget authority (gross)		58	160
23.95	Total new obligations		−58	−160
	New budget authority (gross), detail:			
	Discretionary:			
40.00	Appropriation		58	160
	Change in unpaid obligations:			
73.10	Total new obligations		58	160
73.20	Total outlays (gross)		−58	−160
	Outlays (gross), detail:			
86.90	Outlays from new discretionary authority		58	160
	Net budget authority and outlays:			
89.00	Budget authority		58	160
90.00	Outlays		58	160

Funding for the Pacific Coastal Salmon Recovery within this account is proposed as part of a new Lands Legacy discretionary spending category to provide dedicated and protected funding for the President's Lands Legacy Initiative. See the Environment Chapter in the Budget for a summary of the Initiative.

This account funds Pacific Coastal Salmon Recovery for the purpose of helping share the costs of State, Tribal and local conservation initiatives. This account supports NOAA's contribution to a broad interdepartmental initiative bolstering and deploying existing and new Federal capabilities to assist in the conservation of at-risk Pacific salmon runs in the western States of California, Oregon, Washington, and Alaska. These Federal dollars would be matched dollar for dollar with non-Federal contributions. In addition, funds would be available to coastal tribes (not to exceed 10 percent) that do not require matching dollars. The account has been established under existing authorities by the Secretary of Commerce and made available through agreements with the Governors of each of the four States for distribution to assist State, Tribal and local conservation efforts. The Secretary will establish terms and conditions for the effective use of the funds and specific reporting requirements appropriate for ensuring full accountability of the available funds to meet the purpose of the account. An increase is requested to provide for continued implementation of the Pacific Salmon Agreement. This request will provide funds to capitalize the Southern Boundary Restoration and Enhancement Fund and the Northern Boundary and Transboundary Restoration and Enhancement Fund plus provide grants to the states of Washington and Alaska. The two endowment funds are administered jointly by the United States and Canada to invest in habitat, stock enhancement, science, and salmon management initiatives in both countries.

FISHERIES ASSISTANCE

For necessary expenses associated with vessel buyouts and other activities to address overfishing or overcapitalization in fisheries that are not sustainable, $10,000,000, to remain available until expended, as authorized by the Magnuson-Stevens Fishery Conservation and Management Act (16 U.S.C. 1861a).

Program and Financing (in millions of dollars)

Identification code 13–1461–0–1–302	1999 actual	2000 est.	2001 est.
Obligations by program activity:			
10.00 Total new obligations (object class 41.0)			10
Budgetary resources available for obligation:			
22.00 New budget authority (gross)			10
23.95 Total new obligations			−10
New budget authority (gross), detail:			
Discretionary:			
40.00 Appropriation			10
Change in unpaid obligations:			
73.10 Total new obligations			10
73.20 Total outlays (gross)			−10
Outlays (gross), detail:			
86.90 Outlays from new discretionary authority			10
Net budget authority and outlays:			
89.00 Budget authority			10
90.00 Outlays			10

This account is proposed to fund the Fisheries Assistance Fund to address overfishing or overcapitalization in fisheries that are not sustainable through capacity reduction (vessel buyouts and other means). The funds would be used to complement the fishing industry's funding of overall buyback costs in 2001.

The fishing industry funds buyback costs through long-term loans from the Fisheries Finance Program (FFP). Post-buyback harvesters repay FFP buyback loans by landing fees equal to up to 5% of the landed value of all post-buyback harvests. Fish buyers collect these fees by deducting them from fish purchase proceeds before paying harvesters. Buyback loans are possible only if two-thirds of harvesters voting in special referenda approve the necessary loan repayment fees. The Fisheries Assistance Fund would help realize the economic and conservation benefits associated with fishing capacity reduction.

COASTAL IMPACT ASSISTANCE

For grants to states to protect and sustainably manage coastal resources, $100,000,000 for Lands Legacy, to remain available until expended, as authorized by the Coastal Zone Management Act of 1972, as amended.

Program and Financing (in millions of dollars)

Identification code 13–1462–0–1–302	1999 actual	2000 est.	2001 est.
Obligations by program activity:			
00.01 Coastal Community Grants			100
10.00 Total new obligations (object class 41.0)			100
Budgetary resources available for obligation:			
22.00 New budget authority (gross)			100
23.95 Total new obligations			−100
New budget authority (gross), detail:			
Discretionary:			
40.00 Appropriation			100
Change in unpaid obligations:			
73.10 Total new obligations			100
73.20 Total outlays (gross)			−50
74.40 Unpaid obligations, end of year: Obligated balance, end of year			50
Outlays (gross), detail:			
86.90 Outlays from new discretionary authority			50
Net budget authority and outlays:			
89.00 Budget authority			100
90.00 Outlays			50

Funding for this account is proposed as part of a new Lands Legacy discretionary spending category to provide dedicated and protected funding for the President's Lands Legacy Initiative. See the Environment chapter in the Budget for a summary of the initiative. This account is proposed to provide coastal States currently involved in offshore oil and gas production with additional resources needed to protect and sustainably use ocean and coastal resources. Funds from this account will provide grants to coastal states to implement activities consistent with Coastal Zone Management Plans and that increase protection and sustainable management of coastal resources such as habitat protection, community revitalization, improved coastal access, and public education on coastal issues. The account will be administered by the Secretary of Commerce and made available through agreements with eligible coastal states for distribution. The Secretary will establish terms and conditions for the effective use of funds and specific reporting requirements appropriate for ensuring full accountability of the available funds to meet the purposes of the account.

PROMOTE AND DEVELOP FISHERY PRODUCTS AND RESEARCH PERTAINING TO AMERICAN FISHERIES

FISHERIES PROMOTIONAL FUND

[(RESCISSION)**]**

[All unobligated balances available in the Fisheries Promotional Fund are rescinded: *Provided,* That all obligated balances are transferred to the "Operations, Research, and Facilities" account.**]** *(Department of Commerce and Related Agencies Appropriations Act, 2000,*

General and special funds—Continued

FISHERIES PROMOTIONAL FUND—Continued

[(RESCISSION)]—Continued

as enacted by section 1000(a)(1) of the Consolidated Appropriations Act, 2000 (P.L. 106–113).).

Program and Financing (in millions of dollars)

Identification code 13–5139–0–2–376	1999 actual	2000 est.	2001 est.
Obligations by program activity:			
10.00 Total new obligations	4	3	2
Budgetary resources available for obligation:			
21.40 Unobligated balance available, start of year	2	2	
22.00 New budget authority (gross)	3	1	2
23.90 Total budgetary resources available for obligation	5	3	2
23.95 Total new obligations	−4	−3	−2
24.40 Unobligated balance available, end of year	2		
New budget authority (gross), detail:			
Discretionary:			
40.36 Unobligated balance rescinded		−1	
41.00 Transferred to other accounts	−63	−68	−68
43.00 Appropriation (total discretionary)	−63	−69	−68
Mandatory:			
62.00 Transferred from other accounts	66	70	70
70.00 Total new budget authority (gross)	3	1	2
Change in unpaid obligations:			
72.40 Unpaid obligations, start of year: Obligated balance, start of year	7	5	2
73.10 Total new obligations	4	3	2
73.20 Total outlays (gross)	−5	−6	−3
74.40 Unpaid obligations, end of year: Obligated balance, end of year	5	2	
Outlays (gross), detail:			
86.97 Outlays from new mandatory authority	3	1	1
86.98 Outlays from mandatory balances	2	5	2
87.00 Total outlays (gross)	5	6	3
Net budget authority and outlays:			
89.00 Budget authority	3	1	2
90.00 Outlays	5	6	3

Promote and Develop Fishery Products and Research Pertaining to American Fisheries.—An amount equal to 30 percent of the gross receipts from customs duties on imported fishery products is transferred to the Department of Commerce annually from the U.S. Department of Agriculture.

The American Fisheries Promotion Act (AFPA) of 1980 authorized a grants program for fisheries research and development projects and a National Fisheries Research and Development Program to be carried out with Saltonstall-Kennedy (S–K) funds. These funds are used to enhance the productivity and improve the sustainable yield of domestic marine fisheries resources.

Object Classification (in millions of dollars)

Identification code 13–5139–0–2–376	1999 actual	2000 est.	2001 est.
25.2 Other services	2	1	2
41.0 Grants, subsidies, and contributions	2	2	
99.9 Total new obligations	4	3	2

Personnel Summary

Identification code 13–5139–0–2–376	1999 actual	2000 est.	2001 est.
1001 Total compensable workyears: Full-time equivalent employment	4	4	4

FISHERMEN'S CONTINGENCY FUND

For carrying out the provisions of title IV of Public Law 95–372, not to exceed [$953,000] *$951,000*, to be derived from receipts collected pursuant to that Act, to remain available until expended. *(Department of Commerce and Related Agencies Appropriations Act, 2000, as enacted by section 10001(a)(1) of the Consolidated Appropriations Act, 2000 (P.L. 106–113).).*

Unavailable Collections (in millions of dollars)

Identification code 13–5120–0–2–376	1999 actual	2000 est.	2001 est.
Balance, start of year:			
01.99 Balance, start of year	1	2	2
Receipts:			
02.02 Fees, Fishermen's contingency fund		1	
04.00 Total: Balances and collections	1	3	2
Appropriation:			
05.01 Fishermen's contingency fund		−1	−1
07.99 Total balance, end of year	2	2	1

Program and Financing (in millions of dollars)

Identification code 13–5120–0–2–376	1999 actual	2000 est.	2001 est.
Obligations by program activity:			
00.01 Object Class 42.0		2	1
10.00 Total new obligations (object class 42.0)		2	1
Budgetary resources available for obligation:			
21.40 Unobligated balance available, start of year	2	1	
22.00 New budget authority (gross)		1	1
23.90 Total budgetary resources available for obligation	2	2	1
23.95 Total new obligations		−2	−1
24.40 Unobligated balance available, end of year	1		
New budget authority (gross), detail:			
Discretionary:			
40.25 Appropriation (special fund, indefinite)		1	1
Change in unpaid obligations:			
73.10 Total new obligations		2	1
73.20 Total outlays (gross)		−2	−1
Outlays (gross), detail:			
86.90 Outlays from new discretionary authority		1	1
86.93 Outlays from discretionary balances		1	
87.00 Total outlays (gross)		2	1
Net budget authority and outlays:			
89.00 Budget authority		1	1
90.00 Outlays		2	1
Memorandum (non-add) entries:			
92.01 Total investments, start of year: U.S. securities: Par value	1	1	1
92.02 Total investments, end of year: U.S. securities: Par value	1	1	1

Fishermen's Contingency Fund.—This program provides compensation to commercial fishermen for damages to or loss of fishing gear, including loss of profits, related to oil and gas exploration, development, and production on the Outer Continental Shelf. The fund is supported by assessments to holders of leases, permits, easements, and rights of way in areas of the Outer Continental Shelf. The fund was established in 1978.

Personnel Summary

Identification code 13–5120–0–2–376	1999 actual	2000 est.	2001 est.
1001 Total compensable workyears: Full-time equivalent employment	1	1	1

Coastal Zone Management Fund

Of amounts collected pursuant to section 308 of the Coastal Zone Management Act of 1972 (16 U.S.C. 1456a), not to exceed [$4,000,000, for purposes set forth in sections 308(b)(2)(A), 308(b)(2)(B)(v), and 315(e) of such Act] *$3,200,000 shall be transferred to the Operations, Research, and Facilities account, to offset the costs of implementing such Act. (Department of Commerce and Related Agencies Appropriations Act, 2000, as enacted by section 1000(a)(1) of the Consolidated Appropriations Act, 2000 (P.L. 106–113).)*

Unavailable Collections (in millions of dollars)

Identification code 13–4313–0–3–306	1999 actual	2000 est.	2001 est.
Balance, start of year:			
01.99 Balance, start of year			
03.00 Offsetting Collections	1	1	1
Appropriation:			
05.01 Coastal zone management fund	−1	−1	−1
07.99 Total balance, end of year			

Program and Financing (in millions of dollars)

Identification code 13–4313–0–3–306	1999 actual	2000 est.	2001 est.
Obligations by program activity:			
10.00 Total new obligations	4	4	
Budgetary resources available for obligation:			
21.40 Unobligated balance available, start of year	1	1	
22.00 New budget authority (gross)	4	4	
23.90 Total budgetary resources available for obligation	5	5	
23.95 Total new obligations	−4	−4	
24.40 Unobligated balance available, end of year	1		
New budget authority (gross), detail:			
Discretionary:			
41.00 Transferred to other accounts			−3
Spending authority from offsetting collections:			
68.00 Offsetting collections (cash)	4	4	3
68.26 Offsetting collections (unavailable balances)	1	1	1
68.45 Portion not available for obligation (limitation on obligations)	−1	−1	−1
68.90 Spending authority from offsetting collections (total discretionary)	4	4	3
70.00 Total new budget authority (gross)	4	4	
Change in unpaid obligations:			
72.40 Unpaid obligations, start of year: Obligated balance, start of year	4	2	
73.10 Total new obligations	4	4	
73.20 Total outlays (gross)	−7	−6	
74.40 Unpaid obligations, end of year: Obligated balance, end of year	2		
Outlays (gross), detail:			
86.90 Outlays from new discretionary authority	4	4	
86.93 Outlays from discretionary balances	3	3	
87.00 Total outlays (gross)	7	6	
Offsets:			
Against gross budget authority and outlays:			
88.40 Offsetting collections (cash) from: Non-Federal sources	−4	−4	−3
Net budget authority and outlays:			
89.00 Budget authority			−3
90.00 Outlays	2	2	−3

This fund was established by the Coastal Zone Act Reauthorization Amendments of 1990 (CZARA). The fund consists of loan repayments from the former Coastal Energy Impact Program. The proceeds are to be used to offset the Operations, Research, and Facilities account for the costs of implementing the Coastal Zone Management Act of 1972, as amended.

Object Classification (in millions of dollars)

Identification code 13–4313–0–3–306	1999 actual	2000 est.	2001 est.
11.1 Personnel compensation: Full-time permanent	2		
12.1 Civilian personnel benefits	2		
41.0 Grants, subsidies, and contributions		4	
99.9 Total new obligations	4	4	

Personnel Summary

Identification code 13–4313–0–3–306	1999 actual	2000 est.	2001 est.
1001 Total compensable workyears: Full-time equivalent employment	18		

Damage Assessment and Restoration Revolving Fund

Program and Financing (in millions of dollars)

Identification code 13–4316–0–3–306	1999 actual	2000 est.	2001 est.
Obligations by program activity:			
10.00 Total new obligations (object class 25.2)		22	4
Budgetary resources available for obligation:			
21.40 Unobligated balance available, start of year	8	16	
22.00 New budget authority (gross)	10	6	4
22.21 Unobligated balance transferred to other accounts	−5		
22.22 Unobligated balance transferred from other accounts	4		
23.90 Total budgetary resources available for obligation	17	22	4
23.95 Total new obligations		−22	−4
24.40 Unobligated balance available, end of year	16		
New budget authority (gross), detail:			
Mandatory:			
62.00 Transferred from other accounts		4	2
69.00 Offsetting collections (cash)	13	2	2
69.61 Transferred to other accounts	−3		
69.90 Spending authority from offsetting collections (total mandatory)	10	2	2
70.00 Total new budget authority (gross)	10	6	4
Change in unpaid obligations:			
73.10 Total new obligations		22	4
73.20 Total outlays (gross)		−22	−4
Outlays (gross), detail:			
86.97 Outlays from new mandatory authority		6	4
86.98 Outlays from mandatory balances		16	
87.00 Total outlays (gross)		22	4
Offsets:			
Against gross budget authority and outlays:			
88.40 Offsetting collections (cash) from: Non-Federal sources	−13	−2	−2
Net budget authority and outlays:			
89.00 Budget authority	−3	4	2
90.00 Outlays	−13	20	2

The Oil Pollution Act of 1990 stipulates that sums recovered from awards or settlements for natural resource damages to NOAA trust resources shall be retained in a revolving trust account to permit NOAA to carry out (1) oil and hazardous materials contingency planning and response, (2) natural resource damage assessment, and (3) restoration or replacement of injured or lost natural resources. For a comprehensive description of the Prince William Sound Restoration Program, refer to the U.S. Fish and Wildlife Service's Natural Resource Damage Assessment account. The 2000 and 2001 estimates of budget authority transferred from other accounts are preliminary and subject to change. NOAA will utilize funds transferred to this account to respond to haz-

186-484 00 - 8

General and special funds—Continued

DAMAGE ASSESSMENT AND RESTORATION REVOLVING FUND—Continued

ardous materials spills in the coastal and marine environments, by conducting damage assessments, providing scientific support during litigation, and using recovered damages to restore injured resources.

Credit accounts:

FISHERIES FINANCE PROGRAM ACCOUNT

For the cost of direct loans, [$338,000] *$6,628,000*, as authorized by the Merchant Marine Act of 1936, as amended: *Provided*, That such costs, including the cost of modifying such loans, shall be as defined in section 502 of the Congressional Budget Act of 1974: *Provided further*, That none of the funds made available under this heading may be used for direct loans for any new fishing vessel that will increase the harvesting capacity in any United States fishery. *(Department of Commerce and Related Agencies Appropriations Act, 2000, as enacted by section 1000(a)(1) of the Consolidated Appropriations Act, 2000 (P.L. 106–113).)*

Program and Financing (in millions of dollars)

Identification code 13–1456–0–1–376	1999 actual	2000 est.	2001 est.
Obligations by program activity:			
00.01 Vessel buy out	22		
00.02 American Fisheries Act Implementation	6		
00.03 Cost of Loan Subsidy	1	1	5
00.04 Program Administration			2
10.00 Total new obligations	29	1	7
Budgetary resources available for obligation:			
22.00 New budget authority (gross)	28		7
23.95 Total new obligations	−29	−1	−7
New budget authority (gross), detail:			
Discretionary:			
40.00 Appropriation	28		7
Change in unpaid obligations:			
72.40 Unpaid obligations, start of year: Obligated balance, start of year		6	
73.10 Total new obligations	29	1	7
73.20 Total outlays (gross)	−23	−6	−7
74.40 Unpaid obligations, end of year: Obligated balance, end of year	6		
Outlays (gross), detail:			
86.90 Outlays from new discretionary authority	23		7
86.93 Outlays from discretionary balances		6	
87.00 Total outlays (gross)	23	6	7
Net budget authority and outlays:			
89.00 Budget authority	28		7
90.00 Outlays	23	6	7

Summary of Loan Levels, Subsidy Budget Authority and Outlays by Program (in millions of dollars)

Identification code 13–1456–0–1–376	1999 actual	2000 est.	2001 est.
Direct loan levels supportable by subsidy budget authority:			
1150 Pollack/Crab Buyout	175		
1150 IFQ Loans	5	5	
1150 Traditional Loan Program	24	23	75
1150 Offshore Mariculture			30
1150 CDQ Loans			19
1150 Industry Funded Buyback Loans			200
1150 Community Development Loans	25		
1159 Total direct loan levels	229	28	324
Direct loan subsidy (in percent):			
1320 Pollack/Crab Buyout	1.00	0.00	0.00
1320 IFQ Loans	1.00	1.00	0.00
1320 Traditional Direct Loans	1.00	1.00	1.00
1320 Offshore Mariculture	0.00	0.00	5.00
1320 CDQ Loans	0.00	0.00	5.00
1320 Industry Funded Buyback Loans	0.00	0.00	1.00
1320 Community Development Loans	1.00	0.00	0.00
1329 Weighted average subsidy rate	0.96	1.00	1.00
Direct loan subsidy budget authority:			
1330 Pollack/Crab Buyouts	2	1	
1330 IFQ Loans			
1330 Traditional Loan Program			
1330 Offshore Mariculture			2
1330 CDQ Loans			1
1330 Industry Funded Buyback Loans			2
1330 Community Development Loans			
1339 Total subsidy budget authority	2	1	5
Direct loan subsidy outlays:			
1340 Pollack/Crab Buyouts	1	1	
1340 IFQ Loans			
1340 Traditional Loan Program			
1340 Offshore Mariculture			2
1340 CDQ Loans			1
1340 Industry Funded Buyback Loans			2
1340 Community Development Loans			
1349 Total subsidy outlays	1	1	5
Administrative expense data:			
3510 Budget authority, administrative expenses	6		2
3580 Outlays from balances		4	
3590 Outlays from new authority, administrative expenses	2		2

This account covers the subsidy costs of guaranteed loans (pre-1997) and direct loans (post-1996) obligated or committed subsequent to October 1, 1991, as authorized by the Merchant Marine Act of 1936 as amended. Increases are requested to administer additional responsibilities including Community Development Quota Loans and industry funded buyback loans and direct payments.

Object Classification (in millions of dollars)

Identification code 13–1456–0–1–376	1999 actual	2000 est.	2001 est.
25.2 Other services	21	1	2
33.0 Investments and loans	6		
41.0 Grants, subsidies, and contributions	2		5
99.9 Total new obligations	29	1	7

Personnel Summary

Identification code 13–1456–0–1–376	1999 actual	2000 est.	2001 est.
1001 Total compensable workyears: Full-time equivalent employment	5	5	5

FISHERIES FINANCE, DIRECT LOAN FINANCING ACCOUNT

Program and Financing (in millions of dollars)

Identification code 13–4324–0–3–376	1999 actual	2000 est.	2001 est.
Obligations by program activity:			
00.01 Direct loans	229	30	324
00.02 Interest payment to Treasury	9	11	9
10.00 Total new obligations	238	41	333
Budgetary resources available for obligation:			
22.00 New financing authority (gross)	237	41	333
22.10 Resources available from recoveries of prior year obligations	1		
23.90 Total budgetary resources available for obligation	238	41	333
23.95 Total new obligations	−238	−41	−333
New financing authority (gross), detail:			
Mandatory:			
67.10 Authority to borrow	227	28	320

	1999 actual	2000 est.	2001 est.
Discretionary:			
68.00 Spending authority from offsetting collections: Offsetting collections (cash)	10	13	13
70.00 Total new financing authority (gross)	237	41	333
Change in unpaid obligations:			
72.40 Unpaid obligations, start of year: Obligated balance, start of year	28	156	38
73.10 Total new obligations	238	41	333
73.20 Total financing disbursements (gross)	−108	−159	−160
73.45 Adjustments in unexpired accounts	−1	....	....
74.40 Unpaid obligations, end of year: Obligated balance, end of year	156	38	211
87.00 Total financing disbursements (gross)	108	159	160
Offsets:			
Against gross financing authority and financing disbursements:			
Offsetting collections (cash) from:			
88.00 Federal sources	−1	−1	−5
88.25 Interest on uninvested funds	−4	−1	−1
Non-Federal sources:			
88.40 Non-Federal sources, interest	−3	−11	−7
88.40 Non-Federal sources, principal	−2	....	....
88.90 Total, offsetting collections (cash)	−10	−13	−13
Net financing authority and financing disbursements:			
89.00 Financing authority	227	28	320
90.00 Financing disbursements	98	146	147

Status of Direct Loans (in millions of dollars)

Identification code 13–4324–0–3–376	1999 actual	2000 est.	2001 est.
Position with respect to appropriations act limitation on obligations:			
1111 Limitation on direct loans	229	28	324
Cumulative balance of direct loans outstanding:			
1210 Outstanding, start of year	26	122	277
1231 Disbursements: Direct loan disbursements	98	159	160
1251 Repayments: Repayments and prepayments	−2	−4	−7
1290 Outstanding, end of year	122	277	430

This account covers the financing of direct loans as authorized by the Magnuson-Stevens Fishery Conservation and Management Act. Funds are not used for purposes that would contribute to the overcapitalization of the fishing industry.

Balance Sheet (in millions of dollars)

Identification code 13–4324–0–3–376	1998 actual	1999 actual	2000 est.	2001 est.
ASSETS:				
1101 Federal assets: Fund balances with Treasury	29	20	20	20
1206 Non-Federal assets: Receivables, net	27	140	140	140
1999 Total assets	56	160	160	160
LIABILITIES:				
2101 Federal liabilities: Accounts payable	56	160	160	160
2999 Total liabilities	56	160	160	160
NET POSITION:				
3999 Total net position	....	....	....	....
4999 Total liabilities and net position	56	160	160	160

Fisheries Finance, Guaranteed Loan Financing Account

Program and Financing (in millions of dollars)

Identification code 13–4314–0–3–376	1999 actual	2000 est.	2001 est.
Obligations by program activity:			
00.01 Loan default costs	....	2	2
00.02 Interest Payments to Treasury	1	1	1
10.00 Total new obligations	1	3	3
Budgetary resources available for obligation:			
21.40 Unobligated balance available, start of year	2	3	3
22.00 New financing authority (gross)	2	3	3
23.90 Total budgetary resources available for obligation	4	6	6
23.95 Total new obligations	−1	−3	−3
24.40 Unobligated balance available, end of year	3	3	3
New financing authority (gross), detail:			
Discretionary:			
68.00 Spending authority from offsetting collections (gross): Offsetting collections (cash)	2	3	3
Change in unpaid obligations:			
73.10 Total new obligations	1	3	3
73.20 Total financing disbursements (gross)	−1	−3	−3
87.00 Total financing disbursements (gross)	1	3	3
Offsets:			
Against gross financing authority and financing disbursements:			
88.40 Offsetting collections (cash) from: Non-Federal sources	−2	−3	−3
Net financing authority and financing disbursements:			
89.00 Financing authority	....	....	....
90.00 Financing disbursements	−1	....	....

Status of Guaranteed Loans (in millions of dollars)

Identification code 13–4314–0–3–376	1999 actual	2000 est.	2001 est.
Position with respect to appropriations act limitation on commitments:			
2111 Limitation on guaranteed loans made by private lenders	....	....	....
Cumulative balance of guaranteed loans outstanding:			
2210 Outstanding, start of year	80	71	47
2231 Disbursements of new guaranteed loans	....	....	....
2251 Repayments and prepayments	−9	−22	−22
2263 Adjustments: Terminations for default that result in claim payments	....	−2	−2
2290 Outstanding, end of year	71	47	23
Memorandum:			
2299 Guaranteed amount of guaranteed loans outstanding, end of year	71	47	23

This account covers the financing of guaranteed loans obligated or committed subsequent to October 1, 1991 as authorized by the Merchant Marine Act of 1936 as amended. Funds are not used for purposes which would contribute to the overcapitalization of the fishing industry.

Balance Sheet (in millions of dollars)

Identification code 13–4314–0–3–376	1998 actual	1999 actual	2000 est.	2001 est.
ASSETS:				
Federal assets:				
1101 Fund balances with Treasury	2	3	3	3
Investments in US securities:				
1106 Receivables, net	....	1	1	1
1206 Non-Federal assets: Receivables, net	14	15	15	15
1999 Total assets	16	19	19	19
LIABILITIES:				
Federal liabilities:				
2101 Accounts payable	....	9	9	9
2103 Debt	6	10	10	10
2204 Non-Federal liabilities: Liabilities for loan guarantees	10	....	....	....
2999 Total liabilities	16	19	19	19
NET POSITION:				
3999 Total net position	....	....	....	....
4999 Total liabilities and net position	16	19	19	19

Credit accounts—Continued

FEDERAL SHIP FINANCING FUND, FISHING VESSELS LIQUIDATING ACCOUNT

Program and Financing (in millions of dollars)

Identification code 13–4417–0–3–376	1999 actual	2000 est.	2001 est.
Obligations by program activity:			
10.00 Total new obligations (object class 33.0)	2	....	....
Budgetary resources available for obligation:			
21.40 Unobligated balance available, start of year	3	8	....
22.00 New budget authority (gross)	10	1	....
22.40 Capital transfer to general fund	−3	−8	....
23.90 Total budgetary resources available for obligation	10	1	....
23.95 Total new obligations	−2	....	....
24.40 Unobligated balance available, end of year	8	....	....
New budget authority (gross), detail:			
Mandatory:			
60.05 Appropriation (indefinite)	2	1	....
69.00 Offsetting collections (cash)	8	....	....
70.00 Total new budget authority (gross)	10	1	....
Change in unpaid obligations:			
72.40 Unpaid obligations, start of year: Obligated balance, start of year	10	9	8
73.10 Total new obligations	2	....	....
73.20 Total outlays (gross)	−2	−1	....
74.40 Unpaid obligations, end of year: Obligated balance, end of year	9	8	7
Outlays (gross), detail:			
86.97 Outlays from new mandatory authority	2	1	....
Offsets:			
Against gross budget authority and outlays:			
88.40 Offsetting collections (cash) from: Non-Federal sources	−8	....	....
Net budget authority and outlays:			
89.00 Budget authority	2	1	....
90.00 Outlays	−5	1	....
Memorandum (non-add) entries:			
92.01 Total investments, start of year: U.S. securities: Par value	13	8	8
92.02 Total investments, end of year: U.S. securities: Par value	8	8	8

Status of Guaranteed Loans (in millions of dollars)

Identification code 13–4417–0–3–376	1999 actual	2000 est.	2001 est.
Cumulative balance of guaranteed loans outstanding:			
2210 Outstanding, start of year	68	54	44
2251 Repayments and prepayments	−14	−10	−9
2290 Outstanding, end of year	54	44	35
Memorandum:			
2299 Guaranteed amount of guaranteed loans outstanding, end of year	54	44	35
Addendum:			
Cumulative balance of defaulted guaranteed loans that result in loans receivable:			
2310 Outstanding, start of year	24	24	24
2390 Outstanding, end of year	24	24	24

Premiums and fees collected under the Fishing Vessel Obligations Guarantee program for loan commitments made prior to October 1, 1991 are deposited in this fund for operations of this program, loans, and for use in case of default. Proceeds from the sale of collateral also are deposited in the fund for defaults on loans committed prior to October 1, 1991 (46 U.S.C. 1272, 1273(f), and 1274).

Statement of Operations (in millions of dollars)

Identification code 13–4417–0–3–376	1998 actual	1999 actual	2000 est.	2001 est.
0101 Revenue	5	5	5	....
0102 Expense	−5	−5	−5	....
0105 Net income or loss (−)	....	....	....	....
0199 Total comprehensive income	....	....	....	....

Balance Sheet (in millions of dollars)

Identification code 13–4417–0–3–376	1998 actual	1999 actual	2000 est.	2001 est.
ASSETS:				
1101 Federal assets: Fund balances with Treasury	13	17	17	17
1701 Net value of assets related to pre–1992 direct loans receivable and acquired defaulted guaranteed loans receivable: Defaulted guaranteed loans, gross	38	27	27	27
1999 Total assets	51	44	44	44
LIABILITIES:				
2104 Federal liabilities: Resources payable to Treasury	40	44	44	44
2201 Non-Federal liabilities: Accounts payable	11	....	....	....
2999 Total liabilities	51	44	44	44
4999 Total liabilities and net position	51	44	44	44

PATENT AND TRADEMARK OFFICE

Federal Funds

General and special funds:

SALARIES AND EXPENSES

For necessary expenses of the Patent and Trademark Office provided for by law, including defense of suits instituted against the [Commissioner] *Director* of Patents and Trademarks, [$755,000,000] *$783,843,000*, to remain available until expended: *Provided*, That of this amount, [$755,000,000] *$783,843,000* shall be derived from offsetting collections assessed and collected pursuant to 15 U.S.C. 1113 and 35 U.S.C. 41 and 376, and shall be retained and used for necessary expenses in this appropriation: *Provided further*, That the sum herein appropriated from the general fund shall be reduced as such offsetting collections are received during fiscal year [2000] *2001*, so as to result in a final fiscal year [2000] *2001* appropriation from the general fund estimated at $0: *Provided further*, That, during fiscal year [2000] *2001*, should the total amount of offsetting fee collections be less than [$755,000,000] *$783,843,000*, the total amounts available to the Patent and Trademark Office shall be reduced accordingly: *Provided further*, That any amount received in excess of [$755,000,000] *$783,843,000* in fiscal year [2000] *2001* shall remain available until expended: *Provided further*, That of the amount in excess of [$755,000,000] *$783,843,000* referred to in the previous proviso, [$229,000,000] *$367,744,000* shall not be available for obligation until October 1, [2000: *Provided further*, That not to exceed $116,000,000 from fees collected in fiscal year 1999 shall be made available for obligation in fiscal year 2000] *2001: Provided further, That $25,889,000 from fees collected in fiscal year 1999 and $229,000,000 from fees collected in fiscal year 2000 shall be made available for obligation in fiscal year 2001. (Department of Commerce and Related Agencies Appropriations Act, 2000, as enacted by section 1000(a)(1) of the Consolidated Appropriations Act, 2000 (P.L. 106–113).)*

Unavailable Collections (in millions of dollars)

Identification code 13–1006–0–1–376	1999 actual	2000 est.	2001 est.
Balance, start of year:			
01.99 Balance, start of year	397	431	544
03.00 Offsetting Collections	142	229	368
04.00 Total: Balances and collections	539	660	912
Appropriation:			
05.01 Salaries and expenses	−108	−116	−255

07.99	Total balance, end of year	431	544	657

Program and Financing (in millions of dollars)

Identification code 13–1006–0–1–376		1999 actual	2000 est.	2001 est.
	Obligations by program activity:			
	Reimbursable Program:			
09.01	Patents	627	685	809
09.02	Trademarks	101	109	124
09.03	Information Dissemination	60	58	63
09.09	Reimbursable program—subtotal line	788	852	996
09.20	Policy	16	19	23
09.30	Indirect Cost Transfer to OPM			20
09.99	Total reimbursable program	804	871	1,039
10.00	Total new obligations	804	871	1,039
	Budgetary resources available for obligation:			
21.40	Unobligated balance available, start of year	13	3	
22.00	New budget authority (gross)	781	868	1,039
22.10	Resources available from recoveries of prior year obligations	11		
23.90	Total budgetary resources available for obligation	805	871	1,039
23.95	Total new obligations	−804	−871	−1,039
24.40	Unobligated balance available, end of year	3		
	New budget authority (gross), detail:			
	Discretionary:			
40.20	Appropriation (special fund, definite)			
40.35	Appropriation rescinded	−71		
40.75	Reduction pursuant to P.L. 106–51	−1		
40.76	Reduction pursuant to P.L. 106–113		−3	
43.00	Appropriation (total discretionary)	−72	−3	
	Spending authority from offsetting collections:			
68.00	Offsetting collections (cash)	887	984	1,152
	Offsetting collections (unavailable balances):			
68.26	Offsetting collections (PY available balances)	108	116	229
68.26	Offsetting collections (PY–1 available balances)			26
68.45	Portion not available for obligation (limitation on obligations) CY	−142	−229	−368
68.90	Spending authority from offsetting collections (total discretionary)	853	871	1,039
70.00	Total new budget authority (gross)	781	868	1,039
	Change in unpaid obligations:			
72.40	Unpaid obligations, start of year: Obligated balance, start of year	293	245	435
73.10	Total new obligations	804	871	1,039
73.20	Total outlays (gross)	−840	−681	−865
73.45	Adjustments in unexpired accounts	−11		
74.40	Unpaid obligations, end of year: Obligated balance, end of year	245	435	608
	Outlays (gross), detail:			
86.90	Outlays from new discretionary authority	634	547	662
86.93	Outlays from discretionary balances	206	134	203
87.00	Total outlays (gross)	840	681	865
	Offsets:			
	Against gross budget authority and outlays:			
88.40	Offsetting collections (cash) from: Non-Federal sources	−887	−984	−1,152
	Net budget authority and outlays:			
89.00	Budget authority	−106	−116	−113
90.00	Outlays	−48	−303	−287

The Patent and Trademark Office (PTO) is one of the 32 High Impact agencies that have the most extensive interaction with the American people, represent most of the Federal Budget, and employ most of the Federal workforce. In response to the Vice President, the PTO developed bold performance goals that will improve service in the year 2001 and beyond.

On November 29, 1999, President Clinton signed a consolidated spending bill that included the "American Inventors Protection Act of 1999". This Act reforms the U.S. patent system in a number of significant ways, including adjusting patent and trademark fees to reflect the results of an activity-based costing effort; providing an optional reexamination process for reviewing patent validity; extending patent terms if processing of a patent application is delayed for reasons beyond the inventor's control; publishing certain patent applications 18 months after filing date; and providing personnel and procurement flexibilities to ensure more effective and modern management of PTO.

Fee collections in fiscal year 2000 are estimated to be $984 million. In fiscal year 2001, total fee collections are estimated to be $1,152 million.

During 2001, the Office will continue to operate through three distinct business lines:

Patent Business.—The Patent Business supports the Department's strategic goal to stimulate innovation for competitiveness. The Patent Business grants exclusive rights, for limited times, to inventors for their discoveries. The activities under this business include all functions in the patent application processing pipeline, including the initial administrative examination of patent applications, the processing of patent applications filed under the Patent Cooperation Treaty, the formal examination of patent applications to determine the patentability of a claimed invention, the post-examination processing and printing of allowed patents, the review for quality, and the quasi-judicial review in appeal and interference proceedings. Other ancillary functions of the Patent Business are the classification, documentation and search systems, and the maintenance of a scientific and technical library.

The 2001 program level provides resources to improve the quality of our products and services through enhancement of training, classification, and examiner searcher programs. Additionally, specific programs geared toward improving weaknesses identified by our customers will be implemented. Finally, funds are provided for implementation of the American Inventors Protection Act of 1999.

Key Patent Business quantity and quality performance measures are:

	1999 actual	*2000 est.*	*2001 est.*
Applications received	272,221	299,400	335,400
Original inventions filed	228,766	251,600	281,900
Application disposals by examiners	219,556	235,700	264,100
Patents issued	143,604	154,700	170,600
Average pendency (months)	25.0	20.9	19.5
Average cycle time of original inventions processed (months)	12.9	10.2	10.0
Percent of original inventions achieving 12 month or less cycle time	62	80	85
Percent of customers satisfied	57	70	75

Trademark Business.—The Trademark Business supports the Department's strategic goal to stimulate innovation for competitiveness. The Trademark Business has the mission to enhance trademark protection. The activities under this business include the examination of trademark applications to determine whether the statutory criteria for the Federal registration of a trade or service mark are met. The Office issues notices of allowance and certificates of registration based on a trademark attorney's determination. Trademark application processing functions also include *inter parte* proceedings involving oppositions, cancellations, and *ex parte* proceedings.

The 2001 program level provides resources to fund fiscal year 2000 trademark programs and staff levels, including inflationary adjustments.

Key Trademark Business quantity and quality performance measures are:

	1999 actual	*2000 est.*	*2001 est.*
Applications received (includes amendments and combined classes)	295,165	324,700	363,700
Trademark registrations printed	104,324	154,000	169,500

General and special funds—Continued

SALARIES AND EXPENSES—Continued

	1999 actual	2000 est.	2001 est.
Pending time to first action (in months)	4.6	3.0	3.0
Pending time to registration/abandonment (in months)	18.9	13.8	13.8
Percent of customers' satisfied	69	80	80

Information Dissemination Business.—The Information Dissemination Business supports the Department's strategic goal to stimulate innovation for competitiveness. The goal of the Information Dissemination Business is to promote awareness of, and provide effective access to, patent and trademark information. The activities under this business serve the fundamental purpose of patent and trademark laws to disclose new technologies and to provide public notice concerning intellectual property rights. Information dissemination functions include the maintenance of public search rooms, the provision of copies and certified copies of patents, trademark registrations, and other official documents and the recordation of assignments of patent and trademark rights.

The 2001 program level provides resources to fund fiscal year 2000 information dissemination programs and staff levels, including inflationary adjustment.

Key Information Dissemination Business performance measures are:

	1999 actual	2000 est.	2001 est.
Percent of key products and services meeting schedules or cycle time of standards	64	80	80
Percent of total customers satisfied with key products and services	75	**	90

**This survey is conducted every two years. 1999 survey results reflect a change in the scale used when administering the survey.

Policy.—The Policy function supports the Department's strategic goal to stimulate innovation for competitiveness. The Policy function is organized to help protect, promote, and expand intellectual property rights systems throughout the United States and abroad. The primary function of this activity is to advise, assist, promote, and provide expertise, in the area of intellectual property rights. The 2001 program level provides resources to fund fiscal year 2000 policy programs and staff levels, including inflationary adjustment.

A key Policy performance measures is:

	1999 actual	2000 est.	2001 est.
Number of countries provided technical assistance in intellectual property rights systems	99	102	104

Corporate Support.—Planned obligations for administrative and infrastructure functions in support of the businesses and policy operations are included in the respective budget activity and line items. The 2001 program level provides resources to fund fiscal year 2000 corporate support and staff levels, including inflationary adjustment.

Object Classification (in millions of dollars)

Identification code 13–1006–0–1–376	1999 actual	2000 est.	2001 est.
99.0 Reimbursable obligations: Subtotal, reimbursable obligations	804	871	1,039
99.9 Total new obligations	804	871	1,039

Personnel Summary

Identification code 13–1006–0–1–376	1999 actual	2000 est.	2001 est.
2001 Total compensable workyears: Full-time equivalent employment	5,860	6,801	7,449

TECHNOLOGY ADMINISTRATION

Federal Funds

General and special funds:

UNDER SECRETARY FOR TECHNOLOGY/OFFICE OF TECHNOLOGY POLICY

SALARIES AND EXPENSES

For necessary expenses for the Undersecretary for Technology/Office of Technology Policy, [$7,972,000] *$8,716,000. (15 U.S.C. 1511(e), 1533, 3704, 3711; Department of Commerce and Related Agencies Appropriations Act, 2000, as enacted by section 1000(a)(1) of the Consolidated Appropriations Act, 2000 (P.L. 106–113).)*

Program and Financing (in millions of dollars)

Identification code 13–1100–0–1–376	1999 actual	2000 est.	2001 est.
Obligations by program activity:			
00.01 Direct program	11	8	9
09.00 Reimbursable program		1	1
10.00 Total new obligations	11	9	10
Budgetary resources available for obligation:			
21.40 Unobligated balance available, start of year	2		
22.00 New budget authority (gross)	9	9	10
23.90 Total budgetary resources available for obligation	11	9	10
23.95 Total new obligations	−11	−9	−10
New budget authority (gross), detail:			
Discretionary:			
40.00 Appropriation	9	8	9
68.00 Spending authority from offsetting collections: Offsetting collections (cash)		1	1
70.00 Total new budget authority (gross)	9	9	10
Change in unpaid obligations:			
72.40 Unpaid obligations, start of year: Obligated balance, start of year	14	16	3
73.10 Total new obligations	11	9	10
73.20 Total outlays (gross)	−9	−22	−9
74.40 Unpaid obligations, end of year: Obligated balance, end of year	16	3	3
Outlays (gross), detail:			
86.90 Outlays from new discretionary authority	5	6	7
86.93 Outlays from discretionary balances	4	16	3
87.00 Total outlays (gross)	9	22	9
Offsets:			
Against gross budget authority and outlays:			
88.00 Offsetting collections (cash) from: Federal sources		−1	−1
Net budget authority and outlays:			
89.00 Budget authority	9	8	9
90.00 Outlays	9	21	8

The Technology Administration (TA) is the focal point for civilian technology and competitiveness issues within the Administration. TA's sole mission is to work in partnership with the private sector to improve U.S. industrial competitiveness and to exercise leadership as the private sector's advocate.

TA administers the National Medal of Technology, a Presidential award program that recognizes excellence in technological innovation and commercialization.

The Under Secretary for Technology oversees three agencies within TA: the Office of Technology Policy (OTP), the National Institute of Standards and Technology, and the National Technical Information Service.

TA also houses the Office of Air and Space Commercialization which coordinates the Department's efforts to foster commercial space development and encourages private sector investment in space.

The Under Secretary and the Office of Technology Policy are responsible for coordinating a national technology policy.

The Under Secretary fulfills this role in part by chairing the high-level coordinating committee overseeing the Partnership for a New Generation of Vehicles Initiative (PNGV), a unique Government-wide, 10-year partnership between the Federal Government and the big three automakers. The Under Secretary also serves on the Executive Committee of the Committee on Technology within the President's National Science and Technology Council. This committee pursues industry defined and led activities relating to research and development in the areas of materials, construction and building, manufacturing infrastructure, electronics, and automotive technologies.

OTP provides advice and analysis for industrial competitiveness and civilian technology issues.

Performance Measures.—The activities under this account support the Commerce strategic goal involving promotion of economic growth:

Stimulate Innovation for Competitiveness

Goal: To improve technology's contribution to U.S. competitiveness, economic growth, and job creation through the analysis, development, advocacy, and implementation of national technology policies and programs.

	1999 act.	*2000 est.*	*2001 est.*
Number of roundtables, seminars, and negotiations held with industry, government and academia to advance TA policy goals	25	25	25

Object Classification (in millions of dollars)

Identification code 13–1100–0–1–376		1999 actual	2000 est.	2001 est.
	Direct obligations:			
11.1	Personnel compensation: Full-time permanent	3	3	3
12.1	Civilian personnel benefits	1	1	1
23.1	Rental payments to GSA	1	1	1
25.2	Other services	2	2	2
41.0	Grants, subsidies, and contributions	4		
99.0	Subtotal, direct obligations	11	7	7
99.0	Reimbursable obligations		1	1
99.5	Below reporting threshold		1	2
99.9	Total new obligations	11	9	10

Personnel Summary

Identification code 13–1100–0–1–376		1999 actual	2000 est.	2001 est.
	Direct:			
1001	Total compensable workyears: Full-time equivalent employment	43	50	50
	Reimbursable:			
2001	Total compensable workyears: Full-time equivalent employment	1	1	1

NATIONAL TECHNICAL INFORMATION SERVICE

Federal Funds

Intragovernmental funds:

NTIS Revolving Fund

Program and Financing (in millions of dollars)

Identification code 13–4295–0–3–376		1999 actual	2000 est.	2001 est.
	Obligations by program activity:			
00.01	Direct Program Activity	1		
09.01	Reimbursable program	32	40	
10.00	Total new obligations	33	40	
	Budgetary resources available for obligation:			
21.40	Unobligated balance available, start of year	3	5	
22.00	New budget authority (gross)	35	35	
23.90	Total budgetary resources available for obligation	38	40	
23.95	Total new obligations	−33	−40	
24.40	Unobligated balance available, end of year	5		
	New budget authority (gross), detail:			
	Discretionary:			
42.00	Transferred from other accounts	1		
68.00	Spending authority from offsetting collections: Offsetting collections (cash)	34	35	
70.00	Total new budget authority (gross)	35	35	
	Change in unpaid obligations:			
72.40	Unpaid obligations, start of year: Obligated balance, start of year	37	34	16
73.10	Total new obligations	33	40	
73.20	Total outlays (gross)	−36	−58	−16
74.40	Unpaid obligations, end of year: Obligated balance, end of year	34	16	
	Outlays (gross), detail:			
86.90	Outlays from new discretionary authority	34	19	
86.93	Outlays from discretionary balances	2	39	16
87.00	Total outlays (gross)	36	58	16
	Offsets:			
	Against gross budget authority and outlays:			
	Offsetting collections (cash) from:			
88.00	Federal sources	−15	−16	
88.40	Non-Federal sources	−19	−19	
88.90	Total, offsetting collections (cash)	−34	−35	
	Net budget authority and outlays:			
89.00	Budget authority	1		
90.00	Outlays	2	23	16

Summary of Budget Authority and Outlays

(in millions of dollars)

Enacted/requested:	*1999 actual*	*2000 est.*	*2001 est.*
Budget Authority	1		
Outlays	2	23	16
Supplemental proposal:			
Budget Authority		4	
Outlays		4	
Total:			
Budget Authority	1	4	
Outlays	2	27	16

The National Technical Information Service (NTIS), a component of the Technology Administration, operates this revolving fund for the payment of all expenses incurred in performing the activities of the NTIS, which historically included the acquisition and public sale of domestic and foreign federally funded research, development, and engineering reports.

The Department has proposed to Congress the abolishment of the National Technical Information Service in 2000. These schedules reflect the Department's proposal to shutdown NTIS. A supplemental is proposed to provide for costs associated with the shutdown. This request is included in the supplemental chapter of this volume.

Statement of Operations (in millions of dollars)

Identification code 13–4295–0–3–376		1998 actual	1999 actual	2000 est.	2001 est.
0101	Revenue	37	35	35	
0102	Expense	–41	–35	–35	
0105	Net income or loss (–)	–4			

Balance Sheet (in millions of dollars)

Identification code 13–4295–0–3–376		1998 actual	1999 actual	2000 est.	2001 est.
	ASSETS:				
1101	Federal assets: Fund balances with Treasury	40	39	39	
1206	Non-Federal assets: Receivables, net	1	1	1	
	Other Federal assets:				
1802	Inventories and related properties	3			

Intragovernmental funds—Continued

NTIS REVOLVING FUND—Continued

Balance Sheet (in millions of dollars)—Continued

Identification code 13–4295–0–3–376		1998 actual	1999 actual	2000 est.	2001 est.
1803	Property, plant and equipment, net	6	1	1	....
1901	Other assets	....	7	7	....
1999	Total assets	50	48	48	....
	LIABILITIES:				
	Federal liabilities:				
2101	Accounts payable	13	11	11	....
2105	Other	....	15	15	....
	Non-Federal liabilities:				
2201	Accounts payable	2	2	2	....
2207	Other	24	8	8	....
2999	Total liabilities	39	36	36	....
	NET POSITION:				
3300	Cumulative results of operations	11	11	11	....
3999	Total net position	11	11	11	....
4999	Total liabilities and net position	50	47	47	....

Object Classification (in millions of dollars)

Identification code 13–4295–0–3–376		1999 actual	2000 est.	2001 est.
11.1	Personnel compensation: Full-time permanent	14	12	....
12.1	Civilian personnel benefits	3	3	....
22.0	Transportation of things	1	2	....
23.1	Rental payments to GSA	1	1	....
23.2	Rental payments to others	....	1	....
23.3	Communications, utilities, and miscellaneous charges	2	2	....
24.0	Printing and reproduction	2	3	....
25.2	Other services	4	12	....
25.3	Purchases of goods and services from Government accounts	2	1	....
25.7	Operation and maintenance of equipment	1	1	....
26.0	Supplies and materials	1	1	....
31.0	Equipment	2	1	....
99.0	Subtotal, reimbursable obligations	33	40	....
99.9	Total new obligations	33	40	....

Personnel Summary

Identification code 13–4295–0–3–376		1999 actual	2000 est.	2001 est.
2001	Total compensable workyears: Full-time equivalent employment	322	260	....

SCIENCE AND TECHNOLOGY

NATIONAL INSTITUTE OF STANDARDS AND TECHNOLOGY

Federal Funds

General and special funds:

SCIENTIFIC AND TECHNICAL RESEARCH AND SERVICES

For necessary expenses of the National Institute of Standards and Technology, [$283,132,000] *$337,508,000*, to remain available until expended, of which not to exceed [$282,000] *$6,200,000* may be transferred to the "Working Capital Fund". *(15 U.S.C. 272, 273, 278b–e, 278g–h, 278p, 290b–f, 1151–57, 1454(d), 1454(e), 1501, 1512, 3711a; 40 U.S.C. 759(f); Department of Commerce and Related Agencies Appropriations Act, 2000, as enacted by section 1000(a)(1) of the Consolidated Appropriations Act, 2000 (P.L. 106–113).)*

Program and Financing (in millions of dollars)

Identification code 13–0500–0–1–376		1999 actual	2000 est.	2001 est.
	Obligations by program activity:			
	Operating expenses:			
	Measurement and engineering research and standards:			
00.01	Electronics and electrical engineering	38	39	40
00.02	Manufacturing engineering	19	19	24
00.03	Chemical science and technology	32	32	32
00.04	Physics	29	29	38
00.05	Materials science and engineering	50	53	58
00.06	Building and fire research	15	15	14
00.07	Computer science and applied mathematics	42	45	56
00.08	Technology assistance	18	18	17
00.09	National quality program	4	6	5
00.10	Research support activities	32	34	48
10.00	Total new obligations	279	290	332
	Budgetary resources available for obligation:			
21.40	Unobligated balance available, start of year	6	7	....
22.00	New budget authority (gross)	280	282	332
22.10	Resources available from recoveries of prior year obligations	1	1	1
23.90	Total budgetary resources available for obligation	287	290	333
23.95	Total new obligations	−279	−290	−332
24.40	Unobligated balance available, end of year	7	....	....
	New budget authority (gross), detail:			
	Discretionary:			
40.00	Appropriation	280	283	338
40.76	Reduction pursuant to P.L. 106–113	....	−1	....
41.00	Transferred to other accounts	....	....	−6
43.00	Appropriation (total discretionary)	280	282	332
	Change in unpaid obligations:			
72.40	Unpaid obligations, start of year: Obligated balance, start of year	78	74	72
73.10	Total new obligations	279	290	332
73.20	Total outlays (gross)	−283	−290	−322
73.45	Adjustments in unexpired accounts	−1	−1	−1
74.40	Unpaid obligations, end of year: Obligated balance, end of year	74	72	82
	Outlays (gross), detail:			
86.90	Outlays from new discretionary authority	223	217	256
86.93	Outlays from discretionary balances	60	73	66
87.00	Total outlays (gross)	283	290	322
	Net budget authority and outlays:			
89.00	Budget authority	280	282	332
90.00	Outlays	283	290	322

Summary of Budget Authority and Outlays

(in millions of dollars)

Enacted/requested:	*1999 actual*	*2000 est.*	*2001 est.*
Budget Authority	280	282	332
Outlays	283	290	322
Supplemental proposal:			
Budget Authority	....	1	....
Outlays	....	1	....
Total:			
Budget Authority	280	283	332
Outlays	283	291	322

The National Institute of Standards and Technology (NIST) is responsible for the measurement foundation that supports U.S. industry, Government, and scientific establishments. NIST's intramural research program is funded by the Scientific and Technical Research and Services appropriation.

Measurement and engineering research and standards.—

Electronics and electrical engineering.—Includes infrastructure research efforts to support the fundamental electronic technologies of semiconductors, magnetics, and superconductors; information and communications technologies, such as fiber optics, photonics, microwaves, and video; electrical power systems; the advanced manufacturing of electronic products; electronic measurement instrumentation; and, provision of the physical standards for electricity.

Manufacturing engineering.—Encompasses research in high-precision dimensional measurement and precision engineering; robotics and intelligent machines; manufacturing data description, data administration, and information processing; and, advanced sensors for manufacturing processes.

Chemical science and technology.—Covers fundamental investigations of measurement-based phenomena related to the composition and behavior of chemical and biochemical systems. This research includes developing and improving measurement capability and quantitative understanding of the underlying physical principles of measurement science.

Physics.—Includes investigation of the structure and dynamics of atoms, molecules, and micro- or nanoscale structures and the development of high performance sensors, instrumentation, measurement methods, and standards for time, frequency, and optical and ionizing radiation.

Materials science and engineering.—Covers research in materials characterization, nondestructive evaluation, metallurgy, polymers, and ceramics and addresses the measurement, standards and technological issues required to stimulate the more effective production and use of materials.

Building and fire research.—Includes research and development of technologies to predict, measure, and test the performance of construction materials, components, systems, and practices, and to investigate the scientific principles that govern the phenomena of fire initiation, propagation, and suppression.

Computer science and applied mathematics.—Includes development and demonstration of evaluation techniques, testing methods, and standards to enable usable, reliable, and interoperable computer and telecommunications systems; and provides leadership and collaborative research in the application and use of mathematics, statistics and computer science, and support of computing and telecommunications services.

Technology assistance.—Provides a central source of information and assistance for U.S. industry, academia, and Government regarding national and international standardization certification and conformity assessment activities and provides, on a reimbursable basis, centralized access to critically needed services, including Standard Reference Materials, Standard Reference Data, calibration and legal metrology services, and laboratory accreditation programs.

National Quality Program.—Extends U.S. competitiveness through performance excellence criteria and other information transfer, and administration of the Malcolm Baldrige National Quality Award.

Research support activities.—Includes centrally managed activities that provide support to all other NIST programs. This support includes competence development in NIST mission-oriented areas of research, high caliber postdoctoral scientists and engineers, and computing support for research programs, and financial management systems development.

These program activities are included in the 21st Century Research Fund.

Performance Measures.—The activities under this account support two Commerce strategic goals: promote economic growth and stimulate innovation for competitiveness.

1. Provide technical leadership for the Nation's measurement and standards infrastructure and assure the availability of essential reference data and measurement capability. NIST evaluates the perfomance of its laboratories through external peer review (conducted by the National Research Council), economic impact studies, and evaluation of numerous scientific and technical outputs.

2. Assist U.S. businesses and other organizations in continuously improving their productivity and efficiency by adopting performance and quality management practices.

	1999 actual	*2000 est.*	*2001 est.*
Standard Reference Materials available	1,288	1,300	1,315
Standard Reference Database title available	60	63	66
Number of items calibrated	3,118	3,200	3,100
Number of technical publications	2,414	2,450	2,450
Total number of applications to the MBNQA and Baldrige-based State and local programs	892 (est.)	916	935

Object Classification (in millions of dollars)

Identification code 13–0500–0–1–376		1999 actual	2000 est.	2001 est.
	Personnel compensation:			
11.1	Full-time permanent	122	126	137
11.3	Other than full-time permanent	11	11	12
11.5	Other personnel compensation	4	4	4
11.9	Total personnel compensation	137	141	153
12.1	Civilian personnel benefits	29	31	34
21.0	Travel and transportation of persons	6	6	7
22.0	Transportation of things	1	1	1
23.2	Rental payments to others	3	3	3
23.3	Communications, utilities, and miscellaneous charges	11	12	13
24.0	Printing and reproduction	1	1	1
25.1	Advisory and assistance services	4	4	4
25.2	Other services	23	21	29
25.3	Purchases of goods and services from Government accounts	9	12	14
25.5	Research and development contracts	1	2	9
25.7	Operation and maintenance of equipment	3	3	4
26.0	Supplies and materials	15	17	17
31.0	Equipment	23	23	24
32.0	Land and structures	1	1	1
41.0	Grants, subsidies, and contributions	12	12	18
99.9	Total new obligations	279	290	332

Personnel Summary

Identification code 13–0500–0–1–376		1999 actual	2000 est.	2001 est.
1001	Total compensable workyears: Full-time equivalent employment	2,062	2,048	2,113

INDUSTRIAL TECHNOLOGY SERVICES

For necessary expenses of the Manufacturing Extension Partnership of the National Institute of Standards and Technology, [$104,836,000] *$114,137,000*, to remain available until expended.

In addition, for necessary expenses of the Advanced Technology Program of the National Institute of Standards and Technology, [$142,600,000] *$175,467,000*, to remain available until expended, of which not to exceed [$50,700,000] *$65,000,000* shall be available for the award of new grants[, and of which not to exceed $500,000 may be transferred to the "Working Capital Fund"].

In addition, for necessary expenses of the Institute for Information Infrastructure Protection of the National Institute of Standards and Technology, $50,000,000, to remain available until expended, of which not to exceed $1,600,000 may be transferred to the "Working Capital Fund". (15 U.S.C. 278k, 278l, 278n; Department of Commerce and Related Agencies Appropriations Act, 2000, as enacted by section 1000(a)(1) of the Consolidated Appropriations Act, 2000 (P.L. 106–113).)

Program and Financing (in millions of dollars)

Identification code 13–0525–0–1–376		1999 actual	2000 est.	2001 est.
	Obligations by program activity:			
	Extramural programs:			
00.01	Advanced technology program	190	211	199
00.02	Manufacturing extension partnership	128	105	114
00.03	Institute for Information Infrastructure Protection			48
10.00	Total new obligations	318	316	361
	Budgetary resources available for obligation:			
21.40	Unobligated balance available, start of year	33	69	24
22.00	New budget authority (gross)	325	247	338
22.10	Resources available from recoveries of prior year obligations	28	24	4
23.90	Total budgetary resources available for obligation	386	340	366
23.95	Total new obligations	–318	–316	–361
24.40	Unobligated balance available, end of year	69	24	4
	New budget authority (gross), detail:			
	Discretionary:			
40.00	Appropriation	310	247	340
40.36	Unobligated balance rescinded	–6		
40.76	Reduction pursuant to P.L. 106–113		–1	

General and special funds—Continued

INDUSTRIAL TECHNOLOGY SERVICES—Continued

Program and Financing (in millions of dollars)—Continued

Identification code 13–0525–0–1–376	1999 actual	2000 est.	2001 est.
41.00 Transferred to other accounts			–2
42.00 Transferred from other accounts	21		
43.00 Appropriation (total discretionary)	325	247	338
Change in unpaid obligations:			
72.40 Unpaid obligations, start of year: Obligated balance, start of year	529	492	516
73.10 Total new obligations	318	316	361
73.20 Total outlays (gross)	–327	–268	–285
73.45 Adjustments in unexpired accounts	–28	–24	–4
74.40 Unpaid obligations, end of year: Obligated balance, end of year	492	516	588
Outlays (gross), detail:			
86.90 Outlays from new discretionary authority	56	25	34
86.93 Outlays from discretionary balances	271	243	251
87.00 Total outlays (gross)	327	268	285
Net budget authority and outlays:			
89.00 Budget authority	325	247	338
90.00 Outlays	327	268	285

Summary of Budget Authority and Outlays

(in millions of dollars)

	1999 actual	2000 est.	2001 est.
Enacted/requested:			
Budget Authority	325	247	338
Outlays	327	268	285
Supplemental proposal:			
Budget Authority			
Outlays			1
Total:			
Budget Authority	325	247	338
Outlays	327	268	286

This appropriation supports the extension of technology to American industry and fosters the development of broad-based, high-risk technology by industry.

Extramural programs.

Advanced technology program (ATP).—The ATP is the focus of a national effort to help accelerate the commercialization of high-risk, broad benefit enabling technologies with significant commercial potential. ATP is a merit-based, rigorously competitive, cost-shared partnership program that provides assistance to U.S. businesses and joint R&D ventures to help them improve their competitive position. The program resources will be used for technology areas having significant potential for stimulating U.S. economic growth. This program is included in the 21st Century Research Fund.

Manufacturing extension partnership (MEP).—The MEP program emphasizes NIST's role in transferring developed technologies to small- and medium-sized manufacturers through Government-industry partnerships and extension services and by improving the competitiveness of existing American business.

Institute for Information Infrastructure Protection (IIIP).—This program will establish and operate an institute to support research and development of technologies to protect the Nation's critical information infrastructures by working directly with industry and universities through the provision of research grants.

Performance Measures.—The activities under this account support two Commerce strategic goals: Promote economic growth and stimulate innovation for competitiveness. The performance of these activities is evaluated through a combination of external review, economic impact studies, and evaluation of numerous quantitative outcomes and outputs.

1. Accelerate technological innovation and the development of new technologies that underpin future economic growth (ATP).

2. Improve the technological capability, productivity, and competitiveness of small manufacturers (MEP).

3. Increase the security, reliability, and survivability of the information technology systems and networks that comprise the Nation's Information Infrastructure (IIIP).

	1999 est.	2000 est.	2001 est.
Cumulative number of technologies under commercialization	120	170	200
Increased sales attributed to MEP (millions of dollars)	443	595	748

Object Classification (in millions of dollars)

Identification code 13–0525–0–1–376	1999 actual	2000 est.	2001 est.
Personnel compensation:			
11.1 Full-time permanent	22	25	28
11.3 Other than full-time permanent	2	2	2
11.5 Other personnel compensation			1
11.9 Total personnel compensation	24	27	31
12.1 Civilian personnel benefits	5	5	6
21.0 Travel and transportation of persons	1	1	2
23.2 Rental payments to others	1	1	1
23.3 Communications, utilities, and miscellaneous charges	3	3	3
25.1 Advisory and assistance services	4	4	4
25.2 Other services	11	10	15
25.3 Purchases of goods and services from Government accounts	6	6	10
26.0 Supplies and materials	2	2	2
31.0 Equipment	3	3	3
41.0 Grants, subsidies, and contributions	258	254	282
99.0 Subtotal, direct obligations	318	316	359
99.5 Below reporting threshold			2
99.9 Total new obligations	318	316	361

Personnel Summary

Identification code 13–0525–0–1–376	1999 actual	2000 est.	2001 est.
1001 Total compensable workyears: Full-time equivalent employment	360	393	425

CONSTRUCTION OF RESEARCH FACILITIES

For construction of new research facilities, including architectural and engineering design, and for renovation of existing facilities, not otherwise provided for the National Institute of Standards and Technology, as authorized by 15 U.S.C. 278c–278e, **[**$108,414,000**]** *$35,879,000*, to remain available until expended**[**: *Provided*, That of the amounts provided under this heading, $84,916,000 shall be available for obligation and expenditure only after submission of a plan for the expenditure of these funds, in accordance with section 605 of this Act**]**. *(Department of Commerce and Related Agencies Appropriations Act, 2000, as enacted by section 1000(a)(1) of the Consolidated Appropriations Act, 2000 (P.L. 106–113).)*

Program and Financing (in millions of dollars)

Identification code 13–0515–0–1–376	1999 actual	2000 est.	2001 est.
Obligations by program activity:			
10.00 Total new obligations	20	226	36
Budgetary resources available for obligation:			
21.40 Unobligated balance available, start of year	82	120	
22.00 New budget authority (gross)	57	106	36
23.90 Total budgetary resources available for obligation	139	226	36
23.95 Total new obligations	–20	–226	–36
24.40 Unobligated balance available, end of year	120		
New budget authority (gross), detail:			
Discretionary:			
40.00 Appropriation	57	108	36
40.76 Reduction pursuant to P.L. 106–113		–2	
43.00 Appropriation (total discretionary)	57	106	36

	Change in unpaid obligations:			
72.40	Unpaid obligations, start of year: Obligated balance, start of year	32	16	210
73.10	Total new obligations	20	226	36
73.20	Total outlays (gross)	−36	−32	−41
74.40	Unpaid obligations, end of year: Obligated balance, end of year	16	210	205
	Outlays (gross), detail:			
86.90	Outlays from new discretionary authority	2	13	4
86.93	Outlays from discretionary balances	34	19	37
87.00	Total outlays (gross)	36	32	41
	Net budget authority and outlays:			
89.00	Budget authority	57	106	36
90.00	Outlays	36	32	41

This appropriation supports the renovation of NIST's current buildings and laboratories to comply with more stringent science and engineering requirements and is included in the 21st Century Research Fund.

The request includes $15,000,000 for the fit-up and relocation costs associated with the Advanced Measurement Laboratory at NIST's main campus in Gaithersburg, Maryland. The 5-wing complex will provide stringent controls for particulate matter, temperature, vibration, and humidity that are unattainable in current NIST buildings, and equal to or better than similar labs overseas. Such conditions are vital for NIST to keep pace with rapid developments in semiconductors, precision instruments, industrial robots, computers, chemicals, pharmaceuticals, building materials, and emerging technologies requiring molecular and atomic-level precision. NIST will award a contract for construction in 2000 and projected completion is in late 2004.

To improve the safety and performance of existing NIST facilities, the remaining balance of funds in this account will be used to address the highest-priority maintenance and repair projects, as outlined in the NIST Facilities Improvement Plan.

Object Classification (in millions of dollars)

Identification code 13–0515–0–1–376		1999 actual	2000 est.	2001 est.
11.1	Personnel compensation: Full-time permanent	1	2	2
25.2	Other services	11	5	15
26.0	Supplies and materials	1	1	1
31.0	Equipment	1	1	1
32.0	Land and structures	5	206	17
41.0	Grants, subsidies, and contributions		11	
99.0	Subtotal, direct obligations	19	226	36
99.5	Below reporting threshold	1		
99.9	Total new obligations	20	226	36

Personnel Summary

Identification code 13–0515–0–1–376		1999 actual	2000 est.	2001 est.
1001	Total compensable workyears: Full-time equivalent employment	27	33	33

Intragovernmental funds:

WORKING CAPITAL FUND

Program and Financing (in millions of dollars)

Identification code 13–4650–0–4–376		1999 actual	2000 est.	2001 est.
	Obligations by program activity:			
	Extramural Programs:			
00.01	National Institute for Information Infrastructure Protection			2
	Measurement and engineering research and standards:			
09.01	Electronics and electrical engineering	15	13	13
09.02	Manufacturing engineering	6	6	6
09.03	Chemical science and technology	15	15	16
09.04	Physics	13	13	15
09.05	Material science and engineering	7	6	7
09.06	Building and fire research	9	12	12
09.07	Computer science and applied mathematics	9	14	14
09.08	Technology Assistance	19	18	18
09.11	National quality program	2	2	2
09.12	Research support activities	27	8	11
09.14	Manufacturing extension partnership	3	1	
10.00	Total new obligations	125	108	116
	Budgetary resources available for obligation:			
21.40	Unobligated balance available, start of year	32	41	41
22.00	New budget authority (gross)	133	108	116
23.90	Total budgetary resources available for obligation	165	149	157
23.95	Total new obligations	−125	−108	−116
24.40	Unobligated balance available, end of year	41	41	41
	New budget authority (gross), detail:			
	Discretionary:			
42.00	Transferred from other accounts			8
43.00	Appropriation (total discretionary)			8
68.00	Spending authority from offsetting collections: Offsetting collections (cash)	133	108	108
70.00	Total new budget authority (gross)	133	108	116
	Change in unpaid obligations:			
72.40	Unpaid obligations, start of year: Obligated balance, start of year	42	21	27
73.10	Total new obligations	125	108	116
73.20	Total outlays (gross)	−147	−102	−112
74.40	Unpaid obligations, end of year: Obligated balance, end of year	21	27	31
	Outlays (gross), detail:			
86.90	Outlays from new discretionary authority	133	83	87
86.93	Outlays from discretionary balances	14	19	25
87.00	Total outlays (gross)	147	102	112
	Offsets:			
	Against gross budget authority and outlays:			
	Offsetting collections (cash) from:			
88.00	Federal sources	−103	−84	−84
88.40	Non-Federal sources	−30	−24	−24
88.90	Total, offsetting collections (cash)	−133	−108	−108
	Net budget authority and outlays:			
89.00	Budget authority			8
90.00	Outlays	14	−6	4

The Working capital fund finances research and technical services performed for other Government agencies and the public. These activities are funded through advances and reimbursements. The fund also finances the acquisition of equipment and standard reference materials and storeroom inventories until issued or sold.

Object Classification (in millions of dollars)

Identification code 13–4650–0–4–376		1999 actual	2000 est.	2001 est.
	Personnel compensation:			
11.1	Full-time permanent	42	43	44
11.3	Other than full-time permanent	4	4	4
11.5	Other personnel compensation	1	1	1
11.9	Total personnel compensation	47	48	49
12.1	Civilian personnel benefits	10	10	10
21.0	Travel and transportation of persons	2	2	2
22.0	Transportation of things	1		
23.2	Rental payments to others	1	1	3
23.3	Communications, utilities, and miscellaneous charges	4	4	4
25.1	Advisory and assistance services	2	2	2
25.2	Other services	14	12	10
25.3	Purchases of goods and services from Government accounts	5	5	5
25.5	Research and development contracts	2	2	3
25.7	Operation and maintenance of equipment	1	1	1

Intragovernmental funds—Continued

WORKING CAPITAL FUND—Continued

Object Classification (in millions of dollars)—Continued

Identification code 13–4650–0–4–376	1999 actual	2000 est.	2001 est.
26.0 Supplies and materials	4	6	6
31.0 Equipment	28	9	17
41.0 Grants, subsidies, and contributions	4	4	4
99.0 Subtotal, reimbursable obligations	125	106	116
99.5 Below reporting threshold		2	
99.9 Total new obligations	125	108	116

Personnel Summary

Identification code 13–4650–0–4–376	1999 actual	2000 est.	2001 est.
2001 Total compensable workyears: Full-time equivalent employment	732	722	714

NATIONAL TELECOMMUNICATIONS AND INFORMATION ADMINISTRATION

Federal Funds

General and special funds:

SALARIES AND EXPENSES

For necessary expenses, as provided for by law, of the National Telecommunications and Information Administration (NTIA), [$10,975,000] *$20,315,000*, to remain available until expended: *Provided*, That, notwithstanding 31 U.S.C. 1535(d), the Secretary of Commerce shall charge Federal agencies for costs incurred in spectrum management, analysis, and operations, and related services and such fees shall be retained and used as offsetting collections for costs of such spectrum services, to remain available until expended: *Provided further*, That hereafter, notwithstanding any other provision of law, NTIA shall not authorize spectrum use or provide any spectrum functions pursuant to the National Telecommunications and Information Administration Organization Act, 47 U.S.C. 902–903, to any Federal entity without reimbursement as required by NTIA for such spectrum management costs, and Federal entities withholding payment of such cost shall not use spectrum: *Provided further*, That the Secretary of Commerce is authorized to retain and use as offsetting collections all funds transferred, or previously transferred, from other Government agencies for all costs incurred in telecommunications research, engineering, and related activities by the Institute for Telecommunication Sciences of NTIA, in furtherance of its assigned functions under this paragraph, and such funds received from other Government agencies shall remain available until expended. *(15 U.S.C. 1512, 1532; 47 U.S.C. §§305, 606, 701 et seq., 721, and 744; Department of Commerce and Related Agencies Appropriations Act, 2000, as enacted by section 1000(a)(1) of the Consolidated Appropriations Act, 2000 (P.L. 106–113).)*

Program and Financing (in millions of dollars)

Identification code 13–0550–0–1–376	1999 actual	2000 est.	2001 est.
Obligations by program activity:			
Direct program:			
00.01 Domestic and International Policy	4	4	4
00.02 Spectrum Management	4	4	8
00.03 Telecommunication Science Research	3	4	8
01.00 Total, direct program	11	12	20
Reimbursable Program:			
09.01 Spectrum Management	12	14	17
09.02 Telecommunications Science Research	6	7	7
09.99 Total reimbursable program	18	21	24
10.00 Total new obligations	29	33	44
Budgetary resources available for obligation:			
21.40 Unobligated balance available, start of year	1	3	
22.00 New budget authority (gross)	29	31	44
23.90 Total budgetary resources available for obligation	30	34	44
23.95 Total new obligations	−29	−33	−44
24.40 Unobligated balance available, end of year	3		
New budget authority (gross), detail:			
Discretionary:			
40.00 Appropriation	11	11	20
68.00 Spending authority from offsetting collections: Offsetting collections (cash)	18	20	24
70.00 Total new budget authority (gross)	29	31	44
Change in unpaid obligations:			
72.40 Unpaid obligations, start of year: Obligated balance, start of year	5	3	3
73.10 Total new obligations	29	33	44
73.20 Total outlays (gross)	−31	−34	−43
74.40 Unpaid obligations, end of year: Obligated balance, end of year	3	3	5
Outlays (gross), detail:			
86.90 Outlays from new discretionary authority	27	29	40
86.93 Outlays from discretionary balances	4	5	3
87.00 Total outlays (gross)	31	34	43
Offsets:			
Against gross budget authority and outlays:			
88.00 Offsetting collections (cash) from: Federal sources	−18	−20	−24
Net budget authority and outlays:			
89.00 Budget authority	11	11	20
90.00 Outlays	13	14	19

The National Telecommunications and Information Administration (NTIA) is the principal executive branch adviser to the President on domestic and international telecommunications policy. Additionally, it manages the Federal Government's use of the radio frequency spectrum and performs extensive research in telecommunications sciences.

Domestic and international policies.—NTIA develops and advocates policies to improve and expand domestic telecommunications services and markets so that the benefits of telecommunications are more widely available to consumers. NTIA provides advice to White House officials, coordinates with other Executive Branch agencies, and participates in relevant Congressional actions and interagency and Federal Communications Commission (FCC) proceedings on a host of issues. NTIA's focus is on current and emerging issues such as implementation of specific provisions of the 1996 Telecommunications Act. NTIA develops policies promoting universal service to all Americans, competition in telecommunications and information markets, and development of new technologies. NTIA makes policy recommendations in such areas as traditional common carrier networks, wireless services and products, the mass media (including advanced television), as well as issues arising from the Internet and electronic commerce, such as the Digital Divide.

NTIA advocates the advancement of U.S. priorities in the international telecommunications policy and regulatory areas. NTIA will continue to encourage forcefully the broad liberalization of telecommunication regulations now taking hold across the globe that create significant opportunities for U.S. telecommunications interests and enterprises including emphasis on the international development of electronic commerce as an essential element of today's information society. NTIA supports U.S. interests in international and regional fora affecting telecommunications standards, infrastructure development and market access. NTIA also represents executive branch concerns related to international telecommunications regulation before the FCC. In coordination with the Department of State and the FCC, the agency also discharges statutory responsibilities for oversight of the Communications Satellite Corporation in its role as U.S. Signatory to INTELSAT and INMARSAT as these two organizations consider options for restructuring.

Spectrum Management.—NTIA manages the Federal Government's use of the spectrum, both domestically and internationally. In coordination with the FCC and with the advice of the Interdepartment Radio Advisory Committee (IRAC), NTIA supports the spectrum requirements of the Federal Government, makes plans to satisfy the Government's future spectrum needs, coordinates Federal spectrum requirements in shared spectrum bands, and develops and implements policy to use the spectrum effectively and efficiently. NTIA prepares for, participates in, and implements the results of regional, national, and international conferences on spectrum use and allocations. NTIA also is responsible for emergency communications and Federal Government continuity of operations planning for communications during emergency conditions. NTIA coordinates its activities with the private sector through its spectrum openness program and its Internet web site and apprises private sector entities of Government spectrum use and rules and regulations governing this use. NTIA reviews major Federal communications systems to certify that spectrum will be available; conducts frequency band studies to define spectrum issues and makes plans to prevent future interference; and, processes approximately 80,000 annual requests for frequency assignments to meet the communications needs of the Federal Government and support analysis and engineering aspects of spectrum management. NTIA also strives to identify and apply new spectrum saving technologies, identify adjacent band effects for use by designers of future communications, and address the public safety community's need for spectrum and interoperability at the Federal, State, and local levels.

Telecommunications Sciences Research.—NTIA develops improved spectrum measurement techniques to address the increasing use of broadband technologies, including digital signals, spread-spectrum, and frequency agile systems. NTIA supports the development of wireless technologies by studying the behavior of broadband radio waves in indoor and outdoor environments in order to create more accurate modeling of radio propagation that will lead to improved methods of spectrum sharing among users. Additionally, NTIA prepares and coordinates proposed domestic and international telecommunications standards, develops and demonstrates user-friendly ways to assess the performance of industry and Government telecommunications networks, evaluates future technologies that may facilitate competition in the U.S. telecommunications industry, promotes international trade opportunities for U.S. telecommunications firms and improves the cost effectiveness of Government telecommunications use. Also, NTIA will initiate a program to analyze the Nation's telecommunications and information infrastructure protection needs and formulate outputs that will enhance the ability of the U.S. to protect this critical infrastructure.

Performance measures.—Activities under this account support the Commerce strategic goal involving stimulation of innovation for American competitiveness.

Goal: Ensure spectrum provides the greatest benefit to all people.

	1999 actual	*2000 est.*	*2001 est.*
Performance Measure:			
Number of authorized spectrum assignments	437,313	505,000	510,000

A more detailed presentation of goals, performance measures and targets is found in the Commerce Annual Performance Plan.

Object Classification (in millions of dollars)

Identification code 13–0550–0–1–376		1999 actual	2000 est.	2001 est.
	Direct obligations:			
11.1	Personnel compensation: Full-time permanent	6	6	8
12.1	Civilian personnel benefits	2	2	2
23.1	Rental payments to GSA	1	1	2
25.2	Other services			3
25.3	Purchases of goods and services from Government accounts	2	2	3
99.0	Subtotal, direct obligations	11	11	18
99.0	Reimbursable obligations	15	20	22
99.5	Below reporting threshold	3	2	4
99.9	Total new obligations	29	33	44

Personnel Summary

Identification code 13–0550–0–1–376		1999 actual	2000 est.	2001 est.
	Direct:			
1001	Total compensable workyears: Full-time equivalent employment	90	96	127
	Reimbursable:			
2001	Total compensable workyears: Full-time equivalent employment	132	148	148

Public Telecommunications Facilities, Planning and Construction

For grants authorized by [section] *Sections 391 and* 392 of the Communications Act of 1934, as amended, [$26,500,000], to *become available on October 1 of the fiscal year specified and* remain available until expended [as authorized by section 391 of the Act, as amended] *$110,075,000 in fiscal year 2001; $110,000,000 in fiscal year 2002; and $87,500,000 in fiscal year 2003*: *Provided*, That not to exceed [$1,800,000] *$4,075,000* shall be available for program administration as authorized by section 391 of the Act: *Provided further*, That notwithstanding the provisions of section 391 of the Act, the prior year unobligated balances may be made available for grants for projects for which applications have been submitted and approved during any fiscal year: *Provided further, That these funds shall be used for grants to support acquisition of core digital transmission capabilities and ensure public broadcasters' transition to digital broadcasting by 2003, as well as for necessary equipment and facilities to maintain public television and radio service: Provided further*, That, hereafter, notwithstanding any other provision of law, the Pan-Pacific Education and Communication Experiments by Satellite (PEACESAT) Program is eligible to compete for Public Telecommunications Facilities, Planning and Construction funds. *(Department of Commerce and Related Agencies Appropriations Act, 2000, as enacted by section 1000(a)(1) of the Consolidated Appropriations Act, 2000 (P.L. 106–113).)*

Program and Financing (in millions of dollars)

Identification code 13–0551–0–1–503		1999 actual	2000 est.	2001 est.
	Obligations by program activity:			
00.01	Grants	22	25	106
00.02	Program management	2	2	4
10.00	Total new obligations	24	27	110
	Budgetary resources available for obligation:			
21.40	Unobligated balance available, start of year	3	1	
22.00	New budget authority (gross)	20	26	110
22.10	Resources available from recoveries of prior year obligations	1		
23.90	Total budgetary resources available for obligation	24	27	110
23.95	Total new obligations	–24	–27	–110
24.40	Unobligated balance available, end of year	1		
	New budget authority (gross), detail:			
	Discretionary:			
40.00	Public Telecommunications Facilities, Planning and Construction	21	26	110
40.36	Unobligated balance rescinded-Endowment for Children's Educational TV	–1		

General and special funds—Continued

PUBLIC TELECOMMUNICATIONS FACILITIES, PLANNING AND CONSTRUCTION—Continued

Program and Financing (in millions of dollars)—Continued

Identification code 13–0551–0–1–503		1999 actual	2000 est.	2001 est.
43.00	Appropriation (total discretionary)	20	26	110
	Change in unpaid obligations:			
72.40	Unpaid obligations, start of year: Obligated balance, start of year	36	42	41
73.10	Total new obligations	24	27	110
73.20	Total outlays (gross)	−17	−27	−37
73.45	Adjustments in unexpired accounts	−1		
74.40	Unpaid obligations, end of year: Obligated balance, end of year	42	41	116
	Outlays (gross), detail:			
86.90	Outlays from new discretionary authority	3	3	13
86.93	Outlays from discretionary balances	14	24	24
87.00	Total outlays (gross)	17	27	37
	Net budget authority and outlays:			
89.00	Budget authority	20	26	110
90.00	Outlays	17	27	37

In April 1997, the Federal Communications Commission issued regulations requiring broadcasters to transition from analog to digital broadcasting. Public broadcasters must convert to digital broadcasting by May 1, 2003. Advance appropriations are requested for a multi-year program to allow advance planning and certainty in the public broadcasting system's transition to digital broadcasting. Funds made available from this program to the Public Telecommunications Facilities, Planning and Construction program (PTFP) will facilitate public broadcasters' transition to digital broadcasting. $110 million is requested in 2001 as part of a $450 million, five-year initiative now in its third year. The initiative is funded in both the Corporation for Public Broadcasting and the Department of Commerce. Funding through PTFP will be targeted for digital transmission equipment, while funding for the Corporation for Public Broadcasting will support necessary expenses related to digital program production and development.

PTFP grants strengthen and extend service delivery by the public broadcasting system and assist public broadcasters and non-commercial entities with facilities purchases to demonstrate innovative, replicable applications of digital broadcasting. To facilitate the public broadcasting's transition to digital technology, PTFP will fund broadcasters' acquisition of core digital transmission and base equipment through merit- and need-based grants.

Performance measure.—Activities under this account contribute to the Commerce's strategic goals of supporting the development of an advanced information infrastructure that will be accessible to all Americans.

Performance Measure:	*1999 actual*	*2000 est.*	*2001 est.*
Digital Conversion projects awarded:	7	18	120

A more detailed presentation of goals, performance measures and targets is found in the Commerce Strategic Plan.

Summary of Funding Levels, 1999–2003

(in millions of dollars)

	1999 actual	*2000 est.*	*2001 est.*	*2002 est.*	*2003 est.*
PTFP	21	26	110	110	88

Object Classification (in millions of dollars)

Identification code 13–0551–0–1–503		1999 actual	2000 est.	2001 est.
11.1	Personnel compensation: Full-time permanent	1	1	2
25.3	Purchases of goods and services from Government accounts	1		
41.0	Grants—Public facilities	22	25	106
99.0	Subtotal, direct obligations	24	26	108
99.5	Below reporting threshold		1	2
99.9	Total new obligations	24	27	110

Personnel Summary

Identification code 13–0551–0–1–503		1999 actual	2000 est.	2001 est.
1001	Total compensable workyears: Full-time equivalent employment	12	13	21

[INFORMATION INFRASTRUCTURE GRANTS] *TECHNOLOGY OPPORTUNITY GRANTS*

For grants authorized by section 392 of the Communications Act of 1934, as amended, [$15,500,000] *$45,119,000*, to remain available until expended as authorized by section 391 of the Act, as amended: *Provided*, That not to exceed [$3,000,000] *$4,119,000* shall be available for program administration and other support activities as authorized by section 391: *Provided further*, That, of the funds appropriated herein, not to exceed 5 percent may be available for telecommunications research activities for projects related directly to the development of a national information infrastructure: *Provided further*, That, notwithstanding the requirements of sections 392(a) and 392(c) of the Act, these funds may be used for the planning and construction of telecommunications networks for the provision of educational, cultural, health care, public information, public safety, or other social services: *Provided further*, That notwithstanding any other provision of law, no entity that receives telecommunications services at preferential rates under section 254(h) of the Act (47 U.S.C. 254(h)) or receives assistance under the regional information sharing systems grant program of the Department of Justice under part M of title I of the Omnibus Crime Control and Safe Streets Act of 1968 (42 U.S.C. 3796h) may use funds under a grant under this heading to cover any costs of the entity that would otherwise be covered by such preferential rates or such assistance, as the case may be. *(Department of Commerce and Related Agencies Appropriations Act, 2000, as enacted by section 1000(a)(1) of the Consolidated Appropriations Act, 2000 (P.L. 106–113).)*

Program and Financing (in millions of dollars)

Identification code 13–0552–0–1–503		1999 actual	2000 est.	2001 est.
	Obligations by program activity:			
00.01	Grants	18	13	41
00.02	Program management	4	4	4
10.00	Total new obligations	22	17	45
	Budgetary resources available for obligation:			
21.40	Unobligated balance available, start of year	2	1	
22.00	New budget authority (gross)	18	16	45
22.10	Resources available from recoveries of prior year obligations	3		
23.90	Total budgetary resources available for obligation	23	17	45
23.95	Total new obligations	−22	−17	−45
24.40	Unobligated balance available, end of year	1		
	New budget authority (gross), detail:			
	Discretionary:			
40.00	Appropriation	18	16	45
	Change in unpaid obligations:			
72.40	Unpaid obligations, start of year: Obligated balance, start of year	44	47	36
73.10	Total new obligations	22	17	45
73.20	Total outlays (gross)	−17	−28	−24
73.45	Adjustments in unexpired accounts	−3		
74.40	Unpaid obligations, end of year: Obligated balance, end of year	47	36	56
	Outlays (gross), detail:			
86.90	Outlays from new discretionary authority	1	1	3
86.93	Outlays from discretionary balances	16	27	20
87.00	Total outlays (gross)	17	28	24

Net budget authority and outlays:			
89.00 Budget authority	18	16	45
90.00 Outlays	17	28	24

The Technology Opportunities Program (formerly the Telecommunications and Information Infrastructure Assistance program) facilitates the development of the national telecommunications and information infrastructure by promoting the widespread availability and use of advanced telecommunications technologies to enhance the delivery of social services, such as education, health care, and public safety. The program greatly leverages the Federal investment by providing grants for outstanding projects that can serve as national models, evaluating the projects, and broadly disseminating the project findings. By focusing on underserved communities in both rural and urban areas, the program helps to reduce disparities in access to the developing national information infrastructure.

Performance measures.—Activities under this account support the Commerce strategic goal involving stimulation of innovation for American competitiveness.

	1999 actual	2000 est.	2001 est.
Performance Measure:			
Number of models/grants available for non-profit or public sector organizations	43	50	55

A detailed presentation of goals, performance measures and targets is found in the Commerce Annual Plan.

Object Classification (in millions of dollars)

Identification code 13–0552–0–1–503	1999 actual	2000 est.	2001 est.
11.1 Personnel compensation: Full-time permanent	1	1	2
25.2 Other services	1	1	1
41.0 Grants, subsidies, and contributions	18	13	41
99.0 Subtotal, direct obligations	20	15	44
99.5 Below reporting threshold	2	2	1
99.9 Total new obligations	22	17	45

Personnel Summary

Identification code 13–0552–0–1–503	1999 actual	2000 est.	2001 est.
1001 Total compensable workyears: Full-time equivalent employment	22	24	29

Home Internet Access

For grants authorized by sections 391 and 392 of the Communications Act of 1934, as amended, $50,000,000, to remain available until expended, of which not to exceed $4,000,000 shall be for program administration and other support activities as authorized by section 391: Provided, That notwithstanding sections 392(a) and 392(c) of the Act, these funds may be used to support activities to provide low-income individuals and families with access to the Internet in their homes.

Program and Financing (in millions of dollars)

Identification code 13–0553–0–1–451	1999 actual	2000 est.	2001 est.
Obligations by program activity:			
00.01 Grants			46
00.02 Program management			4
10.00 Total new obligations			50
Budgetary resources available for obligation:			
22.00 New budget authority (gross)			50
23.95 Total new obligations			−50
New budget authority (gross), detail:			
Discretionary:			
40.00 Appropriation			50
Change in unpaid obligations:			
73.10 Total new obligations			50
73.20 Total outlays (gross)			−4
74.40 Unpaid obligations, end of year: Obligated balance, end of year			46
Outlays (gross), detail:			
86.90 Outlays from new discretionary authority			4
Net budget authority and outlays:			
89.00 Budget authority			50
90.00 Outlays			4

The Administration proposes $50 million for a new grants program that would provide low-income individuals and families with the connections, training, and support necessary for full participation in today's increasingly online society. The National Telecommunications and Information Administration will encourage community-based partnerships between local organizations, academia, and private industry to devise solutions that address the needs of low-income populations in gaining access to technology and online resources at home.

Object Classification (in millions of dollars)

Identification code 13–0553–0–1–451	1999 actual	2000 est.	2001 est.
11.1 Personnel compensation: Full-time permanent			1
25.2 Other services			1
41.0 Grants, subsidies, and contributions			46
99.0 Subtotal, direct obligations			48
99.5 Below reporting threshold			2
99.9 Total new obligations			50

Personnel Summary

Identification code 13–0553–0–1–451	1999 actual	2000 est.	2001 est.
1001 Total compensable workyears: Full-time equivalent employment			15

GENERAL FUND RECEIPT ACCOUNTS

(in millions of dollars)

	1999 actual	2000 est.	2001 est.
Offsetting receipts from the public:			
13–225200 Fees for maps and charts, public, NOAA, Commerce	13	8	8
General Fund Offsetting receipts from the public	13	8	8

GENERAL PROVISIONS—DEPARTMENT OF COMMERCE

Sec. 201. During the current fiscal year, applicable appropriations and funds made available to the Department of Commerce by this Act shall be available for the activities specified in the Act of October 26, 1949 (15 U.S.C. 1514), to the extent and in the manner prescribed by the Act, and, notwithstanding 31 U.S.C. 3324, may be used for advanced payments not otherwise authorized only upon the certification of officials designated by the Secretary of Commerce that such payments are in the public interest.

Sec. 202. During the current fiscal year, appropriations made available to the Department of Commerce by this Act for salaries and expenses shall be available for hire of passenger motor vehicles as authorized by 31 U.S.C. 1343 and 1344; services as authorized by 5 U.S.C. 3109; and uniforms or allowances therefore, as authorized by law (5 U.S.C. 5901–5902).

Sec. 203. None of the funds made available by this Act may be used to support the hurricane reconnaissance aircraft and activities that are under the control of the United States Air Force or the United States Air Force Reserve.

SEC. 204. None of the funds provided in this or any previous Act, or hereinafter made available to the Department of Commerce, shall be available to reimburse the Unemployment Trust Fund or any other fund or account of the Treasury to pay for any expenses authorized by section 8501 of title 5, United States Code, for services performed by individuals appointed to temporary positions within the Bureau of the Census for purposes relating to the decennial censuses of population.

SEC. 205. Not to exceed 5 percent of any appropriation made available for the current fiscal year for the Department of Commerce in this Act may be transferred between such appropriations, but no such appropriation shall be increased by more than 10 percent by any such transfers: *Provided*, That any transfer pursuant to this section shall be treated as a reprogramming of funds under section 605 of this Act and shall not be available for obligation or expenditure except in compliance with the procedures set forth in that section.

SEC. 206. (a) Should legislation be enacted to dismantle or reorganize the Department of Commerce, or any portion thereof, the Secretary of Commerce, no later than 90 days thereafter, shall submit to the Committees on Appropriations of the House of Representatives and the Senate a plan for transferring funds provided in this Act to the appropriate successor organizations: *Provided*, That the plan shall include a proposal for transferring or rescinding funds appropriated herein for agencies or programs terminated under such legislation: *Provided further*, That such plan shall be transmitted in accordance with section 605 of this Act.

(b) The Secretary of Commerce or the appropriate head of any successor organization(s) may use any available funds to carry out legislation dismantling or reorganizing the Department of Commerce, or any portion thereof, to cover the costs of actions relating to the abolishment, reorganization, or transfer of functions and any related personnel action, including voluntary separation incentives if authorized by such legislation: *Provided*, That the authority to transfer funds between appropriations accounts that may be necessary to carry out this section is provided in addition to authorities included under section 205 of this Act: *Provided further*, That use of funds to carry out this section shall be treated as a reprogramming of funds under section 605 of this Act and shall not be available for obligation or expenditure except in compliance with the procedures set forth in that section.

SEC. 207. Any costs incurred by a department or agency funded under this title resulting from personnel actions taken in response to funding reductions included in this title or from actions taken for the care and protection of loan collateral or grant property shall be absorbed within the total budgetary resources available to such department or agency: *Provided*, That the authority to transfer funds between appropriations accounts as may be necessary to carry out this section is provided in addition to authorities included elsewhere in this Act: *Provided further*, That use of funds to carry out this section shall be treated as a reprogramming of funds under section 605 of this Act and shall not be available for obligation or expenditure except in compliance with the procedures set forth in that section.

SEC. 208. The Secretary of Commerce may award contracts for hydrographic, geodetic, and photogrammetric surveying and mapping services in accordance with title IX of the Federal Property and Administrative Services Act of 1949 (40 U.S.C. 541 et seq.).

SEC. 209. The Secretary of Commerce may use the Commerce franchise fund for expenses and equipment necessary for the maintenance and operation of such administrative services as the Secretary determines may be performed more advantageously as central services, pursuant to section 403 of Public Law 103–356: *Provided*, That any inventories, equipment, and other assets pertaining to the services to be provided by such fund, either on hand or on order, less the related liabilities or unpaid obligations, and any appropriations made for the purpose of providing capital shall be used to capitalize such fund: *Provided further*, That such fund shall be paid in advance from funds available to the department and other Federal agencies for which such centralized services are performed, at rates which will return in full all expenses of operation, including accrued leave, depreciation of fund plant and equipment, amortization of automated data processing (ADP) software and systems (either acquired or donated), and an amount necessary to maintain a reasonable operating reserve, as determined by the Secretary: *Provided further*, That such fund shall provide services on a competitive basis: *Provided further*, That an amount not to exceed 4 percent of the total annual income to such fund may be retained in the fund for fiscal year [2000] *2001* and each fiscal year thereafter, to remain available until expended, to be used for the acquisition of capital equipment, and for the improvement and implementation of department financial management, ADP, and other support systems: *Provided further*, That such amounts retained in the fund for fiscal year [2000] *2001* and each fiscal year thereafter shall be available for obligation and expenditure only in accordance with section 605 of this Act: *Provided further*, That no later than 30 days after the end of each fiscal year, amounts in excess of this reserve limitation shall be deposited as miscellaneous receipts in the Treasury: *Provided further*, That such franchise fund pilot program shall terminate pursuant to section 403(f) of Public Law 103–356.

[SEC. 210. Section 302(a)(1)(A) of the Magnuson-Stevens Fishery Conservation and Management Act (16 U.S.C. 1852(a)(1)(A)) is amended—

(1) by striking "17" and inserting "18"; and

(2) by striking "11" and inserting "12".]

[SEC. 211. Notwithstanding any other provision of law, of the amounts made available elsewhere in this title to the "National Institute of Standards and Technology, Construction of Research Facilities", $2,000,000 is appropriated to the Institute at Saint Anselm College, $700,000 is appropriated to the New Hampshire State Library, and $9,000,000 is appropriated to fund a cooperative agreement with the Medical University of South Carolina.] *(Department of Commerce and Related Agencies Appropriations Act, 2000, as enacted by section 1000(a)(1) of the Consolidated Appropriations Act, 2000 (P.L. 106–113).)*

TITLE VI—GENERAL PROVISIONS

SEC. 601. No part of any appropriation contained in this Act shall be used for publicity or propaganda purposes not authorized by the Congress.

SEC. 602. No part of any appropriation contained in this Act shall remain available for obligation beyond the current fiscal year unless expressly so provided herein.

SEC. 603. The expenditure of any appropriation under this Act for any consulting service through procurement contract, pursuant to 5 U.S.C. 3109, shall be limited to those contracts where such expenditures are a matter of public record and available for public inspection, except where otherwise provided under existing law, or under existing Executive order issued pursuant to existing law.

SEC. 604. If any provision of this Act or the application of such provision to any person or circumstances shall be held invalid, the remainder of the Act and the application of each provision to persons or circumstances other than those as to which it is held invalid shall not be affected thereby.

SEC. 605. (a) None of the funds provided under this Act, or provided under previous appropriations Acts to the agencies funded by this Act that remain available for obligation or expenditure in fiscal year [2000] *2001*, or provided from any accounts in the Treasury of the United States derived by the collection of fees available to the agencies funded by this Act, shall be available for obligation or expenditure through a reprogramming of funds which: (1) creates new programs; (2) eliminates a program, project, or activity; (3) increases funds or personnel by any means for any project or activity for which funds have been denied or restricted; (4) relocates an office or employees; (5) reorganizes offices, programs, or activities; or (6) contracts out or privatizes any functions, or activities presently performed by Federal employees; unless the Appropriations Committees of both Houses of Congress are notified 15 days in advance of such reprogramming of funds.

(b) None of the funds provided under this Act, or provided under previous appropriations Acts to the agencies funded by this Act that remain available for obligation or expenditure in fiscal year [2000] *2001*, or provided from any accounts in the Treasury of the United States derived by the collection of fees available to the agencies funded by this Act, shall be available for obligation or expenditure for activities, programs, or projects through a reprogramming of funds in excess of $500,000 or 10 percent, whichever is less, that: (1) augments existing programs, projects, or activities; (2) reduces by 10 percent funding for any existing program, project, or activity, or numbers of personnel by 10 percent as approved by Congress; or (3) results from any general savings from a reduction in personnel which would result in a change in existing programs, activities, or projects as approved by Congress; unless the Appropriations Committees of both Houses of Congress are notified 15 days in advance of such reprogramming of funds.

SEC. 606. None of the funds made available in this Act may be used for the construction, repair (other than emergency repair), overhaul, conversion, or modernization of vessels for the National Oceanic and Atmospheric Administration in shipyards located outside of the United States.

SEC. 607. (a) PURCHASE OF AMERICAN-MADE EQUIPMENT AND PRODUCTS.—It is the sense of the Congress that, to the greatest extent practicable, all equipment and products purchased with funds made available in this Act should be American-made.

(b) NOTICE REQUIREMENT.—In providing financial assistance to, or entering into any contract with, any entity using funds made available in this Act, the head of each Federal agency, to the greatest extent practicable, shall provide to such entity a notice describing the statement made in subsection (a) by the Congress.

(c) PROHIBITION OF CONTRACTS WITH PERSONS FALSELY LABELING PRODUCTS AS MADE IN AMERICA.—If it has been finally determined by a court or Federal agency that any person intentionally affixed a label bearing a "Made in America" inscription, or any inscription with the same meaning, to any product sold in or shipped to the United States that is not made in the United States, the person shall be ineligible to receive any contract or subcontract made with funds made available in this Act, pursuant to the debarment, suspension, and ineligibility procedures described in sections 9.400 through 9.409 of title 48, Code of Federal Regulations.

[SEC. 608. None of the funds made available in this Act may be used to implement, administer, or enforce any guidelines of the Equal Employment Opportunity Commission covering harassment based on religion, when it is made known to the Federal entity or official to which such funds are made available that such guidelines do not differ in any respect from the proposed guidelines published by the Commission on October 1, 1993 (58 Fed. Reg. 51266).]

[SEC. 609. None of the funds made available by this Act may be used for any United Nations undertaking when it is made known to the Federal official having authority to obligate or expend such funds: (1) that the United Nations undertaking is a peacekeeping mission; (2) that such undertaking will involve United States Armed Forces under the command or operational control of a foreign national; and (3) that the President's military advisors have not submitted to the President a recommendation that such involvement is in the national security interests of the United States and the President has not submitted to the Congress such a recommendation.]

[SEC. 610. (a) None of the funds appropriated or otherwise made available by this Act shall be expended for any purpose for which appropriations are prohibited by section 609 of the Departments of Commerce, Justice, and State, the Judiciary, and Related Agencies Appropriations Act, 1999.

(b) The requirements in subparagraphs (A) and (B) of section 609 of that Act shall continue to apply during fiscal year 2000.]

[SEC. 611. Notwithstanding any other provision of law, not more than 20 percent of the amount allocated to any account from an appropriation made by this Act that is available for obligation only in the current fiscal year may be obligated during the last 2 months of the fiscal year unless the Committees on Appropriations of the House of Representatives and the Senate are notified prior to such obligation in accordance with section 605 of this Act: *Provided*, That this section shall not apply to the obligation of funds under grant programs.]

SEC. [612] *608*. None of the funds made available in this Act shall be used to provide the following amenities or personal comforts in the Federal prison system—

(1) in-cell television viewing except for prisoners who are segregated from the general prison population for their own safety;

(2) the viewing of R, X, and NC–17 rated movies, through whatever medium presented;

(3) any instruction (live or through broadcasts) or training equipment for boxing, wrestling, judo, karate, or other martial art, or any bodybuilding or weightlifting equipment of any sort;

(4) possession of in-cell coffee pots, hot plates or heating elements; or

(5) the use or possession of any electric or electronic musical instrument.

SEC. [613] *609*. None of the funds made available in title II for the National Oceanic and Atmospheric Administration (NOAA) under the headings "Operations, Research, and Facilities" and "Procurement, Acquisition and Construction" may be used to implement sections 603, 604, and 605 of Public Law 102–567: *Provided*, That NOAA may develop a modernization plan for its fisheries research vessels that takes fully into account opportunities for contracting for fisheries surveys.

SEC. [614] *610*. Any costs incurred by a department or agency funded under this Act resulting from personnel actions taken in response to funding reductions included in this Act shall be absorbed within the total budgetary resources available to such department or agency: *Provided*, That the authority to transfer funds between appropriations accounts as may be necessary to carry out this section is provided in addition to authorities included elsewhere in this Act: *Provided further*, That use of funds to carry out this section shall be treated as a reprogramming of funds under section 605 of this Act and shall not be available for obligation or expenditure except in compliance with the procedures set forth in that section.

SEC. [615] *611*. None of the funds made available in this Act to the Federal Bureau of Prisons may be used to distribute or make available any commercially published information or material to a prisoner when it is made known to the Federal official having authority to obligate or expend such funds that such information or material is sexually explicit or features nudity.

SEC. [616] *612*. Of the funds appropriated in this Act under the heading "Office of Justice Programs—State and Local Law Enforcement Assistance", not more than 90 percent of the amount to be awarded to an entity under the Local Law Enforcement Block Grant shall be made available to such an entity when it is made known to the Federal official having authority to obligate or expend such funds that the entity that employs a public safety officer (as such term is defined in section 1204 of title I of the Omnibus Crime Control and Safe Streets Act of 1968) does not provide such a public safety officer who retires or is separated from service due to injury suffered as the direct and proximate result of a personal injury sustained in the line of duty while responding to an emergency situation or a hot pursuit (as such terms are defined by State law) with the same or better level of health insurance benefits at the time of retirement or separation as they received while on duty.

SEC. [617] *613*. None of the funds provided by this Act shall be available to promote the sale or export of tobacco or tobacco products, or to seek the reduction or removal by any foreign country of restrictions on the marketing of tobacco or tobacco products, except for restrictions which are not applied equally to all tobacco or tobacco products of the same type.

[SEC. 618. (a) None of the funds appropriated or otherwise made available by this Act shall be expended for any purpose for which appropriations are prohibited by section 616 of the Departments of Commerce, Justice, and State, the Judiciary, and Related Agencies Appropriations Act, 1999.

(b) Subsection (a)(1) of section 616 of that Act is amended—

(1) by striking "and" after "Gonzalez"; and

(2) by inserting before the semicolon at the end of the subsection, ", Jean-Yvon Toussaint, and Jimmy Lalanne".

(c) The requirements in subsections (b) and (c) of section 616 of that Act shall continue to apply during fiscal year 2000.]

[SEC. 619. None of the funds appropriated pursuant to this Act or any other provision of law may be used for: (1) the implementation of any tax or fee in connection with the implementation of 18 U.S.C. 922(t); and (2) any system to implement 18 U.S.C. 922(t) that does not require and result in the destruction of any identifying information submitted by or on behalf of any person who has been determined not to be prohibited from owning a firearm.]

[SEC. 620. Notwithstanding any other provision of law, amounts deposited in the Fund established under 42 U.S.C. 10601 in fiscal year 1999 in excess of $500,000,000 shall not be available for obligation until October 1, 2000.]

[SEC. 621. None of the funds appropriated by this Act shall be used to propose or issue rules, regulations, decrees, or orders for the purpose of implementation, or in preparation for implementation, of the Kyoto Protocol which was adopted on December 11, 1997, in Kyoto, Japan at the Third Conference of the Parties to the United Nations Framework Convention on Climate Change, which has not been submitted to the Senate for advice and consent to ratification pursuant to article II, section 2, clause 2, of the United States Constitution, and which has not entered into force pursuant to article 25 of the Protocol.]

[SEC. 622. For an additional amount for "Small Business Administration, Salaries and Expenses", $30,000,000, of which $2,500,000 shall be available for a grant to the NTTC at Wheeling Jesuit University to continue the outreach program to assist small business development; $2,000,000 shall be available for a grant for Western Carolina University to develop a facility to assist in small business and rural economic development; $3,000,000 shall be available for a grant to the Bronx Museum of the Arts, New York, to develop a facility; $750,000 shall be available for a grant to Soundview Community in Action for a technology access and business improvement project; $2,500,000 shall be available for a grant for the City of Hazard, Kentucky for a Center for Rural Law Enforcement Technology and Training; $1,000,000 shall be available for a grant to the State University of New York to develop a facility and operate the Institute of Entrepreneurship for small business and workforce development; $1,000,000 shall be available for a grant for Pikeville College, School of Osteopathic Medicine for a telemedicine and medical education network; $1,000,000 shall be available for a grant to Operation Hope in Maywood, California for a business incubator project; $1,900,000 shall be available for a grant to the Southern Kentucky Tourism Development Association to develop a facility for regional tourism promotion; $1,000,000 shall be available for a grant to the Southern Kentucky Economic Development Corporation to support a science and technology business loan fund; $500,000 shall be available for a grant for the Moundsville Economic Development Council to work in conjunction with the Office of Law Enforcement Technology Commercialization for the establishment of the National Corrections and Law Enforcement Training and Technology Center, and for infrastructure improvements associated with this initiative; $8,550,000 shall be available for a grant to Somerset Community College to develop a facility to support workforce development and skills training; $200,000 shall be available for a grant for the Vandalia Heritage Foundation to fulfill its charter purposes; $2,000,000 shall be available for a grant for the Illinois Coalition to establish and operate a national demonstration project in the DuPage County Research Park providing one-stop access for technology startup businesses; $200,000 shall be available for a grant to Rural Enterprises, Inc., in Durant, Oklahoma to support a resource center for rural businesses; $500,000 shall be available for a grant for the City of Chicago to establish and operate a program for technology-based business growth; $500,000 shall be available for a grant for the Illinois Department of Commerce and Community Affairs to develop strategic plans for technology-based business growth; $200,000 shall be available for a grant to the Long Island Bay Shore Aquarium to develop a facility; $150,000 shall be available for a grant to Miami-Dade Community College for an Entrepreneurial Education Center; $300,000 shall be available for a grant for the Western Massachusetts Enterprise Fund for a microenterprise loan program; and $250,000 shall be available for a grant for the Johnstown Area Regional Industries Center to develop a small business incubator facility.]

[SEC. 623. (a) NORTHERN FUND AND SOUTHERN FUND.—

(1) As provided in the June 30, 1999, Agreement of the United States and Canada on the Treaty Between the Government of the United States and the Government of Canada Concerning Pacific Salmon, 1985 (hereafter referred to as the "1999 Pacific Salmon Treaty Agreement") there are hereby established a Northern Boundary and Transboundary Rivers Restoration and Enhancement Fund (hereafter referred to as the "Northern Fund") and a Southern Boundary Restoration and Enhancement Fund (hereafter referred to as the "Southern Fund") to be held by the Pacific Salmon Commission. The Northern Fund and Southern Fund shall be invested in interest bearing accounts, bonds, securities, or other investments in order to achieve the highest annual yield consistent with protecting the principal of each Fund. The Northern Fund and Southern Fund shall each receive $10,000,000, of the amounts authorized by this section. Income from investments made pursuant to this paragraph shall be available until expended, without appropriation or fiscal year limitation, for programs and activities relating to salmon restoration and enhancement, salmon research, the conservation of salmon habitat, and implementation of the Pacific Salmon Treaty and related agreements. Amounts provided by grants under this subsection may be held in interest bearing accounts prior to the disbursement of such funds for program purposes, and any interest earned may be retained for program purposes without further appropriation. The Northern Fund and Southern Fund are subject to the laws governing Federal appropriations and funds and to unrestricted circulars of the Office of Management and Budget. Recipients of amounts from either Fund shall keep separate accounts and such records as are reasonably necessary to disclose the use of the funds as well as to facilitate effective audits.

(2) FUND MANAGEMENT.—

(A) As provided in the 1999 Pacific Salmon Treaty Agreement, amounts made available from the Northern Fund pursuant to paragraph (1) shall be administered by a Northern Fund Committee, which shall be comprised of three representatives of the Government of Canada, and three representatives of the United States. The three United States representatives shall be the United States Commissioner and Alternate Commissioner appointed (or designated) from a list submitted by the Governor of Alaska for appointment to the Pacific Salmon Commission and the Regional Administrator of the National Marine Fisheries Service for the Alaska Region. Only programs and activities consistent with the purposes in paragraph (1) which affect the geographic area from Cape Caution, Canada to Cape Suckling, Alaska may be approved for funding by the Northern Fund Committee.

(B) As provided in the 1999 Pacific Salmon Treaty Agreement, amounts made available from the Southern Fund pursuant to paragraph (1) shall be administered by a Southern Fund Committee, which shall be comprised of three representatives of Canada and three representatives of the United States. The United States representatives shall be appointed by the Secretary of Commerce: one shall be selected from a list of three qualified individuals submitted by the Governors of the States of Washington and Oregon; one shall be selected from a list of three qualified individuals submitted by the treaty Indian tribes (as defined by the Secretary of Commerce); and one shall be the Regional Administrator of the National Marine Fisheries Service for the Northwest Region. Only programs and activities consistent with the purposes in paragraph (1) which affect the geographic area south of Cape Caution, Canada may be approved for funding by the Southern Fund Committee.

(b) PACIFIC SALMON TREATY IMPLEMENTATION.—(1) None of the funds authorized by this section for implementation of the 1999 Pacific Salmon Treaty Agreement shall be made available until each of the following conditions to the 1999 Pacific Salmon Treaty Agreement has been fulfilled—

(A) stipulations are revised and court orders requested as set forth in the letter of understanding of the United States negotiators dated June 22, 1999. If such orders are not requested by December 31, 1999, this condition shall be considered unfulfilled; and

(B) a determination is made that—

(i) the entry by the United States into the 1999 Pacific Salmon Treaty Agreement;

(ii) the conduct of the Alaskan fisheries pursuant to the 1999 Pacific Salmon Treaty Agreement, without further clarification or modification of the management regimes contained therein; and

(iii) the decision by the North Pacific Fisheries Management Council to continue to defer its management authority over salmon to the State of Alaska are not likely to cause jeopardy to, or adversely modify designated critical habitat of, any salmonid species listed under Public Law 93–205, as amended, in any fishery subject to the Pacific Salmon Treaty.

(2) If the requests for orders in subparagraph (1)(A) are withdrawn after December 31, 1999, or if such orders are not entered by March 1, 2000, amounts in the Northern Fund and the Southern Fund shall be transferred to the general fund of the United States Treasury.

(3) During the term of the 1999 Pacific Salmon Treaty Agreement, the Secretary of Commerce shall determine whether Southern United States fisheries are likely to cause jeopardy to, or adversely modify designated critical habitat of, any salmonid species listed under Public Law 93–205, as amended, before the Secretary of Commerce may initiate or reinitiate consultation on Alaska fisheries under such Act.

(4) During the term of the 1999 Pacific Salmon Treaty Agreement, the Secretary of Commerce may not initiate or reinitiate consultation on Alaska fisheries under section 7 of Public Law 93–205, as amended, until—

(A) the Pacific Salmon Commission has had a reasonable opportunity to implement the provisions of the 1999 Pacific Salmon Treaty Agreement, including the harvest responses pursuant to paragraph 9, chapter 3 of Annex IV to the Pacific Salmon Treaty; and

(B) he determines, in consultation with the United States Section of the Pacific Salmon Commission, that implementation actions under the 1999 Agreement will not return escapements as expeditiously as possible to maximum sustainable yield or other biologically-based escapement objectives agreed to by the Pacific Salmon Commission.

(5) The Secretary of Commerce shall notify the Committee on Commerce, Science, and Transportation of the Senate and the Committee on Resources of the House of Representatives of his intent to initiate or reinitiate consultation on Alaska fisheries.

(6)(A) For purposes of this section, "Alaska fisheries" means all directed Pacific salmon fisheries off the coast of Alaska that are subject to the Pacific Salmon Treaty.

(B) For purposes of this section, "Southern United States fisheries" means all directed Pacific salmon fisheries in Washington, Oregon, and the Snake River basin of Idaho that are subject to the Pacific Salmon Treaty.

(c) IMPROVED SALMON MANAGEMENT.—Section 3(g) of Public Law 99–5, as amended, is amended—

(1) in paragraph (1) by striking "The" and inserting "Except as provided in paragraph (2), the";

(2) by inserting after paragraph (1) the following new paragraph:

"(2) A decision of the United States Section with respect to any salmon fishery regime covered by chapter 1 or 2 (except paragraph 4 of chapter 2) of Annex IV to the Pacific Salmon Treaty of 1985 shall be taken upon the affirmative vote of the United States Commissioner appointed from the list submitted by the Governor of Alaska pursuant to subsection (a). A decision of the United States Section with respect to any salmon fishery regime covered by chapter 4, 5 (except paragraph 2(b) of chapter 5), or 6 of the Pacific Salmon Treaty of 1985 shall be taken upon the affirmative vote of both the United States Commissioner appointed from the list submitted by the Governors of Washington and Oregon pursuant to subsection (a) and the United States Commissioner appointed from the list submitted by the treaty Indian tribes of the State of Idaho, Oregon, or Washington pursuant to subsection (a). Before a decision of the United States Section is made under this paragraph, the voting Commissioner or Commissioners shall consult with the Commissioner who is an official of the United States Government under subsection (a)"; and

(3) by renumbering the existing paragraphs.

(d) AUTHORIZATION OF APPROPRIATIONS.—

(1) For capitalizing the Northern Fund and the Southern Fund, there is authorized to be appropriated in fiscal year 2000, $20,000,000.

(2) For salmon habitat restoration, salmon stock enhancement, salmon research, and implementation of the 1999 Pacific Salmon Treaty Agreement and related agreements, there is authorized to be appropriated in fiscal year 2000, $50,000,000 to the States of California, Oregon, Washington, and Alaska. The State of Alaska may allocate a portion of any funds it receives under this subsection to eligible activities outside Alaska.

(3) For salmon habitat restoration, salmon stock enhancement, salmon research, and implementation of the 1999 Pacific Salmon Treaty Agreement and related agreements, there is authorized to be appropriated $6,000,000 in fiscal year 2000 to the Pacific Coastal tribes (as defined by the Secretary of Commerce) and $2,000,000 in fiscal year 2000 to the Columbia River tribes (as defined by the Secretary of Commerce).

Funds appropriated to the States under the authority of this section shall be subject to a 25 percent non-Federal match requirement. In addition, not more than 3 percent of such funds shall be available for administrative expenses, with the exception of funds used in the Washington State for the Forest and Fish Agreement.]

SEC. [624] *614.* Funds made available under Public Law 105–277 for costs associated with implementation of the American Fisheries Act of 1998 (division C, title II, of Public Law 105–277) for vessel documentation activities shall remain available until expended.

[SEC. 625. Effective as of October 1, 1999, section 635 of Public Law 106–58 is amended—

(1) in subsection (b)(2), by inserting "the carrier for" after "if"; and

(2) in subsection (c), by inserting "or otherwise provide for" after "to prescribe".]

[SEC. 626. None of the funds made available to the Department of Justice in this Act may be used to discriminate against or denigrate the religious or moral beliefs of students who participate in programs for which financial assistance is provided from those funds, or of the parents or legal guardians of such students.]

[SEC. 627. None of the funds appropriated in this Act shall be available for the purpose of granting either immigrant or nonimmigrant visas, or both, consistent with the Secretary's determination under section 243(d) of the Immigration and Nationality Act, to citizens, subjects, nationals, or residents of countries that the Attorney General has determined deny or unreasonably delay accepting the return of citizens, subjects, nationals, or residents under that section.]

SEC. [628] *615.* None of the funds made available to the Department of Justice in this Act may be used for the purpose of transporting an individual who is a prisoner pursuant to conviction for crime under State or Federal law and is classified as a maximum or high security prisoner, other than to a prison or other facility certified by the Federal Bureau of Prisons as appropriately secure for housing such a prisoner.

[SEC. 629. Beginning 60 days from the date of the enactment of this Act, none of the funds appropriated or otherwise made available by this Act may be made available for the participation by delegates of the United States to the Standing Consultative Commission unless the President certifies and so reports to the Committees on Appropriations that the United States Government is not implementing the Memorandum of Understanding Relating to the Treaty Between the United States of America and the Union of Soviet Socialist Republics on the limitation of Anti-Ballistic Missile Systems of May 26, 1972, entered into in New York on September 26, 1997, by the United States, Russia, Kazakhstan, Belarus, and Ukraine, or until the Senate provides its advice and consent to the Memorandum of Understanding.]

[SEC. 630. None of the funds made available in this Act may be used for any activity in support of adding or maintaining any World Heritage Site in the United States on the List of World Heritage in Danger as maintained under the Convention Concerning the Protection of the World Cultural and Natural Heritage.]

SEC. 616. Notwithstanding section 1005(d) of the Legal Services Act, 42 U.S.C. 2996d(d), the President of the Legal Services Corporation may be paid at an annual rate of basic pay of not more than the maximum rate of basic pay for the Senior Executive Service under 5 U.S.C. 5382. (Departments of Commerce, Justice, and State, the Judiciary, and Related Agencies Appropriations Act, 2000, as enacted by section 1000(a)(1) of the Consolidated Appropriations Act, 2000 (P.L. 106–113).).

DEPARTMENT OF DEFENSE—MILITARY

MILITARY PERSONNEL

Resources presented under the Military Personnel title contribute primarily to achieving the Department's corporate goal 1 (Shape). A detailed description of the corporate goals is contained in the FY 2001 Performance Plan in the Department's 2000 Annual Report to the President and Congress. This performance plan is required by the Government Performance and Results Act of 1993.

ACTIVE FORCES

These appropriations finance the personnel costs of the active duty forces of the Army, Navy, Marine Corps, and Air Force. This includes pay and allowances of officers, enlisted personnel, cadets and midshipmen, permanent change of station travel and other military personnel costs. Changes in financial requirements are primarily related to military personnel strengths. In addition, these appropriations finance the future retirement benefits of the current active forces. While most of the entitlements financed by these appropriations are set by statute, the estimates reflect continuing efforts to improve management, including implementation of audit recommendations, improved management of military travel, prudent use of bonus programs, and other pay programs.

Included in the 2001 request is funding for a 3.7% pay raise. This raise will help ensure that military compensation remains attractive and competitive with private sector pay and that the military services continue to attract and retain highly qualified people. Illustrative of the high quality of service members is their educational achievements. Almost 93% of the individuals recruited into the military services in 1999 were high school graduates compared to 81% of the youth of the same age in the general population. Over 95% of personnel entering the services as commissioned officers are college graduates. Over 43% of the officers on active duty have advanced college degrees compared to less than 8% in the general population.

The numbers of active duty military personnel provided for are shown in the following table.

YEAR-END NUMBER

	1999 actual	2000 est.	2001 est.
Defense total	1,385,703	1,382,218	1,381,600
Officers	218,905	218,599	219,255
Enlisted	1,154,231	1,151,619	1,150,345
Academy cadets and midshipmen	12,567	12,000	12,000
Army	479,426	480,000	480,000
Officers	77,152	77,800	77,800
Enlisted	398,138	398,200	398,200
Military Academy cadets	4,136	4,000	4,000
Navy	373,046	371,800	372,000
Officers	53,538	53,350	53,367
Enlisted	315,180	314,450	314,633
Naval Academy midshipmen	4,328	4,000	4,000
Marine Corps	172,641	172,518	172,600
Officers	17,897	17,860	17,888
Enlisted	154,744	154,658	154,712
Air Force	360,590	357,900	357,000
Officers	70,318	69,589	70,200
Enlisted	286,169	284,311	282,800
Air Force Academy cadets	4,103	4,000	4,000

AVERAGE NUMBER

	1999 actual	2000 est.	2001 est.
Defense total	1,387,270	1,379,070	1,379,500
Officers	222,341	219,998	220,222
Enlisted	1,153,003	1,147,268	1,147,350
Academy cadets and midshipmen	11,926	11,804	11,928
Army	475,289	476,368	477,835
Officers	78,492	78,333	77,964
Enlisted	392,738	394,088	395,871
Military Academy cadets	4,059	3,947	4,000
Navy	372,806	368,720	368,306
Officers	54,111	53,206	53,482
Enlisted	314,759	311,668	310,975
Naval Academy midshipmen	3,936	3,846	3,849
Marine Corps	172,084	171,761	171,163
Officers	18,087	18,039	18,046
Enlisted	153,997	153,722	153,117
Air Force	367,091	362,221	362,196
Officers	71,651	70,420	70,730
Enlisted	291,509	287,790	287,387
Air Force Academy cadets	3,931	4,011	4,079

Federal Funds

General and special funds:

Military Personnel, Army

For pay, allowances, individual clothing, subsistence, interest on deposits, gratuities, permanent change of station travel (including all expenses thereof for organizational movements), and expenses of temporary duty travel between permanent duty stations, for members of the Army on active duty (except members of reserve components provided for elsewhere), cadets, and aviation cadets; and for payments pursuant to section 156 of Public Law 97–377, as amended (42 U.S.C. 402 note), to section 229(b) of the Social Security Act (42 U.S.C. 429(b)), and to the Department of Defense Military Retirement Fund, **[**$22,006,361,000**]** *$22,198,457,000. (10 U.S.C. 701–04, 744, 956, 1035, 1037, 1047–49, 1212, 1475–80, 2389, 2421, 2634, 3687, 4561, 4562, 4741; chapters 3, 5, 7, and 9 of title 37, United States Code; Department of Defense Appropriations Act, 2000.)*

Program and Financing (in millions of dollars)

Identification code 21–2010–0–1–051		1999 actual	2000 est.	2001 est.
	Obligations by program activity:			
	Direct program:			
00.01	Pay and allowances of officers	5,889	6,165	6,313
00.02	Pay and allowances of enlisted personnel	12,439	13,183	13,482
00.03	Pay and allowances of cadets	41	40	42
00.04	Subsistence of enlisted personnel	1,205	1,243	1,156
00.05	Permanent change of station travel	1,083	1,088	1,083
00.06	Other military personnel costs	204	134	123
09.01	Reimbursable program	193	213	181
10.00	Total new obligations	21,054	22,064	22,380

General and special funds—Continued

MILITARY PERSONNEL, ARMY—Continued

Program and Financing (in millions of dollars)—Continued

Identification code 21–2010–0–1–051		1999 actual	2000 est.	2001 est.
	Budgetary resources available for obligation:			
22.00	New budget authority (gross)	21,003	22,064	22,380
22.22	Unobligated balance transferred from other DoD accounts	49		
23.90	Total budgetary resources available for obligation	21,054	22,064	22,380
23.95	Total new obligations	–21,054	–22,064	–22,380
	New budget authority (gross), detail:			
	Discretionary:			
40.00	Appropriation	20,836	21,428	22,198
40.15	Appropriation (emergency)	13		
40.74	Reduction pursuant to P.L. 106–79		–16	
41.00	Transferred to other DoD accounts	–359	–120	
42.00	Transferred from other DoD accounts	321		
43.00	Appropriation (total discretionary)	20,811	21,292	22,198
55.00	Advance appropriation		560	
	Spending authority from offsetting collections:			
68.00	Offsetting collections (cash)	159	213	181
68.10	From Federal sources: Change in receivables and unpaid, unfilled orders	–28		
68.15	From Federal sources: Adjustments to receivables and unpaid, unfilled orders	61		
68.90	Spending authority from offsetting collections (total discretionary)	192	213	181
70.00	Total new budget authority (gross)	21,003	22,065	22,379
	Change in unpaid obligations:			
	Unpaid obligations, start of year:			
72.40	Obligated balance, start of year	1,976	2,400	2,370
72.95	From Federal sources: Receivables and unpaid, unfilled orders	289	261	261
72.99	Total unpaid obligations, start of year	2,264	2,661	2,631
73.10	Total new obligations	21,054	22,064	22,380
73.20	Total outlays (gross)	–20,491	–22,094	–22,243
73.40	Adjustments in expired accounts (net)	–166		
	Unpaid obligations, end of year:			
74.40	Obligated balance, end of year	2,400	2,370	2,507
74.95	From Federal sources: Receivables and unpaid, unfilled orders	261	261	261
74.99	Total unpaid obligations, end of year	2,661	2,631	2,768
	Outlays (gross), detail:			
86.90	Outlays from new discretionary authority	19,080	20,514	20,803
86.93	Outlays from discretionary balances	1,411	1,582	1,440
87.00	Total outlays (gross)	20,491	22,094	22,243
	Offsets:			
	Against gross budget authority and outlays:			
	Offsetting collections (cash) from:			
88.00	Federal sources	–119	–173	–151
88.40	Non-Federal sources	–40	–40	–30
88.90	Total, offsetting collections (cash)	–159	–213	–181
	Against gross budget authority only:			
88.95	From Federal sources: Change in receivables and unpaid, unfilled orders	28		
88.96	From Federal sources: Adjustment to receivables and unpaid, unfilled orders	–61		
	Net budget authority and outlays:			
89.00	Budget authority	20,811	21,851	22,198
90.00	Outlays	20,332	21,882	22,062

Object Classification (in millions of dollars)

Identification code 21–2010–0–1–051		1999 actual	2000 est.	2001 est.
	Direct obligations:			
11.7	Personnel compensation: Military personnel	13,836	14,511	14,977
	Military personnel benefits:			
12.2	Accrued retirement benefits	3,251	3,571	3,486
12.2	Other personnel benefits	2,175	2,144	2,213
13.0	Benefits for former personnel	124	110	98
21.0	Travel and transportation of persons	292	296	295
22.0	Transportation of things	539	525	523
25.7	Operation and maintenance of equipment	137	146	144
26.0	Supplies and materials	505	545	459
42.0	Insurance claims and indemnities	2	3	3
99.0	Subtotal, direct obligations	20,861	21,851	22,198
99.0	Reimbursable obligations	193	213	181
99.9	Total new obligations	21,054	22,064	22,380

MILITARY PERSONNEL, NAVY

For pay, allowances, individual clothing, subsistence, interest on deposits, gratuities, permanent change of station travel (including all expenses thereof for organizational movements), and expenses of temporary duty travel between permanent duty stations, for members of the Navy on active duty (except members of the Reserve provided for elsewhere), midshipmen, and aviation cadets; and for payments pursuant to section 156 of Public Law 97–377, as amended (42 U.S.C. 402 note), to section 229(b) of the Social Security Act (42 U.S.C. 429(b)), and to the Department of Defense Military Retirement Fund, [$17,258,823,000] *$17,742,897,000. (10 U.S.C. 600, 683–4, 701–4, 744, 956, 1035, 1037, 1047–49, 1212, 1475–80, 2421, 2634, 5413–14, 5441–42, 5444, 5446, 5450–51, 5454, 5501, 5503, 6081–86, 6221, 6911–12, 6960, 6969; 26 U.S.C. 3121; chapters 3, 5, 7, 9, and 10 of title 37, United States Code; Department of Defense Appropriations Act, 2000.)*

Program and Financing (in millions of dollars)

Identification code 17–1453–0–1–051		1999 actual	2000 est.	2001 est.
	Obligations by program activity:			
	Direct program:			
00.01	Pay and allowances of officers	4,377	4,546	4,643
00.02	Pay and allowances of enlisted personnel	10,768	11,201	11,590
00.03	Pay and allowances of cadets	39	38	39
00.04	Subsistence of enlisted personnel	737	765	780
00.05	Permanent change of station travel	634	634	617
00.06	Other military personnel costs	100	70	73
09.01	Reimbursable program	248	237	219
10.00	Total new obligations	16,903	17,491	17,961
	Budgetary resources available for obligation:			
22.00	New budget authority (gross)	16,859	17,491	17,961
22.22	Unobligated balance transferred from other DoD accounts	50		
23.90	Total budgetary resources available for obligation	16,909	17,491	17,961
23.95	Total new obligations	–16,903	–17,491	–17,961
23.98	Unobligated balance expiring or withdrawn	–6		
	New budget authority (gross), detail:			
	Discretionary:			
40.00	Appropriation	16,559	16,820	17,743
40.15	Appropriation (emergency)	41		
40.74	Reduction pursuant to P.L. 106–79		–12	
41.00	Transferred to other DoD accounts	–32		
42.00	Transferred from other DoD accounts	43	10	
43.00	Appropriation (total discretionary)	16,611	16,817	17,743
55.00	Advance appropriation		437	
	Spending authority from offsetting collections:			
68.00	Offsetting collections (cash)	272	237	219
68.10	From Federal sources: Change in receivables and unpaid, unfilled orders	–21		
68.15	From Federal sources: Adjustments to receivables and unpaid, unfilled orders	–3		
68.90	Spending authority from offsetting collections (total discretionary)	248	237	219
70.00	Total new budget authority (gross)	16,859	17,492	17,962
	Change in unpaid obligations:			
	Unpaid obligations, start of year:			
72.40	Obligated balance, start of year	1,175	1,459	1,418
72.95	From Federal sources: Receivables and unpaid, unfilled orders	133	112	112
72.99	Total unpaid obligations, start of year	1,308	1,571	1,530

73.10	Total new obligations	16,903	17,491	17,961
73.20	Total outlays (gross)	−16,603	−17,532	−17,844
73.40	Adjustments in expired accounts (net)	−37		
	Unpaid obligations, end of year:			
74.40	Obligated balance, end of year	1,459	1,418	1,537
74.95	From Federal sources: Receivables and unpaid, unfilled orders	112	112	112
74.99	Total unpaid obligations, end of year	1,571	1,530	1,649
	Outlays (gross), detail:			
86.90	Outlays from new discretionary authority	15,767	16,508	16,880
86.93	Outlays from discretionary balances	836	1,024	964
87.00	Total outlays (gross)	16,603	17,532	17,844
	Offsets:			
	Against gross budget authority and outlays:			
	Offsetting collections (cash) from:			
88.00	Federal sources	−116	−237	−219
88.40	Non-Federal sources	−156		
88.90	Total, offsetting collections (cash)	−272	−237	−219
	Against gross budget authority only:			
88.95	From Federal sources: Change in receivables and unpaid, unfilled orders	21		
88.96	From Federal sources: Adjustment to receivables and unpaid, unfilled orders	3		
	Net budget authority and outlays:			
89.00	Budget authority	16,611	17,254	17,743
90.00	Outlays	16,331	17,295	17,625

Object Classification (in millions of dollars)

Identification code 17–1453–0–1–051		1999 actual	2000 est.	2001 est.
	Direct obligations:			
11.7	Personnel compensation: Military personnel	11,615	12,074	12,559
	Military personnel benefits:			
12.2	Accrued retirement benefits	2,533	2,719	2,651
12.2	Other personnel benefits	1,812	1,770	1,824
13.0	Benefits for former personnel	63	58	64
21.0	Travel and transportation of persons	163	159	203
22.0	Transportation of things	389	396	364
25.7	Operation and maintenance of equipment	14	14	13
26.0	Supplies and materials	66	63	65
99.0	Subtotal, direct obligations	16,655	17,253	17,743
99.0	Reimbursable obligations	248	238	219
99.9	Total new obligations	16,903	17,491	17,961

MILITARY PERSONNEL, MARINE CORPS

For pay, allowances, individual clothing, subsistence, interest on deposits, gratuities, permanent change of station travel (including all expenses thereof for organizational movements), and expenses of temporary duty travel between permanent duty stations, for members of the Marine Corps on active duty (except members of the Reserve provided for elsewhere); and for payments pursuant to section 156 of Public Law 97–377, as amended (42 U.S.C. 402 note), to section 229(b) of the Social Security Act (42 U.S.C. 429(b)), and to the Department of Defense Military Retirement Fund, [$6,555,403,000] *$6,822,300,000. (10 U.S.C. 956, 1035, 1047–49, 1212, 1475–80, 2634, 5413–14, 5441, 5443, 5446, 5451, 5454, 5456, 5458, 5502–03, 6032, 6081–86, 6148, 6222; 12 U.S.C. 1715m; chapters 3, 5, 7, and 9 of title 37, United States Code; 41 U.S.C. 1594d; Department of Defense Appropriations Act, 2000.)*

Program and Financing (in millions of dollars)

Identification code 17–1105–0–1–051		1999 actual	2000 est.	2001 est.
	Obligations by program activity:			
	Direct program:			
00.01	Pay and allowances of officers	1,314	1,388	1,437
00.02	Pay and allowances of enlisted personnel	4,269	4,547	4,708
00.04	Subsistence of enlisted personnel	356	367	408
00.05	Permanent change of station travel	227	235	238
00.06	Other military personnel costs	44	29	32
09.01	Reimbursable program	30	31	32
10.00	Total new obligations	6,241	6,597	6,854
	Budgetary resources available for obligation:			
22.00	New budget authority (gross)	6,230	6,597	6,854
22.22	Unobligated balance transferred from other DoD accounts	20		
23.90	Total budgetary resources available for obligation	6,251	6,597	6,854
23.95	Total new obligations	−6,241	−6,597	−6,854
23.98	Unobligated balance expiring or withdrawn	−10		
	New budget authority (gross), detail:			
	Discretionary:			
40.00	Appropriation	6,259	6,377	6,822
40.15	Appropriation (emergency)	11		
41.00	Transferred to other DoD accounts	−78		
42.00	Transferred from other DoD accounts	8	11	
43.00	Appropriation (total discretionary)	6,200	6,388	6,822
55.00	Advance appropriation		178	
	Spending authority from offsetting collections:			
68.00	Offsetting collections (cash)	17	31	32
68.10	From Federal sources: Change in receivables and unpaid, unfilled orders	4		
68.15	From Federal sources: Adjustments to receivables and unpaid, unfilled orders	9		
68.90	Spending authority from offsetting collections (total discretionary)	30	31	32
70.00	Total new budget authority (gross)	6,230	6,597	6,854
	Change in unpaid obligations:			
	Unpaid obligations, start of year:			
72.40	Obligated balance, start of year	412	427	459
72.95	From Federal sources: Receivables and unpaid, unfilled orders	39	43	43
72.99	Total unpaid obligations, start of year	451	469	502
73.10	Total new obligations	6,241	6,597	6,854
73.20	Total outlays (gross)	−6,217	−6,564	−6,854
73.40	Adjustments in expired accounts (net)	−7		
	Unpaid obligations, end of year:			
74.40	Obligated balance, end of year	427	459	461
74.95	From Federal sources: Receivables and unpaid, unfilled orders	43	43	43
74.99	Total unpaid obligations, end of year	469	502	504
	Outlays (gross), detail:			
86.90	Outlays from new discretionary authority	5,937	6,242	6,513
86.93	Outlays from discretionary balances	280	322	340
87.00	Total outlays (gross)	6,217	6,564	6,854
	Offsets:			
	Against gross budget authority and outlays:			
	Offsetting collections (cash) from:			
88.00	Federal sources	−17	−31	−32
88.40	Non-Federal sources			
88.90	Total, offsetting collections (cash)	−17	−31	−32
	Against gross budget authority only:			
88.95	From Federal sources: Change in receivables and unpaid, unfilled orders	−4		
88.96	From Federal sources: Adjustment to receivables and unpaid, unfilled orders	−9		
	Net budget authority and outlays:			
89.00	Budget authority	6,200	6,566	6,822
90.00	Outlays	6,200	6,533	6,822

Object Classification (in millions of dollars)

Identification code 17–1105–0–1–051		1999 actual	2000 est.	2001 est.
	Direct obligations:			
11.7	Personnel compensation: Military personnel	4,405	4,630	4,791
	Military personnel benefits:			
12.2	Accrued retirement benefits	1,020	1,127	1,101
12.2	Other personnel benefits	516	533	566
13.0	Benefits for former personnel	26	26	28
21.0	Travel and transportation of persons	76	74	76
22.0	Transportation of things	128	134	134
25.8	Subsistence and support of persons	5	4	86
26.0	Supplies and materials	34	37	40

General and special funds—Continued

MILITARY PERSONNEL, MARINE CORPS—Continued

Object Classification (in millions of dollars)—Continued

Identification code 17–1105–0–1–051	1999 actual	2000 est.	2001 est.
42.0 Insurance claims and indemnities	1	1	1
99.0 Subtotal, direct obligations	6,211	6,566	6,822
99.0 Reimbursable obligations	30	31	32
99.9 Total new obligations	6,241	6,597	6,854

MILITARY PERSONNEL, AIR FORCE

For pay, allowances, individual clothing, subsistence, interest on deposits, gratuities, permanent change of station travel (including all expenses thereof for organizational movements), and expenses of temporary duty travel between permanent duty stations, for members of the Air Force on active duty (except members of reserve components provided for elsewhere), cadets, and aviation cadets; and for payments pursuant to section 156 of Public Law 97–377, as amended (42 U.S.C. 402 note), to section 229(b) of the Social Security Act (42 U.S.C. 429(b)), and to the Department of Defense Military Retirement Fund, [$17,861,803,000] *$18,282,834,000. (10 U.S.C. 503, 504–09, 518–19, 600, 683–84, 687, 701–04, 744, 956, 1035–37, 1047–49, 1211–12, 1331, 1475–80, 2632, 2634, 8033, 8036, 8066, 8201–15, 8281, 8284–89, 8293–8303, 8305–10, 8312–13, 8441–49, 8451–52, 8491, 8494–8504, 8531, 8687, 8722, 9306, 9331–37, 9341–55, 9441, 9561–63, 9741–43; 12 U.S.C. 1715m; 33 U.S.C. 855, 858; chapters 3, 5, 7, 9, 10, and 11 of title 37, United States Code; 49 U.S.C. 1657; Department of Defense Appropriations Act, 2000.)*

Program and Financing (in millions of dollars)

Identification code 57–3500–0–1–051	1999 actual	2000 est.	2001 est.
Obligations by program activity:			
Direct program:			
00.01 Pay and allowances of officers	5,710	6,071	6,126
00.02 Pay and allowances of enlisted personnel	9,666	9,994	10,433
00.03 Pay and allowances of cadets	37	38	38
00.04 Subsistence of enlisted personnel	767	771	776
00.05 Permanent change of station travel	846	899	870
00.06 Other military personnel costs	41	40	40
09.01 Reimbursable program	205	248	190
10.00 Total new obligations	17,274	18,061	18,473
Budgetary resources available for obligation:			
22.00 New budget authority (gross)	17,253	18,061	18,473
22.22 Unobligated balance transferred from other DoD accounts	71		
23.90 Total budgetary resources available for obligation	17,324	18,061	18,473
23.95 Total new obligations	−17,274	−18,061	−18,473
23.98 Unobligated balance expiring or withdrawn	−50		
New budget authority (gross), detail:			
Discretionary:			
40.00 Appropriation	17,204	17,380	18,283
40.15 Appropriation (emergency)	4		
40.74 Reduction pursuant to P.L. 106–79		−35	
41.00 Transferred to other DoD accounts	−308	−3	
42.00 Transferred from other DoD accounts	148		
43.00 Appropriation (total discretionary)	17,048	17,342	18,283
55.00 Advance appropriation		472	
Spending authority from offsetting collections:			
68.00 Offsetting collections (cash)	249	248	190
68.10 From Federal sources: Change in receivables and unpaid, unfilled orders	−161		
68.15 From Federal sources: Adjustments to receivables and unpaid, unfilled orders	117		
68.90 Spending authority from offsetting collections (total discretionary)	205	248	190
70.00 Total new budget authority (gross)	17,253	18,062	18,473
Change in unpaid obligations:			
Unpaid obligations, start of year:			
72.40 Obligated balance, start of year	1,450	1,216	1,292
72.95 From Federal sources: Receivables and unpaid, unfilled orders	184	23	23
72.99 Total unpaid obligations, start of year	1,634	1,239	1,315
73.10 Total new obligations	17,274	18,061	18,473
73.20 Total outlays (gross)	−17,104	−17,985	−18,244
73.40 Adjustments in expired accounts (net)	−566		
Unpaid obligations, end of year:			
74.40 Obligated balance, end of year	1,216	1,292	1,521
74.95 From Federal sources: Receivables and unpaid, unfilled orders	23	23	23
74.99 Total unpaid obligations, end of year	1,239	1,315	1,544
Outlays (gross), detail:			
86.90 Outlays from new discretionary authority	16,195	16,868	17,248
86.93 Outlays from discretionary balances	909	1,117	996
87.00 Total outlays (gross)	17,104	17,985	18,244
Offsets:			
Against gross budget authority and outlays:			
Offsetting collections (cash) from:			
88.00 Federal sources	−219	−175	−125
88.40 Non-Federal sources	−30	−73	−65
88.90 Total, offsetting collections (cash)	−249	−247	−190
Against gross budget authority only:			
88.95 From Federal sources: Change in receivables and unpaid, unfilled orders	161		
88.96 From Federal sources: Adjustment to receivables and unpaid, unfilled orders	−117		
Net budget authority and outlays:			
89.00 Budget authority	17,048	17,814	18,283
90.00 Outlays	16,854	17,738	18,054

Object Classification (in millions of dollars)

Identification code 57–3500–0–1–051	1999 actual	2000 est.	2001 est.
Direct obligations:			
11.7 Personnel compensation: Military personnel	11,673	12,077	12,597
Military personnel benefits:			
12.2 Accrued retirement benefits	2,719	2,917	2,879
12.2 Other personnel benefits	1,885	1,991	2,002
13.0 Benefits for former personnel	35	33	33
21.0 Travel and transportation of persons	209	222	215
22.0 Transportation of things	483	507	494
25.3 Payments to foreign national indirect hire personnel	26	25	23
26.0 Supplies and materials	38	39	38
42.0 Insurance claims and indemnities	1	2	2
43.0 Interest and dividends	1	1	1
99.0 Subtotal, direct obligations	17,069	17,814	18,283
99.0 Reimbursable obligations	205	247	190
99.9 Total new obligations	17,274	18,061	18,473

RESERVE FORCES

These appropriations finance the personnel costs of the National Guard and Reserve forces, including the future retirement benefits of the current Reserve forces. The estimates reflect continuing efforts to improve management efficiency including, for example, more economical use of training and recruiting resources as well as the undertaking of active missions at lower costs.

The number of National Guard and Reserve personnel estimated to participate in the Selected Reserve training programs and the number of full-time active duty military personnel provided for are summarized in the following table.

YEAR-END NUMBER

	1999 actual	2000 est.	2001 est.
Defense total	870,917	864,144	865,700

Trained inactive duty	761,909	758,672	756,237
Training pipeline	43,967	40,665	44,931
Full-time active duty	65,041	64,807	64,532
Army Reserve	206,836	205,000	205,000
Trained inactive duty	181,650	179,197	177,148
Training pipeline	12,203	12,999	15,046
Full-time active duty	12,983	12,804	12,806
Navy Reserve	89,172	89,134	88,900
Trained inactive duty	73,297	74,124	74,251
Training pipeline			
Full-time active duty	15,875	15,010	14,649
Marine Corps Reserve	39,953	39,624	39,500
Trained inactive duty	34,640	34,325	34,280
Training pipeline	2,996	3,027	3,017
Full-time active duty	2,317	2,272	2,203
Air Force Reserve	71,772	73,708	74,300
Trained inactive duty	70,397	71,803	72,251
Training pipeline	394	771	771
Full-time active duty	981	1,134	1,278
Army National Guard	357,469	350,000	350,000
Trained inactive duty	310,786	306,500	304,121
Training pipeline	24,771	21,070	23,431
Full-time active duty	21,912	22,430	22,448
Air National Guard	105,715	106,678	108,000
Trained inactive duty	91,139	92,723	94,186
Training pipeline	3,603	2,798	2,666
Full-time active duty	10,973	11,157	11,148
Planned QDR actions (Army Reserve/Guard)			
Trained inactive duty			

The Reserve Officers' Training Corps program provides training for reserve and regular officer candidates who have enrolled in the course while attending a college at which an ROTC unit has been established. College graduates who satisfactorily complete the advanced course of the program are commissioned and may be ordered to active duty for a minimum of 3 years.

The Reserve Officers' Training Corps Vitalization Act of 1964, as amended, authorizes a limited number of scholarships for ROTC students on a competitive basis. Successful candidates for the scholarships generally serve a minimum period of 4 years on active duty upon graduation and appointment as a commissioned officer. A number of scholarship recipients will fulfill their entire obligation in the Reserve components.

The Armed Forces health professions scholarship program provides a source of active duty commissioned officers for the various health professions.

The numbers of commissioned officers graduated from these programs are summarized below:

	1999 actual	2000 est.	2001 est.
ROTC:			
Army	3,281	3,147	3,257
Navy	776	1,050	1,050
Air Force	1,830	1,932	1,876
Total	5,887	6,129	6,183
Marine Corps officer candidates	187	175	175
Total	6,074	6,304	6,358
Health professions scholarship:			
Army	363	369	375
Navy	338	362	363
Air Force	25	25	25
Total	726	756	763

Federal Funds

General and special funds:

RESERVE PERSONNEL, ARMY

For pay, allowances, clothing, subsistence, gratuities, travel, and related expenses for personnel of the Army Reserve on active duty under sections 10211, 10302, and 3038 of title 10, United States Code, or while serving on active duty under section 12301(d) of title 10, United States Code, in connection with performing duty specified in section 12310(a) of title 10, United States Code, or while undergoing reserve training, or while performing drills or equivalent duty or other duty, and for members of the Reserve Officers' Training Corps, and expenses authorized by section 16131 of title 10, United States Code; and for payments to the Department of Defense Military Retirement Fund, [$2,289,996,000] *$2,433,880,000. (10 U.S.C. 683, 1475–80, 2101–11, 3722; 37 U.S.C. 204, 206, 209, 301, 305, 402–04, 414–18, 1002; Department of Defense Appropriations Act, 2000.)*

Program and Financing (in millions of dollars)

Identification code 21–2070–0–1–051		1999 actual	2000 est.	2001 est.
	Obligations by program activity:			
	Direct program:			
00.01	Unit and individual training	1,021	1,064	1,158
00.02	Other training and support	1,159	1,228	1,276
09.01	Reimbursable program	14	20	20
10.00	Total new obligations	2,193	2,312	2,454
	Budgetary resources available for obligation:			
22.00	New budget authority (gross)	2,197	2,312	2,454
23.95	Total new obligations	−2,193	−2,312	−2,454
23.98	Unobligated balance expiring or withdrawn	−4		
	New budget authority (gross), detail:			
	Discretionary:			
40.00	Appropriation	2,167	2,249	2,434
40.15	Appropriation (emergency)	8		
42.00	Transferred from other DoD accounts	8	2	
43.00	Appropriation (total discretionary)	2,183	2,251	2,434
55.00	Advance appropriation		41	
	Spending authority from offsetting collections:			
68.00	Offsetting collections (cash)	12	20	20
68.15	From Federal sources: Adjustments to receivables and unpaid, unfilled orders	2		
68.90	Spending authority from offsetting collections (total discretionary)	14	20	20
70.00	Total new budget authority (gross)	2,197	2,312	2,454
	Change in unpaid obligations:			
	Unpaid obligations, start of year:			
72.40	Obligated balance, start of year	302	264	294
72.95	From Federal sources: Receivables and unpaid, unfilled orders	3	3	3
72.99	Total unpaid obligations, start of year	305	268	298
73.10	Total new obligations	2,193	2,312	2,454
73.20	Total outlays (gross)	−2,159	−2,282	−2,407
73.40	Adjustments in expired accounts (net)	−72		
	Unpaid obligations, end of year:			
74.40	Obligated balance, end of year	264	294	341
74.95	From Federal sources: Receivables and unpaid, unfilled orders	3	3	3
74.99	Total unpaid obligations, end of year	268	298	344
	Outlays (gross), detail:			
86.90	Outlays from new discretionary authority	1,990	2,106	2,220
86.93	Outlays from discretionary balances	168	176	187
87.00	Total outlays (gross)	2,159	2,282	2,407

General and special funds—Continued

RESERVE PERSONNEL, ARMY—Continued

Program and Financing (in millions of dollars)—Continued

Identification code 21–2070–0–1–051		1999 actual	2000 est.	2001 est.
	Offsets:			
	Against gross budget authority and outlays:			
	Offsetting collections (cash) from:			
88.00	Federal sources	–12	–20	–20
88.40	Non-Federal sources			
88.90	Total, offsetting collections (cash)	–12	–20	–20
	Against gross budget authority only:			
88.96	From Federal sources: Adjustment to receivables and unpaid, unfilled orders	–2		
	Net budget authority and outlays:			
89.00	Budget authority	2,183	2,292	2,434
90.00	Outlays	2,147	2,262	2,387

Object Classification (in millions of dollars)

Identification code 21–2070–0–1–051		1999 actual	2000 est.	2001 est.
	Direct obligations:			
11.7	Personnel compensation: Military personnel	1,491	1,511	1,580
	Military personnel benefits:			
12.2	Accrued retirement benefits	199	229	267
12.2	Other personnel benefits	219	249	268
21.0	Travel and transportation of persons	158	171	177
22.0	Transportation of things	12	11	12
25.2	Other services	1	1	1
25.3	Purchases of goods and services from Government accounts	2	2	2
25.8	Subsistence and support of persons	45	52	55
26.0	Supplies and materials	52	65	71
99.0	Subtotal, direct obligations	2,179	2,292	2,434
99.0	Reimbursable obligations	14	20	20
99.9	Total new obligations	2,193	2,312	2,454

RESERVE PERSONNEL, NAVY

For pay, allowances, clothing, subsistence, gratuities, travel, and related expenses for personnel of the Navy Reserve on active duty under section 10211 of title 10, United States Code, or while serving on active duty under section 12301(d) of title 10, United States Code, in connection with performing duty specified in section 12310(a) of title 10, United States Code, or while undergoing reserve training, or while performing drills or equivalent duty, and for members of the Reserve Officers' Training Corps, and expenses authorized by section 16131 of title 10, United States Code; and for payments to the Department of Defense Military Retirement Fund, [$1,473,388,000] *$1,528,385,000. (10 U.S.C. 600, 683–4, 1475–80, 2031, 2101–11, 5456–57, 6081–86, 6148; 26 U.S.C. 3121; 37 U.S.C. 204, 206, 301, 305, 402–4, 415–18, 427, 1002; 38 U.S.C. 701–12; Department of Defense Appropriations Act, 2000.)*

Program and Financing (in millions of dollars)

Identification code 17–1405–0–1–051		1999 actual	2000 est.	2001 est.
	Obligations by program activity:			
	Direct program:			
00.01	Unit and individual training	580	591	636
00.02	Other training and support	868	883	893
09.01	Reimbursable program	15	17	18
10.00	Total new obligations	1,463	1,491	1,546
	Budgetary resources available for obligation:			
22.00	New budget authority (gross)	1,466	1,491	1,546
23.95	Total new obligations	–1,463	–1,491	–1,546
23.98	Unobligated balance expiring or withdrawn	–2		
	New budget authority (gross), detail:			
	Discretionary:			
40.00	Appropriation	1,427	1,444	1,528
40.15	Appropriation (emergency)	10		
42.00	Transferred from other DoD accounts	14		
43.00	Appropriation (total discretionary)	1,451	1,444	1,528
55.00	Advance appropriation		30	
	Spending authority from offsetting collections:			
68.00	Offsetting collections (cash)	14	17	18
68.15	From Federal sources: Adjustments to receivables and unpaid, unfilled orders	1		
68.90	Spending authority from offsetting collections (total discretionary)	15	17	18
70.00	Total new budget authority (gross)	1,466	1,491	1,546
	Change in unpaid obligations:			
	Unpaid obligations, start of year:			
72.40	Obligated balance, start of year	265	276	292
72.95	From Federal sources: Receivables and unpaid, unfilled orders	7	7	7
72.99	Total unpaid obligations, start of year	271	283	299
73.10	Total new obligations	1,463	1,491	1,546
73.20	Total outlays (gross)	–1,436	–1,475	–1,502
73.40	Adjustments in expired accounts (net)	–15		
	Unpaid obligations, end of year:			
74.40	Obligated balance, end of year	276	292	337
74.95	From Federal sources: Receivables and unpaid, unfilled orders	7	7	7
74.99	Total unpaid obligations, end of year	283	299	344
	Outlays (gross), detail:			
86.90	Outlays from new discretionary authority	1,333	1,351	1,387
86.93	Outlays from discretionary balances	104	124	115
87.00	Total outlays (gross)	1,436	1,475	1,502
	Offsets:			
	Against gross budget authority and outlays:			
88.00	Offsetting collections (cash) from: Federal sources	–14	–17	–18
	Against gross budget authority only:			
88.96	From Federal sources: Adjustment to receivables and unpaid, unfilled orders	–1		
	Net budget authority and outlays:			
89.00	Budget authority	1,451	1,473	1,528
90.00	Outlays	1,422	1,457	1,484

Object Classification (in millions of dollars)

Identification code 17–1405–0–1–051		1999 actual	2000 est.	2001 est.
	Direct obligations:			
11.7	Personnel compensation: Military personnel	985	1,021	1,037
	Military personnel benefits:			
12.2	Accrued retirement benefits	151	161	175
12.2	Other personnel benefits	128	109	117
21.0	Travel and transportation of persons	139	130	136
22.0	Transportation of things	20	20	21
25.8	Subsistence and support of persons		9	9
26.0	Supplies and materials	22	21	30
42.0	Insurance claims and indemnities	3	3	3
99.0	Subtotal, direct obligations	1,448	1,473	1,528
99.0	Reimbursable obligations	15	17	18
99.9	Total new obligations	1,463	1,491	1,546

RESERVE PERSONNEL, MARINE CORPS

For pay, allowances, clothing, subsistence, gratuities, travel, and related expenses for personnel of the Marine Corps Reserve on active duty under section 10211 of title 10, United States Code, or while serving on active duty under section 12301(d) of title 10, United States Code, in connection with performing duty specified in section 12310(a) of title 10, United States Code, or while undergoing reserve training, or while performing drills or equivalent duty, and for members of the Marine Corps platoon leaders class, and expenses authorized by section 16131 of title 10, United States Code; and for payments to the Department of Defense Military Retirement Fund, [$412,650,000] *$436,386,000. (10 U.S.C. 600, 683, 1475–80, 2031, 2101–11, 5456, 5458, 6081–86, 6148; 37 U.S.C. 206, 301, 305, 402–04, 415–18, 1002; Department of Defense Appropriations Act, 2000.)*

Program and Financing (in millions of dollars)

Identification code 17–1108–0–1–051		1999 actual	2000 est.	2001 est.
	Obligations by program activity:			
	Direct program:			
00.01	Unit and individual training	216	225	245
00.02	Other training and support	183	188	192
09.01	Reimbursable program		1	1
10.00	Total new obligations	399	414	437
	Budgetary resources available for obligation:			
22.00	New budget authority (gross)	402	414	437
23.95	Total new obligations	−399	−414	−437
23.98	Unobligated balance expiring or withdrawn	−3		
	New budget authority (gross), detail:			
	Discretionary:			
40.00	Appropriation	407	405	436
41.00	Transferred from other DoD accounts	−8		
42.00	Transferred from other DoD accounts	2		
43.00	Appropriation (total discretionary)	401	405	436
55.00	Advance appropriation		8	
	Spending authority from offsetting collections:			
68.00	Offsetting collections (cash)	1	1	1
68.10	From Federal sources: Change in receivables and unpaid, unfilled orders	−1		
68.15	From Federal sources: Adjustments to receivables and unpaid, unfilled orders	1		
68.90	Spending authority from offsetting collections (total discretionary)	1	1	1
70.00	Total new budget authority (gross)	402	414	437
	Change in unpaid obligations:			
	Unpaid obligations, start of year:			
72.40	Obligated balance, start of year	46	59	63
72.95	From Federal sources: Receivables and unpaid, unfilled orders	2	1	1
72.99	Total unpaid obligations, start of year	47	59	63
73.10	Total new obligations	399	414	437
73.20	Total outlays (gross)	−389	−409	−426
73.40	Adjustments in expired accounts (net)	3		
	Unpaid obligations, end of year:			
74.40	Obligated balance, end of year	59	63	74
74.95	From Federal sources: Receivables and unpaid, unfilled orders	1	1	1
74.99	Total unpaid obligations, end of year	59	63	75
	Outlays (gross), detail:			
86.90	Outlays from new discretionary authority	361	378	399
86.93	Outlays from discretionary balances	28	31	27
87.00	Total outlays (gross)	389	409	426
	Offsets:			
	Against gross budget authority and outlays:			
	Offsetting collections (cash) from:			
88.00	Federal sources	−1	−1	−1
88.40	Non-Federal sources			
88.90	Total, offsetting collections (cash)	−1	−1	−1
	Against gross budget authority only:			
88.95	From Federal sources: Change in receivables and unpaid, unfilled orders	1		
88.96	From Federal sources: Adjustment to receivables and unpaid, unfilled orders	−1		
	Net budget authority and outlays:			
89.00	Budget authority	401	413	436
90.00	Outlays	388	408	425

Object Classification (in millions of dollars)

Identification code 17–1108–0–1–051		1999 actual	2000 est.	2001 est.
	Direct obligations:			
11.7	Personnel compensation: Military personnel	300	307	319
	Military personnel benefits:			
12.2	Accrued retirement benefits	32	36	45
12.2	Other personnel benefits	19	25	26
21.0	Travel and transportation of persons	35	30	31
22.0	Transportation of things	1	1	1
26.0	Supplies and materials	11	14	14
99.0	Subtotal, direct obligations	398	413	436
99.0	Reimbursable obligations	1	1	1
99.9	Total new obligations	399	414	437

Reserve Personnel, Air Force

For pay, allowances, clothing, subsistence, gratuities, travel, and related expenses for personnel of the Air Force Reserve on active duty under sections 10211, 10305, and 8038 of title 10, United States Code, or while serving on active duty under section 12301(d) of title 10, United States Code, in connection with performing duty specified in section 12310(a) of title 10, United States Code, or while undergoing reserve training, or while performing drills or equivalent duty or other duty, and for members of the Air Reserve Officers' Training Corps, and expenses authorized by section 16131 of title 10, United States Code; and for payments to the Department of Defense Military Retirement Fund, **[**$892,594,000**]** *$981,710,000. (10 U.S.C. 261–80, 591–95, 597–600, 651, 671–85, 687, 715, 1475–80, 2031, 2101–11, 2120–27, 2131–33, 2511, 8062, 8076, 8221–23, 8259–60, 8351–54, 8356–63, 8365–68, 8371–81, 8392–95, 8491, 8687, 8722, 9301, 9411–14, 9561–63, 9741, 9743; 37 U.S.C. 204, 206, 209, 301, 309, 402–11, 415–18, 1002; Department of Defense Appropriations Act, 2000.)*

Program and Financing (in millions of dollars)

Identification code 57–3700–0–1–051		1999 actual	2000 est.	2001 est.
	Obligations by program activity:			
	Direct program:			
00.01	Unit and individual training	494	524	567
00.02	Other training and support	351	369	415
09.01	Reimbursable program	1	2	3
10.00	Total new obligations	846	895	985
	Budgetary resources available for obligation:			
22.00	New budget authority (gross)	857	895	985
23.95	Total new obligations	−846	−895	−985
23.98	Unobligated balance expiring or withdrawn	−12		
	New budget authority (gross), detail:			
	Discretionary:			
40.00	Appropriation	852	879	982
42.00	Transferred from other DoD accounts	4		
43.00	Appropriation (total discretionary)	856	879	982
55.00	Advance appropriation		13	
	Spending authority from offsetting collections:			
68.00	Offsetting collections (cash)	1	2	3
68.10	From Federal sources: Change in receivables and unpaid, unfilled orders	−1		
68.15	From Federal sources: Adjustments to receivables and unpaid, unfilled orders	1		
68.90	Spending authority from offsetting collections (total discretionary)	1	2	3
70.00	Total new budget authority (gross)	857	894	985
	Change in unpaid obligations:			
	Unpaid obligations, start of year:			
72.40	Obligated balance, start of year	75	86	99
72.95	From Federal sources: Receivables and unpaid, unfilled orders	2	1	1
72.99	Total unpaid obligations, start of year	77	86	100
73.10	Total new obligations	846	895	985
73.20	Total outlays (gross)	−822	−881	−970
73.40	Adjustments in expired accounts (net)	−14		
	Unpaid obligations, end of year:			
74.40	Obligated balance, end of year	86	99	113
74.95	From Federal sources: Receivables and unpaid, unfilled orders	1	1	1
74.99	Total unpaid obligations, end of year	86	100	114
	Outlays (gross), detail:			
86.90	Outlays from new discretionary authority	774	827	911

General and special funds—Continued

RESERVE PERSONNEL, AIR FORCE—Continued

Program and Financing (in millions of dollars)—Continued

Identification code 57–3700–0–1–051		1999 actual	2000 est.	2001 est.
86.93	Outlays from discretionary balances	48	54	59
87.00	Total outlays (gross)	822	881	970
	Offsets:			
	Against gross budget authority and outlays:			
88.00	Offsetting collections (cash) from: Federal sources	−1	−2	−3
	Against gross budget authority only:			
88.95	From Federal sources: Change in receivables and unpaid, unfilled orders	1		
88.96	From Federal sources: Adjustment to receivables and unpaid, unfilled orders	−1		
	Net budget authority and outlays:			
89.00	Budget authority	857	893	982
90.00	Outlays	822	879	967

Object Classification (in millions of dollars)

Identification code 57–3700–0–1–051		1999 actual	2000 est.	2001 est.
	Direct obligations:			
11.7	Personnel compensation: Military personnel	587	617	648
	Military personnel benefits:			
12.2	Accrued retirement benefits	47	53	84
12.2	Other personnel benefits	56	64	74
21.0	Travel and transportation of persons	121	119	136
22.0	Transportation of things	1	1	1
26.0	Supplies and materials	29	35	35
41.0	Grants, subsidies, and contributions	4	4	4
99.0	Subtotal, direct obligations	845	893	982
99.0	Reimbursable obligations	1	2	3
99.9	Total new obligations	846	895	985

NATIONAL GUARD PERSONNEL, ARMY

For pay, allowances, clothing, subsistence, gratuities, travel, and related expenses for personnel of the Army National Guard while on duty under section 10211, 10302, or 12402 of title 10 or section 708 of title 32, United States Code, or while serving on duty under section 12301(d) of title 10 or section 502(f) of title 32, United States Code, in connection with performing duty specified in section 12310(a) of title 10, United States Code, or while undergoing training, or while performing drills or equivalent duty or other duty, and expenses authorized by section 16131 of title 10, United States Code; and for payments to the Department of Defense Military Retirement Fund, [$3,610,479,000] *$3,747,636,000. (10 U.S.C. 683, 1475–80, 3722; 37 U.S.C. 301, 305, 402–04, 418, 1002; Department of Defense Appropriations Act, 2000.)*

Program and Financing (in millions of dollars)

Identification code 21–2060–0–1–051		1999 actual	2000 est.	2001 est.
	Obligations by program activity:			
	Direct program:			
00.01	Unit and individual training	1,771	1,768	1,923
00.02	Other training and support	1,842	1,837	1,825
09.01	Reimbursable program	9	9	9
10.00	Total new obligations	3,622	3,614	3,757
	Budgetary resources available for obligation:			
22.00	New budget authority (gross)	3,645	3,614	3,757
22.22	Unobligated balance transferred from other DoD accounts	2		
23.90	Total budgetary resources available for obligation	3,647	3,614	3,757
23.95	Total new obligations	−3,622	−3,614	−3,757
23.98	Unobligated balance expiring or withdrawn	−25		
	New budget authority (gross), detail:			
	Discretionary:			
40.00	Appropriation	3,490	3,540	3,748
40.15	Appropriation (emergency)	7		
41.00	Transferred to Other DoD accounts		−7	
42.00	Transferred from other DoD accounts	139	2	
43.00	Appropriation (total discretionary)	3,636	3,535	3,748
55.00	Advance appropriation		70	
	Spending authority from offsetting collections:			
68.00	Offsetting collections (cash)	2	9	9
68.10	From Federal sources: Change in receivables and unpaid, unfilled orders	5		
68.15	From Federal sources: Adjustments to receivables and unpaid, unfilled orders	2		
68.90	Spending authority from offsetting collections (total discretionary)	9	9	9
70.00	Total new budget authority (gross)	3,645	3,614	3,757
	Change in unpaid obligations:			
	Unpaid obligations, start of year:			
72.40	Obligated balance, start of year	559	420	484
72.95	From Federal sources: Receivables and unpaid, unfilled orders	17	22	22
72.99	Total unpaid obligations, start of year	576	442	506
73.10	Total new obligations	3,622	3,614	3,757
73.20	Total outlays (gross)	−3,561	−3,550	−3,673
73.40	Adjustments in expired accounts (net)	−195		
	Unpaid obligations, end of year:			
74.40	Obligated balance, end of year	420	484	568
74.95	From Federal sources: Receivables and unpaid, unfilled orders	22	22	22
74.99	Total unpaid obligations, end of year	442	506	590
	Outlays (gross), detail:			
86.90	Outlays from new discretionary authority	3,319	3,290	3,427
86.93	Outlays from discretionary balances	242	261	246
87.00	Total outlays (gross)	3,561	3,550	3,673
	Offsets:			
	Against gross budget authority and outlays:			
	Offsetting collections (cash) from:			
88.00	Federal sources	1	−9	−9
88.40	Non-Federal sources	−3		
88.90	Total, offsetting collections (cash)	−2	−9	−9
	Against gross budget authority only:			
88.95	From Federal sources: Change in receivables and unpaid, unfilled orders	−5		
88.96	From Federal sources: Adjustment to receivables and unpaid, unfilled orders	−2		
	Net budget authority and outlays:			
89.00	Budget authority	3,636	3,605	3,748
90.00	Outlays	3,559	3,541	3,664

Object Classification (in millions of dollars)

Identification code 21–2060–0–1–051		1999 actual	2000 est.	2001 est.
	Direct obligations:			
11.7	Personnel compensation: Military personnel	2,561	2,615	2,706
	Military personnel benefits:			
12.2	Accrued retirement benefits	356	378	430
12.2	Other personnel benefits	381	348	358
21.0	Travel and transportation of persons	174	132	118
22.0	Transportation of things	3	5	5
25.2	Other services	5	5	5
25.8	Subsistence and support of persons	22	22	22
26.0	Supplies and materials	111	100	104
99.0	Subtotal, direct obligations	3,613	3,605	3,748
99.0	Reimbursable obligations	9	9	9
99.9	Total new obligations	3,622	3,614	3,757

NATIONAL GUARD PERSONNEL, AIR FORCE

For pay, allowances, clothing, subsistence, gratuities, travel, and related expenses for personnel of the Air National Guard on duty under section 10211, 10305, or 12402 of title 10 or section 708 of title 32, United States Code, or while serving on duty under section

12301(d) of title 10 or section 502(f) of title 32, United States Code, in connection with performing duty specified in section 12310(a) of title 10, United States Code, or while undergoing training, or while performing drills or equivalent duty or other duty, and expenses authorized by section 16131 of title 10, United States Code; and for payments to the Department of Defense Military Retirement Fund, [$1,533,196,000] *$1,627,181,000. (10 U.S.C. 261–812, 510, 591–95, 597–600, 651, 671–85, 2132–33, 2511, 3015, 8062, 8077–78, 8080, 8224–25, 8261, 8351–54, 8356, 8358–63, 8365–68, 8371–81, 8392–95, 8491, 8722, 9301, 9561–63, 9741, 18233a; 32 U.S.C. 101–11, 301–05, 307–08, 312–33, 501–07, 701, 37 U.S.C. 201, 203–06, 301, 309, 402–11, 414–18, 501–02, 1002; Department of Defense Appropriations Act, 2000.)*

Program and Financing (in millions of dollars)

Identification code 57–3850–0–1–051	1999 actual	2000 est.	2001 est.
Obligations by program activity:			
Direct program:			
00.01 Unit and individual training	621	662	722
00.02 Other training and support	831	867	905
09.01 Reimbursable program	20	22	22
10.00 Total new obligations	1,472	1,551	1,649
Budgetary resources available for obligation:			
22.00 New budget authority (gross)	1,472	1,551	1,649
23.95 Total new obligations	−1,472	−1,551	−1,649
New budget authority (gross), detail:			
Discretionary:			
40.00 Appropriation	1,377	1,504	1,627
40.15 Appropriation (emergency)	1		
41.00 Transferred to Other DoD accounts		−5	
42.00 Transferred from other DoD accounts	74		
43.00 Appropriation (total discretionary)	1,452	1,499	1,627
55.00 Advance appropriation		30	
Spending authority from offsetting collections:			
68.00 Offsetting collections (cash)	24	22	22
68.15 From Federal sources: Adjustments to receivables and unpaid, unfilled orders	−4		
68.90 Spending authority from offsetting collections (total discretionary)	20	22	22
70.00 Total new budget authority (gross)	1,472	1,551	1,649
Change in unpaid obligations:			
72.40 Unpaid obligations, start of year: Obligated balance, start of year	72	69	87
73.10 Total new obligations	1,472	1,551	1,649
73.20 Total outlays (gross)	−1,472	−1,533	−1,627
73.40 Adjustments in expired accounts (net)	−3		
74.40 Unpaid obligations, end of year: Obligated balance, end of year	69	87	109
Outlays (gross), detail:			
86.90 Outlays from new discretionary authority	1,417	1,485	1,571
86.93 Outlays from discretionary balances	55	48	56
87.00 Total outlays (gross)	1,472	1,533	1,627
Offsets:			
Against gross budget authority and outlays:			
88.00 Offsetting collections (cash) from: Federal sources	−24	−22	−22
Against gross budget authority only:			
88.96 From Federal sources: Adjustment to receivables and unpaid, unfilled orders	4		
Net budget authority and outlays:			
89.00 Budget authority	1,452	1,529	1,627
90.00 Outlays	1,448	1,511	1,605

Object Classification (in millions of dollars)

Identification code 57–3850–0–1–051	1999 actual	2000 est.	2001 est.
Direct obligations:			
11.7 Personnel compensation: Military personnel	929	1,007	1,063
Military personnel benefits:			
12.2 Accrued retirement benefits	147	174	198
12.2 Other personnel benefits	278	248	260
21.0 Travel and transportation of persons	73	68	72
22.0 Transportation of things	1	1	1
26.0 Supplies and materials	24	30	32
42.0 Insurance claims and indemnities		1	1
99.0 Subtotal, direct obligations	1,452	1,529	1,627
99.0 Reimbursable obligations	20	22	22
99.9 Total new obligations	1,472	1,551	1,649

OPERATION AND MAINTENANCE

These appropriations finance the cost of operating and maintaining the Armed Forces, including the Reserve components and related support activities of the Department of Defense, except military personnel pay, allowances and travel costs. Included are amounts for pay of civilians, contract services for maintenance of equipment and facilities, fuel, supplies, and repair parts for weapons and equipment. Financial requirements are influenced by many factors, including the number of aircraft squadrons, Army and Marine Corps divisions, installations, military strength and deployments, rates of operational activity, and the quantity and complexity of major equipment (aircraft, ships, missiles, tanks, et cetera) in operation. Special emphasis is placed on ensuring adequate funding for all programs that contribute directly or indirectly to the readiness of our armed forces. As such, the Department has undertaken important efforts to better assess our military readiness and the relationship between readiness and operation and maintenance program funding levels.

Resources presented under the Operation and Maintenance title contribute primarily to achieving the Department's corporate goals 1 (Shape and Respond) and 2 (Prepare). A detailed description of the corporate goals is contained in the FY 2001 Performance Plan in the Department's 2000 Annual Report to the President and Congress. This performance plan is required by the Government Performance and Results Act of 1993.

Federal Funds

General and special funds:

Operation and Maintenance, Army

(including transfer of funds)

For expenses, not otherwise provided for, necessary for the operation and maintenance of the Army, as authorized by law; and not to exceed [$10,624,000] *$10,616,000* can be used for emergencies and extraordinary expenses, to be expended on the approval or authority of the Secretary of the Army, and payments may be made on his certificate of necessity for confidential military purposes, [$19,256,152,000] *$19,073,731,000* and, in addition, $50,000,000 shall be derived by transfer from the National Defense Stockpile Transaction Fund[: *Provided*, That of the funds made available under this heading, $5,000,000, to remain available until expended, shall be transferred to "National Park Service—Construction" within 30 days of the enactment of this Act, only for necessary infrastructure repair improvements at Fort Baker, under the management of the Golden Gate Recreation Area: *Provided further*, That of the funds appropriated in this paragraph, not less than $355,000,000 shall be made available only for conventional ammunition care and maintenance: *Provided further*, That of the funds appropriated under this heading, $4,000,000 shall not be available until 30 days after the Secretary of the Army provides to the congressional defense committees the results of an assessment, solicited by means of a competitive bid, on the prospects of recovering costs associated with the environmental restoration of the Department of the Army's government-owned, contractor-operated facilities: *Provided further*, That of the funds made available under this heading, $7,000,000 shall only be available to the Secretary of the Army, acting through the Chief of Engineers, only for demolition and removal of facilities, buildings, and structures used at MOTBY (a Military Traffic Management Command facility): *Provided further*, That notwithstanding section 2215 of title 10, United States Code, of the funds appropriated in this

General and special funds—Continued

OPERATION AND MAINTENANCE, ARMY—Continued

(INCLUDING TRANSFER OF FUNDS)—Continued

paragraph, $975,666 is authorized to be transferred to the Presidential Advisory Commission on Holocaust Assets in the United States, to remain available until March 31, 2001]. *(Department of Defense Appropriations Act, 2000.)*

Program and Financing (in millions of dollars)

Identification code 21–2020–0–1–051		1999 actual	2000 est.	2001 est.
	Obligations by program activity:			
	Direct program:			
00.01	Operating forces	11,439	9,346	9,581
00.02	Mobilization	585	603	527
00.03	Training and recruiting	3,239	3,294	3,454
00.04	Administration and servicewide activities	5,928	5,676	5,562
09.01	Reimbursable program	5,852	5,858	6,056
10.00	Total new obligations	27,043	24,777	25,179
	Budgetary resources available for obligation:			
21.40	Unobligated balance available, start of year		71	
22.00	New budget authority (gross)	26,623	24,643	25,180
22.10	Resources available from recoveries of prior year obligations	1		
22.22	Unobligated balance transferred from other DoD accounts	494	62	
23.90	Total budgetary resources available for obligation	27,118	24,776	25,180
23.95	Total new obligations	−27,043	−24,777	−25,179
23.98	Unobligated balance expiring or withdrawn	−5		
24.40	Unobligated balance available, end of year	71		
	New budget authority (gross), detail:			
	Discretionary:			
40.00	Appropriation	17,014	17,292	19,074
40.15	Appropriation (emergency)	595	1,573	
40.74	Reduction pursuant to P.L. 106–79		−12	
40.76	Reduction pursuant to P.L. 106–113		−98	
40.77	Reduction pursuant to P.L. 105–262	−16		
41.00	Transferred to other accounts	−442	−373	
42.00	Transferred from other DoD accounts	3,570	354	
43.00	Appropriation (total discretionary)	20,721	18,737	19,074
	Spending authority from offsetting collections:			
68.00	Offsetting collections (cash)	5,743	5,857	6,056
68.10	From Federal sources: Change in receivables and unpaid, unfilled orders	3		
68.15	From Federal sources: Adjustments to receivables and unpaid, unfilled orders	106		
68.62	Transferred from National Defense Stockpile	50	50	50
68.90	Spending authority from offsetting collections (total discretionary)	5,902	5,907	6,106
70.00	Total new budget authority (gross)	26,623	24,643	25,180
	Change in unpaid obligations:			
	Unpaid obligations, start of year:			
72.40	Obligated balance, start of year	7,857	9,065	8,597
72.95	From Federal sources: Receivables and unpaid, unfilled orders	2,676	2,679	2,679
72.99	Total unpaid obligations, start of year	10,532	11,744	11,276
73.10	Total new obligations	27,043	24,777	25,179
73.20	Total outlays (gross)	−25,600	−25,243	−25,690
73.40	Adjustments in expired accounts (net)	−230		
73.45	Adjustments in unexpired accounts	−1		
	Unpaid obligations, end of year:			
74.40	Obligated balance, end of year	9,065	8,597	8,086
74.95	From Federal sources: Receivables and unpaid, unfilled orders	2,679	2,679	2,679
74.99	Total unpaid obligations, end of year	11,744	11,276	10,765
	Outlays (gross), detail:			
86.90	Outlays from new discretionary authority	20,016	19,083	19,730
86.93	Outlays from discretionary balances	5,584	6,160	5,960
87.00	Total outlays (gross)	25,600	25,243	25,690
	Offsets:			
	Against gross budget authority and outlays:			
	Offsetting collections (cash) from:			
88.00	Federal sources	−5,333	−5,353	−5,543
88.40	Non-Federal sources	−410	−504	−513
88.90	Total, offsetting collections (cash)	−5,743	−5,857	−6,056
	Against gross budget authority only:			
88.95	From Federal sources: Change in receivables and unpaid, unfilled orders	−3		
88.96	From Federal sources: Adjustment to receivables and unpaid, unfilled orders	−106		
	Net budget authority and outlays:			
89.00	Budget authority	20,771	18,787	19,124
90.00	Outlays	19,857	19,386	19,634

Note: The "National Board for Promotion of Rifle Practice" is consolidated in this presentation.

Object Classification (in millions of dollars)

Identification code 21–2020–0–1–051		1999 actual	2000 est.	2001 est.
	Direct obligations:			
	Personnel compensation:			
11.1	Full-time permanent	2,896	2,965	3,032
11.3	Other than full-time permanent	484	415	424
11.5	Other personnel compensation	171	172	174
11.9	Total personnel compensation	3,551	3,552	3,630
12.1	Civilian personnel benefits	995	958	982
13.0	Benefits for former personnel	86	91	58
21.0	Travel and transportation of persons	860	688	668
22.0	Transportation of things	968	890	838
23.1	Rental payments to GSA	134	131	138
23.2	Rental payments to others	139	127	126
23.3	Communications, utilities, and miscellaneous charges	677	785	810
24.0	Printing and reproduction	41	49	48
25.1	Advisory and assistance services	161	105	103
25.2	Other services	1,575	1,106	1,008
	Purchases of goods and services from Government accounts:			
25.3	Purchases of goods and services from other Federal accounts	1,936	1,642	1,630
25.3	Payments to foreign national indirect hire personnel	431	388	347
25.3	Purchases from revolving funds	2,440	1,968	1,361
25.4	Operation and maintenance of facilities	929	860	1,668
25.6	Medical care	661	436	400
25.7	Operation and maintenance of equipment	1,215	1,196	1,219
26.0	Supplies and materials	3,599	3,236	3,372
31.0	Equipment	696	617	632
32.0	Land and structures	33	32	29
41.0	Grants, subsidies, and contributions	7	6	6
42.0	Insurance claims and indemnities	57	56	50
99.0	Subtotal, direct obligations	21,191	18,919	19,123
99.0	Reimbursable obligations	5,852	5,858	6,056
99.9	Total new obligations	27,043	24,777	25,179

Personnel Summary

Identification code 21–2020–0–1–051		1999 actual	2000 est.	2001 est.
	Direct:			
1001	Total compensable workyears: Full-time equivalent employment	82,190	78,770	77,066
	Reimbursable:			
2001	Total compensable workyears: Full-time equivalent employment	42,206	41,884	41,965

OPERATION AND MAINTENANCE, NAVY

(INCLUDING TRANSFER OF FUNDS)

For expenses, not otherwise provided for, necessary for the operation and maintenance of the Navy and the Marine Corps, as authorized by law; and not to exceed [$5,155,000] *$5,146,000* can be used for emergencies and extraordinary expenses, to be expended on the approval or authority of the Secretary of the Navy, and payments may be made on his certificate of necessity for confidential military purposes, [$22,958,784,000] *$23,250,154,000,* and, in addition, $50,000,000 shall be derived by transfer from the National Defense

Stockpile Transaction Fund. *(Department of Defense Appropriations Act, 2000.)*

Program and Financing (in millions of dollars)

Identification code 17–1804–0–1–051		1999 actual	2000 est.	2001 est.
	Obligations by program activity:			
	Direct program:			
00.01	Operating forces	16,297	16,143	16,693
00.02	Mobilization	971	760	669
00.03	Training and recruiting	1,789	1,868	1,966
00.04	Administration and servicewide activities	4,175	3,820	3,973
09.01	Reimbursable program	3,677	3,712	3,712
10.00	Total new obligations	26,909	26,303	27,012
	Budgetary resources available for obligation:			
21.40	Unobligated balance available, start of year		48	
22.00	New budget authority (gross)	26,966	26,234	27,012
22.22	Unobligated balance transferred from other DoD accounts	40	22	
23.90	Total budgetary resources available for obligation	27,007	26,303	27,012
23.95	Total new obligations	–26,909	–26,303	–27,012
23.98	Unobligated balance expiring or withdrawn	–50		
24.40	Unobligated balance available, end of year	48		
	New budget authority (gross), detail:			
	Discretionary:			
40.00	Appropriation	21,662	20,641	23,250
40.15	Appropriation (emergency)	340	1,875	
40.74	Reduction pursuant to P.L. 106–79		–6	
40.76	Reduction pursuant to P.L. 106–113		–116	
40.77	Reduction pursuant to P.L. 105–262	–21		
41.00	Transferred to other DoD accounts	–296	–265	
42.00	Transferred from other DoD accounts	1,554	343	
43.00	Appropriation (total discretionary)	23,239	22,471	23,250
	Spending authority from offsetting collections:			
68.00	Offsetting collections (cash)	3,446	3,712	3,712
68.10	From Federal sources: Change in receivables and unpaid, unfilled orders	–4		
68.15	From Federal sources: Adjustments to receivables and unpaid, unfilled orders	235		
68.62	Transferred from National Defense Stockpile	50	50	50
68.90	Spending authority from offsetting collections (total discretionary)	3,727	3,762	3,762
70.00	Total new budget authority (gross)	26,966	26,234	27,012
	Change in unpaid obligations:			
	Unpaid obligations, start of year:			
72.40	Obligated balance, start of year	5,750	7,642	7,989
72.95	From Federal sources: Receivables and unpaid, unfilled orders	2,613	2,609	2,609
72.99	Total unpaid obligations, start of year	8,363	10,251	10,599
73.10	Total new obligations	26,909	26,303	27,012
73.20	Total outlays (gross)	–24,431	–25,955	–27,025
73.40	Adjustments in expired accounts (net)	–590		
	Unpaid obligations, end of year:			
74.40	Obligated balance, end of year	7,642	7,989	7,976
74.95	From Federal sources: Receivables and unpaid, unfilled orders	2,609	2,609	2,609
74.99	Total unpaid obligations, end of year	10,251	10,599	10,585
	Outlays (gross), detail:			
86.90	Outlays from new discretionary authority	20,980	20,783	22,002
86.93	Outlays from discretionary balances	3,451	5,173	5,023
87.00	Total outlays (gross)	24,431	25,955	27,025
	Offsets:			
	Against gross budget authority and outlays:			
	Offsetting collections (cash) from:			
88.00	Federal sources	–3,322	–3,712	–3,712
88.40	Non-Federal sources	–124		
88.90	Total, offsetting collections (cash)	–3,446	–3,712	–3,712
	Against gross budget authority only:			
88.95	From Federal sources: Change in receivables and unpaid, unfilled orders	4		
88.96	From Federal sources: Adjustment to receivables and unpaid, unfilled orders	–235		
	Net budget authority and outlays:			
89.00	Budget authority	23,290	22,521	23,300
90.00	Outlays	20,986	22,244	23,314

Object Classification (in millions of dollars)

Identification code 17–1804–0–1–051		1999 actual	2000 est.	2001 est.
	Direct obligations:			
	Personnel compensation:			
11.1	Full-time permanent	2,487	2,625	2,590
11.3	Other than full-time permanent	123	112	115
11.5	Other personnel compensation	142	149	149
11.8	Special personal services payments			6
11.9	Total personnel compensation	2,752	2,885	2,859
12.1	Civilian personnel benefits	780	824	826
13.0	Benefits for former personnel	46	42	56
21.0	Travel and transportation of persons	452	391	394
22.0	Transportation of things	257	219	219
23.1	Rental payments to GSA	55	59	29
23.2	Rental payments to others	68	70	70
23.3	Communications, utilities, and miscellaneous charges	404	496	494
24.0	Printing and reproduction	72	70	71
25.1	Advisory and assistance services	198	182	198
25.2	Contracts with the private sector	1,686	1,274	1,396
	Purchases of goods and services from Government accounts:			
25.3	Purchases of goods and services from Government accounts	788	704	695
25.3	Payments to foreign national indirect hire personnel	39	49	49
25.3	Purchases from revolving funds	6,307	6,483	6,376
25.4	Operation and maintenance of facilities	1,088	797	1,293
25.6	Medical care		7	6
25.7	Operation and maintenance of equipment	3,007	3,326	3,263
25.8	Subsistence and support of persons	16	14	14
26.0	Supplies and materials	2,558	2,371	2,441
31.0	Equipment	2,396	2,315	2,541
32.0	Land and structures	263	12	9
99.0	Subtotal, direct obligations	23,233	22,591	23,300
99.0	Reimbursable obligations	3,677	3,712	3,712
99.9	Total new obligations	26,909	26,303	27,012

Personnel Summary

Identification code 17–1804–0–1–051		1999 actual	2000 est.	2001 est.
	Direct:			
1001	Total compensable workyears: Full-time equivalent employment	57,047	57,300	54,155
	Reimbursable:			
2001	Total compensable workyears: Full-time equivalent employment	23,208	21,456	21,033

OPERATION AND MAINTENANCE, MARINE CORPS

For expenses, not otherwise provided for, necessary for the operation and maintenance of the Marine Corps, as authorized by law, [$2,808,354,000] *$2,705,658,000. (Department of Defense Appropriations Act, 2000.)*

Program and Financing (in millions of dollars)

Identification code 17–1106–0–1–051		1999 actual	2000 est.	2001 est.
	Obligations by program activity:			
	Direct program:			
00.01	Operating forces	1,962	2,014	1,995
00.03	Training and recruiting	433	441	433
00.04	Administration and servicewide activities	280	258	278
09.01	Reimbursable program	480	412	412
10.00	Total new obligations	3,155	3,125	3,118
	Budgetary resources available for obligation:			
21.40	Unobligated balance available, start of year		18	
22.00	New budget authority (gross)	3,169	3,099	3,118
22.22	Unobligated balance transferred from DoD other accounts	6	7	
23.90	Total budgetary resources available for obligation	3,175	3,125	3,118

General and special funds—Continued

OPERATION AND MAINTENANCE, MARINE CORPS—Continued

Program and Financing (in millions of dollars)—Continued

Identification code 17–1106–0–1–051		1999 actual	2000 est.	2001 est.
23.95	Total new obligations	−3,155	−3,125	−3,118
23.98	Unobligated balance expiring or withdrawn	−2		
24.40	Unobligated balance available, end of year	18		
	New budget authority (gross), detail:			
	Discretionary:			
40.00	Appropriation	2,563	2,518	2,706
40.15	Appropriation (emergency)	91	229	
40.76	Reduction pursuant to P.L. 106–113		−14	
40.77	Reduction pursuant to P.L. 105–262	−2		
41.00	Transferred to other DoD accounts	−96	−109	
42.00	Transferred from other DoD accounts	133	63	
43.00	Appropriation (total discretionary)	2,689	2,687	2,706
	Spending authority from offsetting collections:			
68.00	Offsetting collections (cash)	483	412	412
68.10	From Federal sources: Change in receivables and unpaid, unfilled orders	30		
68.15	From Federal sources: Adjustments to receivables and unpaid, unfilled orders	−33		
68.90	Spending authority from offsetting collections (total discretionary)	480	412	412
70.00	Total new budget authority (gross)	3,169	3,099	3,118
	Change in unpaid obligations:			
	Unpaid obligations, start of year:			
72.40	Obligated balance, start of year	934	1,055	1,137
72.95	From Federal sources: Receivables and unpaid, unfilled orders	173	203	203
72.99	Total unpaid obligations, start of year	1,108	1,258	1,339
73.10	Total new obligations	3,155	3,125	3,118
73.20	Total outlays (gross)	−2,969	−3,043	−3,104
73.40	Adjustments in expired accounts (net)	−36		
	Unpaid obligations, end of year:			
74.40	Obligated balance, end of year	1,055	1,137	1,150
74.95	From Federal sources: Receivables and unpaid, unfilled orders	203	203	203
74.99	Total unpaid obligations, end of year	1,258	1,339	1,353
	Outlays (gross), detail:			
86.90	Outlays from new discretionary authority	2,260	2,199	2,252
86.93	Outlays from discretionary balances	710	843	852
87.00	Total outlays (gross)	2,969	3,043	3,104
	Offsets:			
	Against gross budget authority and outlays:			
	Offsetting collections (cash) from:			
88.00	Federal sources	−457	−412	−412
88.40	Non-Federal sources	−26		
88.90	Total, offsetting collections (cash)	−483	−412	−412
	Against gross budget authority only:			
88.95	From Federal sources: Change in receivables and unpaid, unfilled orders	−30		
88.96	From Federal sources: Adjustment to receivables and unpaid, unfilled orders	33		
	Net budget authority and outlays:			
89.00	Budget authority	2,689	2,687	2,706
90.00	Outlays	2,486	2,630	2,692

Object Classification (in millions of dollars)

Identification code 17–1106–0–1–051		1999 actual	2000 est.	2001 est.
	Direct obligations:			
	Personnel compensation:			
11.1	Full-time permanent	451	452	452
11.3	Other than full-time permanent	14	12	13
11.5	Other personnel compensation	19	18	18
11.9	Total personnel compensation	484	482	483
12.1	Civilian personnel benefits	136	140	143
13.0	Benefits for former personnel	6		
21.0	Travel and transportation of persons	135	133	134
22.0	Transportation of things	68	69	71
23.1	Rental payments to GSA	2		
23.2	Rental payments to others	30	31	31
23.3	Communications, utilities, and miscellaneous charges	131	139	142
24.0	Printing and reproduction	40	36	40
25.1	Advisory and assistance services	20	24	25
25.2	Other services	131	79	81
	Purchases of goods and services from Government accounts:			
25.3	Purchases of goods and services from Government accounts	54	45	46
25.3	Purchases from revolving funds	267	434	364
25.4	Operation and maintenance of facilities	232	172	319
25.7	Operation and maintenance of equipment	129	125	118
25.8	Subsistence and support of persons	28	47	48
26.0	Supplies and materials	566	510	436
31.0	Equipment	110	155	134
32.0	Land and structures	106	92	91
99.0	Subtotal, direct obligations	2,675	2,713	2,706
99.0	Reimbursable obligations	480	412	412
99.9	Total new obligations	3,155	3,125	3,118

Personnel Summary

Identification code 17–1106–0–1–051		1999 actual	2000 est.	2001 est.
	Direct:			
1001	Total compensable workyears: Full-time equivalent employment	11,449	11,097	10,769
	Reimbursable:			
2001	Total compensable workyears: Full-time equivalent employment	1,520	1,432	1,366

OPERATION AND MAINTENANCE, AIR FORCE

(INCLUDING TRANSFER OF FUNDS)

For expenses, not otherwise provided for, necessary for the operation and maintenance of the Air Force, as authorized by law; and not to exceed [$7,882,000] *$7,878,000* can be used for emergencies and extraordinary expenses, to be expended on the approval or authority of the Secretary of the Air Force, and payments may be made on his certificate of necessity for confidential military purposes, [$20,896,959,000] *$22,297,277,000* and, in addition, [$50,000,000] *$50,000,000,* shall be derived by transfer from the National Defense Stockpile Transaction Fund[: *Provided*, That, notwithstanding any other provision of law, that of the funds available under this heading, $950,000 shall only be available to the Secretary of the Air Force for a grant to Florida Memorial College for the purpose of funding minority aviation training]. *(Department of Defense Appropriations Act, 2000.)*

Program and Financing (in millions of dollars)

Identification code 57–3400–0–1–051		1999 actual	2000 est.	2001 est.
	Obligations by program activity:			
	Direct program:			
00.01	Operating forces	11,404	10,799	11,490
00.02	Mobilization	3,553	2,678	3,160
00.03	Training and recruiting	1,870	2,037	2,242
00.04	Administration and servicewide activities	5,249	5,138	5,455
09.01	Reimbursable program	2,738	2,354	2,291
10.00	Total new obligations	24,814	23,006	24,638
	Budgetary resources available for obligation:			
21.40	Unobligated balance available, start of year	1	34	
22.00	New budget authority (gross)	24,836	22,812	24,638
22.22	Unobligated balance transferred from other DoD accounts	48	161	
23.90	Total budgetary resources available for obligation	24,885	23,006	24,638
23.95	Total new obligations	−24,814	−23,006	−24,638
23.98	Unobligated balance expiring or withdrawn	−37		
24.40	Unobligated balance available, end of year	34		
	New budget authority (gross), detail:			
	Discretionary:			
40.00	Appropriation	18,721	18,707	22,297

40.15	Appropriation (emergency)	417	1,707	
40.74	Reduction pursuant to P.L. 106–79		−13	
40.76	Reduction pursuant to P.L. 106–113		−105	
40.77	Reduction pursuant to P.L. 105–262	−20		
41.00	Transferred to other accounts	−434	−324	
42.00	Transferred from other DoD accounts	3,366	436	
43.00	Appropriation (total discretionary)	22,050	20,408	22,297
	Spending authority from offsetting collections:			
68.00	Offsetting collections (cash)	2,918	2,354	2,291
68.10	From Federal sources: Change in receivables and unpaid, unfilled orders	−217		
68.15	From Federal sources: Adjustments to receivables and unpaid, unfilled orders	35		
68.62	Transferred from National Defense Stockpile	50	50	50
68.90	Spending authority from offsetting collections (total discretionary)	2,786	2,404	2,341
70.00	Total new budget authority (gross)	24,836	22,812	24,638
	Change in unpaid obligations:			
	Unpaid obligations, start of year:			
72.40	Obligated balance, start of year	6,599	7,737	8,125
72.95	From Federal sources: Receivables and unpaid, unfilled orders	746	529	529
72.99	Total unpaid obligations, start of year	7,345	8,265	8,654
73.10	Total new obligations	24,814	23,006	24,638
73.20	Total outlays (gross)	−23,597	−22,617	−24,904
73.40	Adjustments in expired accounts (net)	−296		
	Unpaid obligations, end of year:			
74.40	Obligated balance, end of year	7,737	8,125	7,860
74.95	From Federal sources: Receivables and unpaid, unfilled orders	529	529	529
74.99	Total unpaid obligations, end of year	8,265	8,654	8,389
	Outlays (gross), detail:			
86.90	Outlays from new discretionary authority	18,834	16,900	19,163
86.93	Outlays from discretionary balances	4,763	5,718	5,741
87.00	Total outlays (gross)	23,597	22,617	24,904
	Offsets:			
	Against gross budget authority and outlays:			
	Offsetting collections (cash) from:			
88.00	Federal sources	−2,803	−2,252	−2,197
88.40	Non-Federal sources	−115	−102	−94
88.90	Total, offsetting collections (cash)	−2,918	−2,354	−2,291
	Against gross budget authority only:			
88.95	From Federal sources: Change in receivables and unpaid, unfilled orders	217		
88.96	From Federal sources: Adjustment to receivables and unpaid, unfilled orders	−35		
	Net budget authority and outlays:			
89.00	Budget authority	22,101	20,458	22,347
90.00	Outlays	20,679	20,263	22,613

Object Classification (in millions of dollars)

Identification code 57–3400–0–1–051		1999 actual	2000 est.	2001 est.
	Direct obligations:			
	Personnel compensation:			
11.1	Full-time permanent	2,652	2,840	2,820
11.3	Other than full-time permanent	328	349	349
11.5	Other personnel compensation	162	141	140
11.9	Total personnel compensation	3,142	3,330	3,309
12.1	Civilian personnel benefits	737	793	800
13.0	Benefits for former personnel	31	108	180
21.0	Travel and transportation of persons	813	471	558
22.0	Transportation of things	419	268	360
23.1	Rental payments to GSA	13	17	13
23.2	Rental payments to others	38	46	46
23.3	Communications, utilities, and miscellaneous charges	715	756	759
24.0	Printing and reproduction	37	39	40
25.1	Advisory and assistance services	277	270	272
25.2	Contracts with the private sector	2,160	1,464	1,692
	Purchases of goods and services from Government accounts:			
25.3	Purchases of goods and services from Government accounts	338	710	634
25.3	Payments to foreign national indirect hire personnel	78	87	84
25.3	Purchases from revolving funds	3,351	2,902	3,376
25.4	Operation and maintenance of facilities	2,507	1,935	2,334
25.7	Operation and maintenance of equipment	2,238	2,556	3,242
26.0	Supplies and materials	4,601	4,453	4,120
31.0	Equipment	478	304	377
32.0	Land and structures		43	42
41.0	Grants, subsidies, and contributions	1		1
42.0	Insurance claims and indemnities	95	99	107
43.0	Interest and dividends	7	1	1
99.0	Subtotal, direct obligations	22,076	20,652	22,347
99.0	Reimbursable obligations	2,738	2,354	2,291
99.9	Total new obligations	24,814	23,006	24,638

Personnel Summary

Identification code 57–3400–0–1–051		1999 actual	2000 est.	2001 est.
	Direct:			
1001	Total compensable workyears: Full-time equivalent employment	72,585	73,452	71,910
	Reimbursable:			
2001	Total compensable workyears: Full-time equivalent employment	14,293	10,819	10,654

Operation and Maintenance, Defense-Wide

For expenses, not otherwise provided for, necessary for the operation and maintenance of activities and agencies of the Department of Defense (other than the military departments), as authorized by law, [$11,489,483,000] *$11,920,069,000*, of which not to exceed $25,000,000 may be available for the CINC initiative fund account; and of which not to exceed [$32,300,000] *$32,700,000* can be used for emergencies and extraordinary expenses, to be expended on the approval or authority of the Secretary of Defense, and payments may be made on his certificate of necessity for confidential military purposes[: *Provided*, That of the amount appropriated under the heading "Operation and Maintenance, Defense-Wide" in division B, title I, of Public Law 105–277, the amount of $202,000,000 not covered as of July 12, 1999, by an official budget request under the fifth proviso of that section is available, subject to such an official budget request for that entire amount, only for the following accounts in the specified amounts:

"Other Procurement, Air Force", $102,000,000; and

"Procurement, Defense-Wide", $100,000,000:

Provided further, That none of the amount of $202,000,000 described in the preceding proviso may be made available for obligation unless the entire amount is released to the Department of Defense and made available for obligation for the accounts, and in the amounts, specified in the preceding proviso: *Provided further*, That of the amounts provided under this heading, $20,000,000 to remain available until expended, is available only for expenses relating to certain classified activities, and may be transferred as necessary by the Secretary of Defense to operation and maintenance, procurement, and research, development, test and evaluation appropriations accounts, to be merged with and to be available for the same time period as the appropriations to which transferred: *Provided further*, That the transfer authority provided under this heading is in addition to any other transfer authority provided in this Act: *Provided further*, That of the funds made available under this heading, $10,000,000 shall be available only for retrofitting security containers that are under the control of, or that are accessible by, defense contractors.] *(Department of Defense Appropriations Act, 2000.)*

Program and Financing (in millions of dollars)

Identification code 97–0100–0–1–051		1999 actual	2000 est.	2001 est.
	Obligations by program activity:			
	Direct program:			
	Operating Forces:			
00.01	The Joint Staff	442	376	396
00.02	Special Operations Command	1,251	1,205	1,264
	Mobilization:			
00.06	Defense Logistics Agency	35	35	46
	Training and Recruiting:			
00.14	Defense Threat Reduction Agency	1	1	1
00.15	Defense Finance and Accounting Service		17	15

General and special funds—Continued

OPERATION AND MAINTENANCE, DEFENSE-WIDE—Continued

Program and Financing (in millions of dollars)—Continued

Identification code 97–0100–0–1–051		1999 actual	2000 est.	2001 est.
00.16	Defense Acquisition University	95	101	100
00.17	Armed Forces Information Services	9	11	11
00.18	Special Operations Command	34	49	49
00.19	Defense Security Service	8	7	7
00.20	DoD Human Resources Activity	28	60	78
	Administration and Servicewide Activities:			
00.21	Armed Forces Information Services	98	93	95
00.22	Department of Defense Dependents Education	1,406	1,425	1,434
00.23	Defense POW/MIA Office	14	14	15
00.25	Intelligence and communications activities	4,843	4,912	4,962
00.27	Defense Contract Audit Agency	310	329	349
00.28	Defense Logistics Agency	1,200	1,206	1,143
00.29	Secretary of Defense	462	475	417
00.31	Washington Headquarters Services	214	248	299
00.33	Defense Human Resources Activity	184	164	185
00.34	Defense Legal Services Agency	9	11	13
00.35	Office of Economic Adjustment	34	76	22
00.36	Defense Security Service	77	128	127
00.43	The Joint Staff	129	132	158
00.45	Special Operations Command	45	42	44
00.46	Defense Finance and Accounting Service	96	27	1
00.48	Civil Military Program	75	91	88
00.49	Defense Security Cooperation Agency	49	62	68
00.50	Defense Threat Reduction and Treaty Compliance Agency	232	186	216
00.51	FY 1999 Supplemental		297	
00.52	Other Defense Agencies			200
00.53	Special Activities		75	115
09.01	Reimbursable program	648	823	831
10.00	Total new obligations	12,028	12,680	12,749
	Budgetary resources available for obligation:			
21.40	Unobligated balance available, start of year	10	22	
22.00	New budget authority (gross)	12,101	12,655	12,751
22.21	Unobligated balance transferred to other DoD Accounts	−7		
22.22	Unobligated balance transferred from other DoD accounts	13	2	
23.90	Total budgetary resources available for obligation	12,117	12,680	12,751
23.95	Total new obligations	−12,028	−12,680	−12,749
23.98	Unobligated balance expiring or withdrawn	−66		
24.40	Unobligated balance available, end of year	22		
	New budget authority (gross), detail:			
	Discretionary:			
40.00	Appropriation	10,818	10,545	11,920
40.15	Appropriation (emergency)	1,876	939	
40.60	Contingent emergency appropriation not available for obligations	−559		
40.65	Contingent emergency appropriation released		559	
40.76	Reduction pursuant to P.L. 106–113		−59	
40.77	Reduction pursuant to P.L. 105–262	−13		
41.00	Transferred to other DoD accounts	−1,398	−219	
42.00	Transferred from other DoD accounts	729	66	
43.00	Appropriation (total discretionary)	11,453	11,832	11,920
	Spending authority from offsetting collections:			
68.00	Offsetting collections (cash)	264	824	831
68.10	From Federal sources: Change in receivables and unpaid, unfilled orders	349		
68.15	From Federal sources: Adjustments to receivables and unpaid, unfilled orders	35		
68.90	Spending authority from offsetting collections (total discretionary)	648	824	831
70.00	Total new budget authority (gross)	12,101	12,655	12,751
	Change in unpaid obligations:			
	Unpaid obligations, start of year:			
72.40	Obligated balance, start of year	4,019	4,321	4,628
72.95	From Federal sources: Receivables and unpaid, unfilled orders	756	1,105	1,105
72.99	Total unpaid obligations, start of year	4,775	5,426	5,733
73.10	Total new obligations	12,028	12,680	12,749
73.20	Total outlays (gross)	−11,021	−12,373	−12,751
73.40	Adjustments in expired accounts (net)	−356		
	Unpaid obligations, end of year:			
74.40	Obligated balance, end of year	4,321	4,628	4,626
74.95	From Federal sources: Receivables and unpaid, unfilled orders	1,105	1,105	1,105
74.99	Total unpaid obligations, end of year	5,426	5,733	5,731
	Outlays (gross), detail:			
86.90	Outlays from new discretionary authority	8,618	9,438	9,662
86.93	Outlays from discretionary balances	2,402	2,935	3,089
87.00	Total outlays (gross)	11,021	12,373	12,751
	Offsets:			
	Against gross budget authority and outlays:			
	Offsetting collections (cash) from:			
88.00	Federal sources	−116	−680	−691
88.40	Non-Federal sources	−148	−144	−140
88.90	Total, offsetting collections (cash)	−264	−824	−831
	Against gross budget authority only:			
88.95	From Federal sources: Change in receivables and unpaid, unfilled orders	−349		
88.96	From Federal sources: Adjustment to receivables and unpaid, unfilled orders	−35		
	Net budget authority and outlays:			
89.00	Budget authority	11,453	11,832	11,920
90.00	Outlays	10,757	11,549	11,920

Summary of Budget Authority and Outlays

(in millions of dollars)

	1999 actual	2000 est.	2001 est.
Enacted/requested:			
Budget Authority	11,453	11,832	11,920
Outlays	10,756	11,549	11,920
Supplemental proposal:			
Budget Authority		24	
Outlays		18	5
Total:			
Budget Authority	11,453	11,856	11,920
Outlays	10,756	11,567	11,925

Object Classification (in millions of dollars)

Identification code 97–0100–0–1–051		1999 actual	2000 est.	2001 est.
	Direct obligations:			
	Personnel compensation:			
11.1	Full-time permanent	2,345	2,434	2,533
11.3	Other than full-time permanent	116	109	109
11.5	Other personnel compensation	59	57	60
11.9	Total personnel compensation	2,520	2,600	2,702
12.1	Civilian personnel benefits	599	663	680
13.0	Benefits for former personnel	11	9	10
21.0	Travel and transportation of persons	439	495	508
22.0	Transportation of things	492	455	479
23.1	Rental payments to GSA	83	78	84
23.2	Rental payments to others	94	125	157
23.3	Communications, utilities, and miscellaneous charges	288	335	333
24.0	Printing and reproduction	30	35	34
25.1	Advisory and assistance services	292	410	368
25.2	Other services	2,458	1,771	1,789
	Purchases of goods and services from Government accounts:			
25.3	Purchases of goods and services from Government accounts	2,065	2,211	2,370
25.3	Payments to foreign national indirect hire personnel	18	19	20
25.3	Purchases from revolving funds	54	63	59
25.4	Operation and maintenance of facilities	237	190	167
25.7	Operation and maintenance of equipment	628	804	881
25.8	Subsistence and support of persons	2	1	1
26.0	Supplies and materials	645	919	763
31.0	Equipment	332	520	464
32.0	Land and structures	20	19	19
41.0	Grants, subsidies, and contributions	64	121	17
91.0	Unvouchered	9	14	15
99.0	Subtotal, direct obligations	11,380	11,856	11,920
99.0	Reimbursable obligations	648	823	829
99.9	Total new obligations	12,028	12,680	12,749

This table reflects the reduction in the balances of contingent emergency funding resulting from proposed supplemental action. These balances are available for obligation only after the President designates them to the Congress as an emergency requirement, in accordance with the Balanced Budget and Emergency Control Act of 1985, as amended.

Personnel Summary

Identification code 97–0100–0–1–051	1999 actual	2000 est.	2001 est.
Direct:			
1001 Total compensable workyears: Full-time equivalent employment	44,333	44,566	44,431
Reimbursable:			
2001 Total compensable workyears: Full-time equivalent employment	3,270	3,191	3,051

OFFICE OF THE INSPECTOR GENERAL

For expenses and activities of the Office of the Inspector General in carrying out the provisions of the Inspector General Act of 1978, as amended, [$137,544,000] *$147,545,000*, of which [$136,244,000] *$144,245,000* shall be for Operation and maintenance, of which not to exceed $700,000 is available for emergencies and extraordinary expenses to be expended on the approval or authority of the Inspector General, and payments may be made on the Inspector General's certificate of necessity for confidential military purposes; and of which [$1,300,000] *$3,300,000* to remain available until September 30, [2002] *2003*, shall be for Procurement. *(Department of Defense Appropriations Act, 2000.)*

Program and Financing (in millions of dollars)

Identification code 97–0107–0–1–051	1999 actual	2000 est.	2001 est.
Obligations by program activity:			
00.01 Operation and Maintenance	131	135	144
00.02 Procurement	1	1	3
10.00 Total new obligations	132	137	148
Budgetary resources available for obligation:			
22.00 New budget authority (gross)	132	137	148
23.95 Total new obligations	–132	–137	–148
23.98 Unobligated balance expiring or withdrawn	–1		
New budget authority (gross), detail:			
Discretionary:			
40.00 Appropriation	132	138	148
40.76 Reduction pursuant to P.L. 106–113		–1	
43.00 Appropriation (total discretionary)	132	137	148
Spending authority from offsetting collections:			
68.10 From Federal sources: Change in receivables and unpaid, unfilled orders	1		
68.15 From Federal sources: Adjustments to receivables and unpaid, unfilled orders	–1		
68.90 Spending authority from offsetting collections (total discretionary)			
70.00 Total new budget authority (gross)	132	137	148
Change in unpaid obligations:			
Unpaid obligations, start of year:			
72.40 Obligated balance, start of year	29	23	23
72.95 From Federal sources: Receivables and unpaid, unfilled orders		1	1
72.99 Total unpaid obligations, start of year	30	23	24
73.10 Total new obligations	132	137	148
73.20 Total outlays (gross)	–134	–137	–147
73.40 Adjustments in expired accounts (net)	–5		
Unpaid obligations, end of year:			
74.40 Obligated balance, end of year	23	23	25
74.95 From Federal sources: Receivables and unpaid, unfilled orders	1	1	1
74.99 Total unpaid obligations, end of year	23	24	26
Outlays (gross), detail:			
86.90 Outlays from new discretionary authority	117	121	130
86.93 Outlays from discretionary balances	17	16	16
87.00 Total outlays (gross)	134	137	147
Offsets:			
Against gross budget authority only:			
88.95 From Federal sources: Change in receivables and unpaid, unfilled orders	–1		
88.96 From Federal sources: Adjustment to receivables and unpaid, unfilled orders	1		
Net budget authority and outlays:			
89.00 Budget authority	132	137	148
90.00 Outlays	134	136	147

Object Classification (in millions of dollars)

Identification code 97–0107–0–1–051	1999 actual	2000 est.	2001 est.
Personnel compensation:			
11.1 Full-time permanent	75	78	82
11.5 Other personnel compensation	7	7	7
11.9 Total personnel compensation	82	85	89
12.1 Civilian personnel benefits	20	22	23
13.0 Benefits for former personnel	1		
21.0 Travel and transportation of persons	6	6	6
23.1 Rental payments to GSA	10	10	10
23.3 Communications, utilities, and miscellaneous charges	2	2	2
25.2 Other services	1	1	1
Purchases of goods and services from Government accounts:			
25.3 Purchases of goods and services from other Federal agencies	2	2	2
25.3 Purchases from revolving funds	1	1	1
25.7 Operation and maintenance of equipment	1	2	4
26.0 Supplies and materials	3	2	2
31.0 Equipment	3	2	6
91.0 Unvouchered		1	1
99.0 Subtotal, direct obligations	132	136	147
99.5 Below reporting threshold		1	1
99.9 Total new obligations	132	137	148

Personnel Summary

Identification code 97–0107–0–1–051	1999 actual	2000 est.	2001 est.
Direct:			
1001 Total compensable workyears: Full-time equivalent employment	1,188	1,209	1,210
Reimbursable:			
2001 Total compensable workyears: Full-time equivalent employment	2	3	2

OPERATION AND MAINTENANCE, ARMY RESERVE

For expenses, not otherwise provided for, necessary for the operation and maintenance, including training, organization, and administration, of the Army Reserve; repair of facilities and equipment; hire of passenger motor vehicles; travel and transportation; care of the dead; recruiting; procurement of services, supplies, and equipment; and communications, [$1,469,176,000] *$1,521,418,000. (10 U.S.C. 1481–88, 3013–14, 3062, 4302, 4411–14, 4741; 37 U.S.C. 404; Department of Defense Appropriations Act, 2000.)*

Program and Financing (in millions of dollars)

Identification code 21–2080–0–1–051	1999 actual	2000 est.	2001 est.
Obligations by program activity:			
Direct program:			
00.01 Operating forces	1,072	1,296	1,353
00.04 Administration and servicewide activities	174	174	168
09.01 Reimbursable program	68	68	72
10.00 Total new obligations	1,314	1,539	1,594
Budgetary resources available for obligation:			
21.40 Unobligated balance available, start of year		9	
22.00 New budget authority (gross)	1,327	1,529	1,593
23.90 Total budgetary resources available for obligation	1,327	1,539	1,594

General and special funds—Continued

OPERATION AND MAINTENANCE, ARMY RESERVE—Continued

Program and Financing (in millions of dollars)—Continued

Identification code 21–2080–0–1–051		1999 actual	2000 est.	2001 est.
23.95	Total new obligations	–1,314	–1,539	–1,594
23.98	Unobligated balance expiring or withdrawn	–4		
24.40	Unobligated balance available, end of year	9		
	New budget authority (gross), detail:			
	Discretionary:			
40.00	Appropriation	1,199	1,349	1,521
40.15	Appropriation (emergency)	33	120	
40.76	Reduction pursuant to P.L. 106–113		–8	
40.77	Reduction pursuant to P.L. 105–262	–1		
42.00	Transferred from other DoD accounts	28		
43.00	Appropriation (total discretionary)	1,259	1,462	1,521
	Spending authority from offsetting collections:			
68.00	Offsetting collections (cash)	62	68	72
68.10	From Federal sources: Change in receivables and unpaid, unfilled orders	6		
68.90	Spending authority from offsetting collections (total discretionary)	68	68	72
70.00	Total new budget authority (gross)	1,327	1,529	1,593
	Change in unpaid obligations:			
	Unpaid obligations, start of year:			
72.40	Obligated balance, start of year	448	415	484
72.95	From Federal sources: Receivables and unpaid, unfilled orders	29	35	35
72.99	Total unpaid obligations, start of year	477	450	519
73.10	Total new obligations	1,314	1,539	1,594
73.20	Total outlays (gross)	–1,320	–1,470	–1,560
73.40	Adjustments in expired accounts (net)	–21		
	Unpaid obligations, end of year:			
74.40	Obligated balance, end of year	415	484	518
74.95	From Federal sources: Receivables and unpaid, unfilled orders	35	35	35
74.99	Total unpaid obligations, end of year	450	519	553
	Outlays (gross), detail:			
86.90	Outlays from new discretionary authority	982	1,113	1,160
86.93	Outlays from discretionary balances	338	356	400
87.00	Total outlays (gross)	1,320	1,470	1,560
	Offsets:			
	Against gross budget authority and outlays:			
	Offsetting collections (cash) from:			
88.00	Federal sources	–59	–68	–72
88.40	Non-Federal sources	–3		
88.90	Total, offsetting collections (cash)	–62	–68	–72
	Against gross budget authority only:			
88.95	From Federal sources: Change in receivables and unpaid, unfilled orders	–6		
	Net budget authority and outlays:			
89.00	Budget authority	1,258	1,462	1,521
90.00	Outlays	1,258	1,401	1,488

Object Classification (in millions of dollars)

Identification code 21–2080–0–1–051		1999 actual	2000 est.	2001 est.
	Direct obligations:			
	Personnel compensation:			
11.1	Full-time permanent	376	370	372
11.3	Other than full-time permanent	8	10	10
11.5	Other personnel compensation	11	9	9
11.9	Total personnel compensation	395	389	391
12.1	Civilian personnel benefits	103	104	102
13.0	Benefits for former personnel	3	6	5
21.0	Travel and transportation of persons	79	92	87
22.0	Transportation of things	11	17	18
23.1	Rental payments to GSA	8	8	8
23.3	Communications, utilities, and miscellaneous charges	71	78	69
24.0	Printing and reproduction	8	10	10
25.1	Advisory and assistance services	2	12	13
25.2	Other services	99	62	65
	Purchases of goods and services from Government accounts:			
25.3	Purchases of goods and services from other Federal agencies	79	81	84
25.3	Purchases from revolving funds	48	75	86
25.4	Operation and maintenance of facilities	29	75	99
25.7	Operation and maintenance of equipment	9	10	11
25.8	Subsistence and support of persons	129	186	198
26.0	Supplies and materials	131	189	241
31.0	Equipment	41	45	33
32.0	Land and structures	1	32	2
99.0	Subtotal, direct obligations	1,246	1,470	1,522
99.0	Reimbursable obligations	68	68	72
99.9	Total new obligations	1,314	1,539	1,594

Personnel Summary

Identification code 21–2080–0–1–051		1999 actual	2000 est.	2001 est.
	Direct:			
1001	Total compensable workyears: Full-time equivalent employment	10,383	10,186	9,861
	Reimbursable:			
2001	Total compensable workyears: Full-time equivalent employment	218	254	307

OPERATION AND MAINTENANCE, NAVY RESERVE

For expenses, not otherwise provided for, necessary for the operation and maintenance, including training, organization, and administration, of the Navy Reserve; repair of facilities and equipment; hire of passenger motor vehicles; travel and transportation; care of the dead; recruiting; procurement of services, supplies, and equipment; and communications, [$958,978,000] *$960,946,000. (10 U.S.C. 262, 503, 1481–88, 2110, 2202, 2631–34, 5013, 5062, 5251, 6022, 18233a; Department of Defense Appropriations Act, 2000.)*

Program and Financing (in millions of dollars)

Identification code 17–1806–0–1–051		1999 actual	2000 est.	2001 est.
	Obligations by program activity:			
	Direct program:			
00.01	Operating forces	866	825	855
00.04	Administration and servicewide activities	104	139	106
09.01	Reimbursable program	77	73	74
10.00	Total new obligations	1,047	1,037	1,035
	Budgetary resources available for obligation:			
21.40	Unobligated balance available, start of year		9	
22.00	New budget authority (gross)	1,058	1,027	1,035
22.22	Unobligated balance transferred from other DoD accounts		1	
23.90	Total budgetary resources available for obligation	1,058	1,037	1,035
23.95	Total new obligations	–1,047	–1,037	–1,035
23.98	Unobligated balance expiring or withdrawn	–3		
24.40	Unobligated balance available, end of year	9		
	New budget authority (gross), detail:			
	Discretionary:			
40.00	Appropriation	947	881	961
40.15	Appropriation (emergency)	13	78	
40.76	Reduction pursuant to P.L. 106–113		–5	
40.77	Reduction pursuant to P.L. 105–262	–1		
42.00	Transferred from other DoD accounts	23		
43.00	Appropriation (total discretionary)	982	954	961
	Spending authority from offsetting collections:			
68.00	Offsetting collections (cash)	59	73	74
68.10	From Federal sources: Change in receivables and unpaid, unfilled orders	16		
68.15	From Federal sources: Adjustments to receivables and unpaid, unfilled orders	1		
68.90	Spending authority from offsetting collections (total discretionary)	76	73	74

70.00	Total new budget authority (gross)	1,058	1,027	1,035
	Change in unpaid obligations:			
	Unpaid obligations, start of year:			
72.40	Obligated balance, start of year	440	387	402
72.95	From Federal sources: Receivables and unpaid, unfilled orders	28	44	44
72.99	Total unpaid obligations, start of year	468	431	446
73.10	Total new obligations	1,047	1,037	1,035
73.20	Total outlays (gross)	−1,040	−1,022	−1,032
73.40	Adjustments in expired accounts (net)	−44		
	Unpaid obligations, end of year:			
74.40	Obligated balance, end of year	387	402	405
74.95	From Federal sources: Receivables and unpaid, unfilled orders	44	44	44
74.99	Total unpaid obligations, end of year	431	446	449
	Outlays (gross), detail:			
86.90	Outlays from new discretionary authority	731	716	727
86.93	Outlays from discretionary balances	308	306	304
87.00	Total outlays (gross)	1,040	1,022	1,032
	Offsets:			
	Against gross budget authority and outlays:			
	Offsetting collections (cash) from:			
88.00	Federal sources	−58	−73	−74
88.40	Non-Federal sources	−1		
88.90	Total, offsetting collections (cash)	−59	−73	−74
	Against gross budget authority only:			
88.95	From Federal sources: Change in receivables and unpaid, unfilled orders	−16		
88.96	From Federal sources: Adjustment to receivables and unpaid, unfilled orders	−1		
	Net budget authority and outlays:			
89.00	Budget authority	982	954	961
90.00	Outlays	980	949	958

Object Classification (in millions of dollars)

Identification code 17–1806–0–1–051		1999 actual	2000 est.	2001 est.
	Direct obligations:			
	Personnel compensation:			
11.1	Full-time permanent	69	74	72
11.3	Other than full-time permanent	1	1	1
11.5	Other personnel compensation	4	4	3
11.9	Total personnel compensation	74	79	76
12.1	Civilian personnel benefits	19	20	20
13.0	Benefits for former personnel	2	1	
21.0	Travel and transportation of persons	28	28	28
22.0	Transportation of things	1	1	1
23.1	Rental payments to GSA	1		
23.2	Rental payments to others	7	7	3
23.3	Communications, utilities, and miscellaneous charges	22	32	29
24.0	Printing and reproduction	1	1	2
25.1	Advisory and assistance services	1	1	1
25.2	Other services	66	58	46
	Purchases of goods and services from Government accounts:			
25.3	Purchases of goods and services from Government accounts	60	48	50
25.3	Purchases from revolving funds	88	77	78
25.4	Operation and maintenance of facilities	30	26	67
25.6	Medical care	1	1	1
25.7	Operation and maintenance of equipment	196	206	185
26.0	Supplies and materials	219	242	224
31.0	Equipment	150	133	147
32.0	Land and structures	4	3	3
99.0	Subtotal, direct obligations	970	964	961
99.0	Reimbursable obligations	77	73	74
99.9	Total new obligations	1,047	1,037	1,035

Personnel Summary

Identification code 17–1806–0–1–051		1999 actual	2000 est.	2001 est.
	Direct:			
1001	Total compensable workyears: Full-time equivalent employment	1,927	1,917	1,796
	Reimbursable:			
2001	Total compensable workyears: Full-time equivalent employment	126	49	43

OPERATION AND MAINTENANCE, MARINE CORPS RESERVE

For expenses, not otherwise provided for, necessary for the operation and maintenance, including training, organization, and administration, of the Marine Corps Reserve; repair of facilities and equipment; hire of passenger motor vehicles; travel and transportation; care of the dead; recruiting; procurement of services, supplies, and equipment; and communications, [$138,911,000] *$133,959,000. (10 U.S.C. 503, 1481–88, 2110, 2202, 2631–34, 5013, 5062, 5252, 6022, 18233a; Department of Defense Appropriations Act, 2000.)*

Program and Financing (in millions of dollars)

Identification code 17–1107–0–1–051		1999 actual	2000 est.	2001 est.
	Obligations by program activity:			
	Direct program:			
00.01	Operating forces	94	102	99
00.04	Administration and servicewide activities	33	37	35
09.01	Reimbursable program	4	5	5
10.00	Total new obligations	131	143	139
	Budgetary resources available for obligation:			
22.00	New budget authority (gross)	131	143	139
23.95	Total new obligations	−131	−143	−139
	New budget authority (gross), detail:			
	Discretionary:			
40.00	Appropriation	118	128	134
40.15	Appropriation (emergency)	3	11	
40.76	Reduction pursuant to P.L. 106–113		−1	
41.00	Transferred to other DoD accounts	−2		
42.00	Transferred from other DoD accounts	8		
43.00	Appropriation (total discretionary)	127	138	134
	Spending authority from offsetting collections:			
68.00	Offsetting collections (cash)	7	5	5
68.10	From Federal sources: Change in receivables and unpaid, unfilled orders	−5		
68.15	From Federal sources: Adjustments to receivables and unpaid, unfilled orders	2		
68.90	Spending authority from offsetting collections (total discretionary)	4	5	5
70.00	Total new budget authority (gross)	131	143	139
	Change in unpaid obligations:			
	Unpaid obligations, start of year:			
72.40	Obligated balance, start of year	67	69	64
72.95	From Federal sources: Receivables and unpaid, unfilled orders	4	−1	−1
72.99	Total unpaid obligations, start of year	71	69	63
73.10	Total new obligations	131	143	139
73.20	Total outlays (gross)	−128	−148	−136
73.40	Adjustments in expired accounts (net)	−5		
	Unpaid obligations, end of year:			
74.40	Obligated balance, end of year	69	64	67
74.95	From Federal sources: Receivables and unpaid, unfilled orders	−1	−1	−1
74.99	Total unpaid obligations, end of year	69	63	66
	Outlays (gross), detail:			
86.90	Outlays from new discretionary authority	82	94	89
86.93	Outlays from discretionary balances	46	54	47
87.00	Total outlays (gross)	128	148	136
	Offsets:			
	Against gross budget authority and outlays:			
88.00	Offsetting collections (cash) from: Federal sources	−7	−5	−5

General and special funds—Continued

OPERATION AND MAINTENANCE, MARINE CORPS RESERVE—Continued

Program and Financing (in millions of dollars)—Continued

Identification code 17–1107–0–1–051	1999 actual	2000 est.	2001 est.
Against gross budget authority only:			
88.95 From Federal sources: Change in receivables and unpaid, unfilled orders	5	....	....
88.96 From Federal sources: Adjustment to receivables and unpaid, unfilled orders	–2	....	....
Net budget authority and outlays:			
89.00 Budget authority	127	138	134
90.00 Outlays	121	144	131

Object Classification (in millions of dollars)

Identification code 17–1107–0–1–051	1999 actual	2000 est.	2001 est.
Direct obligations:			
11.1 Personnel compensation: Full-time permanent	6	6	6
12.1 Civilian personnel benefits	1	1	1
21.0 Travel and transportation of persons	15	16	14
22.0 Transportation of things	5	4	4
23.3 Communications, utilities, and miscellaneous charges	13	11	11
24.0 Printing and reproduction	1	1	1
25.1 Advisory and assistance services	3	3	3
25.2 Other services	5	7	7
25.3 Purchases from revolving funds	18	24	24
25.4 Operation and maintenance of facilities	8	9	9
25.7 Operation and maintenance of equipment	17	19	17
26.0 Supplies and materials	29	34	34
31.0 Equipment	6	3	3
99.0 Subtotal, direct obligations	127	138	134
99.0 Reimbursable obligations	4	5	5
99.9 Total new obligations	131	143	139

Personnel Summary

Identification code 17–1107–0–1–051	1999 actual	2000 est.	2001 est.
1001 Total compensable workyears: Full-time equivalent employment	152	160	157

OPERATION AND MAINTENANCE, AIR FORCE RESERVE

For expenses, not otherwise provided for, necessary for the operation and maintenance, including training, organization, and administration, of the Air Force Reserve; repair of facilities and equipment; hire of passenger motor vehicles; travel and transportation; care of the dead; recruiting; procurement of services, supplies, and equipment; and communications, [$1,782,591,000] *$1,885,859,000. (10 U.S.C. 264, 510–11, 1124, 1481–88, 2232–37, 8013, 8541–42, 8721–23, 9301–04, 9315, 9411–14, 9531, 9536, 9561–63, 9593, 9741, 9743, 18233a; 37 U.S.C. 404–11; Department of Defense Appropriations Act, 2000.)*

Program and Financing (in millions of dollars)

Identification code 57–3740–0–1–051	1999 actual	2000 est.	2001 est.
Obligations by program activity:			
Direct program:			
00.01 Operating forces	1,682	1,685	1,800
00.04 Administration and servicewide activities	97	89	86
09.01 Reimbursable program	80	51	51
10.00 Total new obligations	1,859	1,825	1,937
Budgetary resources available for obligation:			
22.00 New budget authority (gross)	1,870	1,825	1,937
23.95 Total new obligations	–1,859	–1,825	–1,937
23.98 Unobligated balance expiring or withdrawn	–11	....	....
New budget authority (gross), detail:			
Discretionary:			
40.00 Appropriation	1,734	1,637	1,886
40.15 Appropriation (emergency)	9	145	....
40.76 Reduction pursuant to P.L. 106–113	....	–9	....
40.77 Reduction pursuant to P.L. 105–262	–2	....	....
42.00 Transferred from other DoD accounts	49	....	....
43.00 Appropriation (total discretionary)	1,790	1,773	1,886
Spending authority from offsetting collections:			
68.00 Offsetting collections (cash)	77	51	51
68.10 From Federal sources: Change in receivables and unpaid, unfilled orders	4	....	....
68.15 From Federal sources: Adjustments to receivables and unpaid, unfilled orders	–1	....	....
68.90 Spending authority from offsetting collections (total discretionary)	80	51	51
70.00 Total new budget authority (gross)	1,870	1,824	1,937
Change in unpaid obligations:			
Unpaid obligations, start of year:			
72.40 Obligated balance, start of year	352	470	430
72.95 From Federal sources: Receivables and unpaid, unfilled orders	17	21	21
72.99 Total unpaid obligations, start of year	369	491	450
73.10 Total new obligations	1,859	1,825	1,937
73.20 Total outlays (gross)	–1,722	–1,865	–1,919
73.40 Adjustments in expired accounts (net)	–15	....	....
Unpaid obligations, end of year:			
74.40 Obligated balance, end of year	470	430	446
74.95 From Federal sources: Receivables and unpaid, unfilled orders	21	21	21
74.99 Total unpaid obligations, end of year	491	450	467
Outlays (gross), detail:			
86.90 Outlays from new discretionary authority	1,456	1,452	1,575
86.93 Outlays from discretionary balances	266	413	345
87.00 Total outlays (gross)	1,722	1,865	1,919
Offsets:			
Against gross budget authority and outlays:			
Offsetting collections (cash) from:			
88.00 Federal sources	–76	–51	–51
88.40 Non-Federal sources	–1	....	....
88.90 Total, offsetting collections (cash)	–77	–51	–51
Against gross budget authority only:			
88.95 From Federal sources: Change in receivables and unpaid, unfilled orders	–4	....	....
88.96 From Federal sources: Adjustment to receivables and unpaid, unfilled orders	1	....	....
Net budget authority and outlays:			
89.00 Budget authority	1,790	1,773	1,886
90.00 Outlays	1,645	1,814	1,868

Object Classification (in millions of dollars)

Identification code 57–3740–0–1–051	1999 actual	2000 est.	2001 est.
Direct obligations:			
11.1 Personnel compensation: Full-time permanent	758	846	920
21.0 Travel and transportation of persons	19	19	19
22.0 Transportation of things	1	3	3
23.2 Rental payments to others	14	17	17
23.3 Communications, utilities, and miscellaneous charges	8	10	10
24.0 Printing and reproduction	2	2	2
25.1 Advisory and assistance services	2	2	2
Purchases of goods and services from Government accounts:			
25.3 Purchases of goods and services from Government accounts	248	229	239
25.3 Purchases from revolving funds	288	273	287
26.0 Supplies and materials	383	338	368
31.0 Equipment	49	34	19
42.0 Insurance claims and indemnities	7	....	....
99.0 Subtotal, direct obligations	1,779	1,773	1,886
99.0 Reimbursable obligations	80	51	51
99.9 Total new obligations	1,859	1,825	1,937

Personnel Summary

Identification code 57–3740–0–1–051	1999 actual	2000 est.	2001 est.
Direct:			
1001 Total compensable workyears: Full-time equivalent employment	14,041	14,724	14,569
Reimbursable:			
2001 Total compensable workyears: Full-time equivalent employment	284	299	299

Operation and Maintenance, Army National Guard

For expenses of training, organizing, and administering the Army National Guard, including medical and hospital treatment and related expenses in non-Federal hospitals; maintenance, operation, and repairs to structures and facilities; hire of passenger motor vehicles; personnel services in the National Guard Bureau; travel expenses (other than mileage), as authorized by law for Army personnel on active duty, for Army National Guard division, regimental, and battalion commanders while inspecting units in compliance with National Guard Bureau regulations when specifically authorized by the Chief, National Guard Bureau; supplying and equipping the Army National Guard as authorized by law; and expenses of repair, modification, maintenance, and issue of supplies and equipment (including aircraft), [$3,161,378,000] *$3,182,335,000. (10 U.S.C. 261–80, 2231–38, 2511, 4651; 32 U.S.C. 701–02, 709, 18233a; Department of Defense Appropriations Act, 2000.)*

Program and Financing (in millions of dollars)

Identification code 21–2065–0–1–051	1999 actual	2000 est.	2001 est.
Obligations by program activity:			
Direct program:			
00.01 Operating forces	2,575	2,964	2,987
00.04 Administration and servicewide activities	205	197	195
09.01 Reimbursable program	117	159	162
10.00 Total new obligations	2,897	3,320	3,344
Budgetary resources available for obligation:			
21.40 Unobligated balance available, start of year		16	
22.00 New budget authority (gross)	2,924	3,304	3,344
23.90 Total budgetary resources available for obligation	2,924	3,320	3,344
23.95 Total new obligations	−2,897	−3,320	−3,344
23.98 Unobligated balance expiring or withdrawn	−10		
24.40 Unobligated balance available, end of year	16		
New budget authority (gross), detail:			
Discretionary:			
40.00 Appropriation	2,671	2,903	3,182
40.15 Appropriation (emergency)	95	258	
40.76 Reduction pursuant to P.L. 106–113		−16	
40.77 Reduction pursuant to P.L. 105–262	−3		
41.00 Transferred to other DoD accounts	−12		
42.00 Transferred from other DoD accounts	55		
43.00 Appropriation (total discretionary)	2,806	3,145	3,182
Spending authority from offsetting collections:			
68.00 Offsetting collections (cash)	114	159	162
68.10 From Federal sources: Change in receivables and unpaid, unfilled orders			
68.15 From Federal sources: Adjustments to receivables and unpaid, unfilled orders	4		
68.90 Spending authority from offsetting collections (total discretionary)	118	159	162
70.00 Total new budget authority (gross)	2,924	3,304	3,344
Change in unpaid obligations:			
Unpaid obligations, start of year:			
72.40 Obligated balance, start of year	722	875	891
72.95 From Federal sources: Receivables and unpaid, unfilled orders	40	40	40
72.99 Total unpaid obligations, start of year	762	915	931
73.10 Total new obligations	2,897	3,320	3,344
73.20 Total outlays (gross)	−2,694	−3,305	−3,272
73.40 Adjustments in expired accounts (net)	−50		
Unpaid obligations, end of year:			
74.40 Obligated balance, end of year	875	891	963
74.95 From Federal sources: Receivables and unpaid, unfilled orders	40	40	40
74.99 Total unpaid obligations, end of year	915	931	1,003
Outlays (gross), detail:			
86.90 Outlays from new discretionary authority	2,137	2,527	2,517
86.93 Outlays from discretionary balances	556	777	755
87.00 Total outlays (gross)	2,694	3,305	3,272
Offsets:			
Against gross budget authority and outlays:			
Offsetting collections (cash) from:			
88.00 Federal sources	−111	−157	−160
88.40 Non-Federal sources	−3	−2	−2
88.90 Total, offsetting collections (cash)	−114	−159	−162
Against gross budget authority only:			
88.95 From Federal sources: Change in receivables and unpaid, unfilled orders			
88.96 From Federal sources: Adjustment to receivables and unpaid, unfilled orders	−4		
Net budget authority and outlays:			
89.00 Budget authority	2,806	3,145	3,182
90.00 Outlays	2,580	3,145	3,110

Object Classification (in millions of dollars)

Identification code 21–2065–0–1–051	1999 actual	2000 est.	2001 est.
Direct obligations:			
Personnel compensation:			
11.1 Full-time permanent	797	845	880
11.3 Other than full-time permanent	79	82	83
11.5 Other personnel compensation	15	16	17
11.9 Total personnel compensation	891	943	980
12.1 Civilian personnel benefits	244	259	263
13.0 Benefits for former personnel	18	19	20
21.0 Travel and transportation of persons	58	37	38
22.0 Transportation of things	31	32	32
23.1 Rental payments to GSA	4	4	4
23.2 Rental payments to others	2	3	3
23.3 Communications, utilities, and miscellaneous charges	104	106	107
24.0 Printing and reproduction	8	9	9
25.1 Advisory and assistance services	12	15	16
25.2 Other services	278	203	102
Purchases of goods and services from Government accounts:			
25.3 Purchases of goods and services from Government accounts	48	75	78
25.3 Purchases from revolving funds	33	101	103
25.4 Operation and maintenance of facilities	167	266	270
25.5 Research and development contracts	4	5	6
25.6 Medical care	6	13	16
25.7 Operation and maintenance of equipment	61	84	89
26.0 Supplies and materials	749	925	983
31.0 Equipment	45	46	47
32.0 Land and structures	17	16	16
99.0 Subtotal, direct obligations	2,780	3,161	3,182
99.0 Reimbursable obligations	117	159	162
99.9 Total new obligations	2,897	3,320	3,344

Personnel Summary

Identification code 21–2065–0–1–051	1999 actual	2000 est.	2001 est.
Direct:			
1001 Total compensable workyears: Full-time equivalent employment	23,647	23,715	23,893
Reimbursable:			
2001 Total compensable workyears: Full-time equivalent employment	183	93	93

Operation and Maintenance, Air National Guard

For operation and maintenance of the Air National Guard, including medical and hospital treatment and related expenses in non-Federal hospitals; maintenance, operation, repair, and other nec-

General and special funds—Continued

OPERATION AND MAINTENANCE, AIR NATIONAL GUARD—Continued

essary expenses of facilities for the training and administration of the Air National Guard, including repair of facilities, maintenance, operation, and modification of aircraft; transportation of things, hire of passenger motor vehicles; supplies, materials, and equipment, as authorized by law for the Air National Guard; and expenses incident to the maintenance and use of supplies, materials, and equipment, including such as may be furnished from stocks under the control of agencies of the Department of Defense; travel expenses (other than mileage) on the same basis as authorized by law for Air National Guard personnel on active Federal duty, for Air National Guard commanders while inspecting units in compliance with National Guard Bureau regulations when specifically authorized by the Chief, National Guard Bureau, [$3,241,138,000] *$3,446,375,000. (10 U.S.C. 261–80, 2232–38, 2511, 8012, 8721–22, 9741, 9743; 32 U.S.C. 106, 107, 320, 701–03, 709, 18233a; 37 U.S.C. 404–11; Department of Defense Appropriations Act, 2000.)*

Program and Financing (in millions of dollars)

Identification code 57–3840–0–1–051		1999 actual	2000 est.	2001 est.
	Obligations by program activity:			
	Direct program:			
00.01	Operating forces	3,196	3,206	3,434
00.04	Administration and servicewide activities	17	19	12
09.01	Reimbursable program	223	200	205
10.00	Total new obligations	3,437	3,425	3,651
	Budgetary resources available for obligation:			
21.40	Unobligated balance available, start of year		1	
22.00	New budget authority (gross)	3,439	3,424	3,651
22.22	Unobligated balance transferred from other DoD accounts	1		
23.90	Total budgetary resources available for obligation	3,440	3,425	3,651
23.95	Total new obligations	−3,437	−3,425	−3,651
23.98	Unobligated balance expiring or withdrawn	−3		
24.40	Unobligated balance available, end of year	1		
	New budget authority (gross), detail:			
	Discretionary:			
40.00	Appropriation	3,080	2,976	3,446
40.15	Appropriation (emergency)	25	265	
40.76	Reduction pursuant to P.L. 106–113		−17	
40.77	Reduction pursuant to P.L. 105–262	−3		
42.00	Transferred from other DoD accounts	114		
43.00	Appropriation (total discretionary)	3,216	3,224	3,446
	Spending authority from offsetting collections:			
68.00	Offsetting collections (cash)	200	200	205
68.10	From Federal sources: Change in receivables and unpaid, unfilled orders	23		
68.90	Spending authority from offsetting collections (total discretionary)	223	200	205
70.00	Total new budget authority (gross)	3,439	3,424	3,651
	Change in unpaid obligations:			
	Unpaid obligations, start of year:			
72.40	Obligated balance, start of year	666	727	693
72.95	From Federal sources: Receivables and unpaid, unfilled orders	61	84	84
72.99	Total unpaid obligations, start of year	727	811	776
73.10	Total new obligations	3,437	3,425	3,651
73.20	Total outlays (gross)	−3,327	−3,459	−3,593
73.40	Adjustments in expired accounts (net)	−26		
	Unpaid obligations, end of year:			
74.40	Obligated balance, end of year	727	693	750
74.95	From Federal sources: Receivables and unpaid, unfilled orders	84	84	84
74.99	Total unpaid obligations, end of year	811	776	834
	Outlays (gross), detail:			
86.90	Outlays from new discretionary authority	2,771	2,795	2,996
86.93	Outlays from discretionary balances	557	664	597
87.00	Total outlays (gross)	3,327	3,459	3,593
	Offsets:			
	Against gross budget authority and outlays:			
	Offsetting collections (cash) from:			
88.00	Federal sources	−197	−198	−203
88.40	Non-Federal sources	−3	−2	−2
88.90	Total, offsetting collections (cash)	−200	−200	−205
	Against gross budget authority only:			
88.95	From Federal sources: Change in receivables and unpaid, unfilled orders	−23		
	Net budget authority and outlays:			
89.00	Budget authority	3,216	3,224	3,446
90.00	Outlays	3,127	3,259	3,388

Object Classification (in millions of dollars)

Identification code 57–3840–0–1–051		1999 actual	2000 est.	2001 est.
	Direct obligations:			
	Personnel compensation:			
11.1	Full-time permanent	950	985	1,006
11.3	Other than full-time permanent	6	6	7
11.5	Other personnel compensation	16	17	17
11.9	Total personnel compensation	972	1,008	1,029
12.1	Civilian personnel benefits	253	270	281
13.0	Benefits for former personnel	3	3	3
21.0	Travel and transportation of persons	48	43	39
22.0	Transportation of things	14	8	7
23.2	Rental payments to others	3	2	2
23.3	Communications, utilities, and miscellaneous charges	47	58	59
24.0	Printing and reproduction	1	2	2
25.1	Advisory and assistance services	8	9	10
25.2	Other services	38	58	48
	Purchases of goods and services from Government accounts:			
25.3	Purchases of goods and services from Government accounts	4	12	12
25.3	Purchases from revolving funds	409	442	453
25.4	Operation and maintenance of facilities	272	294	286
25.6	Medical care	2	3	3
25.7	Operation and maintenance of equipment	89	98	94
26.0	Supplies and materials	961	837	1,043
31.0	Equipment	79	64	61
42.0	Insurance claims and indemnities	11	13	13
99.0	Subtotal, direct obligations	3,214	3,225	3,446
99.0	Reimbursable obligations	223	200	205
99.9	Total new obligations	3,437	3,425	3,651

Personnel Summary

Identification code 57–3840–0–1–051		1999 actual	2000 est.	2001 est.
	Direct:			
1001	Total compensable workyears: Full-time equivalent employment	23,632	23,407	23,012
	Reimbursable:			
2001	Total compensable workyears: Full-time equivalent employment	844	818	818

MORALE, WELFARE AND RECREATION AND PERSONNEL SUPPORT FOR CONTINGENCY DEPLOYMENTS

(INCLUDING TRANSFER OF FUNDS)

Program and Financing (in millions of dollars)

Identification code 97–0844–0–1–051		1999 actual	2000 est.	2001 est.
	New budget authority (gross), detail:			
	Discretionary:			
40.15	Appropriation (emergency)	50		
41.00	Transfers to other DoD accounts	−50		
43.00	Appropriation (total discretionary)			
	Net budget authority and outlays:			
89.00	Budget authority			
90.00	Outlays			

[QUALITY OF LIFE ENHANCEMENTS, DEFENSE]

[For expenses, not otherwise provided for, resulting from unfunded shortfalls in the repair and maintenance of real property of the Department of Defense (including military housing and barracks), $300,000,000, for the maintenance of real property of the Department of Defense (including minor construction and major maintenance and repair), which shall remain available for obligation until September 30, 2001, as follows:

Army, $77,000,000;
Navy, $77,000,000;
Marine Corps, $58,500,000;
Air Force, $77,000,000; and
Defense-Wide, $10,500,000:

Provided, That notwithstanding any other provision of law, of the funds appropriated under this heading for Defense-Wide activities, the entire amount shall only be available for grants by the Secretary of Defense to local educational authorities which maintain primary and secondary educational facilities located within Department of Defense installations, and which are used primarily by Department of Defense military and civilian dependents, for facility repairs and improvements to such educational facilities: *Provided further*, That such grants to local educational authorities may be made for repairs and improvements to such educational facilities as required to meet classroom size requirements: *Provided further*, That the cumulative amount of any grant or grants to any single local educational authority provided pursuant to the provisions under this heading shall not exceed $1,500,000.2] *(Department of Defense Appropriations Act, 2000.)*

Program and Financing (in millions of dollars)

Identification code 97–0839–0–1–051	1999 actual	2000 est.	2001 est.
Obligations by program activity:			
10.00 Total new obligations	414	392	....
Budgetary resources available for obligation:			
21.40 Unobligated balance available, start of year	52	94	....
22.00 New budget authority (gross)	455	298	....
22.10 Resources available from recoveries of prior year obligations	5	....	....
23.90 Total budgetary resources available for obligation	512	392	....
23.95 Total new obligations	–414	–392	....
23.98 Unobligated balance expiring or withdrawn	–4	....	....
24.40 Unobligated balance available, end of year	94	....	....
New budget authority (gross), detail:			
Discretionary:			
40.00 Appropriation	455	300	....
40.76 Reduction pursuant to P.L. 106–113	....	–2	....
43.00 Appropriation (total discretionary)	455	298	....
Change in unpaid obligations:			
72.40 Unpaid obligations, start of year: Obligated balance, start of year	457	508	468
73.10 Total new obligations	414	392	....
73.20 Total outlays (gross)	–366	–433	–297
73.40 Adjustments in expired accounts (net)	8	....	....
73.45 Adjustments in unexpired accounts	–5	....	....
74.40 Unpaid obligations, end of year: Obligated balance, end of year	508	468	171
Outlays (gross), detail:			
86.90 Outlays from new discretionary authority	51	33	....
86.93 Outlays from discretionary balances	315	400	297
87.00 Total outlays (gross)	366	433	297
Net budget authority and outlays:			
89.00 Budget authority	455	298	....
90.00 Outlays	366	433	297

Budget Plan (in millions of dollars)
Outlays

Identification code 97–0839–0–1–051	1999 actual	2000 est.	2001 est.
0701 Quality of life activities	455	298	....
0893 Total budget plan	455	298	....

[PENTAGON RENOVATION TRANSFER FUND]

[For expenses, not otherwise provided for, resulting from the Department of Defense renovation of the Pentagon Reservation, $222,800,000, for the renovation of the Pentagon Reservation, which shall remain available for obligation until September 30, 2001.] *(Department of Defense Appropriations Act, 2000.)*

Program and Financing (in millions of dollars)

Identification code 97–0841–0–1–051	1999 actual	2000 est.	2001 est.
Obligations by program activity:			
10.00 Total new obligations (object class 26.0)	280	222	....
Budgetary resources available for obligation:			
22.00 New budget authority (gross)	280	222	....
23.95 Total new obligations	–280	–222	....
New budget authority (gross), detail:			
Discretionary:			
40.00 Appropriation	....	223	....
40.76 Reduction pursuant to P.L. 106–113	....	–1	....
42.00 Transferred from other DoD accounts	280	....	....
43.00 Appropriation (total discretionary)	280	222	....
Change in unpaid obligations:			
73.10 Total new obligations	280	222	....
73.20 Total outlays (gross)	–280	–222	....
Outlays (gross), detail:			
86.90 Outlays from new discretionary authority	280	222	....
Net budget authority and outlays:			
89.00 Budget authority	280	222	....
90.00 Outlays	280	222	....

Budget Plan (in millions of dollars)
Outlays

Identification code 97–0841–0–1–051	1999 actual	2000 est.	2001 est.
0701 Renovation	280	222	....

DEPOT LEVEL MAINTENANCE AND REPAIR TRANSFER FUND

Program and Financing (in millions of dollars)

Identification code 97–0136–0–1–051	1999 actual	2000 est.	2001 est.
Budgetary resources available for obligation:			
21.40 Unobligated balance available, start of year	....	455	....
22.00 New budget authority (gross)	455	–400	....
22.21 Unobligated balance transferred to other DoD accounts	....	–55	....
23.90 Total budgetary resources available for obligation	455	....	....
24.40 Unobligated balance available, end of year	455	....	....
New budget authority (gross), detail:			
Discretionary:			
40.15 Appropriation (emergency)	743	....	....
41.00 Transferred to other DoD accounts	–288	–400	....
43.00 Appropriation (total discretionary)	455	–400	....
Outlays (gross), detail:			
86.90 Outlays from new discretionary authority	....	–400	....
86.93 Outlays from discretionary balances	....	400	....
87.00 Total outlays (gross)	....	....	....
Net budget authority and outlays:			
89.00 Budget authority	455	–400	....
90.00 Outlays	....	....	....

General and special funds—Continued

OVERSEAS CONTINGENCY OPERATIONS TRANSFER ACCOUNT

(INCLUDING TRANSFER OF FUNDS)

For expenses directly relating to Overseas Contingency Operations by United States military forces, [$1,722,600,000] *$4,100,577,000*, to remain available until expended: *Provided*, That the Secretary of Defense may transfer these funds only to *military personnel accounts;* operation and maintenance accounts [within this title,], *including the Overseas Humanitarian, Disaster Assistance, and Civic Aid appropriation*; the Defense Health Program appropriation*; procurement accounts; research, development, test, and evaluation accounts;* and to working capital funds: *Provided further*, That the funds transferred shall be merged with and shall be available for the same purposes and for the same time period, as the appropriation to which transferred: *Provided further*, That upon a determination that all or part of the funds transferred from this appropriation are not necessary for the purposes provided herein, such amounts may be transferred back to this appropriation: *Provided further*, That the transfer authority provided in this paragraph is in addition to any other transfer authority contained elsewhere in this Act. *(Department of Defense Appropriations Act, 2000.)*

Program and Financing (in millions of dollars)

Identification code 97–0118–0–1–051	1999 actual	2000 est.	2001 est.
Obligations by program activity:			
00.01 Overseas Contingency Operations Transfer Fund		2,258	4,101
10.00 Total new obligations (object class 26.0)		2,258	4,101
Budgetary resources available for obligation:			
21.40 Unobligated balance available, start of year	343	544	
22.00 New budget authority (gross)	544	1,714	4,101
22.21 Unobligated balance transferred to other DoD accounts	–343		
23.90 Total budgetary resources available for obligation	544	2,258	4,101
23.95 Total new obligations		–2,258	–4,101
24.40 Unobligated balance available, end of year	544		
New budget authority (gross), detail:			
Discretionary:			
40.00 Appropriation	439	1,723	4,101
40.15 Appropriation (emergency)	6,866		
40.60 Contingent emergency appropriation not available for obligations	–1,100		
40.65 Contingent emergency appropriation released		1,100	
40.76 Reduction pursuant to P.L. 106–113		–9	
41.00 Transferred to other DoD accounts	–5,818	–1,100	
42.00 Transferred from other DoD accounts	157		
43.00 Appropriation (total discretionary)	544	1,714	4,101
Change in unpaid obligations:			
72.40 Unpaid obligations, start of year: Obligated balance, start of year			467
73.10 Total new obligations		2,258	4,101
73.20 Total outlays (gross)		–1,791	–3,414
74.40 Unpaid obligations, end of year: Obligated balance, end of year		467	1,154
Outlays (gross), detail:			
86.90 Outlays from new discretionary authority		1,277	3,055
86.93 Outlays from discretionary balances		514	359
87.00 Total outlays (gross)		1,791	3,414
Net budget authority and outlays:			
89.00 Budget authority	544	1,714	4,101
90.00 Outlays		1,790	3,413

Summary of Budget Authority and Outlays

(in millions of dollars)

Enacted/requested:	*1999 actual*	*2000 est.*	*2001 est.*
Budget Authority	544	1,714	4,101
Outlays		1,791	3,414
Supplemental proposal:			
Budget Authority		2,050	
Outlays		1,527	408
Total:			
Budget Authority	544	3,764	4,101
Outlays		3,318	3,822

MILITARY TRAINING EQUIPMENT AND ASSOCIATED SUPPORT TRANSFER FUND

Program and Financing (in millions of dollars)

Identification code 97–0135–0–1–051	1999 actual	2000 est.	2001 est.
Budgetary resources available for obligation:			
21.40 Unobligated balance available, start of year		57	
22.00 New budget authority (gross)	57		
22.21 Unobligated balance transferred to other DoD accounts		–57	
23.90 Total budgetary resources available for obligation	57		
24.40 Unobligated balance available, end of year	57		
New budget authority (gross), detail:			
Discretionary:			
40.15 Appropriation (emergency)	200		
41.00 Transferred to other DoD accounts	–143		
43.00 Appropriation (total discretionary)	57		
Net budget authority and outlays:			
89.00 Budget authority	57		
90.00 Outlays			

OPLAN 34A–35 P.O.W. PAYMENTS

Program and Financing (in millions of dollars)

Identification code 97–0840–0–1–051	1999 actual	2000 est.	2001 est.
Obligations by program activity:			
10.00 Total new obligations		7	5
Budgetary resources available for obligation:			
21.40 Unobligated balance available, start of year	17	17	10
23.95 Total new obligations		–7	–5
24.40 Unobligated balance available, end of year	17	10	5
Change in unpaid obligations:			
72.40 Unpaid obligations, start of year: Obligated balance, start of year			3
73.10 Total new obligations		7	5
73.20 Total outlays (gross)		–4	–4
74.40 Unpaid obligations, end of year: Obligated balance, end of year		3	3
Outlays (gross), detail:			
86.93 Outlays from discretionary balances		4	4
Net budget authority and outlays:			
89.00 Budget authority			
90.00 Outlays		4	4

This account provides funding for payments to certain individuals who served time in prisoner of war camps, and their families. The payments are required by section 657 of Public Law 104–201 as amended by section 658 of Public Law 105–261.

SPARES, REPAIRS, AND ASSOCIATED LOGISTICAL SUPPORT TRANSFER FUND

Program and Financing (in millions of dollars)

Identification code 97–0137–0–1–051	1999 actual	2000 est.	2001 est.
Budgetary resources available for obligation:			
21.40 Unobligated balance available, start of year		779	
22.00 New budget authority (gross)	779	–550	

22.21 Unobligated balance transferred to other DoD accounts		−229	
23.90 Total budgetary resources available for obligation	779		
24.40 Unobligated balance available, end of year	779		
New budget authority (gross), detail:			
Discretionary:			
40.15 Appropriation (emergency)	1,125		
41.00 Transferred to other DoD accounts	−346	−550	
43.00 Appropriation (total discretionary)	779	−550	
Outlays (gross), detail:			
86.90 Outlays from new discretionary authority		−550	
86.93 Outlays from discretionary balances		550	
87.00 Total outlays (gross)			
Net budget authority and outlays:			
89.00 Budget authority	779	−550	
90.00 Outlays			

United States Courts of Appeals for the Armed Forces

For salaries and expenses necessary for the United States Court of Appeals for the Armed Forces, [$7,621,000] *$8,574,000*, of which not to exceed $2,500 can be used for official representation purposes. *(10 U.S.C. 867; Department of Defense Appropriations Act, 2000.)*

Program and Financing (in millions of dollars)

Identification code 97–0104–0–1–051	1999 actual	2000 est.	2001 est.
Obligations by program activity:			
10.00 Total new obligations	7	8	9
Budgetary resources available for obligation:			
22.00 New budget authority (gross)	7	8	9
23.95 Total new obligations	−7	−8	−9
New budget authority (gross), detail:			
Discretionary:			
40.00 Appropriation	7	8	9
Change in unpaid obligations:			
72.40 Unpaid obligations, start of year: Obligated balance, start of year	2	5	1
73.10 Total new obligations	7	8	9
73.20 Total outlays (gross)	−5	−11	−9
74.40 Unpaid obligations, end of year: Obligated balance, end of year	5	1	1
Outlays (gross), detail:			
86.90 Outlays from new discretionary authority	6	7	8
86.93 Outlays from discretionary balances	−1	5	1
87.00 Total outlays (gross)	5	11	9
Net budget authority and outlays:			
89.00 Budget authority	7	8	9
90.00 Outlays	5	11	9

Object Classification (in millions of dollars)

Identification code 97–0104–0–1–051	1999 actual	2000 est.	2001 est.
11.1 Personnel compensation: Full-time permanent	5	5	5
12.1 Civilian personnel benefits	1	1	1
23.1 Rental payments to GSA	1	1	1
26.0 Supplies and materials			1
99.0 Subtotal, direct obligations	7	7	8
99.5 Below reporting threshold		1	1
99.9 Total new obligations	7	8	9

Personnel Summary

Identification code 97–0104–0–1–051	1999 actual	2000 est.	2001 est.
1001 Total compensable workyears: Full-time equivalent employment	53	59	59

Drug Interdiction and Counter-Drug Activities, Defense

(INCLUDING TRANSFER OF FUNDS)

For drug interdiction and counter-drug activities of the Department of Defense, for transfer to appropriations available to the Department of Defense for military personnel of the reserve components serving under the provisions of title 10 and title 32, United States Code; for Operation and maintenance; for Procurement; and for Research, development, test and evaluation, [$847,800,000] *$836,300,000: Provided*, [That of the funds appropriated under this heading, $10,800,000 is hereby transferred to appropriations available for "Military Construction, Air Force" for fiscal year 2000, and the transferred funds shall be available for study, planning, design, architect and engineer services at forward operating locations in the area of responsibility of the United States Southern Command: *Provided further*,] That the funds appropriated under this heading shall be available for obligation for the same time period and for the same purpose as the appropriation to which transferred: *Provided further*, That the transfer authority provided under this heading is in addition to any transfer authority contained elsewhere in this Act. *(Department of Defense Appropriations Act, 2000.)*

Program and Financing (in millions of dollars)

Identification code 97–0105–0–1–051	1999 actual	2000 est.	2001 est.
Obligations by program activity:			
10.00 Total new obligations		833	836
Budgetary resources available for obligation:			
22.00 New budget authority (gross)		833	836
22.21 Unobligated balance transferred to other DoD accounts	−45		
22.22 Unobligated balance transferred from other DoD accounts	45		
23.90 Total budgetary resources available for obligation		833	836
23.95 Total new obligations		−833	−836
New budget authority (gross), detail:			
Discretionary:			
40.00 Appropriation	734	848	836
40.15 Appropriation (emergency)	42		
40.76 Reduction pursuant to P.L. 106–113		−4	
41.00 Transferred to other DoD accounts	−776	−11	
43.00 Appropriation (total discretionary)		833	836
Change in unpaid obligations:			
72.40 Unpaid obligations, start of year: Obligated balance, start of year			546
73.10 Total new obligations		833	836
73.20 Total outlays (gross)		−286	−648
74.40 Unpaid obligations, end of year: Obligated balance, end of year		546	734
Outlays (gross), detail:			
86.90 Outlays from new discretionary authority		287	288
86.93 Outlays from discretionary balances			361
87.00 Total outlays (gross)		286	648
Net budget authority and outlays:			
89.00 Budget authority		833	836
90.00 Outlays		286	648

Summary of Budget Authority and Outlays

(in millions of dollars)

	1999 actual	*2000 est.*	*2001 est.*
Enacted/requested:			
Budget Authority		833	836
Outlays		287	649
Supplemental proposal:			
Budget Authority		98	
Outlays		34	43
Total:			
Budget Authority		931	836
Outlays		321	692

General and special funds—Continued

DRUG INTERDICTION AND COUNTER-DRUG ACTIVITIES, DEFENSE—Continued

(INCLUDING TRANSFER OF FUNDS)—Continued

Object Classification (in millions of dollars)

Identification code 97–0105–0–1–051	1999 actual	2000 est.	2001 est.
21.0 Travel and transportation of persons	....	81	91
22.0 Transportation of things	....	20	22
23.2 Rental payments to others	....	5	5
23.3 Communications, utilities, and miscellaneous charges	....	13	13
24.0 Printing and reproduction	....	1	1
25.1 Advisory and assistance services	....	19	20
25.2 Other services	....	102	99
25.3 Purchases of goods and services from Government accounts	....	170	179
25.4 Operation and maintenance of facilities	....	9	10
25.7 Operation and maintenance of equipment	....	34	35
26.0 Supplies and materials	....	367	349
31.0 Equipment	....	12	12
99.9 Total new obligations	....	833	836

SUPPORT FOR INTERNATIONAL SPORTING COMPETITIONS, DEFENSE

Program and Financing (in millions of dollars)

Identification code 97–0838–0–1–051	1999 actual	2000 est.	2001 est.
Obligations by program activity:			
10.00 Total new obligations	1	11	3
Budgetary resources available for obligation:			
21.40 Unobligated balance available, start of year	14	14	3
23.95 Total new obligations	−1	−11	−3
24.40 Unobligated balance available, end of year	14	3	....
Change in unpaid obligations:			
72.40 Unpaid obligations, start of year: Obligated balance, start of year	2	2	−1
73.10 Total new obligations	1	11	3
73.20 Total outlays (gross)	−1	−13	−2
74.40 Unpaid obligations, end of year: Obligated balance, end of year	2	−1	....
Outlays (gross), detail:			
86.93 Outlays from discretionary balances	1	13	2
Net budget authority and outlays:			
89.00 Budget authority	....	....	....
90.00 Outlays	....	13	3

Object Classification (in millions of dollars)

Identification code 97–0838–0–1–051	1999 actual	2000 est.	2001 est.
25.2 Other services	....	3	3
26.0 Supplies and materials	1	8	....
99.9 Total new obligations	1	11	3

FOREIGN CURRENCY FLUCTUATIONS, DEFENSE

Program and Financing (in millions of dollars)

Identification code 97–0801–0–1–051	1999 actual	2000 est.	2001 est.
Budgetary resources available for obligation:			
21.40 Unobligated balance available, start of year	722	647	647
22.00 New budget authority (gross)	354	....	....
22.21 Unobligated balance transferred to other DoD accounts	−428	....	....
23.90 Total budgetary resources available for obligation	647	647	647
24.40 Unobligated balance available, end of year	647	647	647
New budget authority (gross), detail:			
Discretionary:			
50.00 Reappropriation	354	....	....
Net budget authority and outlays:			
89.00 Budget authority	354	....	....
90.00 Outlays	....	....	....

This account transfers funds to operation and maintenance and military personnel appropriations available for Defense activities in foreign countries to finance upward adjustment of recorded obligations due to foreign currency fluctuations above the budget rate. Transfers are made as needed to meet disbursement requirements in excess of funds otherwise available for obligation adjustment. Net gains resulting from favorable exchange rates are returned to this appropriation and are available for subsequent transfer when needed.

REAL PROPERTY MAINTENANCE, DEFENSE

Program and Financing (in millions of dollars)

Identification code 97–0131–0–1–051	1999 actual	2000 est.	2001 est.
Budgetary resources available for obligation:			
23.95 Total new obligations	....	....	....
Change in unpaid obligations:			
72.40 Unpaid obligations, start of year: Obligated balance, start of year	41	....	....
73.10 Total new obligations	....	....	....
73.20 Total outlays (gross)	−13	....	....
73.40 Adjustments in expired accounts (net)	−27	....	....
74.40 Unpaid obligations, end of year: Obligated balance, end of year	....	....	....
Outlays (gross), detail:			
86.93 Outlays from discretionary balances	13	....	....
Net budget authority and outlays:			
89.00 Budget authority	....	....	....
90.00 Outlays	13	....	....

DISASTER RELIEF

Program and Financing (in millions of dollars)

Identification code 97–0132–0–1–051	1999 actual	2000 est.	2001 est.
Budgetary resources available for obligation:			
21.40 Unobligated balance available, start of year	3	2	2
24.40 For completion of prior year budget plans	2	2	2
Change in unpaid obligations:			
72.40 Unpaid obligations, start of year: Obligated balance, start of year	1	1	1
74.40 Unpaid obligations, end of year: Obligated balance, end of year	1	1	1
Net budget authority and outlays:			
89.00 Budget authority	....	....	....
90.00 Outlays	....	....	....

DEFENSE HEALTH PROGRAM

For expenses, not otherwise provided for, for medical and health care programs of the Department of Defense, as authorized by law, [$11,154,617,000] *$11,600,429,000*, of which [$10,522,647,000] *$11,244,543,000* shall be for Operation and maintenance, of which not[,] to exceed 2 percent shall remain available until September 30, [2001] *2002*; of which [$356,970,000] *$290,006,000*, to remain available [for obligation] until September 30, [2002] *2003*, shall be for Procurement; [and] of which [$275,000,000] *$65,880,000*, to remain available [for obligation] until September 30, [2001] *2002*, shall be for Research, development, test and evaluation, *and of which*

$10,000,000 shall be available for HIV prevention educational activities undertaken in connection with U.S. military training, exercises, and humanitarian assistance activities conducted in African nations. (Department of Defense Appropriations Act, 2000.)

Program and Financing (in millions of dollars)

Identification code 97–0130–0–1–051		1999 actual	2000 est.	2001 est.
	Obligations by program activity:			
	Direct program:			
00.01	Operation and Maintenance	10,084	10,740	11,245
00.02	Procurement	388	284	263
00.03	Research, Development, Test and Evaluation	10	278	83
09.01	Reimbursable program	716	700	700
10.00	Total new obligations	11,199	12,002	12,291
	Budgetary resources available for obligation:			
21.40	For completion of prior year budget plans	54	108	127
22.00	New budget authority (gross)	11,248	12,020	12,300
22.10	Resources available from recoveries of prior year obligations	17		
22.22	Unobligated balance transferred from other DoD accounts	11		
23.90	Total budgetary resources available for obligation	11,330	12,128	12,427
23.95	Total new obligations	−11,199	−12,002	−12,291
23.98	Unobligated balance expiring or withdrawn	−24		
24.40	For completion of prior year budget plans	108	127	136
	New budget authority (gross), detail:			
	Discretionary:			
40.00	Appropriation	10,114	11,145	11,600
40.15	Appropriation (emergency)	204		
40.76	Reduction pursuant to P.L. 106–113		−58	
41.00	Transferred to other DoD accounts	−30		
42.00	Transferred from other DoD accounts	211	233	
43.00	Appropriation (total discretionary)	10,499	11,320	11,600
	Spending authority from offsetting collections:			
68.00	Offsetting collections (cash)	463	700	700
68.10	From Federal sources: Change in receivables and unpaid, unfilled orders	321		
68.15	From Federal sources: Adjustments to receivables and unpaid, unfilled orders	−35		
68.90	Spending authority from offsetting collections (total discretionary)	749	700	700
70.00	Total new budget authority (gross)	11,248	12,020	12,300
	Change in unpaid obligations:			
	Unpaid obligations, start of year:			
72.40	Obligated balance, start of year	3,257	3,233	3,413
72.95	From Federal sources: Receivables and unpaid, unfilled orders	2,181	2,502	2,502
72.99	Total unpaid obligations, start of year	5,438	5,736	5,915
73.10	Total new obligations	11,199	12,002	12,291
73.20	Total outlays (gross)	−10,909	−11,823	−12,299
73.40	Adjustments in expired accounts (net)	25		
73.45	Adjustments in unexpired accounts	−17		
	Unpaid obligations, end of year:			
74.40	Obligated balance, end of year	3,233	3,413	3,404
74.95	From Federal sources: Receivables and unpaid, unfilled orders	2,502	2,502	2,502
74.99	Total unpaid obligations, end of year	5,736	5,915	5,906
	Outlays (gross), detail:			
86.90	Outlays from new discretionary authority	8,673	9,428	9,849
86.93	Outlays from discretionary balances	2,236	2,394	2,450
87.00	Total outlays (gross)	10,909	11,823	12,299
	Offsets:			
	Against gross budget authority and outlays:			
	Offsetting collections (cash) from:			
88.00	Federal sources	−252	−638	−637
88.40	Non-Federal sources	−211	−62	−63
88.90	Total, offsetting collections (cash)	−463	−700	−700
	Against gross budget authority only:			
88.95	From Federal sources: Change in receivables and unpaid, unfilled orders	−321		
88.96	From Federal sources: Adjustment to receivables and unpaid, unfilled orders	35		
	Net budget authority and outlays:			
89.00	Budget authority	10,499	11,320	11,600
90.00	Outlays	10,445	11,123	11,599

Budget Plan (in millions of dollars)
Outlays

Identification code 97–0130–0–1–051		1999 actual	2000 est.	2001 est.
	Direct:			
0701	Operation and Maintenance	10,084	10,728	11,245
0702	Procurement	403	322	290
0703	Research, Development, Test and Evaluation	38	270	66
0791	Total direct program	10,525	11,320	11,600
0801	Reimbursable program	716	700	700
0893	Total budget plan	11,241	12,020	12,300

The Defense Health Program provides care to present and retired members of the armed forces, their dependents, and other eligible beneficiaries. Beneficiaries may obtain care from Army, Navy, and Air Force facilities or, for those beneficiaries under age 65, through TRICARE (formerly CHAMPUS).

The Defense Health Program also manages Research and Development funds appropriated by Congress. These funds permit the Defense Department to conduct research into several areas relevant to the health of military personnel.

Medical care is provided in military facilities as follows:

	1999	*2000*	*2001*	*2002*
Hospitals/Medical Centers	94	78	78	78
Clinics	489	501	495	495

These hospitals, medical centers, and clinics are staffed by:

	Staff in thousands			
	1999	*2000*	*2001*	*2002*
Civilian work years	40	39	38	38
Military personnel	99	92	92	92
Percent of all active duty military personnel	7	7	7	7

The number of beneficiaries using the Defense Health Program is estimated as follows:

	Beneficiaries in thousands			
	1999	*2000*	*2001*	*2002*
Active Duty Personnel	1,549	1,531	1,520	1,513
Dependents of Active Duty Personnel	2,082	2,091	2,079	2,072
Retirees and dependents of retirees under age 65	1,895	1,877	1,858	1,843
Retirees and dependents of retirees over age 65	340	352	365	377
Total estimated Defense Health Program user population	5,866	5,851	5,822	5,805

Changes over time in the estimated number of users of the Defense Health Program largely reflect changes in the eligible population.

Object Classification (in millions of dollars)

Identification code 97–0130–0–1–051		1999 actual	2000 est.	2001 est.
	Direct obligations:			
	Personnel compensation:			
11.1	Full-time permanent	18	19	20
11.5	Other personnel compensation	1	1	1
11.9	Total personnel compensation	19	21	22
12.1	Civilian personnel benefits	4	4	4
21.0	Travel and transportation of persons	153	157	157
22.0	Transportation of things	7	7	7
23.1	Rental payments to GSA	14	14	14
23.2	Rental payments to others	20	20	20
23.3	Communications, utilities, and miscellaneous charges	114	114	118
24.0	Printing and reproduction	13	6	6
25.1	Advisory and assistance services	56	56	57

General and special funds—Continued

DEFENSE HEALTH PROGRAM—Continued

Object Classification (in millions of dollars)—Continued

Identification code 97–0130–0–1–051		1999 actual	2000 est.	2001 est.
25.2	Other services	256	263	267
25.3	Purchases of goods and services from Government accounts	1,750	1,840	1,881
25.4	Operation and maintenance of facilities	109	129	133
25.5	Research and development contracts	10	291	68
25.6	Medical care	5,734	6,144	6,639
25.7	Operation and maintenance of equipment	80	85	90
26.0	Supplies and materials	1,542	1,593	1,444
31.0	Equipment	584	552	658
41.0	Grants, subsidies, and contributions	18	7	7
99.0	Subtotal, direct obligations	10,483	11,302	11,591
99.0	Reimbursable obligations	716	700	700
99.9	Total new obligations	11,199	12,002	12,291

Personnel Summary

Identification code 97–0130–0–1–051		1999 actual	2000 est.	2001 est.
1001	Total compensable workyears: Full-time equivalent employment	321	297	297

THE DEPARTMENT OF DEFENSE ENVIRONMENTAL RESTORATION ACCOUNTS

ENVIRONMENTAL RESTORATION, ARMY

(INCLUDING TRANSFER OF FUNDS)

For the Department of the Army, [$378,170,000] *$389,932,000*, to remain available until transferred: *Provided*, That the Secretary of the Army shall, upon determining that such funds are required for environmental restoration, reduction and recycling of hazardous waste, removal of unsafe buildings and debris of the Department of the Army, or for similar purposes, transfer the funds made available by this appropriation to other appropriations made available to the Department of the Army, to be merged with and to be available for the same purposes and for the same time period as the appropriations to which transferred: *Provided further*, That upon a determination that all or part of the funds transferred from this appropriation are not necessary for the purposes provided herein, such amounts may be transferred back to this appropriation. *(Department of Defense Appropriations Act, 2000.)*

ENVIRONMENTAL RESTORATION, NAVY

(INCLUDING TRANSFER OF FUNDS)

For the Department of the Navy, [$284,000,000] *$294,038,000*, to remain available until transferred: *Provided*, That the Secretary of the Navy shall, upon determining that such funds are required for environmental restoration, reduction and recycling of hazardous waste, removal of unsafe buildings and debris of the Department of the Navy, or for similar purposes, transfer the funds made available by this appropriation to other appropriations made available to the Department of the Navy, to be merged with and to be available for the same purposes and for the same time period as the appropriations to which transferred: *Provided further*, That upon a determination that all or part of the funds transferred from this appropriation are not necessary for the purposes provided herein, such amounts may be transferred back to this appropriation. *(Department of Defense Apropriations Act, 2000.)*

ENVIRONMENTAL RESTORATION, AIR FORCE

(INCLUDING TRANSFER OF FUNDS)

For the Department of the Air Force, [$376,800,000] *$376,300,000*, to remain available until transferred: *Provided*, That the Secretary of the Air Force shall, upon determining that such funds are required for environmental restoration, reduction and recycling of hazardous waste, removal of unsafe buildings and debris of the Department of the Air Force, or for similar purposes, transfer the funds made available by this appropriation to other appropriations made available to the Department of the Air Force, to be merged with and to be available for the same purposes and for the same time period as the appropriations to which transferred: *Provided further*, That upon a determination that all or part of the funds transferred from this appropriation are not necessary for the purposes provided herein, such amounts may be transferred back to this appropriation. *(Department of Defense Apropriations Act, 2000.)*

ENVIRONMENTAL RESTORATION, DEFENSE-WIDE

(INCLUDING TRANSFER OF FUNDS)

For the Department of Defense, [$25,370,000] *$23,412,000*, to remain available until transferred: *Provided*, That the Secretary of Defense shall, upon determining that such funds are required for environmental restoration, reduction and recycling of hazardous waste, removal of unsafe buildings and debris of the Department of Defense, or for similar purposes, transfer the funds made available by this appropriation to other appropriations made available to the Department of Defense, to be merged with and to be available for the same purposes and for the same time period as the appropriations to which transferred: *Provided further*, That upon a determination that all or part of the funds transferred from this appropriation are not necessary for the purposes provided herein, such amounts may be transferred back to this appropriation. *(Department of Defense Appropriations Act, 2000.)*

ENVIRONMENTAL RESTORATION, FORMERLY USED DEFENSE SITES

(INCLUDING TRANSFER OF FUNDS)

For the Department of the Army, [$239,214,000] *$186,499,000*, to remain available until transferred: *Provided*, That the Secretary of the Army shall, upon determining that such funds are required for environmental restoration, reduction and recycling of hazardous waste, removal of unsafe buildings and debris at sites formerly used by the Department of Defense, transfer the funds made available by this appropriation to other appropriations made available to the Department of the Army, to be merged with and to be available for the same purposes and for the same time period as the appropriations to which transferred: *Provided further*, That upon a determination that all or part of the funds transferred from this appropriation are not necessary for the purposes provided herein, such amounts may be transferred back to this appropriation. *(Department of Defense Appropriations Act, 2000.)*

Program and Financing (in millions of dollars)

Identification code 97–0810–0–1–051		1999 actual	2000 est.	2001 est.
	Obligations by program activity:			
00.01	Department of Army		376	390
00.02	Department of Navy		283	294
00.03	Department of Air Force		375	376
00.04	Defense-wide		25	23
00.05	Formerly used defense sites		238	186
10.00	Total new obligations (object class 32.0)		1,297	1,270
	Budgetary resources available for obligation:			
22.00	New budget authority (gross)		1,297	1,270
22.10	Resources available from recoveries of prior year obligations	4		
22.21	Unobligated balance transferred to other DoD accounts	−4		
23.90	Total budgetary resources available for obligation		1,297	1,270
23.95	Total new obligations		−1,297	−1,270
	New budget authority (gross), detail:			
	Discretionary:			
40.00	Appropriation	1,264	1,304	1,270
40.76	Reduction pursuant to P.L. 106–113		−7	
41.00	Transferred to other DoD accounts	−1,264		
43.00	Appropriation (total discretionary)		1,297	1,270
	Change in unpaid obligations:			
72.40	Unpaid obligations, start of year: Obligated balance, start of year			1,012
73.10	Total new obligations		1,297	1,270
73.20	Total outlays (gross)	4	−286	−863
73.45	Adjustments in unexpired accounts	−4		
74.40	Unpaid obligations, end of year: Obligated balance, end of year		1,012	1,419

		1999 actual	2000 est.	2001 est.
	Outlays (gross), detail:			
86.90	Outlays from new discretionary authority		285	279
86.93	Outlays from discretionary balances	−4		584
87.00	Total outlays (gross)	−4	286	863
	Net budget authority and outlays:			
89.00	Budget authority		1,297	1,270
90.00	Outlays	−4	286	863

The defense environmental restoration program provides for the identification, investigation, and cleanup of contamination resulting from past DoD activities. The Department has 16,003 previously identified contaminated sites requiring no further action, leaving 8,547 active sites at 678 military installations and over 2000 formerly used Defense properties. For the active sites, DoD is engaged in either a study to determine the extent of the contamination or the actual clean-up.

The Department's environmental restoration program is funded by five separate environmental restoration accounts, one for each military department, one for defense agencies and one for formerly used defense sites. These five decentralized accounts include restoration activities from preliminary assessment and site planning to studies, then clean-up and finally closeout of a site, functions formerly funded in the defense environmental restoration account.

Overseas Humanitarian, Disaster, and Civic Aid

For expenses relating to the Overseas Humanitarian, Disaster, and Civic Aid programs of the Department of Defense (consisting of the programs provided under sections 401, 402, 404, 2547, and 2551 of title 10, United States Code), [$55,800,000] *$64,900,000*, to remain available until September 30, [2001] *2002. (Department of Defense Appropriations Act, 2000.)*

Program and Financing (in millions of dollars)

Identification code 97–0819–0–1–051		1999 actual	2000 est.	2001 est.
	Obligations by program activity:			
10.00	Total new obligations	77	98	64
	Budgetary resources available for obligation:			
21.40	For completion of prior year budget plans	18	48	6
22.00	New budget authority (gross)	105	56	65
22.10	Resources available from recoveries of prior year obligations	5		
23.90	Total budgetary resources available for obligation	127	104	71
23.95	Total new obligations	−77	−98	−64
23.98	Unobligated balance expiring or withdrawn	−2		
24.40	Unobligated balance available, end of year	48	6	7
	New budget authority (gross), detail:			
	Discretionary:			
40.00	Appropriation	50	56	65
40.15	Appropriation (emergency)	38		
42.00	Transferred from other DoD accounts	17		
43.00	Appropriation (total discretionary)	105	56	65
	Change in unpaid obligations:			
	Unpaid obligations, start of year:			
72.40	Obligated balance, start of year	127	87	62
72.95	From Federal sources: Receivables and unpaid, unfilled orders			
72.99	Total unpaid obligations, start of year	127	87	62
73.10	Total new obligations	77	98	64
73.20	Total outlays (gross)	−106	−122	−59
73.40	Adjustments in expired accounts (net)	−6		
73.45	Adjustments in unexpired accounts	−5		
	Unpaid obligations, end of year:			
74.40	Obligated balance, end of year	87	62	67
74.95	From Federal sources: Receivables and unpaid, unfilled orders			
74.99	Total unpaid obligations, end of year	87	62	67
	Outlays (gross), detail:			
86.90	Outlays from new discretionary authority	46	12	14
86.93	Outlays from discretionary balances	60	111	46
87.00	Total outlays (gross)	106	122	59
	Net budget authority and outlays:			
89.00	Budget authority	104	56	65
90.00	Outlays	106	122	59

Budget Plan (in millions of dollars)

Outlays

Identification code 97–0819–0–1–051		1999 actual	2000 est.	2001 est.
0701	Overseas humanitarian, disaster and civic aid	104	56	65

New Horizons Transfer Fund

Program and Financing (in millions of dollars)

Identification code 97–0138–0–1–051		1999 actual	2000 est.	2001 est.
	New budget authority (gross), detail:			
	Discretionary:			
40.15	Appropriation (emergency)	46		
41.00	Transferred to other DoD accounts	−46		
43.00	Appropriation (total discretionary)			
	Net budget authority and outlays:			
89.00	Budget authority			
90.00	Outlays			

Defense Reinvestment for Economic Growth

Program and Financing (in millions of dollars)

Identification code 97–0828–0–1–051		1999 actual	2000 est.	2001 est.
	Change in unpaid obligations:			
72.40	Unpaid obligations, start of year: Obligated balance, start of year	99	50	50
73.20	Total outlays (gross)	−20		
73.40	Adjustments in expired accounts (net)	−28		
74.40	Unpaid obligations, end of year: Obligated balance, end of year	50	50	50
	Outlays (gross), detail:			
86.93	Outlays from discretionary balances	20		
	Net budget authority and outlays:			
89.00	Budget authority			
90.00	Outlays	20		

Former Soviet Union Threat Reduction

For assistance to the republics of the former Soviet Union, including assistance provided by contract or by grants, for facilitating the elimination and the safe and secure transportation and storage of nuclear, chemical and other weapons; for establishing programs to prevent the proliferation of weapons, weapons components, and weapon-related technology and expertise; for programs relating to the training and support of defense and military personnel for demilitarization and protection of weapons, weapons components and weapons technology and expertise, [$460,500,000] *$458,400,000*, to remain available until September 30, [2002: *Provided*, That of the amounts provided under this heading, $25,000,000 shall be available only to support the dismantling and disposal of nuclear submarines and submarine reactor components in the Russian Far East] *2003. (Department of Defense Appropriations Act, 2000.)*

General and special funds—Continued

FORMER SOVIET UNION THREAT REDUCTION—Continued

Program and Financing (in millions of dollars)

Identification code 97–0134–0–1–051	1999 actual	2000 est.	2001 est.
Obligations by program activity:			
10.00 Total new obligations	320	379	598
Budgetary resources available for obligation:			
21.40 Unobligated balance available, start of year	405	569	648
22.00 New budget authority (gross)	440	458	458
22.10 Resources available from recoveries of prior year obligations	45		
23.90 Total budgetary resources available for obligation	890	1,027	1,106
23.95 Total new obligations	−320	−379	−598
24.40 Unobligated balance available, end of year	569	648	508
New budget authority (gross), detail:			
Discretionary:			
40.00 Appropriation	440	460	458
40.76 Reduction pursuant to P.L. 106–113		−2	
43.00 Appropriation (total discretionary)	440	458	458
Change in unpaid obligations:			
72.40 Unpaid obligations, start of year: Obligated balance, start of year	564	518	233
73.10 Total new obligations	320	379	598
73.20 Total outlays (gross)	−321	−665	−359
73.45 Adjustments in unexpired accounts	−45		
74.40 Unpaid obligations, end of year: Obligated balance, end of year	518	233	472
Outlays (gross), detail:			
86.90 Outlays from new discretionary authority		16	16
86.93 Outlays from discretionary balances	321	648	342
87.00 Total outlays (gross)	321	665	359
Net budget authority and outlays:			
89.00 Budget authority	440	458	458
90.00 Outlays	321	665	359

Budget Plan (in millions of dollars)
Outlays

Identification code 97–0134–0–1–051	1999 actual	2000 est.	2001 est.
0701 Threat reduction activities	440	458	458

Object Classification (in millions of dollars)

Identification code 97–0134–0–1–051	1999 actual	2000 est.	2001 est.
21.0 Travel and transportation of persons	5	3	3
25.1 Advisory and assistance services	61		1
25.2 Other services	220	237	476
25.3 Purchases of goods and services from Government accounts		107	105
31.0 Equipment	34	32	13
99.9 Total new obligations	320	379	598

DEFENSE AGAINST WEAPONS OF MASS DESTRUCTION

Program and Financing (in millions of dollars)

Identification code 97–0837–0–1–051	1999 actual	2000 est.	2001 est.
New budget authority (gross), detail:			
Discretionary:			
40.00 Appropriation		35	
40.15 Appropriation (emergency)	50		
41.00 Transferred to other DoD accounts	−50	−35	
43.00 Appropriation (total discretionary)			
Net budget authority and outlays:			
89.00 Budget authority			
90.00 Outlays			

PAYMENT TO KAHO'OLAWE

For payment to Kaho'olawe Island Conveyance, Remediation, and Environmental Restoration Fund, as authorized by law, [$35,000,000] *$25,000,000*, to remain available until expended. *(Department of Defense Appropriations Act, 2000.)*

Program and Financing (in millions of dollars)

Identification code 17–1236–0–1–051	1999 actual	2000 est.	2001 est.
Obligations by program activity:			
10.00 Total new obligations (object class 32.0)	25	35	25
Budgetary resources available for obligation:			
21.40 Unobligated balance available, start of year	21	21	21
22.00 New budget authority (gross)	25	35	25
23.90 Total budgetary resources available for obligation	46	56	46
23.95 Total new obligations	−25	−35	−25
24.40 Unobligated balance available, end of year	21	21	21
New budget authority (gross), detail:			
Discretionary:			
40.00 Appropriation	25	35	25
Change in unpaid obligations:			
72.40 Unpaid obligations, start of year: Obligated balance, start of year	26	26	26
73.10 Total new obligations	25	35	25
73.20 Total outlays (gross)	−25	−35	−25
74.40 Unpaid obligations, end of year: Obligated balance, end of year	26	26	26
Outlays (gross), detail:			
86.90 Outlays from new discretionary authority	25	35	25
Net budget authority and outlays:			
89.00 Budget authority	25	35	25
90.00 Outlays	25	35	25

EMERGENCY RESPONSE FUND

Program and Financing (in millions of dollars)

Identification code 97–0833–0–1–051	1999 actual	2000 est.	2001 est.
Obligations by program activity:			
10.00 Total new obligations (object class 26.0)	22		
Budgetary resources available for obligation:			
21.40 Unobligated balance available, start of year	33	12	12
22.10 Resources available from recoveries of prior year obligations	1		
23.90 Total budgetary resources available for obligation	34	12	12
23.95 Total new obligations	−22		
24.40 Unobligated balance available, end of year	12	12	12
Change in unpaid obligations:			
72.40 Unpaid obligations, start of year: Obligated balance, start of year	3	17	17
73.10 Total new obligations	22		
73.20 Total outlays (gross)	−7		
73.45 Adjustments in unexpired accounts	−1		
74.40 Unpaid obligations, end of year: Obligated balance, end of year	17	17	17
Outlays (gross), detail:			
86.93 Outlays from discretionary balances	7		
Net budget authority and outlays:			
89.00 Budget authority			
90.00 Outlays	7		

INFORMATION TECHNOLOGY SYSTEMS AND SECURITY TRANSFER ACCOUNT

Program and Financing (in millions of dollars)

Identification code 97–0843–0–1–051	1999 actual	2000 est.	2001 est.
New budget authority (gross), detail:			
Discretionary:			
40.15 Appropriation (emergency)	1,100		
41.00 Transferred to other DoD accounts	–1,100		
43.00 Appropriation (total discretionary)			
Net budget authority and outlays:			
89.00 Budget authority			
90.00 Outlays			

This account was created in Public Law 105–277, the Omnibus Consolidated and Emergency Supplemental Act, 1999, to address requirements associated with Year 2000 (Y2K) computer conversion. A total of $1,100 million in contingent emergency funding was provided, to be transferred to the Department of Defense as unforeseen requirements are identified. All funds have been transferred to accounts throughout the Department.

ALLIED CONTRIBUTIONS AND COOPERATION ACCOUNT

Unavailable Collections (in millions of dollars)

Identification code 97–9927–0–2–051	1999 actual	2000 est.	2001 est.
Balance, start of year:			
01.99 Balance, start of year			
Receipts:			
02.03 Contributions for burdensharing and other cooperative activites	208	210	215
Appropriation:			
05.01 Allied contributions and cooperation account	–208	–210	–215
07.99 Total balance, end of year			

Program and Financing (in millions of dollars)

Identification code 97–9927–0–2–051	1999 actual	2000 est.	2001 est.
Obligations by program activity:			
10.00 Total new obligations (object class 26.0)	208	210	215
Budgetary resources available for obligation:			
22.00 New budget authority (gross)	208	210	215
23.95 Total new obligations	–208	–210	–215
New budget authority (gross), detail:			
Mandatory:			
60.25 Appropriation (special fund, indefinite)	208	210	215
Change in unpaid obligations:			
72.40 Unpaid obligations, start of year: Obligated balance, start of year	–65	17	3
73.10 Total new obligations	208	210	215
73.20 Total outlays (gross)	–126	–224	–216
74.40 Unpaid obligations, end of year: Obligated balance, end of year	17	3	2
Outlays (gross), detail:			
86.97 Outlays from new mandatory authority	208	210	215
86.98 Outlays from mandatory balances	–82	14	1
87.00 Total outlays (gross)	126	224	216
Net budget authority and outlays:			
89.00 Budget authority	208	210	215
90.00 Outlays	126	224	216
Memorandum (non-add) entries:			
92.01 Total investments, start of year: U.S. securities: Par value	1	1	
92.02 Total investments, end of year: U.S. securities: Par value	1		

Cash contributions from allied countries and individuals are deposited into this account for reallocation to other DoD appropriations. Contributions are used to offset costs of DoD's overseas presence.

MISCELLANEOUS SPECIAL FUNDS

Unavailable Collections (in millions of dollars)

Identification code 97–9922–0–2–051	1999 actual	2000 est.	2001 est.
Balance, start of year:			
01.99 Balance, start of year	13	32	32
Receipts:			
02.01 Lease and Disposal of DoD Real Property	28	27	24
02.02 Restoration of Rocky Mountain Arsenal	5	6	6
02.03 Kaho'olawe Island Restoration Fund	25	35	25
02.04 Transfer Commissary Facilities, National Science Center and Korean War Fund	18		
02.99 Total receipts	76	68	55
04.00 Total: Balances and collections	89	100	87
Appropriation:			
05.01 Discretionary Appropriations	–57	–68	–31
05.99 Subtotal appropriation	–57	–68	–31
07.99 Total balance, end of year	32	32	56

Program and Financing (in millions of dollars)

Identification code 97–9922–0–2–051	1999 actual	2000 est.	2001 est.
Obligations by program activity:			
00.01 Restoration of Rocky Mountain Arsenal	24	6	6
00.02 Disposal of DoD real property	7	10	
00.03 Lease of DoD real property	11	15	
00.04 Kaho'olawe Island Restoration Fund	21	35	25
10.00 Total new obligations	63	66	31
Budgetary resources available for obligation:			
21.40 Unobligated balance available, start of year	138	134	135
22.00 New budget authority (gross)	57	68	31
22.10 Resources available from recoveries of prior year obligations	2		
23.90 Total budgetary resources available for obligation	197	202	166
23.95 Total new obligations	–63	–66	–31
24.40 Unobligated balance available, end of year	134	135	135
New budget authority (gross), detail:			
Discretionary:			
40.25 Appropriation (special fund, indefinite)	52	62	25
Mandatory:			
60.25 Appropriation (special fund, indefinite)	5	6	6
70.00 Total new budget authority (gross)	57	68	31
Change in unpaid obligations:			
72.40 Unpaid obligations, start of year: Obligated balance, start of year	94	87	70
73.10 Total new obligations	63	66	31
73.20 Total outlays (gross)	–68	–84	–30
73.45 Adjustments in unexpired accounts	–2		
74.40 Unpaid obligations, end of year: Obligated balance, end of year	87	70	70
Outlays (gross), detail:			
86.90 Outlays from new discretionary authority	25	41	22
86.93 Outlays from discretionary balances	23	37	2
86.97 Outlays from new mandatory authority		6	6
86.98 Outlays from mandatory balances	20		
87.00 Total outlays (gross)	68	84	30
Net budget authority and outlays:			
89.00 Budget authority	57	68	31
90.00 Outlays	68	84	30

These special funds include: receipts from the disposal and lease of DoD real property which are applied to real property

General and special funds—Continued

MISCELLANEOUS SPECIAL FUNDS—Continued

maintenance efforts at DoD installations; receipts used to operate the National Science Center; and, funds for the restoration of Kaho'olawe Island and Rocky Mountain Arsenal.

Object Classification (in millions of dollars)

Identification code 97–9922–0–2–051	1999 actual	2000 est.	2001 est.
25.2 Other services	7		
25.3 Purchases of goods and services from Government accounts	2		
25.4 Operation and maintenance of facilities	33	31	6
32.0 Land and structures	21	35	25
99.9 Total new obligations	63	66	31

OVERSEAS MILITARY FACILITY INVESTMENT RECOVERY

Unavailable Collections (in millions of dollars)

Identification code 97–5193–0–2–051	1999 actual	2000 est.	2001 est.
Balance, start of year:			
01.99 Balance, start of year			
Receipts:			
02.01 Overseas military facility, investment and recovery	4	3	3
Appropriation:			
05.01 Overseas military facility, investment and recovery	–4	–3	
07.99 Total balance, end of year			3

Program and Financing (in millions of dollars)

Identification code 97–5193–0–2–051	1999 actual	2000 est.	2001 est.
Obligations by program activity:			
10.00 Total new obligations (object class 25.4)	2	3	
Budgetary resources available for obligation:			
21.40 Unobligated balance available, start of year	3	5	5
22.00 New budget authority (gross)	4	3	
23.90 Total budgetary resources available for obligation	7	9	5
23.95 Total new obligations	–2	–3	
24.40 Unobligated balance available, end of year	5	5	5
New budget authority (gross), detail:			
Discretionary:			
40.25 Appropriation (special fund, indefinite)	4	3	
Change in unpaid obligations:			
72.40 Unpaid obligations, start of year: Obligated balance, start of year	71	43	24
73.10 Total new obligations	2	3	
73.20 Total outlays (gross)	–29	–22	–18
74.40 Unpaid obligations, end of year: Obligated balance, end of year	43	24	7
Outlays (gross), detail:			
86.93 Outlays from discretionary balances	29	22	18
Net budget authority and outlays:			
89.00 Budget authority	4	3	
90.00 Outlays	30	23	17

DEFENSE EXPORT LOAN GUARANTEE FINANCING ACCOUNT

Program and Financing (in millions of dollars)

Identification code 97–4168–0–3–051	1999 actual	2000 est.	2001 est.
Budgetary resources available for obligation:			
21.40 Unobligated balance available, start of year	3	3	3
22.00 New financing authority (gross)	1		
23.90 Total budgetary resources available for obligation	4	3	3
23.95 Total new obligations			
24.40 Unobligated balance available, end of year	3	3	3
New financing authority (gross), detail:			
Discretionary:			
68.00 Spending authority from offsetting collections (gross): Offsetting collections (cash)	1		
Offsets:			
Against gross financing authority and financing disbursements:			
88.40 Offsetting collections (cash) from: Non-Federal sources	–1		
Net financing authority and financing disbursements:			
89.00 Financing authority			
90.00 Financing disbursements	–1		

Status of Guaranteed Loans (in millions of dollars)

Identification code 97–4168–0–3–051	1999 actual	2000 est.	2001 est.
Position with respect to appropriations act limitation on commitments:			
2111 Limitation on guaranteed loans made by private lenders	14,980	14,980	14,980
2112 Uncommitted loan guarantee limitation	–14,980	–14,980	–14,980
2113 Uncommitted limitation carried forward			
2150 Total guaranteed loan commitments			
2199 Guaranteed amount of guaranteed loan commitments			
Cumulative balance of guaranteed loans outstanding:			
2210 Outstanding, start of year	15	16	12
2231 Disbursements of new guaranteed loans	5		
2251 Repayments and prepayments	–4	–4	–4
2263 Adjustments: Terminations for default that result in claim payments			–1
2290 Outstanding, end of year	16	12	7
Memorandum:			
2299 Guaranteed amount of guaranteed loans outstanding, end of year	14	11	7

Balance Sheet (in millions of dollars)

Identification code 97–4168–0–3–051	1998 actual	1999 actual	2000 est.	2001 est.
ASSETS:				
1101 Federal assets: Fund balances with Treasury	3	4	4	4
1999 Total assets	3	4	4	4
LIABILITIES:				
2204 Non-Federal liabilities: Liabilities for loan guarantees	3	4	4	4
2999 Total liabilities	3	4	4	4
4999 Total liabilities and net position	3	4	4	4

As required by the Federal Credit Reform Act of 1990, this non-budgetary account records all cash flows to and from the Government resulting from loan guarantees committed in 1992 and beyond (including modifications of loan guarantees that resulted from commitments in any year). The amounts in this account are a means of financing and are not included in the budget totals.

DEFENSE VESSEL TRANSFER PROGRAM ACCOUNT

Program and Financing (in millions of dollars)

Identification code 97–0842–0–1–051	1999 actual	2000 est.	2001 est.
Budgetary resources available for obligation:			
21.40 Unobligated balance available, start of year		107	
22.00 New budget authority (gross)	107		
23.90 Total budgetary resources available for obligation	107	107	

23.95	Total new obligations			
23.98	Unobligated balance expiring or withdrawn		−107	
24.40	Unobligated balance available, end of year	107		
	New budget authority (gross), detail:			
	Discretionary:			
40.00	Appropriation	107		
	Net budget authority and outlays:			
89.00	Budget authority	107		
90.00	Outlays			

As required by the Federal Credit Reform Act of 1990, this non-budgetary account records all cash flows to and from the Government resulting from loan guarantees committed in 1992 and beyond (including modifications of loan guarantees that resulted from commitments in any year). The amounts in this account are a means of financing and are not included in the budget totals.

PROCUREMENT

Appropriations in this title support the acquisition of weapons, equipment, munitions, spares, and modification of existing equipment. Resources presented under the Procurement title contribute primarily to achieving the Department's corporate goal 2 (Prepare). A detailed description of the corporate goals is contained in the FY 2001 Performance Plan in the Department's 2000 Annual Report to the President and Congress. This performance plan is required by the Government Performance and Results Act of 1993.

Procurement to improve the capability of U.S. ground forces continues in 2001 and includes Army wheeled and tracked combat systems, missile systems, and tactical trucks. Major upgrade programs are also included for the ABRAMS tank, the Bradley Fighting Vehicle, and the AH–64 Apache Longbow attack helicopter. Marine Corps modernization emphasizes procurement of communications and electronic equipment and the V–22 Osprey tilt-rotor aircraft.

Modernization of our naval forces in 2001 is highlighted by continued procurement of the improved E/F version of the F/A–18 multi-role fighter. Procurement of the CH–60 helicopter, the T–45 trainer aircraft and remanufacture and upgrade of the AV–8B vertical/short takeoff and landing close air support aircraft continues. Procurement of Trident strategic missiles, and Standard surface-to-air missiles also continues. Procurement of DDG–51 guided missile destroyers continues, along with funding for LPD–17 amphibious transport dock ships, procurement of the CVN–77 aircraft carrier, a Virginia class attack submarine, and advance procurement of the CVN(X) aircraft carrier.

Significant Air Force programs include procurement of the low rate initial production lot of ten F–22 fighter aircraft, continued procurement of C–17 airlift aircraft, the Advanced Medium Range Air-to-Air Missile (AMRAAM), the Joint Standoff Weapon (JSOW) precision munition, the Joint Direct Attack Munition (JDAM), satellites, and space launch vehicles. Procurement continues for the JPATS trainer aircraft, a joint Navy/Air Force program.

The budget plan for each appropriation is shown as a separate table immediately following the program and financing schedules for those appropriations that are available for obligation for more than one year. In all years, it presents, by budget activity, the value of the program requested for the life of the multiple-year appropriation.

Federal Funds

General and special funds:

AIRCRAFT PROCUREMENT, ARMY

For construction, procurement, production, modification, and modernization of aircraft, equipment, including ordnance, ground handling equipment, spare parts, and accessories therefor; specialized equipment and training devices; expansion of public and private plants, including the land necessary therefor, for the foregoing purposes, and such lands and interests therein, may be acquired, and construction prosecuted thereon prior to approval of title; and procurement and installation of equipment, appliances, and machine tools in public and private plants; reserve plant and Government and contractor-owned equipment layaway; and other expenses necessary for the foregoing purposes, [$1,451,688,000] *$1,323,262,000*, to remain available for obligation until September 30, [2002] *2003, of which $84,069,000 shall be available for the Army National Guard and Army Reserve. (10 U.S.C. 3013, 4532; Department of Defense Appropriations Act, 2000.)*

Program and Financing (in millions of dollars)

Identification code 21–2031–0–1–051		1999 actual	2000 est.	2001 est.
	Obligations by program activity:			
	Direct program:			
00.01	Aircraft	334	230	57
00.02	Modification of aircraft	1,035	1,008	1,135
00.03	Spares and repair parts	33	19	15
00.04	Support equipment and facilities	127	113	115
09.01	Reimbursable program	18	16	18
10.00	Total new obligations	1,547	1,386	1,340
	Budgetary resources available for obligation:			
	Unobligated balance available, start of year:			
21.40	For completion of prior year budget plans	236	161	245
21.40	Available to finance new budget plans		8	
21.99	Total unobligated balance, start of year	236	169	245
22.00	New budget authority (gross)	1,398	1,462	1,342
22.10	Resources available from recoveries of prior year obligations	82		
23.90	Total budgetary resources available for obligation	1,716	1,630	1,586
23.95	Total new obligations	−1,547	−1,386	−1,340
	Unobligated balance available, end of year:			
24.40	Unobligated balance available, end of year	161	245	247
24.40	Available to finance subsequent year budget plans	8		
24.99	Total unobligated balance, end of year	169	245	247
	New budget authority (gross), detail:			
	Discretionary:			
40.00	Appropriation	1,384	1,452	1,323
40.36	Unobligated balance rescinded		−8	
40.76	Reduction pursuant to P.L. 106–113		−7	
41.00	Transferred to other DoD accounts		−7	
42.00	Transferred from other DoD accounts	7	15	
43.00	Appropriation (total discretionary)	1,391	1,444	1,323
	Spending authority from offsetting collections:			
68.00	Offsetting collections (cash)	11	17	18
68.10	From Federal sources: Change in receivables and unpaid, unfilled orders	−5		
68.90	Spending authority from offsetting collections (total discretionary)	6	17	18
70.00	Total new budget authority (gross)	1,397	1,462	1,341
	Change in unpaid obligations:			
	Unpaid obligations, start of year:			
72.40	Obligated balance, start of year	1,519	1,436	1,415
72.95	From Federal sources: Receivables and unpaid, unfilled orders	14	9	9
72.99	Total unpaid obligations, start of year	1,532	1,445	1,424
73.10	Total new obligations	1,547	1,386	1,340
73.20	Total outlays (gross)	−1,544	−1,407	−1,328
73.40	Adjustments in expired accounts (net)	−8		
73.45	Adjustments in unexpired accounts	−82		
	Unpaid obligations, end of year:			
74.40	Obligated balance, end of year	1,436	1,415	1,427

General and special funds—Continued

AIRCRAFT PROCUREMENT, ARMY—Continued

Program and Financing (in millions of dollars)—Continued

Identification code 21–2031–0–1–051		1999 actual	2000 est.	2001 est.
74.95	From Federal sources: Receivables and unpaid, unfilled orders	9	9	9
74.99	Total unpaid obligations, end of year	1,445	1,424	1,436
	Outlays (gross), detail:			
86.90	Outlays from new discretionary authority	478	362	343
86.93	Outlays from discretionary balances	1,065	1,045	984
87.00	Total outlays (gross)	1,544	1,407	1,328
	Offsets:			
	Against gross budget authority and outlays:			
88.00	Offsetting collections (cash) from: Federal sources	−11	−17	−18
	Against gross budget authority only:			
88.95	From Federal sources: Change in receivables and unpaid, unfilled orders	5		
88.96	From Federal sources: Adjustment to receivables and unpaid, unfilled orders			
	Net budget authority and outlays:			
89.00	Budget authority	1,392	1,444	1,323
90.00	Outlays	1,533	1,390	1,309

Budget Plan (in millions of dollars)
Outlays

Identification code 21–2031–0–1–051		1999 actual	2000 est.	2001 est.
	Direct:			
0701	Aircraft	318	221	87
0702	Modification of aircraft	936	1,100	1,130
0703	Spares and repair parts	27	16	15
0704	Support equipment and facilities	103	115	91
0791	Total direct	1,384	1,452	1,323
0801	Reimbursable	9	17	18
0893	Total budget plan	1,393	1,470	1,342

Object Classification (in millions of dollars)

Identification code 21–2031–0–1–051		1999 actual	2000 est.	2001 est.
	Direct obligations:			
21.0	Travel and transportation of persons	1	1	1
25.1	Advisory and assistance services	76	60	62
25.2	Other services	118	47	48
	Purchases of goods and services from Government accounts:			
25.3	Purchases of goods and services from Government accounts	73	75	77
25.3	Purchases from revolving funds	2	2	2
25.4	Operation and maintenance of facilities	1	1	1
25.5	Research and development contracts	20	21	22
25.7	Operation and maintenance of equipment	104	106	109
26.0	Supplies and materials	40	31	32
31.0	Equipment	1,092	1,024	966
32.0	Land and structures	2	2	2
99.0	Subtotal, direct obligations	1,529	1,370	1,322
99.0	Reimbursable obligations	18	16	18
99.9	Total new obligations	1,547	1,386	1,340

MISSILE PROCUREMENT, ARMY

For construction, procurement, production, modification, and modernization of missiles, equipment, including ordnance, ground handling equipment, spare parts, and accessories therefor; specialized equipment and training devices; expansion of public and private plants, including the land necessary therefor, for the foregoing purposes, and such lands and interests therein, may be acquired, and construction prosecuted thereon prior to approval of title; and procurement and installation of equipment, appliances, and machine tools in public and private plants; reserve plant and Government and contractor-owned equipment layaway; and other expenses necessary for the foregoing purposes, [$1,322,305,000] *$1,295,728,000* to remain available for obligation until September 30, [2002] *2003, of which $127,093,000 shall be available for the Army National Guard and Army Reserve. (10 U.S.C. 2353, 3013; Department of Defense Appropriations Act, 2000.)*

Program and Financing (in millions of dollars)

Identification code 21–2032–0–1–051		1999 actual	2000 est.	2001 est.
	Obligations by program activity:			
	Direct program:			
00.01	Other missiles	1,111	1,108	1,126
00.02	Modification of missiles	120	142	125
00.03	Spares and repair parts	11	27	24
00.04	Support equipment and facilities	10	7	7
09.01	Reimbursable program	54	437	158
10.00	Total new obligations	1,306	1,721	1,440
	Budgetary resources available for obligation:			
	Unobligated balance available, start of year:			
21.40	For completion of prior year budget plans	143	120	206
21.40	Available to finance new budget plans		7	
21.99	Total unobligated balance, start of year	143	127	206
22.00	New budget authority (gross)	1,272	1,799	1,411
22.10	Resources available from recoveries of prior year obligations	20		
23.90	Total budgetary resources available for obligation	1,435	1,926	1,617
23.95	Total new obligations	−1,306	−1,721	−1,440
23.98	Unobligated balance expiring or withdrawn	−1		
	Unobligated balance available, end of year:			
24.40	For completion of prior year budget plans	120	206	177
24.40	Available to finance subsequent year budget plans	7		
24.99	Total unobligated balance, end of year	127	206	177
	New budget authority (gross), detail:			
	Discretionary:			
40.00	Appropriation	1,222	1,324	1,296
40.36	Unobligated balance rescinded	−13	−7	
40.76	Reduction pursuant to P.L. 106–113		−7	
41.00	Transferred to other DoD accounts		−7	
43.00	Appropriation (total discretionary)	1,210	1,303	1,296
	Spending authority from offsetting collections:			
68.00	Offsetting collections (cash)	98	496	115
68.10	From Federal sources: Change in receivables and unpaid, unfilled orders	−37		
68.15	From Federal sources: Adjustments to receivables and unpaid, unfilled orders	2		
68.90	Spending authority from offsetting collections (total discretionary)	63	496	115
70.00	Total new budget authority (gross)	1,272	1,799	1,411
	Change in unpaid obligations:			
	Unpaid obligations, start of year:			
72.40	Obligated balance, start of year	1,277	1,710	1,876
72.95	From Federal sources: Receivables and unpaid, unfilled orders	116	79	79
72.99	Total unpaid obligations, start of year	1,392	1,788	1,954
73.10	Total new obligations	1,306	1,721	1,440
73.20	Total outlays (gross)	−881	−1,554	−1,257
73.40	Adjustments in expired accounts (net)	−10		
73.45	Adjustments in unexpired accounts	−20		
	Unpaid obligations, end of year:			
74.40	Obligated balance, end of year	1,710	1,876	2,059
74.95	From Federal sources: Receivables and unpaid, unfilled orders	79	79	79
74.99	Total unpaid obligations, end of year	1,788	1,954	2,138
	Outlays (gross), detail:			
86.90	Outlays from new discretionary authority	115	587	215
86.93	Outlays from discretionary balances	766	967	1,041
87.00	Total outlays (gross)	881	1,554	1,257

		1999 actual	2000 est.	2001 est.
	Offsets:			
	Against gross budget authority and outlays:			
	Offsetting collections (cash) from:			
88.00	Federal sources	−91	−123	−70
88.40	Non-Federal sources	−7	−373	−45
88.90	Total, offsetting collections (cash)	−98	−496	−115
	Against gross budget authority only:			
88.95	From Federal sources: Change in receivables and unpaid, unfilled orders	37		
88.96	From Federal sources: Adjustment to receivables and unpaid, unfilled orders	−2		
	Net budget authority and outlays:			
89.00	Budget authority	1,210	1,303	1,296
90.00	Outlays	783	1,058	1,141

Budget Plan (in millions of dollars)
Outlays

Identification code 21–2032–0–1–051		1999 actual	2000 est.	2001 est.
	Direct:			
0701	Other missiles	1,086	1,133	1,134
0702	Modification of missiles	102	150	133
0703	Spares and repair parts	19	19	21
0704	Support equipment and facilities	8	8	8
0720	Program activities			
0791	Total direct	1,215	1,310	1,296
0801	Reimbursable	66	496	116
0893	Total budget plan	1,282	1,806	1,411

Object Classification (in millions of dollars)

Identification code 21–2032–0–1–051		1999 actual	2000 est.	2001 est.
	Direct obligations:			
22.0	Transportation of things		7	149
25.1	Advisory and assistance services	10	4	5
25.2	Other services	105	1	1
	Purchases of goods and services from Government accounts:			
25.3	Purchases of goods and services from Government accounts	100		
25.3	Purchases from revolving funds	1		
25.4	Operation and maintenance of facilities	1		
25.5	Research and development contracts	129		
25.7	Operation and maintenance of equipment	8		
26.0	Supplies and materials	21	246	98
31.0	Equipment	877	1,026	1,029
99.0	Subtotal, direct obligations	1,252	1,284	1,282
99.0	Reimbursable obligations	54	437	158
99.9	Total new obligations	1,306	1,721	1,440

Procurement of Weapons and Tracked Combat Vehicles, Army

For construction, procurement, production, and modification of weapons and tracked combat vehicles, equipment, including ordnance, spare parts, and accessories therefor; specialized equipment and training devices; expansion of public and private plants, including the land necessary therefor, for the foregoing purposes, and such lands and interests therein, may be acquired, and construction prosecuted thereon prior to approval of title; and procurement and installation of equipment, appliances, and machine tools in public and private plants; reserve plant and Government and contractor-owned equipment layaway; and other expenses necessary for the foregoing purposes, [$1,586,490,000] *$1,874,638,000* to remain available for obligation until September 30, [2002] *2003, of which $41,832,000 shall be available for the Army National Guard and Army Reserve. (10 U.S.C. 2353, 3013; Department of Defense Appropriations Act, 2000.)*

Program and Financing (in millions of dollars)

Identification code 21–2033–0–1–051		1999 actual	2000 est.	2001 est.
	Obligations by program activity:			
	Direct program:			
00.01	Tracked combat vehicles	1,418	1,371	1,719
00.02	Weapons and other combat vehicles	81	113	86
00.03	Spare and repair parts	18	21	27
09.01	Reimbursable program	30	33	53
10.00	Total new obligations	1,547	1,538	1,886
	Budgetary resources available for obligation:			
	Unobligated balance available, start of year:			
21.40	For completion of prior year budget plans	291	347	414
21.40	Available to finance new budget plans		9	
21.99	Total unobligated balance, start of year	291	356	414
22.00	New budget authority (gross)	1,562	1,596	1,936
22.10	Resources available from recoveries of prior year obligations	49		
23.90	Total budgetary resources available for obligation	1,902	1,952	2,350
23.95	Total new obligations	−1,547	−1,538	−1,886
23.98	Unobligated balance expiring or withdrawn			
	Unobligated balance available, end of year:			
24.40	For completion of prior year budget plans	347	414	464
24.40	Unobligated balance available, end of year	9		
24.99	Total unobligated balance, end of year	356	414	464
	New budget authority (gross), detail:			
	Discretionary:			
40.00	Appropriation	1,544	1,586	1,875
40.36	Unobligated balance rescinded	−7	−9	
40.76	Reduction pursuant to P.L. 106–113		−8	
41.00	Transferred to other DoD accounts		−7	
42.00	Transferred from other DoD accounts	1		
43.00	Appropriation (total discretionary)	1,538	1,562	1,875
	Spending authority from offsetting collections:			
68.00	Offsetting collections (cash)	10	34	61
68.10	From Federal sources: Change in receivables and unpaid, unfilled orders	11		
68.15	From Federal sources: Adjustments to receivables and unpaid, unfilled orders	3		
68.90	Spending authority from offsetting collections (total discretionary)	24	34	61
70.00	Total new budget authority (gross)	1,562	1,596	1,936
	Change in unpaid obligations:			
	Unpaid obligations, start of year:			
72.40	Obligated balance, start of year	1,640	1,486	1,599
72.95	From Federal sources: Receivables and unpaid, unfilled orders	34	45	45
72.99	Total unpaid obligations, start of year	1,673	1,531	1,644
73.10	Total new obligations	1,547	1,538	1,886
73.20	Total outlays (gross)	−1,615	−1,425	−1,619
73.40	Adjustments in expired accounts (net)	−26		
73.45	Adjustments in unexpired accounts	−49		
	Unpaid obligations, end of year:			
74.40	Obligated balance, end of year	1,486	1,599	1,866
74.95	From Federal sources: Receivables and unpaid, unfilled orders	45	45	45
74.99	Total unpaid obligations, end of year	1,531	1,644	1,912
	Outlays (gross), detail:			
86.90	Outlays from new discretionary authority	302	282	372
86.93	Outlays from discretionary balances	1,312	1,143	1,246
87.00	Total outlays (gross)	1,615	1,425	1,619
	Offsets:			
	Against gross budget authority and outlays:			
	Offsetting collections (cash) from:			
88.00	Federal sources	−9	−24	−44
88.40	Non-Federal sources	−1	−10	−17
88.90	Total, offsetting collections (cash)	−10	−34	−61
	Against gross budget authority only:			
88.95	From Federal sources: Change in receivables and unpaid, unfilled orders	−11		
88.96	From Federal sources: Adjustment to receivables and unpaid, unfilled orders	−3		
	Net budget authority and outlays:			
89.00	Budget authority	1,538	1,562	1,875
90.00	Outlays	1,604	1,391	1,557

General and special funds—Continued

PROCUREMENT OF WEAPONS AND TRACKED COMBAT VEHICLES, ARMY—Continued

Budget Plan (in millions of dollars)
Outlays

Identification code 21–2033–0–1–051	1999 actual	2000 est.	2001 est.
Direct:			
0701 Tracked combat vehicles	1,443	1,420	1,761
0702 Weapons and other combat vehicles	73	129	84
0703 Spare and repair parts	20	23	29
0791 Total direct	1,536	1,571	1,875
0801 Reimbursable	24	34	61
0893 Total budget plan	1,560	1,605	1,936

Object Classification (in millions of dollars)

Identification code 21–2033–0–1–051	1999 actual	2000 est.	2001 est.
Direct obligations:			
22.0 Transportation of things	2	2	2
25.1 Advisory and assistance services	24	12	7
25.2 Other services	92	54	53
Purchases of goods and services from Government accounts:			
25.3 Purchases of goods and services from Government accounts	135	173	183
25.3 Purchases from revolving funds	71	106	113
25.5 Research and development contracts	54		
25.7 Operation and maintenance of equipment	18		
26.0 Supplies and materials	38	66	69
31.0 Equipment	1,079	1,092	1,406
32.0 Land and structures	4		
99.0 Subtotal, direct obligations	1,517	1,505	1,833
99.0 Reimbursable obligations	30	33	53
99.9 Total new obligations	1,547	1,538	1,886

PROCUREMENT OF AMMUNITION, ARMY

For construction, procurement, production, and modification of ammunition, and accessories therefor; specialized equipment and training devices; expansion of public and private plants, including ammunition facilities authorized by section 2854 of title 10, United States Code, and the land necessary therefor, for the foregoing purposes, and such lands and interests therein, may be acquired, and construction prosecuted thereon prior to approval of title; and procurement and installation of equipment, appliances, and machine tools in public and private plants; reserve plant and Government and contractor-owned equipment layaway; and other expenses necessary for the foregoing purposes, [$1,204,120,000] *$1,131,323,000*, to remain available for obligation until September 30, [2002] *2003, of which $173,534,000 shall be available for the Army National Guard and Army Reserve. (10 U.S.C. 2353, 3013; Department of Defense Appropriations Act, 2000.)*

Program and Financing (in millions of dollars)

Identification code 21–2034–0–1–051	1999 actual	2000 est.	2001 est.
Obligations by program activity:			
Direct program:			
00.01 Ammunition	1,024	917	1,015
00.02 Ammunition production base support	208	196	156
09.01 Reimbursable program	261	480	400
10.00 Total new obligations	1,493	1,594	1,571
Budgetary resources available for obligation:			
Unobligated balance available, start of year:			
21.40 For completion of prior year budget plans	192	314	318
21.40 Available to finance new budget plans		6	
21.99 Total unobligated balance, start of year	192	320	318
22.00 New budget authority (gross)	1,568	1,592	1,531
22.10 Resources available from recoveries of prior year obligations	53		
23.90 Total budgetary resources available for obligation	1,813	1,912	1,849
23.95 Total new obligations	−1,493	−1,594	−1,571
23.98 Unobligated balance expiring or withdrawn	−1		
Unobligated balance available, end of year:			
24.40 For completion of prior year budget plans	314	318	278
24.40 Available to finance subsequent year budget plans	6		
24.99 Total unobligated balance, end of year	320	318	278
New budget authority (gross), detail:			
Discretionary:			
40.00 Appropriation	1,063	1,204	1,131
40.36 Unobligated balance rescinded		−6	
40.76 Reduction pursuant to P.L. 106–113		−6	
41.00 Transferred to other accounts		−5	
42.00 Transferred from other DoD accounts	126		
43.00 Appropriation (total discretionary)	1,189	1,187	1,131
Spending authority from offsetting collections:			
68.00 Offsetting collections (cash)	34	405	400
68.10 From Federal sources: Change in receivables and unpaid, unfilled orders	345		
68.90 Spending authority from offsetting collections (total discretionary)	380	405	400
70.00 Total new budget authority (gross)	1,568	1,592	1,531
Change in unpaid obligations:			
Unpaid obligations, start of year:			
72.40 Obligated balance, start of year	1,351	1,198	1,217
72.95 From Federal sources: Receivables and unpaid, unfilled orders	13	358	358
72.99 Total unpaid obligations, start of year	1,364	1,556	1,575
73.10 Total new obligations	1,493	1,594	1,571
73.20 Total outlays (gross)	−1,248	−1,574	−1,461
73.45 Adjustments in unexpired accounts	−53		
Unpaid obligations, end of year:			
74.40 Obligated balance, end of year	1,198	1,217	1,327
74.95 From Federal sources: Receivables and unpaid, unfilled orders	358	358	358
74.99 Total unpaid obligations, end of year	1,556	1,575	1,685
Outlays (gross), detail:			
86.90 Outlays from new discretionary authority	302	756	743
86.93 Outlays from discretionary balances	946	818	718
87.00 Total outlays (gross)	1,248	1,574	1,461
Offsets:			
Against gross budget authority and outlays:			
Offsetting collections (cash) from:			
88.00 Federal sources	−30	−387	−400
88.40 Non-Federal sources	−4	−18	
88.90 Total, offsetting collections (cash)	−34	−405	−400
Against gross budget authority only:			
88.95 From Federal sources: Change in receivables and unpaid, unfilled orders	−345		
Net budget authority and outlays:			
89.00 Budget authority	1,189	1,187	1,131
90.00 Outlays	1,214	1,170	1,061

Budget Plan (in millions of dollars)
Outlays

Identification code 21–2034–0–1–051	1999 actual	2000 est.	2001 est.
Direct:			
0701 Ammunition	1,007	1,012	979
0702 Ammunition production base support	175	181	153
0791 Total direct	1,183	1,193	1,131
0801 Reimbursable	380	405	400
0893 Total budget plan	1,562	1,598	1,531

Object Classification (in millions of dollars)

Identification code 21–2034–0–1–051	1999 actual	2000 est.	2001 est.
Direct obligations:			
22.0 Transportation of things	12	7	4

25.1	Advisory and assistance services	9	1	
25.2	Other services	129	31	20
	Purchases of goods and services from Government accounts:			
25.3	Purchases of goods and services from Government accounts	102	63	39
25.3	Purchases from revolving funds	71	44	31
25.4	Operation and maintenance of facilities	118	68	62
25.5	Research and development contracts	1		
26.0	Supplies and materials	790	898	1,014
31.0	Equipment		2	1
99.0	Subtotal, direct obligations	1,232	1,114	1,171
99.0	Reimbursable obligations	261	480	400
99.9	Total new obligations	1,493	1,594	1,571

OTHER PROCUREMENT, ARMY

For construction, procurement, production, and modification of vehicles, including tactical, support, and non-tracked combat vehicles; the purchase of not to exceed [36] *35* passenger motor vehicles for replacement only; and the purchase of [three] *12* vehicles required for physical security of personnel, notwithstanding price limitations applicable to passenger vehicles but not to exceed $200,000 per vehicle; communications and electronic equipment; other support equipment; spare parts, ordnance, and accessories therefor; specialized equipment and training devices; expansion of public and private plants, including the land necessary therefor, for the foregoing purposes, and such lands and interests therein, may be acquired, and construction prosecuted thereon prior to approval of title; and procurement and installation of equipment, appliances, and machine tools in public and private plants; reserve plant and Government and contractor-owned equipment layaway; and other expenses necessary for the foregoing purposes, [$3,738,934,000] *$3,795,870,000*, to remain available for obligation until September 30, [2002] *2003, of which $805,740,000 shall be available for the Army National Guard and Army Reserve. (10 U.S.C. 2353, 3013, 4532; Department of Defense Appropriations Act, 2000.)*

Program and Financing (in millions of dollars)

Identification code 21–2035–0–1–051		1999 actual	2000 est.	2001 est.
	Obligations by program activity:			
	Direct program:			
00.01	Tactical and support vehicles	828	879	916
00.02	Communications and electronics equipment	1,744	1,816	1,886
00.03	Other support equipment	835	860	932
00.04	Spare and repair parts	57	47	44
09.01	Reimbursable program	19	63	62
10.00	Total new obligations	3,483	3,664	3,840
	Budgetary resources available for obligation:			
	Unobligated balance available, start of year:			
21.40	For completion of prior year budget plans	291	352	520
21.40	Available to finance new budget plans		33	
21.99	Total unobligated balance, start of year	291	384	520
22.00	New budget authority (gross)	3,428	3,800	3,858
22.10	Resources available from recoveries of prior year obligations	149		
22.21	Unobligated balance transferred to other DoD accounts	−2		
22.22	Unobligated balance transferred from other DoD accounts	2		
23.90	Total budgetary resources available for obligation	3,868	4,185	4,379
23.95	Total new obligations	−3,483	−3,664	−3,840
23.98	Unobligated balance expiring or withdrawn	−1		
	Unobligated balance available, end of year:			
24.40	For completion of prior year budget plans	352	520	539
24.40	Available to finance subsequent year budget plans	33		
24.99	Total unobligated balance, end of year	384	520	539
	New budget authority (gross), detail:			
	Discretionary:			
40.00	Appropriation	3,330	3,739	3,796
40.36	Unobligated balance rescinded	−24	−33	
40.76	Reduction pursuant to P.L. 106–113		−19	
40.77	Reduction pursuant to P.L. 105–262	−35		
41.00	Transferred to other DoD accounts		−16	
42.00	Transferred from other DoD accounts	154	66	
43.00	Appropriation (total discretionary)	3,425	3,737	3,796
	Spending authority from offsetting collections:			
68.00	Offsetting collections (cash)	32	63	63
68.10	From Federal sources: Change in receivables and unpaid, unfilled orders	−32		
68.15	From Federal sources: Adjustments to receivables and unpaid, unfilled orders	2		
68.90	Spending authority from offsetting collections (total discretionary)	2	63	63
70.00	Total new budget authority (gross)	3,427	3,800	3,859
	Change in unpaid obligations:			
	Unpaid obligations, start of year:			
72.40	Obligated balance, start of year	3,317	3,478	3,903
72.95	From Federal sources: Receivables and unpaid, unfilled orders	94	62	62
72.99	Total unpaid obligations, start of year	3,411	3,540	3,965
73.10	Total new obligations	3,483	3,664	3,840
73.20	Total outlays (gross)	−3,156	−3,239	−3,470
73.40	Adjustments in expired accounts (net)	−48		
73.45	Adjustments in unexpired accounts	−149		
	Unpaid obligations, end of year:			
74.40	Obligated balance, end of year	3,478	3,903	4,272
74.95	From Federal sources: Receivables and unpaid, unfilled orders	62	62	62
74.99	Total unpaid obligations, end of year	3,540	3,965	4,334
	Outlays (gross), detail:			
86.90	Outlays from new discretionary authority	961	930	970
86.93	Outlays from discretionary balances	2,195	2,309	2,501
87.00	Total outlays (gross)	3,156	3,239	3,470
	Offsets:			
	Against gross budget authority and outlays:			
	Offsetting collections (cash) from:			
88.00	Federal sources	−31	−63	−63
88.40	Non-Federal sources	−1		
88.90	Total, offsetting collections (cash)	−32	−63	−63
	Against gross budget authority only:			
88.95	From Federal sources: Change in receivables and unpaid, unfilled orders	32		
88.96	From Federal sources: Adjustment to receivables and unpaid, unfilled orders	−2		
	Net budget authority and outlays:			
89.00	Budget authority	3,425	3,737	3,796
90.00	Outlays	3,124	3,176	3,408

Budget Plan (in millions of dollars)

Outlays

Identification code 21–2035–0–1–051		1999 actual	2000 est.	2001 est.
	Direct:			
0701	Tactical and support vehicles	808	936	942
0702	Communications and electronics equipment	1,717	1,889	1,848
0703	Other support equipment	834	902	963
0704	Spare and repair parts	59	44	43
0791	Total direct	3,417	3,770	3,796
0801	Reimbursable	13	63	63
0893	Total budget plan	3,430	3,833	3,858

Object Classification (in millions of dollars)

Identification code 21–2035–0–1–051		1999 actual	2000 est.	2001 est.
	Direct obligations:			
21.0	Travel and transportation of persons	2	1	1
22.0	Transportation of things	7	12	12
23.3	Communications, utilities, and miscellaneous charges	20		
25.1	Advisory and assistance services	116	36	36
25.2	Other services	253	2	3

General and special funds—Continued

OTHER PROCUREMENT, ARMY—Continued

Object Classification (in millions of dollars)—Continued

Identification code 21–2035–0–1–051		1999 actual	2000 est.	2001 est.
	Purchases of goods and services from Government accounts:			
25.3	Purchases of goods and services from Government accounts	275	393	453
25.3	Purchases from revolving funds	7	12	13
25.4	Operation and maintenance of facilities	1		
25.5	Research and development contracts	150		
25.7	Operation and maintenance of equipment	48		
26.0	Supplies and materials	82	67	79
31.0	Equipment	2,496	3,078	3,181
32.0	Land and structures	7		
99.0	Subtotal, direct obligations	3,463	3,601	3,778
99.0	Reimbursable obligations	19	63	62
99.9	Total new obligations	3,483	3,664	3,840

AIRCRAFT PROCUREMENT, NAVY

For construction, procurement, production, modification, and modernization of aircraft, equipment, including ordnance, spare parts, and accessories therefor; specialized equipment; expansion of public and private plants, including the land necessary therefor, and such lands and interests therein, may be acquired, and construction prosecuted thereon prior to approval of title; and procurement and installation of equipment, appliances, and machine tools in public and private plants; reserve plant and Government and contractor-owned equipment layaway, [$8,662,655,000] *$7,963,858,000*, to remain available for obligation until September 30, [2002] *2003, of which $30,666,000, shall be available for the Navy Reserve and Marine Corps Reserve. (10 U.S.C. 5013, 5063, 7201, 7341; Department of Defense Appropriations Act, 2000.)*

Program and Financing (in millions of dollars)

Identification code 17–1506–0–1–051		1999 actual	2000 est.	2001 est.
	Obligations by program activity:			
	Direct program:			
00.01	Combat aircraft	3,997	4,734	5,145
00.02	Airlift aircraft	114	353	302
00.03	Trainer aircraft	314	314	331
00.04	Other aircraft	147	63	133
00.05	Modification of aircraft	1,709	1,715	1,055
00.06	Aircraft spares and repair parts	720	763	883
00.07	Aircraft support equipment and facilities	343	418	376
09.01	Reimbursable program		7	7
10.00	Total new obligations	7,344	8,367	8,232
	Budgetary resources available for obligation:			
	Unobligated balance available, start of year:			
21.40	For completion of prior year budget plans	757	949	1,412
21.40	Available to finance new budget plans		86	
21.99	Total unobligated balance, start of year	757	1,034	1,412
22.00	New budget authority (gross)	7,633	8,657	7,971
22.10	Resources available from recoveries of prior year obligations	5		
22.22	Unobligated balances transferred from other DoD accounts	3	88	
23.90	Total budgetary resources available for obligation	8,397	9,779	9,383
23.95	Total new obligations	−7,344	−8,367	−8,232
23.98	Unobligated balance expiring or withdrawn	−17		
	Unobligated balance available, end of year:			
24.40	For completion of prior year budget plans	949	1,412	1,150
24.40	Available to finance subsequent year budget plans	86		
24.99	Total unobligated balance, end of year	1,034	1,412	1,150
	New budget authority (gross), detail:			
	Discretionary:			
40.00	Appropriation	7,520	8,663	7,964
40.36	Unobligated balance rescinded		−86	
40.76	Reduction pursuant to P.L. 106–113		−44	
41.00	Transferred to other DoD accounts	−53	−9	
42.00	Transferred from other DoD accounts	165	126	
43.00	Appropriation (total discretionary)	7,632	8,650	7,964
	Spending authority from offsetting collections:			
68.00	Offsetting collections (cash)	3	7	7
68.10	From Federal sources: Change in receivables and unpaid, unfilled orders	2		
68.15	From Federal sources: Adjustments to receivables and unpaid, unfilled orders	−4		
68.90	Spending authority from offsetting collections (total discretionary)	1	7	7
70.00	Total new budget authority (gross)	7,633	8,657	7,971
	Change in unpaid obligations:			
	Unpaid obligations, start of year:			
72.40	Obligated balance, start of year	9,072	10,376	11,525
72.95	From Federal sources: Receivables and unpaid, unfilled orders	−2		
72.99	Total unpaid obligations, start of year	9,070	10,376	11,525
73.10	Total new obligations	7,344	8,367	8,232
73.20	Total outlays (gross)	−6,027	−7,217	−7,486
73.40	Adjustments in expired accounts (net)	−6		
73.45	Adjustments in unexpired accounts	−5		
	Unpaid obligations, end of year:			
74.40	Obligated balance, end of year	10,376	11,525	12,272
74.95	From Federal sources: Receivables and unpaid, unfilled orders			
74.99	Total unpaid obligations, end of year	10,376	11,525	12,272
	Outlays (gross), detail:			
86.90	Outlays from new discretionary authority	1,144	1,287	1,241
86.93	Outlays from discretionary balances	4,883	5,930	6,245
87.00	Total outlays (gross)	6,027	7,217	7,486
	Offsets:			
	Against gross budget authority and outlays:			
88.00	Offsetting collections (cash) from: Federal sources	−3	−7	−7
	Against gross budget authority only:			
88.95	From Federal sources: Change in receivables and unpaid, unfilled orders	−2		
88.96	From Federal sources: Adjustment to receivables and unpaid, unfilled orders	4		
	Net budget authority and outlays:			
89.00	Budget authority	7,632	8,650	7,964
90.00	Outlays	6,024	7,210	7,479

Budget Plan (in millions of dollars)
Outlays

Identification code 17–1506–0–1–051		1999 actual	2000 est.	2001 est.
	Direct:			
0701	Combat aircraft	4,196	4,661	4,840
0702	Airlift aircraft	134	426	296
0703	Trainer aircraft	300	388	348
0704	Other aircraft	111	77	155
0705	Modification of aircraft	1,732	1,804	998
0706	Aircraft spares and repair parts	730	965	942
0707	Aircraft support equipment and facilities	345	502	385
0791	Total direct	7,549	8,823	7,964
0801	Reimbursable		7	7
0893	Total budget plan	7,549	8,830	7,971

Object Classification (in millions of dollars)

Identification code 17–1506–0–1–051		1999 actual	2000 est.	2001 est.
	Direct obligations:			
25.1	Advisory and assistance services	95	107	114
25.3	Purchases from other Govt acct—revolving funds	569	473	409
26.0	Supplies and materials		12	13
31.0	Equipment	6,680	7,767	7,689
99.0	Subtotal, direct obligations	7,344	8,359	8,225
99.0	Reimbursable obligations		8	7
99.9	Total new obligations	7,344	8,367	8,232

WEAPONS PROCUREMENT, NAVY

For construction, procurement, production, modification, and modernization of missiles, torpedoes, other weapons, and related support equipment including spare parts, and accessories therefor; expansion of public and private plants, including the land necessary therefor, and such lands and interests therein, may be acquired, and construction prosecuted thereon prior to approval of title; and procurement and installation of equipment, appliances, and machine tools in public and private plants; reserve plant and Government and contractor-owned equipment layaway, [$1,383,413,000] *$1,434,250,000*, to remain available for obligation until September 30, [2002] *2003. (10 U.S.C. 5013, 5062; Department of Defense Appropriations Act, 2000.)*

Program and Financing (in millions of dollars)

Identification code 17–1507–0–1–051		1999 actual	2000 est.	2001 est.
	Obligations by program activity:			
	Direct program:			
00.01	Ballistic missiles	299	459	389
00.02	Other missiles	1,033	718	891
00.03	Torpedoes and related equipment	96	104	97
00.04	Other weapons	47	47	15
00.06	Spares and repair parts	43	43	50
09.01	Reimbursable program	3	10	11
10.00	Total new obligations	1,521	1,381	1,454
	Budgetary resources available for obligation:			
	Unobligated balance available, start of year:			
21.40	For completion of prior year budget plans	203	266	296
21.40	Available to finance new budget plans		8	
21.99	Total unobligated balance, start of year	203	274	296
22.00	New budget authority (gross)	1,596	1,404	1,444
22.10	Resources available from recoveries of prior year obligations	4		
23.90	Total budgetary resources available for obligation	1,804	1,677	1,740
23.95	Total new obligations	–1,521	–1,381	–1,454
23.98	Unobligated balance expiring or withdrawn	–10		
	Unobligated balance available, end of year:			
24.40	For completion of prior year budget plans	266	296	287
24.40	Available to finance subsequent year budget plans	8		
24.99	Total unobligated balance, end of year	274	296	287
	New budget authority (gross), detail:			
	Discretionary:			
40.00	Appropriation	1,207	1,333	1,434
40.15	Appropriation (emergency)	431		
40.36	Unobligated balance rescinded	–2	–8	
40.76	Reduction pursuant to P.L. 106–113		–7	
41.00	Transferred to other DoD accounts	–23	–22	
42.00	Transferred from other DOD accounts		98	
43.00	Appropriation (total discretionary)	1,614	1,394	1,434
	Spending authority from offsetting collections:			
68.00	Offsetting collections (cash)	52	10	10
68.10	From Federal sources: Change in receivables and unpaid, unfilled orders	–69		
68.90	Spending authority from offsetting collections (total discretionary)	–17	10	10
70.00	Total new budget authority (gross)	1,596	1,404	1,444
	Change in unpaid obligations:			
	Unpaid obligations, start of year:			
72.40	Obligated balance, start of year	1,991	2,147	2,184
72.95	From Federal sources: Receivables and unpaid, unfilled orders	72	3	3
72.99	Total unpaid obligations, start of year	2,063	2,150	2,187
73.10	Total new obligations	1,521	1,381	1,454
73.20	Total outlays (gross)	–1,331	–1,344	–1,367
73.40	Adjustments in expired accounts (net)	–99		
73.45	Adjustments in unexpired accounts	–4		
	Unpaid obligations, end of year:			
74.40	Obligated balance, end of year	2,147	2,184	2,272
74.95	From Federal sources: Receivables and unpaid, unfilled orders	3	3	3
74.99	Total unpaid obligations, end of year	2,150	2,187	2,274
	Outlays (gross), detail:			
86.90	Outlays from new discretionary authority	231	244	261
86.93	Outlays from discretionary balances	1,100	1,099	1,106
87.00	Total outlays (gross)	1,331	1,344	1,367
	Offsets:			
	Against gross budget authority and outlays:			
88.00	Offsetting collections (cash) from: Federal sources	–52	–10	–10
	Against gross budget authority only:			
88.95	From Federal sources: Change in receivables and unpaid, unfilled orders	69		
88.96	From Federal sources: Adjustment to receivables and unpaid, unfilled orders			
	Net budget authority and outlays:			
89.00	Budget authority	1,614	1,394	1,434
90.00	Outlays	1,279	1,334	1,357

Budget Plan (in millions of dollars)
Outlays

Identification code 17–1507–0–1–051		1999 actual	2000 est.	2001 est.
	Direct:			
0701	Ballistic missiles	310	489	464
0702	Other missiles	1,107	712	818
0703	Torpedoes and related equipment	92	116	92
0704	Other weapons	54	38	7
0706	Spares and repair parts	45	47	53
0791	Total direct	1,608	1,402	1,434
0801	Reimbursable	1	10	10
0893	Total budget plan	1,609	1,412	1,444

Object Classification (in millions of dollars)

Identification code 17–1507–0–1–051		1999 actual	2000 est.	2001 est.
	Direct obligations:			
25.1	Advisory and assistance services	15	14	14
25.3	Purchases from revolving funds	166	169	170
26.0	Supplies and materials		20	29
31.0	Equipment	1,337	1,168	1,230
99.0	Subtotal, direct obligations	1,518	1,371	1,443
99.0	Reimbursable obligations	3	10	11
99.9	Total new obligations	1,521	1,381	1,454

PROCUREMENT OF AMMUNITION, NAVY AND MARINE CORPS

For construction, procurement, production, and modification of ammunition, and accessories therefor; specialized equipment and training devices; expansion of public and private plants, including ammunition facilities authorized by section 2854 of title 10, United States Code, and the land necessary therefor, for the foregoing purposes, and such lands and interests therein, may be acquired, and construction prosecuted thereon prior to approval of title; and procurement and installation of equipment, appliances, and machine tools in public and private plants; reserve plant and Government and contractor-owned equipment layaway; and other expenses necessary for the foregoing purposes, [$525,200,000] *$429,649,000*, to remain available for obligation until September 30, [2002] *2003, of which $13,304,000 shall be available for the Navy Reserve and Marine Corps Reserve. (Department of Defense Appropriations Act, 2000.)*

Program and Financing (in millions of dollars)

Identification code 17–1508–0–1–051		1999 actual	2000 est.	2001 est.
	Obligations by program activity:			
	Direct program:			
00.01	Ammunition, Navy	284	349	302
00.02	Ammunition, Marine Corps	172	212	141
09.01	Reimbursable program	11	10	10
10.00	Total new obligations	468	571	453
	Budgetary resources available for obligation:			
	Unobligated balance available, start of year:			
21.40	For completion of prior year budget plans	67	66	93

General and special funds—Continued

PROCUREMENT OF AMMUNITION, NAVY AND MARINE CORPS—Continued

Program and Financing (in millions of dollars)—Continued

Identification code 17–1508–0–1–051		1999 actual	2000 est.	2001 est.
21.40	Available to finance new budget plans		3	
21.99	Total unobligated balance, start of year	67	69	93
22.00	New budget authority (gross)	469	595	440
22.10	Resources available from recoveries of prior year obligations	2		
23.90	Total budgetary resources available for obligation	539	664	532
23.95	Total new obligations	–468	–571	–453
23.98	Unobligated balance expiring or withdrawn	–2		
	Unobligated balance available, end of year:			
24.40	For completion of prior year budget plans	66	93	79
24.40	Available to finance subsequent year budget plans	3		
24.99	Total unobligated balance, end of year	69	93	79
	New budget authority (gross), detail:			
	Discretionary:			
40.00	Appropriation	483	412	430
40.36	Unobligated balance rescinded	–13	–3	
40.76	Reduction pursuant to P.L. 106–113		–2	
41.00	Transferred to other DoD accounts	–13		
42.00	Transferred from other DoD accounts		178	
43.00	Appropriation (total discretionary)	458	585	430
	Spending authority from offsetting collections:			
68.00	Offsetting collections (cash)	11	10	10
68.10	From Federal sources: Change in receivables and unpaid, unfilled orders	1		
68.90	Spending authority from offsetting collections (total discretionary)	12	10	10
70.00	Total new budget authority (gross)	469	595	440
	Change in unpaid obligations:			
	Unpaid obligations, start of year:			
72.40	Obligated balance, start of year	516	576	707
72.95	From Federal sources: Receivables and unpaid, unfilled orders	–9	–8	–8
72.99	Total unpaid obligations, start of year	508	568	699
73.10	Total new obligations	468	571	453
73.20	Total outlays (gross)	–406	–440	–425
73.45	Adjustments in unexpired accounts	–2		
	Unpaid obligations, end of year:			
74.40	Obligated balance, end of year	576	707	735
74.95	From Federal sources: Receivables and unpaid, unfilled orders	–8	–8	–8
74.99	Total unpaid obligations, end of year	568	699	727
	Outlays (gross), detail:			
86.90	Outlays from new discretionary authority	74	132	103
86.93	Outlays from discretionary balances	332	308	322
87.00	Total outlays (gross)	406	440	425
	Offsets:			
	Against gross budget authority and outlays:			
88.00	Offsetting collections (cash) from: Federal sources	–11	–10	–10
	Against gross budget authority only:			
88.95	From Federal sources: Change in receivables and unpaid, unfilled orders	–1		
	Net budget authority and outlays:			
89.00	Budget authority	458	585	430
90.00	Outlays	395	430	415

Budget Plan (in millions of dollars)
Outlays

Identification code 17–1508–0–1–051		1999 actual	2000 est.	2001 est.
	Direct:			
0701	Ammunition, Navy	288	396	296
0702	Ammunition, Marine Corps	179	192	134
0791	Subtotal	467	588	430
0801	Reimbursable program	3	10	10
0893	Total budget plan	470	598	440

Object Classification (in millions of dollars)

Identification code 17–1508–0–1–051		1999 actual	2000 est.	2001 est.
	Direct obligations:			
25.1	Advisory and assistance services		5	5
	Purchases of goods and services from Government accounts:			
25.3	Purchases of goods and services from Government accounts	7	38	36
25.3	Purchases from revolving funds	136	106	121
25.7	Operation and maintenance of equipment	26	24	18
31.0	Equipment	288	388	263
99.0	Subtotal, direct obligations	457	561	443
99.0	Reimbursable obligations	11	10	10
99.9	Total new obligations	468	571	453

SHIPBUILDING AND CONVERSION, NAVY

For expenses necessary for the construction, acquisition, or conversion of vessels as authorized by law, including armor and armament thereof, plant equipment, appliances, and machine tools and installation thereof in public and private plants; reserve plant and Government and contractor-owned equipment layaway; procurement of critical, long leadtime components and designs for vessels to be constructed or converted in the future; and expansion of public and private plants, including land necessary therefor, and such lands and interests therein, may be acquired, and construction prosecuted thereon prior to approval of title, [as follows:

NSSN (AP), $748,497,000;

CVN–77 (AP), $751,540,000;

CVN Refuelings (AP), $345,565,000;

DDG–51 destroyer program, $2,681,653,000;

LPD–17 amphibious transport dock ship, $1,508,338,000;

LHD–8 (AP), $375,000,000;

ADC(X), $439,966,000;

LCAC landing craft air cushion program, $31,776,000; and

For craft, outfitting, post delivery, conversions, and first destination transportation, $171,119,000;

In all: $7,053,454,000] *$12,296,919,000*, to remain available for obligation until September 30, [2004] *2005*: *Provided*, That additional obligations may be incurred after September 30, [2004] *2005*, for engineering services, tests, evaluations, and other such budgeted work that must be performed in the final stage of ship construction: *Provided further*, That none of the funds provided under this heading for the construction or conversion of any naval vessel to be constructed in shipyards in the United States shall be expended in foreign facilities for the construction of major components of such vessel: *Provided further*, That none of the funds provided under this heading shall be used for the construction of any naval vessel in foreign shipyards[: *Provided further*, That the Secretary of the Navy is hereby granted the authority to enter into a contract for an LHD–1 Amphibious Assault Ship which shall be funded on an incremental basis]. *(10 U.S.C. 5013, 5062; Department of Defense Appropriations Act, 2000.)*

Program and Financing (in millions of dollars)

Identification code 17–1611–0–1–051		1999 actual	2000 est.	2001 est.
	Obligations by program activity:			
	Direct Program:			
00.01	Fleet ballistic missile ships	3	12	
00.02	Other warships	5,244	5,071	8,841
00.03	Amphibious ships	535	1,425	1,418
00.04	Mine warfare and patrol ships	35	4	1
00.05	Auxiliaries, craft, and prior-year program costs	330	565	699
09.01	Reimbursable program	17		
10.00	Total new obligations	6,162	7,077	10,959
	Budgetary resources available for obligation:			
	Unobligated balance available, start of year:			
21.40	For completion of prior year budget plans	6,510	6,229	6,299

21.40	Available to finance new budget plans		210	
21.99	Total unobligated balance, start of year	6,510	6,439	6,299
22.00	New budget authority (gross)	5,918	6,936	12,297
22.10	Resources available from recoveries of prior year obligations	174		
23.90	Total budgetary resources available for obligation	12,601	13,375	18,596
23.95	Total new obligations	−6,162	−7,077	−10,959
	Unobligated balance available, end of year:			
24.40	For completion of prior year budget plans	6,229	6,299	7,637
24.40	Available to finance subsequent year budget plans	210		
24.99	Total unobligated balance, end of year	6,439	6,299	7,637
	New budget authority (gross), detail:			
	Discretionary:			
40.00	Appropriation	6,018	7,053	12,297
40.36	Unobligated balance rescinded	−100	−81	
40.76	Reduction pursuant to P.L. 106–113		−36	
41.00	Transferred to other DoD accounts	−181	−129	
42.00	Transferred from other DoD accounts	181	129	
43.00	Appropriation (total discretionary)	5,918	6,936	12,297
	Spending authority from offsetting collections:			
68.00	Offsetting collections (cash)	215		
68.10	From Federal sources: Change in receivables and unpaid, unfilled orders	−215		
68.90	Spending authority from offsetting collections (total discretionary)			
70.00	Total new budget authority (gross)	5,918	6,936	12,297
	Change in unpaid obligations:			
	Unpaid obligations, start of year:			
72.40	Obligated balance, start of year	15,121	14,186	15,440
72.95	From Federal sources: Receivables and unpaid, unfilled orders	647	432	432
72.99	Total unpaid obligations, start of year	15,768	14,618	15,872
73.10	Total new obligations	6,162	7,077	10,959
73.20	Total outlays (gross)	−6,912	−5,823	−6,399
73.40	Adjustments in expired accounts (net)	−226		
73.45	Adjustments in unexpired accounts	−174		
	Unpaid obligations, end of year:			
74.40	Obligated balance, end of year	14,186	15,440	20,000
74.95	From Federal sources: Receivables and unpaid, unfilled orders	432	432	432
74.99	Total unpaid obligations, end of year	14,618	15,872	20,432
	Outlays (gross), detail:			
86.90	Outlays from new discretionary authority	485	460	729
86.93	Outlays from discretionary balances	6,427	5,363	5,669
87.00	Total outlays (gross)	6,912	5,823	6,399
	Offsets:			
	Against gross budget authority and outlays:			
88.00	Offsetting collections (cash) from: Federal sources	−215		
	Against gross budget authority only:			
88.95	From Federal sources: Change in receivables and unpaid, unfilled orders	215		
	Net budget authority and outlays:			
89.00	Budget authority	5,917	6,936	12,297
90.00	Outlays	6,698	5,823	6,399

Budget Plan (in millions of dollars)

Outlays

Identification code 17–1611–0–1–051		1999 actual	2000 est.	2001 est.
0702	Other warships	5,152	4,515	9,868
0703	Amphibious ships	677	1,861	1,510
0704	Mine warfare and patrol ships	6		
0705	Auxiliaries, craft, and prior-year program costs	283	771	919
0893	Total budget plan	6,118	7,147	12,297

Object Classification (in millions of dollars)

Identification code 17–1611–0–1–051		1999 actual	2000 est.	2001 est.
	Direct obligations:			
25.1	Advisory and assistance services	55	57	54
25.2	Other services	792	733	749
	Purchases of goods and services from Government accounts:			
25.3	Purchases of goods and services from Government accounts	56	48	37
25.3	Purchases from revolving funds	466	463	452
26.0	Supplies and materials	5	25	34
31.0	Equipment	4,771	5,751	9,633
99.0	Subtotal, direct obligations	6,145	7,077	10,959
99.0	Reimbursable obligations	17		
99.9	Total new obligations	6,162	7,077	10,959

Other Procurement, Navy

For procurement, production, and modernization of support equipment and materials not otherwise provided for, Navy ordnance (except ordnance for new aircraft, new ships, and ships authorized for conversion); the purchase of not to exceed [50] *63* passenger motor vehicles for replacement only, *and the purchase of one vehicle required for physical security of personnel, notwithstanding price limitations applicable to passenger vehicles but not to exceed $200,000*; expansion of public and private plants, including the land necessary therefor, and such lands and interests therein, may be acquired, and construction prosecuted thereon prior to approval of title; and procurement and installation of equipment, appliances, and machine tools in public and private plants; reserve plant and Government and contractor-owned equipment layaway, [$4,320,238,000] *$3,334,611,000*, to remain available for obligation until September 30, [2002] *2003, of which $4,054,000, shall be available for the Navy Reserve. (10 U.S.C. 5013, 5063; Department of Defense Appropriations Act, 2000.)*

Program and Financing (in millions of dollars)

Identification code 17–1810–0–1–051		1999 actual	2000 est.	2001 est.
	Obligations by program activity:			
	Direct program:			
00.01	Ships support equipment	940	771	609
00.02	Communications and electronics equipment	1,598	2,135	1,537
00.03	Aviation support equipment	255	203	204
00.04	Ordinance support equipment	674	580	510
00.05	Civil engineering support equipment	43	68	94
00.06	Supply support equipment	95	114	151
00.07	Personnel and command support equipment	109	76	98
00.08	Spares and repair parts	235	235	211
09.01	Reimbursable program	46	54	42
10.00	Total new obligations	3,995	4,236	3,456
	Budgetary resources available for obligation:			
	Unobligated balance available, start of year:			
21.40	For completion of prior year budget plans	466	543	649
21.40	Available to finance new budget plans		39	
21.99	Total unobligated balance, start of year	466	582	649
22.00	New budget authority (gross)	4,109	4,304	3,377
22.10	Resources available from recoveries of prior year obligations	9		
23.90	Total budgetary resources available for obligation	4,584	4,886	4,026
23.95	Total new obligations	−3,995	−4,236	−3,456
23.98	Unobligated balance expiring or withdrawn	−6		
	Unobligated balance available, end of year:			
24.40	For completion of prior year budget plans	543	649	569
24.40	Available to finance subsequent year budget plans	39		
24.99	Total unobligated balance, end of year	582	649	569
	New budget authority (gross), detail:			
	Discretionary:			
40.00	Appropriation	4,061	4,320	3,335
40.36	Unobligated balance rescinded	−29	−39	
40.76	Reduction pursuant to P.L. 106–113		−22	
40.77	Reduction pursuant to P.L. 105–262	−55		
41.00	Transferred to other DoD accounts	−3		
42.00	Transferred from other DoD accounts	81	3	
43.00	Appropriation (total discretionary)	4,055	4,262	3,335
	Spending authority from offsetting collections:			
68.00	Offsetting collections (cash)	58	42	42
68.10	From Federal sources: Change in receivables and unpaid, unfilled orders	−12		

General and special funds—Continued

OTHER PROCUREMENT, NAVY—Continued

Program and Financing (in millions of dollars)—Continued

Identification code 17–1810–0–1–051		1999 actual	2000 est.	2001 est.
68.15	From Federal sources: Adjustments to receivables and unpaid, unfilled orders	8		
68.90	Spending authority from offsetting collections (total discretionary)	54	42	42
70.00	Total new budget authority (gross)	4,109	4,304	3,377
	Change in unpaid obligations:			
	Unpaid obligations, start of year:			
72.40	Obligated balance, start of year	3,116	3,616	3,937
72.95	From Federal sources: Receivables and unpaid, unfilled orders	78	66	66
72.99	Total unpaid obligations, start of year	3,194	3,682	4,003
73.10	Total new obligations	3,995	4,236	3,456
73.20	Total outlays (gross)	−3,421	−3,915	−3,828
73.40	Adjustments in expired accounts (net)	−76		
73.45	Adjustments in unexpired accounts	−9		
	Unpaid obligations, end of year:			
74.40	Obligated balance, end of year	3,616	3,937	3,565
74.95	From Federal sources: Receivables and unpaid, unfilled orders	66	66	66
74.99	Total unpaid obligations, end of year	3,682	4,003	3,631
	Outlays (gross), detail:			
86.90	Outlays from new discretionary authority	1,437	1,470	1,183
86.93	Outlays from discretionary balances	1,984	2,445	2,645
87.00	Total outlays (gross)	3,421	3,915	3,828
	Offsets:			
	Against gross budget authority and outlays:			
	Offsetting collections (cash) from:			
88.00	Federal sources	−6	−42	−42
88.40	Non-Federal sources	−52		
88.90	Total, offsetting collections (cash)	−58	−42	−42
	Against gross budget authority only:			
88.95	From Federal sources: Change in receivables and unpaid, unfilled orders	12		
88.96	From Federal sources: Adjustment to receivables and unpaid, unfilled orders	−8		
	Net budget authority and outlays:			
89.00	Budget authority	4,055	4,262	3,335
90.00	Outlays	3,363	3,873	3,786

Budget Plan (in millions of dollars)

Outlays

Identification code 17–1810–0–1–051		1999 actual	2000 est.	2001 est.
	Direct:			
0701	Ship support equipment	946	910	573
0702	Communications and electronics equipment	1,642	1,949	1,490
0703	Aviation support equipment	251	238	205
0704	Ordnance support equipment	715	652	498
0705	Civil engineering support equipment	54	69	98
0706	Supply support equipment	89	140	162
0707	Personnel and command support equipment	105	71	99
0708	Spares and repair parts	244	273	209
0791	Total direct	4,047	4,302	3,335
0801	Reimbursable	53	42	42
0893	Total budget plan	4,100	4,344	3,377

Object Classification (in millions of dollars)

Identification code 17–1810–0–1–051		1999 actual	2000 est.	2001 est.
	Direct obligations:			
25.1	Advisory and assistance services	21	23	22
25.2	Other services	8	132	160
	Purchases of goods and services from Government accounts:			
25.3	Purchases of goods and services from Government accounts	127	139	131
25.3	Purchases from revolving funds	909	951	877
26.0	Supplies and materials	111	119	69
31.0	Equipment	2,773	2,818	2,155
99.0	Subtotal, direct obligations	3,949	4,182	3,414
99.0	Reimbursable obligations	46	54	42
99.9	Total new obligations	3,995	4,236	3,456

COASTAL DEFENSE AUGMENTATION

Program and Financing (in millions of dollars)

Identification code 17–0380–0–1–051		1999 actual	2000 est.	2001 est.
	Budgetary resources available for obligation:			
21.40	For completion of prior year budget plans	1	1	1
24.40	Unobligated balance available, end of year	1	1	1
	Change in unpaid obligations:			
72.40	Unpaid obligations, start of year: Obligated balance, start of year	56	56	50
73.20	Total outlays (gross)		−6	−6
73.40	Adjustments in expired accounts (net)			
74.40	Unpaid obligations, end of year: Obligated balance, end of year	56	50	44
	Outlays (gross), detail:			
86.93	Outlays from discretionary balances		6	6
	Net budget authority and outlays:			
89.00	Budget authority			
90.00	Outlays		6	6

PROCUREMENT, MARINE CORPS

For expenses necessary for the procurement, manufacture, and modification of missiles, armament, military equipment, spare parts, and accessories therefor; plant equipment, appliances, and machine tools, and installation thereof in public and private plants; reserve plant and Government and contractor-owned equipment layaway; vehicles for the Marine Corps, including the purchase of not to exceed [43] *33* passenger motor vehicles for replacement only; and expansion of public and private plants, including land necessary therefor, and such lands and interests therein, may be acquired, and construction prosecuted thereon prior to approval of title, [$1,300,920,000] *$1,171,935,000*, to remain available for obligation until September 30, [2002] *2003, of which $27,959,000 shall be available for the Marine Corps Reserve. (10 U.S.C. 5013; Department of Defense Appropriations Act, 2000.)*

Program and Financing (in millions of dollars)

Identification code 17–1109–0–1–051		1999 actual	2000 est.	2001 est.
	Obligations by program activity:			
	Direct program:			
00.02	Weapons and combat vehicles	104	150	188
00.03	Guided missiles and equipment	86	79	82
00.04	Communications and electronics equipment	368	535	314
00.05	Support vechicles	161	234	420
00.06	Engineer and other equipment	131	136	114
00.07	Spares and repair parts	24	38	28
09.01	Reimbursable program		9	9
10.00	Total new obligations	874	1,181	1,155
	Budgetary resources available for obligation:			
	Unobligated balance available, start of year:			
21.40	For completion of prior year budget plans	165	166	289
21.40	Available to finance new budget plans		5	
21.99	Total unobligated balance, start of year	165	171	289
22.00	New budget authority (gross)	863	1,299	1,181
22.10	Resources available from recoveries of prior year obligations	22		

23.90	Total budgetary resources available for obligation	1,050	1,470	1,470
23.95	Total new obligations	−874	−1,181	−1,155
23.98	Unobligated balance expiring or withdrawn	−5		
	Unobligated balance available, end of year:			
24.40	For completion of prior year budget plans	166	289	315
24.40	Unobligated balance available, end of year	5		
24.99	Total unobligated balance, end of year	171	289	315
	New budget authority (gross), detail:			
	Discretionary:			
40.00	Appropriation	872	1,302	1,172
40.36	Unobligated balance rescinded		−5	
40.76	Reduction pursuant to P.L. 106–113		−7	
40.77	Reduction pursuant to P.L. 105–262	−16		
41.00	Transferred to other DoD accounts	−10		
42.00	Transferred from other DoD accounts	16		
43.00	Appropriation (total discretionary)	862	1,290	1,172
	Spending authority from offsetting collections:			
68.00	Offsetting collections (cash)		9	9
68.15	From Federal sources: Adjustments to receivables and unpaid, unfilled orders	1		
68.90	Spending authority from offsetting collections (total discretionary)	1	9	9
70.00	Total new budget authority (gross)	863	1,299	1,181
	Change in unpaid obligations:			
72.40	Unpaid obligations, start of year: Obligated balance, start of year	583	841	1,198
73.10	Total new obligations	874	1,181	1,155
73.20	Total outlays (gross)	−593	−826	−1,026
73.40	Adjustments in expired accounts (net)	−1		
73.45	Adjustments in unexpired accounts	−22		
74.40	Unpaid obligations, end of year: Obligated balance, end of year	841	1,198	1,327
	Outlays (gross), detail:			
86.90	Outlays from new discretionary authority	193	252	238
86.93	Outlays from discretionary balances	400	574	788
87.00	Total outlays (gross)	593	826	1,026
	Offsets:			
	Against gross budget authority and outlays:			
88.00	Offsetting collections (cash) from: Federal sources		−9	−9
	Against gross budget authority only:			
88.96	From Federal sources: Adjustment to receivables and unpaid, unfilled orders	−1		
	Net budget authority and outlays:			
89.00	Budget authority	862	1,289	1,172
90.00	Outlays	592	817	1,017

Budget Plan (in millions of dollars)
Outlays

Identification code 17–1109–0–1–051		1999 actual	2000 est.	2001 est.
	Direct:			
0702	Weapons and combat vehicles	103	173	177
0703	Guided missiles and equipment	86	96	88
0704	Communications and electronics equipment	406	545	272
0705	Support vehicles	156	283	487
0706	Engineer and other equipment	70	166	123
0707	Spares and repair parts	36	31	25
0791	Total direct	857	1,294	1,172
0801	Reimbursable		9	9
0893	Total budget plan	858	1,304	1,181

Object Classification (in millions of dollars)

Identification code 17–1109–0–1–051		1999 actual	2000 est.	2001 est.
	Direct obligations:			
25.1	Advisory and assistance services	6	8	8
25.3	Purchases from revolving funds	47	76	74
26.0	Supplies and materials	24		
31.0	Equipment	797	1,088	1,064
99.0	Subtotal, direct obligations	874	1,172	1,146
99.0	Reimbursable obligations		9	9
99.9	Total new obligations	874	1,181	1,155

Aircraft Procurement, Air Force

For construction, procurement, lease, and modification of aircraft and equipment, including armor and armament, specialized ground handling equipment, and training devices, spare parts, and accessories therefor; specialized equipment; expansion of public and private plants, Government-owned equipment and installation thereof in such plants, erection of structures, and acquisition of land, for the foregoing purposes, and such lands and interests therein, may be acquired, and construction prosecuted thereon prior to approval of title; reserve plant and Government and contractor-owned equipment layaway; and other expenses necessary for the foregoing purposes including rents and transportation of things, [$8,228,630,000] *$9,539,602,000*, to remain available for obligation until September 30, [2002] *2003, of which $341,400,000 shall be available for the Air National Guard and Air Force Reserve. (10 U.S.C. 2271–79, 2353, 2386, 2663, 2672, 2672a, 8013, 8062, 9501–02, 9532, 9741–42; 50 U.S.C. 451, 453, 455; Department of Defense Appropriations Act, 2000.)*

Program and Financing (in millions of dollars)

Identification code 57–3010–0–1–051		1999 actual	2000 est.	2001 est.
	Obligations by program activity:			
	Direct program:			
00.01	Combat aircraft	883	769	2,617
00.02	Airlift aircraft	3,050	3,056	3,308
00.03	Trainer aircraft	101	113	92
00.04	Other aircraft	768	625	638
00.05	Modification of in-service aircraft	1,575	2,075	1,609
00.06	Aircraft spares and repair parts	526	421	287
00.07	Aircraft support equipment and facilities	877	1,002	721
09.01	Reimbursable program	35	51	50
10.00	Total new obligations	7,815	8,113	9,321
	Budgetary resources available for obligation:			
	Unobligated balance available, start of year:			
21.40	For completion of prior year budget plans	1,061	1,486	1,952
21.40	Available to finance new budget plans		92	
21.99	Total unobligated balance, start of year	1,061	1,578	1,952
22.00	New budget authority (gross)	8,345	8,487	9,590
22.10	Resources available from recoveries of prior year obligations	42		
22.21	Unobligated balance transferred to other DoD accounts	−21		
23.90	Total budgetary resources available for obligation	9,425	10,065	11,542
23.95	Total new obligations	−7,815	−8,113	−9,321
23.98	Unobligated balance expiring or withdrawn	−32		
	Unobligated balance available, end of year:			
24.40	For completion of prior year budget plans	1,486	1,952	2,221
24.40	Available to finance subsequent year budget plans	92		
24.99	Total unobligated balance, end of year	1,578	1,952	2,221
	New budget authority (gross), detail:			
	Discretionary:			
40.00	Appropriation	8,073	8,208	9,540
40.15	Appropriation (emergency)	160		
40.36	Unobligated balance rescinded	−9	−92	
40.76	Reduction pursuant to P.L. 106–113		−42	
40.77	Reduction pursuant to P.L. 105–262			
41.00	Transferred to other DoD accounts	−13	−49	
42.00	Transferred from other DoD accounts	92	417	
43.00	Appropriation (total discretionary)	8,303	8,442	9,540
	Spending authority from offsetting collections:			
68.00	Spending authority from offsetting collections (new)	15	45	50
68.10	From Federal sources: Change in receivables and unpaid, unfilled orders	−1		
68.15	From Federal sources: Adjustments to receivables and unpaid, unfilled orders	28		
68.90	Spending authority from offsetting collections (total discretionary)	42	45	50
70.00	Total new budget authority (gross)	8,345	8,487	9,590

General and special funds—Continued

AIRCRAFT PROCUREMENT, AIR FORCE—Continued

Program and Financing (in millions of dollars)—Continued

Identification code 57–3010–0–1–051		1999 actual	2000 est.	2001 est.
	Change in unpaid obligations:			
	Unpaid obligations, start of year:			
72.40	Obligated balance, start of year	11,075	9,756	10,771
72.95	From Federal sources: Receivables and unpaid, unfilled orders	16	15	15
72.99	Total unpaid obligations, start of year	11,091	9,771	10,787
73.10	Total new obligations	7,815	8,113	9,321
73.20	Total outlays (gross)	−8,943	−7,097	−8,333
73.40	Adjustments in expired accounts (net)	−150		
73.45	Adjustments in unexpired accounts	−42		
	Unpaid obligations, end of year:			
74.40	Obligated balance, end of year	9,756	10,771	11,760
74.95	From Federal sources: Receivables and unpaid, unfilled orders	15	15	15
74.99	Total unpaid obligations, end of year	9,771	10,787	11,775
	Outlays (gross), detail:			
86.90	Outlays from new discretionary authority	2,134	1,531	1,796
86.93	Outlays from discretionary balances	6,809	5,567	6,537
87.00	Total outlays (gross)	8,943	7,097	8,333
	Offsets:			
	Against gross budget authority and outlays:			
	Offsetting collections (cash) from:			
88.00	Federal sources	−14	−5	−5
88.40	Non-Federal sources	−1	−40	−45
88.90	Total, offsetting collections (cash)	−15	−45	−50
	Against gross budget authority only:			
88.95	From Federal sources: Change in receivables and unpaid, unfilled orders	1		
88.96	From Federal sources: Adjustment to receivables and unpaid, unfilled orders	−28		
	Net budget authority and outlays:			
89.00	Budget authority	8,302	8,442	9,540
90.00	Outlays	8,928	7,052	8,283

Budget Plan (in millions of dollars)

Outlays

Identification code 57–3010–0–1–051		1999 actual	2000 est.	2001 est.
	Direct:			
0701	Combat aircraft	806	831	2,546
0702	Airlift aircraft	3,067	3,488	3,099
0703	Trainer aircraft	108	111	114
0704	Other aircraft	982	485	704
0705	Modification of inservice aircraft	1,774	2,182	1,875
0706	Aircraft spares and repair parts	513	441	357
0707	Aircraft support equipment and facilities	984	994	845
0791	Total direct	8,235	8,533	9,540
0801	Reimbursable	39	45	50
0893	Total budget plan	8,274	8,578	9,590

Summary of Budget Authority and Outlays

(in millions of dollars)

	1999 actual	*2000 est.*	*2001 est.*
Enacted/requested:			
Budget Authority	8,303	8,442	9,540
Outlays	8,928	7,053	8,283
Supplemental proposal:			
Budget Authority		73	
Outlays		13	29
Total:			
Budget Authority	8,303	8,515	9,540
Outlays	8,928	7,066	8,312

Object Classification (in millions of dollars)

Identification code 57–3010–0–1–051		1999 actual	2000 est.	2001 est.
	Direct obligations:			
25.1	Advisory and assistance services	47	42	33
31.0	Equipment	7,733	8,020	9,238
99.0	Subtotal, direct obligations	7,780	8,062	9,271
99.0	Reimbursable obligations	35	51	50
99.9	Total new obligations	7,815	8,113	9,321

MISSILE PROCUREMENT, AIR FORCE

For construction, procurement, and modification of missiles, spacecraft, rockets, and related equipment, including spare parts and accessories therefor, ground handling equipment, and training devices; expansion of public and private plants, Government-owned equipment and installation thereof in such plants, erection of structures, and acquisition of land, for the foregoing purposes, and such lands and interests therein, may be acquired, and construction prosecuted thereon prior to approval of title; reserve plant and Government and contractor-owned equipment layaway; and other expenses necessary for the foregoing purposes including rents and transportation of things, [$2,211,407,000] *$3,061,715,000*, to remain available for obligation until September 30, [2002] *2003. (10 U.S.C. 1905, 2271–79, 2363, 2386, 2653, 2672, 2672a, 8013, 8062, 9501–02, 9531–32, 9741–42; 50 U.S.C. 451, 453, 455; Department of Defense Appropriations Act, 2000.)*

Program and Financing (in millions of dollars)

Identification code 57–3020–0–1–051		1999 actual	2000 est.	2001 est.
	Obligations by program activity:			
	Direct program:			
00.01	Ballistic missiles	7	16	34
00.02	Other missiles	189	124	179
00.03	Modification of inservice missiles	199	335	430
00.04	Spares and repair parts	44	23	41
00.05	Other support	1,484	1,572	2,204
09.01	Reimbursable program	22	86	75
10.00	Total new obligations	1,946	2,157	2,963
	Budgetary resources available for obligation:			
	Unobligated balance available, start of year:			
21.40	For completion of prior year budget plans	293	477	595
21.40	Available to finance new budget plans		144	
21.99	Total unobligated balance, start of year	293	621	595
22.00	New budget authority (gross)	2,251	2,131	3,137
22.10	Resources available from recoveries of prior year obligations	42		
22.21	Unobligated balance transferred to other DoD accounts	−3		
23.90	Total budgetary resources available for obligation	2,585	2,752	3,732
23.95	Total new obligations	−1,946	−2,157	−2,963
23.98	Unobligated balance expiring or withdrawn	−18		
	Unobligated balance available, end of year:			
24.40	For completion of prior year budget plans	477	595	769
24.40	Available to finance subsequent year budget plans	144		
24.99	Total unobligated balance, end of year	621	595	769
	New budget authority (gross), detail:			
	Discretionary:			
40.00	Appropriation	2,063	2,211	3,062
40.15	Appropriation (emergency)	178		
40.36	Unobligated balance rescinded	−12	−144	
40.76	Reduction pursuant to P.L. 106–113		−11	
40.77	Reduction pursuant to P.L. 105–262	−6		
41.00	Transferred to other DoD accounts		−24	
42.00	Transferred from other DoD accounts		24	
43.00	Appropriation (total discretionary)	2,223	2,056	3,062
	Spending authority from offsetting collections:			
68.00	Offsetting collections (cash)	62	75	75
68.10	From Federal sources: Change in receivables and unpaid, unfilled orders	−37		
68.15	From Federal sources: Adjustments to receivables and unpaid, unfilled orders	4		

68.90	Spending authority from offsetting collections (total discretionary)	29	75	75
70.00	Total new budget authority (gross)	2,252	2,131	3,137
	Change in unpaid obligations:			
	Unpaid obligations, start of year:			
72.40	Obligated balance, start of year	3,372	2,855	2,745
72.95	From Federal sources: Receivables and unpaid, unfilled orders	77	40	40
72.99	Total unpaid obligations, start of year	3,450	2,895	2,785
73.10	Total new obligations	1,946	2,157	2,963
73.20	Total outlays (gross)	−2,360	−2,267	−2,365
73.40	Adjustments in expired accounts (net)	−98		
73.45	Adjustments in unexpired accounts	−42		
	Unpaid obligations, end of year:			
74.40	Obligated balance, end of year	2,855	2,745	3,343
74.95	From Federal sources: Receivables and unpaid, unfilled orders	40	40	40
74.99	Total unpaid obligations, end of year	2,895	2,785	3,383
	Outlays (gross), detail:			
86.90	Outlays from new discretionary authority	648	561	819
86.93	Outlays from discretionary balances	1,713	1,705	1,546
87.00	Total outlays (gross)	2,360	2,267	2,365
	Offsets:			
	Against gross budget authority and outlays:			
	Offsetting collections (cash) from:			
88.00	Federal sources	−62	−59	−59
88.40	Non-Federal sources		−16	−16
88.90	Total, offsetting collections (cash)	−62	−75	−75
	Against gross budget authority only:			
88.95	From Federal sources: Change in receivables and unpaid, unfilled orders	37		
88.96	From Federal sources: Adjustment to receivables and unpaid, unfilled orders	−4		
	Net budget authority and outlays:			
89.00	Budget authority	2,223	2,056	3,062
90.00	Outlays	2,298	2,192	2,290

Budget Plan (in millions of dollars)
Outlays

Identification code 57–3020–0–1–051		1999 actual	2000 est.	2001 est.
	Direct:			
0701	Ballistic missiles	6	15	42
0702	Other missiles	167	135	197
0703	Modification of inservice missiles	312	304	410
0704	Spares and repair parts	47	18	44
0705	Other support	1,560	1,729	2,369
0791	Total direct	2,091	2,200	3,062
0801	Reimbursable	27	75	75
0893	Total budget plan	2,119	2,275	3,137

Object Classification (in millions of dollars)

Identification code 57–3020–0–1–051		1999 actual	2000 est.	2001 est.
	Direct obligations:			
25.1	Advisory and assistance services	23	20	19
31.0	Equipment	1,901	2,051	2,869
99.0	Subtotal, direct obligations	1,924	2,071	2,888
99.0	Reimbursable obligations	22	86	75
99.9	Total new obligations	1,946	2,157	2,963

PROCUREMENT OF AMMUNITION, AIR FORCE

For construction, procurement, production, and modification of ammunition, and accessories therefor; specialized equipment and training devices; expansion of public and private plants, including ammunition facilities authorized by section 2854 of title 10, United States Code, and the land necessary therefor, for the foregoing purposes, and such lands and interests therein, may be acquired, and construction prosecuted thereon prior to approval of title; and procurement and installation of equipment, appliances, and machine tools in public and private plants; reserve plant and Government and contractor-owned equipment layaway; and other expenses necessary for the foregoing purposes, [$442,537,000] *$638,808,000*, to remain available for obligation until September 30, [2002] *2003, of which $51,023,000 shall be available for the Air National Guard and Air Force Reserve. (Department of Defense Appropriations Act, 2000.)*

Program and Financing (in millions of dollars)

Identification code 57–3011–0–1–051		1999 actual	2000 est.	2001 est.
	Obligations by program activity:			
	Direct program:			
00.01	Ammunition	373	533	615
00.02	Weapons	9	3	4
09.01	Reimbursable program	2	17	13
10.00	Total new obligations	385	553	632
	Budgetary resources available for obligation:			
	Unobligated balance available, start of year:			
21.40	For completion of prior year budget plans	60	77	120
21.40	Unobligated balance available, start of year		2	
21.99	Total unobligated balance, start of year	60	79	120
22.00	New budget authority (gross)	408	595	652
23.90	Total budgetary resources available for obligation	467	674	772
23.95	Total new obligations	−385	−553	−632
23.98	Unobligated balance expiring or withdrawn	−3		
	Unobligated balance available, end of year:			
24.40	For completion of prior year budget plans	77	120	140
24.40	Unobligated balance available, end of year	2		
24.99	Total unobligated balance, end of year	79	120	140
	New budget authority (gross), detail:			
	Discretionary:			
40.00	Appropriation	378	271	639
40.15	Appropriation (emergency)	35		
40.36	Unobligated balance rescinded	−14	−2	
40.76	Reduction pursuant to P.L. 106–113		−1	
42.00	Transfer from other DoD accounts		314	
43.00	Appropriation (total discretionary)	399	582	639
	Spending authority from offsetting collections:			
68.00	Offsetting collections (cash)	4	13	13
68.10	From Federal sources: Change in receivables and unpaid, unfilled orders	2		
68.15	From Federal sources: Adjustments to receivables and unpaid, unfilled orders	3		
68.90	Spending authority from offsetting collections (total discretionary)	8	13	13
70.00	Total new budget authority (gross)	408	595	652
	Change in unpaid obligations:			
	Unpaid obligations, start of year:			
72.40	Obligated balance, start of year	542	532	657
72.95	From Federal sources: Receivables and unpaid, unfilled orders	−2		
72.99	Total unpaid obligations, start of year	540	532	657
73.10	Total new obligations	385	553	632
73.20	Total outlays (gross)	−392	−429	−471
	Unpaid obligations, end of year:			
74.40	Obligated balance, end of year	532	657	818
74.95	From Federal sources: Receivables and unpaid, unfilled orders			
74.99	Total unpaid obligations, end of year	532	657	818
	Outlays (gross), detail:			
86.90	Outlays from new discretionary authority	24	96	109
86.93	Outlays from discretionary balances	369	332	363
87.00	Total outlays (gross)	392	429	471
	Offsets:			
	Against gross budget authority and outlays:			
	Offsetting collections (cash) from:			
88.00	Federal sources	−4		
88.40	Non-Federal sources		−13	−13

General and special funds—Continued

PROCUREMENT OF AMMUNITION, AIR FORCE—Continued

Program and Financing (in millions of dollars)—Continued

Identification code 57–3011–0–1–051		1999 actual	2000 est.	2001 est.
88.90	Total, offsetting collections (cash)	−4	−13	−13
	Against gross budget authority only:			
88.95	From Federal sources: Change in receivables and unpaid, unfilled orders	−2		
88.96	From Federal sources: Adjustment to receivables and unpaid, unfilled orders	−3		
	Net budget authority and outlays:			
89.00	Budget authority	399	582	639
90.00	Outlays	388	416	458

Budget Plan (in millions of dollars)
Outlays

Identification code 57–3011–0–1–051		1999 actual	2000 est.	2001 est.
	Direct:			
0701	Ammunition	406	580	635
0702	Weapons	6	3	4
0791	Total direct	411	584	639
0801	Reimbursable	4	13	13
0893	Total budget plan	416	597	652

Object Classification (in millions of dollars)

Identification code 57–3011–0–1–051		1999 actual	2000 est.	2001 est.
	Direct obligations:			
25.1	Advisory and assistance services	2	3	2
31.0	Equipment	381	533	617
99.0	Subtotal, direct obligations	383	536	619
99.0	Reimbursable obligations	2	17	13
99.9	Total new obligations	385	553	632

OTHER PROCUREMENT, AIR FORCE

For procurement and modification of equipment (including ground guidance and electronic control equipment, and ground electronic and communication equipment), and supplies, materials, and spare parts therefor, not otherwise provided for; the purchase of not to exceed [53] *173*, passenger motor vehicles for replacement only, *and the purchase of one vehicle required for physical security of personnel, notwithstanding price limitations applicable to passenger vehicles but not to exceed $230,000*; lease of passenger motor vehicles; and expansion of public and private plants, Government-owned equipment and installation thereof in such plants, erection of structures, and acquisition of land, for the foregoing purposes, and such lands and interests therein, may be acquired, and construction prosecuted thereon, prior to approval of title; reserve plant and Government and contractor-owned equipment layaway, [$7,146,157,000] *$7,699,127,000*, to remain available for obligation until September 30, [2002] *2003*, *of which $113,100,000 shall be available for the Air National Guard and Air Force Reserve. (10 U.S.C. 2110, 2353, 2386, 8013, 9505, 9531–32; 50 U.S.C. 491–94; Department of Defense Appropriations Act, 2000.)*

Program and Financing (in millions of dollars)

Identification code 57–3080–0–1–051		1999 actual	2000 est.	2001 est.
	Obligations by program activity:			
	Direct program:			
00.02	Vehicular equipment	195	214	234
00.03	Electronics and telecommunications equipment	833	982	1,276
00.04	Other base maintenance and support equipment	6,162	5,816	6,124
00.05	Spares and repair parts	32	55	39
09.01	Reimbursable program	81	304	300
10.00	Total new obligations	7,303	7,371	7,973
	Budgetary resources available for obligation:			
	Unobligated balance available, start of year:			
21.40	For completion of prior year budget plans	433	689	840
21.40	Available to finance new budget plans		44	
21.99	Total unobligated balance, start of year	433	734	840
22.00	New budget authority (gross)	7,590	7,477	7,999
22.10	Resources available from recoveries of prior year obligations	23		
22.22	Unobligated balance transferred from other DoD accounts	2		
23.90	Total budgetary resources available for obligation	8,050	8,211	8,839
23.95	Total new obligations	−7,303	−7,371	−7,973
23.98	Unobligated balance expiring or withdrawn	−12		
	Unobligated balance available, end of year:			
24.40	For completion of prior year budget plans	689	840	865
24.40	Available to finance subsequent year budget plans	44		
24.99	Total unobligated balance, end of year	734	840	865
	New budget authority (gross), detail:			
	Discretionary:			
40.00	Appropriation	6,943	7,146	7,699
40.36	Unobligated balance rescinded	−4	−44	
40.76	Reduction pursuant to P.L. 106–113		−37	
40.77	Reduction pursuant to P.L. 105–262	−38		
41.00	Transferred to other DoD accounts	−36	−7	
42.00	Transferred from other DoD accounts	644	119	
43.00	Appropriation (total discretionary)	7,509	7,177	7,699
	Spending authority from offsetting collections:			
68.00	Spending authority from offsetting collections (cash)	78	300	300
68.10	From Federal sources: Change in receivables and unpaid, unfilled orders	−7		
68.15	From Federal sources: Adjustments to receivables and unpaid, unfilled orders	10		
68.90	Spending authority from offsetting collections (total discretionary)	81	300	300
70.00	Total new budget authority (gross)	7,590	7,477	7,999
	Change in unpaid obligations:			
	Unpaid obligations, start of year:			
72.40	Obligated balance, start of year	3,231	3,413	3,279
72.95	From Federal sources: Receivables and unpaid, unfilled orders	47	40	40
72.99	Total unpaid obligations, start of year	3,278	3,454	3,320
73.10	Total new obligations	7,303	7,371	7,973
73.20	Total outlays (gross)	−6,849	−7,505	−7,840
73.40	Adjustments in expired accounts (net)	−257		
73.45	Adjustments in unexpired accounts	−23		
	Unpaid obligations, end of year:			
74.40	Obligated balance, end of year	3,413	3,279	3,413
74.95	From Federal sources: Receivables and unpaid, unfilled orders	40	40	40
74.99	Total unpaid obligations, end of year	3,454	3,320	3,453
	Outlays (gross), detail:			
86.90	Outlays from new discretionary authority	4,562	4,570	4,944
86.93	Outlays from discretionary balances	2,287	2,934	2,894
87.00	Total outlays (gross)	6,849	7,505	7,840
	Offsets:			
	Against gross budget authority and outlays:			
	Offsetting collections (cash) from:			
88.00	Federal sources	−78	−109	−109
88.40	Non-Federal sources		−191	−191
88.90	Total, offsetting collections (cash)	−78	−300	−300
	Against gross budget authority only:			
88.95	From Federal sources: Change in receivables and unpaid, unfilled orders	7		
88.96	From Federal sources: Adjustment to receivables and unpaid, unfilled orders	−10		
	Net budget authority and outlays:			
89.00	Budget authority	7,510	7,177	7,699
90.00	Outlays	6,770	7,205	7,540

Budget Plan (in millions of dollars)
Outlays

Identification code 57–3080–0–1–051	1999 actual	2000 est.	2001 est.
Direct:			
0702 Vehicular equipment	187	215	262
0703 Electronics and telecommunications equipment	876	1,043	1,105
0704 Other base maintenance and support equipment	6,363	5,925	6,300
0705 Spares and repair parts	44	38	32
0791 Total direct	7,471	7,221	7,699
0801 Reimbursable	82	300	300
0893 Total budget plan	7,552	7,521	7,999

Object Classification (in millions of dollars)

Identification code 57–3080–0–1–051	1999 actual	2000 est.	2001 est.
Direct obligations:			
25.1 Advisory and assistance services	30	28	27
31.0 Equipment	7,192	7,039	7,646
99.0 Subtotal, direct obligations	7,223	7,067	7,673
99.0 Reimbursable obligations	81	304	300
99.9 Total new obligations	7,303	7,371	7,973

Procurement, Defense-Wide

[INCLUDING TRANSFER OF FUNDS**]**

For expenses of activities and agencies of the Department of Defense (other than the military departments) necessary for procurement, production, and modification of equipment, supplies, materials, and spare parts therefor, not otherwise provided for; the purchase of not to exceed **[**103**]** *115* passenger motor vehicles for replacement only; the purchase of **[**seven**]** *10* vehicles required for physical security of personnel, notwithstanding price limitations applicable to passenger vehicles but not to exceed $250,000 per vehicle; expansion of public and private plants, equipment, and installation thereof in such plants, erection of structures, and acquisition of land for the foregoing purposes, and such lands and interests therein, may be acquired, and construction prosecuted thereon prior to approval of title; reserve plant and Government and contractor-owned equipment layaway, **[**$2,249,566,000**]** *$2,275,308,000*, to remain available for obligation until September 30, **[**2002: *Provided*, That of the funds available under this heading, not less than $39,491,000, including $6,000,000 derived by transfer from "Research, Development, Test and Evaluation, Defense-Wide", shall be available only to support Electronic Commerce Resource Centers**]** *2003. (Department of Defense Appropriations Act, 2000.)*

Program and Financing (in millions of dollars)

Identification code 97–0300–0–1–051	1999 actual	2000 est.	2001 est.
Obligations by program activity:			
Direct program:			
00.01 Major equipment	1,288	1,280	1,210
00.02 Special Operations Command	544	713	557
00.03 Chemical/Biological Defense	517	338	444
09.01 Reimbursable program	85	149	108
10.00 Total new obligations	2,435	2,480	2,318
Budgetary resources available for obligation:			
Unobligated balance available, start of year:			
21.40 For completion of prior year budget plans	589	524	510
21.40 Available to finance new budget plans	....	5	....
21.99 Total unobligated balance, start of year	589	529	510
22.00 New budget authority (gross)	2,133	2,461	2,383
22.10 Resources available from recoveries of prior year obligations	256	....	....
22.22 Unobligated balance transferred from other DoD accounts	3	....	....
23.90 Total budgetary resources available for obligation	2,982	2,990	2,893
23.95 Total new obligations	−2,435	−2,480	−2,318
23.98 Unobligated balance expiring or withdrawn	−18	....	....
Unobligated balance available, end of year:			
24.40 For completion of prior year budget plans	524	510	575
24.40 Available to finance subsequent year budget plans	5	....	....
24.99 Total unobligated balance, end of year	529	510	575
New budget authority (gross), detail:			
Discretionary:			
40.00 Appropriation	1,947	2,258	2,275
40.36 Unobligated balance rescinded	....	−6	....
40.76 Reduction pursuant to P.L. 106–113	....	−12	....
41.00 Transferred to other DoD accounts	−88	−22	....
42.00 Transferred from other DoD accounts	200	135	....
43.00 Appropriation (total discretionary)	2,059	2,354	2,275
Spending authority from offsetting collections:			
68.00 Offsetting collections (cash)	50	108	108
68.10 From Federal sources: Change in receivables and unpaid, unfilled orders	22	....	....
68.15 From Federal sources: Adjustments to receivables and unpaid, unfilled orders	2	....	....
68.90 Spending authority from offsetting collections (total discretionary)	74	108	108
70.00 Total new budget authority (gross)	2,133	2,461	2,383
Change in unpaid obligations:			
Unpaid obligations, start of year:			
72.40 Obligated balance, start of year	2,349	2,207	2,486
72.95 From Federal sources: Receivables and unpaid, unfilled orders	109	131	131
72.99 Total unpaid obligations, start of year	2,459	2,338	2,617
73.10 Total new obligations	2,435	2,480	2,318
73.20 Total outlays (gross)	−2,218	−2,201	−2,348
73.40 Adjustments in expired accounts (net)	−81	....	....
73.45 Adjustments in unexpired accounts	−256	....	....
Unpaid obligations, end of year:			
74.40 Obligated balance, end of year	2,207	2,486	2,456
74.95 From Federal sources: Receivables and unpaid, unfilled orders	131	131	131
74.99 Total unpaid obligations, end of year	2,338	2,617	2,587
Outlays (gross), detail:			
86.90 Outlays from new discretionary authority	733	823	816
86.93 Outlays from discretionary balances	1,485	1,378	1,533
87.00 Total outlays (gross)	2,218	2,201	2,348
Offsets:			
Against gross budget authority and outlays:			
Offsetting collections (cash) from:			
88.00 Federal sources	−33	−108	−108
88.40 Non-Federal sources	−17	....	....
88.90 Total, offsetting collections (cash)	−50	−108	−108
Against gross budget authority only:			
88.95 From Federal sources: Change in receivables and unpaid, unfilled orders	−22	....	....
88.96 From Federal sources: Adjustment to receivables and unpaid, unfilled orders	−2	....	....
Net budget authority and outlays:			
89.00 Budget authority	2,059	2,354	2,275
90.00 Outlays	2,168	2,094	2,240

Budget Plan (in millions of dollars)
Outlays

Identification code 97–0300–0–1–051	1999 actual	2000 est.	2001 est.
Direct:			
0701 Major equipment	1,241	1,248	1,276
0702 Special Operations Command	508	729	525
0703 Chemical/Biological Defense	301	381	474
0791 Total direct	2,050	2,359	2,275
0801 Reimbursable	76	108	108
0893 Total budget plan	2,126	2,466	2,383

186-484 00 - 10

General and special funds—Continued

PROCUREMENT, DEFENSE-WIDE—Continued

[INCLUDING TRANSFER OF FUNDS]—Continued

Object Classification (in millions of dollars)

Identification code 97–0300–0–1–051		1999 actual	2000 est.	2001 est.
	Direct obligations:			
23.3	Communications, utilities, and miscellaneous charges	1	1	1
25.1	Advisory and assistance services	8	6	6
25.2	Other services	192	134	131
	Purchases of goods and services from Government accounts:			
25.3	Purchases of goods and services from Government accounts	25	17	17
25.3	Purchases from revolving funds	1		
25.5	Research and development contracts	34	24	23
25.7	Operation and maintenance of equipment	30	21	20
26.0	Supplies and materials	11	8	8
31.0	Equipment	2,048	2,120	2,004
99.0	Subtotal, direct obligations	2,350	2,331	2,210
99.0	Reimbursable obligations	85	149	108
99.9	Total new obligations	2,435	2,480	2,318

[NATIONAL GUARD AND RESERVE EQUIPMENT]

[For procurement of aircraft, missiles, tracked combat vehicles, ammunition, other weapons, and other procurement for the reserve components of the Armed Forces, $150,000,000, to remain available for obligation until September 30, 2002: *Provided*, That the Chiefs of the Reserve and National Guard components shall, not later than 30 days after the enactment of this Act, individually submit to the congressional defense committees the modernization priority assessment for their respective Reserve or National Guard component.] *(Department of Defense Appropriations Act, 2000.)*

Program and Financing (in millions of dollars)

Identification code 97–0350–0–1–051		1999 actual	2000 est.	2001 est.
	Obligations by program activity:			
00.01	Reserve equipment	329	109	40
00.02	National Guard equipment	272	171	21
10.00	Total new obligations	601	280	62
	Budgetary resources available for obligation:			
21.40	For completion of prior year budget plans	402	210	80
22.00	New budget authority (gross)	358	149	
22.10	Resources available from recoveries of prior year obligations	54		
23.90	Total budgetary resources available for obligation	813	359	80
23.95	Total new obligations	−601	−280	−62
23.98	Unobligated balance expiring or withdrawn	−2		
24.40	For completion of prior year budget plans	210	80	18
	New budget authority (gross), detail:			
	Discretionary:			
40.00	Appropriation	352	150	
40.76	Reduction pursuant to P.L. 106–113		−1	
42.00	Transferred from other DoD accounts	6		
43.00	Appropriation (total discretionary)	358	149	
	Change in unpaid obligations:			
	Unpaid obligations, start of year:			
72.40	Obligated balance, start of year	964	743	491
72.95	From Federal sources: Receivables and unpaid, unfilled orders			
72.99	Total unpaid obligations, start of year	964	743	492
73.10	Total new obligations	601	280	62
73.20	Total outlays (gross)	−716	−531	−288
73.40	Adjustments in expired accounts (net)	−53		
73.45	Adjustments in unexpired accounts	−54		
	Unpaid obligations, end of year:			
74.40	Obligated balance, end of year	743	491	265
74.95	From Federal sources: Receivables and unpaid, unfilled orders			
74.99	Total unpaid obligations, end of year	743	492	265
	Outlays (gross), detail:			
86.90	Outlays from new discretionary authority	86	22	
86.93	Outlays from discretionary balances	630	509	288
87.00	Total outlays (gross)	716	531	288
	Net budget authority and outlays:			
89.00	Budget authority	358	149	
90.00	Outlays	716	531	288

Budget Plan (in millions of dollars)
Outlays

Identification code 97–0350–0–1–051		1999 actual	2000 est.	2001 est.
0701	Reserve equipment	120	90	
0702	National Guard equipment	238	60	
0720	Program activities			
0893	Total budget plan	358	149	

OPERATIONAL RAPID RESPONSE TRANSFER FUND

Program and Financing (in millions of dollars)

Identification code 97–0139–0–1–051		1999 actual	2000 est.	2001 est.
	Budgetary resources available for obligation:			
23.95	Total new obligations			
	New budget authority (gross), detail:			
	Discretionary:			
40.15	Appropriation (emergency)	300		
41.00	Transferred to other DoD accounts	−300		
43.00	Appropriation (total discretionary)			
	Net budget authority and outlays:			
89.00	Budget authority			
90.00	Outlays			

[DEFENSE PRODUCTION ACT PURCHASES]

[For activities by the Department of Defense pursuant to sections 108, 301, 302, and 303 of the Defense Production Act of 1950 (50 U.S.C. App. 2078, 2091, 2092, and 2093), $3,000,000 only for microwave power tubes and to remain available until expended.] *(Department of Defense Appropriations Act, 2000.)*

Program and Financing (in millions of dollars)

Identification code 97–0360–0–1–051		1999 actual	2000 est.	2001 est.
	Obligations by program activity:			
10.00	Total new obligations (object class 26.0)	10	2	1
	Budgetary resources available for obligation:			
21.40	For completion of prior year budget plans	24	15	16
22.00	New budget authority (gross)		3	
22.10	Resources available from recoveries of prior year obligations	2		
23.90	Total budgetary resources available for obligation	26	18	16
23.95	Total new obligations	−10	−2	−1
24.40	For completion of prior year budget plans	15	16	15
	New budget authority (gross), detail:			
	Discretionary:			
40.00	Appropriation		3	
	Change in unpaid obligations:			
72.40	Unpaid obligations, start of year: Obligated balance, start of year	45	41	36
73.10	Total new obligations	10	2	1
73.20	Total outlays (gross)	−11	−7	−7

73.40 Adjustments in expired accounts (net)	−2		
73.45 Adjustments in unexpired accounts	−2		
74.40 Unpaid obligations, end of year: Obligated balance, end of year	41	36	31
Outlays (gross), detail:			
86.93 Outlays from discretionary balances	11	7	7
Net budget authority and outlays:			
89.00 Budget authority		3	
90.00 Outlays	11	7	7

The Defense Production Act (50 U.S.C. App. 2061, *et seq.*) authorizes the use of Federal funds to correct industrial resource shortfalls and promote critical technology items which are essential to the national defense. This budget includes a FY 2000 project, funded from existing balances, to establish a high-volume production capacity for dielectric thin film coatings on polycarbonate substrates for laser protective eyewear. This project meets the requirements of subsection (a)(3) of Title III of this Act.

Budget Plan (in millions of dollars)
Outlays

Identification code 97–0360–0–1–051	1999 actual	2000 est.	2001 est.
0701 Defense Production Act Purchases		3	
0893 Total budget plan		3	

Chemical Agents and Munitions Destruction, Army

For expenses, not otherwise provided for, necessary for the destruction of the United States stockpile of lethal chemical agents and munitions in accordance with the provisions of section 1412 of the Department of Defense Authorization Act, 1986 (50 U.S.C. 1521), and for the destruction of other chemical warfare materials that are not in the chemical weapon stockpile, [$1,029,000,000] *$1,003,500,000*, of which [$543,500,000] *$607,200,000* shall be for Operation and maintenance to remain available until September 30, [2001] *2002*, [$191,500,000] *$121,900,000* shall be for Procurement to remain available until September 30, [2002] *2003*, and [$294,000,000] *$274,400,000* shall be for Research, development, test and evaluation to remain available until September 30, [2001: *Provided*, That of the funds available under this heading, $1,000,000 shall be available until expended each year only for a Johnston Atoll off-island leave program: *Provided further*, That the Secretaries concerned shall, pursuant to uniform regulations, prescribe travel and transportation allowances for travel by participants in the off-island leave program] *2002: Provided, That of the funds available under this heading, not to exceed $22,500,000 may be transferred between budget activities under this heading, to be merged with and to be available for the same purposes, and for the same time period, as the budget activity to which transferred: Provided further, That the transfer authority provided in this paragraph is in addition to any other transfer authority contained elsewhere in this Act. (Department of Defense Appropriations Act, 2000.)*

Program and Financing (in millions of dollars)

Identification code 21–0390–0–1–051	1999 actual	2000 est.	2001 est.
Obligations by program activity:			
Direct program:			
00.01 Research, development, test, and evaluation	188	276	291
00.02 Procurement	99	162	130
00.03 Operation and maintenance	487	543	607
09.01 Reimbursable program	3	5	5
10.00 Total new obligations	778	986	1,033
Budgetary resources available for obligation:			
Unobligated balance available, start of year:			
21.40 For completion of prior year budget plans	26	61	104
21.40 Available to finance new budget plans		2	
21.99 Total unobligated balance, start of year	26	63	104
22.00 New budget authority (gross)	780	1,027	1,008
22.10 Resources available from recoveries of prior year obligations	37		
23.90 Total budgetary resources available for obligation	843	1,090	1,112
23.95 Total new obligations	−778	−986	−1,033
23.98 Unobligated balance expiring or withdrawn	−3		
Unobligated balance available, end of year:			
24.40 Unobligated balance available, end of year	61	104	79
24.40 Available to finance subsequent year budget plans	2		
24.99 Total unobligated balance, end of year	63	104	79
New budget authority (gross), detail:			
Discretionary:			
40.00 Appropriation	777	1,029	1,003
40.36 Unobligated balance rescinded		−2	
40.76 Reduction pursuant to P.L. 106–113		−5	
43.00 Appropriation (total discretionary)	777	1,022	1,004
Spending authority from offsetting collections:			
68.00 Offsetting collections (cash)	5	5	5
68.10 From Federal sources: Change in receivables and unpaid, unfilled orders	−2		
68.90 Spending authority from offsetting collections (total discretionary)	3	5	5
70.00 Total new budget authority (gross)	780	1,027	1,008
Change in unpaid obligations:			
Unpaid obligations, start of year:			
72.40 Obligated balance, start of year	925	717	909
72.95 From Federal sources: Receivables and unpaid, unfilled orders	4	2	2
72.99 Total unpaid obligations, start of year	929	720	912
73.10 Total new obligations	778	986	1,033
73.20 Total outlays (gross)	−941	−793	−894
73.40 Adjustments in expired accounts (net)	−9		
73.45 Adjustments in unexpired accounts	−37		
Unpaid obligations, end of year:			
74.40 Obligated balance, end of year	717	909	1,048
74.95 From Federal sources: Receivables and unpaid, unfilled orders	2	2	2
74.99 Total unpaid obligations, end of year	720	912	1,051
Outlays (gross), detail:			
86.90 Outlays from new discretionary authority	377	394	437
86.93 Outlays from discretionary balances	564	400	457
87.00 Total outlays (gross)	941	793	894
Offsets:			
Against gross budget authority and outlays:			
88.00 Offsetting collections (cash) from: Federal sources	−5	−5	−5
Against gross budget authority only:			
88.95 From Federal sources: Change in receivables and unpaid, unfilled orders	2		
88.96 From Federal sources: Adjustment to receivables and unpaid, unfilled orders			
Net budget authority and outlays:			
89.00 Budget authority	777	1,022	1,004
90.00 Outlays	936	788	889

P.L. 99–145 authorized an appropriation to the Chemical Agents and Munitions Destruction account to destroy the U.S. inventory of lethal chemical agents and munitions and related (non-stockpile) materiel thus avoiding future risks and costs associated with the continued storage of chemical warfare materiel. The program supports the Chemical Weapons Convention initiatives to rid the world of chemical weapons.

Budget Plan (in millions of dollars)
Outlays

Identification code 21–0390–0–1–051	1999 actual	2000 est.	2001 est.
Direct:			
0701 Research, development, test, and evaluation	171	292	274
0702 Procurement	114	190	122
0703 Operation and maintenance	487	542	607
0791 Total direct	772	1,024	1,004

General and special funds—Continued

CHEMICAL AGENTS AND MUNITIONS DESTRUCTION, ARMY—Continued

Budget Plan (in millions of dollars)—Continued
Outlays

Identification code 21–0390–0–1–051		1999 actual	2000 est.	2001 est.
0801	Reimbursable	3	5	5
0893	Total budget plan	775	1,029	1,008

Object Classification (in millions of dollars)

Identification code 21–0390–0–1–051		1999 actual	2000 est.	2001 est.
	Direct obligations:			
21.0	Travel and transportation of persons	2	4	3
24.0	Printing and reproduction	1	1	1
25.1	Advisory and assistance services	25	24	25
25.2	Other services	99	97	101
25.3	Purchases of goods and services from Government accounts	146	143	150
25.4	Operation and maintenance of facilities	254	315	488
25.5	Research and development contracts	57	169	188
25.7	Operation and maintenance of equipment	8	9	10
26.0	Supplies and materials	7	20	12
31.0	Equipment	174	196	47
41.0	Grants, subsidies, and contributions	3	3	3
99.0	Subtotal, direct obligations	774	981	1,028
99.0	Reimbursable obligations	3	5	5
99.9	Total new obligations	778	986	1,033

ARMS INITIATIVE GUARANTEED LOAN FINANCING ACCOUNT

This program, first authorized in PL 102–484 (the FY 1992 Authorization Act), is to encourage commercial firms to use idle government owned, contractor-operated Army ammunition manufacturing facilities to ensure a viable industrial base for the manufacture of ammunition.

As required by the Federal Credit Reform Act of 1990, this non-budgetary account records all cash flows to and from the Government resulting from loan guarantees committed in 1992 and beyond (including modifications of loan guarantees that resulted from commitments in any year). The amounts in this account are a means of financing and are not included in the budget totals.

Status of Guaranteed Loans (in millions of dollars)

Identification code 21–4275–0–3–051		1999 actual	2000 est.	2001 est.
	Position with respect to appropriations act limitation on commitments:			
2111	Limitation on guaranteed loans made by private lenders	....	8	....
2150	Total guaranteed loan commitments	....	8	....
2199	Guaranteed amount of guaranteed loan commitments	....	8	....
	Cumulative balance of guaranteed loans outstanding:			
2210	Outstanding, start of year	10	10	17
2231	Disbursements of new guaranteed loans	....	8	....
2251	Repayments and prepayments	....	−1	−2
2290	Outstanding, end of year	10	17	15
	Memorandum:			
2299	Guaranteed amount of guaranteed loans outstanding, end of year	10	17	15

RESEARCH, DEVELOPMENT, TEST, AND EVALUATION

Appropriations in this title support modernization through basic and applied research, fabrication of technology-demonstration devices, and development and testing of prototypes and full-scale preproduction hardware. This work is performed by contractors, government laboratories and facilities, universities and nonprofit organizations. Research and development programs are funded to cover annual needs. Resources presented under the Research, Development, Test, and Evaluation title contribute primarily to achieving the Department's corporate goal 2 (Prepare). A detailed description of the corporate goals is contained in the FY 2001 Performance Plan in the Department's 2000 Annual Report to the President and Congress. This performance plan is required by the Government Performance and Results Act of 1993.

The budget plan for each appropriation is shown as a separate table immediately following the program and financing schedules for that appropriation. Funds for each fiscal year are available for obligation for a two-year period beginning on the first day of that fiscal year.

The 2001 budget provides for major technology and development efforts. These include science and technology programs emphasizing information technology and nanotechnology, counterproliferation, defense against chemical and biological warfare, ballistic missile defense, Army digitization initiatives, advanced anti-tank weapons, the RAH–66 Comanche Helicopter, the F–22 Advanced Tactical Fighter, the Joint Strike Fighter program, development of a new attack submarine and new classes of aircraft carriers and surface combatants, the Advanced Amphibious Assault Vehicle, the Evolved Expendable Launch Vehicle program, the Airborne Laser and a new space-based warning system.

The Department will continue to emphasize technology efforts that ensure that the Nation will maintain a technological advantage over potential adversaries. Advanced Concept Technology Demonstrations will continue to receive particular emphasis. Development and evaluation of technologies will be pursued through prototyping, with further development and production based on identifiable threats and maturity of the technology. The Department's funding in the basic and applied research budget activities, below, is included in the 21st Century Research Fund.

Federal Funds

General and special funds:

RESEARCH, DEVELOPMENT, TEST AND EVALUATION, ARMY

For expenses necessary for basic and applied scientific research, development, test and evaluation, including maintenance, rehabilitation, lease, and operation of facilities and equipment, [$5,266,601,000] *$5,260,346,000*, to remain available for obligation until September 30, [2001] *2002*. *(10 U.S.C. 2353; Department of Defense Appropriations Act, 2000.)*

Program and Financing (in millions of dollars)

Identification code 21–2040–0–1–051		1999 actual	2000 est.	2001 est.
	Obligations by program activity:			
	Direct program:			
00.01	Basic research	180	196	201
00.02	Applied research	708	800	612
00.03	Advanced technology development	663	850	501
00.04	Demonstration/validation	502	395	650
00.05	Engineering and manufacturing development	1,231	1,496	1,757
00.06	Management support	1,358	742	699
00.07	Operational system development	637	831	837
09.01	Reimbursable program	1,675	1,648	1,320
10.00	Total new obligations	6,954	6,957	6,576
	Budgetary resources available for obligation:			
	Unobligated balance available, start of year:			
21.40	Unobligated balance available, start of year	604	789	325
21.40	Available to finance new budget plans	....	25	....
21.99	Total unobligated balance, start of year	604	814	325

22.00	New budget authority (gross)	6,779	6,468	6,580
22.10	Resources available from recoveries of prior year obligations	376		
22.21	Unobligated balance transferred to other DoD accounts	−2		
22.22	Unobligated balance transferred from other DoD accounts	12		
23.90	Total budgetary resources available for obligation	7,769	7,282	6,905
23.95	Total new obligations	−6,954	−6,957	−6,576
23.98	Unobligated balance expiring or withdrawn	−2		
	Unobligated balance available, end of year:			
24.40	For completion of prior year budget plans	789		
24.40	For completion of prior year budget plans	25	325	329
24.99	Total unobligated balance, end of year	814	325	329
	New budget authority (gross), detail:			
	Discretionary:			
40.00	Appropriation	5,022	5,267	5,260
40.36	Unobligated balance rescinded		−25	
40.76	Reduction pursuant to P.L. 106–113		−27	
40.77	Reduction pursuant to P.L. 105–262	−5		
41.00	Transferred to other DoD accounts	−7	−21	
42.00	Transferred from other DoD accounts	44	6	
43.00	Appropriation (total discretionary)	5,054	5,200	5,260
55.00	Advance appropriation			
	Spending authority from offsetting collections:			
68.00	Offsetting collections (cash)	1,567	1,268	1,320
68.10	From Federal sources: Change in receivables and unpaid, unfilled orders	149		
68.15	From Federal sources: Adjustments to receivables and unpaid, unfilled orders	9		
68.90	Spending authority from offsetting collections (total discretionary)	1,725	1,268	1,320
70.00	Total new budget authority (gross)	6,779	6,468	6,580
	Change in unpaid obligations:			
	Unpaid obligations, start of year:			
72.40	Obligated balance, start of year	2,543	2,331	2,982
72.95	From Federal sources: Receivables and unpaid, unfilled orders	962	1,111	1,111
72.99	Total unpaid obligations, start of year	3,505	3,442	4,093
73.10	Total new obligations	6,954	6,957	6,576
73.20	Total outlays (gross)	−6,593	−6,307	−6,571
73.40	Adjustments in expired accounts (net)	−48		
73.45	Adjustments in unexpired accounts	−376		
	Unpaid obligations, end of year:			
74.40	Obligated balance, end of year	2,331	2,982	2,987
74.95	From Federal sources: Receivables and unpaid, unfilled orders	1,111	1,111	1,111
74.99	Total unpaid obligations, end of year	3,442	4,093	4,098
	Outlays (gross), detail:			
86.90	Outlays from new discretionary authority	4,461	4,222	4,345
86.93	Outlays from discretionary balances	2,133	2,085	2,226
87.00	Total outlays (gross)	6,593	6,307	6,571
	Offsets:			
	Against gross budget authority and outlays:			
	Offsetting collections (cash) from:			
88.00	Federal sources	−1,501	−1,268	−1,320
88.40	Non-Federal sources	−66		
88.90	Total, offsetting collections (cash)	−1,567	−1,268	−1,320
	Against gross budget authority only:			
88.95	From Federal sources: Change in receivables and unpaid, unfilled orders	−149		
88.96	From Federal sources: Adjustment to receivables and unpaid, unfilled orders	−9		
	Net budget authority and outlays:			
89.00	Budget authority	5,054	5,200	5,260
90.00	Outlays	5,027	5,038	5,251

Budget Plan (in millions of dollars)
Outlays

Identification code 21–2040–0–1–051		1999 actual	2000 est.	2001 est.
	Direct:			
0701	Basic research	177	204	201
0702	Applied research	612	791	602
0703	Advanced technology development	634	684	491
0704	Demonstration/validation	489	476	661
0705	Engineering manufacturing development	1,247	1,503	1,770
0706	Management support	1,263	739	697
0707	Operational system development	609	827	837
0791	Total direct	5,031	5,225	5,260
0801	Reimbursable	1,728	1,268	1,320
0893	Total budget plan	6,759	6,493	6,581

Object Classification (in millions of dollars)

Identification code 21–2040–0–1–051		1999 actual	2000 est.	2001 est.
	Direct obligations:			
	Personnel compensation:			
11.1	Full-time permanent	587	407	410
11.3	Other than full-time permanent	30	39	37
11.5	Other personnel compensation	35	19	19
11.9	Total personnel compensation	652	465	466
12.1	Civilian personnel benefits	144	92	92
13.0	Benefits for former personnel	6	11	22
21.0	Travel and transportation of persons	60	49	54
22.0	Transportation of things	9	6	7
23.1	Rental payments to GSA	3	2	2
23.2	Rental payments to others	2		
23.3	Communications, utilities, and miscellaneous charges	36	26	29
24.0	Printing and reproduction	2	2	2
25.1	Advisory and assistance services	177	85	89
25.2	Other services	622	541	597
	Purchases of goods and services from Government accounts:			
25.3	Purchases of goods and services from Government accounts	230	448	512
25.3	Purchases from revolving funds	30	37	43
25.4	Operation and maintenance of facilities	12		
25.5	Research and development contracts	2,710	3,256	3,023
25.6	Medical care	1		
25.7	Operation and maintenance of equipment	37		
25.8	Subsistence and support of persons	28		
26.0	Supplies and materials	130	89	99
31.0	Equipment	70	50	55
32.0	Land and structures	7	2	2
41.0	Grants, subsidies, and contributions	311	149	163
99.0	Subtotal, direct obligations	5,279	5,309	5,257
99.0	Reimbursable obligations	1,675	1,648	1,320
99.9	Total new obligations	6,954	6,957	6,576

Personnel Summary

Identification code 21–2040–0–1–051		1999 actual	2000 est.	2001 est.
	Direct:			
1001	Total compensable workyears: Full-time equivalent employment	11,444	8,430	8,127
	Reimbursable:			
2001	Total compensable workyears: Full-time equivalent employment	9,235	9,135	8,573

Research, Development, Test and Evaluation, Navy

For expenses necessary for basic and applied scientific research, development, test and evaluation, including maintenance, rehabilitation, lease, and operation of facilities and equipment, [$9,110,326,000] *$8,476,677,000*, to remain available for obligation until September 30, [2001] *2002*: *Provided*, That funds appropriated in this paragraph which are available for the V–22 may be used to meet unique requirements of the Special Operation Forces[: *Provided further*, That of the funds available under this heading, no more than $7,000,000 shall be available only to initiate a cost improvement program for the Intercooled Recuperated Gas Turbine Engine program: *Provided further*, That the funds identified in the immediately preceding proviso shall be made available only if the Secretary of the Navy certifies to the congressional defense committees that binding commitments to finance the remaining cost of the ICR cost improvement program have been secured from non-federal sources: *Provided further*, That should the Secretary of the Navy

General and special funds—Continued

RESEARCH, DEVELOPMENT, TEST AND EVALUATION, NAVY—Continued

fail to make the certification required in the immediately preceding proviso by July 31, 2000, the Secretary shall make the funds subject to such certification available for DD–21 ship propulsion risk reduction: *Provided further*, That the Department of Defense shall not pay more than one-third of the cost of the Intercooled Recuperated Gas Turbine Engine cost improvement program]. *(10 U.S.C. 174, 2352–54, 7522; Department of Defense Appropriations Act, 2000.)*

Program and Financing (in millions of dollars)

Identification code 17–1319–0–1–051		1999 actual	2000 est.	2001 est.
	Obligations by program activity:			
	Direct program:			
00.01	Basic research	356	355	396
00.02	Applied research	517	632	533
00.03	Advanced technology development	571	746	551
00.04	Demonstration/validation	2,388	2,358	2,280
00.05	Engineering and manufacturing development	2,171	2,272	2,161
00.06	Management support	731	635	632
00.07	Operational system development	1,910	2,173	2,000
09.01	Reimbursable program	193	176	185
10.00	Total new obligations	8,837	9,347	8,739
	Budgetary resources available for obligation:			
	Unobligated balance available, start of year:			
21.40	For completion of prior year budget plans	415	702	597
21.40	Available to finance new budget plans		56	
21.99	Total unobligated balance, start of year	415	758	597
22.00	New budget authority (gross)	9,174	9,186	8,662
22.10	Resources available from recoveries of prior year obligations	4		
22.21	Unobligated balance transferred to other DoD accounts	−5		
22.22	Unobligated balance transferred from other DoD accounts	15		
23.90	Total budgetary resources available for obligation	9,603	9,944	9,258
23.95	Total new obligations	−8,837	−9,347	−8,739
23.98	Unobligated balance expiring or withdrawn	−8		
	Unobligated balance available, end of year:			
24.40	For completion of prior year budget plans	702	597	520
24.40	Available to finance subsequent year budget plans	56		
24.99	Total unobligated balance, end of year	758	597	520
	New budget authority (gross), detail:			
	Discretionary:			
40.00	Appropriation	8,617	9,110	8,477
40.36	Unobligated balance rescinded	−22	−55	
40.76	Reduction pursuant to P.L. 106–113		−47	
40.77	Reduction pursuant to P.L. 105–262	−4		
41.00	Transferred to other DoD accounts	−6	−18	
42.00	Transferred from other DoD accounts	392	11	
43.00	Appropriation (total discretionary)	8,977	9,001	8,477
	Spending authority from offsetting collections:			
68.00	Offsetting collections (cash)	151	185	185
68.10	From Federal sources: Change in receivables and unpaid, unfilled orders	30		
68.15	From Federal sources: Adjustments to receivables and unpaid, unfilled orders	16		
68.90	Spending authority from offsetting collections (total discretionary)	197	185	185
70.00	Total new budget authority (gross)	9,174	9,186	8,662
	Change in unpaid obligations:			
	Unpaid obligations, start of year:			
72.40	Obligated balance, start of year	3,783	4,245	4,333
72.95	From Federal sources: Receivables and unpaid, unfilled orders	146	176	176
72.99	Total unpaid obligations, start of year	3,930	4,421	4,509
73.10	Total new obligations	8,837	9,347	8,739
73.20	Total outlays (gross)	−8,203	−9,258	−8,902
73.40	Adjustments in expired accounts (net)	−139		
73.45	Adjustments in unexpired accounts	−4		
	Unpaid obligations, end of year:			
74.40	Obligated balance, end of year	4,245	4,333	4,170
74.95	From Federal sources: Receivables and unpaid, unfilled orders	176	176	176
74.99	Total unpaid obligations, end of year	4,421	4,509	4,346
	Outlays (gross), detail:			
86.90	Outlays from new discretionary authority	5,305	5,523	5,229
86.93	Outlays from discretionary balances	2,898	3,736	3,673
87.00	Total outlays (gross)	8,203	9,258	8,902
	Offsets:			
	Against gross budget authority and outlays:			
88.00	Offsetting collections (cash) from: Federal sources	−151	−185	−185
	Against gross budget authority only:			
88.95	From Federal sources: Change in receivables and unpaid, unfilled orders	−30		
88.96	From Federal sources: Adjustment to receivables and unpaid, unfilled orders	−16		
	Net budget authority and outlays:			
89.00	Budget authority	8,977	9,001	8,477
90.00	Outlays	8,052	9,073	8,717

Budget Plan (in millions of dollars)
Outlays

Identification code 17–1319–0–1–051		1999 actual	2000 est.	2001 est.
	Direct:			
0701	Basic research	354	374	397
0702	Applied research	551	622	527
0703	Advanced technology development	570	754	539
0704	Demonstration/validation	2,424	2,367	2,230
0705	Engineering manufacturing support	2,154	2,302	2,152
0706	Management support	733	641	632
0707	Operational system development	2,157	1,997	2,000
0791	Total direct	8,942	9,057	8,477
0801	Reimbursable	211	185	185
0893	Total budget plan	9,153	9,242	8,662

Object Classification (in millions of dollars)

Identification code 17–1319–0–1–051		1999 actual	2000 est.	2001 est.
	Direct obligations:			
	Personnel compensation:			
11.1	Full-time permanent	36	34	38
11.3	Other than full-time permanent	3	3	2
11.5	Other personnel compensation	1	1	3
11.9	Total personnel compensation	40	38	43
12.1	Civilian personnel benefits	8	8	9
13.0	Benefits for former personnel		1	
21.0	Travel and transportation of persons	28	26	26
22.0	Transportation of things	1	1	1
23.2	Rental payments to others	10	10	10
23.3	Communications, utilities, and miscellaneous charges	4	4	4
24.0	Printing and reproduction	1	1	1
25.1	Advisory and assistance services	189	188	177
25.2	Other services	7	1	1
	Purchases of goods and services from Government accounts:			
25.3	Purchases of goods and services from Government accounts	765	581	602
25.3	Purchases from revolving funds	2,284	2,076	1,999
25.4	Operation and maintenance of facilities	1	9	13
25.5	Research and development contracts	5,276	6,197	5,629
26.0	Supplies and materials	4	4	4
31.0	Equipment	26	26	35
99.0	Subtotal, direct obligations	8,644	9,171	8,554
99.0	Reimbursable obligations	193	176	185
99.9	Total new obligations	8,837	9,347	8,739

Personnel Summary

Identification code 17–1319–0–1–051		1999 actual	2000 est.	2001 est.
	Direct:			
1001	Total compensable workyears: Full-time equivalent employment	742	630	669

	Reimbursable:			
2001	Total compensable workyears: Full-time equivalent employment	1,074	900	899

Research, Development, Test and Evaluation, Air Force

For expenses necessary for basic and applied scientific research, development, test and evaluation, including maintenance, rehabilitation, lease, and operation of facilities and equipment, [$13,674,537,000] *$13,685,576,000*, to remain available for obligation until September 30, [2001] *2002. (10 U.S.C. 174, 1581, 1584, 2271–79, 2352–54, 2386, 2663, 2672, 2672a, 8012, 9503–04, 9532; 42 U.S.C. 1891–92; 50 U.S.C. App. 2093(g); Department of Defense Appropriations Act, 2000.)*

Program and Financing (in millions of dollars)

Identification code 57–3600–0–1–051		1999 actual	2000 est.	2001 est.
	Obligations by program activity:			
	Direct program:			
00.01	Basic research	191	202	209
00.02	Applied research	574	563	596
00.03	Advanced technology development	465	240	607
00.04	Demonstration/validation	1,188	869	910
00.05	Engineering and manufacturing development	3,746	3,822	3,659
00.06	Management support	800	564	601
00.07	Operational system development	7,064	7,706	7,164
09.01	Reimbursable program	1,761	2,072	2,050
10.00	Total new obligations	15,789	16,038	15,796
	Budgetary resources available for obligation:			
	Unobligated balance available, start of year:			
21.40	For completion of prior year budget plans	1,654	1,335	1,634
21.40	Available to finance new budget plans		93	
21.99	Total unobligated balance, start of year	1,654	1,428	1,634
22.00	New budget authority (gross)	15,582	16,244	15,736
22.10	Resources available from recoveries of prior year obligations	5		
22.21	Unobligated balance transferred to other DoD accounts	–2		
22.22	Unobligated balance transferred from other DoD accounts	21		
23.90	Total budgetary resources available for obligation	17,260	17,671	17,370
23.95	Total new obligations	–15,789	–16,038	–15,796
23.98	Unobligated balance expiring or withdrawn	–43		
	Unobligated balance available, end of year:			
24.40	For completion of prior year budget plans	1,335	1,634	1,574
24.40	Available to finance subsequent year budget plans	93		
24.99	Total unobligated balance, end of year	1,428	1,634	1,574
	New budget authority (gross), detail:			
	Discretionary:			
40.00	Appropriation	13,720	13,675	13,686
40.36	Unobligated balance rescinded	–18	–93	
40.76	Reduction pursuant to P.L. 106–113		–70	
40.77	Reduction pursuant to P.L. 105–262	–19		
41.00	Transferred to other DoD accounts	–5	–114	
42.00	Transferred from other DoD accounts	129	796	
43.00	Appropriation (total discretionary)	13,807	14,194	13,686
	Spending authority from offsetting collections:			
68.00	Offsetting collections (cash)	1,695	2,050	2,050
68.10	From Federal sources: Change in receivables and unpaid, unfilled orders	12		
68.15	From Federal sources: Adjustments to receivables and unpaid, unfilled orders	68		
68.90	Spending authority from offsetting collections (total discretionary)	1,775	2,050	2,050
70.00	Total new budget authority (gross)	15,582	16,244	15,736
	Change in unpaid obligations:			
	Unpaid obligations, start of year:			
72.40	Obligated balance, start of year	5,637	5,386	5,923
72.95	From Federal sources: Receivables and unpaid, unfilled orders	775	787	787
72.99	Total unpaid obligations, start of year	6,413	6,173	6,710
73.10	Total new obligations	15,789	16,038	15,796
73.20	Total outlays (gross)	–15,867	–15,501	–15,605
73.40	Adjustments in expired accounts (net)	–156		
73.45	Adjustments in unexpired accounts	–5		
	Unpaid obligations, end of year:			
74.40	Obligated balance, end of year	5,386	5,923	6,114
74.95	From Federal sources: Receivables and unpaid, unfilled orders	787	787	787
74.99	Total unpaid obligations, end of year	6,173	6,710	6,901
	Outlays (gross), detail:			
86.90	Outlays from new discretionary authority	10,042	10,389	10,198
86.93	Outlays from discretionary balances	5,825	5,112	5,406
87.00	Total outlays (gross)	15,867	15,501	15,605
	Offsets:			
	Against gross budget authority and outlays:			
	Offsetting collections (cash) from:			
88.00	Federal sources	–1,629	–2,050	–2,050
88.40	Non-Federal sources	–66		
88.90	Total, offsetting collections (cash)	–1,695	–2,050	–2,050
	Against gross budget authority only:			
88.95	From Federal sources: Change in receivables and unpaid, unfilled orders	–12		
88.96	From Federal sources: Adjustment to receivables and unpaid, unfilled orders	–68		
	Net budget authority and outlays:			
89.00	Budget authority	13,807	14,194	13,686
90.00	Outlays	14,171	13,451	13,555

Budget Plan (in millions of dollars)

Outlays

Identification code 57–3600–0–1–051		1999 actual	2000 est.	2001 est.
	Direct:			
0701	Basic research	198	214	206
0702	Applied research	582	597	590
0703	Advanced technology development	430	577	495
0704	Demonstration/validation	1,200	926	888
0705	Engineering manufacturing development	3,596	4,073	3,554
0706	Management support	794	585	590
0707	Operational system development	6,932	7,315	7,362
0791	Total direct	13,732	14,286	13,686
0801	Reimbursable	1,744	2,050	2,050
0893	Total budget plan	15,476	16,336	15,736

Object Classification (in millions of dollars)

Identification code 57–3600–0–1–051		1999 actual	2000 est.	2001 est.
	Direct obligations:			
	Personnel compensation:			
11.1	Full-time permanent	292	262	269
11.3	Other than full-time permanent	24	21	22
11.5	Other personnel compensation	8	8	8
11.9	Total personnel compensation	324	290	299
12.1	Civilian personnel benefits	71	65	68
13.0	Benefits for former personnel	6	7	7
21.0	Travel and transportation of persons	41	52	53
22.0	Transportation of things	1	2	2
23.2	Rental payments to others	1	1	1
23.3	Communications, utilities, and miscellaneous charges	3	14	15
24.0	Printing and reproduction		1	1
25.1	Advisory and assistance services	177	160	168
25.2	Other services	1,158	1,047	1,063
25.3	Purchases of goods and services from Government accounts	22	141	148
25.4	Operation and maintenance of facilities	19	66	70
25.5	Research and development contracts	12,118	12,018	11,743
26.0	Supplies and materials	60	75	79
31.0	Equipment	27	26	27
99.0	Subtotal, direct obligations	14,028	13,965	13,744
99.0	Reimbursable obligations	1,761	2,072	2,050
99.9	Total new obligations	15,789	16,038	15,796

General and special funds—Continued

RESEARCH, DEVELOPMENT, TEST AND EVALUATION, AIR FORCE—Continued

Personnel Summary

Identification code 57–3600–0–1–051	1999 actual	2000 est.	2001 est.
Direct:			
1001 Total compensable workyears: Full-time equivalent employment	5,852	4,646	4,697
Reimbursable:			
2001 Total compensable workyears: Full-time equivalent employment	2,143	2,824	2,419

F–22 TRANSFER ACCOUNT

Program and Financing (in millions of dollars)

Identification code 57–3012–0–1–051	1999 actual	2000 est.	2001 est.
Obligations by program activity:			
10.00 Total new obligations (object class 31.0)		293	
Budgetary resources available for obligation:			
22.00 New budget authority (gross)		293	
23.95 Total new obligations		−293	
New budget authority (gross), detail:			
Discretionary:			
40.00 Appropriation		1,300	
40.76 Reduction pursuant to P.L. 106–113		−7	
41.00 Transferred to other DoD accounts		−1,000	
43.00 Appropriation (total discretionary)		293	
Change in unpaid obligations:			
72.40 Unpaid obligations, start of year: Obligated balance, start of year			293
73.10 Total new obligations		293	
73.20 Total outlays (gross)			−179
74.40 Unpaid obligations, end of year: Obligated balance, end of year		293	114
Outlays (gross), detail:			
86.93 Outlays from discretionary balances			179
Net budget authority and outlays:			
89.00 Budget authority		293	
90.00 Outlays			179

RESEARCH, DEVELOPMENT, TEST AND EVALUATION, DEFENSE-WIDE

For expenses of activities and agencies of the Department of Defense (other than the military departments), necessary for basic and applied scientific research, development, test and evaluation; advanced research projects as may be designated and determined by the Secretary of Defense, pursuant to law; maintenance, rehabilitation, lease, and operation of facilities and equipment, [$9,256,705,000] *$10,238,242,000*, to remain available for obligation until September 30, [2001: *Provided*, That of the amount appropriated in section 102 of division B, title I, of Public Law 105–277 (112 Stat. 2681–558), the amount of $230,000,000 not covered as of July 12, 1999, by an official budget request under the third proviso of that section is available, subject to such an official budget request for that entire amount, only for the following programs in the specified amounts:

"Theater High-Altitude Area Defense System—TMD–EMD", $38,000,000;

"PATRIOT PAC–3 Theater Missile Defense Acquisition—EMD", $75,000,000; and

"National Missile Defense Dem/Val", $117,000,000:

Provided further, That none of the amount of $230,000,000 described in the preceding proviso may be made available for obligation unless the entire amount is released to the Department of Defense and made available for obligation for the programs, and in the amounts, specified in the preceding proviso] *2002. (Department of Defense Appropriations Act, 2000.)*

Program and Financing (in millions of dollars)

Identification code 97–0400–0–1–051	1999 actual	2000 est.	2001 est.
Obligations by program activity:			
Direct program:			
00.01 Basic research	299	371	407
00.02 Applied research	1,299	1,311	1,421
00.03 Advanced technology development	1,862	1,612	1,662
00.04 Demonstration/validation	2,840	3,168	2,988
00.05 Engineering and manufacturing development	648	739	1,127
00.06 Management support	429	313	307
00.07 Operational system development	2,315	1,837	2,202
09.01 Reimbursable program	377	452	506
10.00 Total new obligations	10,070	9,805	10,622
Budgetary resources available for obligation:			
Unobligated balance available, start of year:			
21.40 For completion of prior year budget plans	972	1,413	1,481
21.40 Available to finance new budget plans		52	
21.99 Total unobligated balance, start of year	972	1,465	1,481
22.00 New budget authority (gross)	10,526	9,821	10,753
22.10 Resources available from recoveries of prior year obligations	90		
22.21 Unobligated balance transferred to other DoD accounts	−15		
22.22 Unobligated balance transferred from other DoD accounts	7		
23.90 Total budgetary resources available for obligation	11,580	11,286	12,235
23.95 Total new obligations	−10,070	−9,805	−10,622
23.98 Unobligated balance expiring or withdrawn	−45		
Unobligated balance available, end of year:			
24.40 For completion of prior year budget plans	1,413	1,481	1,613
24.40 Available to finance subsequent year budget plans	52		
24.99 Total unobligated balance, end of year	1,465	1,481	1,613
New budget authority (gross), detail:			
Discretionary:			
40.00 Appropriation	9,010	9,257	10,238
40.15 Appropriation (emergency)	1,000		
40.36 Unobligated balance rescinded		−52	
40.60 Contingent emergency appropriation not available for obligations	−230		
40.65 Contingent emergency appropriation released		230	
40.76 Reduction pursuant to P.L. 106–113		−48	
40.77 Reduction pursuant to P.L. 105–262	−16		
41.00 Transferred to other DoD accounts	−24	−52	
42.00 Transferred from other DoD accounts	406	53	
43.00 Appropriation (total discretionary)	10,146	9,388	10,238
Spending authority from offsetting collections:			
68.00 Offsetting collections (cash)	260	433	515
68.10 From Federal sources: Change in receivables and unpaid, unfilled orders	119		
68.15 From Federal sources: Adjustments to receivables and unpaid, unfilled orders	1		
68.90 Spending authority from offsetting collections (total discretionary)	380	433	515
70.00 Total new budget authority (gross)	10,526	9,821	10,753
Change in unpaid obligations:			
Unpaid obligations, start of year:			
72.40 Obligated balance, start of year	6,275	6,022	5,843
72.95 From Federal sources: Receivables and unpaid, unfilled orders	336	455	455
72.99 Total unpaid obligations, start of year	6,612	6,477	6,298
73.10 Total new obligations	10,070	9,805	10,622
73.20 Total outlays (gross)	−10,087	−9,984	−10,266
73.40 Adjustments in expired accounts (net)	−28		
73.45 Adjustments in unexpired accounts	−90		
Unpaid obligations, end of year:			
74.40 Obligated balance, end of year	6,022	5,843	6,198
74.95 From Federal sources: Receivables and unpaid, unfilled orders	455	455	455
74.99 Total unpaid obligations, end of year	6,477	6,298	6,653
Outlays (gross), detail:			
86.90 Outlays from new discretionary authority	4,838	4,564	5,091
86.93 Outlays from discretionary balances	5,249	5,420	5,174

87.00	Total outlays (gross)	10,087	9,984	10,266
	Offsets:			
	Against gross budget authority and outlays:			
	Offsetting collections (cash) from:			
88.00	Federal sources	−260	−433	−515
88.40	Non-Federal sources			
88.90	Total, offsetting collections (cash)	−260	−433	−515
	Against gross budget authority only:			
88.95	From Federal sources: Change in receivables and unpaid, unfilled orders	−119		
88.96	From Federal sources: Adjustment to receivables and unpaid, unfilled orders	−1		
	Net budget authority and outlays:			
89.00	Budget authority	10,146	9,388	10,238
90.00	Outlays	9,827	9,551	9,750

Budget Plan (in millions of dollars)

Outlays

Identification code 97–0400–0–1–051		1999 actual	2000 est.	2001 est.
	Direct:			
0701	Basic research	340	375	413
0702	Applied research	1,307	1,405	1,424
0703	Advanced technology development	1,775	1,825	1,657
0704	Demonstration/validation	3,251	2,760	3,028
0705	Engineering manufacturing development	651	803	1,185
0706	Management support	434	272	314
0707	Operational system development	2,337	2,001	2,217
0791	Total direct	10,093	9,440	10,238
0801	Reimbursable	380	433	516
0893	Total budget plan	10,473	9,873	10,753

Summary of Budget Authority and Outlays

(in millions of dollars)

Enacted/requested:	1999 actual	2000 est.	2001 est.
Budget Authority	10,146	9,388	10,238
Outlays	9,827	9,551	9,750
Supplemental proposal:			
Budget Authority		−15	
Outlays		−7	−6
Total:			
Budget Authority	10,146	9,373	10,238
Outlays	9,827	9,544	9,744

Object Classification (in millions of dollars)

Identification code 97–0400–0–1–051		1999 actual	2000 est.	2001 est.
	Direct obligations:			
	Personnel compensation:			
11.1	Full-time permanent	73	77	85
11.5	Other personnel compensation	2	3	5
11.9	Total personnel compensation	75	80	90
12.1	Civilian personnel benefits	15	17	19
21.0	Travel and transportation of persons	21	17	19
22.0	Transportation of things		3	
23.1	Rental payments to GSA	5	10	7
23.2	Rental payments to others	5		
23.3	Communications, utilities, and miscellaneous charges	13	18	12
25.1	Advisory and assistance services	261	291	289
25.2	Other services	11	213	213
25.3	Purchases of goods and services from Government accounts	308	235	222
25.5	Research and development contracts	8,722	8,288	9,020
25.7	Operation and maintenance of equipment	2	2	2
26.0	Supplies and materials	20	17	18
31.0	Equipment	224	156	197
32.0	Land and structures	1		1
41.0	Grants, subsidies, and contributions	10	6	7
99.0	Subtotal, direct obligations	9,693	9,353	10,116
99.0	Reimbursable obligations	377	452	506
99.9	Total new obligations	10,070	9,805	10,622

Personnel Summary

Identification code 97–0400–0–1–051		1999 actual	2000 est.	2001 est.
	Direct:			
1001	Total compensable workyears: Full-time equivalent employment	1,041	1,210	1,192
	Reimbursable:			
2001	Total compensable workyears: Full-time equivalent employment	3	5	7

[DEVELOPMENTAL TEST AND EVALUATION, DEFENSE]

[For expenses, not otherwise provided for, of independent activities of the Director, Test and Evaluation in the direction and supervision of developmental test and evaluation, including performance and joint developmental testing and evaluation; and administrative expenses in connection therewith, $265,957,000, to remain available for obligation until September 30, 2001]. *(Department of Defense Appropriations Act, 2000.)*

Program and Financing (in millions of dollars)

Identification code 97–0450–0–1–051		1999 actual	2000 est.	2001 est.
	Obligations by program activity:			
00.06	Total direct obligations: Defensewide mission support	262	261	26
09.01	Reimbursable program	9		
10.00	Total new obligations	271	261	26
	Budgetary resources available for obligation:			
21.40	For completion of prior year budget plans	27	23	26
22.00	New budget authority (gross)	264	265	
22.10	Resources available from recoveries of prior year obligations	5		
23.90	Total budgetary resources available for obligation	295	287	26
23.95	Total new obligations	−271	−261	−26
23.98	Unobligated balance expiring or withdrawn	−1		
24.40	For completion of prior year budget plans	23	26	
	New budget authority (gross), detail:			
	Discretionary:			
40.00	Appropriation	259	266	
40.76	Reduction pursuant to P.L. 106–113		−1	
43.00	Appropriation (total discretionary)	259	265	
	Spending authority from offsetting collections:			
68.00	Offsetting collections (cash)	7		
68.10	From Federal sources: Change in receivables and unpaid, unfilled orders	−2		
68.15	From Federal sources: Adjustments to receivables and unpaid, unfilled orders			
68.90	Spending authority from offsetting collections (total discretionary)	5		
70.00	Total new budget authority (gross)	264	265	
	Change in unpaid obligations:			
	Unpaid obligations, start of year:			
72.40	Obligated balance, start of year	207	198	206
72.95	From Federal sources: Receivables and unpaid, unfilled orders	19	17	17
72.99	Total unpaid obligations, start of year	227	214	223
73.10	Total new obligations	271	261	26
73.20	Total outlays (gross)	−260	−253	−144
73.40	Adjustments in expired accounts (net)	−18		
73.45	Adjustments in unexpired accounts	−5		
	Unpaid obligations, end of year:			
74.40	Obligated balance, end of year	198	206	88
74.95	From Federal sources: Receivables and unpaid, unfilled orders	17	17	17
74.99	Total unpaid obligations, end of year	214	223	105
	Outlays (gross), detail:			
86.90	Outlays from new discretionary authority	117	114	
86.93	Outlays from discretionary balances	143	139	144
87.00	Total outlays (gross)	260	253	144

General and special funds—Continued

[DEVELOPMENTAL TEST AND EVALUATION, DEFENSE]—Continued

Program and Financing (in millions of dollars)—Continued

Identification code 97–0450–0–1–051	1999 actual	2000 est.	2001 est.
Offsets:			
Against gross budget authority and outlays:			
88.00 Offsetting collections (cash) from: Federal sources	–7		
Against gross budget authority only:			
88.95 From Federal sources: Change in receivables and unpaid, unfilled orders	2		
88.96 From Federal sources: Adjustment to receivables and unpaid, unfilled orders			
Net budget authority and outlays:			
89.00 Budget authority	259	265	
90.00 Outlays	253	253	144

Budget Plan (in millions of dollars)
Outlays

Identification code 97–0450–0–1–051	1999 actual	2000 est.	2001 est.
Direct:			
0706 Defensewide mission support	259	265	
0801 Reimbursable	8		
0893 Total budget plan	266	265	

Object Classification (in millions of dollars)

Identification code 97–0450–0–1–051	1999 actual	2000 est.	2001 est.
Direct obligations:			
25.1 Advisory and assistance services	10	16	
25.2 Other services	19	7	
25.3 Purchases of goods and services from Government accounts		236	26
25.4 Operation and maintenance of facilities		2	
25.5 Research and development contracts	233		
99.0 Subtotal, direct obligations	262	261	26
99.0 Reimbursable obligations	9		
99.9 Total new obligations	271	261	26

OPERATIONAL TEST AND EVALUATION, DEFENSE

For expenses, not otherwise provided for, necessary for the independent activities of the Director, Operational Test and Evaluation in the direction and supervision of operational test and evaluation, including initial operational test and evaluation which is conducted prior to, and in support of, production decisions; joint operational testing and evaluation; *policy and guidance for the Department's overall test and evaluation functions; test and evaluation infrastructure investment and oversight; specialized assessment capabilities;* and administrative expenses in connection therewith, [$31,434,000] *$201,560,000*, to remain available for obligation until September 30, [2001] *2002. (Department of Defense Appropriations Act, 2000.)*

Program and Financing (in millions of dollars)

Identification code 97–0460–0–1–051	1999 actual	2000 est.	2001 est.
Obligations by program activity:			
10.00 Defensewide mission support—Total obligations	41	35	185
Budgetary resources available for obligation:			
21.40 Unobligated balance available, start of year	1	7	3
22.00 New budget authority (gross)	47	31	202
23.90 Total budgetary resources available for obligation	48	38	205
23.95 Total new obligations	–41	–35	–185
24.40 Unobligated balance available, end of year	7	3	20
New budget authority (gross), detail:			
Discretionary:			
40.00 Appropriation	34	31	202
42.00 Transferred from other DoD accounts	13		
43.00 Appropriation (total discretionary)	47	31	202
Change in unpaid obligations:			
72.40 Unpaid obligations, start of year: Obligated balance, start of year	20	29	24
73.10 Total new obligations	41	35	185
73.20 Total outlays (gross)	–32	–40	–107
74.40 Unpaid obligations, end of year: Obligated balance, end of year	29	24	102
Outlays (gross), detail:			
86.90 Outlays from new discretionary authority	18	13	89
86.93 Outlays from discretionary balances	14	26	18
87.00 Total outlays (gross)	32	40	107
Net budget authority and outlays:			
89.00 Budget authority	47	31	202
90.00 Outlays	32	40	107

Budget Plan (in millions of dollars)
Outlays

Identification code 97–0460–0–1–051	1999 actual	2000 est.	2001 est.
0706 Defensewide mission support	47	31	202

Object Classification (in millions of dollars)

Identification code 97–0460–0–1–051	1999 actual	2000 est.	2001 est.
25.1 Advisory and assistance services	23	23	24
25.3 Purchases of goods and services from Government accounts	18	12	161
99.9 Total new obligations	41	35	185

MILITARY CONSTRUCTION

The budget plan for each appropriation is shown as a separate table immediately following the program and financing schedules for those appropriations that are available for obligation for more than one year. In 2001 it presents, by budget activity, the value of the program requested for the life of the multiple-year appropriations, with comparable amounts in 1999 and 2000. Resources presented under the Military Construction title contribute primarily to achieving the Department's corporate goal 2 (Prepare). A detailed description of the corporate goals is contained in the FY 2001 Performance Plan in the Department's 2000 Annual Report to the President and Congress. This performance plan is required by the Government Performance and Results Act of 1993.

The budget authority for military construction programs for the Armed Forces, both Active and Reserve, shown in the individual schedules of this title is summarized in the following table:

MILITARY CONSTRUCTION PROGRAM

[In millions of dollars]

	1999 actual	*2000 est.*	*2001 est.*
Active Forces	2,242	2,717	2,182
Reserve Forces	505	702	222
Interservice activities	2,658	1,335	2,145
Total	5,405	4,754	4,549

The Military Construction programs are intended to provide facilities required as a result of new weapon systems entering the inventory including aircraft and naval vessels, to support chemical demilitarization and other high priority initiatives. The program continues initiatives to improve living and working conditions, reduce operating costs, increase productivity, and conserve energy by upgrading or replacing facilities which have become functionally obsolete or can be made more efficient through relatively modest investments in improvements. Also included in this request are resources required to realign and close bases consistent with the four closure rounds required by the Base Closure Acts of 1988 and 1990, and the expected land revenues which partially offset the one-time costs of closures.

Federal Funds

General and special funds:

MILITARY CONSTRUCTION, ARMY

For acquisition, construction, installation, and equipment of temporary or permanent public works, military installations, facilities, and real property for the Army as currently authorized by law, including personnel in the Army Corps of Engineers and other personal services necessary for the purposes of this appropriation, and for construction and operation of facilities in support of the functions of the Commander in Chief, [$1,042,033,000] *$897,938,000*, to remain available until September 30, [2004] *2005*: *Provided*, That of this amount, not to exceed [$91,605,000] *$94,706,000* shall be available for study, planning, design, architect and engineer services, and host nation support, as authorized by law, unless the Secretary of Defense determines that additional obligations are necessary for such purposes and notifies the Committees on Appropriations of both Houses of Congress of his determination and the reasons therefor.

In addition, for the foregoing purposes, $210,250,000 to become available on October 1, 2001 and to remain available until September 30, 2006; $83,400,000 to become available on October 1, 2002 and remain available until September 30, 2007; and $10,890,000 to become available on October 1, 2003 and remain available until September 30, 2008. (Military Construction Appropriations Act, 2000.)

Program and Financing (in millions of dollars)

Identification code 21–2050–0–1–051		1999 actual	2000 est.	2001 est.
	Obligations by program activity:			
	Direct program:			
00.01	Major construction	964	881	786
00.02	Minor construction	14	14	14
00.03	Planning	64	89	89
00.04	Supporting Activites		17	1
09.01	Reimbursable program	2,927	2,041	1,961
10.00	Total new obligations	3,969	3,042	2,851
	Budgetary resources available for obligation:			
21.40	For completion of prior year budget plans	820	693	737
22.00	New budget authority (gross)	3,594	3,037	2,898
22.10	Resources available from recoveries of prior year obligations	268		
22.21	Unobligated balance transferred to DoD other accounts	−30		
22.22	Unobligated balance transferred from other DoD accounts	25	49	
23.90	Total budgetary resources available for obligation	4,677	3,779	3,635
23.95	Total new obligations	−3,969	−3,042	−2,851
23.98	Unobligated balance expiring or withdrawn	−14		
24.40	For completion of prior year budget plans	693	737	784
	New budget authority (gross), detail:			
	Discretionary:			
40.00	Appropriation	869	1,042	898
40.15	Appropriation (emergency)	118		
40.35	Appropriation rescinded	−3		
40.76	Reduction pursuant to P.L. 106–113		−5	
42.00	Transferred from other DoD accounts	8		
43.00	Appropriation (total discretionary)	992	1,037	898
	Spending authority from offsetting collections:			
68.00	Offsetting collections (cash)	2,369	2,000	2,000
68.10	From Federal sources: Change in receivables and unpaid, unfilled orders	225		
68.15	From Federal sources: Adjustments to receivables and unpaid, unfilled orders	8		
68.90	Spending authority from offsetting collections (total discretionary)	2,602	2,000	2,000
70.00	Total new budget authority (gross)	3,594	3,037	2,898
	Change in unpaid obligations:			
	Unpaid obligations, start of year:			
72.40	Obligated balance, start of year	478	794	1,019
72.95	From Federal sources: Receivables and unpaid, unfilled orders	2,854	3,079	3,079
72.99	Total unpaid obligations, start of year	3,331	3,874	4,098
73.10	Total new obligations	3,969	3,042	2,851
73.20	Total outlays (gross)	−3,157	−2,817	−2,958
73.40	Adjustments in expired accounts (net)	−2		
73.45	Adjustments in unexpired accounts	−268		
	Unpaid obligations, end of year:			
74.40	Obligated balance, end of year	794	1,019	910
74.95	From Federal sources: Receivables and unpaid, unfilled orders	3,079	3,079	3,079
74.99	Total unpaid obligations, end of year	3,874	4,098	3,989
	Outlays (gross), detail:			
86.90	Outlays from new discretionary authority	2,435	2,058	2,046
86.93	Outlays from discretionary balances	722	761	912
87.00	Total outlays (gross)	3,157	2,817	2,958
	Offsets:			
	Against gross budget authority and outlays:			
	Offsetting collections (cash) from:			
88.00	Federal sources	−2,324	−2,000	−2,000
88.40	Non-Federal sources	−45		
88.90	Total, offsetting collections (cash)	−2,369	−2,000	−2,000
	Against gross budget authority only:			
88.95	From Federal sources: Change in receivables and unpaid, unfilled orders	−225		
88.96	From Federal sources: Adjustment to receivables and unpaid, unfilled orders	−8		
	Net budget authority and outlays:			
89.00	Budget authority	992	1,037	898
90.00	Outlays	788	817	958

Budget Plan (in millions of dollars)

Outlays

Identification code 21–2050–0–1–051		1999 actual	2000 est.	2001 est.
	Direct:			
0701	Major construction	899	960	788
0702	Minor construction	12	15	15
0703	Planning	71	92	95
0704	Supporting Activities		19	
0791	Total direct	983	1,085	898
0801	Reimbursable	2,667	2,000	2,000
0893	Total budget plan	3,650	3,085	2,898

Object Classification (in millions of dollars)

Identification code 21–2050–0–1–051		1999 actual	2000 est.	2001 est.
	Direct obligations:			
	Personnel compensation:			
11.1	Full-time permanent	24	1	1
11.3	Other than full-time permanent	2		
11.9	Total personnel compensation	26	1	1
12.1	Civilian personnel benefits	5		
21.0	Travel and transportation of persons	2	1	1
23.1	Rental payments to GSA		1	1
24.0	Printing and reproduction		1	1
25.2	Other services	38	77	39
25.3	Purchases of goods and services from Government accounts	110	179	218
25.4	Operation and maintenance of facilities		1	1
31.0	Equipment	1	1	1
32.0	Land and structures	860	739	627
99.0	Subtotal, direct obligations	1,042	1,001	890
99.0	Reimbursable obligations	2,927	2,041	1,961
99.9	Total new obligations	3,969	3,042	2,851

General and special funds—Continued

MILITARY CONSTRUCTION, ARMY—Continued

Personnel Summary

Identification code 21–2050–0–1–051	1999 actual	2000 est.	2001 est.
Direct:			
1001 Total compensable workyears: Full-time equivalent employment	919	25	23
Reimbursable:			
2001 Total compensable workyears: Full-time equivalent employment	4,738	5,734	5,742

MILITARY CONSTRUCTION, NAVY

For acquisition, construction, installation, and equipment of temporary or permanent public works, naval installations, facilities, and real property for the Navy as currently authorized by law, including personnel in the Naval Facilities Engineering Command and other personal services necessary for the purposes of this appropriation, [$901,531,000] *$753,422,000*, to remain available until September 30, [2004] *2005*: *Provided*, That of this amount, not to exceed [$72,630,000] *$63,335,000* shall be available for study, planning, design, architect and engineer services, as authorized by law, unless the Secretary of Defense determines that additional obligations are necessary for such purposes and notifies the Committees on Appropriations of both Houses of Congress of his determination and the reasons therefor.

In addition, for the foregoing purposes, $69,064,000 to become available on October 1, 2001 and to remain available until September 30, 2006. (Military Construction Appropriations Act, 2000.)

Program and Financing (in millions of dollars)

Identification code 17–1205–0–1–051	1999 actual	2000 est.	2001 est.
Obligations by program activity:			
Direct program:			
00.01 Major construction	585	623	652
00.02 Minor construction	17	7	7
00.03 Planning	56	61	60
09.01 Reimbursable program	364	354	354
10.00 Total new obligations	1,022	1,045	1,074
Budgetary resources available for obligation:			
21.40 For completion of prior year budget plans	223	148	387
22.00 New budget authority (gross)	971	1,251	1,107
22.10 Resources available from recoveries of prior year obligations	5		
22.22 Unobligated balance transerred from other DoD accounts	1	33	
23.90 Total budgetary resources available for obligation	1,200	1,432	1,495
23.95 Total new obligations	−1,022	−1,045	−1,074
23.98 Unobligated balance expiring or withdrawn	−28		
24.40 For completion of prior year budget plans	148	387	421
New budget authority (gross), detail:			
Discretionary:			
40.00 Appropriation	605	902	753
40.15 Appropriation (emergency)	6		
40.35 Appropriation rescinded	−2		
40.76 Reduction pursuant to P.L. 106–113		−5	
43.00 Appropriation (total discretionary)	609	897	753
Spending authority from offsetting collections:			
68.00 Offsetting collections (cash)	373	354	354
68.10 From Federal sources: Change in receivables and unpaid, unfilled orders	−11		
68.90 Spending authority from offsetting collections (total discretionary)	362	354	354
70.00 Total new budget authority (gross)	971	1,251	1,107
Change in unpaid obligations:			
Unpaid obligations, start of year:			
72.40 Obligated balance, start of year	856	827	881
72.95 From Federal sources: Receivables and unpaid, unfilled orders	419	408	408
72.99 Total unpaid obligations, start of year	1,275	1,235	1,289
73.10 Total new obligations	1,022	1,045	1,074
73.20 Total outlays (gross)	−1,047	−990	−1,141
73.40 Adjustments in expired accounts (net)	−10		
73.45 Adjustments in unexpired accounts	−5		
Unpaid obligations, end of year:			
74.40 Obligated balance, end of year	827	881	813
74.95 From Federal sources: Receivables and unpaid, unfilled orders	408	408	408
74.99 Total unpaid obligations, end of year	1,235	1,289	1,221
Outlays (gross), detail:			
86.90 Outlays from new discretionary authority	384	381	369
86.93 Outlays from discretionary balances	664	611	773
87.00 Total outlays (gross)	1,047	990	1,141
Offsets:			
Against gross budget authority and outlays:			
88.00 Offsetting collections (cash) from: Federal sources	−373	−354	−354
Against gross budget authority only:			
88.95 From Federal sources: Change in receivables and unpaid, unfilled orders	11		
Net budget authority and outlays:			
89.00 Budget authority	608	897	753
90.00 Outlays	674	636	787

Budget Plan (in millions of dollars)

Outlays

Identification code 17–1205–0–1–051	1999 actual	2000 est.	2001 est.
Direct:			
0701 Major construction	539	849	682
0702 Minor construction	10	8	8
0703 Planning	60	72	63
0791 Total direct	608	930	753
0801 Reimbursable	220	354	354
0893 Total budget plan	828	1,284	1,107

Object Classification (in millions of dollars)

Identification code 17–1205–0–1–051	1999 actual	2000 est.	2001 est.
Direct obligations:			
Personnel compensation:			
11.1 Full-time permanent	97	113	115
11.3 Other than full-time permanent	4	4	4
11.5 Other personnel compensation	4	4	4
11.9 Total personnel compensation	105	121	123
12.1 Civilian personnel benefits	22	29	30
13.0 Benefits for former personnel	3	3	14
21.0 Travel and transportation of persons	6	7	8
22.0 Transportation of things	1	2	2
23.2 Rental payments to others	1	2	2
23.3 Communications, utilities, and miscellaneous charges	3	4	4
24.0 Printing and reproduction	1	2	2
25.7 Operation and maintenance of equipment	1	1	1
26.0 Supplies and materials	3	3	3
31.0 Equipment	6	3	3
32.0 Land and structures	506	514	528
99.0 Subtotal, direct obligations	658	691	720
99.0 Reimbursable obligations	364	354	354
99.9 Total new obligations	1,022	1,045	1,074

Personnel Summary

Identification code 17–1205–0–1–051	1999 actual	2000 est.	2001 est.
Direct:			
1001 Total compensable workyears: Full-time equivalent employment	2,002	2,106	2,039
Reimbursable:			
2001 Total compensable workyears: Full-time equivalent employment	658	657	376

MILITARY CONSTRUCTION, AIR FORCE

For acquisition, construction, installation, and equipment of temporary or permanent public works, military installations, facilities, and real property for the Air Force as currently authorized by law, [$777,238,000] *$530,969,000*, to remain available until September 30, [2004] *2005*: *Provided*, That of this amount, not to exceed [$36,412,000] *$54,237,000* shall be available for study, planning, design, architect and engineer services, as authorized by law, unless the Secretary of Defense determines that additional obligations are necessary for such purposes and notifies the Committees on Appropriations of both Houses of Congress of his determination and the reasons therefor. *(Military Construction Appropriations Act, 2000.)*

Program and Financing (in millions of dollars)

Identification code 57–3300–0–1–051	1999 actual	2000 est.	2001 est.
Obligations by program activity:			
00.01 Major construction	600	597	502
00.02 Minor construction	10	7	9
00.03 Planning	44	35	52
00.04 Supporting Activities			2
10.00 Total new obligations (object class 32.0)	655	639	565
Budgetary resources available for obligation:			
21.40 For completion of prior year budget plans	152	139	327
22.00 New budget authority (gross)	642	784	531
22.10 Resources available from recoveries of prior year obligations	1		
22.21 Unobligated balance transferred to other DoD accounts	–5		
22.22 Unobligated balance transferred from other DoD accounts	5	44	
23.90 Total budgetary resources available for obligation	795	967	858
23.95 Total new obligations	–655	–639	–565
23.98 Unobligated balance expiring or withdrawn	–1		
24.40 For completion of prior year budget plans	139	327	294
New budget authority (gross), detail:			
Discretionary:			
40.00 Appropriation	616	777	531
40.15 Appropriation (emergency)	29		
40.35 Appropriation rescinded	–3		
40.76 Reduction pursuant to P.L. 106–113		–4	
42.00 Transferred from other DoD accounts		11	
43.00 Appropriation (total discretionary)	642	784	531
Change in unpaid obligations:			
72.40 Unpaid obligations, start of year: Obligated balance, start of year	838	782	723
73.10 Total new obligations	655	639	565
73.20 Total outlays (gross)	–713	–698	–718
73.40 Adjustments in expired accounts (net)	4		
73.45 Adjustments in unexpired accounts	–1		
74.40 Unpaid obligations, end of year: Obligated balance, end of year	782	723	570
Outlays (gross), detail:			
86.90 Outlays from new discretionary authority	85	113	74
86.93 Outlays from discretionary balances	627	585	643
87.00 Total outlays (gross)	713	698	718
Net budget authority and outlays:			
89.00 Budget authority	642	784	531
90.00 Outlays	713	698	718

Budget Plan (in millions of dollars)

Outlays

Identification code 57–3300–0–1–051	1999 actual	2000 est.	2001 est.
0701 Major construction	598	770	465
0702 Minor construction	8	11	10
0703 Planning	38	47	54
0704 Supporting Activities			2
0893 Total budget plan	644	828	531

MILITARY CONSTRUCTION, DEFENSE-WIDE

(INCLUDING TRANSFER OF FUNDS)

For acquisition, construction, installation, and equipment of temporary or permanent public works, installations, facilities, and real property for activities and agencies of the Department of Defense (other than the military departments), as currently authorized by law, [$593,615,000] *$784,753,000*, to remain available until September 30, [2004] *2005*: *Provided*, That such amounts of this appropriation as may be determined by the Secretary of Defense may be transferred to such appropriations of the Department of Defense available for military construction or family housing as he may designate, to be merged with and to be available for the same purposes, and for the same time period, as the appropriation or fund to which transferred: *Provided further*, That of the amount appropriated, not to exceed [$48,324,000] *$78,605,000* shall be available for study, planning, design, architect and engineer services, as authorized by law, unless the Secretary of Defense determines that additional obligations are necessary for such purposes and notifies the Committees on Appropriations of both Houses of Congress of his determination and the reasons therefor.

In addition, for the foregoing purposes, $230,800,000 to become available on October 1, 2001 and to remain available until September 30, 2006; $147,400,000 to become available on October 1, 2002 and remain available until September 30, 2007; $50,000,000 to become available on October 1, 2003 and remain available until September 30, 2008; and $18,900,000 to become available on October 1, 2004 and remain available until September 30, 2009. (Military Construction Appropriations Act, 2000.)

Program and Financing (in millions of dollars)

Identification code 97–0500–0–1–051	1999 actual	2000 est.	2001 est.
Obligations by program activity:			
00.01 Major construction	533	520	648
00.02 Minor construction	15	12	7
00.03 Planning	54	27	43
10.00 Total new obligations	602	559	698
Budgetary resources available for obligation:			
21.40 For completion of prior year budget plans	430	391	478
22.00 New budget authority (gross)	551	591	785
22.10 Resources available from recoveries of prior year obligations	21		
22.21 Unobligated balance transferred to other DoD accounts	–6		
22.22 Unobligated balance transferred from other DoD accounts	5	55	
23.90 Total budgetary resources available for obligation	1,000	1,037	1,263
23.95 Total new obligations	–602	–559	–698
23.98 Unobligated balance expiring or withdrawn	–7		
24.40 For completion of prior year budget plans	391	478	565
New budget authority (gross), detail:			
Discretionary:			
40.00 Appropriation	553	594	785
40.35 Appropriation rescinded	–2		
40.76 Reduction pursuant to P.L. 106–113		–3	
43.00 Appropriation (total discretionary)	551	591	785
Change in unpaid obligations:			
72.40 Unpaid obligations, start of year: Obligated balance, start of year	790	738	693
73.10 Total new obligations	602	559	698
73.20 Total outlays (gross)	–631	–603	–625
73.40 Adjustments in expired accounts (net)	–3		
73.45 Adjustments in unexpired accounts	–21		
74.40 Unpaid obligations, end of year: Obligated balance, end of year	738	693	766
Outlays (gross), detail:			
86.90 Outlays from new discretionary authority	59	60	85
86.93 Outlays from discretionary balances	572	543	541
87.00 Total outlays (gross)	631	603	625
Net budget authority and outlays:			
89.00 Budget authority	551	591	785
90.00 Outlays	631	603	625

General and special funds—Continued

MILITARY CONSTRUCTION, DEFENSE-WIDE—Continued

(INCLUDING TRANSFER OF FUNDS)—Continued

Budget Plan (in millions of dollars)
Outlays

Identification code 97–0500–0–1–051	1999 actual	2000 est.	2001 est.
0701 Major construction	502	579	689
0702 Minor construction	10	19	17
0703 Planning	40	48	79
0893 Total budget plan	552	646	785

Summary of Budget Authority and Outlays

(in millions of dollars)

Enacted/requested:	1999 actual	2000 est.	2001 est.
Budget Authority	551	591	785
Outlays	631	603	626
Supplemental proposal:			
Budget Authority		39	
Outlays		4	15
Total:			
Budget Authority	551	630	785
Outlays	631	607	641

Object Classification (in millions of dollars)

Identification code 97–0500–0–1–051	1999 actual	2000 est.	2001 est.
21.0 Travel and transportation of persons	1	1	1
25.1 Advisory and assistance services	2	2	2
25.2 Other services	10	9	10
Purchases of goods and services from Government accounts:			
25.3 Purchases of goods and services from Government accounts	34	30	36
25.3 Purchases from revolving funds	2	2	1
26.0 Supplies and materials	1	1	1
32.0 Land and structures	552	514	647
99.9 Total new obligations	602	559	698

NORTH ATLANTIC TREATY ORGANIZATION

SECURITY INVESTMENT PROGRAM

For the United States share of the cost of the North Atlantic Treaty Organization Security Investment Program for the acquisition and construction of military facilities and installations (including international military headquarters) and for related expenses for the collective defense of the North Atlantic Treaty Area as authorized in Military Construction Authorization Acts and section 2806 of title 10, United States Code, [$81,000,000] *$190,000,000*, to remain available until expended. *(Military Construction Appropriations Act, 2000.)*

Program and Financing (in millions of dollars)

Identification code 97–0804–0–1–051	1999 actual	2000 est.	2001 est.
Obligations by program activity:			
00.01 NATO Infrastructure	170	92	189
00.02 NATO Expansion			12
10.00 Total new obligations (object class 32.0)	170	92	201
Budgetary resources available for obligation:			
21.40 Unobligated balance available, start of year	29	105	105
22.00 New budget authority (gross)	245	92	201
22.10 Resources available from recoveries of prior year obligations	1		
23.90 Total budgetary resources available for obligation	275	196	306
23.95 Total new obligations	−170	−92	−201
24.40 Unobligated balance available, end of year	105	105	105
New budget authority (gross), detail:			
Discretionary:			
40.00 Appropriation	154	81	190
42.00 Transferred from other DoD accounts	91		
43.00 Appropriation (total discretionary)	245	81	190
Spending authority from offsetting collections:			
68.00 Offsetting collections (cash)	17	11	11
68.10 From Federal sources: Change in receivables and unpaid, unfilled orders	−16		
68.15 From Federal sources: Adjustments to receivables and unpaid, unfilled orders	−1		
68.90 Spending authority from offsetting collections (total discretionary)		11	11
70.00 Total new budget authority (gross)	245	92	201
Change in unpaid obligations:			
Unpaid obligations, start of year:			
72.40 Obligated balance, start of year	241	342	348
72.95 From Federal sources: Receivables and unpaid, unfilled orders	12	−4	−4
72.99 Total unpaid obligations, start of year	254	338	343
73.10 Total new obligations	170	92	201
73.20 Total outlays (gross)	−85	−86	−299
73.45 Adjustments in unexpired accounts	−1		
Unpaid obligations, end of year:			
74.40 Obligated balance, end of year	342	348	250
74.95 From Federal sources: Receivables and unpaid, unfilled orders	−4	−4	−4
74.99 Total unpaid obligations, end of year	338	343	246
Outlays (gross), detail:			
86.90 Outlays from new discretionary authority	68	21	34
86.93 Outlays from discretionary balances	17	65	264
87.00 Total outlays (gross)	85	86	299
Offsets:			
Against gross budget authority and outlays:			
88.40 Offsetting collections (cash) from: Non-Federal sources	−17	−11	−11
Against gross budget authority only:			
88.95 From Federal sources: Change in receivables and unpaid, unfilled orders	16		
88.96 From Federal sources: Adjustment to receivables and unpaid, unfilled orders	1		
Net budget authority and outlays:			
89.00 Budget authority	245	81	190
90.00 Outlays	68	75	288

MILITARY CONSTRUCTION, ARMY NATIONAL GUARD

For construction, acquisition, expansion, rehabilitation, and conversion of facilities for the training and administration of the Army National Guard, and contributions therefor, as authorized by chapter 1803 of title 10, United States Code, and Military Construction Authorization Acts, [$227,456,000] *$59,130,000*, to remain available until September 30, [2004] *2005*. *(Military Construction Appropriations Act, 2000.)*

Program and Financing (in millions of dollars)

Identification code 21–2085–0–1–051	1999 actual	2000 est.	2001 est.
Obligations by program activity:			
00.01 Major construction	147	163	93
00.02 Minor construction	5	10	5
00.03 Planning	13	12	8
10.00 Total new obligations	165	185	105
Budgetary resources available for obligation:			
21.40 For completion of prior year budget plans	91	101	152
22.00 New budget authority (gross)	151	236	59
22.10 Resources available from recoveries of prior year obligations	25		
23.90 Total budgetary resources available for obligation	267	337	212
23.95 Total new obligations	−165	−185	−105
23.98 Unobligated balance expiring or withdrawn	−1		
24.40 For completion of prior year budget plans	101	152	106
New budget authority (gross), detail:			
Discretionary:			
40.00 Appropriation	142	237	59

40.15	Appropriation (emergency)	9		
40.76	Reduction pursuant to P.L. 106–113		–1	
43.00	Appropriation (total discretionary)	151	236	59
	Change in unpaid obligations:			
72.40	Unpaid obligations, start of year: Obligated balance, start of year	192	181	222
73.10	Total new obligations	165	185	105
73.20	Total outlays (gross)	–153	–144	–164
73.45	Adjustments in unexpired accounts	–25		
74.40	Unpaid obligations, end of year: Obligated balance, end of year	181	222	163
	Outlays (gross), detail:			
86.90	Outlays from new discretionary authority	16	17	4
86.93	Outlays from discretionary balances	137	127	159
87.00	Total outlays (gross)	153	144	164
	Net budget authority and outlays:			
89.00	Budget authority	151	236	59
90.00	Outlays	153	144	164

Budget Plan (in millions of dollars)
Outlays

Identification code 21–2085–0–1–051		1999 actual	2000 est.	2001 est.
0701	Major construction	137	204	53
0702	Minor construction	5	16	2
0703	Planning	9	16	4
0893	Total budget plan	151	236	59

Object Classification (in millions of dollars)

Identification code 21–2085–0–1–051		1999 actual	2000 est.	2001 est.
25.2	Other services	1	1	
25.3	Purchases of goods and services from Government accounts	2	2	2
32.0	Land and structures	162	182	103
99.9	Total new obligations	165	185	105

Military Construction, Air National Guard

For construction, acquisition, expansion, rehabilitation, and conversion of facilities for the training and administration of the Air National Guard, and contributions therefor, as authorized by chapter 1803 of title 10, United States Code, and Military Construction Authorization Acts, **[**$263,724,000**]** *$50,179,000*, to remain available until September 30, **[**2004**]** *2005. (Military Construction Appropriations Act, 2000.)*

Program and Financing (in millions of dollars)

Identification code 57–3830–0–1–051		1999 actual	2000 est.	2001 est.
	Obligations by program activity:			
00.01	Major construction	177	131	110
00.02	Minor construction	12	2	2
00.03	Planning	12	6	6
10.00	Total new obligations	200	140	118
	Budgetary resources available for obligation:			
21.40	For completion of prior year budget plans	101	87	209
22.00	New budget authority (gross)	186	262	50
23.90	Total budgetary resources available for obligation	287	349	259
23.95	Total new obligations	–200	–140	–118
24.40	For completion of prior year budget plans	87	209	141
	New budget authority (gross), detail:			
	Discretionary:			
40.00	Appropriation	170	264	50
40.15	Appropriation (emergency)	16		
40.76	Reduction pursuant to P.L. 106–113		–1	
43.00	Appropriation (total discretionary)	186	262	50
	Change in unpaid obligations:			
72.40	Unpaid obligations, start of year: Obligated balance, start of year	218	204	158
73.10	Total new obligations	200	140	118
73.20	Total outlays (gross)	–214	–187	–210
73.40	Adjustments in expired accounts (net)	1		
74.40	Unpaid obligations, end of year: Obligated balance, end of year	204	158	65
	Outlays (gross), detail:			
86.90	Outlays from new discretionary authority	29	24	4
86.93	Outlays from discretionary balances	186	163	206
87.00	Total outlays (gross)	214	187	210
	Net budget authority and outlays:			
89.00	Budget authority	186	262	50
90.00	Outlays	214	187	210

Budget Plan (in millions of dollars)
Outlays

Identification code 57–3830–0–1–051		1999 actual	2000 est.	2001 est.
0701	Major construction	170	252	37
0702	Minor construction	8	4	4
0703	Planning	9	7	9
0893	Total budget plan	186	262	50

Object Classification (in millions of dollars)

Identification code 57–3830–0–1–051		1999 actual	2000 est.	2001 est.
32.0	Direct obligations: Land and structures	177	131	111
32.0	Allocation Account: Land and structures	23	9	7
99.9	Total new obligations	200	140	118

Military Construction, Army Reserve

For construction, acquisition, expansion, rehabilitation, and conversion of facilities for the training and administration of the Army Reserve as authorized by chapter 1803 of title 10, United States Code, and Military Construction Authorization Acts, **[**$111,340,000**]** *$81,713,000*, to remain available until September 30, **[**2004**]** *2005. (Military Construction Appropriations Act, 2000.)*

Program and Financing (in millions of dollars)

Identification code 21–2086–0–1–051		1999 actual	2000 est.	2001 est.
	Obligations by program activity:			
00.01	Major construction	96	99	76
00.02	Minor construction	1	2	2
00.03	Planning	7	8	7
10.00	Total new obligations	104	110	85
	Budgetary resources available for obligation:			
21.40	Unobligated balance available, start of year	38	41	42
22.00	New budget authority (gross)	102	111	82
22.10	Resources available from recoveries of prior year obligations	4		
23.90	Total budgetary resources available for obligation	145	152	123
23.95	Total new obligations	–104	–110	–85
23.98	Unobligated balance expiring or withdrawn	–1		
24.40	For completion of prior year budget plans	41	42	39
	New budget authority (gross), detail:			
	Discretionary:			
40.00	Appropriation	102	111	82
40.76	Reduction pursuant to P.L. 106–113		–1	
43.00	Appropriation (total discretionary)	102	111	82
	Change in unpaid obligations:			
72.40	Unpaid obligations, start of year: Obligated balance, start of year	84	109	130
73.10	Total new obligations	104	110	85
73.20	Total outlays (gross)	–76	–89	–91
73.40	Adjustments in expired accounts (net)	2		

General and special funds—Continued

MILITARY CONSTRUCTION, ARMY RESERVE—Continued

Program and Financing (in millions of dollars)—Continued

Identification code 21–2086–0–1–051	1999 actual	2000 est.	2001 est.
73.45 Adjustments in unexpired accounts	–4		
74.40 Unpaid obligations, end of year: Obligated balance, end of year	109	130	122
Outlays (gross), detail:			
86.90 Outlays from new discretionary authority	11	12	10
86.93 Outlays from discretionary balances	65	77	82
87.00 Total outlays (gross)	76	89	91
Net budget authority and outlays:			
89.00 Budget authority	102	111	82
90.00 Outlays	76	89	91

Budget Plan (in millions of dollars)
Outlays

Identification code 21–2086–0–1–051	1999 actual	2000 est.	2001 est.
0701 Major construction	95	100	73
0702 Minor construction		3	2
0703 Planning	7	8	6
0893 Total budget plan	102	111	82

Object Classification (in millions of dollars)

Identification code 21–2086–0–1–051	1999 actual	2000 est.	2001 est.
23.2 Rental payments to others		2	2
25.2 Other services	2		
25.3 Purchases of goods and services from Government accounts	4		
32.0 Land and structures	98	108	83
99.9 Total new obligations	104	110	85

MILITARY CONSTRUCTION, NAVAL RESERVE

For construction, acquisition, expansion, rehabilitation, and conversion of facilities for the training and administration of the reserve components of the Navy and Marine Corps as authorized by chapter 1803 of title 10, United States Code, and Military Construction Authorization Acts, [$28,457,000] *$16,103,000*, to remain available until September 30, [2004] *2005*. *(Military Construction Appropriations Act, 2000.)*

Program and Financing (in millions of dollars)

Identification code 17–1235–0–1–051	1999 actual	2000 est.	2001 est.
Obligations by program activity:			
00.01 Major construction	33	21	16
00.02 Minor construction	1	3	1
00.03 Planning	2	4	2
10.00 Total new obligations (object class 32.0)	35	28	18
Budgetary resources available for obligation:			
21.40 For completion of prior year budget plans	14	11	12
22.00 New budget authority (gross)	32	28	16
23.90 Total budgetary resources available for obligation	46	39	28
23.95 Total new obligations	–35	–28	–18
24.40 Unobligated balance available, end of year	11	12	9
New budget authority (gross), detail:			
Discretionary:			
40.00 Appropriation	32	28	16
Change in unpaid obligations:			
72.40 Unpaid obligations, start of year: Obligated balance, start of year	64	52	48
73.10 Total new obligations	35	28	18
73.20 Total outlays (gross)	–47	–31	–28
74.40 Unpaid obligations, end of year: Obligated balance, end of year	52	48	38
Outlays (gross), detail:			
86.90 Outlays from new discretionary authority	5	2	2
86.93 Outlays from discretionary balances	43	29	27
87.00 Total outlays (gross)	47	31	28
Net budget authority and outlays:			
89.00 Budget authority	32	28	16
90.00 Outlays	47	31	28

Budget Plan (in millions of dollars)
Outlays

Identification code 17–1235–0–1–051	1999 actual	2000 est.	2001 est.
0701 Major construction	28	23	15
0702 Minor construction	1	3	
0703 Planning	3	3	2
0893 Total budget plan	32	28	16

MILITARY CONSTRUCTION, AIR FORCE RESERVE

For construction, acquisition, expansion, rehabilitation, and conversion of facilities for the training and administration of the Air Force Reserve as authorized by chapter 1803 of title 10, United States Code, and Military Construction Authorization Acts, [$64,404,000] *$14,851,000*, to remain available until September 30, [2004] *2005*. *(Military Construction Appropriations Act, 2000.)*

Program and Financing (in millions of dollars)

Identification code 57–3730–0–1–051	1999 actual	2000 est.	2001 est.
Obligations by program activity:			
00.01 Major construction	29	38	21
00.02 Minor construction	3	3	4
00.03 Planning	5	2	2
10.00 Total new obligations	37	44	27
Budgetary resources available for obligation:			
Unobligated balance available, start of year:			
21.40 For completion of prior year budget plans	10	8	28
21.40 For completion of prior year budget plans			
21.99 Total unobligated balance, start of year	10	8	28
22.00 New budget authority (gross)	34	64	15
23.90 Total budgetary resources available for obligation	45	72	43
23.95 Total new obligations	–37	–44	–27
Unobligated balance available, end of year:			
24.40 For completion of prior year budget plans	8	28	16
24.40 Unobligated balance available, end of year			
24.99 Total unobligated balance, end of year	8	28	16
New budget authority (gross), detail:			
Discretionary:			
40.00 Appropriation	34	64	15
Change in unpaid obligations:			
72.40 Unpaid obligations, start of year: Obligated balance, start of year	39	38	46
73.10 Total new obligations	37	44	27
73.20 Total outlays (gross)	–37	–36	–44
73.40 Adjustments in expired accounts (net)			
74.40 Unpaid obligations, end of year: Obligated balance, end of year	38	46	29
Outlays (gross), detail:			
86.90 Outlays from new discretionary authority	4	9	2
86.93 Outlays from discretionary balances	34	27	42
87.00 Total outlays (gross)	37	36	44
Net budget authority and outlays:			
89.00 Budget authority	34	64	15
90.00 Outlays	37	36	44

Budget Plan (in millions of dollars)
Outlays

Identification code 57–3730–0–1–051	1999 actual	2000 est.	2001 est.
0701 Major construction	29	58	8
0702 Minor construction	3	4	4
0703 Planning	2	2	2
0893 Total budget plan	34	64	15

Military Construction Transfer Fund

Program and Financing (in millions of dollars)

Identification code 97–0140–0–1–051	1999 actual	2000 est.	2001 est.
Budgetary resources available for obligation:			
21.40 Unobligated balance available, start of year		181	
22.00 New budget authority (gross)	181		
22.21 Unobligated balance transferred to other DoD MILCON accounts		–181	
23.90 Total budgetary resources available for obligation	181		
24.40 Unobligated balance available, end of year	181		
New budget authority (gross), detail:			
Discretionary:			
40.15 Appropriation (emergency)	475		
40.60 Contingent emergency appropriation not available for obligations	–203		
41.00 Transferred to other DoD MILCON accounts	–91		
43.00 Appropriation (total discretionary)	181		
Net budget authority and outlays:			
89.00 Budget authority	181		
90.00 Outlays			

Base Realignment and Closure Account

For deposit into the Department of Defense Base Closure Account 1990 established by section 2906(a)(1) of the Department of Defense Authorization Act, 1991 (Public Law 101–510), $1,764,369,000, to remain available until expended[: *Provided*, That not more than $346,403,000 of the funds appropriated herein shall be available solely for environmental restoration, unless the Secretary of Defense determines that additional obligations are necessary for such purposes and notifies the Committees on Appropriations of both Houses of Congress of his determination and the reasons therefor]. *(Military Construction Appropriations Act, 2000.)*

Program and Financing (in millions of dollars)

Identification code 97–0103–0–1–051	1999 actual	2000 est.	2001 est.
Obligations by program activity:			
Direct program:			
00.02 Base Closure (II)	34		
00.03 Base Closure (III)	556	206	80
00.04 Base Closure (IV)	1,298	400	848
10.00 Total obligations—Base closure program	1,888	606	928
Budgetary resources available for obligation:			
21.40 Available to finance new budget plans	467	361	426
22.00 New budget authority (gross)	1,625	672	1,178
22.10 Resources available from recoveries of prior year obligations	166		
22.21 Unobligated balance transferred to other DoD accounts	–8		
23.90 Total budgetary resources available for obligation	2,249	1,032	1,604
23.95 Total new obligations	–1,888	–606	–928
24.40 Available to finance subsequent year budget plans	361	426	677
New budget authority (gross), detail:			
Discretionary:			
40.00 Appropriation	1,631	672	1,174
40.35 Appropriation rescinded	–6		
40.76 Reduction pursuant to P.L. 106–113		–3	
41.00 Transferred to other DoD accounts	–7	–5	–4
43.00 Appropriation (total discretionary)	1,618	664	1,170
Spending authority from offsetting collections:			
68.00 Offsetting collections (cash)		8	8
68.10 From Federal sources: Change in receivables and unpaid, unfilled orders	7		
68.90 Spending authority from offsetting collections (total discretionary)	7	8	8
70.00 Total new budget authority (gross)	1,625	672	1,178
Change in unpaid obligations:			
Unpaid obligations, start of year:			
72.40 Obligated balance, start of year	2,743	2,331	1,489
72.95 From Federal sources: Receivables and unpaid, unfilled orders	11	18	18
72.99 Total unpaid obligations, start of year	2,754	2,349	1,507
73.10 Total new obligations	1,888	606	928
73.20 Total outlays (gross)	–2,116	–1,450	–1,059
73.40 Adjustments in expired accounts (net)	–11		
73.45 Adjustments in unexpired accounts	–166		
Unpaid obligations, end of year:			
74.40 Obligated balance, end of year	2,331	1,489	1,357
74.95 From Federal sources: Receivables and unpaid, unfilled orders	18	18	18
74.99 Total unpaid obligations, end of year	2,349	1,507	1,375
Outlays (gross), detail:			
86.90 Outlays from new discretionary authority	368	205	369
86.93 Outlays from discretionary balances	1,749	1,246	691
87.00 Total outlays (gross)	2,116	1,450	1,059
Offsets:			
Against gross budget authority and outlays:			
Offsetting collections (cash) from:			
88.00 Federal sources	7		
88.40 Non-Federal sources	–7	–8	–8
88.90 Total, offsetting collections (cash)		–8	–8
Against gross budget authority only:			
88.95 From Federal sources: Change in receivables and unpaid, unfilled orders	–7		
Net budget authority and outlays:			
89.00 Budget authority	1,617	664	1,170
90.00 Outlays	2,117	1,441	1,051

Budget Plan (in millions of dollars)
Outlays

Identification code 97–0103–0–1–051	1999 actual	2000 est.	2001 est.
0703 Base Closure (III)	368		
0704 Base Closure (IV)	1,317	672	1,178
0893 Total budget plan	1,685	672	1,178

Object Classification (in millions of dollars)

Identification code 97–0103–0–1–051	1999 actual	2000 est.	2001 est.
Personnel compensation:			
11.5 Other personnel compensation	170	85	128
11.7 Military personnel	2		5
11.9 Total personnel compensation	172	85	133
21.0 Travel and transportation of persons	12		1
22.0 Transportation of things	11		2
23.3 Communications, utilities, and miscellaneous charges	190	2	2
25.1 Advisory and assistance services	19	12	10
25.2 Other services		8	19
Purchases of goods and services from Government accounts:			
25.3 Purchases of goods and services from Government accounts	321	248	169
25.3 Purchases from revolving funds	70	11	27
25.4 Operation and maintenance of facilities	87	18	45
25.5 Research and development contracts	1		
25.7 Operation and maintenance of equipment	13	1	3
26.0 Supplies and materials	85	11	28
31.0 Equipment	15	1	2
32.0 Land and structures	888	207	485

General and special funds—Continued

BASE REALIGNMENT AND CLOSURE ACCOUNT—Continued

Object Classification (in millions of dollars)—Continued

Identification code 97–0103–0–1–051	1999 actual	2000 est.	2001 est.
41.0 Grants, subsidies, and contributions	4	1	2
99.9 Total new obligations	1,888	606	928

FOREIGN CURRENCY FLUCTUATIONS, CONSTRUCTION

Program and Financing (in millions of dollars)

Identification code 97–0803–0–1–051	1999 actual	2000 est.	2001 est.
Budgetary resources available for obligation:			
21.40 Unobligated balance available, start of year	143	171	171
22.00 New budget authority (gross)	63		
22.21 Unobligated balance transferred to other DoD accounts	−183		
22.22 Unobligated balance transferred from other DoD accounts	148		
23.90 Total budgetary resources available for obligation	171	171	171
24.40 Unobligated balance available, end of year	171	171	171
New budget authority (gross), detail:			
Discretionary:			
50.00 Reappropriation	63		
Net budget authority and outlays:			
89.00 Budget authority	63		
90.00 Outlays			

FAMILY HOUSING, DEFENSE

These appropriations finance all costs associated with construction, improvements, operations, maintenance and leasing of all military family housing. In addition to quality of life enhancements, the program contains initiatives to reduce operating costs and conserve energy by upgrading or replacing facilities which can be made more efficient through relatively modest investments in improvements.

The Family Housing Improvement Fund (FHIF) was created to finance the use of innovative methods authorized in the Housing Revitalization Act (HRA), P.L. 104–106, to meet the Department's housing needs. The HRA authorizes the Department to use limited partnerships, make direct and guaranteed loans, and convey Department-owned property to stimulate the private sector to increase the availability of affordable, quality housing for military personnel. The Department's goal is to increase its reliance on the private sector to provide quality housing for all military personnel much sooner than possible with traditional family housing programs at currently planned funding levels.

The budget plan for each appropriation is shown as a separate table immediately following the program and financing schedules for those appropriations that are available for obligation for more than one year. In 2001 it presents, by budget activity, the value of the program requested for the life of the multiple-year appropriation, with comparable amounts in 1999 and 2000.

Resources presented under the Family Housing, Defense title contribute primarily to achieving the Department's corporate goals 1 (Shape) and 2 (Prepare). A detailed description of the corporate goals is contained in the FY 2001 Performance Plan in the Department's 2000 Annual Report to the President and Congress. This performance plan is required by the Government Performance and Results Act of 1993.

Federal Funds

General and special funds:

FAMILY HOUSING, ARMY

For expenses of family housing for the Army for construction, including acquisition, replacement, addition, expansion, extension and alteration and for operation and maintenance, including debt payment, leasing, minor construction, principal and interest charges, and insurance premiums, as authorized by law, as follows: for Construction, [$80,700,000] *$162,106,000*, to remain available until September 30, [2004] *2005*; for Operation and Maintenance, and for debt payment, [$1,086,312,000] *$978,275,000*; in all [$1,167,012,000] *$1,140,381,000. (10 U.S.C. 2824, 2827–29, 2831, 2851–54, 2857; Military Construction Appropriations Act, 2000.)*

Program and Financing (in millions of dollars)

Identification code 21–0702–0–1–051	1999 actual	2000 est.	2001 est.
Obligations by program activity:			
Direct program:			
Construction:			
01.01 Construction of new housing	74	34	76
01.02 Construction improvements	90	52	58
01.03 Planning and Design	5	5	6
01.91 Total construction	169	91	140
Operation, maintenance, and interest payment:			
Operation:			
02.01 Operating expenses	416	398	378
02.02 Leasing	196	222	202
02.03 Maintenance of real property	490	460	398
02.91 Total operation, maintenance, and interest payment	1,102	1,080	978
09.01 Reimbursable program	16	19	22
10.00 Total new obligations	1,287	1,190	1,140
Budgetary resources available for obligation:			
Unobligated balance available, start of year:			
21.40 For completion of prior year budget plans	119	59	39
21.40 Available to finance new budget plans		52	30
21.99 Total unobligated balance, start of year	119	111	69
22.00 New budget authority (gross)	1,268	1,180	1,162
22.10 Resources available from recoveries of prior year obligations	14		
22.21 Unobligated balance transferred to other DoD accounts	−122	−31	−30
22.22 Unobligated balance transferred from other DoD accounts	131		
23.90 Total budgetary resources available for obligation	1,411	1,260	1,202
23.95 Total new obligations	−1,287	−1,190	−1,140
23.98 Unobligated balance expiring or withdrawn	−13		
Unobligated balance available, end of year:			
24.40 For completion of prior year budget plans	59	39	61
24.40 Unobligated balance available, end of year	52	30	
24.99 Total unobligated balance, end of year	111	69	61
New budget authority (gross), detail:			
Discretionary:			
40.00 Appropriation	1,230	1,167	1,140
40.15 Appropriation (emergency)	30		
40.35 Appropriation rescinded	−8		
40.76 Reduction pursuant to P.L. 106–113		−6	
43.00 Appropriation (total discretionary)	1,252	1,161	1,140
Spending authority from offsetting collections:			
68.00 Offsetting collections (cash)	15	19	22
68.10 From Federal sources: Change in receivables and unpaid, unfilled orders	1		
68.90 Spending authority from offsetting collections (total discretionary)	16	19	22
70.00 Total new budget authority (gross)	1,268	1,180	1,162
Change in unpaid obligations:			
Unpaid obligations, start of year:			
72.40 Obligated balance, start of year	650	639	545
72.95 From Federal sources: Receivables and unpaid, unfilled orders	4	5	5

		1999 actual	2000 est.	2001 est.
72.99	Total unpaid obligations, start of year	654	644	550
73.10	Total new obligations	1,287	1,190	1,140
73.20	Total outlays (gross)	–1,269	–1,285	–1,170
73.40	Adjustments in expired accounts (net)	–14		
73.45	Adjustments in unexpired accounts	–14		
	Unpaid obligations, end of year:			
74.40	Obligated balance, end of year	639	545	515
74.95	From Federal sources: Receivables and unpaid, unfilled orders	5	5	5
74.99	Total unpaid obligations, end of year	644	550	520
	Outlays (gross), detail:			
86.90	Outlays from new discretionary authority	806	793	725
86.93	Outlays from discretionary balances	463	491	446
87.00	Total outlays (gross)	1,269	1,285	1,170
	Offsets:			
	Against gross budget authority and outlays:			
	Offsetting collections (cash) from:			
88.00	Federal sources	–15	–3	–4
88.40	Non-Federal sources		–16	–18
88.90	Total, offsetting collections (cash)	–15	–19	–22
	Against gross budget authority only:			
88.95	From Federal sources: Change in receivables and unpaid, unfilled orders	–1		
	Net budget authority and outlays:			
89.00	Budget authority	1,252	1,161	1,140
90.00	Outlays	1,255	1,266	1,148

Budget Plan (in millions of dollars)
Outlays

Identification code 21–0702–0–1–051		1999 actual	2000 est.	2001 est.
	Direct:			
	Construction:			
0601	Construction of new housing	59	32	92
0602	Construction improvements	64	35	64
0603	Planning and Design	6	4	7
0691	Total construction	130	71	162
	Operation, maintenance, and interest payment:			
	Operation:			
0701	Operating expenses	417	398	378
0702	Leasing	196	222	202
0703	Maintenance of real property	490	460	398
0791	Total operation, maintenance, and interest payment	1,103	1,081	978
0801	Reimbursable	16	19	22
0893	Total budget plan	1,248	1,171	1,162

Object Classification (in millions of dollars)

Identification code 21–0702–0–1–051		1999 actual	2000 est.	2001 est.
	Direct obligations:			
	Personnel compensation:			
11.1	Full-time permanent	24	27	26
11.3	Other than full-time permanent	5	4	4
11.5	Other personnel compensation	1	2	2
11.9	Total personnel compensation	30	33	32
12.1	Civilian personnel benefits	8	8	8
13.0	Benefits for former personnel		2	1
21.0	Travel and transportation of persons	2	2	2
22.0	Transportation of things	4	4	4
23.1	Rental payments to GSA	1	1	1
23.2	Rental payments to others	11	12	12
23.3	Communications, utilities, and miscellaneous charges	188	196	182
25.1	Advisory and assistance services	3	2	2
25.2	Other services	252	122	109
	Purchases of goods and services from Government accounts:			
25.3	Purchases of goods and services from other Government accounts	275	402	365
25.3	Payments to foreign national indirect hire personnel	15	15	14
25.3	Purchases from revolving funds	36	25	23
25.4	Operation and maintenance of facilities	248	226	203
25.7	Operation and maintenance of equipment	10	11	9
26.0	Supplies and materials	21	12	10
31.0	Equipment	15	14	13
32.0	Land and structures	152	84	129
99.0	Subtotal, direct obligations	1,271	1,171	1,118
99.0	Reimbursable obligations	16	19	22
99.9	Total new obligations	1,287	1,190	1,140

Personnel Summary

Identification code 21–0702–0–1–051		1999 actual	2000 est.	2001 est.
1001	Total compensable workyears: Full-time equivalent employment	810	821	770

FAMILY HOUSING, NAVY AND MARINE CORPS

For expenses of family housing for the Navy and Marine Corps for construction, including acquisition, replacement, addition, expansion, extension and alteration and for operation and maintenance, including debt payment, leasing, minor construction, principal and interest charges, and insurance premiums, as authorized by law, as follows: for Construction, [$341,071,000] *$362,822,000*, to remain available until September 30, [2004] *2005*; for Operation and Maintenance, and for debt payment, [$891,470,000] *$882,638,000*; in all [$1,232,541,000] *$1,245,460,000. (10 U.S.C. 2824, 2827–29, 2831, 2851–54, 2857; Military Construction Appropriations Act, 2000.)*

Program and Financing (in millions of dollars)

Identification code 17–0703–0–1–051		1999 actual	2000 est.	2001 est.
	Obligations by program activity:			
	Direct program:			
	Construction:			
01.01	Construction of new housing	70	224	271
01.02	Construction improvements	174	173	176
01.03	Planning and Design	10	14	17
01.91	Total construction	254	412	464
	Operation, maintenance, and interest payment:			
	Operation:			
02.01	Operating expenses	294	350	346
02.02	Leasing	92	145	143
02.03	Maintenance of real property	517	392	394
02.91	Total operation, maintenance, and interest payment	903	887	883
09.01	Reimbursable program	7	21	21
10.00	Total new obligations	1,164	1,320	1,367
	Budgetary resources available for obligation:			
	Unobligated balance available, start of year:			
21.40	For completion of prior year budget plans	458	467	394
21.40	Unobligated balance available, start of year		16	8
21.99	Total unobligated balance, start of year	458	483	403
22.00	New budget authority (gross)	1,229	1,247	1,266
22.21	Unobligated balance transferred to other DoD accounts	–15	–8	–9
22.22	Unobligated balance transferred from other DoD accounts	2		
23.90	Total budgetary resources available for obligation	1,673	1,722	1,661
23.95	Total new obligations	–1,164	–1,320	–1,367
23.98	Unobligated balance expiring or withdrawn	–26		
	Unobligated balance available, end of year:			
24.40	For completion of prior year budget plans	467	394	293
24.40	Unobligated balance available, end of year	16	8	
24.99	Total unobligated balance, end of year	483	403	293
	New budget authority (gross), detail:			
	Discretionary:			
40.00	Appropriation	1,208	1,233	1,245
40.15	Appropriation (emergency)	11		
40.35	Appropriation rescinded	–3		
40.76	Reduction pursuant to P.L. 106–113		–6	
43.00	Appropriation (total discretionary)	1,216	1,226	1,245
	Spending authority from offsetting collections:			
68.00	Offsetting collections (cash)	17	21	21

General and special funds—Continued

FAMILY HOUSING, NAVY AND MARINE CORPS—Continued

Program and Financing (in millions of dollars)—Continued

Identification code 17–0703–0–1–051		1999 actual	2000 est.	2001 est.
68.15	From Federal sources: Adjustments to receivables and unpaid, unfilled orders	–4		
68.90	Spending authority from offsetting collections (total discretionary)	13	21	21
70.00	Total new budget authority (gross)	1,229	1,248	1,266
	Change in unpaid obligations:			
	Unpaid obligations, start of year:			
72.40	Obligated balance, start of year	1,118	902	897
72.95	From Federal sources: Receivables and unpaid, unfilled orders	–2	–2	–2
72.99	Total unpaid obligations, start of year	1,116	900	896
73.10	Total new obligations	1,164	1,320	1,367
73.20	Total outlays (gross)	–1,347	–1,324	–1,259
73.40	Adjustments in expired accounts (net)	–33		
	Unpaid obligations, end of year:			
74.40	Obligated balance, end of year	902	897	1,005
74.95	From Federal sources: Receivables and unpaid, unfilled orders	–2	–2	–2
74.99	Total unpaid obligations, end of year	900	896	1,003
	Outlays (gross), detail:			
86.90	Outlays from new discretionary authority	588	549	551
86.93	Outlays from discretionary balances	760	775	708
87.00	Total outlays (gross)	1,347	1,324	1,259
	Offsets:			
	Against gross budget authority and outlays:			
	Offsetting collections (cash) from:			
88.00	Federal sources	–4	–21	–21
88.40	Non-Federal sources	–13		
88.90	Total, offsetting collections (cash)	–17	–21	–21
	Against gross budget authority only:			
88.96	From Federal sources: Adjustment to receivables and unpaid, unfilled orders	4		
	Net budget authority and outlays:			
89.00	Budget authority	1,216	1,226	1,245
90.00	Outlays	1,330	1,303	1,238

Note: Section 125 of the FY 1999 Military Construction Appropriations Act appropriated receipts ($6 million) for the construction of housing at Naval Station Puget Sound.

Budget Plan (in millions of dollars)
Outlays

Identification code 17–0703–0–1–051		1999 actual	2000 est.	2001 est.
	Direct:			
	Construction:			
0601	Construction of new housing	46	134	159
0602	Construction improvements	226	188	184
0603	Planning and Design	16	18	20
0691	Total construction	287	339	363
	Operation, maintenance, and interest payment:			
	Operation:			
0701	Operating expenses	294	350	346
0702	Leasing	92	145	143
0703	Maintenance of real property	522	392	394
0791	Total operation, maintenance, and interest payment	908	887	883
0801	Reimbursable	2	21	21
0893	Total budget plan	1,197	1,247	1,266

Object Classification (in millions of dollars)

Identification code 17–0703–0–1–051		1999 actual	2000 est.	2001 est.
	Direct obligations:			
21.0	Travel and transportation of persons	3		
23.2	Rental payments to others	102	144	143
23.3	Communications, utilities, and miscellaneous charges	219	412	411
	Purchases of goods and services from Government accounts:			
25.3	Purchases of goods and services from Government accounts	75	5	5
25.3	Purchases from revolving funds	149	180	178
25.4	Operation and maintenance of facilities	319	125	125
25.7	Operation and maintenance of equipment	5	4	5
26.0	Supplies and materials		14	11
31.0	Equipment	30	3	4
32.0	Land and structures	255	412	464
99.0	Subtotal, direct obligations	1,157	1,299	1,346
99.0	Reimbursable obligations	7	21	21
99.9	Total new obligations	1,164	1,320	1,367

FAMILY HOUSING, AIR FORCE

For expenses of family housing for the Air Force for construction, including acquisition, replacement, addition, expansion, extension and alteration and for operation and maintenance, including debt payment, leasing, minor construction, principal and interest charges, and insurance premiums, as authorized by law, as follows: for Construction, **[**$349,456,000**]** *$223,483,000*, to remain available until September 30, **[**2004**]** *2005*; for Operation and Maintenance, and for debt payment, **[**$818,392,000**]** *$826,271,000*; in all **[**$1,167,848,000**]** *$1,049,754,000. (10 U.S.C. 2824, 2827–29, 2831, 2852–54, 2857; Military Construction Appropriations Act, 2000.)*

Program and Financing (in millions of dollars)

Identification code 57–0704–0–1–051		1999 actual	2000 est.	2001 est.
	Obligations by program activity:			
	Direct program:			
	Construction:			
01.01	Construction of new housing	149	157	115
01.02	Construction improvements	97	76	124
01.03	Planning and Design	9	13	13
01.91	Total construction	255	246	252
	Operation, maintenance, and interest payment:			
	Operation:			
02.01	Operating expenses	282	288	283
02.02	Leasing	98	119	115
02.03	Maintenance of real property	410	409	428
02.91	Total operation, maintenance, and interest payment	790	814	826
09.01	Reimbursable program	10	11	11
10.00	Total new obligations	1,055	1,072	1,089
	Budgetary resources available for obligation:			
	Unobligated balance available, start of year:			
21.40	For completion of prior year budget plans	139	118	219
21.40	Unobligated balance available, start of year		66	39
21.99	Total unobligated balance, start of year	139	184	258
22.00	New budget authority (gross)	1,093	1,172	1,061
22.21	Unobligated balance transferred to other DoD accounts		–27	–39
22.22	Unobligated balance transferred from other DoD accounts	14		
23.90	Total budgetary resources available for obligation	1,247	1,329	1,279
23.95	Total new obligations	–1,055	–1,072	–1,089
23.98	Unobligated balance expiring or withdrawn	–8		
	Unobligated balance available, end of year:			
24.40	For completion of prior year budget plans	118	219	190
24.40	Unobligated balance available, end of year	66	39	
24.99	Total unobligated balance, end of year	184	258	190
	New budget authority (gross), detail:			
	Discretionary:			
40.00	Appropriation	1,064	1,168	1,050
40.15	Appropriation (emergency)	22		
40.35	Appropriation rescinded	–4		
40.76	Reduction pursuant to P.L. 106–113		–6	
43.00	Appropriation (total discretionary)	1,082	1,162	1,050

		1999 actual	2000 est.	2001 est.
68.00	Spending authority from offsetting collections: Offsetting collections (cash)	11	11	11
70.00	Total new budget authority (gross)	1,093	1,173	1,061
	Change in unpaid obligations:			
	Unpaid obligations, start of year:			
72.40	Obligated balance, start of year	612	606	557
72.95	From Federal sources: Receivables and unpaid, unfilled orders	2	2	2
72.99	Total unpaid obligations, start of year	614	608	559
73.10	Total new obligations	1,055	1,072	1,089
73.20	Total outlays (gross)	−1,040	−1,121	−1,146
73.40	Adjustments in expired accounts (net)	−20		
	Unpaid obligations, end of year:			
74.40	Obligated balance, end of year	606	557	500
74.95	From Federal sources: Receivables and unpaid, unfilled orders	2	2	2
74.99	Total unpaid obligations, end of year	608	559	502
	Outlays (gross), detail:			
86.90	Outlays from new discretionary authority	597	616	622
86.93	Outlays from discretionary balances	443	505	524
87.00	Total outlays (gross)	1,040	1,121	1,146
	Offsets:			
	Against gross budget authority and outlays:			
	Offsetting collections (cash) from:			
88.00	Federal sources	−1	−1	−1
88.40	Non-Federal sources	−10	−10	−10
88.90	Total, offsetting collections (cash)	−11	−11	−11
	Net budget authority and outlays:			
89.00	Budget authority	1,082	1,162	1,050
90.00	Outlays	1,029	1,110	1,135

Budget Plan (in millions of dollars)

Outlays

Identification code 57–0704–0–1–051		1999 actual	2000 est.	2001 est.
	Direct:			
	Construction:			
0601	Construction of new housing	154	202	37
0602	Construction improvements	103	129	174
0603	Planning and Design	12	17	13
0691	Total construction	269	348	224
	Operation, maintenance, and interest payment:			
	Operation:			
0701	Operating expenses	282	288	283
0702	Leasing	98	119	115
0703	Maintenance of real property	410	408	428
0791	Total operation, maintenance, and interest payment	789	814	826
0801	Reimbursable program	10	11	11
0893	Total budget plan	1,068	1,172	1,061

Object Classification (in millions of dollars)

Identification code 57–0704–0–1–051		1999 actual	2000 est.	2001 est.
	Direct obligations:			
21.0	Travel and transportation of persons	8	8	8
22.0	Transportation of things	7	8	8
23.2	Rental payments to others	100	102	99
25.2	Other services	117	121	124
26.0	Supplies and materials	353	364	372
31.0	Equipment	196	203	207
32.0	Land and structures	264	255	260
99.0	Subtotal, direct obligations	1,045	1,061	1,078
99.0	Reimbursable obligations	10	11	11
99.9	Total new obligations	1,055	1,072	1,089

Family Housing, Defense-wide

For expenses of family housing for the activities and agencies of the Department of Defense (other than the military departments) for construction, including acquisition, replacement, addition, expansion, extension and alteration, and for operation and maintenance, leasing, and minor construction, as authorized by law, [as follows: for Construction, $50,000, to remain available until September 30, 2004;] for Operation and Maintenance, [$41,440,000; in all $41,490,000] *$44,886,000. (Military Construction Appropriations Act, 2000.)*

Program and Financing (in millions of dollars)

Identification code 97–0706–0–1–051		1999 actual	2000 est.	2001 est.
	Obligations by program activity:			
	Direct program:			
	Construction:			
01.01	Construction of new housing		1	
	Operation, maintenance, and interest payment:			
02.01	Operating Expenses	5	5	6
02.02	Leasing	29	34	38
02.03	Maintenance of real property	1	1	1
02.91	Total operation, maintenance, and interest payment	35	41	45
09.01	Reimbursable program	1	3	3
10.00	Total new obligations	36	44	48
	Budgetary resources available for obligation:			
21.40	Unobligated balance available, start of year	2	1	
22.00	New budget authority (gross)	38	44	48
23.90	Total budgetary resources available for obligation	40	46	48
23.95	Total new obligations	−36	−44	−48
23.98	Unobligated balance expiring or withdrawn	−2		
24.40	Unobligated balance available, end of year	1		
	New budget authority (gross), detail:			
	Discretionary:			
40.00	Appropriation	37	41	45
68.00	Spending authority from offsetting collections: Offsetting collections (cash)	2	3	3
70.00	Total new budget authority (gross)	39	44	48
	Change in unpaid obligations:			
72.40	Unpaid obligations, start of year: Obligated balance, start of year	34	31	32
73.10	Total new obligations	36	44	48
73.20	Total outlays (gross)	−37	−44	−47
73.40	Adjustments in expired accounts (net)	−3		
74.40	Unpaid obligations, end of year: Obligated balance, end of year	31	32	33
	Outlays (gross), detail:			
86.90	Outlays from new discretionary authority	27	29	32
86.93	Outlays from discretionary balances	10	15	15
87.00	Total outlays (gross)	37	44	47
	Offsets:			
	Against gross budget authority and outlays:			
88.00	Offsetting collections (cash) from: Federal sources	−2	−3	−3
	Net budget authority and outlays:			
89.00	Budget authority	37	41	45
90.00	Outlays	35	41	44

Budget Plan (in millions of dollars)

Outlays

Identification code 97–0706–0–1–051		1999 actual	2000 est.	2001 est.
	Direct:			
	Operation, maintenance, and interest payment:			
	Operation:			
0701	Operating expenses	5	5	5
0702	Leasing	29	35	38
0703	Maintenance of real property	1	1	1
0791	Total operation, maintenance, and interest payment	35	41	45

General and special funds—Continued

FAMILY HOUSING, DEFENSE-WIDE—Continued

Budget Plan (in millions of dollars)—Continued
Outlays

Identification code 97–0706–0–1–051	1999 actual	2000 est.	2001 est.
0801 Reimbursable program	1	3	3
0893 Total budget plan	36	44	48

Object Classification (in millions of dollars)

Identification code 97–0706–0–1–051	1999 actual	2000 est.	2001 est.
Direct obligations:			
22.0 Transportation of things	1	1	1
23.2 Rental payments to others	14	23	26
23.3 Communications, utilities, and miscellaneous charges	3	2	2
25.2 Other services	....	....	1
25.3 Purchases of goods and services from Government accounts	10	9	10
25.4 Operation and maintenance of facilities	1	1	1
26.0 Supplies and materials	....	3	3
31.0 Equipment	4	1	1
32.0 Land and structures	2	1	....
99.0 Subtotal, direct obligations	35	41	45
99.0 Reimbursable obligations	1	3	3
99.9 Total new obligations	36	44	48

Public enterprise funds:

HOMEOWNERS ASSISTANCE FUND, DEFENSE

Program and Financing (in millions of dollars)

Identification code 97–4090–0–3–051	1999 actual	2000 est.	2001 est.
Obligations by program activity:			
09.01 Payment to homeowners (private sale and foreclosure assistance)	33	15	7
09.02 Other operating costs	16	14	12
09.03 Capital Investment: Acquisition of real property	33	26	10
10.00 Total new obligations	82	55	29
Budgetary resources available for obligation:			
21.40 Unobligated balance available, start of year	42	29	9
22.00 New budget authority (gross)	53	35	29
22.10 Resources available from recoveries of prior year obligations	7	....	....
22.22 Unobligated balance transferred from other DoD accounts	8	....	....
23.90 Total budgetary resources available for obligation	110	64	38
23.95 Total new obligations	−82	−55	−29
24.40 Unobligated balance available, end of year	29	9	9
New budget authority (gross), detail:			
Discretionary:			
42.00 Transferred from other DoD accounts	7	5	4
Spending authority from offsetting collections:			
68.00 Offsetting collections (cash)	44	30	25
68.10 From Federal sources: Change in receivables and unpaid, unfilled orders	2	....	....
68.90 Spending authority from offsetting collections (total discretionary)	46	30	25
70.00 Total new budget authority (gross)	53	35	29
Change in unpaid obligations:			
Unpaid obligations, start of year:			
72.40 Obligated balance, start of year	14	7	19
72.95 From Federal sources: Receivables and unpaid, unfilled orders	3	5	5
72.99 Total unpaid obligations, start of year	16	12	24
73.10 Total new obligations	82	55	29
73.20 Total outlays (gross)	−80	−43	−36
73.45 Adjustments in unexpired accounts	−7	....	....
Unpaid obligations, end of year:			
74.40 Obligated balance, end of year	7	19	12
74.95 From Federal sources: Receivables and unpaid, unfilled orders	5	5	5
74.99 Total unpaid obligations, end of year	12	24	17
Outlays (gross), detail:			
86.90 Outlays from new discretionary authority	51	31	25
86.93 Outlays from discretionary balances	29	12	10
87.00 Total outlays (gross)	80	43	36
Offsets:			
Against gross budget authority and outlays:			
Offsetting collections (cash) from:			
88.00 Federal sources	2	....	....
88.40 Non-Federal sources	−46	−30	−25
88.90 Total, offsetting collections (cash)	−44	−30	−25
Against gross budget authority only:			
88.95 From Federal sources: Change in receivables and unpaid, unfilled orders	−2	....	....
Net budget authority and outlays:			
89.00 Budget authority	7	5	4
90.00 Outlays	36	13	11

Object Classification (in millions of dollars)

Identification code 97–4090–0–3–051	1999 actual	2000 est.	2001 est.
26.0 Supplies and materials	49	25	7
32.0 Land and structures	33	30	22
99.0 Subtotal, reimbursable obligations	82	55	29
99.9 Total new obligations	82	55	29

[DEPARTMENT OF DEFENSE FAMILY HOUSING IMPROVEMENT FUND]

[For the Department of Defense Family Housing Improvement Fund, $2,000,000, to remain available until expended, as the sole source of funds for planning, administrative, and oversight costs relating to family housing initiatives undertaken pursuant to 10 U.S.C. 2883, pertaining to alternative means of acquiring and improving military family housing, and supporting facilities.] *(Military Construction Appropriations Act, 2000.)*

Program and Financing (in millions of dollars)

Identification code 97–0834–0–1–051	1999 actual	2000 est.	2001 est.
Obligations by program activity:			
10.00 Total new obligations (object class 25.2)	3	96	90
Budgetary resources available for obligation:			
21.40 Unobligated balance available, start of year	28	57	28
22.00 New budget authority (gross)	2	2	....
22.22 Unobligated balance transferred from other DoD accounts	30	66	78
23.90 Total budgetary resources available for obligation	60	125	106
23.95 Total new obligations	−3	−96	−90
24.40 Unobligated balance available, end of year	57	28	16
New budget authority (gross), detail:			
Discretionary:			
40.00 Appropriation	2	2	....
Change in unpaid obligations:			
72.40 Unpaid obligations, start of year: Obligated balance, start of year	6	2	77
73.10 Total new obligations	3	96	90
73.20 Total outlays (gross)	−7	−22	−13
74.40 Unpaid obligations, end of year: Obligated balance, end of year	2	77	153
Outlays (gross), detail:			
86.90 Outlays from new discretionary authority	2	1	....
86.93 Outlays from discretionary balances	5	20	13

87.00 Total outlays (gross)	7	22	13
Net budget authority and outlays:			
89.00 Budget authority	2	2	
90.00 Outlays	7	22	13

As required by he Federal Credit Reform Act of 1990, this account records, for this program, the subsidy costs associated with the direct loans obligated and loan guarantees committed in 1992 and beyond (including modifications of direct loans on loan guarantees that resulted from obligations or commitments in any year), as well as administrative expenses of this program. The subsidy amounts are estimated on a present value basis; the administrative expenses are estimated on a cash basis.

Budget Plan (in millions of dollars)
Outlays

Identification code 97–0834–0–1–051	1999 actual	2000 est.	2001 est.
0701 Improvements	32	2	

Summary of Loan Levels, Subsidy Budget Authority and Outlays by Program (in millions of dollars)

Identification code 97–0834–0–1–051	1999 actual	2000 est.	2001 est.
Direct loan levels supportable by subsidy budget authority:			
1150 Direct loan levels		74	99
1159 Total direct loan levels		74	99
Direct loan subsidy (in percent):			
1320 Subsidy rate	63.00	38.80	38.80
1329 Weighted average subsidy rate	63.00	38.80	38.80
Direct loan subsidy budget authority:			
1330 Subsidy budget authority		29	38
1339 Total subsidy budget authority		29	38
Direct loan subsidy outlays:			
1340 Subsidy outlays		4	
1349 Total subsidy outlays		4	
Guaranteed loan levels supportable by subsidy budget authority:			
2150 Loan guarantee levels		563	507
2159 Total loan guarantee levels		563	507
Guaranteed loan subsidy (in percent):			
2320 Subsidy rate	0.00	8.42	8.86
2329 Weighted average subsidy rate	0.00	8.42	8.86
Guaranteed loan subsidy budget authority:			
2330 Subsidy budget authority		47	45
2339 Total subsidy budget authority		47	45
Guaranteed loan subsidy outlays:			
2340 Subsidy outlays		2	
2349 Total subsidy outlays		2	
Administrative expense data:			
3510 Budget authority			
3580 Outlays from balances		1	1

Department of Defense, Family Housing Improvement, Direct Loan Financing Account

Program and Financing (in millions of dollars)

Identification code 97–4166–0–3–051	1999 actual	2000 est.	2001 est.
Obligations by program activity:			
00.01 Direct Loans		74	99
10.00 Total new obligations		74	99
Budgetary resources available for obligation:			
22.00 New financing authority (gross)		74	99
23.95 Total new obligations		−74	−99
New financing authority (gross), detail:			
Mandatory:			
67.10 Authority to borrow		45	61
69.00 Offsetting collections (cash)		4	
69.10 From Federal sources: Change in receivables and unpaid, unfilled orders		25	38
69.47 Portion applied to repay debt			
69.90 Spending authority from offsetting collections (total mandatory)		29	38
70.00 Total new financing authority (gross)		74	99
Change in unpaid obligations:			
Unpaid obligations, start of year:			
72.40 Obligated balance, start of year	7	7	45
72.95 Receivables from program account	4	4	29
72.99 Total unpaid obligations, start of year	11	11	74
73.10 Total new obligations		74	99
73.20 Total financing disbursements (gross)		−11	
Unpaid obligations, end of year:			
74.40 Obligated balance, end of year	7	45	106
74.95 Receivables from program account	4	29	67
74.99 Total unpaid obligations, end of year	11	74	173
87.00 Total financing disbursements (gross)		11	
Offsets:			
Against gross financing authority and financing disbursements:			
Offsetting collections (cash) from:			
88.00 Federal sources		−4	
Non-Federal sources:			
88.40 Non-Federal sources: Pepayments of principal			
88.40 Non-Federal sources: Interest received on loans			
88.90 Total, offsetting collections (cash)		−4	
Against gross financing authority only:			
88.95 Change in receivables from program accounts		−25	−38
Net financing authority and financing disbursements:			
89.00 Financing authority		45	61
90.00 Financing disbursements		7	

As required by the Federal Credit Reform Act of 1990, this non-budgetary account records all cash flows to and from the Government resulting from direct loans obligated in 1992 and beyond (including modifications of direct loans that resulted from obligations in any year). The amounts in this account are a means of financing and are not included in the budget totals.

Status of Direct Loans (in millions of dollars)

Identification code 97–4166–0–3–051	1999 actual	2000 est.	2001 est.
Position with respect to appropriations act limitation on obligations:			
1111 Limitation on direct loans			
1131 Direct loan obligations exempt from limitation		74	99
1150 Total direct loan obligations		74	99
Cumulative balance of direct loans outstanding:			
1210 Outstanding, start of year			11
1231 Disbursements: Direct loan disbursements		11	
1251 Repayments: Repayments and prepayments			
1263 Write-offs for default: Direct loans			
1290 Outstanding, end of year		11	11

Balance Sheet (in millions of dollars)

Identification code 97–4166–0–3–051	1998 actual	1999 actual	2000 est.	2001 est.
ASSETS:				
Investments in US securities:				
1106 Federal assets: Receivables, net		4	29	67
Net value of assets related to post-1991 direct loans receivable:				
1401 Direct loans receivable, gross			11	10

Public enterprise funds—Continued

DEPARTMENT OF DEFENSE, FAMILY HOUSING IMPROVEMENT, DIRECT LOAN FINANCING ACCOUNT—Continued

Balance Sheet (in millions of dollars)—Continued

Identification code 97–4166–0–3–051	1998 actual	1999 actual	2000 est.	2001 est.
1405 Allowance for subsidy cost (–)			–4	–4
1499 Net present value of assets related to direct loans			7	6
1999 Total assets		4	36	73
LIABILITIES:				
2103 Federal liabilities: Debt			6	6
2999 Total liabilities			6	6
NET POSITION:				
3100 Appropriated capital		4	29	67
3300 Cumulative results of operations				
3999 Total net position		4	29	67
4999 Total liabilities and net position		4	35	73

DEPARTMENT OF DEFENSE, FAMILY HOUSING IMPROVEMENT GUARANTEED LOAN FINANCING ACCOUNT

Program and Financing (in millions of dollars)

Identification code 97–4167–0–3–051	1999 actual	2000 est.	2001 est.
Budgetary resources available for obligation:			
21.40 Unobligated balance available, start of year			2
22.00 New financing authority (gross)		2	
23.90 Total budgetary resources available for obligation		2	2
23.95 Total new obligations			
24.40 Unobligated balance available, end of year		2	2
New financing authority (gross), detail:			
Mandatory:			
69.00 Offsetting collections (cash)		2	
Offsets:			
Against gross financing authority and financing disbursements:			
88.00 Offsetting collections (cash) from: Federal sources		−2	
Net financing authority and financing disbursements:			
89.00 Financing authority			
90.00 Financing disbursements		−2	

As required by the Federal Credit Reform Act of 1990, this non-budgetary account records all cash flows to and from the government resulting from loan guarantees committed in 1992 and beyond (including modifications of loan guarantees that resulted from commitments in any year). The amounts in this account are a means of financing and are not included in the budget totals.

Status of Guaranteed Loans (in millions of dollars)

Identification code 97–4167–0–3–051	1999 actual	2000 est.	2001 est.
Position with respect to appropriations act limitation on commitments:			
2111 Limitation on guaranteed loans made by private lenders			
2131 Guaranteed loan commitments exempt from limitation		563	507
2150 Total guaranteed loan commitments		563	507
2199 Guaranteed amount of guaranteed loan commitments		563	507
Cumulative balance of guaranteed loans outstanding:			
2210 Outstanding, start of year			29
2231 Disbursements of new guaranteed loans		29	
2251 Repayments and prepayments			
2263 Adjustments: Terminations for default that result in claim payments			
2290 Outstanding, end of year		29	29
Memorandum:			
2299 Guaranteed amount of guaranteed loans outstanding, end of year		29	29

Balance Sheet (in millions of dollars)

Identification code 97–4167–0–3–051	1998 actual	1999 actual	2000 est.	2001 est.
ASSETS:				
1101 Federal assets: Fund balances with Treasury			2	2
1999 Total assets			2	2
LIABILITIES:				
2204 Non-Federal liabilities: Liabilities for loan guarantees			2	2
2999 Total liabilities			2	2
NET POSITION:				
3999 Total net position				
4999 Total liabilities and net position			2	2

DEPARTMENT OF DEFENSE MILITARY UNACCOMPANIED HOUSING IMPROVEMENT FUND

Program and Financing (in millions of dollars)

Identification code 97–0836–0–1–051	1999 actual	2000 est.	2001 est.
Obligations by program activity:			
10.00 Total new obligations (object class 25.1)			
Budgetary resources available for obligation:			
21.40 Unobligated balance available, start of year	5		
22.00 New budget authority (gross)	−5		
23.90 Total budgetary resources available for obligation			
New budget authority (gross), detail:			
Discretionary:			
40.05 Appropriation (indefinite)			
40.36 Unobligated balance rescinded	−5		
43.00 Appropriation (total discretionary)	−5		
Net budget authority and outlays:			
89.00 Budget authority	−5		
90.00 Outlays			

REVOLVING AND MANAGEMENT FUNDS

Federal Funds

Resources presented under the Revolving and Management Funds title contribute primarily to achieving the Department's corporate goal 1 (Shape). A detailed description of the corporate goals is contained in the FY 2000 Performance Plan in the Department's 2000 Annual Report to the President and Congress. This performance plan is required by the Government Performance and Results Act of 1993.

Public enterprise funds:

NATIONAL DEFENSE STOCKPILE TRANSACTION FUND

Unavailable Collections (in millions of dollars)

Identification code 97–4555–0–3–051	1999 actual	2000 est.	2001 est.
Balance, start of year:			
01.99 Balance, start of year	774	774	774
07.99 Total balance, end of year	774	774	774

Program and Financing (in millions of dollars)

Identification code 97–4555–0–3–051	1999 actual	2000 est.	2001 est.
Obligations by program activity:			
09.04 Stockpile operations	71	74	71
09.07 Payment to receipt account (FMS)	66	62	62
09.08 Payment to receipt account (HHS)	3	22	28
09.10 Payment to receipt account (general fund, FY99 authorization)	102	75	99
09.11 Payment to receipt account (general fund, FY00 authorization)		10	30
10.00 Total new obligations	242	243	290
Budgetary resources available for obligation:			
21.40 Unobligated balance available, start of year	100	162	217
22.00 New budget authority (gross)	299	298	306
22.10 Resources available from recoveries of prior year obligations	5		
23.90 Total budgetary resources available for obligation	404	460	523
23.95 Total new obligations	−242	−243	−290
24.40 Unobligated balance available, end of year	162	217	233
New budget authority (gross), detail:			
Spending authority from offsetting collections:			
Discretionary:			
68.00 Offsetting collections (cash)	449	448	456
68.61 Transferred to other accounts	−150	−150	−150
68.90 Spending authority from offsetting collections (total discretionary)	299	298	306
Change in unpaid obligations:			
72.40 Unpaid obligations, start of year: Obligated balance, start of year	27	24	22
73.10 Total new obligations	242	243	290
73.20 Total outlays (gross)	−240	−245	−299
73.45 Adjustments in unexpired accounts	−5		
74.40 Unpaid obligations, end of year: Obligated balance, end of year	24	22	13
Outlays (gross), detail:			
86.90 Outlays from new discretionary authority	240	245	299
Offsets:			
Against gross budget authority and outlays:			
Offsetting collections (cash) from:			
88.00 Federal sources	−32	−17	−21
88.40 Non-Federal sources	−417	−431	−435
88.90 Total, offsetting collections (cash)	−449	−448	−456
Net budget authority and outlays:			
89.00 Budget authority	−150	−150	−150
90.00 Outlays	−209	−203	−157

The National Defense Stockpile is planned and operated under the authority of the Strategic and Critical Materials Stockpiling Act. The purpose of the Stockpile is to decrease or preclude a dangerous and costly dependence by the United States upon foreign sources for supplies of strategic and critical materials in times of national emergency. The quantities of the materials stockpiled as required by the Stockpiling Act are to be sufficient to sustain the United States during a national emergency involving military conflict that necessitates an expansion of the Armed Forces together with a significant mobilization of the economy of the United States.

The National Defense Stockpile Transaction Fund provides for the financing of acquisition, disposal and upgrading of strategic and critical stockpile materials, and all related expenses such as transportation, development of specifications, testing, quality studies, and relocation of materials, and operation of the Defense National Stockpile Center.

The FY 2001 budget proposes transferring $50 million to the operation and maintenance accounts of the Navy, Army, and Air Force to provide funding for readiness-related programs.

Object Classification (in millions of dollars)

Identification code 97–4555–0–3–051	1999 actual	2000 est.	2001 est.
11.1 Personnel compensation: Full-time permanent	15	14	14
12.1 Civilian personnel benefits	3	3	3
21.0 Travel and transportation of persons	1	1	1
22.0 Transportation of things	1		
23.1 Rental payments to GSA	8	9	8
23.2 Rental payments to others	10	10	7
23.3 Communications, utilities, and miscellaneous charges	1	1	1
25.2 Other services	4	4	5
Purchases of goods and services from Government accounts:			
25.3 Purchases of goods and services from Government accounts	15	18	17
25.3 Purchases from revolving funds		2	2
25.4 Operation and maintenance of facilities	8	8	10
26.0 Supplies and materials	2	2	2
31.0 Equipment	3	2	1
92.0 Undistributed	171	169	219
99.0 Subtotal, reimbursable obligations	242	243	290
99.9 Total new obligations	242	243	290

Personnel Summary

Identification code 97–4555–0–3–051	1999 actual	2000 est.	2001 est.
2001 Total compensable workyears: Full-time equivalent employment	267	298	280

Reserve Mobilization Income Insurance Fund

Program and Financing (in millions of dollars)

Identification code 97–4179–0–3–051	1999 actual	2000 est.	2001 est.
Obligations by program activity:			
10.00 Total new obligations (object class 42.0)	5		
Budgetary resources available for obligation:			
21.40 Unobligated balance available, start of year	21	17	17
22.00 New budget authority (gross)	1		
23.90 Total budgetary resources available for obligation	22	17	17
23.95 Total new obligations	−5		
24.40 Unobligated balance available, end of year	17	17	17
New budget authority (gross), detail:			
Discretionary:			
68.00 Spending authority from offsetting collections (gross): Offsetting collections (cash)	1		
Change in unpaid obligations:			
73.10 Total new obligations	5		
73.20 Total outlays (gross)	−5		
Outlays (gross), detail:			
86.90 Outlays from new discretionary authority	1		
86.93 Outlays from discretionary balances	4		
87.00 Total outlays (gross)	5		
Offsets:			
Against gross budget authority and outlays:			
88.00 Offsetting collections (cash) from: Federal sources	−1		
Net budget authority and outlays:			
89.00 Budget authority			
90.00 Outlays	4		
Memorandum (non-add) entries:			
92.01 Total investments, start of year: U.S. securities: Par value	21	17	17
92.02 Total investments, end of year: U.S. securities: Par value	17	17	17

This fund pays claims and administrative costs for participating members of the insurance program. The program provided insurance coverage for Ready Reservists who elected

Public enterprise funds—Continued

RESERVE MOBILIZATION INCOME INSURANCE FUND—Continued

to participate and who were involuntarily ordered to active duty in excess of 30 days. The program became operational on October 1, 1996. The program was terminated on November 18, 1997 by the National Defense Authorization Act of 1998 (P.L. 105–85). The FY 1998 Supplemental provided funding to complete benefit payments and close out the program.

Object Classification (in millions of dollars)

Identification code 97–4179–0–3–051		1999 actual	2000 est.	2001 est.
42.0	Insurance claims and indemnities	5		
99.0	Subtotal, reimbursable obligations	5		

PENTAGON RESERVATION MAINTENANCE REVOLVING FUND

Program and Financing (in millions of dollars)

Identification code 97–4950–0–4–051		1999 actual	2000 est.	2001 est.
	Obligations by program activity:			
09.01	Operations	158	170	142
09.02	Renovation	280	204	250
10.00	Total new obligations	438	374	392
	Budgetary resources available for obligation:			
21.40	Unobligated balance available, start of year	25	16	21
22.00	New budget authority (gross)	386	379	384
22.10	Resources available from recoveries of prior year obligations	42		
23.90	Total budgetary resources available for obligation	453	395	405
23.95	Total new obligations	−438	−374	−392
24.40	Unobligated balance available, end of year	16	21	13
	New budget authority (gross), detail:			
	Mandatory:			
69.00	Offsetting collections (cash)	112	382	389
69.10	From Federal sources: Change in receivables and unpaid, unfilled orders	274	−3	−5
69.15	From Federal sources: Adjustments to receivables and unpaid, unfilled orders	1		
69.90	Spending authority from offsetting collections (total mandatory)	386	379	384
	Change in unpaid obligations:			
	Unpaid obligations, start of year:			
72.40	Obligated balance, start of year	173	259	373
72.95	From Federal sources: Receivables and unpaid, unfilled orders	82	356	353
72.99	Total unpaid obligations, start of year	255	615	726
73.10	Total new obligations	438	374	392
73.20	Total outlays (gross)	−35	−263	−264
73.45	Adjustments in unexpired accounts	−42		
	Unpaid obligations, end of year:			
74.40	Obligated balance, end of year	259	373	506
74.95	From Federal sources: Receivables and unpaid, unfilled orders	356	353	348
74.99	Total unpaid obligations, end of year	615	726	854
	Outlays (gross), detail:			
86.97	Outlays from new mandatory authority	35	188	164
86.98	Outlays from mandatory balances		75	100
87.00	Total outlays (gross)	35	263	264
	Offsets:			
	Against gross budget authority and outlays:			
	Offsetting collections (cash) from:			
88.00	Federal sources	−112	−380	−387
88.40	Non-Federal sources		−2	−2
88.90	Total, offsetting collections (cash)	−112	−382	−389
	Against gross budget authority only:			
88.95	From Federal sources: Change in receivables and unpaid, unfilled orders	−274	3	5
88.96	From Federal sources: Adjustment to receivables and unpaid, unfilled orders	−1		
	Net budget authority and outlays:			
89.00	Budget authority			
90.00	Outlays	−77	−119	−125

Object Classification (in millions of dollars)

Identification code 97–4950–0–4–051		1999 actual	2000 est.	2001 est.
	Personnel compensation:			
11.1	Full-time permanent	28	25	31
11.5	Other personnel compensation	6	6	7
11.9	Total personnel compensation	34	31	38
12.1	Civilian personnel benefits	10	9	9
22.0	Transportation of things	1	1	1
23.3	Communications, utilities, and miscellaneous charges	35	29	30
25.4	Operation and maintenance of facilities	131	127	101
26.0	Supplies and materials	9	8	8
31.0	Equipment	16	18	19
32.0	Land and structures	202	151	186
99.0	Subtotal, reimbursable obligations	438	374	392
99.9	Total new obligations	438	374	392

Personnel Summary

Identification code 97–4950–0–4–051		1999 actual	2000 est.	2001 est.
2001	Total compensable workyears: Full-time equivalent employment	651	696	696

NATIONAL DEFENSE SEALIFT FUND

[(INCLUDING TRANSFER OF FUNDS)]

For National Defense Sealift Fund programs, projects, and activities, and for expenses of the National Defense Reserve Fleet, as established by section 11 of the Merchant Ship Sales Act of 1946 (50 U.S.C. App. 1744), [$717,200,000] *$388,158,000*, to remain available until expended[: *Provided*, That none of the funds provided in this paragraph shall be used to award a new contract that provides for the acquisition of any of the following major components unless such components are manufactured in the United States: auxiliary equipment, including pumps, for all shipboard services; propulsion system components (that is; engines, reduction gears, and propellers); shipboard cranes; and spreaders for shipboard cranes: *Provided further*, That the exercise of an option in a contract awarded through the obligation of previously appropriated funds shall not be considered to be the award of a new contract: *Provided further*, That the Secretary of the military department responsible for such procurement may waive the restrictions in the first proviso on a case-by-case basis by certifying in writing to the Committees on Appropriations of the House of Representatives and the Senate that adequate domestic supplies are not available to meet Department of Defense requirements on a timely basis and that such an acquisition must be made in order to acquire capability for national security purposes]. *(Department of Defense Appropriations Act, 2000.)*

Program and Financing (in millions of dollars)

Identification code 17–4557–0–4–051		1999 actual	2000 est.	2001 est.
	Obligations by program activity:			
09.01	Strategic sealift operations	468	321	119
09.02	Strategic sealift O&M	632	768	805
09.03	Ready Reserve Force	260	257	258
09.05	Research and Development	7	2	5
10.00	Total new obligations	1,367	1,348	1,187
	Budgetary resources available for obligation:			
21.40	Unobligated balance available, start of year	561	500	622
22.00	New budget authority (gross)	1,237	1,469	1,193
22.10	Resources available from recoveries of prior year obligations	68		
23.90	Total budgetary resources available for obligation	1,866	1,970	1,815
23.95	Total new obligations	−1,367	−1,348	−1,187

24.40	Unobligated balance available, end of year	500	622	628
	New budget authority (gross), detail:			
	Discretionary:			
40.00	Appropriation	708	717	388
40.36	Unobligated balance rescinded	−85		
40.76	Reduction pursuant to P.L. 106–113		−4	
41.00	Transferred to other accounts	−29	−12	
43.00	Appropriation (total discretionary)	594	702	388
	Spending authority from offsetting collections:			
68.00	Offsetting collections (cash)	762	768	805
68.10	From Federal sources: Change in receivables and unpaid, unfilled orders	−119		
68.90	Spending authority from offsetting collections (total discretionary)	643	768	805
70.00	Total new budget authority (gross)	1,237	1,469	1,193
	Change in unpaid obligations:			
	Unpaid obligations, start of year:			
72.40	Obligated balance, start of year	1,649	1,149	986
72.95	From Federal sources: Receivables and unpaid, unfilled orders	765	646	646
72.99	Total unpaid obligations, start of year	2,414	1,795	1,632
73.10	Total new obligations	1,367	1,348	1,187
73.20	Total outlays (gross)	−1,916	−1,511	−1,465
73.40	Adjustments in expired accounts (net)	−2		
73.45	Adjustments in unexpired accounts	−68		
	Unpaid obligations, end of year:			
74.40	Obligated balance, end of year	1,149	986	708
74.95	From Federal sources: Receivables and unpaid, unfilled orders	646	646	646
74.99	Total unpaid obligations, end of year	1,795	1,632	1,354
	Outlays (gross), detail:			
86.90	Outlays from new discretionary authority	874	998	985
86.93	Outlays from discretionary balances	1,042	513	480
87.00	Total outlays (gross)	1,916	1,511	1,465
	Offsets:			
	Against gross budget authority and outlays:			
88.00	Offsetting collections (cash) from: Federal sources	−762	−768	−805
	Against gross budget authority only:			
88.95	From Federal sources: Change in receivables and unpaid, unfilled orders	119		
	Net budget authority and outlays:			
89.00	Budget authority	594	701	388
90.00	Outlays	1,154	743	660

In 2000, the Department of Defense will continue to reimburse the Department of Transportation for operations and maintenance of the Ready Reserve Force from funds appropriated to DOD.

Object Classification (in millions of dollars)

Identification code 17–4557–0–4–051		1999 actual	2000 est.	2001 est.
25.1	Advisory and assistance services	13		
	Purchases of goods and services from Government accounts:			
25.3	Purchases of goods and services from Government accounts	350		
25.3	Purchases from revolving funds	20	768	805
31.0	Equipment	984	580	382
99.0	Subtotal, reimbursable obligations	1,367	1,348	1,187
99.9	Total new obligations	1,367	1,348	1,187

Defense Working Capital Funds

For the Defense Working Capital Funds; [$90,344,000] *$916,276,000*: *Provided,* That during fiscal year [2000] *2001*, funds in the Defense Working Capital Funds may be used for the purchase of not to exceed [295] *330* passenger carrying motor vehicles for replacement only for the Defense Security Service. *(Department of Defense Appropriations Act, 2000.)*

Working Capital Fund, Army

Program and Financing (in millions of dollars)

Identification code 97–493001–0–4–051		1999 actual	2000 est.	2001 est.
	Obligations by program activity:			
	Operating Expenses:			
09.01	Ordnance	460	688	638
09.02	Depot Maintenance	1,418	1,156	1,136
09.03	Information Sevices	111	159	106
09.04	Supply Management	6,626	6,835	4,869
09.09	Total operating expenses	8,615	8,838	6,749
	Capital Investment:			
09.11	Ordnance	14	22	29
09.12	Depot Maintenance	23	17	16
09.13	Reimbursable program	1		
09.14	Supply Management	59	65	60
09.19	Total capital investment	97	104	105
10.00	Total new obligations	8,712	8,942	6,854
	Budgetary resources available for obligation:			
21.40	Unobligated balance available, start of year	1,139	1,277	
22.00	New budget authority (gross)	8,827	7,665	6,854
22.10	Resources available from recoveries of prior year obligations	218		
22.21	Unobligated balance transferred to other DoD accounts	−70		
22.22	Unobligated balance transferred from other DoD accounts	12		
22.75	Balance of contract authority withdrawn	−138		
23.90	Total budgetary resources available for obligation	9,989	8,942	6,854
23.95	Total new obligations	−8,712	−8,942	−6,854
24.40	Unobligated balance available, end of year	1,277		
	New budget authority (gross), detail:			
	Discretionary:			
40.00	Appropriation		62	
	Mandatory:			
66.15	Contract authority (indefinite)	9		
	Spending authority from offsetting collections:			
	Discretionary:			
68.00	Offsetting collections (cash)	8,518	8,632	6,797
68.10	From Federal sources: Change in receivables and unpaid, unfilled orders	301	−1,028	57
68.15	From Federal sources: Adjustments to receivables and unpaid, unfilled orders	−1		
68.90	Spending authority from offsetting collections (total discretionary)	8,818	7,604	6,854
70.00	Total new budget authority (gross)	8,827	7,666	6,854
	Change in unpaid obligations:			
	Unpaid obligations, start of year:			
72.40	Obligated balance, start of year	−775	−744	693
72.49	Obligated balance, start of year: Contract authority	1,362	1,233	1,233
72.95	From Federal sources: Receivables and unpaid, unfilled orders	3,208	3,509	2,481
72.99	Total unpaid obligations, start of year	3,795	3,997	4,407
73.10	Total new obligations	8,712	8,942	6,854
73.20	Total outlays (gross)	−8,292	−8,533	−6,803
73.45	Adjustments in unexpired accounts	−218		
	Unpaid obligations, end of year:			
74.40	Obligated balance, end of year	−744	693	687
74.49	Obligated balance, end of year: Contract authority	1,233	1,233	1,233
74.95	From Federal sources: Receivables and unpaid, unfilled orders	3,509	2,481	2,538
74.99	Total unpaid obligations, end of year	3,997	4,407	4,458
	Outlays (gross), detail:			
86.90	Outlays from new discretionary authority	4,992	5,033	3,803
86.93	Outlays from discretionary balances	3,300	3,500	3,000
87.00	Total outlays (gross)	8,292	8,533	6,803
	Offsets:			
	Against gross budget authority and outlays:			
	Offsetting collections (cash) from:			
88.00	Federal sources	−8,490	−8,246	−6,467
88.40	Non-Federal sources	−28	−386	−330

Public enterprise funds—Continued

DEFENSE WORKING CAPITAL FUNDS—Continued

WORKING CAPITAL FUND, ARMY—Continued

Program and Financing (in millions of dollars)—Continued

Identification code 97–493001–0–4–051	1999 actual	2000 est.	2001 est.
88.90 Total, offsetting collections (cash)	–8,518	–8,632	–6,797
Against gross budget authority only:			
88.95 From Federal sources: Change in receivables and unpaid, unfilled orders	–301	1,028	–57
88.96 From Federal sources: Adjustment to receivables and unpaid, unfilled orders	1		
Net budget authority and outlays:			
89.00 Budget authority	9	62	
90.00 Outlays	–226	–99	6

The Army Working Capital Fund finances the operations of Army industrial, commercial and support-type activities. The separate Working Capital Fund emphasizes the Component's functional and financial management responsibilities for its operations. The Fund finances, in accordance with section 2208 of 10 U.S.C. through receipt of funded customer reimbursable orders, operating and capital expenses (excluding Military Construction), and uses cost accounting-type techniques to provide DoD managers with information that can be used to monitor, control, and minimize its cost of operations.

Status of Contract Authority (in millions of dollars)

Identification code 97–493001–0–4–051	1999 actual	2000 est.	2001 est.
0100 Balance, start of year	1,362	1,233	1,233
Contract authority:			
0200 Contract authority	9		
0600 Balance of contract authority withdrawn	–138		
0700 Balance, end of year	1,233	1,233	1,233

Object Classification (in millions of dollars)

Identification code 97–493001–0–4–051	1999 actual	2000 est.	2001 est.
Personnel compensation:			
11.1 Full-time permanent	938	948	917
11.3 Other than full-time permanent	28		
11.5 Other personnel compensation	86		
11.7 Military personnel		6	6
11.9 Total personnel compensation	1,052	954	924
12.1 Civilian personnel benefits	250	195	182
13.0 Benefits for former personnel	40	2	
21.0 Travel and transportation of persons	22	26	21
22.0 Transportation of things	91	81	80
23.1 Rental payments to GSA	2	11	11
23.2 Rental payments to others	9	1	2
23.3 Communications, utilities, and miscellaneous charges	40	51	45
25.1 Advisory and assistance services	53	22	22
25.2 Other services	207	113	103
Purchases of goods and services from Government accounts:			
25.3 Purchases of goods and services from other Federal Agencies	318	146	135
25.3 Payments to foreign national indirect hire personnel	10		
25.3 Purchases from revolving funds	586	363	345
25.4 Operation and maintenance of facilities including GOCOs	38	82	63
25.7 Contract operation and maintenance of equipment including ADP hard/software	207	29	25
26.0 Supplies and materials	5,681	6,695	4,723
31.0 Equipment	102	171	174
32.0 Land and structures	4		
99.0 Subtotal, reimbursable obligations	8,712	8,942	6,854
99.9 Total new obligations	8,712	8,942	6,854

Personnel Summary

Identification code 97–493001–0–4–051	1999 actual	2000 est.	2001 est.
2001 Total compensable workyears: Full-time equivalent employment	23,313	22,439	20,938

WORKING CAPITAL FUND, NAVY

Program and Financing (in millions of dollars)

Identification code 97–493002–0–4–051	1999 actual	2000 est.	2001 est.
Obligations by program activity:			
Operating expenses:			
09.01 Distribution Depots		168	165
09.02 Depot Maintenance—Shipyards	2,101	1,842	1,850
09.03 Depot Maintenance—Aviation	1,581	1,751	1,661
09.04 Ordnance	196	47	
09.05 Depot Maintenance	166	197	190
09.06 Base Support	2,127	1,593	1,590
09.07 Transportation	1,194	1,239	1,299
09.08 Research and Development Activities	7,245	6,589	6,696
09.09 Subtotal operating expenses	14,610	13,426	13,451
Additional operating expenses:			
09.10 Information Services	248	209	91
09.11 Supply Management	5,253	5,865	6,150
09.19 Total operating expenses	5,501	6,074	6,241
Capital Investment:			
09.20 Supply Management	35	41	53
09.21 Depot Maintenance—Shipyards	41	58	61
09.22 Depot Maintenance—Aviation	46	41	50
09.23 Ordnance	3		
09.24 Depot Maintenance	4	3	4
09.25 Base Support	19	20	18
09.26 Transportation	3	9	7
09.27 Research and Development Activities	116	126	126
09.28 Information Services	1	1	
09.29 Total capital investment	268	299	319
10.00 Total new obligations	20,379	19,799	20,011
Budgetary resources available for obligation:			
21.40 Unobligated balance available, start of year	2,633	2,462	2,390
22.00 New budget authority (gross)	20,490	19,799	20,011
22.22 Unobligated balance transferred from other DoD accounts			
22.60 Portion applied to repay debt	–69	–73	–78
22.75 Balance of contract authority withdrawn	–212		
23.90 Total budgetary resources available for obligation	22,842	22,188	22,322
23.95 Total new obligations	–20,379	–19,799	–20,011
24.40 Unobligated balance available, end of year	2,462	2,390	2,312
New budget authority (gross), detail:			
Discretionary:			
40.15 Appropriation (emergency)	2		
Mandatory:			
66.15 Contract authority (indefinite)	13		
Spending authority from offsetting collections:			
Discretionary:			
68.00 Offsetting collections (cash)	20,128	19,458	18,845
68.10 From Federal sources: Change in receivables and unpaid, unfilled orders	347	340	1,166
68.90 Spending authority from offsetting collections (total discretionary)	20,475	19,798	20,011
70.00 Total new budget authority (gross)	20,490	19,798	20,011
Change in unpaid obligations:			
Unpaid obligations, start of year:			
72.40 Obligated balance, start of year	–1,424	–1,282	–969
72.49 Obligated balance, start of year: Contract authority	3,926	3,727	3,727
72.95 From Federal sources: Receivables and unpaid, unfilled orders	6,177	6,524	6,864
72.99 Total unpaid obligations, start of year	8,679	8,969	9,622
73.10 Total new obligations	20,379	19,799	20,011
73.20 Total outlays (gross)	–20,089	–19,145	–18,944
Unpaid obligations, end of year:			
74.40 Obligated balance, end of year	–1,282	–969	–1,068

74.49	Obligated balance, end of year: Contract authority	3,727	3,727	3,727
74.95	From Federal sources: Receivables and unpaid, unfilled orders	6,524	6,864	8,030
74.99	Total unpaid obligations, end of year	8,969	9,622	10,689
	Outlays (gross), detail:			
86.90	Outlays from new discretionary authority	15,089	14,145	13,944
86.93	Outlays from discretionary balances	5,000	5,000	5,000
87.00	Total outlays (gross)	20,089	19,145	18,944
	Offsets:			
	Against gross budget authority and outlays:			
	Offsetting collections (cash) from:			
88.00	Federal sources	–19,804	–19,458	–18,845
88.40	Non-Federal sources	–324		
88.90	Total, offsetting collections (cash)	–20,128	–19,458	–18,845
	Against gross budget authority only:			
88.95	From Federal sources: Change in receivables and unpaid, unfilled orders	–347	–340	–1,166
	Net budget authority and outlays:			
89.00	Budget authority	15		
90.00	Outlays	–39	–313	99

The Navy Working Capital Fund finances the operations of Navy industrial, commercial and support-type activities. The separate Working Capital Fund emphasizes the Component's functional and financial management responsibilities for its operations. The Fund finances, in accordance with section 2208 of 10 U.S.C. through receipt of funded customer reimbursable orders, operating and capital expenses (excluding Military Construction), and uses cost accounting-type techniques to provide DoD managers with information that can be used to monitor, control, and minimize its cost of operations.

Status of Contract Authority (in millions of dollars)

Identification code 97–493002–0–4–051		1999 actual	2000 est.	2001 est.
0100	Balance, start of year	3,926	3,727	3,727
	Contract authority:			
0200	Contract authority	13		
0600	Balance of contract authority withdrawn	–212		
0700	Balance, end of year	3,727	3,727	3,727

Object Classification (in millions of dollars)

Identification code 97–493002–0–4–051		1999 actual	2000 est.	2001 est.
	Personnel compensation:			
11.1	Full-time permanent	4,472	4,455	4,520
11.3	Other than full-time permanent	57	72	77
11.5	Other personnel compensation	472	418	438
11.7	Military personnel	147	130	113
11.8	Special personal services payments	5	2	2
11.9	Total personnel compensation	5,153	5,077	5,151
12.1	Civilian personnel benefits	1,122	1,131	1,156
13.0	Benefits for former personnel	73	78	38
21.0	Travel and transportation of persons	293	292	288
22.0	Transportation of things	127	149	155
23.1	Rental payments to GSA	1	2	2
23.2	Rental payments to others	429	455	454
23.3	Communications, utilities, and miscellaneous charges	617	623	623
24.0	Printing and reproduction	30	25	24
25.1	Advisory and assistance services	80	68	61
25.2	Other services	828	636	606
	Purchases of goods and services from Government accounts:			
25.3	Purchases of goods and services from other Federal Agencies	519	434	411
25.3	Payments to foreign national indirect hire personnel	9	10	10
25.3	Purchases from revolving funds	714	729	688
25.4	Operation and maintenance of facilities including GOCOs	822	617	627
25.5	Research and development contracts	1,775	1,287	1,292
25.7	Contract operation and maintenance of equipment including ADP hard/software	860	794	764
26.0	Supplies and materials	6,507	6,724	6,971
31.0	Equipment	420	668	691
99.0	Subtotal, reimbursable obligations	20,379	19,799	20,011
99.9	Total new obligations	20,379	19,799	20,011

Personnel Summary

Identification code 97–493002–0–4–051		1999 actual	2000 est.	2001 est.
2001	Total compensable workyears: Full-time equivalent employment	92,759	89,893	88,367

WORKING CAPITAL FUND, AIR FORCE

Program and Financing (in millions of dollars)

Identification code 97–493003–0–4–051		1999 actual	2000 est.	2001 est.
	Obligations by program activity:			
	Operating Expenses:			
09.00	Depot Maintenance—Aviation	4,656	4,900	4,970
09.01	Transportation	4,300	4,000	4,320
09.02	Information Services	368	524	532
09.03	Supply Management	9,903	9,138	10,065
09.09	Total operating expenses	19,227	18,562	19,887
	Capital Investment:			
09.10	Depot Maintenance—Aviation	52	138	129
09.11	Transportation	189	183	196
09.12	Information Services	7	7	7
09.13	Supply Management	63	52	39
09.19	Total capital investment	311	380	371
10.00	Total new obligations	19,538	18,942	20,258
	Budgetary resources available for obligation:			
21.40	Unobligated balance available, start of year	–732	364	345
22.00	New budget authority (gross)	20,585	18,941	20,229
22.10	Resources available from recoveries of prior year obligations	33		
22.22	Unobligated balance transferred from other DoD accounts	58		
22.60	Portion applied to repay debt	–17	–18	–28
22.75	Balance of contract authority withdrawn	–25		
23.90	Total budgetary resources available for obligation	19,902	19,287	20,546
23.95	Total new obligations	–19,538	–18,942	–20,258
24.40	Unobligated balance available, end of year	364	345	288
	New budget authority (gross), detail:			
	Discretionary:			
40.00	Appropriation	31	28	
	Mandatory:			
66.15	Contract authority (indefinite)	1,480		
	Spending authority from offsetting collections:			
	Discretionary:			
68.00	Offsetting collections (cash)	19,281	19,104	19,759
68.10	From Federal sources: Change in receivables and unpaid, unfilled orders	–207	–191	470
68.90	Spending authority from offsetting collections (total discretionary)	19,074	18,913	20,229
70.00	Total new budget authority (gross)	20,585	18,941	20,229
	Change in unpaid obligations:			
	Unpaid obligations, start of year:			
72.40	Obligated balance, start of year	1,434	131	428
72.49	Obligated balance, start of year: Contract authority	1,842	3,297	3,297
72.95	From Federal sources: Receivables and unpaid, unfilled orders	5,542	5,335	5,144
72.99	Total unpaid obligations, start of year	8,818	8,763	8,870
73.10	Total new obligations	19,538	18,942	20,258
73.20	Total outlays (gross)	–19,560	–18,835	–19,756
73.45	Adjustments in unexpired accounts	–33		
	Unpaid obligations, end of year:			
74.40	Obligated balance, end of year	131	428	459
74.49	Obligated balance, end of year: Contract authority	3,297	3,297	3,297
74.95	From Federal sources: Receivables and unpaid, unfilled orders	5,335	5,144	5,614
74.99	Total unpaid obligations, end of year	8,763	8,870	9,371

Public enterprise funds—Continued

DEFENSE WORKING CAPITAL FUNDS—Continued

WORKING CAPITAL FUND, AIR FORCE—Continued

Program and Financing (in millions of dollars)—Continued

Identification code 97–493003–0–4–051	1999 actual	2000 est.	2001 est.
Outlays (gross), detail:			
86.90 Outlays from new discretionary authority	13,560	13,035	13,656
86.93 Outlays from discretionary balances	6,000	5,800	6,100
87.00 Total outlays (gross)	19,560	18,835	19,756
Offsets:			
Against gross budget authority and outlays:			
Offsetting collections (cash) from:			
88.00 Federal sources	−19,017	−19,079	−19,734
88.40 Non-Federal sources	−264	−25	−25
88.90 Total, offsetting collections (cash)	−19,281	−19,104	−19,759
Against gross budget authority only:			
88.95 From Federal sources: Change in receivables and unpaid, unfilled orders	207	191	−470
Net budget authority and outlays:			
89.00 Budget authority	1,511	28	....
90.00 Outlays	280	−269	−2

The Air Force Working Capital Fund finances the operations of Air Force and USTRANSCOM industrial, commercial and support-type activities. The separate Working Capital Fund emphasizes the Component's functional and financial management responsibilities for their operations. The Fund finances, in accordance with section 2208 of 10 U.S.C. through receipt of funded customer reimbursable orders, operating and capital expenses (excluding Military Construction), and uses cost accounting-type techniques to provide DoD managers with information that can be used to monitor, control, and minimize its cost of operations.

Status of Contract Authority (in millions of dollars)

Identification code 97–493003–0–4–051	1999 actual	2000 est.	2001 est.
0100 Balance, start of year	1,842	3,297	3,297
Contract authority:			
0200 Contract authority	1,480	....	....
0600 Balance of contract authority withdrawn	−25	....	....
0700 Balance, end of year	3,297	3,297	3,297

Object Classification (in millions of dollars)

Identification code 97–493003–0–4–051	1999 actual	2000 est.	2001 est.
Personnel compensation:			
11.1 Full-time permanent	786	778	782
11.3 Other than full-time permanent	704	781	764
11.5 Other personnel compensation	142	141	135
11.7 Military personnel	110	96	105
11.9 Total personnel compensation	1,742	1,796	1,786
12.1 Civilian personnel benefits	49	2	1
21.0 Travel and transportation of persons	115	111	115
22.0 Transportation of things	1,504	1,722	1,734
23.1 Rental payments to GSA	1	....	....
23.2 Rental payments to others	7	6	5
23.3 Communications, utilities, and miscellaneous charges	112	71	68
24.0 Printing and reproduction	7	4	4
25.1 Advisory and assistance services	18	25	24
25.2 Other services	1,642	1,033	1,032
Purchases of goods and services from Government accounts:			
25.3 Purchases of goods and services from other Federal Agencies	203	226	261
25.3 Payments to foreign national indirect hire personnel	13	11	11
25.3 Purchases from revolving funds	8,488	5,824	6,471
25.4 Operation and maintenance of facilities including GOCOs	82	102	99
25.7 Contract operation and maintenance of equipment including ADP hard/software	1,147	1,635	1,707
26.0 Supplies and materials	4,109	5,975	6,548
31.0 Equipment	299	399	392
99.0 Subtotal, reimbursable obligations	19,538	18,942	20,258
99.9 Total new obligations	19,538	18,942	20,258

Personnel Summary

Identification code 97–493003–0–4–051	1999 actual	2000 est.	2001 est.
2001 Total compensable workyears: Full-time equivalent employment	28,332	25,025	25,446

WORKING CAPITAL FUND, DEFENSE-WIDE

Program and Financing (in millions of dollars)

Identification code 97–493005–0–4–051	1999 actual	2000 est.	2001 est.
Obligations by program activity:			
Operating Expenses:			
Operating expenses:			
09.01 Distribution Depots	1,316	1,371	1,242
09.02 Defense Reutilization and Marketing	331	343	317
09.03 Defense Automated Printing Service	187	366	357
09.04 Defense Financial Operations	1,426	1,455	1,373
09.05 Information Services	2,876	3,053	2,980
09.06 Supply Management	12,884	14,055	13,842
09.07 Defense Security Service	211	308	312
09.09 Subtotal Operating Expenses	19,231	20,951	20,423
Capital investment:			
09.10 Distribution Depots	44	36	44
09.11 Defense Reutilization and Marketing	8	9	7
09.12 Defense Automated Printing Service	3	9	6
09.13 Defense Financial Operations	218	217	192
09.14 Information Services	36	27	28
09.15 Supply Management	66	107	148
09.16 Defense Security Service	....	12	29
10.00 Total new obligations	19,606	21,368	20,877
Budgetary resources available for obligation:			
21.40 Unobligated balance available, start of year	1,332	2,079	231
22.00 New budget authority (gross)	22,089	19,521	20,243
22.10 Resources available from recoveries of prior year obligations	8	....	....
22.21 Unobligated balance transferred to other DoD accounts	....	−2	....
22.22 Unobligated balance transferred from other DoD accounts	452	....	....
22.75 Balance of contract authority withdrawn	−2,196	....	....
23.90 Total budgetary resources available for obligation	21,685	21,598	20,474
23.95 Total new obligations	−19,606	−21,368	−20,877
24.40 Unobligated balance available, end of year	2,079	231	−403
New budget authority (gross), detail:			
Discretionary:			
41.00 Transferred to other DoD accounts	−569	....	....
Mandatory:			
66.15 Contract authority (indefinite)	2,660	....	....
Spending authority from offsetting collections:			
Discretionary:			
68.00 Offsetting collections (cash)	19,807	19,480	20,100
68.10 From Federal sources: Change in receivables and unpaid, unfilled orders	191	41	144
68.90 Spending authority from offsetting collections (total discretionary)	19,998	19,521	20,244
70.00 Total new budget authority (gross)	22,089	19,521	20,244
Change in unpaid obligations:			
Unpaid obligations, start of year:			
72.40 Obligated balance, start of year	163	170	609
72.49 Obligated balance, start of year: Contract authority	4,982	5,446	5,446
72.95 From Federal sources: Receivables and unpaid, unfilled orders	4,131	4,322	4,363
72.99 Total unpaid obligations, start of year	9,276	9,937	10,418
73.10 Total new obligations	19,606	21,368	20,877
73.20 Total outlays (gross)	−18,937	−20,887	−20,245

73.45	Adjustments in unexpired accounts	–8		
	Unpaid obligations, end of year:			
74.40	Obligated balance, end of year	170	609	1,098
74.49	Obligated balance, end of year: Contract authority	5,446	5,446	5,446
74.95	From Federal sources: Receivables and unpaid, unfilled orders	4,322	4,363	4,507
74.99	Total unpaid obligations, end of year	9,937	10,418	11,050
	Outlays (gross), detail:			
86.90	Outlays from new discretionary authority	16,724	19,480	18,139
86.93	Outlays from discretionary balances	2,213	1,407	2,106
87.00	Total outlays (gross)	18,937	20,887	20,245
	Offsets:			
	Against gross budget authority and outlays:			
	Offsetting collections (cash) from:			
88.00	Federal sources	–19,455	–19,410	–20,029
88.40	Non-Federal sources	–352	–70	–71
88.90	Total, offsetting collections (cash)	–19,807	–19,480	–20,100
	Against gross budget authority only:			
88.95	From Federal sources: Change in receivables and unpaid, unfilled orders	–191	–41	–144
	Net budget authority and outlays:			
89.00	Budget authority	2,091		
90.00	Outlays	–870	1,407	145

The Defense-Wide Working Capital Fund finances the operations of Defense Logistics Agency, Defense Finance and Accounting Service, Defense Information Services Agency, and Defense Security Service commercial and support-type activities. The separate Working Capital Fund emphasizes the Components' functional and financial management responsibilities for their operations. The Fund finances, in accordance with section 2208 of 10 U.S.C. through receipt of funded customer reimbursable orders, operating and capital expenses (excluding Military Construction), and uses cost accounting-type techniques to provide DoD managers with information that can be used to monitor, control, and minimize its cost of operations.

Status of Contract Authority (in millions of dollars)

Identification code 97–493005–0–4–051		1999 actual	2000 est.	2001 est.
0100	Balance, start of year	4,982	5,446	5,446
	Contract authority:			
0200	Contract authority	2,660		
0600	Balance of contract authority withdrawn	–2,196		
0700	Balance, end of year	5,446	5,446	5,446

Object Classification (in millions of dollars)

Identification code 97–493005–0–4–051		1999 actual	2000 est.	2001 est.
	Personnel compensation:			
11.1	Full-time permanent	2,046	2,184	2,141
11.3	Other than full-time permanent	43	60	61
11.5	Other personnel compensation	92	101	97
11.7	Military personnel	46	41	44
11.9	Total personnel compensation	2,227	2,386	2,343
12.1	Civilian personnel benefits	469	356	345
13.0	Benefits for former personnel	57	54	46
21.0	Travel and transportation of persons	87	84	85
22.0	Transportation of things	920	589	556
23.1	Rental payments to GSA	46	52	50
23.2	Rental payments to others	25	23	20
23.3	Communications, utilities, and miscellaneous charges	1,400	1,591	1,541
24.0	Printing and reproduction	96	199	200
25.1	Advisory and assistance services	36	25	29
25.2	Other services	1,316	404	379
	Purchases of goods and services from Government accounts:			
25.3	Purchases of goods and services from other Federal Agencies	299	469	445
25.3	Payments to foreign national indirect hire personnel	17	30	32
25.3	Purchases from revolving funds	1,747	1,878	1,768
25.4	Operation and maintenance of facilities including GOCOs	54	52	51
25.7	Contract operation and maintenance of equipment including ADP hard/software	59	83	78
26.0	Supplies and materials	10,102	12,507	12,325
31.0	Equipment	621	520	518
32.0	Land and structures	23	66	66
41.0	Grants, subsidies, and contributions	1		
43.0	Interest and dividends	4		
99.0	Subtotal, reimbursable obligations	19,606	21,368	20,877
99.9	Total new obligations	19,606	21,368	20,877

Personnel Summary

Identification code 97–493005–0–4–051		1999 actual	2000 est.	2001 est.
2001	Total compensable workyears: Full-time equivalent employment	49,920	49,184	46,390

Working Capital Fund, Defense Commissary Agency

Program and Financing (in millions of dollars)

Identification code 97–493004–0–4–051		1999 actual	2000 est.	2001 est.
	Obligations by program activity:			
	Operating Expenses:			
09.01	Commissary Resale Stocks	5,001	5,000	5,000
09.02	Commissary Operations	998	1,020	1,020
10.00	Total new obligations	5,999	6,020	6,020
	Budgetary resources available for obligation:			
21.40	Unobligated balance available, start of year	45	–141	53
22.00	New budget authority (gross)	6,301	6,214	6,109
22.10	Resources available from recoveries of prior year obligations	9		
22.21	Unobligated balances transferred to other DoD accounts	–497		
23.90	Total budgetary resources available for obligation	5,858	6,073	6,162
23.95	Total new obligations	–5,999	–6,020	–6,020
24.40	Unobligated balance available, end of year	–141	53	141
	New budget authority (gross), detail:			
	Discretionary:			
40.00	Appropriation	64		916
42.00	Transferred from other DoD accounts	987	1,009	
43.00	Appropriation (total discretionary)	1,051	1,009	916
	Mandatory:			
66.15	Contract authority (indefinite)	259		
	Spending authority from offsetting collections:			
	Discretionary:			
68.00	Offsetting collections (cash)	5,013	4,973	5,069
68.10	From Federal sources: Change in receivables and unpaid, unfilled orders	–23	232	124
68.15	From Federal sources: Adjustments to receivables and unpaid, unfilled orders	1		
68.90	Spending authority from offsetting collections (total discretionary)	4,991	5,205	5,193
70.00	Total new budget authority (gross)	6,301	6,214	6,109
	Change in unpaid obligations:			
	Unpaid obligations, start of year:			
72.40	Obligated balance, start of year	432	250	23
72.49	Obligated balance, start of year: Contract authority	50	309	309
72.95	From Federal sources: Receivables and unpaid, unfilled orders	208	185	417
72.99	Total unpaid obligations, start of year	689	744	750
73.10	Total new obligations	5,999	6,020	6,020
73.20	Total outlays (gross)	–5,934	–6,014	–6,048
73.45	Adjustments in unexpired accounts	–9		
	Unpaid obligations, end of year:			
74.40	Obligated balance, end of year	250	23	–128
74.49	Obligated balance, end of year: Contract authority	309	309	309
74.95	From Federal sources: Receivables and unpaid, unfilled orders	185	417	541
74.99	Total unpaid obligations, end of year	744	750	723

Public enterprise funds—Continued

WORKING CAPITAL FUND, DEFENSE COMMISSARY AGENCY—Continued

Program and Financing (in millions of dollars)—Continued

Identification code 97–493004–0–4–051	1999 actual	2000 est.	2001 est.
Outlays (gross), detail:			
86.90 Outlays from new discretionary authority	5,701	5,530	5,485
86.93 Outlays from discretionary balances	233	482	563
87.00 Total outlays (gross)	5,934	6,014	6,048
Offsets:			
Against gross budget authority and outlays:			
Offsetting collections (cash) from:			
88.00 Federal sources	−46	26	−70
88.40 Non-Federal sources	−4,967	−4,999	−4,999
88.90 Total, offsetting collections (cash)	−5,013	−4,973	−5,069
Against gross budget authority only:			
88.95 From Federal sources: Change in receivables and unpaid, unfilled orders	23	−232	−124
88.96 From Federal sources: Adjustment to receivables and unpaid, unfilled orders	−1		
Net budget authority and outlays:			
89.00 Budget authority	1,310	1,009	916
90.00 Outlays	922	1,041	979

The Defense Commissary Agency Working Capital Fund finances the cost of Commissary Operations and Resale Stocks activities. Commissary Operations pays the operating costs of about 300 commissaries worldwide, agency and region headquarters, and support services. Costs include civilian pay, transportation of commissary goods overseas, rewarehousing, shelf stocking, janitorial services in each commissary, and base support as a tenant organization. Resale Stocks pays for the purchase of inventory for resale to commissary patrons.

Status of Contract Authority (in millions of dollars)

Identification code 97–493004–0–4–051	1999 actual	2000 est.	2001 est.
0100 Balance, start of year	50	309	309
Contract authority:			
0200 Contract authority	259		
0700 Balance, end of year	309	309	309

Object Classification (in millions of dollars)

Identification code 97–493004–0–4–051	1999 actual	2000 est.	2001 est.
Personnel compensation:			
11.1 Full-time permanent	339	288	287
11.3 Other than full-time permanent	117	179	179
11.5 Other personnel compensation	23	22	22
11.7 Military personnel	1	1	1
11.9 Total personnel compensation	480	490	488
12.1 Civilian personnel benefits	123	120	116
21.0 Travel and transportation of persons	11	9	10
22.0 Transportation of things	108	126	109
25.1 Advisory and assistance services		1	1
25.2 Other services	15	10	11
Purchases of goods and services from Government accounts:			
25.3 Purchases of goods and services from Government accounts	83	77	78
25.3 Payments to foreign national indirect hire personnel	36	41	44
25.3 Purchases from revolving funds	28	36	38
25.4 Operation and maintenance of facilities	108	108	122
26.0 Supplies and materials	5,007	5,002	5,002
99.0 Subtotal, reimbursable obligations	5,999	6,020	6,020
99.9 Total new obligations	5,999	6,020	6,020

Personnel Summary

Identification code 97–493004–0–4–051	1999 actual	2000 est.	2001 est.
2001 Total compensable workyears: Full-time equivalent employment	15,928	15,608	14,962

BUILDINGS MAINTENANCE FUND

Program and Financing (in millions of dollars)

Identification code 97–4931–0–4–051	1999 actual	2000 est.	2001 est.
Obligations by program activity:			
09.01 Operation and Maintenance	22	24	28
09.02 Administration	6	5	5
10.00 Total new obligations	27	29	33
Budgetary resources available for obligation:			
21.40 Unobligated balance available, start of year	13	12	10
22.00 New budget authority (gross)	23	27	29
22.10 Resources available from recoveries of prior year obligations	3		
23.90 Total budgetary resources available for obligation	39	39	39
23.95 Total new obligations	−27	−29	−33
24.40 Unobligated balance available, end of year	12	10	6
New budget authority (gross), detail:			
Mandatory:			
69.00 Offsetting collections (cash)	12	27	29
69.10 From Federal sources: Change in receivables and unpaid, unfilled orders	11		
69.90 Spending authority from offsetting collections (total mandatory)	23	27	29
Change in unpaid obligations:			
Unpaid obligations, start of year:			
72.40 Obligated balance, start of year	−9	−2	−10
72.95 From Federal sources: Receivables and unpaid, unfilled orders	39	50	50
72.99 Total unpaid obligations, start of year	30	48	40
73.10 Total new obligations	27	29	33
73.20 Total outlays (gross)	−6	−37	−29
73.45 Adjustments in unexpired accounts	−3		
Unpaid obligations, end of year:			
74.40 Obligated balance, end of year	−2	−10	−6
74.95 From Federal sources: Receivables and unpaid, unfilled orders	50	50	50
74.99 Total unpaid obligations, end of year	48	40	44
Outlays (gross), detail:			
86.97 Outlays from new mandatory authority	6	27	29
86.98 Outlays from mandatory balances		10	
87.00 Total outlays (gross)	6	37	29
Offsets:			
Against gross budget authority and outlays:			
88.00 Offsetting collections (cash) from: Federal sources	−12	−27	−29
Against gross budget authority only:			
88.95 From Federal sources: Change in receivables and unpaid, unfilled orders	−11		
Net budget authority and outlays:			
89.00 Budget authority			
90.00 Outlays	−6	10	

The Buildings Maintenance Fund was established in accordance with direction from Congress in the 1994 Appropriations Conference Report for the General Services Administration and under authority in 10 U.S.C., section 2208. It provides for operation and maintenance of over 30 leased and owned facilities occupied by DoD in the Washington Metropolitan area.

Object Classification (in millions of dollars)

Identification code 97–4931–0–4–051	1999 actual	2000 est.	2001 est.
11.1 Personnel compensation: Full-time permanent	4	4	4
12.1 Civilian personnel benefits		1	1
23.3 Communications, utilities, and miscellaneous charges	2	2	2
25.7 Operation and maintenance of equipment	20	22	26
31.0 Equipment	1		
99.0 Subtotal, reimbursable obligations	27	29	33
99.9 Total new obligations	27	29	33

Personnel Summary

Identification code 97–4931–0–4–051	1999 actual	2000 est.	2001 est.
2001 Total compensable workyears: Full-time equivalent employment	63	66	66

NAVY MANAGEMENT FUND

Program and Financing (in millions of dollars)

Identification code 17–3980–0–4–051	1999 actual	2000 est.	2001 est.
Budgetary resources available for obligation:			
21.40 Unobligated balance available, start of year	1		
23.95 Total new obligations			
23.98 Unobligated balance expiring or withdrawn	–1		
New budget authority (gross), detail:			
Mandatory:			
69.00 Offsetting collections (cash)			
Offsets:			
Against gross budget authority and outlays:			
88.00 Offsetting collections (cash) from: Federal sources			
Net budget authority and outlays:			
89.00 Budget authority			
90.00 Outlays			

ARMY CONVENTIONAL AMMUNITION WORKING CAPITAL FUND

Program and Financing (in millions of dollars)

Identification code 21–4528–0–4–051	1999 actual	2000 est.	2001 est.
Obligations by program activity:			
09.01 Load, assemble and pack	140	122	50
09.02 Components	34	33	14
09.03 Quality assurance, proof and acceptance testing	12	16	6
09.04 Rework cost	65	3	1
10.00 Total new obligations	251	174	72
Budgetary resources available for obligation:			
21.40 Unobligated balance available, start of year	186	59	10
22.00 New budget authority (gross)	–18	125	72
22.10 Resources available from recoveries of prior year obligations	143		
22.21 Unobligated balance transferred to other DoD accounts	–12		
22.22 Unobligated balance transferred from other DoD accounts	12		
23.90 Total budgetary resources available for obligation	310	184	82
23.95 Total new obligations	–251	–174	–72
24.40 Unobligated balance available, end of year	59	10	10
New budget authority (gross), detail:			
Mandatory:			
69.00 Offsetting collections (cash)	833	282	72
69.10 From Federal sources: Change in receivables and unpaid, unfilled orders	–851	–157	
69.90 Spending authority from offsetting collections (total mandatory)	–18	125	72
Change in unpaid obligations:			
Unpaid obligations, start of year:			
72.40 Obligated balance, start of year	55	228	10
72.95 From Federal sources: Receivables and unpaid, unfilled orders	1,008	157	
72.99 Total unpaid obligations, start of year	1,063	385	10
73.10 Total new obligations	251	174	72
73.20 Total outlays (gross)	–786	–549	–70
73.45 Adjustments in unexpired accounts	–143		
Unpaid obligations, end of year:			
74.40 Obligated balance, end of year	228	10	12
74.95 From Federal sources: Receivables and unpaid, unfilled orders	157		
74.99 Total unpaid obligations, end of year	385	10	12
Outlays (gross), detail:			
86.97 Outlays from new mandatory authority	–18	125	70
86.98 Outlays from mandatory balances	804	424	
87.00 Total outlays (gross)	786	549	70
Offsets:			
Against gross budget authority and outlays:			
88.00 Offsetting collections (cash) from: Federal sources	–833	–282	–72
Against gross budget authority only:			
88.95 From Federal sources: Change in receivables and unpaid, unfilled orders	851	157	
Net budget authority and outlays:			
89.00 Budget authority			
90.00 Outlays	–47	267	–2

The Army Conventional Ammunition Working Capital Fund (CAWCF) financed the procurement and assembly of conventional ammunition for all the Services and other customers. It provided for payment of loading, assembling and packing (LAP) operations, component purchases for metal parts and explosive materials, and quality assurance and rework effort. The CAWCF ceased operations as a working capital fund at the end of FY 1998. All unfinished orders on hand as of that date will be processed through the fund until completed.

Object Classification (in millions of dollars)

Identification code 21–4528–0–4–051	1999 actual	2000 est.	2001 est.
22.0 Transportation of things	1	2	2
25.2 Other services	14	17	6
Purchases of goods and services from Government accounts:			
25.3 Purchases of goods and services from Government accounts	63		
25.3 Purchases from revolving funds	3		
26.0 Supplies and materials	170	155	64
99.0 Subtotal, reimbursable obligations	251	174	72
99.9 Total new obligations	251	174	72

TRUST FUNDS

Trust Funds

VOLUNTARY SEPARATION INCENTIVE FUND

Unavailable Collections (in millions of dollars)

Identification code 97–8335–0–7–051	1999 actual	2000 est.	2001 est.
Balance, start of year:			
01.99 Balance, start of year	787	786	786
Receipts:			
02.01 Payment to voluntary separation incentive fund	102	86	23
02.02 Earnings on investments	70	57	53
02.99 Total receipts	172	143	76

186-484 00 - 11

VOLUNTARY SEPARATION INCENTIVE FUND—Continued

Unavailable Collections (in millions of dollars)—Continued

Identification code 97–8335–0–7–051	1999 actual	2000 est.	2001 est.
04.00 Total: Balances and collections	959	929	862
Appropriation:			
05.01 Voluntary separation incentive fund	–173	–143	–76
07.99 Total balance, end of year	786	786	786

Program and Financing (in millions of dollars)

Identification code 97–8335–0–7–051	1999 actual	2000 est.	2001 est.
Obligations by program activity:			
10.00 Total new obligations	157	159	159
Budgetary resources available for obligation:			
21.40 Unobligated balance available, start of year	84	100	84
22.00 New budget authority (gross)	173	143	76
23.90 Total budgetary resources available for obligation	257	243	160
23.95 Total new obligations	–157	–159	–159
24.40 Unobligated balance available, end of year	100	84	1
New budget authority (gross), detail:			
Mandatory:			
60.27 Appropriation (trust fund, indefinite)	173	143	76
Change in unpaid obligations:			
72.40 Unpaid obligations, start of year: Obligated balance, start of year	6	7	7
73.10 Total new obligations	157	159	159
73.20 Total outlays (gross)	–157	–159	–159
74.40 Unpaid obligations, end of year: Obligated balance, end of year	7	7	7
Outlays (gross), detail:			
86.97 Outlays from new mandatory authority	66	143	76
86.98 Outlays from mandatory balances	90	16	83
87.00 Total outlays (gross)	157	159	159
Net budget authority and outlays:			
89.00 Budget authority	173	143	76
90.00 Outlays	157	159	159
Memorandum (non-add) entries:			
92.01 Total investments, start of year: U.S. securities: Par value	873	889	889
92.02 Total investments, end of year: U.S. securities: Par value	889	889	889

Section 662 of the Defense Authorization Act for 1992 and 1993, Public Law 102–190, established the Voluntary Separation Incentive (VSI) Fund to help manage the ongoing military force drawdown. VSI provides annual payments to selected active-duty Service members with more than six but less than 20 years of service who leave the service voluntarily. The Act provided that after January 1, 1993, all voluntary separation incentive payments shall be made from the fund. The fund is financed through actuarially-determined Government contributions from the Department of Defense personnel appropriations to cover the unfunded liability and the present value of future benefits for those separating and interest on the investments. The Act, as amended by Section 561 of Public Law 105–261 requires that the total present value costs of VSI benefit payments be deposited in the fund by September 30, 2001, when the authority to approve VSI benefits ends. Permanent authority to make these payments is contained in section 8044 of the 1997 Defense Appropriations Act.

HOST NATION SUPPORT FUND FOR RELOCATION

Unavailable Collections (in millions of dollars)

Identification code 97–8337–0–7–051	1999 actual	2000 est.	2001 est.
Balance, start of year:			
01.99 Balance, start of year	....	....	....
Receipts:			
02.01 Contributions	....	6	6
Appropriation:			
05.01 Host Nation support fund for relocation	....	–6	–6
07.99 Total balance, end of year	....	....	....

Program and Financing (in millions of dollars)

Identification code 97–8337–0–7–051	1999 actual	2000 est.	2001 est.
Obligations by program activity:			
10.00 Total new obligations	....	6	6
Budgetary resources available for obligation:			
22.00 New budget authority (gross)	....	6	6
23.95 Total new obligations	....	–6	–6
New budget authority (gross), detail:			
Mandatory:			
60.27 Appropriation (trust fund, indefinite)	....	6	6
Change in unpaid obligations:			
73.10 Total new obligations	....	6	6
73.20 Total outlays (gross)	....	–6	–6
Outlays (gross), detail:			
86.97 Outlays from new mandatory authority	....	6	6
Net budget authority and outlays:			
89.00 Budget authority	....	6	6
90.00 Outlays	....	6	6

Section 2350k of U.S.C. Title 10 established a trust fund for cash contributions from any nation in support of relocation of elements of the Armed Forces within that nation. The Host Nation Support for Relocation Account is financed through these cash contributions and interest accrued on the cash balances. Funds may be used to defray costs incurred in connection with the relocation for which the contribution was made.

OTHER DOD TRUST FUNDS

Unavailable Collections (in millions of dollars)

Identification code 21–9971–0–7–051	1999 actual	2000 est.	2001 est.
Balance, start of year:			
01.99 Balance, start of year	2	....	1
Receipts:			
02.01 Deposits, other DOD trust funds	16	10	10
02.02 Profits from sale of ships' stores	18	20	20
02.03 Interest, other DOD trust funds	1	1	1
02.04 The Fisher House trust fund	–2	....	....
02.99 Total receipts	33	31	31
04.00 Total: Balances and collections	35	31	32
Appropriation:			
05.01 Other DOD trust funds	–35	–30	–30
07.99 Total balance, end of year	....	1	2

Program and Financing (in millions of dollars)

Identification code 21–9971–0–7–051	1999 actual	2000 est.	2001 est.
Obligations by program activity:			
02.11 Army trust funds	8	5	5
02.12 Air Force trust funds	1	1	1
02.13 Ships Stores Profit, Navy trust fund	19	20	20
02.14 Other Navy trust funds	6	5	5

		1999 actual	2000 est.	2001 est.
10.00	Total new obligations	34	31	31
	Budgetary resources available for obligation:			
21.40	Unobligated balance available, start of year	22	23	22
22.00	New budget authority (gross)	35	30	30
23.90	Total budgetary resources available for obligation	57	53	52
23.95	Total new obligations	−34	−31	−31
24.40	Unobligated balance available, end of year	23	22	21
	New budget authority (gross), detail:			
	Mandatory:			
60.27	Appropriation (trust fund, indefinite)	35	30	30
	Change in unpaid obligations:			
72.40	Unpaid obligations, start of year: Obligated balance, start of year	8	3	4
73.10	Total new obligations	34	31	31
73.20	Total outlays (gross)	−39	−30	−30
74.40	Unpaid obligations, end of year: Obligated balance, end of year	3	4	5
	Outlays (gross), detail:			
86.97	Outlays from new mandatory authority	18	30	30
86.98	Outlays from mandatory balances	21		
87.00	Total outlays (gross)	39	30	30
	Net budget authority and outlays:			
89.00	Budget authority	35	30	30
90.00	Outlays	39	30	30
	Memorandum (non-add) entries:			
92.01	Total investments, start of year: U.S. securities: Par value	12	12	12
92.02	Total investments, end of year: U.S. securities: Par value	12	12	12

This fund includes gifts and bequests limited to specific purposes by the donor. In addition, it accounts for gifts and bequests, not limited to specific use by the donor, which may be used for purposes as determined by the Secretaries of the Army, Navy and Air Force.

Object Classification (in millions of dollars)

Identification code 21–9971–0–7–051		1999 actual	2000 est.	2001 est.
24.0	Printing and reproduction	1	1	1
26.0	Supplies and materials	8	8	8
31.0	Equipment	3	3	3
33.0	Investments and loans	1	1	1
41.0	Grants, subsidies, and contributions	21	18	18
99.9	Total new obligations	34	31	31

National Security Education Trust Fund

For the purposes of title VIII of Public Law 102–183, [$8,000,000] *$6,950,000*, to be derived from the National Security Education Trust Fund, to remain available until expended. *(Department of Defense Appropriations Act, 2000.)*

Unavailable Collections (in millions of dollars)

Identification code 97–8168–0–7–051		1999 actual	2000 est.	2001 est.
	Balance, start of year:			
01.99	Balance, start of year	44	44	40
	Receipts:			
02.02	Earnings on investments	3	4	4
04.00	Total: Balances and collections	47	48	44
	Appropriation:			
05.01	National security education trust fund	−3	−8	−7
07.99	Total balance, end of year	44	40	37

Program and Financing (in millions of dollars)

Identification code 97–8168–0–7–051		1999 actual	2000 est.	2001 est.
	Obligations by program activity:			
10.00	Total new obligations (object class 41.0)	7	8	8
	Budgetary resources available for obligation:			
21.40	Unobligated balance available, start of year	5	1	1
22.00	New budget authority (gross)	3	8	7
22.10	Resources available from recoveries of prior year obligations			
23.90	Total budgetary resources available for obligation	8	9	8
23.95	Total new obligations	−7	−8	−8
24.40	Unobligated balance available, end of year	1	1	
	New budget authority (gross), detail:			
	Discretionary:			
40.26	Appropriation (trust fund, definite)	3	8	7
	Change in unpaid obligations:			
72.40	Unpaid obligations, start of year: Obligated balance, start of year	7	7	7
73.10	Total new obligations	7	8	8
73.20	Total outlays (gross)	−6	−8	−7
73.40	Adjustments in expired accounts (net)			
73.45	Adjustments in unexpired accounts			
74.40	Unpaid obligations, end of year: Obligated balance, end of year	7	7	8
	Outlays (gross), detail:			
86.90	Outlays from new discretionary authority	3	8	7
86.93	Outlays from discretionary balances	3		
87.00	Total outlays (gross)	6	8	7
	Net budget authority and outlays:			
89.00	Budget authority	3	8	7
90.00	Outlays	6	8	7
	Memorandum (non-add) entries:			
92.01	Total investments, start of year: U.S. securities: Par value	52	48	48
92.02	Total investments, end of year: U.S. securities: Par value	48	48	48

The National Security Education Act of 1991 established a program for undergraduate scholarships, graduate fellowships, and grants to educational institutions in critical area studies, foreign languages and other international fields.

This program enhances the quality of U.S. educational programs in these fields by making it possible for more U.S.-citizen students to study abroad. The programs will develop a larger pool of potential U.S. Government employees with knowledge of particular cultures, languages, and governments. The program is carried out by the Secretary of Defense in consultation with the National Security Education Board. The Board establishes the criteria for awards.

Foreign National Employees Separation Pay

Unavailable Collections (in millions of dollars)

Identification code 97–8165–0–7–051		1999 actual	2000 est.	2001 est.
	Balance, start of year:			
01.99	Balance, start of year			
	Receipts:			
02.01	Foreign national employees separation pay trust fund	15	12	12
	Appropriation:			
05.01	Foreign national employees separation pay	−15	−12	−12
07.99	Total balance, end of year			

FOREIGN NATIONAL EMPLOYEES SEPARATION PAY—Continued

Program and Financing (in millions of dollars)

Identification code 97–8165–0–7–051	1999 actual	2000 est.	2001 est.
Obligations by program activity:			
10.00 Total new obligations (object class 13.0)	14	12	12
Budgetary resources available for obligation:			
21.40 Unobligated balance available, start of year	35	36	36
22.00 New budget authority (gross)	15	12	12
22.10 Resources available from recoveries of prior year obligations			
23.90 Total budgetary resources available for obligation	50	48	48
23.95 Total new obligations	–14	–12	–12
24.40 Unobligated balance available, end of year	36	36	36
New budget authority (gross), detail:			
Mandatory:			
60.27 Appropriation (trust fund, indefinite)	15	12	12
Change in unpaid obligations:			
72.40 Unpaid obligations, start of year: Obligated balance, start of year	281	268	268
73.10 Total new obligations	14	12	12
73.20 Total outlays (gross)	–26	–12	–12
73.40 Adjustments in expired accounts (net)			
73.45 Adjustments in unexpired accounts			
74.40 Unpaid obligations, end of year: Obligated balance, end of year	268	268	268
Outlays (gross), detail:			
86.97 Outlays from new mandatory authority		12	12
86.98 Outlays from mandatory balances	27		
87.00 Total outlays (gross)	26	12	12
Net budget authority and outlays:			
89.00 Budget authority	15	12	12
90.00 Outlays	26	12	12

This account funds separation payments for former Department of Defense employees who are not United States citizens and who worked outside the United States. The payments are determined according to the applicable labor laws of the various countries.

OTHER DOD TRUST REVOLVING FUNDS

Program and Financing (in millions of dollars)

Identification code 97–9981–0–8–051	1999 actual	2000 est.	2001 est.
Obligations by program activity:			
10.00 Total new obligations (object class 44.0)	17	15	15
Budgetary resources available for obligation:			
21.40 Unobligated balance available, start of year	1	1	1
22.00 New budget authority (gross)	17	14	14
23.90 Total budgetary resources available for obligation	18	15	15
23.95 Total new obligations	–17	–15	–15
24.40 Unobligated balance available, end of year	1	1	1
New budget authority (gross), detail:			
Mandatory:			
69.00 Offsetting collections (cash)	17	16	15
69.10 From Federal sources: Change in receivables and unpaid, unfilled orders		–1	
69.90 Spending authority from offsetting collections (total mandatory)	17	15	15
Change in unpaid obligations:			
Unpaid obligations, start of year:			
72.40 Obligated balance, start of year	–1	–1	–1
72.95 From Federal sources: Receivables and unpaid, unfilled orders	1	1	
72.99 Total unpaid obligations, start of year		1	–1
73.10 Total new obligations	17	15	15
73.20 Total outlays (gross)	–17	–16	–14
Unpaid obligations, end of year:			
74.40 Obligated balance, end of year	–1	–1	–1
74.95 From Federal sources: Receivables and unpaid, unfilled orders	1		
74.99 Total unpaid obligations, end of year	1	–1	–1
Outlays (gross), detail:			
86.97 Outlays from new mandatory authority	17	15	14
86.98 Outlays from mandatory balances		1	
87.00 Total outlays (gross)	17	16	14
Offsets:			
Against gross budget authority and outlays:			
88.40 Offsetting collections (cash) from: Non-Federal sources	–17	–16	–15
Against gross budget authority only:			
88.95 From Federal sources: Change in receivables and unpaid, unfilled orders		1	
Net budget authority and outlays:			
89.00 Budget authority			
90.00 Outlays			

SURCHARGE COLLECTIONS, SALES OF COMMISSARY STORES, DEFENSE

Program and Financing (in millions of dollars)

Identification code 97–8164–0–8–051	1999 actual	2000 est.	2001 est.
Obligations by program activity:			
09.01 Total Obligations	340	300	250
10.00 Total new obligations	340	300	250
Budgetary resources available for obligation:			
22.00 New budget authority (gross)	327	300	262
22.10 Resources available from recoveries of prior year obligations	13		
23.90 Total budgetary resources available for obligation	340	300	262
23.95 Total new obligations	–340	–300	–250
24.40 Unobligated balance available, end of year			13
New budget authority (gross), detail:			
Mandatory:			
66.15 Contract authority (indefinite)	68	37	
69.00 Offsetting collections (cash)	284	238	262
69.10 From Federal sources: Change in receivables and unpaid, unfilled orders	–25	25	
69.90 Spending authority from offsetting collections (total mandatory)	259	263	262
70.00 Total new budget authority (gross)	327	300	262
Change in unpaid obligations:			
Unpaid obligations, start of year:			
72.40 Obligated balance, start of year	282	216	101
72.49 Obligated balance, start of year: Contract authority	25	93	130
72.95 From Federal sources: Receivables and unpaid, unfilled orders	3	–22	3
72.99 Total unpaid obligations, start of year	310	287	234
73.10 Total new obligations	340	300	250
73.20 Total outlays (gross)	–351	–353	–288
73.45 Adjustments in unexpired accounts	–13		
Unpaid obligations, end of year:			
74.40 Obligated balance, end of year	216	101	62
74.49 Obligated balance, end of year: Contract authority	93	130	130
74.95 From Federal sources: Receivables and unpaid, unfilled orders	–22	3	3
74.99 Total unpaid obligations, end of year	287	234	195
Outlays (gross), detail:			
86.97 Outlays from new mandatory authority	259	241	262
86.98 Outlays from mandatory balances	91	112	26
87.00 Total outlays (gross)	351	353	288

		1999 actual	2000 est.	2001 est.
	Offsets:			
	Against gross budget authority and outlays:			
	Offsetting collections (cash) from:			
88.00	Federal sources	−44	22	−2
88.40	Non-Federal sources	−240	−260	−260
88.90	Total, offsetting collections (cash)	−284	−238	−262
	Against gross budget authority only:			
88.95	From Federal sources: Change in receivables and unpaid, unfilled orders	25	−25	
	Net budget authority and outlays:			
89.00	Budget authority	68	37	
90.00	Outlays	66	115	26

Status of Contract Authority (in millions of dollars)

Identification code 97–8164–0–8–051		1999 actual	2000 est.	2001 est.
0100	Balance, start of year	25	93	130
	Contract authority:			
0200	Contract authority	68	37	
0700	Balance, end of year	93	130	130

This fund was established in 1992 as a result of the consolidation of Defense Commissaries. The trust fund pays for certain commissary store operating equipment and supplies, utilities of Commissaries in the Continental United States, laundry services, and inventory losses. Surcharge funds are also utilized for both minor and major construction of commissaries. Title 10 of the United States Code prescribes costs which may be financed by the Trust Fund.

Object Classification (in millions of dollars)

Identification code 97–8164–0–8–051		1999 actual	2000 est.	2001 est.
22.0	Transportation of things	1	1	1
23.3	Communications, utilities, and miscellaneous charges	34	35	36
25.1	Advisory and assistance services	1		
25.2	Other services	1	1	1
25.3	Purchases of goods and services from Government accounts	1	47	3
25.7	Operation and maintenance of equipment	32	35	35
26.0	Supplies and materials	49	49	51
31.0	Equipment	133	84	75
32.0	Land and structures	88	48	48
99.9	Total new obligations	340	300	250

GENERAL FUND RECEIPT ACCOUNTS

(in millions of dollars)

	1999 actual	2000 est.	2001 est.
Offsetting receipts from the public:			
17–304117 Recoveries under the Foreign Military Sales Program, Navy	296	247	247
17–321017 General fund proprietary receipts, Department of Defense, Not otherwise classified, Navy	−370		
21–301900 Recoveries for Government property lost or damaged	6	7	7
21–304121 Recoveries under the Foreign Military Sales Program, Army	133	133	133
21–321021 General fund proprietary receipts, Department of Defense, Not otherwise classified, Army	62	62	62
57–304157 Recoveries under the Foreign Military Sales Program, Air Force	199	233	233
57–321057 General fund proprietary receipts, Department of Defense, Not otherwise classified, Air Force	49	55	55
97–184000 Rent of equipment and other personal property	3	3	3
97–223600 Sale of certain materials in National Defense Stockpile, Defense	171	169	219
97–246200 Deposits for survivor annuity benefits	16	17	17
97–265197 Sale of scrap and salvage materials, Defense agencies	1	1	1
97–304197 Recoveries under the Foreign Military Sales Program, Defense agencies	18	19	19
97–321097 General fund proprietary receipts, Department of Defense, Not otherwise classified, Defense agencies	116	128	128
General Fund Offsetting receipts from the public	700	1,074	1,124

GENERAL PROVISIONS—DEPARTMENT OF DEFENSE

SEC. 8001. *Propaganda Prohibition.* No part of any appropriation contained in this Act shall be used for publicity or propaganda purposes not authorized by the Congress.

[SEC. 8002. During the current fiscal year, provisions of law prohibiting the payment of compensation to, or employment of, any person not a citizen of the United States shall not apply to personnel of the Department of Defense: *Provided*, That salary increases granted to direct and indirect hire foreign national employees of the Department of Defense funded by this Act shall not be at a rate in excess of the percentage increase authorized by law for civilian employees of the Department of Defense whose pay is computed under the provisions of section 5332 of title 5, United States Code, or at a rate in excess of the percentage increase provided by the appropriate host nation to its own employees, whichever is higher: *Provided further*, That this section shall not apply to Department of Defense foreign service national employees serving at United States diplomatic missions whose pay is set by the Department of State under the Foreign Service Act of 1980: *Provided further*, That the limitations of this provision shall not apply to foreign national employees of the Department of Defense in the Republic of Turkey.]

SEC. [8003.] *8002. One-Year Limitation.* No part of any appropriation contained in this Act shall remain available for obligation beyond the current fiscal year, unless expressly so provided herein.

SEC. [8004.] *8003. 20% Obligation Limitation.* No more than 20 percent of the appropriations in this Act which are limited for obligation during the current fiscal year shall be obligated during the last 2 months of the fiscal year: *Provided*, That this section shall not apply to obligations for support of active duty training of reserve components or summer camp training of the Reserve Officers' Training Corps.

(TRANSFER OF FUNDS)

SEC. [8005.] *8004. General Transfer Authority.* Upon determination by the Secretary of Defense that such action is necessary in the national interest, he may, with the approval of the Office of Management and Budget, transfer not to exceed [$1,600,000,000] *$2,000,000,000* of working capital funds of the Department of Defense or funds made available in this Act to the Department of Defense for military functions (except military construction) between such appropriations or funds or any subdivision thereof, to be merged with and to be available for the same purposes, and for the same time period, as the appropriation or fund to which transferred: *Provided*, That such authority to transfer may not be used unless for higher priority items, based on unforeseen military requirements, than those for which originally appropriated and in no case where the item for which funds are requested has been denied by the Congress: *Provided further*, That the Secretary of Defense shall notify the Congress promptly of all transfers made pursuant to this authority or any other authority in this Act: *Provided further*, That no part of the funds in this Act shall be available to prepare or present a request to the Committees on Appropriations for reprogramming of funds, unless for higher priority items, based on unforeseen military requirements, than those for which originally appropriated and in no case where the item for which reprogramming is requested has been denied by the Congress.

(TRANSFER OF FUNDS)

SEC. [8006.] *8005. Working Capital Fund Balances.* During the current fiscal year, cash balances in working capital funds of the Department of Defense established pursuant to section 2208 of title 10, United States Code, may be maintained in only such amounts as are necessary at any time for cash disbursements to be made from such funds: *Provided*, That transfers may be made between such funds: *Provided further*, That transfers may be made between working capital funds and the "Foreign Currency Fluctuations, Defense" appropriation and the "Operation and Maintenance" appropriation accounts in such amounts as may be determined by the Secretary of Defense, with the approval of the Office of Management and Budget, except that such transfers may not be made unless the Secretary

(TRANSFER OF FUNDS)—Continued

of Defense has notified the Congress of the proposed transfer. Except in amounts equal to the amounts appropriated to working capital funds in this Act, no obligations may be made against a working capital fund to procure or increase the value of war reserve material inventory, unless the Secretary of Defense has notified the Congress prior to any such obligation.

[SEC. 8007. Funds appropriated by this Act may not be used to initiate a special access program without prior notification 30 calendar days in session in advance to the congressional defense committees.]

SEC. [8008] *8006. Multiyear Contract Limitation.* [None of the funds provided in this Act shall be available to initiate: (1) a multiyear contract that employs economic order quantity procurement in excess of $20,000,000 in any 1 year of the contract or that includes an unfunded contingent liability in excess of $20,000,000; or (2) a contract for advance procurement leading to a multiyear contract that employs economic order quantity procurement in excess of $20,000,000 in any 1 year, unless the congressional defense committees have been notified at least 30 days in advance of the proposed contract award: *Provided*, That no part of any appropriation contained in this Act shall be available to initiate a multiyear contract for which the economic order quantity advance procurement is not funded at least to the limits of the Government's liability: *Provided further*, That no part of any appropriation contained in this Act shall be available to initiate multiyear procurement contracts for any systems or component thereof if the value of the multiyear contract would exceed $500,000,000 unless specifically provided in this Act: *Provided further*, That no multiyear procurement contract can be terminated without 10-day prior notification to the congressional defense committees: *Provided further*, That the execution of multiyear authority shall require the use of a present value analysis to determine lowest cost compared to an annual procurement.]

Funds appropriated in title III of this Act may be used for multiyear procurement contracts as follows:

[Longbow Apache Helicopter; Javelin missile; Abrams M1A2 Upgrade; F/A–18E/F aircraft; C–17 aircraft; and F–16 aircraft] *M2A3 Bradley fighting vehicle; DDG–51 destroyer; and UH–60/CH–60 aircraft.*

SEC. [8009.] *8007. Humanitarian Fund Appropriation.* Within the funds appropriated for the operation and maintenance of the Armed Forces, funds are hereby appropriated pursuant to section 401 of title 10, United States Code, for humanitarian and civic assistance costs under chapter 20 of title 10, United States Code. Such funds may also be obligated for humanitarian and civic assistance costs incidental to authorized operations and pursuant to authority granted in section 401 of chapter 20 of title 10, United States Code, and these obligations shall be reported to the Congress on September 30 of each year: *Provided*, That funds available for operation and maintenance shall be available for providing humanitarian and similar assistance by using Civic Action Teams in the Trust Territories of the Pacific Islands and freely associated states of Micronesia, pursuant to the Compact of Free Association as authorized by Public Law 99–239: *Provided further*, That upon a determination by the Secretary of the Army that such action is beneficial for graduate medical education programs conducted at Army medical facilities located in Hawaii, the Secretary of the Army may authorize the provision of medical services at such facilities and transportation to such facilities, on a nonreimbursable basis, for civilian patients from American Samoa, the Commonwealth of the Northern Mariana Islands, the Marshall Islands, the Federated States of Micronesia, Palau, and Guam.

[SEC. 8010. (a) During fiscal year 2000, the civilian personnel of the Department of Defense may not be managed on the basis of any end-strength, and the management of such personnel during that fiscal year shall not be subject to any constraint or limitation (known as an end-strength) on the number of such personnel who may be employed on the last day of such fiscal year.

(b) The fiscal year 2001 budget request for the Department of Defense as well as all justification material and other documentation supporting the fiscal year 2001 Department of Defense budget request shall be prepared and submitted to the Congress as if subsections (a) and (b) of this provision were effective with regard to fiscal year 2001.

(c) Nothing in this section shall be construed to apply to military (civilian) technicians.]

[SEC. 8011. Notwithstanding any other provision of law, none of the funds made available by this Act shall be used by the Department of Defense to exceed, outside the 50 United States, its territories, and the District of Columbia, 125,000 civilian workyears: *Provided*, That workyears shall be applied as defined in the Federal Personnel Manual: *Provided further*, That workyears expended in dependent student hiring programs for disadvantaged youths shall not be included in this workyear limitation.]

SEC. [8012.] *8008. Lobbying Prohibition.* None of the funds made available by this Act shall be used in any way, directly or indirectly, to influence congressional action on any legislation or appropriation matters pending before the Congress.

SEC. [8013.] *8009. Defense Education Fund.* (a) None of the funds appropriated by this Act shall be used to make contributions to the Department of Defense Education Benefits Fund pursuant to section 2006(g) of title 10, United States Code, representing the normal cost for future benefits under section 3015(d) of title 38, United States Code, for any member of the armed services who, on or after the date of the enactment of this Act, enlists in the armed services for a period of active duty of less than 3 years, nor shall any amounts representing the normal cost of such future benefits be transferred from the Fund by the Secretary of the Treasury to the Secretary of Veterans Affairs pursuant to section 2006(d) of title 10, United States Code; nor shall the Secretary of Veterans Affairs pay such benefits to any such member: *Provided*, That these limitations shall not apply to members in combat arms skills or to members who enlist in the armed services on or after July 1, 1989, under a program continued or established by the Secretary of Defense in fiscal year 1991 to test the cost-effective use of special recruiting incentives involving not more than 19 noncombat arms skills approved in advance by the Secretary of Defense: *Provided further*, That this subsection applies only to active components of the Army.

(b) None of the funds appropriated by this Act shall be available for the basic pay and allowances of any member of the Army participating as a full-time student and receiving benefits paid by the Secretary of Veterans Affairs from the Department of Defense Education Benefits Fund when time spent as a full-time student is credited toward completion of a service commitment: *Provided*, That this subsection shall not apply to those members who have reenlisted with this option prior to October 1, 1987: *Provided further*, That this subsection applies only to active components of the Army.

[SEC. 8014. None of the funds appropriated by this Act shall be available to convert to contractor performance an activity or function of the Department of Defense that, on or after the date of the enactment of this Act, is performed by more than 10 Department of Defense civilian employees until a most efficient and cost-effective organization analysis is completed on such activity or function and certification of the analysis is made to the Committees on Appropriations of the House of Representatives and the Senate: *Provided*, That this section and subsections (a), (b), and (c) of 10 U.S.C. 2461 shall not apply to a commercial or industrial type function of the Department of Defense that: (1) is included on the procurement list established pursuant to section 2 of the Act of June 25, 1938 (41 U.S.C. 47), popularly referred to as the Javits-Wagner-O'Day Act; (2) is planned to be converted to performance by a qualified nonprofit agency for the blind or by a qualified nonprofit agency for other severely handicapped individuals in accordance with that Act; or (3) is planned to be converted to performance by a qualified firm under 51 percent Native American ownership.]

(TRANSFER OF FUNDS)

SEC. [8015.] *8010. Mentor-Protegé Program.* Funds appropriated in title III of this Act for the Department of Defense Pilot Mentor-Protege Program may be transferred to any other appropriation contained in this Act solely for the purpose of implementing a Mentor-Protege Program developmental assistance agreement pursuant to section 831 of the National Defense Authorization Act for Fiscal Year 1991 (Public Law 101–510; 10 U.S.C. 2301 note), as amended, under the authority of this provision or any other transfer authority contained in this Act.

[SEC. 8016. None of the funds in this Act may be available for the purchase by the Department of Defense (and its departments and agencies) of welded shipboard anchor and mooring chain 4 inches in diameter and under unless the anchor and mooring chain are manufactured in the United States from components which are substantially manufactured in the United States: *Provided*, That for the purpose of this section manufactured will include cutting, heat treating, quality control, testing of chain and welding (including the forging and shot blasting process): *Provided further*, That for the purpose of this section substantially all of the components of anchor and mooring chain shall be considered to be produced or manufactured in the United States if the aggregate cost of the components produced or manufactured in the United States exceeds the aggregate cost of the components produced or manufactured outside the United States: *Provided further*, That when adequate domestic supplies are not available to meet Department of Defense requirements on a timely basis, the Secretary of the service responsible for the procurement may waive this restriction on a case-by-case basis by certifying in writing to the Committees on Appropriations that such an acquisition must be made in order to acquire capability for national security purposes.]

SEC. [8017.] *8011. Mental Health Payments.* None of the funds appropriated by this Act available for the Civilian Health and Medical Program of the Uniformed Services (CHAMPUS) *or Tricare* shall be available for the reimbursement of any health care provider for inpatient mental health service for care received when a patient is referred to a provider of inpatient mental health care or residential treatment care by a medical or health care professional having an economic interest in the facility to which the patient is referred: *Provided*, That this limitation does not apply in the case of inpatient mental health services provided under the program for [the handicapped] *persons with disabilities* under subsection (d) of section 1079 of title 10, United States Code, provided as partial hospital care, or provided pursuant to a waiver authorized by the Secretary of Defense because of medical or psychological circumstances of the patient that are confirmed by a health professional who is not a Federal employee after a review, pursuant to rules prescribed by the Secretary, which takes into account the appropriate level of care for the patient, the intensity of services required by the patient, and the availability of that care.

SEC. [8018.] *8012. Vietnam POW/MIA's.* Funds available in this Act may be used to provide transportation for the next-of-kin of individuals who have been prisoners of war or missing in action from the Vietnam era to an annual meeting in the United States, under such regulations as the Secretary of Defense may prescribe.

SEC. [8019.] *8013. Residual Value Accounts.* Notwithstanding any other provision of law, during the current fiscal year, the Secretary of Defense may, by executive agreement, establish with host nation governments in NATO member states a separate account into which such residual value amounts negotiated in the return of United States military installations in NATO member states may be deposited, in the currency of the host nation, in lieu of direct monetary transfers to the United States Treasury: *Provided*, That such credits may be utilized only for the construction of facilities to support United States military forces in that host nation, or such real property maintenance and base operating costs that are currently executed through monetary transfers to such host nations[: *Provided further*, That the Department of Defense's budget submission for fiscal year 2001 shall identify such sums anticipated in residual value settlements, and identify such construction, real property maintenance or base operating costs that shall be funded by the host nation through such credits: *Provided further*, That all military construction projects to be executed from such accounts must be previously approved in a prior Act of Congress: *Provided further*, That each such executive agreement with a NATO member host nation shall be reported to the congressional defense committees, the Committee on International Relations of the House of Representatives and the Committee on Foreign Relations of the Senate 30 days prior to the conclusion and endorsement of any such agreement established under this provision].

[SEC. 8020. None of the funds available to the Department of Defense may be used to demilitarize or dispose of M–1 Carbines, M–1 Garand rifles, M–14 rifles, .22 caliber rifles, .30 caliber rifles, or M–1911 pistols.]

[SEC. 8021. Notwithstanding any other provision of law, none of the funds appropriated by this Act shall be available to pay more than 50 percent of an amount paid to any person under section 308 of title 37, United States Code, in a lump sum.]

[SEC. 8022. No more than $500,000 of the funds appropriated or made available in this Act shall be used during a single fiscal year for any single relocation of an organization, unit, activity or function of the Department of Defense into or within the National Capital Region: *Provided*, That the Secretary of Defense may waive this restriction on a case-by-case basis by certifying in writing to the congressional defense committees that such a relocation is required in the best interest of the Government.]

[SEC. 8023. A member of a reserve component whose unit or whose residence is located in a State which is not contiguous with another State is authorized to travel in a space required status on aircraft of the Armed Forces between home and place of inactive duty training, or place of duty in lieu of unit training assembly, when there is no road or railroad transportation (or combination of road and railroad transportation between those locations): *Provided*, That a member traveling in that status on a military aircraft pursuant to the authority provided in this section is not authorized to receive travel, transportation, or per diem allowances in connection with that travel.]

[SEC. 8024. In addition to the funds provided elsewhere in this Act, $8,000,000 is appropriated only for incentive payments authorized by section 504 of the Indian Financing Act of 1974 (25 U.S.C. 1544): *Provided*, That contractors participating in the test program established by section 854 of Public Law 101–189 (15 U.S.C. 637 note) shall be eligible for the program established by section 504 of the Indian Financing Act of 1974 (25 U.S.C. 1544).]

SEC. [8025.] *8014. Military Leave for Reserves in Public Emergencies.* During the current fiscal year, funds appropriated or otherwise available for any Federal agency, the Congress, the judicial branch, or the District of Columbia may be used for the pay, allowances, and benefits of an employee as defined by section 2105 of title 5, United States Code, or an individual employed by the government of the District of Columbia, permanent or temporary indefinite, who—

(1) is a member of a Reserve component of the Armed Forces, as described in section 10101 of title 10, United States Code, or the National Guard, as described in section 101 of title 32, United States Code;

(2) performs, for the purpose of providing military aid to enforce the law or providing assistance to civil authorities in the protection or saving of life or property or prevention of injury—

(A) Federal service under sections 331, 332, 333, or 12406 of title 10, United States Code, or other provision of law, as applicable; or

(B) full-time military service for his or her State, the District of Columbia, the Commonwealth of Puerto Rico, or a territory of the United States; and

(3) requests and is granted—

(A) leave under the authority of this section; or

(B) annual leave, which may be granted without regard to the provisions of sections 5519 and 6323(b) of title 5, United States Code, if such employee is otherwise entitled to such annual leave:

Provided, That any employee who requests leave under subsection (3)(A) for service described in subsection (2) of this section is entitled to such leave, subject to the provisions of this section and of the last sentence of section 6323(b) of title 5, United States Code, and such leave shall be considered leave under section 6323(b) of title 5, United States Code.

[SEC. 8026. None of the funds appropriated by this Act shall be available to perform any cost study pursuant to the provisions of OMB Circular A–76 if the study being performed exceeds a period of 24 months after initiation of such study with respect to a single function activity or 48 months after initiation of such study for a multi-function activity.]

SEC. [8027.] *8015. AFIS Limitation.* Funds appropriated by this Act for the American Forces Information Service shall not be used for any national or international political or psychological activities.

SEC. [8028.] *8016. Health Care Wage Rates.* Notwithstanding any other provision of law or regulation, the Secretary of Defense may adjust wage rates for civilian employees hired for certain health care occupations as authorized for the Secretary of Veterans Affairs by section 7455 of title 38, United States Code.

[Sec. 8029. None of the funds appropriated or made available in this Act shall be used to reduce or disestablish the operation of the 53rd Weather Reconnaissance Squadron of the Air Force Reserve, if such action would reduce the WC–130 Weather Reconnaissance mission below the levels funded in this Act.]

SEC. [8030.] *8017. Contracts with Agencies for the Blind or Other Severely Handicapped.* (a) Of the funds for the procurement of supplies or services appropriated by this Act, qualified nonprofit agencies for the blind or other severely handicapped shall be afforded the maximum practicable opportunity to participate as subcontractors and suppliers in the performance of contracts let by the Department of Defense.

(TRANSFER OF FUNDS)—Continued

(b) During the current fiscal year, a business concern which has negotiated with a military service or defense agency a subcontracting plan for the participation by small business concerns pursuant to section 8(d) of the Small Business Act (15 U.S.C. 637(d)) shall be given credit toward meeting that subcontracting goal for any purchases made from qualified nonprofit agencies for the blind or other severely handicapped.

(c) For the purpose of this section, the phrase "qualified nonprofit agency for the blind or other severely handicapped" means a nonprofit agency for the blind or other severely handicapped that has been approved by the Committee for the Purchase from the Blind and Other Severely Handicapped under the Javits-Wagner-O'Day Act (41 U.S.C. 46–48).

SEC. [8031.] *8018. Third Party Collections.* During the current fiscal year, net receipts pursuant to collections from third party payers pursuant to section 1095 of title 10, United States Code, shall be made available to the local facility of the uniformed services responsible for the collections and shall be over and above the facility's direct budget amount.

SEC. [8032.] *8019. Kuwait Contributions.* During the current fiscal year, the Department of Defense is authorized to incur obligations of not to exceed $350,000,000 for purposes specified in section 2350j(c) of title 10, United States Code, in anticipation of receipt of contributions, only from the Government of Kuwait, under that section: *Provided*, That upon receipt, such contributions from the Government of Kuwait shall be credited to the appropriations or fund which incurred such obligations.

[SEC. 8033. Of the funds made available in this Act, not less than $26,588,000 shall be available for the Civil Air Patrol Corporation, of which $22,888,000 shall be available for Civil Air Patrol Corporation operation and maintenance to support readiness activities which includes $1,418,000 for the Civil Air Patrol counterdrug program: *Provided*, That funds identified for "Civil Air Patrol" under this section are intended for and shall be for the exclusive use of the Civil Air Patrol Corporation and not for the Air Force or any unit thereof.]

SEC. [8034.] *8020. FFRDC Limitations.* [(a) None of the funds appropriated in this Act are available to establish a new Department of Defense (department) federally funded research and development center (FFRDC), either as a new entity, or as a separate entity administrated by an organization managing another FFRDC, or as a nonprofit membership corporation consisting of a consortium of other FFRDCs and other non-profit entities.]

[(b)] No member of a Board of Directors, Trustees, Overseers, Advisory Group, Special Issues Panel, Visiting Committee, or any similar entity of a defense FFRDC, and no paid consultant to any defense FFRDC, except when acting in a technical advisory capacity, may be compensated for his or her services as a member of such entity, or as a paid consultant by more than one FFRDC in a fiscal year: *Provided*, That a member of any such entity referred to previously in this subsection shall be allowed travel expenses and per diem as authorized under the Federal Joint Travel Regulations, when engaged in the performance of membership duties.

[(c) Notwithstanding any other provision of law, none of the funds available to the department from any source during fiscal year 2000 may be used by a defense FFRDC, through a fee or other payment mechanism, for construction of new buildings, for payment of cost sharing for projects funded by Government grants, for absorption of contract overruns, or for certain charitable contributions, not to include employee participation in community service and/or development.]

[(d) Notwithstanding any other provision of law, of the funds available to the department during fiscal year 2000, not more than 6,206 staff years of technical effort (staff years) may be funded for defense FFRDCs: *Provided*, That of the specific amount referred to previously in this subsection, not more than 1,105 staff years may be funded for the defense studies and analysis FFRDCs.]

[(e) The Secretary of Defense shall, with the submission of the department's fiscal year 2001 budget request, submit a report presenting the specific amounts of staff years of technical effort to be allocated for each defense FFRDC during that fiscal year.]

[SEC. 8035. None of the funds appropriated or made available in this Act shall be used to procure carbon, alloy or armor steel plate for use in any Government-owned facility or property under the control of the Department of Defense which were not melted and rolled in the United States or Canada: *Provided*, That these procurement restrictions shall apply to any and all Federal Supply Class 9515, American Society of Testing and Materials (ASTM) or American Iron and Steel Institute (AISI) specifications of carbon, alloy or armor steel plate: *Provided further*, That the Secretary of the military department responsible for the procurement may waive this restriction on a case-by-case basis by certifying in writing to the Committees on Appropriations of the House of Representatives and the Senate that adequate domestic supplies are not available to meet Department of Defense requirements on a timely basis and that such an acquisition must be made in order to acquire capability for national security purposes: *Provided further*, That these restrictions shall not apply to contracts which are in being as of the date of the enactment of this Act.]

[SEC. 8036. For the purposes of this Act, the term "congressional defense committees" means the Armed Services Committee of the House of Representatives, the Armed Services Committee of the Senate, the Subcommittee on Defense of the Committee on Appropriations of the Senate, and the Subcommittee on Defense of the Committee on Appropriations of the House of Representatives.]

SEC. [8037.] *8021. Depot Maintenance Competition.* During the current fiscal year, the Department of Defense may acquire the modification, depot maintenance and repair of aircraft, vehicles and vessels as well as the production of components and other Defense-related articles, through competition between Department of Defense depot maintenance activities and private firms: *Provided*, That the Senior Acquisition Executive of the military department or defense agency concerned, with power of delegation, shall certify that successful bids include comparable estimates of all direct and indirect costs for both public and private bids: *Provided further*, That Office of Management and Budget Circular A–76 shall not apply to competitions conducted under this section.

[SEC. 8038. (a)(1) If the Secretary of Defense, after consultation with the United States Trade Representative, determines that a foreign country which is party to an agreement described in paragraph (2) has violated the terms of the agreement by discriminating against certain types of products produced in the United States that are covered by the agreement, the Secretary of Defense shall rescind the Secretary's blanket waiver of the Buy American Act with respect to such types of products produced in that foreign country.

(2) An agreement referred to in paragraph (1) is any reciprocal defense procurement memorandum of understanding, between the United States and a foreign country pursuant to which the Secretary of Defense has prospectively waived the Buy American Act for certain products in that country.

(b) The Secretary of Defense shall submit to the Congress a report on the amount of Department of Defense purchases from foreign entities in fiscal year 2000. Such report shall separately indicate the dollar value of items for which the Buy American Act was waived pursuant to any agreement described in subsection (a)(2), the Trade Agreement Act of 1979 (19 U.S.C. 2501 et seq.), or any international agreement to which the United States is a party.

(c) For purposes of this section, the term "Buy American Act" means title III of the Act entitled "An Act making appropriations for the Treasury and Post Office Departments for the fiscal year ending June 30, 1934, and for other purposes", approved March 3, 1933 (41 U.S.C. 10a et seq.).]

SEC. [8039.] *8022. Energy Cost Savings.* Appropriations contained in this Act that remain available at the end of the current fiscal year as a result of energy cost savings realized by the Department of Defense shall remain available for obligation for the next fiscal year to the extent, and for the purposes, provided in section 2865 of title 10, United States Code.

(INCLUDING TRANSFER OF FUNDS)

SEC. [8040.] *8023. Utilization of Amounts Deposited for Non-excess Property Leases.* Amounts deposited during the current fiscal year to the special account established under 40 U.S.C. 485(h)(2) and to the special account established under 10 U.S.C. 2667(d)(1) are appropriated and shall be available until transferred by the Secretary of Defense to current applicable appropriations or funds of the Department of Defense under the terms and conditions specified by 40 U.S.C. 485(h)(2)(A) and (B) and 10 U.S.C. 2667(d)(1)(B), to be merged with and to be available for the same time period and the same purposes as the appropriation to which transferred.

[SEC. 8041. During the current fiscal year, appropriations available to the Department of Defense may be used to reimburse a member of a reserve component of the Armed Forces who is not otherwise entitled to travel and transportation allowances and who occupies transient Government housing while performing active duty for training or inactive duty training: *Provided*, That such members may be provided lodging in kind if transient Government quarters are unavailable as if the member was entitled to such allowances under subsection (a) of section 404 of title 37, United States Code: *Provided further*, That if lodging in kind is provided, any authorized service charge or cost of such lodging may be paid directly from funds appropriated for operation and maintenance of the reserve component of the member concerned.]

[SEC. 8042. The President shall include with each budget for a fiscal year submitted to the Congress under section 1105 of title 31, United States Code, materials that shall identify clearly and separately the amounts requested in the budget for appropriation for that fiscal year for salaries and expenses related to administrative activities of the Department of Defense, the military departments, and the defense agencies.]

SEC. [8043.] *8024. Young Marines Program.* Notwithstanding any other provision of law, funds available for "Drug Interdiction and Counter-Drug Activities, Defense" may be obligated for the Young Marines program.

SEC. [8044.] *8025. Overseas Military Facility Investment Recovery Account.* During the current fiscal year, amounts contained in the Department of Defense Overseas Military Facility Investment Recovery Account established by section 2921(c)(1) of the National Defense Authorization Act of 1991 (Public Law 101–510; 10 U.S.C. 2687 note) shall be available until expended for the payments specified by section 2921(c)(2) of that Act[: *Provided*, That none of the funds made available for expenditure under this section may be transferred or obligated until 30 days after the Secretary of Defense submits a report which details the balance available in the Overseas Military Facility Investment Recovery Account, all projected income into the account during fiscal years 2000 and 2001, and the specific expenditures to be made using funds transferred from this account during fiscal year 2000].

[SEC. 8045. Of the funds appropriated or otherwise made available by this Act, not more than $119,200,000 shall be available for payment of the operating costs of NATO Headquarters: *Provided*, That the Secretary of Defense may waive this section for Department of Defense support provided to NATO forces in and around the former Yugoslavia.]

[SEC. 8046. During the current fiscal year, appropriations which are available to the Department of Defense for operation and maintenance may be used to purchase items having an investment item unit cost of not more than $100,000.]

[SEC. 8047. (a) During the current fiscal year, none of the appropriations or funds available to the Department of Defense Working Capital Funds shall be used for the purchase of an investment item for the purpose of acquiring a new inventory item for sale or anticipated sale during the current fiscal year or a subsequent fiscal year to customers of the Department of Defense Working Capital Funds if such an item would not have been chargeable to the Department of Defense Business Operations Fund during fiscal year 1994 and if the purchase of such an investment item would be chargeable during the current fiscal year to appropriations made to the Department of Defense for procurement.

(b) The fiscal year 2001 budget request for the Department of Defense as well as all justification material and other documentation supporting the fiscal year 2001 Department of Defense budget shall be prepared and submitted to the Congress on the basis that any equipment which was classified as an end item and funded in a procurement appropriation contained in this Act shall be budgeted for in a proposed fiscal year 2001 procurement appropriation and not in the supply management business area or any other area or category of the Department of Defense Working Capital Funds.]

SEC. [8048.] *8026. CIA Funding Limit.* None of the funds appropriated by this Act for programs of the Central Intelligence Agency shall remain available for obligation beyond the current fiscal year, except for funds appropriated for the Reserve for Contingencies, which shall remain available until September 30, [2001] *2002*: *Provided*, That funds appropriated, transferred, or otherwise credited to the Central Intelligence Agency Central Services Working Capital Fund during this or any prior or subsequent fiscal year shall remain available until expended.

SEC. [8049.] *8027. General Defense Intelligence Program Systems.* Notwithstanding any other provision of law, funds made available in this Act for the Defense Intelligence Agency may be used for the design, development, and deployment of General Defense Intelligence Program intelligence communications and intelligence information systems for the Services, the Unified and Specified Commands, and the component commands.

[SEC. 8050. Of the funds appropriated by the Department of Defense under the heading "Operation and Maintenance, Defense-Wide", not less than $8,000,000 shall be made available only for the mitigation of environmental impacts, including training and technical assistance to tribes, related administrative support, the gathering of information, documenting of environmental damage, and developing a system for prioritization of mitigation and cost to complete estimates for mitigation, on Indian lands resulting from Department of Defense activities.]

SEC. [8051.] *8028. National Science Center.* Amounts collected for the use of the facilities of the National Science Center for Communications and Electronics during the current fiscal year pursuant to section 1459(g) of the Department of Defense Authorization Act, 1986, and deposited to the special account established under subsection 1459(g)(2) of that Act are appropriated and shall be available until expended for the operation and maintenance of the Center as provided for in subsection 1459(g)(2).

SEC. [8052.] *8029. Medical Facility Commanders.* None of the funds appropriated in this Act may be used to fill the commander's position at any military medical facility with a health care professional unless the prospective candidate can demonstrate professional administrative skills.

[SEC. 8053. (a) None of the funds appropriated in this Act may be expended by an entity of the Department of Defense unless the entity, in expending the funds, complies with the Buy American Act. For purposes of this subsection, the term "Buy American Act" means title III of the Act entitled "An Act making appropriations for the Treasury and Post Office Departments for the fiscal year ending June 30, 1934, and for other purposes", approved March 3, 1933 (41 U.S.C. 10a et seq.).

(b) If the Secretary of Defense determines that a person has been convicted of intentionally affixing a label bearing a "Made in America" inscription to any product sold in or shipped to the United States that is not made in America, the Secretary shall determine, in accordance with section 2410f of title 10, United States Code, whether the person should be debarred from contracting with the Department of Defense.

(c) In the case of any equipment or products purchased with appropriations provided under this Act, it is the sense of the Congress that any entity of the Department of Defense, in expending the appropriation, purchase only American-made equipment and products, provided that American-made equipment and products are cost-competitive, quality-competitive, and available in a timely fashion.]

SEC. [8054.] *8030. Unsolicited Proposals for Study, Analysis, or Consulting Services Contracts.* None of the funds appropriated by this Act shall be available for a contract for studies, analysis, or consulting services entered into without competition on the basis of an unsolicited proposal unless the head of the activity responsible for the procurement determines—

(1) as a result of thorough technical evaluation, only one source is found fully qualified to perform the proposed work;

(2) the purpose of the contract is to explore an unsolicited proposal which offers significant scientific or technological promise, represents the product of original thinking, and was submitted in confidence by one source; or

(3) the purpose of the contract is to take advantage of unique and significant industrial accomplishment by a specific concern, or to insure that a new product or idea of a specific concern is given financial support:

Provided, That this limitation shall not apply to contracts in an amount of less than $25,000, contracts related to improvements of equipment that is in development or production, or contracts as to which a civilian official of the Department of Defense, who has been confirmed by the Senate, determines that the award of such contract is in the interest of the national defense.

[SEC. 8055. (a) Except as provided in subsections (b) and (c), none of the funds made available by this Act may be used—

(1) to establish a field operating agency; or

(2) to pay the basic pay of a member of the Armed Forces or civilian employee of the department who is transferred or reassigned from a headquarters activity if the member or employee's place of duty remains at the location of that headquarters.

(b) The Secretary of Defense or Secretary of a military department may waive the limitations in subsection (a), on a case-by-case basis, if the Secretary determines, and certifies to the Committees on Appropriations of the House of Representatives and Senate that the grant-

(TRANSFER OF FUNDS)—Continued

ing of the waiver will reduce the personnel requirements or the financial requirements of the department.

(c) This section does not apply to field operating agencies funded within the National Foreign Intelligence Program.]

SEC. [8056.] *8031. Intelligence Authorization.* Funds appropriated by this Act and in Public Law 105–277, or made available by the transfer of funds in this Act and in Public Law 105–277 for intelligence activities are deemed to be specifically authorized by the Congress for purposes of section 504 of the National Security Act of 1947 (50 U.S.C. 414) during fiscal year [2000] *2001* until the enactment of the Intelligence Authorization Act for Fiscal Year 2000] *2001.*

SEC. [8057.] *8032. Adak Leasing.* Notwithstanding section 303 of Public Law 96–487 or any other provision of law, the Secretary of the Navy is authorized to lease real and personal property at Naval Air Facility, Adak, Alaska, pursuant to 10 U.S.C. 2667(f), for commercial, industrial or other purposes: *Provided,* That notwithstanding any other provision of law, the Secretary of the Navy may remove hazardous materials from facilities, buildings, and structures at Adak, Alaska, and may demolish or otherwise dispose of such facilities, buildings, and structures[: *Provided further,* That notwithstanding any other provision of law, not more than $4,650,000 of the funds provided under the heading "Operation and Maintenance, Army" in title II of this Act shall be available to the Secretary of the Army, acting through the Chief of Engineers, only for demolition and removal of facilities, buildings, and structures formerly used as a District Headquarters Office by the Corps of Engineers (Northwest Division, CENWW, Washington State), as described in the study conducted regarding the headquarters pursuant to the Energy and Water Development Appropriations Act, 1992 (Public Law 102–104; 105 Stat. 511)].

[*(RESCISSIONS)*]

[SEC. 8058. Of the funds provided in Department of Defense Appropriations Acts, the following funds are hereby rescinded as of the date of the enactment of this Act, from the following accounts and programs in the specified amounts:

"Other Procurement, Navy, 1998/2000", $2,167,000;

"Aircraft Procurement, Air Force, 1998/2000", $15,800,000;

"Other Procurement, Army, 1999/2001", $13,700,000;

"Aircraft Procurement, Navy, 1999/2001", $41,500,000;

Under the heading, "Shipbuilding and Conversion, Navy, 1999/2003":

New Attack Submarine, $32,400,000;

CVN–69, $11,400,000;

"Other Procurement, Navy, 1999/2001", $13,784,000;

"Aircraft Procurement, Air Force, 1999/2001", $29,729,000;

"Missile Procurement, Air Force, 1999/2001", $130,000,000;

"Research, Development, Test and Evaluation, Army, 1999/2000", $5,400,000;

"Research, Development, Test and Evaluation, Navy, 1999/2000", $14,900,000;

"Research, Development, Test and Evaluation, Air Force, 1999/2000", $15,900,000; and

"Research, Development, Test and Evaluation, Defense-Wide, 1999/2000", $23,500,000.]

[SEC. 8059. None of the funds available in this Act may be used to reduce the authorized positions for military (civilian) technicians of the Army National Guard, the Air National Guard, Army Reserve and Air Force Reserve for the purpose of applying any administratively imposed civilian personnel ceiling, freeze, or reduction on military (civilian) technicians, unless such reductions are a direct result of a reduction in military force structure.]

[SEC. 8060. None of the funds appropriated or otherwise made available in this Act may be obligated or expended for assistance to the Democratic People's Republic of North Korea unless specifically appropriated for that purpose.]

SEC. [8061.] *8033. National Guard Pay on State Duty.* During the current fiscal year, funds appropriated in this Act are available to compensate members of the National Guard for duty performed pursuant to a plan submitted by a Governor of a State and approved by the Secretary of Defense under section 112 of title 32, United States Code: *Provided,* That during the performance of such duty, the members of the National Guard shall be under State command and control: *Provided further,* That such duty shall be treated as full-time National Guard duty for purposes of sections 12602(a)(2) and (b)(2) of title 10, United States Code.

SEC. [8062] *8034. Reimbursements for Reserve Intelligence Personnel* Funds appropriated in this Act for operation and maintenance of the Military Departments, [Unified and Specified] *Combatant* Commands and Defense Agencies shall be available for reimbursement of pay, allowances and other expenses which would otherwise be incurred against appropriations for the National Guard and Reserve when members of the National Guard and Reserve provide intelligence or counterintelligence support to [Unified] *Combatant* Commands, Defense Agencies and Joint Intelligence Activities, including the activities and programs included within the National Foreign Intelligence Program (NFIP), the Joint Military Intelligence Program (JMIP), and the Tactical Intelligence and Related Activities (TIARA) aggregate: *Provided,* That nothing in this section authorizes deviation from established Reserve and National Guard personnel and training procedures.

[SEC. 8063. During the current fiscal year, none of the funds appropriated in this Act may be used to reduce the civilian medical and medical support personnel assigned to military treatment facilities below the September 30, 1999 level: *Provided,* That the Service Surgeons General may waive this section by certifying to the congressional defense committees that the beneficiary population is declining in some catchment areas and civilian strength reductions may be consistent with responsible resource stewardship and capitation-based budgeting.]

(INCLUDING TRANSFER OF FUNDS)

SEC. [8064. (a)] *8035. Pentagon Reservation Renovation Certification.* None of the funds appropriated in this Act may be transferred to or obligated from the Pentagon Reservation Maintenance Revolving Fund, unless the Secretary of Defense certifies that the total cost for the planning, design, construction and installation of equipment for the renovation of the Pentagon Reservation will not exceed $1,222,000,000.

[(b) The Secretary shall, in conjunction with the Pentagon Renovation, design and construct secure secretarial offices and support facilities and security-related changes to the subway entrance at the Pentagon Reservation.]

SEC. [8065.] *8036. Counter-drug Activity Fund Transfers.* (a) None of the funds available to the Department of Defense for any fiscal year for drug interdiction or counter-drug activities may be transferred to any other department or agency of the United States except as specifically provided in an appropriations law.

(b) None of the funds available to the Central Intelligence Agency for any fiscal year for drug interdiction and counter-drug activities may be transferred to any other department or agency of the United States except as specifically provided in an appropriations law.

(TRANSFER OF FUNDS)

SEC. [8066.] *8037. Transfers.* Appropriations available in this Act under the heading "Operation and Maintenance, Defense-Wide" for increasing energy and water efficiency in Federal buildings may, during their period of availability, be transferred to other appropriations or funds of the Department of Defense for projects related to increasing energy and water efficiency, to be merged with and to be available for the same general purposes, and for the same time period, as the appropriation or fund to which transferred.

[SEC. 8067. None of the funds appropriated by this Act may be used for the procurement of ball and roller bearings other than those produced by a domestic source and of domestic origin: *Provided,* That the Secretary of the military department responsible for such procurement may waive this restriction on a case-by-case basis by certifying in writing to the Committees on Appropriations of the House of Representatives and the Senate, that adequate domestic supplies are not available to meet Department of Defense requirements on a timely basis and that such an acquisition must be made in order to acquire capability for national security purposes.]

SEC. [8068.] *8038. Transportation of Relief Supplies.* Notwithstanding any other provision of law, funds available to the Department of Defense shall be made available to provide transportation of medical supplies and equipment, on a nonreimbursable basis, to American Samoa, and funds available to the Department of Defense shall be made available to provide transportation of medical supplies and equipment, on a nonreimbursable basis, to the Indian Health Service when it is in conjunction with a civil-military project.

[SEC. 8069. None of the funds in this Act may be used to purchase any supercomputer which is not manufactured in the United States, unless the Secretary of Defense certifies to the congressional defense committees that such an acquisition must be made in order to acquire capability for national security purposes that is not available from United States manufacturers.]

SEC. [8070.] *8039. Shipyard Manufacturing Program.* Notwithstanding any other provision of law, the Naval shipyards of the United States shall be eligible to participate in any manufacturing extension program financed by funds appropriated in this or any other Act.

[SEC. 8071. Notwithstanding any other provision of law, each contract awarded by the Department of Defense during the current fiscal year for construction or service performed in whole or in part in a State (as defined in section 381(d) of title 10, United States Code) which is not contiguous with another State and has an unemployment rate in excess of the national average rate of unemployment as determined by the Secretary of Labor, shall include a provision requiring the contractor to employ, for the purpose of performing that portion of the contract in such State that is not contiguous with another State, individuals who are residents of such State and who, in the case of any craft or trade, possess or would be able to acquire promptly the necessary skills: *Provided*, That the Secretary of Defense may waive the requirements of this section, on a case-by-case basis, in the interest of national security.]

[SEC. 8072. During the current fiscal year, the Army shall use the former George Air Force Base as the airhead for the National Training Center at Fort Irwin: *Provided*, That none of the funds in this Act shall be obligated or expended to transport Army personnel into Edwards Air Force Base for training rotations at the National Training Center.]

[SEC. 8073. (a) The Secretary of Defense shall submit, on a quarterly basis, a report to the congressional defense committees, the Committee on International Relations of the House of Representatives and the Committee on Foreign Relations of the Senate setting forth all costs (including incremental costs) incurred by the Department of Defense during the preceding quarter in implementing or supporting resolutions of the United Nations Security Council, including any such resolution calling for international sanctions, international peacekeeping operations, and humanitarian missions undertaken by the Department of Defense. The quarterly report shall include an aggregate of all such Department of Defense costs by operation or mission.

(b) The Secretary of Defense shall detail in the quarterly reports all efforts made to seek credit against past United Nations expenditures and all efforts made to seek compensation from the United Nations for costs incurred by the Department of Defense in implementing and supporting United Nations activities.]

[SEC. 8074. (a) LIMITATION ON TRANSFER OF DEFENSE ARTICLES AND SERVICES.—Notwithstanding any other provision of law, none of the funds available to the Department of Defense for the current fiscal year may be obligated or expended to transfer to another nation or an international organization any defense articles or services (other than intelligence services) for use in the activities described in subsection (b) unless the congressional defense committees, the Committee on International Relations of the House of Representatives, and the Committee on Foreign Relations of the Senate are notified 15 days in advance of such transfer.

(b) COVERED ACTIVITIES.—This section applies to—

(1) any international peacekeeping or peace-enforcement operation under the authority of chapter VI or chapter VII of the United Nations Charter under the authority of a United Nations Security Council resolution; and

(2) any other international peacekeeping, peace-enforcement, or humanitarian assistance operation.

(c) REQUIRED NOTICE.—A notice under subsection (a) shall include the following:

(1) A description of the equipment, supplies, or services to be transferred.

(2) A statement of the value of the equipment, supplies, or services to be transferred.

(3) In the case of a proposed transfer of equipment or supplies—

(A) a statement of whether the inventory requirements of all elements of the Armed Forces (including the reserve components) for the type of equipment or supplies to be transferred have been met; and

(B) a statement of whether the items proposed to be transferred will have to be replaced and, if so, how the President proposes to provide funds for such replacement.]

SEC. [8075.] *8040. Defense Export Loan Guarantees.* To the extent authorized by subchapter VI of chapter 148 of title 10, United States Code, the Secretary of Defense may issue loan guarantees in support of United States defense exports not otherwise provided for: *Provided*, That the total contingent liability of the United States for guarantees issued under the authority of this section may not exceed $15,000,000,000: *Provided further*, That the exposure fees charged and collected by the Secretary for each guarantee, shall be paid by the country involved and shall not be financed as part of a loan guaranteed by the United States: *Provided further*, That the Secretary shall provide quarterly reports to the Committees on Appropriations, Armed Services, and Foreign Relations of the Senate and the Committees on Appropriations, Armed Services, and International Relations in the House of Representatives on the implementation of this program: *Provided further*, That amounts charged for administrative fees and deposited to the special account provided for under section 2540c(d) of title 10, shall be available for paying the costs of administrative expenses of the Department of Defense that are attributable to the loan guarantee program under subchapter VI of chapter 148 of title 10, United States Code.

SEC. [8076.] *8041. Contractor Bonus.* None of the funds available to the Department of Defense under this Act shall be obligated or expended to pay a contractor under a contract with the Department of Defense for costs of any amount paid by the contractor to an employee when—

(1) such costs are for a bonus or otherwise in excess of the normal salary paid by the contractor to the employee; and

(2) such bonus is part of restructuring costs associated with a business combination.

[SEC. 8077. (a) None of the funds appropriated or otherwise made available in this Act may be used to transport or provide for the transportation of chemical munitions or agents to the Johnston Atoll for the purpose of storing or demilitarizing such munitions or agents.

(b) The prohibition in subsection (a) shall not apply to any obsolete World War II chemical munition or agent of the United States found in the World War II Pacific Theater of Operations.

(c) The President may suspend the application of subsection (a) during a period of war in which the United States is a party.]

[SEC. 8078. None of the funds provided in title II of this Act for "Former Soviet Union Threat Reduction" may be obligated or expended to finance housing for any individual who was a member of the military forces of the Soviet Union or for any individual who is or was a member of the military forces of the Russian Federation.]

(INCLUDING TRANSFER OF FUNDS)

SEC. [8079.] *8042. Reserve Pilot and Community Program Transfers.* During the current fiscal year, no more than $10,000,000 of appropriations made in this Act under the heading "Operation and Maintenance, Defense-Wide" may be transferred to appropriations available for the pay of military personnel, to be merged with, and to be available for the same time period as the appropriations to which transferred, to be used in support of such personnel in connection with support and services for eligible organizations and activities outside the Department of Defense pursuant to section 2012 of title 10, United States Code.

SEC. [8080.] *8043. Shipbuilding and Conversion.* For purposes of section 1553(b) of title 31, United States Code, any subdivision of appropriations made in this Act under the heading "Shipbuilding and Conversion, Navy" shall be considered to be for the same purpose as any subdivision under the heading "Shipbuilding and Conversion, Navy" appropriations in any prior year, and the 1 percent limitation shall apply to the total amount of the appropriation.

[SEC. 8081. During the current fiscal year, in the case of an appropriation account of the Department of Defense for which the period of availability for obligation has expired or which has closed under the provisions of section 1552 of title 31, United States Code, and which has a negative unliquidated or unexpended balance, an obligation or an adjustment of an obligation may be charged to any current appropriation account for the same purpose as the expired or closed account if—

(1) the obligation would have been properly chargeable (except as to amount) to the expired or closed account before the end of the period of availability or closing of that account;

(2) the obligation is not otherwise properly chargeable to any current appropriation account of the Department of Defense; and

(3) in the case of an expired account, the obligation is not chargeable to a current appropriation of the Department of Defense under the provisions of section 1405(b)(8) of the National Defense Authorization Act for Fiscal Year 1991, Public Law 101–510, as amended (31 U.S.C. 1551 note): *Provided*, That in the case of an expired account, if subsequent review or investigation discloses that there

(TRANSFER OF FUNDS)—Continued

was not in fact a negative unliquidated or unexpended balance in the account, any charge to a current account under the authority of this section shall be reversed and recorded against the expired account: *Provided further*, That the total amount charged to a current appropriation under this section may not exceed an amount equal to 1 percent of the total appropriation for that account.]

[*(TRANSFER OF FUNDS)*]

[SEC. 8082. Upon the enactment of this Act, the Secretary of Defense shall make the following transfers of funds: *Provided*, That the amounts transferred shall be available for the same purposes as the appropriations to which transferred, and for the same time period as the appropriation from which transferred: *Provided further*, That the amounts shall be transferred between the following appropriations in the amount specified:

From:

Under the heading, "Shipbuilding and Conversion, Navy, 1988/2001":

SSN–688 attack submarine program, $6,585,000;
CG–47 cruiser program, $12,100,000;
Aircraft carrier service life extension program, $202,000;
LHD–1 amphibious assault ship program, $2,311,000;
LSD–41 cargo variant ship program, $566,000;
T–AO fleet oiler program, $3,494,000;
AO conversion program, $133,000;
Craft, outfitting, and post delivery, $1,688,000;

To:

Under the heading, "Shipbuilding and Conversion, Navy, 1995/2001":

DDG–51 destroyer program, $27,079,000;

From:

Under the heading, "Shipbuilding and Conversion, Navy, 1989/2000":

DDG–51 destroyer program, $13,200,000;
Aircraft carrier service life extension program, $186,000;
LHD–1 amphibious assault ship program, $3,621,000;
LCAC landing craft, air cushioned program, $1,313,000;
T–AO fleet oiler program, $258,000;
AOE combat support ship program, $1,078,000;
AO conversion program, $881,000;
T–AGOS drug interdiction conversion, $407,000;
Outfitting and post delivery, $219,000;

To:

Under the heading, "Shipbuilding and Conversion, Navy, 1996/2000":

LPD–17 amphibious transport dock ship, $21,163,000;

From:

Under the heading, "Shipbuilding and Conversion, Navy, 1990/2002":

SSN–688 attack submarine program, $5,606,000;
DDG–51 destroyer program, $6,000,000;
ENTERPRISE refueling/modernization program, $2,306,000;
LHD–1 amphibious assault ship program, $183,000;
LSD–41 dock landing ship cargo variant program, $501,000;
LCAC landing craft, air cushioned program, $345,000;
MCM mine countermeasures program, $1,369,000;
Moored training ship demonstration program, $1,906,000;
Oceanographic ship program, $1,296,000;
AOE combat support ship program, $4,086,000;
AO conversion program, $143,000;
Craft, outfitting, post delivery, and ship special support equipment, $1,209,000;

To:

Under the heading, "Shipbuilding and Conversion, Navy, 1990/2002":

T–AGOS surveillance ship program, $5,000,000;
Coast Guard icebreaker program, $8,153,000;

Under the heading, "Shipbuilding and Conversion, Navy, 1996/2002":

LPD–17 amphibious transport dock ship, $7,192,000;

Under the heading, "Shipbuilding and Conversion, Navy, 1998/2002":

CVN refuelings, $4,605,000;

From:

Under the heading, "Shipbuilding and Conversion, Navy, 1991/2001":

SSN–21(AP) attack submarine program, $1,614,000;
LHD–1 amphibious assault ship program, $5,647,000;
LSD–41 dock landing ship cargo variant program, $1,389,000;
LCAC landing craft, air cushioned program, $330,000;
AOE combat support ship program, $1,435,000;

To:

Under the heading, "Shipbuilding and Conversion, Navy, 1998/2001":

CVN refuelings, $10,415,000;

From:

Under the heading, "Shipbuilding and Conversion, Navy, 1992/2001":

SSN–21 attack submarine program, $11,983,000;
Craft, outfitting, post delivery, and DBOF transfer, $836,000;
Escalation, $5,378,000;

To:

Under the heading, "Shipbuilding and Conversion, Navy, 1998/2001":

CVN refuelings, $18,197,000;

From:

Under the heading, "Shipbuilding and Conversion, Navy, 1993/2002":

Carrier replacement program (AP), $30,332,000;
LSD–41 cargo variant ship program, $676,000;
AOE combat support ship program, $2,066,000;
Craft, outfitting, post delivery, and first destination transportation, and inflation adjustments, $2,127,000;

To:

Under the heading, "Shipbuilding and Conversion, Navy, 1998/2002":

CVN refuelings, $29,844,000;

Under the heading, "Shipbuilding and Conversion, Navy, 1999/2002":

Craft, outfitting, post delivery, conversions, and first destination transportation, $5,357,000;

From:

Under the heading, "Shipbuilding and Conversion, Navy, 1994/2003":

LHD–1 amphibious assault ship program, $23,900,000;
Oceanographic ship program, $9,000;

To:

Under the heading, "Shipbuilding and Conversion, Navy, 1994/2003":

DDG–51 destroyer program, $18,349,000;

Under the heading, "Shipbuilding and Conversion, Navy, 1995/1999":

DDG–51 destroyer program, $5,383,000;

Under the heading, "Shipbuilding and Conversion, Navy, 1996/2000":

LPD–17 amphibious transport dock ship, $168,000;

Under the heading, "Shipbuilding and Conversion, Navy, 1999/2003":

Craft, outfitting, post delivery, conversions, and first destination transportation, $9,000;

From:

Under the heading, "Shipbuilding and Conversion, Navy, 1996/2000":

SSN–21 attack submarine program, $10,100,000;
LHD–1 amphibious assault ship program, $7,100,000;

To:

Under the heading, "Shipbuilding and Conversion, Navy, 1996/2000":

DDG–51 destroyer program, $3,723,000;
LPD–17 amphibious transport dock ship, $13,477,000.]

[SEC. 8083. The Under Secretary of Defense (Comptroller) shall submit to the congressional defense committees by February 1, 2000, a detailed report identifying, by amount and by separate budget activity, activity group, subactivity group, line item, program element, program, project, subproject, and activity, any activity for which the fiscal year 2001 budget request was reduced because the Congress appropriated funds above the President's budget request for that specific activity for fiscal year 2000.]

SEC. [8084.] *8044. Supervision and Administrative Cost Obligations.* Funds appropriated in title II of this Act and for the Defense Health Program in title VI of this Act for supervision and administration costs for facilities maintenance and repair, minor construction, or design projects may be obligated at the time the reimbursable order is accepted by the performing activity: *Provided*, That for the purpose of this section, supervision and administration costs includes all in-house Government cost.

SEC. [8085.] *8045. Asia Pacific Center.* During the current fiscal year, the Secretary of Defense may waive reimbursement of the cost of conferences, seminars, courses of instruction, or similar educational activities of the Asia-Pacific Center for Security Studies for military officers and civilian officials of foreign nations if the Secretary determines that attendance by such personnel, without reimbursement, is in the national security interest of the United States: *Provided,* That costs for which reimbursement is waived pursuant to this subsection shall be paid from appropriations available for the Asia-Pacific Center.

SEC. [8086.] *8046. National Guard Distance Learning Equipment.* (a) Notwithstanding any other provision of law, the Chief of the National Guard Bureau may permit the use of equipment of the National Guard Distance Learning Project by any person or entity on a space-available, reimbursable basis. The Chief of the National Guard Bureau shall establish the amount of reimbursement for such use on a case-by-case basis.

(b) Amounts collected under subsection (a) shall be credited to funds available for the National Guard Distance Learning Project and be available to defray the costs associated with the use of equipment of the project under that subsection. Such funds shall be available for such purposes without fiscal year limitation.

[SEC. 8087. Using funds available by this Act or any other Act, the Secretary of the Air Force, pursuant to a determination under section 2690 of title 10, United States Code, may implement cost-effective agreements for required heating facility modernization in the Kaiserslautern Military Community in the Federal Republic of Germany: *Provided,* That in the City of Kaiserslautern such agreements will include the use of United States anthracite as the base load energy for municipal district heat to the United States Defense installations: *Provided further,* That at Landstuhl Army Regional Medical Center and Ramstein Air Base, furnished heat may be obtained from private, regional or municipal services, if provisions are included for the consideration of United States coal as an energy source.]

SEC. [8088.] *8047. Interest Penalties.* Notwithstanding 31 U.S.C. 3902, during the current fiscal year, interest penalties may be paid by the Department of Defense from funds financing the operation of the military department or defense agency with which the invoice or contract payment is associated.

[SEC. 8089. None of the funds appropriated in title IV of this Act may be used to procure end-items for delivery to military forces for operational training, operational use or inventory requirements: *Provided,* That this restriction does not apply to end-items used in development, prototyping, and test activities preceding and leading to acceptance for operational use: *Provided further,* That this restriction does not apply to programs funded within the National Foreign Intelligence Program: *Provided further,* That the Secretary of Defense may waive this restriction on a case-by-case basis by certifying in writing to the Committees on Appropriations of the House of Representatives and the Senate that it is in the national security interest to do so.]

[*(RESCISSIONS)*]

[SEC. 8090. Of the funds provided in the Department of Defense Appropriations Act, 1999 (Public Law 105–262), $452,100,000, to reflect savings from revised economic assumptions, is hereby rescinded as of the date of the enactment of this Act, or October 1, 1999, whichever is later, from the following accounts in the specified amounts:

"Aircraft Procurement, Army", $8,000,000;
"Missile Procurement, Army", $7,000,000;
"Procurement of Weapons and Tracked Combat Vehicles, Army", $9,000,000;
"Procurement of Ammunition, Army", $6,000,000;
"Other Procurement, Army", $19,000,000;
"Aircraft Procurement, Navy", $44,000,000;
"Weapons Procurement, Navy", $8,000,000;
"Procurement of Ammunition, Navy and Marine Corps", $3,000,000;
"Shipbuilding and Conversion, Navy", $37,000,000;
"Other Procurement, Navy", $23,000,000;
"Procurement, Marine Corps", $5,000,000;
"Aircraft Procurement, Air Force", $46,000,000;
"Missile Procurement, Air Force", $14,000,000;
"Procurement of Ammunition, Air Force", $2,000,000;
"Other Procurement, Air Force", $44,400,000;
"Procurement, Defense-Wide", $5,200,000;
"Chemical Agents and Munitions Destruction, Army", $5,000,000;
"Research, Development, Test and Evaluation, Army", $20,000,000;
"Research, Development, Test and Evaluation, Navy", $40,900,000;
"Research, Development, Test and Evaluation, Air Force", $76,900,000; and
"Research, Development, Test and Evaluation, Defense-Wide", $28,700,000:

Provided, That these reductions shall be applied proportionally to each budget activity, activity group and subactivity group and each program, project, and activity within each appropriation account.]

[SEC. 8091. The budget of the President for fiscal year 2001 submitted to the Congress pursuant to section 1105 of title 31, United States Code, and each annual budget request thereafter, shall include budget activity groups (known as "subactivities") in all appropriations accounts provided in this Act, as may be necessary, to separately identify all costs incurred by the Department of Defense to support the North Atlantic Treaty Organization and all Partnership For Peace programs and initiatives. The budget justification materials submitted to the Congress in support of the budget of the Department of Defense for fiscal year 2001, and subsequent fiscal years, shall provide complete, detailed estimates for all such costs.]

[SEC. 8092. None of the funds made available in this Act may be used to approve or license the sale of the F–22 advanced tactical fighter to any foreign government.]

SEC. [8093.] *8048. Buy America Waiver.* (a) The Secretary of Defense may, on a case-by-case basis, waive with respect to a foreign country each limitation on the procurement of defense items from foreign sources provided in law if the Secretary determines that the application of the limitation with respect to that country would invalidate cooperative programs entered into between the Department of Defense and the foreign country, or would invalidate reciprocal trade agreements for the procurement of defense items entered into under section 2531 of title 10, United States Code, and the country does not discriminate against the same or similar defense items produced in the United States for that country.

(b) Subsection (a) applies with respect to—

(1) contracts and subcontracts entered into on or after the date of the enactment of this Act; and

(2) options for the procurement of items that are exercised after such date under contracts that are entered into before such date if the option prices are adjusted for any reason other than the application of a waiver granted under subsection (a).

(c) Subsection (a) does not apply to a limitation regarding construction of public vessels, ball and roller bearings, food, and clothing or textile materials as defined by section 11 (chapters 50–65) of the Harmonized Tariff Schedule and products classified under headings 4010, 4202, 4203, 6401 through 6406, 6505, 7019, 7218 through 7229, 7304.41 through 7304.49, 7306.40, 7502 through 7508, 8105, 8108, 8109, 8211, 8215, and 9404.

[(d) None of the funds appropriated or otherwise provided for the Department of Defense in this or any other Act for any fiscal year may be obligated or expended for procurement of a nuclear-capable shipyard crane from a foreign source. Subsection (a) does not apply to the limitation in the preceding sentence.]

(d) Section 8093(d) of the Department of Defense Appropriations Act, 2000 (P.L. 106–79) is repealed.

[SEC. 8094. Funds made available to the Civil Air Patrol in this Act under the heading "Drug Interdiction and Counter-Drug Activities, Defense" may be used for the Civil Air Patrol Corporation's counterdrug program, including its demand reduction program involving youth programs, as well as operational and training drug reconnaissance missions for Federal, State, and local government agencies; for administrative costs, including the hiring of Civil Air Patrol Corporation employees; for travel and per diem expenses of Civil Air Patrol Corporation personnel in support of those missions; and for equipment needed for mission support or performance: *Provided,* That of these funds, $300,000 shall be made available to establish and operate a distance learning program: *Provided further,* That the Department of the Air Force should waive reimbursement from the Federal, State, and local government agencies for the use of these funds.]

SEC. [8095. Notwithstanding any other provision of law, the] *8049. TRICARE Contract Extension. The* TRICARE managed care support contracts in effect, or in final stages of acquisition as of September 30, [1999] *2000,* may be extended for 2 years: *Provided,* That any such extension may only take place if the Secretary of Defense deter-

(*TRANSFER OF FUNDS*)—Continued

mines that it is in the best interest of the Government *or is necessary to allow the Department sufficient time to reassess the structure and content of the managed care support contract program*: *Provided further*, That any contract extension shall be based on the price in the final best and final offer for the last year of the existing contract as adjusted for inflation and other factors mutually agreed to by the contractor and the Government[: *Provided further*, That notwithstanding any other provision of law, all future TRICARE managed care support contracts replacing contracts in effect, or in the final stages of acquisition as of September 30, 1999, may include a base contract period for transition and up to seven 1-year option periods].

[SEC. 8096. None of the funds in this Act may be used to compensate an employee of the Department of Defense who initiates a new start program without notification to the Office of the Secretary of Defense, the Office of Management and Budget, and the congressional defense committees, as required by Department of Defense financial management regulations.]

[SEC. 8097. In addition to the amounts provided elsewhere in this Act, notwithstanding any other provision of law, $5,000,000 is hereby appropriated to the Office of the Secretary of Defense, and is available only for a grant to the Women in Military Service for America Memorial Foundation, Inc., only for costs associated with completion of the "Women in Military Service For America" memorial at Arlington National Cemetery.]

SEC. [8098.] *8050*. TRAINING AND OTHER PROGRAMS. (a) PROHIBITION.—None of the funds made available by this Act may be used to support any training program involving a unit of the security forces of a foreign country if the Secretary of Defense has received credible information from the Department of State that the unit has committed a gross violation of human rights, unless all necessary corrective steps have been taken.

(b) MONITORING.—The Secretary of Defense, in consultation with the Secretary of State, shall ensure that prior to a decision to conduct any training program referred to in subsection (a), full consideration is given to all credible information available to the Department of State relating to human rights violations by foreign security forces.

(c) WAIVER.—The Secretary of Defense, after consultation with the Secretary of State, may waive the prohibition in subsection (a) if he determines that such waiver is required by extraordinary circumstances.

(d) REPORT.—Not more than 15 days after the exercise of any waiver under subsection (c), the Secretary of Defense shall submit a report to the congressional defense committees describing the extraordinary circumstances, the purpose and duration of the training program, the United States forces and the foreign security forces involved in the training program, and the information relating to human rights violations that necessitates the waiver.

SEC. [8099.] *8051. Surplus Dental Equipment.* The Secretary of Defense, in coordination with the Secretary of Health and Human Services, may carry out a program to distribute surplus dental equipment of the Department of Defense, at no cost to the Department of Defense, to Indian health service facilities and to federally-qualified health centers (within the meaning of section 1905(l)(2)(B) of the Social Security Act (42 U.S.C. 1396d(l)(2)(B))).

[SEC. 8100. Notwithstanding any other provision in this Act, the total amount appropriated in this Act is hereby reduced by $123,200,000 to reflect savings from the pay of civilian personnel, to be distributed as follows:

"Operation and Maintenance, Army", $30,900,000;
"Operation and Maintenance, Navy", $66,600,000;
"Operation and Maintenance, Air Force", $9,200,000; and
"Operation and Maintenance, Defense-Wide", $16,500,000.]

[SEC. 8101. Notwithstanding any other provision in this Act, the total amount appropriated in this Act is hereby reduced by $171,000,000 to reflect savings from favorable foreign currency fluctuations, to be distributed as follows:

"Military Personnel, Army", $19,100,000;
"Military Personnel, Navy", $2,200,000;
"Military Personnel, Air Force", $9,900,000;
"Operation and Maintenance, Army", $80,700,000;
"Operation and Maintenance, Navy", $13,700,000;
"Operation and Maintenance, Air Force," $26,900,000;
"Operation and Maintenance, Defense-Wide", $8,700,000; and
"Defense Health Program", $9,800,000.]

[SEC. 8102. Notwithstanding any other provision of law, the Secretary of Defense may retain all or a portion of the family housing at Fort Buchanan, Puerto Rico, as the Secretary deems necessary to meet military family housing needs arising out of the relocation of elements of the United States Army South to Fort Buchanan.]

[SEC. 8103. From within amounts made available in title II of this Act, under the heading "Operation and Maintenance, Army", and notwithstanding any other provision of law, $12,500,000 shall be available only for repairs and safety improvements to the segment of Fort Irwin Road which extends from Interstate 15 northeast toward the boundary of Fort Irwin, California and the originating intersection of Irwin Road: *Provided*, That these funds shall remain available until expended: *Provided further*, That the authorized scope of work includes, but is not limited to, environmental documentation and mitigation, engineering and design, improving safety, resurfacing, widening lanes, enhancing shoulders, and replacing signs and pavement markings: *Provided further*, That these funds may be used for advances to the Federal Highway Administration, Department of Transportation, for the authorized scope of work.]

[SEC. 8104. Funds appropriated to the Department of the Navy in title II of this Act may be available to replace lost and canceled Treasury checks issued to Trans World Airlines in the total amount of $255,333.24 for which timely claims were filed and for which detailed supporting records no longer exist.]

[SEC. 8105. None of the funds appropriated or made available in this Act to the Department of the Navy shall be used to develop, lease or procure the ADC(X) class of ships unless the main propulsion diesel engines and propulsors are manufactured in the United States by a domestically operated entity: *Provided*, That the Secretary of Defense may waive this restriction on a case-by-case basis by certifying in writing to the Committees on Appropriations of the House of Representatives and the Senate that adequate domestic supplies are not available to meet Department of Defense requirements on a timely basis and that such an acquisition must be made in order to acquire capability for national security purposes or there exists a significant cost or quality difference.]

[SEC. 8106. From within amounts made available in title II of this Act under the heading "Operation and Maintenance, Defense-Wide", and notwithstanding any other provision of law, $2,500,000 shall be available only for a grant for "America's Promise—The Alliance for Youth, Inc.", only to support, on a dollar-for-dollar matching basis with non-departmental funds, efforts to mobilize individuals, groups and organizations to build and strengthen the character and competence of the Nation's youth.]

[SEC. 8107. Of the funds made available in this Act, not less than $47,100,000 shall be available to maintain an attrition reserve force of 23 B–52 aircraft, of which $3,100,000 shall be available from "Military Personnel, Air Force", $34,500,000 shall be available from "Operation and Maintenance, Air Force", and $9,600,000 shall be available from "Aircraft Procurement, Air Force": *Provided*, That the Secretary of the Air Force shall maintain a total force of 94 B–52 aircraft, including 23 attrition reserve aircraft, during fiscal year 2000: *Provided further*, That the Secretary of Defense shall include in the Air Force budget request for fiscal year 2001 amounts sufficient to maintain a B–52 force totaling 94 aircraft.]

[SEC. 8108. Notwithstanding any other provision in this Act, the total amount appropriated in title II is hereby reduced by $100,000,000 to reflect savings resulting from reviews of Department of Defense missions and functions conducted pursuant to Office of Management and Budget Circular A–76, to be distributed as follows:

"Operation and Maintenance, Army", $34,300,000;
"Operation and Maintenance, Navy", $22,800,000;
"Operation and Maintenance, Marine Corps", $1,400,000; and
"Operation and Maintenance, Air Force", $41,500,000:

Provided, That none of the funds appropriated or otherwise made available by this Act may be obligated or expended for the purpose of contracting out functions directly related to the award of Department of Defense contracts, oversight of contractors with the Department of Defense, or the payment of such contractors including, but not limited to: contracting technical officers, contact administration officers, accounting and finance officers, and budget officers.]

[SEC. 8109. (a) REPORT ON OMB CIRCULAR A–76 REVIEWS OF WORK PERFORMED BY DOD EMPLOYEES.—The Secretary of Defense shall submit a report not later than 90 days after the enactment of this Act which lists all instances since 1995 in which missions or functions of the Department of Defense have been reviewed by the Department of Defense pursuant to OMB Circular A–76. The report shall list the disposition of each such review and indicate whether the review resulted in the performance of such missions or functions by Department of Defense civilian and military personnel, or whether such reviews resulted in performance by contractors. The report shall include a description of the types of missions or functions, the locations where the missions or functions are performed, the name of the contractor performing the work (if applicable), the cost to perform the missions or functions at the time the review was conducted, and the current cost to perform the missions or functions.

(b) REPORT ON OMB CIRCULAR A–76 REVIEWS OF WORK PERFORMED BY DOD CONTRACTORS.—The report shall also identify those instances in which work performed by a contractor has been converted to performance by civilian or military employees of the Department of Defense. For each instance of contracting in, the report shall include a description of the types of work, the locations where the work was performed, the name of the contractor that was performing the work, the cost of contractor performance at the time the work was contracted in, and the current cost of performance by civilian or military employees of the Department of Defense. In addition, the report shall include recommendations for maximizing the possibility of effective public-private competition for work that has been contracted out.

(c) COMPTROLLER GENERAL REVIEW.—Not later than 90 days after the date on which the Secretary submits the annual report, the Comptroller General shall submit to the House and Senate Committees on Appropriations the Comptroller General's views on whether the department has complied with the requirements for the report.]

[SEC. 8110. The budget of the President for fiscal year 2001 submitted to the Congress pursuant to section 1105 of title 31, United States Code, and each annual budget request thereafter, shall include separate budget justification documents for costs of United States Armed Forces' participation in contingency operations for the Military Personnel accounts, the Procurement accounts, and the Overseas Contingency Operations Transfer Fund: *Provided*, That these budget justification documents shall include a description of the funding requested for each anticipated contingency operation, for each military service, to include active duty and Guard and Reserve components, and for each appropriation account: *Provided further*, That these documents shall include estimated costs for each element of expense or object class, a reconciliation of increases and decreases for ongoing contingency operations, and programmatic data including, but not limited to troop strength for each active duty and Guard and Reserve component, and estimates of the major weapons systems deployed in support of each contingency.]

[*(INCLUDING TRANSFER OF FUNDS)*]

[SEC. 8111. In addition to amounts appropriated or otherwise made available in this Act, $35,000,000 is hereby appropriated, only to initiate and expand activities of the Department of Defense to prevent, prepare for, and respond to a terrorist attack in the United States involving weapons of mass destruction: *Provided*, That funds made available under this section shall be transferred to the following accounts:

"Reserve Personnel, Army", $2,000,000;

"National Guard Personnel, Army", $2,000,000;

"National Guard Personnel, Air Force", $500,000;

"Operation and Maintenance, Army", $24,500,000; and

"Research, Development, Test and Evaluation, Army", $6,000,000: *Provided further*, That funds transferred pursuant to this section shall be merged with and be available for the same purposes and for the same time period as the appropriation to which transferred: *Provided further*, That the transfer authority provided in this section is in addition to any other transfer authority available to the Department of Defense: *Provided further*, That of the funds transferred to "Operation and Maintenance, Army", not less than $3,000,000 shall be made available only to establish a cost effective counter-terrorism training program for first responders and concurrent testing of response apparatus and equipment at the Memorial Tunnel Facility: *Provided further*, That of the funds transferred to "Operation and Maintenance, Army", not less than $2,000,000 shall be made available only to support development of a structured undergraduate research program for chemical and biological warfare defense designed to produce graduates with specialized laboratory training and scientific skills required by military and industrial laboratories engaged in combating the threat of biological and chemical terrorism: *Provided further*, That of the funds transferred to "Operation and Maintenance, Army", not less than $3,500,000 shall be made available for a National Guard Bureau and Department of Justice collaborative training program only to enhance distance learning technologies and develop related courseware to provide training for counter-terrorism and related concerns: *Provided further*, That of the funds transferred to "Research, Development, Test and Evaluation, Army", not less than $3,000,000 shall be made available only to continue development and presentation of advanced distributed learning consequence management response courses and conventional courses.]

[SEC. 8112. (a) The Secretary of Defense shall, along with submission of the fiscal year 2001 budget request for the Department of Defense, submit to the congressional defense committees a report, in both unclassified and classified versions, which contains an assessment of the advantages or disadvantages of deploying a ground-based National Missile Defense system at more than one site.

(b) This report shall include, but not be limited to, an assessment of the following issues:

(1) The ability of a single site, versus multiple sites, to counter the expected ballistic missile threat.

(2) The optimum basing locations for a single and multiple site National Missile Defense system.

(3) The survivability and redundancy of potential National Missile Defense systems under a single or multiple site architecture.

(4) The estimated costs (including development, construction and infrastructure, and procurement of equipment) associated with different site deployment options.

(5) Other issues bearing on deploying a National Missile Defense system at one or more sites.]

[SEC. 8113. The Secretary of the Navy and the Secretary of the Air Force each shall submit a report to the congressional defense committees within 90 days of the enactment of this Act in both classified and unclassified form which shall provide a detailed description of the dedicated aggressor squadrons used to conduct combat flight training for the Navy, Marine Corps and Air Force covering the period from fiscal year 1990 through the present. For each year of the specified time period, each report shall provide a detailed description of the following: the assets which comprise dedicated aggressor squadrons including both aircrews, and the types and models of aircraft assigned to these squadrons; the number of training sorties for all forms of combat flight training which require aggressor aircraft, and the number of sorties that the dedicated aggressor squadrons can generate to meet these requirements; the ratio of the total inventory of attack and fighter aircraft to the number of aircraft available for dedicated aggressor squadrons; a comparison of the performance characteristics of the aircraft assigned to dedicated aggressor squadrons compared to the performance characteristics of the aircraft they are intended to represent in training scenarios; an assessment of pilot proficiency by year from 1986 to the present; service recommendations to enhance aggressor squadron proficiency to include number of dedicated aircraft, equipment, facilities, and personnel; and a plan that proposes improvements in dissimilar aircraft air combat training.]

SEC. [8114.] *8052. Family Housing Repair.* None of the funds appropriated or otherwise made available by this or other Department of Defense Appropriations Acts may be obligated or expended for the purpose of performing repairs or maintenance to military family housing units of the Department of Defense, including areas in such military family housing units that may be used for the purpose of conducting official Department of Defense business[: *Provided*, That the Department of Defense Office of the Inspector General shall provide a report to the House and Senate Committees on Appropriations not later than 90 days after the enactment of this Act which assesses the compliance of each of the military services with applicable appropriations law, Office of Management and Budget circulars, and Undersecretary of Defense (Comptroller) directives which govern funding for maintenance and repairs to flag officer quarters: *Provided further*, That this report shall include an assessment as to whether there have been violations of the Anti-Deficiency Act resulting from instances of improper funding of such maintenance and repair projects].

[SEC. 8115. Notwithstanding any other provision of law, funds appropriated in this Act under the heading "Research, Development, Test and Evaluation, Defense-Wide" for any advanced concept technology demonstration project may only be obligated 30 days after a report, including a description of the project and its estimated annual and total cost, has been provided in writing to the congressional defense committees: *Provided*, That the Secretary of Defense may waive this restriction on a case-by-case basis by certifying to the congressional defense committees that it is in the national interest to do so: *Provided further*, That none of the funds appropriated under the heading "Research, Development, Test and Evaluation, Defense-Wide" in the Department of Defense Appropriations Act, 1999 (Public Law 105–262) which remain available for obligation

(*TRANSFER OF FUNDS*)—Continued

are available for the Line of Sight Anti-Tank Program: *Provided further*, That of the funds appropriated under the heading "Research, Development, Test and Evaluation, Defense-Wide" in Public Law 105–262, $10,027,000 shall be available only for the Air Directed Surface to Air Missile.]

[SEC. 8116. None of the funds appropriated under the heading "Research, Development, Test and Evaluation, Defense-Wide" in the Department of Defense Appropriations Act, 1999 (Public Law 105–262) which remain available for obligation are available for the Medium Extended Air Defense System or successor systems.]

[SEC. 8117. Of the funds appropriated in title II of this Act under the heading "Operation and Maintenance, Army", $250,000 shall be available only for a grant to the Nebraska Game and Parks Commission for the purpose of locating, identifying the boundaries of, acquiring, preserving, and memorializing the cemetery site that is located in close proximity to Fort Atkinson, Nebraska. The Secretary of the Army shall require as a condition of such grant that the Nebraska Game and Parks Commission, in carrying out the purposes of which the grant is made, work in conjunction with the Nebraska State Historical Society. The grant under this section shall be made without regard to section 1301 of title 31, United States Code, or any other provision of law.]

[SEC. 8118. Notwithstanding any other provision of law, for the purpose of establishing all Department of Defense policies governing the provision of care provided by and financed under the military health care system's case management program under 10 U.S.C. 1079(a)(17), the term "custodial care" shall be defined as care designed essentially to assist an individual in meeting the activities of daily living and which does not require the supervision of trained medical, nursing, paramedical or other specially trained individuals: *Provided*, That the case management program shall provide that members and retired members of the military services, and their dependents and survivors, have access to all medically necessary health care through the health care delivery system of the military services regardless of the health care status of the person seeking the health care: *Provided further*, That the case management program shall be the primary obligor for payment of medically necessary services and shall not be considered as secondarily liable to title XIX of the Social Security Act, other welfare programs or charity based care.]

SEC. [8119.] *8053. Travel Card and Purchase Card Refunds.* During the current fiscal year—

(1) refunds attributable to the use of the Government travel card and refunds attributable to official Government travel arranged by Government Contracted Travel Management Centers may be credited to operation and maintenance accounts of the Department of Defense which are current when the refunds are received; and

(2) refunds attributable to the use of the Government Purchase Card by military personnel and civilian employees of the Department of Defense may be credited to accounts of the Department of Defense that are current when the refunds are received and that are available for the same purposes as the accounts originally charged.

[SEC. 8120. During the current fiscal year and hereafter, any Federal grant of funds to an institution of higher education to be available solely for student financial assistance or related administrative costs may be used for the purpose for which the grant is made without regard to any provision to the contrary in section 514 of the Departments of Labor, Health and Human Services, Education, and Related Agencies Appropriations Act, 1997 (10 U.S.C. 503 note), or section 983 of title 10, United States Code.]

[SEC. 8121. (a) REGISTERING INFORMATION TECHNOLOGY SYSTEMS WITH DOD CHIEF INFORMATION OFFICER.—After March 31, 2000, none of the funds appropriated in this Act may be used for a mission critical or mission essential information technology system (including a system funded by the defense working capital fund) that is not registered with the Chief Information Officer of the Department of Defense. A system shall be considered to be registered with that officer upon the furnishing to that officer of notice of the system, together with such information concerning the system as the Secretary of Defense may prescribe. An information technology system shall be considered a mission critical or mission essential information technology system as defined by the Secretary of Defense.

(b) CERTIFICATIONS AS TO COMPLIANCE WITH CLINGER-COHEN ACT.—(1) During fiscal year 2000, a major automated information system may not receive Milestone I approval, Milestone II approval, or Milestone III approval within the Department of Defense until the Chief Information Officer certifies, with respect to that milestone, that the system is being developed in accordance with the Clinger-Cohen Act of 1996 (40 U.S.C. 1401 et seq.). The Chief Information Officer may require additional certifications, as appropriate, with respect to any such system.

(2) The Chief Information Officer shall provide the congressional defense committees timely notification of certifications under paragraph (1). Each such notification shall include, at a minimum, the funding baseline and milestone schedule for each system covered by such a certification and confirmation that the following steps have been taken with respect to the system:

(A) Business process reengineering.

(B) An analysis of alternatives.

(C) An economic analysis that includes a calculation of the return on investment.

(D) Performance measures.

(E) An information assurance strategy consistent with the Department's Command, Control, Communications, Computers, Intelligence, Surveillance, and Reconnaissance (C4ISR) Architecture Framework.

(c) DEFINITIONS.—For purposes of this section:

(1) The term "Chief Information Officer" means the senior official of the Department of Defense designated by the Secretary of Defense pursuant to section 3506 of title 44, United States Code.

(2) The term "information technology system" has the meaning given the term "information technology" in section 5002 of the Clinger-Cohen Act of 1996 (40 U.S.C. 1401).

(3) The term "major automated information system" has the meaning given that term in Department of Defense Directive 5000.1.]

SEC. [8122.] *8054. Payment of Arrears to DoD.* During the current fiscal year, none of the funds available to the Department of Defense may be used to provide support to another department or agency of the United States if such department or agency is more than 90 days in arrears in making payment to the Department of Defense for goods or services previously provided to such department or agency on a reimbursable basis: *Provided*, That this restriction shall not apply if the department is authorized by law to provide support to such department or agency on a nonreimbursable basis, and is providing the requested support pursuant to such authority: *Provided further*, That the Secretary of Defense may waive this restriction on a case-by-case basis by certifying in writing to the Committees on Appropriations of the House of Representatives and the Senate that it is in the national security interest to do so.

[SEC. 8123. (a) RECOVERY OF CERTAIN DOD ADMINISTRATIVE EXPENSES IN CONNECTION WITH FOREIGN MILITARY SALES PROGRAM.—Charges for administrative services calculated under section 21(e) of the Arms Export Control Act (22 U.S.C. 2761(e)) in connection with the sale of defense articles or defense services shall (notwithstanding paragraph (3) of section 43(b) of such Act (22 U.S.C. 2792(b))) include recovery of administrative expenses incurred by the Department of Defense during fiscal year 2000 that are attributable to: (1) salaries of members of the Armed Forces; and (2) unfunded estimated costs of civilian retirement and other benefits.

(b) REIMBURSEMENT OF APPLICABLE MILITARY PERSONNEL ACCOUNTS.—During the current fiscal year, amounts in the Foreign Military Sales Trust Fund shall be available in an amount not to exceed $63,000,000 to reimburse the applicable military personnel accounts in title I of this Act for the value of administrative expenses referred to in subsection (a)(1).

(c) REDUCTIONS TO REFLECT AMOUNTS EXPECTED TO BE RECOVERED.—(1) The amounts in title I of this Act are hereby reduced by an aggregate of $63,000,000 (such amount being the amount expected to be recovered by reason of subsection (a)(1)).

(2) The amounts in title II of this Act are hereby reduced by an aggregate of $31,000,000 (such amount being that amount expected to be recovered by reason of subsection (a)(2)).]

[SEC. 8124. (a) The Communications Act of 1934 is amended in section 337(b) (47 U.S.C. 337(b)), by deleting paragraph (2). Upon the enactment of this provision, the Federal Communications Commission shall initiate the competitive bidding process in fiscal year 1999 and shall conduct the competitive bidding in a manner that ensures that all proceeds of such bidding are deposited in accordance with section 309(j)(8) of the Act not later than September 30, 2000. To expedite the assignment by competitive bidding of the frequencies identified in section 337(a)(2) of the Act, the rules governing such frequencies shall be effective immediately upon publication in the Federal Register, notwithstanding 5 U.S.C. 553(d), 801(a)(3), 804(2), and 806(a). Chapter 6 of such title, 15 U.S.C. 632, and 44 U.S.C. 3507 and 3512, shall not apply to the rules and competitive bidding procedures governing such frequencies. Notwithstanding section 309(b) of the Act, no application for an instrument of authorization for such frequencies shall be granted by the Commission earlier than 7 days following issuance of public notice by the Commission of the acceptance for filing of such application or of any substantial amendment thereto. Notwithstanding section 309(d)(1) of such Act, the Commission may specify a period (no less than 5 days following issuance of such public notice) for the filing of petitions to deny any application for an instrument of authorization for such frequencies.

(b)(1) Not later than 15 days after the date of the enactment of this Act, the Director of the Office of Management and Budget and the Federal Communications Commission shall each submit to the appropriate congressional committees a report which shall—

(A) set forth the anticipated schedule (including specific dates) for—

(i) preparing and conducting the competitive bidding process required by subsection (a); and

(ii) depositing the receipts of the competitive bidding process;

(B) set forth each signficant milestone in the rulemaking process with respect to the competitive bidding process;

(C) include an explanation of the effect of each requirement in subsection (a) on the schedule for the competitive bidding process and any post-bidding activities (including the deposit of receipts) when compared with the schedule for the competitive bidding and any post-bidding activities (including the deposit of receipts) that would otherwise have occurred under section 337(b)(2) of the Communications Act of 1934 (47 U.S.C. 337(b)(2)) if not for the enactment of subsection (a);

(D) set forth for each spectrum auction held by the Federal Communications Commission since 1993 information on—

(i) the time required for each stage of preparation for the auction;

(ii) the date of the commencement and of the completion of the auction;

(iii) the time which elapsed between the date of the completion of the auction and the date of the first deposit of receipts from the auction in the Treasury; and

(iv) the dates of all subsequent deposits of receipts from the auction in the Treasury; and

(E) include an assessment of how the stages of the competitive bidding process required by subsection (a), including preparation, commencement and completion, and deposit of receipts, will differ from similar stages in the auctions referred to in subparagraph (D).

(2) Not later than October 5, 2000, the Director of the Office of Management and Budget and the Federal Communications Commission shall each submit to the appropriate congressional committees the report which shall—

(A) describe the course of the competitive bidding process required by subsection (a) through September 30, 2000, including the amount of any receipts from the competitive bidding process deposited in the Treasury as of September 30, 2000; and

(B) if the course of the competitive bidding process has included any deviations from the schedule set forth under paragraph (1)(A), an explanation for such deviations from the schedule.

(3) The Federal Communications Commission may not consult with the Director in the preparation and submittal of the reports required of the Commission by this subsection.

(4) In this subsection, the term "appropriate congressional committees" means the following:

(A) The Committees on Appropriations, the Budget, and Commerce of the Senate.

(B) The Committees on Appropriations, the Budget, and Commerce of the House of Representatives.

(c) Nothing in this section shall be construed to supercede the requirements placed on the Federal Communications Commission by 47 U.S.C. 337(d)(4).]

[SEC. 8125. (a) REPORT REQUIRED.—Not later than January 31, 2000, the Secretary of Defense shall submit to the congressional defense committees in both classified and unclassified form a report on the conduct of Operation Desert Fox and Operation Allied Force (also referred to as Operation Noble Anvil). The Secretary of Defense shall submit to such committees a preliminary report on the conduct of these operations not later than December 15, 1999. The report (including the preliminary report) should be prepared in consultation with the Chairman of the Joint Chiefs of Staff, the Commander in Chief of the United States Central Command, and the Commander in Chief of the United States European Command.

(b) REVIEW OF SUCCESSES AND DEFICIENCIES.—The report should contain a thorough review of the successes and deficiencies of these operations, with respect to the following matters:

(1) United States military objectives in these operations.

(2) With respect to Operation Allied Force, the military strategy of the North Atlantic Treaty Organization (NATO) to obtain said military objectives.

(3) The command structure for the execution of Operation Allied Force.

(4) The process for identifying, nominating, selecting, and verifying targets to be attacked during Operation Desert Fox and Operation Allied Force.

(5) A comprehensive battle damage assessment of targets prosecuted during the conduct of the air campaigns in these operations, to include—

(A) fixed targets, both military and civilian, to include bridges, roads, rail lines, airfields, power generating plants, broadcast facilities, oil refining infrastructure, fuel and munitions storage installations, industrial plants producing military equipment, command and control nodes, civilian leadership bunkers and military barracks;

(B) mobile military targets such as tanks, armored personnel carriers, artillery pieces, trucks, and air defense assets;

(C) with respect to Operation Desert Fox, research and production facilities associated with Iraq's weapons of mass destruction and ballistic missile programs, and any military units or organizations associated with such activities within Iraq; and

(D) a discussion of decoy, deception and counter-intelligence techniques employed by the Iraqi and Serbian military.

(6) The use and performance of United States military equipment, weapon systems, munitions, and national and tactical reconnaissance and surveillance assets (including items classified under special access procedures) and an analysis of—

(A) any equipment or capabilities that were in research and development and if available could have been used in these operations' respective theater of operations;

(B) any equipment or capabilities that were available and could have been used but were not introduced into these operations' respective theater of operations; and

(C) any equipment or capabilities that were introduced to these operations' respective theater of operations that could have been used but were not.

(7) Command, control, communications and operational security of NATO forces as a whole and United States forces separately during Operation Allied Force, including the ability of United States aircraft to operate with aircraft of other nations without degradation of capabilities or protection of United States forces.

(8) The deployment of United States forces and supplies to the theater of operations, including an assessment of airlift and sealift (to include a specific assessment of the deployment of Task Force Hawk during Operation Allied Force, to include detailed explanations for the delay in initial deployment, the suitability of equipment deployed compared to other equipment in the United States inventory that was not deployed, and a critique of the training provided to operational personnel prior to and during the deployment).

(9) The use of electronic warfare assets, in particular an assessment of the adequacy of EA–6B aircraft in terms of inventory, capabilities, deficiencies, and ability to provide logistics support.

(10) The effectiveness of reserve component forces including their use and performance in the theater of operations.

(11) The contributions of United States (and with respect to Operation Allied Force, NATO) intelligence and counterintelligence systems and personnel, including an assessment of the targeting selection and bomb damage assessment process.

(c) The report should also contain:

(1) An analysis of the transfer of operational assets from other United States Unified Commands to these operations' theater of operations and the impact on the readiness, warfighting capability and deterrence value of those commands.

(2) An analysis of the implications of these operations as regards the ability of United States Armed Forces and intelligence capabilities to carry out the current national security strategy, including—

(TRANSFER OF FUNDS)—Continued

(A) whether the Department of Defense and its components, and the intelligence community and its components, have sufficient force structure and manning as well as equipment (to include items such as munitions stocks) to deploy, prosecute and sustain operations in a second major theater of war as called for under the current national security strategy;

(B) which, if any aspects, of currently programmed manpower, operations, training and other readiness programs, and weapons and other systems are found to be inadequate in terms of supporting the national military strategy; and

(C) what adjustments need to be made to current defense planning and budgets, and specific programs to redress any deficiencies identified by this analysis.]

SEC. [8126.] *8053. Transfer of Ammunitiion.* None of the funds provided in this Act may be used to transfer to any nongovernmental entity ammunition held by the Department of Defense that has a center-fire cartridge and a United States military nomenclature designation of "armor penetrator", "armor piercing (AP)", "armor piercing incendiary (API)", or "armor-piercing incendiary-tracer (API–T)", except to an entity performing demilitarization services for the Department of Defense under a contract that requires the entity to demonstrate to the satisfaction of the Department of Defense that armor piercing projectiles are either: (1) rendered incapable of reuse by the demilitarization process; or (2) used to manufacture ammunition pursuant to a contract with the Department of Defense or the manufacture of ammunition for export pursuant to a License for Permanent Export of Unclassified Military Articles issued by the Department of State.

SEC. [8127]. *8055. National Guard Equipment Lease.* Notwithstanding any other provision of law, the Chief of the National Guard Bureau, or his designee, may waive payment of all or part of the consideration that otherwise would be required under 10 U.S.C. 2667, in the case of a lease of personal property for a period not in excess of 1 year to any organization specified in 32 U.S.C. 508(d), or any other youth, social, or fraternal non-profit organization as may be approved by the Chief of the National Guard Bureau, or his designee, on a case-by-case basis.

[SEC. 8128. In the current fiscal year and hereafter, funds appropriated for the Pacific Disaster Center may be obligated to carry out such missions as the Secretary of Defense may specify for disaster information management and related supporting activities in the geographic area of responsibility of the Commander in Chief, Pacific and beyond in support of a global disaster information network: *Provided*, That the Secretary may enable the Pacific Disaster Center and its derivatives to enter into flexible public-private cooperative arrangements for the delegation or implementation of some or all of its missions and accept and provide grants, or other remuneration to or from any agency of the Federal Government, State or local government, private source or foreign government to carry out any of its activities: *Provided further*, That the Pacific Disaster Center may not accept any remuneration or provide any service or grant which could compromise national security.]

[SEC. 8129. Notwithstanding any other provision in this Act, the total amount appropriated in title I of this Act is hereby reduced by $1,838,426,000 to reflect amounts appropriated in Public Law 106–31. This amount is to be distributed as follows:

"Military Personnel, Army", $559,533,000;
"Military Personnel, Navy", $436,773,000;
"Military Personnel, Marine Corps", $177,980,000;
"Military Personnel, Air Force", $471,892,000;
"Reserve Personnel, Army", $40,574,000;
"Reserve Personnel, Navy", $29,833,000;
"Reserve Personnel, Marine Corps", $7,820,000;
"Reserve Personnel, Air Force", $13,143,000;
"National Guard Personnel, Army", $70,416,000; and
"National Guard Personnel, Air Force", $30,462,000.]

[SEC. 8130. Notwithstanding any other provision of law, that not more than 35 percent of funds provided in this Act, may be obligated for environmental remediation under indefinite delivery/indefinite quantity contracts with a total contract value of $130,000,000 or higher.]

[SEC. 8131. Of the funds made available under the heading "Operation and Maintenance, Air Force", $5,000,000 shall be transferred to the Department of Transportation to enable the Secretary of Transportation to realign railroad track on Elmendorf Air Force Base.]

[SEC. 8132. None of the funds appropriated by this Act shall be used for the support of any nonappropriated funds activity of the Department of Defense that procures malt beverages and wine with nonappropriated funds for resale (including such alcoholic beverages sold by the drink) on a military installation located in the United States unless such malt beverages and wine are procured within that State, or in the case of the District of Columbia, within the District of Columbia, in which the military installation is located: *Provided*, That in a case in which the military installation is located in more than one State, purchases may be made in any State in which the installation is located: *Provided further*, That such local procurement requirements for malt beverages and wine shall apply to all alcoholic beverages only for military installations in States which are not contiguous with another State: *Provided further*, That alcoholic beverages other than wine and malt beverages, in contiguous States and the District of Columbia shall be procured from the most competitive source, price and other factors considered.]

[SEC. 8133. MULTI-YEAR AIRCRAFT LEASE PILOT PROGRAM. (a) The Secretary of the Air Force may establish a multi-year pilot program for leasing aircraft for operational support purposes, including transportation for the combatant Commanders in Chief, on such terms and conditions as the Secretary may deem appropriate, consistent with this section.

(b) Sections 2401 and 2401a of title 10, United States Code, shall not apply to any aircraft lease authorized by this section.

(c) Under the aircraft lease Pilot Program authorized by this section:

(1) The Secretary may include terms and conditions in lease agreements that are customary in aircraft leases by a non-Government lessor to a non-Government lessee.

(2) The term of any individual lease agreement into which the Secretary enters under this section shall not exceed 10 years.

(3) The Secretary may provide for special payments to a lessor if either the Secretary terminates or cancels the lease prior to the expiration of its term or aircraft are damaged or destroyed prior to the expiration of the term of the lease. Such special payments shall not exceed an amount equal to the value of one year's lease payment under the lease. The amount of special payments shall be subject to negotiation between the Air Force and lessors.

(4) Notwithstanding any other provision of law, any payments required under a lease under this section, and any payments made pursuant to subsection (3) above may be made from:

(A) appropriations available for the performance of the lease at the time the lease takes effect;

(B) appropriations for the operation and maintenance available at the time which the payment is due; and

(C) funds appropriated for those payments.

(5) The Secretary may lease aircraft, on such terms and conditions as the Secretary may deem appropriate, consistent with this section, through an operating lease consistent with OMB Circular A–11.

(6) The Secretary may exchange or sell existing aircraft and apply the exchange allowance or sale proceeds in whole or in part toward the cost of leasing replacement aircraft under this section.

(7) Lease arrangements authorized by this section may not commence until:

(A) The Secretary submits a report to the congressional defense committees outlining the plans for implementing the Pilot Program. The report shall describe the terms and conditions of proposed contracts and the savings in operations and support costs expected to be derived from retiring older aircraft as compared to the expected cost of leasing newer replacement aircraft.

(B) A period of not less than 30 calendar days has elapsed after submitting the report.

(8) Not later than 1 year after the date on which the first aircraft is delivered under this Pilot Program, and yearly thereafter on the anniversary of the first delivery, the Secretary shall submit a report to the congressional defense committees describing the status of the Pilot Program. The Report will be based on at least 6 months of experience in operating the Pilot Program.

(9) No lease of operational support aircraft may be entered into under this section after September 30, 2004.

(d) The authority granted to the Secretary of the Air Force by this section is separate from and in addition to, and shall not be construed to impair or otherwise affect, the authority of the Secretary to procure transportation or enter into leases under a provision of law other than this section.

(e) The authority provided under this section may be used to lease not more than a total of six aircraft for the purposes of providing operational support.]

[SEC. 8134. Notwithstanding any other provision in this Act, the total amount appropriated in this Act for "Operation and Maintenance, Air Force" is hereby reduced by $100,000,000 to reflect supplemental appropriations provided under Public Law 106–31 for Readiness/Munitions.]

[SEC. 8135. Section 8106(a) of the Department of Defense Appropriations Act, 1997 (titles I through VIII of the matter under section 101(b) of Public Law 104–208; 110 Stat. 3009–111; 10 U.S.C. 113 note), is amended—

(1) by striking "not later than June 30, 1997,"; and

(2) by striking "$1,000,000" and inserting "$500,000".]

[SEC. 8136. None of the funds provided for the Joint Warfighting Experimentation Program may be obligated until the Vice Chairman of the Joint Chiefs of Staff reports to the congressional defense committees on the role and participation of all unified and specified commands in the Joint Warfighting Experimentation Program.]

[SEC. 8137. In addition to the amounts appropriated or otherwise made available elsewhere in this Act for the Department of Defense, $5,000,000, to remain available until September 30, 2000 is hereby appropriated to the Department of Defense: *Provided*, That the Secretary of Defense shall make a grant in the amount of $5,000,000 to the American Red Cross for Armed Forces Emergency Services.]

[SEC. 8138. The Department of the Army is directed to conduct a live fire, side-by-side operational test of the air-to-air Starstreak and air-to-air Stinger missiles from the AH–64D Longbow helicopter. The operational test is to be completed utilizing funds provided for in this Act in addition to funding provided for this purpose in the Fiscal Year 1999 Defense Appropriations Act (Public Law 105–262): *Provided*, That notwithstanding any other provision of law, the department is to ensure that the development, procurement or integration of any missile for use on the AH–64 or RAH–66 helicopters, as an air-to-air missile, is subject to a full and open competition which includes the conduct of a live-fire, side-by-side test as an element of the source selection criteria: *Provided further*, That the Undersecretary of Defense (Acquisition and Technology) will conduct an independent review of the need, and the merits of acquiring an air-to-air missile to provide self-protection for the AH–64 and RAH–66 from the threat of hostile forces. The Secretary is to provide his findings in a report to the congressional defense committees, no later than March 31, 2000.]

[SEC. 8139. During the current fiscal year, under regulations prescribed by the Secretary of Defense, the Center of Excellence for Disaster Management and Humanitarian Assistance may also pay, or authorize payment for, the expenses of providing or facilitating education and training for appropriate military and civilian personnel of foreign countries in disaster management and humanitarian assistance: *Provided*, That not later than April 1, 2001, the Secretary of Defense shall submit to the congressional defense committees a report regarding the training of foreign personnel conducted under this authority during the preceding fiscal year for which expenses were paid under the section: *Provided further*, That the report shall specify the countries in which the training was conducted, the type of training conducted, and the foreign personnel trained.]

[SEC. 8140. Of the funds appropriated in title II under the heading "OPERATION AND MAINTENANCE, DEFENSE-WIDE" for the Office of the Special Assistant to the Deputy Secretary of Defense for Gulf War Illnesses, up to $10,000,000 may be made available for carrying out the first-year actions under the 5-year research plan outlined in the report entitled "Department of Defense Strategy to Address Low-Level Exposures to Chemical Warfare Agents (CWAs)", dated May 1999, that was submitted to committees of the Congress pursuant to section 247(d) of the Strom Thurmond National Defense Authorization Act for Fiscal Year 1999 (Public Law 105–261; 112 Stat. 1957).]

[SEC. 8141. (a) The Department of Defense is authorized to enter into agreements with the Veterans Administration and federally-funded health agencies providing services to Native Hawaiians for the purpose of establishing a partnership similar to the Alaska Federal Health Care Partnership, in order to maximize Federal resources in the provision of health care services by federally-funded health agencies, applying telemedicine technologies. For the purpose of this partnership, Native Hawaiians shall have the same status as other Native Americans who are eligible for the health care services provided by the Indian Health Service.

(b) The Department of Defense is authorized to develop a consultation policy, consistent with Executive Order No. 13084 (issued May 14, 1998), with Native Hawaiians for the purpose of assuring maximum Native Hawaiian participation in the direction and administration of governmental services so as to render those services more responsive to the needs of the Native Hawaiian community.

(c) For purposes of this section, the term "Native Hawaiian" means any individual who is a descendant of the aboriginal people who, prior to 1778, occupied and exercised sovereignty in the area that now comprises the State of Hawaii.]

[SEC. 8142. None of the funds appropriated or otherwise made available by this Act or any other Act may be made available for reconstruction activities in the Republic of Serbia (excluding the province of Kosovo) as long as Slobodan Milosevic remains the President of the Federal Republic of Yugoslavia (Serbia and Montenegro).]

[SEC. 8143. In addition to the amounts provided elsewhere in this Act, the amount of $5,000,000 is hereby appropriated for "OPERATION AND MAINTENANCE, DEFENSE-WIDE", to be available, notwithstanding any other provision of law, only for a grant to the United Service Organizations Incorporated, a federally chartered corporation under chapter 2201 of title 36, United States Code. The grant provided for by this section is in addition to any grant provided for under any other provision of law.]

[SEC. 8144. None of the funds in this Act shall be available to initiate a multi-year procurement contract for the Abrams M1A2 Tank Upgrade Program until 30 days after the Department of the Army has submitted a report to the Congress detailing its efforts to reduce the costs of the tank upgrade program, to include the effects and potential savings that would result from any alternate fixed price or fixed quantity option contracts.]

[SEC. 8145. The multi-year authority for the C–17 granted in this Act shall become effective once the Secretary of the Air Force certifies to the congressional defense committees that the average unit flyaway price of C–17 aircraft P121 through P180 purchased under a multi-year contract will be at least 25 percent below the average unit flyaway price of the C–17 under the current 80 aircraft multi-year procurement program, with both prices calculated in fiscal year 1999 dollars.]

[*(INCLUDING TRANSFER OF FUNDS)*]

[SEC. 8146. (a) In addition to amounts appropriated elsewhere in this Act, $1,000,000,000 is hereby appropriated for the F–22 program: *Provided*, That these funds shall only be available for transfer to the appropriate F–22 program R–1 and P–1 line items of titles IV and III of this Act for the purposes of F–22 program research, development, test and evaluation, and advance procurement: *Provided further*, That of this amount, not more than $277,100,000 may be transferred to the "Aircraft Procurement, Air Force" account only for advance procurement of F–22 aircraft: *Provided further*, That any funds transferred for F–22 advance procurement shall not be available for obligation until the Secretary of Defense certifies to the congressional defense committees that all 1999 Defense Acquisition Board exit criteria have been met: *Provided further*, That the transfer authority provided in this section is in addition to any other transfer authority contained elsewhere in this Act.

(b) Notwithstanding any other provision of law, the Secretary of Defense may use funds provided under this section and transferred to titles IV and III of this Act to continue acquisition of F–22 test aircraft for which procurement funding has been previously provided.

(c) The Secretary of the Air Force shall adjust the amounts of the limitations set forth in subsections (a) and (b) of section 217, Public Law 105–85 accordingly, and may modify any F–22 contracts to implement the requirements of this section.

(d) Funds appropriated in this Act or any other prior Act for "Research, Development, Test and Evaluation, Air Force" and "Aircraft Procurement, Air Force" may not be used for acquisition of more than a total of 17 flight-capable test vehicles for the F–22 aircraft program.

(e) The Secretary of the Air Force may not award a full funding contract for low-rate initial production for the F–22 aircraft program until—

(1) the first flight of an F–22 aircraft incorporating Block 3.0 software has been conducted;

(2) the Secretary of Defense certifies to the congressional defense committees that all Defense Acquisition Board exit criteria for the award of low-rate initial production of the aircraft have been met; and

(3) upon completion of the requirements under (e)(1) and (e)(2) the Director of Operational Test and Evaluation submits to the congressional defense committees a report assessing the adequacy

(TRANSFER OF FUNDS)—Continued

of testing to date to measure and predict performance of F–22 avionics systems, stealth characteristics, and weapons delivery systems.

(f) The funds transferred under the authority provided within this section shall be merged with and shall be available for the same purposes, and for the same time period, as the appropriation to which transferred.]

[*(INCLUDING TRANSFER OF FUNDS)*]

[SEC. 8147. (a) In addition to the amounts appropriated elsewhere in this Act, $300,000,000 is hereby appropriated for F–22 program termination liability or for other F–22 program contractual requirements in lieu of termination liability obligations: *Provided*, That these funds shall only be available for transfer to the appropriate F–22 program R–1 and P–1 line items of titles IV and III of this Act for the purposes specified in this section: *Provided further*, That the transfer authority provided in this section is in addition to any other transfer authority contained elsewhere in this Act: *Provided further*, That these funds shall not be available for expenditure until October 1, 2000.

(b) The funds transferred under the authority provided within this section shall be merged with and shall be available for the same purposes, and for the same time period, as the appropriation to which transferred.]

[SEC. 8148. In addition to the amounts provided elsewhere in this Act, the amount of $5,500,000 is hereby appropriated for "OPERATION AND MAINTENANCE, DEFENSE-WIDE", to be available, notwithstanding any other provision of law, only for a grant to the High Desert Partnership in Academic Excellence Foundation, Inc., for the purpose of developing, implementing, and evaluating a standards and performance based academic model at schools administered by the Department of Defense Education Activity.]

[SEC. 8149. None of the funds appropriated in this Act may be used for the payment of a fine or penalty that is imposed against the Department of Defense or a military department arising from an environmental violation at a military installation or facility unless the payment of the fine or penalty has been specifically authorized by law. For purposes of this section, expenditure of funds to carry out a supplemental environmental project that is required to be carried out as part of such a penalty shall be considered to be a payment of the penalty.]

[SEC. 8150. Section 8145 of the Department of Defense Appropriations Act, 1999 (Public Law 105–262; 112 Stat. 2340), is amended by inserting before the period at the end the following: ", and for such additional environmental restoration activities at such former base as may be accomplished within such total amount".]

[SEC. 8151. Of the funds made available in this Act under the heading "Operation and Maintenance, Defense-Wide", up to $5,000,000 shall be available to provide assistance, by grant or otherwise, to public school systems that have unusually high concentrations of special needs military dependents enrolled: *Provided*, That in selecting school systems to receive such assistance, special consideration shall be given to school systems in States that are considered overseas assignments.]

[SEC. 8152. Funds appropriated by the paragraph under the heading "MILITARY CONSTRUCTION TRANSFER FUND" in the 1999 Emergency Supplemental Appropriations Act (Public Law 106–31; 113 Stat. 85) may be transferred to military construction accounts, as authorized by that paragraph, and shall be merged with and shall be available for the same purposes and for the same time period as the account to which transferred.]

[SEC. 8153. Section 127 of the Military Construction Appropriations Act, 1995 (Public Law 103–307; 108 Stat. 1666) is amended—

(1) in subsection (B)(1), by striking "an amount" and all that follows and inserting "$3,400,000."; and

(2) by adding at the end the following:

"(i) COMPLETION OF CONVEYANCE BY END OF FISCAL YEAR 2000.—The Secretary shall endeavor to complete any conveyance under this section not later than September 30, 2000.".]

[SEC. 8154. Notwithstanding any other provision of law, funds appropriated in this Act under the heading "Operation and Maintenance, Army" shall be available for expenses associated with characterization and remediation activities at the Massachusetts Military Reservation, Cape Cod, Massachusetts, resulting from environmental problems pertaining to use of Camp Edwards as a training range and impact area and any administrative orders issued by the United States Environmental Protection Agency to address those problems.]

SEC. [8155.] *8056. Conveyance of Relocatable Housing Units.* (a) IN GENERAL.—Notwithstanding any other provision of law, the Secretary of the Air Force may convey at no cost to the Air Force, without consideration, to Indian tribes located in the States of North Dakota, South Dakota, Montana, and Minnesota relocatable military housing units located at Grand Forks Air Force Base and Minot Air Force Base that are excess to the needs of the Air Force.

(b) PROCESSING OF REQUESTS.—The Secretary of the Air Force shall convey, at no cost to the Air Force, military housing units under subsection (a) in accordance with the request for such units that are submitted to the Secretary by the Operation Walking Shield Program on behalf of Indian tribes located in the States of North Dakota, South Dakota, Montana, and Minnesota.

(c) RESOLUTION OF HOUSING UNIT CONFLICTS.—The Operation Walking Shield program shall resolve any conflicts among request of Indian tribes for housing units under subsection (a) before submitting requests to the Secretary of the Air Force under paragraph (b).

(d) INDIAN TRIBE DEFINED.—In this section, the term "Indian tribe" means any recognized Indian tribe included on the current list published by the Secretary of Interior under section 104 of the Federally Recognized Indian Tribe Act of 1994 (Public Law 103–454; 108 Stat. 4792; 25 U.S.C. 479a–1).

SEC. [8156.] *8057. Arrow Program.* Of the amounts appropriated in the Act under the heading "Research, Development, Test and Evaluation, Defense-Wide", $45,000,000 shall be available for the purpose of adjusting the cost-share of the parties under the Agreement between the Department of Defense and the Ministry of Defence of Israel for the Arrow Deployability Program.

[SEC. 8157. The Secretary of Defense shall fully identify and determine the validity of healthcare contract additional liabilities, requests for equitable adjustment, and claims for unanticipated healthcare contract costs: *Provided*, That the Secretary of Defense shall establish an equitable and timely process for the adjudication of claims, and recognize actual liabilities during the Department's planning, programming and budgeting process, including fiscal year 2000 supplemental appropriation requests if appropriate: *Provided further*, That not later than December 1, 1999, the Secretary of Defense shall submit a report to the congressional defense committees on the scope and extent of healthcare contract claims, and on the action taken to implement the provisions of this section: *Provided further*, That nothing in this section should be construed as congressional direction to liquidate or pay any claims that otherwise would not have been adjudicated in favor of the claimant.]

[SEC. 8158. Of the funds appropriated in title II of this Act under the heading "Operation and Maintenance, Defense-Wide", $8,000,000 shall be available only for a community retraining, reinvestment, and manufacturing initiative to be conducted by an academic consortia with existing programs in manufacturing and retraining: *Provided*, That the $8,000,000 made available in this section shall be obligated by grant not later than 15 days after the enactment of this Act.]

[SEC. 8159. (a) REPORT REQUIRED.—Not later than 90 days after the date of the enactment of this Act, the Secretary of Defense shall submit to the congressional defense committees a report on the management of the chemical weapons demilitarization program.

(b) REPORT ELEMENTS.—The report under subsection (a) shall include the following:

(1) A description and assessment of the current management structure of the chemical weapons demilitarization program, including the management of the assembled chemical weapons assessment (ACWA) program.

(2) An assessment of the feasibility and advisability for the management of the chemical weapons demilitarization program of the assignment of a panel for oversight of the management of program, which panel would—

(A) consist of officials of the Department of Defense and of other departments and agencies of the Federal Government having an interest in the safe and timely demilitarization of chemical weapons; and

(B) prepare annual reports on the schedule, cost, and effectiveness of the program.

(3) Any other matters relating to the management of the chemical weapons demilitarization program, including the improvement of the management of the program, that the Secretary considers appropriate.]

[SEC. 8160. Notwithstanding any other provision of law, all military construction projects for which funds were appropriated in Public Law 106–52 are hereby authorized.]

[SEC. 8161. The Secretary of Defense may treat the opening of the National D-Day Museum in New Orleans, Louisiana, as an official event of the Department of Defense for the purposes of the provision of support for ceremonies and activities related to that opening.]

[SEC. 8162. DWIGHT D. EISENHOWER MEMORIAL. (a) FINDINGS.—Congress finds that—

(1) the people of the United States feel a deep debt of gratitude to Dwight D. Eisenhower, who served as Supreme Commander of the Allied Forces in Europe in World War II and subsequently as 34th President of the United States; and

(2) an appropriate permanent memorial to Dwight D. Eisenhower should be created to perpetuate his memory and his contributions to the United States.

(b) COMMISSION.—There is established a commission to be known as the "Dwight D. Eisenhower Memorial Commission" (referred to in this section as the "Commission").

(c) MEMBERSHIP.—The Commission shall be composed of—

(1) four persons appointed by the President, not more than two of whom may be members of the same political party;

(2) four Members of the Senate appointed by the President Pro Tempore of the Senate in consultation with the Majority Leader and Minority Leader of the Senate, of which not more than two appointees may be members of the same political party; and

(3) four Members of the House of Representatives appointed by the Speaker of the House of Representatives in consultation with the Majority Leader and Minority Leader of the House of Representatives, of which not more than two appointees may be members of the same political party.

(d) CHAIR AND VICE CHAIR.—The members of the Commission shall select a Chair and Vice Chair of the Commission. The Chair and Vice Chair shall not be members of the same political party.

(e) VACANCIES.—Any vacancy in the Commission shall not affect its powers if a quorum is present, but shall be filled in the same manner as the original appointment.

(f) MEETINGS.—

(1) INITIAL MEETING.—Not later than 45 days after the date on which a majority of the members of the Commission have been appointed, the Commission shall hold its first meeting.

(2) SUBSEQUENT MEETINGS.—The Commission shall meet at the call of the Chair.

(g) QUORUM.—A majority of the members of the Commission shall constitute a quorum but a lesser number of members may hold hearings.

(h) NO COMPENSATION.—A member of the Commission shall serve without compensation, but may be reimbursed for expenses incurred in carrying out the duties of the Commission.

(i) DUTIES.—The Commission shall consider and formulate plans for such a permanent memorial to Dwight D. Eisenhower, including its nature, design, construction, and location.

(j) POWERS.—The Commission may—

(1) make such expenditures for services and materials for the purpose of carrying out this section as the Commission considers advisable from funds appropriated or received as gifts for that purpose;

(2) accept gifts to be used in carrying out this section or to be used in connection with the construction or other expenses of the memorial; and

(3) hold hearings, enter into contracts for personal services and otherwise, and do such other things as are necessary to carry out this section.

(k) REPORTS.—The Commission shall—

(1) report the plans under subsection (i), together with recommendations, to the President and the Congress at the earliest practicable date; and

(2) in the interim, make annual reports on its progress to the President and the Congress.

(l) APPLICABILITY OF OTHER LAWS.—The Federal Advisory Committee Act (5 U.S.C. App.) shall not apply to the Commission.

(m) APPROPRIATION OF FUNDS.—In addition to amounts provided elsewhere in this Act, there is appropriated to the Commission $300,000, to remain available until expended.]

SEC. [8163. (a)] *8058.* The Secretary of the Air Force may accept contributions from the State of New York for the project at Rome Research Site, Rome, New York authorized in section 2301(a) of the National Defense Authorization Act for Fiscal Year 2000, for purposes of carrying out military construction relating to the consolidation of Air Force Research Laboratory facilities at the Rome Research Site, Rome, New York. Any contributions received from the State of New York shall be in addition to the funds authorized for the project in section 2304(a)(1) of the National Defense Authorization Act for Fiscal Year 2000.

[(b) The item for "New York, Rome Research Site", in the table in section 2301(a) of the National Defense Authorization Act for Fiscal Year 2000 is amended by striking "12,800,000" and inserting "25,800,000".]

[SEC. 8164. Chapter 1 of title I of division B of the Omnibus Consolidated and Emergency Supplemental Appropriations Act, 1999 (Public Law 105–277; 112 Stat. 2681–553) is amended in the paragraph under the heading "Operation and Maintenance, Defense-Wide" by inserting before the period at the end the following: ": *Provided further*, That an amount not to exceed $75,000,000 of the funds provided under this heading shall remain available without fiscal year limitation after transfer from this account: *Provided further*, That, notwithstanding any other provision of law, the Secretary of Defense is authorized to transfer the funds referred to in the immediately preceding proviso to other activities of the Federal Government pursuant to section 1535 of title 31, United States Code (referred to as the 'Economy Act')".]

[SEC. 8165. REVIEW OF LOW DENSITY, HIGH DEMAND ASSETS. (a) REPORT TO CONGRESSIONAL DEFENSE COMMITTEES.—The Secretary of Defense shall submit to the congressional defense committees a report assessing the requirements, plans, and resources needed to maintain, update, modernize, restore, and expand the Department of Defense fleet of specialized aircraft and related equipment commonly described as "Low Density, High Demand Assets". The report shall be submitted no later than May 15, 2000 and shall be submitted in both classified and unclassified versions.

(b) ASSETS TO BE COVERED.—The report shall cover the following aircraft and equipment:

(1) Electronic warfare aircraft and specialized jamming equipment.

(2) Intelligence, surveillance, and reconnaissance (ISR) platforms and major systems, including—

(A) U–2 aircraft;

(B) AWACS aircraft;

(C) JSTARS aircraft;

(D) RIVET JOINT aircraft;

(E) tactical unmanned aerial vehicles (UAVs);

(F) interoperable/secure communications;

(G) command and control systems;

(H) new data links; and

(I) data fusion capability.

(3) Strategic and tactical airlift aircraft.

(4) Aerial refueling aircraft.

(5) Strategic bomber aircraft.

(c) REPORT ELEMENTS.—The report shall include for each asset specified in subsection (b) the following:

(1) A description of—

(A) inventory, age, capabilities, current deficiencies, usage rates, current and remaining service life, and expected rates of fatigue;

(B) ability to provide logistical support;

(C) planned replacement dates; and

(D) number of sorties, percentage of inventory used, and overall effectiveness in Operation Desert Fox and in Operation Allied Force.

(2) A comparison of the Department's plans and resource requirements to update, replace, modernize, or restore the asset as contained in the Future Years Defense Plan for fiscal year 2000 with those plans and resource requirements for that asset as contained in the Future Years Defense Plan for fiscal year 2001, and an explanation for any significant difference in those plans and requirements.

(3) A detailed listing, by fiscal year, of—

(A) the total amount required to fulfill mission needs statements and documented inventory objectives for the asset in order to improve critical warfighting capabilities over the next 10 years; and

(B) of that total amount for each such year, the portion (stated as an amount and as a percentage) that is not included in the fiscal year 2001 Future Years Defense Plan.]

[SEC. 8166. Of the funds appropriated in title II of this Act under the heading "Operation and Maintenance, Army", $5,000,000 shall

(TRANSFER OF FUNDS)—Continued

be available only for a grant to the Chicago Public Schools for conversion and expansion of the former Eighth Regiment National Guard Armory (Bronzeville).]

[SEC. 8167. Notwithstanding any other provision of law, $10,000,000, is hereby appropriated and authorized for "Military Construction, Army National Guard", to remain available until September 30, 2004, for construction, and, contributions therefor, of an Army Aviation Support Facility at West Bend, Wisconsin.]

[SEC. 8168. (a) PURPOSE.—The purpose of this section is to evaluate and demonstrate methods for more efficient operation of military installations through improved capital asset management and greater reliance on the public or private sector for less-costly base support services, where available.

(b) AUTHORITY.—(1) The Secretary of the Air Force may carry out at Brooks Air Force Base, Texas, a demonstration project to be known as the "Base Efficiency Project" to improve mission effectiveness and reduce the cost of providing quality installation support at Brooks Air Force Base.

(2) The Secretary may carry out the Project in consultation with the Community to the extent the Secretary determines such consultation is necessary and appropriate.

(3) The authority provided in this section is in addition to any other authority vested in or delegated to the Secretary, and the Secretary may exercise any authority or combination of authorities provided under this section or elsewhere to carry out the purposes of the Project.

(c) EFFICIENT PRACTICES.—(1) The Secretary may convert services at or for the benefit of the Base from accomplishment by military personnel or by Department civilian employees (appropriated fund or non-appropriated fund), to services performed by contract or provided as consideration for the lease, sale, or other conveyance or transfer of property.

(2) Notwithstanding section 2462 of title 10, United States Code, a contract for services may be awarded based on "best value" if the Secretary determines that the award will advance the purposes of a joint activity conducted under the Project and is in the best interest of the Department.

(3) Notwithstanding that such services are generally funded by local and State taxes and provided without specific charge to the public at large, the Secretary may contract for public services at or for the benefit of the Base in exchange for such consideration, if any, the Secretary determines to be appropriate.

(4)(A) The Secretary may conduct joint activities with the Community, the State, and any private parties or entities on or for the benefit of the Base.

(B) Payments or reimbursements received from participants for their share of direct and indirect costs of joint activities, including the costs of providing, operating, and maintaining facilities, shall be in an amount and type determined to be adequate and appropriate by the Secretary.

(C) Such payments or reimbursements received by the Department shall be deposited into the Project Fund.

(d) LEASE AUTHORITY.—(1) The Secretary may lease real or personal property located on the Base and not required at other Air Force installations to any lessee upon such terms and conditions as the Secretary considers appropriate and in the interest of the United States, if the Secretary determines that the lease would facilitate the purposes of the Project.

(2) Consideration for a lease under this subsection shall be determined in accordance with subsection (g).

(3) A lease under this subsection—

(A) may be for such period as the Secretary determines is necessary to accomplish the goals of the Project; and

(B) may give the lessee the first right to purchase the property at fair market value if the lease is terminated to allow the United States to sell the property under any other provision of law.

(4)(A) The interest of a lessee of property leased under this subsection may be taxed by the State or the Community.

(B) A lease under this subsection shall provide that, if and to the extent that the leased property is later made taxable by State governments or local governments under Federal law, the lease shall be renegotiated.

(5) The Department may furnish a lessee with utilities, custodial services, and other base operation, maintenance, or support services performed by Department civilian or contract employees, in exchange for such consideration, payment, or reimbursement as the Secretary determines appropriate.

(6) All amounts received from leases under this subsection shall be deposited into the Project Fund.

(7) A lease under this subsection shall not be subject to the following provisions of law:

(A) Section 2667 of title 10, United States Code, other than subsection (b)(1) of that section.

(B) Section 321 of the Act of June 30, 1932 (40 U.S.C. 303b).

(C) The Federal Property and Administrative Services Act of 1949 (40 U.S.C. 471 et seq.).

(e) PROPERTY DISPOSAL.—(1) The Secretary may sell or otherwise convey or transfer real and personal property located at the Base to the Community or to another public or private party during the Project, upon such terms and conditions as the Secretary considers appropriate for purposes of the Project.

(2) Consideration for a sale or other conveyance or transfer of property under this subsection shall be determined in accordance with subsection (g).

(3) The sale or other conveyance or transfer of property under this subsection shall not be subject to the following provisions of law:

(A) Section 2693 of title 10, United States Code.

(B) The Federal Property and Administrative Services Act of 1949 (40 U.S.C. 471 et seq.).

(4) Cash payments received as consideration for the sale or other conveyance or transfer of property under this subsection shall be deposited into the Project Fund.

(f) LEASEBACK OF PROPERTY LEASED OR DISPOSED.—(1) The Secretary may lease, sell, or otherwise convey or transfer real property at the Base under subsections (b) and (e), as applicable, which will be retained for use by the Department or by another military department or other Federal agency, if the lessee, purchaser, or other grantee or transferee of the property agrees to enter into a leaseback to the Department in connection with the lease, sale, or other conveyance or transfer of one or more portions or all of the property leased, sold, or otherwise conveyed or transferred, as applicable.

(2) A leaseback of real property under this subsection shall be an operating lease for no more than 20 years unless the Secretary of the Air Force determines that a longer term is appropriate.

(3)(A) Consideration, if any, for real property leased under a leaseback entered into under this subsection shall be in such form and amount as the Secretary considers appropriate.

(B) The Secretary may use funds in the Project Fund or other funds appropriated or otherwise available to the Department for use at the Base for payment of any such cash rent.

(4) Notwithstanding any other provision of law, the Department or other military department or other Federal agency using the real property leased under a leaseback entered into under this subsection may construct and erect facilities on or otherwise improve the leased property using funds appropriated or otherwise available to the Department or other military department or other Federal agency for such purpose.

(g) CONSIDERATION.—(1) The Secretary shall determine the nature, value, and adequacy of consideration required or offered in exchange for a lease, sale, or other conveyance or transfer of real or personal property or for other actions taken under the Project.

(2) Consideration may be in cash or in-kind or any combination thereof. In-kind consideration may include the following:

(A) Real property.

(B) Personal property.

(C) Goods or services, including operation, maintenance, protection, repair, or restoration (including environmental restoration) of any property or facilities (including non-appropriated fund facilities).

(D) Base operating support services.

(E) Improvement of Department facilities.

(F) Provision of facilities, including office, storage, or other usable space, for use by the Department on or off the Base.

(G) Public services.

(3) Consideration may not be for less than the fair market value.

(h) PROJECT FUND.—(1) There is established on the books of the Treasury a fund to be known as the "Base Efficiency Project Fund" into which all cash rents, proceeds, payments, reimbursements, and other amounts from leases, sales, or other conveyances or transfers, joint activities, and all other actions taken under the Project shall be deposited. All amounts deposited into the Project Fund are without fiscal year limitation.

(2) Amounts in the Project Fund may be used only for operation, base operating support services, maintenance, repair, or improvement

of Department facilities, payment of consideration for acquisitions of interests in real property (including payment of rentals for lease-backs), and environmental protection or restoration, in addition to or in combination with other amounts appropriated for these purposes.

(3) Subject to generally prescribed financial management regulations, the Secretary shall establish the structure of the Project Fund and such administrative policies and procedures as the Secretary considers necessary to account for and control deposits into and disbursements from the Project Fund effectively.

(4) All amounts in the Project Fund shall be available for use for the purposes authorized in paragraph (2) at the Base.

(i) FEDERAL AGENCIES.—(1)(A) Any Federal agency, its contractors, or its grantees shall pay rent, in cash or services, for the use of facilities or property at the Base, in an amount and type determined to be adequate by the Secretary.

(B) Such rent shall generally be the fair market rental of the property provided, but in any case shall be sufficient to compensate the Base for the direct and overhead costs incurred by the Base due to the presence of the tenant agency on the Base.

(2) Transfers of real or personal property at the Base to other Federal agencies shall be at fair market value consideration. Such consideration may be paid in cash, by appropriation transfer, or in property, goods, or services.

(3) Amounts received from other Federal agencies, their contractors, or grantees, including any amounts paid by appropriation transfer, shall be deposited in the Project Fund.

(j) REPORTS TO CONGRESS.—(1) Section 2662 of title 10, United States Code, shall not apply to transactions at the Base during the Project.

(2)(A) Not later than March 1 each year, the Secretary shall submit to the appropriate committees of the Congress a report on any transactions at the Base during the preceding fiscal year that would be subject to such section 2662.

(B) The report shall include a detailed cost analysis of the financial savings and gains realized through joint activities and other actions under the Project authorized by this section and a description of the status of the Project.

(k) LIMITATION.—None of the authorities in this section shall create any legal rights in any person or entity except rights embodied in leases, deeds, or contracts.

(l) EXPIRATION OF AUTHORITY.—The authority to enter into a lease, deed, permit, license, contract, or other agreement under this section shall expire on September 30, 2004.

(m) DEFINITIONS.—In this section:

(1) The term "Project" means the Base Efficiency Project authorized by this section.

(2) The term "Base" means Brooks Air Force Base, Texas.

(3) The term "Community" means the City of San Antonio, Texas.

(4) The term "Department" means the Department of the Air Force.

(5) The term "facility" means a building, structure, or other improvement to real property (except a military family housing unit as that term is used in subchapter IV of chapter 169 of title 10, United States Code).

(6) The term "joint activity" means an activity conducted on or for the benefit of the Base by the Department, jointly with the Community, the State, or any private entity, or any combination thereof.

(7) The term "Project Fund" means the Base Efficiency Project Fund established by subsection (h).

(8) The term "public services" means public services (except public schools, fire protection, and police protection) that are funded by local and State taxes and provided without specific charge to the public at large.

(9) The term "Secretary" means the Secretary of the Air Force or the Secretary's designee, who shall be a civilian official of the Department appointed by the President with the advice and consent of the Senate.

(10) The term "State" means the State of Texas.

(n) The authorities provided in this section shall not take effect until June 15, 2000.]

[SEC. 8169. Notwithstanding any other provision of this Act, the total amount appropriated in this Act is hereby reduced by $400,000,000, to be distributed as follows:

"Operation and Maintenance, Army", $115,000,000;

"Operation and Maintenance, Navy", $150,000,000;

"Operation and Maintenance, Marine Corps", $20,000,000; and

"Operation and Maintenance, Air Force", $115,000,000:

Provided, That of the unobligated amounts made available in section 2008 of title II, chapter 3 of Public Law 106–31, $400,000,000 shall be made available only for depot level maintenance and repair, as follows:

"Operation and Maintenance, Army", $115,000,000;

"Operation and Maintenance, Navy", $150,000,000;

"Operation and Maintenance, Marine Corps", $20,000,000; and

"Operation and Maintenance, Air Force", $115,000,000.]

[SEC. 8170. Notwithstanding any other provision of this Act, the total amount appropriated in this Act is hereby reduced by $550,000,000, to be distributed as follows:

"Operation and Maintenance, Army", $170,000,000;

"Operation and Maintenance, Navy", $170,000,000;

"Operation and Maintenance, Marine Corps", $40,000,000; and

"Operation and Maintenance, Air Force", $170,000,000:

Provided, That of the unobligated amounts made available in section 2007 of title II, chapter 3 of Public Law 106–31, $550,000,000 shall be made available only for spare and repair parts and associated logistical support necessary for the maintenance of weapons systems and equipment, as follows:

"Operation and Maintenance, Army", $170,000,000;

"Operation and Maintenance, Navy", $170,000,000;

"Operation and Maintenance, Marine Corps", $40,000,000; and

"Operation and Maintenance, Air Force", $170,000,000.]

[SEC. 8171. Notwithstanding any other provision of this Act, the total amount appropriated in this Act is hereby reduced by $100,000,000, to be distributed as follows:

"Operation and Maintenance, Army", $60,000,000;

"Operation and Maintenance, Navy", $20,000,000; and

"Operation and Maintenance, Air Force", $20,000,000:

Provided, That of the unobligated amounts made available in section 2011 of title II, chapter 3 of Public Law 106–31, $100,000,000 shall be made available only for base operations support costs at Department of Defense facilities, as follows:

"Operation and Maintenance, Army", $60,000,000;

"Operation and Maintenance, Navy", $20,000,000; and

"Operation and Maintenance, Air Force", $20,000,000.]

[SEC. 8172. Notwithstanding any other provision of this Act, the total amount appropriated in this Act is hereby reduced by $356,400,000, to be distributed as follows:

"Weapons Procurement, Navy", $50,900,000;

"Procurement of Ammunition, Navy and Marine Corps", $113,500,000;

"Aircraft Procurement, Air Force", $20,800,000; and

"Procurement of Ammunition, Air Force", $171,200,000:

Provided, That the Secretary of Defense shall allocate these reductions to reflect savings available as a result of the increased procurement of munitions resulting from funds made available in title II, chapter 3 of Public Law 106–31.]

[SEC. 8173. (a) Notwithstanding any other provision of this Act, amounts otherwise provided by this Act in title II for the following accounts and activities are reduced by the following amounts:

"Operation and Maintenance, Army", $1,572,947,000;

"Operation and Maintenance, Navy", $1,874,598,000;

"Operation and Maintenance, Marine Corps", $228,709,000;

"Operation and Maintenance, Air Force", $1,707,150,000;

"Operation and Maintenance, Defense-Wide", $939,341,000;

"Operation and Maintenance, Army Reserve", $120,072,000;

"Operation and Maintenance, Navy Reserve", $77,598,000;

"Operation and Maintenance, Marine Corps Reserve", $11,346,000;

"Operation and Maintenance, Air Force Reserve", $145,393,000;

"Operation and Maintenance, Army National Guard", $258,115,000;

"Operation and Maintenance, Air National Guard", $264,731,000;

in all: $7,200,000,000.

(b) In addition to amounts appropriated elsewhere in this Act there are hereby appropriated the following amounts for the following accounts:

"Operation and Maintenance, Army", $1,572,947,000;

"Operation and Maintenance, Navy", $1,874,598,000;

"Operation and Maintenance, Marine Corps", $228,709,000;

"Operation and Maintenance, Air Force", $1,707,150,000;

"Operation and Maintenance, Defense-Wide", $939,341,000;

"Operation and Maintenance, Army Reserve", $120,072,000;

"Operation and Maintenance, Navy Reserve", $77,598,000;

"Operation and Maintenance, Marine Corps Reserve", $11,346,000;

(TRANSFER OF FUNDS)—Continued

"Operation and Maintenance, Air Force Reserve", $145,393,000;

"Operation and Maintenance, Army National Guard", $258,115,000;

"Operation and Maintenance, Air National Guard", $264,731,000; in all; $7,200,000,000:

Provided, That the entire amount shall be available only to the extent an official budget request for $7,200,000,000, that includes designation of the entire amount of the request as an emergency requirement as defined in the Balanced Budget and Emergency Deficit Control Act of 1985, as amended, is transmitted by the President to the Congress: *Provided further*, That the entire amount is designated by the Congress as an emergency requirement pursuant to section 251(b)(2)(A) of such Act.]

[SEC. 8174. None of the funds appropriated or otherwise made available in this Act may be used for the American Heritage Rivers Initiative.]

[SEC. 8175. Notwithstanding any other provision of law, the Department of Defense shall make progress payments based on progress no less than 12 days after receiving a valid billing and the Department of Defense shall make progress payments based on cost no less than 19 days after receiving a valid billing.]

[SEC. 8176. Notwithstanding any other provision of law, the Department of Defense shall make adjustments in payment procedures and policies to ensure that payments are made no less than 29 days after receipt of a proper invoice.] *(Department of Defense Appropriations Act, 2000.)*

SEC. 8059. GLOBAL POSITIONING SYSTEM CIVIL REQUIREMENTS. Funds available to the Department of Defense for the Global Positioning System during the current fiscal year may be used to fund civil requirements associated with the satellite and ground control segments of such system's modernization program.

SEC. 8060. Of the amounts appropriated in this Act under the heading, "Operation and Maintenance, Defense-Wide," $115,000,000 shall remain available until expended: Provided, That notwithstanding any other provision of law, the Secretary of Defense is authorized to transfer such funds to other activities of the Federal Government.

GENERAL PROVISIONS—MILITARY CONSTRUCTION

SEC. 101. None of the funds appropriated in Military Construction Appropriations Acts shall be expended for payments under a cost-plus-a-fixed-fee contract for construction, where cost estimates exceed $25,000, to be performed within the United States, except Alaska, without the specific approval in writing of the Secretary of Defense setting forth the reasons therefor.

SEC. 102. Funds appropriated to the Department of Defense for construction shall be available for hire of passenger motor vehicles.

SEC. 103. Funds appropriated to the Department of Defense for construction may be used for advances to the Federal Highway Administration, Department of Transportation, for the construction of access roads as authorized by section 210 of title 23, United States Code, when projects authorized therein are certified as important to the national defense by the Secretary of Defense.

SEC. 104. None of the funds appropriated in this Act may be used to begin construction of new bases inside the continental United States for which specific appropriations have not been made.

SEC. 105. No part of the funds provided in Military Construction Appropriations Acts shall be used for purchase of land or land easements in excess of 100 percent of the value as determined by the Army Corps of Engineers or the Naval Facilities Engineering Command, except: (1) where there is a determination of value by a Federal court; (2) purchases negotiated by the Attorney General or his designee; (3) where the estimated value is less than $25,000; or (4) as otherwise determined by the Secretary of Defense to be in the public interest.

SEC. 106. None of the funds appropriated in Military Construction Appropriations Acts shall be used to: (1) acquire land; (2) provide for site preparation; or (3) install utilities for any family housing, except housing for which funds have been made available in annual Military Construction Appropriations Acts.

SEC. 107. None of the funds appropriated in Military Construction Appropriations Acts for minor construction may be used to transfer or relocate any activity from one base or installation to another, without prior notification to the Committees on Appropriations.

SEC. 108. No part of the funds appropriated in Military Construction Appropriations Acts may be used for the procurement of steel for any construction project or activity for which American steel producers, fabricators, and manufacturers have been denied the opportunity to compete for such steel procurement.

SEC. 109. None of the funds available to the Department of Defense for military construction or family housing during the current fiscal year may be used to pay real property taxes in any foreign nation.

SEC. 110. None of the funds appropriated in Military Construction Appropriations Acts may be used to initiate a new installation overseas without prior notification to the Committees on Appropriations.

[SEC. 111. None of the funds appropriated in Military Construction Appropriations Acts may be obligated for architect and engineer contracts estimated by the Government to exceed $500,000 for projects to be accomplished in Japan, in any NATO member country, or in countries bordering the Arabian Gulf, unless such contracts are awarded to United States firms or United States firms in joint venture with host nation firms.]

SEC. [112] *111.* None of the funds appropriated in Military Construction Appropriations Acts for military construction in the United States territories and possessions in the Pacific and on Kwajalein Atoll, or in countries bordering the Arabian Gulf, may be used to award any contract estimated by the Government to exceed $1,000,000 to a foreign contractor: *Provided*, That this section shall not be applicable to contract awards for which the lowest responsive and responsible bid of a United States contractor exceeds the lowest responsive and responsible bid of a foreign contractor by greater than 20 percent: *Provided further*, That this section shall not apply to contract awards for military construction on Kwajalein Atoll for which the lowest responsive and responsible bid is submitted by a Marshallese contractor.

[SEC. 113. The Secretary of Defense is to inform the appropriate committees of Congress, including the Committees on Appropriations, of the plans and scope of any proposed military exercise involving United States personnel 30 days prior to its occurring, if amounts expended for construction, either temporary or permanent, are anticipated to exceed $100,000.]

SEC. [114] *112.* Not more than 20 percent of the appropriations in Military Construction Appropriations Acts which are limited for obligation during the current fiscal year shall be obligated during the last 2 months of the fiscal year.

(TRANSFER OF FUNDS)

SEC. [115] *113.* Funds appropriated to the Department of Defense for construction in prior years shall be available for construction authorized for each such military department by the authorizations enacted into law during the current session of Congress.

SEC. [116] *114.* For military construction or family housing projects that are being completed with funds otherwise expired or lapsed for obligation, expired or lapsed funds may be used to pay the cost of associated supervision, inspection, overhead, engineering and design on those projects and on subsequent claims, if any.

SEC. [117] *115.* Notwithstanding any other provision of law, any funds appropriated to a military department or defense agency for the construction of military projects may be obligated for a military construction project or contract, or for any portion of such a project or contract, at any time before the end of the fourth fiscal year after the fiscal year for which funds for such project were appropriated if the funds obligated for such project: (1) are obligated from funds available for military construction projects; and (2) do not exceed the amount appropriated for such project, plus any amount by which the cost of such project is increased pursuant to law.

(TRANSFER OF FUNDS)

SEC. [118] *116.* During the 5-year period after appropriations available to the Department of Defense for military construction and family housing operation and maintenance and construction have expired for obligation, upon a determination that such appropriations will not be necessary for the liquidation of obligations or for making authorized adjustments to such appropriations for obligations incurred during the period of availability of such appropriations, unobligated balances of such appropriations may be transferred into the appropriation "Foreign Currency Fluctuations, Construction, Defense" to be merged with and to be available for the same time period and for the same purposes as the appropriation to which transferred.

[SEC. 119. The Secretary of Defense is to provide the Committees on Appropriations of the Senate and the House of Representatives with an annual report by February 15, containing details of the specific actions proposed to be taken by the Department of Defense during the current fiscal year to encourage other member nations of the North Atlantic Treaty Organization, Japan, Korea, and United States allies bordering the Arabian Gulf to assume a greater share of the common defense burden of such nations and the United States.]

(TRANSFER OF FUNDS)

SEC. [120] *117.* During the current fiscal year, in addition to any other transfer authority available to the Department of Defense, proceeds deposited to the Department of Defense Base Closure Account established by section 207(a)(1) of the Defense Authorization Amendments and Base Closure and Realignment Act (Public Law 100–526) pursuant to section 207(a)(2)(C) of such Act, may be transferred to the account established by section 2906(a)(1) of the Department of Defense Authorization Act, 1991, to be merged with, and to be available for the same purposes and the same time period as that account.

[SEC. 121. No funds appropriated pursuant to this Act may be expended by an entity unless the entity agrees that in expending the assistance the entity will comply with sections 2 through 4 of the Act of March 3, 1933 (41 U.S.C. 10a–10c, popularly known as the "Buy American Act").]

[SEC. 122. (a) In the case of any equipment or products that may be authorized to be purchased with financial assistance provided under this Act, it is the sense of the Congress that entities receiving such assistance should, in expending the assistance, purchase only American-made equipment and products.

(b) In providing financial assistance under this Act, the Secretary of the Treasury shall provide to each recipient of the assistance a notice describing the statement made in subsection (a) by the Congress.]

(TRANSFER OF FUNDS)

SEC. [123] *118.* Subject to 30 days prior notification to the Committees on Appropriations, such additional amounts as may be determined by the Secretary of Defense may be transferred to the Department of Defense Family Housing Improvement Fund from amounts appropriated for construction in "Family Housing" accounts, to be merged with and to be available for the same purposes and for the same period of time as amounts appropriated directly to the Fund: *Provided,* That appropriations made available to the Fund shall be available to cover the costs, as defined in section 502(5) of the Congressional Budget Act of 1974, of direct loans or loan guarantees issued by the Department of Defense pursuant to the provisions of subchapter IV of chapter 169, title 10, United States Code, pertaining to alternative means of acquiring and improving military family housing and supporting facilities.

[SEC. 124. None of the funds appropriated or made available by this Act may be obligated for Partnership for Peace Programs in the New Independent States of the former Soviet Union.]

[SEC. 125. (a) Not later than 60 days before issuing any solicitation for a contract with the private sector for military family housing the Secretary of the military department concerned shall submit to the congressional defense committees the notice described in subsection (b).

(b)(1) A notice referred to in subsection (a) is a notice of any guarantee (including the making of mortgage or rental payments) proposed to be made by the Secretary to the private party under the contract involved in the event of—

(A) the closure or realignment of the installation for which housing is provided under the contract;

(B) a reduction in force of units stationed at such installation; or

(C) the extended deployment overseas of units stationed at such installation.

(2) Each notice under this subsection shall specify the nature of the guarantee involved and assess the extent and likelihood, if any, of the liability of the Federal Government with respect to the guarantee.

(c) In this section, the term "congressional defense committees" means the following:

(1) The Committee on Armed Services and the Military Construction Subcommittee, Committee on Appropriations of the Senate.

(2) The Committee on Armed Services and the Military Construction Subcommittee, Committee on Appropriations of the House of Representatives.]

(TRANSFER OF FUNDS)

SEC. [126] *119.* During the current fiscal year, in addition to any other transfer authority available to the Department of Defense, amounts may be transferred from the account established by section 2906(a)(1) of the Department of Defense Authorization Act, 1991, to the fund established by section 1013(d) of the Demonstration Cities and Metropolitan Development Act of 1966 (42 U.S.C. 3374) to pay for expenses associated with the Homeowners Assistance Program. Any amounts transferred shall be merged with and be available for the same purposes and for the same time period as the fund to which transferred.

[SEC. 127. Not later than April 30, 2000, the Secretary of Defense shall submit to the congressional defense committees a report examining the adequacy of special education facilities and services available to the dependent children of uniformed personnel stationed in the United States. The report shall identify the following:

(1) The schools on military installations in the United States that are operated by the Department of Defense, other entities of the Federal Government, or local school districts.

(2) School districts in the United States that have experienced an increase in enrollment of 20 percent or more in the past five years resulting from base realignments or consolidations.

(3) The impact of increased special education requirements on student populations, student-teacher ratios, and financial requirements in school districts supporting installations designated by the military departments as compassionate assignment posts.

(4) The adequacy of special education services and facilities for dependent children of uniformed personnel within the United States, particularly at compassionate assignment posts.

(5) Corrective measures that are needed to adequately support the special education needs of military families, including such improvements as the renovation of existing schools or the construction of new schools.

(6) An estimate of the cost of needed improvements, and a recommended source of funding within the Department of Defense.]

SEC. [128] *120.* Notwithstanding this or any other provision of law, funds appropriated in Military Construction Appropriations Acts for operations and maintenance of family housing shall be the exclusive source of funds for repair and maintenance of all family housing units, including flag and general officer quarters: *Provided,* That not more than $25,000 per unit may be spent annually for the maintenance and repair of any general or flag officer quarters without 30 days advance prior notification of the appropriate committees of Congress[: *Provided further,* That beginning January 15, 2000 the Under Secretary of Defense (Comptroller) is to report annually to the Committees on Appropriations all operations and maintenance expenditures for each individual flag and general officer quarters for the prior fiscal year].

[SEC. 129. The first proviso under the heading "MILITARY CONSTRUCTION TRANSFER FUND" in chapter 6 of title II of the 1999 Emergency Supplemental Appropriations Act (Public Law 106–31) is amended by inserting "and to the North Atlantic Treaty Organization Security Investment Program as provided in section 2806 of title 10, United States Code" after "to military construction accounts": *Provided,* That funds transferred to the North Atlantic Treaty Organization Security Investment Program from the Military Construction Transfer Fund pursuant to such authority shall be available for all purposes of the Security Investment Program and shall remain available until expended.]

[SEC. 130. The Army, Navy, Marine Corps, and Air Force are directed to submit to the appropriate committees of the Congress by July 1, 2000, a Family Housing Master Plan demonstrating how they plan to meet the year 2010 housing goals with traditional construction, operation and maintenance support, as well as privatization initiative proposals. Each plan shall include projected life cycle costs for family housing construction, basic allowance for housing, operation and maintenance, other associated costs, and a time line for housing completions each year.]

[SEC. 131. Notwithstanding any other provision of law, no funds appropriated or otherwise made available by this Act or any other Act may be obligated or expended for any purpose relating to the construction at Bluegrass Army Depot, Kentucky, of any facility employing a specific technology for the demilitarization of assembled chemical munitions until the date on which the Secretary of Defense certifies to the Committees on Appropriations that the Department of Defense will complete a demonstration of the six alternatives to baseline incineration for the destruction of chemical agents and munitions as identified by the Program Evaluation Team of the Assembled Chemical Weapons Assessment program.]

SEC. 121. Upon a determination by the Secretary of Defense that such action is necessary in the national interest, he may, with the approval of the Office of Management and Budget, transfer not to exceed $67,000,000, of funds appropriated in this Act between appropriations, funds, or accounts, or any subdivision thereof contained in this Act, to be merged with and to be available for the same purposes, and for the same time period, as the appropriation, fund, or account to which transferred: Provided, That such authority to transfer may not be used unless for higher priority items, based on unforeseen military requirements, than those for which originally appropriated and in no case where the item for which funds are requested has been denied by Congress: Provided further, That the Secretary of Defense shall notify the Congress promptly of all transfers made pursuant to this authority. (Military Construction Appropriations Act, 2000.)

[SEC. 214. (a) Section 8175 of the Department of Defense Appropriations Act, 2000 (Public Law 106–79) is amended by striking section 8175 and inserting the following new section 8175:

"SEC. 8175. Notwithstanding any other provision of law, the Department of Defense shall make progress payments based on progress no less than 12 days after receiving a valid billing and the Department of Defense shall make progress payments based on cost no less than 19 days after receiving a valid billing: *Provided,* That this provision shall be effective only with respect to billings received during the last month of the fiscal year.".

(b) The amendment made by subsection (a) shall take effect as if included in the Department of Defense Appropriations Act, 2000 (Public Law 106–79), to which such amendment relates.]

[SEC. 215. (a) Section 8176 of the Department of Defense Appropriations Act, 2000 (Public Law 106–79) is amended by striking section 8176 and inserting the following new section 8176:

"SEC. 8176. Notwithstanding any other provision of law, the Department of Defense shall make adjustments in payment procedures and policies to ensure that payments are made no earlier than one day before the date on which the payments would otherwise be due under any other provision of law: *Provided,* That this provision shall be effective only with respect to invoices received during the last month of the fiscal year.".

(b) The amendment made by subsection (a) shall take effect as if included in the Department of Defense Appropriations Act, 2000 (Public Law 106–79), to which such amendment relates.]

[SEC. 216. The Office of Net Assessment in the Office of the Secretary of Defense, jointly with the United States Pacific Command, shall submit, through the Under Secretary of Defense (Policy), a report to Congress no later than 270 days after the enactment of this Act which addresses the following issues: (1) A review of the operational planning and other preparations of the United States Department of Defense, including but not limited to the United States Pacific Command, to implement the relevant sections of the Taiwan Relations Act since its enactment in 1979; and (2) a review of evaluation of all gaps in relevant knowledge about the People's Republic of China's capabilities and intentions as they might affect the current and future military balance between Taiwan and the People's Republic of China, including both classified United States intelligence information and Chinese open source writing. The report shall be submitted in classified form, with an unclassified summary.]

[SEC. 217. The Secretary of Defense, jointly with the Secretary of Veterans Affairs, shall submit a report to Congress no later than 90 days after the enactment of this Act assessing the adequacy of medical research activities currently underway or planned to commence in fiscal year 2000 to investigate the health effects of low-level chemical exposures of Persian Gulf military forces while serving in the Southwest Asia theater of operations. This report shall also identify and assess valid proposals (including the cost of such proposals) to accelerate medical research in this area, especially those aimed at studying, diagnosing, and developing treatment protocols for Gulf War veterans with multi-system symptoms and multiple chemical intolerances.]

[*(INCLUDING TRANSFER OF FUNDS)*]

[SEC. 218. In addition to amounts appropriated or otherwise made available in Public Law 106–79, $100,000,000 is hereby appropriated to the Department of the Army and shall be made available only for transfer to titles II, III, IV, and V of Public law 106–79 to meet readiness needs: *Provided,* That these funds may be used to initiate the fielding and equipping, to include leasing of vehicles for test and evaluation, of two prototype brigade combat teams at Fort Lewis, Washington: *Provided further,* That funds transferred pursuant to this section shall be merged with and be available for the same purposes and for the same time period as the appropriation to which transferred: *Provided further,* That the transfer authority provided in this section is in addition to any transfer authority available to the Department of Defense: *Provided further,* That none of the funds made available under this section may be obligated or expended until 30 days after the Chief of Staff of the Army submits a detailed plan for the expenditure of the funds to the congressional defense committees.]

[*(TRANSFER OF FUNDS)*]

[SEC. 219. Of the funds appropriated in Public Law 106–79, $500,000 shall be transferred from "Research, Development, Test, and Evaluation, Army" to "Operation and Maintenance, Defense-Wide": *Provided,* That funds transferred pursuant to this section shall be merged with and be available for the same purposes and for the same time period as the appropriation to which transferred.]

(Miscellaneous Appropriations, 2000, as enacted by section 1000(a)(5) of the Consolidated Appropriations Act, 2000 (P.L. 106–113).)

DEPARTMENT OF EDUCATION

OFFICE OF ELEMENTARY AND SECONDARY EDUCATION

Federal Funds

General and special funds:

EDUCATION REFORM

[For carrying out activities authorized by titles III and IV of the Goals 2000: Educate America Act, the School-to-Work Opportunities Act, and sections 3122, 3132, 3136, and 3141, parts B, C, and D of title III, and part I of title X of the Elementary and Secondary Education Act of 1965, $1,768,370,000, of which $456,500,000 for the Goals 2000: Educate America Act and $55,000,000 for the School-to-Work Opportunities Act shall become available on July 1, 2000 and remain available through September 30, 2001, and of which $109,500,000 shall be for section 3122: *Provided*, That none of the funds appropriated under this heading shall be obligated or expended to carry out section 304(a)(2)(A) of the Goals 2000: Educate America Act, except that no more than $1,500,000 may be used to carry out activities under section 314(a)(2) of that Act: *Provided further*, That section 315(a)(2) of the Goals 2000: Educate America Act shall not apply: *Provided further*, That up to one-half of 1 percent of the amount available under section 3132 shall be set aside for the outlying areas, to be distributed on the basis of their relative need as determined by the Secretary in accordance with the purposes of the program: *Provided further*, That if any State educational agency does not apply for a grant under section 3132, that State's allotment under section 3131 shall be reserved by the Secretary for grants to local educational agencies in that State that apply directly to the Secretary according to the terms and conditions published by the Secretary in the Federal Register: *Provided further*, That of the funds made available to carry out section 3136 and notwithstanding any other provision of law, $500,000 shall be awarded to the Houston Independent School District for technology infrastructure, $8,000,000 shall be awarded to the I CAN LEARN program, $3,000,000 shall be awarded to the Linking Education Technology and Educational Reform (LINKS) project for educational technology, $1,000,000 shall be awarded to the Center for Advanced Research and Technology (CART) for comprehensive secondary education reform, $250,000 shall be awarded to the Vaughn Reno Starks Community Center in Elizabethtown, Kentucky for a technology program, $125,000 shall be awarded to the Wyandanch Compel Youth Academy Educational Assistance Program in New York, $3,000,000 shall be awarded to Hi-Technology High School in San Bernardino County, California for technology enhancement, $300,000 shall be awarded to the Long Island 21st Century Technology and E-Commerce Alliance, $800,000 shall be awarded to Montana State University-Billings for a distance learning initiative, $2,000,000 for the Tupelo School District in Tupelo, Mississippi for technology innovation in education, $900,000 for the University of Alaska at Anchorage for distance learning education, $1,000,000 shall be awarded to the Seton Hill College in Greensburg, Pennsylvania for a model education technology training program, $500,000 shall be awarded to the University of Alaska-Fairbanks, in Fairbanks, Alaska for a teacher technology training program, $200,000 shall be awarded to the Alaska Department of Education for the Alaska State Distance Education Technology Consortium, $1,000,000 shall be awarded to the North East Vocational Area Cooperative in Washington State for a multi-district technology education center, $400,000 shall be awarded to the University of Vermont for the Vermont Learning Gateway Program, $2,500,000 shall be awarded to the State University of New Jersey for the RUNet 2000 project at Rutgers for an integrated voice-video-data network to link students, faculty and administration via a high-speed, broad band fiber optic network, $500,000 shall be awarded to the Iowa Area Education Agency 13 for a public/private partnership to demonstrate the effective use of technology in grades 1–3, $235,000 shall be for the Louisville Deaf Oral School for technology enhancements: *Provided further*, That in the State of Alabama $50,000 shall be awarded to the Bibb County Board of Education for technology enhancements, $50,000 shall be awarded to the Calhoun County Board of Education for technology enhancements, $50,000 shall be awarded to the Chambers County Board of Education for technology enhancements, $50,000 shall be awarded to the Chilton County Board of Education for technology enhancements, $50,000 shall be awarded to the Clay County Board of Education for technology enhancements, $50,000 shall be awarded to the Cleburne County Board of Education for technology enhancements, $50,000 shall be awarded to the Coosa County Board of Education for technology enhancements, $50,000 shall be awarded to the Lee County Board of Education for technology enhancements, $50,000 shall be awarded to the Macon County Board of Education for technology enhancements, $50,000 shall be awarded to the St. Clair County Board of Education for technology enhancements, $50,000 shall be awarded to the Talladega County Board of Education for technology enhancements, $50,000 shall be awarded to the Tallapoosa County Board of Education for technology enhancements, $50,000 shall be awarded to the Randolph County Board of Education for technology enhancements, $50,000 shall be awarded to the Russell County Board of Education for technology enhancements, $50,000 shall be awarded to the Alexander City Board of Education for technology enhancements, $50,000 shall be awarded to the Anniston City Board of Education for technology enhancements, $50,000 shall be awarded to the Lanett City Board of Education for technology enhancements, $50,000 shall be awarded to the Pell City Board of Education for technology enhancements, $50,000 shall be awarded to the Roanoke City Board of Education for technology enhancements, $50,000 shall be awarded to the Talledega City Board of Education for technology enhancements, $500,000 shall be to continue a state-of-the-art information technology system at Mansfield University, Mansfield, Pennsylvania, $250,000 shall be awarded to the Chicago Public School Science and Technology Academy to establish a curriculum of math, science, and technology, $500,000 shall be awarded to Prairie Hills, Illinois Elementary School District 144 for a public/private teacher technology training program, $1,000,000 shall be awarded to Adelphi University in New York for the Information Commons project, $250,000 shall be awarded to the Oakland School District in California to support a distance education initiative, $800,000 shall be awarded to the Kennedy Krieger Career and Technology Center in Maryland for a distance learning project, $1,000,000 shall be awarded to Augsburg College and Twin Cities Public Television to demonstrate interactive technology to assist teachers and parents in effectively using emerging innovations in education, $100,000 shall be awarded to the Santa Barbara Industry Education Council in California to provide technology education to area students and teachers, $200,000 shall be awarded to the Nebraska Community College for technology training, and $250,000 shall be awarded to the Providence Public School System, in partnership with the Metropolitan Regional Career and Technical Center, for Project Family Net to provide computer technology training to children and their parents: *Provided further*, That of the funds made available to carry out title III, part B of the Elementary and Secondary Education Act of 1965 and notwithstanding any other provision of law, $750,000 shall be awarded to the Technology Literacy Center at the Museum of Science and Industry, Chicago, $1,000,000 shall be awarded to an on-line math and science training program at Oklahoma State University, $4,000,000 shall be awarded to continue and expand the Iowa Communications Network State-wide fiber optic demonstration project, and $250,000 shall be awarded to the WinstonNet distance learning project in Winston Salem, North Carolina: *Provided further*, That of the funds made available for title X, part I of the Elementary and Secondary Education Act of 1965 and notwithstanding any other provision of law, $6,000 shall be awarded to the Study Partners Program, Inc., in Louisville, Kentucky, $12,000 shall be awarded to the Shawnee Gardens Tenants Association Inc., in Louisville, Kentucky for a tutorial program, $12,000 shall be awarded to the 100 Black Men of Louisville, Kentucky for a mentoring and leadership training program, $500,000 shall be awarded to the Omaha, Nebraska Public Schools for the OPS 21st Century Learning Grant, $25,000 shall be for the Plymouth Renewal Center in Kentucky for a tutoring program, $25,000 shall be for the Canaan Community Development Corporation's Village Learning Center Program, $25,000 shall be for the St. Stephen Life Center

General and special funds—Continued

EDUCATION REFORM—Continued

After School Program, $25,000 shall be for the Louisville Central Community Centers Youth Education Program, $15,000 shall be for the Trinity Family Life Center tutoring program, $15,000 shall be for the New Zion Community Development Foundation, Inc., after school mentoring program, $20,000 shall be for the St. Joseph Catholic Orphan Society program for abused and neglected children, $25,000 shall be for the Portland Neighborhood House after school program, $25,000 shall be for the St. Anthony Community Outreach Center, Inc., for the Education PAYs program, $250,000 shall be awarded to the Harvey Public School District 152 in Chicago, Illinois for the "Project CAFE" after-school program, $200,000 shall be awarded to the St. Clair County, Michigan Intermediate School District for after-school programs, $400,000 shall be awarded to the Macomb County, Michigan Intermediate School District for after-school programs, $200,000 shall be awarded to the Danbury Public School System in Connecticut for an ESCAPE Arts after-school program, $50,000 shall be awarded to the Tuckahoe School District for an after-school program in Eastchester, New York, $100,000 shall be awarded to Innovative Directions, an Educational Alliance (IDEA), based at the City Island School (P.S. 175) in the Bronx, New York City, New York, $250,000 shall be awarded to the New York Hall of Science in Queens, New York for after-school education programs, $60,000 shall be awarded to the Mamaroneck School District in Mamaroneck, New York for expansion of an after-school program, $250,000 shall be awarded to the White Plains School District for an after-school program in White Plains, New York, $200,000 shall be awarded to the New Rochelle School District for an after-school program in New Rochelle, New York, $250,000 shall be awarded to the Community School District 30 in Queens, New York for the expansion of after-school activities, $500,000 shall be awarded to the Jefferson Elementary School for a joint after-school program with the Madison Elementary School in Stevens Point, Wisconsin, $400,000 shall be awarded to the School District of Superior in Wisconsin for an after-school center, $100,000 shall be awarded to the Independence School District in Kansas City, Missouri for an after-school program, and $500,000 shall be awarded to the Clark County School District in Nevada for an after-school program.] *(Department of Education Appropriations Act, 2000, as enacted by section 1000(a)(4) of the Consolidated Appropriations Act, 2000 (P.L. 106–113).)*

Program and Financing (in millions of dollars)

Identification code 91–0500–0–1–501		1999 actual	2000 est.	2001 est.
	Obligations by program activity:			
	Goals 2000:			
00.01	State and local education systemic improvement	469	457	9
00.02	Parental assistance	30	33	
00.91	Total, goals 2000	499	490	9
01.01	School-to-work opportunities	128	125	55
	Educational technology:			
02.01	Technology literacy challenge fund	425	425	
02.02	Technology innovation challenge grants	115	146	
02.03	Regional technology in education consortia	10	10	
	National activities:			
02.04	Teacher training in technology	75	75	
02.05	Community-based technology	10	33	
02.06	Technology leadership activities	2	2	
02.07	Star schools	45	51	
02.08	Ready to learn television	11	16	
02.09	Telecommunications demonstration project for mathematics	5	8	
02.91	Total, educational technology	698	766	
03.01	21st Century community learning centers		453	
10.00	Total new obligations	1,325	1,834	64
	Budgetary resources available for obligation:			
21.40	Unobligated balance available, start of year	204	133	64
22.00	New budget authority (gross)	1,314	1,765	
22.21	Unobligated balance transferred to other accounts	−64		
22.22	Unobligated balance transferred from other accounts	5		
23.90	Total budgetary resources available for obligation	1,459	1,898	64
23.95	Total new obligations	−1,325	−1,834	−64
23.98	Unobligated balance expiring or withdrawn	−1		
24.40	Unobligated balance available, end of year	133	64	
	New budget authority (gross), detail:			
	Discretionary:			
40.00	Appropriation	1,314	1,768	
40.76	Reduction pursuant to P.L. 106–113		−3	
43.00	Appropriation (total discretionary)	1,314	1,765	
	Change in unpaid obligations:			
72.40	Unpaid obligations, start of year: Obligated balance, start of year	1,409	1,847	2,556
73.10	Total new obligations	1,325	1,834	64
73.20	Total outlays (gross)	−887	−1,125	−1,385
74.40	Unpaid obligations, end of year: Obligated balance, end of year	1,847	2,556	1,235
	Outlays (gross), detail:			
86.90	Outlays from new discretionary authority	124	88	
86.93	Outlays from discretionary balances	763	1,037	1,385
87.00	Total outlays (gross)	887	1,125	1,385
	Net budget authority and outlays:			
89.00	Budget authority	1,314	1,765	
90.00	Outlays	887	1,125	1,385

The Administration has proposed legislation reauthorizing programs included in the expiring Elementary and Secondary Education Act. When new authorizing legislation is enacted, resources for the affected programs will be requested. See the "Legislative proposal, not subject to PAYGO" schedule for additional details.

Summary of Budget Authority and Outlays

(in millions of dollars)

Enacted/requested:	*1999 actual*	*2000 est.*	*2001 est.*
Budget Authority	1,314	1,765	
Outlays	887	1,125	1,385
Legislative proposal, not subject to PAYGO:			
Budget Authority			2,073
Outlays			104
Total:			
Budget Authority	1,314	1,765	2,073
Outlays	887	1,125	1,489

Object Classification (in millions of dollars)

Identification code 91–0500–0–1–501		1999 actual	2000 est.	2001 est.
25.1	Advisory and assistance services	15	21	
25.2	Other services	4	5	
25.3	Purchases of goods and services from Government accounts	6	8	
25.5	Research and development contracts	3	4	
41.0	Grants, subsidies, and contributions	1,297	1,796	64
99.9	Total new obligations	1,325	1,834	64

EDUCATION REFORM

(Legislative proposal, not subject to PAYGO)

Of the funds to be made available under this heading, $120,000,000 shall be available to support activities under section 10105 of part A, title X of the Elementary and Secondary Education Act of 1965, of which up to 5 percent may be available for evaluation, technical assistance, and school networking activities: Provided, That funds made available to local educational agencies under section 10105 shall be used only for activities related to establishing smaller learning communities in high schools: Provided further, That funds to be made available for section 10105 shall become available on July 1, 2001, and remain available through September 30, 2002.

Program and Financing (in millions of dollars)

Identification code 91–0500–2–1–501		1999 actual	2000 est.	2001 est.
	Obligations by program activity:			
00.01	21st century community learning centers			1,000
00.02	Small, safe and successful high schools			120

00.91	Direct Program Subtotal			1,120
	Educational technology:			
01.01	Technology literacy challenge fund			450
01.02	Regional technology in education consortia			170
01.03	Next generation technology innovation			10
01.04	Technology leadership activities			2
01.05	Ready to learn digital television			16
01.06	Telecommunications program for professional development			5
01.07	Community technology centers			100
01.08	Preparing tomorrow's teachers to use technology			150
01.91	Subtotal, educational technology			903
02.01	Recognition and reward			50
10.00	Total new obligations			2,073
	Budgetary resources available for obligation:			
22.00	New budget authority (gross)			2,073
23.95	Total new obligations			−2,073
	New budget authority (gross), detail:			
	Discretionary:			
40.00	Appropriation			2,073
	Change in unpaid obligations:			
73.10	Total new obligations			2,073
73.20	Total outlays (gross)			−104
74.40	Unpaid obligations, end of year: Obligated balance, end of year			1,969
	Outlays (gross), detail:			
86.90	Outlays from new discretionary authority			104
	Net budget authority and outlays:			
89.00	Budget authority			2,073
90.00	Outlays			104

The resources in this schedule are proposed for later transmittal under proposed legislation to revise and reauthorize programs currently authorized under the Elementary and Secondary Education Act of 1965 and the Goals 2000: Educate America Act, as amended. Proposed appropriations language for Small, Safe and Successful Schools is provided to continue appropriations policy established in FY 2000. Appropriations language for the remainder of the account will be transmitted at a later date.

21st Century community learning centers.—Funds would support grants to centers providing school-based academic and recreational services for youths and other members of the community. The budget expands this program dramatically to provide more high-quality extended learning opportunities for children and to make after or summer school programs universally available to help turn around failing schools.

Small, safe and successful high schools.—Funds would be used to assist high schools to create smaller, safer learning environments through such strategies as schools-within-schools, career academies, or magnet schools.

Educational Technology

Technology Literacy Challenge Fund.—Funds would be provided by formula to States, which in turn award grants competitively to local educational agencies to acquire computers, connections, training, and software to achieve the President's four goals for fully integrating technology into classrooms.

Next generation technology innovation.—The proposal would combine the Technology Innovation Challenge Grants and the Star Schools program into a new program designed to develop and expand cutting-edge technologies such as Web-based instruction to improve instruction. Funds would be used for competitive awards to consortia that include at least one State or local educational agency and at least one institution of higher education, for-profit business, museum, library, or other entity with relevant experience.

Regional technology in education consortia.—Under the proposal, funds would continue to support technical assistance to promote the effective use of technology in education.

Technology leadership activities.—Funds would support leadership activities designed to promote the effective use of educational technology, and to strengthen and coordinate the Department's technology initiatives and other Federal and private sector efforts.

Ready to learn digital television.—Under the proposal, funds would continue to support the development of educational programming and outreach activities promoting literacy and school readiness for preschool and elementary school children and their parents.

Telecommunications program for professional development.—Currently, funds support a national telecommunications-based demonstration project to improve teaching in mathematics. The reauthorization proposal would expand the program to include teaching in core content areas, not just in mathematics.

Community technology centers.—Funds support computer learning centers for students and adults in low-income neighborhoods.

Preparing tomorrow's teachers to use technology.—Funds would support grants to consortia of States, colleges of education, and other public and private entities to prepare new teachers to use technology effectively in their classrooms.

Recognition and reward.—Funds would be used to reward States that are improving student achievement; narrowing the achievement gap between high- and low-performing students; and that have strategies in place for continuous improvement.

Object Classification (in millions of dollars)

Identification code 91–0500–2–1–501		1999 actual	2000 est.	2001 est.
25.1	Advisory and assistance services			23
25.2	Other services			5
25.5	Research and development contracts			9
41.0	Grants, subsidies, and contributions			2,036
99.9	Total new obligations			2,073

Education for the Disadvantaged

For carrying out [title I of the Elementary and Secondary Education Act of 1965, and] section 418A of the Higher Education Act of 1965, *$30,000,000* [$8,700,986,000, of which $2,461,823,000 shall become available on July 1, 2000, and shall remain available through September 30, 2001, and of which $6,204,763,000 shall become available on October 1, 2000 and shall remain available through September 30, 2001, for academic year 2000–2001: *Provided*, That $6,783,000,000 shall be available for basic grants under section 1124: *Provided further*, That $134,000,000 shall be allocated among the States in the same proportion as funds are allocated among the States under section 1122, to carry out section 1116(c): *Provided further*, That 100 percent of these funds shall be allocated to local educational agencies for the purposes of carrying out section 1116(c) and that local educational agencies shall provide all students enrolled in a school identified under section 1116(c) with the option to transfer to another public school within the local educational agency, including a public charter school, that has not been identified for school improvement under section 1116(c): *Provided further*, That if the local educational agency demonstrates to the satisfaction of the State educational agency that the local educational agency lacks the capacity to provide all students with the option to transfer to another public school, and after giving notice to the parents of children affected that it is not possible, consistent with State and local law, to accommodate the transfer request of every student, the local educational agency shall permit as many students as possible (who shall be selected by the local educational agency on an equitable basis) to transfer to a public school that has not been identified for school improvement under section 1116(c): *Provided further*, That up to $3,500,000 of these funds shall be available to the Secretary on October 1, 1999, to obtain updated local-educational-agency-level census poverty data from the Bureau of the Census: *Provided further*, That $1,158,397,000 shall be available for concentration grants under sec-

General and special funds—Continued

EDUCATION FOR THE DISADVANTAGED—Continued

tion 1124A: *Provided further*, That $8,900,000 shall be available for evaluations under section 1501 and not more than $8,500,000 shall be reserved for section 1308, of which not more than $3,000,000 shall be reserved for section 1308(d): *Provided further*, That grant awards under sections 1124 and 1124A of title I of the Elementary and Secondary Education Act of 1965 shall be made to each State and local educational agency at no less than 100 percent of the amount such State or local educational agency received under this authority for fiscal year 1999: *Provided further*, That notwithstanding any other provision of law, grant awards under section 1124A of title I of the Elementary and Secondary Education Act of 1965 shall be made to those local educational agencies that received a Concentration Grant under the Department of Education Appropriations Act, 1998, but are not eligible to receive such a grant for fiscal year 2000: *Provided further*, That each such local educational agency shall receive an amount equal to the Concentration Grant the agency received in fiscal year 1998, ratably reduced, if necessary, to ensure that these local educational agencies receive no greater share of their hold-harmless amounts than other local educational agencies: *Provided further*, That the Secretary shall not take into account the hold harmless provisions in this section in determining State allocations under any other program administered by the Secretary in any fiscal year: *Provided further*, That $170,000,000 shall be available under section 1002(g)(2) to demonstrate effective approaches to comprehensive school reform to be allocated and expended in accordance with the instructions relating to this activity in the statement of the managers on the conference report accompanying Public Law 105–78 and in the statement of the managers on the conference report accompanying Public Law 105–277: *Provided further*, That in carrying out this initiative, the Secretary and the States shall support only approaches that show the most promise of enabling children served by title I to meet challenging State content standards and challenging State student performance standards based on reliable research and effective practices, and include an emphasis on basic academics and parental involvement]. *(Department of Education Appropriations Act, 2000, as enacted by section 1000(a)(4) of the Consolidated Appropriations Act, 2000 (P.L. 106–113).)*

Program and Financing (in millions of dollars)

Identification code 91–0900–0–1–501		1999 actual	2000 est.	2001 est.
	Obligations by program activity:			
	Direct program:			
	Grants to local educational agencies:			
00.01	Basic grants	2,965	6,786	5,058
00.02	Concentration grants	11	1,160	1,147
00.03	Capital expenses	24	12	
00.04	Even start	134	154	
00.05	State agency programs	393	403	
00.06	Evaluation	7	9	
00.07	Demonstrations of comprehensive school reform	176	171	
00.08	Migrant education projects	13	22	30
10.00	Total new obligations	3,723	8,717	6,235
	Budgetary resources available for obligation:			
21.40	Unobligated balance available, start of year	71	16	
22.00	New budget authority (gross)	3,670	8,701	6,235
22.10	Resources available from recoveries of prior year obligations	1		
23.90	Total budgetary resources available for obligation	3,742	8,717	6,235
23.95	Total new obligations	−3,723	−8,717	−6,235
23.98	Unobligated balance expiring or withdrawn	−1		
24.40	Unobligated balance available, end of year	16		
	New budget authority (gross), detail:			
	Discretionary:			
40.00	Appropriation	2,222	2,496	30
55.00	Advance appropriation	1,448	6,205	6,205
70.00	Total new budget authority (gross)	3,670	8,701	6,235
	Change in unpaid obligations:			
72.40	Unpaid obligations, start of year: Obligated balance, start of year	7,304	3,472	3,811
73.10	Total new obligations	3,723	8,717	6,235
73.20	Total outlays (gross)	−7,554	−8,378	−8,108
73.40	Adjustments in expired accounts (net)	−2		
73.45	Adjustments in unexpired accounts	−1		
74.40	Unpaid obligations, end of year: Obligated balance, end of year	3,472	3,811	1,938
	Outlays (gross), detail:			
86.90	Outlays from new discretionary authority	1,425	5,399	4,966
86.93	Outlays from discretionary balances	6,129	2,980	3,143
87.00	Total outlays (gross)	7,554	8,378	8,108
	Net budget authority and outlays:			
89.00	Budget authority	3,670	8,701	6,235
90.00	Outlays	7,554	8,378	8,108

SUMMARY OF PROGRAM LEVEL

(in millions of dollars)

	1999–2000 academic year	2000–2001 academic year	2001–2002 academic year
Current Budget Authority	2,222	2,496	2,935
Advance appropriation	6,205	6,205	6,205
Total program level	8,427	8,701	9,140
Increase in advance appropriation over previous year			

Title I programs.—The Administration has proposed legislation reauthorizing programs under Title I of the Elementary and Secondary Education Act. When new authorizing legislation is enacted, resources will be requested for these programs. See the "Legislative proposal, not subject to PAYGO" schedule for additional details.

Migrant education projects.—Funds support grants to institutions of higher education and other nonprofit agencies that assist migrant students to earn a high school equivalency certificate or to complete their first year of college.

Summary of Budget Authority and Outlays

(in millions of dollars)

	1999 actual	2000 est.	2001 est.
Enacted/requested:			
Budget Authority	3,670	8,701	6,235
Outlays	7,554	8,379	8,109
Legislative proposal, not subject to PAYGO:			
Budget Authority			2,915
Outlays			456
Total:			
Budget Authority	3,670	8,701	9,150
Outlays	7,554	8,379	8,565

Object Classification (in millions of dollars)

Identification code 91–0900–0–1–501		1999 actual	2000 est.	2001 est.
25.1	Advisory and assistance services	9	11	
25.2	Other services	8	9	
25.3	Purchases of goods and services from Government accounts	4	4	
41.0	Grants, subsidies, and contributions	3,702	8,693	6,235
99.9	Total new obligations	3,723	8,717	6,235

EDUCATION FOR THE DISADVANTAGED

(Legislative proposal, not subject to PAYGO)

Of the funds to be made available under this heading, $250,000,000 of funds for part A of title I of the Elementary and Secondary Education Act of 1965 shall be allocated among the States in the same proportion as funds are allocated among them under section 1122, to carry out sections 1116(c), 1116(d), and 1117 of that Act: Provided, That each State shall allocate at least 70 percent of such funds to local educational agencies to carry out section 1116(c), giving priority first to local educational agencies with schools identified for corrective action under section 1116(c)(5) and second to local educational agencies with schools identified for program improvement under section 1116(c)(1) that are farthest from meeting State standards, which those agencies shall use for the benefit of students in those schools: Provided further, That each State shall use the remainder of such funds in the following priority: (1) to take corrective action, under section

1116(c)(6)(B), with respect to schools and local educational agencies described in that section; (2) to take corrective action with respect to local educational agencies in accordance with section 1116(d)(6); and (3) to provide technical assistance to remaining schools that are farthest from meeting State standards: Provided further, That a State educational agency shall require any local educational agency receiving funds under part A, title I, except where prohibited by State or local law (including school board-approved local educational agency policy), to permit students attending any school identified for corrective action under section 1116(c)(5) to transfer, at no cost to the student, to another public school of the agency that has not been so identified, in addition to taking at least one other action described in section 1116(c)(5)(B), except that no agency may use more than 10 percent of the funds, if any, it receives from the $250,000,000 reserved above for the costs of transportation.

Program and Financing (in millions of dollars)

Identification code 91–0900–2–1–501		1999 actual	2000 est.	2001 est.
	Obligations by program activity:			
	Direct program:			
	Grants to local educational agencies:			
00.01	Basic grants			2,120
00.02	Concentration grants			12
00.03	Targeted grants			21
00.04	Even start			150
00.05	State agency programs			422
00.08	Demonstrations of comprehensive school reform			190
10.00	Total new obligations			2,915
	Budgetary resources available for obligation:			
22.00	New budget authority (gross)			2,915
23.95	Total new obligations			−2,915
	New budget authority (gross), detail:			
	Discretionary:			
40.00	Appropriation			2,915
	Change in unpaid obligations:			
73.10	Total new obligations			2,915
73.20	Total outlays (gross)			−456
74.40	Unpaid obligations, end of year: Obligated balance, end of year			2,459
	Outlays (gross), detail:			
86.90	Outlays from new discretionary authority			456
	Net budget authority and outlays:			
89.00	Budget authority			2,915
90.00	Outlays			456

The resources in this schedule are proposed for later transmittal under proposed legislation to revise and reauthorize programs currently authorized under the Elementary and Secondary Education Act (ESEA), as amended. Proposed appropriations language for the Title I Accountability Fund is provided to continue and modify appropriations policy established in 2000. Appropriations language for the remainder of the account will be transmitted at a later date.

Under the Administration's proposal for Title I of that Act, funds would be provided to States and to local school districts for the activities shown below.

Grants to local education agencies.—Funds would be allocated through the Basic, Concentration, and Targeted grants formulas for local programs that help Title I students meet high standards, hold school districts and schools accountable for improved student achievement and reduce the number of failing schools, support schoolwide reforms and the use of research-based strategies for improving teaching and learning, dedicate more resources to professional development, and target funds to high-poverty schools. To improve Title I accountability, funds would be included to help turn around low-achieving schools in all States.

Even start.—Funds would be provided by formula to States, which would award grants for local projects to partnerships of local educational agencies and other organizations to operate family literacy projects integrating early childhood education, adult literacy, and parenting education for low-income families with children under age 8.

State agency migrant program.—Funds would be provided by formula to States for educational services to children of migratory farmworkers and fishers. Funds and services would be concentrated on children who have moved within the past 36 months.

State agency neglected and delinquent program.—Funds would be provided by formula to States for educational services to children and youth under age 21 in State neglected, delinquent, or adult correction facilities. Services would help institutionalized youth achieve to the same challenging standards established for students in local public schools.

Demonstrations of comprehensive school reform.—Funds would be provided by formula to States, which in turn award grants to local educational agencies to help participating schools initiate and implement comprehensive school reforms based on approaches and methods grounded in reliable research and practice.

Object Classification (in millions of dollars)

Identification code 91–0900–2–1–501		1999 actual	2000 est.	2001 est.
25.1	Advisory and assistance services			20
25.2	Other services			9
25.3	Purchases of goods and services from Government accounts			4
41.0	Grants, subsidies, and contributions			2,882
99.9	Total new obligations			2,915

IMPACT AID

[For carrying out programs of financial assistance to federally affected schools authorized by title VIII of the Elementary and Secondary Education Act of 1965, $910,500,000, of which $737,200,000 shall be for basic support payments under section 8003(b), $50,000,000 shall be for payments for children with disabilities under section 8003(d), $76,000,000, to remain available until expended, shall be for payments under section 8003(f), $10,300,000 shall be for construction under section 8007, $32,000,000 shall be for Federal property payments under section 8002 and $5,000,000 to remain available until expended shall be for facilities maintenance under section 8008: *Provided*, That of the funds available for section 8007 and notwithstanding any other provision of law, $500,000 shall be awarded to the Fort Sam Houston Independent School District, Texas, $800,000 shall be awarded to the Hays Lodgepole School District, Montana, and $2,000,000 shall be awarded to the North Chicago Community Unit SD 187: *Provided further*, That these funds shall remain available until expended: *Provided further*, That the Secretary of Education shall treat as timely filed, and shall process for payment, an application for a fiscal year 1999 payment from the local educational agency for Brookeland, Texas under section 8002 of the Elementary and Secondary Education Act of 1965 if the Secretary has received that application not later than 30 days after the enactment of this Act: *Provided further*, That section 8002(f) of the Elementary and Secondary Education Act of 1965 is amended by adding a new paragraph "(3)" at the end to read as follows:

"(3) For each fiscal year beginning with fiscal year 2000, the Secretary shall treat the Central Union, California; Island, California; Hill City, South Dakota; and Wall, South Dakota local educational agencies as meeting the eligibility requirements of subsection (a)(1)(C) of this section.":

Provided further, That the Secretary of Education shall consider all payments received by the educational agency for Hatboro-Horsham and Delaware Valley, Pennsylvania for fiscal year 1995 under section 8002(a) of the Elementary and Secondary Education Act of 1965 (20 U.S.C. 7702(a)), and all payments under section 8002(h)(2)(A) for subsequent years through fiscal year 1999, to be correct: *Provided further*, That section 8002(f) of the Elementary and Secondary Education Act of 1965 is amended by adding at the end thereof a new paragraph (4) to read as follows:

"(4) For the purposes of payments under this section for each fiscal year beginning with fiscal year 2000, the Secretary shall

General and special funds—Continued

IMPACT AID—Continued

treat the Hot Springs, South Dakota local educational agency as if it had filed a timely application under section 8002 of the Elementary and Secondary Education Act of 1965 for fiscal year 1994 if the Secretary has received the fiscal year 1994 application, as well as Exhibits A and B not later than December 1, 1999.": *Provided further*, That section 8002(f) of the Elementary and Secondary Education Act of 1965 is amended by adding at the end thereof a new paragraph (5) to read as follows:

"(5) For purposes of payments under this section for each fiscal year beginning with fiscal year 2000, the Secretary shall treat the Hueneme, California local educational agency as if it had filed a timely application under section 8002 of the Elementary and Secondary Education Act of 1965 if the Secretary has received the fiscal year 1995 application not later than December 1, 1999.": *Provided further*, That the Secretary of Education shall treat as timely filed, and shall process for payment, an application for a fiscal year 1998 payment from the local educational agency for Hydaburg, Alaska, under section 8003 of the Elementary and Secondary Education Act of 1965 if the Secretary has received that application not later than 30 days after the enactment of this Act: *Provided further*, That the Secretary of Education shall treat as timely, and process for payment, an application for fiscal years 1996 and 1997 payment from the local education agency for Fallbrook Unified High School District, California, under section 8002 of the Elementary and Secondary Education Act of 1965, if the Secretary has received that application not later than 30 days after the enactment of this Act: *Provided further*, That for the purpose of computing the amount of a payment for a local educational agency for children identified under section 8003 of the Elementary and Secondary Education Act of 1965, children residing in housing initially acquired or constructed under section 801 of the Military Construction Authorization Act of 1984 (Public Law 98–115) ("Build to Lease" program) shall be considered as children described under section 8003(a)(1)(B) if the property described is within the fenced security perimeter of the military facility upon which such housing is situated: *Provided further*, That if such property is not owned by the Federal Government, is subject to taxation by a State or political subdivision of a State, and thereby generates revenues for a local educational agency which received a payment from the Secretary under section 8003, the Secretary shall: (1) require such local educational agency to provide certification from an appropriate official of the Department of Defense that such property is being used to provide military housing; and (2) reduce the amount of such payment by an amount equal to the amount of revenue from such taxation received in the second preceding fiscal year by such local educational agency, unless the amount of such revenue was taken into account by the State for such second preceding fiscal year and already resulted in a reduction in the amount of State aid paid to such local educational agency.] *(Department of Education Appropriations Act, 2000, as enacted by section 1000(a)(4) of the Consolidated Appropriations Act, 2000 (P.L. 106–113).)*

Program and Financing (in millions of dollars)

Identification code 91–0102–0–1–501		1999 actual	2000 est.	2001 est.
	Obligations by program activity:			
	Payments for federally connected children:			
00.01	Basic support payments	704	737	
00.02	Supplemental payments for children with disabilities	50	50	
00.03	Payments for heavily impacted districts	106	78	
00.91	Subtotal, payments for federally connected children	860	865	
01.01	Facilities maintenance	12	4	3
02.01	Construction (formula)	7	7	
03.01	Payments for Federal property	28	32	
04.01	Special construction	5	3	2
10.00	Total new obligations	912	911	5
	Budgetary resources available for obligation:			
21.40	Unobligated balance available, start of year	73	24	19
22.00	New budget authority (gross)	864	906	
23.90	Total budgetary resources available for obligation	937	930	19
23.95	Total new obligations	−912	−911	−5
24.40	Unobligated balance available, end of year	24	19	14
	New budget authority (gross), detail:			
	Discretionary:			
40.00	Appropriation	864	910	
40.76	Reduction pursuant to P.L. 106–113		−4	
43.00	Appropriation (total discretionary)	864	906	
	Change in unpaid obligations:			
72.40	Unpaid obligations, start of year: Obligated balance, start of year	407	249	126
73.10	Total new obligations	912	911	5
73.20	Total outlays (gross)	−1,081	−1,034	−102
73.40	Adjustments in expired accounts (net)	11		
74.40	Unpaid obligations, end of year: Obligated balance, end of year	249	126	29
	Outlays (gross), detail:			
86.90	Outlays from new discretionary authority	790	809	
86.93	Outlays from discretionary balances	291	225	102
87.00	Total outlays (gross)	1,081	1,034	102
	Net budget authority and outlays:			
89.00	Budget authority	864	906	
90.00	Outlays	1,081	1,034	102

The Administration has proposed legislation reauthorizing Impact Aid programs included in the expiring Elementary and Secondary Education Act. When new authorizing legislation is enacted, resources will be requested for these programs. See the "Legislative proposal, not subject to PAYGO" schedule for additional details.

Summary of Budget Authority and Outlays

(in millions of dollars)

	1999 actual	2000 est.	2001 est.
Enacted/requested:			
Budget Authority	864	906	
Outlays	1,081	1,034	102
Legislative proposal, not subject to PAYGO:			
Budget Authority			770
Outlays			689
Total:			
Budget Authority	864	906	770
Outlays	1,081	1,034	791

Object Classification (in millions of dollars)

Identification code 91–0102–0–1–501		1999 actual	2000 est.	2001 est.
25.3	Purchases of goods and services from Government accounts	1		
32.0	Land and structures	10	7	3
41.0	Grants, subsidies, and contributions	901	904	2
99.9	Total new obligations	912	911	5

IMPACT AID

(Legislative proposal, not subject to PAYGO)

Program and Financing (in millions of dollars)

Identification code 91–0102–2–1–501		1999 actual	2000 est.	2001 est.
	Obligations by program activity:			
	Payments for federally connected children:			
00.01	Basic support payments			720
00.02	Supplemental payments for children with disabilities			40
00.91	Subtotal, payments for federally connected children			760
01.01	Facilities maintenance			3
01.02	Construction			5
01.91	Subtotal			8
10.00	Total new obligations			768
	Budgetary resources available for obligation:			
22.00	New budget authority (gross)			770

23.95	Total new obligations			−768
24.40	Unobligated balance available, end of year			3
	New budget authority (gross), detail:			
	Discretionary:			
40.00	Appropriation			770
	Change in unpaid obligations:			
73.10	Total new obligations			768
73.20	Total outlays (gross)			−689
74.40	Unpaid obligations, end of year: Obligated balance, end of year			79
	Outlays (gross), detail:			
86.90	Outlays from new discretionary authority			689
	Net budget authority and outlays:			
89.00	Budget authority			770
90.00	Outlays			689

The resources in this schedule are proposed for later transmittal under the proposed legislation to revise and reauthorize programs currently authorized under the Elementary and Secondary Education Act, as amended. Under the Administration proposal for Impact Aid, funds would be provided to assist local educational agencies that are affected by Federal activities. Payments would be made to local educational agencies that educate (1) children of members of the uniformed services living on Federal property; (2) children living on Indian lands; (3) children of Federal employees who both live and work on Federal property; and (4) children of foreign military officers living on Federal property.

Basic support payments.—Payments would be made on behalf of approximately 292,000 federally connected children enrolled in approximately 950 local educational agencies across the country. The request would provide an average payment of approximately $2,500 for each of these federally connected children.

Payments for children with disabilities.—Payments would be made for additional assistance to local educational agencies educating federally connected children with disabilities. Approximately 33,000 such children are enrolled in school districts across the country. The request would provide approximately $1,200 in additional assistance for the education of each of these children.

Facilities maintenance.—Funds would be used to provide emergency repairs for school facilities that serve federally connected military students and are owned by the Department of Education. Funds would also be used to transfer the facilities to local educational agencies.

Construction.—Payments would provide assistance for school construction for local educational agencies in which at least 50 percent of the students reside on Indian lands.

Object Classification (in millions of dollars)

Identification code 91–0102–2–1–501		1999 actual	2000 est.	2001 est.
32.0	Land and structures			3
41.0	Grants, subsidies, and contributions			765
99.9	Total new obligations			768

School Improvement Programs

For carrying out school improvement activities authorized by [titles II, IV, V–A and B, VI, IX,] *title* X–*C*, [and XIII] of the Elementary and Secondary Education Act of 1965 ("ESEA"); [the Stewart B. McKinney Homeless Assistance Act; and] the Civil Rights Act of 1964 and part B of title VIII of the Higher Education Act of 1965[; $3,026,884,000, of which $975,300,000 shall become available on July 1, 2000, and remain available through September 30, 2001, and of which $1,515,000,000 shall become available on October 1, 2000 and shall remain available through September 30, 2001 for academic year 2000–2001: *Provided*, That of the amount appropriated, $335,000,000 shall be for Eisenhower professional development State grants under title II–B and $1,680,000,000 shall be for title VI and up to $750,000 shall be for an evaluation of comprehensive regional assistance centers under title XIII of ESEA: *Provided further*, That of the amount made available for title VI $1,300,000,000 shall be available, notwithstanding any other provision of law, to carry out title VI of Elementary and Secondary Education Act of 1965 in accordance with section 310 of this Act, in order to reduce class size, particularly in the early grades, using highly qualified teachers to improve educational achievement for regular and special needs children], *$202,334,000. (Department of Education Appropriations Act, 2000, as enacted by section 1000(a)(4) of the Consolidated Appropriations Act, 2000 (P.L. 106–113).)*

Program and Financing (in millions of dollars)

Identification code 91–1000–0–1–501		1999 actual	2000 est.	2001 est.
	Direct program:			
	Obligations by program activity:			
	Professional development and program innovation:			
00.01	Eisenhower professional development State grants	337	336	
00.02	Innovative education program strategies State grants	375	81	285
00.03	Class size reduction	1,199	401	900
	Safe and drug-free schools and communities:			
00.04	State grants	441	111	330
00.05	National programs	90	111	
00.06	Coordinator Initiative	35	50	
00.08	Inexpensive book distribution	18	20	
00.09	Arts in education	11	12	
00.10	Magnet schools assistance	104	110	
00.11	Education for homeless children and youth	29	29	
00.12	Women's educational equity	3	3	
00.13	Training and advisory services	7	7	7
00.14	Ellender fellowships	2	2	
00.15	Education for Native Hawaiians	20	23	
00.16	Alaska Native education equity	10	13	
00.17	Charter schools	100	145	175
00.18	Advanced placement incentives	4	15	20
00.19	Comprehensive regional assistance centers	28	28	
01.00	Total direct program	2,813	1,497	1,717
09.01	Reimbursable program	36		
10.00	Total new obligations	2,849	1,497	1,717
	Budgetary resources available for obligation:			
21.40	Unobligated balance available, start of year	5	4	
22.00	New budget authority (gross)	2,847	1,492	1,717
23.90	Total budgetary resources available for obligation	2,852	1,496	1,717
23.95	Total new obligations	−2,849	−1,497	−1,717
24.40	Unobligated balance available, end of year	4		
	New budget authority (gross), detail:			
	Discretionary:			
40.00	Appropriation	2,811	1,512	202
40.76	Reduction pursuant to P.L. 106–113		−20	
43.00	Appropriation (total discretionary)	2,811	1,492	202
55.00	Advance appropriation			1,515
68.00	Spending authority from offsetting collections: Offsetting collections (cash)	36		
70.00	Total new budget authority (gross)	2,847	1,492	1,717
	Change in unpaid obligations:			
72.40	Unpaid obligations, start of year: Obligated balance, start of year	1,941	3,423	2,393
73.10	Total new obligations	2,849	1,497	1,717
73.20	Total outlays (gross)	−1,362	−2,527	−2,627
73.40	Adjustments in expired accounts (net)	−4		
74.40	Unpaid obligations, end of year: Obligated balance, end of year	3,423	2,393	1,483
	Outlays (gross), detail:			
86.90	Outlays from new discretionary authority	155	150	1,026
86.93	Outlays from discretionary balances	1,207	2,377	1,602
87.00	Total outlays (gross)	1,362	2,527	2,627
	Offsets:			
	Against gross budget authority and outlays:			
88.00	Offsetting collections (cash) from: Federal sources	−36		

General and special funds—Continued

SCHOOL IMPROVEMENT PROGRAMS—Continued

Program and Financing (in millions of dollars)—Continued

Identification code 91–1000–0–1–501	1999 actual	2000 est.	2001 est.
Net budget authority and outlays:			
89.00 Budget authority	2,811	1,492	1,717
90.00 Outlays	1,326	2,527	2,627

Note.—Includes $15 million in budget authority in 2001 for Eisenhower regional mathematics and science education consortia previously financed from:

(in millions of dollars)	1999 actual	2000 est.
Office of Educational Research and Improvement, Education Research, Statistics, and Improvement	15	15

The Administration has proposed legislation to reauthorize the Elementary and Secondary Education Act and portions of the Stewart B. McKinney Homeless Assistance Act. When new authorizing legislation is enacted, resources will be requested for most programs in the School Improvement Programs account. See the "Legislative proposal, not subject to PAYGO".

Training and advisory services.—Grants are made to regional equity assistance centers that provide technical assistance to school districts in addressing equity in education related to issues of race, gender, and national origin.

Charter schools.—Grants are awarded to State educational agencies and charter schools to support the planning, design, initial implementation, and dissemination of information regarding model charter schools. These schools are created by teachers, parents, and members of the community, and are exempt from certain local, State, and Federal regulations.

Advanced placement incentives.—Funds are used by States to pay for advanced placement test fees for low-income students who are enrolled in advanced placement classes. In States in which no eligible low-income individual is required to pay more than a nominal fee to take advanced placement tests, funds may be used for other purposes to increase the number of low-income students taking these tests, such as curriculum development and training of teachers for advanced placement courses.

Summary of Budget Authority and Outlays

(in millions of dollars)

Enacted/requested:	1999 actual	2000 est.	2001 est.
Budget Authority	2,811	1,492	1,717
Outlays	1,326	2,527	2,628
Legislative proposal, not subject to PAYGO:			
Budget Authority	....	....	2,200
Outlays	....	....	186
Total:			
Budget Authority	2,811	1,492	3,917
Outlays	1,326	2,527	2,814

Object Classification (in millions of dollars)

Identification code 91–1000–0–1–501	1999 actual	2000 est.	2001 est.
Direct obligations:			
25.1 Advisory and assistance services	4	2	1
25.2 Other services	30	11	4
25.3 Purchases of goods and services from Government accounts	1	....	....
41.0 Grants, subsidies, and contributions	2,777	1,484	1,712
99.0 Subtotal, direct obligations	2,812	1,497	1,717
99.0 Reimbursable obligations	36	....	....
99.5 Below reporting threshold	1	....	....
99.9 Total new obligations	2,849	1,497	1,717

SCHOOL IMPROVEMENT PROGRAMS

(Legislative proposal, not subject to PAYGO)

Program and Financing (in millions of dollars)

Identification code 91–1000–2–1–501	1999 actual	2000 est.	2001 est.
Obligations by program activity:			
High standards in the classroom:			
00.01 Teaching to high standards	....	....	405
National programs:			
00.02 School leadership initiative	....	....	40
00.03 National activities for the improvement of teaching and school leadership	....	....	25
00.04 Eisenhower regional mathematics and science education consortia	....	....	15
00.05 Hometown teachers initiative	....	....	75
00.06 Higher standards, higher pay	....	....	50
00.07 Teacher quality incentives	....	....	50
00.08 Transition to teaching: Troops to teachers	....	....	25
00.09 Early childhood educator professional development	....	....	30
00.10 Class size reduction	....	....	850
Safe and drug-free schools and communities:			
00.11 State grants	....	....	109
00.12 National programs	....	....	201
00.13 Project SERV	....	....	10
00.14 Inexpensive book distribution	....	....	20
00.15 Arts in education	....	....	23
00.16 Magnet schools assistance	....	....	110
00.17 Education for homeless children and youth	....	....	32
00.18 Women's educational equity	....	....	3
00.19 Education for Native Hawaiians	....	....	23
00.20 Alaska Native education equity	....	....	13
00.21 Opportunities to improve our Nation's schools (OPTIONS)	....	....	20
00.22 Strengthening technical assistance capacity grants	....	....	38
00.23 Parental information resource centers	....	....	33
10.00 Total new obligations	....	....	2,200
Budgetary resources available for obligation:			
22.00 New budget authority (gross)	....	....	2,200
23.95 Total new obligations	....	....	−2,200
New budget authority (gross), detail:			
Discretionary:			
40.00 Appropriation	....	....	2,200
Change in unpaid obligations:			
73.10 Total new obligations	....	....	2,200
73.20 Total outlays (gross)	....	....	−186
74.40 Unpaid obligations, end of year: Obligated balance, end of year	....	....	2,014
Outlays (gross), detail:			
86.90 Outlays from new discretionary authority	....	....	186
Net budget authority and outlays:			
89.00 Budget authority	....	....	2,200
90.00 Outlays	....	....	186

SUMMARY OF PROGRAM LEVEL

(in millions of dollars)

	1999–2000 academic year	2000–2001 academic year	2001–2002 academic year
Current Budget Authority	2,811	1,492	2,402
Advance appropriation	0	1,515	1,515
Total program level	2,811	3,007	3,917
Increase in advance appropriation over previous year	+0	+1,515	+0

The resources in this schedule are proposed for later transmittal under proposed legislation to revise and reauthorize programs currently authorized under the Elementary and Secondary Education Act of 1965 and the Stewart B. McKinney Homeless Assistance Act.

Teaching to high standards State grants.—Under this new program, funds would be allocated by formula to States, outlying areas, and the Bureau of Indian Affairs to support standards-based reform and sustained and intensive high-quality professional development for educators in the core academic subjects.

School leadership initiative.—This new program would fund centers that would provide professional development to principals and other school and district level administrators.

National activities for the improvement of teaching and school leadership.—This program will continue to support projects previously funded by Eisenhower Professional Development Federal activities, including the National Clearinghouse for Mathematics and Science Education and the National Board for Professional Teaching Standards.

Eisenhower regional mathematics and science education consortia.—This program would continue to support regional consortia to disseminate exemplary mathematics and science instructional materials and provide technical assistance to help teachers and administrators implement new teaching methods and assessment tools.

Hometown teachers initiative.—This new program would encourage high school students to become teachers and support them in their undergraduate teacher training programs and their first years in the classroom.

Higher standards, higher pay.—This initiative would award competitive grants to high-poverty school districts that implement peer review systems to attract and retain high-quality teachers and principals through better pay.

Teacher quality incentives.—This new program would encourage the use of fully certified and licensed teachers and discourage out-of-field teaching.

Transition to teaching: Troops to teachers.—This program would fund the Troops to Teachers program, which encourages and supports former members of the military to become teachers, and would expand the program to encourage other mid-career professionals to become teachers.

Early childhood educator professional development.—Under this new program, funds would be awarded competitively to partnerships of higher education institutions and other entities to create high-quality professional development for early childhood educators and caregivers working in communities with high concentrations of young children living in poverty.

Class size reduction.—Formula grants would be provided to local school districts to help them carry out effective approaches to reducing class sizes with highly qualified teachers. School districts give particular consideration to reducing class sizes in the early elementary grades.

Safe and Drug-Free Schools and Communities:

State grants.—Formula grants would be made to States, outlying areas, and the Bureau of Indian Affairs to help create and maintain drug-free, safe, and orderly environments for learning in and around schools by supporting effective, research-based approaches to drug and violence prevention

National programs.—Funds would support activities to promote drug-free, safe, and orderly learning environments for students at all educational levels. Such activities may include programs implemented in conjunction with other Federal agencies, such as the Safe Schools/Healthy Students initiative, that support local educational agencies and communities in developing and implementing comprehensive programs that create safe, disciplined, and drug-free learning environments and promote healthy childhood development; recruiting, hiring, and training program coordinators to assist school districts in implementing high-quality, effective, research-based drug and violence prevention programs; and other forms of training and technical assistance, demonstrations, and direct services to school districts, as well as developing and disseminating prevention and education materials and evaluating the effectiveness of drug and violence prevention programs.

Project SERV (School Emergency Response to Violence).—A new Federal response to violent deaths and other crises in schools under which the Department of Education, in collaboration with the Departments of Justice and Health and Human Services and the Federal Emergency Management Administration, would provide immediate emergency assistance to a community following a school-related violent or traumatic incident to help identify and meet urgent and unplanned local needs, such as additional security personnel, emergency mental health crisis counseling, and longer-term counseling to students, faculty, and families.

Other Programs.—

Inexpensive book distribution.—Funds would support reading motivation activities, including the distribution of free books to children.

Arts in education.—Funds would support education activities of the Kennedy Center and VSA arts, as well as collaborative, arts education programs with the National Endowment for the Arts.

Magnet schools assistance.—Grants would be made to local educational agencies to establish and operate magnet school programs that are part of approved desegregation plans.

Education for homeless children and youth.—Formula grants would be provided to States, outlying areas, and the Bureau of Indian Affairs to provide educational and support services that enable homeless children and youth to enroll in, attend, and achieve success in school.

Women's educational equity.—Funds would support implementation of gender-equity practices at schools and colleges, as well as the development and dissemination of educational materials that promote educational equity for women and girls.

Education for Native Hawaiians.—Grants would provide supplemental education services to Native Hawaiians in the areas of family-based education, special education, gifted and talented education, higher education, curriculum development, teacher training and recruitment, and community-based learning.

Alaska Native education equity.—Grants would provide supplemental education services to Alaska Natives in the areas of educational planning, curriculum development, teacher training, teacher recruitment, student enrichment, and home-based instruction for pre-school children.

Opportunities to improve our Nation's schools (OPTIONS).—Under this new program, grants would be awarded to States and local educational agencies to support the planning, design, and implementation of public school choice projects.

Strengthening technical assistance capacity grants.—Under this new program, funds would be allocated by formula to States and large school districts to purchase, and to strengthen their capacity to acquire and use, technical assistance that best fits their needs to increase opportunities for all children to achieve the State's academic performance standards and to implement the State's or district's plan or policies for comprehensive standards-based education reform.

Parental information resource centers.—Funds would be provided for centers in all States to provide training, information, and support to State and local educational agencies and schools—particularly high-poverty, low-performing schools—to remove barriers to parent involvement in their child's education.

Object Classification (in millions of dollars)

Identification code 91–1000–2–1–501		1999 actual	2000 est.	2001 est.
25.2	Other services			2
41.0	Grants, subsidies, and contributions			2,198
99.9	Total new obligations			2,200

General and special funds—Continued

READING EXCELLENCE

[For necessary expenses to carry out the Reading Excellence Act, $65,000,000, which shall become available on July 1, 2000 and shall remain available through September 30, 2001 and $195,000,000 which shall become available on October 1, 2000 and remain available through September 30, 2001.] *(Department of Education Appropriations Act, 2000, as enacted by section 1000(a)(4) of the Consolidated Appropriations Act, 2000 (P.L. 106–113).)*

Program and Financing (in millions of dollars)

Identification code 91–0011–0–1–501	1999 actual	2000 est.	2001 est.
Obligations by program activity:			
00.01 Reading Excellence	233	92	195
10.00 Total new obligations	233	92	195
Budgetary resources available for obligation:			
21.40 Unobligated balance available, start of year		27	
22.00 New budget authority (gross)	260	65	195
23.90 Total budgetary resources available for obligation	260	92	195
23.95 Total new obligations	−233	−92	−195
24.40 Unobligated balance available, end of year	27		
New budget authority (gross), detail:			
Discretionary:			
40.00 Appropriation	260	65	
41.00 Transferred to other accounts	−210		
43.00 Appropriation (total discretionary)	50	65	
55.00 Advance appropriation	210		195
70.00 Total new budget authority (gross)	260	65	195
Change in unpaid obligations:			
72.40 Unpaid obligations, start of year: Obligated balance, start of year		233	192
73.10 Total new obligations	233	92	195
73.20 Total outlays (gross)		−133	−205
74.40 Unpaid obligations, end of year: Obligated balance, end of year	233	192	182
Outlays (gross), detail:			
86.90 Outlays from new discretionary authority		3	98
86.93 Outlays from discretionary balances		130	108
87.00 Total outlays (gross)		133	205
Net budget authority and outlays:			
89.00 Budget authority	260	65	195
90.00 Outlays		133	205

Reading Excellence.—The Administration has proposed legislation to reauthorize the Reading Excellence program included in the Elementary and Secondary Education Act. When new authorizing legislation is enacted, resources will be requested for this program. See the "Legislative proposal, not subject to PAYGO" schedule for additional details.

Summary of Budget Authority and Outlays

(in millions of dollars)

	1999 actual	2000 est.	2001 est.
Enacted/requested:			
Budget Authority	260	65	195
Outlays		133	206
Legislative proposal, not subject to PAYGO:			
Budget Authority			91
Outlays			3
Total:			
Budget Authority	260	65	286
Outlays		133	209

Object Classification (in millions of dollars)

Identification code 91–0011–0–1–501	1999 actual	2000 est.	2001 est.
25.1 Advisory and assistance services		5	
25.2 Other services	1	4	
41.0 Grants, subsidies, and contributions	232	83	195
99.9 Total new obligations	233	92	195

READING EXCELLENCE

(Legislative proposal, not subject to PAYGO)

Program and Financing (in millions of dollars)

Identification code 91–0011–2–1–501	1999 actual	2000 est.	2001 est.
Obligations by program activity:			
00.01 Reading Excellence			91
10.00 Total new obligations			91
Budgetary resources available for obligation:			
22.00 New budget authority (gross)			91
23.95 Total new obligations			−91
New budget authority (gross), detail:			
Discretionary:			
40.00 Appropriation			91
Change in unpaid obligations:			
73.10 Total new obligations			91
73.20 Total outlays (gross)			−3
74.40 Unpaid obligations, end of year: Obligated balance, end of year			88
Outlays (gross), detail:			
86.90 Outlays from new discretionary authority			3
Net budget authority and outlays:			
89.00 Budget authority			91
90.00 Outlays			3

SUMMARY OF PROGRAM LEVEL

(in millions of dollars)

	1999–2000 academic year	*2000–2001 academic year*	*2001–2002 academic year*
Current Budget Authority	260	65	91
Advance appropriation		195	195
Total program level	260	260	286
Increase in advance appropriation over previous year		195	

The resources in this schedule are proposed for later transmittal under proposed legislation to revise and reauthorize programs currently authorized under the Elementary and Secondary Education Act.

Reading Excellence.—The Reading Excellence Act funds programs to provide children with the readiness skills and support they need in early childhood to learn to read once they enter school, to help ensure that all children read well and independently by the end of the third grade, to support programs to assist kindergarten children who are not ready for the transition to first grade, and to improve the instructional practices of teachers and other instructional staff in elementary schools. States that receive competitive grants will make subgrants on a competitive basis to school districts to help them provide professional development opportunities for professional staff, operate tutoring programs, and provide family literacy services.

Object Classification (in millions of dollars)

Identification code 91–0011–2–1–501	1999 actual	2000 est.	2001 est.
25.1 Advisory and assistance services			5
25.2 Other services			4
41.0 Grants, subsidies, and contributions			82
99.9 Total new obligations			91

CHICAGO LITIGATION SETTLEMENT

Program and Financing (in millions of dollars)

Identification code 91–0220–0–1–501	1999 actual	2000 est.	2001 est.
Obligations by program activity:			
10.00 Total new obligations (object class 41.0)	3	2	
Budgetary resources available for obligation:			
21.40 Unobligated balance available, start of year	5	2	
23.95 Total new obligations	−3	−2	
24.40 Unobligated balance available, end of year	2		
Change in unpaid obligations:			
72.40 Unpaid obligations, start of year: Obligated balance, start of year	3	3	3
73.10 Total new obligations	3	2	
73.20 Total outlays (gross)	−2	−3	−3
74.40 Unpaid obligations, end of year: Obligated balance, end of year	3	3	1
Outlays (gross), detail:			
86.93 Outlays from discretionary balances	2	3	3
Net budget authority and outlays:			
89.00 Budget authority			
90.00 Outlays	2	3	3

Funds made available under this account were reappropriated by the Supplemental Appropriations Act, 1987 (Public Law 100–71) from funds enjoined in *United States of America* v. *Board of Education of the City of Chicago.* The funds were reappropriated for the specific purpose of settling this case. The funds are used by the Chicago Board of Education to implement Project CANAL (Creating A New Approach to Learning), the project approved by the court to support the Board's desegregation efforts.

The Department of Education provides these funds to the Chicago Board of Education in annual increments upon receipt and approval of an annual plan for Project CANAL activities.

INDIAN EDUCATION

[For expenses necessary to carry out, to the extent not otherwise provided, title IX, part A of the Elementary and Secondary Education Act of 1965, as amended, $77,000,000.] *(Department of Education Appropriations Act, 2000, as enacted by section 1000(a)(4) of the Consolidated Appropriations Act, 2000 (P.L. 106–113).)*

Program and Financing (in millions of dollars)

Identification code 91–0101–0–1–501	1999 actual	2000 est.	2001 est.
Obligations by program activity:			
00.01 Grants to local educational agencies	62	62	
00.02 Special programs for Indian children	3	13	
00.03 National activities	1	2	
10.00 Total new obligations	66	77	
Budgetary resources available for obligation:			
22.00 New budget authority (gross)	66	77	
23.95 Total new obligations	−66	−77	
New budget authority (gross), detail:			
Discretionary:			
40.00 Appropriation	66	77	
Change in unpaid obligations:			
72.40 Unpaid obligations, start of year: Obligated balance, start of year	77	86	82
73.10 Total new obligations	66	77	
73.20 Total outlays (gross)	−57	−81	−65
74.40 Unpaid obligations, end of year: Obligated balance, end of year	86	82	17
Outlays (gross), detail:			
86.90 Outlays from new discretionary authority	2	9	
86.93 Outlays from discretionary balances	55	71	65
87.00 Total outlays (gross)	57	81	65
Net budget authority and outlays:			
89.00 Budget authority	66	77	
90.00 Outlays	57	81	65

The administration has proposed legislation reauthorizing programs included in the expiring Elementary and Secondary Education Act. When new authorizing legislation is enacted, resources for Indian Education programs will be requested. See the "Legislative proposal, not subject to PAYGO" schedule for additional details.

Summary of Budget Authority and Outlays

(in millions of dollars)

Enacted/requested:	*1999 actual*	*2000 est.*	*2001 est.*
Budget Authority	66	77	
Outlays	57	80	65
Legislative proposal, not subject to PAYGO:			
Budget Authority			116
Outlays			14
Total:			
Budget Authority	66	77	116
Outlays	57	80	79

Object Classification (in millions of dollars)

Identification code 91–0101–0–1–501	1999 actual	2000 est.	2001 est.
25.2 Other services	1	2	
41.0 Grants, subsidies, and contributions	65	75	
99.9 Total new obligations	66	77	

INDIAN EDUCATION

(Legislative proposal, not subject to PAYGO)

Program and Financing (in millions of dollars)

Identification code 91–0101–2–1–501	1999 actual	2000 est.	2001 est.
Obligations by program activity:			
00.01 Grants to local educational agencies			93
00.02 Special programs for Indian children			20
00.03 National activities			3
10.00 Total new obligations			116
Budgetary resources available for obligation:			
22.00 New budget authority (gross)			116
23.95 Total new obligations			−116
New budget authority (gross), detail:			
Discretionary:			
40.00 Appropriation			116
Change in unpaid obligations:			
72.40 Unpaid obligations, start of year: Obligated balance, start of year			
73.10 Total new obligations			116
73.20 Total outlays (gross)			−14
74.40 Unpaid obligations, end of year: Obligated balance, end of year			102
Outlays (gross), detail:			
86.90 Outlays from new discretionary authority			14
Net budget authority and outlays:			
89.00 Budget authority			116
90.00 Outlays			14

The resources in this schedule are proposed for later transmittal under proposed legislation to revise and reauthorize Indian Education programs currently authorized under the Elementary and Secondary Education Act of 1965.

Grants to local education agencies.—Formula grants support local educational agencies in their efforts to reform elemen-

General and special funds—Continued

INDIAN EDUCATION—Continued

tary and secondary school programs that serve Indian students, with the goal of ensuring that such programs are based on challenging State standards that are used for all students. In 1999, 1,274 formula grants were made to local educational agencies and certain tribal schools enrolling approximately 460,782 students.

Special Programs for Indian Children.—Competitive grants are made for a demonstration grants program, a professional development program, and to support the American Indian Teacher Corps, an initiative to train and recruit 1,000 new Indian teachers for positions in school districts with high concentrations of Indian students. Increased funding in 2001 will support an initiative to train and recruit 500 new Indian school administrators for positions in school districts with high concentrations of Indian students.

National activities.—Funds support research, evaluation, data collection, and related activities.

Object Classification (in millions of dollars)

Identification code 91–0101–2–1–501	1999 actual	2000 est.	2001 est.
25.2 Other services			3
41.0 Grants, subsidies, and contributions			113
99.9 Total new obligations			116

SCHOOL RENOVATION PROGRAM ACCOUNT

For grants and loans to carry out school renovation under Title XII of the Elementary and Secondary Education Act of 1965, $1,300,000,000, to become available on July 1, 2001 and remain available until expended, of which (1) $50,000,000 shall be for grants to local educational agencies (as defined in section 8013(9) of such Act) in which the number of children determined under section 8003(a)(1)(C) of such Act constituted at least 50 percent of the number of children who were in average daily attendance in the schools of such agency during the preceding school year; (2) $125,000,000 shall be for grants to local educational agencies (other than those under (1)); and (3) $1,125,000,000 shall be for the costs of loans to local educational agencies: Provided, That such costs, including the cost of modifying such loans, shall be as defined in section 502 of the Congressional Budget Act of 1974: Provided further, That these funds are available to subsidize gross obligations for the principal amount of direct loans not to exceed $7,000,000,000: Provided further, That notwithstanding any provision of titles XII and XIV, the Secretary shall make these grants and loans subject to such terms and conditions as the Secretary shall establish.

Program and Financing (in millions of dollars)

Identification code 91–0009–0–1–501	1999 actual	2000 est.	2001 est.
Obligations by program activity:			
School renovation:			
00.01 Grants to Indian LEAs			50
00.02 Grants to other high-need LEAs			125
00.03 School renovation loan subsidies			1,125
10.00 Total new obligations (object class 41.0)			1,300
Budgetary resources available for obligation:			
21.40 Unobligated balance available, start of year			
22.00 New budget authority (gross)			1,300
23.90 Total budgetary resources available for obligation			1,300
23.95 Total new obligations			−1,300
24.40 Unobligated balance available, end of year			
New budget authority (gross), detail:			
Discretionary:			
40.00 Appropriation			1,300
Change in unpaid obligations:			
72.40 Unpaid obligations, start of year: Obligated balance, start of year			
73.10 Total new obligations			1,300
73.20 Total outlays (gross)			−74
74.40 Unpaid obligations, end of year: Obligated balance, end of year			1,226
Outlays (gross), detail:			
86.90 Outlays from new discretionary authority			74
Net budget authority and outlays:			
89.00 Budget authority			1,300
90.00 Outlays			74

School Renovation.—Under the Administration's proposal, grants and loans would be provided to high-need local educational agencies (LEAs) that have little or no capacity to fund urgent repairs. Grants would be provided to the neediest LEAs, including $50 million to LEAs in which 50 percent or more of the students reside on certain Indian lands, and $125 million to other school districts. The loan subsidy would generate approximately $6.5 billion in 7-year, no-interest loans for school renovation in high-need LEAs. Renovation funded through these loans and grants could include such projects as repairs to roofs, climate control systems, or plumbing.

Summary of Loan Levels, Subsidy Budget Authority and Outlays by Program (in millions of dollars)

Identification code 91–0009–0–1–501	1999 actual	2000 est.	2001 est.
Direct loan levels supportable by subsidy budget authority:			
1150 Direct loan levels			6,541
1159 Total direct loan levels			6,541
Direct loan subsidy (in percent):			
1320 Subsidy rate			17.20
1329 Weighted average subsidy rate			17.20
Direct loan subsidy budget authority:			
1330 Subsidy budget authority			1,125
1339 Total subsidy budget authority			1,125
Direct loan subsidy outlays:			
1340 Subsidy outlays			56
1349 Total subsidy outlays			56

SCHOOL RENOVATION, DIRECT LOAN FINANCING ACCOUNT

Program and Financing (in millions of dollars)

Identification code 91–4247–0–3–501	1999 actual	2000 est.	2001 est.
Obligations by program activity:			
00.01 Direct program activity			6,541
00.02 Interest payments to Treasury			6
10.00 Total new obligations			6,547
Budgetary resources available for obligation:			
22.00 New financing authority (gross)			6,546
23.95 Total new obligations			−6,547
New financing authority (gross), detail:			
Discretionary:			
47.00 Authority to borrow			6,485
Spending authority from offsetting collections:			
68.00 Offsetting collections (cash)			102
68.47 Portion applied to repay debt			−41
68.90 Spending authority from offsetting collections (total discretionary)			61
70.00 Total new financing authority (gross)			6,546
Change in unpaid obligations:			
73.10 Total new obligations			6,547
73.20 Total financing disbursements (gross)			−333
74.40 Unpaid obligations, end of year: Obligated balance, end of year			6,214

87.00	Total financing disbursements (gross)			333

	Offsets:			
	Against gross financing authority and financing disbursements:			
	Offsetting collections (cash) from:			
88.00	Federal sources			−56
88.40	Non-Federal sources			−46
88.90	Total, offsetting collections (cash)			−102

	Net financing authority and financing disbursements:			
89.00	Financing authority			6,444
90.00	Financing disbursements			231

Status of Direct Loans (in millions of dollars)

Identification code 91–4247–0–3–501		1999 actual	2000 est.	2001 est.
	Position with respect to appropriations act limitation on obligations:			
1111	Limitation on direct loans			
1131	Direct loan obligations exempt from limitation			6,541
1150	Total direct loan obligations			6,541
	Cumulative balance of direct loans outstanding:			
1210	Outstanding, start of year			
1231	Disbursements: Direct loan disbursements			327
1251	Repayments: Repayments and prepayments			−46
1290	Outstanding, end of year			281

Balance Sheet (in millions of dollars)

Identification code 91–4247–0–3–501		1998 actual	1999 actual	2000 est.	2001 est.
	ASSETS:				
1101	Federal assets: Fund balances with Treasury				6,214
	Net value of assets related to post–1991 direct loans receivable:				
1401	Direct loans receivable, gross				281
1405	Allowance for subsidy cost (–)				–4
1499	Net present value of assets related to direct loans				277
1999	Total assets				6,491
	LIABILITIES:				
2103	Federal liabilities: Debt				6,444
2999	Total liabilities				6,444
	NET POSITION:				
3100	Appropriated capital				46
3999	Total net position				46
4999	Total liabilities and net position				6,490

Object Classification (in millions of dollars)

Identification code 91–4247–0–3–501		1999 actual	2000 est.	2001 est.
33.0	Investments and loans			5,241
41.0	Grants, subsidies, and contributions			1,300
43.0	Interest and dividends			6
99.9	Total new obligations			6,547

OFFICE OF BILINGUAL EDUCATION AND MINORITY LANGUAGES AFFAIRS

Federal Funds

General and special funds:

BILINGUAL AND IMMIGRANT EDUCATION

[For carrying out, to the extent not otherwise provided, bilingual, foreign language and immigrant education activities authorized by parts A and C and section 7203 of title VII of the Elementary and Secondary Education Act of 1965, without regard to section 7103(b), $406,000,000: *Provided*, That State educational agencies may use all, or any part of, their part C allocation for competitive grants to local educational agencies.] *(Department of Education Appropriations Act, 2000, as enacted by section 1000(a)(4) of the Consolidated Appropriations Act, 2000 (P.L. 106–113).)*

Program and Financing (in millions of dollars)

Identification code 91–1300–0–1–501		1999 actual	2000 est.	2001 est.
	Obligations by program activity:			
00.01	Instructional services	160	162	
00.02	Support services	14	14	
00.03	Training grants	49	72	
00.04	Foreign language assistance	6	8	
00.05	Immigrant education	150	150	
10.00	Total new obligations	379	406	
	Budgetary resources available for obligation:			
22.00	New budget authority (gross)	380	406	
23.95	Total new obligations	−379	−406	
23.98	Unobligated balance expiring or withdrawn	−1		
	New budget authority (gross), detail:			
	Discretionary:			
40.00	Appropriation	380	406	
	Change in unpaid obligations:			
72.40	Unpaid obligations, start of year: Obligated balance, start of year	465	531	440
73.10	Total new obligations	379	406	
73.20	Total outlays (gross)	−311	−497	−351
73.40	Adjustments in expired accounts (net)	−2		
74.40	Unpaid obligations, end of year: Obligated balance, end of year	531	440	89
	Outlays (gross), detail:			
86.90	Outlays from new discretionary authority	16	49	
86.93	Outlays from discretionary balances	295	448	351
87.00	Total outlays (gross)	311	497	351
	Net budget authority and outlays:			
89.00	Budget authority	380	406	
90.00	Outlays	311	497	351

Bilingual and Immigrant Education.—The Administration has proposed legislation to reauthorize the Elementary and Secondary Education Act. When the new authorizing legislation is enacted, resources will be requested for bilingual, foreign language, and immigrant education programs. See the "Legislative proposal, not subject to PAYGO" schedule for additional details.

Summary of Budget Authority and Outlays

(in millions of dollars)

	1999 actual	*2000 est.*	*2001 est.*
Enacted/requested:			
Budget Authority	380	406	
Outlays	311	497	351
Legislative proposal, not subject to PAYGO:			
Budget Authority			460
Outlays			55
Total:			
Budget Authority	380	406	460
Outlays	311	497	406

Object Classification (in millions of dollars)

Identification code 91–1300–0–1–501		1999 actual	2000 est.	2001 est.
25.1	Advisory and assistance services	4	5	
25.2	Other services	2	2	
41.0	Grants, subsidies, and contributions	373	399	
99.9	Total new obligations	379	406	

General and special funds—Continued

BILINGUAL AND IMMIGRANT EDUCATION

(Legislative proposal, not subject to PAYGO)

Program and Financing (in millions of dollars)

Identification code 91–1300–2–1–501	1999 actual	2000 est.	2001 est.
Obligations by program activity:			
00.01 Instructional services			180
00.02 Support services			16
00.03 Training grants			100
00.04 Foreign language assistance			14
00.05 Immigrant education			150
10.00 Total new obligations			460
Budgetary resources available for obligation:			
22.00 New budget authority (gross)			460
23.95 Total new obligations			−460
New budget authority (gross), detail:			
Discretionary:			
40.00 Appropriation			460
Change in unpaid obligations:			
73.10 Total new obligations			460
73.20 Total outlays (gross)			−55
74.40 Unpaid obligations, end of year: Obligated balance, end of year			407
Outlays (gross), detail:			
86.90 Outlays from new discretionary authority			55
Net budget authority and outlays:			
89.00 Budget authority			460
90.00 Outlays			55

The resources in this schedule are proposed for later transmittal under proposed legislation to revise and reauthorize programs currently authorized under the Elementary and Secondary Education Act of 1965.

Bilingual education.—The bilingual education programs would provide assistance to local educational agencies and other entities to develop and enhance their capacity to provide high-quality instructional programs to children and youth of limited English proficiency. Projects would be designed to teach English and to assist these students in achieving the same challenging State content and performance standards expected of all children and youth. Aid would also support training education personnel to serve limited English proficient children, building State capacity to improve educational services for these children, and information dissemination, studies, and evaluations.

Foreign language assistance.—The foreign language assistance program would provide competitive grants to States and local educational agencies that are linked to State foreign language standards and are designed to improve the quality of foreign language instruction for elementary and secondary school students.

Immigrant education.—The immigrant education program would provide grants to school districts to help finance educational services for immigrant students. Participation would be limited to districts with at least 500 immigrant students or districts in which immigrant children represent at least 3 percent of the enrollment. Awards would be made to State educational agencies, which would make subgrants to local educational agencies. States would be authorized to distribute these funds on either a formula or discretionary grant basis.

Object Classification (in millions of dollars)

Identification code 91–1300–2–1–501	1999 actual	2000 est.	2001 est.
25.1 Advisory and assistance services			2
25.2 Other services			5
41.0 Grants, subsidies, and contributions			453
99.9 Total new obligations			460

OFFICE OF SPECIAL EDUCATION AND REHABILITATIVE SERVICES

Federal Funds

General and special funds:

SPECIAL EDUCATION

For carrying out the Individuals with Disabilities Education Act, [$6,036,646,000] *$6,368,841,000*, of which [$2,047,885,000] *$2,356,452,000* shall become available for obligation on July 1, [2000] *2001*, and shall remain available through September 30, [2001] *2002*, and of which $3,742,000,000 shall become available on October 1, [2000] *2001* and shall remain available through September 30, [2001] *2002*, for academic year [2000–2001] *2001–2002*: *Provided*, That [$1,500,000 shall be for the recipient of funds provided by Public Law 105–78 under section 687(b)(2)(G) of the Act to provide information on diagnosis, intervention, and teaching strategies for children with disabilities: *Provided further*, That $1,500,000 shall be awarded to the Organizing Committee for the 2001 Special Olympics World Winter Games in Alaska and $1,000,000 shall be awarded to the Salt Lake City Organizing Committee for the VIII Paralympic Winter Games: *Provided further*, That $1,000,000 shall be for the Early Childhood Development Project of the National Easter Seal Society for the Mississippi Delta Region, which funds shall be used to provide training, technical support, services and equipment to address personnel and other needs: *Provided further*, That $1,000,000 shall be awarded to the Center for Literacy and Assessment at the University of Southern Mississippi for research dissemination and teacher and parent training] *the amount for section 611(c) of the Act shall be equal to the amount available for that section under Public Law 106–113, increased by the rate of inflation as specified in section 611(f)(1)(B)(ii) of the Act. (Department of Education Appropriations Act, 2000, as enacted by section 1000(a)(4) of the Consolidated Appropriations Act, 2000 (P.L. 106–113).)*

Program and Financing (in millions of dollars)

Identification code 91–0300–0–1–501	1999 actual	2000 est.	2001 est.
Direct program:			
Obligations by program activity:			
State grants:			
00.01 Grants to States	4,315	1,273	5,280
00.02 Preschool grants	374	390	390
00.03 Grants for infants and families	373	441	384
00.91 Subtotal, State grants	5,062	2,104	6,054
National activities:			
01.01 State improvement	31	61	45
01.02 Research and innovation	64	64	74
01.03 Technical assistance and dissemination	45	45	53
01.04 Personnel preparation	81	83	82
01.05 Parent information centers	19	19	26
01.06 Technology and media services	35	36	35
01.91 Subtotal, National activities	275	308	315
02.00 Total Direct Program	5,337	2,412	6,369
09.01 Reimbursable program	1		
10.00 Total new obligations	5,338	2,412	6,369
Budgetary resources available for obligation:			
21.40 Unobligated balance available, start of year	118	119	1
22.00 New budget authority (gross)	5,335	2,294	6,369
22.10 Resources available from recoveries of prior year obligations	4		
23.90 Total budgetary resources available for obligation	5,457	2,413	6,370
23.95 Total new obligations	−5,338	−2,412	−6,369
23.98 Unobligated balance expiring or withdrawn	−1	−1	
24.40 Unobligated balance available, end of year	119	1	1
New budget authority (gross), detail:			
Discretionary:			
40.00 Appropriation	5,124	2,294	2,627
42.00 Transferred from other accounts	210		

43.00 Appropriation (total discretionary)	5,334	2,294	2,627
55.00 Advance appropriation			3,742
68.00 Spending authority from offsetting collections: Offsetting collections (cash)	1		
70.00 Total new budget authority (gross)	5,335	2,294	6,369
Change in unpaid obligations:			
72.40 Unpaid obligations, start of year: Obligated balance, start of year	5,990	6,855	3,835
73.10 Total new obligations	5,338	2,412	6,369
73.20 Total outlays (gross)	−4,445	−5,432	−5,816
73.40 Adjustments in expired accounts (net)	−23		
73.45 Adjustments in unexpired accounts	−4		
74.40 Unpaid obligations, end of year: Obligated balance, end of year	6,855	3,835	4,388
Outlays (gross), detail:			
86.90 Outlays from new discretionary authority	115	302	2,937
86.93 Outlays from discretionary balances	4,330	5,130	2,878
87.00 Total outlays (gross)	4,445	5,432	5,816
Offsets:			
Against gross budget authority and outlays:			
88.00 Offsetting collections (cash) from: Federal sources	−1		
Net budget authority and outlays:			
89.00 Budget authority	5,334	2,294	6,369
90.00 Outlays	4,444	5,432	5,816

SUMMARY OF PROGRAM LEVEL

[In millions of dollars]

	1999–2000 academic year	*2000–2001 academic year*	*2001–2002 academic year*
Current Budget Authority	5,334	2,294	2,627
Advance appropriation	0	3,742	3,742
Total program level	5,334	6,036	6,369
Increase in advance appropriation over previous year	+0	+3,742	+0

State Grants:

Grants to States.—Formula grants are provided to States to assist them in providing special education and related services to children with disabilities ages 3 through 21.

Preschool grants.—Formula grants provide additional funds to States to further assist them in providing special education and related services to children with disabilities ages 3 through 5 served under the Grants to States program.

The goal of both of these programs is to improve results for children with disabilities by assisting State and local educational agencies to provide children with disabilities with access to high quality education that will help them meet challenging standards and prepare them for employment and independent living.

Grants for infants and families.—Formula grants are provided to assist States to implement statewide systems of coordinated, comprehensive, multi-disciplinary interagency programs to provide early intervention services to children with disabilities, birth through age 2, and their families.

The goal of this program is to help States provide a comprehensive system of early intervention services that will enhance family and child outcomes.

National activities.—These activities include research, demonstration, personnel preparation, technical assistance, grants to States to promote systems change, and other activities to support State efforts to improve results for children with disabilities under the State grants programs.

The goal of National activities is to link States, school systems, and families to best practices to improve results for infants, toddlers, and children with disabilities.

Performance data related to these goals include:

Number of children served in first quarter of fiscal year:	1999 actual	2000 est.	2001 est.
Ages 3 through 21	6,133,000	6,262,000	6,368,000
Ages 3 through 5	574,713	577,600	580,500
Birth through 2	186,819	191,489	196,276

	1994–1995 actual	1995–1996 actual	1996–1997 actual
Educational Environment			
Percent of children ages 6 through 21 provided special education in:			
Regular classrooms	44.5	45.3	45.7
Resource rooms	28.8	28.7	28.5
Separate classes	22.4	21.7	21.4
Separate schools	3.0	3.1	3.1
Residential facilities	.7	.7	.7
Home or hospital	.6	.6	.5
Status of Exiting Students			
Percent of students with disabilities aged 14–21 leaving school:			
Graduated with a diploma	52.3	52.6	53.5
Graduated through certification	11.1	10.9	11.4
Reached maximum age and other	2.5	2.4	2.4
Dropped out of school	34.2	34.1	32.7

Object Classification (in millions of dollars)

Identification code 91–0300–0–1–501	1999 actual	2000 est.	2001 est.
25.2 Other services	8	8	8
41.0 Grants, subsidies, and contributions	5,330	2,404	6,361
99.9 Total new obligations	5,338	2,412	6,369

REHABILITATION SERVICES AND DISABILITY RESEARCH

For carrying out, to the extent not otherwise provided, the Rehabilitation Act of 1973, the Assistive Technology Act of 1998, and the Helen Keller National Center Act, [$2,707,522,000] *$2,798,651,000*: *Provided*, [That notwithstanding section 105(b)(1) of the Assistive Technology Act of 1998 ("the AT Act"), each State shall be provided $50,000 for activities under section 102 of the AT Act: *Provided further*, That of the funds available for section 303 of the Rehabilitation Act of 1973 and notwithstanding any other provision of law, $750,000 shall be awarded to the Krasnow Institute at George Mason University for a Receptive Language Disorders research center, $1,000,000 shall be awarded to the University of Central Florida for a virtual reality-based education and training program for the deaf, $2,000,000 shall be awarded to the Seattle Lighthouse for the Blind for interpreter, orientation, mobility, and education services for deaf, blind and other visually impaired adults, $1,000,000 shall be awarded to the Professional Development and Research Institute on Blindness in Louisiana for the training of professionals in the field of education and rehabilitation of blind adults and children, $600,000 shall be awarded to the Alaska Center for Independent Living in Anchorage, Alaska to develop capacity to implement a self-directed model for personal assistance services, including training of self-employed personal assistants and their clients, and $250,000 shall be awarded to the Center for Discovery International Family Institute in Sullivan County, New York to provide educational opportunities and support to individuals with severe mental and physical disabilities: *Provided further*, That of the funds available for section 305 of the Rehabilitation Act of 1973 and notwithstanding any other provision of law, $1,000,000 shall be awarded to the California State University at Northridge for a Western Center for Adaptive Therapy: *Provided further*, That of the funds available for title II of the Rehabilitation Act of 1973 and notwithstanding any other provision of law, $500,000 shall be awarded to the Albert Einstein Medical Center healthcare network in Philadelphia for research on post polio syndrome] *That the funds for Title I of the Assistive Technology Act of 1998 ("the AT Act") shall be allocated notwithstanding section 105(b)(1) of the AT Act: Provided further, That $15,000,000 shall be used to support grants for up to three years to States under title III of the AT Act, of which the Federal share shall not exceed 75 percent in the first year, 50 percent in the second year, and 25 percent in the third year, and that the requirements in section 302 of the AT Act shall not apply to such grants. (Department of Education Appropriations Act, 2000, as enacted by section 1000(a)(4) of the Consolidated Appropriations Act, 2000 (P.L. 106–113).)*

General and special funds—Continued

REHABILITATION SERVICES AND DISABILITY RESEARCH—Continued

Program and Financing (in millions of dollars)

Identification code 91–0301–0–1–506	1999 actual	2000 est.	2001 est.
Obligations by program activity:			
Direct program:			
00.01 Vocational rehabilitation State grants	2,304	2,339	2,400
00.02 Client assistance State grants	11	11	11
00.03 Training	40	40	40
00.04 Demonstration and training programs	15	22	22
00.05 Migrant and seasonal farmworkers	2	2	3
00.06 Recreational programs	2	3	2
00.07 Protection and advocacy of individual rights	11	12	12
00.08 Projects with industry	22	22	22
00.09 Supported employment State grants	38	38	38
00.10 Independent living	79	85	95
00.11 Program improvement	2	2	2
00.12 Evaluation	2	2	2
00.13 Helen Keller National Center	9	9	9
00.14 National Institute on Disability and Rehabilitation Research	81	86	100
00.15 Assistive technology	34	34	41
01.00 Total direct program	2,652	2,707	2,799
09.01 Reimbursable program	3	3	3
10.00 Total new obligations	2,655	2,710	2,802
Budgetary resources available for obligation:			
22.00 New budget authority (gross)	2,655	2,710	2,802
23.95 Total new obligations	−2,655	−2,710	−2,802
New budget authority (gross), detail:			
Discretionary:			
40.00 Appropriation	348	369	399
40.76 Reduction pursuant to P.L. 106–113	....	−1	....
43.00 Appropriation (total discretionary)	348	368	399
Mandatory:			
60.00 Appropriation	2,304	2,339	2,400
Discretionary:			
68.00 Spending authority from offsetting collections: Offsetting collections (cash)	3	3	3
70.00 Total new budget authority (gross)	2,655	2,710	2,802
Change in unpaid obligations:			
72.40 Unpaid obligations, start of year: Obligated balance, start of year	1,100	1,028	893
73.10 Total new obligations	2,655	2,710	2,802
73.20 Total outlays (gross)	−2,715	−2,845	−2,772
73.40 Adjustments in expired accounts (net)	−12	....	....
74.40 Unpaid obligations, end of year: Obligated balance, end of year	1,028	893	923
Outlays (gross), detail:			
86.90 Outlays from new discretionary authority	61	260	281
86.93 Outlays from discretionary balances	119	308	110
86.97 Outlays from new mandatory authority	1,728	1,637	1,680
86.98 Outlays from mandatory balances	808	641	701
87.00 Total outlays (gross)	2,715	2,845	2,772
Offsets:			
Against gross budget authority and outlays:			
88.00 Offsetting collections (cash) from: Federal sources	−3	−3	−3
Net budget authority and outlays:			
89.00 Budget authority	2,652	2,707	2,799
90.00 Outlays	2,713	2,842	2,769

Vocational rehabilitation State grants.—The basic State grants program provides Federal matching funds to State vocational rehabilitation (VR) agencies to assist individuals with physical or mental impairments to become gainfully employed. Services are tailored to the specific needs of the individual. Priority is given to serving those with the most significant disabilities. Current law requires that between 1.0 percent and 1.5 percent of the funds appropriated for the VR State grants program be set aside for Grants for Indians in 2001.

The table below presents national data on selected performance measures for the VR State grants program. The data are based on the number of individuals whose service records were closed in fiscal years 1997 (347,601) and 1998 (359,877). The 2001 target is to increase the number of individuals with disabilities achieving an employment outcome by one percent over the previous year and to increase the employment outcome rate to 63 percent.

CONSUMER OUTCOMES (CASES CLOSED)

	1997 actual	1998 actual
Individuals achieving employment outcomes	211,503	223,668
Percent with significant disabilities	79.6%	82.6%
Employment outcomes as a percent all of individuals receiving services	60.8%	62.1%

Client assistance State grants.—Formula grants are made to States to provide assistance in informing and advising clients and applicants of benefits available under the Rehabilitation Act and, if requested, to pursue legal or administrative remedies to ensure the protection of the rights of individuals with disabilities.

Training.—Grants are made to States and public or nonprofit agencies and organizations, including institutions of higher education, to increase the number of skilled personnel available for employment in the field of rehabilitation and to upgrade the skills of those already employed.

Demonstration and training programs.—Grants are made for programs that expand, improve, or further the purpose of activities supported under the Rehabilitation Act.

Migrant and seasonal farmworkers.—Grants are made to State VR agencies and other nonprofit or local agencies to provide comprehensive vocational rehabilitation services to migrant and seasonal farmworkers with disabilities. Data for 1998 indicate that more than 9,200 migrant and seasonal farmworkers were served.

Recreational programs.—Grants are made to provide individuals with disabilities with recreational and related activities to aid in their employment, mobility, independence, socialization, and community integration.

Protection and advocacy of individual rights.—Formula grants are made to State protection and advocacy systems to protect the legal and human rights of individuals with disabilities.

Projects with industry (PWI).—Grants are made to a variety of public and private organizations to facilitate the establishment of partnerships between rehabilitation service providers and business and industry in order to create and expand employment and career advancement opportunities for individuals with disabilities. In 1998, PWI projects placed in competitive employment approximately 49 percent (6,792) of the 13,811 individuals with disabilities served by the 104 projects. The 2001 target for this program is to place 62 percent of the individuals served in competitive employment.

Supported employment State grants.—Formula grants are made to assist States in developing programs with public and nonprofit organizations to provide supported employment services for individuals with the most significant disabilities who require on-going support services to enter or retain competitive employment. In 1998, 74 percent of individuals with a supported employment goal achieved a competitive employment outcome. The 2001 target for this program is for 76 percent to achieve competitive employment outcomes.

Independent living.—Grants are awarded to States and nonprofit agencies to assist individuals with significant disabilities in their achievement of self-determined independent living goals. Grants are also awarded to provide support services to older blind individuals to increase their ability to care for their own needs. Performance indicators focus on customer satisfaction, achievement of individual goals, and broader systemic reforms in the community.

Program improvement.—Funds are used to promote broad-based planning and coordination, improve accountability, and enhance the Department's ability to address critical areas of national significance in achieving the goals of the Rehabilitation Act. Examples of program improvement activities include technical assistance, dissemination, and performance measurement activities.

Evaluation.—Studies are conducted to evaluate the impact and effectiveness of various programs authorized under the Rehabilitation Act. The multi-year national longitudinal study of the Vocational Rehabilitation State grants program is scheduled for completion in 2000. Expanded study findings on employment retention will be available in 2002.

Helen Keller National Center for Deaf-Blind Youths and Adults.—The Center provides services to deaf-blind youths and adults and provides training and technical assistance to professional and allied personnel at its national headquarters center and through its regional representatives and affiliate agencies.

National Institute on Disability and Rehabilitation Research.—The Institute carries out a comprehensive and coordinated program of rehabilitation research and related activities. Through grants and contracts, it supports the conduct and dissemination of research aimed at improving the lives of individuals with disabilities.

Assistive technology.—Activities include the Assistive Technology State grant program, protection and advocacy services, and technical assistance designed to develop and implement consumer-responsive comprehensive statewide programs of technology-related assistance for individuals with disabilities. Grants also are made to States to establish alternative loan financing programs to increase access to assistive technology for individuals with disabilities.

Object Classification (in millions of dollars)

Identification code 91–0301–0–1–506	1999 actual	2000 est.	2001 est.
Direct obligations:			
25.1 Advisory and assistance services	5	5	5
25.2 Other services	1	1	1
25.3 Purchases of goods and services from Government accounts	1	1	1
25.5 Research and development contracts	1	2	2
41.0 Grants, subsidies, and contributions	2,644	2,698	2,790
99.0 Subtotal, direct obligations	2,652	2,707	2,799
99.0 Reimbursable obligations	3	3	3
99.9 Total new obligations	2,655	2,710	2,802

SPECIAL INSTITUTIONS FOR PERSONS WITH DISABILITIES

AMERICAN PRINTING HOUSE FOR THE BLIND

For carrying out the Act of March 3, 1879, as amended (20 U.S.C. 101 et seq.), [$10,100,000] *$10,265,000*. *(Department of Education Appropriations Act, 2000, as enacted by section 1000(a)(4) of the Consolidated Appropriations Act, 2000 (P.L. 106–113).)*

Program and Financing (in millions of dollars)

Identification code 91–0600–0–1–501	1999 actual	2000 est.	2001 est.
Obligations by program activity:			
10.00 Total new obligations (object class 41.0)	9	10	10
Budgetary resources available for obligation:			
22.00 New budget authority (gross)	9	10	10
23.95 Total new obligations	−9	−10	−10
New budget authority (gross), detail:			
Discretionary:			
40.00 Appropriation	9	10	10
Change in unpaid obligations:			
72.40 Unpaid obligations, start of year: Obligated balance, start of year	2	3	1
73.10 Total new obligations	9	10	10
73.20 Total outlays (gross)	−8	−13	−10
74.40 Unpaid obligations, end of year: Obligated balance, end of year	3	1	1
Outlays (gross), detail:			
86.90 Outlays from new discretionary authority	6	9	9
86.93 Outlays from discretionary balances	2	3	1
87.00 Total outlays (gross)	8	13	10
Net budget authority and outlays:			
89.00 Budget authority	9	10	10
90.00 Outlays	8	13	10

The Federal appropriation supports the production of free educational materials for students below the college level who are blind, research related to developing and improving products, and advisory services to consumer organizations on the availability and use of materials. In 1999, the portion of the Federal appropriation allocated to educational materials represented approximately 49.3 percent of the Printing House's total sales. The full appropriation represented approximately 36.1 percent of the Printing House's total budget.

NATIONAL TECHNICAL INSTITUTE FOR THE DEAF

For the National Technical Institute for the Deaf under titles I and II of the Education of the Deaf Act of 1986 (20 U.S.C. 4301 et seq.), [$48,151,000] *$51,786,000*, of which [$2,651,000] *$5,376,000* shall be for construction and shall remain available until expended: *Provided*, That from the total amount available, the Institute may at its discretion use funds for the endowment program as authorized under section 207. *(Department of Education Appropriations Act, 2000, as enacted by section 1000(a)(4) of the Consolidated Appropriations Act, 2000 (P.L. 106–113).)*

Program and Financing (in millions of dollars)

Identification code 91–0601–0–1–502	1999 actual	2000 est.	2001 est.
Obligations by program activity:			
00.01 Operations	46	45	46
00.02 Construction		3	5
10.00 Total new obligations (object class 41.0)	46	48	51
Budgetary resources available for obligation:			
22.00 New budget authority (gross)	46	48	51
23.95 Total new obligations	−46	−48	−51
New budget authority (gross), detail:			
Discretionary:			
40.00 Appropriation	46	48	51
Change in unpaid obligations:			
72.40 Unpaid obligations, start of year: Obligated balance, start of year	1	1	5
73.10 Total new obligations	46	48	51
73.20 Total outlays (gross)	−45	−44	−48
74.40 Unpaid obligations, end of year: Obligated balance, end of year	1	5	9
Outlays (gross), detail:			
86.90 Outlays from new discretionary authority	46	43	44
86.93 Outlays from discretionary balances		1	4
87.00 Total outlays (gross)	45	44	48
Net budget authority and outlays:			
89.00 Budget authority	46	48	51
90.00 Outlays	45	44	48

This residential program provides postsecondary technical and professional education for people who are deaf to prepare them for employment, provides training, and conducts applied research into employment related aspects of deafness. In 1999, Federal appropriations represented 81 percent of the Institute's operating budget. The Institute may use appro-

General and special funds—Continued

SPECIAL INSTITUTIONS FOR PERSONS WITH DISABILITIES—Continued

NATIONAL TECHNICAL INSTITUTE FOR THE DEAF—Continued

priated funds for the Endowment Grant program. The request also includes funds for the second phase of a construction project to renovate the Institute's dormitories.

GALLAUDET UNIVERSITY

For the Kendall Demonstration Elementary School, the Model Secondary School for the Deaf, and the partial support of Gallaudet University under titles I and II of the Education of the Deaf Act of 1986 (20 U.S.C. 4301 et seq.), [$85,980,000, of which $2,500,000 shall be for construction and shall remain available until expended] *$87,650,000*: *Provided*, That from the total amount available, the University may at its discretion use funds for the endowment program as authorized under section 207. *(Department of Education Appropriations Act, 2000, as enacted by section 1000(a)(4) of the Consolidated Appropriations Act, 2000 (P.L. 106–113).)*

Program and Financing (in millions of dollars)

Identification code 91–0602–0–1–502	1999 actual	2000 est.	2001 est.
Obligations by program activity:			
00.01 Operations	83	83	88
00.02 Construction		3	
10.00 Total new obligations (object class 41.0)	83	86	88
Budgetary resources available for obligation:			
22.00 New budget authority (gross)	83	86	88
23.95 Total new obligations	−83	−86	−88
New budget authority (gross), detail:			
Discretionary:			
40.00 Appropriation	83	86	88
Change in unpaid obligations:			
72.40 Unpaid obligations, start of year: Obligated balance, start of year	2	3	7
73.10 Total new obligations	83	86	88
73.20 Total outlays (gross)	−82	−82	−88
74.40 Unpaid obligations, end of year: Obligated balance, end of year	3	7	7
Outlays (gross), detail:			
86.90 Outlays from new discretionary authority	83	78	83
86.93 Outlays from discretionary balances	−2	3	6
87.00 Total outlays (gross)	82	82	88
Net budget authority and outlays:			
89.00 Budget authority	83	86	88
90.00 Outlays	82	82	88

This institution provides undergraduate and continuing education programs for persons who are deaf, and graduate programs related to deafness for students who are deaf and students who are hearing. The University also conducts basic and applied research and provides public service programs for persons who are deaf and persons who work with them.

Gallaudet operates two elementary and secondary education programs on the main campus of the University. The Kendall Demonstration Elementary School serves students who are deaf from infancy through age 15, and the Model Secondary School for the Deaf serves high school age students who are deaf. Both schools also develop and disseminate information on effective educational techniques and strategies for teachers and professionals working with students who are deaf or hard of hearing.

In 1999, the Federal appropriation represented 63 percent of the University's operating budget, excluding Federal financial aid, vocational rehabilitation, and competitive grants, and 97.9 percent of the operating budgets of the related elementary and secondary schools. The University may also use appropriated funds for the Endowment Grant program.

OFFICE OF VOCATIONAL AND ADULT EDUCATION

Federal Funds

General and special funds:

VOCATIONAL AND ADULT EDUCATION

For carrying out, to the extent not otherwise provided, the Carl D. Perkins Vocational and Technical Education Act, the Adult Education and Family Literacy Act, and title VIII–D of the Higher Education Act of 1965, as amended, and Public Law 102–73, [$1,681,750,000] *$1,751,250,000*, of which [$3,500,000] *$1,000,000* shall remain available until expended, and of which [$858,150,000] *$942,650,000* shall become available on July 1, [2000] *2001* and shall remain available through September 30, [2001] *2002* and of which $791,000,000 shall become available on October 1, [2000] *2001* and shall remain available through September 30, [2001] *2002*: *Provided*, That of the amounts made available for the Carl D. Perkins Vocational and Technical Education Act, $4,600,000 shall be for tribally controlled vocational institutions under section 117: [*Provided further*, That of the $450,000,000 for Adult Education State Grants, 30 percent of the amount exceeding the amount appropriated in fiscal year 1999 shall be made available for integrated English literacy and civics education services to immigrants and other limited English proficient populations: *Provided further*, That of the amount reserved for integrated English literacy and civics education, half shall be allocated to the States with the largest absolute need for such services and half shall be allocated to the States with the largest recent growth in need for such services, based on the best available data, notwithstanding section 211 of the Adult Education and Family Literacy Act: *Provided further*, That $9,000,000 shall be for carrying out section 118 of such act for all activities conducted by and through the National Occupational Information Coordinating Committee:]: *Provided further, That of the funds made available to carry out section 204 of the Perkins Act, all funds that a State receives in excess of its prior-year allocation shall be competitively awarded: Provided further, That in making these awards, each State shall give priority to consortia whose applications most effectively integrate all components under section 204(c): Provided further*, That of the amounts made available for the Adult Education and Family Literacy Act, [$14,000,000] *$89,000,000* shall be for national leadership activities under section 243 and [$6,000,000] *$6,500,000* shall be for the National Institute for Literacy under section 242: [*Provided further*, That $19,000,000 shall be for Youth Offender Grants, of which $5,000,000, which shall become available on July 1, 2000, and remain available through September 30, 2001, shall be used in accordance with section 601 of Public Law 102–73 as that section was in effect prior to the enactment of Public Law 105–220] *Provided further, That of the amounts made available for title I of the Perkins Act, the Secretary may reserve up to 0.54 percent for incentive grants under section 503 of the Workforce Investment Act, without regard to section 111(a)(1)(C) of the Perkins Act: Provided further, That of the amounts made available for the Adult Education and Family Literacy Act, the Secretary may reserve up to 0.54 percent for incentive grants under section 503 of the Workforce Investment Act, without regard to section 211(a)(3) of the Adult Education and Family Literacy Act. (Department of Education Appropriations Act, 2000, as enacted by section 1000(a)(4) of the Consolidated Appropriations Act, 2000 (P.L. 106–113).)*

Program and Financing (in millions of dollars)

Identification code 91–0400–0–1–501	1999 actual	2000 est.	2001 est.
Obligations by program activity:			
Vocational education:			
Annual appropriations:			
Vocational education:			
00.01 Basic grants	1,023	284	1,056
00.02 National programs	13	13	17
00.03 Occupational and employment information		9	
00.04 Tribally controlled postsecondary vocational institutions	4	5	5
00.05 Tech-prep education	105	107	106

00.91	Total, Vocational education	1,145	418	1,184
	Adult education:			
01.01	State grants	364	451	460
01.02	National Institute for Literacy	5	6	6
01.03	National leadership activities	5	14	14
01.91	Total, adult education	374	471	480
02.01	State grants for incarcerated youth offenders		14	12
03.01	Literacy programs for prisoners	5		5
10.00	Total new obligations	1,524	903	1,681
	Budgetary resources available for obligation:			
21.40	Unobligated balance available, start of year	45	60	48
22.00	New budget authority (gross)	1,539	891	1,751
23.90	Total budgetary resources available for obligation	1,584	951	1,799
23.95	Total new obligations	−1,524	−903	−1,681
24.40	Unobligated balance available, end of year	60	48	119
	New budget authority (gross), detail:			
	Discretionary:			
40.00	Appropriation	1,539	891	960
55.00	Advance appropriation			791
70.00	Total new budget authority (gross)	1,539	891	1,751
	Change in unpaid obligations:			
72.40	Unpaid obligations, start of year: Obligated balance, start of year	1,781	1,939	1,295
73.10	Total new obligations	1,524	903	1,681
73.20	Total outlays (gross)	−1,364	−1,547	−1,641
73.40	Adjustments in expired accounts (net)	−3		
74.40	Unpaid obligations, end of year: Obligated balance, end of year	1,939	1,295	1,334
	Outlays (gross), detail:			
86.90	Outlays from new discretionary authority	64	85	642
86.93	Outlays from discretionary balances	1,298	1,462	1,000
86.98	Outlays from mandatory balances	2		
87.00	Total outlays (gross)	1,364	1,547	1,641
	Net budget authority and outlays:			
89.00	Budget authority	1,539	891	1,751
90.00	Outlays	1,364	1,547	1,641

Program levels for activities in this account are as follows:

(in millions of dollars)

	1999–2000 academic year	2000–2001 academic year	2001–2002 academic year
1. Vocational education:			
a. Basic grants:			
Annual appropriation	1,031	265	265
Advance appropriation		791	591
Subtotal, basic grants	1,031	1,056	856
b. National programs	13	17	17
c. Occupational & employment information		9	
d. Tribally controlled postsecondary vocational institutions	4	5	5
e. Tech-prep education:			
Annual appropriation	106	106	106
Advance appropriation			200
Subtotal, tech-prep	106	106	306
Total, vocational education	1,154	1,193	1,184
2. Adult education:			
a. State grants	365	450	460
b. National Institute for Literacy	6	6	6
c. National leadership activities	14	14	89
Total, adult education	385	470	555
3. State grants for incarcerated youth offenders		14	12
4. Literacy programs for prisoners		5	
Total	1,539	1,682	1,751

SUMMARY OF PROGRAM LEVEL

(in millions of dollars)

	1999–2000 academic year	2000–2001 academic year	2001–2002 academic year
Current Budget Authority	1,539	891	960
Advance appropriation	0	791	791
Total program level	1,539	1,682	1,751
Increase in advance appropriation over previous year		791	

Vocational education.—

Basic grants.—Formula grants provide funds to States and localities to expand and improve their programs of vocational education and promote equal opportunity in vocational education programs for historically underserved populations. Funds under the Indian program are awarded to federally recognized Indian tribes and are in addition to services provided under other provisions of the Perkins Act. Funds under the Hawaiian Natives program are awarded to organizations primarily serving and representing Hawaiian Natives. Funds under the Territorial set-aside support the expansion and improvement of vocational education programs in American Samoa, Guam, the Northern Marianas, and the Freely Associated States.

National programs.—Funds are awarded on a competitive basis for activities that contribute to knowledge of how to improve access to vocational education for underserved populations and how to improve vocational education nationally. Activities include two national centers for research and dissemination in vocational education and a program of discretionary research and development projects, including a national assessment of vocational education.

Tribally controlled postsecondary vocational and technical institutions.—Grants support the operation and improvement of tribally controlled postsecondary vocational institutions, to ensure continued and expanded educational opportunities for Indian students.

Tech-prep education.—Formula grants to States support planning and demonstration grants to consortia of local educational agencies and postsecondary institutions to develop and operate model 4-year programs. Programs begin in high school and provide students with the mathematical, scientific, communications, and technological skills needed to earn a 2-year associate degree or a 2-year certificate in a specific occupational field.

Adult Education.—

State programs.—Formula grants are made to States to help eliminate functional illiteracy among the Nation's adults, to assist adults in obtaining a high school diploma or its equivalent, and to promote family literacy.

National Institute for Literacy.—Funds support the Institute's national leadership activities to improve and expand the Nation's system for delivery of literacy services.

National leadership activities.—Funds support discretionary activities to evaluate the effectiveness of Federal, State, and local adult education programs and to test and demonstrate methods of improving program quality. Activities will include development of model programs for providing English language and citizenship education to recent immigrants.

State Grants for Incarcerated Youth Offenders.—Formula grants are made to State correctional agencies to assist and encourage incarcerated youths to acquire functional literacy skills and life and job skills.

Object Classification (in millions of dollars)

Identification code 91–0400–0–1–501		1999 actual	2000 est.	2001 est.
	Personnel compensation:			
11.1	Full-time permanent			1
11.3	Other than full-time permanent	1	1	1
11.9	Total personnel compensation	1	1	2
25.1	Advisory and assistance services	6	5	4
25.2	Other services	1		1
25.5	Research and development contracts	7	9	9
41.0	Grants, subsidies, and contributions	1,509	887	1,664
99.0	Subtotal, direct obligations	1,524	902	1,680
99.5	Below reporting threshold		1	1

General and special funds—Continued

VOCATIONAL AND ADULT EDUCATION—Continued

Object Classification (in millions of dollars)—Continued

Identification code 91–0400–0–1–501	1999 actual	2000 est.	2001 est.
99.9 Total new obligations	1,524	903	1,681

Personnel Summary

Identification code 91–0400–0–1–501	1999 actual	2000 est.	2001 est.
1001 Total compensable workyears: Full-time equivalent employment	13	14	16

OFFICE OF POSTSECONDARY EDUCATION

Federal Funds

General and special funds:

HIGHER EDUCATION

For carrying out, to the extent not otherwise provided, section 121 and titles II, III, IV, V, VI, VII, and VIII of the Higher Education Act of 1965, as amended, and the Mutual Educational and Cultural Exchange Act of 1961; [$1,533,659,000] *$1,755,973,000*, of which [$12,000,000] *$10,000,000* for interest subsidies authorized by section 121 of the Higher Education Act of 1965, shall remain available until expended: *Provided*, That [of the funds available for part A, subpart 2 of title VII of the Higher Education Act of 1965, $10,000,000 shall be available to fund awards for academic year 2000–2001, and] $10,000,000, to remain available through September 30, [2001] *2002*, shall be available to fund [awards] *fellowships* for academic year [2001–2002] *2002–2003*[, for fellowships] under part A, subpart 1 of title VII of said Act, under the terms and conditions of part A, subpart 1: [*Provided further*, That section 852(b)(1) of the Higher Education Amendments of 1998 is amended—

(1) in the matter preceding subparagraph (A), by striking "14" and inserting "16";

(2) in subparagraph (E), by striking "and" after the semicolon;

(3) in subparagraph (F), by striking the period and inserting a semicolon; and

(4) by adding at the end the following:

"(G) one member shall be appointed by the Chairperson of the Committee on Health, Education, Labor, and Pensions of the Senate from among members of the Senate; and

"(H) one member shall be appointed by the Chairperson of the Committee on Education and the Workforce of the House of Representatives from among members of the House of Representatives.":

Provided further, That the matter preceding paragraph (1) of section 853(b) of the Higher Education Amendments of 1998 is amended by striking "6 months" and inserting "12 months": *Provided further*, That the amounts provided under this heading in division A, section 101(f) of Public Law 105–277 for the Web-Based Education Commission, authorized by part J of title VIII of the Higher Education Amendments of 1998, shall remain available through September 30, 2000:] *Provided further*, That $3,000,000 is for data collection and evaluation activities for programs under the Higher Education Act of 1965, including such activities needed to comply with the Government Performance and Results Act of 1993: *Provided further*, That [of the funds available for title IV, part A, subpart 8 of the Higher Education Act of 1965 and notwithstanding any other provision of law, $3,000,000 shall be awarded to the University of South Florida for a distance learning program, $190,000 shall be awarded to the New York Global Communication Center in West Islip, New York for a distance learning program, $2,000,000 shall be awarded to the Alliance for Technology, Learning and Society (ATLAS) at the University of Colorado for technology-enhanced learning, $2,500,000 shall be awarded to the Illinois Community College Board to develop a systemwide, on-line virtual degree program for the community college system in Illinois, and $1,250,000 shall be made available to the University of Idaho Interactive Learning Environments to develop and improve Internet-based delivery of education programs] *section 404F(a) of the Higher Education Amendments of 1998 is amended by striking out "using funds appropriated under section 404H that do not exceed $200,000" and inserting in lieu thereof "using not more than 0.2 percent of the funds appropriated under section 404H".* (Department of Education Appropriations Act, 2000, as enacted by section 1000(a)(4) of the Consolidated Appropriations Act, 2000 (P.L. 106–113).)

Program and Financing (in millions of dollars)

Identification code 91–0201–0–1–502	1999 actual	2000 est.	2001 est.
Obligations by program activity:			
Aid for institutional development:			
00.01 Strengthening institutions	60	60	63
00.02 Strengthening tribally controlled colleges and universities	3	6	9
00.03 Strengthening Alaska Native and Native Hawaiian-serving institutions	3	5	5
00.04 Strengthening historically black colleges and universities	136	149	169
00.05 Strengthening historically black graduate institutions	30	31	40
00.06 Minority science and engineering improvement	8	8	9
00.91 Subtotal, aid for institutional development	240	259	295
Other aid for institutions:			
01.01 Developing Hispanic-serving institutions	28	42	63
01.02 International education and foreign language studies	67	70	72
01.03 Fund for the Improvement of Postsecondary Education	50	74	31
01.04 Urban community service	5		
01.05 Demonstration projects to ensure quality higher education for students with disabilities	5	5	5
01.06 Interest subsidy grants	11	12	10
01.91 Subtotal, other aid for institutions	166	203	181
Assistance for students:			
02.01 Federal TRIO programs	600	645	725
02.02 Gaining early awareness and readiness for undergraduate programs (GEAR UP)	120	200	325
02.03 Byrd honors scholarships	39	40	41
02.04 Javits fellowships	7	20	10
02.05 Graduate assistance in areas of national need	24	31	31
02.06 Child care access means parents in school	5	5	15
02.07 Learning anytime anywhere partnerships	10	23	30
02.08 State grants for incarcerated youth offenders	12	5	
02.91 Subtotal, assistance for students	817	969	1,177
Other Aid:			
03.01 Teacher quality enhancement	77	98	98
03.02 Underground railroad program	2	2	2
03.03 GPRA data/program evaluation		3	3
03.04 Endowment Grants	1		
03.05 Community scholarship mobilization		1	
03.91 Subtotal, Other Aid	80	104	103
10.00 Total new obligations	1,303	1,535	1,756
Budgetary resources available for obligation:			
21.40 Unobligated balance available, start of year	5	11	6
22.00 New budget authority (gross)	1,310	1,529	1,756
23.90 Total budgetary resources available for obligation	1,315	1,540	1,762
23.95 Total new obligations	–1,303	–1,535	–1,756
23.98 Unobligated balance expiring or withdrawn	–1		
24.40 Unobligated balance available, end of year	11	6	6
New budget authority (gross), detail:			
Discretionary:			
40.00 Appropriation	1,308	1,533	1,756
40.76 Reduction pursuant to P.L. 106–113		–4	
42.00 Transferred from other accounts	2		
43.00 Appropriation (total discretionary)	1,310	1,529	1,756
Change in unpaid obligations:			
72.40 Unpaid obligations, start of year: Obligated balance, start of year	1,095	1,533	1,599
73.10 Total new obligations	1,303	1,535	1,756
73.20 Total outlays (gross)	–855	–1,469	–1,504
73.40 Adjustments in expired accounts (net)	–10		
74.40 Unpaid obligations, end of year: Obligated balance, end of year	1,533	1,599	1,851
Outlays (gross), detail:			
86.90 Outlays from new discretionary authority	61	192	218

86.93 Outlays from discretionary balances	794	1,276	1,285
87.00 Total outlays (gross)	855	1,469	1,504
Net budget authority and outlays:			
89.00 Budget authority	1,310	1,529	1,756
90.00 Outlays	855	1,469	1,504

Aid for institutional development.—

Strengthening institutions.—Funds will support planning and development grants for improving academic programs and financial management at schools that enroll high proportions of disadvantaged students and have low per-student expenditures.

Strengthening tribally controlled colleges and universities.—Funds will support grants to American Indian tribally controlled colleges and universities with scarce resources to enable them to improve and expand their capacity to serve Indian students.

Strengthening Alaska Native and Native Hawaiian-serving institutions.—Funds will support Alaska Native and Native Hawaiian-serving institutions to enable them to improve and expand their capacity to serve Alaska Native and Native Hawaiian students.

Strengthening historically black colleges and universities.—Funds will support grants to help historically black undergraduate institutions to improve and expand their capacity to serve students, and to strengthen management and fiscal operations.

Strengthening historically black graduate institutions.—Funds will support grants to help historically black graduate institutions to improve and expand their capacity to serve students, and to strengthen management and fiscal operations.

Minority science and engineering improvement.—Funds will support grants to predominantly minority institutions to help them make long-range improvements in science and engineering education and to increase the participation of minorities in scientific and technological careers.

Other aid for institutions.—

Developing Hispanic-serving institutions.—Funds will support Hispanic-serving institutions to enable them to improve and expand their capacity to serve students.

International education and foreign language studies programs.—Funds will promote the development and improvement of international and foreign language programs.

Fund for the improvement of postsecondary education.—Funds will support flexible, field-initiated postsecondary improvement projects in a broad range of activities, as well as special focus programs.

Demonstration projects to ensure quality higher education for students with disabilities.—Funds will support model demonstration projects to provide technical assistance or professional development for faculty and administrators in institutions of higher education in order to provide students with disabilities a quality postsecondary education.

Interest subsidy grants.—Funds will meet mandatory interest subsidy costs of construction loan commitments made prior to 1974.

Assistance for students.—

Federal TRIO programs.—Funds will support postsecondary education outreach and student support services through 5 major programs designed to help individuals from disadvantaged backgrounds enter and complete college and graduate studies.

Gaining early awareness and readiness for undergraduate programs.—Funds will support early college preparation and awareness activities at the State and local levels to ensure that low-income elementary and secondary school students are prepared for and pursue postsecondary education.

Byrd honors scholarships.—Funds will support merit-based scholarships to students who have demonstrated outstanding academic achievement and who show promise of continued academic excellence for study at an institution of higher education.

Javits fellowships.—Funds will support fellowships to students of superior ability who are pursuing doctoral degrees in the arts, humanities, and social sciences.

Graduate assistance in areas of national need.—Funds will support fellowships to graduate students of superior ability who have financial need and who are from traditionally under-represented backgrounds for study in areas of national need.

Child care access means parents in school.—Funds will support a program designed to bolster the participation of low-income parents in postsecondary education through the provision of campus-based child care services.

Learning anytime anywhere partnerships.—Funds will support projects using distance learning technology and other innovations to promote and enhance the delivery of postsecondary education and lifelong learning opportunities.

Other aid.—

Teacher quality enhancement.—Funds will support programs that seek to make lasting changes in the ways our Nation recruits, prepares, licenses, and supports teachers.

Underground railroad program.—Funds will support grants to one or more nonprofit educational organizations to establish facilities to house, display, and interpret artifacts relating to the history of the Underground Railroad.

GPRA data/HEA program evaluation.—Funds will support data collection and evaluation activities for programs under the Higher Education Act of 1965, including such activities needed to comply with the Government Performance and Results Act of 1993.

Summary of Budget Authority and Outlays
(in millions of dollars)

Enacted/requested:	*1999 actual*	*2000 est.*	*2001 est.*
Budget Authority	1,310	1,529	1,756
Outlays	855	1,468	1,503
Legislative proposal, not subject to PAYGO:			
Budget Authority			40
Outlays			5
Total:			
Budget Authority	1,310	1,529	1,796
Outlays	855	1,468	1,508

Object Classification (in millions of dollars)

Identification code 91–0201–0–1–502	1999 actual	2000 est.	2001 est.
25.1 Advisory and assistance services	3	6	7
25.2 Other services	4	5	6
25.3 Purchases of goods and services from Government accounts	1	1	2
25.7 Operation and maintenance of equipment	1	1	1
41.0 Grants, subsidies, and contributions	1,293	1,522	1,740
99.0 Subtotal, direct obligations	1,302	1,535	1,756
99.5 Below reporting threshold	1		
99.9 Total new obligations	1,303	1,535	1,756

HIGHER EDUCATION

(Legislative proposal, not subject to PAYGO)

Program and Financing (in millions of dollars)

Identification code 91–0201–2–1–502	1999 actual	2000 est.	2001 est.
Obligations by program activity:			
Other aid for institutions:			
00.01 Dual Degree			40
10.00 Total new obligations (object class 41.0)			40

General and special funds—Continued

HIGHER EDUCATION—Continued

Program and Financing (in millions of dollars)—Continued

Identification code 91–0201–2–1–502	1999 actual	2000 est.	2001 est.
Budgetary resources available for obligation:			
21.40 Unobligated balance available, start of year			
22.00 New budget authority (gross)			40
23.90 Total budgetary resources available for obligation			40
23.95 Total new obligations			−40
New budget authority (gross), detail:			
Discretionary:			
40.00 Appropriation			40
Change in unpaid obligations:			
72.40 Unpaid obligations, start of year: Obligated balance, start of year			
73.10 Total new obligations			40
73.20 Total outlays (gross)			−5
74.40 Unpaid obligations, end of year: Obligated balance, end of year			35
Outlays (gross), detail:			
86.90 Outlays from new discretionary authority			5
Net budget authority and outlays:			
89.00 Budget authority			40
90.00 Outlays			5

The Administration will propose legislation that will authorize the use of funds for the following purpose:

Dual degree programs for minority-serving institutions.—Funds will support a new program to enable students at Hispanic-serving institutions, historically black colleges and universities, and tribally controlled colleges and universities to earn dual degrees in five years: one degree from the minority-serving institution, and one from a partner institution in a field in which the minority-serving institution does not offer a program and in which minorities are underrepresented.

HOWARD UNIVERSITY

For partial support of Howard University (20 U.S.C. 121 et seq.), [$219,444,000] *$224,000,000*, of which not less than $3,530,000 shall be for a matching endowment grant pursuant to the Howard University Endowment Act (Public Law 98–480) and shall remain available until expended. *(Department of Education Appropriations Act, 2000, as enacted by section 1000(a)(4) of the Consolidated Appropriations Act, 2000 (P.L. 106–113).)*

Program and Financing (in millions of dollars)

Identification code 91–0603–0–1–502	1999 actual	2000 est.	2001 est.
Obligations by program activity:			
00.01 General support	182	193	194
00.02 Howard University Hospital	29	30	30
10.00 Total new obligations (object class 41.0)	211	223	224
Budgetary resources available for obligation:			
21.40 Unobligated balance available, start of year		4	
22.00 New budget authority (gross)	214	219	224
23.90 Total budgetary resources available for obligation	214	223	224
23.95 Total new obligations	−211	−223	−224
24.40 Unobligated balance available, end of year	4		
New budget authority (gross), detail:			
Discretionary:			
40.00 Appropriation	214	219	224
Change in unpaid obligations:			
72.40 Unpaid obligations, start of year: Obligated balance, start of year	10	1	13
73.10 Total new obligations	211	223	224
73.20 Total outlays (gross)	−220	−210	−224
74.40 Unpaid obligations, end of year: Obligated balance, end of year	1	13	13
Outlays (gross), detail:			
86.90 Outlays from new discretionary authority	211	206	211
86.93 Outlays from discretionary balances	9	4	13
87.00 Total outlays (gross)	220	210	224
Net budget authority and outlays:			
89.00 Budget authority	214	219	224
90.00 Outlays	220	210	224

Howard University is a private, nonprofit educational institution consisting of 12 schools and colleges. Federal funds are used to provide partial support for university programs as well as for the teaching hospital facilities. In 1999, direct Federal appropriations for general support represented approximately 54 percent of the university's educational and general expenditures.

COLLEGE HOUSING AND ACADEMIC FACILITIES LOANS PROGRAM

For Federal administrative expenses authorized under section 121 of the Higher Education Act of 1965, $737,000 to carry out activities related to existing facility loans entered into under the Higher Education Act of 1965. *(Department of Education Appropriations Act, 2000, as enacted by section 1000(a)(4) of the Consolidated Appropriations Act, 2000 (P.L. 106–113).)*

HISTORICALLY BLACK COLLEGE AND UNIVERSITY CAPITAL FINANCING PROGRAM ACCOUNT

The total amount of bonds insured pursuant to section 344 of title III, part D of the Higher Education Act of 1965 shall not exceed $357,000,000, and the cost, as defined in section 502 of the Congressional Budget Act of 1974, of such bonds shall not exceed zero.

For administrative expenses to carry out the Historically Black College and University Capital Financing Program entered into pursuant to title III, part D of the Higher Education Act of 1965, as amended, [$207,000] *$208,000*. *(Department of Education Appropriations Act, 2000, as enacted by section 1000(a)(4) of the Consolidated Appropriations Act, 2000 (P.L. 106–113).)*

Program and Financing (in millions of dollars)

Identification code 91–0241–0–1–502	1999 actual	2000 est.	2001 est.
Obligations by program activity:			
00.09 Federal administration	1	1	1
10.00 Total new obligations (object class 99.5)	1	1	1
Budgetary resources available for obligation:			
22.00 New budget authority (gross)	1	1	1
23.95 Total new obligations	−1	−1	−1
New budget authority (gross), detail:			
Discretionary:			
40.00 Appropriation (Federal administration)	1	1	1
Change in unpaid obligations:			
72.95 Unpaid obligations, start of year: From Federal sources: Receivables and unpaid, unfilled orders	1	1	
73.10 Total new obligations	1	1	1
73.20 Total outlays (gross)	−1	−1	−1
74.95 Unpaid obligations, end of year: From Federal sources: Receivables and unpaid, unfilled orders	1		
Outlays (gross), detail:			
86.90 Outlays from new discretionary authority		1	1
86.93 Outlays from discretionary balances	1		
87.00 Total outlays (gross)	1	1	1
Net budget authority and outlays:			
89.00 Budget authority	1	1	1
90.00 Outlays	1	1	1

Summary of Loan Levels, Subsidy Budget Authority and Outlays by Program (in millions of dollars)

Identification code 91–0241–0–1–502	1999 actual	2000 est.	2001 est.
Direct loan subsidy outlays:			
1340 Subsidy outlays	....	....	....
Administrative expense data:			
3510 Budget authority	1	1	1
3580 Outlays from balances	1	....	....

The College Housing and Academic Facilities Loan (CHAFL) Program account and the Historically Black College and University (HBCU) Capital Financing Program account are consolidated for presentation purposes only. The College Housing and Academic Facilities Loans and Historically Black College and University Capital Financing programs will continue to be administered separately.

The College Housing and Academic Facilities Loans (CHAFL) Program.—The Department began issuing CHAFL facility loans in 1987 and made its last awards in 1993. Prior to 1987, loans were made under two separate loan programs: Higher Education Facilities Loans (HEFL) and College Housing Loans (CHL). The loans support financing for the reconstruction, renovation, and construction of academic facilities, housing and other postsecondary education facilities for students and faculty. Although the Department no longer makes new loans, the Department continues to be responsible for conducting architectural and engineering reviews before disbursing payments to institutions and servicing the outstanding loans under an agreement with the Federal Reserve Bank.

In prior years, funding for CHAFL administration was in this account, and funding for CHL and HEFL administration was split between the Department's Program Administration account and the liquidating accounts for these two programs. Beginning in 1998, the Department consolidated funding for administrative activities for CHAFL, HEFL, and CHL under a single account. The 2001 request includes funding for personnel and other discretionary costs for all three programs. Loan servicing and architectural and engineering services for the HEFL and CHL programs are funded from their respective liquidating accounts.

Historically Black College and University Capital Financing Program.—The Historically Black College and University (HBCU) Capital Financing Program provides HBCUs with access to capital financing for the repair, renovation, and construction of classrooms, libraries, laboratories, dormitories, instructional equipment, and research instrumentation. The Higher Education Amendments of 1992 granted the Department authority to enter into insurance agreements with a private for-profit Designated Bonding Authority to guarantee no more than $375,000,000 in outstanding principal and unpaid accrued interest combined. The bonding authority issues the bonds and maintains an escrow account in which 5 percent of each institution's principal is deposited. This amount is estimated to be sufficient to cover all potential delinquencies and defaults.

Since the first loan was issued in 1996, a total of 7 loans for $46 million have been made. Additional loans are expected in 2000 and 2001. No subsidy appropriations are required. The 2001 budget provides funds for continuing Federal administrative activities only.

Personnel Summary

Identification code 91–0241–0–1–502	1999 actual	2000 est.	2001 est.
1001 Total compensable workyears: Full-time equivalent employment	7	7	7

College Housing and Academic Facilities Loans Financing Account

Note.—The financing account includes all cash flows to and from the Government from college housing and academic facilities loans committed after 1991.

Program and Financing (in millions of dollars)

Identification code 91–4252–0–3–502	1999 actual	2000 est.	2001 est.
Obligations by program activity:			
00.02 Interest paid to Treasury	2	2	2
10.00 Total new obligations	2	2	2
Budgetary resources available for obligation:			
22.00 New financing authority (gross)	2	2	2
22.70 Balance of authority to borrow withdrawn	−1	....	....
23.90 Total budgetary resources available for obligation	1	2	2
23.95 Total new obligations	−2	−2	−2
New financing authority (gross), detail:			
Discretionary:			
68.00 Spending authority from offsetting collections (gross): Offsetting collections (cash)	2	2	2
Change in unpaid obligations:			
Unpaid obligations, start of year:			
Obligated balance, start of year:			
72.40 Obligated balance: Borrowing Authority	8	5	4
72.40 Obligated balance, Treasury Interest	2	1	....
72.95 Receivables from program account	1	1	1
72.99 Total unpaid obligations, start of year	11	7	5
73.10 Total new obligations	2	2	2
73.20 Total financing disbursements (gross)	−6	−4	−7
Unpaid obligations, end of year:			
Obligated balance, end of year:			
74.40 Obligated balance: Borrowing Authority	5	4	....
74.40 Obligated balance: Treasury Interest	1	....	....
74.95 Receivables from program account	1	1	....
74.99 Total unpaid obligations, end of year	7	5	....
87.00 Total financing disbursements (gross)	6	4	7
Offsets:			
Against gross financing authority and financing disbursements:			
Offsetting collections (cash) from:			
88.25 Interest on uninvested funds	−1	−1	−1
88.40 Interest repayments	−1	−1	−1
88.90 Total, offsetting collections (cash)	−2	−2	−2
Net financing authority and financing disbursements:			
89.00 Financing authority	....	....	....
90.00 Financing disbursements	4	2	5

Status of Direct Loans (in millions of dollars)

Identification code 91–4252–0–3–502	1999 actual	2000 est.	2001 est.
Position with respect to appropriations act limitation on obligations:			
1111 Limitation on direct loans	....	....	....
1150 Total direct loan obligations	....	....	....
Cumulative balance of direct loans outstanding:			
1210 Outstanding, start of year	21	25	26
1231 Disbursements: Direct loan disbursements	4	1	4
1290 Outstanding, end of year	25	26	30

The reestimate of the subsidy from prior year obligations may require the Department to exercise its permanent indefinite authority to borrow funds to cover outstanding Treasury interest expenses due on September 30, 2001.

General and special funds—Continued

College Housing and Academic Facilities Loans Financing Account—Continued

Balance Sheet (in millions of dollars)

Identification code 91–4252–0–3–502	1998 actual	1999 actual	2000 est.	2001 est.
ASSETS:				
Investments in US securities:				
1106 Federal assets: Receivables, net	2	3	3	3
Net value of assets related to post-1991 direct loans receivable:				
1401 Direct loans receivable, gross	21	22	25	26
1402 Interest receivable	1	1	1	1
1405 Allowance for subsidy cost (–)	....	....	....	....
1499 Net present value of assets related to direct loans	22	23	26	27
1999 Total assets	24	26	29	30
LIABILITIES:				
Federal liabilities:				
2102 Interest payable	1	2	2	2
2103 Debt	27	22	26	27
2999 Total liabilities	28	24	28	29
NET POSITION:				
3100 Appropriated capital	–2	....	....	....
3999 Total net position	–2	....	....	....
4999 Total liabilities and net position	26	24	28	29

College Housing and Academic Facilities Loans Liquidating Account

Program and Financing (in millions of dollars)

Identification code 91–0242–0–1–502	1999 actual	2000 est.	2001 est.
Obligations by program activity:			
10.00 Total new obligations (object class 43.0)	16	20	17
Budgetary resources available for obligation:			
21.40 Unobligated balance available, start of year	15	33	....
22.00 New budget authority (gross)	66	60	58
22.40 Capital transfer to general fund	–32	–73	–41
23.90 Total budgetary resources available for obligation	49	20	17
23.95 Total new obligations	–16	–20	–17
24.40 Unobligated balance available, end of year	33	....	....
New budget authority (gross), detail:			
Mandatory:			
69.00 Offsetting collections (cash)	66	60	58
Change in unpaid obligations:			
72.40 Unpaid obligations, start of year: Obligated balance, start of year	29	23	20
73.10 Total new obligations	16	20	17
73.20 Total outlays (gross)	–22	–23	–23
74.40 Unpaid obligations, end of year: Obligated balance, end of year	23	20	14
Outlays (gross), detail:			
86.97 Outlays from new mandatory authority	22	23	23
Offsets:			
Against gross budget authority and outlays:			
Offsetting collections (cash) from:			
Non-Federal sources:			
88.40 Repayments of principal	–47	–43	–42
88.40 Interest received on loans	–19	–17	–16
88.90 Total, offsetting collections (cash)	–66	–60	–58
Net budget authority and outlays:			
89.00 Budget authority	....	....	....
90.00 Outlays	–44	–37	–35

The College Housing and Academic Facilities Loans Liquidating Account records all cash flows to and from the Government resulting from direct loans made prior to 1992 to schools and colleges for the reconstruction, renovation, and construction of academic facilities, housing and other postsecondary education facilities. Loans were made under three separate loan programs: Higher Education Facilities Loans, College Housing Loans, and College Housing and Academic Facilities Loans. Beginning in 1998, the Department consolidated the three loan programs into the CHAFL Liquidating account for budget presentation purposes only. The three individual programs continue to be administered separately.

Status of Direct Loans (in millions of dollars)

Identification code 91–0242–0–1–502	1999 actual	2000 est.	2001 est.
CHAFL LIQUIDATING			
Cumulative balance of direct loans outstanding:			
1210 Outstanding, start of year	151	142	134
1231 Disbursements: Direct loan disbursements	....	....	....
1251 Repayments: Repayments and prepayments	–9	–8	–7
1290 Outstanding, end of year	142	134	127
HIGHER EDUCATION FACILITIES LOANS			
Cumulative balance of direct loans outstanding:			
1210 Outstanding, start of year	35	30	25
1251 Repayments: Repayments and prepayments	–5	–5	–5
1290 Outstanding, end of year	30	25	20
COLLEGE HOUSING LOANS			
Cumulative balance of direct loans outstanding:			
1210 Outstanding, start of year	380	347	317
1251 Repayments: Repayments and prepayments	–33	–30	–31
1290 Outstanding, end of year	347	317	286

Historically Black College and University Capital Financing Direct Loan Financing Account

Program and Financing (in millions of dollars)

Identification code 91–4255–0–3–502	1999 actual	2000 est.	2001 est.
Obligations by program activity:			
00.01 Direct Loan Disbursements	6	25	25
10.00 Total new obligations	6	25	25
Budgetary resources available for obligation:			
22.00 New financing authority (gross)	6	25	25
23.95 Total new obligations	–6	–25	–25
24.40 Unobligated balance available, end of year	....	....	....
New financing authority (gross), detail:			
Mandatory:			
67.15 Authority to borrow (indefinite)	6	25	25
Change in unpaid obligations:			
73.10 Total new obligations	6	25	25
73.20 Total financing disbursements (gross)	–6	–25	–25
87.00 Total financing disbursements (gross)	6	25	25
Net financing authority and financing disbursements:			
89.00 Financing authority	6	25	25
90.00 Financing disbursements	6	25	25

In 1997, the Federal Financing Bank (FFB) began purchasing bonds issued by the HBCU Designated Bonding Authority. Under the policies governing Federal credit programs, bonds purchased by the FFB and supported by the Department of Education with a letter of credit create the equivalent of a Federal direct loan. For Budget purposes, all FFB loans shall be treated as direct loans. HBCU bonds are still available for purchase by the private sector, and these will be treated as loan guarantees. However, the Department anticipates that all HBCU loans will be financed by the FFB.

Status of Direct Loans (in millions of dollars)

Identification code 91–4255–0–3–502	1999 actual	2000 est.	2001 est.
Position with respect to appropriations act limitation on obligations:			
1111 Limitation on direct loans	375	364	339
1112 Unobligated direct loan limitation	−364	339	−314
1150 Total direct loan obligations	11	25	25
Cumulative balance of direct loans outstanding:			
1210 Outstanding, start of year	5	11	36
1231 Disbursements: Direct loan disbursements	6	25	25
1251 Repayments: Repayments and prepayments			
1290 Outstanding, end of year	11	36	61

Balance Sheet (in millions of dollars)

Identification code 91–4255–0–3–502	1998 actual	1999 actual	2000 est.	2001 est.
ASSETS:				
Net value of assets related to post–1991 direct loans receivable:				
1401 Direct loans receivable, gross		11	36	61
1499 Net present value of assets related to direct loans		11	36	61
1999 Total assets		11	36	61
LIABILITIES:				
2103 Federal liabilities: Debt		11	36	61
2999 Total liabilities		11	36	61
4999 Total liabilities and net position		11	36	61

OFFICE OF STUDENT FINANCIAL ASSISTANCE

Federal Funds

General and special funds:

STUDENT FINANCIAL ASSISTANCE

For carrying out subparts 1, 3 and 4 of part A, part C and part E of title IV of the Higher Education Act of 1965, as amended, [$9,435,000,000] *$10,258,000,000*, which shall remain available through September 30, [2001] *2002*.

The maximum Pell Grant for which a student shall be eligible during award year [2000–2001] *2001–2002* shall be [$3,300] *$3,500*: *Provided*, That notwithstanding section 401(g) of the Act, if the Secretary determines, prior to publication of the payment schedule for such award year, that the amount included within this appropriation for Pell Grant awards in such award year, and any funds available from the fiscal year [1999] *2000* appropriation for Pell Grant awards, are insufficient to satisfy fully all such awards for which students are eligible, as calculated under section 401(b) of the Act, the amount paid for each such award shall be reduced by either a fixed or variable percentage, or by a fixed dollar amount, as determined in accordance with a schedule of reductions established by the Secretary for this purpose.

[For an additional amount for "STUDENT FINANCIAL ASSISTANCE" for payment of allocations to institutions of higher education for Federal Supplemental Educational Opportunity Grants for award years 1999–2000 and 2000–2001, made under title IV, part A, subpart 3, of the Higher Education Act of 1965, as amended, $10,000,000: *Provided*, That notwithstanding any other provision of law, the Secretary of Education may waive or modify any statutory or regulatory provision applicable to the Federal Supplemental Educational Opportunity Grant program and the determination of need for such grants, that the Secretary deems necessary to assist individuals who suffered financial harm resulting from the hurricanes, and the flooding associated with the hurricanes, that struck the eastern United States in August and September 1999, and who, at the time of the disaster were residing, attending an institution of higher education, or employed within an area affected by such a disaster on the date which the President declared the existence of a major disaster (or, in the case of an individual who is a dependent student, whose parent or stepparent suffered financial harm from such disaster, and who resided, or was employed in such an area at that time): *Provided further*, That notwithstanding section 437 of the General Education Provisions Act (20 U.S.C. 1232) and section 553 of title 5, United States Code, the Secretary shall, by notice in the Federal Register, exercise this authority, through publication of waivers or modifications of statutory and regulatory provisions, as the Secretary deems necessary to assist such individuals: *Provided further*, That notwithstanding section 413D of the Higher Education Act of 1965, allocations from such additional amount shall not be taken into account in determining institutional allocations under such section in future years: *Provided further*, That the entire amount made available under this paragraph is designated by the Congress as an emergency requirement pursuant to section 251(b)(2)(A) of the Balanced Budget and Emergency Deficit Control Act of 1985, and that the entire amount shall be available only to the extent an official budget request for the entire amount, that includes designation of the entire amount as an emergency requirement pursuant to the Balanced Budget and Emergency Deficit Control Act of 1985, is transmitted by the President to the Congress.] *(Department of Education Appropriations Act, 2000, as enacted by section 1000(a)(4) of the Consolidated Appropriations Act, 2000 (P.L. 106–113).)*

Program and Financing (in millions of dollars)

Identification code 91–0200–0–1–502	1999 actual	2000 est.	2001 est.
Obligations by program activity:			
Federal Pell grants:			
01.01 Federal Pell grants	6,044	9,285	8,084
Campus-based aid:			
02.01 Federal supplemental educational opportunity grants (SEOG)	619	633	691
02.02 Federal work-study	876	937	1,011
02.03 Federal Perkins loans: Federal capital contributions	102	100	100
02.05 Federal Perkins loans: Loan cancellations	30	30	60
02.91 Subtotal, Campus-based activities	1,627	1,700	1,862
03.01 Leveraging educational assistance partnership	25	40	40
10.00 Total new obligations (object class 41.0)	7,696	11,025	9,986
Budgetary resources available for obligation:			
21.40 Unobligated balance available, start of year	2,891	4,554	2,903
22.00 New budget authority (gross)	9,348	9,375	10,258
22.10 Resources available from recoveries of prior year obligations	10		
23.90 Total budgetary resources available for obligation	12,249	13,929	13,161
23.95 Total new obligations	−7,696	−11,025	−9,986
24.40 Unobligated balance available, end of year	4,554	2,903	3,175
New budget authority (gross), detail:			
Discretionary:			
40.00 Appropriation	9,348	9,435	10,258
40.15 Appropriation (emergency)		10	
40.76 Reduction pursuant to P.L. 106–113		−70	
43.00 Appropriation (total discretionary)	9,348	9,375	10,258
Change in unpaid obligations:			
72.40 Unpaid obligations, start of year: Obligated balance, start of year	4,704	3,176	4,838
73.10 Total new obligations	7,696	11,025	9,986
73.20 Total outlays (gross)	−9,125	−9,363	−9,829
73.40 Adjustments in expired accounts (net)	−88		
73.45 Adjustments in unexpired accounts	−10		
74.40 Unpaid obligations, end of year: Obligated balance, end of year	3,176	4,838	4,995
Outlays (gross), detail:			
86.90 Outlays from new discretionary authority	1,936	1,828	2,297
86.93 Outlays from discretionary balances	7,189	7,535	7,532
87.00 Total outlays (gross)	9,125	9,363	9,829
Net budget authority and outlays:			
89.00 Budget authority	9,348	9,375	10,258
90.00 Outlays	9,125	9,363	9,829

General and special funds—Continued

STUDENT FINANCIAL ASSISTANCE—Continued

Status of Direct Loans (in millions of dollars)

Identification code 91–0200–0–1–502	1999 actual	2000 est.	2001 est.
Cumulative balance of direct loans outstanding:			
1210 Outstanding, start of year	137	64	58
1251 Repayments: Repayments and prepayments	−66	−25	−26
Write-offs for default:			
1263 Direct loans	−15	−9	−10
1264 Other adjustments, net	8	28	34
1290 Outstanding, end of year	64	58	56

[1] Includes in all years institutional matching share of defaulted notes assigned from institutions to the Education Department.

The Administration's 2001 budget for the SFA account is $10.258 billion, an increase of $883 million, or 9.4 percent, over the 2000 appropriation, which together with matching funds (less allowable administrative costs) would provide more than $11.7 billion in aid available to an estimated 8.6 million students.

Federal Pell Grants.—Undergraduate students establish eligibility for these grants under award and need determination rules set out in the authorizing statute and the annual appropriations act.

The Administration proposes $8.356 billion, an increase of $716 million or 9.4 percent over the 2000 appropriation level, for the Pell Grant program in 2001, to raise the maximum award for the 2001–2002 award year to $3,500—the highest ever and an increase of $200 from the 2000–2001 level of $3,300. Approximately 3.9 million students would receive grants under the program in the 2001–2002 award year.

Campus-based programs.—The Federal Supplemental Educational Opportunity Grants, Federal Work-Study, and Federal Perkins Loan programs are called the "campus-based" programs because participating institutions are responsible for administering the programs on their own campuses. These programs provide aid administrators with considerable flexibility in the packaging of financial aid awards to best meet the needs of students.

Federal Supplemental Educational Opportunity Grants.—Federal funds are awarded by formula to qualifying institutions, which use these funds to award grants to undergraduate students. While institutions have discretion in awarding these funds, they are required to give priority to Pell Grant recipients and other students with exceptional need. The Federal share of such grants may not exceed 75 percent of the total grant. The Administration proposes $691 million for the SEOG program in 2001, an increase of $60 million or 9.5 percent over the 2000 level. This level of funding would provide approximately $875 million in available aid to an estimated 1.2 million needy students.

Federal Work-Study.—Federal funds are awarded by formula to qualifying institutions, which develop and provide part-time jobs for eligible undergraduate and graduate students with demonstrated need. Hourly earnings under the program must be at least equal to the Federal minimum wage. Federal funding in most cases pays 75 percent of a student's hourly wages, with the remaining 25 percent paid by the employer. An institution must use at least 7 percent of its Federal allocation to compensate students employed in community service activities. An institution's community service activities must include at least one tutoring or family literacy project. The Secretary has waived the required 25 percent employer funding match for students working in the America Reads Challenge as reading tutors of children and in family literacy programs, and for students working as math tutors for children in kindergarten through 9th grade in support of the America Counts Challenge. To continue to provide 1 million students the opportunity to work their way through college, the Administration proposes $1.011 billion, an increase of $77 million over the 2000 appropriation, for the Work-Study program.

Perkins Loan Program.—Institutions award low-interest loans from institutional revolving funds, which are comprised of Federal Capital Contributions, institutional matching funds, and student repayments on outstanding loans. The Administration proposes $100 million in new budget authority for the Perkins loan program, the same as the 2000 level. This level of funding would provide nearly $1.1 billion in available aid to some 676,000 needy undergraduate and graduate students in the 2001–2002 award year.

Perkins Loan Program—Cancellations.—Under the Perkins Loan cancellation program, institutional revolving funds are reimbursed for indebtedness canceled as a result of a borrower engaging in certain public service activities, as specified in the Higher Education Act. Amendments to the Higher Education Act in 1992 and 1998 greatly expanded the number of borrowers with loans eligible for cancellation. The resulting increase in demand for these benefits has created a significant funding shortfall. The Administration's budget proposal for Perkins Loan cancellations is $60 million, double the 2000 level.

Leveraging Educational Assistance Partnership Program.—Under this program, formerly known as the State Student Incentive Grant (SSIG) Program, Federal matching funds are awarded to assist States in providing programs of grants and work-study assistance to needy students attending qualifying institutions. When appropriations are $30 million or less, States must match these Federal funds on at least a dollar-for-dollar basis and comply with statutory maintenance of effort requirements. State awards to students may not exceed $5,000 per academic year.

When appropriations exceed $30 million, those funds in excess of $30 million are reserved for the Special Leveraging Educational Assistance Partnership Program. Under Special LEAP, States may use the grant funds for several new authorized activities including increasing the dollar amount of LEAP grants to students who demonstrate financial need. The Federal share of the cost of the authorized activities may not exceed 33⅓ percent. The Administration proposes $40 million for LEAP in 2001, the same as the 2000 appropriation.

Funding Tables.—The following tables display student aid funds available, the number of aid awards, average awards, and the unduplicated count of recipients from any Federal student aid program. The tables include the aid from programs in the Student Financial Assistance account, as well as aid from the Federal Family Education Loan (FFEL) program, and the William D. Ford Federal Direct Loan program. Loan amounts reflect the capital actually loaned, not the Federal cost of those loans. The data in these tables include the effects of matching funds wherever applicable.

AID FUNDS AVAILABLE FOR POSTSECONDARY EDUCATION AND TRAINING

(in millions of dollars)

	1999 actual	*2000 est.*	*2001 est.*
Pell grants	7,326	7,940	8,469
Student loans:			
Guaranteed student loans:			
Stafford loans	10,427	10,529	10,901
Unsubsidized Stafford loans	7,771	8,223	8,813
PLUS	1,908	2,207	2,442
Direct student loans:			
Stafford loans	5,318	5,568	5,770
Unsubsidized Stafford loans	3,437	3,798	4,068
PLUS	1,198	1,239	1,372
Consolidation:			
FFEL	4,720	4,581	4,745
Direct Loans	8,006	4,250	4,403
Student loans, subtotal	42,786	40,395	42,516
Work-study	1,044	1,123	1,216
Supplemental educational opportunity grants	784	799	875

Perkins loans	1,058	1,058	1,058
Leveraging Educational Assistance Partnership	50	90	90
Total aid available	53,048	51,405	54,224

Note: Detail may not add to totals due to rounding.

NUMBER OF AID AWARDS

[In thousands]

	1999 actual	2000 est.	2001 est.
Pell grants	3,810	3,849	3,885
Student loans:			
Guaranteed student loans:			
Stafford loans	3,091	3,198	3,291
Unsubsidized Stafford loans	1,970	2,124	2,237
PLUS	293	345	371
Direct student loans:			
Stafford loans	1,659	1,652	1,701
Unsubsidized Stafford loans	1,027	1,029	1,085
PLUS	205	191	205
Consolidation:			
FFEL	266	261	268
Direct Loans	412	207	213
Student loans, subtotal	8,922	9,007	9,371
Work-study	930	1,000	1,000
Supplemental educational opportunity grants	1,118	1,139	1,203
Perkins loans	698	698	676
Leveraging Educational Assistance Partnership	83	120	120
Total awards	15,562	15,813	16,254

Note: Detail may not add to totals due to rounding.

AVERAGE AID AWARDS

[In whole dollars]

	1999 actual	2000 est.	2001 est.
Pell grants	1,923	2,063	2,180
Student loans:			
Guaranteed student loans:			
Stafford loans	3,373	3,292	3,312
Unsubsidized Stafford loans	3,945	3,872	3,939
PLUS	6,522	6,401	6,590
Direct student loans:			
Stafford loans	3,206	3,370	3,393
Unsubsidized Stafford loans	3,346	3,690	3,751
PLUS	5,837	6,497	6,690
Consolidation:			
FFEL	17,754	17,582	17,696
Direct Loans	19,449	20,520	20,653
Work-study	1,123	1,215	1,215
Supplemental educational opportunity grants	701	727	727
Perkins loans	1,516	1,564	1,564
Leveraging Educational Assistance Partnership	600	750	750

NUMBER OF STUDENTS AIDED

[In thousands]

	1999 actual	2000 est.	2001 est.
Unduplicated student count	8,162	8,406	8,623

The following table displays institutional administrative costs paid from program funds.

ADMINISTRATIVE PAYMENTS TO INSTITUTIONS

[In millions of dollars]

	1999 actual	2000 est.	2001 est.
Pell grants	20	20	20
Work-study	65	70	76
Supplemental educational opportunity grants	31	32	32
Perkins loans	42	42	42

The following table displays the status of defaulted Perkins loans held by the Department and by institutions.

DEFAULTED PERKINS LOANS

[In millions of dollars]

	1999 actual	2000 est.	2001 est.
Outstanding defaulted loans, beginning of year:			
Assigned defaulted loans [1]	137	64	58
Unassigned defaulted loans [2]	948	987	1,029
New defaulted loans	147	168	176
Collections on assigned loans	–66	–25	–26
Collections on unassigned loans	–93	–94	–96
Write-offs for assigned loans	–15	–9	–10
Write-offs for unassigned loans	–7	–4	–3
Outstanding defaulted loans, end of year	1,051	1,087	1,128

[1] Permanently assigned to the Federal Government for collection. Does not include the following amounts in loans made to institutions to establish Perkins revolving funds: $94 thousand in 1999, $94 thousand in 2000, and $94 thousand in 2001. These amounts are recorded as outstanding loans in the "Status of Direct Loans" schedule.

[2] Unassigned loans at institutions.

Perkins Loan Revolving Fund

Program and Financing (in millions of dollars)

Identification code 91–4248–0–1–502		1999 actual	2000 est.	2001 est.
	Budgetary resources available for obligation:			
21.40	Unobligated balance available, start of year	53		
22.10	Resources available from recoveries of prior year obligations	1		
22.40	Capital transfer to general fund	–54		
23.90	Total budgetary resources available for obligation			
	Change in unpaid obligations:			
72.40	Unpaid obligations, start of year: Obligated balance, start of year	3		
73.10	Total new obligations			
73.20	Total outlays (gross)	–1		
73.45	Adjustments in unexpired accounts	–1		
74.40	Unpaid obligations, end of year: Obligated balance, end of year			
	Outlays (gross), detail:			
86.98	Outlays from mandatory balances	1		
	Net budget authority and outlays:			
89.00	Budget authority			
90.00	Outlays	1		

The Higher Education Amendments of 1998 repealed the Perkins Loan Revolving fund. Pursuant to section 467 of the Higher Education Amendments of 1998, these funds have been returned to the general fund of the Treasury.

Federal Family Education Loan Insurance Fund

Program and Financing (in millions of dollars)

Identification code 91–4256–0–3–502		1999 actual	2000 est.	2001 est.
	Budgetary resources available for obligation:			
21.40	Unobligated balance available, start of year	47		
22.40	Capital transfer to general fund	–47		
23.90	Total budgetary resources available for obligation			
	Net budget authority and outlays:			
89.00	Budget authority			
90.00	Outlays			

The Federal Family Education Loan Insurance Fund was established under Section 431 of the Higher Education Act of 1965, as amended, for use by the Secretary of Education to pay administrative costs related to default management and prevention, guaranty agency oversight, and related expenses.

Credit accounts:

Federal Direct Student Loan Program, Program Account

Program and Financing (in millions of dollars)

Identification code 91–0243–0–1–502		1999 actual	2000 est.	2001 est.
	Obligations by program activity:			
07.09	Student loan administrative expenses	610	735	770
10.00	Total new obligations	610	735	770

Credit accounts—Continued

FEDERAL DIRECT STUDENT LOAN PROGRAM, PROGRAM ACCOUNT—Continued

Program and Financing (in millions of dollars)—Continued

Identification code 91–0243–0–1–502	1999 actual	2000 est.	2001 est.
Budgetary resources available for obligation:			
21.40 Unobligated balance available, start of year	4	12	12
22.00 New budget authority (gross)	619	735	770
22.10 Resources available from recoveries of prior year obligations	5		
23.90 Total budgetary resources available for obligation	628	747	782
23.95 Total new obligations	−610	−735	−770
23.98 Unobligated balance expiring or withdrawn	−5		
24.40 Unobligated balance available, end of year	12	12	12
New budget authority (gross), detail:			
Discretionary:			
42.00 Transferred from other accounts	1		
Mandatory:			
60.00 Appropriation	618	735	770
60.05 Appropriation (indefinite)			
62.50 Appropriation (total mandatory)	618	735	770
69.00 Offsetting collections (cash)	720	3,432	607
69.10 From Federal sources: Change in receivables and unpaid, unfilled orders			
69.27 Capital transfer to general fund	−720	−3,432	−607
69.90 Spending authority from offsetting collections (total mandatory)			
70.00 Total new budget authority (gross)	619	735	770
Change in unpaid obligations:			
72.40 Unpaid obligations, start of year: Obligated balance, start of year	303	281	335
73.10 Total new obligations	610	735	770
73.20 Total outlays (gross)	−627	−681	−722
73.45 Adjustments in unexpired accounts	−5		
74.40 Unpaid obligations, end of year: Obligated balance, end of year	281	335	383
Outlays (gross), detail:			
86.97 Outlays from new mandatory authority	392	468	481
86.98 Outlays from mandatory balances	235	213	241
87.00 Total outlays (gross)	627	681	722
Offsets:			
Against gross budget authority and outlays:			
88.00 Offsetting collections (cash) from: Federal sources	−720	−3,432	−607
Against gross budget authority only:			
88.95 From Federal sources: Change in receivables and unpaid, unfilled orders			
Net budget authority and outlays:			
89.00 Budget authority	−101	−2,697	163
90.00 Outlays	−93	−2,751	115

Summary of Loan Levels, Subsidy Budget Authority and Outlays by Program (in millions of dollars)

Identification code 91–0243–0–1–502	1999 actual	2000 est.	2001 est.
Direct loan levels supportable by subsidy budget authority:			
1150 Stafford	5,318	6,129	6,354
1150 Unsubsidized Stafford	3,437	4,235	4,537
1150 PLUS	1,198	1,459	1,615
1150 Consolidated	8,006	4,312	4,466
1159 Total direct loan levels	17,959	16,135	16,972
Direct loan subsidy (in percent):			
1320 Stafford	8.17	3.39	8.03
1320 Unsubsidized Stafford	−11.74	−20.49	−14.36
1320 PLUS	−10.40	−16.39	−12.36
1320 Consolidated	−3.95	−9.59	−3.92
1329 Weighted average subsidy rate	−2.15	−8.14	−3.04
Direct loan subsidy budget authority:			
1330 Stafford	169	−918	510
1330 Unsubsidized Stafford	−685	−1,623	−652
1330 PLUS	−104	−387	−200
1330 Consolidated	−119	−827	−175
1339 Total subsidy budget authority	−739	−3,755	−517
Direct loan subsidy outlays:			
1340 Stafford	236	−863	385
1340 Unsubsidized Stafford	−657	−1,428	−639
1340 PLUS	−94	−320	−180
1340 Consolidated	−123	−822	−173
1349 Total subsidy outlays	−638	−3,433	−607
Student loan administrative expense data:			
3510 Budget authority	618	735	770
3590 Outlays	544	681	721

The Federal Government operates two major student loan programs: the Federal Family Education Loan (FFEL) program—formerly the Guaranteed Student Loan (GSL) program—and the William D. Ford Federal Direct Loan (Direct Loan) program. The President is committed to improving the efficiency of both programs and allowing individual institutions to choose which of these two programs best meets their needs and the needs of their students.

This summary section outlines the structure of these two programs, highlights their differences and similarities, and provides text tables displaying program cost data; loan volume, subsidy, default, and interest rates; and other descriptive information. As part of his 2001 Budget, the President is proposing a number of changes for the Direct Loan and FFEL programs. These changes are discussed as part of this program description.

From its inception in 1965 through 1999, the FFEL program has provided over $300 billion in loans to postsecondary students and their parents. Since July 1, 1994, the Direct Loan program has provided almost $57 billion in new and consolidation loans to students and parents. Taken together, the FFEL and Direct Loan programs will make almost $32 billion in new loans available in 2000. Because funding for these two programs is provided on a permanent indefinite basis, for budget purposes they are considered separately from other Federal student financial assistance programs. The FFEL and Direct Loan programs should be viewed in combination with these other programs, however, and with Perkins Loans in particular, as part of the overall Federal effort to ensure access to higher education.

Loan capital in the FFEL program is provided by private lenders. State and private nonprofit guaranty agencies act as agents of the Federal Government, providing a variety of services including collection of some defaulted loans, default avoidance activities, and counseling to schools, students, and lenders. The Government provides substantial payments to these guaranty agencies. The Government also pays interest subsidies to lenders for certain borrowers, as well as most costs associated with loan defaults and other write-offs.

The Higher Education Amendments of 1998 (HEA) fundamentally restructured the guaranty agency system, reducing the need for agencies to hold Federal reserve funds. Accordingly, the Administration is proposing to bring forward $359 million in reserve recalls included in the HEA. In addition, the Administration is proposing $950 million in new recalls for 2001. (Amounts recalled in 2001 will be used to offset discretionary spending.) To provide guaranty agencies the maximum flexibility under this new structure, the Administration is also proposing to allow the Secretary of Education to expand the use of voluntary flexible agreements. These agreements, a limited number of which were authorized in the HEA, afford agencies greater discretion in their financial and operational organization.

The Direct Loan program was created by the Student Loan Reform Act (SLRA) of 1993. Under this program, the Federal Government provides loan funds to postsecondary institutions directly or through an alternative originator. Direct Loans offer a streamlined system that is simpler for student and parent borrowers, less prone to waste and abuse, and less expensive for the Federal taxpayer than the FFEL program. The program also offers income-contingent repayment options that allow borrowers to consider lower-paying careers, such as public service, without fear of default.

The Direct Loan program began operation in academic year 1994–1995 with 7 percent of overall loan volume. The program grew to 31 percent of overall volume in academic year 1995–1996, and is expected to account for 33 percent in academic year 1999–2000. All eligible institutions are free to participate in either the Direct Loan or FFEL program.

The Direct Loan and FFEL programs share many basic elements. Each program offers four types of loans: Stafford, Unsubsidized Stafford, PLUS for parents, and Consolidation. Evidence of financial need is required for a student to receive a subsidized Stafford loan. The other three loan programs are available to borrowers at all income levels. Loans can be used only to meet qualified educational expenses.

The borrower interest rate for new Stafford Loans equals the 91-day Treasury bill rate plus 1.7 percent during in-school, grace, and deferment periods, and the 91-day Treasury bill plus 2.3 percent at all other times, with a cap of 8.25 percent, adjusted annually. Interest payments for these loans are fully subsidized by the Government while a student is in school and during grace and deferment periods. Unsubsidized Stafford loans carry the same borrower interest rate as Stafford loans, but have no interest subsidy. For new PLUS loans, the borrower interest rate equals the 91-day Treasury bill rate plus 3.1 percent, with a cap of 9 percent and no interest subsidy.

In the FFEL program, lenders may receive an interest subsidy, called a special allowance, from the Government to ensure a guaranteed rate of return on their loans. Special allowance payments vary by loan type, are determined quarterly, and are based on current borrower interest rates and market-yield formulas. For new Stafford and Unsubsidized Stafford loans, for example, the Federal Government must pay lenders a special allowance if the average 3-month commercial paper rate for a given quarter plus 2.34 percent—or 1.74 percent during in-school, grace, or deferment periods—is higher than the current interest rate charged borrowers.

The basis for interest subsidies to FFEL lenders was changed to 3-month commercial paper rates from the 91-day Treasury bill—the instrument upon which student interest rates are based—as part of the Ticket to Work and Work Incentives Improvement Act 1999. This change was not intended to increase lender returns. In fact, however, the change has increased lender yields in two ways. Under current economic forecasts, Federal interest subsidies to lenders are 11 basis points higher than would have been the case under the previous formula. In addition, the move to commercial paper also reduces lender costs by 20 basis points by eliminating the need for hedging—insurance against future interest rate changes. In order to reestablish the cost-neutrality of the change to commercial paper, the Administration is therefore proposing to reduce lender subsidies by a total of 31 basis points, setting the special allowance formula at the 3-month commercial paper rate plus 2.03 percent during repayment and plus 1.43 percent during in-school, grace, or deferment periods.

The Administration is also proposing to eliminate interest subsidy payments on FFEL loans funded through tax-exempt securities that are currently subject to a 9.5 percent interest rate floor. Lenders with access to tax-exempt financing have a lower cost of funding than their private competitors; the proposed elimination of Federal interest subsidies on loans subject to this unnecessary floor provision will bring the return on tax-exempt-funded loans roughly in line with those realized on loans funded with private capital.

Consolidation loans allow borrowers to combine loans made under Title IV of the Higher Education Act—FFEL, Direct Loans, and Perkins Loans—as well as some loans made under the Public Health Service Act. The interest rate for new FFEL and Direct Consolidation loans equals the weighted average of the interest rate on the loans consolidated, rounded up to the nearest one-eighth of one percent. Lenders may choose to offer a lower rate. Interest rates for all new FFEL and Direct Consolidation Loans are capped at 8.25 percent.

FFEL borrowers pay an origination fee to the Government equal to 3 percent of principal, and are also liable for a guaranty agency insurance premium of up to 1 percent of principal. Guaranty agencies have the option of waiving this premium and FFEL lenders have the option of paying some or all of a borrower's origination fee for Stafford Loan borrowers. Direct Loan borrowers are charged an origination fee equal to 3 percent of principal, which partially offsets Federal program operation costs.

Loan limits are also identical across the two programs. In addition, loans made under both programs are discharged when borrowers die, are totally and permanently disabled, or, under some circumstances, declare bankruptcy. The HEA limited discharges due to bankruptcy to borrowers who can demonstrate that repayment would constitute an "undue hardship."

Borrowers under Direct Loans may choose from among five repayment plans including income-contingent repayment ("pay-as-you-can"), under which annual repayment amounts vary based on the income of the borrower and the amount borrowed, and payments can be made over 25 years. Borrowers may switch between repayment plans at any time. (Income-contingent repayment is not available to Direct PLUS borrowers).

FFEL borrowers may choose from among four repayment plans. Repayment periods under standard, graduated, and income-sensitive repayment may not exceed 10 years. The HEA created an extended repayment plan of up to 25 years for new borrowers with outstanding loans totalling more than $30,000. FFEL borrowers may change repayment plans annually.

The Administration is proposing a number of changes to improve the management and collection of defaulted loans which build on provisions enacted in the HEA. The amount guaranty agencies may retain on default collections will be reduced from 24 percent to 18.5 percent—approximately the rate paid on loans collected by the Department of Education through competitively awarded contracts. (The HEA lowered the guaranty agency retention rate from 27 percent to 24 percent through 2003, and to 23 percent thereafter.) Second, the rate guaranty agencies may retain on collections stemming from the consolidation of a defaulted loan will be further reduced to 12 percent to reflect the lower costs associated with this type of collection.

In order to ensure the uninterrupted availability of aid funds for students and parents, Congress provided permanent funding to support student aid administration and expenses. These funds support Department personnel and contractors for Direct Loan origination and servicing, payments to guaranty agencies, as well as certain costs associated with activities common to Direct Loans, FFEL and other student assistance programs, such as application printing and processing. Discretionary funds requested for the FFEL program support additional Department personnel and administrative activities associated with operating the program.

Performance indicators have been developed on a broad spectrum of policy objectives in both the Direct Loan and FFEL programs. These indicators measure program efficiency,

Credit accounts—Continued

FEDERAL DIRECT STUDENT LOAN PROGRAM, PROGRAM ACCOUNT—Continued

Federal costs, and financial management, as well as borrower and institutional satisfaction.

The following tables display performance indicators and program data; including projected overall Direct Loan and FFEL costs; loan volume, number of loans, and average loan amount; descriptive data, and program activity under the President's budget and legislative request.

Funding Levels (In thousands of dollars)

	1999 actual	2000 est.	2001 est.
Program Cost:			
FFEL:			
Liquidating [1]	–550,000	–691,237	–599,901
Program [2]	3,421,720	3,643,377	3,277,052
Reestimate of Prior Year Costs	–687,572	1,105,545	
Non-Contractual Modifications [3]			–502,297
Subtotal, FFEL [2]	2,184,148	4,057,685	2,124,854
Direct Loans:			
Program [2]	–67,846	–899,266	–341,106
Reestimate of Prior Year Costs	–552,730	–2,028,650	
Subtotal, Direct Loans [2]	–620,576	–2,927,916	–341,106
Consolidation Loans:			
FFEL:	63,666	87,839	123,249
Reestimate of Prior Year Costs	534,438	–329,544	
Non-Contractual Modifications [3]			–87,703
Direct Loans	–310,366	–413,490	–175,085
Reestimate of Prior Year Costs	191,850	–413,636	
Subtotal, Consolidation Loans	479,589	–1,068,829	–139,539
Administration:			
FFEL [4]	47,276	48,000	48,000
Student Aid [5]	617,591	735,000	770,000
Subtotal, Administration	664,867	783,000	818,000
Total, FFEL and Direct Loans	2,708,028	843,939	2,462,210
Program Cost Outlays:			
FFEL:			
Liquidating [1]	–1,163,000	–706,100	–615,772
Program [2]	2,812,329	3,120,968	2,994,621
Reestimate of Prior Year Costs [2]	–687,572	1,105,545	
Non-Contractual Modifications [3]			–502,297
Subtotal, FFEL [2]	961,757	3,520,412	1,876,553
Direct Loans:			
Program [2]	38,566	–581,786	–434,554
Reestimate of Prior Year Costs [2]	–552,730	–2,028,650	
Subtotal, Direct Loans [2]	–514,164	–2,610,437	–434,554
Consolidation Loans:			
FFEL	94,044	86,582	121,485
Reestimate of Prior Year Costs	534,438	–329,544	
Non-Contractual Modifications [3]			–87,703
Direct Loans	–314,479	–407,586	–172,586
Reestimate of Prior Year Costs	191,850	–413,636	
Subtotal, Consolidation Loans	505,854	–1,064,184	–138,804
Administration:			
FFEL [4]	52,248	47,198	49,921
Student Aid [5]	543,409	681,353	721,944
Subtotal, Administration	595,657	728,551	771,865
Total, FFEL and Direct Loans	1,549,104	574,342	2,075,060

[1] Liquidating account reflects loans made prior to 1992.

[2] Because these figures do not include consolidation loans, they do not correspond with those shown in account-specific schedules.

[3] Reflect costs and savings associated with policy changes that do not change the terms of existing or future loans.

[4] Reflects annual discretionary appropriation. Amount for 1999 reflects transfer from Treasury of $794,000 for Year 2000-related activities.

[5] Supports account maintenance fee payments to FFEL guaranty agencies, as well as a range of administrative activities such as application printing, mailing, and processing that are common to all Federal student financial assistance programs. Amount for 1999 reflects transfer from Treasury of $591,000 for Year 2000-related activities.

Summary of Loans Available (net commitments in millions of dollars) [1]

	1999 actual	2000 est.	2001 est.
FFEL:			
Stafford	10,427	10,529	10,901
Unsubsidized Stafford	7,771	8,223	8,813
PLUS	1,908	2,207	2,442
Total, FFEL	20,106	20,959	22,156
Direct Loans:			
Stafford	5,318	5,568	5,770
Unsubsidized Stafford	3,437	3,798	4,068
PLUS	1,198	1,239	1,372
Total, Direct Loans	9,953	10,605	11,210
Consolidation Loans:			
FFEL	4,720	4,581	4,745
Direct Loans	8,006	4,250	4,403
Subtotal, Consolidation Loans	12,726	8,831	9,148
Total, All Loans	42,786	40,395	42,516

[1] Net commitments equal gross commitments minus loan cancellations.

Number of Loans (In thousands)

	1999 actual	2000 est.	2001 est.
FFEL:			
Stafford	3,091	3,198	3,291
Unsubsidized Stafford	1,970	2,124	2,237
PLUS	293	345	371
Total, FFEL	5,354	5,667	5,899
Direct Loans:			
Stafford	1,659	1,652	1,701
Unsubsidized Stafford	1,027	1,029	1,085
PLUS	205	191	205
Total, Direct Loans	2,891	2,872	2,991
Consolidation Loans:			
FFEL	266	261	268
Direct Loans	412	207	213
Subtotal, Consolidation Loans	677	468	481
Total, All Loans	8,922	9,007	9,371

Average Loan Size (in whole dollars)

	1999 actual	2000 est.	2001 est.
FFEL:			
Stafford	3,373	3,292	3,312
Unsubsidized Stafford	3,945	3,872	3,939
PLUS	6,522	6,401	6,590
Weighted Average, FFEL	3,756	3,699	3,756
Direct Loans:			
Stafford	3,206	3,370	3,393
Unsubsidized Stafford	3,346	3,690	3,751
PLUS	5,837	6,497	6,690
Weighted Average, Direct Loans	3,443	3,692	3,749
Consolidation Loans:			
FFEL	17,754	17,582	17,696
Direct Loans	19,449	20,520	20,653
Subtotal, Consolidation Loans	18,784	18,883	19,006
Weighted Average, All Loans	4,795	4,485	4,537

Composition of Consolidation Loans

	1999 actual	2000 est.	2001 est.
Net commitments (in millions of dollars):			
FFEL:			
Standard consolidations	4,160	3,965	4,108
Consolidations from Default	560	616	638
Subtotal, FFEL	4,720	4,581	4,745
Direct Loans:			
Standard consolidations	6,637	2,473	2,561
Consolidations from Default	1,369	1,778	1,841
Subtotal, Direct Loans	8,006	4,250	4,403
Total:			
Standard consolidations	6,637	2,473	2,561

Consolidations from Default	1,369	1,778	1,841
Total, Consolidated Loans	12,726	8,831	9,148

Summary of Subsidy Rates, Default Rates, Interest Rates, and Discount Rates

	1999 actual	2000 est.	2001 est.
Subsidy Rates (in percent) [1]			
FFEL:			
Stafford	22.16	23.21	20.84
Unsubsidized Stafford	7.63	8.20	5.36
PLUS	5.47	5.49	5.17
Weighted Average, FFEL [2]	14.89	15.39	12.89
Direct Loans:			
Stafford	3.73	3.39	8.03
Unsubsidized Stafford	−19.35	−20.49	−14.36
PLUS	−15.61	−16.39	−12.36
Weighted Average, Direct Loans [2]	−6.70	−7.61	−2.73
Consolidation Loans:			
FFEL	2.79	1.89	2.56
Direct Loans	−6.84	−9.59	−3.92
Weighted Average, Consolidation Loans	−3.26	−3.63	−0.56
Default Rates (in percent) [3]			
FFEL:			
Stafford	16.79	16.94	16.97
Unsubsidized Stafford	15.76	15.80	15.80
PLUS	10.09	10.05	10.05
Weighted Average, FFEL [2]	15.76	15.77	15.74
Direct Loans:			
Stafford	16.33	16.30	16.32
Unsubsidized Stafford	15.88	15.91	15.78
PLUS	9.36	9.44	9.42
Weighted Average, Direct Loans [2]	15.34	15.31	15.28
Consolidation Loans:			
FFEL	22.02	21.96	21.96
Direct Loans	22.02	21.96	21.96
Weighted Average, Consolidation Loans	22.02	21.96	21.96
Borrower Interest Rates (in percent)			
FFEL:			
Stafford [4]	7.46	6.92	7.78
Unsubsidized Stafford [4]	7.46	6.92	7.78
PLUS [4]	8.26	7.72	8.58
Direct Loans:			
Stafford [4]	7.46	6.92	7.78
Unsubsidized Stafford [4]	7.46	6.92	7.78
PLUS [4]	8.26	7.72	8.58
Federal Borrowing Rate for Direct Loans (in percent)	5.67	5.01	6.25

[1] Subsidy rates represent the Federal portion of non-administrative costs—principally interest subsidies and defaults—associated with each borrowed dollar. For example, a $1,000 loan with Federal subsidy costs of $100 would have a subsidy rate of 10 percent.

[2] Because these figures do not include totals for consolidation loans, they do not correspond with totals shown in account-specific schedules.

[3] Default rates displayed in this table, which reflect projected defaults over the life of a loan cohort, are used in developing program cost estimates. The Department uses other rates based on defaults occurring in the first three years of repayment to determine institutional eligibility to participate in Federal loan programs. These three-year rates tend to be lower than those included in this table.

[4] Rates shown are those set beginning July 1st of the previous fiscal year.

[5] Consolidation Loan interest rates are set at the weighted average of the rates of the loans consolidated, rounded up to the nearest eighth of a percent.

Composition of Loan Collections (In thousands of dollars)

	1999 actual	2000 est.	2001 est.
FFEL:			
Collections by Guaranty Agencies [1]	2,438,858	1,398,596	1,454,052
Collections by Department of Education	892,109	428,392	439,804
Internal Revenue Service Tax Refund Offsets	1,347,153	565,011	577,016
Total, FFEL	4,678,120	2,391,999	2,470,872
Direct Loans:			
Collections by Department of Education	49,022	153,086	255,385
Internal Revenue Service Tax Refund Offsets	15,265	26,768	49,880
Total, Direct Loans	64,286	179,854	305,265
Total, FFEL and Direct Loan	4,742,406	2,571,852	2,776,136

[1] These figures show total collections by guaranty agencies. Actual Federal revenues resulting from these collections are lower than the amount shown because agencies retain a portion of the amount collected.

Projected Participation in Repayment Plans [1] (in percent)

	1999 cohort	2000 cohort	2001 cohort
FFEL: [1]			
Standard:			
Percent of Loan Volume: [2]			
Stafford	100.00	100.00	100.00
Unsubsidized Stafford	100.00	100.00	100.00
PLUS	100.00	100.00	100.00
Consolidation	100.00	100.00	100.00
Subsidy Rate (in percent):			
Stafford	22.16	23.21	20.84
Unsubsidized Stafford	7.63	8.20	5.36
PLUS	5.47	5.49	5.17
Consolidation	2.79	1.89	2.56
Direct Loans [1]			
Standard			
Percent of Loan Volume [2]			
Stafford	78.60	74.36	70.35
Unsubsidized Stafford	74.99	70.97	67.16
PLUS	78.56	78.56	78.56
Consolidation	33.09	33.09	33.09
Subsidy Rate (in percent):			
Stafford	9.25	5.84	9.67
Unsubsidized Stafford	−10.50	−17.36	−12.45
PLUS	−8.08	−12.82	−9.95
Consolidation	1.14	−2.50	0.29
Graduated: [3]			
Percent of Loan Volume: [2]			
Stafford	15.67	18.98	22.10
Unsubsidized Stafford	17.76	20.79	23.67
PLUS	15.51	15.51	15.51
Consolidation	21.80	21.80	21.80
Subsidy Rate (in percent):			
Stafford	4.37	−4.13	3.92
Unsubsidized Stafford	−16.45	−29.87	−19.57
PLUS	−17.97	−29.73	−21.36
Consolidation	−6.74	−15.42	−8.23
Extended: [3]			
Percent of Loan Volume: [2]			
Stafford	4.44	5.38	6.26
Unsubsidized Stafford	5.79	6.78	7.72
PLUS	5.94	5.94	5.94
Consolidation	20.98	20.98	20.98
Subsidy Rate (in percent):			
Stafford	4.44	−3.50	4.37
Unsubsidized Stafford	−16.35	−29.11	−19.05
PLUS	−18.08	−29.15	−20.82
Consolidation	−6.62	−14.56	−7.59
Income-Contingent:			
Percent of Loan Volume [2]			
Stafford	1.29	1.29	1.29
Unsubsidized Stafford	1.46	1.46	1.46
Consolidation	24.13	24.13	24.13
Subsidy Rate (in percent):			
Stafford	2.72	0.24	6.86
Unsubsidized Stafford	2.70	0.14	6.79
Consolidation	−4.09	−12.50	−4.05

[1] No data is included for the Alternative repayment plan under either FFEL or Direct Loans. Borrowers are not expected to participate in this plan due to the flexibility available under the other options. For FFEL, no data is included for income-sensitive repayment. This option, which has been available for a number of years, has never made up more than a tiny portion of overall loan volume. For Direct Loans, income-contingent repayment is not available for PLUS borrowers.

[2] Percent of Loan Volume represents aggregate data. Individual borrowers may move between plans over time.

[3] Maximum terms under the Extended and Graduated repayment plans reflect the following "classes" based on borrower debt levels.

Credit accounts—Continued

FEDERAL DIRECT STUDENT LOAN PROGRAM, PROGRAM ACCOUNT—Continued

Debt Level	Maximum Term (in years)	Percent of Volume Within Direct Extended and Graduated Plans (Stafford) FY 00
Below $10,000	12	5.65
$10,000–$20,000	15	15.79
$20,000–$40,000	20	31.39
$40,000–$60,000	25	20.02
Above $60,000	30	27.15

The Higher Education Amendments of 1998 broadened the availability of alternative repayment plans in the FFEL program. Data on the extent to which FFEL borrowers will take advantage of these plans is not yet available.

Subsidy costs for the FFEL and Direct Loan programs are estimated in accordance with procedures set out in the Credit Reform Act of 1990. Subsidy costs for each loan type are estimated separately and, because costs can vary widely within a program depending on the characteristics of the individual borrower, cost estimates are aggregated from data for homogeneous groups within risk categories.

Risk categories for Stafford and Unsubsidized Stafford Loans are based on the type of school attended by the borrower. Since PLUS loan borrowers are all parents, they are assumed to share similar risk profiles and are grouped together in a single category. For Consolidation Loans, risk categories distinguish between standard Consolidation Loans—in which borrowers in repayment consolidate a number of outstanding loans—and loans consolidated out of default.

Default rates are a major cause of differences in subsidy between risk categories. The default rates in the following tables reflect estimates of the percent of borrowers who will default over the lifetime of the loans. These estimates are revised annually based on an analysis of default trends prepared each year by an independent auditor. Within each risk group, it is assumed that borrowers choosing similar repayment plans will have similar default rates, regardless of whether they borrow under the FFEL or Direct Loan program.

The risk group data below also reflect proposed policy changes and interest rate projections in the President's 2001 Budget. These factors substantially decrease subsidy rates across years in the FFEL program.

FFEL RISK CATEGORIES: STAFFORD LOANS

Subsidy Rate (as a percentage of loan commitments)

Risk Categories:	1999 actual	2000 est.	2001 est.
Category 1: 4 year college, 1st and 2nd year students	26.04	28.04	25.64
Category 2: 4 year college, 3rd and 4th year students	18.25	19.79	17.75
Category 3: 2 year college, all students	21.96	22.85	21.24
Category 4: Proprietary school, all students	23.83	23.88	22.92
Category 5: Graduate students	20.28	22.33	19.98

Gross Default Rates (in percent)

Risk Categories:	1999 actual	2000 est.	2001 est.
Category 1: 4 year college, 1st and 2nd year students	19.67	19.68	19.66
Category 2: 4 year college, 3rd and 4th year students	13.17	13.18	13.17
Category 3: 2 year college, all students	32.69	32.68	32.67
Category 4: Proprietary school, all students	49.25	49.25	49.26
Category 5: Graduate students	8.86	8.87	8.87

UNSUBSIDIZED STAFFORD LOANS

Subsidy Rate (as a percentage of loan commitments)

Risk Categories:	1999 actual	2000 est.	2001 est.
Category 1: 4 year college, 1st and 2nd year students	8.76	8.97	6.25
Category 2: 4 year college, 3rd and 4th year students	5.86	6.20	3.81
Category 3: 2 year college, all students	11.94	11.66	9.69
Category 4: Proprietary school, all students	16.99	16.42	15.26
Category 5: Graduate students	5.92	6.51	3.84

Gross Default Rates (in percent)

Risk Categories:	1999 actual	2000 est.	2001 est.
Category 1: 4 year college, 1st and 2nd year students	20.01	20.04	20.02
Category 2: 4 year college, 3rd and 4th year students	13.08	13.09	13.09
Category 3: 2 year college, all students	32.07	32.07	32.06
Category 4: Proprietary school, all students	48.16	48.21	48.21
Category 5: Graduate students	8.74	8.75	8.75

PLUS LOANS

Subsidy Rate (as a percentage of loan commitments)

	1999 actual	2000 est.	2001 est.
All PLUS Loans	5.47	5.49	5.17

Gross Default Rates (in percent)

	1999 actual	2000 est.	2001 est.
All PLUS Loans	10.09	10.05	10.05

DIRECT LOAN RISK CATEGORIES: STAFFORD LOANS

Subsidy Rate (as a percentage of loan commitments)

Risk Categories:	1999 actual	2000 est.	2001 est.
Category 1: 4 year college, 1st and 2nd year students	12.51	7.69	12.68
Category 2: 4 year college, 3rd and 4th year students	5.30	0.45	4.92
Category 3: 2 year college, all students	10.69	4.94	9.96
Category 4: Proprietary school, all students	15.83	10.67	15.03
Category 5: Graduate students	7.13	2.65	7.00

Gross Default Rates (in percent)

Risk Categories:	1999 actual	2000 est.	2001 est.
Category 1: 4 year college, 1st and 2nd year students	20.02	20.03	20.00
Category 2: 4 year college, 3rd and 4th year students	13.16	13.15	13.14
Category 3: 2 year college, all students	33.25	33.24	33.23
Category 4: Proprietary school, all students	49.49	49.42	49.42
Category 5: Graduate students	8.84	8.83	8.82

UNSUBSIDIZED STAFFORD LOANS

Subsidy Rate (as a percentage of loan commitments)

Risk Categories:	1999 actual	2000 est.	2001 est.
Category 1: 4 year college, 1st and 2nd year students	–10.96	–20.63	–13.59
Category 2: 4 year college, 3rd and 4th year students	–13.47	–21.98	–16.14
Category 3: 2 year college, all students	–6.72	–15.97	–9.79
Category 4: Proprietary school, all students	1.09	–7.38	–1.87
Category 5: Graduate students	–13.44	–21.50	–15.77

Gross Default Rates (in percent)

Risk Categories:	1999 actual	2000 est.	2001 est.
Category 1: 4 year college, 1st and 2nd year students	20.02	20.04	20.02
Category 2: 4 year college, 3rd and 4th year students	13.04	13.03	13.03
Category 3: 2 year college, all students	32.45	32.45	32.44
Category 4: Proprietary school, all students	48.35	48.30	48.30
Category 5: Graduate students	8.73	8.72	8.72

PLUS LOANS

Subsidy Rate (as a percentage of loan commitments)

	1999 actual	2000 est.	2001 est.
All PLUS Loans	–15.61	–16.39	–12.36

Gross Default Rates (in percent)

	1999 actual	2000 est.	2001 est.
All PLUS Loans	9.36	9.44	9.42

Summary of Program Costs and Offsets (in thousands of dollars)

	1999 actual	2000 est.	2001 est.
Interest costs:			
Interest benefits:			
FFEL Liquidating	29,205	2,014	....
FFEL Program	3,629,000	1,845,606	1,968,452
Direct Loans [1]	884,326	881,577	980,630
	4,542,531	2,729,197	2,949,082
Special allowance:			
FFEL Liquidating	20,499	65,889	32,033
FFEL Program	837,528	822,719	573,388
	858,027	888,608	605,421

Default costs and offsets:			
Default costs[2]:			
FFEL Liquidating	413,325	167,886	94,348
FFEL Program	3,225,804	3,306,394	3,585,518
Direct Loans	642,037	1,365,850	1,679,715
	4,281,166	4,840,130	5,359,582
Gross default collections:			
FFEL Liquidating	2,803,024	1,095,176	876,097
FFEL Program	1,875,096	1,296,823	1,594,775
Direct Loans	64,286	179,854	305,265
	4,742,406	2,571,852	2,776,136
Default collection costs:			
FFEL Liquidating:			
Contract collection costs	20,254	46,163	40,669
Guaranty agency retention	121,024	99,446	53,526
	141,278	145,609	94,194
FFEL Program:			
Contract collection costs	73,000	19,846	31,781
Guaranty agency retention	136,096	190,765	159,412
	209,096	210.612	191,192
Direct Loans:			
Collection costs[3]	246	885	2,325
Net default costs:[4]			
FFEL Liquidating	–2,248,421	–781,681	–687,554
FFEL Program	1,559,804	2,220,183	2,181,935
Direct Loans	577,996	1,186,882	1,376,775
	–110,621	2,265,384	2,871,156
Death, disability, and bankruptcy costs:			
FFEL Liquidating	80,768	26,910	18,821
FFEL Program	424,453	251,536	279,518
Direct Loans	39,284	80,725	108,464
	544,505	359,172	406,803
Administrative Costs:			
Federal administration:			
FFEL[5]	47,276	48,000	48,000
Student Aid Management[6]	617,591	735,000	770,000
Guaranty agency administrative payments:			
Account Maintenance Fee	177,000	180,000	170,000
Loan Issuance and Processing Fee	253,000	153,910	162,749
Supplemental preclaims assistance	6,607		
Lender-paid default prevention fee			
Fees:			
Borrower origination fees:			
FFEL	636,857	620,412	651,824
Direct Loans	386,626	348,292	344,129
Lender origination fee[7]	106,143	126,307	132,365
Sallie Mae offset fee[7]	26,000	53,600	51,100
Consolidation loan holder fees[7]	196,000	220,695	253,119

[1] This represents net interest costs associated with Direct Loans.

[2] Default costs under FFEL reflect claims paid to guaranty agencies. Default costs under Direct Loans reflect outstanding balances at time of default.

[3] In the budget schedules, Direct Loan collections are displayed net of collection costs.

[4] Net default costs equal default claims minus net collections (gross collections minus contract collection costs and guaranty agency retention).

[5] Amount for 1999 reflects transfer from Treasury of $794,000 for Year 2000-related activities.

[6] A number of expenses related to the administration of the student assistance programs are paid out of Student Aid Management funds. One of these expenses, account maintenance fee payments to guaranty agencies, is shown as a separate line. Amount for 1999 includes transfer from Treasury of $591,000 for Year 2000-related activities.

[7] Applies to FFEL Program only.

Object Classification (in millions of dollars)

Identification code 91–0243–0–1–502		1999 actual	2000 est.	2001 est.
	Personnel compensation:			
11.1	Full-time permanent	31	37	38
11.3	Other than full-time permanent	1		
11.5	Other personnel compensation	1	1	1
11.9	Total personnel compensation	33	38	39
12.1	Civilian personnel benefits	7	8	9
21.0	Travel and transportation of persons	3	4	3
23.1	Rental payments to GSA	5	5	5
23.3	Communications, utilities, and miscellaneous charges	36	43	45
24.0	Printing and reproduction	7	6	7
25.1	Advisory and assistance services	6	1	1
25.2	Other services	21	12	17
25.3	Purchases of goods and services from Government accounts	4	1	2
25.7	Operation and maintenance of equipment	307	417	455
31.0	Equipment	4	1	2
32.0	Land and structures		19	15
41.0	Grants, subsidies, and contributions	177	180	170
99.9	Total new obligations	610	735	770

Personnel Summary

Identification code 91–0243–0–1–502		1999 actual	2000 est.	2001 est.
1001	Total compensable workyears: Full-time equivalent employment	551	571	571

FEDERAL DIRECT STUDENT LOAN PROGRAM, FINANCING ACCOUNT

Program and Financing (in millions of dollars)

Identification code 91–4253–0–3–502		1999 actual	2000 est.	2001 est.
	Obligations by program activity:			
	Direct loans:			
01.01	Stafford	6,072	6,129	6,354
01.02	Unsubsidized Stafford	3,925	4,235	4,537
01.03	PLUS	1,296	1,459	1,615
01.04	Consolidated	7,950	4,312	4,466
01.91	Subtotal, direct loans obligations	19,243	16,135	16,972
	Payment for consolidations:			
02.04	Consolidated	29	15	15
03.01	Payment of contract collections		1	2
04.01	Interest payment to Treasury	3,483	3,364	4,093
	Other obligations:			
08.01	Payment of negative subsidy to program account	378	1,200	607
08.02	Payment of downward reestimate to program account	361	2,442	
08.91	Subtotal, other obligations	739	3,642	607
10.00	Total new obligations	23,494	23,157	21,689
	Budgetary resources available for obligation:			
21.40	Unobligated balance available, start of year	5		
22.00	New financing authority (gross)	23,489	23,157	21,689
23.90	Total budgetary resources available for obligation	23,494	23,157	21,689
23.95	Total new obligations	−23,494	−23,157	−21,689
24.40	Unobligated balance available, end of year			
	New financing authority (gross), detail:			
	Mandatory:			
67.15	Authority to borrow (indefinite)	19,977	19,778	17,579
69.00	Offsetting collections (cash)	8,199	5,863	8,044
69.10	From Federal sources: Change in receivables and unpaid, unfilled orders	−88		
69.47	Portion applied to repay debt	−4,599	−2,484	−3,934
69.90	Spending authority from offsetting collections (total mandatory)	3,512	3,379	4,110
70.00	Total new financing authority (gross)	23,489	23,157	21,689
	Change in unpaid obligations:			
	Unpaid obligations, start of year:			
72.40	Obligated balance, start of year	5,396	6,718	3,415
72.95	Receivables from program account	88		
72.99	Total unpaid obligations, start of year	5,484	6,718	3,415
73.10	Total new obligations	23,494	23,157	21,689
73.20	Total financing disbursements (gross)	−22,256	−26,460	−21,489
73.40	Adjustments in expired accounts (net)	−5		
	Unpaid obligations, end of year:			
74.40	Obligated balance, end of year	6,718	3,415	3,614
74.95	Receivables from program account			
74.99	Total unpaid obligations, end of year	6,718	3,415	3,614
87.00	Total financing disbursements (gross)	22,256	26,460	21,489
	Offsets:			
	Against gross financing authority and financing disbursements:			
	Offsetting collections (cash) from:			
	Federal sources:			
	Payments from subsidy account:			
88.00	Stafford	−196		
88.00	Unsubsidized Stafford	85		

Credit accounts—Continued

FEDERAL DIRECT STUDENT LOAN PROGRAM, FINANCING ACCOUNT—Continued

Program and Financing (in millions of dollars)—Continued

Identification code 91–4253–0–3–502		1999 actual	2000 est.	2001 est.
88.00	PLUS	24		
88.00	Consolidated	4		
88.00	Downward reestimate			
88.25	Interest on uninvested funds	−1,088		
	Non-Federal sources:			
	Stafford loans:			
88.40	Repayment of principal, Stafford	−2,229	−1,012	−1,445
88.40	Interest received on loans, Stafford	−284	−961	−1,348
88.40	Fees, Stafford	−221	−179	−171
88.40	Repayment of principal, Unsubsidized Stafford	−1,527	−612	−909
88.40	Interest received on loans, Unsubsidized Stafford	−237	−608	−895
88.40	Fees, Unsubsidized Stafford	−131	−120	−120
88.40	Repayment of principal, PLUS	−519	−267	−348
88.40	Interest received on loans, PLUS	−193	−322	−432
88.40	Fees, PLUS	−36	−50	−53
88.40	Payment of principal, Consolidated	−1,283	−680	−959
88.40	Interest received on loans, Consolidated	−368	−1,052	−1,364
88.90	Total, offsetting collections (cash)	−8,199	−5,863	−8,044
	Against gross financing authority only:			
88.95	Change in receivables from program accounts	88		
	Net financing authority and financing disbursements:			
89.00	Financing authority	15,378	17,294	13,645
90.00	Financing disbursements	14,056	20,597	13,445

Status of Direct Loans (in millions of dollars)

Identification code 91–4253–0–3–502		1999 actual	2000 est.	2001 est.
	STAFFORD			
	Position with respect to appropriations act limitation on obligations:			
1111	Limitation on direct loans			
1131	Direct loan obligations exempt from limitation	6,072	6,129	6,353
1150	Total direct loan obligations	6,072	6,129	6,353
	Cumulative balance of direct loans outstanding:			
1210	Outstanding, start of year	16,844	19,699	24,153
1231	Disbursements: Direct loan disbursements	5,502	5,469	5,705
1251	Repayments: Repayments and prepayments	−2,228	−981	−1,382
1261	Adjustments: Capitalized interest	88		
	Write-offs for default:			
1263	Direct loans	−14	−34	−44
1264	Other adjustments, net	−493		
1290	Outstanding, end of year	19,699	24,153	28,432
	UNSUBSIDIZED STAFFORD			
	Position with respect to appropriations act limitation on obligations:			
1111	Limitation on direct loans			
1131	Direct loan obligations exempt from limitation	3,925	4,235	4,537
1150	Total direct loan obligations	3,925	4,235	4,537
	Cumulative balance of direct loans outstanding:			
1210	Outstanding, start of year	9,239	11,216	14,857
1231	Disbursements: Direct loan disbursements	3,432	3,676	3,992
1251	Repayments: Repayments and prepayments	−1,526	−593	−870
1261	Adjustments: Capitalized interest	360	576	721
	Write-offs for default:			
1263	Direct loans	−8	−18	−25
1264	Other adjustments, net	−281		
1290	Outstanding, end of year	11,216	14,857	18,675
	PLUS			
	Position with respect to appropriations act limitation on obligations:			
1111	Limitation on direct loans			
1131	Direct loan obligations exempt from limitation	1,296	1,459	1,615
1150	Total direct loan obligations	1,296	1,459	1,615
	Cumulative balance of direct loans outstanding:			
1210	Outstanding, start of year	2,296	2,848	3,792
1231	Disbursements: Direct loan disbursements	1,039	1,241	1,330
1251	Repayments: Repayments and prepayments	−519	−276	−358
1261	Adjustments: Capitalized interest	111		
	Write-offs for default:			
1263	Direct loans	−8	−21	−26
1264	Other adjustments, net	−71		
1290	Outstanding, end of year	2,848	3,792	4,738
	CONSOLIDATED			
	Position with respect to appropriations act limitation on obligations:			
1111	Limitation on direct loans			
1131	Direct loan obligations exempt from limitation	7,950	4,312	4,466
1150	Total direct loan obligations	7,950	4,312	4,466
	Cumulative balance of direct loans outstanding:			
1210	Outstanding, start of year	4,986	12,067	15,674
1231	Disbursements: Direct loan disbursements	8,097	4,250	4,402
1251	Repayments: Repayments and prepayments	−1,282	−666	−929
1261	Adjustments: Capitalized interest	579	36	42
	Write-offs for default:			
1263	Direct loans	−11	−13	−23
1264	Other adjustments, net	−302		
1290	Outstanding, end of year	12,067	15,674	19,166

Balance Sheet (in millions of dollars)

Identification code 91–4253–0–3–502		1998 actual	1999 actual	2000 est.	2001 est.
	ASSETS:				
1101	Federal assets: Fund balances with Treasury	5,396	−6,718	3,415	3,614
	Net value of assets related to post–1991 direct loans receivable:				
	Direct loans receivable, gross:				
1401	Stafford	15,988	19,698	24,152	28,432
1401	Unsubsidized Stafford	8,769	11,216	14,857	18,675
1401	PLUS	2,180	2,848	3,792	4,738
1401	Consolidated	4,733	12,067	15,638	19,165
	Interest receivable:				
1402	Interest receivable, Stafford	80	333	408	480
1402	Interest receivable, Unsub Stafford	462	405	516	649
1402	Interest receivable, PLUS	3	1,965	2,616	3,268
1402	Interest receivable, Consolidated	77	427	554	678
1405	Allowance for subsidy cost (–)	–1,575	–1,558	–1,306	–1,374
1499	Net present value of assets related to direct loans	30,717	47,401	61,227	74,711
1999	Total assets	36,113	40,683	64,642	78,325
	LIABILITIES:				
2103	Federal liabilities: Debt	35,097	52,070	69,364	83,009
2999	Total liabilities	35,097	52,070	69,364	83,009
	NET POSITION:				
3100	Appropriated capital	1,016	–11,386	–4,721	–4,682
3999	Total net position	1,016	–11,386	–4,721	–4,682
4999	Total liabilities and net position	36,113	40,684	64,643	78,327

As required by the Federal Credit Reform Act of 1990, this non-budgetary account records all cash flows to and from the Government resulting from Direct Loans. The amounts in this account are a means of financing and are not included in the budget totals.

FEDERAL FAMILY EDUCATION LOAN PROGRAM ACCOUNT

For Federal administrative expenses to carry out guaranteed student loans authorized by title IV, part B, of the Higher Education Act of 1965, as amended, $48,000,000. *(Department of Education Appropriations Act, 2000, as enacted by section 1000(a)(4) of the Consolidated Appropriations Act, 2000 (P.L. 106–113).)*

Note.—The following tables display the program account which includes the subsidy costs and administrative expenses associated with guaranteed student loan commitments beginning in 1992.

Program and Financing (in millions of dollars)

Identification code 91–0231–0–1–502		1999 actual	2000 est.	2001 est.
	Obligations by program activity:			
00.02	Guaranteed Loan Net Subsidy	3,485	3,731	4,004

00.07	Upward Reestimate	21	627	....
00.08	Interest on Reestimate	−174	187	....
	Administrative expenses:			
00.09	Administrative expenses due to limitations	47	48	48
10.00	Total new obligations	3,379	4,593	4,052
	Budgetary resources available for obligation:			
22.00	New budget authority (gross)	3,379	4,592	4,052
23.95	Total new obligations	−3,379	−4,593	−4,052
	New budget authority (gross), detail:			
	Discretionary:			
40.00	Appropriation (Federal administration)	46	48	48
42.00	Transferred from other accounts	1	....	....
43.00	Appropriation (total discretionary)	47	48	48
	Mandatory:			
60.05	Appropriation (indefinite)	3,332	4,507	4,004
69.00	Offsetting collections (cash)	....	37	....
70.00	Total new budget authority (gross)	3,379	4,592	4,052
	Change in unpaid obligations:			
72.40	Unpaid obligations, start of year: Obligated balance, start of year	859	1,433	1,959
73.10	Total new obligations	3,379	4,593	4,052
73.20	Total outlays (gross)	−2,805	−4,067	−3,549
74.40	Unpaid obligations, end of year: Obligated balance, end of year	1,433	1,959	2,464
	Outlays (gross), detail:			
86.90	Outlays from new discretionary authority	33	35	23
86.93	Outlays from discretionary balances	19	11	22
86.97	Outlays from new mandatory authority	1,926	3,015	2,378
86.98	Outlays from mandatory balances	827	1,006	1,125
87.00	Total outlays (gross)	2,805	4,067	3,549
	Offsets:			
	Against gross budget authority and outlays:			
88.00	Offsetting collections (cash) from: Federal sources	....	−37	....
	Net budget authority and outlays:			
89.00	Budget authority	3,379	4,555	4,052
90.00	Outlays	2,805	4,030	3,549

Summary of Budget Authority and Outlays

(in millions of dollars)

Enacted/requested:	*1999 actual*	*2000 est.*	*2001 est.*
Budget Authority	3,379	4,555	4,052
Outlays	2,805	4,030	3,548
Legislative proposal, subject to PAYGO:			
Budget Authority	....	....	....
Outlays	....	....	....
Legislative proposal, discretionary offset:			
Budget Authority	....	....	−1,244
Outlays	....	....	−977
Total:			
Budget Authority	3,379	4,555	2,808
Outlays	2,805	4,030	2,571

Summary of Loan Levels, Subsidy Budget Authority and Outlays by Program (in millions of dollars)

Identification code 91–0231–0–1–502		1999 actual	2000 est.	2001 est.
	Guaranteed loan levels supportable by subsidy budget authority:			
2150	Stafford	11,671	11,791	12,210
2150	Unsubsidized Stafford	8,836	9,351	10,023
2150	PLUS	2,195	2,536	2,806
2150	Consolidated	4,795	4,648	4,814
2159	Total loan guarantee levels	27,497	28,326	29,853
	Guaranteed loan subsidy (in percent):			
2320	Stafford	21.55	23.21	23.53
2320	Unsubsidized Stafford	7.84	8.20	8.38
2320	PLUS	5.94	5.49	5.38
2320	Consolidated	1.35	1.89	2.91
2329	Weighted average subsidy rate	12.51	13.17	13.41
	Guaranteed loan subsidy budget authority:			
2330	Stafford	2,199	3,578	2,873
2330	Unsubsidized Stafford	175	1,062	840
2330	PLUS	158	83	151
2330	Consolidated	598	−242	140
2330	SLS	203	26	....
2339	Total subsidy budget authority	3,333	4,507	4,004
	Guaranteed loan subsidy outlays:			
2340	Stafford	1,821	3,204	2,520
2340	Unsubsidized Stafford	−15	932	717
2340	PLUS	116	64	128
2340	Consolidated	628	−243	138
2340	SLS	203	26	....
2349	Total subsidy outlays	2,753	3,983	3,503
	Administrative expense data:			
3510	Budget authority	46	48	48
3590	Outlays	52	47	45

As required by the Federal Credit Reform Act of 1990, this program account records for this program the subsidy costs associated with Federal Family Education Loans (FFEL), formerly guaranteed student loans (GSL), committed in 1992 and beyond, as well as certain administrative expenses of the program. Administrative expenses include discretionary expenses for salaries, expenses and overhead of employees working directly on the program. Beginning with the 1993 cohort, mandatory administrative costs, specifically contract collection costs, are included in the FFEL subsidy estimates of each year's cohort. Another mandatory administrative cost, supplemental pre-claims assistance, was repealed by the Higher Education Amendments of 1998. Subsidy amounts are estimated on a net present value basis.

A description of the FFEL program and accompanying tables are included under the Federal Direct Student Loan program account.

Object Classification (in millions of dollars)

Identification code 91–0231–0–1–502		1999 actual	2000 est.	2001 est.
11.1	Personnel compensation: Full-time permanent	20	23	22
12.1	Civilian personnel benefits	5	5	6
21.0	Travel and transportation of persons	....	1	1
23.1	Rental payments to GSA	2	5	5
23.3	Communications, utilities, and miscellaneous charges	1	2	1
25.2	Other services	1	1	2
25.3	Purchases of goods and services from Government accounts	1	1	2
25.7	Operation and maintenance of equipment	15	9	6
31.0	Equipment	1	1	1
32.0	Land and structures	1	....	....
41.0	Grants, subsidies, and contributions	3,332	4,545	4,006
99.9	Total new obligations	3,379	4,593	4,052

Personnel Summary

Identification code 91–0231–0–1–502		1999 actual	2000 est.	2001 est.
1001	Total compensable workyears: Full-time equivalent employment	356	356	356

FEDERAL FAMILY EDUCATION LOAN PROGRAM ACCOUNT

(Legislative proposal, discretionary offset)

Program and Financing (in millions of dollars)

Identification code 91–0231–6–1–502		1999 actual	2000 est.	2001 est.
	Obligations by program activity:			
	Guaranteed loan subsidy:			
02.01	Stafford	....	....	−328
02.02	Unsubsidized Stafford	....	....	−303
02.03	PLUS	....	....	−6
02.05	Consolidated	....	....	−17
02.07	Upward reestimate	....	....	....
02.08	Interest on reestimate	....	....	....
02.91	Subtotal, subsidy cost	....	....	−654
	Administrative expenses:			
07.01	Administrative expenses due to limitations	....	....	....

Credit accounts—Continued

FEDERAL FAMILY EDUCATION LOAN PROGRAM ACCOUNT—Continued

Program and Financing (in millions of dollars)—Continued

Identification code 91–0231–6–1–502		1999 actual	2000 est.	2001 est.
10.00	Total new obligations (object class 41.0)			−654
	Budgetary resources available for obligation:			
22.00	New budget authority (gross)			−654
23.95	Total new obligations			654
	New budget authority (gross), detail:			
	Mandatory:			
60.05	Appropriation (indefinite)			−654
69.00	Offsetting collections (cash)			590
69.27	Capital transfer to general fund			−590
69.90	Spending authority from offsetting collections (total mandatory)			
70.00	Total new budget authority (gross)			−654
	Change in unpaid obligations:			
73.10	Total new obligations			−654
73.20	Total outlays (gross)			387
74.40	Unpaid obligations, end of year: Obligated balance, end of year			−267
	Outlays (gross), detail:			
86.97	Outlays from new mandatory authority			−387
	Offsets:			
	Against gross budget authority and outlays:			
88.00	Offsetting collections (cash) from: Federal sources			−590
	Net budget authority and outlays:			
89.00	Budget authority			−1,244
90.00	Outlays			−977

Summary of Loan Levels, Subsidy Budget Authority and Outlays by Program (in millions of dollars)

Identification code 91–0231–6–1–502		1999 actual	2000 est.	2001 est.
	Guaranteed loan subsidy (in percent):			
2320	Stafford			−0.03
2320	Unsubsidized Stafford			−0.03
2320	PLUS			0.00
2320	Consolidated			0.00
2329	Weighted average subsidy rate			−0.02
	Guaranteed loan subsidy budget authority:			
2330	Stafford			−328
2330	Unsubsidized Stafford			−303
2330	PLUS			−6
2330	Consolidated			−17
2339	Total subsidy budget authority			−654
	Guaranteed loan subsidy outlays:			
2340	Stafford			−191
2340	Unsubsidized Stafford			−176
2340	PLUS			−3
2340	Consolidated			−17
2340	SLS			
2340	Contractual Modification			−590
2349	Total subsidy outlays			−977
	Administrative expense data:			
3510	Budget authority			
3590	Outlays			

FEDERAL FAMILY EDUCATION LOAN PROGRAM, FINANCING ACCOUNT

Note.—The financing account includes all cash flows to and from the Government from guaranteed student loans committed after 1991.

Program and Financing (in millions of dollars)

Identification code 91–4251–0–3–502		1999 actual	2000 est.	2001 est.
	Obligations by program activity:			
	Stafford loans:			
01.01	Interest benefits	3,629	1,845	1,969
01.02	Special allowance	524	481	311
01.03	Default claims	1,477	1,588	1,649
01.04	Death, disability, and bankruptcy claims	103	112	120
01.06	Supplemental preclaims assistance	2		
01.07	Contract collection costs	44	13	18
01.08	Loan Processing Fee	131	77	79
01.91	Subtotal, Stafford loans	5,910	4,116	4,146
	Unsubsidized Stafford loans:			
02.02	Special allowance	165	260	211
02.03	Default claims	591	864	1,013
02.04	Death, disability, and bankruptcy claims	44	50	60
02.06	Supplemental preclaims assistance	1		
02.07	Contract collection costs	6	2	3
02.08	Loan Processing Fee	98	61	65
02.91	Subtotal, Unsubsidized Stafford loans	905	1,237	1,352
	PLUS loans:			
03.02	Special allowance	42	21	19
03.03	Default claims	41	147	166
03.04	Death, disability, and bankruptcy claims	39	50	56
03.07	Loan Processing Fee	24	16	18
03.91	Subtotal, PLUS loans	146	234	259
	SLS loans:			
04.02	Special allowance	15	2	1
04.03	Default claims	130	105	79
04.04	Death, disability and bankruptcy claims	50	9	7
04.06	Supplemental preclaims assistance	2		
04.07	Contract collection costs	17	4	5
04.91	Subtotal, SLS loans	214	120	92
	Consolidation loans:			
05.02	Special allowance	92	59	61
05.03	Default claims	987	602	678
05.04	Death, disability, and bankruptcy claims	187	30	37
05.06	Supplemental preclaims assistance	1		
05.07	Contract collection costs	6	2	3
05.91	Subtotal, Consolidations loans	1,273	693	779
07.01	Interest paid to Treasury	9		
08.02	Downward reestimate	−21	19	
08.04	Interest on downward reestimate	174	120	
08.91	Direct Program by Activities—Subtotal (1 level)	153	139	
10.00	Total new obligations	8,610	6,539	6,628
	Budgetary resources available for obligation:			
21.40	Unobligated balance available, start of year	8,657	5,338	5,528
22.00	New financing authority (gross)	5,290	6,730	6,471
23.90	Total budgetary resources available for obligation	13,947	12,068	11,999
23.95	Total new obligations	−8,610	−6,539	−6,628
24.40	Unobligated balance available, end of year	5,338	5,528	5,371
	New financing authority (gross), detail:			
	Spending authority from offsetting collections:			
	Discretionary:			
68.00	Offsetting collections (cash)	6,234	6,551	6,352
68.10	From Federal sources: Change in receivables and unpaid, unfilled orders	−827	179	119
68.47	Portion applied to repay debt	−117		
68.90	Spending authority from offsetting collections (total discretionary)	5,290	6,730	6,471
	Change in unpaid obligations:			
	Unpaid obligations, start of year:			
72.40	Obligated balance, start of year	−557	3,539	−687
72.95	Receivables from program account	827		179
72.99	Total unpaid obligations, start of year	270	3,539	−508
73.10	Total new obligations	8,610	6,539	6,628
73.20	Total financing disbursements (gross)	−5,341	−10,587	−6,618

73.40	Adjustments in expired accounts (net)			
	Unpaid obligations, end of year:			
74.40	Obligated balance, end of year	3,539	−687	−796
74.95	Receivables from program account		179	298
74.99	Total unpaid obligations, end of year	3,539	−508	−498
87.00	Total financing disbursements (gross)	5,341	10,587	6,618
	Offsets:			
	Against gross financing authority and financing disbursements:			
	Offsetting collections (cash) from:			
	Federal sources:			
	Payment from subsidy account:			
88.00	Stafford loans	−2,204	−2,364	−2,520
88.00	Unsubsidized Stafford	−459	−637	−717
88.00	PLUS loans	−98	−120	−128
88.00	SLS loans	−37		
88.00	Consolidated loans	−108	−87	−138
88.00	Scheduled payments from Liquidating account for noncontractual modifications	−125		
88.00	Upward reestimate		−828	
88.25	Interest on uninvested funds: Stafford loans	−441	−387	−392
	Non-Federal sources:			
	Student Loans: Stafford, Unsubsidized Stafford, PLUS, SLS & Consolidation:			
88.40	Stafford recoveries on defaults	−1,088	−636	−758
88.40	Stafford origination fees	−392	−368	−377
88.40	Stafford Sallie Mae offset fees	−15	−30	−28
88.40	Stafford other fees	−54		
88.40	Unsubsidized Stafford recoveries on defaults	−173	−178	−252
88.40	Unsubsidized Stafford origination fees	−282	−283	−301
88.40	Unsubsidized Stafford Sallie Mae offset fees	−7	−16	−17
88.40	PLUS recoveries on defaults	−100	−48	−58
88.40	PLUS origination fees	−69	−73	−82
88.40	PLUS Sallie Mae offset fees	−3	−6	−6
88.40	PLUS other fees	−1		
88.40	SLS recoveries on defaults	−137	−102	−105
88.40	SLS Sallie Mae offset fees	−1	−1	−1
88.40	SLS other fees	−2		
88.40	Consolidation recoveries on defaults	−241	−143	−196
88.40	Consolidation other fees	−1		
88.40	Consolidation origination fees		−23	−24
88.40	Consolidated loan holders fee	−196	−221	−252
88.90	Total, offsetting collections (cash)	−6,234	−6,551	−6,352
	Against gross financing authority only:			
88.95	Change in receivables from program accounts	827	−179	−119
	Net financing authority and financing disbursements:			
89.00	Financing authority	−117		
90.00	Financing disbursements	−893	4,036	266

Status of Guaranteed Loans (in millions of dollars)

Identification code 91–4251–0–3–502		1999 actual	2000 est.	2001 est.
	STAFFORD			
	Position with respect to appropriations act limitation on commitments:			
2111	Limitation on guaranteed loans made by private lenders			
2131	Guaranteed loan commitments exempt from limitation	11,671	11,791	12,210
2150	Total guaranteed loan commitments	11,671	11,791	12,210
	Cumulative balance of guaranteed loans outstanding:			
2210	Outstanding, start of year	50,168	55,035	57,428
2231	Disbursements of new guaranteed loans	9,919	10,508	10,759
2251	Repayments and prepayments	−4,092	−6,404	−7,636
	Adjustments:			
2261	Terminations for default that result in loans receivable	−1,056	−1,599	−1,668
2263	Terminations for default that result in claim payments	−61	−112	−120
2264	Other adjustments, net	157		
2290	Outstanding, end of year	55,035	57,428	58,763
	Memorandum:			
2299	Guaranteed amount of guaranteed loans outstanding, end of year	55,035	57,428	58,763
	Addendum:			
	Cumulative balance of defaulted guaranteed loans that result in loans receivable:			
2310	Outstanding, start of year	4,701	4,596	5,481
2331	Disbursements for guaranteed loan claims	1,056	1,599	1,668
2351	Repayments of loans receivable	−1,045	−638	−758
2361	Write-offs of loans receivable	−116	−76	−91
2390	Outstanding, end of year	4,596	5,481	6,300
	UNSUBSIDIZED STAFFORD			
	Position with respect to appropriations act limitation on commitments:			
2131	Guaranteed loan commitments exempt from limitation	8,836	9,351	10,023
2150	Total guaranteed loan commitments	8,836	9,351	10,023
	Cumulative balance of guaranteed loans outstanding:			
2210	Outstanding, start of year	23,397	28,565	33,256
2231	Disbursements of new guaranteed loans	7,120	8,090	8,614
2251	Repayments and prepayments	−1,809	−2,511	−3,361
	Adjustments:			
2261	Terminations for default that result in loans receivable	−392	−838	−1,007
2263	Terminations for default that result in claim payments	−20	−50	−60
2264	Other adjustments, net	269		
2290	Outstanding, end of year	28,565	33,256	37,442
	Memorandum:			
2299	Guaranteed amount of guaranteed loans outstanding, end of year	28,565	33,256	37,442
	Addendum:			
	Cumulative balance of defaulted guaranteed loans that result in loans receivable:			
2310	Outstanding, start of year	924	1,115	1,754
2331	Disbursements for guaranteed loan claims	392	838	1,007
2351	Repayments of loans receivable	−178	−178	−252
2361	Write-offs of loans receivable	−23	−21	−30
2390	Outstanding, end of year	1,115	1,754	2,479
	PLUS			
	Position with respect to appropriations act limitation on commitments:			
2131	Guaranteed loan commitments exempt from limitation	2,195	2,536	2,806
2150	Total guaranteed loan commitments	2,195	2,536	2,806
	Cumulative balance of guaranteed loans outstanding:			
2210	Outstanding, start of year	5,745	6,693	7,554
2231	Disbursements of new guaranteed loans	1,816	2,082	2,354
2251	Repayments and prepayments	−947	−1,039	−1,230
	Adjustments:			
2261	Terminations for default that result in loans receivable	−70	−132	−165
2263	Terminations for default that result in claim payments	−20	−50	−56
2264	Other adjustments, net	169		
2290	Outstanding, end of year	6,693	7,554	8,457
	Memorandum:			
2299	Guaranteed amount of guaranteed loans outstanding, end of year	6,693	7,554	8,457
	Addendum:			
	Cumulative balance of defaulted guaranteed loans that result in loans receivable:			
2310	Outstanding, start of year	327	315	393
2331	Disbursements for guaranteed loan claims	70	132	165
2351	Repayments of loans receivable	−74	−48	−58
2361	Write-offs of loans receivable	−8	−6	−7
2390	Outstanding, end of year	315	393	493
	SLS			
	Cumulative balance of guaranteed loans outstanding:			
2210	Outstanding, start of year	3,034	2,467	1,522
2251	Repayments and prepayments	−400	−825	−711
	Adjustments:			
2261	Terminations for default that result in loans receivable	−104	−111	−85
2263	Terminations for default that result in claim payments	−8	−9	−7

Credit accounts—Continued

Federal Family Education Loan Program, Financing Account—Continued

Status of Guaranteed Loans (in millions of dollars)—Continued

Identification code 91–4251–0–3–502		1999 actual	2000 est.	2001 est.
2264	Other adjustments, net	−55		
2290	Outstanding, end of year	2,467	1,522	719
	Memorandum:			
2299	Guaranteed amount of guaranteed loans outstanding, end of year	2,467	1,522	719
	Addendum:			
	Cumulative balance of defaulted guaranteed loans that result in loans receivable:			
2310	Outstanding, start of year	987	907	904
2331	Disbursements for guaranteed loan claims	104	111	85
2351	Repayments of loans receivable	−160	−102	−105
2361	Write-offs of loans receivable	−24	−12	−13
2390	Outstanding, end of year	907	904	871
	CONSOLIDATED			
	Position with respect to appropriations act limitation on commitments:			
2131	Guaranteed loan commitments exempt from limitation	4,795	4,648	4,814
2150	Total guaranteed loan commitments	4,795	4,648	4,814
	Cumulative balance of guaranteed loans outstanding:			
2210	Outstanding, start of year	17,164	20,008	22,532
2231	Disbursements of new guaranteed loans	3,059	4,581	4,745
2251	Repayments and prepayments	270	−1,355	−1,692
	Adjustments:			
2261	Terminations for default that result in loans receivable	−423	−672	−679
2263	Terminations for default that result in claim payments	−49	−30	−37
2264	Other adjustments, net	−13		
2290	Outstanding, end of year	20,008	22,532	24,869
	Memorandum:			
2299	Guaranteed amount of guaranteed loans outstanding, end of year	20,008	22,532	24,869
	Addendum:			
	Cumulative balance of defaulted guaranteed loans that result in loans receivable:			
2310	Outstanding, start of year	1,507	1,768	2,280
2331	Disbursements for guaranteed loan claims	423	672	679
2351	Repayments of loans receivable	−125	−143	−196
2361	Write-offs of loans receivable	−37	−17	−23
2390	Outstanding, end of year	1,768	2,280	2,740

Balance Sheet (in millions of dollars)

Identification code 91–4251–0–3–502		1998 actual	1999 actual	2000 est.	2001 est.
	ASSETS:				
1101	Federal assets: Fund balances with Treasury	7,830	6,384	6,867	6,871
	Net value of assets related to post-1991 acquired defaulted guaranteed loans receivable:				
1501	Defaulted guaranteed loans receivable, gross	6,083	8,701	10,812	12,883
1599	Net present value of assets related to defaulted guaranteed loans	6,083	8,701	10,812	12,883
1999	Total assets	13,913	15,085	17,679	19,754
	LIABILITIES:				
2103	Federal liabilities: Debt	354	117		
2999	Total liabilities	354	117		
	NET POSITION:				
3100	Appropriated capital	13,559	14,968	17,679	19,754
3999	Total net position	13,559	14,968	17,679	19,754
4999	Total liabilities and net position	13,913	15,085	17,679	19,754

As required by the Federal Credit Reform Act of 1990, this nonbudgetary account records all cash flows to and from the Government resulting from Federal Family Education Loans (FFEL), formerly guaranteed student loans (GSL), committed in 1992 and beyond. The amounts in this account are a means of financing and are not included in the budget totals.

Federal Family Education Loan Program, Financing Account

(Legislative proposal, discretionary offset)

Program and Financing (in millions of dollars)

Identification code 91–4251–6–3–502		1999 actual	2000 est.	2001 est.
	Obligations by program activity:			
	Stafford loans:			
01.02	Special allowance			−16
01.07	Contract collection costs			1
01.91	Subtotal, Stafford loans			−15
	Unsubsidized Stafford loans:			
02.02	Special allowance			−13
08.03	Contractural modification to program account			550
10.00	Total new obligations			522
	Budgetary resources available for obligation:			
21.40	Unobligated balance available, start of year			
22.00	New financing authority (gross)			−562
23.90	Total budgetary resources available for obligation			−562
23.95	Total new obligations			−522
24.40	Unobligated balance available, end of year			−1,086
	New financing authority (gross), detail:			
	Discretionary:			
68.00	Spending authority from offsetting collections (gross): Offsetting collections (cash)			−562
	Change in unpaid obligations:			
73.10	Total new obligations			522
73.20	Total financing disbursements (gross)			−497
74.40	Unpaid obligations, end of year: Obligated balance, end of year			26
87.00	Total financing disbursements (gross)			497
	Offsets:			
	Against gross financing authority and financing disbursements:			
	Offsetting collections (cash) from:			
	Federal sources:			
	Payment from subsidy account:			
88.00	Stafford loans			293
88.00	Unsubsidized Stafford			266
88.00	PLUS loans			5
88.00	Consolidated loans			17
88.25	Interest on uninvested funds: Stafford loans			47
	Non-Federal sources:			
	Stafford loans:			
88.40	Recoveries on defaults			−36
88.40	Recoveries on defaults			−13
88.40	Recoveries on defaults			−3
88.40	Recoveries on defaults			−4
88.40	Recoveries on defaults			−10
88.90	Total, offsetting collections (cash)			562
	Net financing authority and financing disbursements:			
89.00	Financing authority			
90.00	Financing disbursements			1,059

Status of Guaranteed Loans (in millions of dollars)

Identification code 91–4251–6–3–502	1999 actual	2000 est.	2001 est.
STAFFORD			
Position with respect to appropriations act limitation on commitments:			
2111 Limitation on guaranteed loans made by private lenders			
2150 Total guaranteed loan commitments			
Addendum:			
Cumulative balance of defaulted guaranteed loans that result in loans receivable:			
2310 Outstanding, start of year			
2351 Repayments of loans receivable			−36
2361 Write-offs of loans receivable			−4
2390 Outstanding, end of year			−40
UNSUBSIDIZED STAFFORD			
Addendum:			
Cumulative balance of defaulted guaranteed loans that result in loans receivable:			
2310 Outstanding, start of year			
2351 Repayments of loans receivable			−13
2361 Write-offs of loans receivable			−2
2390 Outstanding, end of year			−15
PLUS			
Addendum:			
Cumulative balance of defaulted guaranteed loans that result in loans receivable:			
2310 Outstanding, start of year			
2351 Repayments of loans receivable			−3
2390 Outstanding, end of year			−3
SLS			
Addendum:			
Cumulative balance of defaulted guaranteed loans that result in loans receivable:			
2310 Outstanding, start of year			
2351 Repayments of loans receivable			−4
2390 Outstanding, end of year			−4
CONSOLIDATED			
Addendum:			
Cumulative balance of defaulted guaranteed loans that result in loans receivable:			
2310 Outstanding, start of year			
2351 Repayments of loans receivable			−10
2361 Write-offs of loans receivable			−1
2390 Outstanding, end of year			−11

Balance Sheet (in millions of dollars)

Identification code 91–4251–6–3–502	1998 actual	1999 actual	2000 est.	2001 est.
ASSETS:				
1101 Federal assets: Fund balances with Treasury				−1,086
Net value of assets related to post–1991 acquired defaulted guaranteed loans receivable:				
1501 Defaulted guaranteed loans receivable, gross				−74
1599 Net present value of assets related to defaulted guaranteed loans				−74
1999 Total assets				−1,160
LIABILITIES:				
2103 Federal liabilities: Debt				
2999 Total liabilities				
NET POSITION:				
3100 Appropriated capital				−1,160
3999 Total net position				−1,160
4999 Total liabilities and net position				−1,160

Federal Family Education Loan Liquidating Account

Note.—The following tables display the liquidating account, which includes all cash flows to and from the Government from guaranteed student loan commitments prior to 1992.

Program and Financing (in millions of dollars)

Identification code 91–0230–0–1–502	1999 actual	2000 est.	2001 est.
Obligations by program activity:			
Stafford loans:			
01.01 Interest benefits, net of origination fees	29	2	
01.02 Special allowance net of origination fees	18	63	29
01.03 Default claims	336	141	88
01.04 Death, disability, and bankruptcy claims	65	23	17
01.07 Contract collection costs	17	37	30
01.91 Subtotal, Stafford loans	465	266	164
PLUS/SLS loans:			
02.01 Default claims	77	26	7
02.02 Death, disability, and bankruptcy claims	16	4	2
02.05 Contract collection costs	3	9	8
02.06 Special allowance net of origination fees	3	3	3
02.91 Subtotal, PLUS/SLS loans	99	42	20
Miscellaneous costs:			
03.01 Scheduled payments to finance account for noncontractual modifications	125		
10.00 Total new obligations	689	308	184
Budgetary resources available for obligation:			
21.40 Unobligated balance available, start of year	149	209	
22.00 New budget authority (gross)	2,147	308	184
22.10 Resources available from recoveries of prior year obligations	−1,400		
22.40 Capital transfer to general fund		−209	
23.90 Total budgetary resources available for obligation	896	308	184
23.95 Total new obligations	−689	−308	−184
24.40 Unobligated balance available, end of year	209		
New budget authority (gross), detail:			
Mandatory:			
69.00 Offsetting collections (cash)	2,697	1,001	803
69.27 Capital transfer to general fund	−548	−693	−619
69.75 Reduction pursuant to P.L. 106–51	−2		
69.90 Spending authority from offsetting collections (total mandatory)	2,147	308	184
Change in unpaid obligations:			
72.40 Unpaid obligations, start of year: Obligated balance, start of year	741	1,296	1,310
73.10 Total new obligations	689	308	184
73.20 Total outlays (gross)	−1,534	−294	−174
73.45 Adjustments in unexpired accounts	1,400		
74.40 Unpaid obligations, end of year: Obligated balance, end of year	1,296	1,310	1,320
Outlays (gross), detail:			
86.97 Outlays from new mandatory authority	793	85	−49
86.98 Outlays from mandatory balances	741	209	223
87.00 Total outlays (gross)	1,534	294	174
Offsets:			
Against gross budget authority and outlays:			
Offsetting collections (cash) from:			
Non-Federal sources:			
Federal student loans:			
88.40 Federal collections on defaulted loans	−625	−232	−185
88.40 Federal collections on bankruptcies	−13	−5	−3
88.40 Offsets against Federal tax refunds	−768	−285	−240
88.40 Reimbursements from guaranty agencies	−881	−327	−250

186-484 00 - 13

Credit accounts—Continued

Federal Family Education Loan Liquidating Account—Continued

Program and Financing (in millions of dollars)—Continued

Identification code 91–0230–0–1–502		1999 actual	2000 est.	2001 est.
88.40	Federal collections on defaulted loans, PLUS/SLS	−168	−62	−55
88.40	Federal collections on bankruptcies, PLUS/SLS	−2	−1	
88.40	Offsets against Federal tax refunds, PLUS/SLS	−97	−36	−30
88.40	Reimbursements from guaranty agencies, PLUS/SLS	−143	−53	−40
88.90	Total, offsetting collections (cash)	−2,697	−1,001	−803
	Net budget authority and outlays:			
89.00	Budget authority	−550	−693	−619
90.00	Outlays	−1,163	−707	−629

Summary of Budget Authority and Outlays

(in millions of dollars)

	1999 actual	2000 est.	2001 est.
Enacted/requested:			
Budget Authority	−550	−693	−619
Outlays	−1,163	−707	−629
Legislative proposal, not subject to PAYGO:			
Budget Authority			21
Outlays			14
Total:			
Budget Authority	−550	−693	−598
Outlays	−1,163	−707	−615

Status of Guaranteed Loans (in millions of dollars)

Identification code 91–0230–0–1–502		1999 actual	2000 est.	2001 est.
	STAFFORD LOANS			
	Cumulative balance of guaranteed loans outstanding:			
2210	Outstanding, start of year	14,127	10,364	6,749
2251	Repayments and prepayments	−3,519	−3,430	−2,404
	Adjustments:			
2261	Terminations for default that result in loans receivable	−218	−158	−99
2263	Terminations for default that result in claim payments	−26	−27	−19
2290	Outstanding, end of year	10,364	6,749	4,227
	Memorandum:			
2299	Guaranteed amount of guaranteed loans outstanding, end of year	10,408	5,938	3,416
	Addendum:			
	Cumulative balance of defaulted guaranteed loans that result in loans receivable:			
2310	Outstanding, start of year	12,237	10,394	9,743
2331	Disbursements for guaranteed loan claims	218	158	99
2351	Repayments of loans receivable	−1,661	−482	−374
2361	Write-offs of loans receivable	−303	−250	−230
2364	Other adjustments, net	−97	−77	−59
2390	Outstanding, end of year	10,394	9,743	9,179
	PLUS/SLS LOANS			
	Cumulative balance of guaranteed loans outstanding:			
2210	Outstanding, start of year	4,170	3,546	3,077
2251	Repayments and prepayments	−516	−433	−247
	Adjustments:			
2261	Terminations for default that result in loans receivable	−96	−32	−10
2263	Terminations for default that result in claim payments	−12	−4	−2
2290	Outstanding, end of year	3,546	3,077	2,818
	Memorandum:			
2299	Guaranteed amount of guaranteed loans outstanding, end of year	3,546	705	446
	Addendum:			
	Cumulative balance of defaulted guaranteed loans that result in loans receivable:			
2310	Outstanding, start of year	3,072	2,793	2,649
2331	Disbursements for guaranteed loan claims	96	32	10
2351	Repayments of loans receivable	−283	−86	−69
2361	Write-offs of loans receivable	−76	−77	−72
2364	Other adjustments, net	−16	−13	−9
2390	Outstanding, end of year	2,793	2,649	2,509

Statement of Operations (in millions of dollars)

Identification code 91–0230–0–1–502		1998 actual	1999 actual	2000 est.	2001 est.
	Stafford:				
0111	Revenue	699	1,019	842	842
0112	Expense	−889	−585	−410	−410
0115	Net income or loss (−)	−190	434	432	432
	PLUS/SLS:				
0121	Revenue	91	169	147	147
0122	Expense	−67	−66	−40	−40
0125	Net income or loss (−)	24	103	107	107
0191	Total revenues	790	1,188	989	989
0192	Total expenses	−956	−651	−450	−450
0195	Total income or loss (−)	−166	537	539	539
0199	Total comprehensive income	−166	537	539	539

Balance Sheet (in millions of dollars)

Identification code 91–0230–0–1–502		1998 actual	1999 actual	2000 est.	2001 est.
	ASSETS:				
1101	Federal assets: Fund balances with Treasury	741	116	68	68
	Net value of assets related to pre–1992 direct loans receivable and acquired defaulted guaranteed loans receivable:				
1701	Defaulted guaranteed loans, gross	11,458	10,591	9,807	9,807
1704	Defaulted guaranteed loans and interest receivable, net	11,458	10,591	9,807	9,807
1799	Value of assets related to loan guarantees	11,458	10,591	9,807	9,807
1999	Total assets	12,199	10,707	9,875	9,875
	NET POSITION:				
3100	Appropriated capital	12,199	10,707	9,875	9,875
3999	Total net position	12,199	10,707	9,875	9,875

[1] Excludes interest and premium collections on insured loans.

As required by the Federal Credit Reform Act of 1990, this liquidating account records, for this program, all cash flows to and from the Government resulting from guaranteed student loans committed prior to 1992. This account is shown on a cash basis. All new loan activity in this program in 1992 and beyond is recorded in corresponding program and financing accounts.

Object Classification (in millions of dollars)

Identification code 91–0230–0–1–502		1999 actual	2000 est.	2001 est.
25.2	Other services	20	46	38
33.0	Investments and loans	413	167	95
41.0	Grants, subsidies, and contributions	175	68	32
42.0	Insurance claims and indemnities	81	27	19
99.9	Total new obligations	689	308	184

FEDERAL FAMILY EDUCATION LOAN LIQUIDATING ACCOUNT

(Legislative proposal, not subject to PAYGO)

Program and Financing (in millions of dollars)

Identification code 91–0230–2–1–502		1999 actual	2000 est.	2001 est.
	Obligations by program activity:			
	Stafford loans:			
01.07	Contract collection costs			2
	PLUS/SLS loans:			
02.05	Contract collection costs			1
	Miscellaneous costs:			
03.01	Scheduled payments to finance account for non-contractual modifications			40
10.00	Total new obligations			43
	Budgetary resources available for obligation:			
21.40	Unobligated balance available, start of year			
22.00	New budget authority (gross)			43
23.90	Total budgetary resources available for obligation			43
23.95	Total new obligations			–43
24.40	Unobligated balance available, end of year			
	New budget authority (gross), detail:			
	Mandatory:			
69.00	Offsetting collections (cash)			22
69.27	Capital transfer to general fund			21
69.90	Spending authority from offsetting collections (total mandatory)			43
	Change in unpaid obligations:			
72.40	Unpaid obligations, start of year: Obligated balance, start of year			
73.10	Total new obligations			43
73.20	Total outlays (gross)			–36
74.40	Unpaid obligations, end of year: Obligated balance, end of year			7
	Outlays (gross), detail:			
86.97	Outlays from new mandatory authority			36
	Offsets:			
	Against gross budget authority and outlays:			
	Offsetting collections (cash) from:			
	Federal student loans:			
	Non-Federal sources:			
88.40	Reimbursements from guaranty agencies			–19
88.40	Reimbursements from guaranty agencies, PLUS/SLS			–3
88.90	Total, offsetting collections (cash)			–22
	Net budget authority and outlays:			
89.00	Budget authority			21
90.00	Outlays			14

Status of Guaranteed Loans (in millions of dollars)

Identification code 91–0230–2–1–502		1999 actual	2000 est.	2001 est.
	STAFFORD LOANS			
	Addendum:			
	Cumulative balance of defaulted guaranteed loans that result in loans receivable:			
2310	Outstanding, start of year			
2331	Disbursements for guaranteed loan claims			
2351	Repayments of loans receivable			–12
2361	Write-offs of loans receivable			
2364	Other adjustments, net			–5
2390	Outstanding, end of year			–17
	PLUS/SLS LOANS			
	Addendum:			
	Cumulative balance of defaulted guaranteed loans that result in loans receivable:			
2310	Outstanding, start of year			
2331	Disbursements for guaranteed loan claims			
2351	Repayments of loans receivable			–2
2364	Other adjustments, net			–1
2390	Outstanding, end of year			–3

Object Classification (in millions of dollars)

Identification code 91–0230–2–1–502		1999 actual	2000 est.	2001 est.
25.2	Other services			3
41.0	Grants, subsidies, and contributions			40
99.9	Total new obligations			43

OFFICE OF EDUCATIONAL RESEARCH AND IMPROVEMENT

Federal Funds

General and special funds:

EDUCATION RESEARCH, STATISTICS, AND IMPROVEMENT

[For carrying out activities authorized by the Educational Research, Development, Dissemination, and Improvement Act of 1994, including part E; the National Education Statistics Act of 1994, including sections 411 and 412; section 2102 of title II, and parts A, B, and K and section 10102, section 10105, and 10601 of title X, and part C of title XIII of the Elementary and Secondary Education Act of 1965, as amended, and title VI of Public Law 103–227, $596,892,000: *Provided*, That $50,000,000 shall be available to demonstrate effective approaches to comprehensive school reform, to be allocated and expended in accordance with the instructions relating to this activity in the statement of managers on the conference report accompanying Public Law 105–78 and in the statement of the managers on the conference report accompanying Public Law 105–277: *Provided further*, That the funds made available for comprehensive school reform shall become available on July 1, 2000, and remain available through September 30, 2001, and in carrying out this initiative, the Secretary and the States shall support only approaches that show the most promise of enabling children to meet challenging State content standards and challenging State student performance standards based on reliable research and effective practices, and include an emphasis on basic academics and parental involvement: *Provided further*, That $30,000,000 of the funds provided for the national education research institutes shall be allocated notwithstanding section 912(m)(1)(B–F) and subparagraphs (B) and (C) of section 931(c)(2) of Public Law 103–227: *Provided further*, That of the funds appropriated under section 10601 of title X of the Elementary and Secondary Education Act of 1965, as amended, $1,500,000 shall be used to conduct a violence prevention demonstration program: *Provided further*, That $45,000,000 shall be available to support activities under section 10105 of part A of title X of the Elementary and Secondary Education Act of 1965, of which up to $2,250,000 may be available for evaluation, technical assistance, and school networking activities: *Provided further*, That funds made available to local educational agencies under this section shall be used only for activities related to establishing smaller learning communities in high schools: *Provided further*, That funds made available for section 10105 of part A of title X of the Elementary and Secondary Education Act of 1965 shall become available on July 1, 2000, and remain available through September 30, 2001: *Provided further*, That of the funds available for part A of title X of the Elementary and Secondary Education Act of 1965, $10,000,000 shall be awarded to the National Constitution Center, established by Public Law 100–433, for exhibition design, program planning and operation of the center, $10,000,000 shall be provided to continue a demonstration of public school facilities to the Iowa Department of Education, $1,000,000 shall be made available to the New Mexico Department of Education for school performance improvement and drop-out prevention, $300,000 shall be made available to Semos Unlimited, Inc., in New Mexico to support bilingual education and literacy programs, $700,000 shall be awarded to Loyola University Chicago for recruitment and preparation of new teacher candidates for employment in rural and inner-city schools, $500,000 shall be awarded to Shedd Aquarium/Brookfield Zoo for science education/exposure programs for local elementary school students, $3,000,000 shall be awarded to Big Brothers/Big Sisters of America to expand school-based mentoring, $2,500,000 shall be awarded to the Chicago Public School System to support a substance abuse pilot program in conjunction with Elgin and East Aurora School Systems, $1,000,000 shall be awarded to

General and special funds—Continued

EDUCATION RESEARCH, STATISTICS, AND IMPROVEMENT—Continued

the University of Virginia Center for Governmental Studies for the Youth Leadership Initiative, $800,000 shall be awarded to the Institute for Student Achievement at Holmes Middle School and Annandale High School in Virginia for academic enrichment programs, $100,000 shall be awarded to the Mountain Arts Center for educational programming, $1,500,000 shall be awarded to the University of Louisville for research in the area of academic readiness, $500,000 shall be awarded to the West Ed Regional Educational Laboratory for the 24 Challenge and Jumping Levels Math Demonstration Project, $1,000,000 shall be awarded to Central Michigan University for a charter schools development and performance institute, $950,000 shall be awarded to the Living Science Interactive Learning Model partnership in Indian River, Florida for a science education program, $825,000 shall be awarded to the North Babylon Community Youth Services for an educational program, $1,000,000 shall be awarded to the Los Angeles County Office of Education/Educational Telecommunications and Technology for a pilot program for teachers, $650,000 shall be awarded to the University of Northern Iowa for an institute of technology for inclusive education, $500,000 shall be awarded to Youth Crime Watch of America to expand a program to prevent crime, drugs and violence in schools, $892,000 shall be awarded to Muhlenberg College in Pennsylvania for an environmental science program, $560,000 shall be awarded to the Western Suffolk St. Johns-LaSalle Academy Science and Technology Mentoring Program, $4,000,000 shall be awarded to the National Teaching Academy of Chicago for a model teacher recruitment, preparation and professional development program, $2,000,000 shall be awarded to the University of West Florida for a teacher enhancement program, $1,000,000 shall be awarded to Delta State University in Mississippi for innovative teacher training, $1,000,000 shall be awarded to the Alaska Humanities Forum, Inc., in Anchorage, Alaska, $250,000 shall be awarded to An Achievable Dream in Newport News, Virginia to improve academic performance of at-risk youths, $250,000 shall be awarded to the Rock School of Ballet in Philadelphia, Pennsylvania, to expand its community-outreach programs for inner-city children and underprivileged youth in Camden, New Jersey and southern New Jersey, $1,000,000 shall be awarded to the University of Maryland Center for Quality and Productivity to provide a link for the Blue Ribbon Schools, $1,000,000 shall be awarded to the Continuing Education Center and Teachers' Institute in South Boston, Virginia to promote participation among youth in the United States democratic process, $1,000,000 shall be for the National Museum of Women in the Arts to expand its "Discovering Art" program to elementary and secondary schools and other educational organizations, $400,000 shall be awarded to the Alaska Department of Education's summer reading program, $400,000 shall be awarded to the Partners in Education, Inc., to foster successful business-school partnerships, $250,000 shall be for the Kodiak Island Borough School District for development of an environmental education program, $2,000,000 shall be for the Reach Out and Read Program to expand literacy and health awareness for at-risk families, $1,000,000 shall be for the Virginia Living Museum in Newport News, Virginia for an educational program, $450,000 shall be for the Challenger Learning Center in Hardin County, Kentucky for technology assistance and teacher training, $250,000 shall be for the Crawford County School System in Georgia for technology and curriculum support, $500,000 shall be for the Berrien County School System in Georgia for technology development, $35,000 shall be for the Louisville Salvation Army Boys and Girls Club Diversion Enhancement Program, $100,000 shall be awarded to the Philadelphia Orchestra's Philly Pops to operate the Jazz in the Schools program in the Philadelphia school district, $500,000 for the Mississippi Delta Education for a teacher incentive program initiative, $500,000 shall be for A Community of Agile Partners in Education and the Pennsylvania Telecommunications Exchange Network for a technology resource sharing initiative, $500,000 shall be for enhanced teacher training in reading in the District of Columbia, $100,000 shall be awarded to the Project 2000 D.C. mentoring project, and $1,250,000 shall be awarded to Helen Keller World Wide to expand the ChildSight vision screening program and provide eyeglasses to additional children whose educational performance may be hindered by poor vision, $750,000 shall be awarded to the Explornet Technology Learning Project in North Carolina, $1,750,000 shall be awarded to the Connecticut Early Reading Success Institute to broaden the training of professionals in best practices in reading instruction, $400,000 shall be awarded to the National Academy of Recording Artists and Sciences Foundation for the GRAMMY in the Schools program to provide music education to high school students, $1,000,000 shall be awarded to the Rosa and Raymond Parks Institute for Self-Development for the Pathways to Freedom program for civil rights education for young people and for community learning centers, $500,000 shall be awarded to the Milton S. Eisenhower Foundation to replicate and scientifically evaluate full-service community schools, $500,000 shall be awarded to the Henry Abbott Technical High School in Danbury, Connecticut for workforce education and training activities, $1,000,000 shall be awarded to the Educational Performance Foundation, CPI music education program called "From the Top", $250,000 shall be awarded to the Mount Vernon School District in Mount Vernon, New York for the Institute of Student Achievement program, $2,000,000 shall be awarded to the National Council of La Raza for a project to improve educational outcomes and opportunities for Hispanic children, $250,000 shall be awarded to the Oakland Unified School District in California for an African American Literacy and Culture Project, $300,000 shall be awarded to the Vasona Center Youth Science Institute, $750,000 shall be awarded to the Life Learning Academy Charter School in San Francisco, California, $250,000 shall be awarded to the National Urban Coalition Say YES To A Youngster's Future Program to provide math and science education, $750,000 shall be awarded to the Wisconsin Academy Staff Development Initiative in Chippewa Falls, Wisconsin to provide math, science, and technology teacher training, $500,000 shall be awarded to the University of Missouri-St. Louis to develop a plan to improve the education system in the City of St. Louis, Missouri, $313,000 shall be awarded to the City of Houston for the ASPIRE after-school program, $900,000 shall be awarded to the Boston Music Education Collaborative comprehensive interdisciplinary music program and teacher resource center in Boston, Massachusetts, $250,000 shall be awarded to the Baltimore Reads after-school tutoring program in Baltimore, Maryland, $300,000 shall be awarded to the School of International Training in Brattleboro, Vermont to develop an education curriculum addressing child labor issues in collaboration with the Brattleboro Union High School, $750,000 shall be awarded to the University of Puerto Rico for the continuation and expansion of the Hispanic Educational Linkages Program in New York City, including the South Bronx, New York, $250,000 shall be awarded to the Community Service Society of New York for mentoring, tutoring and technology activities in New York City public schools, including schools in the South Bronx, $250,000 shall be awarded to the Smithsonian Institution for a jazz music education program in Washington, D.C., $500,000 shall be awarded to Johnson Elementary School in Cedar Rapids, Iowa, to develop an innovative arts education model which could be replicated in other schools, $2,000,000 shall be awarded to the Boys and Girls Clubs of America for after-school programs, $500,000 shall be for the University of New Orleans for a teacher preparation and educational technology initiative, and $250,000 shall be for the Florida Department of Education for an Internet-based teacher recruitment model, $250,000 shall be awarded to the Kennedy Center for the Performing Arts for the "Make a Ballet" arts education program in the New York City area: *Provided further*, That of the funds available for section 10601 of title X of such Act, $2,000,000 shall be awarded to the Center for Educational Technologies for production and distribution of an effective CD-ROM product that would complement the "We the People: The Citizen and the Constitution" curriculum: *Provided further*, That, in addition to the funds for title VI of Public Law 103–227 and notwithstanding the provisions of section 601(c)(1)(C) of that Act, $1,000,000 shall be available to the Center for Civic Education to conduct a civic education program with Northern Ireland and the Republic of Ireland and, consistent with the civics and Government activities authorized in section 601(c)(3) of Public Law 103–227, to provide civic education assistance to democracies in developing countries. The term "developing countries" shall have the same meaning as the term "developing country" in the Education for the Deaf Act.] *(Department of Education Appropriations Act, 2000, as enacted by section 1000(a)(4) of the Consolidated Appropriations Act, 2000 (P.L. 106–113).)*

Program and Financing (in millions of dollars)

Identification code 91–1100–0–1–503		1999 actual	2000 est.	2001 est.
	Direct program:			
	Obligations by program activity:			
	Research, development and dissemination:			
00.01	National education research institutes	64	85	....

00.02 Regional educational laboratories	61	65	....
00.03 National dissemination activities	19	19	....
00.04 Statistics	68	68	....
00.05 Assessment	40	40	....
00.06 Eisenhower professional development federal activities	23	23	....
00.07 Fund for the improvement of education	150	244	....
00.08 Javits gifted and talented education	6	6	....
00.09 Eisenhower regional mathematics and science education consortia	15	15	....
00.10 21st Century community learning centers	200	....	....
00.11 National writing project	7	9	....
00.12 Civic education	8	10	....
00.13 International education exchange	7	7	....
01.00 Total direct program	668	591	....
09.01 Reimbursable program	7	7	....
10.00 Total new obligations	675	598	....
Budgetary resources available for obligation:			
21.40 Unobligated balance available, start of year	12	....	....
22.00 New budget authority (gross)	664	598	....
23.90 Total budgetary resources available for obligation	676	598	....
23.95 Total new obligations	−675	−598	....
23.98 Unobligated balance expiring or withdrawn	−1	....	....
New budget authority (gross), detail:			
Discretionary:			
40.00 Appropriation	659	597	....
40.76 Reduction pursuant to P.L. 106–113	....	−6	....
41.00 Transferred to other accounts	−2	....	....
43.00 Appropriation (total discretionary)	657	591	....
68.00 Spending authority from offsetting collections: Offsetting collections (cash)	7	7	....
70.00 Total new budget authority (gross)	664	598	....
Change in unpaid obligations:			
72.40 Unpaid obligations, start of year: Obligated balance, start of year	496	682	582
73.10 Total new obligations	675	598	....
73.20 Total outlays (gross)	−485	−698	−455
73.40 Adjustments in expired accounts (net)	−2	....	....
74.40 Unpaid obligations, end of year: Obligated balance, end of year	682	582	127
Outlays (gross), detail:			
86.90 Outlays from new discretionary authority	103	152	....
86.93 Outlays from discretionary balances	383	545	455
87.00 Total outlays (gross)	485	698	455
Offsets:			
Against gross budget authority and outlays:			
88.00 Offsetting collections (cash) from: Federal sources	−7	−7	....
Net budget authority and outlays:			
89.00 Budget authority	657	591	....
90.00 Outlays	479	691	455

Note.—Excludes $15 million in budget authority in 2001 that the Eisenhower regional mathematics and science education consortia transferred to the School Improvement Programs account. Comparable amounts for 1999 ($15 million) and 2000 ($15 million) are included above.

The Administration has proposed legislation to revise and reauthorize programs currently authorized under the Education Research, Development, Dissemination, and Improvement Act, the National Education Statistics Act, the Elementary and Secondary Education Act, and the Goals 2000: Educate America Act. When new authorizing legislation is enacted, resources will be requested for the Education Research, Statistics and Improvement account. See the "Legislative proposal, not subject to PAYGO" schedule for additional details.

Summary of Budget Authority and Outlays

(in millions of dollars)

	1999 actual	*2000 est.*	*2001 est.*
Enacted/requested:			
Budget Authority	657	591	....
Outlays	479	690	455
Legislative proposal, not subject to PAYGO:			
Budget Authority	....	....	503
Outlays	....	....	149
Total:			
Budget Authority	657	591	503
Outlays	479	690	604

Object Classification (in millions of dollars)

Identification code 91–1100–0–1–503	1999 actual	2000 est.	2001 est.
Direct obligations:			
11.3 Personnel compensation: Other than full-time permanent	1	1	....
24.0 Printing and reproduction	3	3	....
25.1 Advisory and assistance services	4	4	....
25.2 Other services	119	121	....
25.3 Purchases of goods and services from Government accounts	16	16	....
25.5 Research and development contracts	29	31	....
25.7 Operation and maintenance of equipment	4	4	....
41.0 Grants, subsidies, and contributions	492	411	....
99.0 Subtotal, direct obligations	668	591	....
99.0 Reimbursable obligations	7	7	....
99.9 Total new obligations	675	598	....

Personnel Summary

Identification code 91–1100–0–1–503	1999 actual	2000 est.	2001 est.
1001 Total compensable workyears: Full-time equivalent employment	14	15	....

Educational Research, Statistics and Improvement

(Legislative proposal, not subject to PAYGO)

Program and Financing (in millions of dollars)

Identification code 91–1100–2–1–503	1999 actual	2000 est.	2001 est.
Direct program:			
Obligations by program activity:			
00.01 Research, development, and dissemination	....	....	199
00.02 Statistics	....	....	84
00.03 Assessment	....	....	42
00.04 America's tests	....	....	5
00.05 Fund for the Improvement of Education	....	....	137
00.06 Javits gifted and talented education	....	....	8
00.07 National writing project	....	....	10
00.08 Civic education	....	....	10
00.09 International education exchange	....	....	8
01.00 Total direct program	....	....	503
09.01 Reimbursable program	....	....	7
10.00 Total new obligations	....	....	510
Budgetary resources available for obligation:			
21.40 Unobligated balance available, start of year	....	....	....
22.00 New budget authority (gross)	....	....	510
23.90 Total budgetary resources available for obligation	....	....	510
23.95 Total new obligations	....	....	−510
23.98 Unobligated balance expiring or withdrawn	....	....	....
New budget authority (gross), detail:			
Discretionary:			
40.00 Appropriation	....	....	503
68.00 Spending authority from offsetting collections: Offsetting collections (cash)	....	....	7
70.00 Total new budget authority (gross)	....	....	510
Change in unpaid obligations:			
72.40 Unpaid obligations, start of year: Obligated balance, start of year	....	....	....
73.10 Total new obligations	....	....	510
73.20 Total outlays (gross)	....	....	−156
74.40 Unpaid obligations, end of year: Obligated balance, end of year	....	....	354
Outlays (gross), detail:			
86.90 Outlays from new discretionary authority	....	....	156

General and special funds—Continued

EDUCATIONAL RESEARCH, STATISTICS AND IMPROVEMENT—Continued

Program and Financing (in millions of dollars)—Continued

Identification code 91–1100–2–1–503		1999 actual	2000 est.	2001 est.
	Offsets:			
	Against gross budget authority and outlays:			
88.00	Offsetting collections (cash) from: Federal sources			−7
	Net budget authority and outlays:			
89.00	Budget authority			503
90.00	Outlays			149

Research, development, and dissemination.—The proposal would establish a national institute of education research to improve education in the United States by supporting education research, development, and dissemination activities designed to improve teaching and learning; improve the ability of schools, school districts, and States to implement reforms; and use new knowledge from research to design and implement effective improvement strategies. Funds would support national research and development centers, field-initiated studies, directed studies, interagency initiatives, expert study panels, regional educational laboratories, information clearinghouses, and a national library of education.

Statistics.—Funds would support the collection of statistics on educational institutions and on individuals to monitor trends in education. Funds also would support a coordinated program of statistical services to assist States in the development of comparable databases and analyses of the implications of data.

Assessment.—Funds would support the National Assessment of Educational Progress, which surveys young Americans to provide reliable information about educational attainments in important skill areas. Both national- and State-representative data are collected.

America's Tests.—Funds would support the development and field testing of voluntary national tests in reading for fourth grade students and in mathematics for eighth grade students. The tests will provide parents, teachers, and policymakers with information needed to assess student achievement and improve instruction.

Fund for the improvement of education (FIE).—Funds would support nationally significant projects to improve the quality of education, help all students meet challenging standards, and contribute to the achievement of the National Education Goals.

Javits gifted and talented education.—Funds would support projects designed to help educators identify and meet the special educational needs of gifted and talented students and, where appropriate, to adapt strategies successful with those students to improve instruction for all students.

National writing project.—Funds would support a national professional development project to improve the teaching of writing by teachers of all subject areas to improve the quality of student writing and learning.

Civic education.—Funds would support a program to educate students about the history and principles of the Constitution of the United States, including the Bill of Rights, and to foster civic competence and responsibility.

International education exchange.—Funds would support international exchange programs to help improve civics and economics education in central and eastern European countries, countries that were part of the former Soviet Union, and the United States. Funds would also be used to conduct civic education programs with Northern Ireland, the Republic of Ireland, and democracies in other developing countries.

Object Classification (in millions of dollars)

Identification code 91–1100–2–1–503		1999 actual	2000 est.	2001 est.
	Direct obligations:			
11.3	Personnel compensation: Other than full-time permanent			1
24.0	Printing and reproduction			3
25.1	Advisory and assistance services			4
25.2	Other services			139
25.3	Purchases of goods and services from Government accounts			16
25.5	Research and development contracts			30
25.7	Operation and maintenance of equipment			4
41.0	Grants, subsidies, and contributions			306
99.0	Subtotal, direct obligations			503
99.0	Reimbursable obligations			7
99.9	Total new obligations			510

Personnel Summary

Identification code 91–1100–2–1–503		1999 actual	2000 est.	2001 est.
1001	Total compensable workyears: Full-time equivalent employment			15

DEPARTMENTAL MANAGEMENT

Federal Funds

General and special funds:

PROGRAM ADMINISTRATION

For carrying out, to the extent not otherwise provided, the Department of Education Organization Act, including rental of conference rooms in the District of Columbia and hire of two passenger motor vehicles, [$383,184,000] *$413,184,000. (Department of Education Appropriations Act, 2000, as enacted by section 1000(a)(4) of the Consolidated Appropriations Act, 2000 (P.L. 106–113).)*

Program and Financing (in millions of dollars)

Identification code 91–0800–0–1–503		1999 actual	2000 est.	2001 est.
	Obligations by program activity:			
00.01	Program Administration	357	383	413
00.02	Y2K Activities	7	1	
09.01	Reimbursable program	1	1	1
10.00	Total new obligations	365	385	414
	Budgetary resources available for obligation:			
21.40	Unobligated balance available, start of year		2	
22.00	New budget authority (gross)	368	384	414
23.90	Total budgetary resources available for obligation	368	386	414
23.95	Total new obligations	−365	−385	−414
23.98	Unobligated balance expiring or withdrawn	−1		
24.40	Unobligated balance available, end of year	2		
	New budget authority (gross), detail:			
	Discretionary:			
40.00	Appropriation	363	383	413
42.00	Transferred from other accounts	4		
43.00	Appropriation (total discretionary)	367	383	413
68.00	Spending authority from offsetting collections: Offsetting collections (cash)	1	1	1
70.00	Total new budget authority (gross)	368	384	414
	Change in unpaid obligations:			
72.40	Unpaid obligations, start of year: Obligated balance, start of year	128	138	120
73.10	Total new obligations	365	385	414
73.20	Total outlays (gross)	−346	−403	−401
73.40	Adjustments in expired accounts (net)	−9		
74.40	Unpaid obligations, end of year: Obligated balance, end of year	138	120	134
	Outlays (gross), detail:			
86.90	Outlays from new discretionary authority	280	292	314

86.93	Outlays from discretionary balances	67	111	87
87.00	Total outlays (gross)	346	403	401
	Offsets:			
	Against gross budget authority and outlays:			
88.00	Offsetting collections (cash) from: Federal sources	−1	−1	−1
	Net budget authority and outlays:			
89.00	Budget authority	367	383	413
90.00	Outlays	345	402	400

The Program Administration account includes the direct Federal costs of providing grants and administering elementary and secondary education, bilingual education, Indian education, higher education, vocational and adult education, and special education programs, programs for persons with disabilities and a portion of the direct Federal costs for administering student financial aid programs. It also supports assessment, statistics, research and improvement activities, and costs for the Year 2000 computer conversion process.

In addition, this account includes the cost of providing centralized support and administrative services, overall policy development, and strategic planning for the Department. Included in the centralized activities are rent and mail services; telecommunciations; contractual services; financial management and accounting, including payments to schools, education agencies and other grant recipients, and preparation of auditable financial statements; information technology services; personnel management; budget formulation and execution; program evaluation; legal services; congressional and public relations; and intergovernmental affairs.

Also included in this account are contributions from the public. Activities supported include the Millennium Project, Satellite Town Meetings, Goals 2000 Teachers' Forum, School Recognition, and the Gifts and Bequests Miscellaneous Fund.

Reimbursable program.—Reimbursements to this account are for providing administrative services to other agencies, recycling activities, and other non-Federal sources for in-kind travel.

Object Classification (in millions of dollars)

Identification code 91–0800–0–1–503		1999 actual	2000 est.	2001 est.
	Direct obligations:			
	Personnel compensation:			
11.1	Full-time permanent	140	170	182
11.3	Other than full-time permanent	24	11	10
11.5	Other personnel compensation	3	3	3
11.9	Total personnel compensation	167	184	195
12.1	Civilian personnel benefits	35	40	44
21.0	Travel and transportation of persons	6	8	8
23.1	Rental payments to GSA	30	29	31
23.3	Communications, utilities, and miscellaneous charges	12	12	12
24.0	Printing and reproduction	4	6	6
25.1	Advisory and assistance services	3	5	5
25.2	Other services	27	19	21
25.3	Purchases of goods and services from Government accounts	9	7	6
25.7	Operation and maintenance of equipment	52	61	67
26.0	Supplies and materials	3	3	3
31.0	Equipment	15	8	13
32.0	Land and structures	1	2	2
99.0	Subtotal, direct obligations	364	384	413
99.0	Reimbursable obligations	1	1	1
99.9	Total new obligations	365	385	414

Personnel Summary

Identification code 91–0800–0–1–503		1999 actual	2000 est.	2001 est.
1001	Total compensable workyears: Full-time equivalent employment	2,600	2,733	2,763

Office for Civil Rights

For expenses necessary for the Office for Civil Rights, as authorized by section 203 of the Department of Education Organization Act, [$71,200,000] *$76,000,000. (Department of Education Appropriations Act, 2000, as enacted by section 1000(a)(4) of the Consolidated Appropriations Act, 2000 (P.L. 106–113).)*

Program and Financing (in millions of dollars)

Identification code 91–0700–0–1–751		1999 actual	2000 est.	2001 est.
	Obligations by program activity:			
00.01	Civil rights	66	71	76
10.00	Total new obligations	66	71	76
	Budgetary resources available for obligation:			
22.00	New budget authority (gross)	66	71	76
23.95	Total new obligations	−66	−71	−76
	New budget authority (gross), detail:			
	Discretionary:			
40.00	Appropriation	66	71	76
	Change in unpaid obligations:			
72.40	Unpaid obligations, start of year: Obligated balance, start of year	18	20	15
73.10	Total new obligations	66	71	76
73.20	Total outlays (gross)	−63	−76	−74
74.40	Unpaid obligations, end of year: Obligated balance, end of year	20	15	17
	Outlays (gross), detail:			
86.90	Outlays from new discretionary authority	52	60	63
86.93	Outlays from discretionary balances	11	16	11
87.00	Total outlays (gross)	63	76	74
	Net budget authority and outlays:			
89.00	Budget authority	66	71	76
90.00	Outlays	63	76	74

The Office for Civil Rights is responsible for ensuring that no person is unlawfully discriminated against on the basis of race, color, national origin, sex, disability, or age in the delivery of services or the provision of benefits in programs or activities of schools and institutions receiving financial assistance from the Department of Education. The authorities under which the Office for Civil Rights operates are title VI of the Civil Rights Act of 1964 (racial and ethnic discrimination), title IX of the Education Amendments of 1972 (sex discrimination), section 504 of the Rehabilitation Act of 1973 (discrimination against individuals with a disability), the Age Discrimination Act of 1975, and the Americans with Disabilities Act of 1990.

Object Classification (in millions of dollars)

Identification code 91–0700–0–1–751		1999 actual	2000 est.	2001 est.
	Personnel compensation:			
11.1	Full-time permanent	40	42	44
11.3	Other than full-time permanent	2	2	2
11.9	Total personnel compensation	42	44	46
12.1	Civilian personnel benefits	9	10	10
21.0	Travel and transportation of persons	1	1	1
23.1	Rental payments to GSA	5	5	5
23.3	Communications, utilities, and miscellaneous charges	1	2	2
25.2	Other services	1	1	1
25.3	Purchases of goods and services from Government accounts	1	1	2
25.7	Operation and maintenance of equipment	3	4	5
31.0	Equipment	1	2	3
32.0	Land and structures	1	....	....
99.0	Subtotal, direct obligations	65	70	75
99.5	Below reporting threshold	1	1	1
99.9	Total new obligations	66	71	76

General and special funds—Continued

OFFICE FOR CIVIL RIGHTS—Continued

Personnel Summary

Identification code 91–0700–0–1–751	1999 actual	2000 est.	2001 est.
1001 Total compensable workyears: Full-time equivalent employment	727	724	724

OFFICE OF THE INSPECTOR GENERAL

For expenses necessary for the Office of Inspector General, as authorized by section 212 of the Department of Education Organization Act, [$34,000,000] *$36,500,000. (Department of Education Appropriations Act, 2000, as enacted by section 1000(a)(4) of the Consolidated Appropriations Act, 2000 (P.L. 106–113).)*

Program and Financing (in millions of dollars)

Identification code 91–1400–0–1–751	1999 actual	2000 est.	2001 est.
Obligations by program activity:			
00.01 Inspector General	31	34	37
10.00 Total new obligations	31	34	37
Budgetary resources available for obligation:			
22.00 New budget authority (gross)	31	34	37
23.95 Total new obligations	−31	−34	−37
New budget authority (gross), detail:			
Discretionary:			
40.00 Appropriation	31	34	37
Change in unpaid obligations:			
72.40 Unpaid obligations, start of year: Obligated balance, start of year	11	9	7
73.10 Total new obligations	31	34	37
73.20 Total outlays (gross)	−33	−36	−35
74.40 Unpaid obligations, end of year: Obligated balance, end of year	9	7	9
Outlays (gross), detail:			
86.90 Outlays from new discretionary authority	27	28	30
86.93 Outlays from discretionary balances	6	8	5
87.00 Total outlays (gross)	33	36	35
Net budget authority and outlays:			
89.00 Budget authority	31	34	37
90.00 Outlays	33	36	35

The Inspector General is responsible for the quality, coverage, and coordination of audit, investigation, and security functions relating to Federal education activities. The Inspector General has the authority to inquire into all activities of the Department including those performed under Federal education contracts, grants, or other agreements. Under the Chief Financial Officers Act of 1990, the Inspector General is also responsible for internal reviews of the Department's financial systems and audits of its financial statements.

Object Classification (in millions of dollars)

Identification code 91–1400–0–1–751	1999 actual	2000 est.	2001 est.
Personnel compensation:			
11.1 Full-time permanent	16	17	18
11.3 Other than full-time permanent	1	1	1
11.5 Other personnel compensation	1	1	1
11.9 Total personnel compensation	18	19	20
12.1 Civilian personnel benefits	4	5	5
21.0 Travel and transportation of persons	1	2	2
23.1 Rental payments to GSA	2	2	2
23.3 Communications, utilities, and miscellaneous charges	1	1	1
25.1 Advisory and assistance services	1	1	2
25.3 Purchases of goods and services from Government accounts	1	1	1
25.7 Operation and maintenance of equipment	1	1	2
31.0 Equipment	1	1	1
99.0 Subtotal, direct obligations	30	33	36
99.5 Below reporting threshold	1	1	1
99.9 Total new obligations	31	34	37

Personnel Summary

Identification code 91–1400–0–1–751	1999 actual	2000 est.	2001 est.
1001 Total compensable workyears: Full-time equivalent employment	281	285	285

HEADQUARTERS RENOVATION

Program and Financing (in millions of dollars)

Identification code 91–1500–0–1–503	1999 actual	2000 est.	2001 est.
Change in unpaid obligations:			
72.40 Unpaid obligations, start of year: Obligated balance, start of year	2	3	
73.20 Total outlays (gross)		−3	
74.40 Unpaid obligations, end of year: Obligated balance, end of year	3		
Outlays (gross), detail:			
86.93 Outlays from discretionary balances		3	
Net budget authority and outlays:			
89.00 Budget authority			
90.00 Outlays		3	

This account provided the Department of Education's portion of funds to renovate its headquarters building, including costs for administrative services, information technology, telecommunications cabling, and systems furniture. The remaining funds required for the renovation, which was completed in 1998, were provided by the General Services Administration.

GENERAL FUND RECEIPT ACCOUNTS

(in millions of dollars)

	1999 actual	2000 est.	2001 est.
Offsetting receipts from the public:			
91–022100 FFEL Guarantee agency reserve recoveries			
Legislative proposal, subject to PAYGO			
91–291500 Repayment of loans, capital contributions, higher education activities, Education	66	50	50
91–310900 HEAF reserve recoveries		27	
General Fund Offsetting receipts from the public	66	77	50

GENERAL PROVISIONS

SEC. 301. No funds appropriated in this Act may be used for the transportation of students or teachers (or for the purchase of equipment for such transportation) in order to overcome racial imbalance in any school or school system, or for the transportation of students or teachers (or for the purchase of equipment for such transportation) in order to carry out a plan of racial desegregation of any school or school system.

SEC. 302. None of the funds contained in this Act shall be used to require, directly or indirectly, the transportation of any student to a school other than the school which is nearest the student's home, except for a student requiring special education, to the school offering such special education, in order to comply with title VI of the Civil Rights Act of 1964. For the purpose of this section an indirect requirement of transportation of students includes the transportation of students to carry out a plan involving the reorganization of the grade structure of schools, the pairing of schools, or the clustering of schools, or any combination of grade restructuring, pairing or clustering. The prohibition described in this section does not include the establishment of magnet schools.

SEC. 303. No funds appropriated under this Act may be used to prevent the implementation of programs of voluntary prayer and meditation in the public schools.

(TRANSFER OF FUNDS)

SEC. 304. Not to exceed 1 percent of any discretionary funds (pursuant to the Balanced Budget and Emergency Deficit Control Act of 1985, as amended) which are appropriated for the Department of Education in this Act may be transferred between appropriations, but no such appropriation shall be increased by more than 3 percent by any such transfer: *Provided*, That the Appropriations Committees of both Houses of Congress are notified at least 15 days in advance of any transfer.

[SEC. 305. (a) From the funds appropriated for payments to local educational agencies under section 8003(f) of the Elementary and Secondary Education Act of 1965 ("ESEA") for fiscal year 2000, the Secretary of Education shall distribute supplemental payments for certain local educational agencies, as follows:

(1) First, from the amount of $74,000,000, the Secretary shall make supplemental payments to the following agencies under section 8003(f) of ESEA:

(A) Local educational agencies that received assistance under section 8003(f) for fiscal year 1999—

(i) in fiscal year 1997 had at least 40 percent federally connected children described in section 8003(a)(1) in average daily attendance; and in fiscal year 1997 had a tax rate for general fund purposes which was at least 95 percent of the State average tax rate for general fund purposes; or

(ii) whose boundary is coterminous with the boundary of a Federal military installation.

(B) Local educational agencies that received assistance under section 8003(f) for fiscal year 1999; and in fiscal year 1997 had at least 30 percent federally connected children described in section 8003(a)(1) in average daily attendance; and in fiscal year 1997 had a tax rate for general fund purposes which was at least 125 percent of the State average tax rate for general fund purposes.

(C) Any eligible local educational agency that in fiscal year 1997, which had at least 25,000 children in average daily attendance, at least 50 percent federally connected children described in section 8003(a)(1) in average daily attendance, and at least 6,000 children described in subparagraphs (A) and (B) of section 8003(a)(1) in average daily attendance.

(2) From the remaining $2,000,000 and any amounts available after making payments under paragraph (1), the Secretary shall then make supplemental payments to local educational agencies that are not described in paragraph (1) of this subsection, but that meet the requirements of paragraphs (2) and (4) of section 8003(f) of ESEA for fiscal year 2000.

(3) After making payments to all eligible local educational agencies described in paragraph (2) of subsection (a), the Secretary shall use any remaining funds from paragraph (2) for making payments to the eligible local educational agencies described in paragraph (1) of subsection (a) if the amount available under paragraph (1) is insufficient to fully fund all eligible local educational agencies.

(4) After making payments to all eligible local educational agencies as described in paragraphs 1 through 3, the Secretary shall use any remaining funds to increase basic support payments under section 8003(b) for fiscal year 2000 for all eligible applicants.

(b) In calculating the amounts of supplemental payments for agencies described in subparagraphs (1)(A) and (B) and paragraph (2) of subsection (a), the Secretary shall use the formula contained in section 8003(b)(1)(C) of ESEA, except that—

(1) eligible local educational agencies may count all children described in section 8003(a)(1) in computing the amount of those payments;

(2) maximum payments for any of those agencies that use local contribution rates identified in section 8003(b)(1)(C) (i) or (ii) shall be computed by using four-fifths instead of one-half of those rates;

(3) the learning opportunity threshold percentage of all such agencies under section 8003(b)(2)(B) shall be deemed to be 100;

(4) for an eligible local educational agency with 35 percent or more of its children in average daily attendance described in either subparagraph (D) or (E) of section 8003(a)(1) in fiscal year 1997, the weighted student unit figure from its regular basic support payment shall be recomputed by using a factor of 0.55 for such children;

(5) for an eligible local educational agency with fewer than 100 children in average daily attendance in fiscal year 1997, the weighted student unit figure from its regular basic support payment shall be recomputed by multiplying the total number of children described in section 8003(a)(1) by a factor of 1.75; and

(6) for an eligible local educational agency whose total number of children in average daily attendance in fiscal year 1997 was at least 100, but fewer than 750, the weighted student unit figure from its regular basic support payment shall be recomputed by multiplying the total number of children described in section 8003(a)(1) by a factor of 1.25.

(c) For a local educational agency described in subsection (a)(1)(C) above, the Secretary shall use the formula contained in section 8003(b)(1)(C) of ESEA, except that the weighted student unit total from its regular basic support payment shall be recomputed by using a factor of 1.35 for children described in subparagraphs (A) and (B) of section 8003(a)(1) and its learning opportunity threshold percentage shall be deemed to be 100.

(d) For each eligible local educational agency, the calculated supplemental section 8003(f) payment shall be reduced by subtracting the agency's fiscal year 2000 section 8003(b) basic support payment.

(e) If the sums described in subsections (a)(1) and (2) above are insufficient to pay in full the calculated supplemental payments for the local educational agencies identified in those subsections, the Secretary shall ratably reduce the supplemental section 8003(f) payment to each local educational agency.]

[SEC. 306. (a) Section 1204(b)(1)(A) of the Elementary and Secondary Education Act of 1965 (20 U.S.C. 6364(b)(1)(a)) is amended—

(1) in clause (iv), by striking "and" after the semicolon;

(2) by striking clause (v) and adding the following:

"(v) 50 percent in the fifth, sixth, seventh, and eighth such years; and

"(vi) 35 percent in any subsequent such year.".

(b) Section 1208(b) of the Elementary and Secondary Education Act of 1965 is amended—

(1) by striking paragraph (3) and inserting the following:

"(3) CONTINUING ELIGIBILITY.—In awarding subgrant funds to continue a program under this part after the first year, the State educational agency shall review the progress of each eligible entity in meeting the goals of the program referred to in section 1207(c)(1)(A) and shall evaluate the program based on the indicators of program quality developed by the State under section 1210."; and

(2) in paragraph (5)(A), by striking the last sentence.]

[SEC. 307. (a) Notwithstanding sections 401(j) and 435(a)(2) of the Higher Education Act of 1965 (20 U.S.C. 1070a(j) and 1085(a)(2)) and subject to the requirements of subsection (b), the Secretary of Education shall—

(1) recalculate the official fiscal year 1996 cohort default rate for Jacksonville College of Jacksonville, Texas, on the basis of data corrections confirmed by the Texas Guaranteed Student Loan Corporation; and

(2) restore the eligibility of Jacksonville College to participate in the Federal Pell Grant Program for the 1999–2000 award year and succeeding award years.

(b) Jacksonville College shall implement a default management plan that is satisfactory to the Secretary of Education.

(c) For purposes of determining its Federal Pell Grant Program eligibility, Jacksonville College shall be deemed to have withdrawn from the Federal Family Education Loan program as of October 6, 1998.]

[SEC. 308. An amount of $14,500,000 from the balances of returned reserve funds, formerly held by the Higher Education Assistance Foundation, that are currently held in Higher Education Assistance Foundation Claims Reserves, Treasury account number 91X6192, and $12,000,000 from funds formerly held by the Higher Education Assistance Foundation, that are currently held in trust, shall be deposited in the general fund of the Treasury.]

[SEC. 309. Of the funds provided in title III of this Act, under the heading "Higher Education", for title VII, part B of the Higher Education Act of 1965, $250,000 shall be awarded to the Snelling Center for Government at the University of Vermont for a model school program, $750,000 shall be awarded to Texas A&M University,

(TRANSFER OF FUNDS)—Continued

Corpus Christi, for operation of the Early Childhood Development Center, $1,000,000 shall be awarded to Southeast Missouri State University for equipment and curriculum development associated with the University's Polytechnic Institute, $800,000 shall be awarded to the Washington Virtual Classroom Consortium to develop, equip and implement an ecosystem curriculum, $500,000 shall be provided to the Puget Sound Center for Technology for faculty development activities for the use of technology in the classroom, $500,000 shall be awarded to the Center for the Advancement of Distance Education in Rural America, $3,000,000, to be available until expended, shall be awarded to the University Center of Lake County, Illinois and $1,000,000, to be available until expended, shall be awarded to the Oregon University System for activities authorized under title III, part A, section 311(c)(2), of the Higher Education Act of 1965, as amended, $500,000 shall be awarded to Columbia College Illinois for a freshman retention program, $1,500,000 shall be awarded to the University of Hawaii at Manoa for a Globalization Research Center, $2,000,000 shall be awarded to the University of Arkansas at Pine Bluff for technology infrastructure, $1,000,000 shall be awarded to the I Have a Dream Foundation, $1,000,000 shall be awarded to a demonstration program for activities authorized under part G of title VIII of the Higher Education Act of 1965, as amended, $3,000,000 shall be awarded to the Daniel J. Evans School of Public Policy at the University of Washington, $200,000 shall be awarded to North Dakota State University for the Career Program for Dislocated Farmers and Ranchers, $350,000 shall be awarded to North Dakota State University for the Tech-based Industry Traineeship Program, $3,000,000 shall be awarded to Washington State University for the Thomas S. Foley Institute to support programs in congressional studies, public policy, voter education, and to ensure community access and outreach, $200,000 shall be awarded to Minot State University for the Rural Communications Disabilities Program, $300,000 shall be awarded to Bryant College for the Linking International Trade Education Program (LITE), $1,000,000 shall be awarded to Concord College, West Virginia for a technology center to further enhance the technical skills of West Virginia teachers and students, $200,000 shall be awarded to Peirce College in Philadelphia, Pennsylvania for education and training programs, $250,000 shall be awarded to the Philadelphia Zoo for educational programs, $800,000 shall be awarded to Spelman College in Georgia for educational operations, $1,000,000 shall be awarded to the Philadelphia University Education Center for technology education, $725,000 shall be awarded to Lock Haven University for technology innovations, $250,000 for Middle Georgia College for an advanced distributed learning center demonstration program, $1,000,000 for the University of the Incarnate Word in San Antonio, Texas, to improve teacher capabilities in technology, $1,000,000 for Elmira College in New York for a technology enhancement initiative, $1,000,000 shall be awarded to the Southeastern Pennsylvania Consortium on Higher Education for education programs, $400,000 shall be awarded to Lehigh University Iacocca Institute for educational training, $250,000 shall be awarded to Lafayette College for arts education, $1,000,000 shall be awarded to Lewis and Clark College for the Crime Victims Law Institute, $1,650,000 for Rust College in Mississippi for technology infrastructure, $500,000 for the University of Notre Dame for a teacher quality initiative, $2,400,000 shall be awarded to the Western Governors University for a distance learning initiative, $1,000,000 shall be awarded to the Alabama A&M University for the development of a research institute, $1,000,000 shall be awarded to Tarleton State University in Stephenville, Texas for the Center for Astronomy Education and Research summer science programs for students and teachers, $1,500,000 shall be awarded to the Great Plains Network at Kansas University, $350,000 shall be awarded to the Science Education and Literacy Center at Rider University in New Jersey, $1,500,000 shall be awarded to the Indiana State University DegreeLink Partnership for a distance learning program, $1,000,000 shall be awarded to the Ivy Technical State College in Indiana for a machine tool training program, $1,250,000 shall be awarded to the Connecticut State University System Center for Education Technology Assessment, $400,000 shall be awarded to Monmouth University in New Jersey for the 21st Century Science Teachers Skills Project, $58,000 shall be awarded to the Black Hawk College International Business Education Center in Moline, Illinois for training in international economics, $325,000 shall be awarded to the World Learning School of International Training in Brattleboro, Vermont for the expansion of a language study program, $500,000 shall be awarded to the Diablo Valley Community College at Contra-Costa Community College District for a model teacher program to foster interest in teaching careers among high school and community college students, $1,000,000 shall be awarded to the Urban College of Boston, Massachusetts, for tutoring and mentoring services for educationally disadvantaged students, $1,000,000 shall be awarded to the University of Rhode Island Center for Environmental Design, Planning, and Policy in Kingston, Rhode Island to foster environmental education, $800,000 shall be awarded to the Wisconsin Indianhead Technical College at Ashland and Superior to provide high technology education and training, $400,000 shall be for an award to the University of Wisconsin at Superior for Project SPARKS to link faculty with schools in the Superior School District in Wisconsin, and $100,000 shall be awarded to the University of Nevada at Las Vegas for the Nevada Institute for Children Children's literacy program.]

[SEC. 310. (a) From the amount appropriated for title VI of the Elementary and Secondary Education Act of 1965 in accordance with this section, the Secretary of Education—(1) shall make available a total of $6,000,000 to the Secretary of the Interior (on behalf of the Bureau of Indian Affairs) and the outlying areas for activities under this section; and (2) shall allocate the remainder by providing each State the same percentage of that remainder as it received of the funds allocated to States under section 307(a)(2) of the Department of Education Appropriations Act, 1999.

(b)(1) Each State that receives funds under this section shall distribute 100 percent of such funds to local educational agencies, of which—

(A) 80 percent of such amount shall be allocated to such local educational agencies in proportion to the number of children, aged 5 to 17, who reside in the school district served by such local educational agency from families with incomes below the poverty line (as defined by the Office of Management and Budget and revised annually in accordance with section 673(2) of the Community Services Block Grant Act (42 U.S.C. 9902(2))) applicable to a family of the size involved for the most recent fiscal year for which satisfactory data are available compared to the number of such individuals who reside in the school districts served by all the local educational agencies in the State for that fiscal year; and

(B) 20 percent of such amount shall be allocated to such local educational agencies in accordance with the relative enrollments of children, aged 5 to 17, in public and private nonprofit elementary and secondary schools within the boundaries of such agencies.

(2) Notwithstanding paragraph (1), if the award to a local educational agency under this section is less than the starting salary for a new fully qualified teacher in that agency who is certified within the State (which may include certification through State or local alternative routes), has a baccalaureate degree, and demonstrates the general knowledge, teaching skills, and subject matter knowledge required to teach in his or her content areas, that agency may use funds under this section to (A) help pay the salary of a full- or part-time teacher hired to reduce class size, which may be in combination with other Federal, State, or local funds; or (B) pay for activities described in subsection (c)(2)(A)(iii) which may be related to teaching in smaller classes.

(c)(1) The basic purpose and intent of this section is to reduce class size with fully qualified teachers. Each local educational agency that receives funds under this section shall use such funds to carry out effective approaches to reducing class size with fully qualified teachers who are certified within the State, including teachers certified through State or local alternative routes, and who demonstrate competency in the areas in which they teach, to improve educational achievement for both regular and special needs children, with particular consideration given to reducing class size in the early elementary grades for which some research has shown class size reduction is most effective.

(2)(A) Each such local educational agency may use funds under this section for

(i) recruiting (including through the use of signing bonuses, and other financial incentives), hiring, and training fully qualified regular and special education teachers (which may include hiring special education teachers to team-teach with regular teachers in classrooms that contain both children with disabilities and non-disabled children) and teachers of special-needs children, who are certified within the State, including teachers certified through State or local alternative routes, have a baccalaureate degree and demonstrate the general knowledge, teaching skills, and subject matter knowledge required to teach in their content areas;

(ii) testing new teachers for academic content knowledge, and to meet State certification requirements that are consistent with title II of the Higher Education Act of 1965; and

(iii) providing professional development (which may include such activities as promoting retention and mentoring) to teachers, including special education teachers and teachers of special-needs children, in order to meet the goal of ensuring that all instructional staff have the subject matter knowledge, teaching knowledge, and teaching skills necessary to teach effectively in the content area or areas in which they provide instruction, consistent with title II of the Higher Education Act of 1965.

(B)(i) Except as provided under clause (ii) a local educational agency may use not more than a total of 25 percent of the award received under this section for activities described in clauses (ii) and (iii) of subparagraph (A).

(ii) A local educational agency in an Ed-Flex Partnership State under Public Law 106–25, the Education Flexibility Partnership Act, and in which 10 percent or more of teachers in elementary schools as defined by section 14101(14) of the Elementary and Secondary Education Act of 1965 have not met applicable State and local certification requirements (including certification through State or local alternative routes), or if such requirements have been waived, may apply to the State educational agency for a waiver that would permit it to use more than 25 percent of the funds it receives under this section for activities described in subparagraph (A)(iii) for the purpose of helping teachers who have not met the certification requirements become certified.

(iii) If the State educational agency approves the local educational agency's application for a waiver under clause (ii), the local educational agency may use the funds subject to the waiver for activities described in subparagraph (A)(iii) that are needed to ensure that at least 90 percent of the teachers in elementary schools are certified within the State.

(C) A local educational agency that has already reduced class size in the early grades to 18 or less children (or has already reduced class size to a State or local class size reduction goal that was in effect on the day before the enactment of the Department of Education Appropriations Act, 2000, if that State or local educational agency goal is 20 or fewer children) may use funds received under this section—

(i) to make further class size reductions in grades kindergarten through 3;

(ii) to reduce class size in other grades; or

(iii) to carry out activities to improve teacher quality, including professional development.

(D) If a local educational agency has already reduced class size in the early grades to 18 or fewer children and intends to use funds provided under this section to carry out professional development activities, including activities to improve teacher quality, then the State shall make the award under subsection (b) to the local educational agency.

(3) Each such agency shall use funds under this section only to supplement, and not to supplant, State and local funds that, in the absence of such funds, would otherwise be spent for activities under this section.

(4) No funds made available under this section may be used to increase the salaries or provide benefits, other than participation in professional development and enrichment programs, to teachers who are not hired under this section. Funds under this section may be used to pay the salary of teachers hired under section 307 of the Department of Education Appropriations Act, 1999.

(d)(1) Each State receiving funds under this section shall report on activities in the State under this section, consistent with section 6202(a)(2) of the Elementary and Secondary Education Act of 1965.

(2) Each State and local educational agency receiving funds under this section shall publicly report to parents on its progress in reducing class size, increasing the percentage of classes in core academic areas taught by fully qualified teachers who are certified within the State and demonstrate competency in the content areas in which they teach, and on the impact that hiring additional highly qualified teachers and reducing class size, has had, if any, on increasing student academic achievement.

(3) Each school receiving funds under this section shall provide to parents upon request, the professional qualifications of their child's teacher.

(e) If a local educational agency uses funds made available under this section for professional development activities, the agency shall ensure for the equitable participation of private nonprofit elementary and secondary schools in such activities. Section 6402 of the Elementary and Secondary Education Act of 1965 shall not apply to other activities under this section.

(f) ADMINISTRATIVE EXPENSES.—A local educational agency that receives funds under this section may use not more than 3 percent of such funds for local administrative costs.

(g) REQUEST FOR FUNDS.—Each local educational agency that desires to receive funds under this section shall include in the application required under section 6303 of the Elementary and Secondary Education Act of 1965 a description of the agency's program to reduce class size by hiring additional highly qualified teachers.

(h) No funds under this section may be used to pay the salary of any teacher hired with funds under section 307 of the Department of Education Appropriations Act, 1999, unless, by the start of the 2000–2001 school year, the teacher is certified within the State (which may include certification through State or local alternative routes) and demonstrates competency in the subject areas in which he or she teaches.

(i) Titles III and IV of the Goals 2000: Educate America Act are repealed on September 30, 2000.]

[LIMITATION ON PUNITIVE DAMAGES AWARDED AGAINST INSTITUTIONS OF HIGHER EDUCATION]

[SEC. 311. Section 5 of the Y2K Act (15 U.S.C. 6604) is amended by adding at the end the following:

"(d) INSTITUTIONS OF HIGHER EDUCATION.—

"(1) IN GENERAL.—Subject to paragraph (2), punitive damages in a Y2K action may not be awarded against an instituion of higher education as defined in section 101(a) of the Higher Education Act of 1965 (20 U.S.C. 1001(a)).

"(2) EXCEPTION.—Paragraph (1) shall not apply to an institution of higher education if the Y2K failure in the Y2K action occurred in a computer-based student financial aid system of that institution of higher education, and the institution—

"(A) has not passed Y2K data exchange testing with the Department of Education; or

"(B) is not or was not in the process of performing data exchange testing with the Department of Education at the time the Department terminates such testing.".]

[SEC. 312. Section 4 of P.L. 106–71 is amended by striking subsection (c).]

[SEC. 313. HOLD HARMLESS.

(a) LOCAL CONTRIBUTION RATE.—For purposes of calculating a payment under section 8003(b) of the Elementary and Secondary Education Act of 1965 for fiscal year 1999 or 2000 with respect to any local educational agency described in subsection (b), the Secretary of Education shall not use a local contribution rate for the fiscal year that is less than the local contribution rate used for the local educational agency for fiscal year 1998.

(b) LOCAL EDUCATIONAL AGENCIES.—A local educational agency referred to in subsection (a) is any local educational agency that—

(1) is eligible to receive a payment under section 8003(b) of the Elementary and Secondary Education Act of 1965 for fiscal year 1999 or 2000, as the case may be; and

(2) received a payment under such section for fiscal year 1998 that was calculated on the basis of a local contribution rate based on generally comparable school districts using the special additional factors method.

(c) EFFECTIVE DATE.—This section shall be effective for fiscal years 1999 and 2000.]

[SEC. 314. VOTER REGISTRATION OF COLLEGE STUDENTS.

Subparagraph (C) of section 487(a)(23) of the Higher Education Act of 1965 (20 U.S.C. 1094(a)(23)) is amended to read as follows:

"(C) This paragraph shall apply to general and special elections for Federal office, as defined in section 301(3) of the Federal Election Campaign Act of 1971 (2 U.S.C. 431(3)), and to the elections for Governor or other chief executive within such State).".] *(Department of Education Appropriations Act, 2000, as enacted by section 1000(a)(4) of the Consolidated Appropriations Act, 2000 (P.L. 106–113).)*

DEPARTMENT OF ENERGY

NATIONAL NUCLEAR SECURITY ADMINISTRATION

Federal Funds

General and special funds:

WEAPONS ACTIVITIES

For Department of Energy expenses, including the purchase, construction and acquisition of plant and capital equipment and other incidental expenses necessary for atomic energy defense weapons activities in carrying out the purposes of the Department of Energy Organization Act (42 U.S.C. 7101 et seq.), including the acquisition or condemnation of any real property or any facility or for plant or facility acquisition, construction, or expansion; and the purchase of passenger motor vehicles (not to exceed [three] *12* for replacement only), [$4,443,939,000] *$4,594,000,000*, to remain available until expended[: *Provided*, That funding for any ballistic missile defense program undertaken by the Department of Energy for the Department of Defense shall be provided by the Department of Defense according to procedures established for Work for Others by the Department of Energy]. *(Energy and Water Development Appropriations Act, 2000.)*

Program and Financing (in millions of dollars)

Identification code 89–0240–0–1–053		1999 actual	2000 est.	2001 est.
	Obligations by program activity:			
	Direct program:			
00.01	Stockpile stewardship	2,103	2,210	
00.02	Stockpile management	2,025	1,979	
00.03	Directed stockpile work			837
00.04	Campaigns			1,050
00.05	Readiness in technical base and facilities			1,953
00.06	Secure Transportation Asset		91	116
00.07	Construction			414
00.08	Program direction	251	209	224
01.00	Subtotal, direct program	4,379	4,489	4,594
09.01	Reimbursable program	980	1,500	1,350
10.00	Total new obligations	5,359	5,989	5,944
	Budgetary resources available for obligation:			
	Unobligated balance available, start of year:			
21.40	Unobligated balance available, start of year	47	61	
21.40	Unobligated balance available, start of year	405	483	483
21.99	Total unobligated balance, start of year	452	544	483
22.00	New budget authority (gross)	5,453	5,927	5,944
22.10	Resources available from recoveries of prior year obligations	1		
22.21	Unobligated balance transferred to other accounts	−2		
23.90	Total budgetary resources available for obligation	5,904	6,471	6,427
23.95	Total new obligations	−5,359	−5,989	−5,944
	Unobligated balance available, end of year:			
24.40	Unobligated balance available, end of year	61		
24.40	Unobligated balance available, end of year	483	483	483
24.99	Total unobligated balance, end of year	544	483	483
	New budget authority (gross), detail:			
	Discretionary:			
40.00	Appropriation	4,400	4,444	4,594
40.76	Reduction pursuant to P.L. 106–113		−17	
41.00	Transferred to other accounts	−4		
43.00	Appropriation (total discretionary)	4,396	4,427	4,594
68.00	Spending authority from offsetting collections: Offsetting collections (cash)	1,057	1,500	1,350
70.00	Total new budget authority (gross)	5,453	5,927	5,944
	Change in unpaid obligations:			
72.40	Unpaid obligations, start of year: Obligated balance, start of year	1,356	1,050	1,134
73.10	Total new obligations	5,359	5,989	5,944
73.20	Total outlays (gross)	−5,661	−5,905	−5,884
73.31	Obligated balance transferred to other accounts	−3		
73.45	Adjustments in unexpired accounts	−1		
74.40	Unpaid obligations, end of year: Obligated balance, end of year	1,050	1,134	1,194
	Outlays (gross), detail:			
86.90	Outlays from new discretionary authority	3,914	4,378	4,336
86.93	Outlays from discretionary balances	1,747	1,526	1,548
87.00	Total outlays (gross)	5,661	5,905	5,884
	Offsets:			
	Against gross budget authority and outlays:			
	Offsetting collections (cash) from:			
88.00	Federal sources	−950	−1,368	−1,225
88.40	Non-Federal sources	−107	−132	−125
88.90	Total, offsetting collections (cash)	−1,057	−1,500	−1,350
	Net budget authority and outlays:			
89.00	Budget authority	4,396	4,427	4,594
90.00	Outlays	4,604	4,405	4,534

Summary of Budget Authority and Outlays

(in millions of dollars)

	1999 actual	*2000 est.*	*2001 est.*
Enacted/requested:			
Budget Authority	4,396	4,427	4,594
Outlays	4,604	4,404	4,534
Supplemental proposal:			
Budget Authority		55	
Outlays		36	17
Total:			
Budget Authority	4,396	4,482	4,594
Outlays	4,604	4,440	4,551

Beginning in FY 2001, Weapons activities appears under the National Nuclear Security Administration (NNSA), reflecting its transfer within DOE to the newly established NNSA. Also beginning in FY 2001, changes in the structure of Weapons activities are proposed. The changes reflect maturation of the stockpile stewardship programs without underground nuclear testing, and are a result of numerous management studies that have recommended a more unified program management approach that includes closer integration of research, development, and production activities.

Weapons activities provides for the maintenance and refurbishment of nuclear weapons to sustain confidence in their safety, reliability, and performance; expansion of scientific, engineering, and manufacturing capabilities to enable certification of the enduring nuclear weapons stockpile; and manufacture of nuclear weapon components under a comprehensive test ban. Weapons activities also provide for continued maintenance and investment in the Department's enterprise of nuclear stewardship, including maintaining the capability to return to the design and production of new weapons and to underground nuclear testing, if so directed by the President. The major elements of the program include the following:

Directed stockpile work.—Encompasses all activities that directly support specific weapons in the stockpile. These activities include maintenance and day-to-day care; planned refurbishment as outlined by the Stockpile Life Extension Program (SLEP); reliability assessments; weapon dismantlement and

General and special funds—Continued

WEAPONS ACTIVITIES—Continued

disposal; and research, development, and certification technology efforts to meet future stockpile requirements.

Campaigns.—Focuses on scientific and technical efforts to develop and maintain critical capabilities and tools needed to support continued assessment and certification of the stockpile for the long term.

Readiness in technical base and facilities (RTBF).—Provides the underlying physical infrastructure and operational readiness for the Directed Stockpile Work and Campaign activities. These activities include ensuring that facilities are operational, safe, secure, and compliant with regulatory requirements, and that a defined level of readiness is sustained at facilities funded by the Office of Defense programs. The Department is still reviewing the budget structure changes associated with RTBF, and may offer revisions as technical amendments to the Weapons Activities budget request.

Secure transportation asset.—Provides for the safe, secure movement of nuclear weapons, special nuclear material, and weapon components between military locations and nuclear complex facilities within the United States.

Construction.—Includes line item construction projects to establish, maintain, and preserve the physical infrastructure of the national security enterprise. Construction projects provide production capability as well as state-of-the-art research and development capabilities to enable continued maintenance and certification of the nuclear weapons stockpile under a comprehensive test ban treaty.

Weapons program direction.—This activity provides personnel and contractual services for the Federal management, direction, and administration of Defense Programs' missions.

Object Classification (in millions of dollars)

Identification code 89–0240–0–1–053		1999 actual	2000 est.	2001 est.
	Direct obligations:			
	Personnel compensation:			
11.1	Full-time permanent	110	107	120
11.3	Other than full-time permanent	2	3	3
11.5	Other personnel compensation	7	8	8
11.9	Total personnel compensation	119	118	131
12.1	Civilian personnel benefits	29	41	45
13.0	Benefits for former personnel	1	1	1
21.0	Travel and transportation of persons	7	10	10
23.2	Rental payments to others	1	1	1
23.3	Communications, utilities, and miscellaneous charges	3	3	3
25.1	Advisory and assistance services	40	36	36
25.2	Other services	198	153	148
25.3	Purchases of goods and services from Government accounts	11	10	7
25.4	Operation and maintenance of facilities	3,198	3,397	3,530
25.5	Research and development contracts	50	53	54
25.7	Operation and maintenance of equipment	2	2	2
26.0	Supplies and materials	2	2	3
31.0	Equipment	152	169	185
32.0	Land and structures	544	469	414
41.0	Grants, subsidies, and contributions	22	24	24
99.0	Subtotal, direct obligations	4,379	4,489	4,594
99.0	Reimbursable obligations	980	1,500	1,350
99.9	Total new obligations	5,359	5,989	5,944

Personnel Summary

Identification code 89–0240–0–1–053		1999 actual	2000 est.	2001 est.
1001	Total compensable workyears: Full-time equivalent employment	1,772	1,754	1,753

OTHER NUCLEAR SECURITY ACTIVITIES

For Department of Energy expenses necessary for atomic energy defense and other national security activities to carry out the Department of Energy Organization Act (42 U.S.C. 7101 et seq.), including acquisition (by purchase, condemnation, construction, or otherwise) of real property, plant and capital equipment, facilities, and facility expansion, to remain available until expended $1,583,635,000, and in addition, $49,000,000, to become available on October 1, 2003: Provided, That not to exceed $5,000 may be used for official reception and representation expenses for national security and nonproliferation (including transparency) activities in fiscal year 2001.

Program and Financing (in millions of dollars)

Identification code 89–0309–0–1–053		1999 actual	2000 est.	2001 est.
	Obligations by program activity:			
00.01	Nonproliferation and national security	750	723	683
00.02	Fissile materials disposition	145	199	268
00.04	Naval reactors	664	677	678
00.07	Other	11	11	
10.00	Total new obligations	1,570	1,610	1,629
	Budgetary resources available for obligation:			
21.40	Unobligated balance available, start of year	47	257	151
22.00	New budget authority (gross)	1,781	1,504	1,584
22.10	Resources available from recoveries of prior year obligations	2		
22.21	Unobligated balance transferred to other accounts	−2		
23.90	Total budgetary resources available for obligation	1,828	1,761	1,735
23.95	Total new obligations	−1,570	−1,610	−1,629
24.40	Unobligated balance available, end of year	257	151	106
	New budget authority (gross), detail:			
	Discretionary:			
40.00	Appropriation	1,736	1,509	1,584
40.76	Reduction pursuant to P.L. 106–113		−5	
41.00	Transferred to other accounts	−5		
42.00	Transferred from other accounts	50		
43.00	Appropriation (total discretionary)	1,781	1,504	1,584
	Change in unpaid obligations:			
72.40	Unpaid obligations, start of year: Obligated balance, start of year	570	618	682
73.10	Total new obligations	1,570	1,610	1,629
73.20	Total outlays (gross)	−1,520	−1,546	−1,604
73.45	Adjustments in unexpired accounts	−2		
74.40	Unpaid obligations, end of year: Obligated balance, end of year	618	682	707
	Outlays (gross), detail:			
86.90	Outlays from new discretionary authority	990	978	1,030
86.93	Outlays from discretionary balances	530	568	574
87.00	Total outlays (gross)	1,520	1,546	1,604
	Net budget authority and outlays:			
89.00	Budget authority	1,781	1,504	1,584
90.00	Outlays	1,520	1,546	1,604

Note.—BY estimate is for activities previously financed from Department of Energy, Other Defense Activities.

Summary of Budget Authority and Outlays

(in millions of dollars)

	1999 actual	*2000 est.*	*2001 est.*
Enacted/requested:			
Budget Authority	1,781	1,504	1,584
Outlays	1,520	1,546	1,604
Supplemental proposal:			
Budget Authority		−40	
Outlays			
Total:			
Budget Authority	1,781	1,464	1,584
Outlays	1,520	1,546	1,604

This account includes the following activities that were included in past fiscal years under Other defense activities, but in FY 2001 are proposed to be included within this new account under the National Nuclear Security Administration:

Nonproliferation and national security.—The Department's nonproliferation and national security activities consist of the following areas: nonproliferation and verification, research and development, arms control and nonproliferation, international nuclear safety, highly enriched uranium transparency implementation, and program direction. These activities provide policy, direction, technology development and implementation, and leadership in national and international efforts to reduce the danger to U.S. national security posed by weapons of mass destruction. FY 2001 activities include increases for the DOE portion of the Expanded Threat Reduction Initiative to enhance protection and control of fissile material and prevent further plutonium separation within Russia. Key mission areas are: (1) preventing the spread of weapons of mass destruction materials, technology, and expertise; (2) detecting the proliferation of weapons of mass destruction worldwide; (3) reversing the proliferation of nuclear weapons capabilities; and (4) reducing the national security and environmental threats posed by the operation of unsafe nuclear facilities worldwide.

Fissile materials disposition.—The program is responsible for disposition of U.S. surplus weapons-useable fissile materials, providing key negotiation and technical support for efforts to attain reciprocal actions for the disposition of surplus Russian plutonium, and storage of surplus U.S. fissile materials pending disposition. Highly enriched uranium (HEU) will be blended down to low enriched uranium for use as commercial reactor fuel. Plutonium will be immobilized with ceramic material and burned as mixed oxide (MOX) fuel in existing domestic commercial reactors. Near term efforts include the design of U.S. disposition facilities, the pit disassembly and conversion facility, the MOX fuel fabrication facility, and the immobilization and associated process facility. Negotiation of a bilateral agreement with Russia to begin disposition of plutonium in the Russian Federation is expected to be completed in spring of 2000. In FY 2001, DOE will continue production mode testing and technology demonstrations for plutonium disposition; perform detailed design of two disposition facilities; start design of the immobilization facility; ship HEU for blend-down; and proceed with facilities in Russia in the initial phase of U.S.-Russia cooperation as defined in a bilateral agreement on plutonium disposition.

Naval reactors.—This program performs the design, development, and testing necessary to provide the Navy with safe, militarily effective nuclear propulsion plants in keeping with the Nation's nuclear-powered fleet defense requirements. During 2001, the program expects to reach 5,400 cumulative reactor-years of safe operation, and will continue to support and improve operating reactors and plant components, carry out test activities and verification, develop nuclear reactor plant components and systems for the Navy's new attack submarine and next-generation aircraft carriers, and maintain or shut down aging facilities as appropriate.

Other.—This category includes obligations for a portion of the projects reviewed under the independent assessment of DOE projects funding. In addition, obligations are included for the close out of the new production reactor program.

Object Classification (in millions of dollars)

Identification code 89–0309–0–1–053		1999 actual	2000 est.	2001 est.
	Personnel compensation:			
11.1	Full-time permanent	49	55	34
11.3	Other than full-time permanent	1	1	1
11.5	Other personnel compensation	1	1	1
11.9	Total personnel compensation	51	57	36
12.1	Civilian personnel benefits	11	12	7
21.0	Travel and transportation of persons	4	4	4
23.3	Communications, utilities, and miscellaneous charges	1	1	1
25.1	Advisory and assistance services	48	35	40
25.2	Other services	72	147	118
25.3	Purchases of goods and services from Government accounts	16	18	16
25.4	Operation and maintenance of facilities	1,251	1,207	1,289
25.5	Research and development contracts	6	7	6
25.7	Operation and maintenance of equipment	3	3	3
26.0	Supplies and materials	2	2	2
31.0	Equipment	51	57	52
32.0	Land and structures	51	57	52
41.0	Grants, subsidies, and contributions	3	3	3
99.9	Total new obligations	1,570	1,610	1,629

Personnel Summary

Identification code 89–0309–0–1–053		1999 actual	2000 est.	2001 est.
1001	Total compensable workyears: Full-time equivalent employment	624	663	396

ENVIRONMENTAL AND OTHER DEFENSE ACTIVITIES

Federal Funds

General and special funds:

DEFENSE ENVIRONMENTAL RESTORATION AND WASTE MANAGEMENT

For Department of Energy expenses, including the purchase, construction and acquisition of plant and capital equipment and other expenses necessary for atomic energy defense environmental restoration and waste management activities in carrying out the purposes of the Department of Energy Organization Act (42 U.S.C. 7101 et seq.), including the acquisition or condemnation of any real property or any facility or for plant or facility acquisition, construction, or expansion; and the purchase of [35] *67* passenger motor vehicles for replacement only, [$4,484,349,000] *$4,551,527,000,* to remain available until expended: *Provided,* That any amounts appropriated under this heading that are used to provide economic assistance under section 15 of the Waste Isolation Pilot Plant Land Withdrawal Act (Public Law 102–579) shall be utilized to the extent necessary to reimburse costs of financial assurances required of a contractor by any permit or license of the Waste Isolation Pilot Plant issued by the State of New Mexico. *(Energy and Water Development Appropriations Act, 2000.)*

Program and Financing (in millions of dollars)

Identification code 89–0242–0–1–053		1999 actual	2000 est.	2001 est.
	Obligations by program activity:			
00.01	Site/project completion	1,038	977	971
00.02	Post 2006 completion	2,695	2,932	3,108
00.03	Science and technology	231	228	197
00.04	Program direction	345	338	360
00.05	EH health studies	12		
10.00	Total new obligations	4,321	4,475	4,636
	Budgetary resources available for obligation:			
21.40	Unobligated balance available, start of year	313	33	34
22.00	New budget authority (gross)	4,316	4,476	4,602
22.10	Resources available from recoveries of prior year obligations	2		
22.21	Unobligated balance transferred to other accounts	−279		
22.22	Unobligated balance transferred from other accounts	2		
23.90	Total budgetary resources available for obligation	4,354	4,509	4,636
23.95	Total new obligations	−4,321	−4,475	−4,636
24.40	Unobligated balance available, end of year	33	34	
	New budget authority (gross), detail:			
	Discretionary:			
40.00	Appropriation	4,310	4,484	4,552
40.76	Reduction pursuant to P.L. 106–113		−17	
41.00	Transferred to other accounts	−4		
42.00	Transferred from other accounts	10		
43.00	Appropriation (total discretionary)	4,316	4,467	4,552
68.00	Spending authority from offsetting collections: Offsetting collections (cash)		9	50
70.00	Total new budget authority (gross)	4,316	4,476	4,602

General and special funds—Continued

DEFENSE ENVIRONMENTAL RESTORATION AND WASTE MANAGEMENT—Continued

Program and Financing (in millions of dollars)—Continued

Identification code 89–0242–0–1–053	1999 actual	2000 est.	2001 est.
Change in unpaid obligations:			
72.40 Unpaid obligations, start of year: Obligated balance, start of year	1,751	1,468	1,508
73.10 Total new obligations	4,321	4,475	4,636
73.20 Total outlays (gross)	−4,341	−4,435	−4,569
73.31 Obligated balance transferred to other accounts	−261		
73.32 Obligated balance transferred from other accounts	1		
73.45 Adjustments in unexpired accounts	−2		
74.40 Unpaid obligations, end of year: Obligated balance, end of year	1,468	1,508	1,575
Outlays (gross), detail:			
86.90 Outlays from new discretionary authority	2,816	3,136	3,236
86.93 Outlays from discretionary balances	1,525	1,299	1,333
87.00 Total outlays (gross)	4,341	4,435	4,569
Offsets:			
Against gross budget authority and outlays:			
88.40 Offsetting collections (cash) from: Non-Federal sources		−9	−50
Net budget authority and outlays:			
89.00 Budget authority	4,316	4,467	4,552
90.00 Outlays	4,341	4,426	4,519

Summary of Budget Authority and Outlays

(in millions of dollars)

	1999 actual	*2000 est.*	*2001 est.*
Enacted/requested:			
Budget Authority	4,316	4,467	4,552
Outlays	4,341	4,426	4,519
Rescission proposal:			
Budget Authority		−13	
Outlays		−9	−3
Total:			
Budget Authority	4,316	4,454	4,552
Outlays	4,341	4,417	4,516

Environmental management.—The Environmental Management (EM) program is responsible for addressing the environmental legacy resulting from the production of nuclear weapons. The nuclear weapons complex generated waste, pollution, and contamination that pose unique problems, including unprecedented volumes of contaminated soil and water, radiological hazards from special nuclear material, and a vast number of contaminated structures. Factories, laboratories and thousands of square miles of land were devoted to producing tens of thousands of nuclear weapons. Much of this infrastructure, waste, and contamination still exists and is largely maintained, decommissioned, managed, and remediated by the EM program, which is sometimes referred to as the "cleanup program." EM's responsibilities include facilities and sites in 30 states and one territory, and occupy an area equal to that of Rhode Island and Delaware combined—or about 2.1 million acres.

EM activities performed include: environmental restoration, which provides for assessments, characterization, remediation, and decontamination and decommissioning of contaminated DOE facilities and sites; waste management, which provides for the safe treatment, storage, and disposal of wastes generated by defense activities; and, nuclear material and facility stabilization, which provides for stabilization, safeguarding, interim storage, and stewardship of excess nuclear materials, including spent nuclear fuel, awaiting ultimate disposition.

EM will continue to improve the efficiency of its programs through a variety of management and contracting strategies with emphasis on the reduction of support costs and implementation of performance-based contracts.

The EM program has established a goal of cleaning up as many of its contaminated sites as possible by 2006, in a manner that is safe and protects the environment. By working towards this goal, EM can reduce the hazards presently facing its workforce and the public, and reduce the financial burden on the taxpayer. The FY 2001 budget request continues to reflect the program's emphasis on site closure and project completion.

The FY 2001 budget request will support the following major program areas:

Site/project completion.—Includes sites and/or projects planned to be completed by 2006 at EM laboratories or other facilities where DOE will continue to have a presence beyond the year 2006. Examples of sites with projects included in this account are Sandia National Laboratories, New Mexico; Argonne National Laboratory—East, Illinois; and Lawrence Livermore National Laboratory, California.

Post 2006 completion.—Includes projects that will continue after 2006. Included are various projects at Albuquerque, New Mexico; Hanford, Washington; Savannah River, South Carolina; Idaho National Engineering and Environmental Laboratory, Idaho; Nevada Test Site, Nevada; Oak Ridge Reservation, Tennessee; and the Waste Isolation Pilot Plant in Carlsbad, New Mexico.

Office of Science and Technology.—Conducts research and development programs to provide solutions to the Department's major environmental management problems. The activities are focused on technology development and deployment assistance; in partnership with DOE's Office of Science, managing the Environmental Management Science Program which conducts a targeted basic research program to address Environmental Management's most intractable problems.

EM program direction.—Provides salaries and benefits, travel and other contractual support costs for the Federal workforce at Headquarters and in the field which support the Environmental Management Program.

Object Classification (in millions of dollars)

Identification code 89–0242–0–1–053	1999 actual	2000 est.	2001 est.
Personnel compensation:			
11.1 Full-time permanent	179	186	193
11.3 Other than full-time permanent	6	6	6
11.5 Other personnel compensation	4	4	4
11.9 Total personnel compensation	189	196	203
12.1 Civilian personnel benefits	43	45	46
13.0 Benefits for former personnel	1	1	1
21.0 Travel and transportation of persons	8	8	9
23.1 Rental payments to GSA	7	7	8
23.2 Rental payments to others	1	1	1
23.3 Communications, utilities, and miscellaneous charges	3	3	3
25.1 Advisory and assistance services	108	112	116
25.2 Other services	747	774	803
25.3 Purchases of goods and services from Government accounts	31	32	33
25.4 Operation and maintenance of facilities	2,733	2,829	2,929
25.5 Research and development contracts	49	51	53
26.0 Supplies and materials	3	3	3
31.0 Equipment	49	51	53
32.0 Land and structures	244	253	262
41.0 Grants, subsidies, and contributions	105	109	113
99.9 Total new obligations	4,321	4,475	4,636

Personnel Summary

Identification code 89–0242–0–1–053	1999 actual	2000 est.	2001 est.
1001 Total compensable workyears: Full-time equivalent employment	2,666	2,778	2,674

DEFENSE FACILITIES CLOSURE PROJECTS

For expenses of the Department of Energy to accelerate the closure of defense environmental management sites, including the purchase, construction and acquisition of plant and capital equipment and other necessary expenses, [$1,064,492,000] *$1,082,297,000*, to remain available until expended. *(Energy and Water Development Appropriations Act, 2000.)*

Program and Financing (in millions of dollars)

Identification code 89–0251–0–1–053	1999 actual	2000 est.	2001 est.
Obligations by program activity:			
10.00 Total new obligations	1,042	1,061	1,082
Budgetary resources available for obligation:			
21.40 Unobligated balance available, start of year		1	
22.00 New budget authority (gross)	1,042	1,060	1,082
22.10 Resources available from recoveries of prior year obligations	1		
22.22 Unobligated balance transferred from other accounts			
23.90 Total budgetary resources available for obligation	1,043	1,061	1,082
23.95 Total new obligations	–1,042	–1,061	–1,082
24.40 Unobligated balance available, end of year	1		
New budget authority (gross), detail:			
Discretionary:			
40.00 Appropriation	1,038	1,064	1,082
40.76 Reduction pursuant to P.L. 106–113		–4	
42.00 Transferred from other accounts	4		
43.00 Appropriation (total discretionary)	1,042	1,060	1,082
Change in unpaid obligations:			
72.40 Unpaid obligations, start of year: Obligated balance, start of year	290	327	342
73.10 Total new obligations	1,042	1,061	1,082
73.20 Total outlays (gross)	–1,014	–1,046	–1,074
73.32 Obligated balance transferred from other accounts	10		
73.45 Adjustments in unexpired accounts	–1		
74.40 Unpaid obligations, end of year: Obligated balance, end of year	327	342	350
Outlays (gross), detail:			
86.90 Outlays from new discretionary authority	723	742	757
86.93 Outlays from discretionary balances	291	304	317
87.00 Total outlays (gross)	1,014	1,046	1,074
Net budget authority and outlays:			
89.00 Budget authority	1,042	1,060	1,082
90.00 Outlays	1,014	1,046	1,074

These funds are managed by the Department of Energy's Environmental Management Program.

Site closure.—Provides funding for completing cleanup and closing facilities with no enduring Federal presence on site, except for stewardship activities. Example of sites included under this account are the Rocky Flats site in Colorado, and the Fernald, Mound, Battelle Columbus, and Ashtabula sites in Ohio. The Department has established a goal of completing cleanup activities budgeted for in this account by 2006.

EM activities performed include: environmental restoration, which provides for assessments, characterization, remediation, and decontamination and decommissioning of contaminated DOE facilities and sites; waste management, which provides for the safe treatment, storage, and disposal of wastes generated by defense activities; and, nuclear material and facility stabilization, which provides for stabilization, safeguarding, interim storage, and stewardship of excess nuclear materials, awaiting ultimate disposition.

Object Classification (in millions of dollars)

Identification code 89–0251–0–1–053	1999 actual	2000 est.	2001 est.
23.3 Communications, utilities, and miscellaneous charges	7	7	8
25.2 Other services	31	32	32
25.4 Operation and maintenance of facilities	967	984	1,004
32.0 Land and structures	31	32	32
41.0 Grants, subsidies, and contributions	6	6	6
99.9 Total new obligations	1,042	1,061	1,082

DEFENSE ENVIRONMENTAL MANAGEMENT PRIVATIZATION

For Department of Energy expenses for privatization projects necessary for atomic energy defense environmental management activities authorized by the Department of Energy Organization Act (42 U.S.C. 7101 et seq.), [$189,000,000] *$515,000,000*, to remain available until expended. *(Energy and Water Development Appropriations Act, 2000.)*

Program and Financing (in millions of dollars)

Identification code 89–0249–0–1–053	1999 actual	2000 est.	2001 est.
Obligations by program activity:			
10.00 Total new obligations (object class 25.2)	110	585	515
Budgetary resources available for obligation:			
21.40 Unobligated balance available, start of year		397	
22.00 New budget authority (gross)	228	188	515
22.22 Unobligated balance transferred from other accounts	279		
23.90 Total budgetary resources available for obligation	507	585	515
23.95 Total new obligations	–110	–585	–515
24.40 Unobligated balance available, end of year	397		
New budget authority (gross), detail:			
Discretionary:			
40.00 Appropriation	228	189	515
40.76 Reduction pursuant to P.L. 106–113		–1	
43.00 Appropriation (total discretionary)	228	188	515
Change in unpaid obligations:			
72.40 Unpaid obligations, start of year: Obligated balance, start of year		361	915
73.10 Total new obligations	110	585	515
73.20 Total outlays (gross)		–31	–45
73.32 Obligated balance transferred from other accounts	251		
74.40 Unpaid obligations, end of year: Obligated balance, end of year	361	915	1,385
Outlays (gross), detail:			
86.93 Outlays from discretionary balances		31	45
Net budget authority and outlays:			
89.00 Budget authority	228	188	515
90.00 Outlays		31	45

Environmental management privatization.—Provides funding necessary to proceed with privatization of various DOE environmental management projects that will treat some of DOE's most contaminated soil and highly radioactive waste, as well as deactivate contaminated nuclear facilities that are excess to DOE's needs. This contracting approach to cleanup relies on the private sector to construct and operate facilities or proceed with cleanup actions on a fixed-price, fee-for-service basis. These competitively awarded projects are expected to result in substantial savings over the life-cycle of the projects, when compared to DOE's traditional approach of designing, constructing and operating a government-owned facility. Funds in this account will allow DOE to enter into these contracts and assures private investors that funds will be available to pay for services once the facilities are built.

OTHER DEFENSE ACTIVITIES

For Department of Energy expenses, including the purchase, construction and acquisition of plant and capital equipment and other expenses necessary for atomic energy defense, other defense activities, in carrying out the purposes of the Department of Energy Organization Act (42 U.S.C. 7101 et seq.), including the acquisition or condemnation of any real property or any facility or for plant or facility acquisition, construction, or expansion, [$1,722,444,000] *$555,122,000*, to remain available until expended[: *Provided*, That not to exceed $5,000 may be used for official reception and representation expenses for transparency, national security and nonproliferation activities]. *(Energy and Water Development Appropriations Act, 2000.)*

General and special funds—Continued

OTHER DEFENSE ACTIVITIES—Continued

Program and Financing (in millions of dollars)

Identification code 89–0243–0–1–053	1999 actual	2000 est.	2001 est.
Obligations by program activity:			
00.01 Intelligence		35	38
00.02 Counterintelligence	7	37	45
00.03 Security and emergency operations			320
00.04 Worker and community transition	34	29	25
00.05 Environment, safety and health (defense)	92	99	109
00.06 Independent oversight		5	15
00.07 Purchase of Russian uranium	325		
00.08 Other	45	21	3
10.00 Total new obligations	503	226	555
Budgetary resources available for obligation:			
21.40 Unobligated balance available, start of year	23	14	
22.00 New budget authority (gross)	491	212	555
22.10 Resources available from recoveries of prior year obligations	1		
22.22 Unobligated balance transferred from other accounts	2		
23.90 Total budgetary resources available for obligation	517	226	555
23.95 Total new obligations	–503	–226	–555
24.40 Unobligated balance available, end of year	14		
New budget authority (gross), detail:			
Discretionary:			
40.00 Appropriation	486	214	555
40.76 Reduction pursuant to P.L. 106–113		–2	
42.00 Transferred from other accounts	5		
43.00 Appropriation (total discretionary)	491	212	555
Change in unpaid obligations:			
72.40 Unpaid obligations, start of year: Obligated balance, start of year	133	120	150
73.10 Total new obligations	503	226	555
73.20 Total outlays (gross)	–517	–196	–432
73.32 Obligated balance transferred from other accounts	2		
73.45 Adjustments in unexpired accounts	–1		
74.40 Unpaid obligations, end of year: Obligated balance, end of year	120	150	273
Outlays (gross), detail:			
86.90 Outlays from new discretionary authority	432	138	361
86.93 Outlays from discretionary balances	85	58	72
87.00 Total outlays (gross)	517	196	432
Net budget authority and outlays:			
89.00 Budget authority	491	212	555
90.00 Outlays	517	196	432

Note.—Excludes –$1,584 million in budget authority in BY for activities transferred to:

	PY	CY
Other Nuclear Security Activities, Department of Energy	–$1,736	–$1,509

Comparable amounts for PY and CY are included above.

Summary of Budget Authority and Outlays

(in millions of dollars)

	1999 actual	2000 est.	2001 est.
Enacted/requested:			
Budget Authority	491	212	555
Outlays	517	196	433
Supplemental proposal:			
Budget Authority		18	
Outlays		12	5
Total:			
Budget Authority	491	230	555
Outlays	517	208	438

Intelligence.—The Department's intelligence activities consist of providing the Department, other U.S. Government policy makers, and the Intelligence Community with timely, accurate high impact foreign intelligence analyses including support to counterintelligence; providing quick-turnaround, specialized technology applications and operational support to the intelligence, special operations, and law enforcement communities; and ensuring that the Department's technical, analytical and research expertise is made available to the Intelligence Community in accordance with executive Order 12333, "United States Intelligence Activities."

Counterintelligence.—The Office of Counterintelligence was established as an independent office as the result of classified Presidential Decision Directive NSC–61, "U.S. DOE Counterintelligence Program", dated February 11, 1998. Its mission is to develop and implement an effective Counterintelligence Program throughout the Department of Energy to identify, neutralize and deter foreign government or industrial intelligence activities directed at or involving DOE programs, personnel, facilities, technologies, classified information and unclassified sensitive information. This program serves six core functions: analysis; investigations; counterintelligence cyber; counterintelligence evaluation board; inspections; and training. This program is also responsible for approving, conducting, coordinating all counterintelligence policy and investigative matters with the Federal Bureau of Investigation at Headquarters and in the field.

Security and Emergency Operations.—Security and Emergency Operations consists of the following programs: Nuclear Safeguards and Security, Security Investigations, Emergency Management, and Program Direction. Key mission areas are: physical, information, cyber and personnel security; technology development; materials control and accountability; critical infrastructure; declassification/classification; emergency management and emergency response; foreign visits and assignments; plutonium, uranium, and special nuclear material inventory; and security investigations. These programs provide policy, programmatic direction and training for the protection of the Department's nuclear weapons, nuclear materials, classified and unclassified information, and facilities. The programs: ensure protection of certain critical national infrastructures against physical and cyber attacks; provide security clearances for federal and contractor personnel; and ensures an integrated response to emergencies affecting Departmental operations.

Worker and community transition.—This program provides for the development, implementation, and funding of plans under section 3161 of the National Defense Authorization Act of 1993, to provide options to assist workers affected by workforce restructuring including preference in hiring, outplacement assistance, relocation assistance, and incentives for early retirement or separation. This program also provides impact assistance to local communities, as well as disposition of assets excess to current Department needs.

Environment, safety and health (Defense).—The Office of Environment, Safety and Health is a corporate resource that provides Departmental leadership and management to protect the workers, public, and environment. The programs in the other defense activities are oversight, health studies, gaseous diffusion plants, and radiation effects research foundation support as well as program direction.

Independent oversight.—The Office of Independent Oversight and Performance Assurance provides an independent assessment of the effectiveness of Departmental policies and site performance in the areas of safeguards, security, emergency management, cyber security, and other critical functions. Appraisals are performed to determine whether site programs are effectively implemented and achieving Department-wide and site specific objectives.

Other.—This category includes obligations for a portion of the projects reviewed under the Independent Assessment of DOE project funding. In addition, obligations are included for the National Security Programs Administrative Support and the Office of Hearings and Appeals. Responsibilities of the office of Hearings and Appeals include adjudications of matters involving employees' eligibility for security clearances, appeals of adverse determinations under the Freedom of Information and Privacy Acts, complaints of reprisals by contractor-employees for "whistleblowing", and requests for exception from DOE orders, rules, and regulations.

Object Classification (in millions of dollars)

Identification code 89–0243–0–1–053		1999 actual	2000 est.	2001 est.
	Personnel compensation:			
11.1	Full-time permanent	18	31	148
11.3	Other than full-time permanent	1	1	3
11.5	Other personnel compensation	1	1	3
11.9	Total personnel compensation	20	33	154
12.1	Civilian personnel benefits	4	8	27
21.0	Travel and transportation of persons	2	2	6
25.1	Advisory and assistance services	3	23	36
25.2	Other services	373	56	142
25.3	Purchases of goods and services from Government accounts	40	39	39
25.4	Operation and maintenance of facilities	35	35	74
26.0	Supplies and materials	1	1	3
41.0	Grants, subsidies, and contributions	25	29	74
99.9	Total new obligations	503	226	555

Personnel Summary

Identification code 89–0243–0–1–053		1999 actual	2000 est.	2001 est.
1001	Total compensable workyears: Full-time equivalent employment	258	369	802

DEFENSE NUCLEAR WASTE DISPOSAL

For nuclear waste disposal activities to carry out the purposes of Public Law 97–425, as amended, including the acquisition of real property or facility construction or expansion, $112,000,000, to remain available until expended. *(Energy and Water Development Appropriations Act, 2000.)*

Program and Financing (in millions of dollars)

Identification code 89–0244–0–1–053		1999 actual	2000 est.	2001 est.
	Obligations by program activity:			
10.00	Total new obligations	189	112	112
	Budgetary resources available for obligation:			
21.40	Unobligated balance available, start of year	85	85	85
22.00	New budget authority (gross)	189	112	112
22.21	Unobligated balance transferred to other accounts			−85
23.90	Total budgetary resources available for obligation	274	197	112
23.95	Total new obligations	−189	−112	−112
24.40	Unobligated balance available, end of year	85	85	
	New budget authority (gross), detail:			
	Discretionary:			
40.00	Appropriation	189	112	112
	Change in unpaid obligations:			
72.40	Unpaid obligations, start of year: Obligated balance, start of year	6	3	28
73.10	Total new obligations	189	112	112
73.20	Total outlays (gross)	−192	−87	−112
74.40	Unpaid obligations, end of year: Obligated balance, end of year	3	28	28
	Outlays (gross), detail:			
86.90	Outlays from new discretionary authority	186	84	84
86.93	Outlays from discretionary balances	6	3	28
87.00	Total outlays (gross)	192	87	112
	Net budget authority and outlays:			
89.00	Budget authority	189	112	112
90.00	Outlays	192	87	112

This appropriation was established by Congress as part of the 1993 Energy and Water Development Appropriation (P.L. 102–377) in lieu of payment from the Department of Energy into the Nuclear Waste Fund for activities related to the disposal of defense high-level waste.

The program's cost estimates reflect DOE's best projections, given the scope of work identified and planned schedule of required activities. Future budget requests for the Program have yet to be established and will be determined through the annual executive and congressional budget process.

Since passage of the Nuclear Waste Policy Act of 1982, as amended, the Nuclear Waste Fund has incurred costs for activities related to disposal of high-level waste generated from the atomic energy defense activities of the Department of Energy. At the end of fiscal year 1999 the balance owed by the Federal Government to the Nuclear Waste Fund was approximately $1,500,000,000 (including principal and interest). The "Defense Nuclear Waste Disposal" appropriation was established to ensure payment of the Federal Government's contribution to the nuclear waste repository program. Through fiscal year 1999, a total of approximately $2,276,830,000 has been appropriated to support nuclear waste repository activities attributed to atomic energy defense activities.

Object Classification (in millions of dollars)

Identification code 89–0244–0–1–053		1999 actual	2000 est.	2001 est.
25.1	Advisory and assistance services	13	7	7
25.2	Other services	1	1	1
25.3	Purchases of goods and services from Government accounts	11	7	7
25.4	Operation and maintenance of facilities	164	97	97
99.9	Total new obligations	189	112	112

ENERGY EMPLOYEES COMPENSATION INITIATIVE

(Legislative proposal, not subject to PAYGO)

Program and Financing (in millions of dollars)

Identification code 89–9911–2–1–053		1999 actual	2000 est.	2001 est.
	Obligations by program activity:			
00.01	Energy employees beryllium compensation fund			13
00.02	Energy employees pilot project			2
00.03	Paducah employees exposure compensation fund			2
10.00	Total new obligations (object class 25.2)			17
	Budgetary resources available for obligation:			
22.00	New budget authority (gross)			17
23.95	Total new obligations			−17
	New budget authority (gross), detail:			
	Discretionary:			
40.00	Appropriation			17
	Change in unpaid obligations:			
72.40	Unpaid obligations, start of year: Obligated balance, start of year			
73.10	Total new obligations			17
73.20	Total outlays (gross)			−11
74.40	Unpaid obligations, end of year: Obligated balance, end of year			6
	Outlays (gross), detail:			
86.90	Outlays from new discretionary authority			11
	Net budget authority and outlays:			
89.00	Budget authority			17
90.00	Outlays			11

General and special funds—Continued

ENERGY EMPLOYEES COMPENSATION INITIATIVE—Continued

[Dollars in millions]

	1999	2000	2001
Distribution of budget authority by account:			
Energy employees beryllium compensation fund			13
Energy employees pilot project			2
Paducah employees exposure compensation fund			2
Total Budget Authority, Energy employees compensation initiative			17

[Dollars in millions]

	1999	2000	2001
Distribution of outlays by account:			
Energy employees beryllium compensation fund			9
Energy employees pilot project			1
Paducah employees exposure compensation fund			1
Total Outlays, Energy employees compensation initiative			11

The Administration has transmitted legislation to Congress that would establish a program to compensate current and former Department of Energy (DOE) employees and contractors who are ill because of beryllium exposure at DOE nuclear facilities, because of workplace exposure to plutonium and other highly radioactive materials at DOE's gaseous diffusion facility at Paducah, Kentucky, and because of workplace exposure to radiation and hazardous materials and for occupational illnesses at the DOE Oak Ridge site.

ENERGY PROGRAMS

Federal Funds

General and special funds:

SCIENCE

For Department of Energy expenses including the purchase, construction and acquisition of plant and capital equipment, and other expenses necessary for science activities in carrying out the purposes of the Department of Energy Organization Act (42 U.S.C. 7101 et seq.), including the acquisition or condemnation of any real property or facility or for plant or facility acquisition, construction, or expansion, and purchase of not to exceed [six] *58* passenger motor vehicles for replacement only, [$2,799,851,000] *$3,151,065,000*, to remain available until expended. *In addition, to become available on October 1 of the fiscal year specified and to remain available until expended for the Spallation Neutron Source project: for fiscal year 2002, $300,000,000; for fiscal year 2003, $232,500,000; for fiscal year 2004, $150,000,000; and for fiscal year 2005, $115,000,000. (Energy and Water Development Appropriations Act, 2000.)*

Program and Financing (in millions of dollars)

Identification code 89–0222–0–1–251		1999 actual	2000 est.	2001 est.
	Obligations by program activity:			
00.01	High energy physics	678	699	715
00.03	Nuclear physics	326	349	370
00.05	Biological and environmental research	396	456	445
00.06	Basic energy sciences	778	774	1,016
00.07	Advanced scientific computing research	151	129	182
00.08	Energy research analyses	1	1	1
00.09	Multiprogram energy labs—facility support	21	33	34
00.11	Program direction	50	133	141
00.12	Small business innovation research	81		
00.13	Small business technology transfer	4		
00.14	Fusion energy sciences	216	245	247
10.00	Total new obligations	2,702	2,819	3,151
	Budgetary resources available for obligation:			
21.40	Unobligated balance available, start of year	12	31	
22.00	New budget authority (gross)	2,721	2,788	3,151
22.10	Resources available from recoveries of prior year obligations	1		
22.22	Unobligated balance transferred from other accounts	1		
23.90	Total budgetary resources available for obligation	2,735	2,819	3,151
23.95	Total new obligations	–2,702	–2,819	–3,151
24.40	Unobligated balance available, end of year	31		
	New budget authority (gross), detail:			
	Discretionary:			
	Appropriation:			
40.00	Appropriation	2,683	2,800	3,151
40.00	Appropriation (Omnibus- Next Generation Internet)	15		
40.76	Reduction pursuant to P.L. 106–113		–12	
42.00	Transferred from other accounts	23		
43.00	Appropriation (total discretionary)	2,721	2,788	3,151
	Change in unpaid obligations:			
72.40	Unpaid obligations, start of year: Obligated balance, start of year	1,047	1,336	1,436
73.10	Total new obligations	2,702	2,819	3,151
73.20	Total outlays (gross)	–2,449	–2,719	–2,993
73.32	Obligated balance transferred from other accounts	37		
73.45	Adjustments in unexpired accounts	–1		
74.40	Unpaid obligations, end of year: Obligated balance, end of year	1,336	1,436	1,594
	Outlays (gross), detail:			
86.90	Outlays from new discretionary authority	1,565	1,617	1,828
86.93	Outlays from discretionary balances	884	1,102	1,165
87.00	Total outlays (gross)	2,449	2,719	2,993
	Net budget authority and outlays:			
89.00	Budget authority	2,721	2,788	3,151
90.00	Outlays	2,449	2,719	2,993

High energy physics.—This research program focuses on gaining insights into the fundamental constituents of matter, the fundamental forces in nature, and the transformations between matter and energy at the most elementary level. The program encompasses both experimental and theoretical particle physics research and related advanced accelerator and detector technology R&D. The primary mode of experimental research involves the study of collisions of energetic particles using large particle accelerators or colliding beam facilities.

Research in 2001 will continue to focus on studies of known fundamental particle constituents, the search for new particle constituents, and the pursuit of a unified description of the four fundamental forces in nature.

In addition to contributing to breakthrough discoveries such as the existence of the top quark, high energy physics research enhances national economic competitiveness. State-of-the-art technology developed for accelerators and detectors contribute to progress in fields such as fast electronics, high-speed computing, superconducting magnet technology, and high-power radio frequency devices. High energy physics research also continues to make major contributions to accelerator technology and provides the expertise necessary for the expansion of such technology into fields such as medical diagnostics, and applied research using synchrotron light sources.

The 2001 high energy physics budget request will support the continued operation of two of the Department's major high energy physics facilities: the Fermilab Tevatron and the Stanford B-Factory. In addition, $70 million is provided for the Department's FY 2001 contribution to continued U.S. participation in the large hadron collider project at the European Center for Nuclear Research.

The high energy physics R&D request provides funding for advanced accelerator and detector R&D that is necessary for next-generation high energy particle accelerators. The request also includes $23.0 million for the neutrinos at the main injector project and $4.2 million for Wilson Hall safety improvements, and $5.2 million for the SLAC research office building.

Superconducting Super Collider.—The Department will continue the orderly termination of the Superconducting Super Collider (SSC) in 2001, as directed by Congress in the 1994 Energy and Water Development Appropriations Act. No additional funding for such activities is requested in 2001.

Nuclear Physics.—The goal of the nuclear physics program is to understand the interactions and structure of atomic nuclei and to investigate fundamental particles and forces of nature as manifested in nuclear matter. In 2001, the program will continue to focus on the role of quarks in the composition and interactions of nuclei, the application of nuclear physics methods to astrophysical problems, the properties of neutrinos, and the mechanisms by which colliding nuclei exchange mass, energy, and angular momentum.

The nuclear physics program supports and provides experimental equipment to qualified scientists and research groups conducting experiments at nuclear physics accelerator facilities. In addition, nuclear physics accelerators generate many of the radioisotopes used for medical diagnosis and treatments; support several cooperative programs in biomedical research and atomic physics; and provide training opportunities for health physicists concerned with radiation effects on humans.

The Thomas Jefferson National Accelerator Facility/Continuous Electron Beam Accelerator Facility experimental program began in FY 1996 and will continue in FY 2001 with the conduct of research in all three experimental halls. Preparations at the MIT/Bates accelerator for a new program of research utilizing the BLAST large acceptance detector will continue. Experimental operations at the Radioactive Ion Beam facility in Oak Ridge National Laboratory will continue in 2001. Operation of ATLAS (ANL), AGS (BNL), and the 88-inch cyclotron (LBNL) will be supported, as will the operation of the university-based accelerator laboratories.

The Relativistic Heavy Ion Collider (RHIC) research program will reach full data production capabilities in FY 2001.

Biological and environmental research.—This program develops the knowledge base necessary to identify, understand, and anticipate the long-term health and environmental consequences of energy use and development and utilizes the Department's unique scientific and technological capabilities to solve major scientific problems in the environment, medicine, and biology. Planned 2001 activities include programs in global climate change; terrestrial, atmospheric and marine environmental processes; molecular, cellular and systemic studies on the biological effects of radiation; structural biology; and medical applications of nuclear technology and the Human Genome Program. Funding for the Human Genome Program is provided to allow for high throughput human DNA sequencing. The Climate Change Technology Initiative continues in FY 2001, focusing on science related to carbon sequestration and sequencing of genomes of microbes that use carbon dioxide to produce methane and hydrogen. In conjunction with the ASCR program a global systems application is continued to accelerate progress in coupled general circulation model development through use of enhanced computer simulation and modeling. An accelerated life sciences program is included for microbial cell ($10 million) and biomedical engineering ($5 million) research. The request also includes $2.5 million to initiate construction of the Laboratory for Comparative and Functional Genomics at Oak Ridge National Laboratory.

Basic Energy Sciences.—The basic energy sciences (BES) program funds basic research in the physical, biological and engineering sciences that support the Department's nuclear and non-nuclear technology programs. The BES program is responsible for operating large national user research facilities, including synchrotron light and neutron sources, and a combustion research facility, as well as smaller user facilities such as materials preparation and electron microscopy centers.

The BES program supports a substantial basic research budget for materials sciences, chemical sciences, energy biosciences, engineering and geosciences. The program supports a number of research areas that are unique within the Federal government; in many basic research areas, such as materials science, funding provided by the BES program represents a large percentage, or even the sole source, of Federal funding.

The 2001 BES budget request includes continued support to maintain utilization of the Department's large state-of-the-art science facilities. The proposed funding will maintain the quality of service and availability of facility resources to users, including university and government scientists, as well as private companies who rely on unique BES facilities for their basic research needs. Research areas that will benefit from the facilities funding include structural biology, materials science, superconductor technology, and medical research and technology development. The request also includes funding to continue an instrumentation enhancement of the Department's neutron source at the Los Alamos Neutron Scattering Center.

In addition, the BES request includes $281 million in FY 2001 to continue construction at Oak Ridge National Laboratory for the Spallation Neutron Source (SNS) to meet the Nation's neutron scattering needs. The SNS will provide significant scientific, technical, and economic benefits that derive from neutron scattering and materials irradiation research. This world class Neutron source will enable the Nation to carry out major research activities in areas such as biology, materials science, superconductivity, pharmaceuticals, electronic materials, and many other technological areas that are critical for future U.S. economic competitiveness and national security. This activity also funds a small portion of the Climate Change Technology Initiative (CCTI). The multi-agency national nanotechnology program is funded in FY 2001 with $36.2 million of new funding. The request also includes $2.5 million for microbial cell research as part of an enhanced life sciences program.

Fusion Energy Sciences Program.—The fusion energy sciences program for FY 2001 is designed to incorporate the results of the Secretary of Energy Advisory Board and recommendations of the Fusion Energy Science Advisory committee. The mission of the program is to advance plasma science, fusion science, and fusion technology. The program emphasizes the underlying basic research in plasma and fusion sciences, with the long-term goal of harnessing fusion as a viable energy source. The program centers on the following goals: understanding the physics of plasmas; identification and exploration of innovative and cost effective development paths to fusion energy; and exploration of the science and technology of energy producing plasmas, as a partner in an international effort.

The budget request provides for support of basic research in plasma science, plasma containment research, and investigation of tokamak alternatives, along with continued operation of DIII–D, Alcator C-Mod, and the National Spherical Torus Experiment. Research on alternate concepts is continued to identify approaches that may improve the economical and environmental attractiveness of fusion. The inertial fusion energy activity is exploring an alternative path for fusion energy that would capitalize on the major R&D effort in inertial confinement fusion which is carried out for stockpile stewardship purposes. Theory and modeling efforts also will be supported.

General and special funds—Continued

SCIENCE—Continued

Energy research analyses.—This activity involves objective assessments to evaluate the quality and impact of DOE research programs and projects.

Multiprogram energy laboratories facilities support.—The goal of the multiprogram energy laboratories facilities support program is to provide funds for rehabilitating, replacing or demolishing deficient common-use utilities, roads, and buildings and to correct Environment, Safety and Health deficiencies at the multiprogram laboratories. The Oak Ridge Landlord activity is now funded in MELFS.

Advanced Scientific Computing Research (ASCR).—This program includes research in mathematical, information, and computational sciences and laboratory technology research activities. The purpose of the ASCR program is to support advanced computational research—applied mathematics, computer science, and networking—to enable the analysis, simulation and prediction of complex physical phenomena. The program also supports the operation of large supercomputer user facilities. The request includes research integrated with other science programs, on application of computer simulation and modeling to science problems.

21st Century Research Fund.—The Science programs are included in the 21st Century Research Fund.

Object Classification (in millions of dollars)

Identification code 89–0222–0–1–251		1999 actual	2000 est.	2001 est.
	Personnel compensation:			
11.1	Full-time permanent	23	77	72
11.3	Other than full-time permanent	1	2	3
11.5	Other personnel compensation	1	2	4
11.9	Total personnel compensation	25	81	79
12.1	Civilian personnel benefits	5	16	24
21.0	Travel and transportation of persons	1	3	3
23.1	Rental payments to GSA		2	2
23.3	Communications, utilities, and miscellaneous charges		2	3
25.1	Advisory and assistance services	9	9	7
25.2	Other services	2	11	12
25.3	Purchases of goods and services from Government accounts	18	18	14
25.4	Operation and maintenance of facilities	796	812	854
25.5	Research and development contracts	886	988	1,046
26.0	Supplies and materials			1
31.0	Equipment	223	205	234
32.0	Land and structures	222	205	387
41.0	Grants, subsidies, and contributions	515	467	485
99.9	Total new obligations	2,702	2,819	3,151

Personnel Summary

Identification code 89–0222–0–1–251		1999 actual	2000 est.	2001 est.
1001	Total compensable workyears: Full-time equivalent employment	311	1,092	1,078

ENERGY SUPPLY

(INCLUDING TRANSFER OF FUNDS)

For Department of Energy expenses including the purchase, construction and acquisition of plant and capital equipment, and other expenses necessary for energy supply, and uranium supply and enrichment activities in carrying out the purposes of the Department of Energy Organization Act (42 U.S.C. 7101 et seq.), including the acquisition or condemnation of any real property or any facility or for plant or facility acquisition, construction, or expansion; and the purchase of not to exceed [one] *17* passenger motor vehicles for replacement only, [$644,937,953, of which $820,953 shall be derived by transfer from the Geothermal Resources Development Fund, and of which $5,000,000 shall be derived by transfer from the United States Enrichment Corporation Fund] *$764,895,000 to remain available until September 30, 2002, of which $12,000,000 shall be derived by transfer from the United States Enrichment Corporation Fund: Provided, That, in addition, royalties received to compensate the Department of Energy for its participation in the First-Of-A-Kind-Engineering program shall be credited to this account to be available until September 30, 2002 for the purposes of Nuclear Energy, Science and Technology activities. (Energy and Water Development Appropriations Act, 2000.)*

Program and Financing (in millions of dollars)

Identification code 89–0224–0–1–271		1999 actual	2000 est.	2001 est.
	Obligations by program activity:			
	Direct program:			
00.01	Solar and renewable energy	335	353	
00.02	Solar and renewable resources			334
00.03	Hydrogen research and development			23
00.04	Electric energy systems			48
00.05	Departmental energy management			5
00.06	Nuclear energy research and development	281	324	308
00.07	Environment, safety and health	48	47	40
00.08	Technical information management program	9	10	9
00.09	Oak Ridge landlord	11		
00.10	Field operations	103		
00.11	Small business innovation	5		
01.00	Total, direct program	792	734	767
09.10	Reimbursable program	899	1,350	1,350
10.00	Total new obligations	1,691	2,084	2,117
	Budgetary resources available for obligation:			
21.40	Unobligated balance available, start of year	138	90	
22.00	New budget authority (gross)	1,639	1,994	2,117
22.10	Resources available from recoveries of prior year obligations	2		
22.21	Unobligated balance transferred to other accounts	−1		
22.22	Unobligated balance transferred from other accounts	3		
23.90	Total budgetary resources available for obligation	1,781	2,084	2,117
23.95	Total new obligations	−1,691	−2,084	−2,117
24.40	Unobligated balance available, end of year	90		
	New budget authority (gross), detail:			
	Discretionary:			
	Appropriation:			
40.00	Appropriation	727	639	753
40.00	Appropriation (Omnibus appropriations)	60		
40.75	Reduction pursuant to P.L. 106–51	−1		
40.76	Reduction pursuant to P.L. 106–113		−1	
42.00	Transferred from other accounts		6	12
43.00	Appropriation (total discretionary)	786	644	765
	Spending authority from offsetting collections:			
68.00	Offsetting collections (cash)	835	1,350	1,352
68.10	From Federal sources: Change in receivables and unpaid, unfilled orders	18		
68.90	Spending authority from offsetting collections (total discretionary)	853	1,350	1,352
70.00	Total new budget authority (gross)	1,639	1,994	2,117
	Change in unpaid obligations:			
	Unpaid obligations, start of year:			
72.40	Obligated balance, start of year	361	248	235
72.95	From Federal sources: Receivables and unpaid, unfilled orders	283	301	301
72.99	Total unpaid obligations, start of year	644	549	536
73.10	Total new obligations	1,691	2,084	2,117
73.20	Total outlays (gross)	−1,773	−2,097	−2,071
73.31	Obligated balance transferred to other accounts	−37		
73.32	Obligated balance transferred from other accounts	26		
73.45	Adjustments in unexpired accounts	−2		
	Unpaid obligations, end of year:			
74.40	Obligated balance, end of year	248	235	279
74.95	From Federal sources: Receivables and unpaid, unfilled orders	301	301	301
74.99	Total unpaid obligations, end of year	549	536	580
	Outlays (gross), detail:			
86.90	Outlays from new discretionary authority	1,189	1,640	1,695
86.93	Outlays from discretionary balances	584	457	376
87.00	Total outlays (gross)	1,773	2,097	2,071

	Offsets:			
	Against gross budget authority and outlays:			
	Offsetting collections (cash) from:			
88.00	Federal sources	−283	−562	−562
88.40	Non-Federal sources	−552	−788	−790
88.90	Total, offsetting collections (cash)	−835	−1,350	−1,352
	Against gross budget authority only:			
88.95	From Federal sources: Change in receivables and unpaid, unfilled orders	−18		
	Net budget authority and outlays:			
89.00	Budget authority	786	644	765
90.00	Outlays	938	747	719

The purpose of energy supply research and development activities is to develop new energy technologies and improve existing energy technologies. Included in this mission are basic and applied research and targeted programs in technology development and market deployment.

This account provides funds for operating expenses, and capital equipment for the advancement of the various energy technologies under examination in the energy supply, research and development mission.

Solar and Renewable Resources.—A strong, balanced program is proposed for FY 2001 that will contribute to strengthening the Nation's energy security, providing a cleaner environment, enhancing global sales of U.S. energy products, and increasing industrial competitiveness and federal technology transfer. The solar and renewable resources program is a major component of the Administration's activities to address global climate change. Program activities range from basic cost-shared research in universities and national laboratories to cost-shared applied research, development, and field validations in full partnership with private sector manufacturers.

The FY 2001 program continues to work in partnership with industry to develop and facilitate the use of renewable energy and power delivery system technologies. Specific goals or activities of the various programs include: (1) in photovoltaics: an industry-driven effort in research, advanced processing and manufacturing, systems engineering and reliability, and market development; (2) in solar buildings: a focus on cooperative industry and utility efforts to effectively use advanced solar technology for water heating; (3) in Concentrating Solar Power: working with industry to develop reliable and efficient dish/engine systems, while reducing the costs of these emerging technologies and existing parabolic trough systems; (4) in wind energy a program focus on developing and testing utility-grade wind turbines in collaboration with utilities and industry and encouraging the use of wind energy as an opportunity to address rural and agricultural economic needs; and (5) in Biomass Power and Biofuels Energy Systems: continued R&D to achieve further reductions in biopower and biofuels production costs, and to develop high-efficiency thermochemical and biochemical conversion technologies. Additionally, a multi-sectoral approach is being pursued to take advantage of the emerging technology synergies between biomass power, biofuels and the manufacture of bio-based products. These developments raise the prospect of profitable "energy crop" farming early in the next century, accompanied by improved rural economic development, increased environmental benefits in both urban and rural areas, and new global market opportunities for U.S. industry; (6) in geothermal energy, begin development of an enhanced geothermal system (EGS) that will allow the broader use of geothermal energy throughout the western United States, and conduct cooperative research with industry to reduce the cost of geothermal wells; and (7) in hydropower, continue development of a "fish-friendly" turbine to address the primary environmental mitigation issues associated with licensing and sustaining hydropower production.

The solar and renewable resource program also includes ongoing support for international solar energy programs such as the U.S. initiative on joint implementation, renewable energy outreach information, and technical assistance and in FY 2001 a significant increase is provided to support adoption in developing countries of technologies that can help address the threat of global climate change.

Electric energy systems.—(Formerly included in solar and renewable energy.) These activities focus on the development of technologies that will enable the efficient and reliable delivery of electric services for consumer use in competitive, restructured electric markets. The high-temperature superconductivity program, with its world-record R&D accomplishments, will provide additional power delivery system efficiency and capability benefits. A key element of the effort is the superconductivity partnership initiative, and industry-DOE collaboration intended to speed the commercialization of superconductivity products.

Hydrogen research and development.—(Formerly included in solar and renewable energy.) In the hydrogen program, R&D efforts are focused on reducing the cost of hydrogen production, increasing the capability of hydrogen storage, and validating the benefits of using hydrogen by integrating advanced technologies.

Departmental energy management.—Funding will also be provided to allow the Department to meet the requirements of Executive Order 13123, "Greening the Government Through Efficient Energy Management." The objective of this program is to enable the Department to demonstrate leadership as a model program for energy management within the Federal Government.

Nuclear fission.—Nuclear fission programs represent much of the federal government's core competency in nuclear technology. This expertise is critical in assuring that, through its unique research and development activities, the United States government can respond to nuclear energy resource, national security, and safety issues. Because of the nation's reliance on these vital technologies, the Department of Energy continues to invest in services, products, and technologies that are beyond the capability of private industry to fund alone.

The FY 2001 budget request continues to support the Nuclear Energy Research Initiative (NERI), an investigator-initiated, peer-reviewed research and development program, which will include an international component in 2001, that addresses key issues affecting the future of nuclear energy, including nuclear waste storage and disposal, nuclear plant economics and operational safety, and potential for weapons proliferation, that currently impede nuclear energy from becoming a viable and acceptable energy option in the United States. Projects proposed by universities, national laboratories, and industry are selected competitively, and partnerships and industry cost-sharing are encouraged. The Administration's proposal continues to support the PCAST recommendation for a cost-shared program, nuclear energy plant optimization (NEPO), with industry to address issues that could impact the continued operation of the nation's 103 nuclear power plants.

Nuclear fission programs also include ongoing support to: (1) build and deliver advanced nuclear power systems to NASA and other federal agencies; (2) provide radioisotopes for medical and other research purposes; (3) support nuclear education; (4) oversee the legacy of the nation's uranium supply and enrichment activities; and (5) ensure that the Department's nuclear facilities are maintained in an environmentally compliant condition.

Management of depleted uranium hexafluoride.—The Department is committed to proper management of its inventory of depleted uranium hexafluoride (DUF_6), including eventual conversion of DUF_6 to a more stable form. The Department views DUF_6 as an asset and will continue to research beneficial uses for depleted uranium products. The FY 2001 budget request supports the award of one or more contracts to ini-

General and special funds—Continued

ENERGY SUPPLY—Continued

(INCLUDING TRANSFER OF FUNDS)—Continued

tiate design of two conversion facilities: one at Paducah, Kentucky and one at Portsmouth, Ohio.

Environment, safety and health.—The Office of Environment, Safety and Health is a corporate resource that fosters Departmental excellence through innovative leadership in the protection of workers, the public, and the environment. This commitment to excellence will be demonstrated by striving for improvement in programs and policies; conducting independent oversight of environment, safety, and health performance; and providing assistance, resources and information sharing.

The 2001 budget request for the Office of Environment, Safety and Health reflects these priorities. It is important to note that the budget request for the Office of Environment, Safety and Health programs is contained in two accounts: this and other defense activities. The funding in this account supports policy, standards and guidance and corporate programs as well as Program Direction.

Technical information management program.—This program provides timely, accurate technical information to DOE's researchers and the public by collecting, preserving, and disseminating scientific and technical information, the principal product resulting from the multi-billion dollar Department of Energy research and development (R&D) program. The TIM program also provides worldwide energy scientific and technical information to the Department of Energy (DOE, the United States (U.S.), industry, academia, and the public through interagency and international scientific and technical information exchange agreements and coordinates technical information-related activities across DOE and its laboratories.

Policy and management.—Provides executive direction, management assistance, and administrative support to all programs within energy supply activities.

21st Century Research Fund.—The solar and renewable resources, hydrogen R&D, electric energy systems, and departmental energy management programs, all formerly included within "solar and renewable energy," are included in the 21st Century Research Fund.

Object Classification (in millions of dollars)

Identification code 89–0224–0–1–271	1999 actual	2000 est.	2001 est.
Direct obligations:			
Personnel compensation:			
11.1 Full-time permanent	92	34	36
11.3 Other than full-time permanent	2	1	1
11.5 Other personnel compensation	2	1	1
11.9 Total personnel compensation	96	36	38
12.1 Civilian personnel benefits	20	7	8
13.0 Benefits for former personnel	12	4	5
21.0 Travel and transportation of persons	4	4	4
23.1 Rental payments to GSA	2	2	2
23.2 Rental payments to others	2	2	2
23.3 Communications, utilities, and miscellaneous charges	303	314	326
24.0 Printing and reproduction	1	1	1
25.1 Advisory and assistance services	44	46	47
25.2 Other services	95	98	104
25.3 Purchases of goods and services from Government accounts	26	27	28
25.4 Operation and maintenance of facilities	31	32	34
25.5 Research and development contracts	22	23	24
26.0 Supplies and materials	2	2	2
31.0 Equipment	7	7	8
32.0 Land and structures	14	14	15
41.0 Grants, subsidies, and contributions	111	115	119
99.0 Subtotal, direct obligations	792	734	767
99.0 Reimbursable obligations	899	1,350	1,350
99.9 Total new obligations	1,691	2,084	2,117

Personnel Summary

Identification code 89–0224–0–1–271	1999 actual	2000 est.	2001 est.
Direct:			
Total compensable workyears:			
Full-time equivalent employment:			
1001 Full-time equivalent employment	107	121	121
1001 Full-time equivalent employment	170	166	171
1001 Full-time equivalent employment	128	122	122
1001 Full-time equivalent employment	844	83	87
1001 Full-time equivalent employment	126		
Reimbursable:			
2001 Total compensable workyears: Full-time equivalent employment	4	15	15

NON-DEFENSE ENVIRONMENTAL MANAGEMENT

For Department of Energy expenses, including the purchase, construction and acquisition of plant and capital equipment and other expenses necessary for non-defense environmental management activities in carrying out the purposes of the Department of Energy Organization Act (42 U.S.C. 7101 et seq.), including the acquisition or condemnation of any real property or any facility or for plant or facility acquisition, construction or expansion, [$333,618,000] *$286,001,000*, to remain available until expended, *of which, not to exceed $10,000,000 shall be available for the Atlas site in Moab, Utah. (Energy and Water Development Appropriations Act, 2000.)*

Program and Financing (in millions of dollars)

Identification code 89–0250–0–1–271	1999 actual	2000 est.	2001 est.
Obligations by program activity:			
00.04 Site closure	105	218	82
00.05 Site/project completion	83	98	65
00.06 Post 2006 completion	246	19	139
10.00 Total new obligations	434	335	286
Budgetary resources available for obligation:			
21.40 Unobligated balance available, start of year	6	3	
22.00 New budget authority (gross)	430	332	286
23.90 Total budgetary resources available for obligation	436	335	286
23.95 Total new obligations	−434	−335	−286
24.40 Unobligated balance available, end of year	3		
New budget authority (gross), detail:			
Discretionary:			
40.00 Appropriation	431	333	286
40.75 Reduction pursuant to P.L. 106–51	−1		
40.76 Reduction pursuant to P.L. 106–113		−1	
43.00 Appropriation (total discretionary)	431	332	286
Change in unpaid obligations:			
72.40 Unpaid obligations, start of year: Obligated balance, start of year	160	139	110
73.10 Total new obligations	434	335	286
73.20 Total outlays (gross)	−447	−364	−305
73.31 Obligated balance transferred to other accounts	−8		
74.40 Unpaid obligations, end of year: Obligated balance, end of year	139	110	91
Outlays (gross), detail:			
86.90 Outlays from new discretionary authority	303	232	200
86.93 Outlays from discretionary balances	144	132	105
87.00 Total outlays (gross)	447	364	305
Net budget authority and outlays:			
89.00 Budget authority	430	332	286
90.00 Outlays	447	364	305

Environmental management.—The Environmental management (EM) program is responsible for addressing the environmental legacy resulting from nuclear energy and energy research activities. The nuclear energy research and development efforts of the Department of Energy and its predecessors focused on peaceful uses of nuclear energy and generated waste, pollution, and contamination that pose unique problems, including unprecedented volumes of contaminated soil and water, radiological hazards from special nuclear material, and a vast number of contaminated structures. Much of this infrastructure, waste, and contamination still exists and is largely maintained, decommissioned, managed, and remediated by the EM program, which is sometimes referred to as the "cleanup program." EM's responsibilities include facilities and sites in 30 states and one territory, and occupy an area equal to that of Rhode Island and Delaware combined—or about 2.1 million acres.

EM activities performed include: environmental restoration, which provides for assessments, characterization, remediation, and decontamination and decommissioning of contaminated DOE facilities and sites; waste management, which provides for the safe, treatment, storage, and disposal of wastes generated by defense activities; and, nuclear material and facility stabilization, which provides for stabilization, safeguarding, interim storage, and stewardship of excess nuclear materials, awaiting ultimate disposition.

EM will continue to improve the efficiency of its programs through a variety of management and contracting strategies with emphasis on the reduction of support costs and implementation of performance-based contracts.

The EM program has established a goal of cleaning up as many of its contaminated sites as possible by 2006, in a manner that is safe and protects the environment. By working towards this goal, EM can reduce the hazards presently facing its workforce and the public, and reduce the financial burden on the taxpayer. The FY 2001 budget request continues to reflect the program's emphasis on site closure and project completion—in other words, finishing the work as quickly as possible.

The FY 2001 budget request will support the following major program areas:

Site closure.—This account provides funding for completing cleanup and closing facilities with no enduring Federal presence on site, except for stewardship activities. This account includes the following sites: Grand Junction, Colorado, Weldon Spring, Missouri, and Battelle Columbus Laboratory and Mound Plant, Ohio. The Department has established a goal of completing cleanup activities budgeted for in this account by 2006.

Site/project completion.—This account provides funding for environmental management projects that will be completed by 2006 at (1) EM sites where overall site cleanup will not be fully accomplished by 2006; and (2) DOE sites where all EM projects will be completed by 2006 (except for long-term stewardship activities), but where there will be a continuing federal workforce at the site to carry out enduring non-EM missions, such as nuclear weapons support or scientific research, and the necessary waste management to handle newly generated wastes from these missions. This account includes projects and sites under the following operations offices: Albuquerque, Chicago, Idaho, Oakland, and Richland.

Post 2006 completion.—This account funds projects that are expected to require work beyond FY 2006. This includes projects at the following operations offices and sites: Albuquerque, Oak Ridge, West Valley, New York, as well as multi-site and Headquarters activities.

Object Classification (in millions of dollars)

Identification code 89–0250–0–1–271	1999 actual	2000 est.	2001 est.
25.1 Advisory and assistance services	60	46	39
25.2 Other services	71	54	46
25.4 Operation and maintenance of facilities	279	212	181
25.5 Research and development contracts	24	18	16
32.0 Land and structures	−6		
41.0 Grants, subsidies, and contributions	6	5	4
99.9 Total new obligations	434	335	286

Uranium Supply and Enrichment Activities

Program and Financing (in millions of dollars)

Identification code 89–0226–0–1–271	1999 actual	2000 est.	2001 est.
Budgetary resources available for obligation:			
21.40 Unobligated balance available, start of year	3		
22.21 Unobligated balance transferred to other accounts	−3		
23.90 Total budgetary resources available for obligation			
Change in unpaid obligations:			
72.40 Unpaid obligations, start of year: Obligated balance, start of year	18		
73.31 Obligated balance transferred to other accounts	−18		
Net budget authority and outlays:			
89.00 Budget authority			
90.00 Outlays			

Uranium programs.—Beginning in fiscal year 1998, these programs were funded in the Energy supply account.

Fossil Energy Research and Development

(INCLUDING TRANSFER OF FUNDS)

For necessary expenses in carrying out fossil energy research and development activities, under the authority of the Department of Energy Organization Act (Public Law 95–91), including the acquisition of interest, including defeasible and equitable interests in any real property or any facility or for plant or facility acquisition or expansion, and for conducting inquiries, technological investigations and research concerning the extraction, processing, use, and disposal of mineral substances without objectionable social and environmental costs (30 U.S.C. 3, 1602, and 1603), performed under the minerals and materials science programs at the Albany Research Center in Oregon, **[**$419,025,000**]** *$384,570,000*, to remain available until expended, of which **[**$24,000,000 shall be derived by transfer from unobligated balances in the Biomass Energy Development account**]** *$9,000,000 shall be derived from available prior year balances*: *Provided*, That no part of the sum herein made available shall be used for the field testing of nuclear explosives in the recovery of oil and gas. *(Department of the Interior and Related Agencies Appropriations Act, 2000, as enacted by section 1000(a)(3) of the Consolidated Appropriations Act, 2000 (P.L. 106–113).)*

Program and Financing (in millions of dollars)

Identification code 89–0213–0–1–271	1999 actual	2000 est.	2001 est.
Obligations by program activity:			
00.01 Coal and power systems	205	222	194
00.02 Oil and gas research and development	71	93	91
00.03 Program direction and management support	71	75	75
00.05 Environmental restoration	12	10	9
00.06 Cooperative research and development ventures	7	7	6
00.07 Fuels conversion (natural gas and electricity)	2	2	2
00.08 Plant and capital equipment	3	3	2
00.09 Advanced metallurgical process	5	5	5
00.10 Black liquor gasification		14	
10.00 Total new obligations	376	431	384
Budgetary resources available for obligation:			
21.40 Unobligated balance available, start of year	23	23	9
22.00 New budget authority (gross)	376	417	376
23.90 Total budgetary resources available for obligation	399	440	385
23.95 Total new obligations	−376	−431	−384
24.40 Unobligated balance available, end of year	23	9	1
New budget authority (gross), detail:			
Discretionary:			
40.00 Appropriation	384	395	376
40.75 Reduction pursuant to P.L. 106–51	−1		
40.76 Reduction pursuant to P.L. 106–113		−2	
41.00 Transferred to other accounts	−7		
42.00 Transferred from other accounts		24	
43.00 Appropriation (total discretionary)	376	417	376

General and special funds—Continued

FOSSIL ENERGY RESEARCH AND DEVELOPMENT—Continued

(INCLUDING TRANSFER OF FUNDS)—Continued

Program and Financing (in millions of dollars)—Continued

Identification code 89–0213–0–1–271	1999 actual	2000 est.	2001 est.
Change in unpaid obligations:			
72.40 Unpaid obligations, start of year: Obligated balance, start of year	296	318	360
73.10 Total new obligations	376	431	384
73.20 Total outlays (gross)	−353	−389	−392
74.40 Unpaid obligations, end of year: Obligated balance, end of year	318	360	352
Outlays (gross), detail:			
86.90 Outlays from new discretionary authority	150	167	150
86.93 Outlays from discretionary balances	203	222	242
87.00 Total outlays (gross)	353	389	392
Net budget authority and outlays:			
89.00 Budget authority	376	417	376
90.00 Outlays	353	389	392

The Fossil Energy Research and Development program supports high-priority, high risk and cross-cutting research that will improve the Nation's ability to use coal, oil and natural gas cleanly and efficiently, and enhance the economic recovery of our oil and gas reserves. The program funds research and development that strengthens the technology base industry uses in developing new products and processes to support these national goals. Fossil Energy R&D supports activities ranging from early concept research in universities and national laboratories to applied R&D and proof-of-concept projects in private sector firms.

Coal and Power R&D.—The Coal and Power R&D program will focus on addressing the energy and environmental demands of the post-2000 domestic market, and includes five elements: (1) Central systems which includes technologies for advanced coal-fueled and gas-fired power systems (including advanced turbines) and innovations for existing plants; (2) Distributed systems including fuel cell technology; (3) Sequestration R&D which focuses on greenhouse gas capture and reduction; (4) Fuels R&D for the production of ultra-clean transportation fuels, chemicals and premium carbon products; and (5) Advanced research which, through early concept research, bridges fundamental research and engineering development. The program goals of these elements are integrated through the Vision 21 concept, aimed at doubling the existing power plant efficiency with the flexibility to produce high value products from coal and other fuels while achieving near-zero pollution and reducing energy costs.

Oil and gas.—The oil program encompasses advanced exploration and production technology, industry cost-shared demonstrations of improved and advanced oil recovery methods, petroleum-derived ultra clean fuels, and environmental research activities.

The natural gas program emphasizes advanced gas exploration and production technology, gas hydrates, infrastructure, and emerging processing technology (upgrading and gas-to-liquids). As in all other programs, cost-sharing by industry is a key feature. The national laboratory partnership focuses on the transfer of National Laboratory-developed technology to the oil and gas industry.

Program direction and management support.—The program provides the funding for all headquarters and indirect field personnel and overhead expenses in Fossil Energy. In addition, it provides support for day-to-day project management functions.

Environmental restoration.—The Department of Energy is managing the environmental cleanup of former and present Fossil Energy project sites. Activities include environmental protection, on-site cleanup, and cleanup at several former off-site research and development locations in Wyoming and Connecticut and environmental efforts at the National Energy Technology Laboratory (NETL) Morgantown and Pittsburgh sites, and the Albany Research Center (ARC).

Fuels conversion.—This program will continue regulatory reviews and oversight of the transmission of natural gas and electricity across the U.S. borders.

Object Classification (in millions of dollars)

Identification code 89–0213–0–1–271	1999 actual	2000 est.	2001 est.
Personnel compensation:			
11.1 Full-time permanent	40	42	41
11.3 Other than full-time permanent	1	1	1
11.5 Other personnel compensation	1	1	1
11.9 Total personnel compensation	42	44	43
12.1 Civilian personnel benefits	9	10	9
21.0 Travel and transportation of persons	3	4	3
23.3 Communications, utilities, and miscellaneous charges	3	3	3
25.1 Advisory and assistance services	44	45	44
25.2 Other services	57	58	57
25.3 Purchases of goods and services from Government accounts	8	8	8
25.4 Operation and maintenance of facilities	38	39	38
25.5 Research and development contracts	151	195	156
26.0 Supplies and materials	7	7	7
31.0 Equipment		2	2
32.0 Land and structures	3	3	3
41.0 Grants, subsidies, and contributions	11	13	11
99.9 Total new obligations	376	431	384

Personnel Summary

Identification code 89–0213–0–1–271	1999 actual	2000 est.	2001 est.
1001 Total compensable workyears: Full-time equivalent employment	641	685	705

NAVAL PETROLEUM AND OIL SHALE RESERVES

The requirements of 10 U.S.C. 7430(b)(2)(B) shall not apply to fiscal year [2000] *2001 and any fiscal year thereafter: Provided*, That, notwithstanding any other provision of law, unobligated funds remaining from prior years shall be available for all naval petroleum and oil shale reserve activities. *(Department of the Interior and Related Agencies Appropriations Act, 2000, as enacted by section 1000(a)(3) of the Consolidated Appropriations Act, 2000 (P.L. 106–113).)*

Program and Financing (in millions of dollars)

Identification code 89–0219–0–1–271	1999 actual	2000 est.	2001 est.
Obligations by program activity:			
10.00 Total new obligations	4	21	21
Budgetary resources available for obligation:			
21.40 Unobligated balance available, start of year	39	52	31
22.00 New budget authority (gross)	16		
22.10 Resources available from recoveries of prior year obligations	1		
23.90 Total budgetary resources available for obligation	56	52	31
23.95 Total new obligations	−4	−21	−21
24.40 Unobligated balance available, end of year	52	31	10
New budget authority (gross), detail:			
Discretionary:			
40.00 Appropriation	14		
68.00 Spending authority from offsetting collections: Offsetting collections (cash)	2		
70.00 Total new budget authority (gross)	16		
Change in unpaid obligations:			
72.40 Unpaid obligations, start of year: Obligated balance, start of year	59	32	32

73.10	Total new obligations	4	21	21
73.20	Total outlays (gross)	−30	−21	−21
73.45	Adjustments in unexpired accounts	−1		
74.40	Unpaid obligations, end of year: Obligated balance, end of year	32	32	32
	Outlays (gross), detail:			
86.90	Outlays from new discretionary authority	10		
86.93	Outlays from discretionary balances	20	21	21
87.00	Total outlays (gross)	30	21	21
	Offsets:			
	Against gross budget authority and outlays:			
88.40	Offsetting collections (cash) from: Non-Federal sources	−2		
	Net budget authority and outlays:			
89.00	Budget authority	14		
90.00	Outlays	30	21	21

The mission of the Naval petroleum and oil shale reserves is to manage, operate, maintain and produce the remaining Reserves to achieve the greatest value and benefit to the Government. To that end, the program has historically produced oil and related hydrocarbons from the Naval petroleum reserves at the maximum efficient rates of production pursuant to the Naval Petroleum Reserves Production Act of 1976. Petroleum products were most frequently sold competitively in the open market. NPOSR activities generated a net income of $13.8 billion for the U.S. Treasury from FY 1976 through FY 1998. In addition, another $3.65 billion in gross receipts was generated from the divestment of NPR–1 (or Elk Hills) during FY 1998, when the field was sold to Occidental Petroleum Corporation as mandated by the National Defense Authorization Act for FY 1996. A number of post-sale activities remain. The most significant is the settlement of ownership equity shares with the former unit partner in the NPR–1 field, Chevron USA, Inc. Geologic, petroleum and reservoir engineering services are required to prepare and support the Government's equity position before an independent petroleum engineer and the Assistant Secretary for Fossil Energy, who is to impartially determine final equity shares. Each percentage point change in equity is worth millions of dollars to the Government. Other important close-out activities include environmental assessment and remediation work.

The primary objective of NPR–3 is to operate and produce the Reserve to maximize profitability while preparing for the orderly abandonment of the oil field when it is no longer profitable. FY 2001 activities consist of continued conventional oil field management and operating activities. Management initiatives which have contributed to cost savings in prior years will be continued, and new initiatives evaluated. Although no future development activities are planned, NPR–3 should continue operating economically through at least FY 2005 depending upon the price of oil and stabilization of production levels. Emphasis is on continuation of routine maintenance activities, plugging and abandonment of uneconomic wells, and environmental remediation of the site in anticipation of its eventual divestment. Divestment may consist of transfer to the private sector or abandonment, consistent with congressional authorization.

Under the Rocky Mountain Oilfield Testing Center (RMOTC) program, the naval petroleum reserves offers Naval Petroleum Reserve No. 3 (Teapot Dome) to the oil industry for use as a working laboratory on a cost-sharing basis. Teapot Dome is a unique opportunity for the industry to test and evaluate innovation production techniques in an impartial setting. The naval petroleum reserve program anticipates privatizing the RMOTC program during 2001.

Object Classification (in millions of dollars)

Identification code 89–0219–0–1–271		1999 actual	2000 est.	2001 est.
11.1	Personnel compensation: Full-time permanent	4	3	3
12.1	Civilian personnel benefits	1	1	1
25.1	Advisory and assistance services	4	3	4
25.2	Other services	−5	7	5
25.4	Operation and maintenance of facilities	−1	7	8
99.0	Subtotal, direct obligations	3	21	21
99.5	Below reporting threshold	1		
99.9	Total new obligations	4	21	21

Personnel Summary

Identification code 89–0219–0–1–271		1999 actual	2000 est.	2001 est.
1001	Total compensable workyears: Full-time equivalent employment	48	54	39

ENERGY CONSERVATION

(INCLUDING TRANSFER OF FUNDS)

For necessary expenses in carrying out energy conservation activities, [$745,242,000] *$850,500,000*, to remain available until expended, of which [$25,000,000] *$2,000,000* shall be derived by transfer from unobligated balances in the Biomass Energy Development account: *Provided*, That [$168,500,000] *$191,000,000* shall be for use in energy conservation *grant* programs [as defined in section 3008(3) of Public Law 99–509 (15 U.S.C. 4507)]: *Provided further*, That [notwithstanding section 3003(d)(2) of Public Law 99–509,] such sums shall be allocated [to the eligible programs] as follows: [$135,000,000] *$154,000,000* for weatherization assistance grants and [$33,500,000] *$37,000,000* for State energy [conservation] *program* grants: *Provided further*, That[, notwithstanding any other provision of law, in fiscal year 2001 and thereafter sums appropriated for weatherization assistance grants shall be contingent on a cost share of 25 percent by each participating State or other qualified participant] *the last proviso under this heading in the Department of the Interior and Related Agencies Appropriations Act, 2000, is repealed. (Department of the Interior and Related Agencies Appropriations Act, 2000, as enacted by section 1000(a)(3) of the Consolidated Appropriations Act, 2000 (P.L. 106–113).)*

Program and Financing (in millions of dollars)

Identification code 89–0215–0–1–272		1999 actual	2000 est.	2001 est.
	Obligations by program activity:			
00.01	Building technology, State and community programs—non-grant	93	120	149
00.02	Building technology, State and community programs – grants	165	174	191
00.03	Federal energy management program	24	25	30
00.04	Industrial sector	161	167	184
00.05	Transportation sector	197	237	251
00.06	Policy and management	38	44	46
10.00	Total new obligations	678	767	851
	Budgetary resources available for obligation:			
21.40	Unobligated balance available, start of year	15	22	
22.00	New budget authority (gross)	683	745	850
22.10	Resources available from recoveries of prior year obligations	1		
23.90	Total budgetary resources available for obligation	699	767	850
23.95	Total new obligations	−678	−767	−851
24.40	Unobligated balance available, end of year	22		
	New budget authority (gross), detail:			
	Discretionary:			
40.00	Appropriation	628	720	848
40.75	Reduction pursuant to P.L. 106–51	−1		
41.00	Transferred to other accounts	−8		
42.00	Transferred from other accounts		25	2
43.00	Appropriation (total discretionary)	619	745	850
68.00	Spending authority from offsetting collections: Offsetting collections (cash)	64		

General and special funds—Continued

ENERGY CONSERVATION—Continued

(INCLUDING TRANSFER OF FUNDS)—Continued

Program and Financing (in millions of dollars)—Continued

Identification code 89–0215–0–1–272		1999 actual	2000 est.	2001 est.
70.00	Total new budget authority (gross)	683	745	850
	Change in unpaid obligations:			
72.40	Unpaid obligations, start of year: Obligated balance, start of year	522	548	626
73.10	Total new obligations	678	767	851
73.20	Total outlays (gross)	−650	−690	−767
73.45	Adjustments in unexpired accounts	−1		
74.40	Unpaid obligations, end of year: Obligated balance, end of year	548	626	710
	Outlays (gross), detail:			
86.90	Outlays from new discretionary authority	205	224	255
86.93	Outlays from discretionary balances	445	466	512
87.00	Total outlays (gross)	650	690	767
	Offsets:			
	Against gross budget authority and outlays:			
88.40	Offsetting collections (cash) from: Non-Federal sources	−64		
	Net budget authority and outlays:			
89.00	Budget authority	619	745	850
90.00	Outlays	586	690	767

The Administration's energy efficiency programs produce substantial benefits for the Nation—both now and in the future—in terms of economic growth, increased national security and a cleaner environment through the research and development of energy efficiency and pollution prevention technologies. These programs carry out the Department's responsibility under the bipartisan Energy Policy Act of 1992 and other major pieces of authorizing legislation.

The dollar benefits of our carefully constructed programs—to industries, homeowners, and commercial firms—far exceed program costs. Furthermore, the technologies developed in these programs create jobs and global market opportunities for U.S. firms. These programs are a major component of the Administration's climate change response, and when the benefits to energy security and the environment are included, it is clear that these programs represent important investments in a clean, productive future.

In total, the Department's energy efficiency programs are projected to save consumers and businesses over $30 billion per year by the year 2010. Our transportation technologies research is designed to reduce oil consumption, thus reducing pollution and vulnerability to oil price shocks.

The activities and programs contained in the 2001 budget request represent a balanced portfolio of research and development, applied research and demonstration, and market introduction. Virtually all of the research and development programs are conducted jointly with industrial partners who share significantly in research costs, often paying 20 percent or more. Similarly, demonstration and deployment programs are specifically designed to leverage the existing programs and the efforts of utilities and existing state and local government programs in energy efficiency and pollution prevention.

Building technology, State, and community sector.—In partnership with industry, the program will continue to develop, promote, and integrate energy technologies and practices to make buildings more efficient and affordable and communities more livable. The program accelerates the introduction of highly efficient buildings technologies and practices through research and development; increases the minimum efficiency of buildings and equipment through building codes, appliance standards, and guidelines; and encourages the use of energy-efficient and renewable energy technologies and practices through state grant programs and community partnerships. The buildings research and standards program integrates research and development activities to improve the energy efficiency of appliances, building equipment, and the building envelope by developing test procedures and building efficiency codes an standards.

The building technology assistance program complements the Research and Standards program by moving advanced technologies into the marketplace, producing near-term energy savings with associated economic and environmental benefits. The building technology assistance program, is designed to promote the adoption of energy efficient and renewable energy technologies among States, municipalities, institutions, and by private citizens through community outreach and energy star programs. These voluntary partnerships help lower the barriers to adoption of cost-effective technologies advanced through collaborations with manufacturers, utilities, state and local government and community organizations. Conservation grants programs—the weatherization assistance program and the State energy program—assist States and localities in promoting energy efficiency. The FY 2001 budget also includes funds to promote adoption of efficient buildings and appliances in developing countries, and to adapt American design tools for developing-country markets.

Federal energy management program.—The Federal energy management program (FEMP) will continue to reduce the cost of government by advancing energy efficiency and water conservation, the use of solar and other renewable energy sources, and by managing utility costs. FEMP's major emphasis will be on creating and sustaining a core level of federal energy management as an institutionalized activity at all federal agencies and leveraging both Federal and private resources to provide technical and financial assistance to other Federal agencies, which take actions and make investments that increase energy efficiency and renewable energy utilization, and reduce water consumption in their buildings, facilities, and operations.

Industrial sector.—The program focuses on funding cost-shared research in critical technology areas identified by industry. Through its "Industries of the Future" initiative, the Office of Industrial Technologies (OIT) encourages the most energy-intensive industries to develop a strategic vision and a "technology roadmap" to help achieve that vision. By identifying and prioritizing their technology needs, the industries help OIT target its R&D resources toward where they can do the most good. The energy-intensive and environmentally sensitive industries targeted by OIT include chemicals, petroleum refining, forest products, steel, aluminum, metal casting, agriculture, mining, and glass. The focus is on high risk but promising technologies that decrease these industries' use of raw materials and depletable energy resources and reduce generation of wastes and pollutants. A significant budget increase is provided in FY 2001 for the agriculture and forest products industries as part of a multi-agency initiative on bioproducts and biofuels. The Industries of the Future (Crosscutting) develops technologies that are useful to multiple industries simultaneously, such as power generation equipment, combustion equipment, and sensors and controls. It delivers information and tools to help plant managers make informed decisions on technology choices today that result in energy, waste and dollar savings. In addition, these programs develop advanced materials which address a multitude of wear and corrosion problems, support new ideas from inventors, and fund grants for demonstration of near-term viable technologies. In FY 2001, a small amount of funding is also included to promote the adoption of energy efficient practices by industries in developing countries.

Transportation sector.—The program continues development and commercialization of technologies which can radically alter current projections of U.S. and world demand for energy, particularly oil. The program represents a major portion of the Partnership for the Next Generation of Vehicles with its significant improvements in fuel economy and environmental emissions including criteria pollutants and carbon dioxide. Program priorities reflect work on technologies which are most critical to achieve a tripling of light duty vehicle fuel economy, including hybrid vehicles, fuel cells, compression ignition direct injection diesel engines, and advanced materials technologies that improve engine efficiency and reduce weight. In addition, the program will enhance the development of cleaner and alternative fuels, and pursue research of advanced batteries that enable the use of electricity as an alternative fuel, and technologies for enabling fuel flexibility and fuel economy in heavy trucks. These activities include demonstrating advanced alternative fuel vehicles that provide improved range and reduced emissions, with performance equivalent to conventional vehicles; accelerating the use of alternative fuels and vehicles through implementation of Energy Policy Act programs; and continuing support for the U.S. Advanced Battery Consortium and demonstrating continued progress in improving range and performance for electric and hybrid vehicles.

Policy and management.—This activity provides program management for all of the Energy Conservation programs, and supports management in the development of policy and crosscutting activities such as program evaluations for energy conservation programs to ensure program effectiveness.

21st Century Research Fund.—The Energy Conservation R&D programs (i.e. all except Conservation Grants) are included in the 21st Century Research Fund.

Object Classification (in millions of dollars)

Identification code 89–0215–0–1–272		1999 actual	2000 est.	2001 est.
	Personnel compensation:			
11.1	Full-time permanent	28	31	32
11.3	Other than full-time permanent	2	2	2
11.5	Other personnel compensation	1	1	1
11.9	Total personnel compensation	31	34	35
12.1	Civilian personnel benefits	6	7	7
13.0	Benefits for former personnel		1	1
21.0	Travel and transportation of persons	3	3	3
22.0	Transportation of things		1	1
23.1	Rental payments to GSA	2	2	2
23.3	Communications, utilities, and miscellaneous charges	1	2	2
25.1	Advisory and assistance services	44	49	54
25.2	Other services	14	17	19
25.3	Purchases of goods and services from Government accounts	6	7	8
25.4	Operation and maintenance of facilities	233	265	292
25.5	Research and development contracts	51	60	66
26.0	Supplies and materials	1	2	2
31.0	Equipment	5	6	7
41.0	Grants, subsidies, and contributions	281	311	352
99.9	Total new obligations	678	767	851

Personnel Summary

Identification code 89–0215–0–1–272		1999 actual	2000 est.	2001 est.
1001	Total compensable workyears: Full-time equivalent employment	415	470	470

Strategic Petroleum Reserve

For necessary expenses for Strategic Petroleum Reserve facility development and operations and program management activities pursuant to the Energy Policy and Conservation Act of 1975, as amended (42 U.S.C. 6201 et seq.), **[**$159,000,000**]** *$158,000,000*, to remain available until expended**[**: *Provided*, That the Secretary of Energy hereafter may transfer to the SPR Petroleum Account such funds as may be necessary to carry out drawdown and sale operations of the Strategic Petroleum Reserve initiated under section 161 of the Energy Policy and Conservation Act (42 U.S.C. 6241) from any funds available to the Department of Energy under this or any other Act: *Provided further*, That all funds transferred pursuant to this authority must be replenished as promptly as possible from oil sale receipts pursuant to the drawdown and sale**]**. *(Department of the Interior and Related Agencies Appropriations Act, 2000, as enacted by section 1000(a)(3) of the Consolidated Appropriations Act, 2000 (P.L. 106–113).)*

Program and Financing (in millions of dollars)

Identification code 89–0218–0–1–274		1999 actual	2000 est.	2001 est.
	Obligations by program activity:			
00.01	Storage facilities operations	166	157	145
00.02	Management	14	18	15
10.00	Total new obligations	180	175	160
	Budgetary resources available for obligation:			
21.40	Unobligated balance available, start of year	37	19	2
22.00	New budget authority (gross)	160	158	158
22.10	Resources available from recoveries of prior year obligations	2		
23.90	Total budgetary resources available for obligation	199	177	160
23.95	Total new obligations	−180	−175	−160
24.40	Unobligated balance available, end of year	19	2	
	New budget authority (gross), detail:			
	Discretionary:			
40.00	Appropriation	160	159	158
40.76	Reduction pursuant to P.L. 106–113		−1	
43.00	Appropriation (total discretionary)	160	158	158
	Change in unpaid obligations:			
72.40	Unpaid obligations, start of year: Obligated balance, start of year	131	84	95
73.10	Total new obligations	180	175	160
73.20	Total outlays (gross)	−225	−164	−158
73.45	Adjustments in unexpired accounts	−2		
74.40	Unpaid obligations, end of year: Obligated balance, end of year	84	95	97
	Outlays (gross), detail:			
86.90	Outlays from new discretionary authority	88	87	87
86.93	Outlays from discretionary balances	137	77	71
87.00	Total outlays (gross)	225	164	158
	Net budget authority and outlays:			
89.00	Budget authority	160	158	158
90.00	Outlays	225	164	158

The object of this program is to reduce the vulnerability of the United States to energy supply disruptions by maintaining a crude oil stockpile capable of rapid deployment at the direction of the President. This program enables the President to meet the Nation's membership commitments within the International Energy Agency's coordinated energy emergency response plans and programs to deter the use of energy supply disruptions and to take effective, co-ordinated action should such an energy supply disruption occur.

The account provides for petroleum reserve storage facility construction, ongoing operations and maintenance activities, planning studies, and program administration.

The key measure of program performance is expressed as capability to comply with Level 1 Performance Criteria. These criteria are specific engineered performance and reliability standards applied to critical inventory storage, drawdown, and distribution systems required for drawing down and distributing crude oil inventory.

Object Classification (in millions of dollars)

Identification code 89–0218–0–1–274		1999 actual	2000 est.	2001 est.
11.1	Personnel compensation: Full-time permanent	8	9	9
12.1	Civilian personnel benefits	2	2	2
21.0	Travel and transportation of persons	1	1	1

General and special funds—Continued

STRATEGIC PETROLEUM RESERVE—Continued

Object Classification (in millions of dollars)—Continued

Identification code 89–0218–0–1–274	1999 actual	2000 est.	2001 est.
23.2 Rental payments to others	2	2	2
23.3 Communications, utilities, and miscellaneous charges	1	1	1
25.1 Advisory and assistance services	2	2	2
25.2 Other services	15	16	17
25.4 Operation and maintenance of facilities	149	142	126
99.9 Total new obligations	180	175	160

Personnel Summary

Identification code 89–0218–0–1–274	1999 actual	2000 est.	2001 est.
1001 Total compensable workyears: Full-time equivalent employment	127	128	128

SPR PETROLEUM ACCOUNT

From funds appropriated in prior years under this head, $7,000,000 is hereby rescinded.

Program and Financing (in millions of dollars)

Identification code 89–0233–0–1–274	1999 actual	2000 est.	2001 est.
Budgetary resources available for obligation:			
21.40 Unobligated balance available, start of year	33	33	33
22.00 New budget authority (gross)			−7
23.90 Total budgetary resources available for obligation	33	33	26
24.40 Unobligated balance available, end of year	33	33	26
New budget authority (gross), detail:			
Discretionary:			
40.36 Unobligated balance rescinded			−7
Change in unpaid obligations:			
72.40 Unpaid obligations, start of year: Obligated balance, start of year	3	3	3
74.40 Unpaid obligations, end of year: Obligated balance, end of year	3	3	3
Net budget authority and outlays:			
89.00 Budget authority			−7
90.00 Outlays			

Summary of Budget Authority and Outlays

(in millions of dollars)

	1999 actual	2000 est.	2001 est.
Enacted/requested:			
Budget Authority			−7
Outlays			
Rescission proposal:			
Budget Authority		−12	
Outlays			
Total:			
Budget Authority		−12	−7
Outlays			

This account provides for the acquisition, transportation, and injection of petroleum into the Strategic Petroleum Reserve and for its drawdown and distribution. The budget proposes no additional appropriations in FY 2001 for SPR oil purchases. The small remaining balance will support drawdown/distribution readiness, miscellaneous costs associated with the oil delivered from Department of Energy/Department of Interior royalty-in-kind agreement during FY 1999 and FY 2000, and the incremental costs of drawdown in the event of an energy emergency. The budget proposes rescissions of $12 million in FY 2000 and $7 million in FY 2001 from prior year balances which are no longer needed.

ENERGY INFORMATION ADMINISTRATION

For necessary expenses in carrying out the activities of the Energy Information Administration, [$72,644,000] *$75,000,000*, to remain available until expended. *(Department of the Interior and Related Agencies Appropriations Act, 2000, as enacted by section 1000(a)(3) of the Consolidated Appropriations Act, 2000 (P.L. 106–113).)*

Program and Financing (in millions of dollars)

Identification code 89–0216–0–1–276	1999 actual	2000 est.	2001 est.
Obligations by program activity:			
10.00 Total new obligations	73	74	75
Budgetary resources available for obligation:			
21.40 Unobligated balance available, start of year	5	2	
22.00 New budget authority (gross)	70	72	75
23.90 Total budgetary resources available for obligation	75	74	75
23.95 Total new obligations	−73	−74	−75
24.40 Unobligated balance available, end of year	2		
New budget authority (gross), detail:			
Discretionary:			
40.00 Appropriation	70	72	75
Change in unpaid obligations:			
72.40 Unpaid obligations, start of year: Obligated balance, start of year	19	25	28
73.10 Total new obligations	73	74	75
73.20 Total outlays (gross)	−67	−71	−74
74.40 Unpaid obligations, end of year: Obligated balance, end of year	25	28	29
Outlays (gross), detail:			
86.90 Outlays from new discretionary authority	44	47	49
86.93 Outlays from discretionary balances	23	24	25
87.00 Total outlays (gross)	67	71	74
Net budget authority and outlays:			
89.00 Budget authority	70	72	75
90.00 Outlays	67	71	74

This program supports energy information activities which are designed to provide timely, accurate and relevant energy information for use by the Administration, the Congress, and the general public. The activities funded in this program include the design, development and maintenance of information systems on petroleum, natural gas, coal, nuclear, electricity, alternate fuel sources, and energy consumption. This includes collecting data and ensuring its accuracy; preparing forecasts of alternative energy futures; and preparing reports on energy sources, end-uses, prices, supply and demand, and associated environmental, economic, international, and financial matters. In addition, the National Energy Information Center disseminates statistical and analytical publications, reports, and data files in hard-copy and electronic formats, and responds to public inquiries. Finally, this activity provides survey and statistical design standards, documentation standards, and energy data public-use forms clearance and burden control services.

Funding for the climate change technology initiative is continued.

Object Classification (in millions of dollars)

Identification code 89–0216–0–1–276	1999 actual	2000 est.	2001 est.
Personnel compensation:			
11.1 Full-time permanent	26	27	28
11.3 Other than full-time permanent	1	1	1
11.5 Other personnel compensation	1	1	1
11.9 Total personnel compensation	28	29	30
12.1 Civilian personnel benefits	5	5	5
25.2 Other services	26	21	22
25.3 Purchases of goods and services from Government accounts	7	12	11
26.0 Supplies and materials	7	7	7

99.9 Total new obligations	73	74	75

Personnel Summary

Identification code 89–0216–0–1–276	1999 actual	2000 est.	2001 est.
1001 Total compensable workyears: Full-time equivalent employment	373	375	375

ECONOMIC REGULATION

For necessary expenses in carrying out the activities of the Office of Hearings and Appeals, $2,000,000, to remain available until expended. *(Department of the Interior and Related Agencies Appropriations Act, 2000, as enacted by section 1000(a)(3) of the Consolidated Appropriations Act, 2000 (P.L. 106–113).)*

Program and Financing (in millions of dollars)

Identification code 89–0217–0–1–276	1999 actual	2000 est.	2001 est.
Obligations by program activity:			
10.00 Total new obligations	2	2	2
Budgetary resources available for obligation:			
22.00 New budget authority (gross)	2	2	2
23.95 Total new obligations	−2	−2	−2
New budget authority (gross), detail:			
Discretionary:			
40.00 Appropriation	2	2	2
Change in unpaid obligations:			
73.10 Total new obligations	2	2	2
73.20 Total outlays (gross)	−2	−2	−2
Outlays (gross), detail:			
86.90 Outlays from new discretionary authority	2	2	2
Net budget authority and outlays:			
89.00 Budget authority	2	2	2
90.00 Outlays	2	2	2

Compliance.—This program, administered by the Office of General Counsel, is responsible for resolving all remaining enforcement actions to ensure that oil companies complied with petroleum regulations in effect prior to decontrol of oil in January 1981.

Hearings and appeals.—The Office of Hearings and Appeals issues all final orders of an adjudicatory nature other than those over which the Federal Energy Regulatory Commission or the Board of Contract Appeals have jurisdiction. It decides appeals of petroleum enforcement actions and administers refund proceedings involving funds obtained as a result of petroleum enforcement actions. This funding request is limited to expenses related to petroleum overcharge cases.

Object Classification (in millions of dollars)

Identification code 89–0217–0–1–276	1999 actual	2000 est.	2001 est.
11.1 Personnel compensation: Full-time permanent	1	1	1
25.3 Purchases of goods and services from Government accounts	1	1	1
99.9 Total new obligations	2	2	2

Personnel Summary

Identification code 89–0217–0–1–276	1999 actual	2000 est.	2001 est.
1001 Total compensable workyears: Full-time equivalent employment	26	16	14

FEDERAL ENERGY REGULATORY COMMISSION

SALARIES AND EXPENSES

For necessary expenses of the Federal Energy Regulatory Commission to carry out the provisions of the Department of Energy Organization Act (42 U.S.C. 7101 et seq.), including services as authorized by 5 U.S.C. 3109, the hire of passenger motor vehicles, and official reception and representation expenses (not to exceed $3,000), [$174,950,000] *$175,200,000*, to remain available until expended: *Provided*, That notwithstanding any other provision of law, not to exceed [$174,950,000] *$175,200,000* of revenues from fees and annual charges, and other services and collections in fiscal year [2000] *2001* shall be retained and used for necessary *2001* expenses in this account, and shall remain available until expended: *Provided further*, That the sum herein appropriated from the General Fund shall be reduced as revenues are received during fiscal year [2000] *2001* so as to result in a final fiscal year [2000] *2001* appropriation from the General Fund estimated at not more than $0. *(Energy and Water Development Appropriations Act, 2000.)*

Program and Financing (in millions of dollars)

Identification code 89–0212–0–1–276	1999 actual	2000 est.	2001 est.
Obligations by program activity:			
Reimbursable program:			
09.01 Energy markets	55	60	62
09.02 Energy projects	44	42	43
09.03 Program support	68	73	70
09.99 Total reimbursable program	167	175	175
10.00 Total new obligations	167	175	175
Budgetary resources available for obligation:			
22.00 New budget authority (gross)	168	175	175
23.95 Total new obligations	−167	−175	−175
New budget authority (gross), detail:			
Discretionary:			
68.00 Spending authority from offsetting collections (gross): Offsetting collections (cash)	168	175	175
Change in unpaid obligations:			
72.40 Unpaid obligations, start of year: Obligated balance, start of year	21	20	29
73.10 Total new obligations	167	175	175
73.20 Total outlays (gross)	−168	−166	−174
74.40 Unpaid obligations, end of year: Obligated balance, end of year	20	29	28
Outlays (gross), detail:			
86.90 Outlays from new discretionary authority	150	149	149
86.93 Outlays from discretionary balances	18	17	25
87.00 Total outlays (gross)	168	166	174
Offsets:			
Against gross budget authority and outlays:			
88.40 Offsetting collections (cash) from: Non-Federal sources	−168	−175	−175
Net budget authority and outlays:			
89.00 Budget authority			
90.00 Outlays		−9	−1

The Federal Energy Regulatory Commission (FERC) is charged with regulating certain interstate aspects of the natural gas, oil pipeline, hydropower, and electric industries. Such regulation includes issuing licenses and certificates for construction of facilities, approving rates, inspecting dams, implementing compliance and enforcement activities, and providing other services to regulated businesses. These businesses will pay fees and charges sufficient to recover the Government's full costs of operations.

Energy markets.—The Commission is responsible for setting rates for the interstate transmission and wholesale sales of electric energy and for authorizing certain public utility corporate transactions. The Commission approves rates for all Federal power marketing administrations except TVA. Since

General and special funds—Continued

FEDERAL ENERGY REGULATORY COMMISSION—Continued

SALARIES AND EXPENSES—Continued

enactment of the Energy Policy Act of 1992, the Commission has introduced a number of initiatives to foster competition in the generation sector of the electric utility industry while continuing to ensure system reliability. In 1996, the Commission issued Order Nos. 888 and 889, which require all jurisdictional public utilities to provide open access transmission service to all customers under standard terms and conditions. In the wake of Order Nos. 888 and 889, new market institutions are developing. For example, many utilities are turning over control of their transmission systems to independent system operators, which requires Commission approval. The Commission also certifies three special classes of power generators: cogeneration facilities, small power production facilities, and exempt whole sale generators. Further, the Commission determines just and reasonable rates for the interstate transportation of natural gas and oil on the pipelines subject to the Commission's jurisdiction. The Commission authorizes tariff provisions, as appropriate, to allow the gas and oil pipelines to adjust their services to meet their customers' needs and the pipelines' needs to meet competition in their markets. The Commission has and will continue to develop creative and flexible pricing policies and new and innovative services to address the changing competitive marketplace in both the gas and oil industries.

Energy projects.—The Commission issues preliminary permits, exemptions, and licenses, including relicenses, for nonfederal hydroelectric projects, enforces their terms and conditions, and performs dam safety inspections. The Commission regulates over 1,660 hydroelectric projects which supply about 5 percent of the electric energy generated in the United States. The Commission investigates to determine the amount of headwater benefits derived from federally-owned and FERC-licensed headwater improvements and returned approximately $6 million in revenues to the U.S. Treasury in 1999. The Commission also issues certificates authorizing natural gas pipelines to construct and operate new facilities and to provide new services. The Commission will continue to assure that environmental concerns involving energy projects, whether from pipeline construction or hydropower operations, are properly addressed and that the public interest is protected when new hydropower projects are licensed or relicensed, or when new natural gas pipeline services are authorized.

Program support.—Program support facilitates the Commission's ability to accomplish its regulatory mission. The Commission's support work includes human resources management and development, financial management, procurement, strategic management, information technology, external communications, dispute resolution, and general legal services. Through support activities, the Commission realizes its central values, since they determine how the Commission does its work. In the long run, the Commission's core programs can only be as good as the support programs and central values that stand behind them.

Object Classification (in millions of dollars)

Identification code 89–0212–0–1–276	1999 actual	2000 est.	2001 est.
99.0 Reimbursable obligations: Subtotal, reimbursable obligations	166	173	174
99.5 Below reporting threshold	1	2	1
99.9 Total new obligations	167	175	175

Personnel Summary

Identification code 89–0212–0–1–276	1999 actual	2000 est.	2001 est.
2001 Total compensable workyears: Full-time equivalent employment	1,299	1,250	1,250

GEOTHERMAL RESOURCES DEVELOPMENT FUND

Program and Financing (in millions of dollars)

Identification code 89–0206–0–1–271	1999 actual	2000 est.	2001 est.
Budgetary resources available for obligation:			
21.40 Unobligated balance available, start of year	1	1	
22.00 New budget authority (gross)		–1	
23.90 Total budgetary resources available for obligation	1		
24.40 Unobligated balance available, end of year	1		
New budget authority (gross), detail:			
Discretionary:			
41.00 Transferred to other accounts		–1	
Net budget authority and outlays:			
89.00 Budget authority		–1	
90.00 Outlays			

This loan guarantee program was started in 1979 to subsidize loans for geothermal energy projects too risky to acquire private sector financing on their own. The fund is no longer in operation, and has been closed pursuant to 31 U.S.C. 1555. The balances remaining on the Fund were transferred to the Energy Supply account in FY 2000.

CLEAN COAL TECHNOLOGY

(RESCISSION AND DEFERRAL)

Of the funds made available under this heading for obligation in prior years, [$156,000,000] *$105,000,000 is hereby rescinded; and an additional $221,000,000* shall not be available until October 1, [2000] *2001*: *Provided*, That funds made available in previous appropriations Acts shall be available for any ongoing project regardless of the separate request for proposal under which the project was selected*: Provided further, That all such projects are executed in accordance with the Nonnuclear Energy Research Act, as amended. (42 U.S.C. 5901–20; Department of the Interior and Related Agencies Appropriations Act, 2000, as enacted by section 1000(a)(3) of the Consolidated Appropriations Act, 2000 (P.L. 106–113).)*

Program and Financing (in millions of dollars)

Identification code 89–0235–0–1–271	1999 actual	2000 est.	2001 est.
Obligations by program activity:			
10.00 Total new obligations	16	14	74
Budgetary resources available for obligation:			
21.40 Unobligated balance available, start of year	427	372	212
22.00 New budget authority (gross)	–40	–146	–155
22.10 Resources available from recoveries of prior year obligations	1		20
23.90 Total budgetary resources available for obligation	388	226	77
23.95 Total new obligations	–16	–14	–74
24.40 Unobligated balance available, end of year	372	212	3
New budget authority (gross), detail:			
Discretionary:			
Unobligated balance rescinded:			
40.36 Unobligated balance rescinded			–105
40.36 Unobligated balance deferred	–40	–156	–221
43.00 Appropriation (total discretionary)	–40	–156	–326
55.00 Advance appropriation		10	171
70.00 Total new budget authority (gross)	–40	–146	–155

	Change in unpaid obligations:			
72.40	Unpaid obligations, start of year: Obligated balance, start of year	433	391	334
73.10	Total new obligations	16	14	74
73.20	Total outlays (gross)	−57	−71	−105
73.45	Adjustments in unexpired accounts	−1		−20
74.40	Unpaid obligations, end of year: Obligated balance, end of year	391	334	283
	Outlays (gross), detail:			
86.93	Outlays from discretionary balances	57	71	105
	Net budget authority and outlays:			
89.00	Budget authority	−40	−146	−155
90.00	Outlays	57	71	105

Public Law 99–190, making continuing appropriations for 1986, provided $400 million from funds in the Energy Security Reserve in the Department of the Treasury for a new clean coal technology program in the Department of Energy. This program was authorized under the clean coal technology reserve proviso of Public Law 98–473 to subsidize the construction and operation of facilities to demonstrate the potential commercial feasibility of such technologies.

Termination of the domestic clean coal technology program, after completion of projects now underway, is part of the President's realignment of the Department of Energy. The Administration's policy calls for limiting the program's existing domestic projects which have been selected under contract. If a project is canceled, the canceled project's funding will either be used to meet the needs of remaining on-going projects, or will be rescinded if the funds are not needed by the program.

Object Classification (in millions of dollars)

Identification code 89–0235–0–1–271		1999 actual	2000 est.	2001 est.
11.1	Personnel compensation: Full-time permanent	6	6	6
12.1	Civilian personnel benefits	1	1	1
25.1	Advisory and assistance services	3	3	3
25.2	Other services	6	3	3
25.4	Operation and maintenance of facilities	1	1	1
25.5	Research and development contracts	−1		
41.0	Grants, subsidies, and contributions			60
99.9	Total new obligations	16	14	74

Personnel Summary

Identification code 89–0235–0–1–271		1999 actual	2000 est.	2001 est.
1001	Total compensable workyears: Full-time equivalent employment	66	66	66

Alternative Fuels Production

(including transfer of funds)

Moneys received as investment income on the principal amount in the Great Plains Project Trust at the Norwest Bank of North Dakota, in such sums as are earned as of October 1, [1999] *2000*, shall be deposited in this account and immediately transferred to the general fund of the Treasury. Moneys received as revenue sharing from operation of the Great Plains Gasification Plant and settlement payments shall be immediately transferred to the general fund of the Treasury. *Of the unobligated balances under this head, $1,000,000 are rescinded. (Department of the Interior and Related Agencies Appropriations Act, 2000, as enacted by section 1000(a)(3) of the Consolidated Appropriations Act, 2000 (P.L. 106–113).)*

Program and Financing (in millions of dollars)

Identification code 89–5180–0–2–271		1999 actual	2000 est.	2001 est.
	Budgetary resources available for obligation:			
21.40	Unobligated balance available, start of year	3	3	3
22.00	New budget authority (gross)			−1
23.90	Total budgetary resources available for obligation	3	3	2
24.40	Unobligated balance available, end of year	3	3	2
	New budget authority (gross), detail:			
	Discretionary:			
40.36	Unobligated balance rescinded			−1
	Spending authority from offsetting collections:			
68.00	Offsetting collections (cash)	1		
68.27	Capital transfer to general fund	−1		
68.90	Spending authority from offsetting collections (total discretionary)			
70.00	Total new budget authority (gross)			−1
	Change in unpaid obligations:			
72.40	Unpaid obligations, start of year: Obligated balance, start of year	10	10	10
74.40	Unpaid obligations, end of year: Obligated balance, end of year	10	10	10
	Offsets:			
	Against gross budget authority and outlays:			
88.40	Offsetting collections (cash) from: Interest from principal in the Great Plains Project Trust	−1		
	Net budget authority and outlays:			
89.00	Budget authority	−1		−1
90.00	Outlays			

This program was established in 1980 for the purpose of expediting the development and production of alternative fuels.

When the Synthetic Fuels Corporation was declared to be operational in 1982, the uncommitted and unobligated funds remaining in the program were transferred to the Energy Security Reserve for use by the Synthetic Fuels Corporation, with the exception of the loan guarantee for the Great Plains gasification project, which remained under the jurisdiction of the Department of Energy. The Department exercised its authority to borrow from the Treasury to repay the Federal Financing Bank upon default of the borrower in 1985. This loan was repaid, along with accrued interest, by a supplemental appropriation in 1986. The Department acquired ownership of the Great Plains plant by foreclosure, which was completed on July 14, 1986, and continued operation of the plant without the expenditure of appropriated funds. On October 31, 1988, the Department completed the process of establishing an asset purchase agreement for the Great Plains Gasification Plant by settlement with Basin Electric Power Cooperative Association. Responsibilities for other related agreements—trust agreement, gas transportation agreement, gas purchase agreement—were also settled. Under the terms of the asset purchase agreement a check for $85 million was provided to the Government as an initial payment. These agreements were the subject of litigation between the Department, Dakota Gasification Company (DGC) and the four pipeline companies which purchased synthetic gas from the plant. Future revenue sharing payments to the Department are dependent upon natural gas prices.

The parties to litigation negotiated settlement agreements in principle in December 1993. Settlement agreements dated February 16, 1994, have been signed. These settlement agreements resolve all past disputes as well as restructure the Gas Purchase Agreements pricing provisions. The settlement agreements have received final Federal Energy Regulatory Commission (FERC) approval. In a separate agreement with DOE, DGC agreed to pay DOE $25 million over the 7 year period of time DGC receives the demand payments from the pipeline companies.

Elk Hills School Lands Fund

For necessary expenses in fulfilling [the second] installment [payment] *payments* under the Settlement Agreement entered into by

General and special funds—Continued

ELK HILLS SCHOOL LANDS FUND—Continued

the United States and the State of California on October 11, 1996, as authorized by section 3415 of Public Law 104–106, [$36,000,000, to become available on October 1, 2000] for payment to the State of California for the State Teachers' Retirement Fund from the Elk Hills School Lands Fund, *to become available on October 1 of the fiscal year specified and to remain available until expended, as follows: for fiscal year 2002, $36,000,000; for fiscal year 2003, $36,000,000; for fisal year 2004, $36,000,000; for fiscal year 2005, $60,000,000; and for fiscal year 2006, $60,000,000. (Department of the Interior and Related Agencies Appropriations Act, 2000, as enacted by section 1000(a)(3) of the Consolidated Appropriations Act, 2000 (P.L. 106–113).)*

Unavailable Collections (in millions of dollars)

Identification code 89–5428–0–2–271	1999 actual	2000 est.	2001 est.
Balance, start of year:			
01.99 Balance, start of year	298	262	262
Appropriation:			
05.01 Elk Hills school lands fund	−36		
07.99 Total balance, end of year	262	262	262

Program and Financing (in millions of dollars)

Identification code 89–5428–0–2–271	1999 actual	2000 est.	2001 est.
Obligations by program activity:			
10.00 Total new obligations (object class 41.0)	36		36
Budgetary resources available for obligation:			
22.00 New budget authority (gross)	36		36
23.95 Total new obligations	−36		−36
24.40 Unobligated balance available, end of year			
New budget authority (gross), detail:			
Discretionary:			
40.20 Appropriation (special fund, definite)	36		
55.00 Advance appropriation			36
70.00 Total new budget authority (gross)	36		36
Change in unpaid obligations:			
73.10 Total new obligations	36		36
73.20 Total outlays (gross)	−36		−36
Outlays (gross), detail:			
86.90 Outlays from new discretionary authority	36		36
Net budget authority and outlays:			
89.00 Budget authority	36		36
90.00 Outlays	36		36

Title XXXIV, Subtitle B of Public Law 104–106 required the Department to sell the government's interest in Naval Petroleum Reserve No. 1 (Elk Hills) pursuant to the terms of the Act. The sale occurred in February 1998, following a statutorily-required 31-day congressional review period.

Section 3415 of the Act required, among other things, that the Department make an offer of settlement based on the fair value of the State of California's longstanding claims to two parcels of land ("school lands") within the Reserve. Under the Act, nine percent of the net proceeds were reserved in contingent fund in the Treasury for payment to the State. In compliance with the Act and in order to remove any cloud over title which could diminish the sales value of the Reserve, the Department entered into a settlement agreement with the State on October 11, 1996. That agreement calls for payment to the State, subject to appropriations, of nine percent of the net proceeds of sale, payable over a seven-year period (without interest), commencing in fiscal year 1999. Under the settlement agreement and provided that funds are appropriated, the first five installments are for $36,000,000 each year, and the remaining balance is to be paid in two equal installments in years six and seven, FY 2004 and FY 2005. The Budget requests advance appropriations for FY 2002 through FY 2006 to fully fund the settlement agreement.

PAYMENTS TO STATES UNDER FEDERAL POWER ACT

Unavailable Collections (in millions of dollars)

Identification code 89–5105–0–2–806	1999 actual	2000 est.	2001 est.
Balance, start of year:			
01.99 Balance, start of year			
Receipts:			
02.01 Licenses under Federal Power Act from public lands and national forests, payment to States (37 1/2%),Energy	3	3	3
Appropriation:			
05.01 Payments to States under Federal Power Act	−3	−3	−3
07.99 Total balance, end of year			

Program and Financing (in millions of dollars)

Identification code 89–5105–0–2–806	1999 actual	2000 est.	2001 est.
Obligations by program activity:			
10.00 Total new obligations (object class 41.0)	3	3	3
Budgetary resources available for obligation:			
21.40 Unobligated balance available, start of year	3	3	3
22.00 New budget authority (gross)	3	3	3
23.90 Total budgetary resources available for obligation	6	6	6
23.95 Total new obligations	−3	−3	−3
24.40 Unobligated balance available, end of year	3	3	3
New budget authority (gross), detail:			
Mandatory:			
60.25 Appropriation (special fund, indefinite)	3	3	3
Change in unpaid obligations:			
73.10 Total new obligations	3	3	3
73.20 Total outlays (gross)	−3	−3	−3
Outlays (gross), detail:			
86.97 Outlays from new mandatory authority	3	3	3
Net budget authority and outlays:			
89.00 Budget authority	3	3	3
90.00 Outlays	3	3	3

The States are paid 37.5 percent of the receipts from licenses for occupancy and use of national forests and public lands within their boundaries issued by the Federal Energy Regulatory Commission (16 U.S.C. 810).

NUCLEAR WASTE DISPOSAL

For nuclear waste disposal activities to carry out the purposes of Public Law 97–425, as amended, including the acquisition of real property or facility construction or expansion, [$240,500,000] *$325,500,000, to remain available until expended and* to be derived from the Nuclear Waste Fund: *Provided,* That not to exceed [$500,000] *$4,648,000* may be provided to the State of Nevada solely for expenditures[, other than salaries and expenses of State employees,] to conduct scientific oversight responsibilities pursuant to the Nuclear Waste Policy Act of 1982, (Public Law 97–425) as amended: *Provided further,* That not to exceed [$5,432,000] *$5,887,000* may be provided to affected units of local governments, as defined in Public Law 97–425, to conduct appropriate activities pursuant to the Act: *Provided further,* That the distribution of the funds as determined by the units of local government shall be approved by the Department of Energy: *Provided further,* That the funds shall be made available to the State and units of local government by direct payment: *Provided further,* That within 90 days of the completion of each Federal fiscal year, the State and each local entity shall provide certification to the Department of Energy, that all funds expended from such payments have been expended for activities [as defined in] *authorized by* Public Law [97–425] *97–425 and this Act.* Failure to provide such certification shall cause such entity to be prohibited from any further funding provided for similar activities: *Provided further,* That none of the funds herein appropriated may be: (1) used directly or indirectly to influence legislative action on any matter pending before Congress or a State legislature or for lobbying activity as provided in 18 U.S.C. 1913; (2) used for litigation expenses; or (3) used to support multi-state efforts or other coalition building activities [inconsistent with the restrictions contained in this Act]: *Provided further, That all proceeds and recoveries by the Secretary in carrying out activities authorized by the Nuclear Waste Policy Act of 1982 in Public Law 97–425, as amended, including but not limited to, any proceeds from the sale of assets, shall be available without further appropriation and shall remain available until expended.*

[RESCISSION]

[Of the funds made available under the heading "Department of Energy—Energy Programs—Nuclear Waste Disposal Fund" in the Energy and Water Development Appropriations Act, 1998 (Public Law 105–62), $4,000,000 is rescinded, to be derived from the amount specified under such heading for the Nuclear Regulatory Commission to license a multi-purpose canister design.] *(Energy and Water Development Appropriations Act, 2000.)*

Unavailable Collections (in millions of dollars)

Identification code 89–5227–0–2–271	1999 actual	2000 est.	2001 est.
Balance, start of year:			
01.99 Balance, start of year	7,237	7,821	8,917
Receipts:			
02.01 Receipts from nuclear powered electric utilities	662	663	550
02.02 Net earnings on investments	106	695	767
02.99 Total receipts	768	1,358	1,317
04.00 Total: Balances and collections	8,005	9,179	10,234
Appropriation:			
05.01 Nuclear waste fund	−165	−241	−326
05.02 Nuclear Regulatory Commission	−17	−19	−22
05.04 Nuclear Waste Technical Review Board	−3	−3	−3
05.99 Subtotal appropriation	−185	−263	−351
06.20 Reduction pursuant to Public Law 106–51	1	1	
07.99 Total balance, end of year	7,821	8,917	9,883

Program and Financing (in millions of dollars)

Identification code 89–5227–0–2–271	1999 actual	2000 est.	2001 est.
Obligations by program activity:			
00.01 Nuclear waste disposal fund	118	188	266
00.02 Program direction	57	60	60
10.00 Total new obligations	175	248	326
Budgetary resources available for obligation:			
21.40 Unobligated balance available, start of year	16	89	81
22.00 New budget authority (gross)	249	236	326
22.22 Unobligated balance transferred from other accounts		4	
23.90 Total budgetary resources available for obligation	265	329	407
23.95 Total new obligations	−175	−248	−326
24.40 Unobligated balance available, end of year	89	81	81
New budget authority (gross), detail:			
Discretionary:			
40.00 Appropriation	4		
40.20 Appropriation (special fund, definite)	165	241	326
40.36 Unobligated balance rescinded		−4	
40.75 Reduction pursuant to P.L. 106–51	−1		
40.76 Reduction pursuant to P.L. 106–113		−1	
43.00 Appropriation (total discretionary)	168	236	326
68.10 Spending authority from offsetting collections: From Federal sources: Change in receivables and unpaid, unfilled orders	81		
70.00 Total new budget authority (gross)	249	236	326
Change in unpaid obligations:			
Unpaid obligations, start of year:			
72.40 Obligated balance, start of year	92	17	126
72.95 From Federal sources: Receivables and unpaid, unfilled orders		81	81
72.99 Total unpaid obligations, start of year	92	98	207
73.10 Total new obligations	175	248	326
73.20 Total outlays (gross)	−169	−140	−281
Unpaid obligations, end of year:			
74.40 Obligated balance, end of year	17	126	172
74.95 From Federal sources: Receivables and unpaid, unfilled orders	81	81	81
74.99 Total unpaid obligations, end of year	98	207	253
Outlays (gross), detail:			
86.90 Outlays from new discretionary authority	146	118	163
86.93 Outlays from discretionary balances	23	22	118
87.00 Total outlays (gross)	169	140	281
Offsets:			
Against gross budget authority only:			
88.95 From Federal sources: Change in receivables and unpaid, unfilled orders	−81		
Net budget authority and outlays:			
89.00 Budget authority	168	236	326
90.00 Outlays	169	140	281
Memorandum (non-add) entries:			
92.01 Total investments, start of year: U.S. securities: Par value	11,169	15,195	9,128
92.02 Total investments, end of year: U.S. securities: Par value	15,195	9,128	10,140

The nuclear waste disposal program consists of efforts related to the development, acquisition, and operation of facilities for the disposal of civilian and defense high level nuclear waste. These activities are funded by appropriations from the nuclear waste fund, which is paid for by the users of the disposal service, and the Defense nuclear waste disposal account, which was established by Congress as part of the 1993 Energy and Water Development Appropriation (P.L. 102–377) in lieu of a payment from the Department of Energy into the Nuclear waste fund for activities related to the disposal of defense high-level waste.

In FY 2001, the Office of Civilian Radioactive Waste Management program will focus on the activities necessary to make a decision on the suitability of the Yucca Mountain site as a repository; develop the documentation, including a final Environmental Impact Statement, needed for a Secretarial decision whether to recommend the site to the President in FY 2001; and conduct other activities associated with the Federal government's waste acceptance obligations.

Following the issuance of the site recommendation in late FY 2001, the program, through the Yucca Mountain Site Characterization Office, will evaluate the repository system against the Department's suitability criteria; validate data and update process models using data from scientific tests and evolving designs; conduct an iteration of total system performance assessment for use in license application; continue to develop the draft license application and supporting documents; and refine repository and waste package design.

The program's cost estimates reflect DOE's best projections, given the scope of work identified and planned schedule of required activities. Future budget requests for the program have yet to be established and will be determined through the annual executive and congressional budget process.

Status of Funds (in millions of dollars)

Identification code 89–5227–0–2–271	1999 actual	2000 est.	2001 est.
Unexpended balance, start of year:			
0100 Uninvested balance		1	
U.S. Securities:			
0101 Par value	11,169	15,195	9,128
0102 Unrealized discounts	−3,824	−7,267	−4
0199 Total balance, start of year	7,345	7,927	9,124

General and special funds—Continued

NUCLEAR WASTE DISPOSAL—Continued

[RESCISSION]—Continued

Status of Funds (in millions of dollars)—Continued

Identification code 89–5227–0–2–271		1999 actual	2000 est.	2001 est.
	Cash income during the year:			
	Proprietary receipts:			
0220	Nuclear waste disposal fund , Energy	662	663	550
	Intragovernmental transactions:			
0240	Earnings on investments, Nuclear waste disposal fund , Energy	106	695	767
0299	Total cash income	768	1,358	1,317
	Cash outgo during year:			
0500	Nuclear waste disposal fund	−169	−140	−281
0502	Nuclear Waste Technical Review Board,	−2	−3	−3
0503	Nuclear Regulatory Commission(−)	−17	−18	−21
0599	Total cash outgo (−)	−188	−161	−305
0625	Balances expired or permanently cancelled		−4	
0645	Balance transferred, net		4	
0699	Total adjustments			
	Unexpended balance, end of year:			
0700	Uninvested balance	1		
	U.S. Securities:			
0701	Par value	15,195	9,128	10,140
0702	Unrealized discounts	−7,267	−4	−4
0799	Total balance, end of year	7,927	9,124	10,136

Object Classification (in millions of dollars)

Identification code 89–5227–0–2–271		1999 actual	2000 est.	2001 est.
	Personnel compensation:			
11.1	Full-time permanent	14	15	16
11.5	Other personnel compensation	1	1	2
11.9	Total personnel compensation	15	16	18
12.1	Civilian personnel benefits	3	4	5
21.0	Travel and transportation of persons	1	1	2
23.2	Rental payments to others	1	1	2
25.1	Advisory and assistance services	35	35	37
25.2	Other services	11	15	20
25.3	Purchases of goods and services from Government accounts	8	11	15
25.4	Operation and maintenance of facilities	83	141	194
26.0	Supplies and materials	1	1	2
41.0	Grants, subsidies, and contributions	17	23	31
99.9	Total new obligations	175	248	326

Personnel Summary

Identification code 89–5227–0–2–271		1999 actual	2000 est.	2001 est.
1001	Total compensable workyears: Full-time equivalent employment	183	200	200

URANIUM ENRICHMENT DECONTAMINATION AND DECOMMISSIONING FUND

For necessary expenses in carrying out uranium enrichment facility decontamination and decommissioning, remedial actions and other activities of title II of the Atomic Energy Act of 1954 and title X, subtitle A of the Energy Policy Act of 1992, [$250,198,000] *$303,038,000*, to be derived from the Fund, to remain available until expended: *Provided,* That $30,000,000 of amounts derived from the Fund for such expenses shall be available in accordance with title X, subtitle A, of the Energy Policy Act of 1992. *(Energy and Water Development Appropriations Act, 2000.)*

Unavailable Collections (in millions of dollars)

Identification code 89–5231–0–2–271		1999 actual	2000 est.	2001 est.
	Balance, start of year:			
01.99	Balance, start of year	1,224	1,612	1,987
	Receipts:			
02.01	Assessments	171	175	179
02.02	Earnings on investments	39	45	52
02.03	General fund payment	398	420	420
02.99	Total receipts	608	640	651
04.00	Total: Balances and collections	1,832	2,252	2,638
	Appropriation:			
05.01	Uranium enrichment decontamination and decommissioning fund	−220	−250	−303
05.02	Supplemental proposal		−16	
05.99	Subtotal appropriation	−220	−266	−303
06.20	Reduction pursuant to Public Law 106–113		1	
07.99	Total balance, end of year	1,612	1,987	2,335

Program and Financing (in millions of dollars)

Identification code 89–5231–0–2–271		1999 actual	2000 est.	2001 est.
	Obligations by program activity:			
00.01	Environmental restoration and waste management	190	219	273
00.02	Uranium / thorium reimbursements	30	30	30
10.00	Total new obligations	220	249	303
	Budgetary resources available for obligation:			
22.00	New budget authority (gross)	220	249	303
23.95	Total new obligations	−220	−249	−303
	New budget authority (gross), detail:			
	Discretionary:			
40.20	Appropriation (special fund, definite)	220	250	303
40.76	Reduction pursuant to P.L. 106–113		−1	
43.00	Appropriation (total discretionary)	220	249	303
	Change in unpaid obligations:			
72.40	Unpaid obligations, start of year: Obligated balance, start of year	47	39	79
73.10	Total new obligations	220	249	303
73.20	Total outlays (gross)	−228	−209	−287
74.40	Unpaid obligations, end of year: Obligated balance, end of year	39	79	95
	Outlays (gross), detail:			
86.90	Outlays from new discretionary authority	185	174	212
86.93	Outlays from discretionary balances	43	35	75
87.00	Total outlays (gross)	228	209	287
	Net budget authority and outlays:			
89.00	Budget authority	220	249	303
90.00	Outlays	228	209	287
	Memorandum (non-add) entries:			
92.01	Total investments, start of year: U.S. securities: Par value	1,280	1,655	2,071
92.02	Total investments, end of year: U.S. securities: Par value	1,655	2,071	2,430

Summary of Budget Authority and Outlays

(in millions of dollars)

	1999 actual	2000 est.	2001 est.
Enacted/requested:			
Budget Authority	220	249	303
Outlays	228	209	287
Supplemental proposal:			
Budget Authority		16	
Outlays		11	5
Total:			
Budget Authority	220	265	303
Outlays	228	220	292

The uranium enrichment decontamination and decommissioning fund will cover D&D, remedial action and other costs associated with environmental cleanup activities at sites leased and operated by the United States Enrichment Corporation, as well as DOE facilities at these and other sites. A portion of the fund will be used to reimburse current owners of uranium and thorium sites for a portion of their remediation costs for tailings attributable to the sale of uranium or thorium to the Federal government.

This fund includes projects at the East Tennessee Technology Park and Oak Ridge Reservation, Tennessee; Paducah gaseous diffusion plant, Kentucky; and Portsmouth gaseous diffusion plant, Ohio.

Status of Funds (in millions of dollars)

Identification code 89–5231–0–2–271	1999 actual	2000 est.	2001 est.
Unexpended balance, start of year:			
U.S. Securities:			
0101 Par value	1,280	1,655	2,071
0102 Unrealized discounts	–9	–4	
0199 Total balance, start of year	1,271	1,651	2,071
Cash income during the year:			
Governmental receipts:			
0200 Assessments, Decontamination and Decommissioning Fund	171	175	179
Intragovernmental transactions:			
0240 Earnings on investments, Decontamination and Decommissioning Fund	39	45	52
0241 General fund payment—Defense, Decontamination and Decommissioning Fund	398	420	420
0299 Total cash income	608	640	651
Cash outgo during year:			
0500 Uranium enrichment decontamination and decommissioning fund	–228	–209	–287
0501 Supplemental proposal		–11	–5
0597 Outgo under present law (–)	–228	–209	–287
0598 Outgo under proposed legislation (–)		–11	–5
0599 Total cash outgo (–)	–228	–220	–292
0625 Balances expired or permanently cancelled		–1	
Unexpended balance, end of year:			
U.S. Securities:			
0701 Par value	1,654	2,071	2,430
0702 Unrealized discounts	–4		
0799 Total balance, end of year	1,651	2,071	2,430

Object Classification (in millions of dollars)

Identification code 89–5231–0–2–271	1999 actual	2000 est.	2001 est.
25.2 Other services	81	92	112
25.4 Operation and maintenance of facilities	136	154	187
41.0 Grants, subsidies, and contributions	3	3	4
99.9 Total new obligations	220	249	303

Public enterprise funds:

Isotope Production and Distribution Program Fund

Program and Financing (in millions of dollars)

Identification code 89–4180–0–3–271	1999 actual	2000 est.	2001 est.
Obligations by program activity:			
09.01 Isotope production and distribution	27	22	27
09.02 Isotope production facility project	6	8	
10.00 Total new obligations	33	30	27
Budgetary resources available for obligation:			
21.40 Unobligated balance available, start of year	5	3	3
22.00 New budget authority (gross)	31	30	27
23.90 Total budgetary resources available for obligation	36	33	30
23.95 Total new obligations	–33	–30	–27
24.40 Unobligated balance available, end of year	3	3	3
New budget authority (gross), detail:			
Discretionary:			
68.00 Spending authority from offsetting collections (gross): Offsetting collections (cash)	31	30	27
Change in unpaid obligations:			
72.40 Unpaid obligations, start of year: Obligated balance, start of year	6	8	8
73.10 Total new obligations	33	30	27
73.20 Total outlays (gross)	–31	–30	–27
74.40 Unpaid obligations, end of year: Obligated balance, end of year	8	8	8
Outlays (gross), detail:			
86.90 Outlays from new discretionary authority	31	30	27
Offsets:			
Against gross budget authority and outlays:			
Offsetting collections (cash) from:			
88.00 Federal sources—Expenditure transfers	–22	–20	–19
88.40 Non-Federal sources	–9	–10	–8
88.90 Total, offsetting collections (cash)	–31	–30	–27
Net budget authority and outlays:			
89.00 Budget authority			
90.00 Outlays			

The charter of the Department of Energy (DOE) isotope production and distribution program covers the production and sale of isotope products and related services to the user community utilizing Government-owned facilities. The isotopes produced by the Department are those that can be produced in existing DOE production and research facilities dedicated to the products required by the isotope production and distribution program. The isotopes are sold at their market value or at a price determined to be in the best interest of the government for use in medical diagnoses and therapy, medical and scientific research, and industrial applications.

Object Classification (in millions of dollars)

Identification code 89–4180–0–3–271	1999 actual	2000 est.	2001 est.
25.4 Operation and maintenance of facilities	26	24	21
32.0 Land and structures	6	5	5
41.0 Grants, subsidies, and contributions	1	1	1
99.9 Total new obligations	33	30	27

Trust Funds

Advances for Cooperative Work

Program and Financing (in millions of dollars)

Identification code 89–8575–0–7–271	1999 actual	2000 est.	2001 est.
Change in unpaid obligations:			
72.40 Unpaid obligations, start of year: Obligated balance, start of year	7	5	5
74.40 Unpaid obligations, end of year: Obligated balance, end of year	5	5	5
Net budget authority and outlays:			
89.00 Budget authority			
90.00 Outlays	2		

In past years, this account received advances from domestic and foreign sources, to fund research and development activities for civilian reactor, magnetic fusion, and basic energy sciences. Sources also provided funds for defense programs, the technical information management program. The account will be terminated when balances have been expended.

POWER MARKETING ADMINISTRATIONS

Federal Funds

General and special funds:

Operation and Maintenance, Alaska Power Administration

Program and Financing (in millions of dollars)

Identification code 89–0304–0–1–271	1999 actual	2000 est.	2001 est.
Obligations by program activity:			
00.02 Program direction	2		

General and special funds—Continued

OPERATION AND MAINTENANCE, ALASKA POWER ADMINISTRATION—Continued

Program and Financing (in millions of dollars)—Continued

Identification code 89–0304–0–1–271	1999 actual	2000 est.	2001 est.
00.03 Transition and termination	4		
10.00 Total new obligations (object class 25.2)	6		
Budgetary resources available for obligation:			
21.40 Unobligated balance available, start of year	8		
22.40 Capital transfer to general fund	−2		
23.90 Total budgetary resources available for obligation	6		
23.95 Total new obligations	−6		
Change in unpaid obligations:			
72.40 Unpaid obligations, start of year: Obligated balance, start of year	10	11	11
73.10 Total new obligations	6		
73.20 Total outlays (gross)	−5		
74.40 Unpaid obligations, end of year: Obligated balance, end of year	11	11	11
Outlays (gross), detail:			
86.93 Outlays from discretionary balances	5		
Net budget authority and outlays:			
89.00 Budget authority			
90.00 Outlays	5		

The Alaska Power Administration (APA) was created in 1967 by the Secretary of the Interior to assume the functions of the Bureau of Reclamation in Alaska—the operations, maintenance, transmission, and power marketing of the two Federal hydroelectric projects (Eklutna and Snettisham), and the investigation of future water and power development programs.

The Alaska Power Administration Asset Sale and Termination Act (Public Law 104–58), signed into law on November 28, 1995, authorizes and directs the sale of all Alaska Power Administration assets and the subsequent termination of APA. The Eklutna project was sold on October 2, 1997, for a cash payment of $5,953,000. The Snettisham project was sold on August 18, 1998, for $81,966,177.

All remaining Alaska activities of APA, including the Juneau headquarters office, were terminated on September 30, 1998. Unobligated transition and termination balances were used to complete remaining close-out activities and report preparation in Washington, D.C. in 1999.

Personnel Summary

Identification code 89–0304–0–1–271	1999 actual	2000 est.	2001 est.
1001 Total compensable workyears: Full-time equivalent employment	1		

OPERATION AND MAINTENANCE, SOUTHEASTERN POWER ADMINISTRATION

For necessary expenses of operation and maintenance of power transmission facilities and of marketing electric power and energy, including transmission wheeling and ancillary services, pursuant to the provisions of section 5 of the Flood Control Act of 1944 (16 U.S.C. 825s), as applied to the southeastern power area, [$11,594,000] *$3,900,000, to remain available until expended*; in addition, notwithstanding the provisions of 31 U.S.C. 3302, [not to exceed $28,000,000 in reimbursements for transmission wheeling and ancillary services and for power purchases, to remain available until expended] *amounts collected by the Southeastern Power Administration pursuant to the Flood Control Act to recover purchase power and wheeling expenses shall be credited to this account as offsetting collections, to remain available until expended for the sole purpose of making purchase power and wheeling expenditures as follows: for fiscal year 2001, up to $34,463,000; for fiscal year 2002, up to $26,463,000; for fiscal year 2003, up to $20,000,000; and for fiscal year 2004, up to $15,000,000.*

[(RESCISSION)]

[Of the funds made available under this heading in Public Law 105–245 and prior Energy and Water Development Acts, $3,000,000, are rescinded.] *(Energy and Water Development Appropriations Act, 2000.)*

Program and Financing (in millions of dollars)

Identification code 89–0302–0–1–271	1999 actual	2000 est.	2001 est.
Obligations by program activity:			
Direct program:			
00.01 Program direction	4	6	5
00.02 Purchase power and wheeling	7	7	
09.01 Reimbursable program	19	28	34
10.00 Total new obligations	30	41	39
Budgetary resources available for obligation:			
21.40 Unobligated balance available, start of year	8	6	1
22.00 New budget authority (gross)	27	36	38
22.10 Resources available from recoveries of prior year obligations	1		
23.90 Total budgetary resources available for obligation	36	42	39
23.95 Total new obligations	−30	−41	−39
24.40 Unobligated balance available, end of year	6	1	
New budget authority (gross), detail:			
Discretionary:			
40.00 Appropriation	8	9	4
41.00 Transferred to other accounts		−1	
43.00 Appropriation (total discretionary)	8	8	4
Spending authority from offsetting collections:			
Offsetting collections (cash):			
68.00 Offsetting collections (cash)	19	28	
68.00 Offsetting collections (cash) – Purchase Power and Wheeling			34
68.90 Spending authority from offsetting collections (total discretionary)	19	28	34
70.00 Total new budget authority (gross)	27	36	38
Change in unpaid obligations:			
72.40 Unpaid obligations, start of year: Obligated balance, start of year	3	1	5
73.10 Total new obligations	30	41	39
73.20 Total outlays (gross)	−30	−36	−39
73.45 Adjustments in unexpired accounts	−1		
74.40 Unpaid obligations, end of year: Obligated balance, end of year	1	5	5
Outlays (gross), detail:			
86.90 Outlays from new discretionary authority	26	35	38
86.93 Outlays from discretionary balances	4	1	1
87.00 Total outlays (gross)	30	36	39
Offsets:			
Against gross budget authority and outlays:			
Offsetting collections (cash) from:			
Non-Federal sources:			
88.40 Non-Federal sources	−19	−28	
88.40 Non-Federal sources-Purchase Power and Wheeling Offsetting Collections			−34
88.90 Total, offsetting collections (cash)	−19	−28	−34
Net budget authority and outlays:			
89.00 Budget authority	8	8	4
90.00 Outlays	11	8	5

The Southeastern Power Administration (SEPA) markets power generated at Corps of Engineers hydroelectric generating plants in an eleven-State area of the Southeast. Deliveries are made by means of transmission facilities owned by others. There are 23 projects now in operation.

SEPA sells wholesale power primarily to publicly and cooperatively-owned electric distribution utilities. SEPA does not own or operate any transmission facilities. Its long-term contracts provide for periodic electric rate adjustments to ensure that the Federal Government recovers costs of operation and capital invested in power, with interest, in keeping with statutory requirements.

Program direction.—Provision is made for negotiation and administration of power contracts, collection of revenues, development of wholesale power rates, the amortization of power investment, energy efficiency and competitiveness program, investigation and planning of proposed water resources projects, scheduling and dispatch of power generation, scheduling storage and release of water, administration of contractual operation requirements, and determination of methods of operating generating plants individually and in coordination with others to obtain maximum utilization of resources. Proprietary receipts deposited in the Treasury were $116 million for fiscal year 1999 and are estimated to be $139 million for fiscal year 2000 and $173 million for fiscal year 2001.

Purchase power and wheeling.—Between FY 2001 and FY 2004, the Southeastern Power Administration will phase-out Federal financing of purchase power and wheeling activities. Authority to spend power revenues to pay for purchase of power and wheeling activities will end after FY 2004. Industry restructuring and resulting competition now make it attractive for Southeastern's customers to shop for power and transmission services. Southeastern may continue to support customer bill crediting, net billing and other alternative financing arrangements for these activities.

Based on Administration policy, the Southeastern Power Administration will set rates consistent with current law to recover the full cost of the Civil Service Retirement System and post-retirement health benefits for its employees.

Object Classification (in millions of dollars)

Identification code 89–0302–0–1–271	1999 actual	2000 est.	2001 est.
Direct obligations:			
11.1 Personnel compensation: Full-time permanent	3	3	3
25.2 Other services	8	10	2
99.0 Subtotal, direct obligations	11	13	5
99.0 Reimbursable obligations	19	28	34
99.9 Total new obligations	30	41	39

Personnel Summary

Identification code 89–0302–0–1–271	1999 actual	2000 est.	2001 est.
1001 Total compensable workyears: Full-time equivalent employment	40	42	42

CONTINUING FUND, SOUTHEASTERN POWER ADMINISTRATION

Unavailable Collections (in millions of dollars)

Identification code 89–5653–0–2–271	1999 actual	2000 est.	2001 est.
Balance, start of year:			
01.99 Balance, start of year			
Receipts:			
02.01 Deposits from sale and transmission of electric energy, Southeastern Power Administration	2		
Appropriation:			
05.01 Continuing fund, Southeastern Power Administration	−2		
07.99 Total balance, end of year			

Program and Financing (in millions of dollars)

Identification code 89–5653–0–2–271	1999 actual	2000 est.	2001 est.
Obligations by program activity:			
10.00 Total new obligations (object class 25.2)	2		
Budgetary resources available for obligation:			
22.00 New budget authority (gross)	2		
23.95 Total new obligations	−2		
New budget authority (gross), detail:			
Mandatory:			
60.25 Appropriation (special fund, indefinite)	2		
Change in unpaid obligations:			
72.40 Unpaid obligations, start of year: Obligated balance, start of year		2	2
73.10 Total new obligations	2		
74.40 Unpaid obligations, end of year: Obligated balance, end of year	2	2	2
Net budget authority and outlays:			
89.00 Budget authority	2		
90.00 Outlays			

A continuing fund of $50 thousand, maintained from receipts from the sale and transmission of electric power in the southeastern area, is available to defray expenses necessary to ensure continuity of service (16 U.S.C. 825s–2). The fund was activitated during FY 1999 to finance power purchases associated with below normal hydro power generation due to drought.

OPERATION AND MAINTENANCE, SOUTHWESTERN POWER ADMINISTRATION

(INCLUDING TRANSFER OF FUNDS)

For necessary expenses of operation and maintenance of power transmission facilities and of marketing electric power and energy, and for construction and acquisition of transmission lines, substations and appurtenant facilities, and for administrative expenses, including official reception and representation expenses in an amount not to exceed $1,500 in carrying out the provisions of section 5 of the Flood Control Act of 1944 (16 U.S.C. 825s), as applied to the southwestern power area, [$28,773,000] *$28,100,000*, to remain available until expended[, of which $773,000 shall be derived by transfer from unobligated balances in "Operation and Maintenance, Southeastern Power Administration"]; in addition, notwithstanding the provisions of 31 U.S.C. 3302, not to exceed $4,200,000 in reimbursements, to remain available until expended*: Provided, That amounts collected by the Southwestern Power Administration pursuant to the Flood Control Act to recover purchase power and wheeling expenses shall be credited to this account as offsetting collections, to remain available until expended for the sole purpose of making purchase power and wheeling expenditures as follows: for fiscal year 2001, up to $288,000; for fiscal year 2002, up to $288,000; for fiscal year 2003, up to $288,000; and for fiscal year 2004, up to $288,000. (Energy and Water Development Appropriations Act, 2000.)*

Program and Financing (in millions of dollars)

Identification code 89–0303–0–1–271	1999 actual	2000 est.	2001 est.
Obligations by program activity:			
Direct program:			
00.01 Systems operation and maintenance	3	4	4
00.03 Construction	7	7	7
00.04 Program direction	16	17	18
09.01 Reimbursable program	7	11	12
10.00 Total new obligations	33	39	41
Budgetary resources available for obligation:			
21.40 Unobligated balance available, start of year			1
22.00 New budget authority (gross)	33	40	40
23.90 Total budgetary resources available for obligation	33	40	41
23.95 Total new obligations	−33	−39	−41

General and special funds—Continued

OPERATION AND MAINTENANCE, SOUTHWESTERN POWER ADMINISTRATION—Continued

(INCLUDING TRANSFER OF FUNDS)—Continued

Program and Financing (in millions of dollars)—Continued

Identification code 89–0303–0–1–271	1999 actual	2000 est.	2001 est.
24.40 Unobligated balance available, end of year		1	
New budget authority (gross), detail:			
Discretionary:			
40.00 Appropriation	26	28	28
42.00 Transferred from other accounts		1	
43.00 Appropriation (total discretionary)	26	29	28
Spending authority from offsetting collections:			
68.00 Offsetting collections (cash)	4	11	12
68.10 From Federal sources: Change in receivables and unpaid, unfilled orders	3		
68.90 Spending authority from offsetting collections (total discretionary)	7	11	12
70.00 Total new budget authority (gross)	33	40	40
Change in unpaid obligations:			
Unpaid obligations, start of year:			
72.40 Obligated balance, start of year	13	9	11
72.95 From Federal sources: Receivables and unpaid, unfilled orders	2	5	5
72.99 Total unpaid obligations, start of year	15	14	16
73.10 Total new obligations	33	39	41
73.20 Total outlays (gross)	−34	−39	−40
Unpaid obligations, end of year:			
74.40 Obligated balance, end of year	9	11	13
74.95 From Federal sources: Receivables and unpaid, unfilled orders	5	5	5
74.99 Total unpaid obligations, end of year	14	16	18
Outlays (gross), detail:			
86.90 Outlays from new discretionary authority	21	29	29
86.93 Outlays from discretionary balances	13	10	11
87.00 Total outlays (gross)	34	39	40
Offsets:			
Against gross budget authority and outlays:			
Offsetting collections (cash) from:			
88.00 Federal sources	−4	−7	−8
88.40 Non-Federal sources		−4	−4
88.90 Total, offsetting collections (cash)	−4	−11	−12
Against gross budget authority only:			
88.95 From Federal sources: Change in receivables and unpaid, unfilled orders	−3		
Net budget authority and outlays:			
89.00 Budget authority	26	29	28
90.00 Outlays	30	28	28

The Southwestern Power Administration (Southwestern) operates in a six-State area as a marketing agent for hydroelectric power produced at Corps of Engineers dams. It also operates and maintains some 2,225 kilometers (1,380 miles) of high voltage transmission line, 24 substations and switching stations, and 46 VHF radio and microwave stations. Southwestern sells its power at wholesale primarily to publicly and cooperatively owned electric distribution utilities. Its power sales contracts provide for periodic rate adjustments to ensure that the Federal Government recovers all costs of operation and all capital invested in power, with interest, in keeping with statutory requirements.

Southwestern also is responsible for scheduling and dispatching power, negotiating power sales contracts, and constructing facilities required to meet changing customer load requirements.

Program direction.—This activity provides for the overall direction and support of Southwestern's program activities and includes salaries and benefits, travel, support services and other related expenses such as rent, utilities, communications, supplies, materials and building maintenance.

Systems operation and maintenance.—Provision is made for engineering assessments of issues and alternatives that could adversely impact or optimize the operation of Southwestern's hydroelectric resources. Provision also is made for maintenance and improvement of the transmission system and related facilities to ensure reliable service, negotiation and administration of power contracts, collection of revenue, development of wholesale power rates and the amortization of the power investment. Actual proprietary receipts in the amount of $95 million were deposited in the Treasury in 1999. Estimated proprietary receipts in the amount of $92 million in 2000 and $96 million in FY 2001 are expected.

Purchase power and wheeling.—Between FY 2001 and FY 2004, the Southwestern Power Administration will phase-out Federal financing of purchase power and wheeling activities. Authority to spend power revenues to pay for purchase of power and wheeling activities will end after FY 2004. Industry restructuring and resulting competition now make it attractive for Southwestern's customers to shop for power and transmission services. Southwestern may continue to support customer bill crediting, net billing and other alternative financing arrangements for these activities.

Construction.—The construction program provides for transmission, substation, switching and control facility replacements and improvements to transmit power generated at Corps of Engineers' hydroelectric projects in the Southwest. This program is coordinated with the Corps of Engineers' construction program and customer requirements.

Reimbursable program.—This program involves services provided by Southwestern Power Administration to others under various types of reimbursable arrangements.

Based on Administration policy the Southwestern Power Administration will set rates consistent with current law to recover the full cost of the civil service retirement system and post-retirement health benefits for its employees.

Object Classification (in millions of dollars)

Identification code 89–0303–0–1–271	1999 actual	2000 est.	2001 est.
Direct obligations:			
11.1 Personnel compensation: Full-time permanent	10	10	10
12.1 Civilian personnel benefits	2	2	2
21.0 Travel and transportation of persons	1	1	1
23.1 Rental payments to GSA	1	1	1
25.2 Other services	8	9	10
26.0 Supplies and materials	1	1	1
31.0 Equipment	3	4	4
99.0 Subtotal, direct obligations	26	28	29
99.0 Reimbursable obligations	7	11	12
99.9 Total new obligations	33	39	41

Personnel Summary

Identification code 89–0303–0–1–271	1999 actual	2000 est.	2001 est.
1001 Total compensable workyears: Full-time equivalent employment	170	177	177

CONTINUING FUND, SOUTHWESTERN POWER ADMINISTRATION

Unavailable Collections (in millions of dollars)

Identification code 89–5649–0–2–271	1999 actual	2000 est.	2001 est.
Balance, start of year:			
01.99 Balance, start of year			

Receipts:			
02.01 Deposits from sale and transmission of electric energy, Southwest Power Administration	2		
Appropriation:			
05.01 Continuing fund, Southwest Power Administration	−2		
07.99 Total balance, end of year			

Program and Financing (in millions of dollars)

Identification code 89–5649–0–2–271	1999 actual	2000 est.	2001 est.
Obligations by program activity:			
10.00 Total new obligations (object class 25.2)	1		
Budgetary resources available for obligation:			
21.40 Unobligated balance available, start of year	−1		
22.00 New budget authority (gross)	2		
23.90 Total budgetary resources available for obligation	1		
23.95 Total new obligations	−1		
New budget authority (gross), detail:			
Mandatory:			
60.25 Appropriation (special fund, indefinite)	2		
Change in unpaid obligations:			
72.40 Unpaid obligations, start of year: Obligated balance, start of year	2		
73.10 Total new obligations	1		
73.20 Total outlays (gross)	−2		
Outlays (gross), detail:			
86.97 Outlays from new mandatory authority	1		
86.98 Outlays from mandatory balances	1		
87.00 Total outlays (gross)	2		
Net budget authority and outlays:			
89.00 Budget authority	2		
90.00 Outlays	2		

This fund, replenished from power receipts, is available permanently for emergency expenses that would be necessary to ensure continuity of service (16 U.S.C. 825s-1: 63 Stat. 767: 65 Stat. 249). The fund was activated in FY 1999 to finance power purchases associated with below normal hydropower generation due to drought and increased demand resulting from an unusually warm summer.

CONSTRUCTION, REHABILITATION, OPERATION AND MAINTENANCE, WESTERN AREA POWER ADMINISTRATION

For carrying out the functions authorized by title III, section 302(a)(1)(E) of the Act of August 4, 1977 (42 U.S.C. 7152), and other related activities including conservation and renewable resources programs as authorized, including official reception and representation expenses in an amount not to exceed $1,500, **[**$193,357,000**]** *$164,916,000*, to remain available until expended, of which **[**$182,172,000**]** *$154,616,000* shall be derived from the Department of the Interior Reclamation Fund: *Provided*, That of the amount herein appropriated, $5,036,000 is for deposit into the Utah Reclamation Mitigation and Conservation Account pursuant to title IV of the Reclamation Projects Authorization and Adjustment Act of 1992: *Provided further, That amounts collected by the Western Area Power Administration pursuant to the Flood Control Act of 1944 and the Reclamation Project Act of 1939 to recover purchase power and wheeling expenses shall be credited to this account as offsetting collections, to remain available until expended for the sole purpose of making purchase power and wheeling expenditures as follows: for fiscal year 2001, up to $35,500,000; for fiscal year 2002, up to $33,500,000;* for fiscal year 2003, up to $30,000,000; and for fiscal year 2004, up to $20,000,000. *(Energy and Water Development Appropriations Act, 2000.)*

Program and Financing (in millions of dollars)

Identification code 89–5068–0–2–271	1999 actual	2000 est.	2001 est.
Obligations by program activity:			
Operating expenses:			
00.01 Systems operation and maintenance	32	36	36
00.02 Purchase power and wheeling	53	27	
00.04 Program direction	105	105	107
00.05 Utah mitigation and conservation fund	5	5	5
00.91 Total operating expenses	195	173	148
01.01 Capital investment	20	22	23
09.01 Reimbursable program	65	200	236
10.00 Total new obligations	280	395	407
Budgetary resources available for obligation:			
21.40 Unobligated balance available, start of year	29	30	7
22.00 New budget authority (gross)	276	372	401
22.10 Resources available from recoveries of prior year obligations	1		
22.22 Unobligated balance transferred from other accounts	4		
23.90 Total budgetary resources available for obligation	310	402	408
23.95 Total new obligations	−280	−395	−407
24.40 Unobligated balance available, end of year	30	7	1
New budget authority (gross), detail:			
Discretionary:			
40.00 Appropriation	9	11	10
40.20 Appropriation (special fund, definite)	194	182	155
40.76 Reduction pursuant to P.L. 106–113		−1	
43.00 Appropriation (total discretionary)	203	192	165
Spending authority from offsetting collections:			
Offsetting collections (cash):			
68.00 Offsetting collections (cash)	63	180	200
68.00 Offsetting collections (cash)—Purchase Power and Wheeling			36
68.10 From Federal sources: Change in receivables and unpaid, unfilled orders	10		
68.90 Spending authority from offsetting collections (total discretionary)	73	180	236
70.00 Total new budget authority (gross)	276	372	401
Change in unpaid obligations:			
Unpaid obligations, start of year:			
72.40 Obligated balance, start of year	137	138	155
72.95 From Federal sources: Receivables and unpaid, unfilled orders	4	14	14
72.99 Total unpaid obligations, start of year	141	152	169
73.10 Total new obligations	280	395	407
73.20 Total outlays (gross)	−269	−378	−416
73.45 Adjustments in unexpired accounts	−1		
Unpaid obligations, end of year:			
74.40 Obligated balance, end of year	138	155	146
74.95 From Federal sources: Receivables and unpaid, unfilled orders	14	14	14
74.99 Total unpaid obligations, end of year	152	169	160
Outlays (gross), detail:			
86.90 Outlays from new discretionary authority	154	266	310
86.93 Outlays from discretionary balances	114	112	106
87.00 Total outlays (gross)	269	378	416
Offsets:			
Against gross budget authority and outlays:			
Offsetting collections (cash) from:			
88.00 Federal sources	−35	−100	−100
Non-Federal sources:			
88.40 Non-Federal sources	−28	−80	−100
88.40 Non-Federal sources-Purchase Power and Wheeling			−36
88.90 Total, offsetting collections (cash)	−63	−180	−236
Against gross budget authority only:			
88.95 From Federal sources: Change in receivables and unpaid, unfilled orders	−10		
Net budget authority and outlays:			
89.00 Budget authority	203	192	165

General and special funds—Continued

CONSTRUCTION, REHABILITATION, OPERATION AND MAINTENANCE, WESTERN AREA POWER ADMINISTRATION—Continued

Program and Financing (in millions of dollars)—Continued

Identification code 89–5068–0–2–271	1999 actual	2000 est.	2001 est.
90.00 Outlays	206	198	180

The Western Area Power Administration (Western) markets electric power in 15 western States from federally-owned power plants operated primarily by the Bureau of Reclamation, Corps of Engineers, and the International Boundary and Water Commission. Western operates and maintains approximately 16,850 circuit-miles of high-voltage transmission line, 256 substations/switchyards, associated power system control, communication and electrical facilities for 15 separate power projects. Western also constructs additions and modifications to existing facilities.

In keeping with statutory requirements, Western's long-term power contracts allow for periodic rate adjustments to ensure that the Federal Government recovers costs of operation, other costs allocated to power, and the capital investment in power facilities, with interest.

Power is sold to wholesale customers such as municipalities, cooperatives, irrigation districts, public utility districts, State and Federal Government agencies, and private utilities. Receipts are deposited in the Reclamation fund, the Falcon and Amistad operating and maintenance fund, the general fund, the Colorado River dam fund, the Central Valley project restoration Fund, and the Colorado River basins power marketing fund.

Systems operation and maintenance.—The systems operation and maintenance activity provides essential electrical and communication equipment replacements, and upgrades, capitalized moveable equipment, technical services, and supplies and materials necessary for safe reliable operation and cost-effective maintenance of the power systems.

Purchase power and wheeling.—Between FY 2001 and FY 2004, the Western Area Power Administration will phase-out Federal financing of purchase power and wheeling activities. Authority to spend power revenues to pay for purchase power and wheeling activities will end after FY 2004. Industry restructuring and resulting competition now make it attractive for Western's customers to shop for power and transmission services. Western may continue to support customer bill crediting, net billing and other alternative financing arrangements for these activities.

System construction.—Western's construction and rehabilitation activity emphasizes replacement and upgrades of existing infrastructure to sustain reliable power delivery to our customers, to contain annual maintenance costs, and to improve overall operational efficiency. Western will continue to participate in joint construction projects to encourage more widespread transmission access.

Program direction.—This activity provides compensation and all related expenses for the workforce that operates and maintains Western's high voltage interconnected transmission system (systems operation and maintenance program), and those that plan design, and supervise the construction of replacements, upgrades and additions (system construction program) to the transmission facilities.

Utah mitigation and conservation.—The request includes $5,036,000 for deposit into the Utah reclamation mitigation and conservation account in the U.S. Treasury, pursuant to Title IV of the Reclamation Projects Authorization and Adjustment Act of 1992. The account is earmarked primarily for environmental mitigation expenditures in the State of Utah covering fish and wildlife, and recreation resources impacted by the Colorado River Storage Project.

Reimbursable program.—This program involves services provided by Western to others under various types of reimbursable arrangements.

Western will continue to spend directly out of the Colorado River dam fund for operations and maintenance activities associated with the Boulder Canyon Project. The Colorado River dam fund is a revolving fund operated by the Interior Department's Bureau of Reclamation. Authority for Western to obligate directly from the Colorado River dam fund comes from section 104(a) of the Hoover Power Plant Act of 1984.

Based on Administration policy, the Western Area Power Administration will set rates consistent with current law to recover the full cost of the Civil Service Retirement System and post-retirement health benefits, for its employees.

For display purposes only, the unobligated balances of this account include a continuing fund of $500 thousand, which is maintained from deposits to the Reclamation Fund, and is available to ensure continuous operation of power systems in the event of below normal hydropower generation, equipment failure, or other damage caused by acts of God, flood, drought, strikes, embargoes, or other conditions which might cause interruptions in service.

Object Classification (in millions of dollars)

Identification code 89–5068–0–2–271	1999 actual	2000 est.	2001 est.
Direct obligations:			
Personnel compensation:			
11.1 Full-time permanent	54	56	56
11.3 Other than full-time permanent	1	1	1
11.5 Other personnel compensation	3	3	3
11.9 Total personnel compensation	58	60	60
12.1 Civilian personnel benefits	15	15	16
21.0 Travel and transportation of persons	6	5	7
22.0 Transportation of things	2	3	3
23.1 Rental payments to GSA	3	3	3
23.3 Communications, utilities, and miscellaneous charges	4	5	4
25.2 Other services	79	57	28
25.3 Purchases of goods and services from Government accounts	3	1	2
26.0 Supplies and materials	8	7	7
31.0 Equipment	10	11	11
32.0 Land and structures	22	23	25
41.0 Grants, subsidies, and contributions	5	5	5
99.0 Subtotal, direct obligations	215	195	171
99.0 Reimbursable obligations	65	200	236
99.9 Total new obligations	280	395	407

Personnel Summary

Identification code 89–5068–0–2–271	1999 actual	2000 est.	2001 est.
1001 Total compensable workyears: Full-time equivalent employment	1,057	1,075	1,075

FALCON AND AMISTAD OPERATING AND MAINTENANCE FUND

For operation, maintenance, and emergency costs for the hydroelectric facilities at the Falcon and Amistad Dams, [$1,309,000] *$2,670,000*, to remain available until expended, and to be derived from the Falcon and Amistad Operating and Maintenance Fund of the Western Area Power Administration, as provided in section 423 of the Foreign Relations Authorization Act, Fiscal Years 1994 and 1995. *(Energy and Water Development Appropriations Act, 2000.)*

Unavailable Collections (in millions of dollars)

Identification code 89–5178–0–2–271	1999 actual	2000 est.	2001 est.
Balance, start of year:			
01.99 Balance, start of year	2	2	2
Receipts:			
02.01 Falcon and Amistad operating and maintenance fund	1	1	3
04.00 Total: Balances and collections	3	3	5

Appropriation:			
05.01 Falcon and Amistad operating and maintenance fund	−1	−1	−3
07.99 Total balance, end of year	2	2	2

Program and Financing (in millions of dollars)

Identification code 89–5178–0–2–271	1999 actual	2000 est.	2001 est.
Obligations by program activity:			
10.00 Total new obligations (object class 25.3)	1	1	3
Budgetary resources available for obligation:			
22.00 New budget authority (gross)	1	1	3
23.95 Total new obligations	−1	−1	−3
New budget authority (gross), detail:			
Discretionary:			
40.20 Appropriation (special fund, definite)	1	1	3
Change in unpaid obligations:			
73.10 Total new obligations	1	1	3
73.20 Total outlays (gross)	−1	−1	2
Outlays (gross), detail:			
86.90 Outlays from new discretionary authority	1	1	2
Net budget authority and outlays:			
89.00 Budget authority	1	1	3
90.00 Outlays	1	1	2

Pursuant to section 423(c) of the Foreign Relations Authorization Act, Fiscal Years 1994 and 1995, Western Area Power Administration is requesting an appropriation from the Falcon and Amistad operating and maintenance fund, to defray operations, maintenance, and emergency (O,M&E) expenses for the hydroelectric facilities at Falcon and Amistad dams on the Rio Grande river. Most of these funds will be made available to the United States Section of the International Boundary and Water Commission through a reimbursable agreement. $200,000 in the fund is for an emergency reserve that will remain unobligated unless unanticipated expenses arise. Revenues in excess of O,M&E will be paid to the General Fund to repay the costs of replacements and the original investment with interest. Revenues resulting from the Falcon and Amistad dams power system operations are deposited to the Falcon and Amistad operating and maintenance fund.

Public enterprise funds:

BONNEVILLE POWER ADMINISTRATION FUND

Expenditures from the Bonneville Power Administration Fund, established pursuant to Public Law 93–454, are approved for the [Northeast Oregon Hatchery Master Plan] *Nez Perce Tribe Resident Fish Substitution Program, the Cour D'Alene Tribe Trout Production facility,* and for official reception and representation expenses in an amount not to exceed $1,500.

During fiscal year [2000] *2001,* no new direct loan obligations may be made. *Section 511 of the Energy and Water Development Appropriations Act, 1997 (Public Law 104–206), is amended by striking the last sentence and inserting, "This authority shall expire September 30, 2005.". (Energy and Water Development Appropriations Act, 2000.)*

Program and Financing (in millions of dollars)

Identification code 89–4045–0–3–271	1999 actual	2000 est.	2001 est.
Obligations by program activity:			
Operating expenses:			
Operating expenses:			
00.01 Power business line	1,236	1,088	1,087
00.02 Residential exchange	63	63	68
00.05 Bureau of Reclamation	42	46	48
00.06 Corps of Engineers	99	101	102
00.07 Colville settlement	14	15	15
00.19 U.S. Fish & Wildlife	13	15	15
00.20 Planning council	7	7	7
00.21 Fish and wildlife	108	110	105
00.23 Transmission business line	190	218	219
00.24 Conservation and energy efficiency	34	35	34
00.25 Interest	420	412	439
00.26 Pension and health benefits	4	6	8
00.91 Total operating expenses	2,230	2,116	2,147
Capital investment:			
01.01 Power business line	59	80	76
01.02 Transmission services	97	168	207
01.03 Conservation and energy efficiency		1	
01.04 Fish and wildlife	15	27	27
01.05 Capital equipment	14	18	15
01.06 Capitalized bonds premiums		16	6
01.91 Total capital investment	185	310	331
02.01 Projects funded in advance	11	25	25
10.00 Total new obligations	2,426	2,451	2,503
Budgetary resources available for obligation:			
21.40 Unobligated balance available, start of year	579	800	800
22.00 New budget authority (gross)	2,647	2,451	2,503
23.90 Total budgetary resources available for obligation	3,226	3,251	3,303
23.95 Total new obligations	−2,426	−2,451	−2,503
24.40 Unobligated balance available, end of year	800	800	800
New budget authority (gross), detail:			
Mandatory:			
67.15 Authority to borrow (indefinite)	185	217	231
69.00 Offsetting collections (cash)	2,629	2,399	2,435
69.47 Portion applied to repay debt	−167	−165	−163
69.90 Spending authority from offsetting collections (total mandatory)	2,462	2,234	2,272
70.00 Total new budget authority (gross)	2,647	2,451	2,503
Change in unpaid obligations:			
72.40 Unpaid obligations, start of year: Obligated balance, start of year	197	197	197
73.10 Total new obligations	2,426	2,451	2,503
73.20 Total outlays (gross)	−2,426	−2,451	−2,503
74.40 Unpaid obligations, end of year: Obligated balance, end of year	197	197	197
Outlays (gross), detail:			
86.97 Outlays from new mandatory authority	2,408	2,399	2,423
86.98 Outlays from mandatory balances	18	53	80
87.00 Total outlays (gross)	2,426	2,451	2,503
Offsets:			
Against gross budget authority and outlays:			
Offsetting collections (cash) from:			
88.00 Federal sources	−90	−90	−90
88.40 Non-Federal sources	−2,539	−2,309	−2,345
88.90 Total, offsetting collections (cash)	−2,629	−2,399	−2,435
Net budget authority and outlays:			
89.00 Budget authority	18	52	68
90.00 Outlays	−203	52	68

Status of Direct Loans (in millions of dollars)

Identification code 89–4045–0–3–271	1999 actual	2000 est.	2001 est.
Cumulative balance of direct loans outstanding:			
1210 Outstanding, start of year	2	2	2
1290 Outstanding, end of year	2	2	2

Bonneville Power Administration (BPA) is the Federal electric power marketing agency in the Pacific Northwest. BPA markets hydroelectric power from 21 multipurpose water resource projects of the U.S. Army Corps of Engineers and 8 projects of the U.S. Bureau of Reclamation, plus some energy from non-Federal generating projects in the region. These generating resources and BPA's transmission system, planned by the end of 2001 to consist of an estimated 15,000

Public enterprise funds—Continued

BONNEVILLE POWER ADMINISTRATION FUND—Continued

circuit miles of high-voltage transmission lines and 324 substations, are operated as an integrated power system with operating and financial results combined and reported as the Federal Columbia River Power System (FCRPS). BPA is the largest power wholesaler in the Northwest and provides about forty percent of the region's electric energy supply and about three-fourths of the region's electric power transmission capacity.

BPA is responsible for meeting the net firm power requirements of its requesting customers through a variety of means, including energy conservation programs, acquisition of renewable and other resources, and power exchanges with utilities both in and outside the region.

BPA will finance its operations on the basis of the self-financing authority provided by Federal Columbia River Transmission System Act of 1974 (Transmission Act) (Public Law 93–454) and the new borrowing authority provided by the Pacific Northwest Electric Power Planning and Conservation Act (Pacific Northwest Power Act) (Public Law 96–501) for energy conservation, renewable energy resources and capital fish facilities. Authority to borrow is available to the BPA on a permanent, indefinite basis. The amount of borrowing outstanding at any time cannot exceed $3.75 billion.

Operating expenses: Transmission services business line.—Provides funding from revenues for electric transmission research and development and program support of the capital investment program described below for transmission services. Provides for operating an estimated 15,000 miles of line and 324 substations, and for maintaining the facilities and equipment of the Bonneville transmission system in 2001.

Power business line.—Provides for the planning, contractual acquisition and oversight of reliable, cost effective resources. These resources are needed to serve BPA's portion of the region's forecasted net electric load requirements. Also includes protection, mitigation and enhancement of fish and wildlife affected by hydroelectric facilities on the Columbia River and its tributaries in accordance with the Pacific Northwest Power Act. Provides for payment of the operation and maintenance (O&M) costs of the 29 U.S. Army Corps of Engineers and U.S. Bureau of Reclamation power generation projects, and amortization on the U.S. Bureau of Reclamation capital investment in power generating facilities and irrigation assistance at Bureau facilities. Provides for the planning, contractual acquisition and oversight of reliable, cost effective conservation. Also provides for extending the benefits of low cost Federal power to the residential and small farm customers of investor-owned and publicly-owned utilities, in accordance with the Pacific Northwest Power Act and for activities of the Pacific Northwest Electric Power and Conservation Planning Council required by the Pacific Northwest Power Act.

Interest.—Provides for payments to the U.S. Treasury for interest on borrowings to finance BPA's transmission services, conservation, capital equipment, fish and wildlife, and associated projects capital programs under $3.75 billion borrowing authority provided by the Transmission Act as amended by the Pacific Northwest Power Act and replenished by Public Law 98–50. This category also includes interest on Corps of Engineers, BPA and U.S. Bureau of Reclamation appropriated debt.

Capital Investments: Transmission services business line.—Provides for the planning, design and construction of transmission lines, substation and control system additions, replacements, and enhancements to the FCRPS transmission system for a reliable, efficient and cost-effective regional transmission system. Provides for planning, design, and construction work to repair or replace existing transmission lines, substations, control systems, and general facilities of the FCRPS transmission system.

Power business line.—Provides for direct funding of additions, improvements, and replacements at existing Federal hydroelectric projects in the Northwest. Also provides for capital investments to implement environmental activities, and protect, mitigate, and enhance fish and wildlife affected by hydroelectric facilities on the Columbia River and its tributaries, in accordance with the Pacific Northwest Power Act. Also provides for the planning, contractual acquisition and oversight of reliable, cost effective conservation.

Capital equipment/Capitalized bond premium.—Provides for general purpose ADP equipment, office furniture and equipment, and software capital development in support of all BPA programs. Also provides for bond premiums incurred for refinancing of bonds.

Contingencies.—Although contingencies are not specifically funded, the need may arise to provide for purchase of power in low-water years; for repair and/or replacement of facilities affected by natural and man-made emergencies, including the resulting additional costs for contracting, construction, and operation and maintenance work; for unavoidable increased costs for the planned program due to necessary but unforeseen adjustments, including engineering and design changes, contractor and other claims and relocations, or for payment of a retrospective premium adjustment in excess nuclear property insurance.

Financing.—The Transmission Act provides for the use by BPA of all receipts, collections, and recoveries in cash from all sources, including the sale of bonds, to finance the annual budget programs of BPA. These receipts result primarily from the sale of power and wheeling services. The Transmission Act also provides for authority to borrow from the U.S. Treasury at rates comparable to borrowings at open market rates for similar issues. As amended by the Pacific Northwest Power Act and replenished by Public Law 98–50, it allows for $3.75 billion of borrowing to be outstanding at any time. The fiscal year 2001 capital obligations are estimated to be $331 million. To the extent BPA capital borrowing authority is insufficient in 2001, BPA would use cash reserves generated by revenues from customers, if available, to finance some of these investments.

In FY 1999, BPA made payments to the Treasury of $628 million and also expects to make payments of $594 million in 2000 and $620 million in 2001. The 2001 payment will be distributed as follows: interest on bonds and appropriations ($447 million), Bureau of Reclamation irrigation assistance ($10 million), and amortization ($163 million).

Direct loans.—During FY 2001, no new direct loan obligations may be made.

Operating results.—Total revenues are forecast at approximately $2.4 billion in FY 2001.

It should be noted that BPA's revenue forecasts are based on several critical assumptions about both the supply of and demand for Federal energy. During the operating year, deviation from the conditions assumed in a rate case may result in a variation in actual revenues of several hundred million dollars from the forecast.

Consistent with Administration policy, BPA will continue to fully recover, from the sale of electric power and transmission, funds sufficient to cover the full cost of Civil Service Retirement System and Post-Retirement Health Benefits for their employees. The entire cost of BPA employees working under the Federal Employees Retirement System is already fully recovered in wholesale electric power and transmission rates.

Statement of Operations (in millions of dollars)

Identification code 89–4045–0–3–271	1998 actual	1999 actual	2000 est.	2001 est.
0101 Revenue	2,323	2,619	2,330	2,330

0102	Expense	−2,282	−2,434	−2,055	−2,055
0105	Net income or loss (−)	41	185	275	275

Balance Sheet (in millions of dollars)

Identification code 89–4045–0–3–271		1998 actual	1999 actual	2000 est.	2001 est.
	ASSETS:				
	Federal assets:				
1101	Fund balances with Treasury	526	614	650	691
	Investments in US securities:				
1106	Receivables, net	3	3	3	3
1206	Non-Federal assets: Receivables, net	186	197	197	197
1601	Net value of assets related to pre–1992 direct loans receivable and acquired defaulted guaranteed loans receivable: Direct loans, gross	2	2	2	2
	Other Federal assets:				
1802	Inventories and related properties	66	63	63	63
1803	Property, plant and equipment, net	3,244	3,227	3,257	3,354
1901	Other assets	7,999	7,704	7,325	6,947
1999	Total assets	12,026	11,810	11,497	11,257
	LIABILITIES:				
2102	Federal liabilities: Interest payable	35	32	32	32
	Non-Federal liabilities:				
2201	Accounts payable	253	158	158	158
2203	Debt	10,708	10,339	10,057	9,853
2207	Other	407	447	447	447
2999	Total liabilities	11,403	10,976	10,694	10,490
	NET POSITION:				
3300	Cumulative results of operations	623	834	803	767
3999	Total net position	623	834	803	767
4999	Total liabilities and net position	12,026	11,810	11,497	11,257

Object Classification (in millions of dollars)

Identification code 89–4045–0–3–271		1999 actual	2000 est.	2001 est.
	Personnel compensation:			
11.1	Full-time permanent	166	168	173
11.3	Other than full-time permanent	3	3	3
11.5	Other personnel compensation	16	16	17
11.9	Total personnel compensation	185	187	193
	Civilian personnel benefits:			
12.1	Civilian personnel benefits	4	6	8
12.1	Civilian personnel benefits	39	38	37
21.0	Travel and transportation of persons	8	8	9
22.0	Transportation of things	6	6	6
23.1	Rental payments to GSA	10	10	10
23.2	Rental payments to others	10	10	10
23.3	Communications, utilities, and miscellaneous charges	5	5	5
25.1	Advisory and assistance services	11	11	11
25.2	Other services	1,404	1,414	1,439
25.3	Purchases of goods and services from Government accounts	217	221	226
25.5	Research and development contracts	2	2	2
26.0	Supplies and materials	38	39	39
31.0	Equipment	22	22	23
32.0	Land and structures	20	21	21
41.0	Grants, subsidies, and contributions	22	21	23
43.0	Interest and dividends	423	430	441
99.9	Total new obligations	2,426	2,451	2,503

Personnel Summary

Identification code 89–4045–0–3–271		1999 actual	2000 est.	2001 est.
1001	Total compensable workyears: Full-time equivalent employment	2,738	2,800	2,755

Colorado River Basins Power Marketing Fund, Western Area Power Administration

Program and Financing (in millions of dollars)

Identification code 89–4452–0–3–271		1999 actual	2000 est.	2001 est.
	Obligations by program activity:			
09.01	Program direction	27	29	31
09.02	Colorado River storage project	42	72	73
09.03	Fort Peck project	6	10	10
09.04	Other projects		3	1
10.00	Total new obligations	75	114	115
	Budgetary resources available for obligation:			
21.40	Unobligated balance available, start of year	30	58	58
22.00	New budget authority (gross)	103	114	115
23.90	Total budgetary resources available for obligation	133	172	173
23.95	Total new obligations	−75	−114	−115
24.40	Unobligated balance available, end of year	58	58	58
	New budget authority (gross), detail:			
	Spending authority from offsetting collections:			
	Discretionary:			
68.00	Offsetting collections (cash)	104	135	136
68.10	From Federal sources: Change in receivables and unpaid, unfilled orders	−1		
68.27	Capital transfer to general fund		−21	−21
68.90	Spending authority from offsetting collections (total discretionary)	103	114	115
	Change in unpaid obligations:			
	Unpaid obligations, start of year:			
72.40	Obligated balance, start of year	8	9	9
72.95	From Federal sources: Receivables and unpaid, unfilled orders	1		
72.99	Total unpaid obligations, start of year	9	9	9
73.10	Total new obligations	75	114	115
73.20	Total outlays (gross)	−75	−114	−115
74.40	Unpaid obligations, end of year: Obligated balance, end of year	9	9	9
	Outlays (gross), detail:			
86.90	Outlays from new discretionary authority	75	114	115
	Offsets:			
	Against gross budget authority and outlays:			
	Offsetting collections (cash) from:			
88.00	Federal sources	−9	−8	−8
88.40	Non-Federal sources	−95	−127	−128
88.90	Total, offsetting collections (cash)	−104	−135	−136
	Against gross budget authority only:			
88.95	From Federal sources: Change in receivables and unpaid, unfilled orders	1		
	Net budget authority and outlays:			
89.00	Budget authority		−21	−21
90.00	Outlays	−29	−21	−21

Western's operation and maintenance and power marketing expenses for the Colorado River storage project, the Colorado River basin project, the Seedskadee project, the Dolores project and the Fort Peck project are financed from power revenues.

Program direction.—Western operates and maintains approximately 4,000 miles of transmission lines, substations, switchyards, communications and control equipment associated with this Fund. The personnel compensation and related expenses for all these activities are quantified under Program Direction. Wholesale power is provided to utilities over interconnected high-voltage transmission systems. In keeping with statutory requirements, long-term power contracts provide for periodic rate adjustments to ensure that the Federal Government recovers all costs of operation and all capital invested in power, with interest.

Colorado River storage project.—Western markets power and operates and maintains the power transmission facilities of the Colorado River Storage Project. Western also purchases electricity and pays wheeling fees to meet firm and nonfirm commitments.

Colorado River basin project.—The Colorado River Basin Project includes Western's expenses associated with the Central Arizona Project and the United States entitlement from the Navajo coal-fired powerplant. Revenues in excess of oper-

Public enterprise funds—Continued

COLORADO RIVER BASINS POWER MARKETING FUND, WESTERN AREA POWER ADMINISTRATION—Continued

ating expenses are transferred to the Lower Colorado River Basin Development Fund.

Fort Peck project.—Revenue collected by Western is used to defray operation and maintenance and power marketing expenses associated with the power generation and transmission facilities of the Fort Peck Project, Corps of Engineers—Civil, to defray emergency expenses, and to ensure continuous operation. The Corps operates and maintains the power generating facilities, and Western operates and maintains the transmission system and performs power marketing functions.

Seedskadee project.—This activity includes Western's expenses for O/M, power marketing, and transmission of hydroelectric power from Fontenelle Dam's powerplant in Southwestern Wyoming.

Dolores project.—This activity includes Western's expenses for O/M, power marketing, and transmission of hydroelectric power from powerplants at McPhee Dam Towaoc Canal in Southwestern Colorado.

Based on Administration policy, the Western Area Power Administration will set rates consistent with current law to recover the full cost of the civil service retirement system and post-retirement health benefits for its employees.

Balance Sheet (in millions of dollars)

Identification code 89–4452–0–3–271	1998 actual	1999 actual	2000 est.	2001 est.
ASSETS:				
Federal assets:				
1101 Fund balances with Treasury	38	67	67	67
Investments in US securities:				
1106 Receivables, net	1	8	8	8
1206 Non-Federal assets: Receivables, net	31	−3	−3	−3
Other Federal assets:				
1802 Inventories and related properties	3	3	3	3
1803 Property, plant and equipment, net	100	72	72	72
1901 Other assets	42	89	89	89
1999 Total assets	215	236	236	236
LIABILITIES:				
Federal liabilities:				
2101 Accounts payable	2			
2105 Other		217	217	217
Non-Federal liabilities:				
2201 Accounts payable		3	3	3
2207 Other	214	2	2	2
2999 Total liabilities	216	222	222	222
NET POSITION:				
3300 Cumulative results of operations	−1	14	14	14
3999 Total net position	−1	14	14	14
4999 Total liabilities and net position	215	236	236	236

Object Classification (in millions of dollars)

Identification code 89–4452–0–3–271	1999 actual	2000 est.	2001 est.
Personnel compensation:			
11.1 Full-time permanent	10	12	13
11.5 Other personnel compensation	1	1	1
11.9 Total personnel compensation	11	13	14
12.1 Civilian personnel benefits	2	3	3
21.0 Travel and transportation of persons	1	1	1
22.0 Transportation of things		1	1
23.1 Rental payments to GSA	1	1	1
23.3 Communications, utilities, and miscellaneous charges	1	1	1
25.2 Other services	27	60	62
25.3 Purchases of goods and services from Government accounts	3	3	4
26.0 Supplies and materials	2	3	4
31.0 Equipment	5	4	4
32.0 Land and structures	6	5	5
43.0 Interest and dividends	16	19	15
99.9 Total new obligations	75	114	115

Personnel Summary

Identification code 89–4452–0–3–271	1999 actual	2000 est.	2001 est.
2001 Total compensable workyears: Full-time equivalent employment	202	189	185

DEPARTMENTAL ADMINISTRATION

Federal Funds

General and special funds:

DEPARTMENTAL ADMINISTRATION

For salaries and expenses of the Department of Energy necessary for departmental administration in carrying out the purposes of the Department of Energy Organization Act (42 U.S.C. 7101 et seq.), including the hire of passenger motor vehicles and official reception and representation expenses (not to exceed $35,000), [$206,365,000] *$213,339,000*, to remain available until expended, plus such additional amounts as necessary to cover increases in the estimated amount of cost of work for others notwithstanding the provisions of the Anti-Deficiency Act (31 U.S.C. 1511 et seq.): *Provided*, That such increases in cost of work are offset by revenue increases of the same or greater amount, to remain available until expended: *Provided further*, That moneys received by the Department for miscellaneous revenues estimated to total [$106,887,000] *$128,762,000* in fiscal year [2000] *2001* may be retained and used for operating expenses within this account, and may remain available until expended, as authorized by section 201 of Public Law 95–238, notwithstanding the provisions of 31 U.S.C. 3302: *Provided further*, That the sum herein appropriated shall be reduced by the amount of miscellaneous revenues received during fiscal year [2000] *2001* so as to result in a final fiscal year [2000] *2001* appropriation from the General Fund estimated at not more than [$99,478,000] *$84,577,000*. *(Energy and Water Development Appropriations Act, 2000.)*

Program and Financing (in millions of dollars)

Identification code 89–0228–0–1–276	1999 actual	2000 est.	2001 est.
Obligations by program activity:			
00.01 Office of Policy	16	17	8
00.02 Management and administration	76	103	91
00.03 Chief Financial Officer	22	26	31
00.04 Office of Congressional and Intergovernmental Affairs	5	5	5
00.05 Office of Public Affairs	4	4	4
00.06 Field management	7	2	
00.07 General Counsel	20	21	23
00.08 Office of the Secretary	5	5	6
00.09 Board of Contract Appeals	1	1	1
00.10 Economic impact and diversity	6	7	7
00.12 Contract reform and privatization	2	3	3
00.13 International Affairs			10
09.01 Reimbursable program	33	33	34
10.00 Total new obligations	197	227	223
Budgetary resources available for obligation:			
21.40 Unobligated balance available, start of year	17	31	10
22.00 New budget authority (gross)	210	206	214
23.90 Total budgetary resources available for obligation	227	237	224
23.95 Total new obligations	−197	−227	−223
24.40 Unobligated balance available, end of year	31	10	1
New budget authority (gross), detail:			
Discretionary:			
40.00 Appropriation	126	100	85
40.76 Reduction pursuant to P.L. 106–113		−1	
42.00 Transferred from other accounts	10		
43.00 Appropriation (total discretionary)	136	99	85
68.00 Spending authority from offsetting collections: Offsetting collections (cash)	74	107	129
70.00 Total new budget authority (gross)	210	206	214
Change in unpaid obligations:			
72.40 Unpaid obligations, start of year: Obligated balance, start of year	61	73	93

73.10	Total new obligations	197	227	223
73.20	Total outlays (gross)	−184	−207	−213
74.40	Unpaid obligations, end of year: Obligated balance, end of year	73	93	103
	Outlays (gross), detail:			
86.90	Outlays from new discretionary authority	173	170	176
86.93	Outlays from discretionary balances	11	37	36
87.00	Total outlays (gross)	184	207	213
	Offsets:			
	Against gross budget authority and outlays:			
	Offsetting collections (cash) from:			
88.00	Federal sources	−43	−71	−76
88.40	Non-Federal sources	−31	−36	−53
88.90	Total, offsetting collections (cash)	−74	−107	−129
	Net budget authority and outlays:			
89.00	Budget authority	136	99	85
90.00	Outlays	110	100	84

Departmental administration.—This account funds a wide array of policy development and analysis activities, institutional and public liaison functions, and other program support requirements necessary to ensure effective operation and management. Specific activities provided for are:

Office of Policy.—This organization is the principal advisor to the Secretary, Deputy Secretary and Under Secretary on energy and technology policy issues, including the environmental consequences of energy use. Policy has primary responsibility for the formulation and development of national energy policy and for the conduct of policy analyses. The Policy Office has the lead role in the Department for international negotiations on environmental issues, such as climate change. Policy also analyzes, develops and coordinates departmental science and technology policy, environmental policy, including global change policy, and economic policy. This office is responsible for advising the Department's senior management on issues related to the Department's national and environmental security and energy emergency policies.

Office of International Affairs.—This organization serves as the principal advisor to the Secretary and senior Departmental officials, on international energy affairs, including international energy policy. Other responsibilities are to: lead the Department's bilateral and multilateral cooperation with other nations and international organizations, including participation in international negotiations; coordinate the implementation of international cooperative agreements; advance energy, environmental, climate change and non-proliferation policies in international agreements; promote positive relationships with foreign nations that support U.S. policy goals; and, promote policy and regulatory reforms in foreign countries that will remove barriers and open markets for U.S. firms abroad. International Affairs also coordinate the Department's international energy, science and technology relations with other countries. In these activities, International Affairs, works closely with the Department of State and other Departments and agencies.

Management and administration.—This office provides management and oversight and institutional support services to headquarters organizations and to the Department as a whole. Areas of responsibility include: organization and management systems; human resources management; procurement; facilities planning; aviation management and safety; headquarters administrative services; and procurement and assistance management and oversight.

Chief Financial Officer (CFO).—This office provides centralized direction and oversight of financial activities including departmental budgeting, accounting, financial policy, compliance, and financial management. The CFO provides oversight at the Department of government-wide efforts to improve financial management as mandated by recent legislation, for example, Government Performance and Results Act and Government Management Reform Act, through such means as the audited financial statements. The CFO also operates and maintains payroll and financial accounting systems and performs financial management functions including accounting, cash management and reporting. In addition, in FY 2000 the CFO organization acquired two new functions which are responsible for the Department's strategic planning process and corporate oversight for engineering and construction. In FY 2000, the CFO began implementation of a comprehensive business management information system that will replace the departmental primary accounting system.

Congressional and intergovernmental affairs.—This office is responsible for coordinating, directing, and promoting the Secretary's and the Department's policies and legislative initiatives with the Congress, State, territorial, Tribal and local government officials, and other Federal agencies. The office is also responsible for managing and overseeing the Department's liaison with members of Congress, the White House and other levels of government and stakeholders which includes public interest groups representing state, local and tribal governments.

Office of Public Affairs.—This office is responsible for directing and managing the Secretary's, Department's, and Administration's policies and initiatives with the public, news media and other stakeholders on energy issues and also serves as the Department's chief spokesperson. The office manages and oversees all public affairs efforts, which includes public information, press and media services, the departmental newsletter *DOE This Month,* speech writing, special projects, editorial services, the Department's home page, and review of proposed publications and audiovisuals.

General Counsel.—This office is responsible for providing legal services to all energy activities except for those functions belonging exclusively to the Federal Energy Regulatory Commission, which is served by its own General Counsel. Its responsibilities entail the provision of legal opinion, advice and services to administrative and program offices, and the conduct of both administrative and judicial litigation, as well as legal advice and support for enforcement activities. Further, the General Counsel appears before State and Federal agencies in defense of national energy policies and activities. The office is responsible for the coordination and clearance of proposed legislation affecting energy activities and testimony before Congress. The General Counsel is also responsible for ensuring consistency and legal sufficiency of all energy regulations; administering and monitoring standards of conduct requirements; and conducting the patents program.

Office of the Secretary.—Directs and supervises the staff and provides policy guidance to line and staff organizations in the accomplishment of agency objectives.

Board of Contract Appeals.—Adjudicates disputes arising out of the Department's contracts and financial assistance programs and provides for neutral services and facilities for alternative dispute resolution.

Economic impact and diversity.—This office is responsible for: advising the Secretary on the effects of the Department's policies, regulations and actions on underrepresented population groups, communities, and business enterprises; conducting research to determine energy consumption and use patterns of minorities; and providing technical assistance to minority educational institutions and minority business enterprises to enable them to participate more fully in departmental activities. The office is also responsible for initiatives on minority educational institutions for the Department; administering a departmental small and disadvantaged business program; serves as the Department's enforcer to ensure that the civil rights of employees are protected and complaints are processed within applicable regulatory timeframes; implements the Department's environmental justice strategy; and

General and special funds—Continued

DEPARTMENTAL ADMINISTRATION—Continued

responsible for the Office of Employee Concerns which manages the whistle blower reform initiative.

Cost of work for others.—This activity covers the cost of work performed under orders placed with the Department by non-DOE entities which are precluded by law from making advance payments and certain revenue programs. Reimbursement for these costs is made through deposits of offsetting collections to this account.

Contract Reform and Privatization Project Office.—This office is the principle advisor to the Secretary in the formulation, guidance and implementation of the Department's privatization and contract reform initiatives. The office represents the Department on privatization and contract reform matters in dealing with Congress, other Federal agencies, and various stakeholders. It participates in reviews at various stages of privatization projects including acquisition planning, budgeting and the development of requests for proposals and contracts, and has concurrence authority on all major procurement actions.

Corporate management information program (CMIP).—This initiative began in FY 1998 and supports the objectives of the National Performance Review to provide better delivery of information and more efficient support to DOE's customers through modernized corporate information systems using more cost effective and current information technology. Funding in the amount of $12.0 million is provided to support modernization of corporate administrative systems at DOE. A corporate human resources information system is under development to support activities such as position management, processing personnel actions, and applicant/employee tracking of awards and benefits through a user-friendly, automated information technology system. Additionally, CMIP funding will be used to update and replace a number of independent, antiquated financial management systems with compatible, user-friendly business systems providing real time financial and management data to managers throughout the Department. Finally, some funds will be provided for procurement modernization activities and for technology infrastructure needs.

Object Classification (in millions of dollars)

Identification code 89–0228–0–1–276		1999 actual	2000 est.	2001 est.
	Direct obligations:			
	Personnel compensation:			
11.1	Full-time permanent	82	83	81
11.3	Other than full-time permanent	7	7	7
11.5	Other personnel compensation	2	2	2
11.8	Special personal services payments	2	2	2
11.9	Total personnel compensation	93	94	92
12.1	Civilian personnel benefits	17	18	18
21.0	Travel and transportation of persons	4	4	4
23.3	Communications, utilities, and miscellaneous charges	2	2	2
25.1	Advisory and assistance services	10	10	10
25.2	Other services	1	1	1
25.3	Purchases of goods and services from Government accounts	11	28	25
25.4	Operation and maintenance of facilities	19	30	30
25.6	Medical care	1	1	1
26.0	Supplies and materials	6	6	6
99.0	Subtotal, direct obligations	164	194	189
99.0	Reimbursable obligations	33	33	34
99.9	Total new obligations	197	227	223

Personnel Summary

Identification code 89–0228–0–1–276		1999 actual	2000 est.	2001 est.
1001	Total compensable workyears: Full-time equivalent employment	1,247	1,245	1,165

OFFICE OF THE INSPECTOR GENERAL

For necessary expenses of the Office of the Inspector General in carrying out the provisions of the Inspector General Act of 1978, as amended, [$29,500,000] *$33,000,000*, to remain available until expended. *(Energy and Water Development Appropriations Act, 2000.)*

Program and Financing (in millions of dollars)

Identification code 89–0236–0–1–276		1999 actual	2000 est.	2001 est.
	Obligations by program activity:			
10.00	Total new obligations	29	30	33
	Budgetary resources available for obligation:			
21.40	Unobligated balance available, start of year	1	1	
22.00	New budget authority (gross)	29	30	33
23.90	Total budgetary resources available for obligation	30	31	33
23.95	Total new obligations	−29	−30	−33
24.40	Unobligated balance available, end of year	1		
	New budget authority (gross), detail:			
	Discretionary:			
40.00	Appropriation	29	30	33
	Change in unpaid obligations:			
72.40	Unpaid obligations, start of year: Obligated balance, start of year	5	6	6
73.10	Total new obligations	29	30	33
73.20	Total outlays (gross)	−28	−30	−33
74.40	Unpaid obligations, end of year: Obligated balance, end of year	6	6	6
	Outlays (gross), detail:			
86.90	Outlays from new discretionary authority	25	26	28
86.93	Outlays from discretionary balances	4	4	5
87.00	Total outlays (gross)	28	30	33
	Net budget authority and outlays:			
89.00	Budget authority	29	30	33
90.00	Outlays	28	30	33

This appropriation provides agencywide audit, inspection, and investigative functions to identify and correct management and administrative deficiencies which create conditions for existing or potential instances of fraud, waste, and mismanagement. The audit function provides financial and performance audits of programs and operations. Financial audits include financial statement and financial related audits. Performance audits include economy and efficiency and program results audits. The inspection function provides independent inspections and analyses of the effectiveness, efficiency, and economy of programs and operations. The investigative function provides for the detection and investigation of improper and illegal activities involving programs, personnel, and operations.

Object Classification (in millions of dollars)

Identification code 89–0236–0–1–276		1999 actual	2000 est.	2001 est.
	Personnel compensation:			
11.1	Full-time permanent	16	17	19
11.5	Other personnel compensation	1	1	1
11.9	Total personnel compensation	17	18	20
12.1	Civilian personnel benefits	4	5	5
21.0	Travel and transportation of persons	1	1	1
25.1	Advisory and assistance services	5	2	4
25.3	Purchases of goods and services from Government accounts	2	4	3

99.9	Total new obligations	29	30	33

Personnel Summary

Identification code 89–0236–0–1–276		1999 actual	2000 est.	2001 est.
1001	Total compensable workyears: Full-time equivalent employment	254	265	277

INTERIM STORAGE ACTIVITIES

Of the funds appropriated in Public Law 104–46 for interim storage of nuclear waste, $85,000,000 are transferred to this heading: Provided, That such amount is hereby rescinded.

Program and Financing (in millions of dollars)

Identification code 89–0311–0–1–053		1999 actual	2000 est.	2001 est.
	Budgetary resources available for obligation:			
22.00	New budget authority (gross)			–85
22.22	Unobligated balance transferred from other accounts			85
23.90	Total budgetary resources available for obligation			
	New budget authority (gross), detail:			
	Discretionary:			
40.36	Unobligated balance rescinded			–85
	Net budget authority and outlays:			
89.00	Budget authority			–85
90.00	Outlays			

Intragovernmental funds:

WORKING CAPITAL FUND

Program and Financing (in millions of dollars)

Identification code 89–4563–0–4–276		1999 actual	2000 est.	2001 est.
	Obligations by program activity:			
09.01	Telephones	6	7	7
09.02	Networking	3	3	3
09.03	Desktop	1	2	1
09.04	Electronic services	1	1	1
09.05	Building occupancy	56	56	54
09.06	Supplies	3	3	3
09.07	Copiers	2	2	2
09.08	Mail services	2	2	2
09.10	Printing and graphics	3	3	3
09.11	Contract closeout	1	1	1
09.12	Payroll and personnel	2	2	3
10.00	Total new obligations	80	82	80
	Budgetary resources available for obligation:			
21.40	Unobligated balance available, start of year	5	7	2
22.00	New budget authority (gross)	82	77	82
23.90	Total budgetary resources available for obligation	87	84	84
23.95	Total new obligations	–80	–82	–80
24.40	Unobligated balance available, end of year	7	2	4
	New budget authority (gross), detail:			
	Discretionary:			
68.00	Spending authority from offsetting collections (gross): Offsetting collections (cash)	82	77	82
	Change in unpaid obligations:			
72.40	Unpaid obligations, start of year: Obligated balance, start of year	21	20	20
73.10	Total new obligations	80	82	80
73.20	Total outlays (gross)	–81	–82	–82
74.40	Unpaid obligations, end of year: Obligated balance, end of year	20	20	20
	Outlays (gross), detail:			
86.90	Outlays from new discretionary authority	78	74	79
86.93	Outlays from discretionary balances	3	8	3
87.00	Total outlays (gross)	81	82	82
	Offsets:			
	Against gross budget authority and outlays:			
88.00	Offsetting collections (cash) from: Federal sources	–82	–77	–82
	Net budget authority and outlays:			
89.00	Budget authority			
90.00	Outlays	–1	5	

The Department's Working Capital Fund (WCF), established in FY 1997, provides the following common administrative services: rent and building operations, telecommunications, automated office systems, executive information systems, payroll processing, supplies, printing, copying, mail, and contract closeout. Establishment of the WCF has helped the Department reduce waste and improve efficiency, since funding for the goods and services is requested by the program office consumers who purchase what they need through the WCF.

Object Classification (in millions of dollars)

Identification code 89–4563–0–4–276		1999 actual	2000 est.	2001 est.
23.1	Rental payments to GSA	42	42	40
23.3	Communications, utilities, and miscellaneous charges	22	23	23
24.0	Printing and reproduction	3	3	3
25.1	Advisory and assistance services	2	2	2
25.2	Other services	6	7	7
25.3	Purchases of goods and services from Government accounts	1	1	1
25.6	Medical care	1	1	1
26.0	Supplies and materials	3	3	3
99.9	Total new obligations	80	82	80

GENERAL FUND RECEIPT ACCOUNTS

(in millions of dollars)

	1999 actual	2000 est.	2001 est.
Offsetting receipts from the public:			
89–089400 Fees and Recoveries, Federal Energy Regulatory Commissions, Energy	25	21	28
89–223000 Oil and gas sale proceeds at NPRs.	18	6	6
89–223300 Proceeds from uranium sales	1		
89–224500 Sale and transmission of electric energy, Falcon Dam	2	2	2
89–224700 Sale and transmission of electric energy, Southwestern Power Administration	95	92	96
89–224800 Sale and transmission of electric energy, Southeastern Power Administration	116	139	173
89–224900 Sale of power and other utilities, not otherwise classified		177	43
89–288900 Repayments on miscellaneous recoverable costs, not otherwise classified	17	18	22
General Fund Offsetting receipts from the public	274	455	370

GENERAL PROVISIONS

SEC. 301. (a) None of the funds appropriated by this Act may be used to award a management and operating contract unless such contract is awarded using competitive procedures or the Secretary of Energy grants, on a case-by-case basis, a waiver to allow for such a deviation. The Secretary may not delegate the authority to grant such a waiver.

(b) At least 60 days before a contract award, amendment, or modification for which the Secretary intends to grant such a waiver, the Secretary shall submit to the Subcommittees on Energy and Water Development of the Committees on Appropriations of the House of Representatives and the Senate a report notifying the subcommittees of the waiver and setting forth the reasons for the waiver.

SEC. 302. (a) None of the funds appropriated by this Act may be used to award, amend, or modify a contract in a manner that deviates from the Federal Acquisition Regulation, unless the Secretary of Energy grants, on a case-by-case basis, a waiver to allow for such a deviation. The Secretary may not delegate the authority to grant such a waiver.

(b) At least 60 days before a contract award, amendment, or modification for which the Secretary intends to grant such a waiver, the Secretary shall submit to the Subcommittees on Energy and Water Development of the Committees on Appropriations of the House of Representatives and the Senate a report notifying the subcommittees of the waiver and setting forth the reasons for the waiver.

[SEC. 303. None of the funds appropriated by this Act may be used to—

(1) develop or implement a workforce restructuring plan that covers employees of the Department of Energy; or

(2) provide enhanced severance payments or other benefits for employees of the Department of Energy,

under section 3161 of the National Defense Authorization Act for Fiscal Year 1993 (Public Law 102–484; 106 Stat. 2644; 42 U.S.C. 7274h).]

[SEC. 304. None of the funds appropriated by this Act may be used to augment the $24,500,000 made available for obligation by this Act for severance payments and other benefits and community assistance grants under section 3161 of the National Defense Authorization Act for Fiscal Year 1993 (Public Law 102–484; 106 Stat. 2644; 42 U.S.C. 7274h).]

SEC. [305] *303.* None of the funds appropriated by this Act may be used to prepare or initiate Requests For Proposals (RFPs) for a program if the program has not been funded by Congress.

(TRANSFERS OF UNEXPENDED BALANCES)

SEC. [306] *304.* The unexpended balances of prior appropriations provided for activities in this Act may be transferred to appropriation accounts for such activities established pursuant to this title. Balances so transferred may be merged with funds in the applicable established accounts and thereafter may be accounted for as one fund for the same time period as originally enacted.

[SEC. 307. Notwithstanding 41 U.S.C. 254c(a), the Secretary of Energy may use funds appropriated by this Act to enter into or continue multi-year contracts for the acquisition of property or services under the head, "Energy Supply" without obligating the estimated costs associated with any necessary cancellation or termination of the contract. The Secretary of Energy may pay costs of termination or cancellation from—

(1) appropriations originally available for the performance of the contract concerned;

(2) appropriations currently available for procurement of the type of property or services concerned, and not otherwise obligated; or

(3) funds appropriated for those payments.]

SEC. [308] *305.* Of the funds in this Act provided to government-owned, contractor-operated laboratories, not to exceed 6 percent shall be available to be used for Laboratory Directed Research and Development: *Provided*, That none of the funds in the Environmental Management programs are available for Laboratory Directed Research and Development.

SEC. [309] *306.* (a) Of the funds appropriated by this title to the Department of Energy, not more than $200,000,000 shall be available for reimbursement of management and operating contractor travel expenses.

(b) Funds appropriated by this title to the Department of Energy may be used to reimburse a Department of Energy management and operating contractor for travel costs of its employees under the contract only to the extent that the contractor applies to its employees the same rates and amounts as those that apply to Federal employees under subchapter I of chapter 57 of title 5, United States Code, or rates and amounts established by the Secretary of Energy. The Secretary of Energy may provide exceptions to the reimbursement requirements of this section as the Secretary considers appropriate.

[SEC. 310. (a) None of the funds in this Act or any future Energy and Water Development Appropriations Act may be expended after December 31 of each year under a covered contract unless the funds are expended in accordance with a Laboratory Funding Plan that has been approved by the Secretary of Energy. At the beginning of each fiscal year, the Secretary shall issue directions to the laboratories for the programs, projects, and activities to be conducted in that fiscal year. The Secretary and the Laboratories shall devise a Laboratory Funding Plan that identifies the resources needed to carry out these programs, projects, and activities. Funds shall be released to the Laboratories only after the Secretary has approved the Laboratory Funding Plan. The Secretary of Energy may provide exceptions to this requirement as the Secretary considers appropriate.

(b) For purposes of this section, "covered contract" means a contract for the management and operation of the following laboratories: Argonne National Laboratory, Brookhaven National Laboratory, Idaho National Engineering and Environmental Laboratory, Lawrence Berkeley National Laboratory, Lawrence Livermore National Laboratory, Los Alamos National Laboratory, Oak Ridge National Laboratory, Pacific Northwest National Laboratory, and Sandia National Laboratories.]

[SEC. 311. As part of the Department of Energy's approval of laboratory funding for prime contractors responsible for management of Department of Energy sites and facilities, the Secretary shall review and approve the incentive structure for contractor fees, the amounts of award fees to be made available for next year, the allowable salaries of first and second tier laboratory management, and the overhead expenditures. The Secretary of Energy may provide exceptions to this requirement as the Secretary considers appropriate.]

SEC. [312] *307.* None of the funds provided in this Act may be used to establish or maintain independent centers at a Department of Energy laboratory or facility unless such funds have been specifically identified in the budget submission.

[SEC. 313. None of the funds made available in this or any other Act may be used to restart the High Flux Beam Reactor.]

SEC. [314] *308.* No funds are provided in this Act or any other Act for the Administrator of the Bonneville Power Administration to enter into any agreement to perform energy efficiency services outside the legally defined Bonneville service territory, with the exception of services provided internationally, including services provided on a reimbursable basis, unless the Administrator certifies that such services are not available from private sector businesses.

SEC. [315] *309.* None of the funds in this Act may be used to dispose of transuranic waste in the Waste Isolation Pilot Plant which contains concentrations of plutonium in excess of 20 percent by weight for the aggregate of any material category on the date of the enactment of this Act, or is generated after such date.

[SEC. 316. LIMITING THE INCLUSION OF COSTS OF PROTECTION OF, MITIGATION OF DAMAGE TO, AND ENHANCEMENT OF FISH AND WILDLIFE, WITHIN RATES CHARGED BY THE BONNEVILLE POWER ADMINISTRATION, TO THE RATE PERIOD IN WHICH THE COSTS ARE INCURRED. Section 7 of the Pacific Northwest Electric Power Planning and Conservation Act (16 U.S.C. 839e) is amended by adding at the end the following:

"(n) LIMITING THE INCLUSION OF COSTS OF PROTECTION OF, MITIGATION OF DAMAGE TO, AND ENHANCEMENT OF FISH AND WILDLIFE, WITHIN RATES CHARGED BY THE BONNEVILLE POWER ADMINISTRATION, TO THE RATE PERIOD IN WHICH THE COSTS ARE INCURRED.—Notwithstanding any other provision of this section, rates established by the Administrator, under this section shall recover costs for protection, mitigation and enhancement of fish and wildlife, whether under the Pacific Northwest Electric Power Planning and Conservation Act or any other Act, not to exceed such amounts the Administrator forecasts will be expended during the fiscal year 2002–2006 rate period, while preserving the Administrator's ability to establish appropriate reserves and maintain a high Treasury payment probability for the subsequent rate period.".] *(Energy and Water Development Appropriations Act, 2000.)*

TITLE VI—GENERAL PROVISIONS

SEC. 601. None of the funds appropriated by this Act may be used in any way, directly or indirectly, to influence congressional action on any legislation or appropriation matters pending before Congress, other than to communicate to Members of Congress as described in section 1913 of title 18, United States Code.

SEC. 602. (a) PURCHASE OF AMERICAN-MADE EQUIPMENT AND PRODUCTS.—It is the sense of the Congress that, to the greatest extent practicable, all equipment and products purchased with funds made available in this Act should be American-made.

(b) NOTICE REQUIREMENT.—In providing financial assistance to, or entering into any contract with, any entity using funds made available in this Act, the head of each Federal agency, to the greatest extent practicable, shall provide to such entity a notice describing the statement made in subsection (a) by the Congress.

(c) PROHIBITION OF CONTRACTS WITH PERSONS FALSELY LABELING PRODUCTS AS MADE IN AMERICA.—If it has been finally determined by a court or Federal agency that any person intentionally affixed a label bearing a "Made in America" inscription, or any inscription with the same meaning, to any product sold in or shipped to the United States that is not made in the United States, the person shall be ineligible to receive any contract or subcontract made with funds made available in this Act, pursuant to the debarment, suspension, and ineligibility procedures described in sections 9.400 through 9.409 of title 48, Code of Federal Regulations.

SEC. 603. (a) None of the funds appropriated or otherwise made available by this Act may be used to determine the final point of discharge for the interceptor drain for the San Luis Unit until development by the Secretary of the Interior and the State of California of a plan, which shall conform to the water quality standards of the State of California as approved by the Administrator of the Environmental Protection Agency, to minimize any detrimental effect of the San Luis drainage waters.

(b) The costs of the Kesterson Reservoir Cleanup Program and the costs of the San Joaquin Valley Drainage Program shall be classified by the Secretary of the Interior as reimbursable or nonreimbursable and collected until fully repaid pursuant to the "Cleanup Program—Alternative Repayment Plan" and the "SJVDP—Alternative Repayment Plan" described in the report entitled "Repayment Report, Kesterson Reservoir Cleanup Program and San Joaquin Valley Drainage Program, February 1995", prepared by the Department of the Interior, Bureau of Reclamation. Any future obligations of funds by the United States relating to, or providing for, drainage service or drainage studies for the San Luis Unit shall be fully reimbursable by San Luis Unit beneficiaries of such service or studies pursuant to Federal Reclamation law.

[SEC. 604. Section 6101(a)(3) of the Omnibus Budget Reconciliation Act of 1990, as amended (42 U.S.C. 2214(a)(3)) is amended by striking "September 30, 1999" and inserting "September 30, 2000".]

[SEC. 605. Title VI, division C, of Public Law 105–277, Making Omnibus Consolidated and Emergency Supplemental Appropriations for Fiscal Year 1999, is repealed.]

[SEC. 606. Section 211(e)(2)(A) of the Water Resources Development Act of 1996 (Public Law 104–303, 110 Stat. 3682) is amended by striking "in advance in appropriations Acts".]

[SEC. 607. None of the funds appropriated by this Act shall be used to propose or issue rules, regulations, decrees, or orders for the purpose of implementation, or in preparation for implementation, of the Kyoto Protocol which was adopted on December 11, 1997, in Kyoto, Japan at the Third Conference of the Parties to the United Nations Framework Convention on Climate Change, which has not been submitted to the Senate for advice and consent to ratification pursuant to article II, section 2, clause 2, of the United States Constitution, and which has not entered into force pursuant to article 25 of the Protocol.]

[SEC. 608. UNITED STATES ENRICHMENT CORPORATION FUND. (a) WITHDRAWALS.—Subsections (b) and (c) of section 1 of Public Law 105–204 (112 Stat. 681) are amended by striking "fiscal year 2000" and inserting "fiscal year 2002".

(b) INVESTMENT OF AMOUNTS IN THE UNITED STATES ENRICHMENT CORPORATION FUND.—

(1) IN GENERAL.—The Secretary of the Treasury shall invest such portion of the United States Enrichment Corporation Fund as is not, in the judgment of the Secretary, required to meet current withdrawals. Investments may be made only in interest-bearing obligations of the United States.

(2) ACQUISITION OF OBLIGATIONS.—For the purpose of investments under paragraph (1), obligations may be acquired—

(A) on original issue at the issue price; or

(B) by purchase of outstanding obligations at the market price.

(3) SALE OF OBLIGATIONS.—Any obligation acquired by the Fund may be sold by the Secretary of the Treasury at the market price.

(4) CREDITS TO FUND.—The interest on, and the proceeds from the sale or redemption of, any obligations held in the Fund shall be credited to and form a part of the Fund.]

[SEC. 609. LAKE CASCADE. (a) DESIGNATION.—The reservoir commonly known as the "Cascade Reservoir", created as a result of the building of the Cascade Dam authorized by the matter under the heading "BUREAU OF RECLAMATION" of the fifth section of the Interior Department Appropriation Act, 1942 (55 Stat. 334, chapter 259) for the Boise Project, Idaho, Payette division, is redesignated as "Lake Cascade".

(b) REFERENCES.—Any reference in any law, regulation, document, record, map, or other paper of the United States to "Cascade Reservoir" shall be considered to be a reference to "Lake Cascade".]

[SEC. 610. Section 4(h)(10)(D) of the Pacific Northwest Electric Power Planning and Conservation Act (16 U.S.C. 839b(h)(10)(D)) is amended by striking clauses (vii) and (viii) and inserting the following:

"(vii) COST LIMITATION.—The annual cost of this provision shall not exceed $500,000 in 1997 dollars.".]

[SEC. 611. (a) The Secretary of the Army, acting through the Chief of Engineers, in carrying out the program known as the Formerly Utilized Sites Remedial Action Program, shall undertake the following functions and activities to be performed at eligible sites where remediation has not been completed:

(1) Sampling and assessment of contaminated areas.

(2) Characterization of site conditions.

(3) Determination of the nature and extent of contamination.

(4) Selection of the necessary and appropriate response actions as the lead Federal agency.

(5) Cleanup and closeout of sites.

(6) Any other functions and activities determined by the Secretary of the Army, acting through the Chief of Engineers, as necessary for carrying out that program, including the acquisition of real estate interests where necessary, which may be transferred upon completion of remediation to the administrative jurisdiction of the Secretary of Energy.

(b) Any response action under that program by the Secretary of the Army, acting through the Chief of Engineers, shall be subject to the Comprehensive Environmental Response, Compensation, and Liability Act of 1980 (42 U.S.C. 9601 et seq.) (in this section referred to as "CERCLA"), and the National Oil and Hazardous Substances Pollution Contingency Plan (40 CFR 300).

(c) Any sums recovered under CERCLA or other authority from a liable party, contractor, insurer, surety, or other person for any expenditures by the Army Corps of Engineers or the Department of Energy for response actions under that program shall be credited to the amounts made available to carry out that program and shall be available until expended for costs of response actions for any eligible site.

(d) The Secretary of Energy may exercise the authority under section 168 of the Atomic Energy Act of 1954 (42 U.S.C. 2208) to make payments in lieu of taxes for federally owned property at which activities under that program are carried out, regardless of which Federal agency has administrative jurisdiction over the property and notwithstanding any reference to "the activities of the Commission" in that section.

(e) This section does not alter, curtail, or limit the authorities, functions, or responsibilities of other agencies under CERCLA or, except as stated in this section, under the Atomic Energy Act of 1954 (42 U.S.C. 2011 et seq.).

(f) This section shall apply to fiscal year 2000 and each succeeding fiscal year.] *(Energy and Water Development Appropriations Act, 2000.)*

DEPARTMENT OF HEALTH AND HUMAN SERVICES

FOOD AND DRUG ADMINISTRATION

Federal Funds

General and special funds:

SALARIES AND EXPENSES

For necessary expenses of the Food and Drug Administration, including hire and purchase of passenger motor vehicles; for payment of space rental and related costs pursuant to Public Law 92–313 for programs and activities of the Food and Drug Administration which are included in this Act; for rental of special purpose space in the District of Columbia or elsewhere; and for miscellaneous and emergency expenses of enforcement activities, authorized and approved by the Secretary and to be accounted for solely on the Secretary's certificate, not to exceed $25,000; [$1,186,072,000] *$1,306,178,000*, of which not to exceed [$145,434,000] *$149,273,000* in prescription drug user fees authorized by 21 U.S.C. 379(h) may be credited to this appropriation and remain available until expended: *Provided*, That [fees derived from applications received during fiscal year 2000 shall be subject to the fiscal year 2000 limitation: *Provided further*, That none of these funds shall be used to develop, establish, or operate any program of user fees authorized by 31 U.S.C. 9701: *Provided further*, That of the total amount appropriated: (1) $269,245,000 shall be for the Center for Food Safety and Applied Nutrition and related field activities in the Office of Regulatory Affairs; (2) $309,026,000 shall be for the Center for Drug Evaluation and Research and related field activities in the Office of Regulatory Affairs, of which no less than $11,542,000 shall be available for grants and contracts awarded under section 5 of the Orphan Drug Act (21 U.S.C. 360ee); (3) $132,092,000 shall be for the Center for Biologics Evaluation and Research and for related field activities in the Office of Regulatory Affairs; (4) $48,821,000 shall be for the Center for Veterinary Medicine and for related field activities in the Office of Regulatory Affairs; (5) $154,271,000 shall be for the Center for Devices and Radiological Health and for related field activities in the Office of Regulatory Affairs, of which $1,000,000 shall be for premarket review, enforcement and oversight activities related to users and manufacturers of all reprocessed medical devices as authorized by the Federal Food, Drug, and Cosmetic Act (21 U.S.C. 321 et seq.), and of which no less than $55,500,000 and 522 full-time equivalent positions shall be for premarket application review activities to meet statutory review times; (6) $34,536,000 shall be for the National Center for Toxicological Research; (7) $34,000,000 shall be for the Office of Tobacco; (8) $25,855,000 shall be for Rent and Related activities, other than the amounts paid to the General Services Administration; (9) $100,180,000 shall be for payments to the General Services Administration for rent and related costs; and (10) $78,046,000 shall be for other activities, including the Office of the Commissioner; the Office of Policy; the Office of the Senior Associate Commissioner; the Office of International and Constituent Relations; the Office of Policy, Legislation, and Planning; and central services for these offices: *Provided further*, That funds may be transferred from one specified activity to another with the prior approval of the Committee on Appropriations of both Houses of Congress] *no more than $104,954,000 shall be for payments to the General Services Administration for rent and related costs.*

In addition, mammography user fees authorized by 42 U.S.C. 263(b) may be credited to this account, to remain available until expended.

In addition, export certification user fees authorized by 21 U.S.C. 381, *as amended,* may be credited to this account, to remain available until expended.

BUILDINGS AND FACILITIES

For plans, construction, repair, improvement, extension, alteration, and purchase of fixed equipment or facilities of or used by the Food and Drug Administration, where not otherwise provided, [$11,350,000,] to remain available until expended *$31,350,000, and to become available on October 1, 2001, $23,000,000.* (7 U.S.C. 2209b). *(Agriculture, Rural Development, Food and Drug Administration, and Related Agencies Appropriations Act, 2000.)*

Unavailable Collections (in millions of dollars)

Identification code 75–9911–0–1–554	1999 actual	2000 est.	2001 est.
Balance, start of year:			
01.99 Balance, start of year			
Receipts:			
02.01 Cooperative research and development agreements	1	1	1
Appropriation:			
05.01 Salaries and expenses	−1	−1	−1
07.99 Total balance, end of year			

Program and Financing (in millions of dollars)

Identification code 75–9911–0–1–554	1999 actual	2000 est.	2001 est.
Obligations by program activity:			
Direct program:			
00.01 Foods	235	267	303
00.02 Drugs	338	357	414
00.03 Devices and radiological products	146	154	172
00.04 National center for toxicological research	32	34	38
00.05 Tobacco	34	34	39
00.06 Other activities	75	72	66
00.07 Other rent and rent related activities	26	26	26
00.08 Rental payments	83	94	99
00.09 Buildings and facilities	16	11	31
00.10 CRADAs	1	1	1
09.01 Reimbursable program	156	181	200
10.00 Total new obligations	1,142	1,231	1,389
Budgetary resources available for obligation:			
21.40 Unobligated balance available, start of year	95	106	106
22.00 New budget authority (gross)	1,147	1,231	1,389
22.10 Resources available from recoveries of prior year obligations	6		
23.90 Total budgetary resources available for obligation	1,248	1,337	1,495
23.95 Total new obligations	−1,142	−1,231	−1,389
24.40 Unobligated balance available, end of year	106	106	108
New budget authority (gross), detail:			
Discretionary:			
40.00 Appropriation	982	1,052	1,188
40.75 Reduction pursuant to P.L. 106–51	−2		
40.76 Reduction pursuant to P.L. 106–113		−3	
43.00 Appropriation (total discretionary)	980	1,049	1,188
Mandatory:			
60.25 Appropriation (special fund, indefinite)	1	1	1
Spending authority from offsetting collections:			
Discretionary:			
68.00 Offsetting collections (cash)	164	181	200
68.10 From Federal sources: Change in receivables and unpaid, unfilled orders	2		
68.90 Spending authority from offsetting collections (total discretionary)	166	181	200
70.00 Total new budget authority (gross)	1,147	1,231	1,389
Change in unpaid obligations:			
Unpaid obligations, start of year:			
72.40 Obligated balance, start of year	324	330	333
72.95 From Federal sources: Receivables and unpaid, unfilled orders		2	2
72.99 Total unpaid obligations, start of year	324	332	335
73.10 Total new obligations	1,142	1,231	1,389
73.20 Total outlays (gross)	−1,112	−1,228	−1,393
73.40 Adjustments in expired accounts (net)	−18		
73.45 Adjustments in unexpired accounts	−6		
Unpaid obligations, end of year:			
74.40 Obligated balance, end of year	330	333	329
74.95 From Federal sources: Receivables and unpaid, unfilled orders	2	2	2

General and special funds—Continued

BUILDINGS AND FACILITIES—Continued

Program and Financing (in millions of dollars)—Continued

Identification code 75–9911–0–1–554		1999 actual	2000 est.	2001 est.
74.99	Total unpaid obligations, end of year	332	335	331
	Outlays (gross), detail:			
86.90	Outlays from new discretionary authority	930	958	1,098
86.93	Outlays from discretionary balances	182	269	294
86.97	Outlays from new mandatory authority		1	1
87.00	Total outlays (gross)	1,112	1,228	1,393
	Offsets:			
	Against gross budget authority and outlays:			
88.40	Offsetting collections (cash) from: Non-Federal sources	−164	−181	−200
	Against gross budget authority only:			
88.95	From Federal sources: Change in receivables and unpaid, unfilled orders	−2		
	Net budget authority and outlays:			
89.00	Budget authority	981	1,050	1,189
90.00	Outlays	948	1,047	1,193

[In millions of dollars]

	1999	2000	2001
Distribution of budget authority by account:			
Salaries and expenses	886	944	1,058
Rental payments (FDA)	83	94	99
Buildings and facilities	16	11	31
Distribution of outlays by account:			
Salaries and expenses	839	926	1,074
Rental payments (FDA)	83	98	99
Buildings and facilities	26	23	18

Summary of Budget Authority and Outlays

(in millions of dollars)

	1999 actual	2000 est.	2001 est.
Enacted/requested:			
Budget Authority	981	1,050	1,189
Outlays	948	1,047	1,193
Legislative proposal, not subject to PAYGO:			
Budget Authority			
Outlays			
Total:			
Budget Authority	981	1,050	1,189
Outlays	948	1,047	1,193

The Food and Drug Administration (FDA) administers laws concerning misbranded and adulterated foods, drugs, human biologics, medical devices, cosmetics, and human-made sources of radiation. The Budget provides a $163.2 million (+13 percent) increase over the FY 2000 enacted program level. The Budget includes $1,156.9 million for Salaries and expenses, which includes funding for the food safety initiative and tobacco regulation, as well as initiatives for the reporting of medical errors and the prevention of illegal sales of prescription drugs over the Internet. Of the Salaries and expenses amount, $99.1 million will be used for payments to the General Services Administration for rent and rent related costs (an additional $5.9 million will be derived from fees). The Budget reflects the transfer of the Seafood Inspection Division of the National Oceanic and Atmospheric Administration of the Department of Commerce to the FDA, which will be financed with $12.7 million in currently authorized fees. In addition, the Budget includes $189.9 million for user fees, an increase of $24.7 million in user fees over FY 2000, which will be used to finance FDA activities. Of the $189.9 million in user fees, $19.5 million consists of new user fees related to the review of direct food additive petitions, food export certificates, and for the review of medical device applications, which are represented in the legislative proposal schedule. The buildings and facilities appropriation of $31.4 million provides funds for projects related to the repair, construction, alteration, and improvement of all buildings and facilities of FDA, including a replacement laboratory in Los Angeles.

Object Classification (in millions of dollars)

Identification code 75–9911–0–1–554		1999 actual	2000 est.	2001 est.
	Direct obligations:			
	Personnel compensation:			
11.1	Full-time permanent	443	480	522
11.3	Other than full-time permanent	28	30	32
11.5	Other personnel compensation	16	17	19
11.9	Total personnel compensation	487	527	573
12.1	Civilian personnel benefits	112	121	132
21.0	Travel and transportation of persons	19	19	21
22.0	Transportation of things	2	2	3
23.1	Rental payments to GSA	83	94	99
23.2	Rental payments to others	5	5	7
23.3	Communications, utilities, and miscellaneous charges	20	20	20
24.0	Printing and reproduction	2	3	3
25.1	Advisory and assistance services	12	12	19
25.2	Other services	62	62	90
25.3	Purchases of goods and services from Government accounts	43	44	55
25.4	Operation and maintenance of facilities	24	24	25
25.5	Research and development contracts	16	16	17
25.7	Operation and maintenance of equipment	19	19	20
26.0	Supplies and materials	14	14	18
31.0	Equipment	29	30	41
32.0	Land and structures	15	15	23
41.0	Grants, subsidies, and contributions	20	21	21
42.0	Insurance claims and indemnities	2	2	2
99.0	Subtotal, direct obligations	986	1,050	1,189
99.0	Reimbursable obligations	156	181	200
99.9	Total new obligations	1,142	1,231	1,389

Personnel Summary

Identification code 75–9911–0–1–554		1999 actual	2000 est.	2001 est.
	Direct:			
1001	Total compensable workyears: Full-time equivalent employment	7,851	7,994	8,203
	Reimbursable:			
2001	Total compensable workyears: Full-time equivalent employment	1,013	978	1,164
	Allocation account:			
3001	Total compensable workyears: Full-time equivalent employment	14	2	

SALARIES AND EXPENSES

(Legislative proposal, not subject to PAYGO)

Contingent upon the enactment of authorizing legislation, up to $19,483,000 derived from fees assessed for activities related to the review of direct food additive petitions, the issuing of food export certificates, and the review of medical device applications may be collected and credited to this appropriation, to remain available until expended for those activities.

Program and Financing (in millions of dollars)

Identification code 75–9911–2–1–554		1999 actual	2000 est.	2001 est.
	Obligations by program activity:			
09.01	Additive user fees			19
10.00	Total new obligations			19
	Budgetary resources available for obligation:			
22.00	New budget authority (gross)			19
23.95	Total new obligations			−19
	New budget authority (gross), detail:			
	Discretionary:			
68.00	Spending authority from offsetting collections (gross): Offsetting collections (cash)			19

		1999 actual	2000 est.	2001 est.
	Change in unpaid obligations:			
73.10	Total new obligations			19
73.20	Total outlays (gross)			−19
	Outlays (gross), detail:			
86.90	Outlays from new discretionary authority			19
	Offsets:			
	Against gross budget authority and outlays:			
88.40	Offsetting collections (cash) from: Non-Federal sources			−19
	Net budget authority and outlays:			
89.00	Budget authority			
90.00	Outlays			

The Budget includes $189.9 million in user fees, of which $19.5 million are new user fees to finance FDA activities as reflected in the legislative proposal schedule. Additional appropriations language is being proposed contingent upon the enactment of authorizing legislation. The authorizing legislation will be proposed to authorize the collection and spending of the fees subject to appropriations action.

Object Classification (in millions of dollars)

Identification code 75–9911–2–1–554		1999 actual	2000 est.	2001 est.
99.0	Reimbursable obligations: Subtotal, reimbursable obligations			19
99.9	Total new obligations			19

Personnel Summary

Identification code 75–9911–2–1–554		1999 actual	2000 est.	2001 est.
2001	Total compensable workyears: Full-time equivalent employment			108

Public enterprise funds:

Revolving Fund for Certification and Other Services

Program and Financing (in millions of dollars)

Identification code 75–4309–0–3–554		1999 actual	2000 est.	2001 est.
	Obligations by program activity:			
10.00	Total new obligations	7	4	4
	Budgetary resources available for obligation:			
21.40	Unobligated balance available, start of year	6	3	3
22.00	New budget authority (gross)	4	4	4
23.90	Total budgetary resources available for obligation	10	7	7
23.95	Total new obligations	−7	−4	−4
24.40	Unobligated balance available, end of year	3	3	3
	New budget authority (gross), detail:			
	Mandatory:			
69.00	Offsetting collections (cash)	4	4	4
	Change in unpaid obligations:			
72.40	Unpaid obligations, start of year: Obligated balance, start of year	2	1	1
73.10	Total new obligations	7	4	4
73.20	Total outlays (gross)	−7	−4	−4
74.40	Unpaid obligations, end of year: Obligated balance, end of year	1	1	1
	Outlays (gross), detail:			
86.97	Outlays from new mandatory authority	4	4	4
86.98	Outlays from mandatory balances	3		
87.00	Total outlays (gross)	7	4	4
	Offsets:			
	Against gross budget authority and outlays:			
88.40	Offsetting collections (cash) from: Non-Federal sources	−4	−4	−4
	Net budget authority and outlays:			
89.00	Budget authority			
90.00	Outlays	3		

FDA certifies color additives for use in foods, drugs, and cosmetics. It also lists color additives for use in foods, drugs, medical devices, and cosmetics (21 U.S.C. 346a, 356, 357, 376). These services are financed wholly by fees paid by the industries affected.

Object Classification (in millions of dollars)

Identification code 75–4309–0–3–554		1999 actual	2000 est.	2001 est.
11.1	Personnel compensation: Full-time permanent	2	2	2
12.1	Civilian personnel benefits		1	1
23.1	Rental payments to GSA	1		
25.2	Other services	3	1	1
31.0	Equipment	1		
99.9	Total new obligations	7	4	4

Personnel Summary

Identification code 75–4309–0–3–554		1999 actual	2000 est.	2001 est.
2001	Total compensable workyears: Full-time equivalent employment	32	35	35

Administrative Provision, Food and Drug Administration

Effective October 1, 2000, (1) the functions and authorities related to fish or fishery products under the Agricultural Marketing Act of 1946, including inspections and other activities authorized under section 203(h) of that Act, are transferred from the Secretary of Commerce to the Secretary of Health and Human Services ("HHS"); (2) the Secretary of Commerce shall transfer to the Secretary of HHS (A) all personnel of the Seafood Inspection Division of the National Oceanic and Atmospheric Administration and such other employees of the Department of Commerce as may be designated by the Secretary of Commerce, with the concurrence of the Secretary of HHS, all of whom shall become personnel of a voluntary seafood inspection unit within the Food and Drug Administration ("FDA"); and (B) all assets and liabilities of the Department of Commerce pertaining to the activities specified in clause (1), which shall become assets and liabilities of such seafood inspection unit, including facilities, contracts, property, records, accounts payable and receivable, and unexpended and unobligated balances of funds; (3) all rules, regulations, administrative directives, grants, contracts, and other determinations and agreements in effect on such date relating to the activities specified in clause (1) shall remain in effect until modified by the Secretary of HHS; (4) the Secretary of HHS is authorized to promulgate, without comment, a final rule transferring to title 21, Code of Federal Regulations, regulations of the Secretary of Commerce necessary to carry out the activities specified in clause (1); (5) all activities of such seafood inspection unit shall be funded exclusively from fees charged for, and other amounts specifically appropriated for, such activities, and fees collected and amounts appropriated for such activities shall not be used for any other purpose; and (6) for purposes of any reduction in the personnel complement of the FDA on or before September 30, 2005, such unit will be deemed a distinct competitive area within the FDA, under 5 CFR 351.402.

HEALTH RESOURCES AND SERVICES ADMINISTRATION

Federal Funds

General and special funds:

HEALTH RESOURCES AND SERVICES

For carrying out titles II, III, VII, VIII, X, XII, XIX, and XXVI of the Public Health Service Act, section 427(a) of the Federal Coal Mine Health and Safety Act, title V and section 1820 of the Social Security Act, the Health Care Quality Improvement Act of 1986, as amended, and the Native Hawaiian Health Care Act of 1988, as amended, [$4,584,721,000, of which $150,000 shall remain available until expended for interest subsidies on loan guarantees made prior to fiscal year 1981 under part B of title VII of the Public Health Service Act, and of which $122,182,000 shall be available for the construction and renovation of health care and other facilities, and] *$4,681,337,000,* of which $25,000,000 from general revenues, notwithstanding section 1820(j) of the Social Security Act, shall be available for carrying out the Medicare rural hospital flexibility grants program under section 1820 of such Act: *Provided*, That the Division of Federal Occupational Health may utilize personal services contracting to employ professional management/administrative and occupational health professionals: *Provided further*, That of the funds made available under this heading, $250,000 shall be available until expended for facilities renovations at the Gillis W. Long Hansen's Disease Center: *Provided further*, That in addition to fees authorized by section 427(b) of the Health Care Quality Improvement Act of 1986, fees shall be collected for the full disclosure of information under the Act sufficient to recover the full costs of operating the National Practitioner Data Bank, and shall remain available until expended to carry out that Act: *Provided further*, That no more than $5,000,000 is available for carrying out the provisions of Public Law 104–73: *Provided further*, That of the funds made available under this heading, [$238,932,000] *$273,932,000* shall be for the program under title X of the Public Health Service Act to provide for voluntary family planning projects: *Provided further*, That amounts provided to said projects under such title shall not be expended for abortions, that all pregnancy counseling shall be nondirective, and that such amounts shall not be expended for any activity (including the publication or distribution of literature) that in any way tends to promote public support or opposition to any legislative proposal or candidate for public office: *Provided further*, That [$528,000,000] *$554,000,000* shall be for State AIDS Drug Assistance Programs authorized by section 2616 of the Public Health Service Act: *Provided further, That of the funds made available under this heading, $90,000,000 shall be for grants for reducing infant mortality consistent with the methods used in the Healthy Start Infant Mortality Demonstration Project grants from 1991 through 2000: Provided further, That such funds will be available first to continue making grants to Healthy Start grantees that were awarded funds on or before January 15, 2000, whose current grant award continues in FY 2001: Provided further, That if the total amount of such grant awards is less than $90,000,000, at least 95% of the remaining funds shall be available for States, under the cost sharing provisions of section 503 of such Act, according to the ratio that infant mortality in each State bears to the total of infant mortality in the United States, as measured by the Centers for Disease Control and Prevention for the most recently available calendar year, and up to 5% of remaining funds shall be available for States for technical assistance: Provided further, That these grants use those Healthy Start methods that have been proven successful and are designed to reduce infant mortality within high-incidence areas by 50% over 5 years: Provided further, That each State shall include in its annual audit report, as required by section 506 of such Act, an additional section reporting on Healthy Start: Provided further, That sections 507, 508, and 509 of such Act apply to said State allotments: Provided further*, That, notwithstanding section 502(a)(1) of the Social Security Act, not to exceed [$109,307,000] *$109,148,000* is available for carrying out special projects of regional and national significance pursuant to section 501(a)(2) of such Act: [*Provided further*, That of the amount provided under this heading, $40,000,000 shall be available for children's hospitals graduate medical education payments, subject to authorization: *Provided further*, That of the amount provided under this heading, $900,000 shall be for the American Federation of Negro Affairs Education and Research Fund.] *Provided further, That notwithstanding section 757(b)2 of the Public Health Service Act, $28,587,000 shall be available under section 751, $3,765,000 under section 752, $4,720,000 under section 754, and $3,838,000 under section 755. (Department of Health and Human Services Appropriations Act, 2000, as enacted by section 1000(a)(4) of the Consolidated Appropriations Act, 2000 (P.L. 106–113).)*

Program and Financing (in millions of dollars)

Identification code 75–0350–0–1–550		1999 actual	2000 est.	2001 est.
	Obligations by program activity:			
	Direct program:			
00.01	Health centers	919	1,014	1,064
00.02	National Health Service Corps	37	38	38
00.03	National Health Service Corps recruitment	78	79	79
00.04	Hansen's disease center	22	20	17
00.09	Payment to Hawaii for the treatment of Hansen's disease	2	2	2
00.10	Black lung clinics	5	6	6
00.11	Nursing loan repayment	2	2	2
00.12	Health professions	302	342	298
00.13	Maternal and child health block grant	700	709	799
00.14	Healthy start	105	90	
00.15	Universal newborn hearing		3	3
00.16	Emergency medical services	15	17	15
00.17	Poison control centers		3	1
00.18	HIV/AIDS	1,411	1,595	1,720
00.19	Organ transplantation	10	10	15
00.20	Health care facilities	65	112	
00.21	Bone marrow donor registry	18	18	18
00.22	Rural health policy development	12	33	6
00.23	Rural health outreach grants	38	36	38
00.24	Rural health flexiblity grants	25	25	25
00.25	Office for the advancement of telehealth			6
00.26	Program management	119	125	124
00.27	Family planning	215	239	274
00.28	Abstinence education	49	50	50
00.29	Health care access for the uninsured		25	125
00.30	One-time access demos		15	
00.31	Health centers tort claims fund	5	5	5
00.32	Health centers guarantee program account		3	1
03.00	Total direct programs	4,154	4,616	4,731
09.01	Reimbursable program	100	124	127
10.00	Total new obligations	4,254	4,740	4,858
	Budgetary resources available for obligation:			
21.40	Unobligated balance available, start of year	47	50	48
22.00	New budget authority (gross)	4,257	4,738	4,858
22.10	Resources available from recoveries of prior year obligations	2		
23.90	Total budgetary resources available for obligation	4,306	4,788	4,906
23.95	Total new obligations	−4,254	−4,740	−4,858
23.98	Unobligated balance expiring or withdrawn	−2		
24.40	Unobligated balance available, end of year	50	48	48
	New budget authority (gross), detail:			
	Discretionary:			
40.00	Appropriation	4,108	4,585	4,681
40.75	Reduction pursuant to P.L. 106–51	−1		
40.76	Reduction pursuant to P.L. 106–113		−21	
41.00	Transferred to other accounts	−1		
43.00	Appropriation (total discretionary)	4,106	4,564	4,681
	Mandatory:			
60.00	Appropriation	50	50	50
	Discretionary:			
68.00	Spending authority from offsetting collections: Offsetting collections (cash)	101	121	123
	Mandatory:			
69.00	Offsetting collections (cash)		3	4
70.00	Total new budget authority (gross)	4,257	4,738	4,858
	Change in unpaid obligations:			
72.40	Unpaid obligations, start of year: Obligated balance, start of year	2,726	3,078	3,353
73.10	Total new obligations	4,254	4,740	4,858
73.20	Total outlays (gross)	−3,859	−4,444	−4,746
73.40	Adjustments in expired accounts (net)	−41	−21	4
73.45	Adjustments in unexpired accounts	−2		
74.40	Unpaid obligations, end of year: Obligated balance, end of year	3,078	3,353	3,469
	Outlays (gross), detail:			
86.90	Outlays from new discretionary authority	1,611	1,837	1,922
86.93	Outlays from discretionary balances	2,218	2,562	2,771

86.97	Outlays from new mandatory authority	10	15	16
86.98	Outlays from mandatory balances	20	30	38
87.00	Total outlays (gross)	3,859	4,444	4,746
	Offsets:			
	Against gross budget authority and outlays:			
	Offsetting collections (cash) from:			
88.00	Federal sources	−85	−106	−106
88.40	Non-Federal sources	−16	−18	−21
88.90	Total, offsetting collections (cash)	−101	−124	−127
	Net budget authority and outlays:			
89.00	Budget authority	4,156	4,614	4,731
90.00	Outlays	3,758	4,320	4,619

[Dollars in millions]

	1999	*2000*	*2001*
Distribution of budget authority by account:			
Health resources and services	4,151	4,609	4,726
Health centers malpractice claims	5	5	5
Distribution of outlays by account:			
Health resources and services	3,753	4,315	4,614
Health centers malpractice claims	5	5	5

Summary of Loan Levels, Subsidy Budget Authority and Outlays by Program (in millions of dollars)

Identification code 75–0350–0–1–550		1999 actual	2000 est.	2001 est.
	Guaranteed loan levels supportable by subsidy budget authority:			
2150	Health centers: Facilities renovation loan guarantee levels		54	34
2150	Health centers: Managed care network development loan guarantee levels		20	7
2150	Health centers: Managed care plan loan guarantee levels		26	10
2159	Total loan guarantee levels		100	51
	Guaranteed loan subsidy (in percent):			
2320	Facilities loan subsidy rate	2.26	0.71	0.43
2320	Managed care network development loan subsidy rate	8.59	8.19	7.71
2320	Managed care plan loan subsidy rate	5.11	4.16	3.93
2329	Weighted average subsidy rate	4.27	3.10	2.11
	Guaranteed loan subsidy budget authority:			
2330	Facilities loan subsidy budget authority			
2330	Managed care network development loan subsidy budget authority		2	1
2330	Managed care plan loan subsidy budget authority		1	
2339	Total subsidy budget authority		3	1
	Guaranteed loan subsidy outlays:			
2340	Facilities loan subsidy outlays			
2340	Managed care network development loan subsidy outlays		2	1
2340	Managed care plan loan subsidy outlays		1	
2349	Total subsidy outlays		3	1
	Administrative expense data:			
3510	Administrative expenses	1	1	1
3580	Outlays from balances			
3590	Outlays for administrative expenses	1	1	1

Activities displayed here support categorical health resources and services grants and the Medical malpractice claims fund, which pays malpractice claims filed against employees of federally-supported health centers. In FY 2001, Healthy Start will become a separate grant program within the maternal and child health block grant.

Object Classification (in millions of dollars)

Identification code 75–0350–0–1–550		1999 actual	2000 est.	2001 est.
	Direct obligations:			
	Personnel compensation:			
11.1	Full-time permanent	97	103	105
11.3	Other than full-time permanent	3	4	4
11.5	Other personnel compensation	4	4	4
11.9	Total personnel compensation	104	111	113
12.1	Civilian personnel benefits	26	28	28
21.0	Travel and transportation of persons	4	5	6
22.0	Transportation of things	1	1	1
23.1	Rental payments to GSA	10	12	12
23.3	Communications, utilities, and miscellaneous charges	5	5	5
24.0	Printing and reproduction	1	1	1
25.1	Advisory and assistance services	45	50	50
25.2	Other services	51	87	124
25.3	Purchases of goods and services from Government accounts	55	60	62
25.4	Operation and maintenance of facilities	2	1	1
25.6	Medical care	1	1	1
25.7	Operation and maintenance of equipment	3	4	3
26.0	Supplies and materials	2	3	3
31.0	Equipment	3	4	4
41.0	Grants, subsidies, and contributions	3,836	4,238	4,312
42.0	Insurance claims and indemnities	5	5	5
99.0	Subtotal, direct obligations	4,154	4,616	4,731
99.0	Reimbursable obligations	100	124	127
99.9	Total new obligations	4,254	4,740	4,858

Personnel Summary

Identification code 75–0350–0–1–550		1999 actual	2000 est.	2001 est.
	Direct:			
	Total compensable workyears:			
1001	Full-time equivalent employment	1,607	1,744	1,681
1011	Exempt Full-time equivalent employment	82		
	Reimbursable:			
2001	Total compensable workyears: Full-time equivalent employment	199	241	241
	Allocation account:			
3001	Total compensable workyears: Full-time equivalent employment	5	11	11

Vaccine Injury Compensation

Program and Financing (in millions of dollars)

Identification code 75–0320–0–1–551		1999 actual	2000 est.	2001 est.
	Obligations by program activity:			
10.00	Total new obligations (object class 42.0)	47	52	
	Budgetary resources available for obligation:			
21.40	Unobligated balance available, start of year	61	115	64
22.00	New budget authority (gross)	100		
22.10	Resources available from recoveries of prior year obligations	1		
23.90	Total budgetary resources available for obligation	162	115	64
23.95	Total new obligations	−47	−52	
24.40	Unobligated balance available, end of year	115	64	64
	New budget authority (gross), detail:			
	Mandatory:			
60.00	Appropriation	100		
	Change in unpaid obligations:			
72.40	Unpaid obligations, start of year: Obligated balance, start of year	2	5	
73.10	Total new obligations	47	52	
73.20	Total outlays (gross)	−43	−57	
73.45	Adjustments in unexpired accounts	−1		
74.40	Unpaid obligations, end of year: Obligated balance, end of year	5		
	Outlays (gross), detail:			
86.98	Outlays from mandatory balances	43	57	
	Net budget authority and outlays:			
89.00	Budget authority	100		
90.00	Outlays	43	57	

The Vaccine improvement program was established pursuant to Public Law 99–660 and Public Law 100–203, and serves as a source of funds to pay claims for compensation for vaccine related injury or death. Payment of claims associated with vaccine related injury or death occurring before

General and special funds—Continued

VACCINE INJURY COMPENSATION—Continued

October 1, 1988 are financed from the General Fund and are reflected in this account. Given sufficient carry-over funds from prior years' appropriations to pay for the balance of the pre-1988 backlog of claims yet to be adjudicated, no appropriation is requested in FY 2001 to cover payment of pre-1988 claims. Payment of claims associated with vaccine related injury or death occurring after October 1, 1988 are reflected in the Vaccine improvement trust fund account.

PAYMENT TO THE RICKY RAY HEMOPHILIA RELIEF FUND

For payment to the Ricky Ray Hemophilia Relief Fund, as provided by Public Law 105–369, and for administrative expenses, $100,000,000, of which up to $10,000,000 may be used for administrative expenses.

Program and Financing (in millions of dollars)

Identification code 75–0355–0–1–551	1999 actual	2000 est.	2001 est.
Obligations by program activity:			
10.00 Total new obligations (object class 92.0)			100
Budgetary resources available for obligation:			
22.00 New budget authority (gross)			100
23.95 Total new obligations			−100
New budget authority (gross), detail:			
Discretionary:			
40.00 Appropriation			100
Change in unpaid obligations:			
73.10 Total new obligations			100
73.20 Total outlays (gross)			−100
Outlays (gross), detail:			
86.90 Outlays from new discretionary authority			100
Net budget authority and outlays:			
89.00 Budget authority			100
90.00 Outlays			100

These amounts will be paid to the Ricky Ray hemophilia relief fund. The Ricky Ray hemophilia relief fund was established pursuant to Public Law 105–369 and serves as a source of funds to pay claims to eligible individuals on behalf of persons with HIV and a blood clotting disorder, who were treated with an anti-hemophiliac factor between July 1982 and December 1987.

Credit accounts:

HEALTH CENTER GUARANTEED LOAN FINANCING ACCOUNT

Program and Financing (in millions of dollars)

Identification code 75–4442–0–3–551	1999 actual	2000 est.	2001 est.
Budgetary resources available for obligation:			
21.40 Unobligated balance available, start of year	1	1	5
22.00 New financing authority (gross)		4	2
23.90 Total budgetary resources available for obligation	1	5	7
24.40 Unobligated balance available, end of year	1	5	7
New financing authority (gross), detail:			
Discretionary:			
68.00 Spending authority from offsetting collections (gross): (Federal sources: From program account)		4	3
Offsets:			
Against gross financing authority and financing disbursements:			
Offsetting collections (cash) from:			
88.00 Federal sources		−3	−1
88.40 Premium income		−1	−2
88.90 Total, offsetting collections (cash)		−4	−3
Net financing authority and financing disbursements:			
89.00 Financing authority			−1
90.00 Financing disbursements		−4	−3

Status of Guaranteed Loans (in millions of dollars)

Identification code 75–4442–0–3–551	1999 actual	2000 est.	2001 est.
Position with respect to appropriations act limitation on commitments:			
2111 Limitation on guaranteed loans made by private lenders		100	51
2150 Total guaranteed loan commitments		100	51
Cumulative balance of guaranteed loans outstanding:			
2210 Outstanding, start of year	9	9	109
2231 Disbursements of new guaranteed loans		100	51
2261 Adjustments: Terminations for default that result in loans receivable			
2290 Outstanding, end of year	9	109	160
Memorandum:			
2299 Guaranteed amount of guaranteed loans outstanding, end of year	9	109	160
Addendum:			
Cumulative balance of defaulted guaranteed loans that result in loans receivable:			
2331 Disbursements for guaranteed loan claims			
2351 Repayments of loans receivable			

P.L. 104–299 and P.L. 104–208 authorize HRSA to guarantee up to $80 million in private loans to health centers for the costs of developing and operating managed care networks or plans and for the construction, renovation and modernization of medical facilities. Since this program has only used $9 million of its available $160 million in loan guarantee authority, HRSA will use the remaining existing loan guarantee limit over FY 2000 and FY 2001. As required by the Federal Credit Reform Act of 1990, this financing account records all cash flows to and from the Government resulting from the Health center loan guarantee program. The program account for this activity is displayed in the Health resources and services account (75–0350) as a line in the program and financing schedule.

Balance Sheet (in millions of dollars)

Identification code 75–4442–0–3–551	1998 actual	1999 actual	2000 est.	2001 est.
ASSETS:				
Investments in US securities:				
1106 Federal assets: Receivables, net	9	9	109	160
1999 Total assets	9	9	109	160
LIABILITIES:				
2204 Non-Federal liabilities: Liabilities for loan guarantees	9	9	109	160
2999 Total liabilities	9	9	109	160
4999 Total liabilities and net position	9	9	109	160

HEALTH EDUCATION ASSISTANCE LOANS PROGRAM ACCOUNT

Such sums as may be necessary to carry out the purpose of the program, as authorized by title VII of the Public Health Service Act, as amended. For administrative expenses to carry out the guaranteed loan program, including section 709 of the Public Health Service Act, [$3,688,000] *$3,679,000*. *(Department of Health and Human Services Appropriations Act, 2000, as enacted by section 1000(a)(4) of the Consolidated Appropriations Act, 2000 (P.L. 106–113).)*

Program and Financing (in millions of dollars)

Identification code 75–0340–0–1–552	1999 actual	2000 est.	2001 est.
Obligations by program activity:			
00.09 Administrative expenses subject to limitation	4	4	4
10.00 Total new obligations	4	4	4
Budgetary resources available for obligation:			
22.00 New budget authority (gross)	4	4	4
23.95 Total new obligations	–4	–4	–4
New budget authority (gross), detail:			
Discretionary:			
40.00 Appropriation	4	4	4
Change in unpaid obligations:			
72.40 Unpaid obligations, start of year: Obligated balance, start of year	2	2	
73.10 Total new obligations	4	4	4
73.20 Total outlays (gross)	–3	–6	–4
74.40 Unpaid obligations, end of year: Obligated balance, end of year	2		
Outlays (gross), detail:			
86.90 Outlays from new discretionary authority	2	4	4
86.93 Outlays from discretionary balances	1	2	
87.00 Total outlays (gross)	3	6	4
Net budget authority and outlays:			
89.00 Budget authority	4	4	4
90.00 Outlays	3	6	4

Summary of Loan Levels, Subsidy Budget Authority and Outlays by Program (in millions of dollars)

Identification code 75–0340–0–1–552	1999 actual	2000 est.	2001 est.
Guaranteed loan levels supportable by subsidy budget authority:			
2150 Loan guarantee levels			
2159 Total loan guarantee levels			
Guaranteed loan subsidy (in percent):			
2320 Subsidy rate	0.00	0.00	0.00
2329 Weighted average subsidy rate	0.00	0.00	0.00
Guaranteed loan subsidy budget authority:			
2330 Subsidy budget authority			
2339 Total subsidy budget authority			
Guaranteed loan subsidy outlays:			
2340 Subsidy outlays			
2349 Total subsidy outlays			
Administrative expense data:			
3510 Budget authority	4	4	4
3580 Outlays from balances	1	2	
3590 Outlays from new authority	2	4	

The Health education assistance loan (HEAL) program guarantees loans from private lenders to health professions students to help pay for the costs of their training. As required by the Federal Credit Reform Act of 1990, this account records, for the HEAL program, the subsidy costs associated with HEAL loan guarantees committed in 1992 and beyond (including modifications of HEAL loan guarantees that resulted from obligations or commitments in any year), as well as administrative expenses of the program. The administrative expenses are estimated on a cash basis.

Object Classification (in millions of dollars)

Identification code 75–0340–0–1–552	1999 actual	2000 est.	2001 est.
11.1 Personnel compensation: Full-time permanent	2	2	2
25.3 Purchases of goods and services from Government accounts	1	1	1
99.0 Subtotal, direct obligations	3	3	3
99.5 Below reporting threshold	1	1	1
99.9 Total new obligations	4	4	4

Personnel Summary

Identification code 75–0340–0–1–552	1999 actual	2000 est.	2001 est.
Total compensable workyears:			
1001 Full-time equivalent employment	17	24	24
1011 Exempt Full-time equivalent employment	7		

Health Education Assistance Loans Financing Account

Program and Financing (in millions of dollars)

Identification code 75–4304–0–3–552	1999 actual	2000 est.	2001 est.
Obligations by program activity:			
00.01 Death and disability claims	2	1	1
00.02 Default claims	9	22	28
10.00 Total new obligations	11	23	29
Budgetary resources available for obligation:			
21.40 Unobligated balance available, start of year	259	295	303
22.00 New financing authority (gross)	48	31	33
23.90 Total budgetary resources available for obligation	307	326	336
23.95 Total new obligations	–11	–23	–29
24.40 Unobligated balance available, end of year	295	303	307
New financing authority (gross), detail:			
Discretionary:			
68.00 Spending authority from offsetting collections (gross): Offsetting collections (cash)	48	31	33
Change in unpaid obligations:			
73.10 Total new obligations	11	23	29
73.20 Total financing disbursements (gross)	–11	–23	–29
87.00 Total financing disbursements (gross)	11	23	29
Offsets:			
Against gross financing authority and financing disbursements:			
Offsetting collections (cash) from:			
88.25 Interest on uninvested funds	–45	–29	–29
88.40 Recoveries of defaulted loans	–3	–2	–4
88.90 Total, offsetting collections (cash)	–48	–31	–33
Net financing authority and financing disbursements:			
89.00 Financing authority			
90.00 Financing disbursements	–37	–8	–4

Status of Guaranteed Loans (in millions of dollars)

Identification code 75–4304–0–3–552	1999 actual	2000 est.	2001 est.
Position with respect to appropriations act limitation on commitments:			
2111 Limitation on guaranteed loans made by private lenders			
2150 Total guaranteed loan commitments			
Cumulative balance of guaranteed loans outstanding:			
2210 Outstanding, start of year	1,562	1,551	1,528
Adjustments:			
2261 Terminations for default that result in loans receivable	–9	–22	–28
2263 Terminations for default that result in claim payments	–2	–1	–2
2290 Outstanding, end of year	1,551	1,528	1,498
Memorandum:			
2299 Guaranteed amount of guaranteed loans outstanding, end of year	1,551	1,528	1,498

Credit accounts—Continued

HEALTH EDUCATION ASSISTANCE LOANS FINANCING ACCOUNT—Continued

Status of Guaranteed Loans (in millions of dollars)—Continued

Identification code 75–4304–0–3–552	1999 actual	2000 est.	2001 est.
Addendum:			
Cumulative balance of defaulted guaranteed loans that result in loans receivable:			
2310 Outstanding, start of year	32	38	57
2331 Disbursements for guaranteed loan claims	9	22	28
2351 Repayments of loans receivable	−3	−3	−4
2390 Outstanding, end of year	38	57	81

This account records all cash flows to and from the Government resulting from HEAL loan guarantees committed between 1992 and 1998.

Balance Sheet (in millions of dollars)

Identification code 75–4304–0–3–552	1998 actual	1999 actual	2000 est.	2001 est.
ASSETS:				
1101 Federal assets: Fund balances with Treasury	247	295	303	307
Non-Federal assets:				
1201 Investments in non-Federal securities, net	22	45	29	29
1206 Receivables, net	5	3	2	4
1999 Total assets	274	343	334	340
LIABILITIES:				
2204 Non-Federal liabilities: Liabilities for loan guarantees	1,562	1,551	1,528	1,498
2999 Total liabilities	1,562	1,551	1,528	1,498
NET POSITION:				
3300 Cumulative results of operations	−1,287	−1,208	−1,194	−1,158
3999 Total net position	−1,287	−1,208	−1,194	−1,158
4999 Total liabilities and net position	275	343	334	340

HEALTH EDUCATION ASSISTANCE LOANS LIQUIDATING ACCOUNT

Program and Financing (in millions of dollars)

Identification code 75–4305–0–3–552	1999 actual	2000 est.	2001 est.
Obligations by program activity:			
00.01 Death and disability claims	4	5	5
00.02 Defaulted loans	20	23	18
00.03 Debt collection	3	7	7
10.00 Total new obligations	27	35	30
Budgetary resources available for obligation:			
21.40 Unobligated balance available, start of year	18		
22.00 New budget authority (gross)	57	35	30
22.40 Capital transfer to general fund	−48		
23.90 Total budgetary resources available for obligation	27	35	30
23.95 Total new obligations	−27	−35	−30
New budget authority (gross), detail:			
Mandatory:			
60.05 Appropriation (indefinite)	37	15	10
69.00 Offsetting collections (cash)	20	20	20
70.00 Total new budget authority (gross)	57	35	30
Change in unpaid obligations:			
72.40 Unpaid obligations, start of year: Obligated balance, start of year	5	13	
73.10 Total new obligations	27	35	30
73.20 Total outlays (gross)	−20	−48	−30
74.40 Unpaid obligations, end of year: Obligated balance, end of year	13		
Outlays (gross), detail:			
86.97 Outlays from new mandatory authority	20	35	30
86.98 Outlays from mandatory balances		13	
87.00 Total outlays (gross)	20	48	30
Offsets:			
Against gross budget authority and outlays:			
88.40 Offsetting collections (cash) from: Non-Federal sources	−20	−20	−20
Net budget authority and outlays:			
89.00 Budget authority	37	15	10
90.00 Outlays		28	10

Status of Guaranteed Loans (in millions of dollars)

Identification code 75–4305–0–3–552	1999 actual	2000 est.	2001 est.
Cumulative balance of guaranteed loans outstanding:			
2210 Outstanding, start of year	1,412	1,343	1,260
2251 Repayments and prepayments	−58	−69	−75
Adjustments:			
2261 Terminations for default that result in loans receivable	−9	−12	−9
2263 Terminations for default that result in claim payments	−2	−2	−3
2290 Outstanding, end of year	1,343	1,260	1,173
Memorandum:			
2299 Guaranteed amount of guaranteed loans outstanding, end of year	1,343	1,260	1,173
Addendum:			
Cumulative balance of defaulted guaranteed loans that result in loans receivable:			
2310 Outstanding, start of year	494	496	475
2331 Disbursements for guaranteed loan claims	20	23	18
2351 Repayments of loans receivable	−15	−15	−15
2361 Write-offs of loans receivable	−29	−29	−29
2364 Other adjustments, net	26		
2390 Outstanding, end of year	496	475	449

Note.—Includes carryover commitments from prior years.

Note.—The adjustment to loans receivable represents interest, which had not previously been reflected in cumulative outstanding balances.

This account records all cash flows to and from the Government resulting from HEAL loan guarantees committed prior to 1992.

Statement of Operations (in millions of dollars)

Identification code 75–4305–0–3–552	1998 actual	1999 actual	2000 est.	2001 est.
0101 Revenue	48	45	35	30
0102 Expense	−38	−27	−35	−30
0105 Net income or loss (−)	10	18		

Balance Sheet (in millions of dollars)

Identification code 75–4305–0–3–552	1998 actual	1999 actual	2000 est.	2001 est.
ASSETS:				
Net value of assets related to pre–1992 direct loans receivable and acquired defaulted guaranteed loans receivable:				
1701 Defaulted guaranteed loans, gross	470	496	475	449
1702 Interest receivable	5	6	6	6
1704 Defaulted guaranteed loans and interest receivable, net	475	502	481	455
1799 Value of assets related to loan guarantees	475	502	481	455
1801 Other Federal assets: Cash and other monetary assets	38	27	35	30
1999 Total assets	513	529	516	485
LIABILITIES:				
2104 Federal liabilities: Resources payable to Treasury	2	2	6	6
2201 Non-Federal liabilities: Accounts payable	29	20	23	18
2999 Total liabilities	31	22	29	24

NET POSITION:				
3300 Cumulative results of operations	482	507	487	461
3999 Total net position	482	507	487	461
4999 Total liabilities and net position	513	529	516	485

Object Classification (in millions of dollars)

Identification code 75–4305–0–3–552	1999 actual	2000 est.	2001 est.
25.2 Other services	8	8	8
42.0 Insurance claims and indemnities	19	27	22
99.9 Total new obligations	27	35	30

Medical Facilities Guarantee and Loan Fund

FEDERAL INTEREST SUBSIDIES FOR MEDICAL FACILITIES

[For carrying out subsections (d) and (e) of section 1602 of the Public Health Service Act, $1,000,000, together with any amounts received by the Secretary in connection with loans and loan guarantees under title VI of the Public Health Service Act, to be available without fiscal year limitation for the payment of interest subsidies. During the fiscal year, no commitments for direct loans or loan guarantees shall be made.] *(Department of Health and Human Services Appropriations Act, 2000, as enacted by section 1000(a)(4) of the Consolidated Appropriations Act, 2000 (P.L. 106–113).)*

Program and Financing (in millions of dollars)

Identification code 75–9931–0–3–551	1999 actual	2000 est.	2001 est.
Obligations by program activity:			
00.01 Operating expenses: Interest subsidies, private	2	3	3
10.00 Total new obligations (object class 41.0)	2	3	3
Budgetary resources available for obligation:			
21.40 Unobligated balance available, start of year	50	48	40
22.00 New budget authority (gross)	4	7	5
22.60 Portion applied to repay debt	−4	−12	−12
23.90 Total budgetary resources available for obligation	50	43	33
23.95 Total new obligations	−2	−3	−3
24.40 Unobligated balance available, end of year	48	40	30
New budget authority (gross), detail:			
Mandatory:			
60.00 Appropriation	1	1	
60.36 Unobligated balance rescinded	−3		
62.50 Appropriation (total mandatory)	−2	1	
69.00 Offsetting collections (cash)	6	6	5
70.00 Total new budget authority (gross)	4	7	5
Change in unpaid obligations:			
72.40 Unpaid obligations, start of year: Obligated balance, start of year	15	15	14
73.10 Total new obligations	2	3	3
73.20 Total outlays (gross)	−3	−4	−4
74.40 Unpaid obligations, end of year: Obligated balance, end of year	15	14	13
Outlays (gross), detail:			
86.97 Outlays from new mandatory authority	1	1	
86.98 Outlays from mandatory balances	2	3	4
87.00 Total outlays (gross)	3	4	4
Offsets:			
Against gross budget authority and outlays:			
Offsetting collections (cash) from:			
Non-Federal sources:			
88.40 Principal repaid on loans not sold	−2	−2	−1
88.40 Principal collections from FFB	−4	−4	−4
88.90 Total, offsetting collections (cash)	−6	−6	−5
Net budget authority and outlays:			
89.00 Budget authority	−2	1	
90.00 Outlays	−4	−2	−1

Status of Direct Loans (in millions of dollars)

Identification code 75–9931–0–3–551	1999 actual	2000 est.	2001 est.
Cumulative balance of direct loans outstanding:			
1210 Outstanding, start of year	17	15	8
1251 Repayments: Repayments and prepayments	−6	−7	−8
1264 Write-offs for default: Other adjustments, net	4		
1290 Outstanding, end of year	15	8	

Status of Guaranteed Loans (in millions of dollars)

Identification code 75–9931–0–3–551	1999 actual	2000 est.	2001 est.
Cumulative balance of guaranteed loans outstanding:			
2210 Outstanding, start of year	82	45	15
2251 Repayments and prepayments	−37	−30	−15
2290 Outstanding, end of year	45	15	
Memorandum:			
2299 Guaranteed amount of guaranteed loans outstanding, end of year	45	15	

Title VII, part C of the Public Health Service Act established a revolving fund from which health professions schools could borrow in order to provide loans to their students.

Public Law 89–751, the Allied Health Professions Personnel Training Act of 1966, amended the Public Health Service Act to authorize the Federal Government to pay the difference between the interest paid by students to the schools and the interest payable by the schools to the Government National Mortgage Association (GNMA) and the Treasury.

Title VI and subsequently title XVI of the Public Health Service Act established a loan and loan guarantee fund for medical facilities with a maximum amount allowable for the Government's liability. Direct loans were made available for public facilities and guaranteed loans for private, nonprofit facilities. Funds under this authority were established in the amount of $50 million for use in fulfilling guarantees in event of default, $30 million as a revolving fund for direct loans and an amount for interest subsidy payments on guaranteed loans. Unobligated balances will be used to pay defaults and interest subsidy payments.

Trust Funds

Vaccine Injury Compensation Program Trust Fund

For payments from the Vaccine Injury Compensation Program Trust Fund, such sums as may be necessary for claims associated with vaccine-related injury or death with respect to vaccines administered after September 30, 1988, pursuant to subtitle 2 of title XXI of the Public Health Service Act, to remain available until expended: *Provided*, That for necessary administrative expenses, not to exceed [$3,000,000] *$2,992,000* shall be available from the Trust Fund to the Secretary of Health and Human Services. *(Department of Health and Human Services Appropriations Act, 2000, as enacted by section 1000(a)(4) of the Consolidated Appropriations Act, 2000 (P.L. 106–113).)*

Unavailable Collections (in millions of dollars)

Identification code 20–8175–0–7–551	1999 actual	2000 est.	2001 est.
Balance, start of year:			
01.99 Balance, start of year	1,264	1,398	1,528
Receipts:			
02.01 Deposits	130	131	134
02.03 Interest income	64	71	77
02.99 Total receipts	194	202	211
04.00 Total: Balances and collections	1,458	1,600	1,739
Appropriation:			
05.01 Vaccine injury compensation program trust fund	−60	−72	−124
05.99 Subtotal appropriation	−60	−72	−124

VACCINE INJURY COMPENSATION PROGRAM TRUST FUND—Continued

Unavailable Collections (in millions of dollars)—Continued

Identification code 20–8175–0–7–551	1999 actual	2000 est.	2001 est.
07.99 Total balance, end of year	1,398	1,528	1,615

Program and Financing (in millions of dollars)

Identification code 20–8175–0–7–551	1999 actual	2000 est.	2001 est.
Obligations by program activity:			
00.01 Compensation: Claims for post—FY 1989 injuries	53	62	114
Administrative expenses:			
01.03 Claims processing (Claims Court)	2	3	3
01.04 Claims processing (Public Health Service)	3	3	3
01.05 Claims processing (Dept. of Justice)	2	4	4
01.91 Total, administrative expenses	7	10	10
10.00 Total new obligations	60	72	124
Budgetary resources available for obligation:			
21.40 Unobligated balance available, start of year	2	1	
22.00 New budget authority (gross)	60	72	124
23.90 Total budgetary resources available for obligation	62	73	124
23.95 Total new obligations	−60	−72	−124
24.40 Unobligated balance available, end of year	1		
New budget authority (gross), detail:			
Discretionary:			
40.26 Appropriation (trust fund, definite)	7	10	10
Mandatory:			
60.27 Appropriation (trust fund, indefinite)	53	62	114
70.00 Total new budget authority (gross)	60	72	124
Change in unpaid obligations:			
72.40 Unpaid obligations, start of year: Obligated balance, start of year		1	
73.10 Total new obligations	60	72	124
73.20 Total outlays (gross)	−60	−73	−124
74.40 Unpaid obligations, end of year: Obligated balance, end of year	1		
Outlays (gross), detail:			
86.90 Outlays from new discretionary authority	5	10	10
86.93 Outlays from discretionary balances	2	1	
86.97 Outlays from new mandatory authority	53	62	114
87.00 Total outlays (gross)	60	73	124
Net budget authority and outlays:			
89.00 Budget authority	60	72	124
90.00 Outlays	60	73	124
Memorandum (non-add) entries:			
92.01 Total investments, start of year: U.S. securities: Par value	1,285	1,431	1,528
92.02 Total investments, end of year: U.S. securities: Par value	1,431	1,528	1,615

The Vaccine improvement program was established pursuant to Public Law 99–660 and Public Law 100–203, and serves as a source of funds to pay claims for compensation for vaccine related injury or death. This account reflects payments for claims for vaccine related injury or death occurring after October 1, 1988.

Object Classification (in millions of dollars)

Identification code 20–8175–0–7–551	1999 actual	2000 est.	2001 est.
25.2 Other services	3	3	3
25.3 Purchases of goods and services from Government accounts	4	7	7
42.0 Insurance claims and indemnities	53	62	114
99.9 Total new obligations	60	72	124

RICKY RAY HEMOPHILIA RELIEF FUND

Unavailable Collections (in millions of dollars)

Identification code 75–8074–0–7–551	1999 actual	2000 est.	2001 est.
Balance, start of year:			
01.99 Balance, start of year			
Receipts:			
02.01 Payments from the general fund		75	100
Appropriation:			
05.01 Ricky Ray hemophilia relief fund		−75	−100
07.99 Total balance, end of year			

Program and Financing (in millions of dollars)

Identification code 75–8074–0–7–551	1999 actual	2000 est.	2001 est.
Obligations by program activity:			
10.00 Total new obligations		75	100
Budgetary resources available for obligation:			
22.00 New budget authority (gross)		75	100
23.95 Total new obligations		−75	−100
New budget authority (gross), detail:			
Discretionary:			
40.27 Appropriation (trust fund, indefinite)		75	100
Change in unpaid obligations:			
73.10 Total new obligations		75	100
73.20 Total outlays (gross)		−75	−100
Outlays (gross), detail:			
86.90 Outlays from new discretionary authority		75	100
Net budget authority and outlays:			
89.00 Budget authority		75	100
90.00 Outlays		75	100

These amounts will be paid to the Ricky Ray hemophilia relief fund. The Ricky Ray hemophilia relief fund was established pursuant to Public Law 105–369 and serves as a source of funds to pay claims to eligible individuals on behalf of persons with HIV and a blood clotting disorder, who were treated with an anti-hemophiliac factor between July 1982 and December 1987.

Object Classification (in millions of dollars)

Identification code 75–8074–0–7–551	1999 actual	2000 est.	2001 est.
25.2 Other services		5	5
42.0 Insurance claims and indemnities		70	95
99.9 Total new obligations		75	100

INDIAN HEALTH SERVICE

Federal Funds

General and special funds:

INDIAN HEALTH SERVICES

For expenses necessary to carry out the Act of August 5, 1954 (68 Stat. 674), the Indian Self-Determination Act, the Indian Health Care Improvement Act, and titles II and III of the Public Health Service Act with respect to the Indian Health Service, **[**$2,078,967,000**]**, *$2,271,055,000* together with payments received during the fiscal year pursuant to 42 U.S.C. 238(b) for services furnished by the Indian Health Service: *Provided*, That funds made available to tribes and tribal organizations through contracts, grant agreements, or any other agreements or compacts authorized by the Indian Self-Determination and Education Assistance Act of 1975 (25 U.S.C. 450), shall be deemed to be obligated at the time of the grant or contract award and thereafter shall remain available to the tribe or tribal organization without fiscal year limitation: *Provided further*, That **[**$12,000,000**]** *$18,000,000* shall remain available until expended, for the Indian Catastrophic Health Emergency Fund: *Provided further*, That [$395,290,000] *$429,672,000* for contract medical care shall remain available for obligation until September 30, [2001] *2002*: *Provided further*, That of the funds provided, up to $17,000,000 shall be used to carry out the loan repayment program under section 108 of the Indian Health Care Improvement Act: *Provided further*, That funds provided in this Act may be used for 1-year contracts and grants which are to be performed in two fiscal years, so long as the total obligation is recorded in the year for which the funds are appropriated: *Provided further*, That the amounts collected by the Secretary of Health and Human Services under the authority of title IV of the Indian Health Care Improvement Act shall remain available until expended for the purpose of achieving compliance with the applicable conditions and requirements of titles XVIII and XIX of the Social Security Act (exclusive of planning, design, or construction of new facilities): *Provided further*, That funding contained herein, and in any earlier appropriations Acts for scholarship programs under the Indian Health Care Improvement Act (25 U.S.C. 1613) shall remain available for obligation until September 30, [2001] *2002*: *Provided further*, That amounts received by tribes and tribal organizations under title IV of the Indian Health Care Improvement Act shall be reported and accounted for and available to the receiving tribes and tribal organizations until expended: *Provided further*, That, notwithstanding any other provision of law, of the amounts provided herein, not to exceed [$228,781,000] *$268,781,000* shall be for payments to tribes and tribal organizations for contract or grant support costs associated with contracts, grants, self-governance compacts or annual funding agreements *(herein "contracts/compacts")* between the Indian Health Service and a tribe or tribal organization pursuant to the Indian Self-Determination Act of 1975, as amended, prior to or during fiscal year [2000] *2001*, of which not to exceed [$10,000,000 may be used for such costs associated with] *$40,000,000 is available first for* new and expanded [contracts, grants, self-governance compacts or annual funding agreements] *contracts/compacts, which shall receive contract support costs at, and not greater than, the minimum percentage of need funded for existing contracts/compacts in fiscal year 2001: Provided further, That any remaining portion of the $40,000,000 shall be used for contract support costs for existing contracts/compacts*: *Provided further*, That funds available for the Indian Health Care Improvement Fund may be used, as needed, to carry out activities typically funded under the Indian Health Facilities account. *(Department of the Interior and Related Agencies Appropriations Act, 2000, as enacted by section 1000(a)(3) of the Consolidated Appropriations Act, 2000 (P.L. 106–113).)*

Program and Financing (in millions of dollars)

Identification code 75–0390–0–1–551		1999 actual	2000 est.	2001 est.
	Obligations by program activity:			
	Direct program:			
00.01	Clinical services	1,524	1,632	1,769
00.02	Preventive health	86	92	103
00.03	Urban health	27	28	31
00.04	Indian health professions	29	30	33
00.05	Tribal management	2	2	2
00.06	Direct operations	48	51	54
00.07	Self-governance	9	10	10
00.08	Contract support costs	204	229	269
00.09	Diabetes funds	34	30	30
09.01	Reimbursable program	561	582	582
10.00	Total new obligations	2,524	2,686	2,883
	Budgetary resources available for obligation:			
21.40	Unobligated balance available, start of year	103	115	115
22.00	New budget authority (gross)	2,539	2,686	2,883
22.10	Resources available from recoveries of prior year obligations	1		
23.90	Total budgetary resources available for obligation	2,643	2,801	2,998
23.95	Total new obligations	−2,524	−2,686	−2,883
23.98	Unobligated balance expiring or withdrawn	−4		
24.40	Unobligated balance available, end of year	115	115	115
	New budget authority (gross), detail:			
	Discretionary:			
40.00	Appropriation	1,950	2,079	2,271
40.75	Reduction pursuant to P.L. 106–51	−2		
40.76	Reduction pursuant to P.L. 106–113		−5	
43.00	Appropriation (total discretionary)	1,948	2,074	2,271
	Mandatory:			
62.00	Transferred from HCFA for Diabetes	30	30	30
	Discretionary:			
68.00	Spending authority from offsetting collections: Offsetting collections (cash)	561	582	582
70.00	Total new budget authority (gross)	2,539	2,686	2,883
	Change in unpaid obligations:			
72.40	Unpaid obligations, start of year: Obligated balance, start of year	484	481	514
73.10	Total new obligations	2,524	2,686	2,883
73.20	Total outlays (gross)	−2,490	−2,653	−2,882
73.40	Adjustments in expired accounts (net)	−36		
73.45	Adjustments in unexpired accounts	−1		
74.40	Unpaid obligations, end of year: Obligated balance, end of year	481	514	515
	Outlays (gross), detail:			
86.90	Outlays from new discretionary authority	2,061	2,154	2,331
86.93	Outlays from discretionary balances	399	469	521
86.97	Outlays from new mandatory authority	23	23	23
86.98	Outlays from mandatory balances	7	7	7
87.00	Total outlays (gross)	2,490	2,653	2,882
	Offsets:			
	Against gross budget authority and outlays:			
	Offsetting collections (cash) from:			
88.00	Federal sources	−286	−288	−288
88.40	Non-Federal sources	−275	−294	−294
88.90	Total, offsetting collections (cash)	−561	−582	−582
	Net budget authority and outlays:			
89.00	Budget authority	1,978	2,104	2,301
90.00	Outlays	1,930	2,071	2,300

The Indian health services account provides medical care, public health services, and health professions training opportunities to American Indians and Alaska Natives. An estimated $592 million will be administered by tribal governments under self-governance compacts in FY 2001.

Object Classification (in millions of dollars)

Identification code 75–0390–0–1–551		1999 actual	2000 est.	2001 est.
	Direct obligations:			
	Personnel compensation:			
11.1	Full-time permanent	312	334	357
11.3	Other than full-time permanent	14	15	16
11.5	Other personnel compensation	29	36	38
11.9	Total personnel compensation	355	385	411
12.1	Civilian personnel benefits	99	105	114
13.0	Benefits for former personnel	2	3	4
21.0	Travel and transportation of persons	28	31	31
22.0	Transportation of things	10	11	11
23.1	Rental payments to GSA	8	8	8
23.2	Rental payments to others	3	9	9
23.3	Communications, utilities, and miscellaneous charges	21	24	24
24.0	Printing and reproduction	1	1	1
25.1	Advisory and assistance services	7	13	13
25.2	Other services	66	25	30
25.3	Purchases of goods and services from Government accounts	24	25	25
25.4	Operation and maintenance of facilities	−5	4	4
25.5	Research and development contracts		1	1
25.6	Medical care	182	191	232
25.7	Operation and maintenance of equipment	−2	16	16
25.8	Subsistence and support of persons	1	5	5
26.0	Supplies and materials	95	139	139
31.0	Equipment	24	9	10
32.0	Land and structures	1	1	1
41.0	Grants, subsidies, and contributions	1,043	1,098	1,212
99.0	Subtotal, direct obligations	1,963	2,104	2,301
99.0	Reimbursable obligations	561	582	582
99.9	Total new obligations	2,524	2,686	2,883

General and special funds—Continued

INDIAN HEALTH SERVICES—Continued

Personnel Summary

Identification code 75–0390–0–1–551	1999 actual	2000 est.	2001 est.
Direct:			
Total compensable workyears:			
1001 Full-time equivalent employment	10,376	10,433	10,546
1011 Exempt Full-time equivalent employment	1		
Reimbursable:			
2001 Total compensable workyears: Full-time equivalent employment	2,916	2,916	2,916
Allocation account:			
3001 Total compensable workyears: Full-time equivalent employment	2		

INDIAN HEALTH FACILITIES

For construction, repair, maintenance, improvement, and equipment of health and related auxiliary facilities, including quarters for personnel; preparation of plans, specifications, and drawings; acquisition of sites, purchase and erection of modular buildings, and purchases of trailers; and for provision of domestic and community sanitation facilities for Indians, as authorized by section 7 of the Act of August 5, 1954 (42 U.S.C. 2004a), the Indian Self-Determination Act, and the Indian Health Care Improvement Act, and for expenses necessary to carry out such Acts and titles II and III of the Public Health Service Act with respect to environmental health and facilities support activities of the Indian Health Service, [$318,580,000] *$290,795,000*, to remain available until expended: *Provided*, That notwithstanding any other provision of law, funds appropriated for the planning, design, construction or renovation of health facilities for the benefit of an Indian tribe or tribes may be used to purchase land for sites to construct, improve, or enlarge health or related facilities: [*Provided further*, That notwithstanding any provision of law governing Federal construction, $3,000,000 of the funds provided herein shall be provided to the Hopi Tribe to reduce the debt incurred by the Tribe in providing staff quarters to meet the housing needs associated with the new Hopi Health Center:] *Provided further*, That not to exceed $500,000 shall be used by the Indian Health Service to purchase TRANSAM equipment from the Department of Defense for distribution to the Indian Health Service and tribal facilities: *Provided further*, That not to exceed $500,000 shall be used by the Indian Health Service to obtain ambulances for the Indian Health Service and tribal facilities in conjunction with an existing interagency agreement between the Indian Health Service and the General Services Administration: *Provided further*, That not to exceed $500,000 shall be placed in a Demolition Fund, available until expended, to be used by the Indian Health Service for demolition of Federal buildings[: *Provided further*, That from within existing funds, the Indian Health Service may purchase up to 5 acres of land for expanding the parking facilities at the Indian Health Service hospital in Tahlequah, Oklahoma].

In addition, to remain available until expended: for construction of a replacement health facility at Fort Defiance, Arizona, up to $38,715,000; for construction of a replacement health facility at Parker, Arizona, up to $7,578,000; and for construction of a replacement health facility at Winnebago, Nebraska, up to $12,286,000 and, to become available October 1, 2001 and remain available until expended, up to $17,541,000. (Department of the Interior and Related Agencies Appropriations Act, 2000, as enacted by section 1000(a)(3) of the Consolidated Appropriations Act, 2000 (P.L. 106–113).)

Unavailable Collections (in millions of dollars)

Identification code 75–0391–0–1–551	1999 actual	2000 est.	2001 est.
Balance, start of year:			
01.99 Balance, start of year			
Receipts:			
02.01 Rent and charges for quarters, Indian health service, HHS	5	5	5
Appropriation:			
05.01 Indian health facilities	−5	−5	−5
07.99 Total balance, end of year			

Program and Financing (in millions of dollars)

Identification code 75–0391–0–1–551	1999 actual	2000 est.	2001 est.
Obligations by program activity:			
Direct program:			
00.01 Sanitation and health facilities	122	143	162
00.02 Maintenance	40	48	50
00.03 Facilities and environmental health	95	117	130
00.04 Equipment	12	14	12
01.00 Total direct program	269	322	354
09.01 Reimbursable program	11	12	12
10.00 Total new obligations	280	334	366
Budgetary resources available for obligation:			
21.40 Unobligated balance available, start of year	22	72	72
22.00 New budget authority (gross)	318	334	366
22.10 Resources available from recoveries of prior year obligations	11		
23.90 Total budgetary resources available for obligation	351	406	438
23.95 Total new obligations	−280	−334	−366
24.40 Unobligated balance available, end of year	72	72	72
New budget authority (gross), detail:			
Discretionary:			
40.00 Appropriation	292	319	349
40.76 Reduction pursuant to P.L. 106–113		−2	
43.00 Appropriation (total discretionary)	292	317	349
Mandatory:			
60.25 Appropriation (special fund, indefinite)	5	5	5
Discretionary:			
68.00 Spending authority from offsetting collections: Offsetting collections (cash)	21	12	12
70.00 Total new budget authority (gross)	318	334	366
Change in unpaid obligations:			
72.40 Unpaid obligations, start of year: Obligated balance, start of year	356	335	346
73.10 Total new obligations	280	334	366
73.20 Total outlays (gross)	−290	−323	−340
73.45 Adjustments in unexpired accounts	−11		
74.40 Unpaid obligations, end of year: Obligated balance, end of year	335	346	372
Outlays (gross), detail:			
86.90 Outlays from new discretionary authority	109	105	117
86.93 Outlays from discretionary balances	176	212	218
86.97 Outlays from new mandatory authority	5	5	5
87.00 Total outlays (gross)	290	323	340
Offsets:			
Against gross budget authority and outlays:			
88.00 Offsetting collections (cash) from: Federal sources	−21	−12	−12
Net budget authority and outlays:			
89.00 Budget authority	297	322	354
90.00 Outlays	269	311	328

The Indian health facilities account supports construction, repair and improvement, equipment, and environmental health and facilities support for the Indian health services.

Object Classification (in millions of dollars)

Identification code 75–0391–0–1–551	1999 actual	2000 est.	2001 est.
Direct obligations:			
Personnel compensation:			
11.1 Full-time permanent	46	50	54
11.3 Other than full-time permanent	3	4	4
11.5 Other personnel compensation	1	1	1
11.9 Total personnel compensation	50	55	59
12.1 Civilian personnel benefits	13	14	15
21.0 Travel and transportation of persons	4	5	5
22.0 Transportation of things	3	3	3
23.3 Communications, utilities, and miscellaneous charges	11	11	11
25.1 Advisory and assistance services	1	1	1

25.2	Other services	115	146	169
25.3	Purchases of goods and services from Government accounts	5	5	5
25.4	Operation and maintenance of facilities	12	10	10
25.7	Operation and maintenance of equipment	2	1	1
26.0	Supplies and materials	6	7	7
31.0	Equipment	7	2	2
32.0	Land and structures	2	17	17
41.0	Grants, subsidies, and contributions	38	45	49
99.0	Subtotal, direct obligations	269	322	354
99.0	Reimbursable obligations	11	12	12
99.9	Total new obligations	280	334	366

Personnel Summary

Identification code 75–0391–0–1–551		1999 actual	2000 est.	2001 est.
1001	Total compensable workyears: Full-time equivalent employment	1,231	1,264	1,301

ADMINISTRATIVE PROVISIONS, INDIAN HEALTH SERVICE

Appropriations in this Act to the Indian Health Service shall be available for services as authorized by 5 U.S.C. 3109 but at rates not to exceed the per diem rate equivalent to the maximum rate payable for senior-level positions under 5 U.S.C. 5376; hire of passenger motor vehicles and aircraft; purchase of medical equipment; purchase of reprints; purchase, renovation and erection of modular buildings and renovation of existing facilities; payments for telephone service in private residences in the field, when authorized under regulations approved by the Secretary; and for uniforms or allowances therefore as authorized by 5 U.S.C. 5901–5902; and for expenses of attendance at meetings which are concerned with the functions or activities for which the appropriation is made or which will contribute to improved conduct, supervision, or management of those functions or activities: *Provided*, That in accordance with the provisions of the Indian Health Care Improvement Act, non-Indian patients may be extended health care at all tribally administered or Indian Health Service facilities, subject to charges, and the proceeds along with funds recovered under the Federal Medical Care Recovery Act (42 U.S.C. 2651–2653) shall be credited to the account of the facility providing the service and shall be available without fiscal year limitation: *Provided further*, That notwithstanding any other law or regulation, funds transferred from the Department of Housing and Urban Development to the Indian Health Service shall be administered under Public Law 86–121 (the Indian Sanitation Facilities Act) and Public Law 93–638, as amended: *Provided further*, That funds appropriated to the Indian Health Service in this Act, except those used for administrative and program direction purposes, shall not be subject to limitations directed at curtailing Federal travel and transportation: *Provided further*, That notwithstanding any other provision of law, funds previously or herein made available to a tribe or tribal organization through a contract, grant, or agreement authorized by title I or title III of the Indian Self-Determination and Education Assistance Act of 1975 (25 U.S.C. 450), may be deobligated and reobligated to a self-determination contract under title I, or a self-governance agreement under title III of such Act and thereafter shall remain available to the tribe or tribal organization without fiscal year limitation: *Provided further*, That none of the funds made available to the Indian Health Service in this Act shall be used to implement the final rule published in the Federal Register on September 16, 1987, by the Department of Health and Human Services, relating to the eligibility for the health care services of the Indian Health Service until the Indian Health Service has submitted a budget request reflecting the increased costs associated with the proposed final rule, and such request has been included in an appropriations Act and enacted into law: *Provided further*, That funds made available in this Act are to be apportioned to the Indian Health Service as appropriated in this Act, and accounted for in the appropriation structure set forth in this Act: *Provided further*, That with respect to functions transferred by the Indian Health Service to tribes or tribal organizations, the Indian Health Service is authorized to provide goods and services to those entities, on a reimbursable basis, including payment in advance with subsequent adjustment, and the reimbursements received therefrom, along with the funds received from those entities pursuant to the Indian Self-Determination Act, may be credited to the same or subsequent appropriation account which provided the funding, said amounts to remain available until expended: *Provided further*, That reimbursements for training, technical assistance, or services provided by the Indian Health Service will contain total costs, including direct, administrative, and overhead associated with the provision of goods, services, or technical assistance: *Provided further*, That the appropriation structure for the Indian Health Service may not be altered without advance [approval of] *notice submitted to* the House and Senate Committees on Appropriations. *(Department of the Interior and Related Agencies Appropriations Act, 2000, as enacted by section 1000(a)(3) of the Consolidated Appropriations Act, 2000 (P.L. 106–113).)*

CENTERS FOR DISEASE CONTROL AND PREVENTION

Federal Funds

General and special funds:

DISEASE CONTROL, RESEARCH, AND TRAINING

To carry out titles II, III, VII, XI, XV, XVII, XIX and XXVI of the Public Health Service Act, sections 101, 102, 103, 201, 202, 203, 301, and 501 of the Federal Mine Safety and Health Act of 1977, sections 20, 21, and 22 of the Occupational Safety and Health Act of 1970, title IV of the Immigration and Nationality Act and section 501 of the Refugee Education Assistance Act of 1980; including insurance of official motor vehicles in foreign countries; and hire, maintenance, and operation of aircraft, [$2,910,761,000] *$3,239,487,000*, of which [$60,000,000] *$127,074,000* shall remain available until expended for equipment and construction and renovation of facilities, and in addition, such sums as may be derived from authorized user fees, which shall be credited to this account: *Provided*, That in addition to amounts provided herein, up to [$71,690,000] *$76,690,000* shall be available from amounts available under section 241 of the Public Health Service Act, to carry out the National Center for Health Statistics surveys: *Provided further*, That none of the funds made available for injury prevention and control at the Centers for Disease Control and Prevention may be used to advocate or promote gun control: *Provided further*, That the Director may redirect the total amount made available under authority of Public Law 101–502, section 3, dated November 3, 1990, to activities the Director may so designate: *Provided further*, That the Congress is to be notified promptly of any such transfer[: *Provided further*, That notwithstanding any other provision of law, a single contract or related contracts for the development and construction of the infectious disease laboratory through the General Services Administration may be employed which collectively include the full scope of the project: *Provided further*, That the solicitation and contract shall contain the clause "availability of funds" found at 48 CFR 52.232–18]: *Provided further*, That not to exceed $10,000,000 may be available for making grants under section 1509 of the Public Health Service Act to not more than 10 States[: *Provided further*, That of the amount provided under this heading, $3,000,000 shall be for the Center for Environmental Medicine and Toxicology at the University of Mississippi Medical Center at Jackson; $2,000,000 shall be for the University of Mississippi phytomedicine project; $500,000 shall be for the Alaska aviation safety initiative; and $1,000,000 shall be for the University of South Alabama birth defects monitoring and prevention activities.

In addition, $51,000,000, to be derived from the Violent Crime Reduction Trust Fund, for carrying out sections 40151 and 40261 of Public Law 103–322]. *In addition, to become available on October 1 of the fiscal year specified and remain available until expended for construction of Laboratory Building 18: $20,840,000 for fiscal year 2002 and $20,840,000 for fiscal year 2003. (Department of Health and Human Services Appropriations Act, 2000, as enacted by section 1000(a)(4) of the Consolidated Appropriations Act, 2000 (P.L. 106–113).)*

Unavailable Collections (in millions of dollars)

Identification code 75–0943–0–1–999		1999 actual	2000 est.	2001 est.
	Balance, start of year:			
01.99	Balance, start of year			
	Receipts:			
02.01	Cooperative research and development agreements, Centers for Disease Control	2	2	2

General and special funds—Continued

DISEASE CONTROL, RESEARCH, AND TRAINING—Continued

Unavailable Collections (in millions of dollars)—Continued

Identification code 75–0943–0–1–999		1999 actual	2000 est.	2001 est.
	Appropriation:			
05.01	Disease control, research, and training	–2	–2	–2
07.99	Total balance, end of year			

Program and Financing (in millions of dollars)

Identification code 75–0943–0–1–999		1999 actual	2000 est.	2001 est.
	Obligations by program activity:			
	Direct program:			
00.01	Preventive health block grant	150	135	179
00.02	Prevention centers	13	18	15
00.03	Sexually transmitted diseases	124	136	151
00.04	Immunization	420	490	530
00.05	Infectious diseases	257	294	329
00.06	Other chronic and environmental diseases	475	553	583
00.07	Tobacco	74	101	106
00.08	Occupational safety and health	200	215	220
00.10	Epidemic services	86	86	86
00.11	Health statistics	27	33	33
00.12	HIV	657	695	795
00.13	Prevention research	15	15	15
00.14	Buildings and facilities	45	100	127
00.15	Office of the director	30	38	36
00.16	Violent crime reduction programs	51	50	
00.17	Eliminating racial and ethnic disparities	10	30	35
09.01	Reimbursable program	180	189	195
10.00	Total new obligations	2,814	3,178	3,435
	Budgetary resources available for obligation:			
21.40	Unobligated balance available, start of year	56	43	22
22.00	New budget authority (gross)	2,791	3,157	3,439
22.10	Resources available from recoveries of prior year obligations	11		
23.90	Total budgetary resources available for obligation	2,858	3,200	3,461
23.95	Total new obligations	–2,814	–3,178	–3,435
23.98	Unobligated balance expiring or withdrawn	–1		
24.40	Unobligated balance available, end of year	43	22	27
	New budget authority (gross), detail:			
	Discretionary:			
40.00	Appropriation	2,559	2,911	3,239
40.75	Reduction pursuant to P.L. 106–51	–3		
40.76	Reduction pursuant to P.L. 106–113		–19	
41.00	Transferred to other accounts	–1		
42.00	Transferred from other accounts	51	71	
43.00	Appropriation (total discretionary)	2,606	2,963	3,239
	Mandatory:			
60.25	Appropriation (special fund, indefinite)	2	2	2
62.00	Transferred from other accounts	3	3	3
62.50	Appropriation (total mandatory)	5	5	5
	Discretionary:			
68.00	Spending authority from offsetting collections: Offsetting collections (cash)	180	189	195
70.00	Total new budget authority (gross)	2,791	3,157	3,439
	Change in unpaid obligations:			
72.40	Unpaid obligations, start of year: Obligated balance, start of year	2,042	2,223	2,518
73.10	Total new obligations	2,814	3,178	3,435
73.20	Total outlays (gross)	–2,610	–2,881	–3,228
73.40	Adjustments in expired accounts (net)	–13		
73.45	Adjustments in unexpired accounts	–11		
74.40	Unpaid obligations, end of year: Obligated balance, end of year	2,223	2,518	2,724
	Outlays (gross), detail:			
86.90	Outlays from new discretionary authority	1,133	1,211	1,329
86.93	Outlays from discretionary balances	1,470	1,664	1,893
86.97	Outlays from new mandatory authority	5	5	5
86.98	Outlays from mandatory balances	2	1	1
87.00	Total outlays (gross)	2,610	2,881	3,228
	Offsets:			
	Against gross budget authority and outlays:			
	Offsetting collections (cash) from:			
88.00	Federal sources	–178	–187	–193
88.40	Non-Federal sources	–2	–2	–2
88.90	Total, offsetting collections (cash)	–180	–189	–195
	Net budget authority and outlays:			
89.00	Budget authority	2,611	2,968	3,244
90.00	Outlays	2,430	2,692	3,033

[Dollars in millions]

	1999	*2000*	*2001*
Distribution of budget authority by account:			
Disease control, research and training	2,560	2,918	3,244
Violent crime reduction programs	51	50	
Distribution of outlays by account:			
Disease control, research and training	2,382	2,658	2,996
Violent crime reduction programs	48	34	37

The Centers for Disease Control and Prevention (CDC) supports a number of categorical programs including grants for immunizations, control of sexually transmitted diseases, HIV prevention, and control of other infectious and chronic diseases. CDC also supports the Preventive health block grant.

This display also includes amounts derived from the Violent crime reduction trust fund in FY 1999 and FY 2000. In FY 2001, the activities funded through the trust fund in FY 2000 are maintained at the same funding level of $51 million, and displayed in FY 2001 within the activity lines for the preventive health block grant ($45 million) and other chronic and environmental diseases ($6 million).

Object Classification (in millions of dollars)

Identification code 75–0943–0–1–999		1999 actual	2000 est.	2001 est.
	Direct obligations:			
	Personnel compensation:			
11.1	Full-time permanent	304	335	368
11.3	Other than full-time permanent	7	9	10
11.5	Other personnel compensation	16	17	18
11.9	Total personnel compensation	327	361	396
12.1	Civilian personnel benefits	97	104	112
21.0	Travel and transportation of persons	26	31	34
22.0	Transportation of things	5	6	7
23.1	Rental payments to GSA	19	22	24
23.2	Rental payments to others	2	3	3
23.3	Communications, utilities, and miscellaneous charges	24	26	28
24.0	Printing and reproduction	7	9	10
25.1	Advisory and assistance services	24	29	31
25.2	Other services	50	56	60
25.3	Purchases of goods and services from Government accounts	71	80	87
25.4	Operation and maintenance of facilities	12	57	62
25.5	Research and development contracts	123	133	145
25.6	Medical care	3	5	5
25.7	Operation and maintenance of equipment	10	13	14
26.0	Supplies and materials	23	30	39
31.0	Equipment	38	43	47
32.0	Land and structures	14	38	41
41.0	Grants, subsidies, and contributions	1,759	1,943	2,095
99.0	Subtotal, direct obligations	2,634	2,989	3,240
99.0	Reimbursable obligations	180	189	195
99.9	Total new obligations	2,814	3,178	3,435

Personnel Summary

Identification code 75–0943–0–1–999		1999 actual	2000 est.	2001 est.
	Direct:			
	Total compensable workyears:			
1001	Full-time equivalent employment	6,381	6,582	6,796
1011	Exempt Full-time equivalent employment	4		
	Reimbursable:			
2001	Total compensable workyears: Full-time equivalent employment	972	1,114	1,124

	Allocation account:			
3001	Total compensable workyears: Full-time equivalent employment	133	226	140

ALLOCATIONS RECEIVED FROM OTHER ACCOUNTS

Note.—Obligations incurred under allocations from other accounts are included in the schedules of the parent appropriation as follows:

Environmental Protection Agency: "Hazardous substance response trust fund."

NATIONAL INSTITUTES OF HEALTH

Federal Funds

General and special funds:

NATIONAL CANCER INSTITUTE

For carrying out section 301 and title IV of the Public Health Service Act with respect to cancer, [$3,332,317,000] *$3,249,730,000. (Department of Health and Human Services Appropriations Act, 2000, as enacted by section 1000(a)(4) of the Consolidated Appropriations Act, 2000 (P.L. 106–113).)*

NATIONAL HEART, LUNG, AND BLOOD INSTITUTE

For carrying out section 301 and title IV of the Public Health Service Act with respect to cardiovascular, lung, and blood diseases, and blood and blood products, [$2,040,291,000] *$2,069,582,000. (Department of Health and Human Services Appropriations Act, 2000, as enacted by section 1000(a)(4) of the Consolidated Appropriations Act, 2000 (P.L. 106–113).)*

NATIONAL INSTITUTE OF DENTAL AND CRANIOFACIAL RESEARCH

For carrying out section 301 and title IV of the Public Health Service Act with respect to dental disease, [$270,253,000] *$263,075,000. (Department of Health and Human Services Appropriations Act, 2000, as enacted by section 1000(a)(4) of the Consolidated Appropriations Act, 2000 (P.L. 106–113).)*

NATIONAL INSTITUTE OF DIABETES AND DIGESTIVE AND KIDNEY DISEASES

For carrying out section 301 and title IV of the Public Health Service Act with respect to diabetes and digestive and kidney disease, [$1,147,588,000] *$1,186,266,000. (Department of Health and Human Services Appropriations Act, 2000, as enacted by section 1000(a)(4) of the Consolidated Appropriations Act, 2000 (P.L. 106–113).)*

NATIONAL INSTITUTE OF NEUROLOGICAL DISORDERS AND STROKE

For carrying out section 301 and title IV of the Public Health Service Act with respect to neurological disorders and stroke, [$1,034,886,000] *$1,050,412,000. (Department of Health and Human Services Appropriations Act, 2000, as enacted by section 1000(a)(4) of the Consolidated Appropriations Act, 2000 (P.L. 106–113).)*

NATIONAL INSTITUTE OF ALLERGY AND INFECTIOUS DISEASES

For carrying out section 301 and title IV of the Public Health Service Act with respect to allergy and infectious diseases, [$1,803,063,000] *$935,166,000. (Department of Health and Human Services Appropriations Act, 2000, as enacted by section 1000(a)(4) of the Consolidated Appropriations Act, 2000 (P.L. 106–113).)*

NATIONAL INSTITUTE OF GENERAL MEDICAL SCIENCES

For carrying out section 301 and title IV of the Public Health Service Act with respect to general medical sciences, [$1,361,668,000] *$1,389,492,000. (Department of Health and Human Services Appropriations Act, 2000, as enacted by section 1000(a)(4) of the Consolidated Appropriations Act, 2000 (P.L. 106–113).)*

NATIONAL INSTITUTE OF CHILD HEALTH AND HUMAN DEVELOPMENT

For carrying out section 301 and title IV of the Public Health Service Act with respect to child health and human development, [$862,884,000] *$810,501,000. (Department of Health and Human Services Appropriations Act, 2000, as enacted by section 1000(a)(4) of the Consolidated Appropriations Act, 2000 (P.L. 106–113).)*

NATIONAL EYE INSTITUTE

For carrying out section 301 and title IV of the Public Health Service Act with respect to eye diseases and visual disorders, [$452,706,000] *$462,776,000. (Department of Health and Human Services Appropriations Act, 2000, as enacted by section 1000(a)(4) of the Consolidated Appropriations Act, 2000 (P.L. 106–113).)*

NATIONAL INSTITUTE OF ENVIRONMENTAL HEALTH SCIENCES

For carrying out sections 301 and 311 and title IV of the Public Health Service Act with respect to environmental health sciences, [$444,817,000] *$460,971,000. (Department of Health and Human Services Appropriations Act, 2000, as enacted by section 1000(a)(4) of the Consolidated Appropriations Act, 2000 (P.L. 106–113).)*

NATIONAL INSTITUTE ON AGING

For carrying out section 301 and title IV of the Public Health Service Act with respect to aging, [$690,156,000] *$721,651,000. (Department of Health and Human Services Appropriations Act, 2000, as enacted by section 1000(a)(4) of the Consolidated Appropriations Act, 2000 (P.L. 106–113).)*

NATIONAL INSTITUTE OF ARTHRITIS AND MUSCULOSKELETAL AND SKIN DISEASES

For carrying out section 301 and title IV of the Public Health Service Act with respect to arthritis and musculoskeletal and skin diseases, [$351,840,000] *$363,479,000. (Department of Health and Human Services Appropriations Act, 2000, as enacted by section 1000(a)(4) of the Consolidated Appropriations Act, 2000 (P.L. 106–113).)*

NATIONAL INSTITUTE ON DEAFNESS AND OTHER COMMUNICATION DISORDERS

For carrying out section 301 and title IV of the Public Health Service Act with respect to deafness and other communication disorders, [$265,185,000] *$276,418,000. (Department of Health and Human Services Appropriations Act, 2000, as enacted by section 1000(a)(4) of the Consolidated Appropriations Act, 2000 (P.L. 106–113).)*

NATIONAL INSTITUTE OF NURSING RESEARCH

For carrying out section 301 and title IV of the Public Health Service Act with respect to nursing research, [$90,000,000] *$84,714,000. (Department of Health and Human Services Appropriations Act, 2000, as enacted by section 1000(a)(4) of the Consolidated Appropriations Act, 2000 (P.L. 106–113).)*

NATIONAL INSTITUTE ON ALCOHOL ABUSE AND ALCOHOLISM

For carrying out section 301 and title IV of the Public Health Service Act with respect to alcohol abuse and alcoholism, [$293,935,000] *$288,578,000. (Department of Health and Human Services Appropriations Act, 2000, as enacted by section 1000(a)(4) of the Consolidated Appropriations Act, 2000 (P.L. 106–113).)*

NATIONAL INSTITUTE ON DRUG ABUSE

For carrying out section 301 and title IV of the Public Health Service Act with respect to drug abuse, [$689,448,000] *$496,294,000. (Department of Health and Human Services Appropriations Act, 2000, as enacted by section 1000(a)(4) of the Consolidated Appropriations Act, 2000 (P.L. 106–113).)*

NATIONAL INSTITUTE OF MENTAL HEALTH

For carrying out section 301 and title IV of the Public Health Service Act with respect to mental health, [$978,360,000] *$896,059,000. (Department of Health and Human Services Appropriations Act, 2000, as enacted by section 1000(a)(4) of the Consolidated Appropriations Act, 2000 (P.L. 106–113).)*

NATIONAL HUMAN GENOME RESEARCH INSTITUTE

For carrying out section 301 and title IV of the Public Health Service Act with respect to human genome research, [$337,322,000] *$353,427,000. (Department of Health and Human Services Appropriations Act, 2000, as enacted by section 1000(a)(4) of the Consolidated Appropriations Act, 2000 (P.L. 106–113).)*

NATIONAL CENTER FOR RESEARCH RESOURCES

For carrying out section 301 and title IV of the Public Health Service Act with respect to research resources and general research support grants, [$680,176,000] *$602,728,000*: *Provided*, That none of these funds shall be used to pay recipients of the general research support grants program any amount for indirect expenses in connection with such grants: *Provided further*, That *$72,500,000* shall be for extramural facilities construction grants. *(Department of Health and Human Services ppropriations Act, 2000, as enacted by section*

General and special funds—Continued

NATIONAL CENTER FOR RESEARCH RESOURCES—Continued

1000(a)(4) of the Consolidated Appropriations Act, 2000 (P.L. 106–113).)

NATIONAL CENTER FOR COMPLEMENTARY AND ALTERNATIVE MEDICINE

For carrying out section 301 and title IV of the Public Health Service Act with respect to complementary and alternative medicine, [$68,753,000] *$71,362,000*. *(Department of Health and Human Services ppropriations Act, 2000, as enacted by section 1000(a)(4) of the Consolidated Appropriations Act, 2000 (P.L. 106–113).)*

JOHN E. FOGARTY INTERNATIONAL CENTER

For carrying out the activities at the John E. Fogarty International Center, [$43,723,000] *$32,532,000*. *(Department of Health and Human Services Appropriations Act, 2000, as enacted by section 1000(a)(4) of the Consolidated Appropriations Act, 2000 (P.L. 106–113).)*

NATIONAL LIBRARY OF MEDICINE

For carrying out section 301 and title IV of the Public Health Service Act with respect to health information communications, [$215,214,000] *$224,942,000*, of which $4,000,000 shall be available until expended for improvement of information systems: *Provided*, That in fiscal year [2000] *2001*, the Library may enter into personal services contracts for the provision of services in facilities owned, operated, or constructed under the jurisdiction of the National Institutes of Health. *(Department of Health and Human Services Appropriations Act, 2000, as enacted by section 1000(a)(4) of the Consolidated Appropriations Act, 2000 (P.L. 106–113).)*

OFFICE OF THE DIRECTOR

(INCLUDING TRANSFER OF FUNDS)

For carrying out the responsibilities of the Office of the Director, National Institutes of Health, [$283,509,000, of which $44,953,000 shall be for the Office of AIDS Research] *$262,456,000*: *Provided*, That funding shall be available for the purchase of not to exceed [29] *20* passenger motor vehicles for replacement only: *Provided further*, That the Director may direct up to 1 percent of the total amount made available in this or any other Act to all National Institutes of Health appropriations to activities the Director may so designate: *Provided further*, That no such appropriation shall be decreased by more than 1 percent by any such transfers and that the Congress is promptly notified of the transfer: *Provided further*, That the National Institutes of Health is authorized to collect third party payments for the cost of clinical services that are incurred in National Institutes of Health research facilities and that such payments shall be credited to the National Institutes of Health Management Fund: *Provided further*, That all funds credited to the National Institutes of Health Management Fund shall remain available for one fiscal year after the fiscal year in which they are deposited: [*Provided further*, That up to $500,000 shall be available to carry out section 499 of the Public Health Service Act: *Provided further*, That, notwithstanding section 499(k)(10) of the Public Health Service Act, funds from the Foundation for the National Institutes of Health may be transferred to the National Institutes of Health] *Provided further, That the Director of NIH may establish an extramural clinical loan repayment program in order to provide recruitment and retention incentives for clinical researchers: Provided further, That the Director of the Office of Research on Minority Health, in consultation with the Advisory Council for the Office of Research on Minority Health and the Institutes and Centers, may, in exceptional circumstances, fund peer-reviewed grants for innovative projects that address high priority areas of minority health. (Department of Health and Human Services Appropriations Act, 2000, as enacted by section 1000(a)(4) of the Consolidated Appropriations Act, 2000 (P.L. 106–113).)*

OFFICE OF AIDS RESEARCH

(INCLUDING TRANSFER OF FUNDS)

For carrying out part D of title XXIII of the Public Health Service Act, $2,111,224,000: Provided, That the Director of the Office of AIDS Research shall transfer funds from this appropriation as authorized by subsection 2353(d) of such Act.

BUILDINGS AND FACILITIES

For the study of, construction of, and acquisition of equipment for, facilities of or used by the National Institutes of Health, including the acquisition of real property, [$135,376,000] *$148,900,000*, to remain available until expended, *of which $47,300,000 shall be for the neuroscience research center.*

In addition, to become available on October 1, 2001 and remain available until expended, for the neuroscience research center, $26,000,000. (Department of Health and Human Services Appropriations Act, 2000, as enacted by section 1000(a)(4) of the Consolidated Appropriations Act, 2000 (P.L. 106–113).)

Unavailable Collections (in millions of dollars)

Identification code 75–9915–0–1–552	1999 actual	2000 est.	2001 est.
Balance, start of year:			
01.99 Balance, start of year			
Receipts:			
02.01 Cooperative research and development agreements, NIH	13	13	13
Appropriation:			
05.01 National Institutes of Health	−13	−13	−13
07.99 Total balance, end of year			

Program and Financing (in millions of dollars)

Identification code 75–9915–0–1–552	1999 actual	2000 est.	2001 est.
Obligations by program activity:			
Direct program:			
00.01 National Cancer Institute	2,918	3,315	3,250
00.02 National Heart, Lung, and Blood Institute	1,788	2,029	2,070
00.03 National Institute of Dental and Craniofacial Research	234	269	263
00.04 National Institute of Diabetes and Digestive and Kidney Disease	1,018	1,168	1,213
00.05 National Institute of Neurological Disorders and Stroke	900	1,029	1,050
00.06 National Institute of Allergy and Infectious Diseases	1,565	1,778	935
00.07 National Institute of General Medical Sciences	1,203	1,354	1,390
00.08 National Institute of Child Health and Human Development	749	858	811
00.09 National Eye Institute	395	450	463
00.10 National Institute of Environmental Health Sciences	374	442	461
00.11 National Institute on Aging	594	686	722
00.12 National Institute of Arthritis and Musculoskeletal and Skin Disease	307	350	364
00.13 National Institute on Deafness and Other Communication Disorder	229	264	276
00.14 National Institute of Mental Health	858	973	896
00.15 National Institute on Drug Abuse	611	687	496
00.16 Natinal Institute on Alcohol Abuse and Alcoholism	259	292	289
00.17 National Institute of Nursing Research	70	90	85
00.18 National Human Genome Research Institute	279	336	353
00.19 National Center for Research Resources	562	677	603
00.20 National Center for Complementary and Alternative Medicine	40	68	71
00.21 John F. Fogarty International Center	35	44	33
00.22 National Library of Medicine	181	214	225
00.23 Office of the Director	256	282	262
00.24 Office of AIDS Research			2,111
00.25 Buildings and facilities	217	165	148
00.26 Cooperative research and development agreements	16	13	13
00.27 Royalities	45		
09.00 Reimbursable program	1,038	1,187	1,215
10.00 Total new obligations	16,741	19,020	20,068
Budgetary resources available for obligation:			
21.40 Unobligated balance available, start of year	147	161	161
22.00 New budget authority (gross)	16,756	19,020	20,068
23.90 Total budgetary resources available for obligation	16,903	19,181	20,229
23.95 Total new obligations	−16,741	−19,020	−20,068
23.98 Unobligated balance expiring or withdrawn	−1		
24.40 Unobligated balance available, end of year	161	161	161
New budget authority (gross), detail:			
Discretionary:			
40.00 Appropriation	15,612	17,913	18,813
40.75 Reduction pursuant to P.L. 106–51	−10		
40.76 Reduction pursuant to P.L. 106–113		−100	

		1999	2000	2001
41.00	Transferred to other accounts	−5	−20	
42.00	Transferred from other accounts	10		
43.00	Appropriation (total discretionary)	15,607	17,793	18,813
	Mandatory:			
60.25	Appropriation (special fund, indefinite)	13	13	13
62.00	Transferred from other accounts	27	27	27
62.50	Appropriation (total mandatory)	40	40	40
	Spending authority from offsetting collections:			
	Discretionary:			
68.00	Offsetting collections (cash)	949	1,187	1,215
68.10	From Federal sources: Change in receivables and unpaid, unfilled orders	160		
68.90	Spending authority from offsetting collections (total discretionary)	1,109	1,187	1,215
70.00	Total new budget authority (gross)	16,756	19,020	20,068
	Change in unpaid obligations:			
	Unpaid obligations, start of year:			
72.40	Obligated balance, start of year	12,119	13,898	16,194
72.95	From Federal sources: Receivables and unpaid, unfilled orders	3,984	4,144	4,144
72.99	Total unpaid obligations, start of year	16,103	18,042	20,338
73.10	Total new obligations	16,741	19,020	20,068
73.20	Total outlays (gross)	−14,764	−16,725	−19,080
73.40	Adjustments in expired accounts (net)	−38		
	Unpaid obligations, end of year:			
74.40	Obligated balance, end of year	13,898	16,194	17,182
74.95	From Federal sources: Receivables and unpaid, unfilled orders	4,144	4,144	4,144
74.99	Total unpaid obligations, end of year	18,042	20,338	21,326
	Outlays (gross), detail:			
86.90	Outlays from new discretionary authority	5,549	5,998	6,606
86.93	Outlays from discretionary balances	9,190	10,692	12,435
86.97	Outlays from new mandatory authority	14	14	14
86.98	Outlays from mandatory balances	11	21	25
87.00	Total outlays (gross)	14,764	16,725	19,080
	Offsets:			
	Against gross budget authority and outlays:			
88.00	Offsetting collections (cash) from: Federal sources	−949	−1,187	−1,215
	Against gross budget authority only:			
88.95	From Federal sources: Change in receivables and unpaid, unfilled orders	−160		
	Net budget authority and outlays:			
89.00	Budget authority	15,647	17,833	18,853
90.00	Outlays	13,815	15,538	17,865

[Dollars in millions]

	1999	*2000*	*2001*
Distribution of budget authority by account:			
National Cancer Institute	2,918	3,315	3,250
National Heart, Lung, and Blood Institute	1,788	2,029	2,070
National Institute of Dental and Craniofacial Research	234	269	263
National Institute of Diabetes and Digestive and Kidney Diseases	1,018	1,168	1,213
National Institute of Neurological Disorder and Stroke	900	1,029	1,050
National Institute of Allergy and Infectious Diseases	1,565	1,778	935
National Institute of General Medical Sciences	1,203	1,354	1,390
National Institute of Child Health and Human Development	749	858	811
National Eye Institute	395	450	463
National Institute of Environmental Health Sciences	374	442	461
National Institute on Aging	595	686	722
National Institute of Arthritis and Musculoskeletal and Skin Diseases	307	350	364
National Institute on Deafness and Other Communication Disorders	229	264	276
National Institute of Nursing Research	70	90	85
National Institute on Alcohol Abuse and Alcoholism	259	292	289
National Institute on Drug Abuse	611	687	496
National Institute of Mental Health	858	973	896
National Center for Research Resources	562	677	603
National Human Genome Research Institute	279	336	353
National Center for Complementary and Alternative Medicine	50	68	71
John E. Fogarty International Center	35	44	33
National Library of Medicine	181	214	225
Office of the Director	256	282	262
Office of AIDS Research			2,111
Buildings and Facilities	197	165	148
Subtotal	15,633	17,820	18,840
Cooperative Research and Development Agreements	13	13	13
Total Budget Authority, NIH	15,646	17,833	18,853

[Dollars in millions]

	1999	*2000*	*2001*
Distribution of outlays by account:			
National Cancer Institute	2,617	2,906	3,110
National Heart, Lung, and Blood Institute	1,539	1,749	1,949
National Institute of Dental and Craniofacial Research	212	234	248
National Institute of Diabetes and Digestive and Kidney Diseases	903	1,014	1,145
National Institute of Neurological Disorders and Stroke	776	899	996
National Institute of Allergy and Infectious Diseases	1,375	1,549	871
National Institute of General Medical Sciences	1,076	1,202	1,322
National Institute of Child Health and Human Development	675	755	771
National Eye Institute	352	391	440
National Institute of Environmental Health Sciences	335	380	441
National Institute on Aging	518	592	676
National Institute of Arthritis and Musculoskeletal and Skin Diseases	267	309	345
National Institute on Deafness and Other Communication Disorders	197	226	261
National Institute of Nursing Research	63	70	79
National Institute on Alcohol Abuse and Alcoholism	228	254	272
National Institute on Drug Abuse	539	596	464
National Institute of Mental Health	738	849	841
National Center for Research Resources	460	557	554
National Human Genome Research Institute	228	280	330
National Center for Complementary and Alternative Medicine	3	40	65
John E. Fogarty International Center	24	35	29
National Library of Medicine	161	193	215
Office of the Director	309	247	240
Office of AIDS Research			1,981
Buildings and Facilities	198	198	208
Service and Supply Fund/Management Fund	3		
Subtotal Outlays	13,796	15,525	17,853
Cooperative Research and Development Agreements	19	13	13
Total Outlays, NIH	13,815	15,538	17,866

Note: The total amount for FY 2000 AIDS research was $2,006,368,000 which was jointly determined by the Director of NIH and the Director of the Office of AIDS Research pursuant to section 208 of P.L. 106–113. $1,961,654,000 was made available to OAR. This amount is net of the $44,714,000 in AIDS funds earmarked in P.L. 106–113 in the Office of the Director account. Amounts available under section 4921 of P.L. 105–33 for research on diabetes are included in the National Institute of Diabetes and Digestive and Kidney Disorders.

This program funds biomedical research and research training. These accounts will continue to be appropriated separately, and are displayed in a consolidated format to improve the readability of the presentation. Detailed information is available through the Department of Health and Human Services.

NIH research and related activities are included in the 21st Century research fund.

Object Classification (in millions of dollars)

Identification code 75–9915–0–1–552		1999 actual	2000 est.	2001 est.
	Direct obligations:			
	Personnel compensation:			
11.1	Full-time permanent	520	602	647
11.3	Other than full-time permanent	123	142	153
11.5	Other personnel compensation	36	32	34
11.8	Special personal services payments	89	106	114
11.9	Total personnel compensation	768	882	948
12.1	Civilian personnel benefits	170	196	215
21.0	Travel and transportation of persons	26	27	28
22.0	Transportation of things	4	4	4
23.1	Rental payments to GSA	7	8	9
23.2	Rental payments to others	19	18	19
23.3	Communications, utilities, and miscellaneous charges	36	39	40
24.0	Printing and reproduction	15	16	17
25.1	Advisory and assistance services	47	39	40
25.2	Other services	313	503	493
25.3	Purchases of goods and services from Government accounts	1,116	1,014	1,151
25.4	Operation and maintenance of facilities	224	118	120
25.5	Research and development contracts	857	958	986

General and special funds—Continued

BUILDINGS AND FACILITIES—Continued

Object Classification (in millions of dollars)—Continued

Identification code 75–9915–0–1–552		1999 actual	2000 est.	2001 est.
25.6	Medical care	11	13	12
25.7	Operation and maintenance of equipment	39	33	34
26.0	Supplies and materials	162	156	159
31.0	Equipment	154	158	163
41.0	Grants, subsidies, and contributions	11,735	13,651	14,415
99.0	Subtotal, direct obligations	15,703	17,833	18,853
99.0	Reimbursable obligations	1,038	1,187	1,215
99.9	Total new obligations	16,741	19,020	20,068

Personnel Summary

Identification code 75–9915–0–1–552		1999 actual	2000 est.	2001 est.
	Direct:			
	Total compensable workyears:			
1001	Full-time equivalent employment	10,986	12,058	12,432
1011	Exempt Full-time equivalent employment	22		
	Reimbursable:			
2001	Total compensable workyears: Full-time equivalent employment	4,321	4,615	4,638

SUBSTANCE ABUSE AND MENTAL HEALTH SERVICES ADMINISTRATION

Federal Funds

General and special funds:

SUBSTANCE ABUSE AND MENTAL HEALTH SERVICES

For carrying out titles V and XIX of the Public Health Service Act with respect to substance abuse and mental health services, the Protection and Advocacy for Mentally Ill Individuals Act of 1986, and section 301 of the Public Health Service Act with respect to program management, [$2,654,953,000] *$2,823,016,000: Provided, That in addition to amounts provided herein, $12,000,000 shall be available from amounts available under section 241 of the Public Health Services Act, to carry out the National Household Survey on Drug Abuse. (Department of Health and Human Services Appropriations Act, 2000, as enacted by section 1000(a)(4) of the Consolidated Appropriations Act, 2000 (P.L. 106–113).)*

Program and Financing (in millions of dollars)

Identification code 75–1362–0–1–551		1999 actual	2000 est.	2001 est.
	Obligations by program activity:			
	Direct program:			
00.01	Mental health and substance abuse activities	556	637	716
00.02	Mental health partnership	289	356	416
00.03	Substance abuse partnership	1,585	1,600	1,631
00.05	Program management	56	59	60
09.01	Reimbursable program	33	40	40
10.00	Total new obligations	2,519	2,692	2,863
	Budgetary resources available for obligation:			
22.00	New budget authority (gross)	2,520	2,692	2,863
23.95	Total new obligations	−2,519	−2,692	−2,863
23.98	Unobligated balance expiring or withdrawn	−1		
	New budget authority (gross), detail:			
	Discretionary:			
40.00	Appropriation	2,488	2,655	2,823
40.76	Reduction pursuant to P.L. 106–113		−3	
41.00	Transferred to other accounts	−1		
43.00	Appropriation (total discretionary)	2,487	2,652	2,823
68.00	Spending authority from offsetting collections: Offsetting collections (cash)	33	40	40
70.00	Total new budget authority (gross)	2,520	2,692	2,863
	Change in unpaid obligations:			
72.40	Unpaid obligations, start of year: Obligated balance, start of year	1,620	1,852	2,053
73.10	Total new obligations	2,519	2,692	2,863
73.20	Total outlays (gross)	−2,247	−2,491	−2,688
73.40	Adjustments in expired accounts (net)	−40		
74.40	Unpaid obligations, end of year: Obligated balance, end of year	1,852	2,053	2,228
	Outlays (gross), detail:			
86.90	Outlays from new discretionary authority	1,086	1,109	1,164
86.93	Outlays from discretionary balances	1,161	1,382	1,524
87.00	Total outlays (gross)	2,247	2,491	2,688
	Offsets:			
	Against gross budget authority and outlays:			
88.00	Offsetting collections (cash) from: Federal sources	−33	−40	−40
	Net budget authority and outlays:			
89.00	Budget authority	2,487	2,652	2,823
90.00	Outlays	2,214	2,451	2,648

This program provides Federal support for treatment and prevention in the areas of alcoholism, drug abuse, and mental health.

Object Classification (in millions of dollars)

Identification code 75–1362–0–1–551		1999 actual	2000 est.	2001 est.
	Direct obligations:			
	Personnel compensation:			
11.1	Full-time permanent	35	40	42
11.3	Other than full-time permanent	1	1	1
11.5	Other personnel compensation	1	1	1
11.9	Total personnel compensation	37	42	44
12.1	Civilian personnel benefits	8	9	10
21.0	Travel and transportation of persons	1	1	1
23.1	Rental payments to GSA	5	5	6
23.3	Communications, utilities, and miscellaneous charges	1	1	1
24.0	Printing and reproduction	4	4	4
25.1	Advisory and assistance services	11	16	18
25.2	Other services	152	169	175
25.3	Purchases of goods and services from Government accounts	46	50	52
31.0	Equipment	1	2	2
41.0	Grants, subsidies, and contributions	2,218	2,351	2,508
42.0	Insurance claims and indemnities	2	2	2
99.0	Subtotal, direct obligations	2,486	2,652	2,823
99.0	Reimbursable obligations	33	40	40
99.9	Total new obligations	2,519	2,692	2,863

Personnel Summary

Identification code 75–1362–0–1–551		1999 actual	2000 est.	2001 est.
	Direct:			
1001	Total compensable workyears: Full-time equivalent employment	559	612	612
	Reimbursable:			
	Total compensable workyears:			
2001	Full-time equivalent employment	2	74	74
2011	Exempt Full-time equivalent employment	71		

AGENCY FOR HEALTHCARE RESEARCH AND QUALITY

Federal Funds

General and special funds:

[HEALTH CARE POLICY AND RESEARCH] *HEALTHCARE RESEARCH AND QUALITY*

For carrying out titles III and IX of the Public Health Service Act, and part A of title XI of the Social Security Act, [$111,424,000; in addition,] amounts received from Freedom of Information Act fees, reimbursable and interagency agreements, and the sale of data [tapes] shall be credited to this appropriation and shall remain available until expended: *Provided*, That the amount made available pursuant to section 926(b) of the Public Health Service Act shall not exceed [$88,576,000] *$249,943,000. (Department of Health and Human Services Appropriations Act, 2000, as enacted by section 1000(a)(4) of the Consolidated Appropriations Act, 2000 (P.L. 106–113).)*

Program and Financing (in millions of dollars)

Identification code 75–1700–0–1–552		1999 actual	2000 est.	2001 est.
	Obligations by program activity:			
	Direct program:			
01.01	Research on health costs, quality, and outcomes	98	108	....
01.04	Program support	2	2	....
09.00	Reimbursable program	82	100	261
10.00	Total new obligations	182	210	261
	Budgetary resources available for obligation:			
21.40	Unobligated balance available, start of year	2	2	2
22.00	New budget authority (gross)	182	210	261
23.90	Total budgetary resources available for obligation	184	212	263
23.95	Total new obligations	–182	–210	–261
23.98	Unobligated balance expiring or withdrawn	....	....	....
24.40	Unobligated balance available, end of year	2	2	....
	New budget authority (gross), detail:			
	Discretionary:			
40.00	Appropriation	100	111	....
40.76	Reduction pursuant to P.L. 106–113	....	–1	....
43.00	Appropriation (total discretionary)	100	110	....
68.00	Spending authority from offsetting collections: Offsetting collections (cash)	82	100	261
70.00	Total new budget authority (gross)	182	210	261
	Change in unpaid obligations:			
	Unpaid obligations, start of year:			
72.40	Obligated balance, start of year	139	154	138
72.95	From Federal sources: Receivables and unpaid, unfilled orders	7	7	7
72.99	Total unpaid obligations, start of year	146	161	145
73.10	Total new obligations	182	210	261
73.20	Total outlays (gross)	–161	–220	–353
73.40	Adjustments in expired accounts (net)	–6	–6	–2
	Unpaid obligations, end of year:			
74.40	Obligated balance, end of year	154	138	46
74.95	From Federal sources: Receivables and unpaid, unfilled orders	7	7	7
74.99	Total unpaid obligations, end of year	161	145	53
	Outlays (gross), detail:			
86.90	Outlays from new discretionary authority	65	110	261
86.93	Outlays from discretionary balances	96	110	92
87.00	Total outlays (gross)	161	220	353
	Offsets:			
	Against gross budget authority and outlays:			
88.00	Offsetting collections (cash) from: Federal sources	–82	–100	–261
	Net budget authority and outlays:			
89.00	Budget authority	100	110	....
90.00	Outlays	79	120	92

This activity supports the development of scientific evidence and tools to improve the quality, safety, and effectiveness of all aspects of the health care system, and initiatives to disseminate and translate scientific findings into health care practice.

Object Classification (in millions of dollars)

Identification code 75–1700–0–1–552		1999 actual	2000 est.	2001 est.
	Direct obligations:			
	Personnel compensation:			
11.1	Full-time permanent	11	13	....
11.3	Other than full-time permanent	2	2	....
11.9	Total personnel compensation	13	15	....
12.1	Civilian personnel benefits	3	4	....
21.0	Travel and transportation of persons	....	1	....
23.1	Rental payments to GSA	3	2	....
23.3	Communications, utilities, and miscellaneous charges	1	1	....
24.0	Printing and reproduction	1	1	....
25.2	Other services	7	7	....
25.3	Purchases of goods and services from Government accounts	3	3	....
25.5	Research and development contracts	26	21	....
31.0	Equipment	1	1	....
41.0	Grants, subsidies, and contributions	42	54	....
99.0	Subtotal, direct obligations	100	110	....
99.0	Reimbursable obligations	82	100	261
99.9	Total new obligations	182	210	261

Personnel Summary

Identification code 75–1700–0–1–552		1999 actual	2000 est.	2001 est.
	Direct:			
1001	Total compensable workyears: Full-time equivalent employment	194	226	....
	Reimbursable:			
2001	Total compensable workyears: Full-time equivalent employment	59	59	294

HEALTH CARE FINANCING ADMINISTRATION

Federal Funds

General and special funds:

GRANTS TO STATES FOR MEDICAID

For carrying out, except as otherwise provided, titles XI and XIX of the Social Security Act, [$86,087,393,000] *$93,586,251,000*, to remain available until expended.

For making, after May 31, [2000] *2001*, payments to States under title XIX of the Social Security Act for the last quarter of fiscal year [2000] *2001* for unanticipated costs, incurred for the current fiscal year, such sums as may be necessary.

For making payments to States or in the case of section 1928 on behalf of States under title XIX of the Social Security Act for the first quarter of fiscal year [2001, $30,589,003,000] *2002, $36,207,551,000*, to remain available until expended.

Payment under title XIX may be made for any quarter with respect to a State plan or plan amendment in effect during such quarter, if submitted in or prior to such quarter and approved in that or any subsequent quarter. *(Department of Health and Human Services Appropriations Act, 2000, as enacted by section 1000(a)(4) of the Consolidated Appropriations Act, 2000 (P.L. 106–113).)*

Program and Financing (in millions of dollars)

Identification code 75–0512–0–1–551		1999 actual	2000 est.	2001 est.
	Obligations by program activity:			
00.01	Medicaid vendor payments	104,775	109,272	116,448
00.02	State and local administration	5,836	6,380	7,258
00.03	Vaccine purchases	531	465	469
09.00	Medicare Part B premium transfer	....	50	60
10.00	Total new obligations	111,142	116,167	124,235
	Budgetary resources available for obligation:			
21.40	Unobligated balance available, start of year	6,012	1,117	....
22.00	New budget authority (gross)	102,394	115,050	124,235
22.10	Resources available from recoveries of prior year obligations	3,852	....	....
23.90	Total budgetary resources available for obligation	112,258	116,167	124,235
23.95	Total new obligations	–111,142	–116,167	–124,235
24.40	Unobligated balance available, end of year	1,117	....	....
	New budget authority (gross), detail:			
	Mandatory:			
60.00	Appropriation	74,594	86,087	93,586

General and special funds—Continued

GRANTS TO STATES FOR MEDICAID—Continued

Program and Financing (in millions of dollars)—Continued

Identification code 75–0512–0–1–551	1999 actual	2000 est.	2001 est.
60.05 Appropriation (indefinite)		179	
62.50 Appropriation (total mandatory)	74,594	86,266	93,586
65.00 Advance appropriation	27,801	28,734	30,589
69.00 Offsetting collections (cash)		50	60
70.00 Total new budget authority (gross)	102,395	115,050	124,235
Change in unpaid obligations:			
72.40 Unpaid obligations, start of year: Obligated balance, start of year	5,504	4,751	4,751
73.10 Total new obligations	111,142	116,167	124,235
73.20 Total outlays (gross)	–108,043	–116,167	–124,235
73.45 Adjustments in unexpired accounts	–3,852		
74.40 Unpaid obligations, end of year: Obligated balance, end of year	4,751	4,751	4,751
Outlays (gross), detail:			
86.97 Outlays from new mandatory authority	96,526	115,050	124,235
86.98 Outlays from mandatory balances	11,516	1,117	
87.00 Total outlays (gross)	108,043	116,167	124,235
Offsets:			
Against gross budget authority and outlays:			
88.00 Offsetting collections (cash) from: Federal sources		–50	–60
Net budget authority and outlays:			
89.00 Budget authority	102,394	115,000	124,175
90.00 Outlays	108,043	116,117	124,175

Summary of Budget Authority and Outlays

(in millions of dollars)

Enacted/requested:	*1999 actual*	*2000 est.*	*2001 est.*
Budget Authority	102,395	115,000	124,175
Outlays	108,042	116,117	124,175
Legislative proposal, subject to PAYGO:			
Budget Authority			663
Outlays			663
Total:			
Budget Authority	102,395	115,000	124,838
Outlays	108,042	116,117	124,838

Medicaid assists States in providing medical care to their low-income population by granting Federal matching payments under title XIX of the Social Security Act to States with approved plans.

Object Classification (in millions of dollars)

Identification code 75–0512–0–1–551	1999 actual	2000 est.	2001 est.
41.0 Direct obligations: Grants, subsidies, and contributions	111,142	116,117	124,175
99.0 Reimbursable obligations: Subtotal, reimbursable obligations		50	60
99.9 Total new obligations	111,142	116,167	124,235

GRANTS TO STATES FOR MEDICAID

(Legislative proposal, subject to PAYGO)

Program and Financing (in millions of dollars)

Identification code 75–0512–4–1–551	1999 actual	2000 est.	2001 est.
Obligations by program activity:			
10.00 Total new obligations (object class 41.0)			663
Budgetary resources available for obligation:			
22.00 New budget authority (gross)			663
23.95 Total new obligations			–663
New budget authority (gross), detail:			
Mandatory:			
60.00 Appropriation			663
Change in unpaid obligations:			
73.10 Total new obligations			663
73.20 Total outlays (gross)			–663
Outlays (gross), detail:			
86.97 Outlays from new mandatory authority			663
Net budget authority and outlays:			
89.00 Budget authority			663
90.00 Outlays			663

This schedule reflects the effects of proposals contained in the Budget on the Grants to States for Medicaid account.

STATE GRANTS AND DEMONSTRATIONS

Program and Financing (in millions of dollars)

Identification code 75–0897–0–1–551	1999 actual	2000 est.	2001 est.
Obligations by program activity:			
00.01 Infrastructure grants			20
00.02 Coverage demonstrations			42
10.00 Total new obligations (object class 41.0)			62
Budgetary resources available for obligation:			
22.00 New budget authority (gross)			62
23.95 Total new obligations			–62
24.40 Unobligated balance available, end of year			
New budget authority (gross), detail:			
Mandatory:			
60.00 Appropriation			62
Change in unpaid obligations:			
73.10 Total new obligations			62
73.20 Total outlays (gross)			–16
74.40 Unpaid obligations, end of year: Obligated balance, end of year			46
Outlays (gross), detail:			
86.97 Outlays from new mandatory authority			16
Net budget authority and outlays:			
89.00 Budget authority			62
90.00 Outlays			16

Summary of Budget Authority and Outlays

(in millions of dollars)

Enacted/requested:	*1999 actual*	*2000 est.*	*2001 est.*
Budget Authority			62
Outlays			16
Legislative proposal, subject to PAYGO:			
Budget Authority			10
Outlays			10
Total:			
Budget Authority			72
Outlays			26

This account includes funds for: grants to develop and establish State infrastructures to support working individuals with disabilities (sec. 203 of P.L. 106–170), and demonstration of health care coverage of workers with potentially severe disabilities (sec. 204 of P.L. 106–170).

STATE GRANTS AND DEMONSTRATIONS

(Legislative proposal, subject to PAYGO)

Program and Financing (in millions of dollars)

Identification code 75–0897–4–1–551	1999 actual	2000 est.	2001 est.
Obligations by program activity:			
10.00 Total new obligations (object class 41.0)			10
Budgetary resources available for obligation:			
22.00 New budget authority (gross)			10
23.95 Total new obligations			−10
New budget authority (gross), detail:			
Mandatory:			
60.00 Appropriation			10
Change in unpaid obligations:			
73.10 Total new obligations			10
73.20 Total outlays (gross)			−10
Outlays (gross), detail:			
86.97 Outlays from new mandatory authority			10
Net budget authority and outlays:			
89.00 Budget authority			10
90.00 Outlays			10

The Budget contains $10 million in FY 2001 for competitive demonstration grants to States. The demonstrations will assess eligible individuals' access to programs addressing the needs of the homeless and improve coordination among these programs.

PAYMENTS TO HEALTH CARE TRUST FUNDS

For payment to the Federal Hospital Insurance and the Federal Supplementary Medical Insurance Trust Funds, as provided under sections 217(g) and 1844 of the Social Security Act, sections 103(c) and 111(d) of the Social Security Amendments of 1965, section 278(d) of Public Law 97–248, and for administrative expenses incurred pursuant to section 201(g) of the Social Security Act, [$69,289,100,000] *$70,381,600,000*. *(Department of Health and Human Services Appropriations Act, 2000, as enacted by section 1000(a)(4) of the Consolidated Appropriations Act, 2000 (P.L. 106–113).)*

Program and Financing (in millions of dollars)

Identification code 75–0580–0–1–571	1999 actual	2000 est.	2001 est.
Obligations by program activity:			
00.01 Supplementary medical insurance (SMI)	62,171	65,063	69,777
00.02 Hospital insurance for uninsured (HI)	555	349	321
00.03 Federal uninsured payment (HI)	97	121	132
00.04 Program management (HI)	96	129	152
00.06 Federal payments from taxation of OASDI benefits (HI)	6,552	7,190	6,878
00.08 Fraud and abuse control, FBI	66	76	88
00.10 Fraud and abuse control, criminal fines	36	40	44
00.13 Fraud and abuse, civil monetary penalties		5	6
00.14 Fraud and abuse control, administrative fees	2		
00.15 Other (SMI)	14		
10.00 Total new obligations	69,589	72,973	77,398
Budgetary resources available for obligation:			
21.40 Unobligated balance available, start of year	14		
22.00 New budget authority (gross)	69,609	76,600	77,398
23.90 Total budgetary resources available for obligation	69,623	76,600	77,398
23.95 Total new obligations	−69,589	−72,973	−77,398
23.98 Unobligated balance expiring or withdrawn	−34	−3,627	
New budget authority (gross), detail:			
Mandatory:			
Appropriation:			
60.00 Appropriation	66	76	88
60.00 Appropriation	62,953	69,289	70,382
60.05 Appropriation (indefinite)	6,590	7,235	6,928
62.50 Appropriation (total mandatory)	69,609	76,600	77,398
Change in unpaid obligations:			
73.10 Total new obligations	69,589	72,973	77,398
73.20 Total outlays (gross)	−69,589	−72,973	−77,398
Outlays (gross), detail:			
86.97 Outlays from new mandatory authority	69,589	72,973	77,398
Net budget authority and outlays:			
89.00 Budget authority	69,609	76,600	77,398
90.00 Outlays	69,589	72,973	77,398

Summary of Budget Authority and Outlays

(in millions of dollars)

	1999 actual	*2000 est.*	*2001 est.*
Enacted/requested:			
Budget Authority	69,609	76,600	77,398
Outlays	69,589	72,973	77,398
Legislative proposal, not subject to PAYGO:			
Budget Authority			15,120
Outlays			15,120
Total:			
Budget Authority	69,609	76,600	92,518
Outlays	69,589	72,973	92,518

Payments are made (1) to the Federal Supplementary Medical Insurance trust fund; and (2) to the Federal hospital insurance trust fund for individuals aged 65 and over who meet certain transitional insured status requirements, and for civil service employees and annuitants who worked before 1983 and who were employed during January 1983. Since 1992, amounts have been included for non-Medicare activities of HCFA program management.

Object Classification (in millions of dollars)

Identification code 75–0580–0–1–571	1999 actual	2000 est.	2001 est.
41.0 Grants, subsidies, and contributions	69,033	72,374	76,793
42.0 Insurance claims and indemnities	460	470	453
92.0 Undistributed	96	129	152
99.9 Total new obligations	69,589	72,973	77,398

PAYMENTS TO THE HEALTH CARE TRUST FUNDS

(Legislative proposal, not subject to PAYGO)

Program and Financing (in millions of dollars)

Identification code 75–0580–2–1–571	1999 actual	2000 est.	2001 est.
Obligations by program activity:			
00.02 SMI premium match match—savings proposals			−280
00.03 Surplus transfer for HI solvency			15,400
10.00 Total new obligations			15,120
Budgetary resources available for obligation:			
22.00 New budget authority (gross)			15,120
23.95 Total new obligations			−15,120
New budget authority (gross), detail:			
Mandatory:			
60.00 Appropriation			−280
60.05 Appropriation (indefinite)			15,400
62.50 Appropriation (total mandatory)			15,120
Change in unpaid obligations:			
73.10 Total new obligations			15,120
73.20 Total outlays (gross)			−15,120
Outlays (gross), detail:			
86.97 Outlays from new mandatory authority			15,120
Net budget authority and outlays:			
89.00 Budget authority			15,120

General and special funds—Continued

PAYMENTS TO THE HEALTH CARE TRUST FUNDS—Continued

Program and Financing (in millions of dollars)—Continued

Identification code 75–0580–2–1–571	1999 actual	2000 est.	2001 est.
90.00 Outlays	....	....	15,120

This schedule reflects the effects of the Medicare proposals contained in the Budget on the Payments to the health care trust funds account.

Object Classification (in millions of dollars)

Identification code 75–0580–2–1–571	1999 actual	2000 est.	2001 est.
41.0 Grants, subsidies, and contributions	....	....	−280
92.0 Undistributed	....	....	15,400
99.9 Total new obligations	....	....	15,120

PROGRAM MANAGEMENT

For carrying out, except as otherwise provided, titles XI, XVIII, XIX, and XXI of the Social Security Act, titles XIII and XXVII of the Public Health Service Act, and the Clinical Laboratory Improvement Amendments of 1988, not to exceed [$1,994,548,000] *$2,086,302,000*, to be transferred from the Federal Hospital Insurance and the Federal Supplementary Medical Insurance Trust Funds, as authorized by section 201(g) of the Social Security Act; together with all funds collected in accordance with section 353 of the Public Health Service Act and such sums as may be collected from authorized user fees and the sale of data, which shall remain available until expended[, and together with administrative fees collected relative to Medicare overpayment recovery activities, which shall remain available until expended]: *Provided*, That all funds derived in accordance with 31 U.S.C. 9701 from organizations established under title XIII of the Public Health Service Act shall be credited to and available for carrying out the purposes of this appropriation: *Provided further*, That $18,000,000 appropriated under this heading for the managed care system redesign shall remain available until expended: [*Provided further*, That $2,000,000 of the amount available for research, demonstration, and evaluation activities shall be available to continue carrying out demonstration projects on Medicaid coverage of community-based attendant care services for people with disabilities which ensures maximum control by the consumer to select and manage their attendant care services: *Provided further*, That $3,000,000 of the amount available for research, demonstration, and evaluation activities shall be awarded to an application from the University of Pennsylvania Medical Center, the University of Louisville Sciences Center, and St. Vincent's Hospital in Montana to conduct a demonstration to reduce hospitalizations among high-risk patients with congestive heart failure: *Provided further*, That $2,000,000 of the amount available for research, demonstration, and evaluation activities shall be awarded to the AIDS Healthcare Foundation in Los Angeles: *Provided further*, That $100,000 of the amount available for research, demonstration, and evaluation activities shall be awarded to Littleton Regional Hospital in New Hampshire, to assist in the development of rural emergency medical services: *Provided further*, That $250,000 of the amount available for research, demonstration, and evaluation activities shall be awarded to the University of Missouri-Kansas City to test behavorial interventions of nursing home residents with moderate to severe dementia: *Provided further*, That $1,000,000 of the amount available for research, demonstration, and evaluation activities shall be awarded for a children's hospice care demonstration program in Virginia, Florida, Kentucky, New York, and Utah: *Provided further*, That $150,000 of the amount available for research, demonstration, and evaluation activities shall be awarded to L.A. Care Health Plan in Los Angeles, California for a Medicaid outreach demonstration project to provide access to medical care for uninsured workers: *Provided further*, That $500,000 of the amount available for research, demonstration, and evaluation activities shall be awarded to the Baystate Medical Center in Springfield, Massachusetts for the Partners for a Healthier Community childhood immunization demonstration project: *Provided further*, That $250,000 shall be awarded to the Shelby County Regional Medical Center to establish a Master Patient Index to determine patient Medicaid/TennCare eligibility:] *Provided further*, That the Secretary of Health and Human Services is directed to collect[, in aggregate, $95,000,000 in] fees in fiscal year [2000] *2001* from Medicare+Choice organizations pursuant to section 1857(e)(2) of the Social Security Act and from eligible organizations with risk-sharing contracts under section 1876 of that Act pursuant to section 1876(k)(4)(D) of that Act*: Provided further, That administrative fees collected relative to Medicare overpayment recovery activities shall be transferred to the Health Care Fraud and Abuse Control (HCFAC) account, to be used for Medicare Integrity Program (MIP) activities in addition to the amounts already specified, and shall remain available until expended*. (*Department of Health and Human Services Appropriations Act, 2000, as enacted by section 1000(a)(4) of the Consolidated Appropriations Act, 2000 (P.L. 106–113).*)

Program and Financing (in millions of dollars)

Identification code 75–0511–0–1–550	1999 actual	2000 est.	2001 est.
Obligations by program activity:			
Direct program:			
00.01 Medicare contractors	1,256	1,264	1,301
00.02 Federal administration	455	483	496
00.03 State survey and certification	175	205	234
00.04 Research, demonstrations, and evaluation projects	50	62	55
01.00 Total direct program	1,936	2,014	2,086
09.01 CLIA	34	43	43
09.03 Other reimbursements	3	1	2
09.06 Medicare+Choice	91	95	19
09.09 Total reimbursable program	128	139	64
10.00 Total new obligations	2,063	2,153	2,150
Budgetary resources available for obligation:			
21.40 Unobligated balance available, start of year	15	88	67
22.00 New budget authority (gross)	2,082	2,133	2,150
22.10 Resources available from recoveries of prior year obligations	64	....	....
23.90 Total budgetary resources available for obligation	2,161	2,221	2,217
23.95 Total new obligations	−2,063	−2,153	−2,150
23.98 Unobligated balance expiring or withdrawn	−10	....	....
24.40 Unobligated balance available, end of year	88	67	67
New budget authority (gross), detail:			
Spending authority from offsetting collections:			
Discretionary:			
Offsetting collections (cash):			
68.00 Offsetting collections (cash)	1,812	1,993	2,086
68.00 Offsetting collections (cash)	134	140	64
68.10 From Federal sources: Change in receivables and unpaid, unfilled orders	286	....	....
68.15 From Federal sources: Adjustments to receivables and unpaid, unfilled orders	−149	....	....
68.75 Reduction pursuant to P.L. 106–51	−1	....	....
68.90 Spending authority from offsetting collections (total discretionary)	2,082	2,133	2,150
Change in unpaid obligations:			
Unpaid obligations, start of year:			
72.40 Obligated balance, start of year	280	74	74
72.95 From Federal sources: Receivables and unpaid, unfilled orders	377	663	663
72.99 Total unpaid obligations, start of year	657	737	737
73.10 Total new obligations	2,063	2,153	2,150
73.20 Total outlays (gross)	−1,914	−2,153	−2,150
73.40 Adjustments in expired accounts (net)	−5	....	....
73.45 Adjustments in unexpired accounts	−64	....	....
Unpaid obligations, end of year:			
74.40 Obligated balance, end of year	74	74	74
74.95 From Federal sources: Receivables and unpaid, unfilled orders	663	663	663
74.99 Total unpaid obligations, end of year	737	737	737
Outlays (gross), detail:			
86.90 Outlays from new discretionary authority	1,524	2,133	2,150
86.93 Outlays from discretionary balances	389	20	....
87.00 Total outlays (gross)	1,914	2,153	2,150

		1999 actual	2000 est.	2001 est.
	Offsets:			
	Against gross budget authority and outlays:			
	Offsetting collections (cash) from:			
88.00	Federal sources	−1,812	−1,993	−2,086
88.40	Non-Federal sources	−134	−140	−64
88.90	Total, offsetting collections (cash)	−1,946	−2,133	−2,150
	Against gross budget authority only:			
88.95	From Federal sources: Change in receivables and unpaid, unfilled orders	−286		
88.96	From Federal sources: Adjustment to receivables and unpaid, unfilled orders	149		
	Net budget authority and outlays:			
89.00	Budget authority	−1		
90.00	Outlays	−32	20	

Summary of Budget Authority and Outlays

(in millions of dollars)

	1999 actual	2000 est.	2001 est.
Enacted/requested:			
Budget Authority	−1		
Outlays	−33	20	
Legislative proposal, not subject to PAYGO:			
Budget Authority			
Outlays			
Legislative proposal, subject to PAYGO:			
Budget Authority			250
Outlays			250
Total:			
Budget Authority	−1		250
Outlays	−33	20	250

Program management activities include funding for research, Medicare contractors, survey and certification, CLIA, Medicare+Choice, and administrative costs.

Object Classification (in millions of dollars)

Identification code 75–0511–0–1–550		1999 actual	2000 est.	2001 est.
	Direct obligations:			
	Personnel compensation:			
11.1	Full-time permanent	246	280	291
11.3	Other than full-time permanent	8	5	8
11.5	Other personnel compensation	5	4	5
11.9	Total personnel compensation	259	289	304
12.1	Civilian personnel benefits	51	55	59
21.0	Travel and transportation of persons	11	11	8
23.1	Rental payments to GSA	19	21	22
23.3	Communications, utilities, and miscellaneous charges	22	6	8
24.0	Printing and reproduction	8	9	8
25.1	Advisory and assistance services	6	1	1
25.2	Other services	443	318	349
25.3	Purchases of goods and services from Government accounts	9	17	8
25.6	Medical care	1,055	1,260	1,297
26.0	Supplies and materials	3	1	1
31.0	Equipment	31	2	2
32.0	Land and structures	10	10	10
41.0	Grants, subsidies, and contributions	8	13	9
99.0	Subtotal, direct obligations	1,935	2,013	2,086
99.0	Reimbursable obligations	128	140	64
99.9	Total new obligations	2,063	2,153	2,150

Personnel Summary

Identification code 75–0511–0–1–550		1999 actual	2000 est.	2001 est.
	Direct:			
1001	Total compensable workyears: Full-time equivalent employment	4,139	4,233	4,353
	Reimbursable:			
2001	Total compensable workyears: Full-time equivalent employment	80	80	82
	Allocation account:			
3001	Total compensable workyears: Full-time equivalent employment		50	

PROGRAM MANAGEMENT

(Legislative proposal, not subject to PAYGO)

Contingent upon enactment of authorization to establish fees to cover administrative costs of the Health Care Financing Administration and its contractors, such fees may be collected and credited to this account as offsetting collections, to remain available until expended for authorized purposes: Provided, That upon enactment of such authorizing legislation, the amount appropriated for fiscal year 2001 from the Federal Hospital Insurance and Federal Supplementary Medical Insurance Trust Funds shall be reduced by $220,000,000: Provided further, That contingent upon enactment of an amendment to section 1857(e)(2) of the Social Security Act which increases the aggregate amount of user fees from Medicare+Choice organizations, the Secretary of Health and Human Services is directed to collect up to $150,000,000 in fiscal year 2001 which shall be credited to this account as offsetting collections and remain available until expended to implement the Medicare+Choice education campaign: Provided further, That contingent upon enactment of authorizing legislation, the Secretary is directed to collect up to $4,300,000 in fiscal year 2001 which shall be credited to this account as offsetting collections and remain available until expended for the purposes of operating a nursing home criminal abuse registry.

Program and Financing (in millions of dollars)

Identification code 75–0511–2–1–550		1999 actual	2000 est.	2001 est.
	Obligations by program activity:			
	Direct program:			
00.01	Medicare contractor appropriation			−136
00.02	Federal administration appropriation			−21
00.03	State survey and certification appropriation			−63
01.00	Total direct program			−220
09.01	User fee for duplicate and unprocessable claims			53
09.02	User fee for paper claims			83
09.03	User fee for initial survey and certification			13
09.04	User fee for recertification (survey)			50
09.05	User fee for processing health plan applications			21
09.06	HMO user fee: Medicare+Choice beneficiary information campaign			131
09.07	User fee for background checks in nursing home patient abuse registry			4
09.09	Total reimbursable program			355
10.00	Total new obligations			135
	Budgetary resources available for obligation:			
22.00	New budget authority (gross)			135
23.95	Total new obligations			−135
	New budget authority (gross), detail:			
	Spending authority from offsetting collections:			
	Discretionary:			
	Offsetting collections (cash):			
68.00	Offsetting collections (cash)			−220
68.00	Offsetting collections (cash)			355
68.90	Spending authority from offsetting collections (total discretionary)			135
	Change in unpaid obligations:			
73.10	Total new obligations			135
73.20	Total outlays (gross)			−135
	Outlays (gross), detail:			
86.90	Outlays from new discretionary authority			135
	Offsets:			
	Against gross budget authority and outlays:			
	Offsetting collections (cash) from:			
88.00	Federal sources			220
88.40	Non-Federal sources			−355
88.90	Total, offsetting collections (cash)			−135
	Net budget authority and outlays:			
89.00	Budget authority			
90.00	Outlays			

The Budget includes $220 million in new user fees to finance HCFA activities. Proposed fees include: a duplicate or

General and special funds—Continued

PROGRAM MANAGEMENT—Continued

unprocessable claims fee, a paper claims fee, a managed care organization application and renewal fee, an initial survey and certification fee, and a recertification fee. If the authorizing legislation is enacted, the amount appropriated from the Federal hospital insurance and Federal supplementary medical insurance trust funds will be reduced by $220 million. Additional appropriations language is being proposed contingent upon the enactment of authorizing legislation. The authorizing legislation will be proposed to authorize the collection and spending of the fee subject to appropriations action. Contingent upon the enactment of authorizing legislation, the budget also authorizes the Secretary to collect up to $150 million in user fees to finance the Medicare+Choice education campaign. Additional appropriations language is being proposed contingent upon the enactment of authorizing legislation. The authorizing legislation will be proposed to authorize the collection and spending of the fee subject to appropriations action. Contingent upon the enactment of authorizing legislation, the Budget also authorizes the Secretary to collect up to $4.3 million in user fees to finance the operation of a nursing home criminal abuse registry. Additional appropriations language is being proposed contingent upon the enactment of authorizing legislation. The authorizing legislation will be proposed to authorize the collection and spending of the fee subject to appropriations action.

Object Classification (in millions of dollars)

Identification code 75–0511–2–1–550	1999 actual	2000 est.	2001 est.
Direct obligations:			
25.2 Other services			−84
25.6 Medical care			−136
99.0 Subtotal, direct obligations			−220
99.0 Reimbursable obligations			355
99.9 Total new obligations			135

PROGRAM MANAGEMENT

(Legislative proposal, subject to PAYGO)

Program and Financing (in millions of dollars)

Identification code 75–0511–4–1–550	1999 actual	2000 est.	2001 est.
Obligations by program activity:			
Direct program:			
00.04 Research, demonstrations, and evaluation projects			250
10.00 Total new obligations (object class 41.0)			250
Budgetary resources available for obligation:			
22.00 New budget authority (gross)			250
23.95 Total new obligations			−250
New budget authority (gross), detail:			
Mandatory:			
60.00 Appropriation			250
Change in unpaid obligations:			
73.10 Total new obligations			250
73.20 Total outlays (gross)			−250
Outlays (gross), detail:			
86.97 Outlays from new mandatory authority			250
Net budget authority and outlays:			
89.00 Budget authority			250
90.00 Outlays			250

This schedule reflects the effects on the Program management account of the Administration's proposal to create a time-limited demonstration that would cover the patient care costs associated with Medicare beneficiary participation in certain clinical trials for cancer.

STATE CHILDREN'S HEALTH INSURANCE FUND

Program and Financing (in millions of dollars)

Identification code 75–0515–0–1–551	1999 actual	2000 est.	2001 est.
Obligations by program activity:			
00.01 Grants, subsidies, and contributions	4,732	4,249	4,249
00.02 Advisory and assistance services		10	
10.00 Total new obligations (object class 41.0)	4,732	4,259	4,249
Budgetary resources available for obligation:			
21.40 Unobligated balance available, start of year	485		
22.00 New budget authority (gross)	4,247	4,259	4,249
23.90 Total budgetary resources available for obligation	4,732	4,259	4,249
23.95 Total new obligations	−4,732	−4,259	−4,249
24.40 Unobligated balance available, end of year			
New budget authority (gross), detail:			
Mandatory:			
Appropriation:			
60.00 Appropriation, BBRA Sec. 702	4,307	4,275	4,275
60.00 Appropriation, BBRA for territories		34	34
60.00 Appropriation, BBRA Sec. 703		10	
61.00 Transferred to other accounts	−60	−60	−60
62.50 Appropriation (total mandatory)	4,247	4,259	4,249
Change in unpaid obligations:			
72.40 Unpaid obligations, start of year: Obligated balance, start of year	3,745	7,912	10,871
73.10 Total new obligations	4,732	4,259	4,249
73.20 Total outlays (gross)	−565	−1,300	−1,905
74.40 Unpaid obligations, end of year: Obligated balance, end of year	7,912	10,871	13,215
Outlays (gross), detail:			
86.97 Outlays from new mandatory authority	43	200	
86.98 Outlays from mandatory balances	522	1,100	1,905
87.00 Total outlays (gross)	565	1,300	1,905
Net budget authority and outlays:			
89.00 Budget authority	4,247	4,259	4,249
90.00 Outlays	565	1,300	1,905

Summary of Budget Authority and Outlays

(in millions of dollars)

	1999 actual	*2000 est.*	*2001 est.*
Enacted/requested:			
Budget Authority	4,247	4,259	4,249
Outlays	565	1,300	1,905
Legislative proposal, subject to PAYGO:			
Budget Authority			212
Outlays			212
Total:			
Budget Authority	4,247	4,259	4,461
Outlays	565	1,300	2,117

The Balanced Budget Act of 1997 established the State children's health insurance program (SCHIP) under Title XXI of the Social Security Act. Title XXI provides Federal matching funds to States to enable them to extend coverage to uninsured children from low-income families. States are able to use Title XXI funds for obtaining health benefit coverage for uninsured children through a SCHIP program, a SCHIP Medicaid expansion program, or a combination of both.

STATE CHILDREN'S HEALTH INSURANCE FUND

(Legislative proposal, subject to PAYGO)

Program and Financing (in millions of dollars)

Identification code 75–0515–4–1–551	1999 actual	2000 est.	2001 est.
Obligations by program activity:			
10.00 Total new obligations (object class 41.0)			212
Budgetary resources available for obligation:			
22.00 New budget authority (gross)			212
23.95 Total new obligations			−212
New budget authority (gross), detail:			
Mandatory:			
60.00 Appropriation			212
Change in unpaid obligations:			
73.10 Total new obligations			212
73.20 Total outlays (gross)			−212
Outlays (gross), detail:			
86.97 Outlays from new mandatory authority			212
Net budget authority and outlays:			
89.00 Budget authority			212
90.00 Outlays			212

This schedule reflects the effects of the SCHIP proposals contained in the Budget on the State children's health insurance fund.

HEALTH MAINTENANCE ORGANIZATION LOAN AND LOAN GUARANTEE FUND

For carrying out subsections (d) and (e) of section 1308 of the Public Health Service Act, any amounts received by the Secretary in connection with loans and loan guarantees under title XIII of the Public Health Service Act, to be available without fiscal year limitation for the payment of outstanding obligations. During fiscal year [2000] *2001*, no commitments for direct loans or loan guarantees shall be made. *(Department of Health and Human Services Appropriations Act, 2000, as enacted by section 1000(a)(4) of the Consolidated Appropriations Act, 2000 (P.L. 106–113).)*

Program and Financing (in millions of dollars)

Identification code 75–4420–0–3–551	1999 actual	2000 est.	2001 est.
Budgetary resources available for obligation:			
21.40 Unobligated balance available, start of year	11	11	11
22.00 New budget authority (gross)	2	1	
22.60 Portion applied to repay debt	−1	−1	−1
23.90 Total budgetary resources available for obligation	12	11	10
24.40 Unobligated balance available, end of year	11	11	10
New budget authority (gross), detail:			
Mandatory:			
69.00 Offsetting collections (cash)	2	1	
Offsets:			
Against gross budget authority and outlays:			
88.40 Offsetting collections (cash) from: Other	−2	−1	
Net budget authority and outlays:			
89.00 Budget authority			
90.00 Outlays	−2	−1	

The last loan commitments from the HMO loan fund were made in 1983. The schedule above reflects receipts on outstanding loans and payments to the Federal Financing Bank.

Trust Funds

FEDERAL HOSPITAL INSURANCE TRUST FUND

Unavailable Collections (in millions of dollars)

Identification code 20–8005–0–7–571	1999 actual	2000 est.	2001 est.
Balance, start of year:			
01.99 Balance, start of year	116,434	137,807	162,730
Receipts:			
02.00 Interest on investments, legislative proposal, not subject to PAYGO			264
02.01 Transfers from general fund (FICA taxes)	123,360	126,602	133,621
02.02 Receipts from Railroad Retirement Board	388	388	393
02.03 Transfers from general fund (SECA taxes)	8,520	9,525	9,681
02.04 Federal employer contributions (FICA)	1,894	1,980	2,029
02.05 Postal service employer contributions (FICA)	611	633	659
02.07 Interest received by trust funds	9,244	11,010	12,242
02.08 Other proprietary receipts from the public	2		
02.10 Taxation on OASDI benefits	6,552	7,190	6,878
02.12 Interest payments by Railroad Retirement Board	42	36	38
02.13 Payments from the general fund (uninsured and program management)	749	599	605
02.14 Payments for military service credits	71	63	64
02.15 Premiums collected for uninsured individuals not otherwise eligible	1,401	1,379	1,426
02.16 FBI, Payment from the general fund	66	76	88
02.17 Criminal fines, transfers from the general fund	41	40	44
02.18 Civil monetary penalties, transfers from the general fund	5	5	6
02.20 Civil penalties and damages	69	81	90
02.21 Transfers from DOD, HI		11	14
02.23 Payment to extend solvency, legislative proposal not subject to PAYGO			15,400
02.99 Total receipts	153,015	159,618	183,542
04.00 Total: Balances and collections	269,449	297,425	346,272
Appropriation:			
05.01 Federal hospital insurance trust fund	−130,873	−133,832	−144,750
05.02 Health care fraud and abuse control account	−764	−864	−950
05.04 Proposed legislation subject to PAYGO			185
05.06 Proposed legislation not subject to PAYGO			74
05.99 Subtotal appropriation	−131,637	−134,696	−145,441
06.10 Unobligated balance returned to receipts	−5		
06.20 Reduction pursuant to Public Law 106–113		1	
07.99 Total balance, end of year	137,807	162,730	200,831

Program and Financing (in millions of dollars)

Identification code 20–8005–0–7–571	1999 actual	2000 est.	2001 est.
Obligations by program activity:			
00.01 Benefit payments, HI	129,221	129,216	139,869
00.02 Administration, HI	1,264	1,360	1,428
00.03 Peer review organizations, HI	177	495	71
00.04 Research, HI	32	41	37
00.05 HI partial transfer of home health to SMI	179	2,718	3,345
10.00 Total new obligations	130,873	133,830	144,750
Budgetary resources available for obligation:			
22.00 New budget authority (gross)	130,873	133,831	144,750
23.95 Total new obligations	−130,873	−133,830	−144,750
New budget authority (gross), detail:			
Discretionary:			
40.26 Appropriation (trust fund, definite)	1,297	1,363	1,425
40.76 Reduction pursuant to P.L. 106–113		−1	
43.00 Appropriation (total discretionary)	1,297	1,361	1,425
Mandatory:			
60.27 Appropriation (trust fund, indefinite)	150,954	157,393	165,502
60.28 Appropriation (unavailable balances)	−21,378	−24,924	−22,177
62.50 Appropriation (total mandatory)	129,576	132,469	143,325
70.00 Total new budget authority (gross)	130,873	133,831	144,750
Change in unpaid obligations:			
72.40 Unpaid obligations, start of year: Obligated balance, start of year	352	465	564
73.10 Total new obligations	130,873	133,830	144,750
73.20 Total outlays (gross)	−130,759	−133,731	−145,023

FEDERAL HOSPITAL INSURANCE TRUST FUND—Continued

Program and Financing (in millions of dollars)—Continued

Identification code 20–8005–0–7–571	1999 actual	2000 est.	2001 est.
74.40 Unpaid obligations, end of year: Obligated balance, end of year	465	564	291
Outlays (gross), detail:			
86.90 Outlays from new discretionary authority	1,118	1,168	1,225
86.93 Outlays from discretionary balances	130	170	186
86.97 Outlays from new mandatory authority	129,289	132,097	143,234
86.98 Outlays from mandatory balances	221	295	378
87.00 Total outlays (gross)	130,759	133,731	145,023
Net budget authority and outlays:			
89.00 Budget authority	130,873	133,831	144,750
90.00 Outlays	130,759	133,731	145,023
Memorandum (non-add) entries:			
92.01 Total investments, start of year: U.S. securities: Par value	118,250	153,767	163,444
92.02 Total investments, end of year: U.S. securities: Par value	153,767	163,444	185,612

Summary of Budget Authority and Outlays

(in millions of dollars)

Enacted/requested:	*1999 actual*	*2000 est.*	*2001 est.*
Budget Authority	130,873	133,830	144,750
Outlays	130,758	133,730	145,023
Legislative proposal, not subject to PAYGO:			
Budget Authority			–74
Outlays			–74
Legislative proposal, subject to PAYGO:			
Budget Authority			–185
Outlays			–185
Total:			
Budget Authority	130,873	133,830	144,491
Outlays	130,758	133,730	144,764

The Hospital Insurance (HI) program funds the costs of hospital and related care for individuals age 65 or older and for eligible disabled people.

The status of the trust fund is as follows:

Status of Funds (in millions of dollars)

Identification code 20–8005–0–7–571	1999 actual	2000 est.	2001 est.
Unexpended balance, start of year:			
0100 Treasury balance	–1,343	–15,346	
0101 U.S. Securities: Par value	118,250	153,767	163,444
0199 Total balance, start of year	116,909	138,421	163,443
Cash income during the year:			
Governmental receipts:			
0200 FHI trust fund, transfers from general fund (FICA taxes)	123,360	126,602	133,621
0201 FHI trust fund, transfers from general fund (SECA taxes)	8,520	9,525	9,681
0205 FHI trust fund, receipts from Railroad Retirement Board	388	388	393
0206 HCFAC: Civil penalties and damages	69	81	90
Proprietary receipts:			
0221 FHI trust fund, premiums collected for uninsured individuals not otherwise eligible	1,401	1,379	1,426
0222 Other proprietary receipts	2		
Intragovernmental transactions:			
0240 FHI trust fund, Federal employer contributions (FICA)	1,894	1,980	2,029
0241 FHI trust fund, Postal Service employer contributions (FICA)	611	633	659
0242 FHI trust fund, Federal payment for transitional coverage for uninsured Federal employees	97	121	132
0243 FHI trust fund, Federal payment for transitional coverage for the uninsured	555	349	321
0245 FHI trust fund, general fund transfer, program management (HI)	96	129	152
0246 FHI trust fund, Federal payments for OASDI taxes	6,552	7,190	6,878
0248 FHI trust fund, interest payment from Railroad Retirement Board	42	36	38
0249 FHI trust fund, interest on investments	9,244	11,010	12,242
0250 Interest on investments, legislative proposal not subject to PAYGO			264
0251 FHI trust fund, transfer from Department of Defense for military service credits	71	63	64
0252 HCFAC: FBI	66	76	88
0253 HCFAC: Criminal fines	41	40	44
0254 HCFAC: Civil monetary penalties	5	5	6
0255 Other intragovernmental transactions		11	14
0256 Payment to extend solvency, legislative proposal not subject to PAYGO			15,400
Offsetting collections:			
0280 HCFAC user fees	3	4	
0297 Income under present law	153,017	159,622	167,878
0298 Income under proposed legislation			15,664
0299 Total cash income	153,018	159,622	183,542
Cash outgo during year:			
0500 Benefit Payments	–129,107	–129,216	–139,869
0501 Benefit payments, legislative proposal subject to PAYGO			185
0502 Administration	–1,264	–1,344	–1,415
0503 Administration, legislative proposal not subject to PAYGO			74
0504 Peer Review Organizations	–177	–418	–358
0505 Research	–32	–35	–37
0506 HCFAC	–744	–868	–950
0507 HI Partial Transfer of Home Health to SMI	–179	–2,718	–3,345
0597 Outgo under present law (–)	–131,503	–134,599	–145,974
0598 Outgo under proposed legislation (–)			259
0599 Total cash outgo (–)	–131,503	–134,599	–145,714
Unexpended balance, end of year:			
0700 Treasury Balance	–15,346		
0701 U.S. Securities: Par value	153,767	163,444	201,271
0799 Total balance, end of year	138,421	163,443	201,271

Object Classification (in millions of dollars)

Identification code 20–8005–0–7–571	1999 actual	2000 est.	2001 est.
Grants, subsidies, and contributions:			
41.0 Payment for health insurance experiments and demonstration projects	32	41	37
41.0 Payment for peer review organization (PRO) activities	177	495	71
42.0 Insurance claims and indemnities	129,221	129,216	139,869
Undistributed:			
92.0 HI Partial Transfer of Home Health to SMI	179	2,718	3,345
92.0 Reimbursement for administrative expenses for other than SSA LAE	48	40	40
92.0 Purchases of goods and services	720	764	807
93.0 Administrative expenses: Portion of limitation on salaries and expenses: Social Security Administration	496	556	581
99.9 Total new obligations	130,873	133,830	144,750

FEDERAL HOSPITAL INSURANCE TRUST FUND
(Legislative proposal, not subject to PAYGO)

Program and Financing (in millions of dollars)

Identification code 20–8005–2–7–571	1999 actual	2000 est.	2001 est.
Obligations by program activity:			
00.02 Administration			–74
10.00 Total new obligations (object class 92.0)			–74
Budgetary resources available for obligation:			
22.00 New budget authority (gross)			–74
23.95 Total new obligations			74
New budget authority (gross), detail:			
Discretionary:			
40.26 Appropriation (trust fund, definite)			–74
Mandatory:			
60.27 Appropriation (trust fund, indefinite)			15,400
60.28 Appropriation (unavailable balances)			–15,400
62.50 Appropriation (total mandatory)			

		1999 actual	2000 est.	2001 est.
70.00	Total new budget authority (gross)	....	....	−74
	Change in unpaid obligations:			
73.10	Total new obligations	....	....	−74
73.20	Total outlays (gross)	....	....	74
	Outlays (gross), detail:			
86.90	Outlays from new discretionary authority	....	....	−74
	Net budget authority and outlays:			
89.00	Budget authority	....	....	−74
90.00	Outlays	....	....	−74
	Memorandum (non-add) entries:			
92.02	Total investments, end of year: U.S. securities: Par value	....	....	15,474

This schedule reflects the effects of the HCFA user fees proposed in the Budget on the Hospital Insurance trust fund.

FEDERAL HOSPITAL INSURANCE TRUST FUND

(Legislative proposal, subject to PAYGO)

Program and Financing (in millions of dollars)

Identification code 20–8005–4–7–571		1999 actual	2000 est.	2001 est.
	Obligations by program activity:			
10.00	Total new obligations (object class 42.0)	....	....	−185
	Budgetary resources available for obligation:			
22.00	New budget authority (gross)	....	....	−185
23.95	Total new obligations	....	....	185
	New budget authority (gross), detail:			
	Mandatory:			
60.28	Appropriation (unavailable balances)	....	....	−185
	Change in unpaid obligations:			
73.10	Total new obligations	....	....	−185
73.20	Total outlays (gross)	....	....	185
	Outlays (gross), detail:			
86.97	Outlays from new mandatory authority	....	....	−185
	Net budget authority and outlays:			
89.00	Budget authority	....	....	−185
90.00	Outlays	....	....	−185
	Memorandum (non-add) entries:			
92.02	Total investments, end of year: U.S. securities: Par value	....	....	185

This schedule reflects the effects of Medicare proposals contained in the Budget on the Hospital Insurance trust fund.

HEALTH CARE FRAUD AND ABUSE CONTROL ACCOUNT

(FEDERAL HOSPITAL INSURANCE TRUST FUND)

Program and Financing (in millions of dollars)

Identification code 75–8393–0–7–571		1999 actual	2000 est.	2001 est.
	Obligations by program activity:			
00.01	Medicare integrity program	551	630	680
00.02	FBI fraud and abuse control	66	76	88
00.03	Other fraud and abuse control	135	158	182
09.01	Reimbursable	3	4	....
10.00	Total new obligations	755	868	950
	Budgetary resources available for obligation:			
22.00	New budget authority (gross)	767	868	950
23.95	Total new obligations	−755	−868	−950
23.98	Unobligated balance expiring or withdrawn	−11	....	....
	New budget authority (gross), detail:			
	Mandatory:			
60.26	Appropriation (trust fund, definite)	764	864	950
69.00	Offsetting collections (cash)	3	4	....
70.00	Total new budget authority (gross)	767	868	950
	Change in unpaid obligations:			
72.40	Unpaid obligations, start of year: Obligated balance, start of year	123	149	149
73.10	Total new obligations	755	868	950
73.20	Total outlays (gross)	−744	−868	−950
73.40	Adjustments in expired accounts (net)	16	....	....
74.40	Unpaid obligations, end of year: Obligated balance, end of year	149	149	149
	Outlays (gross), detail:			
86.97	Outlays from new mandatory authority	663	868	950
86.98	Outlays from mandatory balances	82	....	....
87.00	Total outlays (gross)	744	868	950
	Offsets:			
	Against gross budget authority and outlays:			
88.00	Offsetting collections (cash) from: Federal sources	−3	−4	....
	Net budget authority and outlays:			
89.00	Budget authority	764	864	950
90.00	Outlays	742	864	950

P.L. 104–191 established the Health Care Fraud and Abuse Control (HCFAC) account within the Federal hospital insurance trust fund and appropriated funds, to be available without further appropriation, from the trust fund to the HCFAC account for specified health care fraud and abuse control activities of the Department of Health and Human Services (HHS), the Department of Justice, and other agencies.

Object Classification (in millions of dollars)

Identification code 75–8393–0–7–571		1999 actual	2000 est.	2001 est.
	Direct obligations:			
25.6	Medical care (HCFA)	551	630	680
92.0	Undistributed (FBI)	66	76	88
99.0	Subtotal, direct obligations	617	706	768
	Allocation Account:			
	Personnel compensation:			
	Full-time permanent:			
11.1	Full-time permanent (OIG)	54	70	74
11.1	Full-time permanent (DoJ)	14	16	18
11.1	Full-time permanent (OGC)	1	2	2
	Other than full-time permanent:			
11.3	Other than full-time permanent (DOJ)	....	1	1
11.3	Other than full-time permanent (OIG)	....	....	1
11.5	Other personnel compensation (OIG)	....	....	1
	Special personal services payments:			
11.8	Special personal services payments (DOJ)	1	....	1
11.8	Special personal services payments (AoA)	1	....	1
11.9	Total personnel compensation	71	89	99
	Civilian personnel benefits:			
12.1	Civilian personnel benefits (OIG)	13	15	17
12.1	Civilian personnel benefits (DoJ)	4	4	4
	Travel and transportation of persons:			
21.0	Travel and transportation of persons (OIG)	5	6	6
21.0	Travel and transportation of persons (DoJ)	....	1	1
22.0	Transportation of things (OIG)	....	....	1
	Rental payments to GSA:			
23.1	Rental payments to GSA (OIG)	8	8	8
23.1	Rental payments to GSA (DoJ)	3	3	3
23.1	Rental payments to GSA (OGC)	1	....	1
23.3	Communications, utilities, and miscellaneous charges (OIG)	1	1	2
	Other services:			
25.2	Other services (DoJ)	6	8	16
25.2	Other services (OIG)	....	....	2
25.2	Other services (HRSA)	2	....	....
	Purchases of goods and services from Government accounts:			
25.3	Purchases of goods and services from Government accounts (OIG)	1	2	12
25.3	Purchases of goods and services from Government accounts (DoJ)	....	2	1
25.5	Research and development contracts (OIG)	12	17	....
25.7	Operation and maintenance of equipment (HRSA)	4	....	....
26.0	Supplies and materials (OIG)	1	1	2

HEALTH CARE FRAUD AND ABUSE CONTROL ACCOUNT—Continued
(FEDERAL HOSPITAL INSURANCE TRUST FUND)—Continued

Object Classification (in millions of dollars)—Continued

Identification code 75–8393–0–7–571	1999 actual	2000 est.	2001 est.
Equipment:			
31.0 Equipment (OIG)	5	4	4
31.0 Equipment (DOJ)			1
41.0 Grants, subsidies, and contributions (AoA)	1	1	2
99.0 Subtotal, allocation account	138	162	182
99.9 Total new obligations	755	868	950

This schedule reflects estimated distribution of the allocation account. This allocation assumes $12.5 million within HCFAC would be used for oversight of HCFA's contractor initiative and $3.5 million would fund incentive grants for States to develop Medicaid error rates. The non-HHS/DoJ amounts would be distributed based on competitive criteria established by HHS and DoJ.

	1999 actual	2000 est.	2001 est.
Department of Justice (DOJ)	28	34	34
Office of the Inspector General, HHS	100	124	124
Health Care Financing Administration	551	630	680
Office of General Counsel, HHS	2	2	0
Other HHS	8	2	2
Other non-HHS/non-DOJ	0	0	22
Total	689	794	862

FEDERAL SUPPLEMENTARY MEDICAL INSURANCE TRUST FUND

Unavailable Collections (in millions of dollars)

Identification code 20–8004–0–7–571	1999 actual	2000 est.	2001 est.
Balance, start of year:			
01.99 Balance, start of year	40,875	45,615	44,386
Receipts:			
02.00 Interest on investments, legislative proposal not subject to PAYGO			9
02.01 Federal contributions	62,185	65,063	69,777
02.02 Interest received by trust fund	2,926	3,080	2,940
02.03 Other proprietary receipts from the public	7		
02.05 Premiums collected for the aged	17,722	17,773	19,065
02.06 Premiums collected for the disabled	2,438	2,583	2,849
02.07 Transfers from DOD, SMI		11	14
02.09 Premiums collected for the aged, legislative proposal subject to PAYGO			−160
02.10 Premiums collected for the disabled, legislative proposal subject to PAYGO			−20
02.12 Federal contributions, legislative proposal not subject to PAYGO			−280
02.99 Total receipts	85,278	88,510	94,194
04.00 Total: Balances and collections	126,153	134,125	138,580
Appropriation:			
05.01 Federal supplementary medical insurance trust fund	−80,538	−89,740	−98,782
05.03 Legislative proposal subject to PAYGO			685
05.04 Legislative proposal not subject to PAYGO			146
05.99 Subtotal appropriation	−80,538	−89,740	−97,951
06.20 Reduction pursuant to Public Law xx-xxx		1	
07.99 Total balance, end of year	45,615	44,386	40,629

Program and Financing (in millions of dollars)

Identification code 20–8004–0–7–571	1999 actual	2000 est.	2001 est.
Obligations by program activity:			
00.01 Benefit payments, SMI	78,972	87,856	96,928
00.02 Administration, SMI	1,494	1,690	1,758
00.03 Peer review organizations, SMI	56	124	18
00.04 Research, SMI	16	20	18
00.06 Transfer to Medicaid for payment of SMI premiums		50	60
09.01 HI partial transfer of home health	179	2,718	3,345
10.00 Total new obligations	80,717	92,458	102,127
Budgetary resources available for obligation:			
22.00 New budget authority (gross)	80,717	92,457	102,127
23.95 Total new obligations	−80,717	−92,458	−102,127
New budget authority (gross), detail:			
Discretionary:			
40.26 Appropriation (trust fund, definite)	1,506	1,706	1,772
40.76 Reduction pursuant to P.L. 106–113		−1	
43.00 Appropriation (total discretionary)	1,506	1,706	1,772
Mandatory:			
60.27 Appropriation (trust fund, indefinite)	83,772	86,804	92,873
60.28 Appropriation (unavailable balances)		1,230	4,137
60.45 Portion precluded from obligation	−4,740		
62.50 Appropriation (total mandatory)	79,032	88,034	97,010
69.00 Offsetting collections (cash)	179	2,718	3,345
70.00 Total new budget authority (gross)	80,717	92,457	102,127
Change in unpaid obligations:			
72.40 Unpaid obligations, start of year: Obligated balance, start of year	14	34	98
73.10 Total new obligations	80,717	92,458	102,127
73.20 Total outlays (gross)	−80,697	−92,394	−102,165
74.40 Unpaid obligations, end of year: Obligated balance, end of year	34	98	60
Outlays (gross), detail:			
86.90 Outlays from new discretionary authority	1,506	1,697	1,763
86.93 Outlays from discretionary balances		3	
86.97 Outlays from new mandatory authority	79,191	90,694	100,359
86.98 Outlays from mandatory balances			43
87.00 Total outlays (gross)	80,697	92,394	102,165
Offsets:			
Against gross budget authority and outlays:			
88.00 Offsetting collections (cash) from: Federal sources	−179	−2,718	−3,345
Net budget authority and outlays:			
89.00 Budget authority	80,538	89,739	98,782
90.00 Outlays	80,518	89,676	98,820
Memorandum (non-add) entries:			
92.01 Total investments, start of year: U.S. securities: Par value	39,502	26,528	44,484
92.02 Total investments, end of year: U.S. securities: Par value	26,528	44,484	40,318

Summary of Budget Authority and Outlays

(in millions of dollars)

	1999 actual	2000 est.	2001 est.
Enacted/requested:			
Budget Authority	80,538	89,740	98,782
Outlays	80,518	89,676	98,820
Legislative proposal, not subject to PAYGO:			
Budget Authority			−146
Outlays			−146
Legislative proposal, subject to PAYGO:			
Budget Authority			−685
Outlays			−685
Total:			
Budget Authority	80,538	89,740	97,951
Outlays	80,518	89,676	97,989

The Supplementary Medical Insurance (SMI) program is a voluntary program which affords protection against the costs of physician and certain other medical services. The program also covers treatment of end-stage renal disease for eligible enrollees. SMI costs are financed by premium payments from enrollees and contributions from the general revenues.

The status of the trust fund is as follows:

Status of Funds (in millions of dollars)

Identification code 20–8004–0–7–571	1999 actual	2000 est.	2001 est.
Unexpended balance, start of year:			
0100 Treasury balance	1,387	19,120	

		1999 actual	2000 est.	2001 est.
0101	U.S. Securities: Par value	39,502	26,528	44,484
0199	Total balance, start of year	40,889	45,649	44,484
	Cash income during the year:			
	Proprietary receipts:			
0221	Premiums collected for the aged, FSMI fund	17,722	17,773	19,065
0222	Premiums collected for the aged, legislative proposal subject to PAYGO			−160
	Proprietary receipts:			
0223	Premiums collected for the disabled, FSMI fund	2,438	2,583	2,849
0223	Premiums collected for the disabled, legislative proposal subject to PAYGO			−20
0225	Other proprietary receipts	7		
	Intragovernmental transactions:			
	Intragovernmental transactions:			
0240	Federal contributions, FSMI fund	62,185	65,063	69,777
0240	Interest received by trust fund, legislative proposal not subject to PAYGO			9
0241	Federal contributions, legislative proposal not subject to PAYGO			−280
0242	Interest received by trust fund, FSMI fund	2,926	3,080	2,940
0243	Intragovernmental transactions		11	14
	Offsetting collections:			
0280	HI partial transfer of home health	179	2,718	3,345
0297	Income under present law	85,457	91,228	97,990
0298	Income under proposed legislation			−451
0299	Total cash income	85,457	91,228	97,539
	Cash outgo during year:			
	Cash outgo during the year (−):			
0501	Benefit payments & ESRD	−78,972	−87,856	−96,928
0501	Benefit payments & ESRD, legislative proposal subject to PAYGO			685
0502	Administration	−1,494	−1,687	−1,749
0503	Administration, legislative proposal not subject to PAYGO			146
0504	Peer review organizations	−36	−66	−65
0505	Research	−16	−17	−18
0506	HI partial transfer of home health	−179	−2,718	−3,345
0507	Transfer to Medicaid for payment of SMI premiums		−50	−60
0597	Outgo under present law (−)	−80,697	−92,394	−102,165
0598	Outgo under proposed legislation (−)			831
0599	Total cash outgo (−)	−80,697	−92,394	−101,334
	Unexpended balance, end of year:			
0700	Treasury balance	19,120		
0701	U.S. Securities: Par value	26,528	44,484	40,689
0799	Total balance, end of year	45,649	44,484	40,689

Object Classification (in millions of dollars)

Identification code 20–8004–0–7–571		1999 actual	2000 est.	2001 est.
	Direct obligations:			
	Grants, subsidies, and contributions:			
41.0	Payment for peer review organization (PRO) activity	56	124	18
41.0	Payment for health insurance experiments and demonstration projects	16	20	18
42.0	Insurance claims and indemnities	78,972	87,910	96,992
92.0	Undistributed	1,064	1,204	1,241
93.0	Administrative expenses: Portion of limitation on salaries and expenses: Social Security Administration	430	482	513
99.0	Subtotal, direct obligations	80,538	89,740	98,782
99.0	Reimbursable obligations	179	2,718	3,345
99.9	Total new obligations	80,717	92,458	102,127

Federal Supplementary Medical Insurance Trust Fund

(Legislative proposal, not subject to PAYGO)

Program and Financing (in millions of dollars)

Identification code 20–8004–2–7–571		1999 actual	2000 est.	2001 est.
	Obligations by program activity:			
00.02	Administration, SMI			−146
10.00	Total new obligations (object class 92.0)			−146
	Budgetary resources available for obligation:			
22.00	New budget authority (gross)			−146
23.95	Total new obligations			146
	New budget authority (gross), detail:			
	Discretionary:			
40.26	Appropriation (trust fund, definite)			−146
	Change in unpaid obligations:			
73.10	Total new obligations			−146
73.20	Total outlays (gross)			146
	Outlays (gross), detail:			
86.90	Outlays from new discretionary authority			−146
	Net budget authority and outlays:			
89.00	Budget authority			−146
90.00	Outlays			−146
	Memorandum (non-add) entries:			
92.02	Total investments, end of year: U.S. securities: Par value			146

This schedule reflects the effects of the HCFA user fees proposed in the Budget on the Supplemental Medical Insurance trust fund.

Federal Supplementary Medical Insurance Trust Fund

(Legislative proposal, subject to PAYGO)

Program and Financing (in millions of dollars)

Identification code 20–8004–4–7–571		1999 actual	2000 est.	2001 est.
	Obligations by program activity:			
10.00	Total new obligations (object class 42.0)			−685
	Budgetary resources available for obligation:			
22.00	New budget authority (gross)			−685
23.95	Total new obligations			685
	New budget authority (gross), detail:			
	Mandatory:			
60.27	Appropriation (trust fund, indefinite)			−460
60.28	Appropriation (unavailable balances)			−225
62.50	Appropriation (total mandatory)			−685
	Change in unpaid obligations:			
73.10	Total new obligations			−685
73.20	Total outlays (gross)			685
	Outlays (gross), detail:			
86.97	Outlays from new mandatory authority			−685
	Net budget authority and outlays:			
89.00	Budget authority			−685
90.00	Outlays			−685
	Memorandum (non-add) entries:			
92.02	Total investments, end of year: U.S. securities: Par value			225

This schedule reflects the effects of Medicare proposals contained in the Budget on the Supplemental Medical Insurance trust fund.

Allocation Received From Other Accounts

Note.—Obligations incurred under allocations from other accounts are included in the schedule of the parent appropriation as follows: Health Care Financing Administration: "Health Care Fraud and Abuse Control Account."

ADMINISTRATION FOR CHILDREN AND FAMILIES

Federal Funds

General and special funds:

TEMPORARY ASSISTANCE FOR NEEDY FAMILIES

Program and Financing (in millions of dollars)

Identification code 75–1552–0–1–609	1999 actual	2000 est.	2001 est.
Obligations by program activity:			
00.01 State family assistance grant	16,489	16,489	16,489
00.02 State penalties			–10
00.03 Territories—family assistance grants	78	78	78
00.04 Matching grants to territories	3	15	15
00.05 Bonus to reward decrease in illegitimacy	100	100	100
00.06 Supplemental grants for population increases	160	239	319
00.07 Bonus to reward high performance States		200	200
00.08 Tribal work programs	7	7	7
10.00 Total new obligations (object class 41.0)	16,837	17,128	17,198
Budgetary resources available for obligation:			
21.40 Unobligated balance available, start of year	721	1,561	1,122
22.00 New budget authority (gross)	17,693	16,689	16,679
23.90 Total budgetary resources available for obligation	18,414	18,250	17,801
23.95 Total new obligations	–16,837	–17,128	–17,198
23.98 Unobligated balance expiring or withdrawn	–16		–3
24.40 Unobligated balance available, end of year	1,561	1,122	600
New budget authority (gross), detail:			
Mandatory:			
60.05 Appropriation (indefinite)	17,693	16,689	16,679
Change in unpaid obligations:			
72.40 Unpaid obligations, start of year: Obligated balance, start of year	7,212	10,056	12,084
73.10 Total new obligations	16,837	17,128	17,198
73.20 Total outlays (gross)	–14,161	–14,996	–15,742
73.40 Adjustments in expired accounts (net)	168	–104	
74.40 Unpaid obligations, end of year: Obligated balance, end of year	10,056	12,084	13,540
Outlays (gross), detail:			
86.97 Outlays from new mandatory authority	9,924	9,160	8,661
86.98 Outlays from mandatory balances	4,237	5,836	7,081
87.00 Total outlays (gross)	14,161	14,996	15,742
Net budget authority and outlays:			
89.00 Budget authority	17,693	16,689	16,679
90.00 Outlays	14,161	14,996	15,742

Summary of Budget Authority and Outlays

(in millions of dollars)

Enacted/requested:	*1999 actual*	*2000 est.*	*2001 est.*
Budget Authority	17,693	16,689	16,679
Outlays	14,161	14,996	15,742
Legislative proposal, subject to PAYGO:			
Budget Authority			
Outlays			208
Legislative proposal, discretionary offset:			
Budget Authority			–240
Outlays			–122
Total:			
Budget Authority	17,693	16,689	16,439
Outlays	14,161	14,996	15,828

This account provides funding for activities established by the Personal Responsibility and Work Opportunity Reconciliation Act of 1996 (P.L. 104–193). The Temporary assistance for needy families block grant provides funding to States for aid to low-income families with children.

This account also includes Federal loans for State welfare programs, established by section 406 of the Social Security Act as amended.

TEMPORARY ASSISTANCE FOR NEEDY FAMILIES

(Legislative proposal, subject to PAYGO)

Program and Financing (in millions of dollars)

Identification code 75–1552–4–1–609	1999 actual	2000 est.	2001 est.
Change in unpaid obligations:			
73.20 Total outlays (gross)			–208
74.40 Unpaid obligations, end of year: Obligated balance, end of year			–208
Outlays (gross), detail:			
86.98 Outlays from mandatory balances			208
Net budget authority and outlays:			
89.00 Budget authority			
90.00 Outlays			208

This reflects interactions with the Administration's proposal on the allocation of common State administrative costs between the Medicaid and Temporary Assistance for Needy Families programs.

TEMPORARY ASSISTANCE FOR NEEDY FAMILIES

(Legislative proposal, discretionary offset)

Program and Financing (in millions of dollars)

Identification code 75–1552–6–1–609	1999 actual	2000 est.	2001 est.
Obligations by program activity:			
10.00 Total new obligations (object class 41.0)			–240
Budgetary resources available for obligation:			
22.00 New budget authority (gross)			–240
23.95 Total new obligations			240
New budget authority (gross), detail:			
Mandatory:			
60.36 Unobligated balance rescinded			–240
Change in unpaid obligations:			
73.10 Total new obligations			–240
73.20 Total outlays (gross)			122
74.40 Unpaid obligations, end of year: Obligated balance, end of year			–118
Outlays (gross), detail:			
86.98 Outlays from mandatory balances			–122
Net budget authority and outlays:			
89.00 Budget authority			–240
90.00 Outlays			–122

The Administration will propose legislation that reduces TANF supplemental grant funds in 2001 to the 1998 level for all eligible States, and will apply the offset to discretionary spending.

CONTINGENCY FUND

Program and Financing (in millions of dollars)

Identification code 75–1522–0–1–609	1999 actual	2000 est.	2001 est.
Budgetary resources available for obligation:			
21.40 Unobligated balance available, start of year	1,958	1,958	1,958
24.40 Unobligated balance available, end of year	1,958	1,958	1,958
Net budget authority and outlays:			
89.00 Budget authority			
90.00 Outlays			

PAYMENTS TO STATES FOR CHILD SUPPORT ENFORCEMENT AND FAMILY SUPPORT PROGRAMS

For making payments to States or other non-Federal entities under titles I, IV–D, X, XI, XIV, and XVI of the Social Security Act and the Act of July 5, 1960 (24 U.S.C. ch. 9), *$2,442,000,000, to remain available until expended; and for such purposes* for the first quarter of fiscal year [2001, $650,000,000] *2002, $1,000,000,000, to remain available until expended.*

For making payments to each State for carrying out the program of Aid to Families with Dependent Children under title IV–A of the Social Security Act before the effective date of the program of Temporary Assistance to Needy Families (TANF) with respect to such State, such sums as may be necessary: *Provided*, That the sum of the amounts available to a State with respect to expenditures under such title IV–A in fiscal year 1997 under this appropriation and under such title IV–A as amended by the Personal Responsibility and Work Opportunity Reconciliation Act of 1996 shall not exceed the limitations under section 116(b) of such Act.

For making, after May 31 of the current fiscal year, payments to States or other non-Federal entities under titles I, IV–D, X, XI, XIV, and XVI of the Social Security Act and the Act of July 5, 1960 (24 U.S.C. ch. 9), for the last 3 months of the current year for unanticipated costs, incurred for the current fiscal year, such sums as may be necessary. *(Department of Health and Human Services Appropriations Act, 2000, as enacted by section 1000(a)(4) of the Consolidated Appropriations Act, 2000 (P.L. 106–113).)*

Program and Financing (in millions of dollars)

Identification code 75–1501–0–1–609		1999 actual	2000 est.	2001 est.
	Obligations by program activity:			
	Child support enforcement (CSE):			
	Benefit payments:			
00.01	State child support administrative costs	2,513	2,819	3,058
00.02	Federal incentive/hold harmless payments to States	400	382	415
00.03	Access and visitation grants	10	10	10
00.91	Subtotal, child support enforcement	2,923	3,211	3,483
01.02	Payments to territories	16	23	23
01.03	Repatriation	1	1	1
01.91	Subtotal, other payments	17	24	24
	Aid to families with dependent children (AFDC) payments:			
02.01	AFDC benefit payments	95	98	
02.03	State and local welfare administration	13	2	
02.04	AFDC/JOBS child care	6		
02.91	Subtotal, AFDC programs	114	100	
10.00	Total new obligations (object class 41.0)	3,054	3,335	3,507
	Budgetary resources available for obligation:			
21.40	Unobligated balance available, start of year	1,564	1,920	
22.00	New budget authority (gross)	3,049	1,415	3,507
22.10	Resources available from recoveries of prior year obligations	361		
23.90	Total budgetary resources available for obligation	4,974	3,335	3,507
23.95	Total new obligations	−3,054	−3,335	−3,507
24.40	Unobligated balance available, end of year	1,920		
	New budget authority (gross), detail:			
	Mandatory:			
60.00	Appropriation	1,989	283	2,442
65.00	Advance appropriation	660	750	650
69.00	Offsetting collections (cash)	400	382	415
70.00	Total new budget authority (gross)	3,049	1,415	3,507
	Change in unpaid obligations:			
72.40	Unpaid obligations, start of year: Obligated balance, start of year	1,520	1,057	957
73.10	Total new obligations	3,054	3,335	3,507
73.20	Total outlays (gross)	−3,156	−3,435	−3,474
73.45	Adjustments in unexpired accounts	−361		
74.40	Unpaid obligations, end of year: Obligated balance, end of year	1,057	957	990
	Outlays (gross), detail:			
86.97	Outlays from new mandatory authority	3,049	1,415	2,978
86.98	Outlays from mandatory balances	107	2,020	496
87.00	Total outlays (gross)	3,156	3,435	3,474
	Offsets:			
	Against gross budget authority and outlays:			
88.40	Offsetting collections (cash) from: Non-Federal sources	−400	−382	−415
	Net budget authority and outlays:			
89.00	Budget authority	2,649	1,033	3,092
90.00	Outlays	2,756	3,053	3,059

Summary of Budget Authority and Outlays

(in millions of dollars)

	1999 actual	2000 est.	2001 est.
Enacted/requested:			
Budget Authority	2,649	1,033	3,092
Outlays	2,756	3,053	3,059
Legislative proposal, subject to PAYGO:			
Budget Authority			32
Outlays			32
Total:			
Budget Authority	2,649	1,033	3,124
Outlays	2,756	3,053	3,091

This account provides for payments to States for child support enforcement and other family support programs including access and visitation programs for families. Spending authority from the Federal share of child support collections is used to pay incentive payments and, for a limited time, hold harmless payments to States. The remaining net Federal share of collections is returned to the Treasury in a receipt account. The text table below shows the traditional display of child support enforcement costs:

Net Federal Costs of Child Support Enforcement

(In millions of dollars)

	1999	2000	2001
Gross Federal share of collections	(1268)	(1233)	(1265)
Federal incentive payments to States	362	371	404
Hold harmless payments	38	11	11
State child support administrative costs	2513	2819	3058
Access and visitation grants	10	10	10
Subtotal	1655	1978	2218

PAYMENTS TO STATES FOR CHILD SUPPORT ENFORCEMENT AND FAMILY SUPPORT PROGRAMS

(Legislative proposal, subject to PAYGO)

Program and Financing (in millions of dollars)

Identification code 75–1501–4–1–609		1999 actual	2000 est.	2001 est.
	Obligations by program activity:			
	Child support enforcement (CSE):			
	Benefit payments:			
00.01	State child support administrative costs			32
10.00	Total new obligations (object class 41.0)			32
	Budgetary resources available for obligation:			
22.00	New budget authority (gross)			32
23.95	Total new obligations			−32
	New budget authority (gross), detail:			
	Mandatory:			
60.00	Appropriation			32
	Change in unpaid obligations:			
73.10	Total new obligations			32
73.20	Total outlays (gross)			−32
	Outlays (gross), detail:			
86.97	Outlays from new mandatory authority			32
	Net budget authority and outlays:			
89.00	Budget authority			32

General and special funds—Continued

PAYMENTS TO STATES FOR CHILD SUPPORT ENFORCEMENT AND FAMILY SUPPORT PROGRAMS—Continued

Program and Financing (in millions of dollars)—Continued

Identification code 75–1501–4–1–609	1999 actual	2000 est.	2001 est.
90.00 Outlays	....	....	32

This legislative proposal includes several provisions to increase child support collections and to direct more of these payments to families. The proposal would also conform the match rate for paternity testing with the basic administrative match rate.

LOW INCOME HOME ENERGY ASSISTANCE

For making payments under title XXVI of the Omnibus Budget Reconciliation Act of 1981, $1,100,000,000, to be available for obligation in the period October 1, [2000] *2001* through September 30, [2001] *2002*.

For making payments under title XXVI of such Act, $300,000,000: *Provided*, That these funds are hereby designated by Congress to be emergency requirements pursuant to section 251(b)(2)(A) of the Balanced Budget and Emergency Deficit Control Act of 1985: *Provided further*, That these funds shall be made available only after submission to Congress of a formal budget request by the President that includes designation of the entire amount of the request as an emergency requirement as defined in [the Balanced Budget and Emergency Deficit Control] *such* Act [of 1985].

[The $1,100,000,000 provided in the first paragraph under this heading in the Departments of Labor, Health and Human Services, and Education, and Related Agencies Appropriations Act, 1999 (as contained in section 101(f) of division A of Public Law 105–277) is hereby designated by the Congress as an emergency requirement pursuant to section 251(b)(2)(A) of the Balanced Budget and Emergency Deficit Control Act of 1985: *Provided*, That such funds shall be available only if the President submits to the Congress one official budget request for $1,100,000,000 that includes designation of the entire amount as an emergency requirement pursuant to such section: *Provided further*, That such funds shall be distributed in accordance with section 2604 of the Omnibus Budget Reconciliation Act of 1981 (42 U.S.C. 8623), other than subsection (e) of such section.] *(Department of Health and Human Services Appropriations Act, 2000, as enacted by section 1000(a)(4) of the Consolidated Appropriations Act, 2000 (P.L. 106–113).)*

Program and Financing (in millions of dollars)

Identification code 75–1502–0–1–609	1999 actual	2000 est.	2001 est.
Obligations by program activity:			
10.00 Total new obligations (object class 41.0)	1,277	1,105	1,100
Budgetary resources available for obligation:			
22.00 New budget authority (gross)	1,277	1,400	1,400
23.95 Total new obligations	−1,277	−1,105	−1,100
23.98 Unobligated balance expiring or withdrawn	....	−295	−300
New budget authority (gross), detail:			
Discretionary:			
40.15 Appropriation (emergency)	300	300	300
40.60 Contingent emergency appropriation not available for obligations	−125	....	....
43.00 Appropriation (total discretionary)	175	300	300
50.00 Reappropriation	2	....	....
55.00 Advance appropriation	1,100	1,100	1,100
70.00 Total new budget authority (gross)	1,277	1,400	1,400
Change in unpaid obligations:			
72.40 Unpaid obligations, start of year: Obligated balance, start of year	377	474	337
73.10 Total new obligations	1,277	1,105	1,100
73.20 Total outlays (gross)	−1,176	−1,242	−1,105
73.40 Adjustments in expired accounts (net)	−4	....	....
74.40 Unpaid obligations, end of year: Obligated balance, end of year	474	337	332
Outlays (gross), detail:			
86.90 Outlays from new discretionary authority	859	818	814
86.93 Outlays from discretionary balances	317	424	291
87.00 Total outlays (gross)	1,176	1,242	1,105
Net budget authority and outlays:			
89.00 Budget authority	1,275	1,400	1,400
90.00 Outlays	1,176	1,242	1,105

This program makes grants to States and Indian tribes to aid low-income households with high energy costs through payments to eligible households, energy suppliers, and weatherization providers.

REFUGEE AND ENTRANT ASSISTANCE

For making payments for refugee and entrant assistance activities authorized by title IV of the Immigration and Nationality Act and section 501 of the Refugee Education Assistance Act of 1980 (Public Law 96–422), [$419,005,000] *$422,804,000*, to remain available through September 30, 2003: *Provided*, That funds appropriated pursuant to section 414(a) of the Immigration and Nationality Act under Public Law [105–78] *106–113* for fiscal year [1998 and under Public Law 105–277 for fiscal year 1999] *2000* shall be available for the costs of assistance provided and other activities through September 30, [2001] *2002*.

For carrying out section 5 of the Torture Victims Relief Act of 1998 (Public Law 105–320), [$7,500,000] *$9,765,000*.

[The $426,505,000 provided under this heading is hereby designated by the Congress as an emergency requirement pursuant to section 251(b)(2)(A) of the Balanced Budget and Emergency Deficit Control Act of 1985: *Provided*, That such funds shall be available only if the President submits to the Congress one official budget request for $426,505,000 that includes designation of the entire amount as an emergency requirement pursuant to such section.] *(Department of Health and Human Services Appropriations Act, 2000, as enacted by section 1000(a)(4) of the Consolidated Appropriations Act, 2000 (P.L. 106–113).)*

Program and Financing (in millions of dollars)

Identification code 75–1503–0–1–609	1999 actual	2000 est.	2001 est.
Obligations by program activity:			
00.01 Refugee and entrant assistance	465	447	423
00.02 Assistance for treatment of torture victims	....	7	10
10.00 Total new obligations	465	454	433
Budgetary resources available for obligation:			
21.40 Unobligated balance available, start of year	2	2	2
22.00 New budget authority (gross)	481	454	433
23.90 Total budgetary resources available for obligation	483	454	433
23.95 Total new obligations	−465	−454	−433
23.98 Unobligated balance expiring or withdrawn	−16	....	....
24.40 Unobligated balance available, end of year	2	2	2
New budget authority (gross), detail:			
Discretionary:			
40.00 Appropriation	415	....	433
40.15 Appropriation (emergency)	....	427	....
40.76 Reduction pursuant to P.L. 106–113	....	−1	....
43.00 Appropriation (total discretionary)	415	426	433
50.00 Reappropriation	66	28	....
70.00 Total new budget authority (gross)	481	454	433
Change in unpaid obligations:			
72.40 Unpaid obligations, start of year: Obligated balance, start of year	511	587	574
73.10 Total new obligations	465	454	433
73.20 Total outlays (gross)	−332	−444	−446
73.40 Adjustments in expired accounts (net)	−57	−23	....
74.40 Unpaid obligations, end of year: Obligated balance, end of year	587	574	561

	Outlays (gross), detail:			
86.90	Outlays from new discretionary authority	122	123	117
86.93	Outlays from discretionary balances	210	321	329
87.00	Total outlays (gross)	332	444	446
	Net budget authority and outlays:			
89.00	Budget authority	481	454	433
90.00	Outlays	332	444	446

States are subsidized for administering the refugee assistance program. Funds are also provided to assist in the rehabilitation of victims of torture.

Object Classification (in millions of dollars)

Identification code 75–1503–0–1–609		1999 actual	2000 est.	2001 est.
25.1	Advisory and assistance services	1	1	1
25.2	Other services	1	1	1
25.3	Purchases of goods and services from Government accounts	29	1	1
41.0	Grants, subsidies, and contributions	434	451	430
99.9	Total new obligations	465	454	433

PROMOTING SAFE AND STABLE FAMILIES

For carrying out section 430 of the Social Security Act, [$295,000,000.] *$305,000,000. (Department of Health and Human Services Appropriations Act, 2000, as enacted by section 1000(a)(4) of the Consolidated Appropriations Act, 2000 (P.L. 106–113).)*

Program and Financing (in millions of dollars)

Identification code 75–1512–0–1–506		1999 actual	2000 est.	2001 est.
	Obligations by program activity:			
00.01	Grants to States and Tribes	241	279	289
00.02	Training and technical assistance	6	6	6
00.03	State court assessment activities	10	10	10
10.00	Total new obligations	257	295	305
	Budgetary resources available for obligation:			
22.00	New budget authority (gross)	275	295	305
23.95	Total new obligations	−257	−295	−305
23.98	Unobligated balance expiring or withdrawn	−18		
	New budget authority (gross), detail:			
	Mandatory:			
60.00	Appropriation	275	295	305
	Change in unpaid obligations:			
72.40	Unpaid obligations, start of year: Obligated balance, start of year	274	322	331
73.10	Total new obligations	257	295	305
73.20	Total outlays (gross)	−248	−286	−288
73.40	Adjustments in expired accounts (net)	39		−13
74.40	Unpaid obligations, end of year: Obligated balance, end of year	322	331	335
	Outlays (gross), detail:			
86.97	Outlays from new mandatory authority	46	50	52
86.98	Outlays from mandatory balances	202	236	236
87.00	Total outlays (gross)	248	286	288
	Net budget authority and outlays:			
89.00	Budget authority	275	295	305
90.00	Outlays	248	286	288

This program provides funds for a broad range of child welfare services, including family preservation and family support services.

Object Classification (in millions of dollars)

Identification code 75–1512–0–1–506		1999 actual	2000 est.	2001 est.
25.1	Advisory and assistance services	6	6	6
41.0	Grants, subsidies, and contributions	251	289	299
99.9	Total new obligations	257	295	305

JOB OPPORTUNITIES AND BASIC SKILLS TRAINING PROGRAM

Program and Financing (in millions of dollars)

Identification code 75–1509–0–1–504		1999 actual	2000 est.	2001 est.
	Change in unpaid obligations:			
72.40	Unpaid obligations, start of year: Obligated balance, start of year	77	62	47
73.20	Total outlays (gross)	−9	−8	−5
73.40	Adjustments in expired accounts (net)	−6	−7	−42
74.40	Unpaid obligations, end of year: Obligated balance, end of year	62	47	
	Outlays (gross), detail:			
86.98	Outlays from mandatory balances	9	8	5
	Net budget authority and outlays:			
89.00	Budget authority			
90.00	Outlays	9	8	5

This activity is replaced by Temporary assistance for needy families.

STATE LEGALIZATION IMPACT-ASSISTANCE GRANTS

Program and Financing (in millions of dollars)

Identification code 75–1508–0–1–506		1999 actual	2000 est.	2001 est.
	Change in unpaid obligations:			
72.40	Unpaid obligations, start of year: Obligated balance, start of year	11	7	7
73.20	Total outlays (gross)	1		
73.40	Adjustments in expired accounts (net)	−5		
74.40	Unpaid obligations, end of year: Obligated balance, end of year	7	7	7
	Outlays (gross), detail:			
86.98	Outlays from mandatory balances	−1		
	Net budget authority and outlays:			
89.00	Budget authority			
90.00	Outlays	−1		

CHILD CARE ENTITLEMENT TO STATES

Program and Financing (in millions of dollars)

Identification code 75–1550–0–1–609		1999 actual	2000 est.	2001 est.
	Obligations by program activity:			
00.01	Mandatory child care	1,221	1,225	1,229
00.02	Matching child care	941	1,136	1,332
00.03	Training and technical assistance	5	6	6
10.00	Total new obligations	2,167	2,367	2,567
	Budgetary resources available for obligation:			
22.00	New budget authority (gross)	2,167	2,367	2,567
23.95	Total new obligations	−2,167	−2,367	−2,567
	New budget authority (gross), detail:			
	Mandatory:			
60.00	Appropriation	2,167	2,367	2,567
	Change in unpaid obligations:			
72.40	Unpaid obligations, start of year: Obligated balance, start of year	608	522	465
73.10	Total new obligations	2,167	2,367	2,567
73.20	Total outlays (gross)	−2,254	−2,420	−2,556
73.40	Adjustments in expired accounts (net)	1	−4	
74.40	Unpaid obligations, end of year: Obligated balance, end of year	522	465	476

General and special funds—Continued

CHILD CARE ENTITLEMENT TO STATES—Continued

Program and Financing (in millions of dollars)—Continued

Identification code 75–1550–0–1–609	1999 actual	2000 est.	2001 est.
Outlays (gross), detail:			
86.97 Outlays from new mandatory authority	1,742	1,988	2,168
86.98 Outlays from mandatory balances	512	432	388
87.00 Total outlays (gross)	2,254	2,420	2,556
Net budget authority and outlays:			
89.00 Budget authority	2,167	2,367	2,567
90.00 Outlays	2,254	2,420	2,556

Summary of Budget Authority and Outlays

(in millions of dollars)

Enacted/requested:	*1999 actual*	*2000 est.*	*2001 est.*
Budget Authority	2,167	2,367	2,567
Outlays	2,254	2,420	2,556
Legislative proposal, subject to PAYGO:			
Budget Authority			600
Outlays			402
Total:			
Budget Authority	2,167	2,367	3,167
Outlays	2,254	2,420	2,958

This account provides child care funding for welfare recipients and low-income working families and was established by the Personal Responsibility and Work Opportunity Reconciliation Act of 1996 (P.L. 104–193).

Object Classification (in millions of dollars)

Identification code 75–1550–0–1–609	1999 actual	2000 est.	2001 est.
25.1 Advisory and assistance services	5	6	6
41.0 Grants, subsidies, and contributions	2,162	2,361	2,561
99.9 Total new obligations	2,167	2,367	2,567

CHILD CARE ENTITLEMENT TO STATES

(Legislative proposal, subject to PAYGO)

Program and Financing (in millions of dollars)

Identification code 75–1550–4–1–609	1999 actual	2000 est.	2001 est.
Obligations by program activity:			
00.01 Early learning fund			600
10.00 Total new obligations			600
Budgetary resources available for obligation:			
22.00 New budget authority (gross)			600
23.95 Total new obligations			−600
New budget authority (gross), detail:			
Mandatory:			
60.00 Appropriation			600
Change in unpaid obligations:			
72.40 Unpaid obligations, start of year: Obligated balance, start of year			
73.10 Total new obligations			600
73.20 Total outlays (gross)			−402
74.40 Unpaid obligations, end of year: Obligated balance, end of year			198
Outlays (gross), detail:			
86.97 Outlays from new mandatory authority			402
Net budget authority and outlays:			
89.00 Budget authority			600
90.00 Outlays			402

This legislative proposal will provide challenge grants to communities to support early childhood education for children under five, with a focus on language acquisition, emergent literacy, reading, numeracy, and other cognitive, physical, social, and emotional development activities aimed at improving readiness for school.

Object Classification (in millions of dollars)

Identification code 75–1550–4–1–609	1999 actual	2000 est.	2001 est.
25.1 Advisory and assistance services			6
41.0 Grants, subsidies, and contributions			594
99.9 Total new obligations			600

PAYMENTS TO STATES FOR THE CHILD CARE AND DEVELOPMENT BLOCK GRANT

For carrying out sections 658A through 658R of the Omnibus Budget Reconciliation Act of 1981 (The Child Care and Development Block Grant Act of 1990), *in addition to amounts already appropriated for fiscal year 2001, $817,328,000; and* to become available on October 1, [2000] *2001* and remain available through September 30, [2001, $1,182,672,000] *2002, $2,000,000,000*: *Provided*, That *of the funds appropriated for each of fiscal years 2001 and 2002,* $19,120,000 shall be available for child care resource and referral and school-aged child care activities, *of which $500,000 shall be for a toll-free child care services program hotline to be operated by Child Care Aware*: *Provided further*, That of the funds [provided for fiscal year 2001, $172,672,000] *appropriated for each of fiscal years 2001 and 2002, in addition to the amounts required to be reserved by the States under section 658G, $222,672,000* shall be reserved by the States for activities authorized under section 658G [of the Omnibus Budget Reconciliation Act of 1981 (The Child Care and Development Block Grant Act of 1990), such funds to be in addition to the amounts required to be reserved by the States under section 658G], *of which $50,000,000 shall be for activities that improve the quality of infant and toddler child care*: *Provided further, That of the funds appropriated for each of fiscal years 2001 and 2002, $10,000,000 shall be for use by the Secretary for child care research, demonstration, and evaluation activities*[: *Provided further*, That of the funds provided for fiscal year 2000 under Public Law 105–277, $500,000 shall be for a toll-free child care services program hotline to be operated by Child Care Aware]. *(Department of Health and Human Services Appropriations Act, 2000, as enacted by section 1000(a)(4) of the Consolidated Appropriations Act, 2000 (P.L. 106–113).)*

Program and Financing (in millions of dollars)

Identification code 75–1515–0–1–609	1999 actual	2000 est.	2001 est.
Obligations by program activity:			
00.01 Block grant payments to States	997	1,170	1,985
00.02 Advisory and assistance services	3	3	5
00.03 Research and evaluation fund		10	10
10.00 Total new obligations	1,000	1,183	2,000
Budgetary resources available for obligation:			
22.00 New budget authority (gross)	1,000	1,183	2,000
23.95 Total new obligations	−1,000	−1,183	−2,000
New budget authority (gross), detail:			
Discretionary:			
40.00 Appropriation	1,000		817
55.00 Advance appropriation		1,183	1,183
70.00 Total new budget authority (gross)	1,000	1,183	2,000
Change in unpaid obligations:			
72.40 Unpaid obligations, start of year: Obligated balance, start of year	410	390	426
73.10 Total new obligations	1,000	1,183	2,000
73.20 Total outlays (gross)	−1,032	−1,147	−1,720
73.40 Adjustments in expired accounts (net)	12		
74.40 Unpaid obligations, end of year: Obligated balance, end of year	390	426	706
Outlays (gross), detail:			
86.90 Outlays from new discretionary authority	668	787	1,335

86.93 Outlays from discretionary balances	364	360	385
87.00 Total outlays (gross)	1,032	1,147	1,720
Net budget authority and outlays:			
89.00 Budget authority	1,000	1,183	2,000
90.00 Outlays	1,032	1,147	1,720

This appropriation helps low-income families pay for child care and related services and supports grants to States for child care quality activities.

Object Classification (in millions of dollars)

Identification code 75–1515–0–1–609	1999 actual	2000 est.	2001 est.
25.1 Advisory and assistance services	3	5	7
41.0 Grants, subsidies, and contributions	997	1,178	1,993
99.9 Total new obligations	1,000	1,183	2,000

Social Services Block Grant

[For making grants to States pursuant to section 2002 of the Social Security Act, $1,775,000,000: *Provided*, That notwithstanding section 2003(c) of such Act, as amended, the amount specified for allocation under such section for fiscal year 2000 shall be $1,775,000,000.] *(Department of Health and Human Services Appropriations Act, 2000, as enacted by section 1000(a)(4) of the Consolidated Appropriations Act, 2000 (P.L. 106–113).)*

Program and Financing (in millions of dollars)

Identification code 75–1534–0–1–506	1999 actual	2000 est.	2001 est.
Obligations by program activity:			
10.00 Total new obligations (object class 41.0)	1,909	1,775	1,700
Budgetary resources available for obligation:			
22.00 New budget authority (gross)	1,909	1,775	1,700
23.95 Total new obligations	−1,909	−1,775	−1,700
New budget authority (gross), detail:			
Mandatory:			
60.00 Appropriation	1,909	1,775	1,700
Change in unpaid obligations:			
72.40 Unpaid obligations, start of year: Obligated balance, start of year	1,007	927	1,079
73.10 Total new obligations	1,909	1,775	1,700
73.20 Total outlays (gross)	−1,993	−1,623	−1,932
73.40 Adjustments in expired accounts (net)	4		−2
74.40 Unpaid obligations, end of year: Obligated balance, end of year	927	1,079	845
Outlays (gross), detail:			
86.97 Outlays from new mandatory authority	1,677	1,349	1,496
86.98 Outlays from mandatory balances	316	274	436
87.00 Total outlays (gross)	1,993	1,623	1,932
Net budget authority and outlays:			
89.00 Budget authority	1,909	1,775	1,700
90.00 Outlays	1,993	1,623	1,932

Summary of Budget Authority and Outlays

(in millions of dollars)

	1999 actual	*2000 est.*	*2001 est.*
Enacted/requested:			
Budget Authority	1,909	1,775	1,700
Outlays	1,993	1,623	1,932
Legislative proposal, subject to PAYGO:			
Budget Authority			75
Outlays			66
Total:			
Budget Authority	1,909	1,775	1,775
Outlays	1,993	1,623	1,998

Social services block grant.—The proposed level will support grants to States for social services.

Social Service Block Grant

(Legislative proposal, subject to PAYGO)

Program and Financing (in millions of dollars)

Identification code 75–1534–4–1–506	1999 actual	2000 est.	2001 est.
Obligations by program activity:			
10.00 Total new obligations (object class 41.0)			75
Budgetary resources available for obligation:			
22.00 New budget authority (gross)			75
23.95 Total new obligations			−75
New budget authority (gross), detail:			
Mandatory:			
60.00 Appropriation			75
Change in unpaid obligations:			
72.40 Unpaid obligations, start of year: Obligated balance, start of year			
73.10 Total new obligations			75
73.20 Total outlays (gross)			−66
74.40 Unpaid obligations, end of year: Obligated balance, end of year			9
Outlays (gross), detail:			
86.97 Outlays from new mandatory authority			66
Net budget authority and outlays:			
89.00 Budget authority			75
90.00 Outlays			66

This proposal increases FY 2001 funding for the Social services block grant by $75 million for a total of $1,775 million. Of this amount, $25 million will be available to support second-chance homes for teen-age parents.

Children and Families Services Programs

(INCLUDING RESCISSIONS)

For carrying out, except as otherwise provided, the Runaway and Homeless Youth Act, the Developmental Disabilities Assistance and Bill of Rights Act, the Head Start Act, the Child Abuse Prevention and Treatment Act, the Native American Programs Act of 1974, title II of Public Law 95–266 (adoption opportunities), the Adoption and Safe Families Act of 1997 (Public Law 105–89), the Abandoned Infants Assistance Act of 1988, part B(1) of title IV and sections 413, 429A, 1110, and 1115 of the Social Security Act; for making payments under the Community Services Block Grant Act, section 473A of the Social Security Act, and title IV of Public Law 105–285; and for necessary administrative expenses to carry out said Acts and titles I, IV, X, XI, XIV, XVI, and XX of the Social Security Act, the Act of July 5, 1960 (24 U.S.C. ch. 9), the Omnibus Budget Reconciliation Act of 1981, title IV of the Immigration and Nationality Act, section 501 of the Refugee Education Assistance Act of 1980, section 5 of the Torture Victims Relief Act of 1998 (Public Law 105–320), sections 40155, 40211, and 40241 of Public Law 103–322 and section 126 and titles IV and V of Public Law 100–485, [$6,734,133,000] *$7,671,590,000*, of which [$43,000,000] *$41,791,000*, to remain available until September 30, [2001] *2002*, shall be for grants to States for adoption incentive payments, as authorized by section 473A of title IV of the Social Security Act (42 U.S.C. 670–679); of which [$587,065,000] *$540,500,000* shall be for making payments under the Community Services Block Grant Act; and of which [$5,267,000,000] *$6,267,000,000* shall be for making payments under the Head Start Act, of which $1,400,000,000 shall become available October 1, [2000] *2001* and remain available through September 30, [2001: *Provided*, That to the extent Community Services Block Grant funds are distributed as grant funds by a State to an eligible entity as provided under the Act, and have not been expended by such entity, they shall remain with such entity for carryover into the next fiscal year for expenditure by such entity consistent with program purposes: *Provided further*, That the Secretary shall establish procedures regarding the disposition of intangible property which permits grant funds, or intangible assets acquired with funds authorized under section 680 of the Community Services Block Grant Act, as amended, to become the sole property

General and special funds—Continued

CHILDREN AND FAMILIES SERVICES PROGRAMS—Continued

(INCLUDING RESCISSIONS)—Continued

of such grantees after a period of not more than 12 years after the end of the grant for purposes and uses consistent with the original grant: *Provided further,* That $1,700,000,000 of the amount provided for making payments under the Head Start Act is hereby designated by Congress as an emergency requirement pursuant to section 251(b)(2)(A) of the Balanced Budget and Emergency Deficit Control Act of 1985: *Provided further,* That such funds shall be available only if the President submits to the Congress one official budget request for $1,700,000,000 that includes designation of the entire amount as an emergency requirement pursuant to such section] *2002.*

[In addition, $101,000,000, to be derived from the Violent Crime Reduction Trust Fund for carrying out sections 40155, 40211, and 40241 of Public Law 103–322.]

[Funds appropriated for fiscal year 2000 under section 429A(e), part B of title IV of the Social Security Act shall be reduced by $6,000,000.

Funds appropriated for fiscal year 2000 under section 413(h)(1) of the Social Security Act shall be reduced by $15,000,000.] *(Department of Health and Human Services Appropriations Act, 2000, as enacted by section 1000(a)(4) of the Consolidated Appropriations Act, 2000 (P.L. 106–113).)*

Program and Financing (in millions of dollars)

Identification code 75–1536–0–1–506		1999 actual	2000 est.	2001 est.
	Obligations by program activity:			
00.01	Head Start	4,658	3,867	6,267
	Social services programs:			
	Children, youth, and families:			
01.03	Runaway and homeless youth	44	44	44
01.04	Runaway youth transitional living	15	21	21
01.05	Strengthening of parent-adolescent relationships			10
01.07	Child abuse state grants	21	21	21
01.08	Child abuse discretionary grants	14	18	18
01.09	Community based resource centers	33	33	33
01.11	Abandoned infants assistance	12	12	12
01.14	Child welfare services	292	292	292
01.15	Child welfare training	7	7	7
01.16	Adoption initiative	20	42	42
01.17	Adoption opportunities	25	27	27
01.19	Family violence grants		17	
01.20	Social services and income maintenance research	26	28	7
	Developmental disabilities:			
01.23	State grants	65	66	66
01.24	Protection and advocacy	27	28	28
01.25	Special projects	10	10	10
01.26	University affiliated projects	17	18	18
01.28	Native American programs	36	35	44
01.91	Subtotal social services programs	664	719	701
02.01	ACF Federal administration	144	148	165
02.93	Total Head Start, social services programs, Federal administration	5,466	4,734	7,132
	Community services programs:			
03.01	Community services block grants	500	528	510
03.03	Community food and nutrition	5	6	
03.04	Community services discretionary	33	35	5
03.05	National youth sports	15	15	
03.06	Individual development accounts	10	10	25
03.91	Subtotal, community services	563	594	540
04.00	Total direct programs	6,029	5,328	7,672
09.01	Reimbursable program	14	14	14
10.00	Total new obligations	6,043	5,342	7,686
	Budgetary resources available for obligation:			
21.40	Unobligated balance available, start of year		1	
22.00	New budget authority (gross)	6,045	5,342	7,686
23.90	Total budgetary resources available for obligation	6,045	5,343	7,686
23.95	Total new obligations	−6,043	−5,342	−7,686
23.98	Unobligated balance expiring or withdrawn	−2		
24.40	Unobligated balance available, end of year	1		
	New budget authority (gross), detail:			
	Discretionary:			
40.00	Appropriation	6,032	3,634	6,272
40.15	Appropriation (emergency)		1,700	
40.75	Reduction pursuant to P.L. 106–51	−1		
40.76	Reduction pursuant to P.L. 106–113		−6	
41.00	Transferred to other accounts	−2		
43.00	Appropriation (total discretionary)	6,029	5,328	6,272
55.00	Advance appropriation			1,400
	Spending authority from offsetting collections:			
68.00	Offsetting collections (cash)	20	14	14
68.10	From Federal sources: Change in receivables and unpaid, unfilled orders	−4		
68.90	Spending authority from offsetting collections (total discretionary)	16	14	14
70.00	Total new budget authority (gross)	6,045	5,342	7,686
	Change in unpaid obligations:			
	Unpaid obligations, start of year:			
72.40	Obligated balance, start of year	3,951	4,261	3,322
72.95	From Federal sources: Receivables and unpaid, unfilled orders	4		
72.99	Total unpaid obligations, start of year	3,955	4,261	3,322
73.10	Total new obligations	6,043	5,342	7,686
73.20	Total outlays (gross)	−5,723	−6,228	−7,027
73.40	Adjustments in expired accounts (net)	−15	−53	
	Unpaid obligations, end of year:			
74.40	Obligated balance, end of year	4,261	3,322	3,981
74.95	From Federal sources: Receivables and unpaid, unfilled orders			
74.99	Total unpaid obligations, end of year	4,261	3,322	3,981
	Outlays (gross), detail:			
86.90	Outlays from new discretionary authority	2,442	2,668	4,106
86.93	Outlays from discretionary balances	3,281	3,560	2,921
87.00	Total outlays (gross)	5,723	6,228	7,027
	Offsets:			
	Against gross budget authority and outlays:			
88.00	Offsetting collections (cash) from: Federal sources	−20	−14	−14
	Against gross budget authority only:			
88.95	From Federal sources: Change in receivables and unpaid, unfilled orders	4		
	Net budget authority and outlays:			
89.00	Budget authority	6,029	5,328	7,672
90.00	Outlays	5,703	6,214	7,013

Head Start.—The proposed level will enable Head Start projects to continue comprehensive early childhood development services and is consistent with the President's goal to serve one million children by 2002, including a doubling of the number of infants and toddlers in Early Head Start. The proposed level will allow Head Start to expand beyond the 2000 enrollment level of 880,000 slots, adding approximately 60,000 pre-school slots and 10,000 Early Head Start slots in 2001, for total enrollment of nearly 950,000.

Social services.—The proposed level will continue to support State, local, and private efforts to provide developmental and other services for children and youth, grants to improve support networks for persons with developmental disabilities, and economic development assistance to Native American populations.

Adoption incentive payments.—The proposed level includes almost $42 million for bonus payments to States that increase the number of children adopted from the foster care system.

Individual development accounts (IDAs).—The Administration will transmit legislation to allow low-income working families to use IDAs to save for a car that helps them get or keep a job.

Object Classification (in millions of dollars)

Identification code 75–1536–0–1–506		1999 actual	2000 est.	2001 est.
	Direct obligations:			
	Personnel compensation:			
11.1	Full-time permanent	90	94	104
11.3	Other than full-time permanent	1	1	1
11.5	Other personnel compensation	1	1	1
11.9	Total personnel compensation	92	96	106
12.1	Civilian personnel benefits	17	18	19
21.0	Travel and transportation of persons	2	3	4
23.1	Rental payments to GSA	13	14	15
23.3	Communications, utilities, and miscellaneous charges	2	2	2
24.0	Printing and reproduction	1	2	2
25.1	Advisory and assistance services	76	78	67
25.2	Other services	3	4	5
25.3	Purchases of goods and services from Government accounts	22	16	17
25.7	Operation and maintenance of equipment		1	1
26.0	Supplies and materials	1		1
31.0	Equipment	1		1
41.0	Grants, subsidies, and contributions	5,799	5,094	7,432
99.0	Subtotal, direct obligations	6,029	5,328	7,672
99.0	Reimbursable obligations	14	14	14
99.9	Total new obligations	6,043	5,342	7,686

Personnel Summary

Identification code 75–1536–0–1–506		1999 actual	2000 est.	2001 est.
	Direct:			
1001	Total compensable workyears: Full-time equivalent employment	1,507	1,498	1,560
	Allocation account:			
3001	Total compensable workyears: Full-time equivalent employment	2	2	

VIOLENT CRIME REDUCTION PROGRAMS

For activities authorized by sections 40155, 40211, and 40241 of Public Law 103–322, $134,074,000, to remain available until expended, of which $116,918,000 shall be for Family Violence (including Battered Women's Shelters); $14,999,000 for Education and Prevention grants to reduce sexual abuse of runaway, homeless and street youth; and $2,157,000 for the National Domestic Violence Hotline.

Program and Financing (in millions of dollars)

Identification code 75–8605–0–1–754		1999 actual	2000 est.	2001 est.
	Obligations by program activity:			
00.01	Family violence/battered women's shelters and domestic violence hotline	89	86	119
00.02	Education and prevention grants to reduce sexual abuse of runaway, homeless and street youth	15	15	15
10.00	Total new obligations	104	101	134
	Budgetary resources available for obligation:			
22.00	New budget authority (gross)	105	101	134
23.95	Total new obligations	−104	−101	−134
23.98	Unobligated balance expiring or withdrawn	−1		
	New budget authority (gross), detail:			
	Discretionary:			
40.00	Appropriation			134
42.00	Transferred from other accounts	105	101	
43.00	Appropriation (total discretionary)	105	101	134
	Change in unpaid obligations:			
72.40	Unpaid obligations, start of year: Obligated balance, start of year	82	116	114
73.10	Total new obligations	104	101	134
73.20	Total outlays (gross)	−70	−103	−112
74.40	Unpaid obligations, end of year: Obligated balance, end of year	116	114	136
	Outlays (gross), detail:			
86.90	Outlays from new discretionary authority	19	32	43
86.93	Outlays from discretionary balances	51	71	69
87.00	Total outlays (gross)	70	103	112
	Net budget authority and outlays:			
89.00	Budget authority	105	101	134
90.00	Outlays	70	103	112

Object Classification (in millions of dollars)

Identification code 75–8605–0–1–754		1999 actual	2000 est.	2001 est.
25.1	Advisory and assistance services	2	2	3
41.0	Grants, subsidies, and contributions	102	99	131
99.9	Total new obligations	104	101	134

CHILDREN'S RESEARCH AND TECHNICAL ASSISTANCE

Program and Financing (in millions of dollars)

Identification code 75–1553–0–1–609		1999 actual	2000 est.	2001 est.
	Obligations by program activity:			
00.01	Training and technical assistance	13	15	12
00.02	Federal parent locator service	23	30	25
00.03	Child welfare study			6
00.04	Welfare research			15
00.05	Evaluation of welfare to work	9		
00.06	Evaluation of abstinence education	3		
09.01	Reimbursable program	4	9	13
09.09	Reimbursable program—subtotal line	4	9	13
10.00	Total new obligations	52	54	71
	Budgetary resources available for obligation:			
21.40	Unobligated balance available, start of year	3	8	2
22.00	New budget authority (gross)	56	48	71
22.10	Resources available from recoveries of prior year obligations	1		
23.90	Total budgetary resources available for obligation	60	56	73
23.95	Total new obligations	−52	−54	−71
24.40	Unobligated balance available, end of year	8	2	2
	New budget authority (gross), detail:			
	Mandatory:			
60.00	Appropriation	52	39	58
69.00	Offsetting collections (cash)	4	9	13
70.00	Total new budget authority (gross)	56	48	71
	Change in unpaid obligations:			
72.40	Unpaid obligations, start of year: Obligated balance, start of year	65	59	44
73.10	Total new obligations	52	54	71
73.20	Total outlays (gross)	−57	−71	−68
73.40	Adjustments in expired accounts (net)	1		
73.45	Adjustments in unexpired accounts	−1		
74.40	Unpaid obligations, end of year: Obligated balance, end of year	59	44	47
	Outlays (gross), detail:			
86.97	Outlays from new mandatory authority	42	32	33
86.98	Outlays from mandatory balances	15	39	35
87.00	Total outlays (gross)	57	71	68
	Offsets:			
	Against gross budget authority and outlays:			
88.40	Offsetting collections (cash) from: Non-Federal sources	−4	−9	−13
	Net budget authority and outlays:			
89.00	Budget authority	52	39	58
90.00	Outlays	53	62	55

Summary of Budget Authority and Outlays

(in millions of dollars)

Enacted/requested:	*1999 actual*	*2000 est.*	*2001 est.*
Budget Authority	52	39	58

General and special funds—Continued

CHILDREN'S RESEARCH AND TECHNICAL ASSISTANCE—Continued

Summary of Budget Authority and Outlays—Continued

(in millions of dollars)

	1999 actual	2000 est.	2001 est.
Outlays	53	62	55
Legislative proposal, subject to PAYGO:			
Budget Authority			1
Outlays			3
Total:			
Budget Authority	52	39	59
Outlays	53	62	58

This account provides funding for research and technical assistance activities established in P.L. 104–193. Amounts for child welfare study and welfare research are in addition to research amounts in the Children and families services program account.

Object Classification (in millions of dollars)

Identification code 75–1553–0–1–609		1999 actual	2000 est.	2001 est.
	Direct obligations:			
21.0	Travel and transportation of persons	1	1	1
23.1	Rental payments to GSA		1	1
23.3	Communications, utilities, and miscellaneous charges	1	1	1
24.0	Printing and reproduction	1	1	1
25.1	Advisory and assistance services	3	5	13
25.2	Other services	11	14	11
25.3	Purchases of goods and services from Government accounts	26	15	14
25.7	Operation and maintenance of equipment	1	1	1
26.0	Supplies and materials	1	1	1
31.0	Equipment	1	1	1
41.0	Grants, subsidies, and contributions	2	4	13
99.0	Subtotal, direct obligations	48	45	58
99.0	Reimbursable obligations	4	9	13
99.9	Total new obligations	52	54	71

CHILDREN'S RESEARCH AND TECHNICAL ASSISTANCE

(Legislative proposal, subject to PAYGO)

Program and Financing (in millions of dollars)

Identification code 75–1553–4–1–609		1999 actual	2000 est.	2001 est.
	Obligations by program activity:			
00.02	Federal parent locator service			3
10.00	Total new obligations			3
	Budgetary resources available for obligation:			
21.40	Unobligated balance available, start of year			2
22.00	New budget authority (gross)			1
23.90	Total budgetary resources available for obligation			3
23.95	Total new obligations			−3
24.40	Unobligated balance available, end of year		2	
	New budget authority (gross), detail:			
	Mandatory:			
60.00	Appropriation			1
	Change in unpaid obligations:			
72.40	Unpaid obligations, start of year: Obligated balance, start of year			
73.10	Total new obligations			3
73.20	Total outlays (gross)			−3
	Outlays (gross), detail:			
86.97	Outlays from new mandatory authority			1
86.98	Outlays from mandatory balances			2
87.00	Total outlays (gross)			3
	Net budget authority and outlays:			
89.00	Budget authority			1
90.00	Outlays			3

The legislative proposals for the child support enforcement program impact this account by changing the estimated funding levels for child support training and technical assistance and the Federal parent locator service. In addition, these proposals increase Federal administrative costs.

Object Classification (in millions of dollars)

Identification code 75–1553–4–1–609		1999 actual	2000 est.	2001 est.
25.2	Other services			1
31.0	Equipment			2
99.9	Total new obligations			3

PAYMENTS TO STATES FOR FOSTER CARE AND ADOPTION ASSISTANCE

For making payments to States or other non-Federal entities under title IV–E of the Social Security Act, [$4,307,300,000] *$4,863,100,000*. [of which $105,000,000 shall be for making payments under sections 470 and 477 of title IV–E of the Social Security Act;]

For making payments to States or other non-Federal entities under title IV–E of the Social Security Act, for the first quarter of fiscal year [2001, $1,538,000,000] *2002, $1,735,900,000. (Department of Health and Human Services Appropriations Act, 2000, as enacted by section 1000(a)(4) of the Consolidated Appropriations Act, 2000 (P.L. 106–113).)*

Program and Financing (in millions of dollars)

Identification code 75–1545–0–1–506		1999 actual	2000 est.	2001 est.
	Obligations by program activity:			
00.01	Foster care	3,982	4,537	5,063
00.02	Independent living	70	105	140
00.03	Adoption assistance	826	1,020	1,198
10.00	Total new obligations (object class 41.0)	4,878	5,662	6,401
	Budgetary resources available for obligation:			
22.00	New budget authority (gross)	4,922	5,662	6,401
23.95	Total new obligations	−4,878	−5,662	−6,401
23.98	Unobligated balance expiring or withdrawn	−43		
	New budget authority (gross), detail:			
	Mandatory:			
60.00	Appropriation	3,764	4,307	4,863
65.00	Advance appropriation	1,158	1,355	1,538
70.00	Total new budget authority (gross)	4,922	5,662	6,401
	Change in unpaid obligations:			
72.40	Unpaid obligations, start of year: Obligated balance, start of year	688	853	1,025
73.10	Total new obligations	4,878	5,662	6,401
73.20	Total outlays (gross)	−4,707	−5,490	−6,272
73.40	Adjustments in expired accounts (net)	−6		
74.40	Unpaid obligations, end of year: Obligated balance, end of year	853	1,025	1,153
	Outlays (gross), detail:			
86.97	Outlays from new mandatory authority	4,231	4,911	5,596
86.98	Outlays from mandatory balances	476	579	676
87.00	Total outlays (gross)	4,707	5,490	6,272
	Net budget authority and outlays:			
89.00	Budget authority	4,922	5,662	6,401
90.00	Outlays	4,707	5,490	6,272

Summary of Budget Authority and Outlays

(in millions of dollars)

	1999 actual	2000 est.	2001 est.
Enacted/requested:			
Budget Authority	4,922	5,662	6,401
Outlays	4,707	5,490	6,272
Supplemental proposal:			
Budget Authority		35	

Outlays		5	21
Legislative proposal, subject to PAYGO:			
Budget Authority			5
Outlays			1
Total:			
Budget Authority	4,922	5,697	6,406
Outlays	4,707	5,495	6,294

Foster care.—The proposed level will support eligible low-income children who must be placed outside the home. An average of 341,700 children per month will be served in 2001.

Adoption assistance.—The proposed funding level will support subsidies for families adopting eligible low-income children with special needs. An average of 256,400 children per month will be served in 2001.

PAYMENTS TO STATES FOR FOSTER CARE AND ADOPTION ASSISTANCE

(Legislative proposal, subject to PAYGO)

Program and Financing (in millions of dollars)

Identification code 75–1545–4–1–506	1999 actual	2000 est.	2001 est.
Obligations by program activity:			
00.01 Foster care			5
10.00 Total new obligations (object class 41.0)			5
Budgetary resources available for obligation:			
22.00 New budget authority (gross)			5
23.95 Total new obligations			−5
New budget authority (gross), detail:			
Mandatory:			
60.00 Appropriation			5
Change in unpaid obligations:			
72.40 Unpaid obligations, start of year: Obligated balance, start of year			
73.10 Total new obligations			5
73.20 Total outlays (gross)			−1
74.40 Unpaid obligations, end of year: Obligated balance, end of year			4
Outlays (gross), detail:			
86.97 Outlays from new mandatory authority			1
Net budget authority and outlays:			
89.00 Budget authority			5
90.00 Outlays			1

This proposal supports a five-year project to enhance Tribal management of child welfare services.

ADMINISTRATION ON AGING

Federal Funds

General and special funds:

AGING SERVICES PROGRAMS

For carrying out, to the extent not otherwise provided, the Older Americans Act of 1965, as amended, and section 398 of the Public Health Service Act, [$934,285,000: *Provided*, That notwithstanding section 308(b)(1) of the Older Americans Act of 1965, as amended, the amounts available to each State for administration of the State plan under title III of such Act shall be reduced not more than 5 percent below the amount that was available to such State for such purpose for fiscal year 1995:] *$1,083,619,000, of which not less than $125,000,000 shall be for an expanded focus on respite and other assistance for families of vulnerable elderly, as authorized by section 341 of the Older Americans Act: Provided* [*further*], That in considering grant applications for nutrition services for elder Indian recipients, the Assistant Secretary shall provide maximum flexibility to applicants who seek to take into account subsistence, local customs, and other characteristics that are appropriate to the unique cultural, regional, and geographic needs of the American Indian, Alaska and Hawaiian Native communities to be served. *(Department of Health and Human Services Appropriations Act, 2000, as enacted by section 1000(a)(4) of the Consolidated Appropriations Act, 2000 (P.L. 106–113).)*

Program and Financing (in millions of dollars)

Identification code 75–0142–0–1–506	1999 actual	2000 est.	2001 est.
Obligations by program activity:			
01.01 Supportive services and centers	300	310	450
01.02 Preventive health	16	16	16
01.05 Congregate meals	374	374	374
01.06 Home-delivered meals	112	147	147
01.07 In home services for the frail elderly	10		
01.08 Grants to Indian tribes	18	18	23
01.09 State and local innovations and projects of national significance	18	32	36
01.10 Federal administration	15	17	17
01.13 Alzheimer's disease demonstration grants to States	6	6	6
01.14 Grants to States for the protection of vulnerable older Americans	12	13	13
10.00 Total new obligations	882	933	1,084
Budgetary resources available for obligation:			
22.00 New budget authority (gross)	882	933	1,084
23.95 Total new obligations	−882	−933	−1,084
New budget authority (gross), detail:			
Discretionary:			
40.00 Appropriation	882	934	1,084
40.76 Reduction pursuant to P.L. 106–113		−1	
43.00 Appropriation (total discretionary)	882	933	1,084
Change in unpaid obligations:			
72.40 Unpaid obligations, start of year: Obligated balance, start of year	259	260	307
73.10 Total new obligations	882	933	1,084
73.20 Total outlays (gross)	−879	−887	−1,020
73.40 Adjustments in expired accounts (net)	−2		
74.40 Unpaid obligations, end of year: Obligated balance, end of year	260	307	371
Outlays (gross), detail:			
86.90 Outlays from new discretionary authority	639	649	745
86.93 Outlays from discretionary balances	240	237	275
87.00 Total outlays (gross)	879	887	1,020
Net budget authority and outlays:			
89.00 Budget authority	882	933	1,084
90.00 Outlays	879	887	1,020

Administration on Aging.—The proposed level will provide continued funding for core formula grant programs that provide nutrition and supportive services through the aging network. Funding will also support an expanded focus on respite and other assistance for families of vulnerable elderly as authorized by section 341 of the Older Americans Act. These programs and the State and local innovations and projects of national significance are part of a comprehensive system of support for older people and their families.

Object Classification (in millions of dollars)

Identification code 75–0142–0–1–506	1999 actual	2000 est.	2001 est.
11.1 Personnel compensation: Full-time permanent	8	10	11
12.1 Civilian personnel benefits	1	2	2
23.1 Rental payments to GSA	1	1	1
25.2 Other services	5	5	6
41.0 Grants, subsidies, and contributions	867	915	1,064
99.9 Total new obligations	882	933	1,084

General and special funds—Continued

AGING SERVICES PROGRAMS—Continued

Personnel Summary

Identification code 75–0142–0–1–506	1999 actual	2000 est.	2001 est.
Direct:			
1001 Total compensable workyears: Full-time equivalent employment	116	142	154
Allocation account:			
3001 Total compensable workyears: Full-time equivalent employment	4	5	13

DEPARTMENTAL MANAGEMENT

Federal Funds

General and special funds:

GENERAL DEPARTMENTAL MANAGEMENT

For necessary expenses, not otherwise provided, for general departmental management, including hire of six sedans, and for carrying out titles III, XVII, and XX of the Public Health Service Act, and the United States-Mexico Border Health Commission Act, [$227,051,000, of which $20,000,000 shall become available on October 1, 2000, and shall remain available until September 30, 2001] *$223,741,000*, together with $5,851,000, to be transferred and expended as authorized by section 201(g)(1) of the Social Security Act from the Hospital Insurance Trust Fund and the Supplemental Medical Insurance Trust Fund: *Provided*, That [$450,000 shall be for a contract with the National Academy of Sciences to conduct a study of the proposed tuberculosis standard promulgated by the Occupational Safety and Health Administration: *Provided further*, That said contract shall be awarded not later than 60 days after the enactment of this Act: *Provided further*, That said study shall be submitted to the Congress not later than 12 months after award of the contract: *Provided further*, That of the funds made available under this heading for carrying out title XX of the Public Health Service Act, $10,569,000 shall be for activities specified under section 2003(b)(2), of which $9,131,000 shall be for prevention service demonstration grants under section 510(b)(2) of title V of the Social Security Act, as amended, without application of the limitation of section 2010(c) of said title XX: *Provided further*, That $500,000 shall be available to the Office of the Surgeon General, within the Office of Public Health and Science, to prepare and disseminate the findings of the Surgeon General's report on youth violence, and to coordinate activities across the Department of Health and Human Services: *Provided further*, That the Secretary may transfer a portion of such funds to other Federal entities for youth violence prevention coordination activities: *Provided further*, That $2,000,000 shall be available to the Lawton Chiles Foundation] *$20,000,000 appropriated under this heading in Public Law 106–113, to become available October 1, 2000, are hereby rescinded. (Department of Health and Human Services Appropriations Act, 2000, as enacted by section 1000(a)(4) of the Consolidated Appropriations Act, 2000 (P.L. 106–113).)*

OFFICE FOR CIVIL RIGHTS

For expenses necessary for the Office for Civil Rights, [$18,838,000] *$20,742,000*, together with not to exceed $3,314,000, to be transferred and expended as authorized by section 201(g)(1) of the Social Security Act from the Hospital Insurance Trust Fund and the Supplemental Medical Insurance Trust Fund. *(Department of Health and Human Services Appropriations Act, 2000, as enacted by section 1000(a)(4) of the Consolidated Appropriations Act, 2000 (P.L. 106–113).)*

POLICY RESEARCH

For carrying out, to the extent not otherwise provided, research studies under section 1110 of the Social Security Act, [$17,000,000] *$16,738,000. (Department of Health and Human Services Appropriations Act, 2000, as enacted by section 1000(a)(4) of the Consolidated Appropriations Act, 2000 (P.L. 106–113).)*

PUBLIC HEALTH AND SOCIAL SERVICES EMERGENCY FUND

For *public health and social services, $264,600,000, of which $208,600,000 is for* expenses necessary to support activities related to countering potential biological, disease and chemical threats to civilian populations[, $214,600,000]: *Provided*, That this amount is distributed as follows: Centers for Disease Control and Prevention, [$155,000,000, of which $30,000,000 shall be for the Health Alert Network, $1,000,000 shall be for the Carnegie Mellon Research Institute, $1,000,000 shall be for the St. Louis University School of Public Health, $1,000,000 shall be for the University of Texas Medical Branch at Galveston, $1,000,000 shall be for the Noble Army Hospital of Alabama bioterrorism program and $1,000,000 shall be for the Johns Hopkins University Center for Civilian Biodefense] *$148,500,000*; Office of the Secretary, $30,000,000; [Agency for Health Care Policy and Research, $5,000,000,] and Office of Emergency Preparedness, [$24,600,000. In addition, for expenses necessary for the portion of the Global Health Initiative conducted by the Centers for Disease Control and Prevention, $69,000,000: *Provided further*, That this amount is distributed as follows: $35,000,000 shall be for international HIV/AIDS programs, $9,000,000 shall be for malaria programs, $5,000,000 shall be for global micronutrient malnutrition programs and $20,000,000 shall be for carrying out polio eradication activities. In addition, $150,000,000 for carrying out the Department's Year 2000 computer conversion activities, $5,000,000 for the environmental health laboratory at the Centers for Disease Control and Prevention, $50,000,000] *$30,100,000: Provided further, That $50,000,000 of this amount is* for minority AIDS prevention and treatment activities[, $20,000,000 for the National Institutes of Health challenge grant program, and $75,000,000 to support the Ricky Ray Hemophilia Relief Fund Act of 1998: *Provided further*, That notwithstanding any other provision of law, up to $10,000,000 of the amount provided for the Ricky Ray Hemophilia Relief Fund Act may be available for administrative expenses: *Provided further*, That the entire amount under this heading is hereby designated by the Congress to be emergency requirements pursuant to section 251(b)(2)(A) of the Balanced Budget and Emergency Deficit Control Act of 1985, as amended: *Provided further*, That the entire amount under this heading shall be made available only after submission to the Congress of a formal budget request by the President that includes designation of the entire amount of the request as an emergency requirement as defined in the Balanced Budget and Emergency Deficit Control Act of 1985, as amended: *Provided further*, That no funds shall be obligated until the Department of Health and Human Services submits an operating plan to the House and Senate Committees on Appropriations]. *(Department of Health and Human Services Appropriations Act, 2000, as enacted by section 1000(a)(4) of the Consolidated Appropriations Act, 2000 (P.L. 106–113).)*

Program and Financing (in millions of dollars)

Identification code 75–9912–0–1–551	1999 actual	2000 est.	2001 est.
Obligations by program activity:			
Direct activities:			
00.01 General departmental management	196	205	230
00.02 Office for Civil Rights	21	22	24
00.03 Policy research	14	17	17
00.04 Public health and social services emergency fund	465	688	265
09.01 Reimbursable program	98	98	103
10.00 Total new obligations	794	1,030	639
Budgetary resources available for obligation:			
21.40 Unobligated balance available, start of year	21	105	....
22.00 New budget authority (gross)	881	925	637
22.10 Resources available from recoveries of prior year obligations	2	....	....
22.21 Unobligated balance transferred to other accounts	....	....	....
23.90 Total budgetary resources available for obligation	904	1,030	637
23.95 Total new obligations	−794	−1,030	−639
23.98 Unobligated balance expiring or withdrawn	−5	....	....
24.40 Unobligated balance available, end of year	105	....	....
New budget authority (gross), detail:			
Discretionary:			
40.00 Appropriation	221	826	526
40.15 Appropriation (emergency)	217	....	....
40.75 Reduction pursuant to P.L. 106–51	−1	....	....
40.76 Reduction pursuant to P.L. 106–113	....	−2	....
41.00 Transferred to other accounts	−1	....	....
42.00 Transferred from other accounts	337	....	....
43.00 Appropriation (total discretionary)	773	824	526
55.00 Advance appropriation	....	....	20
55.35 Advance appropriation rescinded	....	....	−20

		1999 actual	2000 est.	2001 est.
55.90	Advance appropriation (total discretionary)	....	....	....
	Spending authority from offsetting collections:			
68.00	Offsetting collections (cash)	106	101	111
68.10	From Federal sources: Change in receivables and unpaid, unfilled orders	2	....	....
68.90	Spending authority from offsetting collections (total discretionary)	109	101	111
70.00	Total new budget authority (gross)	881	925	637
	Change in unpaid obligations:			
	Unpaid obligations, start of year:			
72.40	Obligated balance, start of year	191	514	638
72.95	From Federal sources: Receivables and unpaid, unfilled orders	109	111	111
72.99	Total unpaid obligations, start of year	300	625	749
73.10	Total new obligations	794	1,030	639
73.20	Total outlays (gross)	−449	−906	−618
73.40	Adjustments in expired accounts (net)	−17	....	....
73.45	Adjustments in unexpired accounts	−2	....	....
	Unpaid obligations, end of year:			
74.40	Obligated balance, end of year	514	638	659
74.95	From Federal sources: Receivables and unpaid, unfilled orders	111	111	111
74.99	Total unpaid obligations, end of year	625	749	770
	Outlays (gross), detail:			
86.90	Outlays from new discretionary authority	363	508	285
86.93	Outlays from discretionary balances	86	398	333
87.00	Total outlays (gross)	449	906	618
	Offsets:			
	Against gross budget authority and outlays:			
88.00	Offsetting collections (cash) from: Federal sources	−106	−101	−111
	Against gross budget authority only:			
88.95	From Federal sources: Change in receivables and unpaid, unfilled orders	−2	....	....
	Net budget authority and outlays:			
89.00	Budget authority	773	824	526
90.00	Outlays	343	805	507

[Dollars in millions]

	1999 actual	*2000 est.*	*2001 est.*
Distribution of budget authority by account:			
General departmental management	193	206	224
Office for Civil Rights	17	19	21
Policy research	14	17	17
Public Health and Social Services Emergency Fund	547	583	265
Year 2000 computer conversion	324	150	0
Bioterrorism	140	214	209
Minority AIDS	50	50	50
Other	33	169	6
Distribution of outlays by account:			
General departmental management	179	182	213
Office for Civil Rights	18	21	24
Policy research	15	13	16
Public Health and Social Services Emergency Fund	131	589	254

Departmental management (DM) is a consolidated display of accounts that fund activities which provide leadership, policy, legal, and administrative guidance to HHS components; carry out the Department's civil rights and nondiscrimination enforcement programs; and support research to develop policy initiatives and improve existing HHS programs. DM also includes the activities of the Office of Public Health and Science, including adolescent family life, disease prevention and health promotion, physical fitness and sports, minority health, research integrity, women's health, and emergency preparedness. These accounts will continue to be appropriated separately, and are being displayed in a consolidated format to improve the readability of the presentation. Detailed information will continue to be available through the Department of Health and Human Services.

The Public health and social services emergency fund supports two main activities: preparing for and responding to the medical and public health consequences of potential bioterrorist events and minority AIDS prevention and treatment. In FY 2000 it also supported Year 2000 computer conversion activities and some activities that are being requested within HHS operating divisions in FY 2001.

Object Classification (in millions of dollars)

Identification code 75–9912–0–1–551		1999 actual	2000 est.	2001 est.
	Direct obligations:			
	Personnel compensation:			
11.1	Full-time permanent	80	93	102
11.3	Other than full-time permanent	6	7	8
11.5	Other personnel compensation	2	2	2
11.9	Total personnel compensation	88	102	112
12.1	Civilian personnel benefits	18	21	23
21.0	Travel and transportation of persons	3	4	4
23.1	Rental payments to GSA	11	13	14
23.3	Communications, utilities, and miscellaneous charges	4	4	4
24.0	Printing and reproduction	1	1	1
25.1	Advisory and assistance services	7	1	1
25.2	Other services	36	34	51
25.3	Purchases of goods and services from Government accounts	28	23	27
25.4	Operation and maintenance of facilities	4	3	3
25.5	Research and development contracts	2	35	34
25.7	Operation and maintenance of equipment	3	5	5
26.0	Supplies and materials	3	4	4
31.0	Equipment	4	6	7
41.0	Grants, subsidies, and contributions	49	101	41
99.0	Subtotal, direct obligations	261	357	331
99.0	Reimbursable obligations	98	98	103
	Allocation Account:			
	Personnel compensation:			
11.1	Full-time permanent	17	17	9
11.3	Other than full-time permanent	....	2	....
11.5	Other personnel compensation	....	1	....
11.9	Total personnel compensation	17	20	9
12.1	Civilian personnel benefits	7	6	2
21.0	Travel and transportation of persons	3	5	1
22.0	Transportation of things	....	1	....
23.1	Rental payments to GSA	....	2	2
23.3	Communications, utilities, and miscellaneous charges	4	12	....
24.0	Printing and reproduction	1	4	....
25.1	Advisory and assistance services	12	1	....
25.2	Other services	125	220	65
25.3	Purchases of goods and services from Government accounts	4	....	....
25.5	Research and development contracts	7	2	2
25.6	Medical care	54	154	....
25.7	Operation and maintenance of equipment	18	....	....
26.0	Supplies and materials	1	2	1
31.0	Equipment	49	10	8
41.0	Grants, subsidies, and contributions	133	136	115
99.0	Subtotal, allocation account	435	575	205
99.9	Total new obligations	794	1,030	639

Personnel Summary

Identification code 75–9912–0–1–551		1999 actual	2000 est.	2001 est.
	Direct:			
1001	Total compensable workyears: Full-time equivalent employment	1,250	1,412	1,498
	Reimbursable:			
2001	Total compensable workyears: Full-time equivalent employment	177	184	201
	Allocation account:			
3001	Total compensable workyears: Full-time equivalent employment	56	63	66

ALLOCATIONS RECEIVED FROM OTHER ACCOUNTS

Note.—Obligations incurred under allocations from other accounts are included in the schedules of the parent appropriation as follows: Health Care Financing Administration: "Health Care Fraud and Abuse Control Account."

PROGRAM SUPPORT CENTER

General and special funds:

Retirement Pay and Medical Benefits for Commissioned Officers

For retirement pay and medical benefits of Public Health Service Commissioned Officers as authorized by law, for payments under the Retired Serviceman's Family Protection Plan and Survivor Benefit Plan, for medical care of dependents and retired personnel under the Dependents' Medical Care Act (10 U.S.C. ch. 55), and for payments pursuant to section 229(b) of the Social Security Act (42 U.S.C. 429(b)), such amounts as may be required during the current fiscal year. *(Department of Health and Human Services Appropriations Act, 2000, as enacted by section 1000(a)(4) of the Consolidated Appropriations Act, 2000 (P.L. 106–113).)*

Program and Financing (in millions of dollars)

Identification code 75–0379–0–1–551	1999 actual	2000 est.	2001 est.
Obligations by program activity:			
00.01 Retirement payments	159	172	176
00.02 Survivors' benefits	12	12	12
00.03 Medical care	29	30	31
00.04 Military service credits	2	1	1
10.00 Total new obligations	202	215	220
Budgetary resources available for obligation:			
22.00 New budget authority (gross)	202	215	220
23.95 Total new obligations	−202	−215	−220
New budget authority (gross), detail:			
Mandatory:			
60.05 Appropriation (indefinite)	202	215	220
Change in unpaid obligations:			
72.40 Unpaid obligations, start of year: Obligated balance, start of year	23	23	23
73.10 Total new obligations	202	215	220
73.20 Total outlays (gross)	−202	−213	−219
74.40 Unpaid obligations, end of year: Obligated balance, end of year	23	23	24
Outlays (gross), detail:			
86.97 Outlays from new mandatory authority	184	197	201
86.98 Outlays from mandatory balances	18	18	18
87.00 Total outlays (gross)	202	213	219
Net budget authority and outlays:			
89.00 Budget authority	202	215	220
90.00 Outlays	202	213	219

This activity funds annuities of retired Public Health Service (PHS) commissioned officers and survivors of retirees, and medical care to active duty PHS commissioned officers, retirees, and dependents of members and retirees of the PHS Commissioned Corps.

Object Classification (in millions of dollars)

Identification code 75–0379–0–1–551	1999 actual	2000 est.	2001 est.
13.0 Benefits for former personnel	171	184	188
25.2 Other services	29	30	31
25.3 Purchases of goods and services from Government accounts	2	1	1
99.9 Total new obligations	202	215	220

Health Activities Funds

Program and Financing (in millions of dollars)

Identification code 75–9913–0–1–552	1999 actual	2000 est.	2001 est.
Change in unpaid obligations:			
72.40 Unpaid obligations, start of year: Obligated balance, start of year	10	10	10
74.40 Unpaid obligations, end of year: Obligated balance, end of year	10	10	10
Net budget authority and outlays:			
89.00 Budget authority	....	....	....
90.00 Outlays	....	....	....

This display shows activities in support of St. Elizabeths Hospital and scientific activities overseas that were supported by foreign currencies by the United States abroad.

Intragovernmental funds:

HHS Service and Supply Fund

Program and Financing (in millions of dollars)

Identification code 75–9941–0–4–551	1999 actual	2000 est.	2001 est.
Obligations by program activity:			
09.01 Program support center	307	311	326
09.02 Federal employee occupational health	85	93	101
09.03 OS activities	7	7	7
10.00 Total new obligations	399	411	434
Budgetary resources available for obligation:			
21.40 Unobligated balance available, start of year	35	57	57
22.00 New budget authority (gross)	421	411	434
23.90 Total budgetary resources available for obligation	456	468	491
23.95 Total new obligations	−399	−411	−434
24.40 Unobligated balance available, end of year	57	57	57
New budget authority (gross), detail:			
Mandatory:			
69.00 Offsetting collections (cash)	376	411	434
69.10 From Federal sources: Change in receivables and unpaid, unfilled orders	45	....	....
69.90 Spending authority from offsetting collections (total mandatory)	421	411	434
Change in unpaid obligations:			
Unpaid obligations, start of year:			
72.40 Obligated balance, start of year	−41	−108	−108
72.95 From Federal sources: Receivables and unpaid, unfilled orders	218	263	263
72.99 Total unpaid obligations, start of year	177	155	155
73.10 Total new obligations	399	411	434
73.20 Total outlays (gross)	−421	−411	−434
Unpaid obligations, end of year:			
74.40 Obligated balance, end of year	−108	−108	−108
74.95 From Federal sources: Receivables and unpaid, unfilled orders	263	263	263
74.99 Total unpaid obligations, end of year	155	155	155
Outlays (gross), detail:			
86.97 Outlays from new mandatory authority	421	411	434
Offsets:			
Against gross budget authority and outlays:			
88.00 Offsetting collections (cash) from: Federal sources	−376	−411	−434
Against gross budget authority only:			
88.95 From Federal sources: Change in receivables and unpaid, unfilled orders	−45	....	....
Net budget authority and outlays:			
89.00 Budget authority	....	....	....
90.00 Outlays	44	....	....

The HHS Service and supply fund (SSF) provides common centralized services to HHS components. The Program support center (PSC) line includes activities such as personnel and payroll administration, financial management operations, and a wide array of administrative services, including acquisitions management, building and property management, and technical support. The Office of the Secretary (OS) activities line includes the fund manager, departmental contracts and grants, audit resolution, OS graphics, and the regional health administrators. The Federal employee occupational health (FOH) program is also funded through the SSF. FOH includes clinical services, environmental health services and employee assistance programs.

Object Classification (in millions of dollars)

Identification code 75–9941–0–4–551	1999 actual	2000 est.	2001 est.
Personnel compensation:			
11.1 Full-time permanent	56	60	64
11.3 Other than full-time permanent	9	10	10
11.5 Other personnel compensation	3	3	3
11.9 Total personnel compensation	68	73	77
12.1 Civilian personnel benefits	12	14	15
21.0 Travel and transportation of persons	2	2	3
22.0 Transportation of things	2	2	2
23.1 Rental payments to GSA	9	10	10
23.3 Communications, utilities, and miscellaneous charges	38	43	44
24.0 Printing and reproduction	2	2	2
25.1 Advisory and assistance services	2	3	3
25.2 Other services	86	93	98
25.3 Purchases of goods and services from Government accounts	57	36	36
26.0 Supplies and materials	113	128	138
31.0 Equipment	8	5	6
99.9 Total new obligations	399	411	434

Personnel Summary

Identification code 75–9941–0–4–551	1999 actual	2000 est.	2001 est.
Reimbursable:			
2001 Total compensable workyears: Full-time equivalent employment	1,179	1,284	1,290
Allocation account:			
3001 Total compensable workyears: Full-time equivalent employment	29	....	....

Trust Funds

Miscellaneous Trust Funds

Unavailable Collections (in millions of dollars)

Identification code 75–9971–0–7–551	1999 actual	2000 est.	2001 est.
Balance, start of year:			
01.99 Balance, start of year	....	....	....
Receipts:			
02.01 Contributions, Indian health facilities, Health Services Administration	25	25	25
02.02 Gifts and contributions, miscellaneous trust funds	26	26	26
02.03 Interest, miscellaneous trust funds	1	1	1
02.99 Total receipts	52	52	52
Appropriation:			
05.01 Miscellaneous trust funds	–52	–52	–52
07.99 Total balance, end of year	....	....	....

Program and Financing (in millions of dollars)

Identification code 75–9971–0–7–551	1999 actual	2000 est.	2001 est.
Obligations by program activity:			
00.02 Gifts	23	27	27
00.03 Contributions, Indian health facilities	12	25	25
10.00 Total new obligations	35	52	52
Budgetary resources available for obligation:			
21.40 Unobligated balance available, start of year	27	47	47
22.00 New budget authority (gross)	52	52	52
22.10 Resources available from recoveries of prior year obligations	3	....	....
23.90 Total budgetary resources available for obligation	82	99	99
23.95 Total new obligations	–35	–52	–52
24.40 Unobligated balance available, end of year	47	47	47
New budget authority (gross), detail:			
Mandatory:			
60.27 Appropriation (trust fund, indefinite)	52	52	52
Change in unpaid obligations:			
72.40 Unpaid obligations, start of year: Obligated balance, start of year	96	68	65
73.10 Total new obligations	35	52	52
73.20 Total outlays (gross)	–60	–55	–53
73.45 Adjustments in unexpired accounts	–3	....	....
74.40 Unpaid obligations, end of year: Obligated balance, end of year	68	65	64
Outlays (gross), detail:			
86.97 Outlays from new mandatory authority	8	13	13
86.98 Outlays from mandatory balances	52	42	40
87.00 Total outlays (gross)	60	55	53
Net budget authority and outlays:			
89.00 Budget authority	52	52	52
90.00 Outlays	60	55	53
Memorandum (non-add) entries:			
92.01 Total investments, start of year: U.S. securities: Par value	13	15	15
92.02 Total investments, end of year: U.S. securities: Par value	15	15	15

[Dollars in millions]	*1999*	*2000*	*2001*
Distribution of budget authority by account:			
Gifts	27	27	27
Contributions, Indian health facilities	25	25	25
Distribution of outlays by account:			
Gifts	24	20	24
Contributions, Indian health facilities	36	35	29

Gifts to the Public health service are for the benefit of patients and for research. Contributions are made for the construction, improvement, extension, and provision of sanitation facilities.

Object Classification (in millions of dollars)

Identification code 75–9971–0–7–551	1999 actual	2000 est.	2001 est.
11.3 Personnel compensation: Other than full-time permanent	2	2	2
12.1 Civilian personnel benefits	1	1	1
21.0 Travel and transportation of persons	1	2	2
22.0 Transportation of things	1	2	2
25.2 Other services	2	3	3
25.3 Purchases of goods and services from Government accounts	1	2	2
25.4 Operation and maintenance of facilities	2	3	3
25.5 Research and development contracts	5	8	8
25.7 Operation and maintenance of equipment	4	6	6
26.0 Supplies and materials	2	3	3
31.0 Equipment	1	1	1
32.0 Land and structures	4	5	5
41.0 Grants, subsidies, and contributions	9	14	14
99.9 Total new obligations	35	52	52

Personnel Summary

Identification code 75–9971–0–7–551	1999 actual	2000 est.	2001 est.
1001 Total compensable workyears: Full-time equivalent employment	61	61	61

OFFICE OF THE INSPECTOR GENERAL

General and special funds:

Office of Inspector General

For expenses necessary for the Office of Inspector General in carrying out the provisions of the Inspector General Act of 1978, as amended, [$31,500,000] *$33,849,000*. *(Department of Health and Human Services Appropriations Act, 2000, as enacted by section*

General and special funds—Continued

OFFICE OF INSPECTOR GENERAL—Continued

1000(a)(4) of the Consolidated Appropriations Act, 2000 (P.L. 106–113).)

Program and Financing (in millions of dollars)

Identification code 75–0128–0–1–551	1999 actual	2000 est.	2001 est.
Obligations by program activity:			
00.01 Direct program	29	31	34
09.01 Reimbursable program	14	22	23
10.00 Total new obligations	43	53	57
Budgetary resources available for obligation:			
21.40 Unobligated balance available, start of year	1	1	1
22.00 New budget authority (gross)	43	53	57
23.90 Total budgetary resources available for obligation	44	54	58
23.95 Total new obligations	−43	−53	−57
24.40 Unobligated balance available, end of year	1	1	1
New budget authority (gross), detail:			
Discretionary:			
40.00 Appropriation	29	31	34
Spending authority from offsetting collections:			
68.00 Offsetting collections (cash)	24	22	23
68.10 From Federal sources: Change in receivables and unpaid, unfilled orders	−10	....	....
68.90 Spending authority from offsetting collections (total discretionary)	14	22	23
70.00 Total new budget authority (gross)	43	53	57
Change in unpaid obligations:			
Unpaid obligations, start of year:			
72.40 Obligated balance, start of year	3	−3	5
72.95 From Federal sources: Receivables and unpaid, unfilled orders	14	4	4
72.99 Total unpaid obligations, start of year	17	1	9
73.10 Total new obligations	43	53	57
73.20 Total outlays (gross)	−58	−45	−58
Unpaid obligations, end of year:			
74.40 Obligated balance, end of year	−3	5	4
74.95 From Federal sources: Receivables and unpaid, unfilled orders	4	4	4
74.99 Total unpaid obligations, end of year	1	9	8
Outlays (gross), detail:			
86.90 Outlays from new discretionary authority	40	49	54
86.93 Outlays from discretionary balances	18	−4	4
87.00 Total outlays (gross)	58	45	58
Offsets:			
Against gross budget authority and outlays:			
88.00 Offsetting collections (cash) from: Federal sources	−24	−22	−23
Against gross budget authority only:			
88.95 From Federal sources: Change in receivables and unpaid, unfilled orders	10	....	....
Net budget authority and outlays:			
89.00 Budget authority	29	31	34
90.00 Outlays	34	23	35

The Office of Inspector General (OIG) identifies and recommends actions to correct fraud, waste, and abuse in HHS administered and assisted programs and operations through audits and investigations.

In addition to the discretionary resources appropriated to the OIG, the Health Insurance Portability and Accountability Act of 1996 makes available mandatory funding for use by the OIG to combat Medicare fraud and abuse through a coordinated Health care fraud and abuse control (HCFAC) program with the Department of Justice. The following table shows total funding resources for the OIG:

(In millions of dollars)

	1999 actual	2000 est.	2001 est.
Budget Authority:			
Discretionary appropriations	29	31	34
Mandatory (HCFAC Account)	100	124	124
Total	129	155	158
Outlays:			
Discretionary appropriations	34	23	35
Mandatory (HCFAC Account)	84	124	124
Total	118	147	159

This schedule reflects estimated distribution of mandatory funds from the HCFAC account in FY 2001. Actual FY 2001 distribution will be determined by the Secretary of HHS and the Attorney General.

Object Classification (in millions of dollars)

Identification code 75–0128–0–1–551	1999 actual	2000 est.	2001 est.
Direct obligations:			
11.1 Personnel compensation: Full-time permanent	16	18	20
12.1 Civilian personnel benefits	4	4	5
21.0 Travel and transportation of persons	2	2	2
23.1 Rental payments to GSA	2	2	2
25.3 Purchases of goods and services from Government accounts	4	4	4
31.0 Equipment	1	1	1
99.0 Subtotal, direct obligations	29	31	34
99.0 Reimbursable obligations	14	22	23
99.9 Total new obligations	43	53	57

Personnel Summary

Identification code 75–0128–0–1–551	1999 actual	2000 est.	2001 est.
Direct:			
1001 Total compensable workyears: Full-time equivalent employment	275	285	306
Reimbursable:			
2001 Total compensable workyears: Full-time equivalent employment	56	93	90
Allocation account:			
Total compensable workyears:			
Full-time equivalent employment:			
3001 Full-time equivalent employment	882	1,054	1,143
3001 Full-time equivalent employment	60	....	....

ALLOCATIONS RECEIVED FROM OTHER ACCOUNTS

Note.—Obligations incurred under allocations from other accounts are included in the schedules of the parent appropriations as follows: Health Care Financing Administration: "Health Care Fraud and Abuse Control Account."

GENERAL FUND RECEIPT ACCOUNTS

(in millions of dollars)

	1999 actual	2000 est.	2001 est.
Offsetting receipts from the public:			
75–310700 Federal share of child support collections	868	851	850
Legislative proposal, subject to PAYGO	....	....	22
General Fund Offsetting receipts from the public	868	851	872

GENERAL PROVISIONS

SEC. 201. Funds appropriated in this title shall be available for not to exceed $37,000 for official reception and representation expenses when specifically approved by the Secretary.

SEC. 202. The Secretary shall make available through assignment not more than 60 employees of the Public Health Service to assist in child survival activities and to work in AIDS programs through and with funds provided by the Agency for International Development, the United Nations International Children's Emergency Fund or the World Health Organization.

SEC. 203. None of the funds appropriated under this Act may be used to implement section 399L(b) of the Public Health Service Act or section 1503 of the National Institutes of Health Revitalization Act of 1993, Public Law 103–43.

SEC. 204. None of the funds appropriated in this Act for the National Institutes of Health and the Substance Abuse and Mental Health Services Administration shall be used to pay the salary of an individual, through a grant or other extramural mechanism, at a rate in excess of Executive Level II.

SEC. 205. [None of the funds appropriated in this Act may be expended pursuant to section 241 of the Public Health Service Act, except for funds specifically provided for in this Act, or for other taps and assessments made by any office located in the Department of Health and Human Services, prior to the Secretary's preparation and submission of a report to the Committee on Appropriations of the Senate and of the House detailing the planned uses of such funds.] *Notwithstanding section 241(a) of the Public Health Service Act, such portion as the Secretary shall determine, but not more than 1.6 percent, of any amounts appropriated for programs authorized under the PHS Act shall be made available for the evaluation (directly or by grants or contracts) of the implementation and effectiveness of such programs.*

(TRANSFER OF FUNDS)

SEC. 206. Not to exceed 1 percent of any discretionary funds (pursuant to the Balanced Budget and Emergency Deficit Control Act of 1985, as amended) which are appropriated for the current fiscal year for the Department of Health and Human Services in this Act may be transferred between appropriations, but no such appropriation shall be increased by more than 3 percent by any such transfer: *Provided*, That the Appropriations Committees of both Houses of Congress are notified at least 15 days in advance of any transfer.

SEC. 207. The Director of the National Institutes of Health, jointly with the Director of the Office of AIDS Research, may transfer up to 3 percent among institutes, centers, and divisions from the total amounts identified by these two Directors as funding for research pertaining to the human immunodeficiency virus: *Provided*, That the Congress is promptly notified of the transfer.

[SEC. 208. Of the amounts made available in this Act for the National Institutes of Health, the amount for research related to the human immunodeficiency virus, as jointly determined by the Director of the National Institutes of Health and the Director of the Office of AIDS Research, shall be made available to the "Office of AIDS Research" account. The Director of the Office of AIDS Research shall transfer from such account amounts necessary to carry out section 2353(d)(3) of the Public Health Service Act.]

SEC. [209] *208.* None of the funds appropriated in this Act may be made available to any entity under title X of the Public Health Service Act unless the applicant for the award certifies to the Secretary that it encourages family participation in the decision of minors to seek family planning services and that it provides counseling to minors on how to resist attempts to coerce minors into engaging in sexual activities.

[SEC. 210. The final rule entitled "Organ Procurement and Transplantation Network", promulgated by the Secretary of Health and Human Services on April 2, 1998 (63 Fed. Reg. 16295 et seq.) (relating to part 121 of title 42, Code of Federal Regulations), together with the amendments to such rules promulgated on October 20, 1999 (64 Fed. Reg. 56649 et seq.) shall not become effective before the expiration of the 42 day period beginning on the date of the enactment of this Act.]

SEC. [211] *209.* None of the funds appropriated by this Act (including funds appropriated to any trust fund) may be used to carry out the Medicare+Choice program if the Secretary denies participation in such program to an otherwise eligible entity (including a Provider Sponsored Organization) because the entity informs the Secretary that it will not provide, pay for, provide coverage of, or provide referrals for abortions: *Provided*, That the Secretary shall make appropriate prospective adjustments to the capitation payment to such an entity (based on an actuarially sound estimate of the expected costs of providing the service to such entity's enrollees): *Provided further*, That nothing in this section shall be construed to change the Medicare program's coverage for such services and a Medicare+Choice organization described in this section shall be responsible for informing enrollees where to obtain information about all Medicare covered services.

[SEC. 212. (a) MENTAL HEALTH.—Section 1918(b) of the Public Health Service Act (42 U.S.C. 300x–7(b)) is amended to read as follows:

"(b) MINIMUM ALLOTMENTS FOR STATES.—With respect to fiscal year 2000, the amount of the allotment of a State under section 1911 shall not be less than the amount the State received under section 1911 for fiscal year 1998.".

(b) SUBSTANCE ABUSE.—Section 1933(b) of the Public Health Service Act (42 U.S.C. 300x–33(b)) is amended to read as follows:

"(b) MINIMUM ALLOTMENTS FOR STATES.—Each State's allotment for fiscal year 2000 for programs under this subpart shall be equal to such State's allotment for such programs for fiscal year 1999, except that, if the amount appropriated in fiscal year 2000 is less than the amount appropriated in fiscal year 1999, then the amount of a State's allotment under section 1921 shall be equal to the amount that the State received under section 1921 in fiscal year 1999 decreased by the percentage by which the amount appropriated for fiscal year 2000 is less than the amount appropriated for such section for fiscal year 1999.".]

SEC. [213] *210.* Notwithstanding any other provision of law, no provider of services under title X of the Public Health Service Act shall be exempt from any State law requiring notification or the reporting of child abuse, child molestation, sexual abuse, rape, or incest.

[SEC. 214. EXTENSION OF CERTAIN ADJUDICATION PROVISIONS.—The Foreign Operations, Export Financing, and Related Programs Appropriations Act, 1990 (Public Law 101–167) is amended—

(1) in section 599D (8 U.S.C. 1157 note)—

(A) in subsection (b)(3), by striking "1997, 1998, and 1999" and inserting "1997, 1998, 1999, and 2000"; and

(B) in subsection (e), by striking "October 1, 1999" each place it appears and inserting "October 1, 2000"; and

(2) in section 599E (8 U.S.C. 1255 note) in subsection (b)(2), by striking "September 30, 1999" and inserting "September 30, 2000".]

[SEC. 215. None of the funds provided in this Act or in any other Act making appropriations for fiscal year 2000 may be used to administer or implement in Arizona or in the Kansas City, Missouri or in the Kansas City, Kansas area the Medicare Competitive Pricing Demonstration Project (operated by the Secretary of Health and Human Services under authority granted in section 4011 of the Balanced Budget Act of 1997 (Public Law 105–33)).]

[SEC. 216. Of the funds appropriated for the National Institutes of Health for fiscal year 2000, $3,000,000,000 shall not be available for obligation until September 29, 2000. Of the funds appropriated for the Health Resources and Services Administration for fiscal year 2000, $450,000,000 shall not be available for obligation until September 29, 2000. Of the funds appropriated for the Centers for Disease Control and Prevention for fiscal year 2000, $500,000,000 shall not be available for obligation until September 29, 2000. Of the funds appropriated for the Children and Families Services Programs for fiscal year 2000, $400,000,000 shall not be available for obligation until September 29, 2000. Of the funds appropriated for the Social Services Block Grant for fiscal year 2000, $425,000,000 shall not be available for obligation until September 29, 2000. Of the funds appropriated for the Substance Abuse and Mental Health Services Administration for fiscal year 2000, $200,000,000 shall not be available for obligation until September 29, 2000. Such funds delayed by this section shall be available for obligation until October 15, 2000.]

[SEC. 217. STUDY AND REPORT ON THE GEOGRAPHIC ADJUSTMENT FACTORS UNDER THE MEDICARE PROGRAM. (a) STUDY.—The Secretary of Health and Human Services shall conduct a study on—

(1) the reasons why, and the appropriateness of the fact that, the geographic adjustment factor (determined under paragraph (2) of section 1848(e) (42 U.S.C. 1395w–4(e)) used in determining the amount of payment for physicians' services under the Medicare program is less for physicians' services provided in New Mexico than for physicians' services provided in Arizona, Colorado, and Texas; and

(2) the effect that the level of the geographic cost-of-practice adjustment factor (determined under paragraph (3) of such section) has on the recruitment and retention of physicians in small rural States, including New Mexico, Iowa, Louisiana, and Arkansas.

(b) REPORT.—Not later than 3 months after the date of the enactment of this Act, the Secretary of Health and Human Services shall submit a report to Congress on the study conducted under subsection (a), together with any recommendations for legislation that the Secretary determines to be appropriate as a result of such study.]

[SEC. 218. WITHHOLDING OF SUBSTANCE ABUSE FUNDS. (a) IN GENERAL.—None of the funds appropriated by this Act may be used to withhold substance abuse funding from a State pursuant to section 1926 of the Public Health Service Act (42 U.S.C. 300x–26) if such State certifies to the Secretary of Health and Human Services that the State will commit additional State funds, in accordance with subsection (b), to ensure compliance with State laws prohibiting the sale of tobacco products to individuals under 18 years of age.

(b) AMOUNT OF STATE FUNDS.—The amount of funds to be committed by a State under subsection (a) shall be equal to 1 percent of such State's substance abuse block grant allocation for each percentage point by which the State misses the retailer compliance rate goal established by the Secretary of Health and Human Services under section 1926 of such Act, except that the Secretary may agree to a smaller commitment of additional funds by the State.

(c) SUPPLEMENT NOT SUPPLANT.—Amounts expended by a State pursuant to a certification under subsection (a) shall be used to supplement and not supplant State funds used for tobacco prevention programs and for compliance activities described in such subsection in the fiscal year preceding the fiscal year to which this section applies.

(d) ENFORCEMENT OF STATE EXPENDITURE.—The Secretary shall exercise discretion in enforcing the timing of the State expenditure required by the certification described in subsection (a) as late as July 31, 2000.] [1]

[SEC. 219. None of the funds made available under this title may be used to carry out the transmittal of August 13, 1997 (relating to self-administered drugs) of the Deputy Director of the Division of Acute Care of the Health Care Financing Administration to regional offices of such Administration or to promulgate any regulation or other transmittal or policy directive that has the effect of imposing (or clarifying the imposition of) a restriction on the coverage of injectable drugs under section 1861(s)(2) of the Social Security Act beyond the restrictions applied before the date of such transmittal.]

[1] The Administration proposes to delete this provision and will work with the Congress to address this issue.

[SEC. 220. In accordance with section 1557 of title 31, United States Code, funds obligated and awarded in fiscal years 1994 and 1995 under the heading "National Cancer Institute" for the Cancer Therapy and Research Center in San Antonio, Texas, grant numbers 1 C06 CA58690–01 and 3 C06 CA58690–01S1, shall be exempt from subchapter IV of chapter 15 of such title and the obligated unexpended dollars shall remain available to the grantee for expenditure without fiscal year limitation to fulfill the purpose of the award.]

[SEC. 221. Not later than January 15, 2000, the Secretary of Health and Human Services shall transfer $20,000,000 from the appropriation in this Act for "National Institutes of Health—National Institute of Allergy and Infectious Diseases" to the appropriation in this Act for "Centers for Disease Control and Prevention—Disease Control, Research, and Training".]

SEC. 211. Funds provided in Public Law 106–31 under the heading, "Refugee and Entrant Assistance," shall be available until expended, remain subject to the first and second provisos under that heading, and are available for costs of assisting in the resettlement of refugees and entrants—

(1)(A) under section 412(b)(3) of the Immigration and Nationality Act, and 45 CFR 400.205 and 45 CFR 400.207;

(B) under 45 CFR 400.203(b) and 45 CFR 400.204(b), to maintain the period of time-eligibility in effect under 45 CFR 400.211 as of the end of the preceding fiscal year; and

(C) under section 412(c)(1) of the Immigration and Nationality Act and section 7 of Public Law 99–605 (8 USC 1522 note) in the event of refugee arrivals in excess of those anticipated in the annual consultation under section 207(d) of the Immigration and Nationality Act; and

(2) under section 501(a)(1) of the Refugee Education Assistance Act of 1980 for costs comparable to costs specified in paragraph (1): Provided, That an unanticipated mass migration of eligible populations may be considered for purposes of paragraph 1(C) to be comparable to refugee arrivals in excess of those anticipated in the annual consultation under section 207(d) of the Immigration and Nationality Act. (Department of Health and Human Services Appropriations Act, 2000, as enacted by section 1000(a)(4) of the Consolidated Appropriations Act, 2000 (P.L. 106–113).)

DEPARTMENT OF HOUSING AND URBAN DEVELOPMENT

This chapter presents the budget estimates and program justifications for the Department of Housing and Urban Development (HUD). HUD's core mission is to promote adequate and affordable housing, economic opportunity and a suitable living environment free from discrimination. The 2001 Budget for HUD reflects the successful implementation of a multi-year comprehensive reform effort which has helped restore the effectiveness and financial integrity of the Department's critical affordable housing and economic development initiatives. Building on the success of these reforms, Congress and the Administration have provided significant increases in key HUD programs over the past two years. The 2001 Budget will continue these historic successes by providing the Department with the tools to fulfill its fundamental strategic goals: increasing the availability of decent, safe and affordable housing in American communities (including the enhancement of homeownership opportunities, especially for minorities and first-time homebuyers, the transformation of public housing and the expansion of housing assistance to alleviate severe housing needs); ensuring equal housing opportunity; promoting self-sufficiency and asset development of families and individuals (including moving homeless families to self-sufficiency through locally-developed continuum of care strategies and contributing to the success of welfare-to-work efforts); and improving community quality of life and economic vitality through locally-driven initiatives and programs.

The 2001 budget provides increases for two successful block grant programs which serve HUD's fundamental affordable housing and economic development missions—the Community Development Block Grant (CDBG) and the HOME Investment Partnerships programs. These programs provide states and localities with formula funding pursuant to locally-developed consolidated plans for a wide variety of activities which benefit low and moderate-income families. The Community Development Loan Guarantee program (under Section 108 of the Housing and Community Development Act of 1974) will be continued with level funding and a slightly increased loan guarantee limitation. The Economic Development Initiative will also be maintained. Grants for Urban Empowerment Zones will continue support for ten-year plans to provide new job opportunities and community revitalization in 15 urban areas. The Rural Housing and Economic Development program will be continued at an increased level.

HUD's Homeless Assistance programs will be funded at an increased level to enable communities to continue their development and implementation of comprehensive coordinated continuum of care systems to address the needs of homeless people and families. This funding includes 18,000 rental assistance vouchers designed to provide affordable permanent housing for formerly homeless individuals and families in order to provide a stable living environment, a critical necessity for maintaining access to needed services and providing access to employment opportunities. HUD's Continuum of Care approach recently received the prestigious 1999 Innovations in Government award from the Harvard University's John F. Kennedy School of Government and the Ford Foundation.

The 2001 Budget maintains the Federal commitment to replacing distressed and obsolete public housing with attractive, mixed-income communities and creating new economic opportunities for residents. Consistent with this commitment and with a special focus on replacing projects that have been determined to be non-viable, the HOPE VI program will receive a significant increase from last year's enacted level. The 2001 Budget provides $3,192 million for the Public Housing Operating Fund, which helps to maintain good quality housing, and provides a slight increase for the Public Housing Capital Fund, which helps modernize and improve the housing stock.

The 2001 budget includes 120,000 incremental vouchers that will help address the severe housing needs of low-income households. These vouchers are necessary to address the continued increase in the number of families nationwide which have worst case needs for housing assistance, including extremely-low income families currently paying more than half their income for rent or living in severely inadequate living conditions. The Administration reaffirms its long-held commitment to renew all expiring Section 8 contracts, to protect residents from displacement by substantially increasing funding for Section 8 renewals, to provide Section 8 tenant-based assistance for displaced families, and for the replacement of affordable housing due to opt-outs from the project-based Section 8 program.

The Administration also continues its support for the Department's successful Housing for Persons With HIV/AIDS program (HOPWA) by providing increased funding to prevent thousands of persons with HIV/AIDS from becoming homeless. This increase is necessary to continue to provide stable housing and services in existing local programs and fund new jurisdictions as they become eligible for formula funding due to the continued increase in the number of AIDS cases.

Building on last year's successful adoption of the Housing Security Plan for Older Americans, the Housing for the Elderly program (under Section 202 of the Housing Act of 1959) will receive a substantial increase, including an increase in capital funding to convert existing housing to assisted living with services and an increase for construction of new affordable assisted living. The Housing for Persons with Disabilities (under Section 811 of the National Affordable Housing Act of 1990) will receive additional funding.

In support of the Administration's strong commitment to increase homeownership opportunities, the 2001 budget includes major support to help low- and moderate-income American families become homebuyers. The budget will increase the Federal Housing Administration's (FHA) maximum mortgage loan limits, allowing Single Family insurance to cover loans up to the same level as the Fannie Mae and Freddie Mac (GSEs) limits. (Currently FHA can insure home mortgages only up to 87 percent of the GSE limits in high cost areas and only up to 48 percent in low-cost areas, including approximately 2,200 rural counties throughout the Nation). In addition, the budget authorizes FHA to develop new adjustable rate mortgage products. These provisions will provide much-needed assistance to first-time homebuyers, minorities, and other underserved populations.

Increased funding for the Fair Housing Assistance and Fair Housing Initiatives programs (FHAP and FHIP) will strengthen the ability of public and private fair housing groups, and partnerships between them, to enforce the laws protecting all Americans against illegal housing discrimination.

In order to ensure the effective implementation of its programs, the Department's Office of Policy Development and Research (PD&R) will be provided with a budget increase. These additional funds are necessary to ensure timely provision of data, research and analysis of national housing and economic conditions, and to measure the performance of programs consistent with the Government Performance and Results Act of 1994. Also, an increase is included for the Partnerships for Advancing Technology in Housing (PATH) initiative, which is designed to develop and disseminate technologies that will result in housing that is more affordable, durable, disaster resistant, safer and energy/resource efficient.

PUBLIC AND INDIAN HOUSING

Federal Funds

General and special funds:

HOUSING CERTIFICATE FUND

[(INCLUDING TRANSFERS OF FUNDS)]

For activities and assistance to prevent the involuntary displacement of low-income families, the elderly and the disabled because of the loss of affordable housing stock, expiration of subsidy contracts (other than contracts for which amounts are provided under another heading in this Act) or expiration of use restrictions, or other changes in housing assistance arrangements, and for other purposes, [$11,376,695,000] *$14,127,824,459* and amounts that are recaptured in this account, [and recaptured under the appropriation for "Annual contributions for assisted housing",] to remain available until expended: *Provided*, That of the total amount provided under this heading, [$10,990,135,000] *$13,484,388,459*, of which [$6,790,135,000] *$9,284,388,459* shall be available on October 1, [1999] *2000* and $4,200,000,000 shall be available on October 1, [2000] *2001*, shall be for assistance under the United States Housing Act of 1937 ("the Act" herein) (42 U.S.C. 1437) for use in connection with expiring or terminating section 8 subsidy contracts, for amendments to section 8 subsidy contracts, for enhanced vouchers (including amendments and renewals) under any provision of law authorizing such assistance under section 8(t) of the [United States Housing] Act [of 1937] (47 U.S.C. 1437f(t)), [as added by section 538 of title V of this Act,] and contracts entered into pursuant to section 441 *and, for terms of one year, section 473* of the Stewart B. McKinney Homeless Assistance Act: *Provided further*, That amounts available under the first proviso under this heading may be available for section 8 rental assistance under the [United States Housing] Act [of 1937: (1) to relocate residents of properties: (A) that are owned by the Secretary and being disposed of; or (B) that are discontinuing section 8 project-based assistance; (2) for relocation and replacement housing for units that are demolished or disposed of: (A) from the public housing inventory (in addition to amounts that may be available for such purposes under this and other headings); or (B)]*:(1)* pursuant to section 24 of the [United States Housing] Act [of 1937] or to other authority for the revitalization of severely distressed public housing, as set forth in the Appropriations Acts for the Departments of Veterans Affairs and Housing and Urban Development, and Independent Agencies for fiscal years 1993, 1994, 1995, and 1997, and in the Omnibus Consolidated Rescissions and Appropriations Act of 1996; [(3)] *(2)* for the conversion of section 23 projects to assistance under section 8; [(4)] *(3)* for funds to carry out the family unification program; [(5)] *(4)* for the relocation of witnesses in connection with efforts to combat crime in public and assisted housing pursuant to a request from a law enforcement or prosecution agency; and [(6)] *(5) tenant protection assistance, including replacement and relocation assistance; (6)* for the [1-year] renewal of section 8 contracts for units in a project that is subject to an approved plan of action under the Emergency Low Income Housing Preservation Act of 1987 or the Low-Income Housing Preservation and Resident Homeownership Act of 1990: *Provided further, That of the amounts provided under this heading, $50,000,000 shall be available for a Voucher Success Fund to improve the operation of the section 8 voucher program, to be administered by HUD and to remain available until expended: Provided further, That HUD shall use funding for communities experiencing problems in utilizing section 8 vouchers, identified by criteria such as difficult market conditions, low rates of success for families attempting to use voucher assistance, concentrations of assisted families in high poverty neighborhoods, and other evidence of program difficulty determined by the Secretary: Provided further, That activities allowed under the Voucher Success Fund may include: (1) technical assistance to the local public housing authority or community to improve the success of the voucher program, (2) assistance for families in using vouchers, including mobility counseling, assistance with security deposits, transportation, and other activities intended to increase the likelihood that families will succeed in leasing units or leasing them outside areas of concentrated poverty, and (3) further outreach to landlords and community groups to encourage participation in the voucher program: Provided further, That the Secretary may use up to one percent of the amount available under this paragraph to establish monitoring systems for the Voucher Success Fund and to conduct detailed evaluations of the effect of providing assistance under such Fund: Provided further,* That of the total amount provided under this heading, [$40,000,000] *up to $25,000,000* shall be made available to nonelderly disabled families affected by the designation of a public housing development under section 7 of such Act, the establishment of preferences in accordance with section 651 of the Housing and Community Development Act of 1992 (42 U.S.C. 1361l), or the restriction of occupancy to elderly families in accordance with section 658 of such Act, and to the extent the Secretary determines that such amount is not needed to fund applications for such affected families, to other nonelderly disabled families: *Provided further*, That amounts available under this heading may be made available for administrative fees and other expenses to cover the cost of administering rental assistance programs under section 8 of the [United States Housing] Act [of 1937: *Provided further*, That the fee otherwise authorized under section 8(q) of such Act shall be determined in accordance with section 8(q), as in effect immediately before the enactment of the Quality Housing and Work Responsibility Act of 1998: *Provided further*, That all balances for the section 8 rental assistance, section 8 counseling, section 8 new construction, section 8 substantial rehabilitation, relocation/replacement/demolition, section 23 conversions, rental and disaster vouchers, loan management set-aside, section 514 technical assistance, and other programs previously funded within the "Annual Contributions" account shall be transferred to this account, to be available for the purposes for which they were originally appropriated: *Provided further*, That all balances in the "Section 8 Reserve Preservation" account shall be transferred to this account, to be available for the purposes for which they were originally appropriated: *Provided further*, That the unexpended amounts previously appropriated for special purpose grants within the "Annual Contributions for Assisted Housing" account shall be recaptured and transferred to this account, to be available for assistance under the Act for use in connection with expiring or terminating section 8 subsidy contracts: *Provided further*, That of the amounts previously appropriated for property disposition within the "Annual Contributions for Assisted Housing" account, up to $79,000,000 shall be transferred to this account, to be available for assistance under the Act for use in connection with expiring or terminating section 8 subsidy contracts: *Provided further*, That of the unexpended amounts previously appropriated for carrying out the Low-Income Housing Preservation and Resident Homeownership Act of 1990 and the Emergency Low Income Housing Preservation Act of 1987, other than amounts made available for rental assistance, within the "Annual Contributions for Assisted Housing" and "Preserving Existing Housing Investments" accounts, shall be recaptured and transferred to this account, to be available for assistance under the Act for use in connection with expiring or terminating section 8 subsidy contracts]: *Provided further*, That of the total amount provided under this heading, [$346,560,000] *$343,980,000* shall be made available for incremental vouchers under section 8 of the [United States Housing] Act [of 1937 on a fair share basis and administered by public housing agencies]; *and $66,000,000 shall be available for the Housing Production Program as authorized under this Act*[: *Provided further*, That of the balances remaining from funds appropriated under this heading or the heading "Annual Contributions for Assisted Housing" during fiscal year 2000 and prior years, $2,243,000,000 is rescinded: *Provided further*, That of the amount rescinded under the previous proviso, $1,300,000,000 shall be from amounts recaptured and the Secretary shall have discretion to specify the amounts to be rescinded from each of the foregoing accounts, $505,000,000 shall be from unobligated balances, and $438,000,000 shall be from amounts that were appropriated in fiscal year 1999 and prior years for section 8 assistance including assistance to relocate residents of properties that are owned by the Secretary and being disposed of or that are discontinuing section 8 project-based assistance, for relocation and replacement housing for units that are demolished or disposed of from the public housing inventory, and for enhanced vouchers as provided under the "Preserving Existing Housing Investment" account in the Departments of Veterans Affairs and Housing and Urban Development, and Independent Agencies Appropriations Act, 1997 (Public Law 104–204)].

For tenant-based assistance under the Act to help eligible families make the transition from welfare to work, $183,456,000 from the total amount provided under this heading, to be administered by public housing agencies (including Indian tribes and their tribally designated housing entities, as defined by the Secretary of HUD), to remain available until expended: Provided, That families initially selected to receive assistance under this paragraph: (1) shall be eligible to receive, shall be currently receiving, or shall have received within the preceding two years, assistance or services funded under the Temporary Assistance for Needy Families (TANF) program under part A of title IV of the Social Security Act or as part of a State's qualified State expenditure under section 409(a)(7)(B)(i) of such Act; (2) shall be determined by the agency to be families for which tenant-based housing assistance is critical to successfully obtaining or retaining employment; and (3) shall not already be receiving tenant-based assistance under the Act: Provided further, That each application shall: (1) describe the proposed program, which shall be developed by the public housing agency and the State, local or Tribal entity administering the TANF program and the entity, if any, administering the Welfare-to-Work grants allocated by the United States Department of Labor pursuant to section 403(a)(5)(A) of the Social Security Act, and which shall take into account the particular circumstances of the community; (2) demonstrate that tenant-based housing assistance is critical to the success of assisting eligible families to obtain or retain employment; (3) specify the criteria for selecting among eligible families to receive housing assistance under this paragraph; (4) describe the proposed strategy for tenant counseling and housing search assistance and landlord outreach; (5) include any requests for waivers of any administrative requirements or any provisions of the Act, with a demonstration of how approval of the waivers would substantially further the objective of this paragraph; (6) include certifications from the State, local, or Tribal entity administering assistance under the TANF program and from the entity, if any, administering the Welfare-to-Work grants allocated by the United States Department of Labor, that the entity has participated in developing the proposed program and will cooperate with the public housing agency that administers the housing assistance to assure that such assistance is coordinated with other welfare reform and welfare to work initiatives; and (7) include such other information as the Secretary may require and meet such other requirements as the Secretary may establish: Provided further, That the Secretary, after consultation with the Secretary of Health and Human Services and the Secretary of Labor, shall select public housing agencies to receive assistance under this paragraph on the basis of a national competition, taking into account the need for and quality of the proposed program (including innovative approaches), the extent to which the assistance will be coordinated with welfare reform and welfare to work initiatives, the extent to which the application demonstrates that tenant-based assistance is critical to the success of assisting eligible families to obtain or retain employment; and other appropriate criteria established by the Secretary: Provided further, That seven Public Housing Agencies (PHAs) selected by the Secretary for the Jobs Plus Initiative of the Moving to Work (MTW) Demonstration (P.L. 104–134, sec. 204) may use up to $7,000,000 of their Section 8 project reserves, or funds which otherwise would be transferred to such reserves after year-end settlement, as reimbursement for the cost of providing rent incentives to families participating in MTW: Provided further, That any obligated balances of contract authority that have been terminated shall be canceled. (Departments of Veterans Affairs and Housing and Urban Development, and Independent Agencies Appropriations Act, 2000.)

Program and Financing (in millions of dollars)

Identification code 86–0319–0–1–604		1999 actual	2000 est.	2001 est.
	Obligations by program activity:			
00.01	Contract renewals	10,830	9,889	14,513
00.02	Section 8 amendments	454		
00.03	Relocation & other	193	237	266
00.04	Preservation Amendments	11	25	
00.05	Section 514 Technical Assistance		4	
00.06	Non-Elderly Disabled	74	80	25
00.07	Welfare to Work	1	282	183
00.08	Regional Opportunity Counseling		10	
00.09	Voucher Success Fund			50
00.10	Preservation Prepayments	33	8	
00.11	Housing Production Program Premium			8
00.12	Incremental vouchers		352	377
00.13	Section 8 Counseling		11	
00.14	Section 8 Conversions		2	
00.15	Property Disposition		131	
10.00	Total new obligations (object class 41.0)	11,596	11,031	15,422
	Budgetary resources available for obligation:			
21.40	Unobligated balance available, start of year	3,477	3,185	103
22.00	New budget authority (gross)	9,411	4,963	14,128
22.10	Resources available from recoveries of prior year obligations	1,894	2,345	1,295
22.22	Unobligated balance transferred from other accounts		641	
23.90	Total budgetary resources available for obligation	14,782	11,134	15,526
23.95	Total new obligations	−11,596	−11,031	−15,422
24.40	Unobligated balance available, end of year	3,185	103	103
	New budget authority (gross), detail:			
	Discretionary:			
40.00	Appropriation	10,327	7,177	9,928
40.05	Appropriation (indefinite)			1,000
40.36	Unobligated balance rescinded	−916	−2,246	
40.49	Portion applied to liquidate contract authority			−1,000
40.76	Reduction pursuant to P.L. 106–113		−72	
42.00	Transferred from other accounts		104	
43.00	Appropriation (total discretionary)	9,411	4,963	9,928
55.00	Advance appropriation			4,200
70.00	Total new budget authority (gross)	9,411	4,963	14,128
	Change in unpaid obligations:			
	Unpaid obligations, start of year:			
72.40	Obligated balance, start of year	10,330	12,174	5,615
72.49	Obligated balance, start of year: Contract authority			43,430
72.99	Total unpaid obligations, start of year	10,330	12,174	49,045
73.10	Total new obligations	11,596	11,031	15,422
73.20	Total outlays (gross)	−7,858	−16,090	−16,579
73.32	Obligated balance transferred from other accounts		44,275	
73.45	Adjustments in unexpired accounts	−1,894	−2,345	−1,295
	Unpaid obligations, end of year:			
74.40	Obligated balance, end of year	12,174	5,615	4,163
74.49	Obligated balance, end of year: Contract authority		43,430	42,430
74.99	Total unpaid obligations, end of year	12,174	49,045	46,593
	Outlays (gross), detail:			
86.90	Outlays from new discretionary authority	2,953	2,107	6,889
86.93	Outlays from discretionary balances	4,905	13,983	9,690
87.00	Total outlays (gross)	7,858	16,090	16,579
	Net budget authority and outlays:			
89.00	Budget authority	9,411	4,963	14,128
90.00	Outlays	7,858	16,090	16,579

Summary of Budget Authority and Outlays

(in millions of dollars)

	1999 actual	2000 est.	2001 est.
Enacted/requested:			
Budget Authority	9,411	4,963	14,128
Outlays	7,858	16,090	16,579
Rescission proposal:			
Budget Authority		−103	
Outlays			
Total:			
Budget Authority	9,411	4,860	14,128
Outlays	7,858	16,090	16,579

The funds requested will support the following activities for 2001, as shown in the below table.

HOUSING CERTIFICATE FUND

[Budget Authority Request for FY 2001, $ in Millions]

	Units	Per Unit Cost	Contract Term	BA
FY 2001:				
Incremental Rental Assistance	60,000	5,733	1 year	343,980,000
Non-Elderly Disabled	[5,000]	5,043	1 year	[25,215,000]
Family Unification	[2,000]	5,733	1 year	[11,466,000]
Tenant Protections—Housing	30,300	NA	1 year	198,671,611
Tenant Protections—PIH	10,000	6,733	1 year	67,330,000
Contract Administrators	NA	NA	NA	209,000,000
Welfare-to-Work	32,000	5,733	1 year	183,456,000
Voucher Success Fund	NA	NA	NA	50,000,000
Housing Production Program	10,000		1 year	58,000,000

General and special funds—Continued

HOUSING CERTIFICATE FUND—Continued

[(INCLUDING TRANSFERS OF FUNDS)]—Continued

HOUSING CERTIFICATE FUND—Continued

[Budget Authority Request for FY 2001, $ in Millions]

	Units	Per Unit Cost	Contract Term	BA
Housing Production Program Premium	NA	NA	NA	8,000,000
Contract Renewals:				
PIH	1,764,243	5,733	1 year	10,089,530,963
HOPE VI and 202 Conversion	10,000	5,733	1 year	57,330,000
Welfare-to-Work Vouchers	50,000	5,733	1 year	286,650,000
CPD-Mod. Rehab. SRO	1,702	4,427	1 year	7,534,754
Shelter Plus Care	6,454	5,733	1 year	37,000,782
Housing	761,807	NA	1 year	3,781,340,349
Recaptures and Reuse	NA	NA	NA	(1,295,000,000)
Family Self-Sufficiency Coordinators	NA	NA	NA	45,000,000
Subtotal, contract renewals	2,594,206			13,009,386,848
Administrative Fees [non-add]				Approx. [1,100,000,000]
Advance Appropriation for FY 2002				(4,200,000,000)
Advance Appropriation Enacted in FY 2000				4,200,000,000
Total, FY 2001 Housing Certificate Fund	2,736,506			14,127,824,459

Contract Renewals. Contract renewals provide funding to renew expiring Section 8 rental assistance contracts covering certificates, vouchers, and moderate rehabilitation (renewed as certificates or vouchers), Loan Management, New Construction/Substantial Rehabilitation, Property Disposition, and Preservation, and Shelter Plus Care contracts authorized under section 441 of the Stewart B. McKinney Homeless Assistance Act.

Incremental Rental Assistance. For 2001, the Department is requesting 120,000 vouchers as follows: $585 million in budget authority for 60,000 incremental vouchers, 32,000 Welfare to Work vouchers, and 10,000 vouchers for a Housing Production Program, along with an additional $105 million for 18,000 vouchers which are proposed within the Homeless Assistance Grants Program.

Welfare to Work.—The lack of affordable, stable housing, or housing located close to employment, impedes the efforts of families moving from welfare to work. To help families who need housing assistance in order to achieve self-sufficiency, the Department is requesting $183 million to fund 32,000 Welfare to Work Housing Vouchers to supplement the program enacted in 1999. Additionally, waiver authority is requested to allow applicants to receive waivers of administrative provisions or statutory provisions of the United States Housing Act of 1937 that are needed to substantially further the objectives of the program.

Housing Production Voucher Program. The Administration proposes a program that combines and strengthens a number of existing housing production tools to spur the production of housing affordable to the lowest income Americans in neighborhoods that will provide strong job opportunities and other benefits. 10,000 incremental vouchers would be linked to two existing multifamily housing productions tools: the Low-Income Housing Tax Credit (LIHTC) and FHA insurance. FHA multifamily insurance would be used to finance the properties through the 221(d)(4) or risk-sharing programs. Pending completion and occupancy of new projects, vouchers allocated to the local administering authority can be used for regular tenant-based assistance. Funding for 2001 is proposed at $58 million for vouchers and $8 million for one-time incentive payments to developers who build units for targeted needs, such as large families.

Voucher Success Fund. This Fund provides a flexible tool for the Department to address situations in which difficult market conditions, concentrations of assisted families in high-poverty neighborhoods, or other forces that make it difficult for tenants to use vouchers or to use them in a wide variety of locations. The Department will use $50 million for communities experiencing problems in utilizing Section 8 vouchers for technical assistance to the local public housing authority or the community, for assistance to families to help them use vouchers, and for increased outreach to landlords.

Status of Contract Authority (in millions of dollars)

Identification code 86–0319–0–1–604		1999 actual	2000 est.	2001 est.
0100	Balance, start of year			43,430
0340	Unobligated balance transferred		43,430	
0400	Appropriation to liquidate contract authority			−1,000
0700	Balance, end of year		43,430	42,430

Public and Indian Housing

Family Self-Sufficiency (FSS) Coordinators. In 1990, the National Affordable Housing Act established the Family Self-Sufficiency Program. In establishing the program, Congress mandated that any housing agency that received any funding for rental vouchers and certificates in 1993 and subsequent would be required to establish a self-sufficiency program equal to the number of rental vouchers or certificates received.

Since that time, Congress has appropriated funds to support approximately one service coordinator in approximately 530 Public Housing Authorities each year. The PHAs that receive the special funding for FSS coordinators were the smallest agencies that administered less than 1,500 rental vouchers and certificates. Starting in 1999, the program was expanded to all PHAs.

The Department is committed to administering the FSS program for families receiving assistance under the rental voucher and certificate programs. The request for this account includes $45 million to allow the smallest housing agencies to hire FSS coordinators. Under the FSS program, families will receive job training and employment that should lead to a decrease in their dependency on welfare programs and move them toward economic self-sufficiency.

In 2001, seven Public Housing Agencies (PHAs) previously selected by the Secretary for the Jobs Plus component of the Moving to Work (MTW) Demonstration (Section 204 of the Omnibus Consolidated Rescissions and Appropriations Act of 1996, P.L. 104–134) may use a total of up to $7 million of their Section 8 project reserves, or funds which otherwise would be transferred to such reserves after year-end settlement, as reimbursement for the cost of providing rent incentives to families participating at eight MTW sites. The Jobs-Plus PHAs would be reimbursed of incurred costs upon HUD approval of a Plan submitted by the PHAs. Each rent incentive proposal will be approved by the Department in advance and be reasonable in terms of amount and duration.

Tenant Protection Vouchers. The Housing Certificate fund supports families living in public and assisted housing units affected by changes in the status of the units. Income-eligible families who are affected by the demolition, disposition, revitalization or other capital improvement through no fault of their own, receive relocation/replacement vouchers through the Housing Certificate Fund.

Housing

Tenant Protection Set-Asides. The Housing Certificate Fund also serves a role in supporting families in FHA-insured, privately owned assisted housing projects affected by changes in project status. It is intended that income-eligible families who, through no fault of their own, are affected by HUD's management of the multifamily inventory be aided through the Housing Certificate Fund.

Verifying the right person gets the right benefit.—In 2000, HUD will begin verifying tenant reported income against other Federal income and other wage data, as authorized under existing statutes. This will help ensure that housing assistance is only provided to the extent entitled. It will provide greater assurance that tenants pay the proper amount of rent as provided under law.

While tenant income is a major factor affecting eligibility and the amount of federal rental subsidies, admission and subsidy determinations are almost entirely dependent on self-reporting. HUD research has determined that there is a significant level of under-reporting. HUD statistically sampled tenants from its automated data bases and matched their reported income with federal tax data in Social Security Administration (SSA) and Internal Revenue Service (IRS) data bases in CY 1995 and CY 1996. Based on the result of this computer income matching project, HUD statistically projected that the amount of excess rental subsidies when projected to the entire universe would total as much as hundreds of millions of dollars. HUD projects an estimated savings of $80 million from this matching effort in 2001.

The verification program will reinforce incentives for voluntary reporting of income and the corresponding determination of the rent payment. Actions will include interest charges on under-payment of rent, additional financial penalties for very large amounts of under-payments, and routine notification to credit bureaus when amounts remain unpaid. HUD will amend its administrative procedures to standardized interim reporting policies for when a tenant must report increases and decreases in income. HUD will also streamline its procedures to easily reconcile these mismatches to actual income. When new verification procedures are fully implemented, HUD will reduce the existing administrative burden of paper verification of employment with employers to a sampling basis.

Tenants assessed back rent will be asked to repay the amount over a reasonable period of time in order to ease the burden of reimbursement. In subsequent years, HUD envisions a system of reconciliation where tenant reporting would be routinely reconciled with actual income. Any significant overpayment or underpayment of rent would be adjusted in the tenant's future rental payment over the following year. In 2000, HUD will focus primarily on tenants with the very large discrepancies between income reported to HUD and income reported to other sources.

In 2001, The Department is seeking legislation to modify the existing statutes that require 50 percent of any back rent collection to be shared with HUD's agent in project-based housing. This sharing is no longer appropriate in instances where HUD background checks discover the deficiency.

SECTION 8 RESERVE PRESERVATION ACCOUNT

Program and Financing (in millions of dollars)

Identification code 86–0316–0–1–604		1999 actual	2000 est.	2001 est.
	Obligations by program activity:			
00.01	Contract Renewals	988		
10.00	Total new obligations (object class 41.0)	988		
	Budgetary resources available for obligation:			
21.40	Unobligated balance available, start of year	995	11	
22.10	Resources available from recoveries of prior year obligations	4		
22.21	Unobligated balance transferred to other accounts		−11	
23.90	Total budgetary resources available for obligation	999		
23.95	Total new obligations	−988		
24.40	Unobligated balance available, end of year	11		
	New budget authority (gross), detail:			
	Discretionary:			
40.36	Unobligated balance rescinded			
	Change in unpaid obligations:			
72.40	Unpaid obligations, start of year: Obligated balance, start of year	289	845	
73.10	Total new obligations	988		
73.20	Total outlays (gross)	−429		
73.31	Obligated balance transferred to other accounts		−845	
73.45	Adjustments in unexpired accounts	−4		
74.40	Unpaid obligations, end of year: Obligated balance, end of year	845		
	Outlays (gross), detail:			
86.93	Outlays from discretionary balances	429		
	Net budget authority and outlays:			
89.00	Budget authority			
90.00	Outlays	429		

The Section 8 Reserve Preservation Account was authorized by P.L. 105–18. This account contains funds which were recaptured from project reserve accounts maintained by Housing Authorities nationwide. These funds will be used to renew expiring contracts during 2000.

All balances in this account will be transferred to the Housing Certificate Fund in 2000.

ANNUAL CONTRIBUTIONS FOR ASSISTED HOUSING

Program and Financing (in millions of dollars)

Identification code 86–0164–0–1–604		1999 actual	2000 est.	2001 est.
	Obligations by program activity:			
00.01	Lower income housing	802		
10.00	Total new obligations (object class 41.0)	802		
	Budgetary resources available for obligation:			
	Unobligated balance available, start of year:			
21.40	Unobligated balance available, start of year	1,794	231	
21.40	Authority to Borrow	16	522	
21.99	Total unobligated balance, start of year	1,810	753	
22.00	New budget authority (gross)	−1,089	−120	
22.10	Resources available from recoveries of prior year obligations	834		
22.21	Unobligated balance transferred to other accounts		−632	
23.90	Total budgetary resources available for obligation	1,555	1	
23.95	Total new obligations	−802		
	Unobligated balance available, end of year:			
24.40	Unobligated balance available, end of year	231		
24.40	Unobligated balance available, end of year	522		
24.99	Total unobligated balance, end of year	753		
	New budget authority (gross), detail:			
	Discretionary:			
40.05	Appropriation (indefinite)	2,737		
40.36	Unobligated balance rescinded	−1,084	−16	
40.49	Portion applied to liquidate contract authority	−2,737		
41.00	Transferred to other accounts	−5	−104	
43.00	Appropriation (total discretionary)	−1,089	−120	
	Change in unpaid obligations:			
	Unpaid obligations, start of year:			
72.40	Obligated balance, start of year	11,523	6,864	
72.49	Obligated balance, start of year: Contract authority	46,167	43,430	
72.99	Total unpaid obligations, start of year	57,690	50,294	
73.10	Total new obligations	802		
73.20	Total outlays (gross)	−7,365		
73.31	Obligated balance transferred to other accounts		−50,293	
73.45	Adjustments in unexpired accounts	−834		
	Unpaid obligations, end of year:			
74.40	Obligated balance, end of year	6,864		
74.49	Obligated balance, end of year: Contract authority	43,430		
74.99	Total unpaid obligations, end of year	50,294		

General and special funds—Continued

ANNUAL CONTRIBUTIONS FOR ASSISTED HOUSING—Continued

Program and Financing (in millions of dollars)—Continued

Identification code 86–0164–0–1–604	1999 actual	2000 est.	2001 est.
Outlays (gross), detail:			
86.93 Outlays from discretionary balances	7,365		
Net budget authority and outlays:			
89.00 Budget authority	–1,089	–120	
90.00 Outlays	7,364		

Status of Contract Authority (in millions of dollars)

Identification code 86–0164–0–1–604	1999 actual	2000 est.	2001 est.
0100 Balance, start of year	46,167	43,430	
0340 Unobligated balance transferred		–43,430	
0400 Appropriation to liquidate contract authority	–2,737		
0700 Balance, end of year	43,430		

The Annual Contributions for Assisted Housing account provided assistance for low-income housing and various other programs.

This account has not received an appropriation for several years. The 2000 Appropriations Act (P.L. 106–74) transferred the unexpended balances from this account to other accounts.

MOVING TO WORK

Note.—Section 210 of the Department of Veterans Affairs and Housing and Urban Development, and Independent Agencies Appropriations Act, 2000, provided $5 million for the Jobs-Plus Initiative within the Moving-to-Work Demonstration.

Program and Financing (in millions of dollars)

Identification code 86–0331–0–1–451	1999 actual	2000 est.	2001 est.
Obligations by program activity:			
00.01 JOBS PLUS Initiative		5	
10.00 Total new obligations (object class 41.0)		5	
Budgetary resources available for obligation:			
22.00 New budget authority (gross)		5	
23.95 Total new obligations		–5	
New budget authority (gross), detail:			
Discretionary:			
40.00 Appropriation		5	
Change in unpaid obligations:			
72.40 Unpaid obligations, start of year: Obligated balance, start of year			2
73.10 Total new obligations		5	
73.20 Total outlays (gross)		–3	–2
74.40 Unpaid obligations, end of year: Obligated balance, end of year		2	
Outlays (gross), detail:			
86.90 Outlays from new discretionary authority		3	
86.93 Outlays from discretionary balances			2
87.00 Total outlays (gross)		3	2
Net budget authority and outlays:			
89.00 Budget authority		5	
90.00 Outlays		3	2

The Moving-to-Work demonstration provides unprecedented autonomy and flexibility to a select group of high-performing public housing authorities (PHAs) in order to assess the potential impacts of Federal deregulation on resident households, housing developments, and local housing programs. Through waivers of requirements of the 1937 Housing Act, as amended, and related Federal regulations, participating PHAs can combine Federal funding allocated for public housing operating subsidy, capital subsidy, and Section 8 certificates and vouchers into a flexible housing assistance fund. By providing incentives to families that work, are seeking work, or are preparing for work, PHAs are also allowed to change administrative procedures and management policies so they can reallocate resources to better address local housing needs and priorities.

PUBLIC HOUSING CAPITAL FUND

(INCLUDING TRANSFERS OF FUNDS)

For the Public Housing Capital Fund Program to carry out capital and management activities for public housing agencies, as authorized under section 9 of the United States Housing Act of 1937, as amended (42 U.S.C. 1437), [$2,900,000,000]*$2,955,000,000*, to remain available until expended[: *Provided*, That of the total amount, up to $75,000,000]; *of which, up to $100,000,000* shall be for carrying out activities under section 9(h) of such Act, and for lease adjustments to section 23 projects[: *Provided further*, That no funds may be used under this heading for the purposes specified in section 9(k) of the United States Housing Act of 1937: *Provided further*, That of the total amount, up to $75,000,000 shall be available for the Secretary of Housing and Urban Development to make grants to public housing agencies for emergency capital needs resulting from emergencies and natural disasters in fiscal year 2000:]; *$55,000,000 shall be for the Resident Opportunity and Self-Sufficiency Program for grants for supportive services for public housing residents, as authorized by section 34 of such Act, and for service coordinators and congregate services for the elderly and disabled residents of public and assisted housing; up to $10,000,000 shall be for promoting consortia or other consolidations among housing authorities; and up to $1,000,000 shall be for the design of a capital financing program: Provided* [*further*], That all balances for [debt service for Public and Indian Housing and Public and Indian Housing Grants previously] *the Economic Development and Supportive Services program, the Tenant Opportunity program, and the Resident Opportunities and Self-Sufficiency program (section 34 of such Act)*, funded within the ["Annual Contributions for Assisted Housing"] *"Community Development Block Grants"* account, shall be transferred to this account, to be available for the purposes for which they were originally appropriated. *(Departments of Veterans Affairs and Housing and Urban Development, and Independent Agencies Appropriations Act, 2000.)*

Program and Financing (in millions of dollars)

Identification code 86–0304–0–1–604	1999 actual	2000 est.	2001 est.
Obligations by program activity:			
00.01 Capital Grants	2,173	3,044	2,911
10.00 Total new obligations (object class 41.0)	2,173	3,044	2,911
Budgetary resources available for obligation:			
21.40 Unobligated balance available, start of year	1,608	2,464	2,289
22.00 New budget authority (gross)	3,000	2,869	2,955
22.10 Resources available from recoveries of prior year obligations	29		
23.90 Total budgetary resources available for obligation	4,637	5,333	5,244
23.95 Total new obligations	–2,173	–3,044	–2,911
24.40 Unobligated balance available, end of year	2,464	2,289	2,333
New budget authority (gross), detail:			
Discretionary:			
40.00 Appropriation	3,000	2,900	2,955
40.36 Unobligated balance rescinded		–31	
43.00 Appropriation (total discretionary)	3,000	2,869	2,955
Change in unpaid obligations:			
72.40 Unpaid obligations, start of year: Obligated balance, start of year	6,137	5,201	11,566
73.10 Total new obligations	2,173	3,044	2,911
73.20 Total outlays (gross)	–3,080	–3,159	–3,346
73.32 Obligated balance transferred from other accounts		6,480	
73.45 Adjustments in unexpired accounts	–29		
74.40 Unpaid obligations, end of year: Obligated balance, end of year	5,201	11,566	11,131

	Outlays (gross), detail:			
86.90	Outlays from new discretionary authority		65	70
86.93	Outlays from discretionary balances	3,080	3,094	3,275
87.00	Total outlays (gross)	3,080	3,159	3,346
	Net budget authority and outlays:			
89.00	Budget authority	3,000	2,869	2,955
90.00	Outlays	3,080	3,159	3,346

The Public Housing Capital Fund, a comprehensive formula-driven program based on need, is designed to respond to the capital and management improvement requirements of public housing. The fund is a consolidation of the following programs: public housing modernization; public housing development; Major Reconstruction of Obsolete Public Housing Projects (MROP); public housing amendments; lease adjustments; Family Investment Centers; and the resident opportunities and self sufficiency program.

Of the $2.955 billion requested for the Public Housing Capital Fund, $2.79 billion will assist housing authorities in carrying out capital and management activities and is sufficient to cover the accrual of additional capital needs which has been estimated at $2.1 billion annually. In addition, of the requested amount, up to $100 million is set aside for technical assistance including inspection of public housing units. Further, of the requested amount, $55 million will be for the Resident Opportunities and Self Sufficiency Program. In addition, up to $10 million is provided to promote consortia or other consolidations among housing authorities and up to $1 million will be for the design of a capital financing program.

During 1999, the Department modified its formula for allocating capital subsidies to housing authorities through negotiated rulemaking with representatives of public housing authorities, public housing residents, and other stakeholders. The new formula will be implemented in 2000.

Pursuant to P.L. 106–74, all balances for debt service for Public and Indian Housing and Public and Indian Grants previously funded under the Annual Contributions for Assisted Housing account were transferred to the Public Housing Capital Fund in 2000.

The 2001 Budget proposes to transfer all balances reflected in the Community Development Block Grant account for the Tenant Opportunities, the Economic Development and Supportive Services, and the Resident Opportunities and Self Sufficiency programs to the Public Housing Capital Fund.

Public Housing Operating Fund

(INCLUDING TRANSFERS OF FUNDS)

For payments to public housing agencies for the operation and management of public housing, as authorized by section 9(e) of the United States Housing Act of 1937, as amended (42 U.S.C. 1437g), [$3,138,000,000] *$3,192,000,000*, to remain available until expended [: *Provided*, That no funds may be used under this heading for the purposes specified in section 9(k) of the United States Housing Act of 1937]. *(Departments of Veterans Affairs and Housing and Urban Development, and Independent Agencies Appropriations Act, 2000.)*

Program and Financing (in millions of dollars)

Identification code 86–0163–0–1–604		1999 actual	2000 est.	2001 est.
	Obligations by program activity:			
00.01	Operating subsidies	2,852	3,150	3,192
10.00	Total new obligations (object class 41.0)	2,852	3,150	3,192
	Budgetary resources available for obligation:			
21.40	Unobligated balance available, start of year	41	12	
22.00	New budget authority (gross)	2,818	3,138	3,192
22.10	Resources available from recoveries of prior year obligations	5		
23.90	Total budgetary resources available for obligation	2,864	3,150	3,192
23.95	Total new obligations	−2,852	−3,150	−3,192
24.40	Unobligated balance available, end of year	12		
	New budget authority (gross), detail:			
	Discretionary:			
40.00	Appropriation	2,818	3,138	3,192
	Change in unpaid obligations:			
72.40	Unpaid obligations, start of year: Obligated balance, start of year	1,441	1,412	1,590
73.10	Total new obligations	2,852	3,150	3,192
73.20	Total outlays (gross)	−2,876	−2,972	−3,160
73.45	Adjustments in unexpired accounts	−5		
74.40	Unpaid obligations, end of year: Obligated balance, end of year	1,412	1,590	1,622
	Outlays (gross), detail:			
86.90	Outlays from new discretionary authority	1,454	1,600	1,628
86.93	Outlays from discretionary balances	1,422	1,372	1,532
87.00	Total outlays (gross)	2,876	2,972	3,160
	Net budget authority and outlays:			
89.00	Budget authority	2,818	3,138	3,192
90.00	Outlays	2,876	2,972	3,160

Operating subsidies are provided to public housing authorities (PHAs) to assist in funding the operation and maintenance expenses of public housing units in accordance with Section 9(e) of the United States Housing Act of 1937, as amended. The annual subsidy requirements shown reflect efforts to date to develop a new formula for the allocation of operating subsidies using regulatory negotiations as required by the Quality Housing and Work Responsibility Act of 1998. It is anticipated that sufficient funds will be available to provide 100 percent of PFS requirements in 2001.

The following tables display the sources of housing authorities' expected revenue and expenditures by category for 2001. The distribution is based on historical data reported by housing authorities to HUD on the Statement of Operating Receipts and Expenditures.

Table 1. Sources of Housing Authorities' Operating Revenue (in millions of dollars)

Category	*Annual income*	*Percent of total*
Operating Subsidies	$3,192	51
Dwelling Rental	$2,752	44
Investment	$125	2
Other Income	$188	3
Total, Operating Revenue	6,259	

Operating Subsidies.—Represent HUD's contributions to a housing authority's operating budget. Under the current PFS, HUD sets a formula-determined allowable expense level (AEL) for each PHA and separately computes utility and audit costs. The PHA's dwelling rental income is also projected and the subsidy is the difference between the projected expenses and projected dwelling rental income.

Dwelling Rental.—Income derived from tenants' rents.

Investment Income.—Income from interest earned on general fund investments.

Other Income.—Includes income from other sources such as renting rooftop space for signs or broadcasting and from operating services for tenants, such as laundromats or day care centers.

Table 2. Housing Authorities' Operating Expenditures (in millions of dollars)

Category	*Annual expenditures*	*Percent of total*
Utilities	$1,377	22
Administration	1,189	19
General Operating Expenses	1,127	18
Maintenance	1,815	29
Tenant Services	63	1
Protective Services	125	2
Capital Expenditures	125	2

General and special funds—Continued

PUBLIC HOUSING OPERATING FUND—Continued

(INCLUDING TRANSFERS OF FUNDS)—Continued

Table 2. Housing Authorities' Operating Expenditures (in millions of dollars)—Continued

Category	*Annual expenditures*	*Percent of total*
Operating Reserve	438	7
Total, Operating Expenses	6,259	

Utilities.—Includes water, sewer, electricity, gas, fuel, and related labor expenses.

Administration.—Includes administrative salaries, legal expenses, staff training, travel, accounting fees, auditing fees, sundry, and outside management costs.

General Operating Expenses.—Includes insurance, payments made to local governments in lieu of taxes, terminal leave payments, employees benefit contributions, collection losses, interest on administrative and sundry notes, and other general expenses.

Ordinary Maintenance and Operations.—Consists of expenses for labor, materials, contracts and garbage fees associated with the day-to-day operation of the public housing authority.

Tenant Services.—Cover salaries, recreation, publication, contract costs, training, and other expenses.

Protective Services.—Includes expenses for labor, materials, and contract costs.

Capital Expenditures.—Includes extraordinary maintenance, casualty losses, and property betterments (e.g. roofs and furnaces).

Operating reserves.—Provides working capital funds and is a reserve for emergencies.

The Budget also projects that additional funds for operating subsidies will be available to housing authorities from increased rent collections from improved income matching.

Pursuant to the requirements of the Quality Housing and Work Responsibility Act of 1998, during 2000, the Department will continue to modify its approach to the operating subsidy calculation through negotiated rulemaking with public housing authority representatives, public housing tenants, and other stakeholders. The operating subsidy negotiated rulemaking committee will base the new formula on the following four principles:

- Provide incentives for good management and rewards for performance.
- Reward cost-effective use of resources to improve housing services, housing quality, and mobility.
- Be administratively simple.
- Result in increased accountability for delivering quality housing services at reasonable cost.

These principles build on the Secretary's existing management proposals to restore the public trust in HUD's programs and the Administration's principles for performance-based service contracting (PBSC). The PBSC guidelines have been demonstrated to significantly save money and result in improved performance.

The Administration proposes collecting security deposits in public housing beginning October 1, 2000. To improve incentives for resident upkeep of units, this administrative change would require a one-month security deposit from all public housing residents. This parallels management practices in HUD's Section 8 program and in the private rental market. Deposits will be placed in interest-bearing escrow accounts. PHAs have discretion to decide how the security deposit will be paid, either in monthly installments, up-front, or a combination of the two.

DRUG ELIMINATION GRANTS FOR LOW-INCOME HOUSING

For grants to public housing agencies and Indian tribes and their tribally designated housing entities for use in eliminating crime in public housing projects authorized by 42 U.S.C. 11901–11908, for grants for federally assisted low-income housing authorized by 42 U.S.C. 11909, and for drug information clearinghouse services authorized by 42 U.S.C. 11921–11925, [$310,000,000] *$345,000,000*, to remain available until expended[: *Provided*, That of the total amount provided under this heading, up to $4,500,000]*; of which $10,000,000* shall be solely for technical assistance, technical assistance grants, training, and program assessment for or on behalf of public housing agencies, resident organizations, and Indian tribes and their tribally designated housing entities (including up to [$150,000] *$250,000* for the cost of necessary travel for participants in such training)[: *Provided further*, That of the amount provided under this heading,]*;* $10,000,000 shall be used in connection with efforts to combat violent crime in public and assisted housing under the Operation Safe Home Program administered by the Inspector General of the Department of Housing and Urban Development: *Provided further*, That of the amount under this heading; $10,000,000 shall be provided to the Office of Inspector General for Operation Safe Home[: *Provided further*, That of the amount under this heading,]*;* $20,000,000 shall be available for [a program named] the New Approach Anti-Drug program which will provide competitive grants to entities managing or operating public housing developments, federally assisted multifamily housing developments, or other multifamily housing developments for low-income families supported by non-Federal governmental entities or similar housing developments supported by nonprofit private sources in order to provide or augment security (including personnel costs), to assist in the investigation and/or prosecution of drug related criminal activity in and around such developments, and to provide assistance for the development of capital improvements at such developments directly relating to the security of such developments: *Provided [further]*, That grants for the New Approach Anti-Drug program shall be made on a competitive basis as specified in section 102 of the Department of Housing and Urban Development Reform Act of 1989: *Provided further, That of the amount under this heading, $30,000,000 shall be for the Community Gun Safety and Violence Reduction Initiative, which will include (1) competitive grants to public or private nonprofit organizations and other appropriate entities as determined by the Secretary, including consortia of such organizations and entities, for community-based education and outreach programs to address gun violence, both criminal and accidental; (2) competitive matching grants and technical assistance to units of general local government, law enforcement agencies, pubic housing agencies, recipients under the Native American Housing Assistance and Self-Determination Act of 1996, public and private for-profit and nonprofit organizations, and civic associations, including consortia of such entities, to support gun safety and violence reduction activities, including gun buy-back programs, gun-tracing efforts, youth diversion programs that offer alternatives to crime, violence counseling programs, and gun-violence hotlines and training; (3) competitive grants and technical assistance to law enforcement agencies who have partnered with public and private entities to develop and support computer crime-tracking and mapping databases on gun-related crimes and violence; and (4) an evaluation and report on the initiative that sets forth which elements or combination of elements are most effective at reducing gun-related crime and violence. (Departments of Veterans Affairs and Housing and Urban Development, and Independent Agencies Appropriations Act, 2000.)*

Program and Financing (in millions of dollars)

Identification code 86–0197–0–1–604		1999 actual	2000 est.	2001 est.
	Obligations by program activity:			
00.01	Direct program	296	517	259
00.02	Federally Assisted Housing	16	35	16
00.03	Operation Safe Home	17	31	20
00.04	New Approach Anti-Drug Program	11	49	20
00.05	Community Gun Safety and Violence Reduction			30
10.00	Total new obligations (object class 41.0)	340	632	345
	Budgetary resources available for obligation:			
	Unobligated balance available, start of year:			
21.40	Unobligated balance available, start of year	336	81	
21.40	Administrative Authority	10	241	
21.99	Total unobligated balance, start of year	346	322	

22.00 New budget authority (gross)	310	310	345
22.10 Resources available from recoveries of prior year obligations	6		
23.90 Total budgetary resources available for obligation	662	632	345
23.95 Total new obligations	−340	−632	−345
Unobligated balance available, end of year:			
24.40 Unobligated balance available, end of year	81		
24.40 Administrative Commitments	241		
24.99 Total unobligated balance, end of year	322		
New budget authority (gross), detail:			
Discretionary:			
40.00 Appropriation	310	310	345
Change in unpaid obligations:			
72.40 Unpaid obligations, start of year: Obligated balance, start of year	266	316	623
73.10 Total new obligations	340	632	345
73.20 Total outlays (gross)	−283	−325	−315
73.45 Adjustments in unexpired accounts	−6		
74.40 Unpaid obligations, end of year: Obligated balance, end of year	316	623	653
Outlays (gross), detail:			
86.93 Outlays from discretionary balances	283	325	315
Net budget authority and outlays:			
89.00 Budget authority	310	310	345
90.00 Outlays	283	325	315

The Public Housing Drug Elimination Grants program has been authorized since 1988 and provides funds to Public Housing Authorities (PHAs) and Tribally Designated Housing Entities (TDHEs) for their anti-drug, anti-crime efforts. To combat the concentration of crime in and around assisted housing communities, staff and residents use these resources to increase police coverage and security as well as to provide alternative activities to residents. Eligible activities include reimbursing local law enforcement for additional services, security contracts, investigators, and training residents for volunteer resident programs. The 1998 Amendments have expanded the definition of crime prevention activities beyond drug-related patrols, physical changes to enhance security, drug prevention, and intervention and treatment, thus allowing housing authorities greater scope in targeting crime and developing successful alternatives. In 1999, HUD completed rulemaking to implement the 1998 amendments and to distribute grant awards through a simple formula.

The $345 million requested for this program in 2001 also includes funding for the Community Gun Safety and Violence Reduction Initiative. With more than 30,000 people killed and 100,000 injured by guns each year in our Nation, gun-related violence poses a major threat to HUD's obligation to help ensure "a decent home and a suitable living environment for every American family." Through such programs as the Drug Elimination Program, the Gun Buyback Violence Reduction Initiative, Operation Safe Home, the Peacemakers Corp, the Youth Violence Prevention Program, Crime Prevention Through Environmental Design, Safe Futures and Others, HUD has targeted crime and violence in our Nation's communities, but more must be done about the distinctive program of gun-related violence, both criminal and accidental. The Community Gun Safety and Violence Reduction Initiative will help address this problem with three program elements. The Initiative will fund public education programs that will use a variety of media to address the hazards posed by the presence of firearms in the community as well as actions associated with responsible gun ownership. The Initiative will also provide technical assistance and matching funds to implement gun violence reduction programs, building upon or complementing existing community safety programs where they exist. Finally, the Initiative will fund state-of-the-art computerized gun-violence tracking and gun tracing efforts to close the knowledge gap and assist communities and law enforcement agencies in planning gun-violence reduction initiatives. An evaluation of the program will be included.

The budget proposes to allocate the $345 million requested in 2001 as follows: (1) $248.75 million for Drug Elimination Grants and clearinghouse information services; (2) $20 million for the New Approach Anti-Drug program; (3) $20 million for Operation Safe Home; (4) $16.25 million for other Federally assisted low-income housing grants; (5) $10 million for technical assistance, training, and information dissemination; and (6) $30 million for the Community Gun Safety and Violence Reduction initiative.

Revitalization of Severely Distressed Public Housing (HOPE VI)

For grants to public housing agencies for demolition, site revitalization, replacement housing, and tenant-based assistance grants to projects as authorized by section 24 of the United States Housing Act of 1937, [$575,000,000] *$625,000,000,* to remain available until expended; of which the Secretary may use up to [$10,000,000] *$15,000,000* for technical assistance and contract expertise, to be provided directly or indirectly by grants, contracts or cooperative agreements, including training and cost of necessary travel for participants in such training, by or to officials and employees of the department and of public housing agencies and to residents[: *Provided*, That none of such funds shall be used directly or indirectly by granting competitive advantage in awards to settle litigation or pay judgments, unless expressly permitted herein: *Provided further*, That of the amount provided under this heading, $1,200,000 shall be contracted through the Secretary to be used by the Urban Institute to conduct an independent study on the long-term effects of the HOPE VI program on former residents of distressed public housing developments]*; and of which the Secretary shall use up to $180,000,000 for grants to address sites: (1) that are subject to conversion or assessment under section 202 of the Departments of Veterans Affairs and Housing and Urban Development and Independent Agencies Appropriations Act of 1996, and (2) for which no applicable approval under that section or other approval for demolition, disposition, or HOPE VI has been provided prior to January 1, 2000: Provided That the Secretary may allocate grants under the preceding clause in any manner the Secretary deems appropriate to assure to the maximum extent possible that such sites are addressed satisfactorily: Provided further, That of the amount in the preceding proviso, up to $50,000,000 shall be used for demolition grants and up to $5,000,000 shall be used for capacity building in communities receiving grants to address sites described above. (Departments of Veterans Affairs and Housing and Urban Development, and Independent Agencies Appropriations Act, 2000.)*

Program and Financing (in millions of dollars)

Identification code 86–0218–0–1–604	1999 actual	2000 est.	2001 est.
Obligations by program activity:			
00.01 Direct Program Activity	577	1,255	625
10.00 Total new obligations (object class 41.0)	577	1,255	625
Budgetary resources available for obligation:			
21.40 Unobligated balance available, start of year	630	680	
22.00 New budget authority (gross)	625	575	625
23.90 Total budgetary resources available for obligation	1,255	1,255	625
23.95 Total new obligations	−577	−1,255	−625
24.40 Unobligated balance available, end of year	680		
New budget authority (gross), detail:			
Discretionary:			
40.00 Appropriation	625	575	625
Change in unpaid obligations:			
72.40 Unpaid obligations, start of year: Obligated balance, start of year	1,943	2,198	2,865
73.10 Total new obligations	577	1,255	625
73.20 Total outlays (gross)	−321	−588	−597
74.40 Unpaid obligations, end of year: Obligated balance, end of year	2,198	2,865	2,893

General and special funds—Continued

REVITALIZATION OF SEVERELY DISTRESSED PUBLIC HOUSING (HOPE VI)—Continued

Program and Financing (in millions of dollars)—Continued

Identification code 86–0218–0–1–604	1999 actual	2000 est.	2001 est.
Outlays (gross), detail:			
86.93 Outlays from discretionary balances	321	588	597
Net budget authority and outlays:			
89.00 Budget authority	625	575	625
90.00 Outlays	321	588	597

This program utilizes Federal resources to rehabilitate and restore severely distressed public housing projects, thereby expanding the supply of decent, safe, and affordable housing for low-income renters. The funds may also be used for project demolition, hard replacement units, as well as tenant-based rental assistance.

For the 2001 Budget, HUD will use up to $180 million of HOPE VI funds to address sites subject to the "mandatory conversion" law. That law requires that sites which would cost more to operate and modernize than vouchers and cannot be reasonably revitalized must be removed from the inventory. By devoting funds to the resolution of issues regarding sites subject to this law, HUD will be removing nearly 30,000 of the worst public housing units in the country and providing a positive alternative over the next three years. The balance of funds will be used for general HOPE VI competition, demolition-only grants, and technical assistance.

[NATIVE AMERICAN] *INDIAN* HOUSING BLOCK GRANTS

(INCLUDING TRANSFER OF FUNDS)

For the [Native American] *Indian* Housing Block Grants program, as authorized under title I of the Native American Housing Assistance and Self-Determination Act of 1996 (NAHASDA) (Public Law 104–330), [$620,000,000] *$650,000,000*, to remain available until expended, of which [$2,000,000 shall be contracted through the Secretary as technical assistance and capacity building to be used by the National American Indian Housing Council in support of the implementation of NAHASDA and] up to [$4,000,000 by the Secretary] *$6,000,000 shall be* to support the inspection of Indian housing units, contract expertise, training, and technical assistance in the oversight and management of Indian housing and tenant-based assistance, including up to [$200,000] *$300,000* for related travel[: *Provided*, That of the amount provided under this heading, [$6,000,000]; *$5,000,000 shall be for the Indian Homeownership Intermediary Initiative; and $5,000,000* shall be made available for the cost of guaranteed notes and other obligations, as authorized by title VI of NAHASDA: *Provided* [*further*], That such costs, including the costs of modifying such notes and other obligations, shall be as defined in section 502 of the Congressional Budget Act of 1974, as amended: *Provided further*, That these funds are available to subsidize the total principal amount of any notes and other obligations, any part of which is to be guaranteed, not to exceed [$54,600,000] *$43,360,000*: *Provided further*, That for administrative expenses to carry out the guaranteed loan program, up to $200,000 from amounts in the first proviso, which shall be transferred to and merged with the appropriation for "Salaries and expenses", to be used only for the administrative costs of these guarantees. *(Departments of Veterans Affairs and Housing and Urban Development, and Independent Agencies Appropriations Act, 2000.)*

Program and Financing (in millions of dollars)

Identification code 86–0313–0–1–604	1999 actual	2000 est.	2001 est.
Obligations by program activity:			
00.01 Indian Housing Block Grants	577	789	644
00.02 Technical Assistance	5	6	6
10.00 Total new obligations (object class 41.0)	582	795	650
Budgetary resources available for obligation:			
21.40 Unobligated balance available, start of year	136	175	
22.00 New budget authority (gross)	620	620	650
23.90 Total budgetary resources available for obligation	756	795	650
23.95 Total new obligations	−582	−795	−650
24.40 Unobligated balance, end of year	175		
New budget authority (gross), detail:			
Discretionary:			
40.00 Appropriation	620	620	650
Change in unpaid obligations:			
72.40 Unpaid obligations, start of year: Obligated balance, start of year	1,121	1,105	1,235
73.10 Total new obligations	582	795	650
73.20 Total outlays (gross)	−597	−665	−699
74.40 Unpaid obligations, end of year: Obligated balance, end of year	1,105	1,235	1,186
Outlays (gross), detail:			
86.90 Outlays from new discretionary authority	59	192	202
86.93 Outlays from discretionary balances	538	473	497
87.00 Total outlays (gross)	597	665	699
Net budget authority and outlays:			
89.00 Budget authority	620	620	650
90.00 Outlays	597	665	699

Summary of Loan Levels, Subsidy Budget Authority and Outlays by Program (in millions of dollars)

Identification code 86–0313–0–1–604	1999 actual	2000 est.	2001 est.
Guaranteed loan levels supportable by subsidy budget authority:			
2150 Loan guarantee levels		55	43
2159 Total loan guarantee levels		55	43
Guaranteed loan subsidy (in percent):			
2320 Subsidy rate	11.07	11.07	11.07
2329 Weighted average subsidy rate	11.07	11.07	11.07
Guaranteed loan subsidy budget authority:			
2330 Subsidy budget authority	6	6	5
2339 Total subsidy budget authority	6	6	5
Guaranteed loan subsidy outlays:			
2340 Subsidy outlays		3	2
2349 Total subsidy outlays		3	2

Title I of the Native American Housing Assistance and Self-Determination Act (NAHASDA) of 1996 (P.L. 104–330) authorized the Indian Housing Block Grant (IHBG) program. This program provides an allocation of funds on a formula basis to Indian tribes and their tribally designated housing entities to help them address housing needs within their communities. Indian tribes use performance measures and benchmarks that are consistent with the national goals of the program but can base these measures on the needs and priorities they establish in their own Indian housing plan.

The Indian Housing Block Grant program includes $5 million to create an Indian Homeownership Intermediary with specific expertise in Indian country. The purpose of this initiative is to provide a catalyst for a homeownership market by providing homeownership and homeownership-related services on Indian reservations and other Indian areas.

The Indian Housing Block Grant program also includes a guaranteed loan provision (Title VI). A guarantee level of $43 million is proposed for this loan guarantee program for 2001. The subsidy rate for this program is set at 11.07 percent with a federal guarantee of 80 percent. A primary goal of the Title VI program is to encourage private lenders to provide financing in Indian country. Therefore, the program provides for the federal guarantee of notes or other obligations issued by Indian tribes or tribally designated housing entities for the purpose of financing affordable housing activities described in section 202 of the Act. A tribe or its tribally designated housing entity can pledge up to five times its future IHBG funds to collaterize the loan.

As required by the Federal Credit Reform Act of 1990, this account records, for this program, the subsidy costs associated with the loan guarantees committed in 1998 and beyond (including modifications of guarantees that resulted from obligations in any given year), as well as administrative expenses of this program. The subsidy amounts are estimated on a present value basis; the administrative expenses are estimated on a cash basis.

Public enterprise funds:

LOW-RENT PUBLIC HOUSING—LOANS AND OTHER EXPENSES

Program and Financing (in millions of dollars)

Identification code 86–4098–0–3–604	1999 actual	2000 est.	2001 est.
Obligations by program activity:			
09.01 Reimbursable program: Capital investment loans to PHAs	17	40	40
10.00 Total new obligations (object class 33.0)	17	40	40
Budgetary resources available for obligation:			
21.40 Unobligated balance available, start of year	17	20	20
22.00 New budget authority (gross)	108	111	111
22.60 Portion applied to repay debt	–88	–71	–71
23.90 Total budgetary resources available for obligation	37	60	60
23.95 Total new obligations	–17	–40	–40
24.40 Unobligated balance available, end of year	20	20	20
New budget authority (gross), detail:			
Mandatory:			
67.15 Authority to borrow (indefinite)	25	40	40
69.00 Offsetting collections (cash)	83	71	71
70.00 Total new budget authority (gross)	108	111	111
Change in unpaid obligations:			
72.40 Unpaid obligations, start of year: Obligated balance, start of year	965	866	790
73.10 Total new obligations	17	40	40
73.20 Total outlays (gross)	–116	–116	–116
74.40 Unpaid obligations, end of year: Obligated balance, end of year	866	790	714
Outlays (gross), detail:			
86.97 Outlays from new mandatory authority	28	40	40
86.98 Outlays from mandatory balances	88	76	76
87.00 Total outlays (gross)	116	116	116
Offsets:			
Against gross budget authority and outlays:			
Offsetting collections (cash) from:			
88.00 Federal sources	–12	....	....
88.40 Non-Federal sources	–71	–71	–71
88.90 Total, offsetting collections (cash)	–83	–71	–71
Net budget authority and outlays:			
89.00 Budget authority	25	40	40
90.00 Outlays	32	45	45

Status of Direct Loans (in millions of dollars)

Identification code 86–4098–0–3–604	1999 actual	2000 est.	2001 est.
Cumulative balance of direct loans outstanding:			
1210 Outstanding, start of year	1,492	1,421	1,350
1251 Repayments: Repayments and prepayments	–71	–71	–71
1290 Outstanding, end of year	1,421	1,350	1,279

Status of Guaranteed Loans (in millions of dollars)

Identification code 86–4098–0–3–604	1999 actual	2000 est.	2001 est.
Cumulative balance of guaranteed loans outstanding:			
2210 Outstanding, start of year	3,307	3,026	2,745
2251 Repayments and prepayments	–281	–281	–281
2290 Outstanding, end of year	3,026	2,745	2,464
Memorandum:			
2299 Guaranteed amount of guaranteed loans outstanding, end of year	3,026	2,745	2,464

The Low-Rent Public Housing Loan Fund provides direct Federal loans to fund remaining Public Housing Agency and Indian Housing Authority construction, acquisition, and modernization activities reserved under the Annual Contributions appropriation through 1986. These loans are made from borrowings from the Treasury. Under legislation enacted during 1986 (Public Law 99–272), the borrowings from the Treasury are forgiven at the end of each fiscal year and the loans to PHAs/IHAs are forgiven as construction, acquisition, and modernization activities are completed. Under the provisions of this legislation, $25 million of borrowings from the Treasury were forgiven in 1999, an estimated $40 million will be borrowed from the Treasury and forgiven in 2000, and an estimated $40 million will be borrowed from the Treasury and forgiven in 2001.

Since 1987, new reservations of capital funds for construction, acquisition, and modernization activities have been provided directly from the Annual Contributions and Public Housing Capital Fund appropriations.

Operating results.—The actual and estimated net operating income for 1998, 1999, 2000 and 2001 follows:

Statement of Operations (in millions of dollars)

Identification code 86–4098–0–3–604	1998 actual	1999 actual	2000 est.	2001 est.
0101 Revenue	104	100	100	100
0102 Expense	–95	–91	–91	–91
0105 Net income or loss (–)	9	9	9	9

Balance Sheet (in millions of dollars)

Identification code 86–4098–0–3–604	1998 actual	1999 actual	2000 est.	2001 est.
ASSETS:				
Federal assets:				
1101 Fund balances with Treasury	968	886	886	886
Investments in US securities:				
1106 Receivables, net	1,585	....	....	....
Net value of assets related to pre–1992 direct loans receivable and acquired defaulted guaranteed loans receivable:				
1601 Direct loans, gross	35	1,447	1,447	1,447
1602 Interest receivable	3	89	89	89
1603 Allowance for estimated uncollectible loans and interest (–)	–12	–12	–12	–12
1604 Direct loans and interest receivable, net	26	1,524	1,524	1,524
1699 Value of assets related to direct loans	26	1,524	1,524	1,524
1999 Total assets	2,579	2,410	2,410	2,410
LIABILITIES:				
Federal liabilities:				
2102 Interest payable	181	173	173	173
2104 Resources payable to Treasury	1,491	1,420	1,420	1,420
2207 Non-Federal liabilities: Other	1	–15	–15	–15
2999 Total liabilities	1,673	1,578	1,578	1,578
NET POSITION:				
3100 Appropriated capital	866	821	821	821
3300 Cumulative results of operations	40	11	11	11
3999 Total net position	906	832	832	832
4999 Total liabilities and net position	2,579	2,410	2,410	2,410

Credit accounts:

INDIAN HOUSING LOAN GUARANTEE FUND PROGRAM ACCOUNT

(INCLUDING TRANSFER OF FUNDS)

For the cost of guaranteed loans, as authorized by section 184 of the Housing and Community Development Act of 1992 (106 Stat. 3739), $6,000,000, to remain available until expended: *Provided*, That such costs, including the costs of modifying such loans, shall be as defined in section 502 of the Congressional Budget Act of 1974, as amended: *Provided further*, That these funds are available to subsidize total loan principal, any part of which is to be guaranteed, not to exceed $71,956,000.

In addition, for administrative expenses to carry out the guaranteed loan program, up to $150,000 from amounts in the first paragraph, which shall be transferred to and merged with the appropriation for "Salaries and expenses", to be used only for the administrative costs of these guarantees. *(Departments of Veterans Affairs and Housing and Urban Development, and Independent Agencies Appropriations Act, 2000.)*

Program and Financing (in millions of dollars)

Identification code 86–0223–0–1–371	1999 actual	2000 est.	2001 est.
Obligations by program activity:			
00.02 Guaranteed loan subsidy	1	6	6
10.00 Total new obligations (object class 41.0)	1	6	6
Budgetary resources available for obligation:			
21.40 Unobligated balance available, start of year	4	13	13
22.00 New budget authority (gross)	10	6	6
22.10 Resources available from recoveries of prior year obligations	1		
23.90 Total budgetary resources available for obligation	15	19	19
23.95 Total new obligations	−1	−6	−6
24.40 Unobligated balance available, end of year	13	13	13
New budget authority (gross), detail:			
Discretionary:			
40.00 Appropriation	6	6	6
50.00 Reappropriation	4		
70.00 Total new budget authority (gross)	10	6	6
Change in unpaid obligations:			
72.40 Unpaid obligations, start of year: Obligated balance, start of year	6	3	2
73.10 Total new obligations	1	6	6
73.20 Total outlays (gross)	−2	−7	−7
73.40 Adjustments in expired accounts (net)	−2		
73.45 Adjustments in unexpired accounts	−1		
74.40 Unpaid obligations, end of year: Obligated balance, end of year	3	2	1
Outlays (gross), detail:			
86.90 Outlays from new discretionary authority	1	1	1
86.93 Outlays from discretionary balances	1	6	6
87.00 Total outlays (gross)	2	7	7
Net budget authority and outlays:			
89.00 Budget authority	10	6	6
90.00 Outlays	2	7	7

Summary of Loan Levels, Subsidy Budget Authority and Outlays by Program (in millions of dollars)

Identification code 86–0223–0–1–371	1999 actual	2000 est.	2001 est.
Guaranteed loan levels supportable by subsidy budget authority:			
2150 Loan guarantee levels	12	72	72
2159 Total loan guarantee levels	12	72	72
Guaranteed loan subsidy (in percent):			
2320 Subsidy rate	8.13	8.13	8.13
2329 Weighted average subsidy rate	8.13	8.13	8.13
Guaranteed loan subsidy budget authority:			
2330 Subsidy budget authority	10	6	6
2339 Total subsidy budget authority	10	6	6
Guaranteed loan subsidy outlays:			
2340 Subsidy outlays	2	7	7
2349 Total subsidy outlays	2	7	7

As required by the Federal Credit Reform Act of 1990, this account records, for this program, the subsidy costs associated with the loan guarantees committed in 1992 and beyond (including modifications of guarantees that resulted from obligations in any year). The subsidy amounts are estimated on a net present value basis. The administrative expenses are shown on a cash basis.

This program provides access to sources of private financing for Indian families, Indian tribes and their tribally designated housing entities who otherwise could not acquire housing financing because of the unique legal status of Indian trust land.

It is anticipated that the funding requested for 2001 will be used to guarantee approximately 450 loans.

INDIAN HOUSING LOAN GUARANTEE FUND FINANCING ACCOUNT

Program and Financing (in millions of dollars)

Identification code 86–4104–0–3–604	1999 actual	2000 est.	2001 est.
Budgetary resources available for obligation:			
21.40 Unobligated balance available, start of year	4	6	13
22.00 New financing authority (gross)	2	7	7
23.90 Total budgetary resources available for obligation	6	13	20
24.40 Unobligated balance available, end of year	6	13	20
New financing authority (gross), detail:			
Discretionary:			
68.00 Spending authority from offsetting collections (gross): Federal sources	2	7	7
Offsets:			
Against gross financing authority and financing disbursements:			
88.00 Offsetting collections (cash) from: Federal sources: Payments from program account	−2	−7	−7
Net financing authority and financing disbursements:			
89.00 Financing authority			
90.00 Financing disbursements	−2	−7	−7

Status of Guaranteed Loans (in millions of dollars)

Identification code 86–4104–0–3–604	1999 actual	2000 est.	2001 est.
Position with respect to appropriations act limitation on commitments:			
2111 Limitation on guaranteed loans made by private lenders	81	72	72
2112 Uncommitted loan guarantee limitation	−69		
2150 Total guaranteed loan commitments	12	72	72
2199 Guaranteed amount of guaranteed loan commitments	12	72	72
Cumulative balance of guaranteed loans outstanding:			
2210 Outstanding, start of year	38	47	84
2231 Disbursements of new guaranteed loans	17	40	40
2251 Repayments and prepayments	−8	−3	−3
2290 Outstanding, end of year	47	84	121
Memorandum:			
2299 Guaranteed amount of guaranteed loans outstanding, end of year	47	84	121

As required by the Federal Credit Reform Act of 1990, this non-budgetary account records all cash flows to and from the Government resulting from the loan guarantees committed in 1992 and beyond (including modifications of loan guarantees that resulted from obligations in any year). The amounts in this account are a means of financing and are not included in the budget totals. As required by the Federal Credit Reform Act of 1990, no administrative expenses can be recorded in the financing account.

Balance Sheet (in millions of dollars)

Identification code 86–4104–0–3–604	1998 actual	1999 actual	2000 est.	2001 est.
ASSETS:				
1101 Federal assets: Fund balances with Treasury	4	6	4	4
1999 Total assets	4	6	4	4
LIABILITIES:				
2204 Non-Federal liabilities: Liabilities for loan guarantees	4	6	3	3
2999 Total liabilities	4	6	3	3
4999 Total liabilities and net position	4	6	3	3

Title VI Indian Federal Guarantees Financing Account

Program and Financing (in millions of dollars)

Identification code 86–4244–0–3–604	1999 actual	2000 est.	2001 est.
Budgetary resources available for obligation:			
21.40 Unobligated balance available, start of year			3
22.00 New financing authority (gross)		3	2
23.90 Total budgetary resources available for obligation		3	5
23.95 Total new obligations			
24.40 Unobligated balance available, end of year		3	5
New financing authority (gross), detail:			
Discretionary:			
68.00 Spending authority from offsetting collections (gross): Offsetting collections (cash)		3	2
Offsets:			
Against gross financing authority and financing disbursements:			
88.00 Offsetting collections (cash) from: Federal sources		−3	−2
Net financing authority and financing disbursements:			
89.00 Financing authority			
90.00 Financing disbursements		−3	−2

Status of Guaranteed Loans (in millions of dollars)

Identification code 86–4244–0–3–604	1999 actual	2000 est.	2001 est.
Position with respect to appropriations act limitation on commitments:			
2111 Limitation on guaranteed loans made by private lenders	55	55	43
2112 Uncommitted loan guarantee limitation	−55		
2150 Total guaranteed loan commitments		55	43
Cumulative balance of guaranteed loans outstanding:			
2210 Outstanding, start of year			52
2231 Disbursements of new guaranteed loans		55	43
2251 Repayments and prepayments		−3	−3
2290 Outstanding, end of year		52	92
Memorandum:			
2299 Guaranteed amount of guaranteed loans outstanding, end of year		52	92

As required by the Federal Credit Reform Act of 1990, this non-budgetary account records all cash flows to and from the Government resulting from loan guarantees committed in 1992 and beyond (including modifications of loan guarantees that resulted from commitments in any year). The amounts in this account are a means of financing and are not included in the budget totals. As required by the Federal Credit Reform Act of 1990, no administrative expenses can be recorded in the financing account.

COMMUNITY PLANNING AND DEVELOPMENT

Federal Funds

General and special funds:

Housing Opportunities for Persons with AIDS

For carrying out the Housing Opportunities for Persons with AIDS program, as authorized by the AIDS Housing Opportunity Act (42 U.S.C. 12901), [$232,000,000] *$260,000,000*, to remain available until expended: *Provided*, That the Secretary may use up to [0.75] *1* percent of the funds under this heading for technical assistance. *(Departments of Veterans Affairs and Housing and Urban Development, and Independent Agencies Appropriations Act, 2000.)*

Program and Financing (in millions of dollars)

Identification code 86–0308–0–1–604	1999 actual	2000 est.	2001 est.
Obligations by program activity:			
00.01 Housing for AIDs victims	208	289	260
10.00 Total new obligations (object class 41.0)	208	289	260
Budgetary resources available for obligation:			
21.40 Unobligated balance available, start of year	40	57	
22.00 New budget authority (gross)	225	232	260
23.90 Total budgetary resources available for obligation	265	289	260
23.95 Total new obligations	−208	−289	−260
24.40 Unobligated balance available, end of year	57		
New budget authority (gross), detail:			
Discretionary:			
40.00 Appropriation	225	232	260
Change in unpaid obligations:			
72.40 Unpaid obligations, start of year: Obligated balance, start of year	440	436	513
73.10 Total new obligations	208	289	260
73.20 Total outlays (gross)	−211	−212	−213
74.40 Unpaid obligations, end of year: Obligated balance, end of year	436	513	560
Outlays (gross), detail:			
86.90 Outlays from new discretionary authority	2	5	5
86.93 Outlays from discretionary balances	209	207	207
87.00 Total outlays (gross)	211	212	213
Net budget authority and outlays:			
89.00 Budget authority	225	232	260
90.00 Outlays	211	212	213

The Housing Opportunities for Persons with AIDS program provides States and localities with resources and incentives to devise long-term comprehensive strategies for meeting the housing needs of persons with HIV/AIDS and their families.

One percent of funds is used for technical assistance to grantees and up to 0.5 percent is used for management information systems support. States and metropolitan areas receive 90 percent of the remaining funds by formula based on the incidence of HIV/AIDS in their jurisdictions. The final 10 percent is awarded competitively to States, local governments, and private nonprofit entities for projects of national significance. Awards are also made to States and local governments for projects in jurisdictions which do not qualify for a formula allocation. The requested funding for 2001 will support approximately 48,000 housing units for persons with HIV/AIDS and their families.

Community Development Block Grants

(including transfers of funds)

For grants to States and units of general local government and for related expenses, not otherwise provided for, to carry out a community development grants program as authorized by title I of the Housing and Community Development Act of 1974, as amended (the

General and special funds—Continued

COMMUNITY DEVELOPMENT BLOCK GRANTS—Continued

(INCLUDING TRANSFERS OF FUNDS)—Continued

"Act" herein) (42 U.S.C. 5301), [$4,800,000,000] *$4,900,000,000*, to remain available until September 30, [2002] *2003*: *Provided*, That [$67,000,000] *$69,000,000* shall be for *flexible* grants to Indian tribes notwithstanding section 106(a)(1) of such Act, *of which $2,000,000 shall be for the Native American Economic Development Access Center*, $3,000,000 shall be available as a grant to the Housing Assistance Council, $2,200,000 shall be available as a grant to the National American Indian Housing Council, *and $5,000,000 for Tribal Colleges and Universities*; and [$41,500,000] *$68,500,000* shall be for grants pursuant to section 107 of the Act, *including $5,000,000 for New Markets University Partnership pilot grants*, including $2,000,000 to support Alaska Native serving institutions and native Hawaiian serving institutions, as defined under the Higher Education Act, as amended: *Provided further*, That [$20,000,000] *$17,500,000* shall be for grants pursuant to the Self Help Housing Opportunity Program: *Provided further, That $22,000,000 shall be for grants for economic revitalization and community development initiatives in the Mississippi Delta Region (as such region is defined in P.L. 100–460): Provided further*, That not to exceed 20 percent of any grant made with funds appropriated herein (other than a grant made available in this paragraph to the Housing Assistance Council or the National American Indian Housing Council, or a grant using funds under section 107(b)(3) of the Housing and Community Development Act of 1974, as amended) shall be expended for "Planning and Management Development" and "Administration" as defined in regulations promulgated by the department[: *Provided further*, That all balances for the Economic Development Initiative grants program, the John Heinz Neighborhood Development program, grants to Self Help Housing Opportunity program, and the Moving to Work Demonstration program previously funded within the "Annual Contributions for Assisted Housing" account shall be transferred to this account, to be available for the purposes for which they were originally appropriated].

Of the amount made available under this heading, [$23,750,000] *$31,500,000* shall be made available for capacity building[, of which $20,000,000 shall be made available for "Capacity Building for Community Development and Affordable Housing",] for LISC and the Enterprise Foundation for activities as authorized by section 4 of the HUD Demonstration Act of 1993 (Public Law 103–120), as in effect immediately before June 12, 1997, with not less than $4,000,000 of the funding to be used in rural areas, including tribal areas, and of which [$3,750,000] *$7,500,000* shall be [made available] *for capacity building activities administered by* [to] Habitat for Humanity International.

[Of the amount made available under this heading, the Secretary of Housing and Urban Development may use up to $55,000,000 for supportive services for public housing residents, as authorized by section 34 of the United States Housing Act of 1937, as amended, and for grants for service coordinators and congregate services for the elderly and disabled residents of public and assisted housing: *Provided further*, That amounts made available for congregate services and service coordinators for the elderly and disabled under this heading and in prior fiscal years may be used by grantees to reimburse themselves for costs incurred in connection with providing service coordinators previously advanced by grantees out of other funds due to delays in the granting by or receipt of funds from the Secretary, and the funds so made available to grantees for congregate services or service coordinators under this heading or in prior years shall be considered as expended by the grantees upon such reimbursement. The Secretary shall not condition the availability of funding made available under this heading or in prior years for congregate services or service coordinators upon any grantee's obligation or expenditure of any prior funding.]

[Of the amount made available under this heading, $30,000,000 shall be available for neighborhood initiatives that are utilized to improve the conditions of distressed and blighted areas and neighborhoods, to stimulate investment, economic diversification, and community revitalization in areas with population outmigration or a stagnating or declining economic base, or to determine whether housing benefits can be integrated more effectively with welfare reform initiatives: *Provided*, that any unobligated balances of amounts set aside for neighborhood initiatives in fiscal years 1998 and 1999 may be utilized for any of the foregoing purposes: *Provided further*, That of the amount set aside for fiscal year 2000 under this paragraph, $23,000,000 shall be used for grants specified in the statement of the managers of the committee of conference accompanying this Act.]

Of the amount made available under this heading, notwithstanding any other provision of law, [$42,500,000] *$75,000,000* shall be available for YouthBuild program activities authorized by subtitle D of title IV of the Cranston-Gonzalez National Affordable Housing Act, as amended, and such activities shall be an eligible activity with respect to any funds made available under this heading: *Provided*, That local YouthBuild programs that demonstrate an ability to leverage private and nonprofit funding shall be given a priority for YouthBuild funding[: *Provided further*, That of the amount provided under this paragraph, [$2,500,000] *$3,750,000* shall be set aside and made available for a grant to Youthbuild USA for capacity building for community development and affordable housing activities as specified in section 4 of the HUD Demonstration Act of 1993, as amended].

Of the amount made available under this heading, [$275,000,000] *$100,000,000* shall be available for grants for the Economic Development Initiative (EDI), *as authorized by section 108(q) of the Act*, to finance a variety of economic development efforts[, including $240,000,000 for making individual grants for targeted economic investments in accordance with the terms and conditions specified for such grants in the statement of the managers of the committee of conference accompanying this Act].

Of the amount made available under this heading, $20,000,000 shall be available to assist community-based (including religiously affiliated) non-profit organizations in their efforts to supply affordable housing, create economic opportunity, promote the goals of fair housing, and increase the effectiveness of other programs and initiatives administered in distressed high poverty areas by the Secretary: Provided, That these amounts for technical assistance and capacity building activities for community-based (including religiously affiliated) non-profit organizations shall be administered by the Center for Community and Interfaith Partnerships at the Department of Housing and Urban Development.

For the cost of guaranteed loans, [$29,000,000] *$28,000,000*, as authorized by section 108 of the Housing and Community Development Act of 1974: *Provided*, That such costs, including the cost of modifying such loans, shall be as defined in section 502 of the Congressional Budget Act of 1974, as amended: *Provided further*, That these funds are available to subsidize total loan principal, any part of which is to be guaranteed, not to exceed [$1,261,000,000] *$1,217,000,000*, notwithstanding any aggregate limitation on outstanding obligations guaranteed in section 108(k) of the Housing and Community Development Act of 1974: *Provided further*, That in addition, *up to $2,000,000* for administrative expenses to carry out the guaranteed loan program[, $1,000,000], which shall be transferred to and merged with the appropriation for "Salaries and expenses".

[The Secretary is directed to transfer the administration of the small cities component of the Community Development Block Grant Program for the funds allocated for the State of New York under section 106(d) of the Housing and Community Development Act of 1974 for fiscal year 2000 and all fiscal years thereafter to the State of New York to be administered by the Governor of New York]. *(Departments of Veterans Affairs and Housing and Urban Development, and Independent Agencies Appropriations Act, 2000.)*

Program and Financing (in millions of dollars)

Identification code 86–0162–0–1–451	1999 actual	2000 est.	2001 est.
Obligations by program activity:			
00.01 Community development	4,797	5,712	4,895
10.00 Total new obligations (object class 41.0)	4,797	5,712	4,895
Budgetary resources available for obligation:			
21.40 Unobligated balance available, start of year	832	931	
22.00 New budget authority (gross)	4,893	4,781	4,895
22.10 Resources available from recoveries of prior year obligations	4		
23.90 Total budgetary resources available for obligation	5,729	5,712	4,895
23.95 Total new obligations	−4,797	−5,712	−4,895
23.98 Unobligated balance expiring or withdrawn	−2		
24.40 Unobligated balance available, end of year	931		
New budget authority (gross), detail:			
Discretionary:			
40.00 Appropriation	4,750	4,800	4,895

40.15	Appropriation (emergency)	150		
40.76	Reduction pursuant to P.L. 106–113		−19	
41.00	Transferred to other accounts	−7		
43.00	Appropriation (total discretionary)	4,893	4,781	4,895
	Change in unpaid obligations:			
72.40	Unpaid obligations, start of year: Obligated balance, start of year	9,031	9,013	10,046
73.10	Total new obligations	4,797	5,712	4,895
73.20	Total outlays (gross)	−4,804	−4,856	−4,826
73.31	Obligated balance transferred to other accounts		−100	
73.32	Obligated balance transferred from other accounts		277	
73.40	Adjustments in expired accounts (net)	−7		
73.45	Adjustments in unexpired accounts	−4		
74.40	Unpaid obligations, end of year: Obligated balance, end of year	9,013	10,046	10,115
	Outlays (gross), detail:			
86.90	Outlays from new discretionary authority	98	96	98
86.93	Outlays from discretionary balances	4,706	4,760	4,728
87.00	Total outlays (gross)	4,804	4,856	4,826
	Net budget authority and outlays:			
89.00	Budget authority	4,893	4,781	4,895
90.00	Outlays	4,804	4,856	4,826

Summary of Budget Authority and Outlays

(in millions of dollars)

	1999 actual	*2000 est.*	*2001 est.*
Enacted/requested:			
Budget Authority	4,893	4,781	4,895
Outlays	4,804	4,856	4,826
Legislative proposal, not subject to PAYGO:			
Budget Authority			5
Outlays			
Total:			
Budget Authority	4,893	4,781	4,900
Outlays	4,804	4,856	4,826

Title I of the Housing and Community Development Act of 1974, as amended, authorizes the Secretary to make grants to units of general local government and States to fund local community development programs.

The 2001 Budget allocates $69 million to Indian tribes as authorized by Section 106(a)(1) of the Housing and Community Development Act of 1974. Since its inception, funds made available to Native American communities have supported a wide variety of community development activities, predominantly, but not exclusively, community facilities, infrastructure and buildings to help meet the basic needs of low and moderate income community members. Since the vast majority of eligible tribes and Alaska Native Villages have nonexistent tax bases, this program has helped to finance those public facilities needed to maintain or establish community viability. While it has had a significant impact on many Native American communities throughout the Nation, basic community development needs throughout Indian Country remain substantial.

Seventy percent of formula funds are allocated to metropolitan cities and urban counties that receive their grants using the higher of two objective formulas. States and small cities receive 30 percent of the formula funds. The proposed level of funding for CDBG and the Section 108 Loan Guarantee Program will support an estimated 256,500 jobs. These funds will also help to rehabilitate 169,300 housing units.

Section 107 Grants include funding for Insular Areas, technical assistance, management information systems support, Historically Black Colleges and Universities, a New Markets University Partnerships pilot program, Hispanic serving Institutions, Alaska and Hawaiian serving Institutions, the Community Development Work Study and Community Outreach Partnership Centers (COPC) programs.

As authorized by Section 4 of the HUD Demonstration Act of 1993, the National Community Development Initiative (NCDI) will help build capacity of community-based development corporations and housing development organizations, and assist such corporations and organizations to carry out community development and affordable housing activities. The 2001 Budget includes $24 million for this program.

The Youthbuild program provides resources to educate, train and supply stipends for economically disadvantaged young adults through their participation in the construction and rehabilitation of housing for low-income and homeless persons. The program expands the supply of affordable housing and, at the same time, enables high school drop-outs to obtain the education and employment skills necessary to achieve self-sufficiency. The 2001 request for $75 million will provide more than 5,100 young people with skills they need to obtain jobs and will provide approximately 750 families in distressed communities with homes.

The 2001 Budget proposes $100 million for the Economic Development Initiative (EDI) program within the new Community Empowerment Fund to support an estimated 100,000 jobs in distressed areas. CEF will support the financing of critical economic development efforts, in tandem with the existing Section 108 guaranteed loan program. EDI funds provide enhanced security for Section 108 loans, and improve the viability of projects financed with these loans. The CEF, including a new trust mechanism that is being piloted in 2000, will facilitate and encourage the use of the Section 108 program by State and local governments.

HUD's Section 108 guaranteed loan program, when combined with EDI grants, supports jobs in distressed communities. Over the past six years, we have committed to 711 projects and completed the financing on 429 of those for a total of $1.7 billion—projects such as supermarkets in Washington, DC, and Houston, TX, industrial parks, and other business ventures. When all 711 projects are completed, an estimated 338,000 jobs will have been created or retained.

Funding of $22 million is requested for HUD's participation in the Mississippi Delta Regional Initiative. This initiative will provide funds and technical assistance for economic revitalization in the Delta region.

Up to $2 million is included for the development of a toll-free telephone assistance service center at HUD to Native Americans to provide information and answer inquiries about economic development assistance. The center will feature the following components: (1) a comprehensive inventory of Federal, state and private programs available to support economic development in Indian Country; (2) a comprehensive inventory of credit enhancements available to the financial community for lending and investing in Indian Country; and (3) a comprehensive inventory of private market incentives for companies doing business in Indian Country.

The 2001 Budget also includes $5 million in competitive grants to Tribal Colleges and Universities (TCU) to address community development needs in their communities. The TCUs funded would assist communities with neighborhood revitalization and housing and economic development. The predominant activities to be accomplished under this program would be to create partnerships, create community development corporations, develop supportive services for welfare to work initiatives, rehabilitate housing, promote economic development through small business incubators and job training programs and rehabilitate commercial properties. The target service population would be low- and moderate-income families within the communities served by the TCU.

The Community and Interfaith Partnerships set-aside initiative seeks to empower community-based (including religiously affiliated) non-profit organizations in their efforts to supply affordable housing and create economic opportunity, promote the goal of fair housing, and assist HUD in the disposition of foreclosed properties and increase the effectiveness of HUD programs in distressed high poverty areas. Eligi-

General and special funds—Continued

COMMUNITY DEVELOPMENT BLOCK GRANTS—Continued

(INCLUDING TRANSFERS OF FUNDS)—Continued

ble entities for these capacity building and technical assistance grants would include social service and community development (including religiously affiliated) organizations. The initiative would be funded through a $20 million set-aside within the HUD Community Development Block Grant Program and administered by the Center for Community and Interfaith Partnerships. No funds provided to a community-based organization under this heading shall be expended for sectarian worship, instruction, or proselytization.

The Department is finalizing an Optional Entitlement Communities (OEC) proposal under which cities as small as 25,000, that are not currently part of an entitlement county, and urban counties as small as 100,000 population could opt for "entitlement" status within a three year period. These new OEC's would receive formula grants directly from HUD.

COMMUNITY DEVELOPMENT BLOCK GRANTS

(Legislative proposal, not subject to PAYGO)

Program and Financing (in millions of dollars)

Identification code 86–0162–2–1–451	1999 actual	2000 est.	2001 est.
Obligations by program activity:			
00.02 New Markets University Partnership Initiative			5
10.00 Total new obligations (object class 41.0)			5
Budgetary resources available for obligation:			
22.00 New budget authority (gross)			5
23.95 Total new obligations			−5
New budget authority (gross), detail:			
Discretionary:			
40.00 Appropriation			5
Change in unpaid obligations:			
73.10 Total new obligations			5
74.40 Unpaid obligations, end of year: Obligated balance, end of year			5
Net budget authority and outlays:			
89.00 Budget authority			5
90.00 Outlays			

REGIONAL CONNECTIONS

(Legislative proposal, not subject to PAYGO)

Program and Financing (in millions of dollars)

Identification code 86–0325–2–1–452	1999 actual	2000 est.	2001 est.
Obligations by program activity:			
00.01 Grants for Regional Activities			25
10.00 Total new obligations (object class 41.0)			25
Budgetary resources available for obligation:			
22.00 New budget authority (gross)			25
23.95 Total new obligations			−25
New budget authority (gross), detail:			
Discretionary:			
40.00 Appropriation			25
Change in unpaid obligations:			
73.10 Total new obligations			25
73.20 Total outlays (gross)			−1
74.40 Unpaid obligations, end of year: Obligated balance, end of year			24
Outlays (gross), detail:			
86.90 Outlays from new discretionary authority			1
Net budget authority and outlays:			
89.00 Budget authority			25
90.00 Outlays			1

Regional Connections will provide $25 million to fund local partnerships to design and implement smarter growth strategies across jurisdictional lines. Such strategies may include: (a) compact development rules and incentives for new growth areas; and (b) coordinated reinvestment in already built-up and infrastructure-rich areas of participating regions. Participating regions will also be asked to outline strategies for managing economic and workforce development in ways that reinforce the overall development strategy. Eligible lead applicants will include states and groups of localities (cities, counties, towns), and partnerships of groups of localities and their state or states but these will demonstrate active partnerships with private and nonprofit stakeholders. Where formally designated by eligible lead applicants, existing regional institutions, such as Councils of Government (COGs), regional councils, and Metropolitan Planning Organizations (MPOs), will also be eligible as lead applicants.

The solutions to challenges produced by new development patterns extend far beyond individual jurisdictional boundaries. Cities and suburbs are increasingly inter-connected. Many communities recognize this and are developing strategies to improve cooperation to make communities more livable. Civic, business and government leaders are forging partnerships that transcend jurisdictional and sectional boundaries to address the critical issues; yet, many of these strategies require assistance to move them to implementation.

Regional Connections will complement existing Federal programs that direct growth and investment patterns. Competing localities will be asked to demonstrate how Regional Connections activities will build on: Transportation Department (DOT)-funded TEA21 transportation planning and investment; HUD/EPA Brownfields; HUD-required Consolidated Plans for CDBG, HOME and other funds; Empowerment Zones/Enterprise Communities (EZs/ECs); and other inter-jurisdictional strategies developed with Federal funds.

[URBAN EMPOWERMENT ZONES]

[For grants in connection with a second round of the empowerment zones program in urban areas, designated by the Secretary of Housing and Urban Development in fiscal year 1999 pursuant to the Taxpayer Relief Act of 1997, $55,000,000 to the Secretary of Housing and Urban Development for "Urban Empowerment Zones", including $3,666,000 for each empowerment zone for use in conjunction with economic development activities consistent with the strategic plan of each empowerment zone, to remain available until expended.] *(Departments of Veterans Affairs and Housing and Urban Development, and Independent Agencies Appropriations Act, 2000.)*

Program and Financing (in millions of dollars)

Identification code 86–0315–0–1–451	1999 actual	2000 est.	2001 est.
Obligations by program activity:			
00.01 Develop urban sites	42	62	
10.00 Total new obligations (object class 41.0)	42	62	
Budgetary resources available for obligation:			
21.40 Unobligated balance available, start of year	4	7	
22.00 New budget authority (gross)	45	55	
23.90 Total budgetary resources available for obligation	49	62	
23.95 Total new obligations	−42	−62	
24.40 Unobligated balance available, end of year	7		
New budget authority (gross), detail:			
Discretionary:			
40.00 Appropriation	45	55	

	1999 actual	2000 est.	2001 est.
Change in unpaid obligations:			
72.40 Unpaid obligations, start of year: Obligated balance, start of year	1	39	84
73.10 Total new obligations	42	62	....
73.20 Total outlays (gross)	−3	−17	−37
74.40 Unpaid obligations, end of year: Obligated balance, end of year	39	84	47
Outlays (gross), detail:			
86.90 Outlays from new discretionary authority	....	1	....
86.93 Outlays from discretionary balances	3	16	37
87.00 Total outlays (gross)	3	17	37
Net budget authority and outlays:			
89.00 Budget authority	45	55	....
90.00 Outlays	3	17	37

Summary of Budget Authority and Outlays

(in millions of dollars)

Enacted/requested:	1999 actual	2000 est.	2001 est.
Budget Authority	45	55	....
Outlays	3	17	37
Legislative proposal, subject to PAYGO:			
Budget Authority	....	....	150
Outlays	....	....	3
Total:			
Budget Authority	45	55	150
Outlays	3	17	40

The goal of the Empowerment Zone (EZ) initiative is to revitalize city neighborhoods in a way that will retain and attract middle-class residents and provide employment opportunities that will move people from welfare to work. Grant funds will allow the 15 new urban EZs that were authorized by the Taxpayer Relief Act of 1997, in accordance with their strategic plans, to create economic opportunity in America's distressed communities, with a special emphasis on stimulating job creation linked to welfare reform. Flexible grant funds will be used to integrate human capital needs with economic development initiatives. Empowerment Zone principals include a strategic vision for change, a community-based partnership, providing economic opportunity and sustainable community development.

The 2001 budget proposes legislation to authorize mandatory funding for the 15 urban Empowerment Zones designated in January 1999, for a nine year commitment of $1.5 billion. In addition, $100 million in discretionary funds was provided for Round II EZs in the 1999 and 2000 Appropriations Act (P.L. 105–276 and P.L. 106–74).

Funding will be available for a broad range of activities aimed at assisting residents, businesses and organizations in urban EZs, including: community policing; health care; neighborhood development; brownfields clean-up and redevelopment; support for financing of capital projects; education; work force preparation and job creation efforts linked to welfare reform; leveraging private sector resources, repayment of debt financing by municipal bonds; financing of projects in conjunction with the Section 108 loan guarantee program and other economic development projects; support for project-based rental assistance; and, financing other housing activities.

EZs are helping to stimulate billions of dollars in private investment, reviving inner city neighborhoods once given up for dead, and supporting jobs and helping families move from welfare to work.

Urban Empowerment Zones

(Legislative proposal, subject to PAYGO)

Program and Financing (in millions of dollars)

Identification code 86–0315–4–1–451	1999 actual	2000 est.	2001 est.
Obligations by program activity:			
00.01 Develop urban sites	....	....	150
10.00 Total new obligations (object class 41.0)	....	....	150
Budgetary resources available for obligation:			
22.00 New budget authority (gross)	....	....	150
23.95 Total new obligations	....	....	−150
New budget authority (gross), detail:			
Mandatory:			
60.00 Appropriation	....	....	150
Change in unpaid obligations:			
73.10 Total new obligations	....	....	150
73.20 Total outlays (gross)	....	....	−3
74.40 Unpaid obligations, end of year: Obligated balance, end of year	....	....	147
Outlays (gross), detail:			
86.97 Outlays from new mandatory authority	....	....	3
Net budget authority and outlays:			
89.00 Budget authority	....	....	150
90.00 Outlays	....	....	3

Brownfields Redevelopment

For Economic Development Grants, as authorized by section 108(q) of the Housing and Community Development Act of 1974, as amended, for Brownfields redevelopment projects, [$25,000,000] *$50,000,000*, to remain available until expended: *Provided*, That the Secretary of Housing and Urban Development shall make these grants available on a competitive basis as specified in section 102 of the Department of Housing and Urban Development Reform Act of 1989. *(Departments of Veterans Affairs and Housing and Urban Development, and Independent Agencies Appropriations Act, 2000.)*

Program and Financing (in millions of dollars)

Identification code 86–0314–0–1–451	1999 actual	2000 est.	2001 est.
Obligations by program activity:			
00.01 Cleanup and develop contaminated sites	....	75	50
10.00 Total new obligations (object class 41.0)	....	75	50
Budgetary resources available for obligation:			
21.40 Unobligated balance available, start of year	25	50	....
22.00 New budget authority (gross)	25	25	50
23.90 Total budgetary resources available for obligation	50	75	50
23.95 Total new obligations	....	−75	−50
24.40 Unobligated balance available, end of year	50	....	....
New budget authority (gross), detail:			
Discretionary:			
40.00 Appropriation	25	25	50
Change in unpaid obligations:			
72.40 Unpaid obligations, start of year: Obligated balance, start of year	....	....	65
73.10 Total new obligations	....	75	50
73.20 Total outlays (gross)	....	−10	−28
74.40 Unpaid obligations, end of year: Obligated balance, end of year	....	65	87
Outlays (gross), detail:			
86.90 Outlays from new discretionary authority	....	1	1
86.93 Outlays from discretionary balances	....	9	27
87.00 Total outlays (gross)	....	10	28

General and special funds—Continued

BROWNFIELDS REDEVELOPMENT—Continued

Program and Financing (in millions of dollars)—Continued

Identification code 86–0314–0–1–451	1999 actual	2000 est.	2001 est.
Net budget authority and outlays:			
89.00 Budget authority	25	25	50
90.00 Outlays	....	10	28

The Brownfields Redevelopment program provides competitive economic development grants in conjunction with Section 108 loan guarantees for qualified brownfield projects. Eligible communities are invited to submit proposals to return contaminated sites to productive and employment-generating uses, with an emphasis on creating substantial numbers of jobs for lower-income people in physically and economically distressed neighborhoods.

Grants are made in accordance with section 108(q) selection criteria and such other criteria deemed appropriate for brownfield projects, including the extent to which an applicant is currently operating a brownfields program and is working with appropriate environmental regulatory agencies.

The Brownfields Redevelopment program was funded at $25 million in 1998, 1999 and 2000. The 2001 request of $50 million accelerates and expands the President's commitment to help communities clean up and redevelop the approximately 450,000 brownfields sites nationwide. This level of funding is expected to leverage $200 million in Section 108 loan guarantee commitments, which will support the creation of 20,000 to 25,000 jobs.

YOUTHBUILD PROGRAM

Program and Financing (in millions of dollars)

Identification code 86–0219–0–1–604	1999 actual	2000 est.	2001 est.
Change in unpaid obligations:			
72.40 Unpaid obligations, start of year: Obligated balance, start of year	4	2	....
73.20 Total outlays (gross)	−2	−2	....
74.40 Unpaid obligations, end of year: Obligated balance, end of year	2	....	....
Outlays (gross), detail:			
86.93 Outlays from discretionary balances	2	2	....
Net budget authority and outlays:			
89.00 Budget authority	....	....	....
90.00 Outlays	2	2	....

This program provides resources to educate, train, and provide stipends for economically disadvantaged young adults through their participation in the construction and rehabilitation of housing for low-income and homeless persons. The program expands the supply of affordable housing and, at the same time, enables high school dropouts to obtain the education and employment skills necessary to achieve self-sufficiency. The 2001 request of $75 million will provide more than 5,100 young people with skills they need to get jobs and will provide 750 families in distressed communities with homes. The Youthbuild program has been funded at a set-aside within the CDBG program since 1996. The obligated balance and outlays shown above represent activity in the separate youthbuild account.

HOME INVESTMENT PARTNERSHIPS PROGRAM

For the HOME investment partnerships program, as authorized under title II of the Cranston-Gonzalez National Affordable Housing Act (Public Law 101–625), as amended, [$1,600,000,000], *$1,650,000,000* to remain available until expended[: *Provided*, That up to $15,000,000 of these funds], *of which up to $24,000,000* shall be available for Housing Counseling under section 106 of the Housing and Urban Development Act of 1968[: *Provided further*, That $2,000,000 of these funds shall be made available as a grant to the National Housing Development Corporation for a program of housing acquisition and rehabilitation: *Provided further*, That all Housing Counseling program balances previously appropriated in the "Housing Counseling Assistance" account shall be transferred to this account, to be available for the purposes for which they were originally appropriated; *3 percent shall be for Native Americans and up to $5,000,000 shall be for the development and operation of integrated community development management information systems. (Departments of Veterans Affairs and Housing and Urban Development, and Independent Agencies Appropriations Act, 2000.)*

Program and Financing (in millions of dollars)

Identification code 86–0205–0–1–604	1999 actual	2000 est.	2001 est.
Obligations by program activity:			
00.01 HOME grants	1,647	1,791	1,650
10.00 Total new obligations (object class 41.0)	1,647	1,791	1,650
Budgetary resources available for obligation:			
21.40 Unobligated balance available, start of year	236	191	....
22.00 New budget authority (gross)	1,600	1,600	1,650
22.10 Resources available from recoveries of prior year obligations	2	....	....
23.90 Total budgetary resources available for obligation	1,838	1,791	1,650
23.95 Total new obligations	−1,647	−1,791	−1,650
24.40 Unobligated balance available, end of year	191	....	....
New budget authority (gross), detail:			
Discretionary:			
40.00 Appropriation	1,600	1,600	1,650
Change in unpaid obligations:			
72.40 Unpaid obligations, start of year: Obligated balance, start of year	3,650	3,947	4,081
73.10 Total new obligations	1,647	1,791	1,650
73.20 Total outlays (gross)	−1,347	−1,657	−1,734
73.45 Adjustments in unexpired accounts	−2	....	....
74.40 Unpaid obligations, end of year: Obligated balance, end of year	3,947	4,081	3,997
Outlays (gross), detail:			
86.90 Outlays from new discretionary authority	14	32	33
86.93 Outlays from discretionary balances	1,333	1,625	1,701
87.00 Total outlays (gross)	1,347	1,657	1,734
Net budget authority and outlays:			
89.00 Budget authority	1,600	1,600	1,650
90.00 Outlays	1,347	1,657	1,734

The HOME Investment Partnership program is authorized by the National Affordable Housing Act (P.L. 101–625). This program provides assistance to States and units of local government, through formula allocation, for the purpose of expanding the supply and affordability of housing. Eligible activities include acquisition, rehabilitation, and new construction of housing and tenant-based rental assistance. The 2001 request will result in the production of 92,064 units of affordable housing through new construction, rehabilitation, or acquisition. In addition, tenant-based rental assistance will be provided for 10,883 units.

The HOME request also includes up to $5 million to continue to develop, implement and refine integrated community development management information systems in order to establish a national database of local programs. Funding for technical assistance is also included.

Funding of $24 million for the Housing Counseling Assistance program is also included in this account. This program provides comprehensive housing counseling services, including pre-purchase, default, and renter counseling, to eligible homeowners and tenants. Up to three percent of these funds are set aside for housing counseling assistance for Native Americans. The Housing Counseling program was funded at $17.5 million in 1999, and $15 million in 2000 as set-asides in the HOME account.

HOMELESS ASSISTANCE GRANTS

For the emergency shelter grants program (as authorized under subtitle B of title IV of the Stewart B. McKinney Homeless Assistance Act, as amended); the supportive housing program (as authorized under subtitle C of title IV of such Act); the section 8 moderate rehabilitation single room occupancy program (as authorized under the United States Housing Act of 1937, as amended) to assist homeless individuals pursuant to section 441 of the Stewart B. McKinney Homeless Assistance Act; and the shelter plus care program (as authorized under subtitle F of title IV of such Act), [$1,020,000,000] *$1,200,000,000*, to remain available until expended, *of which $105,000,000 shall be for section 8 rental assistance under the Housing Act of 1937: Provided*, That [not less than 30 percent of these funds shall be used for permanent housing, and] all funding for services must be matched by 25 percent in funding by each grantee: [*Provided further*, That the Secretary of Housing and Urban Development shall conduct a review of any balances of amounts provided under this heading in any previous appropriations Acts that have been obligated but remain unexpended and shall deobligate any such amounts that the Secretary determines were obligated for contracts that are unlikely to be performed and award such amounts during this fiscal year:]*: Provided further, That all awards of assistance under this heading shall take into account proposed strategies to expand access to McKinney and non-McKinney-funded programs by coordinating and integrating homeless programs with other mainstream health, social services, and employment progams for which homeless populations may be eligible. These include Medicaid, State Children's Health Insurance Program, Temporary Assistance for Needy Families, Food Stamps, and services funding through the Mental Health and Substance Abuse Block Grant, Workforce Investment Act, and the Welfare-to-Work grant program: Provided further*, That up to 1 percent of the funds appropriated under this heading may be used for technical assistance *and management information systems*: [*Provided further*, That all balances previously appropriated in the "Emergency Shelter Grants", "Supportive Housing", "Supplemental Assistance for Facilities to Assist the Homeless", "Shelter Plus Care", "Section 8 Moderate Rehabilitation Single Room Occupancy", and "Innovative Homeless Initiatives Demonstration" accounts shall be transferred to and merged with this account, to be available for any authorized purpose under this heading]. *(Departments of Veterans Affairs and Housing and Urban Development, and Independent Agencies Appropriations Act, 2000.)*

Program and Financing (in millions of dollars)

Identification code 86–0192–0–1–604		1999 actual	2000 est.	2001 est.
	Obligations by program activity:			
00.01	Homeless assistance grants	934	2,197	1,095
00.02	Homeless assistance vouchers			105
10.00	Total new obligations (object class 41.0)	934	2,197	1,200
	Budgetary resources available for obligation:			
21.40	Unobligated balance available, start of year	1,019	1,072	
22.00	New budget authority (gross)	975	1,020	1,200
22.10	Resources available from recoveries of prior year obligations	12		
22.22	Unobligated balance transferred from other accounts		105	
23.90	Total budgetary resources available for obligation	2,006	2,197	1,200
23.95	Total new obligations	−934	−2,197	−1,200
24.40	Unobligated balance available, end of year	1,072		
	New budget authority (gross), detail:			
	Discretionary:			
	Appropriation:			
40.00	Appropriation	975	1,020	1,095
40.00	Appropriation			105
43.00	Appropriation (total discretionary)	975	1,020	1,200
	Change in unpaid obligations:			
72.40	Unpaid obligations, start of year: Obligated balance, start of year	1,588	1,867	3,774
73.10	Total new obligations	934	2,197	1,200
73.20	Total outlays (gross)	−643	−961	−1,112
73.32	Obligated balance transferred from other accounts		671	
73.45	Adjustments in unexpired accounts	−12		
74.40	Unpaid obligations, end of year: Obligated balance, end of year	1,867	3,774	3,862
	Outlays (gross), detail:			
86.90	Outlays from new discretionary authority	9	31	43
86.93	Outlays from discretionary balances	634	930	1,069
87.00	Total outlays (gross)	643	961	1,112
	Net budget authority and outlays:			
89.00	Budget authority	975	1,020	1,200
90.00	Outlays	643	961	1,112

The Homeless Assistance Grants program funds the Shelter Plus Care, Supportive Housing, Emergency Shelter Grants, and Section 8 Moderate Rehabilitation Single Room Occupancy programs. These funds will enable localities to continue to shape and implement comprehensive, flexible, coordinated "continuum of care" approaches to solving rather than institutionalizing homelessness. In fact, in recent years, many communities have made great strides in developing holistic continuum of care approaches to solving homelessness. A community-based process is required as part of the application process. Communities are required to include in their applications performance measures that contain specific goals that would accrue from the community's efforts, and are required to demonstrate tangible results on an annual basis. Requested funding would be available for a wide range of activities to assist homeless persons and prevent future homelessness. The 2001 request will fund 14,500 transitional beds and 11,000 permanent beds, all linked to supportive services.

Funding is also requested for technical assistance to provide needed assistance to grantees to resolve problems that hinder successful project completion and implementation, and for management information systems support, including the continuing operation of tracking systems required by House Report 105–610.

Finally, $105 million is for 18,000 housing vouchers for homeless families or individuals who have achieved a sufficient level of independence to move to permanent housing linked to services. These vouchers will offer the ongoing assistance so desperately needed to help move homeless people into the housing mainstream when they are ready to do so. These vouchers are intended for homeless individuals and families who would otherwise have the most difficult time in securing permanent housing resources, as determined through the approved Continuum of Care strategy. Helping them secure permanent housing will allow HUD to assist even more homeless persons through existing emergency and transitional programs.

RURAL HOUSING AND ECONOMIC DEVELOPMENT

(INCLUDING TRANSFER OF FUNDS)

For the Office of Rural Housing and Economic Development in the Department of Housing and Urban Development, [$25,000,000], *$27,000,000* to remain available until expended[: *Provided*, That of the amount under this heading, up to $3,000,000 shall be used to develop capacity at the State and local level for developing rural housing and for rural economic development and for maintaining a clearinghouse of ideas for innovative strategies for rural housing and economic development and revitalization: *Provided further*, That of the amount under this heading, at least $22,000,000], *which amount* shall be awarded [by June 1, 2000] to Indian tribes, State housing finance agencies, State community and/or economic development agencies, local rural nonprofits and community development corporations to support innovative housing and economic development

General and special funds—Continued

RURAL HOUSING AND ECONOMIC DEVELOPMENT—Continued

(INCLUDING TRANSFER OF FUNDS)—Continued

activities in rural areas: *Provided further*, That all grants shall be awarded on a competitive basis as specified in section 102 of the HUD Reform Act. *(Departments of Veterans Affairs and Housing and Urban Development, and Independent Agencies Appropriations Act, 2000.)*

Program and Financing (in millions of dollars)

Identification code 86–0324–0–1–604	1999 actual	2000 est.	2001 est.
Obligations by program activity:			
00.01 Rural Housing	....	57	27
10.00 Total new obligations (object class 41.0)	....	57	27
Budgetary resources available for obligation:			
21.40 Unobligated balance available, start of year	....	32	....
22.00 New budget authority (gross)	32	25	27
23.90 Total budgetary resources available for obligation	32	57	27
23.95 Total new obligations	....	−57	−27
24.40 Unobligated balance available, end of year	32	....	....
New budget authority (gross), detail:			
Discretionary:			
40.00 Appropriation	25	25	27
42.00 Transferred from other accounts	7	....	....
43.00 Appropriation (total discretionary)	32	25	27
Change in unpaid obligations:			
72.40 Unpaid obligations, start of year: Obligated balance, start of year	....	....	46
73.10 Total new obligations	....	57	27
73.20 Total outlays (gross)	....	−11	−22
74.40 Unpaid obligations, end of year: Obligated balance, end of year	....	46	51
Outlays (gross), detail:			
86.90 Outlays from new discretionary authority	....	1	1
86.93 Outlays from discretionary balances	....	10	21
87.00 Total outlays (gross)	....	11	22
Net budget authority and outlays:			
89.00 Budget authority	32	25	27
90.00 Outlays	....	11	22

The 2000 VA–HUD and Independent Agencies Appropriations Act (P.L. 106–74) provided $25 million to the Rural Housing and Economic Development program. This program is located in the Office of Community Planning and Development and is used to encourage new and innovative approaches to serving the housing and economic development needs of the nation's rural communities.

URBAN DEVELOPMENT ACTION GRANTS

Program and Financing (in millions of dollars)

Identification code 86–0170–0–1–451	1999 actual	2000 est.	2001 est.
Change in unpaid obligations:			
72.40 Unpaid obligations, start of year: Obligated balance, start of year	96	78	68
73.20 Total outlays (gross)	−18	−10	−10
74.40 Unpaid obligations, end of year: Obligated balance, end of year	78	68	58
Outlays (gross), detail:			
86.93 Outlays from discretionary balances	18	10	10
Net budget authority and outlays:			
89.00 Budget authority	....	....	....
90.00 Outlays	18	10	10

Title I of the Housing and Community Development Act of 1974, as amended, authorized grants to distressed cities and distressed urban counties to fund economic development projects. The program was terminated in 1990.

CAPACITY BUILDING FOR COMMUNITY DEVELOPMENT AND AFFORDABLE HOUSING

Program and Financing (in millions of dollars)

Identification code 86–0222–0–1–451	1999 actual	2000 est.	2001 est.
Obligations by program activity:			
00.01 Build capacity of community development organizations	8	....	....
10.00 Total new obligations (object class 41.0)	8	....	....
Budgetary resources available for obligation:			
21.40 Unobligated balance available, start of year	8	....	....
23.95 Total new obligations	−8	....	....
Change in unpaid obligations:			
72.40 Unpaid obligations, start of year: Obligated balance, start of year	21	19	10
73.10 Total new obligations	8	....	....
73.20 Total outlays (gross)	−9	−9	−7
74.40 Unpaid obligations, end of year: Obligated balance, end of year	19	10	3
Outlays (gross), detail:			
86.93 Outlays from discretionary balances	9	9	7
Net budget authority and outlays:			
89.00 Budget authority	....	....	....
90.00 Outlays	9	9	7

As authorized by section 4 of the HUD Demonstration Act of 1993, this program provides funding to the National Community Development Initiative to build the capacity of community-based development corporations and housing development organizations and to assist such corporations and organizations to carry out community development and affordable housing activities. Funding for this program was provided under the Annual Contributions for Assisted Housing account in 1996. Public Law 105–18 amended authorizing legislation to include additional eligible recipients and provided funding for this program through a transfer from the Homeownership and Opportunity for People Everywhere Grants account in 1997. Public Law 105–65 provided funding for this program under the Community Development Block Grant Account in 1998. P.L. 105–276 provided $15 million for this program in 1999 for the two organizations eligible prior to the enactment of P.L. 105–18. Funding of $20 million was provided for this program in 2000 in Public Law 106–74 as a set-aside within the CDBG program. $24 million is being requested in 2001, again as a set-aside within CDBG.

EMERGENCY SHELTER GRANTS PROGRAM

Program and Financing (in millions of dollars)

Identification code 86–0181–0–1–604	1999 actual	2000 est.	2001 est.
Budgetary resources available for obligation:			
21.40 Unobligated balance available, start of year	1	1	....
22.21 Unobligated balance transferred to other accounts	....	−1	....
23.90 Total budgetary resources available for obligation	1	....	....
24.40 Unobligated balance available, end of year	1	....	....
Net budget authority and outlays:			
89.00 Budget authority	....	....	....
90.00 Outlays	....	....	....

Title IV, subtitle B, of the Stewart B. McKinney Homeless Assistance Act (Public Law 100–77) authorizes the Secretary to make Emergency Shelter Grants to States and units of local government to provide emergency shelter and other support for the homeless. Since 1995, this assistance has been funded under the Homeless Assistance Grants account. The 2000 Appropriations Act transferred all balances in this account to the Homeless Assistance Grants account.

SUPPORTIVE HOUSING PROGRAM

Program and Financing (in millions of dollars)

Identification code 86–0188–0–1–604	1999 actual	2000 est.	2001 est.
Obligations by program activity:			
00.01 Homelessness prevention	2		
10.00 Total new obligations (object class 41.0)	2		
Budgetary resources available for obligation:			
21.40 Unobligated balance available, start of year	17	35	
22.10 Resources available from recoveries of prior year obligations	20		
22.21 Unobligated balance transferred to other accounts		−35	
23.90 Total budgetary resources available for obligation	37		
23.95 Total new obligations	−2		
24.40 Unobligated balance available, end of year	35		
Change in unpaid obligations:			
72.40 Unpaid obligations, start of year: Obligated balance, start of year	177	96	
73.10 Total new obligations	2		
73.20 Total outlays (gross)	−63		
73.31 Obligated balance transferred to other accounts		−96	
73.45 Adjustments in unexpired accounts	−20		
74.40 Unpaid obligations, end of year: Obligated balance, end of year	96		
Outlays (gross), detail:			
86.93 Outlays from discretionary balances	63		
Net budget authority and outlays:			
89.00 Budget authority			
90.00 Outlays	63		

Title IV, subtitle C, of the Stewart B. McKinney Homeless Assistance Act authorizes assistance to promote the development of supportive housing and services, especially for: deinstitutionalized homeless individuals; homeless families with children; homeless individuals with mental disabilities; and other persons including those with AIDS. Such assistance is available for the acquisition, rehabilitation, construction, or leasing of structures to be used for homeless persons as well as to pay for operating costs and supportive services. Since 1995, this type of assistance has been funded under the Homeless Assistance Grants account. The 2000 Appropriations Act transferred all balances in this account to the Homeless Assistance Grants account.

SUPPLEMENTAL ASSISTANCE FOR FACILITIES TO ASSIST THE HOMELESS

Program and Financing (in millions of dollars)

Identification code 86–0187–0–1–451	1999 actual	2000 est.	2001 est.
Budgetary resources available for obligation:			
21.40 Unobligated balance available, start of year	1	1	
22.21 Unobligated balance transferred to other accounts		−1	
23.90 Total budgetary resources available for obligation	1		
24.40 Unobligated balance available, end of year	1		
Change in unpaid obligations:			
72.40 Unpaid obligations, start of year: Obligated balance, start of year	1	1	
73.31 Obligated balance transferred to other accounts		−1	
74.40 Unpaid obligations, end of year: Obligated balance, end of year	1		
Net budget authority and outlays:			
89.00 Budget authority			
90.00 Outlays			

Title IV, subtitle D, of the Stewart B. McKinney Homeless Assistance Act authorized the Supplemental Assistance for Facilities To Assist the Homeless program (SAFAH) to provide comprehensive assistance for particularly innovative programs or alternative methods of meeting the immediate and long-term needs of the homeless. The authority for the SAFAH program was terminated by section 1403 of the Housing and Community Development Act of 1992. The 2000 Appropriations Act transferred all balances in this account to the Homeless Assistance Grants account.

SHELTER PLUS CARE

Program and Financing (in millions of dollars)

Identification code 86–0204–0–1–604	1999 actual	2000 est.	2001 est.
Obligations by program activity:			
00.01 Homelessness prevention	4		
10.00 Total new obligations (object class 41.0)	4		
Budgetary resources available for obligation:			
21.40 Unobligated balance available, start of year	6	3	
22.10 Resources available from recoveries of prior year obligations	1		
22.21 Unobligated balance transferred to other accounts		−3	
23.90 Total budgetary resources available for obligation	7		
23.95 Total new obligations	−4		
24.40 Unobligated balance available, end of year	3		
Change in unpaid obligations:			
72.40 Unpaid obligations, start of year: Obligated balance, start of year	300	228	
73.10 Total new obligations	4		
73.20 Total outlays (gross)	−75		
73.31 Obligated balance transferred to other accounts		−228	
73.45 Adjustments in unexpired accounts	−1		
74.40 Unpaid obligations, end of year: Obligated balance, end of year	228		
Outlays (gross), detail:			
86.93 Outlays from discretionary balances	75		
Net budget authority and outlays:			
89.00 Budget authority			
90.00 Outlays	75		

Title IV, subtitle F, of the Stewart B. McKinney Homeless Assistance Act authorizes the Secretary to provide rental assistance to persons with disabilities. Supportive services at least equal in value to the aggregate rental assistance must also be provided by grant recipients using other Federal, State, local and private resources. Eligible recipients include States and units of general local government.

Since 1995, this type of assistance has been funded under the Homeless Assistance Grants account.

The 2000 Appropriations Act transferred all balances in this account to the Homeless Assistance Grants account.

General and special funds—Continued

INNOVATIVE HOMELESS INITIATIVES DEMONSTRATION PROGRAM

Program and Financing (in millions of dollars)

Identification code 86–0221–0–1–604	1999 actual	2000 est.	2001 est.
Change in unpaid obligations:			
72.40 Unpaid obligations, start of year: Obligated balance, start of year	18	9	
73.20 Total outlays (gross)	–9		
73.31 Obligated balance transferred to other accounts		–9	
74.40 Unpaid obligations, end of year: Obligated balance, end of year	9		
Outlays (gross), detail:			
86.93 Outlays from discretionary balances	9		
Net budget authority and outlays:			
89.00 Budget authority			
90.00 Outlays	9		

Section 2 of the HUD Demonstration Act of 1993 authorized assistance for projects intended to provide a continuum of care for homeless persons and for innovative programs to assist homeless persons. Eligible recipients included States, units of local government, Indian tribes, and nonprofit organizations. Authorization for this program expired at the end of 1994. The 2000 Appropriations Act transferred all balances in this account to the Homeless Assistance Grants account.

[NATIONAL CITIES] *COMMUNITIES* IN SCHOOLS COMMUNITY DEVELOPMENT PROGRAM

Note.—Section 209 provides $5,000,000 for this account.

For grants for the Communities in Schools Community Development Program, $5,000,000, as authorized by section 930 of the Housing and Community Development Act of 1992.

Program and Financing (in millions of dollars)

Identification code 86–0220–0–1–451	1999 actual	2000 est.	2001 est.
Obligations by program activity:			
00.01 Grants for Schools	5	5	5
10.00 Total new obligations (object class 41.0)	5	5	5
Budgetary resources available for obligation:			
22.00 New budget authority (gross)	5	5	5
23.95 Total new obligations	–5	–5	–5
New budget authority (gross), detail:			
Discretionary:			
40.00 Appropriation		5	5
42.00 Transferred from other accounts	5		
43.00 Appropriation (total discretionary)	5	5	5
Change in unpaid obligations:			
72.40 Unpaid obligations, start of year: Obligated balance, start of year		1	3
73.10 Total new obligations	5	5	5
73.20 Total outlays (gross)	–4	–4	–5
74.40 Unpaid obligations, end of year: Obligated balance, end of year	1	3	3
Outlays (gross), detail:			
86.90 Outlays from new discretionary authority	4	3	3
86.93 Outlays from discretionary balances		1	3
87.00 Total outlays (gross)	4	4	5
Net budget authority and outlays:			
89.00 Budget authority	5	5	5
90.00 Outlays	4	4	5

The Communities in Schools program, formerly known as the National Cities in Schools program, provides funding to empower local communities to work through collaborative public/private partnerships involving schools, public housing communities, and community organizations to prevent youngsters from dropping out of school, while involving youth in local community building, job training and neighborhood revitalization projects. P.L. 105–276 authorized the transfer of $5,000,000 in Annual Contributions for Assisted Housing recaptures to this account in 1999. The 2000 Appropriations Act (P.L. 106–74) provided $5 million; an additional $5 million is requested for 2001.

Public enterprise funds:

REVOLVING FUND (LIQUIDATING PROGRAMS)

Program and Financing (in millions of dollars)

Identification code 86–4015–0–3–451	1999 actual	2000 est.	2001 est.
Obligations by program activity:			
09.01 Loan servicing	5	10	9
09.03 Administrative expenses	1	1	1
10.00 Total new obligations	6	11	10
Budgetary resources available for obligation:			
21.40 Unobligated balance available, start of year	100	93	76
22.00 New budget authority (gross)	53	44	42
22.10 Resources available from recoveries of prior year obligations	2		
22.40 Capital transfer to general fund	–55	–50	–45
23.90 Total budgetary resources available for obligation	100	87	73
23.95 Total new obligations	–6	–11	–10
24.40 Unobligated balance available, end of year	93	76	63
New budget authority (gross), detail:			
Mandatory:			
69.00 Offsetting collections (cash)	53	44	42
Change in unpaid obligations:			
72.40 Unpaid obligations, start of year: Obligated balance, start of year	12	9	4
73.10 Total new obligations	6	11	10
73.20 Total outlays (gross)	–7	–16	–14
73.45 Adjustments in unexpired accounts	–2		
74.40 Unpaid obligations, end of year: Obligated balance, end of year	9	4	
Outlays (gross), detail:			
86.98 Outlays from mandatory balances	7	16	14
Offsets:			
Against gross budget authority and outlays:			
88.40 Offsetting collections (cash) from: Non-Federal sources	–53	–44	–42
Net budget authority and outlays:			
89.00 Budget authority			
90.00 Outlays	–45	–28	–28

Status of Direct Loans (in millions of dollars)

Identification code 86–4015–0–3–451	1999 actual	2000 est.	2001 est.
Cumulative balance of direct loans outstanding:			
1210 Outstanding, start of year	220	175	140
1251 Repayments: Repayments and prepayments	–39	–35	–30
1263 Write-offs for default: Direct loans	–6		
1290 Outstanding, end of year	175	140	110

Status of Guaranteed Loans (in millions of dollars)

Identification code 86–4015–0–3–451	1999 actual	2000 est.	2001 est.
Cumulative balance of guaranteed loans outstanding:			
2210 Outstanding, start of year	2	1	
2251 Repayments and prepayments	–1	–1	
2290 Outstanding, end of year	1		

Memorandum:				
2299 Guaranteed amount of guaranteed loans outstanding, end of year		1		

The Revolving fund (liquidating programs) was established by the Independent Offices Appropriations Act of 1955 for the efficient liquidation of assets acquired under a number of housing and urban development programs.

Statement of Operations (in millions of dollars)

Identification code 86–4015–0–3–451	1998 actual	1999 actual	2000 est.	2001 est.
0101 Revenue	11	11	10	9
0102 Expense	–4	–1	–1	–1
0105 Net income or loss (–)	7	10	9	8

Balance Sheet (in millions of dollars)

Identification code 86–4015–0–3–451	1998 actual	1999 actual	2000 est.	2001 est.
ASSETS:				
1101 Federal assets: Fund balances with Treasury	112	103	85	60
Non-Federal assets:				
1206 Receivables, net	10	20	18	16
1207 Advances and prepayments	2			
Net value of assets related to pre–1992 direct loans receivable and acquired defaulted guaranteed loans receivable:				
1601 Direct loans, gross	220	175	157	135
1602 Interest receivable	17	16	15	11
1603 Allowance for estimated uncollectible loans and interest (–)	–20	–7	–7	–7
1604 Direct loans and interest receivable, net	217	184	165	139
1699 Value of assets related to direct loans	217	184	165	139
1801 Other Federal assets: Cash and other monetary assets	1	1		
1999 Total assets	342	308	268	215
LIABILITIES:				
Non-Federal liabilities:				
2201 Accounts payable	1	1	1	1
2207 Other	7	8	5	4
2999 Total liabilities	8	9	6	5
NET POSITION:				
3100 Appropriated capital	197	193	170	140
3300 Cumulative results of operations	138	106	92	70
3999 Total net position	335	299	262	210
4999 Total liabilities and net position	343	308	268	215

Object Classification (in millions of dollars)

Identification code 86–4015–0–3–451	1999 actual	2000 est.	2001 est.
25.2 Other services	3	5	5
32.0 Land and structures	3	6	5
99.9 Total new obligations	6	11	10

Credit accounts:

Community Development Loan Guarantees Program Account

Program and Financing (in millions of dollars)

Identification code 86–0198–0–1–451	1999 actual	2000 est.	2001 est.
Obligations by program activity:			
00.02 Community development loan guarantee credit subsidy	10	29	28
00.09 Administrative expense	1	1	2
10.00 Total new obligations (object class 33.0)	11	30	30
Budgetary resources available for obligation:			
22.00 New budget authority (gross)	30	30	30
23.95 Total new obligations	–11	–30	–30
23.98 Unobligated balance expiring or withdrawn	–19		
New budget authority (gross), detail:			
Discretionary:			
40.00 Appropriation	30	30	30
Change in unpaid obligations:			
72.40 Unpaid obligations, start of year: Obligated balance, start of year	18	18	32
73.10 Total new obligations	11	30	30
73.20 Total outlays (gross)	–9	–16	–21
73.40 Adjustments in expired accounts (net)	–2		
74.40 Unpaid obligations, end of year: Obligated balance, end of year	18	32	41
Outlays (gross), detail:			
86.90 Outlays from new discretionary authority	3	5	6
86.93 Outlays from discretionary balances	6	11	15
87.00 Total outlays (gross)	9	16	21
Net budget authority and outlays:			
89.00 Budget authority	30	30	30
90.00 Outlays	9	16	21

Guaranteed Loans.—The Community Development Block Grant program includes a guaranteed loan provision (Section 108). A commitment level of $1.2 billion is proposed for the Community Development Loan Guarantees (Section 108) program for 2001. The credit subsidy/administrative cost estimate for the guaranteed loan program is $30 million in 2001.

Section 108 loan guarantees are used by entitlement and nonentitlement communities (assisted by their State) to cover the cost of: acquiring real property; rehabilitating publicly owned real property; housing rehabilitation; and, certain other economic development activities. In addition, Section 108 has, in some cases, been used to finance the construction of housing by nonprofit organizations.

Summary of Loan Levels, Subsidy Budget Authority and Outlays by Program (in millions of dollars)

Identification code 86–0198–0–1–451	1999 actual	2000 est.	2001 est.
Guaranteed loan levels supportable by subsidy budget authority:			
2150 Loan guarantee levels	432	1,261	1,217
2159 Total loan guarantee levels	432	1,261	1,217
Guaranteed loan subsidy (in percent):			
2320 Subsidy rate	2.30	2.30	2.30
2329 Weighted average subsidy rate	2.30	2.30	2.30
Guaranteed loan subsidy budget authority:			
2330 Subsidy budget authority	10	29	28
2339 Total subsidy budget authority	10	29	28
Guaranteed loan subsidy outlays:			
2340 Subsidy outlays	8	15	19
2349 Total subsidy outlays	8	15	19
Administrative expense data:			
3510 Budget authority	1	1	2
3590 Outlays from new authority	1	1	2

As required by the Federal Credit Reform Act of 1990, this account records, for this program, the subsidy costs associated with the loan guarantees committed in 1992 and beyond (including modifications of direct loans or loan guarantees that resulted from obligations or commitments in any year), as well as administrative expenses of this program. The subsidy amounts are estimated on a present value basis; the administrative expenses are estimated on a cash basis.

Credit accounts—Continued

COMMUNITY DEVELOPMENT LOAN GUARANTEES FINANCING ACCOUNT

Program and Financing (in millions of dollars)

Identification code 86–4096–0–3–451	1999 actual	2000 est.	2001 est.
Budgetary resources available for obligation:			
21.40 Unobligated balance available, start of year	7	16	32
22.00 New financing authority (gross)	9	16	21
23.90 Total budgetary resources available for obligation	16	32	53
24.40 Unobligated balance available, end of year	16	32	53
New financing authority (gross), detail:			
Discretionary:			
68.00 Spending authority from offsetting collections (gross): Offsetting collections (cash)	9	16	21
Offsets:			
Against gross financing authority and financing disbursements:			
Offsetting collections (cash) from:			
88.00 Federal sources	−8	−15	−19
88.25 Interest on uninvested funds	−1	−1	−2
88.90 Total, offsetting collections (cash)	−9	−16	−21
Net financing authority and financing disbursements:			
89.00 Financing authority			
90.00 Financing disbursements	−9	−16	−21

Status of Guaranteed Loans (in millions of dollars)

Identification code 86–4096–0–3–451	1999 actual	2000 est.	2001 est.
Position with respect to appropriations act limitation on commitments:			
2111 Limitation on guaranteed loans made by private lenders	1,261	1,261	1,217
2112 Uncommitted loan guarantee limitation	−829		
2150 Total guaranteed loan commitments	432	1,261	1,217
Cumulative balance of guaranteed loans outstanding:			
2210 Outstanding, start of year	1,189	1,509	1,959
2231 Disbursements of new guaranteed loans	468	650	825
2251 Repayments and prepayments	−148	−200	−250
2290 Outstanding, end of year	1,509	1,959	2,534
Memorandum:			
2299 Guaranteed amount of guaranteed loans outstanding, end of year	1,509	1,959	2,534

Balance Sheet (in millions of dollars)

Identification code 86–4096–0–3–451	1998 actual	1999 actual	2000 est.	2001 est.
ASSETS:				
1101 Federal assets: Fund balances with Treasury	7	16	32	53
1999 Total assets	7	16	32	53
LIABILITIES:				
2204 Non-Federal liabilities: Liabilities for loan guarantees	8	16	32	53
2999 Total liabilities	8	16	32	53
4999 Total liabilities and net position	8	16	32	53

Guaranteed loans.—The Community Development Loan Guarantees program provides a mechanism for the Federal guarantee of private loans. There is an accompanying liquidating account which shows activity for Federal Financing Bank (FFB) direct loan activity, obligated prior to July 1, 1986. Also following is a status of privately financed guaranteed loan commitments made prior to 1992.

As required by the Federal Credit Reform Act of 1990, this non-budgetary account records all cash flows to and from the Government resulting from loan guarantees committed in 1992 and beyond (including modifications of loan guarantees that resulted from commitments in any year). The amounts in this account are a means of financing and are not included in the budget totals. As required by the Federal Credit Reform Act of 1990, no administrative expenses can be recorded in the financing account.

COMMUNITY DEVELOPMENT LOAN GUARANTEES LIQUIDATING ACCOUNT

Program and Financing (in millions of dollars)

Identification code 86–4097–0–3–451	1999 actual	2000 est.	2001 est.
Budgetary resources available for obligation:			
22.00 New budget authority (gross)	24	4	4
22.60 Portion applied to repay debt	−17	−4	−4
23.90 Total budgetary resources available for obligation	7		
23.95 Total new obligations			
23.98 Unobligated balance expiring or withdrawn	−7		
New budget authority (gross), detail:			
Mandatory:			
69.00 Offsetting collections (cash)	24	4	4
Change in unpaid obligations:			
Unpaid obligations, start of year:			
72.40 Obligated balance, start of year	138	134	134
72.95 From Federal sources: Receivables and unpaid, unfilled orders	10	10	10
72.99 Total unpaid obligations, start of year	148	144	144
73.20 Total outlays (gross)	−4		
Unpaid obligations, end of year:			
74.40 Obligated balance, end of year	134	134	134
74.95 From Federal sources: Receivables and unpaid, unfilled orders	10	10	10
74.99 Total unpaid obligations, end of year	144	144	144
Outlays (gross), detail:			
86.98 Outlays from mandatory balances	4		
Offsets:			
Against gross budget authority and outlays:			
88.40 Offsetting collections (cash) from: Non-Federal sources	−24	−4	−4
Net budget authority and outlays:			
89.00 Budget authority			
90.00 Outlays	−20	−4	−4

Status of Direct Loans (in millions of dollars)

Identification code 86–4097–0–3–451	1999 actual	2000 est.	2001 est.
Cumulative balance of direct loans outstanding:			
1210 Outstanding, start of year	30	13	9
1251 Repayments: Repayments and prepayments	−17	−4	−4
1290 Outstanding, end of year	13	9	5

Status of Guaranteed Loans (in millions of dollars)

Identification code 86–4097–0–3–451	1999 actual	2000 est.	2001 est.
Cumulative balance of guaranteed loans outstanding:			
2210 Outstanding, start of year	165	134	109
2251 Repayments and prepayments	−31	−25	−25
2290 Outstanding, end of year	134	109	84
Memorandum:			
2299 Guaranteed amount of guaranteed loans outstanding, end of year	134	109	84

Statement of Operations (in millions of dollars)

Identification code 86–4097–0–3–451	1998 actual	1999 actual	2000 est.	2001 est.
0101 Revenue	8	8	6	6

0102	Expense	–8	–8	–6	–6

Balance Sheet (in millions of dollars)

Identification code 86–4097–0–3–451		1998 actual	1999 actual	2000 est.	2001 est.
	ASSETS:				
	Federal assets:				
1101	Fund balances with Treasury	–8	–4	–4	–4
	Investments in US securities:				
1106	Receivables, net	9	11	7	7
	Net value of assets related to pre–1992 direct loans receivable and acquired defaulted guaranteed loans receivable:				
1701	Defaulted guaranteed loans, gross	31	13	12	11
1702	Interest receivable	4	4	4	4
1799	Value of assets related to loan guarantees	35	17	16	15
1901	Other Federal assets: Other assets	149	139	135	130
1999	Total assets	185	163	154	148
	LIABILITIES:				
2105	Federal liabilities: Other	155	14	14	13
2201	Non-Federal liabilities: Accounts payable	30	149	140	135
2999	Total liabilities	185	163	154	148
4999	Total liabilities and net position	185	163	154	148

As required by the Federal Credit Reform Act of 1990, this account records all cash flows to and from the Government resulting from Federal Financing Bank (FFB) direct loans for which loan guarantees were committed prior to 1992. This account is shown on a cash basis.

Guaranteed loans.—Guaranteed loan assistance under the Community Development Loan Guarantees program is provided to eligible communities to finance economic development activities, housing rehabilitation, public facilities, acquisition of real property, rehabilitation of publicly owned real property, and certain related expenses. In the past, the FFB financed these guaranteed loans. The Consolidated Omnibus Budget Reconciliation Act of 1985 required private financing of all loan guarantees committed after July 1, 1986. FFB will continue disbursing loans for commitments approved prior to July 1, 1986. The activity shown in the above account reflects privately financed guaranteed loans for which commitments were made prior to 1992.

America's Private Investment Companies Program Account

[INCLUDING TRANSFER OF FUNDS]

For the cost of guaranteed loans under the America's Private Investment Companies Program, [$20,000,000], *$37,000,000* to remain available until September 30, [2002] *2003, of which not to exceed $1,000,000 shall be for administrative expenses to carry out such a loan program, to be transferred to and merged with "Salaries and Expenses": Provided*, That such costs, including the cost of modifying loans, shall be as defined in section 502 of the Congressional Budget Act of 1974, as amended: *Provided further*, That these funds are available to subsidize total loan principal, any part of which is guaranteed, not to exceed [$541,000,000: *Provided further*, That the funds appropriated under this heading shall not be available for obligation until the America's Private Investment Companies Program is authorized by subsequent legislation and the program is developed subject to notice and comment rulemaking: *Provided further*, That if the authorizing legislation is not enacted by June 30, 2000, all funds under this heading shall be transferred to and merged with the appropriation for the "Community development financial institutions fund program account" to be available for use as grants and loans under that account] *$1,000,000,000. (Departments of Veterans Affairs and Housing and Urban Development, and Independent Agencies Appropriations Act, 2000.)*

Program and Financing (in millions of dollars)

Identification code 86–0326–0–1–451		1999 actual	2000 est.	2001 est.
	Obligations by program activity:			
00.02	Credit Subsidy		19	36
00.09	Administrative Expense		1	1
10.00	Total new obligations (object class 33.0)		20	37
	Budgetary resources available for obligation:			
22.00	New budget authority (gross)		20	37
23.95	Total new obligations		–20	–37
	New budget authority (gross), detail:			
	Discretionary:			
40.00	Appropriation		20	37
	Change in unpaid obligations:			
72.40	Unpaid obligations, start of year: Obligated balance, start of year			5
73.10	Total new obligations		20	37
73.20	Total outlays (gross)		–15	–28
74.40	Unpaid obligations, end of year: Obligated balance, end of year		5	14
	Outlays (gross), detail:			
86.90	Outlays from new discretionary authority		15	27
86.93	Outlays from discretionary balances			1
87.00	Total outlays (gross)		15	28
	Net budget authority and outlays:			
89.00	Budget authority		20	37
90.00	Outlays		15	28

The America's Private Investment Companies (APIC) is a vehicle for increasing the private equity capital invested in distressed urban and rural areas. The difficulty in obtaining equity-type financing, which is harder to come by than debt financing, worsens the overall shortage of investment capital in distressed inner city and rural areas. This Budget proposes $36 million in credit subsidy, which is expected to leverage $1 billion in loan commitments and an additional $500 million in private equity capital.

APIC is administered by the Department of Housing and Urban Development (HUD) with support from the Small Business Administration (SBA), drawing on the dual expertise of these two agencies. The SBA's Small Business Investment Companies (SBIC) program also supports the effective investment of private equity and can be targeted to distressed areas. However, SBICs are capped in size of companies eligible for investment and therefore may not be able to serve large projects such as manufacturing facilities that can have significant impact on distressed areas. APICs provide a financing mechanism for venture capital funds that would be able to invest in larger businesses which could relocate or expand into distressed areas. An APIC venture funds issue debentures and takes equity positions in businesses needing equity-type capital of $10 million or more.

As required by the Federal Credit Reform Act of 1990, this account records, for this program, the subsidy costs associated with the loan guarantees committed in 1992 and beyond, as well as administrative expenses of this program. The subsidy amounts are estimated on a present value basis, the administrative expenses are estimated on a cash basis.

Summary of Loan Levels, Subsidy Budget Authority and Outlays by Program (in millions of dollars)

Identification code 86–0326–0–1–451		1999 actual	2000 est.	2001 est.
	Guaranteed loan levels supportable by subsidy budget authority:			
2150	Loan guarantee levels		541	1,000
2159	Total loan guarantee levels		541	1,000
	Guaranteed loan subsidy (in percent):			
2320	Subsidy rate		3.60	3.60

Credit accounts—Continued

AMERICA'S PRIVATE INVESTMENT COMPANIES PROGRAM ACCOUNT—Continued

[INCLUDING TRANSFER OF FUNDS]—Continued

Summary of Loan Levels, Subsidy Budget Authority and Outlays by Program (in millions of dollars)—Continued

Identification code 86–0326–0–1–451	1999 actual	2000 est.	2001 est.
2329 Weighted average subsidy rate	....	3.60	3.60
Guaranteed loan subsidy budget authority:			
2330 Subsidy budget authority	....	20	36
2339 Total subsidy budget authority	....	20	36
Guaranteed loan subsidy outlays:			
2340 Subsidy outlays	....	14	27
2349 Total subsidy outlays	....	14	27
Administrative expense data:			
3510 Budget authority	....	1	1
3590 Outlays from new authority	....	1	1

AMERICA'S PRIVATE INVESTMENT COMPANIES LOAN GUARANTEE FINANCING ACCOUNT

Program and Financing (in millions of dollars)

Identification code 86–4102–0–3–451	1999 actual	2000 est.	2001 est.
Budgetary resources available for obligation:			
21.40 Unobligated balance available, start of year	....	....	14
22.00 New financing authority (gross)	....	14	29
23.90 Total budgetary resources available for obligation	....	14	43
24.40 Unobligated balance available, end of year	....	14	43
New financing authority (gross), detail:			
Discretionary:			
68.00 Spending authority from offsetting collections (gross): Offsetting collections (cash)	....	14	29
Offsets:			
Against gross financing authority and financing disbursements:			
Offsetting collections (cash) from:			
88.00 Federal sources	....	–14	–27
88.25 Interest on uninvested funds	....	....	–2
88.90 Total, offsetting collections (cash)	....	–14	–29
Net financing authority and financing disbursements:			
89.00 Financing authority	....	....	....
90.00 Financing disbursements	....	–14	–29

Status of Guaranteed Loans (in millions of dollars)

Identification code 86–4102–0–3–451	1999 actual	2000 est.	2001 est.
Position with respect to appropriations act limitation on commitments:			
2111 Limitation on guaranteed loans made by private lenders	....	541	1,000
2150 Total guaranteed loan commitments	....	541	1,000
Cumulative balance of guaranteed loans outstanding:			
2210 Outstanding, start of year	....	....	395
2231 Disbursements of new guaranteed loans	....	395	771
2290 Outstanding, end of year	....	395	1,166
Memorandum:			
2299 Guaranteed amount of guaranteed loans outstanding, end of year	....	395	1,166

Balance Sheet (in millions of dollars)

Identification code 86–4102–0–3–451	1998 actual	1999 actual	2000 est.	2001 est.
ASSETS:				
1101 Federal assets: Fund balances with Treasury	....	....	14	29
1999 Total assets	....	....	14	29
LIABILITIES:				
2204 Non-Federal liabilities: Liabilities for loan guarantees	....	....	14	29
2999 Total liabilities	....	....	14	29
4999 Total liabilities and net position	....	....	14	29

As required by the Federal Credit Reform Act of 1990, this non-budgetary account records all cash flows to and from the Government resulting from loan guarantees committed in 1992 and beyond (including modifications of direct loans that resulted from obligations in any year). The amounts in this account are a means of financing and are not included in the budget totals.

HOUSING PROGRAMS

Federal Funds

General and special funds:

HOUSING FOR SPECIAL POPULATIONS

For assistance for the purchase, construction, acquisition, or development of additional public and subsidized housing units for low income families not otherwise provided for, [$911,000,000], *$989,000,000,* to remain available until expended: *Provided*, That [$710,000,000] *$779,000,000* shall be for capital advances, including amendments to capital advance contracts, for housing for the elderly, as authorized by section 202 of the Housing Act of 1959, as amended, and for project rental assistance, and amendments to contracts for project rental assistance, for the elderly under such section 202(c)(2), and for supportive services associated with the housing, of which [amount $50,000,000 shall be for service coordinators and continuation of existing congregate services grants for residents of assisted housing projects, and of which amount $50,000,000 shall be for grants for conversion of existing section 202 projects, or portions thereof, to assisted living or related use, consistent with the relevant provision of title V of this Act] *$50,000,000 shall be for service coordinators and the continuation of existing congregate service grants for residents of assisted housing projects and for other eligible elderly persons residing in the neighborhood in which such projects are located on an exception basis; $50,000,000 shall be for the conversion of existing projects for the elderly, or portions of such projects, to assisted living or related use, as authorized by section 202b (including up to $5,000,000 for intergenerational learning centers); and $50,000,000 shall be for grants for up to 20 percent of the units in any new assisted living facility which is developed with new constsruction or substantial rehabilitation loan guarantee financing under section 232 of the National Housing Act: Provided further, That such units shall be occupied by low-income elderly families with at least one member who is frail: Provided further, That such grants shall be awarded, at the discretion of the Secretary, based on an approved plan of the State or political subdivision thereof to supplement the grants with appropriate supportive services funding for those frail elderly occupying such units: Provided further,* That of the amount under this heading, [$201,000,000] *$210,000,000* shall be for capital advances, including amendments to capital advance contracts, for supportive housing for persons with disabilities, as authorized by section 811 of the Cranston-Gonzalez National Affordable Housing Act, for project rental assistance, for amendments to contracts for project rental assistance, and supportive services associated with the housing for persons with disabilities as authorized by section 811 of such Act: *Provided further*, That the Secretary [may] *shall* designate [up to 25 percent] *at least 25 percent but no more than 50 percent* of the amounts earmarked under this paragraph for section 811 of such Act for tenant-based assistance, as authorized under that section, including such authority as may be waived under the next proviso, which assistance is 5 years in duration: *Provided further*, That the Secretary may waive any provision of such section 202 and such section 811 (including the provisions governing the terms and conditions of project rental assistance and tenant-based assistance) that the Secretary determines is not necessary to achieve the objectives of these programs, or that otherwise impedes the ability to develop, operate or administer projects assisted under these programs, and may make provision for alternative conditions or terms where appropriate. *(Departments of Veterans Affairs and Housing and Urban Development, and Independent Agencies Appropriations Act, 2000.)*

Program and Financing (in millions of dollars)

Identification code 86–0320–0–1–604	1999 actual	2000 est.	2001 est.
Obligations by program activity:			
00.01 Direct Program Activity	972	1,280	1,355
10.00 Total new obligations (object class 41.0)	972	1,280	1,355
Budgetary resources available for obligation:			
21.40 Unobligated balance available, start of year	2,864	2,749	2,380
22.00 New budget authority (gross)	854	911	989
22.10 Resources available from recoveries of prior year obligations	3		
23.90 Total budgetary resources available for obligation	3,721	3,660	3,369
23.95 Total new obligations	−972	−1,280	−1,355
24.40 Unobligated balance available, end of year	2,749	2,380	2,014
New budget authority (gross), detail:			
Discretionary:			
40.00 Appropriation	854	911	989
Change in unpaid obligations:			
72.40 Unpaid obligations, start of year: Obligated balance, start of year	3,591	3,799	4,295
73.10 Total new obligations	972	1,280	1,355
73.20 Total outlays (gross)	−761	−784	−1,014
73.45 Adjustments in unexpired accounts	−3		
74.40 Unpaid obligations, end of year: Obligated balance, end of year	3,799	4,295	4,636
Outlays (gross), detail:			
86.93 Outlays from discretionary balances	761	784	1,014
Net budget authority and outlays:			
89.00 Budget authority	854	911	989
90.00 Outlays	761	784	1,014

This account consolidates activity under the Section 202 Housing for the Elderly Program and the Section 811 Housing for the Disabled Program. Program activity prior to 1997 was reflected in the Annual Contributions for Assisted Housing account. Renewal of prior year contracts is reflected in the Housing Certificate Fund. In 2001, a total of $989 million is requested for the Housing for Special Populations account.

Housing for the Disabled.—$210 million is proposed for housing for persons with disabilities, including language to permit at least 25 percent and up to 50 percent of these funds to be earmarked for tenant-based assistance which increases the number of persons that can be assisted by maximizing the use of the private market.

Housing for the Elderly.—A total of $779 million is proposed for housing for the elderly. Of this amount $50 million is for the capital grant program to convert existing 202 properties to assisted living under appropriate conditions. These funds for capital grants are available to existing HUD elderly subsidized (Section 202) projects that convert some or all units to Assisted Living. These competitive grants are available to current project owners who agree to several specified conditions. These conditions would include: (1) a tight cap on operating expenses and HUD subsidy; (2) Medicaid home and community-based services or personal care services for Medicaid-eligible residents; and accessible services for non-Medicaid eligible residents through local and community service providers; (3) at least two meals per day; and (4) 24-hour staff. Preference will be given to grant applicants who demostrate a strong commitment to (1) serve extremely low income frail, disabled elderly residents, (2) promote resident autonomy, independence choice and control.

This initiative will make available to low-income elderly, a new type of housing that Americans with higher incomes already benefit from in increasing numbers. Converting some Section 202 projects to assisted living brings this successful innovation to a population that includes a much higher proportion of frail elderly than when subsidized apartment projects were first constructed. These elderly need additional help with various tasks in order to continue living as independently as possible. Projects need to be reconfigured to provide more congregate areas and room for additional services. As a result of this investment, people who otherwise would be confined to nursing homes and receive a higher level of care can enjoy a much greater degree of independence.

$50 million is provided for an expanded service coordinator program that will serve both residents of HUD-assisted elderly housing and other eligible elderly residing in the neighborhood in which such projects are located on an exception basis. These new grants and an expanded 202 program will address the growing housing needs of the nation's elderly.

This initiative will begin to address in a more comprehensive way the changing and expanding long-term care needs of the elderly population including: the lack of decent affordable housing for low-income elderly people. The Administration proposes to expand assistance to low income elderly people by providing more accessible decent affordable housing, and by coordinating and ensuring the existence and accessibility of supportive services provided by the community, non-profits, and through the Federal health programs to residents of the projects. Together these efforts will establish a Continuum of Care for the elderly.

Additionally, in the 2001 budget, the Administration includes funding for the Housing Security Plan, and to continue to implement the Continuum of Care for America's seniors. The budget this year proposes an initiative to increase assisted living opportunities for the elderly. $50 million is provided for the production of new affordable assisted living units for the low-income elderly. The Administration proposes that HUD partner with HHS and states and localities to better integrate housing assistance with Medicaid funding for services.

Other Assisted Housing Programs

Rental Housing Assistance

Program and Financing (in millions of dollars)

Identification code 86–0206–0–1–999	1999 actual	2000 est.	2001 est.
Obligations by program activity:			
00.01 Rent supplement	8	5	5
00.02 Homeownership and rental housing assistance (Sections 235 and 236)	21	25	25
00.03 College Housing	6		
00.04 IRP Rehab Grants		190	300
10.00 Total new obligations (object class 41.0)	35	220	330
Budgetary resources available for obligation:			
21.40 Unobligated balance available, start of year	8	7	
21.49 Unobligated balance available, start of year: Contract authority	950	1,053	1,083
21.99 Total unobligated balance, start of year	958	1,060	1,083
22.00 New budget authority (gross)		−7	
22.10 Resources available from recoveries of prior year obligations	130	250	266
22.75 Balance of contract authority withdrawn	6		
23.90 Total budgetary resources available for obligation	1,094	1,303	1,349
23.95 Total new obligations	−35	−220	−330
24.40 Unobligated balance available, end of year	7		
24.49 Unobligated balance, end of year: Contract authority	1,053	1,083	1,019

General and special funds—Continued

RENTAL HOUSING ASSISTANCE—Continued

Program and Financing (in millions of dollars)—Continued

Identification code 86–0206–0–1–999	1999 actual	2000 est.	2001 est.
24.99 Total unobligated balance, end of year	1,060	1,083	1,019
New budget authority (gross), detail:			
Discretionary:			
40.05 Appropriation (indefinite)	676	664	711
40.36 Preservation prepayment rescission		−7	
40.49 Portion applied to liquidate contract authority	−676	−664	−711
43.00 Appropriation (total discretionary)		−7	
Change in unpaid obligations:			
Unpaid obligations, start of year:			
72.40 Obligated balance, start of year	127	39	
72.49 Obligated balance, start of year: Contract authority	11,332	10,616	9,915
72.99 Total unpaid obligations, start of year	11,459	10,655	9,915
73.10 Total new obligations	35	220	330
73.20 Total outlays (gross)	−708	−710	−711
73.45 Adjustments in unexpired accounts	−130	−250	−266
Unpaid obligations, end of year:			
74.40 Obligated balance, end of year	39		
74.49 Obligated balance, end of year: Contract authority	10,616	9,915	9,268
74.99 Total unpaid obligations, end of year	10,655	9,915	9,268
Outlays (gross), detail:			
86.93 Outlays from discretionary balances	708	710	711
Net budget authority and outlays:			
89.00 Budget authority		−7	
90.00 Outlays	708	710	711

Status of Contract Authority (in millions of dollars)

Identification code 86–0206–0–1–999	1999 actual	2000 est.	2001 est.
0100 Balance, start of year	12,282	11,669	10,998
Contract authority:			
0200 Contract authority		−7	
0400 Appropriation to liquidate contract authority	−676	−664	−711
0600 Balance of contract authority withdrawn	6		
0700 Balance, end of year	11,669	10,998	10,287

OTHER ASSISTED HOUSING

Summary of Administrative Commitments

(in millions of dollars)

	1999 actual	2000 est.	2001 est.
Assistance contracts:			
College Housing	6		
Rent supplement	8	5	5
Homeownership and rental housing assistance (sections 235 and 236)	21	25	25
IRP Rehab Grants		190	300
Administrative commitments, start of year	16	16	16
Administrative commitments, end of year	−16	−16	−16
Total obligations	35	220	330

The Other Assisted Housing Account contains the programs listed below:

Rent supplement.—Rent supplement assistance payments will continue to be made on behalf of qualified low-income tenants in approximately 20,000 units which have not converted to section 8.

Section 235.—The Housing and Urban-Rural Recovery Act of 1983 (Public Law 98–181) authorized a restructured section 235 (Homeownership Assistance) program based on a 10-year interest reduction subsidy. This replaced earlier versions of the program, the original and the revised versions. All were below interest rate mortgages for single family homes.

Section 236.—The Housing and Urban Development Act of 1968, as amended, authorizes the section 236 Rental Housing Assistance Program which subsidizes the monthly mortgage payment that an owner of a rental or cooperative project is required to make. This interest subsidy reduces rents for lower income tenants.

IRP Rehab Grants.—Title V of the 1998 Appropriations Act (P.L. 105–65) establishes a program of rehabilitation grants for owners of eligible projects. An estimated $300 million of such grants are expected in 2001.

The table below reflects the consolidated outlay total for: the Annual Contributions for Assisted Housing account; the Housing Certificate Fund; the Public Housing Capital Fund; the Section 8 Reserve Preservation account; and the Other Assisted Housing account, for 1999, 2000 and 2001.

SUMMARY OF OUTLAYS [1]

(in millions of dollars)

	1999 actual	*2000 est.*	*2001 est.*
Subsidized housing programs, total	19,438	19,959	20,636
Low-income housing assistance (sec. 8)	15,560	16,090	16,579
Public housing capital fund	3,080	3,159	3,346
Rent supplement	55	56	56
Homeownership assistance (sec. 235)	28	28	28
Rental housing assistance (sec. 236)	609	610	610
College housing grants	15	16	16

[1] Includes outlays for contract renewals.

HOMEOWNERSHIP AND OPPORTUNITY FOR PEOPLE EVERYWHERE GRANTS (HOPE GRANTS)

Program and Financing (in millions of dollars)

Identification code 86–0196–0–1–604	1999 actual	2000 est.	2001 est.
Budgetary resources available for obligation:			
21.40 Unobligated balance available, start of year	11	14	3
22.00 New budget authority (gross)		−11	
22.10 Resources available from recoveries of prior year obligations	3		
23.90 Total budgetary resources available for obligation	14	3	3
24.40 Unobligated balance available, end of year	14	3	3
New budget authority (gross), detail:			
Discretionary:			
40.36 Unobligated balance rescinded		−11	
Change in unpaid obligations:			
72.40 Unpaid obligations, start of year: Obligated balance, start of year	102	81	63
73.20 Total outlays (gross)	−18	−18	−18
73.45 Adjustments in unexpired accounts	−3		
74.40 Unpaid obligations, end of year: Obligated balance, end of year	81	63	45
Outlays (gross), detail:			
86.93 Outlays from discretionary balances	18	18	18
Net budget authority and outlays:			
89.00 Budget authority		−11	
90.00 Outlays	18	18	18

The Homeownership and Opportunity for People Everywhere Program provided affordable homeownership opportunities for low-income families. Units were converted to homeownership from public and Indian housing properties in HOPE 1, from FHA-insured and Government-held multifamily properties in HOPE 2, and from Government-owned or -held single family properties in HOPE 3. HOPE Grants were used for property acquisition, rehabilitation, mortgage subsidies, security measures, and technical assistance. In addition, grants have been devoted to counseling and training of residents, and other activities intended to help them become economically self-sufficient homeowners. No funding is being requested for 2001. This schedule reflects the liquidation of prior year balances.

Congregate Services

Program and Financing (in millions of dollars)

Identification code 86–0178–0–1–604	1999 actual	2000 est.	2001 est.
Change in unpaid obligations:			
72.40 Unpaid obligations, start of year: Obligated balance, start of year	9	2	
73.20 Total outlays (gross)	–5	–2	
73.40 Adjustments in expired accounts (net)	–1		
74.40 Unpaid obligations, end of year: Obligated balance, end of year	2		
Outlays (gross), detail:			
86.93 Outlays from discretionary balances	5	2	
Net budget authority and outlays:			
89.00 Budget authority			
90.00 Outlays	5	2	

Under the Congregate Services program, HUD contracted directly with local public housing agencies and section 202 housing for the elderly or disabled sponsors to supply support services, including meals and other services. Funding for this activity will be requested in the supportive services set-aside within the Public Housing Capital Fund for 2001. Renewals of congregate services contracts for assisted housing are funded within the Housing for Special Populations account. This schedule reflects the liquidation of prior year balances from the separately appropriated Congregate Services Program.

Housing Counseling Assistance

Program and Financing (in millions of dollars)

Identification code 86–0156–0–1–506	1999 actual	2000 est.	2001 est.
Change in unpaid obligations:			
72.40 Unpaid obligations, start of year: Obligated balance, start of year	2		
73.20 Total outlays (gross)			
73.40 Adjustments in expired accounts (net)	–2		
Net budget authority and outlays:			
89.00 Budget authority			
90.00 Outlays			

The Housing Counseling Assistance program provides comprehensive housing counseling services to eligible homeowners and tenants, including pre-purchase, default and renter counseling.

In 1998, housing counseling was appropriated as a $20 million set-aside in the HOME Investment Partnerships Program. The program was funded at $17.5 million as a HOME set-aside in 1999 and at $15 million in 2000. The Budget proposes Housing Counseling as a $24 million HOME set-aside for 2001.

Section 8 Moderate Rehabilitation

single room occupancy

Program and Financing (in millions of dollars)

Identification code 86–0195–0–1–604	1999 actual	2000 est.	2001 est.
Obligations by program activity:			
00.01 Homelessness prevention	20		
10.00 Total new obligations (object class 41.0)	20		
Budgetary resources available for obligation:			
21.40 Unobligated balance available, start of year	85	65	
22.21 Unobligated balance transferred to other accounts		–65	
23.90 Total budgetary resources available for obligation	85		
23.95 Total new obligations	–20		
24.40 Unobligated balance available, end of year	65		
Change in unpaid obligations:			
72.40 Unpaid obligations, start of year: Obligated balance, start of year	348	337	
73.10 Total new obligations	20		
73.20 Total outlays (gross)	–31		
73.31 Obligated balance transferred to other accounts		–337	
74.40 Unpaid obligations, end of year: Obligated balance, end of year	337		
Outlays (gross), detail:			
86.93 Outlays from discretionary balances	31		
Net budget authority and outlays:			
89.00 Budget authority			
90.00 Outlays	31		

Section 8 assistance for single room occupancy dwellings is authorized by Title IV, subtitle E, of the Stewart B. McKinney Homeless Assistance Act, as amended by the Housing and Community Development Act of 1992. Since 1995, these activities have been funded in the Homeless Assistance Grants account. The 2000 Appropriations Act transferred all balances in this account to the Homeless Assistance Grants account.

Manufactured Home Inspection and Monitoring

Unavailable Collections (in millions of dollars)

Identification code 86–5271–0–2–376	1999 actual	2000 est.	2001 est.
Balance, start of year:			
01.99 Balance, start of year			
Receipts:			
02.01 Manufactured home inspection and monitoring	15	16	17
Appropriation:			
05.01 Manufactured home inspection and monitoring	–15	–16	–17
07.99 Total balance, end of year			

Program and Financing (in millions of dollars)

Identification code 86–5271–0–2–376	1999 actual	2000 est.	2001 est.
Obligations by program activity:			
00.01 Transfer to salaries and expenses	1	1	1
00.02 Other program costs	14	15	16
10.00 Total new obligations (object class 25.2)	15	16	17
Budgetary resources available for obligation:			
21.40 Unobligated balance available, start of year	8	9	9
22.00 New budget authority (gross)	15	16	17
22.10 Resources available from recoveries of prior year obligations	1		
23.90 Total budgetary resources available for obligation	24	25	26
23.95 Total new obligations	–15	–16	–17
24.40 Unobligated balance available, end of year	9	9	8
New budget authority (gross), detail:			
Mandatory:			
60.25 Appropriation (special fund, indefinite)	15	16	17
Change in unpaid obligations:			
72.40 Unpaid obligations, start of year: Obligated balance, start of year	2	1	2
73.10 Total new obligations	15	16	17
73.20 Total outlays (gross)	–15	–15	–16
73.45 Adjustments in unexpired accounts	–1		
74.40 Unpaid obligations, end of year: Obligated balance, end of year	1	2	3
Outlays (gross), detail:			
86.97 Outlays from new mandatory authority	14	14	15
86.98 Outlays from mandatory balances	1	1	1
87.00 Total outlays (gross)	15	15	16

General and special funds—Continued

MANUFACTURED HOME INSPECTION AND MONITORING—Continued

Program and Financing (in millions of dollars)—Continued

Identification code 86–5271–0–2–376	1999 actual	2000 est.	2001 est.
Net budget authority and outlays:			
89.00 Budget authority	15	16	17
90.00 Outlays	15	15	16

Section 620 of the National Manufactured Housing Construction and Safety Standards Act of 1974, as amended, authorizes enforcement of appropriate construction standards for the construction, design and performance of manufactured homes to assure their quality, durability, and safety. All manufactured homes produced since the standards took effect on June 15, 1976 must comply with Federal construction and safety standards. The States are actively encouraged to participate in the program under compliance plans approved by HUD.

A fee of $24 per transportable section is charged to the manufacturers for each manufactured home produced. The fee is used to cover the costs of the monitoring and enforcement activities by HUD and its contract agents. Fees are deposited in a special fund administered by the Department, and a portion of the fee receipts are transferred to the salaries and expenses account to defray the direct administrative expenses of the program. In 1999, an estimated 375,000 manufactured homes and 631,828 transportable sections were produced.

This account also presents activities formerly shown under the Interstate Land Sales account.

The Interstate Land Sales Full Disclosure Act provides protection to the public with respect to purchases or leases of subdivision lots. Statements of record must be filed with the Secretary before subdivisions with 100 or more lots may be sold in interstate commerce, except when the subdivision is eligible for exemption.

The Secretary is authorized to charge a fee, to be paid by the developer when filing a statement of record. The fee receipts are permanently appropriated and have helped finance a portion of the direct administrative expenses incurred in program operations.

The estimated annual program activity level will continue at 1,020 filings, approximately the same estimated level as in recent years.

Public enterprise funds:

RENTAL HOUSING ASSISTANCE FUND

Program and Financing (in millions of dollars)

Identification code 86–4041–0–3–604	1999 actual	2000 est.	2001 est.
Obligations by program activity:			
09.00 Reimbursable program	34	31	28
10.00 Total new obligations (object class 25.2)	34	31	28
Budgetary resources available for obligation:			
21.40 Unobligated balance available, start of year	1	1	1
22.00 New budget authority (gross)	34	31	28
23.90 Total budgetary resources available for obligation	35	32	29
23.95 Total new obligations	−34	−31	−28
24.40 Unobligated balance available, end of year	1	1	1
New budget authority (gross), detail:			
Mandatory:			
69.00 Offsetting collections (cash)	34	31	28
Change in unpaid obligations:			
72.40 Unpaid obligations, start of year: Obligated balance, start of year	7	7	6
73.10 Total new obligations	34	31	28
73.20 Total outlays (gross)	−34	−31	−28
74.40 Unpaid obligations, end of year: Obligated balance, end of year	7	6	6
Outlays (gross), detail:			
86.97 Outlays from new mandatory authority	34	31	28
Offsets:			
Against gross budget authority and outlays:			
88.40 Offsetting collections (cash) from: Non-Federal sources	−34	−31	−28
Net budget authority and outlays:			
89.00 Budget authority			
90.00 Outlays			

The Housing and Urban Development Act of 1968 authorized the Secretary to establish a revolving fund into which rental collections in excess of the established basic rents for units in section 236 subsidized projects would be deposited.

The Housing and Community Development Amendment of 1978 authorized the Secretary, subject to approval in appropriation acts, to transfer excess rent collections received after 1978 to the Troubled Projects Operating Subsidy program, renamed the Flexible Subsidy Fund. Prior to that time, collections were used for paying tax and utility increases in section 236 projects. The Housing and Community Development Act of 1980 amended the 1978 Act by authorizing the transfer of excess rent collections regardless of when collected. This Budget proposes that the resources from the Rental Housing Assistance Fund continue to be transferred to the Flexible Subsidy Fund.

FLEXIBLE SUBSIDY FUND

(TRANSFER OF FUNDS)

From the Rental Housing Assistance Fund, all uncommitted balances of excess rental charges as of September 30, [1999] *2000*, and any collections made during fiscal year [2000] *2001*, shall be transferred to the Flexible Subsidy Fund, as authorized by section 236(g) of the National Housing Act, as amended. *(Departments of Veterans Affairs and Housing and Urban Development, and Independent Agencies Appropriations Act, 2000.)*

Program and Financing (in millions of dollars)

Identification code 86–4044–0–3–604	1999 actual	2000 est.	2001 est.
Obligations by program activity:			
09.00 Reimbursable program	18	17	18
10.00 Total new obligations (object class 41.0)	18	17	18
Budgetary resources available for obligation:			
21.40 Unobligated balance available, start of year	235	264	286
22.00 New budget authority (gross)	48	39	36
23.90 Total budgetary resources available for obligation	283	303	322
23.95 Total new obligations	−18	−17	−18
24.40 Unobligated balance available, end of year	264	286	305
New budget authority (gross), detail:			
Discretionary:			
68.00 Spending authority from offsetting collections (gross): Offsetting collections (cash)	48	39	36
Change in unpaid obligations:			
72.40 Unpaid obligations, start of year: Obligated balance, start of year	27	28	31
73.10 Total new obligations	18	17	18
73.20 Total outlays (gross)	−17	−14	−20
74.40 Unpaid obligations, end of year: Obligated balance, end of year	28	31	29
Outlays (gross), detail:			
86.93 Outlays from discretionary balances	17	14	20

		1999 actual	2000 est.	2001 est.
	Offsets:			
	Against gross budget authority and outlays:			
	Offsetting collections (cash) from:			
88.00	Federal sources	−41	−31	−28
88.40	Non-Federal sources	−7	−8	−8
88.90	Total, offsetting collections (cash)	−48	−39	−36
	Net budget authority and outlays:			
89.00	Budget authority			
90.00	Outlays	−31	−25	−16
	Memorandum (non-add) entries:			
92.01	Total investments, start of year: U.S. securities: Par value	150	205	205
92.02	Total investments, end of year: U.S. securities: Par value	205	205	205

Status of Direct Loans (in millions of dollars)

Identification code 86–4044–0–3–604		1999 actual	2000 est.	2001 est.
	Cumulative balance of direct loans outstanding:			
1210	Outstanding, start of year	769	786	796
1231	Disbursements: Direct loan disbursements	17	14	20
1251	Repayments: Repayments and prepayments		−4	−4
1290	Outstanding, end of year	786	796	812

The Flexible Subsidy Fund assisted financially troubled subsidized projects under certain FHA authorities. The subsidies were intended to prevent potential losses to the FHA fund resulting from project insolvency and to preserve these projects as a viable source of housing for low and moderate-income tenants. Priority was given to projects with Federal insurance-in-force and then to those with mortgages that had been assigned to the Department of Housing and Urban Development.

The budget assumes that the account will continue to serve as a repository of excess rental charges appropriated from the Rental Housing Assistance Fund. Since 1996, these resources have not been used for new reservations but they continue to offset Flexible Subsidy outlays and other discretionary expenditures.

Statement of Operations (in millions of dollars)

Identification code 86–4044–0–3–604		1998 actual	1999 actual	2000 est.	2001 est.
0101	Revenue	66	54	50	47
0102	Expense	−90	−1		
0105	Net income or loss (−)	−24	53	50	47

Balance Sheet (in millions of dollars)

Identification code 86–4044–0–3–604		1998 actual	1999 actual	2000 est.	2001 est.
	ASSETS:				
	Federal assets:				
1101	Fund balances with Treasury	131	108	184	200
	Investments in US securities:				
1102	Treasury securities, par	150	205	205	205
1106	Receivables, net	4			
	Net value of assets related to pre–1992 direct loans receivable and acquired defaulted guaranteed loans receivable:				
1601	Direct loans, gross	769	786	796	812
1603	Allowance for estimated uncollectible loans and interest (−)	−692	−692	−717	−731
1699	Value of assets related to direct loans	77	94	79	81
1999	Total assets	362	407	468	486
	NET POSITION:				
3100	Appropriated capital	217	217	217	217
3300	Cumulative results of operations	145	190	251	269
3999	Total net position	362	407	468	486
4999	Total liabilities and net position	362	407	468	486

Homeownership Assistance Fund

Program and Financing (in millions of dollars)

Identification code 86–4043–0–3–604		1999 actual	2000 est.	2001 est.
	Budgetary resources available for obligation:			
21.40	Unobligated balance available, start of year	23	23	23
21.49	Unobligated balance available, start of year: Contract authority	61	61	61
21.99	Total unobligated balance, start of year	84	84	84
22.00	New budget authority (gross)	1		
22.10	Resources available from recoveries of prior year obligations	1		
23.90	Total budgetary resources available for obligation	86	84	84
24.40	Unobligated balance available, end of year	23	23	23
24.49	Unobligated balance, end of year: Contract authority	61	61	61
24.99	Total unobligated balance, end of year	84	84	84
	New budget authority (gross), detail:			
	Mandatory:			
69.00	Offsetting collections (cash)	1		
	Change in unpaid obligations:			
72.40	Unpaid obligations, start of year: Obligated balance, start of year	−1		
73.45	Adjustments in unexpired accounts	−1		
	Offsets:			
	Against gross budget authority and outlays:			
88.40	Offsetting collections (cash) from: Non-Federal sources	−1		
	Net budget authority and outlays:			
89.00	Budget authority			
90.00	Outlays	−1		
	Memorandum (non-add) entries:			
92.01	Total investments, start of year: U.S. securities: Par value	18		

Status of Contract Authority (in millions of dollars)

Identification code 86–4043–0–3–604		1999 actual	2000 est.	2001 est.
0100	Balance, start of year	61	61	61
0700	Balance, end of year	61	61	61

The Homeownership Assistance Fund was established by the Housing and Urban-Rural Recovery Act of 1983. It provided for the receipt of recaptures of budget authority, cash, and interest earnings under the restructured section 235 program. The funds were authorized to be used, to the extent approved in Appropriation Acts, by the Secretary to provide additional section 235 assistance payments for mortgagors who are unable to assume the full payment due under the mortgage after the termination of the original 10-year assistance payments contract.

Nehemiah Housing Opportunity Fund

Program and Financing (in millions of dollars)

Identification code 86–4071–0–3–604		1999 actual	2000 est.	2001 est.
	Obligations by program activity:			
09.00	Reimbursable program		3	
10.00	Total new obligations (object class 33.0)		3	
	Budgetary resources available for obligation:			
21.40	Unobligated balance available, start of year	1	3	
22.10	Resources available from recoveries of prior year obligations	2		
23.90	Total budgetary resources available for obligation	3	3	
23.95	Total new obligations		−3	
24.40	Unobligated balance available, end of year	3		

Public enterprise funds—Continued

NEHEMIAH HOUSING OPPORTUNITY FUND—Continued

Program and Financing (in millions of dollars)—Continued

Identification code 86–4071–0–3–604	1999 actual	2000 est.	2001 est.
Change in unpaid obligations:			
72.40 Unpaid obligations, start of year: Obligated balance, start of year	26	21	16
73.10 Total new obligations		3	
73.20 Total outlays (gross)	−2	−8	−8
73.45 Adjustments in unexpired accounts	−2		
74.40 Unpaid obligations, end of year: Obligated balance, end of year	21	16	8
Outlays (gross), detail:			
86.93 Outlays from discretionary balances	2	8	8
Net budget authority and outlays:			
89.00 Budget authority			
90.00 Outlays	2	8	8

The Nehemiah grants program was authorized by the Housing and Community Development Act of 1987 to provide loans to eligible families to assist in the purchase of new or substantially rehabilitated units. This schedule reflects the liquidation of remaining reserved and obligated balances.

Credit accounts:

FHA—MUTUAL MORTGAGE INSURANCE PROGRAM ACCOUNT

(INCLUDING TRANSFERS OF FUNDS)

During fiscal year [2000], *2001* commitments to guarantee loans to carry out the purposes of section 203(b) of the National Housing Act, as amended, shall not exceed a loan principal of [$140,000,000,000] *$160,000,000,000*.

During fiscal year [2000], *2001* obligations to make direct loans to carry out the purposes of section 204(g) of the National Housing Act, as amended, shall not exceed [$100,000,000] *$250,000,000*: *Provided*, That the foregoing amount shall be for loans to nonprofit and governmental entities in connection with sales of single family real properties owned by the Secretary and formerly insured under the Mutual Mortgage Insurance Fund.

For administrative expenses necessary to carry out the guaranteed and direct loan program, $330,888,000, of which not to exceed $324,866,000 shall be transferred to the appropriation for "Salaries and expenses"; not to exceed $4,022,000 shall be transferred to the appropriation for the Office of Inspector General*; and not to exceed $2,000,000 shall be to support a data warehouse operated by the Federal Housing Credit Consortium*. In addition, for administrative contract expenses, $160,000,000: *Provided*, That to the extent guaranteed loan commitments exceed [$49,664,000,000] *$65,500,000,000* on or before April 1, [2000], *2001* an additional $1,400 for administrative contract expenses shall be available for each $1,000,000 in additional guaranteed loan commitments (including a pro rata amount for any amount below $1,000,000), but in no case shall funds made available by this proviso exceed $16,000,000. *(Departments of Veterans Affairs and Housing and Urban Development, and Independent Agencies Appropriations Act, 2000.)*

Unavailable Collections (in millions of dollars)

Identification code 86–0183–0–1–371	1999 actual	2000 est.	2001 est.
Balance, start of year:			
01.99 Balance, start of year	1,264		
Receipts:			
02.01 FHA Mutual Mortgage Insurance Guaranteed Loan, negative subsidies	3,559		
04.00 Total: Balances and collections	4,823		
Appropriation:			
05.01 FHA mutual mortgage insurance program account	−4,823		
05.99 Subtotal appropriation	−4,823		
07.99 Total balance, end of year			

Program and Financing (in millions of dollars)

Identification code 86–0183–0–1–371	1999 actual	2000 est.	2001 est.
Obligations by program activity:			
00.07 Reestimates of loan guarantee negative subsidy	3,789		
00.08 Interest on reestimates of loan guarantee subsidy	705		
00.09 Administrative expenses, salaries & expenses transfer	329	329	329
00.12 Non-overhead administrative expenses for FHA contracts		160	160
00.13 Transfer to Federal Housing Credit Consortium		2	2
10.00 Total new obligations	4,823	491	491
Budgetary resources available for obligation:			
22.00 New budget authority (gross)	4,823	491	491
23.95 Total new obligations	−4,823	−491	−491
New budget authority (gross), detail:			
Discretionary:			
40.00 Appropriation		491	491
40.20 Appropriation (special fund, definite)	329		
43.00 Appropriation (total discretionary)	329	491	491
Mandatory:			
60.25 Appropriation (special fund, indefinite)	4,494		
70.00 Total new budget authority (gross)	4,823	491	491
Change in unpaid obligations:			
72.40 Unpaid obligations, start of year: Obligated balance, start of year			40
73.10 Total new obligations	4,823	491	491
73.20 Total outlays (gross)	−4,823	−451	−491
74.40 Unpaid obligations, end of year: Obligated balance, end of year		40	40
Outlays (gross), detail:			
86.90 Outlays from new discretionary authority	329	451	451
86.93 Outlays from discretionary balances			40
Outlays from permanent authority:			
86.97 Outlays from new mandatory authority	4,494		
87.00 Total outlays (gross)	4,823	451	491
Net budget authority and outlays:			
89.00 Budget authority	4,823	491	491
90.00 Outlays	4,823	451	491

Summary of Loan Levels, Subsidy Budget Authority and Outlays by Program (in millions of dollars)

Identification code 86–0183–0–1–371	1999 actual	2000 est.	2001 est.
Direct loan levels supportable by subsidy budget authority:			
1150 Direct loan levels	1	100	250
1159 Total direct loan levels	1	100	250
Guaranteed loan levels supportable by subsidy budget authority:			
2150 MMI Fund, Section 203(b)	123,546	122,658	158,993
2150 Standby commitment authority			
2150 Standby commitment authority	16,454	17,342	1,007
2159 Total loan guarantee levels	140,000	140,000	160,000
Guaranteed loan subsidy (in percent):			
2320 Subsidy rate	−2.62	−1.99	−2.57
2329 Weighted average subsidy rate	−2.62	−1.99	−2.57
Guaranteed loan subsidy budget authority:			
2330 MMI Section 203(b) negative subsidy	−3,129	−2,628	−3,675
2330 Subsidy budget authority—reestimates	4,494		
2339 Total subsidy budget authority	1,365	−2,628	−3,675
Guaranteed loan subsidy outlays:			
2340 Subsidy outlays—MMI 203(b) negative subsidy	−3,129	−2,628	−3,675
2340 Subsidy outlays—reestimates	4,494		
2349 Total subsidy outlays	1,365	−2,628	−3,675
Administrative expense data:			
3510 Budget authority	329	491	491
3580 Outlays from balances			40
3590 Outlays from new authority	329	451	451

The Federal Housing Administration (FHA) provides mortgage insurance to encourage lenders to make credit available to expand homeownership and to predominantly serve borrowers that the conventional market does not adequately provide for including: first-time homebuyers; minorities; lower-income families; and, residents of underserved areas (central cities and rural areas).

The Budget proposes to increase the FHA limitation on individual mortgages to insure single family loans with a principal balance at or below the conforming loan limits established by Freddie Mac and Fannie Mae. Under current law FHA cannot insure loans with a principal balance over 87 percent of the conforming loan limit. Raising the FHA loan limit to 100 percent of the Freddie Mac/Fannie Mae conforming loan limit will help approximately 55,000 families purchase their first homes, especially large families and families in high cost areas. These additional loans will generate $241 million in negative subsidy in the MMI Fund in 2001.

In addition, the Budget proposes legislation to allow FHA to insure a relatively new product on the mortgage market—hybrid adjustable-rate mortgages (ARMs). Using the conventional market as a prototype, hybrid ARMs are defined as adjustable-rate loans that carry an initial fixed interest rate for longer than one year. After the initial fixed-rate period ends, these loans are subject to interest rate adjustments, typically on an annual basis and indexed to the corresponding term Treasury bond yield. FHA intends to develop ARMs with a set interest rate for an initial period of 3, 5, 7, or 10 years, and annual interest rate adjustments thereafter. Hybrid ARMs will substantially enhance FHA's product line, offering a sound mortgage product to borrowers who do not qualify for a fixed-rate mortgage or cannot afford the fixed-rate pricing, but who want to avoid the volatility associated with traditional ARMs. This new product will increase loan endorsement activity by approximately 40,000 loans, resulting in an additional $114 million in negative subsidy in 2001.

The Budget proposes an aggregate limitation of $160 billion on commitments to guarantee loans in 2001. The $20 billion increase over 2000 reflects, in part, the increased volume of business associated with the proposals to increase the FHA mortgage limit and to offer hybrid ARMs.

As required by the Federal Credit Reform Act of 1990, this account records administrative expenses for this program, as well as the subsidy costs, if any, associated with the loan guarantees committed in 1992 and thereafter. The subsidy amounts are estimated on a present value basis; the administrative expenses are estimated on a cash basis.

FHA will contribute $2,000,000 from the FHA–MMI fund to fund efforts by the Federal Housing Credit Consortium to develop a pilot data warehouse for use by the four major housing credit agencies.

Object Classification (in millions of dollars)

Identification code 86–0183–0–1–371	1999 actual	2000 est.	2001 est.
25.2 Other services		160	160
25.3 Purchases of goods and services from Government accounts	329	331	331
41.0 Grants, subsidies, and contributions	4,494		
99.9 Total new obligations	4,823	491	491

FHA—Mutual Mortgage Insurance Direct Loan Financing Account

Program and Financing (in millions of dollars)

Identification code 86–4242–0–3–371	1999 actual	2000 est.	2001 est.
Obligations by program activity:			
00.01 Direct loans	1	100	250
00.02 Interest paid to Treasury		6	15
00.03 Claims & other		4	8
10.00 Total new obligations	1	110	273
Budgetary resources available for obligation:			
21.40 Unobligated balance available, start of year	3	5	
22.00 New financing authority (gross)	3	110	273
22.60 Portion applied to repay debt		−5	
23.90 Total budgetary resources available for obligation	6	110	273
23.95 Total new obligations	−1	−110	−273
24.40 Unobligated balance available, end of year	5		
New financing authority (gross), detail:			
Mandatory:			
67.15 Authority to borrow (indefinite)		100	250
Spending authority from offsetting collections:			
Discretionary:			
68.00 Offsetting collections (cash)	3	10	51
68.47 Portion applied to repay debt			−28
68.90 Spending authority from offsetting collections (total discretionary)	3	10	23
70.00 Total new financing authority (gross)	3	110	273
Change in unpaid obligations:			
72.40 Unpaid obligations, start of year: Obligated balance, start of year	3	3	13
73.10 Total new obligations	1	110	273
73.20 Total financing disbursements (gross)	−2	−100	−250
74.40 Unpaid obligations, end of year: Obligated balance, end of year	3	13	36
87.00 Total financing disbursements (gross)	2	100	250
Offsets:			
Against gross financing authority and financing disbursements:			
Offsetting collections (cash) from:			
88.25 Interest on uninvested funds		−1	−1
Non-Federal sources:			
88.40 Repayment of principal	−3	−8	−47
88.40 Repayment of interest		−1	−3
88.90 Total, offsetting collections (cash)	−3	−10	−51
Net financing authority and financing disbursements:			
89.00 Financing authority		100	222
90.00 Financing disbursements	−2	90	199

As required by the Federal Credit Reform Act of 1990, this non-budgetary account records all cash flows to and from the Government resulting from direct loans obligated in 1992 and thereafter (including modifications of direct loans that resulted from obligations in any year). The amounts in this account are a means of financing and are not included in the budget totals.

The $250 million in 2001 direct loan limitation in the MMI Fund would permit the Department to use Purchase Money Mortgages (PMMs) to help finance the sale of acquired single family properties. HUD would extend credit for these single-family homes to community nonprofit organizations or local government entities who would be expected to sell the properties to low- and moderate-income buyers. The use of PMMs provides a tool for State and local nonprofit organizations to use in revitalizing communities, and creates enhanced homeownership opportunities for low- and moderate-income families.

Status of Direct Loans (in millions of dollars)

Identification code 86–4242–0–3–371	1999 actual	2000 est.	2001 est.
Position with respect to appropriations act limitation on obligations:			
1111 Limitation on direct loans	100	100	250
1112 Unobligated direct loan limitation	−99		
1150 Total direct loan obligations	1	100	250
Cumulative balance of direct loans outstanding:			
1210 Outstanding, start of year	5	3	87

Credit accounts—Continued

FHA—MUTUAL MORTGAGE INSURANCE DIRECT LOAN FINANCING ACCOUNT—Continued

Status of Direct Loans (in millions of dollars)—Continued

Identification code 86–4242–0–3–371	1999 actual	2000 est.	2001 est.
1231 Disbursements: Direct loan disbursements	1	90	227
1251 Repayments: Repayments and prepayments	−3	−6	−28
1263 Write-offs for default: Direct loans	....	....	−2
1290 Outstanding, end of year	3	87	284

Balance Sheet (in millions of dollars)

Identification code 86–4242–0–3–371	1998 actual	1999 actual	2000 est.	2001 est.
ASSETS:				
1101 Federal assets: Fund balances with Treasury	7	8	10	36
Net value of assets related to post-1991 direct loans receivable:				
1401 Direct loans receivable, gross	5	3	87	284
1499 Net present value of assets related to direct loans	5	3	87	284
1999 Total assets	12	11	97	320
LIABILITIES:				
Federal liabilities:				
2103 Treasury borrowing	7	7	88	302
2105 Other liabilites—intragovernmental	3	3	3	6
2207 Non-Federal liabilities: Other liabilites with the public	2	1	6	12
2999 Total liabilities	12	11	97	320
4999 Total liabilities and net position	12	11	97	320

FHA—MUTUAL MORTGAGE INSURANCE GUARANTEED LOAN FINANCING ACCOUNT

Program and Financing (in millions of dollars)

Identification code 86–4587–0–3–371	1999 actual	2000 est.	2001 est.
Obligations by program activity:			
00.08 Interest payments to Treasury	426	460	280
00.09 Administrative expenses (payment of negative subsidy to receipt account)	329	....	....
00.11 Default claims and other	4,948	4,131	4,772
00.12 Payment to liquidating account of value of assets sold	....	169	....
00.91 Subtotal, capital/operating expenses	5,703	4,760	5,052
08.01 Payment of negative subsidy to liquidating account for new business	2,729	2,628	3,674
08.14 Negative subsidy to liquidating account, new legislation	400	....	....
08.91 Subtotal, subsidy activity	3,129	2,628	3,674
10.00 Total new obligations	8,832	7,388	8,726
Budgetary resources available for obligation:			
21.40 Unobligated balance available, start of year	541	2,980	3,377
22.00 New financing authority (gross)	11,271	8,385	8,628
22.60 Portion applied to repay debt	....	−600	−2,900
23.90 Total budgetary resources available for obligation	11,812	10,765	9,105
23.95 Total new obligations	−8,832	−7,388	−8,726
24.40 Unobligated balance available, end of year	2,980	3,377	379
New financing authority (gross), detail:			
Mandatory:			
67.15 Authority to borrow (indefinite)	900	200	200
Discretionary:			
68.00 Spending authority from offsetting collections: Offsetting collections (cash)	10,371	8,185	8,428
70.00 Total new financing authority (gross)	11,271	8,385	8,628
Change in unpaid obligations:			
72.40 Unpaid obligations, start of year: Obligated balance, start of year	−128	−78	−78
73.10 Total new obligations	8,832	7,388	8,726
73.20 Total financing disbursements (gross)	−8,782	−7,388	−8,726
74.40 Unpaid obligations, end of year: Obligated balance, end of year	−78	−78	−78
87.00 Total financing disbursements (gross)	8,782	7,388	8,726
Offsets:			
Against gross financing authority and financing disbursements:			
Offsetting collections (cash) from:			
88.00 Transfer of Reestimates from reserves in Liquidating account	−4,494	....	....
88.25 Interest on uninvested funds	−92	−224	−212
Non-Federal sources:			
88.40 Fees and premiums	−3,171	−3,733	−4,658
88.40 Recoveries on defaults	−2,614	−3,838	−3,558
88.40 Gross proceeds from asset sales	....	−390	....
88.90 Total, offsetting collections (cash)	−10,371	−8,185	−8,428
Net financing authority and financing disbursements:			
89.00 Financing authority	900	200	200
90.00 Financing disbursements	−1,589	−797	298

Status of Guaranteed Loans (in millions of dollars)

Identification code 86–4587–0–3–371	1999 actual	2000 est.	2001 est.
Position with respect to appropriations act limitation on commitments:			
2111 Limitation on guaranteed loans made by private lenders	140,000	140,000	160,000
2112 Uncommitted loan guarantee limitation	−16,454	−17,342	−1,007
2150 Total guaranteed loan commitments	123,546	122,658	158,993
Cumulative balance of guaranteed loans outstanding:			
2210 Outstanding, start of year	309,309	355,608	429,966
2231 Disbursements of new guaranteed loans	113,174	122,341	149,883
2251 Repayments and prepayments	−62,098	−44,493	−59,708
Adjustments:			
2261 Terminations for default that result in loans receivable	−35	−14	−26
2262 Terminations for default that result in acquisition of property	−4,664	−3,440	−4,273
2263 Terminations for default that result in claim payments	−78	−36	−46
2290 Outstanding, end of year	355,608	429,966	515,796
Memorandum:			
2299 Guaranteed amount of guaranteed loans outstanding, end of year	355,608	429,966	515,796
Addendum:			
Cumulative balance of defaulted guaranteed loans that result in loans receivable:			
2310 Outstanding, start of year	348	369	35
2331 Disbursements for guaranteed loan claims	35	14	26
2351 Repayments of loans receivable	−9	−1	−1
2364 Other adjustments, net	−5	−347	−3
2390 Outstanding, end of year	369	35	57

As required by the Federal Credit Reform Act of 1990, this non-budgetary account records all cash flows to and from the Government resulting from loans insured in 1992 and thereafter. The amounts in this account are considered a means of financing and are not included in the budget totals.

Balance Sheet (in millions of dollars)

Identification code 86–4587–0–3–371	1998 actual[1]	1999 actual	2000 est.	2001 est.
ASSETS:				
1101 Federal assets: Fund balances with Treasury	730	3,228	3,586	588
Net value of assets related to post-1991 acquired defaulted guaranteed loans receivable:				
1501 Defaulted guaranteed loans receivable, gross	258	369	35	57

1504	Foreclosed property	2,045	2,820	1,425	1,299
1505	Allowance for subsidy cost	–880	–1,363	–1,249	–1,249
1599	Net value of assets related to defaulted guaranteed loan	1,423	1,826	211	107
1901	Other Federal assets: Other assets	4,713	388		
1999	Total assets	6,866	5,442	3,797	695
	LIABILITIES:				
	Federal liabilities:				
2103	Federal liabilities, Debt	5,482	6,382	5,982	3,282
2105	Other liabilites –intragovernmental	34	1,571		
	Non-Federal liabilities:				
2201	Accounts payable	205	34		
2204	Liabilities for loan guarantees	873	–2,692	–2,694	–3,604
2207	Other	67	147	509	1,017
2999	Total liabilities	6,661	5,442	3,797	695
	NET POSITION:				
3300	Cumulative results of operations	205			
3999	Total net position	205			
4999	Total liabilities and net position	6,866	5,442	3,797	695

[1] As reflected in the 2000 Budget.

FHA—Mutual Mortgage and Cooperative Housing Insurance Funds Liquidating Account

Unavailable Collections (in millions of dollars)

Identification code 86–4070–0–3–371		1999 actual	2000 est.	2001 est.
	Balance, start of year:			
01.99	Balance, start of year			
	Appropriation:			
05.01	Mutual mortgage and cooperative housing insurance funds liquidating account			355
07.99	Total balance, end of year			355

Program and Financing (in millions of dollars)

Identification code 86–4070–0–3–371		1999 actual	2000 est.	2001 est.
	Obligations by program activity:			
00.02	Transfer of Reestimates amount	3,230		
	Operating expenses:			
00.03	Other operating costs	6	6	6
00.04	Administrative contract expenses	118		
00.91	Total operating expenses	3,354	6	6
	Capital investment:			
01.02	Assignment of defaulted mortgages	11		
01.03	Acquisition of real properties	1,078	273	183
01.05	Acquisition of other assets	6	6	6
01.07	Capitalized property expenses	142	113	39
01.08	Loss mitigation activities	6	9	5
01.09	Preforeclosure sale claims	11	7	5
01.91	Total capital investment	1,254	408	238
10.00	Total new obligations	4,608	414	244
	Budgetary resources available for obligation:			
21.40	Unobligated balance available, start of year	14,392	14,736	18,973
22.00	New budget authority (gross)	4,939	4,651	4,986
22.10	Resources available from recoveries of prior year obligations	13		
23.90	Total budgetary resources available for obligation	19,344	19,387	23,959
23.95	Total new obligations	–4,608	–414	–244
24.40	Unobligated balance available, end of year	14,736	18,973	23,716
	New budget authority (gross), detail:			
	Spending authority from offsetting collections:			
	Discretionary:			
68.00	Offsetting collections (cash)			355
68.26	Offsetting collections (unavailable balances)			–355
	Mandatory:			
69.00	Offsetting collections (cash)	4,939	4,651	4,986
70.00	Total new budget authority (gross)	4,939	4,651	4,986
	Change in unpaid obligations:			
72.40	Unpaid obligations, start of year: Obligated balance, start of year	706	681	381
73.10	Total new obligations	4,608	414	244
73.20	Total outlays (gross)	–4,620	–714	–444
73.45	Adjustments in unexpired accounts	–13		
74.40	Unpaid obligations, end of year: Obligated balance, end of year	681	381	181
	Outlays (gross), detail:			
86.97	Outlays from new mandatory authority	3,914	5	63
86.98	Outlays from mandatory balances	706	709	381
87.00	Total outlays (gross)	4,620	714	444
	Offsets:			
	Against gross budget authority and outlays:			
	Offsetting collections (cash) from:			
	Federal sources:			
88.00	Payment from financing account	–2,729	–2,628	–3,674
88.00	Legislative savings	–400		
88.20	Interest on U.S. securities	–983	–1,095	–1,354
	Non-Federal sources:			
88.40	Fees and premiums	–65	–55	–47
88.40	Rebate of unearned prepaid premiums collected		13	
88.40	Proceeds from sale of real property	–762	–690	–263
88.40	Proceeds from sale of mortgage notes		–169	
88.40	Repayment of mortgage notes and sales contracts	–1	–1	
88.40	Interest and operating income	–14	–6	
88.40	Recoveries on defaulted mortgages	–18	–17	
88.40	Miscellaneous collections	–32		
88.40	Other income	65	–3	–3
88.90	Total, offsetting collections (cash)	–4,939	–4,651	–5,341
	Net budget authority and outlays:			
89.00	Budget authority			–355
90.00	Outlays	–319	–3,937	–4,897
	Memorandum (non-add) entries:			
92.01	Total investments, start of year: U.S. securities: Par value	14,344	14,942	18,642
92.02	Total investments, end of year: U.S. securities: Par value	14,942	18,642	23,242

Status of Direct Loans (in millions of dollars)

Identification code 86–4070–0–3–371		1999 actual	2000 est.	2001 est.
	Cumulative balance of direct loans outstanding:			
1210	Outstanding, start of year	5	4	
1251	Repayments: Repayments and prepayments	–1	–1	
1264	Write-offs for default: Other adjustments, net		–3	
1290	Outstanding, end of year	4		

Status of Guaranteed Loans (in millions of dollars)

Identification code 86–4070–0–3–371		1999 actual	2000 est.	2001 est.
	Cumulative balance of guaranteed loans outstanding:			
2210	Outstanding, start of year	71,030	55,866	47,384
2251	Repayments and prepayments	–14,065	–8,193	–6,704
	Adjustments:			
2261	Terminations for default that result in loans receivable	–11	–5	–3
2262	Terminations for default that result in acquisition of property	–1,076	–273	–183
2263	Terminations for default that result in claim payments	–12	–11	–7
2264	Other adjustments, net			
2290	Outstanding, end of year	55,866	47,384	40,487
	Memorandum:			
2299	Guaranteed amount of guaranteed loans outstanding, end of year	55,866	47,384	40,487
	Addendum:			
	Cumulative balance of defaulted guaranteed loans that result in loans receivable:			
2310	Outstanding, start of year	294	270	4
2331	Disbursements for guaranteed loan claims	11	5	3
2351	Repayments of loans receivable	–18	–186	

Credit accounts—Continued

FHA—MUTUAL MORTGAGE AND COOPERATIVE HOUSING INSURANCE FUNDS LIQUIDATING ACCOUNT—Continued

Status of Guaranteed Loans (in millions of dollars)—Continued

Identification code 86–4070–0–3–371	1999 actual	2000 est.	2001 est.
2361 Write-offs of loans receivable	–17	–85	–1
2390 Outstanding, end of year	270	4	6

The Federal Housing Administration Fund currently consists of four separate insurance funds.

In order to present more clearly the operations of the various funds, FHA's budget transactions are separated into two major business segments. The basic single-family insurance programs in the Mutual Mortgage Insurance (MMI) fund and the multifamily Cooperative Management Housing Insurance (CMHI) funds form one segment. All other multifamily and other specialized insurance programs in the General Insurance and Special Risk Insurance funds (GI/SRI) form the other segment.

The Federal Credit Reform Act of 1990 creates a structure of three accounts for existing credit program. For each of the FHA business segments (MMI/CMHI and GI/SRI) there is a liquidating account, which records the revenues and costs associated with loan insurance committed prior to October 1, 1991, a financing account which records the revenues and costs associated with commitments to insure loans made after September 30, 1991, and, a program account which records the transactions associated with the program subsidy costs, if any, and the costs of administering the program.

This liquidating account records, for this program, all cash flows to and from the Government resulting from MMI/CMHI loans insured prior to fiscal year 1992, and is shown on a cash basis. All new activity in this program in 1992 and thereafter (including modifications of loans insured in any year) is recorded in the corresponding program (86–0183) and financing (86–4587 and 86–4242) accounts.

The program activity in the "Program Highlights" table shown below reflects only the activity in the MMI/CMHI liquidating and financing accounts. The GI/SRI program activity can be found with the GI/SRI liquidating account (86–4072).

PROGRAM HIGHLIGHTS

(in millions of dollars)

	1999 actual[1]	*2000 est.*	*2001 est.*
Insurance initiation:			
Mortgage insurance commitments (units)	1,287,654	1,191,988	1,473,620
Mortgage insurance written (in fiscal year):			
Units	1,219,469	1,206,533	1,401,626
Amount	$113,174	$122,341	$149,883
Insurance maintenance: Outstanding balance of insurance in force, end of year:			
Mortgage insurance	$411,474	$477,351	$556,283

[1] Unaudited preliminary results.

Financial condition.—The following tables reflect the revenues, expenses and financial condition of the MMI/CMHI liquidating funds based on Generally Accepted Accounting Principles.

Statement of Operations (in millions of dollars)

Identification code 86–4070–0–3–371	1998 actual[1]	1999 actual[2]	2000 est.	2001 est.
0101 Revenue	3,927	5,768	3,812	4,157
0102 Expense	–5,130	–382	–1,351	–279
0105 Net income or loss (–)	–1,203	5,386	2,461	3,878

[1] As reflected in the 2000 Budget.
[2] Estimated result on GAAP basis pending final audit.

Balance Sheet (in millions of dollars)

Identification code 86–4070–0–3–371	1998 actual[1]	1999 actual	2000 est.	2001 est.
ASSETS:				
Federal assets:				
1101 Fund balances with Treasury	561	346	277	575
Investments in US securities:				
Treasury securities, par:				
1102 Treasury securities, par	14,344	14,942	18,642	23,242
1102 Unamortized net premium/discount	–236	–309	–307	–383
1106 Receivables, net	174	298	175	175
Net value of assets related to pre–1992 direct loans receivable and acquired defaulted guaranteed loans receivable:				
1601 Direct loans, gross	5	4		
1603 Allowance for estimated uncollectible loans and interest (–)	–4	–2		
1699 Value of assets related to direct loans	1	2		
1701 Defaulted guaranteed loans, gross	655	647	6	6
1703 Allowance for estimated uncollectible loans and interest (–)	–333	–339	–6	–6
1704 Defaulted guaranteed loans and interest receivable, net	322	308		
1705 Allowance for uncollectables from foreclosed property	–316	–367	–103	–39
1706 Foreclosed property	779	899	252	96
1799 Value of assets related to loan guarantees	785	840	149	57
1901 Other Federal assets: Other assets	95	1,636	1,639	1,642
1999 Total assets	15,724	17,755	20,575	25,308
LIABILITIES:				
2105 Federal liabilities: Other Intragovernmental liabilites	3,384	356		
Non-Federal liabilities:				
2201 Accounts payable	153	205	164	131
2206 Pension and other actuarial liabilities	1,039	667	533	427
2207 Unearned revenue and advances, and other	1,024	1,017	813	651
2999 Total liabilities	5,600	2,245	1,510	1,209
NET POSITION:				
3100 Appropriated capital	18	18	18	18
3300 Cumulative results of operations	10,106	15,492	19,048	24,081
3999 Total net position	10,124	15,510	19,066	24,099
4999 Total liabilities and net position	15,724	17,755	20,576	25,308

[1] As reflected in the 2000 Budget.

Object Classification (in millions of dollars)

Identification code 86–4070–0–3–371	1999 actual	2000 est.	2001 est.
25.2 Other services	124	6	6
32.0 Land and structures	1,223	386	222
33.0 Investments and loans	17	11	9
41.0 Grants, subsidies, and contributions	3,230		
42.0 Insurance claims and indemnities	14	11	7
99.9 Total new obligations	4,608	414	244

FHA—GENERAL AND SPECIAL RISK PROGRAM ACCOUNT

(INCLUDING TRANSFERS OF FUNDS)

For the cost of guaranteed loans, as authorized by sections 238 and 519 of the National Housing Act (12 U.S.C. 1715z–3 and 1735c), including the cost of loan guarantee modifications (as that term is defined in section 502 of the Congressional Budget Act of 1974, as amended), **[**$153,000,000, including not to exceed $153,000,000 from unobligated balances previously appropriated under this heading**]** *$101,000,000*, to remain available until expended: *Provided*, That these funds are available to subsidize total loan principal, any part of which is to be guaranteed, of up to **[**$18,100,000,000**]** *$21,000,000,000*: *Provided further,* That any amounts made available in any prior appropriations Act for the cost (as such term is defined in section 502 of the Congressional Budget Act of 1974) of guaranteed loans that are obligations of the funds established under section 238 or 519 of the National Housing Act that have not been obligated or that are deobligated shall be available to the Secretary of Housing and Urban Development in connection with the making of such guarantees and shall remain available until expended, notwithstanding the expiration of any period of availability otherwise applicable to such amounts.

Gross obligations for the principal amount of direct loans, as authorized by sections 204(g), 207(l), 238, and 519(a) of the National Housing Act, shall not exceed $50,000,000; of which not to exceed $30,000,000 shall be for bridge financing in connection with the sale of multifamily real properties owned by the Secretary and formerly insured under such Act; and of which not to exceed $20,000,000 shall be for loans to nonprofit and governmental entities in connection with the sale of single-family real properties owned by the Secretary and formerly insured under such Act.

In addition, for administrative expenses necessary to carry out the guaranteed and direct loan programs, $211,455,000 [(including not to exceed $147,000,000 from unobligated balances previously appropriated under this heading)], of which $193,134,000, shall be transferred to the appropriation for "Salaries and expenses"; and of which $18,321,000 shall be transferred to the appropriation for the Office of Inspector General. In addition, for administrative contract expenses necessary to carry out the guaranteed and direct loan programs, $144,000,000: *Provided*, That to the extent guaranteed loan commitments exceed [$7,263,000,000] *$8,426,000,000* on or before April 1, [2000] *2001*, an additional $19,800 for administrative contract expenses shall be available for each $1,000,000 in additional guaranteed loan commitments over [$7,263,000,000] *$8,426,000,000* (including a pro rata amount for any increment below $1,000,000), but in no case shall funds made available by this proviso exceed $14,400,000. *(Departments of Veterans Affairs and Housing and Urban Development, and Independent Agencies Appropriations Act, 2000.)*

General Fund Credit Receipt Accounts (in millions of dollars)

Identification code 86–0200–0–1–371		1999 actual	2000 est.	2001 est.
0101	FHA-General and special risk, negative subsidies	159	229	149
0102	FHA-General and special risk, downward reestimates of subsidies	154		

Program and Financing (in millions of dollars)

Identification code 86–0200–0–1–371		1999 actual	2000 est.	2001 est.
	Obligations by program activity:			
00.02	Prior year adjustment	108		
00.04	Guaranteed loan subsidy	182	153	101
00.07	Reestimate of credit subsidy	233		
00.09	Administrative expenses, salaries & expenses transfer	211	211	211
00.10	Administrative contract expenses		144	144
10.00	Total new obligations	734	508	456
	Budgetary resources available for obligation:			
21.40	Unobligated balance available, start of year	443	250	4
22.00	New budget authority (gross)	541	262	456
23.90	Total budgetary resources available for obligation	984	512	460
23.95	Total new obligations	−734	−508	−456
24.40	Unobligated balance available, end of year	250	4	4
	New budget authority (gross), detail:			
	Discretionary:			
40.00	Appropriation	292	262	456
50.05	Reappropriation (indefinite)	16		
	Mandatory:			
60.05	Appropriation (indefinite)	233		
70.00	Total new budget authority (gross)	541	262	456
	Change in unpaid obligations:			
72.40	Unpaid obligations, start of year: Obligated balance, start of year	−15	78	105
73.10	Total new obligations	734	508	456
73.20	Total outlays (gross)	−638	−479	−469
73.40	Adjustments in expired accounts (net)	−3		
74.40	Unpaid obligations, end of year: Obligated balance, end of year	78	105	93
	Outlays (gross), detail:			
86.90	Outlays from new discretionary authority	272	226	395
86.93	Outlays from discretionary balances	133	253	74
86.97	Outlays from new mandatory authority	233		
87.00	Total outlays (gross)	638	479	469
	Net budget authority and outlays:			
89.00	Budget authority	541	262	456
90.00	Outlays	638	479	469

Summary of Budget Authority and Outlays

(in millions of dollars)

	1999 actual	*2000 est.*	*2001 est.*
Enacted/requested:			
Budget Authority	541	262	456
Outlays	638	479	469
Supplemental proposal:			
Budget Authority		49	
Outlays		37	12
Total:			
Budget Authority	541	311	456
Outlays	638	516	481

Summary of Loan Levels, Subsidy Budget Authority and Outlays by Program (in millions of dollars)

Identification code 86–0200–0–1–371		1999 actual	2000 est.	2001 est.
	Direct loan levels supportable by subsidy budget authority:			
1150	Single-family PMMs	20	20	20
1150	Multifamily bridge loans	30	30	30
1159	Total direct loan levels	50	50	50
	Guaranteed loan levels supportable by subsidy budget authority:			
2150	Apartments NC/SC	2,214	1,442	2,304
2150	Mobile Home Parks	1		
2150	221d3 NP/Coop owned apts	49	35	49
2150	Tax Credits NC	29	102	105
2150	Mixed Income (Hope d4)	6	4	9
2150	Apartments Refinance	981	886	912
2150	241a Supplemental Loans for Apts	51	38	54
2150	Operating Loss Loans for Apts (plus 232)	11	9	13
2150	HFA Risk Sharing		661	678
2150	HFA NC@50 (542c)	145		
2150	HFA NC@90 (542c)	20		
2150	GSE Risk Sharing	19	792	816
2150	FHA Full Insurance for Health Care Facilities (plus 241/232)	816	409	421
2150	Health Care Refinances		326	336
2150	Hospitals	230	1,030	1,030
2150	Single Family Programs			
2150	Section 234: Condominiums	10,397	5,984	8,137
2150	Section 203(k): Rehabilitation Mortgages	1,430	985	1,339
2150	Section 221(d)(2): Low Income Housing	30	19	
2150	Title I Programs			
2150	Property Improvements	482	340	464
2150	Manufactured housing	13	8	10
2150	Standby authority	1,176	5,030	4,323
2159	Total loan guarantee levels	18,100	18,100	21,000
	Guaranteed loan subsidy (in percent):			
2320	Apartments NC/SR	7.09	7.12	3.35
2320	Mobile Home Parks	7.09	0.00	0.00
2320	221d3 NP/Coop owned apts	17.99	15.44	17.22
2320	Tax Credits NC	−0.88	−0.57	−1.75
2320	Mixed Income (Hope IV)	12.13	11.81	3.35
2320	Apartmentst Refinance	−0.78	−1.34	−1.11
2320	241a Supplemental Loans for Apts	17.06	13.88	22.08
2320	Operating Loss Loans for Apts (plus 232's)	25.15	25.10	22.55
2320	HFA Risk Sharing	0.00	−0.45	−1.14
2320	HFA NC@50% (542c)	−0.23	0.00	0.00
2320	HFA NC@90% (542c)	−0.88	0.00	0.00
2320	GSE Risk Sharing	−1.01	−1.88	−1.52
2320	FHA Full Insurance for Health Care Facilities (plus 241/232)	−0.70	−2.79	−2.07
2320	Health Care Refinance	0.00	−1.90	−1.38
2320	Hospital	1.53	−1.60	−1.77
2320	Single Family Programs	0.00	0.00	0.00
2320	Section234: Condominiums	−1.32	0.26	−0.69
2320	Section 203(k): Rehabilitation Mortgages	−1.32	1.75	−0.11
2320	Section 221(d)(2): Low Income Housing	−1.32	4.49	0.00
2320	Title I Programs	0.00	0.00	0.00

Credit accounts—Continued

FHA—GENERAL AND SPECIAL RISK PROGRAM ACCOUNT—Continued
(INCLUDING TRANSFERS OF FUNDS)—Continued

Summary of Loan Levels, Subsidy Budget Authority and Outlays by Program (in millions of dollars)—Continued

Identification code 86–0200–0–1–371		1999 actual	2000 est.	2001 est.
2320	Property Improvements	–1.22	0.87	–0.06
2320	Manufactured housing	–3.13	0.97	0.14
2329	Weighted average subsidy rate	0.03	0.67	–0.12
	Guaranteed loan subsidy budget authority:			
2330	Subsidy budget authority	97		101
2330	Subsidy rate reestimate	233		
2330	Negative Subsidy Receipts	–159	–83	–122
2339	Total subsidy budget authority	171	–83	–21
	Guaranteed loan subsidy outlays:			
2340	Subsidy outlays	194	160	114
2340	Subsidy reestimate outlays	233		
2340	Negative Subsidy Receipts	–159	–83	–122
2349	Total subsidy outlays	268	77	–8
	Administrative expense data:			
3510	Budget authority, S&E Transfer	211	117	211
3510	Budget authority, FHA		144	144
3580	Outlays from balances		94	
3590	Outlays from new authority	211	225	355

Multifamily Products.—This account includes budget authority for multifamily insurance programs requiring positive credit subsidies, as well as for salaries and expenses for all General and Special Risk Insurance Fund programs.

As required by the Federal Credit Reform Act of 1990, this account records, for the single family, multifamily, hospital, and Title I insurance programs of FHA's General Insurance and Special Risk Insurance Funds, the subsidy costs associated with the loan guarantees committed or direct loans obligated in 1992 and thereafter (including modifications of loan guarantees or direct loans that resulted from obligations or commitments in any year), as well as administrative expenses of these programs. The subsidy amounts are estimated on a present value basis; the administrative expenses are accounted for on a cash basis.

Object Classification (in millions of dollars)

Identification code 86–0200–0–1–371		1999 actual	2000 est.	2001 est.
25.1	Advisory and assistance services		144	144
25.3	Purchases of goods and services from Government accounts	211	211	211
41.0	Grants, subsidies, and contributions	523	153	101
99.9	Total new obligations	734	508	456

FHA—GENERAL AND SPECIAL RISK GUARANTEED LOAN FINANCING ACCOUNT

Program and Financing (in millions of dollars)

Identification code 86–4077–0–3–371		1999 actual	2000 est.	2001 est.
	Obligations by program activity:			
	Capital investment, claims and other:			
00.01	Default claims and other	819	714	796
00.05	Interest paid to Treasury	118		
00.08	Asset sale negative subsidy payment to the receipt account			146
00.09	Asset sale payment to liquidating account		118	110
00.10	Value paid to liquidating account for guarantees refinanced under 223(a)(7)	2	3	3
08.01	Payment of negative subsidy to receipt account	159	83	122
08.02	Downward subsidy rate reestimate	154		
10.00	Total new obligations	1,252	918	1,177
	Budgetary resources available for obligation:			
21.40	Unobligated balance available, start of year	1,095	1,907	2,394
22.00	New financing authority (gross)	2,291	1,651	1,534
22.10	Resources available from recoveries of prior year obligations	6		
22.60	Portion applied to repay debt	–233	–246	–246
23.90	Total budgetary resources available for obligation	3,159	3,312	3,682
23.95	Total new obligations	–1,252	–918	–1,177
24.40	Unobligated balance available, end of year	1,907	2,394	2,505
	New financing authority (gross), detail:			
	Mandatory:			
67.15	Authority to borrow (indefinite)	750	200	200
	Discretionary:			
68.00	Spending authority from offsetting collections: Offsetting collections (cash)	1,541	1,451	1,334
70.00	Total new financing authority (gross)	2,291	1,651	1,534
	Change in unpaid obligations:			
72.40	Unpaid obligations, start of year: Obligated balance, start of year	–15	–36	–15
73.10	Total new obligations	1,252	918	1,177
73.20	Total financing disbursements (gross)	–1,267	–897	–1,162
73.45	Adjustments in unexpired accounts	–6		
74.40	Unpaid obligations, end of year: Obligated balance, end of year	–36	–15	
87.00	Total financing disbursements (gross)	1,267	897	1,162
	Offsets:			
	Against gross financing authority and financing disbursements:			
	Offsetting collections (cash) from:			
	Federal sources:			
88.00	Payments from program account	–210	–153	–101
88.00	Repayment of principal and interest from liquidating account	–273	–273	–273
88.00	Subsidy reestimate from program account	–233		
88.25	Interest on uninvested funds	–119	–81	–81
	Non-Federal sources:			
88.40	Fees and premiums	–340	–397	–445
88.40	Recoveries on defaulted mortgages	–45	–1	–2
88.40	Title I recoveries	–17	–24	–6
88.40	Single family property recoveries	–314	–307	–182
88.40	Other recoveries	–6		
88.40	Gross Proceeds from sale of mortgage notes (liquidating)		–118	–110
88.40	Gross Proceeds from Mortgage Note Sales		–104	–143
88.40	Multifamily property recoveries	–1	7	9
88.40	Prior Period Adjustment- Subsidy	17		
88.90	Total, offsetting collections (cash)	–1,541	–1,451	–1,334
	Net financing authority and financing disbursements:			
89.00	Financing authority	750	200	200
90.00	Financing disbursements	–274	–554	–172

Status of Guaranteed Loans (in millions of dollars)

Identification code 86–4077–0–3–371		1999 actual	2000 est.	2001 est.
	Position with respect to appropriations act limitation on commitments:			
2111	Limitation on guaranteed loans made by private lenders	18,100	18,100	21,000
2112	Uncommitted loan guarantee limitation	–1,176	–5,030	–4,323
2150	Total guaranteed loan commitments	16,924	13,070	16,677
	Cumulative balance of guaranteed loans outstanding:			
2210	Outstanding, start of year	52,697	59,692	67,406
2231	Disbursements of new guaranteed loans	16,074	13,070	16,429
2251	Repayments and prepayments	–8,331	–4,642	–4,602
	Adjustments:			
2261	Terminations for default that result in loans receivable	–243	–407	–508
2262	Terminations for default that result in acquisition of property	–494	–307	–289
2263	Terminations for default that result in claim payments	–11		
2290	Outstanding, end of year	59,692	67,406	78,436

	Memorandum:			
2299	Guaranteed amount of guaranteed loans outstanding, end of year	59,692	67,406	78,436
	Addendum:			
	Cumulative balance of defaulted guaranteed loans that result in loans receivable:			
2310	Outstanding, start of year	381	491	793
2331	Disbursements for guaranteed loan claims	243	407	508
2351	Repayments of loans receivable	–17	–105	–145
2361	Write-offs of loans receivable	–116		
2390	Outstanding, end of year	491	793	1,156

As required by the Federal Credit Reform Act of 1990, this non-budgetary account records all cash flows to and from the Government resulting from loan guarantees committed in 1992 and thereafter (including modifications of loan guarantees that resulted from commitments in any year) for FHA's General and Special Risk Insurance Fund programs. The amounts in this account are a means of financing and are not included in the budget totals. As required by the Federal Credit Reform Act of 1990, no administrative expenses can be recorded in the financing account.

Balance Sheet[1] (in millions of dollars)

Identification code 86–4077–0–3–371		1998 actual	1999 actual	2000 est.	2001 est.
	ASSETS:				
	Federal assets:				
1101	Fund balances with Treasury	1,080	1,897	1,633	1,633
	Investments in US securities:				
1107	Borrowings receivable from liquidating account			202	202
	Net value of assets related to post-1991 acquired defaulted guaranteed loans receivable:				
1501	Defaulted guaranteed loans receivable, gross	381	491	793	1,156
1504	Foreclosed property	308	347	598	598
1505	Allowance for subsidy cost	–443	–539	–1,061	–1,061
1599	Net value of assets related to defaulted guaranteed loan	246	299	330	693
1901	Other Federal assets: Other assets		787		
1999	Total assets	1,326	2,983	2,165	2,528
	LIABILITIES:				
	Federal liabilities:				
2101	Accounts payable Intragovernmental		4		
2103	Debt	1,089	1,606	1,555	1,386
2105	Payable to Special Receipt Account for Subsidy Reestimate		303		
	Non-Federal liabilities:				
2204	Liabilities for loan guarantees	237	1,056	610	1,142
2207	Other		14		
2999	Total liabilities	1,326	2,983	2,165	2,528
4999	Total liabilities and net position	1,326	2,983	2,165	2,528

[1] Preliminary results pending final audit. Subsidy reestimates for fiscal year 1999 disbursements will be performed for the Mid-Session review of the Budget.

FHA—General and Special Risk Direct Loan Financing Account

Program and Financing (in millions of dollars)

Identification code 86–4105–0–3–371		1999 actual	2000 est.	2001 est.
	Obligations by program activity:			
00.01	Direct loans		15	15
00.02	Interest paid to Treasury		2	2
10.00	Total new obligations		17	17
	Budgetary resources available for obligation:			
21.40	Unobligated balance available, start of year		1	1
22.00	New financing authority (gross)	1	16	16
23.90	Total budgetary resources available for obligation	1	17	17
23.95	Total new obligations		–17	–17
24.40	Unobligated balance available, end of year	1	1	1
	New financing authority (gross), detail:			
	Mandatory:			
67.15	Authority to borrow (indefinite)		15	15
	Spending authority from offsetting collections:			
	Discretionary:			
68.00	Offsetting collections (cash)	1	2	2
68.47	Portion applied to repay debt		–1	–1
68.90	Spending authority from offsetting collections (total discretionary)	1	1	1
70.00	Total new financing authority (gross)	1	16	16
	Change in unpaid obligations:			
73.10	Total new obligations		17	17
73.20	Total financing disbursements (gross)	–1	–17	–17
87.00	Total financing disbursements (gross)	1	17	17
	Offsets:			
	Against gross financing authority and financing disbursements:			
88.40	Offsetting collections (cash) from: Interest received on loans	–1	–2	–2
	Net financing authority and financing disbursements:			
89.00	Financing authority		14	14
90.00	Financing disbursements	–1	15	15

Status of Direct Loans (in millions of dollars)

Identification code 86–4105–0–3–371		1999 actual	2000 est.	2001 est.
	Position with respect to appropriations act limitation on obligations:			
1111	Limitation on direct loans	50	50	50
1112	Unobligated direct loan limitation	–50	–33	–33
1150	Total direct loan obligations		17	17
	Cumulative balance of direct loans outstanding:			
1210	Outstanding, start of year		1	17
1231	Disbursements: Direct loan disbursements	1	17	17
1251	Repayments: Repayments and prepayments		–1	–1
1290	Outstanding, end of year	1	17	33

As required by the Federal Credit Reform Act of 1990, this non-budgetary account records all cash flows to and from the Government resulting from direct loans obligated in 1992 and thereafter (including loan modifications) for FHA's General Insurance and Special Risk Insurance Fund programs. The amounts in this account are a means of financing and are not included in the budget totals. As required by the Federal Credit Reform Act of 1990, no administrative expenses can be recorded in the financing account.

This schedule includes two direct loan programs. One provides bridge loan financing to facilitate the disposition of multifamily housing owned by the Department to non-profit organizations who agree to preserve it as affordable rental or cooperative housing. The second is a single-family direct loan program for purchase money mortgages, as discussed in the preceding section for the Mutual Mortgage Insurance Fund.

Balance Sheet (in millions of dollars)

Identification code 86–4105–0–3–371		1998 actual	1999 actual	2000 est.	2001 est.
	ASSETS:				
	Net value of assets related to post-1991 direct loans receivable:				
1401	Direct loans receivable, gross	1	1	17	33
1499	Net present value of assets related to direct loans	1	1	17	33
1999	Total assets	1	1	17	33
	LIABILITIES:				
	Federal liabilities:				
2103	Treasury borrowing	1	1	16	32
2104	Resources payable to Treasury			1	1

Credit accounts—Continued

FHA—General and Special Risk Direct Loan Financing Account—Continued

Balance Sheet (in millions of dollars)—Continued

Identification code 86–4105–0–3–371	1998 actual	1999 actual	2000 est.	2001 est.
2999 Total liabilities	1	1	17	33
4999 Total liabilities and net position	1	1	17	33

FHA—Loan Guarantee Recovery Fund—Financing Account

Program and Financing (in millions of dollars)

Identification code 86–4106–0–3–371	1999 actual	2000 est.	2001 est.
Budgetary resources available for obligation:			
21.40 Unobligated balance available, start of year	1	1	3
22.00 New financing authority (gross)		2	2
23.90 Total budgetary resources available for obligation	1	3	5
23.95 Total new obligations			
24.40 Unobligated balance available, end of year	1	3	5
New financing authority (gross), detail:			
Discretionary:			
68.00 Spending authority from offsetting collections (gross): Offsetting collections (cash)		2	2
Offsets:			
Against gross financing authority and financing disbursements:			
88.00 Offsetting collections (cash) from: Federal sources		−2	−2
Net financing authority and financing disbursements:			
89.00 Financing authority			
90.00 Financing disbursements		−2	−2

Status of Guaranteed Loans (in millions of dollars)

Identification code 86–4106–0–3–371	1999 actual	2000 est.	2001 est.
Position with respect to appropriations act limitation on commitments:			
2111 Limitation on guaranteed loans made by private lenders	8	7	
2113 Uncommitted limitation carried forward	−7		
2150 Total guaranteed loan commitments	1	7	
Cumulative balance of guaranteed loans outstanding:			
2210 Outstanding, start of year	1	2	6
2231 Disbursements of new guaranteed loans	1	4	4
2290 Outstanding, end of year	2	6	10
Memorandum:			
2299 Guaranteed amount of guaranteed loans outstanding, end of year	2	6	10

Balance Sheet (in millions of dollars)

Identification code 86–4106–0–3–371	1998 actual	1999 actual	2000 est.	2001 est.
ASSETS:				
Investments in US securities:				
1102 Federal assets: Treasury securities, par	1	1	3	5
1999 Total assets	1	1	3	5
LIABILITIES:				
2204 Non-Federal liabilities: Liabilities for loan guarantees	1	1	3	5
2999 Total liabilities	1	1	3	5
4999 Total liabilities and net position	1	1	3	5

Section 4 of the Church Arson Prevention Act of 1996 (P.L. 104–155), entitled "Loan Guarantee Recovery Fund," authorizes the Secretary of Housing and Urban Development to guarantee loans made by financial institutions to assist certain nonprofit organizations that were damaged as a result of acts of arson or terrorism.

FHA—General and Special Risk Insurance Funds Liquidating Account

Unavailable Collections (in millions of dollars)

Identification code 86–4072–0–3–371	1999 actual	2000 est.	2001 est.
Balance, start of year:			
01.99 Balance, start of year		7	7
06.20 Reduction pursuant to Public Law 106–51	7		
07.99 Total balance, end of year	7	7	7

Program and Financing (in millions of dollars)

Identification code 86–4072–0–3–371	1999 actual	2000 est.	2001 est.
Obligations by program activity:			
Operating expenses:			
00.02 Interest on debentures	22	22	22
00.03 Other operating costs	18	18	18
00.04 Administrative Contract Expenses	126		
00.05 Legislative savings repayments	273	273	273
00.06 PAE & 3rd party restructuring fees		101	101
00.91 Total operating expenses	439	414	414
Capital investment: Claims and other:			
01.01 Acquisition of defaulted Title I notes	−14	12	11
01.02 Assignment of mortgages	161	149	181
01.03 Acquisition of real properties	126	115	97
01.04 Rehabilitation of real properties	62	42	65
01.05 Rehabitation Grants	59	43	65
01.07 Capitalized property expenses	118	79	69
01.08 Loss on defaulted guaranteed loans	3	3	3
01.10 Tax advances on held mortgages	66	66	66
01.11 Mark-To-Market Restructures	24	229	2,010
01.12 Mark-to-market rehabilitation		18	18
01.91 Total capital investment	605	756	2,585
10.00 Total new obligations	1,044	1,170	2,999
Budgetary resources available for obligation:			
21.40 Unobligated balance available, start of year	2,029	393	
22.00 New budget authority (gross)	628	1,216	3,045
22.10 Resources available from recoveries of prior year obligations	10		
22.40 Capital transfer to general fund	−1,094	−393	
22.60 Portion applied to repay debt	−135	−46	−46
23.90 Total budgetary resources available for obligation	1,438	1,170	2,999
23.95 Total new obligations	−1,044	−1,170	−2,999
24.40 Unobligated balance available, end of year	393		
New budget authority (gross), detail:			
Mandatory:			
60.05 Appropriation (indefinite)		502	2,346
67.15 Authority to borrow (indefinite)	76	46	46
69.00 Offsetting collections (cash)	559	668	653
69.75 Reduction pursuant to P.L. 106–51	−7		
69.90 Spending authority from offsetting collections (total mandatory)	552	668	653
70.00 Total new budget authority (gross)	628	1,216	3,045
Change in unpaid obligations:			
72.40 Unpaid obligations, start of year: Obligated balance, start of year	523	499	499
73.10 Total new obligations	1,044	1,170	2,999
73.20 Total outlays (gross)	−1,057	−1,170	−2,999
73.45 Adjustments in unexpired accounts	−10		
74.40 Unpaid obligations, end of year: Obligated balance, end of year	499	499	499
Outlays (gross), detail:			
86.97 Outlays from new mandatory authority	628	1,170	2,999
86.98 Outlays from mandatory balances	429		

87.00	Total outlays (gross)	1,057	1,170	2,999
	Offsets:			
	Against gross budget authority and outlays:			
	Offsetting collections (cash) from:			
	Non-Federal sources:			
88.40	Fees and premiums	−177	−160	−160
88.40	Rebates of insurance premiums	10	10	10
88.40	Multifamily foreclosure sales		−95	−97
88.40	Proceeds from sale of real property	−100	−96	−105
88.40	Proceeds from sale of mortgage notes	−11	−118	−110
88.40	MTM second mortgage repayments		−12	−16
88.40	Prior year adjustment	17		
88.40	Recoveries on defaulted mortgages	−196	−158	−137
88.40	Interest and operating income	−70	−6	−5
88.40	Other interest, dividends and revenue	−29	−30	−30
88.40	Modification subsidy & transfers from financing acct.	−2	−3	−3
88.40	Payment from the Finanacing Account	−1		
88.90	Total, offsetting collections (cash)	−559	−668	−653
	Net budget authority and outlays:			
89.00	Budget authority	69	548	2,392
90.00	Outlays	499	502	2,346
	Memorandum (non-add) entries:			
92.01	Total investments, start of year: U.S. securities: Par value	6	5	6
92.02	Total investments, end of year: U.S. securities: Par value	5	6	6

Status of Direct Loans (in millions of dollars)

Identification code 86–4072–0–3–371		1999 actual	2000 est.	2001 est.
	Cumulative balance of direct loans outstanding:			
1210	Outstanding, start of year	72	68	64
1251	Repayments: Repayments and prepayments	−2	−2	−2
1264	Write-offs for default: Other adjustments, net	−2	−2	−2
1290	Outstanding, end of year	68	64	60

Status of Guaranteed Loans (in millions of dollars)

Identification code 86–4072–0–3–371		1999 actual	2000 est.	2001 est.
	Cumulative balance of guaranteed loans outstanding:			
2210	Outstanding, start of year	36,590	32,905	30,053
2251	Repayments and prepayments	−3,377	−2,017	−651
	Adjustments:			
2261	Terminations for default that result in loans receivable	−172	−136	−170
2262	Terminations for default that result in acquisition of property	−126	−115	−97
2263	Terminations for default that result in claim payments	−24	−571	−1,222
2264	Other adjustments, net	14	−13	−11
2290	Outstanding, end of year	32,905	30,053	27,902
	Memorandum:			
2299	Guaranteed amount of guaranteed loans outstanding, end of year	32,905	30,053	27,902
	Addendum:			
	Cumulative balance of defaulted guaranteed loans that result in loans receivable:			
2310	Outstanding, start of year	1,989	1,890	1,497
2331	Disbursements for guaranteed loan claims	172	136	170
2351	Repayments of loans receivable	−215	−300	−294
2361	Write-offs of loans receivable	−56	−229	−652
2390	Outstanding, end of year	1,890	1,497	721

The General Insurance fund provides for a large number of specialized mortgage insurance programs, including the insurance of loans for property improvements as well as for cooperatives, condominiums, housing for the elderly, rental housing and nonprofit hospitals.

The Special Risk Insurance fund provides insurance on behalf of mortgagors who otherwise would not be eligible for mortgage insurance. In addition, the fund provides insurance on mortgages covering experimental housing where strict adherence to State or local building regulations was not observed.

As required by the Federal Credit Reform Act of 1990, this account records, for this program, all cash flows to and from the Government resulting from loan guarantees committed and direct loans obligated prior to 1992. This account is shown on a cash basis. New insurance and direct loan activity in 1992 and thereafter in the GI/SRI programs is recorded in corresponding program (86–0200) and financing (86–4077 and 86–4105) accounts.

Section 571 of the Departments of Veterans Affairs and Housing and Urban Development, and Independent Agencies Appropriations Act, 1998 established the Office of Multifamily Housing Assistance Restructuring within HUD to administer the program of mortgage and rental assistance restructuring. Included in the budget estimates for this account are projections for the financial operations of the office.

Financial Condition.—The following tables reflect the revenues, expenses, and financial condition of the GI/SRI Liquidating Account based on Generally Accepted Accounting Principles.

Statement of Operations (in millions of dollars)

Identification code 86–4072–0–3–371		1998 actual[1]	1999 actual[2]	2000 est.	2001 est.
0101	Revenue	1,393	640	304	556
0102	Expense	−1,649	−1,143	−1,393	−1,321
0105	Net income or loss (−)	−256	−503	−1,089	−765

[1] As reflected in the 1998 Budget.
[2] Preliminary results pending final audit.

Balance Sheet (in millions of dollars)

Identification code 86–4072–0–3–371		1998 actual[1]	1999 actual	2000 est.	2001 est.
	ASSETS:				
	Federal assets:				
1101	Fund balances with Treasury	2,545	845		
	Investments in US securities:				
	Treasury securities, par:				
1102	Treasury securities, par		5		
1102	Unamortized net premium/discount		−2		
1106	Receivables, net	3	4	3	3
1206	Non-Federal assets: Receivables, net	51		86	86
	Net value of assets related to pre–1992 direct loans receivable and acquired defaulted guaranteed loans receivable:				
1601	Direct loans, gross	72	68	64	60
1603	Allowance for estimated uncollectible loans and interest (−)	−56	−43	−51	−47
1699	Value of assets related to direct loans	16	25	13	13
1701	Defaulted guaranteed loans, gross	2,044	2,492	1,701	1,701
1703	Allowance for estimated uncollectible loans and interest (−)	−1,464	−1,771	−1,208	−1,208
1704	Defaulted guaranteed loans and interest receivable, net	580	721	493	493
1705	Allowance for uncollectables from foreclosed property	−384	−561	−150	−150
1706	Foreclosed property	255	651	244	244
1799	Value of assets related to loan guarantees	451	811	587	587
1901	Other Federal assets: Other assets	270	150	330	330
1999	Total assets	3,336	1,838	1,019	1,019
	LIABILITIES:				
2101	Federal liabilities: Accounts payable	136	499	363	363
	Non-Federal liabilities:				
2201	Accounts payable	561		443	443
2206	Pension and other actuarial liabilities	6,810	6,372	6,000	6,000
2207	Unearned revenue and advances	123	598	124	124
2999	Total liabilities	7,630	7,469	6,930	6,930
	NET POSITION:				
3100	Appropriated capital	7,264		8,532	8,532

Credit accounts—Continued

FHA—GENERAL AND SPECIAL RISK INSURANCE FUNDS LIQUIDATING ACCOUNT—Continued

Balance Sheet (in millions of dollars)—Continued

Identification code 86–4072–0–3–371	1998 actual[1]	1999 actual	2000 est.	2001 est.
3300 Cumulative results of operations	–11,558	–5,632	–14,443	–14,443
3999 Total net position	–4,294	–5,632	–5,911	–5,911
4999 Total liabilities and net position	3,336	1,837	1,019	1,019

[1] As reflected in 1999 Budget.
[2] Preliminary pending final audit.

Object Classification (in millions of dollars)

Identification code 86–4072–0–3–371	1999 actual	2000 est.	2001 est.
25.1 Advisory and assistance services	126		
25.2 Other services	18	119	119
32.0 Land and structures	365	279	296
33.0 Investments and loans	171	408	2,220
42.0 Insurance claims and indemnities	69	69	69
43.0 Interest and dividends	22	22	22
44.0 Repayments to financing account	273	273	273
99.9 Total new obligations	1,044	1,170	2,999

HOUSING FOR THE ELDERLY OR HANDICAPPED FUND LIQUIDATING ACCOUNT

Program and Financing (in millions of dollars)

Identification code 86–4115–0–3–371	1999 actual	2000 est.	2001 est.
Obligations by program activity:			
Capital investment:			
00.01 Housing for the elderly or handicapped loans	1	3	3
00.02 Maintenance security and collateral	1	1	2
00.91 Subtotal, capital investment	2	4	5
01.01 Operating expenses: Interest on borrowings	402	274	232
10.00 Total new obligations	404	278	237
Budgetary resources available for obligation:			
21.40 Unobligated balance available, start of year	1,189	900	
22.00 New budget authority (gross)	772	751	751
22.10 Resources available from recoveries of prior year obligations	9		
22.60 Portion applied to repay debt	–665	–1,372	–514
23.90 Total budgetary resources available for obligation	1,305	279	237
23.95 Total new obligations	–404	–278	–237
24.40 Unobligated balance available, end of year	900		
New budget authority (gross), detail:			
Mandatory:			
69.00 Offsetting collections (cash)	772	751	751
Change in unpaid obligations:			
72.40 Unpaid obligations, start of year: Obligated balance, start of year	200	214	127
73.10 Total new obligations	404	278	237
73.20 Total outlays (gross)	–382	–365	–267
73.45 Adjustments in unexpired accounts	–9		
74.40 Unpaid obligations, end of year: Obligated balance, end of year	214	127	97
Outlays (gross), detail:			
86.97 Outlays from new mandatory authority	382	365	267
Offsets:			
Against gross budget authority and outlays:			
88.40 Offsetting collections (cash) from: Non-Federal sources	–772	–751	–751
Net budget authority and outlays:			
89.00 Budget authority			
90.00 Outlays	–389	–386	–484

Status of Direct Loans (in millions of dollars)

Identification code 86–4115–0–3–371	1999 actual	2000 est.	2001 est.
Cumulative balance of direct loans outstanding:			
1210 Outstanding, start of year	8,143	8,045	7,958
1231 Disbursements: Direct loan disbursements	3		
1251 Repayments: Repayments and prepayments	–99	–87	–86
1264 Write-offs for default: Other adjustments, net	–2		
1290 Outstanding, end of year	8,045	7,958	7,872

Note.—Amounts for direct loan obligations reflect reservations of section 202 funds. Loan obligations shown under the program and financing schedule reflect loans that have reached the initial closing stage of processing.

The Housing for the Elderly or Handicapped Fund was established pursuant to section 202 of the Housing Act of 1959, as amended. The fund provided direct loans to nonprofit organizations building and managing housing projects for lower income persons who are elderly or disabled.

Projects included an assured range of necessary services for the occupants of such projects. In addition, the section 8 lower income housing assistance payments program has been used in conjunction with the section 202 program. Applications under the two programs have been processed simultaneously.

The data included in these schedules represent direct loan activities funded under the Housing for the Elderly or Handicapped Loan Fund. Further, activities in support of the needs of the elderly and disabled have been carried out under a grant program funded in the 1991 Appropriations Act (P.L. 101–507) and authorized in the National Affordable Housing Act (P.L. 101–625).

After April 1, 1992, all projects for which there were administrative reservations converted to the capital advance assistance program.

The program and financing schedule for this account summarizes the Federal government's obligations for this loan program.

Financing.—Repayments and interest income from loans continue to be available to pay for commitments of the fund.

Statement of Operations (in millions of dollars)

Identification code 86–4115–0–3–371	1998 actual	1999 actual	2000 est.	2001 est.
0101 Revenue	691	685	664	665
0102 Expense	–489	–403	–275	–234
0105 Net income or loss (–)	202	282	389	431

Balance Sheet (in millions of dollars)

Identification code 86–4115–0–3–371	1998 actual	1999 actual	2000 est.	2001 est.
ASSETS:				
1101 Federal assets: Fund balances with Treasury	1,389	1,114	127	97
Non-Federal assets:				
1206 Receivables, net	82	84	84	84
1207 Advances and prepayments		8		
Net value of assets related to pre-1992 direct loans receivable and acquired defaulted guaranteed loans receivable:				
1601 Direct loans, gross	8,143	8,044	7,957	7,872
1603 Allowance for estimated uncollectible loans and interest (–)	–20	–20	–20	–20
1604 Direct loans and interest receivable, net	8,123	8,024	7,937	7,852
1606 Acquired Real Property	1	3		
1699 Value of assets related to direct loans	8,124	8,027	7,937	7,852
1999 Total assets	9,595	9,233	8,148	8,033
LIABILITIES:				
Federal liabilities:				
2102 Interest payable	166	203	138	117

2103	Debt	5,293	4,628	2,978	2,464
2104	Resources payable to Treasury	4,126	4,395	5,027	5,446
2207	Non-Federal liabilities: Other	9	6	6	6
2999	Total liabilities	9,594	9,232	8,149	8,033
4999	Total liabilities and net position	9,594	9,232	8,149	8,033

Object Classification (in millions of dollars)

Identification code 86–4115–0–3–371		1999 actual	2000 est.	2001 est.
32.0	Land and structures	1	1	2
33.0	Investments and loans	1	3	3
43.0	Interest and dividends	402	274	232
99.9	Total new obligations	404	278	237

NONPROFIT SPONSOR ASSISTANCE LIQUIDATING ACCOUNT

Program and Financing (in millions of dollars)

Identification code 86–4042–0–3–604		1999 actual	2000 est.	2001 est.
	Budgetary resources available for obligation:			
21.40	Unobligated balance available, start of year	6	6	
22.00	New budget authority (gross)		–6	
23.90	Total budgetary resources available for obligation	6		
24.40	Unobligated balance available, end of year	6		
	New budget authority (gross), detail:			
	Discretionary:			
40.36	Unobligated balance rescinded		–6	
	Net budget authority and outlays:			
89.00	Budget authority		–6	
90.00	Outlays			

Status of Direct Loans (in millions of dollars)

Identification code 86–4042–0–3–604		1999 actual	2000 est.	2001 est.
	Cumulative balance of direct loans outstanding:			
1210	Outstanding, start of year	1	1	1
1290	Outstanding, end of year	1	1	1

As required by the Federal Credit Reform Act of 1990, this account records, for this program, all cash flows to and from the Government resulting from direct loans obligated prior to 1992. This account is shown on a cash basis.

The Nonprofit Sponsor Assistance fund provided interest-free loans to nonprofit organizations to plan housing projects to be financed under the section 202 housing for the elderly or disabled program.

Balance Sheet (in millions of dollars)

Identification code 86–4042–0–3–604		1998 actual	1999 actual	2000 est.	2001 est.
	ASSETS:				
1101	Federal assets: Fund balances with Treasury		6	6	6
	Net value of assets related to pre–1992 direct loans receivable and acquired defaulted guaranteed loans receivable:				
1601	Direct loans, gross	1	1	1	1
1603	Allowance for estimated uncollectible loans and interest (–)	–1	–1	–1	–1
1999	Total assets		6	6	6
	NET POSITION:				
3100	Appropriated capital		6	6	6
3999	Total net position		6	6	6
4999	Total liabilities and net position		6	6	6

GOVERNMENT NATIONAL MORTGAGE ASSOCIATION

Federal Funds

The Housing and Urban Development Act of 1968 authorized the Government National Mortgage Association (Ginnie Mae) to guarantee the timely payment of principal and interest on privately issued securities that are backed by pools of FHA, Veterans Affairs (VA) and Rural Housing Service mortgages. The Ginnie Mae guarantee gives lenders access to the capital markets for funds to originate new loans. New FHA and VA loans are currently pooled into Ginnie Mae securities.

Financing.—Ginnie Mae issuers are assessed commitment, guarantee and other fees to cover costs incurred by Ginnie Mae and to fund a reserve against possible future payments under the guarantee.

Operating results.—Fee collections, interest, and other income are expected to exceed expenses by $779 million in 2000 and $783 million in 2001.

Credit accounts:

GUARANTEES OF MORTGAGE-BACKED SECURITIES LOAN GUARANTEE PROGRAM ACCOUNT

(INCLUDING TRANSFER OF FUNDS)

[During fiscal year 2000, new] *New* commitments to issue guarantees to carry out the purposes of section 306 of the National Housing Act, as amended (12 U.S.C. 1721(g)), shall not exceed $200,000,000,000, *to remain available until September 30, 2002.*

For administrative expenses necessary to carry out the guaranteed mortgage-backed securities program, $9,383,000 to be derived from the GNMA guarantees of mortgage-backed securities guaranteed loan receipt account, of which not to exceed $9,383,000 shall be transferred to the appropriation for departmental "Salaries and expenses". *In addition, for administrative contract expenses, $40,000,000, to remain available until September 30, 2002: Provided, That to the extent guarantee commitments exceed $42,460,000,000 on or before April 1, 2001, an additional $400 for administrative contract expenses shall be available for each $1,000,000 in additional guarantee commitments (including a pro-rata amount for any amount below $1,000,000), but in no case shall funds made available by this proviso exceed $10,000,000. (Departments of Veterans Affairs and Housing and Urban Development, and Independent Agencies Appropriations Act, 2000.)*

Unavailable Collections (in millions of dollars)

Identification code 86–0186–0–1–371		1999 actual	2000 est.	2001 est.
	Balance, start of year:			
01.99	Balance, start of year	355	701	7,222
	Receipts:			
02.01	Guarantees of mortgage backed securities guarantee loans, negative subsidies	355	6,530	721
04.00	Total: Balances and collections	710	7,231	7,943
	Appropriation:			
05.01	Guarantees of mortgage-backed securities loan guarantee program account	–9	–9	–9
07.99	Total balance, end of year	701	7,222	7,934

Program and Financing (in millions of dollars)

Identification code 86–0186–0–1–371		1999 actual	2000 est.	2001 est.
	Obligations by program activity:			
00.01	Administrative expenses, salaries and expenses	9	9	9
00.02	Administrative Contract Expenses			40
10.00	Total new obligations	9	9	49
	Budgetary resources available for obligation:			
22.00	New budget authority (gross)	9	9	49
23.95	Total new obligations	–9	–9	–49

Credit accounts—Continued

GUARANTEES OF MORTGAGE-BACKED SECURITIES LOAN GUARANTEE PROGRAM ACCOUNT—Continued

(INCLUDING TRANSFER OF FUNDS)—Continued

Program and Financing (in millions of dollars)—Continued

Identification code 86–0186–0–1–371	1999 actual	2000 est.	2001 est.
New budget authority (gross), detail:			
Discretionary:			
40.00 Appropriation			40
40.20 Appropriation (special fund, definite)	9	9	9
43.00 Appropriation (total discretionary)	9	9	49
Change in unpaid obligations:			
73.10 Total new obligations	9	9	49
73.20 Total outlays (gross)	−9	−9	−49
Outlays (gross), detail:			
86.90 Outlays from new discretionary authority	9	9	49
Net budget authority and outlays:			
89.00 Budget authority	9	9	49
90.00 Outlays	9	9	49
Memorandum (non-add) entries:			
92.01 Total Investments, start of year: U.S. securities: Par value [1]			6,189
92.02 Total Investments, end of year: U.S. securities: Par value [1]		6,189	6,554

[1] These invested balances are shown in the program account for presentation purposes only. Actual balances are in the receipt account.

Summary of Loan Levels, Subsidy Budget Authority and Outlays by Program (in millions of dollars)

Identification code 86–0186–0–1–371	1999 actual	2000 est.	2001 est.
Guaranteed loan levels supportable by subsidy budget authority:			
2150 Loan guarantee levels	163,508	114,311	96,262
2150 Standby commitment authority	36,492	85,689	103,738
2159 Total loan guarantee levels	200,000	200,000	200,000
Guaranteed loan subsidy (in percent):			
2320 Subsidy rate	−0.42	−0.33	−0.36
2329 Weighted average subsidy rate	−0.42	−0.33	−0.36
Guaranteed loan subsidy budget authority:			
2330 Subsidy budget authority	−355	−341	−356
2339 Total subsidy budget authority	−355	−341	−356
Guaranteed loan subsidy outlays:			
2340 Subsidy outlays	−355	−341	−356
2349 Total subsidy outlays	−355	−341	−356
Administrative expense data:			
3510 Budget authority	9	9	49
3590 Outlays from new authority	9	9	49

As required by the Federal Credit Reform Act of 1990, this account records the administrative expenses of this program. The administrative expenses are estimated on a cash basis.

Object Classification (in millions of dollars)

Identification code 86–0186–0–1–371	1999 actual	2000 est.	2001 est.
25.2 Other services			40
25.3 Purchases of goods and services from Government accounts	9	9	9
99.9 Total new obligations	9	9	49

GUARANTEES OF MORTGAGE-BACKED SECURITIES FINANCING ACCOUNT

Program and Financing (in millions of dollars)

Identification code 86–4240–0–3–371	1999 actual	2000 est.	2001 est.
Obligations by program activity:			
00.01 Operating expenses	39	51	54
00.02 Capital investment		140	133
08.01 Payment to receipt account for negative subsidy	355	341	356
10.00 Total new obligations	394	532	543
Budgetary resources available for obligation:			
21.40 Unobligated balance available, start of year	415	496	570
22.00 New financing authority (gross)	475	606	604
23.90 Total budgetary resources available for obligation	890	1,102	1,174
23.95 Total new obligations	−394	−532	−543
24.40 Unobligated balance available, end of year	496	570	631
New financing authority (gross), detail:			
Discretionary:			
68.00 Spending authority from offsetting collections (gross): Offsetting collections (cash)	475	606	604
Change in unpaid obligations:			
72.40 Unpaid obligations, start of year: Obligated balance, start of year	8	11	16
73.10 Total new obligations	394	532	543
73.20 Total financing disbursements (gross)	−392	−527	−540
74.40 Unpaid obligations, end of year: Obligated balance, end of year	11	16	18
87.00 Total financing disbursements (gross)	392	527	540
Offsets:			
Against gross financing authority and financing disbursements:			
Offsetting collections (cash) from:			
88.25 Interest on uninvested funds	−38	−29	−29
Non-Federal sources:			
88.40 Guarantee Fees	−362	−365	−369
88.40 Commitment and other fees	−55	−49	−46
88.40 Multiclass fees	−20	−29	−32
88.40 Repayment of advances		−134	−128
88.90 Total, offsetting collections (cash)	−475	−606	−604
Net financing authority and financing disbursements:			
89.00 Financing authority			
90.00 Financing disbursements	−83	−79	−64

Status of Guaranteed Loans (in millions of dollars)

Identification code 86–4240–0–3–371	1999 actual	2000 est.	2001 est.
Position with respect to appropriations act limitation on commitments:			
2111 Limitation on guaranteed loans made by private lenders	200,000	200,000	200,000
2112 Uncommitted loan guarantee limitation	−36,492	−85,689	−103,738
2150 Total guaranteed loan commitments	163,508	114,311	96,262
Cumulative balance of guaranteed loans outstanding:			
2210 Outstanding, start of year	445,615	569,312	599,567
2231 Disbursements of new guaranteed loans	163,508	114,311	96,262
2251 Repayments and prepayments	−39,811	−84,056	−88,825
2290 Outstanding, end of year	569,312	599,567	607,004
Memorandum:			
2299 Guaranteed amount of guaranteed loans outstanding, end of year	569,312	599,567	607,004

Operating Results.—Fee collections, interest, and other income are expected to exceed expenses by $79 million in 1999; $82 million in 2000 and $67 million in 2001. These amounts will be retained against losses that may be incurred on guarantees.

Balance Sheet (in millions of dollars)

Identification code 86–4240–0–3–371	1998 actual	1999 actual	2000 est.	2001 est.
ASSETS:				
1101 Federal assets: Fund balances with Treasury	423	507	586	650
1206 Non-Federal assets: Receivables, net	2	30	27	26
Net value of assets related to pre-1992 direct loans receivable and acquired defaulted guaranteed loans receivable:				
1601 Direct loans, gross			4	7
1699 Value of assets related to direct loans			4	7
1999 Total assets	425	537	617	683
LIABILITIES:				
Non-Federal liabilities:				
2201 Accounts payable	10	40	43	45
2207 Other			201	253
2999 Total liabilities	10	40	244	298
NET POSITION:				
3300 Cumulative results of operations	415	496	373	386
3999 Total net position	415	496	373	386
4999 Total liabilities and net position	425	536	617	684

Note.—Ginnie Mae guarantees the timely payment of principal and interest installments on securities which are backed by FHA-insured, Rural Housing Service-insured, and VA-guaranteed mortgages. Such guarantees are excluded from the Government total of guaranteed obligations duplicating FHA, Rural Housing Service, and VA guarantees.

Guarantees of Mortgage-Backed Securities Liquidating Account

Unavailable Collections (in millions of dollars)

Identification code 86–4238–0–3–371	1999 actual	2000 est.	2001 est.
Balance, start of year:			
01.99 Balance, start of year			
03.00 Offsetting collections			50
07.99 Total balance, end of year			50

Program and Financing (in millions of dollars)

Identification code 86–4238–0–3–371	1999 actual	2000 est.	2001 est.
Obligations by program activity:			
00.01 Functional services	1	2	2
Operating expenses:			
00.02 Default expenses	3	3	3
00.03 Servicing expenses	3	3	3
00.04 Other expenses	2	2	2
00.05 Administrative contract expenses		50	
00.91 Total operating expenses	9	60	10
Capital investment:			
01.01 Advances of guaranty payments	101	111	100
Other:			
02.01 Transfer to Receipt Account		6,189	
10.00 Total new obligations	110	6,360	110
Budgetary resources available for obligation:			
21.40 Unobligated balance available, start of year	5,508	5,826	
22.00 New budget authority (gross)	428	532	109
23.90 Total budgetary resources available for obligation	5,936	6,358	109
23.95 Total new obligations	−110	−6,360	−110
24.40 Unobligated balance available, end of year	5,826		
New budget authority (gross), detail:			
Discretionary:			
Mandatory:			
69.00 Offsetting collections (cash)	428	532	159
	428	532	109
Change in unpaid obligations:			
72.40 Unpaid obligations, start of year: Obligated balance, start of year[1]	−74	−57	−55
73.10 Total new obligations	110	6,360	110
73.20 Total outlays (gross)	−93	−6,358	−35
74.40 Unpaid obligations, end of year: Obligated balance, end of year	−57	−55	20
Outlays (gross), detail:			
86.90 Outlays from new discretionary authority			−50
86.97 Outlays from new mandatory authority	93	532	85
86.98 Outlays from mandatory balances		5,826	
87.00 Total outlays (gross)	93	6,358	35
Offsets:			
Against gross budget authority and outlays:			
Offsetting collections (cash) from:			
88.00 Federal sources (financing account)		−50	−50
88.20 Interest on U.S. securities	−323	−364	
Non-Federal sources:			
88.40 Repayments of guaranteed payments	−95	−106	−95
88.40 Servicing income	−8	−8	−8
88.40 Repayments on mortgages	−1	−1	−1
88.40 Other Fees	−1	−3	−5
88.90 Total, offsetting collections (cash)	−428	−532	−159
Net budget authority and outlays:			
89.00 Budget authority			−50
90.00 Outlays	−336	5,826	−124
Memorandum (non-add) entries:			
92.01 Total investments, start of year: U.S. securities: Par value	5,449	5,781	
92.02 Total investments, end of year: U.S. securities: Par value	5,781		

[1] This line nets unpaid obligations and offsetting collections from new Federal sources.

Status of Direct Loans (in millions of dollars)

Identification code 86–4238–0–3–371	1999 actual	2000 est.	2001 est.
Cumulative balance of direct loans outstanding:			
1210 Outstanding, start of year	358	360	342
1232 Disbursements: Purchase of loans assets from the public	101	112	101
1252 Repayments: Proceeds from loan asset sales to the public or discounted	−95	−108	−98
1264 Write-offs for default: Other adjustments, net	−4	−22	−20
1290 Outstanding, end of year	360	342	325

Status of Guaranteed Loans (in millions of dollars)

Identification code 86–4238–0–3–371	1999 actual	2000 est.	2001 est.
Cumulative balance of guaranteed loans outstanding:			
2210 Outstanding, start of year	96,009	156	156
2251 Repayments and prepayments	−95,853		−2
2290 Outstanding, end of year	156	156	154
Memorandum:			
2299 Guaranteed amount of guaranteed loans outstanding, end of year	156	156	154

Operating results.—Fee collections, interest, and other income are expected to exceed expenses by $326 million in 1999, $365 million in 2000 and $4 million in 2001. These amounts will be retained to cover future year expenses and as a reserve against losses that may be incurred on guarantees.

Statement of Operations (in millions of dollars)

Identification code 86–4238–0–3–371	1998 actual	1999 actual	2000 est.	2001 est.
0101 Revenue	112	329	374	13
0102 Expense	−52	−3	−9	−9
0105 Net income or loss (−)	60	326	365	4
0199 Total comprehensive income	60	326	365	4

Credit accounts—Continued

GUARANTEES OF MORTGAGE-BACKED SECURITIES LIQUIDATING ACCOUNT—Continued

Balance Sheet (in millions of dollars)

Identification code 86–4238–0–3–371		1998 actual	1999 actual	2000 est.	2001 est.
	ASSETS:				
	Federal assets:				
1101	Fund balances with Treasury	1	3	3	4
	Investments in US securities:				
1102	Treasury securities, par	5,449	5,778	....	....
1106	Receivables, net	73	70	75	6
1206	Non-Federal assets: Receivables, net	31	1	2	....
	Net value of assets related to pre–1992 direct loans receivable and acquired defaulted guaranteed loans receivable:				
1601	Direct loans, gross	358	360	340	323
1603	Allowance for estimated uncollectible loans and interest (–)	–325	–326	–192	–181
1699	Value of assets related to direct loans	33	34	148	142
1999	Total assets	5,587	5,886	228	152
	LIABILITIES:				
	Non-Federal liabilities:				
2201	Accounts payable	35	17	20	24
2207	Other	512	512	101	15
2999	Total liabilities	547	529	121	39
	NET POSITION:				
3300	Cumulative results of operations	5,039	5,357	107	112
3999	Total net position	5,039	5,357	107	112
4999	Total liabilities and net position	5,586	5,886	228	151

Note.—Ginnie Mae guarantees the timely payment of principal and interest installments on securities which are backed by FHA-insured, Rural Housing Service, and VA-guaranteed mortgages. Such guarantees are excluded from the Government total of guaranteed obligations duplicating FHA, Rural Housing Service, and VA guarantees.

Object Classification (in millions of dollars)

Identification code 86–4238–0–3–371		1999 actual	2000 est.	2001 est.
25.2	Other services	9	60	10
33.0	Investments and loans	101	111	100
92.0	Undistributed	....	6,189	....
99.9	Total new obligations	110	6,360	110

POLICY DEVELOPMENT AND RESEARCH

Federal Funds

General and special funds:

RESEARCH AND TECHNOLOGY

For contracts, grants, and necessary expenses of programs of research and studies relating to housing and urban problems, not otherwise provided for, as authorized by title V of the Housing and Urban Development Act of 1970, as amended (12 U.S.C. 1701z–1 et seq.), including carrying out the functions of the Secretary under section 1(a)(1)(i) of Reorganization Plan No. 2 of 1968 [$45,000,000] *$62,000,000*, to remain available until September 30, [2001: *Provided*, That of the amount provided under this heading, $10,000,000] *2002, of which $12,000,000* shall be for the Partnership for Advancing Technology in Housing (PATH) Initiative [and $500,000 shall be for a commission established in section 525 of title V of this Act]. *(Departments of Veterans Affairs and Housing and Urban Development, and Independent Agencies Appropriations Act, 2000.)*

Program and Financing (in millions of dollars)

Identification code 86–0108–0–1–451		1999 actual	2000 est.	2001 est.
	Obligations by program activity:			
00.01	Housing Research	47	36	50
00.02	PATH	10	10	12
00.03	International Activities	....	10	....
00.04	Commission on Affordable Housing	....	1	....
10.00	Total new obligations	57	57	62
	Budgetary resources available for obligation:			
21.40	Unobligated balance available, start of year	11	12	....
22.00	New budget authority (gross)	58	45	62
23.90	Total budgetary resources available for obligation	69	57	62
23.95	Total new obligations	–57	–57	–62
24.40	Unobligated balance available, end of year	12	....	....
	New budget authority (gross), detail:			
	Discretionary:			
40.00	Appropriation	48	45	62
42.00	Transferred from other accounts	10	....	....
43.00	Appropriation (total discretionary)	58	45	62
	Change in unpaid obligations:			
72.40	Unpaid obligations, start of year: Obligated balance, start of year	22	52	56
73.10	Total new obligations	57	57	62
73.20	Total outlays (gross)	–27	–53	–56
74.40	Unpaid obligations, end of year: Obligated balance, end of year	52	56	62
	Outlays (gross), detail:			
86.90	Outlays from new discretionary authority	11	18	25
86.93	Outlays from discretionary balances	16	35	31
87.00	Total outlays (gross)	27	53	56
	Net budget authority and outlays:			
89.00	Budget authority	58	45	62
90.00	Outlays	27	53	56

The Housing and Urban Development Act of 1970 directs the Secretary to undertake programs of research, studies, testing, and demonstrations related to the HUD mission. These functions are carried out internally and through contracts with industry, nonprofit research organizations, and educational institutions, and through agreements with State and local governments and other Federal agencies.

In 2001, the research program will focus on activities to support research examining the implications of significant changes in public and assisted housing policy and the impacts of welfare reform on HUD-assisted households and HUD-subsidized developments. National Housing Surveys will continue in 2001. Research and evaluation will support the Department in carrying out its responsibilities under the Government Performance and Results Act.

The 2001 request includes $12 million to continue the Partnership for Advancing Technologies in Housing (PATH). Launched by President Clinton on May 4, 1998, PATH is a key component of the President's program to improve the housing technology infrastructure of the United States and to reduce carbon emissions. A public/private partnership, PATH joins together key Federal agencies, with leaders from the home building, product manufacturing, insurance, and financial industries to develop and deploy the technologies for the next generation of American housing.

Object Classification (in millions of dollars)

Identification code 86–0108–0–1–451		1999 actual	2000 est.	2001 est.
25.2	Other services	52	52	56
41.0	Grants, subsidies, and contributions	5	5	6
99.9	Total new obligations	57	57	62

FAIR HOUSING AND EQUAL OPPORTUNITY

Federal Funds

General and special funds:

FAIR HOUSING ACTIVITIES

For contracts, grants, and other assistance, not otherwise provided for, as authorized by title VIII of the Civil Rights Act of 1968, as amended by the Fair Housing Amendments Act of 1988, and section 561 of the Housing and Community Development Act of 1987, as amended, [$44,000,000] *$50,000,000*, to remain available until September 30, [2001] *2002*, of which [$24,000,000] *$29,000,000* shall be to carry out activities pursuant to such section 561: *Provided*, That no funds made available under this heading shall be used to lobby the executive or legislative branches of the Federal Government in connection with a specific contract, grant or loan. *(Departments of Veterans Affairs and Housing and Urban Development, and Independent Agencies Appropriations Act, 2000.)*

Program and Financing (in millions of dollars)

Identification code 86–0144–0–1–751	1999 actual	2000 est.	2001 est.
Obligations by program activity:			
00.01 Fair housing assistance	13	30	21
00.02 Fair housing initiatives	22	40	29
10.00 Total new obligations (object class 41.0)	35	70	50
Budgetary resources available for obligation:			
21.40 Unobligated balance available, start of year	22	26	
22.00 New budget authority (gross)	40	44	50
23.90 Total budgetary resources available for obligation	62	70	50
23.95 Total new obligations	–35	–70	–50
23.98 Unobligated balance expiring or withdrawn	–1		
24.40 Unobligated balance available, end of year	26		
New budget authority (gross), detail:			
Discretionary:			
40.00 Appropriation	40	44	50
Change in unpaid obligations:			
72.40 Unpaid obligations, start of year: Obligated balance, start of year	30	34	68
73.10 Total new obligations	35	70	50
73.20 Total outlays (gross)	–31	–36	–31
74.40 Unpaid obligations, end of year: Obligated balance, end of year	34	68	87
Outlays (gross), detail:			
86.90 Outlays from new discretionary authority	3		
86.93 Outlays from discretionary balances	28	36	31
87.00 Total outlays (gross)	31	36	31
Net budget authority and outlays:			
89.00 Budget authority	40	44	50
90.00 Outlays	31	36	31

The Budget proposes an appropriation of $50 million in 2001 for fair housing activities to fund programs, consistent with the President's "One America" policy, which will continue to support efforts to end housing discrimination. Of the amount requested, $21 million is for the Fair Housing Assistance Program and $29 million is for the Fair Housing Initiatives Program.

The Fair Housing Assistance Program (FHAP), authorized by title VIII of the Civil Rights Act of 1968 as amended, provides funding to State and local agencies to assure prompt and effective processing of Title VIII (Civil Rights Act of 1968) complaints.

The funding requested for FHAP will support the President's fair housing enforcement initiative by increasing funding to support additional State and local fair housing organizations to meet the needs of currently underserved populations. These funds will be used for joint investigations and enforcement activities with State and local fair housing agencies that will contribute to the Department's goal of doubling enforcement actions and will result in other enforcement outcomes that are a critical component of the Administration's attack on discrimination. It is estimated that the number of new State and local agencies with laws equivalent to the Fair Housing Act will increase to 93 in 2001 from 88 in 2000. Of the $21 million requested for FHAP, $3.5 million will be used to fund an innovative Fair Housing Partnership between State and local fair housing enforcement agencies and private fair housing groups. The partnership will require its participants to focus their fair housing activities to foster substantial and new fair housing results that individual organizations could not achieve alone.

The Fair Housing Initiatives Program (FHIP), authorized by the Housing and Community Development Act of 1987, as amended by the Housing and Community Development Act of 1992, provides support to public and private organizations for the purpose of eliminating or preventing discrimination in housing and for enhancing fair housing opportunities.

Of the $29 million requested, $7.5 million will be used to fund the final year of a three-year audit-based enforcement initiative which will continue to address the existence of both blatant and subtle forms of housing discrimination confirmed through testing experience.

$2.5 million will be used to fund the Project for Accessbility Training and Technical Assistance (PATTA). PATTA will provide training and technical assistance to housing providers on designing and constructing properties to be in compliance with the accessibility requirements of the Fair Housing Act. $1 million will be used to establish an academy to conduct HUD-approved training, primarily in the areas of testing and self-monitoring, to fair housing organizations and industry. It will be a joint venture combining an institution of higher learning and a private fair housing group. Additional FHIP funding will support extended testing and other anti-discrimination activities by private fair housing groups. Funding for FHIP will also include $3.5 million for the Fair Housing Partnership, as discussed above.

OFFICE OF LEAD HAZARD CONTROL

Federal Funds

General and Special Funds:

LEAD HAZARD REDUCTION

(INCLUDING TRANSFER OF FUNDS)

For the Lead Hazard Reduction Program, as authorized by sections 1011 and 1053 of the Residential Lead-Based Hazard Reduction Act of 1992, [$80,000,000] *$120,000,000* to remain available until expended, of which [$1,000,000 shall be for CLEARCorps and] $10,000,000 shall be for a Healthy Homes Initiative, which shall be a program pursuant to sections 501 and 502 of the Housing and Urban Development Act of 1970 that shall include research, studies, testing, and demonstration efforts, including education and outreach concerning lead-based paint poisoning and other housing-related environmental diseases and hazards[: *Provided*, That all balances for the Lead Hazard Reduction Programs previously funded in the Annual Contributions for Assisted Housing and Community Development Block Grant accounts shall be transferred to this account, to be available for the purposes for which they were originally appropriated]. *(Departments of Veterans Affairs and Housing and Urban Development, and Independent Agencies Appropriations Act, 2000.)*

Program and Financing (in millions of dollars)

Identification code 86–0174–0–1–451	1999 actual	2000 est.	2001 est.
Obligations by program activity:			
00.01 Lead abatement	18	144	120
10.00 Total new obligations (object class 41.0)	18	144	120
Budgetary resources available for obligation:			
21.40 Unobligated balance available, start of year		62	

General and Special Funds—Continued

LEAD HAZARD REDUCTION—Continued

(INCLUDING TRANSFER OF FUNDS)—Continued

Program and Financing (in millions of dollars)—Continued

Identification code 86–0174–0–1–451	1999 actual	2000 est.	2001 est.
22.00 New budget authority (gross)	80	80	120
22.22 Unobligated balance transferred from other accounts	....	2	....
23.90 Total budgetary resources available for obligation	80	144	120
23.95 Total new obligations	–18	–144	–120
24.40 Unobligated balance available, end of year	62	....	....
New budget authority (gross), detail:			
Discretionary:			
40.00 Appropriation	80	80	120
Change in unpaid obligations:			
72.40 Unpaid obligations, start of year: Obligated balance, start of year	....	16	286
73.10 Total new obligations	18	144	120
73.20 Total outlays (gross)	–2	–80	–81
73.32 Obligated balance transferred from other accounts	....	206	....
74.40 Unpaid obligations, end of year: Obligated balance, end of year	16	286	325
Outlays (gross), detail:			
86.90 Outlays from new discretionary authority	2	2	2
86.93 Outlays from discretionary balances	....	78	79
87.00 Total outlays (gross)	2	80	81
Net budget authority and outlays:			
89.00 Budget authority	80	80	120
90.00 Outlays	2	80	81

Title X of the Housing and Community Development Act of 1992 (Public Law 102–550), known as the Residential Lead-Based Paint Hazard Reduction Act, authorized the Secretary to establish the Lead-Based Paint Hazard Control Grant Program. The primary purpose of the program is to reduce the exposure of young children to lead-based paint hazards in their homes.

The President's Task Force on Children's Environmental Health and Safety Risk has developed a ten-year, interagency strategy to eliminate lead poisoning in children. The 2001 Budget includes a 50 percent increase, to $90 million, for HUD's Lead Hazard Control Grant program as a major part of this ambitious strategy.

The Lead Hazard Control Grant Program provides grants of $1 to $4 million to State and local governments for control of lead-based paint hazards in privately owned, low-income owner-occupied and rental housing. The grants are also designed to stimulate the development of a trained and certified hazard evaluation and control industry by requiring all contractors to be certified and all workers to be trained through a State-accredited program. In awarding grants, HUD promotes the use of new, low cost approaches to hazard control that can be replicated across the nation.

The Healthy Homes Initiative will enable the Department to control additional childhood diseases and injuires that are caused by housing related factors. The initative will allow for a demonstration that evaluates the methods of controlling two or more housing related diseases through a single intervention. A public education/outreach effort, to enable the public to act effectively to protect their children, will also be conducted.

The Office of Lead Hazard Control will continue its Technical Assistance Program which will include a program to conduct lead-based paint compliance checks, provide technical assistance for State and local agencies, private property owners, HUD programs and field offices, and professional organizations; provide quality control to ensure that the evaluation and control of lead-based paint hazards is done properly in HUD associated housing; provide for the development of standards, technical guidance material and regulations; and provide for the development of streamlined measures of testing, hazard control, cleanup, clearance, and public education.

Prior to 1997, funding for the lead hazard control grant program was provided under the Annual Contributions for Assisted Housing Account. In 1997 and 1998, the program was funded as a set-aside under the Community Development Block Grant (CDBG) account. Starting in 1999 the program was funded as a separate, stand-alone program.

MANAGEMENT AND ADMINISTRATION

Federal Funds

General and special funds:

SALARIES AND EXPENSES

(INCLUDING TRANSFER OF FUNDS)

For necessary administrative and non-administrative expenses of the Department of Housing and Urban Development, not otherwise provided for, including not to exceed $7,000 for official reception and representation expenses, [$1,005,733,000] *$1,094,733,000*, of which $518,000,000 shall be provided from the various funds of the Federal Housing Administration, $9,383,000 shall be provided from funds of the Government National Mortgage Association, $1,000,000 shall be provided from the "Community development block grants program" account, *up to $1,000,000 shall be provided from the "America's Private Investment Companies Program" account,* $150,000 shall be provided by transfer from the "Title VI Indian federal guarantees program" account, and $200,000 shall be provided by transfer from the "Indian housing loan guarantee fund program" account: [*Provided*, That the Secretary is prohibited from using any funds under this heading or any other heading in this Act from employing more than 77 schedule C and 20 noncareer Senior Executive Service employees: *Provided further*, That the Secretary is prohibited from using funds under this heading or any other heading in this Act to employ more than 9,300 employees: *Provided further*, That the Secretary is prohibited from using funds under this heading or any other heading in this Act to convert any external community builders to career employees, and after September 1, 2000 to employ any external community builders: *Provided further*, That the Secretary is prohibited from using funds under this heading or any other heading in this Act to employ more than 14 employees in the Office of Public Affairs: *Provided further*, That of the amount made available under this heading, $2,000,000 shall be for the Millennial Housing Commission as established under section 206.] *(Departments of Veterans Affairs and Housing and Urban Development, and Independent Agencies Appropriations Act, 2000.)*

Program and Financing (in millions of dollars)

Identification code 86–0143–0–1–999	1999 actual	2000 est.	2001 est.
Obligations by program activity:			
Direct program:			
00.01 Housing, mortgage credit, regulatory and energy conservation	174	174	206
00.02 Community planning and development programs	29	29	35
00.03 Equal opportunity and research programs	32	32	38
00.04 Departmental management, legal and audit services	28	28	34
00.05 Field direction and administration	206	214	252
09.01 Reimbursable program	534	529	530
09.99 Total reimbursable program	534	529	530
10.00 Total new obligations	1,003	1,006	1,095
Budgetary resources available for obligation:			
22.00 New budget authority (gross)	1,006	1,006	1,095
23.95 Total new obligations	–1,003	–1,006	–1,095
23.98 Unobligated balance expiring or withdrawn	–3	....	....
New budget authority (gross), detail:			
Discretionary:			
40.00 Appropriation	457	477	565
42.00 Transferred from other accounts	15	....	....

		1999 actual	2000 est.	2001 est.
43.00	Appropriation (total discretionary)	472	477	565
68.00	Spending authority from offsetting collections: Offsetting collections (cash)	534	529	530
70.00	Total new budget authority (gross)	1,006	1,006	1,095
	Change in unpaid obligations:			
72.40	Unpaid obligations, start of year: Obligated balance, start of year	185	163	160
73.10	Total new obligations	1,003	1,006	1,095
73.20	Total outlays (gross)	−1,028	−1,006	−1,073
73.40	Adjustments in expired accounts (net)	3	−3	12
74.40	Unpaid obligations, end of year: Obligated balance, end of year	163	160	193
	Outlays (gross), detail:			
86.90	Outlays from new discretionary authority	915	897	965
86.93	Outlays from discretionary balances	113	109	109
87.00	Total outlays (gross)	1,028	1,006	1,073
	Offsets:			
	Against gross budget authority and outlays:			
88.00	Offsetting collections (cash) from: Federal sources	−534	−529	−530
	Net budget authority and outlays:			
89.00	Budget authority	472	477	565
90.00	Outlays	493	477	543

This appropriation finances all salaries and related costs associated with administering the programs of the Department of Housing and Urban Development, including: housing and mortgage credit programs; community planning and development programs; equal opportunity, research, regulatory and insurance programs; departmental management, and legal services; and, field direction and administration.

Object Classification (in millions of dollars)

Identification code 86–0143–0–1–999		1999 actual	2000 est.	2001 est.
	Direct obligations:			
	Personnel compensation:			
11.1	Full-time permanent	233	255	294
11.3	Other than full-time permanent	17	18	21
11.5	Other personnel compensation	6	7	8
11.9	Total personnel compensation	256	280	323
12.1	Civilian personnel benefits	56	61	69
21.0	Travel and transportation of persons	7	7	11
22.0	Transportation of things	1	....	1
23.1	Rental payments to GSA	38	40	48
23.3	Communications, utilities, and miscellaneous charges	15	16	19
24.0	Printing and reproduction	2	2	2
25.1	Advisory and assistance services	69	51	68
25.2	Other services	6	5	6
25.3	Purchases of goods and services from Government accounts	10	8	10
25.4	Operation and maintenance of facilities	5	4	5
26.0	Supplies and materials	3	2	2
31.0	Equipment	3	1	1
99.0	Subtotal, direct obligations	471	477	565
99.0	Reimbursable obligations	532	529	530
99.9	Total new obligations	1,003	1,006	1,095

Personnel Summary

Identification code 86–0143–0–1–999		1999 actual	2000 est.	2001 est.
	Direct:			
1001	Total compensable workyears: Full-time equivalent employment	4,210	4,363	4,804
	Reimbursable:			
2001	Total compensable workyears: Full-time equivalent employment	4,747	4,837	4,496

OFFICE OF INSPECTOR GENERAL

(INCLUDING TRANSFER OF FUNDS)

For necessary expenses of the Office of Inspector General in carrying out the Inspector General Act of 1978, as amended, [$83,000,000] *$84,000,000*, of which $22,343,000 shall be provided from the various funds of the Federal Housing Administration and $10,000,000 shall be provided from the amount earmarked for Operation Safe Home in the appropriation for "Drug elimination grants for low-income housing": *Provided*, That the Inspector General shall have independent authority over all personnel issues within the Office of Inspector General. *(Departments of Veterans Affairs and Housing and Urban Development, and Independent Agencies Appropriations Act, 2000.)*

Program and Financing (in millions of dollars)

Identification code 86–0189–0–1–451		1999 actual	2000 est.	2001 est.
	Obligations by program activity:			
00.01	Direct program	38	61	52
09.01	Reimbursable program	33	32	32
10.00	Total new obligations	71	93	84
	Budgetary resources available for obligation:			
21.40	Unobligated balance available, start of year	....	10	....
22.00	New budget authority (gross)	83	83	84
23.90	Total budgetary resources available for obligation	83	93	84
23.95	Total new obligations	−71	−93	−84
23.98	Unobligated balance expiring or withdrawn	−1	....	....
24.40	Unobligated balance available, end of year	10	....	....
	New budget authority (gross), detail:			
	Discretionary:			
40.00	Appropriation	50	51	52
68.00	Spending authority from offsetting collections: Offsetting collections (cash)	33	32	32
70.00	Total new budget authority (gross)	83	83	84
	Change in unpaid obligations:			
72.40	Unpaid obligations, start of year: Obligated balance, start of year	24	52	32
73.10	Total new obligations	71	93	84
73.20	Total outlays (gross)	−42	−112	−87
74.40	Unpaid obligations, end of year: Obligated balance, end of year	52	32	29
	Outlays (gross), detail:			
86.90	Outlays from new discretionary authority	41	71	72
86.93	Outlays from discretionary balances	1	41	15
87.00	Total outlays (gross)	42	112	87
	Offsets:			
	Against gross budget authority and outlays:			
88.00	Offsetting collections (cash) from: Federal sources	−33	−32	−32
	Net budget authority and outlays:			
89.00	Budget authority	50	51	52
90.00	Outlays	9	80	55

Summary of Budget Authority and Outlays

(in millions of dollars)

	1999 actual	*2000 est.*	*2001 est.*
Enacted/requested:			
Budget Authority	50	51	52
Outlays	9	80	55
Supplemental proposal:			
Budget Authority	....	−6	6
Outlays	....	−5	4
Total:			
Budget Authority	50	45	58
Outlays	9	75	59

This appropriation provides agencywide audit and investigative functions to identify and correct management and administrative deficiencies that create conditions for existing or potential instances of fraud, waste and mismanagement. The audit function provides internal audit and contract audit.

General and special funds—Continued

OFFICE OF INSPECTOR GENERAL—Continued

(INCLUDING TRANSFER OF FUNDS)—Continued

Internal audits review and evaluate all facets of agency operations. The investigative function provides for the detection and investigation of improper and illegal activities involving programs, personnel, and operations.

Object Classification (in millions of dollars)

Identification code 86–0189–0–1–451		1999 actual	2000 est.	2001 est.
	Direct obligations:			
	Personnel compensation:			
11.1	Full-time permanent	19	26	26
11.5	Other personnel compensation	2	3	3
11.9	Total personnel compensation	21	29	29
12.1	Civilian personnel benefits	5	8	6
21.0	Travel and transportation of persons	3	5	5
23.1	Rental payments to GSA	2	3	3
23.3	Communications, utilities, and miscellaneous charges	1	3	3
25.1	Advisory and assistance services	1	7	2
25.3	Purchases of goods and services from Government accounts	3	3	2
31.0	Equipment	2	3	2
99.0	Subtotal, direct obligations	38	61	52
99.0	Reimbursable obligations	33	32	32
99.9	Total new obligations	71	93	84

Personnel Summary

Identification code 86–0189–0–1–451		1999 actual	2000 est.	2001 est.
	Direct:			
1001	Total compensable workyears: Full-time equivalent employment	312	374	329
	Reimbursable:			
2001	Total compensable workyears: Full-time equivalent employment	266	331	331

OFFICE OF FEDERAL HOUSING ENTERPRISE OVERSIGHT

SALARIES AND EXPENSES

(INCLUDING TRANSFER OF FUNDS)

For carrying out the Federal Housing Enterprise Financial Safety and Soundness Act of 1992, including not to exceed $500 for official reception and representation expenses, [$19,493,000] *$25,800,000*, to remain available until expended, to be derived from the Federal Housing Enterprise Oversight Fund: *Provided*, That not to exceed such amount shall be available from the General Fund of the Treasury to the extent necessary to incur obligations and make expenditures pending the receipt of collections to the Fund: *Provided further*, That the General Fund amount shall be reduced as collections are received during the fiscal year so as to result in a final appropriation from the General Fund estimated at not more than $0. *(Departments of Veterans Affairs and Housing and Urban Development, and Independent Agencies Appropriations Act, 2000.)*

Unavailable Collections (in millions of dollars)

Identification code 86–5272–0–2–371		1999 actual	2000 est.	2001 est.
	Balance, start of year:			
01.99	Balance, start of year	....	....	....
	Receipts:			
02.01	Office of federal housing enterprise oversight	16	19	26
	Appropriation:			
05.01	Office of federal housing enterprise oversight	−16	−19	−26
07.99	Total balance, end of year	....	....	....

Program and Financing (in millions of dollars)

Identification code 86–5272–0–2–371		1999 actual	2000 est.	2001 est.
	Obligations by program activity:			
00.01	Direct program	16	19	26
10.00	Total new obligations	16	19	26
	Budgetary resources available for obligation:			
22.00	New budget authority (gross)	16	19	26
23.95	Total new obligations	−16	−19	−26
	New budget authority (gross), detail:			
	Discretionary:			
40.20	Appropriation (special fund, definite)	16	19	26
	Change in unpaid obligations:			
72.40	Unpaid obligations, start of year: Obligated balance, start of year	5	4	4
73.10	Total new obligations	16	19	26
73.20	Total outlays (gross)	−16	−19	−25
74.40	Unpaid obligations, end of year: Obligated balance, end of year	4	4	5
	Outlays (gross), detail:			
86.90	Outlays from new discretionary authority	12	15	21
86.93	Outlays from discretionary balances	4	4	4
87.00	Total outlays (gross)	16	19	25
	Net budget authority and outlays:			
89.00	Budget authority	16	19	26
90.00	Outlays	16	19	25

This appropriation funds the Office of Federal Housing Enterprise Oversight (the Office), which was established in 1992 to regulate the financial safety and soundness of two housing Government Sponsored Enterprises (GSEs)—Fannie Mae and Freddie Mac. The Office was authorized in the Federal Housing Enterprise Safety and Soundness Act of 1992, which also instituted a risk-based capital standard for the GSEs, and gave the regulator enhanced authority to enforce those standards. The office is also required by statute to conduct onsite annual examinations at the GSEs to determine the condition of each enterprise for the purpose of ensuring their financial safety and soundness.

Object Classification (in millions of dollars)

Identification code 86–5272–0–2–371		1999 actual	2000 est.	2001 est.
11.1	Personnel compensation: Personnel Compensation	7	10	12
12.1	Civilian personnel benefits	1	2	3
23.2	Rental payments to others	2	2	3
25.2	Other services	4	4	6
31.0	Equipment	1	1	2
99.0	Subtotal, direct obligations	15	19	26
99.5	Below reporting threshold	1	....	....
99.9	Total new obligations	16	19	26

Personnel Summary

Identification code 86–5272–0–2–371		1999 actual	2000 est.	2001 est.
1001	Total compensable workyears: Full-time equivalent employment	73	95	118

Intragovernmental funds:

WORKING CAPITAL FUND

Program and Financing (in millions of dollars)

Identification code 86–4586–0–4–451		1999 actual	2000 est.	2001 est.
	Obligations by program activity:			
09.01	Reimbursable program	348	266	390

10.00	Total new obligations	348	266	390
	Budgetary resources available for obligation:			
21.40	Unobligated balance available, start of year	57	32	
22.00	New budget authority (gross)	319	266	390
22.10	Resources available from recoveries of prior year obligations	5	−32	
23.90	Total budgetary resources available for obligation	381	266	390
23.95	Total new obligations	−348	−266	−390
24.40	Unobligated balance available, end of year	32		
	New budget authority (gross), detail:			
	Mandatory:			
69.00	Offsetting collections (cash)	305	266	390
69.10	From Federal sources: Change in receivables and unpaid, unfilled orders	12		
69.15	From Federal sources: Adjustments to receivables and unpaid, unfilled orders	2		
69.90	Spending authority from offsetting collections (total mandatory)	319	266	390
	Change in unpaid obligations:			
	Unpaid obligations, start of year:			
72.40	Obligated balance, start of year	−13	21	34
72.95	From Federal sources: Receivables and unpaid, unfilled orders	9	21	21
72.99	Total unpaid obligations, start of year	−4	42	55
73.10	Total new obligations	348	266	390
73.20	Total outlays (gross)	−296	−285	−390
73.45	Adjustments in unexpired accounts	−5	32	
	Unpaid obligations, end of year:			
74.40	Obligated balance, end of year	21	34	34
74.95	From Federal sources: Receivables and unpaid, unfilled orders	21	21	21
74.99	Total unpaid obligations, end of year	42	55	55
	Outlays (gross), detail:			
86.97	Outlays from new mandatory authority	296	285	390
	Offsets:			
	Against gross budget authority and outlays:			
88.00	Offsetting collections (cash) from: Federal sources	−305	−266	−390
	Against gross budget authority only:			
88.95	From Federal sources: Change in receivables and unpaid, unfilled orders	−12		
88.96	From Federal sources: Adjustment to receivables and unpaid, unfilled orders	−2		
	Net budget authority and outlays:			
89.00	Budget authority			
90.00	Outlays	−9	19	

The Working Capital Fund, authorized by the Department of Housing and Urban Development Act of 1965, finances information technology and office automation initiatives which can be performed more efficiently on a centralized basis. The fund is financed from fees charged for services performed.

Object Classification (in millions of dollars)

Identification code 86–4586–0–4–451		1999 actual	2000 est.	2001 est.
11.1	Personnel compensation: Full-time permanent	24	18	27
12.1	Civilian personnel benefits	5	4	6
21.0	Travel and transportation of persons	1	1	1
23.3	Communications, utilities, and miscellaneous charges	54	42	59
25.1	Advisory and assistance services	223	170	252
26.0	Supplies and materials	1	1	1
31.0	Equipment	40	30	44
99.9	Total new obligations	348	266	390

Personnel Summary

Identification code 86–4586–0–4–451		1999 actual	2000 est.	2001 est.
2001	Total compensable workyears: Full-time equivalent employment	355	462	462

Administrative Provisions

Sec. 201. Fifty percent of the amounts of budget authority, or in lieu thereof 50 percent of the cash amounts associated with such budget authority, that are recaptured from projects described in section 1012(a) of the Stewart B. McKinney Homeless Assistance Amendments Act of 1988 (Public Law 100–628; 102 Stat. 3224, 3268) shall be rescinded, or in the case of cash, shall be remitted to the Treasury, and such amounts of budget authority or cash recaptured and not rescinded or remitted to the Treasury shall be used by State housing finance agencies or local governments or local housing agencies with projects approved by the Secretary of Housing and Urban Development for which settlement occurred after January 1, 1992, in accordance with such section. Notwithstanding the previous sentence, the Secretary may award up to 15 percent of the budget authority or cash recaptured and not rescinded or remitted to the Treasury to provide project owners with incentives to refinance their project at a lower interest rate.

Fair Housing and Free Speech

Sec. 202. None of the amounts made available under this Act may be used during fiscal year [2000] *2001* to investigate or prosecute under the Fair Housing Act any otherwise lawful activity engaged in by one or more persons, including the filing or maintaining of a nonfrivolous legal action, that is engaged in solely for the purpose of achieving or preventing action by a Government official or entity, or a court of competent jurisdiction.

Housing Opportunities for Persons With AIDS Grants

Sec. 203. [Section 207 of the Departments of Veterans Affairs and Housing and Urban Development, and Independent Agencies Appropriations Act, 1999, is amended by striking wherever it occurs "fiscal year 1999 *and 2000*" and inserting "fiscal years 1999 and 2000".]

(a) Eligibility. Notwithstanding section 854(c)(1)(A) of the AIDS Housing Opportunity Act (42 U.S.C. 12903(c)(1)(A)), from any amounts made available under this title for fiscal year 2001 that are allocated under such section, the Secretary of Housing and Urban Development shall allocate and make a grant, in the amount determined under subsection (b), for any State that—

(1) received an allocation in a prior fiscal year under clause (ii) of such section; and

(2) is not otherwise eligible for an allocation for fiscal year 2001 under such clause (ii) because the areas in the State outside of the metropolitan statistical areas that qualify under clause (i) in fiscal year 2000 do not have the number of cases of acquired immunodeficiency syndrome required under such clause.

(b) Amount.—The amount of the allocation and grant for any State described in subsection (a) shall be an amount based on the cumulative number of AIDS cases in the areas of that State that are outside of metropolitan statistical areas that qualify under clause (i) of such section 845(c)(1)(A) in fiscal year 2000, in proportion to AIDS cases among cities and States that qualify under clauses (i) and (ii) of such section and States deemed eligible under subsection (a).

(c) Environmental Review. Section 856 of the Act is amended by adding the following new subsection at the end:

"(h) Environmental Review.—For purposes of environmental review, a grant under this subtitle shall be treated as assistance for a special project that is subject to section 305(c) of the Multifamily Housing Property Disposition Reform Act of 1994, and shall be subject to the regulations issued by the Secretary to implement such section.".

[Reprogramming]

[Sec. 204. Of the amounts made available under the sixth undesignated paragraph under the heading "Community Planning and Development—community development block grants" in title II of the Departments of Veterans Affairs and Housing and Urban Development, and Independent Agencies Appropriations Act, 1999 (Public Law 105–276; 112 Stat. 2477) for the Economic Development Initiative (EDI) for grants for targeted economic investments, the $1,000,000 to be made available (pursuant to the related provisions of the joint explanatory statement in the conference report to accompany such Act (House Report No. 105–769, 105th Congress, 2d session)) to the City of Redlands, California, for the redevelopment initiatives near the historic Fox Theater shall, notwithstanding such provisions, be made available to such city for the following purposes:

(1) $700,000 shall be for renovation of the City of Redlands Fire Station No. 1;

[REPROGRAMMING]—Continued

(2) $200,000 shall be for renovation of the Mission Gables House at the Redlands Bowl historic outdoor amphitheater; and

(3) $100,000 shall be for the preservation of historic Hillside Cemetery.]

[ADJUSTMENTS TO INCOME ELIGIBILITY FOR UNUSUALLY HIGH OR LOW FAMILIES INCOMES IN ASSISTED HOUSING]

[SEC. 205. Section 16 of the United States Housing Act of 1937 is amended—

(1) in subsection (a)(2)(A), by inserting before the period the following: "; except that the Secretary may establish income ceilings higher or lower than 30 percent of the area median income on the basis of the Secretary's findings that such variations are necessary because of unusually high or low family incomes"; and

(2) in subsection (c)(3), by inserting before the period the following: "; except that the Secretary may establish income ceilings higher or lower than 30 percent of the area median income on the basis of the Secretary's findings that such variations are necessary because of unusually high or low family incomes".]

[MILLENNIAL HOUSING COMMISSION]

[SEC. 206. (a) ESTABLISHMENT.—There is hereby established a commission to be known as the Millennial Housing Commission (in this section referred to as the "Commission").

(b) STUDY.—The duty of the Commission shall be to conduct a study that examines, analyzes, and explores—

(1) the importance of housing, particularly affordable housing which includes housing for the elderly, to the infrastructure of the United States;

(2) the various possible methods for increasing the role of the private sector in providing affordable housing in the United States, including the effectiveness and efficiency of such methods; and

(3) whether the existing programs of the Department of Housing and Urban Development work in conjunction with one another to provide better housing opportunities for families, neighborhoods, and communities, and how such programs can be improved with respect to such purpose.

(c) MEMBERSHIP.—

(1) NUMBER AND APPOINTMENT.—The Commission shall be composed of 22 members, appointed not later than January 1, 2000, as follows:

(A) Two co-chairpersons appointed by—

(i) one co-chairperson appointed by a committee consisting of the chairmen of the Subcommittees on the Departments of Veterans Affairs and Housing and Urban Development, and Independent Agencies of the Committees on Appropriations of the House of Representatives and the Senate, and the chairman of the Subcommittee on Housing and Community Opportunities of the House of Representatives and the chairman of the Subcommittee on Housing and Transportation of the Senate; and

(ii) one co-chairperson appointed by a committee consisting of the ranking minority members of the Subcommittees on the Departments of Veterans Affairs and Housing and Urban Development, and Independent Agencies of the Committees on Appropriations of the House of Representatives and the Senate, and the ranking minority member of the Subcommittee on Housing and Community Opportunities of the House of Representatives and the ranking minority member of the Subcommittee on Housing and Transportation of the Senate.

(B) Ten members appointed by the Chairman and Ranking Minority Member of the Committee on Appropriations of the House of Representatives and the Chairman and Ranking Minority Member of the Committee on Banking and Financial Services of the House of Representatives.

(C) Ten members appointed by the Chairman and Ranking Minority Member of the Committee on Appropriations of the Senate and the Chairman and Ranking Minority Member of the Committee on Banking, Housing, and Urban Affairs of the Senate.

(2) QUALIFICATIONS.—Appointees should have proven expertise in directing, assemblying, or applying capital resources from a variety of sources to the successful development of affordable housing or the revitalization of communities, including economic and job development.

(3) VACANCIES.—Any vacancy on the Commission shall not affect its powers and shall be filled in the manner in which the original appointment was made.

(4) CHAIRPERSONS.—The members appointed pursuant to paragraph (1)(A) shall serve as co-chairpersons of the Commission.

(5) PROHIBITION OF PAY.—Members of the Commission shall serve without pay.

(6) TRAVEL EXPENSES.—Each member of the Commission shall receive travel expenses, including per diem in lieu of subsistence, in accordance with sections 5702 and 5703 of title 5, United States Code.

(7) QUORUM.—A majority of the members of the Commission shall constitute a quorum but a lesser number may hold hearings.

(8) MEETINGS.—The Commission shall meet at the call of the Chairpersons.

(d) DIRECTOR AND STAFF.—

(1) DIRECTOR.—The Commission shall have a Director who shall be appointed by the Chairperson. The Director shall be paid at a rate not to exceed the rate of basic pay payable for level V of the Executive Schedule.

(2) STAFF.—The Commission may appoint personnel as appropriate. The staff of the Commission shall be appointed subject to the provisions of title 5, United States Code, governing appointments in the competitive service, and shall be paid in accordance with the provisions of chapter 51 and subchapter III of chapter 53 of that title relating to classification and General Schedule pay rates.

(3) EXPERTS AND CONSULTANTS.—The Commission may procure temporary and intermittent services under section 3109(b) of title 5, United States Code, but at rates for individuals not to exceed the daily equivalent of the maximum annual rate of basic pay payable for the General Schedule.

(4) STAFF OF FEDERAL AGENCIES.—Upon request of the Commission, the head of any Federal department or agency may detail, on a reimbursable basis, any of the personnel of that department or agency to the Commission to assist it in carrying out its duties under this Act.

(e) POWERS.—

(1) HEARINGS AND SESSIONS.—The Commission may, for the purpose of carrying out this section, hold hearings, sit and act at times and places, take testimony, and receive evidence as the Commission considers appropriate.

(2) POWERS OF MEMBERS AND AGENTS.—Any member or agent of the Commission may, if authorized by the Commission, take any action which the Commission is authorized to take by this section.

(3) OBTAINING OFFICIAL DATA.—The Commission may secure directly from any department or agency of the United States information necessary to enable it to carry out this Act. Upon request of the Chairpersons of the Commission, the head of that department or agency shall furnish that information to the Commission.

(4) GIFTS, BEQUESTS, AND DEVISES.—The Commission may accept, use, and dispose of gifts, bequests, or devises of services or property, both real and personal, for the purpose of aiding or facilitating the work of the Commission. Gifts, bequests, or devises of money and proceeds from sales of other property received as gifts, bequests, or devises shall be deposited in the Treasury and shall be available for disbursement upon order of the Commission.

(5) MAILS.—The Commission may use the United States mails in the same manner and under the same conditions as other departments and agencies of the United States.

(6) ADMINISTRATIVE SUPPORT SERVICES.—Upon the request of the Commission, the Administrator of General Services shall provide to the Commission, on a reimbursable basis, the administrative support services necessary for the Commission to carry out its responsibilities under this section.

(7) CONTRACT AUTHORITY.—The Commission may contract with and compensate Government and private agencies or persons for services, without regard to section 3709 of the Revised Statutes (41 U.S.C. 5).

(f) REPORT.—The Commission shall submit to the Committees on Appropriations and Banking and Financial Services of the House of Representatives and the Committees on Appropriations and Banking, Housing, and Urban Affairs of the Senate a final report not later than March 1, 2002. The report shall contain a detailed statement of the findings and conclusions of the Commission with respect to the study conducted under subsection (b), together with its recommendations for legislation, administrative actions, and any other actions the Commission considers appropriate.

(g) TERMINATION.—The Commission shall terminate on June 30, 2002. Section 14(a)(2)(B) of the Federal Advisory Committee Act (5

U.S.C. App.; relating to the termination of advisory committees) shall not apply to the Commission.]

[FHA TECHNICAL CORRECTION]

[SEC. 207. Section 203(b)(2)(A)(ii) of the National Housing Act (12 U.S.C. 1709(b)(2)(A)(ii)) is amended by adding before "48 percent" the following: "the greater of the dollar amount limitation in effect under this section for the area on the date of the enactment of the Departments of Veterans Affairs and Housing and Urban Development, and Independent Agencies Appropriations Act for Fiscal Year 1999 or".]

[RESCISSIONS]

[SEC. 208. Of the balances remaining from funds appropriated to the Department of Housing and Urban Development in Public Law 105–65 and prior appropriations Acts, $74,400,000 is rescinded: *Provided*, That the amount rescinded shall be comprised of—

(1) $30,552,000 of the amounts that were appropriated for the modernization of public housing unit; under the heading "Annual contributions for assisted housing", including an amount equal to the amount transferred from such account to, and merged with amounts under the heading "Public housing capital fund";

(2) $3,048,000 of the amounts from which no disbursements have been made within five successive fiscal years beginning after September 30, 1993, that were appropriated under the heading "Annual contributions for assisted housing", including an amount equal to the amount transferred from such account to the account under the heading "Housing certificate fund";

(3) $22,975,000 of amounts appropriated for homeownership assistance under section 235(r) of the National Housing Act, including $6,875,000 appropriated in Public Law 103–327 (approved September 28, 1994, 104 Stat. 2305) for such purposes;

(4) $11,400,000 of the amounts appropriated for the Homeownership and Opportunity for People Everywhere programs (HOPE programs), as authorized by the Cranston-Gonzalez National Affordable Housing Act; and

(5) $6,400,000 of the balances remaining in the account under the heading "Nonprofit Sponsor Assistance Account".]

[GRANT FOR NATIONAL CITIES IN SCHOOLS]

[SEC. 209. For a grant to the National Cities in Schools Community Development program under section 930 of the Housing and Community Development Act of 1992, $5,000,000.]

[MOVING TO WORK DEMONSTRATION]

[SEC. 210. For the Jobs-Plus Initiative of the Moving to Work Demonstration, $5,000,000 to cover the cost of rent-based work incentives to families in selected public housing developments, who shall be encouraged to go to work under work incentive plans approved by the Secretary and carefully tracked as part of the research and demonstration effort.]

[REPEALER]

[SEC. 211. Section 218 of Public Law 104–204 is repealed.]

[FHA ADMINISTRATIVE CONTRACT EXPENSE AUTHORITY]

[SEC. 212. Section 1 of the National Housing Act (12 U.S.C. 1702) is amended by inserting the following new sentence after the first proviso: "Except with respect to title III, for the purposes of this section, the term 'nonadministrative' shall not include contract expenses that are not capitalized or routinely deducted from the proceeds of sales, and such expenses shall not be payable from funds made available by this Act.".]

[FULL PAYMENT OF CLAIMS]

[SEC. 213. (a) Section 541 of the National Housing Act is amended—

(1) by amending the heading to read as follows: "PARTIAL PAYMENT OF CLAIMS ON DEFAULTED MORTGAGES AND IN CONNECTION WITH MORTGAGE RESTRUCTURING"; and

(2) in subsection (b), by striking "partial payment of the claim under the mortgage insurance contract" and inserting "partial or full payment of claim under one or more mortgage insurance contracts".

(b) Section 517 of the Multifamily Assisted Housing Reform and Affordability Act of 1997 is amended by adding a new subsection (a)(6) to read as follows: "(6) The second mortgage under this section may be a first mortgage if no restructured or new first mortgage will meet the requirement of paragraph (1)(A).".]

[AVAILABILITY OF INCOME MATCHING INFORMATION]

[SEC. 214. (a) Section 3(f) of the United States Housing Act of 1937 (42 U.S.C. 1437a), as amended by section 508(d)(1) of the Quality Housing and Work Responsibility Act of 1998, is further amended—

(1) in paragraph (1)—

(A) after the first appearance of "public housing agency" by inserting ", or the owner responsible for determining the participant's eligibility or level of benefits,"; and

(B) after "as applicable" by inserting ", or to the owner responsible for determining the participant's eligibility or level of benefits"; and

(2) in paragraph (2)—

(A) in subparagraph (A) by striking "or";

(B) in subparagraph (B) by striking the period and inserting ", or"; and

(C) by inserting at the end the following new subparagraph:

"(C) for which project-based assistance is provided under section 8, section 202, or section 811.".

(b) Section 904(b) of the Stewart B. McKinney Homeless Assistance Amendments Act of 1988 (42 U.S.C. 3544), as amended by section 508(d)(2) of the Quality Housing and Work Responsibility Act of 1998, is further amended in paragraph (4)—

(1) by inserting after "public housing agency" the first time it appears the following: ", or the owner responsible for determining the participant's eligibility or level of benefits,"; and

(2) by striking "the public housing agency verifying income" and inserting "verifying income".]

EXEMPTION FOR ALASKA AND MISSISSIPPI FROM REQUIREMENT OF RESIDENT ON BOARD

SEC. [215] *204*. Public housing agencies in the States of Alaska and Mississippi shall not be required to comply with section 2(b) of the United States Housing Act of 1937, as amended, during fiscal year [2000] *2001*.

[ADMINISTRATION OF THE CDBG PROGRAM BY NEW YORK STATE]

[SEC. 216. The Secretary of Housing and Urban Development shall transfer on the date of the enactment of this Act the administration of the Small Cities component of the Community Development Block Grants program for all funds allocated for the State of New York under section 106(d) of the Housing and Community Development Act of 1974 for fiscal year 2000 and all fiscal years thereafter, to the State of New York to be administered by the Governor of such State.]

[SECTION 202 EXEMPTION]

[SEC. 217. Notwithstanding section 202 of the Housing Act of 1959 or any other provision of law, Peggy A. Burgin may not be disqualified on the basis of age from residing at Clark's Landing in Groton, Vermont.]

[DARLINTON PRESERVATION AMENDMENT]

[SEC. 218. Notwithstanding any other provision of law, upon prepayment of the FHA-insured section 236 mortgage, the Secretary shall continue to provide interest reduction payment in accordance with the existing amortization schedule for Darlinton Manor Apartments, a 100-unit project located at 606 North 5th Street, Bozemen, Montana, which will continue as affordable housing pursuant to a use agreement with the State of Montana.]

[RISK-SHARING PRIORITY]

[SEC. 219. Section 517(b)(3) of the Departments of Veterans Affairs and Housing and Urban Development, and Independent Agencies Appropriations Act, 1998 is amended by inserting after "1992." the following: "The Secretary shall use risk-shared financing under section 542(c) of the Housing and Community Development Act of 1992 for any mortgage restructuring, rehabilitation financing, or debt refinancing included as part of a mortgage restructuring and rental assistance sufficiency plan if the terms and conditions are considered to be the best available financing in terms of financial savings to the FHA insurance funds and will result in reduced risk of loss to the Federal Government.".]

[TREATMENT OF EXPIRING ECONOMIC DEVELOPMENT INITIATIVE GRANTS]

[SEC. 220. (a) AVAILABILITY.—Notwithstanding section 1552 of title 31, United States Code, the grant amounts identified in subsection

[TREATMENT OF EXPIRING ECONOMIC DEVELOPMENT INITIATIVE GRANTS]—Continued

(b) shall remain available to the grantees for the purposes for which such amounts were obligated through September 30, 2000.

(b) GRANTS.—The grant amounts identified in this subsection are the amounts provided under the following grants made by the Secretary of Housing and Urban Development under the economic development initiative under section 108(q) of the Housing and Community Development Act of 1974 (42 U.S.C. 5308(q)):

(1) The grant for Miami, Florida, designated as B–92–ED–12–013.

(2) The grant for Miami Beach, Florida, designated as B–92–ED–12–014.

(c) EFFECTIVE DATE.—This section shall be considered to have taken effect on September 30, 1999. The Secretary of the Treasury and the Secretary of Housing and Urban Development shall take such actions as may be necessary to carry out this section, notwithstanding any actions taken previously pursuant to section 1552 of title 31, United States Code.]

[USE OF TRUSTS WITH REGARD TO COOPERATIVE HOUSING SECTION]

[SEC. 221. Section 213(a) of the National Housing Act (12 U.S.C. 1715e(a)) is amended by adding at the end the following new sentence: "Nothing in this section may be construed to prevent membership in a nonprofit housing cooperative from being held in the name of a trust, the beneficiary of which shall occupy the dwelling unit in accordance with rules and regulations prescribed by the Secretary.".]

[GRANT TECHNICAL CORRECTION]

[SEC. 222. Notwithstanding any other provision of law, the amount made available under the Departments of Veterans Affairs and Housing and Urban Development, and Independent Agencies Appropriations Act, 1991 (Public Law 101–507) for a special purpose grant under section 107 of the Housing and Community Development Act of 1974 to the County of Hawaii for the purpose of an environmental impact statement for the development of a water resource system in Kohala, Hawaii, that is unobligated on the date of the enactment of this Act, may be used to fund water system improvements, including exploratory wells, well drillings, pipeline replacements, water system planning and design, and booster pump and reservoir development.]

[REUSE OF CERTAIN BUDGET AUTHORITY]

[SEC. 223. Section 8(z) of the United States Housing Act of 1937 is amended—

(1) in paragraph (1)—

(A) by inserting after "on account of" the following: "expiration or"; and

(B) by striking the parenthetical phrase; and

(2) by striking paragraph (3).]

[SECTION 108 WAIVER]

[SEC. 224. With respect to the $6,700,000 commitment in connection with guaranteed obligations for the Sandtown-Winchester Home Ownership Zone under section 108 of the Housing and Community Development Act of 1974, the Secretary shall not require security in excess of that authorized under section 108(d)(1)(B).]

[HOPWA TECHNICAL]

[SEC. 225. (a) Notwithstanding any other provision of law, the amount allocated for fiscal year 2000, and the amounts that would otherwise be allocated for fiscal year 2001, to the City of Philadelphia, Pennsylvania on behalf of the Philadelphia, PA–NJ Primary Metropolitan Area (hereafter "metropolitan area"), under section 854(c) of the AIDS Housing Opportunity Act (42 U.S.C. 12903(c)), the Secretary of Housing and Urban Development shall adjust such amounts by allocating to the State of New Jersey the proportion of the metropolitan area's amount that is based on the number of cases of AIDS reported in the portion of the metropolitan area that is located in New Jersey.

(b) The State of New Jersey shall use amounts allocated to the State under this section to carry out eligible activities under section 855 of the AIDS Housing Opportunity Act (42 U.S.C. 12904) in the portion of the metropolitan area that is located in New Jersey.]

EXPANSION OF ENVIRONMENTAL ASSUMPTION AUTHORITY FOR HOMELESS ASSISTANCE PROGRAMS

SEC. 205. Section 443 of the Stewart B. McKinney Homeless Assistance Act is amended to read as follows:

"SEC. 443. ENVIRONMENTAL REVIEW.

For purposes of environmental review, assistance and projects under this title shall be treated as assistance for special projects that are subject to section 305(c) of the Multifamily Housing Property Disposition Reform Act of 1994, and shall be subject to the regulations issued by the Secretary to implement such section.".

PERMANENT EXTENSION OF FHA MULTIFAMILY MORTGAGE CREDIT DEMONSTRATIONS

SEC. 206. Section 542 of the Housing and Community Development Act of 1992 is amended—

(1) by revising subsection (b)(5) to read as follows:

"(5) INSURANCE AUTHORITY.—Using any authority provided in appropriation Acts to insure mortgages under the National Housing Act, the Secretary may enter into commitments under this subsection for risk-sharing units.";

(2) by revising subsection (c)(4) to read as follows:

"(4) INSURANCE AUTHORITY.—Using any authority provided in appropriation Acts to insure mortgages under the National Housing Act, the Secretary may enter into commitments under this subsection for risk-sharing units.";

(3) in the heading, by striking "DEMONSTRATIONS" and inserting "PROGRAMS";

(4) in the first sentence of subsection (a), by striking "demonstrate the effectiveness of providing" and inserting "provide";

(5) in the second sentence of subsection (a), by striking "demonstration";

(6) in subsection (b)(1), by striking "determine the effectiveness of" and inserting "provide";

(7) in subsection (c)(1), by striking "test the effectiveness of" and inserting "provide";

(8) by striking subsection (d); and

(9) by striking "pilot" and "PILOT" each place it appears.

SEC. 207. PERMANENT EXTENSION OF STREAMLINED DOWNPAYMENT REQUIREMENTS.—Section 203(b)(2) of the National Housing Act is amended by striking subparagraph (B) and all that follows in the paragraph through "applicability of this requirement," and inserting the following:

"(B) not to exceed an amount equal to—

"(i) 98.75 percent of the appraised value of the property, if such value is equal to or less than $50,000;

"(ii) 97.65 percent of the appraised value of the property, if such value is in excess of $50,000 but not in excess of $125,000;

"(iii) 97.15 percent of the appraised value of the property, if such value is in excess of $125,000; or

"(iv) Notwithstanding clauses (ii) and (iii), 97.75 percent of the appraised value of the property, if such value is in excess of $50,000 and the property is in a State for which the average closing cost exceeds 2.10 percent of the average, for the State, of the sales price of properties located in the State for which mortgages have been executed, as determined by the Secretary.

"For purposes of this subparagraph, the term 'average closing cost' means, with respect to a State, the average, for mortgages executed for properties in the State, of the total amounts (as determined by the Secretary) of initial service charges, appraisal, inspection, and other fees and costs (as the Secretary shall approve) that are paid in connection with such mortgages.".

ENHANCED DISPOSITION AUTHORITY

SEC. 208. Section 204 of the Departments of Veterans Affairs and Housing and Urban Development, and Independent Agencies Appropriations Act, 1997, is amended by striking "and 2000" and inserting "2000, and thereafter".

GINNIE MAE ADMINISTRATIVE CONTRACT AUTHORITY

SEC. 209. Section 1 of the National Housing Act (12 U.S.C. 1702) is amended in the first sentence following the first proviso by striking "Except with respect to title III," and inserting "Except with respect to the Federal National Mortgage Association,".

FHA MORTGAGE LIMIT INCREASE

SEC. 210. INCREASE IN FHA SINGLE FAMILY MAXIMUM MORTGAGE AMOUNT.

(a) INCREASE IN MAXIMUM MORTGAGE AMOUNTS TO UNIFORM NATIONAL MAXIMUM.—Section 203(b)(2)(A) of the National Housing Act is amended to read as follows:

"(A) not to exceed the average of the dollar amounts determined under section 305(a)(2) of the Federal Home Loan Mortgage Corporation Act and section 302(b)(2) of the National Housing Act for a residence of the applicable size; and"

(b) CONFORMING AMENDMENT FOR TITLE I MANUFACTURED HOME LOANS IN HIGH-COST AREAS.—Section 2(b)(2) of such Act is amended by—

(1) striking "the lesser of (A)"; and

(2) striking ", or (B)" and all that follows up to the period.

(c) CONFORMING AMENDMENT FOR HECMS.—Section 255(g) of such Act is amended by striking "in the area" and all that follows up to the period.

SEC. 211. Rental Assistance Fraud Recoveries. Section 326(b) of the Housing and Community Development Act of 1992, Public Law 102–550, is repealed.

FHA INSURANCE FOR HYBRID ARMS

SEC. 212. FHA INSURANCE FOR HYBRID ARMS.—Section 251 of the National Housing Act is amended—

(1) in subsection (b), by striking "issue regulations" and all that follows and inserting the following: "require that the mortgagee make available to the mortgagor, at the time of loan application, a written explanation of the features of an adjustable rate mortgage consistent with the disclosure requirements applicable to variable rate mortgages secured by a principal dwelling under the Truth in Lending Act.";

(2) in subsection (c), by striking "30" and inserting "40"; and

(3) by adding the following new subsection at the end:

"(d)(1) The Secretary may insure under this subsection a mortgage that meets the requirements of subsection (a), except that the effective rate of interest—

"(A) shall be fixed for a period of not less than the first 3 years of the mortgage term;

"(B) shall be adjusted by the mortgagee initially upon the expiration of such period and annually thereafter; and

"(C) in the case of the initial interest rate adjustment, is subject to the 1 percent limitation only if the interest rate remained fixed for 5 or fewer years.

"(2) The disclosure required under subsection (b) shall be required for a mortgage insured under this subsection.

"(3) The Secretary may implement this subsection in advance of rulemaking.".

SEC. 213.—MIXED FINANCING FOR SECTION 202.

Section 202 of the Housing Act of 1959 is amended—

(1) in subsection (h)(6), by striking "non-Federal sources" and inserting "sources other than this section"; and

(2) in subsection (k)(4), by inserting after and below subparagraph (C) the following new sentence:

"Such term includes: (1) a limited partnership the sole general partner of which is an organization meeting the requirements of subparagraphs (A), (B), and (C); and (2) a corporation wholly owned by an organization meeting the requirements under subparagraphs (A), (B), and (C).".

SEC. 214.—MAXIMUM PAYMENT STANDARD FOR ENHANCED VOUCHERS.

Section 8(t)(1)(B) of the United States Housing Act of 1937 is amended by inserting "and any other reasonable limit prescribed by the Secretary" immediately before the semi-colon. (Departments of Veterans Affairs and Housing and Urban Development, and Independent Agencies Appropriations Act, 2000.)

SEC. 215. TECHNICAL AMENDMENTS AND CORRECTIONS TO THE NATIONAL HOUSING ACT.

(a) SECTION 203 SUBSECTION DESIGNATIONS.—Section 203 of the National Housing Act is amended by—

(1) redesignating subsection (t) as subsection (u);

(2) redesignating subsection (s), as added by section 329 of the Cranston-Gonzalez National Affordable Housing Act, as subsection (t); and

(3) redesignating subsection (v), as added by section 504 of the Housing and Community Development Act of 1992, as subsection (w).

(b) MORTGAGE AUCTIONS.—The first sentence of section 221(g)(4)(C)(viii) of the National Housing Act is amended by inserting after "December 31, 2002" the following: ", except that this subparagraph shall continue to apply if the Secretary receives a mortgagee's written notice of intent to assign its mortgage to the Secretary on or before such date".

(c) MORTGAGEE REVIEW BOARD.—Section 202(c)(2) of the National Housing Act is amended—

(1) in subparagraph (E), by striking "and";

(2) in subparagraph (F), by striking "or their designees." and inserting "and";

(3) by adding the following new subparagraph at the end:

"(G) the Director of the Enforcement Center; or their designees.".

SEC. 216. CLARIFICATION OF RULEMAKING AUTHORITY FOR RENEWALS OF PROJECT-BASED ASSISTANCE WITHOUT RESTRUCTURING.—Section 522(a) of the Multifamily Assisted Housing Reform and Affordability Act of 1997 is amended by inserting the following new paragraph (4) at the end:

"(4) RULEMAKING AFTER INITIAL IMPLEMENTATION.—After the Director issues final regulations under paragraph (2), the Secretary shall have the authority to issue all regulations concerning contract renewals under section 524 of this Act, including amendment, revision and removal of such regulations previously issued by the Director.".

SEC. 217. HOUSING PRODUCTION ASSISTANCE.

(a) TYPES OF ASSISTANCE.

(1) VOUCHER AUTHORITY.—In addition to assistance otherwise available under section 8 of the United States Housing Act of 1937, the Secretary of Housing and Urban Development shall make up to an additional 10,000 housing vouchers available to public housing agencies, under such terms and conditions as the Secretary determines. Such vouchers shall be for extremely low-income families.

(2) INCENTIVE GRANTS.—Of the amounts appropriated for this section for fiscal year 2001, the Secretary may use up to $8,000,000 for one-time grants to developers who produce housing units that satisfy such unmet needs as the Secretary may identify, such as a need for an increase in units to house large families.

(b) HUD ALLOCATION OF VOUCHERS.—Notwithstanding section 213(d) of the Housing and Community Development Act of 1974, the Secretary shall allocate the vouchers described in subsection (a) to States in the same proportions as low-income housing tax credits pursuant to 26 U.S.C. 42 are allocated. Allocation of these vouchers shall be subject to the per capita tax credit amount established for such credits for fiscal year 2001. The Secretary may reallocate any vouchers that a State housing credit agency does not designate for use at a particular building pursuant to subsection (c) in the same manner as such tax credits are reallocated.

(c) DISTRIBUTION OF VOUCHERS.

(1) The housing credit agency shall select the buildings or housing at which the vouchers made available for each State under subsection (b) shall be used. Such buildings or housing may include—

(A) new buildings with a mortgage insured under section 221(d)(4) of the National Housing Act which is allocated a housing credit dollar amount pursuant to 26 U.S.C. 42 and is not located in a qualified census tract; and

(B) new multifamily housing with a mortgage insured under section 542(c) of the Housing and Community Development Act of 1992 which may or may not be allocated a housing credit dollar amount pursuant to 26 U.S.C. 42 and is not located in a qualified census tract.

(2) The housing credit agency shall determine the number of vouchers the Secretary shall distribute for use at the buildings or housing selected under paragraph (1), but in no case shall such number be more than 25 percent of the total number of units in the building or housing.

(3) The housing credit agency shall select a public housing agency to administer these vouchers, and subject to paragraph (4), any public housing agency that has jurisdiction over the building or multifamily housing for which these vouchers have been distributed for use may be so selected.

(4) The Secretary shall decline to make the requested vouchers available to any public housing agency that—

(A)(i) the Secretary determines is not administering tenant-based assistance under section 8 of the United States Housing Act of 1937 in a satisfactory manner; and

(ii) has not proposed an alternative administrator of vouchers under this section satisfactory to the Secretary;

(B) does not comply with title VI of the Civil Rights Act of 1964, the Fair Housing Act, section 504 of the Rehabilitation Act of 1973, or title II of the Americans with Disabilities Act of 1990, or other applicable civil rights laws; or

FHA INSURANCE FOR HYBRID ARMS—Continued

(C) is otherwise determined by the Secretary to be ineligible for receipt of such vouchers.

(d) PUBLIC HOUSING AGENCY ALLOCATION OF VOUCHERS.

(1) IN GENERAL.—The public housing agency receiving housing vouchers under this section shall make the vouchers available for use in accordance with subsection (e) to extremely low-income households that agree to move into the buildings or multifamily housing selected by the housing credit agency under subsection (c)(1).

(2) INTERIM USE.—Notwithstanding this section, prior to such time as the housing vouchers made available under this section may be used pursuant to paragraph (1), the public housing agency receiving the vouchers may administer such vouchers in accordance with the provisions of section 8(o) of the United States Housing Act of 1937 and such other terms and conditions as the Secretary may determine. In the event of such use, the Secretary shall reserve authority in future fiscal years to provide housing assistance under section 8(o) in furtherance of this section such that the same number of families receive assistance under this section as would have been assisted absent any interim use of vouchers under this paragraph.

(3) LIHTC BUILDING STANDARDS UNAFFECTED.—No vouchers shall be made available under this section for use at a building allocated a housing credit dollar amount pursuant to 26 U.S.C. 42, unless the building at which the vouchers would be used meets all standards for tax credit financing under such section, without taking into account the vouchers made available under this section.

(e) USE RESTRICTIONS.—The vouchers described in subsection (a) shall be administered in accordance with the provisions of section 8(o) of the United States Housing Act of 1937, except that—

(1) public housing agencies administering these vouchers shall initially make these vouchers available to extremely low-income households that agree to move into buildings or housing selected by a housing credit agency pursuant to subsection (c)(1) of this section, for initial use of at least one year at such buildings or housing;

(2) subject to the availability of appropriations, after the initial 1-year use of these vouchers, the household receiving the voucher—

(A) may elect to remain in place with the voucher assistance for up to 14 additional years; or

(B) may elect to relocate with the voucher assistance to another dwelling unit eligible under section 8(o); and

(3) the payment standard for each size of dwelling unit shall be equal to the lesser of comparable market rents or rents available pursuant to 26 U.S.C. 42 for the selected building or housing, but in no event shall the payment standard be higher than 150 percent of the fair market rent of the area in which the building or multifamily housing is located, except that the Secretary may adjust such percentage on an exception basis.

(f) FUNDING.—In addition to any amounts appropriated in this Act for fiscal year 2001, there are hereby authorized to be appropriated such sums as may be necessary in ensuing years to carry out this section. Any amounts appropriated shall remain available until expended.

(g) DEFINITION.—For purposes of this section, the term "extremely low-income family" means a family whose income does not exceed 30 percent of the median family income for the area, as determined by the Secretary with adjustments for smaller or larger families, except that the Secretary may establish income ceilings higher or lower than 30 percent of the median for the area on the basis of the Secretary's findings that such variations are necessary because of unusually high or low family income, but such income ceilings shall not exceed the minimum set-asides under 26 U.S.C. 42(g).

SEC. 218. REPEAL OF INDEPENDENT ASSESSMENT FOR TROUBLED AGENCIES.

Section 6(j)(2) of the United States Housing Act of 1937 is amended—

(1) by repealing subparagraph (B); and

(2) in subparagraph (C), by revising the first sentence to read as follows: "The Secretary shall seek to enter into an agreement with each troubled public housing agency.".

INDIAN HOUSING BLOCK GRANT PROGRAM

SEC. 219. DEFINES CERTAIN LAW ENFORCEMENT OFFICERS AS ELIGIBLE FAMILIES FOR HOUSING ASSISTANCE UNDER THE INDIAN HOUSING BLOCK GRANT PROGRAM.

Section 201(b) of the Native American Housing Assistance and Self-Determination Act of 1996 is amended—

(1) by redesignating paragraphs (4) and (5) as paragraphs (5) and (6) respectively; and

(2) by inserting after paragraph (3) the following new paragraph:

"(4) LAW ENFORCEMENT OFFICERS.—Notwithstanding paragraph (1), a recipient may provide housing or housing assistance provided through affordable housing activities assisted with grant amounts under this Act to a law enforcement officer on the reservation or other Indian area, who is employed full-time by a Federal, state, county or tribal government, and in implementing such full-time employment is sworn to uphold, and make arrests for violations of Federal, state, county or tribal law, if the recipient determines that the presence of the law enforcement officer on the Indian reservation or other Indian area may deter crime.".

GENERAL FUND RECEIPT ACCOUNTS

(in millions of dollars)

	1999 actual	2000 est.	2001 est.
Offsetting receipts from the public:			
86–271910 FHA-General and Special Risk, Negative Subsidies	159	229	149
86–271930 FHA-General and Special Risk, Downward reestimates of subsidies	154		
General Fund Offsetting receipts from the public	313	229	149

DEPARTMENT OF THE INTERIOR

LAND AND MINERALS MANAGEMENT

BUREAU OF LAND MANAGEMENT

The Bureau of Land Management (BLM) is charged with the multiple use management of natural resources on 264 million acres of public land. It also supervises mineral leasing and operations on an additional 300 million acres of Federal mineral estate that underlie other surface ownerships. The lands managed by BLM provide important natural resources, recreational and scenic values to the American people, as well as resource commodities and revenue to the Federal Government, States, and counties. It is the mission of the BLM to sustain the health, diversity, and productivity of the public lands for the use and enjoyment of present and future generations.

Federal Funds

General and special funds:

MANAGEMENT OF LANDS AND RESOURCES

For expenses necessary for protection, use, improvement, development, disposal, cadastral surveying, classification, acquisition of easements and other interests in lands, and performance of other functions, including maintenance of facilities, as authorized by law, in the management of lands and their resources under the jurisdiction of the Bureau of Land Management, including the general administration of the Bureau, and assessment of mineral potential of public lands pursuant to Public Law 96–487 (16 U.S.C. 3150(a)), [$646,218,000] *$715,191,000*, to remain available until expended, of which [$2,147,000] *$2,198,000* shall be available for assessment of the mineral potential of public lands in Alaska pursuant to section 1010 of Public Law 96–487 (16 U.S.C. 3150); and of which not to exceed $1,000,000 shall be derived from the special receipt account established by the Land and Water Conservation Act of 1965, as amended (16 U.S.C. 460l–6a(i)); and of which $2,500,000 shall be available in fiscal year [2000] *2001* subject to a match by at least an equal amount by the National Fish and Wildlife Foundation, to such Foundation for cost-shared projects supporting conservation of Bureau lands and such funds shall be advanced to the Foundation as a lump sum grant without regard to when expenses are incurred; in addition, [$33,529,000] *$34,328,000* for Mining Law Administration program operations, including the cost of administering the mining claim fee program; to remain available until expended, to be reduced by amounts collected by the Bureau and credited to this appropriation from annual mining claim fees so as to result in a final appropriation estimated at not more than [$646,218,000] *$715,191,000*, and $2,000,000, to remain available until expended, from communication site rental fees established by the Bureau for the cost of administering communication site activities[, and of which $2,500,000, to remain available until expended, is for coalbed methane Applications for Permits to Drill in the Powder River Basin: *Provided*, That unless there is a written agreement in place between the coal mining operator and a gas producer, the funds available herein shall not be used to process or approve coalbed methane Applications for Permits to Drill for well sites that are located within an area, which as of the date of the coalbed methane Application for Permit to Drill, are covered by: (1) a coal lease; (2) a coal mining permit; or (3) an application for a coal mining lease]: *Provided further*, That appropriations herein made shall not be available for the destruction of healthy, unadopted, wild horses and burros in the care of the Bureau or its contractors. *(Department of the Interior and Related Agencies Appropriations Act, 2000, as enacted by section 1000(a)(3) of the Consolidated Appropriations Act, 2000 (P.L. 106–113).)*

Unavailable Collections (in millions of dollars)

Identification code 14–1109–0–1–302	999 actual	2000 est.	2001 est.
Balance, start of year:			
01.99 Balance, start of year	2		
Receipts:			
02.01 Recreation, entrance and use fees	1	1	1
04.00 Total: Balances and collections	3	1	1
Appropriation:			
05.01 Management of public lands and resources	–3	–1	–1
07.99 Total balance, end of year			

Program and Financing (in millions of dollars)

Identification code 14–1109–0–1–302	1999 actual	2000 est.	2001 est.
Obligations by program activity:			
Direct program:			
00.11 Land resources	145	164	191
00.12 Wildlife and fisheries	32	38	41
00.13 Threatened and endangered species	17	19	24
00.14 Recreation management	51	53	63
00.15 Energy and minerals	71	76	80
00.16 Realty and ownership management	74	80	81
00.17 Resource protection	66	35	39
00.18 Transportation and facilities maintenance	8	48	51
00.19 Land and resource information systems	39	24	21
00.20 Workforce and organizational support	119	125	128
00.21 Alaska minerals assessment	3	2	2
09.01 Reimbursable program	66	60	54
10.00 Total new obligations	691	724	775
Budgetary resources available for obligation:			
21.40 Unobligated balance available, start of year	29	32	6
22.00 New budget authority (gross)	684	698	769
22.10 Resources available from recoveries of prior year obligations	10		
23.90 Total budgetary resources available for obligation	723	730	775
23.95 Total new obligations	–691	–724	–775
24.40 Unobligated balance available, end of year	32	6	
New budget authority (gross), detail:			
Discretionary:			
40.00 Appropriation (general fund)	617	645	714
40.20 Appropriation (special fund, definite)	3	1	1
40.75 Reduction pursuant to P.L. 106–51	–1		
40.76 Reduction pursuant to P.L. 106–113		–3	
42.00 Transferred from other accounts		1	
43.00 Appropriation (total discretionary)	619	644	715
Spending authority from offsetting collections:			
Offsetting collections (cash):			
68.00 Offsetting collections (cash)	52	60	56
68.00 Offsetting collections (cash)	7	5	
From Federal sources: Change in receivables and unpaid, unfilled orders:			
68.10 From Federal sources: Change in receivables and unpaid, unfilled orders	1	–6	–2
68.10 From Federal sources: Change in receivables and unpaid, unfilled orders	5	–5	
68.90 Spending authority from offsetting collections (total discretionary)	65	54	54
70.00 Total new budget authority (gross)	684	698	769
Change in unpaid obligations:			
Unpaid obligations, start of year:			
72.40 Obligated balance, start of year	124	139	176
From Federal sources: Receivables and unpaid, unfilled orders:			
72.95 From Federal sources: Receivables and unpaid, unfilled orders	13	14	8

General and special funds—Continued

MANAGEMENT OF LANDS AND RESOURCES—Continued

Program and Financing (in millions of dollars)—Continued

Identification code 14–1109–0–1–302		1999 actual	2000 est.	2001 est.
72.95	From Federal sources: Receivables and unpaid, unfilled orders		5	
72.99	Total unpaid obligations, start of year	137	158	184
73.10	Total new obligations	691	724	775
73.20	Total outlays (gross)	−661	−698	−761
73.40	Adjustments in expired accounts (net)	1		
73.45	Adjustments in unexpired accounts	−10		
	Unpaid obligations, end of year:			
74.40	Obligated balance, end of year	139	176	192
	From Federal sources: Receivables and unpaid, unfilled orders:			
74.95	From Federal sources: Receivables and unpaid, unfilled orders	14	8	6
74.95	From Federal sources: Receivables and unpaid, unfilled orders	5		
74.99	Total unpaid obligations, end of year	158	184	198
	Outlays (gross), detail:			
86.90	Outlays from new discretionary authority	543	556	612
86.93	Outlays from discretionary balances	118	142	151
87.00	Total outlays (gross)	661	698	761
	Offsets:			
	Against gross budget authority and outlays:			
	Offsetting collections (cash) from:			
88.00	Federal sources	−7	−5	
88.45	Offsetting governmental collections from the public	−52	−60	−56
88.90	Total, offsetting collections (cash)	−59	−65	−56
	Against gross budget authority only:			
88.95	From Federal sources: Change in receivables and unpaid, unfilled orders	−6	11	2
	Net budget authority and outlays:			
89.00	Budget authority	619	644	715
90.00	Outlays	602	633	705

Land resources.—Provides for management of rangeland and forest resources; riparian areas; soil, water, and air activities; wild horses and burros; and, cultural resources.

Wildlife and fisheries management.—Provides for maintenance, improvement, or enhancement of fish and wildlife habitats as part of the management of public lands and ecosystems.

Threatened and endangered species management.—Provides for protection, conservation, consultation, recovery, and evaluation of populations and habitats of threatened, endangered and special status animal and plant species.

Recreation management.—Provides for management and protection of recreational resource values, designated and potential wilderness areas, and collection and expenditure of recreation user fees.

Energy and minerals management.—Provides for management of: onshore oil and gas, coal, and geothermal resources; and, other leasable minerals, mineral materials activities, and the administration of encumbrances on the mineral estate on Federal and Indian lands.

Realty and ownership management.—Provides for management and non-reimbursable processing of authorizations and compliance for realty actions and rights-of-way (including Alaska), administration of land title records and performing cadastral surveys on public lands.

Transportation and Facilities Maintenance.—Provides for maintenance of administrative and recreation sites, roads, trails, bridges and dams including compliance with building codes and standards and environmental protection requirements. Funding for Transportation and Facilities Maintenance is proposed as part of the third year of the Administration's facilities restoration initiative. These funds emphasize the Administration's commitment to the long-term stewardship of Federal lands and facilities.

Resource protection.—Provides for management of the land use planning and National Environmental Policy Act processes. Also ensures the health and safety of users or activities on public lands through: protection from criminal and other non-lawful activities; protection from the effects of hazardous material and/or waste; and from physical safety hazards.

Land and Resource Information Systems.—Provides for the development and bureau-wide implementation of the Land and Resource Information Systems.

Workforce and organizational support.—Provides for management of specified bureau business practices, such as human resources, EEO, financial resources, procurement, property, general use automated systems, and fixed costs.

Alaska minerals.—Provides for the identification, inventory, and evaluation of mineral resources on Federal lands within the State of Alaska.

PERFORMANCE MEASURES

	1999 actual	*2000 est.*	*2001 est.*
Number of abandoned mine sites that are being remediated	120	130	134
Number of wild horses and burros removed from public lands	6,024	6,200	12,855
Riparian areas assessed against health standards (mi)	6,301	6,184	5,850
Shrub grassland, pinyon juniper, and aquatic, riparian, and wetland treatments (acres)	N/A	2,735,000	2,768,300
Acres treated to prevent the spread of noxious weeds and undesirable plants (acres)	120,496	199,999	213,700
Dollars Contributed by non-Federal partners for BLM challenge cost share project ($000)	10,664,000	9,217,000	9,200,000
Number of oil and gas applications for permit to drill processed	2,503	3,438	3,500
Number of mining claim filings	124	125	125
Miles of road maintained	9,278	11,787	12,000
Percent of users satisfied with the condition of BLM rec. areas	95	93	93
Percent of customers satisfied with BLMs protection of significant historical, cultural and other heritage resources (percent)	84	82	82
Percent of BOR withdrawn acreage reviewed	44	N/A	N/A

Object Classification (in millions of dollars)

Identification code 14–1109–0–1–302		1999 actual	2000 est.	2001 est.
	Direct obligations:			
	Personnel compensation:			
11.1	Full-time permanent	272	286	309
11.3	Other than full-time permanent	13	14	15
11.5	Other personnel compensation	8	8	9
11.9	Total personnel compensation	293	308	333
12.1	Civilian personnel benefits	74	78	84
21.0	Travel and transportation of persons	18	19	20
22.0	Transportation of things	11	12	13
23.1	Rental payments to GSA	22	23	25
23.2	Rental payments to others	19	20	22
23.3	Communications, utilities, and miscellaneous charges	16	18	18
24.0	Printing and reproduction	2	3	3
25.2	Other services	107	115	130
26.0	Supplies and materials	22	23	26
31.0	Equipment	34	37	38
32.0	Land and structures	4	4	4
41.0	Grants, subsidies, and contributions	3	4	5
99.0	Subtotal, direct obligations	625	664	721
99.0	Reimbursable obligations	66	60	54
99.9	Total new obligations	691	724	775

Personnel Summary

Identification code 14–1109–0–1–302		1999 actual	2000 est.	2001 est.
	Direct:			
1001	Total compensable workyears: Full-time equivalent employment	5,926	5,954	6,197
	Reimbursable:			
2001	Total compensable workyears: Full-time equivalent employment	509	509	509

Allocation account:			
3001 Total compensable workyears: Full-time equivalent employment	54	61	61

CONSTRUCTION

For construction of buildings, recreation facilities, roads, trails, and appurtenant facilities, **[**$11,425,000**]** *$11,200,000*, to remain available until expended. *(Department of the Interior and Related Agencies Appropriations Act, 2000, as enacted by section 1000(a)(3) of the Consolidated Appropriations Act, 2000 (P.L. 106–113).)*

Program and Financing (in millions of dollars)

Identification code 14–1110–0–1–302	1999 actual	2000 est.	2001 est.
Obligations by program activity:			
10.00 Total new obligations	7	11	11
Budgetary resources available for obligation:			
21.40 Unobligated balance available, start of year	9	14	14
22.00 New budget authority (gross)	11	11	11
23.90 Total budgetary resources available for obligation	20	25	25
23.95 Total new obligations	–7	–11	–11
24.40 Unobligated balance available, end of year	14	14	14
New budget authority (gross), detail:			
Discretionary:			
40.00 Appropriation	11	11	11
Change in unpaid obligations:			
72.40 Unpaid obligations, start of year: Obligated balance, start of year	4	5	9
73.10 Total new obligations	7	11	11
73.20 Total outlays (gross)	–6	–7	–10
74.40 Unpaid obligations, end of year: Obligated balance, end of year	5	9	10
Outlays (gross), detail:			
86.90 Outlays from new discretionary authority	2	3	3
86.93 Outlays from discretionary balances	4	4	7
87.00 Total outlays (gross)	6	7	10
Net budget authority and outlays:			
89.00 Budget authority	11	11	11
90.00 Outlays	6	7	10

Construction.—Provides for the construction of buildings, recreation facilities, bridges, roads, and trails necessary for effective multiple use management of the public lands and resources.

Funding for the Construction account is proposed as part of the third year of the Administration's facilities restoration initiative. These funds emphasize the Administration's commitment to halt infrastructure decay and allow for systematic protection of critical health and safety, natural and cultural resources, and the environment.

Object Classification (in millions of dollars)

Identification code 14–1110–0–1–302	1999 actual	2000 est.	2001 est.
11.1 Personnel compensation: Full-time permanent	1	1	1
25.2 Other services	2	4	3
26.0 Supplies and materials	1	1	1
32.0 Land and structures	3	5	6
99.9 Total new obligations	7	11	11

Personnel Summary

Identification code 14–1110–0–1–302	1999 actual	2000 est.	2001 est.
1001 Total compensable workyears: Full-time equivalent employment	11	13	13

PAYMENTS IN LIEU OF TAXES

For expenses necessary to implement the Act of October 20, 1976, as amended (31 U.S.C. 6901–6907), $135,000,000, of which not to exceed $400,000 shall be available for administrative expenses: *Provided,* That no payment shall be made to otherwise eligible units of local government if the computed amount of the payment is less than $100. *(Department of the Interior and Related Agencies Appropriations Act, 2000, as enacted by section 1000(a)(3) of the Consolidated Appropriations Act, 2000 (P.L. 106–113).)*

Program and Financing (in millions of dollars)

Identification code 14–1114–0–1–806	1999 actual	2000 est.	2001 est.
Obligations by program activity:			
10.00 Total new obligations (object class 41.0)	125	134	135
Budgetary resources available for obligation:			
22.00 New budget authority (gross)	125	134	135
23.95 Total new obligations	–125	–134	–135
New budget authority (gross), detail:			
Discretionary:			
40.00 Appropriation	125	135	135
40.76 Reduction pursuant to P.L. 106–113		–1	
43.00 Appropriation (total discretionary)	125	134	135
Change in unpaid obligations:			
73.10 Total new obligations	125	134	135
73.20 Total outlays (gross)	–125	–134	–135
Outlays (gross), detail:			
86.90 Outlays from new discretionary authority	125	134	135
Net budget authority and outlays:			
89.00 Budget authority	125	134	135
90.00 Outlays	125	134	135

Public Law 94–565 (31 U.S.C. 6901–07), as amended, authorizes payments in lieu of taxes to counties and other units of local government for lands within their boundaries that are administered by the Bureau of Land Management, Forest Service, National Park Service, Fish and Wildlife Service, and certain other agencies.

Personnel Summary

Identification code 14–1114–0–1–806	1999 actual	2000 est.	2001 est.
1001 Total compensable workyears: Full-time equivalent employment	1	1	1

OREGON AND CALIFORNIA GRANT LANDS

For expenses necessary for management, protection, and development of resources and for construction, operation, and maintenance of access roads, reforestation, and other improvements on the revested Oregon and California Railroad grant lands, on other Federal lands in the Oregon and California land-grant counties of Oregon, and on adjacent rights-of-way; and acquisition of lands or interests therein including existing connecting roads on or adjacent to such grant lands; **[**$99,225,000**]** *$104,267,000*, to remain available until expended: *Provided,* That 25 percent of the aggregate of all receipts during the current fiscal year from the revested Oregon and California Railroad grant lands is hereby made a charge against the Oregon and California land-grant fund and shall be transferred to the General Fund in the Treasury in accordance with the second paragraph of subsection (b) of title II of the Act of August 28, 1937 (50 Stat. 876). *(Department of the Interior and Related Agencies Appropriations Act, 2000, as enacted by section 1000(a)(3) of the Consolidated Appropriations Act, 2000 (P.L. 106–113).)*

Program and Financing (in millions of dollars)

Identification code 14–1116–0–1–302	1999 actual	2000 est.	2001 est.
Obligations by program activity:			
00.01 Western Oregon construction and acquisition		1	

General and special funds—Continued

OREGON AND CALIFORNIA GRANT LANDS—Continued

Program and Financing (in millions of dollars)—Continued

Identification code 14–1116–0–1–302	1999 actual	2000 est.	2001 est.
00.02 Western Oregon facilities maintenance	10		
00.03 Western Oregon transportation and facilities maintenance		11	10
00.04 Western Oregon resource management	80	82	86
00.05 Western Oregon information and resource data system	2	2	2
00.06 Jobs-in-the-woods	5	6	6
10.00 Total new obligations	97	102	104
Budgetary resources available for obligation:			
21.40 Unobligated balance available, start of year	1	3	
22.00 New budget authority (gross)	97	99	104
22.10 Resources available from recoveries of prior year obligations	2		
23.90 Total budgetary resources available for obligation	100	102	104
23.95 Total new obligations	−97	−102	−104
24.40 Unobligated balance available, end of year	3		
New budget authority (gross), detail:			
Discretionary:			
40.00 Appropriation	97	99	104
Change in unpaid obligations:			
72.40 Unpaid obligations, start of year: Obligated balance, start of year	45	36	39
73.10 Total new obligations	97	102	104
73.20 Total outlays (gross)	−104	−99	−104
73.45 Adjustments in unexpired accounts	−2		
74.40 Unpaid obligations, end of year: Obligated balance, end of year	36	39	39
Outlays (gross), detail:			
86.90 Outlays from new discretionary authority	64	65	69
86.93 Outlays from discretionary balances	40	34	35
87.00 Total outlays (gross)	104	99	104
Net budget authority and outlays:			
89.00 Budget authority	97	99	104
90.00 Outlays	104	99	104

Western Oregon resources management.—Provides for the management of 2.4 million acres of lands that are primarily forested ecosystems in western Oregon. These lands support a number of resource management activities including timber management, grazing management, and recreation management. In support of these management activities, BLM is involved in improving critical watersheds, restoring wildlife and fish habitat, providing safe recreation opportunities, and preserving cultural resources.

Western Oregon information and resource data systems.—Provides for the acquisition, operation and maintenance of the automated data support systems required for the management of the O&C programs.

Western Oregon transportation and facilities maintenance.—Provides for the maintenance of office buildings, warehouse and storage structures, shops, greenhouses, recreation sites and the transportation system that is necessary to assure public safety and effective management of the lands in western Oregon. Funding for Western Oregon transportation and facilities maintenance is proposed as part of the third year of the Administration's facilities restoration initiative. These funds emphasize the Administration's commitment to the long-term stewardship of Federal lands and facilities.

Western Oregon construction and acquisition.—Provides for the acquisition of road easements and road use agreements for timber site access and for other resource management activities including recreation use. This activity also provides for transportation planning, survey and design of access and other resource management roads; and, construction projects.

Jobs in the Woods.—Provides for the "Jobs in the Woods" program offering resource-based job opportunities to displaced timber workers in the Pacific Northwest to improve water quality and restore Oregon's coastal salmon populations. Projects include: improving fish passage structures, improving instream habitat, reducing sedimentation runoff, and improving road conditions.

PERFORMANCE MEASURES

	1999 actual	*2000 est.*	*2001 est.*
Volume of Timber Offered for Sale (MMBF)	62	70	211
Job Opportunities Created (Jobs-in-the-Woods)	168	165	165
Forest Restoration Treatments Applied (acres)	16,121	12,300	11,000

Object Classification (in millions of dollars)

Identification code 14–1116–0–1–302	1999 actual	2000 est.	2001 est.
Personnel compensation:			
11.1 Full-time permanent	39	41	43
11.3 Other than full-time permanent	6	7	7
11.5 Other personnel compensation	2	2	2
11.9 Total personnel compensation	47	50	52
12.1 Civilian personnel benefits	10	11	11
21.0 Travel and transportation of persons	1	2	2
22.0 Transportation of things	3	3	3
23.3 Communications, utilities, and miscellaneous charges	1	2	2
25.2 Other services	27	26	25
26.0 Supplies and materials	4	4	5
31.0 Equipment	3	3	3
32.0 Land and structures	1	1	1
99.9 Total new obligations	97	102	104

Personnel Summary

Identification code 14–1116–0–1–302	1999 actual	2000 est.	2001 est.
1001 Total compensable workyears: Full-time equivalent employment	992	993	1,000

WILDLAND FIRE MANAGEMENT

For necessary expenses for fire preparedness, suppression operations, emergency rehabilitation and hazardous fuels reduction by the Department of the Interior, [$292,282,000] *$297,197,000*, to remain available until expended, of which not to exceed $9,300,000 shall be for the renovation or construction of fire facilities: *Provided*, That such funds are also available for repayment of advances to other appropriation accounts from which funds were previously transferred for such purposes: *Provided further*, That unobligated balances of amounts previously appropriated to the "Fire Protection" and "Emergency Department of the Interior Firefighting Fund" may be transferred and merged with this appropriation: *Provided further*, That persons hired pursuant to 43 U.S.C. 1469 may be furnished subsistence and lodging without cost from funds available from this appropriation: *Provided further*, That notwithstanding 42 U.S.C. 1856d, sums received by a bureau or office of the Department of the Interior for fire protection rendered pursuant to 42 U.S.C. 1856 et seq., protection of United States property, may be credited to the appropriation from which funds were expended to provide that protection, and are available without fiscal year limitation[: *Provided further*, That not more than $58,000 shall be available to the Bureau of Land Management to reimburse Trinity County for expenses incurred as part of the July 2, 1999 Lowden Fire]. *(Department of the Interior and Related Agencies Appropriations Act, 2000, as enacted by section 1000(a)(3) of the Consolidated Appropriations Act, 2000 (P.L. 106–113).)*

Program and Financing (in millions of dollars)

Identification code 14–1125–0–1–302	1999 actual	2000 est.	2001 est.
Obligations by program activity:			
Direct program:			
00.02 Wildland Fire Preparedness	169	179	182
00.03 Wildland Fire Operations	209	127	125
09.01 Reimbursable program	12	92	22

10.00	Total new obligations	390	398	329
	Budgetary resources available for obligation:			
21.40	Unobligated balance available, start of year	59	55	18
22.00	New budget authority (gross)	378	361	312
22.10	Resources available from recoveries of prior year obligations	8		
23.90	Total budgetary resources available for obligation	445	416	330
23.95	Total new obligations	−390	−398	−329
24.40	Unobligated balance available, end of year	55	18	
	New budget authority (gross), detail:			
	Discretionary:			
40.00	Appropriation	287	292	297
40.15	Appropriation (emergency)	50		
40.76	Reduction pursuant to P.L. 106–113		−1	
43.00	Appropriation (total discretionary)	337	291	297
	Spending authority from offsetting collections:			
68.00	Offsetting collections (cash)	22	80	24
68.10	From Federal sources: Change in receivables and unpaid, unfilled orders	19	−10	−9
68.90	Spending authority from offsetting collections (total discretionary)	41	70	15
70.00	Total new budget authority (gross)	378	361	312
	Change in unpaid obligations:			
	Unpaid obligations, start of year:			
72.40	Obligated balance, start of year	73	87	91
72.95	From Federal sources: Receivables and unpaid, unfilled orders	4	23	13
72.99	Total unpaid obligations, start of year	77	110	104
73.10	Total new obligations	390	398	329
73.20	Total outlays (gross)	−349	−404	−329
73.45	Adjustments in unexpired accounts	−8		
	Unpaid obligations, end of year:			
74.40	Obligated balance, end of year	87	91	100
74.95	From Federal sources: Receivables and unpaid, unfilled orders	23	13	4
74.99	Total unpaid obligations, end of year	110	104	104
	Outlays (gross), detail:			
86.90	Outlays from new discretionary authority	255	265	214
86.93	Outlays from discretionary balances	93	139	115
87.00	Total outlays (gross)	349	404	329
	Offsets:			
	Against gross budget authority and outlays:			
88.00	Offsetting collections (cash) from: Federal sources	−22	−80	−24
	Against gross budget authority only:			
88.95	From Federal sources: Change in receivables and unpaid, unfilled orders	−19	10	9
	Net budget authority and outlays:			
89.00	Budget authority	337	291	297
90.00	Outlays	327	324	305

Summary of Budget Authority and Outlays

(in millions of dollars)

	1999 actual	*2000 est.*	*2001 est.*
Enacted/requested:			
Budget Authority	337	291	297
Outlays	326	324	305
Supplemental proposal:			
Budget Authority		100	
Outlays			
Total:			
Budget Authority	337	391	297
Outlays	326	324	305

Wildland fire preparedness.—This activity funds the non-emergency and predictable aspects of the Department's wildland fire program. Preparedness includes readiness, operational planning, oversight, procurement, training, supervision, and deployment of wildland fire suppression personnel and equipment prior to wildland fire occurrence. It also includes activities related to program monitoring and evaluation, integration of fire into land-use planning, fire facility construction and maintenance, and fire research and fire science program activities.

Wildland fire operations.—This activity funds the emergency and unpredictable aspects of the Department's wildland fire management program. Wildland fire operations include emergency suppression, emergency rehabilitation, and hazardous fuels reduction. Suppression operations include the total spectrum of management actions taken on wildland fires in a safe, cost-effective manner, considering public benefits and values to be protected and consistent with resource objectives and land management plans. Suppression operations also include severity funding used to improve initial attack preparedness response capabilities when abnormal fire conditions occur resulting in fire seasons starting earlier than normal, lasting longer than normal, or exceeding average fire danger rating for prolonged periods. Emergency rehabilitation of wildland fire areas is carried out to prevent land degradation and resource damages and to stabilize soils, structures, or other conditions or damage caused by wildland fires. Hazardous fuels reduction operations include all operational aspects of applying prescribed fire to reduce fuel loadings and for ecosystem diversity. It also includes mechanical treatments. Funding requests are guided by the historical 10-year average of suppression and rehabilitation expenditures adjusted for inflation, and a target level for hazardous fuels reduction operations.

PERFORMANCE MEASURES

	1999 actual	*2000 est.*	*2001 est.*
Acres treated, fuels management (000s)	254	300	325

Object Classification (in millions of dollars)

Identification code 14–1125–0–1–302		1999 actual	2000 est.	2001 est.
	Direct obligations:			
	Personnel compensation:			
11.1	Full-time permanent	41	46	48
11.3	Other than full-time permanent	8	9	9
11.5	Other personnel compensation	27	28	29
11.9	Total personnel compensation	76	83	86
12.1	Civilian personnel benefits	16	17	18
21.0	Travel and transportation of persons	7	7	6
22.0	Transportation of things	4	4	3
23.2	Rental payments to others	1	1	1
23.3	Communications, utilities, and miscellaneous charges	4	4	4
25.2	Other services	57	8	6
26.0	Supplies and materials	35	15	15
31.0	Equipment	3	4	4
32.0	Land and structures	1	1	1
41.0	Grants, subsidies, and contributions	4	3	4
99.0	Subtotal, direct obligations	208	147	148
99.0	Reimbursable obligations	12	92	22
	Allocation Account:			
	Personnel compensation:			
11.1	Full-time permanent	30	35	37
11.3	Other than full-time permanent	8	10	11
11.5	Other personnel compensation	16	22	23
11.8	Special personal services payments	26	30	31
11.9	Total personnel compensation	80	97	102
12.1	Civilian personnel benefits	11	14	14
21.0	Travel and transportation of persons	7	6	5
22.0	Transportation of things	3	3	4
23.3	Communications, utilities, and miscellaneous charges	7	7	6
24.0	Printing and reproduction		1	1
25.2	Other services	41	8	5
26.0	Supplies and materials	10	10	10
31.0	Equipment	6	6	6
32.0	Land and structures	1	2	2
41.0	Grants, subsidies, and contributions	4	5	4
99.0	Subtotal, allocation account	170	159	159
99.9	Total new obligations	390	398	329

General and special funds—Continued

WILDLAND FIRE MANAGEMENT—Continued

Personnel Summary

Identification code 14–1125–0–1–302	1999 actual	2000 est.	2001 est.
Direct:			
1001 Total compensable workyears: Full-time equivalent employment	1,671	1,810	1,810
Reimbursable:			
2001 Total compensable workyears: Full-time equivalent employment	40	40	40

CENTRAL HAZARDOUS MATERIALS FUND

For necessary expenses of the Department of the Interior and any of its component offices and bureaus for the remedial action, including associated activities, of hazardous waste substances, pollutants, or contaminants pursuant to the Comprehensive Environmental Response, Compensation, and Liability Act, as amended (42 U.S.C. 9601 et seq.), $10,000,000, to remain available until expended: *Provided*, That notwithstanding 31 U.S.C. 3302, sums recovered from or paid by a party in advance of or as reimbursement for remedial action or response activities conducted by the Department pursuant to section 107 or 113(f) of such Act, shall be credited to this account to be available until expended without further appropriation: *Provided further*, That such sums recovered from or paid by any party are not limited to monetary payments and may include stocks, bonds or other personal or real property, which may be retained, liquidated, or otherwise disposed of by the Secretary and which shall be credited to this account. *(Department of the Interior and Related Agencies Appropriations Act, 2000, as enacted by section 1000(a)(3) of the Consolidated Appropriations Act, 2000 (P.L. 106–113).)*

Program and Financing (in millions of dollars)

Identification code 14–1121–0–1–304	1999 actual	2000 est.	2001 est.
Obligations by program activity:			
00.01 Remedial action	6	10	10
10.00 Total new obligations	6	10	10
Budgetary resources available for obligation:			
21.40 Unobligated balance available, start of year	5	9	9
22.00 New budget authority (gross)	10	10	10
23.90 Total budgetary resources available for obligation	15	19	19
23.95 Total new obligations	−6	−10	−10
24.40 Unobligated balance available, end of year	9	9	9
New budget authority (gross), detail:			
Discretionary:			
40.00 Appropriation	10	10	10
Change in unpaid obligations:			
72.40 Unpaid obligations, start of year: Obligated balance, start of year	11	9	8
73.10 Total new obligations	6	10	10
73.20 Total outlays (gross)	−8	−11	−13
74.40 Unpaid obligations, end of year: Obligated balance, end of year	9	8	6
Outlays (gross), detail:			
86.90 Outlays from new discretionary authority	3	5	5
86.93 Outlays from discretionary balances	5	6	8
87.00 Total outlays (gross)	8	11	13
Net budget authority and outlays:			
89.00 Budget authority	10	10	10
90.00 Outlays	8	11	13

The Central Hazardous Materials Fund is used to fund remedial investigations/feasibility studies and cleanups of hazardous waste sites for which the Department of the Interior is liable. Authority is provided for amounts recovered from responsible parties to be credited to this account. Thus, the account may be composed of both annual appropriations of no-year funds and of offsetting collections. The Comprehensive Environmental Response, Compensation and Liability Act, as amended (42 U.S.C. Section 9601 *et seq.*) requires responsible parties, including Federal landowners, to investigate and clean up releases of hazardous substances.

Object Classification (in millions of dollars)

Identification code 14–1121–0–1–304	1999 actual	2000 est.	2001 est.
25.2 Direct obligations: Other services	1	1	1
Allocation Account:			
11.1 Personnel compensation: Full-time permanent	1	1	1
25.2 Other services	4	8	8
99.0 Subtotal, allocation account	5	9	9
99.9 Total new obligations	6	10	10

LAND ACQUISITION

For expenses necessary to carry out sections 205, 206, and 318(d) of Public Law 94–579, including administrative expenses and acquisition of lands or waters, or interests therein, [$15,500,000] *$60,900,000 for Lands Legacy*, to be derived from the Land and Water Conservation Fund, to remain available until expended. *(Department of the Interior and Related Agencies Appropriations Act, 2000, as enacted by section 1000(a)(3) of the Consolidated Appropriations Act, 2000 (P.L. 106–113).)*

Program and Financing (in millions of dollars)

Identification code 14–5033–0–2–302	1999 actual	2000 est.	2001 est.
Obligations by program activity:			
00.01 Land acquisition	11	16	56
00.02 Acquisition management	3	4	3
09.01 Reimbursable program	276	48	
10.00 Total new obligations	290	68	59
Budgetary resources available for obligation:			
21.40 Unobligated balance available, start of year	15	40	12
22.00 New budget authority (gross)	315	40	61
23.90 Total budgetary resources available for obligation	330	80	73
23.95 Total new obligations	−290	−68	−59
24.40 Unobligated balance available, end of year	40	12	12
New budget authority (gross), detail:			
Discretionary:			
40.20 Appropriation (special fund, definite)	15	16	61
Spending authority from offsetting collections:			
Offsetting collections (cash):			
68.00 Offsetting collections (cash)	300		
68.00 Offsetting collections (cash)		24	
68.90 Spending authority from offsetting collections (total discretionary)	300	24	
70.00 Total new budget authority (gross)	315	40	61
Change in unpaid obligations:			
72.40 Unpaid obligations, start of year: Obligated balance, start of year	1	2	14
73.10 Total new obligations	290	68	59
73.20 Total outlays (gross)	−289	−56	−28
74.40 Unpaid obligations, end of year: Obligated balance, end of year	2	14	45
Outlays (gross), detail:			
86.90 Outlays from new discretionary authority	288	29	18
86.93 Outlays from discretionary balances	1	27	10
87.00 Total outlays (gross)	289	56	28
Offsets:			
Against gross budget authority and outlays:			
Offsetting collections (cash) from:			
Federal sources:			
88.00 Federal sources	−300		
88.00 Federal sources		−24	

88.90	Total, offsetting collections (cash)	−300	−24	
	Net budget authority and outlays:			
89.00	Budget authority	15	16	61
90.00	Outlays	−11	32	28

This appropriation provides for the acquisition of lands or interests in lands, by exchange or purchase, when necessary for public recreation use, resource protection and other purposes related to the management of public lands.

Funding for this account is proposed as part of a new Lands Legacy discretionary spending category to provide dedicated and protected funding for the President's Lands Legacy Initiative. See the Environment chapter in the Budget for a Summary of the Lands Legacy Initiative.

Object Classification (in millions of dollars)

Identification code 14–5033–0–2–302		1999 actual	2000 est.	2001 est.
	Direct obligations:			
11.1	Personnel compensation: Full-time permanent	2	2	2
25.2	Other services	1	2	2
32.0	Land and structures	11	16	55
99.0	Subtotal, direct obligations	14	20	59
99.0	Reimbursable obligations	276	48	
99.9	Total new obligations	290	68	59

Personnel Summary

Identification code 14–5033–0–2–302		1999 actual	2000 est.	2001 est.
	Direct:			
1001	Total compensable workyears: Full-time equivalent employment	32	35	35
	Reimbursable:			
2001	Total compensable workyears: Full-time equivalent employment	1		

RANGE IMPROVEMENTS

For rehabilitation, protection, and acquisition of lands and interests therein, and improvement of Federal rangelands pursuant to section 401 of the Federal Land Policy and Management Act of 1976 (43 U.S.C. 1701), notwithstanding any other Act, sums equal to 50 percent of all moneys received during the prior fiscal year under sections 3 and 15 of the Taylor Grazing Act (43 U.S.C. 315 et seq.) and the amount designated for range improvements from grazing fees and mineral leasing receipts from Bankhead-Jones lands transferred to the Department of the Interior pursuant to law, but not less than $10,000,000, to remain available until expended: *Provided,* That not to exceed $600,000 shall be available for administrative expenses. *(Department of the Interior and Related Agencies Appropriations Act, 2000, as enacted by section 1000(a)(3) of the Consolidated Appropriations Act, 2000 (P.L. 106–113).)*

Unavailable Collections (in millions of dollars)

Identification code 14–5132–0–2–302		1999 actual	2000 est.	2001 est.
	Balance, start of year:			
01.99	Balance, start of year			
	Receipts:			
02.01	Grazing fees for range improvements, Taylor Grazing Act	8	8	8
	Appropriation:			
05.01	Range improvements	−8	−8	−8
07.99	Total balance, end of year			

Program and Financing (in millions of dollars)

Identification code 14–5132–0–2–302		1999 actual	2000 est.	2001 est.
	Obligations by program activity:			
00.01	Improvements to Public Lands	9	10	8
00.02	Farm Tenant Act Lands	1	1	1
00.03	Administrative Expenses	1	1	1
10.00	Total new obligations	11	12	10
	Budgetary resources available for obligation:			
21.40	Unobligated balance available, start of year	3	2	
22.00	New budget authority (gross)	10	10	10
23.90	Total budgetary resources available for obligation	13	12	10
23.95	Total new obligations	−11	−12	−10
24.40	Unobligated balance available, end of year	2		
	New budget authority (gross), detail:			
	Mandatory:			
60.05	Appropriation (indefinite)	2	2	2
60.25	Appropriation (special fund, indefinite)	8	8	8
62.50	Appropriation (total mandatory)	10	10	10
	Change in unpaid obligations:			
72.40	Unpaid obligations, start of year: Obligated balance, start of year	3	4	4
73.10	Total new obligations	11	12	10
73.20	Total outlays (gross)	−10	−12	−11
74.40	Unpaid obligations, end of year: Obligated balance, end of year	4	4	3
	Outlays (gross), detail:			
86.97	Outlays from new mandatory authority	7	7	7
86.98	Outlays from mandatory balances	3	5	3
87.00	Total outlays (gross)	10	12	11
	Net budget authority and outlays:			
89.00	Budget authority	10	10	10
90.00	Outlays	10	12	11

Note.—Payments to States and to the Range Improvements Fund are derived from statutory percentages of collections in the prior fiscal year.

This appropriation is derived from a percentage of receipts from grazing of livestock on the public lands, and from grazing and mineral leasing receipts on Bankhead-Jones Farm Tenant Act lands transferred from the Department of Agriculture by various Executive Orders. These funds are used for the planning, construction, development, and monitoring of range improvements when appropriated.

Object Classification (in millions of dollars)

Identification code 14–5132–0–2–302		1999 actual	2000 est.	2001 est.
11.1	Personnel compensation: Full-time permanent	3	3	3
12.1	Civilian personnel benefits	1	1	1
22.0	Transportation of things	1	1	1
25.2	Other services	2	3	2
26.0	Supplies and materials	2	2	2
32.0	Land and structures	2	2	1
99.9	Total new obligations	11	12	10

Personnel Summary

Identification code 14–5132–0–2–302		1999 actual	2000 est.	2001 est.
1001	Total compensable workyears: Full-time equivalent employment	72	72	72

SERVICE CHARGES, DEPOSITS, AND FORFEITURES

For administrative expenses and other costs related to processing application documents and other authorizations for use and disposal of public lands and resources, for costs of providing copies of official public land documents, for monitoring construction, operation, and termination of facilities in conjunction with use authorizations, and for rehabilitation of damaged property, such amounts as may be collected under Public Law 94–579, as amended, and Public Law 93–153, to remain available until expended: *Provided,* That notwithstanding any provision to the contrary of section 305(a) of Public Law 94–579 (43 U.S.C. 1735(a)), any moneys that have been or will be received pursuant to that section, whether as a result of forfeiture, compromise, or settlement, if not appropriate for refund pursuant to section 305(c) of that Act (43 U.S.C. 1735(c)), shall be available

186-484 00 - 18

General and special funds—Continued

SERVICE CHARGES, DEPOSITS, AND FORFEITURES—Continued

and may be expended under the authority of this Act by the Secretary to improve, protect, or rehabilitate any public lands administered through the Bureau of Land Management which have been damaged by the action of a resource developer, purchaser, permittee, or any unauthorized person, without regard to whether all moneys collected from each such action are used on the exact lands damaged which led to the action: *Provided further,* That any such moneys that are in excess of amounts needed to repair damage to the exact land for which funds were collected may be used to repair other damaged public lands. *(Department of the Interior and Related Agencies Appropriations Act, 2000, as enacted by section 1000(a)(3) of the Consolidated Appropriations Act, 2000 (P.L. 106–113).)*

Unavailable Collections (in millions of dollars)

Identification code 14–5017–0–2–302	1999 actual	2000 est.	2001 est.
Balance, start of year:			
01.99 Balance, start of year			
Receipts:			
02.01 Service charges, deposits, and forfeitures, BLM	12	9	8
Appropriation:			
05.01 Service charges, deposits, and forfeitures	−12	−9	−8
07.99 Total balance, end of year			

Program and Financing (in millions of dollars)

Identification code 14–5017–0–2–302	1999 actual	2000 est.	2001 est.
Obligations by program activity:			
00.01 Right-of-way processing	6	5	4
00.02 Adopt-a-horse program	1	1	2
00.03 Repair of lands and facilities	2	2	3
00.04 Cost recoverable realty cases		1	1
00.05 Copy fees	2	2	2
10.00 Total new obligations	11	11	12
Budgetary resources available for obligation:			
21.40 Unobligated balance available, start of year	8	9	7
22.00 New budget authority (gross)	12	9	8
23.90 Total budgetary resources available for obligation	20	18	15
23.95 Total new obligations	−11	−11	−12
24.40 Unobligated balance available, end of year	9	7	3
New budget authority (gross), detail:			
Discretionary:			
40.25 Appropriation (special fund, indefinite)	12	9	8
Change in unpaid obligations:			
72.40 Unpaid obligations, start of year: Obligated balance, start of year	2	2	5
73.10 Total new obligations	11	11	12
73.20 Total outlays (gross)	−11	−8	−11
74.40 Unpaid obligations, end of year: Obligated balance, end of year	2	5	6
Outlays (gross), detail:			
86.90 Outlays from new discretionary authority	9	5	4
86.93 Outlays from discretionary balances	2	3	6
87.00 Total outlays (gross)	11	8	11
Net budget authority and outlays:			
89.00 Budget authority	12	9	8
90.00 Outlays	11	8	11

This appropriation is derived from: (1) revenues received to offset administrative and other costs incurred to process applications for rights-of-way, and the monitoring of construction, operation, and termination of rights-of-ways; (2) recovery of costs associated with the adopt-a-horse program; (3) revenues received for rehabilitation of damages to lands, resources, and facilities; (4) fees for processing specified categories of realty actions under FLPMA; (5) deposits received from contractors in lieu of completing contract requirements such as slash burning and timber extension expenses; and (6) fees for costs of reproduction and administrative services involved in providing requested copies of materials.

Object Classification (in millions of dollars)

Identification code 14–5017–0–2–302	1999 actual	2000 est.	2001 est.
11.1 Personnel compensation: Full-time permanent	4	4	4
12.1 Civilian personnel benefits	1	1	2
22.0 Transportation of things	1	1	1
25.2 Other services	4	3	3
26.0 Supplies and materials	1	2	2
99.9 Total new obligations	11	11	12

Personnel Summary

Identification code 14–5017–0–2–302	1999 actual	2000 est.	2001 est.
1001 Total compensable workyears: Full-time equivalent employment	84	84	84

PERMANENT OPERATING FUNDS

FOREST ECOSYSTEMS HEALTH AND RECOVERY FUND

(REVOLVING FUND, SPECIAL ACCOUNT)

In addition to the purposes authorized in Public Law 102–381, funds made available in the Forest Ecosystem Health and Recovery Fund can be used for the purpose of planning, preparing, and monitoring salvage timber sales and forest ecosystem health and recovery activities such as release from competing vegetation and density control treatments. The Federal share of receipts (defined as the portion of salvage timber receipts not paid to the counties under 43 U.S.C. 1181f and 43 U.S.C. 1181–1 et seq., and Public Law 103–66) derived from treatments funded by this account shall be deposited into the Forest Ecosystem Health and Recovery Fund. *(Department of the Interior and Related Agencies Appropriations Act, 2000, as enacted by section 1000(a)(3) of the Consolidated Appropriations Act, 2000 (P.L. 106–113).)*

Unavailable Collections (in millions of dollars)

Identification code 14–9926–0–2–302	1999 actual	2000 est.	2001 est.
Balance, start of year:			
01.99 Balance, start of year			
Receipts:			
02.01 Deposits for road maintenance and reconstruction	2	2	2
02.03 Forest ecosystem health and recovery, disposal of salvage timber	5	6	9
02.05 Timber sale pipeline restoration fund	3	3	2
02.06 Recreational fee demonstration program	5	6	7
02.07 Southern Nevada public land management	2	13	22
02.08 Earnings on investments, Southern Nevada public land management			1
02.09 Surplus land sales			2
02.10 Land sale, Deschutes County, Oregon		1	
02.99 Total receipts	17	31	45
Appropriation:			
05.01 Permanent operating funds	−17	−31	−43
05.02 Permanent operating funds, legislative proposal			−2
05.99 Subtotal appropriation	−17	−31	−45
07.99 Total balance, end of year			

Program and Financing (in millions of dollars)

Identification code 14–9926–0–2–302	1999 actual	2000 est.	2001 est.
Obligations by program activity:			
00.01 Forest ecosystems health and recovery	10	10	9
00.02 Recreation fee demonstration	4	6	7
00.03 Expenses, road maintenance deposits	2	2	2
00.04 Timber sale pipeline restoration fund	10	2	2
00.05 Southern Nevada public land sales (85%)		9	22
00.06 Land sales, Deschutes County, Oregon		1	
10.00 Total new obligations	26	30	42

	Budgetary resources available for obligation:			
21.40	Unobligated balance available, start of year	43	39	41
22.00	New budget authority (gross)	21	31	43
22.10	Resources available from recoveries of prior year obligations	1		
23.90	Total budgetary resources available for obligation	65	70	84
23.95	Total new obligations	−26	−30	−42
24.40	Unobligated balance available, end of year	39	41	42
	New budget authority (gross), detail:			
	Mandatory:			
60.25	Appropriation (special fund, indefinite)	17	31	43
62.00	Transferred from other accounts	4		
62.50	Appropriation (total mandatory)	21	31	43
	Change in unpaid obligations:			
72.40	Unpaid obligations, start of year: Obligated balance, start of year	6	8	2
73.10	Total new obligations	26	30	42
73.20	Total outlays (gross)	−24	−35	−44
73.45	Adjustments in unexpired accounts	−1		
74.40	Unpaid obligations, end of year: Obligated balance, end of year	8	2	
	Outlays (gross), detail:			
86.97	Outlays from new mandatory authority	14	31	43
86.98	Outlays from mandatory balances	10	4	1
87.00	Total outlays (gross)	24	35	44
	Net budget authority and outlays:			
89.00	Budget authority	21	31	43
90.00	Outlays	24	35	44
	Memorandum (non-add) entries:			
92.01	Total investments, start of year: U.S. securities: Par value	1	1	1
92.02	Total investments, end of year: U.S. securities: Par value	1	1	1

Summary of Budget Authority and Outlays

(in millions of dollars)

	1999 actual	2000 est.	2001 est.
Enacted/requested:			
Budget Authority	21	31	43
Outlays	24	35	44
Legislative proposal, subject to PAYGO:			
Budget Authority			2
Outlays			2
Total:			
Budget Authority	21	31	45
Outlays	24	35	46

Permanent operating funds accounts include:

Operations and maintenance of quarters.—Funds in this account are used to maintain and repair BLM employee-occupied quarters from which rental charges are collected. Agencies are required to collect quarter rentals from employees who occupy Government-owned housing and quarters. This housing is provided only in isolated areas or where an employee is required to live on-site at a Federally owned facility or reservation.

Forest ecosystems health and recovery.—Funds in this account are derived from revenue generated from the Federal share of receipts from the sale of salvage timber from the Oregon and California grant lands, public domain lands, and Coos Bay Wagon Road lands. This account was established to allow the Bureau of Land Management to more efficiently and effectively address forest health. Funds can be used for other forest health purposes, including release from competing vegetation and density control treatments.

Timber sale pipeline restoration fund.—This fund provides for the deposit and use of fees collected by the BLM for sales of non-salvage timber pursuant to the timber salvage provisions of Public Law 104–19 and Public Law 105–83. Of the total deposited into this account, 75 percent is to be used for preparation of timber sales to fill the timber pipeline on lands administered by the BLM, and 25 percent is to be expended on the backlog of recreation projects on BLM lands.

Recreation fees.—This account holds funds that enable the BLM to retain and spend up to 15 percent of recreation receipts collected during the current year to offset fee collection costs.

Expenses, road maintenance deposits.—Users of certain roads under jurisdiction of the Bureau of Land Management (BLM) make deposits for maintenance purposes. Moneys collected are appropriated for necessary road maintenance. Moneys collected on Oregon and California grant lands are available only for those lands (43 U.S.C. 1762(c), 43 U.S.C. 1735(b)).

Recreational fee demonstration program.—Fees collected by the BLM at recreation sites identified pursuant to provisions of the 1996 Interior and Related Agencies Appropriations Act are deposited to this account. BLM returns 100 percent of these receipts back to the site where the fees were generated.

Acquisitions in Deschutes, OR from land sale receipts.—Pursuant to Public Law 105–221, the Oregon Public Lands Transfer Act, the Secretary of the Interior is authorized to use the proceeds from sales in Deschutes County to purchase envrironmentally sensitive lands.

Operations and Acquisitions in Nevada from land sale receipts.—Pursuant to Public Law 105–263, 85% of receipts from sales of public domain lands in southern Nevada are used to acquire envrionmentally sensitive land in the state, and to make capital improvements to areas administered by the NPS, FWS, and BLM in Clark County, NV. Included in this account is earnings on investments.

Object Classification (in millions of dollars)

Identification code 14–9926–0–2–302		1999 actual	2000 est.	2001 est.
	Personnel compensation:			
11.1	Full-time permanent	7	7	7
11.3	Other than full-time permanent	4	4	4
11.9	Total personnel compensation	11	11	11
12.1	Civilian personnel benefits	2	2	2
22.0	Transportation of things	1	1	1
25.2	Other services	9	9	13
26.0	Supplies and materials	2	2	2
31.0	Equipment	1	1	1
32.0	Land and structures		3	10
41.0	Grants, subsidies, and contributions		1	2
99.9	Total new obligations	26	30	42

Personnel Summary

Identification code 14–9926–0–2–302		1999 actual	2000 est.	2001 est.
1001	Total compensable workyears: Full-time equivalent employment	288	270	270

Permanent Operating Funds

(Legislative proposal, subject to PAYGO)

Program and Financing (in millions of dollars)

Identification code 14–9926–4–2–302		1999 actual	2000 est.	2001 est.
	Obligations by program activity:			
00.01	Lands acquired from disposal of public domain lands			2
10.00	Total new obligations (object class 32.0)			2
	Budgetary resources available for obligation:			
22.00	New budget authority (gross)			2
23.95	Total new obligations			−2

General and special funds—Continued

PERMANENT OPERATING FUNDS—Continued

Program and Financing (in millions of dollars)—Continued

Identification code 14–9926–4–2–302	1999 actual	2000 est.	2001 est.
New budget authority (gross), detail:			
Mandatory:			
60.25 Appropriation (special fund, indefinite)			2
Change in unpaid obligations:			
73.10 Total new obligations			2
Outlays (gross), detail:			
86.97 Outlays from new mandatory authority			2
Net budget authority and outlays:			
89.00 Budget authority			2
90.00 Outlays			2

Land acquisition from certain land sales.—The Administration will propose new authority to conduct sales of lands that have been classified as suitable for disposal under current resource management plans. This proposal will provide that receipts from such sales may be used to acquire non-Federal lands with significant resource values that fall within the boundaries of areas now managed by the Department of the Interior.

MISCELLANEOUS PERMANENT PAYMENT ACCOUNTS

Unavailable Collections (in millions of dollars)

Identification code 14–9921–0–2–999	1999 actual	2000 est.	2001 est.
Balance, start of year:			
01.99 Balance, start of year	103	87	89
Receipts:			
02.01 Receipts from grazing, etc., public lands outside grazing districts	2	1	1
02.02 Receipts from grazing, etc., public lands within grazing districts	1	1	1
02.06 Sale of public land and materials, 5% fund to States	1	3	6
02.10 Sale of public lands and materials	11		
02.11 Oregon and California land-grant fund	10		
02.13 Coos Bay wagon road grant fund	2		
02.15 Sale of natural gas and oil shale, Naval Oil Shale Reserves 1 and 3	7	1	1
02.99 Total receipts	34	6	9
04.00 Total: Balances and collections	137	93	98
Appropriation:			
05.01 Miscellaneous permanent payment accounts	–50	–4	–5
07.99 Total balance, end of year	87	89	93

Program and Financing (in millions of dollars)

Identification code 14–9921–0–2–999	1999 actual	2000 est.	2001 est.
Obligations by program activity:			
00.01 Payments to Coos and Douglas Counties, Oregon, from Coos Bay Wagon Road Receipts	1	1	
00.02 Payments to counties, Oregon and California grant lands	64	62	59
Payments to States, Proceeds from sales:			
00.03 Proceeds of sales	1	1	1
00.04 From grazing fees, etc., public lands outside grazing districts	1	1	1
00.05 From grazing fees, etc., public lands within grazing districts	1	2	2
00.06 Payments to counties, national grasslands (Farm Tenant Act lands)	1		
00.07 Payments to Nevada from receipts on land sales (15%)		2	5
00.08 Native Alaskan groups' property		5	5
00.09 Utah School land exchange	50		
10.00 Total new obligations (object class 41.0)	119	74	73
Budgetary resources available for obligation:			
21.40 Unobligated balance available, start of year	2	2	2
22.00 New budget authority (gross)	119	73	73
23.90 Total budgetary resources available for obligation	121	75	75
23.95 Total new obligations	–119	–74	–73
24.40 Unobligated balance available, end of year	2	2	2
New budget authority (gross), detail:			
Mandatory:			
60.05 Appropriation (indefinite)	69	69	68
60.25 Appropriation (special fund, indefinite)	50	4	5
62.50 Appropriation (total mandatory)	119	73	73
Change in unpaid obligations:			
72.40 Unpaid obligations, start of year: Obligated balance, start of year		1	
73.10 Total new obligations	119	74	73
73.20 Total outlays (gross)	–118	–75	–73
74.40 Unpaid obligations, end of year: Obligated balance, end of year	1		
Outlays (gross), detail:			
86.97 Outlays from new mandatory authority	117	73	73
86.98 Outlays from mandatory balances	1		
87.00 Total outlays (gross)	118	75	73
Net budget authority and outlays:			
89.00 Budget authority	119	73	73
90.00 Outlays	118	75	73

Summary of Budget Authority and Outlays

(in millions of dollars)

Enacted/requested:	*1999 actual*	*2000 est.*	*2001 est.*
Budget Authority	119	73	73
Outlays	118	73	73
Legislative proposal, subject to PAYGO:			
Budget Authority			11
Outlays			11
Total:			
Budget Authority	119	73	84
Outlays	118	73	84

Miscellaneous permanent payments include:

Payments to Oklahoma (royalties).—The State of Oklahoma is paid 37½ percent of the Red River oil and gas royalties in lieu of State and local taxes on Kiowa, Comanche, and Apache Tribal lands, to be used for construction and maintenance of public roads and support of public schools (65 Stat. 252).

Payments to Coos and Douglas Counties, Oreg., from receipts, Coos Bay Wagon Road grant lands.—Under provisions of the Omnibus Budget Reconciliation Act of 1993, Coos and Douglas Counties receive payments under established formulas related to values of past timber sales for schools, roads, highways, bridges, and port districts.

Payments to counties, Oregon and California grant lands.—Under provisions of the Omnibus Budget Reconciliation Act of 1993, counties in Western Oregon receive payments under established formulas related to values of past timber sales.

Payments to States (proceeds of sales).—The States are paid 5 percent of the net proceeds from sale of public land and public land products (31 U.S.C. 1305).

Payments to States from grazing receipts, etc., public lands outside grazing districts.—The States are paid 50 percent of the grazing receipts from public lands outside of grazing districts (43 U.S.C. 315i, 315m).

Payments to States from grazing receipts, etc., public lands within districts.—The States are paid 12½ percent of grazing receipts from public lands inside grazing districts (43 U.S.C. 315b, 315i).

Payments to States from grazing receipts, etc., public lands within grazing districts, miscellaneous.—The States are paid specifically determined amounts from grazing receipts derived from miscellaneous lands within grazing districts when payment is not feasible on a percentage basis (43 U.S.C. 315).

Payments to counties, National Grasslands.—Of the revenues received from the use of Bankhead-Jones Act lands administered by the Bureau of Land Management, 25 percent is paid to the counties in which such lands are situated, for school and road purposes (7 U.S.C. 1012).

Payments to Nevada from receipts on land sales.—(A) Public Law 96–586 authorizes and directs the Secretary to sell not more than 700 acres of public lands per calendar year in and around Las Vegas, Nevada, the proceeds of which are to be used to acquire environmentally sensitive lands in the Lake Tahoe Basin of California and Nevada. Annual revenues are distributed to the State of Nevada (5 percent) and the county in which the land is located (10 percent). (B) Public Law 105–263 authorizes the disposal through sale of approximately 27,000 acres in Clark City Nevada, the proceeds of which are to be distributed as follows: (a) 5% for use in the general education program of the State of Nevada (b) 10% for use by Southern Nevada Water Authority for water treatment and transmission facility infrastructure in Clark County, Nevada and (c) The remaining 85% to be used to acquire environmentally sensitive lands in Nevada, capital improvements to areas administered by NPS, FWS and BLM in Clark County, Nevada, development of multispecies habitat plan in Clark County, Nevada; development of parks, trails and natural areas in Clark County, Nevada; and reimbursements of BLM costs incurred arranging sales and exchanges under the Act.

Cook Inlet Region Inc. property.—This account received funding appropriated by section 9102 of the fiscal year 1990 Department of Defense Appropriations Act for the acquisition of Federal real properties, improvements on such lands or rights to their use or exploitation, and any personal property related to the land purchased by the Cook Inlet Region, Incorporated as authorized by the provisions of section 12(b) of Public Law 94–204 (43 U.S.C. 1611). Funds are made available to the Bureau of Land Management for administration and subsequent payment to accounts accepting Cook Inlet Region, Incorporated offers for Federal properties.

Native Alaskan groups' properties.—Funds were appropriated by Public Law 102–172 for the Calista Corporation, and by Public Law 102–415 for the Haida Corporation and the Gold Creek Susitna Association, Incorporated, for the acquisition by those groups of Federal real properties in fulfillment of claims originally settled in 43 U.S.C. 1617, the Alaska Native Claims Settlement Act.

Miscellaneous Permanent Payment Accounts

(Legislative proposal, subject to PAYGO)

Program and Financing (in millions of dollars)

Identification code 14–9921–4–2–999	1999 actual	2000 est.	2001 est.
Obligations by program activity:			
00.01 Payments to counties and States, Federal timber programs			11
10.00 Total new obligations (object class 41.0)			11
Budgetary resources available for obligation:			
22.00 New budget authority (gross)			11
23.95 Total new obligations			−11
New budget authority (gross), detail:			
Mandatory:			
60.05 Appropriation (indefinite)			11
Change in unpaid obligations:			
73.10 Total new obligations			11
73.20 Total outlays (gross)			−11
Outlays (gross), detail:			
86.97 Outlays from new mandatory authority			11
Net budget authority and outlays:			
89.00 Budget authority			11
90.00 Outlays			11

Payments to States and Western Oregon Counties for Harvested Timber.—The Administration proposes to permanently stabilize payments to states, to Coos and Douglas Counties, and to the Oregon and California grant land counties for timber harvested on those lands, rather than permit such payments to fluctuate based on unpredictable harvest levels.

HELIUM FUND

Program and Financing (in millions of dollars)

Identification code 14–4053–0–3–306	1999 actual	2000 est.	2001 est.
Obligations by program activity:			
09.01 Production and sales	3	3	3
09.02 Transmission and storage operations	2	2	2
09.03 Administrative and other expenses	1	1	1
09.11 Capital Investment: land, structures, and equipment	1	1	1
10.00 Total new obligations	7	7	7
Budgetary resources available for obligation:			
21.40 Unobligated balance available, start of year	35	36	36
22.00 New budget authority (gross)	18	15	15
22.40 Capital transfer to general fund	−10	−8	−8
23.90 Total budgetary resources available for obligation	43	43	43
23.95 Total new obligations	−7	−7	−7
24.40 Unobligated balance available, end of year	36	36	36
New budget authority (gross), detail:			
Mandatory:			
69.00 Offsetting collections (cash)	16	15	15
69.10 From Federal sources: Change in receivables and unpaid, unfilled orders	2		
69.90 Spending authority from offsetting collections (total mandatory)	18	15	15
Change in unpaid obligations:			
Unpaid obligations, start of year:			
72.40 Obligated balance, start of year	−4	−5	−2
72.95 From Federal sources: Receivables and unpaid, unfilled orders	1	3	3
72.99 Total unpaid obligations, start of year	−3	−2	1
73.10 Total new obligations	7	7	7
73.20 Total outlays (gross)	−6	−4	−7
Unpaid obligations, end of year:			
74.40 Obligated balance, end of year	−5	−2	−2
74.95 From Federal sources: Receivables and unpaid, unfilled orders	3	3	3
74.99 Total unpaid obligations, end of year	−2	1	1
Outlays (gross), detail:			
86.97 Outlays from new mandatory authority	6		
86.98 Outlays from mandatory balances		4	7
87.00 Total outlays (gross)	6	4	7
Offsets:			
Against gross budget authority and outlays:			
Offsetting collections (cash) from:			
88.40 Non-Federal sources	−10	−10	−10
88.45 Offsetting governmental collections from the public	−6	−5	−5
88.90 Total, offsetting collections (cash)	−16	−15	−15
Against gross budget authority only:			
88.95 From Federal sources: Change in receivables and unpaid, unfilled orders	−2		
Net budget authority and outlays:			
89.00 Budget authority			

General and special funds—Continued

MISCELLANEOUS PERMANENT PAYMENT ACCOUNTS—Continued

HELIUM FUND—Continued

Program and Financing (in millions of dollars)—Continued

Identification code 14–4053–0–3–306	1999 actual	2000 est.	2001 est.
90.00 Outlays	–10	–11	–8

The Helium Act Amendments of 1960, Public Law 86–777 (50 U.S.C. 167), authorized activities necessary to provide sufficient helium to meet the current and foreseeable future needs of essential government activities.

The Helium Privatization Act of 1996, Public Law 104–273, provides for the eventual privatization of the program and its functions. In FY 2000, the Helium program will consist of:

(a) continued storage and transmission of crude helium;

(b) complete disposal of helium refining facilities and other excess property not needed for storage and transmission of crude helium;

(c) oversight of the production of helium on Federal lands;

(d) administration of in kind crude helium gas sale program.

The estimates assume that the helium program will continue to fund full implementation of the Helium Privatization Act.

Statement of Operations (in millions of dollars)

Identification code 14–4053–0–3–306	1998 actual	1999 actual	2000 est.	2001 est.
0101 Revenue	20	18	15	15
0102 Expense	–18	–10	–10	–8
0105 Net income or loss (–)	2	8	5	7

Balance Sheet (in millions of dollars)

Identification code 14–4053–0–3–306	1998 actual	1999 actual	2000 est.	2001 est.
ASSETS:				
1101 Federal assets: Fund balances with Treasury	36	41	31	23
Other Federal assets:				
1802 Inventories and related properties	367	364	340	336
1803 Property, plant and equipment, net	8	10	10	10
1999 Total assets	411	415	381	369
LIABILITIES:				
Federal liabilities:				
2102 Interest payable	1,060	1,060	1,052	1,042
2103 Debt	289	289	289	289
2999 Total liabilities	1,349	1,349	1,341	1,331
NET POSITION:				
3300 Cumulative results of operations	–936	–934	–960	–962
3999 Total net position	–936	–934	–960	–962
4999 Total liabilities and net position	413	415	381	369

Object Classification (in millions of dollars)

Identification code 14–4053–0–3–306	1999 actual	2000 est.	2001 est.
Personnel compensation:			
11.1 Full-time permanent	3	3	3
11.5 Other personnel compensation	1	1	1
11.9 Total personnel compensation	4	4	4
12.1 Civilian personnel benefits	1	1	1
25.2 Other services	1	1	1
99.0 Subtotal, reimbursable obligations	6	6	6
99.5 Below reporting threshold	1	1	1
99.9 Total new obligations	7	7	7

Personnel Summary

Identification code 14–4053–0–3–306	1999 actual	2000 est.	2001 est.
2001 Total compensable workyears: Full-time equivalent employment	67	65	65

Intragovernmental funds:

WORKING CAPITAL FUND

Program and Financing (in millions of dollars)

Identification code 14–4525–0–4–302	1999 actual	2000 est.	2001 est.
Obligations by program activity:			
Land management related supplies and support:			
09.01 Operating expenses	7	8	8
09.02 Capital investment	11	12	20
10.00 Total new obligations	18	20	28
Budgetary resources available for obligation:			
21.40 Unobligated balance available, start of year	13	19	23
22.00 New budget authority (gross)	23	24	24
23.90 Total budgetary resources available for obligation	36	43	47
23.95 Total new obligations	–18	–20	–28
24.40 Unobligated balance available, end of year	19	23	19
New budget authority (gross), detail:			
Discretionary:			
68.00 Spending authority from offsetting collections (gross): Offsetting collections (cash)	23	24	24
Change in unpaid obligations:			
72.40 Unpaid obligations, start of year: Obligated balance, start of year	10	8	4
73.10 Total new obligations	18	20	28
73.20 Total outlays (gross)	–20	–23	–27
74.40 Unpaid obligations, end of year: Obligated balance, end of year	8	4	4
Outlays (gross), detail:			
86.90 Outlays from new discretionary authority	18	24	24
86.93 Outlays from discretionary balances	2		3
87.00 Total outlays (gross)	20	23	27
Offsets:			
Against gross budget authority and outlays:			
88.00 Offsetting collections (cash) from: Federal sources	–23	–24	–24
Net budget authority and outlays:			
89.00 Budget authority			
90.00 Outlays	–3	–1	3

Section 306 of the Federal Land Policy and Management Act of 1976 authorizes a BLM working capital fund. The fund is managed as a self-sustaining revolving fund for purchase and maintenance of vehicles and equipment, purchase of materials for resource conservation projects, purchase of uniforms, and other business-type functions.

Balance Sheet (in millions of dollars)

Identification code 14–4525–0–4–302	1998 actual	1999 actual	2000 est.	2001 est.
ASSETS:				
1101 Federal assets: Fund balances with Treasury	23	26	30	31
1803 Other Federal assets: Property, plant and equipment, net	55	57	59	62
1999 Total assets	78	83	89	93
NET POSITION:				
3100 Appropriated capital	55	57	59	62
3300 Cumulative results of operations	23	26	30	31
3999 Total net position	78	83	89	93
4999 Total liabilities and net position	78	83	89	93

Object Classification (in millions of dollars)

Identification code 14–4525–0–4–302	1999 actual	2000 est.	2001 est.
11.1 Personnel compensation: Full-time permanent	1	1	1
25.2 Other services	3	3	3
26.0 Supplies and materials	4	4	4
31.0 Equipment	10	12	20
99.9 Total new obligations	18	20	28

Personnel Summary

Identification code 14–4525–0–4–302	1999 actual	2000 est.	2001 est.
2001 Total compensable workyears: Full-time equivalent employment	18	18	18

Trust Funds

MISCELLANEOUS TRUST FUNDS

In addition to amounts authorized to be expended under existing laws, there is hereby appropriated such amounts as may be contributed under section 307 of the Act of October 21, 1976 (43 U.S.C. 1701), and such amounts as may be advanced for administrative costs, surveys, appraisals, and costs of making conveyances of omitted lands under section 211(b) of that Act, to remain available until expended. *(Department of the Interior and Related Agencies Appropriations Act, 2000, as enacted by section 1000(a)(3) of the Consolidated Appropriations Act, 2000 (P.L. 106–113).)*

Unavailable Collections (in millions of dollars)

Identification code 14–9971–0–7–302	1999 actual	2000 est.	2001 est.
Balance, start of year:			
01.99 Balance, start of year	....	....	....
Receipts:			
02.01 Contributions and deposits, BLM	13	9	9
Appropriation:			
05.01 Miscellaneous trust funds	–13	–9	–9
07.99 Total balance, end of year	....	....	....

Program and Financing (in millions of dollars)

Identification code 14–9971–0–7–302	1999 actual	2000 est.	2001 est.
Obligations by program activity:			
00.01 Land and resource management trust fund	12	13	12
10.00 Total new obligations	12	13	12
Budgetary resources available for obligation:			
21.40 Unobligated balance available, start of year	11	12	8
22.00 New budget authority (gross)	13	9	9
23.90 Total budgetary resources available for obligation	24	21	17
23.95 Total new obligations	–12	–13	–12
24.40 Unobligated balance available, end of year	12	8	5
New budget authority (gross), detail:			
Mandatory:			
60.27 Appropriation (trust fund, indefinite)	13	9	9
Change in unpaid obligations:			
72.40 Unpaid obligations, start of year: Obligated balance, start of year	3	3	3
73.10 Total new obligations	12	13	12
73.20 Total outlays (gross)	–12	–13	–12
74.40 Unpaid obligations, end of year: Obligated balance, end of year	3	3	3
Outlays (gross), detail:			
86.97 Outlays from new mandatory authority	9	7	7
86.98 Outlays from mandatory balances	3	6	3
87.00 Total outlays (gross)	12	13	12
Net budget authority and outlays:			
89.00 Budget authority	13	9	9
90.00 Outlays	12	13	12

Current Trust Fund includes:

Land and Resource Management Trust Fund.—Provides for the acceptance of contributed money or services for: (1) resource development, protection and management; (2) conveyance or acquisition of public lands (including omitted lands or islands) to States, their political subdivisions or individuals; and (3) conducting cadastral surveys; provided that estimated costs are paid prior to project initiation. (The Federal Land Policy and Management Act of 1976 (43 U.S.C. 1721, 1737).)

Permanent Trust Funds include:

Range improvement.—Acceptance of contributions for rangeland improvements is authorized by the Taylor Grazing Act (43 U.S.C. 315h and 315i). These funds are permanently appropriated as trust funds to the Secretary for such uses as specified by those Acts.

Public surveys.—Acceptance of contributions for public surveys is authorized by 43 U.S.C. 759, 761, and 31 U.S.C. 1321(a). These contributions are permanently appropriated as trust funds to the Secretary for such uses as specified by those Acts.

Trustee funds, Alaska townsites.—Amounts received from sale of Alaska town lots are available for expenses incident to the maintenance and sale of townsites (31 U.S.C. 1321; Comp. Gen. Dec. of Nov. 18, 1935).

Object Classification (in millions of dollars)

Identification code 14–9971–0–7–302	1999 actual	2000 est.	2001 est.
Personnel compensation:			
11.1 Full-time permanent	2	2	2
11.5 Other personnel compensation	1	1	1
11.9 Total personnel compensation	3	3	3
12.1 Civilian personnel benefits	1	1	1
23.3 Communications, utilities, and miscellaneous charges	1	1	1
25.2 Other services	4	4	3
26.0 Supplies and materials	1	2	2
31.0 Equipment	1	1	1
32.0 Land and structures	1	1	1
99.9 Total new obligations	12	13	12

Personnel Summary

Identification code 14–9971–0–7–302	1999 actual	2000 est.	2001 est.
1001 Total compensable workyears: Full-time equivalent employment	75	75	75

ADMINISTRATIVE PROVISIONS

Appropriations for the Bureau of Land Management shall be available for purchase, erection, and dismantlement of temporary structures, and alteration and maintenance of necessary buildings and appurtenant facilities to which the United States has title; up to $100,000 for payments, at the discretion of the Secretary, for information or evidence concerning violations of laws administered by the Bureau; miscellaneous and emergency expenses of enforcement activities authorized or approved by the Secretary and to be accounted for solely on his certificate, not to exceed $10,000: *Provided,* That notwithstanding 44 U.S.C. 501, the Bureau may, under cooperative cost-sharing and partnership arrangements authorized by law, procure printing services from cooperators in connection with jointly produced publications for which the cooperators share the cost of printing either in cash or in services, and the Bureau determines the cooperator is capable of meeting accepted quality standards. *(Department of the Interior and Related Agencies Appropriations Act, 2000, as enacted by section 1000(a)(3) of the Consolidated Appropriations Act, 2000 (P.L. 106–113).)*

MINERALS MANAGEMENT SERVICE

Federal Funds

General and special funds:

ROYALTY AND OFFSHORE MINERALS MANAGEMENT

For expenses necessary for minerals leasing and environmental studies, regulation of industry operations, and collection of royalties, as authorized by law; for enforcing laws and regulations applicable to oil, gas, and other minerals leases, permits, licenses and operating contracts; and for matching grants or cooperative agreements; including the purchase of not to exceed eight passenger motor vehicles for replacement only; **[**$110,682,000**]** *$134,128,000*, of which **[**$84,569,000**]** *$86,257,000*, shall be available for royalty management activities; and an amount not to exceed **[**$124,000,000**]** *$107,410,000*, to be credited to this appropriation and to remain available until expended, from additions to receipts resulting from increases to rates in effect on August 5, 1993, from rate increases to fee collections for Outer Continental Shelf administrative activities performed by the Minerals Management Service over and above the rates in effect on September 30, 1993, and from additional fees for Outer Continental Shelf administrative activities established after September 30, 1993**[**: *Provided*, That to the extent $124,000,000 in additions to receipts are not realized from the sources of receipts stated above, the amount needed to reach $124,000,000 shall be credited to this appropriation from receipts resulting from rental rates for Outer Continental Shelf leases in effect before August 5, 1993**]**: *Provided further*, That $3,000,000 for computer acquisitions shall remain available until September 30, **[**2001**]** *2002*: *Provided further*, That funds appropriated under this Act shall be available for the payment of interest in accordance with 30 U.S.C. 1721(b) and (d): *Provided further*, That not to exceed $3,000 shall be available for reasonable expenses related to promoting volunteer beach and marine cleanup activities: *Provided further*, That notwithstanding any other provision of law, $15,000 under this heading shall be available for refunds of overpayments in connection with certain Indian leases in which the Director of the Minerals Management Service concurred with the claimed refund due, to pay amounts owed to Indian allottees or tribes, or to correct prior unrecoverable erroneous payments**[**: *Provided further*, That not to exceed $198,000 shall be available to carry out the requirements of section 215(b)(2) of the Water Resources Development Act of 1999**]**. *(Department of the Interior and Related Agencies Appropriations Act, 2000, as enacted by section 1000(a)(3) of the Consolidated Appropriations Act, 2000 (P.L. 106–113).)*

Program and Financing (in millions of dollars)

Identification code 14–1917–0–1–302		1999 actual	2000 est.	2001 est.
	Obligations by program activity:			
	Direct program:			
00.01	OCS lands	42	36	44
00.02	Royalty management	54	58	70
00.03	General administration	19	16	20
09.00	Reimbursable program	100	124	107
10.00	Total new obligations	215	234	241
	Budgetary resources available for obligation:			
21.40	Unobligated balance available, start of year	5	3	3
22.00	New budget authority (gross)	218	234	241
22.10	Resources available from recoveries of prior year obligations	–3		
22.22	Unobligated balance transferred from other accounts		1	
23.90	Total budgetary resources available for obligation	220	238	244
23.95	Total new obligations	–215	–234	–241
23.98	Unobligated balance expiring or withdrawn	–1		
24.40	Unobligated balance available, end of year	3	3	3
	New budget authority (gross), detail:			
	Discretionary:			
40.00	Appropriation	118	111	134
40.76	Reduction pursuant to P.L. 106–113		–1	
43.00	Appropriation (total discretionary)	118	110	134
68.00	Spending authority from offsetting collections: Offsetting collections (cash)	100	124	107
70.00	Total new budget authority (gross)	218	234	241
	Change in unpaid obligations:			
72.40	Unpaid obligations, start of year: Obligated balance, start of year	65	70	70
73.10	Total new obligations	215	234	241
73.20	Total outlays (gross)	–214	–233	–238
73.45	Adjustments in unexpired accounts	3		
74.40	Unpaid obligations, end of year: Obligated balance, end of year	70	70	72
	Outlays (gross), detail:			
86.90	Outlays from new discretionary authority	152	160	173
86.93	Outlays from discretionary balances	62	73	65
87.00	Total outlays (gross)	214	233	238
	Offsets:			
	Against gross budget authority and outlays:			
88.40	Offsetting collections (cash) from: Non-Federal sources	–100	–124	–107
	Net budget authority and outlays:			
89.00	Budget authority	118	110	134
90.00	Outlays	114	109	131

Summary of Budget Authority and Outlays

(in millions of dollars)

Enacted/requested:	1999 actual	2000 est.	2001 est.
Budget Authority	118	110	134
Outlays	114	109	131
Legislative proposal, not subject to PAYGO:			
Budget Authority			–10
Outlays			–10
Total:			
Budget Authority	118	110	124
Outlays	114	109	121

The Minerals Management Service supervises exploration for, and the development and production of, gas, oil, and other minerals on the Outer Continental Shelf (OCS) lands; and collects royalties, rentals, and bonuses due the Federal Government and Indian lessors from minerals produced on Federal, Indian, and OCS lands.

Outer Continental Shelf (OCS) lands.—The program provides for: (1) performance of environmental assessments to ensure compliance with the National Environmental Policy Act (NEPA); (2) conduct of lease offerings; (3) selection and evaluation of tracts offered for lease by competitive bidding; (4) assurance that the Federal Government receives fair market value for leased lands; and (5) regulation and supervision of energy and mineral exploration, development, and production operations on the OCS lands.

Royalty management.—The Royalty management program provides accounting, auditing, and compliance activities for royalties, rentals, and bonuses due from minerals produced on Federal, Indian, allotted and OCS lands. The program includes an automated accounting system to ensure that all royalties are properly collected.

General administration.—General administrative expenses provide for management, executive direction and coordination, administrative support, Federal building space and general support services.

The following are key performance measures for the Royalty and offshore minerals management account.

PERFORMANCE MEASURES

	1999 actual	2000 est.	2001 est.
Compliance Index	98.1%	97.7%	98%
Percent of on-time State disbursements	98.2%	98%	98%
Production of OCS oil (millions of barrels)	499	571	586
Production of OCS gas (trillion cubic feet)	5.2	4.9	4.7
Number of leases drilled	240	514	610

Object Classification (in millions of dollars)

Identification code 14–1917–0–1–302		1999 actual	2000 est.	2001 est.
	Direct obligations:			
	Personnel compensation:			
11.1	Full-time permanent	75	72	78
11.5	Other personnel compensation	17	17	18
11.9	Total personnel compensation	92	89	96
21.0	Travel and transportation of persons	2	2	2
23.3	Communications, utilities, and miscellaneous charges	3	3	3
25.2	Other services	15	13	30
26.0	Supplies and materials	1	1	1
31.0	Equipment	2	2	2
99.0	Subtotal, direct obligations	115	110	134
99.0	Reimbursable obligations	100	124	107
99.9	Total new obligations	215	234	241

Personnel Summary

Identification code 14–1917–0–1–302		1999 actual	2000 est.	2001 est.
	Direct:			
1001	Total compensable workyears: Full-time equivalent employment	1,357	1,372	1,377
	Reimbursable:			
2001	Total compensable workyears: Full-time equivalent employment	365	365	365

ROYALTY AND OFFSHORE MINERALS MANAGEMENT

(Legislative proposal, not subject to PAYGO)

Contingent upon the enactment of authorizing legislation, the Secretary shall establish and adjust user fees for the Minerals Management Service and such user fees shall be deposited as additional offsetting collections to this appropriation, to remain available until expended for the purpose of such services: Provided, That upon enactment of such authorizing legislation, the amount appropriated above from the General Fund shall be reduced by $10,000,000.

Program and Financing (in millions of dollars)

Identification code 14–1917–2–1–302		1999 actual	2000 est.	2001 est.
	Obligations by program activity:			
00.01	Direct Program			−10
09.01	Reimbursable program			10
10.00	Total new obligations			
	New budget authority (gross), detail:			
	Discretionary:			
40.00	Appropriation			−10
68.00	Spending authority from offsetting collections: Offsetting collections (cash)			10
70.00	Total new budget authority (gross)			
	Offsets:			
	Against gross budget authority and outlays:			
88.40	Offsetting collections (cash) from: Non-Federal sources			−10
	Net budget authority and outlays:			
89.00	Budget authority			−10
90.00	Outlays			−10

This Administration will propose legislation to authorize the collection and spending of new and expansion of existing user fees for the Minerals Management Service program that supports energy and mineral exploration, development, and production on the Outer Continental Shelf lands, contingent upon the enactment of the appropriations proviso above. If the proposed authorizing legislation is enacted, the proviso will reduce the General Fund appropriation by the amount of the estimated user fee collections. This will allow total discretionary resources to not exceed the amount allowed under the discretionary spending caps. The proviso will allow the Minerals Management Service to spend up to the specified reduction in the General Fund appropriation.

Object Classification (in millions of dollars)

Identification code 14–1917–2–1–302		1999 actual	2000 est.	2001 est.
25.2	Direct obligations: Other services			−10
99.0	Reimbursable obligations: Subtotal, reimbursable obligations			10
99.9	Total new obligations			

MINERAL LEASING AND ASSOCIATED PAYMENTS

Unavailable Collections (in millions of dollars)

Identification code 14–5003–0–2–999		1999 actual	2000 est.	2001 est.
	Balance, start of year:			
01.99	Balance, start of year			
	Receipts:			
02.01	Receipts from mineral leasing, public lands	478	678	583
	Appropriation:			
05.01	Mineral leasing and associated payments	−478	−678	−583
07.99	Total balance, end of year			

Program and Financing (in millions of dollars)

Identification code 14–5003–0–2–999		1999 actual	2000 est.	2001 est.
	Obligations by program activity:			
10.00	Total new obligations (object class 41.0)	478	678	583
	Budgetary resources available for obligation:			
22.00	New budget authority (gross)	478	678	583
23.95	Total new obligations	−478	−678	−583
	New budget authority (gross), detail:			
	Mandatory:			
60.25	Appropriation (special fund, indefinite)	478	678	583
	Change in unpaid obligations:			
73.10	Total new obligations	478	678	583
73.20	Total outlays (gross)	−478	−678	−583
	Outlays (gross), detail:			
86.97	Outlays from new mandatory authority	478	678	583
	Net budget authority and outlays:			
89.00	Budget authority	478	678	583
90.00	Outlays	478	678	583

Alaska is paid 90 percent (50 percent for NPR–A area) and other States 50 percent of the receipts from bonuses, royalties, payor late payment interest, and rentals of public lands within those States resulting from the leasing and development of mineral resources under: the Mineral Leasing Act (30 U.S.C. 191); the Mineral Leasing Act for Acquired Lands (30 U.S.C. 351); the Geothermal Steam Act of 1970 (30 U.S.C. 1001); and, from leases of potash deposits (30 U.S.C. 285), on both public domain and certain acquired lands.

The Omnibus Reconciliation Act of 1993 (OBRA) requires 50 percent of the Federal Government's mineral leasing administrative program costs to be recovered before disbursement to the United States Treasury and States. The Act also requires that a State's share of program costs be the lesser amount as determined under two different methods (revenue versus cost-based) as is prescribed in the Act.

General and special funds—Continued

ENVIRONMENTAL IMPROVEMENT AND RESTORATION FUND

Unavailable Collections (in millions of dollars)

Identification code 14–5425–0–2–302	1999 actual	2000 est.	2001 est.
Balance, start of year:			
01.99 Balance, start of year			
Receipts:			
02.01 Court award, OCS rent and bonuses			221
02.02 Interest earned			46
02.03 Court award, OCS escrow account interest			671
02.99 Total receipts			938
07.99 Total balance, end of year			938

Title IV of the Department of the Interior and Related Agencies Appropriations Act, 1998 (P.L. 105–83) established the Environmental Improvement and Restoration Fund account. Under section 352(a) of the Department of the Interior and Related Agencies Appropriations Act, 2000 (P.L. 106–113), the fund is to be invested. Twenty percent of the interest earned is permanently appropriated to the Department of Commerce and the unappropriated balance of interest will remain in the fund. No budget authority is requested.

NATIONAL FORESTS FUND, PAYMENT TO STATES

Unavailable Collections (in millions of dollars)

Identification code 14–5243–0–2–302	1999 actual	2000 est.	2001 est.
Balance, start of year:			
01.99 Balance, start of year			
Receipts:			
02.01 National forests fund, payments to states—Interior	3	5	3
Appropriation:			
05.01 National forests fund, payment to states	−3	−5	−3
07.99 Total balance, end of year			

Program and Financing (in millions of dollars)

Identification code 14–5243–0–2–302	1999 actual	2000 est.	2001 est.
Obligations by program activity:			
10.00 Total new obligations (object class 41.0)	3	5	3
Budgetary resources available for obligation:			
22.00 New budget authority (gross)	3	5	3
23.95 Total new obligations	−3	−5	−3
New budget authority (gross), detail:			
Mandatory:			
60.25 Appropriation (special fund, indefinite)	3	5	3
Change in unpaid obligations:			
73.10 Total new obligations	3	5	3
73.20 Total outlays (gross)	−3	−5	−3
Outlays (gross), detail:			
86.97 Outlays from new mandatory authority	3	5	3
Net budget authority and outlays:			
89.00 Budget authority	3	5	3
90.00 Outlays	3	5	3

The Omnibus Reconciliation Act of 1993 (OBRA) requires that 50 percent of the Federal Government's mineral leasing administrative program costs to be recovered before disbursement to the United States Treasury and States. The Act also requires that a State's share of program costs be the lesser amount as determined under two different methods (revenue versus cost-based) as is prescribed in the Act.

LEASES OF LANDS ACQUIRED FOR FLOOD CONTROL, NAVIGATION, AND ALLIED PURPOSES

Unavailable Collections (in millions of dollars)

Identification code 14–5248–0–2–302	1999 actual	2000 est.	2001 est.
Balance, start of year:			
01.99 Balance, start of year			
Receipts:			
02.01 Leases of lands acquired for flood control, navigation, and allied purposes	1	1	1
Appropriation:			
05.01 Leases of lands acquired for flood control, navigation, and allied purposes	−1	−1	−1
07.99 Total balance, end of year			

Program and Financing (in millions of dollars)

Identification code 14–5248–0–2–302	1999 actual	2000 est.	2001 est.
Obligations by program activity:			
10.00 Total new obligations (object class 41.0)	1	1	1
Budgetary resources available for obligation:			
22.00 New budget authority (gross)	1	1	1
23.95 Total new obligations	−1	−1	−1
New budget authority (gross), detail:			
Mandatory:			
60.25 Appropriation (special fund, indefinite)	1	1	1
Change in unpaid obligations:			
73.10 Total new obligations	1	1	1
73.20 Total outlays (gross)	−1	−1	−1
Outlays (gross), detail:			
86.97 Outlays from new mandatory authority	1	1	1
Net budget authority and outlays:			
89.00 Budget authority	1	1	1
90.00 Outlays	1	1	1

The Omnibus Reconciliation Act of 1993 (OBRA) requires 50 percent of the Federal Government's mineral leasing administrative program costs to be recovered before disbursement to the United States Treasury and States. The Act also requires that a State's share of program costs be the lesser amount as determined under two different methods (revenue versus cost-based) as is prescribed in the Act.

Trust Funds

OIL SPILL RESEARCH

For necessary expenses to carry out title I, section 1016, title IV, sections 4202 and 4303, title VII, and title VIII, section 8201 of the Oil Pollution Act of 1990, $6,118,000, which shall be derived from the Oil Spill Liability Trust Fund, to remain available until expended. *(Department of the Interior and Related Agencies Appropriations Act, 2000, as enacted by section 1000(a)(3) of the Consolidated Appropriations Act, 2000 (P.L. 106–113).)*

Program and Financing (in millions of dollars)

Identification code 14–8370–0–7–302	1999 actual	2000 est.	2001 est.
Obligations by program activity:			
10.00 Total new obligations	6	6	6
Budgetary resources available for obligation:			
22.00 New budget authority (gross)	6	6	6
23.95 Total new obligations	−6	−6	−6
New budget authority (gross), detail:			
Discretionary:			
40.26 Appropriation (trust fund, definite)	6	6	6
Change in unpaid obligations:			
72.40 Unpaid obligations, start of year: Obligated balance, start of year	6	6	6

73.10	Total new obligations	6	6	6
73.20	Total outlays (gross)	−6	−6	−6
74.40	Unpaid obligations, end of year: Obligated balance, end of year	6	6	6
	Outlays (gross), detail:			
86.90	Outlays from new discretionary authority	6	5	5
86.93	Outlays from discretionary balances		1	1
87.00	Total outlays (gross)	6	6	6
	Net budget authority and outlays:			
89.00	Budget authority	6	6	6
90.00	Outlays	6	6	6

The Oil Pollution Act of 1990 authorizes use of the Oil Spill Liability Trust Fund, established by section 9509 of the Internal Revenue Code of 1986, to perform oil pollution research and other duties related to oil spill prevention and financial responsibility. The moneys provided will be used to carry out the purposes for which the fund is established.

Object Classification (in millions of dollars)

Identification code 14–8370–0–7–302		1999 actual	2000 est.	2001 est.
11.1	Personnel compensation: Full-time permanent	1	1	1
25.2	Other services	5	5	5
99.9	Total new obligations	6	6	6

Personnel Summary

Identification code 14–8370–0–7–302		1999 actual	2000 est.	2001 est.
1001	Total compensable workyears: Full-time equivalent employment	23	23	23

Office of Surface Mining Reclamation and Enforcement

Federal Funds

General and special funds:

REGULATION AND TECHNOLOGY

For necessary expenses to carry out the provisions of the Surface Mining Control and Reclamation Act of 1977, Public Law 95–87, as amended, including the purchase of not to exceed 10 passenger motor vehicles, for replacement only; [$95,891,000] *$97,801,000*: *Provided*, That the Secretary of the Interior, pursuant to regulations, may use directly or through grants to States, moneys collected in fiscal year [2000] *2001* for civil penalties assessed under section 518 of the Surface Mining Control and Reclamation Act of 1977 (30 U.S.C. 1268), to reclaim lands adversely affected by coal mining practices after August 3, 1977, to remain available until expended: *Provided further*, That appropriations for the Office of Surface Mining Reclamation and Enforcement may provide for the travel and per diem expenses of State and tribal personnel attending Office of Surface Mining Reclamation and Enforcement sponsored training. *(Department of the Interior and Related Agencies Appropriations Act, 2000, as enacted by section 1000(a)(3) of the Consolidated Appropriations Act, 2000 (P.L. 106–113).)*

Program and Financing (in millions of dollars)

Identification code 14–1801–0–1–302		1999 actual	2000 est.	2001 est.
	Obligations by program activity:			
	Direct program:			
00.02	Environmental protection	70	71	73
00.03	Technology development & transfer	11	11	11
00.04	Financial management	1	1	1
00.05	Executive direction & administration	11	12	12
09.01	Reimbursable program	1	1	1
10.00	Total new obligations	94	96	98
	Budgetary resources available for obligation:			
21.40	Unobligated balance available, start of year	1	1	3
22.00	New budget authority (gross)	95	98	100
23.90	Total budgetary resources available for obligation	96	99	103
23.95	Total new obligations	−94	−96	−98
24.40	Unobligated balance available, end of year	1	3	5
	New budget authority (gross), detail:			
	Discretionary:			
40.00	Appropriation (general fund)	93	96	98
68.00	Spending authority from offsetting collections: Offsetting collections (cash)	2	2	2
70.00	Total new budget authority (gross)	95	98	100
	Change in unpaid obligations:			
72.40	Unpaid obligations, start of year: Obligated balance, start of year	29	29	32
73.10	Total new obligations	94	96	98
73.20	Total outlays (gross)	−92	−95	−100
73.40	Adjustments in expired accounts (net)	−2		
74.40	Unpaid obligations, end of year: Obligated balance, end of year	29	32	30
	Outlays (gross), detail:			
86.90	Outlays from new discretionary authority	66	66	67
86.93	Outlays from discretionary balances	25	29	33
87.00	Total outlays (gross)	92	95	100
	Offsets:			
	Against gross budget authority and outlays:			
88.40	Offsetting collections (cash) from: Non-Federal sources	−2	−2	−2
	Net budget authority and outlays:			
89.00	Budget authority	93	96	98
90.00	Outlays	91	93	98

Environmental protection.—This activity funds those functions that directly contribute to ensuring that the environment is protected during surface coal mining operations. It also addresses those activities that ensure that coal operators adequately reclaim the land after mining is completed.

Under this activity, OSM provides regulatory grants to States to operate enforcement programs under the terms of the Surface Mining Control and Reclamation Act of 1977 (SMCRA). It also provides for the operation of Federal and Indian land programs and the oversight of State programs. This activity also supports State regulatory program development and maintenance.

Environmental Restoration.—This activity funds environmental reclamation efforts through the collection of civil penalties for post-SMCRA reclamation and funds from bond forfeitures. It also provides funding for underground and coal outcrop fires.

Technology development and transfer.—This activity provides funding to enhance the technical skills that States and Indian Tribes need to operate their regulatory programs. It provides technical outreach to States and Indian Tribes to solve problems related to the environmental effects of coal mining. The Applicant Violator System is funded from this activity.

Financial Management.—This activity provides the resources for the managing, accounting, and processing of collections and for the pursuit of delinquent civil penalties. This includes developing and maintaining information management systems that support these functions and enhance the agency's ability to deny new mining permits to applicants with unabated State or Federal violations.

Executive direction and administration.—This activity provides funding for executive direction, general administrative support, and the acquisition of certain agency-wide common services, such as rent, telephones, and postage.

The following are key performance measures for the Regulation and technology account:

General and special funds—Continued

REGULATION AND TECHNOLOGY—Continued

PERFORMANCE MEASURES

	1999 actual	2000 est.	2001 est.
Customer satisfaction in the quality of technical training to States, Tribes and OSM staff	91%	89%	89%
Increase in the percent of sites free of offsite impacts	94%	94%	95%

Object Classification (in millions of dollars)

Identification code 14–1801–0–1–302		1999 actual	2000 est.	2001 est.
	Direct obligations:			
11.1	Personnel compensation: Full-time permanent	25	26	26
12.1	Civilian personnel benefits	5	5	5
21.0	Travel and transportation of persons	2	1	1
23.1	Rental payments to GSA	2	2	2
23.2	Rental payments to others	1	1	1
25.2	Other services	4	4	4
25.7	Operation and maintenance of equipment	1	1	1
26.0	Supplies and materials	1	1	1
31.0	Equipment	1	1	1
41.0	Grants, subsidies, and contributions	51	53	55
99.0	Subtotal, direct obligations	93	95	97
99.0	Reimbursable obligations	1	1	1
99.9	Total new obligations	94	96	98

Personnel Summary

Identification code 14–1801–0–1–302		1999 actual	2000 est.	2001 est.
	Direct:			
1001	Total compensable workyears: Full-time equivalent employment	410	412	414
	Reimbursable:			
2001	Total compensable workyears: Full-time equivalent employment	14	14	14

ABANDONED MINE RECLAMATION FUND

For necessary expenses to carry out title IV of the Surface Mining Control and Reclamation Act of 1977, Public Law 95–87, as amended, including the purchase of not more than 10 passenger motor vehicles for replacement only, [$196,208,000] *$211,158,000*, to be derived from receipts of the Abandoned Mine Reclamation Fund and to remain available until expended; of which up to [$8,000,000] *$10,000,000*, to be derived from the Federal Expenses Share of the Fund, shall be for supplemental grants to States for the reclamation of abandoned sites with acid mine rock drainage from coal mines, and for associated activities, through the Appalachian Clean Streams Initiative[: *Provided*, That grants to minimum program States will be $1,500,000 per State in fiscal year 2000: *Provided further*, That of the funds herein provided up to $18,000,000 may be used for the emergency program authorized by section 410 of Public Law 95–87, as amended, of which no more than 25 percent shall be used for emergency reclamation projects in any one State and funds for federally administered emergency reclamation projects under this proviso shall not exceed $11,000,000], *and of which $13,000,000 is to be used only in those states and by those Tribes that are using AML funds to address environmental problems caused by historic abandoned coal sites, and who obligate to grants all of their distributed portion of the fiscal year 2000 AML appropriation*: *Provided further*, That prior year unobligated funds appropriated for the emergency reclamation program shall not be subject to the 25 percent limitation per State and may be used without fiscal year limitation for emergency projects: *Provided further*, That pursuant to Public Law 97–365, the Department of the Interior is authorized to use up to 20 percent from the recovery of the delinquent debt owed to the United States Government to pay for contracts to collect these debts: *Provided further*, That funds made available under title IV of Public Law 95–87 may be used for any required non-Federal share of the cost of projects funded by the Federal Government for the purpose of environmental restoration related to treatment or abatement of acid mine drainage from abandoned mines: *Provided further*, That such projects must be consistent with the purposes and priorities of the Surface Mining Control and Reclamation Act: [*Provided further*, That, in addition to the amount granted to the Commonwealth of Pennsylvania under sections 402(g)(1) and 402(g)(5) of the Surface Mining Control and Reclamation Act (Act), an additional $300,000 will be specifically used for the purpose of conducting a demonstration project in accordance with section 401(c)(6) of the Act to determine the efficacy of improving water quality by removing metals from eligible waters polluted by acid mine drainage:] *Provided further*, That the State of Maryland may set aside the greater of $1,000,000 or 10 percent of the total of the grants made available to the State under title IV of the Surface Mining Control and Reclamation Act of 1977, as amended (30 U.S.C. 1231 et seq.), if the amount set aside is deposited in an acid mine drainage abatement and treatment fund established under a State law, pursuant to which law the amount (together with all interest earned on the amount) is expended by the State to undertake acid mine drainage abatement and treatment projects, except that before any amounts greater than 10 percent of its title IV grants are deposited in an acid mine drainage abatement and treatment fund, the State of Maryland must first complete all Surface Mining Control and Reclamation Act priority one projects. *(Department of the Interior and Related Agencies Appropriations Act, 2000, as enacted by section 1000(a)(3) of the Consolidated Appropriations Act, 2000 (P.L. 106–113).)*

Unavailable Collections (in millions of dollars)

Identification code 14–5015–0–2–999		1999 actual	2000 est.	2001 est.
	Balance, start of year:			
01.99	Balance, start of year	1,351	1,443	1,489
	Receipts:			
02.01	Abandoned mine reclamation fees	276	277	277
02.03	Earnings on investments	83	73	83
02.04	Interest on late payment of coal mining reclamation fees		1	1
02.99	Total receipts	359	351	361
04.00	Total: Balances and collections	1,710	1,794	1,850
	Appropriation:			
05.01	Abandoned mine reclamation fund	−267	−305	−278
05.99	Subtotal appropriation	−267	−305	−278
07.99	Total balance, end of year	1,443	1,489	1,572

Program and Financing (in millions of dollars)

Identification code 14–5015–0–2–999		1999 actual	2000 est.	2001 est.
	Obligations by program activity:			
00.01	Environmental restoration	177	181	191
00.02	Technology development and transfer	7	4	7
00.03	Financial management	6	5	7
00.04	Executive direction and administration	6	6	6
00.06	Transfer to UMWA Combined Benefits Fund	82	109	67
10.00	Total new obligations	278	305	278
	Budgetary resources available for obligation:			
21.40	Unobligated balance available, start of year	43	52	72
22.00	New budget authority (gross)	268	305	278
22.10	Resources available from recoveries of prior year obligations	20	20	20
23.90	Total budgetary resources available for obligation	331	377	370
23.95	Total new obligations	−278	−305	−278
24.40	Unobligated balance available, end of year	52	72	92
	New budget authority (gross), detail:			
	Discretionary:			
40.20	Appropriation (special fund, definite)	185	264	211
	Mandatory:			
60.25	Appropriation (special fund, indefinite)	82	41	67
	Discretionary:			
68.00	Spending authority from offsetting collections: Offsetting collections (cash)	1		
70.00	Total new budget authority (gross)	268	305	278
	Change in unpaid obligations:			
72.40	Unpaid obligations, start of year: Obligated balance, start of year	250	241	233
73.10	Total new obligations	278	305	278
73.20	Total outlays (gross)	−267	−293	−284
73.45	Adjustments in unexpired accounts	−20	−20	−20

74.40 Unpaid obligations, end of year: Obligated balance, end of year	241	233	207
Outlays (gross), detail:			
86.90 Outlays from new discretionary authority	50	121	58
86.93 Outlays from discretionary balances	136	131	159
86.97 Outlays from new mandatory authority	81	41	67
87.00 Total outlays (gross)	267	293	284
Offsets:			
Against gross budget authority and outlays:			
88.00 Offsetting collections (cash) from: Federal sources	–1	....	....
Net budget authority and outlays:			
89.00 Budget authority	267	305	278
90.00 Outlays	266	293	284
Memorandum (non-add) entries:			
92.01 Total investments, start of year: U.S. securities: Par value	1,668	1,765	1,815
92.02 Total investments, end of year: U.S. securities: Par value	1,765	1,815	1,891

Environmental Restoration.—This activity funds those functions that contribute to reclaiming lands affected by past coal mining practices. Funds are used to restore land and water resources and the environment that have been degraded by mining prior to the passage of the Surface Mining Control and Reclamation Act (SMCRA).

This activity provides reclamation grants to qualified States. It also provides for the Federal reclamation program, which includes the Federally-administered emergency reclamation program, and for high priority projects in States that do not have a reclamation program.

Funding is also provided within this account, for the Appalachian Clean Streams Initiative.

Technology development and transfer.—This activity provides funding to enhance the technical skills that the States and Indian Tribes need to operate their reclamation programs. OSM conducts technical studies on mining and reclamation-related problems. This activity also provides resources for the Small operators assistance program.

Financial Management.—This activity provides funds to identify, notify, collect, and audit fees from coal operators for the Abandoned Mine Reclamation Fund. OSM seeks to maximize voluntary compliance with the SMCRA's reclamation fee provisions.

Executive direction and administration.—This activity provides funding for executive direction, general administrative support, and the acquisition of certain agency-wide common services such as rent, telephones, and postage.

The following are the key performance measures for the Abandoned Mine Reclamation Fund account:

PERFORMANCE MEASURES

	1999 actual	*2000 est.*	*2001 est.*
Number of acres reclaimed on all abandoned coal mine sites.	7,400	8,100	9,100
Percent of total funds from outside sources for the Clean Streams Initiative	55%	60%	62%

[1] The 1999 accomplishment for acres reclaimed is a calculated estimate. The accomplishments reported to OSM by States and Tribes for 1999 included more than one year. Also, all estimates reflect the full number of projects funded by the increase; actual project completion may occur one to three years after initiation.

Status of Funds (in millions of dollars)

Identification code 14–5015–0–2–999	1999 actual	2000 est.	2001 est.
Unexpended balance, start of year:			
0100 Treasury balance	7	3	5
U.S. Securities:			
0101 Par value	1,668	1,765	1,815
0102 Unrealized discounts	–31	–30	–25
0199 Total balance, start of year	1,644	1,736	1,794
Cash income during the year:			
Governmental receipts:			
0200 Abandoned mine reclamation fund, reclamation fees	276	277	277
Proprietary receipts:			
0220 Proprietary receipts	....	1	1
Intragovernmental transactions:			
0240 Earnings on investments, Abandoned Mine Reclamation Fund	83	73	83
Offsetting collections:			
0281 Offsetting collections	1	....	....
0299 Total cash income	360	351	361
Cash outgo during year:			
0500 Abandoned Mine Reclamation Fund	–267	–293	–284
Unexpended balance, end of year:			
0700 Uninvested balance	3	5	5
U.S. Securities:			
0701 Par value	1,765	1,815	1,891
0702 Unrealized discounts	–30	–25	–25
0799 Total balance, end of year	1,736	1,794	1,871

Object Classification (in millions of dollars)

Identification code 14–5015–0–2–999	1999 actual	2000 est.	2001 est.
11.1 Personnel compensation: Full-time permanent	15	16	16
12.1 Civilian personnel benefits	3	3	3
21.0 Travel and transportation of persons	1	....	....
23.1 Rental payments to GSA	3	2	2
25.2 Other services	94	53	53
31.0 Equipment	1	1	1
41.0 Grants, subsidies, and contributions	161	230	203
99.9 Total new obligations	278	305	278

Personnel Summary

Identification code 14–5015–0–2–999	1999 actual	2000 est.	2001 est.
1001 Total compensable workyears: Full-time equivalent employment	221	221	222

WATER AND SCIENCE

Bureau of Reclamation

Appropriations to the Bureau are made from the general fund and special funds. The special funds are: (a) the Reclamation Fund, derived from repayments and other revenues from water and power users, receipts from the sale, lease, and rental of Federal lands, and certain oil and mineral revenues; (b) the Central Valley Project Restoration Fund, consisting of revenues from project beneficiaries; and (c) other sources such as the Colorado River Dam Fund, which generates revenue from the sale of Boulder Canyon Power, and the recreation, entrance, and use fee account, consisting of fees collected pursuant to the Land and Water Conservation Fund Act of 1965, as amended. Non-Federal entities also advance funds for operation and maintenance and provide funds under the Contributed Funds Act. The 2001 estimates are summarized by source as follows (in millions of dollars):

Account Title	*Total appropriations*	*General Fund*	*Reclamation Fund*	*Restoration Fund*	*Other*
Appropriated Funds:					
Water and Related Resources (net)	607	57	550	....	....
Transferred from Water and Related Resources to Lower and Upper Colorado Basin Funds	36	36	....	....	....
Policy and Administration	50	....	50	....	....
Loan Program	9	9	....	....	....
Central Valley Project Restoration Fund	38	....	....	38	....
California Bay-Delta Ecosystem	60	60	....	....	....
Gross Current Authority	800	162	600	38	....
Central Valley Project Restoration Fund, current offset	–28	....	....	–28	....
Net Current Appropriations	772	160	602	10	....
Permanent Funds:					
Reclamation Trust Funds	5	....	....	....	5

BUREAU OF RECLAMATION—Continued

Account Title	Total appropriations	General Fund	Reclamation Fund	Restoration Fund	Other
Lower & Upper Colorado Basin Funds	−21	....	....	....	−21
Loan Liquidating Account	−4	....	....	....	−4
Colorado River Dam Fund	66	....	....	....	66
Total Permanent Appropriations	46	....	....	....	46
Grand Total	818	160	602	10	46

Federal Funds

General and special funds:

The following appropriations shall be expended to execute authorized functions of the Bureau of Reclamation:

WATER AND RELATED RESOURCES

(INCLUDING TRANSFER OF FUNDS)

For management, development, and restoration of water and related natural resources and for related activities, including the operation, maintenance and rehabilitation of reclamation and other facilities, participation in fulfilling related Federal responsibilities to Native Americans, and related grants to, and cooperative and other agreements with, State and local governments, Indian tribes, and others, **[**$607,927,000**]** *$643,058,000*, to remain available until expended, of which **[**$2,247,000**]** *$1,916,000* shall be available for transfer to the Upper Colorado River Basin Fund and **[**$24,089,000**]** *$33,667,000* shall be available for transfer to the Lower Colorado River Basin Development Fund**[**, and**]**; of which such amounts as may be necessary may be advanced to the Colorado River Dam Fund*; of which $16,000,000 shall be for on-reservation water development, feasibility studies, and related administrative costs under Public Law 106–163; of which is not to exceed $200,000 for financial assistance for the preparation of cooperative drought contingency plans under Title II of Public Law 102–250; and of which not less than $500,000 is for high priority projects which shall be carried out by the Youth Conservation Corps, as authorized by 16 U.S.C. 1706*: *Provided*, That such transfers may be increased or decreased within the overall appropriation under this heading: *Provided further*, That of the total appropriated, the amount for program activities that can be financed by the Reclamation Fund or the Bureau of Reclamation special fee account established by 16 U.S.C. 460l–6a(i) shall be derived from that Fund or account: *Provided further*, That funds contributed under 43 U.S.C. 395 are available until expended for the purposes for which contributed: *Provided further*, That funds advanced under 43 U.S.C. 397a shall be credited to this account and are available until expended for the same purposes as the sums appropriated under this heading: *Provided further*, That funds available for expenditure for the Departmental Irrigation Drainage Program may be expended by the Bureau of Reclamation for site remediation on a non-reimbursable basis: *Provided further*, That section 301 of Public Law 102–250, Reclamation States Emergency Drought Relief Act of 1991, as amended **[**by Public Law 104–206**]**, is amended further by inserting "1999, **[**and 2000"**]** *2000, and 2001"* in lieu of *"and 2000"* **[**"and 1997": *Provided further*, That the amount authorized for Indian municipal, rural, and industrial water features by section 10 of Public Law 89–108, as amended by section 8 of Public Law 99–294, section 1701(b) of Public Law 102–575, and Public Law 105–245, is increased by $1,000,000 (October 1998 prices)**]**: *Provided further, That the amount authorized for Minidoka Project North Side Pumping Division, Idaho, by section 5 of Public Law 81–864, is increased by $2,805,000. (Energy and Water Development Appropriations Act, 2000.)*

Program and Financing (in millions of dollars)

Identification code 14–0680–0–1–301		1999 actual	2000 est.	2001 est.
	Obligations by program activity:			
	Direct Program:			
00.01	Facility Operations	139	139	147
00.02	Facility Maintenance and Rehabilitation	141	119	142
00.03	Water and Energy Management and Development	256	254	201
00.04	Fish and Wildlife Management and Development	105	85	84
00.05	Land Management and Development	36	37	33
01.00	Total Direct Program	677	634	607
09.01	Reimbursable program	104	192	159
10.00	Total new obligations	781	826	766
	Budgetary resources available for obligation:			
21.40	Unobligated balance available, start of year	128	85	....
22.00	New budget authority (gross)	738	741	766
23.90	Total budgetary resources available for obligation	866	826	766
23.95	Total new obligations	−781	−826	−766
24.40	Unobligated balance available, end of year	85	....	....
	New budget authority (gross), detail:			
	Discretionary:			
40.00	Appropriation	93	70	93
40.20	Appropriation (special fund)	525	538	550
40.76	Reduction pursuant to P.L. 106–113	....	−2	....
41.00	Transferred to other accounts	−44	−23	−36
42.00	Transferred from other accounts	26	1	....
43.00	Appropriation (total discretionary)	600	584	607
	Spending authority from offsetting collections:			
68.00	(cash)	135	160	159
68.10	From Federal sources: Change in receivables and unpaid, unfilled orders	3	−3	....
68.90	Spending authority from offsetting collections (total discretionary)	138	157	159
70.00	Total new budget authority (gross)	738	741	766
	Change in unpaid obligations:			
	Unpaid obligations, start of year:			
72.40	Obligated balance, start of year	261	304	297
72.95	From Federal sources: Receivables and unpaid, unfilled orders	....	3	....
72.99	Total unpaid obligations, start of year	261	307	297
73.10	Total new obligations	781	826	766
73.20	Total outlays (gross)	−736	−836	−756
	Unpaid obligations, end of year:			
74.40	Obligated balance, end of year	304	297	307
74.95	From Federal sources: Receivables and unpaid, unfilled orders	3	....	....
74.99	Total unpaid obligations, end of year	307	297	307
	Outlays (gross), detail:			
86.90	Outlays from new discretionary authority	347	444	459
86.93	Outlays from discretionary balances	389	392	297
87.00	Total outlays (gross)	736	836	756
	Offsets:			
	Against gross budget authority and outlays:			
	Offsetting collections (cash) from:			
88.00	Federal sources	−88	−119	−118
88.40	Non-Federal sources	−47	−41	−41
88.90	Total, offsetting collections (cash)	−135	−160	−159
	Against gross budget authority only:			
88.95	From Federal sources: Change in receivables and unpaid, unfilled orders	−3	3	....
	Net budget authority and outlays:			
89.00	Budget authority	600	584	607
90.00	Outlays	601	676	597

Status of Direct Loans (in millions of dollars)

Identification code 14–0680–0–1–301		1999 actual	2000 est.	2001 est.
	Cumulative balance of direct loans outstanding:			
1210	Outstanding, start of year	3	3	3
1251	Repayments: Repayments and prepayments	....	....	−1
1290	Outstanding, end of year	3	3	2

The water and related resources account supports the development, management, and restoration of water and related natural resources in the 17 Western States. The account includes funds for operating and maintaining existing facilities to obtain the greatest overall level of benefits, to protect public safety, and to conduct studies on ways to improve the use of water and related natural resources. Work will be done in partnership and cooperation with non-Federal entities and other Federal agencies.

Object Classification (in millions of dollars)

Identification code 14–0680–0–1–301		1999 actual	2000 est.	2001 est.
	Direct obligations:			
	Personnel compensation:			
11.1	Full-time permanent	134	137	143
11.3	Other than full-time permanent	6	6	6
11.5	Other personnel compensation	10	10	10
11.9	Total personnel compensation	150	153	159
12.1	Civilian personnel benefits	31	31	31
21.0	Travel and transportation of persons	13	13	13
22.0	Transportation of things	4	4	4
23.1	Rental payments to GSA	1	1	1
23.2	Rental payments to others	1	1	1
23.3	Communications, utilities, and miscellaneous charges	10	10	10
25.2	Other services	225	176	138
26.0	Supplies and materials	22	22	23
31.0	Equipment	19	19	20
32.0	Land and structures	95	96	98
41.0	Grants, subsidies, and contributions	106	108	109
99.0	Subtotal, direct obligations	677	634	607
99.0	Reimbursable obligations	104	192	159
99.9	Total new obligations	781	826	766

Personnel Summary

Identification code 14–0680–0–1–301		1999 actual	2000 est.	2001 est.
	Direct:			
1001	Total compensable workyears: Full-time equivalent employment	2,359	2,307	2,313
	Reimbursable:			
2001	Total compensable workyears: Full-time equivalent employment	155	158	156
	Allocation account:			
	Total compensable workyears:			
	Full-time equivalent employment:			
3001	Full-time equivalent employment	317	325	325
3001	Full-time equivalent employment	66	70	70

CALIFORNIA BAY-DELTA RESTORATION

(INCLUDING TRANSFER OF FUNDS)

For necessary expenses of the Department of the Interior and other participating Federal agencies in carrying out ecosystem restoration activities pursuant to the California Bay-Delta Environmental Enhancement Act and other activities that are in accord with the CALFED Bay-Delta Program, including projects to improve water use efficiency, water quality, groundwater and surface storage, levees, conveyance, and watershed management, consistent with plans to be approved by the Secretary of the Interior, in consultation with such Federal agencies, $60,000,000, to remain available until expended, of which **[**$30,000,000**]** *$36,000,000* shall be used for ecosystem restoration activities and **[**$30,000,000**]** *$24,000,000* shall be used for such other activities, and of which such amounts as may be necessary to conform with such plans shall be transferred to appropriate accounts of such Federal agencies: *Provided*, That no more than $5,000,000 of the funds appropriated herein may be used for planning and management activities associated with developing the overall CALFED Bay-Delta Program and coordinating its staged implementation: *Provided further*, That funds for ecosystem restoration activities may be obligated only as non-Federal sources provide their share in accordance with the cost-sharing agreement required under section 1101(d) of such Act, and that funds for such other activities may be obligated only as non-Federal sources provide their share in a manner consistent with such cost-sharing agreement: *Provided further*, That such funds may be obligated prior to the completion of a final programmatic environmental impact statement only if: (1) consistent with 40 CFR 1506.1(c); and (2) used for purposes that the Secretary finds are of sufficiently high priority to warrant such an expenditure: *Provided further, That section 1101(a) of Public Law 104–333 is amended in the first sentence by striking "For each of the fiscal years 1998, 1999, and 2000 there are authorized to be appropriated an additional $143,300,000" and inserting "For fiscal year 1998 through fiscal year 2003, there is authorized to be appropriated an additional total of $429,900,000". (Energy and Water Development Appropriations Act, 2000.)*

Program and Financing (in millions of dollars)

Identification code 14–0687–0–1–301		1999 actual	2000 est.	2001 est.
	Obligations by program activity:			
10.00	Total new obligations	39	108	60
	Budgetary resources available for obligation:			
21.40	Unobligated balance available, start of year	12	48	....
22.00	New budget authority (gross)	75	60	60
23.90	Total budgetary resources available for obligation	87	108	60
23.95	Total new obligations	−39	−108	−60
24.40	Unobligated balance available, end of year	48	....	....
	New budget authority (gross), detail:			
	Discretionary:			
40.00	Appropriation	75	60	60
	Change in unpaid obligations:			
72.40	Unpaid obligations, start of year: Obligated balance, start of year	69	85	39
73.10	Total new obligations	39	108	60
73.20	Total outlays (gross)	−23	−154	−60
74.40	Unpaid obligations, end of year: Obligated balance, end of year	85	39	39
	Outlays (gross), detail:			
86.90	Outlays from new discretionary authority	....	21	21
86.93	Outlays from discretionary balances	23	133	39
87.00	Total outlays (gross)	23	154	60
	Net budget authority and outlays:			
89.00	Budget authority	75	60	60
90.00	Outlays	23	154	60

Object Classification (in millions of dollars)

Identification code 14–0687–0–1–301		1999 actual	2000 est.	2001 est.
11.1	Personnel compensation: Full-time permanent	1	1	1
25.2	Other services	38	107	59
99.9	Total new obligations	39	108	60

Personnel Summary

Identification code 14–0687–0–1–301		1999 actual	2000 est.	2001 est.
1001	Total compensable workyears: Full-time equivalent employment	9	9	9

This account funds the Federal share of California Bay-Delta restoration activities, which are selected by a State and Federal partnership (CALFED). Although this account is included within the Bureau of Reclamation for budget presentation purposes, these funds are to be transferred to the Federal agencies participating in CALFED, consistent with plans approved by the Secretary of the Interior. In 2001, funds are requested in this account to: (1) continue implementation of the ecosystem restoration program initiated in 1998; (2) undertake high priority projects in other areas covered by the CALFED Bay-Delta Program; and (3) complete development of the program and coordinate its initial implementation.

General and special funds—Continued

RECLAMATION FUND

Unavailable Collections (in millions of dollars)

Identification code 14–5000–0–2–301	1999 actual	2000 est.	2001 est.
Balance, start of year:			
01.99 Balance, start of year	1,849	2,070	2,188
Receipts:			
02.01 Royalties on natural resources	369	504	459
02.02 Sale of power and other utilities	387	195	294
02.03 Other proprietary receipts from the public	191	127	137
02.04 Sale of electric energy, Bonneville	16	26	55
02.05 Miscellaneous interest	15	14	13
02.06 Sale of timber and other products	2	3	4
02.07 Sale of public domain	7	15	15
02.99 Total receipts	987	884	977
04.00 Total: Balances and collections	2,836	2,954	3,165
Appropriation:			
05.01 Water and related resources	−525	−538	−550
05.02 Policy and administration	−47	−47	−50
05.03 Construction, rehabilitation, operation and maintenance (WAPA)	−194	−182	−155
05.99 Subtotal appropriation	−766	−767	−755
06.20 Reduction pursuant to Public Law xx-xxx		1	
07.99 Total balance, end of year	2,070	2,188	2,410

This fund is derived from repayments and other revenues from water and power users, together with certain receipts from the sale, lease, and rental of Federal lands in the 17 Western States and certain oil and mineral revenues, and is available for expenditure pursuant to appropriation acts.

POLICY AND ADMINISTRATION

For necessary expenses of policy, administration, and related functions in the office of the Commissioner, the Denver office, and offices in the five regions of the Bureau of Reclamation, to remain available until expended, [$47,000,000] *$50,224,000*, to be derived from the Reclamation Fund and be nonreimbursable as provided in 43 U.S.C. 377: *Provided*, That no part of any other appropriation in this Act shall be available for activities or functions budgeted as policy and administration expenses. *(Energy and Water Development Appropriations Act, 2000.)*

Program and Financing (in millions of dollars)

Identification code 14–5065–0–2–301	1999 actual	2000 est.	2001 est.
Obligations by program activity:			
10.00 Total new obligations	50	47	50
Budgetary resources available for obligation:			
21.40 Unobligated balance available, start of year	4		
22.00 New budget authority (gross)	47	47	50
23.90 Total budgetary resources available for obligation	51	47	50
23.95 Total new obligations	−50	−47	−50
New budget authority (gross), detail:			
Discretionary:			
40.20 Appropriation (special fund, definite)	47	47	50
Change in unpaid obligations:			
72.40 Unpaid obligations, start of year: Obligated balance, start of year	7	7	5
73.10 Total new obligations	50	47	50
73.20 Total outlays (gross)	−49	−49	−50
74.40 Unpaid obligations, end of year: Obligated balance, end of year	7	5	5
Outlays (gross), detail:			
86.90 Outlays from new discretionary authority	38	42	45
86.93 Outlays from discretionary balances	11	7	5
87.00 Total outlays (gross)	49	49	50
Net budget authority and outlays:			
89.00 Budget authority	47	47	50
90.00 Outlays	49	49	50

The policy and administration account supports the direction and management of all reclamation activities as performed by the Commissioner's office, the Reclamation Service Center, and the five regional offices. Charges attributable to individual projects or specific beneficiaries, including the costs of related administrative and technical services, are covered under other Bureau of Reclamation accounts.

Object Classification (in millions of dollars)

Identification code 14–5065–0–2–301	1999 actual	2000 est.	2001 est.
Personnel compensation:			
11.1 Full-time permanent	20	20	21
11.3 Other than full-time permanent	1	1	1
11.9 Total personnel compensation	21	21	22
12.1 Civilian personnel benefits	3	3	3
21.0 Travel and transportation of persons	4	3	4
23.2 Rental payments to others	1	1	1
25.2 Other services	20	18	19
26.0 Supplies and materials	1	1	1
99.9 Total new obligations	50	47	50

Personnel Summary

Identification code 14–5065–0–2–301	1999 actual	2000 est.	2001 est.
1001 Total compensable workyears: Full-time equivalent employment	340	355	360

CENTRAL VALLEY PROJECT RESTORATION FUND

[For carrying out the programs, projects, plans, and habitat restoration, improvement, and acquisition provisions of the Central Valley Project Improvement Act, $42,000,000, to be derived from such sums as may be collected] *Beginning in fiscal year 2001 and thereafter, such sums as are or have been deposited* in the Central Valley Project Restoration Fund pursuant to sections 3407(d), 3404(c)(3), 3405(f), and 3406(c)(1) of Public Law 102–575, [to remain] *shall be* available until expended *without further appropriation, to carry out the programs, projects, plans, and habitat restoration, improvement, and acquisition provisions of the Central Valley Project Improvement Act*: *Provided*, That the Bureau of Reclamation is directed to assess and collect the full amount of the additional mitigation and restoration payments authorized by section 3407(d) of Public Law 102–575*: Provided further, That the amount available for fiscal year 2001 shall not exceed $38,382,000. (Energy and Water Development Appropriations Act, 2000.)*

Unavailable Collections (in millions of dollars)

Identification code 14–5173–0–2–301	1999 actual	2000 est.	2001 est.
Balance, start of year:			
01.99 Balance, start of year		16	21
Receipts:			
02.01 Total discretionary and mandatory collections	49	47	38
04.00 Total: Balances and collections	49	63	59
Appropriation:			
05.01 Central Valley Project restoration fund	−33	−42	−38
07.99 Total balance, end of year	16	21	21

Program and Financing (in millions of dollars)

Identification code 14–5173–0–2–301	1999 actual	2000 est.	2001 est.
Obligations by program activity:			
10.00 Total new obligations	55	42	38
Budgetary resources available for obligation:			
21.40 Unobligated balance available, start of year	22		
22.00 New budget authority (gross)	33	42	38

23.90	Total budgetary resources available for obligation	55	42	38
23.95	Total new obligations	−55	−42	−38
	New budget authority (gross), detail:			
	Discretionary:			
	Appropriation (special fund, indefinite):			
40.25	Appropriation (special fund, indefinite, restoration fund, other)	8	10	10
40.25	Appropriation (special fund, indefinite, restoration fund, 3407(d))	25	32	28
43.00	Appropriation (total discretionary)	33	42	38
	Change in unpaid obligations:			
72.40	Unpaid obligations, start of year: Obligated balance, start of year	13	31	8
73.10	Total new obligations	55	42	38
73.20	Total outlays (gross)	−38	−65	−38
74.40	Unpaid obligations, end of year: Obligated balance, end of year	31	8	8
	Outlays (gross), detail:			
86.90	Outlays from new discretionary authority	3	34	30
86.93	Outlays from discretionary balances	35	31	8
87.00	Total outlays (gross)	38	65	38
	Net budget authority and outlays:			
89.00	Budget authority	33	42	38
90.00	Outlays	38	65	38

This fund was established to carry out the provisions of the Central Valley Project Improvement Act. Resources are derived from donations, revenues from voluntary water transfers and tiered water pricing, and Friant Division surcharges. The account is also financed through additional mitigation and restoration payments collected on an annual basis from project beneficiaries. Changes in appropriation language have been proposed that would permanently appropriate all collections of these dedicated receipts starting in 2001.

Object Classification (in millions of dollars)

Identification code 14–5173–0–2–301		1999 actual	2000 est.	2001 est.
11.1	Personnel compensation: Full-time permanent	1	1	1
25.2	Other services	50	37	33
32.0	Land and structures	1	1	1
41.0	Grants, subsidies, and contributions	2	2	2
99.0	Subtotal, direct obligations	54	41	37
99.5	Below reporting threshold	1	1	1
99.9	Total new obligations	55	42	38

Personnel Summary

Identification code 14–5173–0–2–301		1999 actual	2000 est.	2001 est.
1001	Total compensable workyears: Full-time equivalent employment	24	24	24

COLORADO RIVER DAM FUND, BOULDER CANYON PROJECT

Unavailable Collections (in millions of dollars)

Identification code 14–5656–0–2–301		1999 actual	2000 est.	2001 est.
	Balance, start of year:			
01.99	Balance, start of year	....	....	....
	Receipts:			
02.01	Revenues, Colorado River Dam fund, Boulder Canyon project, Interior	65	61	66
	Appropriation:			
05.01	Colorado River dam fund, Boulder Canyon project	−65	−61	−66
07.99	Total balance, end of year	....	....	....

Program and Financing (in millions of dollars)

Identification code 14–5656–0–2–301		1999 actual	2000 est.	2001 est.
	Obligations by program activity:			
00.01	Facility operations	22	29	25
00.02	Facility maintenance and rehabilitation	6	4	6
00.03	Payment of interest	13	13	13
00.04	Payments to Arizona and Nevada	1	1	1
00.05	Western Area Power Administration	....	4	4
00.06	Payment to Lower Colorado River Basin Development Fund	15	15	15
10.00	Total new obligations	57	66	64
	Budgetary resources available for obligation:			
21.40	Unobligated balance available, start of year	7	8	1
22.00	New budget authority (gross)	65	61	66
22.21	Unobligated balance transferred to other accounts	−4	....	....
22.40	Capital transfer to general fund	−2	−2	−2
23.90	Total budgetary resources available for obligation	66	67	65
23.95	Total new obligations	−57	−66	−64
24.40	Unobligated balance available, end of year	8	1	1
	New budget authority (gross), detail:			
	Mandatory:			
60.25	Appropriation (special fund, indefinite)	65	61	66
	Change in unpaid obligations:			
72.40	Unpaid obligations, start of year: Obligated balance, start of year	4	4	26
73.10	Total new obligations	57	66	64
73.20	Total outlays (gross)	−58	−45	−62
74.40	Unpaid obligations, end of year: Obligated balance, end of year	4	26	28
	Outlays (gross), detail:			
86.97	Outlays from new mandatory authority	51	33	35
86.98	Outlays from mandatory balances	7	12	27
87.00	Total outlays (gross)	58	45	62
	Net budget authority and outlays:			
89.00	Budget authority	65	61	66
90.00	Outlays	58	45	62

Revenues from the sale of Boulder Canyon power are placed in this fund and are available without further appropriation to pay the operation and maintenance costs of the project including those of the Western Area Power Administration for power marketing, transmission, operation, maintenance, and rehabilitation; to pay interest on amounts advanced from the Treasury; to pay annually not more than $300,000 each to Arizona and Nevada; and to repay advances from the Treasury for construction and other purposes. The rates charged for Boulder Canyon power also include certain amounts for transfer to the Lower Colorado River Basin Development Fund.

Object Classification (in millions of dollars)

Identification code 14–5656–0–2–301		1999 actual	2000 est.	2001 est.
	Personnel compensation:			
11.1	Full-time permanent	13	14	15
11.5	Other personnel compensation	2	2	2
11.9	Total personnel compensation	15	16	17
12.1	Civilian personnel benefits	3	3	3
25.2	Other services	21	24	21
26.0	Supplies and materials	2	3	3
31.0	Equipment	1	1	1
32.0	Land and structures	1	3	3
41.0	Grants, subsidies, and contributions	1	1	1
43.0	Interest and dividends	13	15	15
99.9	Total new obligations	57	66	64

General and special funds—Continued

COLORADO RIVER DAM FUND, BOULDER CANYON PROJECT—Continued

Personnel Summary

Identification code 14–5656–0–2–301	1999 actual	2000 est.	2001 est.
1001 Total compensable workyears: Full-time equivalent employment	212	211	211

DUTCH JOHN COMMUNITY ASSISTANCE

Unavailable Collections (in millions of dollars)

Identification code 14–5455–0–2–806	1999 actual	2000 est.	2001 est.
Balance, start of year:			
01.99 Balance, start of year			
Receipts:			
02.01 Property sales		1	
Appropriation:			
05.01 Dutch John		–1	
07.99 Total balance, end of year			

Program and Financing (in millions of dollars)

Identification code 14–5455–0–2–806	1999 actual	2000 est.	2001 est.
Obligations by program activity:			
10.00 Total new obligations (object class 32.0)		1	
Budgetary resources available for obligation:			
22.00 New budget authority (gross)		1	
23.95 Total new obligations		–1	
New budget authority (gross), detail:			
Mandatory:			
60.25 Appropriation (special fund, indefinite)		1	
Change in unpaid obligations:			
73.10 Total new obligations		1	
Outlays (gross), detail:			
86.97 Outlays from new mandatory authority		1	
Net budget authority and outlays:			
89.00 Budget authority		1	
90.00 Outlays		1	

This account contains receipts from the sale of properties as authorized by P.L. 105–326. Receipts are available without further appropriation in order to make semi-annual payments to Daggett County, Utah, to be used by the County for purposes associated with the provision of governmental and community services to the Dutch John community.

Public enterprise funds:

LOWER COLORADO RIVER BASIN DEVELOPMENT FUND

Program and Financing (in millions of dollars)

Identification code 14–4079–0–3–301	1999 actual	2000 est.	2001 est.
Obligations by program activity:			
09.01 Facility operation	49	157	68
09.02 Water & energy management & development	117	61	50
09.03 Land Management & Development		1	1
09.04 Interest on investment	89	40	39
09.05 Payment to Upper Colorado River Basin Fund	1		
10.00 Total new obligations	256	259	158
Budgetary resources available for obligation:			
21.40 Unobligated balance available, start of year	169	118	5
22.00 New budget authority (gross)	206	149	161
22.40 Capital transfer to general fund	–1	–3	–3
23.90 Total budgetary resources available for obligation	374	264	163
23.95 Total new obligations	–256	–259	–158
24.40 Unobligated balance available, end of year	118	5	5
New budget authority (gross), detail:			
Discretionary:			
42.00 Transferred from Water & related resources	43	22	34
Mandatory:			
69.00 Offsetting collections (cash)	163	144	148
69.27 Capital transfer to general fund		–17	–21
69.90 Spending authority from offsetting collections (total mandatory)	163	127	127
70.00 Total new budget authority (gross)	206	149	161
Change in unpaid obligations:			
72.40 Unpaid obligations, start of year: Obligated balance, start of year	–119	–65	59
73.10 Total new obligations	256	259	158
73.20 Total outlays (gross)	–201	–135	–153
74.40 Unpaid obligations, end of year: Obligated balance, end of year	–65	59	64
Outlays (gross), detail:			
86.90 Outlays from new discretionary authority	23	13	20
86.93 Outlays from discretionary balances	16	20	9
86.97 Outlays from new mandatory authority	128	69	69
86.98 Outlays from mandatory balances	34	33	55
87.00 Total outlays (gross)	201	135	153
Offsets:			
Against gross budget authority and outlays:			
88.40 Offsetting collections (cash) from: Non-Federal sources	–163	–144	–148
Net budget authority and outlays:			
89.00 Budget authority	43	5	13
90.00 Outlays	38	–9	5

Ongoing construction costs of the Central Arizona project are financed through appropriations transferred to this fund. Revenues from the operation of project facilities are available without further appropriation for operation and maintenance expenses, for capital repayment to the general fund, and for the non-Federal share of salinity control projects. The rates charged for Boulder Canyon power include certain amounts for transfer to this fund, some of which may then be transferred to reimburse the Upper Colorado River Basin Fund. The last transfer occurred in 1999.

Object Classification (in millions of dollars)

Identification code 14–4079–0–3–301	1999 actual	2000 est.	2001 est.
11.1 Personnel compensation: Full-time permanent	3	3	2
25.2 Other services	160	212	113
32.0 Land and structures	4	4	4
43.0 Interest and dividends	89	40	39
99.9 Total new obligations	256	259	158

Personnel Summary

Identification code 14–4079–0–3–301	1999 actual	2000 est.	2001 est.
2001 Total compensable workyears: Full-time equivalent employment	32	27	23

UPPER COLORADO RIVER BASIN FUND

Program and Financing (in millions of dollars)

Identification code 14–4081–0–3–301	1999 actual	2000 est.	2001 est.
Obligations by program activity:			
Reimbursable programs:			
09.01 Facility operation	25	59	21
09.02 Facility maintenance & rehabilitation	7	26	10
09.03 Water & energy management & development	11	29	9

09.04	Fish & wildlife management & development	4	35	12
09.05	Land management & development	1	3	1
09.06	Payment to Ute Indian Tribe	2	2	2
09.07	Interest on investment	35	3	4
10.00	Total new obligations	85	157	59
	Budgetary resources available for obligation:			
21.40	Unobligated balance available, start of year	56	112	10
22.00	New budget authority (gross)	181	57	61
22.40	Capital transfer to general fund	−40	−2	−2
23.90	Total budgetary resources available for obligation	197	167	69
23.95	Total new obligations	−85	−157	−59
24.40	Unobligated balance available, end of year	112	10	10
	New budget authority (gross), detail:			
	Discretionary:			
42.00	Transferred from Water & related resources	1	1	2
	Mandatory:			
69.00	Offsetting collections (cash)	180	56	59
70.00	Total new budget authority (gross)	181	57	61
	Change in unpaid obligations:			
72.40	Unpaid obligations, start of year: Obligated balance, start of year	24	28	23
73.10	Total new obligations	85	157	59
73.20	Total outlays (gross)	−81	−162	−56
74.40	Unpaid obligations, end of year: Obligated balance, end of year	28	23	26
	Outlays (gross), detail:			
86.90	Outlays from new discretionary authority	1	1	1
86.93	Outlays from discretionary balances	4	13	
86.97	Outlays from new mandatory authority	13	21	22
86.98	Outlays from mandatory balances	63	127	33
87.00	Total outlays (gross)	81	162	56
	Offsets:			
	Against gross budget authority and outlays:			
88.40	Offsetting collections (cash) from: Non-Federal sources	−180	−56	−59
	Net budget authority and outlays:			
89.00	Budget authority	1	1	2
90.00	Outlays	−99	106	−3

Ongoing construction costs of the Colorado River Storage project are financed through appropriations transferred to this account. Revenues from the operation of project facilities are available without further appropriation for operation and maintenance expenses and for capital repayment to the general fund.

Object Classification (in millions of dollars)

Identification code 14–4081–0–3–301		1999 actual	2000 est.	2001 est.
	Personnel compensation:			
11.1	Full-time permanent	11	13	13
11.3	Other than full-time permanent	1	1	1
11.5	Other personnel compensation	1	1	1
11.9	Total personnel compensation	13	15	15
12.1	Civilian personnel benefits	3	3	3
21.0	Travel and transportation of persons	1	1	1
25.2	Other services	26	128	29
26.0	Supplies and materials	2	2	2
31.0	Equipment	2	2	2
32.0	Land and structures	1	1	1
41.0	Grants, subsidies, and contributions	2	2	2
43.0	Interest and dividends	35	3	4
99.9	Total new obligations	85	157	59

Personnel Summary

Identification code 14–4081–0–3–301		1999 actual	2000 est.	2001 est.
2001	Total compensable workyears: Full-time equivalent employment	183	195	195

Intragovernmental funds:

WORKING CAPITAL FUND

Program and Financing (in millions of dollars)

Identification code 14–4524–0–4–301		1999 actual	2000 est.	2001 est.
	Obligations by program activity:			
09.01	Information resources management	11	18	18
09.03	Administrative expenses	113	179	183
09.04	Technical expenses	54	85	87
10.00	Total new obligations	178	282	288
	Budgetary resources available for obligation:			
21.40	Unobligated balance available, start of year	54	30	20
22.00	New budget authority (gross)	154	272	285
23.90	Total budgetary resources available for obligation	208	302	305
23.95	Total new obligations	−178	−282	−288
24.40	Unobligated balance available, end of year	30	20	17
	New budget authority (gross), detail:			
	Discretionary:			
41.00	Transferred to Water & Related Resources	−26		
68.00	Spending authority from offsetting collections: (cash)	180	272	285
70.00	Total new budget authority (gross)	154	272	285
	Change in unpaid obligations:			
72.40	Unpaid obligations, start of year: Obligated balance, start of year	28	27	54
73.10	Total new obligations	178	282	288
73.20	Total outlays (gross)	−179	−255	−285
74.40	Unpaid obligations, end of year: Obligated balance, end of year	27	54	57
	Outlays (gross), detail:			
86.90	Outlays from new discretionary authority	153	218	228
86.93	Outlays from discretionary balances	26	37	57
87.00	Total outlays (gross)	179	255	285
	Offsets:			
	Against gross budget authority and outlays:			
88.00	Offsetting collections (cash) from: Federal sources	−180	−272	−285
	Net budget authority and outlays:			
89.00	Budget authority	−26		
90.00	Outlays	−1	−17	

This revolving fund enables the Bureau of Reclamation to recover the costs of the administrative and technical services, and facilities used by its programs and by others, and accumulates funds to finance capital equipment purchases.

Object Classification (in millions of dollars)

Identification code 14–4524–0–4–301		1999 actual	2000 est.	2001 est.
	Personnel compensation:			
11.1	Full-time permanent	115	111	115
11.3	Other than full-time permanent	4	4	4
11.5	Other personnel compensation	3	3	3
11.9	Total personnel compensation	122	118	122
12.1	Civilian personnel benefits	16	15	15
13.0	Benefits for former personnel		1	1
21.0	Travel and transportation of persons	2	8	8
22.0	Transportation of things	2	8	8
23.1	Rental payments to GSA	9	30	30
23.3	Communications, utilities, and miscellaneous charges	7	28	29
25.2	Other services	5	17	18
26.0	Supplies and materials	6	28	28
31.0	Equipment	9	29	29
99.9	Total new obligations	178	282	288

Personnel Summary

Identification code 14–4524–0–4–301		1999 actual	2000 est.	2001 est.
2001	Total compensable workyears: Full-time equivalent employment	2,084	1,933	1,928

Credit accounts:

BUREAU OF RECLAMATION LOAN PROGRAM ACCOUNT

For the cost of direct loans and/or grants, [$12,000,000] *$8,944,000*, to remain available until expended, as authorized by the Small Reclamation Projects Act of August 6, 1956, as amended (43 U.S.C. 422a–422l): *Provided*, That such costs, including the cost of modifying such loans, shall be as defined in section 502 of the Congressional Budget Act of 1974, as amended: *Provided further*, That these funds are available to subsidize gross obligations for the principal amount of direct loans not to exceed [$43,000,000] *$27,000,000*.

In addition, for administrative expenses necessary to carry out the program for direct loans and/or grants, $425,000, to remain available until expended: *Provided*, That of the total sums appropriated, the amount of program activities that can be financed by the Reclamation Fund shall be derived from that Fund. *(Energy and Water Development Appropriations Act, 2000.)*

Program and Financing (in millions of dollars)

Identification code 14–0685–0–1–301		1999 actual	2000 est.	2001 est.
	Obligations by program activity:			
00.01	Water and energy management and development (direct loans)	9	13	9
00.05	Upward Reestimate of direct loan subsidy		3	
00.06	Interest on reestimates of direct loan subsidy		1	
10.00	Total new obligations	9	17	9
	Budgetary resources available for obligation:			
21.40	Unobligated balance available, start of year	3	5	
22.00	New budget authority (gross)	11	12	9
23.90	Total budgetary resources available for obligation	14	17	9
23.95	Total new obligations	−9	−17	−9
24.40	Unobligated balance available, end of year	5		
	New budget authority (gross), detail:			
	Discretionary:			
40.00	Appropriation (general fund)	8	12	9
40.76	Reduction pursuant to P.L. 106–113		−1	
43.00	Appropriation (total discretionary)	8	11	9
	Mandatory:			
60.05	Appropriation (indefinite)	3	1	
70.00	Total new budget authority (gross)	11	12	9
	Change in unpaid obligations:			
72.40	Unpaid obligations, start of year: Obligated balance, start of year	2	1	4
73.10	Total new obligations	9	17	9
73.20	Total outlays (gross)	−9	−14	−10
74.40	Unpaid obligations, end of year: Obligated balance, end of year	1	4	3
	Outlays (gross), detail:			
86.90	Outlays from new discretionary authority	4	7	6
86.93	Outlays from discretionary balances	5	3	4
86.97	Outlays from new mandatory authority		1	
86.98	Outlays from mandatory balances		3	
87.00	Total outlays (gross)	9	14	10
	Net budget authority and outlays:			
89.00	Budget authority	11	12	9
90.00	Outlays	9	14	10

Under the Small Reclamation Projects Act, loans and grants can be made to non-Federal organizations for construction of small water resource projects.

As required by the Federal Credit Reform Act of 1990, the loan program account records the subsidy costs associated with the direct loans obligated in 1992 and beyond, as well as administrative expenses of this program. The subsidy amounts are estimated on a present value basis; the administrative expenses are estimated on a cash basis.

Summary of Loan Levels, Subsidy Budget Authority and Outlays by Program (in millions of dollars)

Identification code 14–0685–0–1–301		1999 actual	2000 est.	2001 est.
	Direct loan levels supportable by subsidy budget authority:			
1150	Direct loan levels	38	43	27
1159	Total direct loan levels	38	43	27
	Direct loan subsidy (in percent):			
1320	Subsidy rate	36.68	36.81	52.99
1329	Weighted average subsidy rate	36.68	36.81	52.99
	Direct loan subsidy budget authority:			
1330	Subsidy budget authority	11	12	9
1339	Total subsidy budget authority	11	12	9
	Direct loan subsidy outlays:			
1340	Subsidy outlays	9	14	10
1349	Total subsidy outlays	9	14	10

Object Classification (in millions of dollars)

Identification code 14–0685–0–1–301		1999 actual	2000 est.	2001 est.
33.0	Investments and loans	6	1	1
41.0	Grants, subsidies, and contributions	3	15	7
99.0	Subtotal, direct obligations	9	16	8
99.5	Below reporting threshold		1	1
99.9	Total new obligations	9	17	9

Personnel Summary

Identification code 14–0685–0–1–301		1999 actual	2000 est.	2001 est.
1001	Total compensable workyears: Full-time equivalent employment	3	5	5

BUREAU OF RECLAMATION DIRECT LOAN FINANCING ACCOUNT

Program and Financing (in millions of dollars)

Identification code 14–4547–0–3–301		1999 actual	2000 est.	2001 est.
	Obligations by program activity:			
00.01	Direct loans	25	43	27
00.02	Interest paid to Treasury		7	8
10.00	Total new obligations	25	50	35
	Budgetary resources available for obligation:			
22.00	New financing authority (gross)	25	50	35
23.95	Total new obligations	−25	−50	−35
	New financing authority (gross), detail:			
	Mandatory:			
67.15	Authority to borrow (indefinite)	17	33	26
	Spending authority from offsetting collections:			
	Discretionary:			
68.00	Offsetting collections (cash)	9	15	13
68.10	From Federal sources: Change in receivables and unpaid, unfilled orders	−1	3	−1
68.47	Portion applied to repay debt		−1	−3
68.90	Spending authority from offsetting collections (total discretionary)	8	17	9
70.00	Total new financing authority (gross)	25	50	35
	Change in unpaid obligations:			
	Unpaid obligations, start of year:			
72.40	Obligated balance, start of year	2		13
72.95	Receivables from program account	2	1	4
72.99	Total unpaid obligations, start of year	4	1	17
73.10	Total new obligations	25	50	35
73.20	Total financing disbursements (gross)	−26	−34	−39
	Unpaid obligations, end of year:			
74.40	Obligated balance, end of year		13	9
74.95	Receivables from program account	1	4	3

	1999 actual	2000 est.	2001 est.
74.99 Total unpaid obligations, end of year	1	17	12
87.00 Total financing disbursements (gross)	26	34	39
Offsets:			
Against gross financing authority and financing disbursements:			
Offsetting collections (cash) from:			
88.00 Federal sources	–9	–14	–10
88.40 Repayments of principal	....	–1	–3
88.90 Total, offsetting collections (cash)	–9	–15	–13
Against gross financing authority only:			
88.95 Change in receivables from program accounts	1	–3	1
Net financing authority and financing disbursements:			
89.00 Financing authority	17	32	23
90.00 Financing disbursements	17	19	26

Status of Direct Loans (in millions of dollars)

Identification code 14–4547–0–3–301	1999 actual	2000 est.	2001 est.
Position with respect to appropriations act limitation on obligations:			
1111 Limitation on direct loans	38	43	27
1112 Unobligated direct loan limitation	–13	....	....
1150 Total direct loan obligations	25	43	27
Cumulative balance of direct loans outstanding:			
1210 Outstanding, start of year	120	146	175
1231 Disbursements: Direct loan disbursements	26	30	27
1251 Repayments: Repayments and prepayments	....	–1	–3
1290 Outstanding, end of year	146	175	199

As required by the Federal Credit Reform Act of 1990, the direct loan financing account is a non-budgetary account for recording all cash flows to and from the Government resulting from direct loans obligated in 1992 and beyond. The amounts in this account are a means of financing and are not included in budget totals.

Balance Sheet (in millions of dollars)

Identification code 14–4547–0–3–301	1998 actual	1999 actual	2000 est.	2001 est.
ASSETS:				
Investments in US securities:				
1106 Federal assets: Receivables, net	2	1	4	3
Net value of assets related to post–1991 direct loans receivable:				
1401 Direct loans receivable, gross	120	146	175	199
1405 Allowance for subsidy cost (–)	–57	–66	–80	–90
1499 Net present value of assets related to direct loans	63	80	95	109
1999 Total assets	65	81	99	112
LIABILITIES:				
2103 Federal liabilities: Debt	63	80	95	109
2999 Total liabilities	63	80	95	109
NET POSITION:				
3100 Appropriated capital	2	1	4	3
3999 Total net position	2	1	4	3
4999 Total liabilities and net position	65	81	99	112

BUREAU OF RECLAMATION LOAN LIQUIDATING ACCOUNT

Program and Financing (in millions of dollars)

Identification code 14–0667–0–1–301	1999 actual	2000 est.	2001 est.
New budget authority (gross), detail:			
Mandatory:			
69.00 Offsetting collections (cash)	....	3	4
69.27 Capital transfer to general fund	....	–3	–4
69.90 Spending authority from offsetting collections (total mandatory)	....	....	....
Offsets:			
Against gross budget authority and outlays:			
88.40 Offsetting collections (cash) from: Non-Federal sources	....	–3	–4
Net budget authority and outlays:			
89.00 Budget authority	....	–3	–4
90.00 Outlays	....	–3	–4

Status of Direct Loans (in millions of dollars)

Identification code 14–0667–0–1–301	1999 actual	2000 est.	2001 est.
Cumulative balance of direct loans outstanding:			
1210 Outstanding, start of year	69	66	63
1251 Repayments: Repayments and prepayments	–3	–3	–4
1290 Outstanding, end of year	66	63	59

Statement of Operations (in millions of dollars)

Identification code 14–0667–0–1–301	1998 actual	1999 actual	2000 est.	2001 est.
0111 Revenue	....	....	3	4
0112 Expense	....	....	–3	–4
0115 Net income or loss (–)	....	....	....	....
0195 Total income or loss (–)	....	....	....	....

Balance Sheet (in millions of dollars)

Identification code 14–0667–0–1–301	1998 actual	1999 actual	2000 est.	2001 est.
ASSETS:				
1601 Net value of assets related to pre–1992 direct loans receivable and acquired defaulted guaranteed loans receivable: Direct loans, gross	69	66	63	59
1999 Total assets	69	66	63	59
LIABILITIES:				
2104 Federal liabilities: Resources payable to Treasury	69	66	63	59
2999 Total liabilities	69	66	63	59
NET POSITION:				
3999 Total net position	....	....	....	....
4999 Total liabilities and net position	69	66	63	59

As required by the Federal Credit Reform Act of 1990, the loan liquidating account records all cash flows to and from the Government resulting from direct loans obligated prior to 1992. All loans obligated in 1992 or thereafter are recorded in loan program account No. 14–0685–0–1–301 and loan program financing account No. 14–4547–0–3–301.

Trust Funds

RECLAMATION TRUST FUNDS

Unavailable Collections (in millions of dollars)

Identification code 14–8070–0–7–301	1999 actual	2000 est.	2001 est.
Balance, start of year:			
01.99 Balance, start of year	....	....	....
Receipts:			
02.01 Deposits, reclamation trust funds, Interior	23	14	5
Appropriation:			
05.01 Reclamation trust funds	–23	–14	–5
07.99 Total balance, end of year	....	....	....

Program and Financing (in millions of dollars)

Identification code 14–8070–0–7–301	1999 actual	2000 est.	2001 est.
Obligations by program activity:			
00.01 Facility maintenance and rehabilitation	4	24	2
00.02 Water and energy management and development	8	22	3

RECLAMATION TRUST FUNDS—Continued

Program and Financing (in millions of dollars)—Continued

Identification code 14–8070–0–7–301	1999 actual	2000 est.	2001 est.
10.00 Total new obligations	12	46	5
Budgetary resources available for obligation:			
21.40 Unobligated balance available, start of year	21	32	
22.00 New budget authority (gross)	23	14	5
23.90 Total budgetary resources available for obligation	44	46	5
23.95 Total new obligations	−12	−46	−5
24.40 Unobligated balance available, end of year	32		
New budget authority (gross), detail:			
Mandatory:			
60.27 Appropriation (trust fund, indefinite)	23	14	5
Change in unpaid obligations:			
72.40 Unpaid obligations, start of year: Obligated balance, start of year	11	10	3
73.10 Total new obligations	12	46	5
73.20 Total outlays (gross)	−13	−53	−7
74.40 Unpaid obligations, end of year: Obligated balance, end of year	10	3	1
Outlays (gross), detail:			
86.97 Outlays from new mandatory authority		11	4
86.98 Outlays from mandatory balances	13	42	3
87.00 Total outlays (gross)	13	53	7
Net budget authority and outlays:			
89.00 Budget authority	23	14	5
90.00 Outlays	13	53	7

The Bureau of Reclamation performs work on various projects and activities with funding provided by non-Federal entities under 43 U.S.C. 395 and 396.

Object Classification (in millions of dollars)

Identification code 14–8070–0–7–301	1999 actual	2000 est.	2001 est.
11.1 Personnel compensation: Full-time permanent		1	1
25.2 Other services	12	45	4
99.9 Total new obligations	12	46	5

Personnel Summary

Identification code 14–8070–0–7–301	1999 actual	2000 est.	2001 est.
1001 Total compensable workyears: Full-time equivalent employment	2	15	15

ADMINISTRATIVE PROVISIONS

Sec. 201. Appropriations for the Bureau of Reclamation shall be available for purchase of not to exceed [six] *four* passenger motor vehicles for replacement only.

[Sec. 202. Funds under this title for Drought Emergency Assistance shall be made available primarily for leasing of water for specified drought related purposes from willing lessors, in compliance with existing State laws and administered under State water priority allocation. Such leases may be entered into with an option to purchase: *Provided*, That such purchase is approved by the State in which the purchase takes place and the purchase does not cause economic harm within the State in which the purchase is made.] *(Energy and Water Development Appropriations Act, 2000.)*

CENTRAL UTAH PROJECT

Federal Funds

General and special funds:

CENTRAL UTAH PROJECT COMPLETION ACCOUNT

For carrying out activities authorized by the Central Utah Project Completion Act, [and for activities related to the Uintah and Upalco Units authorized by 43 U.S.C. 620, $38,049,000] *$38,724,000*, to remain available until expended, of which [$15,476,000] *$19,158,000* shall be deposited into the Utah Reclamation Mitigation and Conservation Account: *Provided*, That of the amounts deposited into that account, $5,000,000 shall be considered the Federal contribution authorized by paragraph 402(b)(2) of the Central Utah Project Completion Act and [$10,476,000] *$14,158,000* shall be available to the Utah Reclamation Mitigation and Conservation Commission to carry out activities authorized under that Act.

In addition, for necessary expenses incurred in carrying out related responsibilities of the Secretary of the Interior, [$1,321,000] *$1,216,000*, to remain available until expended. *(Energy and Water Development Appropriations Act, 2000.)*

Program and Financing (in millions of dollars)

Identification code 14–0787–0–1–301	1999 actual	2000 est.	2001 est.
Obligations by program activity:			
00.01 Central Utah project construction	24	26	20
00.02 Mitigation and conservation	5	6	5
00.04 Program administration	1	1	1
10.00 Total new obligations	30	33	26
Budgetary resources available for obligation:			
21.40 Unobligated balance available, start of year	2	4	
22.00 New budget authority (gross)	32	29	26
23.90 Total budgetary resources available for obligation	34	33	26
23.95 Total new obligations	−30	−33	−26
24.40 Unobligated balance available, end of year	4		
New budget authority (gross), detail:			
Discretionary:			
40.00 Appropriation	42	39	40
41.00 Transferred to other accounts	−10	−10	−14
43.00 Appropriation (total discretionary)	32	29	26
Change in unpaid obligations:			
72.40 Unpaid obligations, start of year: Obligated balance, start of year	1	1	1
73.10 Total new obligations	30	33	26
73.20 Total outlays (gross)	−31	−33	−26
74.40 Unpaid obligations, end of year: Obligated balance, end of year	1	1	1
Outlays (gross), detail:			
86.90 Outlays from new discretionary authority	29	28	25
86.93 Outlays from discretionary balances	2	5	1
87.00 Total outlays (gross)	31	33	26
Net budget authority and outlays:			
89.00 Budget authority	32	29	26
90.00 Outlays	31	33	26

Titles II through VI of Public Law 102–575 authorize the completion of the Central Utah project and related activities, including the mitigation, conservation, and enhancement of fish and wildlife and recreational resources. Funds are requested in this account for the Central Utah Water Conservancy District, for transfer to the Utah Reclamation Mitigation and Conservation Commission, and to carry out related responsibilities of the Secretary.

Object Classification (in millions of dollars)

Identification code 14–0787–0–1–301	1999 actual	2000 est.	2001 est.
25.2 Other services	24	27	20

41.0 Grants, subsidies, and contributions	5	5	5
99.0 Subtotal, direct obligations	29	32	25
99.5 Below reporting threshold	1	1	1
99.9 Total new obligations	30	33	26

Personnel Summary

Identification code 14–0787–0–1–301	1999 actual	2000 est.	2001 est.
1001 Total compensable workyears: Full-time equivalent employment	5	5	5

UTAH RECLAMATION MITIGATION AND CONSERVATION ACCOUNT

Unavailable Collections (in millions of dollars)

Identification code 14–5174–0–2–301	1999 actual	2000 est.	2001 est.
Balance, start of year:			
01.99 Balance, start of year	79	96	111
Receipts:			
02.01 State contribution to principal	3	3	3
02.02 Interest on principal	5	5	6
02.03 Federal contribution to principal	5	5	5
02.04 Contributions from project beneficiaries (District)	3	1	1
02.05 Contributions from project beneficiaries (WAPA)	5	5	5
02.99 Total receipts	21	19	20
04.00 Total: Balances and collections	100	115	131
Appropriation:			
05.01 Utah Reclamation Mitigation and Conservation Account (discretionary)	−4	−4	−1
05.99 Subtotal appropriation	−4	−4	−1
07.99 Total balance, end of year	96	111	130

Program and Financing (in millions of dollars)

Identification code 14–5174–0–2–301	1999 actual	2000 est.	2001 est.
Obligations by program activity:			
10.00 Total new obligations	21	14	15
Budgetary resources available for obligation:			
21.40 Unobligated balance available, start of year	10	3	3
22.00 New budget authority (gross)	14	14	15
23.90 Total budgetary resources available for obligation	24	17	18
23.95 Total new obligations	−21	−14	−15
24.40 Unobligated balance available, end of year	3	3	3
New budget authority (gross), detail:			
Discretionary:			
40.25 Appropriation (special fund, indefinite)	2	4	1
42.00 Transferred from other accounts	10	10	14
43.00 Appropriation (total discretionary)	12	14	15
Mandatory:			
60.25 Appropriation (special fund, indefinite)	2		
70.00 Total new budget authority (gross)	14	14	15
Change in unpaid obligations:			
72.40 Unpaid obligations, start of year: Obligated balance, start of year	20	22	7
73.10 Total new obligations	21	14	15
73.20 Total outlays (gross)	−20	−29	−15
74.40 Unpaid obligations, end of year: Obligated balance, end of year	22	7	6
Outlays (gross), detail:			
86.90 Outlays from new discretionary authority	4	4	5
86.93 Outlays from discretionary balances	16	23	10
86.98 Outlays from mandatory balances		2	
87.00 Total outlays (gross)	20	29	15
Net budget authority and outlays:			
89.00 Budget authority	14	14	15
90.00 Outlays	20	29	15
Memorandum (non-add) entries:			
92.01 Total investments, start of year: U.S. securities: Par value	78	95	110
92.02 Total investments, end of year: U.S. securities: Par value	95	110	129

This account was established under Title IV of Public Law 102–575 to reflect contributions from the State of Utah, the Federal Government, and project beneficiaries; annual appropriations for the Utah Reclamation Mitigation and Conservation Commission; and other receipts. Funds deposited in the account as principal may not be expended for any purpose. The Commission may expend other funds in the account for the mitigation, conservation, and enhancement of fish and wildlife and recreational resources.

Object Classification (in millions of dollars)

Identification code 14–5174–0–2–301	1999 actual	2000 est.	2001 est.
11.1 Personnel compensation: Full-time permanent	1	1	1
25.2 Other services	20	13	14
99.9 Total new obligations	21	14	15

Personnel Summary

Identification code 14–5174–0–2–301	1999 actual	2000 est.	2001 est.
1001 Total compensable workyears: Full-time equivalent employment	13	13	13

UNITED STATES GEOLOGICAL SURVEY

Federal Funds

General and special funds:

SURVEYS, INVESTIGATIONS, AND RESEARCH

For expenses necessary for the United States Geological Survey to perform surveys, investigations, and research covering topography, geology, hydrology, biology, and the mineral and water resources of the United States, its territories and possessions, and other areas as authorized by 43 U.S.C. 31, 1332, and 1340; classify lands as to their mineral and water resources; give engineering supervision to power permittees and Federal Energy Regulatory Commission licensees; administer the minerals exploration program (30 U.S.C. 641); and publish and disseminate data relative to the foregoing activities; and to conduct inquiries into the economic conditions affecting mining and materials processing industries (30 U.S.C. 3, 21a, and 1603; 50 U.S.C. 98g(1)) and related purposes as authorized by law and to publish and disseminate data; [$823,833,000] *$895,379,000, of which $50,000,000 is for Lands Legacy; and* of which [$60,856,000] *$62,879,000* shall be available only for cooperation with States or municipalities for water resources investigations; and of which $16,400,000 shall remain available until expended for conducting inquiries into the economic conditions affecting mining and materials processing industries; [and of which $2,000,000 shall remain available until expended for ongoing development of a mineral and geologic data base;] *and of which $32,322,000 shall be available until September 30, 2002 for the operation and maintenance of facilities and deferred maintenance;* and of which [$137,604,000] *$158,781,000* shall be available until September 30, [2001] *2002* for the biological research activity and the operation of the Cooperative Research Units: *Provided*, That none of these funds provided for the biological research activity shall be used to conduct new surveys on private property, unless specifically authorized in writing by the property owner: *Provided further*, That no part of this appropriation shall be used to pay more than one-half the cost of topographic mapping or water resources data collection and investigations carried on in cooperation with States and municipalities. *(Department of the Interior and Related Agencies Appropriations Act, 2000, as enacted by section 1000(a)(3) of the Consolidated Appropriations Act, 2000 (P.L. 106–113).)*

General and special funds—Continued

SURVEYS, INVESTIGATIONS, AND RESEARCH—Continued

Program and Financing (in millions of dollars)

Identification code 14–0804–0–1–300		1999 actual	2000 est.	2001 est.
	Obligations by program activity:			
	Direct program:			
00.01	National mapping program	135	127	155
00.02	Geologic hazards, resources, and processes	230	212	225
00.03	Water resources investigations	209	186	197
00.04	Biological research	155	142	159
00.05	Science support	24	67	71
00.06	Facilities	22	86	88
09.01	Reimbursable program	369	356	347
10.00	Total new obligations	1,144	1,176	1,242
	Budgetary resources available for obligation:			
21.40	Unobligated balance available, start of year	12	21	13
22.00	New budget authority (gross)	1,156	1,167	1,242
23.90	Total budgetary resources available for obligation	1,168	1,188	1,255
23.95	Total new obligations	–1,144	–1,176	–1,242
23.98	Unobligated balance expiring or withdrawn	–3		
24.40	Unobligated balance available, end of year	21	13	13
	New budget authority (gross), detail:			
	Discretionary:			
40.00	Appropriation	798	823	895
40.15	Appropriation (emergency)	1		
40.75	Reduction pursuant to P.L. 106–51	–2		
40.76	Reduction pursuant to P.L. 106–113		–4	
41.00	Transferred to other accounts		–6	
43.00	Appropriation (total discretionary)	797	813	895
	Spending authority from offsetting collections:			
68.00	Offsetting collections (cash)	371	347	340
68.10	From Federal sources: Change in receivables and unpaid, unfilled orders	–12	7	7
68.90	Spending authority from offsetting collections (total discretionary)	359	354	347
70.00	Total new budget authority (gross)	1,156	1,167	1,242
	Change in unpaid obligations:			
	Unpaid obligations, start of year:			
72.40	Obligated balance, start of year	134	113	140
72.95	From Federal sources: Receivables and unpaid, unfilled orders	198	186	193
72.99	Total unpaid obligations, start of year	332	299	333
73.10	Total new obligations	1,144	1,176	1,242
73.20	Total outlays (gross)	–1,166	–1,142	–1,197
73.40	Adjustments in expired accounts (net)	–11		
	Unpaid obligations, end of year:			
74.40	Obligated balance, end of year	113	140	178
74.95	From Federal sources: Receivables and unpaid, unfilled orders	186	193	200
74.99	Total unpaid obligations, end of year	299	333	378
	Outlays (gross), detail:			
86.90	Outlays from new discretionary authority	934	956	1,015
86.93	Outlays from discretionary balances	232	186	182
87.00	Total outlays (gross)	1,166	1,142	1,197
	Offsets:			
	Against gross budget authority and outlays:			
	Offsetting collections (cash) from:			
88.00	Federal sources	–344	–322	–311
88.40	Non-Federal sources	–27	–25	–29
88.90	Total, offsetting collections (cash)	–371	–347	–340
	Against gross budget authority only:			
88.95	From Federal sources: Change in receivables and unpaid, unfilled orders	12	–7	–7
	Net budget authority and outlays:			
89.00	Budget authority	797	813	895
90.00	Outlays	795	795	857

Summary of Budget Authority and Outlays

(in millions of dollars)

Enacted/requested:	1999 actual	2000 est.	2001 est.
Budget Authority	797	813	895
Outlays	795	795	857
Supplemental proposal:			
Budget Authority		2	
Outlays		2	
Total:			
Budget Authority	797	815	895
Outlays	795	797	857

The U.S. Geological Survey conducts research and provides scientific data and information concerning natural hazards and environmental issues as well as on the water, land, and mineral and biological resources of the Nation. It works with other Federal agencies to determine national priorities and to encourage increased data-production partnerships, data sharing, and adherence to standards for production of geographic, geologic, biologic and water data.

This Budget proposes increases for State Planning Partnerships that will make USGS information and analytical tools available to assist State and local communities in managing local resources, planning for urban growth, and identifying sensitive land for acquisition and protection. Funding for the State Planning Partnerships within this account is proposed as part of a new Lands Legacy discretionary spending category to provide dedicated and protected funding for the President's Lands Legacy Initiative. See the Environment chapter in the Budget for a summary of the Initiative.

National mapping program.—The national mapping program ensures a Nationwide geographic information knowledge base by collecting, integrating, and making available, in printed and digital format, cartographic and geographic base data, remotely sensed data, data from classified sources, and multipurpose and special-purpose maps. The USGS is the lead Federal agency for civil mapping. Research is conducted in the mapping sciences, geography, and related disciplines in support of data production and applications. Activities related to the National Spatial Data Infrastructure support interagency and intergovernmental partnerships for establishing a national geospatial data clearinghouse, developing data standards, coordinating regional data production and sharing, and developing a data framework [data set] for the Nation.

Geologic hazards, resources, and processes.—The national program of onshore and offshore geologic research and investigations produces: (1) information on natural hazards of geologic origin such as earthquakes, volcanic eruptions, landslides, and coastal erosions; (2) geologic information for use in the management of public lands and in national policy determinations; (3) information on the chemistry and physics of the Earth, its past climate, and the geologic processes by which it was formed and is being modified; (4) geologic, geophysical, and geochemical maps and analyses to address environmental, resource, and hazards concerns; (5) hazards, resource, and environmental assessments; and (6) improved methods and instrumentation for detecting and monitoring hazards, disseminating hazards information, and conducting assessments.

Water resources investigations.—The national program of water resources monitoring, investigations, and research has the objective of appraising the Nation's water resources and ensuring that the information necessary to develop and manage them efficiently and effectively is available when needed. The program produces data, analyses, assessments, and methodologies to support Federal, State and local government decisions on water planning, water management, water quality, flood forecasting and warning, and enhancement of the quality of the environment.

Biological research.—The national program of biological research: (1) conducts biological research inventory and monitoring; (2) provides scientific information for the management of biological resources; and (3) predicts the consequences of environmental change and the effects of alternative management actions on plants, animals, and their habitats. The program conducts the high priority biological research needed by the Department of the Interior's land management bureaus and operates the Cooperative Research Unit program which provides research and information to resource managers, and trains natural resource professionals in partnership with university and State scientists.

Science support.—Science support provides for Bureauwide management; executive direction and coordination; administrative, human resources, and information resources management services, and the payment to DOI's National Business Center.

Facilities.—This activity finances: (1) USGS rental payments; (2) operation and maintenance for properties, including libraries; and (3) deferred maintenance and capital improvement. The funding for deferred maintenance and capital improvement is proposed as part of the second year of the Administration's facilities restoration initiative. These funds emphasize the Administration's commitment to the long-term stewardship of federal lands and facilities.

Reimbursable program.—Reimbursements from non-Federal sources are from States and municipalities for: cooperative efforts and proceeds from sale to the public of copies of photographs and records; proceeds from sale of personal property; reimbursements from permittees and licensees of the Federal Energy Regulatory Commission; and reimbursements from foreign countries and international organizations for technical assistance. Reimbursements from other Federal agencies are for mission related work performed at the request of the financing agency.

U.S. Geological Survey programs are included in the 21st Century Research Fund.

Object Classification (in millions of dollars)

Identification code 14–0804–0–1–300		1999 actual	2000 est.	2001 est.
	Direct obligations:			
	Personnel compensation:			
11.1	Full-time permanent	311	322	336
11.3	Other than full-time permanent	25	26	27
11.5	Other personnel compensation	8	8	8
11.9	Total personnel compensation	344	356	371
12.1	Civilian personnel benefits	77	80	83
13.0	Benefits for former personnel	1	1	1
21.0	Travel and transportation of persons	23	24	25
22.0	Transportation of things	6	6	7
23.1	Rental payments to GSA	53	53	54
23.2	Rental payments to others	1	2	2
23.3	Communications, utilities, and miscellaneous charges	14	14	15
24.0	Printing and reproduction	3	3	4
25.1	Advisory and assistance services	1	1	1
25.2	Other services	70	79	92
25.3	Purchases of goods and services from Government accounts	33	38	41
25.4	Operation and maintenance of facilities	2	3	4
25.5	Research and development contracts	4	4	4
25.7	Operation and maintenance of equipment	9	10	11
26.0	Supplies and materials	24	28	32
31.0	Equipment	46	54	59
41.0	Grants, subsidies, and contributions	63	63	88
42.0	Insurance claims and indemnities	1	1	1
99.0	Subtotal, direct obligations	775	820	895
99.0	Reimbursable obligations	369	356	347
99.9	Total new obligations	1,144	1,176	1,242

Personnel Summary

Identification code 14–0804–0–1–300		1999 actual	2000 est.	2001 est.
	Direct:			
1001	Total compensable workyears: Full-time equivalent employment	6,442	6,438	6,464
	Reimbursable:			
2001	Total compensable workyears: Full-time equivalent employment	2,799	2,797	2,797

WORKING CAPITAL FUND

Program and Financing (in millions of dollars)

Identification code 14–4556–0–4–306		1999 actual	2000 est.	2001 est.
	Obligations by program activity:			
10.00	Total new obligations	42	42	37
	Budgetary resources available for obligation:			
21.40	Unobligated balance available, start of year	21	44	33
22.00	New budget authority (gross)	54	31	36
22.10	Resources available from recoveries of prior year obligations	11		
23.90	Total budgetary resources available for obligation	86	75	69
23.95	Total new obligations	−42	−42	−37
24.40	Unobligated balance available, end of year	44	33	32
	New budget authority (gross), detail:			
	Mandatory:			
69.00	Offsetting collections (cash)	56	31	36
69.10	From Federal sources: Change in receivables and unpaid, unfilled orders	−2		
69.90	Spending authority from offsetting collections (total mandatory)	54	31	36
	Change in unpaid obligations:			
	Unpaid obligations, start of year:			
72.40	Obligated balance, start of year	30	2	2
72.95	From Federal sources: Receivables and unpaid, unfilled orders	10	8	8
72.99	Total unpaid obligations, start of year	40	10	10
73.10	Total new obligations	42	42	37
73.20	Total outlays (gross)	−60	−42	−37
73.45	Adjustments in unexpired accounts	−11		
	Unpaid obligations, end of year:			
74.40	Obligated balance, end of year	2	2	2
74.95	From Federal sources: Receivables and unpaid, unfilled orders	8	8	8
74.99	Total unpaid obligations, end of year	10	10	10
	Outlays (gross), detail:			
86.97	Outlays from new mandatory authority	48	29	30
86.98	Outlays from mandatory balances	12	13	7
87.00	Total outlays (gross)	60	42	37
	Offsets:			
	Against gross budget authority and outlays:			
88.00	Offsetting collections (cash) from: Federal sources	−56	−31	−36
	Against gross budget authority only:			
88.95	From Federal sources: Change in receivables and unpaid, unfilled orders	2		
	Net budget authority and outlays:			
89.00	Budget authority			
90.00	Outlays	4	11	1

Statement of Operations (in millions of dollars)

Identification code 14–4556–0–4–306		1998 actual	1999 actual	2000 est.	2001 est.
0101	Revenue	50	46	30	31
0102	Expense	−49	−45	−30	−31
0105	Net income or loss (−)	1	1		
0109	Comprehensive income	1	1		

The Working Capital Fund allows for: efficient financial management of the USGS mainframe computer and telecommunications investments; acquisition, replacement, and enhancement of scientific equipment; facilities and laboratory operations, modernization and equipment replacement; and,

General and special funds—Continued

WORKING CAPITAL FUND—Continued

publications. Other USGS activities might also be appropriately managed through such a fund, subject to future determinations by the Department of the Interior.

Balance Sheet (in millions of dollars)

Identification code 14–4556–0–4–306	1998 actual	1999 actual	2000 est.	2001 est.
ASSETS:				
Federal assets:				
1101 Fund balances with Treasury	50	46	22	25
Investments in US securities:				
1106 Receivables, net	6	14	10	10
1803 Other Federal assets: Property, plant and equipment, net	1	3	1	1
1999 Total assets	57	63	33	36
LIABILITIES:				
2101 Federal liabilities: Accounts payable	53	51	29	32
2201 Non-Federal liabilities: Accounts payable	2	10	2	2
2999 Total liabilities	55	61	31	34
NET POSITION:				
3100 Unexpended appropriations	–2	1	1	1
3300 Cumulative results of operations	4	1	1	1
3999 Total net position	2	2	2	2
4999 Total liabilities and net position	57	63	33	36

Object Classification (in millions of dollars)

Identification code 14–4556–0–4–306	1999 actual	2000 est.	2001 est.
Personnel compensation:			
11.1 Full-time permanent	9	9	10
11.3 Other than full-time permanent	1	1	1
11.9 Total personnel compensation	10	10	11
12.1 Civilian personnel benefits	3	3	3
23.1 Rental payments to GSA	3	3	3
23.2 Rental payments to others	....	1	1
24.0 Printing and reproduction	1	....	....
25.2 Other services	6	8	3
25.3 Purchases of goods and services from Government accounts	3	2	2
25.4 Operation and maintenance of facilities	....	2	1
25.7 Operation and maintenance of equipment	1	1	1
26.0 Supplies and materials	3	2	3
31.0 Equipment	9	9	8
99.0 Subtotal, reimbursable obligations	39	41	36
99.5 Below reporting threshold	3	1	1
99.9 Total new obligations	42	42	37

Personnel Summary

Identification code 14–4556–0–4–306	1999 actual	2000 est.	2001 est.
2001 Total compensable workyears: Full-time equivalent employment	241	241	241

CONTRIBUTED FUNDS

Unavailable Collections (in millions of dollars)

Identification code 14–8562–0–7–303	1999 actual	2000 est.	2001 est.
Balance, start of year:			
01.99 Balance, start of year	....	....	....
Receipts:			
02.01 Contributed funds, Geological Survey	....	1	1
Appropriation:			
05.01 Contributed funds, Geological Survey	....	–1	–1
07.99 Total balance, end of year	....	....	....

Program and Financing (in millions of dollars)

Identification code 14–8562–0–7–303	1999 actual	2000 est.	2001 est.
Obligations by program activity:			
10.00 Total new obligations (object class 25.2)	1	1	1
Budgetary resources available for obligation:			
21.40 Unobligated balance available, start of year	1	1	1
22.00 New budget authority (gross)	....	1	1
23.90 Total budgetary resources available for obligation	1	2	2
23.95 Total new obligations	–1	–1	–1
24.40 Unobligated balance available, end of year	1	1	1
New budget authority (gross), detail:			
Mandatory:			
60.25 Appropriation (special fund, indefinite)	....	1	1
Change in unpaid obligations:			
72.40 Unpaid obligations, start of year: Obligated balance, start of year	3	1	1
73.10 Total new obligations	1	1	1
73.20 Total outlays (gross)	–2	–1	–1
74.40 Unpaid obligations, end of year: Obligated balance, end of year	1	1	1
Outlays (gross), detail:			
86.98 Outlays from mandatory balances	2	1	1
Net budget authority and outlays:			
89.00 Budget authority	....	1	1
90.00 Outlays	2	1	1

Funds in this account are provided by States, local governments, and private organizations (pursuant to 43 U.S.C. 36c). This appropriation (a permanent, indefinite, special fund) makes these funds available to the USGS to perform the work desired by the contributor and the USGS. Research and development; data collection and analysis; and services are undertaken when such activities are of mutual interest and benefit and assist the USGS in accomplishing its mandated purposes.

ALLOCATIONS RECEIVED FROM OTHER ACCOUNTS

Note.—Obligations incurred under allocations from other accounts are included in the schedule of the parent appropriation as follows:
Department of State: "American sections, international commissions."

ADMINISTRATIVE PROVISIONS

The amount appropriated for the United States Geological Survey shall be available for the purchase of not to exceed 53 passenger motor vehicles, of which 48 are for replacement only; reimbursement to the General Services Administration for security guard services; *reimbursement to the United States Fish and Wildlife Service (FWS) for Refuge Revenue Sharing payments made by FWS to local entities for the FWS real property transferred to the Geological Survey;* contracting for the furnishing of topographic maps and for the making of geophysical or other specialized surveys when it is administratively determined that such procedures are in the public interest; construction and maintenance of necessary buildings and appurtenant facilities; acquisition of lands for gauging stations and observation wells; expenses of the United States National Committee on Geology; and payment of compensation and expenses of persons on the rolls of the Survey duly appointed to represent the United States in the negotiation and administration of interstate compacts: *Provided,* That activities funded by appropriations herein made may be accomplished through the use of contracts, grants, or cooperative agreements as defined in 31 U.S.C. 6302 et seq.[: *Provided further,* That the United States Geological Survey may hereafter contract directly with individuals or indirectly with institutions or nonprofit organizations, without regard to 41 U.S.C. 5, for the temporary or intermittent services of students or recent graduates, who shall be considered employees for the purposes of chapters 57 and 81 of title 5, United States Code, relating to compensation for travel and work injuries, and chapter 171 of title 28, United States Code, relating to tort claims, but shall not be considered to be Federal employees for any other purposes]. *(Department of the Interior and Related Agencies Appropriations Act, 2000, as enacted by section 1000(a)(3) of the Consolidated Appropriations Act, 2000 (P.L. 106–113).)*

BUREAU OF MINES

Federal Funds

General and special funds:

MINES AND MINERALS

Program and Financing (in millions of dollars)

Identification code 14–0959–0–1–306	1999 actual	2000 est.	2001 est.
Obligations by program activity:			
10.00 Total new obligations (object class 25.2)	1		
Budgetary resources available for obligation:			
21.40 Unobligated balance available, start of year	1		
23.95 Total new obligations	−1		
Change in unpaid obligations:			
72.40 Unpaid obligations, start of year: Obligated balance, start of year	3	2	
73.10 Total new obligations	1		
73.20 Total outlays (gross)	−2	−2	
74.40 Unpaid obligations, end of year: Obligated balance, end of year	2		
Outlays (gross), detail:			
86.93 Outlays from discretionary balances	2	2	
Net budget authority and outlays:			
89.00 Budget authority			
90.00 Outlays	2	2	

In 1996, Congress terminated the United States Bureau of Mines under Public Law 104–99. Expenditures in FY 1999 reflect costs associated with the safe shutdown of remaining facilities, the transfer of certain facilities to non-Federal entities, and remaining estimated costs for employees severed from Federal employment.

FISH AND WILDLIFE AND PARKS

UNITED STATES FISH AND WILDLIFE SERVICE

Federal Funds

General and special funds:

RESOURCE MANAGEMENT

For necessary expenses of the United States Fish and Wildlife Service, for scientific and economic studies, conservation, management, investigations, protection, and utilization of fishery and wildlife resources, except whales, seals, and sea lions, maintenance of the herd of long-horned cattle on the Wichita Mountains Wildlife Refuge, general administration, and for the performance of other authorized functions related to such resources by direct expenditure, contracts, grants, cooperative agreements and reimbursable agreements with public and private entities, [$716,046,000] *$761,938,000*, to remain available until September 30, [2001] *2002*, except as otherwise provided herein, of which [$11,701,000 shall remain available until expended for operation and maintenance of fishery mitigation facilities constructed by the Corps of Engineers under the Lower Snake River Compensation Plan, authorized by the Water Resources Development Act of 1976, to compensate for loss of fishery resources from water development projects on the Lower Snake River, and of which] not less than $2,000,000 shall be provided to local governments in southern California for planning associated with the Natural Communities Conservation Planning (NCCP) program and shall remain available until expended: *Provided*, That not less than [$1,000,000] *$2,000,000* for high priority projects which shall be carried out by the Youth Conservation Corps as authorized by the Act of August 13, 1970, as amended: *Provided further*, That not to exceed [$6,232,000] *$7,192,000* shall be used for implementing subsections (a), (b), (c), and (e) of section 4 of the Endangered Species Act, as amended, for species that are indigenous to the United States (except for processing petitions, developing and issuing proposed and final regulations, and taking any other steps to implement actions described in subsection (c)(2)(A), (c)(2)(B)(i), or (c)(2)(B)(ii)): *Provided further*, That of the amount available for law enforcement, up to $400,000 to remain available until expended, may at the discretion of the Secretary, be used for payment for information, rewards, or evidence concerning violations of laws administered by the Service, and miscellaneous and emergency expenses of enforcement activity, authorized or approved by the Secretary and to be accounted for solely on his certificate: *Provided further*, That of the amount provided for environmental contaminants, up to $1,000,000 may remain available until expended for contaminant sample analyses[: *Provided further*, That hereafter, all fines collected by the United States Fish and Wildlife Service for violations of the Marine Mammal Protection Act (16 U.S.C. 1362–1407) and implementing regulations shall be available to the Secretary, without further appropriation, to be used for the expenses of the United States Fish and Wildlife Service in administering activities for the protection and recovery of manatees, polar bears, sea otters, and walruses, and shall remain available until expended: *Provided further*, That, notwithstanding any other provision of law, in fiscal year 1999 and thereafter, sums provided by private entities for activities pursuant to reimbursable agreements shall be credited to the "Resource Management" account and shall remain available until expended: *Provided further*, That, heretofore and hereafter, in carrying out work under reimbursable agreements with any State, local, or tribal government, the United States Fish and Wildlife Service may, without regard to 31 U.S.C. 1341 and notwithstanding any other provision of law or regulation, record obligations against accounts receivable from such entities, and shall credit amounts received from such entities to this appropriation, such credit to occur within 90 days of the date of the original request by the Service for payment: *Provided further*, That all funds received by the United States Fish and Wildlife Service from responsible parties, heretofore and hereafter, for site-specific damages to National Wildlife Refuge System lands resulting from the exercise of privately-owned oil and gas rights associated with such lands in the States of Louisiana and Texas (other than damages recoverable under the Comprehensive Environmental Response, Compensation and Liability Act (26 U.S.C. 4611 et seq.), the Oil Pollution Act (33 U.S.C. 1301 et seq.), or section 311 of the Clean Water Act (33 U.S.C. 1321 et seq.)), shall be available to the Secretary, without further appropriation and until expended to: (1) complete damage assessments of the impacted site by the Secretary; (2) mitigate or restore the damaged resources; and (3) monitor and study the recovery of such damaged resources]. *(Department of the Interior and Related Agencies Appropriations Act, 2000, as enacted by section 1000(a)(3) of the Consolidated Appropriations Act, 2000 (P.L. 106–113).)*

Program and Financing (in millions of dollars)

Identification code 14–1611–0–1–303	1999 actual	2000 est.	2001 est.
Obligations by program activity:			
Direct program:			
00.01 Ecological services	185	190	199
00.02 Refuges and wildlife	263	284	305
00.03 Law Enforcement	39	39	52
00.04 Fisheries	76	85	83
00.05 General Administration	111	116	123
01.00 Subtotal, direct program	674	714	762
09.00 Reimbursable program	108	108	108
10.00 Total new obligations	782	822	870
Budgetary resources available for obligation:			
21.40 Unobligated balance available, start of year	69	48	49
22.00 New budget authority (gross)	763	823	870
22.10 Resources available from recoveries of prior year obligations	13		
23.90 Total budgetary resources available for obligation	845	871	919
23.95 Total new obligations	−782	−822	−870
23.98 Unobligated balance expiring or withdrawn	−15		
24.40 Unobligated balance available, end of year	48	49	49
New budget authority (gross), detail:			
Discretionary:			
40.00 Appropriation	661	716	762

General and special funds—Continued

RESOURCE MANAGEMENT—Continued

Program and Financing (in millions of dollars)—Continued

Identification code 14–1611–0–1–303		1999 actual	2000 est.	2001 est.
40.75	Reduction pursuant to P.L. 106–51	−1		
40.76	Reduction pursuant to P.L. 106–113		−2	
42.00	Transferred from other accounts		1	
43.00	Appropriation (total discretionary)	660	715	762
	Spending authority from offsetting collections:			
68.00	Offsetting collections (cash)	107	108	108
68.10	From Federal sources: Change in receivables and unpaid, unfilled orders	−15		
68.15	From Federal sources: Adjustments to receivables and unpaid, unfilled orders	11		
68.90	Spending authority from offsetting collections (total discretionary)	103	108	108
70.00	Total new budget authority (gross)	763	823	870
	Change in unpaid obligations:			
	Unpaid obligations, start of year:			
72.40	Obligated balance, start of year	95	162	173
72.95	From Federal sources: Receivables and unpaid, unfilled orders	120	105	105
72.99	Total unpaid obligations, start of year	215	267	278
73.10	Total new obligations	782	822	870
73.20	Total outlays (gross)	−710	−812	−860
73.40	Adjustments in expired accounts (net)	−5		
73.45	Adjustments in unexpired accounts	−13		
	Unpaid obligations, end of year:			
74.40	Obligated balance, end of year	162	173	183
74.95	From Federal sources: Receivables and unpaid, unfilled orders	105	105	105
74.99	Total unpaid obligations, end of year	267	278	288
	Outlays (gross), detail:			
86.90	Outlays from new discretionary authority	623	680	718
86.93	Outlays from discretionary balances	87	132	143
87.00	Total outlays (gross)	710	812	860
	Offsets:			
	Against gross budget authority and outlays:			
	Offsetting collections (cash) from:			
88.00	Federal sources	−90	−69	−68
88.40	Non-Federal sources	−12	−33	−34
88.45	Offsetting governmental collections from the public	−5	−6	−6
88.90	Total, offsetting collections (cash)	−107	−108	−108
	Against gross budget authority only:			
88.95	From Federal sources: Change in receivables and unpaid, unfilled orders	15		
88.96	From Federal sources: Adjustment to receivables and unpaid, unfilled orders	−11		
	Net budget authority and outlays:			
89.00	Budget authority	660	715	762
90.00	Outlays	603	704	752

Note.—Collections contained in this account include amounts that have been legislatively reclassified as intragovernmental funds.

Ecological services.—The Service provides technical assistance to prevent or minimize adverse environmental effects of development projects; restores trust species habitats; and, produces wetland maps of the United States. Financial assistance is provided to private landowners to restore or improve habitat for endangered species. Contaminants are investigated, monitored, and assessed for effects on trust resources. Activities are pursued to prevent species from becoming extinct, and to return them to the point where they are neither threatened nor endangered.

Refuges and wildlife.—The Service maintains the National Wildlife Refuge System consisting of 521 units, with waterfowl production areas in 198 counties and 50 coordination areas, totaling about 93 million acres; and directs and coordinates national migratory bird programs.

Law enforcement.—The Service enforces federal laws, regulations, and international treaties for the protection of fish, wildlife and plants, including inspections of wildlife shipments entering or leaving the United States at ports-of-entry. The Service is authorized 252 special agents and 93 wildlife inspectors, and manages the Clark R. Bavin National Wildlife Forensics Laboratory in Ashland, OR, the National Wildlife Property Repository and the National Eagle Repository, both located in Commerce City, CO.

Fisheries.—The Service manages 66 national hatcheries, 9 health centers, and 8 technology centers for the production of fish species, protects and enhances inter-jurisdictional fishery resources, and provides technical assistance for the restoration and improvement of fish and wildlife populations and their habitats. Projects to improve aquatic resources are implemented through the National Fish and Wildlife Foundation and other partnerships.

General administration.—Provides policy guidance, program coordination, and administrative services to all fish and wildlife programs. The funds also support the Service's international activities, National Conservation Training Center, and projects through the National Fish and Wildlife Foundation to restore and enhance fish and wildlife populations.

Funding for refuge, hatchery and law enforcement maintenance is proposed as part of the third year of the Administration's facilities restoration initiative. These funds emphasize the Administration's commitment to the long-term stewardship of federal lands and facilities.

PERFORMANCE MEASURES

	1999 actual	*2000 est.*	*2001 est.*
Number of listed species	53	35	29
Number of species listed a decade or more	499	532	567
Number of species listed a decade or more improved or stabilized	99	197	210
Number of species delist/downlist	3	6	12
Number of acres protected, restored, and enhanced:			
Service lands	93,628,301	93,883,301	94,138,301
Off Service lands	394,189	172,895	174,293

Object Classification (in millions of dollars)

Identification code 14–1611–0–1–303		1999 actual	2000 est.	2001 est.
	Direct obligations:			
	Personnel compensation:			
11.1	Full-time permanent	251	274	290
11.3	Other than full-time permanent	18	19	20
11.5	Other personnel compensation	14	15	16
11.9	Total personnel compensation	283	308	326
12.1	Civilian personnel benefits	79	86	91
13.0	Benefits for former personnel			1
21.0	Travel and transportation of persons	23	25	27
22.0	Transportation of things	6	6	6
23.1	Rental payments to GSA	28	29	30
23.2	Rental payments to others	1	2	2
23.3	Communications, utilities, and miscellaneous charges	14	15	16
24.0	Printing and reproduction	3	4	4
25.1	Advisory and assistance services	1	1	1
25.2	Other services	102	115	129
25.3	Purchases of goods and services from Government accounts	2	2	2
25.4	Operation and maintenance of facilities	3	3	3
25.5	Research and development contracts	3	3	3
25.7	Operation and maintenance of equipment	11	12	13
26.0	Supplies and materials	31	33	36
31.0	Equipment	37	40	42
32.0	Land and structures	11	12	12
41.0	Grants, subsidies, and contributions	36	18	18
99.0	Subtotal, direct obligations	674	714	762
99.0	Reimbursable obligations	108	106	108
99.5	Below reporting threshold		2	
99.9	Total new obligations	782	822	870

Personnel Summary

Identification code 14–1611–0–1–303	1999 actual	2000 est.	2001 est.
Direct:			
1001 Total compensable workyears: Full-time equivalent employment	6,134	6,387	6,510
Reimbursable:			
2001 Total compensable workyears: Full-time equivalent employment	779	779	779
Allocation account:			
3001 Total compensable workyears: Full-time equivalent employment	424	479	479

CONSTRUCTION

For construction [and], *improvement*, acquisition, *or removal* of buildings and other facilities required in the conservation, management, investigation, protection, and utilization of fishery and wildlife resources, and the acquisition of lands and interests therein; [$54,583,000] *$44,231,000*, to remain available until expended[: *Provided*, That notwithstanding any other provision of law, a single procurement for the construction of facilities at the Alaska Maritime National Wildlife Refuge may be issued which includes the full scope of the project: *Provided further*, That the solicitation and the contract shall contain the clauses "availability of funds" found at 48 CFR 52.232.18]. *(Department of the Interior and Related Agencies Appropriations Act, 2000, as enacted by section 1000(a)(3) of the Consolidated Appropriations Act, 2000 (P.L. 106–113).)*

Program and Financing (in millions of dollars)

Identification code 14–1612–0–1–303	1999 actual	2000 est.	2001 est.
Obligations by program activity:			
Direct program:			
Construction and rehabilitation:			
00.01 Refuges	57	58	57
00.02 Hatcheries	11	7	7
00.03 Dam safety	3	3	3
00.04 Bridge safety	2	3	3
00.05 Nationwide engineering services	6	7	8
01.00 Total, Direct program	79	78	78
09.01 Reimbursable program	21	17	2
10.00 Total new obligations	100	95	80
Budgetary resources available for obligation:			
21.40 Unobligated balance available, start of year	128	157	118
22.00 New budget authority (gross)	125	56	46
22.10 Resources available from recoveries of prior year obligations	4		
23.90 Total budgetary resources available for obligation	257	213	164
23.95 Total new obligations	−100	−95	−80
24.40 Unobligated balance available, end of year	157	118	84
New budget authority (gross), detail:			
Discretionary:			
40.00 Appropriation	50	55	44
40.15 Appropriation (emergency)—Supplemental Funds—Hurricane Floyd	38		
40.76 Reduction pursuant to P.L. 106–113		−1	
43.00 Appropriation (total discretionary)	88	54	44
Spending authority from offsetting collections:			
68.00 Offsetting collections (cash)	38	2	2
68.10 From Federal sources: Change in receivables and unpaid, unfilled orders	−1		
68.90 Spending authority from offsetting collections (total discretionary)	37	2	2
70.00 Total new budget authority (gross)	125	56	46
Change in unpaid obligations:			
Unpaid obligations, start of year:			
72.40 Obligated balance, start of year	82	62	62
72.95 From Federal sources: Receivables and unpaid, unfilled orders	2	1	1
72.99 Total unpaid obligations, start of year	84	63	63
73.10 Total new obligations	100	95	80
73.20 Total outlays (gross)	−117	−95	−63
73.45 Adjustments in unexpired accounts	−4		
Unpaid obligations, end of year:			
74.40 Obligated balance, end of year	62	62	79
74.95 From Federal sources: Receivables and unpaid, unfilled orders	1	1	1
74.99 Total unpaid obligations, end of year	63	63	80
Outlays (gross), detail:			
86.90 Outlays from new discretionary authority	40	13	11
86.93 Outlays from discretionary balances	77	82	52
87.00 Total outlays (gross)	117	95	63
Offsets:			
Against gross budget authority and outlays:			
88.00 Offsetting collections (cash) from: Federal sources	−38	−2	−2
Against gross budget authority only:			
88.95 From Federal sources: Change in receivables and unpaid, unfilled orders	1		
Net budget authority and outlays:			
89.00 Budget authority	88	54	44
90.00 Outlays	79	93	61

Summary of Budget Authority and Outlays

(in millions of dollars)

Enacted/requested:	1999 actual	2000 est.	2001 est.
Budget Authority	88	54	44
Outlays	79	93	61
Supplemental proposal:			
Budget Authority		5	
Outlays		1	3
Total:			
Budget Authority	88	59	44
Outlays	79	94	64

Construction projects focus on facility construction and rehabilitation, energy conservation, environmental compliance, pollution abatement and hazardous materials cleanup, seismic safety, and the repair and inspection of dams and bridges.

Funding for the Construction account is proposed as part of the third year of the Administration's facilities restoration initiative. These funds emphasize the Administration's commitment to the long-term stewardship of Federal lands and facilities.

Object Classification (in millions of dollars)

Identification code 14–1612–0–1–303	1999 actual	2000 est.	2001 est.
Direct obligations:			
Personnel compensation:			
11.1 Full-time permanent	8	9	9
11.3 Other than full-time permanent	2	2	2
11.9 Total personnel compensation	10	11	11
12.1 Civilian personnel benefits	3	3	3
21.0 Travel and transportation of persons	1	1	1
25.1 Advisory and assistance services	1	1	1
25.3 Purchases of goods and services from Government accounts	6	6	6
25.5 Research and development contracts	1		
25.7 Operation and maintenance of equipment	3	3	3
26.0 Supplies and materials	3	3	3
31.0 Equipment	7	7	7
32.0 Land and structures	38	43	43
41.0 Grants, subsidies, and contributions	6		
99.0 Subtotal, direct obligations	79	78	78
99.0 Reimbursable obligations	20	17	2
99.5 Below reporting threshold	1		
99.9 Total new obligations	100	95	80

Personnel Summary

Identification code 14–1612–0–1–303	1999 actual	2000 est.	2001 est.
Direct:			
1001 Total compensable workyears: Full-time equivalent employment	241	241	241

General and special funds—Continued

CONSTRUCTION—Continued

Personnel Summary—Continued

Identification code 14–1612–0–1–303	1999 actual	2000 est.	2001 est.
Reimbursable:			
2001 Total compensable workyears: Full-time equivalent employment	3	3	3

MULTINATIONAL SPECIES CONSERVATION FUND

For expenses necessary to carry out the African Elephant Conservation Act (16 U.S.C. 4201–4203, 4211–4213, 4221–4225, 4241–4245, and 1538), the Asian Elephant Conservation Act of 1997 ([Public Law 105–96;] 16 U.S.C. 4261–4266), and the Rhinoceros and Tiger Conservation Act of 1994 (16 U.S.C. 5301–5306), [$2,400,000] *$3,000,000*, to remain available until expended: *Provided*, That funds made available under this Act, Public Law 105–277, [and Public Law 105–83] *and hereafter in annual appropriations acts* for rhinoceros, tiger, and Asian elephant conservation programs are exempt from any sanctions imposed against any country under section 102 of the Arms Export Control Act (22 U.S.C. 2799aa–1). *(Department of the Interior and Related Agencies Appropriations Act, 2000, as enacted by section 1000(a)(3) of the Consolidated Appropriations Act, 2000 (P.L. 106–113).)*

Program and Financing (in millions of dollars)

Identification code 14–1652–0–1–303	1999 actual	2000 est.	2001 est.
Obligations by program activity:			
00.01 African Elephant	1	1	1
00.02 Asian Elephant		1	1
00.03 Rhinoceros and Tiger	1	1	1
10.00 Total new obligations (object class 41.0)	2	3	3
Budgetary resources available for obligation:			
21.40 Unobligated balance available, start of year	2	2	2
22.00 New budget authority (gross)	2	2	3
23.90 Total budgetary resources available for obligation	4	5	5
23.95 Total new obligations	−2	−3	−3
24.40 Unobligated balance available, end of year	2	2	2
New budget authority (gross), detail:			
Discretionary:			
40.00 Appropriation	2	2	3
Change in unpaid obligations:			
72.40 Unpaid obligations, start of year: Obligated balance, start of year	2	2	2
73.10 Total new obligations	2	3	3
73.20 Total outlays (gross)	−1	−3	−3
74.40 Unpaid obligations, end of year: Obligated balance, end of year	2	2	2
Outlays (gross), detail:			
86.90 Outlays from new discretionary authority	1	1	2
86.93 Outlays from new current authority		1	1
87.00 Total outlays (gross)	1	3	3
Net budget authority and outlays:			
89.00 Budget authority	2	2	3
90.00 Outlays	1	3	3

Personnel Summary

Identification code 14–1652–0–1–303	1999 actual	2000 est.	2001 est.
1001 Total compensable workyears: Full-time equivalent employment	1	1	1

African elephant conservation program.—Provides technical and financial assistance to protect African elephants and their habitats, including elephant population management, public education, and anti-poaching activities.

Rhinoceros and tiger conservation program.—Provides conservation grants to protect rhinoceros and tiger populations and their habitats within African and Asian countries.

Asian elephant conservation program.—Provides financial assistance for Asian elephant conservation projects to protect elephant populations and their habitats within 13 range countries.

COMMERCIAL SALMON FISHERY CAPACITY REDUCTION

[For the Federal share of a capacity reduction program to repurchase Washington State Fraser River Sockeye commercial fishery licenses consistent with the implementation of the "June 30, 1999, Agreement of the United States and Canada on the Treaty Between the Government of the United States and the Government of Canada Concerning Pacific Salmon, 1985", $5,000,000, to remain available until expended, and to be provided in the form of a grant directly to the State of Washington Department of Fish and Wildlife.] *(Department of the Interior and Related Agencies Appropriations Act, 2000, as enacted by section 1000(a)(3) of the Consolidated Appropriations Act, 2000 (P.L. 106–113).)*

Program and Financing (in millions of dollars)

Identification code 14–1658–0–1–302	1999 actual	2000 est.	2001 est.
Obligations by program activity:			
10.00 Total new obligations (object class 41.0)		5	
Budgetary resources available for obligation:			
22.00 New budget authority (gross)		5	
23.95 Total new obligations		−5	
New budget authority (gross), detail:			
Discretionary:			
40.00 Appropriation		5	
Change in unpaid obligations:			
73.10 Total new obligations		5	
73.20 Total outlays (gross)		−5	
Outlays (gross), detail:			
86.90 Outlays from new discretionary authority		5	
Net budget authority and outlays:			
89.00 Budget authority		5	
90.00 Outlays		5	

As part of the 1999 Pacific Salmon Treaty Agreement between the U.S. and Canada, the U.S. agreed to reduce the harvest of Fraser River salmon by the non-Indian fishing fleet. Pursuant to this agreement, the Congress provided the U.S. Fish and Wildlife Service with $5.0 million in 2000 under this account. The funds are to be awarded as a grant to the State of Washington to (1) meet the intent of the Pacific Salmon Treaty; (2) reduce the overall fleet capacity while maintaining a sustainable and economically viable fishery; and (3) provide economic relief to Washington salmon fishers.

The Fish and Wildlife Service account is not proposed for continuation in 2001. Instead, funding to implement this treaty is included in the Administration's Pacific Coastal Salmon Recovery account included in the Budget for the Department of Commerce.

NON-GAME WILDLIFE STATE GRANTS

For non-game conservation grants to the States and to the District of Columbia, Tribes, Puerto Rico, Guam, the Virgin Islands, the Northern Marianas Islands, and American Samoa (including administrative costs), under the provisions of the Fish and Wildlife Act of 1956 and the Fish and Wildlife Coordination Act for wildlife habitat and restoration initiatives and for land acquisition, $100,000,000 for Lands Legacy, to remain available until expended.

Program and Financing (in millions of dollars)

Identification code 14–1694–0–1–302	1999 actual	2000 est.	2001 est.
Obligations by program activity:			
00.01 Non-game wildlife state grants			47
00.02 Administration			3
10.00 Total new obligations			50
Budgetary resources available for obligation:			
22.00 New budget authority (gross)			100
23.95 Total new obligations			–50
24.40 Unobligated balance available, end of year			50
New budget authority (gross), detail:			
Discretionary:			
40.00 Appropriation			100
Change in unpaid obligations:			
73.10 Total new obligations			50
73.20 Total outlays (gross)			–25
74.40 Unpaid obligations, end of year: Obligated balance, end of year			25
Outlays (gross), detail:			
86.90 Outlays from new discretionary authority			25
Net budget authority and outlays:			
89.00 Budget authority			100
90.00 Outlays			25

This account provides grants to States, Tribes, and U.S. territories for non-game related habitat restoration, planning, monitoring, inventories, and recreation. Grants are also awarded to States for land acquisition.

Funding for this account is proposed as part of a new Lands Legacy discretionary spending category to provide dedicated and protected funding for the President's Lands Legacy Initiative. These funds, along with other increases, highlight the Administration's commitment to make new tools available and to work with States, Tribes, local governments, and private partners to protect great places, to conserve and restore open space for non-game related recreation and habitat, and to preserve forest, farmlands, and coastal areas for non-game species. See the Environment chapter in the Budget for a summary of the initiative.

Object Classification (in millions of dollars)

Identification code 14–1694–0–1–302	1999 actual	2000 est.	2001 est.
11.1 Personnel compensation: Full-time permanent			1
25.2 Other services			2
41.0 Grants, subsidies, and contributions			47
99.9 Total new obligations			50

Personnel Summary

Identification code 14–1694–0–1–302	1999 actual	2000 est.	2001 est.
1001 Total compensable workyears: Full-time equivalent employment			10

LAND ACQUISITION

For expenses necessary to carry out the Land and Water Conservation Fund Act of 1965, as amended (16 U.S.C. 460l–4 through 11), including administrative expenses, and for acquisition of land or waters, or interest therein, in accordance with statutory authority applicable to the United States Fish and Wildlife Service, **[**$50,513,000**]** *$111,632,000 for Lands Legacy,* to be derived from the Land and Water Conservation Fund **[**and**]**, to remain available until expended. *(Department of the Interior and Related Agencies Appropriations Act, 2000, as enacted by section 1000(a)(3) of the Consolidated Appropriations Act, 2000 (P.L. 106–113).)*

Program and Financing (in millions of dollars)

Identification code 14–5020–0–2–303	1999 actual	2000 est.	2001 est.
Obligations by program activity:			
00.01 Acquisition management	9	9	10
00.02 Emergencies and hardships	1	1	2
00.03 Exchanges	1	1	1
00.04 Inholdings	1	1	4
00.05 Federal refuges	49	40	71
01.00 total, direct program	61	52	88
09.00 Reimbursable program	50	33	10
10.00 Total new obligations	111	85	98
Budgetary resources available for obligation:			
21.40 Unobligated balance available, start of year	64	74	43
22.00 New budget authority (gross)	121	54	112
22.10 Resources available from recoveries of prior year obligations	1		
23.90 Total budgetary resources available for obligation	186	128	155
23.95 Total new obligations	–111	–85	–98
24.40 Unobligated balance available, end of year	74	43	59
New budget authority (gross), detail:			
Discretionary:			
Appropriation (special fund, definite):			
40.20 Appropriation (special fund, definite)	48	51	112
40.20 Appropriation (special fund, definite)		1	
43.00 Appropriation (total discretionary)	48	52	112
Spending authority from offsetting collections:			
68.00 Offsetting collections (cash)	85	2	
68.10 From Federal sources: Change in receivables and unpaid, unfilled orders	–12		
68.90 Spending authority from offsetting collections (total discretionary)	73	2	
70.00 Total new budget authority (gross)	121	54	112
Change in unpaid obligations:			
Unpaid obligations, start of year:			
72.40 Obligated balance, start of year	6	24	24
72.95 From Federal sources: Receivables and unpaid, unfilled orders	19	7	7
72.99 Total unpaid obligations, start of year	25	31	31
73.10 Total new obligations	111	85	98
73.20 Total outlays (gross)	–104	–85	–86
73.45 Adjustments in unexpired accounts	–1		
Unpaid obligations, end of year:			
74.40 Obligated balance, end of year	24	24	35
74.95 From Federal sources: Receivables and unpaid, unfilled orders	7	7	7
74.99 Total unpaid obligations, end of year	31	31	42
Outlays (gross), detail:			
86.90 Outlays from new discretionary authority	66	24	50
86.93 Outlays from discretionary balances	38	60	36
87.00 Total outlays (gross)	104	85	86
Offsets:			
Against gross budget authority and outlays:			
88.00 Offsetting collections (cash) from: Federal sources	–85	–2	
Against gross budget authority only:			
88.95 From Federal sources: Change in receivables and unpaid, unfilled orders	12		
Net budget authority and outlays:			
89.00 Budget authority	48	52	112
90.00 Outlays	19	83	86

These funds are used to acquire areas which have native fish and/or wildlife values and provide natural resource benefits over a broad geographical area, and for acquisition management activities.

Funding for this account is proposed as part of a new Lands Legacy discretionary spending category to provide dedicated and protected funding for the President's Lands Legacy Initia-

General and special funds—Continued

LAND ACQUISITION—Continued

tive. These funds, along with increases in other accounts, highlight the Administration's commitment to making new tools available, and working with States, Tribes, local governments and private partners to protect great places; conserve open space for recreation and wildlife habitat; and preserve forest, farmlands, and coastal programs. See the Environment chapter in the Budget for a summary of the Initiative.

PERFORMANCE MEASURES

	1999 actual	2000 est.	2001 est.
Number of acres acquired	312,182	255,000	255,000

Object Classification (in millions of dollars)

Identification code 14–5020–0–2–303		1999 actual	2000 est.	2001 est.
	Direct obligations:			
11.1	Personnel compensation: Full-time permanent	7	7	8
12.1	Civilian personnel benefits	2	2	3
21.0	Travel and transportation of persons	1	1	1
23.1	Rental payments to GSA	1	1	1
23.3	Communications, utilities, and miscellaneous charges	1	1	1
25.2	Other services	3	3	3
31.0	Equipment	1	1	1
32.0	Land and structures	44	35	72
41.0	Grants, subsidies, and contributions	1		
99.0	Subtotal, direct obligations	61	51	90
99.0	Reimbursable obligations	50	32	8
99.5	Below reporting threshold		2	
99.9	Total new obligations	111	85	98

Personnel Summary

Identification code 14–5020–0–2–303		1999 actual	2000 est.	2001 est.
	Direct:			
1001	Total compensable workyears: Full-time equivalent employment	135	135	135
	Reimbursable:			
2001	Total compensable workyears: Full-time equivalent employment	47	8	8

WILDLIFE CONSERVATION AND APPRECIATION FUND

For necessary expenses of the Wildlife Conservation and Appreciation Fund, $800,000, to remain available until expended. *(Department of the Interior and Related Agencies Appropriations Act, 2000, as enacted by section 1000(a)(3) of the Consolidated Appropriations Act, 2000 (P.L. 106–113).)*

Program and Financing (in millions of dollars)

Identification code 14–5150–0–2–303		1999 actual	2000 est.	2001 est.
	Obligations by program activity:			
10.00	Total new obligations (object class 41.0)	1	1	1
	Budgetary resources available for obligation:			
21.40	Unobligated balance available, start of year	1	1	1
22.00	New budget authority (gross)	1	1	1
23.90	Total budgetary resources available for obligation	2	2	2
23.95	Total new obligations	−1	−1	−1
24.40	Unobligated balance available, end of year	1	1	1
	New budget authority (gross), detail:			
	Discretionary:			
40.00	Appropriation	1	1	1
	Change in unpaid obligations:			
72.40	Unpaid obligations, start of year: Obligated balance, start of year	2	2	2
73.10	Total new obligations	1	1	1
73.20	Total outlays (gross)	−1	−1	−1
74.40	Unpaid obligations, end of year: Obligated balance, end of year	2	2	2
	Outlays (gross), detail:			
86.90	Outlays from new discretionary authority	1	1	1
	Net budget authority and outlays:			
89.00	Budget authority	1	1	1
90.00	Outlays	1	1	1

The Partnerships for Wildlife Act (16 U.S.C. 3741), authorizes wildlife conservation and appreciation projects to conserve fish and wildlife species and to provide opportunities for the public to enjoy these species through nonconsumptive activities. Grants to States are directed toward nonconsumptive activities and the conservation of species not taken for recreation, fur, or food; not listed as endangered or threatened under the Endangered Species Act of 1973; and not defined as marine mammals under the Marine Mammal Protection Act of 1972. Funding from appropriations is made available to the extent external matching funds are applied to the projects.

Personnel Summary

Identification code 14–5150–0–2–303		1999 actual	2000 est.	2001 est.
1001	Total compensable workyears: Full-time equivalent employment	1	1	1

MIGRATORY BIRD CONSERVATION ACCOUNT

Unavailable Collections (in millions of dollars)

Identification code 14–5137–0–2–303		1999 actual	2000 est.	2001 est.
	Balance, start of year:			
01.99	Balance, start of year			
	Receipts:			
02.01	Migratory bird hunting stamps	25	25	25
02.02	Custom duties on arms and ammunition	40	17	17
02.99	Total receipts	65	42	42
	Appropriation:			
05.01	Migratory bird conservation account	−65	−42	−42
07.99	Total balance, end of year			

Program and Financing (in millions of dollars)

Identification code 14–5137–0–2–303		1999 actual	2000 est.	2001 est.
	Obligations by program activity:			
00.01	Printing and sale of duck stamps	1	1	1
00.02	Duck stamp promotion	1		
00.03	Acquisition of refuges and other areas	51	43	43
10.00	Total new obligations	53	44	44
	Budgetary resources available for obligation:			
21.40	Unobligated balance available, start of year	6	22	22
22.00	New budget authority (gross)	65	42	42
22.10	Resources available from recoveries of prior year obligations	3		
23.90	Total budgetary resources available for obligation	74	64	64
23.95	Total new obligations	−53	−44	−44
24.40	Unobligated balance available, end of year	22	22	20
	New budget authority (gross), detail:			
	Mandatory:			
60.25	Appropriation (special fund, indefinite)	65	42	42
	Change in unpaid obligations:			
72.40	Unpaid obligations, start of year: Obligated balance, start of year	20	16	11
73.10	Total new obligations	53	44	44
73.20	Total outlays (gross)	−54	−49	−42
73.45	Adjustments in unexpired accounts	−3		

74.40 Unpaid obligations, end of year: Obligated balance, end of year	16	11	13
Outlays (gross), detail:			
86.97 Outlays from new mandatory authority	46	30	30
86.98 Outlays from mandatory balances	9	19	12
87.00 Total outlays (gross)	54	49	42
Net budget authority and outlays:			
89.00 Budget authority	65	42	42
90.00 Outlays	54	49	42

The following funds are available for the costs of locating and acquiring migratory bird refuges and waterfowl production areas: receipts in excess of Postal Service expenses from the sale of migratory bird hunting and conservation stamps; 70 percent of entrance fee collections on national wildlife refuges, excepting national wildlife refuges participating in the Recreational Fee Demonstration Program that may retain additional fee collections for operational and maintenance improvements; and import duties on arms and ammunition. The Migratory Bird Hunting and Conservation Stamp Promotion Act authorizes up to $1 million of Duck Stamp receipts to be used annually for stamp sales promotion through fiscal year 2003.

Object Classification (in millions of dollars)

Identification code 14–5137–0–2–303	1999 actual	2000 est.	2001 est.
11.1 Personnel compensation: Full-time permanent	5	5	5
12.1 Civilian personnel benefits	1	1	1
23.3 Communications, utilities, and miscellaneous charges	1	1	1
25.2 Other services	3	3	3
31.0 Equipment	1	1	1
32.0 Land and structures	41	31	31
99.0 Subtotal, direct obligations	52	42	42
99.5 Below reporting threshold	1	2	2
99.9 Total new obligations	53	44	44

Personnel Summary

Identification code 14–5137–0–2–303	1999 actual	2000 est.	2001 est.
1001 Total compensable workyears: Full-time equivalent employment	96	96	96

NORTH AMERICAN WETLANDS CONSERVATION FUND

For expenses necessary to carry out the provisions of the North American Wetlands Conservation Act, Public Law 101–233, as amended, [$15,000,000] *$30,000,000 for Lands Legacy*, to remain available until expended. *(Department of the Interior and Related Agencies Appropriations Act, 2000, as enacted by section 1000(a)(3) of the Consolidated Appropriations Act, 2000 (P.L. 106–113).)*

Unavailable Collections (in millions of dollars)

Identification code 14–5241–0–2–303	1999 actual	2000 est.	2001 est.
Balance, start of year:			
01.99 Balance, start of year	4	1	
Receipts:			
02.01 Fines, penalties, and forfeitures from Migratory Bird Treaty Act	1		
04.00 Total: Balances and collections	5	1	
Appropriation:			
05.01 North American wetlands conservation fund	−4	−1	−1
07.99 Total balance, end of year	1		

Program and Financing (in millions of dollars)

Identification code 14–5241–0–2–303	1999 actual	2000 est.	2001 est.
Obligations by program activity:			
00.01 Wetlands conservation projects	10	23	29
00.02 Administration	1	1	1
10.00 Total new obligations	11	24	30
Budgetary resources available for obligation:			
21.40 Unobligated balance available, start of year	2	12	3
22.00 New budget authority (gross)	19	16	31
22.10 Resources available from recoveries of prior year obligations	1		
23.90 Total budgetary resources available for obligation	22	28	34
23.95 Total new obligations	−11	−24	−30
24.40 Unobligated balance available, end of year	12	3	4
New budget authority (gross), detail:			
Discretionary:			
40.00 Appropriation	15	15	30
Mandatory:			
60.25 Appropriation (special fund, indefinite)	4	1	1
70.00 Total new budget authority (gross)	19	16	31
Change in unpaid obligations:			
72.40 Unpaid obligations, start of year: Obligated balance, start of year	33	28	36
73.10 Total new obligations	11	24	30
73.20 Total outlays (gross)	−14	−17	−27
73.45 Adjustments in unexpired accounts	−1		
74.40 Unpaid obligations, end of year: Obligated balance, end of year	28	36	39
Outlays (gross), detail:			
86.90 Outlays from new discretionary authority	11	11	21
86.93 Outlays from discretionary balances		5	5
86.97 Outlays from new mandatory authority	3	1	1
86.98 Outlays from mandatory balances		1	
87.00 Total outlays (gross)	14	17	27
Net budget authority and outlays:			
89.00 Budget authority	19	16	31
90.00 Outlays	14	17	27

Funds deposited into this account include direct appropriations and fines, penalties, and forfeitures collected under the authority of the Migratory Bird Treaty Act (16 U.S.C. 707) and interest on obligations held in the Federal Aid in Wildlife Restoration Fund. The North American Wetlands Conservation Fund supports wetlands conservation projects approved by the Migratory Bird Conservation Commission. A portion of receipts to the Sport Fish Restoration Account is also available for coastal wetlands conservation projects. In the general provisions section for the Corps of Engineers, the Budget includes proposed appropriations language to extend the authorization for spending these receipts through 2001.

These projects help fulfill the habitat protection, restoration and enhancement goals of the North American Waterfowl Management Plan and the Tripartite Agreement among Mexico, Canada and the United States. These projects may involve partnerships with public agencies and private entities, with non-Federal matching contributions, for the long-term conservation of habitat for migratory birds and other fish and wildlife, including species that are listed, or are candidates to be listed, under the Endangered Species Act (16 U.S.C. 1531).

Wetlands conservation projects include the obtaining of a real property interest in lands or waters, including water rights; the restoration, management or enhancement of habitat; and training and development for conservation management in Mexico. Funding may be provided for assistance for wetlands conservation projects in Canada or Mexico.

Funding for this account is proposed as part of a new Lands Legacy discretionary spending category to provide dedicated and protected funding for the President's Lands Legacy Initiative. These funds, along with increases in other accounts, highlight the Administration's commitment to making new tools available, and working with state, tribes, local governments, and private partners to protect great places; conserve

General and special funds—Continued

NORTH AMERICAN WETLANDS CONSERVATION FUND—Continued

open spaces for recreation and wildlife habitat; and preserve forest, farmlands, and coastal areas. See the Environment chapter in the Budget for a summary of the Initiative.

Object Classification (in millions of dollars)

Identification code 14–5241–0–2–303	1999 actual	2000 est.	2001 est.
11.1 Personnel compensation: Full-time permanent	1	1	1
32.0 Land and structures	1	1	1
41.0 Grants, subsidies, and contributions	9	22	27
99.0 Subtotal, direct obligations	11	24	29
99.5 Below reporting threshold			1
99.9 Total new obligations	11	24	30

Personnel Summary

Identification code 14–5241–0–2–303	1999 actual	2000 est.	2001 est.
1001 Total compensable workyears: Full-time equivalent employment	9	9	18

COOPERATIVE ENDANGERED SPECIES CONSERVATION FUND

For expenses necessary to carry out the provisions of the Endangered Species Act of 1973 (16 U.S.C. 1531–1543), as amended, [$23,000,000] *$65,000,000 for Lands Legacy*, to be derived from the Cooperative Endangered Species Conservation Fund, and to remain available until expended. *(Department of the Interior and Related Agencies Appropriations Act, 2000, as enacted by section 1000(a)(3) of the Consolidated Appropriations Act, 2000 (P.L. 106–113).)*

Unavailable Collections (in millions of dollars)

Identification code 14–5143–0–2–303	1999 actual	2000 est.	2001 est.
Balance, start of year:			
01.99 Balance, start of year	151	166	176
Receipts:			
02.01 Payment from the general fund	29	33	32
04.00 Total: Balances and collections	180	199	208
Appropriation:			
05.01 Cooperative endangered species conservation fund	−14	−23	−65
07.99 Total balance, end of year	166	176	143

Program and Financing (in millions of dollars)

Identification code 14–5143–0–2–303	1999 actual	2000 est.	2001 est.
Obligations by program activity:			
00.01 Grants to States	6	8	41
00.02 Grants to States/Land acquisition/HCPs	5	14	18
00.03 Conservation Planning Assistance			2
00.04 Administration	1		1
00.05 Payment to special fund unavailable receipt account	29	32	30
10.00 Total new obligations	41	55	92
Budgetary resources available for obligation:			
21.40 Unobligated balance available, start of year	1	6	7
22.00 New budget authority (gross)	43	55	95
22.10 Resources available from recoveries of prior year obligations	3		
23.90 Total budgetary resources available for obligation	47	61	102
23.95 Total new obligations	−41	−55	−92
24.40 Unobligated balance available, end of year	6	7	10
New budget authority (gross), detail:			
Discretionary:			
40.20 Appropriation (special fund, definite)	14	23	65
Mandatory:			
60.00 Appropriation	29	32	30
70.00 Total new budget authority (gross)	43	55	95
Change in unpaid obligations:			
72.40 Unpaid obligations, start of year: Obligated balance, start of year	19	19	26
73.10 Total new obligations	41	55	92
73.20 Total outlays (gross)	−38	−48	−55
73.45 Adjustments in unexpired accounts	−3		
74.40 Unpaid obligations, end of year: Obligated balance, end of year	19	26	65
Outlays (gross), detail:			
86.90 Outlays from new discretionary authority	1	2	7
86.93 Outlays from discretionary balances	8	13	16
86.97 Outlays from new mandatory authority	29	32	30
87.00 Total outlays (gross)	38	48	55
Net budget authority and outlays:			
89.00 Budget authority	43	55	95
90.00 Outlays	38	48	55

The Cooperative Endangered Species Conservation Fund provides grants to States and U.S. territories for conservation, recovery, and monitoring projects for species that are listed, or species that are candidates for listing, as threatened or endangered. Grants are also awarded to States for land acquisition in support of Habitat Conservation Plans and species recovery efforts in partnership with local governments and other interested parties to protect species while allowing development to continue. The Fund is partially financed by permanent appropriations from the General Fund of the U.S. Treasury in an amount equal to 5 percent of receipts deposited to the Federal aid in wildlife and sport fish restoration accounts and amounts equal to Lacey Act receipts over $500,000. The actual amount available for grants is subject to annual appropriations.

Funding for this account is proposed as part of a new Lands Legacy discretionary spending category to provide dedicated and protected funding for the President's Lands Legacy Initiative. These funds along with increases in other accounts highlight the Administration's commitment to making new tools available, and working with states, tribes, local governments and private partners to protect great places; conserve open spaces for recreation and wildlife habitat; and preserve forest, farmlands, and coastal areas. See the Environment chapter in the Budget for a summary of the Initiative.

Object Classification (in millions of dollars)

Identification code 14–5143–0–2–303	1999 actual	2000 est.	2001 est.
11.1 Personnel compensation: Full-time permanent			1
41.0 Grants, subsidies, and contributions	11	22	59
92.0 Undistributed	29	32	30
99.0 Subtotal, direct obligations	40	54	90
99.5 Below reporting threshold	1	1	2
99.9 Total new obligations	41	55	92

Personnel Summary

Identification code 14–5143–0–2–303	1999 actual	2000 est.	2001 est.
1001 Total compensable workyears: Full-time equivalent employment	6	6	28

NATIONAL WILDLIFE REFUGE FUND

For expenses necessary to implement the Act of October 17, 1978 (16 U.S.C. 715s), [$10,779,000] *$10,000,000. (Department of the Interior and Related Agencies Appropriations Act, 2000, as enacted by section 1000(a)(3) of the Consolidated Appropriations Act, 2000 (P.L. 106–113).)*

Unavailable Collections (in millions of dollars)

Identification code 14–5091–0–2–806	1999 actual	2000 est.	2001 est.
Balance, start of year:			
01.99 Balance, start of year	....	....	....
Receipts:			
02.01 National wildlife refuge fund	8	9	9
Appropriation:			
05.01 National wildlife refuge fund	−8	−9	−9
07.99 Total balance, end of year	....	....	....

Program and Financing (in millions of dollars)

Identification code 14–5091–0–2–806	1999 actual	2000 est.	2001 est.
Obligations by program activity:			
00.01 Expenses for sales	2	3	3
00.03 Payments to counties	17	16	16
10.00 Total new obligations	19	19	19
Budgetary resources available for obligation:			
21.40 Unobligated balance available, start of year	6	6	6
22.00 New budget authority (gross)	19	20	19
23.90 Total budgetary resources available for obligation	25	26	25
23.95 Total new obligations	−19	−19	−19
24.40 Unobligated balance available, end of year	6	6	6
New budget authority (gross), detail:			
Discretionary:			
40.00 Appropriation (general fund)	11	11	10
Mandatory:			
60.25 Appropriation (special fund, indefinite)	8	9	9
70.00 Total new budget authority (gross)	19	20	19
Change in unpaid obligations:			
73.10 Total new obligations	19	19	19
73.20 Total outlays (gross)	−19	−19	−19
Outlays (gross), detail:			
86.90 Outlays from new discretionary authority	11	11	10
86.97 Outlays from new mandatory authority	2	3	3
86.98 Outlays from mandatory balances	6	6	6
87.00 Total outlays (gross)	19	19	19
Net budget authority and outlays:			
89.00 Budget authority	19	20	19
90.00 Outlays	19	19	19

The Refuge Revenue Sharing Act (16 U.S.C. 715s) authorizes revenues through the sale of products from Service lands, less expenses for producing revenue and activities related to revenue sharing. The Fish and Wildlife Service makes payments to counties in which Service lands are located. If the net revenues are insufficient to make full payments according to the formula contained in the Act, direct appropriations are authorized to make up the difference.

Object Classification (in millions of dollars)

Identification code 14–5091–0–2–806	1999 actual	2000 est.	2001 est.
11.1 Personnel compensation: Full-time permanent	....	....	1
41.0 Grants, subsidies, and contributions	17	17	16
99.0 Subtotal, direct obligations	18	18	17
99.5 Below reporting threshold	1	1	2
99.9 Total new obligations	19	19	19

Personnel Summary

Identification code 14–5091–0–2–806	1999 actual	2000 est.	2001 est.
1001 Total compensable workyears: Full-time equivalent employment	30	30	30

RECREATIONAL FEE DEMONSTRATION PROGRAM

Unavailable Collections (in millions of dollars)

Identification code 14–5252–0–2–303	1999 actual	2000 est.	2001 est.
Balance, start of year:			
01.99 Balance, start of year	....	....	....
Receipts:			
02.01 Recreational fee demonstration program, FWS	3	4	4
Appropriation:			
05.01 Recreational fee demonstration program	−3	−4	−4
07.99 Total balance, end of year	....	....	....

Program and Financing (in millions of dollars)

Identification code 14–5252–0–2–303	1999 actual	2000 est.	2001 est.
Obligations by program activity:			
10.00 Total new obligations	3	4	4
Budgetary resources available for obligation:			
21.40 Unobligated balance available, start of year	2	3	3
22.00 New budget authority (gross)	3	4	4
23.90 Total budgetary resources available for obligation	5	7	7
23.95 Total new obligations	−3	−4	−4
24.40 Unobligated balance available, end of year	3	3	3
New budget authority (gross), detail:			
Mandatory:			
60.25 Appropriation (special fund, indefinite)	3	4	4
Change in unpaid obligations:			
72.40 Unpaid obligations, start of year: Obligated balance, start of year	....	1	....
73.10 Total new obligations	3	4	4
73.20 Total outlays (gross)	−2	−4	−4
74.40 Unpaid obligations, end of year: Obligated balance, end of year	1	....	....
Outlays (gross), detail:			
86.97 Outlays from new mandatory authority	2	3	3
86.98 Outlays from mandatory balances	....	1	1
87.00 Total outlays (gross)	2	4	4
Net budget authority and outlays:			
89.00 Budget authority	3	4	4
90.00 Outlays	2	4	4

In 1997, the U.S. Fish and Wildlife Service initiated the recreational fee demonstration program at selected refuges and other public sites. Entrance fees and other user receipts collected at sites are deposited into the Recreational fee demonstration program account.

The fee program demonstrates the feasibility of user-generated cost recovery for the operation and maintenance of recreation areas or sites and habitat enhancement projects on Federal lands. Fees are used primarily at the site to improve visitor access, enhance public safety and security, address backlogged maintenance needs, and meet other operational needs. Congress has extended this demonstration program through 2001.

Object Classification (in millions of dollars)

Identification code 14–5252–0–2–303	1999 actual	2000 est.	2001 est.
11.3 Personnel compensation: Other than full-time permanent	1	1	1
25.2 Other services	....	1	1
25.7 Operation and maintenance of equipment	....	1	1
26.0 Supplies and materials	....	1	1
99.0 Subtotal, direct obligations	1	4	4
99.5 Below reporting threshold	2	....	....
99.9 Total new obligations	3	4	4

General and special funds—Continued

RECREATIONAL FEE DEMONSTRATION PROGRAM—Continued

Personnel Summary

Identification code 14–5252–0–2–303	1999 actual	2000 est.	2001 est.
1001 Total compensable workyears: Full-time equivalent employment	29	29	29

FEDERAL AID IN WILDLIFE RESTORATION

Unavailable Collections (in millions of dollars)

Identification code 14–5029–0–2–303	1999 actual	2000 est.	2001 est.
Balance, start of year:			
01.99 Balance, start of year	180	207	215
Receipts:			
02.01 Receipts	19	21	23
02.02 Excise taxes, Federal aid to wildlife restoration fund	207	215	224
02.99 Total receipts	226	236	247
04.00 Total: Balances and collections	406	443	462
Appropriation:			
05.01 Federal aid in wildlife restoration	−199	−228	−237
05.99 Subtotal appropriation	−199	−228	−237
07.99 Total balance, end of year	207	215	225

Program and Financing (in millions of dollars)

Identification code 14–5029–0–2–303	1999 actual	2000 est.	2001 est.
Obligations by program activity:			
00.02 Federal aid in wildlife restoration	215	207	214
00.04 Interest on investments North American wetlands conservation	28	21	23
10.00 Total new obligations	243	228	237
Budgetary resources available for obligation:			
21.40 Unobligated balance available, start of year	60	41	41
22.00 New budget authority (gross)	199	228	237
22.10 Resources available from recoveries of prior year obligations	26		
23.90 Total budgetary resources available for obligation	285	269	278
23.95 Total new obligations	−243	−228	−237
24.40 Unobligated balance available, end of year	41	41	41
New budget authority (gross), detail:			
Mandatory:			
60.25 Appropriation (special fund, indefinite)	19	21	23
60.28 Appropriation (unavailable balances)	180	207	214
62.50 Appropriation (total mandatory)	199	228	237
Change in unpaid obligations:			
72.40 Unpaid obligations, start of year: Obligated balance, start of year	184	188	214
73.10 Total new obligations	243	228	237
73.20 Total outlays (gross)	−212	−202	−209
73.45 Adjustments in unexpired accounts	−26		
74.40 Unpaid obligations, end of year: Obligated balance, end of year	188	214	242
Outlays (gross), detail:			
86.97 Outlays from new mandatory authority	30	30	31
86.98 Outlays from mandatory balances	183	172	177
87.00 Total outlays (gross)	212	202	209
Net budget authority and outlays:			
89.00 Budget authority	199	228	237
90.00 Outlays	213	202	209
Memorandum (non-add) entries:			
92.01 Total investments, start of year: U.S. securities: Par value	417	427	439
92.02 Total investments, end of year: U.S. securities: Par value	427	439	451

The Federal Aid in Wildlife Restoration Act, popularly known as the Pittman-Robertson Act, created a program to fund the selection, restoration, rehabilitation and improvement of wildlife habitat, and wildlife management research. Under the program research Under the program, States, Puerto Rico, Guam, the Virgin Islands, American Samoa, and the Northern Mariana Islands are allocated funds from the 11 percent excise tax on sporting arms and ammunition, the 10 percent excise tax on handguns, and the 11 percent tax on certain archery equipment. States are reimbursed up to 75 percent of the cost of approved wildlife and hunter education projects.

Object Classification (in millions of dollars)

Identification code 14–5029–0–2–303	1999 actual	2000 est.	2001 est.
11.1 Personnel compensation: Full-time permanent	4	4	4
12.1 Civilian personnel benefits	1	1	1
21.0 Travel and transportation of persons	1	1	1
23.3 Communications, utilities, and miscellaneous charges	1	1	1
25.2 Other services	3	3	3
25.5 Research and development contracts	1	1	1
31.0 Equipment	1	1	1
41.0 Grants, subsidies, and contributions	229	216	225
99.0 Subtotal, direct obligations	241	228	237
99.5 Below reporting threshold	2		
99.9 Total new obligations	243	228	237

Personnel Summary

Identification code 14–5029–0–2–303	1999 actual	2000 est.	2001 est.
1001 Total compensable workyears: Full-time equivalent employment	73	73	73

MISCELLANEOUS PERMANENT APPROPRIATIONS

Unavailable Collections (in millions of dollars)

Identification code 14–9927–0–2–303	1999 actual	2000 est.	2001 est.
Balance, start of year:			
01.99 Balance, start of year			
Receipts:			
02.01 Rents and charges for quarters, U.S. Fish and Wildlife Service	2	2	2
Appropriation:			
05.01 Miscellaneous permanent appropriations, U.S. Fish and Wildlife Service	−2	−2	−2
07.99 Total balance, end of year			

Program and Financing (in millions of dollars)

Identification code 14–9927–0–2–303	1999 actual	2000 est.	2001 est.
Obligations by program activity:			
10.00 Total new obligations	2	2	2
Budgetary resources available for obligation:			
21.40 Unobligated balance available, start of year	3	3	3
22.00 New budget authority (gross)	2	2	2
23.90 Total budgetary resources available for obligation	5	5	5
23.95 Total new obligations	−2	−2	−2
24.40 Unobligated balance available, end of year	3	3	3
New budget authority (gross), detail:			
Mandatory:			
60.25 Appropriation (special fund, indefinite)	2	2	2
Change in unpaid obligations:			
72.40 Unpaid obligations, start of year: Obligated balance, start of year	1		

73.10	Total new obligations	2	2	2
73.20	Total outlays (gross)	−2	−2	−2
	Outlays (gross), detail:			
86.97	Outlays from new mandatory authority	2	1	1
86.98	Outlays from mandatory balances	2	1	1
87.00	Total outlays (gross)	2	2	2
	Net budget authority and outlays:			
89.00	Budget authority	2	2	2
90.00	Outlays	2	2	2

Operation and maintenance of quarters.—Revenue from rental of government quarters is deposited in this account for use in the operation and maintenance of such quarters for the Fish and Wildlife Service, pursuant to Public Law 98–473, Section 320.

Proceeds from sales, water resources development projects.—Receipts collected from the sale of timber and crops from refuges leased or licensed from the Department of the Army may be used to pay the costs of production of the timber and crops and for managing wildlife habitat.

Lahontan Valley and Pyramid Lake Fish and Wildlife Fund.—Under the Truckee-Carson Pyramid Lake Settlement Act of 1990, the Lahontan Valley and Pyramid Lake Fish and Wildlife Fund receives revenues from non-federal parties to support the restoration and enhancement of wetlands in the Lahontan Valley and to restore and protect Pyramid Lake fisheries. Payments made in excess of operation and maintenance costs of the Stampede Reservoir are available without further appropriations. Donations made for express purposes, state cost-sharing funds, and unexpended interest from the Pyramid Lake Paiute Fisheries Fund are available without further appropriation. The Secretary is also authorized to deposit proceeds from the sale of certain lands, interests in lands, and water rights into the Pyramid Lake Fish and Wildlife Fund.

Federal aid in fish restoration.—Includes unobligated balances from the predecessor account to Sport Fish Restoration.

Object Classification (in millions of dollars)

Identification code 14–9927–0–2–303		1999 actual	2000 est.	2001 est.
25.4	Operation and maintenance of facilities	1	1	1
26.0	Supplies and materials	1	1	1
99.9	Total new obligations	2	2	2

Personnel Summary

Identification code 14–9927–0–2–303		1999 actual	2000 est.	2001 est.
1001	Total compensable workyears: Full-time equivalent employment	6	6	6

Trust Funds

SPORT FISH RESTORATION

Program and Financing (in millions of dollars)

Identification code 14–8151–0–7–303		1999 actual	2000 est.	2001 est.
	Obligations by program activity:			
00.01	Payments to States for sport fish restoration	272	244	230
00.03	North American Wetlands Conservation Grants	8	11	11
00.04	Coastal Wetlands Conservation Grants	9	11	11
00.05	Clean Vessel Act- Pumpout Stations Grants	9	10	10
00.06	Administration	17	16	15
00.07	National Communication & Outreach	1	6	7
00.08	Non-trailerable Recreational Vessel Access		8	8
10.00	Total new obligations	316	306	292
	Budgetary resources available for obligation:			
21.40	Unobligated balance available, start of year	98	92	93
22.00	New budget authority (gross)	279	306	292
22.10	Resources available from recoveries of prior year obligations	31		
23.90	Total budgetary resources available for obligation	408	398	385
23.95	Total new obligations	−316	−306	−292
24.40	Unobligated balance available, end of year	92	93	93
	New budget authority (gross), detail:			
	Mandatory:			
60.27	Appropriation (trust fund, indefinite)	372	423	407
61.00	Transferred to other accounts	−93	−117	−115
62.50	Appropriation (total mandatory)	279	306	292
	Change in unpaid obligations:			
72.40	Unpaid obligations, start of year: Obligated balance, start of year	265	293	306
73.10	Total new obligations	316	306	292
73.20	Total outlays (gross)	−257	−292	−293
73.45	Adjustments in unexpired accounts	−31		
74.40	Unpaid obligations, end of year: Obligated balance, end of year	293	306	305
	Outlays (gross), detail:			
86.97	Outlays from new mandatory authority	78	92	87
86.98	Outlays from mandatory balances	179	200	206
87.00	Total outlays (gross)	257	292	293
	Net budget authority and outlays:			
89.00	Budget authority	279	306	292
90.00	Outlays	257	292	293

The Federal Aid in Sport Fish Restoration Act, commonly referred to as the Dingell-Johnson act (as modified by the Wallop-Breaux amendment) created a fishery resources, conservation, and restoration program funded by an excise tax on fishing and sporting equipment.

Since 1992 the Sport Fish Restoration Fund has supported coastal wetlands grants pursuant to the Coastal Wetlands Planning, Protection and Restoration Act (P.L. 101–646). Additional revenue from small engine fuel taxes was provided under the Surface Transportation Extension Act of 1997.

The Coastal Wetlands Planning, Protection and Restoration Act requires an amount equal to 18 percent of the total deposits into the Sport Fish Restoration Fund, or amounts collected in small engine fuels excise taxes as provided by 26 U.S.C. 9504(b), whichever is greater, to be distributed as follows: 70 percent shall be available to the Corps of Engineers for priority project and conservation planning activities; 15 percent shall be available to the Fish and Wildlife Service for coastal wetlands conservation grants; and 15 percent to the Fish and Wildlife Service for wetlands conservation projects under Section 8 of the North American Wetlands Conservation Act (P.L. 101–233). In the general provisions section for the Corps of Engineers, the Budget includes proposed appropriations language to extend the authorization for spending these receipts through 2001.

The Clean Vessel Act authorizes the Secretary of the Interior to make grants to States, in specified amounts, to carry out projects for the construction, renovation, operation, and maintenance of pumpout stations and waste reception facilities. The Sport Fish Restoration Act, as amended, provides for the transfer of funds from the Sport fish restoration account of the Aquatic Resources Trust Fund for use by the Secretary of the Interior to carry out the purposes of this Act and for use by the Secretary of Transportation for State recreational boating safety programs (46 USC 13106(a)(1)). The Sportfishing and Boating Safety Act authorizes the Secretary of the Interior to develop national and state outreach plans to promote safe fishing and boating opportunities and the conservation of aquatic resources, as well as to make grants to states for developing and maintaining facilities for certain recreational vessels.

SPORT FISH RESTORATION—Continued

Assistance is provided to States, Puerto Rico, Guam, the Virgin Islands, American Samoa, the Northern Mariana Islands, and the District of Columbia for up to 75 percent of the cost of approved projects including: research into fisheries problems, surveys and inventories of fish populations, and acquisition and improvement of fish habitat and provision of access for public use.

Object Classification (in millions of dollars)

Identification code 14–8151–0–7–303	1999 actual	2000 est.	2001 est.
11.1 Personnel compensation: Full-time permanent	5	5	6
12.1 Civilian personnel benefits	1	1	1
21.0 Travel and transportation of persons	1	1	1
23.1 Rental payments to GSA	1	1	1
23.3 Communications, utilities, and miscellaneous charges	1	1	1
25.2 Other services	3	3	3
31.0 Equipment	1	1	1
41.0 Grants, subsidies, and contributions	303	292	278
99.0 Subtotal, direct obligations	316	305	292
99.5 Below reporting threshold		1	
99.9 Total new obligations	316	306	292

Personnel Summary

Identification code 14–8151–0–7–303	1999 actual	2000 est.	2001 est.
1001 Total compensable workyears: Full-time equivalent employment	86	86	86

CONTRIBUTED FUNDS

Unavailable Collections (in millions of dollars)

Identification code 14–8216–0–7–303	1999 actual	2000 est.	2001 est.
Balance, start of year:			
01.99 Balance, start of year			
Receipts:			
02.01 Deposits, contributed funds, U.S. Fish and Wildlife Service	6	4	4
Appropriation:			
05.01 Contributed funds, U.S. Fish and Wildlife Service	−6	−4	−4
07.99 Total balance, end of year			

Program and Financing (in millions of dollars)

Identification code 14–8216–0–7–303	1999 actual	2000 est.	2001 est.
Obligations by program activity:			
10.00 Total new obligations	4	5	5
Budgetary resources available for obligation:			
21.40 Unobligated balance available, start of year	5	7	6
22.00 New budget authority (gross)	6	4	4
23.90 Total budgetary resources available for obligation	11	11	10
23.95 Total new obligations	−4	−5	−5
24.40 Unobligated balance available, end of year	7	6	5
New budget authority (gross), detail:			
Mandatory:			
60.27 Appropriation (trust fund, indefinite)	6	4	4
Change in unpaid obligations:			
72.40 Unpaid obligations, start of year: Obligated balance, start of year	1	1	1
73.10 Total new obligations	4	5	5
73.20 Total outlays (gross)	−5	−5	−4
74.40 Unpaid obligations, end of year: Obligated balance, end of year	1	1	1
Outlays (gross), detail:			
86.97 Outlays from new mandatory authority	1	1	1
86.98 Outlays from mandatory balances	3	3	3
87.00 Total outlays (gross)	5	5	4
Net budget authority and outlays:			
89.00 Budget authority	6	4	4
90.00 Outlays	5	5	4

Donated funds support activities such as endangered species projects, and refuge operations and maintenance.

Object Classification (in millions of dollars)

Identification code 14–8216–0–7–303	1999 actual	2000 est.	2001 est.
25.2 Other services	1	1	1
26.0 Supplies and materials	1	1	1
32.0 Land and structures	1	1	1
41.0 Grants, subsidies, and contributions	1	1	1
99.0 Subtotal, direct obligations	4	4	4
99.5 Below reporting threshold		1	1
99.9 Total new obligations	4	5	5

Personnel Summary

Identification code 14–8216–0–7–303	1999 actual	2000 est.	2001 est.
1001 Total compensable workyears: Full-time equivalent employment	17	17	17

ALLOCATIONS RECEIVED FROM OTHER ACCOUNTS

Note.—Obligations incurred under allocations from other accounts are included in the schedule of the parent appropriation as follows:

The Department of the Interior: Bureau of Land Management: "Wildland Fire Management".

The Department of the Interior: Bureau of Land Management, "Central Hazardous Materials Fund".

The Department of Agriculture: Forest Service: "Forest Pest Management".

The General Services Administration: "Federal Buildings Fund".

The General Services Administration: "Real Property Relocation".

The Department of Labor, Employment and Training Administration: "Training and Employment Services".

The Department of Transportation: Federal Highway Administration: "Federal-Aid Highways."

ADMINISTRATIVE PROVISIONS

Appropriations and funds available to the United States Fish and Wildlife Service shall be available for purchase of not to exceed [70] *79* passenger motor vehicles, of which [61] *72* are for replacement only (including [36] *41* for police-type use); repair of damage to public roads within and adjacent to reservation areas caused by operations of the Service; options for the purchase of land at not to exceed $1 for each option; facilities incident to such public recreational uses on conservation areas as are consistent with their primary purpose; and the maintenance and improvement of aquaria, buildings, and other facilities under the jurisdiction of the Service and to which the United States has title, and which are used pursuant to law in connection with management and investigation of fish and wildlife resources: *Provided*, That notwithstanding 44 U.S.C. 501, the Service may, under cooperative cost sharing and partnership arrangements authorized by law, procure printing services from cooperators in connection with jointly produced publications for which the cooperators share at least one-half the cost of printing either in cash or services and the Service determines the cooperator is capable of meeting accepted quality standards: *Provided further*, That the Service may accept donated aircraft as replacements for existing aircraft: [*Provided further*, That notwithstanding any other provision of law, the Secretary of the Interior may not spend any of the funds appropriated in this Act for the purchase of lands or interests in lands to be used in the establishment of any new unit of the National Wildlife Refuge System unless the purchase is approved in advance by the House and Senate Committees on Appropriations in compliance with the reprogramming procedures contained in Senate Report 105–56]. *(Department of the Interior and Related Agencies Appropriations Act, 2000, as enacted by section 1000(a)(3) of the Consolidated Appropriations Act, 2000 (P.L. 106–113).)*

NATIONAL PARK SERVICE

Federal Funds

General and special funds:

OPERATION OF THE NATIONAL PARK SYSTEM

For expenses necessary for the management, operation, and maintenance of areas and facilities administered by the National Park Service (including special road maintenance service to trucking permittees on a reimbursable basis), and for the general administration of the National Park Service, including not less than [$1,000,000] *$2,000,000* for high priority projects within the scope of the approved budget which shall be carried out by the Youth Conservation Corps as authorized by 16 U.S.C. 1706, [$1,365,059,000] *$1,454,098,000*, of which [$8,800,000 is] *$9,251,000* for research, planning and interagency coordination in support of land acquisition for Everglades restoration shall remain available until expended, and of which not to exceed [$8,000,000] *$7,000,000*, to remain available until expended, is to be derived from the special fee account established pursuant to title V, section 5201 of Public Law 100–203. *(Department of the Interior and Related Agencies Appropriations Act, 2000, as enacted by section 1000(a)(3) of the Consolidated Appropriations Act, 2000 (P.L. 106–113).)*

Unavailable Collections (in millions of dollars)

Identification code 14–1036–0–1–303	1999 actual	2000 est.	2001 est.
Balance, start of year:			
01.99 Balance, start of year	6	7	3
Receipts:			
02.01 Recreation, entrance and use fees	7	3	3
04.00 Total: Balances and collections	13	10	6
Appropriation:			
05.01 Operation of the national park system	–6	–7	–3
07.99 Total balance, end of year	7	3	3

Note: The receipts shown in this schedule are on deposit in Treasury account 14–5107, "Recreation, entrance and use fees".

Program and Financing (in millions of dollars)

Identification code 14–1036–0–1–303	1999 actual	2000 est.	2001 est.
Obligations by program activity:			
Direct program:			
00.01 Park management	1,189	1,263	1,356
00.02 External administrative costs	103	111	98
09.01 Reimbursable program	35	14	14
10.00 Total new obligations	1,327	1,388	1,468
Budgetary resources available for obligation:			
21.40 Unobligated balance available, start of year	18	10	
22.00 New budget authority (gross)	1,321	1,378	1,468
23.90 Total budgetary resources available for obligation	1,339	1,388	1,468
23.95 Total new obligations	–1,327	–1,388	–1,468
23.98 Unobligated balance expiring or withdrawn	–2		
24.40 Unobligated balance available, end of year	10		
New budget authority (gross), detail:			
Discretionary:			
40.00 Appropriation (general fund)	1,280	1,358	1,451
40.15 Appropriation (emergency)	2		
40.20 Appropriation (special fund, definite)	6	7	3
40.75 Reduction pursuant to P.L. 106–51	–2		
40.76 Reduction pursuant to P.L. 106–113		–3	
42.00 Transferred from other accounts		2	
43.00 Appropriation (total discretionary)	1,286	1,364	1,454
Spending authority from offsetting collections:			
68.00 Offsetting collections (cash)	23	26	14
68.10 From Federal sources: Change in receivables and unpaid, unfilled orders	12	–12	
68.90 Spending authority from offsetting collections (total discretionary)	35	14	14
70.00 Total new budget authority (gross)	1,321	1,378	1,468
Change in unpaid obligations:			
Unpaid obligations, start of year:			
72.40 Obligated balance, start of year	276	297	341
72.95 From Federal sources: Receivables and unpaid, unfilled orders		12	
72.99 Total unpaid obligations, start of year	276	309	341
73.10 Total new obligations	1,327	1,388	1,468
73.20 Total outlays (gross)	–1,290	–1,356	–1,446
73.40 Adjustments in expired accounts (net)	–4		
Unpaid obligations, end of year:			
74.40 Obligated balance, end of year	297	341	363
74.95 From Federal sources: Receivables and unpaid, unfilled orders	12		
74.99 Total unpaid obligations, end of year	309	341	363
Outlays (gross), detail:			
86.90 Outlays from new discretionary authority	1,096	1,037	1,105
86.93 Outlays from discretionary balances	194	319	341
87.00 Total outlays (gross)	1,290	1,356	1,446
Offsets:			
Against gross budget authority and outlays:			
Offsetting collections (cash) from:			
88.00 Federal sources	–9	–12	
88.40 Non-Federal sources	–14	–14	–14
88.90 Total, offsetting collections (cash)	–23	–26	–14
Against gross budget authority only:			
88.95 From Federal sources: Change in receivables and unpaid, unfilled orders	–12	12	
Net budget authority and outlays:			
89.00 Budget authority	1,286	1,364	1,454
90.00 Outlays	1,267	1,330	1,432

The National Park System contains 379 areas and 83.6 million acres of land in 49 States, the District of Columbia, Puerto Rico, the U.S. Virgin Islands, Guam, Samoa, and the Northern Marianas. These areas have been established to protect and preserve the cultural and natural heritage of the United States and its territories. Park visits total over 280 million annually. This appropriation funds the operation of individual units of the National Park System as well as planning and administrative support for the entire system. The total appropriation request of $1,454,098,000 includes $3,400,000 in estimated revenue from recreation, user and entrance fees in accordance with 16 U.S.C. 460l–6a(i)–(j), excluding fees credited to other accounts by law, to remain available until expended.

Funding for the facility operations and maintenance subactivity of this account is proposed as part of the third year of the Administration's facilities restoration initiative. These funds emphasize the Administration's commitment to the long-term stewardship of Federal lands and facilities.

PERFORMANCE MEASURES[1]

	1997 act.	*1998 act.*[2]	*1999 act.*[2]
Recreational visitation (1,000)	273,289	288,322	284,107
Overall Quality of Services:			
Very good	48%	66%	62%
Good	31%	29%	32%
Average	15%	4%	5%
Poor	4%	1%	1%
Very poor	2%	0%	0%
Park Personnel:			
Very good	66%	81%	76%
Good	22%	15%	19%
Average	6%	3%	4%
Poor	3%	1%	1%
Very poor	4%	0%	0%
Visitor Centers:			
Very good	50%	67%	64%
Good	32%	26%	28%
Average	12%	6%	7%
Poor	4%	1%	1%
Very poor	2%	0%	0%
Restrooms:			
Very good	37%	50%	46%
Good	29%	31%	34%
Average	23%	14%	15%
Poor	8%	4%	4%
Very poor	4%	1%	1%

General and special funds—Continued

OPERATION OF THE NATIONAL PARK SYSTEM—Continued

PERFORMANCE MEASURES[1]—Continued

	1997 act.	1998 act.[2]	1999 act.[2]
Ranger Programs:			
Very good	66%	72%	69%
Good	20%	21%	24%
Average	7%	5%	6%
Poor	3%	1%	1%
Very poor	4%	0%	0%
Exhibits:			
Very good	45%	62%	57%
Good	34%	29%	33%
Average	15%	8%	9%
Poor	4%	1%	1%
Very poor	2%	0%	0%
Park brochures/maps:			
Very good	53%	69%	64%
Good	32%	25%	29%
Average	11%	6%	6%
Poor	2%	1%	1%
Very poor	2%	0%	0%
Commercial Services:			
Very good	N/A	41%	36%
Good	N/A	33%	35%
Average	N/A	19%	22%
Poor	N/A	5%	6%
Very poor	N/A	2%	2%

[1] Numbers may not add to 100% due to rounding.
[2] In 1998, the NPS improved the methodology and the survey instrument and expanded the sample size from 18 to 281 parks. In 1999, 307 parks were included in the sample.
"N/A" means not available.

Object Classification (in millions of dollars)

Identification code 14–1036–0–1–303		1999 actual	2000 est.	2001 est.
	Direct obligations:			
	Personnel compensation:			
11.1	Full-time permanent	546	582	622
11.3	Other than full-time permanent	75	80	86
11.5	Other personnel compensation	37	39	42
11.8	Special personal services payments	1	1	1
11.9	Total personnel compensation	659	702	751
12.1	Civilian personnel benefits	180	198	212
13.0	Benefits for former personnel	8	11	10
21.0	Travel and transportation of persons	31	32	34
22.0	Transportation of things	17	18	19
23.1	Rental payments to GSA	31	37	40
23.2	Rental payments to others	2	3	3
23.3	Communications, utilities, and miscellaneous charges	36	37	39
24.0	Printing and reproduction	4	4	5
25.1	Advisory and assistance services	1	1	1
25.2	Other services	165	175	176
25.3	Purchases of goods and services from Government accounts	2	12	14
25.4	Operation and maintenance of facilities	9	9	9
25.5	Research and development contracts	3	3	3
25.7	Operation and maintenance of equipment	6	7	7
26.0	Supplies and materials	79	82	86
31.0	Equipment	31	33	35
32.0	Land and structures	9	10	10
41.0	Grants, subsidies, and contributions	18		
99.0	Subtotal, direct obligations	1,291	1,374	1,454
99.0	Reimbursable obligations	35	14	14
32.0	Allocation Account: Land and structures	1		
99.9	Total new obligations	1,327	1,388	1,468

Personnel Summary

Identification code 14–1036–0–1–303		1999 actual	2000 est.	2001 est.
	Direct:			
1001	Total compensable workyears: Full-time equivalent employment	16,653	17,035	17,517
	Reimbursable:			
2001	Total compensable workyears: Full-time equivalent employment	60	60	60
	Allocation account:			
3001	Total compensable workyears: Full-time equivalent employment	605	654	654

NATIONAL RECREATION AND PRESERVATION

For expenses necessary to carry out recreation programs, natural programs, cultural programs, heritage partnership programs, environmental compliance and review, international park affairs, statutory or contractual aid for other activities, and grant administration, not otherwise provided for, [$53,899,000] *$68,648,000*, of which [$2,000,000] *$20,000,000 for Lands Legacy* shall be available *until expended* to carry out the Urban Park and Recreation Recovery Act of 1978 (16 U.S.C. 2501 et seq.)[, and of which $866,000 shall be available until expended for the Oklahoma City National Memorial Trust, notwithstanding 7(1) of Public Law 105–58: *Provided*, That notwithstanding any other provision of law, the National Park Service may hereafter recover all fees derived from providing necessary review services associated with historic preservation tax certification, and such funds shall be available until expended without further appropriation for the costs of such review services: *Provided further*, That no more than $150,000 may be used for overhead and program administrative expenses for the heritage partnership program]. *(Department of the Interior and Related Agencies Appropriations Act, 2000, as enacted by section 1000(a)(3) of the Consolidated Appropriations Act, 2000 (P.L. 106–113).)*

Program and Financing (in millions of dollars)

Identification code 14–1042–0–1–303		1999 actual	2000 est.	2001 est.
	Obligations by program activity:			
00.01	Recreation programs		1	1
00.02	Natural programs	9	10	11
00.03	Cultural programs	19	19	20
00.05	Grant administration	2	2	2
00.06	International park affairs	2	2	2
00.07	Statutory or contractual aid	8	10	4
00.08	Heritage partnership programs	6	7	9
00.09	Urban Park & Recreation Recovery Fund		3	20
10.00	Total new obligations	46	54	69
	Budgetary resources available for obligation:			
21.40	Unobligated balance available, start of year	1	1	
22.00	New budget authority (gross)	46	53	69
23.90	Total budgetary resources available for obligation	47	54	69
23.95	Total new obligations	−46	−54	−69
23.98	Unobligated balance expiring or withdrawn			
24.40	Unobligated balance available, end of year	1		
	New budget authority (gross), detail:			
	Discretionary:			
40.00	Appropriation	46	54	69
40.76	Reduction pursuant to P.L. 106–113			
43.00	Appropriation (total discretionary)	46	53	69
	Change in unpaid obligations:			
72.40	Unpaid obligations, start of year: Obligated balance, start of year	25	25	34
73.10	Total new obligations	46	54	69
73.20	Total outlays (gross)	−45	−45	−59
74.40	Unpaid obligations, end of year: Obligated balance, end of year	25	34	44
	Outlays (gross), detail:			
86.90	Outlays from new discretionary authority	30	33	33
86.93	Outlays from discretionary balances	15	12	26
87.00	Total outlays (gross)	45	45	59
	Net budget authority and outlays:			
89.00	Budget authority	46	53	69
90.00	Outlays	45	45	59

Note.—Prior to FY2000, appropriations for the National Park Service Urban Park and Recreation Fund were presented in a separate account. The activities previously funded under this separate account are presented in these schedules and are proposed to be funded in FY 2001 as part of the National Recreation and Preservation account.

These programs include: maintenance of the National Register of Historic Places; certifications for investment tax credits, management planning of Federally-owned historic properties, and Government-wide archeological programs; documentation of historic properties; the National Center for Preservation Technology and Training; grants under the Native

American Graves Protection and Repatriation Act; matching grants to cities under the Urban Park and Recreation Recovery Act; Nationwide outdoor recreation planning and assistance; transfer of surplus Federal real property; identification and designation of natural landmarks; environmental reviews; heritage partnership programs; the administration of grants; international park affairs; and statutory or contractual aid for other activities.

Funding for the Urban Park and Recreation Recovery Program was appropriated in 2000 and is proposed in 2001 within this account. This provides matching grants to cities for the renovation of urban park and recreation facilities. These funds are part of the new Lands Legacy discretionary spending category to provide dedicated and protected funding for the President's Lands Legacy Initiative. See the Environment chapter in the Budget for a summary of the Initiative. This Initiative highlights the Administration's commitment to making new tools available and working with states, tribes and local governments to protect great places; to conserve open space for recreation and wildlife habitat; and to preserve forests, farmlands, and coastal areas.

Object Classification (in millions of dollars)

Identification code 14–1042–0–1–303		1999 actual	2000 est.	2001 est.
	Personnel compensation:			
11.1	Full-time permanent	13	14	15
11.3	Other than full-time permanent	2	2	2
11.9	Total personnel compensation	15	16	17
12.1	Civilian personnel benefits	3	4	4
21.0	Travel and transportation of persons	2	2	2
24.0	Printing and reproduction	1	1	1
25.2	Other services	8	9	11
26.0	Supplies and materials	1	2	2
41.0	Grants, subsidies, and contributions	16	20	32
99.9	Total new obligations	46	54	69

Personnel Summary

Identification code 14–1042–0–1–303		1999 actual	2000 est.	2001 est.
1001	Total compensable workyears: Full-time equivalent employment	301	310	331

CONSTRUCTION *AND MAJOR MAINTENANCE*

For construction, improvements, repair or replacement of physical facilities, including the modifications authorized by section 104 of the Everglades National Park Protection and Expansion Act of 1989, **[**$225,493,000**]** *$180,000,000*, to remain available until expended**[**, of which $885,000 shall be for realignment of the Denali National Park entrance road, of which not less than $3,000,000 shall be available for modifications to the Franklin Delano Roosevelt Memorial: *Provided*, That $3,000,000 for the Wheeling National Heritage Area, $3,000,000 for the Lincoln Library, and $3,000,000 for the Southwest Pennsylvania Heritage Area shall be derived from the Historic Preservation Fund pursuant to 16 U.S.C. 470a: *Provided further*, That the National Park Service will make available 37 percent, not to exceed $1,850,000, of the total cost of upgrading the Mariposa County, California municipal solid waste disposal system: *Provided further*, That Mariposa County will provide assurance that future use fees paid by the National Park Service will be reflective of the capital contribution made by the National Park Service**]**.

In addition, for completion of ongoing projects, including Elwha River Ecosystem Restoration pursuant to Public Law 102–495, to become available on October 1 of the fiscal year specified and remain available until expended: for fiscal year 2002, $21,400,000; for fiscal year 2003, $17,200,000; and for fiscal year 2004, $11,000,000. (Department of the Interior and Related Agencies Appropriations Act, 2000, as enacted by section 1000(a)(3) of the Consolidated Appropriations Act, 2000 (P.L. 106–113).)

Program and Financing (in millions of dollars)

Identification code 14–1039–0–1–303		1999 actual	2000 est.	2001 est.
	Obligations by program activity:			
	Direct program:			
00.01	Line item construction and maintenance	110	156	109
00.02	Special programs	20	23	28
00.03	Construction planning	11	16	10
00.04	Pre-design and supplementary services	....	5	5
00.05	Construction program management and operations	....	17	17
00.06	General management planning	7	9	11
09.01	Reimbursable program	96	82	85
10.00	Total new obligations	244	308	265
	Budgetary resources available for obligation:			
21.40	Unobligated balance available, start of year	218	460	473
22.00	New budget authority (gross)	491	321	260
22.21	Unobligated balance transferred to other accounts	−5	....	....
23.90	Total budgetary resources available for obligation	704	781	733
23.95	Total new obligations	−244	−308	−265
24.40	Unobligated balance available, end of year	460	473	468
	New budget authority (gross), detail:			
	Discretionary:			
40.00	Appropriation	217	216	180
40.15	Appropriation (emergency)	14	....	....
40.20	Appropriation (special fund, definite)	8	9	....
40.76	Reduction pursuant to P.L. 106–113	....	−4	....
42.00	Transferred from other accounts	....	5	....
43.00	Appropriation (total discretionary)	239	226	180
	Spending authority from offsetting collections:			
	Offsetting collections (cash):			
68.00	Offsetting collections (cash)	252	80	80
68.00	Offsetting collections (cash)	....	2	5
68.10	From Federal sources: Change in receivables and unpaid, unfilled orders	....	13	−5
68.90	Spending authority from offsetting collections (total discretionary)	252	95	80
70.00	Total new budget authority (gross)	491	321	260
	Change in unpaid obligations:			
	Unpaid obligations, start of year:			
72.40	Obligated balance, start of year	189	92	87
72.95	From Federal sources: Receivables and unpaid, unfilled orders	....	....	13
72.99	Total unpaid obligations, start of year	189	92	100
73.10	Total new obligations	244	308	265
73.20	Total outlays (gross)	−342	−300	−247
	Unpaid obligations, end of year:			
74.40	Obligated balance, end of year	92	87	110
74.95	From Federal sources: Receivables and unpaid, unfilled orders	....	13	8
74.99	Total unpaid obligations, end of year	92	100	118
	Outlays (gross), detail:			
86.90	Outlays from new discretionary authority	288	116	107
86.93	Outlays from discretionary balances	54	186	140
87.00	Total outlays (gross)	342	300	247
	Offsets:			
	Against gross budget authority and outlays:			
	Offsetting collections (cash) from:			
	Federal sources:			
88.00	Federal sources	−134	−45	−45
88.00	Federal sources	....	−2	−5
88.40	Non-Federal sources	−118	−35	−35
88.90	Total, offsetting collections (cash)	−252	−82	−85
	Against gross budget authority only:			
88.95	From Federal sources: Change in receivables and unpaid, unfilled orders	....	−13	5
	Net budget authority and outlays:			
89.00	Budget authority	239	226	180
90.00	Outlays	90	218	162

General and special funds—Continued

CONSTRUCTION *AND MAJOR MAINTENANCE*—Continued

Summary of Budget Authority and Outlays

(in millions of dollars)

	1999 actual	2000 est.	2001 est.
Enacted/requested:			
Budget Authority	239	226	180
Outlays	90	220	162
Supplemental proposal:			
Budget Authority	....	4	....
Outlays	....	1	1
Total:			
Budget Authority	239	230	180
Outlays	90	221	163

Status of Direct Loans (in millions of dollars)

Identification code 14–1039–0–1–303	1999 actual	2000 est.	2001 est.
Cumulative balance of direct loans outstanding:			
1210 Outstanding, start of year	6	6	5
1251 Repayments: Repayments and prepayments	....	−1	....
1290 Outstanding, end of year	6	5	5

Line Item Construction.—This activity provides for the construction, rehabilitation, and replacement of those facilities needed to accomplish the management objectives approved for each park. Projects are categorized as facility improvement, utility systems rehabilitation, historic preservation, and natural resource preservation.

Special Programs.—Under this activity several former activity and subactivity components are combined. These include Emergency and Unscheduled Projects, the Seismic Safety of National Park System Buildings Program, Employee Housing, Dam Safety, and Equipment Replacement.

Construction Planning.—This activity includes the project planning function in which funds are used to prepare working drawings, specification documents, and contracts needed to construct or rehabilitate National Park Service facilities.

Pre-Design and Supplementary Services.—Under this activity, provisions are made to undertake workloads in conformance with improvement recommendations of NAPA. Functions include conditions surveys and special reports to acquire archaeological, historical, environmental and engineering design information which represents requisite preliminary stages of the design process.

Construction Program Management and Operations.—This activity complies with NAPA recommendations to base fund Service Center management and operations.

General Management Plans.—Under this activity, funding is used to prepare General Management Plans and keep them up-to-date to guide National Park Service actions for the protection, use, development, and management of each park unit; and to conduct studies of alternatives for the protection of areas that may have potential for addition to the National Park System.

Full funding through advance appropriations.—Full funding of fixed asset acquisitions reduces the risk of cost overruns from delayed funding and increases accountability for cost estimates. Advance appropriations are requested to complete the following construction projects funded through 2000 that require additional funding in the outyears: Olympic National Park; George Washington Parkway (Glen Echo); Virgin Islands National Park; and the Jefferson Memorial.

Funding for the Construction account is proposed as part of the third year of the Administration's facilities restoration initiative. These funds emphasize the Administration's commitment to the long-term stewardship of Federal lands and facilities.

Object Classification (in millions of dollars)

Identification code 14–1039–0–1–303	1999 actual	2000 est.	2001 est.
Direct obligations:			
Personnel compensation:			
11.1 Full-time permanent	24	18	19
11.3 Other than full-time permanent	8	6	7
11.5 Other personnel compensation	1	1	1
11.9 Total personnel compensation	33	25	27
12.1 Civilian personnel benefits	6	5	5
13.0 Benefits for former personnel	2	....	....
21.0 Travel and transportation of persons	3	2	2
23.3 Communications, utilities, and miscellaneous charges	1	1	1
25.2 Other services	6	94	50
25.3 Purchases of goods and services from Government accounts	1	1	1
25.4 Operation and maintenance of facilities	1	1	1
25.7 Operation and maintenance of equipment	3	2	2
26.0 Supplies and materials	9	6	7
31.0 Equipment	17	13	13
32.0 Land and structures	50	50	50
41.0 Grants, subsidies, and contributions	8	6	6
99.0 Subtotal, direct obligations	140	206	165
99.0 Reimbursable obligations	96	82	85
Allocation Account:			
11.1 Personnel compensation: Full-time permanent	....	2	2
25.2 Other services	4	6	5
32.0 Land and structures	4	12	8
99.0 Subtotal, allocation account	8	20	15
99.9 Total new obligations	244	308	265

Obligations are distributed as follows:			
National Park Service	236	288	250
Corps of Engineers	6	18	14
Department of Transportation—Federal Highway Administration	2	2	1

Personnel Summary

Identification code 14–1039–0–1–303	1999 actual	2000 est.	2001 est.
Direct:			
1001 Total compensable workyears: Full-time equivalent employment	600	433	433
Reimbursable:			
2001 Total compensable workyears: Full-time equivalent employment	475	463	463
Allocation account:			
3001 Total compensable workyears: Full-time equivalent employment	76	76	76

LAND ACQUISITION AND STATE ASSISTANCE

For expenses necessary to carry out the Land and Water Conservation Act of 1965, as amended (16 U.S.C. 4601–4 through 11), including administrative expenses, and for acquisition of lands or waters, or interest therein, in accordance with the statutory authority applicable to the National Park Service, [$120,700,000] *$297,468,000 for Lands Legacy*, to be derived from the Land and Water Conservation Fund, to remain available until expended, of which [$21,000,000] *$150,000,000* is for the State assistance program [including $1,000,000 to administer the State assistance program], *of which $8,500,000 is available, subject to authorization, for acquisition of lands for addition to Great Sand Dunes National Monument,* and of which [$10,000,000] *$47,000,000* may be for [State grants for land acquisition in the State of Florida: *Provided*, That funds provided for State grants for land acquisition in the State of Florida are contingent upon the following: (1) submission of detailed legislative language to the House and Senate Committees on Appropriations agreed to by the Secretary of the Interior, the Secretary of the Army and the Governor of Florida that would provide assurances for the guaranteed supply of water to the natural areas in southern Florida, including all National parks, Preserves, Wildlife Refuge lands, and other natural areas to ensure a restored ecosystem; and (2) submission of a complete prioritized non-Federal land acquisition project list: *Provided further*, That after the requirements under this heading have been met, from the funds made available for State grants for land acquisition in the State of Florida] the Secretary [may] *to* provide Federal assistance to the State of Florida for the acquisition of lands or waters, or interests therein, within the Everglades watershed (consisting of lands and waters within the boundaries of the South Florida Water Management District, Florida Bay and the Florida Keys, including the areas known as the Frog Pond, the Rocky Glades and the Eight and One-Half Square Mile Area) under terms and conditions deemed necessary by the Secretary to improve and restore the hydrological function of the Everglades watershed; *and of which $2,000,000 may be provided to the State of Maryland for acquisition of lands, or waters, or interests therein, known as The Holly Beach Farm near Sandy Point State Park in the State of Maryland: Provided* [*further*], That funds provided under this heading [to the] *for assistance to the* State of Florida *to acquire lands within the Everglades watershed* are contingent upon new matching non-Federal funds by the State and shall be subject to an agreement that the lands to be acquired will be managed in perpetuity for the restoration of the Everglades: *Provided further*, That [of the amount provided herein $2,000,000 shall be made available by the National Park Service, pursuant to a grant agreement, to the State of Wisconsin so that the State may acquire land or interest in land for the Ice Age National Scenic Trail: *Provided further*, That of the amount provided herein $500,000 shall be made available by the National Park Service, pursuant to a grant agreement, to the State of Wisconsin so that the State may acquire land or interest in land for the North Country National Scenic Trail: *Provided further*, That funds provided under this heading to the State of Wisconsin are contingent upon matching funds by the State] *the funds provided for the acquisition of Holly Beach Farm are contingent upon matching non-Federal funds by the State of Maryland. (Department of the Interior and Related Agencies Appropriations Act, 2000, as enacted by section 1000(a)(3) of the Consolidated Appropriations Act, 2000 (P.L. 106–113).)*

Program and Financing (in millions of dollars)

Identification code 14–5035–0–2–303		1999 actual	2000 est.	2001 est.
	Obligations by program activity:			
00.01	Land acquisition	77	83	102
00.02	Land acquisition administration	7	10	12
00.04	State grant administration	1	1	5
00.05	Grants to states		20	145
09.01	Reimbursable program		55	
10.00	Total new obligations	85	169	264
	Budgetary resources available for obligation:			
21.40	Unobligated balance available, start of year	85	148	155
22.00	New budget authority (gross)	148	176	297
23.90	Total budgetary resources available for obligation	233	324	452
23.95	Total new obligations	−85	−169	−264
24.40	Unobligated balance available, end of year	148	155	188
	New budget authority (gross), detail:			
	Discretionary:			
40.20	Appropriation (special fund, definite)	148	121	297
49.35	Contract authority rescinded	−30	−30	−30
	Mandatory:			
66.10	Contract authority	30	30	30
	Spending authority from offsetting collections:			
	Discretionary:			
68.00	Offsetting collections (cash)		22	14
68.10	From Federal sources: Change in receivables and unpaid, unfilled orders		33	−14
68.90	Spending authority from offsetting collections (total discretionary)		55	
70.00	Total new budget authority (gross)	148	176	297
	Change in unpaid obligations:			
	Unpaid obligations, start of year:			
72.40	Obligated balance, start of year	88	104	76
72.95	From Federal sources: Receivables and unpaid, unfilled orders			33
72.99	Total unpaid obligations, start of year	88	104	109
73.10	Total new obligations	85	169	264
73.20	Total outlays (gross)	−69	−164	−222
	Unpaid obligations, end of year:			
74.40	Obligated balance, end of year	104	76	132
74.95	From Federal sources: Receivables and unpaid, unfilled orders		33	19
74.99	Total unpaid obligations, end of year	104	109	151
	Outlays (gross), detail:			
86.90	Outlays from new discretionary authority	52	64	104
86.93	Outlays from discretionary balances	17	100	118
87.00	Total outlays (gross)	69	164	222
	Offsets:			
	Against gross budget authority and outlays:			
88.00	Offsetting collections (cash) from: Federal sources		−22	−14
	Against gross budget authority only:			
88.95	From Federal sources: Change in receivables and unpaid, unfilled orders		−33	14
	Net budget authority and outlays:			
89.00	Budget authority	148	121	297
90.00	Outlays	69	142	208

This appropriation provides funds to acquire certain lands, or interests in land, for inclusion in the National Park System in order to preserve nationally important natural and historic resources. Funds are also included to manage and coordinate the Land Acquisition Program, to provide grants to States, and to administer State outdoor recreation grants, both new grants and those awarded in prior years.

Funding for the Land Acquisition and State Assistance account is proposed as part of the new Lands Legacy discretionary spending category to provide dedicated and protected funding for the President's Lands Legacy Initiative. See the Environment chapter in the Budget for a summary of the programs and funding included in Lands Legacy. These funds highlight the Administration's commitment to making new tools available, and working with states, tribes, and local governments to protect great places; to conserve open space for recreation and wildlife habitat; and to preserve forest, farmlands, and coastal areas.

PERFORMANCE MEASURES

	1999 actual	*2000 est.*	*2001 est.*
Land acquired (acres)	88,898	110,663	81,738
Land acquired (tracts)	1,762	5,059	1,665

Object Classification (in millions of dollars)

Identification code 14–5035–0–2–303		1999 actual	2000 est.	2001 est.
	Direct obligations:			
11.1	Personnel compensation: Full-time permanent	6	8	10
12.1	Civilian personnel benefits	1	2	2
25.2	Other services	5	1	3
31.0	Equipment			1
32.0	Land and structures	73	83	102
41.0	Grants, subsidies, and contributions		20	145
42.0	Insurance claims and indemnities			1
99.0	Subtotal, direct obligations	85	114	264
99.0	Reimbursable obligations		55	
99.9	Total new obligations	85	169	264

Personnel Summary

Identification code 14–5035–0–2–303		1999 actual	2000 est.	2001 est.
1001	Total compensable workyears: Full-time equivalent employment	123	158	203

LAND AND WATER CONSERVATION FUND

(RESCISSION)

The contract authority provided for fiscal year [2000] *2001* by 16 U.S.C. 460l–10a is rescinded. *(Department of the Interior and Related Agencies Appropriations Act, 2000, as enacted by section 1000(a)(3) of the Consolidated Appropriations Act, 2000 (P.L. 106–113).)*

General and special funds—Continued

CONSTRUCTION *AND MAJOR MAINTENANCE*—Continued

LAND AND WATER CONSERVATION FUND—Continued

(RESCISSION)—Continued

Unavailable Collections (in millions of dollars)

Identification code 14–5005–0–2–303	1999 actual	2000 est.	2001 est.
Balance, start of year:			
01.99 Balance, start of year	11,792	12,371	12,805
Receipts:			
02.02 Rent receipts, Outer Continental Shelf lands	899	365	588
02.03 Royalty receipts, Outer Continental Shelf lands	....	532	309
02.04 Motorboat fuels tax	1	1	1
02.05 Surplus property sales	8	2	2
02.99 Total receipts	908	900	900
04.00 Total: Balances and collections	12,700	13,271	13,705
Appropriation:			
05.01 Bureau of Land Management, land acquisition	–15	–16	–61
05.02 Fish and Wildlife Service, land acquisition	–48	–52	–112
05.03 National Park Service, land acquisition and State assistance	–178	–151	–327
05.04 Priority Federal land acquisitions and exchanges	....	–116	....
05.05 USDA Forest Service, land acquisition	–118	–156	–130
05.07 State and private forestry	....	–5	....
05.99 Subtotal appropriation	–359	–496	–630
06.10 Unobligated balance returned to receipts	30	30	30
07.99 Total balance, end of year	12,371	12,805	13,105

The Land and Water Conservation Fund (LWCF) includes revenue pursuant to the Land and Water Conservation Fund Act to support land acquisition, State outdoor recreation and conservation grants, other conservation programs and related administrative expenses.

RECREATION FEE PERMANENT APPROPRIATIONS

Unavailable Collections (in millions of dollars)

Identification code 14–9928–0–2–303	1999 actual	2000 est.	2001 est.
Balance, start of year:			
01.99 Balance, start of year	....	....	....
Receipts:			
02.01 National park passport program	....	8	12
02.02 Transportation systems fund	....	1	1
02.03 Recreational fee demonstration program	143	146	150
02.04 Fee collection support	1	1	1
02.05 Deposits for educational expenses, children of employees, Yellowstone National Park	1	1	1
02.99 Total receipts	145	157	165
Appropriation:			
05.01 Recreation fee permanent appropriations	–145	–157	–165
07.99 Total balance, end of year	....	....	....

Program and Financing (in millions of dollars)

Identification code 14–9928–0–2–303	1999 actual	2000 est.	2001 est.
Obligations by program activity:			
00.01 Recreational fee demonstration program	82	146	150
00.02 Fee collection support	1	1	1
00.03 National park passport program	....	8	12
00.04 Transportation systems fund	....	1	1
00.05 Educational expenses, children of employees, Yellowstone National Park	1	1	1
10.00 Total new obligations	84	157	165
Budgetary resources available for obligation:			
21.40 Unobligated balance available, start of year	126	187	187
22.00 New budget authority (gross)	145	157	165
23.90 Total budgetary resources available for obligation	271	344	352
23.95 Total new obligations	–84	–157	–165
24.40 Unobligated balance available, end of year	187	187	187
New budget authority (gross), detail:			
Mandatory:			
60.25 Appropriation (special fund, indefinite)	145	157	165
Change in unpaid obligations:			
72.40 Unpaid obligations, start of year: Obligated balance, start of year	13	29	53
73.10 Total new obligations	84	157	165
73.20 Total outlays (gross)	–68	–132	–161
74.40 Unpaid obligations, end of year: Obligated balance, end of year	29	53	56
Outlays (gross), detail:			
86.97 Outlays from new mandatory authority	24	33	38
86.98 Outlays from mandatory balances	44	99	123
87.00 Total outlays (gross)	68	132	161
Net budget authority and outlays:			
89.00 Budget authority	145	157	165
90.00 Outlays	68	132	161

Recreational fee demonstration program.—The National Park Service and other land management agencies have initiated a demonstration fee program that allows parks and other units to collect new or increased admission and user fees and spend the revenue for park improvements. This temporary authority, provided in section 315 of section 101(c) of Public Law 104–134 as amended or supplemented by section 319 of section 101(d) of Public Law 104–208, section 5001 of Public Law 105–18, sections 107, 320 and 321 of Public Law 105–83, and section 327 of section 101(e) of Public Law 105–277, expires at the end of fiscal year 2001. To ensure that fee revenue remains available for park improvements after 2001, the Administration will propose legislation providing permanent fee authority to take effect once the current authority expires.

Fee collection support, National Park System.—Up to 15 percent of recreation fees collected by parks not included in the Fee Demonstration Program are withheld to cover fee collection costs as authorized by Public Law 103–66, section 10002(b), section 315(c) of section 101(c) of Public Law 104–134, and section 107 of Public Law 105–83.

National park passport program.—Proceeds from the sale of national park passports for admission to all park units are to be used for the national passport program and the National Park System in accordance with section 603 of Public Law 105–391. By law, up to 15 percent of proceeds may be used to administer and promote the national park passport program and the National Park System, and net proceeds are to be used for high priority visitor service or resource management projects throughout the National Park System.

Deed-restricted parks fee program.—Park units where admission fees may not be collected by reason of deed restrictions retain any other recreation fees collected and use them for certain park operation purposes in accordance with Public Law 105–327. This law applies to Great Smoky Mountains National Park, Lincoln Home National Historic Site and Abraham Lincoln Birthplace National Historic Site.

Transportation systems fund.—Fees charged for public use of transportation services at parks are retained and used by each collecting park for costs associated with the transportation systems in accordance with section 501 of Public Law 105–391.

Educational expenses, children of employees, Yellowstone National Park.—Revenues received from the collection of short-term recreation fees to the park are used to provide education facilities to pupils who are dependents of persons engaged in the administration, operation, and maintenance of Yellowstone National Park (16 U.S.C. 40a).

Payment for tax losses on land acquired for Grand Teton National Park.—Revenues received from fees collected from visitors are used to compensate the State of Wyoming for tax losses on Grand Teton National Park lands (16 U.S.C. 406d–3).

Object Classification (in millions of dollars)

Identification code 14–9928–0–2–303	1999 actual	2000 est.	2001 est.
Personnel compensation:			
11.1 Full-time permanent	10	9	6
11.3 Other than full-time permanent	16	16	10
11.5 Other personnel compensation	2	2	1
11.9 Total personnel compensation	28	27	17
12.1 Civilian personnel benefits	5	4	2
21.0 Travel and transportation of persons	1	1	1
22.0 Transportation of things	1	1	
23.3 Communications, utilities, and miscellaneous charges	1	1	1
25.2 Other services	30	112	137
25.3 Purchases of goods and services from Government accounts	1	1	1
25.4 Operation and maintenance of facilities	2	2	1
26.0 Supplies and materials	7	7	4
31.0 Equipment	2	1	1
32.0 Land and structures	4		
41.0 Grants, subsidies, and contributions	2		
99.9 Total new obligations	84	157	165

Personnel Summary

Identification code 14–9928–0–2–303	1999 actual	2000 est.	2001 est.
1001 Total compensable workyears: Full-time equivalent employment	815	736	463

HISTORIC PRESERVATION FUND

For expenses necessary in carrying out the Historic Preservation Act of 1966, as amended (16 U.S.C. 470), and the Omnibus Parks and Public Lands Management Act of 1996 (Public Law 104–333), [$75,212,000] *$72,071,000*, to be derived from the Historic Preservation Fund, to remain available until September 30, [2001] *2002*, of which [$10,722,000] *$7,177,000* pursuant to section 507 of Public Law 104–333 shall remain available until expended: *Provided*, That of the total amount provided, $30,000,000 shall be for Save America's Treasures for priority preservation projects, including preservation of intellectual and cultural artifacts, preservation of historic structures and sites, and buildings to house cultural and historic resources and to provide educational opportunities: *Provided further*, That any individual Save America's Treasures grant shall be matched by non-Federal funds: *Provided further*, That individual projects shall only be eligible for one grant, and *notice of* all projects to be funded shall be [approved by] *transmitted to* the House and Senate Committees on Appropriations prior to the commitment of grant funds: *Provided further*, That Save America's Treasures funds allocated for Federal projects shall be available by transfer to appropriate accounts of individual agencies, after approval of such projects by the Secretary of the Interior: *Provided further*, That none of the funds provided for Save America's Treasures may be used for administrative expenses, and staffing for the program shall be available from the existing staffing levels in the National Park Service. *(Department of the Interior and Related Agencies Appropriations Act, 2000, as enacted by section 1000(a)(3) of the Consolidated Appropriations Act, 2000 (P.L. 106–113).)*

Unavailable Collections (in millions of dollars)

Identification code 14–5140–0–2–303	1999 actual	2000 est.	2001 est.
Balance, start of year:			
01.99 Balance, start of year	2,316	2,086	2,002
Receipts:			
02.01 Rent receipts, Outer Continental Shelf lands	–150		
04.00 Total: Balances and collections	2,166	2,086	2,002
Appropriation:			
05.01 Historic preservation fund	–72	–75	–72
05.02 Construction	–8	–9	
05.99 Subtotal appropriation	–80	–84	–72
07.99 Total balance, end of year	2,086	2,002	1,930

Program and Financing (in millions of dollars)

Identification code 14–5140–0–2–303	1999 actual	2000 est.	2001 est.
Obligations by program activity:			
00.01 Grants-in-aid	40	45	42
00.03 Millennium initiative grants	10	30	30
10.00 Total new obligations (object class 41.0)	50	75	72
Budgetary resources available for obligation:			
21.40 Unobligated balance available, start of year	2	24	24
22.00 New budget authority (gross)	72	75	72
23.90 Total budgetary resources available for obligation	74	99	96
23.95 Total new obligations	–50	–75	–72
24.40 Unobligated balance available, end of year	24	24	24
New budget authority (gross), detail:			
Discretionary:			
40.20 Appropriation (special fund, definite)	72	75	72
Change in unpaid obligations:			
72.40 Unpaid obligations, start of year: Obligated balance, start of year	32	44	46
73.10 Total new obligations	50	75	72
73.20 Total outlays (gross)	–37	–73	–80
74.40 Unpaid obligations, end of year: Obligated balance, end of year	44	46	38
Outlays (gross), detail:			
86.90 Outlays from new discretionary authority	24	32	30
86.93 Outlays from discretionary balances	13	41	50
87.00 Total outlays (gross)	37	73	80
Net budget authority and outlays:			
89.00 Budget authority	72	75	72
90.00 Outlays	37	73	80

This appropriation finances 60 percent of programmatic matching grants-in-aid to the States and certified local governments. This includes grants to Historically Black Colleges and Universities (HBCUs) and to Indian tribes. Pursuant to the Omnibus Parks and Public Lands Management Act (P.L. 104–333) and other authorities, this appropriation includes approximately $8 million in 2001 for grants to specified HBCUs for the preservation and restoration of historic buildings and structures.

The President's budget proposes $30 million in funding for Save America's Treasures in the National Park Service Historic Preservation Fund to provide assistance for commemorating the Millennium by addressing the Nation's most urgent preservation priorities. These funds will support one of the most important tasks facing America at the turn of the century—to preserve America's most threatened historical and cultural heritage for future generations. These treasures include the significant documents, objects, manuscripts, photographs, works of art, maps, journals, still and moving images, sound recordings, historic structures and sites that document and illuminate the history and culture of the United States.

OTHER PERMANENT APPROPRIATIONS

Unavailable Collections (in millions of dollars)

Identification code 14–9924–0–2–303	1999 actual	2000 est.	2001 est.
Balance, start of year:			
01.99 Balance, start of year			
Receipts:			
02.01 Park buildings lease and maintenance fund		1	2
02.05 Glacier Bay National Park resource protection	1		
02.07 Park concessions franchise fees	15	15	16
02.08 Concessions improvement accounts	19	20	22
02.09 Rents and charges for quarters	15	15	15

General and special funds—Continued

RECREATION FEE PERMANENT APPROPRIATIONS—Continued

OTHER PERMANENT APPROPRIATIONS—Continued

Unavailable Collections (in millions of dollars)—Continued

Identification code 14–9924–0–2–303	1999 actual	2000 est.	2001 est.
02.10 Legislative proposal, user fees for filming and photography on public lands	....	....	3
02.99 Total receipts	50	51	58
Appropriation:			
05.01 Other permanent appropriations	−50	−51	−55
05.02 Other permanent appropriations, legislative proposal subject to PAYGO	....	....	−3
05.99 Subtotal appropriation	−50	−51	−58
07.99 Total balance, end of year	....	....	....

Program and Financing (in millions of dollars)

Identification code 14–9924–0–2–303	1999 actual	2000 est.	2001 est.
Obligations by program activity:			
00.01 Park concessions franchise fees	2	15	16
00.02 Concessions improvement accounts	15	20	22
00.03 Park buildings lease and maintenance fund	....	1	2
00.04 Operation and maintenance of quarters	15	15	15
00.05 Glacier Bay National Park resource protection and other accounts	1	....	....
10.00 Total new obligations	33	51	55
Budgetary resources available for obligation:			
21.40 Unobligated balance available, start of year	50	67	67
22.00 New budget authority (gross)	50	51	55
23.90 Total budgetary resources available for obligation	100	118	122
23.95 Total new obligations	−33	−51	−55
24.40 Unobligated balance available, end of year	67	67	67
New budget authority (gross), detail:			
Mandatory:			
60.25 Appropriation (special fund, indefinite)	50	51	55
Change in unpaid obligations:			
72.40 Unpaid obligations, start of year: Obligated balance, start of year	2	4	3
73.10 Total new obligations	33	51	55
73.20 Total outlays (gross)	−30	−52	−55
74.40 Unpaid obligations, end of year: Obligated balance, end of year	4	3	3
Outlays (gross), detail:			
86.97 Outlays from new mandatory authority	1	9	11
86.98 Outlays from mandatory balances	29	43	44
87.00 Total outlays (gross)	30	52	55
Net budget authority and outlays:			
89.00 Budget authority	50	51	55
90.00 Outlays	30	52	55

Park concessions franchise fees.—Franchise fees for concessioner activities in the National Park System are deposited in this account and used for certain park operations activities in accordance with section 407 of Public Law 105–391. By law, 20 percent of franchise fees collected are used to support activities throughout the National Park System generally and 80 percent are retained and used by each collecting park unit for visitor services and for purposes of funding high-priority and urgently necessary resource management programs and operations.

Concessions improvement accounts.—National Park Service agreements with private concessioners providing visitor services within national parks can require concessioners to deposit a portion of gross receipts or a fixed sum of money in a separate bank account. A concessioner may expend funds from such an account at the direction of the park superintendent for facilities that directly support concession visitor services, but would not otherwise be funded through the appropriations process. Concessioners do not accrue possessory interests from improvements funded through these accounts.

Park buildings lease and maintenance fund.—Rental payments for leases to use buildings and associated property in the National Park System are deposited in this account and used for infrastructure needs at park units in accordance with section 802 of Public Law 105–391.

Operation and maintenance of quarters.—Revenues from the rental of Government-owned quarters to park employees are deposited in this account and used to operate and maintain the quarters.

National Maritime Heritage Grants Program.—Of the revenues received from the sale of obsolete vessels in the National Defense Reserve Fleet, 25 percent are used for matching grants to State and local governments and private nonprofit organizations under the National Maritime Heritage Grants Program and for related administrative expenses in accordance with 16 U.S.C. 5401.

Delaware Water Gap, Route 209 operations.—Fees collected for use of Route 209 within the Delaware Water Gap National Recreation Area by commercial vehicles are used for management, operation, and maintenance of the route within the park as authorized by Public Law 98–63 (97 Stat. 329), section 117 of Public Law 98–151 (97 Stat. 977) as amended by Public Law 99–88 (99 Stat. 343), and section 702 of Division I of Public Law 104–333 (110 Stat. 4185). The expired authorization was restored in fiscal year 1997 by Public Law 104–333.

Glacier Bay National Park resource protection.—Of the revenues received from fees paid by tour boat operators or other permittees for entering Glacier Bay National Park, 60 percent are used for certain activities to protect resources of the Park from harm by permittees in accordance with section 703 of Division I of Public Law 104–333 (110 Stat. 4185).

Summary of Budget Authority and Outlays

(in millions of dollars)

	1999 actual	*2000 est.*	*2001 est.*
Enacted/requested:			
Budget Authority	50	51	55
Outlays	30	52	55
Legislative proposal, subject to PAYGO:			
Budget Authority	....	....	3
Outlays	....	....	3
Total:			
Budget Authority	50	51	58
Outlays	30	52	58

Object Classification (in millions of dollars)

Identification code 14–9924–0–2–303	1999 actual	2000 est.	2001 est.
Personnel compensation:			
11.1 Full-time permanent	4	5	5
11.3 Other than full-time permanent	1	1	1
11.9 Total personnel compensation	5	6	6
12.1 Civilian personnel benefits	1	1	1
23.3 Communications, utilities, and miscellaneous charges	2	2	2
25.2 Other services	20	35	39
25.4 Operation and maintenance of facilities	1	1	1
26.0 Supplies and materials	3	4	4
31.0 Equipment	....	1	1
41.0 Grants, subsidies, and contributions	1	1	1
99.9 Total new obligations	33	51	55

Personnel Summary

Identification code 14–9924–0–2–303	1999 actual	2000 est.	2001 est.
1001 Total compensable workyears: Full-time equivalent employment	138	158	158

OTHER PERMANENT APPROPRIATIONS

(Legislative proposal, subject to PAYGO)

Program and Financing (in millions of dollars)

Identification code 14–9924–4–2–303	1999 actual	2000 est.	2001 est.
Obligations by program activity:			
00.06 Filming and Recording Special Use Fee Program			3
10.00 Total new obligations			3
Budgetary resources available for obligation:			
22.00 New budget authority (gross)			3
23.95 Total new obligations			−3
New budget authority (gross), detail:			
Mandatory:			
60.25 Appropriation (special fund, indefinite)			3
Change in unpaid obligations:			
73.10 Total new obligations			3
73.20 Total outlays (gross)			−3
Outlays (gross), detail:			
86.97 Outlays from new mandatory authority			3
Net budget authority and outlays:			
89.00 Budget authority			3
90.00 Outlays			3

Filming and photography special use fee program.—The Administration will offer a legislative proposal to authorize permits and collection of fees for use of lands and facilites for filming, videotaping, sound recording, and still photography under certain conditions in amounts sufficient to cover related Government costs, including permit processing, cleanup and restoration, and a fair return to the Government. Amounts collected will be used in accordance with the formula and purposes established for the Recreational Fee Demonstration Program.

Object Classification (in millions of dollars)

Identification code 14–9924–4–2–303	1999 actual	2000 est.	2001 est.
11.3 Personnel compensation: Other than full-time permanent			1
25.2 Other services			2
99.9 Total new obligations			3

Personnel Summary

Identification code 14–9924–4–2–303	1999 actual	2000 est.	2001 est.
1001 Total compensable workyears: Full-time equivalent employment			20

Trust Funds

CONSTRUCTION

(TRUST FUND)

Program and Financing (in millions of dollars)

Identification code 14–8215–0–7–401	1999 actual	2000 est.	2001 est.
Obligations by program activity:			
00.01 Cumberland Gap Tunnel	1	3	3
00.03 Baltimore-Washington Parkway		1	
10.00 Total new obligations	1	4	3
Budgetary resources available for obligation:			
21.40 Unobligated balance available, start of year	8	7	3
23.95 Total new obligations	−1	−4	−3
24.40 Unobligated balance available, end of year	7	3	
Change in unpaid obligations:			
72.40 Unpaid obligations, start of year: Obligated balance, start of year	3	3	3
73.10 Total new obligations	1	4	3
73.20 Total outlays (gross)	−1	−4	−5
74.40 Unpaid obligations, end of year: Obligated balance, end of year	3	3	1
Outlays (gross), detail:			
86.93 Outlays from discretionary balances	1	4	5
Net budget authority and outlays:			
89.00 Budget authority			
90.00 Outlays	1	4	5

Parkway construction project funds have been derived from the Highway Trust Fund through appropriations to liquidate contract authority, which has been provided under section 104(a)(8) of the Federal Aid Highway Act of 1978, title I of Public Law 95–599, as amended, and appropriation language, which has made the contract authority and the appropriations available until expended.

Reconstruction and relocation of Route 25E through the Cumberland Gap National Historical Park, including construction of a tunnel and the approaches thereto, are authorized without fund limitation by Public Law 93–87, section 160.

Improvements to the George Washington Memorial Parkway and the Baltimore Washington Parkway are authorized and funded by the Department of the Interior and Related Agencies Appropriations Acts, 1987, as included in Public Law 95–591, and 1991, Public Law 101–512. No more significant obligations are expected in this account for improvements to the George Washington Memorial Parkway.

Object Classification (in millions of dollars)

Identification code 14–8215–0–7–401	1999 actual	2000 est.	2001 est.
25.2 Direct obligations: Other services		1	
Allocation Account:			
25.2 Other services		3	3
32.0 Land and structures	1		
99.0 Subtotal, allocation account	1	3	3
99.9 Total new obligations	1	4	3

Personnel Summary

Identification code 14–8215–0–7–401	1999 actual	2000 est.	2001 est.
1001 Total compensable workyears: Full-time equivalent employment	2	2	2

MISCELLANEOUS TRUST FUNDS

Unavailable Collections (in millions of dollars)

Identification code 14–9972–0–7–303	1999 actual	2000 est.	2001 est.
Balance, start of year:			
01.99 Balance, start of year			
Receipts:			
02.01 Donations to National Park Service	15	15	15
Appropriation:			
05.01 Miscellaneous trust funds	−15	−15	−15
07.99 Total balance, end of year			

Program and Financing (in millions of dollars)

Identification code 14–9972–0–7–303	1999 actual	2000 est.	2001 est.
Obligations by program activity:			
10.00 Total new obligations	15	15	15
Budgetary resources available for obligation:			
21.40 Unobligated balance available, start of year	19	20	20

CONSTRUCTION—Continued

MISCELLANEOUS TRUST FUNDS—Continued

Program and Financing (in millions of dollars)—Continued

Identification code 14–9972–0–7–303	1999 actual	2000 est.	2001 est.
22.00 New budget authority (gross)	15	15	15
23.90 Total budgetary resources available for obligation	35	35	35
23.95 Total new obligations	–15	–15	–15
24.40 Unobligated balance available, end of year	20	20	20
New budget authority (gross), detail:			
Mandatory:			
60.27 Appropriation (trust fund, indefinite)	15	15	15
Change in unpaid obligations:			
72.40 Unpaid obligations, start of year: Obligated balance, start of year	5	5	5
73.10 Total new obligations	15	15	15
73.20 Total outlays (gross)	–15	–15	–15
74.40 Unpaid obligations, end of year: Obligated balance, end of year	5	5	5
Outlays (gross), detail:			
86.98 Outlays from mandatory balances	15	15	15
Net budget authority and outlays:			
89.00 Budget authority	15	15	15
90.00 Outlays	14	15	15

National Park Service, donations.—The Secretary of the Interior accepts and uses donated moneys for purposes of the National Park System (16 U.S.C. 6).

Preservation, Birthplace of Abraham Lincoln, National Park Service.—This fund consists of an endowment given by the Lincoln Farm Association, and the interest therefrom is available for preservation of the Abraham Lincoln Birthplace National Historic Site, Kentucky (16 U.S.C. 211, 212).

Object Classification (in millions of dollars)

Identification code 14–9972–0–7–303	1999 actual	2000 est.	2001 est.
Personnel compensation:			
11.1 Full-time permanent	1	1	1
11.3 Other than full-time permanent	2	2	2
11.9 Total personnel compensation	3	3	3
12.1 Civilian personnel benefits	1	1	1
21.0 Travel and transportation of persons	1	1	1
25.2 Other services	7	7	7
26.0 Supplies and materials	1	1	1
31.0 Equipment	1	1	1
41.0 Grants, subsidies, and contributions	1	1	1
99.9 Total new obligations	15	15	15

Personnel Summary

Identification code 14–9972–0–7–303	1999 actual	2000 est.	2001 est.
1001 Total compensable workyears: Full-time equivalent employment	70	70	70

ALLOCATIONS RECEIVED FROM OTHER ACCOUNTS

Note.—Obligations incurred under allocations from other accounts are included in the schedules of the parent appropriations as follows:

Department of Agriculture, Forest Service: "State and Private Forestry "

Department of Labor, Employment and Training Administration: "Training and Employment Services"

Department of Transportation, Federal Highway Administration:

"Federal-Aid Highways (Liquidation of Contract Authorization) (Highway Trust Fund)" and "Highway Studies, Feasibility, Design, Environmental, Engineering"

Department of the Interior, Bureau of Land Management: "Central Hazardous Materials Fund" and "Wildland Fire Management"

Department of the Interior, United States Fish and Wildlife Service: "Natural Resource Damage Assessment and Restoration Fund"

ADMINISTRATIVE PROVISIONS

Appropriations for the National Park Service shall be available for the purchase of not to exceed [384] *340* passenger motor vehicles, of which [298] *273* shall be for replacement only, including not to exceed [312] *319* for police-type use, 12 buses, and [6] *9* ambulances: *Provided*, That none of the funds appropriated to the National Park Service may be used to process any grant or contract documents which do not include the text of 18 U.S.C. 1913[: *Provided further*, That none of the funds appropriated to the National Park Service may be used to implement an agreement for the redevelopment of the southern end of Ellis Island until such agreement has been submitted to the Congress and shall not be implemented prior to the expiration of 30 calendar days (not including any day in which either House of Congress is not in session because of adjournment of more than three calendar days to a day certain) from the receipt by the Speaker of the House of Representatives and the President of the Senate of a full and comprehensive report on the development of the southern end of Ellis Island, including the facts and circumstances relied upon in support of the proposed project].

[None of the funds in this Act may be spent by the National Park Service for activities taken in direct response to the United Nations Biodiversity Convention.]

The National Park Service may distribute to operating units based on the safety record of each unit the costs of programs designed to improve workplace and employee safety, and to encourage employees receiving workers' compensation benefits pursuant to chapter 81 of title 5, United States Code, to return to appropriate positions for which they are medically able. *(Department of the Interior and Related Agencies Appropriations Act, 2000, as enacted by section 1000(a)(3) of the Consolidated Appropriations Act, 2000 (P.L. 106–113).)*

INDIAN AFFAIRS

BUREAU OF INDIAN AFFAIRS

Federal Funds

General and special funds:

OPERATION OF INDIAN PROGRAMS

For expenses necessary for the operation of Indian programs, as authorized by law, including the Snyder Act of November 2, 1921 (25 U.S.C. 13), the Indian Self-Determination and Education Assistance Act of 1975 (25 U.S.C. 450 et seq.), as amended, the Education Amendments of 1978 (25 U.S.C. 2001–2019), and the Tribally Controlled Schools Act of 1988 (25 U.S.C. 2501 et seq.), as amended, [$1,670,444,000] *$1,795,010,000*, to remain available until September 30, [2001] *2002* except as otherwise provided herein, of which not to exceed [$93,684,000] *$93,225,000* shall be for welfare assistance payments and notwithstanding any other provision of law, including but not limited to the Indian Self-Determination Act of 1975, as amended, not to exceed [$120,229,000] *$128,732,000* shall be available for payments to tribes and tribal organizations for contract support costs associated with ongoing contracts, grants, compacts, or annual funding agreements entered into with the Bureau prior to or during fiscal year [2000] *2001*, as authorized by such Act, except that tribes and tribal organizations may use their tribal priority allocations for unmet indirect costs of ongoing contracts, grants, or compacts, or annual funding agreements and for unmet welfare assistance costs; and up to $5,000,000 shall be for the Indian Self-Determination Fund which shall be available for the transitional cost of initial or expanded tribal contracts, grants, compacts or cooperative agreements with the Bureau under such Act; and of which not to exceed [$401,010,000] *$439,132,000* for school operations costs of Bureau-funded schools and other education programs shall become available on July 1, [2000] *2001*, and shall remain available until September 30, [2001] *2002*; and of which not to exceed [$56,991,000] *$78,242,000* shall remain available until expended for housing improvement, road maintenance, attorney fees, litigation support, self-governance grants, the Indian Self-Determination Fund, land records improvement, [and] the Navajo-Hopi Settlement Program, *and the repair and renovation of adult care institutions*: *Provided*, That notwithstanding any other provision of law, including but not limited to the Indian Self-Determination Act of 1975, as amended, and 25 U.S.C. 2008, not to exceed [$42,160,000] *$46,300,000* within and only from such amounts made available for school operations shall be available to tribes and tribal organizations for administrative cost grants associated with the operation of Bureau-funded schools: *Provided further*, That any forestry funds allocated to a tribe which remain unobligated as of September 30, [2001] *2002*, may be transferred during fiscal year [2002] *2003* to an Indian forest land assistance account established for the benefit of such tribe within the tribe's trust fund account: *Provided further*, That any such unobligated balances not so transferred shall expire on September 30, [2002] *2003*. *(Department of the Interior and Related Agencies Appropriations Act, 2000, as enacted by section 1000(a)(3) of the Consolidated Appropriations Act, 2000 (P.L. 106–113).)*

Program and Financing (in millions of dollars)

Identification code 14–2100–0–1–999		1999 actual	2000 est.	2001 est.
	Obligations by program activity:			
	Direct program:			
00.01	Tribal priority allocations	681	692	739
00.02	Other recurring programs	542	557	595
00.03	Non-recurring programs	51	55	59
00.04	Central office operations	50	54	58
00.05	Regional office operations	40	41	54
00.06	Special program and pooled overhead	192	238	259
09.07	Reimbursable program	118	155	170
09.08	Reimbursable program Y2K	21	5	
10.00	Total new obligations	1,695	1,797	1,934
	Budgetary resources available for obligation:			
21.40	Unobligated balance available, start of year	280	345	348
22.00	New budget authority (gross)	1,744	1,799	1,935
22.10	Resources available from recoveries of prior year obligations	20		
22.22	Unobligated balance transferred from other accounts	2	1	
23.90	Total budgetary resources available for obligation	2,046	2,145	2,283
23.95	Total new obligations	−1,695	−1,797	−1,934
23.98	Unobligated balance expiring or withdrawn	−7		
24.40	Unobligated balance available, end of year	345	348	349
	New budget authority (gross), detail:			
	Discretionary:			
40.00	Appropriation	1,584	1,670	1,795
40.75	Reduction pursuant to P.L. 106–51	−1		
40.76	Reduction pursuant to P.L. 106–113		−4	
41.00	Transferred to other accounts		−28	
42.00	Transferred from other accounts	1	1	
43.00	Appropriation (total discretionary)	1,584	1,639	1,795
	Spending authority from offsetting collections:			
68.00	Offsetting collections (cash)	125	160	140
68.10	From Federal sources: Change in receivables and unpaid, unfilled orders	35		
68.90	Spending authority from offsetting collections (total discretionary)	160	160	140
70.00	Total new budget authority (gross)	1,744	1,799	1,935
	Change in unpaid obligations:			
	Unpaid obligations, start of year:			
72.40	Obligated balance, start of year	226	147	243
72.95	From Federal sources: Receivables and unpaid, unfilled orders	50	85	85
72.99	Total unpaid obligations, start of year	276	232	328
73.10	Total new obligations	1,695	1,797	1,934
73.20	Total outlays (gross)	−1,712	−1,701	−1,831
73.40	Adjustments in expired accounts (net)	−7		
73.45	Adjustments in unexpired accounts	−20		
	Unpaid obligations, end of year:			
74.40	Obligated balance, end of year	147	243	346
74.95	From Federal sources: Receivables and unpaid, unfilled orders	85	85	85
74.99	Total unpaid obligations, end of year	232	328	431
	Outlays (gross), detail:			
86.90	Outlays from new discretionary authority	1,211	1,209	1,289
86.93	Outlays from discretionary balances	501	491	541
87.00	Total outlays (gross)	1,712	1,701	1,831
	Offsets:			
	Against gross budget authority and outlays:			
	Offsetting collections (cash) from:			
	Federal sources:			
88.00	Federal sources	−121	−133	−137
88.00	Federal Sources Y2K	−2	−24	
88.40	Non-Federal sources	−2	−3	−3
88.90	Total, offsetting collections (cash)	−125	−160	−140
	Against gross budget authority only:			
88.95	From Federal sources: Change in receivables and unpaid, unfilled orders	−35		
	Net budget authority and outlays:			
89.00	Budget authority	1,584	1,639	1,795
90.00	Outlays	1,587	1,541	1,691

Summary of Budget Authority and Outlays

(in millions of dollars)

	1999 actual	*2000 est.*	*2001 est.*
Enacted/requested:			
Budget Authority	1,584	1,639	1,795
Outlays	1,587	1,540	1,690
Legislative proposal, not subject to PAYGO:			
Budget Authority			
Outlays			
Total:			
Budget Authority	1,584	1,639	1,795
Outlays	1,587	1,540	1,690

The Operation of Indian Programs appropriation consists of a wide range of services and benefits provided to Indian Tribes, Alaskan Native groups, and individual Native Americans. As part of a joint Department of the Interior and Department of Justice initiative to address the serious crime problem on many reservations, an increase of $16 million in new funding for law enforcement is included in Operation of Indian Programs for 2001.

Tribal priority allocations.—This activity includes the majority of funds used to support ongoing programs at the local Tribal level. Funding priorities for base programs included in Tribal Priority Allocations are determined by Tribes. Although budget estimates include specific amounts for individual programs, funds may be shifted among programs within the total available for a Tribe or a BIA agency or regional office at the time of budget execution.

Other recurring programs.—This activity includes ongoing programs for which funds are (1) distributed by formula, such as elementary and secondary school operations and Tribal community colleges; and (2) for resource management activities that carry out specific laws or court-ordered settlements.

Non-recurring programs.—This activity includes programs that support Indian reservation and Tribal projects of limited duration, such as noxious weed eradication, cadastral surveys, and forest development.

Central office operations.—This activity supports the executive, program, and administrative management costs of central office organizations, most of which are located in Washington, DC.

Regional office operations.—The Bureau of Indian Affairs has 12 regional offices located throughout the country. Regional Directors have line authority over agency office superintendents. Most of the agency offices are located on Indian reservations. Virtually all of the staff and related administrative support costs for area and agency offices are included within this activity. Regional Directors have flexibility in aligning their staff and resources to best meet the program requirements of the Tribes within their region.

Special programs and pooled overhead.—Most of the funds in this activity support law enforcement and bureau-wide expenses for items such as unemployment compensation, workers compensation, facilities rentals, telecommunications, and data processing. This activity includes the Bureau's two post-secondary schools, the Indian police academy, the Indian Arts and Crafts Board, the Indian Integrated Resources Informa-

General and special funds—Continued

OPERATION OF INDIAN PROGRAMS—Continued

tion Program, and non-education facilities operation and maintenance.

Object Classification (in millions of dollars)

Identification code 14–2100–0–1–999		1999 actual	2000 est.	2001 est.
	Direct obligations:			
	Personnel compensation:			
11.1	Full-time permanent	200	211	227
11.3	Other than full-time permanent	87	91	98
11.5	Other personnel compensation	13	14	15
11.9	Total personnel compensation	300	316	340
12.1	Civilian personnel benefits	71	75	81
13.0	Benefits for former personnel	11	12	13
21.0	Travel and transportation of persons	14	15	16
22.0	Transportation of things	12	13	14
23.1	Rental payments to GSA	18	19	20
23.2	Rental payments to others	3	3	3
23.3	Communications, utilities, and miscellaneous charges	23	24	26
24.0	Printing and reproduction	1	1	1
25.1	Advisory and assistance services	1	1	1
25.2	Other services	675	710	767
25.3	Purchases of goods and services from Government accounts	24	25	27
25.4	Operation and maintenance of facilities	1	1	1
25.7	Operation and maintenance of equipment	3	3	3
25.8	Subsistence and support of persons	1	1	1
26.0	Supplies and materials	31	33	36
31.0	Equipment	14	15	16
41.0	Grants, subsidies, and contributions	353	370	398
99.0	Subtotal, direct obligations	1,556	1,637	1,764
99.0	Reimbursable obligations	139	160	170
99.9	Total new obligations	1,695	1,797	1,934

Personnel Summary

Identification code 14–2100–0–1–999		1999 actual	2000 est.	2001 est.
	Direct:			
1001	Total compensable workyears: Full-time equivalent employment	7,512	7,400	7,956
	Reimbursable:			
2001	Total compensable workyears: Full-time equivalent employment	191	191	191
	Allocation account:			
3001	Total compensable workyears: Full-time equivalent employment	439	514	534

OPERATION OF INDIAN PROGRAMS

(Legislative proposal, not subject to PAYGO)

Program and Financing (in millions of dollars)

Identification code 14–2100–2–1–999		1999 actual	2000 est.	2001 est.
	Obligations by program activity:			
	Direct program:			
00.01	Special Programs and Pooled Overhead			5
00.02	Special Programs and Pooled Overhead			−5
10.00	Total new obligations			
	New budget authority (gross), detail:			
	Discretionary:			
40.00	Appropriation			−5
42.00	Transferred from other accounts			5
43.00	Appropriation (total discretionary)			
	Net budget authority and outlays:			
89.00	Budget authority			
90.00	Outlays			

The Administration will propose legislation authorizing the FCC to establish a lease fee on the use of analog spectrum by commercial television broadcasters, subject to appropriations. A portion of the amounts collected will be transferred to the Bureau of Indian Affairs to be used for the purposes of promoting and upgrading public safety wireless communications equipment and facilities across Indian reservations.

Object Classification (in millions of dollars)

Identification code 14–2100–2–1–999		1999 actual	2000 est.	2001 est.
	Equipment:			
31.0	Equipment			−5
31.0	Equipment			5
99.9	Total new obligations			

CONSTRUCTION

For construction, repair, improvement, and maintenance of irrigation and power systems, buildings, utilities, and other facilities, including architectural and engineering services by contract; acquisition of lands, and interests in lands; and preparation of lands for farming, and for construction of the Navajo Indian Irrigation Project pursuant to Public Law 87–483, [$169,884,000] *$365,912,000*, to remain available until expended: *Provided*, That such amounts as may be available for the construction of the Navajo Indian Irrigation Project may be transferred to the Bureau of Reclamation: *Provided further*, That not to exceed 6 percent of contract authority available to the Bureau of Indian Affairs from the Federal Highway Trust Fund may be used to cover the road program management costs of the Bureau: *Provided further*, That any funds provided for the Safety of Dams program pursuant to 25 U.S.C. 13 shall be made available on a nonreimbursable basis: *Provided further*, That for fiscal year [2000] *2001*, in implementing new construction or facilities improvement and repair project grants in excess of $100,000 that are provided to tribally controlled grant schools under Public Law 100–297, as amended, the Secretary of the Interior shall use the Administrative and Audit Requirements and Cost Principles for Assistance Programs contained in 43 CFR part 12 as the regulatory requirements: *Provided further*, That such grants shall not be subject to section 12.61 of 43 CFR; the Secretary and the grantee shall negotiate and determine a schedule of payments for the work to be performed: *Provided further*, That in considering applications, the Secretary shall consider whether the Indian tribe or tribal organization would be deficient in assuring that the construction projects conform to applicable building standards and codes and Federal, tribal, or State health and safety standards as required by 25 U.S.C. 2005(a), with respect to organizational and financial management capabilities: *Provided further*, That if the Secretary declines an application, the Secretary shall follow the requirements contained in 25 U.S.C. 2505(f): *Provided further*, That any disputes between the Secretary and any grantee concerning a grant shall be subject to the disputes provision in 25 U.S.C. 2508(e): *Provided further*, That [notwithstanding any other provision of law, collections from the settlements between the United States and the Puyallup tribe concerning Chief Leschi school are made available for school construction in fiscal year 2000 and hereafter] *the Secretary is authorized to enter into agreements with Federally recognized Tribes or tribal consortia issuing qualified school construction bonds or other taxable bonds for the purpose of repairing or replacing Bureau of Indian Affairs-funded elementary and secondary schools; Provided further, That of the amounts provided herein, up to $30,000,000 may be used to defease the principal of such bonds: Provided further, That the term of such bonds issued may not exceed fifteen years: Provided further, That such bonds shall state on their face that they are not guaranteed by the Federal Government of the United States. (Department of the Interior and Related Agencies Appropriations Act, 2000, as enacted by section 1000(a)(3) of the Consolidated Appropriations Act, 2000 (P.L. 106–113).)*

Program and Financing (in millions of dollars)

Identification code 14–2301–0–1–452		1999 actual	2000 est.	2001 est.
	Obligations by program activity:			
	Direct program:			
00.01	Education construction	63	122	282
00.02	Public safety and justice construction	6	8	6
00.03	Resource management construction	42	56	56

00.05	General administration	13	9	9
00.07	Emergency response	3	2	
09.07	Reimbursable program	10	6	6
10.00	Total new obligations	137	203	359
	Budgetary resources available for obligation:			
21.40	Unobligated balance available, start of year	69	72	73
22.00	New budget authority (gross)	141	206	374
23.90	Total budgetary resources available for obligation	210	278	447
23.95	Total new obligations	−137	−203	−359
24.40	Unobligated balance available, end of year	72	73	88
	New budget authority (gross), detail:			
	Discretionary:			
40.00	Appropriation	123	169	366
42.00	Transferred from other accounts		28	
43.00	Appropriation (total discretionary)	123	197	366
68.00	Spending authority from offsetting collections: Offsetting collections (cash)	18	9	8
70.00	Total new budget authority (gross)	141	206	374
	Change in unpaid obligations:			
	Unpaid obligations, start of year:			
72.40	Obligated balance, start of year	124	85	154
72.95	From Federal sources: Receivables and unpaid, unfilled orders	10	10	
72.99	Total unpaid obligations, start of year	134	95	154
73.10	Total new obligations	137	203	359
73.20	Total outlays (gross)	−177	−144	−207
	Unpaid obligations, end of year:			
74.40	Obligated balance, end of year	85	154	306
74.95	From Federal sources: Receivables and unpaid, unfilled orders	10		
74.99	Total unpaid obligations, end of year	95	154	306
	Outlays (gross), detail:			
86.90	Outlays from new discretionary authority	47	54	92
86.93	Outlays from discretionary balances	130	92	117
87.00	Total outlays (gross)	177	144	207
	Offsets:			
	Against gross budget authority and outlays:			
	Offsetting collections (cash) from:			
88.00	Federal sources	−18	−6	−6
88.45	Offsetting governmental collections from the public		−3	−2
88.90	Total, offsetting collections (cash)	−18	−9	−8
	Net budget authority and outlays:			
89.00	Budget authority	123	197	366
90.00	Outlays	159	135	199

Education construction.—This activity provides for the planning, design, construction, maintenance and rehabilitation of Bureau-funded school facilities and the repair needs for employee housing.

As part of the Administration's proposed school modernization initiative to provide school repairs and replacement in needy school districts throughout the country, funding for a portion of the Construction account may be used to defease qualified school construction bonds or other taxable bonds. These funds may be made available to be held in escrow, and at maturity used to defease qualified school construction bonds by ensuring the repayment of principal to bond holders.

In addition, a portion of the funds from the Construction account are proposed as part of the third year of the Administration's facilities restoration initiative. These funds emphasize the Administration's commitment to the long-term stewardship of federal lands and facilities.

Public safety and justice construction.—This activity provides for the planning, design, improvement, repair, and construction of detention centers for Indian youth and adults.

Resources management construction.—This activity provides for the construction, extension, and rehabilitation of irrigation projects, dams, and related power systems on Indian reservations. Funds for the Navajo Indian irrigation project may be transferred to the Bureau of Reclamation.

General administration.—This activity provides for the improvement and repair of the Bureau's non-education facilities, the telecommunications system, the facilities management information system and construction program management.

Tribal government construction.—This activity is used when self-governance annual negotiated agreements include construction resources.

Object Classification (in millions of dollars)

Identification code 14–2301–0–1–452		1999 actual	2000 est.	2001 est.
	Direct obligations:			
	Personnel compensation:			
11.1	Full-time permanent	7	22	24
11.3	Other than full-time permanent	1	2	2
11.9	Total personnel compensation	8	24	26
12.1	Civilian personnel benefits	2	3	7
25.2	Other services	44	65	67
25.3	Purchases of goods and services from Government accounts	8	9	9
25.4	Operation and maintenance of facilities	8	9	9
25.7	Operation and maintenance of equipment	3	4	4
26.0	Supplies and materials	2	3	3
31.0	Equipment	7	8	8
41.0	Grants, subsidies, and contributions	20	45	193
99.0	Subtotal, direct obligations	102	170	326
99.0	Reimbursable obligations	10	6	6
	Allocation Account:			
11.1	Personnel compensation: Full-time permanent	3	3	3
25.2	Other services	11	11	11
32.0	Land and structures	11	13	13
99.0	Subtotal, allocation account	25	27	27
99.9	Total new obligations	137	203	359

Personnel Summary

Identification code 14–2301–0–1–452		1999 actual	2000 est.	2001 est.
	Direct:			
1001	Total compensable workyears: Full-time equivalent employment	150	385	405
	Reimbursable:			
2001	Total compensable workyears: Full-time equivalent employment	42	42	42
	Allocation account:			
3001	Total compensable workyears: Full-time equivalent employment	605	605	605

WHITE EARTH SETTLEMENT FUND

Program and Financing (in millions of dollars)

Identification code 14–2204–0–1–452		1999 actual	2000 est.	2001 est.
	Obligations by program activity:			
10.00	Total new obligations (object class 41.0)	2	2	2
	Budgetary resources available for obligation:			
22.00	New budget authority (gross)	2	2	2
23.95	Total new obligations	−2	−2	−2
	New budget authority (gross), detail:			
	Mandatory:			
60.05	Appropriation (indefinite)	2	2	2
	Change in unpaid obligations:			
73.10	Total new obligations	2	2	2
73.20	Total outlays (gross)	−2	−2	−2
	Outlays (gross), detail:			
86.97	Outlays from new mandatory authority	2	2	2
	Net budget authority and outlays:			
89.00	Budget authority	2	2	2

General and special funds—Continued

WHITE EARTH SETTLEMENT FUND—Continued

Program and Financing (in millions of dollars)—Continued

Identification code 14–2204–0–1–452	1999 actual	2000 est.	2001 est.
90.00 Outlays	2	2	2

The White Earth Reservation Land Settlement Act of 1985 (Public Law 99–264) authorizes the payment of funds to eligible allottees or heirs of the White Earth Reservation, MN, as determined by the Secretary of the Interior. The payment of funds shall be treated as the final judgment, award, or compromise settlement under the provisions of title 31, United States Code, section 1304.

INDIAN LAND AND WATER CLAIM SETTLEMENTS AND MISCELLANEOUS PAYMENTS TO INDIANS

For miscellaneous payments to Indian tribes and individuals and for necessary administrative expenses, [$27,256,000] *$34,026,000*, to remain available until expended; of which [$25,260,000] *$25,025,000* shall be available for implementation of enacted Indian land and water claim settlements pursuant to Public Laws 101–618[,] and 102–575, and for implementation of other enacted water rights settlements; *of which $8,000,000 shall be available for Tribal compact administration, economic development and future water supplies facilities under Public Law 106–163;* and of which [$1,871,000] *$877,000* shall be available pursuant to Public Laws 99–264[, 100–383, 103–402] and 100–580. *(Department of the Interior and Related Agencies Appropriations Act, 2000, as enacted by section 1000(a)(3) of the Consolidated Appropriations Act, 2000 (P.L. 106–113).)*

Program and Financing (in millions of dollars)

Identification code 14–2303–0–1–452	1999 actual	2000 est.	2001 est.
Obligations by program activity:			
00.01 White Earth Reservation Claims Settlement Act		1	1
00.02 Hoopa Yurok Settlement Act	2	3	
00.03 Pyramid Lake Water Rights Settlement	2	5	
00.04 Ute Indian Water Rights Settlement	25	25	25
00.05 Aleution Pribilof Church Restoration		1	
00.06 Rocky Boys			8
10.00 Total new obligations	29	35	34
Budgetary resources available for obligation:			
21.40 Unobligated balance available, start of year	8	8	
22.00 New budget authority (gross)	29	27	34
23.90 Total budgetary resources available for obligation	37	35	34
23.95 Total new obligations	−29	−35	−34
24.40 Unobligated balance available, end of year	8		
New budget authority (gross), detail:			
Discretionary:			
40.00 Appropriation	29	27	34
Change in unpaid obligations:			
72.40 Unpaid obligations, start of year: Obligated balance, start of year	2	2	10
73.10 Total new obligations	29	35	34
73.20 Total outlays (gross)	−29	−27	−34
74.40 Unpaid obligations, end of year: Obligated balance, end of year	2	10	10
Outlays (gross), detail:			
86.90 Outlays from new discretionary authority	26	24	31
86.93 Outlays from discretionary balances	3	3	3
87.00 Total outlays (gross)	29	27	34
Net budget authority and outlays:			
89.00 Budget authority	29	27	34
90.00 Outlays	29	27	34

This account covers expenses associated with the following activities.

White Earth Reservation Claims Settlement Act (Public Law 99–264).—Funds are used to investigate and verify questionable transfers of land by which individual Indian allottees, or their heirs, were divested of ownership and to achieve the payment of compensation to said allottees or heirs in accordance with the Act. A major portion of work is contracted under Public Law 93–638, as amended, to the White Earth Reservation Business Committee. Approximately 1,000 compensation payments will be made in 2000.

Chippewa Cree Tribe of the Rocky Boy's Reservation Indian Reserved Water Rights Settlement and Water Supply Enhancement Act (Public Law 106–163).—Funds are requested for the settlement of the water rights claims of the Chippewa Cree Tribe. Funds will be used for compact administration and economic development and future water supply activities.

Hoopa-Yurok Settlement Act (Public Law 100–580).—The Act provides for the settlement of reservation lands between the Hoopa Valley Tribe and the Yurok Indians in northern California. Funds will be used for administrative expenses related to implementing the settlement.

Truckee-Carson-Pyramid Lake Water Settlement Act (Public Law 101–618).—The Act provides for the settlement of claims of the Pyramid Lake Paiute Tribe (NV). Funds will be used to provide payments to the Truckee-Carson Irrigation District for service of water rights acquired.

Ute Indian Water Rights Settlement (Public Law 102–575).—Funds are requested for the settlement of the water rights claims of the Ute Indian Tribe (UT). Funds are authorized to be appropriated for Tribal farming operations, stream and reservoir improvements, and recreation enhancement.

Object Classification (in millions of dollars)

Identification code 14–2303–0–1–452	1999 actual	2000 est.	2001 est.
25.2 Other services	3	3	3
41.0 Grants, subsidies, and contributions	26	32	31
99.9 Total new obligations	29	35	34

Personnel Summary

Identification code 14–2303–0–1–452	1999 actual	2000 est.	2001 est.
1001 Total compensable workyears: Full-time equivalent employment	3	3	3

OPERATION AND MAINTENANCE OF QUARTERS

Unavailable Collections (in millions of dollars)

Identification code 14–5051–0–2–452	1999 actual	2000 est.	2001 est.
Balance, start of year:			
01.99 Balance, start of year			
Receipts:			
02.01 Rents and charges for quarters, Bureau of Indian Affairs, Interior	5	6	6
Appropriation:			
05.01 Operation and maintenance of quarters	−5	−6	−6
07.99 Total balance, end of year			

Program and Financing (in millions of dollars)

Identification code 14–5051–0–2–452	1999 actual	2000 est.	2001 est.
Obligations by program activity:			
10.00 Total new obligations	4	6	6
Budgetary resources available for obligation:			
21.40 Unobligated balance available, start of year	2	3	2
22.00 New budget authority (gross)	5	6	6
23.90 Total budgetary resources available for obligation	7	9	8
23.95 Total new obligations	−4	−6	−6
24.40 Unobligated balance available, end of year	3	2	2

		1999 actual	2000 est.	2001 est.
	New budget authority (gross), detail:			
	Mandatory:			
60.25	Appropriation (special fund, indefinite)	5	6	6
	Change in unpaid obligations:			
72.40	Unpaid obligations, start of year: Obligated balance, start of year	1	1	2
73.10	Total new obligations	4	6	6
73.20	Total outlays (gross)	−4	−6	−6
74.40	Unpaid obligations, end of year: Obligated balance, end of year	1	2	2
	Outlays (gross), detail:			
86.97	Outlays from new mandatory authority	4	6	6
	Net budget authority and outlays:			
89.00	Budget authority	5	6	6
90.00	Outlays	4	6	6

Public Law 88–459 (Federal Employees Quarters and Facilities Act of 1964) is the basic authority under which the Secretary utilizes funds from the rental of quarters to defer the costs of operation and maintenance incidental to the employee quarters program. Public Law 98–473 established a special fund, to remain available until expended, for the operation and maintenance of quarters.

Object Classification (in millions of dollars)

Identification code 14–5051–0–2–452		1999 actual	2000 est.	2001 est.
11.1	Direct obligations: Personnel compensation: Full-time permanent	1	2	2
99.5	Below reporting threshold	3	4	4
99.9	Total new obligations	4	6	6

Personnel Summary

Identification code 14–5051–0–2–452		1999 actual	2000 est.	2001 est.
1001	Total compensable workyears: Full-time equivalent employment	70	70	70

MISCELLANEOUS PERMANENT APPROPRIATIONS

Unavailable Collections (in millions of dollars)

Identification code 14–9925–0–2–452		1999 actual	2000 est.	2001 est.
	Balance, start of year:			
01.99	Balance, start of year	....	....	....
	Receipts:			
02.02	Deposits, operation and maintenance, Indian irrigation systems	21	28	28
02.03	Earnings on investments, operation and maintenance, Indian irrigation systems, Interior	2	2	2
02.04	Alaska resupply program	1	2	2
02.05	Power revenues, Indian irrigation projects	45	44	44
02.06	Earnings on investments, Indian irrigation projects	3	3	4
02.99	Total receipts	72	79	80
	Appropriation:			
05.01	Miscellaneous permanent appropriations	−73	−79	−80
07.99	Total balance, end of year	....	....	....

Program and Financing (in millions of dollars)

Identification code 14–9925–0–2–452		1999 actual	2000 est.	2001 est.
	Obligations by program activity:			
00.02	Operation and maintenance, Indian irrigation systems	24	27	27
00.03	Power systems, Indian irrigation projects	48	48	49
00.04	Alaska resupply program	1	4	4
10.00	Total new obligations	73	79	80
	Budgetary resources available for obligation:			
21.40	Unobligated balance available, start of year	69	69	69
22.00	New budget authority (gross)	73	79	80
23.90	Total budgetary resources available for obligation	142	148	149
23.95	Total new obligations	−73	−79	−80
24.40	Unobligated balance available, end of year	69	69	69
	New budget authority (gross), detail:			
	Mandatory:			
60.25	Appropriation (special fund, indefinite)	73	79	80
	Change in unpaid obligations:			
72.40	Unpaid obligations, start of year: Obligated balance, start of year	13	14	19
73.10	Total new obligations	73	79	80
73.20	Total outlays (gross)	−72	−74	−79
74.40	Unpaid obligations, end of year: Obligated balance, end of year	14	19	20
	Outlays (gross), detail:			
86.97	Outlays from new mandatory authority	15	16	16
86.98	Outlays from mandatory balances	57	58	63
87.00	Total outlays (gross)	72	74	79
	Net budget authority and outlays:			
89.00	Budget authority	73	79	80
90.00	Outlays	72	74	79
	Memorandum (non-add) entries:			
92.01	Total investments, start of year: U.S. securities: Par value	39	47	47
92.02	Total investments, end of year: U.S. securities: Par value	47	47	47

Claims and treaty obligations.—Payments are made to fulfill treaty obligations with the Senecas of New York (act of February 19, 1831), the Six Nations of New York (act of November 11, 1794), and the Pawnees of Oklahoma (the treaty of September 24, 1857).

Operation and maintenance, Indian irrigation systems.—Revenues derived from charges for operation and maintenance of Indian irrigation projects are used to defray in part the cost of operating and maintaining these projects (60 Stat. 895).

Power systems, Indian irrigation projects.—Revenues collected from the sale of electric power by the Colorado River and Flathead power systems are used to operate and maintain those systems (60 Stat. 895; 65 Stat. 254). This activity also includes Cochiti Wet Field Solution funds that were transferred from the Corps of Engineers to pay for operation and maintenance, repair, and replacement of the ongoing drainage system (P.L. 102–358).

Alaska resupply program.—Revenues collected from operation of the Alaska Resupply Program are used to operate and maintain this program (P.L. 77–457, 56 Stat. 95).

Object Classification (in millions of dollars)

Identification code 14–9925–0–2–452		1999 actual	2000 est.	2001 est.
11.1	Personnel compensation: Full-time permanent	15	16	17
12.1	Civilian personnel benefits	5	5	5
22.0	Transportation of things	1	1	1
23.3	Communications, utilities, and miscellaneous charges	2	3	3
25.2	Other services	26	30	30
25.3	Purchases of goods and services from Government accounts	5	5	5
25.4	Operation and maintenance of facilities	11	12	12
26.0	Supplies and materials	3	4	4
31.0	Equipment	2	2	2
32.0	Land and structures	1	1	1
99.0	Subtotal, direct obligations	71	79	80
99.5	Below reporting threshold	2	....	....
99.9	Total new obligations	73	79	80

Personnel Summary

Identification code 14–9925–0–2–452		1999 actual	2000 est.	2001 est.
1001	Total compensable workyears: Full-time equivalent employment	330	330	330

General and special funds—Continued

INDIAN DIRECT LOAN PROGRAM ACCOUNT

Program and Financing (in millions of dollars)

Identification code 14–2627–0–1–452	1999 actual	2000 est.	2001 est.
Obligations by program activity:			
00.05 Reestimate of Direct Loan Subsidy	1	4	
00.06 Interest on Reestimates of Direct Loan Subsidy		2	
10.00 Total new obligations (object class 41.0)	1	6	
Budgetary resources available for obligation:			
22.00 New budget authority (gross)	1	6	1
23.95 Total new obligations	−1	−6	
23.98 Unobligated balance expiring or withdrawn			−1
New budget authority (gross), detail:			
Mandatory:			
60.05 Appropriation (indefinite)	1	6	1
Change in unpaid obligations:			
73.10 Total new obligations	1	6	
73.20 Total outlays (gross)	−1	−6	−1
Outlays (gross), detail:			
86.97 Outlays from new mandatory authority	1	6	1
Net budget authority and outlays:			
89.00 Budget authority	1	6	1
90.00 Outlays	1	6	1

Summary of Loan Levels, Subsidy Budget Authority and Outlays by Program (in millions of dollars)

Identification code 14–2627–0–1–452	1999 actual	2000 est.	2001 est.
Direct loan subsidy budget authority:			
1330 Subsidy budget authority		6	
1339 Total subsidy budget authority		6	
Direct loan subsidy outlays:			
1340 Subsidy outlays		6	
1349 Total subsidy outlays		6	
Administrative expense data:			
3510 Budget authority			
3580 Outlays from balances			
3590 Outlays from new authority			

Credit accounts:

INDIAN DIRECT LOAN FINANCING ACCOUNT

Program and Financing (in millions of dollars)

Identification code 14–4416–0–3–452	1999 actual	2000 est.	2001 est.
Obligations by program activity:			
00.01 Interest paid to Treasury	1	5	1
00.02 Repayment of Principal to Treasury	1	3	1
10.00 Total new obligations	2	8	2
Budgetary resources available for obligation:			
21.40 Unobligated balance available, start of year	2		
22.00 New financing authority (gross)	3	8	2
22.40 Capital transfer to general fund	−2		
23.90 Total budgetary resources available for obligation	3	8	2
23.95 Total new obligations	−2	−8	−2
New financing authority (gross), detail:			
Discretionary:			
68.00 Spending authority from offsetting collections: Offsetting collections (cash)	3	2	2
Mandatory:			
69.00 Offsetting collections (cash)		6	
70.00 Total new financing authority (gross)	3	8	2
Change in unpaid obligations:			
73.10 Total new obligations	2	8	2
73.20 Total financing disbursements (gross)	−2	−6	−2
87.00 Total financing disbursements (gross)	2	6	2
Offsets:			
Against gross financing authority and financing disbursements:			
Offsetting collections (cash) from:			
88.00 Direct Subsidy from Program Account		−6	
Non-Federal sources:			
88.40 Collections of loans	−2	−1	−1
88.40 Revenues, interest on loans	−1	−1	−1
88.90 Total, offsetting collections (cash)	−3	−8	−2
Net financing authority and financing disbursements:			
89.00 Financing authority			
90.00 Financing disbursements		−2	

As required by the Federal Credit Reform Act of 1990, this non-budgetary account records all cash flows to and from the Government resulting from direct loans obligated in 1992 and beyond (including modifications of direct loans that resulted from obligations in any year). The amounts in this account are a means of financing and are not included in the budget totals.

Status of Direct Loans (in millions of dollars)

Identification code 14–4416–0–3–452	1999 actual	2000 est.	2001 est.
Position with respect to appropriations act limitation on obligations:			
1111 Limitation on direct loans			
1131 Direct loan obligations exempt from limitation			
1150 Total direct loan obligations			
Cumulative balance of direct loans outstanding:			
1210 Outstanding, start of year	29	28	21
1251 Repayments: Repayments and prepayments	−1	−1	−1
1263 Write-offs for default: Direct loans		−6	−1
1290 Outstanding, end of year	28	21	19

Balance Sheet (in millions of dollars)

Identification code 14–4416–0–3–452	1998 actual	1999 actual	2000 est.	2001 est.
ASSETS:				
Net value of assets related to post-1991 direct loans receivable:				
1401 Direct loans receivable, gross	30	28	21	19
1402 Interest receivable	5	5	5	3
1405 Allowance for subsidy cost (–)	–9	–12	–5	–5
1499 Net present value of assets related to direct loans	26	21	21	17
1999 Total assets	26	21	21	17
LIABILITIES:				
2104 Federal liabilities: Resources payable to Treasury	26	21	21	17
2999 Total liabilities	26	21	21	17
NET POSITION:				
3300 Cumulative results of operations				
3999 Total net position				
4999 Total liabilities and net position	26	21	21	17

REVOLVING FUND FOR LOANS LIQUIDATING ACCOUNT

Program and Financing (in millions of dollars)

Identification code 14–4409–0–3–452	1999 actual	2000 est.	2001 est.
Obligations by program activity:			
10.00 Total new obligations (object class 99.5)			
Budgetary resources available for obligation:			
21.40 Unobligated balance available, start of year	8		

		1999 actual	2000 est.	2001 est.
22.00	New budget authority (gross)	6	3	3
22.40	Capital transfer to general fund	−14	−3	−3
23.90	Total budgetary resources available for obligation			
23.95	Total new obligations			
	New budget authority (gross), detail:			
	Mandatory:			
69.00	Offsetting collections (cash)	6	3	3
	Offsets:			
	Against gross budget authority and outlays:			
	Offsetting collections (cash) from:			
	Non-Federal sources:			
88.40	Collections of loans	−4	−2	−2
88.40	Revenues, interest on loans	−2	−1	−1
88.90	Total, offsetting collections (cash)	−6	−3	−3
	Net budget authority and outlays:			
89.00	Budget authority			
90.00	Outlays	−6	−3	−3

Status of Direct Loans (in millions of dollars)

Identification code 14–4409–0–3–452		1999 actual	2000 est.	2001 est.
	Cumulative balance of direct loans outstanding:			
1210	Outstanding, start of year	47	43	40
1251	Repayments: Repayments and prepayments	−3	−2	−2
1263	Write-offs for default: Direct loans	−1	−1	−1
1290	Outstanding, end of year	43	40	37

As required by the Federal Credit Reform Act of 1990, this account records for this program, all cash flows to and from the Government resulting from direct loans obligated prior to 1992. This account is shown on a cash basis. All new activity in this program in 1992 and beyond (including modifications of direct loans that resulted from obligations or commitments in any year) is recorded in corresponding program and financing accounts.

Statement of Operations (in millions of dollars)

Identification code 14–4409–0–3–452		1998 actual	1999 actual	2000 est.	2001 est.
0101	Revenue		3	2	2
0102	Expense		−1	−1	−1
0105	Net income or loss (−)		2	1	1

Balance Sheet (in millions of dollars)

Identification code 14–4409–0–3–452		1998 actual	1999 actual	2000 est.	2001 est.
	ASSETS:				
	Net value of assets related to pre–1992 direct loans receivable and acquired defaulted guaranteed loans receivable:				
1601	Direct loans, gross	47	44	40	36
1602	Interest receivable	10	10	8	−7
1603	Allowance for estimated uncollectible loans and interest (−)	−15	−14	−12	−11
1604	Direct loans and interest receivable, net	42	40	36	18
1699	Value of assets related to direct loans	42	40	36	18
1999	Total assets	42	40	36	18
	LIABILITIES:				
2104	Federal liabilities: Resources payable to Treasury	42	40	36	18
2999	Total liabilities	42	40	36	18
	NET POSITION:				
3999	Total net position				
4999	Total liabilities and net position	42	40	36	18

INDIAN GUARANTEED LOAN PROGRAM ACCOUNT

For the cost of guaranteed loans, [$4,500,000] *$5,520,000*, as authorized by the Indian Financing Act of 1974, as amended: *Provided*, That such costs, including the cost of modifying such loans, shall be as defined in section 502 of the Congressional Budget Act of 1974: *Provided further*, That these funds are available to subsidize total loan principal, any part of which is to be guaranteed, not to exceed [$59,682,00] *$82,020,802*.

In addition, for administrative expenses to carry out the guaranteed loan programs, [$508,000] *$488,000*. *(Department of the Interior and Related Agencies Appropriations Act, 2000, as enacted by section 1000(a)(3) of the Consolidated Appropriations Act, 2000 (P.L. 106–113).)*

General Fund Credit Receipt Accounts (in millions of dollars)

Identification code 14–2628–0–1–452		1999 actual	2000 est.	2001 est.
0101	Indian loan guarantee, downward reestimates of subsidies		21	

Program and Financing (in millions of dollars)

Identification code 14–2628–0–1–452		1999 actual	2000 est.	2001 est.
	Obligations by program activity:			
00.02	Guaranteed loan subsidy	4	4	5
00.04	Subsidy for modifications of loan guarantees			
00.07	Reestimates of Guaranteed loan subsidy			
00.08	Interest on reeestimates of loan guaranty subsidy			
00.09	Administrative expenses	1	1	1
10.00	Total new obligations	5	5	6
	Budgetary resources available for obligation:			
22.00	New budget authority (gross)	5	5	6
23.95	Total new obligations	−5	−5	−6
	New budget authority (gross), detail:			
	Discretionary:			
40.00	Appropriation	5	5	6
	Change in unpaid obligations:			
72.40	Unpaid obligations, start of year: Obligated balance, start of year	10	12	10
73.10	Total new obligations	5	5	6
73.20	Total outlays (gross)	−4	−7	−7
74.40	Unpaid obligations, end of year: Obligated balance, end of year	12	10	9
	Outlays (gross), detail:			
86.90	Outlays from new discretionary authority	1	1	1
86.93	Outlays from discretionary balances	3	4	6
87.00	Total outlays (gross)	4	7	7
	Net budget authority and outlays:			
89.00	Budget authority	5	5	6
90.00	Outlays	4	7	7

As required by the Federal Credit Reform Act of 1990, this account records for this program, the subsidy costs associated with loan guarantees committed in 1992 and beyond (including modifications of loan guarantees that resulted from obligations or commitments in any year), as well as administrative expenses of this program. The subsidy amounts are estimated on a present value basis; the administrative expenses are estimated on a cash basis. Loan guarantees are targeted to projects with an emphasis on manufacturing, business services, and tourism (hotels, motels, restaurants) providing increased economic development on Indian reservations.

Summary of Loan Levels, Subsidy Budget Authority and Outlays by Program (in millions of dollars)

Identification code 14–2628–0–1–452		1999 actual	2000 est.	2001 est.
	Guaranteed loan levels supportable by subsidy budget authority:			
2150	Loan guarantee levels	60	60	82

Credit accounts—Continued

INDIAN GUARANTEED LOAN PROGRAM ACCOUNT—Continued

Summary of Loan Levels, Subsidy Budget Authority and Outlays by Program (in millions of dollars)—Continued

Identification code 14–2628–0–1–452		1999 actual	2000 est.	2001 est.
2159	Total loan guarantee levels	60	60	82
	Guaranteed loan subsidy (in percent):			
2320	Subsidy rate	7.54	7.54	6.73
2329	Weighted average subsidy rate	7.54	7.54	6.73
	Guaranteed loan subsidy budget authority:			
2330	Subsidy budget authority	4	−16	5
2339	Total subsidy budget authority	4	−16	5
	Guaranteed loan subsidy outlays:			
2340	Subsidy outlays	4	4	5
2349	Total subsidy outlays	4	4	5
	Administrative expense data:			
3510	Budget authority	1	1	1
3580	Outlays from balances			
3590	Outlays from new authority		1	1

Object Classification (in millions of dollars)

Identification code 14–2628–0–1–452		1999 actual	2000 est.	2001 est.
41.0	Direct obligations: Grants, subsidies, and contributions	4	4	5
99.5	Below reporting threshold	1	1	1
99.9	Total new obligations	5	5	6

Personnel Summary

Identification code 14–2628–0–1–452		1999 actual	2000 est.	2001 est.
1001	Total compensable workyears: Full-time equivalent employment	1	1	1

INDIAN GUARANTEED LOAN FINANCING ACCOUNT

Program and Financing (in millions of dollars)

Identification code 14–4415–0–3–452		1999 actual	2000 est.	2001 est.
	Obligations by program activity:			
00.01	Interest subsidy		1	1
00.02	Default claims	1	1	1
00.91	Subtotal	1	2	2
08.02	Payment of downward reestimates to receipt account 010–00272930		18	
08.04	Interest on downward reestimates to receipt account 010–00272930		3	
08.91	Subtotal		21	
10.00	Total new obligations	1	23	2
	Budgetary resources available for obligation:			
21.40	Unobligated balance available, start of year	17	27	8
22.00	New financing authority (gross)	10	5	6
23.90	Total budgetary resources available for obligation	27	32	14
23.95	Total new obligations	−1	−23	−2
24.40	Unobligated balance available, end of year	27	8	11
	New financing authority (gross), detail:			
	Discretionary:			
68.00	Spending authority from offsetting collections (gross): Offsetting collections (cash)	10	5	6
	Change in unpaid obligations:			
72.40	Unpaid obligations, start of year: Obligated balance, start of year	4	5	3
73.10	Total new obligations	1	23	2
73.20	Total financing disbursements (gross)	−1	−25	−4
74.40	Unpaid obligations, end of year: Obligated balance, end of year	5	3	1
87.00	Total financing disbursements (gross)	1	25	4
	Offsets:			
	Against gross financing authority and financing disbursements:			
	Offsetting collections (cash) from:			
88.00	Payments from program account	−4	−4	−5
88.40	Non-Federal sources	−6	−1	−1
88.90	Total, offsetting collections (cash)	−10	−5	−6
	Net financing authority and financing disbursements:			
89.00	Financing authority			
90.00	Financing disbursements	−10	20	−2

Status of Guaranteed Loans (in millions of dollars)

Identification code 14–4415–0–3–452		1999 actual	2000 est.	2001 est.
	Position with respect to appropriations act limitation on commitments:			
2111	Limitation on guaranteed loans made by private lenders	60	60	82
2112	Uncommitted loan guarantee limitation	−28		
2150	Total guaranteed loan commitments	32	60	82
	Cumulative balance of guaranteed loans outstanding:			
2210	Outstanding, start of year	113	120	153
2231	Disbursements of new guaranteed loans	32	60	82
2251	Repayments and prepayments	−24	−26	−28
2261	Adjustments: Terminations for default that result in loans receivable	−1	−1	−1
2290	Outstanding, end of year	120	153	206
	Memorandum:			
2299	Guaranteed amount of guaranteed loans outstanding, end of year	120	128	137
	Addendum:			
	Cumulative balance of defaulted guaranteed loans that result in loans receivable:			
2310	Outstanding, start of year	44	41	41
2331	Disbursements for guaranteed loan claims	3	1	1
2351	Repayments of loans receivable	−6	−1	−1
2390	Outstanding, end of year	41	41	41

As required by the Federal Credit Reform Act of 1990, this non-budgetary account records all cash flows to and from the Government resulting from loan guarantees committed in 1992 and beyond (including modifications of loan guarantees that resulted from commitments in any year). The amounts in this account are a means of financing and are not included in the budget totals.

Balance Sheet (in millions of dollars)

Identification code 14–4415–0–3–452		1998 actual	1999 actual	2000 est.	2001 est.
	ASSETS:				
1101	Federal assets: Fund balances with Treasury	23	41	41	41
	Net value of assets related to post-1991 acquired defaulted guaranteed loans receivable:				
1501	Defaulted guaranteed loans receivable, gross	44	41	41	41
1505	Allowance for subsidy cost (–)	–44	–41	–41	–41
1599	Net present value of assets related to defaulted guaranteed loans				
1999	Total assets	23	41	41	41
	LIABILITIES:				
2204	Non-Federal liabilities: Liabilities for loan guarantees	23	41	41	41
2999	Total liabilities	23	41	41	41
	NET POSITION:				
3100	Appropriated capital				
3999	Total net position				

4999 Total liabilities and net position	23	41	41	41

INDIAN LOAN GUARANTY AND INSURANCE FUND LIQUIDATING ACCOUNT

Program and Financing (in millions of dollars)

Identification code 14–4410–0–3–452	1999 actual	2000 est.	2001 est.
Obligations by program activity:			
00.01 Direct Program Activity		1	1
10.00 Total new obligations (object class 41.0)		1	1
Budgetary resources available for obligation:			
21.40 Unobligated balance available, start of year	16		
22.00 New budget authority (gross)	3	3	3
22.40 Capital transfer to general fund	–19	–2	–2
22.60 Portion applied to repay debt			
23.90 Total budgetary resources available for obligation		1	1
23.95 Total new obligations		–1	–1
New budget authority (gross), detail:			
Mandatory:			
60.05 Appropriation (indefinite)	1	1	1
69.00 Offsetting collections (cash)	2	2	2
70.00 Total new budget authority (gross)	3	3	3
Change in unpaid obligations:			
72.40 Unpaid obligations, start of year: Obligated balance, start of year	1		
73.10 Total new obligations		1	1
73.20 Total outlays (gross)	–2	–2	–2
Outlays (gross), detail:			
86.97 Outlays from new mandatory authority	1	3	3
86.98 Outlays from mandatory balances	1		
87.00 Total outlays (gross)	2	2	2
Offsets:			
Against gross budget authority and outlays:			
88.40 Offsetting collections (cash) from: Non-Federal sources	–2	–2	–2
Net budget authority and outlays:			
89.00 Budget authority	1	1	1
90.00 Outlays	–2		

Status of Guaranteed Loans (in millions of dollars)

Identification code 14–4410–0–3–452	1999 actual	2000 est.	2001 est.
Cumulative balance of guaranteed loans outstanding:			
2210 Outstanding, start of year	40	32	25
2251 Repayments and prepayments	–8	–7	–6
2290 Outstanding, end of year	32	25	19
Memorandum:			
2299 Guaranteed amount of guaranteed loans outstanding, end of year	29	23	17
Addendum:			
Cumulative balance of defaulted guaranteed loans that result in loans receivable:			
2310 Outstanding, start of year	32	29	27
2351 Repayments of loans receivable	–1	–2	–2
2361 Write-offs of loans receivable	–2		
2390 Outstanding, end of year	29	27	25

[1] Guarantees canceled.

As required by the Federal Credit Reform Act of 1990, this account records for this program, all cash flows to and from the Government resulting from loan guarantees committed prior to 1992. This account is shown on a cash basis. All new activity in this program in 1992 and beyond (including modifications of loan guarantees that resulted from obligations or commitments in any year) is recorded in corresponding program and financing accounts.

Balance Sheet (in millions of dollars)

Identification code 14–4410–0–3–452	1998 actual	1999 actual	2000 est.	2001 est.
ASSETS:				
1101 Federal assets: Fund balances with Treasury	17	4	3	3
Net value of assets related to pre–1992 direct loans receivable and acquired defaulted guaranteed loans receivable:				
1701 Defaulted guaranteed loans, gross	32	29	27	25
1702 Interest receivable	15	14	13	12
1703 Allowance for estimated uncollectible loans and interest (–)	–24	–27	–25	–23
1704 Defaulted guaranteed loans and interest receivable, net	23	16	15	14
1799 Value of assets related to loan guarantees	23	16	15	14
1999 Total assets	40	20	18	17
LIABILITIES:				
2104 Federal liabilities: Resources payable to Treasury	40	20	18	17
2999 Total liabilities	40	20	18	17
NET POSITION:				
3999 Total net position				
4999 Total liabilities and net position	40	20	18	17

ALLOCATIONS RECEIVED FROM OTHER ACCOUNTS

Note.—Obligations incurred under allocations from other accounts are included in the schedule of the parent appropriation as follows:

The Department of the Interior: Bureau of Land Management: "Firefighting"

ADMINISTRATIVE PROVISIONS

The Bureau of Indian Affairs may carry out the operation of Indian programs by direct expenditure, contracts, cooperative agreements, compacts and grants, either directly or in cooperation with States and other organizations.

Appropriations for the Bureau of Indian Affairs (except the revolving fund for loans, the Indian loan guarantee and insurance fund, and the Indian Guaranteed Loan Program account) shall be available for expenses of exhibits, and purchase of not to exceed 229 passenger motor vehicles, of which not to exceed 187 shall be for replacement only.

Notwithstanding any other provision of law, no funds available to the Bureau of Indian Affairs for central office operations [or], pooled overhead general administration (except facilities operations and maintenance), *or provided to implement the recommendations of the National Academy of Public Administration's August 1999 report* shall be available for tribal contracts, grants, compacts, or cooperative agreements with the Bureau of Indian Affairs under the provisions of the Indian Self-Determination Act or the Tribal Self-Governance Act of 1994 (Public Law 103–413).

In the event any tribe returns appropriations made available by this Act to the Bureau of Indian Affairs for distribution to other tribes, this action shall not diminish the Federal Government's trust responsibility to that tribe, or the government-to-government relationship between the United States and that tribe, or that tribe's ability to access future appropriations.

Notwithstanding any other provision of law, no funds available to the Bureau, other than the amounts provided herein for assistance to public schools under 25 U.S.C. 452 et seq., shall be available to support the operation of any elementary or secondary school in the State of Alaska.

Appropriations made available in this or any other Act for schools funded by the Bureau shall be available only to the schools in the Bureau school system as of September 1, 1996. No funds available to the Bureau shall be used to support expanded grades for any school or dormitory beyond the grade structure in place or approved

Credit accounts—Continued

ADMINISTRATIVE PROVISIONS—Continued

by the Secretary of the Interior at each school in the Bureau school system as of October 1, 1995. Funds made available under this Act may not be used to establish a charter school at a Bureau-funded school (as that term is defined in section 1146 of the Education Amendments of 1978 (25 U.S.C. 2026)), except that a charter school that is in existence on the date of the enactment of this Act and that has operated at a Bureau-funded school before September 1, 1999, may continue to operate during that period, but only if the charter school pays to the Bureau a pro-rata share of funds to reimburse the Bureau for the use of the real and personal property (including buses and vans), the funds of the charter school are kept separate and apart from Bureau funds, and the Bureau does not assume any obligation for charter school programs of the State in which the school is located if the charter school loses such funding. Employees of Bureau-funded schools sharing a campus with a charter school and performing functions related to the charter school's operation and employees of a charter school shall not be treated as Federal employees for purposes of chapter 171 of title 28, United States Code (commonly known as the "Federal Tort Claims Act"). Not later than June 15, [2000] *2001*, the Secretary of the Interior shall evaluate the effectiveness of Bureau-funded schools sharing facilities with charter schools in the manner described in the preceding sentence and prepare and submit a report on the finding of that evaluation to the Committees on Appropriations of the Senate and of the House.

[The Tate Topa Tribal School, the Black Mesa Community School, the Alamo Navajo School, and other Bureau-funded schools subject to the approval of the Secretary of the Interior, may use prior year school operations funds for the replacement or repair of Bureau of Indian Affairs education facilities which are in compliance with 25 U.S.C. 2005(a) and which shall be eligible for operation and maintenance support to the same extent as other Bureau of Indian Affairs education facilities: *Provided*, That any additional construction costs for replacement or repair of such facilities begun with prior year funds shall be completed exclusively with non-Federal funds.] *(Department of the Interior and Related Agencies Appropriations Act, 2000, as enacted by section 1000(a)(3) of the Consolidated Appropriations Act, 2000 (P.L. 106–113).)*

DEPARTMENTAL OFFICES

DEPARTMENTAL MANAGEMENT

Federal Funds

General and special funds:

SALARIES AND EXPENSES

For necessary expenses for management of the Department of the Interior, [$62,864,000] *$64,469,000*, of which not to exceed $8,500 may be for official reception and representation expenses and of which up to $1,000,000 shall be available for workers compensation payments and unemployment compensation payments associated with the orderly closure of the United States Bureau of Mines. *(Department of the Interior and Related Agencies Appropriations Act, 2000, as enacted by section 1000(a)(3) of the Consolidated Appropriations Act, 2000 (P.L. 106–113).)*

Program and Financing (in millions of dollars)

Identification code 14–0102–0–1–306		1999 actual	2000 est.	2001 est.
	Obligations by program activity:			
	Direct program:			
00.01	Departmental direction	12	12	12
00.03	Management and coordination	22	23	23
00.04	Hearings and appeals	7	8	8
00.06	Central services	25	19	20
00.07	USBM workers comp./unemployment	1	1	1
00.08	Glacier Bay fishing buyout	5		
00.09	Glacier Bay (P.L. 106–31)	23		
01.00	Direct program subtotal	95	63	64
	Reimbursable program: above activity:			
09.01	Departmental direction	7	7	7
09.02	Management and coordination	4	4	4
09.03	Central services-	44	44	44
09.04	Building Maintenance	7		
09.99	Total reimbursable program	62	55	55
10.00	Total new obligations	157	118	119
	Budgetary resources available for obligation:			
21.40	Unobligated balance available, start of year		6	6
22.00	New budget authority (gross)	163	120	119
23.90	Total budgetary resources available for obligation	163	126	125
23.95	Total new obligations	−157	−118	−119
24.40	Unobligated balance available, end of year	6	6	6
	New budget authority (gross), detail:			
	Discretionary:			
40.00	Appropriation	90	63	64
42.00	Transferred from other accounts	3		
43.00	Appropriation (total discretionary)	93	63	64
	Spending authority from offsetting collections:			
68.00	Offsetting collections (cash)	66	57	55
68.10	From Federal sources: Change in receivables and unpaid, unfilled orders	4		
68.90	Spending authority from offsetting collections (total discretionary)	70	57	55
70.00	Total new budget authority (gross)	163	120	119
	Change in unpaid obligations:			
	Unpaid obligations, start of year:			
72.40	Obligated balance, start of year	5	8	6
72.95	From Federal sources: Receivables and unpaid, unfilled orders		4	4
72.99	Total unpaid obligations, start of year	5	12	10
73.10	Total new obligations	157	118	119
73.20	Total outlays (gross)	−150	−118	−119
	Unpaid obligations, end of year:			
74.40	Obligated balance, end of year	8	6	6
74.95	From Federal sources: Receivables and unpaid, unfilled orders	4	4	4
74.99	Total unpaid obligations, end of year	12	10	10
	Outlays (gross), detail:			
86.90	Outlays from new discretionary authority	145	114	113
86.93	Outlays from discretionary balances	5	4	6
87.00	Total outlays (gross)	150	118	119
	Offsets:			
	Against gross budget authority and outlays:			
88.00	Offsetting collections (cash) from: Federal sources	−66	−57	−55
	Against gross budget authority only:			
88.95	From Federal sources: Change in receivables and unpaid, unfilled orders	−4		
	Net budget authority and outlays:			
89.00	Budget authority	93	63	64
90.00	Outlays	84	61	64

This appropriation provides overall departmental direction and guidance, including such activities and functions as: congressional liaison, communications, and equal opportunity; activities concerning management and coordination; the Department's quasi-judicial and appellate responsibilities; aviation policy; and general administrative support, such as space and postage for the Secretarial offices; and workers and unemployment compensation payments for former Bureau of Mines employees.

Object Classification (in millions of dollars)

Identification code 14–0102–0–1–306		1999 actual	2000 est.	2001 est.
	Direct obligations:			
	Personnel compensation:			
11.1	Full-time permanent	27	32	33
11.3	Other than full-time permanent	4	3	3
11.9	Total personnel compensation	31	35	36
12.1	Civilian personnel benefits	7	7	7
21.0	Travel and transportation of persons	1	1	1
23.1	Rental payments to GSA	10	9	9

		1999 actual	2000 est.	2001 est.
23.3	Communications, utilities, and miscellaneous charges	2	1	1
24.0	Printing and reproduction	1	1	1
25.2	Other services	6	3	3
25.3	Purchases of goods and services from Government accounts	36	6	6
26.0	Supplies and materials	1		
99.0	Subtotal, direct obligations	95	63	64
99.0	Reimbursable obligations	62	55	55
99.9	Total new obligations	157	118	119

Personnel Summary

Identification code 14–0102–0–1–306		1999 actual	2000 est.	2001 est.
	Direct:			
1001	Total compensable workyears: Full-time equivalent employment	388	408	408
	Reimbursable:			
2001	Total compensable workyears: Full-time equivalent employment	82	78	83
	Allocation account:			
3001	Total compensable workyears: Full-time equivalent employment	19	18	18

SPECIAL FOREIGN CURRENCY PROGRAM

Program and Financing (in millions of dollars)

Identification code 14–0105–0–1–306		1999 actual	2000 est.	2001 est.
	Budgetary resources available for obligation:			
21.40	Unobligated balance available, start of year	2	1	1
23.95	Total new obligations			
24.40	Unobligated balance available, end of year	1	1	1
	Net budget authority and outlays:			
89.00	Budget authority			
90.00	Outlays			

KING COVE ROAD AND AIRSTRIP

Program and Financing (in millions of dollars)

Identification code 14–0125–0–1–451		1999 actual	2000 est.	2001 est.
	Obligations by program activity:			
00.01	King Cove Road	20		
00.02	King Cove Air Strip	15		
10.00	Total new obligations (object class 25.3)	35		
	Budgetary resources available for obligation:			
22.00	New budget authority (gross)	35		
23.95	Total new obligations	−35		
	New budget authority (gross), detail:			
	Discretionary:			
40.00	Appropriation	35		
	Change in unpaid obligations:			
73.10	Total new obligations	35		
73.20	Total outlays (gross)	−35		
	Outlays (gross), detail:			
86.90	Outlays from new discretionary authority	35		
	Net budget authority and outlays:			
89.00	Budget authority	35		
90.00	Outlays	35		

In 1999, to improve access to health care facilities, funds were appropriated to be available to the Aleutians East Borough for the construction of an unpaved road on King Cove Corporation Lands to an improved dock, and marine facilities. Funds were also appropriated to be available to the State of Alaska to improve the airstrip at King Cove.

MANAGEMENT OF FEDERAL LANDS FOR SUBSISTENCE USES

SUBSISTENCE MANAGEMENT, DEPARTMENT OF THE INTERIOR

Program and Financing (in millions of dollars)

Identification code 14–0124–0–1–302		1999 actual	2000 est.	2001 est.
	Obligations by program activity:			
10.00	Total new obligations (object class 25.3)	1	7	
	Budgetary resources available for obligation:			
21.40	Unobligated balance available, start of year		7	
22.00	New budget authority (gross)	8		
23.90	Total budgetary resources available for obligation	8	7	
23.95	Total new obligations	−1	−7	
24.40	Unobligated balance available, end of year	7		
	New budget authority (gross), detail:			
	Discretionary:			
40.00	Appropriation	8		
	Change in unpaid obligations:			
72.40	Unpaid obligations, start of year: Obligated balance, start of year		1	1
73.10	Total new obligations	1	7	
73.20	Total outlays (gross)		−7	−1
74.40	Unpaid obligations, end of year: Obligated balance, end of year	1	1	
	Outlays (gross), detail:			
86.93	Outlays from discretionary balances		7	1
	Net budget authority and outlays:			
89.00	Budget authority	8		
90.00	Outlays		7	1

In 1999, $8 million was provided to the Secretary of the Interior to implement and enforce certain Federal regulations in the state of Alaska dealing with subsistence uses of fish and wildlife on navigable rivers in Alaska consistent with the Alaska National Interest Lands Conservation Act (ANILCA). The 1999 appropriation stated that Federal enforcement actions were to be taken if the Alaska State Legislature failed to take action by October 1, 1999, to amend the Constitution of the State of Alaska to enable implementation of state laws. If the State Legislature had taken such action by October 1, 1999, the Secretary was directed to make a grant of $8 million to the State of Alaska to implement and enforce the applicable ANILCA provisions. The Alaska State legislature failed to take action by the date specified, and therefore, Federal implementation and enforcement has been initiated. In 2001, funds are requested in the budgets of the Fish and Wildlife Service, the Bureau of Land Management, the National Park Service, the Bureau of Indian Affairs, and the Office of the Solicitor to continue this effort.

EVERGLADES WATERSHED PROTECTION

Program and Financing (in millions of dollars)

Identification code 14–0140–0–1–303		1999 actual	2000 est.	2001 est.
	Obligations by program activity:			
10.00	Total new obligations (object class 32.0)		33	
	Budgetary resources available for obligation:			
21.40	Unobligated balance available, start of year		33	
22.10	Resources available from recoveries of prior year obligations	33		
23.90	Total budgetary resources available for obligation	33	33	
23.95	Total new obligations		−33	
24.40	Unobligated balance available, end of year	33		
	Change in unpaid obligations:			
72.40	Unpaid obligations, start of year: Obligated balance, start of year	160	9	

General and special funds—Continued

EVERGLADES WATERSHED PROTECTION—Continued

Program and Financing (in millions of dollars)—Continued

Identification code 14–0140–0–1–303	1999 actual	2000 est.	2001 est.
73.10 Total new obligations		33	
73.20 Total outlays (gross)	–119	–42	
73.45 Adjustments in unexpired accounts	–33		
74.40 Unpaid obligations, end of year: Obligated balance, end of year	9		
Outlays (gross), detail:			
86.98 Outlays from mandatory balances	119	42	
Net budget authority and outlays:			
89.00 Budget authority			
90.00 Outlays	119	42	

The Federal Agriculture Improvement and Reform Act of 1996 (P.L. 104–127) made these funds available to the Secretary to conduct Everglades ecosystem restoration activities until December 31, 1999. These activities include the acquisition of real property, resource protection, and resource maintenance.

EVERGLADES RESTORATION ACCOUNT

Unavailable Collections (in millions of dollars)

Identification code 14–5233–0–2–303	1999 actual	2000 est.	2001 est.
Balance, start of year:			
01.99 Balance, start of year			
Receipts:			
02.01 Everglades restoration account	4	1	1
Appropriation:			
05.01 Everglades restoration account	–4	–1	–1
07.99 Total balance, end of year			

Program and Financing (in millions of dollars)

Identification code 14–5233–0–2–303	1999 actual	2000 est.	2001 est.
Obligations by program activity:			
10.00 Total new obligations (object class 41.0)		4	1
Budgetary resources available for obligation:			
21.40 Unobligated balance available, start of year		4	1
22.00 New budget authority (gross)	4	1	1
23.90 Total budgetary resources available for obligation	4	5	2
23.95 Total new obligations		–4	–1
24.40 Unobligated balance available, end of year	4	1	1
New budget authority (gross), detail:			
Mandatory:			
60.25 Appropriation (special fund, indefinite)	4	1	1
Change in unpaid obligations:			
73.10 Total new obligations		4	1
73.20 Total outlays (gross)		–4	–1
Outlays (gross), detail:			
86.98 Outlays from mandatory balances		4	1
Net budget authority and outlays:			
89.00 Budget authority	4	1	1
90.00 Outlays		4	1

The Federal Agriculture Improvement and Reform Act of 1996 (P.L. 104–127) provides that receipts not exceeding $100 million, from Federal surplus property sales in the State of Florida, shall be deposited in the Everglades restoration account and shall be available to the Secretary to assist in the restoration of the Everglades.

PRIORITY FEDERAL LAND ACQUISITIONS AND EXCHANGES

Program and Financing (in millions of dollars)

Identification code 14–5039–0–2–303	1999 actual	2000 est.	2001 est.
Obligations by program activity:			
00.01 Priority Land—BLM	310	25	
00.02 Priority Land—NPS	127	70	
00.03 Priority Land—FWS	95	2	
00.04 Other Priority Land Acquisitions		19	
10.00 Total new obligations (object class 32.0)	532	116	
Budgetary resources available for obligation:			
21.40 Unobligated balance available, start of year	532		
22.00 New budget authority (gross)		116	
23.90 Total budgetary resources available for obligation	532	116	
23.95 Total new obligations	–532	–116	
New budget authority (gross), detail:			
Discretionary:			
40.20 Appropriation (special fund, definite)		116	
Change in unpaid obligations:			
72.40 Unpaid obligations, start of year: Obligated balance, start of year			65
73.10 Total new obligations	532	116	
73.20 Total outlays (gross)	–532	–51	–24
74.40 Unpaid obligations, end of year: Obligated balance, end of year		65	41
Outlays (gross), detail:			
86.90 Outlays from new discretionary authority		51	
86.93 Outlays from discretionary balances	532		24
87.00 Total outlays (gross)	532	51	24
Net budget authority and outlays:			
89.00 Budget authority		116	
90.00 Outlays	532	51	24

Funds in the amount of $116.5 million were provided by the 2000 appropriations for the Department of the Interior from the Land and Water Conservation Fund for priority land acquisitions and exchanges and other purposes. Funds are to remain available until September 30, 2003.

Of this amount, $20 million is available for the State land assistance program, $5 million to protect and preserve the California desert, $2 million for the Rhode Island National Wildlife Refuge Complex, $19.5 million for mineral rights within the Grand Staircase-Escalante National Monument, $35 million for State grants for land acquisition in the State of Florida, $10 million for Elwha River ecosystem restoration, $5 million for backlog maintenance in the National Park Service, and the remaining $20 million to be used for other priority land acquisitions.

Intragovernmental funds:

WORKING CAPITAL FUND

Program and Financing (in millions of dollars)

Identification code 14–4523–0–4–306	1999 actual	2000 est.	2001 est.
Obligations by program activity:			
00.01 Y2K	111	16	
01.00 Direct program subtotal	111	16	
09.03 National Business Center	89	142	134
09.05 Aircraft Services	90	90	80
09.06 Other goods and services	5	6	6
09.09 Reimbursable program subtotal	184	238	220
10.00 Total new obligations	295	254	220
Budgetary resources available for obligation:			
21.40 Unobligated balance available, start of year	15	51	12

22.00	New budget authority (gross)	330	214	220
22.10	Resources available from recoveries of prior year obligations	1	1	1
23.90	Total budgetary resources available for obligation	346	266	233
23.95	Total new obligations	−295	−254	−220
24.40	Unobligated balance available, end of year	51	12	13
	New budget authority (gross), detail:			
	Discretionary:			
42.00	Transferred from other accounts	124	3	
	Mandatory:			
69.00	Offsetting collections (cash)	186	211	220
69.10	From Federal sources: Change in receivables and unpaid, unfilled orders	20		
69.90	Spending authority from offsetting collections (total mandatory)	206	211	220
70.00	Total new budget authority (gross)	330	214	220
	Change in unpaid obligations:			
	Unpaid obligations, start of year:			
72.40	Obligated balance, start of year	12	77	3
72.95	From Federal sources: Receivables and unpaid, unfilled orders		20	20
72.99	Total unpaid obligations, start of year	12	97	23
73.10	Total new obligations	295	254	220
73.20	Total outlays (gross)	−210	−328	−220
73.45	Adjustments in unexpired accounts	−1	−1	−1
	Unpaid obligations, end of year:			
74.40	Obligated balance, end of year	77	3	1
74.95	From Federal sources: Receivables and unpaid, unfilled orders	20	20	20
74.99	Total unpaid obligations, end of year	97	23	21
	Outlays (gross), detail:			
86.90	Outlays from new discretionary authority	35	3	
86.93	Outlays from discretionary balances		89	
86.97	Outlays from new mandatory authority	162	200	209
86.98	Outlays from mandatory balances	13	36	11
87.00	Total outlays (gross)	210	328	220
	Offsets:			
	Against gross budget authority and outlays:			
88.00	Offsetting collections (cash) from: Federal sources	−186	−211	−220
	Against gross budget authority only:			
88.95	From Federal sources: Change in receivables and unpaid, unfilled orders	−20		
	Net budget authority and outlays:			
89.00	Budget authority	124	3	
90.00	Outlays	23	117	

This fund finances Departmentwide activities that may be performed more advantageously on a reimbursable basis, including services provided by the National Business Center (NBC) and the Office of Aircraft Services (OAS). Departmentwide activities financed through the fund are centrally managed operational services and programs, such as: Department of the Interior telecommunications network (DOINET), Diversity Intern program, Y2K, and safety and health initiatives. Through the National Business Center (NBC), this fund finances the Department's administrative services systems, including: the Federal Personnel and Payroll System (FPPS), Federal Financial System (FFS), and the Interior Department Electronic Acquisitions System (IDEAS). The NBC also provides accounting, acquisition, central reproduction, communications, supplies and health services. (43 U.S.C. 1467).

Statement of Operations (in millions of dollars)

Identification code 14–4523–0–4–306		1998 actual	1999 actual	2000 est.	2001 est.
0101	Revenue	95	345	275	239
0102	Expense	–93	–294	–254	–228
0105	Net income or loss (–)	2	51	21	11

Balance Sheet (in millions of dollars)

Identification code 14–4523–0–4–306		1998 actual	1999 actual	2000 est.	2001 est.
	ASSETS:				
	Federal assets:				
1101	Fund balances with Treasury	27	40	40	40
	Investments in US securities:				
1106	Receivables, Net (From Other Federal Agencies)		14	14	14
	Other Federal assets:				
1802	Inventories and related properties	1	1	1	1
1803	Property, plant and equipment, net	20	28	28	28
1999	Total assets	48	83	83	83
	LIABILITIES:				
	Federal liabilities:				
2101	Accounts payable	8	2	2	2
2105	Other		10	10	10
	Non-Federal liabilities:				
2201	Accounts payable	7	10	10	10
2207	Other	2	2	2	2
2999	Total liabilities	17	24	24	24
	NET POSITION:				
3300	Cumulative results of operations	31	59	59	59
3999	Total net position	31	59	59	59
4999	Total liabilities and net position	48	83	83	83

Object Classification (in millions of dollars)

Identification code 14–4523–0–4–306		1999 actual	2000 est.	2001 est.
25.2	Direct obligations: Other services	111	16	
	Reimbursable obligations:			
11.1	Personnel compensation: Full-time permanent	33	50	52
12.1	Civilian personnel benefits	7	11	12
21.0	Travel and transportation of persons	2	4	4
22.0	Transportation of things	2	3	3
23.3	Communications, utilities, and miscellaneous charges	6	10	10
24.0	Printing and reproduction	1	2	2
25.2	Other services	121	138	117
26.0	Supplies and materials	10	15	15
31.0	Equipment	2	5	5
99.0	Subtotal, reimbursable obligations	184	238	220
99.9	Total new obligations	295	254	220

Personnel Summary

Identification code 14–4523–0–4–306		1999 actual	2000 est.	2001 est.
2001	Total compensable workyears: Full-time equivalent employment	575	882	888

INTERIOR FRANCHISE FUND

Program and Financing (in millions of dollars)

Identification code 14–4229–0–4–306		1999 actual	2000 est.	2001 est.
	Obligations by program activity:			
09.01	DOI Franchise Fund	43	102	157
10.00	Total new obligations (object class 25.2)	43	102	157
	Budgetary resources available for obligation:			
21.40	Unobligated balance available, start of year	17	48	34
22.00	New budget authority (gross)	73	90	150
23.90	Total budgetary resources available for obligation	90	138	184
23.95	Total new obligations	−43	−102	−157
24.40	Unobligated balance available, end of year	48	34	25
	New budget authority (gross), detail:			
	Mandatory:			
69.00	Offsetting collections (cash)	51	90	150
69.10	From Federal sources: Change in receivables and unpaid, unfilled orders	22		

Intragovernmental funds—Continued

INTERIOR FRANCHISE FUND—Continued

Program and Financing (in millions of dollars)—Continued

Identification code 14–4229–0–4–306		1999 actual	2000 est.	2001 est.
69.90	Spending authority from offsetting collections (total mandatory)	73	90	150
	Change in unpaid obligations:			
	Unpaid obligations, start of year:			
72.40	Obligated balance, start of year	−14	−31	−6
72.95	From Federal sources: Receivables and unpaid, unfilled orders	....	22	22
72.99	Total unpaid obligations, start of year	−14	−9	16
73.10	Total new obligations	43	102	157
73.20	Total outlays (gross)	−39	−75	−105
	Unpaid obligations, end of year:			
74.40	Obligated balance, end of year	−31	−6	46
74.95	From Federal sources: Receivables and unpaid, unfilled orders	22	22	22
74.99	Total unpaid obligations, end of year	−9	16	68
	Outlays (gross), detail:			
86.97	Outlays from new mandatory authority	36	36	60
86.98	Outlays from mandatory balances	3	39	45
87.00	Total outlays (gross)	39	75	105
	Offsets:			
	Against gross budget authority and outlays:			
88.00	Offsetting collections (cash) from: Federal sources	−51	−90	−150
	Against gross budget authority only:			
88.95	From Federal sources: Change in receivables and unpaid, unfilled orders	−22	....	....
	Net budget authority and outlays:			
89.00	Budget authority	....	....	....
90.00	Outlays	−12	−15	−45

The Government Management Reform Act, P.L. 103–356, established the Franchise Fund Pilot Program. Pursuant to the Act, the Department of the Interior was designated as one of six executive branch agencies authorized to establish a franchise fund. Section 113 of the General Provisions of the Department of the Interior Related Agencies Appropriation Act of 1997, P.L. 104–208, established in the Treasury a franchise fund pilot. This fund is to be available for the cost of capitalizing and operating administrative services as the Secretary determines may be performed more advantageously as central services.

Statement of Operations (in millions of dollars)

Identification code 14–4229–0–4–306		1998 actual	1999 actual	2000 est.	2001 est.
0101	Revenue	20	90	117	177
0102	Expense	−21	−43	−90	−150
0105	Net income or loss (−)	−1	47	27	27

Balance Sheet (in millions of dollars)

Identification code 14–4229–0–4–306		1998 actual	1999 actual	2000 est.	2001 est.
	ASSETS:				
	Federal assets:				
1101	Fund balances with Treasury	3	16	11	11
	Investments in US securities:				
1106	Accounts receivable: due from Federal agencies	18	11	13	13
1999	Total assets	21	27	24	24
	LIABILITIES:				
	Federal liabilities:				
2101	Accounts payable	4	12	11	11
2105	Deferred revenue:due to Federal agencies	13	15	13	13
2999	Total liabilities	17	27	24	24
4999	Total liabilities and net position	17	27	24	24

Personnel Summary

Identification code 14–4229–0–4–306		1999 actual	2000 est.	2001 est.
2001	Total compensable workyears: Full-time equivalent employment	3	3	3

ALLOCATIONS RECEIVED FROM OTHER ACCOUNTS

Note.—Obligations incurred under allocations from other accounts are included in the schedule of the parent appropriation as follows:

Interior: Bureau of Land Management: "Wildland Fire Management".

Environmental Protection Agency: "Hazardous Subsistence Superfund".

ADMINISTRATIVE PROVISIONS

There is hereby authorized for acquisition from available resources within the Working Capital Fund, 15 aircraft, 10 of which shall be for replacement and which may be obtained by donation, purchase or through available excess surplus property: *Provided*, That notwithstanding any other provision of law, existing aircraft being replaced may be sold, with proceeds derived or trade-in value used to offset the purchase price for the replacement aircraft: *Provided further*, That no programs funded with appropriated funds in the "Departmental Management", "Office of the Solicitor", and "Office of Inspector General" may be augmented through the Working Capital Fund or the Consolidated Working Fund. *(Department of the Interior and Related Agencies Appropriations Act, 2000, as enacted by section 1000(a)(3) of the Consolidated Appropriations Act, 2000 (P.L. 106–113).)*

INSULAR AFFAIRS

The Secretary of the Interior is charged with the responsibility of promoting the economic and political development of those insular areas which are under U.S. jurisdiction and within the responsibility of the Department of the Interior. The Secretary originates and implements Federal policy for the U.S. territories; guides and coordinates certain operating programs and construction projects; provides information services and technical assistance; coordinates certain Federal programs and services provided to the freely associated states, and participates in foreign policy and defense matters concerning the U.S. territories and the freely associated States.

Federal Funds

General and special funds:

ASSISTANCE TO TERRITORIES

For expenses necessary for assistance to territories under the jurisdiction of the Department of the Interior, [$70,171,000] *$73,891,000*, of which: (1) [$66,076,000] *$69,496,000* shall be available until expended for technical assistance, including maintenance assistance, disaster assistance, insular management controls, coral reef initiative activities, and brown tree snake control and research; grants to the judiciary in American Samoa for compensation and expenses, as authorized by law (48 U.S.C. 1661(c)); grants to the Government of American Samoa, in addition to current local revenues, for construction and support of governmental functions; grants to the Government of the Virgin Islands as authorized by law; grants to the Government of Guam, as authorized by law; and grants to the Government of the Northern Mariana Islands as authorized by law (Public Law 94–241; 90 Stat. 272); and (2) [$4,095,000] *$4,395,000* shall be available for salaries and expenses of the Office of Insular Affairs: *Provided*, That all financial transactions of the territorial and local governments herein provided for, including such transactions of all agencies or instrumentalities established or used by such governments, may be audited by the General Accounting Office, at its discretion, in accordance with chapter 35 of title 31, United States Code: *Provided further*, That Northern Mariana Islands Covenant grant funding shall be provided according to those terms of the Agreement of the Special Representatives on Future United States Financial Assistance for the Northern Mariana Islands approved by Public Law 104–134: *Provided further*, That Public Law 94–241, as amended, is further amended[: (1) in section 4(b) by striking "2002" and inserting "1999" and by striking the comma after "$11,000,000 annually" and inserting the following: "and for fiscal year 2000, payments to the Commonwealth of the Northern Mariana Islands shall be $5,580,000, but shall return to the level of $11,000,000 annually for fiscal years 2001 and 2002. In fiscal year 2003, the payment to the Commonwealth of the Northern Mariana Islands shall be $5,420,000. Such payments shall be"; and (2) in section (4)(c) by adding a new subsection as follows: "(4) for fiscal year 2000, $5,420,000 shall be provided to the Virgin Islands for correctional facilities and other projects mandated by Federal law."] *in section 4(c)(1) by deleting "2001" and inserting "2000", and inserting after the words, "4,580,000 annually", the following additional phrase: "and $10,000,000 annually thereafter"*: *Provided further*, That of the amounts provided for technical assistance, sufficient funding shall be made available for a grant to the Close Up Foundation: *Provided further*, That the funds for the program of operations and maintenance improvement are appropriated to institutionalize routine operations and maintenance improvement of capital infrastructure in American Samoa, Guam, the Virgin Islands, the Commonwealth of the Northern Mariana Islands, the Republic of Palau, the Republic of the Marshall Islands, and the Federated States of Micronesia through assessments of long-range operations maintenance needs, improved capability of local operations and maintenance institutions and agencies (including management and vocational education training), and project-specific maintenance (with territorial participation and cost sharing to be determined by the Secretary based on the individual territory's commitment to timely maintenance of its capital assets): *Provided further*, That any appropriation for disaster assistance under this heading in this Act or previous appropriations Acts may be used as non-Federal matching funds for the purpose of hazard mitigation grants provided pursuant to section 404 of the Robert T. Stafford Disaster Relief and Emergency Assistance Act (42 U.S.C. 5170c). *In addition, for assistance to the Virgin Islands in addressing federally ordered or mandated critical infrastructure needs, such as, school construction, wastewater treatment facilities, correctional facilities, and flood control projects, $10,000,000 to become available in FY2002: Provided, That the entire amount shall be available upon certification of the Secretary that the Virgin Islands is substantially complying with mutually agreed upon performance standards to reduce the Virgin Islands' budget deficit, and that the Virgin Islands agrees to a 50 percent match: Provided further, That if the Secretary does not certify by September 30, 2002, these funds shall immediately lapse. (Department of the Interior and Related Agencies Appropriations Act, 2000, as enacted by section 1000(a)(3) of the Consolidated Appropriations Act, 2000 (P.L. 106–113).)*

Program and Financing (in millions of dollars)

Identification code 14–0412–0–1–808		1999 actual	2000 est.	2001 est.
	Obligations by program activity:			
	Direct:			
00.01	American Samoa Operations grants	23	23	23
	Territorial Assistance:			
00.02	Office of insular affairs	4	4	4
00.03	Technical assistance	5	6	7
00.04	Guam impact of compact		3	
00.10	Brown tree snake	2	2	2
00.11	Insular management controls	1	1	2
00.12	Maintenance assistance fund	2	2	2
00.13	Coral reef initiative		1	1
00.91	Direct subtotal, discretionary	37	42	41
01.01	Covenant grants, mandatory	28	28	33
01.92	Direct subtotal	65	70	74
02.01	Direct Loan Subsidy—Amer. Samoa		3	
03.00	Direct subtotal	65	73	74
09.01	Reimbursable program	1	6	1
09.02	Reimbursable program-Y2K		29	
09.09	Reimbursable subtotal	1	35	1
10.00	Total new obligations	66	108	75
	Budgetary resources available for obligation:			
21.40	Unobligated balance available, start of year	7	9	6
22.00	New budget authority (gross)	67	105	75
22.10	Resources available from recoveries of prior year obligations	2		
23.90	Total budgetary resources available for obligation	76	114	81
23.95	Total new obligations	−66	−108	−75
24.40	Unobligated balance available, end of year	9	6	6
	New budget authority (gross), detail:			
	Discretionary:			
40.00	Appropriation	38	42	41
	Mandatory:			
60.00	Appropriation	28	28	33
	Discretionary:			
68.00	Spending authority from offsetting collections: Offsetting collections (cash)	1	35	1
70.00	Total new budget authority (gross)	67	105	75
	Change in unpaid obligations:			
72.40	Unpaid obligations, start of year: Obligated balance, start of year	167	154	160
73.10	Total new obligations	66	108	75
73.20	Total outlays (gross)	−76	−102	−90
73.45	Adjustments in unexpired accounts	−2		
74.40	Unpaid obligations, end of year: Obligated balance, end of year	154	160	145
	Outlays (gross), detail:			
86.90	Outlays from new discretionary authority	31	62	28
86.93	Outlays from discretionary balances	19	12	20
86.97	Outlays from new mandatory authority	3		
86.98	Outlays from mandatory balances	23	28	42
87.00	Total outlays (gross)	76	102	90
	Offsets:			
	Against gross budget authority and outlays:			
88.00	Offsetting collections (cash) from: Federal sources	−1	−35	−1
	Net budget authority and outlays:			
89.00	Budget authority	66	70	74
90.00	Outlays	76	67	89

Status of Direct Loans (in millions of dollars)

Identification code 14–0412–0–1–808		1999 actual	2000 est.	2001 est.
	Cumulative balance of direct loans outstanding:			
1210	Outstanding, start of year	17	16	15
1251	Repayments: Repayments and prepayments	−1	−1	−1
1290	Outstanding, end of year	16	15	14

Summary of Loan Levels, Subsidy Budget Authority and Outlays by Program (in millions of dollars)

Identification code 14–0412–0–1–808		1999 actual	2000 est.	2001 est.
	Direct loan levels supportable by subsidy budget authority:			
1150	Direct loan levels		19	
1159	Total direct loan levels		19	
	Direct loan subsidy (in percent):			
1320	Subsidy rate		0.16	0.00
1329	Weighted average subsidy rate		0.16	0.00
	Direct loan subsidy budget authority:			
1330	Subsidy budget authority		3	
1339	Total subsidy budget authority		3	
	Direct loan subsidy outlays:			
1340	Subsidy outlays		2	1
1349	Total subsidy outlays		2	1

This appropriation provides support for basic government operations for those territories requiring such support, capital infrastructure improvements, special program and economic development assistance, and technical assistance.

General and special funds—Continued

The appropriation provides an additional $5,420,000 impact aid payment to Guam, and a $10,000,000 advance appropriation for the Virgin Islands to help the Virgin Islands address some of their Federally ordered or mandated critical infrastructure needs. The advance appropriation is subject to the Secretary certifying that the Virgin Islands is complying with the Memorandum of Understanding regarding financial performance standards signed in October 1999. If the Secretary does not certify, the appropriation is no longer available. In addition, the Virgin Islands must agree to a 50 percent match.

The following are key performance measures for the Office of Insular Affairs and the Assistance to Territories account:

PERFORMANCE MEASURES

	1999 actual	2000 est.	2001 est.
Multi-year financial mamagement improvement plans completed (cumulative)	3	4	5
Multi-year capital improvement plans completed (cumulative)	2	3	4

Object Classification (in millions of dollars)

Identification code 14–0412–0–1–808		1999 actual	2000 est.	2001 est.
	Direct obligations:			
11.1	Personnel compensation: Full-time permanent	2	2	2
12.1	Civilian personnel benefits	1	1	1
25.2	Other services	1	1	1
	Grants, subsidies, and contributions:			
41.0	Subsidy—Amer. Samoa loan	....	3	3
41.0	Grants, subsidies, and contributions	60	65	66
99.0	Subtotal, direct obligations	64	72	73
99.0	Reimbursable obligations	1	35	1
99.5	Below reporting threshold	1	1	1
99.9	Total new obligations	66	108	75

Personnel Summary

Identification code 14–0412–0–1–808		1999 actual	2000 est.	2001 est.
1001	Total compensable workyears: Full-time equivalent employment	29	32	34

ASSISTANCE TO AMERICAN SAMOA DIRECT LOAN FINANCING ACCOUNT

Program and Financing (in millions of dollars)

Identification code 14–4163–0–3–806		1999 actual	2000 est.	2001 est.
	Obligations by program activity:			
	Direct:			
00.01	Direct Program	....	14	5
00.02	Interest paid to Treasury (6.27 percent on $12 million)	....	1	....
10.00	Total new obligations	....	15	5
	Budgetary resources available for obligation:			
22.00	New financing authority (gross)	....	14	5
23.95	Total new obligations	....	−15	−5
	New financing authority (gross), detail:			
	Mandatory:			
67.10	Authority to borrow	....	12	4
69.00	Offsetting collections (cash)	....	3	2
69.47	Portion applied to repay debt	....	−1	−1
69.90	Spending authority from offsetting collections (total mandatory)	....	2	1
70.00	Total new financing authority (gross)	....	14	5
	Change in unpaid obligations:			
73.10	Total new obligations	....	15	5
73.20	Total financing disbursements (gross)	....	−14	−5
87.00	Total financing disbursements (gross)	....	14	5
	Offsets:			
	Against gross financing authority and financing disbursements:			
	Offsetting collections (cash) from:			
88.00	Federal sources—sudsidy	....	−2	−1
	Non-Federal sources:			
88.40	Non-Federal sources—interest payments fr. Am. Samoa	....	−1	−1
88.40	Non-Federal sources—principal on loan doesn't round to $1 mil.	....	....	....
88.90	Total, offsetting collections (cash)	....	−3	−2
	Net financing authority and financing disbursements:			
89.00	Financing authority	....	11	3
90.00	Financing disbursements	....	11	3

Status of Direct Loans (in millions of dollars)

Identification code 14–4163–0–3–806		1999 actual	2000 est.	2001 est.
	Position with respect to appropriations act limitation on obligations:			
1111	Limitation on direct loans	....	19	....
1150	Total direct loan obligations	....	19	....
	Cumulative balance of direct loans outstanding:			
1210	Outstanding, start of year	....	....	13
1231	Disbursements: Direct loan disbursements	....	14	5
1251	Repayments: Repayments and prepayments—interest payments	....	−1	−1
1290	Outstanding, end of year	....	13	17

The American Samoa Government (ASG) is authorized to borrow $18.6 million from the U.S. Treasury in order to reduce significant past due debts to vendors. Repayment of the loan is secured and accomplished with funds, as they become due and payable to ASG from the Escrow Account established under the terms and conditions of the Tobacco Master Settlement Agreement. ASG must agree to significant financial reforms as a prerequisite to receiving the loan proceeds.

TRUST TERRITORY OF THE PACIFIC ISLANDS

Program and Financing (in millions of dollars)

Identification code 14–0414–0–1–808		1999 actual	2000 est.	2001 est.
	Obligations by program activity:			
10.00	Total new obligations (object class 25.2)	1	1	....
	Budgetary resources available for obligation:			
21.40	Unobligated balance available, start of year	1	1	....
22.10	Resources available from recoveries of prior year obligations	1	....	....
23.90	Total budgetary resources available for obligation	2	1	....
23.95	Total new obligations	−1	−1	....
24.40	Unobligated balance available, end of year	1	....	....
	Change in unpaid obligations:			
72.40	Unpaid obligations, start of year: Obligated balance, start of year	21	18	13
73.10	Total new obligations	1	1	....
73.20	Total outlays (gross)	−3	−6	−6
73.45	Adjustments in unexpired accounts	−1	....	....
74.40	Unpaid obligations, end of year: Obligated balance, end of year	18	13	7
	Outlays (gross), detail:			
86.93	Outlays from discretionary balances	3	6	6
	Net budget authority and outlays:			
89.00	Budget authority	....	....	....
90.00	Outlays	3	6	6

Until October 1, 1994, the United States exercised jurisdiction over the Trust Territory of the Pacific Islands according to the terms of the 1947 Trusteeship Agreement between the United States and the Security Council of the United Nations. These responsibilities were carried out by the Department of the Interior.

The Department of the Interior is seeking no additional appropriations for the Trust Territory of the Pacific Islands. Compacts of Free Association have been implemented with the Federated States of Micronesia, the Republic of the Marshall Islands, and, as of October 1, 1994, the Republic of Palau. Assistance to the Republic of Palau is now contained in the "Compact of Free Association" account.

Remaining funds in the "Trust Territory of the Pacific Islands" account will be used to meet final transition responsibilities of the United States. Outlays from numerous ongoing infrastructure construction projects in the Republic of Palau and the other two entities will continue as provided by the Compacts of Free Association and appropriation laws, and will be reported as Trust Territory expenditures until such time as the activities cease.

COMPACT OF FREE ASSOCIATION

For economic assistance and necessary expenses for the Federated States of Micronesia and the Republic of the Marshall Islands as provided for in sections 122, 221, 223, 232, and 233 of the Compact of Free Association, and for economic assistance and necessary expenses for the Republic of Palau as provided for in sections 122, 221, 223, 232, and 233 of the Compact of Free Association, $20,545,000, to remain available until expended, as authorized by Public Law 99–239 and Public Law 99–658. *(Department of the Interior and Related Agencies Appropriations Act, 2000, as enacted by section 1000(a)(3) of the Consolidated Appropriations Act, 2000 (P.L. 106–113).)*

Program and Financing (in millions of dollars)

Identification code 14–0415–0–1–808		1999 actual	2000 est.	2001 est.
	Obligations by program activity:			
	Discretionary programs:			
00.01	Federal services assistance	7	7	8
00.02	Enewetak support	1	1	1
00.91	Subtotal, discretionary	8	8	9
	Mandatory:			
01.01	Program grant assistance, mandatory	12	12	12
01.92	Subtotal	20	20	21
	Permanent Indefinite:			
02.01	Assistance to the Marshall Islands	36	37	38
02.02	Assistance to the Federated States of Micronesia	72	73	74
02.03	Assistance to the Republic of Palau	12	12	12
02.04	Palau road construction	113		
02.91	Subtotal, permanent indefinite	233	122	124
10.00	Total new obligations	253	142	145
	Budgetary resources available for obligation:			
21.40	Unobligated balance available, start of year	131	19	19
22.00	New budget authority (gross)	141	142	145
23.90	Total budgetary resources available for obligation	272	161	164
23.95	Total new obligations	−253	−142	−145
24.40	Unobligated balance available, end of year	19	19	19
	New budget authority (gross), detail:			
	Discretionary:			
40.00	Appropriation	9	8	9
	Mandatory:			
60.00	Appropriation	12	12	12
60.05	Appropriation (indefinite)	120	122	124
62.50	Appropriation (total mandatory)	132	134	136
70.00	Total new budget authority (gross)	141	142	145
	Change in unpaid obligations:			
72.40	Unpaid obligations, start of year: Obligated balance, start of year	15	125	98
73.10	Total new obligations	253	142	145
73.20	Total outlays (gross)	−143	−169	−195
74.40	Unpaid obligations, end of year: Obligated balance, end of year	125	98	48
	Outlays (gross), detail:			
86.90	Outlays from new discretionary authority	5	7	8
86.93	Outlays from discretionary balances	5	7	8
86.97	Outlays from new mandatory authority	132	134	136
86.98	Outlays from mandatory balances	1	21	43
87.00	Total outlays (gross)	143	169	195
	Net budget authority and outlays:			
89.00	Budget authority	141	142	145
90.00	Outlays	143	169	195

The peoples of the Marshall Islands and the Federated States of Micronesia approved Compacts of Free Association negotiated by the United States and their governments. The Compact of Free Association Act of 1985 (Public Law 99–239) constituted the necessary authorizing legislation to make annual payments to the Republic of the Marshall Islands and the Federated States of Micronesia. Payments began in 1987 and will continue for fifteen years, totalling an estimated $2.3 billion, to aid in the development of these sovereign nations. The Compact of Free Association with the Republic of Palau was implemented under the terms of Public Law 99–658 on October 1, 1994. This compact will provide annual benefits to the Republic totalling an estimated $600 million over the fifteen-year period that began at the implementation date.

Object Classification (in millions of dollars)

Identification code 14–0415–0–1–808		1999 actual	2000 est.	2001 est.
25.2	Other services	4	5	5
41.0	Grants, subsidies, and contributions	249	137	140
99.9	Total new obligations	253	142	145

PAYMENTS TO THE UNITED STATES TERRITORIES, FISCAL ASSISTANCE

Program and Financing (in millions of dollars)

Identification code 14–0418–0–1–806		1999 actual	2000 est.	2001 est.
	Obligations by program activity:			
00.01	Advance payments to Guam of estimated U.S. income tax collections	54	41	41
00.02	Advance payments to the Virgin Islands of estimated U.S. excise tax collections	55	68	65
10.00	Total new obligations (object class 41.0)	109	109	106
	Budgetary resources available for obligation:			
22.00	New budget authority (gross)	109	109	106
23.95	Total new obligations	−109	−109	−106
	New budget authority (gross), detail:			
	Mandatory:			
60.05	Appropriation (indefinite)	109	109	106
	Change in unpaid obligations:			
73.10	Total new obligations	109	109	106
73.20	Total outlays (gross)	−109	−109	−106
	Outlays (gross), detail:			
86.97	Outlays from new mandatory authority	109	109	106
	Net budget authority and outlays:			
89.00	Budget authority	109	109	106
90.00	Outlays	109	109	106

General and special funds—Continued

PAYMENTS TO THE UNITED STATES TERRITORIES, FISCAL ASSISTANCE—Continued

Public Law 95–348 requires that certain revenues collected by the U.S. Treasury involving Guam and the Virgin Islands (income taxes withheld and excise taxes) be paid prior to the start of the fiscal year of collection. The 2001 request is for the 2002 advanced payment.

OFFICE OF THE SOLICITOR

SALARIES AND EXPENSES

Federal Funds

General and special funds:

For necessary expenses of the Office of the Solicitor, [$40,196,000] *$43,952,000. (Department of the Interior and Related Agencies Appropriations Act, 2000, as enacted by section 1000(a)(3) of the Consolidated Appropriations Act, 2000 (P.L. 106–113).)*

Program and Financing (in millions of dollars)

Identification code 14–0107–0–1–306		1999 actual	2000 est.	2001 est.
	Obligations by program activity:			
00.01	Direct program	37	40	44
09.00	Reimbursable program	4	4	2
10.00	Total new obligations	41	44	46
	Budgetary resources available for obligation:			
21.40	Unobligated balance available, start of year	....	1	....
22.00	New budget authority (gross)	42	44	46
23.90	Total budgetary resources available for obligation	42	45	46
23.95	Total new obligations	−41	−44	−46
24.40	Unobligated balance available, end of year	1	....	....
	New budget authority (gross), detail:			
	Discretionary:			
40.00	Appropriation	37	40	44
42.00	Transferred from other accounts	1	....	....
43.00	Appropriation (total discretionary)	38	40	44
68.00	Spending authority from offsetting collections: Offsetting collections (cash)	4	4	2
70.00	Total new budget authority (gross)	42	44	46
	Change in unpaid obligations:			
72.40	Unpaid obligations, start of year: Obligated balance, start of year	2	1	2
73.10	Total new obligations	41	44	46
73.20	Total outlays (gross)	−41	−42	−46
74.40	Unpaid obligations, end of year: Obligated balance, end of year	1	2	2
	Outlays (gross), detail:			
86.90	Outlays from new discretionary authority	41	42	44
86.93	Outlays from discretionary balances	2	....	2
87.00	Total outlays (gross)	41	42	46
	Offsets:			
	Against gross budget authority and outlays:			
88.00	Offsetting collections (cash) from: Federal sources	−4	−4	−2
	Net budget authority and outlays:			
89.00	Budget authority	38	40	44
90.00	Outlays	37	38	44

The Office of the Solicitor provides legal advice and counsel to the Secretary, the Secretariat, and all constituent bureaus and offices of the Department of the Interior. All attorneys employed in the Department for the purposes of providing legal services are under the supervision of the Solicitor, except the Justices of American Samoa and the attorneys in the Office of Congressional and Legislative Affairs, Office of Inspector General, and the Office of Hearings and Appeals. The Office is comprised of the headquarters staff, located in Washington, DC, and 18 regional and field offices.

Object Classification (in millions of dollars)

Identification code 14–0107–0–1–306		1999 actual	2000 est.	2001 est.
	Direct obligations:			
11.1	Personnel compensation: Full-time permanent	24	26	29
12.1	Civilian personnel benefits	6	6	6
23.1	Rental payments to GSA	4	4	4
25.2	Other services	3	4	5
99.0	Subtotal, direct obligations	37	40	44
99.0	Reimbursable obligations	4	4	2
99.9	Total new obligations	41	44	46

Personnel Summary

Identification code 14–0107–0–1–306		1999 actual	2000 est.	2001 est.
	Direct:			
1001	Total compensable workyears: Full-time equivalent employment	339	340	359
	Reimbursable:			
2001	Total compensable workyears: Full-time equivalent employment	39	50	31

OFFICE OF INSPECTOR GENERAL

SALARIES AND EXPENSES

Federal Funds

General and special funds:

OFFICE OF INSPECTOR GENERAL

For necessary expenses of the Office of Inspector General, [$26,086,000] *$28,859,000. (Department of the Interior and Related Agencies Appropriations Act, 2000, as enacted by section 1000(a)(3) of the Consolidated Appropriations Act, 2000 (P.L. 106–113).)*

Program and Financing (in millions of dollars)

Identification code 14–0104–0–1–306		1999 actual	2000 est.	2001 est.
	Obligations by program activity:			
00.01	Direct program	25	26	29
09.01	Reimbursable program	3	3	3
10.00	Total new obligations	28	29	32
	Budgetary resources available for obligation:			
22.00	New budget authority (gross)	28	29	32
23.95	Total new obligations	−28	−29	−32
	New budget authority (gross), detail:			
	Discretionary:			
40.00	Appropriation	25	26	29
	Spending authority from offsetting collections:			
68.00	Offsetting collections (cash)	....	3	3
68.10	From Federal sources: Change in receivables and unpaid, unfilled orders	3	....	....
68.90	Spending authority from offsetting collections (total discretionary)	3	3	3
70.00	Total new budget authority (gross)	28	29	32
	Change in unpaid obligations:			
	Unpaid obligations, start of year:			
72.40	Obligated balance, start of year	3	4	9
72.95	From Federal sources: Receivables and unpaid, unfilled orders	....	3	3
72.99	Total unpaid obligations, start of year	3	7	12
73.10	Total new obligations	28	29	32
73.20	Total outlays (gross)	−22	−26	−32
	Unpaid obligations, end of year:			
74.40	Obligated balance, end of year	4	9	9
74.95	From Federal sources: Receivables and unpaid, unfilled orders	3	3	3

Identification code 14–0104–0–1–306	1999 actual	2000 est.	2001 est.
74.99 Total unpaid obligations, end of year	7	12	12
Outlays (gross), detail:			
86.90 Outlays from new discretionary authority	22	26	29
86.93 Outlays from discretionary balances			3
87.00 Total outlays (gross)	22	26	32
Offsets:			
Against gross budget authority and outlays:			
88.40 Offsetting collections (cash) from: Non-Federal sources		−3	−3
Against gross budget authority only:			
88.95 From Federal sources: Change in receivables and unpaid, unfilled orders	−3		
Net budget authority and outlays:			
89.00 Budget authority	25	26	29
90.00 Outlays	24	23	29

The mission of the Office of Inspector General is to detect and prevent fraud, waste, and abuse and to promote economy, efficiency, and effectiveness in Departmental programs and operations. The Office conducts and supervises all audits and investigations relating to Departmental programs and operations. In addition, the Office keeps the Secretary and the Congress fully and currently informed about fraud, mismanagement, problems, and deficiencies in Departmental administration of these programs, recommends corrective action, and reports on the progress made in correcting identified problems.

Object Classification (in millions of dollars)

Identification code 14–0104–0–1–306	1999 actual	2000 est.	2001 est.
Direct obligations:			
11.1 Personnel compensation: Full-time permanent	15	18	19
12.1 Civilian personnel benefits	4	4	5
21.0 Travel and transportation of persons		1	1
23.1 Rental payments to GSA	2	2	2
25.3 Purchases of goods and services from Government accounts	2	1	2
26.0 Supplies and materials	1		
99.0 Subtotal, direct obligations	25	26	29
99.0 Reimbursable obligations	3	3	3
99.9 Total new obligations	28	29	32

Personnel Summary

Identification code 14–0104–0–1–306	1999 actual	2000 est.	2001 est.
1001 Total compensable workyears: Full-time equivalent employment	238	265	275

Natural Resource Damage Assessment and Restoration

natural resource damage assessment fund

To conduct natural resource damage assessment activities by the Department of the Interior necessary to carry out the provisions of the Comprehensive Environmental Response, Compensation, and Liability Act, as amended (42 U.S.C. 9601 et seq.), Federal Water Pollution Control Act, as amended (33 U.S.C. 1251 et seq.), the Oil Pollution Act of 1990 **[**(Public Law 101–380)**]** *(33 U.S.C. 2701 et seq.)*, and **[**Public Law 101–337, $5,400,000**]** *the Act of July 27, 1990, as amended (16 U.S.C. 19jj et seq.), $5,403,000*, to remain available until expended. *(Department of the Interior and Related Agencies Appropriations Act, 2000, as enacted by section 1000(a)(3) of the Consolidated Appropriations Act, 2000 (P.L. 106–113).)*

Unavailable Collections (in millions of dollars)

Identification code 14–1618–0–1–303	1999 actual	2000 est.	2001 est.
Balance, start of year:			
01.99 Balance, start of year			
Receipts:			
02.01 Natural resources damages from legal actions	58	47	48
02.02 Natural resources damages from legal actions, earnings on investments	3	3	4
02.99 Total receipts	61	50	52
Appropriation:			
05.01 Natural resource damage assessment and restoration fund	−61	−50	−52
07.99 Total balance, end of year			

Program and Financing (in millions of dollars)

Identification code 14–1618–0–1–303	1999 actual	2000 est.	2001 est.
Obligations by program activity:			
00.01 Damage assessments	5	8	8
00.02 Prince William Sound restoration	13	15	20
00.03 Other restoration	3	17	16
00.04 Program management	1	1	1
10.00 Total new obligations	22	41	45
Budgetary resources available for obligation:			
21.40 Unobligated balance available, start of year	68	80	84
22.00 New budget authority (gross)	38	45	49
22.21 Unobligated balance transferred to other accounts	−5	−1	−1
23.90 Total budgetary resources available for obligation	101	124	132
23.95 Total new obligations	−22	−41	−45
24.40 Unobligated balance available, end of year	80	84	87
New budget authority (gross), detail:			
Discretionary:			
40.00 Appropriation	4	5	5
Mandatory:			
60.25 Appropriation (special fund, indefinite)	61	50	52
61.00 Transferred to other accounts	−27	−10	−8
62.50 Appropriation (total mandatory)	34	40	44
70.00 Total new budget authority (gross)	38	45	49
Change in unpaid obligations:			
72.40 Unpaid obligations, start of year: Obligated balance, start of year	7	6	5
73.10 Total new obligations	22	41	45
73.20 Total outlays (gross)	−22	−40	−44
74.40 Unpaid obligations, end of year: Obligated balance, end of year	6	5	5
Outlays (gross), detail:			
86.90 Outlays from new discretionary authority	3	4	4
86.93 Outlays from discretionary balances	1	1	2
86.97 Outlays from new mandatory authority	4	6	7
86.98 Outlays from mandatory balances	13	30	32
87.00 Total outlays (gross)	22	40	44
Net budget authority and outlays:			
89.00 Budget authority	38	45	49
90.00 Outlays	22	40	44
Memorandum (non-add) entries:			
92.01 Total investments, start of year: U.S. securities: Par value	52	72	90
92.02 Total investments, end of year: U.S. securities: Par value	72	90	115

Under the Natural Resource Damage Assessment and Restoration Fund (Restoration Fund), natural resource damage assessments will be performed in order to provide the basis for claims against responsible parties for the restoration of damaged natural resources. Funds are appropriated to conduct damage assessments and for program management. In addition, funds will be received for the restoration of damaged resources and other activities and for natural resource damage assessments from responsible parties through negotiated settlements or other legal actions by the Department of the Interior.

Restoration activities include: (1) the replacement and enhancement of affected resources; (2) acquisition of equivalent resources and services; and, (3) long-term environmental mon-

General and special funds—Continued

NATURAL RESOURCE DAMAGE ASSESSMENT AND RESTORATION—Continued

NATURAL RESOURCE DAMAGE ASSESSMENT FUND—Continued

itoring and research programs directed to the prevention, containment, and amelioration of hazardous substances and oil spill sites.

The Restoration Fund operates as a departmentwide program, incorporating the interdisciplinary expertise of its various bureaus and offices. Natural resource damage assessments and the restoration of damaged natural resources are authorized by the Comprehensive Environmental Response, Compensation, and Liability Act, as amended (42 U.S.C. 9601 *et seq.*), Federal Water Pollution Control Act, as amended (33 U.S.C. 1251 *et seq.*), the Oil Pollution Act of 1990 (33 U.S.C. 2701 *et seq.*), and the Act of July 27, 1990 (16 U.S.C. 19jj *et seq.*). Since 1992, amounts received by the United States from responsible parties for restoration or reimbursement in settlement of natural resource damages may be deposited in the Fund and shall accrue interest.

Object Classification (in millions of dollars)

Identification code 14–1618–0–1–303		1999 actual	2000 est.	2001 est.
41.0	Direct obligations: Grants, subsidies, and contributions	....	1	1
	Allocation Account:			
	Personnel compensation:			
11.1	Full-time permanent	3	4	5
11.3	Other than full-time permanent	1	1	1
11.9	Total personnel compensation	4	5	6
12.1	Civilian personnel benefits	1	1	1
25.2	Other services	4	11	9
25.3	Purchases of goods and services from Government accounts	....	6	6
32.0	Land and structures	11	14	19
41.0	Grants, subsidies, and contributions	1	2	2
99.0	Subtotal, allocation account	21	39	43
99.5	Below reporting threshold	1	1	1
99.9	Total new obligations	22	41	45

Personnel Summary

Identification code 14–1618–0–1–303		1999 actual	2000 est.	2001 est.
1001	Total compensable workyears: Full-time equivalent employment	3	3	3

EXXON VALDEZ RESTORATION PROGRAM

The budget incorporates the receipts and mandatory spending associated with the 1991 Exxon Valdez oil spill civil and criminal settlements. Receipts for restoration activities from 1992 through 2001 are currently estimated to total $687 million. Additionally, $213 million was recovered for past response and damage assessment activities. The Exxon Valdez Oil Spill Trustee Council was formed to act on behalf of the public as trustees in the collection and joint use of all civil settlement recoveries. The criminal settlement funds are managed separately by the Federal and Alaska State governments, although activities are coordinated with the Trustee Council to maximize restoration benefits.

Funding from the settlements, as well as interest, is provided to the Federal and Alaska State governments to restore the resources and services damaged by the 1989 oil spill. Based upon the current assessment of damages, these funds are sufficient to complete the restoration program. Restoration activities were initiated in 1992 and habitat protection was begun in 1993.

Habitat protection and acquisition is one of the principal tools of restoration. The Trustee Council has underway two habitat protection and acquisition programs, a large parcel program that protects blocks of land in excess of 1,000 acres and a small parcel program that recognizes the unique habitat qualities and strategic restoration value that smaller tracts provide. Funding from the Exxon Valdez civil and criminal settlements, the Land and Water Conservation Fund, and private partnerships work together as an integrated approach to the restoration program. The Council has been working with large and small landowners, on a willing-seller basis, in the spill-impacted area to protect approximately 750,000 acres of habitat.

EXXON VALDEZ RESTORATION PROGRAM BUDGET

Civil and Criminal Settlements
[In thousands of dollars]

	1999 actual	2000 est.	2001 est.
National Oceanic and Atmospheric Administration	3,597	3,229	1,862
U.S. Forest Service	27,977	7,027	6,669
Department of the Interior	5,064	4,236	19,230
Subtotal, Federal Government	36,638	14,492	27,761
State of Alaska	8,954	6,906	5,786
Total Restoration Program	45,592	21,398	33,547

OFFICE OF THE SPECIAL TRUSTEE FOR AMERICAN INDIANS

Federal Funds

General and special funds:

OFFICE OF SPECIAL TRUSTEE FOR AMERICAN INDIANS

FEDERAL TRUST PROGRAMS

For operation of trust programs for Indians by direct expenditure, contracts, cooperative agreements, compacts, and grants, **[**$90,025,000**]** *$82,628,000*, to remain available until expended: *Provided*, That funds for trust management improvements may be transferred, as needed, to the Bureau of Indian Affairs "Operation of Indian Programs" account and to the Departmental Management "Salaries and Expenses" account: *Provided further*, That funds made available to Tribes and Tribal organizations through contracts or grants obligated during fiscal year **[**2000**]** *2001*, as authorized by the Indian Self-Determination Act of 1975 (25 U.S.C. 450 et seq.), shall remain available until expended by the contractor or grantee: *Provided further*, That notwithstanding any other provision of law, the statute of limitations shall not commence to run on any claim, including any claim in litigation pending on the date of the enactment of this Act, concerning losses to or mismanagement of trust funds, until the affected tribe or individual Indian has been furnished with an accounting of such funds from which the beneficiary can determine whether there has been a loss: *Provided further*, That notwithstanding any other provision of law, the Secretary shall not be required to provide a quarterly statement of performance for any Indian trust account that has not had activity for at least 18 months and has a balance of $1.00 or less: *Provided further*, That the Secretary shall issue an annual account statement and maintain a record of any such accounts and shall permit the balance in each such account to be withdrawn upon the express written request of the account holder. *(Department of the Interior and Related Agencies Appropriations Act, 2000, as enacted by section 1000(a)(3) of the Consolidated Appropriations Act, 2000 (P.L. 106–113).)*

Program and Financing (in millions of dollars)

Identification code 14–0120–0–1–808		1999 actual	2000 est.	2001 est.
	Obligations by program activity:			
00.01	Executive direction	2	2	2
00.02	Program operations, support, and improvements	56	107	81
10.00	Total new obligations	58	109	83
	Budgetary resources available for obligation:			
21.40	Unobligated balance available, start of year	21	21	....
22.00	New budget authority (gross)	57	90	83
22.10	Resources available from recoveries of prior year obligations	1	....	....
22.21	Unobligated balance transferred to other accounts	....	−2	....

		1999	2000	2001
23.90	Total budgetary resources available for obligation	79	109	83
23.95	Total new obligations	–58	–109	–83
24.40	Unobligated balance available, end of year	21		
	New budget authority (gross), detail:			
	Discretionary:			
40.00	Appropriation	61	90	83
41.00	Transferred to other accounts	–4		
43.00	Appropriation (total discretionary)	57	90	83
	Change in unpaid obligations:			
72.40	Unpaid obligations, start of year: Obligated balance, start of year	14	27	36
73.10	Total new obligations	58	109	83
73.20	Total outlays (gross)	–43	–99	–85
73.45	Adjustments in unexpired accounts	–1		
74.40	Unpaid obligations, end of year: Obligated balance, end of year	27	36	33
	Outlays (gross), detail:			
86.90	Outlays from new discretionary authority	43	63	58
86.93	Outlays from discretionary balances		38	27
87.00	Total outlays (gross)	43	99	85
	Net budget authority and outlays:			
89.00	Budget authority	57	90	83
90.00	Outlays	43	99	85

Executive direction.—This activity supports the Office of Special Trustee for American Indians, the Trustee's advisory board, and other Tribal representative groups. Under the American Indian Trust Fund Management Reform Act of 1994, the Special Trustee for American Indians is charged with general oversight for Indian trust reform efforts departmentwide. Additionally, in 1996, at the direction of the Congress, direct responsibilities and authorities for Indian Trust Fund Management were transferred to the Special Trustee from the Assistant Secretary of Indian Affairs.

Program operations, support, and improvements.—This activity supports the management and investment of approximately $3 billion held in trust for Tribes and individual Indians. Resources support the implementation of trust management reform efforts and the accurate collection, investment, disbursement, and provision of timely financial information to Indian Tribes and individual Indian monies (IIM) account holders.

Object Classification (in millions of dollars)

Identification code 14–0120–0–1–808		1999 actual	2000 est.	2001 est.
	Personnel compensation:			
11.1	Full-time permanent	11	15	17
11.3	Other than full-time permanent	2	2	2
11.9	Total personnel compensation	13	17	19
12.1	Civilian personnel benefits	3	4	4
21.0	Travel and transportation of persons	1	2	2
23.1	Rental payments to GSA	1	1	1
23.3	Communications, utilities, and miscellaneous charges		1	1
25.2	Other services	21	53	30
25.3	Purchases of goods and services from Government accounts	17	27	24
31.0	Equipment	1	3	1
99.0	Subtotal, direct obligations	57	108	82
99.5	Below reporting threshold	1	1	1
99.9	Total new obligations	58	109	83

Personnel Summary

Identification code 14–0120–0–1–808		1999 actual	2000 est.	2001 est.
1001	Total compensable workyears: Full-time equivalent employment	312	346	366

Payments for Trust Accounting Deficiencies

(Legislative proposal, not subject to PAYGO)

Program and Financing (in millions of dollars)

Identification code 14–0121–2–1–306		1999 actual	2000 est.	2001 est.
	Obligations by program activity:			
10.00	Total new obligations (object class 41.0)			7
	Budgetary resources available for obligation:			
22.00	New budget authority (gross)			7
23.95	Total new obligations			–7
	New budget authority (gross), detail:			
	Mandatory:			
60.00	Appropriation			7
	Change in unpaid obligations:			
73.10	Total new obligations			7
73.20	Total outlays (gross)			–7
	Outlays (gross), detail:			
86.97	Outlays from new mandatory authority			7
	Net budget authority and outlays:			
89.00	Budget authority			7
90.00	Outlays			7

This legislative proposal will provide necessary appropriations to increase the individual Indian money (IIM) investment pool to the aggregate total of the positive balances in the underlying IIM accounts. The current estimate of funding required is $6.7 million. The Administration had proposed a similar appropriation in its April 1998 Tribal trust fund settlement legislative proposal.

Indian Land Consolidation [Pilot]

For implementation of a [pilot] program for consolidation of fractional interests in Indian lands *and expenses associated with redetermining and redistributing escalated interests in alloted lands* by direct expenditure or cooperative agreement, [$5,000,000] *$12,501,000* to remain available until expended and which [shall] *may* be transferred to the Bureau of Indian Affairs *and Departmental Management.* [of which not to exceed $500,000 shall be available for administrative expenses]: *Provided,* That the Secretary may enter into a cooperative agreement, which shall not be subject to Public Law 93–638, as amended, with a tribe having jurisdiction over the [pilot] reservation to implement the program to acquire fractional interests on behalf of such tribe: *Provided further,* That the Secretary may develop a reservation-wide system for establishing the fair market value of various types of lands and improvements to govern the amounts offered for acquisition of fractional interests: *Provided further,* That acquisitions shall be limited to one or more [pilot] reservations as determined by the Secretary: *Provided further,* That funds shall be available for acquisition of fractional interests in trust or restricted lands with the consent of its owners and at fair market value, and the Secretary shall hold in trust for such tribe all interests acquired pursuant to this [pilot] program: *Provided further,* That all proceeds from any lease, resource sale contract, right-of-way or other transaction derived from the fractional interest shall be credited to this appropriation, and remain available until expended, until the purchase price paid by the Secretary under this appropriation has been recovered from such proceeds: *Provided further,* That once the purchase price has been recovered, all subsequent proceeds shall be managed by the Secretary for the benefit of the applicable tribe or paid directly to the tribe. *(Department of the Interior and Related Agencies Appropriations Act, 2000, as enacted by section 1000(a)(3) of the Consolidated Appropriations Act, 2000 (P.L. 106–113).)*

Program and Financing (in millions of dollars)

Identification code 14–2103–0–1–452		1999 actual	2000 est.	2001 est.
	Obligations by program activity:			
10.00	Total new obligations (object class 32.0)	2	8	13

General and special funds—Continued

INDIAN LAND CONSOLIDATION [PILOT]—Continued

Program and Financing (in millions of dollars)—Continued

Identification code 14–2103–0–1–452	1999 actual	2000 est.	2001 est.
Budgetary resources available for obligation:			
21.40 Unobligated balance available, start of year		3	
22.00 New budget authority (gross)	5	5	13
23.90 Total budgetary resources available for obligation	5	8	13
23.95 Total new obligations	−2	−8	−13
24.40 Unobligated balance available, end of year	3		
New budget authority (gross), detail:			
Discretionary:			
40.00 Appropriation	5	5	13
Change in unpaid obligations:			
73.10 Total new obligations	2	8	13
73.20 Total outlays (gross)	−2	−8	−12
Outlays (gross), detail:			
86.90 Outlays from new discretionary authority	2	5	13
86.93 Outlays from discretionary balances		2	
87.00 Total outlays (gross)	2	8	12
Net budget authority and outlays:			
89.00 Budget authority	5	5	13
90.00 Outlays	2	8	12

This appropriation will fund a program on one or more Indian reservations to consolidate fractional interests in Indian lands. Funds will be used to purchase small fractional interests from willing individual Indian landowners. Consolidation of these interests is expected to reduce the Government's costs for managing Indian lands and promote economic opportunity on these lands. While appropriated in the Office of the Special Trustee in 2000, this account was funded under BIA in 1999.

MISCELLANEOUS INDIAN TRUST PAYMENTS

Program and Financing (in millions of dollars)

Identification code 14–2311–0–1–452	1999 actual	2000 est.	2001 est.
Obligations by program activity:			
10.00 Total new obligations (object class 41.0)	32		
Budgetary resources available for obligation:			
22.00 New budget authority (gross)	32		
23.95 Total new obligations	−32		
New budget authority (gross), detail:			
Mandatory:			
60.00 Appropriation	32		
Change in unpaid obligations:			
73.10 Total new obligations	32		
73.20 Total outlays (gross)	−32		
Outlays (gross), detail:			
86.97 Outlays from new mandatory authority	32		
Net budget authority and outlays:			
89.00 Budget authority	32		
90.00 Outlays	32		

This account was established to provide for recording of miscellaneous trust payments to Tribes. In 1999, this account included funding for the Menominee Settlement authorized by section 3 of P.L. 106–54. Similar future Tribal payments will be reflected in this account.

TRIBAL SPECIAL FUND

Unavailable Collections (in millions of dollars)

Identification code 14–5265–0–2–452	1999 actual	2000 est.	2001 est.
Balance, start of year:			
01.99 Balance, start of year			
Receipts:			
02.01 Proprietary receipts from the public		22	23
02.02 Earnings on investments		4	4
02.03 Return of principal from private sector investments		3	3
02.04 Trust fund payments		31	
02.99 Total receipts		60	30
Appropriation:			
05.01 Tribal special fund		−60	−30
07.99 Total balance, end of year			

Program and Financing (in millions of dollars)

Identification code 14–5265–0–2–452	1999 actual	2000 est.	2001 est.
Obligations by program activity:			
10.00 Total new obligations (object class 41.0)		30	30
Budgetary resources available for obligation:			
21.40 Unobligated balance available, start of year			30
22.00 New budget authority (gross)		60	30
23.90 Total budgetary resources available for obligation		60	60
23.95 Total new obligations		−30	−30
24.40 Unobligated balance available, end of year		30	30
New budget authority (gross), detail:			
Mandatory:			
60.25 Appropriation (special fund, indefinite)		60	30
Change in unpaid obligations:			
73.10 Total new obligations		30	30
73.20 Total outlays (gross)		−30	−30
Outlays (gross), detail:			
86.97 Outlays from new mandatory authority		30	30
Net budget authority and outlays:			
89.00 Budget authority		60	30
90.00 Outlays		30	30
Memorandum (non-add) entries:			
92.01 Total investments, start of year: U.S. securities: Par value			44
92.02 Total investments, end of year: U.S. securities: Par value		44	14

Commencing with 2000, most Tribal trust funds, including special funds, managed by the Office of Special Trustee will be reclassified as non-budgetary. 1999 will not be restated, hence, only 2000 and 2001 balances are carried above. Ownership of these funds will not change, nor will the Federal Government's management responsibilities; changes made are for presentation purposes only. Some Tribal trust funds will remain budgetary, in either this Tribal Special Fund or the Tribal Trust Fund presented later in this section. Funds in the Tribal Special Fund are those not designated in law as a trust, and generally are funds held and invested to carry out obligations of the Secretary of the Interior.

Effective October 1, 1999, $1.9 billion in Tribal trust funds were reclassified to a non-budgetary account from Miscellaneous Trust Funds. As of October 1, 1999, the Tribal Special Fund account includes $520 million in fund assets that have been classified as budgetary or are pending further review. The unobligated balances reflected above include only those assets invested in U.S. Treasury securities; most of the assets of these funds are in investments held outside Treasury.

For a further discussion of this change in budgetary classification, see the "Trust Funds and Federal Funds" chapter of the 2001 Analytical Perspectives.

MISCELLANEOUS PERMANENT APPROPRIATIONS

Unavailable Collections (in millions of dollars)

Identification code 14–9922–0–2–452	1999 actual	2000 est.	2001 est.
Balance, start of year:			
01.99 Balance, start of year			
Receipts:			
02.02 Interest on investment	23		
Appropriation:			
05.01 Miscellaneous permanent appropriations	–23		
07.99 Total balance, end of year			

Program and Financing (in millions of dollars)

Identification code 14–9922–0–2–452	1999 actual	2000 est.	2001 est.
Obligations by program activity:			
00.01 Tribal economic recovery	9		
10.00 Total new obligations (object class 25.2)	9		
Budgetary resources available for obligation:			
21.40 Unobligated balance available, start of year	33		
22.00 New budget authority (gross)	23		
23.90 Total budgetary resources available for obligation	56		
23.95 Total new obligations	–9		
24.40 Unobligated balance available, end of year	47		
New budget authority (gross), detail:			
Mandatory:			
60.25 Appropriation (special fund, indefinite)	23		
Change in unpaid obligations:			
73.10 Total new obligations	9		
73.20 Total outlays (gross)	–9		
Outlays (gross), detail:			
86.97 Outlays from new mandatory authority	9		
Net budget authority and outlays:			
89.00 Budget authority	23		
90.00 Outlays	9		
Memorandum (non-add) entries:			
92.01 Total investments, start of year: U.S. securities: Par value	40		
92.02 Total investments, end of year: U.S. securities: Par value	39		

Commencing with 2000, most Tribal trust funds, including special funds, managed by the Office of Special Trustee will be reclassified as non-budgetary. 1999 will not be restated, and hence, 2000 and 2001 budget activity and balances are not presented above. Ownership of these funds will not change, nor will the Federal Government's management responsibilities; changes made are for presentation purposes only. Some tribal trust funds will remain classified as budgetary and their balances and activity are presented in two new accounts: a Tribal Special Fund and a Tribal Trust Fund. For a further discussion of this change in budgetary classification, see the "Trust Funds and Federal Funds" chapter of the 2001 Analytical Perspectives.

This consolidated display presents the activities associated with the following accounts:

Cochiti Wetfields Solution.—In 1994, the Army Corps of Engineers transferred $4 million pursuant to PL. 102–358 and the settlement agreement between the Cochiti Tribe, Corps, and Department of Interior. This is a sinking fund with a life expectancy of 50 to 100 years. Funds are used to pay for operation and maintenance, repair, and replacement of the ongoing drainage system for the Cochiti Pueblo. Funds will be invested and principal and interest may be used. It is estimated that it will cost the Tribe approximately $50,000 per year to operate and maintain the drainage system. The $282,000 represents the estimated interest earnings on the fund. This fund is budgetary and is included in the Tribal Special Fund beginning in 2000.

Tribal Economic Recovery Fund.—This fund is authorized by the Three Affiliated Tribes and Standing Rock Sioux Tribe Equitable Compensation Act of 1992 *(Public Law 102–575)* and holds funds which have been appropriated pursuant to the Act.

Beginning in 1998, interest earned on the principal of this fund is available for both Tribes for economic development, education, and social services programs.

TRIBAL TRUST FUND

Unavailable Collections (in millions of dollars)

Identification code 14–8030–0–7–452	1999 actual	2000 est.	2001 est.
Balance, start of year:			
01.99 Balance, start of year			
Receipts:			
02.03 Interest on investments in GSEs		6	6
02.04 Return of principal from private sector investments		25	27
02.99 Total receipts		31	33
Appropriation:			
05.01 Tribal trust fund		–31	–33
07.99 Total balance, end of year			

Program and Financing (in millions of dollars)

Identification code 14–8030–0–7–452	1999 actual	2000 est.	2001 est.
Obligations by program activity:			
10.00 Total new obligations (object class 41.0)		31	33
Budgetary resources available for obligation:			
22.00 New budget authority (gross)		31	33
23.95 Total new obligations		–31	–33
New budget authority (gross), detail:			
Mandatory:			
60.25 Appropriation (special fund, indefinite)		31	33
Change in unpaid obligations:			
73.10 Total new obligations		31	33
73.20 Total outlays (gross)		–31	–33
Outlays (gross), detail:			
86.97 Outlays from new mandatory authority		31	33
Net budget authority and outlays:			
89.00 Budget authority		31	33
90.00 Outlays		31	33
Memorandum (non-add) entries:			
92.01 Total investments, start of year: U.S. securities: Par value			107
92.02 Total investments, end of year: U.S. securities: Par value		107	107

Commencing with 2000, most Tribal trust funds, including special funds, managed by the Office of Special Trustee will be reclassified as non-budgetary. 1999 will not be restated, hence, only 2000 and 2001 balances are carried above. Ownership of these funds will not change, nor will the Federal Government's management responsibilities; changes made are for presentation purposes only. Some Tribal trust funds will remain budgetary, in either this Tribal Trust Fund or the Tribal Special Fund presented in this section. Effective October 1, 1999, $1.9 billion in Tribal trust funds were reclassified to a non-budgetary account from Miscellaneous Trust Funds. As of October 1, 1999, this Tribal Trust Fund account includes $162 million in fund assets that have been classified as budgetary or are pending further review. The unobligated balances reflected above include only those assets invested in U.S. Treasury securities; most of the assets of these funds are

General and special funds—Continued

TRIBAL TRUST FUND—Continued

in investments held outside Treasury. For a further discussion of this change in budgetary classification, see the "Trust Funds and Federal Funds" chapter of the 2001 Analytical Perspectives.

Trust Funds

COOPERATIVE FUND (PAPAGO)

Unavailable Collections (in millions of dollars)

Identification code 14–8366–0–7–452	1999 actual	2000 est.	2001 est.
Balance, start of year:			
01.99 Balance, start of year	....	....	....
Receipts:			
02.01 Cooperative Fund (Papago), Interior, Interest on investments	2	....	....
Appropriation:			
05.01 Cooperative fund (papago)	−2	....	....
07.99 Total balance, end of year	....	....	....

Program and Financing (in millions of dollars)

Identification code 14–8366–0–7–452	1999 actual	2000 est.	2001 est.
Obligations by program activity:			
00.01 Transfer of securities to Tribal special fund	....	31	....
10.00 Total new obligations (object class 92.0)	....	31	....
Budgetary resources available for obligation:			
21.40 Unobligated balance available, start of year	29	31	....
22.00 New budget authority (gross)	2	....	....
23.90 Total budgetary resources available for obligation	31	31	....
23.95 Total new obligations	....	−31	....
24.40 Unobligated balance available, end of year	31	....	....
New budget authority (gross), detail:			
Mandatory:			
60.27 Appropriation (trust fund, indefinite)	2	....	....
Change in unpaid obligations:			
73.10 Total new obligations	....	31	....
73.20 Total outlays (gross)	....	−31	....
Outlays (gross), detail:			
86.98 Outlays from mandatory balances	....	31	....
Net budget authority and outlays:			
89.00 Budget authority	2	....	....
90.00 Outlays	....	31	....
Memorandum (non-add) entries:			
92.01 Total investments, start of year: U.S. securities: Par value	31	....	....
92.02 Total investments, end of year: U.S. securities: Par value	31	....	....

Commencing with 2000, most Tribal trust funds, including special funds, managed by the Office of Special Trustee will be reclassified as non-budgetary. 1999 will not be restated, and hence, 2000 and 2001 budget activity and balances are not presented above. Ownership of these funds will not change, nor will the Federal Government's management responsibilities; changes made are for presentation purposes only. Some Tribal trust funds will remain classified as budgetary and their balances and activity are presented in two new accounts: a Tribal Special Fund and a Tribal Trust Fund. For a further discussion of this change in budgetary classification, see the "Trust Funds and Federal Funds" chapter of the 2001 Analytical Perspectives.

This Cooperative Fund, established by section 313 of the Southern Arizona Water Rights Settlement Act (96 Stat. 1274–1285), provides a source of funds for the Secretary of the Interior to carry out the obligations of the Secretary under sections 303, 304, and 305 of the Act. Only interest accruing to the fund may be expended. This fund is included in the Tribal Special Fund beginning in 2000.

MISCELLANEOUS TRUST FUNDS

Unavailable Collections (in millions of dollars)

Identification code 14–9973–0–7–452	1999 actual	2000 est.	2001 est.
Balance, start of year:			
01.99 Balance, start of year	....	....	....
Receipts:			
02.02 NCIRWRS-TF- Interest on investments	1	....	....
02.03 Indian tribal funds, awards	95	....	....
02.04 Earnings on investments, Indian Tribal funds, Interior	16	....	....
02.05 Indian tribal funds, interest, other	105	....	....
02.06 Indian tribal funds, fines, penalties, and forfeitures	2	....	....
02.07 Indian tribal funds, other proprietary receipts from the publc	217	....	....
02.14 Crow Creek Sioux Tribe infrastructure development trust fund, interest	2	....	....
02.99 Total receipts	438	....	....
Appropriation:			
05.01 Miscellaneous trust funds	−438	....	....
07.99 Total balance, end of year	....	....	....

Program and Financing (in millions of dollars)

Identification code 14–9973–0–7–452	1999 actual	2000 est.	2001 est.
Obligations by program activity:			
10.00 Total new obligations (object class 41.0)	322	....	....
Budgetary resources available for obligation:			
21.40 Unobligated balance available, start of year	188	....	....
22.00 New budget authority (gross)	438	....	....
23.90 Total budgetary resources available for obligation	626	....	....
23.95 Total new obligations	−322	....	....
24.40 Unobligated balance available, end of year	304	....	....
New budget authority (gross), detail:			
Mandatory:			
60.27 Appropriation (trust fund, indefinite)	438	....	....
Change in unpaid obligations:			
73.10 Total new obligations	322	....	....
73.20 Total outlays (gross)	−322	....	....
Outlays (gross), detail:			
86.97 Outlays from new mandatory authority	322	....	....
Net budget authority and outlays:			
89.00 Budget authority	438	....	....
90.00 Outlays	322	....	....
Memorandum (non-add) entries:			
92.01 Total investments, start of year: U.S. securities: Par value	366	....	....
92.02 Total investments, end of year: U.S. securities: Par value	356	....	....

Commencing with 2000, most Tribal trust funds, including special funds, managed by the Office of Special Trustee will be reclassified as non-budgetary. 1999 will not be restated, and hence, 2000 and 2001 budget activity and balances are not presented above. Ownership of these funds will not change, nor will the Federal government's management responsibilities; changes made are for presentation purposes only. Some Tribal trust funds will remain classified as budgetary and their balances and activity are presented in two new accounts: a Tribal Special Fund and a Tribal Trust Fund. Effective October 1, 1999 $1.9 billion in Tribal trust funds were reclassified to a non-budgetary account; remaining balances in these accounts are included in the Tribal Special or Trust Fund accounts beginning in 2000. For a further discussion of this change in budgetary classification, see the "Trust Funds and Federal Funds" chapter of the 2001 Analytical Perspectives.

This consolidated display presents the activities associated with the following accounts:

Tribal Trust Funds.—Tribal funds are deposited into a consolidated account in the U.S. Treasury pursuant to: (1) general or specific acts of Congress and (2) Federal management of Tribal real properties, the titles to which are held in trust for the Tribes by the United States. There are approximately 330 Tribes with approximately 1,500 accounts, which total approximately $2.5 billion held in the trust fund. These funds are available to the respective Tribal groups for various purposes, under various acts of Congress, and are subject to the provisions of Tribal constitutions, bylaws, charters, and resolutions of the various Tribes, bands, or groups.

Funds Contributed for the Advancement of the Indian Race.—This program accounts for any contributions, donations, gifts, etc., which are to be used for the benefit of American Indians in accordance with the donors' wishes (82 Stat. 171).

Bequest of George C. Edgeter.—This program consists of a bequest, the principal of which is invested in U.S. Treasury bonds and notes, and the interest is to be used for the benefit of American Indians (82 Stat. 171), as specified by the donors wishes.

Navajo Rehabilitation Trust Fund.—Funds deposited into this account shall be used to improve the economic, social, and educational conditions of Navajo families and communities affected by the relocation activities.

Northern Cheyenne Indian Reserved Water Rights Settlement Trust Fund.—Funds transferred provide for the establishment of a $21.5 million trust fund for the Northern Cheyenne Indian Tribe. These funds may be used by the Tribe to make $11.5 million available to the state of Montana as a loan to assist in financing Tongue River Dam project costs; land and natural resources administration, planning, and development; land acquisition; and any other purpose determined by the Tribe.

In addition, this fund holds $31.5 million for the enlargement and repair of the Tongue River Dam project.

The Crow Creek Sioux Tribe Infrastructure Development Trust Fund.—The Crow Creek Sioux Tribe Infrastructure Development Trust Fund Act of 1996 *(Public Law 104–223, 110 Stat. 3026)* establishes a Crow Creek Sioux Tribe Infrastructure Development Trust Fund. In 1997, $27,500,000 was deposited into the Fund. The interest earned from the invested principal is available for payment to the Tribe for Tribal educational, health care, recreational, and other projects.

NATIONAL INDIAN GAMING COMMISSION

Federal Funds

General and special funds:

SALARIES AND EXPENSES

Program and Financing (in millions of dollars)

Identification code 14–0118–0–1–806	1999 actual	2000 est.	2001 est.
Obligations by program activity:			
10.00 Total new obligations	7	3	1
Budgetary resources available for obligation:			
21.40 Unobligated balance available, start of year	5	2	
22.00 New budget authority (gross)	4	1	1
23.90 Total budgetary resources available for obligation	9	3	1
23.95 Total new obligations	–7	–3	–1
24.40 Unobligated balance available, end of year	2		
New budget authority (gross), detail:			
Discretionary:			
68.00 Spending authority from offsetting collections (gross): Offsetting collections (cash)	4	1	1
Change in unpaid obligations:			
72.40 Unpaid obligations, start of year: Obligated balance, start of year	8	1	
73.10 Total new obligations	7	3	1
73.20 Total outlays (gross)	–14	–4	–1
73.40 Adjustments in expired accounts (net)		1	
74.40 Unpaid obligations, end of year: Obligated balance, end of year	1		
Outlays (gross), detail:			
86.90 Outlays from new discretionary authority	4	1	1
86.93 Outlays from discretionary balances	10	3	
87.00 Total outlays (gross)	14	4	1
Offsets:			
Against gross budget authority and outlays:			
88.40 Offsetting collections (cash) from: Non-Federal sources	–4	–1	–1
Net budget authority and outlays:			
89.00 Budget authority			
90.00 Outlays	10	3	

The Indian Gaming Regulatory Act (Public Law 100–497) established the National Indian Gaming Commission as an independent agency within the Department of the Interior. The Commission will have a regulatory role over gaming conducted on Indian lands. Operating costs of the Commission will be financed through annual assessments of gaming operations regulated by the Commission.

Object Classification (in millions of dollars)

Identification code 14–0118–0–1–806	1999 actual	2000 est.	2001 est.
99.0 Reimbursable obligations: Subtotal, reimbursable obligations	7	3	1
99.9 Total new obligations	7	3	1

Personnel Summary

Identification code 14–0118–0–1–806	1999 actual	2000 est.	2001 est.
2001 Total compensable workyears: Full-time equivalent employment	47		

NATIONAL INDIAN GAMING COMMISSION, GAMING ACTIVITY FEES

Unavailable Collections (in millions of dollars)

Identification code 14–5141–0–2–806	1999 actual	2000 est.	2001 est.
Balance, start of year:			
01.99 Balance, start of year			
Receipts:			
02.01 National Indian Gaming Commission, gaming activity fees	5	7	7
Appropriation:			
05.01 National Indian Gaming Commission, gaming activity fees	–5	–7	–7
07.99 Total balance, end of year			

Program and Financing (in millions of dollars)

Identification code 14–5141–0–2–806	1999 actual	2000 est.	2001 est.
Obligations by program activity:			
10.00 Total new obligations		7	7
Budgetary resources available for obligation:			
21.40 Unobligated balance available, start of year		5	5
22.00 New budget authority (gross)	5	7	7

General and special funds—Continued

NATIONAL INDIAN GAMING COMMISSION, GAMING ACTIVITY FEES—Continued

Program and Financing (in millions of dollars)—Continued

Identification code 14–5141–0–2–806	1999 actual	2000 est.	2001 est.
23.90 Total budgetary resources available for obligation	5	12	12
23.95 Total new obligations	....	−7	−7
24.40 Unobligated balance available, end of year	5	5	5
New budget authority (gross), detail:			
Mandatory:			
60.25 Appropriation (special fund, indefinite)	5	7	7
Change in unpaid obligations:			
72.40 Unpaid obligations, start of year: Obligated balance, start of year	....	....	1
73.10 Total new obligations	....	7	7
73.20 Total outlays (gross)	....	−6	−7
73.40 Adjustments in expired accounts (net)	....	−1	....
74.40 Unpaid obligations, end of year: Obligated balance, end of year	....	1	1
Outlays (gross), detail:			
86.97 Outlays from new mandatory authority	....	6	6
86.98 Outlays from mandatory balances	....	1	1
87.00 Total outlays (gross)	....	6	7
Net budget authority and outlays:			
89.00 Budget authority	5	7	7
90.00 Outlays	....	6	7

The Indian Gaming Regulatory Act (Public Law 100–497) established the National Indian Gaming Commission as an independent agency within the Department of the Interior. The Commission regulates gaming conducted on Indian lands. The Indian Gaming Regulatory Act, as amended by the 1998 Interior and Related Agencies Appropriations Act (Public Law 105–83), authorizes the Commission to collect and expend gaming activity fees. Commission operations are entirely funded from those fees.

Object Classification (in millions of dollars)

Identification code 14–5141–0–2–806	1999 actual	2000 est.	2001 est.
11.1 Personnel compensation: Full-time permanent	....	3	3
12.1 Civilian personnel benefits	....	1	1
21.0 Travel and transportation of persons	....	1	1
25.2 Other services	....	2	2
99.9 Total new obligations	....	7	7

Personnel Summary

Identification code 14–5141–0–2–806	1999 actual	2000 est.	2001 est.
1001 Total compensable workyears: Full-time equivalent employment	....	65	70

GENERAL FUND RECEIPT ACCOUNTS

(in millions of dollars)

	1999 actual	2000 est.	2001 est.
Offsetting receipts from the public:			
14–149300 Interest received from Outer Continental Shelf escrow account	1	....	671
14–181100 Rent and bonuses from land leases for resource exploration and extraction	17	55	17
14–182000 Rent and bonuses on Outer Continental Shelf lands	42	....	....
14–202000 Royalties on Outer Continental Shelf lands	2,307	2,653	2,573
14–203900 Royalties on natural resources, not otherwise classified	127	152	140
14–222900 Sale of timber, wildlife and other natural land products, not otherwise classified	43	45	68
14–241910 Fees and other charges for program services	2	2	2
14–248400 Receipts from grazing fees, Federal share, Interior	5	5	5
14–272930 Indian loan guarantee, downward reestimates of subsidies	....	21	....
General Fund Offsetting receipts from the public	2,544	2,933	3,476

GENERAL PROVISIONS, DEPARTMENT OF THE INTERIOR

SEC. 101. Appropriations made in this title shall be available for expenditure or transfer (within each bureau or office), with the approval of the Secretary, for the emergency reconstruction, replacement, or repair of aircraft, buildings, utilities, or other facilities or equipment damaged or destroyed by fire, flood, storm, or other unavoidable causes: *Provided*, That no funds shall be made available under this authority until funds specifically made available to the Department of the Interior for emergencies shall have been exhausted: *Provided further*, That all funds used pursuant to this section are hereby designated by Congress to be "emergency requirements" pursuant to section 251(b)(2)(A) of the Balanced Budget and Emergency Deficit Control Act of 1985, and must be replenished by a supplemental appropriation which must be requested as promptly as possible.

SEC. 102. The Secretary may authorize the expenditure or transfer of any no year appropriation in this title, in addition to the amounts included in the budget programs of the several agencies, for the suppression or emergency prevention of [forest or range] *wildland* fires on or threatening lands under the jurisdiction of the Department of the Interior; for the emergency rehabilitation of burned-over lands under its jurisdiction; for emergency actions related to potential or actual earthquakes, floods, volcanoes, storms, or other unavoidable causes; for contingency planning subsequent to actual oil spills; for response and natural resource damage assessment activities related to actual oil spills; for the prevention, suppression, and control of actual or potential grasshopper and Mormon cricket outbreaks on lands under the jurisdiction of the Secretary, pursuant to the authority in section 1773(b) of Public Law 99–198 (99 Stat. 1658); for emergency reclamation projects under section 410 of Public Law 95–87; and shall transfer, from any no year funds available to the Office of Surface Mining Reclamation and Enforcement, such funds as may be necessary to permit assumption of regulatory authority in the event a primacy State is not carrying out the regulatory provisions of the Surface Mining Act: *Provided*, That appropriations made in this title for [fire suppression purposes] *wildland fire operations* shall be available for the payment of obligations incurred during the preceding fiscal year, and for reimbursement to other Federal agencies for destruction of vehicles, aircraft, or other equipment in connection with their use for [fire suppression purposes] *wildland fire operations*, such reimbursement to be credited to appropriations currently available at the time of receipt thereof: *Provided further*, That for [emergency rehabilitation and wildfire suppression activities] *wildland fire operations*, no funds shall be made available under this authority until [funds appropriated to "Wildland Fire Management" shall have been exhausted] *the Secretary determines that funds appropriated for "wildland fire operations" shall be exhausted within thirty days*: *Provided further*, That all funds used pursuant to this section are hereby designated by Congress to be "emergency requirements" pursuant to section 251(b)(2)(A) of the Balanced Budget and Emergency Deficit Control Act of 1985, and must be replenished by a supplemental appropriation which must be requested as promptly as possible: *Provided further*, That such replenishment funds shall be used to reimburse, on a pro rata basis, accounts from which emergency funds were transferred.

SEC. 103. Appropriations made in this title shall be available for operation of warehouses, garages, shops, and similar facilities, wherever consolidation of activities will contribute to efficiency or economy, and said appropriations shall be reimbursed for services rendered to any other activity in the same manner as authorized by sections 1535 and 1536 of title 31, United States Code: *Provided*, That reimbursements for costs and supplies, materials, equipment, and for services rendered may be credited to the appropriation current at the time such reimbursements are received.

SEC. 104. Appropriations made to the Department of the Interior in this title shall be available for services as authorized by 5 U.S.C. 3109, when authorized by the Secretary, in total amount not to exceed $500,000; hire, maintenance, and operation of aircraft; hire of passenger motor vehicles; purchase of reprints; payment for telephone service in private residences in the field, when authorized under regulations approved by the Secretary; and the payment of dues, when authorized by the Secretary, for library membership in societies or associations which issue publications to members only or at a price to members lower than to subscribers who are not members.

SEC. 105. Appropriations available to the Department of the Interior for salaries and expenses shall be available for uniforms or allowances therefor, as authorized by law (5 U.S.C. 5901–5902 and D.C. Code 4–204).

SEC. 106. [Appropriations] *Annual approriations* made in this title shall be available for obligation in connection with contracts issued for services or rentals for periods not in excess of 12 months beginning at any time during the fiscal year.

SEC. 107. No funds provided in this title may be expended by the Department of the Interior for the conduct of offshore leasing and related activities placed under restriction in the President's moratorium statement of June [26, 1990, in] *12, 1998, which includes* the areas of northern, central, and southern California; the North Atlantic; Washington and Oregon; [and] the eastern Gulf of Mexico south of 26 degrees north latitude and east of 86 degrees west longitude; *and any lands located outside Sale 181, as identified in the final Outer Continental Shelf 5-year Oil and Gas Leasing program, 1997–2002; the North Aleutian Basin area; and the Mid-Atlantic and South Atlantic planning areas.*

[SEC. 108. No funds provided in this title may be expended by the Department of the Interior for the conduct of offshore oil and natural gas preleasing, leasing, and related activities, on lands within the North Aleutian Basin planning area.]

[SEC. 109. No funds provided in this title may be expended by the Department of the Interior to conduct offshore oil and natural gas preleasing, leasing and related activities in the eastern Gulf of Mexico planning area for any lands located outside Sale 181, as identified in the final Outer Continental Shelf 5-Year Oil and Gas Leasing Program, 1997–2002.]

[SEC. 110. No funds provided in this title may be expended by the Department of the Interior to conduct oil and natural gas preleasing, leasing and related activities in the Mid-Atlantic and South Atlantic planning areas.]

SEC. [111] *108.* Advance payments made under this title to Indian tribes, tribal organizations, and tribal consortia pursuant to the Indian Self-Determination and Education Assistance Act (25 U.S.C. 450 et seq.) or the Tribally Controlled Schools Act of 1988 (25 U.S.C. 2501 et seq.) may be invested by the Indian tribe, tribal organization, or consortium before such funds are expended for the purposes of the grant, compact, or annual funding agreement so long as such funds are—

(1) invested by the Indian tribe, tribal organization, or consortium only in obligations of the United States, or in obligations or securities that are guaranteed or insured by the United States, or mutual (or other) funds registered with the Securities and Exchange Commission and which only invest in obligations of the United States or securities that are guaranteed or insured by the United States; or

(2) deposited only into accounts that are insured by an agency or instrumentality of the United States, or are fully collateralized to ensure protection of the funds, even in the event of a bank failure.

[SEC. 112. (a) Employees of Helium Operations, Bureau of Land Management, entitled to severance pay under 5 U.S.C. 5595, may apply for, and the Secretary of the Interior may pay, the total amount of the severance pay to the employee in a lump sum. Employees paid severance pay in a lump sum and subsequently reemployed by the Federal Government shall be subject to the repayment provisions of 5 U.S.C. 5595(i)(2) and (3), except that any repayment shall be made to the Helium Fund.]

[(b) Helium Operations employees who elect to continue health benefits after separation shall be liable for not more than the required employee contribution under 5 U.S.C. 8905a(d)(1)(A). The Helium Fund shall pay for 18 months the remaining portion of required contributions.]

[(c) The Secretary of the Interior may provide for training to assist Helium Operations employees in the transition to other Federal or private sector jobs during the facility shut-down and disposition process and for up to 12 months following separation from Federal employment, including retraining and relocation incentives on the same terms and conditions as authorized for employees of the Department of Defense in section 348 of the National Defense Authorization Act for Fiscal Year 1995.]

[(d) For purposes of the annual leave restoration provisions of 5 U.S.C. 6304(d)(1)(B), the cessation of helium production and sales, and other related Helium Program activities shall be deemed to create an exigency of public business under, and annual leave that is lost during leave years 1997 through 2001 because of 5 U.S.C. 6304 (regardless of whether such leave was scheduled in advance) shall be restored to the employee and shall be credited and available in accordance with 5 U.S.C. 6304(d)(2). Annual leave so restored and remaining unused upon the transfer of a Helium Program employee to a position of the executive branch outside of the Helium Program shall be liquidated by payment to the employee of a lump sum from the Helium Fund for such leave.]

[(e) Benefits under this section shall be paid from the Helium Fund in accordance with section 4(c)(4) of the Helium Privatization Act of 1996. Funds may be made available to Helium Program employees who are or will be separated before October 1, 2002 because of the cessation of helium production and sales and other related activities. Retraining benefits, including retraining and relocation incentives, may be paid for retraining commencing on or before September 30, 2002.]

[(f) This section shall remain in effect through fiscal year 2002.]

[SEC. 113. Notwithstanding any other provision of law, including but not limited to the Indian Self-Determination Act of 1975, as amended, hereafter funds available to the Department of the Interior for Indian self-determination or self-governance contract or grant support costs may be expended only for costs directly attributable to contracts, grants and compacts pursuant to the Indian Self-Determination Act of 1975 and hereafter funds appropriated in this title shall not be available for any contract support costs or indirect costs associated with any contract, grant, cooperative agreement, self-governance compact or funding agreement entered into between an Indian tribe or tribal organization and any entity other than an agency of the Department of the Interior.]

SEC. [114] *109.* Notwithstanding any other provisions of law, the National Park Service shall not develop or implement a reduced entrance fee program to accommodate non-local travel through a unit. The Secretary may provide for and regulate local non-recreational passage through units of the National Park System, allowing each unit to develop guidelines and permits for such activity appropriate to that unit.

[SEC. 115. Notwithstanding any other provision of law, in fiscal year 2000 and thereafter, the Secretary is authorized to permit persons, firms or organizations engaged in commercial, cultural, educational, or recreational activities (as defined in section 612a of title 40, United States Code) not currently occupying such space to use courtyards, auditoriums, meeting rooms, and other space of the main and south Interior building complex, Washington, D.C., the maintenance, operation, and protection of which has been delegated to the Secretary from the Administrator of General Services pursuant to the Federal Property and Administrative Services Act of 1949, and to assess reasonable charges therefore, subject to such procedures as the Secretary deems appropriate for such uses. Charges may be for the space, utilities, maintenance, repair, and other services. Charges for such space and services may be at rates equivalent to the prevailing commercial rate for comparable space and services devoted to a similar purpose in the vicinity of the main and south Interior building complex, Washington, D.C., for which charges are being assessed. The Secretary may without further appropriation hold, administer, and use such proceeds within the Departmental Management Working Capital Fund to offset the operation of the buildings under his jurisdiction, whether delegated or otherwise, and for related purposes, until expended.]

[SEC. 116. Notwithstanding any other provision of law, the Steel Industry American Heritage Area, authorized by Public Law 104–333, is hereby renamed the Rivers of Steel National Heritage Area.]

[SEC. 117. (a) In this section—

(1) the term "Huron Cemetery" means the lands that form the cemetery that is popularly known as the Huron Cemetery, located in Kansas City, Kansas, as described in subsection (b)(3); and

(2) the term "Secretary" means the Secretary of the Interior.

(b)(1) The Secretary shall take such action as may be necessary to ensure that the lands comprising the Huron Cemetery (as described in paragraph (3)) are used only in accordance with this subsection.]

[(2) The lands of the Huron Cemetery shall be used only—

(A) for religious and cultural uses that are compatible with the use of the lands as a cemetery; and

(B) as a burial ground.

(3) The description of the lands of the Huron Cemetery is as follows:]

[The tract of land in the NW quarter of sec. 10, T. 11 S., R. 25 E., of the sixth principal meridian, in Wyandotte County, Kansas (as surveyed and marked on the ground on August 15, 1888, by William Millor, Civil Engineer and Surveyor), described as follows:

"Commencing on the Northwest corner of the Northwest Quarter of the Northwest Quarter of said Section 10;

"Thence South 28 poles to the 'true point of beginning';

"Thence South 71 degrees East 10 poles and 18 links;

"Thence South 18 degrees and 30 minutes West 28 poles;

"Thence West 11 and one-half poles;

"Thence North 19 degrees 15 minutes East 31 poles and 15 feet to the 'true point of beginning', containing 2 acres or more.".]

SEC. [118] *110.* Refunds or rebates received on an on-going basis from a credit card services provider under the Department of the Interior's charge card programs may be deposited to and retained without fiscal year limitation in the Departmental Working Capital Fund established under 43 U.S.C. 1467 and used to fund management initiatives of general benefit to the Department of the Interior's bureaus and offices as determined by the Secretary or his designee.

SEC. [119] *111.* Appropriations made in this title under the headings Bureau of Indian Affairs and Office of Special Trustee for American Indians and any available unobligated balances from prior appropriations Acts made under the same headings, shall be available for expenditure or transfer for Indian trust management activities pursuant to the Trust Management Improvement Project High Level Implementation Plan.

[SEC. 120. All properties administered by the National Park Service at Fort Baker, Golden Gate National Recreation Area, and leases, concessions, permits and other agreements associated with those properties, hereafter shall be exempt from all taxes and special assessments, except sales tax, by the State of California and its political subdivisions, including the County of Marin and the City of Sausalito. Such areas of Fort Baker shall remain under exclusive Federal jurisdiction.]

SEC. [121] *112.* Notwithstanding any provision of law, the Secretary of the Interior is authorized to negotiate and enter into agreements and leases, without regard to section 321 of chapter 314 of the Act of June 30, 1932 (40 U.S.C. 303b), with any person, firm, association, organization, corporation, or governmental entity for all or part of the property within Fort Baker administered by the Secretary as part of Golden Gate National Recreation Area. The proceeds of the agreements or leases shall be retained by the Secretary and such proceeds shall be available, without future appropriation, for the preservation, restoration, operation, maintenance and interpretation and related expenses incurred with respect to Fort Baker properties.

[SEC. 122. Section 211(d) of division I of the Omnibus Parks and Public Lands Management Act of 1996 (Public Law 104–333; 110 Stat. 4110; 16 U.S.C. 81p) is amended by striking "depicted on the map dated August 1993, numbered 333/80031A," and inserting "depicted on the map dated August 1996, numbered 333/80031B,".]

[SEC. 123. A grazing permit or lease that expires (or is transferred) during fiscal year 2000 shall be renewed under section 402 of the Federal Land Policy and Management Act of 1976, as amended (43 U.S.C. 1752) or if applicable, section 510 of the California Desert Protection Act (16 U.S.C. 410aaa–50). The terms and conditions contained in the expiring permit or lease shall continue in effect under the new permit or lease until such time as the Secretary of the Interior completes processing of such permit or lease in compliance with all applicable laws and regulations, at which time such permit or lease may be canceled, suspended or modified, in whole or in part, to meet the requirements of such applicable laws and regulations. Nothing in this section shall be deemed to alter the Secretary's statutory authority.]

SEC. [124] *113.* Notwithstanding any other provision of law, for the purpose of reducing the backlog of Indian probate cases in the Department of the Interior, the hearing requirements of chapter 10 of title 25, United States Code, are deemed satisfied by a proceeding conducted by an Indian probate judge, appointed by the Secretary without regard to the provisions of title 5, United States Code, governing the appointments in the competitive service, for such period of time as the Secretary determines necessary: *Provided*, That [the Secretary may only appoint such Indian probate judges if, by January 1, 2000, the Secretary is unable to secure the services of at least 10 qualified Administrative Law Judges on a temporary basis from other agencies and/or through appointing retired Administrative Law Judges: *Provided further*, That] the basic pay of an Indian probate judge so appointed may be fixed by the Secretary without regard to the provisions of chapter 51, and subchapter III of chapter 53 of title 5, United States Code, governing the classification and pay of General Schedule employees, except that no such Indian probate judge may be paid at a level which exceeds the maximum rate payable for the highest grade of the General Schedule, including locality pay.

[SEC. 125. (a) LOAN TO BE GRANTED.—Notwithstanding any other provision of law or of this Act, the Secretary of the Interior (hereinafter the "Secretary"), in consultation with the Secretary of the Treasury, shall make available to the Government of American Samoa (hereinafter "ASG"), the benefits of a loan in the amount of $18,600,000 bearing interest at a rate equal to the United States Treasury cost of borrowing for obligations of similar duration. Repayment of the loan shall be secured and accomplished pursuant to this section with funds, as they become due and payable to ASG from the Escrow Account established under the terms and conditions of the Tobacco Master Settlement Agreement (and the subsequent Enforcing Consent Decree) (hereinafter collectively referred to as "the Agreement") entered into by the parties November 23, 1998, and judgment granted by the High Court of American Samoa on January 5, 1999 (Civil Action 119–98, American Samoa Government v. Philip Morris Tobacco Co., et. al.).]

[(b) CONDITIONS REGARDING LOAN PROCEEDS.—Except as provided under subsection (e), no proceeds of the loan described in this section shall become available until ASG—

(1) has enacted legislation, or has taken such other or additional official action as the Secretary may deem satisfactory to secure and ensure repayment of the loan, irrevocably transferring and assigning for payment to the Department of the Interior (or to the Department of the Treasury, upon agreement between the Secretaries of such departments) all amounts due and payable to ASG under the terms and conditions of the Agreement for a period of 26 years with the first payment beginning in 2000, such repayment to be further secured by a pledge of the full faith and credit of ASG;

(2) has entered into an agreement or memorandum of understanding described in subsection (c) with the Secretary identifying with specificity the manner in which approximately $14,300,000 of the loan proceeds will be used to pay debts of ASG incurred prior to April 15, 1999; and

(3) has provided to the Secretary an initial plan of fiscal and managerial reform as described in subsection (d) designed to bring the ASG's annual operating expenses into balance with projected revenues for the years 2003 and beyond, and identifying the manner in which approximately $4,300,000 of the loan proceeds will be utilized to facilitate implementation of the plan.]

[(c) PROCEDURE AND PRIORITIES FOR DEBT PAYMENTS.—

(1) In structuring the agreement or memorandum of understanding identified in subsection (b)(2), the ASG and the Secretary shall include provisions, which create priorities for the payment of creditors in the following order—

(A) debts incurred for services, supplies, facilities, equipment and materials directly connected with the provision of health, safety and welfare functions for the benefit of the general population of American Samoa (including, but not limited to, health care, fire and police protection, educational programs grades K–12, and utility services for facilities belonging to or utilized by ASG and its agencies), wherein the creditor agrees to compromise and settle the existing debt for a payment not exceeding 75 percent of the amount owed, shall be given the highest priority for payment from the loan proceeds under this section;

(B) debts not exceeding a total amount of $200,000 owed to a single provider and incurred for any legitimate governmental purpose for the benefit of the general population of American Samoa, wherein the creditor agrees to compromise and settle the existing debt for a payment not exceeding 70 percent of the amount owed, shall be given the second highest priority for payment from the loan proceeds under this section;

(C) debts exceeding a total amount of $200,000 owed to a single provider and incurred for any legitimate governmental purpose for the benefit of the general population of American Samoa, wherein the creditor agrees to compromise and settle the existing debt for a payment not exceeding 65 percent of the amount owed, shall be given the third highest priority for payment from the loan proceeds under this section;

(D) other debts regardless of total amount owed or purpose for which incurred, wherein the creditor agrees to compromise and settle the existing debt for a payment not exceeding 60 percent of the amount owed, shall be given the fourth highest priority for payment from the loan proceeds under this section;

(E) debts described in subparagraphs (A), (B), (C), and (D) of this paragraph, wherein the creditor declines to compromise and settle the debt for the percentage of the amount owed as specified under the applicable subparagraph, shall be given the lowest priority for payment from the loan proceeds under this section.

(2) The agreement described in subsection (b)(2) shall also generally provide a framework whereby the Governor of American Samoa shall, from time-to-time, be required to give 10 business days notice to the Secretary that ASG will make payment in accordance with this section to specified creditors and the amount which will be paid to each of such creditors. Upon issuance of payments in accordance with the notice, the Governor shall immediately confirm such payments to the Secretary, and the Secretary shall within three business days following receipt of such confirmation transfer from the loan proceeds an amount sufficient to reimburse ASG for the payments made to creditors.

(3) The agreement may contain such other provisions as are mutually agreeable, and which are calculated to simplify and expedite the payment of existing debt under this section and ensure the greatest level of compromise and settlement with creditors in order to maximize the retirement of ASG debt.]

[(d) FISCAL AND MANAGERIAL REFORM PROGRAM.—

(1) The initial plan of fiscal and managerial reform, designed to bring ASG's annual operating expenses into balance with projected revenues for the years 2003 and beyond as required under subsection (b)(3), should identify specific measures which will be implemented by ASG to accomplish such goal, the anticipated reduction in government operating expense which will be achieved by each measure, and should include a timetable for attainment of each reform measure identified therein.

(2) The initial plan should also identify with specificity the manner in which approximately $4,300,000 of the loan proceeds will be utilized to assist in meeting the reform plan's targets within the timetable specified through the use of incentives for early retirement, severance pay packages, outsourcing services, or any other expenditures for program elements reasonably calculated to result in reduced future operating expenses for ASG on a long term basis.

(3) Upon receipt of the initial plan, the Secretary shall consult with the Governor of American Samoa, and shall make any recommendations deemed reasonable and prudent to ensure the goals of reform are achieved. The reform plan shall contain objective criteria that can be documented by a competent third party, mutually agreeable to the Governor and the Secretary. The plan shall include specific targets for reducing the amounts of ASG local revenues expended on government payroll and overhead (including contracts for consulting services), and may include provisions which allow modest increases in support of the LBJ Hospital Authority reasonably calculated to assist the Authority implement reforms which will lead to an independent audit indicating annual expenditures at or below annual Authority receipts.

(4) The Secretary shall enter into an agreement with the Governor similar to that specified in subsection (c)(2) of this section, enabling ASG to make payments as contemplated in the reform plan and then to receive reimbursement from the Secretary out of the portion of loan proceeds allocated for the implementation of fiscal reforms.

(5) Within 60 days following receipt of the initial plan, the Secretary shall approve an interim final plan reasonably calculated to make substantial progress toward overall reform. The Secretary shall provide copies of the plan, and any subsequent modifications, to the House Committee on Resources, the House Committee on Appropriations Subcommittee on the Department of the Interior and Related Agencies, the Senate Committee on Energy and Natural Resources, and the Senate Committee on Appropriations Subcommittee on the Department of the Interior and Related Agencies.

(6) From time-to-time as deemed necessary, the Secretary shall consult further with the Governor of American Samoa, and shall approve such mutually agreeable modifications to the interim final plan as circumstances warrant in order to achieve the overall goals of ASG fiscal and managerial reforms.

[(e) RELEASE OF LOAN PROCEEDS.—From the total proceeds of the loan described in this section, the Secretary shall make available—

(1) upon compliance by ASG with paragraphs (b)(1) and (b)(2) of this section and in accordance with subsection (c), approximately $14,300,000 in reimbursements as requested from time-to-time by the Governor for payments to creditors;

(2) upon compliance by ASG with paragraphs (b)(1) and (b)(3) of this section and in accordance with subsection (d), approximately $4,300,000 in reimbursements as requested from time-to-time by the Governor for payments associated with implementation of the interim final reform plan; and

(3) notwithstanding paragraphs (1) and (2) of this subsection, at any time the Secretary and the Governor mutually determine that the amount necessary to fund payments under paragraph (2) will total less than $4,300,000 then the Secretary may approve the amount of any unused portion of such sum for additional payments against ASG debt under paragraph (1).]

[(f) EXCEPTION.— Proceeds from the loan under this section shall be used solely for the purposes of debt payments and reform plan implementation as specified herein, except that the Secretary may provide an amount equal to not more than 2 percent of the total loan proceeds for the purpose of retaining the services of an individual or business entity to provide direct assistance and management expertise in carrying out the purposes of this section. Such individual or business entity shall be mutually agreeable to the Governor and the Secretary, may not be a current or former employee of, or contractor for, and may not be a creditor of ASG. Notwithstanding the preceding two sentences, the Governor and the Secretary may agree to also retain the services of any semi-autonomous agency of ASG which has established a record of sound management and fiscal responsibility, as evidenced by audited financial reports for at least three of the past 5 years, to coordinate with and assist any individual or entity retained under this subsection.]

[(g) CONSTRUCTION.—The provisions of this section are expressly applicable only to the utilization of proceeds from the loan described in this section, and nothing herein shall be construed to relieve ASG from any lawful debt or obligation except to the extent a creditor shall voluntarily enter into an arms length agreement to compromise and settle outstanding amounts under subsection (c).]

[(h) TERMINATION.—The payment of debt and the payments associated with implementation of the interim final reform plan shall be completed not later than October 1, 2003. On such date, any unused loan proceeds totaling $1,000,000 or less shall be transferred by the Secretary directly to ASG. If the amount of unused loan proceeds exceeds $1,000,000, then such amount shall be credited to the total of loan repayments specified in paragraph (b)(1). With approval of the Secretary, ASG may designate additional payments from time-to-time from funds available from any source, without regard to the original purpose of such funds.]

[SEC. 126. The Secretary of the Interior, acting through the Director of the United States Fish and Wildlife Service and in consultation with the Director of the National Park Service, shall undertake the necessary activities to designate Midway Atoll as a National Memorial to the Battle of Midway. In pursuing such a designation the Secretary shall consult with organizations with an interest in Midway Atoll. The Secretary shall consult on a regular basis with such organizations, including the International Midway Memorial Foundation, Inc. on the management of the National Memorial.]

[SEC. 127. Notwithstanding any other provision of law, the Secretary of the Interior is authorized to redistribute any Tribal Priority Allocation funds, including tribal base funds, to alleviate tribal funding inequities by transferring funds to address identified, unmet needs, dual enrollment, overlapping service areas or inaccurate distribution methodologies. No tribe shall receive a reduction in Tribal Priority Allocation funds of more than 10 percent in fiscal year 2000. Under circumstances of dual enrollment, overlapping service areas or inaccurate distribution methodologies, the 10 percent limitation does not apply.]

[SEC. 128. None of the Funds provided in this Act shall be available to the Bureau of Indian Affairs or the Department of the Interior to transfer land into trust status for the Shoalwater Bay Indian Tribe in Clark County, Washington, unless and until the tribe and the county reach a legally enforceable agreement that addresses the financial impact of new development on the county, school district, fire district, and other local governments and the impact on zoning and development.]

[SEC. 129. None of the funds provided in this Act may be used by the Department of the Interior to implement the provisions of Principle 3(C)ii and Appendix section 3(B)(4) in Secretarial Order 3206, entitled "American Indian Tribal Rights, Federal-Tribal Trust Responsibilities, and the Endangered Species Act".]

[SEC. 130. Of the funds appropriated in title V of the Fiscal Year 1998 Interior and Related Agencies Appropriation Act, Public Law 105–83, the Secretary shall provide up to $2,000,000 in the form of a grant to the Fairbanks North Star Borough for acquisition of undeveloped parcels along the banks of the Chena River for the purpose of establishing an urban greenbelt within the Borough. The Secretary shall further provide from the funds appropriated in title V up to $1,000,000 in the form of a grant to the Municipality of Anchorage for the acquisition of approximately 34 acres of wetlands adjacent to a municipal park in Anchorage (the Jewel Lake Wetlands).]

[SEC. 131. FUNDING FOR THE OTTAWA NATIONAL WILDLIFE REFUGE AND CERTAIN PROJECTS IN THE STATE OF OHIO. Notwithstanding any other provision of law, from the unobligated balances appropriated for a grant to the State of Ohio for the acquisition of the Howard Farm near Metzger Marsh, Ohio—

(1) $500,000 shall be derived by transfer and made available for the acquisition of land in the Ottawa National Wildlife Refuge;

(2) $302,000 shall be derived by transfer and made available for the Dayton Aviation Heritage Commission, Ohio; and

(3) $198,000 shall be derived by transfer and made available for a grant to the State of Ohio for the preservation and restoration of the birthplace, boyhood home, and schoolhouse of Ulysses S. Grant.]

[SEC. 132. CONVEYANCE TO NYE COUNTY, NEVADA. (a) DEFINITIONS.—In this section:

(1) COUNTY.—The term "County" means Nye County, Nevada.

(2) SECRETARY.—The term "Secretary" means the Secretary of the Interior, acting through the Director of the Bureau of Land Management.]

[(b) PARCELS CONVEYED FOR USE OF THE NEVADA SCIENCE AND TECHNOLOGY CENTER.—

(1) IN GENERAL.—The Secretary shall convey to the County, subject to the requirements of 43 U.S.C. 869 and subject to valid existing rights, all right, title, and interest in and to the parcels of public land described in paragraph (2). Such conveyance shall be made at a price determined to be appropriate for the conveyance of land for educational facilities under the Act of June 14, 1926 (43 U.S.C. 869 et seq.) and in accordance with the Bureau of Land Management Document entitled "Recreation and Public Purposes Act", dated October 1994, under the category of Special Pricing Program Uses for Governmental Entities.

(2) LAND DESCRIPTION.—The parcels of public land referred to in paragraph (1) are the following:

(A) The portion of Sec. 13 north of United States Route 95, T. 15 S., R. 49 E., Mount Diablo Meridian, Nevada.

(B) In Sec. 18, T. 15 S., R. 50 E., Mount Diablo Meridian, Nevada:

(i) W ½ W ½ NW ¼.

(ii) The portion of the W ½ W ½ SW ¼ north of United States Route 95.

(3) USE.—

(A) IN GENERAL.—The parcels described in paragraph (2) shall be used for the construction and operation of the Nevada Science and Technology Center as a nonprofit museum and exposition center, and related facilities and activities.

(B) REVERSION.—The conveyance of any parcel described in paragraph (2) shall be subject to reversion to the United States, at the discretion of Secretary, if the parcel is used for a purpose other than that specified in subparagraph (A).]

[(c) PARCELS CONVEYED FOR OTHER USE FOR A COMMERCIAL PURPOSE.—

(1) RIGHT TO PURCHASE.—For a period of 5 years beginning on the date of the enactment of this Act, the County shall have the exclusive right to purchase the parcels of public land described in paragraph (2) for the fair market value of the parcels, as determined by the Secretary.

(2) LAND DESCRIPTION.—The parcels of public land referred to in paragraph (1) are the following parcels in Sec. 18, T. 15 S., R. 50 E., Mount Diablo Meridian, Nevada:

(A) E ½ NW ¼.

(B) E ½ W ½ NW ¼.

(C) The portion of the E ½ SW ¼ north of United States Route 95.

(D) The portion of the E ½ W ½ SW ¼ north of United States Route 95.

(E) The portion of the SE ¼ north of United States Route 95.

(3) USE OF PROCEEDS.—Proceeds of a sale of a parcel described in paragraph (2)—

(A) shall be deposited in the special account established under section 4(e)(1)(C) of the Southern Nevada Public Land Management Act of 1998 (112 Stat. 2345); and

(B) shall be available for use by the Secretary—

(i) to reimburse costs incurred by the local offices of the Bureau of Land Management in arranging the land conveyances directed by this Act; and

(ii) as provided in section 4(e)(3) of that Act (112 Stat. 2346).]

[SEC. 133. CONVEYANCE OF LAND TO CITY OF MESQUITE, NEVADA. Section 3 of Public Law 99–548 (100 Stat. 3061; 110 Stat. 3009–202) is amended by adding at the end the following:

"(e) FIFTH AREA.—

"(1) RIGHT TO PURCHASE.—

"(A) IN GENERAL.—For a period of 12 years after the date of the enactment of this Act, the City of Mesquite, Nevada, subject to all appropriate environmental reviews, including compliance with the National Environmental Policy Act and the Endangered Species Act, shall have the exclusive right to purchase the parcels of public land described in paragraph (2).

"(B) APPLICABILITY.—Subparagraph (A) shall apply to a parcel of land described in paragraph (2) that has not been identified for disposal in the 1998 Bureau of Land Management Las Vegas Resource Management Plan only if the conveyance is made under subsection (f).

"(2) LAND DESCRIPTION.—The parcels of public land referred to in paragraph (1) are as follows:

"(A) In T. 13 S., R. 70 E., Mount Diablo Meridian, Nevada:

"(i) The portion of sec. 27 north of Interstate Route 15.

"(ii) Sec. 28: NE ¼, S ½ (except the Interstate Route 15 right-of-way).

"(iii) Sec. 29: E ½ NE ¼ SE ¼, SE ¼ SE ¼.

"(iv) The portion of sec. 30 south of Interstate Route 15.

"(v) The portion of sec. 31 south of Interstate Route 15.

"(vi) Sec. 32: NE ¼ NE ¼ (except the Interstate Route 15 right-of-way), the portion of NW ¼ NE ¼ south of Interstate Route 15, and the portion of W ½ south of Interstate Route 15.

"(vii) The portion of sec. 33 north of Interstate Route 15.

"(B) In T. 13 S., R. 69 E., Mount Diablo Meridian, Nevada:

"(i) The portion of sec. 25 south of Interstate Route 15.

"(ii) The portion of sec. 26 south of Interstate Route 15.

"(iii) The portion of sec. 27 south of Interstate Route 15.

"(iv) Sec. 28: SW ¼ SE ¼.

"(v) Sec. 33: E ½.

"(vi) Sec. 34.

"(vii) Sec. 35.

"(viii) Sec. 36.

"(3) NOTIFICATION.—Not later than 10 years after the date of the enactment of this subsection, the city shall notify the Secretary which of the parcels of public land described in paragraph (2) the city intends to purchase.

"(4) CONVEYANCE.—Not later than 1 year after receiving notification from the city under paragraph (3), the Secretary shall convey to the city the land selected for purchase.

"(5) WITHDRAWAL.—Subject to valid existing rights, until the date that is 12 years after the date of the enactment of this subsection, the parcels of public land described in paragraph (2) are withdrawn from all forms of entry and appropriation under the public land laws, including the mining laws, and from operation of the mineral leasing and geothermal leasing laws.

"(6) USE OF PROCEEDS.—The proceeds of the sale of each parcel—

"(A) shall be deposited in the special account established under section 4(e)(1)(C) of the Southern Nevada Public Land Management Act of 1998 (112 Stat. 2345); and

"(B) shall be available for use by the Secretary—

"(i) to reimburse costs incurred by the local offices of the Bureau of Land Management in arranging the land conveyances directed by this Act; and

"(ii) as provided in section 4(e)(3) of that Act (112 Stat. 2346).
"(f) SIXTH AREA.—

"(1) IN GENERAL.—Not later than 1 year after the date of the enactment of this subsection, the Secretary shall convey to the City of Mesquite, Nevada, in accordance with section 47125 of title 49, United States Code, and subject to all appropriate environmental reviews, including compliance with the National Environmental Policy Act and the Endangered Species Act, up to 2,560 acres of public land to be selected by the city from among the parcels of land described in paragraph (2).

"(2) LAND DESCRIPTION.—The parcels of land referred to in paragraph (1) are as follows:

"(A) In T. 13 S., R. 69 E., Mount Diablo Meridian, Nevada:
"(i) The portion of sec. 28 south of Interstate Route 15 (except S ½ SE ¼).
"(ii) The portion of sec. 29 south of Interstate Route 15.
"(iii) The portion of sec. 30 south of Interstate Route 15.
"(iv) The portion of sec. 31 south of Interstate Route 15.
"(v) Sec. 32.
"(vi) Sec. 33: W ½.

"(B) In T. 14 S., R. 69 E., Mount Diablo Meridian, Nevada:
"(i) Sec. 4.
"(ii) Sec. 5.
"(iii) Sec. 6.
"(iv) Sec. 8.

"(C) In T. 14 S., R. 68 E., Mount Diablo Meridian, Nevada:
"(i) Sec. 1.
"(ii) Sec. 12.

"(3) WITHDRAWAL.—Subject to valid existing rights, until the date that is 12 years after the date of the enactment of this subsection, the parcels of public land described in paragraph (2) are withdrawn from all forms of entry and appropriation under the public land laws, including the mining laws, and from operation of the mineral leasing and geothermal leasing laws.

"(4) If the land conveyed pursuant to this section is not utilized by the city as an airport, it shall revert to the United States, at the option of the Secretary.

"(5) Nothing in this section shall preclude the Secretary from applying appropriate terms and conditions as identified by the required environmental review to any conveyance made under this section.".]

[SEC. 134. QUADRICENTENNIAL COMMEMORATION OF THE SAINT CROIX ISLAND INTERNATIONAL HISTORIC SITE. (a) FINDINGS.—The Senate finds that—

(1) in 1604, one of the first European colonization efforts was attempted at St. Croix Island in Calais, Maine;

(2) St. Croix Island settlement predated both the Jamestown and Plymouth colonies;

(3) St. Croix Island offers a rare opportunity to preserve and interpret early interactions between European explorers and colonists and Native Americans;

(4) St. Croix Island is one of only two international historic sites comprised of land administered by the National Park Service;

(5) the quadricentennial commemorative celebration honoring the importance of the St. Croix Island settlement to the countries and people of both Canada and the United States is rapidly approaching;

(6) the 1998 National Park Service management plans and long-range interpretive plan call for enhancing visitor facilities at both Red Beach and downtown Calais;

(7) in 1982, the Department of the Interior and Canadian Department of the Environment signed a memorandum of understanding to recognize the international significance of St. Croix Island and, in an amendment memorandum, agreed to conduct joint strategic planning for the international commemoration with a special focus on the 400th anniversary of settlement in 2004;

(8) the Department of Canadian Heritage has installed extensive interpretive sites on the Canadian side of the border; and

(9) current facilities at Red Beach and Calais are extremely limited or nonexistent for a site of this historic and cultural importance.]

[(b) SENSE OF THE SENATE.—It is the sense of the Senate that—

(1) using funds made available by this Act, the National Park Service should expeditiously pursue planning for exhibits at Red Beach and the town of Calais, Maine; and

(2) the National Park Service should take what steps are necessary, including consulting with the people of Calais, to ensure that appropriate exhibits at Red Beach and the town of Calais are completed by 2004.]

[SEC. 135. No funds appropriated for the Department of the Interior by this Act or any other Act shall be used to study or implement any plan to drain Lake Powell or to reduce the water level of the lake below the range of water levels required for the operation of the Glen Canyon Dam.]

[SEC. 136. None of the funds appropriated or otherwise made available in this Act or any other provision of law, may be used by any officer, employee, department or agency of the United States to impose or require payment of an inspection fee in connection with the export of shipments of fur-bearing wildlife containing 1,000 or fewer raw, crusted, salted or tanned hides or fur skins, or separate parts thereof, including species listed under the Convention on International Trade in Endangered Species of Wild Fauna and Flora done at Washington, March 3, 1973 (27 UST 1027): *Provided*, That this provision shall for the duration of the calendar year in which the shipment occurs, not apply to any person who ships more than 2,500 of such hides, fur skins or parts thereof during the course of such year.]

[SEC. 137. (a) The Secretary of the Interior shall during fiscal year 2000 reorganize and consolidate the Bureau of Indian Affairs' management and administrative functions based on the recommendations of the National Academy of Public Administration.

(b) Bureau of Indian Affairs employees in Central Office West divisions that are moved due to the implementation of the National Academy of Public Administration recommendations, who voluntarily resign or retire from the Bureau of Indian Affairs on or before December 31, 1999, may receive, from the Bureau of Indian Affairs, a lump sum voluntary separation incentive payment that shall be equal to the lesser of an amount equal to the amount the employee would be entitled to receive under section 5595(c) of title 5, United States Code, if the employee were entitled to payment under such section; or $25,000.

(1) The voluntary separation incentive payment—

(A) shall not be a basis for payment, and shall not be included in the computation of any other type of Government benefit; and

(B) shall be paid from appropriations or funds available for the payment of the basic pay of the employee.

(2) Employees receiving a voluntary separation incentive payment and accepting employment with the Federal Government within 5 years of the date of separation shall be required to repay the entire amount of the incentive payment to the Bureau of Indian Affairs.

(3) The Secretary may, at the request of the head of an executive branch agency, waive the repayment under paragraph (2) if the individual involved possesses unique abilities and is the only qualified applicant available for the position.

(4) In addition to any other payment which is required to be made under subchapter III of chapter 83 of title 5, United States Code, the Bureau of Indian Affairs shall remit to the Office of Personnel Management for deposit in the Treasury of the United States to the credit of the Civil Service Retirement and Disability Fund an amount equal to 15 percent of the final basic pay of each employee of the Bureau of Indian Affairs to whom a voluntary separation incentive payment has been or is to be paid under the provisions of this section.]

[(c) Employees of the Bureau of Indian Affairs, in Central Office West divisions that are moved due to the implementation of the National Academy of Public Administration recommendations and who are entitled to severance pay under 5 U.S.C. 5595, may apply for, and the Bureau of Indian Affairs may pay, the total amount of severance pay to the employee in a lump sum. Employees paid severance pay in a lump sum and subsequently reemployed by the Federal Government shall be subject to the repayment provisions of 5 U.S.C. 5595(i)(2) and (3), except that any repayment shall be made to the Bureau of Indian Affairs.]

[(d) Employees of the Bureau of Indian Affairs, in Central Office West divisions that are moved due to the implementation of the National Academy of Public Administration recommendations and who voluntarily resign on or before December 31, 1999, or who are separated, shall be liable for not more than the required employee contribution under 5 U.S.C. 8905a(d)(1)(A) if they elect to continue health benefits after separation. The Bureau of Indian Affairs shall pay for 12 months the remaining portion of required contributions.]

[SEC. 138. Notwithstanding any other provision of law, the Secretary of the Interior is authorized to acquire lands from the Haines Borough, Alaska, consisting of approximately 20 acres, more or less, in four tracts identified for this purpose by the Borough, and contained in an area formerly known as "Duncan's Camp"; the Secretary shall use $340,000 previously allocated from funds appropriated for the Department of the Interior for fiscal year 1998 for acquisition of lands; the Secretary is authorized to convey in fee all land and interests in land acquired pursuant to this section without compensation to the heirs of Peter Duncan in settlement of a claim filed by them against the United States: *Provided*, That the Secretary shall not convey the lands acquired pursuant to this section unless and until a signed release of all claims is executed.]

SEC. [139] *114*. Funds appropriated for the Bureau of Indian Affairs for postsecondary schools for fiscal year [2000] *2001* shall be allocated among the schools proportionate to the unmet need of the schools as determined by the Postsecondary Funding Formula adopted by the Office of Indian Education Programs.

[SEC. 140. Notwithstanding any other provision of law, in conveying the Twin Cities Research Center under the authority provided by Public Law 104–134, as amended by Public Law 104–208, the Secretary may accept and retain land and other forms of reimbursement: *Provided*, That the Secretary may retain and use any such reimbursement until expended and without further appropriation: (1) for the benefit of the National Wildlife Refuge System within the State of Minnesota; and (2) for all activities authorized by Public Law 100–696; 16 U.S.C. 460zz.]

[SEC. 141. None of the funds made available by this Act shall be used to issue a notice of final rulemaking with respect to the valuation of crude oil for royalty purposes until March 15, 2000. The rulemaking must be consistent with existing statutory requirements.]

[SEC. 142. EXTENSION OF AUTHORITY FOR ESTABLISHMENT OF THOMAS PAINE MEMORIAL. (a) IN GENERAL.—Public Law 102–407 (40 U.S.C. 1003 note; 106 Stat. 1991) is amended by adding at the end the following:

"SEC. 4. EXPIRATION OF AUTHORITY.

"Notwithstanding the time period limitation specified in section 10(b) of the Commemorative Works Act (40 U.S.C. 1010(b)) or any other provision of law, the authority for the Thomas Paine National Historical Association to establish a memorial to Thomas Paine in the District of Columbia under this Act shall expire on December 31, 2003.".]

[(b) CONFORMING AMENDMENTS.—

(1) APPLICABLE LAW.—Section 1(b) of Public Law 102–407 (40 U.S.C. 1003 note; 106 Stat. 1991) is amended by striking "The establishment" and inserting "Except as provided in section 4, the establishment".

(2) EXPIRATION OF AUTHORITY.—Section 3 of Public Law 102–407 (40 U.S.C. 1003 note; 106 Stat. 1991) is amended—

(A) by striking "or upon expiration of the authority for the memorial under section 10(b) of that Act," and inserting "or on expiration of the authority for the memorial under section 4,"; and

(B) by striking "section 8(b)(1) of that Act" and inserting "section 8(b)(1) of the Commemorative Works Act (40 U.S.C. 1008(b)(1))".]

[SEC. 143. USE OF NATIONAL PARK SERVICE TRANSPORTATION SERVICE CONTRACT FEES. Section 412 of the National Parks Omnibus Management Act of 1998 (16 U.S.C. 5961) is amended—

(1) by inserting "(a) IN GENERAL.—" before "Notwithstanding"; and

(2) by adding at the end the following:

"(b) OBLIGATION OF FUNDS.—Notwithstanding any other provision of law, with respect to a service contract for the provision solely of transportation services at Zion National Park, the Secretary may obligate the expenditure of fees received in fiscal year 2000 under section 501 before the fees are received.".]

[SEC. 144. EXTENSION OF DEADLINE FOR RED ROCK CANYON NATIONAL CONSERVATION AREA. (a) IN GENERAL.—Section 3(c)(1) of Public Law 103–450 (108 Stat. 4767) is amended by striking "the date 5 years after the date of enactment of this Act" and inserting "May 2, 2000".

(b) EFFECTIVE DATE.—The amendment made by subsection (a) takes effect on November 1, 1999.]

[SEC. 145. NATIONAL PARK PASSPORT PROGRAM. Section 603(c)(1) of the National Park Omnibus Management Act of 1998 (16 U.S.C. 5993(c)(1)) is amended by striking "10" and inserting "15".] *(Department of the Interior and Related Agencies Appropriations Act, 2000, as enacted by section 1000(a)(3) of the Consolidated Appropriations Act, 2000 (P.L. 106–113).)*

TITLE III—GENERAL PROVISIONS

SEC. 301. The expenditure of any appropriation under this Act for any consulting service through procurement contract, pursuant to 5 U.S.C. 3109, shall be limited to those contracts where such expenditures are a matter of public record and available for public inspection, except where otherwise provided under existing law, or under existing Executive order issued pursuant to existing law.

SEC. 302. No part of any appropriation under this Act shall be available to the Secretary of the Interior or the Secretary of Agriculture for the leasing of oil and natural gas by noncompetitive bidding on publicly owned lands within the boundaries of the Shawnee National Forest, Illinois: *Provided*, That nothing herein is intended to inhibit or otherwise affect the sale, lease, or right to access to minerals owned by private individuals.

SEC. 303. No part of any appropriation contained in this Act shall be available for any activity or the publication or distribution of literature that in any way tends to promote public support or opposition to any legislative proposal on which congressional action is not complete.

SEC. 304. No part of any appropriation contained in this Act shall remain available for obligation beyond the current fiscal year unless expressly so provided herein.

SEC. 305. None of the funds provided in this Act to any department or agency shall be obligated or expended to provide a personal cook, chauffeur, or other personal servants to any officer or employee of such department or agency except as otherwise provided by law.

[SEC. 306. No assessments may be levied against any program, budget activity, subactivity, or project funded by this Act unless advance notice of such assessments and the basis therefor are presented to the Committees on Appropriations and are approved by such committees.]

[SEC. 307. (a) COMPLIANCE WITH BUY AMERICAN ACT.—None of the funds made available in this Act may be expended by an entity unless the entity agrees that in expending the funds the entity will comply with sections 2 through 4 of the Act of March 3, 1933 (41 U.S.C. 10a–10c; popularly known as the "Buy American Act").

(b) SENSE OF THE CONGRESS; REQUIREMENT REGARDING NOTICE.—

(1) PURCHASE OF AMERICAN-MADE EQUIPMENT AND PRODUCTS.—In the case of any equipment or product that may be authorized to be purchased with financial assistance provided using funds made available in this Act, it is the sense of the Congress that entities receiving the assistance should, in expending the assistance, purchase only American-made equipment and products.

(2) NOTICE TO RECIPIENTS OF ASSISTANCE.—In providing financial assistance using funds made available in this Act, the head of each Federal agency shall provide to each recipient of the assistance a notice describing the statement made in paragraph (1) by the Congress.

(c) PROHIBITION OF CONTRACTS WITH PERSONS FALSELY LABELING PRODUCTS AS MADE IN AMERICA.—If it has been finally determined by a court or Federal agency that any person intentionally affixed a label bearing a "Made in America" inscription, or any inscription with the same meaning, to any product sold in or shipped to the United States that is not made in the United States, the person shall be ineligible to receive any contract or subcontract made with funds made available in this Act, pursuant to the debarment, suspension, and ineligibility procedures described in sections 9.400 through 9.409 of title 48, Code of Federal Regulations.

(d) EFFECTIVE DATE.—The provisions of this section are applicable in fiscal year 2000 and thereafter.]

SEC. [308] *306*. None of the funds in this Act may be used to plan, prepare, or offer for sale timber from trees classified as giant sequoia (Sequoiadendron giganteum) which are located on National Forest System or Bureau of Land Management lands in a manner different than such sales were conducted in fiscal year 1999.

[SEC. 309. None of the funds made available by this Act may be obligated or expended by the National Park Service to enter into or implement a concession contract which permits or requires the removal of the underground lunchroom at the Carlsbad Caverns National Park.]

[SEC. 310. None of the funds appropriated or otherwise made available by this Act may be used for the AmeriCorps program, unless the relevant agencies of the Department of the Interior and/or Agriculture follow appropriate reprogramming guidelines: *Provided*, That if no funds are provided for the AmeriCorps program by the Departments of Veterans Affairs and Housing and Urban Development, and Independent Agencies Appropriations Act, 2000, then none of the funds appropriated or otherwise made available by this Act may be used for the AmeriCorps programs.]

[SEC. 311. None of the funds made available in this Act may be used: (1) to demolish the bridge between Jersey City, New Jersey, and Ellis Island; or (2) to prevent pedestrian use of such bridge, when it is made known to the Federal official having authority to obligate or expend such funds that such pedestrian use is consistent with generally accepted safety standards.]

SEC. [312] *307.* (a) LIMITATION OF FUNDS.—None of the funds appropriated or otherwise made available pursuant to this Act shall be obligated or expended to accept or process applications for a patent for any mining or mill site claim located under the general mining laws.

(b) EXCEPTIONS.—The provisions of subsection (a) shall not apply if the Secretary of the Interior determines that, for the claim concerned: (1) a patent application was filed with the Secretary on or before September 30, 1994; and (2) all requirements established under sections 2325 and 2326 of the Revised Statutes (30 U.S.C. 29 and 30) for vein or lode claims and sections 2329, 2330, 2331, and 2333 of the Revised Statutes (30 U.S.C. 35, 36, and 37) for placer claims, and section 2337 of the Revised Statutes (30 U.S.C. 42) for mill site claims, as the case may be, were fully complied with by the applicant by that date.

(c) REPORT.—On September 30, [2000] *2001*, the Secretary of the Interior shall file with the House and Senate Committees on Appropriations and the Committee on Resources of the House of Representatives and the Committee on Energy and Natural Resources of the Senate a report on actions taken by the department under the plan submitted pursuant to section 314(c) of the Department of the Interior and Related Agencies Appropriations Act, 1997 (Public Law 104–208).

(d) MINERAL EXAMINATIONS.—In order to process patent applications in a timely and responsible manner, upon the request of a patent applicant, the Secretary of the Interior shall allow the applicant to fund a qualified third-party contractor to be selected by the Bureau of Land Management to conduct a mineral examination of the mining claims or mill sites contained in a patent application as set forth in subsection (b). The Bureau of Land Management shall have the sole responsibility to choose and pay the third-party contractor in accordance with the standard procedures employed by the Bureau of Land Management in the retention of third-party contractors.

SEC. [313] *308.* Notwithstanding any other provision of law, amounts appropriated to or earmarked in committee reports for the Bureau of Indian Affairs and the Indian Health Service by Public Laws 103–138, 103–332, 104–134, 104–208, 105–83, [and] 105–277, *and 106–113* for payments to tribes and tribal organizations for contract support costs associated with self-determination or self-governance contracts, grants, compacts, or annual funding agreements with the Bureau of Indian Affairs or the Indian Health Service as funded by such Acts, are the total amounts available for fiscal years 1994 through [1999] *2000* for such purposes, except that, for the Bureau of Indian Affairs, tribes and tribal organizations may use their tribal priority allocations for unmet indirect costs of ongoing contracts, grants, self-governance compacts or annual funding agreements.

SEC. [314] *309.* Notwithstanding any other provision of law, for fiscal year [2000] *2001* the Secretaries of Agriculture and the Interior are authorized to limit competition for watershed restoration project contracts as part of the "Jobs in the Woods" component of the President's Forest Plan for the Pacific Northwest, or *the area of the Interior Columbia Basin Ecosystem Management Project, or* the Jobs in the Woods Program established in Region 10 of the Forest Service to individuals and entities in historically timber-dependent areas in the States of Washington, Oregon, northern California and Alaska that have been affected by reduced timber harvesting on Federal lands.

[SEC. 315. None of the funds collected under the Recreational Fee Demonstration program may be used to plan, design, or construct a visitor center or any other permanent structure without prior approval of the House and the Senate Committees on Appropriations if the estimated total cost of the facility exceeds $500,000.]

SEC. [316] *310.* All interests created under leases, concessions, permits and other agreements associated with the properties administered by the Presidio Trust shall be exempt from all taxes and special assessments of every kind by the State of California and its political subdivisions.

[SEC. 317. None of the funds made available in this or any other Act for any fiscal year may be used to designate, or to post any sign designating, any portion of Canaveral National Seashore in Brevard County, Florida, as a clothing-optional area or as an area in which public nudity is permitted, if such designation would be contrary to county ordinance.]

SEC. [318] *311.* Of the funds provided to the National Endowment for the Arts—

[(1) The Chairperson shall only award a grant to an individual if such grant is awarded to such individual for a literature fellowship, National Heritage Fellowship, or American Jazz Masters Fellowship.]

[(2)] *(1)* The Chairperson shall establish procedures to ensure that no funding provided through a grant, except a grant made to a State or local arts agency, or regional group, may be used to make a grant to any other organization or individual to conduct activity independent of the direct grant recipient. Nothing in this subsection shall prohibit payments made in exchange for goods and services.

[(3)] *(2)* No grant shall be used for seasonal support to a group, unless the application is specific to the contents of the season, including identified programs and/or projects.

SEC. [319] *312.* The National Endowment for the Arts and the National Endowment for the Humanities are authorized to solicit, accept, receive, and invest in the name of the United States, gifts, bequests, or devises of money and other property or services and to use such in furtherance of the functions of the National Endowment for the Arts and the National Endowment for the Humanities. Any proceeds from such gifts, bequests, or devises, after acceptance by the National Endowment for the Arts or the National Endowment for the Humanities, shall be paid by the donor or the representative of the donor to the Chairman. The Chairman shall enter the proceeds in a special interest-bearing account to the credit of the appropriate endowment for the purposes specified in each case.

SEC. [320] *313.* (a) In providing services or awarding financial assistance under the National Foundation on the Arts and the Humanities Act of 1965 from funds appropriated under this Act, the Chairperson of the National Endowment for the Arts shall ensure that priority is given to providing services or awarding financial assistance for projects, productions, workshops, or programs that serve underserved populations.

(b) In this section:

(1) The term "underserved population" means a population of individuals, including urban minorities, who have historically been outside the purview of arts and humanities programs due to factors such as a high incidence of income below the poverty line or to geographic isolation.

(2) The term "poverty line" means the poverty line (as defined by the Office of Management and Budget, and revised annually in accordance with section 673(2) of the Community Services Block Grant Act (42 U.S.C. 9902(2))) applicable to a family of the size involved.

(c) In providing services and awarding financial assistance under the National Foundation on the Arts and Humanities Act of 1965 with funds appropriated by this Act, the Chairperson of the National Endowment for the Arts shall ensure that priority is given to providing services or awarding financial assistance for projects, productions, workshops, or programs that will encourage public knowledge, education, understanding, and appreciation of the arts.

(d) With funds appropriated by this Act to carry out section 5 of the National Foundation on the Arts and Humanities Act of 1965—

(1) the Chairperson shall establish a grant category for projects, productions, workshops, or programs that are of national impact or availability or are able to tour several States;

(2) the Chairperson shall not make grants exceeding 15 percent, in the aggregate, of such funds to any single State, excluding grants made under the authority of paragraph (1);

(3) the Chairperson shall report to the Congress annually and by State, on grants awarded by the Chairperson in each grant category under section 5 of such Act; and

(4) the Chairperson shall encourage the use of grants to improve and support community-based music performance and education.

[SEC. 321. No part of any appropriation contained in this Act shall be expended or obligated to fund new revisions of national forest land management plans until new final or interim final rules for forest land management planning are published in the Federal Register. Those national forests which are currently in a revision process, having formally published a Notice of Intent to revise prior to October 1, 1997; those national forests having been court-ordered to revise; those national forests where plans reach the 15 year legally mandated date to revise before or during calendar year 2001; national forests within the Interior Columbia Basin Ecosystem study area; and the White Mountain National Forest are exempt from this section and may use funds in this Act and proceed to complete the forest plan revision in accordance with current forest planning regulations.]

SEC. [322] *314.* No part of any appropriation contained in this Act shall be expended or obligated to complete and issue the 5-year program under the Forest and Rangeland Renewable Resources Planning Act.

[SEC. 323. None of the funds in this Act may be used to support Government-wide administrative functions unless such functions are justified in the budget process and funding is approved by the House and Senate Committees on Appropriations.]

[SEC. 324. Notwithstanding any other provision of law, none of the funds in this Act may be used for GSA Telecommunication Centers or the President's Council on Sustainable Development.]

[SEC. 325. None of the funds in this Act may be used for planning, design or construction of improvements to Pennsylvania Avenue in front of the White House without the advance approval of the House and Senate Committees on Appropriations.]

[SEC. 326. (a) SHORT TITLE.—This section may be cited as the "National Park Service Studies Act of 1999".]

[(b) AUTHORIZATION OF STUDIES.—

(1) IN GENERAL.—The Secretary of the Interior ("the Secretary") shall conduct studies of the geographical areas and historic and cultural themes described in subsection (b)(3) to determine the appropriateness of including such areas or themes in the National Park System.

(2) CRITERIA.—In conducting the studies authorized by this Act, the Secretary shall use the criteria for the study of areas for potential inclusion in the National Park System in accordance with section 8 of Public Law 91–383, as amended by section 303 of the National Parks Omnibus Management Act (Public Law 105–391; 112 Stat. 3501).

(3) STUDY AREAS.—The Secretary shall conduct studies of the following:

(A) Anderson Cottage, Washington, District of Columbia.

(B) Bioluminescent Bay, Puerto Rico.

(C) Civil Rights Sites, multi-State.

(D) Crossroads of the American Revolution, Central New Jersey.

(E) Fort Hunter Liggett, California.

(F) Fort King, Florida.

(G) Gaviota Coast Seashore, California.

(H) Kate Mullany House, New York.

(I) Loess Hills, Iowa.

(J) Low Country Gullah Culture, multi-State.

(K) Nan Madol, State of Ponape, Federated States of Micronesia (upon the request of the Government of the Federated States of Micronesia).

(L) Walden Pond and Woods, Massachusetts.

(M) World War II Sites, Commonwealth of the Northern Marianas.

(N) World War II Sites, Republic of Palau (upon the request of the Government of the Republic of Palau).]

[(c) REPORTS.—The Secretary shall submit to the Committee on Energy and Natural Resources of the Senate and the Committee on Resources of the House of Representatives a report on the findings, conclusions, and recommendations of each study under subsection (b) within three fiscal years following the date on which funds are first made available for each study.]

SEC. [327] *315.* Amounts deposited during fiscal year [1999] *2000* in the roads and trails fund provided for in the fourteenth paragraph under the heading "FOREST SERVICE" of the Act of March 4, 1913 (37 Stat. 843; 16 U.S.C. 501), shall be used by the Secretary of Agriculture, without regard to the State in which the amounts were derived, to repair or reconstruct roads, bridges, and trails on National Forest System lands or to carry out and administer projects to improve forest health conditions, which may include the repair or reconstruction of roads, bridges, and trails on National Forest System lands in the wildland-community interface where there is an abnormally high risk of fire. The projects shall emphasize reducing risks to human safety and public health and property and enhancing ecological functions, long-term forest productivity, and biological integrity. The Secretary shall commence the projects during fiscal year [2000] *2001*, but the projects may be completed in a subsequent fiscal year. Funds shall not be expended under this section to replace funds which would otherwise appropriately be expended from the timber salvage sale fund. Nothing in this section shall be construed to exempt any project from any environmental law.

[SEC. 328. None of the funds in this Act may be used to establish a new National Wildlife Refuge in the Kankakee River basin that is inconsistent with the United States Army Corps of Engineers' efforts to control flooding and siltation in that area. Written certification of consistency shall be submitted to the House and Senate Committees on Appropriations prior to refuge establishment.]

[SEC. 329. None of the funds provided in this or previous appropriations Acts for the agencies funded by this Act or provided from any accounts in the Treasury of the United States derived by the collection of fees available to the agencies funded by this Act, shall be transferred to or used to fund personnel, training, or other administrative activities at the Council on Environmental Quality or other offices in the Executive Office of the President for purposes related to the American Heritage Rivers program.]

[SEC. 330. Other than in emergency situations, none of the funds in this Act may be used to operate telephone answering machines during core business hours unless such answering machines include an option that enables callers to reach promptly an individual on-duty with the agency being contacted.]

[SEC. 331. ENHANCING FOREST SERVICE ADMINISTRATION OF RIGHTS-OF-WAY AND LAND USES. (a) The Secretary of Agriculture shall develop and implement a pilot program for the purpose of enhancing forest service administration of rights-of-way and other land uses. The authority for this program shall be for fiscal years 2000 through 2004. Prior to the expiration of the authority for this pilot program, the Secretary shall submit a report to the House and Senate Committees on Appropriations, and the Committee on Energy and Natural Resources of the Senate and the Committee on Resources of the House of Representatives that evaluates whether the use of funds under this section resulted in more expeditious approval of rights-of-way and special use authorizations. This report shall include the Secretary's recommendation for statutory or regulatory changes to reduce the average processing time for rights-of-way and special use permit applications.]

[(b) DEPOSIT OF FEES.—Subject to subsections (a) and (f), during fiscal years 2000 through 2004, the Secretary of Agriculture shall deposit into a special account established in the Treasury all fees collected by the Secretary to recover the costs of processing applications for, and monitoring compliance with, authorizations to use and occupy National Forest System lands pursuant to section 28(l) of the Mineral Leasing Act (30 U.S.C. 185(l)), section 504(g) of the Federal Land Policy and Management Act of 1976 (43 U.S.C. 1764(g)), section 9701 of title 31, United States Code, and section 110(g) of the National Historic Preservation Act (16 U.S.C. 470h–2(g)).]

[(c) USE OF RETAINED AMOUNTS.—Amounts deposited pursuant to subsection (b) shall be available, without further appropriation, for expenditure by the Secretary of Agriculture to cover costs incurred by the Forest Service for the processing of applications for special use authorizations and for monitoring activities undertaken in connection with such authorizations. Amounts in the special account shall remain available for such purposes until expended.]

[(d) REPORTING REQUIREMENT.—In the budget justification documents submitted by the Secretary of Agriculture in support of the President's budget for a fiscal year under section 1105 of title 31, United States Code, the Secretary shall include a description of the purposes for which amounts were expended from the special account during the preceding fiscal year, including the amounts expended for each purpose, and a description of the purposes for which amounts are proposed to be expended from the special account during the next fiscal year, including the amounts proposed to be expended for each purpose.]

[(e) DEFINITION OF AUTHORIZATION.—For purposes of this section, the term "authorizations" means special use authorizations issued under subpart B of part 251 of title 36, Code of Federal Regulations.]

[(f) IMPLEMENTATION.—This section shall take effect upon promulgation of Forest Service regulations for the collection of fees for processing of special use authorizations and for related monitoring activities.]

[SEC. 332. HARDWOOD TECHNOLOGY TRANSFER AND APPLIED RESEARCH. (a) The Secretary of Agriculture (hereinafter the "Secretary") is hereby and hereafter authorized to conduct technology transfer and development, training, dissemination of information and applied research in the management, processing and utilization of the hardwood forest resource. This authority is in addition to any other authorities which may be available to the Secretary including, but not limited to, the Cooperative Forestry Assistance Act of 1978, as amended (16 U.S.C. 2101 et seq.), and the Forest and Rangeland Renewable Resources Act of 1978, as amended (16 U.S.C. 1600–1614).]

[(b) In carrying out this authority, the Secretary may enter into grants, contracts, and cooperative agreements with public and private agencies, organizations, corporations, institutions and individuals. The Secretary may accept gifts and donations pursuant to the Act of October 10, 1978 (7 U.S.C. 2269) including gifts and donations from a donor that conducts business with any agency of the Department of Agriculture or is regulated by the Secretary of Agriculture.]

[(c) The Secretary is hereby and hereafter authorized to operate and utilize the assets of the Wood Education and Resource Center (previously named the Robert C. Byrd Hardwood Technology Center in West Virginia) as part of a newly formed "Institute of Hardwood Technology Transfer and Applied Research" (hereinafter the "Institute"). The Institute, in addition to the Wood Education and Resource Center, will consist of a Director, technology transfer specialists from State and Private Forestry, the Forestry Sciences Laboratory in Princeton, West Virginia, and any other organizational unit of the Department of Agriculture as the Secretary deems appropriate. The overall management of the Institute will be the responsibility of the Forest Service, State and Private Forestry.]

[(d) The Secretary is hereby and hereafter authorized to generate revenue using the authorities provided herein. Any revenue received as part of the operation of the Institute shall be deposited into a special fund in the Treasury of the United States, known as the "Hardwood Technology Transfer and Applied Research Fund", which shall be available to the Secretary until expended, without further appropriation, in furtherance of the purposes of this section, including upkeep, management, and operation of the Institute and the payment of salaries and expenses.]

[(e) There are hereby and hereafter authorized to be appropriated such sums as necessary to carry out the provisions of this section.]

[SEC. 333. No timber sale in Region 10 shall be advertised if the indicated rate is deficit when appraised under the transaction evidence appraisal system using domestic Alaska values for western red cedar: *Provided*, That sales which are deficit when appraised under the transaction evidence appraisal system using domestic Alaska values for western red cedar may be advertised upon receipt of a written request by a prospective, informed bidder, who has the opportunity to review the Forest Service's cruise and harvest cost estimate for that timber. Program accomplishments shall be based on volume sold. Should Region 10 sell, in fiscal year 2000, the annual average portion of the decadal allowable sale quantity called for in the current Tongass Land Management Plan in sales which are not deficit when appraised under the transaction evidence appraisal system using domestic Alaska values for western red cedar, all of the western red cedar timber from those sales which is surplus to the needs of domestic processors in Alaska, shall be made available to domestic processors in the contiguous 48 United States at prevailing domestic prices. Should Region 10 sell, in fiscal year 2000, less than the annual average portion of the decadal allowable sale quantity called for in the current Tongass Land Management Plan in sales which are not deficit when appraised under the transaction evidence appraisal system using domestic Alaska values for western red cedar, the volume of western red cedar timber available to domestic processors at prevailing domestic prices in the contiguous 48 United States shall be that volume: (i) which is surplus to the needs of domestic processors in Alaska; and (ii) is that percent of the surplus western red cedar volume determined by calculating the ratio of the total timber volume which has been sold on the Tongass to the annual average portion of the decadal allowable sale quantity called for in the current Tongass Land Management Plan. The percentage shall be calculated by Region 10 on a rolling basis as each sale is sold (for purposes of this amendment, a "rolling basis" shall mean that the determination of how much western red cedar is eligible for sale to various markets shall be made at the time each sale is awarded). Western red cedar shall be deemed "surplus to the needs of domestic processors in Alaska" when the timber sale holder has presented to the Forest Service documentation of the inability to sell western red cedar logs from a given sale to domestic Alaska processors at price equal to or greater than the log selling value stated in the contract. All additional western red cedar volume not sold to Alaska or contiguous 48 United States domestic processors may be exported to foreign markets at the election of the timber sale holder. All Alaska yellow cedar may be sold at prevailing export prices at the election of the timber sale holder.]

[SEC. 334. Subsection 104(d) of Public Law 104–333 (110 Stat. 4102) is amended—

(1) in paragraph (3) by striking "after determining that the projects to be funded from the proceeds thereof are creditworthy and that a repayment schedule is established and only" and inserting "including a review of the creditworthiness of the loan and establishment of a repayment schedule," after "and subject to such terms and conditions,"; and

(2) in paragraph (4) by inserting "paragraph (3) of" before "this subsection".]

[SEC. 335. The Secretary of Agriculture and the Secretary of the Interior shall:

(1) prepare the report required of them by section 323(a) of the Interior and Related Agencies Appropriations Act, 1998 (Public Law 105–83; 111 Stat. 1543, 1596–7) except that the report describing the estimated production of goods and services for the first 5 years during the course of the decision may be completed for either each individual unit of Federal lands or for each of the Resource Advisory Council or Provincial Advisory Council units that fall within the Basin area;

(2) distribute the report and make such report available for public comment for a minimum of 120 days; and

(3) include detailed responses to the public comment in any final environmental impact statement associated with the Interior Columbia Basin Ecosystem Management Project.]

[SEC. 336. None of the funds appropriated by this Act shall be used to propose or issue rules, regulations, decrees, or orders for the purpose of implementation, or in preparation for implementation, of the Kyoto Protocol which was adopted on December 11, 1997, in Kyoto, Japan at the Third Conference of the Parties to the United Nations Framework Convention on Climate Change, which has not been submitted to the Senate for advice and consent to ratification pursuant to article II, section 2, clause 2, of the United States Constitution, and which has not entered into force pursuant to article 25 of the Protocol.]

[SEC. 337. (a) MILLSITES OPINION.—No funds shall be expended by the Department of the Interior or the Department of Agriculture, for fiscal years 2000 and 2001, to limit the number or acreage of millsites based on the ratio between the number or acreage of millsites and the number or acreage of associated lode or placer claims with respect to any patent application grandfathered pursuant to section 113 of the Department of the Interior and Related Agencies, Appropriations Act, 1995; any operation for which a plan of operations has been previously approved; or any operation for which a plan of operations has been submitted to the Bureau of Land Management or Forest Service prior to November 7, 1997.]

[(b) NO RATIFICATION.—Nothing in this Act or the Emergency Supplemental Act of 1999 shall be construed as an explicit or tacit adoption, ratification, endorsement, approval, rejection or disapproval of the opinion dated November 7, 1997, by the solicitor of the Department of the Interior concerning millsites.]

[SEC. 338. The Forest Service, in consultation with the Department of Labor, shall review Forest Service campground concessions policy to determine if modifications can be made to Forest Service contracts for campgrounds so that such concessions fall within the regulatory exemption of 29 CFR 4.122(b). The Forest Service shall offer in fiscal year 2000 such concession prospectuses under the regulatory exemption, except that, any prospectus that does not meet the requirements of the regulatory exemption shall be offered as a service contract in accordance with the requirements of 41 U.S.C. 351–358.]

[SEC. 339. PILOT PROGRAM OF CHARGES AND FEES FOR HARVEST OF FOREST BOTANICAL PRODUCTS. (a) DEFINITION OF FOREST BOTANICAL PRODUCT.—For purposes of this section, the term "forest botanical product" means any naturally occurring mushrooms, fungi, flowers, seeds, roots, bark, leaves, and other vegetation (or portion thereof) that grow on National Forest System lands. The term does not include trees, except as provided in regulations issued under this section by the Secretary of Agriculture.]

[(b) RECOVERY OF FAIR MARKET VALUE FOR PRODUCTS.—The Secretary of Agriculture shall develop and implement a pilot program to charge and collect not less than the fair market value for forest botanical products harvested on National Forest System lands. The Secretary shall establish appraisal methods and bidding procedures to ensure that the amounts collected for forest botanical products are not less than fair market value.]

[(c) FEES.—

(1) IMPOSITION AND COLLECTION.—Under the pilot program, the Secretary of Agriculture shall also charge and collect fees from

persons who harvest forest botanical products on National Forest System lands to recover all costs to the Department of Agriculture associated with the granting, modifying, or monitoring the authorization for harvest of the forest botanical products, including the costs of any environmental or other analysis.

(2) SECURITY.—The Secretary may require a person assessed a fee under this subsection to provide security to ensure that the Secretary receives the fees imposed under this subsection from the person.]

[(d) SUSTAINABLE HARVEST LEVELS FOR FOREST BOTANICAL PRODUCTS.—The Secretary of Agriculture shall conduct appropriate analyses to determine whether and how the harvest of forest botanical products on National Forest System lands can be conducted on a sustainable basis. The Secretary may not permit under the pilot program the harvest of forest botanical products at levels in excess of sustainable harvest levels, as defined pursuant to the Multiple-Use Sustained-Yield Act of 1960 (16 U.S.C. 528 et seq.). The Secretary shall establish procedures and timeframes to monitor and revise the harvest levels established for forest botanical products.]

[(e) WAIVER AUTHORITY.—

(1) PERSONAL USE.—The Secretary of Agriculture shall establish a personal use harvest level for each forest botanical product, and the harvest of a forest botanical product below that level by a person for personal use shall not be subject to charges and fees under subsections (b) and (c).

(2) OTHER EXCEPTIONS.—The Secretary may also waive the application of subsection (b) or (c) pursuant to such regulations as the Secretary may prescribe.]

[(f) DEPOSIT AND USE OF FUNDS.—

(1) DEPOSIT.—Funds collected under the pilot program in accordance with subsections (b) and (c) shall be deposited into a special account in the Treasury of the United States.

(2) FUNDS AVAILABLE.—Funds deposited into the special account in accordance with paragraph (1) in excess of the amounts collected for forest botanical products during fiscal year 1999 shall be available for expenditure by the Secretary of Agriculture under paragraph (3) without further appropriation, and shall remain available for expenditure until the date specified in subsection (h)(2).

(3) AUTHORIZED USES.—The funds made available under paragraph (2) shall be expended at units of the National Forest System in proportion to the charges and fees collected at that unit under the pilot program to pay for—

(A) in the case of funds collected under subsection (b), the costs of conducting inventories of forest botanical products, determining sustainable levels of harvest, monitoring and assessing the impacts of harvest levels and methods, and for restoration activities, including any necessary vegetation; and

(B) in the case of fees collected under subsection (c), the costs described in paragraph (1) of such subsection.

(4) TREATMENT OF FEES.—Funds collected under subsections (b) and (c) shall not be taken into account for the purposes of the following laws:

(A) The sixth paragraph under the heading "FOREST SERVICE" in the Act of May 23, 1908 (16 U.S.C. 500) and section 13 of the Act of March 1, 1911 (commonly known as the Weeks Act; 16 U.S.C. 500).

(B) The fourteenth paragraph under the heading "FOREST SERVICE" in the Act of March 4, 1913 (16 U.S.C. 501).

(C) Section 33 of the Bankhead-Jones Farm Tenant Act (7 U.S.C. 1012).

(D) The Act of August 8, 1937, and the Act of May 24, 1939 (43 U.S.C. 1181a et seq.).

(E) Section 6 of the Act of June 14, 1926 (commonly known as the Recreation and Public Purposes Act; 43 U.S.C. 869–4).

(F) Chapter 69 of title 31, United States Code.

(G) Section 401 of the Act of June 15, 1935 (16 U.S.C. 715s).

(H) Section 4 of the Land and Water Conservation Fund Act of 1965 (16 U.S.C. 460l–6a).

(I) Any other provision of law relating to revenue allocation.]

[(g) REPORTING REQUIREMENTS.—As soon as practicable after the end of each fiscal year in which the Secretary of Agriculture collects charges and fees under subsections (b) and (c) or expends funds from the special account under subsection (f), the Secretary shall submit to the Congress a report summarizing the activities of the Secretary under the pilot program, including the funds generated under subsections (b) and (c), the expenses incurred to carry out the pilot program, and the expenditures made from the special account during that fiscal year.]

[(h) DURATION OF PILOT PROGRAM.—

(1) CHARGES AND FEES.—The Secretary of Agriculture may collect charges and fees under the authority of subsections (b) and (c) only during fiscal years 2000 through 2004.

(2) USE OF SPECIAL ACCOUNT.—The Secretary may make expenditures from the special account under subsection (f) until September 30 of the fiscal year following the last fiscal year specified in paragraph (1). After that date, amounts remaining in the special account shall be transferred to the general fund of the Treasury.]

[SEC. 340. Title III, section 3001 of Public Law 106–31 is amended by inserting after "Alabama," the following: "in fiscal year 1999 or 2000".]

[SEC. 341. Section 347 of title III of section 101(e) of division A of Public Law 105–277 is hereby amended—

(1) in subsection (a)—

(A) by inserting ", via agreement or contract as appropriate," before "may enter into"; and

(B) by striking "(28) contracts with private persons and" and inserting "(28) stewardship contracting demonstration pilot projects with private persons or other public or private";

(2) in subsection (b), by striking "contract" and inserting "project";

(3) in subsection (c)—

(A) in the heading, by inserting "Agreements or" before "Contracts";

(B) in paragraph (1)—

(i) by striking "a contract" and inserting "an agreement or contract"; and

(ii) by striking "private contracts" and inserting "private agreements or contracts";

(C) in paragraph (3), by inserting "agreement or" before "contracts"; and

(D) in paragraph (4), by inserting "agreement or" before "contracts";

(4) in subsection (d)—

(A) in paragraph (1), by striking "a contract" and inserting "an agreement or contract"; and

(B) in paragraph (2), by striking "a contract" and inserting "an agreement or contract"; and

(5) in subsection (g)—

(A) in the first sentence by striking "contract" and inserting "pilot project"; and

(B) in the last sentence—

(i) by inserting "agreements or" before "contracts"; and

(ii) by inserting "agreements or" before "contract".]

[SEC. 342. Notwithstanding section 343 of Public Law 105–83, increases in recreation residence fees shall be implemented in fiscal year 2000 only to the extent that the fiscal year 2000 fees do not exceed the fiscal year 1999 fee by more than $2,000.]

[SEC. 343. REDESIGNATION OF BLACKSTONE RIVER VALLEY NATIONAL HERITAGE CORRIDOR IN HONOR OF JOHN H. CHAFEE. (a) CORRIDOR.—

(1) IN GENERAL.—The Blackstone River Valley National Heritage Corridor established by section 1 of Public Law 99–647 (16 U.S.C. 461 note) is redesignated as the "John H. Chafee Blackstone River Valley National Heritage Corridor".

(2) REFERENCES.—Any reference in a law, map, regulation, document, paper, or other record of the United States to the Blackstone River Valley National Heritage Corridor shall be deemed to be a reference to the John H. Chafee Blackstone River Valley National Heritage Corridor.]

[(b) COMMISSION.—

(1) IN GENERAL.—The Blackstone River Valley National Heritage Corridor Commission established by section 3 of Public Law 99–647 (16 U.S.C. 461 note) is redesignated as the "John H. Chafee Blackstone River Valley National Heritage Corridor Commission".

(2) REFERENCES.—Any reference in a law, map, regulation, document, paper, or other record of the United States to the Blackstone River Valley National Heritage Corridor Commission shall be deemed to be a reference to the John H. Chafee Blackstone River Valley National Heritage Corridor Commission.]

[(c) CONFORMING AMENDMENTS.—

(1) Section 1 of Public Law 99–647 (16 U.S.C. 461 note) is amended in the first sentence by striking "Blackstone River Valley National Heritage Corridor" and inserting "John H. Chafee Blackstone River Valley National Heritage Corridor".

(2) Section 3 of Public Law 99–647 (16 U.S.C. 461 note) is amended—

(A) in the section heading, by striking "BLACKSTONE RIVER VALLEY NATIONAL HERITAGE CORRIDOR COMMISSION" and inserting "JOHN H. CHAFEE BLACKSTONE RIVER VALLEY NATIONAL HERITAGE CORRIDOR COMMISSION"; and

(B) in subsection (a), by striking "Blackstone River Valley National Heritage Corridor Commission" and inserting "John H. Chafee Blackstone River Valley National Heritage Corridor Commission".]

SEC. [344] *316.* A project undertaken by the Forest Service under the Recreation Fee Demonstration Program as authorized by section 315 of the Department of the Interior and Related Agencies Appropriations Act for Fiscal Year 1996, as amended, shall not result in—

(1) displacement of the holder of an authorization to provide commercial recreation services on Federal lands. Prior to initiating any project, the Secretary shall consult with potentially affected holders to determine what impacts the project may have on the holders. Any modifications to the authorization shall be made within the terms and conditions of the authorization and authorities of the impacted agency.

(2) the return of a commercial recreation service to the Secretary for operation when such services have been provided in the past by a private sector provider, except when—

(A) the private sector provider fails to bid on such opportunities;

(B) the private sector provider terminates its relationship with the agency; or

(C) the agency revokes the permit for non-compliance with the terms and conditions of the authorization.

In such cases, the agency may use the Recreation Fee Demonstration Program to provide for operations until a subsequent operator can be found through the offering of a new prospectus.

[SEC. 345. NATIONAL FOREST-DEPENDENT RURAL COMMUNITIES ECONOMIC DIVERSIFICATION. (a) FINDINGS AND PURPOSES.—Section 2373 of the National Forest-Dependent Rural Communities Economic Diversification Act of 1990 (7 U.S.C. 6611) is amended—

(1) in subsection (a)—

(A) in paragraph (2), by striking "national forests" and inserting "National Forest System land";

(B) in paragraph (4), by striking "the national forests" and inserting "National Forest System land";

(C) in paragraph (5), by striking "forest resources" and inserting "natural resources"; and

(D) in paragraph (6), by striking "national forest resources" and inserting "National Forest System land resources"; and

(2) in subsection (b)(1)—

(A) by striking "national forests" and inserting "National Forest System land"; and

(B) by striking "forest resources" and inserting "natural resources".]

[(b) DEFINITIONS.—Section 2374(1) of the National Forest-Dependent Rural Communities Economic Diversification Act of 1990 (7 U.S.C. 6612(1)) is amended by striking "forestry" and inserting "natural resources".]

[(c) RURAL FORESTRY AND ECONOMIC DIVERSIFICATION ACTION TEAMS.—Section 2375(b) of the National Forest-Dependent Rural Communities Economic Diversification Act of 1990 (7 U.S.C. 6613(b)) is amended—

(1) in the first sentence, by striking "forestry" and inserting "natural resources"; and

(2) in the second and third sentences, by striking "national forest resources" and inserting "National Forest System land resources".]

[(d) ACTION PLAN IMPLEMENTATION.—Section 2376(a) of the National Forest-Dependent Rural Communities Economic Diversification Act of 1990 (7 U.S.C. 6614(a)) is amended—

(1) by striking "forest resources" and inserting "natural resources"; and

(2) by striking "national forest resources" and inserting "National Forest System land resources".]

[(e) TRAINING AND EDUCATION.—Paragraphs (3) and (4) of section 2377(a) of the National Forest-Dependent Rural Communities Economic Diversification Act of 1990 (7 U.S.C. 6615(a)) are amended by striking "national forest resources" and inserting "National Forest System land resources".]

[(f) LOANS TO ECONOMICALLY DISADVANTAGED RURAL COMMUNITIES.—Paragraphs (2) and (3) of section 2378(a) of the National Forest-Dependent Rural Communities Economic Diversification Act of 1990 (7 U.S.C. 6616(a)) are amended by striking "national forest resources" and inserting "National Forest System land resources".]

[SEC. 346. INTERSTATE 90 LAND EXCHANGE AMENDMENT. (a) This section shall be referred to as the "Interstate 90 Land Exchange Amendment".]

[(b) Section 604(a) of the Interstate 90 Land Exchange Act of 1998, Public Law 105–277; 112 Stat. 2681–328 (1998), is hereby amended by adding at the end of the first sentence: "except title to offered lands and interests in lands described as follows: Township 21 North, Range 12 East, Section 15, W.M., Township 21 North, Range 12 East, Section 23, W.M., Township 21 North, Range 12 East, Section 25, W.M., Township 19 North, Range 13 East, Section 7, W.M., Township 19 North, Range 15 East, Section 31, W.M., Township 19 North, Range 14 East, Section 25, W.M., Township 22 North, Range 11 East, Section 3, W.M., and Township 22 North, Range 11 East, Section 19, W.M. must be placed in escrow by Plum Creek, according to terms and conditions acceptable to the Secretary and Plum Creek, for a 3-year period beginning on the later of the date of the enactment of this Act or consummation of the exchange. During the period the lands are held in escrow, Plum Creek shall not undertake any activities on these lands, except for fire suppression and road maintenance, without the approval of the Secretary, which shall not be unreasonably withheld".]

[(c) Section 604(a) is further amended by inserting in section (2) after the words "dated October 1998" the following: "except the following parcels: Township 19 North, Range 15 East, Section 29, W.M., Township 18 North, Range 15 East, Section 3, W.M., Township 19 North, Range 14 East, Section 9, W.M., Township 21 North, Range 14 East, Section 7, W.M., Township 22 North, Range 12 East, Section 35, W.M., Township 22 North, Range 13 East, Section 3, W.M., Township 22 North, Range 13 East, Section 9, W.M., Township 22 North, Range 13 East, Section 11, W.M., Township 22 North, Range 13 East, Section 13, W.M., Township 22 North, Range 13 East, Section 15, W.M., Township 22 North, Range 13 East, Section 25, W.M., Township 22 North, Range 13 East, Section 33, W.M., Township 22 North, Range 13 East, Section 35, W.M., Township 22 North, Range 14 East, Section 7, W.M., Township 22 North, Range 14 East, Section 9, W.M., Township 22 North, Range 14 East, Section 11, W.M., Township 22 North, Range 14 East, Section 15, W.M., Township 22 North, Range 14 East, Section 17, W.M., Township 22 North, Range 14 East, Section 21, W.M., Township 22 North, Range 14 East, Section 31, W.M., Township 22 North, Range 14 East, Section 27, W.M. The appraisal approved by the Secretary of Agriculture on June 14, 1999 (the "Appraisal") shall be adjusted by subtracting the values for the parcels described in the preceding sentence determined during the Appraisal process in the context of the whole estate to be conveyed".]

[(d) Section 604(b) of the Interstate 90 Land Exchange Act of 1998, Public Law 105–277; 112 Stat. 2681–328 (1998), is hereby amended by inserting after the words "offered land" the following: ", as provided in section 604(a), and placement in escrow of acceptable title to Township 22 North, Range 11 East, Section 3, W.M., Township 22 North, Range 11 East, Section 19, W.M., Township 21 North, Range 12 East, Section 15, W.M., Township 21 North, Range 12 East, Section 23, W.M., Township 21 North, Range 12 East, Section 25, W.M., Township 19 North, Range 13 East, Section 7, W.M., Township 19 North, Range 15 East, Section 31, W.M., and Township 19 North, Range 14 East, Section 25, W.M.".]

[(e) Section 604(b) is further amended by inserting the following before the colon: "except Township 19 North, Range 10 East, W.M., Section 4, Township 20 North, Range 10 East, W.M., Section 32, and Township 21 North, Range 14 East, W.M., W½W½ of Section 16, Township 12 North, Range 7 East, Sections 4 and 5, W.M., Township 13 North, Range 7 East, Sections 32 and 33, W.M., Township 8 North, Range 4 East, Section 17 and the S½ of 16, W.M., which shall be retained by the United States". The Appraisal shall be adjusted by subtracting the values determined for Township 19 North, Range 10 East, W.M., Section 4, Township 20 North, Range 10 East, W.M., Section 32, Township 12 North, Range 7 East, Sections 4 and 5, W.M., Township 13 North, Range 7 East, Sections 32 and 33, W.M., Township 8 North, Range 4 East, Section 17 and the S½ of Section 16, W.M. during the Appraisal process in the context of the whole estate to be conveyed.]

[(f) After adjustment of the Appraisal, the values of the offered and selected lands, including the offered lands held in escrow, shall be equalized as follows:

(1) the appraised value of the offered lands, as such lands and appraised value have been adjusted hereby, minus the appraised

value of the offered lands to be placed into escrow, shall be compared to the appraised value of the selected lands, as such lands and appraised value have been adjusted hereby, and the Secretary shall equalize such values by the payment of cash to Plum Creek at the time that deeds are exchanged, such cash to come from currently appropriated funds, or, if necessary, by reprogramming; and

(2) the Secretary shall compensate Plum Creek for the lands placed into escrow, based upon the values determined for each such parcel during the Appraisal process in the context of the whole estate to be conveyed, through the following, including any combination thereof:

(A) conveyance of any other lands under the jurisdiction of the Secretary acceptable to Plum Creek and the Secretary after compliance with all applicable Federal environmental and other laws; and

(B) to the extent sufficient acceptable lands are not available pursuant to paragraph (A) of this subsection, cash payments as and to the extent funds become available through appropriations, private sources, or, if necessary, by reprogramming.

The Secretary shall promptly seek to identify lands acceptable to equalize values under paragraph (A) of this subsection and shall, not later than July 1, 2000, provide a report to the Congress outlining the results of such efforts.]

[(g) As funds or lands are provided to Plum Creek by the Secretary, Plum Creek shall release to the United States deeds for lands and interests in lands held in escrow based on the values determined during the Appraisal process in the context of the whole estate to be conveyed. Deeds shall be released for lands and interests in lands in the following order: Township 21 North, Range 12 East, Section 15, W.M., Township 21 North, Range 12 East, Section 23, W.M., Township 21 North, Range 12 East, Section 25, W.M., Township 19 North, Range 13 East, Section 7, Township 19 North, Range 15 East, Section 31, Township 19 North, Range 14 East, Section 25, Township 22 North, Range 11 East, Section 3, W.M., and Township 22 North, Range 11 East, Section 19, W.M.]

[(h) Section 606(d) is hereby amended to read as follows: "TIMING.—The Secretary and Plum Creek shall make the adjustments directed in section 604(a) and (b) and consummate the land exchange within 30 days of the enactment of the Interstate 90 Land Exchange Amendment, unless the Secretary and Plum Creek mutually agree to extend the consummation date.".]

[(i) The deadline for the Report to Congress required by section 609(c) of the Interstate 90 Land Exchange Act of 1998 is hereby extended. Such Report is due to the Congress 18 months from the date of the enactment of this Interstate 90 Land Exchange Amendment.]

[(j) Section 610 of the Interstate 90 Land Exchange Act of 1998, is hereby amended by striking "date of enactment of this Act" and inserting "first date on which deeds are exchanged to consummate the land exchange".]

[SEC. 347. THE SNOQUALMIE NATIONAL FOREST BOUNDARY ADJUSTMENT ACT OF 1999. (a) IN GENERAL.—The boundary of the Snoqualmie National Forest is hereby adjusted as generally depicted on a map entitled "Snoqualmie National Forest 1999 Boundary Adjustment" dated June 30, 1999. Such map, together with a legal description of all lands included in the boundary adjustment, shall be on file and available for public inspection in the Office of the Chief of the Forest Service in Washington, District of Columbia. Nothing in this subsection shall limit the authority of the Secretary of Agriculture to adjust the boundary pursuant to section 11 of the Weeks Law of March 1, 1911.]

[(b) RULE FOR LAND AND WATER CONSERVATION FUND.—For the purposes of section 7 of the Land and Water Conservation Fund Act of 1965 (16 U.S.C. 4601–9), the boundary of the Snoqualmie National Forest, as adjusted by subsection (a), shall be considered to be the boundary of the Forest as of January 1, 1965.]

[SEC. 348. Section 1770(d) of the Food Security Act of 1985 (7 U.S.C. 2276(d)) is amended by redesignating paragraph (10) as paragraph (11) and by inserting after paragraph (9) the following new paragraph:

"(10) section 3(e) of the Forest and Rangeland Renewable Resources Research Act of 1978 (16 U.S.C. 1642(e));".]

[SEC. 349. None of the funds appropriated or otherwise made available by this Act may be used to implement or enforce any provision in Presidential Executive Order No. 13123 regarding the Federal Energy Management Program which circumvents or contradicts any statutes relevant to Federal energy use and the measurement thereof.]

[SEC. 350. INVESTMENT OF EXXON VALDEZ OIL SPILL COURT RECOVERY IN HIGH YIELD INVESTMENTS AND IN MARINE RESEARCH. (1) Notwithstanding any other provision of law and subject to the provisions of paragraphs (5) and (7), upon the joint motion of the United States and the State of Alaska and the issuance of an appropriate order by the United States District Court for the District of Alaska, the joint trust funds, or any portion thereof, including any interest accrued thereon, previously received or to be received by the United States and the State of Alaska pursuant to the Agreement and Consent Decree issued in United States v. Exxon Corporation, et al. (No. A91–082 CIV) and State of Alaska v. Exxon Corporation, et al. (No. A91–083 CIV) (hereafter referred to as the "Consent Decree"), may be deposited in—

(A) the Natural Resource Damage Assessment and Restoration Fund (hereafter referred to as the "Fund") established in title I of the Department of the Interior and Related Agencies Appropriations Act, 1992 (Public Law 102–154; 43 U.S.C. 1474b);

(B) accounts outside the United States Treasury (hereafter referred to as "outside accounts"); or

(C) both.

Any funds deposited in an outside account may be invested only in income-producing obligations and other instruments or securities that have been determined unanimously by the Federal and State natural resource trustees for the Exxon Valdez oil spill ("trustees") to have a high degree of reliability and security.

(2) Joint trust funds deposited in the Fund or an outside account that have been approved unanimously by the Trustees for expenditure by or through a State or Federal agency shall be transferred promptly from the Fund or the outside account to the State of Alaska or United States upon the joint request of the governments.

(3) The transfer of joint trust funds outside the Court Registry shall not affect the supervisory jurisdiction of the district court under the Consent Decree or the Memorandum of Agreement and Consent Decree in United States v. State of Alaska (No. A91–081–CIV) over all expenditures of the joint trust funds.

(4) Nothing herein shall affect the requirement of section 207 of the dire emergency supplemental appropriations and transfers for relief from the effects of natural disasters, for other urgent needs, and for the incremental cost of "Operation Desert Shield/Desert Storm" Act of 1992 (Public Law 102–229; 42 U.S.C. 1474b note) that amounts received by the United States and designated by the trustees for the expenditure by or through a Federal agency must be deposited into the Fund.

(5) All remaining settlement funds are eligible for the investment authority granted under this section so long as they are managed and allocated consistent with the Resolution of the Trustees adopted March 1, 1999, concerning the Restoration Reserve, as follows:

(A) $55 million of the funds remaining on October 1, 2002, and the associated earnings thereafter shall be managed and allocated for habitat protection programs including small parcel habitat acquisitions. Such sums shall be reduced by—

(i) the amount of any payments made after the date of enactment of this Act from the Joint Trust Funds pursuant to an agreement between the Trustee Council and Koniag, Inc., which includes those lands which are presently subject to the Koniag Non-Development Easement, including, but not limited to, the continuation or modification of such Easement; and

(ii) payments in excess of $6.32 million for any habitat acquisition or protection from the joint trust funds after the date of enactment of this Act and prior to October 1, 2002, other than payments for which the Council is currently obligated through purchase agreements with the Kodiak Island Borough, Afognak Joint Venture and the Eyak Corporation.

(B) All other funds remaining on October 1, 2002, and the associated earnings shall be used to fund a program, consisting of—

(i) marine research, including applied fisheries research;

(ii) monitoring; and

(iii) restoration, other than habitat acquisition, which may include community and economic restoration projects and facilities (including projects proposed by the communities of the EVOS Region or the fishing industry), consistent with the Consent Decree.

(6) The Federal trustees and the State trustees, to the extent authorized by State law, are authorized to issue grants as needed to implement this program.

(7) The authority provided in this section shall expire on September 30, 2002, unless by September 30, 2001, the Trustees have submitted to the Congress a report recommending a structure the Trustees believe would be most effective and appropriate for the administration and expenditure of remaining funds and interest received. Upon the expiration of the authorities granted in this section all monies in the Fund or outside accounts shall be returned to the Court Registry or other account permitted by law.]

[SEC. 351. YOUTH CONSERVATION CORPS AND RELATED PARTNERSHIPS. (a) Notwithstanding any other provision of this Act, there shall be available for high priority projects which shall be carried out by the Youth Conservation Corps as authorized by Public Law 91–378, or related partnerships with non-Federal youth conservation corps or entities such as the Student Conservation Association, up to $1,000,000 of the funds available to the Bureau of Land Management under this Act, in order to increase the number of summer jobs available for youths, ages 15 through 22, on Federal lands.

(b) Within 6 months after the date of the enactment of this Act, the Secretary of Agriculture and the Secretary of the Interior shall jointly submit a report to the House and Senate Committees on Appropriations and the Committee on Energy and Natural Resources of the Senate and the Committee on Resources of the House of Representatives that includes the following—

(1) the number of youths, ages 15 through 22, employed during the summer of 1999, and the number estimated to be employed during the summer of 2000, through the Youth Conservation Corps, the Public Land Corps, or a related partnership with a State, local or nonprofit youth conservation corps or other entities such as the Student Conservation Association;

(2) a description of the different types of work accomplished by youths during the summer of 1999;

(3) identification of any problems that prevent or limit the use of the Youth Conservation Corps, the Public Land Corps, or related partnerships to accomplish projects described in subsection (a);

(4) recommendations to improve the use and effectiveness of partnerships described in subsection (a); and

(5) an analysis of the maintenance backlog that identifies the types of projects that the Youth Conservation Corps, the Public Land Corps, or related partnerships are qualified to complete.]

[SEC. 352. (a) NORTH PACIFIC RESEARCH BOARD.—Section 401 of Public Law 105–83 is amended as follows:

(1) In subsection (c)—

(A) by striking "available for appropriation, to the extent provided in the subsequent appropriations Acts," and inserting "made available";

(B) by inserting "To the extent provided in the subsequent appropriations Acts," at the beginning of paragraph (1);

(C) by inserting "without further appropriation" after "20 percent of such amounts shall be made available"; and

(2) by striking subsection (f).]

[SEC. 353. None of the funds in this Act may be used by the Secretary of the Interior to issue a prospecting permit for hardrock mineral exploration on Mark Twain National Forest land in the Current River/Jack's Fork River—Eleven Point Watershed (not including Mark Twain National Forest land in Townships 31N and 32N, Range 2 and Range 3 West, on which mining activities are taking place as of the date of the enactment of this Act): *Provided*, That none of the funds in this Act may be used by the Secretary of the Interior to segregate or withdraw land in the Mark Twain National Forest, Missouri under section 204 of the Federal Land Policy and Management Act of 1976 (43 U.S.C. 1714).]

[SEC. 354. Public Law 105–83, the Department of the Interior and Related Agencies Appropriations Act of November 17, 1997, title III, section 331 is hereby amended by adding before the period: ": *Provided further*, That to carryout the provisions of this section, the Bureau of Land Management and the Forest Service may establish Transfer Appropriation Accounts (also known as allocation accounts) as needed".]

[SEC. 355. WHITE RIVER NATIONAL FOREST.—The Forest Service shall extend the public comment period on the White River National Forest plan revision for 90 days beyond February 9, 2000.]

[SEC. 356. The first section of Public Law 99–215 (99 Stat. 1724), as amended by section 597 of the Water Resources Development Act of 1999 (Public Law 106–53), is further amended—

(1) by redesignating subsection (c) as subsection (e); and

(2) by inserting after subsection (b) the following new subsections:

"(c) The National Capital Planning Commission shall vacate and terminate an Easement and Declaration of Covenants, dated February 2, 1989, conveyed by the owner of the adjacent real property pursuant to subsection (b)(1)(D) in exchange for, and not later than 30 days after, the vacation and termination of the Deed of Easement, dated January 4, 1989, conveyed by the Maryland National Capital Park and Planning Commission pursuant to subsection (b)(1).

"(d) Effective on the date of the enactment of this subsection, the memorandum of May 7, 1985, and any amendments thereto, shall terminate.".]

[SEC. 357. None of the funds in this Act or any other Act shall be used by the Secretary of the Interior to promulgate final rules to revise 43 CFR subpart 3809, except that the Secretary, following the public comment period required by section 3002 of Public Law 106–31, may issue final rules to amend 43 C.F.R. Subpart 3809 which are not inconsistent with the recommendations contained in the National Research Council report entitled "Hardrock Mining on Federal Lands" so long as these regulations are also not inconsistent with existing statutory authorities. Nothing in this section shall be construed to expand the existing statutory authority of the Secretary.] *(Department of the Interior and Related Agencies Appropriations Act, 2000, as enacted by section 1000(a)(3) of the Consolidated Appropriations Act, 2000 (P.L. 106–113).)*

DEPARTMENT OF JUSTICE

GENERAL ADMINISTRATION

Federal Funds

General and special funds:

SALARIES AND EXPENSES

For expenses necessary for the administration of the Department of Justice, [$79,328,000] *$88,196,000*, of which not to exceed $3,317,000 is for the Facilities Program 2000, to remain available until expended: [*Provided*, That not to exceed 43 permanent positions and 44 full-time equivalent workyears and $8,136,000 shall be expended for the Department Leadership Program exclusive of augmentation that occurred in these offices in fiscal year 1999: *Provided further*, That not to exceed 41 permanent positions and 48 full-time equivalent workyears and $4,811,000 shall be expended for the Offices of Legislative Affairs and Public Affairs: *Provided further*, That the latter two aforementioned offices may utilize non-reimbursable details of career employees within the caps described in the aforementioned proviso:] *Provided* [*further*], That the Attorney General is authorized to transfer, under such terms and conditions as the Attorney General shall specify, forfeited real or personal property of limited or marginal value, as such value is determined by guidelines established by the Attorney General, to a State or local government agency, or its designated contractor or transferee, for use to support drug abuse treatment, drug and crime prevention and education, housing, job skills, and other community-based public health and safety programs: *Provided further*, That any transfer under the preceding proviso shall not create or confer any private right of action in any person against the United States, and shall be treated as a reprogramming under section 605 of this Act.

JOINT AUTOMATED BOOKING SYSTEM

For expenses necessary for the nationwide deployment of a Joint Automated Booking System *including automated capability to transmit fingerprint and image data*, $1,800,000, to remain available until expended. *(Department of Justice Appropriations Act, 2000, as enacted by section 1000(a)(1) of the Consolidated Appropriations Act, 2000 (P.L. 106–113).)*

PUBLIC KEY INFRASTRUCTURE

For expenses necessary to implement a Public Key Infrastructure, $4,376,000, to remain available until expended.

Program and Financing (in millions of dollars)

Identification code 15–0129–0–1–999	1999 actual	2000 est.	2001 est.
Obligations by program activity:			
00.01 Program direction and policy coordination	103	111	117
00.02 Joint Automated Booking System		2	2
00.03 Public Key Infrastructure			4
09.01 Reimbursable program	104	65	65
10.00 Total new obligations	207	178	188
Budgetary resources available for obligation:			
21.40 Unobligated balance available, start of year	12	13	8
22.00 New budget authority (gross)	210	173	186
23.90 Total budgetary resources available for obligation	222	186	194
23.95 Total new obligations	–207	–178	–188
23.98 Unobligated balance expiring or withdrawn	–4		
24.40 Unobligated balance available, end of year	13	8	6
New budget authority (gross), detail:			
Discretionary:			
40.00 Appropriation	79	81	94
42.00 Transferred from other accounts	27	27	27
43.00 Appropriation (total discretionary)	106	108	121
68.00 Spending authority from offsetting collections: Offsetting collections (cash)	104	65	65
70.00 Total new budget authority (gross)	210	173	186
Change in unpaid obligations:			
72.40 Unpaid obligations, start of year: Obligated balance, start of year	14	28	45
73.10 Total new obligations	207	178	188
73.20 Total outlays (gross)	–191	–161	–185
74.40 Unpaid obligations, end of year: Obligated balance, end of year	28	45	48
Outlays (gross), detail:			
86.90 Outlays from new discretionary authority	188	161	173
86.93 Outlays from discretionary balances	3		12
87.00 Total outlays (gross)	191	161	185
Offsets:			
Against gross budget authority and outlays:			
88.00 Offsetting collections (cash) from: Federal sources	–104	–65	–65
Net budget authority and outlays:			
89.00 Budget authority	106	108	121
90.00 Outlays	87	96	120

Program direction and policy coordination.—The Attorney General of the United States is responsible for leading the Department of Justice in accomplishing its missions. The Attorney General is assisted by the Deputy Attorney General, the Associate Attorney General, Department policy-level officials, and the Justice Management Division. The General Administration appropriation provides the resources for the programs and operations of the Attorney General, the Deputy Attorney General, the Associate Attorney General, and their Offices, the several Senior Policy Offices, and the Justice Management Division. In addition, $5.0 million is anticipated to be available from the Assets. Forfeiture Fund to integrate the INS' IDENT fingerprint system with FBI's IAFIS.

Joint Automated Booking System.—The Joint Automated Booking System (JABS) performs three major functions: (1) facilitates rapid identification of individuals under arrest or detention through automation of the booking process and an interface with the Federal Bureau of Investigation (FBI) fingerprint identification system; (2) minimizes duplication of data entry by multiple law enforcement agencies during the booking process, and; (3) promotes data sharing of arrest records among JABS participants and other interested parties. When implemented, JABS will provide a rapid conduit to the FBI for offender identification and a current, nationwide reference for criminal offenders, arrests, cases and related data to aid in criminal investigations and prosecutions.

Public Key Infrastructure.—The Public Key Infrastructure provides the necessary means through which to secure the Department's critical infrastructures. Current law requires the Department of Justice and other Federal agencies to consider alternative means to accept electronic transmissions from the public. The Government Paperwork Elimination Act mandates that Federal agencies provide electronic forms to the public and a secure method for transmitting completed forms back to the Government.

Object Classification (in millions of dollars)

Identification code 15–0129–0–1–999	1999 actual	2000 est.	2001 est.
Direct obligations:			
Personnel compensation:			
11.1 Full-time permanent	44	45	49
11.3 Other than full-time permanent	2	2	3
11.5 Other personnel compensation	1	1	1
11.9 Total personnel compensation	47	48	53
12.1 Civilian personnel benefits	10	12	13

General and special funds—Continued

Public Key Infrastructure—Continued

Object Classification (in millions of dollars)—Continued

Identification code 15–0129–0–1–999		1999 actual	2000 est.	2001 est.
21.0	Travel and transportation of persons	1	1	1
22.0	Transportation of things	1	1	1
23.3	Communications, utilities, and miscellaneous charges	2	2	2
25.2	Other services	5	8	9
	Purchases of goods and services from Government accounts:			
25.3	Rental payments to GSA	8	9	9
25.3	Purchases of goods and services from Government accounts	27	27	28
26.0	Supplies and materials	2	3	3
31.0	Equipment	....	2	4
99.0	Subtotal, direct obligations	103	113	123
99.0	Reimbursable obligations	104	65	65
99.9	Total new obligations	207	178	188

Personnel Summary

Identification code 15–0129–0–1–999		1999 actual	2000 est.	2001 est.
	Direct:			
1001	Total compensable workyears: Full-time equivalent employment	644	668	670
	Reimbursable:			
2001	Total compensable workyears: Full-time equivalent employment	255	306	317

Allocations Received From Other Accounts

Note.—Obligations incurred under allocations from other accounts are included in the schedules of the parent appropriations as follows:

Health Care Financing Administration: "Health Care Fraud and Abuse Control Account."

Narrowband Communications

For the costs of conversion to narrowband communications as mandated by section 104 of the National Telecommunications and Information Administration Organization Act (47 U.S.C. 903(d)(1)), [$10,625,000] *including the costs for operation and maintenance of Land Mobile Radio legacy systems, $205,000,000*, to remain available until expended. *(Department of Justice Appropriations Act, 2000, as enacted by section 1000(a)(1) of the Consolidated Appropriations Act, 2000 (P.L. 106–113).)*

Program and Financing (in millions of dollars)

Identification code 15–0132–0–1–751		1999 actual	2000 est.	2001 est.
	Obligations by program activity:			
00.01	Direct	....	103	205
09.01	Reimbursable	....	13	....
10.00	Total new obligations	....	116	205
	Budgetary resources available for obligation:			
22.00	New budget authority (gross)	....	116	205
23.95	Total new obligations	....	−116	−205
	New budget authority (gross), detail:			
	Discretionary:			
40.00	Appropriation	....	11	205
42.00	Transferred from other accounts	....	92	....
43.00	Appropriation (total discretionary)	....	103	205
68.00	Spending authority from offsetting collections: Offsetting collections (cash)	....	13	....
70.00	Total new budget authority (gross)	....	116	205
	Change in unpaid obligations:			
72.40	Unpaid obligations, start of year: Obligated balance, start of year	....	....	35
73.10	Total new obligations	....	116	205
73.20	Total outlays (gross)	....	−81	−178
74.40	Unpaid obligations, end of year: Obligated balance, end of year	....	35	62
	Outlays (gross), detail:			
86.90	Outlays from new discretionary authority	....	81	144
86.93	Outlays from discretionary balances	....	....	35
87.00	Total outlays (gross)	....	81	178
	Offsets:			
	Against gross budget authority and outlays:			
88.00	Offsetting collections (cash) from: Federal sources	....	−13	....
	Net budget authority and outlays:			
89.00	Budget authority	....	103	205
90.00	Outlays	....	68	178

In 2001, resources are proposed to provide funding for the Department of Justice to accelerate conversion of its wireless radio communications to narrowband operations. Federal Government agencies are required by 47 U.S.C. 903(d)(1) to make more efficient use of their radio spectrum. The National Telecommunications and Information Administration's (NTIA) implementing regulations require that all Federal spectrum users narrow, by one-half, the bandwidth used to transmit radio signals by the year 2005 for Very High Frequency (VHF) allocations and 2008 for Ultra High Frequency (UHF) allocations. The Department's 2001 budget includes $205,000,000 in funding to continue the implementation of the Justice Wireless Network (JWN), and for wireless commercial services. This amount includes $92,545,000 that was appropriated to DOJ components for wireless radio communications in 2000 but earmarked for transfer to the narrowband program. Of the total funding available, $10,625,000 will be provided to the Wireless Management Office in the Justice Management Division to consolidate wireless communications management functions, including procurement, radio site development, and spectrum management.

Object Classification (in millions of dollars)

Identification code 15–0132–0–1–751		1999 actual	2000 est.	2001 est.
	Direct obligations:			
11.1	Personnel compensation: Full-time permanent	....	1	1
25.1	Advisory and assistance services	....	12	44
31.0	Equipment	....	90	160
99.0	Subtotal, direct obligations	....	103	205
99.0	Reimbursable obligations	....	13	....
99.9	Total new obligations	....	116	205

Personnel Summary

Identification code 15–0132–0–1–751		1999 actual	2000 est.	2001 est.
1001	Total compensable workyears: Full-time equivalent employment	....	12	12

Narrowband Communications

(Legislative proposal, not subject to PAYGO)

Program and Financing (in millions of dollars)

Identification code 15–0132–2–1–751		1999 actual	2000 est.	2001 est.
	Obligations by program activity:			
00.01	Improve wireless communications	....	....	138
00.02	Improve wireless communications	....	....	−138
	New budget authority (gross), detail:			
	Discretionary:			
40.00	Appropriation	....	....	−138
42.00	Transferred from other accounts	....	....	138

43.00	Appropriation (total discretionary)	....	....	....
	Net budget authority and outlays:			
89.00	Budget authority	....	....	....
90.00	Outlays	....	....	....

The Administration will propose legislation authorizing the FCC to establish a lease fee on the use of analog spectrum by television broadcasters. The amounts collected will be transferred to the Department of Justice, the Department of the Treasury, and the Bureau of Indian Affairs to be used for the purposes of promoting digital and wireless communications and to ensure the interoperability of public safety communications systems.

Counterterrorism Fund

For necessary expenses, as determined by the Attorney General, [$10,000,000] *$25,000,000*, to remain available until expended, to reimburse any Department of Justice organization for: (1) the costs incurred in reestablishing the operational capability of an office or facility which has been damaged or destroyed as a result of any domestic or international terrorist incident; and (2) the costs of providing support to counter, investigate or prosecute domestic or international terrorism, including payment of rewards in connection with these activities: *Provided*, That any Federal agency may be reimbursed for the costs of detaining in foreign countries individuals accused of acts of terrorism that violate the laws of the United States: *Provided further*, That funds provided under this paragraph shall be available only after the Attorney General notifies the Committees on Appropriations of the House of Representatives and the Senate in accordance with section 605 of this Act. *(Department of Justice Appropriations Act, 2000, as enacted by section 1000(a)(1) of the Consolidated Appropriations Act, 2000 (P.L. 106–113).)*

Program and Financing (in millions of dollars)

Identification code 15–0130–0–1–751		1999 actual	2000 est.	2001 est.
	Obligations by program activity:			
10.00	Total new obligations (object class 25.2)	151	10	25
	Budgetary resources available for obligation:			
21.40	Unobligated balance available, start of year	27	23	24
22.00	New budget authority (gross)	145	10	25
22.10	Resources available from recoveries of prior year obligations	2	1	....
23.90	Total budgetary resources available for obligation	174	34	49
23.95	Total new obligations	–151	–10	–25
24.40	Unobligated balance available, end of year	23	24	24
	New budget authority (gross), detail:			
	Discretionary:			
40.00	Appropriation	145	10	25
	Change in unpaid obligations:			
72.40	Unpaid obligations, start of year: Obligated balance, start of year	45	29	2
73.10	Total new obligations	151	10	25
73.20	Total outlays (gross)	–165	–36	–25
73.45	Adjustments in unexpired accounts	–2	–1	....
74.40	Unpaid obligations, end of year: Obligated balance, end of year	29	2	2
	Outlays (gross), detail:			
86.90	Outlays from new discretionary authority	109	8	19
86.93	Outlays from discretionary balances	56	28	6
87.00	Total outlays (gross)	165	36	25
	Net budget authority and outlays:			
89.00	Budget authority	145	10	25
90.00	Outlays	165	36	25

Counterterrorism Fund.—$25 million is requested for the costs of providing support to counter, investigate, or prosecute domestic or international terrorism.

Telecommunications Carrier Compliance Fund

For payments authorized by section 109 of the Communications Assistance for Law Enforcement Act (47 U.S.C. 1008), [$15,000,000] *$120,000,000*, to remain available until expended. *(Department of Justice Appropriations Act, 2000, as enacted by section 1000(a)(1) of the Consolidated Appropriations Act, 2000 (P.L. 106–113).)*

Program and Financing (in millions of dollars)

Identification code 15–0202–0–1–999		1999 actual	2000 est.	2001 est.
	Obligations by program activity:			
00.02	Direct program: Law enforcement support	17	58	120
09.00	Reimbursable program	3	40	120
10.00	Total new obligations	20	98	240
	Budgetary resources available for obligation:			
21.40	Unobligated balance available, start of year	60	43	....
22.00	New budget authority (gross)	3	55	240
23.90	Total budgetary resources available for obligation	63	98	240
23.95	Total new obligations	–20	–98	–240
24.40	Unobligated balance available, end of year	43	....	....
	New budget authority (gross), detail:			
	Discretionary:			
40.00	Appropriation	....	15	120
	Spending authority from offsetting collections:			
	Offsetting collections (cash):			
68.00	Offsetting collections (cash)	....	40	120
68.00	Offsetting collections (cash)	3	....	....
68.90	Spending authority from offsetting collections (total discretionary)	3	40	120
70.00	Total new budget authority (gross)	3	55	240
	Change in unpaid obligations:			
72.40	Unpaid obligations, start of year: Obligated balance, start of year	1	5	1
73.10	Total new obligations	20	98	240
73.20	Total outlays (gross)	–16	–102	–240
74.40	Unpaid obligations, end of year: Obligated balance, end of year	5	1	....
	Outlays (gross), detail:			
86.90	Outlays from new discretionary authority	3	55	240
86.93	Outlays from discretionary balances	13	47	....
87.00	Total outlays (gross)	16	102	240
	Offsets:			
	Against gross budget authority and outlays:			
88.00	Offsetting collections (cash) from: Federal sources	–3	–40	–120
	Net budget authority and outlays:			
89.00	Budget authority	....	15	120
90.00	Outlays	13	62	120

The Communications Assistance for Law Enforcement Act (CALEA) of 1994 authorizes the Attorney General to reimburse telecommunications carriers for costs associated with modifying digital equipment installed before January 1, 1995, in order that court-authorized wiretaps may be performed.

The Omnibus Consolidated Appropriations Act of 1997 (P.L. 104–208) extended eligibility for reimbursement to telecommunications equipment manufacturers and providers of support services. In addition to direct appropriations to the Fund, Congress authorized Federal agencies with law enforcement and intelligence responsibilities to transfer to the Fund unobligated balances that are available until expended, upon compliance with Congressional notification requirements.

An increase of $105 million in direct appropriations to the Fund is proposed, and will be used to reimburse the telecommunications industry for eligible CALEA activities. An additional $120 million is included in the Department of Defense request in recognition of the contribution of CALEA to national security activities. The Department of Defense

General and special funds—Continued

TELECOMMUNICATIONS CARRIER COMPLIANCE FUND—Continued

will use these funds to reimburse the Department of Justice for payments to the telecommunications industry.

Object Classification (in millions of dollars)

Identification code 15–0202–0–1–999	1999 actual	2000 est.	2001 est.
25.2 Direct obligations: Other services	17	58	120
99.0 Reimbursable obligations: Subtotal, reimbursable obligations	3	40	120
99.9 Total new obligations	20	98	240

ADMINISTRATIVE REVIEW AND APPEALS

For expenses necessary for the administration of pardon and clemency petitions and immigration related activities, [$98,136,000] *$164,549,000*.

[In addition, $50,363,000, for such purposes, to remain available until expended, to be derived from the Violent Crime Reduction Trust Fund.] *(Department of Justice Appropriations Act, 2000, as enacted by section 1000(a)(1) of the Consolidated Appropriations Act, 2000 (P.L. 106–113).)*

Program and Financing (in millions of dollars)

Identification code 15–0339–0–1–751	1999 actual	2000 est.	2001 est.
Obligations by program activity:			
Direct program:			
00.01 Executive Office for Immigration Review (EOIR)	136	147	163
00.02 Office of the Pardon Attorney (OPA)	2	2	2
09.01 Reimbursable program	1	1	1
10.00 Total new obligations	139	150	166
Budgetary resources available for obligation:			
21.40 Unobligated balance available, start of year	3	5	4
22.00 New budget authority (gross)	139	149	166
22.10 Resources available from recoveries of prior year obligations	2		
23.90 Total budgetary resources available for obligation	144	154	170
23.95 Total new obligations	−139	−150	−166
23.98 Unobligated balance expiring or withdrawn	−1		
24.40 Unobligated balance available, end of year	5	4	3
New budget authority (gross), detail:			
Discretionary:			
40.00 Appropriation	75	98	165
42.00 Transferred from other accounts	63	50	
43.00 Appropriation (total discretionary)	138	148	165
68.00 Spending authority from offsetting collections: Offsetting collections (cash)	1	1	1
70.00 Total new budget authority (gross)	139	149	166
Change in unpaid obligations:			
72.40 Unpaid obligations, start of year: Obligated balance, start of year	19	12	19
73.10 Total new obligations	139	150	166
73.20 Total outlays (gross)	−137	−143	−171
73.40 Adjustments in expired accounts (net)	−7		
73.45 Adjustments in unexpired accounts	−2		
74.40 Unpaid obligations, end of year: Obligated balance, end of year	12	19	14
Outlays (gross), detail:			
86.90 Outlays from new discretionary authority	128	126	150
86.93 Outlays from discretionary balances	9	17	21
87.00 Total outlays (gross)	137	143	171
Offsets:			
Against gross budget authority and outlays:			
88.00 Offsetting collections (cash) from: Federal sources	−1	−1	−1
Net budget authority and outlays:			
89.00 Budget authority	138	148	165
90.00 Outlays	137	142	170
Distribution of budget authority by account:			
Salaries and expenses	79	98	165
Violent crime reduction programs, Administrative review and appeals	59	50	0
Distribution of outlays by account:			
Salaries and expenses	70	87	160
Violent crime reduction programs, Administrative review and appeals	67	55	10

This program includes the Office of the Pardon Attorney (OPA) and the Executive Office for Immigration Review (EOIR). The Pardon Attorney receives and reviews all petitions for clemency, i.e., commutation of sentences and pardons. The Executive Office for Immigration Review contains the Immigration Judge function, the Board of Immigration Appeals, the Office of the Chief Administrative Hearing Officer, and the Office of Management and Administration. EOIR was established January 1, 1983, to improve the immigration hearing and appeal process.

Additional funding of $5.0 million is proposed to provide adjudicative support for INS' enforcement activities. This coordination involves hiring additional Immigration Judges, attorneys, and support staff who will allow EOIR to maintain current performance levels. Workload for the activity follows:

PARDON ATTORNEY WORKLOAD

	1999 actual	*2000 est.*	*2001 est.*
Cases:			
Petitions pending, beginning of year	1,512	1,872	1,750
Petitions received	1,009	1,300	1,300
Correspondence processed	6,719	7,000	7,000

EXECUTIVE OFFICE FOR IMMIGRATION REVIEW WORKLOAD

	1999 actual	*2000 est.*	*2001 est.*
Immigration cases, appeals, and related adjudications, pending beginning of year	154,918	151,971	151,971
Received	266,155	280,000	290,000
Completed	269,102	280,000	290,000
Pending, end of year	151,971	151,971	151,971

Object Classification (in millions of dollars)

Identification code 15–0339–0–1–751	1999 actual	2000 est.	2001 est.
Direct obligations:			
Personnel compensation:			
11.1 Full-time permanent	65	67	70
11.3 Other than full-time permanent	4	4	4
11.9 Total personnel compensation	69	71	74
12.1 Civilian personnel benefits	16	16	18
21.0 Travel and transportation of persons	3	3	3
23.3 Communications, utilities, and miscellaneous charges	6	6	6
24.0 Printing and reproduction	1	1	1
25.2 Other services	21	29	39
25.3 Rental payments to GSA	16	17	18
26.0 Supplies and materials	3	3	3
31.0 Equipment	3	3	3
99.0 Subtotal, direct obligations	138	149	165
99.0 Reimbursable obligations	1	1	1
99.9 Total new obligations	139	150	166

Personnel Summary

Identification code 15–0339–0–1–751	1999 actual	2000 est.	2001 est.
1001 Total compensable workyears: Full-time equivalent employment	1,090	1,138	1,162

DETENTION TRUSTEE

For necessary expenses to establish a Federal Detention Trustee who shall exercise all power and functions authorized by law relating to the detention of Federal prisoners in non-federal institutions or *otherwise in the custody of the United States Marshals Service; and the detention of aliens in the custody of the Immigration and Naturalization Service. The Trustee shall be responsible for (1) construction of detention facilities or for housing related to such detention; (2) the management of funds appropriated to the Department for the exercise of any detention functions; and (3) the direction of the United States Marshals Service and Immigration and Naturalization Service with respect to the exercise of detention policy setting and operations for the Department, $26,000,000; of which not to exceed $25,000,000 is made available until expended to fund or reimburse other entities for the costs associated with the care, maintenance, detention, and repatriation of illegal aliens held outside the continental United States.*

Program and Financing (in millions of dollars)

Identification code 15–0136–0–1–753	1999 actual	2000 est.	2001 est.
Obligations by program activity:			
10.00 Total new obligations (object class 25.2)			26
Budgetary resources available for obligation:			
22.00 New budget authority (gross)			26
23.95 Total new obligations			−26
New budget authority (gross), detail:			
Discretionary:			
40.00 Appropriation			26
Change in unpaid obligations:			
73.10 Total new obligations			26
73.20 Total outlays (gross)			−26
Outlays (gross), detail:			
86.90 Outlays from new discretionary authority			26
Net budget authority and outlays:			
89.00 Budget authority			26
90.00 Outlays			26

The Detention Trustee will report to the Deputy Attorney General and be responsible for managing Department detention resource allocations, exercising financial performance overseeing of detention operations, and ensuring the implementation of efficiency and effectiveness improvements in Department detention operations.

Office of Inspector General

For necessary expenses of the Office of Inspector General in carrying out the provisions of the Inspector General Act of 1978, as amended, [$40,275,000] *$42,192,000*; including not to exceed $10,000 to meet unforeseen emergencies of a confidential character, to be expended under the direction of, and to be accounted for solely under the certificate of, the Attorney General; and for the acquisition, lease, maintenance, and operation of motor vehicles, without regard to the general purchase price limitation for the current fiscal year[: *Provided*, That not less than $40,000 shall be transferred to and administered by the Department of Justice Wireless Management Office for the costs of conversion to narrowband communications and for the operations and maintenance of legacy Land Mobile Radio systems]. *(Department of Justice Appropriations Act, 2000, as enacted by section 1000(a)(1) of the Consolidated Appropriations Act, 2000 (P.L. 106–113).)*

Program and Financing (in millions of dollars)

Identification code 15–0328–0–1–751	1999 actual	2000 est.	2001 est.
Obligations by program activity:			
00.01 Direct program	37	40	42
09.01 Reimbursable program	21	11	11
10.00 Total new obligations	58	51	53
Budgetary resources available for obligation:			
21.40 Unobligated balance available, start of year		1	1
22.00 New budget authority (gross)	58	51	53
23.90 Total budgetary resources available for obligation	58	52	54
23.95 Total new obligations	−58	−51	−53
24.40 Unobligated balance available, end of year	1	1	2
New budget authority (gross), detail:			
Discretionary:			
40.00 Appropriation	34	40	42
42.00 Transferred from other accounts	3		
43.00 Appropriation (total discretionary)	37	40	42
68.00 Spending authority from offsetting collections: Offsetting collections (cash)	21	11	11
70.00 Total new budget authority (gross)	58	51	53
Change in unpaid obligations:			
72.40 Unpaid obligations, start of year: Obligated balance, start of year	4	4	3
73.10 Total new obligations	58	51	53
73.20 Total outlays (gross)	−58	−51	−53
74.40 Unpaid obligations, end of year: Obligated balance, end of year	4	3	3
Outlays (gross), detail:			
86.90 Outlays from new discretionary authority	55	49	50
86.93 Outlays from discretionary balances	3	2	3
87.00 Total outlays (gross)	58	51	53
Offsets:			
Against gross budget authority and outlays:			
88.00 Offsetting collections (cash) from: Federal sources	−21	−11	−11
Net budget authority and outlays:			
89.00 Budget authority	37	40	42
90.00 Outlays	37	40	42

The Office of the Inspector General (OIG) was statutorily established in the Department of Justice on April 14, 1989. The OIG investigates alleged violations of criminal and civil laws, regulations, and ethical standards arising from the conduct of the Department's employees. The OIG provides leadership and assists management in promoting integrity, economy, efficiency, and effectiveness within the Department and in its financial, contractual, and grant relationships with others. Also by statute, the OIG reports to the Attorney General, Congress, and the public on a semiannual basis regarding its significant activities.

The Audit function is responsible for independent audits and reviews of Department organizations, programs, functions, computer security and information technology systems, and financial statement audits. The Audit function also conducts or reviews external audits of expenditures made under Department contracts, grants, and other agreements.

The Investigations function investigates allegations of civil rights violations, bribery, fraud, abuse and violations of other laws, rules and procedures that govern Department employees, contractors, and grantees. This function also develops these cases for criminal prosecution, civil action, or administrative action. In some instances the OIG refers allegations to components within the Department and requests notification of their findings and of any disciplinary action taken.

The Inspections function conducts analyses and makes recommendations to decision makers for improvements in Department programs, policies, and procedures. In addition, this function also conducts shorter and more time-sensitive reviews and evaluations to provide managers with early warnings about possible program deficiencies.

The Special Investigations function investigates allegations of significant interest to the American public and Congress and of vital importance to the Department.

The Executive Direction and Control function provides program direction for the OIG. Responsibilities include policy development, legal counsel, Congressional affairs, planning, budget, finance, personnel, procurement, automated data processing, and general support services.

General and special funds—Continued

OFFICE OF INSPECTOR GENERAL—Continued

Object Classification (in millions of dollars)

Identification code 15–0328–0–1–751		1999 actual	2000 est.	2001 est.
	Direct obligations:			
	Personnel compensation:			
11.1	Full-time permanent	21	24	25
11.5	Other personnel compensation	2	2	2
11.9	Total personnel compensation	23	26	27
12.1	Civilian personnel benefits	6	6	6
21.0	Travel and transportation of persons	2	2	2
23.3	Communications, utilities, and miscellaneous charges	1	1	1
25.2	Other services	1	1	2
25.3	Rental payments to GSA	3	4	4
31.0	Equipment	1		
99.0	Subtotal, direct obligations	37	40	42
99.0	Reimbursable obligations	21	11	11
99.9	Total new obligations	58	51	53

Personnel Summary

Identification code 15–0328–0–1–751		1999 actual	2000 est.	2001 est.
	Direct:			
1001	Total compensable workyears: Full-time equivalent employment	319	328	328
	Reimbursable:			
2001	Total compensable workyears: Full-time equivalent employment	122	52	52

Intragovernmental funds:

WORKING CAPITAL FUND

Program and Financing (in millions of dollars)

Identification code 15–4526–0–4–751		1999 actual	2000 est.	2001 est.
	Obligations by program activity:			
09.01	Financial and employee data	55	49	41
09.01	Telecommunications	130	127	130
09.01	Data Processing	130	116	119
09.01	Publication services	5	5	5
09.01	Space management	281	299	305
09.01	Property management	1	1	1
09.01	Justice building services	15	6	6
09.01	Library acquisition services	11	12	12
09.01	Personnel services	5	5	5
09.01	Debt collection management	43	47	46
09.01	Mail services	11	13	13
09.01	Asset forfeiture management staff	1	1	1
09.01	Capital Investment	309	59	
10.00	Total new obligations	997	740	684
	Budgetary resources available for obligation:			
21.40	Unobligated balance available, start of year	382	116	61
22.00	New budget authority (gross)	708	672	652
22.10	Resources available from recoveries of prior year obligations	24	12	12
23.90	Total budgetary resources available for obligation	1,114	800	725
23.95	Total new obligations	−997	−740	−684
24.40	Unobligated balance available, end of year	116	61	41
	New budget authority (gross), detail:			
	Discretionary:			
40.00	Appropriation			
40.36	Unobligated balance rescinded	−99		
40.75	Reduction pursuant to P.L. 106–51	−8		
42.00	Transferred from other accounts	155		
43.00	Appropriation (total discretionary)	48		
	Mandatory:			
69.00	Offsetting collections (cash)	660	672	652
70.00	Total new budget authority (gross)	708	672	652
	Change in unpaid obligations:			
72.40	Unpaid obligations, start of year: Obligated balance, start of year	193	351	407
73.10	Total new obligations	997	740	684
73.20	Total outlays (gross)	−815	−672	−652
73.45	Adjustments in unexpired accounts	−24	−12	−12
74.40	Unpaid obligations, end of year: Obligated balance, end of year	351	407	427
	Outlays (gross), detail:			
86.97	Outlays from new mandatory authority	660	672	652
86.98	Outlays from mandatory balances	155		
87.00	Total outlays (gross)	815	672	652
	Offsets:			
	Against gross budget authority and outlays:			
88.00	Offsetting collections (cash) from: Federal sources	−660	−672	−652
	Net budget authority and outlays:			
89.00	Budget authority	48		
90.00	Outlays	156		

The Working Capital Fund finances, on a reimbursable basis, those administrative services that can be performed more efficiently at the Department level.

Object Classification (in millions of dollars)

Identification code 15–4526–0–4–751		1999 actual	2000 est.	2001 est.
	Personnel compensation:			
11.1	Full-time permanent	37	43	44
11.5	Other personnel compensation	1	1	1
11.9	Total personnel compensation	38	44	45
12.1	Civilian personnel benefits	8	9	9
21.0	Travel and transportation of persons	1	2	2
22.0	Transportation of things	10	11	11
23.1	Rental payments to GSA	264	281	287
23.2	Rental payments to others	13	5	5
25.2	Other services	164	238	171
	Purchases of goods and services from Government accounts:			
25.3	Rental payments to GSA for WCF only	8	9	9
25.3	Purchases of goods and services from Government accounts	452	114	117
26.0	Supplies and materials	14	14	15
31.0	Equipment	25	13	13
99.9	Total new obligations	997	740	684

Personnel Summary

Identification code 15–4526–0–4–751		1999 actual	2000 est.	2001 est.
2001	Total compensable workyears: Full-time equivalent employment	631	723	723

UNITED STATES PAROLE COMMISSION

Federal Funds

General and special funds:

SALARIES AND EXPENSES

For necessary expenses of the United States Parole Commission as authorized by law, [$8,527,000] *$9,183,000. (Department of Justice Appropriations Act, 2000, as enacted by section 1000(a)(1) of the Consolidated Appropriations Act, 2000 (P.L. 106–113).)*

Program and Financing (in millions of dollars)

Identification code 15–1061–0–1–751		1999 actual	2000 est.	2001 est.
	Obligations by program activity:			
00.01	Direct program	7	9	9
10.00	Total new obligations	7	9	9
	Budgetary resources available for obligation:			
22.00	New budget authority (gross)	7	9	9

23.95	Total new obligations	−7	−9	−9
	New budget authority (gross), detail:			
	Discretionary:			
40.00	Appropriation	7	9	9
41.00	Transferred to other accounts	−1		
43.00	Appropriation (total discretionary)	6	9	9
50.00	Reappropriation	1		
70.00	Total new budget authority (gross)	7	9	9
	Change in unpaid obligations:			
72.40	Unpaid obligations, start of year: Obligated balance, start of year	1	1	1
73.10	Total new obligations	7	9	9
73.20	Total outlays (gross)	−7	−8	−8
74.40	Unpaid obligations, end of year: Obligated balance, end of year	1	1	1
	Outlays (gross), detail:			
86.90	Outlays from new discretionary authority	6	8	8
86.93	Outlays from discretionary balances	1		1
87.00	Total outlays (gross)	7	8	8
	Net budget authority and outlays:			
89.00	Budget authority	7	9	9
90.00	Outlays	7	8	8

The United States Parole Commission makes decisions to grant or deny parole to Federal and D.C. Code prisoners serving sentences of one year and a day or more, sets conditions of parole, supervises parolees and mandatory releasees, recommits parolees in the event of violations of the conditions of supervision, and determines the termination of supervision in accordance with the Parole Commission and Reorganization Act of 1976.

In addition, the Commission seeks to improve the rehabilitation process by monitoring an effective parole supervision program through U.S. probation officers and through research studies that evaluate the effectiveness of parole programs. During 1998, the U.S. Parole Commission assumed responsibility for parole hearings and actions on District of Columbia prisoners under the National Capital Revitalization and Self-Government Improvement Act (P.L. 105–33).

WORKLOAD

	1999 actual	*2000 est.*	*2001 est.*
Hearings:			
Initial	1,225	2,254	2,344
Record review	1,708	1,759	1,829
Rescission	139	154	160
Local revocation	185	283	294
Institutional revocation	485	896	2,439
Expedited revocation	404	394	410
Other	56	73	76
Statutory review	455	1,747	1,817
Termination	70	120	140
Appeal decisions:			
National	588	606	630
Administrative review	3	3	3
Original jurisdiction decisions and appeals	12	35	44

Object Classification (in millions of dollars)

Identification code 15–1061–0–1–751		1999 actual	2000 est.	2001 est.
11.1	Personnel compensation: Full-time permanent	4	5	5
12.1	Civilian personnel benefits	1	1	1
25.2	Other services	1	2	2
25.3	Rental payments to GSA	1	1	1
99.9	Total new obligations	7	9	9

Personnel Summary

Identification code 15–1061–0–1–751		1999 actual	2000 est.	2001 est.
1001	Total compensable workyears: Full-time equivalent employment	73	86	92

LEGAL ACTIVITIES AND U.S. MARSHALS

Federal Funds

General and special funds:

Salaries and Expenses, General Legal Activities

For expenses necessary for the legal activities of the Department of Justice, not otherwise provided for, including not to exceed $20,000 for expenses of collecting evidence, to be expended under the direction of, and to be accounted for solely under the certificate of, the Attorney General; and rent of private or Government-owned space in the District of Columbia, [$357,016,000] *$552,239,000*; of which not to exceed $10,000,000 for litigation support contracts shall remain available until expended: *Provided*, That of the funds available in this appropriation, not to exceed [$36,666,000] *$18,877,000* shall remain available until expended for office automation systems for the legal divisions covered by this appropriation, and for the United States Attorneys, the Antitrust Division, *the United States Trustee Program, the Executive Office for Immigration Review, the Community Relations Service,* and offices funded through "Salaries and Expenses", General Administration: [*Provided further*, That of the amount appropriated under this heading $582,000 shall be transferred to, and merged with, funds available to the Presidential Advisory Commission on Holocaust Assets in the United States and shall be made available for the same purposes for which such funds are available:] *Provided further*, That of the total amount appropriated, not to exceed $1,000 shall be available to the United States National Central Bureau, INTERPOL, for official reception and representation expenses.

[In addition, $147,929,000, to be derived from the Violent Crime Reduction Trust Fund, to remain available until expended for such purposes.]

In addition, for reimbursement of expenses of the Department of Justice associated with processing cases under the National Childhood Vaccine Injury Act of 1986, as amended, not to exceed $4,028,000, to be appropriated from the Vaccine Injury Compensation Trust Fund. *(Department of Justice Appropriations Act, 2000, as enacted by section 1000(a)(1) of the Consolidated Appropriations Act, 2000 (P.L. 106–113).)*

Program and Financing (in millions of dollars)

Identification code 15–0128–0–1–752		1999 actual	2000 est.	2001 est.
	Obligations by program activity:			
	Direct program:			
00.01	Conduct of Supreme Court proceedings and review of appellate	7	7	7
00.02	General tax matters	66	69	73
00.03	Criminal matters	103	108	114
00.04	Claims, customs, and general civil matters	140	154	157
00.05	Land, natural resources, and Indian matters	63	69	71
00.06	Legal opinions	5	5	5
00.07	Civil rights matters	75	84	98
00.08	Interpol	8	7	7
00.09	Legal activities office automation	13	26	19
00.10	Dispute resolution			1
09.00	Reimbursable program	232	234	231
10.00	Total new obligations	712	763	783
	Budgetary resources available for obligation:			
21.40	Unobligated balance available, start of year	6	21	
22.00	New budget authority (gross)	724	738	783
22.10	Net transfers prior year balance	9	4	
23.90	Total budgetary resources available for obligation	739	763	783
23.95	Total new obligations	−712	−763	−783
23.98	Unobligated balance expiring or withdrawn	−5		
24.40	Unobligated balance available, end of year	21		
	New budget authority (gross), detail:			
	Discretionary:			
40.00	Appropriation	467	357	552
41.00	Transferred to other accounts		−1	
42.00	Transferred from other accounts	25	148	
43.00	Appropriation (total discretionary)	492	504	552
68.00	Spending authority from offsetting collections: Offsetting collections (cash)	232	234	231
70.00	Total new budget authority (gross)	724	738	783

General and special funds—Continued

SALARIES AND EXPENSES, GENERAL LEGAL ACTIVITIES—Continued

Program and Financing (in millions of dollars)—Continued

Identification code 15–0128–0–1–752	1999 actual	2000 est.	2001 est.
Change in unpaid obligations:			
72.40 Unpaid obligations, start of year: Obligated balance, start of year	38	26	65
73.10 Total new obligations	712	763	783
73.20 Total outlays (gross)	−710	−720	−776
73.40 Adjustments in expired accounts (net)	−5		
73.45 Adjustments in unexpired accounts	−9	−4	
74.40 Unpaid obligations, end of year: Obligated balance, end of year	26	65	72
Outlays (gross), detail:			
86.90 Outlays from new discretionary authority	673	673	711
86.93 Outlays from discretionary balances	36	47	65
87.00 Total outlays (gross)	710	720	776
Offsets:			
Against gross budget authority and outlays:			
Offsetting collections (cash) from:			
Federal sources:			
88.00 Federal sources	−228	−230	−227
88.00 Federal funds (Drug enforcement)	−4	−4	−4
88.90 Total, offsetting collections (cash)	−232	−234	−231
Net budget authority and outlays:			
89.00 Budget authority	492	504	552
90.00 Outlays	478	486	545
Distribution of budget authority by account:			
Salaries and expenses	484	356	552
Violent crime reduction programs, General Legal Activities	8	148	
Distribution of outlays by account:			
Salaries and expenses	469	355	524
Violent crime reduction programs, General Legal Activities	9	131	21

The following legal activities of the Department are financed from this appropriation:

Conduct of Supreme Court proceedings and review of appellate matters.—Through this program, the Solicitor General supervises and processes all appellate matters and represents the Government before the U.S. Supreme Court.

WORKLOAD

	1999 actual	2000 est.	2001 est.
Cases:			
Pending, beginning of term	281	378	392
Received	3,064	3,070	3,076
Terminated	2,967	3,056	3,148
Pending, end of term	378	392	320
Other activities:			
Appellate determinations	864	866	868
Certiorari determinations	629	630	632
Miscellaneous recommendations	732	733	735
Oral arguments participation	61	56	62

General tax matters.—This program is the prosecution and defense of cases arising under the internal revenue laws and other related statutes.

WORKLOAD

	1999 actual	2000 est.	2001 est.
Cases: [1]			
Pending, beginning of year	20,622	14,044	14,563
Received	6,433	8,250	8,700
Terminated	13,011	7,731	8,113
Pending, end of year	14,044	14,563	15,150

[1] 1999 data includes 4,445 cases that were terminated as a result of data review.

Criminal matters.—This program is the enforcement of all Federal criminal statutes except for statutes dealing specifically with tax, antitrust, environmental, and civil rights matters.

WORKLOAD [1]

	1999 actual	2000 est.	2001 est.
Cases:			
Pending, beginning of year	440	463	500
Received	559	588	620
Terminated	536	551	565
Pending, end of year	463	500	555
Matters:			
Pending, beginning of year	10,248	11,563	12,797
Received	5,267	5,827	6,483
Terminated	3,952	4,593	5,068
Pending, end of year	11,563	12,797	14,212

[1] Includes direct operational authority only.

Claims, customs, and general civil matters.—This program asserts the Government's interest in civil litigation involving billions of dollars in monetary claims as well as a wide range of programs.

WORKLOAD [1]

	1999 actual	2000 est.	2001 est.
Cases:			
Pending, beginning of year	19,158	21,992	24,037
Received	9,006	9,081	9,141
Terminated	6,172	7,036	9,784
Pending, end of year	21,992	24,037	23,394
Major cases receiving Automated Litigation Support (ALS) support	12	9	12
ALS funds (in millions)	$7.2	$5.1	$8.3

[1] Excludes delegated and supervised cases.

Environment and natural resource matters.—The Environment and Natural Resources Division enforces the Nation's civil and criminal environmental laws and defends environmental challenges to Government action. Additionally, the Division represents the United States in virtually all matters concerning the use and development of the Nation's natural resources and public lands, wildlife protection, Indian rights and claims, and the acquisition of Federal property.

WORKLOAD

	1999 actual	2000 est.	2001 est.
Cases and tracts:			
Pending, beginning of year	11,521	10,975	11,575
Received	3,203	3,400	3,500
Terminated	3,749	2,800	3,000
Pending, end of year	10,975	11,575	12,075
Matters:			
Pending, beginning of year	1,156	1,336	1,330
Received	1,696	1,978	2,560
Terminated	1,516	1,984	2,520
Pending, end of year	1,336	1,330	1,370

Legal opinions.—This program is the preparation of legal opinions for the President and Executive agencies and the review of proposed Executive Orders and proclamations for form and legality.

WORKLOAD

	1999 actual	2000 est.	2001 est.
Executive orders and proclamations	120	126	128
Opinions	1,302	1,305	1,310
Intradepartmental opinions	2,997	2,998	3,001
Special assignments	2,320	2,335	2,340

Civil rights matters.—This program is the enforcement of the Nation's civil rights laws.

WORKLOAD

	1999 actual	2000 est.	2001 est.
Cases:			
Pending, beginning of year	909	948	1,014
Filed	342	378	475
Terminated	303	312	379
Pending, end of year	948	1,014	1,110
Matters:			
Pending, beginning of year	8,070	8,525	8,812
Received	5,320	5,459	5,709
Terminated	4,865	5,172	6,310
Pending, end of year	8,525	8,812	8,211

INTERPOL (U.S. National Central Bureau).—This program is the United States liaison, on behalf of the Attorney General, to the International Criminal Police Organization. The program facilitates international law enforcement cooperation.

WORKLOAD

	1999 actual	2000 est.	2001 est.
Investigative matters received (IMRS)	44,300	48,700	53,600

Investigative matters opened (IMRS)	39,500	43,500	47,900
Cases opened	18,100	20,000	22,000
Cases reported	24,419	26,900	29,600
Cases closed	14,670	16,200	17,800
Red notices	1,083	1,200	1,350

Legal activities office automation.—This program is the central fund for the development and acquisition of office automation systems for the various legal divisions, the U.S. Attorneys' offices, and the Department's management offices. An additional $50,000,000 for JCON deployment is anticipated to be available from the Working Capital Fund's unobligated balance.

Dispute Resolution.—This program coordinates the Department's use of Alternative Dispute Resolution (ADR), develops ADR policy, conducts ADR training, advises Department personnel on the use of ADR, and evaluates the effectiveness of ADR programs. The office also coordinates the Federal Interagency ADR Working Group, an organization chaired by the Attorney General and created by the President to promote the use of ADR throughout the Federal Government.

Reimbursable program.—This reflects reimbursable funding for the following:

Civil Division—for processing claims under the Radiation Exposure Compensation Act, for litigating cases under the National Childhood Vaccine Injury Act, and for defending claims arising from the enactment and implementation of FIRREA;

Criminal Division—for detailing of staff to provide assistance to other agencies and for other miscellaneous purposes;

Environment Division—from client agencies for litigation support services and from the Environmental Protection Agency for Superfund litigation; and,

Civil Rights Division—for activities related to the Department's Equal Employment Opportunity Program, providing services to client agencies for litigation support and geographic information related requests, and for detailing staff to provide various types of assistance to other DOJ components and agencies.

Object Classification (in millions of dollars)

Identification code 15–0128–0–1–752		1999 actual	2000 est.	2001 est.
	Direct obligations:			
	Personnel compensation:			
11.1	Full-time permanent	227	253	276
11.3	Other than full-time permanent	20	18	18
11.5	Other personnel compensation	3	3	3
11.8	Special personal services payments	4	3	3
11.9	Total personnel compensation	254	277	300
12.1	Civilian personnel benefits	53	60	68
21.0	Travel and transportation of persons	14	16	16
22.0	Transportation of things	2	3	3
23.1	Rental payments to GSA	48	51	54
23.2	Rental payments to others	2	1	1
23.3	Communications, utilities, and miscellaneous charges	8	10	11
24.0	Printing and reproduction	3	3	3
25.1	Advisory and assistance services	53	5	7
25.2	Other services	10	66	55
25.3	Purchases of goods and services from Government accounts	17	10	9
25.4	Operation and maintenance of facilities	1		
25.7	Operation and maintenance of equipment	1	1	2
26.0	Supplies and materials	5	7	7
31.0	Equipment	8	18	15
41.0	Grants, subsidies, and contributions	1	1	1
99.0	Subtotal, direct obligations	480	529	552
99.0	Reimbursable obligations	232	234	231
99.9	Total new obligations	712	763	783

Personnel Summary

Identification code 15–0128–0–1–752		1999 actual	2000 est.	2001 est.
	Direct:			
1001	Total compensable workyears: Full-time equivalent employment	3,499	3,688	3,822
	Reimbursable:			
2001	Total compensable workyears: Full-time equivalent employment	365	396	374

Salaries and Expenses, Antitrust Division

For expenses necessary for the enforcement of antitrust and kindred laws, **[**$81,850,000**]** *$104,966,000*: *Provided*, That, notwithstanding section 3302(b) of title 31, United States Code, not to exceed **[**$81,850,000**]** *$104,966,000* of offsetting collections derived from fees collected in fiscal year **[**2000**]** *2001* for premerger notification filings under the Hart-Scott-Rodino Antitrust Improvements Act of 1976 (15 U.S.C. 18a) shall be retained and used for necessary expenses in this appropriation, and shall remain available until expended: *Provided further*, That the sum herein appropriated from the general fund shall be reduced as such offsetting collections are received during fiscal year **[**2000**]** *2001*, so as to result in a final fiscal year **[**2000**]** *2001* appropriation from the general fund estimated at not more than $0: *Provided further, That fees collected in excess of $104,966,000 in fiscal year 2001 cannot be made available in fiscal year 2001 through a reprogramming pursuant to section 605 of this Act. (Department of Justice Appropriations Act, 2000, as enacted by section 1000(a)(1) of the Consolidated Appropriations Act, 2000 (P.L. 106–113).)*

Unavailable Collections (in millions of dollars)

Identification code 15–0319–0–1–752		1999 actual	2000 est.	2001 est.
	Balance, start of year:			
01.99	Balance, start of year	31	27	29
03.00	Offsetting collections	27	29	60
04.00	Total: Balances and collections	58	56	89
	Appropriation:			
05.01	Salaries and expenses, Antitrust Division	−31	−27	−29
07.99	Total balance, end of year	27	29	60

Program and Financing (in millions of dollars)

Identification code 15–0319–0–1–752		1999 actual	2000 est.	2001 est.
	Obligations by program activity:			
10.00	Total new obligations	102	110	134
	Budgetary resources available for obligation:			
21.40	Unobligated balance available, start of year	22	22	21
22.00	New budget authority (gross)	102	109	134
23.90	Total budgetary resources available for obligation	124	131	155
23.95	Total new obligations	−102	−110	−134
24.40	Unobligated balance available, end of year	22	21	21
	New budget authority (gross), detail:			
	Spending authority from offsetting collections:			
	Discretionary:			
68.00	Offsetting collections (cash)	98	111	165
68.26	Offsetting collections (unavailable balances)	31	27	29
68.45	Portion not available for obligation (limitation on obligations)	−27	−29	−60
68.90	Spending authority from offsetting collections (total discretionary)	102	109	134
	Change in unpaid obligations:			
72.40	Unpaid obligations, start of year: Obligated balance, start of year	−16	−13	8
73.10	Total new obligations	102	110	134
73.20	Total outlays (gross)	−99	−89	−121
74.40	Unpaid obligations, end of year: Obligated balance, end of year	−13	8	21
	Outlays (gross), detail:			
86.90	Outlays from new discretionary authority	97	89	110

General and special funds—Continued

SALARIES AND EXPENSES, ANTITRUST DIVISION—Continued

Program and Financing (in millions of dollars)—Continued

Identification code 15–0319–0–1–752		1999 actual	2000 est.	2001 est.
86.93	Outlays from discretionary balances	2	....	11
87.00	Total outlays (gross)	99	89	121
	Offsets:			
	Against gross budget authority and outlays:			
	Offsetting collections (cash) from:			
88.00	Federal sources	–1	....	....
88.40	Non-Federal sources	–97	–111	–165
88.90	Total, offsetting collections (cash)	–98	–111	–165
	Net budget authority and outlays:			
89.00	Budget authority	4	–2	–31
90.00	Outlays	1	–22	–44

The Antitrust Division administers and enforces antitrust and related statutes. This program primarily involves the investigation of suspected violations of the antitrust laws, the conduct of civil and criminal proceedings in the Federal courts, and the maintenance of competitive conditions.

In 2001, the Antitrust Division will continue to collect filing fees for pre-merger notifications and will retain these fees for expenditure in support of its programs.

WORKLOAD

Cases and investigations:	*1999 actual*	*2000 est.*	*2001 est.*
Pending, beginning of year	410	411	412
Filed and instituted	394	414	434
Terminated	393	413	433
Pending, end of year	411	412	413
Miscellaneous proceedings	4,419	4,640	4,872

Object Classification (in millions of dollars)

Identification code 15–0319–0–1–752		1999 actual	2000 est.	2001 est.
99.0	Reimbursable obligations: Subtotal, reimbursable obligations	102	110	134
99.9	Total new obligations	102	110	134

Personnel Summary

Identification code 15–0319–0–1–752		1999 actual	2000 est.	2001 est.
2001	Total compensable workyears: Full-time equivalent employment	804	811	945

SALARIES AND EXPENSES, UNITED STATES ATTORNEYS

For necessary expenses of the Offices of the United States Attorneys, including inter-governmental and cooperative agreements, [$1,161,957,000] *$1,291,001,000*; of which not to exceed $2,500,000 shall be available until September 30, [2001] *2002*, for: (1) training personnel in debt collection; (2) locating debtors and their property; (3) paying the net costs of selling property; and (4) tracking debts owed to the United States Government: *Provided*, That of the total amount appropriated, not to exceed $8,000 shall be available for official reception and representation expenses: *Provided further*, That not to exceed $10,000,000 of those funds available for automated litigation support contracts shall remain available until expended: *Provided further*, That not to exceed $2,500,000 for the operation of the National Advocacy Center shall remain available until expended[: *Provided further*, That not to exceed $1,000,000 shall remain available until expended for the expansion of existing Violent Crime Task Forces in United States Attorneys Offices into demonstration projects, including inter-governmental, inter-local, cooperative, and task-force agreements, however denominated, and contracts with State and local prosecutorial and law enforcement agencies engaged in the investigation and prosecution of violent crimes: *Provided further*, That, in addition to reimbursable full-time equivalent workyears available to the Offices of the United States Attorneys, not to exceed 9,120 positions and 9,398 full-time equivalent workyears shall be supported from the funds appropriated in this Act for the United States Attorneys]. *(Department of Justice Appropriations Act, 2000, as enacted by section 1000(a)(1) of the Consolidated Appropriations Act, 2000 (P.L. 106–113).)*

Program and Financing (in millions of dollars)

Identification code 15–0322–0–1–752		1999 actual	2000 est.	2001 est.
	Obligations by program activity:			
	Direct program:			
00.01	U.S. attorneys	1,044	1,190	1,291
00.02	VCRP	94	....	....
09.00	Reimbursable program	119	129	133
10.00	Total new obligations	1,257	1,319	1,424
	Budgetary resources available for obligation:			
21.40	Unobligated balance available, start of year	8	27	4
22.00	New budget authority (gross)	1,256	1,296	1,424
22.10	Resources available from recoveries of prior year obligations	28	....	....
23.90	Total budgetary resources available for obligation	1,292	1,323	1,428
23.95	Total new obligations	–1,257	–1,319	–1,424
23.98	Unobligated balance expiring or withdrawn	–8	....	....
24.40	Unobligated balance available, end of year	27	4	4
	New budget authority (gross), detail:			
	Discretionary:			
40.00	Appropriation	1,009	1,162	1,291
41.00	Transferred to other accounts	–3	....	....
42.00	Transferred from other accounts	128	5	....
43.00	Appropriation (total discretionary)	1,134	1,167	1,291
50.00	Reappropriation	3	....	....
68.00	Spending authority from offsetting collections: Offsetting collections (cash)	119	129	133
70.00	Total new budget authority (gross)	1,256	1,296	1,424
	Change in unpaid obligations:			
72.40	Unpaid obligations, start of year: Obligated balance, start of year	88	130	161
73.10	Total new obligations	1,257	1,319	1,424
73.20	Total outlays (gross)	–1,188	–1,288	–1,376
73.45	Adjustments in unexpired accounts	–28	....	....
74.40	Unpaid obligations, end of year: Obligated balance, end of year	130	161	209
	Outlays (gross), detail:			
86.90	Outlays from new discretionary authority	1,124	1,156	1,269
86.93	Outlays from discretionary balances	64	132	107
87.00	Total outlays (gross)	1,188	1,288	1,376
	Offsets:			
	Against gross budget authority and outlays:			
	Offsetting collections (cash) from:			
	Federal sources:			
88.00	Federal sources	–39	–46	–46
88.00	Drug enforcement	–80	–83	–87
88.90	Total, offsetting collections (cash)	–119	–129	–133
	Net budget authority and outlays:			
89.00	Budget authority	1,137	1,167	1,291
90.00	Outlays	1,069	1,159	1,243

	1999 actual	2000 est.	2001 est.
Distribution of budget authority by account:			
Salaries and expenses	1,056	1,167	1,291
Violent crime reduction programs, U.S. Attorneys	81	....	....
Distribution of outlays by account:			
Salaries and expenses	995	1,152	1,241
Violent crime reduction programs, U.S. Attorneys	74	7	2

The Government is represented in each of the 94 judicial districts by a U.S. Attorney. The U.S. Attorneys prosecute criminal offenses against the United States, represent the Government in civil actions in which the United States is concerned, and initiate proceedings for the collection of fines, penalties, and forfeitures owed to the United States.

For 2001, resources are requested to enhance the Administration's efforts on firearms prosecutions, to prosecute violent crime in Indian country, to increase prosecutions of computer crime or those involved with the theft of Intellectual property, to defend the United States against suits, to prosecute those who engage in child exploitation and pornography, to enforce violations of the immigration statutes, to improve the infrastructure of the United States Attorneys, to increase restitution collected on behalf of the child support recovery act, to support the operations of D.C. Superior Court and to expand the coverage of the short-term protection program.

WORKLOAD

	1999 actual	2000 est.	2001 est.
Cases:			
Pending beginning of year	155,065	162,893	170,769
Filed:			
Criminal	50,779	51,547	53,645
Civil	75,603	75,603	76,685
Total received	126,382	127,150	130,330
Terminated:			
Criminal	46,423	47,143	49,078
Civil	72,131	72,131	72,451
Total terminated	118,554	119,274	121,529
Pending end of year	162,893	170,769	179,570
Matters:			
Pending beginning of year	85,118	90,498	95,926
Received:			
Criminal	91,217	92,273	95,400
Civil	88,640	88,640	89,040
Total received	179,857	180,913	184,440
Terminated	174,477	175,485	179,597
Pending end of year	90,498	95,926	100,769

Object Classification (in millions of dollars)

Identification code 15–0322–0–1–752		1999 actual	2000 est.	2001 est.
	Direct obligations:			
	Personnel compensation:			
11.1	Full-time permanent	556	606	656
11.3	Other than full-time permanent	41	44	46
11.5	Other personnel compensation	11	10	10
11.8	Special personal services payments	5	5	5
11.9	Total personnel compensation	613	665	717
12.1	Civilian personnel benefits	140	153	175
21.0	Travel and transportation of persons	23	24	26
22.0	Transportation of things	3	3	3
23.2	Rental payments to others	4	5	5
23.3	Communications, utilities, and miscellaneous charges	37	43	43
24.0	Printing and reproduction	5	6	5
25.1	Advisory and assistance services	8	11	10
25.2	Other services	61	59	59
	Purchases of goods and services from Government accounts:			
25.3	Rental payments to GSA	139	156	161
25.3	Purchases of goods and services from Government accounts	18	16	26
25.4	Operation and maintenance of facilities	9	8	9
25.6	Medical care	1	1	1
25.7	Operation and maintenance of equipment	5	6	7
26.0	Supplies and materials	16	16	18
31.0	Equipment	55	18	26
99.0	Subtotal, direct obligations	1,137	1,190	1,291
99.0	Reimbursable obligations	119	129	133
99.5	Below reporting threshold	1		
99.9	Total new obligations	1,257	1,319	1,424

Personnel Summary

Identification code 15–0322–0–1–752		1999 actual	2000 est.	2001 est.
	Direct:			
1001	Total compensable workyears: Full-time equivalent employment	9,094	9,398	9,726
	Reimbursable:			
2001	Total compensable workyears: Full-time equivalent employment	969	1,041	1,041

SALARIES AND EXPENSES, FOREIGN CLAIMS SETTLEMENT COMMISSION

For expenses necessary to carry out the activities of the Foreign Claims Settlement Commission, including services as authorized by 5 U.S.C. 3109, [$1,175,000] *$1,214,000*. *(Department of Justice Appropriations Act, 2000, as enacted by section 1000(a)(1) of the Consolidated Appropriations Act, 2000 (P.L. 106–113).)*

Program and Financing (in millions of dollars)

Identification code 15–0100–0–1–153		1999 actual	2000 est.	2001 est.
	Obligations by program activity:			
10.00	Total new obligations (object class 99.5)	1	1	1
	Budgetary resources available for obligation:			
22.00	New budget authority (gross)	1	1	1
23.95	Total new obligations	–1	–1	–1
	New budget authority (gross), detail:			
	Discretionary:			
40.00	Appropriation	1	1	1
	Change in unpaid obligations:			
73.10	Total new obligations	1	1	1
73.20	Total outlays (gross)	–1	–1	–1
	Outlays (gross), detail:			
86.90	Outlays from new discretionary authority	1	1	1
	Net budget authority and outlays:			
89.00	Budget authority	1	1	1
90.00	Outlays	1	1	1

The Foreign Claims Settlement Commission adjudicates the claims of American nationals (individuals and corporations) arising out of the nationalization, expropriation or other taking of their property by foreign governments, pursuant to the International Claims Settlement Act of 1949 and other statutes. In 2001, the Commission will provide technical assistance to the Departments of State and the Treasury and to the public in connection with the 45 international and war claims programs previously completed, including, in particular, the Cuban Claims Program. It also will provide policy recommendations, evaluation of pending claims legislation, and liaison with congressional committees considering such legislation.

Personnel Summary

Identification code 15–0100–0–1–153		1999 actual	2000 est.	2001 est.
1001	Total compensable workyears: Full-time equivalent employment	4	11	11

SALARIES AND EXPENSES, UNITED STATES MARSHALS SERVICE

For necessary expenses of the United States Marshals Service; including the acquisition, lease, maintenance, and operation of vehicles, and the purchase of passenger motor vehicles for police-type use, without regard to the general purchase price limitation for the current fiscal year, [$333,745,000] *$586,469,000*, as authorized by 28 U.S.C. 561(i); of which not to exceed $6,000 shall be available for official reception and representation expenses; *and* of which not to exceed $4,000,000 for development, implementation, maintenance

General and special funds—Continued

SALARIES AND EXPENSES, UNITED STATES MARSHALS SERVICE—Continued

and support, and training for an automated prisoner information system shall remain available until expended[; and of which not less than $2,762,000 shall be for the costs of conversion to narrowband communications and for the operations and maintenance of legacy Land Mobile Radio systems: *Provided*, That such amount shall be transferred to and administered by the Department of Justice Wireless Management Office].

[In addition, $209,620,000, for such purposes, to remain available until expended, to be derived from the Violent Crime Reduction Trust Fund.] *(Department of Justice Appropriations Act, 2000, as enacted by section 1000(a)(1) of the Consolidated Appropriations Act, 2000 (P.L. 106–113).)*

Program and Financing (in millions of dollars)

Identification code 15–0324–0–1–752	1999 actual	2000 est.	2001 est.
Obligations by program activity:			
00.01 Direct program	505	544	586
09.00 Reimbursable program	35	16	33
10.00 Total new obligations	540	560	619
Budgetary resources available for obligation:			
21.40 Unobligated balance available, start of year		3	
22.00 New budget authority (gross)	539	557	619
22.10 Resources available from recoveries of prior year obligations	3		
23.90 Total budgetary resources available for obligation	542	560	619
23.95 Total new obligations	−540	−560	−619
24.40 Unobligated balance available, end of year	3		
New budget authority (gross), detail:			
Discretionary:			
40.00 Appropriation	476	333	586
41.00 Transferred to other accounts	−7	−3	
42.00 Transferred from other accounts	28	211	
43.00 Appropriation (total discretionary)	497	541	586
50.00 Reappropriation	7		
68.00 Spending authority from offsetting collections: Offsetting collections (cash)	35	16	33
70.00 Total new budget authority (gross)	539	557	619
Change in unpaid obligations:			
72.40 Unpaid obligations, start of year: Obligated balance, start of year	93	72	62
73.10 Total new obligations	540	560	619
73.20 Total outlays (gross)	−551	−570	−621
73.40 Adjustments in expired accounts (net)	−9		
73.45 Adjustments in unexpired accounts	−3		
74.40 Unpaid obligations, end of year: Obligated balance, end of year	72	62	60
Outlays (gross), detail:			
86.90 Outlays from new discretionary authority	530	503	560
86.93 Outlays from discretionary balances	21	67	61
87.00 Total outlays (gross)	551	570	621
Offsets:			
Against gross budget authority and outlays:			
Offsetting collections (cash) from:			
Federal sources:			
88.00 Federal sources	−30	−11	−28
88.00 Federal funds (Drug enforcement)	−2	−2	−2
88.40 Non-Federal sources	−3	−3	−3
88.90 Total, offsetting collections (cash)	−35	−16	−33
Net budget authority and outlays:			
89.00 Budget authority	504	541	586
90.00 Outlays	515	554	588
Distribution of budget authority by account:			
Salaries and expenses	478	331	586
Violent crime reduction programs, U.S. Marshals Service	26	210	
Distribution of outlays by account:			
Salaries and expenses	488	362	567
Violent crime reduction programs, U.S. Marshals Service	28	192	21

The Federal Government is represented in each of the 94 judicial districts by a U.S. Marshal. The primary missions of the U.S. Marshals Service are protection of the Federal judiciary, protection of witnesses, execution of warrants and court orders, and custody and transportation of unsentenced prisoners. It is the principal support force in the Federal judicial system and an integral part of the Federal law enforcement community.

Reimbursable program.—Federal funds in 2001 are derived primarily from the Administrative Office of the U.S. Courts for the court security program, the Asset Forfeiture Fund for seized assets management, the Organized Crime Drug Enforcement Task Force Program for multi-agency drug investigations, the U.S. Air Force for the Intercontinental Ballistic Missile Program for transportation security services provided by the U.S. Marshals Service and the Office of National Drug Control Policy for security services. Non-Federal funds are derived from State and local governments for witness protection and for the transportation of prisoners pursuant to State writs and from fees collected from service of civil process and sales associated with judicial orders. In addition, $2.0 million, for the replacement of the U.S. Marshals Service financial management system is anticipated to be available from the Assets Forfeiture Fund.

WORKLOAD

	1999 actual	*2000 est.*	*2001 est.*
Fugitive felon warrants received	25,517	27,037	28,817
USMS fugitive felon arrests (Class 1)	27,627	29,000	31,639
Witness security program—new witnesses	134	145	150
Total program principal witnesses	7,081	7,226	7,376
Prisoners produced	482,313	516,075	552,200
Property Disposed	46,021	45,000	45,000

Object Classification (in millions of dollars)

Identification code 15–0324–0–1–752	1999 actual	2000 est.	2001 est.
Direct obligations:			
Personnel compensation:			
11.1 Full-time permanent	204	178	182
11.3 Other than full-time permanent	9	5	5
11.5 Other personnel compensation	42	32	36
11.8 Special personal services payments	8	7	8
11.9 Total personnel compensation	263	222	231
12.1 Civilian personnel benefits	77	126	145
21.0 Travel and transportation of persons	26	29	34
22.0 Transportation of things	1	1	1
23.2 Rental payments to others	4	2	2
23.3 Communications, utilities, and miscellaneous charges	18	25	25
24.0 Printing and reproduction		3	3
25.2 Other services	31	37	37
25.3 Rental payments to GSA	63	81	83
25.4 Operation and maintenance of facilities	1		
26.0 Supplies and materials	10	9	9
31.0 Equipment	11	9	16
99.0 Subtotal, direct obligations	505	544	586
99.0 Reimbursable obligations	35	16	33
99.9 Total new obligations	540	560	619

Personnel Summary

Identification code 15–0324–0–1–752	1999 actual	2000 est.	2001 est.
Direct:			
1001 Total compensable workyears: Full-time equivalent employment	3,892	3,950	4,014
Reimbursable:			
2001 Total compensable workyears: Full-time equivalent employment	61	74	209

CONSTRUCTION

For planning, constructing, renovating, equipping, and maintaining United States Marshals Service prisoner-holding space in United States courthouses and Federal buildings, including the renovation and expansion of prisoner movement areas, elevators, and sallyports, [$6,000,000] *$6,378,000*, to remain available until expended. *(Department of Justice Appropriations Act, 2000, as enacted by section 1000(a)(1) of the Consolidated Appropriations Act, 2000 (P.L. 106–113).)*

Program and Financing (in millions of dollars)

Identification code 15–0133–0–1–751	1999 actual	2000 est.	2001 est.
Obligations by program activity:			
10.00 Total new obligations	5	6	6
Budgetary resources available for obligation:			
22.00 New budget authority (gross)	5	6	6
23.95 Total new obligations	–5	–6	–6
New budget authority (gross), detail:			
Discretionary:			
40.00 Appropriation	5	6	6
Change in unpaid obligations:			
72.40 Unpaid obligations, start of year: Obligated balance, start of year	....	5	10
73.10 Total new obligations	5	6	6
73.20 Total outlays (gross)	....	–1	–5
74.40 Unpaid obligations, end of year: Obligated balance, end of year	5	10	11
Outlays (gross), detail:			
86.90 Outlays from new discretionary authority	....	1	1
86.93 Outlays from discretionary balances	....	....	4
87.00 Total outlays (gross)	....	1	5
Net budget authority and outlays:			
89.00 Budget authority	5	6	6
90.00 Outlays	....	1	5

These funds will be used for the renovation of U.S. Marshals Service prisoner-holding cells and support space in U.S. courthouses and Federal buildings. Funds will be used to expand prisoner movement areas, construct cell blocks, renovate support space, and build prisoner elevators in existing courthouses.

Object Classification (in millions of dollars)

Identification code 15–0133–0–1–751	1999 actual	2000 est.	2001 est.
25.4 Operation and maintenance of facilities	5	3	3
31.0 Equipment	....	3	3
99.9 Total new obligations	5	6	6

Personnel Summary

Identification code 15–0133–0–1–751	1999 actual	2000 est.	2001 est.
1001 Total compensable workyears: Full-time equivalent employment	....	5	9

FEDERAL PRISONER DETENTION

For expenses, related to United States prisoners in the custody of the United States Marshals Service as authorized in 18 U.S.C. 4013, but not including expenses otherwise provided for in appropriations available to the Attorney General, [$525,000,000] *$597,402,000*, as authorized by 28 U.S.C. 561(i), to remain available until expended*: Provided, That, subject to appropriations in advance, the United States Marshals Service may enter into multi-year contracts with private entities for the confinement of Federal prisoners: Provided further, That hereafter amounts appropriated for the Federal Prisoner Detention shall be available to reimburse the Federal Bureau of Prisons for salaries and expenses of transporting, guarding and providing medical care outside of Federal penal and correctional institutions to prisoners awaiting trial or sentencing. (Department of Justice Appropriations Act, 2000, as enacted by section 1000(a)(1) of the Consolidated Appropriations Act, 2000 (P.L. 106–113).)*

Program and Financing (in millions of dollars)

Identification code 15–1020–0–1–752	1999 actual	2000 est.	2001 est.
Obligations by program activity:			
00.01 Direct program: Care of U.S. prisoners in non-Federal institutions	460	547	597
09.01 Reimbursable program	61	36	35
10.00 Total new obligations	521	583	632
Budgetary resources available for obligation:			
21.40 Unobligated balance available, start of year	24	22	....
22.00 New budget authority (gross)	517	561	632
22.10 Resources available from recoveries of prior year obligations	3	....	....
23.90 Total budgetary resources available for obligation	544	583	632
23.95 Total new obligations	–521	–583	–632
24.40 Unobligated balance available, end of year	22	....	....
New budget authority (gross), detail:			
Discretionary:			
40.00 Appropriation	425	525	597
42.00 Transferred from other accounts	31	....	....
43.00 Appropriation (total discretionary)	456	525	597
68.00 Spending authority from offsetting collections: Offsetting collections (cash)	61	36	35
70.00 Total new budget authority (gross)	517	561	632
Change in unpaid obligations:			
72.40 Unpaid obligations, start of year: Obligated balance, start of year	144	89	254
73.10 Total new obligations	521	583	632
73.20 Total outlays (gross)	–573	–418	–584
73.45 Adjustments in unexpired accounts	–3	....	....
74.40 Unpaid obligations, end of year: Obligated balance, end of year	89	254	302
Outlays (gross), detail:			
86.90 Outlays from new discretionary authority	471	351	393
86.93 Outlays from discretionary balances	102	67	191
87.00 Total outlays (gross)	573	418	584
Offsets:			
Against gross budget authority and outlays:			
88.00 Offsetting collections (cash) from: Federal sources	–61	–36	–35
Net budget authority and outlays:			
89.00 Budget authority	456	525	597
90.00 Outlays	512	382	549

Care of U.S. prisoners in non-Federal institutions.—Under this program, the U.S. Marshals Service contracts with State and local jails to board Federal prisoners and detainees for short periods of time. These periods of confinement occur before and during a trial and while awaiting transfer to Federal institutions after conviction. Requested resources will cover the cost of jail days, medical costs, and medical guard services.

Object Classification (in millions of dollars)

Identification code 15–1020–0–1–752	1999 actual	2000 est.	2001 est.
Direct obligations:			
11.8 Personnel compensation: Special personal services payments	12	13	14
25.2 Other services	7	8	9
25.6 Medical care	29	32	36
25.8 Subsistence and support of persons	412	494	538
99.0 Subtotal, direct obligations	460	547	597
99.0 Reimbursable obligations	61	36	35
99.9 Total new obligations	521	583	632

General and special funds—Continued

FEES AND EXPENSES OF WITNESSES

For expenses, mileage, compensation, and per diems of witnesses, for expenses of contracts for the procurement and supervision of expert witnesses, for private counsel expenses, and for per diems in lieu of subsistence, as authorized by law, including advances, [$95,000,000] *$156,145,000*, to remain available until expended; of which not to exceed $6,000,000 may be made available for planning, construction, renovations, maintenance, remodeling, and repair of buildings, and the purchase of equipment incident thereto, for protected witness safesites; [and] of which not to exceed $1,000,000 may be made available for the purchase and maintenance of armored vehicles for transportation of protected witnesses*; and of which not to exceed $5,000,000 may be made available for the purchase, installation, and maintenance of secure telecommunications equipment and a secure automated information network to store and retrieve the identities and locations of protected witnesses. (Department of Justice Appropriations Act, 2000, as enacted by section 1000(a)(1) of the Consolidated Appropriations Act, 2000 (P.L. 106–113).)*

Program and Financing (in millions of dollars)

Identification code 15–0311–0–1–752	1999 actual	2000 est.	2001 est.
Obligations by program activity:			
00.01 Fees and expenses of witnesses	85	99	127
00.02 Protection of witnesses	22	23	25
00.03 Private counsel	3	2	2
00.04 D.C. court informant protection	....	2	2
10.00 Total new obligations	110	126	156
Budgetary resources available for obligation:			
21.40 Unobligated balance available, start of year	19	31	....
22.00 New budget authority (gross)	95	95	156
22.10 Resources available from recoveries of prior year obligations	28	....	....
23.90 Total budgetary resources available for obligation	142	126	156
23.95 Total new obligations	–110	–126	–156
24.40 Unobligated balance available, end of year	31	....	....
New budget authority (gross), detail:			
Mandatory:			
60.00 Appropriation	95	95	156
Change in unpaid obligations:			
72.40 Unpaid obligations, start of year: Obligated balance, start of year	81	63	93
73.10 Total new obligations	110	126	156
73.20 Total outlays (gross)	–102	–96	–137
73.45 Adjustments in unexpired accounts	–28	....	....
74.40 Unpaid obligations, end of year: Obligated balance, end of year	63	93	112
Outlays (gross), detail:			
86.97 Outlays from new mandatory authority	71	67	109
86.98 Outlays from mandatory balances	31	29	28
87.00 Total outlays (gross)	102	96	137
Net budget authority and outlays:			
89.00 Budget authority	95	95	156
90.00 Outlays	102	96	137

This appropriation is used to pay fees and expenses to witnesses who appear on behalf of the Government in litigation in which the United States is a party. Factors over which the Department of Justice has little, or no, control affect the costs incurred. The U.S. Attorneys, the U.S. Marshals, and the Department's six litigating divisions are served by this appropriation.

Fees and expenses of witnesses.—Pays the fees and expenses associated with the preparation and presentation of testimony on behalf of the United States for fact witnesses, who testify as to events or facts about which they have personal knowledge, and for expert witnesses, who provide technical or scientific testimony. This program also pays the fees of physicians and psychiatrists who examine accused persons upon order of the court to determine their mental competency.

Protection of witnesses.—Pays subsistence and other costs to ensure the safety of Government witnesses whose testimony on behalf of the United States places them or their families in jeopardy.

Victim compensation fund.—Pays restitution to any victim of a crime committed by a protected witness who causes or threatens death or serious bodily injury.

Private counsel.—Pays private counsel retained to represent Government employees who are sued, charged, or subpoenaed for actions taken while performing their official duties (private counsel expenditures may be authorized for congressional testimony as well as for litigation in instances where government counsel is precluded from representing the employee or private counsel is otherwise appropriate);

D.C. Court Informant Protection.—Pays for the short term protection and temporary relocation of informants for the District of Columbia Superior Court.

Alternative Dispute Resolution.—Pays the costs of providing Alternative Dispute Resolution (ADR) services in instances wherein the Department has taken the initiative to use such services and in those matters wherein the courts have directed the parties to attempt a settlement using mediation or some other ADR process.

Reimbursable program.—Receives reimbursement from States and localities to cover the costs of maintaining those State and local organized crime witnesses and their families who have been accepted into the witness protection program.

Object Classification (in millions of dollars)

Identification code 15–0311–0–1–752	1999 actual	2000 est.	2001 est.
Personnel compensation:			
Special personal services payments:			
11.8 Fees and expenses of witnesses	80	90	106
11.8 Fees, protection of witnesses	12	19	25
11.9 Total personnel compensation	92	109	131
Travel and transportation of persons:			
21.0 Per diem in lieu of subsistence	2	2	3
21.0 Mileage	3	3	5
21.0 Other	8	7	10
25.2 Other services	5	5	7
99.9 Total new obligations	110	126	156

SALARIES AND EXPENSES, COMMUNITY RELATIONS SERVICE

For necessary expenses of the Community Relations Service, established by title X of the Civil Rights Act of 1964, [$7,199,000] *$9,829,000* and, in addition, up to $1,000,000 of funds made available to the Department of Justice in this Act may be transferred by the Attorney General to this account: *Provided*, That notwithstanding any other provision of law, upon a determination by the Attorney General that emergent circumstances require additional funding for conflict prevention and resolution activities of the Community Relations Service, the Attorney General may transfer such amounts to the Community Relations Service, from available appropriations for the current fiscal year for the Department of Justice, as may be necessary to respond to such circumstances: *Provided further*, That any transfer pursuant to the previous proviso shall be treated as a reprogramming under section 605 of this Act and shall not be available for obligation or expenditure except in compliance with the procedures set forth in that section. *(Department of Justice Appropriations Act, 2000, as enacted by section 1000(a)(1) of the Consolidated Appropriations Act, 2000 (P.L. 106–113).)*

Program and Financing (in millions of dollars)

Identification code 15–0500–0–1–752	1999 actual	2000 est.	2001 est.
Obligations by program activity:			
00.01 Direct program: Conflict prevention and resolution	7	7	10
09.00 Reimbursable program	1	....	....

10.00	Total new obligations	8	7	10
	Budgetary resources available for obligation:			
22.00	New budget authority (gross)	8	7	10
23.95	Total new obligations	−8	−7	−10
	New budget authority (gross), detail:			
	Discretionary:			
40.00	Appropriation	7	7	10
68.00	Spending authority from offsetting collections: Offsetting collections (cash)	1		
70.00	Total new budget authority (gross)	8	7	10
	Change in unpaid obligations:			
72.40	Unpaid obligations, start of year: Obligated balance, start of year		1	1
73.10	Total new obligations	8	7	10
73.20	Total outlays (gross)	−8	−7	−8
74.40	Unpaid obligations, end of year: Obligated balance, end of year	1	1	1
	Outlays (gross), detail:			
86.90	Outlays from new discretionary authority	7	6	9
86.93	Outlays from discretionary balances		1	1
87.00	Total outlays (gross)	8	7	8
	Offsets:			
	Against gross budget authority and outlays:			
88.00	Offsetting collections (cash) from: Federal sources	−1		
	Net budget authority and outlays:			
89.00	Budget authority	7	7	10
90.00	Outlays	7	7	8

Conflict prevention and resolution program.—The Community Relations Service provides assistance to communities in preventing and resolving disputes and difficulties arising from discriminatory practices based on race, color, or national origin or which disrupt or threaten to disrupt peaceful relations among citizens.

Object Classification (in millions of dollars)

Identification code 15–0500–0–1–752		1999 actual	2000 est.	2001 est.
	Direct obligations:			
11.1	Personnel compensation: Full-time permanent	4	4	6
12.1	Civilian personnel benefits	1	1	1
21.0	Travel and transportation of persons	1	1	1
25.3	Rental payments to GSA	1		1
25.4	Operation and maintenance of facilities		1	1
99.0	Subtotal, direct obligations	7	7	10
99.0	Reimbursable obligations	1		
99.9	Total new obligations	8	7	10

Personnel Summary

Identification code 15–0500–0–1–752		1999 actual	2000 est.	2001 est.
1001	Total compensable workyears: Full-time equivalent employment	42	53	68

Independent Counsel

Program and Financing (in millions of dollars)

Identification code 15–0327–0–1–752		1999 actual	2000 est.	2001 est.
	Obligations by program activity:			
10.00	Total new obligations (object class 25.2)	25	10	10
	Budgetary resources available for obligation:			
22.00	New budget authority (gross)	26	10	10
23.95	Total new obligations	−25	−10	−10
	New budget authority (gross), detail:			
	Mandatory:			
60.05	Appropriation (indefinite)	26	10	10
	Change in unpaid obligations:			
72.40	Unpaid obligations, start of year: Obligated balance, start of year	6	1	
73.10	Total new obligations	25	10	10
73.20	Total outlays (gross)	−31	−10	−10
74.40	Unpaid obligations, end of year: Obligated balance, end of year	1		
	Outlays (gross), detail:			
86.97	Outlays from new mandatory authority	25	10	10
86.98	Outlays from mandatory balances	6		
87.00	Total outlays (gross)	31	10	10
	Net budget authority and outlays:			
89.00	Budget authority	26	10	10
90.00	Outlays	31	10	10

A permanent appropriation finances the independent counsel. Pursuant to 28 U.S.C. 591 et seq., as amended, independent counsel were appointed to investigate allegations that senior Executive branch officials violated Federal law. A permanent appropriation funds the continuation of investigations, and the investigations conducted under independent counsel legislation enacted in June 1994.

Civil Liberties Public Education Fund

Program and Financing (in millions of dollars)

Identification code 15–0329–0–1–808		1999 actual	2000 est.	2001 est.
	Change in unpaid obligations:			
72.40	Unpaid obligations, start of year: Obligated balance, start of year	6		
73.20	Total outlays (gross)	−6		
	Outlays (gross), detail:			
86.98	Outlays from mandatory balances	6		
	Net budget authority and outlays:			
89.00	Budget authority			
90.00	Outlays	6		

The Civil Liberties Act of 1988 (P.L. 100–383) authorized payments to Japanese-Americans whom the Government evacuated, relocated or interned during World War II. The Civil Liberties Act Amendments of 1992 (P.L. 102–371) increased the total authorization for this program to $1.65 billion.

The Departments of Commerce, Justice, and State, the Judiciary, and Related Agencies Appropriations Act, 1990, provided advance appropriations for the redress payments. To date, payments have been made on 82,219 Japanese American cases and 145 Japanese Latin American cases.

The Civil Liberties Act of 1988 (P.L. 100–383) requires that the redress program created under the Act sunset 10 years from the date of its enactment (August 10, 1998). Any new cases arising under the Act had to be postmarked by that date and received by the Office of Redress Administration on or before September 4, 1998. The Office of Redress Administration had until February 5, 1999, to reissue remaining payments and has now closed down its operations for payment purposes.

On September 16, 1999, Congress approved a reprogramming of $4,225,000 for the purpose of paying eligible individuals who filed timely claims under the Civil Liberties Act of 1988 as amended, and in the Mochizuki settlement agreement. To date, payments have been made on 466 Japanese Latin American cases and 13 Japanese American cases.

General and special funds—Continued

UNITED STATES TRUSTEE SYSTEM FUND

For necessary expenses of the United States Trustee Program, as authorized by 28 U.S.C. 589a(a), [$112,775,000] *$127,202,000*, to remain available until expended and to be derived from the United States Trustee System Fund: *Provided*, That, notwithstanding any other provision of law, deposits to the Fund shall be available in such amounts as may be necessary to pay refunds due depositors: *Provided further*, That, notwithstanding any other provision of law, [$112,775,000] *$127,202,000* of offsetting collections derived from fees *and interest* collected pursuant to 28 U.S.C. 589a(b) shall be retained and used for necessary expenses in this appropriation and remain available until expended: *Provided further*, That the sum herein appropriated from the Fund shall be reduced as such offsetting collections are received during fiscal year [2000] *2001*, so as to result in a final fiscal year [2000] *2001* appropriation from the Fund estimated at $0: *Provided further*, That [28 U.S.C. 589a is amended by striking "and" in subsection (b)(7); by striking the period in subsection (b)(8) and inserting "; and"; and by adding a new paragraph as follows: "(9) interest earned on Fund investment."] *any such fees collected in excess of $127,202,000 in fiscal year 2001 shall remain available until expended but shall not become available for obligation until October 1, 2001. (Department of Justice Appropriations Act, 2000, as enacted by section 1000(a)(1) of the Consolidated Appropriations Act, 2000 (P.L. 106–113).)*

Unavailable Collections (in millions of dollars)

Identification code 15–5073–0–2–752	1999 actual	2000 est.	2001 est.
Balance, start of year:			
01.99 Balance, start of year	116	118	126
Receipts:			
02.02 Earnings on investments	6		
03.00 Offsetting Collections		8	
04.00 Total: Balances and collections	122	126	126
Appropriation:			
05.01 United States trustee system fund	−4		
07.99 Total balance, end of year	118	126	126

Program and Financing (in millions of dollars)

Identification code 15–5073–0–2–752	1999 actual	2000 est.	2001 est.
Obligations by program activity:			
00.01 Direct program	5		
09.00 Reimbursable program	115	122	127
10.00 Total new obligations	120	122	127
Budgetary resources available for obligation:			
21.40 Unobligated balance available, start of year	11	10	1
22.00 New budget authority (gross)	115	113	127
22.10 Resources available from recoveries of prior year obligations	3		
23.90 Total budgetary resources available for obligation	129	123	128
23.95 Total new obligations	−120	−122	−127
24.40 Unobligated balance available, end of year	10	1	1
New budget authority (gross), detail:			
Discretionary:			
40.20 Appropriation (special fund, definite)	4		
42.00 Transferred from other accounts	1		
43.00 Appropriation (total discretionary)	5		
Spending authority from offsetting collections:			
68.00 Offsetting collections (cash)	110	121	127
68.45 Portion not available for obligation (limitation on obligations)		−8	
68.90 Spending authority from offsetting collections (total discretionary)	110	113	127
70.00 Total new budget authority (gross)	115	113	127
Change in unpaid obligations:			
72.40 Unpaid obligations, start of year: Obligated balance, start of year	15	−5	8
73.10 Total new obligations	120	122	127
73.20 Total outlays (gross)	−138	−109	−114
73.45 Adjustments in unexpired accounts	−3		
74.40 Unpaid obligations, end of year: Obligated balance, end of year	−5	8	20
Outlays (gross), detail:			
86.90 Outlays from new discretionary authority	115	104	108
86.93 Outlays from discretionary balances	23	5	6
87.00 Total outlays (gross)	138	109	114
Offsets:			
Against gross budget authority and outlays:			
Offsetting collections (cash) from:			
88.20 Interest on U.S. securities		−6	−6
88.40 Non-Federal sources	−110	−115	−121
88.90 Total, offsetting collections (cash)	−110	−121	−127
Net budget authority and outlays:			
89.00 Budget authority	5	−8	
90.00 Outlays	28	−12	−13
Memorandum (non-add) entries:			
92.01 Total investments, start of year: U.S. securities: Par value	106	104	130
92.02 Total investments, end of year: U.S. securities: Par value	104	130	130

United States trustee system fund.—The United States trustees supervise the administration of bankruptcy cases and private trustees in the Federal Bankruptcy Courts. The Bankruptcy Judges, U.S. Trustees and Family Farmer Bankruptcy Act of 1986 (Public Law 99–554) expanded the pilot trustee program to a twenty-one region, Nationwide program encompassing 88 judicial districts. This program collects user fees assessed against debtors, which offset the annual appropriation.

BANKRUPTCY MATTERS[1]

	1999 actual	*2000 est.*	*2001 est.*
Chapter 7 cases filed	936,134	860,000	941,000
Chapter 11 cases filed	8,830	8,000	8,000
Chapter 12 cases filed	791	1,000	1,000
Chapter 13 cases filed	351,708	306,000	340,000
Total number of new cases filed	1,297,463	1,175,000	1,290,000

[1] Does not include cases dismissed or converted to other chapters.

Object Classification (in millions of dollars)

Identification code 15–5073–0–2–752	1999 actual	2000 est.	2001 est.
Direct obligations:			
25.2 Other services	4		
25.3 Purchases of goods and services from Government accounts	1		
99.0 Subtotal, direct obligations	5		
99.0 Reimbursable obligations	114	122	127
99.5 Below reporting threshold	1		
99.9 Total new obligations	120	122	127

Personnel Summary

Identification code 15–5073–0–2–752	1999 actual	2000 est.	2001 est.
2001 Total compensable workyears: Full-time equivalent employment	1,033	1,059	1,059

ASSETS FORFEITURE FUND

For expenses authorized by 28 U.S.C. 524(c)(1)(A)(ii), (B), (F), and (G), as amended, $23,000,000, to be derived from the Department of Justice Assets Forfeiture Fund. *(Department of Justice Appropriations Act, 2000, as enacted by Section 1000(a)(1) of the Consolidated Appropriations Act, 2000 (P.L. 106–113).)*

Unavailable Collections (in millions of dollars)

Identification code 15–5042–0–2–752	1999 actual	2000 est.	2001 est.
Balance, start of year:			
01.99 Balance, start of year	84	110	156
Receipts:			
02.01 Forfeited cash and proceeds from the sale of forfeited property	558	503	490
02.02 Interest and profit on investment	53	50	41
02.99 Total receipts	611	553	531
04.00 Total: Balances and collections	695	663	687
Appropriation:			
05.01 Assets forfeiture fund	–591	–507	–486
05.99 Subtotal appropriation	–591	–507	–486
06.20 Reduction pursuant to Public Law xx-xxx	6		
07.99 Total balance, end of year	110	156	201

Program and Financing (in millions of dollars)

Identification code 15–5042–0–2–752	1999 actual	2000 est.	2001 est.
Obligations by program activity:			
00.01 Direct program	568	709	486
09.01 Reimbursable program	2	4	4
10.00 Total new obligations	570	713	490
Budgetary resources available for obligation:			
Unobligated balance available, start of year:			
21.40 Unobligated balance available, start of year, other	169	332	152
21.40 Unobligated balance available, start of year, super surplus	107	22	
21.99 Total unobligated balance, start of year	276	354	152
22.00 New budget authority (gross)	585	511	490
22.10 Resources available from recoveries of prior year obligations	65		
23.90 Total budgetary resources available for obligation	926	865	642
23.95 Total new obligations	–570	–713	–490
Unobligated balance available, end of year:			
24.40 Unobligated balance available, end of year, other	332	152	152
24.40 Unobligated balance available, end of year, super surplus	22		
24.99 Total unobligated balance, end of year	354	152	152
New budget authority (gross), detail:			
Discretionary:			
40.20 Appropriation (special fund, definite)	23	23	23
Mandatory:			
60.25 Appropriation (special fund, indefinite)	568	476	463
60.28 Appropriation (unavailable balances)		8	
60.36 Reduction pursuant to P.L. 105–277	–2		
60.75 Reduction pursuant to P.L. 106–51	–6		
62.50 Appropriation (total mandatory)	560	484	463
Discretionary:			
68.00 Spending authority from offsetting collections: Offsetting collections (cash)	2	4	4
70.00 Total new budget authority (gross)	585	511	490
Change in unpaid obligations:			
72.40 Unpaid obligations, start of year: Obligated balance, start of year	261	264	456
73.10 Total new obligations	570	713	490
73.20 Total outlays (gross)	–502	–521	–429
73.45 Adjustments in unexpired accounts	–65		
74.40 Unpaid obligations, end of year: Obligated balance, end of year	264	456	517
Outlays (gross), detail:			
86.90 Outlays from new discretionary authority	10	13	13
86.93 Outlays from discretionary balances	19	9	18
86.97 Outlays from new mandatory authority	354	203	175
86.98 Outlays from mandatory balances	119	296	223
87.00 Total outlays (gross)	502	521	429
Offsets:			
Against gross budget authority and outlays:			
88.00 Offsetting collections (cash) from: Federal sources	–2	–4	–4
Net budget authority and outlays:			
89.00 Budget authority	583	507	486
90.00 Outlays	498	517	425
Memorandum (non-add) entries:			
92.01 Total investments, start of year: U.S. securities: Par value	455	580	500
92.02 Total investments, end of year: U.S. securities: Par value	580	500	500

The Comprehensive Crime Control Act of 1984 established the Assets Forfeiture Fund, into which forfeited cash and the proceeds of sales of forfeited property are deposited. Authorities of the fund have been amended by various public laws enacted since 1984. Under current law, authority to use the fund for certain investigative expenses shall be specified in annual appropriation acts. Expenses necessary to seize, detain, inventory, safeguard, maintain, advertise or sell property under seizure are funded through a permanent, indefinite appropriation. In addition, beginning in 1993, other general expenses of managing and operating the asset forfeiture program are paid from the permanent, indefinite portion of the fund. Once all expenses are covered, and statutorily mandated transfers are accomplished, the balance is maintained to meet ongoing expenses of the program. Excess unobligated balances may also be allocated by the Attorney General in accordance with 28 U.S.C. 524(c)(8)(E).

Object Classification (in millions of dollars)

Identification code 15–5042–0–2–752	1999 actual	2000 est.	2001 est.
Direct obligations:			
11.8 Personnel compensation: Special personal services payments	5	5	3
12.1 Civilian personnel benefits	1	1	1
21.0 Travel and transportation of persons	13	16	11
22.0 Transportation of things	2	2	2
23.1 Rental payments to GSA	10	12	8
23.2 Rental payments to others	1	1	1
23.3 Communications, utilities, and miscellaneous charges	12	14	10
24.0 Printing and reproduction	6	7	5
25.1 Advisory and assistance services	12	15	10
25.2 Other services	481	604	414
25.3 Purchases of goods and services from Government accounts	3	4	3
25.4 Operation and maintenance of facilities	5	6	4
25.7 Operation and maintenance of equipment	7	9	6
26.0 Supplies and materials	1	1	
31.0 Equipment	9	12	8
99.0 Subtotal, direct obligations	568	709	486
99.0 Reimbursable obligations	2	4	4
99.9 Total new obligations	570	713	490

Justice Prisoner and Alien Transportation System Fund, United States Marshals Service

Beginning in fiscal year 2000 and thereafter, payment shall be made from the Justice Prisoner and Alien Transportation System Fund for necessary expenses related to the scheduling and transportation of United States prisoners and illegal and criminal aliens in the custody of the United States Marshals Service, as authorized in 18 U.S.C. 4013, including, without limitation, salaries and expenses, operations, and the acquisition, lease, and maintenance of aircraft and support facilities: *Provided*, That the Fund shall be reimbursed or credited with advance payments from amounts available to the Department of Justice, other Federal agencies, and other sources at rates that will recover the expenses of Fund operations, including, without limitation, accrual of annual leave and depreciation of plant and equipment of the Fund: *Provided further*, That proceeds from the disposal of Fund aircraft shall be credited to the Fund: *Provided further*, That amounts in the Fund shall be available

General and special funds—Continued

Justice Prisoner and Alien Transportation System Fund, United States Marshals Service—Continued

without fiscal year limitation, and may be used for operating equipment lease agreements that do not exceed [5] *10* years. *(Department of Justice Appropriations Act, 2000, as enacted by section 1000(a)(1) of the Consolidated Appropriations Act, 2000 (P.L. 106–113).)*

Program and Financing (in millions of dollars)

Identification code 15–4575–0–4–752	1999 actual	2000 est.	2001 est.
Obligations by program activity:			
09.00 Reimbursable program	59	70	80
10.00 Total new obligations	59	70	80
Budgetary resources available for obligation:			
21.40 Unobligated balance available, start of year	....	15	21
22.00 New budget authority (gross)	74	76	86
23.90 Total budgetary resources available for obligation	74	91	107
23.95 Total new obligations	−59	−70	−80
24.40 Unobligated balance available, end of year	15	21	27
New budget authority (gross), detail:			
Discretionary:			
68.00 Spending authority from offsetting collections (gross): Offsetting collections (cash)	74	76	86
Change in unpaid obligations:			
72.40 Unpaid obligations, start of year: Obligated balance, start of year	....	−14	−13
73.10 Total new obligations	59	70	80
73.20 Total outlays (gross)	−73	−69	−85
74.40 Unpaid obligations, end of year: Obligated balance, end of year	−14	−13	−18
Outlays (gross), detail:			
86.90 Outlays from new discretionary authority	73	68	77
86.93 Outlays from discretionary balances	....	1	8
87.00 Total outlays (gross)	73	69	85
Offsets:			
Against gross budget authority and outlays:			
88.00 Offsetting collections (cash) from: Federal sources	−74	−76	−86
Net budget authority and outlays:			
89.00 Budget authority	....	....	....
90.00 Outlays	−1	−7	−1

The Justice Prisoner and Alien Transportation System (JPATS) is responsible for transporting by air all Federal prisoners and detainees, including sentenced, pretrial, and illegal aliens, whether in the custody of the U.S. Marshals Service, the Bureau of Prisons, or the Immigration and Naturalization Service. JPATS also provides prisoner transportation to the Departments of Defense and State and local law enforcement on a space available basis. JPATS will transport prisoners and detainees in a cost effective manner without sacrificing the safety of the public, Federal employees, or those in custody. Proceeds from the disposal of aircraft will be deposited into the Fund.

Object Classification (in millions of dollars)

Identification code 15–4575–0–4–752	1999 actual	2000 est.	2001 est.
Personnel compensation:			
11.1 Full-time permanent	6	7	8
11.5 Other personnel compensation	1	1	1
11.8 Special personal services payments	3	4	4
11.9 Total personnel compensation	10	12	13
12.1 Civilian personnel benefits	2	2	2
21.0 Travel and transportation of persons	14	19	25
23.2 Rental payments to others	....	2	2
23.3 Communications, utilities, and miscellaneous charges	2	....	....
25.2 Other services	16	19	20
26.0 Supplies and materials	11	16	18
31.0 Equipment	4	....	....
99.9 Total new obligations	59	70	80

Personnel Summary

Identification code 15–4575–0–4–752	1999 actual	2000 est.	2001 est.
2001 Total compensable workyears: Full-time equivalent employment	183	183	183

RADIATION EXPOSURE COMPENSATION

Federal Funds

Administrative Expenses

For necessary administrative expenses in accordance with the Radiation Exposure Compensation Act, $2,000,000. *(Department of Justice Appropriations Act, 2000, as enacted by section 1000(a)(1) of the Consolidated Appropriations Act, 2000 (P.L. 106–113).)*

Program and Financing (in millions of dollars)

Identification code 15–0105–0–1–054	1999 actual	2000 est.	2001 est.
Obligations by program activity:			
10.00 Total new obligations (object class 25.2)	1	2	2
Budgetary resources available for obligation:			
22.00 New budget authority (gross)	2	2	2
23.95 Total new obligations	−1	−2	−2
23.98 Unobligated balance expiring or withdrawn	−1	....	....
New budget authority (gross), detail:			
Discretionary:			
40.00 Appropriation	2	2	2
Change in unpaid obligations:			
72.40 Unpaid obligations, start of year: Obligated balance, start of year	1	....	1
73.10 Total new obligations	1	2	2
73.20 Total outlays (gross)	−2	−2	−2
74.40 Unpaid obligations, end of year: Obligated balance, end of year	....	1	1
Outlays (gross), detail:			
86.90 Outlays from new discretionary authority	2	2	2
Net budget authority and outlays:			
89.00 Budget authority	2	2	2
90.00 Outlays	1	2	2

This program processes claims under the Radiation Exposure Compensation Act, which authorizes payments to individuals exposed to radiation as a result of atmospheric nuclear tests or underground uranium mining.

Payment to Radiation Exposure Compensation Trust Fund

For payments to the Radiation Exposure Compensation Trust Fund, [$3,200,000] *$13,727,000. (Department of Justice Appropriations Act, 2000, as enacted by section 1000(a)(1) of the Consolidated Appropriations Act, 2000 (P.L. 106–113).)*

Program and Financing (in millions of dollars)

Identification code 15–0333–0–1–054	1999 actual	2000 est.	2001 est.
Obligations by program activity:			
10.00 Total new obligations (object class 25.2)	....	3	14
Budgetary resources available for obligation:			
22.00 New budget authority (gross)	....	3	14
23.95 Total new obligations	....	−3	−14
New budget authority (gross), detail:			
Discretionary:			
40.00 Appropriation	....	3	14

		1999 actual	2000 est.	2001 est.
	Change in unpaid obligations:			
73.10	Total new obligations		3	14
73.20	Total outlays (gross)		−3	−14
	Outlays (gross), detail:			
86.90	Outlays from new discretionary authority		3	14
	Net budget authority and outlays:			
89.00	Budget authority		3	14
90.00	Outlays		3	14

This appropriation transfers funds from the general fund to the Radiation Exposure Compensation Trust Fund for payment of claims.

Trust Funds

RADIATION EXPOSURE COMPENSATION TRUST FUND

Unavailable Collections (in millions of dollars)

Identification code 15–8116–0–7–054		1999 actual	2000 est.	2001 est.
	Balance, start of year:			
01.99	Balance, start of year			1
	Receipts:			
02.01	Payment from the general fund		3	14
02.02	Earnings on investments		1	1
02.99	Total receipts		4	15
04.00	Total: Balances and collections		4	16
	Appropriation:			
05.01	Radiation exposure compensation trust fund		−3	−14
07.99	Total balance, end of year		1	2

Program and Financing (in millions of dollars)

Identification code 15–8116–0–7–054		1999 actual	2000 est.	2001 est.
	Obligations by program activity:			
10.00	Total new obligations (object class 41.0)	13	11	14
	Budgetary resources available for obligation:			
21.40	Unobligated balance available, start of year	21	8	
22.00	New budget authority (gross)		3	14
23.90	Total budgetary resources available for obligation	21	11	14
23.95	Total new obligations	−13	−11	−14
24.40	Unobligated balance available, end of year	8		
	New budget authority (gross), detail:			
	Discretionary:			
40.26	Appropriation (trust fund, definite)		3	14
41.00	Transferred to other accounts	−2		
43.00	Appropriation (total discretionary)	−2	3	14
50.00	Reappropriation	2		
70.00	Total new budget authority (gross)		3	14
	Change in unpaid obligations:			
72.40	Unpaid obligations, start of year: Obligated balance, start of year	1	1	1
73.10	Total new obligations	13	11	14
73.20	Total outlays (gross)	−14	−11	−9
74.40	Unpaid obligations, end of year: Obligated balance, end of year	1	1	6
	Outlays (gross), detail:			
86.90	Outlays from new discretionary authority		2	8
86.93	Outlays from discretionary balances	13	9	1
87.00	Total outlays (gross)	14	11	9
	Net budget authority and outlays:			
89.00	Budget authority		3	14
90.00	Outlays	13	11	9

The Radiation Exposure Compensation Act authorizes payments to individuals exposed to radiation as a result of atmospheric nuclear tests or underground uranium mining. The Act authorizes the appropriation of such sums as may be necessary to carry out its purposes. These sums remain available until expended. An additional $13.7 million is requested for 2001.

WORKLOAD

	1999 actual	2000 est.	2001 est.	2002 est.
Claims and Appeals:				
Pending, beginning of year	316	352	502	474
Filed	405	539	365	312
Approved	227	225	205	184
Denied	142	164	188	225
Pending, end of year	352	502	474	377

INTERAGENCY LAW ENFORCEMENT

Federal Funds

General and special funds:

INTERAGENCY CRIME AND DRUG ENFORCEMENT

For necessary expenses for the detection, investigation, and prosecution of individuals involved in organized crime drug trafficking not otherwise provided for, to include inter-governmental agreements with State and local law enforcement agencies engaged in the investigation and prosecution of individuals involved in organized crime drug trafficking, [$316,792,000] *$328,898,000*, of which $50,000,000 shall remain available until expended: *Provided*, That any amounts obligated from appropriations under this heading may be used under authorities available to the organizations reimbursed from this appropriation: *Provided further*, That any unobligated balances remaining available at the end of the fiscal year shall revert to the Attorney General for reallocation among participating organizations in succeeding fiscal years, subject to the reprogramming procedures described in section 605 of this Act. *(Department of Justice Appropriations Act, 2000, as enacted by section 1000(a)(1) of the Consolidated Appropriations Act, 2000 (P.L. 106–113).)*

Program and Financing (in millions of dollars)

Identification code 15–0323–0–1–751		1999 actual	2000 est.	2001 est.
	Obligations by program activity:			
00.01	Law enforcement	200	216	224
00.02	Drug intelligence	14	15	15
00.03	Prosecution	79	85	89
00.04	Administrative support	2	1	1
10.00	Total new obligations (object class 25.2)	295	317	329
	Budgetary resources available for obligation:			
21.40	Unobligated balance available, start of year		9	9
22.00	New budget authority (gross)	304	317	329
23.90	Total budgetary resources available for obligation	304	326	338
23.95	Total new obligations	−295	−317	−329
24.40	Unobligated balance available, end of year	9	9	9
	New budget authority (gross), detail:			
	Discretionary:			
40.00	Appropriation	304	317	329
	Change in unpaid obligations:			
72.40	Unpaid obligations, start of year: Obligated balance, start of year	126	104	107
73.10	Total new obligations	295	317	329
73.20	Total outlays (gross)	−317	−314	−326
74.40	Unpaid obligations, end of year: Obligated balance, end of year	104	107	110
	Outlays (gross), detail:			
86.90	Outlays from new discretionary authority	228	238	247
86.93	Outlays from discretionary balances	89	76	79
87.00	Total outlays (gross)	317	314	326
	Net budget authority and outlays:			
89.00	Budget authority	304	317	329
90.00	Outlays	317	314	326

General and special funds—Continued

INTERAGENCY CRIME AND DRUG ENFORCEMENT—Continued

This appropriation provides reimbursements to agencies within the Department of Justice that participate in the Organized Crime Drug Enforcement Task Force (OCDETF) Program. The OCDETF Program consists of a nationwide structure of 9 regional task forces that combine the resources and expertise of its 11 member Federal agencies, in cooperation with State and local investigators and prosecutors, to target and destroy major narcotic trafficking and money-laundering organizations. The task forces perform the following activities:

1. *Law Enforcement.*—This activity includes the resources for direct investigative and support activities of the task forces, focusing on the disruption of drug trafficking controlled by various organized crime enterprises. Organizations participating under the law enforcement function are the Drug Enforcement Administration, Federal Bureau of Investigation, U.S. Customs Service, Internal Revenue Service, Bureau of Alcohol, Tobacco and Firearms, U.S. Coast Guard, U.S. Marshals Service, and the Immigration and Naturalization Service.

2. *Drug Intelligence.*—This activity includes the resources to maintain Regional Drug Intelligence Squads (RDIS) in selected regions. The squads gather and disseminate raw data for strategic, operational and tactical intelligence purposes and provide regional intelligence linkage to the National Drug Intelligence Center (NDIC) and member agencies' headquarters.

3. *Prosecution.*—This activity includes the resources for the prosecution of cases generated through the investigative efforts of task force agents. Litigation efforts are targeted selectively on the criminal leadership involved in drug trafficking and are intended to dissolve organized illicit enterprises. This includes activities designed to secure the seizure and forfeiture of the assets of these enterprises. Participating agencies are the U.S. Attorneys, Criminal Division and Tax Division.

4. *Administrative Support.*—This activity includes the resources for a Washington-based administrative staff in the Criminal Division, which provides policy guidance, central coordination, and administrative support to the headquarters of the 11 member Federal agencies and the 9 regional task forces. The administrative staff is also responsible for financial management, records management, and maintenance of a case tracking system.

The planned distribution of obligations for 2000 and 2001 among the participating Federal agencies, as well as the actual distribution for 1999, is as follows:

[In millions of dollars]

Department of Justice:	1999 actual	2000 est.	2001 est.
Drug Enforcement Administration	97	104	108
Federal Bureau of Investigation	105	110	113
Immigration and Naturalization Service	11	15	16
U.S. Marshals Service	1	2	2
U.S. Attorneys	77	82	87
Criminal Division	3	3	2
Tax Division	1	1	1
Total	295	317	329

WORKLOAD

	1999 actual	2000 est.
Investigations	1,484	1,500
Title III's and Extensions	286	310
Cases filed	3,848	3,750

Measures reported in past years, such as arrests, indictments, and convictions, are not considered useful indicators of the outcome or impact of law enforcement activities by the Department of Justice. The Department will continue to develop new and more meaningful performance measures as part of the implementation of the Government Performance and Results Act.

FEDERAL BUREAU OF INVESTIGATION

Federal Funds

General and special funds:

SALARIES AND EXPENSES

For necessary expenses of the Federal Bureau of Investigation [for detection, investigation, and prosecution of crimes against the United States]; including purchase for police-type use of not to exceed [1,236] *1,432* passenger motor vehicles, of which [1,142] *1,225* will be for replacement only, without regard to the general purchase price limitation for the current fiscal year, and hire of passenger motor vehicles; acquisition, lease, maintenance, and operation of aircraft; and not to exceed $70,000 to meet unforeseen emergencies of a confidential character, to be expended under the direction of, and to be accounted for solely under the certificate of, the Attorney General, [$2,337,015,000] *$3,277,562,000*; of which not to exceed [$50,000,000] *$100,000,000* for automated data processing and telecommunications and technical investigative equipment and not to exceed $1,000,000 for undercover operations shall remain available until September 30, [2001] *2002*; of which not less than [$292,473,000] *$300,473,000* shall be for counterterrorism investigations, foreign counterintelligence, and other activities related to our national security; of which not to exceed $10,000,000 is authorized to be made available for making advances for expenses arising out of contractual or reimbursable agreements with State and local law enforcement agencies while engaged in cooperative activities related to violent crime, terrorism, organized crime, and drug investigations; [and of which not less than $50,000,000 shall be for the costs of conversion to narrowband communications, and for the operations and maintenance of legacy Land Mobile Radio systems:] *Provided*, [That such amount shall be transferred to and administered by the Department of Justice Wireless Management Office: *Provided further*,] That not to exceed $45,000 shall be available for official reception and representation expenses[: *Provided further*, That no funds in this Act may be used to provide ballistics imaging equipment to any State or local authority which has obtained similar equipment through a Federal grant or subsidy unless the State or local authority agrees to return that equipment or to repay that grant or subsidy to the Federal Government].

[In addition, $752,853,000 for such purposes, to remain available until expended, to be derived from the Violent Crime Reduction Trust Fund, as authorized by the Violent Crime Control and Law Enforcement Act of 1994, as amended, and the Antiterrorism and Effective Death Penalty Act of 1996.] *(Department of Justice Appropriations Act, 2000, as enacted by section 1000(a)(1) of the Consolidated Appropriations Act, 2000 (P.L. 106–113).)*

Program and Financing (in millions of dollars)

Identification code 15–0200–0–1–999		1999 actual	2000 est.	2001 est.
	Obligations by program activity:			
	Operating expenses:			
	Direct programs:			
00.01	Criminal, security, and other investigations	1,914	2,031	2,144
00.02	Law enforcement support	569	609	621
00.03	Program direction	172	183	193
00.91	Total operating expenses	2,655	2,823	2,958
	Capital investments:			
02.01	Criminal, security and other investigations	94	102	129
02.02	Law enforcement support	189	206	189
02.03	Program direction	2	2	2
02.91	Total capital investment	285	310	320
03.00	Total	2,940	3,133	3,278
09.00	Reimbursable program	528	528	511
10.00	Total new obligations	3,468	3,661	3,789
	Budgetary resources available for obligation:			
21.40	Unobligated balance available, start of year	80	89	1
22.00	New budget authority (gross)	3,484	3,573	3,789
22.10	Resources available from recoveries of prior year obligations	16		
23.90	Total budgetary resources available for obligation	3,580	3,662	3,790
23.95	Total new obligations	−3,468	−3,661	−3,789
23.98	Unobligated balance expiring or withdrawn	−23		

24.40	Unobligated balance available, end of year	89	1	1
	New budget authority (gross), detail:			
	Discretionary:			
40.00	Appropriation	2,737	2,337	3,278
40.15	Appropriation (emergency)	22		
40.36	Unobligated balance rescinded	−9		
41.00	Transferred to other accounts	−47	−50	
42.00	Transferred from other accounts	241	758	
43.00	Appropriation (total discretionary)	2,944	3,045	3,278
50.00	Reappropriation	12		
68.00	Spending authority from offsetting collections: Offsetting collections (cash)	528	528	511
70.00	Total new budget authority (gross)	3,484	3,573	3,789
	Change in unpaid obligations:			
72.40	Unpaid obligations, start of year: Obligated balance, start of year	695	591	776
73.10	Total new obligations	3,468	3,661	3,789
73.20	Total outlays (gross)	−3,550	−3,476	−3,427
73.40	Adjustments in expired accounts (net)	−6		
73.45	Adjustments in unexpired accounts	−16		
74.40	Unpaid obligations, end of year: Obligated balance, end of year	591	776	1,138
	Outlays (gross), detail:			
86.90	Outlays from new discretionary authority	2,824	2,812	2,970
86.93	Outlays from discretionary balances	726	664	457
87.00	Total outlays (gross)	3,550	3,476	3,427
	Offsets:			
	Federal funds:			
	Offsetting collections (cash) from:			
	Federal sources:			
88.00	Drug enforcement	−153	−142	−145
88.00	Health care fraud	−66	−76	−88
88.00	Other Federal funds	−176	−225	−161
88.40	Non-Federal sources	−133	−85	−117
88.90	Total, offsetting collections (cash)	−528	−528	−511
	Net budget authority and outlays:			
89.00	Budget authority	2,956	3,045	3,278
90.00	Outlays	3,022	2,948	2,916

Summary of Budget Authority and Outlays

(in millions of dollars)

	1999 actual	2000 est.	2001 est.
Enacted/requested:			
Budget Authority	2,956	3,045	3,278
Outlays	3,022	2,948	2,916
Legislative proposal, subject to PAYGO:			
Budget Authority			
Outlays			
Total:			
Budget Authority	2,956	3,045	3,278
Outlays	3,022	2,948	2,916
Distribution of budget authority by account:			
Salaries and expenses	2,733	2,292	3,278
Violent crime reduction programs	223	753	0
Distribution of outlays by account:			
Salaries and expenses	2,809	2,332	2,803
Violent crime reduction programs	213	616	113

The mission of the FBI is to uphold the law through the investigation of violations of Federal criminal law; to protect the United States from foreign intelligence and terrorist activities; to provide leadership and law enforcement assistance to Federal, State, local and international agencies; and to perform these responsibilities in a manner that is responsive to the needs of the public and is faithful to the Constitution of the United States.

The *FBI Strategic Plan: 1998–2003* establishes a three-tier framework to achieve this mission: (1) foreign intelligence, terrorist, and criminal activities that directly threaten the national or economic security of the United States; (2) crimes that affect the public safety or undermine the integrity of American society; and (3) crimes that affect individuals and property. Through this framework, the FBI will focus its resources and operational strategies on threats that affect the security of the Nation and crime problems that are national in scope.

National and Economic Security. FBI investigations in this tier encompass threats and criminal acts that are of such importance to the U.S. national interests that they must receive priority attention by the FBI. Within this tier, strategic goals have been established to:

—identify, prevent, and defeat intelligence operations conducted by any foreign power within the United States, or against U.S. interests abroad, that constitute a threat to U.S. national security;

—prevent, disrupt, and defeat terrorist operations before they occur;

—create an effective and ongoing deterrent designed to prevent criminal conspiracies from defrauding major U.S. industries and the U.S. Government; and

—deter the unlawful exploitation of emerging technologies by foreign powers, terrorists, and criminal elements.

Criminal Enterprises and Public Safety. FBI investigations in this tier target criminal organizations, such as the La Cosa Nostra, drug traffickers, violent gangs, and other groups that exploit social, economic or political circumstances at a significant cost to the Nation. Investigations often transcend jurisdictional and national boundaries, and often are conducted by the FBI in partnership with other Federal agencies, such as the Drug Enforcement Administration, and State and local law enforcement. Strategic goals have been established to:

—identify, disrupt, and dismantle existing and emerging organized criminal enterprises whose activities affect the United States;

—identify, disrupt, and dismantle targeted international and national drug trafficking organizations;

—reduce public corruption at all levels of government with special emphasis on law enforcement operations; and

—deter civil rights violations through aggressive investigations and proactive measures.

Individuals and Property. Violent street crimes, interstate theft, crimes against children, and environmental crimes are among the offenses where the FBI is expected to respond quickly and efficiently. Many Federal crimes involving offenses against individuals and property are also State and local crimes and FBI investigative strategies recognize the generally primary role of State and local law enforcement. The FBI works closely with State and local law enforcement through Safe Streets Task Forces and similar working groups and by providing investigative expertise and technical and forensic assistance. In support of this strategy, the FBI has established a strategic goal to reduce the impact of the most significant crimes that affect individuals and property.

FBI investigations and operations are conducted through a world-wide network of 56 major field offices, over 400 resident agencies, and 4 information technology centers located throughout the United States and Puerto Rico; the FBI Academy complex at Quantico, Virginia; a fingerprint identification center in Clarksburg, West Virginia; 37 foreign liaison posts; and, FBI Headquarters in Washington, D.C.

A number of FBI activities are carried out on a reimbursable basis. Since 1997, the FBI has been reimbursed for investigations of health care fraud and abuse as a result of the enactment of the Health Care Portability and Accountability Act of 1996 (P.L. 104–191). Additionally, the FBI is reimbursed for its participation in Interagency Crime and Drug Enforcement programs and by other Federal agencies for certain investigative services, such as preemployment background inquiries and fingerprint and name checks. The FBI also is authorized to conduct fingerprint and name checks for certain non-federal agencies.

General and special funds—Continued

SALARIES AND EXPENSES—Continued

For 2001, $163.8 million in enhancements are proposed, most of which support priority Tier 1 national security and counterterrorism activities. Investments are also proposed in information technology, infrastructure, and law enforcement services for State and local agencies. Highlights of these initiatives include: (1) $25.3 million for digital collection programs; (2) $55.2 million for upgrades to information technology equipment, systems, and telecommunications services; (3) $6.5 million for basic, advanced, analytical, and other specialized training; (4) $13.1 million for counterterrorism research and development, bomb technician training, and related activities; (5) $4.6 million to enhance investigations in Indian Country; (6) $11.4 million to hire data forensics examiners to retrieve and enhance examinations of computer evidence; (7) $5.3 million to establish a federal convicted offender DNA database; (8) $3.1 million to enhance strategic and tactical analytical capabilities; (9) $2.1 million for investigative case expenses and purchases of evidence; (10) $20.4 million for technical equipment and contract translators to support field investigations; and (11) $16.8 million for other field programs. In addition, $10.0 million for FBI's Casa De Web project is anticipated to be available from the Assets Forfeiture Fund.

WORKLOAD

	1999 actual	2000 est.	2001 est.
Investigative matters:			
Pending, beginning of year	105,712	110,773	115,849
Opened	117,661	118,014	118,958
Closed	112,600	112,938	113,841
Pending, end of year	110,773	115,849	120,966
On board FBI Agents, end of year	11,677	11,733	11,828
On board support employees, end of year	16,765	17,080	17,395
Performance measures:			
Terrorist acts prevented	0	TBD	TBD
Cumulative reduction from 1997 level of Medicare expenditures for Home Health Agency equipment, laboratory services and ambulance services by preventing health care fraud	$0.837 billion reduction	$1.256 billion reduction	$1.674 billion reduction
Percent of the LCN membership incarcerated	18%	22%	25%
Number of U.S. based drug organizations affiliated with the twelve national priority targets that have been dismantled	8	50	75
Percentage of 16 targeted cities where the FBI has conducted law enforcement corruption training	38%	63%	100%
Number of persons prosecuted for the sexual exploitation of children facilitated through the use of on-line computers:			
Arrests	195	TBD	TBD
Convictions and pretrial diversions	106	TBD	TBD
Other workload indicators:			
Training, FBI Academy:			
New FBI Special Agents	718	578	595
FBI in-service/advanced	11,250	6,500	12,500
State, local, and international	4,850	3,280	5,000
Training, field:			
FBI Special Agents	10,940	11,012	11,094
State and local	120,000	120,000	120,000
International	4,176	7,105	9,205
Forensic examinations performed:			
Federal	727,354	727,354	727,354
Non-federal	139,354	139,354	139,354
Fingerprint identification services:			
Criminal cards processed	5,926,920	6,400,000	6,600,000
Civil cards processed	6,496,415	7,600,000	8,000,000
Fugitives identified	TBD	TBD	TBD
Civil submissions with criminal record	565,929	661,000	696,000
Civil submissions using false identifies	66,213	77,337	81,432
National Instant Check System transactions:			
Checks performed by States	3,480,832	3,779,684	3,968,668
Checks performed by FBI	3,346,743	4,805,683	5,045,967
Number of FBI Denials	62,189	86,502	90,827

TBD—to be determined; LCN—La Cosa Nostra.

Object Classification (in millions of dollars)

Identification code 15–0200–0–1–999		1999 actual	2000 est.	2001 est.
	Direct obligations:			
	Personnel compensation:			
11.1	Full-time permanent	1,263	1,341	1,386
11.3	Other than full-time permanent	7	3	3
11.5	Other personnel compensation	196	209	215
11.9	Total personnel compensation	1,466	1,553	1,604
12.1	Civilian personnel benefits	422	426	473
21.0	Travel and transportation of persons	75	66	63
22.0	Transportation of things	9	14	14
23.2	Rental payments to others	34	12	14
23.3	Communications, utilities, and miscellaneous charges	85	102	113
24.0	Printing and reproduction	4	3	3
25.1	Advisory and assistance services	7	11	14
25.2	Other services	234	288	295
25.3	Purchases of goods and services from Government accounts	210	239	256
25.4	Operation and maintenance of facilities	27	20	20
25.5	Research and development contracts	5	5	10
25.7	Operation and maintenance of equipment	25	20	20
26.0	Supplies and materials	51	61	57
31.0	Equipment	285	310	319
32.0	Land and structures	....	2	2
42.0	Insurance claims and indemnities	1	1	1
99.0	Subtotal, direct obligations	2,940	3,133	3,278
99.0	Reimbursable obligations	528	528	511
99.9	Total new obligations	3,468	3,661	3,789

Personnel Summary

Identification code 15–0200–0–1–999		1999 actual	2000 est.	2001 est.
	Direct:			
1001	Total compensable workyears: Full-time equivalent employment	24,822	25,021	24,646
	Reimbursable:			
2001	Total compensable workyears: Full-time equivalent employment	2,834	2,832	3,454

SALARIES AND EXPENSES

(Legislative proposal, subject to PAYGO)

Program and Financing (in millions of dollars)

Identification code 15–0200–4–1–999		1999 actual	2000 est.	2001 est.
	Obligations by program activity:			
10.00	Total new obligations (object class 25.2)	....	....	14
	Budgetary resources available for obligation:			
22.00	New budget authority (gross)	....	....	14
23.95	Total new obligations	....	....	−14
	New budget authority (gross), detail:			
	Discretionary:			
68.00	Spending authority from offsetting collections (gross): Offsetting collections (cash)	....	....	14
	Change in unpaid obligations:			
73.10	Total new obligations	....	....	14
73.20	Total outlays (gross)	....	....	−14
	Outlays (gross), detail:			
86.90	Outlays from new discretionary authority	....	....	14
	Offsets:			
	Federal funds:			
88.40	Offsetting collections (cash) from: Non-Federal sources	....	....	−14
	Net budget authority and outlays:			
89.00	Budget authority	....	....	....
90.00	Outlays	....	....	....

The Administration will propose legislation to improve the quality of care at nursing facilities, including a program to prevent abuse of nursing facility residents. This program will include a requirement that criminal background checks be conducted for applicants for positions at nursing facilities. The legislation authorizes the Attorney General to charge a fee for conducting a search against the data base of criminal history records maintained by the Federal Bureau of Investigation. These fees may not exceed actual costs.

CONSTRUCTION

For necessary expenses to construct or acquire buildings and sites by purchase, or as otherwise authorized by law (including equipment for such buildings); conversion and extension of federally-owned buildings; and preliminary planning and design of projects; [$1,287,000] *$3,187,000*. *(Department of Justice Appropriations Act, 2000, as enacted by section 1000(a)(1) of the Consolidated Appropriations Act, 2000 (P.L. 106–113).)*

Program and Financing (in millions of dollars)

Identification code 15–0203–0–1–751	1999 actual	2000 est.	2001 est.
Obligations by program activity:			
00.01 Laboratory	110		
00.02 Command center	1		
00.03 Academy modernization	2	9	1
00.05 Hazardous Device School			
00.06 Los Angeles field office renovations	2	3	
00.07 Firearms Range Modernization		14	2
10.00 Total new obligations	115	26	3
Budgetary resources available for obligation:			
21.40 Unobligated balance available, start of year	143	25	
22.00 New budget authority (gross)	–3	1	3
23.90 Total budgetary resources available for obligation	140	26	3
23.95 Total new obligations	–115	–26	–3
24.40 Unobligated balance available, end of year	25		
New budget authority (gross), detail:			
Discretionary:			
40.00 Appropriation	1	1	3
40.36 Unobligated balance rescinded	–4		
43.00 Appropriation (total discretionary)	–3	1	3
Change in unpaid obligations:			
72.40 Unpaid obligations, start of year: Obligated balance, start of year	18	115	139
73.10 Total new obligations	115	26	3
73.20 Total outlays (gross)	–18	–2	–5
74.40 Unpaid obligations, end of year: Obligated balance, end of year	115	139	137
Outlays (gross), detail:			
86.93 Outlays from discretionary balances	18	2	5
Net budget authority and outlays:			
89.00 Budget authority	–3	1	3
90.00 Outlays	18	2	5

For 2001, the FBI is proposing $1.9 million to continue the modernization of firearms range facilities and $1.3 million to continue necessary improvements and maintenance at the FBI Academy.

Object Classification (in millions of dollars)

Identification code 15–0203–0–1–751	1999 actual	2000 est.	2001 est.
23.3 Communications, utilities, and miscellaneous charges	1		
25.2 Other services	3		
25.4 Operation and maintenance of facilities	4	12	3
32.0 Land and structures	107	14	
99.9 Total new obligations	115	26	3

DRUG ENFORCEMENT ADMINISTRATION

Federal Funds

General and special funds:

SALARIES AND EXPENSES

For necessary expenses of the Drug Enforcement Administration, including not to exceed $70,000 to meet unforeseen emergencies of a confidential character, to be expended under the direction of, and to be accounted for solely under the certificate of, the Attorney General; expenses for conducting drug education and training programs, including travel and related expenses for participants in such programs and the distribution of items of token value that promote the goals of such programs; purchase of not to exceed 1,358 passenger motor vehicles, of which 1,079 will be for replacement only, for police-type use without regard to the general purchase price limitation for the current fiscal year; and acquisition, lease, maintenance, and operation of aircraft, [$933,000,000] *$1,367,766,000,* of which not to exceed $1,800,000 for research shall remain available until expended, and of which not to exceed $4,000,000 for purchase of evidence and payments for information, not to exceed $10,000,000 for contracting for automated data processing and telecommunications equipment, and not to exceed $2,000,000 for laboratory equipment, $4,000,000 for technical equipment, and $2,000,000 for aircraft replacement retrofit and parts, shall remain available until September 30, [2001] *2002*; of which not to exceed $50,000 shall be available for official reception and representation expenses[; and of which not less than $20,733,000 shall be for the costs of conversion to narrowband communications and for the operations and maintenance of legacy Land Mobile Radio systems: *Provided*, That such amount shall be transferred to and administered by the Department of Justice Wireless Management Office].

[In addition, $343,250,000, for such purposes, to remain available until expended, to be derived from the Violent Crime Reduction Trust Fund.] *(Department of Justice Appropriations Act, 2000, as enacted by section 1000(a)(1) of the Consolidated Appropriations Act, 2000 (P.L. 106–113).)*

Program and Financing (in millions of dollars)

Identification code 15–1100–0–1–751	1999 actual	2000 est.	2001 est.
Obligations by program activity:			
Direct program:			
00.01 Enforcement	718	825	867
00.02 Investigative support	369	347	411
00.03 Program direction	140	83	90
01.00 Total direct program	1,227	1,255	1,368
09.00 Reimbursable program	190	214	203
10.00 Total new obligations	1,417	1,469	1,571
Budgetary resources available for obligation:			
21.40 Unobligated balance available, start of year	12	15	33
22.00 New budget authority (gross)	1,426	1,487	1,571
22.10 Resources available from recoveries of prior year obligations	8		
23.90 Total budgetary resources available for obligation	1,446	1,502	1,604
23.95 Total new obligations	–1,417	–1,469	–1,571
23.98 Unobligated balance expiring or withdrawn	–14		
24.40 Unobligated balance available, end of year	15	33	33
New budget authority (gross), detail:			
Discretionary:			
40.00 Appropriation	799	933	1,368
40.15 Supplemental Appropriation [106–31]	10		
41.00 Transferred to other accounts	–13	–21	
42.00 Transferred from other accounts	431	361	
43.00 Appropriation (total discretionary)	1,227	1,273	1,368
50.00 Reappropriation	9		
68.00 Spending authority from offsetting collections: Offsetting collections (cash)	190	214	203
70.00 Total new budget authority (gross)	1,426	1,487	1,571
Change in unpaid obligations:			
72.40 Unpaid obligations, start of year: Obligated balance, start of year	318	408	517
73.10 Total new obligations	1,417	1,469	1,571

General and special funds—Continued

SALARIES AND EXPENSES—Continued

Program and Financing (in millions of dollars)—Continued

Identification code 15–1100–0–1–751	1999 actual	2000 est.	2001 est.
73.20 Total outlays (gross)	−1,315	−1,360	−1,420
73.40 Adjustments in expired accounts (net)	−4		
73.45 Adjustments in unexpired accounts	−8		
74.40 Unpaid obligations, end of year: Obligated balance, end of year	408	517	668
Outlays (gross), detail:			
86.90 Outlays from new discretionary authority	1,115	1,169	1,229
86.93 Outlays from discretionary balances	200	191	191
87.00 Total outlays (gross)	1,315	1,360	1,420
Offsets:			
Against gross budget authority and outlays:			
Offsetting collections (cash) from:			
88.00 Federal sources	−187	−211	−200
88.40 Non-Federal sources	−3	−3	−3
88.90 Total, offsetting collections (cash)	−190	−214	−203
Net budget authority and outlays:			
89.00 Budget authority	1,236	1,273	1,368
90.00 Outlays	1,125	1,146	1,217

Distribution of budget authority by account:			
Salaries and expenses	831	930	1,368
Violent crime reduction programs	405	343	
Distribution of outlays by account:			
Salaries and expenses	784	889	1,166
Violent crime reduction programs	341	257	51

The mission of the DEA is to control abuse of narcotics and dangerous drugs by restricting the aggregate supply of those drugs. In order to safeguard Americans, DEA will disrupt/dismantle the leadership, command, control and infrastructure of drug syndicates, gangs and traffickers of illicit drugs that threaten Americans and erode the quality of life in our communities. At the Federal level, DEA is the lead drug law enforcement agency. DEA accomplishes its objectives through coordination with State, local, and other Federal officials in drug law enforcement activities, development and maintenance of drug intelligence systems, regulation of legitimate controlled substances activities, and enforcement coordination and intelligence-gathering activities with foreign government agencies.

Cooperation among Federal law enforcement agencies is extensive, especially within the nine Interagency Crime and Drug Enforcement (ICDE) regional task forces. DEA's involvement is integral to this nationwide coordinated enforcement strategy. With the ICDE program and the expansion of other agency cooperative efforts, overall drug enforcement capabilities have been significantly strengthened in recent years.

The activities of the DEA are divided into the following general categories:

Enforcement—

Domestic enforcement.—This activity encompasses DEA's general efforts to eliminate or immobilize major drug trafficking organizations and thereby reduce the domestic supply of illicit drugs.

Domestic Enforcement includes the majority of the activities encompassed within DEA's 21 domestic field divisions. These activities include efforts to reduce the availability of illicit drugs by immobilizing targeted organizations that are substantially responsible for importation and distribution of drugs and by focusing enforcement operations on specific drug trafficking problems. This program also includes DEA's Regional Enforcement Teams (RET), an initiative designed to provide a proactive, mobile regional investigative element to better develop intelligence, and investigate and target drug organizations operating in America's smaller communities. DEA's RET program (2 teams) is equipped with the investigative equipment and vehicles needed to ensure a high degree of mobility and to support the performance of even the most complex of investigations.

State and local task forces.—This activity encompasses efforts to reduce drug availability and immobilize major drug trafficking organizations through intergovernmental cooperation with State and local law enforcement agencies and through DEA's Mobile Enforcement Team Program. There are currently 103 program-funded and 52 provisional State and Local Task Forces and 23 Mobile Enforcement Teams participating in the program.

Measures reported in past years, such as arrests, indictments, and convictions, are not considered useful indicators of the outcome or impact of law enforcement activities by the Department of Justice. The Department will continue to develop new and more meaningful performance measures as part of the implementation of the Government Performance and Results Act. The measures below reflect the level of activity performed by this program.

	1999 actual	*2000 est.*	*2001 est.*
Domestic cases initiated	20,223	21,000	21,000
DEA cooperative cases initiated	14,973	15,000	15,000
Title III Facilities	637	650	675

Foreign cooperative investigations.—This activity encompasses efforts to (1) disrupt, as close to the source as possible, production of opium, heroin, cocaine, marijuana, and illicitly produced and diverted legitimate dangerous drugs destined for the United States, and (2) collect and disseminate intelligence regarding narcotics production and trafficking. The measure below reflects the level of activity performed by this program.

	1999 actual	*2000 est.*	*2001 est.*
Foreign cases initiated	1,919	2,100	2,100

Chemical diversion control.—This activity seeks to reduce the diversion of legitimately produced controlled chemicals into illicit channels at all levels of distribution, and to provide the leadership and support necessary to ensure that State and local agencies and the chemical industry establish and maintain programs and policies to control diversion. The Drug Diversion Control activities are funded from the Drug Diversion Control Fee Account.

The measure below reflects the level of activity performed by this program.

	1999 actual	*2000 est.*	*2001 est.*
Chemical diversion investigations initiated	562	550	550

Investigative Support—

Intelligence.—This activity encompasses the collection, analysis, and dissemination of drug intelligence in support of the enforcement operations of DEA and other Federal, State, and local agencies.

DEA laboratory services.—This activity encompasses laboratory analysis of evidence and expert testimony in support of the investigation and prosecution of drug traffickers. The measure below reflects the results of this program.

	1999 actual	*2000 est.*	*2001 est.*
Number of inquiries to Intell. Databases	193,829	195,401	200,000

DEA training.—This activity encompasses entry level training for all special agents, diversion investigators, and intelligence analysts; advanced, in-service and specialized training for investigative and other personnel; executive, mid-level management, and supervisory training for appropriate agency officials; and foreign language training for DEA personnel assigned to overseas and border offices as needed. In 2000, training will focus on basic agent, in-service and specialized training activities. The measures below reflect a portion of the level of activity performed by this program.

	1999 actual	2000 est.	2001 est.
Students graduated Core—Special Agents, Chemists, Diversion Investigators, Intelligence Specialists	609	475	475

Research, engineering, and technical operations.—This activity provides high quality and timely radio communications capability, technical and investigative equipment assistance support, maintenance and operation of an aircraft fleet, and research programs directly related to the DEA law enforcement and intelligence functions.

ADP and telecommunications.—This activity encompasses automated data processing and telecommunication support on a nationwide and worldwide basis.

Records management.—This activity encompasses effective and efficient records management, Freedom of Information/Privacy Act, and library support.

Program Direction—

Management and Administration.—This activity encompasses the overall management, contracting, and direction of DEA to include personnel, general services, and Equal Employment Opportunity functions.

Reimbursable program.—The primary reimbursements to DEA are for the Interagency Crime and Drug Enforcement Task Force program, the training of foreign drug law enforcement officials (funded by the Department of State), and the expenses incurred in managing seized assets and other purposes for which DEA is reimbursed from the Department of Justice Assets Forfeiture Fund.

Object Classification (in millions of dollars)

Identification code 15–1100–0–1–751		1999 actual	2000 est.	2001 est.
	Direct obligations:			
	Personnel compensation:			
11.1	Full-time permanent	377	447	468
11.3	Other than full-time permanent	2	3	3
11.5	Other personnel compensation	60	53	55
11.9	Total personnel compensation	439	503	526
12.1	Civilian personnel benefits	154	142	157
21.0	Travel and transportation of persons	47	46	46
22.0	Transportation of things	13	11	11
23.1	Rental payments to GSA	78	72	77
23.2	Rental payments to others	4	9	10
23.3	Communications, utilities, and miscellaneous charges	57	66	74
24.0	Printing and reproduction	1	1	2
25.1	Advisory and assistance services			1
25.2	Other services	97	90	135
25.3	Purchases of goods and services from Government accounts	156	157	163
25.4	Operation and maintenance of facilities	3	3	3
25.6	Medical care	1	2	2
25.7	Operation and maintenance of equipment	29	23	23
26.0	Supplies and materials	43	41	41
31.0	Equipment	101	89	97
32.0	Land and structures	4		
99.0	Subtotal, direct obligations	1,227	1,255	1,368
99.0	Reimbursable obligations	190	214	203
99.9	Total new obligations	1,417	1,469	1,571

Personnel Summary

Identification code 15–1100–0–1–751		1999 actual	2000 est.	2001 est.
	Direct:			
1001	Total compensable workyears: Full-time equivalent employment	6,959	7,348	7,398
	Reimbursable:			
2001	Total compensable workyears: Full-time equivalent employment	1,024	1,017	1,017

CONSTRUCTION

For necessary expenses to construct or acquire buildings and sites by purchase, or as otherwise authorized by law (including equipment for such buildings); conversion and extension of federally-owned buildings; and preliminary planning and design of projects, $5,500,000, to remain available until expended. *(Department of Justice Appropriations Act, 2000, as enacted by section 1000(a)(1) of the Consolidated Appropriations Act, 2000 (P.L. 106–113).)*

Program and Financing (in millions of dollars)

Identification code 15–1101–0–1–751		1999 actual	2000 est.	2001 est.
	Obligations by program activity:			
10.00	Total new obligations	5	6	6
	Budgetary resources available for obligation:			
21.40	Unobligated balance available, start of year	9	13	13
22.00	New budget authority (gross)	8	6	6
22.10	Resources available from recoveries of prior year obligations	1		
23.90	Total budgetary resources available for obligation	18	19	19
23.95	Total new obligations	−5	−6	−6
24.40	Unobligated balance available, end of year	13	13	13
	New budget authority (gross), detail:			
	Discretionary:			
40.00	Appropriation	8	6	6
	Change in unpaid obligations:			
72.40	Unpaid obligations, start of year: Obligated balance, start of year	18	10	13
73.10	Total new obligations	5	6	6
73.20	Total outlays (gross)	−13	−3	−12
73.45	Adjustments in unexpired accounts	−1		
74.40	Unpaid obligations, end of year: Obligated balance, end of year	10	13	7
	Outlays (gross), detail:			
86.90	Outlays from new discretionary authority	1	1	1
86.93	Outlays from discretionary balances	12	2	11
87.00	Total outlays (gross)	13	3	12
	Net budget authority and outlays:			
89.00	Budget authority	8	6	6
90.00	Outlays	13	3	12

The account funds $5.5 million for the highest priority renovation and upgrade needs at DEA's current forensic laboratory facilities.

Object Classification (in millions of dollars)

Identification code 15–1101–0–1–751		1999 actual	2000 est.	2001 est.
23.3	Communications, utilities, and miscellaneous charges	1		
25.3	Purchases of goods and services from Government accounts	1		
31.0	Equipment	1		
32.0	Land and structures	2	6	6
99.9	Total new obligations	5	6	6

DIVERSION CONTROL FEE ACCOUNT

[(RESCISSION)]

[Amounts otherwise available for obligation in fiscal year 2000 for the Drug Diversion Control Fee Account are reduced by $35,000,000.] *(Department of Justice Appropriations Act, 2000, as enacted by section 1000(a)(1) of the Consolidated Appropriations Act, 2000 (P.L. 106–113).)*

Unavailable Collections (in millions of dollars)

Identification code 15–5131–0–2–751		1999 actual	2000 est.	2001 est.
	Balance, start of year:			
01.99	Balance, start of year	44	44	36

General and special funds—Continued

DIVERSION CONTROL FEE ACCOUNT—Continued

[(RESCISSION)]—Continued

Unavailable Collections (in millions of dollars)—Continued

Identification code 15–5131–0–2–751	1999 actual	2000 est.	2001 est.
Receipts:			
02.01 Diversion control fee account	54	72	63
04.00 Total: Balances and collections	98	116	99
Appropriation:			
05.01 Diversion control fee account	–61	–115	–83
05.99 Subtotal appropriation	–61	–115	–83
06.10 Unobligated balance returned to receipts		35	
06.20 Reduction pursuant to Public Law 106–51	7		
07.99 Total balance, end of year	44	36	16

Program and Financing (in millions of dollars)

Identification code 15–5131–0–2–751	1999 actual	2000 est.	2001 est.
Obligations by program activity:			
10.00 Total new obligations	72	80	83
Budgetary resources available for obligation:			
21.40 Unobligated balance available, start of year	25	7	7
22.00 New budget authority (gross)	54	80	83
23.90 Total budgetary resources available for obligation	79	87	90
23.95 Total new obligations	–72	–80	–83
24.40 Unobligated balance available, end of year	7	7	7
New budget authority (gross), detail:			
Mandatory:			
60.25 Appropriation (special fund, indefinite)	61	108	83
60.28 Appropriation (unavailable balances)		7	
60.35 Appropriation rescinded		–35	
60.75 Reduction pursuant to P.L. 106–51	–7		
62.50 Appropriation (total mandatory)	54	80	83
Change in unpaid obligations:			
72.40 Unpaid obligations, start of year: Obligated balance, start of year	19	26	26
73.10 Total new obligations	72	80	83
73.20 Total outlays (gross)	–63	–80	–79
74.40 Unpaid obligations, end of year: Obligated balance, end of year	26	26	30
Outlays (gross), detail:			
86.97 Outlays from new mandatory authority	38	60	62
86.98 Outlays from mandatory balances	25	20	17
87.00 Total outlays (gross)	63	80	79
Net budget authority and outlays:			
89.00 Budget authority	54	80	83
90.00 Outlays	65	80	79

Public Law 102–395 established the Diversion Control Fee Account in 1993. Fees charged by the Drug Enforcement Administration under the Diversion Control Program are set at a level that ensures the recovery of the full costs of operating the various aspects of the program. The purpose of this program is to prevent, detect, and investigate the diversion of controlled substances from legitimate channels, while at the same time ensuring an adequate and uninterrupted supply of controlled substances required to meet legitimate needs.

The measures below reflect the level of activity performed by this program.

	1999 actual	2000 est.	2001 est.
New applications processed	56,027	53,500	53,500
Drug diversion investigations initiated	2,413	2,400	2,400

Object Classification (in millions of dollars)

Identification code 15–5131–0–2–751	1999 actual	2000 est.	2001 est.
11.1 Personnel compensation: Full-time permanent	31	33	33
12.1 Civilian personnel benefits	8	8	8
21.0 Travel and transportation of persons	2	3	3
23.1 Rental payments to GSA	9	10	10
23.3 Communications, utilities, and miscellaneous charges	2	5	5
25.1 Advisory and assistance services		4	4
25.2 Other services	1	5	5
25.3 Purchases of goods and services from Government accounts	12	2	5
25.4 Operation and maintenance of facilities		1	1
25.7 Operation and maintenance of equipment		1	1
26.0 Supplies and materials	1	1	1
31.0 Equipment	6	7	7
99.9 Total new obligations	72	80	83

Personnel Summary

Identification code 15–5131–0–2–751	1999 actual	2000 est.	2001 est.
1001 Total compensable workyears: Full-time equivalent employment	599	643	656

IMMIGRATION AND NATURALIZATION SERVICE

Federal Funds

General and special funds:

SALARIES AND EXPENSES

For expenses necessary for the administration and enforcement of the laws relating to immigration, naturalization, and alien registration, as follows:

ENFORCEMENT AND BORDER AFFAIRS

For salaries and expenses for the Border Patrol program, the detention and deportation program, the intelligence program, the investigations program, and the inspections program, including not to exceed $50,000 to meet unforeseen emergencies of a confidential character, to be expended under the direction of, and to be accounted for solely under the certificate of, the Attorney General; purchase for police-type use (not to exceed [3,075] *3,165* passenger motor vehicles, of which [2,266] *2,211* are for replacement only), without regard to the general purchase price limitation for the current fiscal year, and hire of passenger motor vehicles; acquisition, lease, maintenance and operation of aircraft; research related to immigration enforcement; for protecting and maintaining the integrity of the borders of the United States including, without limitation, equipping, maintaining, and making improvements to the infrastructure; and for the care and housing of Federal detainees held in the joint Immigration and Naturalization Service and United States Marshals Service's Buffalo Detention Facility, [$1,107,429,000] *$2,580,890,000*; of which not to exceed $10,000,000 shall be available for costs associated with the training program for basic officer training, and $5,000,000 is for payments or advances arising out of contractual or reimbursable agreements with State and local law enforcement agencies while engaged in cooperative activities related to immigration; of which not to exceed $5,000,000 is to fund or reimburse other Federal agencies for the costs associated with the care, maintenance, and repatriation of smuggled illegal aliens[; and of which not less than $18,510,000 shall be for the costs of conversion to narrowband communications and for the operations and maintenance of legacy Land Mobile Radio systems: *Provided*, That such amount shall be transferred to and administered by the Department of Justice Wireless Management Office]: *Provided* [*further*], That none of the funds available to the Immigration and Naturalization Service shall be available to pay any employee overtime pay in an amount in excess of $30,000 during the calendar year beginning January 1, [2000] *2001, except in such circumstances when the Commissioner determines that enforcing this overtime provision would harm enforcement or service activities: Provided further*, That uniforms may be purchased without regard to the general purchase price limitation for the current fiscal year[: *Provided further*, That none of the funds provided in this or any other Act shall be used for the continued operation of the San Clemente and Temecula checkpoints unless the checkpoints are open and traffic is being checked on a continuous 24-hour basis].

CITIZENSHIP AND BENEFITS, IMMIGRATION SUPPORT AND PROGRAM DIRECTION

For all programs of the Immigration and Naturalization Service not included under the heading "Enforcement and Border Affairs", [$535,011,000] *$539,390,000*, of which not to exceed $400,000 for research shall remain available until expended: *Provided*, That not to exceed $5,000 shall be available for official reception and representation expenses: *Provided further*, That the Attorney General may transfer any funds appropriated under this heading and the heading "Enforcement and Border Affairs" between said appropriations notwithstanding any percentage transfer limitations imposed under this appropriation Act and may direct such fees as are collected by the Immigration and Naturalization Service to the activities funded under this heading and the heading "Enforcement and Border Affairs" for performance of the functions for which the fees legally may be expended: [*Provided further*, That not to exceed 40 permanent positions and 40 full-time equivalent workyears and $4,150,000 shall be expended for the Offices of Legislative Affairs and Public Affairs: *Provided further*, That the latter two aforementioned offices shall not be augmented by personnel details, temporary transfers of personnel on either a reimbursable or non-reimbursable basis, or any other type of formal or informal transfer or reimbursement of personnel or funds on either a temporary or long-term basis: *Provided further*, That the number of positions filled through non-career appointment at the Immigration and Naturalization Service, for which funding is provided in this Act or is otherwise made available to the Immigration and Naturalization Service, shall not exceed four permanent positions and four full-time equivalent workyears:] *Provided further*, That none of the funds available to the Immigration and Naturalization Service shall be used to pay any employee overtime pay in an amount in excess of $30,000 during the calendar year beginning January 1, [2000] *2001, except in such circumstances when the Commissioner determines that enforcing this overtime provision would harm enforcement or service activities: Provided further*, That funds may be used, without limitation, for equipping, maintaining, and making improvements to the infrastructure and the purchase of vehicles for police-type use within the limits of the Enforcement and Border Affairs appropriation: *Provided further*, That, notwithstanding any other provision of law, during fiscal year [2000] *2001*, the Attorney General is authorized and directed to impose disciplinary action, including termination of employment, pursuant to policies and procedures applicable to employees of the Federal Bureau of Investigation, for any employee of the Immigration and Naturalization Service who violates policies and procedures set forth by the Department of Justice relative to the granting of citizenship or who willfully deceives the Congress or department leadership on any matter.

[VIOLENT CRIME REDUCTION PROGRAMS]

[In addition, $1,267,225,000, for such purposes, to remain available until expended, to be derived from the Violent Crime Reduction Trust Fund: *Provided*, That the Attorney General may use the transfer authority provided under the heading "Citizenship and Benefits, Immigration Support and Program Direction" to provide funds to any program of the Immigration and Naturalization Service that heretofore has been funded by the Violent Crime Reduction Trust Fund.] *(Department of Justice Appropriations Act, 2000, as enacted by section 1000(a)(1) of the Consolidated Appropriations Act, 2000 (P.L. 106–113).)*

Unavailable Collections (in millions of dollars)

Identification code 15–1217–0–1–751	1999 actual	2000 est.	2001 est.
Balance, start of year:			
01.99 Balance, start of year		1	2
Receipts:			
02.01 H–1B Nonimmigrant petitioner fees	74	89	85
04.00 Total: Balances and collections	74	90	87
Appropriation:			
05.02 Training and employment services, Department of Labor	−41	−50	−48
05.04 Salaries and expenses, Employment Standards Administration	−5	−5	−5
05.05 Education and human resources, National Science Foundation	−27	−33	−31
05.99 Subtotal appropriation	−73	−88	−84
07.99 Total balance, end of year	1	2	3

Program and Financing (in millions of dollars)

Identification code 15–1217–0–1–751	1999 actual	2000 est.	2001 est.
Obligations by program activity:			
Direct program:			
00.01 Enforcement	1,950	2,246	2,562
00.02 Citizenship and benefits	88	98	20
00.03 Immigration support	388	445	376
00.04 Program direction	115	121	111
00.05 Capital investment—Enforcement	6	25	39
00.07 Capital investment—Immigration support	3	2	2
00.08 Capital investment—Program direction		10	10
01.92 Total direct program	2,550	2,947	3,120
09.00 Reimbursable program	1,261	1,301	1,614
10.00 Total new obligations	3,811	4,248	4,734
Budgetary resources available for obligation:			
21.40 Unobligated balance available, start of year	34	54	
22.00 New budget authority (gross)	3,837	4,194	4,734
23.90 Total budgetary resources available for obligation	3,871	4,248	4,734
23.95 Total new obligations	−3,811	−4,248	−4,734
23.98 Unobligated balance expiring or withdrawn	−6		
24.40 Unobligated balance available, end of year	54		
New budget authority (gross), detail:			
Discretionary:			
40.00 Appropriation	1,707	1,642	3,120
40.15 Appropriation (emergency)	10		
41.00 Transferred to other accounts	−8	−18	
42.00 Transferred from other accounts	859	1,269	
43.00 Appropriation (total discretionary)	2,568	2,893	3,120
50.00 Reappropriation	8		
68.00 Spending authority from offsetting collections: Offsetting collections (cash)	1,261	1,301	1,614
70.00 Total new budget authority (gross)	3,837	4,194	4,734
Change in unpaid obligations:			
72.40 Unpaid obligations, start of year: Obligated balance, start of year	1,183	1,168	883
73.10 Total new obligations	3,811	4,248	4,734
73.20 Total outlays (gross)	−3,806	−4,533	−4,836
73.40 Adjustments in expired accounts (net)	−20		
74.40 Unpaid obligations, end of year: Obligated balance, end of year	1,168	883	781
Outlays (gross), detail:			
86.90 Outlays from new discretionary authority	3,621	3,616	4,110
86.93 Outlays from discretionary balances	185	917	726
87.00 Total outlays (gross)	3,806	4,533	4,836
Offsets:			
Against gross budget authority and outlays:			
Offsetting collections (cash) from:			
Federal sources:			
88.00 Federal sources	−1,249	−1,285	−1,598
88.00 Federal sources (Drug enforcement)	−11	−15	−15
88.40 Non-Federal sources	−1	−1	−1
88.90 Total, offsetting collections (cash)	−1,261	−1,301	−1,614
Net budget authority and outlays:			
89.00 Budget authority	2,576	2,893	3,120
90.00 Outlays	2,545	3,232	3,222

The 1999 appropriation shown above is net of reductions made pursuant to section 126 of the Department of Justice Appropriations Act, 1999.

	1999 actual	2000 est.	2001 est.
Distribution of budget authority by account:			
Salaries and expenses	1,733	1,626	3,120
Violent crime reduction programs	843	1,267	0
Distribution of outlays by account:			
Salaries and expenses	1,915	1,903	2,978
Violent crime reduction programs	630	1,329	244

General and special funds—Continued

[VIOLENT CRIME REDUCTION PROGRAMS]—Continued

The mission of the Immigration and Naturalization Service (INS) provides for enforcing provisions of the law which govern lawful entry and presence within the United States, and providing immigration benefits and services to individuals and entities (e.g., employers) entitled under law. The mission is accomplished through INS' operational offices located on the border, in the interior and overseas, and through numerous special facilities (e.g., detention centers, applications processing centers, national records repository, training centers) throughout the United States. Accomplishing the enforcement and benefits/services mission of the INS requires significant investment in physical infrastructure and equipment, administrative support services, and maintenance; and a competent, diversified, motivated and productive workforce. INS addresses its mission through several goals that are used to target and monitor performance.

Enforcement and border affairs.—This account contains resources for preventing illegal entry into the United States, facilitating the entry of qualified persons, and investigating criminal organizations that facilitate illegal migration. This includes inspection of applicants for admission, patrol of the border, and locating aliens who are in the United States following illegal entry or violation of status after legal entry. Apprehensions are made through the inspection of places of employment, by the investigation of information about the location of undocumented aliens, and through investigative case work. Also included are resources for the Service's nationwide anti-smuggling program and for the detention and deportation of illegal aliens. Additional resources requested in 2001 will add 430 new Border Patrol agents, increase Border Patrol productivity by investing in force-multiplying border technology and equipment ($20 million), and providing resources to staff new land ports of entry and to address the increased workload related to the expedited removal process at land POEs ($10 million).

WORKLOAD

	1999 actual	2000 est.	2001 est.
Total persons inspected (land only)	435,347,324	448,000,000	460,000,000
Inadmissable aliens intercepted (land ports)	536,465	552,000	568,000
Deportable aliens apprehended (border patrol)	1,579,010	1,600,000	1,625,000
Smugglers apprehended (border patrol)	15,755	16,000	16,250
Cases Completed (investigations):			
Smuggling cases completed (investigations)	2,031	2,031	2,031
Fraud cases completed (investigations)	894	894	894
Number of detention days	6,206,124	6,765,275	6,935,000

Border Enforcement.—Secure the land border, ports of entry and coasts of the United States against illegal migration to effectively control the border. In coordination with other agencies and through enhanced integration of INS' overseas, border and interior intelligence operations, this activity seeks to (1) prevent illegal entry by comprehensive border protection programs, including increased Border Patrol strength, (2) concentrate resources at the major problem sources, ports of entry and border points, and (3) gather, analyze, and disseminate intelligence regarding illegal migration to target enforcement efforts on criminal activities, smuggling, fraud, and terrorism. The measures below reflect the expected outcomes from these activities.

	1999 actual	2000 est.	2001 est.
Level of operational effectiveness	Baseline	Extend control in additional zones	Extend control in additional zones
Interceptions of mala fide and offshore travelers	9,124	9,224	9,324
Offshore prosecutions assisted by INS personnel	119	119	119

Border Facilitation.—Facilitate lawful travel and commerce across the borders to the United States. This activity seeks to (1) expand the use of techniques and technologies that promote and expedite lawful entry, including cooperative strategies with other agencies and foreign governments, (2) increase the number of pre-registered DCL participants, and (3) work cooperatively with the U.S. Customs Service and other Federal agencies at ports-of-entry. The measures below reflect the expected outcomes from these activities.

	1999 actual	2000 est.	2001 est.
Commercial air flights to clear primary inspection in 30 min.	74%	72%	72%
Land-border wait times that did not exceed 20 minutes	96%	80%	80%

Interior Enforcement.—Maximize deterrence to unlawful migration and enforce immigration laws in the interior through effective and coordinated use of resources to reduce the incentives of unauthorized employment and assistance; remove deportable/inadmissible aliens expeditiously; address interior smuggling and benefit and document fraud; and increase intergovernmental cooperation and the integration of activities among law enforcement entities at all levels of government. In coordination with other agencies and through enhanced integration of INS' overseas, border and interior intelligence operations, this activity seeks to (1) identify, process and remove deportable aliens and those criminal aliens eligible for deportation who are incarcerated in Federal, State and local institutions, (2) increase prosecution and forfeiture activities to disrupt and dismantle criminal, smuggling, and benefit and document fraud organizations, (3) strengthen coordination with federal, state and local law enforcement entities to identify, detain, and remove aliens, particularly those involved in terrorism, violent gangs and criminal activities (4) target worksite enforcement activities toward employers who intentionally hire unauthorized workers in selected industry and geographic areas or engage in related smuggling and fraud ventures, and (5) provide adequate, safe, humane and efficiently run detention bed space and a transportation capability that meets alien detention and removal obligations.

Reimbursable program.—Federal funds in 2001 are derived primarily from the Organized Crime Drug Enforcement Task Force program for multi-agency drug investigations and the Asset Forfeiture Fund for seized assets. The measures below reflect the expected outcomes from these activities.

	1999 actual	2000 est.	2001 est.
Final order removals from the U.S.	178,168	187,500	195,000
Final order criminal alien removals	62,838	67,000	70,300
Final order of non-criminal removals and expedited removals	115,330	120,500	124,700
Principals presented for prosecution for alien smuggling-related violations [1]	1,967	NA	NA
Principals presented for prosecution for benefit and document fraud violations [1]	636	NA	NA
Criminal cases of employers presented for prosecution [1]	182	NA	NA

[1] Performance targets are not specified; actuals are reported for each fiscal year.

Citizenship and benefits, immigration support and program direction.—This account includes the resources for communications, records management, automated data processing, training of personnel, research and development, legal proceedings, and the overall administration and management of the Service. In addition, $4,200,000 for the replacement of the INS financial management system is anticipated to be available from the Assets Forfeiture Fund.

WORKLOAD

	1999 actual	2000 est.	2001 est.
Basic officer training completions	1,708	2,882	2,882
Status verifications completed	5,691,000	5,865,000	6,016,000
Information services inquiries telephone	6,500,000	7,000,000	15,000,000
Information services inquiries by internet	4,795,000	6,000,000	8,000,000

Immigration Services.—Deliver services to the public in a timely, consistent, fair and high quality manner. This activity encompasses efforts to (1) establish and maintain an asylum process that is fair and timely, and that denies meritless claims quickly without discouraging legitimate seekers of asylum, (2) encourage eligible persons to become citizens by establishing and maintaining a naturalization process that is fair, accurate and timely, (3) make "user friendly" customer service an integral, permanent aspect of all INS activities, and (4) provide employers, benefit providers and other appropriate entities with immigration information and alien status, and the assistance and tools needed to allow them to comply with the laws while safeguarding the civil and privacy rights of citizens and aliens alike.

Reimbursable program.—Federal funds in 2001 are derived primarily from the Treasury Department's Federal Law Enforcement Training Center, and from the sale of excess INS-owned vehicles. The measures below reflect the expected outcomes from these activities.

	1999 actual	2000 est.	2001 est.
Naturalization:			
Cases adjudicated	1.2 million	1.3 million	1.05 million
Avg. prospective case processing time	12 months	6 months	6 months
Adjustment of Status:			
Cases adjudicated	301,000	500,000	600,000
Average prospective case processing time	33 months	24 months	14 months
Alien Status Verification Services:			
Status verification average response time for government customers	3 days	3 days	3 days
Status verification average response time for employers	1 day	1 day	1 day
Asylum Cases:			
New asylum cases processed within 60 days	84%	75%	75%
Expedited removal/credible fear cases processed within 14 days	84%	75%	75%
Fingerprinting Services:			
Processing time for fingerprints	3 weeks	1 week	1 week

Object Classification (in millions of dollars)

Identification code 15–1217–0–1–751		1999 actual	2000 est.	2001 est.
	Direct obligations:			
	Personnel compensation:			
11.1	Full-time permanent	827	876	989
11.3	Other than full-time permanent	25	21	23
11.5	Other personnel compensation	268	221	235
11.8	Special personal services payments	1	1	
11.9	Total personnel compensation	1,121	1,119	1,247
12.1	Civilian personnel benefits	362	361	422
13.0	Benefits for former personnel	1	6	6
21.0	Travel and transportation of persons	67	78	80
22.0	Transportation of things	11	17	18
23.1	Rental payments to GSA	87	109	114
23.2	Rental payments to others	11	9	9
23.3	Communications, utilities, and miscellaneous charges	30	43	43
24.0	Printing and reproduction	2	2	2
25.2	Other services	279	305	255
25.3	Purchases of goods and services from Government accounts	250	259	215
25.4	Operation and maintenance of facilities	60	57	62
25.6	Medical care		5	5
25.7	Operation and maintenance of equipment	17	25	24
25.8	Subsistence and support of persons	106	174	247
26.0	Supplies and materials	99	100	95
31.0	Equipment	36	269	266
32.0	Land and structures	1	9	10
41.0	Grants, subsidies, and contributions	9		
42.0	Insurance claims and indemnities	1		
99.0	Subtotal, direct obligations	2,550	2,947	3,120
99.0	Reimbursable obligations	1,261	1,301	1,614
99.9	Total new obligations	3,811	4,248	4,734

Personnel Summary

Identification code 15–1217–0–1–751		1999 actual	2000 est.	2001 est.
	Direct:			
1001	Total compensable workyears: Full-time equivalent employment	20,221	21,469	22,886
	Reimbursable:			
2001	Total compensable workyears: Full-time equivalent employment	9,944	9,786	10,123

CONSTRUCTION

For planning, construction, renovation, equipping, and maintenance of buildings and facilities necessary for the administration and enforcement of the laws relating to immigration, naturalization, and alien registration, not otherwise provided for, [$99,664,000] *$111,135,000*, to remain available until expended: *Provided*, That no funds shall be available for the site acquisition, design, or construction of any Border Patrol checkpoint in the Tucson sector. *(Department of Justice Appropriations Act, 2000, as enacted by section 1000(a)(1) of the Consolidated Appropriations Act, 2000 (P.L. 106–113).)*

Program and Financing (in millions of dollars)

Identification code 15–1219–0–1–751		1999 actual	2000 est.	2001 est.
	Obligations by program activity:			
10.00	Total new obligations	78	118	111
	Budgetary resources available for obligation:			
21.40	Unobligated balance available, start of year	6	18	
22.00	New budget authority (gross)	90	100	111
23.90	Total budgetary resources available for obligation	96	118	111
23.95	Total new obligations	−78	−118	−111
24.40	Unobligated balance available, end of year	18		
	New budget authority (gross), detail:			
	Discretionary:			
40.00	Appropriation	90	100	111
	Change in unpaid obligations:			
72.40	Unpaid obligations, start of year: Obligated balance, start of year	117	148	171
73.10	Total new obligations	78	118	111
73.20	Total outlays (gross)	−47	−95	−91
74.40	Unpaid obligations, end of year: Obligated balance, end of year	148	171	191
	Outlays (gross), detail:			
86.90	Outlays from new discretionary authority	9	10	11
86.93	Outlays from discretionary balances	38	85	80
87.00	Total outlays (gross)	47	95	91
	Net budget authority and outlays:			
89.00	Budget authority	90	100	111
90.00	Outlays	47	95	91

Funds are used for the acquisition, construction and maintenance of Immigration and Naturalization Service facilities. Program enhancements will be used to construct, repair, renovate, and maintain Border Patrol ($51 million) and Detention ($26 million) facilities.

Object Classification (in millions of dollars)

Identification code 15–1219–0–1–751		1999 actual	2000 est.	2001 est.
11.1	Personnel compensation: Full-time permanent	2	3	3
12.1	Civilian personnel benefits	1	1	1
25.2	Other services	34	41	46
25.3	Purchases of goods and services from Government accounts	36	34	22
26.0	Supplies and materials	4	1	1
31.0	Equipment	1	1	1
32.0	Land and structures		37	37
99.9	Total new obligations	78	118	111

Personnel Summary

Identification code 15–1219–0–1–751		1999 actual	2000 est.	2001 est.
1001	Total compensable workyears: Full-time equivalent employment	35	71	81

IMMIGRATION EMERGENCY FUND

[(RESCISSION)]

[Of the unobligated balances available under this heading, $1,137,000 are rescinded.] *(Department of Justice Appropriations Act, 2000, as enacted by section 1000(a)(1) of the Consolidated Appropriations Act, 2000 (P.L. 106–113).)*

General and special funds—Continued

IMMIGRATION EMERGENCY FUND—Continued

[(RESCISSION)]—Continued

Program and Financing (in millions of dollars)

Identification code 15–1218–0–1–751	1999 actual	2000 est.	2001 est.
Obligations by program activity:			
10.00 Total new obligations (object class 25.2)	1		
Budgetary resources available for obligation:			
21.40 Unobligated balance available, start of year	6	1	
22.00 New budget authority (gross)	−5		
23.90 Total budgetary resources available for obligation	1	1	
23.95 Total new obligations	−1		
24.40 Unobligated balance available, end of year	1		
New budget authority (gross), detail:			
Discretionary:			
40.36 Unobligated balance rescinded	−5	−1	
Change in unpaid obligations:			
73.10 Total new obligations	1		
Outlays (gross), detail:			
86.93 Outlays from discretionary balances	1		
Net budget authority and outlays:			
89.00 Budget authority	−5		
90.00 Outlays	1		

The Consolidated Budget Appropriations Act of 1999, (P.L. 106–113) rescinded all remaining balances of the Immigration Emergency Fund established by the Immigration Reform and Control Act and funded by Public Law 101–162. The Immigration Emergency Fund provided reimbursements to States and localities for assistance in meeting immigration emergencies.

IMMIGRATION SUPPORT

IMMIGRATION SERVICES CAPITAL INVESTMENT

For backlog reduction, infrastructure improvements, process improvements, major capital acquisitions, and such other service-related expenses and programs necessary for the administration of the laws relating to immigration, naturalization, and alien registration, $34,800,000, to remain available until expended.

Unavailable Collections (in millions of dollars)

Identification code 15–9921–0–2–751	1999 actual	2000 est.	2001 est.
Balance, start of year:			
01.99 Balance, start of year	143	30	8
Receipts:			
02.02 Immigration enforcement	4	3	3
02.04 Immigration user fee	423	475	602
02.05 Immigration examinations fee	630	744	887
02.06 Land border inspection fee	1	6	6
02.07 Breached bond/Detention fund	84	72	118
02.99 Total receipts	1,142	1,300	1,616
04.00 Total: Balances and collections	1,285	1,330	1,624
Appropriation:			
05.01 Immigration support	−1,255	−1,322	−1,621
05.99 Subtotal appropriation	−1,255	−1,322	−1,621
07.99 Total balance, end of year	30	8	3

Program and Financing (in millions of dollars)

Identification code 15–9921–0–2–751	1999 actual	2000 est.	2001 est.
Obligations by program activity:			
00.01 Immigration examinations fee	639	755	887
00.02 Immigration user fee	454	487	529
00.03 Immigration legalization fund			
00.04 Land Border inspection fee	1	2	2
00.05 Breached bond/Detention fund	157	77	118
00.07 Enforcement fines account	4	1	4
00.08 Immigration services capital investment account			128
10.00 Total new obligations (object class 25.2)	1,255	1,322	1,668
Budgetary resources available for obligation:			
21.40 Unobligated balance available, start of year	46	93	103
22.00 New budget authority (gross)	1,255	1,322	1,656
22.10 Resources available from recoveries of prior year obligations	47	10	
23.90 Total budgetary resources available for obligation	1,348	1,425	1,759
23.95 Total new obligations	−1,255	−1,322	−1,668
24.40 Unobligated balance available, end of year	93	103	91
New budget authority (gross), detail:			
Discretionary:			
40.00 Appropriation			35
40.20 Appropriation (special fund, definite)			322
43.00 Appropriation (total discretionary)			357
Mandatory:			
60.25 Appropriation (special fund, indefinite)	1,255	1,322	1,299
70.00 Total new budget authority (gross)	1,255	1,322	1,656
Change in unpaid obligations:			
72.40 Unpaid obligations, start of year: Obligated balance, start of year	3	29	19
73.10 Total new obligations	1,255	1,322	1,668
73.20 Total outlays (gross)	−1,182	−1,322	−1,656
73.45 Adjustments in unexpired accounts	−47	−10	
74.40 Unpaid obligations, end of year: Obligated balance, end of year	29	19	31
Outlays (gross), detail:			
86.90 Outlays from new discretionary authority			357
86.97 Outlays from new mandatory authority	1,182	1,322	1,299
87.00 Total outlays (gross)	1,182	1,322	1,656
Net budget authority and outlays:			
89.00 Budget authority	1,255	1,322	1,656
90.00 Outlays	1,182	1,322	1,656

Immigration user fee.—Established by Public Laws 99–500 and 99–591. Provides for the reimbursement to the Immigration and Naturalization Service's appropriation the amount paid for certain expenses. These expenses include: (a) providing immigration inspection and preinspection services for commercial aircraft and vessels, (b) providing overtime immigration inspection services for commercial aircraft and vessels, (c) expanding and operating information systems for nonimmigrant control and debt collection, (d) detecting and training of carriers' personnel regarding fraudulent documents, and (e) providing detention and deportation services for excludable aliens arriving on commercial aircraft or vessels.

WORKLOAD

	1999 actual	2000 est.	2001 est.
Total persons inspected (air and sea)	85,661,450	89,000,000	92,000,000
Inadmissable aliens intercepted (air and sea)	239,466	248,000	257,000
Number of detention days	434,429	473,569	485,450
Aliens detained	7,622	7,622	8,517

Land border inspection fee.—Established by Public Law 101–515. Authorizes the Attorney General to establish, by regulation, a project under which a fee may be charged and collected for inspection services at one or more land border ports of entry. All deposits to the account are to be available until expended for expenses incurred in providing inspection services at land border ports of entry.

Breached bond/Detention fund.—Established by Public Law 102–395. Provides for the depositing into a separate U.S. Treasury account all bonds forfeited by aliens in excess of $8 million. All deposits to the account are to be available until expended for the collection of breached bonds and detention and removal activities of the Immigration and Naturalization Service. As of October 1, 1997, the Immigration Detention Account established by Public Law 104–208 for the detention of aliens under Sections 236(c) and 241(a) of the Immigration and Nationality Act (INA) is merged with the Breached Bond Detention Fund.

Immigration examinations fee.—Established by Public Law 100–979. Provides for the depositing into a separate U.S. Treasury account all adjudications fees collected under the regulations governing the Immigration and Naturalization Service. All deposits to the account are to be available until expended for the adjudication of applications and petitions for benefits and for necessary support for the adjudications and naturalization programs, for the International Affairs and Outreach's asylum program, and for Cuban and Haitian resettlement activities. Beginning October 21, 1998, the Immigration Legalization account was merged with the Immigration Examinations Fee account.

Immigration Examinations Fee Account Workload

	1999 actual	*2000 est.*	*2001 est.*
Total Benefits Applications received	5,398,215	5,802,000	5,802,000
Total Benefits Applications completed	5,221,698	5,400,000	5,400,000
Naturalizations Applications received	863,656	700,000	700,000
Naturalizations Applications completed	1,332,651	1,300,000	1,300,000
Adjustments of Status Applications received	456,246	316,000	316,000
Adjustments of Status Applications completed	299,887	500,000	500,000
Asylum Cases received	42,530	41,400	41,400
Asylum Cases completed	57,933	50,000	50,000

Immigration enforcement account.—Established by Public Law 104–208. May be used for: the identification, investigation, apprehension, detention, and removal of criminal aliens; and repair, maintenance, or construction in high-level illegal alien apprehension areas along U.S. borders.

Immigration Services Capital Investment.—The establishment of this account will provide for the depositing into a separate U.S. Treasury account a portion of the receipts generated from immigration adjustment of status penalties, business-related application premium processing revenues and appropriations. All deposits to the account are to be available until expended for initiatives to address application backlogs, infrastructure improvements, process improvements, major capital acquisitions, and such other service-related expenses and programs.

SHARED SUPPORT OPERATIONS FUND

(INCLUDING TRANSFER OF FUNDS)

There is hereby established a Shared Support Operations Fund for the Immigration and Naturalization Service ("INS"), which shall be available without fiscal year limitation, for expenses and equipment necessary for the operation and maintenance of such administrative services as the Commissioner of INS, with the approval of the Department of Justice and Office of Management and Budget, determines may be performed more advantageously as central services. The capital of the fund shall consist of the amount of the fair and reasonable value of such inventories, equipment, and other assets and inventories on order pertaining to the services to be carried on by the Fund as the Commissioner may transfer to the Fund, less related liabilities and unpaid obligations, together with any appropriations made for the purpose of providing capital: Provided, That the Fund shall be reimbursed or credited with advance payments from applicable appropriations and amounts available for INS, other Federal agencies, and other sources as authorized by law for supplies, materials, and services at rates that will recover the expenses of Fund operations including, without limitation, depreciation of plant and equipment of the Fund. The Fund shall also be credited with other receipts from the sale or exchange of property or in payment for loss or damages to property held by the Fund: Provided further, That all retained earnings shall remain available without limitation, for the acquisition of capital equipment, automated systems and to implement financial, personnel, recordkeeping and management system improvements.

Program and Financing (in millions of dollars)

Identification code 15–4517–0–4–751	1999 actual	2000 est.	2001 est.
Obligations by program activity:			
10.00 Total new obligations (object class 25.2)			155
Budgetary resources available for obligation:			
22.00 New budget authority (gross)			155
23.95 Total new obligations			−155
New budget authority (gross), detail:			
Discretionary:			
68.00 Spending authority from offsetting collections (gross): Offsetting collections (cash)			155
Change in unpaid obligations:			
73.10 Total new obligations			155
73.20 Total outlays (gross)			−155
Outlays (gross), detail:			
86.90 Outlays from new discretionary authority			155
Offsets:			
Against gross budget authority and outlays:			
88.00 Offsetting collections (cash) from: Federal sources			−155
Net budget authority and outlays:			
89.00 Budget authority			
90.00 Outlays			

The Shared Support Operations Fund is requested to be established to finance, on a reimbursable basis, those shared administrative functions that serve both enforcement and service operations.

FEDERAL PRISON SYSTEM

Federal Funds

General and special funds:

SALARIES AND EXPENSES

For expenses necessary for the administration, operation, and maintenance of Federal penal and correctional institutions, including purchase (not to exceed [708] *707*, of which [602] *600* are for replacement only) and hire of law enforcement and passenger motor vehicles, and for the provision of technical assistance and advice on corrections related issues to foreign governments, [$3,089,110,000; of which not less than $500,000 shall be transferred to and administered by the Department of Justice Wireless Management Office for the costs of conversion to narrowband communications and for the operations and maintenance of legacy Land Mobile Radio systems] *$3,545,769,000*: *Provided*, That the Attorney General may transfer to the Health Resources and Services Administration such amounts as may be necessary for direct expenditures by that Administration for medical relief for inmates of Federal penal and correctional institutions: *Provided further*, That the Director of the Federal Prison System (FPS), where necessary, may enter into contracts with a fiscal agent/fiscal intermediary claims processor to determine the amounts payable to persons who, on behalf of FPS, furnish health services to individuals committed to the custody of FPS: *Provided further*, That not to exceed $6,000 shall be available for official reception and representation expenses: *Provided further*, That not to exceed $90,000,000 shall remain available for necessary operations until September 30, [2001] *2002*: *Provided further*, That, of the amounts provided for Contract Confinement, not to exceed $20,000,000 shall remain available until expended to make payments in advance for grants, contracts and reimbursable agreements, and other expenses authorized by section 501(c) of the Refugee Education Assistance Act of 1980, as amended, for the care and security in the United States of Cuban and Haitian entrants: *Provided further*, That, notwithstanding section 4(d) of the Service Contract Act of 1965 (41 U.S.C. 353(d)), FPS may enter into contracts and other agreements with private entities for periods of not to exceed 3 years and seven additional option years for the confinement of Federal prisoners.

[In addition, $22,524,000, for such purposes, to remain available until expended, to be derived from the Violent Crime Reduction Trust

General and special funds—Continued

SALARIES AND EXPENSES—Continued

Fund.] *(Department of Justice Appropriations Act, 2000, as enacted by section 1000(a)(1) of the Consolidated Appropriations Act, 2000 (P.L. 106–113).)*

Program and Financing (in millions of dollars)

Identification code 15–1060–0–1–753		1999 actual	2000 est.	2001 est.
	Obligations by program activity:			
	Direct program:			
	Operating expenses:			
00.01	Inmate care and programs	1,009	1,138	1,219
00.02	Institution security and administration	1,352	1,532	1,605
00.03	Contract confinement	260	345	543
00.04	Program direction	121	147	153
00.05	Inmate care and programs (VCRP)	30	27	
00.91	Total operating expenses	2,772	3,189	3,520
01.01	Capital investment: Institutional improvements	42	19	26
01.92	Total direct program	2,814	3,208	3,546
09.01	Reimbursable program	54	22	22
10.00	Total new obligations	2,868	3,230	3,568
	Budgetary resources available for obligation:			
21.40	Unobligated balance available, start of year	110	97	
22.00	New budget authority (gross)	2,901	3,134	3,568
23.90	Total budgetary resources available for obligation	3,011	3,231	3,568
23.95	Total new obligations	−2,868	−3,230	−3,568
23.98	Unobligated balance expiring or withdrawn	−46		
24.40	Unobligated balance available, end of year	97		
	New budget authority (gross), detail:			
	Discretionary:			
40.00	Appropriation	2,862	3,089	3,546
41.00	Transferred to other accounts	−154		
42.00	Transferred from other accounts	26	23	
43.00	Appropriation (total discretionary)	2,734	3,112	3,546
50.00	Reappropriation	113		
68.00	Spending authority from offsetting collections: Offsetting collections (cash)	54	22	22
70.00	Total new budget authority (gross)	2,901	3,134	3,568
	Change in unpaid obligations:			
72.40	Unpaid obligations, start of year: Obligated balance, start of year	373	433	546
73.10	Total new obligations	2,868	3,230	3,568
73.20	Total outlays (gross)	−2,811	−3,118	−3,400
73.40	Adjustments in expired accounts (net)	3		
74.40	Unpaid obligations, end of year: Obligated balance, end of year	433	546	714
	Outlays (gross), detail:			
86.90	Outlays from new discretionary authority	2,401	2,668	3,036
86.93	Outlays from discretionary balances	410	450	365
87.00	Total outlays (gross)	2,811	3,118	3,400
	Offsets:			
	Against gross budget authority and outlays:			
	Offsetting collections (cash) from:			
88.00	Federal sources	−37	−5	−5
88.40	Non-Federal sources	−17	−17	−17
88.90	Total, offsetting collections (cash)	−54	−22	−22
	Net budget authority and outlays:			
89.00	Budget authority	2,847	3,112	3,546
90.00	Outlays	2,757	3,096	3,378

	1999 actual	2000 est.	2001 est.
Distribution of budget authority by account:			
Salaries and expenses	2,821	3,089	3,456
Violent crime reduction programs	26	23	
Distribution of outlays by account:			
Salaries and expenses	2,727	3,069	3,376
Violent crime reduction programs	30	27	2

This appropriation will provide for the custody and care of an average of 129,128 offenders and for the maintenance and operation of 101 penal institutions, 6 regional offices, 3 staff training centers, and a central office located in Washington, D.C.

The appropriation also finances the boarding of sentenced Federal prisoners in State and local jails and therapeutic, community residential and other facilities for short periods of time. An average of 24,639 sentenced prisoners will be in contract facilities in 2001.

The Bureau receives reimbursements for daily care and maintenance of State and local offenders, for utilities used by Federal Prison Industries, Inc., for staff housing, and for meals provided to Bureau staff at institutions.

Inmate care and programs.—This activity covers the cost of all food, medical supplies, clothing, welfare services, release clothing, transportation, gratuities, staff salaries (including salaries of Health Resources and Services Administration commissioned officers), and operational costs of functions directly related to providing inmate care. This activity also finances the costs of academic, social and occupational education courses, religious programs, psychological services, and other inmate programs.

Institution security and administration.—This activity covers costs associated with the maintenance of facilities and institution security. This activity finances institution maintenance, motor pool operations, powerhouse operations, institution security, and other administrative functions.

Contract confinement.—This activity provides for the confinement of sentenced Federal offenders in Government-owned, contractor-operated facilities and contract State and local facilities, and for the care of Federal prisoners in contract community residential centers and assistance by the National Institute of Corrections to State and local corrections.

Management and administration.—This activity covers all costs associated with regional and central office executive direction and management support functions such as research and evaluation, systems support, financial management, human resources management, inmate systems management, safety, and legal counsel.

For 2001, program increases are requested for activation of four new facilities and six expansions (6,250 beds): USP Pollock, LA; USP Atwater, CA; USP Coleman, FL, and FDC Honolulu, HI. The expansions are at: Ft. Dix, NJ; Elkton, OH; Jesup, GA; Yazoo City, MS; Seagoville, TX, and Lompoc, CA. Also included are funds to purchase initial activation equipment for USP Lee County, VA and FCI Petersburg, VA; add 6,000 low security beds to house short-term criminal aliens and females from the South and Western regions; support a contract population increase, and increase inmate enrollment in education programming.

Object Classification (in millions of dollars)

Identification code 15–1060–0–1–753		1999 actual	2000 est.	2001 est.
	Direct obligations:			
	Personnel compensation:			
11.1	Full-time permanent	1,192	1,345	1,420
11.3	Other than full-time permanent	6	7	7
11.5	Other personnel compensation	106	123	131
11.8	Special personal services payments	1	1	2
11.9	Total personnel compensation	1,305	1,476	1,560
12.1	Civilian personnel benefits	509	586	631
13.0	Benefits for former personnel	1	1	1
21.0	Travel and transportation of persons	28	37	38
22.0	Transportation of things	11	12	12
23.1	Rental payments to GSA	13	16	16
23.3	Communications, utilities, and miscellaneous charges	126	135	137
24.0	Printing and reproduction	2	3	3
25.2	Other services	221	316	514
25.4	Operation and maintenance of facilities	52	53	54
25.6	Medical care	75	82	84
25.7	Operation and maintenance of equipment	6	6	6
25.8	Subsistence and support of persons	92	116	116

26.0	Supplies and materials	279	304	300
31.0	Equipment	42	19	26
32.0	Land and structures	1		
41.0	Grants, subsidies, and contributions	9	3	3
99.0	Subtotal, direct obligations	2,772	3,165	3,501
99.0	Reimbursable obligations	54	22	22
	Allocation Account:			
11.1	Personnel compensation: Full-time permanent	28	29	30
12.1	Civilian personnel benefits	12	12	13
25.2	Other services	2	2	2
99.0	Subtotal, allocation account	42	43	45
99.9	Total new obligations	2,868	3,230	3,568

Personnel Summary

Identification code 15–1060–0–1–753		1999 actual	2000 est.	2001 est.
	Direct:			
1001	Total compensable workyears: Full-time equivalent employment	28,238	31,692	32,118
	Reimbursable:			
2001	Total compensable workyears: Full-time equivalent employment	136	136	136

Buildings and Facilities

For planning, acquisition of sites and construction of new facilities; leasing the Oklahoma City Airport Trust Facility; purchase and acquisition of facilities and remodeling, and equipping of such facilities for penal and correctional use, including all necessary expenses incident thereto, by contract or force account; and constructing, remodeling, and equipping necessary buildings and facilities at existing penal and correctional institutions, including all necessary expenses incident thereto, by contract or force account, [$556,791,000] *$835,660,000,* to remain available until expended, of which not to exceed [$14,074,000] *$14,000,000* shall be available to construct areas for inmate work programs: *Provided,* That labor of United States prisoners may be used for work performed under this appropriation: *Provided further,* That not to exceed 10 percent of the funds appropriated to "Buildings and Facilities" in this or any other Act may be transferred to "Salaries and Expenses", Federal Prison System, upon notification by the Attorney General to the Committees on Appropriations of the House of Representatives and the Senate in compliance with provisions set forth in section 605 of this Act. *In addition, for necessary expenses for planning, acquisition of sites and construction of new facilities, to become available on October 1 of the fiscal year specified and remain available until expended: fiscal year 2002, $791,000,000; and fiscal year 2003, $535,000,000. (Department of Justice Appropriations Act, 2000, as enacted by section 1000(a)(1) of the Consolidated Appropriations Act, 2000 (P.L. 106–113).)*

Program and Financing (in millions of dollars)

Identification code 15–1003–0–1–753		1999 actual	2000 est.	2001 est.
	Obligations by program activity:			
00.01	New construction	497	450	638
00.02	Modernization and repair of existing facilities	109	116	120
09.01	Reimbursable program	154	32	2
10.00	Total new obligations	760	598	760
	Budgetary resources available for obligation:			
21.40	Unobligated balance available, start of year	752	473	431
22.00	New budget authority (gross)	481	557	836
23.90	Total budgetary resources available for obligation	1,233	1,030	1,267
23.95	Total new obligations	–760	–598	–760
24.40	Unobligated balance available, end of year	473	431	507
	New budget authority (gross), detail:			
	Discretionary:			
40.00	Appropriation	411	557	836
42.00	Transferred from other accounts	41		
43.00	Appropriation (total discretionary)	452	557	836
68.00	Spending authority from offsetting collections: Offsetting collections (cash)	29		
70.00	Total new budget authority (gross)	481	557	836
	Change in unpaid obligations:			
72.40	Unpaid obligations, start of year: Obligated balance, start of year	554	831	969
73.10	Total new obligations	760	598	760
73.20	Total outlays (gross)	–484	–460	–665
74.40	Unpaid obligations, end of year: Obligated balance, end of year	831	969	1,065
	Outlays (gross), detail:			
86.90	Outlays from new discretionary authority	70	56	84
86.93	Outlays from discretionary balances	414	404	581
87.00	Total outlays (gross)	484	460	665
	Offsets:			
	Against gross budget authority and outlays:			
88.00	Offsetting collections (cash) from: Federal sources	–29		
	Net budget authority and outlays:			
89.00	Budget authority	452	557	836
90.00	Outlays	455	460	665

New construction.—This activity represents costs associated with the acquisition, construction, and leasing of facilities in order to reduce overcrowding and provide a safe and humane environment for staff and inmates. In 2001, resources are requested for partial site and planning of two penitentiaries and three medium security facilities. The balance of funds for these five institutions and for another U.S. Penitentiary with previous funding is requested for 2002 as an advance appropriation. In addition for 2001, this request includes remaining construction funds for one penitentiary and five medium security institutions, with some prior funding. For 2002 and 2003, additional advance appropriations are requested for site, planning and construction for four medium security institutions and a secure female unit.

Modernization and repair of existing facilities.—This activity includes rehabilitation and renovation of buildings, necessary modifications to accommodate new correctional programs, rehabilitation or replacement of utilities systems, and repair projects at existing facilities.

Object Classification (in millions of dollars)

Identification code 15–1003–0–1–753		1999 actual	2000 est.	2001 est.
	Direct obligations:			
	Personnel compensation:			
11.1	Full-time permanent	14	18	20
11.5	Other personnel compensation	1	1	1
11.9	Total personnel compensation	15	19	21
12.1	Civilian personnel benefits	6	8	8
21.0	Travel and transportation of persons	2	2	2
23.2	Rental payments to others	9	11	13
23.3	Communications, utilities, and miscellaneous charges	4	6	8
25.2	Other services	529	473	654
26.0	Supplies and materials	23	24	29
31.0	Equipment	13	15	17
32.0	Land and structures	5	8	6
99.0	Subtotal, direct obligations	606	566	758
99.0	Reimbursable obligations	154	32	2
99.9	Total new obligations	760	598	760

Personnel Summary

Identification code 15–1003–0–1–753		1999 actual	2000 est.	2001 est.
1001	Total compensable workyears: Full-time equivalent employment	243	334	335

Intragovernmental funds:

FEDERAL PRISON INDUSTRIES, INCORPORATED

The Federal Prison Industries, Incorporated, is hereby authorized to make such expenditures, within the limits of funds and borrowing authority available, and in accord with the law, and to make such contracts and commitments, without regard to fiscal year limitations as provided by section 9104 of title 31, United States Code, as may be necessary in carrying out the program set forth in the budget for the current fiscal year for such corporation, including purchase of (not to exceed five for replacement only) and hire of passenger motor vehicles. *(Department of Justice Appropriations Act, 2000, as enacted by section 1000(a)(1) of the Consolidated Appropriations Act, 2000 (P.L. 106–113).)*

Program and Financing (in millions of dollars)

Identification code 15–4500–0–4–753		1999 actual	2000 est.	2001 est.
	Obligations by program activity:			
	Operating expenses:			
09.01	Production expenses	531	537	565
09.02	Administrative expenses	2	3	4
09.03	Other expenses	11	34	34
09.09	Total operating expenses	544	574	603
	Capital Investment:			
09.10	Buildings and improvements	14	21	21
09.11	Machinery and equipment	4	13	13
09.19	Total capital investment	18	34	34
10.00	Total new obligations	562	608	637
	Budgetary resources available for obligation:			
21.40	Unobligated balance available, start of year	149	50	47
22.00	New budget authority (gross)	463	605	608
23.90	Total budgetary resources available for obligation	612	655	655
23.95	Total new obligations	−562	−608	−637
24.40	Unobligated balance available, end of year	50	47	18
	New budget authority (gross), detail:			
	Discretionary:			
68.00	Spending authority from offsetting collections: Offsetting collections (cash)	3	4	4
	Mandatory:			
69.00	Offsetting collections (cash)	460	601	604
70.00	Total new budget authority (gross)	463	605	608
	Change in unpaid obligations:			
72.40	Unpaid obligations, start of year: Obligated balance, start of year	−61	46	49
73.10	Total new obligations	562	608	637
73.20	Total outlays (gross)	−455	−605	−608
74.40	Unpaid obligations, end of year: Obligated balance, end of year	46	49	78
	Outlays (gross), detail:			
86.90	Outlays from new discretionary authority	3	4	4
86.97	Outlays from new mandatory authority	452	601	604
87.00	Total outlays (gross)	455	605	608
	Offsets:			
	Against gross budget authority and outlays:			
88.00	Offsetting collections (cash) from: Federal sources	−463	−605	−608
	Net budget authority and outlays:			
89.00	Budget authority			
90.00	Outlays	−8		
	Memorandum (non-add) entries:			
92.01	Total investments, start of year: U.S. securities: Par value	62	62	62
92.02	Total investments, end of year: U.S. securities: Par value	62	62	62

Federal Prison Industries, Inc., was created by Congress in 1934 and is a wholly-owned Government corporation. Its mission is to employ and train Federal inmates through a diversified program providing products and services to other Federal agencies. These operations are conducted in such a manner as to offer a minimum of competition to private industry and labor. Employment provides inmates with work, occupational knowledge and skills, plus money for personal expenses and family assistance.

The Corporation strives to provide additional industrial employment opportunities at existing and planned institutions.

Budget program.—Federal Prison Industries, Inc., operations are entirely self-sustaining. No appropriations are required. The amounts used by the Corporation for administrative expenses are subject to a congressional limitation. Information regarding this limitation is provided separately following this account.

Financing program.—Revenues are derived entirely from the sale of products and services to other Federal agencies. Operating expenses are applied against these revenues, resulting in operating income or loss. Earnings surplus to the needs of the manufacturing operations, capital improvements and cash reserves are used to pay accident compensation.

Operating results.—To date, Federal Prison Industries, Inc., has returned to the Treasury a total of $82 million of retained income excess to the Corporation's needs. No contributions from budget authority have been made to offset deficits for non-revenue producing outlays since the inception of the fund.

Object Classification (in millions of dollars)

Identification code 15–4500–0–4–753		1999 actual	2000 est.	2001 est.
	Personnel compensation:			
11.1	Full-time permanent	87	82	85
11.3	Other than full-time permanent		1	1
11.5	Other personnel compensation		4	4
11.8	Special personal services payments	34	39	40
11.9	Total personnel compensation	121	126	130
12.1	Civilian personnel benefits	29	50	52
21.0	Travel and transportation of persons	2	5	5
22.0	Transportation of things	2	14	16
23.2	Rental payments to others		2	2
23.3	Communications, utilities, and miscellaneous charges	2	10	11
24.0	Printing and reproduction	2	3	3
25.2	Other services	15	15	15
26.0	Supplies and materials	369	346	366
31.0	Equipment	4	13	13
32.0	Land and structures	14	21	21
93.0	Limitation on expenses	2	3	3
99.0	Subtotal, reimbursable obligations	562	608	637
99.9	Total new obligations	562	608	637

Personnel Summary

Identification code 15–4500–0–4–753		1999 actual	2000 est.	2001 est.
2001	Total compensable workyears: Full-time equivalent employment	1,663	1,844	1,901

LIMITATION ON ADMINISTRATIVE EXPENSES, FEDERAL PRISON INDUSTRIES, INCORPORATED

Not to exceed $3,429,000 of the funds of the corporation shall be available for its administrative expenses, and for services as authorized by 5 U.S.C. 3109, to be computed on an accrual basis to be determined in accordance with the corporation's current prescribed accounting system, and such amounts shall be exclusive of depreciation, payment of claims, and expenditures which the said accounting system requires to be capitalized or charged to cost of commodities acquired or produced, including selling and shipping expenses, and expenses in connection with acquisition, construction, operation, maintenance, improvement, protection, or disposition of facilities and other property belonging to the corporation or in which it has an interest. *(Department of Justice Appropriations Act, 2000, as enacted by section 1000(a)(1) of the Consolidated Appropriations Act, 2000 (P.L. 106–113).)*

Object Classification (in millions of dollars)

Identification code 15–4500–0–4–753	1999 actual	2000 est.	2001 est.
11.1 Personnel compensation: Full-time permanent	1	1	1
26.0 Supplies and materials	1	2	2
93.0 Limitation on expenses	−2	−3	−3
99.0 Subtotal, limitation acct—reimbursable obligations			

Personnel Summary

Identification code 15–4500–0–4–753	1999 actual	2000 est.	2001 est.
7001 Total compensable workyears: Full-time equivalent employment	29	32	32

Trust Funds

Commissary Funds, Federal Prisons

(TRUST REVOLVING FUND)

Program and Financing (in millions of dollars)

Identification code 15–8408–0–8–753	1999 actual	2000 est.	2001 est.
Obligations by program activity:			
09.00 Sales program	194	194	201
09.01 Capital investment and equipment	3	4	4
10.00 Total new obligations	197	198	205
Budgetary resources available for obligation:			
21.40 Unobligated balance available, start of year	96	91	94
22.00 New budget authority (gross)	192	201	209
23.90 Total budgetary resources available for obligation	288	292	303
23.95 Total new obligations	−197	−198	−205
24.40 Unobligated balance available, end of year	91	94	98
New budget authority (gross), detail:			
Mandatory:			
69.00 Offsetting collections (cash)	192	201	209
Change in unpaid obligations:			
72.40 Unpaid obligations, start of year: Obligated balance, start of year	12	17	12
73.10 Total new obligations	197	198	205
73.20 Total outlays (gross)	−192	−203	−205
74.40 Unpaid obligations, end of year: Obligated balance, end of year	17	12	12
Outlays (gross), detail:			
86.97 Outlays from new mandatory authority	191	201	205
86.98 Outlays from mandatory balances	1	2	
87.00 Total outlays (gross)	192	203	205
Offsets:			
Against gross budget authority and outlays:			
88.40 Offsetting collections (cash) from: Non-Federal sources	−192	−201	−209
Net budget authority and outlays:			
89.00 Budget authority			
90.00 Outlays		2	−4
Memorandum (non-add) entries:			
92.01 Total investments, start of year: U.S. securities: Par value	94	22	22
92.02 Total investments, end of year: U.S. securities: Par value	22	22	22

Budget program.—The commissary fund consists of the operation of commissaries for the inmates as an earned privilege.

Financing.—Profits are derived from the sale of goods and services to inmates. Sales for 2001 are estimated at $209 million. Adequate working capital is assured from retained earnings.

Operating results.—Profits received are used for programs, goods, and services for the benefit of inmates.

Object Classification (in millions of dollars)

Identification code 15–8408–0–8–753	1999 actual	2000 est.	2001 est.
Personnel compensation:			
11.1 Full-time permanent	18	20	21
11.5 Other personnel compensation	1		
11.8 Special personal services payments	23	23	24
11.9 Total personnel compensation	42	43	45
12.1 Civilian personnel benefits	7	8	9
25.2 Other services	13	11	12
26.0 Supplies and materials	132	132	135
31.0 Equipment	3	4	4
99.9 Total new obligations	197	198	205

Personnel Summary

Identification code 15–8408–0–8–753	1999 actual	2000 est.	2001 est.
2001 Total compensable workyears: Full-time equivalent employment	444	576	598

OFFICE OF JUSTICE PROGRAMS

Federal Funds

General and special funds:

Justice Assistance

For grants, contracts, cooperative agreements, and other assistance authorized by title I of the Omnibus Crime Control and Safe Streets Act of 1968, as amended ("the 1968 Act"), and the Missing Children's Assistance Act, as amended, including salaries and expenses in connection therewith, and with the Victims of Crime Act of 1984, as amended, [$155,611,000] *$186,260,000*, to remain available until expended, as authorized by section 1001 of title I of the Omnibus Crime Control and Safe Streets Act of 1968, as amended by Public Law 102–534 (106 Stat. 3524).

In addition, for grants, cooperative agreements, and other assistance authorized by sections 819, 821, and 822 of the Antiterrorism and Effective Death Penalty Act of 1996, [$152,000,000] *$185,000,000*, to remain available until expended. *(Department of Justice Appropriations Act, 2000, as enacted by section 1000(a)(1) of the Consolidated Appropriations Act, 2000 (P.L. 106–113).)*

Program and Financing (in millions of dollars)

Identification code 15–0401–0–1–754	1999 actual	2000 est.	2001 est.
Obligations by program activity:			
Direct program:			
00.01 Research, evaluation, and demonstration programs	48	45	49
00.02 Technology centers	10	10	
00.03 Criminal justice statistics program	27	26	33
00.04 National sex offender registry	1		
00.05 Missing children	11	26	20
00.06 Regional information sharing system	20	20	20
00.07 White collar crime and information center	7	9	18
00.08 Local firefighter and emergency services training	3		
00.09 Counterterrorism programs		152	179
00.10 Next generation NCJRS (JOIE)			1
00.11 Police use of force			2
00.14 Crime control		1	
00.15 Management and administration	39	58	56
09.01 Reimbursable program	176	399	265
10.00 Total new obligations	342	746	643
Budgetary resources available for obligation:			
21.40 Unobligated balance available, start of year	32	163	
22.00 New budget authority (gross)	466	580	643
22.10 Resources available from recoveries of prior year obligations	7	3	
23.90 Total budgetary resources available for obligation	505	746	643
23.95 Total new obligations	−342	−746	−643
24.40 Unobligated balance available, end of year	163		

General and special funds—Continued

JUSTICE ASSISTANCE—Continued

Program and Financing (in millions of dollars)—Continued

Identification code 15–0401–0–1–754		1999 actual	2000 est.	2001 est.
	New budget authority (gross), detail:			
	Discretionary:			
40.00	Appropriation	147	308	371
42.00	Transferred from other accounts	9	7	7
43.00	Appropriation (total discretionary)	156	315	378
68.00	Spending authority from offsetting collections: Offsetting collections (cash)	310	265	265
70.00	Total new budget authority (gross)	466	580	643
	Change in unpaid obligations:			
72.40	Unpaid obligations, start of year: Obligated balance, start of year	133	210	429
73.10	Total new obligations	342	746	643
73.20	Total outlays (gross)	−259	−524	−517
73.45	Adjustments in unexpired accounts	−7	−3	....
74.40	Unpaid obligations, end of year: Obligated balance, end of year	210	429	555
	Outlays (gross), detail:			
86.90	Outlays from new discretionary authority	210	334	348
86.93	Outlays from discretionary balances	49	190	169
87.00	Total outlays (gross)	259	524	517
	Offsets:			
	Against gross budget authority and outlays:			
88.00	Offsetting collections (cash) from: Federal sources	−310	−265	−265
	Net budget authority and outlays:			
89.00	Budget authority	156	315	378
90.00	Outlays	−51	259	252

The Office of Justice Programs (OJP) carries out policy coordination and general management responsibilities for the Bureau of Justice Assistance, Bureau of Justice Statistics, National Institute of Justice, Office of Juvenile Justice and Delinquency Prevention, Office for Victims of Crime, and six program offices. The following OJP programs are funded through the Justice Assistance account.

Research, evaluation, and demonstration programs.—Funds provide for and encourage the development of basic and applied research for the improvement of Federal, State, and local criminal, civil, and juvenile justice systems; new methods for the prevention and reduction of crime and the detection, apprehension, and rehabilitation of criminals; and the dissemination of the results of such research efforts. In 2001, $5,000,000 is requested for continued expansion of the Arrestee Drug Abuse Monitoring (ADAM) program, $1,400,000 is requested to expand the services of the International Office, $10,000,000 is to develop gun detection/childproof technologies, and $2,000,000 is for investigative and forensic sciences.

Technology centers.—These technology centers were established to bring technology information directly to law enforcement agencies, principally to State and local levels, and to provide a source of objective technology information. In 2001, these are funded under the COPS Initiative, but will continue to be administered by OJP.

Criminal justice statistical programs.—Funds provide for the collection and analysis of statistical information concerning crime, victims, offenders, criminal justice processes, juvenile delinquency, and civil disputes in support of public and private policy and decisionmaking about society's response to crime; planning, coordination, implementation and provision of technical assistance to States to initiate innovative applications of communications and information systems technology for State and local criminal justice systems; and assurance of conformity with privacy and security regulations.

In 2001, $5,600,000 is requested to expand the collection and analysis of statistical information related to: cybercrime, hate-crimes, Indian Tribes, discrimination, victimization of the disabled and traffic stops by police. In addition, $500,000 is requested to begin converting paper-based data collection to Internet-based electronic data collections.

Missing children.—Funds are used to reduce the incidence of crimes against children, particularly kidnaping and sexual exploitation, by assisting families, citizen groups, law enforcement agencies and government institutions in a national effort to insure the safety and protection of children.

Regional information sharing system.—Funds aid State and local law enforcement agencies in the exchange of intelligence information.

National White Collar Crime Center.—Funds provide assistance to State and local law enforcement and regulatory agencies in addressing multi-jurisdictional white collar crimes. Increased funds are requested to address cybercrime.

Counterterrorism Programs.—In 2001, $185,000,000 is requested for counterterrorism training, equipment, technical assistance and technology development.

Infrastructure improvement.—$1,000,000 is requested to begin establishing an Internet-based information sharing and communications network for all those interested in justice issues. This system is anticipated to begin saving mailing, printing and warehousing costs in 2004.

Police Use of Force.—$2,100,000 is requested to collect data on excessive use of force by police officers and to support research into the underlying issues of excessive force.

Management and administration.—Funds provide executive direction and control, program operation, and administrative support of the Office of Justice Programs.

The planned distribution of budget authority by fiscal year is as follows (in millions of dollars):

JUSTICE ASSISTANCE

[in millions of dollars]

	1999 actual	2000 est.	2001 est.
Research, evaluation, and demonstration programs	46	43	49
Criminal justice statistical programs	25	26	33
Missing children	17	20	20
Regional information sharing system	20	20	20
White collar information center	7	9	18
Development of counter-terrorism technologies	0	152	185
Justice Online Information Exchange	0	0	1
Police Use of Force	0	0	2
Management and administration	41	45	50
Total	156	315	378

Object Classification (in millions of dollars)

Identification code 15–0401–0–1–754		1999 actual	2000 est.	2001 est.
	Direct obligations:			
	Personnel compensation:			
11.1	Full-time permanent	14	24	27
11.3	Other than full-time permanent	2	1	1
11.5	Other personnel compensation	1	....	....
11.9	Total personnel compensation	17	25	28
12.1	Civilian personnel benefits	4	5	6
21.0	Travel and transportation of persons	2	2	4
23.1	Rental payments to GSA	5	10	11
23.3	Communications, utilities, and miscellaneous charges	1	1	2
24.0	Printing and reproduction	3	3	2
25.1	Advisory and assistance services	10	5	3
25.2	Other services	19	36	35
25.3	Purchases of goods and services from Government accounts	20	28	31
26.0	Supplies and materials	1	1	1
31.0	Equipment	3	2	2
41.0	Grants, subsidies, and contributions	81	229	253
99.0	Subtotal, direct obligations	166	347	378
99.0	Reimbursable obligations	176	399	265

99.9	Total new obligations	342	746	643

Personnel Summary

Identification code 15–0401–0–1–754		1999 actual	2000 est.	2001 est.
	Direct:			
1001	Total compensable workyears: Full-time equivalent employment	387	429	466
	Reimbursable:			
2001	Total compensable workyears: Full-time equivalent employment	406	473	500

State and Local Law Enforcement Assistance

For assistance authorized by the Violent Crime Control and Law Enforcement Act of 1994 (Public Law 103–322), as amended ("the 1994 Act")[, $1,634,500,000] *; the Omnibus Crime Control and Safe Streets Act of 1968, as amended ("the 1968 Act"); and the victims of Child Abuse Act of 1990, as amended ("the 1990 Act"), $1,662,200,000 (including amounts for administrative costs, which shall be transferred to and merged with the "Justice Assistance" account),* to remain available until expended[; of which $523,000,000 shall be for Local Law Enforcement Block Grants, pursuant to H.R. 728 as passed by the House of Representatives on February 14, 1995, except that for purposes of this Act, the Commonwealth of Puerto Rico shall be considered a "unit of local government" as well as a "State", for the purposes set forth in paragraphs (A), (B), (D), (F), and (I) of section 101(a)(2) of H.R. 728 and for establishing crime prevention programs involving cooperation between community residents and law enforcement personnel in order to control, detect, or investigate crime or the prosecution of criminals: *Provided*, That no funds provided under this heading may be used as matching funds for any other Federal grant program: *Provided further*, That $50,000,000 of this amount shall be for Boys and Girls Clubs in public housing facilities and other areas in cooperation with State and local law enforcement: *Provided further*, That funds may also be used to defray the costs of indemnification insurance for law enforcement officers: *Provided further*, That $20,000,000 shall be available to carry out section 102(2) of H.R. 728; of which $420,000,000 shall be for the State Criminal Alien Assistance Program, as authorized by section 242(j) of the Immigration and Nationality Act, as amended; of which $686,500,000 shall be for Violent Offender Incarceration and Truth in Sentencing Incentive Grants pursuant to subtitle A of title II of the 1994 Act, of which $165,000,000 shall be available for payments to States for incarceration of criminal aliens, of which $25,000,000 shall be available for the Cooperative Agreement Program, and of which $34,000,000 shall be reserved by the Attorney General for fiscal year 2000 under section 20109(a) of subtitle A of title II of the 1994 Act; and of which $5,000,000 shall be for the Tribal Courts Initiative]*, as follows:*

(1) $600,000,000 for the State Criminal Alien Assistance Program, as authorized by section 242(j) of the Immigration and Nationality Act, as amended;

(2) $75,000,000 for the Prison Grant Program, of which:

(a) $35,000,000 shall be for the Cooperative Agreement Program,

(b) $34,000,000 shall be for grants under section 20109(a) of subtitle A of title II of the 1994 Act, and

(c) $6,000,000 shall be for the Mental Health of Offenders Program;

(3) $15,000,000 for the Tribal Courts Initiative;

(4) $459,500,000 for programs authorized by part E of title I of the 1968 Act, notwithstanding the provisions of section 511 of said Act, including:

(a) $5,000,000 for the National Institute of Justice for program evaluation,

(b) $59,500,000 for discretionary grants under the Edward Byrne Memorial State and Local Law Enforcement Assistance Programs, of which $4,500,000 shall be for the community demonstration grants on alcohol and crime, $4,500,000 shall be for the Executive Office of the United States Attorneys to support the National District Attorneys Association's participation in legal education training at the National Advocacy Center, $10,000,000 shall be for the Kids and Guns Local Media Campaign, and $6,000,000 shall be for strengthening criminal and civil legal assistance programs for Indian Tribes;

(5) $9,000,000 for the Court Appointed Special Advocate Program, as authorized by section 218 of the 1990 Act;

(6) $2,000,000 for Child Abuse Training Programs for Judicial Personnel and Practitioners, as authorized by section 224 of the 1990 Act;

(7) $220,000,000 for Grants to Combat Violence Against Women, to States, units of local government, and Indian tribal governments, as authorized by section 1001(a)(18) of the 1968 Act, including:

(a) $35,250,000 to be used exclusively for the purpose of strengthening civil legal assistance programs for victims of domestic violence,

(b) $5,200,000 for the National Institute of Justice for research and evaluation of violence against women,

(c) $1,000,000 for the Bureau of Justice Statistics for a domestic violence case processing study,

(d) $5,000,000 for the National Institute of Justice for research on family violence, and

(e) $10,000,000 for the Office of Juvenile Justice and Delinquency Prevention for the Safe Start Program, to be administered as authorized by part C of the Juvenile Justice and Delinquency Act of 1974, as amended;

(8) $34,000,000 for Grants to Encourage Arrest Policies to States, units of local government, and Indian tribal governments, as authorized by section 1001(a)(19) of the 1968 Act;

(9) $25,000,000 for Rural Domestic Violence and Child Abuse Enforcement Assistance Grants, as authorized by section 40295 of the 1994 Act;

(10) $5,000,000 for training programs to assist probation and parole officers who work with released sex offenders, as authorized by section 40152(c) of the 1994 Act, and for local demonstration projects;

(11) $1,000,000 for grants for televised testimony, as authorized by section 1001(a)(7) of the 1968 Act;

(12) $65,000,000 for grants for residential substance abuse treatment for State prisoners, as authorized by section 1001(a)(17) of the 1968 Act: Provided, That states that have existing in prison drug treatment programs, in compliance with federal requirements, may use their residential substance abuse grant funds for treatment and sanctions, both during incarceration and after release;

(13) $900,000 for the Missing Alzheimer's Disease Patient Alert Program, as authorized by section 240001(c) of the 1994 Act;

(14) $1,300,000 for Motor Vehicle Theft Prevention Programs, as authorized by section 220002(h) of the 1994 Act;

(15) $50,000,000 for Drug Courts, as authorized by title V of the 1994 Act, of which $2,000,000 shall be for the National Institute of Justice for research into the dependency court system's response to child abuse and neglect;

(16) $1,500,000 for Law Enforcement Family Support Programs, as authorized by section 1001(a)(21) of the 1968 Act;

(17) $2,000,000 for public awareness programs addressing marketing scams aimed at senior citizens, as authorized by section 250005(3) of the 1994 Act;

(18) $21,000,000 for the Indian Country Grants Program, including $8,000,000 for demonstration grants on alcohol and crime in Indian Country, $5,000,000 for the establishment of sexual assault nurse examiner units in Indian Country, and $8,000,000 for a Tribal Youth Mental Health and Behavior Program;

(19) $75,000,000 for the Zero Tolerance Drug Testing and Intervention Initiative, including $10,000,000 for Indian Tribes and $25,000,000 for the Re-entry Initiative:

Provided further, That funds made available in fiscal year 2001 under subpart 1 of part E of title I of the 1968 Act may be obligated for programs to assist States in the litigation processing of death penalty Federal habeas corpus petitions and for drug testing initiatives: Provided further, That balances for these programs may be transferred from the Violent Crime Reduction Programs, State and Local Law Enforcement Assistance account to this account. (Department of Justice Appropriations Act, 2000, as enacted by section 1000(a)(1) of the Consolidated Appropriations Act, 2000 (P.L. 106–113).)

Program and Financing (in millions of dollars)

Identification code 15–0404–0–1–754		1999 actual	2000 est.	2001 est.
	Obligations by program activity:			
	Direct program:			
00.01	Local law enforcement block grant	....	498	15
00.02	State criminal alien assistance	....	585	600
00.03	Correctional facilities	....	489	75
00.04	Tribal courts initiative	....	5	15
00.05	Edward Byrne formula grants	505	1	400

General and special funds—Continued

STATE AND LOCAL LAW ENFORCEMENT ASSISTANCE—Continued

Program and Financing (in millions of dollars)—Continued

Identification code 15–0404–0–1–754		1999 actual	2000 est.	2001 est.
00.06	Edward Byrne discretionary grants	63	30	64
00.07	Court appointed special advocate			9
00.08	Child abuse training programs for judicial personnel			2
00.09	Violence against women act: STOP grants			220
00.10	Violence against women act: Encourage arrest policies			34
00.11	Violence against women act: Rural domestic violence and child abuse enforcement assistance			25
00.12	Violence against women act: Training programs to assist probation and parole officers			5
00.13	Grants for closed circuit televising			1
00.14	Residential substance abuse treatment			65
00.15	Missing alzheimer's program			1
00.16	Motor vehicle theft prevention			1
00.17	Drug courts			50
00.18	Law enforcement family support			2
00.19	Countering telemarketing scams			2
00.20	Indian country grant program			21
00.21	Zero tolerance and drug intervention initiative			75
09.01	Reimbursable program	21	57	33
10.00	Total new obligations	589	1,665	1,715
	Budgetary resources available for obligation:			
21.40	Unobligated balance available, start of year	17	35	
22.00	New budget authority (gross)	597	1,610	1,695
22.10	Resources available from recoveries of prior year obligations	10	20	20
23.90	Total budgetary resources available for obligation	624	1,665	1,715
23.95	Total new obligations	−589	−1,665	−1,715
24.40	Unobligated balance available, end of year	35		
	New budget authority (gross), detail:			
	Discretionary:			
40.00	Appropriation	552	1,635	1,662
40.76	Reduction pursuant to P.L. 106–113		−58	
43.00	Appropriation (total discretionary)	552	1,577	1,662
68.00	Spending authority from offsetting collections: Offsetting collections (cash)	45	33	33
70.00	Total new budget authority (gross)	597	1,610	1,695
	Change in unpaid obligations:			
72.40	Unpaid obligations, start of year: Obligated balance, start of year	677	898	1,958
73.10	Total new obligations	589	1,665	1,715
73.20	Total outlays (gross)	−359	−585	−3,352
73.32	Obligated balance transferred from other accounts			4,055
73.45	Adjustments in unexpired accounts	−10	−20	−20
74.40	Unpaid obligations, end of year: Obligated balance, end of year	898	1,958	4,356
	Outlays (gross), detail:			
86.90	Outlays from new discretionary authority	142	380	399
86.93	Outlays from discretionary balances	217	205	2,953
87.00	Total outlays (gross)	359	585	3,352
	Offsets:			
	Against gross budget authority and outlays:			
88.00	Offsetting collections (cash) from: Federal sources	−45	−33	−33
	Net budget authority and outlays:			
89.00	Budget authority	552	1,577	1,662
90.00	Outlays	314	552	3,319

These programs are described in the Violent Crime Reduction Programs, State and local law enforcement assistance account, where they were appropriated in 2000.

Object Classification (in millions of dollars)

Identification code 15–0404–0–1–754		1999 actual	2000 est.	2001 est.
	Direct obligations:			
25.2	Other services	2	4	5
25.3	Purchases of goods and services from Government accounts	5	57	85
41.0	Grants, subsidies, and contributions	561	1,547	1,592
99.0	Subtotal, direct obligations	568	1,608	1,682
99.0	Reimbursable obligations	21	57	33
99.9	Total new obligations	589	1,665	1,715

[VIOLENT CRIME REDUCTION PROGRAMS, STATE AND LOCAL LAW ENFORCEMENT ASSISTANCE]

[For assistance (including amounts for administrative costs for management and administration, which amounts shall be transferred to and merged with the "Justice Assistance" account) authorized by the Violent Crime Control and Law Enforcement Act of 1994 (Public Law 103–322), as amended ("the 1994 Act"); the Omnibus Crime Control and Safe Streets Act of 1968, as amended ("the 1968 Act"); and the Victims of Child Abuse Act of 1990, as amended ("the 1990 Act"), $1,194,450,000, to remain available until expended, which shall be derived from the Violent Crime Reduction Trust Fund; of which $552,000,000 shall be for grants, contracts, cooperative agreements, and other assistance authorized by part E of title I of the 1968 Act, for State and Local Narcotics Control and Justice Assistance Improvements, notwithstanding the provisions of section 511 of said Act, as authorized by section 1001 of title I of said Act, as amended by Public Law 102–534 (106 Stat. 3524), of which $52,000,000 shall be available to carry out the provisions of chapter A of subpart 2 of part E of title I of said Act, for discretionary grants under the Edward Byrne Memorial State and Local Law Enforcement Assistance Programs; of which $10,000,000 shall be for the Court Appointed Special Advocate Program, as authorized by section 218 of the 1990 Act; of which $2,000,000 shall be for Child Abuse Training Programs for Judicial Personnel and Practitioners, as authorized by section 224 of the 1990 Act; of which $206,750,000 shall be for Grants to Combat Violence Against Women, to States, units of local government, and Indian tribal governments, as authorized by section 1001(a)(18) of the 1968 Act, including $28,000,000 which shall be used exclusively for the purpose of strengthening civil legal assistance programs for victims of domestic violence: *Provided*, That, of these funds, $5,200,000 shall be provided to the National Institute of Justice for research and evaluation of violence against women, $1,196,000 shall be provided to the Office of the United States Attorney for the District of Columbia for domestic violence programs in D.C. Superior Court, $10,000,000 which shall be used exclusively for violence on college campuses, and $10,000,000 shall be available to the Office of Juvenile Justice and Delinquency Prevention for the Safe Start Program, to be administered as authorized by part C of the Juvenile Justice and Delinquency Act of 1974, as amended; of which $34,000,000 shall be for Grants to Encourage Arrest Policies to States, units of local government, and Indian tribal governments, as authorized by section 1001(a)(19) of the 1968 Act; of which $25,000,000 shall be for Rural Domestic Violence and Child Abuse Enforcement Assistance Grants, as authorized by section 40295 of the 1994 Act; of which $5,000,000 shall be for training programs to assist probation and parole officers who work with released sex offenders, as authorized by section 40152(c) of the 1994 Act, and for local demonstration projects; of which $1,000,000 shall be for grants for televised testimony, as authorized by section 1001(a)(7) of the 1968 Act; of which $63,000,000 shall be for grants for residential substance abuse treatment for State prisoners, as authorized by section 1001(a)(17) of the 1968 Act; of which $900,000 shall be for the Missing Alzheimer's Disease Patient Alert Program, as authorized by section 240001(c) of the 1994 Act; of which $1,300,000 shall be for Motor Vehicle Theft Prevention Programs, as authorized by section 220002(h) of the 1994 Act; of which $40,000,000 shall be for Drug Courts, as authorized by title V of the 1994 Act; of which $1,500,000 shall be for Law Enforcement Family Support Programs, as authorized by section 1001(a)(21) of the 1968 Act; of which $2,000,000 shall be for public awareness programs addressing marketing scams aimed at senior citizens, as authorized by section 250005(3) of the 1994 Act; and of which $250,000,000 shall be for Juvenile Accountability Incentive Block Grants, except that such funds shall be subject to the same terms and conditions as set forth in the provisions under this heading for this program in Public Law 105–119, but all references in such provisions to 1998 shall be deemed to refer instead to 2000: *Provided further*, That funds made available in fiscal year 2000 under subpart 1 of part E of title I of the 1968 Act may be obligated for programs to assist States in the litigation processing of death penalty Federal habeas corpus petitions and for drug testing initiatives: *Provided further*, That, if a unit of local government uses any of the funds made available under this title to increase the number of law enforcement officers, the unit of local government will achieve a net gain in the number of law enforcement officers who perform nonadministrative public safety service]. *(Department of Justice Appropriations Act, 2000, as enacted by section 1000(a)(1) of the Consolidated Appropriations Act, 2000 (P.L. 106–113).)*

Program and Financing (in millions of dollars)

Identification code 15–8586–0–1–754	1999 actual	2000 est.	2001 est.
Obligations by program activity:			
00.01 Byrne law enforcement assistance: Formula	....	500	....
00.02 Byrne law enforcement assistance: Discretionary	....	67	....
00.03 Criminal records upgrade	48	2	....
00.04 Correctional facilities	633	4	....
00.05 Drug courts	40	43	....
00.06 Violence Against Women Act: STOP grants	200	216	....
00.07 Violence Against Women Act: Encouraging arrest policies	29	43	....
00.08 Violence Against Women Act: Rural domestic violence and child abuse enforcement	26	29	....
00.09 State criminal alien assistance	1,163	....	....
00.10 State prison drug treatment	62	66	....
00.12 Indian tribal courts	....	5	....
00.13 DNA grants	14	1	....
00.14 Local law enforcement block grant	457	156	....
00.15 Juvenile incentive block grant	250	247	....
00.21 Other crime control programs	20	28	....
09.01 Reimbursable program	10	63	....
10.00 Total new obligations	2,952	1,470	....
Budgetary resources available for obligation:			
21.40 Unobligated balance available, start of year	690	202	....
22.00 New budget authority (gross)	2,380	1,245	....
22.10 Resources available from recoveries of prior year obligations	83	23	....
23.90 Total budgetary resources available for obligation	3,153	1,470	....
23.95 Total new obligations	−2,952	−1,470	....
24.40 Unobligated balance available, end of year	202	....	....
New budget authority (gross), detail:			
Discretionary:			
40.00 Appropriation	....	....	....
40.76 Reduction pursuant to P.L. 106–113	....	−12	....
42.00 Transferred from other accounts	2,370	1,194	....
43.00 Appropriation (total discretionary)	2,370	1,182	....
68.00 Spending authority from offsetting collections: Offsetting collections (cash)	10	63	....
70.00 Total new budget authority (gross)	2,380	1,245	....
Change in unpaid obligations:			
72.40 Unpaid obligations, start of year: Obligated balance, start of year	3,165	3,757	4,055
73.10 Total new obligations	2,952	1,470	....
73.20 Total outlays (gross)	−2,276	−1,149	....
73.31 Obligated balance transferred to other accounts	....	....	−4,055
73.45 Adjustments in unexpired accounts	−83	−23	....
74.40 Unpaid obligations, end of year: Obligated balance, end of year	3,757	4,055	....
Outlays (gross), detail:			
86.90 Outlays from new discretionary authority	531	323	....
86.93 Outlays from discretionary balances	1,745	826	....
87.00 Total outlays (gross)	2,276	1,149	....
Offsets:			
Against gross budget authority and outlays:			
88.00 Offsetting collections (cash) from: Federal sources	−10	−63	....
Net budget authority and outlays:			
89.00 Budget authority	2,370	1,182	....
90.00 Outlays	2,266	1,086	....

In 2001, the authorities of the Violent Crime Control and Law Enforcement Act are expired. Therefore, these programs are reflected in the State and Local Law Enforcement Assistance Account in 2001, unless otherwise noted.

Criminal records upgrade program.—Expands the program established in 1995 under the Brady Handgun Violence Prevention Act and the National Child Protection Act of 1993. The program provides financial and technical assistance to all States to improve their ability to identify criminal histories of felons and other persons ineligible to purchase firearms or hold positions involving children, the elderly, or the disabled. In 2001, this program is requested at $70,000,000 as part of the 21st Century Policing.

Incarceration of undocumented aliens.—Funds provide for a program to reimburse States and political subdivisions of States for a portion of the costs incurred for the imprisonment of criminal aliens.

Correctional facilities grants.—Funds provide assistance to Tribal governments to provide adequate space to incarcerate violent offenders.

State prison drug treatment.—Funds provide assistance to States to establish residential substance abuse treatment programs in State prisons and local correctional and detention facilities, aimed at reducing recidivism by ensuring that offenders are held accountable for their actions by addressing the myriad problems associated with the lifestyle of drug use and addiction.

Byrne formula grants.—Funds provide assistance to States to develop programs to fight drugs, violence, and gangs in a coordinated manner throughout a State.

Drug courts.—Funds provide assistance to States and local units of government to develop and implement programs for non-violent offenders with substance abuse problems. These programs use the power of the courts and continuing supervision to coerce abstinence through graduated sanctions and the integrated administration of other services such as drug testing and drug treatment. In 2001, an increase of $10,000,000 is requested to expand the number of operating drug courts.

Violence against women.—Funds provide assistance to States, local units of government and to other public or private entities to develop and strengthen effective law enforcement and prosecution strategies to combat violence against women, to implement proarrest programs, to establish and expand cooperative efforts to address domestic violence and child abuse in rural areas, and to provide victim services.

Object Classification (in millions of dollars)

Identification code 15–8586–0–1–754	1999 actual	2000 est.	2001 est.
Direct obligations:			
21.0 Travel and transportation of persons	1	1	....
25.1 Advisory and assistance services	2	2	....
25.2 Other services	8	9	....
25.3 Purchases of goods and services from Government accounts	83	25	....
41.0 Grants, subsidies, and contributions	2,848	1,370	....
99.0 Subtotal, direct obligations	2,942	1,407	....
99.0 Reimbursable obligations	10	63	....
99.9 Total new obligations	2,952	1,470	....

WEED AND SEED PROGRAM FUND

For necessary expenses, including salaries and related expenses of the Executive Office for Weed and Seed, to implement "Weed and Seed" program activities, [$33,500,000] *$42,000,000*, to remain available until expended, for inter-governmental agreements, including grants, cooperative agreements, and contracts, with State and local law enforcement agencies engaged in the investigation and prosecution of violent crimes and drug offenses in "Weed and Seed" designated communities, and for either reimbursements or transfers to appropriation accounts of the Department of Justice and other Federal agencies which shall be specified by the Attorney General to

General and special funds—Continued

WEED AND SEED PROGRAM FUND—Continued

execute the "Weed and Seed" program strategy: *Provided*, That funds designated by Congress through language for other Department of Justice appropriation accounts for "Weed and Seed" program activities shall be managed and executed by the Attorney General through the Executive Office for Weed and Seed: *Provided further*, That the Attorney General may direct the use of other Department of Justice funds and personnel in support of "Weed and Seed" program activities only after the Attorney General notifies the Committees on Appropriations of the House of Representatives and the Senate in accordance with section 605 of this Act. *(Department of Justice Appropriations Act, 2000, as enacted by section 1000(a)(1) of the Consolidated Appropriations Act, 2000 (P.L. 106–113).)*

Program and Financing (in millions of dollars)

Identification code 15–0334–0–1–751	1999 actual	2000 est.	2001 est.
Obligations by program activity:			
00.01 Direct program	35	38	42
09.01 Reimbursable program	7	7	
10.00 Total new obligations	42	45	42
Budgetary resources available for obligation:			
21.40 Unobligated balance available, start of year	4	4	
22.00 New budget authority (gross)	41	41	42
22.10 Resources available from recoveries of prior year obligations	1	1	
23.90 Total budgetary resources available for obligation	46	46	42
23.95 Total new obligations	−42	−45	−42
24.40 Unobligated balance available, end of year	4		
New budget authority (gross), detail:			
Discretionary:			
40.00 Appropriation	34	34	42
68.00 Spending authority from offsetting collections: Offsetting collections (cash)	7	7	
70.00 Total new budget authority (gross)	41	41	42
Change in unpaid obligations:			
72.40 Unpaid obligations, start of year: Obligated balance, start of year	58	63	78
73.10 Total new obligations	42	45	42
73.20 Total outlays (gross)	−35	−29	−47
73.45 Adjustments in unexpired accounts	−1	−1	
74.40 Unpaid obligations, end of year: Obligated balance, end of year	63	78	73
Outlays (gross), detail:			
86.90 Outlays from new discretionary authority	14	14	9
86.93 Outlays from discretionary balances	21	15	38
87.00 Total outlays (gross)	35	29	47
Offsets:			
Against gross budget authority and outlays:			
88.00 Offsetting collections (cash) from: Federal sources	−7	−7	
Net budget authority and outlays:			
89.00 Budget authority	34	34	42
90.00 Outlays	28	22	47

Weed and Seed provides training and technical assistance to designated neighborhoods and communities to develop and coordinate crime and drug prevention and enforcement programs.

Object Classification (in millions of dollars)

Identification code 15–0334–0–1–751	1999 actual	2000 est.	2001 est.
Direct obligations:			
21.0 Travel and transportation of persons	1	1	1
25.2 Other services	4	4	4
41.0 Grants, subsidies, and contributions	30	33	37
99.0 Subtotal, direct obligations	35	38	42
99.0 Reimbursable obligations	7	7	
99.9 Total new obligations	42	45	42

COMMUNITY ORIENTED POLICING SERVICES

[For activities authorized by the Violent Crime Control and Law Enforcement Act of 1994, Public Law 103–322 ("the 1994 Act") (including administrative costs), $595,000,000, to remain available until expended, including $45,000,000 which shall be derived from the Violent Crime Reduction Trust Fund; of which $130,000,000 shall be available to the Office of Justice programs to carry out section 102 of the Crime Identification Technology Act of 1998 (42 U.S.C. 14601), of which $35,000,000 is for grants to upgrade criminal records, as authorized by section 106(b) of the Brady Handgun Violence Prevention Act of 1993, as amended, and section 4(b) of the National Child Protection Act of 1993, of which $15,000,000 is for the National Institute of Justice to develop school safety technologies, and of which $30,000,000 shall be for State and local DNA laboratories as authorized by section 1001(a)(22) of the 1968 Act, as well as for improvements to the State and local forensic laboratory general forensic science capabilities and to reduce their DNA convicted offender database sample backlog; of which $419,325,000 is for Public Safety and Community Policing Grants pursuant to title I of the 1994 Act, of which $180,000,000 shall be available for school resource officers; of which $35,675,000 shall be used for policing initiatives to combat methamphetamine production and trafficking and to enhance policing initiatives in drug "hot spots"; and of which $10,000,000 shall be used for the Community Prosecutors program: *Provided*, That of the amount provided for Public Safety and Community Policing Grants, not to exceed $29,825,000 shall be expended for program management and administration: *Provided further*, That of the unobligated balances available in this program, $210,000,000 shall be used for innovative community policing programs, of which $100,000,000 shall be used for a law enforcement technology program, $25,000,000 shall be used for the Matching Grant Program for Law Enforcement Armor Vests pursuant to section 2501 of part Y of the Omnibus Crime Control and Safe Streets Act of 1968 ("the 1968 Act"), as amended, $30,000,000 shall be used for Police Corps education, training, and service as set forth in sections 200101–200113 of the 1994 Act, $40,000,000 shall be available to improve tribal law enforcement including equipment and training, and $15,000,000 shall be used to combat violence in schools.] *For activities authorized by the Violent Crime Control and Law Enforcement Act of 1994, Public Law 103–322 ("the 1994 Act"), $1,335,000,000, to remain available until expended: Provided, That the Attorney General may transfer any of these funds, and balances for programs funded under this heading in fiscal year 2000, to the "State and Local Law Enforcement Assistance" account, to be available for the purposes stated under this heading: Provided further, That administrative expenses associated with such transferred amounts may be transferred to the "Justice Assistance" account. Of the amounts provided:*

(1) for Public Safety and Community Policing Grants pursuant to title I of the 1994 Act, $650,000,000 as follows: not to exceed $36,000,000 for program management and administration; $20,000,000 for programs to combat violence in schools; $25,000,000 for the matching grant program for Law Enforcement Armor Vests pursuant to section 2501 of part Y of the Omnibus Crime Control and Safe Streets Act of 1968, as amended; $17,000,000 for program support for the Court Services and Offender Supervision Agency for the District of Columbia; $45,000,000 to improve tribal law enforcement including equipment and training; $20,000,000 for National Police Officer Scholarships; and $30,000,000 for Police Corps education, training, and service under sections 200101–200113 of the 1994 Act;

(2) for crime-fighting technology, $350,000,000 as follows: $70,000,000 for grants to upgrade criminal records, as authorized under the Crime Identification Technology Act of 1998 (42 U.S.C. 14601; $15,000,000 for State and local forensic labs to reduce their convicted offender DNA sample backlog; $35,000,000 for State, Tribal and local DNA laboratories as authorized by section 1001(a)(22) of the 1968 Act, as well as improvements to State, Tribal and local forensic laboratory general forensic science capabilities; $10,000,000 for the National Institute of Justice Law Enforcement and Corrections Technology Centers; $5,000,000 for DNA technology research and development; $10,000,000 for research, technical assistance, evaluation, grants, and other expenses to utilize and improve crime-solving, data sharing, and crime-forecasting technologies; $6,000,000 to establish regional forensic computer labs; and

$199,000,000 for discretionary grants, including planning grants, to States under section 102 of the Crime Identification Technology Act of 1998 (42 U.S.C. 14601), of which up to $99,000,000 is for grants to law enforcement agencies, and of which not more than 23 percent may be used for salaries, administrative expenses, technical assistance, training, and evaluation;

(3) for a Community Prosecution Program, $200,000,000, of which $150,000,000 shall be for grants to States and units of local government to address gun violence "hot spots";

(4) for grants, training, technical assistance, and other expenses to support community crime prevention efforts, $135,000,000 as follows: $35,000,000 for a youth and school safety program; $5,000,000 for citizens academies and One America race dialogues; $35,000,000 for an offender re-entry program; $25,000,000 for a Building Blocks Program, including $10,000,000 for the Strategic Approaches to Community Safety Initiative; $20,000,000 for police integrity and hate crimes training; $5,000,000 for police recruitment; and $10,000,000 for police gun destruction grants (Department of Justice Appropriations Act, 2000, as enacted by section 1000(a)(1) of the Consolidated Appropriations Act, 2000 (P.L. 106–113).)

Program and Financing (in millions of dollars)

Identification code 15–8594–0–1–754	1999 actual	2000 est.	2001 est.
Obligations by program activity:			
00.01 Public safety and community policing grants	1,302	613	584
00.02 Police Corps grants	83	30	30
00.03 Crime fighting technologies		230	350
00.04 Community based prosecutors		10	200
00.05 Management and administration	34	30	36
00.06 Community crime prevention efforts			135
10.00 Total new obligations	1,419	913	1,335
Budgetary resources available for obligation:			
21.40 Unobligated balance available, start of year	165	318	
22.00 New budget authority (gross)	1,430	595	1,335
22.10 Resources available from recoveries of prior year obligations	142		
23.90 Total budgetary resources available for obligation	1,737	913	1,335
23.95 Total new obligations	–1,419	–913	–1,335
24.40 Unobligated balance available, end of year	318		
New budget authority (gross), detail:			
Discretionary:			
40.00 Appropriation		550	1,335
42.00 Transferred from other accounts VCRTF	1,430	45	
43.00 Appropriation (total discretionary)	1,430	595	1,335
Change in unpaid obligations:			
72.40 Unpaid obligations, start of year: Obligated balance, start of year	3,243	3,359	3,443
73.10 Total new obligations	1,419	913	1,335
73.20 Total outlays (gross)	–1,161	–829	–1,748
73.45 Adjustments in unexpired accounts	–142		
74.40 Unpaid obligations, end of year: Obligated balance, end of year	3,359	3,443	3,030
Outlays (gross), detail:			
86.90 Outlays from new discretionary authority	290	30	67
86.93 Outlays from discretionary balances	871	799	1,681
87.00 Total outlays (gross)	1,161	829	1,748
Net budget authority and outlays:			
89.00 Budget authority	1,430	595	1,335
90.00 Outlays	1,161	829	1,748
Distribution of budget authority by account:			
Community Oriented Policing Services	0	550	1,335
Violent Crime Reduction Programs, Community Oriented Policing Services	1,430	45	
Distribution of outlays by account:			
Community Oriented Policing Services	0	28	177
Violent Crime Reduction Programs, Community Oriented Policing Services	1,161	801	1,571

This program provides grants to States, units of local government, Indian Tribal governments, and other public and private entities to increase police presence, expand cooperation between law enforcement agencies and members of the community, and enhance public safety. Grants may be used for hiring new officers, rehiring officers laid off as a result of State and local budget cuts, procuring equipment and technology, and funding additional grant projects. Funding also supports training and technical assistance, evaluation and other studies in furtherance of these projects. The maximum Federal share per officer is $75,000 for a three-year grant, and may not exceed 75 percent of the total project cost, unless a waiver is granted for severe fiscal distress. The funds requested will also provide grants and cooperative agreements to Indian Tribes as defined in 42 U.S.C. §3796dd–8 for the hiring or rehiring of additional career law enforcement officers for deployment in community policing, for additional grant projects as authorized, and for other purposes including the procurement of equipment, technology and training directly enhancing the capabilities of Tribal law enforcement officers and agencies to perform their duties effectively. The funds requested will also provide resources for the Police Corps program, as set forth in 42 U.S.C. §14091, to increase the number of police with advanced education and training. Funding is included for bullet-proof vests for law enforcement officers, National Police Office Scholarships, program support for the District of Columbia Court Services and Offender Supervision Agency and the District of Columbia Courts.

Resources have also been included to fund innovative programs for criminal justice agencies. These programs will, among other things, promote compatibility among law enforcement telecommunications and computer systems, encourage the use and improvement of DNA technology and other forensic sciences to solve crimes, and promote the use of crime mapping and analysis tools to detect, prevent, and solve crimes. Funding has also been included for a community prosecution program and for grants to establish community-based crime prevention programs.

Object Classification (in millions of dollars)

Identification code 15–8594–0–1–754	1999 actual	2000 est.	2001 est.
11.1 Personnel compensation: Full-time permanent	13	13	13
12.1 Civilian personnel benefits	3	3	3
21.0 Travel and transportation of persons	1	2	3
23.1 Rental payments to GSA	3	3	3
23.3 Communications, utilities, and rental payments to others	1	1	1
24.0 Printing and reproduction		1	1
25.2 Other services	11	12	14
25.3 Purchases of goods and services from Government accounts	90	10	10
41.0 Grants, subsidies, and contributions	1,297	868	1,287
99.9 Total new obligations	1,419	913	1,335

Personnel Summary

Identification code 15–8594–0–1–754	1999 actual	2000 est.	2001 est.
1001 Total compensable workyears: Full-time equivalent employment	229	235	301

Juvenile Justice Programs

For grants, contracts, cooperative agreements, and other assistance authorized by the Juvenile Justice and Delinquency Prevention Act of 1974, as amended, ("the Act"), including salaries and expenses in connection therewith to be transferred to and merged with the appropriations for Justice Assistance, [$269,097,000] *$272,000,000*, to remain available until expended, as authorized by section 299 of part I of title II and section 506 of title V of the Act, as amended by Public Law 102–586, of which: (1) notwithstanding any other provision of law, $6,847,000 shall be available for expenses authorized by part A of title II of the Act, $89,000,000 shall be available for expenses authorized by part B of title II of the Act, *of which $3,000,000 shall be available to the National Institute of Justice for*

General and special funds—Continued

JUVENILE JUSTICE PROGRAMS—Continued

research into the dependency court system's response to child abuse and neglect, and [$42,750,000] *$47,153,000* shall be available for expenses authorized by part C of title II of the Act: *Provided,* That $26,500,000 of the amounts provided for part B of title II of the Act, as amended, is for the purpose of providing additional formula grants under part B to States that provide assurances to the Administrator that the State has in effect (or will have in effect no later than 1 year after date of application) policies and programs, that ensure that juveniles are subject to accountability-based sanctions for every act for which they are adjudicated delinquent; (2) $12,000,000 shall be available for expenses authorized by sections 281 and 282 of part D of title II of the Act for prevention and treatment programs relating to juvenile gangs; (3) $10,000,000 shall be available for expenses authorized by section 285 of part E of title II of the Act; (4) [$13,500,000] *$12,000,000* shall be available for expenses authorized by part G of title II of the Act for juvenile mentoring programs; and (5) $95,000,000 shall be available for expenses authorized by title V of the Act for incentive grants for local delinquency prevention programs; of which [$12,500,000] *$20,000,000* shall be for delinquency prevention, control, and system improvement programs for tribal youth; of which [$25,000,000 shall be available for grants of $360,000 to each State and $6,640,000 shall be available for discretionary grants to States, for programs and activities to enforce State laws prohibiting the sale of alcoholic beverages to minors or the purchase or consumption of alcoholic beverages by minors, prevention and reduction of consumption of alcoholic beverages by minors, and for technical assistance and training;] *$10,000,000 shall be for prevention and reduction of youth gun violence; of which $10,000,000 shall be for developing, testing and demonstrating programs designed to reduce drug use among juveniles;* and of which $15,000,000 shall be [available] for the Safe Schools Initiative: [*Provided further,* That upon the enactment of reauthorization legislation for Juvenile Justice Programs under the Juvenile Justice and Delinquency Prevention Act of 1974, as amended, funding provisions in this Act shall from that date be subject to the provisions of that legislation and any provisions in this Act that are inconsistent with that legislation shall no longer have effect:] *Provided further,* That of amounts made available under the Juvenile Justice Programs of the Office of Justice Programs to carry out part B (relating to Federal Assistance for State and Local Programs), subpart II of part C (relating to Special Emphasis Prevention and Treatment Programs), part D (relating to Gang-Free Schools and Communities and Community-Based Gang Intervention), part E (relating to State Challenge Activities), and part G (relating to Mentoring) of title II of the Juvenile Justice and Delinquency Prevention Act of 1974, and to carry out the At-Risk Children's Program under title V of that Act, not more than 10 percent of each such amount may be used for research, evaluation, and statistics activities designed to benefit the programs or activities authorized under the appropriate part or title, and not more than 2 percent of each such amount may be used for training and technical assistance activities designed to benefit the programs or activities authorized under that part or title.

In addition, for grants, contracts, cooperative agreements, and other assistance, [$11,000,000] *$10,000,000* to remain available until expended, for developing, testing, and demonstrating programs designed to reduce drug use among juveniles.

In addition, for grants, contracts, cooperative agreements, and other assistance authorized by the Victims of Child Abuse Act of 1990, as amended, $7,000,000, to remain available until expended, as authorized by section 214B of the Act. *(Department of Justice Appropriations Act, 2000, as enacted by section 1000(a)(1) of the Consolidated Appropriations Act, 2000 (P.L. 106–113).)*

Program and Financing (in millions of dollars)

Identification code 15–0405–0–1–754	1999 actual	2000 est.	2001 est.
Obligations by program activity:			
Direct program:			
00.01 Title II—Juvenile justice and delinquency prevention	141	161	136
00.02 Part D—Gang-free schools and communities	11	18	12
00.03 Part E—State challenge activities	10	11	10
00.04 Part G—Mentoring	20	15	12
00.05 Title V—Incentive grants for local delinquency prevention	80	113	95
00.06 Victims of child abuse	6	8	7
00.07 Drug reduction program	1	20	10
09.01 Reimbursable program	32	37	35
10.00 Total new obligations	301	383	317
Budgetary resources available for obligation:			
21.40 Unobligated balance available, start of year	48	63	
22.00 New budget authority (gross)	312	315	317
22.10 Resources available from recoveries of prior year obligations	5	4	
23.90 Total budgetary resources available for obligation	365	382	317
23.95 Total new obligations	−301	−383	−317
24.40 Unobligated balance available, end of year	63		
New budget authority (gross), detail:			
Discretionary:			
40.00 Appropriation	285	287	289
41.00 Transferred to other accounts	−7	−7	−7
43.00 Appropriation (total discretionary)	278	280	282
68.00 Spending authority from offsetting collections: Offsetting collections (cash)	34	35	35
70.00 Total new budget authority (gross)	312	315	317
Change in unpaid obligations:			
72.40 Unpaid obligations, start of year: Obligated balance, start of year	359	470	635
73.10 Total new obligations	301	383	317
73.20 Total outlays (gross)	−185	−214	−382
73.45 Adjustments in unexpired accounts	−5	−4	
74.40 Unpaid obligations, end of year: Obligated balance, end of year	470	635	570
Outlays (gross), detail:			
86.90 Outlays from new discretionary authority	93	97	97
86.93 Outlays from discretionary balances	92	117	285
87.00 Total outlays (gross)	185	214	382
Offsets:			
Against gross budget authority and outlays:			
88.00 Offsetting collections (cash) from: Federal sources	−34	−35	−35
Net budget authority and outlays:			
89.00 Budget authority	278	280	282
90.00 Outlays	151	179	347

In 2001, funds will be targeted at juvenile gun violence and drug use, and how school violence impacts juveniles and how to prevent it.

Object Classification (in millions of dollars)

Identification code 15–0405–0–1–754	1999 actual	2000 est.	2001 est.
Direct obligations:			
21.0 Travel and transportation of persons	2	2	2
23.3 Communications, utilities, and miscellaneous charges	1	1	1
24.0 Printing and reproduction	1	1	1
25.1 Advisory and assistance services	2	2	2
25.2 Other services	7	7	7
25.3 Purchases of goods and services from Government accounts	17	18	18
41.0 Grants, subsidies, and contributions	239	315	251
99.0 Subtotal, direct obligations	269	346	282
99.0 Reimbursable obligations	32	37	35
99.9 Total new obligations	301	383	317

PUBLIC SAFETY OFFICERS BENEFITS

To remain available until expended, for payments authorized by part L of title I of the Omnibus Crime Control and Safe Streets Act of 1968 (42 U.S.C. 3796), as amended, such sums as are necessary, as authorized by section 6093 of Public Law 100–690 (102 Stat. 4339–4340); *and, in addition, $4,800,000 for the Public Safety Officers Dependents Assistance Program, as authorized by section 1211 of said Act. (Department of Justice Appropriations Act, 2000, as en-*

acted by section 1000(a)(1) of the Consolidated Appropriations Act, 2000 (P.L. 106–113).)

Program and Financing (in millions of dollars)

Identification code 15–0403–0–1–754	1999 actual	2000 est.	2001 est.
Obligations by program activity:			
10.00 Total new obligations	30	35	40
Budgetary resources available for obligation:			
21.40 Unobligated balance available, start of year	6	8	3
22.00 New budget authority (gross)	32	33	38
23.90 Total budgetary resources available for obligation	38	41	41
23.95 Total new obligations	–30	–35	–40
23.98 Unobligated balance expiring or withdrawn		–2	
24.40 Unobligated balance available, end of year	8	3	1
New budget authority (gross), detail:			
Discretionary:			
40.00 Appropriation			5
Mandatory:			
60.05 Appropriation (indefinite)	32	33	33
70.00 Total new budget authority (gross)	32	33	38
Change in unpaid obligations:			
72.40 Unpaid obligations, start of year: Obligated balance, start of year	1	2	2
73.10 Total new obligations	30	35	40
73.20 Total outlays (gross)	–29	–35	–41
74.40 Unpaid obligations, end of year: Obligated balance, end of year	2	2	1
Outlays (gross), detail:			
86.90 Outlays from new discretionary authority			5
86.93 Outlays from discretionary balances	1	1	3
86.97 Outlays from new mandatory authority	28	33	33
87.00 Total outlays (gross)	29	35	41
Net budget authority and outlays:			
89.00 Budget authority	32	33	38
90.00 Outlays	29	35	41

This program provides payment of death benefits to eligible survivors of public safety officers who die in the line of duty, disability payments to public safety officers who are permanently disabled as a result of injury incurred in the line of duty, and educational assistance to children or spouses of officers who are killed or permanently disabled in the line of duty. Legislation provides for an annual cost of living escalator tied to the Consumer Price Index (CPI) for the death benefit program. On October 1 of every year, this escalator will increase the benefit by the percentage of increase to the CPI.

Object Classification (in millions of dollars)

Identification code 15–0403–0–1–754	1999 actual	2000 est.	2001 est.
41.0 Grants, subsidies, and contributions	1	2	2
42.0 Insurance claims and indemnities	29	33	38
99.9 Total new obligations	30	35	40

Crime Victims Fund

Unavailable Collections (in millions of dollars)

Identification code 15–5041–0–2–754	1999 actual	2000 est.	2001 est.
Balance, start of year:			
01.99 Balance, start of year	324	988	1,060
Receipts:			
02.01 Fines, penalties, and forefeitures	985	575	350
04.00 Total: Balances and collections	1,309	1,563	1,410
Appropriation:			
05.01 Crime victims fund	–324	–503	–1,063
05.99 Subtotal appropriation	–324	–503	–1,063
06.20 Reduction pursuant to Public Law 106–51	3		
07.99 Total balance, end of year	988	1,060	347

Program and Financing (in millions of dollars)

Identification code 15–5041–0–2–754	1999 actual	2000 est.	2001 est.
Obligations by program activity:			
00.01 Direct program	362	538	550
10.00 Total new obligations	362	538	550
Budgetary resources available for obligation:			
21.40 Unobligated balance available, start of year	33	35	
22.00 New budget authority (gross)	321	503	550
22.10 Resources available from recoveries of prior year obligations	42		
22.22 Unobligated balance transferred from other accounts	1		
23.90 Total budgetary resources available for obligation	397	538	550
23.95 Total new obligations	–362	–538	–550
24.40 Unobligated balance available, end of year	35		
New budget authority (gross), detail:			
Discretionary:			
40.00 Appropriation (limitation on obligational authority)			–513
Mandatory:			
60.25 Appropriation (special fund, indefinite)	324	500	1,063
60.28 Appropriation (unavailable balances)		3	
60.75 Reduction pursuant to P.L. 106–51	–3		
62.50 Appropriation (total mandatory)	321	503	1,063
70.00 Total new budget authority (gross)	321	503	550
Change in unpaid obligations:			
72.40 Unpaid obligations, start of year: Obligated balance, start of year	634	606	395
73.10 Total new obligations	362	538	550
73.20 Total outlays (gross)	–348	–749	–698
73.45 Adjustments in unexpired accounts	–42		
74.40 Unpaid obligations, end of year: Obligated balance, end of year	606	395	247
Outlays (gross), detail:			
86.90 Outlays from new discretionary authority			–513
86.97 Outlays from new mandatory authority	161	503	1,063
86.98 Outlays from mandatory balances	187	246	148
87.00 Total outlays (gross)	348	749	698
Net budget authority and outlays:			
89.00 Budget authority	321	503	550
90.00 Outlays	348	749	698

The Victims of Crime Act of 1984 (Public Law 98–473), as amended, established a special fund in the Treasury entitled "The Crime Victims Fund." This fund is credited with criminal fines that are collected from persons convicted of offenses against the United States. Annual grants are made to eligible crime victims compensation and assistance programs.

Amounts collected in the previous year are available for obligation in the subsequent year, subject to the limitations included in authorizing language.

Object Classification (in millions of dollars)

Identification code 15–5041–0–2–754	1999 actual	2000 est.	2001 est.
25.1 Advisory and assistance services	2	2	2
25.3 Purchases of goods and services from Government accounts	8	8	8
41.0 Grants, subsidies, and contributions	352	528	540
99.9 Total new obligations	362	538	550

VIOLENT CRIME REDUCTION TRUST FUND

VIOLENT CRIME REDUCTION TRUST FUND (VCRTF)

Program and Financing (in millions of dollars)

Identification code 15–8585–0–1–754	1999 actual	2000 est.	2001 est.
New budget authority (gross), detail:			
Discretionary:			
40.00 Appropriation	5,800	4,500	....
41.00 Transferred to other accounts	−5,800	−4,500	....
43.00 Appropriation (total discretionary)	....	....	....
Net budget authority and outlays:			
89.00 Budget authority	....	....	....
90.00 Outlays	....	....	....

The Violent Crime Reduction Trust Fund was established by the Violent Crime Control and Law Enforcement Act of 1994, Public Law 103–322. By law, VCRTF monies may be used only for activities authorized by the Violent Crime Control Act of 1994 and shall be expended in amounts for both budget authority and outlays specified for each from year 1995 through 2000. The VCRTF expires at the end of 2000.

GENERAL FUND RECEIPT ACCOUNTS

(in millions of dollars)

	1999 actual	2000 est.	2001 est.
Governmental receipts:			
15–083400 Breached bond penalties	8	8	8
15–085400 Registration fees, DEA	16	15	15
General Fund Governmental receipts	24	23	23

GENERAL PROVISIONS—DEPARTMENT OF JUSTICE

SEC. 101. In addition to amounts otherwise made available in this title for official reception and representation expenses, a total of not to exceed $45,000 from funds appropriated to the Department of Justice in this title shall be available to the Attorney General for official reception and representation expenses in accordance with distributions, procedures, and regulations established by the Attorney General.

SEC. 102. Authorities contained in the Department of Justice Appropriation Authorization Act, Fiscal Year 1980 (Public Law 96–132; 93 Stat. 1040 (1979)), as amended, shall remain in effect until the termination date of this Act or until the effective date of a Department of Justice Appropriation Authorization Act, whichever is earlier.

[SEC. 103. None of the funds appropriated by this title shall be available to pay for an abortion, except where the life of the mother would be endangered if the fetus were carried to term, or in the case of rape: *Provided*, That should this prohibition be declared unconstitutional by a court of competent jurisdiction, this section shall be null and void.] [1]

SEC. [104] *103*. None of the funds appropriated under this title shall be used to require any person to perform, or facilitate in any way the performance of, any abortion.

SEC. [105] *104*. Nothing in the preceding section shall remove the obligation of the Director of the Bureau of Prisons to provide escort services necessary for a female inmate to receive such service outside the Federal facility: *Provided*, That nothing in this section in any way diminishes the effect of section [104] *103* intended to address the philosophical beliefs of individual employees of the Bureau of Prisons.

SEC. [106] *105*. Notwithstanding any other provision of law, not to exceed $10,000,000 of the funds made available in this Act may be used to establish and publicize a program under which publicly advertised, extraordinary rewards may be paid, which shall not be subject to spending limitations contained in sections 3059 and 3072 of title 18, United States Code: *Provided*, That any reward of $100,000 or more, up to a maximum of $2,000,000, may not be made without the personal approval of the President or the Attorney General and such approval may not be delegated.

SEC. [107] *106*. Not to exceed 5 percent of any appropriation made available for the current fiscal year for the Department of Justice in this Act, [including those derived from the Violent Crime Reduction Trust Fund,] may be transferred between such appropriations, but no such appropriation, except as otherwise specifically provided, shall be increased by more than 10 percent by any such transfers: *Provided*, That any transfer pursuant to this section shall be treated as a reprogramming of funds under section 605 of this Act and shall not be available for obligation except in compliance with the procedures set forth in that section.

SEC. [108] *107*. [(a)] Notwithstanding any other provision of law, for fiscal year [2000] *2001 and hereafter*, the Assistant Attorney General for the Office of Justice Programs of the Department of Justice—

(1) may make grants, or enter into cooperative agreements and contracts, for the Office of Justice Programs and the component organizations of that Office; and

(2) shall have final authority over all grants, cooperative agreements and contracts made, or entered into, for the Office of Justice Programs and the component organizations of that Office, except for grants made under the provisions of sections 201, 202, 301, and 302 of the Omnibus Crime Control and Safe Streets Act of 1968, as amended; and sections 204(b)(3), 241(e)(1), 243(a)(1), 243(a)(14) and 287A(3) of the Juvenile Justice and Delinquency Prevention Act of 1974, as amended.

[(b) Notwithstanding any other provision of law, effective August 1, 2000, all functions of the Director of the Bureau of Justice Assistance, other than those enumerated in the Omnibus Crime Control and Safe Streets Act, as amended, 42 U.S.C. 3742(3) through (6), are transferred to the Assistant Attorney General for the Office of Justice Programs.]

[SEC. 109. Sections 115 and 127 of the Departments of Commerce, Justice, and State, the Judiciary, and Related Agencies Appropriations Act, 1999 (as contained in section 101(b) of division A of Public Law 105–277) shall apply to fiscal year 2000 and thereafter.]

[SEC. 110. Hereafter, for payments of judgments against the United States and compromise settlements of claims in suits against the United States arising from the Financial Institutions Reform, Recovery and Enforcement Act and its implementation, such sums as may be necessary, to remain available until expended: *Provided*, That the foregoing authority is available solely for payment of judgments and compromise settlements: *Provided further*, That payment of litigation expenses is available under existing authority and will continue to be made available as set forth in the Memorandum of Understanding between the Federal Deposit Insurance Corporation and the Department of Justice, dated October 2, 1998.]

[SEC. 111. Section 507 of title 28, United States Code, is amended by adding a new subsection (c) as follows:

"(c) Notwithstanding the provisions of section 901 of title 31, United States Code, the Assistant Attorney General for Administration shall be the Chief Financial Officer of the Department of Justice.".]

SEC. [112] *108*. Section 3024 of the Emergency Supplemental Appropriations Act, 1999 (Public Law 106–31) shall apply for fiscal year [2000] *2001*.

[SEC. 113. Effective 30 days after the enactment of this Act, section 1930(a)(1) of title 28, United States Code, is amended in paragraph (1) by striking "$130" and inserting "$155"; section 589a of title 28, United States Code, is amended in subsection (b)(1) by striking "23.08 percent" and inserting "27.42 percent"; and section 406(b) of Public Law 101–162 (103 Stat. 1016), as amended (28 U.S.C. 1931 note), is further amended by striking "30.76 percent" and inserting "33.87 percent".]

[SEC. 114. Section 4006 of title 18, United States Code, is amended—

(1) by striking "The Attorney General" and inserting the following: "(a) IN GENERAL.—The Attorney General"; and

(2) by adding at the end the following:

"(b) HEALTH CARE ITEMS AND SERVICES.—

"(1) IN GENERAL.—Payment for costs incurred for the provision of health care items and services for individuals in the custody of the United States Marshals Service and the Immigration and Naturalization Service shall not exceed the lesser of the amount that would be paid for the provision of similar health care items and services under—

"(A) the Medicare program under title XVIII of the Social Security Act; or

"(B) the Medicaid program under title XIX of such Act of the State in which the services were provided.

"(2) FULL AND FINAL PAYMENT.—Any payment for a health care item or service made pursuant to this subsection, shall be deemed to be full and final payment.".]

[SEC. 115. (a) None of the funds made available by this or any other Act may be used to pay premium pay under title 5, United States Code, sections 5542–5549, to any individual employed as an attorney, including an Assistant United States Attorney, in the Department of Justice for any work performed on or after the date of the enactment of this Act.

(b) Notwithstanding any other provision of law, neither the United States nor any individual or entity acting on its behalf shall be liable for premium pay under title 5, United States Code, sections 5542–5549, for any work performed on or after the date of the enactment of this Act by any individual employed as an attorney in the Department of Justice, including an Assistant United States Attorney.] [2]

[SEC. 116. Section 113 of the Department of Justice Appropriations Act, 1999 (section 101(b) of division A of Public Law 105–277), as amended by section 3028 of the Emergency Supplemental Appropriations Act, 1999 (Public Law 106–31), is further amended by striking the first comma and inserting "for fiscal year 2000 and hereafter,".]

[SEC. 117. Section 203(b)(2)(B) of the Immigration and Nationality Act (8 U.S.C. 1153(b)(2)(B)) is amended to read as follows:

"(B)(i) Subject to clause (ii), the Attorney General may, when the Attorney General deems it to be in the national interest, waive the requirements of subparagraph (A) that an alien's services in the sciences, arts, professions, or business be sought by an employer in the United States.

"(ii)(I) The Attorney General shall grant a national interest waiver pursuant to clause (i) on behalf of any alien physician with respect to whom a petition for preference classification has been filed under subparagraph (A) if—

"(aa) the alien physician agrees to work full time as a physician in an area or areas designated by the Secretary of Health and Human Services as having a shortage of health care professionals or at a health care facility under the jurisdiction of the Secretary of Veterans Affairs; and

"(bb) a Federal agency or a department of public health in any State has previously determined that the alien physician's work in such an area or at such facility was in the public interest.

"(II) No permanent resident visa may be issued to an alien physician described in subclause (I) by the Secretary of State under section 204(b), and the Attorney General may not adjust the status of such an alien physician from that of a nonimmigrant alien to that of a permanent resident alien under section 245, until such time as the alien has worked full time as a physician for an aggregate of 5 years (not including the time served in the status of an alien described in section 101(a)(15)(J)), in an area or areas designated by the Secretary of Health and Human Services as having a shortage of health care professionals or at a health care facility under the jurisdiction of the Secretary of Veterans Affairs.

"(III) Nothing in this subparagraph may be construed to prevent the filing of a petition with the Attorney General for classification under section 204(a), or the filing of an application for adjustment of status under section 245, by an alien physician described in subclause (I) prior to the date by which such alien physician has completed the service described in subclause (II).

"(IV) The requirements of this subsection do not affect waivers on behalf of alien physicians approved under section 203(b)(2)(B) before the enactment date of this subsection. In the case of a physician for whom an application for a waiver was filed under section 203(b)(2)(B) prior to November 1, 1998, the Attorney General shall grant a national interest waiver pursuant to section 203(b)(2)(B) except that the alien is required to have worked full time as a physician for an aggregate of 3 years (not including time served in the status of an alien described in section 101(a)(15)(J)) before a visa can be issued to the alien under section 204(b) or the status of the alien is adjusted to permanent resident under section 245.".]

[SEC. 118. Section 286(q)(1)(A) of the Immigration and Nationality Act of 1953 (8 U.S.C. 1356(q)(1)(A)), as amended, is further amended—

(1) by striking clause (ii);

(2) by redesignating clause (iii) as (ii); and

(3) by striking ", until September 30, 2000," in clause (iv) and redesignating that clause as (iii).]

[SEC. 119. Section 1402(d) of the Victims of Crime Act of 1984 (42 U.S.C. 10601(d)) is amended—

(1) by striking paragraph (5);

(2) by redesignating paragraphs (3) and (4) as paragraphs (4) and (5), respectively; and

(3) by adding a new paragraph (3), as follows:

"(3) Of the sums remaining in the Fund in any particular fiscal year after compliance with paragraph (2), such sums as may be necessary shall be available for the United States Attorneys Offices to improve services for the benefit of crime victims in the Federal criminal justice system.".]

[SEC. 120. Public Law 103–322, the Violent Crime Control and Law Enforcement Act of 1994, subtitle C, section 210304, Index to Facilitate Law Enforcement Exchange of DNA Identification Information (42 U.S.C. 14132), is amended as follows:

(1) in subsection (a)(2), by striking "and";

(2) in subsection (a)(3), by striking the period and inserting "; and" after "remains"; and

(3) by adding after subsection (a)(3) the following new subsection:

"(4) analyses of DNA samples voluntarily contributed from relatives of missing persons.".]

[SEC. 121. (a) Subsection (b)(1) of section 227 of the Victims of Child Abuse Act of 1990 (42 U.S.C. 13032) is amended by inserting after "such facts or circumstances" the following: "to the Cyber Tip Line at the National Center for Missing and Exploited Children, which shall forward that report".

(b) Subsection (b)(2) of that section is amended by striking "made" and inserting "forwarded".]

SEC. 109. Section 151 of the Foreign Relations Authorization Act, fiscal years 1990 and 1991 (5 U.S.C. 5928 note), is amended by inserting "or Federal Bureau of Investigation" after "Drug Enforcement Administration".

SEC. 110. For fiscal year 2001 and thereafter, whenever the Federal Bureau of Investigation participates in a cooperative project to improve law enforcement or national security operations or services with a friendly foreign country on a cost-sharing basis, any reimbursements or contributions received from that foreign country to meet its share of the project may be credited to appropriate current appropriations of the Federal Bureau of Investigation. The amount of a reimbursement or contribution credited to an appropriation account pursuant to this authority shall be available only for payment of the share of the project expenses allocated to the participating foreign country.

SEC. 111. Section 286 of the Immigration and Nationality Act of 1952 (8 U.S.C. 1356), as amended, is further amended as follows:

(a) by striking in subsection (d) "shall charge and collect $6", and inserting "shall charge and collect $8";

(b) by amending subsection (e) as follows:

"The Attorney General is authorized to charge and collect $8 per individual for the immigration inspection or pre-inspection of each commercial vessel passenger whose journey originated in Mexico, Canada, the United States of America, a territory or possession of the United States, or any adjacent island: Provided, That this section shall not apply to immigration inspection at designated ports-of-entry of passengers arriving by Great Lakes international ferries or Great Lakes vessels on the Great Lakes and connecting waterways, when operating on a regular schedule.";

(c) by adding at the end of subsection (m):

"Each fee collected under this subsection shall be used only to fund adjudication or naturalization services, or subject to the availability of funds provided pursuant to paragraph (5), costs of similar services provided without charge to asylum and refugee applicants. No such fee may be transferred to Immigration and Naturalization Service Enforcement and Border Affairs account or to any other agency or department of government, except under 31 U.S.C. 1535. There are authorized to be appropriated such sums as may be necessary to carry out the provisions of sections 207 through 209.";

(d) by adding after the word "subsection" in subsection (q)(2) ", including receipts for services performed in processing forms I–94, I–94W, and I–68, and other similar applications processed at land border ports of entry,";

(e) by adding at the end the following new subsections:

"(s) Immigration Services Capital Investment Account—

(1) There is established in the general fund of the Treasury a separate account, which shall be known as the Immigration Services Capital Investment Account.

(2) There shall be deposited into the Account funds appropriated to the Attorney General, including fee revenue, which shall remain available until expended and may be expended for the purposes of application backlog reduction, infrastructure improvements, process improvements, major capital acquisitions, and such other service-related expenses and programs.

"(t) Genealogy Fee.—(1) There is hereby established the Genealogy Fee for providing genealogy research and information services. This fee shall be deposited as offsetting collections into the Examinations Fee Account. Fees for such research and information services may be set at a level that will ensure the recovery of the full costs of providing all such services. Such fees shall be available without further appropriation for these purposes.

(2) The Attorney General will prepare and submit annually to Congress statements of financial condition of the Genealogy Fee.

(3) Any officer or employee of the Immigration and Naturalization Service shall collect fees prescribed under regulation before disseminating any requested genealogical information.

"(u) The Attorney General is authorized to establish and collect a premium fee for employment-based petitions and applications. This fee shall be used to provide certain premium-processing services to business customers, and to make infrastructure improvements in the adjudications and customer-service processes. For approval of the benefit applied for, the petitioner/applicant must meet the legal criteria for such benefit. This fee shall be set at $1,000, shall be paid in addition to any normal petition/application fee that may be applicable, and shall be deposited as offsetting collections in the Immigration Examinations Fee Account, of which not to exceed $25,000,000 shall be available to fund expedited processing and benefit fraud investigations. All collections in excess of such amount shall be deposited into the Immigration Services Capital Investment Account for infrastructure improvements. The Attorney General may adjust this fee according to the Consumer Price Index.".

SEC. 112. Beginning in fiscal year 2001 and thereafter, funds appropriated to the Federal Prison System may be used to place in privately operated prisons only such persons sentenced to incarceration under the District of Columbia Code as the Director, Bureau of Prisons, may determine to be appropriate for such placement, after consideration of all relevant factors, including the threat of danger to public safety.

SEC. 113. In addition to any amounts otherwise set aside, one percent of the sums appropriated to the programs of the Office of Justice Programs shall be transferred to and merged with the funds for the National Institute of Justice to carry out research and evaluation.

SEC. 114. Amounts in the fund established under 42 U.S.C. 10601 in fiscal year 2001 in excess of $550,000,000 shall not be available for obligation until October 1, 2001.

SEC. 115. Section 506(c) of P.L. 103–317 (108 Stat. 1766) is amended to read as follows:

"(c) The amendment made by subsections (a) and (b) shall take effect on October 1, 1994.".

SEC. 116. Section 245(i)(3)(B) of the Immigration and Nationality Act, 8 USC 1255(i)(3)(B), is amended to read as follows:

"(B) Any remaining portion of such fees remitted under such paragraphs shall be allocated in equal shares to the Breached Bond Detention Fund established under section 286(r) and to the Immigration Services Capital Investment Account.".

SEC. 117. Section 108 of the Department of Justice and Related Agencies Appropriations Act, 1994 (Pub. Law 103–121), is amended—

(a) in the first sentence, by inserting before the period: ", except that, for fiscal year 2001 and thereafter, the Attorney General may credit up to six percent of all amounts collected"; and

(b) in the second sentence—

(1) by striking "only" and inserting "first"; and

(2) by inserting before the period: ", and thereafter for other personnel, administrative, and litigation expenses of civil debt collection litigation activities". (Department of Justice Appropriations Act, 2000, as enacted by section 1000(a)(1) of the Consolidated Appropriations Act, 2000 (P.L. 106–113).)

SEC. 118 (a) Section 5545a of title 5, United States Code, is amended—

(1) in paragraph (a)(2)—

(A) by replacing "subsection (k))" with "subsection (k))—";

(B) by inserting "(A)" before "who is required to—";

(C) by redesignating subparagraphs (A) through (F) as clauses (i) through (vi), respectively;

(D) in paragraph (E), by redesignating clauses (i) through (v) as subclauses (I) through (V), respectively;

(E) in paragraph (F), by inserting "or" after the semi-colon; and

(F) by inserting at the end a new subparagraph as follows: "(B) who is—

"(i) a pilot employed by the United States Customs Service; or

"(ii) a pilot, border-patrol agent, deportation officer, or detention-and-deportation officer employed by the Immigration and Naturalization Service;"

(2) by amending the text of subsection (i) to read as follows: "The Office of Personnel Management may prescribe regulations necessary to administer subparagraph (a)(2)(B)."

(b) This section shall take effect on the first day of the first applicable pay period that begins on or after 120 days after the date of enactment of this Act. Not later than 30 days after such effective date, the certification specified in section 5545a(e) shall be made initially with respect to each person deemed to be a criminal investigator pursuant to section 5545a(a)(2)(B)(ii) (as added by this section). The Attorney General may prescribe procedures necessary to administer this paragraph.

(c) The Attorney General may establish special salary rates for border patrol agents grades 5 through 11 of the General Schedule, without regard to the criteria in section 5305 of title 5, United States Code. The Attorney General, after consultation with the Office of Personnel Management, shall prescribe procedures necessary to administer this subsection in a manner consistent with special salary rates established under such section 5305.

SEC. 119. Notwithstanding 42 U.S.C. 13708(b)(3), up to 5 percent of the funds made available by this Act for the Prison Grant Program may be used for the purposes set forth in such section.

[1] The Administration proposes to delete this provision and will work with the Congress to address this issue.

[2] Proposed for deletion without prejudice on the merits of the provision.

DEPARTMENT OF LABOR

EMPLOYMENT AND TRAINING ADMINISTRATION

Federal Funds

General and special funds:

TRAINING AND EMPLOYMENT SERVICES

For necessary expenses of the Workforce Investment Act, including the purchase and hire of passenger motor vehicles, the construction, alteration, and repair of buildings and other facilities, and the purchase of real property for training centers as authorized by the Workforce Investment Act[; the Stewart B. McKinney Homeless Assistance Act; the Women in Apprenticeship and Nontraditional Occupations Act;] *and* the National Skill Standards Act of 1994; [and the School-to-Work Opportunities Act; $3,002,618,000] *$3,643,062,000* plus reimbursements, of which [$1,650,153,000] *$2,225,222,000* is available for obligation for the period July 1, [2000] *2001* through June 30, [2001] *2002, including $42,000,000 under section 132(a)(2)(A) of chapter 5 of the Workforce Investment Act for competitive grants for dislocated worker employment and training activities*; of which [$1,250,965,000] *$1,397,465,000* is available for obligation for the period April 1, [2000] *2001* through June 30, [2001] *2002, including $1,022,465,000 to carry out chapter 4 of the Workforce Investment Act and $375,000,000 to carry out section 169 of such Act*; and of which [$35,500,000] *$20,375,000* is available for the period July 1, [2000] *2001* through June 30, [2003 including $34,000,000] *2004* for necessary expenses of construction, rehabilitation, and acquisition of Job Corps centers[, and $1,500,000 under authority of section 171(d) of the Workforce Investment Act for use by the Organizing Committee for the 2001 Special Olympics World Winter Games in Alaska to promote employment opportunities for individuals with disabilities and other staffing needs; and of which $55,000,000 shall be available from July 1, 2000 through September 30, 2001, for carrying out activities of the School-to-Work Opportunities Act]: *Provided*, That [$58,800,000;] *$12,098,000* shall be for carrying out section [166] *172* of the Workforce Investment Act, [including $5,000,000 for carrying out section 166(j)(1) of the Workforce Investment Act, including the provision of assistance to American Samoans who reside in Hawaii for the co-location of federally funded and State-funded workforce investment activities,] and [$7,000,000] *$3,500,000* shall be for carrying out the National Skills Standards Act of 1994: *Provided further*, That no funds from any other appropriation shall be used to provide meal services at or for Job Corps centers[: *Provided further*, That funds provided to carry out section 171(d) of such Act may be used for demonstration projects that provide assistance to new entrants in the workforce and incumbent workers: *Provided further*, That funding provided to carry out projects under section 171 of the Workforce Investment Act of 1998 that are identified in the Conference Agreement, shall not be subject to the requirements of section 171(b)(2)(B) of such Act, the requirements of section 171(c)(4)(D) of such Act, or the joint funding requirements of sections 171(b)(2)(A) and 171(c)(4)(A) of such Act: *Provided further*, That funding appropriated herein for Dislocated Worker Employment and Training Activities under section 132(a)(2)(A) of the Workforce Investment Act of 1998 may be distributed for Dislocated Worker Projects under section 171(d) of the Act without regard to the 10 percent limitation contained in section 171(d) of the Act].

For necessary expenses of the Workforce Investment Act, including the purchase and hire of passenger motor vehicles, the construction, alteration, and repair of buildings and other facilities, and the purchase of real property for training centers as authorized by the Workforce Investment Act; $2,463,000,000 plus reimbursements, of which $2,363,000,000 is available for obligation for the period October 1, [2000] *2001* through June 30, [2001] *2002, including $63,000,000 under section 132(a)(2)(A) of chapter 5 of the Workforce Investment Act for competitive grants for dislocated worker employment and training activities*; and of which $100,000,000 is available for the period October 1, [2000] *2001* through June 30, [2003] *2004*, for necessary expenses of construction, rehabilitation, and acquisition of Job Corps centers. *(Department of Labor Appropriations Act, 2000, as enacted by section 1000(a)(4) of the Consolidated Appropriations Act, 2000 (P.L. 106–113).)*

Program and Financing (in millions of dollars)

Identification code 16–0174–0–1–504		1999 actual	2000 est.	2001 est.
	Obligations by program activity:			
	Direct program:			
00.01	Adult employment and training activities	955	238	950
00.02	Fathers work/families win			25
00.03	Dislocated worker employment and training activities	1,419	668	1,740
00.04	Incumbent workers			3
00.05	Youth activities		1,001	1,022
00.06	Youth opportunity grants		250	250
00.07	Job corps	1,253	1,003	1,399
00.08	Responsible reintegration for young offenders			7
00.09	Safe schools/healthy students			4
00.10	Native Americans	55	58	55
00.11	Migrant and seasonal farmworkers	80	74	74
00.12	Veterans workforce investment program	7	7	2
00.13	National programs	108	148	140
00.14	Expired programs	1,257	113	45
09.01	Reimbursable program	1	4	4
10.00	Total new obligations	5,135	3,564	5,720
	Budgetary resources available for obligation:			
21.40	Unobligated balance available, start of year	1,183	1,486	967
22.00	New budget authority (gross)	5,320	3,045	6,158
22.10	Resources available from recoveries of prior year obligations	61		
22.21	Unobligated balance transferred to other accounts	−5		
22.22	Unobligated balance transferred from other accounts	64		
23.90	Total budgetary resources available for obligation	6,623	4,531	7,125
23.95	Total new obligations	−5,135	−3,564	−5,720
23.98	Unobligated balance expiring or withdrawn	−2		
24.40	Unobligated balance available, end of year	1,486	967	1,405
	New budget authority (gross), detail:			
	Discretionary:			
40.00	Appropriation	5,279	3,003	3,643
40.75	Reduction pursuant to P.L. 106–51	−1		
40.76	Reduction pursuant to P.L. 106–113		−12	
41.00	Transferred to other accounts	−2		
42.00	Transferred from other accounts	2		
43.00	Appropriation (total discretionary)	5,278	2,991	3,643
55.00	Advance appropriation			2,463
	Mandatory:			
60.25	Appropriation (special fund, indefinite)	41	50	48
	Discretionary:			
68.00	Spending authority from offsetting collections: Offsetting collections (cash)	1	4	4
70.00	Total new budget authority (gross)	5,320	3,045	6,158
	Change in unpaid obligations:			
72.40	Unpaid obligations, start of year: Obligated balance, start of year	4,293	4,669	2,860
73.10	Total new obligations	5,135	3,564	5,720
73.20	Total outlays (gross)	−4,676	−5,373	−5,725
73.40	Adjustments in expired accounts (net)	−22		
73.45	Adjustments in unexpired accounts	−61		
74.40	Unpaid obligations, end of year: Obligated balance, end of year	4,669	2,860	2,855
	Outlays (gross), detail:			
86.90	Outlays from new discretionary authority	644	452	2,482
86.93	Outlays from discretionary balances	4,032	4,899	3,202
86.98	Outlays from mandatory balances		22	41
87.00	Total outlays (gross)	4,676	5,373	5,725

General and special funds—Continued

TRAINING AND EMPLOYMENT SERVICES—Continued

Program and Financing (in millions of dollars)—Continued

Identification code 16–0174–0–1–504		1999 actual	2000 est.	2001 est.
	Offsets:			
	Against gross budget authority and outlays:			
	Offsetting collections (cash) from:			
88.00	Federal sources	–1	–2	–2
88.40	Non-Federal sources		–2	–2
88.90	Total, offsetting collections (cash)	–1	–4	–4
	Net budget authority and outlays:			
89.00	Budget authority	5,319	3,041	6,154
90.00	Outlays	4,675	5,369	5,721

Note: Excludes budget authority for veterans' workforce investment programs and the homeless veterans reintegration project transferred to the Assistant Secretary for Veterans Employment and Training. Comparable amounts for 1999 ($10.3 million) and 2000 ($16.9 million) are included above.

Summary of Budget Authority and Outlays

(in millions of dollars)

Enacted/requested:	*1999 actual*	*2000 est.*	*2001 est.*
Budget Authority	5,319	3,041	6,154
Outlays	4,675	5,369	5,721
Legislative proposal, not subject to PAYGO:			
Budget Authority			–105
Outlays			–3
Legislative proposal, subject to PAYGO:			
Budget Authority			
Outlays			–102
Total:			
Budget Authority	5,319	3,041	6,049
Outlays	4,675	5,369	5,616

Enacted in 1998, the Workforce Investment Act (WIA), is the primary authorization for this appropriation account. The act revitalized the Nation's job training system to provide workers with the information, advice, job search assistance, and training they need to get and keep good jobs, and provides employers with skilled workers. Funds appropriated for this account generally are available on a July to June program year basis, but beginning in FY 2000, substantial advance appropriation amounts were provided.

Adult employment and training activities.—Grants to provide financial assistance to States and territories to design and operate training programs for adults, including low-income individuals and public assistance recipients.

Fathers work/families win.—This new program, operated under WIA National Programs authority, will provide competitive grants to state and local areas to: (1) help low-income non-custodial fathers increase their employment and earnings and pay more child support and (2) provide resources for case management and skill training for low-income families to help them move up the career ladder and remain off cash assistance.

Dislocated worker employment and training activities.—Grants to provide reemployment services and retraining assistance to individuals dislocated from their employment. Also included in this activity is funding for competitive grants for dislocated worker employment and training activities, to be financed through fees paid by employers for the certification of certain aliens as eligible workers under the Immigration and Nationality Act as included in proposed legislation.

Incumbent workers.—This new program, operated under WIA National Programs authority, will provide competitive grants to States to train and upgrade the skills of incumbent workers to boost skills and wages of the U.S. workforce. Applicants would be required to provide non-Federal matching resources, and employers that receive grant assistance would be expected to demonstrate that training increased participants' earnings.

Youth activities.—Grants to support a wide range of activities and services to prepare low-income youth for academic and employment success, including summer jobs. The program links academic and occupational learning with youth development activities.

Youth opportunity grants.—Competitive grants to increase the long-term employment of youth who live in empowerment zones, enterprise communities, and similar high poverty areas. This activity includes funding for the Rewarding Achievement in Youth program for competitive grants to high poverty areas to provide low income youth with extended summer employment opportunities and end-of-summer bonuses for high academic achievement and job performance.

Job corps.—A system of primarily residential centers offering basic education, training, work experience, and other support, typically to economically disadvantaged youth.

Responsible reintegration for young offenders.—This program, operated under WIA National Programs authority, is a continuation of the Youth Violence initiative begun in FY 2000. It will link offenders under the age of 35 with essential services that can help make a difference in their choices in the future, such as education, training, job placement, drug counseling, and mentoring, in order to reintegrate them into mainstream society. Through states and local competitive grants, this program would establish partnerships between the criminal justice and local workforce investment systems, complementing a similar program in the Department of Justice.

Safe schools/healthy students.—This program, under WIA National Programs authority, will be operated in conjunction with the Departments of Education, Health and Human Services, and Justice, and will provide competitive grants to local communities. The grants will strengthen connections among high schools, post-secondary schools, alternative schools, out-of-school youth programs, and work-based learning programs, in order to promote safe communities and healthy child development. They also will help build local partnerships amoung Youth Councils, business and community organizations, and schools to improve opportunities for at-risk youth.

Native Americans.—Grants to Indian tribes and other Native American groups to provide training, work experience, and other employment-related services to Native Americans.

Migrant and seasonal farmworkers.—Grants to public agencies and nonprofit groups to provide training and other employability development services to economically disadvantaged youth and families whose principal livelihood is gained in migratory and other forms of seasonal farmwork.

Veterans workforce investment programs.—This program of grants or contracts to provide disabled, Vietnam-era, and recently separated veterans with job training and related assistance to meet their unique employment and training needs will be transferred to the Assistant Secretary for Veterans Employment and Training in FY 2001.

National programs.—Provides program support for WIA activities and nationally administered programs for segments of the population that have special disadvantages in the labor market. In addition, this activity includes a demonstration program of grants to regional and local entities to provide technical skills training for unemployed and incumbent workers and is supported by fees paid by employers applying for foreign workers under the H–1b temporary alien labor certification program. This program is authorized by the American Competitiveness and Workforce Improvement Act of 1998.

Expired programs.—Includes programs for which no funding is requested in FY 2001, including Job Training Partnership Act Summer Youth Employment and Training Grants, Youth Training Grants, and School-to-Work.

Object Classification (in millions of dollars)

Identification code 16–0174–0–1–504	1999 actual	2000 est.	2001 est.
Direct obligations:			
23.1 Rental payments to GSA	1	1	1
24.0 Printing and reproduction	1	1	1
25.2 Other services	25	18	34
25.3 Purchases of goods and services from Government accounts	7	6	7
25.5 Research and development contracts	3	3	3
31.0 Equipment	14	9	14
41.0 Grants, subsidies, and contributions	4,925	3,365	5,494
92.0 Undistributed	1	1	1
99.0 Subtotal, direct obligations	4,977	3,404	5,555
99.0 Reimbursable obligations	1	4	4
Allocation Account:			
Personnel compensation:			
11.1 Full-time permanent	53	55	59
11.3 Other than full-time permanent	2	2	2
11.5 Other personnel compensation	3	3	2
11.9 Total personnel compensation	58	60	63
12.1 Civilian personnel benefits	14	15	16
21.0 Travel and transportation of persons	2	2	2
22.0 Transportation of things	2	2	1
23.3 Communications, utilities, and miscellaneous charges	6	6	5
25.2 Other services	35	33	35
26.0 Supplies and materials	34	32	33
31.0 Equipment	....	2	2
32.0 Land and structures	3	....	1
41.0 Grants, subsidies, and contributions	1	3	3
92.0 Undistributed	2	1	....
99.0 Subtotal, allocation account	157	156	161
99.9 Total new obligations	5,135	3,564	5,720
Obligations are distributed as follows:			
Department of Labor	4,978	3,408	5,558
Department of Agriculture	95	99	100
Department of the Interior	62	57	62

Training and Employment Services

(Legislative proposal, not subject to PAYGO)

Program and Financing (in millions of dollars)

Identification code 16–0174–2–1–504	1999 actual	2000 est.	2001 est.
Obligations by program activity:			
Direct program:			
00.03 Dislocated worker employment and training activities	....	....	–16
10.00 Total new obligations (object class 41.0)	....	....	–16
Budgetary resources available for obligation:			
22.00 New budget authority (gross)	....	....	–105
23.95 Total new obligations	....	....	16
24.40 Unobligated balance available, end of year	....	....	–89
New budget authority (gross), detail:			
Discretionary:			
40.00 Appropriation	....	....	–105
Change in unpaid obligations:			
73.10 Total new obligations	....	....	–16
73.20 Total outlays (gross)	....	....	3
74.40 Unpaid obligations, end of year: Obligated balance, end of year	....	....	–13
Outlays (gross), detail:			
86.90 Outlays from new discretionary authority	....	....	–3
Net budget authority and outlays:			
89.00 Budget authority	....	....	–105
90.00 Outlays	....	....	–3

Legislation will be proposed that would authorize the Secretary of Labor to collect fees from employers for the certification of certain aliens as eligible workers under the Immigration and Nationality Act. This schedule reflects the effects of that legislative proposal on discretionary spending. For more detail see the legislative proposal for the Program Administration account.

Training and Employment Services

(Legislative proposal, subject to PAYGO)

Program and Financing (in millions of dollars)

Identification code 16–0174–4–1–504	1999 actual	2000 est.	2001 est.
Obligations by program activity:			
09.01 Reimbursable program	....	....	16
10.00 Total new obligations (object class 41.0)	....	....	16
Budgetary resources available for obligation:			
22.00 New budget authority (gross)	....	....	105
23.95 Total new obligations	....	....	–16
24.40 Unobligated balance available, end of year	....	....	89
New budget authority (gross), detail:			
Mandatory:			
69.00 Offsetting collections (cash)	....	....	105
Change in unpaid obligations:			
73.10 Total new obligations	....	....	16
73.20 Total outlays (gross)	....	....	–3
74.40 Unpaid obligations, end of year: Obligated balance, end of year	....	....	13
Outlays (gross), detail:			
86.97 Outlays from new mandatory authority	....	....	3
Offsets:			
Against gross budget authority and outlays:			
88.40 Offsetting collections (cash) from: Non-Federal sources	....	....	–105
Net budget authority and outlays:			
89.00 Budget authority	....	....	....
90.00 Outlays	....	....	–102

Legislation will be proposed that would authorize the Secretary of Labor to collect fees from employers for the certification of certain aliens as eligible workers under the Immigration and Nationality Act. This schedule reflects the effects of that legislative proposal on mandatory spending. For more detail see the legislative proposal for the Program Administration account.

Welfare-to-Work Jobs

Program and Financing (in millions of dollars)

Identification code 16–0177–0–1–504	1999 actual	2000 est.	2001 est.
Obligations by program activity:			
00.01 Formula grants	957	....	....
00.02 Competitive grants	519	....	....
00.03 Performance grants	....	50	....
10.00 Total new obligations	1,476	50	....
Budgetary resources available for obligation:			
21.40 Unobligated balance available, start of year	248	187	....
22.00 New budget authority (gross)	1,488	–137	....
22.10 Resources available from recoveries of prior year obligations	6	....	....
23.90 Total budgetary resources available for obligation	1,742	50	....
23.95 Total new obligations	–1,476	–50	....
23.98 Unobligated balance expiring or withdrawn	–79	....	....
24.40 Unobligated balance available, end of year	187	....	....

General and special funds—Continued

WELFARE-TO-WORK JOBS—Continued

Program and Financing (in millions of dollars)—Continued

Identification code 16–0177–0–1–504	1999 actual	2000 est.	2001 est.
New budget authority (gross), detail:			
Mandatory:			
60.00 Appropriation	1,488		
60.36 Unobligated balance rescinded		−137	
62.50 Appropriation (total mandatory)	1,488	−137	
Change in unpaid obligations:			
72.40 Unpaid obligations, start of year: Obligated balance, start of year	1,224	2,426	1,516
73.10 Total new obligations	1,476	50	
73.20 Total outlays (gross)	−267	−960	−1,370
73.45 Adjustments in unexpired accounts	−6		
74.40 Unpaid obligations, end of year: Obligated balance, end of year	2,426	1,516	146
Outlays (gross), detail:			
86.97 Outlays from new mandatory authority	12		
86.98 Outlays from mandatory balances	255	960	1,370
87.00 Total outlays (gross)	267	960	1,370
Net budget authority and outlays:			
89.00 Budget authority	1,488	−137	
90.00 Outlays	267	960	1,370

Summary of Budget Authority and Outlays

(in millions of dollars)

Enacted/requested:	*1999 actual*	*2000 est.*	*2001 est.*
Budget Authority	1,488	−137	
Outlays	267	960	1,370
Legislative proposal, subject to PAYGO:			
Budget Authority		−50	
Outlays		−100	−465
Total:			
Budget Authority	1,488	−187	
Outlays	267	860	905

This account provides funding for activities of the Welfare-to-Work Grants program, which was established by the Balanced Budget Act of 1997 (P.L. 105–33) appropriating funding for 1998 and 1999. Funds are available for expenditure for up to 3 years after they are provided. This program provides formula grants to States and federally administered competitive grants to Private Industry Councils, political subdivisions of States, and private entities to assist hard-to-employ welfare recipients to secure lasting, unsubsidized employment.

Object Classification (in millions of dollars)

Identification code 16–0177–0–1–504	1999 actual	2000 est.	2001 est.
41.0 Direct obligations: Grants, subsidies, and contributions	1,473	50	
41.0 Allocation Account: Grants, subsidies, and contributions	3		
99.9 Total new obligations	1,476	50	

WELFARE-TO-WORK JOBS

(Legislative proposal, subject to PAYGO)

Program and Financing (in millions of dollars)

Identification code 16–0177–4–1–504	1999 actual	2000 est.	2001 est.
Obligations by program activity:			
00.03 Performance grants		−50	
10.00 Total new obligations (object class 41.0)		−50	
Budgetary resources available for obligation:			
22.00 New budget authority (gross)		−50	
23.95 Total new obligations		50	
New budget authority (gross), detail:			
Mandatory:			
60.36 Unobligated balance rescinded		−50	
Change in unpaid obligations:			
72.40 Unpaid obligations, start of year: Obligated balance, start of year			50
73.10 Total new obligations		−50	
73.20 Total outlays (gross)		100	465
74.40 Unpaid obligations, end of year: Obligated balance, end of year		50	515
Outlays (gross), detail:			
86.98 Outlays from mandatory balances		−100	−465
Net budget authority and outlays:			
89.00 Budget authority		−50	
90.00 Outlays		−100	−465

Legislation will be proposed to rescind the welfare-to-work successful performance bonus and to extend by two years the period of time in which grant recipients may expend funds.

COMMUNITY SERVICE EMPLOYMENT FOR OLDER AMERICANS

To carry out the activities for national grants or contracts with public agencies and public or private nonprofit organizations under paragraph (1)(A) of section 506(a) of title V of the Older Americans Act of 1965, as amended, or to carry out older worker activities as subsequently authorized, $343,356,000.

To carry out the activities for grants to States under paragraph (3) of section 506(a) of title V of the Older Americans Act of 1965, as amended, or to carry out older worker activities as subsequently authorized, $96,844,000. *(Department of Labor Appropriations Act, 2000, as enacted by section 1000(a)(4) of the Consolidated Appropriations Act, 2000 (P.L. 106–113).)*

Program and Financing (in millions of dollars)

Identification code 16–0175–0–1–504	1999 actual	2000 est.	2001 est.
Obligations by program activity:			
00.01 National programs	343	343	343
00.02 State programs	97	97	97
10.00 Total new obligations (object class 41.0)	440	440	440
Budgetary resources available for obligation:			
22.00 New budget authority (gross)	440	440	440
23.95 Total new obligations	−440	−440	−440
New budget authority (gross), detail:			
Discretionary:			
40.00 Appropriation	440	440	440
Change in unpaid obligations:			
72.40 Unpaid obligations, start of year: Obligated balance, start of year	373	369	369
73.10 Total new obligations	440	440	440
73.20 Total outlays (gross)	−441	−440	−440
73.40 Adjustments in expired accounts (net)	−3		
74.40 Unpaid obligations, end of year: Obligated balance, end of year	369	369	369
Outlays (gross), detail:			
86.90 Outlays from new discretionary authority	83	84	84
86.93 Outlays from discretionary balances	358	356	356
87.00 Total outlays (gross)	441	440	440
Net budget authority and outlays:			
89.00 Budget authority	440	440	440
90.00 Outlays	441	440	440

This program provides part-time work experience in community service activities to unemployed, low-income persons aged 55 and over.

FEDERAL UNEMPLOYMENT BENEFITS AND ALLOWANCES

For payments during the current fiscal year of trade adjustment benefit payments and allowances under part I; and for training, allowances for job search and relocation, and related State administrative expenses under part II, subchapters B and D, chapter 2, title II of the Trade Act of 1974, as amended, [$415,150,000] *$406,550,000*, together with such amounts as may be necessary to be charged to the subsequent appropriation for payments for any period subsequent to September 15 of the current year. *(Department of Labor Appropriations Act, 2000, as enacted by section 1000(a)(4) of the Consolidated Appropriations Act, 2000 (P.L. 106–113).)*

Program and Financing (in millions of dollars)

Identification code 16–0326–0–1–999		1999 actual	2000 est.	2001 est.
	Obligations by program activity:			
	Direct program:			
00.01	Trade adjustment assistance benefits	226	233	248
00.02	Trade adjustment assistance training	94	95	95
00.03	North American Free Trade Agreement adjustment assistance benefits	19	26	27
00.04	North American Free Trade Agreement adjustment assistance training	37	37	37
09.01	Reimbursable program	38	40	40
10.00	Total new obligations	414	431	447
	Budgetary resources available for obligation:			
22.00	New budget authority (gross)	422	455	447
23.95	Total new obligations	–414	–431	–447
23.98	Unobligated balance expiring or withdrawn	–8	–24	
	New budget authority (gross), detail:			
	Mandatory:			
60.00	Appropriation	361	415	407
69.00	Offsetting collections (cash)	61	40	40
70.00	Total new budget authority (gross)	422	455	447
	Change in unpaid obligations:			
72.40	Unpaid obligations, start of year: Obligated balance, start of year	196	202	203
73.10	Total new obligations	414	431	447
73.20	Total outlays (gross)	–387	–429	–446
73.40	Adjustments in expired accounts (net)	–21		
74.40	Unpaid obligations, end of year: Obligated balance, end of year	202	203	203
	Outlays (gross), detail:			
86.97	Outlays from new mandatory authority	316	339	355
86.98	Outlays from mandatory balances	71	90	91
87.00	Total outlays (gross)	387	429	446
	Offsets:			
	Against gross budget authority and outlays:			
88.00	Offsetting collections (cash) from: Federal sources	–61	–40	–40
	Net budget authority and outlays:			
89.00	Budget authority	361	415	407
90.00	Outlays	326	389	406

Summary of Budget Authority and Outlays

(in millions of dollars)

Enacted/requested:	*1999 actual*	*2000 est.*	*2001 est.*
Budget Authority	361	415	407
Outlays	326	389	406
Legislative proposal, subject to PAYGO:			
Budget Authority			47
Outlays			31
Total:			
Budget Authority	361	415	454
Outlays	326	389	437

Trade adjustment assistance.—Adjustment assistance, including cash weekly benefits, training, job search and relocation allowances, is paid to workers as authorized by the Trade Act of 1974, as amended.

North American Free Trade Agreement (NAFTA) transitional adjustment assistance.—Adjustment assistance, including weekly cash benefits, training, job search and relocation allowances, is paid to workers determined to be adversely affected as a result of trade with Canada and Mexico as authorized by the Trade Act of 1974, as amended.

Object Classification (in millions of dollars)

Identification code 16–0326–0–1–999		1999 actual	2000 est.	2001 est.
41.0	Direct obligations: Grants, subsidies, and contributions	376	391	407
99.0	Reimbursable obligations: Subtotal, reimbursable obligations	38	40	40
99.9	Total new obligations	414	431	447

FEDERAL UNEMPLOYMENT BENEFITS AND ALLOWANCES

(Legislative proposal, subject to PAYGO)

Program and Financing (in millions of dollars)

Identification code 16–0326–4–1–999		1999 actual	2000 est.	2001 est.
	Obligations by program activity:			
	Direct program:			
00.01	Trade adjustment assistance benefits			24
00.02	Trade adjustment assistance training			23
10.00	Total new obligations (object class 41.0)			47
	Budgetary resources available for obligation:			
22.00	New budget authority (gross)			47
23.95	Total new obligations			–47
	New budget authority (gross), detail:			
	Mandatory:			
60.00	Appropriation			47
	Change in unpaid obligations:			
73.10	Total new obligations			47
73.20	Total outlays (gross)			–31
74.40	Unpaid obligations, end of year: Obligated balance, end of year			16
	Outlays (gross), detail:			
86.97	Outlays from new mandatory authority			31
	Net budget authority and outlays:			
89.00	Budget authority			47
90.00	Outlays			31

Legislation will be proposed that would consolidate and reform the Trade Adjustment Assistance (TAA) and the NAFTA-Transitional Adjustment Assistance (NAFTA–TAA) programs and extend the combined program through September 30, 2005. As part of the consolidation, the proposed legislation would extend eligibility for TAA to those who lose their jobs due to shifts in production abroad, similar to the current provision under NAFTA–TAA for shifts in production to Canada and Mexico. The legislative cap on TAA training expenditures would be raised to support the expected increase in program participants. The consolidated program would harmonize existing requirements linking training and income support and would provide supportive services as needed. Finally, the proposed legislation would create a contingency funding provision to assure that resources are available to pay for any unexpected increase in benefits costs for eligible workers.

General and special funds—Continued

STATE UNEMPLOYMENT INSURANCE AND EMPLOYMENT SERVICE OPERATIONS

For authorized administrative expenses, [$163,452,000] *$197,452,000*, together with not to exceed [$3,090,288,000] *$3,191,746,000* (including not to exceed $1,228,000 which may be used for amortization payments to States which had independent retirement plans in their State employment service agencies prior to 1980), which may be expended from the Employment Security Administration account in the Unemployment Trust Fund including the cost of administering [section 1201 of the Small Business Job Protection Act of 1996,] *section 51 of the Internal Revenue Code of 1986, as amended,* section 7(d) of the Wagner-Peyser Act, as amended, the Trade Act of 1974, as amended, the Immigration Act of 1990, and the Immigration and Nationality Act, as amended, and of which the sums available in the allocation for activities authorized by title III of the Social Security Act, as amended (42 U.S.C. 502–504), and the sums available in the allocation for necessary administrative expenses for carrying out 5 U.S.C. 8501–8523, shall be available for obligation by the States through December 31, [2000] *2001*, except that funds used for automation acquisitions shall be available for obligation by the States through September 30, [2002] *2003*; and of which [$163,452,000] *$197,452,000*, together with not to exceed [$738,283,000] *$788,283,000* of the amount which may be expended from said trust fund, shall be available for obligation for the period July 1, [2000] *2001* through June 30, [2001] *2002*, to fund activities under the Act of June 6, 1933, as amended, including the cost of penalty mail authorized under 39 U.S.C. 3202(a)(1)(E) made available to States in lieu of allotments for such purpose[, and of which $125,000,000 shall be available only to the extent necessary for additional State allocations to administer unemployment compensation laws to finance increases in the number of unemployment insurance claims filed and claims paid or changes in a State law]: *Provided*, That to the extent that the Average Weekly Insured Unemployment (AWIU) for fiscal year [2000] *2001* is projected by the Department of Labor to exceed [2,638,000] *2,396,000*, an additional $28,600,000 shall be available for obligation for every 100,000 increase in the AWIU level (including a pro rata amount for any increment less than 100,000) from the Employment Security Administration Account of the Unemployment Trust Fund: *Provided further*, That funds appropriated in this Act which are used to establish a national one-stop career center [network] *system, or which are used to support the Federal-State unemployment insurance programs,* may be obligated in contracts, grants or agreements with non-State entities: *Provided further*, That funds appropriated under this Act for activities authorized under the Wagner-Peyser Act, as amended, and title III of the Social Security Act, may be used by the States to fund integrated Employment Service and Unemployment Insurance automation efforts, notwithstanding cost allocation principles prescribed under Office of Management and Budget Circular A–87. *(Department of Labor Appropriations Act, 2000, as enacted by section 1000(a)(4) of the Consolidated Appropriations Act, 2000 (P.L. 106–113).)*

Program and Financing (in millions of dollars)

Identification code 16–0179–0–1–999		1999 actual	2000 est.	2001 est.
	Obligations by program activity:			
	Direct program:			
	Unemployment compensation:			
00.01	State administration	2,328	2,256	2,349
00.02	National activities	10	10	10
	Employment service:			
00.10	Grants to States	790	762	812
00.11	National activities	60	67	44
00.12	One-stop career centers	179	113	134
00.13	Work incentive assistance grants	....	8	20
09.01	Reimbursable program	4	10	10
10.00	Total new obligations	3,371	3,226	3,379
	Budgetary resources available for obligation:			
21.40	Unobligated balance available, start of year	154	94	107
22.00	New budget authority (gross)	3,311	3,239	3,392
23.90	Total budgetary resources available for obligation	3,465	3,333	3,499
23.95	Total new obligations	−3,371	−3,226	−3,379
24.40	Unobligated balance available, end of year	94	107	121
	New budget authority (gross), detail:			
	Discretionary:			
40.00	Appropriation	162	163	197
68.00	Spending authority from offsetting collections: Offsetting collections (cash)	3,149	3,076	3,195
70.00	Total new budget authority (gross)	3,311	3,239	3,392
	Change in unpaid obligations:			
72.40	Unpaid obligations, start of year: Obligated balance, start of year	143	274	239
73.10	Total new obligations	3,371	3,226	3,379
73.20	Total outlays (gross)	−3,194	−3,261	−3,359
73.40	Adjustments in expired accounts (net)	−46	....	....
74.40	Unpaid obligations, end of year: Obligated balance, end of year	274	239	258
	Outlays (gross), detail:			
86.90	Outlays from new discretionary authority	3,128	3,088	3,208
86.93	Outlays from discretionary balances	66	173	151
87.00	Total outlays (gross)	3,194	3,261	3,359
	Offsets:			
	Against gross budget authority and outlays:			
	Offsetting collections (cash) from:			
	Federal sources:			
88.00	Federal sources	−4	−10	−10
88.00	Trust Fund sources	−3,145	−3,066	−3,185
88.90	Total, offsetting collections (cash)	−3,149	−3,076	−3,195
	Net budget authority and outlays:			
89.00	Budget authority	162	163	197
90.00	Outlays	45	185	164

Note.—Excludes budget authority for occupational employment statistics activities transferred to the Bureau of Labor Statistics. Comparable amounts for 1999 ($20.7 million) and 2000 ($20.7 million) are included above.

Summary of Budget Authority and Outlays

(in millions of dollars)

Enacted/requested:	*1999 actual*	*2000 est.*	*2001 est.*
Budget Authority	162	163	197
Outlays	45	185	164
Legislative proposal, not subject to PAYGO:			
Budget Authority	....	....	....
Outlays	....	....	....
Legislative proposal, subject to PAYGO:			
Budget Authority	....	....	....
Outlays	....	....	....
Total:			
Budget Authority	162	163	197
Outlays	45	185	164

Unemployment compensation.—State administration amounts provide administrative grants to State agencies which pay unemployment compensation to eligible workers and collect State unemployment taxes from employers. These agencies also pay unemployment benefits to former Federal personnel as well as trade adjustment assistance to eligible individuals. State administration amounts also provide administrative grants to State agencies to improve the integrity and financial stability of the unemployment compensation program through a comprehensive program, UI Performs, to effect continuous improvement in State performance and related activities designed to assess and reduce errors and prevent fraud, waste, and abuse in the payment of unemployment compensation benefits and the collection of unemployment taxes. National activities relating to the Federal-State unemployment insurance programs are conducted through contracts or agreements with the State agencies or with non-state entities. Contingency funds included in State administration are available to meet increases in the costs of administration resulting from changes in State law, or increases in the number of claims filed and claims paid.

PROGRAM STATISTICS

	1998 actual	*1999 estimate*	*2000 estimate* [1]	*2001 estimate* [1]
Staff years	36,257	35,333	42,059	44,023

Basic workload (in thousands):				
Employer tax accounts	6,425	6,562	6,642	6,552
Employee wage items recorded	518,513	532,107	578,122	601,406
Initial claims taken	17,372	16,740	17,134	18,598
Eligibility interviews	2,497	2,449	8,915	9,639
Weeks claimed	118,656	117,407	115,221	124,575
Nonmonetary determinations	7,430	7,331	7,265	7,384
Appeals	1,120	1,054	1,002	978
Covered employment	121,610	124,160	125,530	126,610

Employment service.—The public employment service is a nationwide system providing no-fee employment services to individuals who are seeking employment and employers who are seeking workers. State employment service activities are financed by allotment to States distributed under a demographically based funding formula established under the Wagner-Peyser Act, as amended. Employment service allotments are funded on a program year basis running from July 1 through June 30 of the following year. The reemployment needs of unemployed workers who lose their jobs through no fault of their own and who need extra job finding help are financed by Reemployment Services grants. These funds will be distributed to States on a program year basis running from July 1 through June 30 the following year.

Employment service activities serving national needs are conducted through specific reimbursable agreements between the States and the Federal Government under the Wagner-Peyser Act, as amended and other legislation. Funding is also provided for amortization payments for States which had independent retirement plans prior to 1980 in their State employment service agencies.

One-stop career centers.—These funds will be used to support voluntary State efforts to create a comprehensive system of One-Stop Career Centers which will provide workers and employers with quick and easy access to a wide array of enhanced career development and labor market information services. In this activity, funds are provided for America's Agricultural Labor Network (AgNet), a new information system that allows growers to find workers and workers to find employment opportunities that meet their needs. Funding for this activity is on a program year basis, running from July 1 through June 30 of the following year.

Work incentive assistance grants.—These funds will provide competitive grants to improve access to and coordination of information, benefits, and services to enable individuals with disabilities to return to work.

PROGRAM STATISTICS

[In thousands]

	1998 actual[1]	1999 estimate[2]	2000 estimate[3]	2001 estimate[4]
Total applicants	17,288	17,100	17,000	17,000
Entered employment	3,265	3,400	3,500	3,700

[1] For the program year, July 1, 1998–June 30, 1999.
[2] For the program year, July 1, 1999–June 30, 2000.
[3] For the program year, July 1, 2000–June 30, 2001.
[4] For the program year, July 1, 2001–June 30, 2002.

Object Classification (in millions of dollars)

Identification code 16–0179–0–1–999		1999 actual	2000 est.	2001 est.
	Direct obligations:			
23.3	Communications, utilities, and miscellaneous charges	99	102	102
41.0	Grants, subsidies, and contributions	3,268	3,114	3,267
99.0	Subtotal, direct obligations	3,367	3,216	3,369
99.0	Reimbursable obligations	4	10	10
99.9	Total new obligations	3,371	3,226	3,379

State Unemployment Insurance and Employment Service Operations

(Legislative proposal, not subject to PAYGO)

Program and Financing (in millions of dollars)

Identification code 16–0179–2–1–999		1999 actual	2000 est.	2001 est.
	Obligations by program activity:			
10.00	Total new obligations (object class 23.3)			–17
	Budgetary resources available for obligation:			
22.00	New budget authority (gross)			–17
23.95	Total new obligations			17
	New budget authority (gross), detail:			
	Discretionary:			
68.00	Spending authority from offsetting collections (gross): Offsetting collections (cash)			–17
	Change in unpaid obligations:			
73.10	Total new obligations			–17
73.20	Total outlays (gross)			17
	Outlays (gross), detail:			
86.90	Outlays from new discretionary authority			–17
	Offsets:			
	Against gross budget authority and outlays:			
88.00	Offsetting collections (cash) from: Trust Fund sources			17
	Net budget authority and outlays:			
89.00	Budget authority			
90.00	Outlays			

Legislation will be proposed that would authorize the Secretary of Labor to collect fees from employers for the certification of certain aliens as eligible workers under the Immigration and Nationality Act. This schedule reflects the effects of that legislative proposal on discretionary spending. For more detail see the legislative proposal for the Program Administration account.

State Unemployment Insurance and Employment Service Operations

(Legislative proposal, subject to PAYGO)

Program and Financing (in millions of dollars)

Identification code 16–0179–4–1–999		1999 actual	2000 est.	2001 est.
	Obligations by program activity:			
10.00	Total new obligations (object class 41.0)			17
	Budgetary resources available for obligation:			
22.00	New budget authority (gross)			17
23.95	Total new obligations			–17
	New budget authority (gross), detail:			
	Mandatory:			
69.00	Offsetting collections (cash)			17
	Change in unpaid obligations:			
73.10	Total new obligations			17
73.20	Total outlays (gross)			–17
	Outlays (gross), detail:			
86.97	Outlays from new mandatory authority			17
	Offsets:			
	Against gross budget authority and outlays:			
88.40	Offsetting collections (cash) from: Non-Federal sources			–17
	Net budget authority and outlays:			
89.00	Budget authority			
90.00	Outlays			

General and special funds—Continued

STATE UNEMPLOYMENT INSURANCE AND EMPLOYMENT SERVICE OPERATIONS—Continued

Legislation will be proposed that would authorize the Secretary of Labor to collect fees from employers for the certification of certain aliens as eligible workers under the Immigration and Nationality Act. This schedule reflects the effects of that legislative proposal on mandatory spending. For more detail see the legislative proposal for the Program Administration account.

PAYMENTS TO THE UNEMPLOYMENT TRUST FUND

Program and Financing (in millions of dollars)

Identification code 16–0178–0–1–603	1999 actual	2000 est.	2001 est.
Budgetary resources available for obligation:			
21.40 Unobligated balance available, start of year	5	5	5
23.95 Total new obligations			
24.40 Unobligated balance available, end of year	5	5	5
Net budget authority and outlays:			
89.00 Budget authority			
90.00 Outlays			

This account was initiated as a result of the amendments to the Emergency Unemployment Compensation law (P.L. 102–164, as amended) which currently provides for general fund financing for administrative costs related to extended benefits under the optional, total unemployment rate trigger. These funds are transferred to a receipt account in the Unemployment Trust Fund (UTF) in order that resources may be transferred to the Employment Security Administration Account in the UTF for administrative costs.

ADVANCES TO THE UNEMPLOYMENT TRUST FUND AND OTHER FUNDS

For repayable advances to the Unemployment Trust Fund as authorized by sections 905(d) and 1203 of the Social Security Act, as amended, and to the Black Lung Disability Trust Fund as authorized by section 9501(c)(1) of the Internal Revenue Code of 1954, as amended; and for nonrepayable advances to the Unemployment Trust Fund as authorized by section 8509 of title 5, United States Code, and to the "Federal unemployment benefits and allowances" account, to remain available until September 30, [2001] *2002*, [$356,000,000] *$435,000,000*.

In addition, for making repayable advances to the Black Lung Disability Trust Fund in the current fiscal year after September 15, [2000] *2001*, for costs incurred by the Black Lung Disability Trust Fund in the current fiscal year, such sums as may be necessary. *(Department of Labor Appropriations Act, 2000, as enacted by section 1000(a)(4) of the Consolidated Appropriations Act, 2000 (P.L. 106–113).)*

Program and Financing (in millions of dollars)

Identification code 16–0327–0–1–600	1999 actual	2000 est.	2001 est.
Obligations by program activity:			
10.00 Total new obligations (object class 92.0)	23		
Budgetary resources available for obligation:			
21.40 Unobligated balance available, start of year			
22.00 New budget authority (gross)	23		
23.90 Total budgetary resources available for obligation	23		
23.95 Total new obligations	–23		
23.98 Unobligated balance expiring or withdrawn			
New budget authority (gross), detail:			
Mandatory:			
60.05 Appropriation (indefinite)	23		
Change in unpaid obligations:			
73.10 Total new obligations	23		
73.20 Total outlays (gross)	–23		
Outlays (gross), detail:			
86.97 Outlays from new mandatory authority	23		
Net budget authority and outlays:			
89.00 Budget authority	23		
90.00 Outlays	23		

Summary of Budget Authority and Outlays

(in millions of dollars)

Enacted/requested:	*1999 actual*	*2000 est.*	*2001 est.*
Budget Authority	23		
Outlays	23		
Legislative proposal, not subject to PAYGO:			
Budget Authority			1,468
Outlays			1,468
Total:			
Budget Authority	23		1,468
Outlays	23		1,468

This account provides repayable advances to the Black Lung Disability Trust Fund for making payments from that fund whenever its balances prove insufficient. The funding requested in this appropriation for FY 2001 is entirely for Black Lung. This spending authority is presented as authority to borrow in the Black Lung Disability Trust Fund. FY 1999 funding shows an advance to the Federal unemployment benefits and allowances account.

This account also provides advances to several other accounts to pay unemployment compensation to eligible individuals under various Federal and State unemployment compensation laws whenever the balances in the funds prove insufficient or whenever reimbursements to certain accounts, as allowed by law, are to be made. Advances made to the Federal employees compensation account in the Unemployment Trust Fund and to the Federal unemployment benefits and allowances account are nonrepayable. All other advances made to the Federal unemployment account and to the Extended unemployment compensation account (both in the Unemployment Trust Fund) are repaid, with interest, to the general fund of the Treasury.

ADVANCES TO THE UNEMPLOYMENT TRUST FUND

(Legislative proposal, not subject to PAYGO)

Program and Financing (in millions of dollars)

Identification code 16–0327–2–1–600	1999 actual	2000 est.	2001 est.
Obligations by program activity:			
10.00 Total new obligations (object class 92.0)			1,468
Budgetary resources available for obligation:			
22.00 New budget authority (gross)			1,468
23.95 Total new obligations			–1,468
New budget authority (gross), detail:			
Mandatory:			
60.05 Appropriation (indefinite)			1,468
Change in unpaid obligations:			
73.10 Total new obligations			1,468
73.20 Total outlays (gross)			–1,468
Outlays (gross), detail:			
86.97 Outlays from new mandatory authority			1,468
Net budget authority and outlays:			
89.00 Budget authority			1,468
90.00 Outlays			1,468

The Black Lung Disability Trust Fund (BLDTF) revenues, which consist primarily of excise taxes on coal, are not sufficient to repay its $7 billion debt to the Treasury or to service the interest on that debt. See discussion in the Black Lung Disability Trust Fund for information on the Administration's proposal to remedy this problem. As a part of this proposal, the Administration will propose legislation that will provide for a $1.5 billion appropriation to permit the BLDTF to compensate the General Fund for the forgone prepayment premium.

PROGRAM ADMINISTRATION

For expenses of administering employment and training programs, [$100,944,000] *$111,276,000*, including [$6,431,000] *$6,655,000* to support up to 75 full-time equivalent staff, the majority of which will be term Federal appointments lasting no more than 1 year, to administer welfare-to-work grants, together with not to exceed [$45,056,000] *$48,035,000*, which may be expended from the Employment Security Administration account in the Unemployment Trust Fund. *(Department of Labor Appropriations Act, 2000, as enacted by section 1000(a)(4) of the Consolidated Appropriations Act, 2000 (P.L. 106–113).)*

Program and Financing (in millions of dollars)

Identification code 16–0172–0–1–504		1999 actual	2000 est.	2001 est.
	Obligations by program activity:			
	Direct program:			
00.01	Adult services	31	33	36
00.02	Youth services	34	34	37
00.03	Workforce security	48	46	49
00.04	Apprenticeship training, employer and labor services	18	19	22
00.05	Executive direction	7	8	8
00.06	Welfare-to-work	6	6	7
10.00	Total new obligations	144	146	159
	Budgetary resources available for obligation:			
22.00	New budget authority (gross)	144	146	159
23.95	Total new obligations	−144	−146	−159
	New budget authority (gross), detail:			
	Discretionary:			
40.00	Appropriation	94	101	111
42.00	Transferred from other accounts	3		
43.00	Appropriation (total discretionary)	97	101	111
	Spending authority from offsetting collections:			
	Offsetting collections (cash):			
68.00	Offsetting collections (cash)	43	45	48
68.00	Trust Fund sources (16–0179)	4		
68.90	Spending authority from offsetting collections (total discretionary)	47	45	48
70.00	Total new budget authority (gross)	144	146	159
	Change in unpaid obligations:			
72.40	Unpaid obligations, start of year: Obligated balance, start of year	15	19	14
73.10	Total new obligations	144	146	159
73.20	Total outlays (gross)	−138	−152	−160
73.40	Adjustments in expired accounts (net)	−2		
74.40	Unpaid obligations, end of year: Obligated balance, end of year	19	14	12
	Outlays (gross), detail:			
86.90	Outlays from new discretionary authority	127	132	148
86.93	Outlays from discretionary balances	11	19	14
87.00	Total outlays (gross)	138	152	160
	Offsets:			
	Against gross budget authority and outlays:			
	Offsetting collections (cash) from:			
	Federal sources:			
88.00	Trust fund sources	−43	−45	−48
88.00	Trust Fund sources (Transfer 16–0179)	−4		
88.90	Total, offsetting collections (cash)	−47	−45	−48
	Net budget authority and outlays:			
89.00	Budget authority	97	101	111
90.00	Outlays	91	106	114

Summary of Budget Authority and Outlays

(in millions of dollars)

Enacted/requested:	*1999 actual*	*2000 est.*	*2001 est.*
Budget Authority	97	101	111
Outlays	91	106	114
Legislative proposal, not subject to PAYGO:			
Budget Authority			
Outlays			
Legislative proposal, subject to PAYGO:			
Budget Authority			
Outlays			
Total:			
Budget Authority	97	101	111
Outlays	91	106	114

Adult services.—Provides leadership, policy direction and administration for a decentralized system of grants to States and locals as well as federally administered programs for job training and employment assistance for low income adults and dislocated workers; provides for training and employment services to special targeted groups; provides for the settlement of trade adjustment petitions; oversees programs helping noncustodial parents and low-income families find and keep jobs; and includes related program operations support activities.

Youth services.—Provides leadership, policy direction and administration for a decentralized system of grants to States and locals as well as federally administered programs for job training and employment assistance for youth, including youth grants, the Job Corps, and Youth Opportunity Grants; tests ways to help young offenders return to work and reduce anti-social or violent behavior; and includes related program operations support activities.

Workforce security.—Provides leadership and policy direction for the administration of the comprehensive nationwide public employment service system; unemployment insurance programs in each State; and for a one-stop career center network, including a comprehensive system of collecting, analyzing and disseminating labor market information; and includes related program operations support activities.

Apprenticeship training, employer and labor services.—Promotes and provides leadership and policy direction for the administration of apprenticeship as a method of skill acquisition through a Federal-State apprenticeship structure. Employer and labor services will facilitate the understanding and responsiveness of workforce development systems to the training needs of employers and the interest of labor organizations in training programs. It provides for the Child Care Apprenticeship Program for increased training of child care providers and for demonstrations of women in non-traditional apprenticeships.

Executive direction.—Provides leadership and policy direction for all training and employment services programs and activities and provides for related program operations support, including research, evaluations, demonstrations and performance standards.

Welfare-to-work.—Provides leadership, policy direction, technical assistance, and administration for a decentralized system of grants to States and federally administered competitive grants to Workforce Investment Boards, political subdivisions of States, and private entities to assist hard-to-employ welfare recipients and certain noncustodial parents to secure lasting, unsubsidized employment.

Object Classification (in millions of dollars)

Identification code 16–0172–0–1–504		1999 actual	2000 est.	2001 est.
	Personnel compensation:			
11.1	Full-time permanent	76	79	83
11.3	Other than full-time permanent	3	3	3

General and special funds—Continued

Program Administration—Continued

Object Classification (in millions of dollars)—Continued

Identification code 16–0172–0–1–504	1999 actual	2000 est.	2001 est.
11.5 Other personnel compensation	2	2	2
11.9 Total personnel compensation	81	84	88
12.1 Civilian personnel benefits	17	18	19
21.0 Travel and transportation of persons	5	5	5
23.1 Rental payments to GSA	10	11	11
23.3 Communications, utilities, and miscellaneous charges	2	2	2
24.0 Printing and reproduction	1	1	1
25.2 Other services	3	3	5
25.3 Purchases of goods and services from Government accounts	12	13	14
25.7 Operation and maintenance of equipment	7	6	10
26.0 Supplies and materials	2	1	1
31.0 Equipment	4	2	3
99.9 Total new obligations	144	146	159

Personnel Summary

Identification code 16–0172–0–1–504	1999 actual	2000 est.	2001 est.
Direct:			
1001 Total compensable workyears: Full-time equivalent employment	1,346	1,368	1,408
Reimbursable:			
2001 Total compensable workyears: Full-time equivalent employment	4	3	3

Program Administration

(Legislative proposal, not subject to PAYGO)

Upon enactment of legislation enabling the Secretary to charge a fee for permanent labor certifications of aliens as eligible workers, the amount appropriated for Program Administration from the Employment Security Administration account in the Unemployment Trust Fund shall be reduced by $4,641,000; the amount appropriated for Training and Employment Services from the General Fund shall be reduced by $105,100,000; the amount appropriated for the Bureau of Labor Statistics from the Employment Security Administration account in the Unemployment Trust Fund shall be reduced by $10,700,000; and the amount appropriated for State Unemployment Insurance and Employment Services Operations from the Employment Security Administration account in the Unemployment Trust Fund shall be reduced by $16,600,000: Provided, That fees collected shall be deposited in each of the above accounts in the stated amounts.

Program and Financing (in millions of dollars)

Identification code 16–0172–2–1–504	1999 actual	2000 est.	2001 est.
Obligations by program activity:			
10.00 Total new obligations			–5
Budgetary resources available for obligation:			
22.00 New budget authority (gross)			–5
23.95 Total new obligations			5
New budget authority (gross), detail:			
Discretionary:			
68.00 Spending authority from offsetting collections (gross): Offsetting collections (cash)			–5
Change in unpaid obligations:			
73.10 Total new obligations			–5
73.20 Total outlays (gross)			5
Outlays (gross), detail:			
86.90 Outlays from new discretionary authority			–5
Offsets:			
Against gross budget authority and outlays:			
88.00 Offsetting collections (cash) from: Trust fund sources			5
Net budget authority and outlays:			
89.00 Budget authority			
90.00 Outlays			

Legislation will be proposed that would authorize the Secretary of Labor to collect fees from employers for the certification of certain aliens as eligible workers under the Immigration and Nationality Act. This schedule reflects the effects of that legislative proposal on discretionary spending. For more detail see the PAYGO legislative proposal for this account, as described below.

Object Classification (in millions of dollars)

Identification code 16–0172–2–1–504	1999 actual	2000 est.	2001 est.
11.1 Personnel compensation: Full-time permanent			–3
12.1 Civilian personnel benefits			–1
99.0 Subtotal, direct obligations			–4
99.5 Below reporting threshold			–1
99.9 Total new obligations			–5

Personnel Summary

Identification code 16–0172–2–1–504	1999 actual	2000 est.	2001 est.
1001 Total compensable workyears: Full-time equivalent employment			–55

Program Administration

(Legislative proposal, subject to PAYGO)

Program and Financing (in millions of dollars)

Identification code 16–0172–4–1–504	1999 actual	2000 est.	2001 est.
Obligations by program activity:			
10.00 Total new obligations			5
Budgetary resources available for obligation:			
22.00 New budget authority (gross)			5
23.95 Total new obligations			–5
New budget authority (gross), detail:			
Mandatory:			
69.00 Offsetting collections (cash)			5
Change in unpaid obligations:			
73.10 Total new obligations			5
73.20 Total outlays (gross)			–5
Outlays (gross), detail:			
86.97 Outlays from new mandatory authority			5
Offsets:			
Against gross budget authority and outlays:			
88.40 Offsetting collections (cash) from: Non-Federal sources			–5
Net budget authority and outlays:			
89.00 Budget authority			
90.00 Outlays			

Legislation will be proposed that would authorize the Secretary of Labor to collect fees from employers for the certification of certain aliens as eligible workers under the Immigration and Nationality Act. The fee proceeds will offset the costs of administering and enforcing the alien labor program, and provide reemployment and training assistance to U.S. workers who have been dislocated from their jobs.

The additional proviso to be included in appropriation language is being proposed in anticipation of the enactment of authorizing legislation. If the authorizing legislation is enacted, the proviso will reduce the amounts available under the Program Administration heading so that total resources will not exceed the amount allowed under the discretionary spending caps. The proviso allows agencies to spend whatever fees are collected, possibly more or possibly less than the estimates in the schedule, or the specified reduction in Program Administration expenditures.

Object Classification (in millions of dollars)

Identification code 16–0172–4–1–504	1999 actual	2000 est.	2001 est.
99.0 Reimbursable obligations: Subtotal, reimbursable obligations			4
99.5 Below reporting threshold			1
99.9 Total new obligations			5

Personnel Summary

Identification code 16–0172–4–1–504	1999 actual	2000 est.	2001 est.
2001 Total compensable workyears: Full-time equivalent employment			55

Unemployment Trust Fund

Unavailable Collections (in millions of dollars)

Identification code 20–8042–0–7–999	1999 actual	2000 est.	2001 est.
Balance, start of year:			
01.99 Balance, start of year	70,220	76,921	85,105
Receipts:			
02.01 General taxes, FUTA	6,475	6,668	6,873
02.02 Deposits by Federal agencies to the Federal Employees Compensation Account	403	399	454
02.05 Interest and profits on investments in public debt securities	4,795	4,935	5,306
02.06 State accounts, deposits by States	19,894	21,453	23,327
02.08 Deposits by Railroad Retirement Board	111	67	54
02.09 CMIA interest, Unemployment trust fund	3	2	2
02.99 Total receipts	31,681	33,524	36,016
04.00 Total: Balances and collections	101,901	110,445	121,121
Appropriation:			
05.01 Unemployment trust fund	–24,892	–25,242	–28,207
05.02 Legislative proposal not subject to PAYGO			33
05.04 Railroad unemployment insurance trust fund	–110	–117	–123
05.99 Subtotal appropriation	–25,002	–25,359	–28,297
06.10 Unobligated balance returned to receipts	22		
06.20 Reduction pursuant to Public Law 106–113		19	
07.99 Total balance, end of year	76,921	85,105	92,824

Program and Financing (in millions of dollars)

Identification code 20–8042–0–7–999	1999 actual	2000 est.	2001 est.
Obligations by program activity:			
Federal-State unemployment insurance:			
Withdrawals:			
00.01 Benefit payments by States	21,027	21,377	24,143
00.02 Federal employees' unemployment compensation	417	393	474
00.03 State administrative expenses	3,154	3,127	3,259
Federal administrative expenses:			
00.10 Direct expenses	51	50	53
00.11 Reimbursements to the Department of the Treasury	34	88	88
00.20 Veterans employment and training	183	184	186
00.21 Interest on refunds	4	4	4
10.00 Total new obligations	24,870	25,223	28,207
Budgetary resources available for obligation:			
22.00 New budget authority (gross)	24,870	25,223	28,207
23.95 Total new obligations	–24,870	–25,223	–28,207
New budget authority (gross), detail:			
Discretionary:			
40.26 Appropriation (trust fund, definite)	3,410	3,378	3,499
40.35 Appropriation rescinded	–22		
40.76 Reduction pursuant to P.L. 106–113		–19	
43.00 Appropriation (total discretionary)	3,388	3,359	3,499
55.26 Advance appropriation (trust fund, definite)	40		
Mandatory:			
60.27 Appropriation (trust fund, indefinite)	31,681	33,524	36,016
60.45 Portion precluded from obligation	–10,239	–11,660	–11,308
62.50 Appropriation (total mandatory)	21,442	21,864	24,708
70.00 Total new budget authority (gross)	24,870	25,223	28,207
Change in unpaid obligations:			
72.40 Unpaid obligations, start of year: Obligated balance, start of year	776	776	749
73.10 Total new obligations	24,870	25,223	28,207
73.20 Total outlays (gross)	–24,870	–25,250	–28,173
74.40 Unpaid obligations, end of year: Obligated balance, end of year	776	749	783
Outlays (gross), detail:			
86.90 Outlays from new discretionary authority	2,662	2,751	2,853
86.93 Outlays from discretionary balances	766	635	612
86.97 Outlays from new mandatory authority	21,442	21,864	24,708
87.00 Total outlays (gross)	24,870	25,250	28,173
Net budget authority and outlays:			
89.00 Budget authority	24,870	25,223	28,207
90.00 Outlays	24,870	25,250	28,173
Memorandum (non-add) entries:			
92.01 Total investments, start of year: U.S. securities: Par value	70,641	77,358	85,400
92.02 Total investments, end of year: U.S. securities: Par value	77,358	85,400	93,116

Summary of Budget Authority and Outlays

(in millions of dollars)

Enacted/requested:	*1999 actual*	*2000 est.*	*2001 est.*
Budget Authority	24,870	25,223	28,207
Outlays	24,870	25,250	28,173
Legislative proposal, not subject to PAYGO:			
Budget Authority			–33
Outlays			–33
Total:			
Budget Authority	24,870	25,223	28,174
Outlays	24,870	25,250	28,140

The financial transactions of the Federal-State and railroad unemployment insurance systems are made through the Unemployment Trust Fund. All State and Federal unemployment tax receipts are deposited in the trust fund and invested in Government securities until needed for benefit payments or administrative costs. States may receive repayable advances from the fund when their balances in the fund are insufficient to pay benefits. The fund may receive repayable advances from the general fund when it has insufficient balances to make advances to States or to pay the Federal share of extended benefits.

State payroll taxes pay for all regular State benefits. During periods of high State unemployment, extended benefits, financed one-half by State payroll taxes and one-half by the Federal unemployment payroll tax, are also paid. The Federal tax pays the costs of Federal and State administration of unemployment insurance and veterans employment services and 97% of the costs of the employment service.

The Federal employees compensation account provides funds to States for unemployment compensation benefits paid to eligible former Federal civilian personnel, Postal Service employees, and ex-servicemembers. Benefits paid are reimbursed to the Federal employees compensation account by the various Federal agencies. Any additional resources necessary to assure that the account can make the required payments to States will be provided from the Advances to the Unemployment Trust Fund and other funds account.

Both the benefit payments and administrative expenses of the separate unemployment insurance program for railroad employees are paid from the unemployment trust fund and

General and special funds—Continued

UNEMPLOYMENT TRUST FUND—Continued

receipts from the tax on railroad payrolls are deposited in the fund to meet expenses.

Status of Funds (in millions of dollars)

Identification code 20–8042–0–7–999	1999 actual	2000 est.	2001 est.
Unexpended balance, start of year:			
0100 Treasury balance	330	341	456
0101 U.S. Securities: Par value	70,641	77,358	85,400
0199 Total balance, start of year	70,971	77,699	85,856
Cash income during the year:			
Governmental receipts:			
0200 General taxes, FUTA, Unemployment trust fund	6,475	6,668	6,873
0201 Unemployment trust fund, State accounts, Deposits by States	19,894	21,453	23,327
0202 Deposits by Railroad Retirement Board	111	67	54
Proprietary receipts:			
0221 CMIA interest, Unemployment trust fund	3	2	2
Intragovernmental transactions:			
0240 Deposits by Federal agencies to the Federal Employees Compensation Account, Unemployment trust fund	403	399	454
0244 Unemployment trust fund, Interest and profits on investments in public debt securities	4,795	4,935	5,306
0299 Total cash income	31,681	33,524	36,016
Cash outgo during year:			
0500 Unemployment trust fund	–24,870	–25,250	–28,173
0503 Railroad unemployment insurance trust fund	–68	–101	–107
0506 Legislative proposal not subject to PAYGO			33
0597 Outgo under present law (–)	–24,938	–25,351	–28,280
0598 Outgo under proposed legislation (–)			33
0599 Total cash outgo (–)	–24,938	–25,351	–28,247
0645 Balance transferred, net	–15	–16	–16
Unexpended balance, end of year:			
0700 Uninvested balance	341	456	493
0701 U.S. Securities: Par value	77,358	85,400	93,116
0799 Total balance, end of year	77,699	85,856	93,609

Object Classification (in millions of dollars)

Identification code 20–8042–0–7–999	1999 actual	2000 est.	2001 est.
25.3 Reimbursements to Department of the Treasury	34	88	88
Insurance claims and indemnities:			
42.0 Federal unemployment benefits	417	393	474
42.0 State unemployment benefits	20,766	21,377	24,143
43.0 Interest and dividends	4	4	4
Undistributed:			
92.0 Payments to States for administrative expenses	3,407	3,127	3,259
92.0 One-Stop, LMI	8		
92.0 Departmental management	4	5	5
92.0 Employment & Training Administration	47	45	48
92.0 Veterans employment and training	183	184	186
99.9 Total new obligations	24,870	25,223	28,207

UNEMPLOYMENT TRUST FUND

(Legislative proposal, not subject to PAYGO)

Program and Financing (in millions of dollars)

Identification code 20–8042–2–7–999	1999 actual	2000 est.	2001 est.
Obligations by program activity:			
10.00 Total new obligations (object class 92.0)			–33
Budgetary resources available for obligation:			
22.00 New budget authority (gross)			–33
23.95 Total new obligations			33
New budget authority (gross), detail:			
Discretionary:			
40.26 Appropriation (trust fund, definite)			–33
Change in unpaid obligations:			
73.10 Total new obligations			–33
73.20 Total outlays (gross)			33
Outlays (gross), detail:			
86.90 Outlays from new discretionary authority			–33
Net budget authority and outlays:			
89.00 Budget authority			–33
90.00 Outlays			–33

Legislation will be proposed that would authorize the Secretary of Labor to collect fees from employers for the certification of certain aliens as eligible workers under the Immigration and Nationality Act. This schedule reflects the effects of that legislative proposal on discretionary spending in the Unemployment Trust Fund attributable to the State Unemployment Insurance and Employment Service Operations, the Bureau of Labor Statistics, and the Program Administration accounts. For more detail see the legislative proposal for the Program Administration account.

PENSION AND WELFARE BENEFITS ADMINISTRATION

Federal Funds

General and special funds:

SALARIES AND EXPENSES

For necessary expenses for the Pension and Welfare Benefits Administration, [$99,000,000] *$107,832,000*. *(Department of Labor Appropriations Act, 2000, as enacted by section 1000(a)(4) of the Consolidated Appropriations Act, 2000 (P.L. 106–113).)*

Program and Financing (in millions of dollars)

Identification code 16–1700–0–1–601	1999 actual	2000 est.	2001 est.
Obligations by program activity:			
Direct program:			
00.01 Enforcement and compliance	74	78	84
00.02 Policy, regulations, and public services	15	17	20
00.03 Program oversight	4	4	4
09.01 Reimbursable program		6	7
10.00 Total new obligations	93	105	115
Budgetary resources available for obligation:			
21.40 Unobligated balance available, start of year	3		
22.00 New budget authority (gross)	90	105	115
23.90 Total budgetary resources available for obligation	93	105	115
23.95 Total new obligations	–93	–105	–115
New budget authority (gross), detail:			
Discretionary:			
40.00 Appropriation	89	99	108
42.00 Transferred from other accounts	1		
43.00 Appropriation (total discretionary)	90	99	108
68.00 Spending authority from offsetting collections: Offsetting collections (cash)		6	7
70.00 Total new budget authority (gross)	90	105	115
Change in unpaid obligations:			
72.40 Unpaid obligations, start of year: Obligated balance, start of year	20	22	24
73.10 Total new obligations	93	105	115
73.20 Total outlays (gross)	–92	–102	–114
74.40 Unpaid obligations, end of year: Obligated balance, end of year	22	24	25
Outlays (gross), detail:			
86.90 Outlays from new discretionary authority	73	84	93
86.93 Outlays from discretionary balances	19	18	21
87.00 Total outlays (gross)	92	102	114
Offsets:			
Against gross budget authority and outlays:			
88.00 Offsetting collections (cash) from: Federal sources		–6	–7

Net budget authority and outlays:			
89.00 Budget authority	90	99	108
90.00 Outlays	92	96	107

Enforcement and compliance.—Conducts criminal and civil investigations and performs reviews to ensure compliance with the fiduciary provisions of the Employee Retirement Income Security Act (ERISA) and the Federal Employees' Retirement System Act of 1986. Assures compliance with applicable reporting requirements, as well as accounting, auditing and actuarial standards. Provides compliance assistance to the public. The 2001 estimates include: (1) expanded compliance and technical assistance capabilities to help ensure employers, practitioners, participants, and beneficiaries understand their rights and responsibilities under ERISA; (2) expanded protection of benefit plan assets in instances where plan sponsors face bankruptcy; (3) enhanced information technology support; and (4) expanded auditing to help implement new law for the Federal employee Thrift Savings Program.

	1999 actual	2000 est.	2001 est.
Plan reviews and investigations conducted	6,934	7,158	7,227
Investigations closed that restored or protected assets	1,347	1,120	1,148
Benefit recoveries from customer assistance:			
Field offices	$55,000,000	$46,000,000	$47,000,000
Inquiries received:			
Field offices	121,787	129,197	131,540

Policy, regulation and public service.—Conducts policy, research, and legislative analyses on pension, health, and other employee benefit issues. Promulgates regulations and interpretations. Issues individual and class exemptions from regulations. Discloses government-required reports and provides compliance assistance to the public. The 2001 estimates include enhanced education and outreach on pension and health plans as well as implementing the law mandating retirement "savings summit" meetings.

	1999 actual	2000 est.	2001 est.
Exemptions, variances, determinations, interpretations, and regulations issued	1,042	1,292	1,312
Average days to process exemption requests	242	207	200
Benefit recoveries from customer assistance:			
National office	$7,000,000	$7,000,000	$7,000,000
Inquiries received:			
National office	33,839	35,000	35,000

Program oversight.—Provides leadership, policy direction, strategic planning, and management of the pension and welfare benefits program. Provides administrative support for budget, debt collection, personnel, labor/employee relations, and other administrative activities, as well as technical program training related to the agency's enforcement, policy, legislative and regulatory functions.

Object Classification (in millions of dollars)

Identification code 16–1700–0–1–601	1999 actual	2000 est.	2001 est.
Direct obligations:			
11.1 Personnel compensation: Full-time permanent	40	47	50
12.1 Civilian personnel benefits	9	10	11
21.0 Travel and transportation of persons	2	3	3
23.1 Rental payments to GSA	5	5	5
23.3 Communications, utilities, and miscellaneous charges		1	1
24.0 Printing and reproduction	1		1
25.2 Other services	2	5	6
25.3 Purchases of goods and services from Government accounts	17	15	7
25.5 Research and development contracts	2	2	3
25.7 Operation and maintenance of equipment	14	10	17
26.0 Supplies and materials			1
31.0 Equipment	1	1	3
99.0 Subtotal, direct obligations	93	99	108
99.0 Reimbursable obligations		6	7
99.9 Total new obligations	93	105	115

Personnel Summary

Identification code 16–1700–0–1–601	1999 actual	2000 est.	2001 est.
1001 Total compensable workyears: Full-time equivalent employment	703	823	850

PENSION BENEFIT GUARANTY CORPORATION

Federal Funds

Public enterprise funds:

PENSION BENEFIT GUARANTY CORPORATION FUND

The Pension Benefit Guaranty Corporation is authorized to make such expenditures, including financial assistance authorized by section 104 of Public Law 96–364, within limits of funds and borrowing authority available to such Corporation, and in accord with law, and to make such contracts and commitments without regard to fiscal year limitations as provided by section 104 of the Government Corporation Control Act, as amended (31 U.S.C. 9104), as may be necessary in carrying out the program through September 30, **[**2000**]** *2001*, for such Corporation: *Provided*, That not to exceed **[**$11,155,000**]** *$11,871,000* shall be available for administrative expenses of the Corporation: *Provided further*, That expenses of such Corporation in connection with the termination of pension plans, for the acquisition, protection or management, and investment of trust assets, and for benefits administration services shall be considered as non-administrative expenses for the purposes hereof, and excluded from the above limitation. *(Department of Labor Appropriations Act, 2000, as enacted by section 1000(a)(4) of the Consolidated Appropriations Act, 2000 (P.L. 106–113).)*

Program and Financing (in millions of dollars)

Identification code 16–4204–0–3–601	1999 actual	2000 est.	2001 est.
Obligations by program activity:			
09.01 Single employer program benefits payments	1,207	963	988
09.02 Multi-employer program financial assistance	6	94	6
09.03 Administrative expenses	11	11	12
09.04 Services related to terminations	148	154	165
10.00 Total new obligations	1,372	1,222	1,171
Budgetary resources available for obligation:			
21.40 Unobligated balance available, start of year	8,721	9,215	10,430
22.00 Budget authority from offsetting collections	1,866	2,437	2,675
23.90 Total budgetary resources available for obligation	10,587	11,652	13,105
23.95 Total new obligations	−1,372	−1,222	−1,171
24.40 Unobligated balance available, end of year	9,215	10,430	11,934
New budget authority (gross), detail:			
Discretionary:			
68.00 Spending authority from offsetting collections: Offsetting collections (cash)	11	11	12
Mandatory:			
69.00 Offsetting collections (cash)	1,855	2,426	2,663
70.00 Total new budget authority (gross)	1,866	2,437	2,675
Change in unpaid obligations:			
72.40 Unpaid obligations, start of year: Obligated balance, start of year	−17	154	63
73.10 Total new obligations	1,372	1,222	1,171
73.20 Total outlays (gross)	−1,201	−1,313	−1,173
74.40 Unpaid obligations, end of year: Obligated balance, end of year	154	63	61
Outlays (gross), detail:			
86.90 Outlays from new discretionary authority	11	11	12
86.97 Outlays from new mandatory authority	1,190	1,302	1,162
87.00 Total outlays (gross)	1,201	1,313	1,173
Offsets:			
Against gross budget authority and outlays:			
Offsetting collections (cash) from:			
88.20 Interest on U.S. securities	−513	−789	−892
Non-Federal sources:			
88.40 Premium income	−681	−968	−936

Public enterprise funds—Continued

PENSION BENEFIT GUARANTY CORPORATION FUND—Continued

Program and Financing (in millions of dollars)—Continued

Identification code 16–4204–0–3–601		1999 actual	2000 est.	2001 est.
88.40	Benefit payment reimbursements	–490	–528	–680
88.40	Reimbursements from trust funds for services related to terminations	–120	–152	–167
88.40	Other Income	–62		
88.90	Total, offsetting collections (cash)	–1,866	–2,437	–2,675
	Net budget authority and outlays:			
89.00	Budget authority			
90.00	Outlays	–665	–1,124	–1,502
	Memorandum (non-add) entries:			
92.01	Total investments, start of year: U.S. securities: Par value	8,697	9,296	10,417
92.02	Total investments, end of year: U.S. securities: Par value	9,296	10,417	11,921

Summary of Budget Authority and Outlays

(in millions of dollars)

	1999 actual	2000 est.	2001 est.
Enacted/requested:			
Budget Authority			
Outlays	–665	–1,124	–1,501
Legislative proposal, subject to PAYGO:			
Budget Authority			
Outlays			1
Total:			
Budget Authority			
Outlays	–665	–1,124	–1,500

Status of Direct Loans (in millions of dollars)

Identification code 16–4204–0–3–601		1999 actual	2000 est.	2001 est.
	Cumulative balance of direct loans outstanding:			
1231	Disbursements: Direct loan disbursements	6	94	6
1263	Write-offs for default: Direct loans	–6	–94	–6

This wholly owned government corporation administers programs of mandatory insurance to prevent loss of pension benefits under covered private, defined-benefit pension plans if single-employer plans terminate or if multiemployer plans are unable to pay benefits.

Single-employer program.—The single-employer program protects about 33 million participants in about 42,000 pension plans. Under this program, a company may voluntarily seek to terminate its plan, or the Pension Benefit Guaranty Corporation (PBGC) may seek termination under certain circumstances. The PBGC must seek termination when a plan cannot pay current benefits.

In a "standard" termination, plan assets must be sufficient to pay all benefits before the plan is allowed to end. That payment is in the form of an annuity purchased from an insurance company or a lump sum payment. After the payment is made, the PBGC guarantee ends. A plan that cannot pay all benefits may be ended by a "distress" termination, but only if the employer meets tests proving severe financial distress; for example, the likelihood that continuing the plan would force the company to shut down. If the terminated plan cannot pay at least the PBGC-guaranteed benefits, the PBGC uses its funds to ensure guaranteed benefits are paid.

	1999 actual	2000 est.	2001 est.
Government trusteeships at end of year	2,737	2,847	2,957
Participants in government trusteeships owed benefits	532,000	572,000	612,000
Retirees receiving monthly benefits	214,890	228,800	244,800

Multiemployer program.—The multiemployer insurance program protects about 8.7 million participants in about 2,000 plans. Multiemployer pension plans are maintained under collectively bargained agreements involving unrelated employers, generally in the same industry. If a PBGC-insured multiemployer plan is unable to pay guaranteed benefits when due, the PBGC will provide the plan with financial assistance to continue paying guaranteed benefits, ordinarily in the form of a loan to the plan. Twenty-five plans are expected to receive assistance in 2001.

Administrative expenses subject to limitation.—Provides for collection of nearly $1 billion in premiums, accounting and auditing services, asset management, executive direction, and other support functions.

Services related to terminations.—This activity provides for needed, but unpredictable, costs related to benefits administration, actuarial services, managing the assets of trusteed plans, and a share of other costs arising from plan termination. Funding includes enhancement in customer services to process final benefit determinations faster.

Plans terminated during the year:	1999 actual	2000 est.	2001 est.
With sufficient assets	1,969	2,000	2,000
Without sufficient assets	122	110	110
Time to replace initial with final benefit levels	5.7 yrs	4–5 yrs	3–4 yrs

Financing.—The primary source of financing is annual premiums paid by sponsors of ongoing covered plans, which vary according to the plans' funding level. Other sources of financing include assets from terminated plans, investment income, and amounts due PBGC from the sponsors of terminating plans. Also, PBGC is authorized to borrow up to $100 million from the U.S. Treasury.

Operating results.—The following tables show the status of PBGC's trust funds and PBGC's operating results.

STATUS OF TRUST FUNDS

[In thousands of dollars]

	1998 actual	1999 actual	2000 est.	2001 est.
Assets:				
Cash	381,650	179,180	179,180	179,180
Investments	6,148,710	7,675,660	8,036,286	8,443,222
Receivables:				
Due from Pension Benefit Guaranty Corporation	5,754,000	3,301,510	3,875,207	4,471,355
Due from employers—terminated plans	1,903,550	1,782,490	1,304,195	1,218,298
Assets of pretrusteed plans	30,200	41,070	315,278	300,008
Other assets	34,540	56,680	56,680	56,680
Total assets	14,252,650	13,036,590	13,766,826	14,668,743
Liabilities:				
Estimate of future benefits—terminated plans	10,891,070	10,033,160	11,610,189	12,681,725
Estimate of probable terminations (net claims for)	3,274,540	2,850,780	2,080,206	1,910,589
Other liabilities	87,040	152,650	76,430	76,430
Total liabilities	14,252,650	13,036,590	13,766,826	14,668,743

CHANGE IN PBGC's LIABILITY UNDER TERMINATED PLANS

[In thousands of dollars]

	1998 actual	1999 actual	2000 est.	2001 est.
Liability, beginning of year	3,720,600	4,361,140	2,214,000	3,060,886
Liability incurred due to plan terminations	265,150	389,600	762,195	566,164
(New liabilities assumed)	463,990	664,600	1,786,213	1,237,058
(Plan assets acquired)	–199,670	–275,060	–969,688	–615,394
(Recoveries from employers, net)	830	60	–54,330	–55,500
Operating loss of trust fund	767,260	–2,014,600	359,346	404,670
Benefit payments	–391,870	–522,140	–274,654	–308,071
Liability, end of year	4,361,140	2,214,000	3,060,886	3,723,648

Statement of Operations (in millions of dollars)

Identification code 16–4204–0–3–601		1998 actual	1999 actual	2000 est.	2001 est.
	Revenue:				
0101	Premium income	989	925	1,053	888
0101	Investment income	2,071	–893	790	892
0101	Other income	5	1		
	Expense:				
0102	Trust fund operating loss	–767	2,015	–359	–405

0102 Net liability due to plan terminations	–265	–384	–762	–566
0102 Provision for probable terminations	–284	340	273	67
0102 Change in allowance for uncollectible financial assistance	–34	–109	–30	–28
0102 Administrative expenses	–26	–12	–12	–12
0105 Net income or loss (–)	1,689	1,883	953	836
0191 Total revenues	3,065	33	1,843	1,780
0192 Total expenses	–1,376	1,850	–890	–944
0199 Total comprehensive income	1,689	1,883	953	836

Balance Sheet (in millions of dollars)

Identification code 16–4204–0–3–601	1998 actual	1999 actual	2000 est.	2001 est.
ASSETS:				
Federal assets:				
1101 Fund balances with Treasury	1	1	1	1
Investments in US securities:				
Treasury securities, par:				
1102 Treasury securities, par	8,697	9,296	10,417	11,921
1102 Treasury securities, unamortized discount (–)/premium (+)	2,577	1,329	1,662	1,684
1106 Receivables, net	127	162	162	162
1206 Non-Federal assets: Receivables, net	104	317	245	173
Net value of assets related to pre-1992 direct loans receivable and acquired defaulted guaranteed loans receivable:				
1601 Direct loans, gross	37	43	....	....
1602 Interest receivable	29	33	....	....
1603 Allowance for estimated uncollectible loans and interest (–)	–66	–76	....	....
1699 Value of assets related to direct loans	....	....	....	....
Other Federal assets:				
1801 Cash and other monetary assets	332	164	164	164
1803 Property, plant and equipment, net	4	....	2	2
1999 Total assets	11,842	11,269	12,653	14,107
LIABILITIES:				
Non-Federal liabilities:				
2201 Accounts payable	311	194	191	191
2206 Pension and other actuarial liabilities	6,143	3,840	4,274	4,891
2999 Total liabilities	6,454	4,034	4,465	5,082
NET POSITION:				
3300 Cumulative results of operations	5,388	7,235	8,188	9,025
3999 Total net position	5,388	7,235	8,188	9,025
4999 Total liabilities and net position	11,842	11,269	12,653	14,107

Object Classification (in millions of dollars)

Identification code 16–4204–0–3–601	1999 actual	2000 est.	2001 est.
Personnel compensation:			
11.1 Full-time permanent	44	47	49
11.3 Other than full-time permanent	2	2	2
11.5 Other personnel compensation	1	1	2
11.9 Total personnel compensation	47	50	53
12.1 Civilian personnel benefits	10	11	11
21.0 Travel and transportation of persons	1	1	1
23.2 Rental payments to others	12	12	13
23.3 Communications, utilities, and miscellaneous charges	3	3	3
24.0 Printing and reproduction	....	1	1
25.2 Other services	80	81	88
25.3 Purchases of goods and services from Government accounts	1	1	1
26.0 Supplies and materials	1	2	2
31.0 Equipment	3	3	5
33.0 Investments and loans	6	94	6
42.0 Insurance claims and indemnities	1,207	963	987
99.0 Subtotal, reimbursable obligations	1,371	1,222	1,171
99.5 Below reporting threshold	1	....	....
99.9 Total new obligations	1,372	1,222	1,171

Personnel Summary

Identification code 16–4204–0–3–601	1999 actual	2000 est.	2001 est.
2001 Total compensable workyears: Full-time equivalent employment	729	754	754

PENSION BENEFIT GUARANTY CORPORATION

(Legislative proposal, subject to PAYGO)

Program and Financing (in millions of dollars)

Identification code 16–4204–4–3–601	1999 actual	2000 est.	2001 est.
Obligations by program activity:			
10.00 Total new obligations (object class 33.0)	....	....	1
Budgetary resources available for obligation:			
23.95 Total new obligations	....	....	–1
24.40 Unobligated balance available, end of year	....	....	–1
Change in unpaid obligations:			
73.10 Total new obligations	....	....	1
73.20 Total outlays (gross)	....	....	–1
Outlays (gross), detail:			
86.98 Outlays from mandatory balances	....	....	1
Net budget authority and outlays:			
89.00 Budget authority	....	....	....
90.00 Outlays	....	....	1

Status of Direct Loans (in millions of dollars)

Identification code 16–4204–4–3–601	1999 actual	2000 est.	2001 est.
Cumulative balance of direct loans outstanding:			
1231 Disbursements: Direct loan disbursements	....	....	1
1263 Write-offs for default: Direct loans	....	....	–1

The Administration will propose legislation to expand pension coverage, improve benefit portability, and strengthen retirement security. Included in the package will be: (1) a new, simplified, defined-benefit pension plan for small businesses that is insured by PBGC at a reduced rate; (2) raising the current guarantee cap on multiemployer pension benefits; (3) extending PBGC's "missing participants" program to terminating defined-contribution and multiemployer plans; (4) eliminating the "partial termination" rules for multiemployer plans; (5) reducing premium charges for certain new plans; and (6) simplifying the guarantee and allocation rules for owners of small businesses.

EMPLOYMENT STANDARDS ADMINISTRATION

Federal Funds

General and special funds:

SALARIES AND EXPENSES

For necessary expenses for the Employment Standards Administration, including reimbursement to State, Federal, and local agencies and their employees for inspection services rendered, [$337,260,000] *$361,491,000*, together with [$1,740,000] *$1,985,000* which may be expended from the Special Fund in accordance with sections 39(c), 44(d) and 44(j) of the Longshore and Harbor Workers' Compensation Act: *Provided*, That $2,000,000 shall be for the development of an alternative system for the electronic submission of reports [as] required to be filed under the Labor-Management Reporting and Disclosure Act of 1959, as amended, and for a computer database of the information for each submission by whatever means, that is indexed and easily searchable by the public via the Internet: *Provided further*, That the Secretary of Labor is authorized to accept, retain, and spend, until expended, in the name of the Department of Labor, all sums of money ordered to be paid to the Secretary of Labor, in accordance with the terms of the Consent Judgment in Civil Action

General and special funds—Continued

SALARIES AND EXPENSES—Continued

No. 91–0027 of the United States District Court for the District of the Northern Mariana Islands (May 21, 1992): *Provided further*, That the Secretary of Labor is authorized to establish and, in accordance with 31 U.S.C. 3302, collect and deposit in the Treasury fees for processing applications and issuing certificates under sections 11(d) and 14 of the Fair Labor Standards Act of 1938, as amended (29 U.S.C. 211(d) and 214) and for processing applications and issuing registrations under title I of the Migrant and Seasonal Agricultural Worker Protection Act (29 U.S.C. 1801 et seq.). *(Department of Labor Appropriations Act, 2000, as enacted by section 1000(a)(4) of the Consolidated Appropriations Act, 2000 (P.L. 106–113).)*

Program and Financing (in millions of dollars)

Identification code 16–0105–0–1–505		1999 actual	2000 est.	2001 est.
	Obligations by program activity:			
	Direct program:			
00.01	Enforcement of wage and hour standards	132	147	158
00.02	Federal contractor EEO standards enforcement	65	73	76
00.03	Federal programs for workers' compensation	107	110	121
00.04	Program direction and support	12	13	13
00.05	Labor-management standards	28	29	31
09.01	Reimbursable program	5	5	5
10.00	Total new obligations	349	377	404
	Budgetary resources available for obligation:			
21.40	Unobligated balance available, start of year		3	3
22.00	New budget authority (gross)	352	377	404
23.90	Total budgetary resources available for obligation	352	380	407
23.95	Total new obligations	−349	−377	−404
23.98	Unobligated balance expiring or withdrawn	−1		
24.40	Unobligated balance available, end of year	3	3	3
	New budget authority (gross), detail:			
	Discretionary:			
40.00	Appropriation	312	337	361
40.75	Reduction pursuant to P.L. 106–51	−1		
42.00	Transferred from other accounts	1		
43.00	Appropriation (total discretionary)	312	337	361
	Mandatory:			
60.25	Appropriation (special fund, indefinite)	5	5	5
	Discretionary:			
68.00	Spending authority from offsetting collections: Offsetting collections (cash)	35	35	38
70.00	Total new budget authority (gross)	352	377	404
	Change in unpaid obligations:			
72.40	Unpaid obligations, start of year: Obligated balance, start of year	27	33	43
73.10	Total new obligations	349	377	404
73.20	Total outlays (gross)	−343	−367	−414
74.40	Unpaid obligations, end of year: Obligated balance, end of year	33	43	33
	Outlays (gross), detail:			
86.90	Outlays from new discretionary authority	318	339	374
86.93	Outlays from discretionary balances	22	23	33
86.97	Outlays from new mandatory authority	2	5	5
87.00	Total outlays (gross)	343	367	414
	Offsets:			
	Against gross budget authority and outlays:			
	Offsetting collections (cash) from:			
88.00	Federal sources	−33	−33	−36
88.40	Non-Federal sources	−2	−2	−2
88.90	Total, offsetting collections (cash)	−35	−35	−38
	Net budget authority and outlays:			
89.00	Budget authority	317	342	366
90.00	Outlays	307	332	376

Enforcement of wage and hour standards.—The Wage and Hour Division works to obtain and encourage compliance with the minimum wage, overtime, child labor, and other employment standards under the Fair Labor Standards Act, Migrant and Seasonal Agricultural Worker Protection Act, the Family and Medical Leave Act, certain provisions of the Immigration and Nationality Act, the wage garnishment provisions in Title III of the Consumer Credit Protection Act, and the Employee Polygraph Protection Act. Prevailing wages are determined and employment standards enforced under various Government contract wage standards. In 2001, approximately 267,000 persons are expected to be aided under the Fair Labor Standards Act through securing agreements with firms to pay back wages owed to their workers. In government contract compliance actions, about 37,000 persons will be aided through securing agreements to pay wages owed to workers. Under the Migrant and Seasonal Agricultural Worker Protection Act program, approximately 2,500 investigations and 900 housing inspections will be completed. In the course of all on-site investigations, investigators will routinely check for employer compliance with child labor standards and, in all "directed" (non-complaint) investigations, for compliance with the employment eligibility verification recordkeeping requirements of the Immigration and Nationality Act. Resources will be earmarked for Davis-Bacon wage survey/wage determination reengineering and reinvention in FY 2001. The reengineering efforts will be substantially completed in 2001. The Budget maintains resources for the Wage and Hour Division which are assigned to areas where employment of illegal immigrants is most prevalent. The targeting of labor standards enforcement efforts in those industries and geographic areas where unauthorized workers are most prevalent will help to reduce the economic incentive for such illegal employment practices and will, in turn, help reduce illegal immigration. FY 2000 and FY 2001 include fees paid by employers applying for foreign workers under the H1–b program.

Federal contractor equal employment opportunity (EEO) standards enforcement.—The Office of Federal Contract Compliance Programs (OFCCP) is responsible for ensuring nondiscrimination in employment based on race, sex, religion, color, national origin, disability or veteran status by Federal contractors and subcontractors at 200,000 worksites with a total workforce of 22 million people. It conducts compliance reviews and complaint investigations. It assures that Federal contractors and subcontractors take affirmative action in the hiring and advancement of minorities and women under the authority of Executive Orders 11246 and 11375. It enforces the affirmative action and nondiscrimination provisions of the Rehabilitation Act of 1973 and, as an agent of the Equal Employment Opportunity Commission, the Americans With Disabilities Act of 1990. It ensures that contractors comply with the provisions of the Vietnam Era Veterans Readjustment Assistance Act of 1974, providing for affirmative action by Federal contractors to employ, and advance in employment, special disabled and Vietnam era veterans.

The Budget includes resources to increase compliance by improving efficiency and customer service in the National Office and in each of the Regional Offices. The resources will give added impetus to the technical assistance effort to assist Federal contractors in understanding the regulatory requirements. Specific emphasis will continue the assistance to smaller companies that may not have the expertise to develop Affirmative Action Programs. It also provides an enhancement to the Equal Pay initiative for an Industry Partnership initiative, which will help improve compliance efforts in glass ceiling issues as well as focus on discrimination in nontraditional occupations. This initiative is part of an overall effort to increase compliance through enhanced compliance assistance. Moreover, OFCCP will maintain reduced reporting requirements. The staff will provide grassroots seminars and technical assistance training sessions for contractors, contracting agencies, government agencies, and constituency groups through continued development and use of existing information technology. In 2001, approximately 1,978,192 individuals will be directly aided through 6,260 compliance reviews, 342 complaint investigations, and 3,066 other compliance actions.

Federal programs for workers' compensation.—Under this income maintenance activity, the Employment Standards Administration administers the Federal Employees' Compensation Act, the Longshore and Harbor Workers' Compensation Act, and the benefit provisions of the Federal Mine Safety and Health Act of 1977. These programs ensure that eligible disabled and injured workers or their survivors receive compensation and medical benefits and a range of services including rehabilitation, supervision of medical care, and technical and advisory counseling to which they are entitled. Monitoring services are provided with respect to State workers' compensation laws.

Program direction and support.—This activity includes planning, personnel management, financial management, and Federal/State liaison programs, management systems implementation, and data processing operations. Major goals in 2001 will include the continued efforts to eliminate internal fraud, waste, and mismanagement; the improvement of management information, automated data processing, and program and fiscal accountability; and legislative and regulatory improvements.

Labor-management standards.—The Office of Labor-Management Standards (OLMS) receives and discloses statutorily required union financial reports; audits union financial records and investigates possible embezzlements of union funds; conducts union officer election investigations; supervises reruns of union officer elections after court determinations that elections were not conducted in accordance with the Labor-Management Reporting and Disclosure Act; and administers the statutory program to certify employee protection provisions under various Federally-sponsored transportation programs. In FY 2001, OLMS expects to process 36,000 reports and conduct a total of 3,701 investigations, audits, and supervised elections.

Object Classification (in millions of dollars)

Identification code 16–0105–0–1–505		1999 actual	2000 est.	2001 est.
	Direct obligations:			
	Personnel compensation:			
11.1	Full-time permanent	190	208	219
11.3	Other than full-time permanent	2	2	2
11.5	Other personnel compensation	3	2	2
11.9	Total personnel compensation	195	212	223
12.1	Civilian personnel benefits	44	48	50
21.0	Travel and transportation of persons	8	9	11
23.1	Rental payments to GSA	25	25	26
23.3	Communications, utilities, and miscellaneous charges	4	4	5
24.0	Printing and reproduction	1	1	1
25.2	Other services	5	6	8
25.3	Purchases of goods and services from Government accounts	28	28	30
25.7	Operation and maintenance of equipment	28	33	37
26.0	Supplies and materials	2	2	2
31.0	Equipment	5	4	6
99.0	Subtotal, direct obligations	345	372	399
99.0	Reimbursable obligations	4	5	5
99.9	Total new obligations	349	377	404

Personnel Summary

Identification code 16–0105–0–1–505		1999 actual	2000 est.	2001 est.
	Direct:			
1001	Total compensable workyears: Full-time equivalent employment	3,712	3,902	3,934
	Reimbursable:			
2001	Total compensable workyears: Full-time equivalent employment	17	17	17

Special Benefits

(including transfer of funds)

For the payment of compensation, benefits, and expenses (except administrative expenses) accruing during the current or any prior fiscal year authorized by title 5, chapter 81 of the United States Code; continuation of benefits as provided for under the heading "Civilian War Benefits" in the Federal Security Agency Appropriation Act, 1947; the Employees' Compensation Commission Appropriation Act, 1944; sections 4(c) and 5(f) of the War Claims Act of 1948 (50 U.S.C. App. 2012); and 50 percent of the additional compensation and benefits required by section 10(h) of the Longshore and Harbor Workers' Compensation Act, as amended, [$79,000,000] *$56,000,000* together with such amounts as may be necessary to be charged to the subsequent year appropriation for the payment of compensation and other benefits for any period subsequent to August 15 of the current year: *Provided*, That amounts appropriated may be used under section 8104 of title 5, United States Code, by the Secretary of Labor to reimburse an employer, who is not the employer at the time of injury, for portions of the salary of a reemployed, disabled beneficiary: *Provided further*, That balances of reimbursements unobligated on September 30, [1999] *2000*, shall remain available until expended for the payment of compensation, benefits, and expenses: *Provided further*, That in addition there shall be transferred to this appropriation from the Postal Service and from any other corporation or instrumentality required under section 8147(c) of title 5, United States Code, to pay an amount for its fair share of the cost of administration, such sums as the Secretary determines to be the cost of administration for employees of such fair share entities through September 30, [2000] *2001*: *Provided further*, That of those funds transferred to this account from the fair share entities to pay the cost of administration, [$21,849,000] *$30,510,000* shall be made available to the Secretary as follows: (1) for the operation of and enhancement to the automated data processing systems, including document imaging [and], medical bill review, *and periodic roll management,* in support of Federal Employees' Compensation Act administration, [$13,433,000] *$19,971,000*; (2) [for program staff training to operate the new imaging system, $1,300,000; (3) for the periodic roll review program, $7,116,000; and (4)] *for conversion to a paperless office, $7,005,000; (3) for communications redesign, $750,000; (4) for information technology maintenance and support, $2,784,000; and (5)* the remaining funds shall be paid into the Treasury as miscellaneous receipts: *Provided further*, That the Secretary may require that any person filing a notice of injury or a claim for benefits under chapter 81 of title 5, United States Code, or 33 U.S.C. 901 et seq., provide as part of such notice and claim, such identifying information (including Social Security account number) as such regulations may prescribe. *(Department of Labor Appropriations Act, 2000, as enacted by section 1000(a)(4) of the Consolidated Appropriations Act, 2000 (P.L. 106–113).)*

Program and Financing (in millions of dollars)

Identification code 16–1521–0–1–600		1999 actual	2000 est.	2001 est.
	Obligations by program activity:			
00.01	Longshore and harbor workers' compensation benefits	3	4	3
00.02	Federal Employees' Compensation Act benefits	2,009	2,032	2,083
10.00	Total new obligations	2,012	2,036	2,086
	Budgetary resources available for obligation:			
21.40	Unobligated balance available, start of year	1,063	1,130	1,096
22.00	New budget authority (gross)	2,080	2,002	2,011
23.90	Total budgetary resources available for obligation	3,143	3,132	3,107
23.95	Total new obligations	−2,012	−2,036	−2,086
24.40	Unobligated balance available, end of year	1,130	1,096	1,021
	New budget authority (gross), detail:			
	Mandatory:			
60.00	Appropriation	179	79	56
69.00	Offsetting collections (cash)	1,901	1,923	1,955
70.00	Total new budget authority (gross)	2,080	2,002	2,011

General and special funds—Continued

SPECIAL BENEFITS—Continued

(INCLUDING TRANSFER OF FUNDS)—Continued

Program and Financing (in millions of dollars)—Continued

Identification code 16–1521–0–1–600	1999 actual	2000 est.	2001 est.
Change in unpaid obligations:			
72.40 Unpaid obligations, start of year: Obligated balance, start of year	35	−4	−4
73.10 Total new obligations	2,012	2,036	2,086
73.20 Total outlays (gross)	−2,051	−2,036	−2,086
74.40 Unpaid obligations, end of year: Obligated balance, end of year	−4	−4	−4
Outlays (gross), detail:			
86.97 Outlays from new mandatory authority	989	910	994
86.98 Outlays from mandatory balances	1,063	1,126	1,092
87.00 Total outlays (gross)	2,051	2,036	2,086
Offsets:			
Against gross budget authority and outlays:			
Offsetting collections (cash) from:			
88.00 Federal sources	−1,314	−1,327	−1,345
88.40 Non-Federal sources	−587	−596	−610
88.90 Total, offsetting collections (cash)	−1,901	−1,923	−1,955
Net budget authority and outlays:			
89.00 Budget authority	179	79	56
90.00 Outlays	150	113	131

Federal Employees' Compensation Act benefits.—Under the Federal Employees' Compensation Act program, income is replaced if a job injury results in time away from work. Medical bills arising from compensable job injuries are also paid. Not all benefits are paid by the program since the first 45 days of disability are usually covered by keeping injured workers in pay status with their employing agencies. In 2001, 165,000 injured federal workers or their survivors will file claims; 53,000 will receive long-term wage replacement benefits for job-related injuries, diseases, or deaths. Most of the costs of this account are charged back to the employing agencies of beneficiaries.

FEDERAL EMPLOYEES' COMPENSATION WORKLOAD

	1999 actual	*2000 est.*	*2001 est.*
Wage-loss claims received	19,759	19,000	19,000
Compensation and medical payments	3,030,915	3,000,000	3,000,000
Cases received	166,544	165,000	165,000
Periodic payment cases	54,897	54,000	53,000

Longshore and harbor workers' compensation benefits.—Under the Longshore and Harbor Workers' Compensation Act, as amended, the Federal Government pays from direct appropriations one-half of the increased benefits provided by the amendments for persons on the rolls prior to 1972. The remainder is provided from the special fund which is financed by private employers assessed at the beginning of each calendar year for their proportionate share of these payments.

Object Classification (in millions of dollars)

Identification code 16–1521–0–1–600	1999 actual	2000 est.	2001 est.
11.1 Personnel compensation: Full-time permanent	4	6	6
12.1 Civilian personnel benefits	1	1	1
25.2 Other services	1	1	1
25.3 Purchases of goods and services from Government accounts	1	1	1
25.7 Operation and maintenance of equipment	9	10	14
31.0 Equipment	4	3	8
42.0 Insurance claims and indemnities	1,992	2,014	2,055
99.9 Total new obligations	2,012	2,036	2,086

Personnel Summary

Identification code 16–1521–0–1–600	1999 actual	2000 est.	2001 est.
1001 Total compensable workyears: Full-time equivalent employment	101	129	129

PANAMA CANAL COMMISSION COMPENSATION FUND

Unavailable Collections (in millions of dollars)

Identification code 16–5155–0–2–602	1999 actual	2000 est.	2001 est.
Balance, start of year:			
01.99 Balance, start of year			
Receipts:			
02.01 Deposits for Panama Commission Compensation Fund, Labor	2	1	
02.02 Interest on investments, Panama Canal Comm., Labor	5	6	6
02.99 Total receipts	7	7	6
Appropriation:			
05.01 Panama Canal Commission compensation fund	−7	−7	−6
07.99 Total balance, end of year			

Program and Financing (in millions of dollars)

Identification code 16–5155–0–2–602	1999 actual	2000 est.	2001 est.
Obligations by program activity:			
10.00 Total new obligations (object class 42.0)	6	6	7
Budgetary resources available for obligation:			
21.40 Unobligated balance available, start of year	78	79	80
22.00 New budget authority (gross)	7	7	6
23.90 Total budgetary resources available for obligation	85	86	86
23.95 Total new obligations	−6	−6	−7
24.40 Unobligated balance available, end of year	79	80	79
New budget authority (gross), detail:			
Mandatory:			
60.25 Appropriation (special fund, indefinite)	7	7	6
Change in unpaid obligations:			
73.10 Total new obligations	6	6	7
73.20 Total outlays (gross)	−6	−6	−7
Outlays (gross), detail:			
86.97 Outlays from new mandatory authority		6	6
86.98 Outlays from mandatory balances	6		1
87.00 Total outlays (gross)	6	6	7
Net budget authority and outlays:			
89.00 Budget authority	7	7	6
90.00 Outlays	6	6	7
Memorandum (non-add) entries:			
92.01 Total investments, start of year: U.S. securities: Par value	79	79	80
92.02 Total investments, end of year: U.S. securities: Par value	79	80	80

Panama Canal Commission Compensation Fund.—This fund was established to provide for the accumulation of funds to meet the Panama Canal Commission's obligations to defray costs of workers' compensation which will accrue pursuant to the Federal Employees' Compensation Act (FECA). On December 31, 1999, the Commission was dissolved as set forth in the Panama Canal Treaty of 1977, and the liability of the Commission for payments beyond that date will not end with its termination. The establishment of this fund, into which funds will be deposited on a regular basis by the Commission, is in conjunction with the transfer of the administration of the FECA program from the Commission to the Department of Labor effective January 1, 1989.

Trust Funds

BLACK LUNG DISABILITY TRUST FUND

(INCLUDING TRANSFER OF FUNDS)

[For payments from the Black Lung Disability Trust Fund, $1,013,633,000, of which $963,506,000 shall be available until September 30, 2001, for payment of all benefits as authorized by section 9501(d) (1), (2), (4), and (7) of the Internal Revenue Code of 1954, as amended, and interest on advances as authorized by section 9501(c)(2) of that Act, and of which $28,676,000 shall be available for transfer to Employment Standards Administration, Salaries and Expenses, $20,783,000 for transfer to Departmental Management, Salaries and Expenses, $312,000 for transfer to Departmental Management, Office of Inspector General, and $356,000 for payment into miscellaneous receipts for the expenses of the Department of Treasury, for expenses of operation and administration of the Black Lung Benefits program as authorized by section 9501(d)(5) of that Act: *Provided*, That, in addition, such amounts as may be necessary may be charged to the subsequent year appropriation for the payment of compensation, interest, or other benefits for any period subsequent to August 15 of the current year.] *Beginning in fiscal year 2001 and thereafter, such sums as may be necessary from the Black Lung Disability Trust Fund, to remain available until expended, for payment of all benefits authorized by section 9501(d)(1) (2) (4) and (7) of the Internal Revenue Code of 1954, as amended; and interest on advances as authorized by section 9501(c)(2) of that Act. In addition, the following amounts shall be available from the Fund for fiscal year 2001 for expenses of operation and administration of the Black Lung Benefits program as authorized by section 9501(d)(5) of that Act: $30,393,000 for transfer to the Employment Standards Administration, "Salaries and Expenses"; $21,590,000 for transfer to Departmental Management, "Salaries and Expenses"; $318,000 for transfer to Departmental Management, "Office of Inspector General"; and $356,000 for payments into Miscellaneous Receipts for the expenses of the Department of Treasury. (Department of Labor Appropriations Act, 2000, as enacted by section 1000(a)(4) of the Consolidated Appropriations Act, 2000 (P.L. 106–113).)*

Unavailable Collections (in millions of dollars)

Identification code 20–8144–0–7–601	1999 actual	2000 est.	2001 est.
Balance, start of year:			
01.99 Balance, start of year	20	21	1
Receipts:			
02.01 Transfer from general fund, Black Lung Benefits Revenue Act taxes	596	577	591
02.02 Miscellaneous interest	3	2	2
02.04 Payment from the general fund for prepayment premium, legislative proposal not subject to PAYGO			1,468
02.99 Total receipts	599	579	2,061
04.00 Total: Balances and collections	619	600	2,062
Appropriation:			
05.01 Administrative Expenses	−598	−599	−593
05.02 Legislative proposal not subject to PAYGO			−1,468
05.99 Subtotal appropriation	−598	−599	−2,061
07.99 Balance, end of year	21	1	1

Program and Financing (in millions of dollars)

Identification code 20–8144–0–7–601	1999 actual	2000 est.	2001 est.
Obligations by program activity:			
00.01 Disabled coal miners benefits	434	431	409
00.02 Administrative expenses	51	50	53
00.03 Interest on advances	515	533	566
10.00 Total new obligations	1,000	1,014	1,028
Budgetary resources available for obligation:			
22.00 New budget authority (gross)	1,000	1,014	1,028
23.95 Total new obligations	−1,000	−1,014	−1,028
New budget authority (gross), detail:			
Mandatory:			
60.26 Appropriation (trust fund, definite)	51	50	53
60.27 Appropriation (trust fund, indefinite)	547	549	540
62.50 Appropriation (total mandatory)	598	599	593
67.15 Authority to borrow (indefinite)	402	415	435
70.00 Total new budget authority (gross)	1,000	1,014	1,028
Change in unpaid obligations:			
73.10 Total new obligations	1,000	1,014	1,028
73.20 Total outlays (gross)	−1,000	−1,014	−1,028
Outlays (gross), detail:			
86.97 Outlays from new mandatory authority	1,000	1,014	1,028
Net budget authority and outlays:			
89.00 Budget authority	1,000	1,014	1,028
90.00 Outlays	1,000	1,014	1,028

Summary of Budget Authority and Outlays

(in millions of dollars)

	1999 actual	2000 est.	2001 est.
Enacted/requested:			
Budget Authority	1,000	1,014	1,028
Outlays	1,000	1,014	1,028
Legislative proposal, not subject to PAYGO:			
Budget Authority			1,468
Outlays			1,468
Total:			
Budget Authority	1,000	1,014	2,496
Outlays	1,000	1,014	2,496

The trust fund consists of all moneys collected from the coal mine industry under the provisions of the Black Lung Benefits Revenue Act of 1981, as amended by the Consolidated Omnibus Budget Reconciliation Act of 1985, in the form of an excise tax on mined coal. These moneys are expended to pay compensation, medical, and survivor benefits to eligible miners and their survivors, where mine employment terminated prior to 1970 or where no mine operator can be assigned liability. In addition, the fund pays all administrative costs incurred in the operation of part C of the Black Lung program. The fund is administered jointly by the Secretaries of Labor, the Treasury, and Health and Human Services. The Benefits Revenue Act provides for repayable advances to the fund in the event fund resources will not be adequate to meet program obligations. Such advances are to be repaid with interest. The outstanding debt at the end of each year was: 1981, $1,510 million; 1982, $1,793 million; 1983, $2,151 million; 1984, $2,497 million; 1985, $2,833 million; 1986, $2,884 million; 1987, $2,952 million; 1988, $2,993 million; 1989, $3,049 million; 1990, $3,049 million; 1991, $3,266 million; 1992, $3,606 million; 1993, $3,949 million; 1994, $4,363 million; 1995, $4,738 million; 1996, $5,112 million; 1997, $5,487 million; 1998, $5,857 million; and 1999, $6,259 million. It is estimated to be $6,673 million in 2000 and $7,108 million in 2001.

BLACK LUNG DISABILITY TRUST FUND WORKLOAD

	1999 actual	2000 est.	2001 est.
Claims received	5,724	7,100	8,100
Claims in payment status	55,057	53,000	50,000
Medical benefits only recipients	11,087	10,200	9,500

Status of Funds (in millions of dollars)

Identification code 20–8144–0–7–601	1999 actual	2000 est.	2001 est.
Unexpended balance, start of year:			
0100 Treasury balance	20	20	
0105 Outstanding debt to Treasury	−5,857	−6,259	−6,673
0199 Total balance, start of year	−5,837	−6,238	−6,672
Cash income during the year:			
Governmental receipts:			
0200 Transfer from general fund, Black Lung Benefits Revenue Act taxes	596	577	591
Proprietary receipts:			
0220 Miscellaneous interest, Black Lung fund	3	2	2

General and special funds—Continued

BLACK LUNG DISABILITY TRUST FUND—Continued
(INCLUDING TRANSFER OF FUNDS)—Continued

Status of Funds (in millions of dollars)—Continued

Identification code 20–8144–0–7–601	1999 actual	2000 est.	2001 est.
Intragovernmental transactions:			
0241 Payment from the general fund for prepayment premium, legislative proposal not subject to PAYGO			1,468
0297 Income under present law	599	579	593
0298 Income under proposed legislation			1,468
0299 Total cash income	599	579	2,061
Cash outgo during year:			
0500 Black lung disability trust fund	–1,000	–1,014	–1,028
0501 Legislative proposal, not subject to PAYGO			–1,468
0597 Outgo under present law (–)	–1,000	–1,014	–1,028
0598 Outgo under proposed legislation (–)			–1,468
0599 Total cash outgo (–)	–1,000	–1,014	–2,496
Unexpended balance, end of year:			
0700 Cash Balance	20		
0705 Outstanding debt to Treasury	–6,259	–6,673	–7,108
0799 Total balance, end of year	–6,238	–6,672	–7,107

Object Classification (in millions of dollars)

Identification code 20–8144–0–7–601	1999 actual	2000 est.	2001 est.
25.2 Other services	51	50	53
42.0 Insurance claims and indemnities	434	431	409
43.0 Interest and dividends	515	533	566
99.9 Total new obligations	1,000	1,014	1,028

BLACK LUNG DISABILITY TRUST FUND
(Legislative proposal, not subject to PAYGO)

Program and Financing (in millions of dollars)

Identification code 20–8144–2–7–601	1999 actual	2000 est.	2001 est.
Obligations by program activity:			
00.03 Interest on advances			1,468
10.00 Total new obligations (object class 43.0)			1,468
Budgetary resources available for obligation:			
22.00 New budget authority (gross)			1,468
23.95 Total new obligations			–1,468
New budget authority (gross), detail:			
Mandatory:			
60.27 Appropriation (trust fund, indefinite)			1,468
Change in unpaid obligations:			
73.10 Total new obligations			1,468
73.20 Total outlays (gross)			–1,468
Outlays (gross), detail:			
86.97 Outlays from new mandatory authority			1,468
Net budget authority and outlays:			
89.00 Budget authority			1,468
90.00 Outlays			1,468

The Black Lung Disability Trust Fund (BLDTF) revenues, which consist primarily of excise taxes on coal, are not sufficient to repay its nearly $7 billion debt to the Treasury or to service the interest on that debt. Under current conditions, this indebtedness will continue to grow, with the BLDTF never becoming solvent, even when benefit outlays have declined to a level approaching zero. To solve this problem, the Administration will propose legislation that will: (1) authorize a refinancing of the outstanding BLDTF debt, (2) extend at current rates BLDTF excise tax levels set to expire in January 2014, and (3) provide for a $1.5 billion appropriation to compensate the General Fund for the forgone prepayment premium.

SPECIAL WORKERS' COMPENSATION EXPENSES

Unavailable Collections (in millions of dollars)

Identification code 16–9971–0–7–601	1999 actual	2000 est.	2001 est.
Balance, start of year:			
01.99 Balance, start of year		1	2
Receipts:			
02.01 Longshoremen's & Harbor Workers Compensation Act, Receipts, Special workers'	133	149	140
02.02 Longshoremen's & Harbor Workers Compensation Act, Earnings on investments, Special workers', Labor	2	2	2
02.03 Workmen's Compensation Act within District of Columbia, Receipts, Special workers'	10	12	11
02.99 Total receipts	145	163	153
04.00 Total: Balances and collections	145	164	155
Appropriation:			
05.01 Special workers' compensation expenses	–144	–162	–153
05.99 Subtotal appropriation	–144	–162	–153
07.99 Total balance, end of year	1	2	2

Program and Financing (in millions of dollars)

Identification code 16–9971–0–7–601	1999 actual	2000 est.	2001 est.
Obligations by program activity:			
00.01 Longshore and Harbor Workers' Compensation Act, as amended	132	146	137
00.02 District of Columbia Compensation Act	12	11	11
10.00 Total new obligations	144	157	148
Budgetary resources available for obligation:			
21.40 Unobligated balance available, start of year	55	56	61
22.00 New budget authority (gross)	144	162	153
23.90 Total budgetary resources available for obligation	199	218	214
23.95 Total new obligations	–144	–157	–148
24.40 Unobligated balance available, end of year	56	61	66
New budget authority (gross), detail:			
Discretionary:			
40.26 Appropriation (trust fund, definite)	2	2	2
Mandatory:			
60.27 Appropriation (trust fund, indefinite)	142	160	151
70.00 Total new budget authority (gross)	144	162	153
Change in unpaid obligations:			
72.40 Unpaid obligations, start of year: Obligated balance, start of year			
73.10 Total new obligations	144	157	148
73.20 Total outlays (gross)	–143	–157	–148
Outlays (gross), detail:			
86.90 Outlays from new discretionary authority	2	2	2
86.97 Outlays from new mandatory authority	86	100	85
86.98 Outlays from mandatory balances	55	55	61
87.00 Total outlays (gross)	143	157	148
Net budget authority and outlays:			
89.00 Budget authority	144	162	153
90.00 Outlays	143	157	148
Memorandum (non-add) entries:			
92.01 Total investments, start of year: U.S. securities: Par value	55	55	61
92.02 Total investments, end of year: U.S. securities: Par value	55	61	66

Distribution of budget authority by account:

Longshore and Harbor Workers' Compensation Act			

District of Columbia Compensation Act			
Distribution of outlays by account:			
Longshore and Harbor Workers' Compensation Act			
District of Columbia Compensation Act			

The trust funds consist of amounts received from employers for the death of an employee where no person is entitled to compensation for such death, for fines and penalty payments, and pursuant to an annual assessment of the industry, for the general expenses of the fund under the Longshore and Harbor Workers' Compensation Act, as amended.

These trust funds are available for payments of additional compensation for second injuries. When a second injury is combined with a previous disability and results in increased permanent partial disability, permanent total disability, or death, the employer's liability for benefits is limited to a specified period of compensation payments after which the fund provides continuing compensation benefits. In addition, the fund pays one-half of the increased benefits provided under the Longshore and Harbor Workers' Compensation Act, as amended, for persons on the rolls prior to 1972. Maintenance payments are made to disabled employees undergoing vocational rehabilitation to enable them to return to remunerative occupations, and the costs of necessary rehabilitation services not otherwise available to disabled workers are defrayed. Payments are made in cases where other circumstances preclude payment by an employer and to provide medical, surgical, and other treatment in disability cases where there has been a default by the insolvency of an uninsured employer.

Object Classification (in millions of dollars)

Identification code 16–9971–0–7–601		1999 actual	2000 est.	2001 est.
25.3	Purchases of goods and services from Government accounts	2	2	2
42.0	Insurance claims and indemnities	142	155	146
99.9	Total new obligations	144	157	148

OCCUPATIONAL SAFETY AND HEALTH ADMINISTRATION

Federal Funds

General and special funds:

SALARIES AND EXPENSES

For necessary expenses for the Occupational Safety and Health Administration, [$382,000,000] *$425,983,000*, including not to exceed [$82,000,000] *$88,493,000* which shall be the maximum amount available for grants to States under section 23(g) of the Occupational Safety and Health Act, which grants shall be no less than 50 percent of the costs of State occupational safety and health programs required to be incurred under plans approved by the Secretary under section 18 of the Occupational Safety and Health Act of 1970; and, in addition, notwithstanding 31 U.S.C. 3302, the Occupational Safety and Health Administration may retain up to $750,000 per fiscal year of training institute course tuition fees, otherwise authorized by law to be collected, and may utilize such sums for occupational safety and health training and education grants: *Provided*, That, notwithstanding 31 U.S.C. 3302, the Secretary of Labor is authorized, during the fiscal year ending September 30, [2000] *2001*, to collect and retain fees for services provided to Nationally Recognized Testing Laboratories, and may utilize such sums, in accordance with the provisions of 29 U.S.C. 9a, to administer national and international laboratory recognition programs that ensure the safety of equipment and products used by workers in the workplace[: *Provided further*, That none of the funds appropriated under this paragraph shall be obligated or expended to prescribe, issue, administer, or enforce any standard, rule, regulation, or order under the Occupational Safety and Health Act of 1970 which is applicable to any person who is engaged in a farming operation which does not maintain a temporary labor camp and employs 10 or fewer employees: *Provided further*, That no funds appropriated under this paragraph shall be obligated or expended to administer or enforce any standard, rule, regulation, or order under the Occupational Safety and Health Act of 1970 with respect to any employer of 10 or fewer employees who is included within a category having an occupational injury lost workday case rate, at the most precise Standard Industrial Classification Code for which such data are published, less than the national average rate as such rates are most recently published by the Secretary, acting through the Bureau of Labor Statistics, in accordance with section 24 of that Act (29 U.S.C. 673), except—

(1) to provide, as authorized by such Act, consultation, technical assistance, educational and training services, and to conduct surveys and studies;

(2) to conduct an inspection or investigation in response to an employee complaint, to issue a citation for violations found during such inspection, and to assess a penalty for violations which are not corrected within a reasonable abatement period and for any willful violations found;

(3) to take any action authorized by such Act with respect to imminent dangers;

(4) to take any action authorized by such Act with respect to health hazards;

(5) to take any action authorized by such Act with respect to a report of an employment accident which is fatal to one or more employees or which results in hospitalization of two or more employees, and to take any action pursuant to such investigation authorized by such Act; and

(6) to take any action authorized by such Act with respect to complaints of discrimination against employees for exercising rights under such Act:

Provided further, That the foregoing proviso shall not apply to any person who is engaged in a farming operation which does not maintain a temporary labor camp and employs 10 or fewer employees]. *(Department of Labor Appropriations Act, 2000, as enacted by section 1000(a)(4) of the Consolidated Appropriations Act, 2000 (P.L. 106–113.))*

Program and Financing (in millions of dollars)

Identification code 16–0400–0–1–554		1999 actual	2000 est.	2001 est.
	Obligations by program activity:			
	Direct program:			
00.01	Safety and health standards	11	12	15
00.02	Federal enforcement	134	141	153
00.03	State programs	80	82	88
00.04	Technical support	19	18	20
00.05	Federal compliance assistance	45	54	67
00.06	State consultation grants	41	43	48
00.07	Safety and health statistics	17	22	26
00.08	Executive direction and administration	7	8	9
09.01	Reimbursable program	2	2	2
10.00	Total new obligations	356	383	428
	Budgetary resources available for obligation:			
22.00	New budget authority (gross)	356	383	428
22.22	Unobligated balance transferred from other accounts			
23.90	Total budgetary resources available for obligation	356	383	428
23.95	Total new obligations	−356	−383	−428
	New budget authority (gross), detail:			
	Discretionary:			
40.00	Appropriation	353	382	426
40.75	Reduction pursuant to P.L. 106–51	−1		
40.76	Reduction pursuant to P.L. 106–113		−1	
42.00	Transferred from other accounts	2		
43.00	Appropriation (total discretionary)	354	381	426
	Spending authority from offsetting collections:			
68.00	Offsetting collections (cash)	3	2	2
68.10	From Federal sources: Change in receivables and unpaid, unfilled orders	−1		
68.90	Spending authority from offsetting collections (total discretionary)	2	2	2
70.00	Total new budget authority (gross)	356	383	428

General and special funds—Continued

SALARIES AND EXPENSES—Continued

Program and Financing (in millions of dollars)—Continued

Identification code 16–0400–0–1–554	1999 actual	2000 est.	2001 est.
Change in unpaid obligations:			
Unpaid obligations, start of year:			
72.40 Obligated balance, start of year	66	67	73
72.95 From Federal sources: Receivables and unpaid, unfilled orders	1		
72.99 Total unpaid obligations, start of year	67	67	73
73.10 Total new obligations	356	383	428
73.20 Total outlays (gross)	−351	−377	−433
73.40 Adjustments in expired accounts (net)	−5		
Unpaid obligations, end of year:			
74.40 Obligated balance, end of year	67	73	69
74.95 From Federal sources: Receivables and unpaid, unfilled orders			
74.99 Total unpaid obligations, end of year	67	73	69
Outlays (gross), detail:			
86.90 Outlays from new discretionary authority	299	317	360
86.93 Outlays from discretionary balances	52	60	72
87.00 Total outlays (gross)	351	377	433
Offsets:			
Against gross budget authority and outlays:			
Offsetting collections (cash) from:			
88.00 Federal sources	−2	−1	−1
88.40 Non-Federal sources	−1	−1	−1
88.90 Total, offsetting collections (cash)	−3	−2	−2
Against gross budget authority only:			
88.95 From Federal sources: Change in receivables and unpaid, unfilled orders	1		
Net budget authority and outlays:			
89.00 Budget authority	354	381	426
90.00 Outlays	349	375	431

Safety and health standards.—The safety and health standards activity provides for the development, promulgation, review and evaluation of occupational safety and health standards under procedures providing opportunity for public comment. Before any standard is proposed or promulgated, a determination is made that: (1) a significant risk of serious injury or health impairment exists; (2) the standard will reduce this risk; (3) the standard is economically and technologically feasible; and (4) the standard is cost-effective when compared with alternative regulatory proposals providing equal levels of protection. Regulatory reform efforts include consensus-based rulemaking, development of common sense regulations, rewriting existing standards in plain language, and regulatory process improvements.

Enforcement.—This activity provides for the enforcement of workplace standards promulgated under the Occupational Safety and Health Act of 1970 through the physical inspection of worksites, and by fostering the voluntary cooperation of employers and employees. This activity also provides grants to assist States in administering and enforcing State standards. Programs are targeted to the investigation of claims of imminent danger and employee complaints, investigation of fatal and catastrophic accidents, programmed inspections of firms with injury-illness rates that are above the national average, and special emphasis inspections for serious safety and health hazards. OSHA's enforcement strategy includes a selective targeting of inspections and related compliance activities to specific high hazard industries and worksites.

Technical support.—This activity provides specialized technical expertise and advice in support of a wide range of program areas, including construction, standards setting, variance determinations, compliance assistance, and enforcement. Areas of expertise include laboratory accreditation, industrial hygiene, ergonomics, occupational health nursing, occupational medicine, and safety engineering.

Compliance assistance—Federal.—This activity supports a variety of employer and employee assistance programs, consistent with OSHA's partnership initiatives. Outreach activities are conducted, including training and information exchanges and technical assistance to employers requesting such help. Grants are awarded to nonprofit organizations to provide employee and employer training programs, targeted to address specific industry needs for safety and health education. Employers are encouraged to establish voluntary employee protection programs, and Federal agencies are assisted in implementing job safety and health programs for their employees. Professional training for compliance personnel and others with related workplace safety and health responsibilities is conducted at the OSHA Training Institute, and further training is provided by education centers selected and sanctioned by the institute.

Compliance assistance—State.—This activity supports 90 percent Federally-funded cooperative agreements with designated State agencies to provide free on-site consultation to employers upon request. State agencies tailor workplans to specific needs in each State while maximizing their impact on injury and illness rates in smaller establishments. These projects offer a variety of services, including safety and health program assessment and assistance, hazard identification and control, and training of employers and their employees.

Safety and health statistics.—Information technology, management information and statistical support for OSHA's programs and field operations are provided through an integrated data network, and statistical analysis and review. OSHA administers and maintains the recordkeeping system which serves as the foundation for the BLS survey on occupational injuries and illnesses, provides guidance on recordkeeping requirements to both the public and private sectors, and develops regulations along with interpretive publications and materials.

Executive direction and administration.—These activities include executive direction, planning and evaluation, management support, legislative liaison, interagency affairs, administrative services, and budgeting and financial control.

PROGRAM STATISTICS

	1999 actual	*2000 est.*	*2001 est.*
Standards promulgated	3	7	5
Inspections:			
Federal inspections	34,342	34,600	35,640
State program inspections	54,989	55,000	56,320
Training and consultations:			
Training grants supported	54	59	70
Consultation visits	23,241	27,500	30,700

Object Classification (in millions of dollars)

Identification code 16–0400–0–1–554	1999 actual	2000 est.	2001 est.
Direct obligations:			
Personnel compensation:			
11.1 Full-time permanent	121	130	142
11.3 Other than full-time permanent	1	1	2
11.5 Other personnel compensation	2	2	2
11.9 Total personnel compensation	124	133	146
12.1 Civilian personnel benefits	28	30	34
21.0 Travel and transportation of persons	8	9	11
23.1 Rental payments to GSA	17	17	18
23.3 Communications, utilities, and miscellaneous charges	3	3	3
24.0 Printing and reproduction	1	1	1
25.1 Advisory and assistance services	4	4	5
25.2 Other services	48	51	61
25.3 Purchases of goods and services from Government accounts	21	19	19
25.7 Operation and maintenance of equipment	9	10	12
26.0 Supplies and materials	3	4	4
31.0 Equipment	3	9	12
41.0 Grants, subsidies, and contributions	85	90	100

99.0	Subtotal, direct obligations	354	380	426
99.0	Reimbursable obligations	1	1	1
99.5	Below reporting threshold	1	2	1
99.9	Total new obligations	356	383	428

Personnel Summary

Identification code 16–0400–0–1–554		1999 actual	2000 est.	2001 est.
1001	Total compensable workyears: Full-time equivalent employment	2,154	2,262	2,384

ALLOCATIONS RECEIVED FROM OTHER ACCOUNTS

Note.—Obligations incurred under allocations from other accounts are included in the schedules of the parent appropriations as follows:

Environmental Protection Agency: Hazardous Substance Response Trust Fund.

MINE SAFETY AND HEALTH ADMINISTRATION

Federal Funds

General and special funds:

SALARIES AND EXPENSES

For necessary expenses for the Mine Safety and Health Administration, [$228,373,000] *$242,247,000,* including purchase and bestowal of certificates and trophies in connection with mine rescue and first-aid work, and the hire of passenger motor vehicles; including *up to $1,000,000 for mine rescue and recovery activities, which shall be available only to the extent that FY 2001 obligations for these activities exceed $1,000,000; in addition,* not to exceed $750,000 may be collected by the National Mine Health and Safety Academy for room, board, tuition, and the sale of training materials, otherwise authorized by law to be collected, to be available for mine safety and health education and training activities, notwithstanding 31 U.S.C. 3302; *and, in addition, the Administration may retain up to $1,000,000 from fees collected for the approval and certification of equipment, materials, and explosives for use in mines, and may utilize such sums for such activities;* the Secretary is authorized to accept lands, buildings, equipment, and other contributions from public and private sources and to prosecute projects in cooperation with other agencies, Federal, State, or private; the Mine Safety and Health Administration is authorized to promote health and safety education and training in the mining community through cooperative programs with States, industry, and safety associations; and any funds available to the department may be used, with the approval of the Secretary, to provide for the costs of mine rescue and survival operations in the event of a major disaster. *(Department of Labor Appropriations Act, 2000, as enacted by section 1000(a)(4) of the Consolidated Appropriations Act, 2000 (P.L. 106–113).)*

Program and Financing (in millions of dollars)

Identification code 16–1200–0–1–554		1999 actual	2000 est.	2001 est.
	Obligations by program activity:			
	Enforcement:			
00.01	Coal	109	111	115
00.02	Metal/non-metal	43	50	55
00.03	Standards development	2	2	2
00.04	Assessments	3	4	4
00.05	Educational policy and development	20	27	27
00.06	Technical support	23	25	27
00.07	Program administration	16	10	12
09.01	Reimbursable program		1	2
10.00	Total new obligations	216	229	244
	Budgetary resources available for obligation:			
21.40	Unobligated balance available, start of year		1	
22.00	New budget authority (gross)	218	229	244
22.21	Unobligated balance transferred to other accounts		–1	
23.90	Total budgetary resources available for obligation	218	229	244
23.95	Total new obligations	–216	–229	–244
23.98	Unobligated balance expiring or withdrawn	–1		
24.40	Unobligated balance available, end of year	1		
	New budget authority (gross), detail:			
	Discretionary:			
40.00	Appropriation	211	228	242
42.00	Transferred from other accounts	7		
43.00	Appropriation (total discretionary)	218	228	242
68.00	Spending authority from offsetting collections: Offsetting collections (cash)		1	2
70.00	Total new budget authority (gross)	218	229	244
	Change in unpaid obligations:			
72.40	Unpaid obligations, start of year: Obligated balance, start of year	21	21	27
73.10	Total new obligations	216	229	244
73.20	Total outlays (gross)	–213	–223	–244
73.40	Adjustments in expired accounts (net)	–1		
74.40	Unpaid obligations, end of year: Obligated balance, end of year	21	27	27
	Outlays (gross), detail:			
86.90	Outlays from new discretionary authority	196	203	222
86.93	Outlays from discretionary balances	17	20	24
87.00	Total outlays (gross)	213	223	244
	Offsets:			
	Against gross budget authority and outlays:			
88.40	Offsetting collections (cash) from: Non-Federal sources		–1	–2
	Net budget authority and outlays:			
89.00	Budget authority	218	228	242
90.00	Outlays	213	222	242

Enforcement.—The Enforcement strategy in 2001 will be an integrated approach that links all actions to preventing occupational injuries and illness. These include inspection of mines as mandated by the Federal Mine Safety and Health Act of 1977, special emphasis initiatives that focus on persistent safety and health hazards, promulgation of safety and health standards, investigation of serious accidents, and on-site education and training assistance. The desired outcome of these enforcement efforts is to lower fatality and injury rates.

Assessments.—This activity assesses and collects civil monetary penalties for violations of safety and health standards.

Educational policy and development.—This activity develops and coordinates MSHA's mine safety and health education and training policies, and provides classroom instruction at the National Academy for MSHA personnel, other governmental personnel, and the mining industry. States provide mine health and safety training materials, and provide technical assistance through the State Grants program.

Technical support.—This activity applies engineering and scientific expertise through field and laboratory forensic investigations to resolve technical problems associated with implementation of the Mine Act. Technical support administers a fee program to approve equipment, materials, and explosives for use in mines and performs field and laboratory audits of equipment previously approved by MSHA. It also collects and analyzes data relative to the cause, frequency, and circumstances of accidents.

Program administration.—This activity provides for general administrative functions.

PROGRAM STATISTICS

	1999 actual	2000 est.	2001 est.
Enforcement:			
Fatality Rates:			
Coal mines	0.034	0.025	0.025
Metal/non-metal mines	0.020	0.024	0.024
Non-fatal lost time injury rates:			
Coal mines	4.87	4.80	4.75
Metal/Non-metal mines	2.80	2.75	2.70
Regulations promulgated	10	14	10
Assessments:			
Violations assessed	109,941	114,000	114,000
Educational policy and development:			
Course days	1,162	1,350	1,540

General and special funds—Continued

SALARIES AND EXPENSES—Continued

PROGRAM STATISTICS—Continued

	1999 actual	2000 est.	2001 est.
Technical support:			
Equipment approvals	873	1,700	1,700
Field investigations	699	400	400
Laboratory samples analyzed	63,439	56,000	56,000

Note.—Incidence rates represent the number of injuries that occur for each 200,000 employee-hours worked.

Object Classification (in millions of dollars)

Identification code 16–1200–0–1–554		1999 actual	2000 est.	2001 est.
	Direct obligations:			
	Personnel compensation:			
11.1	Full-time permanent	117	127	134
11.3	Other than full-time permanent	2	1	1
11.5	Other personnel compensation	4	3	3
11.9	Total personnel compensation	123	131	138
12.1	Civilian personnel benefits	35	36	38
21.0	Travel and transportation of things	10	9	10
22.0	Transportation of things	3	3	3
23.1	Rental payments to GSA	9	9	10
23.3	Communications, utilities, and miscellaneous charges	2	2	2
24.0	Printing and reproduction	1	1	1
25.2	Other services	7	8	7
25.3	Purchases of goods and services from Government accounts	9	10	11
25.4	Operation and maintenance of facilities		1	1
25.7	Operation and maintenance of equipment	3	4	4
26.0	Supplies and materials	3	3	3
31.0	Equipment	5	5	6
41.0	Grants, subsidies, and contributions	6	6	8
99.0	Subtotal, direct obligations	216	228	242
99.0	Reimbursable obligations		1	2
99.9	Total new obligations	216	229	244

Personnel Summary

Identification code 16–1200–0–1–554		1999 actual	2000 est.	2001 est.
1001	Total compensable workyears: Full-time equivalent employment	2,202	2,317	2,357

BUREAU OF LABOR STATISTICS

Federal Funds

General and special funds:

SALARIES AND EXPENSES

For necessary expenses for the Bureau of Labor Statistics, including advances or reimbursements to State, Federal, and local agencies and their employees for services rendered, **[**$357,781,000, of which $6,986,000 shall be for expenses of revising the Consumer Price Index and shall remain available until September 30, 2001**]** *$386,375,000,* together with not to exceed **[**$55,663,000**]** *$67,257,000,* which may be expended from the Employment Security Administration account in the Unemployment Trust Fund. *(Department of Labor Appropriations Act, 2000, as enacted by section 1000(a)(4) of the Consolidated Appropriations Act, 2000 (P.L. 106–113).)*

Program and Financing (in millions of dollars)

Identification code 16–0200–0–1–505		1999 actual	2000 est.	2001 est.
	Obligations by program activity:			
	Direct program:			
00.01	Labor force statistics	170	171	205
00.02	Prices and cost of living	119	128	136
00.03	Compensation and working conditions	61	69	71
00.04	Productivity and technology	7	8	9
00.05	Employment projections	5	5	7
00.06	Executive direction and staff services	24	25	26
00.07	Consumer price index revision	11	12	
09.01	Reimbursable program	19	17	13
10.00	Total new obligations	416	435	467
	Budgetary resources available for obligation:			
21.40	Unobligated balance available, start of year	4	5	
22.00	New budget authority (gross)	417	430	467
22.10	Resources available from recoveries of prior year obligations	1		
23.90	Total budgetary resources available for obligation	422	435	467
23.95	Total new obligations	−416	−435	−467
23.98	Unobligated balance expiring or withdrawn	−1		
24.40	Unobligated balance available, end of year	5		
	New budget authority (gross), detail:			
	Discretionary:			
40.00	Appropriation	345	357	386
40.75	Reduction pursuant to P.L. 106–51	−1		
43.00	Appropriation (total discretionary)	344	357	386
68.00	Spending authority from offsetting collections: Offsetting collections (cash)	73	73	81
70.00	Total new budget authority (gross)	417	430	467
	Change in unpaid obligations:			
72.40	Unpaid obligations, start of year: Obligated balance, start of year	59	70	94
73.10	Total new obligations	416	435	467
73.20	Total outlays (gross)	−399	−411	−453
73.40	Adjustments in expired accounts (net)	−5		
73.45	Adjustments in unexpired accounts	−1		
74.40	Unpaid obligations, end of year: Obligated balance, end of year	70	94	108
	Outlays (gross), detail:			
86.90	Outlays from new discretionary authority	350	357	394
86.93	Outlays from discretionary balances	49	54	59
87.00	Total outlays (gross)	399	411	453
	Offsets:			
	Against gross budget authority and outlays:			
	Offsetting collections (cash) from:			
88.00	Federal sources	−66	−66	−77
88.40	Non-Federal sources	−7	−7	−4
88.90	Total, offsetting collections (cash)	−73	−73	−81
	Net budget authority and outlays:			
89.00	Budget authority	344	357	386
90.00	Outlays	326	338	372

Note: Includes $20.7 million in budget authority in FY 2001 for activities transferred from the Employment and Training Administration of which $10 million are General Funds and $10.7 million are Trust Funds. Comparable amounts for 1999 ($20.7) and 2000 ($20.7) are excluded above.

Summary of Budget Authority and Outlays

(in millions of dollars)

	1999 actual	2000 est.	2001 est.
Enacted/requested:			
Budget Authority	344	357	386
Outlays	326	338	372
Legislative proposal, not subject to PAYGO:			
Budget Authority			
Outlays			
Legislative proposal, subject to PAYGO:			
Budget Authority			
Outlays			
Total:			
Budget Authority	344	357	386
Outlays	326	338	372

Labor force statistics.—Publishes monthly estimates of the labor force, employment, unemployment, and earnings for the nation, states, and local areas. Makes studies of the labor force. Publishes data on covered employment and wages, by industry. Resources are requested in 2001 to develop a time-use survey that will provide nationally representative estimates of how Americans spend their time at work and at home. Resources also are requested for improved state and local labor market information, to help implement the Workforce Investment Act of 1998.

	1999 actual	2000 est.	2001 est.
Labor force statistics (selected items):			
Covered employment and wages (quarterly series)	1,000,201	1,000,201	1,000,201
Employment and unemployment estimates for States and local areas (monthly and annual series)	87,300	87,300	87,300
Occupational employment statistics (annual series)	57,040	57.040	57,040

Prices and cost of living.—Publishes the Consumer Price Index (CPI), the Producer Price Index (PPI), Export and Import Price Indexes, estimates of consumers' expenditures, and studies of price change. Includes the continuation of an initiative to improve the timeliness and accuracy of the CPI. Also includes resources for an initiative to improve the PPI, which may in turn lead to further improvement of the CPI.

	1999 actual	2000 est.	2001 est.
Consumer price indexes published (monthly)	5,400	5,400	5,400
Percentage of CPI statistics released on schedule	100%	100%	100%
Producer prices:			
(a) Commodity indexes published (monthly)	3,267	3,245	3,223
(b) Mining and manufacturing indexes published (monthly)	6,746	6,314	5,909
International prices and price indexes:			
(a) Sample units initiated (annually)	3,200	3,200	3,200
(b) Price quotations collected (monthly)	23,000	23,000	23,000

Compensation and working conditions.—Publishes data on wages and benefits by occupation for major labor markets and industries. Compiles annual information to estimate the incidence and number of work-related injuries, illnesses, and fatalities.

	1999 actual	2000 est.	2001 est.
Compensation and working conditions (major items):			
Employment cost index—number of schedules	10,000	12,000	14,050
Occupational Safety and Health—number of schedules	200,000	200,000	200,000
Federal pay reform—number of schedules	30,600	30,600	30,600

Productivity and technology.—Provides studies of productivity changes for industries and major economic sectors. Develops international comparisons of productivity and cost. Studies the effects of technology change on employment and productivity. Includes resources to improve output and productivity measures.

	1999 actual	2000 est.	2001 est.
Studies, articles, and special reports	34	30	30
Series maintained	4,196	5,110	5,534

Employment projections.—Provides economic projections, including changes in the level and structure of economic growth, and industry employment and occupational projections. Publishes the *Occupational Outlook Handbook and Quarterly.* Resources are requested in 2001 to provide technical guidance for a new Federal-State cooperative employment projections program.

	1999 actual	2000 est.	2001 est.
Industry projections (2 year cycle)	92	92	92
Occupational Outlook Handbook statements (2 year cycle)	125	125	125

Executive direction and staff services.—Provides planning and policy for the Bureau of Labor Statistics (BLS), operates the management information system, coordinates research, and publishes data and reports for government and public use.

Consumer price index revision.—The BLS will complete the revision using remaining funds from 2000. The complete publication of the revised index was for January 1999. The revision includes new market baskets of goods and services as well as improvements in collecting and processing data for the CPI and for surveys which support the CPI and to prepare for future revision.

	1999 actual	2000 est.	2001 est.
Update the CPI to reflect current spending and population patterns	on schedule	on schedule	on schedule

Object Classification (in millions of dollars)

Identification code 16–0200–0–1–505		1999 actual	2000 est.	2001 est.
	Direct obligations:			
	Personnel compensation:			
11.1	Full-time permanent	113	128	134
11.3	Other than full-time permanent	7	8	7
11.5	Other personnel compensation	2	2	2
11.9	Total personnel compensation	122	138	143
12.1	Civilian personnel benefits	26	29	30
21.0	Travel and transportation of persons	6	7	7
23.1	Rental payments to GSA	28	29	31
23.3	Communications, utilities, and miscellaneous charges	3	4	4
24.0	Printing and reproduction	1	2	2
25.2	Other services	52	53	61
25.3	Purchases of goods and services from Government accounts	79	82	90
25.7	Operation and maintenance of equipment	2	2	2
26.0	Supplies and materials	2	1	1
31.0	Equipment	18	11	11
41.0	Grants, subsidies, and contributions	58	60	72
99.0	Subtotal, direct obligations	397	418	454
99.0	Reimbursable obligations	19	17	13
99.9	Total new obligations	416	435	467

Personnel Summary

Identification code 16–0200–0–1–505		1999 actual	2000 est.	2001 est.
	Direct:			
1001	Total compensable workyears: Full-time equivalent employment	2,325	2,419	2,436
	Reimbursable:			
2001	Total compensable workyears: Full-time equivalent employment	81	81	61

Bureau of Labor Statistics

(Legislative proposal, not subject to PAYGO)

Program and Financing (in millions of dollars)

Identification code 16–0200–2–1–505		1999 actual	2000 est.	2001 est.
	Obligations by program activity:			
10.00	Total new obligations (object class 92.0)			−11
	Budgetary resources available for obligation:			
22.00	New budget authority (gross)			−11
23.95	Total new obligations			11
	New budget authority (gross), detail:			
	Discretionary:			
68.00	Spending authority from offsetting collections (gross): Offsetting collections (cash)			−11
	Change in unpaid obligations:			
73.10	Total new obligations			−11
73.20	Total outlays (gross)			11
	Outlays (gross), detail:			
86.90	Outlays from new discretionary authority			−11
	Offsets:			
	Against gross budget authority and outlays:			
88.00	Offsetting collections (cash) from: trust fund sources			11
	Net budget authority and outlays:			
89.00	Budget authority			
90.00	Outlays			

Legislation will be proposed that would authorize the Secretary of Labor to collect fees from employers for the certification of certain aliens as eligible workers under the Immigration and Nationality Act. This schedule reflects the effects of that legislative proposal on discretionary spending. For

General and special funds—Continued

BUREAU OF LABOR STATISTICS—Continued

more detail see the legislative proposal for the Program Administration account.

BUREAU OF LABOR STATISTICS

(Legislative proposal, subject to PAYGO)

Program and Financing (in millions of dollars)

Identification code 16–0200–4–1–505	1999 actual	2000 est.	2001 est.
Obligations by program activity:			
10.00 Total new obligations (object class 92.0)			11
Budgetary resources available for obligation:			
22.00 New budget authority (gross)			11
23.95 Total new obligations			−11
New budget authority (gross), detail:			
Mandatory:			
69.00 Offsetting collections (cash)			11
Change in unpaid obligations:			
73.10 Total new obligations			11
73.20 Total outlays (gross)			−11
Outlays (gross), detail:			
86.97 Outlays from new mandatory authority			11
Offsets:			
Against gross budget authority and outlays:			
88.40 Offsetting collections (cash) from: Non-Federal sources			−11
Net budget authority and outlays:			
89.00 Budget authority			
90.00 Outlays			

Legislation will be proposed that would authorize the Secretary of Labor to collect fees from employers for the certification of certain aliens as eligible workers under the Immigration and Nationality Act. This schedule reflects the effects of that legislative proposal on mandatory spending. For more detail see the legislative proposal for the Program Administration account.

DEPARTMENTAL MANAGEMENT

Federal Funds

General and special funds:

SALARIES AND EXPENSES

For necessary expenses for Departmental Management, including the hire of three sedans, and including [up to $7,250,000 for the President's Committee on Employment of People with Disabilities, and including] the management or operation of Departmental bilateral and multilateral foreign technical assistance, [$241,478,000] *$54,444,000 for the acquisition of Departmental information technology, architecture, infrastructure, equipment, software and related needs which will be allocated by the Department's Chief Information Officer in accordance with the Department's capital investment management process to assure a sound investment strategy; $437,235,000;* together with not to exceed [$310,000] *$319,000*, which may be expended from the Employment Security Administration account in the Unemployment Trust Fund: *Provided*, That no funds made available by this Act may be used by the Solicitor of Labor to participate in a review in any United States court of appeals of any decision made by the Benefits Review Board under section 21 of the Longshore and Harbor Workers' Compensation Act (33 U.S.C. 921) where such participation is precluded by the decision of the United States Supreme Court in Director, Office of Workers' Compensation Programs v. Newport News Shipbuilding, 115 S. Ct. 1278 (1995), notwithstanding any provisions to the contrary contained in Rule 15 of the Federal Rules of Appellate Procedure: *Provided further*, That no funds made available by this Act may be used by the Secretary of Labor to review a decision under the Longshore and Harbor Workers' Compensation Act (33 U.S.C. 901 et seq.) that has been appealed and that has been pending before the Benefits Review Board for more than 12 months: *Provided further*, That any such decision pending a review by the Benefits Review Board for more than 1 year shall be considered affirmed by the Benefits Review Board on the 1-year anniversary of the filing of the appeal, and shall be considered the final order of the Board for purposes of obtaining a review in the United States courts of appeals: *Provided further*, That these provisions shall not be applicable to the review or appeal of any decision issued under the Black Lung Benefits Act (30 U.S.C. 901 et seq.) *Provided further, That beginning in fiscal year 2001, there is established in the Department of Labor an office of disability employment policy which shall, under the overall direction of the Secretary, provide leadership, develop policy and initiatives, and award grants furthering the objective of eliminating barriers to the training and employment of people with disabilities. Such office shall be headed by an assistant secretary: Provided further that of amounts provided under this head, not more than $20,446,000 is for this purpose. (Department of Labor Appropriations Act, 2000, as enacted by section 1000(a)(4) of the Consolidated Appropriations Act, 2000 (P.L. 106–113).)*

Program and Financing (in millions of dollars)

Identification code 16–0165–0–1–505	1999 actual	2000 est.	2001 est.
Obligations by program activity:			
Direct program:			
00.01 Program direction and support	20	26	46
00.02 Legal services	72	76	81
00.03 International labor affairs	40	70	167
00.04 Administration and management	25	28	25
00.05 Adjudication	37	38	40
00.06 Disability policy	8	8	23
00.07 Women's bureau	8	9	10
00.08 Civil rights	5	6	6
00.09 Chief Financial Officer	6	6	6
00.10 Information technology activities			54
00.14 Other			1
09.01 Reimbursable program	12	11	11
10.00 Total new obligations	233	278	470
Budgetary resources available for obligation:			
21.40 Unobligated balance available, start of year	1	2	
22.00 New budget authority (gross)	236	276	470
22.22 Unobligated balance transferred from other accounts			
23.90 Total budgetary resources available for obligation	237	278	470
23.95 Total new obligations	−233	−278	−470
23.98 Unobligated balance expiring or withdrawn	−1		
24.40 Unobligated balance available, end of year	2		
New budget authority (gross), detail:			
Discretionary:			
40.00 Appropriation	191	241	437
42.00 Transferred from other accounts	7	3	
43.00 Appropriation (total discretionary)	198	244	437
68.00 Spending authority from offsetting collections: Offsetting collections (cash)	38	32	33
70.00 Total new budget authority (gross)	236	276	470
Change in unpaid obligations:			
72.40 Unpaid obligations, start of year: Obligated balance, start of year	20	43	70
73.10 Total new obligations	233	278	470
73.20 Total outlays (gross)	−210	−251	−414
74.40 Unpaid obligations, end of year: Obligated balance, end of year	43	70	126
Outlays (gross), detail:			
86.90 Outlays from new discretionary authority	191	233	373
86.93 Outlays from discretionary balances	19	18	41
87.00 Total outlays (gross)	210	251	414
Offsets:			
Against gross budget authority and outlays:			
Offsetting collections (cash) from:			
88.00 Federal sources	−31	−25	−26

88.40	Non-Federal sources	−7	−7	−7
88.90	Total, offsetting collections (cash)	−38	−32	−33
	Net budget authority and outlays:			
89.00	Budget authority	198	244	437
90.00	Outlays	172	219	381

Program direction and support.—Provides leadership and direction for all programs and functions assigned to the Department. Provides guidance for the development and implementation of governmental policy to protect and promote the interests of the American worker, toward achieving better employment and earnings, promoting productivity and economic growth, safety, equity and affirmative action in employment, and collecting and analyzing statistics on the labor force.

Legal services.—Provides the Secretary of Labor and Departmental program officials with the legal services required to accomplish the Department's mission. The major services include litigating cases, providing assistance to the Department of Justice in case preparation and trials, reviewing rules, orders and written interpretations and opinions for DOL program agencies and the public, and coordinating the Department's legislative program.

International labor affairs.—Coordinates the Department of Labor's international responsibilities, including U.S. government participation in international fora dealing with labor issues; publishes reports on international labor issues; assists in the formulation and implementation of international treaties dealing with labor issues; operates technical assistance programs; and works toward the elimination of exploitative child labor around the world.

Administration and management.—Exercises leadership in all Departmental administrative and management programs and services and ensures efficient and effective operation of Departmental programs; provides policy guidance on matters of personnel management, information resource management and procurement; and provides for consistent and constructive internal labor-management relations throughout the Department.

Adjudication.—Conducts formal hearings and renders timely decisions on claims filed under the Black Lung Benefits Act, the Longshore and Harbor Workers' Compensation Act and its extensions, the Federal Employees' Compensation Act and other acts involving complaints to determine violations of minimum wage requirements, overtime payments, health and safety regulations and unfair labor practices.

Disability policy.—This activity includes funding to establish the Office on Disability Policy, Evaluation, and Technical Assistance, within the Department of Labor to be headed by a Presidential appointee. This office will subsume the responsibilities of the President's Committee on Employment of People with Disabilities in terms of providing leadership to eliminate employment barriers to people with disabilities. In addition, the office will work within DOL to ensure that all DOL programs address the needs of the disabled and increase participation of people with disabilities in DOL training programs—particularly those serving youth. Finally, the office would provide grants to One-Stop Centers to finance assistive technology devices that ensure accessibility of the One-Stops to the disabled.

This activity also includes the President's Task Force on the Employment of Adults with Disabilities. The Task Force is developing a national policy to bring adults with disabilities into gainful employment at a rate that is as close as possible to that of the general population. The Task Force is studying the barriers to employment faced by disabled individuals and is reporting its findings and policy recommendations to the President on a periodic basis over its four-year life. The Task Force will work with the new Office of Disability Policy, Evaluation, and Technical Assistance to continue its role of coordinating interagency employment policy for the disabled.

Women's bureau.—Promotes the interests of wage earning women, and seeks to improve their working conditions and advance their opportunities for profitable employment.

Civil rights.—Ensures full compliance with title VI of the Civil Rights Act of 1964 and other regulatory nondiscrimination provisions in programs receiving financial assistance from the Department of Labor and promotes equal opportunity in these programs and activities; and ensures equal employment opportunity to all DOL employees and applicants for employment.

Chief financial officer.—Responsible for enhancing the level of knowledge and skills of Departmental staff working in financial management operations; developing comprehensive accounting and financial management policies; assuring that all DOL financial functions conform to applicable standards; providing leadership and coordination to DOL agencies' trust and benefit fund financial actions; monitoring the financial execution of the budget in relation to actual expenditures; and managing a comprehensive training program for budget, accounting, and financial support staff.

Information technology activities.—This is a new activity which establishes a permanent, centralized IT investment fund for the Department of Labor (DOL) managed by the Chief Information Officer (CIO). As required by the Clinger Cohen Act, in 1996, the Department established a Chief Information Officer accountable for IT management in the DOL, and implemented an IT Capital Investment Management process for selecting, controlling, and evaluating IT investments. The Department also began developing an information technology architecture to establish a baseline of existing information technologies and provide a target environment as a framework for future information technology investments.

Object Classification (in millions of dollars)

Identification code 16–0165–0–1–505		1999 actual	2000 est.	2001 est.
	Direct obligations:			
	Personnel compensation:			
11.1	Full-time permanent	97	112	121
11.3	Other than full-time permanent	2	1	1
11.5	Other personnel compensation	2	1	2
11.9	Total personnel compensation	101	114	124
12.1	Civilian personnel benefits	21	23	25
21.0	Travel and transportation of persons	3	3	5
23.1	Rental payments to GSA	15	16	17
23.3	Communications, utilities, and miscellaneous charges	2	2	2
24.0	Printing and reproduction			1
25.1	Advisory and assistance services	4	5	5
25.2	Other services	7	12	46
25.3	Purchases of goods and services from Government accounts	17	16	18
25.5	Research and development contracts		1	3
25.7	Operation and maintenance of equipment	14	10	35
26.0	Supplies and materials	2	2	2
31.0	Equipment	2	5	35
41.0	Grants, subsidies, and contributions	33	58	141
99.0	Subtotal, direct obligations	221	267	459
99.0	Reimbursable obligations	12	11	11
99.9	Total new obligations	233	278	470

Personnel Summary

Identification code 16–0165–0–1–505		1999 actual	2000 est.	2001 est.
	Direct:			
1001	Total compensable workyears: Full-time equivalent employment	1,522	1,596	1,680
	Reimbursable:			
2001	Total compensable workyears: Full-time equivalent employment	27	45	35

General and special funds—Continued

OFFICE OF INSPECTOR GENERAL

For salaries and expenses of the Office of Inspector General in carrying out the provisions of the Inspector General Act of 1978, as amended, [$48,095,000] *$51,377,000*, together with not to exceed [$3,830,000] *$4,770,000*, which may be expended from the Employment Security Administration account in the Unemployment Trust Fund. *(Department of Labor Appropriations Act, 2000, as enacted by section 1000(a)(4) of the Consolidated Appropriations Act, 2000 (P.L. 106–113).)*

Program and Financing (in millions of dollars)

Identification code 16–0106–0–1–505		1999 actual	2000 est.	2001 est.
	Obligations by program activity:			
	Direct program:			
00.01	Program activities	42	46	49
00.02	Executive direction and management	6	6	7
09.01	Reimbursable program	5	12	12
10.00	Total new obligations	53	64	68
	Budgetary resources available for obligation:			
22.00	New budget authority (gross)	53	64	68
23.95	Total new obligations	–53	–64	–68
	New budget authority (gross), detail:			
	Discretionary:			
40.00	Appropriation	44	48	51
42.00	Transferred from other accounts	1		
43.00	Appropriation (total discretionary)	45	48	51
68.00	Spending authority from offsetting collections: Offsetting collections (cash)	8	16	17
70.00	Total new budget authority (gross)	53	64	68
	Change in unpaid obligations:			
72.40	Unpaid obligations, start of year: Obligated balance, start of year	4	6	7
73.10	Total new obligations	53	64	68
73.20	Total outlays (gross)	–51	–63	–69
74.40	Unpaid obligations, end of year: Obligated balance, end of year	6	7	6
	Outlays (gross), detail:			
86.90	Outlays from new discretionary authority	46	57	62
86.93	Outlays from discretionary balances	4	6	7
87.00	Total outlays (gross)	51	63	69
	Offsets:			
	Against gross budget authority and outlays:			
88.00	Offsetting collections (cash) from: Federal sources	–8	–16	–17
	Net budget authority and outlays:			
89.00	Budget authority	45	48	51
90.00	Outlays	42	47	52

Program activities.—Program activities within the Office of Inspector General (OIG) include audit, program fraud, labor racketeering and special evaluations and inspections of program activities. The Office of Audit performs audits of the Department's financial statements, programs, activities, and systems to determine whether information is reliable, controls are in place, resources are safeguarded, funds are expended in a manner consistent with laws and regulations and managed economically and efficiently, and desired program results are achieved. The Office of Investigations administers an investigative program to detect and deter fraud, waste and abuse in Departmental programs; and to identify and reduce labor racketeering and corruption in employee benefit plans, labor management relations, and internal union affairs. The Office of Analysis, Complaints, and Evaluations conducts DOL program evaluations and special reviews; analyzes complaints involving DOL programs, operations, or functions; and provides strategic planning and Congressional liaison services. The OIG also provides technical assistance to DOL program agencies.

	1999 actual	2000 est.	2001 est.
Audit reports issued	113	60	65
Benefit plan/UI investigations opened	153	162	171
Other investigative cases opened	391	411	431
Benefit plan/UI investigations completed	291	228	240
Other investigative cases completed	417	437	459

Executive direction and management.—This activity includes the management, legal counsel, administrative support, personnel and financial functions for the OIG.

Object Classification (in millions of dollars)

Identification code 16–0106–0–1–505		1999 actual	2000 est.	2001 est.
	Direct obligations:			
	Personnel compensation:			
11.1	Full-time permanent	27	28	29
11.5	Other personnel compensation	2	3	3
11.9	Total personnel compensation	29	31	32
12.1	Civilian personnel benefits	6	7	7
21.0	Travel and transportation of persons	3	3	3
23.1	Rental payments to GSA	3	3	3
23.3	Communications, utilities, and miscellaneous charges	1	1	1
25.2	Other services	4	4	6
25.3	Purchases of goods and services from Government accounts	2	3	3
31.0	Equipment			1
99.0	Subtotal, direct obligations	48	52	56
99.0	Reimbursable obligations	5	12	12
99.9	Total new obligations	53	64	68

Personnel Summary

Identification code 16–0106–0–1–505		1999 actual	2000 est.	2001 est.
1001	Total compensable workyears: Full-time equivalent employment	412	428	428

[ASSISTANT SECRETARY FOR] VETERANS EMPLOYMENT AND TRAINING

Not to exceed [$184,341,000] *$187,913,000* may be derived from the Employment Security Administration account in the Unemployment Trust Fund to carry out the provisions of 38 U.S.C. 4100–4110A, 4212, 4214, and 4321–4327, and Public Law 103–353, and which shall be available for obligation by the States through December 31, [2000] *2001. To carry out the Stewart B. McKinney Homeless Assistance Act and section 168 of the Workforce Investment Act of 1998, $22,300,000, of which $7,300,000 shall be available for obligation for the period July 1, 2001, through June 30, 2002. (Department of Labor Appropriations Act, 2000, as enacted by section 1000(a)(4) of the Consolidated Appropriations Act, 2000 (P.L. 106–113).)*

Program and Financing (in millions of dollars)

Identification code 16–0164–0–1–702		1999 actual	2000 est.	2001 est.
	Obligations by program activity:			
	Direct program:			
	State administration:			
00.01	Disabled veterans outreach program	80	80	82
00.02	Local veterans employment representatives	77	77	77
00.03	Administration	24	25	27
00.04	National Veterans' Training Institute	2	2	2
00.05	Homeless veterans program			15
00.06	Veterans workforce investment program			7
10.00	Total new obligations	183	184	210
	Budgetary resources available for obligation:			
22.00	New budget authority (gross)	183	184	210
23.95	Total new obligations	–183	–184	–210
	New budget authority (gross), detail:			
	Discretionary:			
40.00	Appropriation			22

		1999 actual	2000 est.	2001 est.
	Spending authority from offsetting collections:			
68.00	Offsetting collections (Trust Funds)	186	184	188
68.10	From Federal sources: Change in receivables and unpaid, unfilled orders	−3		
68.90	Spending authority from offsetting collections (total discretionary)	183	184	188
70.00	Total new budget authority (gross)	183	184	210
	Change in unpaid obligations:			
	Unpaid obligations, start of year:			
72.40	Obligated balance, start of year	19	17	18
72.95	From Federal sources: Receivables and unpaid, unfilled orders	3		
72.99	Total unpaid obligations, start of year	22	17	18
73.10	Total new obligations	183	184	210
73.20	Total outlays (gross)	−186	−183	−191
73.40	Adjustments in expired accounts (net)	−1		
	Unpaid obligations, end of year:			
74.40	Obligated balance, end of year	17	18	37
74.95	From Federal sources: Receivables and unpaid, unfilled orders			
74.99	Total unpaid obligations, end of year	17	18	37
	Outlays (gross), detail:			
86.90	Outlays from new discretionary authority	167	167	174
86.93	Outlays from discretionary balances	19	16	17
87.00	Total outlays (gross)	186	183	191
	Offsets:			
	Against gross budget authority and outlays:			
88.00	Offsetting collections (cash) from: Trust fund sources	−186	−184	−188
	Against gross budget authority only:			
88.95	From Federal sources: Change in receivables and unpaid, unfilled orders	3		
	Net budget authority and outlays:			
89.00	Budget authority			22
90.00	Outlays		−1	3

Note.—Beginning in FY 2001, Veterans Employment and Training activities are presented in a new account. The new account includes activities that had been financed from the Unemployment Trust Fund as well as activities that had been financed from the Training and Employment Services account. The schedule above shows the activities financed out of the Unemployment Trust Fund for FY 1999, FY 2000, and FY 2001. The schedule also includes $22.3 million in FY 2001 budget authority for the activities previously financed from Training and Employment Services; the comparable estimates are $10.3 million in FY 1999 and $16.9 million in FY 2000.

State administration.—The Disabled Veterans Outreach Program provides intensive employment and job development services to secure permanent employment for veterans, particularly those with service-connected disabilities and other disadvantages. Local Veterans Employment Representatives provide job development, placement, and supportive services directly to veterans and conduct functional supervision of the services provided veterans by other local office staff to ensure compliance with the performance standards for services to veterans.

Administration.—Identifies policies and programs to serve and meet employment and training needs of veterans. Assures the adequacy of counseling, testing, job training, and job placement services for veterans through monitoring, evaluating, and providing technical assistance and training to those delivering these services. Coordinates with the Department of Defense to ensure the provision of labor market information and other services to military service-members separating from active duty to expedite their transition from military to civilian employment under the Transition Assistance Program. Provides employment, training and supportive services directly or through linkages with other service providers to assist homeless veterans. Provides on-the-job training programs and other specialized services for certain veterans identified as facing serious barriers to employment. Administers veterans employment and training programs under the Workforce Investment Act to provide these services. Promotes compliance of Federal contractors in listing jobs for veterans. Provides information and investigates complaints, to help veterans, reservists, and members of the National Guard obtain employment, and reemployment rights as provided for by law.

National Veterans Training Institute.—This program operates through a contract with the University of Colorado in Denver, Colorado, providing training to Federal and State employees who assist veterans in finding jobs.

Homeless veterans program.—Provides a program of demonstration projects, coordinated with the Veteran's Administration and the Department of Housing and Urban Development to help homeless veterans into jobs. Homeless veterans projects provide for outreach, supportive services, and leveraged funds for housing, transportation and health, and are funded in both urban and rural areas.

Veterans workforce investment program.—Provides for training, retraining and employment opportunities for most at risk veterans, including those with service connected disabilities, those with significant barriers to employment, Vietnam era veterans, and recently separated veterans.

Object Classification (in millions of dollars)

Identification code 16–0164–0–1–702		1999 actual	2000 est.	2001 est.
11.1	Personnel compensation: Full-time permanent	14	15	15
12.1	Civilian personnel benefits	3	3	4
21.0	Travel and transportation of persons	1	1	1
23.1	Rental payments to GSA	1	1	1
23.3	Communications, utilities, and miscellaneous charges	3	2	2
25.2	Other services	3	4	6
25.3	Purchases of goods and services from Government accounts	2	2	2
41.0	Grants, subsidies, and contributions	155	155	178
99.0	Subtotal, direct obligations	182	183	209
99.5	Below reporting threshold	1	1	1
99.9	Total new obligations	183	184	210

Personnel Summary

Identification code 16–0164–0–1–702		1999 actual	2000 est.	2001 est.
1001	Total compensable workyears: Full-time equivalent employment	254	255	255

Intragovernmental funds:

Working Capital Fund

29 U.S.C. 563 is amended by striking the last proviso and inserting, ": Provided further, That the Secretary may transfer annually an additional amount not to exceed $2,500,000 from the unobligated balances of the Department's salaries and expenses accounts to the Working Capital Fund, to be merged with such Funds and to remain available until expended, for litigation support and related expenses for extraordinary case enforcement activities: Provided further, That the unobligated balance of the Fund shall not exceed $22,500,000.".

Program and Financing (in millions of dollars)

Identification code 16–4601–0–4–505		1999 actual	2000 est.	2001 est.
	Obligations by program activity:			
09.01	Financial and administrative services	54	60	60
09.02	Field services	23	24	25
09.04	Human resources services	8	8	9
09.05	Penalty mail and telecommunications	28	30	30
09.06	Investment in reinvention fund	1	2	1
09.07	Non-DOL reimbursements	7	9	10
10.00	Total new obligations	121	133	135
	Budgetary resources available for obligation:			
21.40	Unobligated balance available, start of year	13	13	7
22.00	New budget authority (gross)	119	127	130
22.10	Resources available from recoveries of prior year obligations	2		
23.90	Total budgetary resources available for obligation	134	140	137
23.95	Total new obligations	−121	−133	−135

Intragovernmental funds—Continued

WORKING CAPITAL FUND—Continued

Program and Financing (in millions of dollars)—Continued

Identification code 16–4601–0–4–505	1999 actual	2000 est.	2001 est.
24.40 Unobligated balance available, end of year	13	7	2
New budget authority (gross), detail:			
Discretionary:			
68.00 Spending authority from offsetting collections (gross): Offsetting collections (cash)	119	127	130
Change in unpaid obligations:			
72.40 Unpaid obligations, start of year: Obligated balance, start of year	14	13	18
73.10 Total new obligations	121	133	135
73.20 Total outlays (gross)	−123	−131	−136
73.40 Adjustments in expired accounts (net)	3	3	3
73.45 Adjustments in unexpired accounts	−2		
74.40 Unpaid obligations, end of year: Obligated balance, end of year	13	18	20
Outlays (gross), detail:			
86.90 Outlays from new discretionary authority	111	116	120
86.93 Outlays from discretionary balances	12	14	17
87.00 Total outlays (gross)	123	131	136
Offsets:			
Against gross budget authority and outlays:			
88.00 Offsetting collections (cash) from: Federal sources	−119	−127	−130
Net budget authority and outlays:			
89.00 Budget authority			
90.00 Outlays	4	4	6

Financial and administrative services.—Provides support for financial systems on a Department-wide basis, financial services primarily for DOL national office staff, cost determination activities, maintenance of Departmental host computer systems, procurement and contract services, safety and health services, maintenance and operation of the Frances Perkins Building and general administrative support in the following areas: space and telecommunications, property and supplies, printing and reproduction and energy management.

Field services.—Provides full range of administrative and technical services to all agencies of the Department located in its regional and field offices. These services are primarily in the personnel, financial, information technology and general administrative areas.

Human resources services.—Provides guidance to DOL agencies in Senior Executive Service resource management and in the management of Schedule "C" and expert and consultant services, development and administration of Departmental programs for personnel security and financial disclosure, direct staffing and position management services, and benefits counseling and services to DOL employees.

Penalty mail and telecommunications.—Provides for departmental mail payments to the U.S. Postal Service and telecommunications payments to the General Services Administration.

Non-DOL reimbursements.—Provides for services rendered to any entity or person for use of Departmental facilities and services, including associated utilities and security services, including support for regional consolidated administrative support unit activities. The income received from non-DOL agencies and organizations funds in full the costs of all services provided. This income is credited to and merged with other income received by the Working Capital Fund.

Investment in reinvention fund.—Finances agency reinvention proposals and other investment or capital acquisition projects in order to achieve savings and streamline work processes. The fund is self-sustaining, with agencies paying back the initial investment with savings generated through implementation of efficiencies and reinvention initiatives.

Financing.—The Working Capital Fund is funded by the agencies and organizations for which centralized services are performed at rates that return in full all expenses of operation, including reserves for accrued annual leave and depreciation of equipment.

Object Classification (in millions of dollars)

Identification code 16–4601–0–4–505	1999 actual	2000 est.	2001 est.
Personnel compensation:			
11.1 Full-time permanent	35	37	40
11.3 Other than full-time permanent	1		
11.5 Other personnel compensation	1	1	1
11.9 Total personnel compensation	37	38	41
12.1 Civilian personnel benefits	9	9	10
21.0 Travel and transportation of persons	1	1	1
23.1 Rental payments to GSA	7	7	8
23.3 Communications, utilities, and miscellaneous charges	36	38	38
25.1 Advisory and assistance services	4	4	4
25.2 Other services	7	10	11
25.3 Purchases of goods and services from Government accounts	3	3	3
25.4 Operation and maintenance of facilities	4	5	5
25.7 Operation and maintenance of equipment	7	7	7
26.0 Supplies and materials	2	2	1
31.0 Equipment	4	9	6
99.9 Total new obligations	121	133	135

Personnel Summary

Identification code 16–4601–0–4–505	1999 actual	2000 est.	2001 est.
2001 Total compensable workyears: Full-time equivalent employment	730	700	719

ALLOCATIONS RECEIVED FROM OTHER ACCOUNTS

Note.—Obligations incurred under allocations from other accounts are included in the schedules of the parent appropriations as follows: Agency for International Development, Functional Development Assistance Program. Department of Education: Office of Vocational and Adult Education: "Vocational and Adult Education".

GENERAL PROVISIONS

SEC. 101. None of the funds appropriated in this title for the Job Corps shall be used to pay the compensation of an individual, either as direct costs or any proration as an indirect cost, at a rate in excess of Executive Level II.

(TRANSFER OF FUNDS)

SEC. 102. Not to exceed 1 percent of any discretionary funds (pursuant to the Balanced Budget and Emergency Deficit Control Act of 1985, as amended) which are appropriated for the current fiscal year for the Department of Labor in this Act may be transferred between appropriations, but no such appropriation shall be increased by more than 3 percent by any such transfer: *Provided*, That the Appropriations Committees of both Houses of Congress are notified at least 15 days in advance of any transfer.

[SEC. 103. The Secretary of Labor shall transfer, without charge or consideration, to the City of Salinas in the State of California, all right, title, and interest (including any equitable interest) the United States holds in the real property located at 342 Front Street, Salinas, California (Reference No. SSL–493), to the extent such right, such title, or such interest was acquired as a result of any loan, grant, guarantee, or other benefit provided by the Secretary to or for the benefit of such city.] *(Department of Labor Appropriations Act, 2000, as enacted by section 1000(a)(4) of the Consolidated Appropriations Act, 2000 (P.L. 106–113).)*

TITLE V—GENERAL PROVISIONS

SEC. 501. The Secretaries of Labor, Health and Human Services, and Education are authorized to transfer unexpended balances of prior appropriations to accounts corresponding to current appropriations provided in this Act: *Provided*, That such transferred balances are used for the same purpose, and for the same periods of time, for which they were originally appropriated.

SEC. 502. No part of any appropriation contained in this Act shall remain available for obligation beyond the current fiscal year unless expressly so provided herein.

SEC. 503. (a) No part of any appropriation contained in this Act shall be used, other than for normal and recognized executive-legislative relationships, for publicity or propaganda purposes, for the preparation, distribution, or use of any kit, pamphlet, booklet, publication, radio, television, or video presentation designed to support or defeat legislation pending before the Congress or any State legislature, except in presentation to the Congress or any State legislature itself.

(b) No part of any appropriation contained in this Act shall be used to pay the salary or expenses of any grant or contract recipient, or agent acting for such recipient, related to any activity designed to influence legislation or appropriations pending before the Congress or any State legislature.

SEC. 504. The Secretaries of Labor and Education are authorized to make available not to exceed $20,000 and $15,000, respectively, from funds available for salaries and expenses under titles I and III, respectively, for official reception and representation expenses; the Director of the Federal Mediation and Conciliation Service is authorized to make available for official reception and representation expenses not to exceed $2,500 from the funds available for "Salaries and expenses, Federal Mediation and Conciliation Service"; and the Chairman of the National Mediation Board is authorized to make available for official reception and representation expenses not to exceed $2,500 from funds available for "Salaries and expenses, National Mediation Board".

SEC. 505. Notwithstanding any other provision of this Act, no funds appropriated under this Act shall be used to carry out any program of distributing sterile needles or syringes for the hypodermic injection of any illegal drug *unless the Secretary of Health and Human Services determines that such programs are effective in preventing the spread of HIV and do not encourage the use of illegal drugs*.

SEC. 506. (a) PURCHASE OF AMERICAN-MADE EQUIPMENT AND PRODUCTS.—It is the sense of the Congress that, to the greatest extent practicable, all equipment and products purchased with funds made available in this Act should be American-made.

(b) NOTICE REQUIREMENT.—In providing financial assistance to, or entering into any contract with, any entity using funds made available in this Act, the head of each Federal agency, to the greatest extent practicable, shall provide to such entity a notice describing the statement made in subsection (a) by the Congress.

(c) PROHIBITION OF CONTRACTS WITH PERSONS FALSELY LABELING PRODUCTS AS MADE IN AMERICA.—If it has been finally determined by a court or Federal agency that any person intentionally affixed a label bearing a "Made in America" inscription, or any inscription with the same meaning, to any product sold in or shipped to the United States that is not made in the United States, the person shall be ineligible to receive any contract or subcontract made with funds made available in this Act, pursuant to the debarment, suspension, and ineligibility procedures described in sections 9.400 through 9.409 of title 48, Code of Federal Regulations.

SEC. 507. When issuing statements, press releases, requests for proposals, bid solicitations and other documents describing projects or programs funded in whole or in part with Federal money, all grantees receiving Federal funds included in this Act, including but not limited to State and local governments and recipients of Federal research grants, shall clearly state: (1) the percentage of the total costs of the program or project which will be financed with Federal money; (2) the dollar amount of Federal funds for the project or program; and (3) percentage and dollar amount of the total costs of the project or program that will be financed by non-governmental sources.

[SEC. 508. (a) None of the funds appropriated under this Act, and none of the funds in any trust fund to which funds are appropriated under this Act, shall be expended for any abortion.

(b) None of the funds appropriated under this Act, and none of the funds in any trust fund to which funds are appropriated under this Act, shall be expended for health benefits coverage that includes coverage of abortion.

(c) The term "health benefits coverage" means the package of services covered by a managed care provider or organization pursuant to a contract or other arrangement.] [1]

[SEC. 509. (a) The limitations established in the preceding section shall not apply to an abortion—

(1) if the pregnancy is the result of an act of rape or incest; or

(2) in the case where a woman suffers from a physical disorder, physical injury, or physical illness, including a life-endangering physical condition caused by or arising from the pregnancy itself, that would, as certified by a physician, place the woman in danger of death unless an abortion is performed.

(b) Nothing in the preceding section shall be construed as prohibiting the expenditure by a State, locality, entity, or private person of State, local, or private funds (other than a State's or locality's contribution of Medicaid matching funds).

(c) Nothing in the preceding section shall be construed as restricting the ability of any managed care provider from offering abortion coverage or the ability of a State or locality to contract separately with such a provider for such coverage with State funds (other than a State's or locality's contribution of Medicaid matching funds).] [1]

SEC. [510] *508.* (a) None of the funds made available in this Act may be used for—

(1) the creation of a human embryo or embryos for research purposes; or

(2) research in which a human embryo or embryos are destroyed, discarded, or knowingly subjected to risk of injury or death greater than that allowed for research on fetuses in utero under 45 CFR 46.208(a)(2) and section 498(b) of the Public Health Service Act (42 U.S.C. 289g(b)).

(b) For purposes of this section, the term "human embryo or embryos" includes any organism, not protected as a human subject under 45 CFR 46 as of the date of the enactment of this Act, that is derived by fertilization, parthenogenesis, cloning, or any other means from one or more human gametes or human diploid cells.

SEC. [511] *509.* (a) LIMITATION ON USE OF FUNDS FOR PROMOTION OF LEGALIZATION OF CONTROLLED SUBSTANCES.—None of the funds made available in this Act may be used for any activity that promotes the legalization of any drug or other substance included in schedule I of the schedules of controlled substances established by section 202 of the Controlled Substances Act (21 U.S.C. 812).

(b) EXCEPTIONS.—The limitation in subsection (a) shall not apply when there is significant medical evidence of a therapeutic advantage to the use of such drug or other substance or that federally sponsored clinical trials are being conducted to determine therapeutic advantage.

SEC. [512] *510.* None of the funds made available in this Act may be obligated or expended to enter into or renew a contract with an entity if—

(1) such entity is otherwise a contractor with the United States and is subject to the requirement in section 4212(d) of title 38, United States Code, regarding submission of an annual report to the Secretary of Labor concerning employment of certain veterans; and

(2) such entity has not submitted a report as required by that section for the most recent year for which such requirement was applicable to such entity.

[SEC. 513. Except as otherwise specifically provided by law, unobligated balances remaining available at the end of fiscal year 2000 from appropriations made available for salaries and expenses for fiscal year 2000 in this Act, shall remain available through December 31, 2000, for each such account for the purposes authorized: *Provided*, That the House and Senate Committees on Appropriations shall be notified at least 15 days prior to the obligation of such funds.]

[SEC. 514. None of the funds made available in this Act may be used to promulgate or adopt any final standard under section 1173(b) of the Social Security Act (42 U.S.C. 1320d–2(b)) providing for, or providing for the assignment of, a unique health identifier for an individual (except in an individual's capacity as an employer or a health care provider), until legislation is enacted specifically approving the standard.]

[SEC. 515. Section 520(c)(2)(D) of the Departments of Labor, Health and Human Services, and Education, and Related Agencies Appropriations Act, 1997, as amended, is further amended by striking "December 31, 1997" and inserting "March 31, 2000".]

[SEC. 516. The United States-Mexico Border Health Commission Act (22 U.S.C. 290n et seq.) is amended—

(1) by striking section 2 and inserting the following:

"SEC. 2. APPOINTMENT OF MEMBERS OF BORDER HEALTH COMMISSION.

"Not later than 30 days after the date of the enactment of this section, the President shall appoint the United States members of the United States-Mexico Border Health Commission, and shall attempt to conclude an agreement with Mexico providing for the establishment of such Commission."; and

(2) in section 3—

(A) in paragraph (1), by striking the semicolon and inserting "; and";

(B) in paragraph (2)(B), by striking "; and" and inserting a period; and

(C) by striking paragraph (3).]

SEC. [517] *511.* The applicable time limitations with respect to the giving of notice of injury and the filing of a claim for compensation for disability or death by an individual under the Federal Employees' Compensation Act, as amended, for injuries sustained as a result of the person's exposure to a nitrogen or sulfur mustard agent in the performance of official duties as an employee at the Department of the Army's Edgewood Arsenal before March 20, 1944, shall not begin to run until the date of the enactment of this Act.

[SEC. 518. Section 169(d)(2)(B) of Public Law 105–220, the Workforce Investment Act of 1998, is amended by striking "or Alaska Native villages or Native groups (as such terms are defined in section 3 of the Alaska Native Claims Settlement Act (43 U.S.C. 1602))." and inserting "or Alaska Natives.".] *(Department of Labor, Health and Human Services, and Education, and Related Agencies Appropriations Act, 2000, as enacted by section 1000(a)(4) of the Consolidated Appropriations Act, 2000 (P.L. 106–113).)*

[1] *The Administration proposes to delete this provision and will work with the Congress to address this issue.*

DEPARTMENT OF STATE

ADMINISTRATION OF FOREIGN AFFAIRS

Federal Funds

General and special funds:

DIPLOMATIC AND CONSULAR PROGRAMS

For necessary expenses of the Department of State and the Foreign Service not otherwise provided for, including expenses authorized by the State Department Basic Authorities Act of 1956, as amended, the Mutual Educational and Cultural Exchange Act of 1961, as amended, and the United States Information and Educational Exchange Act of 1948, as amended, including employment, without regard to civil service and classification laws, of persons on a temporary basis (not to exceed $700,000 of this appropriation), as authorized by section 801 of such Act; expenses authorized by section 9 of the Act of August 31, 1964, as amended; representation to certain international organizations in which the United States participates pursuant to treaties, ratified pursuant to the advice and consent of the Senate, or specific Acts of Congress; arms control, nonproliferation and [disarmanent] *disarmament* activities as authorized by the Arms Control and Disarmament Act of September 26, 1961, as amended; acquisition by exchange or purchase of passenger motor vehicles as authorized by law; and for expenses of general administration, [$2,569,825,000] *$3,101,325,000, of which $410,000,000 shall be available until expended for security programs: Provided*, That, of the amount made available under this heading, not to exceed $4,000,000 may be transferred to, and merged with, funds in the "Emergencies in the Diplomatic and Consular Service" appropriations account, to be available only for emergency evacuations and terrorism rewards: [*Provided further*, That, of the amount made available under this heading, not to exceed $4,500,000 may be transferred to, and merged with, funds in the "International Broadcasting Operations" appropriations account only to avoid reductions in force at the Voice of America, subject to the reprogramming procedures described in section 605 of this Act:] *Provided further*, That, in fiscal year [2000] *2001*, all receipts collected from individuals for assistance in the preparation and filing of an affidavit of support pursuant to section 213A of the Immigration and Nationality Act shall be deposited into this account as an offsetting collection and shall remain available until expended: [*Provided further*, That of the amount made available under this heading, $236,291,000 shall be available only for public diplomacy international information programs: *Provided further*, That of the amount made available under this heading, $500,000 shall be available only for the National Law Center for Inter-American Free Trade: *Provided further*, That of the amount made available under this heading, $2,500,000 shall be available only for overseas continuing language education:] *Provided further*, That of the amount made available under this heading, not to exceed $1,162,000 shall be available for transfer to the Presidential Advisory Commission on Holocaust Assets in the United States: *Provided further*, That any amount transferred pursuant to the previous proviso shall not result in a total amount transferred to the Commission from all Federal sources that exceeds the authorized amount: *Provided further*, That notwithstanding section 140(a)(5), and the second sentence of section 140(a)(3), of the Foreign Relations Authorization Act, Fiscal Years 1994 and 1995, fees may be collected during fiscal [years 2000 and] *year* 2001 *and each fiscal year thereafter*, under the authority of section 140(a)(1) of that Act: *Provided further*, That all fees collected under the preceding proviso shall be deposited [in fiscal years 2000 and 2001] as an offsetting collection to appropriations made under this heading to recover costs as set forth under section 140(a)(2) of that Act and shall remain available until expended: *Provided further*, That [of the amount made available under this heading, $10,000,000 is appropriated for a Northern Boundary and Transboundary Rivers Restoration Fund: *Provided further*, That of the amount made available under this heading, not less than $9,000,000 shall be available for the Office of Defense Trade Controls] *advances for services authorized by 22 U.S.C. 3620(c) may be credited to this account, to remain available until expended for such services.*

In addition, not to exceed $1,252,000 shall be derived from fees collected from other executive agencies for lease or use of facilities located at the International Center in accordance with section 4 of the International Center Act, as amended; in addition, as authorized by section 5 of such Act, $490,000, to be derived from the reserve authorized by that section, to be used for the purposes set out in that section; in addition, as authorized by section 810 of the United States Information and Educational Exchange Act, not to exceed $6,000,000, to remain available until expended, may be credited to this appropriation from fees or other payments received from English teaching, library, motion pictures, and publication programs, and from fees from educational advising and counseling, and exchange visitor programs; and, in addition, not to exceed $15,000, which shall be derived from reimbursements, surcharges, and fees for use of Blair House facilities in accordance with section 46 of the State Department Basic Authorities Act of 1956 (22 U.S.C. 2718(a)).

[In addition, for the costs of worldwide security upgrades, $254,000,000, to remain available until expended.] *(Department of State and Related Agencies Appropriations Act, 2000, as enacted by section 1000(a)(1) of the Consolidated Appropriations Act, 2000 (P.L. 106–113).)*

Unavailable Collections (in millions of dollars)

Identification code 19–0113–0–1–153	1999 actual	2000 est.	2001 est.
Balance, start of year:			
01.99 Balance, start of year			11
Appropriation:			
05.01 Diplomatic and consular programs			–11
06.20 Reduction pursuant to Public Law 106–113		11	
07.99 Total balance, end of year		11	

Program and Financing (in millions of dollars)

Identification code 19–0113–0–1–153	1999 actual	2000 est.	2001 est.
Obligations by program activity:			
Direct program:			
00.01 Executive direction and policy formulation	146	155	159
00.02 Conduct of diplomatic relations	391	403	416
00.03 Conduct of public diplomacy		250	258
00.05 Conduct of consular relations	245	252	260
00.06 Professional development and training	48	50	51
00.07 Information management	349	356	367
00.08 Security	608	981	890
00.09 Medical	11	12	12
00.10 Administration and staff activities	646	712	740
09.01 Reimbursable program	777	831	883
10.00 Total new obligations	3,221	4,002	4,036
Budgetary resources available for obligation:			
21.40 Unobligated balance available, start of year	110	517	177
22.00 New budget authority (gross)	3,628	3,654	3,984
22.22 Unobligated balance transferred from other accounts		8	
23.90 Total budgetary resources available for obligation	3,738	4,179	4,161
23.95 Total new obligations	–3,221	–4,002	–4,036
23.98 Unobligated balance expiring or withdrawn	–1		
24.40 Unobligated balance available, end of year	517	177	125
New budget authority (gross), detail:			
Discretionary:			
40.00 Appropriation	2,802	2,824	3,101
41.00 Transferred to other accounts	–1	–1	
43.00 Appropriation (total discretionary)	2,801	2,823	3,101
50.00 Reappropriation	50		
Spending authority from offsetting collections:			
68.00 Offsetting collections (cash)	777	842	872
68.26 Offsetting collections (unavailable balances)			11
68.76 Reduction pursuant to P.L. 106–113		–11	

General and special funds—Continued

DIPLOMATIC AND CONSULAR PROGRAMS—Continued

Program and Financing (in millions of dollars)—Continued

Identification code 19–0113–0–1–153	1999 actual	2000 est.	2001 est.
68.90 Spending authority from offsetting collections (total discretionary)	777	831	883
70.00 Total new budget authority (gross)	3,628	3,654	3,984
Change in unpaid obligations:			
72.40 Unpaid obligations, start of year: Obligated balance, start of year	640	947	730
73.10 Total new obligations	3,221	4,002	4,036
73.20 Total outlays (gross)	−2,914	−4,219	−4,008
74.40 Unpaid obligations, end of year: Obligated balance, end of year	947	730	758
Outlays (gross), detail:			
86.90 Outlays from new discretionary authority	2,632	2,971	3,519
86.93 Outlays from discretionary balances	282	1,248	489
87.00 Total outlays (gross)	2,914	4,219	4,008
Offsets:			
Against gross budget authority and outlays:			
Offsetting collections (cash) from:			
88.00 Federal sources	−412	−420	−432
88.40 Non-Federal sources	−365	−411	−451
88.90 Total, offsetting collections (cash)	−777	−831	−883
Net budget authority and outlays:			
89.00 Budget authority	2,851	2,823	3,101
90.00 Outlays	2,137	3,388	3,125

Summary of Budget Authority and Outlays

(in millions of dollars)

	1999 actual	*2000 est.*	*2001 est.*
Enacted/requested:			
Budget Authority	2,851	2,823	3,101
Outlays	2,137	3,388	3,125
Supplemental proposal:			
Budget Authority	....	24	....
Outlays	....	21	2
Total:			
Budget Authority	2,851	2,847	3,101
Outlays	2,137	3,409	3,127

The program described below is financed by this appropriation, by fees for services, and by reimbursements from other agencies. Those agencies are provided with most of their administrative services overseas by the Department of State. The programs and activities reflect the full integration of the Arms Control and Disarmament Agency and U.S. Information Agency (excluding broadcasting activities) into the Department beginning in 2000.

Executive direction and policy formulation.—This activity identifies resources which provide sound management through the direction of the Secretary and with the assistance of staff offices, specialized offices, and functional and regional bureaus, for policy formulation and in pursuit of regional and global foreign policy objectives including the hosting of various international conferences and meetings in the United States and abroad.

Conduct of diplomatic relations.—Resources of this activity are used to provide for: the political and economic reporting and analysis of interests to the United States; the representation of U.S. diplomatic and national interests to countries abroad; and the bilateral and multilateral negotiation of our foreign policy objectives, including the hosting of and participation in various international conferences, meetings and other multilateral activities in the United States and abroad. These resources also fund the conduct of U.S. diplomatic policy through political and multilateral affairs, economic and social affairs, international budgetary and management affairs, and participation in and hosting various international conferences. Resources also fund the management of U.S. participation in arms control, nonproliferation, and disarmament negotiations and other verification and compliance activities, in addition to funds otherwise available for such purposes.

Conduct of consular relations.—Activities included are: overseas and American citizen services; the issuance of passports to U.S. citizens both here and abroad; and, implementing a coordinated strategy to improve consular systems and processes in support of U.S. border security. Visa services involve: the issuance, denial, and adjudication of immigrant and non-immigrant visas; refugee processing; and visa fraud detection and investigation. American citizen services include the issuance of passports and emergency assistance to American citizens abroad. Passport services include the issuance of passports in the United States and U.S. missions abroad and passport fraud detection and investigation.

Conduct of Public Diplomacy.—Beginning in 2000, resources in this appropriation will support the conduct of international informational, educational, cultural and exchange programs of the United States and advising the President and the National Security Council on these matters. Formerly, these activities were carried out by the U.S. Information Agency. The Department will define, explain and advocate U.S. policies abroad and will seek to increase knowledge and understanding among foreign audiences of U.S. society and its values. Department posts also administer exchange-of-persons programs and conduct informational and cultural activities.

Professional development and training.—The professional development and training activity is a continuous process by which the Department ensures that its professionals have the skills, experience, and judgment to fulfill its functions at all levels. Training programs are designed to provide employees with the specific functional, area, and language skills needed for the conduct of foreign relations in the Department and abroad.

Information management.—This activity identifies resources that are used for the effective and efficient creation, collection, processing, transmission, dissemination, use, storage, and disposition of information required for the formulation and execution of foreign policy and for the conduct of daily business. Its requirements are driven by the informational needs of the President, the Secretary of State, the Department and its 250 missions, and approximately fifty Government agencies. Components of the information management activity include: telecommunications; classified information handling; unclassified data and word processing; pouch, mail, and publishing services; administration of an electronic and archival records management program; document classification and declassification; information security; and, provision of information management services, as appropriate, to all branches of the Government and to the public.

In all of these programs, responsibilities range from policy setting to planning and design, implementation, operation, and maintenance. The Department manages large computer and communications centers to provide administrative, consular, economic, and political information. The computer systems support worldwide consular applications, financial management systems, management of building programs, and intelligence research systems.

Security.—This activity identifies resources that are used in meeting security and counter-terrorism responsibilities, both foreign and domestic. Covered in this activity are: security operations; engineering services, which relate to the technical defense of U.S. Government personnel and establishments against electronic and physical attack; protection of dignitaries; and physical security operations.

Medical.—This activity encompasses medical programs for the Department of State, the Foreign Service, and other U.S. Government departments and agencies overseas. Services are provided in Washington as well as at missions worldwide and cover some 31,000 employees and dependents.

Administration and staff activities.—These activities include normal domestic and overseas administrative services directly related to Department programs. They include:

—The direction and control of administration and management operations, representing and negotiating U.S. Government administrative matters with foreign officials, and reviewing and setting resource levels and priorities for various programs and bureaus financed by this appropriation.

—The budgeting, financial planning, and fiscal operations for bureaus and offices financed by this appropriation and most federal agencies resident abroad.

—The management, recruitment, and performance evaluation of Foreign and Civil Service employees (particularly the recruitment of qualified minorities, including Hispanics and African Americans) and Foreign Service National staff.

—The contracting and procurement of services and supplies, maintenance and repair of equipment and physical property (including the operation and routine maintenance of property directly leased or owned by the Department), vehicle operation, and shipping and customs services.

—Centralized funding for travel and transportation of effects associated with the assignment, transfer, home leave, and separation of the Department's personnel and dependents.

Object Classification (in millions of dollars)

Identification code 19–0113–0–1–153		1999 actual	2000 est.	2001 est.
	Direct obligations:			
	Personnel compensation:			
11.1	Full-time permanent	784	950	980
11.3	Other than full-time permanent	61	72	74
11.5	Other personnel compensation	70	71	72
11.8	Special personal services payments	2	2	2
11.9	Total personnel compensation	917	1,095	1,128
12.1	Civilian personnel benefits	256	276	284
13.0	Benefits for former personnel	2	2	2
21.0	Travel and transportation of persons	106	116	117
22.0	Transportation of things	76	80	80
23.1	Rental payments to GSA	90	107	123
23.3	Communications, utilities, and miscellaneous charges	114	122	126
24.0	Printing and reproduction	14	26	27
25.1	Advisory and assistance services	5	5	5
25.2	Other services	250	543	437
	Purchases of goods and services from Government accounts:			
25.3	Purchases of goods and services from Government accounts	7	8	9
25.3	Purchases of goods and services from Government accounts (ICASS)	410	546	562
25.4	Operation and maintenance of facilities	27	29	30
25.6	Medical care	4	5	5
25.7	Operation and maintenance of equipment	9	18	20
26.0	Supplies and materials	44	66	68
31.0	Equipment	90	98	100
41.0	Grants, subsidies, and contributions	15	25	26
42.0	Insurance claims and indemnities	8	4	4
99.0	Subtotal, direct obligations	2,444	3,171	3,153
99.0	Reimbursable obligations	777	831	883
99.9	Total new obligations	3,221	4,002	4,036

Personnel Summary

Identification code 19–0113–0–1–153		1999 actual	2000 est.	2001 est.
	Direct:			
1001	Total compensable workyears: Full-time equivalent employment	10,881	13,808	13,890
	Reimbursable:			
2001	Total compensable workyears: Full-time equivalent employment	3,859	4,897	4,926

International Information Programs

Program and Financing (in millions of dollars)

Identification code 19–0201–0–1–154		1999 actual	2000 est.	2001 est.
	Obligations by program activity:			
	Direct program:			
00.01	East Asian and Pacific Program	37		
00.02	African Program	30		
00.03	North African, Near Eastern, and South Asia Program	32		
00.04	Western Hemispheric Program	40		
00.05	West European and Canadian Program	50		
00.06	East European and NIS Program	39		
00.07	World-wide Mission Costs	39		
01.00	Subtotal, Overseas Missions	267		
01.02	Bureau of Information	35		
01.03	Agency Direction and Management	64		
01.04	Administrative Support from Other Agencies	97		
01.91	Direct Program by Activities—Subtotal (1 level)	196		
01.92	Subtotal, Direct Program	463		
09.00	Reimbursable program	12		
10.00	Total new obligations	475		
	Budgetary resources available for obligation:			
21.40	Unobligated balance available, start of year	8	8	
22.00	New budget authority (gross)	476		
22.10	Resources available from recoveries of prior year obligations	1		
22.21	Unobligated balance transferred to other accounts	−3	−8	
22.22	Unobligated balance transferred from other accounts	1		
23.90	Total budgetary resources available for obligation	483		
23.95	Total new obligations	−475		
23.98	Unobligated balance expiring or withdrawn	−1		
24.40	Unobligated balance available, end of year	8		
	New budget authority (gross), detail:			
	Discretionary:			
40.00	Appropriation	455		
40.75	Reduction pursuant to P.L. 106–51	−1		
41.00	Transferred to other accounts	−2		
42.00	Transferred from other accounts	12		
43.00	Appropriation (total discretionary)	464		
68.00	Spending authority from offsetting collections: Offsetting collections (cash)	12		
70.00	Total new budget authority (gross)	476		
	Change in unpaid obligations:			
72.40	Unpaid obligations, start of year: Obligated balance, start of year	96	90	11
73.10	Total new obligations	475		
73.20	Total outlays (gross)	−481	−79	−5
73.40	Adjustments in expired accounts (net)	1		
73.45	Adjustments in unexpired accounts	−1		
74.40	Unpaid obligations, end of year: Obligated balance, end of year	90	11	6
	Outlays (gross), detail:			
86.90	Outlays from new discretionary authority	394		
86.93	Outlays from discretionary balances	87	79	5
87.00	Total outlays (gross)	481	79	5
	Offsets:			
	Against gross budget authority and outlays:			
	Offsetting collections (cash) from:			
88.00	Federal sources	−7		
88.40	Non-Federal sources	−5		
88.90	Total, offsetting collections (cash)	−12		
	Net budget authority and outlays:			
89.00	Budget authority	464		

General and special funds—Continued

INTERNATIONAL INFORMATION PROGRAMS—Continued

Program and Financing (in millions of dollars)—Continued

Identification code 19–0201–0–1–154	1999 actual	2000 est.	2001 est.
90.00 Outlays	469	79	5

This appropriation provided for overseas information and cultural programs of the U.S. Information Agency designed to understand, inform, and influence foreign audiences. Starting in 2000, these activities are administered by the Department of State and funded from the Diplomatic and Consular programs and other accounts within the Department of State, except that such activities as are associated with international broadcasting functions are funded from the Broadcasting Board of Governors account. This schedule reflects the spend-out of current and prior year funds.

Object Classification (in millions of dollars)

Identification code 19–0201–0–1–154	1999 actual	2000 est.	2001 est.
Direct obligations:			
Personnel compensation:			
11.1 Full-time permanent	174		
11.3 Other than full-time permanent	3		
11.5 Other personnel compensation	10		
11.9 Total personnel compensation	187		
12.1 Civilian personnel benefits	46		
13.0 Benefits for former personnel	1		
21.0 Travel and transportation of persons	15		
22.0 Transportation of things	8		
23.1 Rental payments to GSA	36		
23.2 Rental payments to others	10		
23.3 Communications, utilities, and miscellaneous charges	15		
24.0 Printing and reproduction	1		
25.2 Other services	30		
25.3 Purchases of goods and services from Government accounts	66		
26.0 Supplies and materials	15		
31.0 Equipment	15		
41.0 Grants, subsidies, and contributions	16		
42.0 Insurance claims and indemnities	2		
99.0 Subtotal, direct obligations	463		
99.0 Reimbursable obligations	12		
99.9 Total new obligations	475		

Personnel Summary

Identification code 19–0201–0–1–154	1999 actual	2000 est.	2001 est.
Direct:			
1001 Total compensable workyears: Full-time equivalent employment	3,539		
Reimbursable:			
2001 Total compensable workyears: Full-time equivalent employment	26		

ARMS CONTROL AND DISARMAMENT ACTIVITIES

Program and Financing (in millions of dollars)

Identification code 94–0100–0–1–153	1999 actual	2000 est.	2001 est.
Obligations by program activity:			
00.01 Program operation	41		
00.02 External research	1		
10.00 Total new obligations	42		
Budgetary resources available for obligation:			
22.00 New budget authority (gross)	42		
23.95 Total new obligations	−42		
New budget authority (gross), detail:			
Discretionary:			
40.00 Appropriation	42		
42.00 Transferred from other accounts			
43.00 Appropriation (total discretionary)	42		
Change in unpaid obligations:			
72.40 Unpaid obligations, start of year: Obligated balance, start of year	25	22	5
73.10 Total new obligations	42		
73.20 Total outlays (gross)	−45	−17	−5
74.40 Unpaid obligations, end of year: Obligated balance, end of year	22	5	
Outlays (gross), detail:			
86.90 Outlays from new discretionary authority	33		
86.93 Outlays from discretionary balances	12	17	5
87.00 Total outlays (gross)	45	17	5
Net budget authority and outlays:			
89.00 Budget authority	42		
90.00 Outlays	45	17	5

This appropriation provided for arms control, nonproliferation, and disarmament activities and participation in negotiations with other countries seeking international agreements to control, reduce, or eliminate arms. These activities are now funded from the Diplomatic and Consular Programs and other accounts within the Department of State. This schedule reflects the spend-out of current and prior year obligations.

Object Classification (in millions of dollars)

Identification code 94–0100–0–1–153	1999 actual	2000 est.	2001 est.
Personnel compensation:			
11.1 Full-time permanent	15		
11.3 Other than full-time permanent	1		
11.8 Special personal services payments	5		
11.9 Total personnel compensation	21		
12.1 Civilian personnel benefits	3		
21.0 Travel and transportation of persons	3		
23.1 Rental payments to GSA	2		
25.2 Other services	12		
31.0 Equipment	1		
99.9 Total new obligations	42		

Personnel Summary

Identification code 94–0100–0–1–153	1999 actual	2000 est.	2001 est.
1001 Total compensable workyears: Full-time equivalent employment	230		

CAPITAL INVESTMENT FUND

For necessary expenses of the Capital Investment Fund, [$80,000,000] *$97,000,000*, to remain available until expended, as authorized in Public Law 103–236, *as amended*: *Provided*, That section 135(e) of Public Law 103–236 shall not apply to funds available under this heading. *(Department of State and Related Agencies Appropriations Act, 2000, as enacted by section 1000(a)(1) of the Consolidated Appropriations Act, 2000 (P.L. 106–113).)*

Program and Financing (in millions of dollars)

Identification code 19–0120–0–1–153	1999 actual	2000 est.	2001 est.
Obligations by program activity:			
00.01 Technology Infrastructure	81	83	47
00.02 Applications and Software Development	31	26	20
00.03 Project Management and Training	6	6	10
00.04 DTS Enhancements	22	20	20
10.00 Total new obligations	140	135	97
Budgetary resources available for obligation:			
21.40 Unobligated balance available, start of year	5	49	

22.00 New budget authority (gross)	184	81	97
22.22 Unobligated balance transferred from other accounts		5	
23.90 Total budgetary resources available for obligation	189	135	97
23.95 Total new obligations	–140	–135	–97
24.40 Unobligated balance available, end of year	49		
New budget authority (gross), detail:			
Discretionary:			
40.00 Appropriation	80	80	97
42.00 Transferred from other accounts	79	1	
43.00 Appropriation (total discretionary)	159	81	97
50.00 Reappropriation	25		
70.00 Total new budget authority (gross)	184	81	97
Change in unpaid obligations:			
72.40 Unpaid obligations, start of year: Obligated balance, start of year	48	84	75
73.10 Total new obligations	140	135	97
73.20 Total outlays (gross)	–104	–143	–89
74.40 Unpaid obligations, end of year: Obligated balance, end of year	84	75	83
Outlays (gross), detail:			
86.90 Outlays from new discretionary authority	70	61	68
86.93 Outlays from discretionary balances	34	83	21
87.00 Total outlays (gross)	104	143	89
Net budget authority and outlays:			
89.00 Budget authority	184	81	97
90.00 Outlays	104	143	89

The Capital Investment Fund provides for the procurement of information technology and other related capital investments for the Department of State and is designed to ensure the efficient management, coordination, operation and utilization of such resources. The fund is used as a tool to acquire and maintain information technology and other related capital investments necessary to improve operational performance in light of the rapidly advancing technological environment. In 2001, resources will be focused on certain technological enhancements recommended by the Overseas Presence Advisory Panel (OPAP). Resources will also be used in 1999 through 2001 to upgrade overseas telecommunications capabilities through the Diplomatic Telecommunications Service (DTS).

Object Classification (in millions of dollars)

Identification code 19–0120–0–1–153	1999 actual	2000 est.	2001 est.
25.2 Other services	107	91	65
31.0 Equipment	33	44	32
99.9 Total new obligations	140	135	97

Technology Fund

Program and Financing (in millions of dollars)

Identification code 19–0400–0–1–154	1999 actual	2000 est.	2001 est.
Obligations by program activity:			
10.00 Total new obligations	8		
Budgetary resources available for obligation:			
21.40 Unobligated balance available, start of year	1	5	
22.00 New budget authority (gross)	12		
22.21 Unobligated balance transferred to other accounts		–5	
23.90 Total budgetary resources available for obligation	13		
23.95 Total new obligations	–8		
24.40 Unobligated balance available, end of year	5		
New budget authority (gross), detail:			
Discretionary:			
42.00 Transferred from other accounts	12		
43.00 Appropriation (total discretionary)	12		
Change in unpaid obligations:			
72.40 Unpaid obligations, start of year: Obligated balance, start of year	4	6	
73.10 Total new obligations	8		
73.20 Total outlays (gross)	–6	–6	
74.40 Unpaid obligations, end of year: Obligated balance, end of year	6		
Outlays (gross), detail:			
86.90 Outlays from new discretionary authority	5		
86.93 Outlays from discretionary balances	1	6	
87.00 Total outlays (gross)	6	6	
Net budget authority and outlays:			
89.00 Budget authority	12		
90.00 Outlays	6	6	

This account provided funding for information technology improvements for non-broadcasting public diplomacy programs and Year 2000 compliance requirements of the U.S. Information Agency. Pursuant to the Foreign Affairs Reform and Restructuring Act of 1998, included in P.L. 105–277, technology improvements for non-broadcasting public diplomacy programs are funded through State Department accounts beginning in 2000.

Object Classification (in millions of dollars)

Identification code 19–0400–0–1–154	1999 actual	2000 est.	2001 est.
25.2 Other services	1		
26.0 Supplies and materials	1		
31.0 Equipment	6		
99.9 Total new obligations	8		

Office of Inspector General

For necessary expenses of the Office of Inspector General in carrying out the provisions of the Inspector General Act of 1978, as amended (5 U.S.C. App.), [$27,495,000] *$29,502,000*, notwithstanding section 209(a)(1) of the Foreign Service Act of 1980, as amended (Public Law 96–465), as it relates to post inspections. *(Department of State and Related Agencies Appropriations Act, 2000, as enacted by section 1000(a)(1) of the Consolidated Appropriations Act, 2000 (P.L. 106–113).)*

Program and Financing (in millions of dollars)

Identification code 19–0529–0–1–153	1999 actual	2000 est.	2001 est.
Obligations by program activity:			
00.02 Inspections and audits	27	26	29
00.03 Administration and staff activities	1	1	1
10.00 Total new obligations	28	27	30
Budgetary resources available for obligation:			
22.00 New budget authority (gross)	28	27	30
23.95 Total new obligations	–28	–27	–30
New budget authority (gross), detail:			
Discretionary:			
40.00 Appropriation	28	27	30
Change in unpaid obligations:			
72.40 Unpaid obligations, start of year: Obligated balance, start of year	4	2	1
73.10 Total new obligations	28	27	30
73.20 Total outlays (gross)	–30	–28	–29
74.40 Unpaid obligations, end of year: Obligated balance, end of year	2	1	2
Outlays (gross), detail:			
86.90 Outlays from new discretionary authority	26	26	28
86.93 Outlays from discretionary balances	4	2	1
87.00 Total outlays (gross)	30	28	29
Net budget authority and outlays:			
89.00 Budget authority	28	27	30

General and special funds—Continued

OFFICE OF INSPECTOR GENERAL—Continued

Program and Financing (in millions of dollars)—Continued

Identification code 19–0529–0–1–153	1999 actual	2000 est.	2001 est.
90.00 Outlays	30	28	29

This appropriation provides for the conduct or supervision of all audits, investigations, and inspections of the Department's programs and operations as mandated by the Inspector General Act of 1978, as amended, and the Foreign Service Act of 1980, as amended. The objectives of the Office of the Inspector General are to: (1) improve the economy, efficiency, and effectiveness of the Department's operations; (2) detect and prevent fraud, waste, abuse and mismanagement, and, (3) evaluate independently the formulation, applicability, and implementation of security standards at all U.S. diplomatic and consular posts. The Office also assesses the implementation of U.S. foreign policy, primarily through its inspection of all overseas posts and domestic offices on a cyclical basis. The State Department's IG also serves as Inspector General of the Broadcasting Board of Governors, as mandated by law.

Object Classification (in millions of dollars)

Identification code 19–0529–0–1–153	1999 actual	2000 est.	2001 est.
Personnel compensation:			
11.1 Full-time permanent	19	19	19
11.5 Other personnel compensation	1	1	2
11.9 Total personnel compensation	20	20	21
12.1 Civilian personnel benefits	3	3	3
21.0 Travel and transportation of persons	3	2	3
23.3 Communications, utilities, and miscellaneous charges		1	1
25.2 Other services	2	1	2
99.9 Total new obligations	28	27	30

Personnel Summary

Identification code 19–0529–0–1–153	1999 actual	2000 est.	2001 est.
1001 Total compensable workyears: Full-time equivalent employment	275	277	277

[SECURITY AND MAINTENANCE OF UNITED STATES MISSIONS]

EMBASSY SECURITY, CONSTRUCTION, AND MAINTENANCE

For necessary expenses for carrying out the Foreign Service Buildings Act of 1926, as amended (22 U.S.C. 292–300), preserving, maintaining, repairing, and planning for, buildings that are owned or directly leased by the Department of State, renovating, in addition to funds otherwise available, the Main State Building, and carrying out the Diplomatic Security Construction Program as authorized by title IV of the Omnibus Diplomatic Security and Antiterrorism Act of 1986 (22 U.S.C. 4851), [$428,561,000] *$431,178,000*, to remain available until expended as authorized by section 24(c) of the State Department Basic Authorities Act of 1956 (22 U.S.C. 2696(c)), of which not to exceed $25,000 may be used for *domestic and overseas* representation as authorized by section 905 of the Foreign Service Act of 1980, as amended (22 U.S.C. 4085): *Provided*, That none of the funds appropriated in this paragraph shall be available for acquisition of furniture and furnishings and generators for other departments and agencies.

In addition, for the costs of worldwide security upgrades, *acquisition, and construction as authorized by the Secure Embassy Construction and Counterterrorism Act of 1999,* [$313,617,000] *$648,000,000,* to remain available until expended.

In addition, for necessary expenses for capital asset acquisition or construction, including alteration, modification, and equipment costs, of diplomatic and consular facilities, to become available on October 1, of the fiscal year specified and remain available until expended: fiscal year 2002, $650,000,000; fiscal year 2003, $800,000,000; fiscal year 2004, $950,000,000; and fiscal year 2005, $950,000,000. (Department of State and Related Agencies Appropriations Act, 2000, as enacted by section 1000(a)(1) of the Consolidated Appropriations Act, 2000 (P.L. 106–113).)

Program and Financing (in millions of dollars)

Identification code 19–0535–0–1–153	1999 actual	2000 est.	2001 est.
Obligations by program activity:			
Direct program:			
00.01 State Department	15	351	323
00.02 Other agencies		2	2
00.03 Leasehold payments	126	138	138
00.04 Functional programs	205	341	429
00.05 Administration	19	21	20
00.06 Reconstruction of Moscow embassy	31	11	
00.07 Security Supplemental	300	213	70
00.09 Real property acquisitions	38	196	34
01.00 Total direct program	734	1,273	1,016
09.01 Reimbursable program	71	50	50
10.00 Total new obligations	805	1,323	1,066
Budgetary resources available for obligation:			
Unobligated balance available, start of year:			
21.40 Unobligated balance available, start of year	133	461	165
21.40 Unobligated balance available, start of year	83	120	37
21.99 Total unobligated balance, start of year	216	581	202
22.00 New budget authority (gross)	1,150	944	1,193
22.10 Resources available from recoveries of prior year obligations	20		
23.90 Total budgetary resources available for obligation	1,386	1,525	1,395
23.95 Total new obligations	–805	–1,323	–1,066
Unobligated balance available, end of year:			
24.40 Unobligated balance available, end of year	461	165	253
24.40 Unobligated balance available, end of year	120	37	76
24.99 Total unobligated balance, end of year	581	202	329
New budget authority (gross), detail:			
Discretionary:			
40.00 Appropriation	404	742	1,079
40.15 Appropriation (emergency)	678		
40.75 Reduction pursuant to P.L. 106–51	–3		
40.76 Reduction pursuant to P.L. 106–113		–3	
41.00 Transferred to other accounts	–17		
43.00 Appropriation (total discretionary)	1,062	739	1,079
Spending authority from offsetting collections:			
Offsetting collections (cash):			
68.00 Offsetting collections from operations (cash)	76	79	79
68.00 Asset Management Program (cash)	12	126	35
68.90 Spending authority from offsetting collections (total discretionary)	88	205	114
70.00 Total new budget authority (gross)	1,150	944	1,193
Change in unpaid obligations:			
72.40 Unpaid obligations, start of year: Obligated balance, start of year	425	505	922
73.10 Total new obligations	805	1,323	1,066
73.20 Total outlays (gross)	–703	–906	–940
73.45 Adjustments in unexpired accounts	–20		
74.40 Unpaid obligations, end of year: Obligated balance, end of year	505	922	1,048
Outlays (gross), detail:			
86.90 Outlays from new discretionary authority	462	382	438
86.93 Outlays from discretionary balances	241	524	502
87.00 Total outlays (gross)	703	906	940
Offsets:			
Against gross budget authority and outlays:			
Offsetting collections (cash) from:			
88.00 Federal sources	–76	–79	–79
88.40 Non-Federal sources	–12	–126	–35
88.90 Total, offsetting collections (cash)	–88	–205	–114
Net budget authority and outlays:			
89.00 Budget authority	1,062	739	1,079
90.00 Outlays	615	701	826

Summary of Budget Authority and Outlays

(in millions of dollars)

	1999 actual	2000 est.	2001 est.
Enacted/requested:			
Budget Authority	1,062	739	1,079
Outlays	615	701	826
Supplemental proposal:			
Budget Authority		239	
Outlays		72	65
Total:			
Budget Authority	1,062	978	1,079
Outlays	615	773	891

Under the direction of the Secretary of State, the overall mission of the Office of Foreign Buildings Operation is to ensure that U.S. Diplomatic and Consular Missions abroad are provided safe, secure and functional facilities which will assist them in achieving the foreign policy objectives of the United States. Specific program functions in support of the mission include: providing guidance concerning overseas facilities to posts, regional bureaus and other foreign affairs agencies; providing expert facilities and space planning to posts; overseeing the design, construction and renovation of diplomatic facilities; incorporating security features into overseas facilities and ensuring the security of facilities during construction or renovation; establishing standards and policies for overseas housing; developing, in conjunction with posts, maintenance programs for post facilities and keeping inventory of maintenance requirements; ensuring the safety of the building occupants through the development of fire/life safety programs; and providing real property management that establishes priorities for the acquisition and disposal of real property, determines the best use for proceeds from the sale of real property, and maintains an inventory of U.S. Government real property holdings overseas.

The objective of the Asset Management Program is to obtain the best use of diplomatic and consular properties overseas through sale, exchange, or redevelopment. Most often, this involves the sale of surplus or underutilized properties and reinvestment of the proceeds in properties that provide a greater return to the U.S. Government. Balances realized are slated for long-term capital investment that contains the growth of U.S. Government leasehold requirements (by acquiring property that reduces the need for leased facilities) or that addresses a high-priority need for new construction in lieu of appropriated resources.

This appropriation also provides for capital expenditures necessary to preserve, maintain, repair, and plan for buildings that are owned or directly leased by the Department of State in the United States and, in addition to funds otherwise made available, the renovation of the Main State building.

Object Classification (in millions of dollars)

Identification code 19–0535–0–1–153		1999 actual	2000 est.	2001 est.
	Direct obligations:			
	Personnel compensation:			
11.1	Full-time permanent	34	37	40
11.5	Other personnel compensation	16	17	18
11.9	Total personnel compensation	50	54	58
12.1	Civilian personnel benefits	17	18	19
21.0	Travel and transportation of persons	13	13	13
22.0	Transportation of things	6	6	6
23.2	Rental payments to others	163	158	158
25.2	Other services	309	446	275
26.0	Supplies and materials	31	32	32
31.0	Equipment	42	60	60
32.0	Land and structures	101	485	394
41.0	Grants, subsidies, and contributions	2	1	1
99.0	Subtotal, direct obligations	734	1,273	1,016
99.0	Reimbursable obligations	71	50	50
99.9	Total new obligations	805	1,323	1,066

Personnel Summary

Identification code 19–0535–0–1–153		1999 actual	2000 est.	2001 est.
	Direct:			
1001	Total compensable workyears: Full-time equivalent employment	481	498	507
	Reimbursable:			
2001	Total compensable workyears: Full-time equivalent employment	10	10	10

Security and Maintenance of United States Missions (Special Foreign Currency Program)

Program and Financing (in millions of dollars)

Identification code 19–0538–0–1–153		1999 actual	2000 est.	2001 est.
	Obligations by program activity:			
00.01	Rents, M&R, Utilities		1	
10.00	Total new obligations		1	
	Budgetary resources available for obligation:			
21.40	Unobligated balance available, start of year	1	1	
23.95	Total new obligations		−1	
24.40	Unobligated balance available, end of year	1		
	Change in unpaid obligations:			
72.40	Unpaid obligations, start of year: Obligated balance, start of year	1	1	
73.10	Total new obligations		1	
73.20	Total outlays (gross)		−2	
74.40	Unpaid obligations, end of year: Obligated balance, end of year	1		
	Outlays (gross), detail:			
86.93	Outlays from discretionary balances		2	
	Net budget authority and outlays:			
89.00	Budget authority			
90.00	Outlays		2	

Amounts in this fund are used to acquire real property by lease, purchase, or construction; and to maintain, repair, or replace facilities in those localities where the U.S. Government owns excess foreign currency. This program will be terminated once balances from previous years have been expended.

Representation Allowances

For representation allowances as authorized by section 905 of the Foreign Service Act of 1980, as amended (22 U.S.C. 4085), [$5,850,000] *$5,973,000. (Department of State and Related Agencies Appropriations Act, 2000, as enacted by section 1000(a)(1) of the Consolidated Appropriations Act, 2000 (P.L. 106–113).)*

Program and Financing (in millions of dollars)

Identification code 19–0545–0–1–153		1999 actual	2000 est.	2001 est.
	Obligations by program activity:			
00.01	Direct program	4	6	6
10.00	Total new obligations	4	6	6
	Budgetary resources available for obligation:			
22.00	New budget authority (gross)	4	6	6
23.95	Total new obligations	−4	−6	−6
	New budget authority (gross), detail:			
	Discretionary:			
40.00	Appropriation	4	6	6
	Change in unpaid obligations:			
72.40	Unpaid obligations, start of year: Obligated balance, start of year	1	1	1
73.10	Total new obligations	4	6	6

General and special funds—Continued

REPRESENTATION ALLOWANCES—Continued

Program and Financing (in millions of dollars)—Continued

Identification code 19–0545–0–1–153	1999 actual	2000 est.	2001 est.
73.20 Total outlays (gross)	–4	–6	–6
74.40 Unpaid obligations, end of year: Obligated balance, end of year	1	1	1
Outlays (gross), detail:			
86.90 Outlays from new discretionary authority	3	5	5
86.93 Outlays from discretionary balances	1	1	1
87.00 Total outlays (gross)	4	6	6
Net budget authority and outlays:			
89.00 Budget authority	4	6	6
90.00 Outlays	4	6	6

Amounts in this fund are used to reimburse, in part, State Department personnel for expenses incurred for official representation activities abroad and at missions to international organizations in the United States.

PROTECTION OF FOREIGN MISSIONS AND OFFICIALS

For expenses, not otherwise provided, to enable the Secretary of State to provide for extraordinary protective services in accordance with the provisions of section 214 of the State Department Basic Authorities Act of 1956 (22 U.S.C. 4314) and 3 U.S.C. 208, [$8,100,000] *$10,490,000*, to remain available until September 30, [2001] *2002*. *(Department of State and Related Agencies Appropriations Act, 2000, as enacted by section 1000(a)(1) of the Consolidated Appropriations Act, 2000 (P.L. 106–113).)*

Program and Financing (in millions of dollars)

Identification code 19–0520–0–1–153	1999 actual	2000 est.	2001 est.
Obligations by program activity:			
00.01 Missions and officials to United Nations	6	7	9
00.02 Missions and officials in United States	1	1	1
10.00 Total new obligations	7	8	10
Budgetary resources available for obligation:			
21.40 Unobligated balance available, start of year		1	1
22.00 New budget authority (gross)	8	8	10
23.90 Total budgetary resources available for obligation	8	9	11
23.95 Total new obligations	–7	–8	–10
24.40 Unobligated balance available, end of year	1	1	1
New budget authority (gross), detail:			
Discretionary:			
40.00 Appropriation	8	8	10
Change in unpaid obligations:			
72.40 Unpaid obligations, start of year: Obligated balance, start of year	9	4	4
73.10 Total new obligations	7	8	10
73.20 Total outlays (gross)	–12	–8	–9
74.40 Unpaid obligations, end of year: Obligated balance, end of year	4	4	5
Outlays (gross), detail:			
86.90 Outlays from new discretionary authority	5	3	4
86.93 Outlays from discretionary balances	7	5	4
87.00 Total outlays (gross)	12	8	9
Net budget authority and outlays:			
89.00 Budget authority	8	8	10
90.00 Outlays	12	8	9

This appropriation provides for extraordinary protection: (1) in New York, of foreign missions and officials (including those accredited to the United Nations and other international organizations), and visiting foreign dignitaries under certain circumstances; and, (2) in certain other metropolitan areas in the United States, of international organizations, foreign missions and officials, and visiting foreign dignitaries under certain circumstances. Funds may also be used to: reimburse State or local authorities, contract for services by private security firms; or, to reimburse Federal agencies for extraordinary protective services.

EMERGENCIES IN THE DIPLOMATIC AND CONSULAR SERVICE

For expenses necessary to enable the Secretary of State to meet unforeseen emergencies arising in the Diplomatic and Consular Service pursuant to the requirement of 31 U.S.C. 3526(e), and as authorized by section 804(3) of the United States Information and Educational Exchange Act of 1948, as amended, [$5,500,000] *$11,000,000*, to remain available until expended as authorized by section 24(c) of the State Department Basic Authorities Act of 1956 (22 U.S.C. 2696(c)), of which not to exceed $1,000,000 may be transferred to and merged with the Repatriation Loans Program Account, subject to the same terms and conditions. *(Department of State and Related Agencies Appropriations Act, 2000, as enacted by section 1000(a)(1) of the Consolidated Appropriations Act, 2000 (P.L. 106–113).)*

Program and Financing (in millions of dollars)

Identification code 19–0522–0–1–153	1999 actual	2000 est.	2001 est.
Obligations by program activity:			
00.01 Rewards	6	1	3
00.02 Other activities	10	7	8
10.00 Total new obligations	16	8	11
Budgetary resources available for obligation:			
21.40 Unobligated balance available, start of year	4	8	6
22.00 New budget authority (gross)	17	6	11
22.10 Resources available from recoveries of prior year obligations	2		
23.90 Total budgetary resources available for obligation	23	14	17
23.95 Total new obligations	–16	–8	–11
24.40 Unobligated balance available, end of year	8	6	6
New budget authority (gross), detail:			
Discretionary:			
40.00 Appropriation	7	6	11
40.15 Appropriation (emergency)	11		
41.00 Transferred to other accounts	–1		
43.00 Appropriation (total discretionary)	17	6	11
Change in unpaid obligations:			
72.40 Unpaid obligations, start of year: Obligated balance, start of year	4	7	5
73.10 Total new obligations	16	8	11
73.20 Total outlays (gross)	–11	–10	–9
73.45 Adjustments in unexpired accounts	–2		
74.40 Unpaid obligations, end of year: Obligated balance, end of year	7	5	6
Outlays (gross), detail:			
86.90 Outlays from new discretionary authority	7	4	8
86.93 Outlays from discretionary balances	4	6	1
87.00 Total outlays (gross)	11	10	9
Net budget authority and outlays:			
89.00 Budget authority	17	6	11
90.00 Outlays	11	10	9

These funds are used primarily for purposes authorized by section 4 of the Department's Basic Authorities Act (22 U.S.C. 2671), for rewards authorized by section 36 of that Act and for purposes authorized by section 804(3) of the United States Information and Educational Exchange Act of 1948, as amended.

Buying Power Maintenance

Program and Financing (in millions of dollars)

Identification code 19–0524–0–1–153	1999 actual	2000 est.	2001 est.
Budgetary resources available for obligation:			
21.40 Unobligated balance available, start of year	12	8	12
22.00 New budget authority (gross)	−4		
22.22 Unobligated balance transferred from other accounts		4	
23.90 Total budgetary resources available for obligation	8	12	12
24.40 Unobligated balance available, end of year	8	12	12
New budget authority (gross), detail:			
Discretionary:			
40.00 Appropriation			
40.75 Reduction pursuant to P.L. 106–51	−4		
43.00 Appropriation (total discretionary)	−4		
Net budget authority and outlays:			
89.00 Budget authority	−4		
90.00 Outlays			

This account is available to offset losses due to exchange rate and overseas wage and price fluctuations unanticipated in the budget. Any gains due to fluctuations will be merged with this account to be available to offset future losses.

U.S. Information Agency Buying Power Maintenance

Program and Financing (in millions of dollars)

Identification code 19–0301–0–1–154	1999 actual	2000 est.	2001 est.
Budgetary resources available for obligation:			
21.40 Unobligated balance available, start of year	26	8	
22.00 New budget authority (gross)	−18		
22.21 Unobligated balance transferred to other accounts		−8	
23.90 Total budgetary resources available for obligation	8		
24.40 Unobligated balance available, end of year	8		
New budget authority (gross), detail:			
Discretionary:			
40.36 Unobligated balance rescinded	−20		
42.00 Transferred from other accounts	2		
43.00 Appropriation (total discretionary)	−18		
Net budget authority and outlays:			
89.00 Budget authority	−18		
90.00 Outlays			

This account provided funding to offset losses of the U.S. Information Agency due to exchange rate and overseas wage and price fluctuations unanticipated in the budget.

In 2000, all amounts were transferred to Department of State, except for amounts associated with the international broadcasting function, which were transferred to the Broadcasting Board of Governors Buying Power Maintenance Fund.

Payment to the American Institute in Taiwan

For necessary expenses to carry out the Taiwan Relations Act, Public Law 96–8, [$15,375,000] *$16,345,000. (Department of State and Related Agencies Appropriations Act, 2000, as enacted by section 1000(a)(1) of the Consolidated Appropriations Act, 2000 (P.L. 106–113).)*

Program and Financing (in millions of dollars)

Identification code 19–0523–0–1–153	1999 actual	2000 est.	2001 est.
Obligations by program activity:			
10.00 Total new obligations	15	15	16
Budgetary resources available for obligation:			
22.00 New budget authority (gross)	15	15	16
23.95 Total new obligations	−15	−15	−16
New budget authority (gross), detail:			
Discretionary:			
40.00 Appropriation	15	15	16
Change in unpaid obligations:			
72.40 Unpaid obligations, start of year: Obligated balance, start of year	8	15	15
73.10 Total new obligations	15	15	16
73.20 Total outlays (gross)	−8	−15	−16
74.40 Unpaid obligations, end of year: Obligated balance, end of year	15	15	15
Outlays (gross), detail:			
86.90 Outlays from new discretionary authority	8	8	8
86.93 Outlays from discretionary balances		7	8
87.00 Total outlays (gross)	8	15	16
Net budget authority and outlays:			
89.00 Budget authority	15	15	16
90.00 Outlays	8	15	16

Object Classification (in millions of dollars)

Identification code 19–0523–0–1–153	1999 actual	2000 est.	2001 est.
11.8 Personnel compensation: Special personal services payments	8	8	8
12.1 Civilian personnel benefits	2	2	2
23.2 Rental payments to others	2	2	3
25.2 Other services	2	2	2
31.0 Equipment	1	1	1
99.9 Total new obligations	15	15	16

The Taiwan Relations Act (Public Law 96–8) requires programs with respect to Taiwan to be carried out by or through the American Institute in Taiwan.

The Department will continue to contract with the Institute to conduct commercial, cultural, and other relations with the people on Taiwan.

Payment to the Foreign Service Retirement and Disability Fund

For payment to the Foreign Service Retirement and Disability Fund, as authorized by law, [$128,541,000] *$131,224,000. (Department of State and Related Agencies Appropriations Act, 2000, as enacted by section 1000(a)(1) of the Consolidated Appropriations Act, 2000 (P.L. 106–113).)*

Program and Financing (in millions of dollars)

Identification code 19–0540–0–1–153	1999 actual	2000 est.	2001 est.
Obligations by program activity:			
10.00 Total new obligations	216	162	166
Budgetary resources available for obligation:			
22.00 New budget authority (gross)	216	162	166
23.95 Total new obligations	−216	−162	−166
New budget authority (gross), detail:			
Mandatory:			
60.00 Appropriation	132	129	131
60.05 Appropriation (indefinite)	84	33	35
62.50 Appropriation (total mandatory)	216	162	166
Change in unpaid obligations:			
73.10 Total new obligations	216	162	166
73.20 Total outlays (gross)	−216	−162	−166
Outlays (gross), detail:			
86.97 Outlays from new mandatory authority	216	162	166
Net budget authority and outlays:			
89.00 Budget authority	216	162	166
90.00 Outlays	216	162	166

General and special funds—Continued

PAYMENT TO THE FOREIGN SERVICE RETIREMENT AND DISABILITY FUND—Continued

The current appropriation finances, by 30 equal annual installments, any unfunded liability created by new or liberalized benefits, new groups of beneficiaries, and salary increases. In addition, the appropriation also finances the annual balance of the Foreign Service normal cost not met by employee and employer contributions.

The 2001 permanent appropriation provides a payment to the fund for disbursements attributable to military and naval services.

Intragovernmental funds:

WORKING CAPITAL FUND

Unavailable Collections (in millions of dollars)

Identification code 19–4519–0–4–153	1999 actual	2000 est.	2001 est.
Balance, start of year:			
01.99 Balance, start of year		3	
Appropriation:			
05.01 Working capital fund		−3	
06.20 Reduction pursuant to Public Law xx-xxx	3		
07.99 Total balance, end of year	3		

Program and Financing (in millions of dollars)

Identification code 19–4519–0–4–153	1999 actual	2000 est.	2001 est.
Obligations by program activity:			
09.01 Publishing services	22	29	29
09.02 Supply sevices	3	3	3
09.03 Central support services	87	100	101
09.04 International cooperative adminstrative support services (ICASS)	703	947	962
10.00 Total new obligations	815	1,079	1,095
Budgetary resources available for obligation:			
21.40 Unobligated balance available, start of year	18	79	76
22.00 New budget authority (gross)	862	1,076	1,095
22.10 Resources available from recoveries of prior year obligations	14		
23.90 Total budgetary resources available for obligation	894	1,155	1,171
23.95 Total new obligations	−815	−1,079	−1,095
24.40 Unobligated balance available, end of year	79	76	76
New budget authority (gross), detail:			
Mandatory:			
69.00 Offsetting collections (cash)	865	1,073	1,095
69.26 Offsetting collections (unavailable balances)		3	
69.75 Reduction pursuant to P.L. 106–51	−3		
69.90 Spending authority from offsetting collections (total mandatory)	862	1,076	1,095
Change in unpaid obligations:			
72.40 Unpaid obligations, start of year: Obligated balance, start of year	15	−6	3
73.10 Total new obligations	815	1,079	1,095
73.20 Total outlays (gross)	−822	−1,070	−1,095
73.45 Adjustments in unexpired accounts	−14		
74.40 Unpaid obligations, end of year: Obligated balance, end of year	−6	3	3
Outlays (gross), detail:			
86.97 Outlays from new mandatory authority	822	1,076	1,095
86.98 Outlays from mandatory balances		−6	
87.00 Total outlays (gross)	822	1,070	1,095
Offsets:			
Against gross budget authority and outlays:			
88.00 Offsetting collections (cash) from: Federal sources	−865	−1,076	−1,095
Net budget authority and outlays:			
89.00 Budget authority	−3		
90.00 Outlays		−43	−6

This fund, authorized by section 13 of the State Department Basic Authorities Act of 1956 (22 U.S.C. 2684), finances on a reimbursable basis, certain administrative services, such as printing and reproduction, editorial material, motor pool operations and dispatch agencies operations, inter-agency cooperative administrative support services, and expenses of carrying out the Foreign Missions Act, including any acquisitions of property under section 204(f) of the State Department Basic Authorities Act of 1956 (22 U.S.C. 4304(f)).

Using the Working Capital Fund, the International Cooperative Administrative Support Services (ICASS) program was fully implemented in 1998. ICASS restructures overseas administrative support activities to allow more decisionmaking and managerial participation by all participating agencies, more equitable cost distribution, and incentives for efficient provision of services. Under ICASS, each agency represented at an overseas post chooses the services it wishes to receive and pays a proportional share of the cost of those services. Working through inter-agency councils at each overseas post, all agencies have a say in determining post administrative budgets and defining service standards, as well as reviewing costs and vendor performance.

Object Classification (in millions of dollars)

Identification code 19–4519–0–4–153	1999 actual	2000 est.	2001 est.
Personnel compensation:			
11.1 Full-time permanent	221	325	327
11.3 Other than full-time permanent	105	135	138
11.5 Other personnel compensation	5	6	6
11.9 Total personnel compensation	331	466	471
12.1 Civilian personnel benefits	91	117	119
13.0 Benefits for former personnel	1	2	2
21.0 Travel and transportation of persons	12	15	15
22.0 Transportation of things	47	58	59
23.2 Rental payments to others	64	82	84
23.3 Communications, utilities, and miscellaneous charges	44	57	58
25.2 Other services	137	171	174
26.0 Supplies and materials	53	67	68
31.0 Equipment	35	44	45
99.9 Total new obligations	815	1,079	1,095

Personnel Summary

Identification code 19–4519–0–4–153	1999 actual	2000 est.	2001 est.
2001 Total compensable workyears: Full-time equivalent employment	6,821	6,821	6,821

Credit accounts:

REPATRIATION LOANS PROGRAM ACCOUNT

For the cost of direct loans, $593,000, as authorized by section 4 of the State Department Basic Authorities Act of 1956 (22 U.S.C. 2671): *Provided*, That such costs, including the cost of modifying such loans, shall be as defined in section 502 of the Congressional Budget Act of 1974. In addition, for administrative expenses necessary to carry out the direct loan program, $607,000, which may be transferred to and merged with the Diplomatic and Consular Programs account under Administration of Foreign Affairs. *(Department of State and Related Agencies Appropriations Act, 2000, as enacted by section 1000(a)(1) of the Consolidated Appropriations Act, 2000 (P.L. 106–113).)*

Program and Financing (in millions of dollars)

Identification code 19–0601–0–1–153	1999 actual	2000 est.	2001 est.
Obligations by program activity:			
00.01 Direct loan subsidy	1	1	1
10.00 Total new obligations	1	1	1

		1999 actual	2000 est.	2001 est.
	Budgetary resources available for obligation:			
22.00	New budget authority (gross)	1	1	1
23.95	Total new obligations	−1	−1	−1
	New budget authority (gross), detail:			
	Discretionary:			
40.00	Appropriation	1	1	1
	Change in unpaid obligations:			
73.10	Total new obligations	1	1	1
73.20	Total outlays (gross)	−1	−1	−1
	Outlays (gross), detail:			
86.90	Outlays from new discretionary authority	1	1	1
	Net budget authority and outlays:			
89.00	Budget authority	1	1	1
90.00	Outlays	1	1	1

Summary of Loan Levels, Subsidy Budget Authority and Outlays by Program (in millions of dollars)

Identification code 19–0601–0–1–153		1999 actual	2000 est.	2001 est.
	Direct loan levels supportable by subsidy budget authority:			
1150	Direct loan levels	1	1	1
1159	Total direct loan levels	1	1	1
	Direct loan subsidy (in percent):			
1320	Subsidy rate	80.00	80.00	80.00
1329	Weighted average subsidy rate	80.00	80.00	80.00
	Direct loan subsidy budget authority:			
1330	Subsidy budget authority	1	1	1
1339	Total subsidy budget authority	1	1	1
	Direct loan subsidy outlays:			
1340	Subsidy outlays	1	1	1
1349	Total subsidy outlays	1	1	1

As required by the Federal Credit Reform Act of 1990, this account records, for this program, the subsidy costs and administrative expenses associated with the direct loans. The subsidy amounts are estimated on a present value basis, the administrative expenses are estimated on a cash basis.

REPATRIATION LOANS FINANCING ACCOUNT

Program and Financing (in millions of dollars)

Identification code 19–4107–0–3–153		1999 actual	2000 est.	2001 est.
	Obligations by program activity:			
00.01	Direct loans	1	1	1
10.00	Total new obligations	1	1	1
	Budgetary resources available for obligation:			
22.00	New financing authority (gross)	1	1	1
23.95	Total new obligations	−1	−1	−1
	New financing authority (gross), detail:			
	Discretionary:			
68.00	Spending authority from offsetting collections (gross): Offsetting collections (cash)	1	1	1
	Change in unpaid obligations:			
72.40	Unpaid obligations, start of year: Obligated balance, start of year	2	2	2
73.10	Total new obligations	1	1	1
73.20	Total financing disbursements (gross)	−1	−1	−1
74.40	Unpaid obligations, end of year: Obligated balance, end of year	2	2	2
87.00	Total financing disbursements (gross)	1	1	1
	Offsets:			
	Against gross financing authority and financing disbursements:			
88.00	Offsetting collections (cash) from: Payments from program account	−1	−1	−1
	Net financing authority and financing disbursements:			
89.00	Financing authority			
90.00	Financing disbursements			

Status of Direct Loans (in millions of dollars)

Identification code 19–4107–0–3–153		1999 actual	2000 est.	2001 est.
	Position with respect to appropriations act limitation on obligations:			
1111	Limitation on direct loans	1	1	1
1150	Total direct loan obligations	1	1	1
	Cumulative balance of direct loans outstanding:			
1210	Outstanding, start of year	4	4	4
1231	Disbursements: Direct loan disbursements	1	1	1
1263	Write-offs for default: Direct loans	−1	−1	−1
1290	Outstanding, end of year	4	4	4

Balance Sheet (in millions of dollars)

Identification code 19–4107–0–3–153		1998 actual	1999 actual	2000 est.	2001 est.
	ASSETS:				
1601	Net value of assets related to pre–1992 direct loans receivable and acquired defaulted guaranteed loans receivable: Direct loans, gross	1	1	1	1
1999	Total assets	1	1	1	1
	NET POSITION:				
3300	Cumulative results of operations	1	1	1	1
3999	Total net position	1	1	1	1

As required by the Federal Credit Reform Act of 1990, this non-budgetary account records all cash flows to and from the Government resulting from direct loans starting with obligations made in 1992 (including modifications of direct loans that resulted from obligations in any year). The amounts in this account are a means of financing and are not included in the budget totals.

Trust Funds

FOREIGN SERVICE RETIREMENT AND DISABILITY FUND

Unavailable Collections (in millions of dollars)

Identification code 19–8186–0–7–602		1999 actual	2000 est.	2001 est.
	Balance, start of year:			
01.99	Balance, start of year	9,550	10,132	10,687
	Receipts:			
02.01	Deductions from employees salaries	28	30	31
02.02	Interest on investments	710	746	768
02.04	Employing agency contributions	121	128	134
02.05	Receipts from civil service retirement and disability fund		1	1
02.06	Federal contributions	261	206	210
02.99	Total receipts	1,120	1,111	1,144
04.00	Total: Balances and collections	10,670	11,243	11,831
	Appropriation:			
05.01	Foreign Service retirement and disability fund	−538	−556	−576
05.99	Subtotal appropriation	−538	−556	−576
07.99	Total balance, end of year	10,132	10,687	11,255

Program and Financing (in millions of dollars)

Identification code 19–8186–0–7–602		1999 actual	2000 est.	2001 est.
	Obligations by program activity:			
00.01	Payments to beneficiaries	525	542	562
00.02	Refunds and gratuities	13	14	14
10.00	Total new obligations	538	556	576

Credit accounts—Continued

FOREIGN SERVICE RETIREMENT AND DISABILITY FUND—Continued

Program and Financing (in millions of dollars)—Continued

Identification code 19–8186–0–7–602		1999 actual	2000 est.	2001 est.
	Budgetary resources available for obligation:			
22.00	New budget authority (gross)	538	556	576
23.95	Total new obligations	−538	−556	−576
	New budget authority (gross), detail:			
	Mandatory:			
60.27	Appropriation (trust fund, indefinite)	1,120	1,111	1,144
60.28	Appropriation (unavailable balances)	9,550	10,132	10,687
60.45	Portion precluded from obligation	−10,132	−10,687	−11,255
62.50	Appropriation (total mandatory)	538	556	576
	Change in unpaid obligations:			
73.10	Total new obligations	538	556	576
73.20	Total outlays (gross)	−538	−556	−576
	Outlays (gross), detail:			
86.97	Outlays from new mandatory authority	538	556	576
	Net budget authority and outlays:			
89.00	Budget authority	538	556	576
90.00	Outlays	538	556	576
	Memorandum (non-add) entries:			
92.01	Total investments, start of year: U.S. securities: Par value	9,550	10,132	10,687
92.02	Total investments, end of year: U.S. securities: Par value	10,132	10,687	11,255

The fund is maintained through: (a) contributions by participants, consisting of all Foreign Service officers, Foreign Service information officers, Foreign Service reserve officers with unlimited tenure, and all Foreign Service staff officers and employees with unlimited appointments; (b) matching Government contributions; (c) special Government contributions from the Payment to the Foreign Service Retirement and Disability Fund; (d) interest on investments (22 U.S.C. 4042); and (e) voluntary contributions.

Approximately 14,700 annuitants will be paid retirement benefits from this fund in 2001, compared with an estimated 14,500 to be paid in 2000 and 14,300 paid in 1999. Gratuities and refunds represent payments to eligible former participants leaving the retirement system.

The status of the fund is as follows:

Status of Funds (in millions of dollars)

Identification code 19–8186–0–7–602		1999 actual	2000 est.	2001 est.
	Unexpended balance, start of year:			
0101	U.S. Securities: Par value	9,550	10,132	10,687
	Cash income during the year:			
	Governmental receipts:			
0200	Deductions from employees salaries, Foreign Service retirement and disability fund	28	30	31
	Intragovernmental transactions:			
0240	Interest on investments, foreign Service retirement and disability fund	710	746	768
0241	Employing agency contributions, foreign service retirement and disability fund	121	128	134
0242	Receipts from civil service retirement and disability fund, foreign service retirement and disability fund	....	1	1
0243	Federal contributions, foreign service retirement and disability fund	261	206	210
0299	Total cash income	1,120	1,111	1,144
	Cash outgo during year:			
0500	Foreign service retirement and disability fund	−538	−556	−576
	Unexpended balance, end of year:			
0701	U.S. Securities: Par value	10,131	10,687	11,255
0799	Total balance, end of year	10,132	10,687	11,255

Object Classification (in millions of dollars)

Identification code 19–8186–0–7–602		1999 actual	2000 est.	2001 est.
42.0	Insurance claims and indemnities	525	542	562
44.0	Refunds	13	14	14
99.9	Total new obligations	538	556	576

FOREIGN SERVICE NATIONAL SEPARATION LIABILITY TRUST FUND

Unavailable Collections (in millions of dollars)

Identification code 19–8340–0–7–602		1999 actual	2000 est.	2001 est.
	Balance, start of year:			
01.99	Balance, start of year	64	63	64
	Receipts:			
02.03	Foreign service national separation liability trust fund, State	8	8	8
02.04	Foreign service national separation liability trust fund, AID	2	3	3
02.06	Foreign service national separation liability trust fund, BIB	....	1	1
02.99	Total receipts	10	12	12
04.00	Total: Balances and collections	74	75	76
	Appropriation:			
05.03	Foreign service national separation liability trust fund, State	−8	−8	−8
05.04	Foreign service national separation liability trust fund, AID	−3	−3	−3
05.99	Subtotal appropriation	−11	−11	−11
07.99	Total balance, end of year	63	64	65

Program and Financing (in millions of dollars)

Identification code 19–8340–0–7–602		1999 actual	2000 est.	2001 est.
	Obligations by program activity:			
10.00	Total new obligations	10	8	8
	Budgetary resources available for obligation:			
21.40	Unobligated balance available, start of year	73	74	77
22.00	New budget authority (gross)	8	8	8
22.10	Resources available from recoveries of prior year obligations	3	....	....
22.22	Unobligated balance transferred from other accounts	....	4	....
23.90	Total budgetary resources available for obligation	84	86	85
23.95	Total new obligations	−10	−8	−8
24.40	Unobligated balance available, end of year	74	77	77
	New budget authority (gross), detail:			
	Mandatory:			
60.27	Appropriation (trust fund, indefinite)	8	8	8
	Change in unpaid obligations:			
72.40	Unpaid obligations, start of year: Obligated balance, start of year	1	2	2
73.10	Total new obligations	10	8	8
73.20	Total outlays (gross)	−6	−8	−8
73.45	Adjustments in unexpired accounts	−3	....	....
74.40	Unpaid obligations, end of year: Obligated balance, end of year	2	2	2
	Outlays (gross), detail:			
86.97	Outlays from new mandatory authority	6	8	8
	Net budget authority and outlays:			
89.00	Budget authority	8	8	8
90.00	Outlays	6	8	8

This fund is maintained to pay separation costs for Foreign Service National employees of the Department of State, in those countries in which such pay is legally authorized. The fund, as authorized by section 151 of Public Law 102–138 (22 U.S.C. 4012a), is maintained by annual government contributions which are appropriated in the Department's operating accounts.

U.S. Information Agency Foreign Service National Separation Liability Trust Fund

Program and Financing (in millions of dollars)

Identification code 19–8341–0–7–602	1999 actual	2000 est.	2001 est.
Budgetary resources available for obligation:			
21.40 Unobligated balance available, start of year	7	7	
22.21 Unobligated balance transferred to other accounts		–7	
23.90 Total budgetary resources available for obligation	7		
24.40 Unobligated balance available, end of year	7		
Change in unpaid obligations:			
72.40 Unpaid obligations, start of year: Obligated balance, start of year	1	1	
73.10 Total new obligations			
73.20 Total outlays (gross)		–1	
74.40 Unpaid obligations, end of year: Obligated balance, end of year	1		
Outlays (gross), detail:			
86.98 Outlays from mandatory balances		1	
Net budget authority and outlays:			
89.00 Budget authority			
90.00 Outlays		1	

This fund paid separation costs for Foreign Service National employees of the United States Information Agency. In 2000, all amounts were transferred to the Department of State, except for amounts associated with the international broadcasting function, which were transferred to the Broadcasting Board of Governors' FSN Separation Liability Trust Fund.

Miscellaneous Trust Funds

Unavailable Collections (in millions of dollars)

Identification code 19–9971–0–7–153	1999 actual	2000 est.	2001 est.
Balance, start of year:			
01.99 Balance, start of year	12	11	
Receipts:			
02.01 Department of State unconditional gift fund	1	2	2
02.02 Deposits, State conditional gift fund	1	1	1
02.99 Total receipts	2	3	3
04.00 Total: Balances and collections	14	14	3
Appropriation:			
05.01 Miscellaneous trust funds	–3	–14	–3
05.99 Subtotal appropriation	–3	–14	–3
07.99 Total balance, end of year	11		

Program and Financing (in millions of dollars)

Identification code 19–9971–0–7–153	1999 actual	2000 est.	2001 est.
Obligations by program activity:			
00.01 Conditional gift fund	2	6	1
00.02 Unconditional gift fund	1	8	2
10.00 Total new obligations (object class 25.2)	3	14	3
Budgetary resources available for obligation:			
22.00 New budget authority (gross)	3	14	3
23.95 Total new obligations	–3	–14	–3
New budget authority (gross), detail:			
Mandatory:			
60.27 Appropriation (trust fund, indefinite)	2	3	3
60.28 Appropriation (unavailable balances)	15	14	3
60.45 Portion precluded from obligation	–14	–3	–3
62.50 Appropriation (total mandatory)	3	14	3
Change in unpaid obligations:			
72.40 Unpaid obligations, start of year: Obligated balance, start of year	3	6	6
73.10 Total new obligations	3	14	3
73.20 Total outlays (gross)		–14	–3
74.40 Unpaid obligations, end of year: Obligated balance, end of year	6	6	6
Outlays (gross), detail:			
86.97 Outlays from new mandatory authority		14	3
Net budget authority and outlays:			
89.00 Budget authority	3	14	3
90.00 Outlays		14	3
Memorandum (non-add) entries:			
92.01 Total investments, start of year: U.S. securities: Par value	3		

Gift fund.—The Department has authority to accept gifts for use in carrying out the Department's functions (22 U.S.C. 809). Among other purposes, funds are used to renovate, furnish, and maintain the Department's diplomatic reception rooms.

Miscellaneous Trust Funds, Information and Exchange Programs

Unavailable Collections (in millions of dollars)

Identification code 19–9972–0–7–154	1999 actual	2000 est.	2001 est.
Balance, start of year:			
01.99 Balance, start of year	4	4	5
Receipts:			
02.01 Proprietary receipts from the public, special international programs		1	1
02.02 Contributions, Educational and Cultural Exchange, USIA	1	1	1
02.03 Interest, Miscellaneous trust funds, USIA	1	1	1
02.99 Total receipts	2	3	3
04.00 Total: Balances and collections	6	7	8
Appropriation:			
05.01 Miscellaneous trust funds	–2	–2	–2
07.99 Total balance, end of year	4	5	6

Program and Financing (in millions of dollars)

Identification code 19–9972–0–7–154	1999 actual	2000 est.	2001 est.
Obligations by program activity:			
10.00 Total new obligations	2	2	2
Budgetary resources available for obligation:			
21.40 Unobligated balance available, start of year	3	3	4
22.00 New budget authority (gross)	2	2	2
23.90 Total budgetary resources available for obligation	5	5	6
23.95 Total new obligations	–2	–2	–2
24.40 Unobligated balance available, end of year	3	4	5
New budget authority (gross), detail:			
Mandatory:			
60.27 Appropriation (trust fund, indefinite)	2	2	2
Change in unpaid obligations:			
72.40 Unpaid obligations, start of year: Obligated balance, start of year	3	3	3
73.10 Total new obligations	2	2	2
73.20 Total outlays (gross)	–2	–2	–2
74.40 Unpaid obligations, end of year: Obligated balance, end of year	3	3	3
Outlays (gross), detail:			
86.97 Outlays from new mandatory authority	2	2	2
Net budget authority and outlays:			
89.00 Budget authority	2	2	2

Credit accounts—Continued

MISCELLANEOUS TRUST FUNDS, INFORMATION AND EXCHANGE PROGRAMS—Continued

Program and Financing (in millions of dollars)—Continued

Identification code 19–9972–0–7–154	1999 actual	2000 est.	2001 est.
90.00 Outlays	2	2	2

Funds advanced by other governments, business concerns, and private organizations to the Department of State are used to send experts abroad to perform requested services; to give foreign nationals scientific, technical, or other training; to purchase films and other products owned or controlled by the Department of State; to replace damaged or destroyed Department of State property; and for international exhibitions (22 U.S.C. 1431–1479; 70 Stat. 778).

Object Classification (in millions of dollars)

Identification code 19–9972–0–7–154	1999 actual	2000 est.	2001 est.
25.2 Other services	1	1	1
41.0 Grants, subsidies, and contributions	1	1	1
99.9 Total new obligations	2	2	2

INTERNATIONAL ORGANIZATIONS AND CONFERENCES

Federal Funds

General and special funds:

CONTRIBUTIONS TO INTERNATIONAL ORGANIZATIONS

For expenses, not otherwise provided for, necessary to meet annual obligations of membership in international multilateral organizations, pursuant to treaties, ratified pursuant to the advice and consent of the Senate, conventions or specific Acts of Congress, [$885,203,000] *$946,060,000*: *Provided*, [That any payment of arrearages under this title shall be directed toward special activities that are mutually agreed upon by the United States and the respective international organization: *Provided further*,] That none of the funds appropriated in this paragraph shall be available for a United States contribution to an international organization for the United States share of interest costs made known to the United States Government by such organization for loans incurred on or after October 1, 1984, through external borrowings: *Provided further*, That funds appropriated under this paragraph may be obligated and expended to pay the full United States assessment to the civil budget of the North Atlantic Treaty Organization. *(Department of State and Related Agencies Appropriations Act, 2000, as enacted by section 1000(a)(1) of the Consolidated Appropriations Act, 2000 (P.L. 106–113).)*

Program and Financing (in millions of dollars)

Identification code 19–1126–0–1–153	1999 actual	2000 est.	2001 est.
Obligations by program activity:			
United Nations and affiliated agencies:			
00.01 Food and Agriculture Organization	81	81	81
00.02 International Atomic Energy Agency	49	49	55
00.03 International Civil Aviation Organization	13	12	12
00.04 International Labor Organization	61	56	59
00.06 International Telecommunications Union	7	7	7
00.07 United Nations	297	256	300
00.08 UN War Crimes Tribunals	21	36	43
00.10 World Health Organization	108	108	108
00.12 World Meteorological Organization	11	10	10
00.13 Other organizations	4	4	4
00.91 Subtotal	652	619	679
Inter-American Organizations:			
01.02 Inter-American Institute for Cooperation on Agriculture	17	17	17
01.03 Organization of American States	55	57	54
01.04 Pan American Health Organization	50	50	51
01.91 Subtotal	122	124	122
Regional Organizations:			
02.02 Asia Pacific Economic Cooperation	1	1	1
02.03 North Atlantic Assembly	1	1	1
02.04 North Atlantic Treaty Organization	40	43	49
02.05 Organization for Economic Cooperation and Development	54	57	57
02.06 South Pacific Commission	1	1	1
02.91 Subtotal	97	103	109
Other International Organizations:			
03.03 World Trade Organization/ General Agreement on Tariffs and Trade	13	13	13
03.26 Organization for Prohibition of Chemical Weapons	12	12	14
03.27 Other International Organizations	10	9	9
03.91 Subtotal	35	34	36
07.01 UN Buydown	28		
10.00 Total new obligations (object class 41.0)	934	880	946
Budgetary resources available for obligation:			
22.00 New budget authority (gross)	934	880	946
23.95 Total new obligations	−934	−880	−946
New budget authority (gross), detail:			
Discretionary:			
40.00 Appropriation	922	885	946
40.76 Reduction pursuant to P.L. 106–113		−5	
42.00 Transferred from other accounts	12		
43.00 Appropriation (total discretionary)	934	880	946
Change in unpaid obligations:			
72.40 Unpaid obligations, start of year: Obligated balance, start of year	119	106	104
73.10 Total new obligations	934	880	946
73.20 Total outlays (gross)	−947	−882	−945
74.40 Unpaid obligations, end of year: Obligated balance, end of year	106	104	105
Outlays (gross), detail:			
86.90 Outlays from new discretionary authority	857	862	927
86.93 Outlays from discretionary balances	90	20	18
87.00 Total outlays (gross)	947	882	945
Net budget authority and outlays:			
89.00 Budget authority	934	880	946
90.00 Outlays	947	882	945

As a member of the organizations listed above, the United States contributes an assessed share of the budgets of those organizations net of certain withholdings. The purpose of this appropriation is to ensure continued American leadership within the United Nations and other international organizations that serve important U.S. interests.

CONTRIBUTIONS FOR INTERNATIONAL PEACEKEEPING ACTIVITIES

For necessary expenses to pay assessed and other expenses of international peacekeeping activities directed to the maintenance or restoration of international peace and security, [$500,000,000, of which not to exceed $20,000,000 shall remain available until September 30, 2001: *Provided*, That none of the funds made available under this Act shall be obligated or expended for any new or expanded United Nations peacekeeping mission unless, at least 15 days in advance of voting for the new or expanded mission in the United Nations Security Council (or in an emergency, as far in advance as is practicable): (1) the Committees on Appropriations of the House of Representatives and the Senate and other appropriate committees of the Congress are notified of the estimated cost and length of the mission, the vital national interest that will be served, and the planned exit strategy; and (2) a reprogramming of funds pursuant to section 605 of this Act is submitted, and the procedures therein followed, setting forth the source of funds that will be used to pay for the cost of the new or expanded mission: *Provided further*, That funds shall be available for peacekeeping expenses only upon a certification by the Secretary of State to the appropriate committees of the Congress that American manufacturers and suppliers are being given opportunities to provide equipment, services, and material for

United Nations peacekeeping activities equal to those being given to foreign manufacturers and suppliers: *Provided further*, That none of the funds made available under this heading are available to pay the United States share of the cost of court monitoring that is part of any United Nations peacekeeping mission] *$738,666,000, to remain available until September 30, 2002. (Department of State and Related Agencies Appropriations Act, 2000, as enacted by section 1000(a)(1) of the Consolidated Appropriations Act, 2000 (P.L. 106–113).)*

Program and Financing (in millions of dollars)

Identification code 19–1124–0–1–153	1999 actual	2000 est.	2001 est.
Obligations by program activity:			
00.01 U.N. disengagement observer force	7	9	18
00.02 U.N. interim force in Lebanon	36	36	37
00.03 U.N. operations in Angola	24		
00.04 U.N. Iraq-Kuwait observer mission	4	4	4
00.05 UN Mission for the referendum in the western Sahara		11	13
00.07 War crimes tribunal—Rwanda	8	11	18
00.08 U.N. operations in the former Yugoslavia	42	45	45
00.09 War crimes tribunal—Yugoslavia	12	13	18
00.11 U.N. mission in East Timor		181	186
00.12 U.N. observer mission in Georgia	7	8	8
00.13 U.N. operations in Haiti		3	
00.16 U.N. force in Cyprus	6	7	7
00.17 U.N. mission in Tajikistan	4	5	5
00.18 U.N. observer mission in Sierra Leone	2	73	118
00.19 U.N. mission in Kosovo	67	87	138
00.20 U.N. liaison mission in the Dem. Republic of the Congo		4	94
00.21 U.N. mission in Ethiopia and Eritria			29
00.22 Angola Monitor Mission		1	1
10.00 Total new obligations (object class 41.0)	219	498	739
Budgetary resources available for obligation:			
22.00 New budget authority (gross)	219	498	739
23.95 Total new obligations	−219	−498	−739
New budget authority (gross), detail:			
Discretionary:			
40.00 Appropriation	231	500	739
40.76 Reduction pursuant to P.L. 106–113		−2	
41.00 Transferred to other accounts	−12		
43.00 Appropriation (total discretionary)	219	498	739
Change in unpaid obligations:			
72.40 Unpaid obligations, start of year: Obligated balance, start of year	137	121	126
73.10 Total new obligations	219	498	739
73.20 Total outlays (gross)	−235	−493	−734
74.40 Unpaid obligations, end of year: Obligated balance, end of year	121	126	131
Outlays (gross), detail:			
86.90 Outlays from new discretionary authority	120	488	724
86.93 Outlays from discretionary balances	115	5	10
87.00 Total outlays (gross)	235	493	734
Net budget authority and outlays:			
89.00 Budget authority	219	498	739
90.00 Outlays	235	493	734

Summary of Budget Authority and Outlays

(in millions of dollars)

	1999 actual	*2000 est.*	*2001 est.*
Enacted/requested:			
Budget Authority	219	498	739
Outlays	235	493	734
Supplemental proposal:			
Budget Authority		107	
Outlays		107	
Total:			
Budget Authority	219	605	739
Outlays	235	600	734

This appropriation provides funds for the United States' share of the expenses associated with United Nations (UN) peacekeeping operations for which costs are distributed among UN members and are based on a scale of assessments. The cost estimates are based on a 25% assessment rate. The purpose of this appropriation is to ensure continued American leadership in support of United Nations peacekeeping activities that serve U.S. interests in promoting international security, stability and democracy.

Arrearage Payments

[For an additional amount for payment of arrearages to meet obligations of authorized membership in international multilateral organizations, and to pay assessed expenses of international peacekeeping activities, $244,000,000, to remain available until expended: *Provided*, That none of the funds appropriated or otherwise made available under this heading for payment of arrearages may be obligated or expended until such time as the share of the total of all assessed contributions for any designated specialized agency of the United Nations does not exceed 22 percent for any single member of the agency, and the designated specialized agencies have achieved zero nominal growth in their biennium budgets for 2000–2001 from the 1998–1999 biennium budget levels of the respective agencies: *Provided futher*, That, notwithstanding the preceding proviso, an additional amount, not to exceed $107,000,000, which is owed by the United Nations to the United States as a reimbursement, including any reimbursement under the Foreign Assistance Act of 1961 or the United Nations Participation Act of 1945, that was owed to the United States before the date of the enactment of this Act shall be applied or used, without fiscal year limitations, to reduce any amount owed by the United States to the United Nations.] *(Department of State and Related Agencies Appropriations Act, 2000, as enacted by section 1000(a)(1) of the Consolidated Appropriations Act, 2000 (P.L. 106–113).)*

Program and Financing (in millions of dollars)

Identification code 19–1130–0–1–153	1999 actual	2000 est.	2001 est.
Obligations by program activity:			
00.01 Direct Program			582
10.00 Total new obligations (object class 41.0)			582
Budgetary resources available for obligation:			
21.40 Unobligated balance available, start of year		475	826
22.00 New budget authority (gross)	475	351	
23.90 Total budgetary resources available for obligation	475	826	826
23.95 Total new obligations			−582
24.40 Unobligated balance available, end of year	475	826	244
New budget authority (gross), detail:			
Discretionary:			
40.00 Appropriation	475	351	
Change in unpaid obligations:			
73.10 Total new obligations			582
73.20 Total outlays (gross)			−582
Outlays (gross), detail:			
86.93 Outlays from discretionary balances			582
Net budget authority and outlays:			
89.00 Budget authority	475	351	
90.00 Outlays			582

This account makes arrears payments to the United Nations and other international organizations.

International Conferences and Contingencies

Program and Financing (in millions of dollars)

Identification code 19–1125–0–1–153	1999 actual	2000 est.	2001 est.
Budgetary resources available for obligation:			
21.40 Unobligated balance available, start of year	1	2	2
24.40 Unobligated balance available, end of year	2	2	2

General and special funds—Continued

INTERNATIONAL CONFERENCES AND CONTINGENCIES—Continued

Program and Financing (in millions of dollars)—Continued

Identification code 19–1125–0–1–153	1999 actual	2000 est.	2001 est.
Change in unpaid obligations:			
72.40 Unpaid obligations, start of year: Obligated balance, start of year	4	3	3
74.40 Unpaid obligations, end of year: Obligated balance, end of year	3	3	3
Net budget authority and outlays:			
89.00 Budget authority			
90.00 Outlays			

INTERNATIONAL COMMISSIONS

Federal Funds

General and special funds:

INTERNATIONAL COMMISSIONS

For necessary expenses, not otherwise provided for, to meet obligations of the United States arising under treaties, or specific Acts of Congress, as follows:

INTERNATIONAL BOUNDARY AND WATER COMMISSION, UNITED STATES AND MEXICO

For necessary expenses for the United States Section of the International Boundary and Water Commission, United States and Mexico, and to comply with laws applicable to the United States Section, including not to exceed $6,000 for representation; as follows:

SALARIES AND EXPENSES

For salaries and expenses, not otherwise provided for, [$19,551,000] *$7,142,000. (Department of State and Related Agencies Appropriations Act, 2000, as enacted by section 1000(a)(1) of the Consolidated Appropriations Act, 2000 (P.L. 106–113).)*

Program and Financing (in millions of dollars)

Identification code 19–1069–0–1–301	1999 actual	2000 est.	2001 est.
Obligations by program activity:			
Direct program:			
00.01 Administration	4	4	5
00.02 Engineering	3	2	2
00.03 Operation and maintenance	13	13	
09.01 Reimbursable program	2	3	
10.00 Total new obligations	22	22	7
Budgetary resources available for obligation:			
22.00 New budget authority (gross)	22	22	7
23.95 Total new obligations	−22	−22	−7
New budget authority (gross), detail:			
Discretionary:			
40.00 Appropriation	20	19	7
68.00 Spending authority from offsetting collections: Offsetting collections (cash)	2	3	
70.00 Total new budget authority (gross)	22	22	7
Change in unpaid obligations:			
72.40 Unpaid obligations, start of year: Obligated balance, start of year	5	5	5
73.10 Total new obligations	22	22	7
73.20 Total outlays (gross)	−22	−22	−9
74.40 Unpaid obligations, end of year: Obligated balance, end of year	5	5	3
Outlays (gross), detail:			
86.90 Outlays from new discretionary authority	18	19	6
86.93 Outlays from discretionary balances	4	4	3
87.00 Total outlays (gross)	22	22	9
Offsets:			
Against gross budget authority and outlays:			
88.00 Offsetting collections (cash) from: Federal sources	−2	−3	
Net budget authority and outlays:			
89.00 Budget authority	20	19	7
90.00 Outlays	20	19	9

Pursuant to treaties between the United States and Mexico and United States law, the U.S. Section of the International Boundary and Water Commission is charged with the identification and solution of boundary and water problems arising along the 1,952-mile common border, including the southern borders of Texas, New Mexico, Arizona and California. Beginning in 2001, the Administration and Engineering are funded by the Salaries and Expenses appropriation. Construction projects and Operations and Maintenance are funded by the Construction, Operations and Maintenance appropriation.

Administration.—Resources under this heading provide for: negotiations and supervision of joint projects—with Mexico to solve international boundary, water, and environmental problems; overall control of the operation of the U.S. section of the Commission; formulation of operating policies and procedures; support to the Border Environmental Cooperation Commission; and, financial management and administrative services to carry out international obligations of the United States, pursuant to treaty and congressional authorization.

Engineering.—Resources under this heading provide for: (a) technical engineering guidance and supervision of the planning, construction, operation and maintenance, and environmental monitoring and compliance of international projects; (b) studies relating to international problems of a continuing nature; and, (c) preliminary surveys and investigations to determine the need for and feasibility of projects for the solution of international problems arising along the boundary.

Operation and maintenance.—This activity is funded under the Construction, Operations and Maintenance appropriation beginning in 2001.

Object Classification (in millions of dollars)

Identification code 19–1069–0–1–301	1999 actual	2000 est.	2001 est.
Direct obligations:			
11.1 Personnel compensation: Full-time permanent	9	8	4
12.1 Civilian personnel benefits	2	2	1
23.3 Communications, utilities, and miscellaneous charges	2	2	1
25.2 Other services	4	4	1
26.0 Supplies and materials	1	1	
31.0 Equipment	1	1	
41.0 Grants, subsidies, and contributions	1	1	
99.0 Subtotal, direct obligations	20	19	7
99.0 Reimbursable obligations	2	3	
99.9 Total new obligations	22	22	7

Personnel Summary

Identification code 19–1069–0–1–301	1999 actual	2000 est.	2001 est.
Direct:			
1001 Total compensable workyears: Full-time equivalent employment	211	232	82
Reimbursable:			
2001 Total compensable workyears: Full-time equivalent employment	18	27	

CONSTRUCTION, *OPERATIONS, AND MAINTENANCE*

For detailed plan preparation and construction of authorized projects, [$5,939,000] *$26,747,000,* to remain available until expended, as authorized by section 24(c) of the State Department Basic Authorities Act of 1956 (22 U.S.C. 2696(c)). *(Department of State and Related Agencies Appropriations Act, 2000, as enacted by section*

1000(a)(1) of the Consolidated Appropriations Act, 2000 (P.L. 106–113).)

Program and Financing (in millions of dollars)

Identification code 19–1078–0–1–301	1999 actual	2000 est.	2001 est.
Obligations by program activity:			
Direct program:			
00.02 San Diego reimbursement	2	....	....
00.03 Rio Grande canalization/flood control/hydraulic studies	1	2	2
00.04 American canal extension	2	2	....
00.05 Boundary-wide radio/equipment replacement	....	....	2
00.07 Facilities renovation/dam safety	1	1	1
00.08 Colorado River boundary/flood control	1	1	1
00.09 Operation and Maintenance			21
01.00 Total, Direct Program	7	6	27
09.01 Reimbursable program	9	25	101
10.00 Total new obligations	16	31	128
Budgetary resources available for obligation:			
21.40 Unobligated balance available, start of year	8	8	8
22.00 New budget authority (gross)	16	31	128
23.90 Total budgetary resources available for obligation	24	39	136
23.95 Total new obligations	−16	−31	−128
24.40 Unobligated balance available, end of year	8	8	8
New budget authority (gross), detail:			
Discretionary:			
40.00 Appropriation	6	6	27
68.00 Spending authority from offsetting collections: Offsetting collections (cash)	10	25	101
70.00 Total new budget authority (gross)	16	31	128
Change in unpaid obligations:			
72.40 Unpaid obligations, start of year: Obligated balance, start of year	22	7	7
73.10 Total new obligations	16	31	128
73.20 Total outlays (gross)	−31	−31	−111
74.40 Unpaid obligations, end of year: Obligated balance, end of year	7	7	24
Outlays (gross), detail:			
86.90 Outlays from new discretionary authority	11	26	106
86.93 Outlays from discretionary balances	20	5	5
87.00 Total outlays (gross)	31	31	111
Offsets:			
Against gross budget authority and outlays:			
88.00 Offsetting collections (cash) from: Federal sources	−10	−25	−101
Net budget authority and outlays:			
89.00 Budget authority	6	6	27
90.00 Outlays	23	6	10

Construction.—This activity provides for the construction of projects to solve international problems of water supply, water quality, sewage treatment, and flood damage reduction. Projects are normally constructed jointly with Mexico. Reimbursements are mostly from EPA to construct or upgrade waste water treatment plants and to provide facilities planning for the Border Environmental Cooperation Commission projects. In 2000, reprogrammed funds for facilities renovation are used to rehabilitate the backwash filter system at the Nogales International Wastewater Treatment Plant.

Operations and Maintenance.—This activity finances the measurement and determination of the national ownership of boundary waters and the distribution thereof, and the U.S. part of the operation and maintenance of sanitation facilities, river channel and levee projects, flood control dams and hydroelectric power, gauging stations, water quality control projects and boundary demarcation, monuments and markers. Through 2000, this activity was funded under the Salaries and Expenses appropriation.

Object Classification (in millions of dollars)

Identification code 19–1078–0–1–301	1999 actual	2000 est.	2001 est.
Direct obligations:			
11.1 Personnel compensation: Full-time permanent	1	1	8
12.1 Civilian personnel benefits			2
23.3 Communications, utilities, and miscellaneous charges			5
25.2 Other services	3	2	7
31.0 Equipment	1	1	3
41.0 Grants, subsidies, and contributions	2	2	2
99.0 Subtotal, direct obligations	7	6	27
99.0 Reimbursable obligations	9	25	101
99.9 Total new obligations	16	31	128

Personnel Summary

Identification code 19–1078–0–1–301	1999 actual	2000 est.	2001 est.
Direct:			
1001 Total compensable workyears: Full-time equivalent employment	14	22	197
Reimbursable:			
2001 Total compensable workyears: Full-time equivalent employment	13	28	48

American Sections, International Commissions

For necessary expenses, not otherwise provided for the International Joint Commission and the International Boundary Commission, United States and Canada, as authorized by treaties between the United States and Canada or Great Britain, and for the Border Environment Cooperation Commission as authorized by Public Law 103–182, [$5,733,000] *$8,891,000*, of which not to exceed $9,000 shall be available for representation expenses incurred by the International Joint Commission. *(Department of State and Related Agencies Appropriations Act, 2000, as enacted by section 1000(a)(1) of the Consolidated Appropriations Act, 2000 (P.L. 106–113).)*

Program and Financing (in millions of dollars)

Identification code 19–1082–0–1–301	1999 actual	2000 est.	2001 est.
Obligations by program activity:			
00.01 International Boundary Commission	1	1	1
00.02 International Joint Commission	3	3	6
00.05 Border Environment Cooperation Commission	2	2	2
10.00 Total new obligations	6	6	9
Budgetary resources available for obligation:			
22.00 New budget authority (gross)	6	6	9
23.95 Total new obligations	−6	−6	−9
New budget authority (gross), detail:			
Discretionary:			
40.00 Appropriation	6	6	9
Change in unpaid obligations:			
72.40 Unpaid obligations, start of year: Obligated balance, start of year	2	2	2
73.10 Total new obligations	6	6	9
73.20 Total outlays (gross)	−6	−6	−8
74.40 Unpaid obligations, end of year: Obligated balance, end of year	2	2	3
Outlays (gross), detail:			
86.90 Outlays from new discretionary authority	5	4	6
86.93 Outlays from discretionary balances	1	2	2
87.00 Total outlays (gross)	6	6	8
Net budget authority and outlays:			
89.00 Budget authority	6	6	9
90.00 Outlays	6	6	8

These funds are used for payment of the U.S. share of the expenses of:

General and special funds—Continued

AMERICAN SECTIONS, INTERNATIONAL COMMISSIONS—Continued

International Boundary Commission.—The Commission, in accordance with existing treaties, maintains the integrity of a well-delineated boundary between the United States and Canada by: surveying, inspecting, and clearing the boundary; repairing or replacing monuments; regulating construction crossing the boundary; and, serving as the official U.S. Government source for boundary-specific positional/cartographic data.

International Joint Commission.—Pursuant to the Boundary Waters Treaty of 1909, the Commission approves, regulates, and monitors structures in boundary waters and transboundary streams and investigates matters referred to it by the United States and Canada that principally include transboundary environmental issues.

Border Environment Cooperation Commission.—This bilateral Commission works with States and local communities to provide technical financial planning assistance and to review and certify project proposals for the purpose of developing effective solutions to environmental problems in the border region.

Object Classification (in millions of dollars)

Identification code 19–1082–0–1–301	1999 actual	2000 est.	2001 est.
11.1 Personnel compensation: Full-time permanent	3	2	3
25.2 Other services	2	2	4
99.0 Subtotal, direct obligations	5	4	7
99.5 Below reporting threshold	1	2	2
99.9 Total new obligations	6	6	9

Personnel Summary

Identification code 19–1082–0–1–301	1999 actual	2000 est.	2001 est.
1001 Total compensable workyears: Full-time equivalent employment	26	26	28

INTERNATIONAL FISHERIES COMMISSIONS

For necessary expenses for [international fisheries commissions] *International Fisheries Commissions*, not otherwise provided for, as authorized by law, [$15,549,000] *$19,392,000*: *Provided*, That the United States' share of such expenses may be advanced to the respective commissions, pursuant to 31 U.S.C. 3324. *(Department of State and Related Agencies Appropriations Act, 2000, as enacted by section 1000(a)(1) of the Consolidated Appropriations Act, 2000 (P.L. 106–113).)*

Program and Financing (in millions of dollars)

Identification code 19–1087–0–1–302	1999 actual	2000 est.	2001 est.
Obligations by program activity:			
00.02 Inter-American Tropical Tuna Commission	3	3	3
00.06 Great Lakes Fishery Commission	8	9	12
00.09 Pacific Salmon Commission	2	1	2
00.10 Other Commissions and Marine Science Organizations	2	2	2
10.00 Total new obligations	15	15	19
Budgetary resources available for obligation:			
22.00 New budget authority (gross)	15	15	19
23.95 Total new obligations	−15	−15	−19
New budget authority (gross), detail:			
Discretionary:			
40.00 Appropriation	15	15	19
Change in unpaid obligations:			
72.40 Unpaid obligations, start of year: Obligated balance, start of year	1	2	2
73.10 Total new obligations	15	15	19
73.20 Total outlays (gross)	−14	−15	−19
74.40 Unpaid obligations, end of year: Obligated balance, end of year	2	2	2
Outlays (gross), detail:			
86.90 Outlays from new discretionary authority	13	15	19
86.93 Outlays from discretionary balances	1		
87.00 Total outlays (gross)	14	15	19
Net budget authority and outlays:			
89.00 Budget authority	15	15	19
90.00 Outlays	14	15	19

This appropriation provides the U.S. share of operating expenses for nine international fisheries commissions and organizations, three international marine science organizations, one sea turtle commission, and travel expenses of the U.S. commissioners and their advisors. These international fisheries organizations conduct continuing scientific studies of fishery stocks and recommend conservation measures to member governments based on the results of these studies. In addition, the Great Lakes Fishery Commission carries on a program of lamprey eradication and control. The marine science organizations propose fishery and oceanographic investigations and disseminate the results to the member governments.

Object Classification (in millions of dollars)

Identification code 19–1087–0–1–302	1999 actual	2000 est.	2001 est.
25.2 Other services	1	1	1
41.0 Grants, subsidies, and contributions	14	14	18
99.9 Total new obligations	15	15	19

OTHER

Federal Funds

General and special funds:

MIGRATION AND REFUGEE ASSISTANCE

For expenses, not otherwise provided for, necessary to enable the Secretary of State to provide, as authorized by law, [a contribution] *contributions* to the International Committee of the Red Cross, assistance to refugees, including contributions to the International Organization for Migration and the United Nations High Commissioner for Refugees, and other activities to meet refugee and migration needs; salaries and expenses of personnel and dependents as authorized by the Foreign Service Act of 1980; allowances as authorized by sections 5921 through 5925 of title 5, United States Code; purchase and hire of passenger motor vehicles; and services as authorized by section 3109 of title 5, United States Code, [$625,000,000, of which $21,000,000 shall become available for obligation on September 30, 2000, and remain available until expended: *Provided*, That] *$658,212,000, of which* not more than [$13,800,000] *$14,852,000* shall be available for administrative expenses[: *Provided further*, That] *, and* not less than $60,000,000 shall be made available for refugees from the former Soviet Union and Eastern Europe and other refugees resettling in Israel. *(Foreign Operations, Export Financing, and Related Programs Appropriations Act, 2000, as enacted by section 1000(a)(2) of the Consolidated Appropriations Act, 2000 (P.L. 106–113).)*

Program and Financing (in millions of dollars)

Identification code 19–1143–0–1–151	1999 actual	2000 est.	2001 est.
Obligations by program activity:			
Direct program:			
00.01 Overseas assistance	552	582	457
00.02 U.S. refugee admissions program	104	133	126
00.03 Refugees to Israel	70	60	60
00.04 Administrative expenses	13	14	15
09.01 Reimbursable program	2	2	2
10.00 Total new obligations	741	791	660

Budgetary resources available for obligation:			
21.40 Unobligated balance available, start of year	3	168	
22.00 New budget authority (gross)	906	623	660
23.90 Total budgetary resources available for obligation	909	791	660
23.95 Total new obligations	−741	−791	−660
24.40 Unobligated balance available, end of year	168		
New budget authority (gross), detail:			
Discretionary:			
40.00 Appropriation	906	623	658
40.76 Reduction pursuant to P.L. 106–113		−2	
41.00 Transferred to other accounts	−2		
43.00 Appropriation (total discretionary)	904	621	658
68.00 Spending authority from offsetting collections: Offsetting collections (cash)	2	2	2
70.00 Total new budget authority (gross)	906	623	660
Change in unpaid obligations:			
72.40 Unpaid obligations, start of year: Obligated balance, start of year	211	294	268
73.10 Total new obligations	741	791	660
73.20 Total outlays (gross)	−658	−817	−709
74.40 Unpaid obligations, end of year: Obligated balance, end of year	294	268	219
Outlays (gross), detail:			
86.90 Outlays from new discretionary authority	473	423	463
86.93 Outlays from discretionary balances	185	394	246
87.00 Total outlays (gross)	658	817	709
Offsets:			
Against gross budget authority and outlays:			
88.00 Offsetting collections (cash) from: Federal sources	−2	−2	−2
Net budget authority and outlays:			
89.00 Budget authority	904	621	658
90.00 Outlays	656	815	707

Overseas Assistance.—This program addresses the protection and assistance needs of refugees, migrants and conflict victims worldwide. Funds are used primarily to support the programs of international organizations, including the United Nations High Commissioner for Refugees, the United Nations Relief and Works Agency for Palestine Refugees, the World Food Program, the International Organization for Migration, and the International Committee of the Red Cross, as well as non-governmental organizations. When possible, funds are used to resolve refugee situations through repatriation or local integration.

Refugees to Israel.—These funds provide a grant to the United Israel Appeal to assist Jewish refugees resettling in Israel.

U.S. Refugee Admissions.—This program provides overseas cultural orientation, processing, transportation, and initial placement for up to 80,000 refugees and Amerasian immigrants resettling in the United States. These activities are carried out primarily by the International Organization for Migration and U.S. private voluntary agencies.

Administrative Expenses.—These funds finance the salaries and operating expenses in Washington and overseas for the Bureau of Population, Refugees, and Migration. (Note: Funds for the salaries and support costs of the six positions dedicated to international population policy and coordination are requested under the Department of State's Diplomatic and Consular Programs appropriation.)

Object Classification (in millions of dollars)

Identification code 19–1143–0–1–151	1999 actual	2000 est.	2001 est.
Direct obligations:			
11.1 Personnel compensation: Full-time permanent	7	7	8
12.1 Civilian personnel benefits	2	2	2
21.0 Travel and transportation of persons	1	1	1
23.2 Rental payments to others	1	1	1
25.2 Other services	3	2	2
41.0 Grants, subsidies, and contributions	725	776	644
99.0 Subtotal, direct obligations	739	789	658
99.0 Reimbursable obligations	2	2	2
99.9 Total new obligations	741	791	660

Personnel Summary

Identification code 19–1143–0–1–151	1999 actual	2000 est.	2001 est.
1001 Total compensable workyears: Full-time equivalent employment	95	109	110

United States Emergency Refugee and Migration Assistance Fund

For necessary expenses to carry out the provisions of section 2(c) of the Migration and Refugee Assistance Act of 1962, as amended (22 U.S.C. 260(c)), [$12,500,000] *$20,000,000*, to remain available until expended: *Provided*, That the funds made available under this heading are appropriated notwithstanding the provisions contained in section 2(c)(2) of the Act which would limit the amount of funds which could be appropriated for this purpose. *(Foreign Operations, Export Financing, and Related Programs Appropriations Act, 2000, as enacted by section 1000(a)(2) of the Consolidated Appropriations Act, 2000 (P.L. 106–113).)*

Program and Financing (in millions of dollars)

Identification code 11–0040–0–1–151	1999 actual	2000 est.	2001 est.
Obligations by program activity:			
10.00 Total new obligations	89	100	70
Budgetary resources available for obligation:			
21.40 Unobligated balance available, start of year	79	185	98
22.00 New budget authority (gross)	195	13	20
23.90 Total budgetary resources available for obligation	274	198	118
23.95 Total new obligations	−89	−100	−70
24.40 Unobligated balance available, end of year	185	98	48
New budget authority (gross), detail:			
Discretionary:			
40.00 Appropriation	195	13	20
Change in unpaid obligations:			
72.40 Unpaid obligations, start of year: Obligated balance, start of year	22	34	30
73.10 Total new obligations	89	100	70
73.20 Total outlays (gross)	−77	−104	−90
74.40 Unpaid obligations, end of year: Obligated balance, end of year	34	30	10
Outlays (gross), detail:			
86.90 Outlays from new discretionary authority	42	1	2
86.93 Outlays from discretionary balances	35	103	88
87.00 Total outlays (gross)	77	104	90
Net budget authority and outlays:			
89.00 Budget authority	195	13	20
90.00 Outlays	77	104	90

The Emergency fund enables the President to provide emergency assistance for unexpected, urgent refugee and migration needs worldwide.

International Narcotics Control and Law Enforcement

For necessary expenses to carry out section 481 of the Foreign Assistance Act of 1961, [$305,000,000, of which $21,000,000 shall become available for obligation on September 30, 2000, and] *$312,000,000, to* remain available until [expended] *September 30, 2002: Provided*, [That of this amount not less than $10,000,000 should be made available for Law Enforcement Training and Demand Reduction: *Provided further*, That any funds made available under this heading for anti-crime programs and activities shall be made

General and special funds—Continued

INTERNATIONAL NARCOTICS CONTROL AND LAW ENFORCEMENT—Continued

available subject to the regular notification procedures of the Committees on Appropriations: *Provided further,*] That during fiscal year [2000] *2001*, the Department of State may also use the authority of section 608 of the Foreign Assistance Act of 1961, without regard to its restrictions, to receive excess property from an agency of the United States Government for the purpose of providing it to a foreign country under chapter 8 of part I of that Act subject to the regular notification procedures of the Committees on Appropriations[: *Provided further,* That in addition to any funds previously made available to establish and operate the International Law Enforcement Academy for the Western Hemisphere, not less than $5,000,000 shall be made available to establish and operate the International Law Enforcement Academy for the Western Hemisphere at the deBremmond Training Center in Roswell, New Mexico]. *(Foreign Operations, Export Financing, and Related Programs Appropriations Act, 2000, as enacted by section 1000(a)(2) of the Consolidated Appropriations Act, 2000 (P.L. 106–113).)*

Program and Financing (in millions of dollars)

Identification code 19–1022–0–1–151		1999 actual	2000 est.	2001 est.
	Obligations by program activity:			
	Country programs:			
00.01	Bahamas	1	1	1
00.02	Bolivia	31	48	52
00.03	Brazil	1	2	2
00.04	Colombia	186	50	35
00.05	Ecuador	1	1	1
00.06	Guatemala	3	3	3
00.07	Jamaica	1	1	1
00.08	Mexico	8	10	10
00.09	Peru	37	48	48
00.10	Venezuela	1	1	1
00.11	Latin American regional programs	24	9	9
00.12	Laos	4	4	4
00.13	Thailand	3	3	3
00.14	Pakistan	2	3	4
00.16	Asia/Africa regional programs	3	6	5
00.18	Inter-regional aviation support	51	50	50
00.91	Subtotal, country programs	357	240	229
01.01	Anticrime programs	57	30	25
01.02	UN Civilian Police Contingent			10
01.03	Bosnia police programs	14		
01.04	Kosovo Civilian Police	41		
01.05	Africa regional anti-crime programs			10
01.91	Subtotal, anti-crime	112	30	45
02.01	Law enforcement training and demand reduction	8	9	10
03.01	Systems support and upgrades	3	5	4
04.01	Program development and support	9	9	12
07.01	International organization programs	9	12	12
08.01	Mycoherbicide	23		
09.01	Reimbursable program	22	4	
10.00	Total new obligations	543	309	312
	Budgetary resources available for obligation:			
21.40	Unobligated balance available, start of year		22	29
22.00	New budget authority (gross)	555	316	312
22.10	Resources available from recoveries of prior year obligations	10		
23.90	Total budgetary resources available for obligation	565	338	341
23.95	Total new obligations	-543	-309	-312
24.40	Unobligated balance available, end of year	22	29	29
	New budget authority (gross), detail:			
	Discretionary:			
40.00	Appropriation	284	305	312
40.15	Appropriation (emergency)	233		
40.76	Reduction pursuant to P.L. 106–113		-1	
41.00	Transferred to other accounts	-71		
42.00	Transferred from other accounts	87	8	
43.00	Appropriation (total discretionary)	533	312	312
68.00	Spending authority from offsetting collections: Offsetting collections (cash)	22	4	
70.00	Total new budget authority (gross)	555	316	312
	Change in unpaid obligations:			
72.40	Unpaid obligations, start of year: Obligated balance, start of year	285	533	456
73.10	Total new obligations	543	309	312
73.20	Total outlays (gross)	-285	-386	-339
73.45	Adjustments in unexpired accounts	-10		
74.40	Unpaid obligations, end of year: Obligated balance, end of year	533	456	429
	Outlays (gross), detail:			
86.90	Outlays from new discretionary authority	159	109	109
86.93	Outlays from discretionary balances	126	277	230
87.00	Total outlays (gross)	285	386	339
	Offsets:			
	Against gross budget authority and outlays:			
	Offsetting collections (cash) from:			
88.00	Federal sources	-7		
88.40	Non-Federal sources	-15	-4	
88.90	Total, offsetting collections (cash)	-22	-4	
	Net budget authority and outlays:			
89.00	Budget authority	533	312	312
90.00	Outlays	265	382	339

This appropriation provides assistance to foreign countries and international organizations to help them develop and implement policies and programs that strengthen institutional counternarcotics law enforcement and judicial capabilities to control illegal narcotics production, processing, and trafficking. This appropriation also provides counternarcotics-related economic development and military assistance, as well as assistance for anti-crime purposes. The funding levels for Bolivia, Colombia, and Peru for 1999 do not reflect funds transferred to AID for alternative development programs in those countries.

Object Classification (in millions of dollars)

Identification code 19–1022–0–1–151		1999 actual	2000 est.	2001 est.
	Direct obligations:			
	Personnel compensation:			
11.1	Full-time permanent	8	8	8
11.3	Other than full-time permanent	1	1	1
11.9	Total personnel compensation	9	9	9
12.1	Civilian personnel benefits	2	2	2
21.0	Travel and transportation of persons	2	2	2
23.2	Rental payments to others	2	2	2
25.2	Other services	118	67	69
31.0	Equipment	2	2	2
41.0	Grants, subsidies, and contributions	386	221	226
99.0	Subtotal, direct obligations	521	305	312
99.0	Reimbursable obligations	22	4	
99.9	Total new obligations	543	309	312

Personnel Summary

Identification code 19–1022–0–1–151		1999 actual	2000 est.	2001 est.
1001	Total compensable workyears: Full-time equivalent employment	133	159	159

ASSISTANCE TO PLAN COLOMBIA

For an additional amount to carry out section 481 of the Foreign Assistance Act of 1961, $256,000,000, to remain available until expended, to support Plan Colombia: Provided, That such funds shall be in addition to amounts otherwise available for such purposes: Provided further, That section 482(b) of such Act shall not apply to such funds: Provided further, That for purposes of supporting Plan Colombia, any agency of the United States to which funds are transferred under any authority of such Act may utilize, in addition to any authorities available for carrying out section 481, any authorities available to that agency for carrying out related activities, including *utilization of such funds for administrative expenses: Provided further, That funds obligated prior to the date of enactment of this Act for administrative expenses in support of Plan Colombia may be finally charged to funds made available for such purposes by this Act: Provided further, That any limitations on amounts that an agency may use for a particular purpose or activity shall not apply to funds made available under this Act to support Plan Colombia.*

Program and Financing (in millions of dollars)

Identification code 19–1154–0–1–151	1999 actual	2000 est.	2001 est.
Obligations by program activity:			
01.01 Push into Southern Colombia			66
01.02 Drug Trafficking Interdiction			61
01.03 Colombian National Police Support			28
01.04 Economic Development			53
01.05 Boost Governing Capacity			48
10.00 Total new obligations			256
Budgetary resources available for obligation:			
22.00 New budget authority (gross)			256
23.95 Total new obligations			−256
New budget authority (gross), detail:			
Discretionary:			
40.00 Appropriation			256
Change in unpaid obligations:			
73.10 Total new obligations			256
73.20 Total outlays (gross)			−81
74.40 Unpaid obligations, end of year: Obligated balance, end of year			175
Outlays (gross), detail:			
86.90 Outlays from new discretionary authority			81
Net budget authority and outlays:			
89.00 Budget authority			256
90.00 Outlays			81

Summary of Budget Authority and Outlays

(in millions of dollars)

Enacted/requested:	*1999 actual*	*2000 est.*	*2001 est.*
Budget Authority			256
Outlays			81
Supplemental proposal:			
Budget Authority		818	
Outlays		249	303
Total:			
Budget Authority		818	256
Outlays		249	384

This account would fund a second year of United States assistance to Plan Colombia. These funds would support the Colombian Army's push into southern Colombia in support of the Colombian National Police, enhance drug interdiction in Colombia and the region, increase support to the Colombian National Police, provide for economic development in Colombia and the Andean region, and boost Colombia's local and national government capacity. A 2000 supplemental package to initiate United States support for these programs is being proposed, as detailed in a separate chapter.

Object Classification (in millions of dollars)

Identification code 19–1154–0–1–151	1999 actual	2000 est.	2001 est.
25.8 Subsistence and support of persons			140
26.0 Supplies and materials			3
31.0 Equipment			36
32.0 Land and structures			5
41.0 Grants, subsidies, and contributions			72
99.9 Total new obligations			256

Anti-Terrorism Assistance

Program and Financing (in millions of dollars)

Identification code 19–0114–0–1–152	1999 actual	2000 est.	2001 est.
Change in unpaid obligations:			
72.40 Unpaid obligations, start of year: Obligated balance, start of year	4	4	2
74.40 Unpaid obligations, end of year: Obligated balance, end of year	4	2	
Outlays (gross), detail:			
86.93 Outlays from discretionary balances		2	2
Net budget authority and outlays:			
89.00 Budget authority			
90.00 Outlays		2	2

This appropriation provided for a program of anti-terrorism assistance and training for foreign civilian law enforcement authorities as part of the President's overall program to combat international terrorism. Starting in 1997, these activities were funded from the Non-Proliferation, Anti-Terrorism, Demining and Related Programs account. This schedule reflects the spend-out of prior year obligations.

Payment to the Asia Foundation

For a grant to the Asia Foundation, as authorized by section 501 of Public Law 101–246, [$8,250,000] *$10,000,000*, to remain available until expended, as authorized by section 24(c) of the State Department Basic Authorities Act of 1956 (22 U.S.C. 2696(c)). *(Department of State and Related Agencies Appropriations Act, 2000, as enacted by section 1000(a)(1) of the Consolidated Appropriations Act, 2000 (P.L. 106–113).)*

Program and Financing (in millions of dollars)

Identification code 19–0525–0–1–154	1999 actual	2000 est.	2001 est.
Obligations by program activity:			
00.01 Program activities and operations	10	8	10
10.00 Total new obligations	10	8	10
Budgetary resources available for obligation:			
21.40 Unobligated balance available, start of year	2		
22.00 New budget authority (gross)	8	8	10
23.90 Total budgetary resources available for obligation	10	8	10
23.95 Total new obligations	−10	−8	−10
New budget authority (gross), detail:			
Discretionary:			
40.00 Appropriation	8	8	10
Change in unpaid obligations:			
72.40 Unpaid obligations, start of year: Obligated balance, start of year	1	4	4
73.10 Total new obligations	10	8	10
73.20 Total outlays (gross)	−7	−8	−10
74.40 Unpaid obligations, end of year: Obligated balance, end of year	4	4	4
Outlays (gross), detail:			
86.90 Outlays from new discretionary authority	7	7	9
86.93 Outlays from discretionary balances		1	1
87.00 Total outlays (gross)	7	8	10
Net budget authority and outlays:			
89.00 Budget authority	8	8	10
90.00 Outlays	7	8	10

The Asia Foundation supports democratic initiatives, economic reform, rule of law programs, and closer U.S.-Asian relations by providing grants to institutions in Asia.

General and special funds—Continued

EDUCATIONAL AND CULTURAL EXCHANGE PROGRAMS

For expenses of educational and cultural exchange programs, as authorized by the Mutual Educational and Cultural Exchange Act of 1961, as amended (22 U.S.C. 2451 et seq.), and Reorganization Plan No. 2 of 1977, as amended (91 Stat. 1636), [$205,000,000] *$225,000,000*, to remain available until expended as authorized by section 105 of such Act of 1961 (22 U.S.C. 2455): *Provided*, That not to exceed $800,000, to remain available until expended, may be credited to this appropriation from fees or other payments received from or in connection with English teaching and educational advising and counseling programs as authorized by section 810 of the United States Information and Educational Exchange Act of 1948 (22 U.S.C. 1475e). *(Department of State and Related Agencies Appropriations Act, 2000, as enacted by section 1000(a)(1) of the Consolidated Appropriations Act, 2000 (P.L. 106–113).)*

Program and Financing (in millions of dollars)

Identification code 19–0209–0–1–154	1999 actual	2000 est.	2001 est.
Obligations by program activity:			
Direct program:			
00.01 Academic Programs	122	124	139
00.02 Professional/Cultural Exchanges	67	63	61
00.03 Freedom Support Act Exchanges	88	17	
00.04 SEED Exchanges	6	3	
00.05 Cyprus	1	1	
00.06 Exchanges Support	22	25	25
01.00 Subtotal, Direct Obligations	306	233	225
09.00 Reimbursable program	4	3	3
10.00 Total new obligations	310	236	228
Budgetary resources available for obligation:			
21.40 Unobligated balance available, start of year	32	29	
22.00 New budget authority (gross)	296	207	228
22.10 Resources available from recoveries of prior year obligations	4		
22.22 Unobligated balance transferred from other accounts	5		
23.90 Total budgetary resources available for obligation	337	236	228
23.95 Total new obligations	–310	–236	–228
24.40 Unobligated balance available, end of year	29		
New budget authority (gross), detail:			
Discretionary:			
40.00 Appropriation	201	205	225
40.76 Reduction pursuant to P.L. 106–113		–1	
41.00 Transferred to other accounts	–2		
42.00 Transferred from other accounts	93		
43.00 Appropriation (total discretionary)	292	204	225
68.00 Spending authority from offsetting collections: Offsetting collections (cash)	4	3	3
70.00 Total new budget authority (gross)	296	207	228
Change in unpaid obligations:			
72.40 Unpaid obligations, start of year: Obligated balance, start of year	213	243	234
73.10 Total new obligations	310	236	228
73.20 Total outlays (gross)	–276	–245	–226
73.40 Adjustments in expired accounts (net)	–1		
73.45 Adjustments in unexpired accounts	–4		
74.40 Unpaid obligations, end of year: Obligated balance, end of year	243	234	236
Outlays (gross), detail:			
86.90 Outlays from new discretionary authority	148	105	116
86.93 Outlays from discretionary balances	128	142	110
87.00 Total outlays (gross)	276	245	226
Offsets:			
Against gross budget authority and outlays:			
Offsetting collections (cash) from:			
88.00 Federal sources		–3	–3
88.40 Non-Federal sources	–4		
88.90 Total, offsetting collections (cash)	–4	–3	–3
Net budget authority and outlays:			
89.00 Budget authority	292	204	225
90.00 Outlays	272	242	223

Summary of Budget Authority and Outlays

(in millions of dollars)

Enacted/requested:	1999 actual	2000 est.	2001 est.
Budget Authority	292	204	225
Outlays	272	244	223
Supplemental proposal:			
Budget Authority		4	
Outlays		2	2
Total:			
Budget Authority	292	208	225
Outlays	272	246	225

This appropriation provides funding for international exchange programs authorized by the Mutual Educational and Cultural Exchange Act of 1961, as amended, to support U.S. foreign, economic, and security policy objectives and to assist in the development of friendly, sympathetic, and peaceful relations between the United States and other countries. These goals are addressed by fostering increased mutual understanding through international exchange and training activities. Programs under this appropriation include:

Academic programs.—Includes the J. William Fulbright Educational Exchange Program for the exchange of students, scholars, and teachers between the United States and foreign countries; the Hubert H. Humphrey Fellowship Program of academic study and internships in the United States for mid-career professionals from developing countries; specially targeted graduate- and postdoctoral-level studies and research activities; U.S. overseas educational advising centers; American overseas research centers; and programs in support of the study of the United States in other countries designed to promote better foreign understanding of the United States.

Professional/Cultural Programs.—Includes the International Visitor Program which supports professional development travel to the United States by current and emerging foreign leaders to obtain firsthand knowledge about the United States, its people, politics and culture; cooperative programs with non-governmental organizations, such as the Citizen Exchange Program which awards grants to U.S. non-profit organizations for professional, cultural, institutional, and grassroots community exchanges with foreign counterparts; and other programs.

Interagency Appropriation Transfers.—Includes democracy and free-market development programs for the exchange of students, scholars, and professionals between the United States and the Newly Independent States of the former Soviet Union (NIS) and Central and Eastern Europe under the Freedom Support Act of 1992 and the Support for East European Democracy Act of 1988 (funded through appropriation transfers from USAID).

Exchanges Support.—Includes all domestic staff and support costs related to exchanges managed by the Bureau of Educational and Cultural Affairs; overseas staff and support costs related to English teaching abroad; government-wide exchanges coordination; and performance measurement of programs in accordance with the Government Performance and Results Act of 1993.

Object Classification (in millions of dollars)

Identification code 19–0209–0–1–154	1999 actual	2000 est.	2001 est.
Direct obligations:			
11.1 Personnel compensation: Full-time permanent	16	17	18
12.1 Civilian personnel benefits	5	6	6
21.0 Travel and transportation of persons	9	9	9
25.2 Other services	15	14	15
41.0 Grants, subsidies, and contributions	261	187	177
99.0 Subtotal, direct obligations	306	233	225

99.0 Reimbursable obligations	4	3	3
99.9 Total new obligations	310	236	228

Personnel Summary

Identification code 19–0209–0–1–154	1999 actual	2000 est.	2001 est.
1001 Total compensable workyears: Full-time equivalent employment	296	296	296

NATIONAL ENDOWMENT FOR DEMOCRACY

For grants made by the Department of State to the National Endowment for Democracy as authorized by the National Endowment for Democracy Act, [$31,000,000] *$32,000,000* to remain available until expended. *(Department of State and Related Agencies Appropriations Act, 2000, as enacted by section 1000(a)(1) of the Consolidated Appropriations Act, 2000 (P.L. 106–113).)*

Program and Financing (in millions of dollars)

Identification code 19–0210–0–1–154	1999 actual	2000 est.	2001 est.
Obligations by program activity:			
10.00 Total new obligations	35	31	32
Budgetary resources available for obligation:			
22.00 New budget authority (gross)	35	31	32
23.95 Total new obligations	−35	−31	−32
New budget authority (gross), detail:			
Discretionary:			
40.00 Appropriation	31	31	32
42.00 Transferred from other accounts	4		
43.00 Appropriation (total discretionary)	34	31	32
Change in unpaid obligations:			
72.40 Unpaid obligations, start of year: Obligated balance, start of year	28	31	29
73.10 Total new obligations	35	31	32
73.20 Total outlays (gross)	−32	−33	−31
74.40 Unpaid obligations, end of year: Obligated balance, end of year	31	29	30
Outlays (gross), detail:			
86.90 Outlays from new discretionary authority	16	15	15
86.93 Outlays from discretionary balances	16	18	16
87.00 Total outlays (gross)	32	33	31
Net budget authority and outlays:			
89.00 Budget authority	35	31	32
90.00 Outlays	32	33	31

The National Endowment for Democracy (NED) is a private, nonprofit corporation established in the District of Columbia to encourage and strengthen the development of democratic institutions and processes internationally. NED supports democratic initiatives in six regions of the world: Africa, Asia, Central and Eastern Europe, Latin America, the Middle East and the NIS.

The National Endowment for Democracy Act provides for an annual grant to the Endowment to fulfill the purposes of the Act. The Endowment does not carry out programs directly but its Board approves annual grants to the American Center for International Solidarity, the Center for International Private Enterprise, the International Republican Institute, the National Democratic Institute for International Affairs, and scores of indigenous organizations working to promote civic education, human rights, independent media, and other democratic processes and values.

EAST-WEST CENTER

To enable the Secretary of State to provide for carrying out the provisions of the Center for Cultural and Technical Interchange Between East and West Act of 1960 (22 U.S.C. 2054–2057), by grant to the Center for Cultural and Technical Interchange Between East and West in the State of Hawaii, $12,500,000: *Provided*, That none of the funds appropriated herein shall be used to pay any salary, or enter into any contract providing for the payment thereof, in excess of the rate authorized by 5 U.S.C. 5376. *(Department of State and Related Agencies Appropriations Act, 2000, as enacted by section 1000(a)(1) of the Consolidated Appropriations Act, 2000 (P.L. 106–113).)*

Program and Financing (in millions of dollars)

Identification code 19–0202–0–1–154	1999 actual	2000 est.	2001 est.
Obligations by program activity:			
10.00 Total new obligations	13	12	13
Budgetary resources available for obligation:			
22.00 New budget authority (gross)	13	12	13
23.95 Total new obligations	−13	−12	−13
New budget authority (gross), detail:			
Discretionary:			
40.00 Appropriation	13	12	13
Change in unpaid obligations:			
72.40 Unpaid obligations, start of year: Obligated balance, start of year	1	1	
73.10 Total new obligations	13	12	13
73.20 Total outlays (gross)	−12	−13	−13
74.40 Unpaid obligations, end of year: Obligated balance, end of year	1		
Outlays (gross), detail:			
86.90 Outlays from new discretionary authority	12	12	13
86.93 Outlays from discretionary balances		1	
87.00 Total outlays (gross)	12	13	13
Net budget authority and outlays:			
89.00 Budget authority	13	12	13
90.00 Outlays	12	13	13

The Center for Cultural and Technical Interchange Between East and West (East-West Center) is a national educational institution administered by a public, nonprofit educational corporation. The Center promotes better relations and understanding between the United States and the nations of Asia and the Pacific through cooperative programs of research, study, and training, which bring qualified persons from the countries of the area to work jointly on problems of mutual concern.

NORTH/SOUTH CENTER

To enable the Secretary of State to provide for carrying out the provisions of the North/South Center Act of 1991 (22 U.S.C. 2075), by grant to an educational institution in Florida known as the North/South Center, $1,750,000, to remain available until expended. *(Department of State and Related Agencies Appropriations Act, 2000, as enacted by section 1000(a)(1) of the Consolidated Appropriations Act, 2000 (P.L. 106–113).)*

Program and Financing (in millions of dollars)

Identification code 19–0203–0–1–154	1999 actual	2000 est.	2001 est.
Obligations by program activity:			
10.00 Total new obligations	2	2	2
Budgetary resources available for obligation:			
22.00 New budget authority (gross)	2	2	2
23.95 Total new obligations	−2	−2	−2
New budget authority (gross), detail:			
Discretionary:			
40.00 Appropriation	2	2	2

General and special funds—Continued

NORTH/SOUTH CENTER—Continued

Program and Financing (in millions of dollars)—Continued

Identification code 19–0203–0–1–154	1999 actual	2000 est.	2001 est.
Change in unpaid obligations:			
72.40 Unpaid obligations, start of year: Obligated balance, start of year	3	2	2
73.10 Total new obligations	2	2	2
73.20 Total outlays (gross)	−2	−2	−2
74.40 Unpaid obligations, end of year: Obligated balance, end of year	2	2	2
Outlays (gross), detail:			
86.90 Outlays from new discretionary authority	1	1	1
86.93 Outlays from discretionary balances	1	1	1
87.00 Total outlays (gross)	2	2	2
Net budget authority and outlays:			
89.00 Budget authority	2	2	2
90.00 Outlays	2	2	2

The Center for Cultural and Technical Interchange Between North and South (North/South Center) is a national educational institution that promotes better relations between the U.S. and the nations of Latin America, the Caribbean, and Canada by bringing together scholars and students from nations of the hemisphere for cooperative study, training, and research.

INTERNATIONAL LITIGATION FUND

Unavailable Collections (in millions of dollars)

Identification code 19–5177–0–2–153	1999 actual	2000 est.	2001 est.
Balance, start of year:			
01.99 Balance, start of year	2	4	4
Receipts:			
02.01 International litigation fund	....	1	1
02.02 Sale and rental of real property	2	....	....
02.99 Total receipts	2	1	1
04.00 Total: Balances and collections	4	5	5
Appropriation:			
05.01 International litigation fund	....	−1	−1
07.99 Total balance, end of year	4	4	4

Program and Financing (in millions of dollars)

Identification code 19–5177–0–2–153	1999 actual	2000 est.	2001 est.
Obligations by program activity:			
10.00 Total new obligations	2	1	1
Budgetary resources available for obligation:			
21.40 Unobligated balance available, start of year	1	1	....
22.00 New budget authority (gross)	2	1	1
23.90 Total budgetary resources available for obligation	3	2	1
23.95 Total new obligations	−2	−1	−1
24.40 Unobligated balance available, end of year	1	....	....
New budget authority (gross), detail:			
Mandatory:			
60.25 Appropriation (special fund, indefinite)	....	1	1
69.00 Offsetting collections (cash)	2	....	....
70.00 Total new budget authority (gross)	2	1	1
Change in unpaid obligations:			
72.40 Unpaid obligations, start of year: Obligated balance, start of year	3	3	1
73.10 Total new obligations	2	1	1
73.20 Total outlays (gross)	−1	−1	−1
74.40 Unpaid obligations, end of year: Obligated balance, end of year	3	1	1
Outlays (gross), detail:			
86.97 Outlays from new mandatory authority	1	1	1
Offsets:			
Against gross budget authority and outlays:			
88.00 Offsetting collections (cash) from: Federal sources	−2	....	....
Net budget authority and outlays:			
89.00 Budget authority	....	1	1
90.00 Outlays	−1	1	1

The International Litigation Fund (ILF) is authorized by section 38(d) of the State Department Basic Authorities Act of 1956 (22 U.S.C. 2710(d)) to pay for expenses incurred by the Department of State relative to preparing or prosecuting a proceeding before an international tribunal or a claim by or against a foreign government or other foreign entity. Monies otherwise available for such purposes are authorized to be deposited in the ILF. In addition, funds received by the Department from other U.S. Government agencies or from private parties for these purposes are also deposited in the ILF.

INTERNATIONAL CENTER, WASHINGTON, DC

Program and Financing (in millions of dollars)

Identification code 19–5151–0–2–153	1999 actual	2000 est.	2001 est.
Obligations by program activity:			
09.01 Reimbursable program	2	1	1
10.00 Total new obligations	2	1	1
Budgetary resources available for obligation:			
21.40 Unobligated balance available, start of year	2	1	1
22.00 New budget authority (gross)	1	1	1
23.90 Total budgetary resources available for obligation	3	2	2
23.95 Total new obligations	−2	−1	−1
24.40 Unobligated balance available, end of year	1	1	1
New budget authority (gross), detail:			
Mandatory:			
69.00 Offsetting collections (cash)	1	1	1
Change in unpaid obligations:			
72.40 Unpaid obligations, start of year: Obligated balance, start of year	3	2	2
73.10 Total new obligations	2	1	1
73.20 Total outlays (gross)	−3	−1	−1
74.40 Unpaid obligations, end of year: Obligated balance, end of year	2	2	2
Outlays (gross), detail:			
86.97 Outlays from new mandatory authority	1	....	....
86.98 Outlays from mandatory balances	2	....	....
87.00 Total outlays (gross)	3	1	1
Offsets:			
Against gross budget authority and outlays:			
88.00 Offsetting collections (cash) from: Federal sources	−1	−1	−1
Net budget authority and outlays:			
89.00 Budget authority	....	....	....
90.00 Outlays	2	....	....

These funds provide for the development, lease or exchange to foreign governments or international organizations of property owned by the United States at the International Center located in the District of Columbia. Funds also provide for operation of the Federal facility located at the International Center, for maintenance and security of those public improvements which have not been conveyed to a government or international organization and for surveys and plans related to development of additional areas within the Nation's Capital for Chancery and Diplomatic purposes.

FISHERMEN'S PROTECTIVE FUND

Program and Financing (in millions of dollars)

Identification code 19–5116–0–2–376	1999 actual	2000 est.	2001 est.
Budgetary resources available for obligation:			
21.40 Unobligated balance available, start of year	1	1	1
23.95 Total new obligations			
24.40 Unobligated balance available, end of year	1	1	1
Net budget authority and outlays:			
89.00 Budget authority			
90.00 Outlays			

The Fishermen's Protective Fund provides for reimbursement to owners of vessels for amounts of fines, fees, and other direct charges which were paid by owners to a foreign country to secure the release of their vessels and crews and for other specified charges. No new budget authority is requested in 2001.

FISHERMEN'S GUARANTY FUND

Program and Financing (in millions of dollars)

Identification code 19–5121–0–2–376	1999 actual	2000 est.	2001 est.
Budgetary resources available for obligation:			
21.40 Unobligated balance available, start of year	3	3	3
23.95 Total new obligations			
24.40 Unobligated balance available, end of year	3	3	3
Net budget authority and outlays:			
89.00 Budget authority			
90.00 Outlays			

This fund provides for payment to vessel owners to compensate for certain financial losses sustained as a result of foreign seizures of American fishing vessels on the basis of claims to jurisdiction not recognized by the United States. No new budget authority is requested for 2001.

Trust Funds

ISRAELI ARAB AND EISENHOWER EXCHANGE FELLOWSHIP PROGRAMS

EISENHOWER EXCHANGE FELLOWSHIP PROGRAM TRUST FUND

For necessary expenses of Eisenhower Exchange Fellowships, Incorporated, as authorized by sections 4 and 5 of the Eisenhower Exchange Fellowship Act of 1990 (20 U.S.C. 5204–5205), all interest and earnings accruing to the Eisenhower Exchange Fellowship Program Trust Fund on or before September 30, [2000] *2001*, to remain available until expended: *Provided*, That none of the funds appropriated herein shall be used to pay any salary or other compensation, or to enter into any contract providing for the payment thereof, in excess of the rate authorized by 5 U.S.C. 5376; or for purposes which are not in accordance with OMB Circulars A–110 (Uniform Administrative Requirements) and A–122 (Cost Principles for Non-profit Organizations), including the restrictions on compensation for personal services. *(Department of State and Related Agencies Appropriations Act, 2000, as enacted by section 1000(a)(1) of the Consolidated Appropriations Act, 2000 (P.L. 106–113).)*

ISRAELI ARAB SCHOLARSHIP PROGRAM

For necessary expenses of the Israeli Arab Scholarship Program as authorized by section 214 of the Foreign Relations Authorization Act, Fiscal Years 1992 and 1993 (22 U.S.C. 2452), all interest and earnings accruing to the Israeli Arab Scholarship Fund on or before September 30, [2000] *2001*, to remain available until expended. *(Department of State and Related Agencies Appropriations Act, 2000, as enacted by section 1000(a)(1) of the Consolidated Appropriations Act, 2000 (P.L. 106–113).)*

Unavailable Collections (in millions of dollars)

Identification code 95–8276–0–7–154	1999 actual	2000 est.	2001 est.
Balance, start of year:			
01.99 Balance, start of year	10	9	8
Appropriation:			
05.01 Israeli Arab and Eisenhower exchange fellowship program	−1	−1	−1
07.99 Total balance, end of year	9	8	7

Program and Financing (in millions of dollars)

Identification code 95–8276–0–7–154	1999 actual	2000 est.	2001 est.
Obligations by program activity:			
10.00 Total new obligations	1	1	1
Budgetary resources available for obligation:			
21.40 Unobligated balance available, start of year	12	12	12
22.00 New budget authority (gross)	1	1	1
23.90 Total budgetary resources available for obligation	13	13	13
23.95 Total new obligations	−1	−1	−1
24.40 Unobligated balance available, end of year	12	12	12
New budget authority (gross), detail:			
Discretionary:			
40.27 Appropriation (trust fund, indefinite)	1	1	1
Change in unpaid obligations:			
73.10 Total new obligations	1	1	1
73.20 Total outlays (gross)	−1	−1	−1
Outlays (gross), detail:			
86.90 Outlays from new discretionary authority	1	1	1
Net budget authority and outlays:			
89.00 Budget authority	1	1	1
90.00 Outlays	1	1	1
Memorandum (non-add) entries:			
92.01 Total investments, start of year: U.S. securities: Par value			12
92.02 Total investments, end of year: U.S. securities: Par value		12	12

This presentation includes interest and earnings from the Eisenhower Exchange Fellowship Trust Fund and the Israeli-Arab Scholarship Trust Fund.

The Eisenhower Exchange Fellowship Trust fund was created in 1992 with an appropriation of $5,000,000. In 1995, an additional payment of $2,500,000 was made to the fund. This exchange program honors the late president and increases educational opportunities for young leaders in preparation for and enhancement of their professional careers and advancement of peace through international understanding.

The Israeli-Arab Scholarship Trust Fund was created in 1992 with an appropriation of $4,978,500 to provide scholarships for Israeli Arabs to attend institutions of higher learning in the United States.

GENERAL FUND RECEIPT ACCOUNTS

(in millions of dollars)

	1999 actual	2000 est.	2001 est.
Governmental receipts:			
20–083000 Immigration, passport, and consular fees	501	600	600
General Fund Governmental receipts	501	600	600

GENERAL PROVISIONS—DEPARTMENT OF STATE AND RELATED AGENCIES

SEC. 401. Funds appropriated under this title shall be available, except as otherwise provided, for allowances and differentials as authorized by subchapter 59 of title 5, United States Code; for services as authorized by 5 U.S.C. 3109; and hire of passenger transportation pursuant to 31 U.S.C. 1343(b).

SEC. 402. Not to exceed 5 percent of any appropriation made available for the current fiscal year for the Department of State in this Act may be transferred between such appropriations, but no such appropriation, except as otherwise specifically provided, shall be increased by more than 10 percent by any such transfers: *Provided*, That not to exceed 5 percent of any appropriation made available for the current fiscal year for the Broadcasting Board of Governors in this Act may be transferred between such appropriations, but no such appropriation, except as otherwise specifically provided, shall be increased by more than 10 percent by any such transfers: *Provided further*, That any transfer pursuant to this section shall be treated as a reprogramming of funds under section 605 of this Act and shall not be available for obligation or expenditure except in compliance with the procedures set forth in that section.

SEC. 403. The Secretary of State is authorized to administer summer travel and work programs without regard to preplacement requirements.

[SEC. 404. Beginning in fiscal year 2000 and thereafter, section 410(a) of the Department of State and Related Agencies Appropriations Act, 1999, as included in Public Law 105–277, shall be in effect.]

[SEC. 405. None of the funds made available in this Act may be used by the Department of State or the Broadcasting Board of Governors to provide equipment, technical support, consulting services, or any other form of assistance to the Palestinian Broadcasting Corporation.]

[SEC. 406. None of the funds appropriated or otherwise made available in this Act for the United Nations may be used by the United Nations for the promulgation or enforcement of any treaty, resolution, or regulation authorizing the United Nations, or any of its specialized agencies or affiliated organizations, to tax any aspect of the Internet.]

[SEC. 407. Funds appropriated by this Act for the Broadcasting Board of Governors and the Department of State may be obligated and expended notwithstanding section 313 of the Foreign Relations Authorization Act, Fiscal Years 1994 and 1995, section 309(g) of the International Broadcasting Act of 1994, and section 15 of the State Department Basic Authorities Act of 1956.] *(Department of State and Related Agencies Appropriations Act, 2000, as enacted by section 1000(a)(1) of the Consolidated Appropriations Act, 2000 (P.L. 106–113).)*

DEPARTMENT OF TRANSPORTATION

OFFICE OF THE SECRETARY

Federal Funds

General and special funds:

SALARIES AND EXPENSES

[IMMEDIATE OFFICE OF THE SECRETARY]

[For necessary expenses of the Immediate Office of the Secretary, $1,867,000.]

[IMMEDIATE OFFICE OF THE DEPUTY SECRETARY]

[For necessary expenses of the Immediate Office of the Deputy Secretary, $600,000.]

[OFFICE OF THE GENERAL COUNSEL]

[For necessary expenses of the Office of the General Counsel, $9,000,000.]

[OFFICE OF THE ASSISTANT SECRETARY FOR POLICY]

[For necessary expenses of the Office of the Assistant Secretary for Policy, $2,824,000.]

[OFFICE OF THE ASSISTANT SECRETARY FOR AVIATION AND INTERNATIONAL AFFAIRS]

[For necessary expenses of the Office of the Assistant Secretary for Aviation and International Affairs, $7,650,000: *Provided*, That notwithstanding any other provision of law, there may be credited to this appropriation up to $1,250,000 in funds received in user fees.]

[OFFICE OF THE ASSISTANT SECRETARY FOR BUDGET AND PROGRAMS]

[For necessary expenses of the Office of the Assistant Secretary for Budget and Programs, $6,870,000, including not to exceed $45,000 for allocation within the Department for official reception and representation expenses as the Secretary may determine.]

[OFFICE OF THE ASSISTANT SECRETARY FOR GOVERNMENTAL AFFAIRS]

[For necessary expenses of the Office of the Assistant Secretary for Governmental Affairs, $2,039,000.]

[OFFICE OF THE ASSISTANT SECRETARY FOR ADMINISTRATION]

[For necessary expenses of the Office of the Assistant Secretary for Administration, $17,767,000.]

[OFFICE OF PUBLIC AFFAIRS]

[For necessary expenses of the Office of Public Affairs, $1,800,000.]

[EXECUTIVE SECRETARIAT]

[For necessary expenses of the Executive Secretariat, $1,102,000.]

[BOARD OF CONTRACT APPEALS]

[For necessary expenses of the Board of Contract Appeals, $520,000.]

[OFFICE OF SMALL AND DISADVANTAGED BUSINESS UTILIZATION]

[For necessary expenses of the Office of Small and Disadvantaged Business Utilization, $1,222,000.]

[OFFICE OF INTELLIGENCE AND SECURITY]

[For necessary expenses of the Office of Intelligence and Security, $1,454,000.]

[OFFICE OF THE CHIEF INFORMATION OFFICER]

[For necessary expenses of the Office of the Chief Information Officer, $5,075,000.]

[OFFICE OF INTERMODALISM]

[For necessary expenses of the Office of Intermodalism, $1,062,000.]

For necessary expenses of the Office of the Secretary, $69,186,000, of which not to exceed $60,000 shall be allocated within the Department for official reception and representation expenses as the Secretary may determine: Provided, That up to $1,250,000 in authorized user fees may be credited to this account, to be available for the purposes of this account. (Department of Transportation and Related Agencies Appropriations Act, 2000.)

Program and Financing (in millions of dollars)

Identification code 69–0102–0–1–407		1999 actual	2000 est.	2001 est.
	Obligations by program activity:			
00.01	General administration	61	66	69
09.01	Reimbursable program	3	11	11
10.00	Total new obligations	64	77	80
	Budgetary resources available for obligation:			
21.40	Unobligated balance available, start of year	1	7	
22.00	New budget authority (gross)	70	70	80
23.90	Total budgetary resources available for obligation	71	77	80
23.95	Total new obligations	−64	−77	−80
24.40	Unobligated balance available, end of year	7		
	New budget authority (gross), detail:			
	Discretionary:			
40.00	Appropriation	60	61	69
40.76	Reduction pursuant to P.L. 105–277	−1		
40.79	Reduction pursuant to P.L. 106–69		−1	
41.00	Transferred to other accounts		−1	
42.00	Transferred from other accounts	8		
43.00	Appropriation (total discretionary)	67	59	69
68.00	Spending authority from offsetting collections: Offsetting collections (cash)	3	11	11
70.00	Total new budget authority (gross)	70	70	80
	Change in unpaid obligations:			
	Unpaid obligations, start of year:			
72.40	Obligated balance, start of year	13	14	6
72.95	From Federal sources: Receivables and unpaid, unfilled orders	8	8	8
72.99	Total unpaid obligations, start of year	21	22	14
73.10	Total new obligations	64	77	80
73.20	Total outlays (gross)	−62	−85	−79
73.40	Adjustments in expired accounts (net)	−1		
	Unpaid obligations, end of year:			
74.40	Obligated balance, end of year	14	6	7
74.95	From Federal sources: Receivables and unpaid, unfilled orders	8	8	8
74.99	Total unpaid obligations, end of year	22	14	15
	Outlays (gross), detail:			
86.90	Outlays from new discretionary authority	59	64	73
86.93	Outlays from discretionary balances	2	21	6
87.00	Total outlays (gross)	62	85	79
	Offsets:			
	Against gross budget authority and outlays:			
88.00	Offsetting collections (cash) from: Federal sources	−3	−11	−11
	Net budget authority and outlays:			
89.00	Budget authority	67	59	69
90.00	Outlays	58	74	68

General administration.—This appropriation finances the costs of policy development and central supervisory and coordinating functions necessary for the overall planning and direction of the Department. It covers the immediate secretarial offices as well as those of the assistant secretaries and the general counsel.

186-484 00 - 24

General and special funds—Continued

[OFFICE OF INTERMODALISM]—Continued

Object Classification (in millions of dollars)

Identification code 69–0102–0–1–407	1999 actual	2000 est.	2001 est.
Direct obligations:			
Personnel compensation:			
11.1 Full-time permanent	29	29	32
11.3 Other than full-time permanent	4	4	4
11.9 Total personnel compensation	33	33	36
12.1 Civilian personnel benefits	6	7	7
21.0 Travel and transportation of persons	1	1	1
23.1 Rental payments to GSA	7	7	7
25.2 Other services	12	18	17
99.0 Subtotal, direct obligations	59	66	68
99.0 Reimbursable obligations	2	11	11
99.5 Below reporting threshold	3	....	1
99.9 Total new obligations	64	77	80

Personnel Summary

Identification code 69–0102–0–1–407	1999 actual	2000 est.	2001 est.
Direct:			
1001 Total compensable workyears: Full-time equivalent employment	424	448	454
Reimbursable:			
2001 Total compensable workyears: Full-time equivalent employment	23	32	34

OFFICE OF CIVIL RIGHTS

For necessary expenses of the Office of Civil Rights, [$7,200,000] *$8,726,000. (Department of Transportation and Related Agencies Appropriations Act, 2000.)*

Program and Financing (in millions of dollars)

Identification code 69–0118–0–1–407	1999 actual	2000 est.	2001 est.
Obligations by program activity:			
10.00 Total new obligations	7	7	9
Budgetary resources available for obligation:			
22.00 New budget authority (gross)	7	7	9
23.95 Total new obligations	−7	−7	−9
New budget authority (gross), detail:			
Discretionary:			
40.00 Appropriation	7	7	9
Change in unpaid obligations:			
72.40 Unpaid obligations, start of year: Obligated balance, start of year	1	1	1
73.10 Total new obligations	7	7	9
73.20 Total outlays (gross)	−6	−8	−9
74.40 Unpaid obligations, end of year: Obligated balance, end of year	1	1	1
Outlays (gross), detail:			
86.90 Outlays from new discretionary authority	6	6	8
86.93 Outlays from discretionary balances	1	1	1
87.00 Total outlays (gross)	6	8	9
Net budget authority and outlays:			
89.00 Budget authority	7	7	9
90.00 Outlays	6	8	9

This appropriation finances the costs of a Departmental Civil Rights office. This office is responsible for enforcing laws and regulations which prohibit discrimination in federally-operated and assisted transportation programs. This office also handles all civil rights cases related to Department of Transportation employees.

Object Classification (in millions of dollars)

Identification code 69–0118–0–1–407	1999 actual	2000 est.	2001 est.
11.1 Personnel compensation: Full-time permanent	4	4	5
12.1 Civilian personnel benefits	1	1	1
25.2 Other services	2	2	2
99.0 Subtotal, direct obligations	7	7	8
99.5 Below reporting threshold	....	....	1
99.9 Total new obligations	7	7	9

Personnel Summary

Identification code 69–0118–0–1–407	1999 actual	2000 est.	2001 est.
1001 Total compensable workyears: Full-time equivalent employment	62	70	70

MINORITY BUSINESS OUTREACH

For necessary expenses of Minority Business Resource Center outreach activities, [$2,900,000] *$3,000,000,* of which $2,635,000 shall remain available until September 30, [2001] *2002: Provided,* That notwithstanding 49 U.S.C. 332, these funds may be used for business opportunities related to any mode of transportation. *(Department of Transportation and Related Agencies Appropriations Act, 2000.)*

Program and Financing (in millions of dollars)

Identification code 69–0119–0–1–407	1999 actual	2000 est.	2001 est.
Obligations by program activity:			
10.00 Total new obligations	3	3	3
Budgetary resources available for obligation:			
21.40 Unobligated balance available, start of year	1	....	....
22.00 New budget authority (gross)	3	3	3
23.90 Total budgetary resources available for obligation	4	3	3
23.95 Total new obligations	−3	−3	−3
24.40 Unobligated balance available, end of year	....	....	....
New budget authority (gross), detail:			
Discretionary:			
40.00 Appropriation	3	3	3
Change in unpaid obligations:			
72.40 Unpaid obligations, start of year: Obligated balance, start of year	2	3	....
73.10 Total new obligations	3	3	3
73.20 Total outlays (gross)	−3	−6	−3
74.40 Unpaid obligations, end of year: Obligated balance, end of year	3	....	....
Outlays (gross), detail:			
86.90 Outlays from new discretionary authority	1	3	3
86.93 Outlays from discretionary balances	2	3	....
87.00 Total outlays (gross)	3	6	3
Net budget authority and outlays:			
89.00 Budget authority	3	3	3
90.00 Outlays	3	6	3

Minority business outreach.—This activity provides contractual support to assist small, women-owned, Native American, and other disadvantaged business firms, in securing contracts and subcontracts resulting from transportation-related Federal support. It also participates in cooperative agreements with historically black and hispanic colleges.

Object Classification (in millions of dollars)

Identification code 69–0119–0–1–407	1999 actual	2000 est.	2001 est.
25.2 Other services	2	2	2
41.0 Grants, subsidies, and contributions	1	1	1
99.9 Total new obligations	3	3	3

RENTAL PAYMENTS

Program and Financing (in millions of dollars)

Identification code 69–0117–0–1–407	1999 actual	2000 est.	2001 est.
Change in unpaid obligations:			
72.40 Unpaid obligations, start of year: Obligated balance, start of year	1		
Net budget authority and outlays:			
89.00 Budget authority			
90.00 Outlays			

Until 1997, payments to GSA for headquarters and field space rental and related services for all modes were consolidated into this account. Beginning in 1998, however, all GSA rental payments are reflected in the modal budgets.

TRANSPORTATION PLANNING, RESEARCH, AND DEVELOPMENT

For necessary expenses for conducting transportation planning, research, systems development, development activities, and making grants, to remain available until expended, [$3,300,000] *$5,258,000. (Department of Transportation and Related Agencies Appropriations Act, 2000.)*

Program and Financing (in millions of dollars)

Identification code 69–0142–0–1–407	1999 actual	2000 est.	2001 est.
Obligations by program activity:			
Direct program:			
00.01 Transportation policy and planning	9	4	4
00.02 Systems development			1
01.00 Total direct program	9	4	5
09.00 Reimbursable program		1	
10.00 Total new obligations	9	5	5
Budgetary resources available for obligation:			
21.40 Unobligated balance available, start of year	1	1	
22.00 New budget authority (gross)	9	4	5
23.90 Total budgetary resources available for obligation	10	5	5
23.95 Total new obligations	−9	−5	−5
24.40 Unobligated balance available, end of year	1		
New budget authority (gross), detail:			
Discretionary:			
40.00 Appropriation	9	3	5
68.00 Spending authority from offsetting collections: Offsetting collections (cash)		1	
70.00 Total new budget authority (gross)	9	4	5
Change in unpaid obligations:			
72.40 Unpaid obligations, start of year: Obligated balance, start of year		6	4
73.10 Total new obligations	9	5	5
73.20 Total outlays (gross)	−4	−7	−6
74.40 Unpaid obligations, end of year: Obligated balance, end of year	6	4	3
Outlays (gross), detail:			
86.90 Outlays from new discretionary authority	4	2	3
86.93 Outlays from discretionary balances		5	3
87.00 Total outlays (gross)	4	7	6
Offsets:			
Against gross budget authority and outlays:			
88.00 Offsetting collections (cash) from: Federal sources		−1	
Net budget authority and outlays:			
89.00 Budget authority	9	3	5
90.00 Outlays	4	6	6

This appropriation finances systems development and those research activities and studies concerned with planning, analysis, and information development needed to support the Secretary's responsibilities in the formulation of national transportation policies.

The program is carried out primarily through contracts with other Federal agencies, educational institutions, non-profit research organizations, and private firms.

Transportation policy and planning.—Activities support the development of transportation policy, coordination of national level transportation planning, and such issues as regulatory modernization, energy conservation, and environmental and safety impacts of transportation. These also enable departmental leadership on aviation economic policy and international transportation issues.

Systems Development.—This activity funds system development of department-wide management systems. In 2001, it includes resources to improve the Dockets management system.

Object Classification (in millions of dollars)

Identification code 69–0142–0–1–407	1999 actual	2000 est.	2001 est.
Direct obligations:			
11.1 Personnel compensation: Full-time permanent	1	1	1
25.2 Other services	8	2	2
99.0 Subtotal, direct obligations	9	3	3
99.0 Reimbursable obligations		1	
99.5 Below reporting threshold		1	2
99.9 Total new obligations	9	5	5

Personnel Summary

Identification code 69–0142–0–1–407	1999 actual	2000 est.	2001 est.
1001 Total compensable workyears: Full-time equivalent employment	22	13	14

ESSENTIAL AIR SERVICE AND RURAL AIRPORT IMPROVEMENT FUND

Program and Financing (in millions of dollars)

Identification code 69–5423–0–2–402	1999 actual	2000 est.	2001 est.
Obligations by program activity:			
00.01 Direct Program		5	22
09.00 Reimbursable program	46	45	28
10.00 Total new obligations	46	50	50
Budgetary resources available for obligation:			
22.00 New budget authority (gross)	48	50	50
23.95 Total new obligations	−46	−50	−50
New budget authority (gross), detail:			
Mandatory:			
62.00 Transferred from FAA Overflight Fees		5	22
Discretionary:			
68.00 Spending authority from offsetting collections: Offsetting collections (cash)	48	45	28
70.00 Total new budget authority (gross)	48	50	50
Change in unpaid obligations:			
72.40 Unpaid obligations, start of year: Obligated balance, start of year	9	13	20
73.10 Total new obligations	46	50	50
73.20 Total outlays (gross)	−42	−43	−50
74.40 Unpaid obligations, end of year: Obligated balance, end of year	13	20	20
Outlays (gross), detail:			
86.90 Outlays from new discretionary authority	33	27	17
86.93 Outlays from discretionary balances	9	13	18
86.97 Outlays from new mandatory authority		3	13
86.98 Outlays from mandatory balances			2
87.00 Total outlays (gross)	42	43	50

General and special funds—Continued

ESSENTIAL AIR SERVICE AND RURAL AIRPORT IMPROVEMENT FUND—Continued

Program and Financing (in millions of dollars)—Continued

Identification code 69–5423–0–2–402	1999 actual	2000 est.	2001 est.
Offsets:			
Against gross budget authority and outlays:			
88.00 Offsetting collections (cash) from: Federal sources	–48	–45	–28
Net budget authority and outlays:			
89.00 Budget authority		5	22
90.00 Outlays	–6	–2	22

The Federal Aviation Reauthorization Act of 1996 (P.L. 104–264) authorized the collection of user fees for services provided by the FAA to aircraft that neither take off nor land in the United States, commonly known as overflight fees. The Act permanently appropriated the first $50 million of such fees for the Essential Air Service program and rural airport improvements. To the extent that fee collections fall below $50 million, current law requires the difference to be covered by appropriated funds of the Federal Aviation Administration. The 2001 budget assumes the collection of $22 million in overflight fees, with the balance of $28 million to be paid from the FAA Airport improvement program.

Object Classification (in millions of dollars)

Identification code 69–5423–0–2–402	1999 actual	2000 est.	2001 est.
41.0 Direct obligations: Grants, subsidies, and contributions		5	22
99.0 Reimbursable obligations: Subtotal, reimbursable obligations	46	45	28
99.9 Total new obligations	46	50	50

Personnel Summary

Identification code 69–5423–0–2–402	1999 actual	2000 est.	2001 est.
2001 Total compensable workyears: Full-time equivalent employment	10	10	10

Intragovernmental funds:

[TRANSPORTATION ADMINISTRATIVE SERVICE CENTER]

[Necessary expenses for operating costs and capital outlays of the Transportation Administrative Service Center, not to exceed $148,673,000, shall be paid from appropriations made available to the Department of Transportation: *Provided*, That the preceding limitation shall not apply to activities associated with departmental Year 2000 conversion activities: *Provided further*, That such services shall be provided on a competitive basis to entities within the Department of Transportation: *Provided further*, That the above limitation on operating expenses shall not apply to non-DOT entities: *Provided further*, That no funds appropriated in this Act to an agency of the Department shall be transferred to the Transportation Administrative Service Center without the approval of the agency modal administrator: *Provided further*, That no assessments may be levied against any program, budget activity, subactivity or project funded by this Act unless notice of such assessments and the basis therefor are presented to the House and Senate Committees on Appropriations and are approved by such Committees.] *(Department of Transportation and Related Agencies Appropriations Act, 2000.)*

Program and Financing (in millions of dollars)

Identification code 69–4520–0–4–407	1999 actual	2000 est.	2001 est.
Obligations by program activity:			
09.01 DOT service center activities	99	134	120
09.02 Non-DOT service center and Y2K activities	102	97	33
09.03 Aeronautical charting and cartography activities			53
10.00 Total new obligations	201	231	206
Budgetary resources available for obligation:			
21.40 Unobligated balance available, start of year	7	9	9
22.00 New budget authority (gross)	198	231	206
22.10 Resources available from recoveries of prior year obligations	4		
23.90 Total budgetary resources available for obligation	209	240	215
23.95 Total new obligations	–201	–231	–206
24.40 Unobligated balance available, end of year	9	9	9
New budget authority (gross), detail:			
Mandatory:			
69.00 Offsetting collections (cash)	174	231	206
69.10 From Federal sources: Change in receivables and unpaid, unfilled orders	24		
69.90 Spending authority from offsetting collections (total mandatory)	199	231	206
Change in unpaid obligations:			
Unpaid obligations, start of year:			
72.40 Obligated balance, start of year	18	11	11
72.95 From Federal sources: Receivables and unpaid, unfilled orders	61	85	85
72.99 Total unpaid obligations, start of year	79	96	96
73.10 Total new obligations	201	231	206
73.20 Total outlays (gross)	–180	–231	–206
73.45 Adjustments in unexpired accounts	–4		
Unpaid obligations, end of year:			
74.40 Obligated balance, end of year	11	11	11
74.95 From Federal sources: Receivables and unpaid, unfilled orders	85	85	85
74.99 Total unpaid obligations, end of year	96	96	96
Outlays (gross), detail:			
86.97 Outlays from new mandatory authority	180	231	206
Offsets:			
Against gross budget authority and outlays:			
88.00 Offsetting collections (cash) from: Federal sources	–174	–231	–206
Against gross budget authority only:			
88.95 From Federal sources: Change in receivables and unpaid, unfilled orders	–24		
Net budget authority and outlays:			
89.00 Budget authority			
90.00 Outlays	6		

The Transportation Administrative Service Center (TASC) finances common administrative services that are centrally performed in the interest of economy and efficiency in the Department. The fund is financed through negotiated agreements with Departmental operating administrations, and other governmental elements requiring the center's capabilities. The budget proposes that the National Oceanic and Atmospheric Administration's Office of Aeronautical Charting and Cartography be transferred to TASC in 2001.

Object Classification (in millions of dollars)

Identification code 69–4520–0–4–407	1999 actual	2000 est.	2001 est.
Personnel compensation:			
11.1 Full-time permanent	16	17	38
11.3 Other than full-time permanent		1	1
11.5 Other personnel compensation		1	1
11.9 Total personnel compensation	16	19	40
12.1 Civilian personnel benefits	3	3	8
13.0 Benefits for former personnel		1	1
21.0 Travel and transportation of persons		1	1
22.0 Transportation of things			1
23.1 Rental payments to GSA	5	5	11
23.3 Communications, utilities, and miscellaneous charges	12	12	15
25.2 Other services	151	180	118
26.0 Supplies and materials	3	3	6
31.0 Equipment	8	6	5
99.0 Subtotal, reimbursable obligations	198	230	206
99.5 Below reporting threshold	3	1	

99.9	Total new obligations	201	231	206

Personnel Summary

Identification code 69–4520–0–4–407		1999 actual	2000 est.	2001 est.
2001	Total compensable workyears: Full-time equivalent employment	285	287	659

Credit accounts:

MINORITY BUSINESS RESOURCE CENTER PROGRAM

For the cost of [direct] *guaranteed* loans, $1,500,000, as authorized by 49 U.S.C. 332: *Provided*, That such costs, including the cost of modifying such loans, shall be as defined in section 502 of the Congressional Budget Act of 1974: *Provided further*, That these funds are available to subsidize [gross obligations for the principal amount of direct loans] *total loan principal, any part of which is to be guaranteed,* not to exceed $13,775,000. In addition, for administrative expenses to carry out the [direct] *guaranteed* loan program, $400,000. *(Department of Transportation and Related Agencies Appropriations Act, 2000.)*

Program and Financing (in millions of dollars)

Identification code 69–0155–0–1–407		1999 actual	2000 est.	2001 est.
	Obligations by program activity:			
00.01	Direct loan subsidy and administrative expenses	2	2	2
10.00	Total new obligations (object class 41.0)	2	2	2
	Budgetary resources available for obligation:			
22.00	New budget authority (gross)	2	2	2
23.95	Total new obligations	–2	–2	–2
	New budget authority (gross), detail:			
	Discretionary:			
40.00	Appropriation	2	2	2
	Change in unpaid obligations:			
72.40	Unpaid obligations, start of year: Obligated balance, start of year	5	6	6
73.10	Total new obligations	2	2	2
73.20	Total outlays (gross)	....	–2	–2
74.40	Unpaid obligations, end of year: Obligated balance, end of year	6	6	6
	Outlays (gross), detail:			
86.90	Outlays from new discretionary authority	....	2	2
	Net budget authority and outlays:			
89.00	Budget authority	2	2	2
90.00	Outlays	....	2	2

Summary of Budget Authority and Outlays

(in millions of dollars)

	1999 actual	*2000 est.*	*2001 est.*
Enacted/requested:			
Budget Authority	2	2	2
Outlays	....	2	2
Legislative proposal, not subject to PAYGO:			
Budget Authority	....	....	....
Outlays	....	....	....
Total:			
Budget Authority	2	2	2
Outlays	....	2	2

Summary of Loan Levels, Subsidy Budget Authority and Outlays by Program (in millions of dollars)

Identification code 69–0155–0–1–407		1999 actual	2000 est.	2001 est.
	Direct loan levels supportable by subsidy budget authority:			
1150	Direct loan levels	14	14	14
1159	Total direct loan levels	14	14	14
	Direct loan subsidy (in percent):			
1320	Subsidy rate	11.00	11.00	11.00
1329	Weighted average subsidy rate	11.00	11.00	11.00
	Direct loan subsidy budget authority:			
1330	Subsidy budget authority	2	2	2
1339	Total subsidy budget authority	2	2	2
	Direct loan subsidy outlays:			
1340	Subsidy outlays	....	2	2
1349	Total subsidy outlays	....	2	2

Office of Small and Disadvantaged Business Utilization (OSDBU)/Minority Business Resource Center (MBRC).—Provides assistance in obtaining short-term working capital and bonding for minority, women-owned and other disadvantaged businesses and Small Business Administration 8(a) Firms.

As required by the Federal Credit Reform Act of 1990, this account records, for this program, the subsidy costs associated with the direct loans obligated in 1992 and beyond (including modifications of direct loans that resulted from obligations or commitments in any year), as well as administrative expenses of this program. In 2001, legislation will be proposed to convert this program from a direct loan program to a guaranteed loan program. The subsidy amounts are estimated on a present value basis; the administrative expenses are estimated on a cash basis.

MINORITY BUSINESS RESOURCE CENTER PROGRAM

(Legislative proposal, not subject to PAYGO)

Program and Financing (in millions of dollars)

Identification code 69–0155–2–1–407		1999 actual	2000 est.	2001 est.
	Obligations by program activity:			
00.01	Direct loan subsidy and administrative expenses	....	....	–2
00.02	Guaranteed loan subsidy and administrative expenses	....	....	2
10.00	Total new obligations	....	....	....
	Net budget authority and outlays:			
89.00	Budget authority	....	....	....
90.00	Outlays	....	....	....

Summary of Loan Levels, Subsidy Budget Authority and Outlays by Program (in millions of dollars)

Identification code 69–0155–2–1–407		1999 actual	2000 est.	2001 est.
	Direct loan levels supportable by subsidy budget authority:			
1150	Direct loan levels	....	....	–14
1159	Total direct loan levels	....	....	–14
	Direct loan subsidy (in percent):			
1320	Subsidy rate	....	....	–11.00
1329	Weighted average subsidy rate	....	....	–11.00
	Direct loan subsidy budget authority:			
1330	Subsidy budget authority	....	....	–2
1339	Total subsidy budget authority	....	....	–2
	Direct loan subsidy outlays:			
1340	Subsidy outlays	....	....	–2
1349	Total subsidy outlays	....	....	–2
	Guaranteed loan levels supportable by subsidy budget authority:			
2150	Loan guarantee levels	....	....	14
2159	Total loan guarantee levels	....	....	14
	Guaranteed loan subsidy (in percent):			
2320	Subsidy rate	....	....	11.00
2329	Weighted average subsidy rate	....	....	11.00
	Guaranteed loan subsidy budget authority:			
2330	Subsidy budget authority	....	....	2
2339	Total subsidy budget authority	....	....	2
	Guaranteed loan subsidy outlays:			
2340	Subsidy outlays	....	....	2

Credit accounts—Continued

MINORITY BUSINESS RESOURCE CENTER PROGRAM—Continued

Summary of Loan Levels, Subsidy Budget Authority and Outlays by Program (in millions of dollars)—Continued

Identification code 69–0155–2–1–407		1999 actual	2000 est.	2001 est.
2349	Total subsidy outlays	....	....	2

This account reflects the effects of the legislative proposal to convert the program from a direct loan program to a guaranteed loan program.

MINORITY BUSINESS RESOURCE CENTER DIRECT LOAN FINANCING ACCOUNT

Program and Financing (in millions of dollars)

Identification code 69–4186–0–3–407		1999 actual	2000 est.	2001 est.
	Obligations by program activity:			
00.01	Direct loans	6	14	14
00.02	Interest to Treasury	1	....	....
10.00	Total new obligations	7	14	14
	Budgetary resources available for obligation:			
21.40	Unobligated balance available, start of year	....	....	....
22.00	New financing authority (gross)	7	14	14
22.10	Resources available from recoveries of prior year obligations	3	....	....
22.40	Capital transfer to general fund	−3	....	....
23.90	Total budgetary resources available for obligation	7	14	14
23.95	Total new obligations	−7	−14	−14
	New financing authority (gross), detail:			
	Mandatory:			
67.15	Authority to borrow (indefinite)	7	12	12
	Spending authority from offsetting collections:			
	Discretionary:			
68.00	Offsetting collections (cash)	2	11	7
68.47	Portion applied to repay debt	−2	−9	−5
68.90	Spending authority from offsetting collections (total discretionary)	....	2	2
70.00	Total new financing authority (gross)	7	14	14
	Change in unpaid obligations:			
72.40	Unpaid obligations, start of year: Obligated balance, start of year	4	4	11
73.10	Total new obligations	7	14	14
73.20	Total financing disbursements (gross)	−4	−7	−9
73.45	Adjustments in unexpired accounts	−3	....	....
74.40	Unpaid obligations, end of year: Obligated balance, end of year	4	11	15
87.00	Total financing disbursements (gross)	4	7	9
	Offsets:			
	Against gross financing authority and financing disbursements:			
	Offsetting collections (cash) from:			
88.00	Federal sources	....	−2	−2
88.40	Non-Federal sources	−2	−9	−5
88.90	Total, offsetting collections (cash)	−2	−11	−7
	Net financing authority and financing disbursements:			
89.00	Financing authority	5	3	7
90.00	Financing disbursements	2	−4	2

Status of Direct Loans (in millions of dollars)

Identification code 69–4186–0–3–407		1999 actual	2000 est.	2001 est.
	Position with respect to appropriations act limitation on obligations:			
1111	Limitation on direct loans	14	14	14
1112	Unobligated direct loan limitation	−8	....	....
1150	Total direct loan obligations	6	14	14
	Cumulative balance of direct loans outstanding:			
1210	Outstanding, start of year	7	8	6
1231	Disbursements: Direct loan disbursements	3	7	7
1251	Repayments: Repayments and prepayments	−2	−9	−5
1290	Outstanding, end of year	8	6	8

As required by the Federal Credit Reform Act of 1990, this non-budgetary account records all cash flows to and from the Government resulting from direct loans obligated in 1992 and beyond (including modifications of direct loans that resulted from obligations in any year). The amounts in this account are a means of financing and are not included in the budget totals.

Balance Sheet (in millions of dollars)

Identification code 69–4186–0–3–407		1998 actual	1999 actual	2000 est.	2001 est.
	ASSETS:				
1101	Federal assets: Fund balances with Treasury	4	7	5	3
	Net value of assets related to post-1991 direct loans receivable:				
1401	Direct loans receivable, gross	6	7	5	3
1405	Allowance for subsidy cost (–)	–1	....	....	....
1499	Net present value of assets related to direct loans	5	7	5	3
1999	Total assets	9	14	10	6
	LIABILITIES:				
2103	Federal liabilities: Debt	9	14	10	6
2999	Total liabilities	9	14	10	6
	NET POSITION:				
3999	Total net position	....	....	....	....
4999	Total liabilities and net position	9	14	10	6

MINORITY BUSINESS RESOURCE CENTER

DIRECT LOAN FINANCING ACCOUNT

(Legislative proposal not subject to PAYGO)

Program and Financing (in millions of dollars)

Identification code 69–4186–2–3–407		1999 actual	2000 est.	2001 est.
	Obligations by program activity:			
00.01	Direct loans	....	....	−14
10.00	Total new obligations	....	....	−14
	Budgetary resources available for obligation:			
22.00	New financing authority (gross)	....	....	−14
23.95	Total new obligations	....	....	14
	New financing authority (gross), detail:			
	Mandatory:			
67.15	Authority to borrow (indefinite)	....	....	−14
	Spending authority from offsetting collections:			
	Discretionary:			
68.00	Offsetting collections (cash)	....	....	−6
68.47	Portion applied to repay debt	....	....	6
68.90	Spending authority from offsetting collections (total discretionary)	....	....	....
70.00	Total new financing authority (gross)	....	....	−14
	Change in unpaid obligations:			
73.10	Total new obligations	....	....	−14
73.20	Total financing disbursements (gross)	....	....	5
74.40	Unpaid obligations, end of year: Obligated balance, end of year	....	....	−9
87.00	Total financing disbursements (gross)	....	....	−5

Offsets:			
Against gross financing authority and financing disbursements:			
Offsetting collections (cash) from:			
88.00 Federal sources			2
88.40 Non-Federal sources			4
88.90 Total, offsetting collections (cash)			6
Net financing authority and financing disbursements:			
89.00 Financing authority			−8
90.00 Financing disbursements			1

Status of Direct Loans (in millions of dollars)

Identification code 69–4186–2–3–407	1999 actual	2000 est.	2001 est.
Position with respect to appropriations act limitation on obligations:			
1111 Limitation on direct loans			−14
1112 Unobligated direct loan limitation			
1150 Total direct loan obligations			−14
Cumulative balance of direct loans outstanding:			
1210 Outstanding, start of year			
1251 Repayments: Repayments and prepayments			−5
1290 Outstanding, end of year			−5

This account reflects the effects of the legislative proposal to convert the program from a direct loan program to a loan guarantee program.

Minority Business Resource Center

guaranteed loan financing account

(Legislative proposal, not subject to PAYGO)

Program and Financing (in millions of dollars)

Identification code 69–4082–2–3–407	1999 actual	2000 est.	2001 est.
Budgetary resources available for obligation:			
22.00 New financing authority (gross)			2
24.40 Unobligated balance available, end of year			2
New financing authority (gross), detail:			
Discretionary:			
68.00 Spending authority from offsetting collections (gross): Offsetting collections (cash)			2
Offsets:			
Against gross financing authority and financing disbursements:			
88.00 Offsetting collections (cash) from: Federal sources			−2
Net financing authority and financing disbursements:			
89.00 Financing authority			
90.00 Financing disbursements			−2

Status of Guaranteed Loans (in millions of dollars)

Identification code 69–4082–2–3–407	1999 actual	2000 est.	2001 est.
Position with respect to appropriations act limitation on commitments:			
2111 Limitation on guaranteed loans made by private lenders			14
2150 Total guaranteed loan commitments			14
2199 Guaranteed amount of guaranteed loan commitments			11
Cumulative balance of guaranteed loans outstanding:			
2210 Outstanding, start of year			
2231 Disbursements of new guaranteed loans			7
2251 Repayments and prepayments			−2
2290 Outstanding, end of year			5
Memorandum:			
2299 Guaranteed amount of guaranteed loans outstanding, end of year			4

This account reflects the effects of the legislative proposal to convert the program from a direct loan program to a loan guarantee program. This account records all the cash flows to and from the Government resulting from guaranteed loan commitments. The amounts in this account are a means of financing and are not included in the budget totals.

Balance Sheet (in millions of dollars)

Identification code 69–4082–2–3–407	1998 actual	1999 actual	2000 est.	2001 est.
ASSETS:				
1101 Federal assets: Fund balances with Treasury				2
1999 Total assets				2
LIABILITIES:				
2204 Non-Federal liabilities: Liabilities for loan guarantees				2
2999 Total liabilities				2
NET POSITION:				
3999 Total net position				
4999 Total liabilities and net position				2

Payments to Air Carriers

Program and Financing (in millions of dollars)

Identification code 69–8304–0–7–402	1999 actual	2000 est.	2001 est.
Obligations by program activity:			
10.00 Total new obligations (object class 41.0)	1		
Budgetary resources available for obligation:			
21.40 Unobligated balance available, start of year	4		
22.00 New budget authority (gross)	−4		
23.90 Total budgetary resources available for obligation			
23.95 Total new obligations	−1		
New budget authority (gross), detail:			
Discretionary:			
40.36 Unobligated balance rescinded	−4		
Change in unpaid obligations:			
72.40 Unpaid obligations, start of year: Obligated balance, start of year	7	7	6
73.10 Total new obligations	1		
73.20 Total outlays (gross)	−1	−1	
74.40 Unpaid obligations, end of year: Obligated balance, end of year	7	6	6
Outlays (gross), detail:			
86.93 Outlays from discretionary balances	1	1	
Net budget authority and outlays:			
89.00 Budget authority	−4		
90.00 Outlays	1	1	

Through 1997, this program was funded from the Airport and Airway Trust Fund. However, starting in 1998, the FAA reauthorization funded it as a mandatory program supported by overflight fees under the Essential Air Service and Rural Airport Improvement Fund.

COAST GUARD

The following table depicts funding for all Coast Guard programs for which detail is furnished in the budget schedules.

[In millions of dollars]

	1999 actual	2000 est.	2001 est.
Budget authority:			
Regular appropriations:			
Operating expenses [1]	2,697	2,779	3,199
Proposed supplemental transfer		18	
Offsetting user fees, operating expenses			−116
Acquisition, construction and improvements [2]	394	388	510
Offsetting user fees, acquisition, construction and improvements			−96
Environmental compliance and restoration	21	17	17
Alteration of bridges [4]	38	15	
Retired pay	684	730	778
Reserve training	69	72	73
Research, development, test and evaluation [3]	12	19	22
Boat safety	64	64	64
Oil spill recovery, Coast Guard, (OSLTF)	66	61	61
Subtotal, budget authority net	4,045	4,163	4,512
Supplemental appropriations	588		
Total, budget authority net	4,633	4,163	4,512
Direct Obligations:			
Operating expenses	2,855	2,966	3,199
Proposed supplemental transfer		18	
Acquisition, construction, and improvements	539	397	530
Environmental compliance and restoration	23	18	18
Alteration of bridges	15	15	27
Retired pay	672	730	778
Reserve training	74	72	73
Research, development, test, and evaluation	19	20	21
Boat safety	59	64	64
Oil spill recovery, Coast Guard, (OSLTF)	69	61	62
Obligation total net	4,325	4,361	4,772

For comparability purposes this table includes:

[1] Includes $25 million in 1999–2001 from the Oil Spill Liability Trust Fund; $300 million excludes in 1999–2000 and $341 million in 2001 from Defense function.

[2] Includes $20 million in 1999–2001 from the Oil Spill Liability Trust Fund and excludes $10 million in asset sales in 2001.

[3] Includes $3.5 million in 1999–2001 from the Oil Spill Liability Trust Fund.

[4] Includes $29 million transferred from Defense pursuant to P.L. 105–262 and $5 million rescission pursuant to P.L. 106–51 in 1999.

Federal Funds

General and special funds:

OPERATING EXPENSES

For necessary expenses for the operation and maintenance of the Coast Guard, not otherwise provided for; purchase of not to exceed five passenger motor vehicles for replacement only; payments pursuant to section 156 of Public Law 97–377, as amended (42 U.S.C. 402 note), and section 229(b) of the Social Security Act (42 U.S.C. 429(b)); and recreation and welfare; [$2,781,000,000] *$3,199,000,000*, of which [$300,000,000] *$341,000,000* shall be available for defense-related activities; and of which $25,000,000 shall be derived from the Oil Spill Liability Trust Fund: *Provided*, That none of the funds appropriated in this or any other Act shall be available for pay for administrative expenses in connection with shipping commissioners in the United States: *Provided further*, That none of the funds provided in this Act shall be available for expenses incurred for yacht documentation under 46 U.S.C. 12109, except to the extent fees are collected from yacht owners and credited to this appropriation[: *Provided further*, That the Commandant shall reduce both military and civilian employment levels for the purpose of complying with Executive Order No. 12839: *Provided further*, That up to $615,000 in user fees collected pursuant to section 1111 of Public Law 104–324 shall be credited to this appropriation as offsetting collections in fiscal year 2000: *Provided further*, That notwithstanding any other provision of law, the Commandant of the Coast Guard may transfer certain parcels of real property located at Sitka, Japonski Island, Alaska to the State of Alaska for the purpose of airport expansion, provided that the Commandant determines that the Coast Guard has been indemnified for any loss, damage, or destruction of any structures or other improvements on the lands to be conveyed. No other provision of law shall otherwise make the real property improvements on Japonski Island ineligible for Federal funding by virtue of any consideration received by the Coast Guard for such improvements: *Provided further*, That none of the funds in this Act shall be available for the Coast Guard to plan, finalize, or implement any regulation that would promulgate new maritime user fees not specifically authorized by law after the date of the enactment of this Act: *Provided further*, That the Secretary of Transportation may use any surplus funds that are made available to the Secretary, to the maximum extent practicable, for drug interdiction activities of the Coast Guard]. *(Department of Transportation and Related Agencies Appropriations Act, 2000.)*

Program and Financing (in millions of dollars)

Identification code 69–0201–0–1–999		1999 actual	2000 est.	2001 est.
	Obligations by program activity:			
	Direct program:			
00.01	Search and rescue	394	345	383
00.02	Aids to navigation	453	457	483
00.03	Marine safety	392	407	440
00.04	Marine environmental protection	303	340	365
00.05	Enforcement of laws and treaties	1,145	1,241	1,334
00.06	Ice operations	93	112	121
00.07	Defense readiness	75	64	73
08.00	Total direct program	2,855	2,966	3,199
09.01	Reimbursable program	81	105	107
10.00	Total new obligations	2,936	3,071	3,306
	Budgetary resources available for obligation:			
21.40	Unobligated balance available, start of year		187	
22.00	New budget authority (gross)	3,126	2,884	3,306
23.90	Total budgetary resources available for obligation	3,126	3,071	3,306
23.95	Total new obligations	−2,936	−3,071	−3,306
23.98	Unobligated balance expiring or withdrawn	−3		
24.40	Unobligated balance available, end of year	187		
	New budget authority (gross), detail:			
	Discretionary:			
40.00	Appropriation	2,675	2,756	3,174
40.15	Appropriation (emergency)	316		
40.78	Reduction pursuant to P.L. 105–277	−3		
40.79	Reduction pursuant to P.L. 106–69		−2	
42.00	Transferred from other accounts	32		
43.00	Appropriation (total discretionary)	3,020	2,754	3,174
	Spending authority from offsetting collections:			
68.00	Offsetting collections (cash)	117	130	132
68.10	From Federal sources: Change in receivables and unpaid, unfilled orders	41		
68.15	From Federal sources: Adjustments to receivables and unpaid, unfilled orders	−52		
68.90	Spending authority from offsetting collections (total discretionary)	106	130	132
70.00	Total new budget authority (gross)	3,126	2,884	3,306
	Change in unpaid obligations:			
	Unpaid obligations, start of year:			
72.40	Obligated balance, start of year	590	571	820
72.95	From Federal sources: Receivables and unpaid, unfilled orders	164	205	205
72.99	Total unpaid obligations, start of year	754	776	1,025
73.10	Total new obligations	2,936	3,071	3,306
73.20	Total outlays (gross)	−2,929	−2,822	−3,256
73.40	Adjustments in expired accounts (net)	16		
	Unpaid obligations, end of year:			
74.40	Obligated balance, end of year	571	820	870
74.95	From Federal sources: Receivables and unpaid, unfilled orders	205	205	205
74.99	Total unpaid obligations, end of year	776	1,025	1,075
	Outlays (gross), detail:			
86.90	Outlays from new discretionary authority	2,492	2,333	2,671
86.93	Outlays from discretionary balances	437	489	585
87.00	Total outlays (gross)	2,929	2,822	3,256
	Offsets:			
	Against gross budget authority and outlays:			
	Offsetting collections (cash) from:			
	Federal sources:			
88.00	Department of Defense	−26	−32	−32
88.00	Other Federal sources	−81	−91	−93
88.40	Non-Federal sources	−10	−7	−7

88.90	Total, offsetting collections (cash)	–117	–130	–132
	Against gross budget authority only:			
88.95	From Federal sources: Change in receivables and unpaid, unfilled orders	–41		
88.96	From Federal sources: Adjustment to receivables and unpaid, unfilled orders	52		
	Net budget authority and outlays:			
89.00	Budget authority	3,020	2,754	3,174
90.00	Outlays	2,812	2,692	3,124

Summary of Budget Authority and Outlays

(in millions of dollars)

	1999 actual	*2000 est.*	*2001 est.*
Enacted/requested:			
Budget Authority	3,020	2,754	3,174
Outlays	2,812	2,692	3,124
Supplemental proposal:			
Budget Authority		18	
Outlays		18	
Legislative proposal, not subject to PAYGO:			
Budget Authority			–116
Outlays			–116
Total:			
Budget Authority	3,020	2,772	3,058
Outlays	2,812	2,710	3,008

To carry out its unique duties as a peacetime operating agency and one of the military services, the Coast Guard employs multipurpose vessels, aircraft, and shore units, strategically located along the coasts and inland waterways of the United States and in selected areas overseas. The 2001 request provides for the safety of the public, and the Coast Guard's work force, with a continued emphasis on critical national security and law enforcement missions. For example, the request includes $565 million for drug interdiction activities. An additional $48 million for drug interdiction capital expenses is requested in the Acquisition, Construction, and Improvements account. The Coast Guard will increase its drug interdiction efforts over 2000 levels by increasing vessel and aircraft operating hours, expanding the use of armed helicopters, and improving intelligence collection.

The request also addresses Coast Guard readiness concerns. It strengthens the workforce, improves recruiting and retention, adds critical search-and-rescue positions, and makes good health care more accessible for active duty dependents.

A supplemental request transmitted with this budget would authorize the Department of Defense to transfer $18 million to the Coast Guard to cover the cost of medical care services for Coast Guard personnel, retirees, and their dependents. The costs of medical care provided through the Department of Defense TRICARE system and military treatment facilities have increased significantly in the past few years. The Coast guard did not have sufficient information to budget for these increased costs in their 2000 Budget. In order to ensure that the Coast Guard has the ability to finance the health care their beneficiaries obtain through the Department of Defense system, the Department of Defense will transfer $18 million in 2000 to the Coast Guard.

Object Classification (in millions of dollars)

Identification code 69–0201–0–1–999		1999 actual	2000 est.	2001 est.
	Direct obligations:			
	Personnel compensation:			
11.1	Full-time permanent	194	214	228
11.3	Other than full-time permanent	6	7	7
11.5	Other personnel compensation	7	8	9
11.7	Military personnel	1,098	1,203	1,278
11.9	Total personnel compensation	1,305	1,432	1,522
12.1	Civilian personnel benefits	48	53	57
12.2	Military personnel benefits	118	129	136
13.0	Benefits for former personnel	1	1	2
21.0	Travel and transportation of persons	86	86	93
22.0	Transportation of things	55	58	62
23.1	Rental payments to GSA	36	35	34
23.2	Rental payments to others	82	83	83
23.3	Communications, utilities, and miscellaneous charges	100	101	101
24.0	Printing and reproduction	10	10	11
25.1	Advisory and assistance services	10	10	11
25.2	Other services	149	133	148
25.3	Purchases of goods and services from Government accounts	2	3	3
25.4	Operation and maintenance of facilities	164	160	181
25.6	Medical care	122	127	164
25.7	Operation and maintenance of equipment	102	97	113
26.0	Supplies and materials	385	367	389
31.0	Equipment	71	72	79
32.0	Land and structures	1	1	2
42.0	Insurance claims and indemnities	8	8	8
99.0	Subtotal, direct obligations	2,855	2,966	3,199
99.0	Reimbursable obligations	81	105	107
99.9	Total new obligations	2,936	3,071	3,306

Personnel Summary

Identification code 69–0201–0–1–999		1999 actual	2000 est.	2001 est.
	Direct:			
	Total compensable workyears:			
1001	Full-time equivalent employment	4,452	4,529	4,523
1101	Full-time equivalent employment	34,332	34,987	35,291
	Reimbursable:			
	Total compensable workyears:			
2001	Full-time equivalent employment	188	202	202
2101	Full-time equivalent employment	140	146	146

Operating Expenses

(Legislative proposal, not subject to PAYGO)

Contingent upon the enactment of authorizing legislation, the Secretary shall establish and adjust user fees for Coast Guard navigation assistance services to commercial cargo and cruise vessels, and 55 percent of such user fees shall be deposited as offsetting collections to this appropriation, and 45 percent shall be deposited as offsetting collections to the "Acquisition, construction, and improvements" account, all such amounts to remain available until expended for the purpose of navigation assistance services: Provided further, That upon enactment of such authorizing legislation, the amount appropriated above from the General Fund shall be reduced by $116,000,000 and the amount appropriated to the "Acquisition, construction, and improvements" account from the General Fund shall be reduced by $96,000,000.

Program and Financing (in millions of dollars)

Identification code 69–0201–2–1–999		1999 actual	2000 est.	2001 est.
	New budget authority (gross), detail:			
	Discretionary:			
40.00	Appropriation			–116
68.00	Spending authority from offsetting collections: Offsetting collections (cash)			116
70.00	Total new budget authority (gross)			
	Offsets:			
	Against gross budget authority and outlays:			
88.45	Offsetting collections (cash) from: Offsetting governmental collections from the public			–116
	Net budget authority and outlays:			
89.00	Budget authority			–116
90.00	Outlays			–116

The Administration will propose legislation to authorize the collection and spending of a user fee for Coast Guard navigational assistance services to commercial cargo and cruise vessels, contingent upon the enactment of the appropriations proviso above. If the proposed authorizing legislation is enacted, the proviso will reduce the General Fund appropriation in two Coast Guard accounts by the amount of the estimated

General and special funds—Continued

Operating Expenses—Continued

user fee collections. This will allow total discretionary resources to not exceed the amount allowed under the discretionary spending caps. The proviso will allow the Coast Guard to spend whatever amounts of user fees are collected, possibly more or less than the estimates in the schedule or the specified reduction in the General Fund appropriation.

Coast Guard navigational assistance services include buoy placement and maintenance, vessel traffic services, radio and satellite navigation systems, and waterways regulation. The 2001 fee collections are estimated to be $212 million, based on four months implementation of the charge. Of this amount, $116 million will offset the Operating Expenses account and $96 million will offset the Acquisition, construction, and improvements account. When fully implemented, fees are expected to recover $636 million of the Coast Guard's costs annually.

Acquisition, Construction, and Improvements

For necessary expenses of acquisition, construction, renovation, and improvement of aids to navigation, shore facilities, vessels, and aircraft, including equipment related thereto, [$389,326,000] *$520,200,000*, of which $20,000,000 shall be derived from the Oil Spill Liability Trust Fund; of which [$134,560,000] *$257,180,000* shall be available to acquire, repair, renovate or improve vessels, small boats and related equipment, to remain available until September 30, [2004; $44,210,000] *2005; $43,650,000* shall be available to acquire new aircraft and increase aviation capability, to remain available until September 30, [2002; $51,626,000] *2003, $60,313,000* shall be available for other equipment, to remain available until September 30, [2002; $63,800,000] *2003; $61,606,000* shall be available for shore facilities and aids to navigation facilities, to remain available until September 30, [2002; $50,930,000] *2003; $55,151,000* shall be available for personnel compensation and benefits and related costs, to remain available until September 30, [2001] *2002;* and [$44,200,000] *$42,300,000* for the Integrated Deepwater Systems program, to remain available until September 30, [2002] *2003: Provided*, That the Commandant of the Coast Guard is authorized to dispose of *surplus real property*, by sale [at fair market value, all rights, title, and interest of any United States entity on behalf of the Coast Guard in HU–25 aircraft and Coast Guard property, and improvements thereto, in South Haven, Michigan; ESMT Manasquan, New Jersey; Petaluma, California; ESMT Portsmouth, New Hampshire; Station Clair Flats, Michigan; and Aids to Navigation Team Huron, Ohio: *Provided further*, That all] *or lease, and the* proceeds [from the sale of properties listed under this heading, and from the sale of HU–25 aircraft,] shall be credited to this appropriation as offsetting collections [and made available only for the Integrated Deepwater Systems program] *of which not more than $10,000,000,* to remain available for obligation until September 30, [2002: *Provided further*, That obligations made pursuant to the provisions of this Act for the Integrated Deepwater Systems program may not exceed $50,000,000 during fiscal year 2000: *Provided further*, That upon initial submission to the Congress of the fiscal year 2001 President's budget, the Secretary of Transportation shall transmit to the Congress a comprehensive capital investment plan for the United States Coast Guard which includes funding for each budget line item for fiscal years 2001 through 2005, with total funding for each year of the plan constrained to the funding targets for those years as estimated and approved by the Office of Management and Budget] *2003, shall be for purposes of this account: Provided further, That the amount herein appropriated from the General Fund shall be reduced by such amount: Provided further, That any such proceeds in excess of $10,000,000 shall be retained and remain available until expended, but shall not be available for obligation until October 1, 2001. (Department of Transportation and Related Agencies Appropriations Act, 2000.)*

Program and Financing (in millions of dollars)

Identification code 69–0240–0–1–403		1999 actual	2000 est.	2001 est.
	Obligations by program activity:			
	Direct program:			
00.01	Search and rescue	65	46	53
00.02	Aids to navigation	162	111	146
00.03	Marine safety	46	36	46
00.04	Marine environmental protection	70	52	69
00.05	Enforcement of laws and treaties	140	95	119
00.06	Ice operations	46	48	87
00.07	Defense readiness	10	9	10
08.00	Total direct program	539	397	530
09.01	Reimbursable program	12	28	28
10.00	Total new obligations	551	425	558
	Budgetary resources available for obligation:			
21.40	Unobligated balance available, start of year	271	356	346
22.00	New budget authority (gross)	632	416	548
22.10	Resources available from recoveries of prior year obligations	6		
23.90	Total budgetary resources available for obligation	909	772	894
23.95	Total new obligations	−551	−425	−558
23.98	Unobligated balance expiring or withdrawn	−2		
24.40	Unobligated balance available, end of year	356	346	336
	New budget authority (gross), detail:			
	Discretionary:			
40.00	Appropriation	374	370	490
40.15	Appropriation (emergency)	230		
40.76	Reduction pursuant to P.L. 106–113		−1	
40.79	Reduction pursuant to P.L. 106–69		−1	
43.00	Appropriation (total discretionary)	604	368	490
	Spending authority from offsetting collections:			
68.00	Offsetting collections (cash)	28	48	58
68.10	From Federal sources: Change in receivables and unpaid, unfilled orders	−14		
68.15	From Federal sources: Adjustments to receivables and unpaid, unfilled orders	14		
68.90	Spending authority from offsetting collections (total discretionary)	28	48	58
70.00	Total new budget authority (gross)	632	416	548
	Change in unpaid obligations:			
	Unpaid obligations, start of year:			
72.40	Obligated balance, start of year	399	518	480
72.95	From Federal sources: Receivables and unpaid, unfilled orders	60	46	46
72.99	Total unpaid obligations, start of year	459	564	526
73.10	Total new obligations	551	425	558
73.20	Total outlays (gross)	−421	−463	−452
73.40	Adjustments in expired accounts (net)	−20		
73.45	Adjustments in unexpired accounts	−6		
	Unpaid obligations, end of year:			
74.40	Obligated balance, end of year	518	480	585
74.95	From Federal sources: Receivables and unpaid, unfilled orders	46	46	46
74.99	Total unpaid obligations, end of year	564	526	631
	Outlays (gross), detail:			
86.90	Outlays from new discretionary authority	173	140	181
86.93	Outlays from discretionary balances	248	323	272
87.00	Total outlays (gross)	421	463	452
	Offsets:			
	Against gross budget authority and outlays:			
88.00	Offsetting collections (cash) from: Federal sources	−28	−48	−58
	Against gross budget authority only:			
88.95	From Federal sources: Change in receivables and unpaid, unfilled orders	14		
88.96	From Federal sources: Adjustment to receivables and unpaid, unfilled orders	−14		
	Net budget authority and outlays:			
89.00	Budget authority	604	368	490
90.00	Outlays	392	415	394

Summary of Budget Authority and Outlays

(in millions of dollars)

	1999 actual	2000 est.	2001 est.
Enacted/requested:			
Budget Authority	604	368	490
Outlays	393	415	395
Legislative proposal, not subject to PAYGO:			
Budget Authority			−96
Outlays			−96
Total:			
Budget Authority	604	368	394
Outlays	393	415	299

The Acquisition, Construction, and Improvements (AC&I) appropriation provides for the acquisition, construction, and improvement of the vessels, aircraft, information management resources, shore facilities, and aids to navigation required to execute the Coast Guard's missions and achieve its performance goals.

The 2001 Budget proposes the establishment and collection of a cost based user fee on commercial cargo and cruise vessels for navigation assistance provided by the Coast Guard.

Vessels.—In 2001, the Coast Guard will acquire multi-mission platforms that use advanced technology to reduce life cycle operating costs. The seagoing buoy tender acquisition will continue with a one-time request for 3 ships. New projects include replacement of the Great Lakes heavy icebreaker and over-the-horizon cutter boats.

Deepwater.—The Deepwater capability replacement analysis continues. This analysis will identify the types of assets and technologies needed to perform basic Deepwater mission functions at minimum cost. Such information will advise future decisions on the scope of the Deepwater project.

Aircraft.—In 2001, the Coast Guard will acquire assets that ensure safety in the performance of missions. Improvements to the HH–65 helicopter and upgrade of the HU–25 sensors will continue. A new project is proposed to acquire 3 helicopters for operations with USCGC HEALY, a new polar icebreaker.

Other Equipment.—In 2001, the Coast Guard will invest in numerous management information and decision support systems that will result in increased efficiencies, future FTE reductions, and operating and maintenance savings. The Marine Information for Safety and Law Enforcement (MISLE), Fleet Logistics System (FLS), National Distress System (NDS), and Commercial Satellite Communications projects will continue.

Shore Facilities.—In 2001, the Coast Guard will invest in modern structures that are more energy-efficient, comply with regulatory codes, minimize follow-on maintenance requirements and replace existing dilapidated structures.

Personnel and Related Costs.—Personnel resources will be utilized to execute the AC&I projects described above.

Object Classification (in millions of dollars)

Identification code 69–0240–0–1–403		1999 actual	2000 est.	2001 est.
	Direct obligations:			
	Personnel compensation:			
11.1	Full-time permanent	15	18	18
11.7	Military personnel	20	20	21
11.9	Total personnel compensation	35	38	39
12.1	Civilian personnel benefits	3	4	6
12.2	Military personnel benefits	2	3	2
21.0	Travel and transportation of persons	6	8	6
22.0	Transportation of things	1	1	1
23.3	Communications, utilities, and miscellaneous charges	3	3	3
25.1	Advisory and assistance services	34		
25.2	Other services	129	74	109
26.0	Supplies and materials	27	42	42
31.0	Equipment	226	157	247
32.0	Land and structures	73	67	75
99.0	Subtotal, direct obligations	539	397	530
99.0	Reimbursable obligations	12	28	28
99.9	Total new obligations	551	425	558

Personnel Summary

Identification code 69–0240–0–1–403		1999 actual	2000 est.	2001 est.
	Total compensable workyears:			
1001	Full-time equivalent employment	254	285	285
1101	Full-time equivalent employment	366	366	366

Acquisition, Construction, and Improvements

(Legislative proposal, not subject to PAYGO)

Program and Financing (in millions of dollars)

Identification code 69–0240–2–1–403		1999 actual	2000 est.	2001 est.
	New budget authority (gross), detail:			
	Discretionary:			
40.00	Appropriation			−96
68.00	Spending authority from offsetting collections: Offsetting collections (cash)			96
70.00	Total new budget authority (gross)			
	Offsets:			
	Against gross budget authority and outlays:			
88.45	Offsetting collections (cash) from: Offsetting governmental collections from the public			−96
	Net budget authority and outlays:			
89.00	Budget authority			−96
90.00	Outlays			−96

The Administration's forthcoming legislative proposal (discussed under the Operating Expenses heading) will authorize fees to offset costs of $96 million in the Coast Guard's capital appropriation.

Environmental Compliance and Restoration

For necessary expenses to carry out the Coast Guard's environmental compliance and restoration functions under chapter 19 of title 14, United States Code, [$17,000,000] *$16,700,000*, to remain available until expended. *(Department of Transportation and Related Agencies Appropriations Act, 2000.)*

Program and Financing (in millions of dollars)

Identification code 69–0230–0–1–304		1999 actual	2000 est.	2001 est.
	Obligations by program activity:			
10.00	Total new obligations	23	18	18
	Budgetary resources available for obligation:			
21.40	Unobligated balance available, start of year	3	3	2
22.00	New budget authority (gross)	21	17	17
22.10	Resources available from recoveries of prior year obligations	2		
23.90	Total budgetary resources available for obligation	26	20	19
23.95	Total new obligations	−23	−18	−18
24.40	Unobligated balance available, end of year	3	2	1
	New budget authority (gross), detail:			
	Discretionary:			
40.00	Appropriation	21	17	17
	Change in unpaid obligations:			
72.40	Unpaid obligations, start of year: Obligated balance, start of year	15	12	16
73.10	Total new obligations	23	18	18
73.20	Total outlays (gross)	−23	−14	−15
73.45	Adjustments in unexpired accounts	−2		
74.40	Unpaid obligations, end of year: Obligated balance, end of year	12	16	18

General and special funds—Continued

ENVIRONMENTAL COMPLIANCE AND RESTORATION—Continued

Program and Financing (in millions of dollars)—Continued

Identification code 69–0230–0–1–304	1999 actual	2000 est.	2001 est.
Outlays (gross), detail:			
86.90 Outlays from new discretionary authority	6	5	5
86.93 Outlays from discretionary balances	17	9	10
87.00 Total outlays (gross)	23	14	15
Net budget authority and outlays:			
89.00 Budget authority	21	17	17
90.00 Outlays	23	14	15

The environmental compliance and restoration account provides resources to the Coast Guard to satisfy environmental compliance and restoration related obligations arising under chapter 19 of title 14 of the United States Code.

Object Classification (in millions of dollars)

Identification code 69–0230–0–1–304	1999 actual	2000 est.	2001 est.
11.1 Personnel compensation: Full-time permanent	3	4	4
12.1 Civilian personnel benefits	1	1	1
25.2 Other services	19	13	13
99.9 Total new obligations	23	18	18

Personnel Summary

Identification code 69–0230–0–1–304	1999 actual	2000 est.	2001 est.
Total compensable workyears:			
1001 Full-time equivalent employment	50	53	52
1101 Full-time equivalent employment	2	2	2

[ALTERATION OF BRIDGES]

[For necessary expenses for alteration or removal of obstructive bridges, $15,000,000, to remain available until expended.] *(Department of Transportation and Related Agencies Appropriations Act, 2000.)*

Program and Financing (in millions of dollars)

Identification code 69–0244–0–1–403	1999 actual	2000 est.	2001 est.
Obligations by program activity:			
10.00 Total new obligations (object class 25.2)	15	15	27
Budgetary resources available for obligation:			
21.40 Unobligated balance available, start of year		27	27
22.00 New budget authority (gross)	38	15	
22.10 Resources available from recoveries of prior year obligations	4		
23.90 Total budgetary resources available for obligation	42	42	27
23.95 Total new obligations	−15	−15	−27
24.40 Unobligated balance available, end of year	27	27	
New budget authority (gross), detail:			
Discretionary:			
40.00 Appropriation	14	15	
40.75 Reduction pursuant to P.L. 106–51	−5		
42.00 Transferred from other accounts	29		
43.00 Appropriation (total discretionary)	38	15	
Change in unpaid obligations:			
72.40 Unpaid obligations, start of year: Obligated balance, start of year	71	70	42
73.10 Total new obligations	15	15	27
73.20 Total outlays (gross)	−12	−43	−31
73.45 Adjustments in unexpired accounts	−4		
74.40 Unpaid obligations, end of year: Obligated balance, end of year	70	42	38
Outlays (gross), detail:			
86.90 Outlays from new discretionary authority	9	3	
86.93 Outlays from discretionary balances	3	40	31
87.00 Total outlays (gross)	12	43	31
Net budget authority and outlays:			
89.00 Budget authority	38	15	
90.00 Outlays	12	43	31

This appropriation provides the Government's share of the costs for altering or removing bridges determined to be obstructions to navigation. Alteration of obstructive highway bridges is eligible for funding from the Federal-Aid Highways program. Up to $11 million from Federal-Aid Highways will reimburse the costs of alterations. The Coast Guard will continue to make the determinations as to whether any bridge presents an unreasonable obstruction to navigation, and to administer the program.

RETIRED PAY

For retired pay, including the payment of obligations therefor otherwise chargeable to lapsed appropriations for this purpose, and payments under the Retired Serviceman's Family Protection and Survivor Benefits Plans, and for payments for medical care of retired personnel and their dependents under the Dependents Medical Care Act (10 U.S.C. ch. 55), [$730,327,000] *$778,000,000. (Department of Transportation and Related Agencies Appropriations Act, 2000.)*

Program and Financing (in millions of dollars)

Identification code 69–0241–0–1–403	1999 actual	2000 est.	2001 est.
Obligations by program activity:			
00.01 Regular military personnel	555	598	633
00.03 Reserve personnel	37	37	40
00.04 Survivor benefit programs	15	18	20
00.05 Medical care	65	77	85
06.00 Total direct program	672	730	778
10.00 Total new obligations	672	730	778
Budgetary resources available for obligation:			
22.00 New budget authority (gross)	684	730	778
23.95 Total new obligations	−672	−730	−778
23.98 Unobligated balance expiring or withdrawn	−12		
New budget authority (gross), detail:			
Mandatory:			
60.00 Appropriation	684	730	778
Change in unpaid obligations:			
72.40 Unpaid obligations, start of year: Obligated balance, start of year	60	62	100
73.10 Total new obligations	672	730	778
73.20 Total outlays (gross)	−669	−693	−761
74.40 Unpaid obligations, end of year: Obligated balance, end of year	62	100	117
Outlays (gross), detail:			
86.97 Outlays from new mandatory authority	609	631	661
86.98 Outlays from mandatory balances	60	62	100
87.00 Total outlays (gross)	669	693	761
Net budget authority and outlays:			
89.00 Budget authority	684	730	778
90.00 Outlays	669	693	761

This program provides for retired pay of military personnel of the Coast Guard and Coast Guard Reserve, members of the former Lighthouse Service, and for annuities payable to beneficiaries of retired military personnel under the retired serviceman's family protection plan (10 U.S.C. 1431–46) and survivor benefits plans (10 U.S.C. 1447–55); and for payments for medical care of retired personnel and their dependents under the Dependents Medical Care Act (10 U.S.C., ch. 55).

The following tabulation shows the average number of personnel on the rolls during 1999 compared with estimated numbers for 2000 and 2001:

AVERAGE NUMBER

Category:	*1999 actual*	*2000 est.*	*2001 est.*
Commissioned officers	5,396	5,502	5,633
Warrant officers	4,365	4,425	4,512
Enlisted personnel	18,476	18,985	19,415
Former Lighthouse Service personnel	11	8	5
Reserve personnel	3,564	3,764	3,934
Total	31,812	32,684	33,499

Object Classification (in millions of dollars)

Identification code 69–0241–0–1–403	1999 actual	2000 est.	2001 est.
13.0 Benefits for former personnel	607	653	693
25.6 Medical care	65	77	85
99.9 Total new obligations	672	730	778

RESERVE TRAINING

[(INCLUDING TRANSFER OF FUNDS)]

For all necessary expenses of the Coast Guard Reserve, as authorized by law; maintenance and operation of facilities; and supplies, equipment, and services; [$72,000,000: *Provided*, That no more than $21,500,000 of funds made available under this heading may be transferred to Coast Guard "Operating expenses" or otherwise made available to reimburse the Coast Guard for financial support of the Coast Guard Reserve: *Provided further*, That none of the funds in this Act may be used by the Coast Guard to assess direct charges on the Coast Guard Reserves for items or activities which were not so charged during fiscal year 1997] *$73,371,000. (Department of Transportation and Related Agencies Appropriations Act, 2000.)*

Program and Financing (in millions of dollars)

Identification code 69–0242–0–1–403	1999 actual	2000 est.	2001 est.
Obligations by program activity:			
00.01 Initial training	2	2	3
00.02 Continuing training	45	44	45
00.03 Operation and maintenance support	15	16	16
00.04 Program management and administration	12	10	9
10.00 Total new obligations	74	72	73
Budgetary resources available for obligation:			
22.00 New budget authority (gross)	74	72	73
23.95 Total new obligations	−74	−72	−73
New budget authority (gross), detail:			
Discretionary:			
40.00 Appropriation	69	72	73
40.15 Appropriation (emergency)	5		
43.00 Appropriation (total discretionary)	74	72	73
Change in unpaid obligations:			
72.40 Unpaid obligations, start of year: Obligated balance, start of year	9	9	9
73.10 Total new obligations	74	72	73
73.20 Total outlays (gross)	−74	−71	−73
74.40 Unpaid obligations, end of year: Obligated balance, end of year	9	9	10
Outlays (gross), detail:			
86.90 Outlays from new discretionary authority	65	63	64
86.93 Total outlays (gross)	8	8	9
87.00 Total outlays (gross)	74	71	73
Net budget authority and outlays:			
89.00 Budget authority	74	72	73
90.00 Outlays	73	71	73

The Coast Guard Reserve Forces provide qualified personnel and trained units for active duty in event of conflict, national emergency, or natural and man-made disasters. The reservists maintain their readiness through mobilization exercises, and duty alongside regular Coast Guard members during routine and emergency operations. Reservists will continue to serve as a cost effective surge force for response to human and natural disasters.

Object Classification (in millions of dollars)

Identification code 69–0242–0–1–403	1999 actual	2000 est.	2001 est.
Personnel compensation:			
11.1 Full-time permanent	3	3	3
11.7 Military personnel	50	53	54
11.9 Total personnel compensation	53	56	57
12.1 Civilian personnel benefits	1	1	1
12.2 Military personnel benefits	5	5	5
21.0 Travel and transportation of persons	3	2	2
22.0 Transportation of things	2	1	1
25.2 Other services	4	3	3
26.0 Supplies and materials	5	3	3
31.0 Equipment	1	1	1
99.9 Total new obligations	74	72	73

Personnel Summary

Identification code 69–0242–0–1–403	1999 actual	2000 est.	2001 est.
Total compensable workyears:			
1001 Full-time equivalent employment	84	87	85
1101 Full-time equivalent employment	394	394	389

RESEARCH, DEVELOPMENT, TEST, AND EVALUATION

For necessary expenses, not otherwise provided for, for applied scientific research, development, test, and evaluation; maintenance, rehabilitation, lease and operation of facilities and equipment, as authorized by law, [$19,000,000] *$21,320,000*, to remain available until expended, of which $3,500,000 shall be derived from the Oil Spill Liability Trust Fund: *Provided*, That there may be credited to and used for the purposes of this appropriation funds received from State and local governments, other public authorities, private sources, and foreign countries, for expenses incurred for research, development, testing, and evaluation. *(Department of Transportation and Related Agencies Appropriations Act, 2000.)*

Program and Financing (in millions of dollars)

Identification code 69–0243–0–1–403	1999 actual	2000 est.	2001 est.
Obligations by program activity:			
Direct program:			
00.01 Search and rescue	2	2	2
00.02 Aids to navigation	3	2	3
00.03 Marine safety	4	7	7
00.04 Marine environmental protection	3	4	3
00.05 Enforcement of laws and treaties	5	5	6
00.06 Ice operations	1		
00.07 Defense readiness	1		
08.00 Total direct program	19	20	21
09.01 Reimbursable program	1	1	1
10.00 Total new obligations	20	21	22
Budgetary resources available for obligation:			
21.40 Unobligated balance available, start of year	3	1	
22.00 New budget authority (gross)	17	19	22
23.90 Total budgetary resources available for obligation	20	20	22
23.95 Total new obligations	−20	−21	−22
24.40 Unobligated balance available, end of year	1		
New budget authority (gross), detail:			
Discretionary:			
40.00 Appropriation	8	15	18
40.15 Appropriation (emergency)	5		
43.00 Appropriation (total discretionary)	13	15	18
68.00 Spending authority from offsetting collections: Offsetting collections (cash)	4	4	4

General and special funds—Continued

Research, Development, Test, and Evaluation—Continued

Program and Financing (in millions of dollars)—Continued

Identification code 69–0243–0–1–403	1999 actual	2000 est.	2001 est.
70.00 Total new budget authority (gross)	17	19	22
Change in unpaid obligations:			
Unpaid obligations, start of year:			
72.40 Obligated balance, start of year	13	13	11
72.95 From Federal sources: Receivables and unpaid, unfilled orders	2	2	2
72.99 Total unpaid obligations, start of year	15	15	13
73.10 Total new obligations	20	21	22
73.20 Total outlays (gross)	–20	–22	–22
Unpaid obligations, end of year:			
74.40 Obligated balance, end of year	13	11	11
74.95 From Federal sources: Receivables and unpaid, unfilled orders	2	2	2
74.99 Total unpaid obligations, end of year	15	13	13
Outlays (gross), detail:			
86.90 Outlays from new discretionary authority	10	12	14
86.93 Outlays from discretionary balances	10	10	8
87.00 Total outlays (gross)	20	22	22
Offsets:			
Against gross budget authority and outlays:			
88.40 Offsetting collections (cash) from: Non-Federal sources	–4	–4	–4
Net budget authority and outlays:			
89.00 Budget authority	13	15	18
90.00 Outlays	16	18	18

The Coast Guard's Research and Development program includes the development of techniques, methods, hardware, and systems which directly contribute to increasing the productivity and effectiveness of Coast Guard's operating missions. Priorities for 2001 include drug interdiction surveillance, fuel cell vessel propulsion, computerized search-and-rescue tools, and more effective oil spill response techniques.

Object Classification (in millions of dollars)

Identification code 69–0243–0–1–403	1999 actual	2000 est.	2001 est.
Personnel compensation:			
11.1 Full-time permanent	4	5	5
11.7 Military personnel	2	2	2
11.9 Total personnel compensation	6	7	7
12.1 Civilian personnel benefits	1	1	2
21.0 Travel and transportation of persons	1	1	1
25.2 Other services	1	1	1
25.5 Research and development contracts	9	9	9
26.0 Supplies and materials	1	1	1
99.0 Subtotal, direct obligations	19	20	21
99.5 Below reporting threshold	1	1	1
99.9 Total new obligations	20	21	22

Personnel Summary

Identification code 69–0243–0–1–403	1999 actual	2000 est.	2001 est.
Total compensable workyears:			
1001 Full-time equivalent employment	68	74	74
1101 Full-time equivalent employment	31	31	31

Intragovernmental funds:

Coast Guard Supply Fund

Program and Financing (in millions of dollars)

Identification code 69–4535–0–4–403	1999 actual	2000 est.	2001 est.
Obligations by program activity:			
10.00 Total new obligations (object class 26.0)	62	63	63
Budgetary resources available for obligation:			
22.00 New budget authority (gross)	62	63	63
23.95 Total new obligations	–62	–63	–63
New budget authority (gross), detail:			
Discretionary:			
68.00 Spending authority from offsetting collections (gross): Offsetting collections (cash)	62	63	63
Change in unpaid obligations:			
72.40 Unpaid obligations, start of year: Obligated balance, start of year	16	7	7
73.10 Total new obligations	62	63	63
73.20 Total outlays (gross)	–70	–63	–63
74.40 Unpaid obligations, end of year: Obligated balance, end of year	7	7	7
Outlays (gross), detail:			
86.90 Outlays from new discretionary authority	61	63	63
86.93 Outlays from discretionary balances	9		
87.00 Total outlays (gross)	70	63	63
Offsets:			
Against gross budget authority and outlays:			
Offsetting collections (cash) from:			
88.00 Federal sources	–53	–54	–54
88.40 Non-Federal sources	–9	–9	–9
88.90 Total, offsetting collections (cash)	–62	–63	–63
Net budget authority and outlays:			
89.00 Budget authority			
90.00 Outlays	9		

The Coast Guard supply fund, in accordance with 14 U.S.C. 650, finances the procurement of uniform clothing, commissary provisions, general stores, technical material, and fuel for vessels over 180 feet in length. The fund is normally financed by reimbursements from sale of goods.

Coast Guard Yard Fund

Program and Financing (in millions of dollars)

Identification code 69–4743–0–4–403	1999 actual	2000 est.	2001 est.
Obligations by program activity:			
09.01 Costs of goods sold	21	21	21
09.02 Other	44	44	44
09.03 Capital investment: Purchase of equipment	1	1	1
10.00 Total new obligations	66	66	66
Budgetary resources available for obligation:			
21.40 Unobligated balance available, start of year	7	3	
22.00 New budget authority (gross)	62	63	67
23.90 Total budgetary resources available for obligation	69	66	67
23.95 Total new obligations	–66	–66	–66
24.40 Unobligated balance available, end of year	3		
New budget authority (gross), detail:			
Discretionary:			
68.00 Spending authority from offsetting collections (gross): Offsetting collections (cash)	62	63	67
Change in unpaid obligations:			
72.40 Unpaid obligations, start of year: Obligated balance, start of year	1	–2	2
73.10 Total new obligations	66	66	66

73.20 Total outlays (gross)	−69	−63	−67
74.40 Unpaid obligations, end of year: Obligated balance, end of year	−2	2	2
Outlays (gross), detail:			
86.90 Outlays from new discretionary authority	62	63	67
86.93 Outlays from discretionary balances	7		
87.00 Total outlays (gross)	69	63	67
Offsets:			
Against gross budget authority and outlays:			
88.00 Offsetting collections (cash) from: Federal sources	−62	−63	−67
Net budget authority and outlays:			
89.00 Budget authority			
90.00 Outlays	7		

This fund finances the industrial operation of the Coast Guard Yard, Curtis Bay, MD (14 U.S.C.). The yard finances its operations out of advances received from Coast Guard appropriations and other agencies for all direct and indirect costs.

ANALYSIS BY TYPE OF WORK

[Percent]

	1999 actual	*2000 est.*	*2001 est.*
Vessel repairs and alterations	32	25	25
Boat repairs and construction	20	22	10
Buoy fabrication	1	1	1
Fabrication of special and miscellaneous items	47	52	64
Total	100	100	100

Object Classification (in millions of dollars)

Identification code 69–4743–0–4–403	1999 actual	2000 est.	2001 est.
Personnel compensation:			
11.1 Full-time permanent	21	22	23
11.3 Other than full-time permanent	3	3	3
11.5 Other personnel compensation	5	5	5
11.7 Military personnel	1	1	1
11.9 Total personnel compensation	30	31	32
12.1 Civilian personnel benefits	6	6	6
23.3 Communications, utilities, and miscellaneous charges	2	2	2
25.2 Other services	3	3	3
26.0 Supplies and materials	24	23	22
31.0 Equipment	1	1	1
99.9 Total new obligations	66	66	66

Personnel Summary

Identification code 69–4743–0–4–403	1999 actual	2000 est.	2001 est.
Total compensable workyears:			
2001 Full-time equivalent employment	606	632	632
2101 Full-time equivalent employment	21	22	22

Trust Funds

BOAT SAFETY

(AQUATIC RESOURCES TRUST FUND)

Program and Financing (in millions of dollars)

Identification code 69–8149–0–7–403	1999 actual	2000 est.	2001 est.
Obligations by program activity:			
00.01 State recreational boating safety programs	54	59	59
00.02 Compliance and boating programs	5	5	5
10.00 Total new obligations	59	64	64
Budgetary resources available for obligation:			
21.40 Unobligated balance available, start of year	4	9	9
22.00 New budget authority (gross)	64	64	64
23.90 Total budgetary resources available for obligation	68	73	73
23.95 Total new obligations	−59	−64	−64
24.40 Unobligated balance available, end of year	9	9	9
New budget authority (gross), detail:			
Mandatory:			
62.00 Transferred from other accounts	64	64	64
Change in unpaid obligations:			
72.40 Unpaid obligations, start of year: Obligated balance, start of year	35	37	47
73.10 Total new obligations	59	64	64
73.20 Total outlays (gross)	−57	−54	−61
74.40 Unpaid obligations, end of year: Obligated balance, end of year	37	47	49
Outlays (gross), detail:			
86.93 Outlays from discretionary balances	21	10	1
86.97 Outlays from new mandatory authority	29	29	29
86.98 Outlays from mandatory balances	7	15	31
87.00 Total outlays (gross)	57	54	61
Net budget authority and outlays:			
89.00 Budget authority	64	64	64
90.00 Outlays	57	54	61

This account provides grants for the development and implementation of a coordinated national recreational boating safety program. Boating safety statistics reflect the success in meeting the program's objectives. No discretionary appropriation is requested for 2001 from the Boat safety account of the Aquatic resources trust fund. The Transportation Equity Act for the 21st Century (TEA–21) includes permanent appropriations from the Aquatic resources trust fund of $64 million annually beginning in 1999. Of this total, $59 million is provided for grants to States and $5 million is available for Coast Guard coordination efforts.

Object Classification (in millions of dollars)

Identification code 69–8149–0–7–403	1999 actual	2000 est.	2001 est.
25.2 Other services	4	5	5
25.3 Purchases of goods and services from Government accounts	1	1	1
41.0 Grants, subsidies, and contributions	54	58	58
99.9 Total new obligations	59	64	64

AQUATIC RESOURCES TRUST FUND

Unavailable Collections (in millions of dollars)

Identification code 20–8147–0–7–403	1999 actual	2000 est.	2001 est.
Balance, start of year:			
01.99 Balance, start of year	753	843	854
Receipts:			
02.01 Excise Taxes, Sport Fish Restoration	348	327	340
02.03 Excise Taxes, Boat Safety	26	9	1
02.05 Customs duties, Sport Fish Restoration	26	34	35
02.06 Interest on investments	62	64	66
02.99 Total receipts	462	434	442
04.00 Total: Balances and collections	1,215	1,277	1,296
Appropriation:			
05.01 Sport fish restoration	−372	−423	−407
07.99 Total balance, end of year	843	854	889

Program and Financing (in millions of dollars)

Identification code 20–8147–0–7–403	1999 actual	2000 est.	2001 est.
Memorandum (non-add) entries:			
92.01 Total investments, start of year: U.S. securities: Par value	1,018	1,140	1,158
92.02 Total investments, end of year: U.S. securities: Par value	1,140	1,158	1,184

AQUATIC RESOURCES TRUST FUND—Continued

The Internal Revenue Code of 1986, as amended by TEA–21, provides for the transfer of Highway Trust Fund revenue derived from the motor boat fuel tax and certain other taxes to the Aquatic Resources Trust Fund. Appropriations are authorized from this fund to meet expenditures for programs specified by law, including sport fish restoration and boat safety. Excise tax receipts for the trust fund include motorboat fuel tax receipts, plus receipts from taxes on sport fishing equipment, sonar and fish finders, and small engine fuel.

EXCISE TAXES, AQUATIC RESOURCES TRUST FUND

(In millions of dollars)

Source	*1999 actual*	*2000 est.*	*2001 est.*
Motorboat Fuel Tax	205	174	176
Fishing Equipment Tax	96	100	102
Electric Sonar Tax	2	2	2
Small Engine Fuel Tax	70	60	61
Total	373	336	341

OIL SPILL LIABILITY TRUST FUND

Unavailable Collections (in millions of dollars)

Identification code 20–8185–0–7–304	1999 actual	2000 est.	2001 est.
Balance, start of year:			
01.99 Balance, start of year	918	839	935
Receipts:			
02.02 Interest on investments	48	55	62
02.03 Fines and penalties	6	6	6
02.04 Recoveries	7	8	9
02.05 Transfers from the trans-Alaska pipeline liability fund		173	
02.07 Interest on investments, legislative proposal, not subject to PAYGO			2
02.99 Total receipts	61	242	79
04.00 Total: Balances and collections	979	1,081	1,014
Appropriation:			
05.03 Trust fund share of expenses	−49	−49	−49
05.04 Environmental Protection Agency	−15	−15	−16
05.05 Minerals Management Service	−6	−6	−6
05.07 Research and special programs administration	−4	−5	−4
05.09 Oil spill recovery, Coast Guard	−66	−61	−61
05.10 Denali Commission trust fund		−10	−10
05.99 Subtotal appropriation	−140	−146	−146
07.99 Total balance, end of year	839	935	868

Program and Financing (in millions of dollars)

Identification code 20–8185–0–7–304	1999 actual	2000 est.	2001 est.
Memorandum (non-add) entries:			
92.01 Total investments, start of year: U.S. securities: Par value	1,119	1,063	1,156
92.02 Total investments, end of year: U.S. securities: Par value	1,063	1,156	1,088

The Omnibus Budget Reconciliation Act of 1989, Public Law 101–239, triggered collection of a 5 cent tax on each barrel of oil produced domestically or imported to be deposited into the Oil Spill Liability Trust Fund. Resources from the Oil Spill Liability Trust Fund are used to finance oil pollution prevention and cleanup activities by various Federal agencies. In accordance with the provisions of the Act, the Fund may finance annually up to $50 million of emergency resources and all valid claims from injured parties resulting from oil spills. For Coast Guard, this funds the following accounts: Trust fund share of expenses, Oil spill recovery, and Payment of claims. The authority to collect the oil barrel tax expired on December 31, 1994. Legislation will be proposed to reinstate the tax and place a $5 billion cap on the Fund's balance.

Status of Funds (in millions of dollars)

Identification code 20–8185–0–7–304	1999 actual	2000 est.	2001 est.
Unexpended balance, start of year:			
0100 Uninvested balance	10	2	5
U.S. Securities:			
0101 Par value	1,119	1,063	1,156
0102 Unrealized discounts	−46	−48	−46
0199 Total balance, start of year	1,083	1,017	1,115
Cash income during the year:			
Governmental receipts:			
0202 Fines and penalties	6	6	6
0203 Transfers from the trans-Alaska pipeline liability fund		173	
0204 Recoveries	7	8	9
Intragovernmental transactions:			
Intragovernmental transactions:			
0240 Earnings on investments, oil spill liability trust fund	48	55	62
0240 Earnings on investments, oil spill liability trust fund			2
Offsetting collections:			
0280 Offsetting collections	14	26	26
0297 Income under present law	75	268	103
0298 Income under proposed legislation			2
0299 Total cash income	75	268	105
Cash outgo during year:			
0500 Oil spill research	−6	−6	−6
0501 Oil spill response	−38	−41	−42
0502 Oil Spill Recovery, Coast Guard	−44	−61	−61
0504 Trust fund share of expenses	−49	−49	−49
0505 Trust fund share of pipeline safety	−4	−6	−5
0508 Denali Commission trust fund		−10	−10
0599 Total cash outgo	−141	−173	−173
Unexpended balance, end of year:			
0700 Uninvested balance	2	5	5
U.S. Securities:			
0701 Par value	1,062	1,156	1,088
0702 Unrealized discounts	−48	−46	−46
0799 Total balance, end of year	1,017	1,115	1,047

OIL SPILL RECOVERY, COAST GUARD

(OIL SPILL LIABILITY TRUST FUND)

Program and Financing (in millions of dollars)

Identification code 69–8349–0–7–304	1999 actual	2000 est.	2001 est.
Obligations by program activity:			
00.01 Emergency fund	53	50	50
00.02 Payment of claims	15	10	10
00.03 Prince William Sound Oil Spill Recovery Institute	1	1	1
10.00 Total new obligations (object class 25.2)	69	61	61
Budgetary resources available for obligation:			
21.40 Unobligated balance available, start of year	77	81	81
22.00 New budget authority (gross)	66	61	61
22.10 Resources available from recoveries of prior year obligations	8		
23.90 Total budgetary resources available for obligation	151	142	142
23.95 Total new obligations	−69	−61	−61
24.40 Unobligated balance available, end of year	81	81	81
New budget authority (gross), detail:			
Mandatory:			
60.26 Appropriation (trust fund, definite)	50	50	50
60.27 Appropriation (trust fund, indefinite)	16	11	11
62.50 Appropriation (total mandatory)	66	61	61
Change in unpaid obligations:			
72.40 Unpaid obligations, start of year: Obligated balance, start of year	76	94	94
73.10 Total new obligations	69	61	61
73.20 Total outlays (gross)	−44	−61	−61
73.45 Adjustments in unexpired accounts	−8		
74.40 Unpaid obligations, end of year: Obligated balance, end of year	94	94	94

Outlays (gross), detail:			
86.97 Outlays from new mandatory authority	44	61	61
Net budget authority and outlays:			
89.00 Budget authority	66	61	61
90.00 Outlays	44	61	61
Distribution of budget authority by account:			
Emergency fund	50	50	50
Oil spill recovery institute	1	1	1
Payment of claims	15	10	10
Distribution of outlays by account:			
Emergency fund	31	50	50
Oil spill recovery institute	1	1	1
Payment of claims	12	10	10

This account provides resources from the Oil Spill Liability Trust Fund for costs associated with the cleanup of oil spills. These include emergency costs associated with oil spill cleanup, the Prince William Sound Oil Spill Recovery Institute, and the payment of claims to those who suffer harm from oil spills where the responsible party is not identifiable or is without resources. The program activities in this account will continue to be funded under separate permanent appropriations, and are being displayed in a consolidated format to enhance presentation.

Trust Fund Share of Expenses

(Oil Spill Liability Trust Fund)

Program and Financing (in millions of dollars)

Identification code 69–8314–0–7–304	1999 actual	2000 est.	2001 est.
Obligations by program activity:			
00.01 Operating expenses	25	25	25
00.02 Acquisition, construction and improvements	20	20	20
00.03 Research, development, test and evaluation	4	4	4
10.00 Total new obligations (object class 92.0)	49	49	49
Budgetary resources available for obligation:			
22.00 New budget authority (gross)	49	49	49
23.95 Total new obligations	−49	−49	−49
New budget authority (gross), detail:			
Discretionary:			
40.26 Appropriation (trust fund, definite)	49	49	49
Change in unpaid obligations:			
73.10 Total new obligations	49	49	49
73.20 Total outlays (gross)	−49	−49	−49
Outlays (gross), detail:			
86.90 Outlays from new discretionary authority	49	49	49
Net budget authority and outlays:			
89.00 Budget authority	49	49	49
90.00 Outlays	48	49	49
Distribution of budget authority by account:			
Operating expenses	25	25	25
Acquisition, construction and improvement	20	20	20
Research, development, test, and evaluation	4	4	4
Distribution of outlays by account:			
Operating expenses	25	25	25
Acquisition, construction and improvements	20	20	20
Research, development, test, and evaluation	4	4	4

This account provides resources from the Oil spill liability trust fund for activities authorized under the Operating expenses; Acquisition, construction, and improvements; and Research, development, test and evaluation accounts.

Coast Guard General Gift Fund

Program and Financing (in millions of dollars)

Identification code 69–8533–0–7–403	1999 actual	2000 est.	2001 est.
Budgetary resources available for obligation:			
21.40 Unobligated balance available, start of year	2	2	2
24.40 Unobligated balance available, end of year	2	2	2
Net budget authority and outlays:			
89.00 Budget authority	....	....	....
90.00 Outlays	....	....	....
Memorandum (non-add) entries:			
92.01 Total investments, start of year: U.S. securities: Par value	2	2	2
92.02 Total investments, end of year: U.S. securities: Par value	2	2	2

This trust fund, maintained from gifts and bequests, is used for purposes as specified by the donor in connection with the Coast Guard training program (10 U.S.C. 2601).

Miscellaneous Trust Revolving Funds

Program and Financing (in millions of dollars)

Identification code 69–9981–0–8–403	1999 actual	2000 est.	2001 est.
Obligations by program activity:			
10.00 Total new obligations (object class 25.2)	7	7	7
Budgetary resources available for obligation:			
22.00 New budget authority (gross)	7	7	7
23.95 Total new obligations	−7	−7	−7
New budget authority (gross), detail:			
Mandatory:			
69.00 Offsetting collections (cash)	7	7	7
Change in unpaid obligations:			
73.10 Total new obligations	7	7	7
73.20 Total outlays (gross)	−7	−7	−7
Outlays (gross), detail:			
86.97 Outlays from new mandatory authority	7	7	7
Offsets:			
Against gross budget authority and outlays:			
88.00 Offsetting collections (cash) from: Federal sources	−7	−7	−7
Net budget authority and outlays:			
89.00 Budget authority	....	....	....
90.00 Outlays	....	....	....

The Coast Guard cadet fund is used by the Superintendent of the Coast Guard Academy to receive, plan, control, and expend funds for personal expenses and obligations of Coast Guard cadets.

The Coast Guard surcharge collections, sales of commissary stores fund is used to finance expenses incurred in connection with the operation of the Coast Guard commissary store in Kodiak, Alaska. Revenue is derived from a surcharge placed on sales (14 U.S.C. 487).

FEDERAL AVIATION ADMINISTRATION

The following table depicts the total funding for all Federal Aviation Administration programs, for which more detail is furnished in the budget schedules:

[In millions of dollars]

	1999 actual	*2000 est.*	*2001 est.*
Budget authority:			
Operations	5,586	5,893	6,592
General fund (memorandum entry)	(1,474)	....	....

	1999 actual	2000 est.	2001 est.
Grants-in-aid for airports (trust)	2,322	1,896	1,950
Facilities and equipment (trust)	2,121	2,045	2,495
Research, engineering, and development (trust)	150	156	184
National Civil Aviation Review Commission	–1		
Total net	10,179	9,991	11,222
Obligations:			
Operations	5,569	5,910	6,592
General fund (memorandum entry)	(1,457)	(17)	(0)
Grants-in-aid for airports (trust)	1,990	[1]1,846	1,950
Facilities and equipment (trust)	2,181	2,040	2,446
Research, engineering, and development (trust)	152	170	184
Total net	9,802	10,016	11,172
Outlays:			
Operations	5,577	5,852	6,524
General fund (memorandum entry)	(1,455)	(659)	(0)
Grants-in-aid for airports (trust)	1,565	1,896	1,899
Facilities and equipment (trust)	2,195	1,805	1,976
Research, engineering, and development (trust)	174	194	199
Aviation insurance revolving fund	–3	–3	–3
Administrative services franchise fund	–1	5	–36
Total net	9,507	9,748	10,558

Note.—The amount shown as Operations includes the general fund share of operations.
[1] Reflects a reduction of $54 million in 2000 as required by P.L. 106–113.

Federal Funds

General and special funds:

OPERATIONS

Program and Financing (in millions of dollars)

Identification code 69–1301–0–1–402		1999 actual	2000 est.	2001 est.
	Obligations by program activity:			
	Direct program:			
00.01	Air traffic services	4,351	8	
00.02	Regulation and certification	619	4	
00.03	Civil aviation security	120		
00.04	Airports	48		
00.05	Research and acquisitions	78	2	
00.06	Commercial space transportation	6		
00.07	Administration	264		
00.08	Staff offices	84	3	
09.01	Reimbursable program	62		
10.00	Total new obligations	5,631	17	
	Budgetary resources available for obligation:			
21.40	Unobligated balance available, start of year	1	17	
22.00	New budget authority (gross)	5,653		
23.90	Total budgetary resources available for obligation	5,654	17	
23.95	Total new obligations	–5,631	–17	
23.98	Unobligated balance expiring or withdrawn	–5		
24.40	Unobligated balance available, end of year	17		
	New budget authority (gross), detail:			
	Discretionary:			
40.00	Appropriation	1,450		
40.36	Unobligated balance rescinded	–1		
40.75	Reduction pursuant to P.L. 106–51	–6		
40.78	Reduction pursuant to P.L. 105–277	–5		
42.00	Transferred from other accounts	34		
43.00	Appropriation (total discretionary)	1,473		
68.00	Spending authority from offsetting collections: Offsetting collections (cash)	4,180		
70.00	Total new budget authority (gross)	5,652		
	Change in unpaid obligations:			
72.40	Unpaid obligations, start of year: Obligated balance, start of year	691	641	
73.10	Total new obligations	5,631	17	
73.20	Total outlays (gross)	–5,635	–658	
73.40	Adjustments in expired accounts (net)	–46		
74.40	Unpaid obligations, end of year: Obligated balance, end of year	641		
	Outlays (gross), detail:			
86.90	Outlays from new discretionary authority	5,084		
86.93	Outlays from discretionary balances	551	659	
87.00	Total outlays (gross)	5,635	658	
	Offsets:			
	Against gross budget authority and outlays:			
	Offsetting collections (cash) from:			
88.00	Federal sources	–4,158		
88.40	Non-Federal sources	–22		
88.90	Total, offsetting collections (cash)	–4,180		
	Net budget authority and outlays:			
89.00	Budget authority	1,473		
90.00	Outlays	1,455	658	

In 2000, all funding for FAA operations is provided from the Airport and Airway Trust Fund, and the 2001 budget proposes to continue this practice. The 1999 data includes balances of the National Civil Aviation Review Commission.

Object Classification (in millions of dollars)

Identification code 69–1301–0–1–402		1999 actual	2000 est.	2001 est.
	Direct obligations:			
	Personnel compensation:			
11.1	Full-time permanent	3,058		
11.3	Other than full-time permanent	28		
11.5	Other personnel compensation	267		
11.9	Total personnel compensation	3,353		
12.1	Civilian personnel benefits	886		
21.0	Travel and transportation of persons	91		
22.0	Transportation of things	21		
23.1	Rental payments to GSA	76		
23.2	Rental payments to others	32		
23.3	Communications, utilities, and miscellaneous charges	317		
24.0	Printing and reproduction	11		
25.2	Other services	660	17	
26.0	Supplies and materials	81		
31.0	Equipment	39		
32.0	Land and structures	1		
42.0	Insurance claims and indemnities	1		
99.0	Subtotal, direct obligations	5,569	17	
99.0	Reimbursable obligations	62		
99.9	Total new obligations	5,631	17	

Personnel Summary

Identification code 69–1301–0–1–402		1999 actual	2000 est.	2001 est.
	Direct:			
1001	Total compensable workyears: Full-time equivalent employment	46,005		
	Reimbursable:			
2001	Total compensable workyears: Full-time equivalent employment	224		

AVIATION USER FEES

Unavailable Collections (in millions of dollars)

Identification code 69–5422–0–2–402		1999 actual	2000 est.	2001 est.
	Balance, start of year:			
01.99	Balance, start of year			
	Receipts:			
02.01	Overflight user fees		5	22
	Appropriation:			
05.01	FAA activities		–5	–22
07.99	Total balance, end of year			

Program and Financing (in millions of dollars)

Identification code 69–5422–0–2–402	1999 actual	2000 est.	2001 est.
New budget authority (gross), detail:			
Mandatory:			
60.25 Appropriation (special fund, indefinite)	....	5	22
61.00 Transferred to other accounts	....	−5	−22
62.50 Appropriation (total mandatory)	....	....	....
Net budget authority and outlays:			
89.00 Budget authority	....	....	....
90.00 Outlays	....	....	....

The Federal Aviation Reauthorization Act of 1996 (P.L. 104–264) authorized the collection of user fees for services provided by the FAA to aircraft that neither takeoff nor land in the United States, commonly known as overflight fees. In addition, the Act permanently appropriated the first $50 million of such fees, or other FAA resources in the event fees are lower than $50 million, to be used for the Essential Air Service (EAS) program and rural airport improvements. Amounts collected in excess of $50 million are permanently appropriated for authorized expenses of the FAA. The Budget estimates that $22 million in overflight fees will be collected in 2001, and transferred to the Essential Air Service and Rural Airport Improvement Fund. As collections are estimated to be below required EAS funding, the Budget proposes $28 million in EAS financing will be provided from the Airport Improvement Program.

Public enterprise funds:

Aviation Insurance Revolving Fund

The Secretary of Transportation is hereby authorized to make such expenditures and investments, within the limits of funds available pursuant to 49 U.S.C. 44307, and in accordance with section 104 of the Government Corporation Control Act, as amended (31 U.S.C. 9104), as may be necessary in carrying out the program for aviation insurance activities under chapter 443 of title 49, United States Code. *(Department of Transportation and Related Agencies Appropriations Act, 2000.)*

Program and Financing (in millions of dollars)

Identification code 69–4120–0–3–402	1999 actual	2000 est.	2001 est.
Budgetary resources available for obligation:			
21.40 Unobligated balance available, start of year	72	76	79
22.00 New budget authority (gross)	4	3	3
23.90 Total budgetary resources available for obligation	76	79	82
24.40 Unobligated balance available, end of year	76	79	82
New budget authority (gross), detail:			
Discretionary:			
68.00 Spending authority from offsetting collections (gross): Offsetting collections (cash)	4	3	3
Offsets:			
Against gross budget authority and outlays:			
88.00 Offsetting collections (cash) from: Federal sources	−4	−3	−3
Net budget authority and outlays:			
89.00 Budget authority	....	....	....
90.00 Outlays	−3	−3	−3
Memorandum (non-add) entries:			
92.01 Total investments, start of year: U.S. securities: Par value	71	76	79
92.02 Total investments, end of year: U.S. securities: Par value	76	79	82

The fund provides direct support for the aviation insurance program (chapter 443 of title 49, U.S. Code). Authorization to issue new insurance coverage expired on August 6, 1999. Income to the fund is derived from premium deposits for premium insurance coverage issued, income from authorized investments, and binder fees for nonpremium coverage issued. The binders provide aviation insurance coverage for U.S. air carrier aircraft used in connection with certain Government contract operations by the Department of Defense and the Department of State. The Administration has proposed reauthorization of the program through 2004.

Personnel Summary

Identification code 69–4120–0–3–402	1999 actual	2000 est.	2001 est.
1001 Total compensable workyears: Full-time equivalent employment	3	3	3

Intragovernmental accounts:

Administrative Services Franchise Fund

Program and Financing (in millions of dollars)

Identification code 69–4562–0–4–402	1999 actual	2000 est.	2001 est.
Obligations by program activity:			
09.01 Accounting	4	19	19
09.02 Payroll	3	3	3
09.03 Travel	1	1	1
09.04 Duplicating services	5	5	5
09.05 Multi-media	1	2	2
09.06 Training	4	4	4
09.07 Logistics	....	....	157
09.08 Aircraft maintenance	....	....	29
10.00 Total new obligations	18	34	220
Budgetary resources available for obligation:			
21.40 Unobligated balance available, start of year	1	1	....
22.00 New budget authority (gross)	18	33	220
23.90 Total budgetary resources available for obligation	19	34	220
23.95 Total new obligations	−18	−34	−220
24.40 Unobligated balance available, end of year	1	....	....
New budget authority (gross), detail:			
Discretionary:			
68.00 Spending authority from offsetting collections (gross): Offsetting collections (cash)	18	33	220
Change in unpaid obligations:			
72.40 Unpaid obligations, start of year: Obligated balance, start of year	4	5	1
73.10 Total new obligations	18	34	220
73.20 Total outlays (gross)	−19	−38	−184
74.40 Unpaid obligations, end of year: Obligated balance, end of year	5	1	37
Outlays (gross), detail:			
86.90 Outlays from new discretionary authority	15	33	184
86.93 Outlays from discretionary balances	4	5	....
87.00 Total outlays (gross)	19	38	184
Offsets:			
Against gross budget authority and outlays:			
88.00 Offsetting collections (cash) from: Federal sources	−18	−33	−220
Net budget authority and outlays:			
89.00 Budget authority	....	....	....
90.00 Outlays	−1	5	−36

In 1997, the Federal Aviation Administration established a franchise fund to finance operations where the costs for goods and services provided are charged to the users on a reimbursable basis. The fund is expected to improve organizational efficiency and provide better support to FAA's internal and external customers. The activities included in this franchise fund are: training, accounting, payroll, travel, duplicating services, multi-media services, and information technology.

Intragovernmental accounts—Continued

ADMINISTRATIVE SERVICES FRANCHISE FUND—Continued

In 2001, there will be a major expansion of the franchise fund, as the activities of the FAA depot at the Mike Monroney Aeronautical Center in Oklahoma City become a franchise fund activity. This expansion will increase the efficiency of the depot by instituting a more rational and economic basis for procuring and distributing replacement parts and spares.

Also added to the fund in 2001 will be aircraft maintenance activities at the Mike Monroney Aeronautical Center. As with other franchise fund activities, the inclusion of the aircraft maintenance function will allow the agency to achieve economies in performance by distributing fixed costs across a larger business base. This will, in time, lead to improved efficiency and reduced unit costs for the service provided.

Object Classification (in millions of dollars)

Identification code 69–4562–0–4–402		1999 actual	2000 est.	2001 est.
11.1	Personnel compensation: Full-time permanent	6	7	53
12.1	Civilian personnel benefits	2	2	12
21.0	Travel and transportation of persons			1
22.0	Transportation of things			3
23.3	Communications, utilities, and miscellaneous charges	1		
24.0	Printing and reproduction	2	2	2
25.2	Other services	7	23	91
26.0	Supplies and materials			56
31.0	Equipment			2
99.9	Total new obligations	18	34	220

Personnel Summary

Identification code 69–4562–0–4–402		1999 actual	2000 est.	2001 est.
2001	Total compensable workyears: Full-time equivalent employment	152	184	1,067

Trust Funds

AIRPORT AND AIRWAY TRUST FUND

Unavailable Collections (in millions of dollars)

Identification code 20–8103–0–7–402		1999 actual	2000 est.	2001 est.
	Balance, start of year:			
01.99	Balance, start of year	4,589	7,310	7,410
	Receipts:			
02.01	Excise taxes	10,391	9,222	9,645
02.02	Interest	698	771	811
02.03	Aviation user fees, legislative proposal, discretionary offset			965
02.06	Interest, legislative proposal not subject to PAYGO		−9	−11
02.99	Total receipts	11,089	9,984	11,410
04.00	Total: Balances and collections	15,678	17,294	18,820
	Appropriation:			
05.01	Trust fund share of FAA operations	−4,112	−5,900	−6,592
05.02	Grants-in-aid for airports liquidating cash	−2,410	−1,896	−1,950
05.03	Facilities and equipment	−2,122	−2,075	−2,495
05.04	Research, engineering and development	−150	−156	−184
05.99	Subtotal appropriation	−8,794	−10,027	−11,221
06.10	Unobligated balance returned to receipts	425	136	
06.20	Reduction pursuant to Public Law 106–69	1	7	
07.99	Total balance, end of year	7,310	7,410	7,599

Program and Financing (in millions of dollars)

Identification code 20–8103–0–7–402		1999 actual	2000 est.	2001 est.
	Memorandum (non-add) entries:			
92.01	Total investments, start of year: U.S. securities: Par value		12,411	13,333
92.02	Total investments, end of year: U.S. securities: Par value	12,411	13,333	14,145

Section 9502 of Title 26, U.S.C., as amended, provides for the receipts received in the Treasury from the passenger ticket tax and certain other taxes paid by airport and airway users to be transferred to the Airport and Airway Trust Fund. The Budget assumes that the current excise taxes will be reduced over time as more efficient, service-based charges are phased in beginning in 2001. Under this proposal, the amount collected each year from the new service-based charges and excise taxes combined would be equal to the total budget resources requested for the FAA in the succeeding year. The Administration has proposed legislation that creates the service-based charges and will apply the offset to discretionary spending.

The status of the fund is as follows (in millions of dollars):

Status of Funds (in millions of dollars)

Identification code 20–8103–0–7–402		1999 actual	2000 est.	2001 est.
	Unexpended balance, start of year:			
0100	Uninvested balance	861	32	
0101	U.S. Securities: Par value	8,550	12,411	13,333
0199	Total balance, start of year	9,411	12,443	13,333
	Cash income during the year:			
	Governmental receipts:			
0201	Passenger ticket tax	5,941	4,850	4,911
0202	Passenger flight segment tax	1,339	1,594	1,809
0203	Waybill tax	412	443	479
0204	Fuel tax	1,009	854	878
0205	International departure/arrival tax	1,484	1,286	1,367
0206	Rural airports tax	57	54	57
0207	Frequent flyer tax	149	141	144
0208	Aviation user fees, Legislative proposal			965
	Intragovernmental transactions:			
	Intragovernmental transactions:			
0240	Interest, Airport and airway trust fund	698	771	811
0240	Interest, legislative proposal not subject to PAYGO		−9	−11
	Offsetting collections:			
0280	Trust fund share of FAA operations		72	74
0281	Facilities and equipment	27	77	77
0282	Research, engineering, and development	5	16	16
0297	Income under present law	11,121	10,158	10,623
0298	Income under proposed legislation		−9	954
0299	Total cash income	11,121	10,149	11,577
	Cash outgo during year:			
	Cash outgo during the year (−):			
0500	Trust fund share of FAA operations (Airport and airway trust fund)	−4,122	−5,194	−6,523
0500	Trust fund share of FAA operations, offsetting collections		−72	−74
0501	Grants-in-aid for airports (Airport and airway trust fund)	−1,565	−1,894	−1,925
	Cash outgo during the year (−):			
0502	Facilities and equipment (Airport and airway trust fund)	−2,195	−1,805	−1,976
0502	Facilities and equipment offsetting collections	−27	−77	−77
	Cash outgo during the year (−):			
0503	Research, engineering and development (Airport and airway trust fund)	−174	−194	−199
0503	Research, engineering and development offsetting collections	−5	−16	−16
0505	Payments to air carriers (Airport and airway trust fund)	−1	−1	
0507	Grants-in-aid for airports, supplemental proposal		−2	26
0510	Trust fund share of FAA operations, supplemental proposal		2	−2
0597	Outgo under present law (−)	−8,089	−9,253	−10,790
0598	Outgo under proposed legislation (−)			24
0599	Total cash outgo (−)	−8,089	−9,255	−10,765
	Unexpended balance, end of year:			
0700	Uninvested balance	32		
0701	U.S. Securities: Par value	12,414	13,333	14,145
0799	Total balance, end of year	12,446	13,333	14,145

Note.—The invested balances shown above include both appropriated and unavailable balances.

GRANTS-IN-AID FOR AIRPORTS

(LIQUIDATION OF CONTRACT AUTHORIZATION)

(AIRPORT AND AIRWAY TRUST FUND)

For liquidation of obligations incurred for grants-in-aid for airport planning and development, and noise compatibility planning and programs as authorized under subchapter I of chapter 471 and subchapter I of chapter 475 of title 49, United States Code, and under other law authorizing such obligations; for administration of such programs; for administration of programs under section 40117; and for inspection activities and administration of airport safety programs, including those related to airport operating certificates under section 44706 of title 49, United States Code, **[**$1,750,000,000**]** *$1,960,000,000*, to be derived from the Airport and Airway Trust Fund and to remain available until expended: *Provided*, That none of the funds under this heading shall be available for the planning or execution of programs the obligations for which are in excess of $1,950,000,000 in fiscal year **[**2000**]** *2001*, notwithstanding section 47117(h) of title 49, United States Code: *Provided further*, That notwithstanding any other provision of law, not more than **[**$45,000,000**]** *$60,413,000* of funds limited under this heading shall be obligated for administration: *Provided further*, **[**That, notwithstanding any other provision of law, in the event of a lapse in authorization of the grants program under this heading, funding available under Federal Aviation Administration, "Operations" may be obligated for administration during the time period of the lapse in authorization, at the rate corresponding to the maximum annual obligation level of $45,000,000: *Provided further*, That total obligations from all sources in fiscal year 2000 for administration may not exceed $45,000,000**]** *That not more than $27,900,000 of funds under this heading shall be available to carry out the essential air service program under subchapter II of chapter 417 of title 49, United States Code, in partial satisfaction of the requirement of section 41742(a) of such title. (Department of Transportation and Related Agencies Appropriations Act, 2000.)*

Program and Financing (in millions of dollars)

Identification code 69–8106–0–7–402		1999 actual	2000 est.	2001 est.
	Obligations by program activity:			
00.01	Grants-in-aid for airports	1,990	1,851	1,600
00.02	Personnel and related expenses	....	45	60
00.03	Essential air services	....	....	28
10.00	Total new obligations	1,990	1,896	1,688
	Budgetary resources available for obligation:			
21.49	Unobligated balance available, start of year: Contract authority	88	136	....
22.00	New budget authority (gross)	2,322	1,896	1,950
22.10	Resources available from recoveries of prior year obligations	46	....	....
23.90	Total budgetary resources available for obligation	2,456	2,032	1,950
23.95	Total new obligations	–1,990	–1,896	–1,688
23.98	Unobligated balance expiring or withdrawn	–330	–136	....
24.49	Unobligated balance, end of year: Contract authority	136	....	262
	New budget authority (gross), detail:			
	Discretionary:			
40.26	Appropriation (trust fund, definite)	1,600	1,750	1,960
40.49	Portion applied to liquidate contract authority	–1,600	–1,750	–1,960
43.00	Appropriation (total discretionary)	....	....	....
	Mandatory:			
66.10	Contract authority	2,410	1,896	1,950
66.35	Contract authority rescinded	–88	....	....
66.90	Contract authority (total mandatory)	2,322	1,896	1,950
70.00	Total new budget authority (gross)	2,322	1,896	1,950
	Change in unpaid obligations:			
	Unpaid obligations, start of year:			
72.40	Obligated balance, start of year	488	524	380
72.49	Obligated balance, start of year: Contract authority	2,015	2,358	2,504
72.99	Total unpaid obligations, start of year	2,503	2,882	2,884
73.10	Total new obligations	1,990	1,896	1,688
73.20	Total outlays (gross)	–1,565	–1,894	–1,925
73.45	Adjustments in unexpired accounts	–46	....	....
	Unpaid obligations, end of year:			
74.40	Obligated balance, end of year	524	380	460
74.49	Obligated balance, end of year: Contract authority	2,358	2,504	2,188
74.99	Total unpaid obligations, end of year	2,882	2,884	2,648
	Outlays (gross), detail:			
86.90	Outlays from new discretionary authority	351	373	416
86.93	Outlays from discretionary balances	1,214	1,521	1,509
87.00	Total outlays (gross)	1,565	1,894	1,925
	Net budget authority and outlays:			
89.00	Budget authority	2,322	1,896	1,950
90.00	Outlays	1,565	1,894	1,925

Summary of Budget Authority and Outlays

(in millions of dollars)

	1999 actual	*2000 est.*	*2001 est.*
Enacted/requested:			
Budget Authority	2,322	1,896	1,950
Outlays	1,565	1,894	1,925
Supplemental proposal:			
Budget Authority	....	....	....
Outlays	....	2	–26
Total:			
Budget Authority	2,322	1,896	1,950
Outlays	1,565	1,896	1,899

Status of Contract Authority (in millions of dollars)

Identification code 69–8106–0–7–402		1999 actual	2000 est.	2001 est.
0100	Balance, start of year	2,103	2,494	2,504
	Contract authority:			
0200	Contract authority	2,322	1,896	1,688
0350	Unfunded balance expiring	–330	–136	....
0400	Appropriation to liquidate contract authority	–1,600	–1,750	–1,960
0700	Balance, end of year	2,494	2,504	2,234

Subchapter I of chapter 471, title 49, U.S. Code (formerly the Airport and Airway Improvement Act of 1982, as amended) provides for airport improvement grants, including those emphasizing capacity development, safety and security needs, and chapter 475 provides for grants for aircraft noise mitigation and planning.

The 2000 appropriations act allows funding under this heading to be provided for administrative costs related to this program. For 2001, the Administration proposes that funds under this heading also be provided for the FAA's airport-related research and to make up for shortfalls in overflight fee collections to fund the Essential Air Service program, consistent with section 41742, title 49 of the U.S. Code.

Object Classification (in millions of dollars)

Identification code 69–8106–0–7–402		1999 actual	2000 est.	2001 est.
	Personnel compensation:			
11.1	Full-time permanent	....	34	38
11.3	Other than full-time permanent	....	1	1
11.9	Total personnel compensation	....	35	39
12.1	Civilian personnel benefits	....	7	8
21.0	Travel and transportation of persons	....	1	2
23.3	Communications, utilities, and miscellaneous charges	....	1	1
25.2	Other services	....	1	10
41.0	Grants, subsidies, and contributions	1,990	1,851	1,628
99.9	Total new obligations	1,990	1,896	1,688

Personnel Summary

Identification code 69–8106–0–7–402		1999 actual	2000 est.	2001 est.
1001	Total compensable workyears: Full-time equivalent employment	....	501	519

FACILITIES AND EQUIPMENT

(AIRPORT AND AIRWAY TRUST FUND)

For necessary expenses, not otherwise provided for, for acquisition, establishment, and improvement by contract or purchase, and hire of air navigation and experimental facilities and equipment as authorized under part A of subtitle VII of title 49, United States Code, including initial acquisition of necessary sites by lease or grant; engineering and service testing, including construction of test facilities and acquisition of necessary sites by lease or grant; and construction and furnishing of quarters and related accommodations for officers and employees of the Federal Aviation Administration stationed at remote localities where such accommodations are not available; and the purchase, lease, or transfer of aircraft from funds available under this head; to be derived from the Airport and Airway Trust Fund, [$2,075,000,000] *$2,495,000,000*, of which [$1,780,000,000] *$2,172,347,400* shall remain available until September 30, [2002] *2003*, and of which [$295,000,000] *$322,652,600* shall remain available until September 30, [2000] *2001*: *Provided*, That there may be credited to this appropriation funds received from States, counties, municipalities, other public authorities, and private sources, for expenses incurred in the establishment and modernization of air navigation facilities[: *Provided further*, That upon initial submission to the Congress of the fiscal year 2001 President's budget, the Secretary of Transportation shall transmit to the Congress a comprehensive capital investment plan for the Federal Aviation Administration which includes funding for each budget line item for fiscal years 2001 through 2005, with total funding for each year of the plan constrained to the funding targets for those years as estimated and approved by the Office of Management and Budget: *Provided further*, That none of the funds in this Act may be used for the Federal Aviation Administration to enter into a capital lease agreement unless appropriations have been provided to fully cover the Federal Government's contingent liabilities at the time the lease agreement is signed].

In addition, for necessary expenses for capital cost acquisition or construction including alteration or modification costs, to be derived from the Airport and Airway Trust Fund, to become available on October 1 of the fiscal year specified and remain available until expended: fiscal year 2002, $638,100,000; fiscal year 2003, $590,200,000; fiscal year 2004, $565,400,000; fiscal year 2005, $537,300,000; fiscal year 2006, $324,900,000; fiscal year 2007, $168,600,000; and fiscal year 2008, $119,600,000. (Department of Transportation and Related Agencies Appropriations Act, 2000.)

Program and Financing (in millions of dollars)

Identification code 69–8107–0–7–402		1999 actual	2000 est.	2001 est.
	Obligations by program activity:			
	Direct program:			
00.01	Engineering, development, test and evaluation	508	544	609
00.02	Procurement and modernization of air traffic control (ATC) facilities and equipment	904	778	1,048
00.03	Procurement and modernization of non-ATC facilities and equipment	161	179	200
00.04	Mission support	363	244	266
00.05	Personnel and related expenses	245	295	323
09.01	Reimbursable program	27	77	77
10.00	Total new obligations	2,208	2,117	2,523
	Budgetary resources available for obligation:			
21.40	Unobligated balance available, start of year	353	355	360
22.00	New budget authority (gross)	2,148	2,122	2,572
22.10	Resources available from recoveries of prior year obligations	69		
23.90	Total budgetary resources available for obligation	2,570	2,477	2,932
23.95	Total new obligations	−2,208	−2,117	−2,523
23.98	Unobligated balance expiring or withdrawn	−7		
24.40	Unobligated balance available, end of year	355	360	409
	New budget authority (gross), detail:			
	Discretionary:			
40.15	Appropriation (emergency)	100		
40.26	Appropriation (trust fund, definite)	2,022	2,075	2,495
40.36	Unobligated balance rescinded		−30	
40.75	Reduction pursuant to P.L. 106–51	−1		
43.00	Appropriation (total discretionary)	2,121	2,045	2,495
68.00	Spending authority from offsetting collections: Offsetting collections (cash)	27	77	77
70.00	Total new budget authority (gross)	2,148	2,122	2,572
	Change in unpaid obligations:			
72.40	Unpaid obligations, start of year: Obligated balance, start of year	1,664	1,530	1,763
73.10	Total new obligations	2,208	2,117	2,523
73.20	Total outlays (gross)	−2,222	−1,884	−2,053
73.40	Adjustments in expired accounts (net)	−50		
73.45	Adjustments in unexpired accounts	−69		
74.40	Unpaid obligations, end of year: Obligated balance, end of year	1,530	1,763	2,233
	Outlays (gross), detail:			
86.90	Outlays from new discretionary authority	902	691	842
86.93	Outlays from discretionary balances	1,320	1,191	1,211
87.00	Total outlays (gross)	2,222	1,884	2,053
	Offsets:			
	Against gross budget authority and outlays:			
	Offsetting collections (cash) from:			
88.00	Federal sources	−24	−68	−68
88.40	Non-Federal sources	−3	−9	−9
88.90	Total, offsetting collections (cash)	−27	−77	−77
	Net budget authority and outlays:			
89.00	Budget authority	2,121	2,045	2,495
90.00	Outlays	2,195	1,807	1,976

Note.—Mission Support has an estimated contingent liability of $79 million (present value) associated with the FAA's long-term lease of facilities at the Mike Monroney Aeronautical Center, Oklahoma City, Oklahoma. This contingent liability will be funded through this account.

The proposed funding sustains the current infrastructure and advances modernization and improvement of the National airspace system. In particular, funds would provide for significant progress in developing the enroute and terminal automation programs, designed to upgrade air traffic control technology, and in implementing Free flight programs.

The Administration supports full funding of multi-year fixed asset projects as part of an ongoing attempt to improve the cost and performance of agency procurements. To implement the Administration's full funding policy, advance appropriations are requested for the following multi-year projects or usable project segments: Aviation weather service improvements, Air traffic control beacon interrogator replacement, Terminal digital radar, Terminal automation (STARS), Wide area augmentation system for GPS, Weather and radar processor, Oceanic automation system, Aeronautical data link, and Operational and supportability implementation system (OASIS).

In 2000, the Department of Transportation will work with the Office of Management and Budget to improve the management of the FAA's modernization program. In 2001, the Department will work with the Department of Defense to ensure that the civilian requirements of the Global Positioning system are met. These activities are proposed to be funded within the Defense Department budget.

Object Classification (in millions of dollars)

Identification code 69–8107–0–7–402		1999 actual	2000 est.	2001 est.
	Direct obligations:			
	Personnel compensation:			
11.1	Full-time permanent	178	185	198
11.3	Other than full-time permanent	1	1	1
11.5	Other personnel compensation	7	6	9
11.9	Total personnel compensation	186	192	208
12.1	Civilian personnel benefits	46	54	58
21.0	Travel and transportation of persons	34	42	45
22.0	Transportation of things	4	4	5
23.2	Rental payments to others	42	38	46
23.3	Communications, utilities, and miscellaneous charges	13	12	14
24.0	Printing and reproduction		1	1
25.2	Other services	1,362	1,290	1,575

		1999 actual	2000 est.	2001 est.
26.0	Supplies and materials	37	34	41
31.0	Equipment	269	246	299
32.0	Land and structures	134	122	148
41.0	Grants, subsidies, and contributions	55	5	6
99.0	Subtotal, direct obligations	2,182	2,040	2,446
99.0	Reimbursable obligations	26	77	77
99.9	Total new obligations	2,208	2,117	2,523

Personnel Summary

Identification code 69–8107–0–7–402		1999 actual	2000 est.	2001 est.
	Direct:			
1001	Total compensable workyears: Full-time equivalent employment	2,588	2,786	2,801
	Reimbursable:			
2001	Total compensable workyears: Full-time equivalent employment	21	55	55

RESEARCH, ENGINEERING, AND DEVELOPMENT

(AIRPORT AND AIRWAY TRUST FUND)

For necessary expenses, not otherwise provided for, for research, engineering, and development, as authorized under part A of subtitle VII of title 49, United States Code, including construction of experimental facilities and acquisition of necessary sites by lease or grant, [$156,495,000] *$184,366,000*, to be derived from the Airport and Airway Trust Fund and to remain available until September 30, [2002] *2003*: *Provided*, That there may be credited to this appropriation funds received from States, counties, municipalities, other public authorities, and private sources, for expenses incurred for research, engineering, and development. *(Department of Transportation and Related Agencies Appropriations Act, 2000.)*

Program and Financing (in millions of dollars)

Identification code 69–8108–0–7–402		1999 actual	2000 est.	2001 est.
	Obligations by program activity:			
	Direct program:			
00.01	System development and infrastructure	16	18	25
00.02	Capacity and air traffic management technology	1	1	
00.04	Weather	19	20	28
00.06	Aircraft safety technology	36	47	49
00.07	System security technology	52	54	49
00.08	Human factors and aviation medicine	24	26	25
00.09	Environment and energy	3	4	8
00.10	Innovative/cooperative research	1		
09.01	Reimbursable program	5	16	16
10.00	Total new obligations	157	186	200
	Budgetary resources available for obligation:			
21.40	Unobligated balance available, start of year	7	13	
22.00	New budget authority (gross)	155	172	200
22.10	Resources available from recoveries of prior year obligations	8		
23.90	Total budgetary resources available for obligation	170	185	200
23.95	Total new obligations	−157	−186	−200
24.40	Unobligated balance available, end of year	13		
	New budget authority (gross), detail:			
	Discretionary:			
40.26	Appropriation (trust fund, definite)	150	156	184
68.00	Spending authority from offsetting collections: Offsetting collections (cash)	5	16	16
70.00	Total new budget authority (gross)	155	172	200
	Change in unpaid obligations:			
72.40	Unpaid obligations, start of year: Obligated balance, start of year	184	154	130
73.10	Total new obligations	157	186	200
73.20	Total outlays (gross)	−179	−210	−215
73.45	Adjustments in unexpired accounts	−8		
74.40	Unpaid obligations, end of year: Obligated balance, end of year	154	130	115
	Outlays (gross), detail:			
86.90	Outlays from new discretionary authority	69	110	126
86.93	Outlays from discretionary balances	110	100	89
87.00	Total outlays (gross)	179	210	215
	Offsets:			
	Against gross budget authority and outlays:			
88.00	Offsetting collections (cash) from: Federal sources	−5	−16	−16
	Net budget authority and outlays:			
89.00	Budget authority	150	156	184
90.00	Outlays	174	194	199

The 2001 budget proposes funding to conduct research, engineering and development programs to improve the national air traffic control system by increasing its safety, security, capacity, and productivity to meet the expected air traffic demands of the future. The agency also administers human factors research aimed at increasing the effectiveness of air traffic controller operations, airway facilities maintenance, aviation medical research aimed at increasing the safety of aircrew members, and environmental research aimed at mitigating aircraft noise and engine emissions.

Object Classification (in millions of dollars)

Identification code 69–8108–0–7–402		1999 actual	2000 est.	2001 est.
	Direct obligations:			
	Personnel compensation:			
11.1	Full-time permanent	24	31	31
11.3	Other than full-time permanent		1	
11.5	Other personnel compensation	1	1	1
11.9	Total personnel compensation	26	33	33
12.1	Civilian personnel benefits	5	8	7
21.0	Travel and transportation of persons	3	2	2
25.5	Research and development contracts	74	84	99
26.0	Supplies and materials	5	5	
31.0	Equipment	3	3	3
41.0	Grants, subsidies, and contributions	36	35	35
99.0	Subtotal, direct obligations	152	170	184
99.0	Reimbursable obligations	5	16	16
99.9	Total new obligations	157	186	200

Personnel Summary

Identification code 69–8108–0–7–402		1999 actual	2000 est.	2001 est.
1001	Total compensable workyears: Full-time equivalent employment	430	455	455

OPERATIONS

(AIRPORT AND AIRWAY TRUST FUND)

For necessary expenses of the Federal Aviation Administration, not otherwise provided for, including operations and research activities related to commercial space transportation, administrative expenses for research and development, establishment of air navigation facilities, the operation (including leasing) and maintenance of aircraft, subsidizing the cost of aeronautical charts and maps sold to the public, and [carrying out the provisions of subchapter I of chapter 471 of title 49, United States Code, or other provisions of law authorizing the obligation of funds for similar programs of airport and airway development or improvement,] lease or purchase of passenger motor vehicles for replacement only, in addition to amounts made available by Public Law 104–264, [$5,900,000,000] *$6,592,235,000* from the Airport and Airway Trust Fund: *Provided*, [That none of the funds in this Act shall be available for the Federal Aviation Administration to plan, finalize, or implement any regulation that would promulgate new aviation user fees not specifically authorized by law after the date of the enactment of this Act: *Provided further*,] That there may be credited to this appropriation funds received from States, counties, municipalities, foreign authorities, other public authorities, and private sources, for expenses incurred in the provision of agency services, including receipts for the maintenance and operation of air navigation facilities, and for issuance, renewal or modification of certificates, including airman, aircraft, and repair station

OPERATIONS—Continued

(AIRPORT AND AIRWAY TRUST FUND)—Continued

certificates, or for tests related thereto, or for processing major repair or alteration forms: [*Provided further*, That of the funds appropriated under this heading, $5,000,000 shall be for the contract tower cost-sharing program and $600,000 shall be for the Centennial of Flight Commission:] *Provided further*, That funds may be used to enter into a grant agreement with a nonprofit standard-setting organization to assist in the development of aviation safety standards: *Provided further*, That none of the funds in this Act shall be available for new applicants for the second career training program: *Provided further*, That none of the funds in this Act shall be available for paying premium pay under 5 U.S.C. 5546(a) to any Federal Aviation Administration employee unless such employee actually performed work during the time corresponding to such premium pay: *Provided further*, That none of the funds in this Act may be obligated or expended to operate a manned auxiliary flight service station in the contiguous United States[: *Provided further*, That none of the funds in this Act may be used for the Federal Aviation Administration to enter into a multiyear lease greater than 5 years in length or greater than $100,000,000 in value unless such lease is specifically authorized by the Congress and appropriations have been provided to fully cover the Federal Government's contingent liabilities: *Provided further*, That no more than $24,162,700 of funds appropriated to the Federal Aviation Administration in this Act may be used for activities conducted by, or coordinated through, the Transportation Administrative Service Center: *Provided further*, That none of the funds in this Act for aeronautical charting and cartography are available for activities conducted by, or coordinated through, the Transportation Administrative Service Center: *Provided further*, That none of the funds in this Act may be used for the Federal Aviation Administration (FAA) to sign a lease for satellite services related to the global positioning system (GPS) wide area augmentation system until the administrator of FAA certifies in writing to the House and Senate Committees on Appropriations that FAA has conducted a lease versus buy analysis which indicates that such lease will result in the lowest overall cost to the agency]. *(Department of Transportation and Related Agencies Appropriations Act, 2000.)*

Program and Financing (in millions of dollars)

Identification code 69–8104–0–7–402	1999 actual	2000 est.	2001 est.
Obligations by program activity:			
00.01 Air traffic services	....	4,636	5,210
00.02 Regulation and certification	....	640	692
00.03 Civil aviation security	....	131	144
00.05 Research and acquisitions	....	174	197
00.06 Commercial space transportation	....	7	13
00.07 Regional coordination	....	95	....
00.08 Human resources	....	53	....
00.09 Financial services	....	39	....
00.10 Staff offices	....	73	336
00.11 Essential air service	....	45	....
00.12 Undistributed	4,112	....	....
09.01 Reimbursable program	....	72	74
10.00 Total new obligations	4,112	5,965	6,666
Budgetary resources available for obligation:			
22.00 New budget authority (gross)	4,112	5,965	6,666
23.95 Total new obligations	−4,112	−5,965	−6,666
New budget authority (gross), detail:			
Discretionary:			
40.26 Appropriation (trust fund, definite)	4,112	5,900	6,592
40.79 Reduction pursuant to P.L. 106–69	....	−7	....
43.00 Appropriation (total discretionary)	4,112	5,893	6,592
68.00 Spending authority from offsetting collections: Offsetting collections (cash)	....	72	74
70.00 Total new budget authority (gross)	4,112	5,965	6,666
Change in unpaid obligations:			
72.40 Unpaid obligations, start of year: Obligated balance, start of year	12	3	702
73.10 Total new obligations	4,112	5,965	6,666
73.20 Total outlays (gross)	−4,122	−5,266	−6,596
74.40 Unpaid obligations, end of year: Obligated balance, end of year	3	702	772
Outlays (gross), detail:			
86.90 Outlays from new discretionary authority	4,112	5,263	5,894
86.93 Outlays from discretionary balances	10	3	702
87.00 Total outlays (gross)	4,122	5,266	6,596
Offsets:			
Against gross budget authority and outlays:			
Offsetting collections (cash) from:			
88.00 Federal sources	....	−52	−53
88.40 Non-Federal sources	....	−20	−21
88.90 Total, offsetting collections (cash)	....	−72	−74
Net budget authority and outlays:			
89.00 Budget authority	4,112	5,893	6,592
90.00 Outlays	4,122	5,194	6,522

Summary of Budget Authority and Outlays

(in millions of dollars)

Enacted/requested:	*1999 actual*	*2000 est.*	*2001 est.*
Budget Authority	4,112	5,893	6,592
Outlays	4,122	5,194	6,522
Supplemental proposal:			
Budget Authority	....	....	....
Outlays	....	−2	2
Total:			
Budget Authority	4,112	5,893	6,592
Outlays	4,122	5,192	6,524

For 2001, $6,592 million is requested to finance the personnel and support costs of operating and maintaining the air traffic control system, and ensuring the safety and security of its operation. The request represents a 12 percent increase over the 2000 enacted level and will provide funding for additional staff in Airway facilities, regulation and certification, and Civil aviation security. The Budget also provides resources to cover the cost of bringing on-line new air traffic control systems designed to improve safety and efficiency. Other funds are provided to ensure information security and cover key personnel and financial initiatives, including implementing personnel reform and developing a cost-accounting system.

Object Classification (in millions of dollars)

Identification code 69–8104–0–7–402	1999 actual	2000 est.	2001 est.
Direct obligations:			
Personnel compensation:			
11.1 Full-time permanent	....	3,269	3,492
11.3 Other than full-time permanent	....	29	30
11.5 Other personnel compensation	....	285	314
11.8 Special personal services payments	....	1	1
11.9 Total personnel compensation	....	3,584	3,837
12.1 Civilian personnel benefits	....	957	1,024
13.0 Benefits for former personnel	....	1	1
21.0 Travel and transportation of persons	....	93	111
22.0 Transportation of things	....	22	20
23.1 Rental payments to GSA	....	82	87
23.2 Rental payments to others	....	37	39
23.3 Communications, utilities, and miscellaneous charges	....	335	380
24.0 Printing and reproduction	....	11	11
25.2 Other services	....	612	827
26.0 Supplies and materials	....	84	187
31.0 Equipment	....	29	67
32.0 Land and structures	....	1	1
92.0 Grants	4,112	45	....
99.0 Subtotal, direct obligations	4,112	5,893	6,592
99.0 Reimbursable obligations	....	72	74
99.9 Total new obligations	4,112	5,965	6,666

Personnel Summary

Identification code 69–8104–0–7–402	1999 actual	2000 est.	2001 est.
Direct:			
1001 Total compensable workyears: Full-time equivalent employment	....	44,872	44,444
Reimbursable:			
2001 Total compensable workyears: Full-time equivalent employment	....	308	283

FEDERAL HIGHWAY ADMINISTRATION

The Transportation Equity Act for the 21st Century (TEA–21), enacted June 9, 1998, reauthorizes surface transportation programs through 2003. TEA–21 provides for increased transportation infrastructure investment, strengthens transportation safety programs and environmental programs, and continues core research activities. TEA–21, along with title 23, U.S.C. ("Highways") and other supporting legislation, provides authority for the various programs of the Federal Highway Administration designed to improve highways throughout the Nation.

On December 9, 1999, the Motor Carrier Safety Improvement Act of 1999 was signed into law, thereby creating the Federal Motor Carrier Safety Administration to oversee commercial motor vehicle, operator, and carrier safety. Accordingly, the schedules of the Federal Highway Administration have been revised to reflect the transfer of the activities to the new administration.

In 2001, the Federal Highway Administration continues major programs, including the Surface Transportation Program, the National Highway System, Interstate Maintenance, the Highway Bridge Replacement and Rehabilitation Program, and the Congestion Mitigation and Air Quality Improvement Program. New programs authorized by TEA–21 include Transportation Infrastructure Finance and Innovation and the National Corridor Planning and Border Infrastructure Programs.

In summary, the 2001 budget consists of $34,051 million in new budget authority and $27,850 million in outlays. The following table reflects program levels (obligations). Because project selection is determined by the States, the 2000 and 2001 program levels are estimates.

FEDERAL HIGHWAY ADMINISTRATION

[In millions of dollars]

	1999 actual	*2000 est.*	*2001 est.*
Obligations:			
Total Federal-aid highways	26,031	28,530	30,374
Federal-aid subject to limitation	24,700	[1] 27,308	29,334
Direct loan subsidy [TIFIA]	35	54	53
Guarantee loan subsidy [TIFIA]	9	39	39
Line of credit [TIFIA]	2	5	5
Administrative expenses [TIFIA]	1	2	2
Surface transportation program	6,227	6,216	6,411
National highway system	4,888	5,319	5,487
Interstate maintenance	3,357	4,419	4,561
Bridge program	2,565	3,785	3,902
Congestion mitigation and air quality improvement	1,145	1,509	1,557
Minimum guarantee	2,167	1,763	1,905
ITS standards, research and development	75	98	100
ITS deployment	71	124	238
Transportation research	208	220	321
Federal lands highways	339	653	701
Emergency relief	....	....	398
National corridor planning and coordinated border infrastructure	118	122	266
Administration	331	304	316
Other programs	2,162	432	318
High priority projects	581	1,560	1,626
Woodrow Wilson memorial bridge	1	139	180
Appalachian development highway system	319	394	405
Safety incentive grants for use of seat belts	54	80	92
Safety incentive to prevent operation of motor carrier by intoxicated persons	43	70	81
Delta initiative	....	....	23
IRS initiative	....	....	20
Revenue aligned budget authority (estimate for allocated programs)	....	....	329
Programs exempt from obligation limitation	1,331	1,221	1,040
Emergency relief supplemental	97	15	....
Emergency relief program	129	111	100
Minimum allocation/guarantee	858	702	664
Demonstration projects	248	393	275
Miscellaneous highways trust funds	29	10	10
State infrastructure banks (GF)	....	4	....
Appalachian development highway system (GF)	84	90	....
Miscellaneous appropriations (GF)	146	58	58
Miscellaneous trust funds	38	38	29
Ellsworth Housing settlement	....	3	....
Total program level	$26,328	$28,733	$30,471
Total discretionary	25,056	27,488	29,402
Total mandatory	1,272	1,245	1,069

[1] Reflects a reduction of $105 million in 2000 as required by P.L. 106–113.

Federal Funds

Miscellaneous Appropriations

Program and Financing (in millions of dollars)

Identification code 69–9911–0–1–401	1999 actual	2000 est.	2001 est.
Obligations by program activity:			
00.04 Rail line consolidation	1	2	2
00.06 Interstate transfer grants	2	2	2
00.09 Bridge improvement demonstration project	1	1	1
00.10 Feasibility, design, environmental and engineering	1	1	1
00.14 Climbing lane demonstration	4	8	8
00.24 Highway demonstration projects	11	15	15
00.26 Corridor D improvement project	3	3	3
00.30 Highway demonstration projects—preliminary engineering	....	3	3
00.45 Highway bypass demonstration	3	3	3
00.46 Railroad highway crossing demonstration	8	10	10
00.79 Surface transportation projects	10	10	10
00.80 Arkansas I–69 Connector	51	....	....
00.81 Miscellaneous Massachusetts projects	51	....	....
10.00 Total new obligations (object class 41.0)	146	58	58
Budgetary resources available for obligation:			
21.40 Unobligated balance available, start of year	200	254	196
22.00 New budget authority (gross)	200	....	....
23.90 Total budgetary resources available for obligation	400	254	196
23.95 Total new obligations	−146	−58	−58
24.40 Unobligated balance available, end of year	254	196	138
New budget authority (gross), detail:			
Discretionary:			
40.00 Appropriation	200	....	....
Change in unpaid obligations:			
72.40 Unpaid obligations, start of year: Obligated balance, start of year	171	252	178
73.10 Total new obligations	146	58	58
73.20 Total outlays (gross)	−65	−132	−99
74.40 Unpaid obligations, end of year: Obligated balance, end of year	252	178	137
Outlays (gross), detail:			
86.90 Outlays from new discretionary authority	40	....	....
86.93 Outlays from discretionary balances	25	132	99
87.00 Total outlays (gross)	65	132	99
Net budget authority and outlays:			
89.00 Budget authority	200	....	....
90.00 Outlays	65	132	99

This consolidated schedule shows the obligation and outlay of amounts made available for programs in prior years. No further appropriation is requested.

APPALACHIAN DEVELOPMENT HIGHWAY SYSTEM

Program and Financing (in millions of dollars)

Identification code 69–0640–0–1–401	1999 actual	2000 est.	2001 est.
Obligations by program activity:			
00.02 Appalachian Highway Development System FY 1999	84	90	
10.00 Total new obligations (object class 25.2)	84	90	
Budgetary resources available for obligation:			
21.40 Unobligated balance available, start of year	42	90	
22.00 New budget authority (gross)	132		
23.90 Total budgetary resources available for obligation	174	90	
23.95 Total new obligations	−84	−90	
24.40 Unobligated balance available, end of year	90		
New budget authority (gross), detail:			
Discretionary:			
40.00 Appropriation	132		
Change in unpaid obligations:			
72.40 Unpaid obligations, start of year: Obligated balance, start of year	185	196	168
73.10 Total new obligations	84	90	
73.20 Total outlays (gross)	−73	−118	−76
74.40 Unpaid obligations, end of year: Obligated balance, end of year	196	168	92
Outlays (gross), detail:			
86.93 Outlays from discretionary balances	73	118	76
Net budget authority and outlays:			
89.00 Budget authority	132		
90.00 Outlays	73	118	76

Funding for this program will be used for the necessary expenses relating to construction of, and improvements to, corridor X of the Appalachian Development Highway System (ADHS) in the State of Alabama, and to the ADHS in the State of West Virginia.

STATE INFRASTRUCTURE BANKS

Program and Financing (in millions of dollars)

Identification code 69–0549–0–1–401	1999 actual	2000 est.	2001 est.
Obligations by program activity:			
10.00 Total new obligations (object class 41.0)		4	
Budgetary resources available for obligation:			
21.40 Unobligated balance available, start of year	3	4	
22.00 New budget authority (gross)	−7		
22.10 Resources available from recoveries of prior year obligations	7		
23.90 Total budgetary resources available for obligation	3	4	
23.95 Total new obligations		−4	
24.40 Unobligated balance available, end of year	4		
New budget authority (gross), detail:			
Discretionary:			
40.36 Unobligated balance rescinded	−7		
Change in unpaid obligations:			
72.40 Unpaid obligations, start of year: Obligated balance, start of year	80	44	33
73.10 Total new obligations		4	
73.20 Total outlays (gross)	−29	−15	−12
73.45 Adjustments in unexpired accounts	−7		
74.40 Unpaid obligations, end of year: Obligated balance, end of year	44	33	21
Outlays (gross), detail:			
86.93 Outlays from discretionary balances	29	15	12
Net budget authority and outlays:			
89.00 Budget authority	−7		
90.00 Outlays	29	15	12

This schedule shows the obligation and outlay of amounts made available in prior years.

ELLSWORTH HOUSING SETTLEMENT

Unavailable Collections (in millions of dollars)

Identification code 69–5460–0–2–401	1999 actual	2000 est.	2001 est.
Balance, start of year:			
01.99 Balance, start of year			3
Receipts:			
02.01 Ellsworth housing settlement		3	
04.00 Total: Balances and collections		3	3
07.99 Total balance, end of year		3	3

Program and Financing (in millions of dollars)

Identification code 69–5460–0–2–401	1999 actual	2000 est.	2001 est.
Obligations by program activity:			
10.00 Total new obligations (object class 25.2)		3	
Budgetary resources available for obligation:			
22.00 New budget authority (gross)		3	
23.95 Total new obligations		−3	
New budget authority (gross), detail:			
Discretionary:			
40.25 Appropriation (special fund, indefinite)		3	
Change in unpaid obligations:			
72.40 Unpaid obligations, start of year: Obligated balance, start of year			2
73.10 Total new obligations		3	
73.20 Total outlays (gross)		−1	−2
74.40 Unpaid obligations, end of year: Obligated balance, end of year		2	
Outlays (gross), detail:			
86.90 Outlays from new discretionary authority		1	
86.93 Outlays from discretionary balances			2
87.00 Total outlays (gross)		1	2
Net budget authority and outlays:			
89.00 Budget authority		3	
90.00 Outlays		1	2

The account reflects a portion of the funds received by the United States in settlement of the claims against the Hunt Building Corporation and Ellsworth Housing Limited Partnership. The funds that are available to the Secretary of Transportation for construction of an access road on Interstate Route 90 at Box Elder, South Dakota.

Credit accounts:

TRANSPORTATION INFRASTRUCTURE FINANCE AND INNOVATION PROGRAM DIRECT LOAN FINANCING ACCOUNT

Program and Financing (in millions of dollars)

Identification code 69–4123–0–3–401	1999 actual	2000 est.	2001 est.
Obligations by program activity:			
00.01 Loan obligations	873	990	1,210
00.02 Interest paid to Treasury		25	79
10.00 Total new obligations	873	1,015	1,289
Budgetary resources available for obligation:			
22.00 New financing authority (gross)	872	1,015	1,288
23.95 Total new obligations	−873	−1,015	−1,289

		1999 actual	2000 est.	2001 est.
	New financing authority (gross), detail:			
	Mandatory:			
67.15	Authority to borrow (indefinite)	837	961	1,220
69.00	Offsetting collections (cash)		55	42
69.10	From Federal sources: Change in receivables and unpaid, unfilled orders	35	−1	26
69.90	Spending authority from offsetting collections (total mandatory)	35	54	68
70.00	Total new financing authority (gross)	872	1,015	1,288
	Change in unpaid obligations:			
	Unpaid obligations, start of year:			
72.40	Obligated balance, start of year		837	837
72.95	Receivables from program account		35	34
72.99	Total unpaid obligations, start of year		872	871
73.10	Total new obligations	873	1,015	1,289
73.20	Total financing disbursements (gross)		−1,018	−937
	Unpaid obligations, end of year:			
74.40	Obligated balance, end of year	837	837	1,163
74.95	Receivables from program account	35	34	60
74.99	Total unpaid obligations, end of year	872	871	1,223
87.00	Total financing disbursements (gross)		1,018	937
	Offsets:			
	Against gross financing authority and financing disbursements:			
88.00	Offsetting collections (cash) from: Federal sources		−55	−42
	Against gross financing authority only:			
88.95	Change in receivables from program accounts	−35	1	−26
	Net financing authority and financing disbursements:			
89.00	Financing authority	837	961	1,220
90.00	Financing disbursements		963	895

Status of Direct Loans (in millions of dollars)

Identification code 69–4123–0–3–401		1999 actual	2000 est.	2001 est.
	Position with respect to appropriations act limitation on obligations:			
1111	Limitation on direct loans	873	990	1,210
1150	Total direct loan obligations	873	990	1,210
	Cumulative balance of direct loans outstanding:			
1210	Outstanding, start of year			992
1231	Disbursements: Direct loan disbursements		992	858
1251	Repayments: Repayments and prepayments			
1290	Outstanding, end of year		992	1,850

As required by the Federal Credit Reform Act of 1990, this non-budgetary account records all cash flows to and from the Government resulting from direct loans made under the Transportation Infrastructure Finance and Innovation Act Program (TIFIA). The amounts in this account are a means of financing and are not included in the budget totals.

Balance Sheet (in millions of dollars)

Identification code 69–4123–0–3–401		1998 actual	1999 actual	2000 est.	2001 est.
	ASSETS:				
	Investments in US securities:				
1106	Federal assets: Receivables, net			69	129
	Net value of assets related to post-1991 direct loans receivable:				
1401	Direct loans receivable, gross			992	1,850
1405	Allowance for subsidy cost (−)			−69	−129
1499	Net present value of assets related to direct loans			923	1,721
1999	Total assets			992	1,850
	LIABILITIES:				
	Federal liabilities:				
2103	Debt			923	1,721
2105	Other			69	129
2999	Total liabilities			992	1,850
4999	Total liabilities and net position			992	1,850

Transportation Infrastructure Finance and Innovation Program Guaranteed Loan Financing Account

Program and Financing (in millions of dollars)

Identification code 69–4145–0–3–401		1999 actual	2000 est.	2001 est.
	Budgetary resources available for obligation:			
21.40	Unobligated balance available, start of year			23
22.00	New financing authority (gross)		24	20
23.90	Total budgetary resources available for obligation		24	43
23.95	Total new obligations			
24.40	Unobligated balance available, end of year: Loan guarantee subsidies		23	41
	New financing authority (gross), detail:			
	Discretionary:			
68.00	Spending authority from offsetting collections (gross): Offsetting collections (cash)		24	20
	Offsets:			
	Against gross financing authority and financing disbursements:			
	Offsetting collections (cash) from:			
88.00	Federal sources: loan guarantee subsidy		−23	−18
88.25	Interest on uninvested funds		−1	−2
88.90	Total, offsetting collections (cash)		−24	−20
	Net financing authority and financing disbursements:			
89.00	Financing authority			
90.00	Financing disbursements		−24	−20

Status of Guaranteed Loans (in millions of dollars)

Identification code 69–4145–0–3–401		1999 actual	2000 est.	2001 est.
	LOAN GUARANTEES			
	Position with respect to appropriations act limitation on commitments:			
2111	Limitation on guaranteed loans made by private lenders	600	720	880
2150	Total guaranteed loan commitments	600	720	880
2199	Guaranteed amount of guaranteed loan commitments	600	720	880
	Cumulative balance of guaranteed loans outstanding:			
2210	Outstanding, start of year			1,320
2231	Disbursements of new guaranteed loans		1,320	880
2290	Outstanding, end of year		1,320	2,200
	Memorandum:			
2299	Guaranteed amount of guaranteed loans outstanding, end of year		1,320	2,200

As required by the Federal Credit Reform Act of 1990, this non-budgetary account records all cash flows to and from the Government resulting from loan guarantees made under the Transportation Infrastructure Finance and Innovation Act Program (TIFIA). The amounts are a means of financing and are not included in the budget totals.

Balance Sheet (in millions of dollars)

Identification code 69–4145–0–3–401		1998 actual	1999 actual	2000 est.	2001 est.
	ASSETS:				
1101	Federal assets: Fund balances with Treasury			23	41
1999	Total assets			23	41
	LIABILITIES:				
2204	Non-Federal liabilities: Liabilities for loan guarantees			23	41
2999	Total liabilities			23	41
4999	Total liabilities and net position			23	41

Credit accounts—Continued

TRANSPORTATION FINANCE AND INNOVATION PROGRAM LINE OF CREDIT FINANCING ACCOUNT

Program and Financing (in millions of dollars)

Identification code 69–4173–0–3–401	1999 actual	2000 est.	2001 est.
Obligations by program activity:			
00.01 Obligations for lines of credit	20	90	110
10.00 Total new obligations	20	90	110
Budgetary resources available for obligation:			
22.00 New financing authority (gross)	20	90	110
23.95 Total new obligations	−20	−90	−110
New financing authority (gross), detail:			
Mandatory:			
67.15 Authority to borrow (indefinite)	18	81	99
Discretionary:			
68.00 Spending authority from offsetting collections: Offsetting collections (cash)	2	9	11
70.00 Total new financing authority (gross)	20	90	110
Change in unpaid obligations:			
72.40 Unpaid obligations, start of year: Obligated balance, start of year	....	20	110
73.10 Total new obligations	20	90	110
74.40 Unpaid obligations, end of year: Obligated balance, end of year	20	110	220
Offsets:			
Against gross financing authority and financing disbursements:			
Offsetting collections (cash) from:			
88.00 Federal sources	−2	−9	−10
88.25 Interest on uninvested funds	....	....	−1
88.90 Total, offsetting collections (cash)	−2	−9	−11
Net financing authority and financing disbursements:			
89.00 Financing authority	18	81	99
90.00 Financing disbursements	....	−9	−11

Status of Direct Loans (in millions of dollars)

Identification code 69–4173–0–3–401	1999 actual	2000 est.	2001 est.
LINES OF CREDIT			
Position with respect to appropriations act limitation on obligations:			
1111 Limitation on direct loans	20	90	110
1150 Total direct loan obligations	20	90	110

As required by the Federal Credit Reform Act of 1990, this non-budgetary account records all cash flows to and from the Government resulting from lines of credit made under the Transportation Infrastructure Finance and Innovation Act Program (TIFIA). The amounts are a means of financing and are not included in the budget totals.

Balance Sheet (in millions of dollars)

Identification code 69–4173–0–3–401	1998 actual	1999 actual	2000 est.	2001 est.
ASSETS:				
1101 Federal assets: Fund balances with Treasury	....	20	110	220
1999 Total assets	....	20	110	220
LIABILITIES:				
2204 Non-Federal liabilities: Liabilities for loan guarantees	....	20	110	220
2999 Total liabilities	....	20	110	220
4999 Total liabilities and net position	....	20	110	220

ORANGE COUNTY (CA) TOLL ROAD DEMONSTRATION PROJECT PROGRAM ACCOUNT

Program and Financing (in millions of dollars)

Identification code 69–0543–0–1–401	1999 actual	2000 est.	2001 est.
Change in unpaid obligations:			
72.40 Unpaid obligations, start of year: Obligated balance, start of year	18	18	18
74.40 Unpaid obligations, end of year: Obligated balance, end of year	18	18	18
Net budget authority and outlays:			
89.00 Budget authority	....	....	....
90.00 Outlays	....	....	....

The Orange County Toll Road Demonstration Project consists of Federal financial assistance for two toll roads in Orange County, California: the San Joaquin Hills Transportation Corridor and the Foothill/Eastern Transportation Corridor Projects. Federal standby lines of credit were made available to the Transportation Corridor Agencies for these two projects. An appropriation of $10 million in Federal funds for the San Joaquin Hills Corridor was appropriated in 1993 to cover the subsidy cost of a $120 million line of credit. Similarly, $8 million in Federal funds for the Foothills/Eastern Corridor was appropriated in 1995 appropriations to cover the subsidy cost of a $120 million line of credit. Both of these credit lines are available for a 10-year period following substantial completion of the project. The San Joaquin Hills corridor was completed in 1996 and the Foothill/Eastern Corridor was completed in 1999. There have been no draws on either line of credit to date.

As required by the Federal Credit Reform Act of 1990, this account records for this program, the subsidy costs associated with the direct loans obligated in 1992 and later years (including modifications of direct loans, loan guarantees, or lines of credit that resulted from obligations or commitments in any year), as well as administrative expenses of this program. The subsidy amounts are estimated on a present value basis; the administrative expenses are estimated on a cash basis.

Future Federal credit enhancements for transportation infrastructure will be made under the Transportation Infrastructure Finance and Innovation Act Program.

ORANGE COUNTY (CA) TOLL ROAD DEMONSTRATION PROJECT DIRECT LOAN FINANCING ACCOUNT

Program and Financing (in millions of dollars)

Identification code 69–4200–0–3–401	1999 actual	2000 est.	2001 est.
Change in unpaid obligations:			
Unpaid obligations, start of year:			
72.40 Obligated balance, start of year	247	247	247
72.95 Receivables from program account	18	18	18
72.99 Total unpaid obligations, start of year	265	265	265
Unpaid obligations, end of year:			
74.40 Obligated balance, end of year	247	247	247
74.95 Receivables from program account	18	18	18
74.99 Total unpaid obligations, end of year	265	265	265
Net financing authority and financing disbursements:			
89.00 Financing authority	....	....	....
90.00 Financing disbursements	....	....	....

As required by the Federal Credit Reform Act of 1990, this non-budgetary account records all cash flows to and from the Government resulting from direct loans obligated in 1992 and later years (including modifications of direct loans that resulted from obligations in any year). The amounts in this account are a means of financing and are not included in the budget totals.

Balance Sheet (in millions of dollars)

Identification code 69–4200–0–3–401	1998 actual	1999 actual	2000 est.	2001 est.
ASSETS:				
Investments in US securities:				
1106 Federal assets: Receivables, net	18	18	18	18
1999 Total assets	18	18	18	18
NET POSITION:				
3300 Cumulative results of operations	18	18	18	18
3999 Total net position	18	18	18	18
4999 Total liabilities and net position	18	18	18	18

Trust Funds

Right-of-Way Revolving Fund Liquidating Account

Program and Financing (in millions of dollars)

Identification code 69–8402–0–8–401	1999 actual	2000 est.	2001 est.
New budget authority (gross), detail:			
Mandatory:			
69.00 Offsetting collections (cash)	24	24	24
69.45 Portion not available for obligation (limitation on obligations)	−24	−24	−24
69.90 Spending authority from offsetting collections (total mandatory)	....	....	....
Change in unpaid obligations:			
72.40 Unpaid obligations, start of year: Obligated balance, start of year	50	30	27
73.20 Total outlays (gross)	−20	−3	−3
74.40 Unpaid obligations, end of year: Obligated balance, end of year	30	27	24
Outlays (gross), detail:			
86.93 Outlays from discretionary balances	20	3	3
Offsets:			
Against gross budget authority and outlays:			
88.40 Offsetting collections (cash) from: Non-Federal sources	−24	−24	−24
Net budget authority and outlays:			
89.00 Budget authority	−24	−24	−24
90.00 Outlays	−4	−21	−21

Status of Direct Loans (in millions of dollars)

Identification code 69–8402–0–8–401	1999 actual	2000 est.	2001 est.
Cumulative balance of direct loans outstanding:			
1210 Outstanding, start of year	182	194	173
1231 Disbursements: Direct loan disbursements	36	3	3
1251 Repayments: Repayments and prepayments	−24	−24	−24
1290 Outstanding, end of year	194	173	152

The Federal-Aid Highway Act of 1968 authorized the establishment of a right-of-way revolving fund. This fund was used to make cash advances to States for the purpose of purchasing right-of-way parcels in advance of highway construction and thereby preventing the inflation of land prices from significantly increasing construction costs.

This program was terminated by TEA–21 but will continue to be shown for reporting purposes as loan balances remain outstanding. The purchase of right-of-way is an eligible expense of the Federal-aid program and therefore a separate program is unnecessary. No further obligations are proposed in 2001.

Statement of Operations (in millions of dollars)

Identification code 69–8402–0–8–401	1998 actual	1999 actual	2000 est.	2001 est.
0101 Revenue	7	4	24	24
0102 Expense	−9	−40	−14	−14
0105 Net income or loss (−)	−2	−36	10	10

Highway Trust Fund

Unavailable Collections (in millions of dollars)

Identification code 20–8102–0–7–401	1999 actual	2000 est.	2001 est.
Balance, start of year:			
01.99 Encumbered balance, start of year	−17,529	−11,831	−14,207
Receipts:			
02.01 Highway trust fund, deposits (highway account)	33,821	29,638	30,368
02.02 Highway trust fund, deposits (mass transit account)	5,478	4,673	4,780
02.05 Cash Management Improvement Act interest, Highway trust fund (highway account)	2	....	....
02.99 Total receipts	39,301	34,311	35,148
03.00 Offsetting Collections	24	24	24
04.00 Total: Balances and collections	21,796	22,504	20,965
Appropriation:			
05.02 Motor carrier safety grants	−100	−105	−187
05.03 Federal-aid highways	−29,307	−31,605	−34,054
05.05 Operations and research (trust fund share)	−161	−74	−286
05.06 Highway traffic safety grants	−200	−207	−214
05.08 Discretionary grants (trust fund)	....	....	....
05.09 Trust fund share of expenses	−4,252	−4,644	−5,089
05.22 Motor carrier safety	....	−76	−92
05.23 Expanded intercity rail passenger service fund	....	....	....
05.99 Subtotal appropriation	−34,020	−36,711	−39,922
06.10 Unobligated balance returned to receipts	393	....	....
07.99 Encumbered balance, end of year	−11,831	−14,207	−18,957

Program and Financing (in millions of dollars)

Identification code 20–8102–0–7–401	1999 actual	2000 est.	2001 est.
Memorandum (non-add) entries:			
92.01 Total investments, start of year: U.S. securities: Par value	18,570	28,083	31,437
92.02 Total investments, end of year: U.S. securities: Par value	28,083	31,437	32,254

The Highway Revenue Act of 1956, as amended, provides for the transfer from the General Fund to the Highway Trust Fund of revenue from the motor fuel tax and certain other taxes paid by highway users. The Secretary of the Treasury estimates the amounts to be transferred. In turn, appropriations are authorized from this fund to meet expenditures for Federal-aid highways and other programs as specified by law.

This table shows the status of the resources of the Highway Trust Fund relative to the obligational authority that has been made available for programs financed by the trust fund. The encumbered balance indicates the degree to which the outstanding obligational authority exceeds the estimated cash balances of the fund each year. Under the laws governing the Highway Trust Fund, the amount of obligational authority available at any time cannot exceed the actual cash balances plus the amount of receipts estimated to be collected during the following two years; for most other trust funds obligational authority is limited to the actual receipts of the fund. Revenues in 1999 reflect delayed deposits from the prior year pursuant to the Taxpayer Relief Act of 1997, P.L. 105–34.

The status of the fund is as follows:

HIGHWAY TRUST FUND—Continued

Status of Funds (in millions of dollars)

Identification code 20–8102–0–7–401	1999 actual	2000 est.	2001 est.
Unexpended balance, start of year:			
0100 Uninvested balance	644	896	
0101 U.S. Securities: Par value	17,926	28,083	31,437
0199 Total balance, start of year	18,570	28,979	31,437
Cash income during the year:			
Governmental receipts:			
Governmental receipts:			
0200 Highway trust fund, deposits (Highway account)	33,821	29,638	30,368
0200 Highway Trust Fund deposits (Transit account)	5,478	4,673	4,780
Proprietary receipts:			
0221 CMIA receipts	2		
Offsetting collections:			
0280 Federal-aid highways	70	92	92
0281 NHTSA Grants	32	12	14
0284 Right-of-way revolving fund liquidating account	24	24	24
0297 Income under present law	39,427	34,439	35,278
0299 Total cash income	39,427	34,439	35,278
Cash outgo during year:			
0500 Federal-aid highways	−22,812	−25,487	−27,719
0504 Motor carrier safety		−68	−91
0505 National motor carrier safety program	−87	−109	−128
0506 Highway-related safety grants	−1	−1	
0507 Right-of-way revolving fund (trust revolving fund)	−20	−3	−3
0508 Miscellaneous highway trust funds	−40	−52	−34
0510 Operations and research (trust fund share)	−108	−102	−218
0511 Highway traffic safety grants	−190	−210	−217
0512 Trust fund share of next generation high speed rail program	−2	−5	
0514 Discretionary grants (trust fund)	−1,524	−1,314	−932
0516 Trust fund share of expenses	−4,252	−4,626	−5,067
0519 Construction, National Park Service, Interior	−1	−4	−5
0527 Expanded intercity rail passenger service fund			−47
0599 Total cash outgo (−)	−29,037	−31,981	−34,461
0650 Other adjustments	19		
Unexpended balance, end of year:			
0700 Uninvested balance	896		
0701 U.S. Securities: Par value	28,083	31,437	32,254
0799 Total balance, end of year	28,979	31,437	32,254

The following table covers that part of the trust fund that pertains to the highway account. It shows the annual income and outlays of highway programs funded by the trust fund.

HIGHWAY TRUST FUND

(HIGHWAY ACCOUNT ONLY)

[In millions of dollars]

	1999 actual	*2000 est.*	*2001 est.*
Unexpended balance, start of year	8,519	19,226	22,951
Cash income during the year:			
Total cash income	33,947	29,766	30,498
Interest [1]	2		
Total annual income	33,949	29,766	30,498
Cash outgo during the year (outlays)	23,261	26,041	28,512
Unexpended balance, end of year	19,226	22,951	24,937

Note.—The invested balances shown above include both appropriated and unavailable balances.
[1] Interest of $2 million shown in 1999 pursuant to the Cash Management Improvement Act.

FEDERAL-AID HIGHWAYS

(LIMITATION ON OBLIGATIONS)

(HIGHWAY TRUST FUND)

None of the funds in this Act shall be available for the implementation or execution of programs, the obligations for which are in excess of [$27,701,350,000] *$29,318,806,000* for Federal-aid highways and highway safety construction programs for fiscal year [2000] *2001*: *Provided*, That within [the $27,701,350,000] *this* obligation limitation on Federal-aid highways and highway safety construction programs, not more than [$391,450,000] *$658,750,000* shall be available for the implementation or execution of programs for transportation research (sections 502, 503, 504, 506, 507, and 508 of title 23, United States Code, as amended; section 5505 of title 49, United States Code, as amended; and sections 5112 and 5204–5209 of Public Law 105–178) for fiscal year [2000] *2001*; not more than [$20,000,000] *$25,000,000* shall be available for the implementation or execution of programs for the Magnetic Levitation Transportation Technology Deployment Program (section 1218 of Public Law 105–178) for fiscal year [2000] *2001*, of which not to exceed [$1,000,000] *$3,500,000* shall be available to the Federal Railroad Administration for administrative expenses and technical assistance in connection with such program; not more than $31,000,000 shall be available for the implementation or execution of programs for the Bureau of Transportation Statistics (section 111 of title 49, United States Code) for fiscal year [2000] *2001*: *Provided further*, That [within the $211,200,000 obligation limitation on Intelligent Transportation Systems, the following sums shall be made available for Intelligent Transportation System projects in the following specified areas:

Albuquerque, New Mexico, $2,000,000;
Arapahoe County, Colorado, $1,000,000;
Branson, Missouri, $1,000,000;
Central Pennsylvania, $1,000,000;
Charlotte, North Carolina, $1,000,000;
Chicago, Illinois, $1,000,000;
City of Superior and Douglas County, Wisconsin, $1,000,000;
Clay County, Missouri, $300,000;
Clearwater, Florida, $3,500,000;
College Station, Texas, $1,000,000;
Central Ohio, $1,000,000;
Commonwealth of Virginia, $4,000,000;
Corpus Christi, Texas, $1,500,000;
Delaware River, Pennsylvania, $1,000,000;
Fairfield, California, $750,000;
Fargo, North Dakota, $1,000,000;
Florida Bay County, Florida, $1,000,000;
Fort Worth, Texas, $2,500,000;
Grand Forks, North Dakota, $500,000;
Greater Metropolitan Capital Region, District of Columbia, $5,000,000;
Greater Yellowstone, Montana, $1,000,000;
Houma, Louisiana, $1,000,000;
Houston, Texas, $1,500,000;
Huntsville, Alabama, $500,000;
Inglewood, California, $1,000,000;
Jefferson County, Colorado, $1,500,000;
Kansas City, Missouri, $1,000,000;
Las Vegas, Nevada, $2,800,000;
Los Angeles, California, $1,000,000;
Miami, Florida, $1,000,000;
Mission Viejo, California, $1,000,000;
Monroe County, New York, $1,000,000;
Nashville, Tennessee, $1,000,000;
Northeast Florida, $1,000,000;
Oakland, California, $500,000;
Oakland County, Michigan, $1,000,000;
Oxford, Mississippi, $1,500,000;
Pennsylvania Turnpike, Pennsylvania, $2,500,000;
Pueblo, Colorado, $1,000,000;
Puget Sound, Washington, $1,000,000;
Reno/Tahoe, California/Nevada, $500,000;
Rensselaer County, New York, $1,000,000;
Sacramento County, California, $1,000,000;
Salt Lake City, Utah, $3,000,000;
San Francisco, California, $1,000,000;
Santa Clara, California, $1,000,000;
Santa Teresa, New Mexico, $1,000,000;
Seattle, Washington, $2,100,000;
Shenandoah Valley, Virginia, $2,500,000;
Shreveport, Louisiana, $1,000,000;
Silicon Valley, California, $1,000,000;
Southeast Michigan, $2,000,000;
Spokane, Washington, $500,000;
St. Louis, Missouri, $1,000,000;
State of Alabama, $1,300,000;
State of Alaska, $3,000,000;
State of Arizona, $1,000,000;
State of Colorado, $1,500,000;
State of Delaware, $2,000,000;

State of Idaho, $2,000,000;
State of Illinois, $1,500,000;
State of Maryland, $2,000,000;
State of Minnesota, $7,000,000;
State of Montana, $1,000,000;
State of Nebraska, $500,000;
State of Oregon, $1,000,000;
State of Texas, $4,000,000;
State of Vermont rural systems, $1,000,000;
States of New Jersey and New York, $2,000,000;
Statewide Transcom/Transmit upgrades, New Jersey, $4,000,000;
Tacoma Puyallup, Washington, $500,000;
Thurston, Washington, $1,000,000;
Towamencin, Pennsylvania, $600,000;
Wausau-Stevens Point-Wisconsin Rapids, Wisconsin, $1,500,000;
Wayne County, Michigan, $1,000,000:

Provided further, That, notwithstanding Public Law 105–178 as amended, funds authorized under section 110 of title 23, United States Code, for fiscal year 2000 shall be apportioned based on each State's percentage share of funding provided for under section 105 of title 23, United States Code, for fiscal year 2000, except that before such apportionments are made, $90,000,000 shall be set aside for projects authorized under section 1602 of Public Law 105–178 as amended, and $8,000,000 shall be set aside for the Woodrow Wilson Memorial Bridge project authorized by section 404 of the Woodrow Wilson Memorial Bridge Authority Act of 1995 as amended. Of the funds to be apportioned under section 110 for fiscal year 2000, the Secretary shall ensure that such funds are apportioned for the Interstate Maintenance program, the National Highway system program, the bridge program, the surface transportation program, and the congestion mitigation and air quality program in the same ratio that each State is apportioned funds for such program in fiscal year 2000 but for this section: *Provided further*, That, notwithstanding any other provision of law, the Secretary shall, at the request of the State of Nevada, transfer up to $10,000,000 of Minimum Guarantee apportionments, and an equal amount of obligation authority, to the State of California for use on High Priority Project No. 829 "Widen I–15 in San Bernardino County", section 1602 of Public Law 105–178] *of the funds for section 140(b) of title 23, U.S. Code, not less than $1,200,000 shall be for training on reservations or training that would benefit Native Americans: Provided further, That within the obligation limitation, an additional $25,000,000 shall be for the implementation of the Transportation and Community and System Preservation Pilot Program; an additional $140,000,000 shall be for the implementation of the National Corridor Planning and Development and the Coordinated Border Infrastructure Programs; an additional $221,500,000 shall be for the implementation of research programs under chapter 5 of title 23, U.S. Code; and $398,000,000 shall be for implementation of an Emergency Relief Reserve Fund: Provided further, That the limitations on credit amounts provided in 23 U.S.C. 188(c) shall remain available until expended.*

(LIQUIDATION OF CONTRACT AUTHORIZATION)

(HIGHWAY TRUST FUND)

For carrying out the provisions of title 23, United States Code, that are attributable to Federal-aid highways, including the National Scenic and Recreational Highway as authorized by 23 U.S.C. 148, not otherwise provided, including reimbursement for sums expended pursuant to the provisions of 23 U.S.C. 308, [$26,000,000,000] *$28,000,000,000* or so much thereof as may be available in and derived from the Highway Trust Fund, to remain available until expended. *(Department of Transportation and Related Agencies Appropriations Act, 2000.)*

Program and Financing (in millions of dollars)

Identification code 69–8083–0–7–401		1999 actual	2000 est.	2001 est.
	Obligations by program activity:			
	Direct program:			
	Programs subject to obligation limitation:			
00.01	Direct loan subsidy—Transportation Infrastructure Finance and Innovation Act (TIFIA)	35	54	53
00.02	Loan guarantee subsidy (TIFIA)	9	40	39
00.03	Line of credit (TIFIA)	2	5	5
00.09	Administrative expenses (TIFIA)	1	2	2
00.11	Surface transportation program	6,227	6,216	6,411
00.12	National highway program	4,888	5,319	5,487
00.13	Interstate maintenance	3,357	4,419	4,561
00.14	Bridge program	2,565	3,785	3,902
00.15	Congestion mitigation and air quality improvement	1,145	1,509	1,557
00.16	Minimum guarantee	2,167	1,763	1,905
00.21	Intelligent transportation systems (ITS) standards, research and development	75	98	100
00.22	ITS deployment	71	124	238
00.23	Transportation research	208	220	321
00.24	Federal lands highways	339	653	701
00.25	Emergency relief	....	....	398
00.26	National corridor planning and coordinated border infrastructure	118	122	266
00.27	Administration [Federal-aid highways]	331	304	323
00.28	Other programs	2,164	432	309
00.29	High priority projects	581	1,560	1,626
00.30	Woodrow Wilson memorial bridge	1	139	180
00.31	Appalachian development highway system	319	394	405
00.32	Safety incentive grants for use of seat belts	54	80	92
00.33	Safety incentive to prevent operation of motor carrier by intoxicated persons	43	70	81
00.34	Delta initiative	....	....	23
00.35	Internal Revenue Service initiative	....	....	20
00.36	Revenue aligned budget authority (estimate for allocated programs)	....	....	329
00.91	Programs subject to obligation limitation	24,700	27,308	29,334
	Programs exempt from obligation limitation:			
	Programs exempt from obligation limitation:			
02.11	Emergency relief program	129	111	100
02.13	Minimum allocation/guarantee	858	702	664
02.14	Demonstration projects	247	394	275
02.91	Programs exempt from obligation limitation	1,234	1,207	1,039
03.01	Emergency supplementals	97	15	....
06.00	Total direct program	26,031	28,530	30,373
09.01	Reimbursable program	70	92	92
10.00	Total new obligations	26,101	28,622	30,465
	Budgetary resources available for obligation:			
21.40	Unobligated balance available, start of year	116	15	....
21.49	Unobligated balance available, start of year: Contract authority	16,716	20,085	23,175
21.99	Total unobligated balance, start of year	16,832	20,100	23,175
22.00	New budget authority (gross)	29,377	31,697	34,146
22.75	Balance of contract authority withdrawn	−8	....	....
23.90	Total budgetary resources available for obligation	46,201	51,797	57,321
23.95	Total new obligations	−26,101	−28,622	−30,465
24.40	Unobligated balance available, end of year	15	....	....
24.49	Unobligated balance, end of year: Contract authority	20,085	23,175	26,856
24.99	Total unobligated balance, end of year	20,100	23,175	26,856
	New budget authority (gross), detail:			
	Discretionary:			
40.26	Appropriation (trust fund, definite)	24,000	26,000	28,000
40.49	Portion applied to liquidate contract authority	−24,000	−26,000	−28,000
43.00	Appropriation (total discretionary)	....	....	....
	Mandatory:			
66.10	Contract authority	29,307	30,149	31,594
	Contract authority (indefinite):			
66.15	Contract authority (indefinite)	....	1,456	3,058
66.15	Contract authority transfer to Expanded intercity rail passenger service fund, Federal Railroad Administration	....	....	−468
66.15	Contract authority transfer to Operations and research, National Highway Traffic Safety Administration	....	....	−70
66.15	Contract authority transfer to National motor carrier safety program, Federal Motor Carrier Safety Administration	....	....	−10
66.15	Contract authority transfer to Trust fund share of expenses, Federal Transit Administration	....	....	−50
66.90	Contract authority (total mandatory)	29,307	31,605	34,054
	Discretionary:			
68.00	Spending authority from offsetting collections: Offsetting collections (cash)	70	92	92
70.00	Total new budget authority (gross)	29,377	31,697	34,146
	Change in unpaid obligations:			
	Unpaid obligations, start of year:			
72.40	Obligated balance, start of year	2,090	3,450	4,070

FEDERAL-AID HIGHWAYS—Continued

(LIQUIDATION OF CONTRACT AUTHORIZATION)—Continued

Program and Financing (in millions of dollars)—Continued

Identification code 69–8083–0–7–401		1999 actual	2000 est.	2001 est.
72.49	Obligated balance, start of year: Contract authority	30,186	32,115	34,630
72.99	Total unpaid obligations, start of year	32,276	35,565	38,700
73.10	Total new obligations	26,101	28,622	30,465
73.20	Total outlays (gross)	–22,812	–25,487	–27,719
	Unpaid obligations, end of year:			
74.40	Obligated balance, end of year	3,450	4,070	4,443
74.49	Obligated balance, end of year: Contract authority	32,115	34,630	37,003
74.99	Total unpaid obligations, end of year	35,565	38,700	41,446
	Outlays (gross), detail:			
86.90	Outlays from new discretionary authority	6,762	7,560	8,056
86.93	Outlays from discretionary balances	14,577	16,481	18,325
86.97	Outlays from new mandatory authority	332	324	280
86.98	Outlays from mandatory balances	1,141	1,121	1,058
87.00	Total outlays (gross)	22,812	25,487	27,719
	Offsets:			
	Against gross budget authority and outlays:			
	Offsetting collections (cash) from:			
88.40	Non-Federal sources	–10	–10	–10
88.45	Offsetting governmental collections from the public	–60	–82	–82
88.90	Total, offsetting collections (cash)	–70	–92	–92
	Net budget authority and outlays:			
89.00	Budget authority	29,307	31,605	34,054
90.00	Outlays	22,742	25,395	27,627

Status of Contract Authority (in millions of dollars)

Identification code 69–8083–0–7–401		1999 actual	2000 est.	2001 est.
0100	Balance, start of year	46,902	52,200	57,805
	Contract authority:			
0200	Contract authority	29,307	31,605	34,054
0400	Appropriation to liquidate contract authority	–24,000	–26,000	–28,000
0600	Balance of contract authority withdrawn	–8		
0700	Balance, end of year	52,200	57,805	63,859

Summary of Loan Levels, Subsidy Budget Authority and Outlays by Program (in millions of dollars)

Identification code 69–8083–0–7–401		1999 actual	2000 est.	2001 est.
	Direct loan levels supportable by subsidy budget authority:			
1150	Direct loan levels	873	990	1,210
1150	Line of credit	20	90	110
1159	Total direct loan levels	893	1,080	1,320
	Direct loan subsidy (in percent):			
1320	Subsidy rate—direct loan	4.04	5.40	5.40
1320	Subsidy rate—line of credit	11.84	9.50	9.50
1329	Weighted average subsidy rate	4.14	5.74	5.74
	Direct loan subsidy budget authority:			
1330	Subsidy budget authority—direct loan	35	53	65
1330	Subsidy budget authority—line of credit	2	9	10
1339	Total subsidy budget authority	37	62	75
	Direct loan subsidy outlays:			
1340	Subsidy outlays—direct loan		55	42
1340	Subsidy outlays—line of credit		9	10
1349	Total subsidy outlays		64	52
	Guaranteed loan levels supportable by subsidy budget authority:			
2150	Loan guarantee levels	600	720	880
2159	Total loan guarantee levels	600	720	880
	Guaranteed loan subsidy (in percent):			
2320	Subsidy rate—guaranteed loans	1.51	2.00	2.00
2329	Weighted average subsidy rate	1.51	2.00	2.00
	Guaranteed loan subsidy budget authority:			
2330	Subsidy budget authority—guaranteed loans	9	14	18
2339	Total subsidy budget authority	9	14	18
	Guaranteed loan subsidy outlays:			
2340	Subsidy outlays—guaranteed loans		23	18
2349	Total subsidy outlays		23	18
	Administrative expense data:			
3510	Budget authority	2	2	2
3580	Outlays from balances		1	
3590	Outlays from new authority	1	3	2

The Federal-Aid Highways (FAH) program is designed to aid in the development, operations and management of an intermodal transportation system that is economically efficient, environmentally sound, provides the foundation for the Nation to compete in the global economy, and moves people and goods safely.

All programs included within FAH are financed from the Highway Trust Fund and most are distributed via apportionments and allocations to States. Liquidating cash appropriations are subsequently requested to fund outlays resulting from obligations incurred under contract authority. The budget proposes to fund most programs from within the Federal-Aid Highway obligation limitation. Emergency Relief and a portion of the Minimum Guarantee program ($639 million) will be exempt from the limitation. The budget also proposes to provide the Indian Reservation Roads ($275 million), on-the-job training ($10 million), transportation research programs, Transportation Community and System Preservation ($50 million), and Borders and Corridors ($280 million) 100 percent obligation authority under the Federal-aid limitation.

The FAH program is funded by contract authority found in the Transportation Equity Act for the 21st Century (TEA–21), which authorizes surface transportation programs through 2003, as described below.

Surface Transportation Program (STP).—STP funds may be used by States and localities for any roads that are not classified as local or rural minor collector roads, bridge projects on any public road, transit capital projects, and intracity and intercity bus terminals and facilities. TEA–21 set aside 10% of STP funds for transportation enhancements and safety and also provides State sub-allocations including the special rule for areas less than 5,000 population. Prior to apportionment, funds are set aside for Railway-Highway Crossing Hazard Elimination in High Speed Rail Corridors and for Operation Lifesaver.

National highway program.—The National Highway System (NHS) Program provides funding for a designated National Highway System consisting of roads that are of primary Federal interest. The National Highway System consists of the current Interstate, other rural principal arterials, urban freeways and connecting urban principal arterials, and facilities on the Defense Department's designated Strategic Highway Network and roads connecting the NHS to intermodal facilities. Legislation designating the 161,000 mile system was enacted in 1995 and TEA–21 added to the system the highways and connections to transportation facilities identified in the May 24, 1996 report to Congress.

Interstate maintenance (IM).—The IM program finances projects to rehabilitate, restore, resurface and reconstruct the Interstate system. Reconstruction that increases capacity, other than HOV lanes, is not eligible for IM funds.

Emergency relief.—The Emergency Relief (ER) program provides funds for the repair or reconstruction of Federal-aid highways and bridges and Federally-owned roads and bridges which have suffered serious damage as the result of natural disasters or catastrophic failures. The ER program supplements the commitment of resources by States, their political subdivisions, or Federal agencies to help pay for unusually heavy expenses resulting from extraordinary conditions. The mandatory portion of the ER program will be funded at $100 million. The budget proposes that an additional $398 million be made available to establish an Emergency Relief Reserve Fund, which is desperately needed to address the ER backlog. This reserve fund would be part of the Federal-aid obligation limitation program.

Bridge replacement and rehabilitation.—The bridge program enables States to respond to the problem of unsafe and inadequate bridges. The funds are available for use on all bridges, including those on roads functionally classified as rural minor collectors and as local. Highway bridges designated as a hazard to navigation by the U.S. Coast Guard will be funded under the bridge program.

Congestion mitigation and air quality improvement program (CMAQ).—The CMAQ program directs funds toward transportation projects and programs to help meet and maintain national ambient air quality standards for ozone, carbon monoxide, and particulate matter. A minimum ½ percent of the apportionment is guaranteed to each State.

Federal lands.—This category includes Public Lands Highways, including Forest Highways; Park Roads and Parkways; Indian Reservation Roads; and Refuge Roads. Roads funded under this program are open to public travel. State and local roads (29,500 miles) that provide important access within the National Forest System are designated Forest Highways. These roads should not be confused with the Forest Development Roads, which are under the jurisdiction of the Forest Service. Park roads and Parkways (8,000 miles) are owned by the National Park Service and provide access within the National Park System. Indian Reservation Roads program consists of the Bureau of Indian Affairs (25,000 miles) and State and local roads (25,000 miles) that provide access within Indian lands. There are approximately 4,250 miles which are under the jurisdiction of the Fish and Wildlife Service. The new category of Refuge Roads consists of public roads that provide access to or within the National Wildlife Refuge System. The budget proposes that an additional $75 million shall be set aside from the Revenue Aligned Budget Authority for the Indian Reservation Roads program.

Border planning and infrastructure program.—The border planning and infrastructure program provides funds to make grants to State and local governments and Federal inspection agencies to facilitate planning and construction of facilities to improve the flow of people and goods in corridors of national significance and at our Nation's borders. The budget proposes that an additional $140 million be made available for the border planning and infrastructure program. This proposal doubles the funding available to this program.

Transportation infrastructure finance and innovation act (TIFIA) program.—The TIFIA program will provide funds to assist in the development of nationally-significant transportation projects. The goal is to encourage the development of large, capital-intensive infrastructure facilities through public-private partnerships consisting of State or local government and one or more private sector firms. It will encourage more private sector and non-Federal participation, and build on the public's willingness to pay user fees to receive the benefits and services of transportation infrastructure sooner than would be possible under traditional funding techniques. Loans, loan guarantees, and stand-by lines of credit may be used to secure junior lien debt or other obligations requiring credit enhancement. The Administration proposes to make the TIFIA credit levels in TEA–21 available until expended.

As required by the Federal Credit Reform Act of 1990, this account records, for this program, the subsidy costs associated with the direct loans obligated in 1992 and beyond (including modifications of direct loans or loan guarantees that resulted from obligations or commitments in any year), as well as administrative expenses of this program. The subsidy amounts are estimated on a present value basis; the administrative expenses are estimated on a cash basis.

Federal highway research and technology.—The research and technology program develops new transportation technology that can be applied nationwide. Activities include surface transportation research, technology deployment, training and education, University Transportation Research, and funding for State research, development, and technology implementation. The budget proposes that an additional $222 million be made available for research activities.

Intelligent Transportation Systems (ITS).—The ITS program is a cooperative, public/private initiative to research, develop, test and evaluate advanced electronic and information systems that can improve the safety, operational efficiency, and productivity of the existing surface transportation infrastructure. It includes the ITS research and development program and the ITS deployment incentives program. The ITS research and development program supports the development of the next generation of ITS technologies, including the Intelligent Vehicle Initiative; the development and maintenance of the National ITS architecture and standards; and the deployment of integrated ITS systems through guidance documents, training, and technical assistance. The budget proposes an additional $120 million for ITS deployment within the increase in research contract authority. The ITS deployment incentive program supports the integration of existing ITS systems in metropolitan areas, integration and infrastructure deployment in rural areas; and the deployment of the commercial vehicle information systems and networks (CVISN).

Revenue Aligned Budget Authority (RABA).—The budget authority and obligation limitation for Federal-aid highway programs funded from the Highway Account (HA) of the Highway Trust Fund (HTF) is adjusted to reflect changes in tax receipt estimates of the HA of the HTF. The budget proposes to provide $3,058 million in RABA funds in 2001. Of these funds, $70 million shall be set aside for the National Highway Traffic Safety Administration, $48 million shall be set aside for the Mississippi Delta Initiative, $20 million shall be set aside for the Internal Revenue Service, $468 million shall be set aside for expanded intercity rail passenger service, $10 million shall be set aside for the Federal Motor Carrier Safety Administration's Commercial Drivers License program, $50 million shall be set aside for the Federal Transit Administration's Job Access and Reverse Commute program, and $75 million shall be set aside for Indian Reservation Roads. RABA funds totaling $2,317 million will be distributed among Federal-aid highway and highway safety construction programs.

Miscellaneous.—This category includes Scenic Byways, Highway Use Tax Evasion Projects, National Recreational Trails, Value Pricing, Ferry Boats, and Transportation and Community and System Preservation. The budget proposes that an additional $25 million be made available for the Transportation and Community and System Preservation program. This proposal doubles the funding level for this program.

In addition, the Administration is seeking an additional $600 million in contract authority for 2004–2007 for the financing of the Woodrow Wilson Bridge project.

Object Classification (in millions of dollars)

Identification code 69–8083–0–7–401		1999 actual	2000 est.	2001 est.
	Direct obligations:			
	Personnel compensation:			
11.1	Full-time permanent	15	16	15
11.5	Other personnel compensation	2	1	1
11.9	Total personnel compensation	17	17	16
12.1	Civilian personnel benefits	3	4	4
21.0	Travel and transportation of persons	3	3	4
25.2	Other services	41	36	39
32.0	Land and structures	219	276	231
41.0	Grants, subsidies, and contributions	25,002	27,403	29,278

FEDERAL-AID HIGHWAYS—Continued

(LIQUIDATION OF CONTRACT AUTHORIZATION)—Continued

Object Classification (in millions of dollars)—Continued

Identification code 69–8083–0–7–401		1999 actual	2000 est.	2001 est.
93.0	Limitation on general operating expenses (see separate schedule)	331	304	316
99.0	Subtotal, direct obligations	25,616	28,043	29,888
99.0	Reimbursable obligations	70	92	92
	Allocation Account:			
	Personnel compensation:			
11.1	Full-time permanent	37	35	40
11.3	Other than full-time permanent	7	7	7
11.5	Other personnel compensation	3	3	3
11.9	Total personnel compensation	47	45	50
12.1	Civilian personnel benefits	10	10	11
21.0	Travel and transportation of persons	4	4	4
22.0	Transportation of things	2	2	2
23.1	Rental payments to GSA	1	1	1
23.3	Communications, utilities, and miscellaneous charges	8	8	8
24.0	Printing and reproduction		1	1
25.2	Other services	213	237	232
25.3	Purchases of goods and services from Government accounts	4	8	5
25.4	Operation and maintenance of facilities	1	2	2
25.7	Operation and maintenance of equipment	1	1	1
26.0	Supplies and materials	15	15	16
31.0	Equipment	3	3	3
32.0	Land and structures	24	24	22
41.0	Grants, subsidies, and contributions	81	126	127
99.0	Subtotal, allocation account	415	487	485
99.9	Total new obligations	26,101	28,622	30,465

Obligations are distributed as follows:	1999 actual	2000 est.	2001 est.
Transportation:			
Federal Highway Administration	25,618	28,044	29,889
Bureau of Transportation Statistics	29	31	31
Federal Railroad Administration	26	29	29
National Highway Traffic Safety Administration	48	88	89
Agriculture:			
Forest Service	27	9	23
Interior:			
Bureau of Indian Affairs	247	273	273
National Park Service	24	35	25
Bureau of Land Management	3	4	3
U.S. Fish and Wildlife Service	8	11	10
Defense:			
Corps of Engineers		6	1
Military Traffic Management Command:			
Transportation Engineering Agency	1	2	1

Personnel Summary

Identification code 69–8083–0–7–401		1999 actual	2000 est.	2001 est.
	Direct:			
1001	Total compensable workyears: Full-time equivalent employment	397	473	466
	Reimbursable:			
2001	Total compensable workyears: Full-time equivalent employment	10	10	8
	Allocation account:			
3001	Total compensable workyears: Full-time equivalent employment	30	27	31

FEDERAL HIGHWAY ADMINISTRATION

LIMITATION ON ADMINISTRATIVE EXPENSES

Necessary expenses for administration and operation of the Federal Highway Administration, *pursuant to 23 U.S.C. 104(n)*, not to exceed [$376,072,000] *$327,352,000* shall be paid in accordance with law from appropriations made available by this Act to the Federal Highway Administration together with advances and reimbursements received by the Federal Highway Administration[: *Provided*, That $70,484,000 shall be available to carry out the functions and operations of the Office of Motor Carriers: *Provided further*, That of the funds available under section 104(a) of title 23, United States Code: $6,000,000 shall be available for Commercial Remote Sensing Products and Spatial Information Technologies under section 5113 of Public Law 105–178, as amended; $5,000,000 shall be available for Nationwide Differential Global Positioning System program, as authorized; $8,000,000 shall be available for National Historic Covered Bridge Preservation Program under section 1224 of Public Law 105–178, as amended; $15,000,000 shall be available to the University of Alabama in Tuscaloosa, Alabama, for research activities at the Transportation Research Institute and to construct a building to house the Institute, and shall remain available until expended; $18,300,000 shall be available for the Indian Reservation Roads Program under section 204 of title 23, United States Code; $16,400,000 shall be available for the Public Lands Highways Program under section 204 of title 23, United States Code; $11,000,000 shall be available for the Park Roads and Parkways Program under section 204 of title 23, United States Code; $1,300,000 shall be available for the Refuge Road Program under section 204 of title 23, United States Code; $10,000,000 shall be available for the Transportation and Community and System Preservation pilot program under section 1221 of Public Law 105–178; and $7,500,000 shall be available for "Child Passenger Protection Education Grants" under section 2003(b) of Public Law 105–178, as amended], *of which $1,317,000 is for the Office of Intermodalism, $3,524,000 is for the Office of the Inspector General; $5,000,000 is for technology sharing and transfer; $1,000,000 is available for Rural Transportation Centers; $1,000,000 is for the Sustainability Climate Change Center; $2,000,000 is for environmental streamlining; $4,750,000 is for the National Personal Transportation Survey; $1,620,000 is for international trade information collection; and $1,000,000 is for the Mississippi Delta initiative. Of the funds available under 23 U.S.C. 104(a), $5,000,000 shall be for design and preliminary engineering of the Four Bears Bridge in North Dakota. (Department of Transportation and Related Agencies Appropriations Act, 2000.)*

Program and Financing (in millions of dollars)

	1999 actual	2000 est.	2001 est.
Program by activities:			
Program direction and coordination:			
Executive direction	2	2	2
Program review	1	1	1
Legal services	5	6	6
Public affairs	1	1	1
Civil rights	2	2	2
General program support:			
Policy	9	8	9
Research and development	11	10	10
Administrative support	104	91	89
Professional development	1	1	1
Career development programs	1		
Highway programs:			
Infrastructure	5	5	5
Planning and environment	13	13	13
Operations	9	8	9
Motor carrier safety	28		
Federal lands highway office	13	11	11
Other highway programs	7	6	23
Field operations and resource centers	131	132	137
Total obligations	343	298	320
Financing:			
Reimbursable programs	−12	−4	−4
Unobligated balance available, start of year	−11	−4	
Unobligated balance available, end of year	5		
Limitation	325	289	316
Relation of obligations to outlays:			
Total obligations	343	298	320
Obligated balance, start of year	517	403	321
Obligated balance, end of year	−403	−321	−279
Outlays from limitation	457	380	362

This limitation provides for the salaries and expenses of the Federal Highway Administration. Resources are allocated from the Federal-aid highways program. The budget proposes to provide funds for the National Rural Development Partnership, the Garrett A. Morgan Program, Small and Disadvantaged Business, the Office of the Chief Information Officer, and the Working Better Together initiative from this account.

Program direction and coordination.—Provides overall management of the highway transportation program, including formulation of multi-year and long-range policy plans and goals for highway programs; safety programs that focus on high risk areas through technical assistance, research, training, analysis, and public information; development of data and analysis for current and long-range programming; administrative support services for all elements of the FHWA; and training opportunities for highway related personnel.

Highway programs.—Provides engineering guidance to Federal and State agencies and to foreign governments, and conducts a program to encourage use of modern traffic engineering procedures to increase the vehicle-carrying capacity of existing highways and urban streets; and finances construction skill training programs for disadvantaged workers hired by contractors on federally aided highway projects.

Field operations.—Provides staff advisory and support services in field offices of the Federal Highway Administration; and provides program and engineering supervision through division offices.

Object Classification (in millions of dollars)

Identification code 69–8083–0–7–401		1999 actual	2000 est.	2001 est.
	Personnel compensation:			
11.1	Full-time permanent	171	153	160
11.3	Other than full-time permanent	3	3	3
11.5	Other personnel compensation	2	3	4
11.9	Total personnel compensation	176	159	166
12.1	Civilian personnel benefits	48	43	45
21.0	Travel and transportation of persons	13	9	9
22.0	Transportation of things	2	1	
23.1	Rental payments to GSA	18	20	17
23.3	Communications, utilities, and miscellaneous charges	10	10	10
24.0	Printing and reproduction	3	2	2
25.2	Other services	46	53	57
25.5	Research and development contracts	6		
26.0	Supplies and materials	4	2	2
31.0	Equipment	4	5	7
41.0	Grants, subsidies, and contributions	1		
93.0	Limitation on expenses	−331	−304	−316
99.0	Subtotal, limitation acct—direct obligations			

Personnel Summary

Identification code 69–8083–0–7–401		1999 actual	2000 est.	2001 est.
6001	Total compensable workyears: Full-time equivalent employment	2,961	2,427	2,439

Highway-Related Safety Grants

(highway trust fund)

Program and Financing (in millions of dollars)

Identification code 69–8019–0–7–401		1999 actual	2000 est.	2001 est.
	Change in unpaid obligations:			
72.40	Unpaid obligations, start of year: Obligated balance, start of year	2	1	
73.20	Total outlays (gross)	−1	−1	
74.40	Unpaid obligations, end of year: Obligated balance, end of year	1		
	Outlays (gross), detail:			
86.93	Outlays from discretionary balances	1	1	
	Net budget authority and outlays:			
89.00	Budget authority			
90.00	Outlays	1	1	

The Highway Safety Act of 1970 authorized grants to States and communities for implementing and maintaining highway-related safety standards. TEA–21 authorizes a consolidated state and community highway safety formula grant program, and therefore this schedule reflects spending of prior year balances.

Miscellaneous Trust Funds

Unavailable Collections (in millions of dollars)

Identification code 69–9971–0–7–999		1999 actual	2000 est.	2001 est.
	Balance, start of year:			
01.99	Balance, start of year			
	Receipts:			
02.01	Advances from other Federal agencies, FHA miscellaneous trust, DOT	24	5	5
02.02	Advances for highway research program	6		
02.03	Contributions from States, etc., cooperative work, forest highways, FHA, Miscellaneous trust, DOT	6	6	6
02.06	Advances from State cooperating agencies and Foreign governments	14	10	10
02.99	Total receipts	50	21	21
	Appropriation:			
05.01	Miscellaneous trust funds	−50	−21	−21
07.99	Total balance, end of year			

Program and Financing (in millions of dollars)

Identification code 69–9971–0–7–999		1999 actual	2000 est.	2001 est.
	Obligations by program activity:			
00.01	Cooperative work, forest highways	7	7	6
00.02	Technical assistance, U.S. dollars advanced from foreign governments	1	1	
00.03	Contributions for highway research programs	3	10	6
00.04	Advances from State cooperating agencies	27	20	17
10.00	Total new obligations	38	38	29
	Budgetary resources available for obligation:			
21.40	Unobligated balance available, start of year	13	25	8
22.00	New budget authority (gross)	50	21	21
23.90	Total budgetary resources available for obligation	63	46	29
23.95	Total new obligations	−38	−38	−29
24.40	Unobligated balance available, end of year	25	8	
	New budget authority (gross), detail:			
	Mandatory:			
60.27	Appropriation (trust fund, indefinite)	50	21	21
	Change in unpaid obligations:			
72.40	Unpaid obligations, start of year: Obligated balance, start of year	34	46	63
73.10	Total new obligations	38	38	29
73.20	Total outlays (gross)	−26	−21	−21
74.40	Unpaid obligations, end of year: Obligated balance, end of year	46	63	71
	Outlays (gross), detail:			
86.97	Outlays from new mandatory authority	26	21	21
	Net budget authority and outlays:			
89.00	Budget authority	50	21	21
90.00	Outlays	26	21	21

Miscellaneous Trust Funds contains the following programs financed out of the highway trust fund and reimbursed by the requesting parties.

Cooperative work, forest highways.—Contributions are received from States and counties in connection with cooperative engineering, survey, maintenance, and construction projects for forest highways.

Technical assistance, U.S. dollars advanced from foreign governments.—The Federal Highway Administration renders technical assistance and acts as agent for the purchase of equipment and materials for carrying out highway programs in foreign countries.

MISCELLANEOUS TRUST FUNDS—Continued

Contributions for highway research programs.—In association with the General Services Administration and the Department of Defense, tests of highway equipment are conducted for the purpose of establishing performance standards upon which to base specifications for use by the Government in purchasing such equipment.

Advances from State cooperating agencies.—Funds are contributed by the State highway departments or local subdivisions thereof for construction and/or maintenance of roads or bridges. The work is performed under the supervision of the Federal Highway Administration.

International highway transportation outreach.—Funds are collected to inform the domestic highway community of technological innovations, promote highway transportation expertise internationally, and increase transfers of transportation technology to foreign countries.

Object Classification (in millions of dollars)

Identification code 69–9971–0–7–999	1999 actual	2000 est.	2001 est.
11.1 Personnel compensation: Full-time permanent	2	2	2
25.2 Other services	36	36	27
99.9 Total new obligations	38	38	29

Personnel Summary

Identification code 69–9971–0–7–999	1999 actual	2000 est.	2001 est.
1001 Total compensable workyears: Full-time equivalent employment	47	40	43

Personnel Summary

Identification code 69–9971–0–7–999	1999 actual	2000 est.	2001 est.
1001 Total compensable workyears: Full-time equivalent employment	14	14	14

MISCELLANEOUS HIGHWAY TRUST FUNDS

Program and Financing (in millions of dollars)

Identification code 69–9972–0–7–401	1999 actual	2000 est.	2001 est.
Obligations by program activity:			
00.02 Intermodal urban demonstration project	8	1	1
00.04 Highway safety improvement demonstration project		1	1
00.13 Climbing lane and safety demonstration project		1	1
00.26 Highway projects	21	7	7
10.00 Total new obligations (object class 41.0)	29	10	10
Budgetary resources available for obligation:			
21.40 Unobligated balance available, start of year	60	31	21
23.95 Total new obligations	−29	−10	−10
24.40 Unobligated balance available, end of year	31	21	11
Change in unpaid obligations:			
72.40 Unpaid obligations, start of year: Obligated balance, start of year	128	117	75
73.10 Total new obligations	29	10	10
73.20 Total outlays (gross)	−40	−52	−34
74.40 Unpaid obligations, end of year: Obligated balance, end of year	117	75	51
Outlays (gross), detail:			
86.93 Outlays from discretionary balances	40	52	34
Net budget authority and outlays:			
89.00 Budget authority			
90.00 Outlays	40	52	34

No further budget authority is requested for 2001. Accounts in this consolidated schedule show the obligation and outlay amounts made available in prior years.

FEDERAL MOTOR CARRIER SAFETY ADMINISTRATION TRUST FUNDS

Trust Funds

MOTOR CARRIER SAFETY

LIMITATION ON OBLIGATIONS

For necessary expenses for administration of motor carrier safety programs and motor carrier safety research, pursuant to section 104(a) of title 23, United States Code, not to exceed $92,194,000 shall be paid in accordance with law from appropriations made available by this Act to the Federal Motor Carrier Safety Administration, together with advances and reimbursements received by the Federal Motor Carrier Safety Administration: Provided, That such amounts shall be available to carry out the functions and operations of the Federal Motor Carrier Safety Administration.

Program and Financing (in millions of dollars)

Identification code 69–8055–0–7–401	1999 actual	2000 est.	2001 est.
Obligations by program activity:			
00.01 Administration		70	82
00.02 Research and development		6	10
10.00 Total new obligations		76	92
Budgetary resources available for obligation:			
22.00 New budget authority (gross)		76	92
23.95 Total new obligations		−76	−92
New budget authority (gross), detail:			
Discretionary:			
40.26 Appropriation (trust fund, definite)		76	92
40.49 Portion applied to liquidate contract authority		−76	−92
43.00 Appropriation (total discretionary)			
Mandatory:			
66.10 Contract authority		76	92
70.00 Total new budget authority (gross)		76	92
Change in unpaid obligations:			
72.40 Unpaid obligations, start of year: Obligated balance, start of year			8
73.10 Total new obligations		76	92
73.20 Total outlays (gross)		−68	−91
74.40 Unpaid obligations, end of year: Obligated balance, end of year		8	9
Outlays (gross), detail:			
86.90 Outlays from new discretionary authority		68	83
86.93 Outlays from discretionary balances			8
87.00 Total outlays (gross)		68	91
Net budget authority and outlays:			
89.00 Budget authority		76	92
90.00 Outlays		68	91

Note.—Administrative expenses for 1999 are included in the Federal Highway Administration schedules. The Federal Motor Carrier Safety Administration was established in 2000 by Public Law 106–159.

Status of Contract Authority (in millions of dollars)

Identification code 69–8055–0–7–401	1999 actual	2000 est.	2001 est.
Contract authority:			
0200 Contract authority		76	92
0400 Appropriation to liquidate contract authority		−76	−92

This limitation provides resources to expand the nationwide motor carrier safety program. Safety program enhancements include enforcement expansion, Federal Motor Carrier Safety regulations development, crash data analysis, and technology development.

Object Classification (in millions of dollars)

Identification code 69–8055–0–7–401	1999 actual	2000 est.	2001 est.
Personnel compensation:			
11.1 Full-time permanent		34	43
11.3 Other than full-time permanent		1	1
11.9 Total personnel compensation		35	44
12.1 Civilian personnel benefits		9	11
21.0 Travel and transportation of persons		4	4
23.1 Rental payments to GSA			5
24.0 Printing and reproduction		1	1
25.2 Other services		19	15
25.5 Research and development contracts		6	10
31.0 Equipment		2	2
99.9 Total new obligations		76	92

Personnel Summary

Identification code 69–8055–0–7–401	1999 actual	2000 est.	2001 est.
1001 Total compensable workyears: Full-time equivalent employment		714	850

National Motor Carrier Safety [Grants] *Program*

(LIQUIDATION OF CONTRACT AUTHORIZATION)

(HIGHWAY TRUST FUND)

For payment of obligations incurred in carrying out 49 U.S.C. 31102, [$105,000,000] *$187,000,000,* to be derived from the Highway Trust Fund and to remain available until expended: *Provided*, That none of the funds in this Act shall be available for the implementation or execution of programs the obligations for which are in excess of [$105,000,000] *$187,000,000* for ["Motor Carrier Safety Grants"] *the National Motor Carrier Safety Program. (P.L. 106–159; Department of Transportation and Related Agencies Appropriations Act, 2000.)*

Program and Financing (in millions of dollars)

Identification code 69–8048–0–7–401	1999 actual	2000 est.	2001 est.
Obligations by program activity:			
00.01 Motor carrier grants	98	104	185
00.02 Administration and research	1	1	2
10.00 Total new obligations	99	105	187
Budgetary resources available for obligation:			
21.40 Unobligated balance available, start of year	1	1	1
22.00 New budget authority (gross)	100	105	187
23.90 Total budgetary resources available for obligation	101	106	188
23.95 Total new obligations	−99	−105	−187
24.40 Unobligated balance available, end of year	1	1	1
New budget authority (gross), detail:			
Discretionary:			
40.26 Appropriation (trust fund, definite)	99	105	187
40.49 Portion applied to liquidate contract authority	−99	−105	−187
43.00 Appropriation (total discretionary)			
Mandatory:			
66.10 Contract authority	100	105	177
66.15 Contract authority transfer from Federal-aid highways, Federal Highway Administration			10
66.90 Contract authority (total mandatory)	100	105	187
70.00 Total new budget authority (gross)	100	105	187
Change in unpaid obligations:			
Unpaid obligations, start of year:			
72.40 Obligated balance, start of year	24	36	34
72.49 Obligated balance, start of year: Contract authority	43	43	42
72.99 Total unpaid obligations, start of year	67	79	76
73.10 Total new obligations	99	105	187
73.20 Total outlays (gross)	−87	−109	−128
Unpaid obligations, end of year:			
74.40 Obligated balance, end of year	36	34	94
74.49 Obligated balance, end of year: Contract authority	43	42	43
74.99 Total unpaid obligations, end of year	79	76	137
Outlays (gross), detail:			
86.90 Outlays from new discretionary authority	28	29	52
86.93 Outlays from discretionary balances	59	80	76
87.00 Total outlays (gross)	87	109	128
Net budget authority and outlays:			
89.00 Budget authority	100	105	187
90.00 Outlays	87	109	128

Status of Contract Authority (in millions of dollars)

Identification code 69–8048–0–7–401	1999 actual	2000 est.	2001 est.
0100 Balance, start of year	43	43	42
Contract authority:			
0200 Contract authority	100	105	187
0400 Appropriation to liquidate contract authority	−99	−105	−187
0700 Balance, end of year	43	42	43

In 2001, $187 million is requested for the motor carrier grants program. This includes $10 million made available from the Federal Highway Administration as part of a reallocation of the increase resulting from revenue aligned budget authority. The $10 million will be made available to states to enhance their driver record information systems. The National Motor Carrier Safety Program (NMCSP) will support a broad range of comprehensive commercial vehicle programs in each State and provide for improving information systems and analysis. Programs will integrate Federal and State activities through a performance-based approach to commercial vehicle safety nationwide, improve driver and vehicle inspections, traffic enforcement, safety performance data collection, analysis and reporting. NMCSP also will continue to support State-conducted compliance reviews, hazardous materials training and enforcement (including border programs), drug interdiction efforts, public education campaigns and a fully implemented SAFETYNET data collection and reporting system. Training of MCSAP officers will also continue.

Object Classification (in millions of dollars)

Identification code 69–8048–0–7–401	1999 actual	2000 est.	2001 est.
25.2 Other services	1	1	2
41.0 Grants, subsidies, and contributions	98	104	185
99.9 Total new obligations	99	105	187

NATIONAL HIGHWAY TRAFFIC SAFETY ADMINISTRATION

The following table depicts the total funding for all National Highway Traffic Safety programs. A total of $70 million of the Operations and Research activity is to be derived from the Revenue Aligned Budget Authority authorized by the Transportation Equity Act for the 21st Century.

[In millions of dollars]

	1999 actual	2000 est.	2001 est.
Budget authority:			
Operations and research	1	86	
Operations and research (Highway trust fund)	161	74	286
Highway traffic safety grants	200	207	214
Total budget authority	362	367	500
Program level (obligations):			
Operations and research	11	86	
Operations and research (Highway trust fund)	153	74	286
Highway traffic safety grants	200	207	213
Total program level	364	367	499

	1999 actual	2000 est.	2001 est.
Outlays:			
Operations and research	66	88	39
Operations and research (Highway trust fund)	75	90	204
Highway traffic safety grants	190	210	217
Total outlays	331	388	460

Federal Funds

General and special funds:

Operations and Research

Program and Financing (in millions of dollars)

Identification code 69–0650–0–1–401		1999 actual	2000 est.	2001 est.
	Obligations by program activity:			
	Direct program:			
00.01	Safety performance standards	1	14	
00.02	Safety assurance	1	20	
00.04	Research and analysis	11	45	
00.05	Office of the Administrator		3	
00.06	General administration	1	6	
09.01	Reimbursable program		13	
10.00	Total new obligations	14	101	
	Budgetary resources available for obligation:			
21.40	Unobligated balance available, start of year	14	2	
22.00	New budget authority (gross)	1	99	
22.10	Resources available from recoveries of prior year obligations	2		
23.90	Total budgetary resources available for obligation	17	101	
23.95	Total new obligations	−14	−101	
24.40	Unobligated balance available, end of year	2		
	New budget authority (gross), detail:			
	Discretionary:			
40.00	Appropriation		87	
40.79	Reduction pursuant to P.L. 106–69		−1	
42.00	Transferred from other accounts	1		
43.00	Appropriation (total discretionary)	1	86	
68.00	Spending authority from offsetting collections: Offsetting collections (cash)		13	
70.00	Total new budget authority (gross)	1	99	
	Change in unpaid obligations:			
72.40	Unpaid obligations, start of year: Obligated balance, start of year	119	61	61
73.10	Total new obligations	14	101	
73.20	Total outlays (gross)	−66	−101	−39
73.40	Adjustments in expired accounts (net)	−4		
73.45	Adjustments in unexpired accounts	−2		
74.40	Unpaid obligations, end of year: Obligated balance, end of year	61	61	22
	Outlays (gross), detail:			
86.90	Outlays from new discretionary authority	1	63	
86.93	Outlays from discretionary balances	65	38	39
87.00	Total outlays (gross)	66	101	39
	Offsets:			
	Against gross budget authority and outlays:			
88.00	Offsetting collections (cash) from: Federal sources		−13	
	Net budget authority and outlays:			
89.00	Budget authority	1	86	
90.00	Outlays	66	88	39

In 2001, $286 million is proposed for Operations and Research. This includes $216 million from the Highway Trust Fund and $70 million made available from the Federal Highway Administration as part of a reallocation of the increase resulting from revenue aligned budget authority.

Object Classification (in millions of dollars)

Identification code 69–0650–0–1–401		1999 actual	2000 est.	2001 est.
	Direct obligations:			
	Personnel compensation:			
11.1	Full-time permanent	1	25	
11.3	Other than full-time permanent		1	
11.5	Other personnel compensation		1	
11.9	Total personnel compensation	1	27	
12.1	Civilian personnel benefits		5	
23.1	Rental payments to GSA		3	
23.3	Communications, utilities, and miscellaneous charges		2	
24.0	Printing and reproduction		3	
25.2	Other services	4	8	
25.5	Research and development contracts	9	30	
26.0	Supplies and materials		6	
31.0	Equipment		4	
99.0	Subtotal, direct obligations	14	88	
99.0	Reimbursable obligations		13	
99.9	Total new obligations	14	101	

Personnel Summary

Identification code 69–0650–0–1–401		1999 actual	2000 est.	2001 est.
1001	Total compensable workyears: Full-time equivalent employment	6	317	

Trust Funds

Operations and Research

(HIGHWAY TRUST FUND)

For expenses necessary to discharge the functions of the Secretary, with respect to traffic and highway safety under chapter 301 of title 49, United States Code, and part C of subtitle VI of title 49, United States Code, [$87,400,000] *$142,475,000*, of which [$62,928,000] *$102,582,000* shall remain available until September 30, [2002: *Provided*, That none of the funds appropriated by this Act may be obligated or expended to plan, finalize, or implement any rulemaking to add to section 575.104 of title 49 of the Code of Federal Regulations any requirement pertaining to a grading standard that is different from the three grading standards (treadwear, traction, and temperature resistance) already in effect] *2003*.

(Liquidation of Contract Authorization)

(LIMITATION ON OBLIGATIONS)

(HIGHWAY TRUST FUND)

For payment of obligations incurred in carrying out the provisions of 23 U.S.C. 403, to remain available until expended, [$72,000,000] *$142,000,000*, to be derived from the Highway Trust Fund, *of which not less than $1,000,000 shall be for Native American programs*: *Provided*, That none of the funds in this Act shall be available for the planning or execution of programs the total obligations for which, in fiscal year [2000] *2001* are in excess of [$72,000,000] *$142,000,000* for programs authorized under 23 U.S.C. 403. *(Department of Transportation and Related Agencies Appropriations Act, 2000.)*

Program and Financing (in millions of dollars)

Identification code 69–8016–0–7–401		1999 actual	2000 est.	2001 est.
	Obligations by program activity:			
	Direct program:			
00.01	Safety performance standards	13		20
00.02	Safety assurance	21		26
00.03	Highway safety programs	57	59	112
00.04	Research and analysis	59	25	121
00.05	Office of the Administrator	4	2	5
00.06	General administration	10	5	12
09.00	Reimbursable program	22	2	4
10.00	Total new obligations	186	93	300

Budgetary resources available for obligation:			
21.40 Unobligated balance available, start of year		7	
22.00 New budget authority (gross)	193	86	300
23.90 Total budgetary resources available for obligation	193	93	300
23.95 Total new obligations	−186	−93	−300
24.40 Unobligated balance available, end of year	7		
New budget authority (gross), detail:			
Discretionary:			
40.26 Appropriation (trust fund, definite)	161	74	286
40.49 Portion applied to liquidate contract authority	−72	−72	−142
43.00 Appropriation (total discretionary)	89	2	144
Mandatory:			
66.10 Contract authority	72	72	72
66.15 Contract authority (tranfer from Highway trust fund)			70
66.90 Contract authority (total mandatory)	72	72	142
Spending authority from offsetting collections:			
Discretionary:			
68.00 Offsetting collections (cash)	32	12	14
68.10 From Federal sources: Change in receivables and unpaid, unfilled orders	19		
68.15 From Federal sources: Adjustments to receivables and unpaid, unfilled orders	−19		
68.90 Spending authority from offsetting collections (total discretionary)	32	12	14
70.00 Total new budget authority (gross)	193	86	300
Change in unpaid obligations:			
Unpaid obligations, start of year:			
72.40 Obligated balance, start of year		78	69
72.95 From Federal sources: Receivables and unpaid, unfilled orders		19	19
72.99 Total unpaid obligations, start of year		97	88
73.10 Total new obligations	186	93	300
73.20 Total outlays (gross)	−108	−102	−218
73.40 Adjustments in expired accounts (net)	19		
Unpaid obligations, end of year:			
74.40 Obligated balance, end of year	78	69	151
74.95 From Federal sources: Receivables and unpaid, unfilled orders	19	19	19
74.99 Total unpaid obligations, end of year	97	88	170
Outlays (gross), detail:			
86.90 Outlays from new discretionary authority	121	55	180
86.93 Outlays from discretionary balances	−14	47	39
87.00 Total outlays (gross)	108	102	218
Offsets:			
Against gross budget authority and outlays:			
88.00 Offsetting collections (cash) from: Federal sources	−32	−12	−14
Against gross budget authority only:			
88.95 From Federal sources: Change in receivables and unpaid, unfilled orders	−19		
88.96 From Federal sources: Adjustment to receivables and unpaid, unfilled orders	19		
Net budget authority and outlays:			
89.00 Budget authority	161	74	286
90.00 Outlays	75	90	204

Status of Contract Authority (in millions of dollars)

Identification code 69–8016–0–7–401	1999 actual	2000 est.	2001 est.
Contract authority:			
0200 Contract authority	72	72	142
0400 Appropriation to liquidate contract authority	−72	−72	−142

A total of $286 million is proposed for Operations and Research, of which $70 million is transferred from Revenue Aligned Budget authority.

Programs funded under the Operations and Research appropriation are described below.

Safety Performance Standards (Rulemaking) Programs.—Supports the promulgation of Federal motor vehicle safety standards for motor vehicles, and safety-related equipment; automotive fuel economy standards required by the Energy Policy and Conservation Act; international harmonization of vehicle standards; and consumer information on motor vehicle safety, including the New Car Assessment Program. New initiatives include data collection systems for documenting and understanding trunk entrapment and research on adapting vehicles for persons with disabilities.

Safety Assurance (Enforcement) Programs.—Provides support to ensure compliance with motor vehicle safety and automotive fuel economy standards, investigate safety-related motor vehicle defects, enforce federal odometer law and encourage enforcement of state odometer law, conduct safety recalls when warranted, and provide safety information via the Auto Safety Hotline. New initiatives for FY 2001 will include compliance testing for new/enhanced occupant protection standards. These include the advanced air bag compliance test program requiring extensive side and frontal crash testing and extensive testing of child restraints. Additionally, the program will conduct dynamic side impact pole tests for testing Free Motion Headform provisions of the upper interior head protection requirements.

Research and Analysis.—Provides motor vehicle safety research and development in support of all NHTSA programs, including the collection and analysis of crash data to identify safety problems, develop alternative solutions, and assess costs, benefits, and effectiveness. Research will continue to concentrate on improving vehicle crash worthiness and crash avoidance, with emphasis on smart air bag technology and on the National Transportation Biomechanics Research Center, which includes the Crash Injury Research and Engineering Network (CIREN). The 2001 budget includes funds to continue a national crash data collection program to identify specific traffic safety problems to aid in regulatory actions and for program evaluation activities. It also includes a new international research effort and supports the safety needs of the Administration's *Partnership for a New Generation of Vehicles* (PNGV) initiative and the Vehicle Research Test Center (VRTC), and supports NHTSA's crash avoidance research under the Intelligent Vehicle Initiative (IVI) program.

Highway Safety Programs.—Provides for research, demonstrations, technical assistance, and national leadership for highway safety programs conducted by state and local governments, the private sector, universities and research units, and various safety associations and organizations. This program emphasizes alcohol and drug countermeasures, vehicle occupant protection, traffic law enforcement, emergency medical and trauma care systems, traffic records and licensing, state and community evaluation, motorcycle riders, pedestrian and bicycle safety, pupil transportation, young and older driver safety programs, and development of improved accident investigation procedures. Special emphasis this year will be given to new initiatives and expanded programs for FY 2001 in the areas of target populations, safe mobility for an aging America, liveable communities, reducing high risk and aggressive driving, and safe passages for youth, applying technology to help solve highway safety problems, and making .08 the national legal limit. The Department has set a national goal to reduce alcohol-related traffic fatalities to no more than 11,000 by the year 2005. The President has established a goal of increasing safety belt use to 90 percent by 2005, and reducing child occupant fatalities (0–4 years) by 25 percent by 2005.

Section 405(b) 2003(b) Child Passenger Protection Education Grant Program.—A new program to encourage states to implement child passenger protection programs that will help states increase proper child safety seat use and reduce child occupant fatalities. States may qualify for grants by carrying out specific child passenger protection education and training activities.

(LIQUIDATION OF CONTRACT AUTHORIZATION)—Continued

(HIGHWAY TRUST FUND)—Continued

General Administration.—Provides program evaluation, strategic planning, and economic analysis for agency programs. Objective quantitative information about NHTSA's regulatory and highway safety programs is gathered to measure their effectiveness in achieving objectives. This activity also funds development of methods to estimate economic consequences of motor vehicle injuries in forms suitable for agency use in problem identification, regulatory analysis, priority setting, and policy analysis.

Object Classification (in millions of dollars)

Identification code 69–8016–0–7–401		1999 actual	2000 est.	2001 est.
	Direct obligations:			
	Personnel compensation:			
11.1	Full-time permanent	39	17	46
11.3	Other than full-time permanent	1	1	1
11.5	Other personnel compensation	1	1	1
11.9	Total personnel compensation	41	19	48
12.1	Civilian personnel benefits	8	3	9
21.0	Travel and transportation of persons	1	1	2
23.1	Rental payments to GSA	4	2	6
23.3	Communications, utilities, and miscellaneous charges	3	1	4
24.0	Printing and reproduction	5	2	5
25.2	Other services	33	23	84
25.5	Research and development contracts	51	26	112
26.0	Supplies and materials	11	4	11
31.0	Equipment	7	3	7
41.0	Grants, subsidies, and contributions		7	8
99.0	Subtotal, direct obligations	164	91	296
99.0	Reimbursable obligations	22	2	4
99.9	Total new obligations	186	93	300

Personnel Summary

Identification code 69–8016–0–7–401		1999 actual	2000 est.	2001 est.
1001	Total compensable workyears: Full-time equivalent employment	594	304	643

NATIONAL DRIVER REGISTER

(HIGHWAY TRUST FUND)

For expenses necessary to discharge the functions of the Secretary with respect to the National Driver Register under chapter 303 of title 49, United States Code, $2,000,000 to be derived from the Highway Trust Fund, and to remain available until expended. *(Department of Transportation and Related Agencies Appropriations Act, 2000.)*

National Driver Register.—Provides funding to implement and operate the Problem Driver Pointer System (PDPS) and improve traffic safety by assisting state motor vehicle administrators in communicating effectively and efficiently with other states to identify drivers whose licenses have been suspended or revoked for serious traffic offenses, such as driving under the influence of alcohol or other drugs.

HIGHWAY TRAFFIC SAFETY GRANTS

(LIQUIDATION OF CONTRACT AUTHORIZATION)

(LIMITATION ON OBLIGATIONS)

(HIGHWAY TRUST FUND)

Notwithstanding any other provision of law, for payment of obligations incurred in carrying out the provisions of 23 U.S.C. 402, 405, 410, and 411 to remain available until expended, [$206,800,000] *$213,000,000*, to be derived from the Highway Trust Fund: *Provided*, That none of the funds in this Act shall be available for the planning or execution of programs the total obligations for which, in fiscal year [2000] *2001*, are in excess of [$206,800,000] *$213,000,000* for programs authorized under 23 U.S.C. 402, 405, 410, and 411, of which [$152,800,000] *$155,000,000* shall be for "Highway Safety Programs" under 23 U.S.C. 402, [$10,000,000] *$13,000,000* shall be for "Occupant Protection Incentive Grants" under 23 U.S.C. 405, $36,000,000 shall be for "Alcohol-Impaired Driving Countermeasures Grants" under 23 U.S.C. 410, [$8,000,000] *$9,000,000* shall be for the "State Highway Safety Data Grants" under 23 U.S.C. 411: *Provided further*, That none of these funds shall be used for construction, rehabilitation, or remodeling costs, or for office furnishings and fixtures for State, local, or private buildings or structures: *Provided further*, That not to exceed [$7,640,000] *$7,098,000* of the funds made available for section 402, not to exceed [$500,000] *$650,000* of the funds made available for section 405, not to exceed $1,800,000 of the funds made available for section 410, and not to exceed [$400,000] *$450,000* of the funds made available for section 411 shall be available to NHTSA for administering highway safety grants under chapter 4 of title 23, United States Code: *Provided further*, That not to exceed $500,000 of the funds made available for section 410 "Alcohol-Impaired Driving Countermeasures Grants" shall be available for technical assistance to the States. *(Department of Transportation and Related Agencies Appropriations Act, 2000.)*

Program and Financing (in millions of dollars)

Identification code 69–8020–0–7–401		1999 actual	2000 est.	2001 est.
	Obligations by program activity:			
00.01	Section 402 formula grants	150	153	155
00.02	Section 405 occupant protection incentive grants	10	10	13
00.03	Section 410 alcohol incentive grants	35	36	36
00.04	Section 411 safety data grants	5	8	9
10.00	Total new obligations	200	207	213
	Budgetary resources available for obligation:			
22.00	New budget authority (gross)	200	207	214
23.95	Total new obligations	−200	−207	−213
24.49	Unobligated balance, end of year: Contract authority			1
	New budget authority (gross), detail:			
	Discretionary:			
40.26	Appropriation (trust fund, definite)	200	207	213
40.49	Portion applied to liquidate contract authority	−200	−207	−213
43.00	Appropriation (total discretionary)			
	Mandatory:			
66.10	Contract authority	200	207	214
70.00	Total new budget authority (gross)	200	207	214
	Change in unpaid obligations:			
72.40	Unpaid obligations, start of year: Obligated balance, start of year	200	210	207
73.10	Total new obligations	200	207	213
73.20	Total outlays (gross)	−190	−210	−217
74.40	Unpaid obligations, end of year: Obligated balance, end of year	210	207	203
	Outlays (gross), detail:			
86.90	Outlays from new discretionary authority	82	85	87
86.93	Outlays from discretionary balances	108	125	130
87.00	Total outlays (gross)	190	210	217
	Net budget authority and outlays:			
89.00	Budget authority	200	207	214
90.00	Outlays	190	210	217

Status of Contract Authority (in millions of dollars)

Identification code 69–8020–0–7–401		1999 actual	2000 est.	2001 est.
	Contract authority:			
0200	Contract authority	200	207	214
0400	Appropriation to liquidate contract authority	−200	−207	−213
0700	Balance, end of year			1

Section 402.—The Section 402 State and Community Grant Program is a performance-based program administered by NHTSA. Grant allocations are determined on the basis of a statutory formula. States use this funding to reduce traffic

crashes, fatalities, and injuries. The grants are used to support State highway safety programs, within national priorities, implemented jointly with all members of the highway safety community. States develop safety goals, performance measures, and strategic plans to manage use of grants for programs to reduce deaths and injuries on the Nation's highways, such as programs associated with excessive speeds, failure to use occupant restraints, alcohol/drug impaired driving, and roadway safety.

Alcohol-Impaired Driving Incentive Grants.—A two-tiered basic and supplemental grant program to reward states that pass new laws and start more effective programs to attack drunk driving. This continues the Department's strong emphasis on impaired drivers that has been addressed by the Section 410 incentive grant program. States may qualify for basic grants by implementing criteria that include: administrative license revocation, stepped-up police enforcement coupled with publicity, and graduated licensing laws with nighttime driving restrictions and Zero Tolerance. States are also awarded basic grants for demonstrating consistently high performance in reducing alcohol-related fatalities. There are six supplemental grant criteria including self-sustaining drunk driving prevention programs, effective DWI tracking systems, and use of passive alcohol sensors by police.

Section 405 Occupant Protection Incentive Grants.—Targets specific laws and programs to help states increase seat belt and child safety seat use. States may qualify for grants by adopting or demonstrating specific laws and programs, such as primary safety belt use laws, minimum fines or penalty points, and special traffic enforcement programs. Grant funds may be used only to implement and enforce occupant protection programs.

Section 411 State Highway Safety Data Improvement Incentive Grants.—Encourages states to take effective actions to improve the timeliness, accuracy, completeness, uniformity, and accessibility of their highway safety data. States may qualify for grants based on the status of development of a multi-year highway safety data and traffic records strategic plan and establishment of a multi-disciplinary data coordinating committee. Grant funds may be used only to implement data improvement programs.

Object Classification (in millions of dollars)

Identification code 69–8020–0–7–401		1999 actual	2000 est.	2001 est.
25.2	Other services	10	10	10
41.0	Grants, subsidies, and contributions	190	197	203
99.9	Total new obligations	200	207	213

FEDERAL RAILROAD ADMINISTRATION

The following tables show the funding for all Federal Railroad Administration programs:

[In millions of dollars]

Budget authority:	*1999 actual*	*2000 est.*	*2001 est.*
Safety and operations [1]	82	94	103
Offsetting rail user fees			–77
Railroad research and development	22	22	27
Offsetting rail user fees			–26
Grants to the National Railroad Passenger Corporation	609	571	521
Expanded intercity rail passenger service fund			468
Amtrak Reform Council		1	1
Rhode Island rail development	5	10	17
Pennsylvania Station redevelopment project			20
Next generation high-speed rail	20	27	22
Alaska Railroad rehabilitation	38	15	
Amtrak corridor improvement loans	–1	–1	–1
Railroad rehabilitation and improvement program liquidating account	–4	–5	–4
Total budget authority	773	734	1,072
Safety and Operations [1]	79	108	102
Offsetting rail user fees			–77
Local rail freight assistance	3	3	
Railroad research and development	22	38	31
Offsetting rail user fees			–26
Conrail commuter transition assistance	5	6	
Grants to the National Railroad Passenger Corporation	244	597	551
Expanded intercity rail passenger service fund			47
Amtrak Reform Council		1	1
Northeast corridor improvement program	26	19	
Rhode Island rail development	3	24	8
Pennsylvania Station redevelopment project			2
Trust fund share of next generation high-speed rail	2	5	
Next generation high-speed rail	18	24	21
Alaska Railroad rehabilitation	11	42	9
Emergency railroad rehabilitation and repair	6	8	
Amtrak corridor improvement loans	–1	–1	–1
Railroad rehabilitation and improvement program liquidating account	–4	–5	–4
Alameda Corridor direct loan financing program	18		
Total outlays	434	869	664

[1] Former title was Office of the Administrator. The account includes the old Office of the Administrator account, Railroad safety account, and administrative funds from the Railroad research and development and Next generation high-speed rail accounts funds.

For presentation purposes, 1999 figures reflect the total of the Office of the Administrator and Railroad safety accounts. Railroad research and development and Next generation high-speed rail administrative funds are included in the Safety and operations account in 2000 and 2001.

Federal Funds

General and special funds:

Safety and Operations

For necessary expenses of the Federal Railroad Administration, not otherwise provided for, **[**$94,288,000**]** *$103,210,500,* of which **[**$6,800,000**]** *$5,249,000* shall remain available until expended: *Provided,* That, as part of the Washington Union Station transaction in which the Secretary assumed the first deed of trust on the property and, where the Union Station Redevelopment Corporation or any successor is obligated to make payments on such deed of trust on the Secretary's behalf, including payments on and after September 30, 1988, the Secretary is authorized to receive such payments directly from the Union Station Redevelopment Corporation, credit them to the appropriation charged for the first deed of trust, and make payments on the first deed of trust with those funds: *Provided further,* That such additional sums as may be necessary for payment on the first deed of trust may be advanced by the Administrator from unobligated balances available to the Federal Railroad Administration, to be reimbursed from payments received from the Union Station Redevelopment Corporation. *(Department of Transportation and Related Agencies Appropriations Act, 2000.)*

Program and Financing (in millions of dollars)

Identification code 69–0700–0–1–401		1999 actual	2000 est.	2001 est.
	Obligations by program activity:			
	Direct program:			
00.01	Salaries and expenses	84	94	103
00.02	Contract support		1	
00.03	Washington Union Station		1	
00.06	Alaska railroad liabilities	1	2	
01.00	Total direct program	85	98	103
	Reimbursable program:			
09.01	Reimbursable services	1	1	1
09.02	Union Station deed payments	1	1	1
09.99	Total reimbursable program	2	2	2
10.00	Total new obligations	87	100	105
	Budgetary resources available for obligation:			
21.40	Unobligated balance available, start of year	7	4	
22.00	New budget authority (gross)	83	96	105
22.10	Resources available from recoveries of prior year obligations	1		
23.90	Total budgetary resources available for obligation	91	100	105

General and special funds—Continued

SAFETY AND OPERATIONS—Continued

Program and Financing (in millions of dollars)—Continued

Identification code 69–0700–0–1–401	1999 actual	2000 est.	2001 est.
23.95 Total new obligations	–87	–100	–105
24.40 Unobligated balance available, end of year	4		
New budget authority (gross), detail:			
Discretionary:			
40.00 Appropriation	82	94	103
68.00 Spending authority from offsetting collections: Offsetting collections (cash)	1	2	2
70.00 Total new budget authority (gross)	83	96	105
Change in unpaid obligations:			
72.40 Unpaid obligations, start of year: Obligated balance, start of year	16	19	9
73.10 Total new obligations	87	100	105
73.20 Total outlays (gross)	–81	–109	–104
73.40 Adjustments in expired accounts (net)	–3		
73.45 Adjustments in unexpired accounts	–1		
74.40 Unpaid obligations, end of year: Obligated balance, end of year	19	9	10
Outlays (gross), detail:			
86.90 Outlays from new discretionary authority	78	87	95
86.93 Outlays from discretionary balances	2	23	9
87.00 Total outlays (gross)	81	109	104
Offsets:			
Against gross budget authority and outlays:			
Offsetting collections (cash) from:			
88.00 Federal sources		–1	–1
88.40 Non-Federal sources	–1	–1	–1
88.90 Total, offsetting collections (cash)	–1	–2	–2
Net budget authority and outlays:			
89.00 Budget authority	82	94	103
90.00 Outlays	79	107	102

Summary of Budget Authority and Outlays

(in millions of dollars)

Enacted/requested:	*1999 actual*	*2000 est.*	*2001 est.*
Budget Authority	82	94	103
Outlays	79	108	102
Legislative proposal, not subject to PAYGO:			
Budget Authority			–77
Outlays			–77
Total:			
Budget Authority	82	94	26
Outlays	79	108	25

The programs under this account are:

Salaries and expenses.—Provides support for FRA rail safety activities and all other administrative and operating activities related to FRA staff and programs.

Contract support.—Provides support for policy oriented economic, industry, and systems analysis.

Washington Union Station.—The Department of Transportation purchased Washington Union Station on November 1, 1988. Lease payments on the property are collected from the Union Station Redevelopment Corporation, credited to the Safety and operations account, and paid from this account to the deed holder. Receipts are estimated to cover the mortgage payments in 2000 and 2001. The deed is expected to be paid in full in 2001.

Alaska Railroad Liabilities.—Provides reimbursement to the Department of Labor for compensation payments to former Federal employees of the Alaska Railroad who were on the rolls during the period of Federal ownership and support for clean-up activities at hazardous waste sites located at properties once owned by the FRA. The 2001 request is for workers' compensation.

Object Classification (in millions of dollars)

Identification code 69–0700–0–1–401	1999 actual	2000 est.	2001 est.
Direct obligations:			
Personnel compensation:			
11.1 Full-time permanent	41	49	52
11.3 Other than full-time permanent	1	1	1
11.5 Other personnel compensation	1	1	1
11.9 Total personnel compensation	43	51	54
12.1 Civilian personnel benefits	11	13	13
21.0 Travel and transportation of persons	7	7	7
23.1 Rental payments to GSA	3	3	3
23.3 Communications, utilities, and miscellaneous charges	1	1	2
25.1 Advisory and assistance services		1	2
25.2 Other services	13	16	15
25.3 Purchases of goods and services from Government accounts	2	2	3
26.0 Supplies and materials	1	1	1
31.0 Equipment	3	2	3
41.0 Grants, subsidies, and contributions	1	1	
99.0 Subtotal, direct obligations	85	98	103
99.0 Reimbursable obligations	2	2	2
99.9 Total new obligations	87	100	105

Personnel Summary

Identification code 69–0700–0–1–401	1999 actual	2000 est.	2001 est.
1001 Total compensable workyears: Full-time equivalent employment	683	750	759

SAFETY AND OPERATIONS
(Legislative proposal, not subject to PAYGO)

Program and Financing (in millions of dollars)

Identification code 69–0700–2–1–401	1999 actual	2000 est.	2001 est.
New budget authority (gross), detail:			
Discretionary:			
40.00 Appropriation			–77
68.00 Spending authority from offsetting collections: Offsetting collections (cash)			77
70.00 Total new budget authority (gross)			
Offsets:			
Against gross budget authority and outlays:			
88.40 Offsetting collections (cash) from: Non-Federal sources			–77
Net budget authority and outlays:			
89.00 Budget authority			–77
90.00 Outlays			–77

The Administration will propose legislation to authorize the collection and spending of a rail safety user fee. If the proposed authorizing legislation is enacted, the proviso for the rail safety user fee contained in the General Provisions will reduce the General Fund appropriation for Safety and Operations by $77 million, the amount of the proposed user fee.

AMTRAK REFORM COUNCIL

Program and Financing (in millions of dollars)

Identification code 69–0152–0–1–407	1999 actual	2000 est.	2001 est.
Obligations by program activity:			
00.09 Direct program		1	1
09.10 Reimbursable program			

		1999 actual	2000 est.	2001 est.
10.00	Total new obligations (object class 99.5)		1	1
	Budgetary resources available for obligation:			
22.00	New budget authority (gross)		1	1
23.95	Total new obligations		−1	−1
	New budget authority (gross), detail:			
	Discretionary:			
40.00	Appropriation		1	1
	Change in unpaid obligations:			
72.40	Unpaid obligations, start of year: Obligated balance, start of year			
73.10	Total new obligations		1	1
73.20	Total outlays (gross)		−1	−1
74.40	Unpaid obligations, end of year: Obligated balance, end of year			
	Outlays (gross), detail:			
86.90	Outlays from new discretionary authority		1	1
	Net budget authority and outlays:			
89.00	Budget authority		1	1
90.00	Outlays	1	1	1

The Amtrak Reform Council was created by the Amtrak Reform and Accountability Act of 1997 (P.L. 105–134) to perform an independent assessment of Amtrak. The 1999 Department of Transportation and Related Agencies Appropriations Act expanded the Council's mandate to include identifying Amtrak routes which are candidates for closure or realignment. Almost $1 million is requested for these activities. The Council is an independent entity and its funding is presented within the Federal Railroad Administration for display purposes only. As such, funding is requested in a General Provision.179

Personnel Summary

Identification code 69–0152–0–1–407		1999 actual	2000 est.	2001 est.
1001	Total compensable workyears: Full-time equivalent employment	2	5	5

Emergency Railroad Rehabilitation and Repair

Program and Financing (in millions of dollars)

Identification code 69–0124–0–1–401		1999 actual	2000 est.	2001 est.
	Change in unpaid obligations:			
72.40	Unpaid obligations, start of year: Obligated balance, start of year	14	8	
73.10	Total new obligations			
73.20	Total outlays (gross)	−6	−8	
74.40	Unpaid obligations, end of year: Obligated balance, end of year	8		
	Outlays (gross), detail:			
86.93	Outlays from discretionary balances	6	8	
	Net budget authority and outlays:			
89.00	Budget authority			
90.00	Outlays	6	8	

This schedule displays emergency funding programs that no longer require appropriations and thus reflects outlays from 1998 appropriations. The funds were used to repair and rebuild freight rail lines of regional and short-line railroads or State-owned railroads damaged by floods in South Dakota, North Dakota, Minnesota, and West Virginia.

Local Rail Freight Assistance

Program and Financing (in millions of dollars)

Identification code 69–0714–0–1–401		1999 actual	2000 est.	2001 est.
	Obligations by program activity:			
10.00	Total new obligations (object class 41.0)		1	
	Budgetary resources available for obligation:			
21.40	Unobligated balance available, start of year		1	
22.10	Resources available from recoveries of prior year obligations	1		
23.90	Total budgetary resources available for obligation	1	1	
23.95	Total new obligations		−1	
24.40	Unobligated balance available, end of year	1		
	Change in unpaid obligations:			
72.40	Unpaid obligations, start of year: Obligated balance, start of year	6	2	
73.10	Total new obligations		1	
73.20	Total outlays (gross)	−3	−3	
73.45	Adjustments in unexpired accounts	−1		
74.40	Unpaid obligations, end of year: Obligated balance, end of year	2		
	Outlays (gross), detail:			
86.93	Outlays from discretionary balances	3	3	
	Net budget authority and outlays:			
89.00	Budget authority			
90.00	Outlays	3	3	

This program provided discretionary and flat-rate grants to States for rail planning, and for acquisition, track rehabilitation, and rail facility construction with respect to light density freight lines. No funds are requested for this account in 2001.

Railroad Research and Development

For necessary expenses for railroad research and development, [$22,464,000] *$26,800,000*, to remain available until expended. *(Department of Transportation and Related Agencies Appropriations Act, 2000.)*

Program and Financing (in millions of dollars)

Identification code 69–0745–0–1–401		1999 actual	2000 est.	2001 est.
	Obligations by program activity:			
00.01	Equipment, operations, and hazardous materials	7	11	12
00.02	Track and vehicle track interaction	6	10	8
00.03	Railroad safety systems	6	6	5
00.05	Research and development facilties and equipment		1	2
00.06	Other	2	1	
10.00	Total new obligations	21	29	27
	Budgetary resources available for obligation:			
21.40	Unobligated balance available, start of year	4	6	
22.00	New budget authority (gross)	22	22	27
22.10	Resources available from recoveries of prior year obligations	1		
23.90	Total budgetary resources available for obligation	27	28	27
23.95	Total new obligations	−21	−29	−27
24.40	Unobligated balance available, end of year	6		
	New budget authority (gross), detail:			
	Discretionary:			
40.00	Appropriation	22	22	27
	Change in unpaid obligations:			
72.40	Unpaid obligations, start of year: Obligated balance, start of year	31	29	20
73.10	Total new obligations	21	29	27
73.20	Total outlays (gross)	−22	−38	−31
73.45	Adjustments in unexpired accounts	−1		
74.40	Unpaid obligations, end of year: Obligated balance, end of year	29	20	15

General and special funds—Continued

Railroad Research and Development—Continued

Program and Financing (in millions of dollars)—Continued

Identification code 69–0745–0–1–401	1999 actual	2000 est.	2001 est.
Outlays (gross), detail:			
86.90 Outlays from new discretionary authority	11	13	16
86.93 Outlays from discretionary balances	11	25	14
87.00 Total outlays (gross)	22	38	31
Net budget authority and outlays:			
89.00 Budget authority	22	22	27
90.00 Outlays	22	38	31

Summary of Budget Authority and Outlays

(in millions of dollars)

Enacted/requested:	*1999 actual*	*2000 est.*	*2001 est.*
Budget Authority	22	22	27
Outlays	22	38	30
Legislative proposal, not subject to PAYGO:			
Budget Authority			–26
Outlays			–26
Total:			
Budget Authority	22	22	1
Outlays	22	38	4

The objective of the Railroad Research and Development (R&D) program is to provide science and technology support for rail safety rulemaking and enforcement and to stimulate technological advances in conventional and high-speed railroads. This activity is conducted with the cooperation of and some cost-sharing from private sector organizations.

Equipment, operations and hazardous materials research.—Provides for research in safety and performance improvements in train occupant protection, rolling stock safety assurance and performance, human factors, transportation of hazardous materials, and grade crossing safety.

Track and vehicle-track interaction.—Provides for research in safety and performance improvements to track structure, track components, railroad bridge and tunnel structures, signal and train control, and track-vehicle interaction.

Railroad systems safety.—Provides for research in the development of safety performance standards, high-speed rail safety (equipment performance, track performance, train control, systems operations, test equipment), and environmental issues related to new high-speed ground transportation systems.

R&D facilities and equipment.—Provides support for the Transportation Technology Center (TTC) near Pueblo, Colorado, which is a government-owned, contractor-operated facility. The Association of American Railroads (AAR) is the private operator under a contract for care, custody and control.

Other.—Provides support for the salaries and related administrative expenses of the Office of Research and Development. Beginning in 2000, funding for this function is included in the Safety and operations account.

Object Classification (in millions of dollars)

Identification code 69–0745–0–1–401	1999 actual	2000 est.	2001 est.
11.1 Personnel compensation: Full-time permanent	1		
25.2 Other services		8	2
25.4 Operation and maintenance of facilities		1	1
25.5 Research and development contracts	17	16	20
41.0 Grants, subsidies, and contributions	2	3	3
99.0 Subtotal, direct obligations	20	28	26
99.5 Below reporting threshold	1	1	1
99.9 Total new obligations	21	29	27

Personnel Summary

Identification code 69–0745–0–1–401	1999 actual	2000 est.	2001 est.
1001 Total compensable workyears: Full-time equivalent employment	18		

Railroad Research and Development

(Legislative proposal, not subject to PAYGO)

Program and Financing (in millions of dollars)

Identification code 69–0745–2–1–401	1999 actual	2000 est.	2001 est.
New budget authority (gross), detail:			
Discretionary:			
40.00 Appropriation			–26
68.00 Spending authority from offsetting collections: Offsetting collections (cash)			26
70.00 Total new budget authority (gross)			
Offsets:			
Against gross budget authority and outlays:			
88.40 Offsetting collections (cash) from: Non-Federal sources			–26
Net budget authority and outlays:			
89.00 Budget authority			–26
90.00 Outlays			–26

The Administration will propose legislation to authorize the collection and spending of a rail safety user fee. If the proposed authorizing legislation is enacted, the proviso for the rail safety user fee contained in the General Provisions will reduce the General Fund appropriation for Railroad Research and Development by $26 million, the amount of the proposed user fee.

Conrail Commuter Transition Assistance

Program and Financing (in millions of dollars)

Identification code 69–0747–0–1–401	1999 actual	2000 est.	2001 est.
Change in unpaid obligations:			
72.40 Unpaid obligations, start of year: Obligated balance, start of year	11	6	
73.20 Total outlays (gross)	–5	–6	
74.40 Unpaid obligations, end of year: Obligated balance, end of year	6		
Outlays (gross), detail:			
86.93 Outlays from discretionary balances	5	6	
Net budget authority and outlays:			
89.00 Budget authority			
90.00 Outlays	5	6	

These funds helped to defray the one-time-only start-up costs of commuter service and other transition expenses connected with the transfer of rail commuter services from Conrail to other operators. Between 1986 and 1993, funds were appropriated to fund commuter rail and bridge improvements in the Philadelphia, Pennsylvania region. No additional funds are requested in 2001.

NORTHEAST CORRIDOR IMPROVEMENT PROGRAM

Program and Financing (in millions of dollars)

Identification code 69–0123–0–1–401	1999 actual	2000 est.	2001 est.
Obligations by program activity:			
00.04 System engineering, program management and administration		3	
00.05 Penn Station project	12		
10.00 Total new obligations	12	3	
Budgetary resources available for obligation:			
21.40 Unobligated balance available, start of year	15	3	
23.95 Total new obligations	−12	−3	
24.40 Unobligated balance available, end of year	3		
Change in unpaid obligations:			
72.40 Unpaid obligations, start of year: Obligated balance, start of year	30	16	
73.10 Total new obligations	12	3	
73.20 Total outlays (gross)	−26	−19	
74.40 Unpaid obligations, end of year: Obligated balance, end of year	16		
Outlays (gross), detail:			
86.93 Outlays from discretionary balances	26	19	
Net budget authority and outlays:			
89.00 Budget authority			
90.00 Outlays	26	19	

Provided funds to continue the upgrade of passenger rail service in the corridor between Washington, D.C. and Boston. In 2001, funding is available within the Amtrak appropriation.

Object Classification (in millions of dollars)

Identification code 69–0123–0–1–401	1999 actual	2000 est.	2001 est.
25.2 Other services		3	
41.0 Grants, subsidies, and contributions	12		
99.9 Total new obligations	12	3	

RHODE ISLAND RAIL DEVELOPMENT

For the costs associated with construction of a third track on the Northeast Corridor between Davisville and Central Falls, Rhode Island, with sufficient clearance to accommodate double stack freight cars, [$10,000,000] *$17,000,000* to be matched by the State of Rhode Island or its designee on a dollar-for-dollar basis and to remain available until expended[: *Provided*, That none of the funds made available under this head shall be obligated until the enactment of authorizing legislation for the "Rhode Island Rail Development" program]. *(Department of Transportation and Related Agencies Appropriations Act, 2000.)*

Program and Financing (in millions of dollars)

Identification code 69–0726–0–1–401	1999 actual	2000 est.	2001 est.
Obligations by program activity:			
10.00 Total new obligations (object class 41.0)	23	10	17
Budgetary resources available for obligation:			
21.40 Unobligated balance available, start of year	18		
22.00 New budget authority (gross)	5	10	17
23.90 Total budgetary resources available for obligation	23	10	17
23.95 Total new obligations	−23	−10	−17
New budget authority (gross), detail:			
Discretionary:			
40.00 Appropriation	5	10	17
Change in unpaid obligations:			
72.40 Unpaid obligations, start of year: Obligated balance, start of year	2	22	8
73.10 Total new obligations	23	10	17
73.20 Total outlays (gross)	−3	−24	−8
74.40 Unpaid obligations, end of year: Obligated balance, end of year	22	8	17
Outlays (gross), detail:			
86.90 Outlays from new discretionary authority	1	2	3
86.93 Outlays from discretionary balances	2	22	5
87.00 Total outlays (gross)	3	24	8
Net budget authority and outlays:			
89.00 Budget authority	5	10	17
90.00 Outlays	3	24	8

Provides funds to continue the construction of a third rail line and related costs between Davisville and Central Falls, RI.

PENNSYLVANIA STATION REDEVELOPMENT PROJECT

Program and Financing (in millions of dollars)

Identification code 69–0723–0–1–401	1999 actual	2000 est.	2001 est.
Obligations by program activity:			
00.01 Direct Program Activity			20
10.00 Total new obligations (object class 41.0)			20
Budgetary resources available for obligation:			
22.00 New budget authority (gross)			20
23.95 Total new obligations			−20
New budget authority (gross), detail:			
Discretionary:			
40.29 Appropriation available in prior year			20
Change in unpaid obligations:			
72.40 Unpaid obligations, start of year: Obligated balance, start of year		1	
73.10 Total new obligations			20
73.20 Total outlays (gross)			−2
74.40 Unpaid obligations, end of year: Obligated balance, end of year			18
Outlays (gross), detail:			
86.90 Outlays from new discretionary authority			2
Net budget authority and outlays:			
89.00 Budget authority			20
90.00 Outlays			2

Funds are used to redevelop the Pennsylvania Station in New York City, which involves renovating the James A. Farley Post Office building as a train station and commercial center, and basic upgrades to Pennsylvania Station. Funding for this project was included in the Grants to the National Railroad Passenger Corporation appropriation in 1995 through 1997, and the Northeast Corridor Improvement Program in 1998. In 2000 an advance appropriation of $20 million was provided for 2001, 2002, and 2003.

RAILROAD REHABILITATION AND IMPROVEMENT PROGRAM

The Secretary of Transportation is authorized to issue to the Secretary of the Treasury notes or other obligations pursuant to section 512 of the Railroad Revitalization and Regulatory Reform Act of 1976 (Public Law 94–210), as amended, in such amounts and at such times as may be necessary to pay any amounts required pursuant to the guarantee of the principal amount of obligations under sections 511 through 513 of such Act, such authority to exist as long as any such guaranteed obligation is outstanding: *Provided*, That pursuant to section 502 of such Act, as amended, no new direct loans or loan guarantee commitments shall be made using Federal funds for the credit risk premium during fiscal year [2000] *2001*. *(Department of Transportation and Related Agencies Appropriations Act, 2000.)*

General and special funds—Continued

RAILROAD REHABILITATION AND IMPROVEMENT PROGRAM—Continued

Included funds for the Railroad Rehabilitation and Improvement and Amtrak Corridor Improvement Loans program accounts. These accounts were funded under separate appropriations, and are displayed in a consolidated format. The two accounts are loan administration accounts. No funding is requested in 2001. No loans are proposed to be supported in 2001 with Federal funds.

TEA–21 expanded the Railroad Rehabilitation and Improvement program to permit non-Federal entities to provide the subsidy budget authority needed to support a loan through the payment of a credit risk premium. A notice of proposed rulemaking implementing the Railroad rehabilitation and improvement financing program was published on May 20, 1999, outlining the structure of the program.

ALASKA RAILROAD REHABILITATION

[To enable the Secretary of Transportation to make grants to the Alaska Railroad, $10,000,000 shall be for capital rehabilitation and improvements benefiting its passenger operations, to remain available until expended.] *(Department of Transportation and Related Agencies Appropriations Act, 2000.)*

Program and Financing (in millions of dollars)

Identification code 69–0730–0–1–401	1999 actual	2000 est.	2001 est.
Obligations by program activity:			
00.01 Alaska railroad rehabilitation	38	10	....
00.02 Transfer from Department of Defense	....	5	....
09.10 Reimbursable program	5	....	....
10.00 Total new obligations	43	15	....
Budgetary resources available for obligation:			
22.00 New budget authority (gross)	43	15	....
23.95 Total new obligations	−43	−15	....
New budget authority (gross), detail:			
Discretionary:			
40.00 Appropriation	38	10	....
42.00 Transferred from other accounts	....	5	....
43.00 Appropriation (total discretionary)	38	15	....
68.00 Spending authority from offsetting collections: Offsetting collections (cash)	5	....	....
70.00 Total new budget authority (gross)	43	15	....
Change in unpaid obligations:			
72.40 Unpaid obligations, start of year: Obligated balance, start of year	9	36	9
73.10 Total new obligations	43	15	....
73.20 Total outlays (gross)	−16	−42	−9
74.40 Unpaid obligations, end of year: Obligated balance, end of year	36	9	....
Outlays (gross), detail:			
86.90 Outlays from new discretionary authority	12	6	....
86.93 Outlays from discretionary balances	4	36	9
87.00 Total outlays (gross)	16	42	9
Offsets:			
Against gross budget authority and outlays:			
88.00 Offsetting collections (cash) from: Federal sources	−5	....	....
Net budget authority and outlays:			
89.00 Budget authority	38	15	....
90.00 Outlays	11	42	9

These funds provided direct payments to the Alaska railroad. No funds are requested for 2001.

Object Classification (in millions of dollars)

Identification code 69–0730–0–1–401	1999 actual	2000 est.	2001 est.
41.0 Direct obligations: Grants, subsidies, and contributions	38	15	....
99.0 Reimbursable obligations: Subtotal, reimbursable obligations	5	....	....
99.9 Total new obligations	43	15	....

CAPITAL GRANTS TO THE NATIONAL RAILROAD PASSENGER CORPORATION

For necessary expenses of capital improvements of the National Railroad Passenger Corporation as authorized by 49 U.S.C. 24104(a), [$571,000,000] *$521,476,000,* to remain available until expended[: *Provided,* That the Secretary shall not obligate more than $228,400,000 prior to September 30, 2000]. *(Department of Transportation and Related Agencies Appropriations Act, 2000.)*

Program and Financing (in millions of dollars)

Identification code 69–0704–0–1–401	1999 actual	2000 est.	2001 est.
Obligations by program activity:			
00.02 General capital grants	243	594	864
10.00 Total new obligations	243	594	864
Budgetary resources available for obligation:			
21.40 Unobligated balance available, start of year	....	366	343
22.00 New budget authority (gross)	609	571	521
23.90 Total budgetary resources available for obligation	609	937	864
23.95 Total new obligations	−243	−594	−864
24.40 Unobligated balance available, end of year	366	343	....
New budget authority (gross), detail:			
Discretionary:			
40.00 Appropriation	609	571	521
Change in unpaid obligations:			
72.40 Unpaid obligations, start of year: Obligated balance, start of year	3	3	....
73.10 Total new obligations	243	594	864
73.20 Total outlays (gross)	−243	−597	−551
74.40 Unpaid obligations, end of year: Obligated balance, end of year	3	....	313
Outlays (gross), detail:			
86.90 Outlays from new discretionary authority	242	228	208
86.93 Outlays from discretionary balances	1	369	343
87.00 Total outlays (gross)	243	597	551
Net budget authority and outlays:			
89.00 Budget authority	609	571	521
90.00 Outlays	244	597	551

The National Railroad Passenger Corporation (Amtrak) was established in 1970 through the Rail Passenger Service Act. Amtrak is operated and managed as a for profit corporation with all Board members appointed by the Executive Branch of the Federal Government, with the advice and consent of the Senate. Amtrak is not an agency or instrumentality of the U.S. Government.

Funding provides support for Amtrak capital requirements, including Northeast Corridor improvements.

The Administration continues to provide Amtrak the same flexibility in spending its capital grant as provided to transit grantees. A capital project would include acquiring, constructing, supervising or inspecting equipment or facilities (and incidental expenses thereto); payments for the capital portion of trackage rights agreements; rehabilitating, remanufacturing or overhauling rail rolling stock; and preventive maintenance.

Object Classification (in millions of dollars)

Identification code 69–0704–0–1–401		1999 actual	2000 est.	2001 est.
25.2	Other services	1	1	1
41.0	Grants, subsidies, and contributions	242	593	863
99.9	Total new obligations	243	594	864

Next Generation High-Speed Rail

For necessary expenses for the Next Generation High-Speed Rail program as authorized under 49 U.S.C. 26101 and 26102, [$27,200,000] *$22,000,000*, to remain available until expended. *(Department of Transportation and Related Agencies Appropriations Act, 2000.)*

Program and Financing (in millions of dollars)

Identification code 69–0722–0–1–401		1999 actual	2000 est.	2001 est.
	Obligations by program activity:			
00.01	High-speed train control systems	4	15	10
00.02	Non-electric locomotives	9	8	7
00.03	Grade crossing and innovative technology	6	5	4
00.04	Track and structures	2	1	1
00.05	Other	1		
10.00	Total new obligations	22	29	22
	Budgetary resources available for obligation:			
21.40	Unobligated balance available, start of year	3	2	
22.00	New budget authority (gross)	20	27	22
23.90	Total budgetary resources available for obligation	23	29	22
23.95	Total new obligations	−22	−29	−22
24.40	Unobligated balance available, end of year	2		
	New budget authority (gross), detail:			
	Discretionary:			
40.00	Appropriation	20	27	22
	Change in unpaid obligations:			
72.40	Unpaid obligations, start of year: Obligated balance, start of year	53	57	61
73.10	Total new obligations	22	29	22
73.20	Total outlays (gross)	−18	−24	−20
74.40	Unpaid obligations, end of year: Obligated balance, end of year	57	61	63
	Outlays (gross), detail:			
86.90	Outlays from new discretionary authority	5	4	3
86.93	Outlays from discretionary balances	13	20	18
87.00	Total outlays (gross)	18	24	20
	Net budget authority and outlays:			
89.00	Budget authority	20	27	22
90.00	Outlays	18	24	20

The Next Generation High-Speed Rail Program will fund: research, development, and technology demonstration programs and the planning and analysis required to evaluate technology proposals under the program.

Object Classification (in millions of dollars)

Identification code 69–0722–0–1–401		1999 actual	2000 est.	2001 est.
25.2	Other services	18	21	19
41.0	Grants, subsidies, and contributions	4	8	3
99.9	Total new obligations	22	29	22

Personnel Summary

Identification code 69–0722–0–1–401		1999 actual	2000 est.	2001 est.
1001	Total compensable workyears: Full-time equivalent employment	6		

Credit accounts:

Alameda Corridor Direct Loan Financing Program

General Fund Credit Receipt Accounts (in millions of dollars)

Identification code 69–0536–0–1–401		1999 actual	2000 est.	2001 est.
0101	Alameda corridor direct loan financing program, downward reestimate of subsidies		62	

Program and Financing (in millions of dollars)

Identification code 69–0536–0–1–401		1999 actual	2000 est.	2001 est.
	Change in unpaid obligations:			
72.40	Unpaid obligations, start of year: Obligated balance, start of year	18		
73.20	Total outlays (gross)	−18		
	Outlays (gross), detail:			
86.93	Outlays from discretionary balances	18		
	Net budget authority and outlays:			
89.00	Budget authority			
90.00	Outlays	18		

The Alameda Transportation Corridor is an intermodal project connecting the Ports of Los Angeles and Long Beach to downtown Los Angeles. The project replaces the current 20 miles of at-grade rail line with a high-speed, below-grade corridor, thereby eliminating over 200 grade crossings. It also widens and improves the adjacent major highway on this alignment and mitigates the impact of increased international traffic transferring through the San Pedro Ports. The loan has permitted construction to continue without interruption through the sale of debt obligations, the proceeds of which funded the majority of the project's costs.

The amount of subsidy budget authority originally provided for the Alameda Corridor Transportation project was $59 million. The Alameda Corridor Transportation Authority (ACTA) has now completely drawn down the DOT loan proceeds totaling $400 million. In January 1999, ACTA received investment grade ratings from three rating agencies on its debt obligations financing construction of the project. Given ACTA's successful financing of over $1 billion through the capital markets and the investment grade ratings on its debt obligations, the DOT has reestimated the subsidy rate (credit risk) at .81 percent or just over $3 million.

As required by the Federal Credit Reform Act of 1990, this account records, for this program, the subsidy costs associated with the direct loan obligated in 1997. The subsidy amounts are estimated on a present value basis. No funds are requested for this account in 2001, as all funds required to complete this project were provided in 1997.

Alameda Corridor Direct Loan Financing Account

Program and Financing (in millions of dollars)

Identification code 69–4183–0–3–401		1999 actual	2000 est.	2001 est.
	Obligations by program activity:			
00.02	Interest paid to Treasury	22	24	25
08.02	Obligations for downward reestimates		55	
08.04	Obligations for interest on the downward reestimates		7	
08.91	Obligations for downward reestimates		62	
10.00	Total new obligations	22	86	25
	Budgetary resources available for obligation:			
22.00	New financing authority (gross)	22	86	26
23.95	Total new obligations	−22	−86	−25
	New financing authority (gross), detail:			
	Mandatory:			
67.15	Authority to borrow (indefinite)	16	86	26

Credit accounts—Continued

ALAMEDA CORRIDOR DIRECT LOAN FINANCING ACCOUNT—Continued

Program and Financing (in millions of dollars)—Continued

Identification code 69–4183–0–3–401		1999 actual	2000 est.	2001 est.
	Spending authority from offsetting collections:			
	Discretionary:			
68.00	Offsetting collections (cash)	24		487
68.10	From Federal sources: Change in receivables and unpaid, unfilled orders	–18		
68.47	Portion applied to repay debt			–487
68.90	Spending authority from offsetting collections (total discretionary)	6		
70.00	Total new financing authority (gross)	22	86	26
	Change in unpaid obligations:			
	Unpaid obligations, start of year:			
72.40	Obligated balance, start of year	102		
72.95	Receivables from program account	18		
72.99	Total unpaid obligations, start of year	120		
73.10	Total new obligations	22	86	25
73.20	Total financing disbursements (gross)	–142	–86	–26
87.00	Total financing disbursements (gross)	142	86	26
	Offsets:			
	Against gross financing authority and financing disbursements:			
	Offsetting collections (cash) from:			
88.00	Program account	–18		
88.25	Interest on uninvested funds	–6		
88.40	Non-Federal sources			–487
88.90	Total, offsetting collections (cash)	–24		–487
	Against gross financing authority only:			
88.95	Change in receivables from program accounts	18		
	Net financing authority and financing disbursements:			
89.00	Financing authority	16	86	–461
90.00	Financing disbursements	119	86	–461

Status of Direct Loans (in millions of dollars)

Identification code 69–4183–0–3–401		1999 actual	2000 est.	2001 est.
	Position with respect to appropriations act limitation on obligations:			
1111	Limitation on direct loans			
1150	Total direct loan obligations			
	Cumulative balance of direct loans outstanding:			
1210	Outstanding, start of year	280	400	400
1231	Disbursements: Direct loan disbursements	120		
1251	Repayments: Repayments and prepayments			–400
1290	Outstanding, end of year	400	400	

As required by the Federal Credit Reform Act of 1990, this non-budgetary account records all cash flows to and from the Government resulting from direct loans. The amounts in this account are a means of financing and are not included in the budget totals.

Balance Sheet (in millions of dollars)

Identification code 69–4183–0–3–401		1998 actual	1999 actual	2000 est.	2001 est.
	ASSETS:				
	Net value of assets related to post–1991 direct loans receivable:				
1401	Direct loans receivable, gross	280	400	400	
1405	Allowance for subsidy cost (–)	–42	–34	–11	
1499	Net present value of assets related to direct loans	238	366	389	
1999	Total assets	238	366	389	
	LIABILITIES:				
2103	Federal liabilities: Debt	238	366	389	
2999	Total liabilities	238	366	389	
4999	Total liabilities and net position	238	366	389	

RAILROAD REHABILITATION AND IMPROVEMENT DIRECT LOAN FINANCING ACCOUNT

Status of Direct Loans (in millions of dollars)

Identification code 69–4420–0–3–401		1999 actual	2000 est.	2001 est.
	Position with respect to appropriations act limitation on obligations:			
1111	Limitation on direct loans			
1150	Total direct loan obligations			
	Cumulative balance of direct loans outstanding:			
1210	Outstanding, start of year	4	4	4
1290	Outstanding, end of year	4	4	4

As required by the Federal Credit Reform Act of 1990, this non-budgetary account records all cash flows to and from the Government resulting from direct loans. The amounts in this account are a means of financing and are not included in the budget totals.

RAILROAD REHABILITATION AND IMPROVEMENT LIQUIDATING ACCOUNT

Program and Financing (in millions of dollars)

Identification code 69–4411–0–3–401		1999 actual	2000 est.	2001 est.
	Obligations by program activity:			
00.01	Interest to Treasury	3	3	2
10.00	Total new obligations (object class 43.0)	3	3	2
	Budgetary resources available for obligation:			
22.00	New budget authority (gross)	3	3	2
23.95	Total new obligations	–3	–3	–2
	New budget authority (gross), detail:			
	Mandatory:			
69.00	Offsetting collections (cash)	7	8	6
69.47	Portion applied to repay debt	–4	–5	–4
69.90	Spending authority from offsetting collections (total mandatory)	3	3	2
	Change in unpaid obligations:			
73.10	Total new obligations	3	3	2
73.20	Total outlays (gross)	–3	–3	–2
	Outlays (gross), detail:			
86.97	Outlays from new mandatory authority	3	3	2
	Offsets:			
	Against gross budget authority and outlays:			
88.40	Offsetting collections (cash) from: Non-Federal sources	–7	–8	–6
	Net budget authority and outlays:			
89.00	Budget authority	–4	–5	–4
90.00	Outlays	–4	–5	–4

Status of Direct Loans (in millions of dollars)

Identification code 69–4411–0–3–401		1999 actual	2000 est.	2001 est.
	Cumulative balance of direct loans outstanding:			
1210	Outstanding, start of year	56	53	48
1251	Repayments: Repayments and prepayments	–3	–5	–4
1290	Outstanding, end of year	53	48	44

Section 505—Redeemable preference shares.—Authority for the section 505 redeemable preference shares program expired

on September 30, 1988. The account reflects actual outlays of –$4 million in 1999, and projected outlays of –$5 million in 2000 and –$4 milliion in 2001 resulting from payments of principal and interest as well as repurchases of redeemable preference shares and the sale of redeemable preference shares to the private sector.

Section 511—Loan repayments.—This program reflects repayments of principal and interest on outstanding borrowings by the railroads to the Federal Financing Bank under the section 511 loan guarantee program.

As required by the Federal Credit Reform Act of 1990, this account records, for this program, all cash flows to and from the Government resulting from direct loans obligated and loan guarantees committed prior to 1992. All new activity in this program (including modifications of direct loans or loan guarantees that resulted from obligations or commitments in any year) is recorded in corresponding program accounts and financing accounts.

Balance Sheet (in millions of dollars)

Identification code 69–4411–0–3–401	1998 actual	1999 actual	2000 est.	2001 est.
ASSETS:				
Net value of assets related to pre–1992 direct loans receivable and acquired defaulted guaranteed loans receivable:				
1601 Direct loans, gross	56	53	47	43
1602 Interest receivable	18	15	13	13
1699 Value of assets related to direct loans	74	68	60	56
1999 Total assets	74	68	60	56
LIABILITIES:				
Federal liabilities:				
2102 Interest payable	18	15	13	13
2103 Debt	56	53	47	43
2999 Total liabilities	74	68	60	56
4999 Total liabilities and net position	74	68	60	56

Amtrak Corridor Improvement Direct Loan Financing Account

Program and Financing (in millions of dollars)

Identification code 69–4164–0–3–401	1999 actual	2000 est.	2001 est.
Change in unpaid obligations:			
72.40 Unpaid obligations, start of year: Obligated balance, start of year	1	1	....
73.20 Total financing disbursements (gross)	....	....	....
74.40 Unpaid obligations, end of year: Obligated balance, end of year	1	....	....
87.00 Total financing disbursements (gross)	....	....	....
Net financing authority and financing disbursements:			
89.00 Financing authority	....	....	....
90.00 Financing disbursements	....	....	....

As required by the Federal Credit Reform Act of 1990, this non-budgetary account records all cash flows to and from the Government resulting from direct loans obligated in 1992 and beyond (including modifications of direct loans that resulted from obligations in any year). The amounts in this account are a means of financing and are not included in the budget totals.

Balance Sheet (in millions of dollars)

Identification code 69–4164–0–3–401	1998 actual	1999 actual	2000 est.	2001 est.
ASSETS:				
1207 Non-Federal assets: Advances and prepayments	....	1	....	....
1999 Total assets	....	1	....	....
LIABILITIES:				
2202 Non-Federal liabilities: Interest payable	....	1	....	....
2999 Total liabilities	....	1	....	....

Amtrak Corridor Improvement Loans Liquidating Account

Program and Financing (in millions of dollars)

Identification code 69–0720–0–1–401	1999 actual	2000 est.	2001 est.
New budget authority (gross), detail:			
Mandatory:			
69.00 Offsetting collections (cash)	1	1	1
69.47 Portion applied to repay debt	–1	–1	–1
69.90 Spending authority from offsetting collections (total mandatory)	....	....	....
Offsets:			
Against gross budget authority and outlays:			
88.40 Offsetting collections (cash) from: Non-Federal sources	–1	–1	–1
Net budget authority and outlays:			
89.00 Budget authority	–1	–1	–1
90.00 Outlays	–1	–1	–1

Status of Direct Loans (in millions of dollars)

Identification code 69–0720–0–1–401	1999 actual	2000 est.	2001 est.
Cumulative balance of direct loans outstanding:			
1210 Outstanding, start of year	6	5	4
1251 Repayments: Repayments and prepayments	–1	–1	–1
1290 Outstanding, end of year	5	4	3

As required by the Federal Credit Reform Act of 1990, this account records, for this program, all cash flows to and from the Government resulting from direct loans obligated prior to 1992. All new activity in this program (including modifications of direct loans or loan guarantees that resulted from obligations or commitments in any year) is recorded in corresponding program accounts and financing accounts.

Statement of Operations (in millions of dollars)

Identification code 69–0720–0–1–401	1998 actual	1999 actual	2000 est.	2001 est.
0111 Revenue	....	1	....	....
0112 Expense	....	–1	....	....
0115 Net income or loss (–)	....	....	....	....

Balance Sheet (in millions of dollars)

Identification code 69–0720–0–1–401	1998 actual	1999 actual	2000 est.	2001 est.
ASSETS:				
1601 Net value of assets related to pre–1992 direct loans receivable and acquired defaulted guaranteed loans receivable: Direct loans, gross	6	5	4	3
1999 Total assets	6	5	4	3

Trust Funds

EXPANDED INTERCITY RAIL PASSENGER SERVICE FUND

(LIQUIDATION OF CONTRACT AUTHORITY)

(HIGHWAY TRUST FUND)

For liquidation of obligations for capital grants for the improvement of intercity rail passenger service, $468,000,000, to be derived from the Highway Trust Fund and to remain available until expended: Provided, That none of the funds under this heading shall be available for implementation or execution of programs the obligations for which are in excess of $468,000,000: Provided further, That the Secretary of Transportation may make capital grants to the National Railroad Passenger Corporation and/or a State or consortium of States to carry out projects the Secretary determines will generate a positive financial contribution for the Corporation and public benefits in excess of the project's public costs: Provided further, That such grants may not exceed fifty percent of the total project cost and must be used for capital expenses (as defined by Generally Accepted Accounting Principles) which directly lead to enhanced intercity passenger rail service.

Program and Financing (in millions of dollars)

Identification code 69–8114–0–7–401	1999 actual	2000 est.	2001 est.
Obligations by program activity:			
10.00 Total new obligations			468
Budgetary resources available for obligation:			
22.00 New budget authority (gross)			468
23.95 Total new obligations			−468
New budget authority (gross), detail:			
Discretionary:			
40.00 Appropriation			468
40.49 Portion applied to liquidate contract authority			−468
43.00 Appropriation (total discretionary)			
Mandatory:			
66.15 Contract authority (transfer from Highway trust fund)			468
70.00 Total new budget authority (gross)			468
Change in unpaid obligations:			
73.10 Total new obligations			468
73.20 Total outlays (gross)			−47
74.40 Unpaid obligations, end of year: Obligated balance, end of year			421
Outlays (gross), detail:			
86.90 Outlays from new discretionary authority			47
Net budget authority and outlays:			
89.00 Budget authority			468
90.00 Outlays			47

Status of Contract Authority (in millions of dollars)

Identification code 69–8114–0–7–401	1999 actual	2000 est.	2001 est.
Contract authority:			
0200 Contract authority			468
0400 Appropriation to liquidate contract authority			−468

The Administration proposes a new grant program to improve intercity passenger rail service nationwide. Under the proposed program, The Secretary of Transportation will award fifty percent matching grants to Amtrak and/or a partner State or State consortium to implement capital projects which enhance intercity rail service. Eligible projects must generate a positive financial contribution for Amtrak and public benefits in excess of public costs, making them sound investments both for the company and the taxpayer. Projects may be located on any current or potential future intercity rail corridor. This funding would go towards the acquisition of equipment, construction of infrastructure improvements including acquisition of right-of-way, and planning and design. Funds could only be used for capital as defined by Generally Accepted Accounting Principles (GAAP). The Federal Government would maintain a lien on the improvements made with these funds. A positive financial contribution shall be measured by Amtrak recovering from the project all variable and attributable fixed/overhead costs associated with the new service. This program will improve overall intercity passenger rail speeds and service, thereby reducing congestion on the nation's highways and improving air quality. This program will be used to improve passenger rail service, including improvements necessary for high speed rail service and other increases in average speeds through rail infrastructure improvements.

This account is funded from higher than anticipated receipts in the Highway trust fund under revenue aligned budget authority.

Object Classification (in millions of dollars)

Identification code 69–8114–0–7–401	1999 actual	2000 est.	2001 est.
25.2 Other services			1
41.0 Grants, subsidies, and contributions			467
99.9 Total new obligations			468

TRUST FUND SHARE OF NEXT GENERATION HIGH-SPEED RAIL

(LIQUIDATION OF CONTRACT AUTHORIZATION)

(HIGHWAY TRUST FUND)

Program and Financing (in millions of dollars)

Identification code 69–9973–0–7–401	1999 actual	2000 est.	2001 est.
Change in unpaid obligations:			
72.40 Unpaid obligations, start of year: Obligated balance, start of year	7	5	
73.20 Total outlays (gross)	−2	−5	
74.40 Unpaid obligations, end of year: Obligated balance, end of year	5		
Outlays (gross), detail:			
86.93 Outlays from discretionary balances	2	5	
Net budget authority and outlays:			
89.00 Budget authority			
90.00 Outlays	2	5	

This account provided funds for research, development, and demonstrations to support the advancement of high-speed rail technology. These activities are now supported through the Next Generation High-Speed Rail general fund account.

FEDERAL TRANSIT ADMINISTRATION

The Federal Transit Administration (FTA) provides funding to transit operators, State and local governments and other recipients for the construction of facilities; the purchase of vehicles and equipment; the improvement of technology, service techniques, and methods; the support of regionwide transportation planning; and transit operations. In addition to improving general mobility, FTA provides financial assistance to help implement other national goals relating to mobility for the elderly, people with disabilities, and economically disadvantaged individuals.

The Transportation Equity Act for the 21st Century reauthorized transit programs through FY 2003, and created the new discretionary Mass Transit Budget Category. The General Fund and Highway Trust Fund funding contained in the mass transit category is referred to as "guaranteed" funding. Approximately 80 percent of transit funding in 2001 is derived from the mass transit account of the Highway Trust Fund.

In 2001, $6,321 million is proposed for transit programs, including $50 million to be made available from the Federal Highway Administration as part of a reallocation of the increase resulting from the revenue aligned budget authority under the highway program.

The following tables show the funding for the Federal Transit Administration programs.

[In millions of dollars]

Obligation Limitations:	1999 actual	2000 est.	2001 est.
Administrative expenses, general fund	10	12	13
Administrative expenses, trust fund	43	48	51
Subtotal, obligation limitation	53	60	64
Transit planning and research, general fund	10	21	22
Transit planning and research, trust fund	78	86	88
Subtotal, obligation limitation	98	107	110
University transportation centers, general fund	1	1	1
University transportation centers, trust fund	5	5	5
Subtotal, obligation limitation	6	6	6
Job access and reverse commute, general fund	35	15	20
Job access and reverse commute, trust fund	40	60	130
Subtotal, obligation limitation	75	75	150
Formula grants, general fund	519	570	669
Formula grants, trust fund	2,280	2,478	2,676
Subtotal, obligation limitation	2,799	3,048	3,345
Capital investment grants, general fund	501	540	529
Capital investment grants, trust fund	1,806	1,949	2,117
Subtotal, obligation limitation	2,307	2,490	2,646
Washington Metropolitan Transit Authority, general fund	50		
Trust fund share of expenses, total budget authority (non-add)	[4,252]	[4,644]	[5,089]
Trust fund share of expenses, available for obligation (non-add)	[4,252]	[4,626]	[5,067]
Total FTA, obligation limitation	5,389	5,785	6,321

Notes.—2000 obligation limitation reflects a reduction of $18 million pursuant to sec. 301, P.L. 106–113. 2001 Trust fund share of expenses, total budget authority reflects restoration of contract authority of $22 million pursuant to sec. 304, P.L. 106–113. Table does not reflect rescissions of unobligated balances.

Federal Funds

General and special funds:

ADMINISTRATIVE EXPENSES

For necessary administrative expenses of the Federal Transit Administration's programs authorized by chapter 53 of title 49, United States Code, [$12,000,000] *$12,800,000*: *Provided*, That no more than [$60,000,000] *$64,000,000* of budget authority shall be available for these purposes: *Provided further*, That the Federal Transit Administration will reimburse the Department of Transportation Inspector General [$1,500,000] *$1,000,000* for costs associated with the audit and review of new fixed guideway systems. *(Department of Transportation and Related Agencies Appropriations Act, 2000.)*

Program and Financing (in millions of dollars)

Identification code 69–1120–0–1–401		1999 actual	2000 est.	2001 est.
	Obligations by program activity:			
00.01	Direct program	53	60	64
01.01	Reimbursable program	2	2	2
10.00	Total new obligations	55	62	66
	Budgetary resources available for obligation:			
22.00	New budget authority (gross)	54	62	66
22.10	Resources available from recoveries of prior year obligations	1		
23.90	Total budgetary resources available for obligation	55	62	66
23.95	Total new obligations	−55	−62	−66
24.40	Unobligated balance available, end of year			1
	New budget authority (gross), detail:			
	Discretionary:			
40.78	Reduction pursuant to P.L. 105–277		−1	
	Mandatory:			
60.00	Appropriation	11	12	13
	Spending authority from offsetting collections:			
	Discretionary:			
68.00	Offsetting collections (cash)	44	50	53
68.10	From Federal sources: Change in receivables and unpaid, unfilled orders	1		
68.15	From Federal sources: Adjustments to receivables and unpaid, unfilled orders	−1		
68.90	Spending authority from offsetting collections (total discretionary)	44	50	53
70.00	Total new budget authority (gross)	54	62	66
	Change in unpaid obligations:			
	Unpaid obligations, start of year:			
72.40	Obligated balance, start of year	2	4	6
72.95	From Federal sources: Receivables and unpaid, unfilled orders	1	2	2
72.99	Total unpaid obligations, start of year	3	6	8
73.10	Total new obligations	55	62	66
73.20	Total outlays (gross)	−52	−60	−65
73.45	Adjustments in unexpired accounts	−1		
	Unpaid obligations, end of year:			
74.40	Obligated balance, end of year	4	6	6
74.95	From Federal sources: Receivables and unpaid, unfilled orders	2	2	2
74.99	Total unpaid obligations, end of year	6	8	8
	Outlays (gross), detail:			
86.90	Outlays from new discretionary authority	50	56	60
86.93	Outlays from discretionary balances	2	4	6
87.00	Total outlays (gross)	52	60	65
	Offsets:			
	Against gross budget authority and outlays:			
88.00	Offsetting collections (cash) from: Federal sources	−44	−50	−53
	Against gross budget authority only:			
88.95	From Federal sources: Change in receivables and unpaid, unfilled orders	−1		
88.96	From Federal sources: Adjustment to receivables and unpaid, unfilled orders	1		
	Net budget authority and outlays:			
89.00	Budget authority	10	12	13
90.00	Outlays	7	10	12

For 2001, $64 million is requested, the guaranteed amount in TEA–21, to fund the personnel and other support costs associated with management and direction of FTA programs. This includes $1.0 million to be reimbursed to the Inspector General for transit-related audits. FTA has been a forerunner in expanding automated systems to provide better access to customers. The Transportation Electronic Award and Management (TEAM) system provides on-line access to grantees for grant awards and disbursements.

Object Classification (in millions of dollars)

Identification code 69–1120–0–1–401		1999 actual	2000 est.	2001 est.
	Direct obligations:			
	Personnel compensation:			
11.1	Full-time permanent	31	34	35
11.3	Other than full-time permanent	1	1	1
11.9	Total personnel compensation	32	35	36
12.1	Civilian personnel benefits	6	7	8
21.0	Travel and transportation of persons	1	1	2
23.1	Rental payments to GSA	4	4	4
23.3	Communications, utilities, and miscellaneous charges	2	2	3
25.2	Other services	7	10	10
31.0	Equipment	1	1	1
99.0	Subtotal, direct obligations	53	60	64
99.0	Reimbursable obligations	2	2	2
99.9	Total new obligations	55	62	66

General and special funds—Continued

ADMINISTRATIVE EXPENSES—Continued

Personnel Summary

Identification code 69–1120–0–1–401	1999 actual	2000 est.	2001 est.
Direct:			
1001 Total compensable workyears: Full-time equivalent employment	478	495	505
Reimbursable:			
2001 Total compensable workyears: Full-time equivalent employment	22	22	22

RESEARCH, TRAINING, AND HUMAN RESOURCES

Program and Financing (in millions of dollars)

Identification code 69–1121–0–1–401	1999 actual	2000 est.	2001 est.
Budgetary resources available for obligation:			
21.40 Unobligated balance available, start of year		1	
22.10 Resources available from recoveries of prior year obligations	1		
22.21 Unobligated balance transferred to other accounts	–1		
23.90 Total budgetary resources available for obligation		1	
24.40 Unobligated balance available, end of year	1		
Change in unpaid obligations:			
72.40 Unpaid obligations, start of year: Obligated balance, start of year	6	4	1
73.20 Total outlays (gross)		–2	–1
73.45 Adjustments in unexpired accounts	–1		
74.40 Unpaid obligations, end of year: Obligated balance, end of year	4	1	1
Outlays (gross), detail:			
86.93 Outlays from discretionary balances		2	1
Net budget authority and outlays:			
89.00 Budget authority			
90.00 Outlays		2	1

Since 1993, the activities of this account have been financed in the Transit Planning and Research.

INTERSTATE TRANSFER GRANTS—TRANSIT

Program and Financing (in millions of dollars)

Identification code 69–1127–0–1–401	1999 actual	2000 est.	2001 est.
Obligations by program activity:			
10.00 Total new obligations (object class 41.0)	4	10	
Budgetary resources available for obligation:			
21.40 Unobligated balance available, start of year	15	10	
22.00 New budget authority (gross)	–1		
23.90 Total budgetary resources available for obligation	14	10	
23.95 Total new obligations	–4	–10	
24.40 Unobligated balance available, end of year	10		
New budget authority (gross), detail:			
Discretionary:			
40.36 Unobligated balance rescinded	–1		
Spending authority from offsetting collections:			
68.00 Offsetting collections (cash)	8		
68.15 From Federal sources: Adjustments to receivables and unpaid, unfilled orders	–8		
68.90 Spending authority from offsetting collections (total discretionary)			
70.00 Total new budget authority (gross)	–1		
Change in unpaid obligations:			
72.40 Unpaid obligations, start of year: Obligated balance, start of year	6		3
73.10 Total new obligations	4	10	
73.20 Total outlays (gross)	–19	–7	–3
73.40 Adjustments in expired accounts (net)	8		
74.40 Unpaid obligations, end of year: Obligated balance, end of year		3	1
Outlays (gross), detail:			
86.93 Outlays from discretionary balances	19	7	3
Offsets:			
Against gross budget authority and outlays:			
88.00 Offsetting collections (cash) from: Federal sources	–8		
Against gross budget authority only:			
88.96 From Federal sources: Adjustment to receivables and unpaid, unfilled orders	8		
Net budget authority and outlays:			
89.00 Budget authority	–1		
90.00 Outlays	11	7	3

This account funds transit capital projects substituted for previously withdrawn segments of the Interstate Highway System under the provisions of 23 U.S.C. 103(e)(4).

WASHINGTON METROPOLITAN AREA TRANSIT AUTHORITY

Program and Financing (in millions of dollars)

Identification code 69–1128–0–1–401	1999 actual	2000 est.	2001 est.
Obligations by program activity:			
10.00 Total new obligations (object class 41.0)		50	
Budgetary resources available for obligation:			
21.40 Unobligated balance available, start of year	1	50	
22.00 New budget authority (gross)	50		
23.90 Total budgetary resources available for obligation	51	50	
23.95 Total new obligations		–50	
24.40 Unobligated balance available, end of year	50		
New budget authority (gross), detail:			
Mandatory:			
60.00 Appropriation	50		
Spending authority from offsetting collections:			
Discretionary:			
68.00 Offsetting collections (cash)	5		
68.15 From Federal sources: Adjustments to receivables and unpaid, unfilled orders	–5		
68.90 Spending authority from offsetting collections (total discretionary)			
70.00 Total new budget authority (gross)	50		
Change in unpaid obligations:			
72.40 Unpaid obligations, start of year: Obligated balance, start of year	457	295	211
73.10 Total new obligations		50	
73.20 Total outlays (gross)	–167	–134	–94
73.40 Adjustments in expired accounts (net)	5		
74.40 Unpaid obligations, end of year: Obligated balance, end of year	295	211	117
Outlays (gross), detail:			
86.93 Outlays from discretionary balances	167	134	94
Offsets:			
Against gross budget authority and outlays:			
88.00 Offsetting collections (cash) from: Federal sources	–5		
Against gross budget authority only:			
88.96 From Federal sources: Adjustment to receivables and unpaid, unfilled orders	5		
Net budget authority and outlays:			
89.00 Budget authority	50		
90.00 Outlays	162	134	94

The National Capital Transportation Amendments of 1979 (Stark-Harris) authorized $1.7 billion in Federal funds to support the construction of the Washington Metrorail system. In addition, the National Capital Transportation Amendments of 1990 authorized another $1.3 billion in Federal capital assistance to complete construction of the planned 103-mile system. The Federal commitment to complete the 103-mile system was fully funded in 1999. No new budget authority is proposed.

FORMULA GRANTS

For necessary expenses to carry out 49 U.S.C. 5307, 5308, 5310, 5311, 5327, and section 3038 of Public Law 105–178, [$619,600,000] *$669,000,000*, to remain available until expended: *Provided*, That no more than [$3,098,000,000] *$3,345,000,000* of budget authority shall be available for these purposes: [*Provided further*, That notwithstanding section 3008 of Public Law 105–178, the $50,000,000 to carry out 49 U.S.C. 5308 shall be transferred to and merged with funding provided for the replacement, rehabilitation, and purchase of buses and related equipment and the construction of bus-related facilities under "Federal Transit Administration, Capital investment grants"]. *(Department of Transportation and Related Agencies Appropriations Act, 2000.)*

Program and Financing (in millions of dollars)

Identification code 69–1129–0–1–401		1999 actual	2000 est.	2001 est.
	Obligations by program activity:			
	Direct program:			
00.01	Urban formula-capital	2,483	2,898	3,109
00.02	Alaska Railroad		5	5
00.03	Clean fuels			50
00.04	Elderly and disabled	64	73	79
00.05	Nonurban formula	183	198	228
00.06	Over-the-road-bus	1	4	5
10.00	Total new obligations	2,731	3,178	3,476
	Budgetary resources available for obligation:			
21.40	Unobligated balance available, start of year	993	1,077	946
22.00	New budget authority (gross)	2,799	3,048	3,345
22.10	Resources available from recoveries of prior year obligations	16		
23.90	Total budgetary resources available for obligation	3,808	4,125	4,291
23.95	Total new obligations	−2,731	−3,178	−3,476
24.40	Unobligated balance available, end of year	1,077	946	815
	New budget authority (gross), detail:			
	Mandatory:			
60.00	Appropriation	570	620	669
61.00	Transferred to other accounts	−51	−50	
62.50	Appropriation (total mandatory)	519	570	669
	Discretionary:			
68.00	Spending authority from offsetting collections: Offsetting collections (cash)	2,280	2,478	2,676
70.00	Total new budget authority (gross)	2,799	3,048	3,345
	Change in unpaid obligations:			
	Unpaid obligations, start of year:			
72.40	Obligated balance, start of year	3,760	4,300	5,122
72.95	From Federal sources: Receivables and unpaid, unfilled orders	1	1	1
72.99	Total unpaid obligations, start of year	3,761	4,301	5,123
73.10	Total new obligations	2,731	3,178	3,476
73.20	Total outlays (gross)	−2,174	−2,356	−2,248
73.45	Adjustments in unexpired accounts	−16		
	Unpaid obligations, end of year:			
74.40	Obligated balance, end of year	4,300	5,122	6,351
74.95	From Federal sources: Receivables and unpaid, unfilled orders	1	1	1
74.99	Total unpaid obligations, end of year	4,301	5,123	6,352
	Outlays (gross), detail:			
86.90	Outlays from new discretionary authority	140	153	167
86.93	Outlays from discretionary balances	2,034	2,203	2,082
87.00	Total outlays (gross)	2,174	2,356	2,248
	Offsets:			
	Against gross budget authority and outlays:			
88.00	Offsetting collections (cash) from: Federal sources	−2,280	−2,478	−2,676
	Net budget authority and outlays:			
89.00	Budget authority	519	570	669
90.00	Outlays	−106	−122	−428

Formula grants is requested at $3,345 million in 2001, the guarantee level in TEA–21. The Formula Grant funds can be used for all transit purposes including planning, bus and railcar purchases, facility repair and construction, maintenance and where eligible, operating expenses. Increased investment levels help transit succeed in alleviating congestion, ensuring basic mobility, promoting more livable communities and helping meet additional needs required as a result of the Americans with Disabilities Act (ADA) and the Clean Air Act (CAA).

In 2001, FTA requests $4.85 million for the Alaska Railroad and $50 million for the Clean Fuels Formula program consistent with the Transportation Equity Act for the 21st Century, TEA–21. A total of $4.7 million for the Rural Transportation Accessibility Incentive Program, commonly referred to as the Over-the-Road Bus Accessibility Program is requested.

Clean Fuels Formula Program.—$50 million will finance the purchase or lease of clean fuel buses and facilities and the improvement of existing facilities to accommodate clean fuel buses.

Over-the-Road Bus Accessibility Program.—$4.7 million for the Rural Transportation Accessibility Incentive Program established in TEA–21 will assist operators of over-the-road buses to finance the incremental capital and training costs of complying with the Department of Transportation's final rule regarding accessibility of over-the-road buses required by the ADA.

Urbanized Area Formula.—$2,997 million in funds will be apportioned to areas with populations of 50,000 or more. Funds may be used for any transit capital purpose, including preventive maintenance for these capital assets, in urban areas over 200,000 in population. Also, in urbanized areas under 200,000 both capital and operating costs are eligible expenditures. This funding will assist public transit agencies in meeting the requirements of the Clean Air Act Amendments and the Americans with Disabilities Act. These funds are critical to preserving mobility in our cities and supporting welfare reform by providing an affordable commute for people making the transition to work.

Nonurbanized Area Formula.—$209 million will be apportioned according to a legislative formula based on each State's nonurban population to areas with populations of less than 50,000. Available funding may be used to support intercity bus service as well as to help meet rural and small urban areas' transit needs.

Formula Grants for Elderly and Individuals with Disabilities.—$79 million will be apportioned to each State according to a legislatively required formula to assist in providing transportation to the elderly and individuals with disabilities. Grants are made for the purchase of vehicles and equipment and for transportation services under a contract, lease or similar arrangement.

Object Classification (in millions of dollars)

Identification code 69–1129–0–1–401		1999 actual	2000 est.	2001 est.
25.2	Other services	18	16	16
41.0	Grants, subsidies, and contributions	2,713	3,162	3,460
99.9	Total new obligations	2,731	3,178	3,476

General and special funds—Continued

UNIVERSITY TRANSPORTATION RESEARCH

For necessary expenses to carry out 49 U.S.C. 5505, $1,200,000, to remain available until expended: *Provided*, That no more than $6,000,000 of budget authority shall be available for these purposes. *(Department of Transportation and Related Agencies Appropriations Act, 2000.)*

Program and Financing (in millions of dollars)

Identification code 69–1136–0–1–401	1999 actual	2000 est.	2001 est.
Obligations by program activity:			
10.00 Total new obligations (object class 41.0)	6	6	6
Budgetary resources available for obligation:			
22.00 New budget authority (gross)	6	6	6
23.95 Total new obligations	−6	−6	−6
New budget authority (gross), detail:			
Mandatory:			
60.00 Appropriation	1	1	1
Discretionary:			
68.00 Spending authority from offsetting collections: Offsetting collections (cash)	5	5	5
70.00 Total new budget authority (gross)	6	6	6
Change in unpaid obligations:			
72.40 Unpaid obligations, start of year: Obligated balance, start of year	12	13	10
73.10 Total new obligations	6	6	6
73.20 Total outlays (gross)	−5	−7	−7
74.40 Unpaid obligations, end of year: Obligated balance, end of year	13	10	10
Outlays (gross), detail:			
86.90 Outlays from new discretionary authority		1	1
86.93 Outlays from discretionary balances	5	6	6
87.00 Total outlays (gross)	5	7	7
Offsets:			
Against gross budget authority and outlays:			
88.00 Offsetting collections (cash) from: Federal sources	−5	−5	−5
Net budget authority and outlays:			
89.00 Budget authority	1	1	1
90.00 Outlays		2	2

For 2001, $6 million is proposed for the University Transportation Research program. This program provides continued support for research, education and technology transfer activities aimed at addressing regional and national transportation problems. These funds are matched with support from non-Federal sources. This program also receives funding from the Federal Highway Administration.

TRANSIT PLANNING AND RESEARCH

For necessary expenses to carry out 49 U.S.C. 5303, 5304, 5305, 5311(b)(2), 5312, 5313(a), 5314, 5315, and 5322, [$21,000,000] *$22,200,000*, to remain available until expended: *Provided*, That no more than [$107,000,000] *$110,000,000* of budget authority shall be available for these purposes: *Provided further*, That $5,250,000 is available to provide rural transportation assistance (49 U.S.C. 5311(b)(2)); $4,000,000 is available to carry out programs under the National Transit Institute (49 U.S.C. 5315); $8,250,000 is available to carry out transit cooperative research programs (49 U.S.C. 5313(a)); [$49,632,000] *$52,113,600* is available for metropolitan planning (49 U.S.C. 5303, 5304, and 5305); [$10,368,000] *$10,886,400* is available for State planning (49 U.S.C. 5313(b)); and $29,500,000 is available for the national planning and research program (49 U.S.C. 5314)[: *Provided further*, That of the total budget authority made available for the national planning and research program, the Federal Transit Administration shall provide the following amounts for the projects and activities listed below:

Zinc-air battery bus technology demonstration, $1,000,000;

Electric vehicle information sharing and technology transfer program, $750,000;

Portland, Maine independent transportation network, $500,000;

Wheeling, West Virginia mobility study, $250,000;

Project ACTION, $3,000,000;

Washoe County, Nevada transit technology, $1,250,000;

Massachusetts Bay Transit Authority advanced electric transit buses and related infrastructure, $1,500,000;

Palm Springs, California fuel cell buses, $1,000,000;

Gloucester, Massachusetts intermodal technology center, $1,500,000;

Southeastern Pennsylvania Transit Authority advanced propulsion control system, $3,000,000;

Advanced transportation and alternative fuel technology consortium (CALSTART), $3,250,000;

Safety and security programs, $5,450,000;

International program, $1,000,000;

Santa Barbara Electric Transit Institute, $500,000;

Hennepin County community transportation, Minnesota, $1,000,000;

Pittsfield economic development authority electric bus program, $1,350,000; and

Citizens for Modern Transit, Missouri, $300,000], *of which $750,000 is available to carry out the national component of the rural transportation assistance program. (Department of Transportation and Related Agencies Appropriations Act, 2000.)*

Program and Financing (in millions of dollars)

Identification code 69–1137–0–1–401	1999 actual	2000 est.	2001 est.
Obligations by program activity:			
00.01 Direct program	90	116	110
09.01 Reimbursable program	6	12	12
10.00 Total new obligations	96	128	122
Budgetary resources available for obligation:			
21.40 Unobligated balance available, start of year	8	18	9
22.00 New budget authority (gross)	104	119	122
22.10 Resources available from recoveries of prior year obligations	1		
22.22 Unobligated balance transferred from other accounts	1		
23.90 Total budgetary resources available for obligation	114	137	131
23.95 Total new obligations	−96	−128	−122
24.40 Unobligated balance available, end of year	18	9	9
New budget authority (gross), detail:			
Mandatory:			
60.00 Appropriation	20	21	22
Spending authority from offsetting collections:			
Discretionary:			
68.00 Offsetting collections (cash)	82	98	100
68.10 From Federal sources: Change in receivables and unpaid, unfilled orders	−1		
68.15 From Federal sources: Adjustments to receivables and unpaid, unfilled orders	3		
68.90 Spending authority from offsetting collections (total discretionary)	84	98	100
70.00 Total new budget authority (gross)	104	119	122
Change in unpaid obligations:			
Unpaid obligations, start of year:			
72.40 Obligated balance, start of year	137	151	185
72.95 From Federal sources: Receivables and unpaid, unfilled orders	16	15	15
72.99 Total unpaid obligations, start of year	153	166	200
73.10 Total new obligations	96	128	122
73.20 Total outlays (gross)	−88	−94	−120
73.40 Adjustments in expired accounts (net)	6		
73.45 Adjustments in unexpired accounts	−1		
Unpaid obligations, end of year:			
74.40 Obligated balance, end of year	151	185	187
74.95 From Federal sources: Receivables and unpaid, unfilled orders	15	15	15
74.99 Total unpaid obligations, end of year	166	200	202
Outlays (gross), detail:			
86.90 Outlays from new discretionary authority	16	22	22

		1999	2000	2001
86.93	Outlays from discretionary balances	72	72	98
87.00	Total outlays (gross)	88	94	120
	Offsets:			
	Against gross budget authority and outlays:			
88.00	Offsetting collections (cash) from: Federal sources	–82	–98	–100
	Against gross budget authority only:			
88.95	From Federal sources: Change in receivables and unpaid, unfilled orders	1		
88.96	From Federal sources: Adjustment to receivables and unpaid, unfilled orders	–3		
	Net budget authority and outlays:			
89.00	Budget authority	20	21	22
90.00	Outlays	6	–4	20

In 2001, a total of $110 million is requested for the transit planning and research activities, including $47 million for research and technology and $63 million for Metropolitan and Statewide Planning.

In 2001, $47 million is requested for a variety of research activities. The National Research and Technology program is funded at $30 million. These funds will be used to cover costs for FTA's essential safety and transit operations data bases including the National Transit Database—$8 million is for Transit Cooperative Research, $4 million for the National Transit Institute, $5 million for the Rural Transit Assistance Program.

Under the national component of the program, the FTA is a catalyst in the research, development and deployment of transportation methods and technologies which address such issues as accessibility for the disabled, air quality, traffic congestion, and transit service and operational improvements. The National Research Program supports the development of innovative transit technologies, such as hybrid electric buses, fuel cells, and battery powered propulsion systems.

For support of metropolitan and statewide planning activities $63 million, the guaranteed level in TEA–21, is requested in 2001. Of this amount, $52 million will be apportioned to States for Metropolitan planning, and $11 million for statewide planning and research activities. These funds support the transportation planning activities that will enable these regional planning agencies to continue to plan for the transportation investments that best meet the needs of the communities they serve, and to comply with Federal statutes.

Object Classification (in millions of dollars)

Identification code 69–1137–0–1–401		1999 actual	2000 est.	2001 est.
	Direct obligations:			
25.1	Advisory and assistance services	1	1	1
25.5	Research and development contracts	7	23	23
41.0	Grants, subsidies, and contributions	82	92	86
99.0	Subtotal, direct obligations	90	116	110
99.0	Reimbursable obligations	6	12	12
99.9	Total new obligations	96	128	122

Job Access and Reverse Commute Grants

For necessary expenses to carry out section 3037 of the Federal Transit Act of 1998, [$15,000,000] *$20,000,000* to remain available until expended: *Provided*, That no more than [$75,000,000] *$150,000,000* of budget authority shall be available for these purposes, *of which $5,000,000 shall be for projects benefiting Native American Tribes, and $5,000,000 shall be for projects benefiting the Delta Region. (Department of Transportation and Related Agencies Appropriation Act, 2000.)*

Program and Financing (in millions of dollars)

Identification code 69–1125–0–1–401		1999 actual	2000 est.	2001 est.
	Obligations by program activity:			
10.00	Total new obligations (object class 41.0)	14	116	170
	Budgetary resources available for obligation:			
21.40	Unobligated balance available, start of year		61	20
22.00	New budget authority (gross)	75	75	150
23.90	Total budgetary resources available for obligation	75	136	170
23.95	Total new obligations	–14	–116	–170
24.40	Unobligated balance available, end of year	61	20	
	New budget authority (gross), detail:			
	Discretionary:			
40.00	Appropriation	25		
	Mandatory:			
60.00	Appropriation	10	15	20
	Discretionary:			
68.00	Spending authority from offsetting collections: Offsetting collections (cash)	40	60	130
70.00	Total new budget authority (gross)	75	75	150
	Change in unpaid obligations:			
72.40	Unpaid obligations, start of year: Obligated balance, start of year		14	110
73.10	Total new obligations	14	116	170
73.20	Total outlays (gross)		–20	–46
74.40	Unpaid obligations, end of year: Obligated balance, end of year	14	110	234
	Outlays (gross), detail:			
86.90	Outlays from new discretionary authority		4	8
86.93	Outlays from discretionary balances		16	38
87.00	Total outlays (gross)		20	46
	Offsets:			
	Against gross budget authority and outlays:			
88.00	Offsetting collections (cash) from: Federal sources	–40	–60	–130
	Net budget authority and outlays:			
89.00	Budget authority	35	15	20
90.00	Outlays	–40	–40	–84

In 2001, $150 million is requested for the Job Access and Reverse Commute Grants Program. This amount includes $50 million made available from the Federal Highway Administration as part of a reallocation of the increase resulting from the revenue aligned budget authority under the highway program. Through grants to states, local governments, and nonprofit organizations, this program is intended to provide transportation services in urban, suburban and rural areas to assist welfare recipients and low income individuals to access employment opportunities. Federal transit funds would provide 50 percent of the project costs, with grant recipients supplying the remaining 50 percent from local or Federal sources other than the Department of Transportation.

Capital Investment Grants

(including transfer of funds)

For necessary expenses to carry out 49 U.S.C. 5308, 5309, 5318, and 5327, [$490,200,000] *$529,200,000*, to remain available until expended: *Provided*, That no more than [$2,451,000,000] *$2,646,000,000* of budget authority shall be available for these purposes: *Provided further*, That notwithstanding any other provision of law, there shall be available for fixed guideway modernization, [$980,400,000] *$1,058,400,000*; there shall be available for the replacement, rehabilitation, and purchase of buses and related equipment and the construction of bus-related facilities, [$490,200,000, together with $50,000,000 transferred from "Federal Transit Administration, Formula grants", to be available for the following projects in amounts specified below:

General and special funds—Continued

CAPITAL INVESTMENT GRANTS—Continued

(INCLUDING TRANSFER OF FUNDS)—Continued

No.	State	Project	Conference
1	Alaska	Anchorage Ship Creek intermodal facility	$4,500,000
2	Alaska	Fairbanks intermodal rail/bus transfer facility	2,000,000
3	Alaska	Juneau downtown mass transit facility	1,500,000
4	Alaska	North Star Borough-Fairbanks intermodal facility	3,000,000
5	Alaska	Wasilla intermodal facility	1,000,000
6	Alaska	Whittier intermodal facility and pedestrian overpass	1,155,000
7	Alabama	Alabama statewide rural bus needs	2,500,000
8	Alabama	Baldwin Rural Area Transportation System buses	1,000,000
9	Alabama	Birmingham intermodal facility	2,000,000
10	Alabama	Birmingham-Jefferson County buses	1,250,000
11	Alabama	Cullman, buses	500,000
12	Alabama	Dothan Wiregrass Transit Authority vehicles and transit facility	1,000,000
13	Alabama	Escambia County buses and bus facility	100,000
14	Alabama	Gees Bend Ferry facilities, Wilcox County	100,000
15	Alabama	Marshall County, buses	500,000
16	Alabama	Huntsville Airport international intermodal center	3,500,000
17	Alabama	Huntsville, intermodal facility	1,250,000
18	Alabama	Huntsville Space and Rocket Center intermodal center	3,500,000
19	Alabama	Jasper buses	50,000
20	Alabama	Jefferson State Community College/University of Montevallo pedestrian walkway	200,000
21	Alabama	Mobile waterfront terminal complex	5,000,000
22	Alabama	Montgomery Union Station intermodal center and buses	3,500,000
23	Alabama	Valley bus and bus facilities	110,000
24	Arkansas	Arkansas Highway and Transit Department buses	2,000,000
25	Arkansas	Arkansas state safety and preventative maintenance facility	800,000
26	Arkansas	Fayetteville, University of Arkansas Transit System buses	500,000
27	Arkansas	Hot Springs, transportation depot and plaza	1,560,000
28	Arkansas	Little Rock, Central Arkansas Transit buses	300,000
29	Arizona	Phoenix bus and bus facilities	3,750,000
30	Arizona	Phoenix South Central Avenue transit facility	500,000
31	Arizona	San Luis, bus	70,000
32	Arizona	Tucson buses	2,555,000
33	Arizona	Yuma paratransit buses	125,000
34	California	California Mountain Area Regional Transit Authority fueling stations	80,000
35	California	Culver City, CityBus buses	1,250,000
36	California	Davis, Unitrans transit maintenance facility	625,000
37	California	Healdsburg, intermodal facility	1,000,000
38	California	I–5 Corridor intermodal transit centers	1,250,000
39	California	Livermore automatic vehicle locator program	1,000,000
40	California	Lodi, multimodal facility	850,000
41	California	Los Angeles County Metropolitan transportation authority buses	3,000,000
42	California	Los Angeles County Foothill Transit buses and HEV vehicles	1,750,000
43	California	Los Angeles Municipal Transit Operators Coalition	2,250,000
44	California	Los Angeles, Union Station Gateway Intermodal Transit Center	1,250,000
45	California	Maywood, Commerce, Bell, Cudahy, California buses and bus facilities	800,000
46	California	Modesto, bus maintenance facility	625,000
47	California	Monterey, Monterey-Salinas buses	625,000
48	California	Orange County, bus and bus facilities	2,000,000
49	California	Perris bus maintenance facility	1,250,000
50	California	Redlands, trolley project	800,000
51	California	Sacramento CNG buses	1,250,000
52	California	San Bernardino Valley, CNG buses	1,000,000
53	California	San Bernardino train station	3,000,000
54	California	San Diego North County buses and CNG fueling station	3,000,000
55	California	Contra Costa County Connection buses	250,000
56	California	San Francisco, Islais Creek maintenance facility	1,250,000
57	California	Santa Barbara buses and bus facility	1,750,000
58	California	Santa Clarita bus maintenance facility	1,250,000
59	California	Santa Cruz buses and bus facilities	1,755,000
60	California	Santa Maria Valley/Santa Barbara County, buses	240,000
61	California	Santa Rosa/Cotati, Intermodal Transportation Facilities	750,000
62	California	Westminster senior citizen vans	150,000
63	California	Windsor, Intermodal Facility	750,000
64	California	Woodland Hills, Warner Center Transportation Hub	625,000
65	Colorado	Boulder/Denver, RTD buses	625,000
66	Colorado	Colorado Association of Transit Agencies	8,000,000
67	Colorado	Denver, Stapleton Intermodal Center	1,250,000
68	Connecticut	New Haven bus facility	2,250,000
69	Connecticut	Norwich buses	2,250,000
70	Connecticut	Waterbury, bus facility	2,250,000
71	Dist. of Columbia	Fuel cell bus and bus facilities program, Georgetown University	4,850,000
72	Dist. of Columbia	Washington, D.C. Intermodal Transportation Center, District	2,500,000
73	Delaware	New Castle County buses and bus facilities	2,000,000
74	Delaware	Delaware buses and bus facility	500,000
75	Florida	Daytona Beach, Intermodal Center	2,500,000
76	Florida	Gainesville hybrid-electric buses and facilities	500,000
77	Florida	Jacksonville buses and bus facilities	1,000,000
78	Florida	Lakeland, Citrus Connection transit vehicles and related equipment	1,250,000
79	Florida	Miami Beach, electric shuttle service	750,000

80	Florida	Miami-Dade Transit buses	2,750,000
81	Florida	Orlando, Lynx buses and bus facilities	2,000,000
82	Florida	Orlando, Downtown Intermodal Facility	2,500,000
83	Florida	Palm Beach, buses	1,000,000
84	Florida	Tampa HARTline buses	500,000
85	Georgia	Atlanta, MARTA buses	13,500,000
86	Georgia	Chatham Area Transit Bus Transfer Center and buses	3,500,000
87	Georgia	Georgia Regional Transportation Authority buses	2,000,000
88	Georgia	Georgia statewide buses and bus-related facilities	2,750,000
89	Hawaii	Hawaii buses and bus facilities	2,250,000
90	Hawaii	Honolulu, bus facility and buses	2,000,000
91	Iowa	Ames transit facility expansion	700,000
92	Iowa	Cedar Rapids intermodal facility	3,500,000
93	Iowa	Clinton transit facility expansion	500,000
94	Iowa	Fort Dodge, Intermodal Facility (Phase II)	885,000
95	Iowa	Iowa City intermodal facility	1,500,000
96	Iowa	Iowa statewide buses and bus facilities	2,500,000
97	Iowa	Iowa/Illinois Transit Consortium bus safety and security	1,000,000
98	Illinois	East Moline transit center	650,000
99	Illinois	Illinois statewide buses and bus-related equipment	8,200,000
100	Indiana	Gary, Transit Consortium buses	1,250,000
101	Indiana	Indianapolis buses	5,000,000
102	Indiana	South Bend Urban Intermodal Transportation Facility	1,250,000
103	Indiana	West Lafayette bus transfer station/terminal (Wabash Landing)	1,750,000
104	Kansas	Girard, buses and vans	700,000
105	Kansas	Johnson County, farebox equipment	250,000
106	Kansas	Kansas City buses	750,000
107	Kansas	Kansas Public Transit Association buses and bus facilities	1,500,000
108	Kansas	Girard Southeast Kansas Community Action Agency maintenance facility	480,000
109	Kansas	Topeka Transit downtown transfer facility	600,000
110	Kansas	Wichita, buses and bus facilities	2,500,000
111	Kentucky	Transit Authority of Northern Kentucky (TANK) buses	2,500,000
112	Kentucky	Kentucky (southern and eastern) transit vehicles	1,000,000
113	Kentucky	Lexington (LexTran), maintenance facility	1,000,000
114	Kentucky	River City, buses	1,500,000
115	Louisiana	Louisiana statewide buses and bus-related facilities	5,000,000
116	Massachusetts	Attleboro intermodal transit facility	500,000
117	Massachusetts	Brockton intermodal transportation center	1,100,000
118	Massachusetts	Greenfield Montague, buses	500,000
119	Massachusetts	Merrimack Valley Regional Transit Authority bus facilities	467,500
120	Massachusetts	Montachusett, bus and park-and-ride facilities	1,250,000
121	Massachusetts	Pioneer Valley, alternative fuel and paratransit vehicles	650,000
122	Massachusetts	Pittsfield intermodal center	3,600,000
123	Massachusetts	Springfield, Union Station	1,250,000
124	Massachusetts	Swampscott, buses	65,000
125	Massachusetts	Westfield, intermodal transportation facility	500,000
126	Massachusetts	Worcester, Union Station Intermodal Transportation Center	2,500,000
127	Maryland	Maryland statewide bus facilities and buses	11,500,000
128	Michigan	Detroit, transfer terminal facilities	3,963,000
129	Michigan	Detroit, EZ Ride program	287,000
130	Michigan	Menominee-Delta-Schoolcraft buses	250,000
131	Michigan	Michigan statewide buses	22,500,000
132	Michigan	Port Huron, CNG fueling station	500,000
133	Minnesota	Duluth, Transit Authority community circulation vehicles	1,000,000
134	Minnesota	Duluth, Transit Authority intelligent transportation systems	500,000
135	Minnesota	Duluth, Transit Authority Transit Hub	500,000
136	Minnesota	Greater Minnesota transit authorities	500,000
137	Minnesota	Northstar Corridor, Intermodal Facilities and buses	10,000,000
138	Minnesota	Twin Cities metropolitan buses and bus facilities	10,000,000
139	Missouri	Columbia buses and vans	500,000
140	Missouri	Southeast Missouri transportation service rural, elderly, disabled service	1,250,000
141	Missouri	Franklin County buses and bus facilities	200,000
142	Missouri	Jackson County buses and bus facilities	500,000
143	Missouri	Kansas City Area Transit Authority buses and Troost transit center	2,500,000
144	Missouri	Missouri statewide bus and bus facilities	3,500,000
145	Missouri	OATS Transit	1,500,000
146	Missouri	St. Joseph buses and vans	500,000
147	Missouri	St. Louis, buses	2,000,000
148	Missouri	St. Louis, Bi-state Intermodal Center	1,250,000
149	Missouri	Southwest Missouri State University park and ride facility	1,000,000
150	Mississippi	Harrison County multimodal center	3,000,000
151	Mississippi	Jackson, maintenance and administration facility project	1,000,000
152	Mississippi	North Delta planning and development district, buses and bus facilities	1,200,000
153	Montana	Missoula urban transportation district buses	600,000
154	North Carolina	Greensboro multimodal center	3,339,000
155	North Carolina	Greensboro, Transit Authority buses	1,500,000
156	North Carolina	North Carolina statewide buses and bus facilities	2,492,000
157	North Dakota	North Dakota statewide buses and bus-related facilities	1,000,000
158	New Hampshire	New Hampshire statewide transit systems	3,000,000
159	New Jersey	New Jersey Transit alternative fuel buses	5,000,000
160	New Jersey	New Jersey Transit jitney shuttle buses	1,750,000
161	New Jersey	Newark intermodal and arena access improvements	1,650,000
162	New Jersey	Newark, Morris & Essex Station access and buses	1,250,000
163	New Jersey	South Amboy, Regional Intermodal Transportation Initiative	1,250,000
164	New Mexico	Albuquerque West Side transit facility	2,000,000
165	New Mexico	Albuquerque, buses	1,250,000
166	New Mexico	Las Cruces buses and bus facilities	750,000
167	New Mexico	Northern New Mexico Transit Express/Park and Ride buses	2,750,000

General and special funds—Continued

CAPITAL INVESTMENT GRANTS—Continued

(INCLUDING TRANSFER OF FUNDS)—Continued

No.	State	Project	Conference
168	New Mexico	Santa Fe, buses and bus facilities	2,000,000
169	Nevada	Clark County Regional Transportation Commission buses and bus facilities	2,500,000
170	Nevada	Lake Tahoe CNG buses	700,000
171	Nevada	Washoe County transit improvements	2,250,000
172	New York	Babylon Intermodal Center	1,250,000
173	New York	Buffalo, Auditorium Intermodal Center	2,000,000
174	New York	Dutchess County, Loop System buses	521,000
175	New York	Ithaca intermodal transportation center	1,125,000
176	New York	Ithaca, TCAT bus technology improvements	1,250,000
177	New York	Long Island, CNG transit vehicles and facilities and bus replacement	1,250,000
178	New York	Mineola/Hicksville, LIRR intermodal centers	1,250,000
179	New York	New York City Midtown West 38th Street ferry terminal	1,000,000
180	New York	New York, West 72nd St. Intermodal Station	1,750,000
181	New York	Putnam County, vans	470,000
182	New York	Rensselaer intermodal bus facility	6,000,000
183	New York	Rochester buses and bus facility	1,000,000
184	New York	Syracuse, buses	3,000,000
185	New York	Utica Union Station	2,100,000
186	New York	Westchester County DOT, articulated buses	1,250,000
187	New York	Westchester County, Bee-Line transit system fareboxes	979,000
188	New York	Westchester County, Bee-Line transit system shuttle buses	1,000,000
189	Ohio	Cleveland, Triskett Garage bus maintenance facility	625,000
190	Ohio	Dayton, Multimodal Transportation Center	4,125,000
191	Ohio	Ohio statewide buses and bus facilities	9,010,250
192	Oklahoma	Oklahoma statewide bus facilities and buses	5,000,000
193	Oregon	Corvallis buses and automated passenger information system	300,000
194	Oregon	Lane County, Bus Rapid Transit, buses and facilities	4,400,000
195	Oregon	Lincoln County Transit District buses	250,000
196	Oregon	Portland, Tri-Met bus maintenance facility	650,000
197	Oregon	Portland, Tri-Met buses	1,750,000
198	Oregon	Salem Area Mass Transit District natural gas buses	500,000
199	Oregon	Sandy buses	100,000
200	Oregon	South Metro Area Rapid Transit (SMART) maintenance facility	200,000
201	Oregon	Sunset Empire Transit District intermodal transit facility	300,000
202	Pennsylvania	Allegheny County buses	1,500,000
203	Pennsylvania	Altoona bus testing	3,000,000
204	Pennsylvania	Altoona, Metro Transit Authority buses and transit system improvements	842,000
205	Pennsylvania	Armstrong County-Mid-County, bus facilities and buses	150,000
206	Pennsylvania	Bethlehem, intermodal facility	1,000,000
207	Pennsylvania	Cambria County, bus facilities and buses	575,000
208	Pennsylvania	Centre Area Transportation Authority buses	1,250,000
209	Pennsylvania	Chester County, Paoli Transportation Center	1,000,000
210	Pennsylvania	Erie, Metropolitan Transit Authority buses	1,000,000
211	Pennsylvania	Fayette County, intermodal facilities and buses	1,270,000
212	Pennsylvania	Lackawanna County Transit System buses	600,000
213	Pennsylvania	Lackawanna County, intermodal bus facility	1,000,000
214	Pennsylvania	Mid-Mon Valley buses and bus facilities	250,000
215	Pennsylvania	Norristown, parking garage (SEPTA)	1,000,000
216	Pennsylvania	Philadelphia, Frankford Transportation Center	5,000,000
217	Pennsylvania	Philadelphia, Intermodal 30th Street Station	1,250,000
218	Pennsylvania	Reading, BARTA Intermodal Transportation Facility	1,750,000
219	Pennsylvania	Robinson, Towne Center Intermodal Facility	1,500,000
220	Pennsylvania	Somerset County bus facilities and buses	175,000
221	Pennsylvania	Towamencin Township, Intermodal Bus Transportation Center	1,500,000
222	Pennsylvania	Washington County intermodal facilities	630,000
223	Pennsylvania	Westmoreland County, Intermodal Facility	200,000
224	Pennsylvania	Wilkes-Barre, Intermodal Facility	1,250,000
225	Pennsylvania	Williamsport bus facility	1,200,000
226	Puerto Rico	San Juan Intermodal access	600,000
227	Rhode Island	Providence, buses and bus maintenance facility	3,294,000
228	South Carolina	Central Midlands COG/Columbia transit system	2,700,000
229	South Carolina	Charleston Area regional transportation authority	1,900,000
230	South Carolina	Clemson Area Transit buses and bus equipment	550,000
231	South Carolina	Greenville transit authority	500,000
232	South Carolina	Pee Dee buses and facilities	900,000
233	South Carolina	Santee-Wateree regional transportation authority	400,000
234	South Carolina	South Carolina Statewide Virtual Transit Enterprise	1,220,000
235	South Carolina	Transit Management of Spartanburg, Incorporated (SPARTA)	600,000
236	South Dakota	South Dakota statewide bus facilities and buses	1,500,000
237	Tennessee	Southern Coalition for Advanced Transportation (SCAT) (TN, GA, FL, AL) electric buses	3,500,000
238	Texas	Austin buses	1,750,000
239	Texas	Beaumont Municipal Transit System buses and bus facilities	1,000,000
240	Texas	Brazos Transit Authority buses and bus facilities	1,000,000
241	Texas	El Paso Sun Metro buses	1,000,000
242	Texas	Fort Worth bus replacement (including CNG vehicles) and paratransit vehicles	2,500,000
243	Texas	Forth Worth intermodal transportation center	3,100,000
244	Texas	Galveston buses and bus facilities	1,000,000
245	Texas	Texas statewide small urban and rural buses	5,000,000
246	Utah	Ogden Intermodal Center	800,000

247	Utah	Salt Lake City Olympics bus facilities	2,500,000
248	Utah	Salt Lake City Olympics regional park and ride lots	2,500,000
249	Utah	Salt Lake City Olympics transit bus loan project	500,000
250	Utah	Utah Transit Authority, intermodal facilities	1,500,000
251	Utah	Utah Transit Authority/Park City Transit, buses	6,500,000
252	Virginia	Alexandria, bus maintenance facility	1,000,000
253	Virginia	Richmond, GRTC bus maintenance facility	1,250,000
254	Virginia	Statewide buses and bus facilities	8,435,000
255	Vermont	Burlington multimodal center	2,700,000
256	Vermont	Chittenden County Transportation Authority buses	800,000
257	Vermont	Essex Junction multimodal station rehabilitation	500,000
258	Vermont	Killington-Sherburne satellite bus facility	250,000
259	Washington	Bremerton multimodal center—Sinclair's Landing	750,000
260	Washington	Sequim Clallam Transit multimodal center	1,000,000
261	Washington	Everett, Multimodal Transportation Center	1,950,000
262	Washington	Grant County, Grant Transit Authority	500,000
263	Washington	Grays Harbor County, buses and equipment	1,250,000
264	Washington	King County Metro King Street Station	2,000,000
265	Washington	King County Metro Atlantic and Central buses	1,500,000
266	Washington	King County park and ride expansion	1,350,000
267	Washington	Mount Vernon, buses and bus related facilities	1,750,000
268	Washington	Pierce County Transit buses and bus facilities	500,000
269	Washington	Seattle, intermodal transportation terminal	1,250,000
270	Washington	Snohomish County, Community Transit buses, equipment and facilities	1,250,000
271	Washington	Spokane, HEV buses	1,500,000
272	Washington	Tacoma Dome Station	250,000
273	Washington	Vancouver Clark County (C–TRAN) bus facilities	1,000,000
274	Washington	Washington State DOT combined small transit system buses and bus facilities	2,000,000
275	Wisconsin	Milwaukee County, buses	6,000,000
276	Wisconsin	Wisconsin statewide bus facilities and buses	14,250,000
277	West Virginia	Huntington intermodal facility	12,000,000
278	West Virginia	Parkersburg, intermodal transportation facility	4,500,000
279	West Virginia	West Virginia Statewide Intermodal Facility and buses	5,000,000;

and] *$529,200,000, of which $50,000,000 will be available for the Los Angeles County Metropolitan Transportation Authority, not to exceed $35,000,000 for Salt Lake City Winter Olympic Games, $15,000,000 for transit service benefiting the Mississippi Delta Region. In addition,* there shall be available for new fixed guideway systems [$980,400,000, to be available as follows:

$10,400,000 for Alaska or Hawaii ferry projects;

$45,142,000 for the Atlanta, Georgia, North line extension project;

$1,000,000 for the Austin, Texas capital metro northwest/north central corridor project;

$4,750,000 for the Baltimore central LRT double track project;

$3,000,000 for the Birmingham, Alabama transit corridor;

$1,000,000 for the Boston Urban Ring project;

$500,000 for the Calais, Maine branch rail line regional transit program;

$2,500,000 for the Canton-Akron-Cleveland commuter rail project;

$2,500,000 for the Charleston, South Carolina Monobeam corridor project;

$4,000,000 for the Charlotte, North Carolina, north-south corridor transitway project;

$25,000,000 for the Chicago METRA commuter rail project;

$3,500,000 for the Chicago Transit Authority Douglas branch line project;

$3,500,000 for the Chicago Transit Authority Ravenswood branch line project;

$1,000,000 for the Cincinnati northeast/northern Kentucky corridor project;

$3,500,000 for the Clark County, Nevada, fixed guideway project, together with unobligated funds provided in Public Law 103–331 for the "Burlington to Gloucester, New Jersey line";

$1,000,000 for the Cleveland Euclid corridor improvement project;

$1,000,000 for the Colorado Roaring Fork Valley project;

$50,000,000 for the Dallas north central light rail extension project;

$1,000,000 for the Dayton, Ohio, light rail study;

$3,000,000 for the Denver Southeast corridor project;

$35,000,000 for the Denver Southwest corridor project;

$25,000,000 for the Dulles corridor project;

$10,000,000 for the Fort Lauderdale, Florida Tri-County commuter rail project;

$1,500,000 for the Galveston, Texas rail trolley extension project;

$10,000,000 for the Girdwood, Alaska commuter rail project;

$7,000,000 for the Greater Albuquerque mass transit project;

$500,000 for the Harrisburg-Lancaster capital area transit corridor 1 commuter rail project;

$3,000,000 for the Houston advanced transit program;

$52,770,000 for the Houston regional bus project;

$1,000,000 for the Indianapolis, Indiana Northeast Downtown corridor project;

$1,000,000 for the Johnson County, Kansas, I–35 commuter rail project;

$1,000,000 for the Kenosha-Racine-Milwaukee rail extension project;

$500,000 for the Knoxville-Memphis commuter rail feasibility study;

$2,000,000 for the Long Island Railroad East Side access project;

$1,000,000 for the Los Angeles-San Diego LOSSAN corridor project;

$4,000,000 for the Los Angeles Mid-City and East Side corridors projects;

$50,000,000 for the Los Angeles North Hollywood extension project;

$1,000,000 for the Lowell, Massachusetts-Nashua, New Hampshire commuter rail project;

$703,000 for the MARC commuter rail project;

$1,500,000 for MARC expansion projects—Silver Spring intermodal and Penn-Camden rail connection;

$1,000,000 for the Massachusetts North Shore corridor project;

$2,500,000 for the Memphis, Tennessee, Medical Center rail extension project;

$1,500,000 for the Miami-Dade Transit east-west multimodal corridor project;

$1,000,000 for the Nashville, Tennessee, commuter rail project;

$99,000,000 for the New Jersey Hudson Bergen project;

$5,000,000 for the New Jersey/New York Trans-Hudson Midtown corridor;

$1,000,000 for the New Orleans Canal Street corridor project;

$12,000,000 for the Newark rail link MOS–1 project;

$1,000,000 for the Norfolk-Virginia Beach corridor project;

$4,000,000 for the Northern Indiana south shore commuter rail project;

$2,000,000 for the Oceanside-Escondido, California light rail system;

$10,000,000 for temporary and permanent Olympic transportation infrastructure investments: *Provided*, That these funds shall be allocated by the Secretary based on the approved transportation management plan for the Salt Lake City 2002 Winter Olympic Games: *Provided further*, That none of these funds shall be available for rail extensions;

$1,000,000 for the Orange County, California, transitway project;

$5,000,000 for the Orlando Lynx light rail project (phase 1);

General and special funds—Continued

CAPITAL INVESTMENT GRANTS—Continued

(INCLUDING TRANSFER OF FUNDS)—Continued

$500,000 for the Palm Beach, Broward and Miami-Dade counties rail corridor;

$4,000,000 for the Philadelphia-Reading SETPA Schuylkill Valley metro project;

$1,000,000 for the Philadelphia SEPTA cross-county metro;

$5,000,000 for the Phoenix metropolitan area transit project;

$2,500,000 for the Pinellas County, Florida, mobility initiative project;

$10,000,000 for the Pittsburgh North Shore-central business district corridor project;

$8,000,000 for the Pittsburgh stage II light rail project;

$11,062,000 for the Portland Westside light rail transit project;

$25,000,000 for the Puget Sound RTA Link light rail project;

$5,000,000 for the Puget Sound RTA Sounder commuter rail project;

$8,000,000 for the Raleigh-Durham-Chapel Hill Triangle transit project;

$25,000,000 for the Sacramento south corridor LRT project;

$37,928,000 for the Utah north/south light rail project;

$1,000,000 for the San Bernardino, California Metrolink project;

$5,000,000 for the San Diego Mid Coast corridor project;

$20,000,000 for the San Diego Mission Valley East light rail transit project;

$65,000,000 for the San Francisco BART extension to the airport project;

$20,000,000 for the San Jose Tasman West light rail project;

$32,000,000 for the San Juan Tren Urbano project;

$3,000,000 for the Santa Fe/El Dorado, New Mexico rail link;

$53,895,000 for the South Boston piers transitway;

$1,000,000 for the South Dekalb-Lindbergh, Georgia, corridor project;

$2,000,000 for the Spokane, Washington, South Valley corridor light rail project;

$2,500,000 for the St. Louis, Missouri, MetroLink cross county corridor project;

$50,000,000 for the St. Louis-St. Clair County MetroLink light rail (phase II) extension project;

$1,000,000 for the Stamford, Connecticut fixed guideway connector;

$1,000,000 for the Stockton, California Altamont commuter rail project;

$1,000,000 for the Tampa Bay regional rail project;

$3,000,000 for the Twin Cities Transitways projects;

$42,800,000 for the Twin Cities Transitways—Hiawatha corridor project;

$2,200,000 for the Virginia Railway Express commuter rail project;

$4,750,000 for the Washington Metro-Blue Line extension-Addison Road (Largo) project;

$1,000,000 for the West Trenton, New Jersey, rail project;

$2,000,000 for the Whitehall ferry terminal reconstruction project;

$1,000,000 for the Wilmington, Delaware downtown transit connector; and

$500,000 for the Wilsonville to Washington County, Oregon connection to Westside] *$1,058,400,000, to be available as follows:*

$10,322,000 for the Alaska or Hawaii ferry projects;

$25,000,000 for Atlanta—North Spring project;

$10,000,000 for Baltimore—Central LRT Double Tracking project;

$35,969,249 for Boston—South Boston Piers Transitway project;

$17,000,000 for Chicago—Douglas Branch Reconstruction project;

$10,000,000 for Chicago—Metra Southwest Corridor Commuter Rail project;

$70,000,000 for Dallas—North Central LRT Extension project;

$20,203,485 for Denver—Southwest Corridor LRT project;

$20,000,000 for Denver—Southeast Corridor LRT project;

$30,000,000 for Fort Lauderdale—Tri-Rail Commuter Rail Upgrade project;

$10,744,873 for Houston—Regional Bus project;

$50,000,000 for Los Angeles—North Hollywood project;

$14,174,990 for Memphis—Medical Center Extension project;

$20,000,000 for Minneapolis—Hiawatha Corridor LRT project;

$10,000,000 for Newark Rail Link MOS-1 project;

$121,000,000 for New Jersey Urban Core—Hudson-Bergen project;

$20,000,000 for Pittsburgh—Stage II LRT Reconstruction project;

$40,000,000 for Portland—Interstate MAX LRT Extension project;

$209,232 for Portland—Westside/Hillsboro project;

$35,199,450 for Sacramento—LRT Extension project;

$15,000,000 for Salt Lake City—CBD to University LRT project;

$718,006 for Salt Lake City—North-South LRT project;

$60,000,000 for St. Louis—Metrolink St. Clair Extension project;

$65,000,000 for San Diego—Mission Valley East LRT Extension project;

$80,000,000 for San Francisco—BART Extension to the Airport project;

$12,248,715 for San Jose—Tasman West LRT project;

$118,000,000 for San Juan—Tren Urbano project;

$35,000,000 for Seattle—Central Link LRT project;

$10,000,000 for Washington, DC/MD—Largo Extension project;

$84,672,000 for activities other than final design and construction as specified in 49 U.S.C. 5309(m)(2); and

$7,938,000 for activities authorized by 49 U.S.C. 5327. (Department of Transportation and Related Agencies Appropriations Act, 2000.)

Program and Financing (in millions of dollars)

Identification code 69–1134–0–1–401	1999 actual	2000 est.	2001 est.
Obligations by program activity:			
10.00 Total new obligations	1,373	2,957	3,113
Budgetary resources available for obligation:			
21.40 Unobligated balance available, start of year	....	934	467
22.00 New budget authority (gross)	2,307	2,489	2,646
23.90 Total budgetary resources available for obligation	2,307	3,423	3,113
23.95 Total new obligations	–1,373	–2,957	–3,113
24.40 Unobligated balance available, end of year	934	467	....
New budget authority (gross), detail:			
Mandatory:			
60.00 Appropriation	451	490	529
62.00 Transferred from other accounts	50	50	....
62.50 Appropriation (total mandatory)	501	540	529
Discretionary:			
68.00 Spending authority from offsetting collections: Offsetting collections (cash)	1,806	1,949	2,117
70.00 Total new budget authority (gross)	2,307	2,489	2,646
Change in unpaid obligations:			
72.40 Unpaid obligations, start of year: Obligated balance, start of year	....	1,124	3,502
73.10 Total new obligations	1,373	2,957	3,113
73.20 Total outlays (gross)	–249	–579	–1,148
74.40 Unpaid obligations, end of year: Obligated balance, end of year	1,124	3,502	5,466
Outlays (gross), detail:			
86.90 Outlays from new discretionary authority	249	124	132
86.93 Outlays from discretionary balances	....	455	1,017
87.00 Total outlays (gross)	249	579	1,148
Offsets:			
Against gross budget authority and outlays:			
88.00 Offsetting collections (cash) from: Federal sources	–1,806	–1,949	–2,117
Net budget authority and outlays:			
89.00 Budget authority	501	540	529
90.00 Outlays	–1,557	–1,370	–969

For 2001, a total of $2,646 million, the guaranteed level in TEA–21, is requested for Capital Investment Grants. The $2,646 million will be allocated among the following activities:

Bus and bus-related facilities.—$529.2 million for the replacement, rehabilitation and purchase of buses and related equipment and the construction of bus-related facilities. This funding will assist public transit authorities in meeting the requirements of the Clean Air Act Amendments and the Americans with Disabilities Act. For 2001, FTA's goal is to continue in its efforts to make the national fixed-route bus system 80 percent accessible to individuals with disabilities.

Within the bus funding level, $50 million will be provided for the Clean Fuels Formula Grants program, as authorized by TEA–21. The Clean Fuels Formula Program will finance the purchase or lease of clean fuel buses and facilities and the improvement of existing facilities to accommodate clean fuel buses. In addition, FTA will fund $50 million in extraordinary costs associated with the Masters decision in Los Angeles County Metropolitan Transportation Authority and $35 million for cost associated with the 2002 Winter Olympic and paralympic games in Salt Lake City, Utah. FTA will provide $15 million for transit service benefiting the Mississippi Delta Region.

Fixed guideway modernization.—$1,058 million for the acquisition, reconstruction and improvement of facilities and equipment for use on fixed guideways including heavy and light rail, commuter rail, and ferryboat operations. Funding for this program will ensure the fixed guideway modernization activity remains the stabilization and restoration factor for remedying the conditions of the Nation's older fixed guideway systems.

New Starts.—$1,058 million for the construction of new fixed guideway systems and extensions to existing fixed guideway systems. This will fund all projects currently under Full Funding Grant Agreements (FFGA) or expected to be under FFGA during 2001. Within the $1,058 million total, FTA is requesting that 8 percent or, $85 million, be provided for preliminary engineering.

Object Classification (in millions of dollars)

Identification code 69–1134–0–1–401	1999 actual	2000 est.	2001 est.
25.2 Other services	10	19	20
41.0 Grants, subsidies, and contributions	1,363	2,938	3,093
99.9 Total new obligations	1,373	2,957	3,113

MISCELLANEOUS EXPIRED ACCOUNTS

Program and Financing (in millions of dollars)

Identification code 69–1122–0–1–401	1999 actual	2000 est.	2001 est.
Budgetary resources available for obligation:			
21.40 Unobligated balance available, start of year	4	4	
22.00 New budget authority (gross)		–4	
23.90 Total budgetary resources available for obligation	4		
24.40 Unobligated balance available, end of year	4		
New budget authority (gross), detail:			
Discretionary:			
40.36 Unobligated balance rescinded		–4	
Net budget authority and outlays:			
89.00 Budget authority		–4	
90.00 Outlays			

This schedule displays program balances that are no longer required.

Trust Funds

DISCRETIONARY GRANTS

(LIQUIDATION OF CONTRACT AUTHORIZATION)

(HIGHWAY TRUST FUND)

Notwithstanding any other provision of law, for payment of previous obligations incurred in carrying out 49 U.S.C. 5338(b), [$1,500,000,000] *$350,000,000*, to remain available until expended and to be derived from the Mass Transit Account of the Highway Trust Fund. *(Department of Transportation and Related Agencies Appropriations Act, 2000.)*

Program and Financing (in millions of dollars)

Identification code 69–8191–0–7–401	1999 actual	2000 est.	2001 est.
Obligations by program activity:			
10.00 Total new obligations	709	340	
Budgetary resources available for obligation:			
21.49 Unobligated balance available, start of year: Contract authority	1,415	340	
22.00 New budget authority (gross)	–392		
22.10 Resources available from recoveries of prior year obligations	26		
23.90 Total budgetary resources available for obligation	1,049	340	
23.95 Total new obligations	–709	–340	
24.49 Unobligated balance, end of year: Contract authority	340		
New budget authority (gross), detail:			
Discretionary:			
40.26 Appropriation (trust fund, definite)	2,000	1,500	312
40.49 Portion applied to liquidate contract authority	–2,000	–1,500	–312
43.00 Appropriation (total discretionary)			
49.36 Unobligated balance rescinded	–392		
70.00 Total new budget authority (gross)	–392		
Change in unpaid obligations:			
Unpaid obligations, start of year:			
72.40 Obligated balance, start of year	924	1,401	1,586
72.49 Obligated balance, start of year: Contract authority	2,789	1,471	312
72.95 From Federal sources: Receivables and unpaid, unfilled orders	1	1	1
72.99 Total unpaid obligations, start of year	3,714	2,873	1,899
73.10 Total new obligations	709	340	
73.20 Total outlays (gross)	–1,524	–1,314	–932
73.45 Adjustments in unexpired accounts	–26		
Unpaid obligations, end of year:			
74.40 Obligated balance, end of year	1,401	1,586	966
74.49 Obligated balance, end of year: Contract authority	1,471	312	
74.95 From Federal sources: Receivables and unpaid, unfilled orders	1	1	1
74.99 Total unpaid obligations, end of year	2,873	1,899	967
Outlays (gross), detail:			
86.93 Outlays from discretionary balances	1,524	1,314	932
Net budget authority and outlays:			
89.00 Budget authority	–392		
90.00 Outlays	1,524	1,314	932

Status of Contract Authority (in millions of dollars)

Identification code 69–8191–0–7–4C1	1999 actual	2000 est.	2001 est.
0100 Balance, start of year	4,204	1,811	312
Contract authority:			
0200 Contract authority	–392		
0400 Appropriation to liquidate contract authority	–2,000	–1,500	–312
0700 Balance, end of year	1,811	312	

In 2001, $350 million in liquidating cash in the Mass Transit Capital Fund will be available to pay previous obligations in the Discretionary Grants account.

Object Classification (in millions of dollars)

Identification code 69–8191–0–7–401	1999 actual	2000 est.	2001 est.
25.2 Other services	5		
41.0 Grants, subsidies, and contributions	704	340	
99.9 Total new obligations	709	340	

TRUST FUND SHARE OF EXPENSES

(LIQUIDATION OF CONTRACT AUTHORIZATION)

(HIGHWAY TRUST FUND)

Notwithstanding any other provision of law, for payment of obligations incurred in carrying out 49 U.S.C. 5303–5308, 5310–5315, 5317(b), 5322, 5327, 5334, 5505, and sections 3037 and 3038 of Public Law 105–178, [$4,929,270,000] *$5,016,600,000*, to remain available until expended, [and] to be derived from the Mass Transit Account of the Highway Trust Fund, *and $50,000,000, to remain available until expended and to be derived from the Highway Account of the Highway Trust Fund*: *Provided*, That [$2,478,400,000] *$2,676,000,000* shall be paid to the Federal Transit Administration's formula grants account: *Provided further*, That [$86,000,000] *$87,800,000* shall be paid to the Federal Transit Administration's transit planning and research account: *Provided further*, That [$48,000,000] *$51,200,000* shall be paid to the Federal Transit Administration's administrative expenses account: *Provided further*, That $4,800,000 shall be paid to the Federal Transit Administration's university transportation research account: *Provided further*, That [$60,000,000] *$130,000,000* shall be paid to the Federal Transit Administration's job access and reverse commute grants program: *Provided further*, That [$1,960,800,000] *$2,116,800,000* shall be paid to the Federal Transit Administration's capital investment grants account. *(Department of Transportation and Related Agencies Appropriations Act, 2000.)*

Program and Financing (in millions of dollars)

Identification code 69–8350–0–7–401	1999 actual	2000 est.	2001 est.
Obligations by program activity:			
00.01 Administrative expenses	43	48	51
00.02 Job access and reverse commute	40	60	130
00.03 Formula programs	2,280	2,478	2,676
00.04 University transportation research	5	5	5
00.05 Transit planning and research	78	86	88
00.06 Capital investment grants	1,806	1,949	2,117
10.00 Total new obligations (object class 92.0)	4,252	4,626	5,067
Budgetary resources available for obligation:			
21.49 Unobligated balance available, start of year: Contract authority	1	....	18
22.00 New budget authority (gross)	4,251	4,644	5,089
23.90 Total budgetary resources available for obligation	4,252	4,644	5,107
23.95 Total new obligations	–4,252	–4,626	–5,067
24.49 Unobligated balance, end of year: Contract authority	....	18	40
New budget authority (gross), detail:			
Discretionary:			
40.26 Appropriation (trust fund, definite)	4,252	4,935	5,067
40.49 Portion applied to liquidate contract authority used	–4,252	–4,929	–5,067
43.00 Appropriation (total discretionary)	....	6	....
49.36 Unobligated balance rescinded	–1	....	....
Mandatory:			
66.10 Contract authority	4,252	4,638	5,039
66.15 Contract authority (Transfer from 69–8083)	....	....	50
66.90 Contract authority (total mandatory)	4,252	4,638	5,089
70.00 Total new budget authority (gross)	4,251	4,644	5,089
Change in unpaid obligations:			
73.10 Total new obligations	4,252	4,626	5,067
73.20 Total outlays (gross)	–4,252	–4,626	–5,067
Outlays (gross), detail:			
86.90 Outlays from new discretionary authority	4,252	4,626	5,067
Net budget authority and outlays:			
89.00 Budget authority	4,251	4,644	5,089
90.00 Outlays	4,252	4,626	5,067

Status of Contract Authority (in millions of dollars)

Identification code 69–8350–0–7–401	1999 actual	2000 est.	2001 est.
0100 Balance, start of year	1	....	18
Contract authority:			
0200 Contract authority	4,251	4,638	5,089
0400 Appropriation to liquidate contract authority	–4,252	–4,929	–5,067
0700 Balance, end of year	....	18	40

For 2001, this account tracks the portion of funds for each of FTA's programs derived from the Mass Transit Account of the Highway Trust Fund.

STATUS OF THE MASS TRANSIT ACCOUNT OF THE HIGHWAY TRUST FUND

[In millions of dollars]

	1999 actual	*2000 est.*	*2001 est.*
Unexpended balance, start of year	10,051	9,753	8,486
Cash income during the year, Governmental receipts:			
Motor fuel taxes	5,478	4,673	4,780
Interest on investments	....	....	....
Total annual income	5,478	4,673	4,780
Cash outlays during the year:			
Discretionary grants/Major Capital Investments (liquidation of contract authorization)	1,524	1,314	932
Trust fund share of transit programs	4,252	4,626	5,017
Total annual outlays	5,776	5,940	5,949
Unexpended balance, end of year	9,753	8,486	7,317

SAINT LAWRENCE SEAWAY DEVELOPMENT CORPORATION

General and special funds:

Federal Funds

OPERATIONS AND MAINTENANCE (HARBOR SERVICES FEE COLLECTIONS)

(Legislative proposal, subject to PAYGO)

Program and Financing (in millions of dollars)

Identification code 69–5299–4–2–403	1999 actual	2000 est.	2001 est.
Obligations by program activity:			
10.00 Total new obligations (object class 25.2)	....	....	13
Budgetary resources available for obligation:			
22.00 New budget authority (gross)	....	....	13
23.95 Total new obligations	....	....	–13
New budget authority (gross), detail:			
Mandatory:			
60.20 Appropriation (special fund, definite)	....	....	13
Change in unpaid obligations:			
73.10 Total new obligations	....	....	13
73.20 Total outlays (gross)	....	....	–13
Outlays (gross), detail:			
86.97 Outlays from new mandatory authority	....	....	13
Net budget authority and outlays:			
89.00 Budget authority	....	....	13
90.00 Outlays	....	....	13

The Administration proposes to fund activities formerly funded from the Harbor maintenance trust fund from Harbor services fee collections.

Public enterprise funds:

[SAINT LAWRENCE SEAWAY DEVELOPMENT CORPORATION]

[The Saint Lawrence Seaway Development Corporation is hereby authorized to make such expenditures, within the limits of funds and borrowing authority available to the Corporation, and in accord with law, and to make such contracts and commitments without regard to fiscal year limitations as provided by section 104 of the

Government Corporation Control Act, as amended, as may be necessary in carrying out the programs set forth in the Corporation's budget for the current fiscal year.] *(Department of Transportation and Related Agencies Appropriations Act, 2000.)*

Program and Financing (in millions of dollars)

Identification code 69–4089–0–3–403	1999 actual	2000 est.	2001 est.
Obligations by program activity:			
00.01 Operations and maintenance	11	11	12
00.02 Replacement and improvements	1	1	2
10.00 Total new obligations	12	12	14
Budgetary resources available for obligation:			
21.40 Unobligated balance available, start of year	13	13	14
22.00 New budget authority (gross)	13	13	14
23.90 Total budgetary resources available for obligation	26	26	28
23.95 Total new obligations	−12	−12	−14
24.40 Unobligated balance available, end of year	13	14	14
New budget authority (gross), detail:			
Mandatory:			
69.00 Offsetting collections (cash)	13	13	14
Change in unpaid obligations:			
72.40 Unpaid obligations, start of year: Obligated balance, start of year	3	3	2
73.10 Total new obligations	12	12	14
73.20 Total outlays (gross)	−13	−13	−14
74.40 Unpaid obligations, end of year: Obligated balance, end of year	3	2	2
Outlays (gross), detail:			
86.97 Outlays from new mandatory authority	13	13	14
Offsets:			
Against gross budget authority and outlays:			
Offsetting collections (cash) from:			
88.00 Federal sources	−12	−11	−12
88.40 Non-Federal sources	−1	−2	−2
88.90 Total, offsetting collections (cash)	−13	−13	−14
Net budget authority and outlays:			
89.00 Budget authority	....	....	....
90.00 Outlays	....	....	....

The Saint Lawrence Seaway Development Corporation (SLSDC) is a wholly owned Government Corporation responsible for the operation, maintenance and development of the United States portion of the St. Lawrence Seaway between Montreal and Lake Erie. Major priorities are to control Seaway Corporation costs and to encourage increased use of the Seaway system.

SLSDC is proposed as a performance-based organization (PBO) for 2001–2005. The PBO will focus on four key performance goals: safety, long and short term reliability, trade development, and management accountability including customer service, fiscal performance and cost effectiveness. No appropriation is requested as financing is proposed to be derived from an automatic annual payment from the Harbor services fund, based on five-year average tonnage through the Seaway.

Statement of Operations (in millions of dollars)

Identification code 69–4089–0–3–403	1998 actual	1999 actual	2000 est.	2001 est.
0101 Revenue	11	11	11	13
0102 Expense	−11	−11	−11	−13
0105 Net income or loss (−)	....	....	....	....

Balance Sheet (in millions of dollars)

Identification code 69–4089–0–3–403	1998 actual	1999 actual	2000 est.	2001 est.
ASSETS:				
1101 Federal assets: Fund balances with Treasury	1	1	1	1
Other Federal assets:				
1801 Cash and other monetary assets	13	13	13	13
1803 Property, plant and equipment, net	86	85	86	87
1901 Other assets	2	2	2	2
1999 Total assets	102	101	102	103
LIABILITIES:				
Non-Federal liabilities:				
2201 Accounts payable	2	2	2	2
2206 Pension and other actuarial liabilities	2	2	2	2
2999 Total liabilities	4	4	4	4
NET POSITION:				
3300 Cumulative results of operations	98	97	98	99
3999 Total net position	98	97	98	99
4999 Total liabilities and net position	102	101	102	103

Object Classification (in millions of dollars)

Identification code 69–4089–0–3–403	1999 actual	2000 est.	2001 est.
11.1 Personnel compensation: Full-time permanent	7	8	8
12.1 Civilian personnel benefits	2	2	2
26.0 Supplies and materials	1	1	1
32.0 Land and structures	....	....	1
99.0 Subtotal, direct obligations	10	11	12
99.5 Below reporting threshold	2	1	2
99.9 Total new obligations	12	12	14

Personnel Summary

Identification code 69–4089–0–3–403	1999 actual	2000 est.	2001 est.
1001 Total compensable workyears: Full-time equivalent employment	149	157	157

Trust Funds

[OPERATIONS AND MAINTENANCE]

[(HARBOR MAINTENANCE TRUST FUND)]

[For necessary expenses for operations and maintenance of those portions of the Saint Lawrence Seaway operated and maintained by the Saint Lawrence Seaway Development Corporation, $12,042,000, to be derived from the Harbor Maintenance Trust Fund, pursuant to Public Law 99–662.] *(Department of Transportation and Related Agencies Appropriations Act, 2000.)*

Program and Financing (in millions of dollars)

Identification code 69–8003–0–7–403	1999 actual	2000 est.	2001 est.
Obligations by program activity:			
10.00 Total new obligations (object class 25.2)	11	12	13
Budgetary resources available for obligation:			
22.00 New budget authority (gross)	11	12	13
23.95 Total new obligations	−11	−12	−13
New budget authority (gross), detail:			
Discretionary:			
40.26 Appropriation (trust fund, definite)	11	12	13
Change in unpaid obligations:			
73.10 Total new obligations	11	12	13
73.20 Total outlays (gross)	−11	−12	−13
Outlays (gross), detail:			
86.90 Outlays from new discretionary authority	11	12	13
Net budget authority and outlays:			
89.00 Budget authority	11	12	13
90.00 Outlays	11	12	13

[OPERATIONS AND MAINTENANCE]—Continued

[(HARBOR MAINTENANCE TRUST FUND)]—Continued

Summary of Budget Authority and Outlays

(in millions of dollars)

	1999 actual	2000 est.	2001 est.
Enacted/requested:			
Budget Authority	11	12	13
Outlays	11	12	13
Legislative proposal, not subject to PAYGO:			
Budget Authority			–13
Outlays			–13
Total:			
Budget Authority	11	12	
Outlays	11	12	

The Water Resources Development Act of 1986 authorizes use of the Harbor maintenance trust fund as the major source of funding for the Corporation's operations and maintenance activities. The Administration proposes to replace the Harbor maintenance trust fund with a Harbor services fund.

OPERATIONS AND MAINTENANCE

(HARBOR SERVICES FUND)

(Legislative proposal, subject to PAYGO)

Program and Financing (in millions of dollars)

Identification code 69–8003–2–7–403	1999 actual	2000 est.	2001 est.
Obligations by program activity:			
10.00 Total new obligations (object class 25.2)			–13
Budgetary resources available for obligation:			
22.00 New budget authority (gross)			–13
23.95 Total new obligations			13
New budget authority (gross), detail:			
Discretionary:			
40.26 Appropriation (trust fund, definite)			–13
Change in unpaid obligations:			
73.10 Total new obligations			–13
73.20 Total outlays (gross)			13
Outlays (gross), detail:			
86.90 Outlays from new discretionary authority			–13
Net budget authority and outlays:			
89.00 Budget authority			–13
90.00 Outlays			–13

Proposed legislation to establish a performance-based organization (PBO) would finance this program using mandatory budget authority. A legislative proposal to establish a PBO was transmitted during the first session of the 106th Congress.

RESEARCH AND SPECIAL PROGRAMS ADMINISTRATION

The following table depicts funding for all the Research and Special Programs Administration programs.

[In millions of dollars]

	1999 actual	2000 est.	2001 est.
Budget authority:			
Research and Special Programs	31	32	43
Offsetting User Fees [1]			–5
Emergency Preparedness Grants	7	14	14
Pipeline Safety	30	31	43
Trust Fund Share of Pipeline Safety	4	5	4
Pipeline Safety, Subtotal	35	37	47
Total budget authority	73	83	99
Program level (obligations):			
Research and Special Programs	32	32	43
Emergency Preparedness Grants	9	14	14
Pipeline Safety	30	31	43
Trust Fund Share of Pipeline Safety	5	5	4
Pipeline Safety, Subtotal	34	37	47
Volpe Transportation Systems Center (reimbursable)	202	205	205
Total program level, net	278	288	309
Outlays:			
Research and Special Programs	29	31	38
Offsetting User Fees [1]	0	0	–19
Emergency Preparedness Grants	7	9	12
Pipeline Safety	30	29	36
Trust Fund Share of Pipeline Safety	4	6	5
Volpe Transportation Systems Center	1		
Total outlays	71	75	73

[1] Reflects that portion of proposed offsetting collections that would be used to finance hazardous materials transportation safety activities in 2001.

Federal Funds

General and special funds:

RESEARCH AND SPECIAL PROGRAMS

For expenses necessary to discharge the functions of the Research and Special Programs Administration, [$32,061,000] *including grants for university conducted marine transportation research, $42,531,000*, of which $645,000 shall be derived from the Pipeline Safety Fund, and of which [$3,704,000] *$9,607,000* shall remain available until September 30, [2002] *2003*: *Provided*, That up to $1,200,000 in fees collected under 49 U.S.C. 5108(g) shall be deposited in the general fund of the Treasury as offsetting receipts: *Provided further*, That there may be credited to this appropriation, to be available until expended, funds received from States, counties, municipalities, other public authorities, and private sources for expenses incurred for training, for reports publication and dissemination, and for travel expenses incurred in performance of hazardous materials exemptions and approvals functions. *(Department of Transportation and Related Agencies Appropriations Act, 2000.)*

Program and Financing (in millions of dollars)

Identification code 69–0104–0–1–407	1999 actual	2000 est.	2001 est.
Obligations by program activity:			
Direct program:			
00.01 Hazardous materials safety	17	18	19
00.03 Emergency transportation	4	1	2
00.04 Research and technology	4	3	9
00.05 Program and administrative support	8	9	12
09.01 Reimbursable program	42	77	77
10.00 Total new obligations	75	108	119
Budgetary resources available for obligation:			
21.40 Unobligated balance available, start of year	3	2	2
22.00 New budget authority (gross)	75	108	119
23.90 Total budgetary resources available for obligation	78	110	121
23.95 Total new obligations	–75	–108	–119
23.98 Unobligated balance expiring or withdrawn	–1		
24.40 Unobligated balance available, end of year	2	2	2
New budget authority (gross), detail:			
Discretionary:			
40.00 Appropriation	29	31	42
40.20 Appropriation (special fund, definite)	1	1	1
42.00 Transferred from other accounts	2		
43.00 Appropriation (total discretionary)	31	32	43
Spending authority from offsetting collections:			
68.00 Offsetting collections (cash)	29	76	76
68.10 From Federal sources: Change in receivables and unpaid, unfilled orders	18		
68.15 From Federal sources: Adjustments to receivables and unpaid, unfilled orders	–4		
68.90 Spending authority from offsetting collections (total discretionary)	43	76	76

		1999 actual	2000 est.	2001 est.
70.00	Total new budget authority (gross)	75	108	119
	Change in unpaid obligations:			
	Unpaid obligations, start of year:			
72.40	Obligated balance, start of year	7	10	11
72.95	From Federal sources: Receivables and unpaid, unfilled orders	31	49	49
72.99	Total unpaid obligations, start of year	38	59	60
73.10	Total new obligations	75	108	119
73.20	Total outlays (gross)	−59	−107	−114
73.40	Adjustments in expired accounts (net)	5		
	Unpaid obligations, end of year:			
74.40	Obligated balance, end of year	10	11	16
74.95	From Federal sources: Receivables and unpaid, unfilled orders	49	49	49
74.99	Total unpaid obligations, end of year	59	60	65
	Outlays (gross), detail:			
86.90	Outlays from new discretionary authority	49	98	105
86.93	Outlays from discretionary balances	9	9	10
87.00	Total outlays (gross)	59	107	114
	Offsets:			
	Against gross budget authority and outlays:			
88.00	Offsetting collections (cash) from: Federal sources	−29	−76	−76
	Against gross budget authority only:			
88.95	From Federal sources: Change in receivables and unpaid, unfilled orders	−18		
88.96	From Federal sources: Adjustment to receivables and unpaid, unfilled orders	4		
	Net budget authority and outlays:			
89.00	Budget authority	31	32	43
90.00	Outlays	29	31	38

Summary of Budget Authority and Outlays

(in millions of dollars)

	1999 actual	2000 est.	2001 est.
Enacted/requested:			
Budget Authority	31	32	43
Outlays	29	31	39
Legislative proposal, not subject to PAYGO:			
Budget Authority			−5
Outlays			−19
Total:			
Budget Authority	31	32	38
Outlays	29	31	20

The Research and Special Programs Administration serves as a research, analytical, and technical development arm of the Department for multimodal research and development, as well as special programs. Particular emphasis is given to transportation of hazardous cargo by all modes of transportation. In 2001, resources are requested for hazardous materials safety programs, including emergency preparedness activities. Funding is also provided for the management and execution of the Office of Emergency Transportation; the Office of Innovation Research and Education; the Transportation Safety Institute; and the Volpe National Transportation Systems Center (VNTSC). The 2001 Budget proposes to increase hazardous materials registration fees to finance hazardous materials safety activities previously financed by general fund appropriations to this account. This proposal is described in the following section.

Object Classification (in millions of dollars)

Identification code 69–0104–0–1–407		1999 actual	2000 est.	2001 est.
	Direct obligations:			
11.1	Personnel compensation: Full-time permanent	13	14	16
12.1	Civilian personnel benefits	2	3	3
21.0	Travel and transportation of persons	1	1	1
23.1	Rental payments to GSA	2	2	2
23.3	Communications, utilities, and miscellaneous charges	1		
25.2	Other services	5	6	8
25.3	Purchases of goods and services from Government accounts	2	1	2
25.5	Research and development contracts	5	4	7
41.0	Grants, subsidies, and contributions	1		3
99.0	Subtotal, direct obligations	32	31	42
99.0	Reimbursable obligations	42	76	76
99.5	Below reporting threshold	1	1	1
99.9	Total new obligations	75	108	119

Personnel Summary

Identification code 69–0104–0–1–407		1999 actual	2000 est.	2001 est.
	Direct:			
1001	Total compensable workyears: Full-time equivalent employment	189	189	196
	Reimbursable:			
2001	Total compensable workyears: Full-time equivalent employment	49	53	56

Research and Special Programs

(Legislative proposal, not subject to PAYGO)

Contingent upon the enactment of authorizing legislation, the Secretary shall charge a fee to carry out chapter 51 of title 49, United States Code (except sections 5108(g)(2), 5109, 5112, 5115, 5116, 5119), and such fee shall be deposited as an offsetting collection to this appropriation, to remain available until expended for this purpose: Provided, That upon the enactment of such authorizing legislation, the amount appropriated above from the General Fund shall be reduced by $4,722,000.

Program and Financing (in millions of dollars)

Identification code 69–0104–2–1–407		1999 actual	2000 est.	2001 est.
	Obligations by program activity:			
	Direct program:			
00.01	Hazardous materials safety			−5
09.01	Reimbursable program			5
10.00	Total new obligations			
	Budgetary resources available for obligation:			
22.00	New budget authority (gross)			14
24.40	Unobligated balance available, end of year			14
	New budget authority (gross), detail:			
	Discretionary:			
40.00	Appropriation			−5
68.00	Spending authority from offsetting collections: Offsetting collections (cash)			19
70.00	Total new budget authority (gross)			14
	Offsets:			
	Against gross budget authority and outlays:			
88.45	Offsetting collections (cash) from: Offsetting governmental collections from the public			−19
	Net budget authority and outlays:			
89.00	Budget authority			−5
90.00	Outlays			−19

Beginning late in 2001, hazardous materials safety activities previously financed by general fund appropriations to this account are proposed to be financed instead by offsetting collections of hazardous materials registration fees. Authorizing legislation will be proposed to increase the fees paid by shippers and carriers of hazardous materials by an estimated $19 million in 2001 to fund these safety activities. Due to the timing of these collections, a general fund appropriation of $14 million is requested to fund the hazardous materials safety program for the first three quarters of 2001. Beginning in the fourth quarter of 2001, this program would become 100 percent fee-financed. Of the $19 million in new fees collected, $5 million would be obligated in 2001. The remainder would be carried over into 2002 to finance the

General and special funds—Continued

RESEARCH AND SPECIAL PROGRAMS—Continued

hazardous materials safety program until the 2002 fee collections are received.

The collection and expenditure of this increase in hazardous materials fees would be contingent on appropriations action. The additional proviso to be included in appropriation language is being proposed in anticipation of the enactment of authorizing legislation. If the authorizing legislation is enacted, the proviso will reduce the amount of the general fund appropriation provided in the body of the language by $5 million, the amount necessary to fund these activities in the last quarter of 2001, so that total resources for this account will not exceed the amount allowed under the discretionary spending caps.

Object Classification (in millions of dollars)

Identification code 69–0104–2–1–407	1999 actual	2000 est.	2001 est.
92.0 Direct obligations: Undistributed	....	....	−5
99.0 Reimbursable obligations: Subtotal, reimbursable obligations	....	....	5
99.9 Total new obligations	....	....	....

PIPELINE SAFETY

(PIPELINE SAFETY FUND)

(OIL SPILL LIABILITY TRUST FUND)

For expenses necessary to conduct the functions of the pipeline safety program, for grants-in-aid to carry out a pipeline safety program, as authorized by 49 U.S.C. 60107, and to discharge the pipeline program responsibilities of the Oil Pollution Act of 1990, [$36,879,000] *$47,137,000*, of which [$5,479,000] *$4,263,000* shall be derived from the Oil Spill Liability Trust Fund and shall remain available until September 30, [2002] *2003*; of which [$30,000,000] *$42,874,000* shall be derived from the Pipeline Safety Fund, of which [$17,394,000] *$25,213,000* shall remain available until September 30, [2002; and of which $1,400,000 shall be derived from amounts previously collected under 49 U.S.C. 60301: *Provided*, That amounts previously collected under 49 U.S.C. 60301 shall be available for damage prevention grants to States and public education activities] *2003. (Department of Transportation and Related Agencies Appropriations Act, 2000.)*

Unavailable Collections (in millions of dollars)

Identification code 69–5172–0–2–407	1999 actual	2000 est.	2001 est.
Balance, start of year:			
01.99 Balance, start of year	18	17	15
Receipts:			
02.01 Pipeline safety user fees	30	30	44
04.00 Total: Balances and collections	48	47	59
Appropriation:			
05.01 Pipeline safety	−30	−31	−43
05.03 Research and special programs	−1	−1	−1
05.99 Subtotal appropriation	−31	−32	−44
07.99 Total balance, end of year	17	15	15

Program and Financing (in millions of dollars)

Identification code 69–5172–0–2–407	1999 actual	2000 est.	2001 est.
Obligations by program activity:			
Direct program:			
00.01 Operations	19	19	21
00.02 Research and development	1	2	2
00.03 Grants	14	16	24
09.01 Reimbursable program	....	5	5
10.00 Total new obligations	35	42	52
Budgetary resources available for obligation:			
21.40 Unobligated balance available, start of year	2	2	3
22.00 New budget authority (gross)	35	42	52
23.90 Total budgetary resources available for obligation	37	44	55
23.95 Total new obligations	−35	−42	−52
24.40 Unobligated balance available, end of year	2	3	3
New budget authority (gross), detail:			
Discretionary:			
40.20 Appropriation (special fund, definite)	30	31	43
Spending authority from offsetting collections:			
68.00 Offsetting collections (cash)	4	11	9
68.10 From Federal sources: Change in receivables and unpaid, unfilled orders	−1	....	....
68.15 From Federal sources: Adjustments to receivables and unpaid, unfilled orders	2	....	....
68.90 Spending authority from offsetting collections (total discretionary)	5	11	9
70.00 Total new budget authority (gross)	35	42	52
Change in unpaid obligations:			
Unpaid obligations, start of year:			
72.40 Obligated balance, start of year	15	14	16
72.95 From Federal sources: Receivables and unpaid, unfilled orders	4	3	3
72.99 Total unpaid obligations, start of year	19	17	19
73.10 Total new obligations	35	42	52
73.20 Total outlays (gross)	−34	−41	−45
73.40 Adjustments in expired accounts (net)	−2	....	....
Unpaid obligations, end of year:			
74.40 Obligated balance, end of year	14	16	23
74.95 From Federal sources: Receivables and unpaid, unfilled orders	3	3	3
74.99 Total unpaid obligations, end of year	17	19	26
Outlays (gross), detail:			
86.90 Outlays from new discretionary authority	19	26	30
86.93 Outlays from discretionary balances	15	14	15
87.00 Total outlays (gross)	34	41	45
Offsets:			
Against gross budget authority and outlays:			
88.00 Offsetting collections (cash) from: Federal sources	−4	−11	−9
Against gross budget authority only:			
88.95 From Federal sources: Change in receivables and unpaid, unfilled orders	1	....	....
88.96 From Federal sources: Adjustment to receivables and unpaid, unfilled orders	−2	....	....
Net budget authority and outlays:			
89.00 Budget authority	30	31	43
90.00 Outlays	31	30	36

The Research and Special Programs Administration is responsible for the Department's pipeline safety program, which takes a risk-based approach to oversee the safety and environmental protection of pipelines, through damage prevention, compliance, research and development, and grants for State pipeline safety programs and one-call centers.

Object Classification (in millions of dollars)

Identification code 69–5172–0–2–407	1999 actual	2000 est.	2001 est.
Direct obligations:			
11.1 Personnel compensation: Full-time permanent	6	7	8
12.1 Civilian personnel benefits	2	2	2
21.0 Travel and transportation	1	1	1
23.1 Rental payments to GSA	1	1	1
25.2 Other services	7	7	7
25.3 Purchases of goods and services from Government accounts	1	1	1
25.5 Research and development contracts	2	2	2
41.0 Grants, subsidies, and contributions	14	16	24
99.0 Subtotal, direct obligations	34	37	46
99.0 Reimbursable obligations	....	5	5
99.5 Below reporting threshold	1	....	1

99.9 Total new obligations	35	42	52

Personnel Summary

Identification code 69–5172–0–2–407	1999 actual	2000 est.	2001 est.
1001 Total compensable workyears: Full-time equivalent employment	93	105	105

EMERGENCY PREPAREDNESS GRANTS

(EMERGENCY PREPAREDNESS FUND)

For necessary expenses to carry out 49 U.S.C. 5127(c), $200,000, to be derived from the Emergency Preparedness Fund, to remain available until September 30, [2002] *2003*: *Provided*, That none of the funds made available by 49 U.S.C. 5116(i) and 5127(d) shall be made available for obligation by individuals other than the Secretary of Transportation, or his designee. *(Department of Transportation and Related Agencies Appropriations Act, 2000.)*

Unavailable Collections (in millions of dollars)

Identification code 69–5282–0–2–407	1999 actual	2000 est.	2001 est.
Balance, start of year:			
01.99 Balance, start of year			
Receipts:			
02.01 Emergency preparedness, hazardous materials	8	14	14
Appropriation:			
05.01 Emergency preparedness grants	−8	−14	−14
07.99 Total balance, end of year			

Program and Financing (in millions of dollars)

Identification code 69–5282–0–2–407	1999 actual	2000 est.	2001 est.
Obligations by program activity:			
00.01 Grants	8	13	13
00.02 Emergency response guidebook	1	1	1
10.00 Total new obligations	9	14	14
Budgetary resources available for obligation:			
21.40 Unobligated balance available, start of year	5	3	3
22.00 New budget authority (gross)	8	14	14
23.90 Total budgetary resources available for obligation	13	17	17
23.95 Total new obligations	−9	−14	−14
24.40 Unobligated balance available, end of year	3	3	3
New budget authority (gross), detail:			
Mandatory:			
60.25 Appropriation (special fund, indefinite)	8	14	14
Change in unpaid obligations:			
72.40 Unpaid obligations, start of year: Obligated balance, start of year	11	14	19
73.10 Total new obligations	9	14	14
73.20 Total outlays (gross)	−7	−10	−12
74.40 Unpaid obligations, end of year: Obligated balance, end of year	14	19	20
Outlays (gross), detail:			
86.97 Outlays from new mandatory authority	1	1	1
86.98 Outlays from mandatory balances	6	9	11
87.00 Total outlays (gross)	7	10	12
Net budget authority and outlays:			
89.00 Budget authority	8	14	14
90.00 Outlays	7	10	12

The Federal Hazardous Materials Transportation law (Federal hazmat law), 49 U.S.C. 5101 *et seq.*, establishes a national registration program of shippers and carriers of hazardous materials. The registrants finance, through fees, emergency preparedness planning and training grants programs, a training curriculum for emergency responders, and monitoring and technical assistance to States, political subdivisions, and Indian tribes. In the Federal hazmat law, there are permanent appropriations for the planning and training grants, monitoring and technical assistance, and for administrative expenses. As enacted for 2000, the Budget proposes to limit 2001 activities to those authorized for the Department of Transportation. Appropriations are requested for the training curriculum.

The Research and Special Programs Administration (RSPA) has proposed a rulemaking to increase the annual level of funding for the Emergency Preparedness Grants program to approximately $14.3 million prior to 2001.

Object Classification (in millions of dollars)

Identification code 69–5282–0–2–407	1999 actual	2000 est.	2001 est.
41.0 Grants, subsidies, and contributions	8	13	13
92.0 Undistributed	1	1	1
99.9 Total new obligations	9	14	14

Intragovernmental funds:

WORKING CAPITAL FUND, VOLPE NATIONAL TRANSPORTATION SYSTEMS CENTER

Program and Financing (in millions of dollars)

Identification code 69–4522–0–4–407	1999 actual	2000 est.	2001 est.
Obligations by program activity:			
10.00 Total new obligations	183	202	205
Budgetary resources available for obligation:			
21.40 Unobligated balance available, start of year	114	134	134
22.00 New budget authority (gross)	194	202	205
22.10 Resources available from recoveries of prior year obligations	9		
23.90 Total budgetary resources available for obligation	317	336	339
23.95 Total new obligations	−183	−202	−205
24.40 Unobligated balance available, end of year	134	134	134
New budget authority (gross), detail:			
Spending authority from offsetting collections:			
Discretionary:			
68.00 Offsetting collections (cash)	182	202	205
68.10 From Federal sources: Change in receivables and unpaid, unfilled orders	12		
68.90 Spending authority from offsetting collections (total discretionary)	194	202	205
Change in unpaid obligations:			
Unpaid obligations, start of year:			
72.40 Obligated balance, start of year	−52	−73	−73
72.95 From Federal sources: Receivables and unpaid, unfilled orders	151	163	163
72.99 Total unpaid obligations, start of year	99	90	90
73.10 Total new obligations	183	202	205
73.20 Total outlays (gross)	−183	−202	−205
73.45 Adjustments in unexpired accounts	−9		
Unpaid obligations, end of year:			
74.40 Obligated balance, end of year	−73	−73	−73
74.95 From Federal sources: Receivables and unpaid, unfilled orders	163	163	163
74.99 Total unpaid obligations, end of year	90	90	90
Outlays (gross), detail:			
86.90 Outlays from new discretionary authority	51	54	62
86.93 Outlays from discretionary balances	132	148	143
87.00 Total outlays (gross)	183	202	205
Offsets:			
Against gross budget authority and outlays:			
Offsetting collections (cash) from:			
88.00 Federal sources	−180	−199	−203
88.40 Non-Federal sources	−2	−3	−2

Intragovernmental funds—Continued

WORKING CAPITAL FUND, VOLPE NATIONAL TRANSPORTATION SYSTEMS CENTER—Continued

Program and Financing (in millions of dollars)—Continued

Identification code 69–4522–0–4–407	1999 actual	2000 est.	2001 est.
88.90 Total, offsetting collections (cash)	–182	–202	–205
Against gross budget authority only:			
88.95 From Federal sources: Change in receivables and unpaid, unfilled orders	–12		
Net budget authority and outlays:			
89.00 Budget authority			
90.00 Outlays	1		

The Working Capital Fund finances multidisciplinary research, evaluation, analytical and related activities undertaken at the Volpe National Transportation Systems Center (VNTSC) in Cambridge, MA. The fund is financed through negotiated agreements with the Office of the Secretary, Departmental operating administrations, and other governmental elements requiring the Center's capabilities. These agreements also define the activities undertaken at VNTSC.

Object Classification (in millions of dollars)

Identification code 69–4522–0–4–407	1999 actual	2000 est.	2001 est.
Personnel compensation:			
11.1 Full-time permanent	33	36	36
11.3 Other than full-time permanent	2	2	2
11.5 Other personnel compensation	1	1	1
11.9 Total personnel compensation	36	39	39
12.1 Civilian personnel benefits	7	8	8
21.0 Travel and transportation of persons	3	3	3
23.3 Communications, utilities, and miscellaneous charges	3	3	3
25.2 Other services	39	42	44
25.3 Purchases of goods and services from Government accounts	1	1	1
25.4 Operation and maintenance of facilities	3	3	3
25.5 Research and development contracts	76	90	91
26.0 Supplies and materials	3	2	2
31.0 Equipment	12	10	10
32.0 Land and structures		1	1
99.9 Total new obligations	183	202	205

Personnel Summary

Identification code 69–4522–0–4–407	1999 actual	2000 est.	2001 est.
2001 Total compensable workyears: Full-time equivalent employment	526	550	550

Trust Funds

TRUST FUND SHARE OF PIPELINE SAFETY

Program and Financing (in millions of dollars)

Identification code 69–8121–0–7–407	1999 actual	2000 est.	2001 est.
Obligations by program activity:			
10.00 Total new obligations (object class 92.0)	5	5	4
Budgetary resources available for obligation:			
21.40 Unobligated balance available, start of year	1	1	1
22.00 New budget authority (gross)	4	5	4
23.90 Total budgetary resources available for obligation	5	6	5
23.95 Total new obligations	–5	–5	–4
24.40 Unobligated balance available, end of year	1	1	1
New budget authority (gross), detail:			
Discretionary:			
40.26 Appropriation (trust fund, definite)	4	5	4
Change in unpaid obligations:			
72.40 Unpaid obligations, start of year: Obligated balance, start of year	5	5	5
73.10 Total new obligations	5	5	4
73.20 Total outlays (gross)	–4	–6	–5
74.40 Unpaid obligations, end of year: Obligated balance, end of year	5	5	4
Outlays (gross), detail:			
86.90 Outlays from new discretionary authority	2	2	2
86.93 Outlays from discretionary balances	2	3	3
87.00 Total outlays (gross)	4	6	5
Net budget authority and outlays:			
89.00 Budget authority	4	5	4
90.00 Outlays	4	6	5

The Oil Pollution Act of 1990 requires the preparation of oil spill response plans by pipeline operators to minimize the environmental impact of oil spills and to improve public and private sector response capabilities. The Office of Pipeline Safety is responsible for the review, approval and testing of these plans, and to ensure that the public and environment is provided with an adequate level of protection from such spills through data analysis, spill monitoring, pipeline mapping, environmental indexing, and advancing technologies to detect and prevent leaks.

OFFICE OF INSPECTOR GENERAL

Federal Funds

General and special funds:

SALARIES AND EXPENSES

For necessary expenses of the Office of Inspector General to carry out the provisions of the Inspector General Act of 1978, as amended, **[**$44,840,000**]** *$48,050,000***[**: *Provided*, That the Inspector General shall have all necessary authority, in carrying out the duties specified in the Inspector General Act, as amended (5 U.S.C. App. 3) to investigate allegations of fraud, including false statements to the Government (18 U.S.C. 1001), by any person or entity that is subject to regulation by the Department: *Provided further*, That the funds made available under this heading shall be used to investigate pursuant to section 41712 of title 49, United States Code, relating to unfair or deceptive practices and unfair methods of competition by domestic and foreign air carriers and ticket agents: *Provided further*, That it is the sense of the Senate, that for purposes of the preceding proviso, the terms "unfair or deceptive practices" and "unfair methods of competition" include the failure to disclose to a passenger or a ticket agent whether the flight on which the passenger is ticketed or has requested to purchase a ticket is overbooked, unless the Secretary certifies such disclosure by a carrier is technologically infeasible: *Provided further*, That the funds made available under this heading shall be used: (1) to investigate pursuant to section 41712 of title 49, United States Code, relating to unfair or deceptive practices and unfair methods of competition by air carriers and foreign air carriers; (2) for monitoring by the Inspector General of the compliance of domestic and foreign air carriers with respect to paragraph (1) of this proviso; and (3) for the submission to the appropriate committees of Congress by the Inspector General, not later than July 15, 2000, of a report on the extent to which actual or potential barriers exist to consumer access to comparative price and service information from independent sources on the purchase of passenger air transportation: *Provided further*, That it is the sense of the Senate, that for purposes of the preceding proviso, the terms "unfair or deceptive practices" and "unfair methods of competition" mean the offering for sale to the public for any route, class, and time of service through any technology or means of communication a fare that is different than that offered through other technology or means of communication: *Provided further*, That it is the sense of the Senate that funds made available under this heading shall be used for the submission to the appropriate committees of Congress by the Inspector General a report on the extent to which air carriers and foreign air carriers deny travel to airline consumers with nonrefundable tickets from one carrier to another**]**. *(Department of Transportation and Related Agencies Appropriations Act, 2000.)*

Program and Financing (in millions of dollars)

Identification code 69–0130–0–1–407	1999 actual	2000 est.	2001 est.
Obligations by program activity:			
01.01 General administration	44	45	48
09.01 Reimbursable program	1	4	5
10.00 Total new obligations	45	49	53
Budgetary resources available for obligation:			
21.40 Unobligated balance available, start of year		1	
22.00 New budget authority (gross)	45	48	53
23.90 Total budgetary resources available for obligation	45	49	53
23.95 Total new obligations	−45	−49	−53
24.40 Unobligated balance available, end of year	1		
New budget authority (gross), detail:			
Discretionary:			
40.00 Appropriation	43	44	48
Mandatory:			
62.00 Transferred from other accounts	1		
Discretionary:			
68.00 Spending authority from offsetting collections: Offsetting collections (cash)	1	4	5
70.00 Total new budget authority (gross)	45	48	53
Change in unpaid obligations:			
72.40 Unpaid obligations, start of year: Obligated balance, start of year	6	5	5
73.10 Total new obligations	45	49	53
73.20 Total outlays (gross)	−46	−48	−52
74.40 Unpaid obligations, end of year: Obligated balance, end of year	5	5	5
Outlays (gross), detail:			
86.90 Outlays from new discretionary authority	41	44	48
86.93 Outlays from discretionary balances	5	5	5
87.00 Total outlays (gross)	46	48	52
Offsets:			
Against gross budget authority and outlays:			
88.00 Offsetting collections (cash) from: Federal sources	−1	−4	−5
Net budget authority and outlays:			
89.00 Budget authority	44	44	48
90.00 Outlays	45	44	47

This appropriation finances the cost of conducting and supervising audits and investigations relating to the programs and operations of the Department to promote economy, efficiency and effectiveness and to prevent and detect fraud, waste, and abuse in such programs and operations. In addition, funding to audit and investigate highway and transit-related issues will be reimbursed from the Federal Highway Administration and the Federal Transit Administration.

Object Classification (in millions of dollars)

Identification code 69–0130–0–1–407	1999 actual	2000 est.	2001 est.
Direct obligations:			
Personnel compensation:			
11.1 Full-time permanent	27	27	28
11.5 Other personnel compensation	1	1	2
11.9 Total personnel compensation	28	28	30
12.1 Civilian personnel benefits	7	8	8
21.0 Travel and transportation of persons	3	3	3
23.1 Rental payments to GSA	3	3	3
25.3 Purchases of goods and services from Government accounts	1	1	1
31.0 Equipment	1		
99.0 Subtotal, direct obligations	43	43	45
99.0 Reimbursable obligations	1	4	5
99.5 Below reporting threshold	1	2	3
99.9 Total new obligations	45	49	53

Personnel Summary

Identification code 69–0130–0–1–407	1999 actual	2000 est.	2001 est.
Direct:			
1001 Total compensable workyears: Full-time equivalent employment	425	420	410
Reimbursable:			
2001 Total compensable workyears: Full-time equivalent employment	8	35	45

SURFACE TRANSPORTATION BOARD

Federal Funds

General and special funds:

SALARIES AND EXPENSES

For necessary expenses of the Surface Transportation Board, including services authorized by 5 U.S.C. 3109, [$17,000,000] *$17,054,000*: *Provided*, That notwithstanding any other provision of law, not to exceed [$1,600,000] *$900,000* from fees established by the Chairman of the Surface Transportation Board shall be credited to this appropriation as offsetting collections and used for necessary and authorized expenses under this heading: *Provided further*, That [the sum herein appropriated from the general fund shall be reduced on a dollar-for-dollar basis as such offsetting collections are received during fiscal year 2000, to result in a final appropriation from the general fund estimated at no more than $15,400,000] *any fees received in excess of $900,000 in fiscal year 2001 shall remain available until expended, but shall not be available for obligation until October 1, 2001. (Department of Transportation and Related Agencies Appropriations Act, 2000.)*

Program and Financing (in millions of dollars)

Identification code 69–0301–0–1–401	1999 actual	2000 est.	2001 est.
Obligations by program activity:			
Direct program:			
00.01 Rail carriers	14	14	15
00.02 Other surface transportation carriers	1	1	2
01.00 Total direct obligations	15	15	17
09.12 Reimbursable rail carriers	1	2	1
10.00 Total new obligations	16	17	18
Budgetary resources available for obligation:			
21.40 Unobligated balance available, start of year	1	1	1
22.00 New budget authority (gross)	16	17	18
23.90 Total budgetary resources available for obligation	17	18	19
23.95 Total new obligations	−16	−17	−18
24.40 Unobligated balance available, end of year	1	1	1
New budget authority (gross), detail:			
Discretionary:			
40.00 Appropriation	15	15	17
Spending authority from offsetting collections:			
68.00 Offsetting collections (cash)	1	2	1
68.10 From Federal sources: Change in receivables and unpaid, unfilled orders	1		
68.15 From Federal sources: Adjustments to receivables and unpaid, unfilled orders	−1		
68.90 Spending authority from offsetting collections (total discretionary)	1	2	1
70.00 Total new budget authority (gross)	16	17	18
Change in unpaid obligations:			
Unpaid obligations, start of year:			
72.40 Obligated balance, start of year	2	3	3
72.95 From Federal sources: Receivables and unpaid, unfilled orders		1	1
72.99 Total unpaid obligations, start of year	2	4	4
73.10 Total new obligations	16	17	18
73.20 Total outlays (gross)	−15	−18	−18
73.40 Adjustments in expired accounts (net)	1		
Unpaid obligations, end of year:			
74.40 Obligated balance, end of year	3	3	2

General and special funds—Continued

SALARIES AND EXPENSES—Continued

Program and Financing (in millions of dollars)—Continued

Identification code 69–0301–0–1–401	1999 actual	2000 est.	2001 est.
74.95 From Federal sources: Receivables and unpaid, unfilled orders	1	1	1
74.99 Total unpaid obligations, end of year	4	4	3
Outlays (gross), detail:			
86.90 Outlays from new discretionary authority	13	16	16
86.93 Outlays from discretionary balances	2	2	2
87.00 Total outlays (gross)	15	18	18
Offsets:			
Against gross budget authority and outlays:			
88.40 Offsetting collections (cash) from: Non-Federal sources	–1	–2	–1
Against gross budget authority only:			
88.95 From Federal sources: Change in receivables and unpaid, unfilled orders	–1		
88.96 From Federal sources: Adjustment to receivables and unpaid, unfilled orders	1		
Net budget authority and outlays:			
89.00 Budget authority	15	15	17
90.00 Outlays	15	16	17

Summary of Budget Authority and Outlays

(in millions of dollars)

Enacted/requested:	1999 actual	2000 est.	2001 est.
Budget Authority	15	15	17
Outlays	14	16	17
Legislative proposal, not subject to PAYGO:			
Budget Authority			–17
Outlays			–17
Total:			
Budget Authority	15	15	
Outlays	14	16	

The Surface Transportation Board was created on January 1, 1996, by P.L. 104–88, the ICC Termination Act of 1995 (ICCTA). The Board is specifically responsible for the regulation of the rail and pipeline industries and certain non-licensing regulation of motor carriers and water carriers.

Rail Carriers.—This regulatory oversight encompasses the regulation of rates, mergers, and acquisitions, construction, and abandonment of railroad lines, as well as the planning, analysis and policy development associated with these activities. Staff ensure compliance with railroad regulations in order to protect the public interest.

Other Surface Transportation Carriers.—This regulatory oversight includes certain regulation of the intercity bus industry and surface pipeline carriers as well as the rate regulation of water transportation in the non-contiguous domestic trade, household good carriers, and collectively determined motor rates and the processing of truck undercharge matters.

2001 Program Request.—A total of $17.954 million is requested to implement rulemakings and adjudicate the ongoing caseload within the directives and deadlines set forth by the ICCTA. The total program request amount is proposed to be derived from user fees collected from the beneficiaries of the Board's activities. This fee financing proposal stems from a proposal put forward by the Board's predecessor, the Interstate Commerce Commission (ICC). That proposal suggested ways of financing the ICC solely with fees and/or industry assessments. Fee financing will relieve the general taxpayer of the burden of supporting the Board. Further, fee financing will emphasize the accountability of the Board as to the value of the activities it provides to its customers.

The following paragraph is presented in compliance with Section 703 of the ICCTA. It is presented without change or correction.

The Board's Request to OMB.—The Board had submitted to the Secretary of Transportation and the Office of Management and Budget a 2001 appropriation request of $17.054 million and a request for $0.9 million from reimbursements from the offsetting collection of user fees. This funding request supports the required staffing, which mirrors the Board's 2000 budgetary authority granted to date, and is necessary for continued expeditious processing of the Board's caseload. The appropriation request included $17.0 million, the current level of funding provided by the 2000 Department of Transportation Appropriations Act, plus $0.954 million for annual pay and non-pay adjustments. The $0.9 million request from the offsetting collection of user fees is commensurate with the Board's projection for fee-related activities. The offsetting collection of user fees is based on the costs incurred by the Board for fee-related activities and is commensurate with the costs of processing parties' submissions. In past fiscal years, the Board received both an appropriation and authorization for offsetting collections to be made available to the appropriation for the Board's expenses. In light of Congressional action on the enacted FY 2000 appropriation act, the FY 2001 request reflects offsetting collections as a credit to the appropriation received, to the extent that they are collected.

This level of funding is necessary to implement rulemakings and adjudicate the ongoing caseload within the deadlines imposed by the ICCTA. The Board requires adequate resources to perform key functions under the ICCTA, including rail rate reasonableness oversight; the processing of rail consolidations, abandonments and other restructuring proposals; and the resolution of motor carrier undercharge matters.

Object Classification (in millions of dollars)

Identification code 69–0301–0–1–401	1999 actual	2000 est.	2001 est.
Direct obligations:			
11.1 Personnel compensation: Full-time permanent	10	10	11
12.1 Civilian personnel benefits	2	2	2
23.1 Rental payments to GSA	2	2	2
25.3 Purchases of goods and services from Government accounts	1	1	2
99.0 Subtotal, direct obligations	15	15	17
99.0 Reimbursable obligations	1	1	1
99.5 Below reporting threshold		1	
99.9 Total new obligations	16	17	18

Personnel Summary

Identification code 69–0301–0–1–401	1999 actual	2000 est.	2001 est.
Direct:			
1001 Total compensable workyears: Full-time equivalent employment	122	126	134
Reimbursable:			
2001 Total compensable workyears: Full-time equivalent employment	9	14	9

SALARIES AND EXPENSES

(Legislative proposal, not subject to PAYGO)

Contingent upon the enactment of authorizing legislation, the Chairman of the Surface Transportation Board (STB) shall charge additional user fees for services provided by the STB, and such fees shall be deposited as an offsetting collection to this appropriation, to remain available until expended: Provided further, That upon the enactment of such authorizing legislation, the amount appropriated above from the General Fund shall be reduced by $17,054,000.

Program and Financing (in millions of dollars)

Identification code 69–0301–2–1–401	1999 actual	2000 est.	2001 est.
Obligations by program activity:			
Direct program:			
00.01 Rail carriers	....	....	–15
00.02 Other surface transportation carriers	....	....	–2
01.00 Total direct obligations	....	....	–17
09.12 Reimbursable rail carriers	....	....	17
10.00 Total new obligations	....	....	....
New budget authority (gross), detail:			
Discretionary:			
40.00 Appropriation	....	....	–17
68.00 Spending authority from offsetting collections: Offsetting collections (cash)	....	....	17
70.00 Total new budget authority (gross)	....	....	....
Offsets:			
Against gross budget authority and outlays:			
88.40 Offsetting collections (cash) from: Non-Federal sources	....	....	–17
Net budget authority and outlays:			
89.00 Budget authority	....	....	–17
90.00 Outlays	....	....	–17

The Administration proposed legislation during the first session of the 106th Congress to authorize the collection and spending of a user fee for Surface Transportation Board services. If the proposed authorizing legislation is enacted, the proviso will reduce the General Fund appropriation by $17.054 million, the amount of the proposed user fee.

Object Classification (in millions of dollars)

Identification code 69–0301–2–1–401	1999 actual	2000 est.	2001 est.
Direct obligations:			
11.1 Personnel compensation: Full-time permanent	....	....	–11
12.1 Civilian personnel benefits	....	....	–2
23.1 Rental payments to GSA	....	....	–2
25.3 Purchases of goods and services from Government accounts	....	....	–2
99.0 Subtotal, direct obligations	....	....	–17
99.0 Reimbursable obligations	....	....	17
99.9 Total new obligations	....	....	....

Personnel Summary

Identification code 69–0301–2–1–401	1999 actual	2000 est.	2001 est.
Direct:			
1001 Total compensable workyears: Full-time equivalent employment	....	....	–134
Reimbursable:			
2001 Total compensable workyears: Full-time equivalent employment	....	....	134

BUREAU OF TRANSPORTATION STATISTICS

The Bureau's mission is to lead in developing transportation data and information of high quality, and to advance their use in both public and private transportation decision making.

The Bureau of Transportation Statistics (BTS) compiles, analyzes and publishes transportation statistics. BTS maintains the National Transportation Library and the National Transportation Atlas Data Base. It collects financial and operating statistics on airlines and motor carriers, and a variety of data on personal travel and freight transportation through national surveys. BTS is developing the Intermodal Transportation Data Base, to include information on the volume and patterns of movement of people and goods, the location and connectivity of transportation facilities and services, and a national accounting of expenditures and capital stocks for transportation.

Financing of the Bureau's operations is authorized as contract authority from the Highway Trust Fund and is included within the overall limitation on obligations for the Federal-aid program. The 2001 funding level is $31 million. Funds are transferred to BTS from Federal-aid Highways, where all obligations and outlays are counted.

MARITIME ADMINISTRATION

The Maritime Administration (MARAD) is responsible for programs authorized by the Merchant Marine Act, 1936, as amended, and other related acts, to promote a strong U.S. Merchant Marine. Emphasis is placed on increasing the competitiveness and productivity of the U.S. maritime industries as well as ensuring adequate seafaring manpower for peacetime and national emergencies. Programs include: providing operating aid to U.S.-flag operators; administering the Maritime Guaranteed Loan (Title XI) portfolio; reimbursing the Commodity Credit Corporation for the expanded cargo preference requirement in the Food Security Act of 1985; preserving and maintaining merchant ships retained in the National Defense Reserve Fleet including the Ready Reserve Force; emergency planning and coordination; promoting port and intermodal development; and conducting Federal technology assessment projects.

The following table shows the funding for the Maritime Administration programs:

[In millions of dollars]

	1999 actual	2000 est.	2001 est.
Budget authority:			
Maritime security program (054)	90	96	99
Ocean freight differential	16	75	26
Operations and training	72	72	80
Maritime guaranteed loan program (Title XI) (403)	10	10	6
Subsidy re-estimate	....	55	....
Rescission, Ship construction	–17	....	....
Total budget authority	171	308	211
Direct obligations:			
Maritime security program (054)	95	99	99
Ocean freight differential	16	75	26
Operations and training	70	73	80
Ready reserve force [1]	14	7	3
Federal ship financing fund	2	7	7
War risk insurance revolving fund	0	1	1
Maritime guaranteed loan program (Title XI) (403)	60	80	6
Subsidy re-estimate	....	55	....
Obligations, total direct	257	397	222
Outlays:			
Operating-differential subsidies	17	15	11
Maritime security program (054)	94	101	99
Ocean freight differential	16	75	26
Operations and training	57	92	85
Ready reserve force [1]	15	12	6
Vessel operations revolving fund	–56	–103	–27
War risk insurance revolving fund	–2	–1	–1
Federal ship financing fund	–5	–7	–7
Maritime guaranteed loan program (Title XI) (403)	–12	120	6
Subsidy re-estimate	....	55	....
Total outlays	124	359	198

[1] Appropriated directly to MARAD prior to 1996.

Federal Funds

General and special funds:

SHIP CONSTRUCTION

Program and Financing (in millions of dollars)

Identification code 69–1708–0–1–403	1999 actual	2000 est.	2001 est.
Budgetary resources available for obligation:			
21.40 Unobligated balance available, start of year	17		
22.00 New budget authority (gross)	−17		
23.90 Total budgetary resources available for obligation			
New budget authority (gross), detail:			
Discretionary:			
40.36 Unobligated balance rescinded	−17		
Net budget authority and outlays:			
89.00 Budget authority	−17		
90.00 Outlays			

The Ship Construction account is currently inactive except for determinations regarding the use of vessels built under the program, final settlement of open contracts, and closing of financial accounts.

OPERATING-DIFFERENTIAL SUBSIDIES
(LIQUIDATION OF CONTRACT AUTHORITY)

Program and Financing (in millions of dollars)

Identification code 69–1709–0–1–403	1999 actual	2000 est.	2001 est.
Change in unpaid obligations:			
72.40 Unpaid obligations, start of year: Obligated balance, start of year	79	55	40
73.20 Total outlays (gross)	−17	−15	−11
73.40 Adjustments in expired accounts (net)	−7		
74.40 Unpaid obligations, end of year: Obligated balance, end of year	55	40	29
Outlays (gross), detail:			
86.93 Outlays from discretionary balances	17	15	11
Net budget authority and outlays:			
89.00 Budget authority			
90.00 Outlays	17	15	11

The Operating-Differential Subsidies (ODS) account helps to maintain a U.S.-flag merchant fleet to serve both the commercial and national security needs of the U.S. by providing operating subsides to U.S.-flag ship operators to offset certain differences between U.S. and foreign operating costs. Appropriations are provided to liquidate contract authority. This program has been replaced by the Maritime Security Program. Existing liquidating cash on hand is expected to be sufficient to honor existing contracts. No new ODS contracts will be entered into and no existing contracts will be modified.

MARITIME SECURITY PROGRAM

For necessary expenses to maintain and preserve a U.S.-flag merchant fleet to serve the national security needs of the United States, [$96,200,000] *$98,700,000*, to remain available until expended. *(Departments of Commerce, Justice, and State, the Judiciary and Related Agencies Appropriations Act, 2000, as enacted by section 1000(a)(1) of the Consolidated Appropriations Act, 2000 (P.L. 106–113).)*

Program and Financing (in millions of dollars)

Identification code 69–1711–0–1–054	1999 actual	2000 est.	2001 est.
Obligations by program activity:			
10.00 Total new obligations (object class 41.0)	95	101	99
Budgetary resources available for obligation:			
21.40 Unobligated balance available, start of year	8	3	
22.00 New budget authority (gross)	90	96	99
23.90 Total budgetary resources available for obligation	98	99	99
23.95 Total new obligations	−95	−101	−99
24.40 Unobligated balance available, end of year	3		
New budget authority (gross), detail:			
Discretionary:			
40.00 Appropriation	90	96	99
Change in unpaid obligations:			
72.40 Unpaid obligations, start of year: Obligated balance, start of year	8	9	8
73.10 Total new obligations	95	101	99
73.20 Total outlays (gross)	−94	−101	−99
74.40 Unpaid obligations, end of year: Obligated balance, end of year	9	8	7
Outlays (gross), detail:			
86.90 Outlays from new discretionary authority	83	89	92
86.93 Outlays from discretionary balances	11	12	7
87.00 Total outlays (gross)	94	101	99
Net budget authority and outlays:			
89.00 Budget authority	90	96	99
90.00 Outlays	94	101	99

The Maritime Security Program provides resources to maintain a U.S.-flag merchant fleet crewed by U.S. citizens to serve both the commercial and national security needs of the United States. The program provides direct payments to U.S.-flag ship operators engaged in U.S.-foreign trade. Participating operators are required to keep the vessels in active commercial service and are required to provide intermodal sealift support to the Department of Defense in times of war or national emergency.

OCEAN FREIGHT DIFFERENTIAL

Program and Financing (in millions of dollars)

Identification code 69–1751–0–1–403	1999 actual	2000 est.	2001 est.
Obligations by program activity:			
10.00 Total new obligations (object class 22.0)	16	75	26
Budgetary resources available for obligation:			
22.00 New budget authority (gross)	16	75	26
23.95 Total new obligations	−16	−75	−26
New budget authority (gross), detail:			
Mandatory:			
60.05 Appropriation (indefinite)	16	75	26
60.47 Portion applied to repay debt	−16	−75	−26
62.50 Appropriation (total mandatory)			
67.15 Authority to borrow (indefinite)	16	75	26
70.00 Total new budget authority (gross)	16	75	26
Change in unpaid obligations:			
73.10 Total new obligations	16	75	26
73.20 Total outlays (gross)	−16	−75	−26
Outlays (gross), detail:			
86.97 Outlays from new mandatory authority	16	75	26
Net budget authority and outlays:			
89.00 Budget authority	16	75	26
90.00 Outlays	16	75	26

Public Law 99–198 amended section 901 of the Merchant Marine Act to increase from 50 to 75 percent the amount of agricultural commodities under specified programs that must be carried on U.S.-flag vessels. The increased cost associated with this expanded U.S.-flag shipping requirement stems from higher rates charged by U.S.-flag carriers compared with foreign-flag carriers. The Maritime Administration is required to reimburse the Department of Agriculture for ocean freight differential costs for the added tonnage above 50 percent. These reimbursements are funded through borrowings from the Treasury. This account has a permanent, indefinite appropriation to liquidate debt provided in Public Law 100–202 to cover these costs.

The Maritime Administration's ocean freight differential costs are one portion of the government's cargo preference program. The ocean transportation subsidy costs related to cargo preference for all relevant agencies are presented in the following schedule.

CARGO PREFERENCE PROGRAM COSTS

[In millions of dollars]

	1999 actual		*2000 est.*		*2001 est.*	
	Obligations	*Outlays*	*Obligations*	*Outlays*	*Obligations*	*Outlays*
AGENCY:						
Department of Agriculture	85	100	212	205	53	67
Department of Transportation—Maritime Administration	16	16	75	75	26	25
Department of Defense (1998 nos.)	303	303	291	291	294	294
Agency for International Development	3	3	3	3	3	3
Export–Import Bank of the U.S.	7	19	21	14	21	15
Department of State	1	1	1	1	1	1
Total	415	442	603	589	398	405

Operations and Training

For necessary expenses of operations and training activities authorized by law, [$72,073,000] *$80,240,000. (Departments of Commerce, Justice, and State, the Judiciary and Related Agencies Appropriations Act, 2000, as enacted by section 1000(a)(1) of the Consolidated Appropriations Act, 2000 (P.L. 106–113).)*

Program and Financing (in millions of dollars)

Identification code 69–1750–0–1–403		1999 actual	2000 est.	2001 est.
	Obligations by program activity:			
	Direct program:			
00.01	Merchant Marine Academy	32	34	37
00.02	State marine schools	7	7	10
00.03	MARAD operations	31	32	33
01.00	Subtotal, Direct program	70	73	80
09.01	Reimbursable program	41	57	57
10.00	Total new obligations	111	130	137
	Budgetary resources available for obligation:			
22.00	New budget authority (gross)	113	130	137
23.95	Total new obligations	−111	−130	−137
23.98	Unobligated balance expiring or withdrawn	−1		
	New budget authority (gross), detail:			
	Discretionary:			
40.00	Appropriation	71	72	80
42.00	Transferred from other accounts	1		
43.00	Appropriation (total discretionary)	72	72	80
50.00	Reappropriation		1	
	Spending authority from offsetting collections:			
68.00	Offsetting collections (cash)	119	57	57
68.10	From Federal sources: Change in receivables and unpaid, unfilled orders	−79		
68.15	From Federal sources: Adjustments to receivables and unpaid, unfilled orders	1		
68.90	Spending authority from offsetting collections (total discretionary)	41	57	57
70.00	Total new budget authority (gross)	113	130	137
	Change in unpaid obligations:			
	Unpaid obligations, start of year:			
72.40	Obligated balance, start of year	26	41	21
72.95	From Federal sources: Receivables and unpaid, unfilled orders	86	7	7
72.99	Total unpaid obligations, start of year	112	48	28
73.10	Total new obligations	111	130	137
73.20	Total outlays (gross)	−175	−149	−143
	Unpaid obligations, end of year:			
74.40	Obligated balance, end of year	41	21	16
74.95	From Federal sources: Receivables and unpaid, unfilled orders	7	7	7
74.99	Total unpaid obligations, end of year	48	28	23
	Outlays (gross), detail:			
86.90	Outlays from new discretionary authority	89	119	125
86.93	Outlays from discretionary balances	86	31	18
87.00	Total outlays (gross)	175	149	143
	Offsets:			
	Against gross budget authority and outlays:			
	Offsetting collections (cash) from:			
	Federal sources:			
88.00	Ready Reserve Force/National Defense Reserve Fleet	−38	−38	−38
88.00	Merchant Marine Academy	−1	−1	−1
88.00	ARPA—Maritech program	−2	−2	−2
88.00	Title XI Administrative expenses	−4	−4	−4
88.00	Marine Board research program and others	−74	−12	−12
88.90	Total, offsetting collections (cash)	−119	−57	−57
	Against gross budget authority only:			
88.95	From Federal sources: Change in receivables and unpaid, unfilled orders	79		
88.96	From Federal sources: Adjustment to receivables and unpaid, unfilled orders	−1		
	Net budget authority and outlays:			
89.00	Budget authority	72	73	80
90.00	Outlays	56	92	86

This appropriation finances costs incurred by headquarters and region staffs in the administration and direction of Maritime Administration programs; the total cost of officer training at the U.S. Merchant Marine Academy as well as Federal financial support to six state maritime academies; planning for coordination of U.S. maritime industry activities under emergency conditions; activities promoting port and intermodal development; activities under the American Fisheries Act; and Federal technology assessment projects designed to achieve advancements in ship design, construction and operations.

Object Classification (in millions of dollars)

Identification code 69–1750–0–1–403		1999 actual	2000 est.	2001 est.
	Direct obligations:			
	Personnel compensation:			
11.1	Full-time permanent	28	29	30
11.3	Other than full-time permanent	3	3	3
11.5	Other personnel compensation	1	1	1
11.9	Total personnel compensation	32	33	34
12.1	Civilian personnel benefits	7	7	7
21.0	Travel and transportation of persons	1	1	1
23.1	Rental payments to GSA	1	3	3
23.3	Communications, utilities, and miscellaneous charges	2	2	2
25.2	Other services	14	13	12
25.3	Purchases of goods and services from Government accounts	3	3	5
25.4	Operation and maintenance of facilities	3	3	8
26.0	Supplies and materials	4	4	4
31.0	Equipment	2	2	2
41.0	Grants, subsidies, and contributions	2	2	2
99.0	Subtotal, direct obligations	71	73	80
99.0	Reimbursable obligations	40	57	57
99.9	Total new obligations	111	130	137

General and special funds—Continued

OPERATIONS AND TRAINING—Continued

Personnel Summary

Identification code 69–1750–0–1–403	1999 actual	2000 est.	2001 est.
Direct:			
1001 Total compensable workyears: Full-time equivalent employment	420	472	477
Reimbursable:			
2001 Total compensable workyears: Full-time equivalent employment	498	498	470

READY RESERVE FORCE

Program and Financing (in millions of dollars)

Identification code 69–1710–0–1–054	1999 actual	2000 est.	2001 est.
Obligations by program activity:			
00.02 Maintenance and operations	14	7	3
10.00 Total new obligations (object class 25.2)	14	7	3
Budgetary resources available for obligation:			
21.40 Unobligated balance available, start of year	21	13	6
22.10 Resources available from recoveries of prior year obligations	7		
23.90 Total budgetary resources available for obligation	28	13	6
23.95 Total new obligations	−14	−7	−3
24.40 Unobligated balance available, end of year	13	6	3
Change in unpaid obligations:			
72.40 Unpaid obligations, start of year: Obligated balance, start of year	17	9	4
73.10 Total new obligations	14	7	3
73.20 Total outlays (gross)	−15	−12	−5
73.45 Adjustments in unexpired accounts	−7		
74.40 Unpaid obligations, end of year: Obligated balance, end of year	9	4	1
Outlays (gross), detail:			
86.93 Outlays from discretionary balances	15	12	5
Net budget authority and outlays:			
89.00 Budget authority			
90.00 Outlays	15	12	5

Funding for the Ready Reserve Force (RRF) account is included in appropriations for the Department of Defense. Management of the RRF remains with MARAD. Reimbursements from the Department of Defense for the RRF account are reflected in MARAD's Vessel Operations Revolving Fund account. Obligations shown above are the spendout of funding appropriated directly to MARAD prior to 1996 for the RRF.

The RRF is comprised of Government-owned, U.S.-flag merchant ships laid up in the National Defense Reserve Fleet (NDRF). The RRF is maintained in an advanced state of readiness to meet surge shipping requirements during a national emergency.

Public enterprise funds:

VESSEL OPERATIONS REVOLVING FUND

Program and Financing (in millions of dollars)

Identification code 69–4303–0–3–403	1999 actual	2000 est.	2001 est.
Obligations by program activity:			
10.00 Total new obligations	302	420	344
Budgetary resources available for obligation:			
21.40 Unobligated balance available, start of year	18	37	37
22.00 New budget authority (gross)	312	420	344
22.10 Resources available from recoveries of prior year obligations	8		
23.90 Total budgetary resources available for obligation	338	457	381
23.95 Total new obligations	−302	−420	−344
24.40 Unobligated balance available, end of year	37	37	37
New budget authority (gross), detail:			
Spending authority from offsetting collections:			
Discretionary:			
68.00 Offsetting collections (cash)	533	420	344
68.10 From Federal sources: Change in receivables and unpaid, unfilled orders	−221		
68.90 Spending authority from offsetting collections (total discretionary)	312	420	344
Change in unpaid obligations:			
Unpaid obligations, start of year:			
72.40 Obligated balance, start of year	−19	18	121
72.95 From Federal sources: Receivables and unpaid, unfilled orders	360	139	139
72.99 Total unpaid obligations, start of year	341	157	260
73.10 Total new obligations	302	420	344
73.20 Total outlays (gross)	−477	−317	−317
73.45 Adjustments in unexpired accounts	−8		
Unpaid obligations, end of year:			
74.40 Obligated balance, end of year	18	121	148
74.95 From Federal sources: Receivables and unpaid, unfilled orders	139	139	139
74.99 Total unpaid obligations, end of year	157	260	287
Outlays (gross), detail:			
86.90 Outlays from new discretionary authority	256	365	241
86.93 Outlays from discretionary balances	221	−48	76
87.00 Total outlays (gross)	477	317	317
Offsets:			
Against gross budget authority and outlays:			
88.00 Offsetting collections (cash) from: Ready Reserve Force	−533	−420	−344
Against gross budget authority only:			
88.95 From Federal sources: Change in receivables and unpaid, unfilled orders	221		
Net budget authority and outlays:			
89.00 Budget authority			
90.00 Outlays	−56	−103	−27

The Maritime Administration is authorized to reactivate, operate, deactivate, and charter merchant vessels. These operations are financed through the Vessel Operations Revolving Fund with reimbursements from sponsoring agencies. In addition, the fund is available to finance the necessary expenses to protect, maintain, preserve, acquire, and use vessels involved in mortgage foreclosure or forfeiture proceedings instituted by the United States other than those financed by the Federal Ship Financing Fund or the Maritime Guaranteed Loan (Title XI) Financing Account; and to process advances received from Federal agencies. Also the acquisition and disposal of ships under the trade-in/scrap-out program is financed through this account.

Reimbursements from other Federal agencies also pay for various DOD/Navy-sponsored activities, such as the operation of activated RRF vessels, installation of sealift enhancement features and other special projects. The Vessel Operations Revolving Fund account includes DOD/Navy reimbursements for the RRF account. DOD/Navy funding for RRF provides for additional RRF vessels, RRF ship activations and deactivations, maintaining RRF ships in an advanced state of readiness, berthing costs, capital improvements at fleet sites, and other RRF support costs.

Object Classification (in millions of dollars)

Identification code 69–4303–0–3–403	1999 actual	2000 est.	2001 est.
21.0 Travel and transportation of persons	1	3	3
23.3 Communications, utilities, and miscellaneous charges	5	11	15
24.0 Printing and reproduction	1	1	1
25.2 Other services	280	378	291

26.0	Supplies and materials	13	25	32
31.0	Equipment	1	1	1
42.0	Insurance claims and indemnities	1	1	1
99.9	Total new obligations	302	420	344

War Risk Insurance Revolving Fund

Program and Financing (in millions of dollars)

Identification code 69–4302–0–3–403		1999 actual	2000 est.	2001 est.
	Obligations by program activity:			
10.00	Total new obligations (object class 25.2)		1	1
	Budgetary resources available for obligation:			
21.40	Unobligated balance available, start of year	29	31	32
22.00	New budget authority (gross)	2	2	2
23.90	Total budgetary resources available for obligation	31	33	34
23.95	Total new obligations		−1	−1
24.40	Unobligated balance available, end of year	31	32	33
	New budget authority (gross), detail:			
	Discretionary:			
68.00	Spending authority from offsetting collections (gross): Offsetting collections (cash)	2	2	2
	Change in unpaid obligations:			
73.10	Total new obligations		1	1
73.20	Total outlays (gross)		−1	−1
	Outlays (gross), detail:			
86.90	Outlays from new discretionary authority	2	2	2
86.93	Outlays from discretionary balances	−1	−1	−1
87.00	Total outlays (gross)		1	1
	Offsets:			
	Against gross budget authority and outlays:			
88.20	Offsetting collections (cash) from: Interest on U.S. securities	−2	−2	−2
	Net budget authority and outlays:			
89.00	Budget authority			
90.00	Outlays	−1	−1	−1
	Memorandum (non-add) entries:			
92.01	Total investments, start of year: U.S. securities: Par value	27	28	30
92.02	Total investments, end of year: U.S. securities: Par value	28	30	31

The Maritime Administration is authorized to insure against loss or damage from marine war risks until commercial insurance can be obtained on reasonable terms and conditions. This insurance includes war risk hull and disbursements interim insurance, war risk protection and indemnity interim insurance, second seamen's war risk interim insurance, and war risk cargo insurance standby program.

Credit accounts:

Federal Ship Financing Fund Liquidating Account

Program and Financing (in millions of dollars)

Identification code 69–4301–0–3–403		1999 actual	2000 est.	2001 est.
	Obligations by program activity:			
00.01	Operating expenses	3	2	2
01.01	Default claims		5	5
10.00	Total new obligations	3	7	7
	Budgetary resources available for obligation:			
21.40	Unobligated balance available, start of year	52		
22.00	New budget authority (gross)	4	7	7
22.40	Capital transfer to general fund	−51	−2	
23.90	Total budgetary resources available for obligation	5	5	7
23.95	Total new obligations	−3	−7	−7
	New budget authority (gross), detail:			
	Mandatory:			
69.00	Offsetting collections (cash)	11	7	7
69.10	From Federal sources: Change in receivables and unpaid, unfilled orders	−7		
69.90	Spending authority from offsetting collections (total mandatory)	4	7	7
	Change in unpaid obligations:			
	Unpaid obligations, start of year:			
72.40	Obligated balance, start of year	−4		7
72.95	From Federal sources: Receivables and unpaid, unfilled orders	7		
72.99	Total unpaid obligations, start of year	3		7
73.10	Total new obligations	3	7	7
73.20	Total outlays (gross)	−6		
	Unpaid obligations, end of year:			
74.40	Obligated balance, end of year		7	14
74.95	From Federal sources: Receivables and unpaid, unfilled orders			
74.99	Total unpaid obligations, end of year		7	14
	Outlays (gross), detail:			
86.97	Outlays from new mandatory authority	4		
86.98	Outlays from mandatory balances	2		
87.00	Total outlays (gross)	6		
	Offsets:			
	Against gross budget authority and outlays:			
	Offsetting collections (cash) from:			
88.20	Interest on U.S. securities	−3	−1	
	Non-Federal sources:			
88.40	Insurance premiums and fees	−3	−2	−2
88.40	Repayment of loans	−3	−2	−3
88.40	Interest and other income	−2	−2	−2
88.90	Total, offsetting collections (cash)	−11	−7	−7
	Against gross budget authority only:			
88.95	From Federal sources: Change in receivables and unpaid, unfilled orders	7		
	Net budget authority and outlays:			
89.00	Budget authority			
90.00	Outlays	−5	−7	−7
	Memorandum (non-add) entries:			
92.01	Total investments, start of year: U.S. securities: Par value	45		

Status of Guaranteed Loans (in millions of dollars)

Identification code 69–4301–0–3–403		1999 actual	2000 est.	2001 est.
	Cumulative balance of guaranteed loans outstanding:			
2210	Outstanding, start of year	397	321	269
2251	Repayments and prepayments	−72	−52	−57
2261	Adjustments: Terminations for default that result in loans receivable	−4		
2290	Outstanding, end of year	321	269	212
	Memorandum:			
2299	Guaranteed amount of guaranteed loans outstanding, end of year	321	269	212
	Addendum:			
	Cumulative balance of defaulted guaranteed loans that result in loans receivable:			
2310	Outstanding, start of year	46	20	15
2331	Disbursements for guaranteed loan claims	4		
2351	Repayments of loans receivable	−30	−5	−5
2390	Outstanding, end of year	20	15	10

The Merchant Marine Act of 1936, as amended, established the Federal Ship Financing Fund to assist in the development of the U.S. merchant marine by guaranteeing construction loans and mortgages on U.S.-flag vessels built in the United

Credit accounts—Continued

FEDERAL SHIP FINANCING FUND LIQUIDATING ACCOUNT—Continued

States. No new commitments for loan guarantees are projected for the Federal Ship Financing Fund as this Fund is used only to underwrite guarantees made under the Title XI loan guarantee program prior to 1992.

Statement of Operations (in millions of dollars)

Identification code 69–4301–0–3–403	1998 actual	1999 actual	2000 est.	2001 est.
0101 Revenue	9	9	6	5
0102 Expense	–9	–9	–6	–5
0105 Net income or loss (–)	....	....	....	....

Balance Sheet (in millions of dollars)

Identification code 69–4301–0–3–403	1998 actual	1999 actual	2000 est.	2001 est.
ASSETS:				
Federal assets:				
1101 Fund balances with Treasury	4	2	....	....
Investments in US securities:				
1102 Treasury securities, par	35	....	....	....
1106 Receivables, net	1	....	....	....
1206 Non-Federal assets: Receivables, net	7	6	5	4
1803 Other Federal assets: Property, plant and equipment, net	4	1	1	1
1999 Total assets	51	9	6	5
LIABILITIES:				
2201 Non-Federal liabilities: Accounts payable	1	1	1	1
2999 Total liabilities	1	1	1	1
NET POSITION:				
3300 Cumulative results of operations	50	8	5	4
3999 Total net position	50	8	5	4
4999 Total liabilities and net position	51	9	6	5

Object Classification (in millions of dollars)

Identification code 69–4301–0–3–403	1999 actual	2000 est.	2001 est.
25.2 Other services	3	2	2
33.0 Investments and loans	....	5	5
99.9 Total new obligations	3	7	7

MARITIME GUARANTEED LOAN (TITLE XI) PROGRAM ACCOUNT

For the cost of guaranteed loans, as authorized by the Merchant Marine Act, 1936, **[**$6,000,000**]** *$2,000,000*, to remain available until expended: *Provided*, That such costs, including the cost of modifying such loans, shall be as defined in section 502 of the Congressional Budget Act of 1974, as amended**[**: *Provided further*, That these funds are available to subsidize total loan principal, any part of which is to be guaranteed, not to exceed $1,000,000,000**]**.

In addition, for administrative expenses to carry out the guaranteed loan program, not to exceed **[**$3,809,000**]** *$4,179,000*, which shall be transferred to and merged with the appropriation for Operations and Training. *(Departments of Commerce, Justice, and State, the Judiciary and Related Agencies Appropriations Act, 2000, as enacted by section 1000(a)(1) of the Consolidated Appropriations Act, 2000 (P.L. 106–113).)*

General Fund Credit Receipt Accounts (in millions of dollars)

Identification code 69–1752–0–1–403	1999 actual	2000 est.	2001 est.
0101 Maritime (Title XI) loan program, downward reestimates of subsidies	84	29	....

Program and Financing (in millions of dollars)

Identification code 69–1752–0–1–403	1999 actual	2000 est.	2001 est.
Obligations by program activity:			
00.02 Loan guarantee subsidy	56	77	2
00.07 Reestimates of loan guarantee subsidy	....	50	....
00.08 Interest on reestimates of loan guarantee subsidy	....	5	....
00.09 Administrative expense	4	4	4
10.00 Total new obligations	60	136	6
Budgetary resources available for obligation:			
21.40 Unobligated balance available, start of year	71	71	....
22.00 New budget authority (gross)	56	65	6
22.10 Resources available from recoveries of prior year obligations	4	....	....
23.90 Total budgetary resources available for obligation	131	136	6
23.95 Total new obligations	–60	–136	–6
24.40 Unobligated balance available, end of year	71	....	....
New budget authority (gross), detail:			
Discretionary:			
40.00 Appropriation	10	10	6
Mandatory:			
60.05 Appropriation (indefinite)	....	55	....
Discretionary:			
68.00 Spending authority from offsetting collections: Offsetting collections (cash)	46	....	....
70.00 Total new budget authority (gross)	56	65	6
Change in unpaid obligations:			
72.40 Unpaid obligations, start of year: Obligated balance, start of year	18	40	....
73.10 Total new obligations	60	136	6
73.20 Total outlays (gross)	–34	–175	–6
73.45 Adjustments in unexpired accounts	–4	....	....
74.40 Unpaid obligations, end of year: Obligated balance, end of year	40	....	....
Outlays (gross), detail:			
86.90 Outlays from new discretionary authority	10	10	6
86.93 Outlays from discretionary balances	24	110	....
86.97 Outlays from new mandatory authority	....	55	....
87.00 Total outlays (gross)	34	175	6
Offsets:			
Against gross budget authority and outlays:			
88.00 Offsetting collections (cash) from: Federal sources	–46	....	....
Net budget authority and outlays:			
89.00 Budget authority	10	65	6
90.00 Outlays	–12	175	6

Summary of Loan Levels, Subsidy Budget Authority and Outlays by Program (in millions of dollars)

Identification code 69–1752–0–1–403	1999 actual	2000 est.	2001 est.
Guaranteed loan levels supportable by subsidy budget authority:			
2150 Risk category 1A	....	90	....
2150 Risk category 1B	....	110	....
2150 Risk category 1C	....	110	....
2150 Risk category 2A	1,714	875	35
2150 Risk category 2B	38	140	5
2150 Risk category 2C	15	125	....
2150 Risk category 3	....	55	....
2159 Total loan guarantee levels	1,767	1,505	40
Guaranteed loan subsidy (in percent):			
2320 Risk category 1A	0.00	2.09	2.12
2320 Risk category 1B	0.00	2.61	2.64
2320 Risk category 1C	0.00	3.10	3.14
2320 Risk category 2A	2.98	4.72	4.77
2320 Risk category 2B	4.62	6.34	6.40
2320 Risk category 2C	7.55	7.92	7.99
2320 Risk category 3	0.00	12.85	12.96
2329 Weighted average subsidy rate	3.05	5.00	4.97
Guaranteed loan subsidy budget authority:			
2330 Risk category 1A	....	2	....
2330 Risk category 1B	....	4	....
2330 Risk category 1C	....	4	....
2330 Risk category 2A	51	39	2
2330 Risk category 2B	2	19	....
2330 Risk category 2C	1	21	....
2330 Risk category 3	....	14	....
2339 Total subsidy budget authority	54	103	2

		1999 actual	2000 est.	2001 est.
	Guaranteed loan subsidy outlays:			
2340	Risk category 1A		2	
2340	Risk category 1B		4	
2340	Risk category 1C		4	
2340	Risk category 2A	21	65	1
2340	Risk category 2B	6	30	1
2340	Risk category 2C	3	23	
2340	Risk category 3		14	
2349	Total subsidy outlays	30	142	2
	Administrative expense data:			
3510	Budget authority	4	4	4
3590	Outlays from new authority	4	4	4

This program provides for guaranteed loans for purchasers of ships from the U.S. shipbuilding industry and for modernization of U.S. shipyards.

As required by the Federal Credit Reform Act of 1990, this account includes the subsidy costs associated with the loan guarantee commitments made in 1992 and beyond (including modifications of direct loans or loan guarantees that resulted from obligations or commitments in any year), as well as administrative expenses of this program. The subsidy amounts are estimated on a present value basis, the administrative expenses are estimated on a cash basis.

Funds for administrative expenses for the Title XI program are appropriated to this account, then transferred by reimbursement to the Operations and Training account to be obligated and outlayed. The schedule above shows the post-transfer amounts for 1999. For 2000 and 2001, the schedule displays pre-transfer amounts in order to comply with the Federal Credit Reform Act of 1990.

Object Classification (in millions of dollars)

Identification code 69–1752–0–1–403		1999 actual	2000 est.	2001 est.
25.2	Other services	4	4	4
41.0	Grants, subsidies, and contributions	56	132	2
99.9	Total new obligations	60	136	6

Maritime Guaranteed Loan (Title XI) Financing Account

Program and Financing (in millions of dollars)

Identification code 69–4304–0–3–999		1999 actual	2000 est.	2001 est.
	Obligations by program activity:			
00.01	Subsidy returned to program account	46		
00.03	Accounting Adjustment	41		
00.91	Subtotal of new obligations	87		
08.02	Obligations for downward reestimates	72	23	
08.04	Interest on reestimates	13	6	
08.91	Subtotal of reestimate obligations	85	29	
10.00	Total new obligations	172	29	
	Budgetary resources available for obligation:			
21.40	Unobligated balance available, start of year	246	190	457
22.00	New financing authority (gross)	72	295	76
22.10	Resources available from recoveries of prior year obligations	45		
23.90	Total budgetary resources available for obligation	363	485	533
23.95	Total new obligations	−172	−29	
24.40	Unobligated balance available, end of year	190	457	533
	New financing authority (gross), detail:			
	Discretionary:			
68.00	Spending authority from offsetting collections (gross): Offsetting collections (cash)	72	295	76
	Change in unpaid obligations:			
73.10	Total new obligations	172	29	
73.20	Total financing disbursements (gross)	−128	−29	
73.45	Adjustments in unexpired accounts	−45		
87.00	Total financing disbursements (gross)	128	29	
	Offsets:			
	Against gross financing authority and financing disbursements:			
	Offsetting collections (cash) from:			
88.00	Program account	−30	−97	−2
88.25	Interest on uninvested funds	−26	−97	−31
88.40	Insurance premiums	−16	−101	−43
88.90	Total, offsetting collections (cash)	−72	−295	−76
	Net financing authority and financing disbursements:			
89.00	Financing authority			
90.00	Financing disbursements	56	−266	−76

Status of Guaranteed Loans (in millions of dollars)

Identification code 69–4304–0–3–999		1999 actual	2000 est.	2001 est.
	Position with respect to appropriations act limitation on commitments:			
2111	Limitation on guaranteed loans made by private lenders	1,767	1,505	40
2150	Total guaranteed loan commitments	1,767	1,505	40
	Cumulative balance of guaranteed loans outstanding:			
2210	Outstanding, start of year	2,457	3,411	4,745
2231	Disbursements of new guaranteed loans	1,767	1,505	40
2251	Repayments and prepayments	−813	−171	−232
2290	Outstanding, end of year	3,411	4,745	4,553
	Memorandum:			
2299	Guaranteed amount of guaranteed loans outstanding, end of year	3,411	4,745	4,553

As required by the Federal Credit Reform Act of 1990, this non-budgetary account records all cash flows to and from the Government resulting from loan guarantees committed in 1992 and beyond (including modifications of loan guarantees that resulted from commitments in any year). The amounts in this account are a means of financing and are not included in the budget totals.

Balance Sheet (in millions of dollars)

Identification code 69–4304–0–3–999		1998 actual	1999 actual	2000 est.	2001 est.
	ASSETS:				
	Federal assets:				
1101	Fund balances with Treasury	246	190	457	533
	Investments in US securities:				
1106	Receivables, net	5	5	6	6
1999	Total assets	251	195	463	539
	LIABILITIES:				
2101	Federal liabilities: Accounts payable		77	195	215
2204	Non-Federal liabilities: Liabilities for loan guarantees	251	118	268	324
2999	Total liabilities	251	195	463	539
4999	Total liabilities and net position	251	195	463	539

Administrative Provisions—Maritime Administration

Notwithstanding any other provision of this Act, the Maritime Administration is authorized to furnish utilities and services and make necessary repairs in connection with any lease, contract, or occupancy involving Government property under control of the Maritime Administration, and payments received therefore shall be credited to the appropriation charged with the cost thereof: *Provided*, That rental payments under any such lease, contract, or occupancy for items other than such utilities, services, or repairs shall be covered into the Treasury as miscellaneous receipts.

No obligations shall be incurred during the current fiscal year from the construction fund established by the Merchant Marine Act, 1936, or otherwise, in excess of the appropriations and limitations contained in this Act or in any prior appropriation Act. *(Departments of Commerce, Justice, and State, the Judiciary and Related Agencies*

Credit accounts—Continued

ADMINISTRATIVE PROVISIONS—MARITIME ADMINISTRATION—Continued

Appropriations Act, 2000, as enacted by section 1000(a)(1) of the Consolidated Appropriations Act, 2000 (P.L. 106–113).)

GENERAL FUND RECEIPT ACCOUNTS

(in millions of dollars)

	1999 actual	2000 est.	2001 est.
Offsetting receipts from the public:			
20–031100 Tonnage duty increases	69	71	73
69–085500 Registration, filing, and permit fees, hazardous materials transportation	1	1	1
69–242100 Marine safety fees	16	21	21
69–272830 Maritime (Title XI) loan program, downward reestimates of subsidies	84	29	....
69–273530 Alameda corridor, downward reestimates of subsidies	....	62	....
69–309900 Miscellaneous recoveries and refunds, not otherwise classified	1	1	1
General Fund Offsetting receipts from the public	171	185	96

OTHER CONSOLIDATED RECEIPT ACCOUNTS

(in millions of dollars)

	1999 actual	2000 est.	2001 est.
69–977110 Proprietary receipts, Miscellaneous trust funds	....	6	6

TITLE III—GENERAL PROVISIONS

(INCLUDING TRANSFERS OF FUNDS)

SEC. 301. During the current fiscal year applicable appropriations to the Department of Transportation shall be available for maintenance and operation of aircraft; hire of passenger motor vehicles and aircraft; purchase of liability insurance for motor vehicles operating in foreign countries on official department business; and uniforms, or allowances therefor, as authorized by law (5 U.S.C. 5901–5902).

SEC. 302. Such sums as may be necessary for fiscal year [2000] *2001* pay raises for programs funded in this Act shall be absorbed within the levels appropriated in this Act or previous appropriations Acts.

SEC. 303. Funds appropriated under this Act for expenditures by the Federal Aviation Administration shall be available: (1) except as otherwise authorized by title VIII of the Elementary and Secondary Education Act of 1965 (20 U.S.C. 7701 et seq.), for expenses of primary and secondary schooling for dependents of Federal Aviation Administration personnel stationed outside the continental United States at costs for any given area not in excess of those of the Department of Defense for the same area, when it is determined by the Secretary that the schools, if any, available in the locality are unable to provide adequately for the education of such dependents; and (2) for transportation of said dependents between schools serving the area that they attend and their places of residence when the Secretary, under such regulations as may be prescribed, determines that such schools are not accessible by public means of transportation on a regular basis.

SEC. 304. Appropriations contained in this Act for the Department of Transportation shall be available for services as authorized by 5 U.S.C. 3109, but at rates for individuals not to exceed the per diem rate equivalent to the rate for an Executive Level IV.

SEC. 305. None of the funds in this Act shall be available for salaries and expenses of more than [100] *113* political and Presidential appointees in the Department of Transportation[: *Provided*, That none of the personnel covered by this provision may be assigned on temporary detail outside the Department of Transportation].

SEC. 306. None of the funds in this Act shall be used for the planning or execution of any program to pay the expenses of, or otherwise compensate, non-Federal parties intervening in regulatory or adjudicatory proceedings funded in this Act.

SEC. 307. None of the funds appropriated in this Act shall remain available for obligation beyond the current fiscal year, nor may any be transferred to other appropriations, unless expressly so provided herein.

[SEC. 308. The Secretary of Transportation may enter into grants, cooperative agreements, and other transactions with any person, agency, or instrumentality of the United States, any unit of State or local government, any educational institution, and any other entity in execution of the Technology Reinvestment Project authorized under the Defense Conversion, Reinvestment and Transition Assistance Act of 1992 and related legislation: *Provided*, That the authority provided in this section may be exercised without regard to section 3324 of title 31, United States Code.]

SEC. [309] *308.* The expenditure of any appropriation under this Act for any consulting service through procurement contract pursuant to section 3109 of title 5, United States Code, shall be limited to those contracts where such expenditures are a matter of public record and available for public inspection, except where otherwise provided under existing law, or under existing Executive order issued pursuant to existing law.

SEC. [310] *309.* (a) For fiscal year [2000] *2001*, the Secretary of Transportation shall—

(1) [not distribute] *set aside* from the obligation limitation for Federal-aid Highways amounts authorized for administrative expenses and programs funded from the administrative takedown authorized by section 104(a) of title 23, United States Code, for the highway use tax evasion program, *for highway research programs under chapter 5 of title 23, U.S.C., for sections 1116, 1101(a)(8)(A), 1101(a)(9) and 1221 of Public Law 105–178, $10,000,000 for section 140(b) of title 23, U.S.C.,* and amounts provided under section 110 of title 23, United States Code *(excluding $128,752,000 pursuant to subsection (e) of section 110), as amended*, and for the Bureau of Transportation Statistics;

(2) [not distribute] *set aside* an amount from the obligation limitation for Federal-aid Highways that is equal to the unobligated balance of amounts made available from the Highway Trust Fund (other than the Mass Transit Account) for Federal-aid highways and highway safety programs for the previous fiscal year the funds for which are allocated by the Secretary;

(3) determine the ratio that—

(A) the obligation limitation for Federal-aid Highways less the aggregate of amounts [not distributed] *set aside* under paragraphs (1) and (2), bears to

(B) the total of the sums authorized to be appropriated for Federal-aid highways and highway safety construction programs (other than sums authorized to be appropriated for sections set forth in paragraphs (1) through (7) of subsection (b) and sums authorized to be appropriated for section 105 of title 23, United States Code, equal to the amount referred to in subsection (b)(8)) for such fiscal year less the aggregate of the amounts [not distributed] *set aside* under paragraph (1) of this subsection;

(4) distribute the obligation limitation for Federal-aid Highways less the aggregate amounts [not distributed] *set aside* under paragraphs (1) and (2) of section 117 of title 23, United States Code (relating to high priority projects program), section 201 of the Appalachian Regional Development Act of 1965, the Woodrow Wilson Memorial Bridge Authority Act of 1995, and $2,000,000,000 for such fiscal year under section 105 of title 23, United States Code (relating to minimum guarantee) so that the amount of obligation authority available for each of such sections is equal to the amount determined by multiplying the ratio determined under paragraph (3) by the sums authorized to be appropriated for such section (except in the case of section 105, $2,000,000,000) for such fiscal year;

(5) distribute the obligation limitation provided for Federal-aid Highways less the aggregate amounts [not distributed] *set aside* under paragraphs (1) and (2) and amounts distributed under paragraph (4) for each of the programs that are allocated by the Secretary under title 23, United States Code (other than activities to which paragraph (1) applies and programs to which paragraph (4) applies) by multiplying the ratio determined under paragraph (3) by the sums authorized to be appropriated for such program for such fiscal year; and

(6) distribute the obligation limitation provided for Federal-aid Highways less the aggregate amounts [not distributed] *set aside* under paragraphs (1) and (2) and amounts distributed under paragraphs (4) and (5) for Federal-aid highways and highway safety construction programs (other than the minimum guarantee program, but only to the extent that amounts apportioned for the minimum guarantee program for such fiscal year exceed $2,639,000,000, and the Appalachian development highway system program) that are apportioned by the Secretary under title 23, United States Code, in the ratio that—

(A) sums authorized to be appropriated for such programs that are apportioned to each State for such fiscal year, bear to

(B) the total of the sums authorized to be appropriated for such programs that are apportioned to all States for such fiscal year.

(b) EXCEPTIONS FROM OBLIGATION LIMITATION.—The obligation limitation for Federal-aid Highways shall not apply to obligations: (1) under section 125 of title 23, United States Code; (2) under section 147 of the Surface Transportation Assistance Act of 1978; (3) under section 9 of the Federal-Aid Highway Act of 1981; (4) under sections 131(b) and 131(j) of the Surface Transportation Assistance Act of 1982; (5) under sections 149(b) and 149(c) of the Surface Transportation and Uniform Relocation Assistance Act of 1987; (6) under sections 1103 through 1108 of the Intermodal Surface Transportation Efficiency Act of 1991; (7) under section 157 of title 23, United States Code, as in effect on the day before the date of the enactment of the Transportation Equity Act for the 21st Century; and (8) under section 105 of title 23, United States Code (but, only in an amount equal to $639,000,000 for such fiscal year).

(c) REDISTRIBUTION OF UNUSED OBLIGATION AUTHORITY.—Notwithstanding subsection (a), the Secretary shall after August 1 for such fiscal year revise a distribution of the obligation limitation made available under subsection (a) if a State will not obligate the amount distributed during that fiscal year and redistribute sufficient amounts to those States able to obligate amounts in addition to those previously distributed during that fiscal year giving priority to those States having large unobligated balances of funds apportioned under sections 104 and 144 of title 23, United States Code, section 160 (as in effect on the day before the enactment of the Transportation Equity Act for the 21st Century) of title 23, United States Code, and under section 1015 of the Intermodal Surface Transportation Act of 1991 (105 Stat. 1943–1945).

(d) APPLICABILITY OF OBLIGATION LIMITATIONS TO TRANSPORTATION RESEARCH PROGRAMS.—The obligation limitation shall apply to transportation research programs carried out under chapter 5 of title 23, United States Code, except that obligation authority made available for such programs under such limitation shall remain available for a period of 3 fiscal years.

(e) REDISTRIBUTION OF CERTAIN AUTHORIZED FUNDS.—Not later than 30 days after the date of the distribution of obligation limitation under subsection (a), the Secretary shall distribute to the States any funds: (1) that are authorized to be appropriated for such fiscal year for Federal-aid highways programs (other than the program under section 160 of title 23, United States Code) and for carrying out subchapter I of chapter 311 of title 49, United States Code, and highway-related programs under chapter 4 of title 23, United States Code; and (2) that the Secretary determines will not be allocated to the States, and will not be available for obligation, in such fiscal year due to the imposition of any obligation limitation for such fiscal year. Such distribution to the States shall be made in the same ratio as the distribution of obligation authority under subsection (a)(6). The funds so distributed shall be available for any purposes described in section 133(b) of title 23, United States Code.

(f) SPECIAL RULE.—Obligation limitation distributed for a fiscal year under subsection (a)(4) of this section for a section set forth in subsection (a)(4) shall remain available until used and shall be in addition to the amount of any limitation imposed on obligations for Federal-aid highway and highway safety construction programs for future fiscal years.

(g) Notwithstanding Public Law 105–178, as amended, of the funds authorized under 23 U.S.C. 110, as amended, for fiscal year 2001: $70,000,000 shall be transferred to "Operations and Research," National Highway Traffic Safety Administration; $48,000,000 shall be to carry out the Federal Highway Administration's Delta Initiative; $20,000,000 shall be to carry out the Federal Highway Administration's Highway Use Tax Evasion Projects; $468,000,000 shall be transferred to "Expanded Intercity Rail Passenger Service Fund," Federal Railroad Administration; $10,000,000 shall be transferred to "National Motor Carrier Safety Program," Federal Motor Carrier Safety Administration; $50,000,000 shall be transferred to "Job Access and Reverse Commute Program," Federal Transit Administration; and $75,000,000 shall be to carry out the Federal Highway Administration's Indian Reservation Roads Program.

SEC. [311] *310.* The limitations on obligations for the programs of the Federal Transit Administration shall not apply to any authority under 49 U.S.C. 5338, previously made available for obligation, or to any other authority previously made available for obligation.

SEC. [312] *311.* None of the funds in this Act shall be used to implement section 404 of title 23, United States Code.

SEC. [313] *312.* None of the funds in this Act shall be available to plan, finalize, or implement regulations that would establish a vessel traffic safety fairway less than five miles wide between the Santa Barbara Traffic Separation Scheme and the San Francisco Traffic Separation Scheme.

SEC. [314] *313.* Notwithstanding any other provision of law, airports may transfer, without consideration, to the Federal Aviation Administration (FAA) instrument landing systems (along with associated approach lighting equipment and runway visual range equipment) which conform to FAA design and performance specifications, the purchase of which was assisted by a Federal airport-aid program, airport development aid program or airport improvement program grant. The Federal Aviation Administration shall accept such equipment, which shall thereafter be operated and maintained by FAA in accordance with agency criteria.

[SEC. 315. None of the funds in this Act shall be available to award a multiyear contract for production end items that: (1) includes economic order quantity or long lead time material procurement in excess of $10,000,000 in any 1 year of the contract; (2) includes a cancellation charge greater than $10,000,000 which at the time of obligation has not been appropriated to the limits of the Government's liability; or (3) includes a requirement that permits performance under the contract during the second and subsequent years of the contract without conditioning such performance upon the appropriation of funds: *Provided*, That this limitation does not apply to a contract in which the Federal Government incurs no financial liability from not buying additional systems, subsystems, or components beyond the basic contract requirements].

SEC. [316] *314.* Notwithstanding any other provision of law, and except for fixed guideway modernization projects, funds made available by this Act under "Federal Transit Administration, Capital investment grants" for projects specified in this Act or identified in reports accompanying this Act not obligated by September 30, [2002] *2003*, and other recoveries, shall be made available for other projects under 49 U.S.C. 5309.

SEC. [317] *315.* Notwithstanding any other provision of law, any funds appropriated before October 1, [1999] *2000*, under any section of chapter 53 of title 49, United States Code, that remain available for expenditure may be transferred to and administered under the most recent appropriation heading for any such section.

[SEC. 318. None of the funds in this Act may be used to compensate in excess of 320 technical staff-years under the federally funded research and development center contract between the Federal Aviation Administration and the Center for Advanced Aviation Systems Development during fiscal year 2000.]

[SEC. 319. Funds provided in this Act for the Transportation Administrative Service Center (TASC) shall be reduced by $15,000,000, which limits fiscal year 2000 TASC obligational authority for elements of the Department of Transportation funded in this Act to no more than $133,673,000: *Provided*, That such reductions from the budget request shall be allocated by the Department of Transportation to each appropriations account in proportion to the amount included in each account for the Transportation Administrative Service Center.]

SEC. [320] *316.* Funds received by the Federal Highway Administration, Federal Transit Administration, and Federal Railroad Administration from States, counties, municipalities, other public authorities, and private sources for expenses incurred for training may be credited respectively to the Federal Highway Administration's "Federal-Aid Highways" account, the Federal Transit Administration's "Transit Planning and Research" account, and to the Federal Railroad Administration's "Safety and Operations" account, except for State rail safety inspectors participating in training pursuant to 49 U.S.C. 20105.

[SEC. 321. None of the funds in this Act shall be available to prepare, propose, or promulgate any regulations pursuant to title

(INCLUDING TRANSFERS OF FUNDS)—Continued

V of the Motor Vehicle Information and Cost Savings Act (49 U.S.C. 32901 et seq.) prescribing corporate average fuel economy standards for automobiles, as defined in such title, in any model year that differs from standards promulgated for such automobiles prior to the enactment of this section.]

SEC. [322] *317.* TEMPORARY AIR SERVICE INTERRUPTIONS. (a) AVAILABILITY OF FUNDS.—Funds appropriated or otherwise made available by this Act to carry out section 47114(c)(1) of title 49, United States Code, may be available for apportionment to an airport sponsor described in subsection (b) in fiscal year [2000] *2001* in an amount equal to the amount apportioned to that sponsor in fiscal year [1999] *2000*.

(b) COVERED AIRPORT SPONSORS.—An airport sponsor referred to in subsection (a) is an airport sponsor with respect to whose primary airport the Secretary of Transportation found that—

(1) passenger boardings at the airport fell below 10,000 in the calendar year used to calculate the apportionment;

(2) the airport had at least 10,000 passenger boardings in the calendar year prior to the calendar year used to calculate apportionments to airport sponsors in a fiscal year; and

(3) the cause of the shortfall in passenger boardings was a temporary but significant interruption in service by an air carrier to that airport due to an employment action, natural disaster, or other event unrelated to the demand for air transportation at the affected airport.

[SEC. 323. Section 3021 of Public Law 105–178 is amended in subsection (a)—

(1) in the first sentence, by striking "single-State"; and

(2) in the second sentence, by striking "Any" and all that follows through "United States Code" and inserting "The funds made available to the State of Oklahoma and the State of Vermont to carry out sections 5307 and 5311 of title 49, United States Code".]

SEC. [324] *318.* [Notwithstanding] *Hereafter, not withstanding* 31 U.S.C. 3302, funds received by the Bureau of Transportation Statistics from the sale of data products, for necessary expenses incurred pursuant to 49 U.S.C. 111 may be credited to the Federal-aid highways account for the purpose of reimbursing the Bureau for such expenses: *Provided*, That such funds shall *not* be subject to the obligation limitation for Federal-aid highways and highway safety construction.

[SEC. 325. None of the funds in this Act may be obligated or expended for employee training which: (a) does not meet identified needs for knowledge, skills and abilities bearing directly upon the performance of official duties; (b) contains elements likely to induce high levels of emotional response or psychological stress in some participants; (c) does not require prior employee notification of the content and methods to be used in the training and written end of course evaluations; (d) contains any methods or content associated with religious or quasi-religious belief systems or "new age" belief systems as defined in Equal Employment Opportunity Commission Notice N–915.022, dated September 2, 1988; (e) is offensive to, or designed to change, participants' personal values or lifestyle outside the workplace; or (f) includes content related to human immunodeficiency virus/acquired immune deficiency syndrome (HIV/AIDS) other than that necessary to make employees more aware of the medical ramifications of HIV/AIDS and the workplace rights of HIV-positive employees.]

[SEC. 326. None of the funds in this Act shall, in the absence of express authorization by Congress, be used directly or indirectly to pay for any personal service, advertisement, telegraph, telephone, letter, printed or written material, radio, television, video presentation, electronic communications, or other device, intended or designed to influence in any manner a Member of Congress or of a State legislature to favor or oppose by vote or otherwise, any legislation or appropriation by Congress or a State legislature after the introduction of any bill or resolution in Congress proposing such legislation or appropriation, or after the introduction of any bill or resolution in a State legislature proposing such legislation or appropriation: *Provided*, That this shall not prevent officers or employees of the Department of Transportation or related agencies funded in this Act from communicating to Members of Congress or to Congress, on the request of any Member, or to members of State legislature, or to a State legislature, through the proper official channels, requests for legislation or appropriations which they deem necessary for the efficient conduct of business.]

[SEC. 327. (a) IN GENERAL.—None of the funds made available in this Act may be expended by an entity unless the entity agrees that in expending the funds the entity will comply with the Buy American Act (41 U.S.C. 10a–10c).

(b) SENSE OF THE CONGRESS; REQUIREMENT REGARDING NOTICE.—

(1) PURCHASE OF AMERICAN-MADE EQUIPMENT AND PRODUCTS.—In the case of any equipment or product that may be authorized to be purchased with financial assistance provided using funds made available in this Act, it is the sense of the Congress that entities receiving the assistance should, in expending the assistance, purchase only American-made equipment and products to the greatest extent practicable.

(2) NOTICE TO RECIPIENTS OF ASSISTANCE.—In providing financial assistance using funds made available in this Act, the head of each Federal agency shall provide to each recipient of the assistance a notice describing the statement made in paragraph (1) by the Congress.

(c) PROHIBITION OF CONTRACTS WITH PERSONS FALSELY LABELING PRODUCTS AS MADE IN AMERICA.—If it has been finally determined by a court or Federal agency that any person intentionally affixed a label bearing a "Made in America" inscription, or any inscription with the same meaning, to any product sold in or shipped to the United States that is not made in the United States, the person shall be ineligible to receive any contract or subcontract made with funds made available in this Act, pursuant to the debarment, suspension, and ineligibility procedures described in sections 9.400 through 9.409 of title 48, Code of Federal Regulations.]

[SEC. 328. Not to exceed $1,000,000 of the funds provided in this Act for the Department of Transportation shall be available for the necessary expenses of advisory committees: *Provided*, That this limitation shall not apply to advisory committees established for the purpose of conducting negotiated rulemaking in accordance with the Negotiated Rulemaking Act, 5 U.S.C. 561–570a, or the Coast Guard's advisory council on roles and missions.]

[SEC. 329. Hereafter, notwithstanding any other provision of law, receipts, in amounts determined by the Secretary, collected from users of fitness centers operated by or for the Department of Transportation shall be available to support the operation and maintenance of those facilities.]

[SEC. 330. None of the funds in this Act shall be available to implement or enforce regulations that would result in the withdrawal of a slot from an air carrier at O'Hare International Airport under section 93.223 of title 14 of the Code of Federal Regulations in excess of the total slots withdrawn from that air carrier as of October 31, 1993 if such additional slot is to be allocated to an air carrier or foreign air carrier under section 93.217 of title 14 of the Code of Federal Regulations.]

[SEC. 331. Notwithstanding any other provision of law, funds made available under this Act, and any prior year unobligated funds, for the Charleston, South Carolina Monobeam Corridor Project shall be transferred to and administered under the Transit Planning and Research account, subject to such terms and conditions as the Secretary deems appropriate.]

[SEC. 332. Hereafter, notwithstanding 49 U.S.C. 41742, no essential air service subsidies shall be provided to communities in the 48 contiguous States that are located fewer than 70 highway miles from the nearest large or medium hub airport, or that require a rate of subsidy per passenger in excess of $200 unless such point is greater than 210 miles from the nearest large or medium hub airport.]

SEC. [333. Rebates] *319. Hereafter, rebates*, refunds, incentive payments, minor fees and other funds received by the Department from travel management centers, charge card programs, the subleasing of building space, and miscellaneous sources are to be credited to appropriations of the Department and allocated to elements of the Department using fair and equitable criteria and such funds shall be available until [December 31, 2000] *expended*.

SEC. [334] *320.* Notwithstanding any other provision of law, rule or regulation, the Secretary of Transportation is authorized to allow the issuer of any preferred stock heretofore sold to the Department to redeem or repurchase such stock upon the payment to the Department of an amount determined by the Secretary.

SEC. [335] *321.* For necessary expenses of the Amtrak Reform Council authorized under section 203 of Public Law 105–134, [$750,000] *$980,000*, to remain available until September 30, [2001: *Provided*, That the duties of the Amtrak Reform Council described in section 203(g)(1) of Public Law 105–134 shall include the identification of Amtrak routes which are candidates for closure or realignment, based on performance rankings developed by Amtrak which incorporate information on each route's fully allocated costs and ridership on core intercity passenger service, and which assume, for purposes of closure or realignment candidate identification, that Federal subsidies for Amtrak will decline over the 4-year period from fiscal year 1999 to fiscal year 2002: *Provided further*, That these closure or realignment recommendations shall be included in the Amtrak Reform Council's annual report to the Congress required by section 203(h) of Public Law 105–134] *2002*.

[SEC. 336. The Secretary of Transportation is authorized to transfer funds appropriated for any office of the Office of the Secretary to any other office of the Office of the Secretary: *Provided*, That no appropriation shall be increased or decreased by more than 12 percent by all such transfers: *Provided further*, That any such transfer shall be submitted for approval to the House and Senate Committees on Appropriations.]

SEC. [337] *322*. None of the funds in this Act shall be available for activities under the Aircraft Purchase Loan Guarantee Program during fiscal year [2000] *2001*.

[SEC. 338. None of the funds appropriated or limited in this Act may be used to carry out the functions and operations of the Office of Motor Carriers within the Federal Highway Administration: *Provided*, That funds available to the Federal Highway Administration shall be transferred with the functions and operations of the Office of Motor Carriers should any of the functions and operations of that office be delegated by the Secretary outside of the Federal Highway Administration: *Provided further*, That notwithstanding section 104(c)(2) of title 49, United States Code, the Federal Highway Administrator shall not carry out the duties and functions vested in the Secretary under 49 U.S.C. 521(b)(5).]

[SEC. 339. Section 3027 of the Transportation Equity Act for the 21st Century (49 U.S.C. 5307 note; 112 Stat. 336) is amended by adding at the end the following:

"(e) GOVERNMENT SHARE FOR OPERATING ASSISTANCE TO CERTAIN SMALLER URBANIZED AREAS.—Notwithstanding 49 U.S.C. 5307(e), a grant of the Government for operating expenses of a project under 49 U.S.C. 5307(b) in fiscal years 1999 and 2000 to any recipient that is providing transit services in an urbanized area with a population between 128,000 and 128,200, as determined in the 1990 census, and that had adopted a 5-year transit plan before September 1, 1998, may not be more than 80 percent of the net project cost.".]

[SEC. 340. Funds provided in Public Law 104–205 for the Griffin light rail project shall be available for alternative analysis and environmental impact studies for other transit alternatives in the Griffin corridor from Hartford to Bradley International Airport.]

[SEC. 341. Section 3030(c)(1)(A)(v) of the Transportation Equity Act for the 21st Century (Public Law 105–178) is amended by striking "Light Rail".]

[SEC. 342. Notwithstanding any other provision of law, the Federal share of projects funded under section 3038(g)(1)(B) of Public Law 105–178 shall not exceed 90 percent of the project cost.]

[SEC. 343. Of the funds made available to the Coast Guard in this Act under "Acquisition, construction, and improvements", $10,000,000 is only for necessary expenses to support a portion of the acquisition costs, currently estimated at $128,000,000, of a multi-mission vessel to replace the Mackinaw icebreaker in the Great Lakes, to remain available until September 30, 2005.]

[SEC. 344. None of the funds made available in this Act may be obligated or expended to extend a single hull tank vessel's double hull compliance date under the Oil Pollution Act of 1990 due to conversion of the vessel's single hull design by adding a double bottom or double side after August 18, 1990, unless specifically authorized by 46 U.S.C. 3703a(e).]

[SEC. 345. None of the funds in this Act may be used for the planning or development of the California State Route 710 Freeway extension project through South Pasadena, California (as approved in the Record of Decision on State Route 710 Freeway, issued by the United States Department of Transportation, Federal Highway Administration, on April 13, 1998).]

[SEC. 346. Hereafter, none of the funds made available under this Act or any other Act, may be used to implement, carry out, or enforce any regulation issued under section 41705 of title 49, United States Code, including any regulation contained in part 382 of title 14, Code of Federal Regulations, or any other provision of law (including any Act of Congress, regulation, or Executive order or any official guidance or correspondence thereto), that requires or encourages an air carrier (as that term is defined in section 40102 of title 49, United States Code) to, on intrastate or interstate air transportation (as those terms are defined in section 40102 of title 49, United States Code)—

(1) provide a peanut-free buffer zone or any other related peanut-restricted area; or

(2) restrict the distribution of peanuts,

until 90 days after submission to the Congress and the Secretary of a peer-reviewed scientific study that determines that there are severe reactions by passengers to peanuts as a result of contact with very small airborne peanut particles of the kind that passengers might encounter in an aircraft.]

[SEC. 347. Section 5309(g)(1)(B) of title 49, United States Code, is amended by inserting after "Committee on Banking, Housing, and Urban Affairs of the Senate" the following: "and the House and Senate Committees on Appropriations".]

[SEC. 348. Section 1212(g) of the Transportation Equity Act for the 21st Century (Public Law 105–178), as amended, is amended—

(1) in the subsection heading, by inserting "and New Jersey" after "Minnesota"; and

(2) by inserting "or the State of New Jersey" after "Minnesota".]

[SEC. 349. (a) REQUIREMENT TO CONVEY.—The Commandant of the Coast Guard shall convey, without consideration, to the University of New Hampshire (in this section referred to as the "University") all right, title, and interest of the United States in and to a parcel of real property (including any improvements thereon) located in New Castle, New Hampshire, consisting of approximately five acres and including a pier.

(b) IDENTIFICATION OF PROPERTY.—The Commandant shall determine, identify, and describe the property to be conveyed under this section.

(c) EASEMENTS, RIGHTS-OF-WAY, AND RIGHTS.—(1) The Commandant shall, in connection with the conveyance required by subsection (a), grant to the University such easements and rights-of-way as the Commandant considers necessary to permit access to the property conveyed under that subsection.

(2) The Commandant shall, in connection with such conveyance, reserve in favor of the United States such easements and rights as the Commandant considers necessary to protect the interests of the United States, including easements or rights regarding access to property and utilities.

(d) CONDITIONS OF CONVEYANCE.—The conveyance required by subsection (a) shall be subject to the following conditions:

(1) That the University not convey, assign, exchange, or encumber the property conveyed, or any part thereof, unless such conveyance, assignment, exchange, or encumbrance—

(A) is made without consideration; or

(B) is otherwise approved by the Commandant.

(2) That the University not interfere or allow interference in any manner with the maintenance or operation of Coast Guard Station Portsmouth Harbor, New Hampshire, without the express written permission of the Commandant.

(3) That the University use the property for educational, research, or other public purposes.

(e) MAINTENANCE OF PROPERTY.—The University, or any subsequent owner of the property conveyed under subsection (a) pursuant to a conveyance, assignment, or exchange referred to in subsection (d)(1), shall maintain the property in a proper, substantial, and workmanlike manner, and in accordance with any conditions established by the Commandant, pursuant to the National Historic Preservation Act of 1966 (16 U.S.C. 470 et seq.), and other applicable laws.

(f) REVERSIONARY INTEREST.—All right, title, and interest in and to the property conveyed under this section (including any improvements thereon) shall revert to the United States, and the United States shall have the right of immediate entry thereon, if—

(1) the property, or any part thereof, ceases to be used for educational, research, or other public purposes by the University;

(2) the University conveys, assigns, exchanges, or encumbers the property conveyed, or part thereof, for consideration or without the approval of the Commandant;

(3) the Commandant notifies the owner of the property that the property is needed for national security purposes and a period of 30 days elapses after such notice; or

(4) any other term or condition established by the Commandant under this section with respect to the property is violated.]

[SEC. 350. (a) No recipient of funds made available in this Act shall disseminate driver's license personal information as defined in 18 U.S.C. 2725(3) except as provided in subsection (b) of this section

(INCLUDING TRANSFERS OF FUNDS)—Continued

or motor vehicle records as defined in 18 U.S.C. 2725(1) for any use not permitted under 18 U.S.C. 2721.

(b) No recipient of funds made available in this Act shall disseminate a person's driver's license photograph, social security number, and medical or disability information from a motor vehicle record as defined in 18 U.S.C. 2725(1) without the express consent of the person to whom such information pertains, except for uses permitted under 18 U.S.C. 2721(1), 2721(4), 2721(6), and 2721(9): *Provided*, That subsection (b) shall not in any way affect the use of organ donation information on an individual's driver's license or affect the administration of organ donation initiatives in the States.

(c) 18 U.S.C. 2721(b)(11) is amended by striking all after "records" and inserting the following: "if the State has obtained the express consent of the person to whom such personal information pertains.".

(d) 18 U.S.C. 2721(b)(12) is amended by striking all after "solicitations" and inserting the following: "if the State has obtained the express consent of the person to whom such personal information pertains.".

(e) No State may condition or burden in any way the issuance of a motor vehicle record as defined in 18 U.S.C. 2725(1) upon the receipt of consent described in paragraphs (b) and (c).

(f) Notwithstanding subsections (a) and (b), the Secretary shall not withhold funds provided in this Act for any grantee if a State is in noncompliance with this provision.

(g) EFFECTIVE DATES.—

(1) Subsections (a) and (e) shall be effective upon the date of the enactment of this Act, excluding the States of Wisconsin, South Carolina, and Oklahoma that shall be in compliance with this subsection within 90 days after the United States Supreme Court has issued a final decision on Reno vs. Condon;

(2) Subsections (b), (c), and (d) shall be effective on June 1, 2000, excluding the States of Arkansas, Montana, Nevada, North Dakota, Oregon, and Texas that shall be in compliance with subsections (b), (c), and (d) within 90 days of the next convening of the State legislature and excluding the States of Wisconsin, South Carolina, and Oklahoma that shall be in compliance within 90 days following the day of issuance of a final decision on Reno vs. Condon by the United States Supreme Court if the State legislature is in session, or within 90 days of the next convening of the State legislature following the issuance of such final decision if the State legislature is not in session.]

[SEC. 351. Notwithstanding any other provision of law, within the funds provided in this Act for the Federal Highway Administration and the National Highway Traffic Safety Administration, $10,000,000 may be made available for completion of the National Advanced Driving Simulator (NADS): *Provided*, That such funds shall be subject to reprogramming guidelines.]

[SEC. 352. Notwithstanding any other provision of law, section 1107(b) of Public Law 102–240 is amended by striking "Construction of a replacement bridge at Watervale Bridge #63, Harford County, MD" and inserting the following: "For improvements to Bottom Road Bridge, Vinegar Hill Road Bridge and Southampton Road Bridge, Harford County, MD".]

[SEC. 353. (a) FINDINGS.—The Senate makes the following findings:

(1) The survival of American culture is dependent upon the survival of the sacred institution of marriage.

(2) The decennial census is required by section 2 of article 1 of the Constitution of the United States, and has been conducted in every decade since 1790.

(3) The decennial census has included marital status among the information sought from every American household since 1880.

(4) The 2000 decennial census will mark the first decennial census since 1880 in which marital status will not be a question included on the census questionnaire distributed to the majority of American households.

(5) The United States Census Bureau has removed marital status from the short form census questionnaire to be distributed to the majority of American households in the 2000 decennial census and placed that category of information on the long form census questionnaire to be distributed only to a sample of the population in that decennial census.

(6) Every year more than $100,000,000,000 in Federal funds are allocated based on the data collected by the Census Bureau.

(7) Recorded data on marital status provides a basic foundation for the development of Federal policy.

(8) Census data showing an exact account of the numbers of persons who are married, single, or divorced provides critical information which serves as an indicator on the prevalence of marriage in society.

(b) SENSE OF THE SENATE.—It is the sense of the Senate that the United States Census Bureau—

(1) has wrongfully decided not to include marital status on the census questionnaire to be distributed to the majority of Americans for the 2000 decennial census; and

(2) should include marital status on the short form census questionnaire to be distributed to the majority of American households for the 2000 decennial census.]

[SEC. 354. It is the sense of the Senate that the Secretary should expeditiously amend title 14, chapter II, part 250, Code of Federal Regulations, so as to double the applicable penalties for involuntary denied boardings and allow those passengers that are involuntarily denied boarding the option of obtaining a prompt cash refund for the full value of their airline ticket.]

[SEC. 355. Section 656(b) of division C of the Omnibus Consolidated Appropriations Act of 1997 is repealed.]

[SEC. 356. Notwithstanding any other provision of law, the amount made available pursuant to Public Law 105–277 for the Pittsburgh North Shore central business district transit options MIS project may be used to fund any aspect of preliminary engineering, costs associated with an environmental impact statement, or a major investment study for that project.]

[SEC. 357. (a) Notwithstanding the January 4, 1977, decision of the Secretary of Transportation that approved construction of Interstate Highway 66 between the Capital Beltway and Rosslyn, Virginia, the Commonwealth of Virginia, in accordance with existing Federal and State law, shall hereafter have authority for operation, maintenance, and construction of Interstate Route 66 between Rosslyn and the Capital Beltway, except as noted in paragraph (b).

(b) The conditions in the Secretary's January 4, 1997 decision, that exclude heavy duty trucks and permit use by vehicles bound to or from Washington Dulles International Airport in the peak direction during peak hours, shall remain in effect.]

[SEC. 358. NOISE BARRIERS, GEORGIA. Notwithstanding any other provision of law, the Secretary of Transportation shall approve the use of funds apportioned under paragraphs (1) and (3) of section 104(b) of title 23, United States Code, for construction of Type II noise barriers at the locations identified in section 1215(h) and items 540 and 967 of the table contained in section 1602 of the Transportation Equity Act for the 21st Century (112 Stat. 211, 292), and at the following locations: On the east side of I–285 extending from Northlake Parkway to Chamblee Tucker Road in Dekalb County, Georgia; and on the east side of I–185 between Macon Road and Airport Thruway.]

[SEC. 359. Item 44 of the table contained in section 1602 of the Transportation Equity Act for the 21st Century (112 Stat. 258) is amended by striking "Saratoga" and inserting "North Creek".]

[SEC. 360. Funds made available for Alaska or Hawaii ferry boats or ferry terminal facilities pursuant to 49 U.S.C. 5309(m)(2)(B) may be used to construct new vessels and facilities or to improve existing vessels and facilities, including both the passenger and vehicle-related elements of such vessels and facilities, and for repair facilities.]

[SEC. 361. HIGH PRIORITY PROJECTS. (a) PROJECT AUTHORIZATIONS.—The table contained in section 1602 of the Transportation Equity Act for the 21st Century (112 Stat. 257–323) is amended—

(1) in item 174 by striking "5.375" and inserting "5.25";
(2) in item 478 by striking "2.375" and inserting "2.25";
(3) in item 948 by striking "5.375" and inserting "5.25";
(4) in item 1008 by striking "3.875" and inserting "3.75";
(5) in item 1210 by striking "6.875" and inserting "6.75";
(6) by striking item 1289 and inserting the following:

"1289.	Arkansas	Improve Highway 167 from Fordyce, Arkansas, to Saline County line	1.0";

(7) in item 1319 by striking "0.875" and inserting "0.75";
(8) in item 1420—

(A) by inserting "and development" after "Conduct planning"; and

(B) by striking "0.875" and inserting "0.75"; and

(9) by adding at the end the following new item:

"1851. Arkansas	Construction of and improvements to highway projects in the corridor designated by section 1105(c)(18)(C)(ii) of the Intermodal Surface Transportation Efficiency Act of 1991	5.25".

(b) HIGH PRIORITY CORRIDORS.—Section 1105(c)(18)(C)(ii) of the Intermodal Surface Transportation Efficiency Act of 1991 (112 Stat. 190) is amended by striking "in the vicinity of" and inserting "east of Wilmar, Arkansas, and west of".]

[SEC. 362. Section 3030(d)(3) of the Transportation Equity Act for the 21st Century (Public Law 105–178) is amended by adding at the end the following:

"(D) Bethlehem, Pennsylvania intermodal facility.".]

[SEC. 363. Section 3030(b) of the Transportation Equity Act for the 21st Century (112 Stat. 373–375) is amended by adding at the end the following:

"(71) Dane County Corridor—East-West Madison Metropolitan Area.".]

[SEC. 364. Notwithstanding the provisions of 49 U.S.C. 5309(e)(6), funds appropriated under this Act for the Douglas Branch project may be used for any purpose except construction: *Provided*, That in evaluating the Douglas Branch project under 5309(e), the Federal Transit Administration shall use a "no-build" alternative that assumes the current Douglas Branch has been closed due to poor condition, and a "TSM" alternative which assumes the Douglas Branch has been closed due to poor condition and enhanced bus service is provided.]

[SEC. 365. (a) The Administrator of the Environmental Protection Agency (in this section referred to as the "Administrator") shall make a grant for the purpose of conducting a study for the following purposes:

(1) To develop and evaluate methods for calculating reductions in emissions of precursors of ground level ozone that are achieved within a geographic area as a result of reduced vehicle-miles-traveled in the geographic area.

(2) To develop a design for the following proposal for a pilot program:

(A) For the purpose of reducing such emissions, employers electing to participate in the pilot program would authorize and encourage telecommuting by their employees. Pursuant to methods developed and evaluated under paragraph (1), credits would be issued to the participating employers reflecting the amount of reductions in such emissions achieved through reduced vehicle-miles-traveled by their telecommuting employees.

(B) For purposes of compliance with the Clean Air Act, entities that are regulated under such Act with respect to such emissions would obtain the credits through a commercial trading and exchange forum (established for such purpose) and through direct trades and exchanges with participating employers and other persons who hold the credits.

(3) To determine whether, if the proposed pilot program were to be carried out, the program—

(A) could provide significant incentives for increasing the use of telecommuting, thereby reducing vehicle-miles-traveled and improving air quality; and

(B) could have positive effects on national, State, and local transportation and infrastructure policies, and on energy conservation and consumption.

(b) The Administrator shall ensure that the design developed under subsection (a)(2) includes recommendations for carrying out the proposed pilot program described in such subsection in each of the following geographic areas (which recommendations for an area shall be developed in consultation with State and local governments and business leaders and organizations in the designated areas): (1) The greater metropolitan region of the District of Columbia (including areas in the State of Maryland and the Commonwealth of Virginia). (2) The greater metropolitan region of Los Angeles, in the State of California. (3) The greater metropolitan region of Philadelphia, in the Commonwealth of Pennsylvania (including areas in the State of New Jersey). (4) Two additional areas to be selected by the grantee under subsection (a), after consultation with the Administrator (or the designee of the Administrator).

(c) The grant under subsection (a) shall be made to the National Environmental Policy Institute (a nonprofit private entity incorporated under the laws of and located in the District of Columbia). The grant may not be made in an amount exceeding $500,000.

(d) The Administrator shall make the grant under subsection (a) not later than 45 days after the date of the enactment of this Act. The Administrator shall require that, not later than 180 days after receiving the first payment under the grant, the grantee under subsection (a) complete the study under such subsection and submit to the Administrator a report describing the methods developed and evaluated under paragraph (1) of such subsection, and containing the design required in paragraph (2) of such subsection and the determinations required in paragraph (3) of such subsection.

(e) The Administrator shall carry out this section (including subsection (b)(3)) in collaboration with the Secretary of Transportation and the Secretary of Energy.

(f) To carry out this section, $500,000 is hereby appropriated to the Department of Transportation, "Office of the Assistant Secretary for Policy", to be transferred to and administered by the Environmental Protection Agency, to be available until expended.]

[SEC. 366. Notwithstanding the Federal Airport Act (as in effect on April 3, 1956) or sections 47125 and 47153 of title 49, United States Code, and subject to subsection (b), the Secretary of Transportation may waive any term contained in the deed of conveyance dated April 3, 1956, by which the United States conveyed lands to the City of Safford, Arizona, for use by the city for airport purposes: *Provided*, That no waiver may be made under subsection (a) if the waiver would result in the closure of an airport.]

[SEC. 367. None of the funds in this Act may be used to make a grant unless the Secretary of Transportation notifies the House and Senate Committees on Appropriations not less than three full business days before any discretionary grant award, letter of intent, or full funding grant agreement totaling $1,000,000 or more is announced by the department or its modal administrations from: (1) any discretionary grant program of the Federal Highway Administration other than the emergency relief program; (2) the airport improvement program of the Federal Aviation Administration; or (3) any program of the Federal Transit Administration other than the formula grants and fixed guideway modernization programs: *Provided*, That no notification shall involve funds that are not available for obligation.]

[SEC. 368. Funds provided in the Department of Transportation and Related Agencies Appropriations Acts for fiscal years 1998 and 1999 for an intermodal facility in Eureka, California, shall be available for the expansion and rehabilitation of a bus maintenance facility in Humboldt County, California.]

[SEC. 369. Notwithstanding any other provision of law, funds previously expended by the City of Moorhead and Moorhead Township on studies related to the 34th Street Corridor Project in Moorhead, Minnesota, shall be considered as the non-Federal match for obligation of funds available under section 1602, item 1404 of the Transportation Equity Act for the 21st Century, as amended, associated with a study of alternatives to rail relocation.]

SEC. 323. Contingent upon enactment of authorizing legislation, the Secretary of Transportation shall charge user fees for services provided by the Federal Railroad Administration in carrying out chapter 51 of title 49, U.S.C., and subtitle V, part A of title 49, U.S.C. Such sums shall be deposited as offsetting collections to the Federal Railroad Administration's "Safety and Operations" account and "Railroad Research and Development" account, respectively, to remain available until expended: Provided further, That upon enactment of such authorizing legislation, the amount appropriated from the General fund for such accounts shall be reduced by $77,300,000 for "Safety and Operations" and $25,500,000 for "Research and Development".

SEC. 324. Section 3037(b)(4) of the Transportation Equity Act for the 21st Century (Public Law 105–178) is amended by deleting the final word "and" of subparagraph 3037(b)(4)(A), and adding the following new subparagraph at the end: "(C) A tribal government.".

SEC. 325. Section 5338(d)(2) of title 49 U.S.C., is amended by adding at the end the following new paragraph: "(D) The Secretary may use not more than ten percent of the amounts made available under subsection (d)(2)(c)(iv) of this section to provide technical direction and documentation of research and technology projects under sections 5312 and 5314.".

SEC. 326. In addition to the authority provided in section 636 of the Treasury, Postal Service, and General Government Appropriations Act, 1997, as included in Public Law 104–208, title I, section 101(f),

(INCLUDING TRANSFERS OF FUNDS)—Continued

as amended, beginning in fiscal year 2001 and thereafter, amounts appropriated for salaries and expenses for the Department of Transportation may be used to reimburse an employee whose position is that of safety inspector for not to exceed one-half the costs incurred by such employee for professional liability insurance. Any payment under this section shall be contingent upon the submission of such information or documentation as the Department may require.

SEC. 327. (a) Section 4109(b)(2) of title 15, United States Code, is amended by striking everything after "research".

(b) Section 2441 of title 16, United States Code, is amended by striking subsection (c).

(Department of Transportation and Related Agencies Appropriations Act, 2000.)

[SEC. 225. In addition to amounts otherwise made available in Public Law 106–69 (Department of Transportation and Related Agencies Appropriations Act, 2000) to carry out 49 United States Code, 5309(m)(1)(C), $1,750,000 is made available from the Mass Transit Account of the Highway Trust Fund for Twin Cities, Minnesota metropolitan buses and bus facilities; $750,000 is made available from the Mass Transit Account of the Highway Trust Fund for Santa Clarita, California bus maintenance facility; $1,000,000 is made available from the Mass Transit Account of the Highway Trust Fund for a Lincoln, Nebraska bus maintenance facility; and $2,500,000 is made available from the Mass Transit Account of the Highway Trust Fund for Anchorage, Alaska 2001 Special Olympics Winter Games buses and bus facilities: *Provided,* That notwithstanding any other provision of law, $2,000,000 of the funds available in fiscal year 2000 under section 1101(a)(9) of Public Law 105–178, as amended, for the National corridor planning and development and coordinated border infrastructure programs shall be made available for the planning and design of a highway corridor between Dothan, Alabama and Panama City, Florida: *Provided further,* That under "Capital Investment Grants" in Public Law 106–69, item number 66 shall be amended by striking "Colorado Association of Transit Agencies" and inserting "Colorado buses and bus facilities", item number 107 shall be amended by striking "Kansas Public Transit Association buses and bus facilities" and inserting "Kansas buses and bus facilities", the figure in item number 92 shall be amended to read "3,340,000", item number 251 shall be amended by inserting after "buses" the following: "and bus facilities", and there shall be inserted after item number 279 under "Capital Investment Grants" the following:

"280. Iowa .... Mason City, bus facility .... 160,000":

Provided further, That Public Law 105–277, 112 Stat. 2681–458, item number 243 shall be amended by inserting after the word "buses" the following: "and bus facilities".]

[SEC. 226. No funds made available in Public Law 106–69 or any other Act shall be used to decommission or otherwise reduce operations of U.S. Coast Guard WYTL harbor tug boats.]

[SEC. 227. Section 351 of Public Law 106–69 is amended by striking "provided" and inserting "appropriated or limited".]

[SEC. 228. For purposes of section 5117(b)(5) of the Transportation Equity Act for the 21st Century, for fiscal years 1998, 1999 and 2000 the cost-sharing provision of section 5001(b) shall not apply.]

[SEC. 229. Section 366 of the Department of Transportation and Related Agencies Appropriations Act, 2000 (Public Law 106–69) is amended—

(1) by striking "and subject to subsection (b),"; and

(2) by striking "under subsection (a)" and inserting "under this section".]

[SEC. 232. In addition to amounts provided to the Federal Railroad Administration in Public Law 106–69, for necessary expenses for engineering, design and construction activities to enable the James A. Farley Post Office in New York City to be used as a train station and commercial center, to become available on October 1 of the fiscal year specified and to remain available until expended: fiscal year 2001, $20,000,000; fiscal year 2002, $20,000,000; fiscal year 2003, $20,000,000.]

(Miscellaneous Appropriations, 2000, as enacted by section 1000(a)(5) of the Consolidated Appropriations Act, 2000 (P.L. 106–113).)

DEPARTMENT OF THE TREASURY

DEPARTMENTAL OFFICES

Salaries and Expenses

For necessary expenses of the Departmental Offices including operation and maintenance of the Treasury Building and Annex; hire of passenger motor vehicles; maintenance, repairs, and improvements of, and purchase of commercial insurance policies for, real properties leased or owned overseas, when necessary for the performance of official business; [not to exceed $2,900,000 for official travel expenses;] *not to exceed $4,813,000, to remain available until expended for information technology modernization requirements;* not to exceed $150,000 for official reception and representation expenses; not to exceed $258,000 for unforeseen emergencies of a confidential nature, to be allocated and expended under the direction of the Secretary of the Treasury and to be accounted for solely on his certificate, [$134,034,000] *$154,582,000. (Treasury Department Appropriations Act, 2000.)*

Program and Financing (in millions of dollars)

Identification code 20–0101–0–1–803		1999 actual	2000 est.	2001 est.
	Obligations by program activity:			
	Direct program:			
00.01	Executive direction	22	23	
00.02	Domestic finance policies and programs	11	11	
00.03	Tax and economic policies and programs	24	26	
00.04	Enforcement policies and programs	15	18	
00.05	International affairs policies and programs	53	47	
00.06	Treasury-wide management policies and programs	22	22	
00.07	Economic policies and programs			53
00.08	Financial policies and programs			40
00.11	Law enforcement policies and programs			30
00.12	Treasury-wide management policies and programs			32
01.00	Subtotal, Direct programs	147	147	155
	Reimbursable program:			
09.01	Executive direction	2	2	
09.02	Fiscal and financial policies and programs	2	2	
09.03	Enforcement policies and programs	2	2	
09.04	International affairs policies and programs	7	6	
09.05	Treasury-wide management policies and programs	3	3	
09.06	Economic policies and programs			8
09.07	Law enforcement policies and programs			2
09.08	Treasury-wide management policies and programs			3
09.10	Financial policies and programs			2
09.99	Subtotal, reimbursable program	16	15	15
10.00	Total new obligations	163	162	170
	Budgetary resources available for obligation:			
21.40	Unobligated balance available, start of year	14	22	9
22.00	New budget authority (gross)	169	149	170
22.10	Resources available from recoveries of prior year obligations	3		
23.90	Total budgetary resources available for obligation	186	171	179
23.95	Total new obligations	–163	–162	–170
24.40	Unobligated balance available, end of year	22	9	9
	New budget authority (gross), detail:			
	Discretionary:			
40.00	Appropriation	126	134	155
40.75	Reduction pursuant to P.L. 106–51	–1		
42.00	Transferred from other accounts	28		
43.00	Appropriation (total discretionary)	153	134	155
68.00	Spending authority from offsetting collections: Offsetting collections (cash)	16	15	15
70.00	Total new budget authority (gross)	169	149	170
	Change in unpaid obligations:			
	Unpaid obligations, start of year:			
72.40	Obligated balance, start of year	45	52	74
72.95	From Federal sources: Receivables and unpaid, unfilled orders	7	7	7
72.99	Total unpaid obligations, start of year	52	59	81
73.10	Total new obligations	163	162	170
73.20	Total outlays (gross)	–153	–140	–168
73.45	Adjustments in unexpired accounts	–3		
	Unpaid obligations, end of year:			
74.40	Obligated balance, end of year	52	74	76
74.95	From Federal sources: Receivables and unpaid, unfilled orders	7	7	7
74.99	Total unpaid obligations, end of year	59	81	83
	Outlays (gross), detail:			
86.90	Outlays from new discretionary authority	131	140	159
86.93	Outlays from discretionary balances	22		9
87.00	Total outlays (gross)	153	140	168
	Offsets:			
	Against gross budget authority and outlays:			
88.00	Offsetting collections (cash) from: Federal sources	–16	–15	–15
	Net budget authority and outlays:			
89.00	Budget authority	153	134	155
90.00	Outlays	138	125	153
	Memorandum (non-add) entries:			
92.01	Total investments, start of year: U.S. securities: Par value		2	
92.02	Total investments, end of year: U.S. securities: Par value	2		

Departmental Offices' function in the Treasury Department is to provide basic support to the Secretary of the Treasury, who is the chief operating executive of the Department. The Secretary of the Treasury maintains the primary role in formulating and managing the domestic and international tax and financial policies of the Federal Government. The Secretary's responsibilities funded by the Salaries and Expenses appropriation include: recommending and implementing United States domestic and international economic and tax policy; fiscal policy; governing the fiscal operations of the Government; maintaining foreign assets control; managing the public debt; overseeing the major law enforcement functions carried out by the Treasury Department; managing development financial policy; representing the United States on international monetary, trade and investment issues; overseeing Treasury Department overseas operations; and directing the administrative operations of the Treasury Department.

In support of the Secretary, the Salaries and Expenses appropriation provides resources for policy formulation and implementation in the areas of domestic and international financial, investment, tax, economic, trade and financial operations and general fiscal policy. This appropriation also provides resources for administrative support to the Secretary and policy components, and coordination of Departmental administrative policies in financial and personnel management, procurement operations, and automated information systems and telecommunications.

Economic Policies and Programs.—The function of the Economic Policies and Programs Activity is to advise the Secretary and Deputy Secretary in economic areas such as: (1) monitors macro- and micro-economic developments and assists in determining appropriate economic policies; collects and analyzes data pertaining to international portfolio investment and foreign exchange positions; develops an overall appraisal of the current state of, and outlook for the economy; provides

SALARIES AND EXPENSES—Continued

written and oral briefing materials for the Secretary, other officials, and outsiders; participates in interagency groups working on economic matters to develop and maintain a coordinated and consistent government-wide economic program; and (2) the formulation and execution of U.S. international economic and financial policies regarding a wide range of international development and analysis functions involving: trade and investment, energy policy, monetary affairs, development financing, and general economic research into international financial issues. The Office of International Affairs works closely with other Federal agencies and international financial institutions, and coordinates international financial and macro-economic policy with the National Economic Council (Annual Economic Summit), the National Security Council, the Council of Economic Advisors, the Office of Management and Budget (foreign country risk review), the United States Trade Representative (financial services, investment, etc.), and all components of the Executive Office of the President. Under Presidential Executive order, the Office of International Affairs participants with the Department of State in the collection and analysis of economic information on foreign countries. In the areas of international monetary and foreign exchange policy, the Office of International Affairs shares responsibility with the Federal Reserve (principally, the Board of Governors, but also the Federal Reserve Bank of New York) in working closely with the International Monetary Fund. In the area of international development, the Office of International Affairs formulates resource needs, notably U.S. contributions, policies and programs for various Multilateral Development Banks. With the Export-Import Bank, the Office of International Affairs has responsibility for export credit finance. This activity includes the Office of the Assistant Secretary (Economic Policy), the immediate offices of the Under Secretary (International Affairs), the Assistant Secretary (International Affairs) and the Office of International Affairs.

Financial Policies and Programs.—The function of the Financial Policies and Programs Activity is to advise the Secretary and Deputy Secretary in areas of domestic finance, banking, fiscal policy and operations, and other related financial matters, including development of policies and guidance in the areas of financial institutions, federal debt finance, financial regulation, and capital markets. Specifically, this activity ensures that the management of the Federal government's cash minimizes risk and strikes a balance between cash needs and short-term investments. This activity provides decision makers and stakeholders with: (1) timely, concise and thorough policies, guidance and analysis in the areas of: financial institutions, financial regulation, the equitable and efficient delivery of financial services, the availability of credit, financial crimes, federal debt finance, capital markets, the privatization of government assets, and any other issues related to domestic finance and financial services; and (2) the development and implementation of tax policies and programs; provides official estimates of all Government receipts for the President's Budget, fiscal policy decisions, and cash management decisions; establishes policy criteria reflected in regulations and rulings and guides preparation of them with the Internal Revenue Service to implement the Internal Revenue Code; negotiates tax treaties for the United States; and provides economic and legal policy analysis for domestic and international tax policy decisions. This activity includes the immediate office of the Under Secretary (Domestic Finance), the Assistant Secretary (Financial Institutions), the DAS Financial Institutions Policy, the Assistant Secretary (Financial Markets), the Fiscal Assistant Secretary, and the Deputy Assistant Secretary for Community Development Policy and the Assistant Secretary for Tax Policy.

Enforcement Policies and Programs.—The function of the Enforcement Policies and Programs activity is to provide policy development, guidance and coordination to Treasury's law enforcement entities to combat money laundering and other financial crime, interdict illegal drugs, reduce violent crime, protect our nation's leaders, and provide quality training for enforcement personnel. Responsibilities include: providing Departmental oversight and supervision of U.S. Customs Service, U.S. Secret Service, Federal Law Enforcement Training Center, Financial Crimes Enforcement Network, Bureau of Alcohol, Tobacco, and Firearms, and Executive Office of Asset Forfeiture; and negotiating international agreements on behalf of the Secretary to engage in joint law enforcement operations for the exchange of financial information and records. The Office of Enforcement administers economic sanctions against selective foreign countries, international narcotics traffickers and international terrorists in furtherance of U.S. foreign policy and national security goals. This activity includes the immediate offices of the Under Secretary for Enforcement and the Assistant Secretary (Enforcement), including the Office of Foreign Assets Control.

Treasury-wide Management Policies and Programs.—The Treasury-wide Management Policies and Programs Activity provides policy advice on matters involving the internal management of the Department and its bureaus; coinage and currency production and security; the sale and retention of savings bonds; financial management, information systems, security, property management, human resources, procurement and contracting, strategic planning; and customer service. This activity is responsible for implementing the functions of the Chief Financial Officer (CFO), the Government Performance Results Act (GPRA), and the Information Technology Management Reform Act which includes efficient and effective use of the Treasury's resources. This activity includes the Office of the Assistant Secretary (Management) and Chief Financial Officer and the Treasurer of the United States.

Performance Measures:	2001 est.
Progress toward achieving Treasury's strategic goals	Quality report by mission area
Index of borrowing policies and borrowing requirements to financial market participants in a timely manner	100%
Economic conditions in developing countries measured by quantitative indicators	Maintain or improve
Economic conditions of foreign countries which are major U.S. trading partners measured by growth rate	Maintain or improve
Audit opinions of consolidated Treasury-Wide Financial Statements	Unqualified opinion
Percentage of Treasury employees serviced by new, modularly developed human resources system (HR connect)	12%

Object Classification (in millions of dollars)

Identification code 20–0101–0–1–803		1999 actual	2000 est.	2001 est.
	Direct obligations:			
	Personnel compensation:			
11.1	Full-time permanent	68	77	79
11.3	Other than full-time permanent	4	3	4
11.5	Other personnel compensation	3	2	3
11.8	Special personal services payments	2	1	1
11.9	Total personnel compensation	77	83	87
12.1	Civilian personnel benefits	16	17	18
21.0	Travel and transportation of persons	5	6	3
23.1	Rental payments to GSA	1	1	2
23.2	Rental payments to others	2	1	
23.3	Communications, utilities, and miscellaneous charges	8	8	9
24.0	Printing and reproduction	1	2	2
25.1	Advisory and assistance services	4		1
25.2	Other services	28	23	25
26.0	Supplies and materials	2	2	2
31.0	Equipment	3	3	3
99.0	Subtotal, direct obligations	147	146	152
99.0	Reimbursable obligations	15	14	14

99.5	Below reporting threshold	1	2	4
99.9	Total new obligations	163	162	170

Personnel Summary

Identification code 20–0101–0–1–803		1999 actual	2000 est.	2001 est.
	Direct:			
1001	Total compensable workyears: Full-time equivalent employment	969	1,069	1,106
	Reimbursable:			
2001	Total compensable workyears: Full-time equivalent employment	106	114	114

United States Community Adjustment and Investment Program

For the United States Community Adjustment and Investment Program authorized by section 543 of the North American Free Trade Agreement Implementation Act, $10,000,000, to remain available until September 30, [2001] *2002*: *Provided*, That the Secretary may transfer such funds to the North American Development Bank and/or to one or more Federal agencies for the purpose of enabling the Bank or such Federal agencies to assist in carrying out the program by providing technical assistance, grants, loans, loan guarantees, and other financial subsidies endorsed by the interagency finance committee established by section 7 of Executive Order No. 12916: *Provided further*, That no portion of such funds may be transferred to the Bank unless the Secretary shall have first entered into an agreement with the Bank that provides that any such funds may not be used for the Bank's administrative expenses: *Provided further*, That any funds transferred to the Bank under this heading will be in addition to the 10 percent of the paid-in capital paid to the Bank by the United States referred to in section 543 of the Act: *Provided further*, That any funds transferred to any Federal agency under this heading will be in addition to amounts otherwise provided to such agency: *Provided further*, That any funds transferred to an agency under this heading shall be subject to the same terms and conditions as the account to which transferred. *(Foreign Operations, Export Financing, and Related Programs Appropriations Act, 2000, as enacted by section 1000(a)(2) of the Consolidated Appropriations Act, 2000 (P.L. 106–113).)*

Program and Financing (in millions of dollars)

Identification code 20–0118–0–1–451		1999 actual	2000 est.	2001 est.
	Obligations by program activity:			
10.00	Total new obligations (object class 41.0)	1	19	10
	Budgetary resources available for obligation:			
21.40	Unobligated balance available, start of year		9	
22.00	New budget authority (gross)	9	10	10
23.90	Total budgetary resources available for obligation	9	19	10
23.95	Total new obligations	–1	–19	–10
24.40	Unobligated balance available, end of year	9		
	New budget authority (gross), detail:			
	Discretionary:			
40.00	Appropriation	10	10	10
41.00	Transferred to other accounts	–1		
43.00	Appropriation (total discretionary)	9	10	10
	Change in unpaid obligations:			
72.40	Unpaid obligations, start of year: Obligated balance, start of year			5
73.10	Total new obligations	1	19	10
73.20	Total outlays (gross)	–1	–14	–10
74.40	Unpaid obligations, end of year: Obligated balance, end of year		5	5
	Outlays (gross), detail:			
86.90	Outlays from new discretionary authority	1	5	5
86.93	Outlays from discretionary balances		9	5
87.00	Total outlays (gross)	1	14	10
	Net budget authority and outlays:			
89.00	Budget authority	9	10	10
90.00	Outlays	1	14	10

This program provides credit to both new and existing businesses within communities that suffered job losses as a result of changing trade patterns with Canada and Mexico associated with NAFTA. The funding will be used to provide technical assistance, grants, loans, loan guarantees, and other financial subsidies endorsed by the inter-agency finance committee established by section 7 of Executive Order 12916. The interagency finance committee is currently composed of the Department of Treasury, the Department of Labor, the Department of Commerce (Economic Development Administration), the Department of Housing and Urban Development, the Small Business Administration, and the Department of Agriculture.

Department-Wide Systems and Capital Investments Programs

(INCLUDING TRANSFER OF FUNDS)

For development and acquisition of automatic data processing equipment, software, and services for the Department of the Treasury, [$43,961,000] *$99,279,000*, to remain available until expended, *of which $55,000,000 shall be for the development of the Integrated Treasury Network for wireless communications, $7,000,000 shall be for the development of six Public Key Infrastructure pilot programs in Federal agencies, and $4,000,000 shall be for critical infrastructure protection research and development projects in the banking and finance sectors*: *Provided*, That these funds shall be transferred to accounts and in amounts as necessary to satisfy the requirements of the Department's offices, bureaus, and other organizations: *Provided further*, That this transfer authority shall be in addition to any other transfer authority provided in this Act: *Provided further*, That *with the exception of amounts for Treasury-wide Human Resources Information System components and the Integrated Treasury Network for law enforcement communications,* none of the funds appropriated shall be used to support or supplement the Internal Revenue Service appropriations for Information Systems. *(Treasury Department Appropriations Act, 2000.)*

Program and Financing (in millions of dollars)

Identification code 20–0115–0–1–803		1999 actual	2000 est.	2001 est.
	Obligations by program activity:			
00.01	Automation enhancement	74	43	99
10.00	Total new obligations	74	43	99
	Budgetary resources available for obligation:			
21.40	Unobligated balance available, start of year	2	9	9
22.00	New budget authority (gross)	78	43	99
22.10	Resources available from recoveries of prior year obligations	4		
23.90	Total budgetary resources available for obligation	84	52	108
23.95	Total new obligations	–74	–43	–99
24.40	Unobligated balance available, end of year	9	9	9
	New budget authority (gross), detail:			
	Discretionary:			
40.00	Appropriation	29	44	99
40.76	Reduction pursuant to P.L. 106–113		–1	
41.00	Transferred to other accounts	–13		
42.00	Transferred from other accounts	62		
43.00	Appropriation (total discretionary)	78	43	99
	Change in unpaid obligations:			
72.40	Unpaid obligations, start of year: Obligated balance, start of year	3	51	35
73.10	Total new obligations	74	43	99
73.20	Total outlays (gross)	–21	–60	–53
73.45	Adjustments in unexpired accounts	–4		
74.40	Unpaid obligations, end of year: Obligated balance, end of year	51	35	81
	Outlays (gross), detail:			
86.90	Outlays from new discretionary authority	18	8	18
86.93	Outlays from discretionary balances	3	52	35

DEPARTMENT-WIDE SYSTEMS AND CAPITAL INVESTMENTS PROGRAMS—Continued

(INCLUDING TRANSFER OF FUNDS)—Continued

Program and Financing (in millions of dollars)—Continued

Identification code 20–0115–0–1–803	1999 actual	2000 est.	2001 est.
87.00 Total outlays (gross)	21	60	53
Net budget authority and outlays:			
89.00 Budget authority	78	43	99
90.00 Outlays	21	60	53

The 1997 Treasury Postal Appropriations Act established this account which is authorized to be used by or on behalf of Treasury bureaus, at the Secretary's discretion, to modernize business processes and increase efficiency through technology investments.

Object Classification (in millions of dollars)

Identification code 20–0115–0–1–803	1999 actual	2000 est.	2001 est.
25.1 Advisory and assistance services	8		
25.2 Other services	60	21	57
31.0 Equipment	6	19	42
41.0 Grants, subsidies, and contributions		3	
99.9 Total new obligations	74	43	99

DEPARTMENT-WIDE SYSTEMS AND CAPITAL INVESTMENTS PROGRAMS

(Proposed for later transmittal, not subject to PAYGO)

Program and Financing (in millions of dollars)

Identification code 20–0115–2–1–803	1999 actual	2000 est.	2001 est.
New budget authority (gross), detail:			
Discretionary:			
40.00 Appropriation			−55
42.00 Transferred from other accounts			55
43.00 Appropriation (total discretionary)			
Net budget authority and outlays:			
89.00 Budget authority			
90.00 Outlays			

This proposal would transfer receipts from the Federal Communications Commission's (FCC's) proposed analog spectrum lease fee. Funds are included in the request to coordinate with the Department of Justice in the development of the Integrated Treasury Network for wireless communications. Upon enactment of authorizing legislation for the FCC fee, the amount requested from the General Fund will be reduced by the amount of the transfer.

OFFICE OF INSPECTOR GENERAL

SALARIES AND EXPENSES

For necessary expenses of the Office of Inspector General in carrying out the provisions of the Inspector General Act of 1978, as amended, not to exceed $2,000,000 for official travel expenses, including hire of passenger motor vehicles; and not to exceed $100,000 for unforeseen emergencies of a confidential nature, to be allocated and expended under the direction of the Inspector General of the Treasury, [$30,716,000] *$33,608,000*. *(Treasury Department Appropriations Act, 2000.)*

Program and Financing (in millions of dollars)

Identification code 20–0106–0–1–803	1999 actual	2000 est.	2001 est.
Obligations by program activity:			
00.01 Direct program: Inspector General	30	31	34
09.01 Reimbursable program			1
10.00 Total new obligations	30	31	35
Budgetary resources available for obligation:			
22.00 New budget authority (gross)	30	31	35
23.95 Total new obligations	−30	−31	−35
New budget authority (gross), detail:			
Discretionary:			
40.00 Appropriation	31	31	34
41.00 Transferred to other accounts	−1		
43.00 Appropriation (total discretionary)	30	31	34
68.00 Spending authority from offsetting collections: Offsetting collections (cash)			1
70.00 Total new budget authority (gross)	30	31	35
Change in unpaid obligations:			
Unpaid obligations, start of year:			
72.40 Obligated balance, start of year	6	6	6
72.95 From Federal sources: Receivables and unpaid, unfilled orders	1	1	1
72.99 Total unpaid obligations, start of year	7	7	7
73.10 Total new obligations	30	31	35
73.20 Total outlays (gross)	−30	−31	−35
Unpaid obligations, end of year:			
74.40 Obligated balance, end of year	6	6	6
74.95 From Federal sources: Receivables and unpaid, unfilled orders	1	1	1
74.99 Total unpaid obligations, end of year	7	7	7
Outlays (gross), detail:			
86.90 Outlays from new discretionary authority	26	26	30
86.93 Outlays from discretionary balances	4	4	5
87.00 Total outlays (gross)	30	31	35
Offsets:			
Against gross budget authority and outlays:			
88.00 Offsetting collections (cash) from: Federal sources			−1
Net budget authority and outlays:			
89.00 Budget authority	30	31	34
90.00 Outlays	30	31	34

The Office of Inspector General conducts and supervises audits, evaluations and investigations designed to: (1) promote economy, efficiency, and effectiveness and prevent fraud, waste, and abuse in Departmental programs and operations; and (2) keep the Secretary and the Congress fully and currently informed of problems and deficiencies in the administration of Departmental programs and operations. The audit function provides program audit, contract audit and financial statement audit services. Contract audits provide professional advice to agency contracting officials on accounting and financial matters relative to negotiation, award, administration, repricing, and settlement of contracts. Program audits review and audit all facets of agency operations. Financial statement audits assess whether financial statements fairly present the agency's financial condition and results of operations, the adequacy of accounting controls, and compliance with laws and regulations. These audits contribute significantly to improved financial management by helping Treasury managers identify improvements needed in their accounting and internal control systems. The evaluations function reviews program performance and issues critical to the mission of the Department, including assessing the Department's implementation of the Government Performance and Results Act. The investigative function provides for the detection and investigation of improper and illegal activities involving programs, personnel, and operations. This appropriation also provides for the oversight of internal investigations made by the Offices of Internal Affairs and Inspection in the Bureau of ATF, the Customs Service, and the Secret Service.

The Inspectors General Auditor Training Institute provides the necessary facilities, equipment, and support services for conducting auditor training for the Federal Government Inspector General community. The Office of Inspector General is the parent organization for this entity, although program and financing data is reported under the Treasury Franchise fund (effective in 1999).

PERFORMANCE MEASURES

	1999 actual	2000 est.	2001 est.
Audit:			
Potential dollar savings identified (in millions)	$83	$46	$50
Percentage of audit recommendations implemented within 12 months of acceptance by departmental and bureau managers	79%	72%	72%
Investigations:			
Percentage of customers expressing satisfaction with products and services	100%	80%	85%
Percentage of Investigations completed within 12 months	62%	75%	75%
Investigative monetary benefits (in millions)	$.708	$0.35	$0.5

Object Classification (in millions of dollars)

Identification code 20–0106–0–1–803		1999 actual	2000 est.	2001 est.
	Direct obligations:			
	Personnel compensation:			
11.1	Full-time permanent	17	19	19
11.5	Other personnel compensation	1	1	2
11.9	Total personnel compensation	18	20	21
12.1	Civilian personnel benefits	5	5	5
21.0	Travel and transportation of persons	1	1	1
23.1	Rental payments to GSA	2	2	3
23.3	Communications, utilities, and miscellaneous charges	1	1	1
25.2	Other services	1	1	1
25.3	Purchases of goods and services from Government accounts	1	1	1
31.0	Equipment	1	1	1
99.0	Subtotal, direct obligations	30	31	34
99.0	Reimbursable obligations			1
99.9	Total new obligations	30	31	35

Personnel Summary

Identification code 20–0106–0–1–803		1999 actual	2000 est.	2001 est.
1001	Total compensable workyears: Full-time equivalent employment	264	282	288

INSPECTOR GENERAL FOR TAX ADMINISTRATION

SALARIES AND EXPENSES

For necessary expenses of the Treasury Inspector General for Tax Administration in carrying out the Inspector General Act of 1978, as amended, including purchase (not to exceed 150 for replacement only for police-type use) and hire of passenger motor vehicles (31 U.S.C. 1343(b)); services authorized by 5 U.S.C. 3109, at such rates as may be determined by the Inspector General for Tax Administration; not to exceed $6,000,000 for official travel expenses; and not to exceed $500,000 for unforeseen emergencies of a confidential nature, to be allocated and expended under the direction of the Inspector General for Tax Administration, [$112,207,000] *$118,427,000*. *(Treasury Department Appropriations Act, 2000.)*

Program and Financing (in millions of dollars)

Identification code 20–0119–0–1–803		1999 actual	2000 est.	2001 est.
	Obligations by program activity:			
00.01	Direct program		112	118
09.01	Reimbursable program		2	2
10.00	Total new obligations		114	120
	Budgetary resources available for obligation:			
22.00	New budget authority (gross)		114	120
23.95	Total new obligations		−114	−120
	New budget authority (gross), detail:			
	Discretionary:			
40.00	Appropriation		112	118
68.00	Spending authority from offsetting collections: Offsetting collections (cash)		2	2
70.00	Total new budget authority (gross)		114	120
	Change in unpaid obligations:			
72.40	Unpaid obligations, start of year: Obligated balance, start of year			11
73.10	Total new obligations		114	120
73.20	Total outlays (gross)		−103	−119
74.40	Unpaid obligations, end of year: Obligated balance, end of year		11	14
	Outlays (gross), detail:			
86.90	Outlays from new discretionary authority		103	108
86.93	Outlays from discretionary balances			11
87.00	Total outlays (gross)		103	119
	Offsets:			
	Against gross budget authority and outlays:			
88.00	Offsetting collections (cash) from: Federal sources		−2	−2
	Net budget authority and outlays:			
89.00	Budget authority		112	118
90.00	Outlays		101	117

The Treasury Inspector General for Tax Administration (TIGTA) conducts audits, investigations, and evaluations to assess the operations and programs of the Internal Revenue Service (IRS) and Related Entities, the IRS Oversight Board and the Office of Chief Counsel to: (1) promote the economic, efficient and effective administration of the nation's tax laws and to detect and deter fraud and abuse in IRS programs and operations; and (2) recommend actions to resolve fraud and other serious problems, abuses, and deficiencies in these programs and operations, and keep the Secretary and the Congress fully and currently informed of these issues and the progress made in resolving them. TIGTA reviews existing and proposed legislation and regulations relating to the programs and operations of the IRS and Related Entities and makes recommendations concerning the impact of such legislation and regulations on the economy and efficiency in the administration of programs and operations of the IRS and Related Entities. The audit function provides program audit, contract audit and financial statement audit services. Program audits review and audit all facets of IRS and Related Entities. Contract audits provide professional advice to IRS contracting officials on accounting and financial matters relative to negotiation, award, administration, repricing, and settlement of contracts. The evaluations function reviews program performance and issues critical to the mission of the IRS. The investigative function provides for the detection and investigation of improper and illegal activities involving IRS programs and operations and protects the IRS and Related Entities against external attempts to corrupt or threaten their employees.

The Treasury Inspector General for Tax Administration was established by the IRS Restructuring and Reform Act of 1998 (P.L. 105–206). Funding was first appropriated for this account in the FY 2000 Treasury Appropriations Act (P.L. 106–58).

PERFORMANCE MEASURES

	1999 actual	2000 est.	2001 est.
Audit:			
Potential monetary benefits expected from IRS' corrective actions to audit recommendations (in millions)	$192	$102	$120
Percentage of recommendations agreed to by IRS management	95%	90%	90%
Investigations:			
Percentage of criminal investigative reports referred for prosecution within one year of initiation	80%	80%	80%

INSPECTOR GENERAL FOR TAX ADMINISTRATION—Continued

SALARIES AND EXPENSES—Continued

PERFORMANCE MEASURES—Continued

	1999 actual	2000 est.	2001 est.
Percentage of misconduct (non-criminal) investigative reports referred to the IRS within four months of initiation	51%	60%	65%

Object Classification (in millions of dollars)

Identification code 20–0119–0–1–803		1999 actual	2000 est.	2001 est.
	Direct obligations:			
	Personnel compensation:			
11.1	Full-time permanent		64	67
11.5	Other personnel compensation		7	7
11.9	Total personnel compensation		71	74
12.1	Civilian personnel benefits		17	19
21.0	Travel and transportation of persons		5	5
23.1	Rental payments to GSA		8	9
23.3	Communications, utilities, and miscellaneous charges		1	1
25.2	Other services		2	2
25.7	Operation and maintenance of equipment		2	2
26.0	Supplies and materials		1	1
31.0	Equipment		5	5
99.0	Subtotal, direct obligations		112	118
99.0	Reimbursable obligations		2	2
99.9	Total new obligations		114	120

Personnel Summary

Identification code 20–0119–0–1–803		1999 actual	2000 est.	2001 est.
	Direct:			
1001	Total compensable workyears: Full-time equivalent employment		1,000	1,006
	Reimbursable:			
2001	Total compensable workyears: Full-time equivalent employment		20	20

TREASURY BUILDING AND ANNEX REPAIR AND RESTORATION

For the repair, alteration, and improvement of the Treasury Building and Annex, [$23,000,000] *$31,000,000*, to remain available until expended. *(Treasury Department Appropriations Act, 2000.)*

Program and Financing (in millions of dollars)

Identification code 20–0108–0–1–803		1999 actual	2000 est.	2001 est.
	Obligations by program activity:			
00.01	Repair and improvement of Main Treasury	27	52	31
10.00	Total new obligations	27	52	31
	Budgetary resources available for obligation:			
21.40	Unobligated balance available, start of year	28	29	
22.00	New budget authority (gross)	27	23	31
22.10	Resources available from recoveries of prior year obligations	1		
23.90	Total budgetary resources available for obligation	56	52	31
23.95	Total new obligations	–27	–52	–31
24.40	Unobligated balance available, end of year	29		
	New budget authority (gross), detail:			
	Discretionary:			
40.00	Appropriation	27	23	31
	Change in unpaid obligations:			
72.40	Unpaid obligations, start of year: Obligated balance, start of year	6	24	54
73.10	Total new obligations	27	52	31
73.20	Total outlays (gross)	–8	–22	–29
73.45	Adjustments in unexpired accounts	–1		
74.40	Unpaid obligations, end of year: Obligated balance, end of year	24	54	56
	Outlays (gross), detail:			
86.90	Outlays from new discretionary authority	5	17	22
86.93	Outlays from discretionary balances	3	5	7
87.00	Total outlays (gross)	8	22	29
	Net budget authority and outlays:			
89.00	Budget authority	27	23	31
90.00	Outlays	8	22	29

This appropriation funds repairs and selected improvements to maintain the Main Treasury and Annex buildings.

Object Classification (in millions of dollars)

Identification code 20–0108–0–1–803		1999 actual	2000 est.	2001 est.
11.1	Personnel compensation: Full-time permanent	1	1	1
23.1	Rental payments to GSA	2	3	2
23.3	Communications, utilities, and miscellaneous charges		6	3
25.2	Other services	23	41	24
31.0	Equipment	1	1	1
99.9	Total new obligations	27	52	31

Personnel Summary

Identification code 20–0108–0–1–803		1999 actual	2000 est.	2001 est.
1001	Total compensable workyears: Full-time equivalent employment	10	10	10

MONEY LAUNDERING STRATEGY

(INCLUDING TRANSFER OF FUNDS)

For carrying out the Department's money laundering strategy, including grants to State and local law enforcement, $15,000,000, to remain available until expended: Provided, That of these amounts such sums as may be necessary may be transferred to accounts of the Department's offices, bureaus, and other organizations: Provided further, That this transfer authority shall be in addition to any other transfer authority provided in this Act. (P.L. 105–310).

Program and Financing (in millions of dollars)

Identification code 20–0120–0–1–751		1999 actual	2000 est.	2001 est.
	Obligations by program activity:			
00.01	Money laundering strategy			15
10.00	Total new obligations			15
	Budgetary resources available for obligation:			
22.00	New budget authority (gross)			15
23.95	Total new obligations			–15
	New budget authority (gross), detail:			
	Discretionary:			
40.00	Appropriation			15
	Change in unpaid obligations:			
73.10	Total new obligations			15
73.20	Total outlays (gross)			–13
74.40	Unpaid obligations, end of year: Obligated balance, end of year			2
	Outlays (gross), detail:			
86.90	Outlays from new discretionary authority			13
	Net budget authority and outlays:			
89.00	Budget authority			15
90.00	Outlays			13

The Money Laundering and Financial Crimes Strategy Act was enacted in 1998 and calls for the development of a five-year anti-money laundering strategy. Funds are requested to support Treasury's role in the National Money Laundering Strategy, for which the first of five annual reports to the Congress was submitted to the Congress in September 1999. The Strategy reflects an increased national commitment to a coordinated and effective fight against money laundering. The Strategy's implementation will depend, in part, on additional resources, which is the basis of this new request.

The overall strategy was released in September 1999 and sets forth a series of action items designed to advance four fundamental goals in the fight against money laundering: strengthening domestic enforcement; enhancing the measures taken by banks and other financial institutions; building stronger partnerships with state and local governments; and bolstering international cooperation. The Strategy calls on the Departments of the Treasury and Justice and, as appropriate, other relevant agencies, to undertake key actions to implement the National Money Laundering Strategy recommendations.

Object Classification (in millions of dollars)

Identification code 20–0120–0–1–751		1999 actual	2000 est.	2001 est.
	Personnel compensation:			
11.1	Full-time permanent			3
11.5	Other personnel compensation			2
11.9	Total personnel compensation			5
12.1	Civilian personnel benefits			1
21.0	Travel and transportation of persons			1
23.1	Rental payments to GSA			1
25.2	Other services			2
31.0	Equipment			1
41.0	Grants, subsidies, and contributions			4
99.9	Total new obligations			15

Personnel Summary

Identification code 20–0120–0–1–751		1999 actual	2000 est.	2001 est.
1001	Total compensable workyears: Full-time equivalent employment			36

Financial Crimes Enforcement Network

SALARIES AND EXPENSES

For necessary expenses of the Financial Crimes Enforcement Network, including hire of passenger motor vehicles; travel expenses of non-Federal law enforcement personnel to attend meetings concerned with financial intelligence activities, law enforcement, and financial regulation; not to exceed $14,000 for official reception and representation expenses; and for assistance to Federal law enforcement agencies, with or without reimbursement, [$27,818,000] *$34,694,000*, of which not to exceed [$1,000,000] *$2,800,000* shall remain available until September 30, [2002] *2003; and of which $2,275,000 shall remain available until September 30, 2002*: *Provided*, That funds appropriated in this account may be used to procure personal services contracts. *(Treasury Department Appropriations Act, 2000.)*

Program and Financing (in millions of dollars)

Identification code 20–0173–0–1–751		1999 actual	2000 est.	2001 est.
	Obligations by program activity:			
	Direct Program:			
00.01	Investigative analysis, regulatory, and international activities	24	28	33
00.02	Money services business regulatory support program			2
09.01	Reimbursable program	2	3	1
10.00	Total new obligations	26	31	36
	Budgetary resources available for obligation:			
21.40	Unobligated balance available, start of year			
22.00	New budget authority (gross)	26	31	36
23.90	Total budgetary resources available for obligation	26	31	36
23.95	Total new obligations	–26	–31	–36
24.40	Unobligated balance available, end of year			
	New budget authority (gross), detail:			
	Discretionary:			
40.00	Appropriation	24	28	35
	Spending authority from offsetting collections:			
68.00	Offsetting collections (cash)	1	4	1
68.10	From Federal sources: Change in receivables and unpaid, unfilled orders	1	–1	
68.90	Spending authority from offsetting collections (total discretionary)	2	3	1
70.00	Total new budget authority (gross)	26	31	36
	Change in unpaid obligations:			
	Unpaid obligations, start of year:			
72.40	Obligated balance, start of year	5	4	6
72.95	From Federal sources: Receivables and unpaid, unfilled orders		1	
72.99	Total unpaid obligations, start of year	5	5	6
73.10	Total new obligations	26	31	36
73.20	Total outlays (gross)	–26	–29	–34
	Unpaid obligations, end of year:			
74.40	Obligated balance, end of year	4	6	8
74.95	From Federal sources: Receivables and unpaid, unfilled orders	1		
74.99	Total unpaid obligations, end of year	5	6	8
	Outlays (gross), detail:			
86.90	Outlays from new discretionary authority	22	25	28
86.93	Outlays from discretionary balances	4	4	6
87.00	Total outlays (gross)	26	29	34
	Offsets:			
	Against gross budget authority and outlays:			
88.00	Offsetting collections (cash) from: Federal sources	–1	–4	–1
	Against gross budget authority only:			
88.95	From Federal sources: Change in receivables and unpaid, unfilled orders	–1	1	
	Net budget authority and outlays:			
89.00	Budget authority	24	28	35
90.00	Outlays	25	25	33

The Financial Crimes Enforcement Network (FinCEN) has responsibility for implementing Treasury's anti-money laundering regulations through administration of the Bank Secrecy Act, 31 U.S.C. section 5311, et. seq., and serves as a United States Government source for the systematic collection and analysis of information to assist in the investigation of money laundering and other financial crimes. FinCEN supports Treasury's goal to 'Combat Financial Crimes and Money Laundering' by: (1) providing focused and sophisticated analysis of the elements of major case law enforcement support including trends and patterns of money laundering; (2) preventing money laundering through its regulatory programs and its outreach efforts to the financial community; and (3) serving as a catalyst to enlist valuable international support by promoting anti-money laundering measures worldwide.

Investigative Analysis, Regulatory and International Activities.—Through our investigative analysis efforts, FinCEN provides assistance to all law enforcement entities, including Federal, state, local and international, as they investigate and prosecute individuals, businesses and organizations involved in money laundering and other financial crimes. In the regulatory area, FinCEN establishes policy for and oversees Bank Secrecy Act (BSA) compliance by financial institutions. FinCEN provides BSA training to law enforcement, bank regulators, and bankers. FinCEN also provides expertise to support policy issues relevant to U.S. Government anti-money laundering and financial crime initiatives carried out through multilateral organizations. FinCEN is a catalyst for the development of Financial Intelligence Units (FIUs) in other countries, and the transfer of information on money laundering issues and financial services worldwide.

Money Services Business (MSB) Regulatory Program.—The Money Service Business Regulatory Support Program will

FINANCIAL CRIMES ENFORCEMENT NETWORK—Continued

SALARIES AND EXPENSES—Continued

provide funding for additional regulatory and enforcement support to ensure compliance by money service businesses to the requirements of the Bank Secrecy Act.

PERFORMANCE MEASURES

	1999 actual	2000 est.	2001 est.
Investigative Analysis:			
Number of participants in Investigative Self-Help Platform Program	73	70–75	70–75
Number of tactical cases completed	6851	6500–7000	7000–7500
Number of interagency alerts issued by the Gateway System	1580	1500–1700	1700–1900
Percent of case support which provided investigative leads that were used to support criminal or regulatory investigations. Baseline FY 2000=Actual	N/A	N/A	70–80%
Regulatory Partnership:			
Percent reduction to the CTR reporting burden by banks resulting from the elimination or reformulation of unnecessarily burdensome information collection rules and compliance requirements from FY 1996 baseline	0%	N/A	N/A
Reduce the average time to process a civil penalty case CY 1997 base is 4.2 years	2 years	2 years	2 years
International Cooperation:			
Percentage of countries/jurisdictions with membership in the Financial Action Task Force (FATF) or FATF-like organizations	41%	42–45%	45–48%
Percentage of countries/jurisdictions having units that meet the Egmont Group financial intelligence unit (FIU) definition	24%	26–27%	27–29%

Object Classification (in millions of dollars)

Identification code 20–0173–0–1–751	1999 actual	2000 est.	2001 est.
Direct obligations:			
Personnel compensation:			
11.1 Full-time permanent	10	12	14
11.5 Other personnel compensation	1	1	1
11.9 Total personnel compensation	11	13	15
12.1 Civilian personnel benefits	2	3	3
21.0 Travel and transportation of persons		1	1
23.1 Rental payments to GSA	2	2	2
25.2 Other services	7	7	10
25.3 Purchases of goods and services from Government accounts	1	1	3
31.0 Equipment	1	1	1
99.0 Subtotal, direct obligations	24	28	35
99.0 Reimbursable obligations	2	3	1
99.9 Total new obligations	26	31	36

Personnel Summary

Identification code 20–0173–0–1–751	1999 actual	2000 est.	2001 est.
Direct:			
1001 Total compensable workyears: Full-time equivalent employment	160	183	199
Reimbursable:			
2001 Total compensable workyears: Full-time equivalent employment	5	1	1

EXPANDED ACCESS TO FINANCIAL SERVICES

(INCLUDING TRANSFER OF FUNDS)

To develop and implement programs to expand access to financial services for low- and moderate-income individuals, $30,000,000, to remain available until expended: Provided, That of these funds, such sums as may be necessary may be transferred to accounts of the Department's offices, bureaus, and other organizations: Provided further, That this transfer authority shall be in addition to any other transfer authority provided in this Act.

Program and Financing (in millions of dollars)

Identification code 20–0121–0–1–808	1999 actual	2000 est.	2001 est.
Obligations by program activity:			
00.01 Expanded access to financial services			30
10.00 Total new obligations (object class 25.2)			30
Budgetary resources available for obligation:			
22.00 New budget authority (gross)			30
23.95 Total new obligations			–30
New budget authority (gross), detail:			
Discretionary:			
40.00 Appropriation			30
Change in unpaid obligations:			
73.10 Total new obligations			30
73.20 Total outlays (gross)			–10
74.40 Unpaid obligations, end of year: Obligated balance, end of year			20
Outlays (gross), detail:			
86.90 Outlays from new discretionary authority			10
Net budget authority and outlays:			
89.00 Budget authority			30
90.00 Outlays			10

The Secretary of the Treasury will develop and implement a pilot program to expand access to financial services to low- and moderate-income individuals who do not currently utilize bank accounts or other financial service opportunities. The Treasury Department will develop and assist in funding private sector provision of low-cost electronic accounts and access to ATMs as a way of encouraging greater efficiency and access to the financial services system; conduct research on the financial services needs of low- and moderate-income persons; and assist in funding financial education for low- and moderate-income persons.

SALLIE MAE ASSESSMENTS

Unavailable Collections (in millions of dollars)

Identification code 20–5407–0–2–808	1999 actual	2000 est.	2001 est.
Balance, start of year:			
01.99 Balance, start of year			
Receipts:			
02.01 Sallie Mae assessments		1	1
Appropriation:			
05.01 Sallie Mae assessments		–1	–1
07.99 Total balance, end of year			

Program and Financing (in millions of dollars)

Identification code 20–5407–0–2–808	1999 actual	2000 est.	2001 est.
Obligations by program activity:			
00.01 Sallie Mae assessments		1	1
10.00 Total new obligations (object class 99.5)		1	1
Budgetary resources available for obligation:			
21.40 Unobligated balance available, start of year			
22.00 New budget authority (gross)		1	1
23.90 Total budgetary resources available for obligation		1	1
23.95 Total new obligations		–1	–1
New budget authority (gross), detail:			
Discretionary:			
40.20 Appropriation (special fund, definite)		1	1
Change in unpaid obligations:			
73.10 Total new obligations		1	1

	1999 actual	2000 est.	2001 est.
Outlays (gross), detail:			
86.90 Outlays from new discretionary authority		1	1
Net budget authority and outlays:			
89.00 Budget authority		1	1
90.00 Outlays		1	1

The Secretary of Treasury is authorized by the Higher Education Act of 1965, as amended to collect from the Student Loan Marketing Association an annual assessment of up to $800,000, adjusted by the Consumer Price Index, to cover the expenses relating to providing financial oversight of the Association.

Personnel Summary

Identification code 20–5407–0–2–808	1999 actual	2000 est.	2001 est.
2001 Total compensable workyears: Full-time equivalent employment	2	4	4

COUNTERTERRORISM FUND

For necessary expenses, as determined by the Secretary, $25,000,000, to remain available until expended, to reimburse any Department of the Treasury organization for the costs of providing support to counter, investigate, or prosecute terrorism, including payment of rewards in connection with these activities: Provided, That the entire amount is designated by the Congress as an emergency requirement pursuant to section 251(b)(2)(A) of the Balanced Budget and Emergency Deficit Control Act of 1985, as amended: Provided further, That the entire amount shall be available only to the extent that an official budget request for a specific dollar amount that includes designation of the entire amount of the request as an emergency requirement as defined in such Act is transmitted by the President to the Congress.

Program and Financing (in millions of dollars)

Identification code 20–0117–0–1–751	1999 actual	2000 est.	2001 est.
Obligations by program activity:			
00.01 Atlanta bombing investigations	1		
00.02 International meeting counter-terrorism support	7		
10.00 Total new obligations (object class 25.2)	8		
Budgetary resources available for obligation:			
21.40 Unobligated balance available, start of year	8		
22.00 New budget authority (gross)			25
23.90 Total budgetary resources available for obligation	8		25
23.95 Total new obligations	−8		
24.40 Unobligated balance available, end of year			25
New budget authority (gross), detail:			
Discretionary:			
40.15 Appropriation (emergency)			25
Change in unpaid obligations:			
72.40 Unpaid obligations, start of year: Obligated balance, start of year	3	3	
73.10 Total new obligations	8		
73.20 Total outlays (gross)	−7	−3	
74.40 Unpaid obligations, end of year: Obligated balance, end of year	3		
Outlays (gross), detail:			
86.93 Outlays from discretionary balances	7	3	
Net budget authority and outlays:			
89.00 Budget authority			25
90.00 Outlays	7	3	

The budget includes $25 million as a contingency to cover unanticipated costs associated with: (1) providing support to counter, investigate, or prosecute domestic or international terrorism, including payment of rewards in connection with these activities; and (2) re-establishing the operational capability of an office, facility or other property damaged or destroyed as a result of any domestic or international terrorist incident. Treasury bureaus have important counterterrorism responsibilities including: protecting the President; designing and implementing security at National Special Security Events; investigating arson, explosives and firearms incidents; conducting financial investigations relating to terrorism; preventing weapons of mass destruction from entering our country; and implementing sanctions against terrorist organizations. Funds would be reimbursed to Treasury bureaus or departmental offices to compensate for costs incurred in areas such as travel, transportation, rentals and communications, print and graphics, other services, supplies, equipment, and unvouchered funds.

Credit accounts:

[COMMUNITY DEVELOPMENT FINANCIAL INSTITUTIONS]

[FUND PROGRAM ACCOUNT]

[For grants, loans, and technical assistance to qualifying community development lenders, and administrative expenses of the Fund,] *To carry out the Community Development Banking and Financial Institutions Act of 1994,* including services authorized by 5 U.S.C. 3109, but at rates for individuals not to exceed the per diem rate equivalent to the rate for ES–3, [$95,000,000] *$125,000,000,* to remain available until September 30, [2001] *2002,* of which *$5,000,000 shall be for technical assistance and training programs designed to benefit Native American Communities, and* up to [$7,860,000] *$9,500,000* may be used for administrative expenses, up to [$16,500,000] *$23,000,000* may be used for the cost of direct loans, and up to $1,000,000 may be used for administrative expenses to carry out the direct loan program: *Provided,* That the cost of direct loans, including the cost of modifying such loans, shall be as defined in section 502 of the Congressional Budget Act of 1974: *Provided further,* That these funds are available to subsidize gross obligations for the principal amount of direct loans not to exceed [$53,140,000] *$53,000,000*: *Provided further,* That not more than [$30,000,000] *$40,000,000* of the funds made available under this heading may be used for programs and activities authorized in section 114 of the Community Development Banking and Financial Institutions Act of 1994: *Provided further, That administrative costs of the Technical Assistance Program under section 108, the Training Program under section 109, and the costs of the Native American Lending Study under section 117 shall not be considered to be administrative expenses of the Fund. (Departments of Veterans Affairs and Housing and Urban Development, and Independent Agencies Appropriations Act, 2000.)*

Program and Financing (in millions of dollars)

Identification code 20–1881–0–1–451	1999 actual	2000 est.	2001 est.
Obligations by program activity:			
00.01 Direct loan subsidy	3	3	4
00.05 Reestimate of direct loan subsidy			
00.06 Interest on reestimates of direct loan subsidy			
00.09 Administrative expenses for direct loans	1	1	1
00.10 General administrative expenses	7	8	10
00.11 Bank enterprise awards program	32	25	40
00.12 Financial assistance to Community Development Financial Institutions (other than direct loans)	68	58	60
00.13 Training and technical assistance	10	11	10
10.00 Total new obligations	121	106	125
Budgetary resources available for obligation:			
21.40 Unobligated balance available, start of year	36	10	
22.00 New budget authority (gross)	95	96	125
23.90 Total budgetary resources available for obligation	131	106	125
23.95 Total new obligations	−121	−106	−125
24.40 Unobligated balance available, end of year	10		
New budget authority (gross), detail:			
Discretionary:			
40.00 Appropriation	95	95	125
Mandatory:			
60.05 Appropriation (indefinite)		1	

Credit accounts—Continued

[COMMUNITY DEVELOPMENT FINANCIAL INSTITUTIONS]—Continued
[FUND PROGRAM ACCOUNT]—Continued

Program and Financing (in millions of dollars)—Continued

Identification code 20–1881–0–1–451	1999 actual	2000 est.	2001 est.
70.00 Total new budget authority (gross)	95	96	125
Change in unpaid obligations:			
72.40 Unpaid obligations, start of year: Obligated balance, start of year	107	142	158
73.10 Total new obligations	121	106	125
73.20 Total outlays (gross)	−86	−90	−110
74.40 Unpaid obligations, end of year: Obligated balance, end of year	142	158	173
Outlays (gross), detail:			
86.90 Outlays from new discretionary authority	3	3	4
86.93 Outlays from discretionary balances	83	86	106
86.97 Outlays from new mandatory authority		1	
87.00 Total outlays (gross)	86	90	110
Net budget authority and outlays:			
89.00 Budget authority	95	96	125
90.00 Outlays	86	90	110

Summary of Loan Levels, Subsidy Budget Authority and Outlays by Program (in millions of dollars)

Identification code 20–1881–0–1–451	1999 actual	2000 est.	2001 est.
Direct loan levels supportable by subsidy budget authority:			
1150 Direct loan levels	8	10	10
1159 Total direct loan levels	8	10	10
Direct loan subsidy (in percent):			
1320 Subsidy rate	39.21	31.09	43.41
1329 Weighted average subsidy rate	39.21	31.09	43.41
Direct loan subsidy budget authority:			
1330 Subsidy budget authority	3	4	4
1339 Total subsidy budget authority	3	4	4
Direct loan subsidy outlays:			
1340 Subsidy outlays	2	2	3
1349 Total subsidy outlays	2	2	3
Administrative expense data:			
3510 Budget authority	1	1	1
3580 Outlays from balances	1	1	1

The Riegle Community Development and Regulatory Improvement Act of 1994 established the Community Development Financial Institutions (CDFI) Fund. The CDFI Fund provides equity investments, grants, loans, and technical assistance to new and existing community development financial institutions (CDFIs) such as community development banks, community development credit unions, community development loan and venture capital funds, and microenterprise loan funds. Funds provided by the CDFI Fund will enhance the capacity of these institutions to finance economic development, including small businesses, community facilities, housing, and other community development initiatives in distressed urban, rural, and Native American communities. The CDFI Fund also provides grants to insured depository institutions to facilitate investment in CDFIs and increase community lending activities. In addition, the CDFI Fund operates a training program to increase the capacity and expertise of CDFIs and other members of the financial services industry to undertake community development finance activities. The Fund is seeking reauthorization of its activities under the Community Development Banking and Financial Institutions Act.

The CDFI Fund helps to address the urgent problems of declining economic and social infrastructure, loss of jobs, lack of private enterprise, and deteriorating housing facing many American communities today. Government investment and technical assistance supplements private funds and expertise to ensure that CDFIs are effective in restoring and creating healthy economies.

PERFORMANCE MEASURES

	1999 actual	2000 est.	2001 est.
Increase the number of CDFIs selected to receive financial assistance (includes Core, and Intermediary)	60	63	65
Increase the number of organizations that receive training and technical assistance over the previous fiscal year	75	80	85
Increase the number of BEA awardees that provide financial and technical assistance to CDFIs or distressed communities	80	85	87

Object Classification (in millions of dollars)

Identification code 20–1881–0–1–451	1999 actual	2000 est.	2001 est.
11.1 Personnel compensation: Full-time permanent	2	3	4
12.1 Civilian personnel benefits	1	1	1
23.1 Rental payments to GSA	1	1	1
25.2 Other services	4	2	4
41.0 Grants, subsidies, and contributions	113	99	115
99.9 Total new obligations	121	106	125

Personnel Summary

Identification code 20–1881–0–1–451	1999 actual	2000 est.	2001 est.
1001 Total compensable workyears: Full-time equivalent employment	45	50	60

COMMUNITY DEVELOPMENT FINANCIAL INSTITUTIONS FUND DIRECT LOAN FINANCING ACCOUNT

Program and Financing (in millions of dollars)

Identification code 20–4088–0–3–451	1999 actual	2000 est.	2001 est.
Obligations by program activity:			
00.01 Direct loans	5	5	7
10.00 Total new obligations	5	5	7
Budgetary resources available for obligation:			
22.00 New financing authority (gross)	5	7	8
23.95 Total new obligations	−5	−5	−7
New financing authority (gross), detail:			
Mandatory:			
67.15 Authority to borrow (indefinite)	3	3	4
69.00 Offsetting collections (cash)	2	2	4
69.10 From Federal sources: Change in receivables and unpaid, unfilled orders		2	1
69.47 Portion applied to repay debt			−1
69.90 Spending authority from offsetting collections (total mandatory)	2	4	4
70.00 Total new financing authority (gross)	5	7	8
Change in unpaid obligations:			
Unpaid obligations, start of year:			
72.40 Obligated balance, start of year	5	9	9
72.95 Receivables from program account	4	4	6
72.99 Total unpaid obligations, start of year	9	13	15
73.10 Total new obligations	5	5	7
73.20 Total financing disbursements (gross)	−5	−5	−7
Unpaid obligations, end of year:			
74.40 Obligated balance, end of year	9	9	9
74.95 Receivables from program account	4	6	7
74.99 Total unpaid obligations, end of year	13	15	16
87.00 Total financing disbursements (gross)	5	5	7

	Offsets:			
	Against gross financing authority and financing disbursements:			
	Offsetting collections (cash) from:			
88.00	Federal sources	−2	−2	−3
88.40	Non-Federal sources—principal			−1
88.90	Total, offsetting collections (cash)	−2	−2	−4
	Against gross financing authority only:			
88.95	Change in receivables from program accounts		−2	−1
	Net financing authority and financing disbursements:			
89.00	Financing authority	3	3	3
90.00	Financing disbursements	3	3	3

As required by the Federal Credit Reform Act of 1990, this non-budgetary account records all cash flows to and from the Government resulting from direct loans obligated in 1992 and beyond (including modifications of direct loans that resulted from obligations in any year). The amounts in this account are a means of financing and are not included in the budget totals.

Status of Direct Loans (in millions of dollars)

Identification code 20–4088–0–3–451		1999 actual	2000 est.	2001 est.
	Position with respect to appropriations act limitation on obligations:			
1111	Limitation on direct loans	32	53	53
1112	Unobligated direct loan limitation	−24	−43	−43
1150	Total direct loan obligations	8	10	10
	Cumulative balance of direct loans outstanding:			
1210	Outstanding, start of year	5	10	15
1231	Disbursements: Direct loan disbursements	5	5	7
1251	Repayments: Repayments and prepayments			−1
1290	Outstanding, end of year	10	15	21

Balance Sheet (in millions of dollars)

Identification code 20–4088–0–3–451		1998 actual	1999 actual	2000 est.	2001 est.
	ASSETS:				
	Investments in US securities:				
1106	Federal assets: Receivables, net	3	4	6	7
	Net value of assets related to post–1991 direct loans receivable:				
1401	Direct loans receivable, gross	5	10	15	21
1405	Allowance for subsidy cost (–)	–3	–5	–6	–9
1499	Net present value of assets related to direct loans	2	5	9	12
1999	Total assets	5	9	15	19
	LIABILITIES:				
	Federal liabilities:				
2103	Debt	3	10	15	21
2104	Resources payable to Treasury				
2105	Other				–2
2999	Total liabilities	3	10	15	19
	NET POSITION:				
3100	Appropriated capital	3			
3999	Total net position	3			
4999	Total liabilities and net position	6	10	15	19

Department of the Treasury Forfeiture Fund

Unavailable Collections (in millions of dollars)

Identification code 20–5697–0–2–751		1999 actual	2000 est.	2001 est.
	Balance, start of year:			
01.99	Balance, start of year			
	Receipts:			
02.01	Forfeited cash and proceeds from the sale of forfeited property	324	225	225
02.02	Earnings on investments	23	15	15
02.99	Total receipts	347	240	240
	Appropriation:			
05.01	Department of the Treasury forfeiture fund	−347	−240	−240
07.99	Total balance, end of year			

Program and Financing (in millions of dollars)

Identification code 20–5697–0–2–751		1999 actual	2000 est.	2001 est.
	Obligations by program activity:			
00.01	Asset forfeiture fund	348	382	240
10.00	Total new obligations	348	382	240
	Budgetary resources available for obligation:			
21.40	Unobligated balance available, start of year	166	191	50
22.00	New budget authority (gross)	347	240	240
22.10	Resources available from recoveries of prior year obligations	26		
23.90	Total budgetary resources available for obligation	539	431	290
23.95	Total new obligations	−348	−382	−240
24.40	Unobligated balance available, end of year	191	50	50
	New budget authority (gross), detail:			
	Mandatory:			
60.25	Appropriation (special fund, indefinite)	347	240	240
	Change in unpaid obligations:			
72.40	Unpaid obligations, start of year: Obligated balance, start of year	201	222	224
73.10	Total new obligations	348	382	240
73.20	Total outlays (gross)	−300	−382	−253
73.45	Adjustments in unexpired accounts	−26		
74.40	Unpaid obligations, end of year: Obligated balance, end of year	222	224	211
	Outlays (gross), detail:			
86.97	Outlays from new mandatory authority	209	216	216
86.98	Outlays from mandatory balances	91	166	37
87.00	Total outlays (gross)	300	382	253
	Net budget authority and outlays:			
89.00	Budget authority	347	240	240
90.00	Outlays	300	382	253
	Memorandum (non-add) entries:			
92.01	Total investments, start of year: U.S. securities: Par value	248	288	288
92.02	Total investments, end of year: U.S. securities: Par value	288	288	288

Public Law 102–393 authorized the establishment of the Treasury Forfeiture Fund. It is available to pay or reimburse certain costs and expenses related to seizures and forfeitures that occur pursuant to the Treasury Department's law enforcement activities. The Coast Guard also participates in the program.

The Fund supports Treasury's Law Enforcement Mission and associated goals by providing funds to participating law enforcement bureaus. The following performance measurements are provided in compliance with the Government Performance and Results Act of 1993 (GPRA).

PERFORMANCE AND WORKLOAD MEASURES

	1999 actual	2000 est.	2001 est.
Days between the forfeiture of real property and the sale of the property	394	365	333
Days required to process equitable sharing payments	219	200	180

Object Classification (in millions of dollars)

Identification code 20–5697–0–2–751		1999 actual	2000 est.	2001 est.
25.2	Other services	190	280	138
41.0	Grants, subsidies, and contributions	153	97	97
44.0	Refunds	5	5	5
99.9	Total new obligations	348	382	240

Credit accounts—Continued

PRESIDENTIAL ELECTION CAMPAIGN FUND

Unavailable Collections (in millions of dollars)

Identification code 20–5081–0–2–808	1999 actual	2000 est.	2001 est.
Balance, start of year:			
01.99 Balance, start of year			
Receipts:			
02.01 Presidential Election Campaign Fund	61	61	61
Appropriation:			
05.01 Presidential election campaign fund	−61	−61	−61
07.99 Total balance, end of year			

Program and Financing (in millions of dollars)

Identification code 20–5081–0–2–808	1999 actual	2000 est.	2001 est.
Obligations by program activity:			
00.01 Matching funds in primaries		67	2
00.02 Nominating conventions for parties	26	3	
00.03 General elections		148	
10.00 Total new obligations (object class 41.0)	26	218	2
Budgetary resources available for obligation:			
21.40 Unobligated balance available, start of year	132	166	9
22.00 New budget authority (gross)	61	61	61
23.90 Total budgetary resources available for obligation	193	227	70
23.95 Total new obligations	−26	−218	−2
24.40 Unobligated balance available, end of year	166	9	68
New budget authority (gross), detail:			
Mandatory:			
60.25 Appropriation (special fund, indefinite)	61	61	61
Change in unpaid obligations:			
73.10 Total new obligations	26	218	2
73.20 Total outlays (gross)	−26	−218	−2
Outlays (gross), detail:			
86.97 Outlays from new mandatory authority		61	2
86.98 Outlays from mandatory balances	26	157	
87.00 Total outlays (gross)	26	218	2
Net budget authority and outlays:			
89.00 Budget authority	61	61	61
90.00 Outlays	26	218	2

Matching funds in primaries.—Upon certification by the Federal Election Commission, every candidate eligible to receive payments is entitled to an amount equal to the contributions each has received on or after the beginning of the calendar year immediately preceding the election year.

Nominating conventions of parties.—Upon certification by the Commission, payments may be made to the national committee of a major party or a minor party which elects to receive its entitlement. The total of such payments will be limited to the amount in the account at the time of payment. The national committee of each party may receive payments beginning on July 1 of the year immediately preceding the calendar year in which a presidential nominating convention of the political party is held. The two major parties will receive $4 million each, plus a cost-of-living increase.

Candidates for general elections.—The eligible candidates of each major party in a presidential election will be entitled to equal payments in an amount which, in the aggregate, shall not exceed $20 million each, plus a cost-of-living increase.

Also, provision is made for new parties, minor parties and candidates, who may receive in excess of 5 percent of the popular vote and therefore be entitled to reimbursement of qualified campaign expenditures.

Public enterprise funds:

EXCHANGE STABILIZATION FUND

Program and Financing (in millions of dollars)

Identification code 20–4444–0–3–155	1999 actual	2000 est.	2001 est.
Budgetary resources available for obligation:			
Unobligated balance available, start of year:			
21.40 Unobligated balance available, start of year (Special drawing rights)	10,106	10,284	10,798
21.40 Unobligated balance available, start of year (Fund balance)	−1,480	476	654
21.40 Unobligated balance available, start of year (US Securities)	15,981	15,232	15,994
21.99 Total unobligated balance, start of year	24,607	25,992	27,446
22.00 New budget authority (gross)	1,385	1,454	1,527
23.90 Total budgetary resources available for obligation	25,992	27,446	28,973
Unobligated balance available, end of year:			
24.40 Unobligated balance available, end of year (Special drawing rights)	10,284	10,798	11,338
24.40 Unobligated balance available, end of year (Fund Balance)	476	654	841
24.40 Unobligated balance available, end of year (US Securities)	15,232	15,994	16,794
24.99 Total unobligated balance, end of year	25,992	27,446	28,973
New budget authority (gross), detail:			
Mandatory:			
69.00 Offsetting collections (cash)	1,385	1,454	1,527
Change in unpaid obligations:			
72.40 Unpaid obligations, start of year: Obligated balance, start of year	13,924	13,924	13,924
74.40 Unpaid obligations, end of year: Obligated balance, end of year	13,924	13,924	13,924
Offsets:			
Against gross budget authority and outlays:			
Offsetting collections (cash) from:			
88.20 Interest on U.S. securities	−801	−841	−883
Non-Federal sources:			
88.40 Special drawing rights holdings	−172	−181	−190
88.40 Net gain on exchange transactions	−412	−432	−454
88.90 Total, offsetting collections (cash)	−1,385	−1,454	−1,527
Net budget authority and outlays:			
89.00 Budget authority			
90.00 Outlays	−1,385	−1,454	−1,527
Memorandum (non-add) entries:			
92.01 Total investments, start of year: U.S. securities: Par value	15,981	15,232	15,994
92.02 Total investments, end of year: U.S. securities: Par value	15,232	15,994	16,794

The Secretary of the Treasury is authorized to deal in gold and foreign exchange and other instruments of credit and securities as deemed necessary, consistent with U.S. obligations in the International Monetary Fund (IMF), regarding orderly exchange arrangements. An Exchange Stabilization Fund, with a capital of $200 million, is authorized by law for this purpose (31 U.S.C. 5302). All earnings and interest accruing to this fund are available for the purposes thereof. Transactions in special drawing rights (SDR's) and U.S. holdings of SDR's are administered by the fund. U.S. drawings from the IMF are also advanced to the fund.

The principal sources of the fund's income have been profits on foreign exchange transactions and earnings on investments held by the fund, including interest earned on fund holdings of U.S. Government securities.

The amounts reflected in the 1999 and 2000 estimates entail only projected net interest earnings on Exchange Stabilization Fund (ESF) assets. The estimates are subject to considerable variance, depending on changes in the amount and composition of assets and the interest rates applied to investments. In addition, exchange rate fluctuations can cause the dollar value of income received on foreign currency and SDR investments to fluctuate. Moreover, estimates make no attempt to forecast valuation gains or losses on SDR holdings or realized gains or losses on foreign currency holdings. As required by Public Law 95–612, the fund no longer is used to meet the administrative expenses.

Statement of Operations (in millions of dollars)

Identification code 20–4444–0–3–155	1998 actual	1999 actual	2000 est.	2001 est.
0101 Revenue	600	2,842	1,380	1,450
0102 Expense				
0105 Net income or loss (–)	600	2,842	1,380	1,450

Balance Sheet (in millions of dollars)

Identification code 20–4444–0–3–155	1998 actual	1999 actual	2000 est.	2001 est.
ASSETS:				
Federal assets:				
Investments in US securities:				
1102 Treasury securities, par	15,981	15,232	15,994	16,794
1106 Receivables, net	3	2	2	2
Non-Federal assets:				
1201 Foreign Currency Investments	14,528	16,036	16,838	17,680
1206 Receivables, net	119	110	115	121
1801 Other Federal assets: Cash and other monetary assets	10,106	10,284	10,798	11,338
1999 Total assets	40,737	41,664	43,747	45,935
LIABILITIES:				
2207 Non-Federal liabilities: Other	15,967	14,052	14,755	15,493
2999 Total liabilities	15,967	14,052	14,755	15,493
NET POSITION:				
3100 Appropriated capital	200	200	200	200
3300 Cumulative results of operations	24,570	27,412	28,792	30,242
3999 Total net position	24,770	27,612	28,992	30,442
4999 Total liabilities and net position	40,737	41,664	43,747	45,935

Intragovernmental funds:

Working Capital Fund

Program and Financing (in millions of dollars)

Identification code 20–4501–0–4–803	1999 actual	2000 est.	2001 est.
Obligations by program activity:			
09.10 Working capital fund	247	236	240
09.11 Administrative overhead	6	8	8
10.00 Total new obligations	253	244	248
Budgetary resources available for obligation:			
22.00 New budget authority (gross)	219	244	248
22.10 Resources available from recoveries of prior year obligations	34		
23.90 Total budgetary resources available for obligation	253	244	248
23.95 Total new obligations	–253	–244	–248
New budget authority (gross), detail:			
Mandatory:			
69.00 Offsetting collections (cash)	246	244	248
69.10 From Federal sources: Change in receivables and unpaid, unfilled orders	–27		
69.90 Spending authority from offsetting collections (total mandatory)	219	244	248
Change in unpaid obligations:			
Unpaid obligations, start of year:			
72.40 Obligated balance, start of year	237	183	183
72.95 From Federal sources: Receivables and unpaid, unfilled orders	173	146	146
72.99 Total unpaid obligations, start of year	410	329	329
73.10 Total new obligations	253	244	248
73.20 Total outlays (gross)	–300	–244	–248
73.45 Adjustments in unexpired accounts	–34		
Unpaid obligations, end of year:			
74.40 Obligated balance, end of year	183	183	183
74.95 From Federal sources: Receivables and unpaid, unfilled orders	146	146	146
74.99 Total unpaid obligations, end of year	329	329	329
Outlays (gross), detail:			
86.97 Outlays from new mandatory authority	116		
86.98 Outlays from mandatory balances	184	244	248
87.00 Total outlays (gross)	300	244	248
Offsets:			
Against gross budget authority and outlays:			
88.00 Offsetting collections (cash) from: Federal sources	–246	–244	–248
Against gross budget authority only:			
88.95 From Federal sources: Change in receivables and unpaid, unfilled orders	27		
Net budget authority and outlays:			
89.00 Budget authority			
90.00 Outlays	54		

Certain central services in the Department of the Treasury, including telecommunications, printing, reproduction, computer support/usage, personnel/payroll, automated financial management systems, training, centralized short-term management assistance, procurement information, information technology services, public education, and printing procurement services, are provided on a reimbursable basis. Transactions are entered into with other Treasury appropriation accounts at rates which will recover the fund's operating expenses, including accrual of annual leave and depreciation of equipment. This presentation includes the Digital Telecommunications System (DTS), Department of Treasury Telecommunication Systems (DOTTS), Wireless/Radio Service Support (WRSS), the Treasury Communications System (TCS), and the Emergency Access Demonstration Project.

Object Classification (in millions of dollars)

Identification code 20–4501–0–4–803	1999 actual	2000 est.	2001 est.
11.1 Personnel compensation: Full-time permanent	17	21	23
12.1 Civilian personnel benefits	4	5	5
21.0 Travel and transportation of persons	1	1	1
23.1 Rental payments to GSA	2	1	1
23.3 Communications, utilities, and miscellaneous charges	14	49	51
25.1 Advisory and assistance services	26	1	1
25.2 Other services	113	105	105
25.3 Purchases of goods and services from Government accounts	51	23	23
26.0 Supplies and materials	1	1	1
31.0 Equipment	24	36	37
99.5 Below reporting threshold		1	
99.9 Total new obligations	253	244	248

Personnel Summary

Identification code 20–4501–0–4–803	1999 actual	2000 est.	2001 est.
2001 Total compensable workyears: Full-time equivalent employment	313	325	325

Treasury Franchise Fund

Program and Financing (in millions of dollars)

Identification code 20–4560–0–4–803	1999 actual	2000 est.	2001 est.
Obligations by program activity:			
10.00 Total new obligations	146	173	180
Budgetary resources available for obligation:			
21.40 Unobligated balance available, start of year	15	29	29

Intragovernmental funds—Continued

TREASURY FRANCHISE FUND—Continued

Program and Financing (in millions of dollars)—Continued

Identification code 20–4560–0–4–803	1999 actual	2000 est.	2001 est.
22.00 New budget authority (gross)	160	172	180
22.10 Resources available from recoveries of prior year obligations		1	
23.90 Total budgetary resources available for obligation	175	202	209
23.95 Total new obligations	−146	−173	−180
24.40 Unobligated balance available, end of year	29	29	29
New budget authority (gross), detail:			
Spending authority from offsetting collections:			
Discretionary:			
68.00 Offsetting collections (cash)	137	162	170
68.10 From Federal sources: Change in receivables and unpaid, unfilled orders	23	10	10
68.90 Spending authority from offsetting collections (total discretionary)	160	172	180
Change in unpaid obligations:			
Unpaid obligations, start of year:			
72.40 Obligated balance, start of year	−5	−10	−6
72.95 From Federal sources: Receivables and unpaid, unfilled orders	25	48	58
72.99 Total unpaid obligations, start of year	20	38	52
73.10 Total new obligations	146	173	180
73.20 Total outlays (gross)	−127	−157	−165
73.45 Adjustments in unexpired accounts		−1	
Unpaid obligations, end of year:			
74.40 Obligated balance, end of year	−10	−6	−2
74.95 From Federal sources: Receivables and unpaid, unfilled orders	48	58	68
74.99 Total unpaid obligations, end of year	38	52	66
Outlays (gross), detail:			
86.90 Outlays from new discretionary authority	113	155	148
86.93 Outlays from discretionary balances	14	2	17
87.00 Total outlays (gross)	127	157	165
Offsets:			
Against gross budget authority and outlays:			
88.00 Offsetting collections (cash) from: Federal sources	−137	−162	−170
Against gross budget authority only:			
88.95 From Federal sources: Change in receivables and unpaid, unfilled orders	−23	−10	−10
Net budget authority and outlays:			
89.00 Budget authority			
90.00 Outlays	−9	−5	−5

Department of Treasury was chosen as a pilot Franchise Fund under P.L. 103–356, the Government Management and Reform Act of 1994. Begun in 1997, financial and administrative services included in the Franchise Fund (Fund) are financed on a fee-for-service basis. Treasury's Fund is a revolving fund used to supply financial and administrative services on the basis of services supplied. For 2001, service activities are expected to have spending authority of $180 million and employ 493 people.

Activities included in the Fund are financial training, accounting cross-servicing, and various administrative support services. The Fund concept is intended to increase competition for government and financial administrative services, resulting in lower costs and higher quality.

Object Classification (in millions of dollars)

Identification code 20–4560–0–4–803	1999 actual	2000 est.	2001 est.
11.1 Personnel compensation: Full-time permanent	21	23	25
12.1 Civilian personnel benefits	5	6	7
21.0 Travel and transportation of persons	1	1	1
23.3 Communications, utilities, and miscellaneous charges	2	2	3
25.2 Other services	115	138	140
31.0 Equipment	2	3	4
99.9 Total new obligations	146	173	180

Personnel Summary

Identification code 20–4560–0–4–803	1999 actual	2000 est.	2001 est.
2001 Total compensable workyears: Full-time equivalent employment	405	437	493

Trust Funds

[VIOLENT CRIME REDUCTION PROGRAMS]

[(INCLUDING TRANSFER OF FUNDS)]

[For activities authorized by Public Law 103–322, to remain available until expended, which shall be derived from the Violent Crime Reduction Trust Fund, as follows:

(1) As authorized by section 190001(e), $119,000,000; of which $27,920,000 shall be available to the Bureau of Alcohol, Tobacco and Firearms, including $3,000,000 for administering the Gang Resistance Education and Training program; of which $4,200,000 shall be available to the United States Secret Service for forensic and related support of investigations of missing and exploited children, of which $2,200,000 shall be available as a grant for activities related to the investigations of exploited children and shall remain available until expended; of which $61,000,000 shall be available for the United States Customs Service; of which $1,863,000 shall be available for the Financial Crimes Enforcement Network; of which $9,200,000 shall be available to the Federal Law Enforcement Training Center; and of which $14,817,000 shall be available for Interagency Crime and Drug Enforcement.

(2) As authorized by section 32401, $13,000,000 to the Bureau of Alcohol, Tobacco and Firearms for disbursement through grants, cooperative agreements, or contracts to local governments for Gang Resistance Education and Training: *Provided*, That notwithstanding sections 32401 and 310001, such funds shall be allocated to State and local law enforcement and prevention organizations.] *(Treasury Department Appropriations Act, 2000.)*

Program and Financing (in millions of dollars)

Identification code 20–8526–0–1–751	1999 actual	2000 est.	2001 est.
Obligations by program activity:			
Direct program:			
00.01 Departmental Offices			
00.02 Financial crimes enforcement network (FinCEN)	1	2	
00.03 Federal Law Enforcement Training Center		10	
00.04 Bureau of Alcohol, Tobacco and Firearms	20	35	4
00.05 Customs Service	15	130	15
00.06 Secret Service	20	4	
01.00 Subtotal, Direct Programs	56	181	19
09.01 Reimbursable program, Customs Service	6		
10.00 Total new obligations	62	181	19
Budgetary resources available for obligation:			
21.40 Unobligated balance available, start of year	31	85	19
22.00 New budget authority (gross)	111	115	
22.10 Resources available from recoveries of prior year obligations	3		
23.90 Total budgetary resources available for obligation	145	200	19
23.95 Total new obligations	−62	−181	−19
24.40 Unobligated balance available, end of year	85	19	
New budget authority (gross), detail:			
Discretionary:			
40.76 Reduction pursuant to P.L. 106–113		−2	
42.00 Transferred from other accounts	105	117	
43.00 Appropriation (total discretionary)	105	115	
Spending authority from offsetting collections:			
68.00 Offsetting collections (cash)	6	11	
68.10 From Federal sources: Change in receivables and unpaid, unfilled orders		−11	

68.90	Spending authority from offsetting collections (total discretionary)	6	....	....
70.00	Total new budget authority (gross)	111	115	....
	Change in unpaid obligations:			
	Unpaid obligations, start of year:			
72.40	Obligated balance, start of year	76	72	144
72.95	From Federal sources: Receivables and unpaid, unfilled orders	11	11	....
72.99	Total unpaid obligations, start of year	87	83	144
73.10	Total new obligations	62	181	19
73.20	Total outlays (gross)	−61	−120	−54
73.40	Adjustments in expired accounts (net)	−1	....	....
73.45	Adjustments in unexpired accounts	−3	....	....
	Unpaid obligations, end of year:			
74.40	Obligated balance, end of year	72	144	109
74.95	From Federal sources: Receivables and unpaid, unfilled orders	11	....	....
74.99	Total unpaid obligations, end of year	83	144	109
	Outlays (gross), detail:			
86.90	Outlays from new discretionary authority	44	61	....
86.93	Outlays from discretionary balances	17	61	54
87.00	Total outlays (gross)	61	120	54
	Offsets:			
	Against gross budget authority and outlays:			
88.00	Offsetting collections (cash) from: Federal sources	−6	−11	....
	Against gross budget authority only:			
88.95	From Federal sources: Change in receivables and unpaid, unfilled orders	....	11	....
	Net budget authority and outlays:			
89.00	Budget authority	105	115	....
90.00	Outlays	55	109	54

Note.—Does not include funding associated with the Interagency crime and drug enforcement account in 1999 and 2000.

Amounts for the Department of the Treasury's portion of Crime Control Programs are derived from transfers from the Violent Crime Reduction Trust Fund (VCRTF) as authorized by the Crime Control and Law Enforcement Act of 1994. The VCRTF was authorized through 2000.

Object Classification (in millions of dollars)

Identification code 20–8526–0–1–751		1999 actual	2000 est.	2001 est.
	Direct obligations:			
11.1	Personnel compensation: Full-time permanent	3	15	....
12.1	Civilian personnel benefits	1	7	....
21.0	Travel and transportation of persons	2	3	....
22.0	Transportation of things	1	1	....
23.2	Rental payments to others	....	2	....
23.3	Communications, utilities, and miscellaneous charges	1	3	....
25.1	Advisory and assistance services	1	....	....
25.2	Other services	23	61	15
25.3	Purchases of goods and services from Government accounts	1	....	....
25.5	Research and development contracts	2	....	....
25.7	Operation and maintenance of equipment	1	....	....
26.0	Supplies and materials	1	2	....
31.0	Equipment	19	76	4
32.0	Land and structures	....	9	....
41.0	Grants, subsidies, and contributions	....	2	....
99.0	Subtotal, direct obligations	56	181	19
99.0	Reimbursable obligations	6	....	....
99.9	Total new obligations	62	181	19

Personnel Summary

Identification code 20–8526–0–1–751		1999 actual	2000 est.	2001 est.
1001	Total compensable workyears: Full-time equivalent employment	68	149	....

FEDERAL LAW ENFORCEMENT TRAINING CENTER

Federal Funds

General and special funds:

SALARIES AND EXPENSES

For necessary expenses of the Federal Law Enforcement Training Center, as a bureau of the Department of the Treasury, including materials and support costs of Federal law enforcement basic training; purchase (not to exceed 52 for police-type use, without regard to the general purchase price limitation) and hire of passenger motor vehicles; for expenses for student athletic and related activities; uniforms without regard to the general purchase price limitation for the current fiscal year; the conducting of and participating in firearms matches and presentation of awards; for public awareness and enhancing community support of law enforcement training; not to exceed [$9,500] *$11,500* for official reception and representation expenses; room and board for student interns; and services as authorized by 5 U.S.C. 3109, [$84,027,000] *$93,483,000*, of which up to [$16,511,000] *$17,043,000* for materials and support costs of Federal law enforcement basic training shall remain available until September 30, [2002] *2003*: *Provided*, That the Center is authorized to accept and use gifts of property, both real and personal, and to accept services, for authorized purposes, including funding of a gift of intrinsic value which shall be awarded annually by the Director of the Center to the outstanding student who graduated from a basic training program at the Center during the previous fiscal year, which shall be funded only by gifts received through the Center's gift authority: *Provided further*, That notwithstanding any other provision of law, students attending training at any Federal Law Enforcement Training Center site shall reside in on-Center or Center-provided housing, insofar as available and in accordance with Center policy: *Provided further*, That funds appropriated in this account shall be available, at the discretion of the Director, for the following: training United States Postal Service law enforcement personnel and Postal police officers; State and local government law enforcement training on a space-available basis; training of foreign law enforcement officials on a space-available basis with reimbursement of actual costs to this appropriation, except that reimbursement may be waived by the Secretary for law enforcement training activities in foreign countries undertaken pursuant to section 801 of the Antiterrorism and Effective Death Penalty Act of 1996, Public Law 104–32; training of private sector security officials on a space-available basis with reimbursement of actual costs to this appropriation; and travel expenses of non-Federal personnel to attend course development meetings and training sponsored by the Center: *Provided further*, That the Center is authorized to obligate funds in anticipation of reimbursements from agencies receiving training sponsored by the Federal Law Enforcement Training Center, except that total obligations at the end of the fiscal year shall not exceed total budgetary resources available at the end of the fiscal year: *Provided further*, That the Federal Law Enforcement Training Center is authorized to provide training for the Gang Resistance Education and Training program to Federal and non-Federal personnel at any facility in partnership with the Bureau of Alcohol, Tobacco and Firearms: *Provided further*, That the Federal Law Enforcement Training Center is authorized to provide short-term medical services for students undergoing training at the Center. *(Treasury Department Appropriations Act, 2000.)*

Program and Financing (in millions of dollars)

Identification code 20–0104–0–1–751		1999 actual	2000 est.	2001 est.
	Obligations by program activity:			
	Direct program:			
00.01	Law enforcement training	50	64	69
00.02	Plant operations	22	28	29
09.01	Reimbursable program	40	35	36
10.00	Total new obligations	112	127	134
	Budgetary resources available for obligation:			
21.40	Unobligated balance available, start of year	9	13	5
22.00	New budget authority (gross)	115	119	129
22.10	Resources available from recoveries of prior year obligations	1	....	....
23.90	Total budgetary resources available for obligation	125	132	134
23.95	Total new obligations	−112	−127	−134

General and special funds—Continued

SALARIES AND EXPENSES—Continued

Program and Financing (in millions of dollars)—Continued

Identification code 20–0104–0–1–751	1999 actual	2000 est.	2001 est.
23.98 Unobligated balance expiring or withdrawn	–1		
24.40 Unobligated balance available, end of year	13	5	
New budget authority (gross), detail:			
Discretionary:			
40.00 Appropriation	75	84	93
68.00 Spending authority from offsetting collections: Offsetting collections (cash)	40	35	36
70.00 Total new budget authority (gross)	115	119	129
Change in unpaid obligations:			
72.40 Unpaid obligations, start of year: Obligated balance, start of year	12	18	29
73.10 Total new obligations	112	127	134
73.20 Total outlays (gross)	–105	–116	–128
73.45 Adjustments in unexpired accounts	–1		
74.40 Unpaid obligations, end of year: Obligated balance, end of year	18	29	35
Outlays (gross), detail:			
86.90 Outlays from new discretionary authority	92	107	116
86.93 Outlays from discretionary balances	13	9	12
87.00 Total outlays (gross)	105	116	128
Offsets:			
Against gross budget authority and outlays:			
88.00 Offsetting collections (cash) from: Federal sources	–40	–35	–36
Net budget authority and outlays:			
89.00 Budget authority	75	84	93
90.00 Outlays	65	81	92

The Federal Law Enforcement Training Center provides the necessary facilities, equipment, and support services for conducting recruit, advanced, specialized, and refresher training for Federal law enforcement personnel. Center personnel conduct the instructional programs for the basic recruit and some of the advanced training. This appropriation is for operating expenses of the Center, for research in law enforcement training methods, and curriculum content. In addition, the Center has a reimbursable program to accommodate the training requirements of various Federal agencies. As funds are available, law enforcement training is provided to certain State, local, and foreign law enforcement personnel on a space-available basis.

PERFORMANCE MEASURES BY BUDGET ACTIVITY

	1999 actual	*2000 est.*	*2001 est.*
Budget Activity: Law Enforcement Training:			
Student Quality of Training Survey—Achieve an 80% rating on the Student Quality of Training Survey.			
Basic Training	99%	80%	80%
Advanced Training	99%	80%	80%
Conduct 100% of actual Basic Training Requested	100%	100%	100%
Variable Unit Cost Per Basic Student-Week of Training Funded	$165	$149	$149
Conduct FLETC Personnel Input Forums	18	4	4
Conduct Training Partnership Organization meetings	10	Discontinued	Discontinued
Budget Activity: Plant Operations:			
Student Quality of Services Survey—Achieve an 80% rating on the Student Quality of Services Survey.			
Basic Training	99%	80%	80%
Assess/modify the FLETC Master Plan by initiating a Comprehensive Development Plan (CDP)	Initiate Plan	Finalize	Implement

Object Classification (in millions of dollars)

Identification code 20–0104–0–1–751	1999 actual	2000 est.	2001 est.
Direct obligations:			
Personnel compensation:			
11.1 Full-time permanent	30	33	36
11.8 Special personal services payments	1	1	1
11.9 Total personnel compensation	31	34	37
12.1 Civilian personnel benefits	9	12	14
21.0 Travel and transportation of persons	2	3	3
22.0 Transportation of things	1	2	1
23.3 Communications, utilities, and miscellaneous charges	3	4	5
24.0 Printing and reproduction	1	1	1
25.2 Other services	13	18	18
26.0 Supplies and materials	7	10	11
31.0 Equipment	5	7	7
32.0 Land and structures		1	1
99.0 Subtotal, direct obligations	72	92	98
99.0 Reimbursable obligations	40	35	36
99.9 Total new obligations	112	127	134

Personnel Summary

Identification code 20–0104–0–1–751	1999 actual	2000 est.	2001 est.
Direct:			
1001 Total compensable workyears: Full-time equivalent employment	529	572	607
Reimbursable:			
2001 Total compensable workyears: Full-time equivalent employment	31	40	50

ACQUISITION, CONSTRUCTION, IMPROVEMENTS, AND RELATED EXPENSES

For expansion of the Federal Law Enforcement Training Center, for acquisition of necessary additional real property and facilities, and for ongoing maintenance, facility improvements, and related expenses, [$21,611,000] *$17,331,000*, to remain available until expended. *(Treasury Department Appropriations Act, 2000.)*

Program and Financing (in millions of dollars)

Identification code 20–0105–0–1–751	1999 actual	2000 est.	2001 est.
Obligations by program activity:			
10.00 Total new obligations	59	32	21
Budgetary resources available for obligation:			
21.40 Unobligated balance available, start of year	36	13	4
22.00 New budget authority (gross)	35	22	17
22.10 Resources available from recoveries of prior year obligations	1	1	
23.90 Total budgetary resources available for obligation	72	36	21
23.95 Total new obligations	–59	–32	–21
24.40 Unobligated balance available, end of year	13	4	
New budget authority (gross), detail:			
Discretionary:			
40.00 Appropriation	35	22	17
Change in unpaid obligations:			
72.40 Unpaid obligations, start of year: Obligated balance, start of year	29	55	54
73.10 Total new obligations	59	32	21
73.20 Total outlays (gross)	–32	–32	–27
73.45 Adjustments in unexpired accounts	–1	–1	
74.40 Unpaid obligations, end of year: Obligated balance, end of year	55	54	48
Outlays (gross), detail:			
86.90 Outlays from new discretionary authority	10	3	2
86.93 Outlays from discretionary balances	22	29	25
87.00 Total outlays (gross)	32	32	27
Net budget authority and outlays:			
89.00 Budget authority	35	22	17
90.00 Outlays	32	32	27

This account provides for the acquisition, construction, improvements, equipment, furnishings and related costs for expansion and maintenance of facilities of the Federal Law Enforcement Training Center.

This includes funding for the Facilities Master Plan, Minor Construction and Maintenance, Firearms Environmental Restoration and Reconstruction, Environmental Compliance, and installation of Fiber Optics. The Master Plan provides the long range blueprint for expansion of facilities to meet the training requirements of the over 73 participating agencies. Minor construction and maintenance provides alterations and maintenance funding for approximately 300 buildings at two locations (Glynco, Georgia and Artesia, New Mexico). The Firearms Environmental Restoration and Reconstruction funds the clean-up of the existing outdoor ranges and reconstruction. The Environmental Compliance funds are to ensure compliance with EPA and State environmental laws and regulations. The fiber optics funding is to replace the existing antiquated twisted copper wire with a state-of-the-art telecommunications cable system.

The appropriations sought in this account, demonstrate the President's commitment to an important step in completing and maintaining the necessary facilities at FLETC to train our Nation's law enforcement personnel. The Treasury Forfeiture Fund will provide $14 million for the construction of dormitories at the Glynco, Georgia, facility and the construction of firearms ranges at the Artesia, New Mexico, facility.

Object Classification (in millions of dollars)

Identification code 20–0105–0–1–751	1999 actual	2000 est.	2001 est.
25.2 Other services	1	1	1
31.0 Equipment	2	2	2
32.0 Land and structures	56	29	18
99.9 Total new obligations	59	32	21

INTERAGENCY LAW ENFORCEMENT

Federal Funds

General and special funds:

INTERAGENCY CRIME AND DRUG ENFORCEMENT

For expenses necessary [for the detection and investigation of individuals] *to conduct investigations and convict offenders* involved in organized crime drug trafficking, including cooperative efforts with State and local law enforcement, [$61,083,000] *as it relates to the Treasury Department law enforcement violations such as money laundering, violent crime, and smuggling, $103,476,000*, of which $7,827,000 shall remain available until expended. *(Treasury Department Appropriations Act, 2000.)*

Program and Financing (in millions of dollars)

Identification code 20–1501–0–1–751	1999 actual	2000 est.	2001 est.
Obligations by program activity:			
00.01 Internal Revenue Service	38	37	63
00.02 Bureau of Alcohol, Tobacco and Firearms	20	10	11
00.03 United States Customs Service	28	28	28
00.04 Departmental Offices			1
10.00 Total new obligations (object class 25.3)	86	75	103
Budgetary resources available for obligation:			
22.00 New budget authority (gross)	76	75	103
22.10 Resources available from recoveries of prior year obligations	10		
23.90 Total budgetary resources available for obligation	86	75	103
23.95 Total new obligations	−86	−75	−103
New budget authority (gross), detail:			
Discretionary:			
40.00 Appropriation	52	61	103
40.76 Reduction pursuant to P.L. 106–113		−1	
42.00 Transferred from other accounts	24	15	
43.00 Appropriation (total discretionary)	76	75	103
Change in unpaid obligations:			
72.40 Unpaid obligations, start of year: Obligated balance, start of year	32	21	15
73.10 Total new obligations	86	75	103
73.20 Total outlays (gross)	−87	−82	−98
73.45 Adjustments in unexpired accounts	−10		
74.40 Unpaid obligations, end of year: Obligated balance, end of year	21	15	19
Outlays (gross), detail:			
86.90 Outlays from new discretionary authority	62	62	84
86.93 Outlays from discretionary balances	25	20	14
87.00 Total outlays (gross)	87	82	98
Net budget authority and outlays:			
89.00 Budget authority	76	75	103
90.00 Outlays	87	82	98

In a 1982 counterdrug effort, the Department of Justice (DOJ) developed the Interagency Crime and Drug Enforcement Task Force (ICDE) program to bring together and integrate the efforts of all levels of law enforcement in the fight against drugs. The ICDE program designated nine domestic regions that deploy the investigative expertise from ten Federal agencies, and state and local law enforcement agencies to dismantle and disrupt major drug trafficking and money laundering organizations and place offenders in jail. Treasury agencies provide specific value-added investigative expertise to these major cases. The U.S. Customs Service provides specific expertise in international smuggling and interdiction; the Bureau of Alcohol, Tobacco and Firearms (ATF) provides expertise on firearms and explosives violence; and the Internal Revenue Service (Criminal Investigative Division) provides expertise on money laundering and tax evasion. Since 1998, the Treasury portion of the ICDE program has been administered by Treasury's Departmental Offices. Treasury's participating bureaus ATF, Customs, and IRS, are reimbursed from this appropriation. Treasury has assigned two special agents to oversee ICDE policy and budget for the three Treasury bureaus. Funding for Treasury components is primarily utilized for full-time equivalent (FTE) employees; however, a portion of funding is used for operating expenses incurred during the investigative phase of the case.

FINANCIAL MANAGEMENT SERVICE

Federal Funds

General and special funds:

SALARIES AND EXPENSES

For necessary expenses of the Financial Management Service, [$201,320,000] *$202,851,000*, of which not to exceed $10,635,000 shall remain available until September 30, [2002] *2003*, for information systems modernization initiatives; and of which not to exceed $2,500 shall be available for official reception and representation expenses. *(Treasury Department Appropriations Act, 2000.)*

Unavailable Collections (in millions of dollars)

Identification code 20–1801–0–1–803	1999 actual	2000 est.	2001 est.
Balance, start of year:			
01.99 Balance, start of year			
Receipts:			
02.01 Debt collection fund	13	13	20
Appropriation:			
05.01 Debt collection fund	−13	−13	−20
07.99 Total balance, end of year			

General and special funds—Continued

SALARIES AND EXPENSES—Continued

Program and Financing (in millions of dollars)

Identification code 20–1801–0–1–803		1999 actual	2000 est.	2001 est.
	Obligations by program activity:			
	Direct program:			
00.05	Payments	142	131	126
00.06	Collections	11	12	13
00.07	Debt collection	30	26	15
00.08	Governmentwide accounting and reporting	44	46	49
09.01	Reimbursable program	105	111	114
10.00	Total new obligations	332	326	317
	Budgetary resources available for obligation:			
21.40	Unobligated balance available, start of year	11	14	13
22.00	New budget authority (gross)	337	324	337
22.10	Resources available from recoveries of prior year obligations	1		
23.90	Total budgetary resources available for obligation	349	338	350
23.95	Total new obligations	−332	−326	−317
23.98	Unobligated balance expiring or withdrawn	−3		
24.40	Unobligated balance available, end of year	14	13	33
	New budget authority (gross), detail:			
	Discretionary:			
40.00	Appropriation	196	201	203
40.76	Reduction pursuant to P.L. 106–113		−1	
42.00	Transferred from other accounts	6		
43.00	Appropriation (total discretionary)	202	200	203
	Mandatory:			
60.25	Appropriation (special fund, indefinite)	13	13	20
	Spending authority from offsetting collections:			
	Discretionary:			
68.00	Offsetting collections (cash)	110	111	114
68.10	From Federal sources: Change in receivables and unpaid, unfilled orders	12		
68.90	Spending authority from offsetting collections (total discretionary)	122	111	114
70.00	Total new budget authority (gross)	337	324	337
	Change in unpaid obligations:			
	Unpaid obligations, start of year:			
72.40	Obligated balance, start of year	50	40	41
72.95	From Federal sources: Receivables and unpaid, unfilled orders	19	31	31
72.99	Total unpaid obligations, start of year	69	71	72
73.10	Total new obligations	332	326	317
73.20	Total outlays (gross)	−316	−325	−337
73.40	Adjustments in expired accounts (net)	−13		
73.45	Adjustments in unexpired accounts	−1		
	Unpaid obligations, end of year:			
74.40	Obligated balance, end of year	40	41	21
74.95	From Federal sources: Receivables and unpaid, unfilled orders	31	31	31
74.99	Total unpaid obligations, end of year	71	72	52
	Outlays (gross), detail:			
86.90	Outlays from new discretionary authority	269	273	278
86.93	Outlays from discretionary balances	48	39	38
86.97	Outlays from new mandatory authority		13	20
87.00	Total outlays (gross)	316	325	337
	Offsets:			
	Against gross budget authority and outlays:			
88.00	Offsetting collections (cash) from: Federal sources	−110	−111	−114
	Against gross budget authority only:			
88.95	From Federal sources: Change in receivables and unpaid, unfilled orders	−12		
	Net budget authority and outlays:			
89.00	Budget authority	215	213	223
90.00	Outlays	207	214	223

1. *Payments.*—FMS implements payment policy and procedures for the Federal Government, issues and distributes payments, promotes the use of electronics in the payment process, and assists agencies in converting payments from paper checks to electronic funds transfer (EFT). The control and financial integrity of the Federal payments and collections process includes reconciliation, accounting, and claims activities. The claims activity settles claims against the United States resulting from Government checks which have been forged, lost, stolen, or destroyed, and collects monies from those parties liable for fraudulent or otherwise improper negotiation of Government checks.

PERFORMANCE MEASURES

	1999 actual	2000 est.	2001 est.
Dollar savings by reducing the number of check payments ($ in millions)	$10.3	$16.3	discontinued
Percentage of check payments released on-time	99.9949%	99.9993%	discontinued
Percentage of payments customers indicating an overall rating of satisfied or better	99.3%	99%	discontinued
Percentage of forgery and non-receipt check claims adjudicated within current FMS standards (14 days or fewer)	93.5%	90%	90%
Percentage of transmissions of value (payments) and associated information made electronically	68.0%	69%	79%
Number of states in which direct Federal EBT is available	8	16	discontinued

WORKLOAD STATISTICS

(Thousands)

	1999 actual	2000 est.	2001 est.
1. Number of check claims submitted	1,391	1,250	1,200
2. Number of check payments	280,973	224,000	187,000
3. Number of electronic payments	597,695	656,000	691,000

2. *Collections.*—FMS implements collections policy, regulations, standards, and procedures for the Federal Government, facilitates collections, promotes the use of electronics in the collections process, and assists agencies in converting collections from paper to electronic media.

PERFORMANCE MEASURES

	1999 actual	2000 est.	2001 est.
Electronic collections as a percentage of total collections	72%	71%	72%
Percentage of corporate withholding taxes collected electronically	89.3%	94%	discontinued

3. *Debt Collection.*—FMS provides debt collection operational services to client agencies which includes collection of delinquent accounts, offset of Federal payments against debts owed the government, post-judgment enforcement, consolidation of information reported to credit bureaus, reporting for discharged debts or vendor payments, Federal Employee Salary Offset Hearings, mortgage servicing, collection of unclaimed financial assets, and disposition of foreclosed property.

PERFORMANCE MEASURES

	1999 actual	2000 est.	2001 est.
Increase collection of the debts referred to Treasury from FY 1998 baseline of $1.988 billion by $93.1 million in 2000 through the addition of more Federal payment types and agency referrals into the centralized administrative offset program by 2000. (Payment types include vendor/miscellaneous, salary payments, tax refunds (including child support), and Federal benefit payments)	$2.631B	$2.081B	$2.3B
Increase the amount of delinquent debt that is referred to Treasury for collection, as compared to the amount of delinquent debt that is eligible for referral. Total percentage will reach at least 75% by 2000. Baseline is FY 1997	71%	75%	75%

4. *Government-wide Accounting and Reporting.*—FMS provides financial accounting, reporting, and financing services to the Federal Government and the Government's agents who participate in the payments and collections process by generating a series of daily, monthly, quarterly and annual Government-wide reports. FMS also works directly with agencies to help reconcile reporting differences.

PERFORMANCE MEASURES

	1999 actual	2000 est.	2001 est.
Percentage of agency reports for the Consolidated Financial Statement (CFS) processed by FMS within the established standard range	data available 3/00	97%	93%
Percentage of days the Daily Treasury Statement is released on time	100%	99.6%	discontinued

Object Classification (in millions of dollars)

Identification code 20–1801–0–1–803		1999 actual	2000 est.	2001 est.
	Direct obligations:			
	Personnel compensation:			
11.1	Full-time permanent	102	102	96
11.3	Other than full-time permanent	2	1	2
11.5	Other personnel compensation	3	3	3
11.9	Total personnel compensation	107	106	101
12.1	Civilian personnel benefits	21	20	19
21.0	Travel and transportation of persons	2	2	2
23.1	Rental payments to GSA	15	16	17
23.3	Communications, utilities, and miscellaneous charges	13	14	14
24.0	Printing and reproduction	1	1	1
25.1	Advisory and assistance services	6	4	4
25.2	Other services	34	24	17
25.3	Purchases of goods and services from Government accounts	3	6	5
25.4	Operation and maintenance of facilities	1	1	1
25.7	Operation and maintenance of equipment	7	6	7
26.0	Supplies and materials	5	4	5
31.0	Equipment	11	11	10
99.0	Subtotal, direct obligations	226	215	203
99.0	Reimbursable obligations	106	111	113
99.5	Below reporting threshold			1
99.9	Total new obligations	332	326	317

Personnel Summary

Identification code 20–1801–0–1–803		1999 actual	2000 est.	2001 est.
	Direct:			
1001	Total compensable workyears: Full-time equivalent employment	1,933	1,986	1,844
	Reimbursable:			
2001	Total compensable workyears: Full-time equivalent employment	110	156	277

Payment to Department of Justice, FIRREA Related Claims

Program and Financing (in millions of dollars)

Identification code 20–0177–0–1–752		1999 actual	2000 est.	2001 est.
	Change in unpaid obligations:			
72.40	Unpaid obligations, start of year: Obligated balance, start of year	28	2	
73.10	Total new obligations			
73.20	Total outlays (gross)	−26	−2	
74.40	Unpaid obligations, end of year: Obligated balance, end of year	2		
	Outlays (gross), detail:			
86.98	Outlays from mandatory balances	26	2	
	Net budget authority and outlays:			
89.00	Budget authority			
90.00	Outlays	26	2	

In 1998, the Secretary of the Treasury was authorized to use funds made available to the FSLIC Resolution Fund to reimburse the Department of Justice for the reasonable expenses of litigation that were incurred in the defense of claims against the U.S. arising from FIRREA and its implementation.

Payment to the Resolution Funding Corporation

Program and Financing (in millions of dollars)

Identification code 20–1851–0–1–908		1999 actual	2000 est.	2001 est.
	Obligations by program activity:			
10.00	Total new obligations (object class 41.0)	2,328	1,072	1,728
	Budgetary resources available for obligation:			
22.00	New budget authority (gross)	2,328	1,072	1,728
23.95	Total new obligations	−2,328	−1,072	−1,728
	New budget authority (gross), detail:			
	Mandatory:			
60.05	Appropriation (indefinite)	2,328	1,072	1,728
	Change in unpaid obligations:			
73.10	Total new obligations	2,328	1,072	1,728
73.20	Total outlays (gross)	−2,328	−1,072	−1,728
	Outlays (gross), detail:			
86.97	Outlays from new mandatory authority	2,328	1,072	1,728
	Net budget authority and outlays:			
89.00	Budget authority	2,328	1,072	1,728
90.00	Outlays	2,328	1,072	1,728

The Financial Institutions Reform, Recovery, and Enforcement Act of 1989 (FIRREA) authorized and appropriated to the Secretary of the Treasury, such sums as may be necessary to cover interest payments on obligations issued by the Resolution Funding Corporation (REFCORP). REFCORP was established under the Act to raise $31.2 billion for the Resolution Trust Corporation (RTC) in order to resolve savings institution insolvencies.

Sources of payment for interest due on REFCORP obligations include REFCORP investment income, proceeds from the sale of assets or warrants acquired by the RTC, and annual contributions by the Federal Home Loan Banks. If these payment sources are insufficient to cover all interest costs, funds appropriated to the Treasury shall be used to meet the shortfall.

Payment to Terrestrial Wildlife Habitat Restoration Trust Fund

Program and Financing (in millions of dollars)

Identification code 20–1738–0–1–306		1999 actual	2000 est.	2001 est.
	Obligations by program activity:			
00.01	Cheyenne River Sioux Tribe Terrestrial Wildlife restoration trust fund	4	4	4
00.02	Lower Brule Sioux Tribe terrestrial restoration trust fund	1	1	1
10.00	Total new obligations (object class 41.0)	5	5	5
	Budgetary resources available for obligation:			
22.00	New budget authority (gross)	5	5	5
23.95	Total new obligations	−5	−5	−5
	New budget authority (gross), detail:			
	Mandatory:			
60.00	Appropriation	5	5	5
	Change in unpaid obligations:			
73.10	Total new obligations	5	5	5
73.20	Total outlays (gross)	−5	−5	−5
	Outlays (gross), detail:			
86.97	Outlays from new mandatory authority	5	5	5
	Net budget authority and outlays:			
89.00	Budget authority	5	5	5
90.00	Outlays	5	5	5

General and special funds—Continued

Payment to Terrestrial Wildlife Habitat Restoration Trust Fund—Continued

Section 604(b) of the Water Resources Development Act of 1999 (P.L. 106–53) requires that the Secretary of the Treasury, beginning in 1999, deposit $5 million annually (74 percent into the Cheyenne River Sioux Tribe Terrestrial Wildlife Restoration Trust Fund and 26 percent into the Lower Brule Sioux Tribe Terrestrial Wildlife Restoration Trust Fund) until a total of $57.4 million has been deposited.

Federal Reserve Bank Reimbursement Fund

Program and Financing (in millions of dollars)

Identification code 20–1884–0–1–803	1999 actual	2000 est.	2001 est.
Obligations by program activity:			
10.00 Total new obligations (object class 25.2)	104	127	129
Budgetary resources available for obligation:			
21.40 Unobligated balance available, start of year	30	51	51
22.00 New budget authority (gross)	124	127	129
22.10 Resources available from recoveries of prior year obligations	2		
23.90 Total budgetary resources available for obligation	156	178	180
23.95 Total new obligations	−104	−127	−129
24.40 Unobligated balance available, end of year	51	51	51
New budget authority (gross), detail:			
Mandatory:			
60.05 Appropriation (indefinite)	124	127	129
Change in unpaid obligations:			
72.40 Unpaid obligations, start of year: Obligated balance, start of year	56	26	26
73.10 Total new obligations	104	127	129
73.20 Total outlays (gross)	−132	−127	−129
73.45 Adjustments in unexpired accounts	−2		
74.40 Unpaid obligations, end of year: Obligated balance, end of year	26	26	26
Outlays (gross), detail:			
86.97 Outlays from new mandatory authority	102	78	99
86.98 Outlays from mandatory balances	30	51	30
87.00 Total outlays (gross)	132	127	129
Net budget authority and outlays:			
89.00 Budget authority	124	127	129
90.00 Outlays	132	127	129

This fund was established as a permanent, indefinite appropriation to allow the Financial Management Service to reimburse the Federal Reserve Banks for services provided in their capacity as depositaries and fiscal agents for the United States.

Interest on Uninvested Funds

Program and Financing (in millions of dollars)

Identification code 20–1860–0–1–908	1999 actual	2000 est.	2001 est.
Obligations by program activity:			
10.00 Total new obligations (object class 43.0)	5	8	8
Budgetary resources available for obligation:			
22.00 New budget authority (gross)	5	8	8
23.95 Total new obligations	−5	−8	−8
New budget authority (gross), detail:			
Mandatory:			
60.05 Appropriation (indefinite)	5	8	8
Change in unpaid obligations:			
72.40 Unpaid obligations, start of year: Obligated balance, start of year	20	21	21
73.10 Total new obligations	5	8	8
73.20 Total outlays (gross)	−5	−8	−8
74.40 Unpaid obligations, end of year: Obligated balance, end of year	21	21	21
Outlays (gross), detail:			
86.97 Outlays from new mandatory authority	5	8	8
Net budget authority and outlays:			
89.00 Budget authority	5	8	8
90.00 Outlays	5	8	8

Under conditions of the law creating each trust, interest accruing and payable from the general fund of the Treasury is appropriated for payment to the proper fund receipt accounts (31 U.S.C. 1321; 2 U.S.C. 158; 20 U.S.C. 74a and 101; 24 U.S.C. 46; and 69 Stat. 533). Pursuant to Public Law 101–510, commencing October 1, 1991, the Soldiers' Home Permanent Fund will be invested in Treasury securities.

Federal Interest Liabilities to the States

Program and Financing (in millions of dollars)

Identification code 20–1877–0–1–908	1999 actual	2000 est.	2001 est.
Obligations by program activity:			
10.00 Total new obligations (object class 25.2)	20	14	13
Budgetary resources available for obligation:			
22.00 New budget authority (gross)	20	14	13
23.95 Total new obligations	−20	−14	−13
New budget authority (gross), detail:			
Mandatory:			
60.05 Appropriation (indefinite)	20	14	13
Change in unpaid obligations:			
72.40 Unpaid obligations, start of year: Obligated balance, start of year		2	
73.10 Total new obligations	20	14	13
73.20 Total outlays (gross)	−18	−16	−13
74.40 Unpaid obligations, end of year: Obligated balance, end of year	2		
Outlays (gross), detail:			
86.97 Outlays from new mandatory authority	18	14	13
86.98 Outlays from mandatory balances		2	
87.00 Total outlays (gross)	18	16	13
Net budget authority and outlays:			
89.00 Budget authority	20	14	13
90.00 Outlays	18	16	13

As provided by statute and regulation, interest is paid to States when Federal funds are not transferred in a timely manner.

Net Interest Paid to Loan Guarantee Financing Accounts

Program and Financing (in millions of dollars)

Identification code 20–1880–0–1–908	1999 actual	2000 est.	2001 est.
Obligations by program activity:			
10.00 Total new obligations (object class 43.0)	3,617	3,795	3,858
Budgetary resources available for obligation:			
22.00 New budget authority (gross)	3,617	3,795	3,858
23.95 Total new obligations	−3,617	−3,795	−3,858

	New budget authority (gross), detail:			
	Mandatory:			
60.05	Appropriation (indefinite)	3,617	3,795	3,858
	Change in unpaid obligations:			
73.10	Total new obligations	3,617	3,795	3,858
73.20	Total outlays (gross)	−3,617	−3,795	−3,858
	Outlays (gross), detail:			
86.97	Outlays from new mandatory authority	3,617	3,795	3,858
	Net budget authority and outlays:			
89.00	Budget authority	3,617	3,795	3,858
90.00	Outlays	3,617	3,795	3,858

Loan guarantee financing accounts receive various payments and fees and make payments on defaults. When cash balances result from an excess of receipts over outlays, these balances are deposited at the Treasury and earn interest. This account pays such interest to credit loan guarantee financing accounts from the general fund of the Treasury in accordance with section 505(c) of the Federal Credit Reform Act of 1990. The estimates of interest paid by this fund are derived from the estimates of interest received in the various financing accounts.

Claims, Judgments, and Relief Acts

Program and Financing (in millions of dollars)

Identification code 20–1895–0–1–808		1999 actual	2000 est.	2001 est.
	Obligations by program activity:			
00.01	Claims for damages	28	25	12
00.03	Claims for contract disputes	686	75	79
00.91	Total claims adjudicated administratively	714	100	91
	Judgments of the Court:			
01.01	Judgments, Court of Claims	587	200	192
01.02	Judgments, U.S. Courts	558	425	429
01.91	Total judgments of the courts	1,145	625	621
10.00	Total new obligations	1,859	725	712
	Budgetary resources available for obligation:			
22.00	New budget authority (gross)	1,859	725	712
23.95	Total new obligations	−1,859	−725	−712
	New budget authority (gross), detail:			
	Mandatory:			
60.05	Appropriation (indefinite)	1,859	725	712
	Change in unpaid obligations:			
72.40	Unpaid obligations, start of year: Obligated balance, start of year		32	
73.10	Total new obligations	1,859	725	712
73.20	Total outlays (gross)	−1,827	−757	−712
74.40	Unpaid obligations, end of year: Obligated balance, end of year	32		
	Outlays (gross), detail:			
86.97	Outlays from new mandatory authority	1,827	725	712
86.98	Outlays from mandatory balances		32	
87.00	Total outlays (gross)	1,827	757	712
	Net budget authority and outlays:			
89.00	Budget authority	1,859	725	712
90.00	Outlays	1,827	757	712

Appropriations are made for payment of claims and interest for damages not chargeable to appropriations of individual agencies and for payment of private and public relief acts. Public Law 95–26 authorized a permanent indefinite appropriation to pay certain judgments from the general funds of the Treasury.

Object Classification (in millions of dollars)

Identification code 20–1895–0–1–808		1999 actual	2000 est.	2001 est.
42.0	Insurance claims and indemnities	1,859	625	612
43.0	Interest and dividends		100	100
99.9	Total new obligations	1,859	725	712

Energy Security Reserve

Program and Financing (in millions of dollars)

Identification code 20–0112–0–1–271		1999 actual	2000 est.	2001 est.
	Budgetary resources available for obligation:			
21.40	Unobligated balance available, start of year	304	304	304
22.40	Capital transfer to general fund			−304
23.90	Total budgetary resources available for obligation	304	304	
24.40	Unobligated balance available, end of year	304	304	
	Change in unpaid obligations:			
72.40	Unpaid obligations, start of year: Obligated balance, start of year	342	342	342
74.40	Unpaid obligations, end of year: Obligated balance, end of year	342	342	342
	Net budget authority and outlays:			
89.00	Budget authority			
90.00	Outlays			

The Energy Security Reserve was created principally to finance the activities of the U.S. Synthetic Fuels Corporation. Public Law 99–190 rescinded the balance of unobligated funds available to the Corporation. The Act left $10 million in the Reserve for the Corporation's liquidation and $400 million for a Clean Coal Technology Demonstration program, which has been transferred to a new account in the Department of Energy. The Act also transferred responsibility for ongoing projects of the Corporation to the Secretary of the Treasury; these projects' activities and financing will continue to be displayed in this account.

Biomass Energy Development

Program and Financing (in millions of dollars)

Identification code 20–0114–0–1–271		1999 actual	2000 est.	2001 est.
	Budgetary resources available for obligation:			
21.40	Unobligated balance available, start of year	51	55	10
22.00	New budget authority (gross)	5	−45	2
23.90	Total budgetary resources available for obligation	56	10	12
23.95	Total new obligations			
24.40	Unobligated balance available, end of year	55	10	14
	New budget authority (gross), detail:			
	Discretionary:			
41.00	Transferred to other accounts		−49	−2
43.00	Appropriation (total discretionary)		−49	−2
68.00	Spending authority from offsetting collections: Offsetting collections (cash)	5	4	4
70.00	Total new budget authority (gross)	5	−45	2
	Change in unpaid obligations:			
72.40	Unpaid obligations, start of year: Obligated balance, start of year	2	2	
74.40	Unpaid obligations, end of year: Obligated balance, end of year	2		
	Offsets:			
	Against gross budget authority and outlays:			
88.40	Offsetting collections (cash) from: Non-Federal sources	−5	−4	−4

General and special funds—Continued

BIOMASS ENERGY DEVELOPMENT—Continued

Program and Financing (in millions of dollars)—Continued

Identification code 20–0114–0–1–271	1999 actual	2000 est.	2001 est.
Net budget authority and outlays:			
89.00 Budget authority		–49	–2
90.00 Outlays	–5	–4	–4

Summary of Budget Authority and Outlays

(in millions of dollars)

Enacted/requested:	1999 actual	2000 est.	2001 est.
Budget Authority		–49	–2
Outlays	–5	–4	–4
Supplemental proposal:			
Budget Authority		–4	
Outlays			
Total:			
Budget Authority		–53	–2
Outlays	–5	–4	–4

This account was created to provide loan guarantees for the construction of biomass-to-ethanol facilities, as authorized under Title II of the Energy Security Act. All of the loans guaranteed by this account went into default. The guarantees have been paid off, and the assets of all but one of the projects have been liquidated. The one remaining project, the New Energy Company of Indiana, continues to make payments to the Treasury on their loan, which the government acquired after paying off the guarantee.

In 2000, $25 million of the balances remaining in this account is proposed to be transferred to the Department of Energy (DOE) Energy Conservation account and $24 million is proposed to be transferred to the DOE Fossil Energy R&D account in order to partially fund the requirements of those programs.

Credit accounts:

PAYMENTS TO THE FARM CREDIT SYSTEM FINANCIAL ASSISTANCE CORPORATION

Program and Financing (in millions of dollars)

Identification code 20–1850–0–1–908	1999 actual	2000 est.	2001 est.
Obligations by program activity:			
10.00 Total new obligations (object class 41.0)	3		
Budgetary resources available for obligation:			
22.00 New budget authority (gross)	3		
23.95 Total new obligations	–3		
New budget authority (gross), detail:			
Mandatory:			
60.00 Appropriation	3		
Change in unpaid obligations:			
73.10 Total new obligations	3		
73.20 Total outlays (gross)	–3		
Outlays (gross), detail:			
86.97 Outlays from new mandatory authority	3		
Net budget authority and outlays:			
89.00 Budget authority	3		
90.00 Outlays	3		

The Agricultural Credit Act of 1987 (Public Law 100–233) authorized such sums as necessary to be appropriated to the Secretary of the Treasury for payment to the Farm Credit System Financial Assistance Corporation (FAC).

Treasury payments annually reimburse the FAC for interest expense on FAC debt, which was authorized to be issued through 1992. Treasury is authorized to pay all or part of FAC interest for the first 10 years on each 15-year FAC debt issuance. Debt proceeds are used to provide assistance to financially troubled Farm Credit System lending institutions. No payments will be made after 1999.

The Agricultural Credit Act of 1987 provided that the Farm Credit System's share of interest assessment for FAC debt would increase if the System's retained earnings exceeded five percent of its assets. For 1997, 1998, and 1999 the Treasury portion of interest assessments was estimated at 9, 7, and 2 percent respectively.

CHECK FORGERY INSURANCE FUND

Program and Financing (in millions of dollars)

Identification code 20–4109–0–3–803	1999 actual	2000 est.	2001 est.
Obligations by program activity:			
00.01 Direct program		8	2
09.01 Reimbursable program	3	5	6
10.00 Total new obligations	3	13	8
Budgetary resources available for obligation:			
21.40 Unobligated balance available, start of year	7	4	
22.00 New budget authority (gross)		9	8
23.90 Total budgetary resources available for obligation	7	13	8
23.95 Total new obligations	–3	–13	–8
24.40 Unobligated balance available, end of year	4		
New budget authority (gross), detail:			
Mandatory:			
60.05 Appropriation (indefinite)		4	2
69.00 Offsetting collections (cash)		5	6
70.00 Total new budget authority (gross)		9	8
Change in unpaid obligations:			
73.10 Total new obligations	3	13	8
73.20 Total outlays (gross)	–3	–13	–8
Outlays (gross), detail:			
86.97 Outlays from new mandatory authority		9	8
86.98 Outlays from mandatory balances	3	4	
87.00 Total outlays (gross)	3	13	8
Offsets:			
Against gross budget authority and outlays:			
88.00 Offsetting collections (cash) from: Federal sources		–5	–6
Net budget authority and outlays:			
89.00 Budget authority		4	2
90.00 Outlays	3	8	2

This fund was established as a permanent, indefinite appropriation in order to maintain adequate funding of the Check Forgery Insurance Fund (Fund). The Fund facilitates timely payments for replacement Treasury checks necessitated due to a claim of forgery. The Fund recoups disbursements through reclamations made against banks negotiating forged checks.

To reduce hardships sustained by payees of Government checks that have been stolen and forged, settlement is made in advance of the receipt of funds from the endorsers of the checks. If the U.S. Treasury is unable to recover funds through reclamation procedures, the Fund sustains the loss.

Object Classification (in millions of dollars)

Identification code 20–4109–0–3–803	1999 actual	2000 est.	2001 est.
42.0 Direct obligations: Insurance claims and indemnities		8	2
42.0 Reimbursable obligations: Insurance claims and indemnities	3	5	6
99.9 Total new obligations	3	13	8

Trust Funds

CHEYENNE RIVER SIOUX TRIBE TERRESTRIAL WILDLIFE HABITAT RESTORATION TRUST FUND

Unavailable Collections (in millions of dollars)

Identification code 20–8209–0–7–306	1999 actual	2000 est.	2001 est.
Balance, start of year:			
01.99 Balance, start of year	....	4	8
Receipts:			
02.01 General fund payments	4	4	4
02.02 Earnings on investments	....	....	1
02.99 Total receipts	4	4	5
04.00 Total: Balances and collections	4	8	13
07.99 Total balance, end of year	4	8	13

This schedule reflects the payments made to the Cheyenne River Sioux Tribe Terrestrial Wildlife Restoration Trust Fund and the Lower Brule Sioux Tribe Terrestrial Wildlife Restoration Trust Fund. After the funds are fully capitalized (at a total level of $57.4 million), interest earned will be available to carry out the purposes of the funds.

FEDERAL FINANCING BANK ACTIVITIES

Federal Funds

Intragovernmental funds:

FEDERAL FINANCING BANK

Program and Financing (in millions of dollars)

Identification code 20–4521–0–4–803	1999 actual	2000 est.	2001 est.
Obligations by program activity:			
09.01 Administrative expenses	2	2	2
09.02 Interest on borrowings from Treasury	2,484	2,412	2,159
09.03 Interest on borrowings from civil service retirement trust fund	1,337	1,337	1,337
09.04 Prepayment premiums	1,155	....	....
09.05 Interest on prepayment premiums	19	....	....
10.00 Total new obligations	4,997	3,752	3,499
Budgetary resources available for obligation:			
21.40 Unobligated balance available, start of year	11	37	37
22.00 New budget authority (gross)	5,023	3,752	3,499
23.90 Total budgetary resources available for obligation	5,034	3,789	3,536
23.95 Total new obligations	−4,997	−3,752	−3,499
24.40 Unobligated balance available, end of year	37	37	37
New budget authority (gross), detail:			
Discretionary:			
40.00 Appropriation	3,317	....	....
40.47 Portion applied to repay debt	−3,317	....	....
43.00 Appropriation (total discretionary)	....	....	....
Mandatory:			
60.05 Appropriation (indefinite)	1,155	....	....
67.15 Authority to borrow (indefinite)	....	21	22
69.00 Offsetting collections (cash)	3,868	3,731	3,477
70.00 Total new budget authority (gross)	5,023	3,752	3,499
Change in unpaid obligations:			
72.40 Unpaid obligations, start of year: Obligated balance, start of year	337	337	337
73.10 Total new obligations	4,997	3,752	3,499
73.20 Total outlays (gross)	−4,997	−3,752	−3,499
74.40 Unpaid obligations, end of year: Obligated balance, end of year	337	337	337
Outlays (gross), detail:			
86.97 Outlays from new mandatory authority	4,986	3,752	3,499
86.98 Outlays from mandatory balances	11	....	....
87.00 Total outlays (gross)	4,997	3,752	3,499
Offsets:			
Against gross budget authority and outlays:			
88.00 Offsetting collections (cash) from: Federal sources	−3,868	−3,731	−3,477
Net budget authority and outlays:			
89.00 Budget authority	1,155	21	22
90.00 Outlays	1,130	21	22

The Federal Financing Bank (FFB) was created in 1973 to reduce the costs of Federal and federally-assisted borrowing and to ensure the coordination of such borrowing from the public in a manner least disruptive to private financial markets and institutions. Prior to that time, many agencies borrowed directly from the private market to finance credit programs involving lending to the public at higher rates than on comparable Treasury securities. With the implementation of the Federal Credit Reform Act in 1992, however, agencies simply finance such loan programs through direct loan financing accounts that borrow directly from the Treasury. Therefore, FFB loans are now used primarily to finance direct agency activities such as construction of Federal buildings by the General Services Administration and meeting the financing requirements of the U.S. Postal Service. In certain cases, the FFB finances Federal direct loans to the public that would otherwise be made by private lenders and fully guaranteed by a Federal agency.

Lending by the FFB is set at ⅛ percent above Treasury rates and may take one of three forms, depending on the authorizing statutes pertaining to a particular agency or program: (1) the FFB may purchase agency financial assets; (2) the FFB may acquire debt securities that the agency is otherwise authorized to issue to the public; and (3) the FFB may originate direct loans on behalf of an agency by disbursing loans directly to private borrowers and receiving repayments from the private borrower on behalf of the agency. Because law requires that transactions by the FFB be treated as a means of financing agency obligations, the budgetary effect of the third type of transaction is reflected in the budget in the following sequence: a loan by the FFB to the agency, a loan by the agency to a private borrower, a repayment by a private borrower to the agency, and a repayment by the agency to the FFB.

The Treasury Department Appropriations Act, 1999 provided a $3.3 billion appropriation to liquidate the FFB's accumulated deficit resulting from unpaid prepayment premiums. This deficit arose because contractually-required prepayment premiums were waived by statute for FFB loans to certain borrowers, but the FFB was still required to pay a prepayment premium on its corresponding loans from the Treasury.

The following table shows the annual net lending by the FFB by agency and program and the amount outstanding at the end of each year.

The table does not include certain securities originally issued to the FFB by the Tennessee Valley Authority and the Postal Service, which the FFB exchanged with the Civil Service Retirement and Disability Fund in 1996 in return for Treasury securities of equal present value. These TVA and Postal Service securities, which continued to be serviced by the FFB, had a remaining face value of $3.2 billion and $0.7 billion respectively as of the end of 1998. TVA prepaid its securities in October 1998, pursuant to a provision in the Omnibus Consolidated and Emergency Supplemental Appropriations Act, 1999 (P.L. 105–277) that permitted TVA to avoid paying the $1.2 billion contractually-required prepayment premium. Under the terms of the provision, the FFB instead received a $1.2 billion appropriation from the general fund to compensate for the waived prepayment premium. The FFB used this appropriation to pay the corresponding prepayment premium to the Civil Service Retirement and Disability Fund.

Intragovernmental funds—Continued

FEDERAL FINANCING BANK—Continued

NET LENDING AND LOANS OUTSTANDING, END OF YEAR

(in millions of dollars)

	1999 actual	2000 est.	2001 est.
A. Department of Agriculture:			
1. Rural housing loans:			
Lending, net	–2,375	–1,585	–385
Loans outstanding	7,125	5,540	5,155
2. Rural development loans:			
Lending, net	–265		–975
Loans outstanding	3,410	3,410	2,435
3. Rural Utilities Service:			
Lending, net	–282	–1,041	285
Loans outstanding	18,484	17,443	17,728
B. Department of Defense:			
1. Defense working capital funds:			
Lending, net	–86	–91	–106
Loans outstanding	1,139	1,048	942
C. Department of Education:			
1. Historically black colleges and universities:			
Lending, net	6	25	25
Loans outstanding	11	36	61
D. Department of Health and Human Services:			
1. Health maintenance organizations:			
Lending, net	–1	–1	–1
Loans outstanding	2	1	
2. Medical facility loans:			
Lending, net	–4	–2	–1
Loans outstanding	3	1	
E. Department of Housing and Urban Development:			
1. Section 108 guaranteed loans:			
Lending, net	–17	–4	–4
Loans outstanding	14	10	6
2. Low-rent public housing:			
Lending, net	–72	–71	–71
Loans outstanding	1,420	1,349	1,278
F. Department of the Interior:			
1. Territory of the Virgin Islands:			
Lending, net	–1	–1	–1
Loans outstanding	16	15	14
G. Department of Transportation:			
1. Railroad Revitalization and Regulatory Reform Act:			
Lending, net	–*		
Loans outstanding	4	4	4
H. General Services Administration:			
1. Federal buildings fund:			
Lending, net	644	–80	–56
Loans outstanding	2,405	2,325	2,269
2. Pennsylvania Avenue Activities:			
Lending, net	–713		
Loans outstanding			
I. International Assistance Programs:			
1. Foreign military sales credit:			
Lending, net	–218	–221	–233
Loans outstanding	2,611	2,390	2,157
J. Small Business Administration:			
1. Section 503 guaranteed loans:			
Lending, net	–40	–23	–20
Loans outstanding	194	171	151
K. Postal Service:			
Lending, net	583	1,923	449
Loans outstanding	6,279	8,202	8,651
Total lending:			
Lending, net	–2,840	–1,172	–1,094
Loans outstanding	43,115	41,943	40,850

* $500 thousand or less.

Balance Sheet (in millions of dollars)

Identification code 20–4521–0–4–803		1998 actual	1999 actual	2000 est.	2001 est.
	ASSETS:				
	Federal assets:				
1101	Fund balances with Treasury	348	610	610	610
	Investments in US securities:				
1104	Agency securities, par	45,919	43,003	41,831	40,738
1106	Receivables, net	1,051	910	796	724
1999	Total assets	47,318	44,523	43,237	42,072
	LIABILITIES:				
	Federal liabilities:				
2101	Accounts payable	1,380	1,235	1,121	1,049
	Debt:				
2103	Borrowing from Treasury	34,217	28,276	27,125	26,054
2103	Debt arising from prepayment premiums				
2103	Borrowing from the Civil Service Retirement Trust Fund	15,000	15,000	15,000	15,000
2999	Total liabilities	50,597	44,511	43,246	42,103
	NET POSITION:				
3300	Cumulative results of operations	–3,279	12	–9	–31
3999	Total net position	–3,279	12	–9	–31
4999	Total liabilities and net position	47,318	44,523	43,237	42,072

Object Classification (in millions of dollars)

Identification code 20–4521–0–4–803		1999 actual	2000 est.	2001 est.
25.2	Other services	2	2	2
43.0	Interest and dividends	4,995	3,750	3,497
99.9	Total new obligations	4,997	3,752	3,499

BUREAU OF ALCOHOL, TOBACCO AND FIREARMS

Federal Funds

General and special funds:

SALARIES AND EXPENSES

For necessary expenses of the Bureau of Alcohol, Tobacco and Firearms, including purchase of not to exceed 812 vehicles for police-type use, of which 650 shall be for replacement only, and hire of passenger motor vehicles; hire of aircraft; services of expert witnesses at such rates as may be determined by the Director; for payment of per diem and/or subsistence allowances to employees where [an assignment to the National Response Team during the investigation of a bombing or arson incident] *a major investigative assignment* requires an employee to work 16 hours or more per day or to remain overnight at his or her post of duty; not to exceed [$15,000] *$20,000* for official reception and representation expenses; for training of State and local law enforcement agencies with or without reimbursement, including training in connection with the training and acquisition of canines for explosives and fire accelerants detection; *not to exceed $50,000 for cooperative research and development programs for Laboratory Services and Fire Research Center activities;* and provision of laboratory assistance to State and local agencies, with or without reimbursement, [$565,959,000] *$755,903,000*, [of which $39,000,000 may be used for the Youth Crime Gun Interdiction Initiative;] of which not to exceed $1,000,000 shall be available for the payment of attorneys' fees as provided by 18 U.S.C. 924(d)(2); and [of which $1,000,000] *that the amount appropriated* shall be available for the equipping of any vessel, vehicle, equipment, or aircraft available for official use by a State or local law enforcement agency if the conveyance will be used in joint law enforcement operations with the Bureau of Alcohol, Tobacco and Firearms and for the payment of overtime [salaries] *and related Federal benefits*, travel, fuel, training, equipment, supplies, and other similar costs of State and local law enforcement personnel, including sworn officers and support personnel, that are incurred in joint operations with the Bureau of Alcohol, Tobacco and Firearms: *Provided*, That no funds made available by this or any other Act may be used to transfer the functions, missions, or activities of the Bureau of Alcohol, Tobacco and Firearms to other agencies or Departments in fiscal year [2000] *2001*: [*Provided further*, That no funds appropriated herein shall be available for salaries or administrative expenses in connection with consolidating or centralizing, within the Department of the Treasury, the records, or any portion thereof, of acquisition and disposition of firearms maintained by Federal firearms licensees: *Provided further*, That no funds appropriated herein shall be used to pay administrative expenses or the compensation of any officer or employee of the United States to implement an amendment or amendments to 27 CFR 178.118 or to change the definition of "Curios or relics" in 27 CFR 178.11 or remove any item from ATF Publication 5300.11 as it existed on January 1, 1994:] *Provided further*, That none of the funds appropriated herein shall be available to investigate or act upon applications for relief from Federal firearms disabilities under 18 U.S.C.

925(c): *Provided further*, That such funds shall be available to investigate and act upon applications filed by corporations for relief from Federal firearms disabilities under 18 U.S.C. 925(c): **[***Provided further*, That no funds in this Act may be used to provide ballistics imaging equipment to any one installation or site of a State or local authority who has obtained similar equipment through a Federal grant or subsidy unless the State or local authority agrees in writing to the original grantor to return that equipment or to repay that grant or subsidy to the Federal Government: *Provided further*, That no funds under this Act may be used to electronically retrieve information gathered pursuant to 18 U.S.C. 923(g)(4) by name or any personal identification code**]**. *(Treasury Department Appropriations Act, 2000.)*

Program and Financing (in millions of dollars)

Identification code 20–1000–0–1–751		1999 actual	2000 est.	2001 est.
	Obligations by program activity:			
	Direct program:			
00.01	Reduce violent crime	418	432	566
00.02	Collect revenue	65	66	101
00.03	Protect the public	70	72	91
01.92	Total direct program	553	570	758
09.01	Reimbursable program	41	51	51
10.00	Total new obligations	594	621	809
	Budgetary resources available for obligation:			
21.40	Unobligated balance available, start of year	10	11	6
22.00	New budget authority (gross)	599	616	807
22.10	Resources available from recoveries of prior year obligations	2		
23.90	Total budgetary resources available for obligation	611	627	813
23.95	Total new obligations	−594	−621	−809
23.98	Unobligated balance expiring or withdrawn	−6		
24.40	Unobligated balance available, end of year	11	6	4
	New budget authority (gross), detail:			
	Discretionary:			
40.00	Appropriation	542	566	756
40.75	Reduction pursuant to P.L. 106–51	−1		
40.76	Reduction pursuant to P.L. 106–113		−1	
42.00	Transferred from other accounts	16		
43.00	Appropriation (total discretionary)	557	565	756
50.00	Reappropriation	1		
	Spending authority from offsetting collections:			
68.00	Offsetting collections (cash)	6	51	51
68.10	From Federal sources: Change in receivables and unpaid, unfilled orders	35		
68.90	Spending authority from offsetting collections (total discretionary)	41	51	51
70.00	Total new budget authority (gross)	599	616	807
	Change in unpaid obligations:			
	Unpaid obligations, start of year:			
72.40	Obligated balance, start of year	86	75	131
72.95	From Federal sources: Receivables and unpaid, unfilled orders		35	35
72.99	Total unpaid obligations, start of year	86	110	166
73.10	Total new obligations	594	621	809
73.20	Total outlays (gross)	−558	−565	−790
73.40	Adjustments in expired accounts (net)	−10		
73.45	Adjustments in unexpired accounts	−2		
	Unpaid obligations, end of year:			
74.40	Obligated balance, end of year	75	131	150
74.95	From Federal sources: Receivables and unpaid, unfilled orders	35	35	35
74.99	Total unpaid obligations, end of year	110	166	185
	Outlays (gross), detail:			
86.90	Outlays from new discretionary authority	503	560	731
86.93	Outlays from discretionary balances	55	5	59
87.00	Total outlays (gross)	558	565	790
	Offsets:			
	Against gross budget authority and outlays:			
	Offsetting collections (cash) from:			
	Federal sources:			
88.00	Drug enforcement	−1	−10	−10
88.00	Other Federal sources	−5	−41	−41
88.90	Total, offsetting collections (cash)	−6	−51	−51
	Against gross budget authority only:			
88.95	From Federal sources: Change in receivables and unpaid, unfilled orders	−35		
	Net budget authority and outlays:			
89.00	Budget authority	558	565	756
90.00	Outlays	552	514	739

The Bureau of Alcohol, Tobacco and Firearms (ATF) is a law enforcement organization within the United States Department of the Treasury with unique responsibilities dedicated to reducing violent crime, collecting revenue, and protecting the public. ATF enforces the Federal laws and regulations relating to alcohol, tobacco, firearms, explosives, and arson by working directly and in cooperation with others to: (1) Effectively contribute to a safer America by reducing the future number and cost of violent crimes: (2) Maintain a sound revenue management and regulatory system that continues reducing taxpayer burden, improving service, collecting the revenue due and preventing illegal diversion; and (3) Protect the public and prevent consumer deception in ATF's regulated commodities.

In 2001, the Treasury Forfeiture Fund will provide $6 million for construction-related costs associated with ATF's National Laboratory and Fire Research facilities and for continued deployment of the integrated ballistics system.

The following performance measurements continue to be refined and improved in order to provide viable output and outcome measures for the Bureau, thus complying with the Government Performance and Results Act of 1993 (GPRA).

PERFORMANCE AND WORKLOAD MEASURES

	1999 actual	*2000 est.*	*2001 est.*
Reduce Violent Crime:			
Crime related costs avoided ($ billions)	$1.05	$1.00	$15.00
Future crimes avoided	542,560	450,000	5,000,000
Number of persons trained/developed	53,385	52,000	n/a
Number of trace requests	209,126	225,000	240,000
Average trace response time (# of days)	11.4	11.5	10.5
Number of personnel trained in IVRS	n/a	n/a	6,000
NRT customer satisfaction rating	n/a	n/a	90%
Collect the Revenue:			
Taxes and fees collected from the alcohol, firearms and explosives industries ($ billion)	$12.1	$12.3	$12.7
Ratio of taxes and fees collected vs. resources expended to collect	$193: $1	$195: $1	$231: $1
Burden hours reduced	484,600	482,000	n/a
Percent of entities filing electronically	n/a	n/a	TBD
Protect the Public:			
Response to unsafe conditions and product deficiencies discovered (explosives)	923	825	850
The number of commodity seminars held	229	175	175
Workload Measures:			
Number of inspections (explosives)	7,443	8,000	9,000
Percent of population inspected (firearms)	10.5	11	12

Object Classification (in millions of dollars)

Identification code 20–1000–0–1–751		1999 actual	2000 est.	2001 est.
	Direct obligations:			
	Personnel compensation:			
11.1	Full-time permanent	222	240	270
11.3	Other than full-time permanent	2	2	3
11.5	Other personnel compensation	32	32	39
11.9	Total personnel compensation	256	274	312
12.1	Civilian personnel benefits	90	93	118
21.0	Travel and transportation of persons	18	21	29
22.0	Transportation of things	3	3	3
23.1	Rental payments to GSA	39	40	44
23.3	Communications, utilities, and miscellaneous charges	18	22	27
24.0	Printing and reproduction	2	2	2

General and special funds—Continued

SALARIES AND EXPENSES—Continued

Object Classification (in millions of dollars)—Continued

Identification code 20–1000–0–1–751	1999 actual	2000 est.	2001 est.
25.2 Other services	78	71	118
26.0 Supplies and materials	11	9	12
31.0 Equipment	38	35	93
99.0 Subtotal, direct obligations	553	570	758
99.0 Reimbursable obligations	41	51	51
99.9 Total new obligations	594	621	809

Personnel Summary

Identification code 20–1000–0–1–751	1999 actual	2000 est.	2001 est.
Direct:			
1001 Total compensable workyears: Full-time equivalent employment	3,969	4,032	4,671
Reimbursable:			
2001 Total compensable workyears: Full-time equivalent employment	119	113	88

LABORATORY FACILITIES AND HEADQUARTERS

Program and Financing (in millions of dollars)

Identification code 20–1003–0–1–751	1999 actual	2000 est.	2001 est.
Change in unpaid obligations:			
72.40 Unpaid obligations, start of year: Obligated balance, start of year	62	61	12
73.10 Total new obligations			
73.20 Total outlays (gross)	−1	−49	−7
74.40 Unpaid obligations, end of year: Obligated balance, end of year	61	12	5
Outlays (gross), detail:			
86.93 Outlays from discretionary balances	1	49	7
Net budget authority and outlays:			
89.00 Budget authority			
90.00 Outlays	1	49	7

In 2001, the budget proposes funding for construction-related costs of a new ATF headquarters building that meets physical protection and security needs. Outlays associated with prior year funding shown above reflects construction costs for the new ATF National Laboratory and Fire Research facilities.

INTERNAL REVENUE COLLECTIONS FOR PUERTO RICO

Unavailable Collections (in millions of dollars)

Identification code 20–5737–0–2–806	1999 actual	2000 est.	2001 est.
Balance, start of year:			
01.99 Balance, start of year			
Receipts:			
02.01 Deposits, internal revenue collections for Puerto Rico	235	253	315
02.02 Legislative proposal subject to PAYGO		32	−32
02.99 Total receipts	235	285	283
Appropriation:			
05.01 Internal revenue collections for Puerto Rico	−235	−253	−315
05.02 Legislative proposal subject to PAYGO		−32	32
05.99 Subtotal appropriation	−235	−285	−283
07.99 Total balance, end of year			

Program and Financing (in millions of dollars)

Identification code 20–5737–0–2–806	1999 actual	2000 est.	2001 est.
Obligations by program activity:			
10.00 Total new obligations (object class 41.0)	235	253	315
Budgetary resources available for obligation:			
22.00 New budget authority (gross)	235	253	315
23.95 Total new obligations	−235	−253	−315
New budget authority (gross), detail:			
Mandatory:			
60.25 Appropriation (special fund, indefinite)	235	253	315
Change in unpaid obligations:			
73.10 Total new obligations	235	253	315
73.20 Total outlays (gross)	−235	−253	−315
Outlays (gross), detail:			
86.97 Outlays from new mandatory authority	235	253	315
Net budget authority and outlays:			
89.00 Budget authority	235	253	315
90.00 Outlays	235	253	315

Summary of Budget Authority and Outlays

(in millions of dollars)

	1999 actual	*2000 est.*	*2001 est.*
Enacted/requested:			
Budget Authority	235	253	315
Outlays	235	253	315
Legislative proposal, subject to PAYGO:			
Budget Authority		32	−32
Outlays		32	−32
Total:			
Budget Authority	235	285	283
Outlays	235	285	283

Excise taxes collected under the Internal Revenue laws of the United States on articles produced in Puerto Rico and either transported to the United States or consumed on the island are paid to Puerto Rico (26 U.S.C. 7652)

INTERNAL REVENUE COLLECTIONS FOR PUERTO RICO

(Legislative proposal, subject to PAYGO)

Program and Financing (in millions of dollars)

Identification code 20–5737–4–2–806	1999 actual	2000 est.	2001 est.
Obligations by program activity:			
10.00 Total new obligations (object class 41.0)		32	−32
Budgetary resources available for obligation:			
22.00 New budget authority (gross)		32	−32
23.95 Total new obligations		−32	32
New budget authority (gross), detail:			
Mandatory:			
60.25 Appropriation (special fund, indefinite)		32	−32
Change in unpaid obligations:			
73.10 Total new obligations		32	−32
73.20 Total outlays (gross)		−32	32
Outlays (gross), detail:			
86.97 Outlays from new mandatory authority		32	−32
Net budget authority and outlays:			
89.00 Budget authority		32	−32
90.00 Outlays		32	−32

The Puerto Rican Federal Relations Act mandates that excise taxes collected under the Internal Revenue laws of the United States on articles produced in Puerto Rico and either transported to the United States or consumed on the island are to be covered over to Puerto Rico (48 U.S.C. 734). The budget proposes to repeal the special cover over transfer rules in section 512(b) of P.L. 106–170, which delay the transfer of a portion of the funds from 2000 to 2001.

UNITED STATES CUSTOMS SERVICE

Federal Funds

General and special funds:

SALARIES AND EXPENSES

For necessary expenses of the United States Customs Service, including purchase and lease of up to 1,050 motor vehicles of which 550 are for replacement only and of which 1,030 are for police-type use and commercial operations; hire of motor vehicles; contracting with individuals for personal services abroad; not to exceed $40,000 for official reception and representation expenses; and awards of compensation to informers, as authorized by any Act enforced by the United States Customs Service, **[**$1,705,364,000**]** *$1,858,932,000*, of which such sums as become available in the Customs User Fee Account, except sums subject to section 13031(f)(3) of the Consolidated Omnibus Budget Reconciliation Act of 1985, as amended (19 U.S.C. 58c(f)(3)), shall be derived from that Account; of the total, not to exceed $150,000 shall be available for payment for rental space in connection with preclearance operations; not to exceed $4,000,000 shall be available until expended for research**[**, of which $725,000 shall be provided to a northern plains agricultural economics program in North and/or South Dakota to conduct a research program on the bilateral United States/Canadian bilateral trade of agricultural commodities and products; of which not less than $100,000 shall be available to promote public awareness of the child pornography tipline; of which not less than $200,000 shall be available for Project Alert**]**; not to exceed $5,000,000 shall be available until expended for conducting special operations pursuant to 19 U.S.C. 2081; not to exceed $8,000,000 shall be available until expended for the procurement of automation infrastructure items, including hardware, software, and installation; and not to exceed $5,000,000 shall be available until expended for repairs to Customs facilities: *Provided*, That uniforms may be purchased without regard to the general purchase price limitation for the current fiscal year: *Provided further*, That notwithstanding any other provision of law, the fiscal year aggregate overtime limitation prescribed in subsection 5(c)(1) of the Act of February 13, 1911 (19 U.S.C. 261 and 267) shall be $30,000. *(Treasury Department Appropriations Act, 2000.)*

Unavailable Collections (in millions of dollars)

Identification code 20–0602–0–1–751	1999 actual	2000 est.	2001 est.
Balance, start of year:			
01.99 Balance, start of year	....	....	....
Receipts:			
02.01 U.S. Customs users fees account, conveyance/passenger/other	274	300	320
02.02 U.S. Customs user fee accounts, merchandise processing, Treasury	934	953	972
02.99 Total receipts	1,208	1,253	1,292
Appropriation:			
05.01 Salaries and expenses	–1,208	–1,253	–1,292
05.99 Subtotal appropriation	–1,208	–1,253	–1,292
07.99 Total balance, end of year	....	....	....

Program and Financing (in millions of dollars)

Identification code 20–0602–0–1–751	1999 actual	2000 est.	2001 est.
Obligations by program activity:			
Direct program:			
00.04 Commercial	1,122	1,200	1,183
00.05 Drug and other enforcement	956	1,028	1,007
09.01 Reimbursable program	462	451	448
10.00 Total new obligations	2,540	2,679	2,638
Budgetary resources available for obligation:			
21.40 Unobligated balance available, start of year	853	877	680
22.00 New budget authority (gross)	2,534	2,482	2,627
22.10 Resources available from recoveries of prior year obligations	28	....	....
22.22 Unobligated balance transferred from other accounts	8	....	....
23.90 Total budgetary resources available for obligation	3,423	3,359	3,307
23.95 Total new obligations	–2,540	–2,679	–2,638
23.98 Unobligated balance expiring or withdrawn	–6	....	....
24.40 Unobligated balance available, end of year	877	680	669
New budget authority (gross), detail:			
Discretionary:			
40.00 Appropriation	710	752	887
40.15 Appropriation (emergency)	106	....	....
40.25 Appropriation (special fund, indefinite)(Customs user fees)	934	953	972
40.75 Reduction pursuant to P.L. 106–51	–2	....	....
40.76 Reduction pursuant to P.L. 106–113	....	–7	....
42.00 Transferred from other accounts	47	4	....
43.00 Appropriation (total discretionary)	1,795	1,702	1,859
Mandatory:			
60.25 Appropriation (special fund, indefinite)(Customs user fee)	274	300	320
Spending authority from offsetting collections:			
Discretionary:			
68.00 Offsetting collections (cash)	474	451	448
68.10 From Federal sources: Change in receivables and unpaid, unfilled orders	–18	29	....
68.15 From Federal sources: Adjustments to receivables and unpaid, unfilled orders	9	....	....
68.90 Spending authority from offsetting collections (total discretionary)	465	480	448
70.00 Total new budget authority (gross)	2,534	2,482	2,627
Change in unpaid obligations:			
Unpaid obligations, start of year:			
72.40 Obligated balance, start of year	292	356	690
72.95 From Federal sources: Receivables and unpaid, unfilled orders	116	98	127
72.99 Total unpaid obligations, start of year	408	454	817
73.10 Total new obligations	2,540	2,679	2,638
73.20 Total outlays (gross)	–2,446	–2,316	–2,629
73.40 Adjustments in expired accounts (net)	–21	....	....
73.45 Adjustments in unexpired accounts	–28	....	....
Unpaid obligations, end of year:			
74.40 Obligated balance, end of year	356	690	699
74.95 From Federal sources: Receivables and unpaid, unfilled orders	98	127	127
74.99 Total unpaid obligations, end of year	454	817	826
Outlays (gross), detail:			
86.90 Outlays from new discretionary authority	1,960	2,012	2,121
86.93 Outlays from discretionary balances	192	4	190
86.97 Outlays from new mandatory authority	274	270	288
86.98 Outlays from mandatory balances	20	30	30
87.00 Total outlays (gross)	2,446	2,316	2,629
Offsets:			
Against gross budget authority and outlays:			
Offsetting collections (cash) from:			
88.00 Federal sources	–462	–440	–437
88.40 Non-Federal sources	–12	–11	–11
88.90 Total, offsetting collections (cash)	–474	–451	–448
Against gross budget authority only:			
88.95 From Federal sources: Change in receivables and unpaid, unfilled orders	18	–29	....
88.96 From Federal sources: Adjustment to receivables and unpaid, unfilled orders	–9	....	....
Net budget authority and outlays:			
89.00 Budget authority	2,069	2,002	2,179
90.00 Outlays	1,972	1,865	2,181

Summary of Budget Authority and Outlays

(in millions of dollars)

	1999 actual	*2000 est.*	*2001 est.*
Enacted/requested:			
Budget Authority	2,069	2,002	2,179
Outlays	1,972	1,865	2,181
Legislative proposal, not subject to PAYGO:			
Budget Authority	....	....	3

General and special funds—Continued

SALARIES AND EXPENSES—Continued

Summary of Budget Authority and Outlays—Continued

(in millions of dollars)

	1999 actual	2000 est.	2001 est.
Outlays			3
Total:			
Budget Authority	2,069	2,002	2,182
Outlays	1,972	1,865	2,184

The United States Customs Service, in partnership with other Federal agencies, is one of the Nation's principal means of border enforcement. Its mission is to ensure that all goods and persons entering and exiting the United States do so in compliance with all United States laws and regulations.

Commercial.—Commercial activities are all process/business area activities (Trade Compliance, Outbound, and Passenger Processing) which occur prior to a violation being confirmed or acceptance of a referral for investigation. This includes intelligence gathering, targeting, analysis and examination activities.

WORKLOAD DATA

	1999 actual	2000 est.	2001 est.
Total Commercial Entry Summaries (millions)	21.7	23.8	25.0
Total Passengers (in millions):			
Land	394.9	399.5	409.5
Air	75.7	79.3	83.5
Sea	9.2	9.3	10.0
Total Carriers (thousands):			
Land	135,804.3	139,199.3	142,679.4
Air	927.8	974.2	1,022.9
Sea	200.6	201.0	205.0

PERFORMANCE MEASURES

	1999 actual	2000 est.	2001 est.
Overall Trade Compliance Rate	85%	90%	90%
Overall Passenger Compliance Rate:			
Land	97.6%	97.8%	98%
Air	97.4%	97.7%	97.8%
Revenue Collection Compliance Rate	99%	99.06%	99%
Collection (billions $)	19.1	18.7	19.2

Drug and Other Enforcement.—Drug and Other Enforcement activities are process activities which occur after confirmation of a violation or acceptance of a referral for investigation. Also included are enforcement strategies to address enforcement issues which impact more than one process, intelligence activities and investigations of drug and money laundering violations, intelligence activities and investigations related to alleged/suspected violations which are independent of process activities, the air and marine interdiction programs, and radio communications management.

PERFORMANCE MEASURES

	1999 actual	2000 est.	2001 est.
Quantity of narcotics seized (thousands of lbs.):			
Heroin	1.9	1.9	1.9
Cocaine	160.4	172.0	172.5
Marijuana	1,147.6	1,300.0	1,320
Number of narcotics seizures:			
Heroin	911	1,000	1,050
Cocaine	2,509	2,600	2,650
Marijuana	15,699	16,500	17,000
Currency/Real Property Seized (millions $)	360.1	374.1	396.4

The North American Free Trade Agreement Implementation Act (Public Law 103–182) extended the collection of existing Customs user fees (merchandise and passenger fees) through September 2003. Legislation will be proposed to extend these fees through 2010.

The Treasury Forfeiture Fund will provide $11 million for Customs enforcement technology in 2001.

Object Classification (in millions of dollars)

Identification code 20–0602–0–1–751		1999 actual	2000 est.	2001 est.
	Direct obligations:			
	Personnel compensation:			
11.1	Full-time permanent	900	917	970
11.3	Other than full-time permanent	17	21	21
11.5	Other personnel compensation	211	218	220
11.9	Total personnel compensation	1,128	1,156	1,211
12.1	Civilian personnel benefits	290	304	319
21.0	Travel and transportation of persons	33	45	50
22.0	Transportation of things	4	6	6
23.1	Rental payments to GSA	156	165	212
23.2	Rental payments to others	2	1	1
23.3	Communications, utilities, and miscellaneous charges	38	43	48
24.0	Printing and reproduction	3	4	4
25.1	Advisory and assistance services	42	40	31
25.2	Other services	119	173	89
25.3	Purchases of goods and services from Government accounts	27	30	20
25.4	Operation and maintenance of facilities	15	18	15
25.5	Research and development contracts	3	5	1
25.7	Operation and maintenance of equipment	28	29	29
26.0	Supplies and materials	27	26	28
31.0	Equipment	160	179	124
32.0	Land and structures		1	
41.0	Grants, subsidies, and contributions	1	1	
42.0	Insurance claims and indemnities		2	2
99.0	Subtotal, direct obligations	2,076	2,228	2,190
99.0	Reimbursable obligations	462	451	448
99.5	Below reporting threshold	2		
99.9	Total new obligations	2,540	2,679	2,638

Personnel Summary

Identification code 20–0602–0–1–751		1999 actual	2000 est.	2001 est.
	Direct:			
1001	Total compensable workyears: Full-time equivalent employment	17,249	17,271	17,559
	Reimbursable:			
2001	Total compensable workyears: Full-time equivalent employment	1,988	2,037	2,041

SALARIES AND EXPENSES

(Legislative proposal, not subject to PAYGO)

For necessary expenses of the United States Customs Service, $3,000,000 to be derived only from the Harbor Services Fund.

Program and Financing (in millions of dollars)

Identification code 20–0602–2–1–751		1999 actual	2000 est.	2001 est.
	Obligations by program activity:			
00.04	Direct program			3
09.01	Reimbursable program			–3
10.00	Total new obligations			
	New budget authority (gross), detail:			
	Discretionary:			
40.25	Appropriation (special fund, indefinite) (Harbor services fund)			3
68.00	Spending authority from offsetting collections: Offsetting collections (cash)			–3
70.00	Total new budget authority (gross)			
	Offsets:			
	Against gross budget authority and outlays:			
88.45	Offsetting collections (cash) from: Offsetting Collections			3
	Net budget authority and outlays:			
89.00	Budget authority			3
90.00	Outlays			3

Customs collects a fee on imports on behalf of the U.S. Army Corps of Engineers. Starting in 2001 the Administration proposes to offset the costs related to collecting this fee with funding derived from the Harbor Services Fund.

Object Classification (in millions of dollars)

Identification code 20–0602–2–1–751		1999 actual	2000 est.	2001 est.
25.2	Direct obligations: Other services			3
99.0	Reimbursable obligations: Subtotal, reimbursable obligations			–3
99.9	Total new obligations			

OPERATION, MAINTENANCE AND PROCUREMENT, AIR AND MARINE INTERDICTION PROGRAMS

For expenses, not otherwise provided for, necessary for the operation and maintenance of marine vessels, aircraft, and other related equipment of the Air and Marine Programs, including operational training and mission-related travel, and rental payments for facilities occupied by the air or marine interdiction and demand reduction programs, the operations of which include the following: the interdiction of narcotics and other goods; the provision of support to Customs and other Federal, State, and local agencies in the enforcement or administration of laws enforced by the Customs Service; and, at the discretion of the Commissioner of Customs, the provision of assistance to Federal, State, and local agencies in other law enforcement and emergency humanitarian efforts, [$108,688,000] *$156,875,000*, which shall remain available until expended: *Provided*, That no aircraft or other related equipment, with the exception of aircraft which is one of a kind and has been identified as excess to Customs requirements and aircraft which has been damaged beyond repair, shall be transferred to any other Federal agency, department, or office outside of the Department of the Treasury, during fiscal year [2000] *2001* without [the prior approval of] *notice to* the Committees on Appropriations. *(Treasury Department Appropriations Act, 2000.)*

Program and Financing (in millions of dollars)

Identification code 20–0604–0–1–751		1999 actual	2000 est.	2001 est.
	Obligations by program activity:			
	Direct program:			
00.01	Air and marine interdiction	162	116	90
00.02	P3 interdiction	22	98	42
00.03	Procurement	6	3	25
09.01	Reimbursable program	5	1	1
10.00	Total new obligations	195	218	158
	Budgetary resources available for obligation:			
21.40	Unobligated balance available, start of year	20	109	1
22.00	New budget authority (gross)	280	110	158
22.10	Resources available from recoveries of prior year obligations	4		
23.90	Total budgetary resources available for obligation	304	219	159
23.95	Total new obligations	–195	–218	–158
24.40	Unobligated balance available, end of year	109	1	1
	New budget authority (gross), detail:			
	Discretionary:			
40.00	Appropriation	114	109	157
40.15	Appropriation (emergency)	163		
40.75	Reduction pursuant to P.L. 106–51	–2		
43.00	Appropriation (total discretionary)	275	109	157
	Spending authority from offsetting collections:			
68.00	Offsetting collections (cash)	2	1	1
68.10	From Federal sources: Change in receivables and unpaid, unfilled orders	3		
68.90	Spending authority from offsetting collections (total discretionary)	5	1	1
70.00	Total new budget authority (gross)	280	110	158
	Change in unpaid obligations:			
	Unpaid obligations, start of year:			
72.40	Obligated balance, start of year	146	177	231
72.95	From Federal sources: Receivables and unpaid, unfilled orders	1	4	4
72.99	Total unpaid obligations, start of year	147	181	235
73.10	Total new obligations	195	218	158
73.20	Total outlays (gross)	–150	–164	–144
73.40	Adjustments in expired accounts (net)	–7		
73.45	Adjustments in unexpired accounts	–4		
	Unpaid obligations, end of year:			
74.40	Obligated balance, end of year	177	231	246
74.95	From Federal sources: Receivables and unpaid, unfilled orders	4	4	4
74.99	Total unpaid obligations, end of year	181	235	250
	Outlays (gross), detail:			
86.90	Outlays from new discretionary authority	74	77	111
86.93	Outlays from discretionary balances	76	87	33
87.00	Total outlays (gross)	150	164	144
	Offsets:			
	Against gross budget authority and outlays:			
88.00	Offsetting collections (cash) from: Federal sources	–2	–1	–1
	Against gross budget authority only:			
88.95	From Federal sources: Change in receivables and unpaid, unfilled orders	–3		
	Net budget authority and outlays:			
89.00	Budget authority	275	109	157
90.00	Outlays	148	163	143

The Customs Air and Marine Interdiction Program combats the illegal entry of narcotics and other goods into the United States. This appropriation provides capital procurement and total operations and maintenance for the Customs air and marine program. This program also provides support for the interdiction of narcotics by other Federal, State and local agencies.

Object Classification (in millions of dollars)

Identification code 20–0604–0–1–751		1999 actual	2000 est.	2001 est.
	Direct obligations:			
21.0	Travel and transportation of persons	6	9	12
22.0	Transportation of things		1	1
23.2	Rental payments to others	2	2	2
23.3	Communications, utilities, and miscellaneous charges	3	4	2
25.2	Other services	9	82	13
25.3	Purchases of goods and services from Government accounts	5		3
25.4	Operation and maintenance of facilities	3		2
25.7	Operation and maintenance of equipment	57		33
26.0	Supplies and materials	36	41	27
31.0	Equipment	68	78	59
99.0	Subtotal, direct obligations	189	217	154
99.0	Reimbursable obligations	6	1	1
99.5	Below reporting threshold			3
99.9	Total new obligations	195	218	158

CUSTOMS FACILITIES, CONSTRUCTION, IMPROVEMENTS AND RELATED EXPENSES

Program and Financing (in millions of dollars)

Identification code 20–0608–0–1–751		1999 actual	2000 est.	2001 est.
	Obligations by program activity:			
10.00	Total new obligations	2	9	7
	Budgetary resources available for obligation:			
21.40	Unobligated balance available, start of year	11	15	7
22.00	New budget authority (gross)	7		
23.90	Total budgetary resources available for obligation	18	15	7
23.95	Total new obligations	–2	–9	–7
24.40	Unobligated balance available, end of year	15	7	

General and special funds—Continued

CUSTOMS FACILITIES, CONSTRUCTION, IMPROVEMENTS AND RELATED EXPENSES—Continued

Program and Financing (in millions of dollars)—Continued

Identification code 20–0608–0–1–751	1999 actual	2000 est.	2001 est.
New budget authority (gross), detail:			
Discretionary:			
40.15 Appropriation (emergency)	7		
Change in unpaid obligations:			
72.40 Unpaid obligations, start of year: Obligated balance, start of year	1	1	5
73.10 Total new obligations	2	9	7
73.20 Total outlays (gross)	−2	−5	−4
74.40 Unpaid obligations, end of year: Obligated balance, end of year	1	5	9
Outlays (gross), detail:			
86.90 Outlays from new discretionary authority	1		
86.93 Outlays from discretionary balances	1	5	4
87.00 Total outlays (gross)	2	5	4
Net budget authority and outlays:			
89.00 Budget authority	7		
90.00 Outlays	2	5	4

This account funds major Customs construction, repair, and facility improvement initiatives.

Object Classification (in millions of dollars)

Identification code 20–0608–0–1–751	1999 actual	2000 est.	2001 est.
25.2 Other services	2	2	2
25.3 Purchases of goods and services from Government accounts		5	4
31.0 Equipment		1	1
99.0 Subtotal, direct obligations	2	8	7
99.5 Below reporting threshold		1	
99.9 Total new obligations	2	9	7

AUTOMATION MODERNIZATION

For expenses not otherwise provided for Customs automated systems, $338,400,000, to remain available until expended, of which $123,000,000 shall be for the operations and maintenance of the Automated Commercial System, $5,400,000 shall be for the International Trade Data System, and $210,000,000 shall be for the development of the Automated Commercial Environment.

Program and Financing (in millions of dollars)

Identification code 20–0610–0–1–751	1999 actual	2000 est.	2001 est.
Obligations by program activity:			
00.04 Commercial			183
00.05 Drug and other enforcement			155
10.00 Total new obligations			338
Budgetary resources available for obligation:			
22.00 New budget authority (gross)			338
23.95 Total new obligations			−338
New budget authority (gross), detail:			
Discretionary:			
40.00 Appropriation			338
Change in unpaid obligations:			
73.10 Total new obligations			338
73.20 Total outlays (gross)			−178
74.40 Unpaid obligations, end of year: Obligated balance, end of year			160
Outlays (gross), detail:			
86.90 Outlays from new discretionary authority			178
Net budget authority and outlays:			
89.00 Budget authority			338
90.00 Outlays			178

Summary of Budget Authority and Outlays

(in millions of dollars)

Enacted/requested:	*1999 actual*	*2000 est.*	*2001 est.*
Budget Authority			338
Outlays			178
Legislative proposal, not subject to PAYGO:			
Budget Authority			−210
Outlays			−210
Total:			
Budget Authority			128
Outlays			−32

Customs is in the process of modernizing its trade data processing system. The current system, the Automated Commercial System (ACS), will be replaced with the new Automated Commercial Environment (ACE). ACE will provide an upgrade to the system which will enable Customs to meet the demands of an increasing volume of trade and convert to a paperless process and an account-based system. These funds will support the ACS legacy system while the conversion to ACE is underway, provide resources for the conversion to the ACE system, and assist Customs in incorporating the development of an International Trade Data System into its overall plan for modernizing the trade data processing system.

Object Classification (in millions of dollars)

Identification code 20–0610–0–1–751	1999 actual	2000 est.	2001 est.
21.0 Travel and transportation of persons			2
23.1 Rental payments to GSA			26
25.2 Other services			79
31.0 Equipment			231
99.9 Total new obligations			338

AUTOMATION MODERNIZATION

(Legislative proposal, not subject to PAYGO)

Contingent upon the enactment of authorizing legislation, the Secretary shall charge a fee, to be deposited as an offsetting collection to this appropriation to remain available until expended, for the purposes of the development of the Automated Commercial Environment: Provided, That upon enactment of such authorizing legislation, the amount appropriated above from the General Fund shall be reduced by $210,000,000.

Program and Financing (in millions of dollars)

Identification code 20–0610–2–1–751	1999 actual	2000 est.	2001 est.
Obligations by program activity:			
Direct program:			
00.04 Commercial			−113
00.05 Drug and other enforcement			−97
09.01 Reimbursable program			210
10.00 Total new obligations			
New budget authority (gross), detail:			
Discretionary:			
40.00 Appropriation			−210
68.00 Spending authority from offsetting collections: Offsetting collections (cash)			210
70.00 Total new budget authority (gross)			
Offsets:			
Against gross budget authority and outlays:			
88.40 Offsetting collections (cash) from: Non-Federal sources			−210

		1999 actual	2000 est.	2001 est.
	Net budget authority and outlays:			
89.00	Budget authority			−210
90.00	Outlays			−210

The Administration proposes to establish a fee. Proceeds of the fee will offset the costs of modernizing the Customs automated commercial operations, specifically the development of the Automated Commercial Environment (ACE), which is critical to maintain the U.S. Customs Service's ability to process the increasing volume of trade data. Legislation will be transmitted to allow the Secretary to establish the fee.

Object Classification (in millions of dollars)

Identification code 20–0610–2–1–751		1999 actual	2000 est.	2001 est.
	Direct obligations:			
23.3	Communications, utilities, and miscellaneous charges			−5
25.5	Research and development contracts			−25
31.0	Equipment			−180
99.0	Subtotal, direct obligations			−210
99.0	Reimbursable obligations			210
99.9	Total new obligations			

Customs Services at Small Airports

Unavailable Collections (in millions of dollars)

Identification code 20–5694–0–2–751		1999 actual	2000 est.	2001 est.
	Balance, start of year:			
01.99	Balance, start of year			
	Receipts:			
02.01	User fees for customs service	2	2	2
	Appropriation:			
05.01	Customs services at small airports	−2	−2	−2
07.99	Total balance, end of year			

Program and Financing (in millions of dollars)

Identification code 20–5694–0–2–751		1999 actual	2000 est.	2001 est.
	Obligations by program activity:			
00.01	Direct program	2	2	2
09.01	Reimbursable program	1	1	1
10.00	Total new obligations	3	3	3
	Budgetary resources available for obligation:			
21.40	Unobligated balance available, start of year	2	2	1
22.00	New budget authority (gross)	3	3	3
23.90	Total budgetary resources available for obligation	5	5	4
23.95	Total new obligations	−3	−3	−3
24.40	Unobligated balance available, end of year	2	1	1
	New budget authority (gross), detail:			
	Discretionary:			
40.25	Appropriation (special fund, indefinite)	2	2	2
68.00	Spending authority from offsetting collections: Offsetting collections (cash)	1	1	1
70.00	Total new budget authority (gross)	3	3	3
	Change in unpaid obligations:			
72.40	Unpaid obligations, start of year: Obligated balance, start of year		1	1
73.10	Total new obligations	3	3	3
73.20	Total outlays (gross)	−3	−3	−3
74.40	Unpaid obligations, end of year: Obligated balance, end of year	1	1	1
	Outlays (gross), detail:			
86.90	Outlays from new discretionary authority	3	3	3
	Offsets:			
	Against gross budget authority and outlays:			
88.40	Offsetting collections (cash) from: Non-Federal sources	−1	−1	−1
	Net budget authority and outlays:			
89.00	Budget authority	2	2	2
90.00	Outlays	2	2	2

Customs charges fees at certain small airports where the volume or value of business is insufficient to justify the availability of Customs services. The funds generated from these fees are applied to expenditures incurred in providing Customs services at each of these designated small airports. (19 U.S.C. 58b.)

The Treasury, Postal Service, and General Government Appropriations Act of 1998 (Public Law 105–284) made permanent the provision that Customs services at small airports may be derived from fees collected.

Object Classification (in millions of dollars)

Identification code 20–5694–0–2–751		1999 actual	2000 est.	2001 est.
11.1	Direct obligations: Personnel compensation: Full-time permanent	2	2	2
99.0	Reimbursable obligations: Subtotal, reimbursable obligations	1	1	1
99.9	Total new obligations	3	3	3

Personnel Summary

Identification code 20–5694–0–2–751		1999 actual	2000 est.	2001 est.
1001	Total compensable workyears: Full-time equivalent employment	63	69	69

Harbor Maintenance Fee Collection

(INCLUDING TRANSFER OF FUNDS)

For administrative expenses related to the collection of the Harbor Maintenance Fee, pursuant to Public Law 103–182, $3,000,000, to be derived from the Harbor Maintenance Trust Fund and to be transferred to and merged with the Customs "Salaries and Expenses" account for such purposes. *(Treasury Department Appropriations Act, 2000.)*

Program and Financing (in millions of dollars)

Identification code 20–8870–0–7–751		1999 actual	2000 est.	2001 est.
	Obligations by program activity:			
10.00	Total new obligations (object class 25.2)	3	3	3
	Budgetary resources available for obligation:			
22.00	New budget authority (gross)	3	3	3
23.95	Total new obligations	−3	−3	−3
	New budget authority (gross), detail:			
	Discretionary:			
40.26	Appropriation (trust fund, definite)	3	3	3
	Change in unpaid obligations:			
73.10	Total new obligations	3	3	3
73.20	Total outlays (gross)	−3	−3	−3
	Outlays (gross), detail:			
86.90	Outlays from new discretionary authority	3	3	3
	Net budget authority and outlays:			
89.00	Budget authority	3	3	3
90.00	Outlays	3	3	3

Summary of Budget Authority and Outlays

(in millions of dollars)

	1999 actual	*2000 est.*	*2001 est.*
Enacted/requested:			
Budget Authority	3	3	3

General and special funds—Continued

HARBOR MAINTENANCE FEE COLLECTION—Continued
(INCLUDING TRANSFER OF FUNDS)—Continued

Summary of Budget Authority and Outlays—Continued
(in millions of dollars)

	1999 actual	2000 est.	2001 est.
Outlays	3	3	3
Legislative proposal, not subject to PAYGO:			
Budget Authority			–3
Outlays			–3
Total:			
Budget Authority	3	3	
Outlays	3	3	

Customs collects a fee on imports on behalf of the U.S. Army Corps of Engineers. In 2000, collections are estimated at $675 million. This appropriation provides funding derived from the Harbor services trust fund to offset costs incurred by Customs in collecting the fee.

HARBOR MAINTENANCE FEE COLLECTION
(INCLUDING TRANSFER OF FUNDS)
(Legislative proposal, not subject to PAYGO)

Program and Financing (in millions of dollars)

Identification code 20–8870–2–7–751	1999 actual	2000 est.	2001 est.
Obligations by program activity:			
10.00 Total new obligations (object class 25.2)			–3
Budgetary resources available for obligation:			
22.00 New budget authority (gross)			–3
23.95 Total new obligations			3
New budget authority (gross), detail:			
Discretionary:			
40.26 Appropriation (trust fund, definite)			–3
Change in unpaid obligations:			
73.10 Total new obligations			–3
73.20 Total outlays (gross)			3
Outlays (gross), detail:			
86.90 Outlays from new discretionary authority			–3
Net budget authority and outlays:			
89.00 Budget authority			–3
90.00 Outlays			–3

The Administration will propose legislation to establish a Harbor services fund to replace the Harbor services trust fund. Starting in 2001, funding will be derived from the Harbor Services Fund to offset customs cost related to the fee collection.

Trust Funds

REFUNDS, TRANSFERS, AND EXPENSES OF OPERATION, PUERTO RICO

Unavailable Collections (in millions of dollars)

Identification code 20–5687–0–2–806	1999 actual	2000 est.	2001 est.
Balance, start of year:			
01.99 Balance, start of year			
Receipts:			
02.01 Deposits, duties and taxes, Puerto Rico, U.S. Customs Service	100	112	114
Appropriation:			
05.01 Refunds, transfers, and expenses of operation, Puerto Rico	–100	–112	–114
07.99 Total balance, end of year			

Program and Financing (in millions of dollars)

Identification code 20–5687–0–2–806	1999 actual	2000 est.	2001 est.
Obligations by program activity:			
00.01 Direct program	102	112	114
09.01 Reimbursable program	4	4	4
10.00 Total new obligations	106	116	118
Budgetary resources available for obligation:			
21.40 Unobligated balance available, start of year	1	1	
22.00 New budget authority (gross)	104	116	118
22.10 Resources available from recoveries of prior year obligations	1		
23.90 Total budgetary resources available for obligation	106	117	118
23.95 Total new obligations	–106	–116	–118
24.40 Unobligated balance available, end of year	1		
New budget authority (gross), detail:			
Mandatory:			
60.25 Appropriation (special fund, indefinite)	100	112	114
69.00 Offsetting collections (cash)	4	4	4
70.00 Total new budget authority (gross)	104	116	118
Change in unpaid obligations:			
72.40 Unpaid obligations, start of year: Obligated balance, start of year	14	17	17
73.10 Total new obligations	106	116	118
73.20 Total outlays (gross)	–100	–116	–118
73.45 Adjustments in unexpired accounts	–1		
74.40 Unpaid obligations, end of year: Obligated balance, end of year	17	17	17
Outlays (gross), detail:			
86.97 Outlays from new mandatory authority	100	116	118
Offsets:			
Against gross budget authority and outlays:			
88.40 Offsetting collections (cash) from: Non-Federal sources	–4	–4	–4
Net budget authority and outlays:			
89.00 Budget authority	100	112	114
90.00 Outlays	97	112	114

Customs duties, taxes, and fees collected in Puerto Rico are deposited in this account. After providing for the expenses of administering Customs activities in Puerto Rico, the remaining amounts are transferred to the Treasurer of Puerto Rico (48 U.S.C. 740, 795).

Object Classification (in millions of dollars)

Identification code 20–5687–0–2–806	1999 actual	2000 est.	2001 est.
Direct obligations:			
Personnel compensation:			
11.1 Full-time permanent	16	16	17
11.3 Other than full-time permanent	1	1	1
11.5 Other personnel compensation	2	2	2
11.9 Total personnel compensation	19	19	20
12.1 Civilian personnel benefits	8	8	8
21.0 Travel and transportation of persons	1	1	1
23.3 Communications, utilities, and miscellaneous charges	1	1	1
25.2 Other services	3	4	4
25.3 Purchases of goods and services from Government accounts	1	1	1
25.4 Operation and maintenance of facilities	2	2	2
25.7 Operation and maintenance of equipment	2	2	2
26.0 Supplies and materials	1	1	1
31.0 Equipment	3	3	3
41.0 Payments to the Treasurer of Puerto Rico	59	66	67
44.0 Refunds	3	4	4
99.0 Subtotal, direct obligations	103	112	114
99.0 Reimbursable obligations	3	4	4
99.9 Total new obligations	106	116	118

Personnel Summary

Identification code 20–5687–0–2–806	1999 actual	2000 est.	2001 est.
1001 Total compensable workyears: Full-time equivalent employment	332	380	380

Refunds, Transfers, and Expenses, Unclaimed and Abandoned Goods

Unavailable Collections (in millions of dollars)

Identification code 20–8789–0–7–751	1999 actual	2000 est.	2001 est.
Balance, start of year:			
01.99 Balance, start of year	....	....	....
Receipts:			
02.01 Proceeds of sales of unclaimed, abandoned, and seized goods, U.S. Customs Service, Treasury	4	5	5
Appropriation:			
05.01 Refunds, transfers and expenses, unclaimed, and abandoned goods	–4	–5	–5
07.99 Total balance, end of year	....	....	....

Program and Financing (in millions of dollars)

Identification code 20–8789–0–7–751	1999 actual	2000 est.	2001 est.
Obligations by program activity:			
10.00 Total new obligations	6	5	5
Budgetary resources available for obligation:			
21.40 Unobligated balance available, start of year	1	1	....
22.00 New budget authority (gross)	4	5	5
22.10 Resources available from recoveries of prior year obligations	2	....	....
23.90 Total budgetary resources available for obligation	7	6	5
23.95 Total new obligations	–6	–5	–5
24.40 Unobligated balance available, end of year	1	....	....
New budget authority (gross), detail:			
Mandatory:			
60.27 Appropriation (trust fund, indefinite)	4	5	5
Change in unpaid obligations:			
72.40 Unpaid obligations, start of year: Obligated balance, start of year	2	....	....
73.10 Total new obligations	6	5	5
73.20 Total outlays (gross)	–7	–5	–5
73.45 Adjustments in unexpired accounts	–2	....	....
74.40 Unpaid obligations, end of year: Obligated balance, end of year	....	....	....
Outlays (gross), detail:			
86.97 Outlays from new mandatory authority	4	5	5
86.98 Outlays from mandatory balances	3	....	....
87.00 Total outlays (gross)	7	5	5
Net budget authority and outlays:			
89.00 Budget authority	4	5	5
90.00 Outlays	7	5	5

Unclaimed and abandoned goods are held in storage under Customs custody for one year from the date of importation. At the end of that period, all merchandise upon which duties, storage, and other charges have not been paid is appraised and sold at public auction. The proceeds of such sales are deposited in this account. The salaries and expenses account is reimbursed for expenses of such sales and the balance is transferred to the general fund. (19 U.S.C. 528, 1491, 1493, 1559, 1613, 1624).

Object Classification (in millions of dollars)

Identification code 20–8789–0–7–751	1999 actual	2000 est.	2001 est.
25.2 Other services	2	2	2
25.7 Operation and maintenance of equipment	3	2	2
44.0 Refunds	1	1	1
99.9 Total new obligations	6	5	5

BUREAU OF ENGRAVING AND PRINTING

Federal Funds

Intragovernmental funds:

Bureau of Engraving and Printing Fund

Program and Financing (in millions of dollars)

Identification code 20–4502–0–4–803	1999 actual	2000 est.	2001 est.
Obligations by program activity:			
Operating expenditures:			
09.01 Currency program	428	469	486
09.02 Postage program	50	49	60
09.03 Other programs	7	7	4
Capital investment:			
09.11 Purchase of operating equipment	34	75	90
09.12 Plant alterations and experimental equipment	1	1	1
10.00 Total new obligations	520	601	641
Budgetary resources available for obligation:			
21.40 Unobligated balance available, start of year	48	147	76
22.00 New budget authority (gross)	567	530	580
22.10 Resources available from recoveries of prior year obligations	52	....	....
23.90 Total budgetary resources available for obligation	667	677	656
23.95 Total new obligations	–520	–601	–641
24.40 Unobligated balance available, end of year	147	76	15
New budget authority (gross), detail:			
Discretionary:			
68.00 Spending authority from offsetting collections (gross): Offsetting collections (cash)	567	530	580
Change in unpaid obligations:			
72.40 Unpaid obligations, start of year: Obligated balance, start of year	89	32	113
73.10 Total new obligations	520	601	641
73.20 Total outlays (gross)	–527	–520	–570
73.45 Adjustments in unexpired accounts	–52	....	....
74.40 Unpaid obligations, end of year: Obligated balance, end of year	32	113	184
Outlays (gross), detail:			
86.90 Outlays from new discretionary authority	567	530	580
86.93 Outlays from discretionary balances	–40	–10	–10
87.00 Total outlays (gross)	527	520	570
Offsets:			
Against gross budget authority and outlays:			
Offsetting collections (cash) from:			
Federal sources:			
88.00 Postage	–58	–51	–53
88.00 Other	–6	–5	–6
Non-Federal sources:			
88.40 Currency	–501	–472	–519
88.40 Other	–2	–2	–2
88.90 Total, offsetting collections (cash)	–567	–530	–580
Net budget authority and outlays:			
89.00 Budget authority	....	....	....
90.00 Outlays	–40	–10	–10

The Bureau of Engraving and Printing designs, manufactures, and supplies Federal Reserve notes, various public debt instruments, as well as most evidences of a financial character issued by the United States, such as postage and internal revenue stamps. The Bureau executes certain printings for various territories administered by the United States, particularly postage and revenue stamps.

Intragovernmental funds—Continued

BUREAU OF ENGRAVING AND PRINTING FUND—Continued

The anticipated work volume is based on estimates of requirements submitted by agencies served. The program comprises the following activities:

Engraving and printing—

Currency.—Total deliveries of currency for 2000 and 2001 are estimated to be 9.0 billion notes each year. During 1999, the Bureau delivered 11.4 billion Federal Reserve notes.

Stamps.—This category of work is comprised of postal and internal revenue stamps. The projected requirements for 2000 and 2001 are estimated to be 15.0 billion each year. In 1999, the Bureau delivered 19.0 billion stamps.

Securities.—This program encompasses the production of a wide variety of bonds, notes, and debentures for the Bureau of Public Debt and certain other agencies of the Government.

Commissions, certificates, etc.—This program is comprised primarily of Presidential and Department of Defense commissions and certificates, White House invitations, and identification cards for various Government agencies. It represents a small portion of the Bureau's total workload.

Space utilized by other agencies.—Other agencies are charged for services provided in the space occupied in the Bureau's buildings.

Other miscellaneous services.—A wide variety of miscellaneous services are performed by Bureau personnel for other agencies, which are charged on an actual cost basis.

Purchase of operating equipment.—This category consists of new purchases and replacement of printing equipment and other related printing items.

Plant alterations and experimental equipment.—This category encompasses alterations made on the Bureau's buildings and purchases of experimental equipment.

The operations of the Bureau are currently financed by means of a revolving fund established in accordance with the provisions of Public Law 656, August 4, 1950 (31 U.S.C. 181), which requires the Bureau to be reimbursed by customer agencies for all costs of manufacturing products and services performed. The Bureau is also authorized to assess amounts to acquire capital equipment and provide for working capital needs. Bureau operations during 1999 resulted in an increase to retained earnings of $38 million.

PERFORMANCE MEASURES

	1999 actual	2000 est.	2001 est.
Manufacturing workyears	2,180	2,057	2,057
Protection and accountability of assets	415	402	402
Resource management workyears	289	291	291
Total workyears	2,884	2,750	2,750
Manufacturing:			
Federal Reserve orders met as requested	100%	100%	100%
USPS orders met as requested	100%	100%	100%
Change in productivity from prior year	15.9%	–15%	0%
Manufacturing cost for currency (cost per 1000 notes)	$25.87	$24.29	$26.50
Manufacturing cost for stamps 100 stamp flag coil pressure sensitive (cost per 1000 stamps)	$1.31	$1.59	$1.65
Notes returned by Federal Reserve due to manufacturing defect (per million notes)	.0219	.0250	.0250
Stamps returned by USPS due to manufacturing defect (per million notes)	.3365	.1000	.1000
Notes returned by Federal Reserve because of counterfeit deterrence defect (per million notes)	.0453	.0500	.0500
Workload Measure:			
Federal Reserve note deliveries (in billions)	11.4	9.0	9.0
Postage stamp deliveries (in billions)	19.0	15.0	15.0
Protection and Accountability of Assets:			
Currency shipment discrepancies (per million notes)	.0092	.0100	.0100
Postage Stamp discrepancies (per million stamps)	14.0	20.0	20.0
Resource Management:			
Annual financial statement audit opinion	(1)	(2)	(2)

[1] Unqualified opinion received.

[2] Unqualified opinion expected.

Statement of Operations (in millions of dollars)

Identification code 20–4502–0–4–803		1998 actual	1999 actual	2000 est.	2001 est.
0101	Revenue	437	567	530	580
0102	Expense	–460	–529	–501	–550
0105	Net income or loss (–)	–23	38	29	30

Balance Sheet (in millions of dollars)

Identification code 20–4502–0–4–803		1998 actual	1999 actual	2000 est.	2001 est.
	ASSETS:				
	Non-Federal assets:				
1206	Receivables, net	41	51	36	38
1207	Advances and prepayments	1	4	1	1
	Other Federal assets:				
1801	Cash and other monetary assets	138	180	190	190
1802	Inventories and related properties	70	72	61	56
1803	Property, plant and equipment, net	351	334	382	412
1901	Other assets—Machinery repair parts	27	29	27	28
1999	Total assets	628	670	697	725
	LIABILITIES:				
2101	Federal liabilities: Accounts payable	23	36	21	20
	Non-Federal liabilities:				
2201	Accounts payable	24	17	28	27
2206	Pension and other actuarial liabilities	41	39	41	41
2999	Total liabilities	88	92	90	88
	NET POSITION:				
3100	Appropriated capital	32	32	32	32
3300	Cumulative results of operations	508	546	575	605
3999	Total net position	540	578	607	637
4999	Total liabilities and net position	628	670	697	725

Object Classification (in millions of dollars)

Identification code 20–4502–0–4–803		1999 actual	2000 est.	2001 est.
	Personnel compensation:			
11.1	Full-time permanent	129	135	142
11.3	Other than full-time permanent	3	3	3
11.5	Other personnel compensation	32	22	23
11.9	Total personnel compensation	164	160	168
12.1	Civilian personnel benefits	34	32	35
21.0	Travel and transportation of persons	1	2	2
22.0	Transportation of things		1	1
23.1	Rental payments to GSA	1	1	1
23.3	Communications, utilities, and miscellaneous charges	10	12	14
24.0	Printing and reproduction	1	1	1
25.2	Other services	45	57	59
26.0	Supplies and materials	231	259	269
31.0	Equipment	33	75	90
42.0	Insurance claims and indemnities		1	1
99.9	Total new obligations	520	601	641

Personnel Summary

Identification code 20–4502–0–4–803		1999 actual	2000 est.	2001 est.
2001	Total compensable workyears: Full-time equivalent employment	2,489	2,590	2,590

UNITED STATES MINT

Federal Funds

Public enterprise revolving funds:

UNITED STATES MINT PUBLIC ENTERPRISE FUND

Program and Financing (in millions of dollars)

Identification code 20–4159–0–3–803		1999 actual	2000 est.	2001 est.
	Obligations by program activity:			
09.01	Circulating coinage	361	399	299
09.02	Commemorative states quarters	120	242	253

09.03 Numismatic and investment products	907	788	556
09.04 Protection	25	28	29
10.00 Total new obligations	1,413	1,457	1,137
Budgetary resources available for obligation:			
21.40 Unobligated balance available, start of year	31	6	6
22.00 New budget authority (gross)	1,399	1,457	1,137
22.10 Resources available from recoveries of prior year obligations	–11	....	....
23.90 Total budgetary resources available for obligation	1,419	1,463	1,143
23.95 Total new obligations	–1,413	–1,457	–1,137
24.40 Unobligated balance available, end of year	6	6	6
New budget authority (gross), detail:			
Discretionary:			
40.05 Appropriation (indefinite)	....	....	18
68.00 Spending authority from offsetting collections: Offsetting collections (cash)	1,399	1,457	1,119
70.00 Total new budget authority (gross)	1,399	1,457	1,137
Change in unpaid obligations:			
72.40 Unpaid obligations, start of year: Obligated balance, start of year	172	177	172
73.10 Total new obligations	1,413	1,457	1,137
73.20 Total outlays (gross)	–1,419	–1,462	–1,119
73.45 Adjustments in unexpired accounts	11	....	....
74.40 Unpaid obligations, end of year: Obligated balance, end of year	177	172	190
Outlays (gross), detail:			
86.90 Outlays from new discretionary authority	1,399	1,437	1,091
86.93 Outlays from discretionary balances	20	25	28
87.00 Total outlays (gross)	1,419	1,462	1,119
Offsets:			
Against gross budget authority and outlays:			
Offsetting collections (cash) from:			
Non-Federal sources:			
88.40 Circulating coinage	–382	–427	–310
88.40 Commemorative quarters	–120	–242	–253
88.40 Numismatic and investment products	–897	–788	–556
88.90 Total, offsetting collections (cash)	–1,399	–1,457	–1,119
Net budget authority and outlays:			
89.00 Budget authority	....	....	18
90.00 Outlays	20	5	....

The United States Mint manufactures coins, sells numismatic and investment products, and provides for security and asset protection. Public Law 104–52, dated November 19, 1995, enacted 5136, of Subchapter III of chapter 51 of subtitle IV of title 31, United States Code established the United States Mint Public Enterprise Fund (the Fund). The new Fund encompasses the previous Salaries and Expenses, Coinage Profit Fund, Coinage Metal Fund, and the Numismatic Public Enterprise Fund. The Mint submits annual audited business-type financial statements to the Secretary of the Treasury and to Congress in support of the operations of the revolving fund.

The operations of the Mint are divided into three major activities: Circulating Coinage; Numismatic and Investment Products; and Protection. The Mint is credited with receipts from its circulating coinage operations, equal to the full cost of producing and distributing coins that are put into circulation, including depreciation of the Mint's plant and equipment on the basis of current replacement value. From that, the Mint pays its cost of operations, which includes the costs of production and distribution. The difference between the face value of the coins and these costs are profit, which is deposited as seigniorage to the general fund. In 1999, the Mint transferred $1,018 million to the general fund. Any seigniorage used to finance the Mint's capital acquisitions is recorded as budget authority in the year that funds are obligated for this purpose, and as receipts over the life of the asset.

Circulating Coinage.—This activity funds the manufacture of circulating coins for sale to the Federal Reserve System as determined by public demand. In 2001, this activity will manufacture 23.5 billion coins for sale to the Federal Reserve System. In 1996, with the merger of the former Coinage Metal Fund into the Mint Public Enterprise Fund, the Mint began including the cost of metal in the Circulating Coinage activity.

Numismatic and Investment Products.—This activity funds the manufacture of numismatic and bullion coins, medals, and other products for sale to collectors and the general public. These coins include annual recurring programs such as proof and uncirculated sets, silver proof coins, the American Eagle gold and silver bullion uncirculated and proof coins, American Eagle platinum coins, and national and historic medals. The activity also includes nonrecurring programs for coins and medals which are legislated to commemorate specific events or individuals. In 2001, this activity will fund the Capitol Visitor Center Commemorative Coin Act of 1999. In addition, the Fifty States Commemorative Coin Program Act authorized, beginning in 1999, the issuance of quarters for sale to the public and to the Federal Reserve System honoring each of the 50 states with a design emblematic of that state. These quarters will be issued in the order of each state's admission to the Union. The Mint will produce five different state quarter designs each year resulting in a 10-year program. All coins produced for this program are considered to be numismatic products (Public Law 105–124).

Protection.—This activity funds protection of the Government's stock of gold and silver bullion, coins, Mint employees and visitors, plant facilities and equipment, and all other Mint property against abuse, theft, damage, disorders, and all other unsafe or illegal practices by utilizing police officers and modern protective devices.

	1999 actual	2000 est.	2001 est.
Circulating Coinage Activity:			
Frequency of time meeting a minimum, seasonal-adjusted, inventory level (beginning July 2000)	N/A	100%	100%
Federal Reserve Board Customer Satisfaction Survey results	N/A	85%	85%
Average cost per 1000 units of circulating clad and nickel coinage (including metal)	$31.27	$34.48	$34.48
Average cost per 1000 units of circulating pennies (including metal)	$8.35	$7.74	$7.74
Clad and nickel coins produced per circulating production payroll dollar	207	170	170
Numismatic and Investment Products:			
American Customer Satisfaction Index score of 85	86	85	85
Percent of commemorative coins shipped within standard	N/A	98%	98%
Percent of recurring coin products shipped within standard	N/A	98%	98%
Numismatic contribution margin for bullion	1.59%	2%	2%
Numismatic contribution margin for non-bullion	22.18%	15%	15%
Protection:			
Dollar losses per billion of Reserve Value	0.000	0.000	0.000

Statement of Operations (in millions of dollars)

Identification code 20–4159–0–3–803	1998 actual	1999 actual	2000 est.	2001 est.
0101 Revenue	1,035	1,419	1,463	1,143
0102 Expense	–1,004	–1,413	–1,457	–1,137
0105 Net income or loss (–)	31	6	6	6

Balance Sheet (in millions of dollars)

Identification code 20–4159–0–3–803	1998 actual	1999 actual	2000 est.	2001 est.
ASSETS:				
Federal assets:				
1101 Fund balances with Treasury	202	183	110	110
Investments in US securities:				
1106 Receivables, net	3	4	3	3
1107 Advances and prepayments	....	3	6	6
Other Federal assets:				
1802 Inventories and related properties	178	248	290	299
1803 Property, plant and equipment, net	154	169	347	357
1901 Other assets	55	35	60	62
1999 Total assets	592	642	816	837
LIABILITIES:				
2101 Federal liabilities: Accounts payable	93	89	125	129

Public enterprise revolving funds—Continued

UNITED STATES MINT PUBLIC ENTERPRISE FUND—Continued

Balance Sheet (in millions of dollars)—Continued

Identification code 20–4159–0–3–803	1998 actual	1999 actual	2000 est.	2001 est.
Non-Federal liabilities:				
2201 Accounts payable	39	27	15	15
2207 Other	45	79	117	121
2999 Total liabilities	177	195	257	265
NET POSITION:				
3300 Cumulative results of operations	415	447	559	572
3999 Total net position	415	447	559	572
4999 Total liabilities and net position	592	642	816	837

Object Classification (in millions of dollars)

Identification code 20–4159–0–3–803	1999 actual	2000 est.	2001 est.
Personnel compensation:			
11.1 Full-time permanent	82	121	126
11.3 Other than full-time permanent	4	9	10
11.5 Other personnel compensation	19	12	12
11.9 Total personnel compensation	105	142	148
12.1 Civilian personnel benefits	25	34	36
13.0 Benefits for former personnel	1	1	1
21.0 Travel and transportation of persons	4	7	6
22.0 Transportation of things	8	36	37
23.1 Rental payments to GSA	4	6	6
23.2 Rental payments to others	3	4	4
23.3 Communications,utilities,and miscellanoues charges	11	15	16
24.0 Printing and reproduction	5	6	7
25.2 Other services	88	149	98
26.0 Supplies and materials	1,053	938	709
31.0 Equipment	81	47	47
32.0 Land and structures	25	72	22
99.9 Total new obligations	1,413	1,457	1,137

Personnel Summary

Identification code 20–4159–0–3–803	1999 actual	2000 est.	2001 est.
2001 Total compensable workyears: Full-time equivalent employment	2,290	3,107	3,068

BUREAU OF THE PUBLIC DEBT

Federal Funds

General and special funds:

ADMINISTERING THE PUBLIC DEBT

For necessary expenses connected with any public-debt issues of the United States, [$182,219,000] *$187,301,000*, of which not to exceed $2,500 shall be available for official reception and representation expenses, and of which not to exceed $2,000,000 shall remain available until expended for systems modernization: *Provided*, That the sum appropriated herein from the General Fund for fiscal year [2000] *2001* shall be reduced by not more than $4,400,000 as definitive security issue fees and Treasury Direct Investor Account Maintenance fees are collected, so as to result in a final fiscal year [2000] *2001* appropriation from the General Fund estimated at [$177,819,000, and in] *$182,901,000. In* addition, [$20,000] *$23,600* to be derived from the Oil Spill Liability Trust Fund to reimburse the Bureau for administrative and personnel expenses for financial management of the Fund, as authorized by section 1012 of Public Law 101–380*; and in addition, to be appropriated from the General Fund, such sums as may be necessary for administrative expenses in association with the South Dakota Trust Fund and the Cheyenne River Sioux Tribe Terrestrial Wildlife Restoration and Lower Brule Sioux Tribe Terrestrial Restoration Trust Fund, as authorized by sections 603(f) and 604(f) of Public Law 106–53. (Treasury Department Appropriations Act, 2000.)*

Program and Financing (in millions of dollars)

Identification code 20–0560–0–1–803	1999 actual	2000 est.	2001 est.
Obligations by program activity:			
Direct program:			
00.01 Savings and retirement securities	134	144	146
00.02 Marketable and special securities	40	40	41
00.03 Reimbursements to Federal Reserve Banks	140	146	162
09.01 Reimbursable program	4	4	4
10.00 Total new obligations	318	334	353
Budgetary resources available for obligation:			
21.40 Unobligated balance available, start of year	8	10	
22.00 New budget authority (gross)	319	324	353
22.10 Resources available from recoveries of prior year obligations	3		
23.90 Total budgetary resources available for obligation	330	334	353
23.95 Total new obligations	−318	−334	−353
23.98 Unobligated balance expiring or withdrawn	−2		
24.40 Unobligated balance available, end of year	10		
New budget authority (gross), detail:			
Discretionary:			
40.00 Appropriation	173	178	183
40.75 Reduction pursuant to P.L. 106–51	−1		
40.76 Reduction pursuant to P.L. 106–113		−1	
42.00 Transferred from other accounts	1		
43.00 Appropriation (total discretionary)	173	177	183
Mandatory:			
60.05 Appropriation (indefinite)	139	139	162
60.75 Reduction pursuant to P.L. 106–51	−1		
62.50 Appropriation (total mandatory)	138	139	162
Spending authority from offsetting collections:			
Discretionary:			
Offsetting collections (cash):			
68.00 Offsetting collections (cash)	4	4	4
68.00 Offsetting collections (user fees)	4	4	4
68.90 Spending authority from offsetting collections (total discretionary)	8	8	8
70.00 Total new budget authority (gross)	319	324	353
Change in unpaid obligations:			
72.40 Unpaid obligations, start of year: Obligated balance, start of year	88	91	63
73.10 Total new obligations	318	334	353
73.20 Total outlays (gross)	−313	−362	−353
73.40 Adjustments in expired accounts (net)	1		
73.45 Adjustments in unexpired accounts	−3		
74.40 Unpaid obligations, end of year: Obligated balance, end of year	91	63	63
Outlays (gross), detail:			
86.90 Outlays from new discretionary authority	160	164	169
86.93 Outlays from discretionary balances	14	21	28
86.97 Outlays from new mandatory authority	67	104	121
86.98 Outlays from mandatory balances	72	71	35
87.00 Total outlays (gross)	313	362	353
Offsets:			
Against gross budget authority and outlays:			
Offsetting collections (cash) from:			
88.00 Federal sources	−4	−4	−4
88.40 Non-Federal sources	−4	−4	−4
88.90 Total, offsetting collections (cash)	−8	−8	−8
Net budget authority and outlays:			
89.00 Budget authority	311	316	345
90.00 Outlays	305	354	345

This appropriation provides funds for the conduct of all public debt operations and the promotion of the sale of U.S. savings-type securities.

Processing and accounting for:

Savings securities.—This activity involves the issuance, servicing, and retirement of savings bonds and notes and retirement-type securities, including: (1) the maintenance and servicing of individual accounts of owners of series H and HH bonds and the authorization of interest payments; and (2) the maintenance of accounting control over financial transactions, securities transactions and accountability, and interest cost. These functions are performed directly by the Bureau of the Public Debt, by the Federal Reserve Banks as fiscal agents of the United States, and by the qualified agents which issue and redeem savings bonds and notes. This activity also consists of sales promotion efforts, using press, radio, other advertising media, and organized groups, augmented by concentrated sales campaigns emphasizing payroll savings plans.

	1999 actual	2000 est.	2001 est.
Number of Savings Securities Redemptions (000)	66,272	70,800	70,800
Number of Savings Securities Issued (000)	49,125	58,350	58,350
Provide quality service to purchasers of savings bonds:			
Percent over-the-counter issued within three weeks	99	95	95
Percent of customer service transactions within four weeks	97.28	90	90

Marketable and special securities.—This activity involves all securities of the United States, other than savings and retirement securities, including securities of Government corporations for which the Bureau of the Public Debt provides services. Functions performed relate to the issuance, servicing, and retirement of these securities, both directly by the Bureau and through the Federal Reserve Banks, as fiscal agents, including: (1) The maintenance and servicing of individual accounts of owners of registered securities and book-entry Treasury bills; (2) the authorization of interest and principal payments; and (3) the maintenance of accounting control over financial transactions, securities transactions and accountability, and interest cost.

	1999 actual	2000 est.	2001 est.
Meet the borrowing needs of the Federal Government:			
Percent of auctions completed without error	100	100	100
Percent completed within one hour	100	95	95
Quality service to investors:			
Percent of TD transactions within 3 weeks	98.32	90	90
Percent of TD payments timely	100	100	100
Percent of TD payments accurately	100	99.9	99.9
Percent CBE payments accurately and timely	100	100	100
Process Government Securities Investment Program transactions timely	100	100	100
Process Government Securities Investment Program transactions accurately	99.992	99.9	99.9

Object Classification (in millions of dollars)

Identification code 20–0560–0–1–803		1999 actual	2000 est.	2001 est.
	Direct obligations:			
	Personnel compensation:			
11.1	Full-time permanent	63	64	67
11.5	Other personnel compensation	2	4	4
11.9	Total personnel compensation	65	68	71
12.1	Civilian personnel benefits	15	15	15
21.0	Travel and transportation of persons	2	2	2
22.0	Transportation of things	1	1	1
23.1	Rental payments to GSA	6	7	7
23.3	Communications, utilities, and miscellaneous charges	16	21	18
24.0	Printing and reproduction	4	4	4
25.2	Other services	33	37	37
25.3	Purchases of goods and services from Government accounts	160	162	181
25.7	Operation and maintenance of equipment	3	3	3
26.0	Supplies and materials	2	3	3
31.0	Equipment	7	7	7
99.0	Subtotal, direct obligations	314	330	349
99.0	Reimbursable obligations	4	4	4
99.9	Total new obligations	318	334	353

Personnel Summary

Identification code 20–0560–0–1–803		1999 actual	2000 est.	2001 est.
	Direct:			
1001	Total compensable workyears: Full-time equivalent employment	1,481	1,568	1,568
	Reimbursable:			
2001	Total compensable workyears: Full-time equivalent employment	5	5	5

Payment of Government Losses in Shipment

Program and Financing (in millions of dollars)

Identification code 20–1710–0–1–803		1999 actual	2000 est.	2001 est.
	Obligations by program activity:			
10.00	Total new obligations (object class 42.0)	....	1	1
	Budgetary resources available for obligation:			
22.00	New budget authority (gross)	1	1	1
23.95	Total new obligations	....	–1	–1
	New budget authority (gross), detail:			
	Mandatory:			
60.00	Appropriation	1	1	1
	Change in unpaid obligations:			
73.10	Total new obligations	....	1	1
73.20	Total outlays (gross)	....	–1	–1
	Outlays (gross), detail:			
86.97	Outlays from new mandatory authority	....	1	1
	Net budget authority and outlays:			
89.00	Budget authority	1	1	1
90.00	Outlays	....	1	1

This account was created as self-insurance to cover losses in shipment of Government property such as coins, currency, securities, certain losses incurred by the Postal Service, and losses in connection with the redemption of savings bonds. Approximately 500 claims are paid annually.

INTERNAL REVENUE SERVICE

The mission of the Internal Revenue Service is to provide America's taxpayers top quality service by helping them understand and meet their tax responsibilities and by applying the tax law with integrity and fairness to all.

To achieve this mission, the Service has established three strategic goals. In order to achieve the first goal "Service to Each Taxpayer," the IRS will make filing easier, provide first quality service to each taxpayer needing help with his or her return or account, provide prompt, professional, helpful treatment to taxpayers in cases where additional taxes may be due, and improve taxpayer access to toll-free telephone assistance. Second, to achieve the goal of "Service to All Taxpayers," the IRS will increase fairness of compliance, and increase overall compliance. The Service will meet its third goal "Productivity Through a Quality Work Environment," by increasing employee job satisfaction and productivity while the economy grows and service improves.

The IRS is changing the way it uses measures to focus attention on priorities, assess organizational performance and identify improvement opportunities. Management processes and activities are being realigned to ensure that they support the mission of the IRS and incorporate the principles of a balanced measurement system. Under this new approach, the framework for measuring organizational performance is aligned with its strategic goals and balances the Service's focus across three major areas: business results, customer satisfaction, and employee satisfaction, with business results being comprised of measures of quality and quantity. Unlike previous measurement efforts, the redesigned measures ensure that customer and employee satisfaction share equal importance with business results in driving the agency's plans and programs.

In planning for 2001, the balanced measures approach has led to a budget proposal, the Staffing Tax Administration for Balance and Equity (STABLE) initiative, to address declining enforcement and customer service activities and to improve employee satisfaction. IRS staffing levels have been declining and shrinking relative to the size of the economy, while, at the same time, the tax code has become more complex. In addition, the passage of the IRS Reform and Restructuring Act of 1998 has required an enormous amount of time and money to implement. STABLE resources will allow IRS to reverse the trend in declining enforcement activity, improve customer service, and provide better tools to employees. The budget includes a supplemental request for 2000 to begin implementing this critical initiative as soon as possible.

The Service's sixteen budget activities represent the Service's various functional components; each activity contributes to the achievement of the Service's mission and strategic goals and objectives.

KEY PERFORMANCE INDICATORS

Strategic Goals:	*1999 actual*	*2000 est.*	*2001 est.*
Service to Each Taxpayer:			
Customer Satisfaction—Toll Free.[1]	6.2	6.3	6.3
Customer Satisfaction—Walk-In.[1]	6.4	6.5	6.5
Customer Satisfaction—Field and Office Examination.[1]	4.1	4.4	4.5
Customer Satisfaction—Field Collection.[1]	3.9	3.9	4.1
Service to All Taxpayers:			
Toll-Free Level of Service	53.3%	58.0%	60.0%
Number of Calls Answered—Includes Automated (millions)—workload projection only[2]	110.3	118.0	118.0
Tax Law Accuracy Rate for Taxpayer Inquiries (Toll Free)	73.3%	80.0%	84.0%
Number of Taxpayers Served—Walk-In (millions)—workload projection only[2]	10.0	10.0	10.0
Field Collection Quality	86%	86%	88%
Field Examination Quality	65%	68%	70%
Office Examination Quality	70%	72%	73%
Total Net Revenue Collected (trillions)—workload projection only[2]	1,746	1,862	1,920
Total Enforcement Revenue Collected—workload projection only[2] (billions)	32.9	34.8	33.0
Total Enforcement Revenue Protected—workload projection only[2] (billions)	5.5	5.5	5.5
Productivity Through a Quality Work Environment			
Employee Satisfaction (Servicewide)	55%	55%	55%

[1] Customer satisfaction scores are based on surveys of calendar year 1998 activities. The scores are based on a scale of 1 to 7, with 7 being the best.

[2] This indicator is not intended to be a performance target but is to be used only as a workload projection.

Federal Funds

General and special funds:

PROCESSING, ASSISTANCE, AND MANAGEMENT

For necessary expenses of the Internal Revenue Service for tax returns processing; revenue accounting; tax law and account assistance to taxpayers by telephone and correspondence; *providing an independent taxpayer advocate within the Service;* programs to match information returns and tax returns; management services; rent and utilities; and services as authorized by 5 U.S.C. 3109, at such rates as may be determined by the Commissioner**[**, $3,312,535,000**]**; *$3,699,499,000*, of which up to $3,950,000 shall be for the Tax Counseling for the Elderly Program, and of which not to exceed $25,000 shall be for official reception and representation expenses. *(Treasury Department, Appropriations Act, 2000.)*

Unavailable Collections (in millions of dollars)

Identification code 20–0912–0–1–803	1999 actual	2000 est.	2001 est.
Balance, start of year:			
01.99 Balance, start of year			
Receipts:			
02.01 New installment agreements fees	69	72	72
02.02 Restructured installment agreements fees	12	13	13
02.03 Enrolled agent fee increase	2		
02.04 General user fees, miscellaneous retained fees	5	5	5
02.99 Total receipts	88	90	90
Appropriation:			
05.01 Processing, assistance, and management	−78	−82	−82
05.02 Tax law enforcement	−10	−8	−8
05.99 Subtotal appropriation	−88	−90	−90
07.99 Total balance, end of year			

Program and Financing (in millions of dollars)

Identification code 20–0912–0–1–803	1999 actual	2000 est.	2001 est.
Obligations by program activity:			
Direct program:			
00.01 Submission processing	920	962	1,060
00.02 Telephone and correspondence	857	955	1,062
00.03 Document matching	61	58	75
00.04 Inspection	103		
00.05 Management services	638	627	703
00.06 Rent and utilities	632	696	736
00.07 Taxpayer advocate service		138	146
01.00 Subtotal, direct programs	3,211	3,436	3,782
09.01 Reimbursable program	29	30	30
10.00 Total new obligations	3,240	3,466	3,812
Budgetary resources available for obligation:			
21.40 Unobligated balance available, start of year	12	13	
22.00 New budget authority (gross)	3,242	3,453	3,811
23.90 Total budgetary resources available for obligation	3,254	3,466	3,811
23.95 Total new obligations	−3,240	−3,466	−3,812
23.98 Unobligated balance expiring or withdrawn	−1		
24.40 Unobligated balance available, end of year	13		
New budget authority (gross), detail:			
Discretionary:			
40.00 Appropriation	3,086	3,313	3,699
40.75 Reduction pursuant to P.L. 106–51	−1		
40.76 Reduction pursuant to P.L. 106–113		−32	
42.00 Transferred from other accounts	41	60	
43.00 Appropriation (total discretionary)	3,126	3,341	3,699
50.00 Reappropriation	9		
Mandatory:			
60.25 Appropriation (special fund, indefinite)	78	82	82
Discretionary:			
68.00 Spending authority from offsetting collections: Offsetting collections (cash)	29	30	30
70.00 Total new budget authority (gross)	3,242	3,453	3,811
Change in unpaid obligations:			
72.40 Unpaid obligations, start of year: Obligated balance, start of year	538	516	530
73.10 Total new obligations	3,240	3,466	3,812
73.20 Total outlays (gross)	−3,231	−3,452	−3,779
73.40 Adjustments in expired accounts (net)	−31		
74.40 Unpaid obligations, end of year: Obligated balance, end of year	516	530	563
Outlays (gross), detail:			
86.90 Outlays from new discretionary authority	2,871	3,069	3,395
86.93 Outlays from discretionary balances	282	302	302
86.97 Outlays from new mandatory authority	78	82	82
87.00 Total outlays (gross)	3,231	3,452	3,779
Offsets:			
Against gross budget authority and outlays:			
88.00 Offsetting collections (cash) from: Federal sources	−29	−30	−30
Net budget authority and outlays:			
89.00 Budget authority	3,213	3,423	3,781
90.00 Outlays	3,202	3,422	3,749

Summary of Budget Authority and Outlays

(in millions of dollars)

Enacted/requested:	*1999 actual*	*2000 est.*	*2001 est.*
Budget Authority	3,213	3,423	3,781

Outlays	3,202	3,423	3,749
Supplemental proposal:			
Budget Authority		20	
Outlays		18	2
Total:			
Budget Authority	3,213	3,443	3,781
Outlays	3,202	3,441	3,751

This appropriation provides for: processing tax returns and related documents; assisting taxpayers in the filing of their returns and in paying taxes that are due; matching information returns with tax returns; conducting background investigations; managing financial resources, rent and utilities; and providing an independent taxpayer advocate within the Service.

Submission Processing.—This activity enables the Internal Revenue Service to develop, publish, and distribute tax forms, publications, and instructions to taxpayers; receive and process paper and electronic income tax returns and supplemental documents; process and account for tax revenues; process information returns such as wage, dividend, and interest statements; provide for payment of refunds and issue notices that payments are overdue; identify possible non-filers for investigation; and assist in the selection of tax returns for audit. This activity also funds the IRS World Wide Web site that enables taxpayers to retrieve federal tax forms, instructions, publications, and other information electronically. Within this activity are all actions associated with Electronic Tax Administration, including receipt of electronically filed tax returns, information documents, and taxes due; electronic refund payments to taxpayers; and electronic communications between the IRS and taxpayers or third parties.

Telephone and Correspondence.—This activity enables the IRS to operate districts' and service centers' toll-free telephone operations, which provide responses to taxpayer requests received via telephone; perform adjustments and taxpayer relations functions which receive and analyze taxpayer inquiries initiated by correspondence; initiate contacts with taxpayers to resolve accounts before District Office action is required; prepare and issue letters proposing assessments; issue statutory notices of deficiency; operate the Automated Collection System; and determine taxpayers' correct income levels and corresponding tax liabilities.

Document Matching.—This activity includes the Underreporter, Combined Annual Wage Reporting (CAWR), and Federal Unemployment Tax Act (FUTA) Programs. The Document Matching Program enables the Service to identify and follow-up on income reporting discrepancies and unsubstantiated deductions and to verify facts and amounts in question through taxpayer contact prior to assessing additional tax or refunding excess credits. These taxpayer contacts are carried out in service centers through correspondence.

Inspection.—This appropriation formerly contained the IRS Inspection activity. Most of the functions of this activity were transferred to the Treasury Inspector General for Tax Administration that was established by the IRS Reform and Restructuring Act of 1988 (P.L. 105–206). The last appropriation for the IRS Inspection activity was included in the Treasury Appropriations Act, 1999 (P.L. 105–277).

Management Services.—This activity sets policies and goals, provides leadership and direction for the Service, and provides Servicewide policy guidance for managing contract administration and procurement programs, conducting the Service's planning, budgeting, and communication strategies, conducting analysis of programs and investments to support strategic decision-making, acquiring resources, and maintaining controls and safeguards over those resources conducting personnel security investigations as required, and developing and managing the human and logistical resources required to fulfill the Service's mission in administering the nation's tax laws. It also provides all administrative services for IRS National Office and field installations.

Rent and Utilities.—This activity provides rent and utilities for the entire Service.

Taxpayer Advocate Service.—This activity provides an independent advocate for taxpayers within the Service, ensuring that the individual interests of the taxpayer are represented in all aspects of the policies and procedures of the Service, resolving taxpayers' problems through prompt identification and settlement, preventing future problems through prompt identification of the underlying causes of taxpayers' problems, identifying and raising the awareness of systemic issues impacting the operating divisions, reporting regularly to Congress on the program's effectiveness and issues adversely affecting taxpayers, maintaining liaisons with Congressional offices, and educating the public on the role of the Advocate. The Taxpayer Advocate Service includes the immediate office of the National Taxpayer Advocate, the headquarters staff, nine Area offices, 74 local/service center offices responsible for resolving Taxpayer Advocate cases, and two Operating Division Taxpayer Advocate Offices responsible for working directly with the operating divisions to identify and recommend solutions to systemic problems. All Taxpayer Advocate employees report directly to the National Taxpayer Advocate.

Object Classification (in millions of dollars)

Identification code 20–0912–0–1–803		1999 actual	2000 est.	2001 est.
	Direct obligations:			
	Personnel compensation:			
11.1	Full-time permanent	1,149	1,365	1,466
11.3	Other than full-time permanent	313	307	344
11.5	Other personnel compensation	109	84	74
11.9	Total personnel compensation	1,571	1,756	1,884
12.1	Civilian personnel benefits	393	428	503
13.0	Benefits for former personnel	26	18	43
21.0	Travel and transportation of persons	43	39	44
22.0	Transportation of things	15	15	16
23.1	Rental payments to GSA	526	612	624
23.3	Communications, utilities, and miscellaneous charges	153	141	143
24.0	Printing and reproduction	83	83	88
25.1	Advisory and assistance services	88	84	97
25.2	Other services	162	149	187
25.4	Operation and maintenance of facilities	64	60	93
25.5	Research and development contracts	1	2	2
25.6	Medical care		1	1
25.7	Operation and maintenance of equipment	18	6	6
26.0	Supplies and materials	20	18	19
31.0	Equipment	44	20	28
41.0	Grants, subsidies, and contributions	4	4	4
99.0	Subtotal, direct obligations	3,211	3,436	3,782
99.0	Reimbursable obligations	29	30	30
99.9	Total new obligations	3,240	3,466	3,812

Personnel Summary

Identification code 20–0912–0–1–803		1999 actual	2000 est.	2001 est.
	Direct:			
1001	Total compensable workyears: Full-time equivalent employment	43,183	46,416	48,076
	Reimbursable:			
2001	Total compensable workyears: Full-time equivalent employment	498	508	508

TAX LAW ENFORCEMENT

For necessary expenses of the Internal Revenue Service for determining and establishing tax liabilities; providing litigation support; issuing technical rulings; *providing top quality service to tax exempt customers, including employee plans, exempt organizations, and government entities;* examining employee plans and exempt organizations; conducting criminal investigation and enforcement activities;

General and special funds—Continued

TAX LAW ENFORCEMENT—Continued

securing unfiled tax returns; collecting unpaid accounts; compiling statistics of income and conducting compliance research; purchase (for police-type use, not to exceed 850) and hire of passenger motor vehicles (31 U.S.C. 1343(b)); and services as authorized by 5 U.S.C. 3109, at such rates as may be determined by the Commissioner[, $3,336,838,000]; *$3,439,020,000,* of which not to exceed $1,000,000 shall remain available until September 30, [2002] *2003,* for research[, and of which not to exceed $150,000 shall be for official reception and representation expenses associated with hosting the Inter-American Center of Tax Administration (CIAT) 2000 Conference]. *(Treasury Department Appropriations Act, 2000.)*

Program and Financing (in millions of dollars)

Identification code 20–0913–0–1–999		1999 actual	2000 est.	2001 est.
	Obligations by program activity:			
	Direct program:			
00.01	Criminal investigations	365	386	400
00.02	Examination	1,696	1,775	1,890
00.03	Collection	694	674	724
00.04	Tax exempt and government entities	138	156	169
00.05	Statistics of income	26	28	30
00.06	Chief counsel	222	226	235
09.01	Reimbursable program	65	66	92
10.00	Total new obligations	3,206	3,311	3,540
	Budgetary resources available for obligation:			
21.40	Unobligated balance available, start of year	11		
22.00	New budget authority (gross)	3,200	3,312	3,539
23.90	Total budgetary resources available for obligation	3,211	3,312	3,539
23.95	Total new obligations	−3,206	−3,311	−3,540
23.98	Unobligated balance expiring or withdrawn	−3		
	New budget authority (gross), detail:			
	Discretionary:			
40.00	Appropriation	3,164	3,337	3,439
40.75	Reduction pursuant to P.L. 106–51	−10		
41.00	Transferred to other accounts	−40	−100	
42.00	Transferred from other accounts	1	1	
43.00	Appropriation (total discretionary)	3,115	3,238	3,439
50.00	Reappropriation	10		
	Mandatory:			
60.25	Appropriation (special fund, indefinite)	10	8	8
	Discretionary:			
68.00	Spending authority from offsetting collections: Offsetting collections (cash)	65	66	92
70.00	Total new budget authority (gross)	3,200	3,312	3,539
	Change in unpaid obligations:			
72.40	Unpaid obligations, start of year: Obligated balance, start of year	288	264	194
73.10	Total new obligations	3,206	3,311	3,540
73.20	Total outlays (gross)	−3,193	−3,381	−3,527
73.40	Adjustments in expired accounts (net)	−36		
74.40	Unpaid obligations, end of year: Obligated balance, end of year	264	194	207
	Outlays (gross), detail:			
86.90	Outlays from new discretionary authority	2,982	3,110	3,325
86.93	Outlays from discretionary balances	201	264	194
86.97	Outlays from new mandatory authority	10	8	8
87.00	Total outlays (gross)	3,193	3,381	3,527
	Offsets:			
	Against gross budget authority and outlays:			
88.00	Offsetting collections (cash) from: Federal sources	−65	−66	−92
	Net budget authority and outlays:			
89.00	Budget authority	3,135	3,246	3,447
90.00	Outlays	3,127	3,315	3,435

Summary of Budget Authority and Outlays

(in millions of dollars)

	1999 actual	2000 est.	2001 est.
Enacted/requested:			
Budget Authority	3,135	3,246	3,447
Outlays	3,128	3,316	3,435
Supplemental proposal:			
Budget Authority		7	
Outlays		7	
Total:			
Budget Authority	3,135	3,253	3,447
Outlays	3,128	3,323	3,435

This appropriation provides for the examination of tax returns, both domestic and international, and the administrative and judicial settlement of taxpayer appeals of examination findings. It also provides for issuing technical rulings, monitoring employee pension plans, determining qualifications of organizations seeking tax-exempt status, examining tax returns of exempt organizations, enforcing statutes relating to detection and investigation of criminal violations of the internal revenue laws and other financial crimes, collecting unpaid accounts, securing unfiled tax returns and payments, analyzing and determining the reasons for delinquent accounts, preventing accounts from becoming delinquent, and preventing nonfiling. This appropriation supports the Statistics of Income activity, which provides annual income, financial, and tax data from tax returns filed by individuals, corporations, and tax-exempt organizations. Likewise, it provides resources for market-based research to identify compliance issues, for conducting tests of treatments to address noncompliance, and for the implementation of successful treatments of taxpayer non-compliant behavior. Finally, this appropriation provides for legal counsel regarding legal interpretation of the law and representation in litigation. This request ensures IRS's ability to provide equitable application and enforcement of the tax laws, to provide information and assistance to taxpayers to help them comply with the tax laws, to identify possible nonfilers for investigations, and to investigate violations of criminal statutes, including both tax and money laundering charges, that fall under the jurisdiction of the Internal Revenue Service.

Criminal Investigation.—This activity provides for enforcement of criminal statutes relating to violations of internal revenue laws and other financial crimes. It investigates cases of suspected intent to defraud, involving both legal and illegal sources of income, and recommends prosecution as warranted. It assists in the preparation and trial of criminal tax and money laundering investigations. This activity also includes the investigation and prosecution of tax and money laundering violations associated with narcotics organizations. The IRS serves as the Treasury Department's primary receiver and processor of statutorily filed Bank Secrecy Act and Title 26 Currency Reports and provides database accessibility to the law enforcement and tax administration communities.

Examination.—This activity encourages voluntary compliance with the internal revenue laws through the determination of the correct tax liability by the selective examination of tax returns, the correction of errors, and the explanation of these corrections to taxpayers. The taxpayer education portion of this activity is designed to assist taxpayers to comply with their Federal Income Tax responsibilities. The Appeals portion of this activity provides staffing, training, and direct support to allow for an administrative review process that provides a channel for impartial case settlement prior to cases being docketed in a court of law.

The international portion of this activity directs the full range of IRS enforcement and assistance programs related to U.S. taxpayers doing business or residing outside the United States as well as non-resident aliens with a U.S. tax obligation. It also provides technical tax training and administrative assistance to foreign governments; provides compliance and taxpayer service support to Puerto Rico, the Virgin Islands and certain Pacific Island jurisdictions; and manages activities related to tax treaties between the United States and other governments. The operations research component of this activity develops and evaluates data on taxpayer filing characteristics based on returns as they are filed and conducts statistical and economic studies.

Collection.—This activity collects unpaid tax accounts and secures delinquent returns; protects the Government's interest in litigation proceedings; develops and implements programs to prevent tax accounts from becoming delinquent; provides resources to service walk-in taxpayers; assists taxpayers in resolving tax account problems; helps taxpayers to comply with tax laws by educating through outreach programs; and takes appropriate enforcement actions when warranted.

Tax Exempt and Government Entities.—This activity has replaced the Employee Plans and Exempt Organizations activity. This activity provides top quality service to Tax Exempt Customers including Employee Plans, Exempt Organizations and Government Entities. The customer organizations represent a large economic sector and are governed by complex, highly specialized provisions of the tax law designed to ensure that the entities fulfill the policy goals their exemption was designed to achieve. It strategically plans and provides an array of processes including education and communication, rulings and agreements, customer account services, and examinations to help its customers understand and comply with their tax liabilities. This activity has end-to-end responsibility and accountability for its distinct customer segments and will continually monitor and develop its processes to meet customer needs. The customers range from local community organizations and municipalities to major universities, large pension funds, and government entities. Government entities include outstanding tax-exempt bond issuances, state and local entities, and federally recognized Indian Tribes.

Statistics of Income.—This activity publishes Statistics of Income Reports on the operation of income tax laws, as required by the Internal Revenue Code for Congress and its committees; for administrative use by the Secretary of the Treasury and the Commissioner of Internal Revenue; and for the Federal benchmark statistical programs on income, wealth, and finance.

Chief Counsel.—This activity provides the correct legal interpretation of the internal revenue laws; represents the Internal Revenue Service in litigation; provides all other legal support for the Internal Revenue Service; and performs these duties in a manner that enhances public confidence in the integrity, efficiency, and fairness of our nation's tax system.

Object Classification (in millions of dollars)

Identification code 20–0913–0–1–999		1999 actual	2000 est.	2001 est.
	Direct obligations:			
	Personnel compensation:			
11.1	Full-time permanent	2,233	2,260	2,407
11.3	Other than full-time permanent	46	46	48
11.5	Other personnel compensation	76	77	80
11.8	Special personal services payments	13	13	13
11.9	Total personnel compensation	2,368	2,396	2,548
12.1	Civilian personnel benefits	531	585	582
13.0	Benefits for former personnel		23	23
21.0	Travel and transportation of persons	93	113	134
22.0	Transportation of things	3	3	3
23.2	Rental payments to others	4		
23.3	Communications, utilities, and miscellaneous charges		5	5
24.0	Printing and reproduction	14		1
25.1	Advisory and assistance services	50	8	9
25.2	Other services		64	78
25.4	Operation and maintenance of facilities	1		6
25.5	Research and development contracts	14	5	5
25.7	Operation and maintenance of equipment	5	8	8
26.0	Supplies and materials	24	16	19
31.0	Equipment	21	10	18
41.0	Grants, subsidies, and contributions		6	6
91.0	Unvouchered	13	3	3
99.0	Subtotal, direct obligations	3,141	3,245	3,448
99.0	Reimbursable obligations	65	66	92
99.9	Total new obligations	3,206	3,311	3,540

Personnel Summary

Identification code 20–0913–0–1–999		1999 actual	2000 est.	2001 est.
	Direct:			
1001	Total compensable workyears: Full-time equivalent employment	43,243	41,275	42,444
	Reimbursable:			
2001	Total compensable workyears: Full-time equivalent employment	380	388	538

Earned Income Tax Credit Compliance Initiative

For funding essential earned income tax credit compliance and error reduction initiatives pursuant to section 5702 of the Balanced Budget Act of 1997 (Public Law 105–33), [$144,000,000] *$145,000,000*, of which not to exceed $10,000,000 may be used to reimburse the Social Security Administration for the costs of implementing section 1090 of the Taxpayer Relief Act of 1997. *(Treasury Department Appropriations Act, 2000.)*

Program and Financing (in millions of dollars)

Identification code 20–0917–0–1–803		1999 actual	2000 est.	2001 est.
	Obligations by program activity:			
00.01	Earned income tax credit	141	144	145
10.00	Total new obligations	141	144	145
	Budgetary resources available for obligation:			
22.00	New budget authority (gross)	143	144	145
23.95	Total new obligations	−141	−144	−145
23.98	Unobligated balance expiring or withdrawn	−3		
	New budget authority (gross), detail:			
	Discretionary:			
40.00	Appropriation	143	144	145
40.75	Reduction pursuant to P.L. 106–51	−1		
43.00	Appropriation (total discretionary)	142	144	145
50.00	Reappropriation	1		
70.00	Total new budget authority (gross)	143	144	145
	Change in unpaid obligations:			
72.40	Unpaid obligations, start of year: Obligated balance, start of year	25	35	35
73.10	Total new obligations	141	144	145
73.20	Total outlays (gross)	−131	−144	−145
74.40	Unpaid obligations, end of year: Obligated balance, end of year	35	35	35
	Outlays (gross), detail:			
86.90	Outlays from new discretionary authority	131	134	135
86.93	Outlays from discretionary balances		10	10
87.00	Total outlays (gross)	131	144	145
	Net budget authority and outlays:			
89.00	Budget authority	143	144	145
90.00	Outlays	131	144	145

This appropriation provides for expanded customer service and public outreach programs, strengthened enforcement activities, and enhanced research efforts to reduce overclaims and erroneous filings associated with the Earned Income Tax Credit (EITC).

Expanded customer service includes dedicated toll-free telephone assistance, increased community-based tax preparation sites and a coordinated marketing and educational effort (including paid advertising and direct mailings) to assist low income taxpayers in determining their eligibility for EITC. Improved compliance includes increased staff and systemic improvements in submission processing, examination and criminal investigation programs. In returns processing, new procedures include expanded use of math error authority and

General and special funds—Continued

EARNED INCOME TAX CREDIT COMPLIANCE INITIATIVE—Continued

the identification of EITC-based refund claims involving invalid or duplicate primary, secondary and dependent taxpayer identification numbers (TINs). Increased examination coverage, prior to issuance of refunds, reduces overpayments and encourages compliance in subsequent filing periods; in addition, post-refund correspondence audits by service center staff aid in the recovery of erroneous refunds. Criminal investigation activities target individuals and practitioners involved in fraudulent refund schemes and generate referrals of suspicious returns for follow-up examination. Examination staff assigned to district offices, audit return preparers and may apply penalties for non-compliance with "due diligence requirements."

Enhanced research activities and projects focus on EITC claimant characteristics and patterns of non-compliance and are designed to improve education and outreach products, strengthen IRS abuse detection capabilities and measure the effects of Servicewide programs on compliance levels for the EITC-eligible taxpayer population. This appropriation also funds the development of specialized research databases and masterfile updates, reimbursement to the Social Security Administration (SSA) for enhancements to the SSA numbering systems and cooperative efforts with State vital statistics offices.

Object Classification (in millions of dollars)

Identification code 20–0917–0–1–803		1999 actual	2000 est.	2001 est.
	Personnel compensation:			
11.1	Full-time permanent	53	67	71
11.3	Other than full-time permanent	27	16	16
11.5	Other personnel compensation	4	8	8
11.9	Total personnel compensation	84	91	95
12.1	Civilian personnel benefits	20	20	20
21.0	Travel and transportation of persons	1	1	1
22.0	Transportation of things	2		
23.3	Communications, utilities, and miscellaneous charges	1		
24.0	Printing and reproduction	2	5	5
25.1	Advisory and assistance services	1	1	1
25.2	Other services	8	19	16
25.5	Research and development contracts			1
26.0	Supplies and materials	1		
31.0	Equipment	21	7	6
99.9	Total new obligations	141	144	145

Personnel Summary

Identification code 20–0917–0–1–803		1999 actual	2000 est.	2001 est.
1001	Total compensable workyears: Full-time equivalent employment	2,386	2,082	2,082

INFORMATION SYSTEMS

For necessary expenses of the Internal Revenue Service for information systems and telecommunications support, including developmental information systems and operational information systems; the hire of passenger motor vehicles (31 U.S.C. 1343(b)); and services as authorized by 5 U.S.C. 3109, at such rates as may be determined by the Commissioner, [$1,455,401,000] *$1,583,565,000* which shall remain available until September 30, [2001] *2002. (Treasury Department Appropriations Act, 2000.)*

Program and Financing (in millions of dollars)

Identification code 20–0919–0–1–803		1999 actual	2000 est.	2001 est.
	Obligations by program activity:			
	Direct program:			
00.01	Operations and maintenance	954	1,244	1,544
00.02	Year 2000	632	250	
00.03	Business line investments	303		40
09.01	Reimbursable program	12	12	12
10.00	Total new obligations	1,901	1,506	1,596
	Budgetary resources available for obligation:			
21.40	Unobligated balance available, start of year	35	22	21
22.00	New budget authority (gross)	1,824	1,507	1,596
22.10	Resources available from recoveries of prior year obligations	69		
23.90	Total budgetary resources available for obligation	1,928	1,529	1,617
23.95	Total new obligations	−1,901	−1,506	−1,596
23.98	Unobligated balance expiring or withdrawn	−5		
24.40	Unobligated balance available, end of year	22	21	20
	New budget authority (gross), detail:			
	Discretionary:			
40.00	Appropriation	1,265	1,455	1,584
42.00	Transferred from other accounts	547	40	
43.00	Appropriation (total discretionary)	1,812	1,495	1,584
68.00	Spending authority from offsetting collections: Offsetting collections (cash)	12	12	12
70.00	Total new budget authority (gross)	1,824	1,507	1,596
	Change in unpaid obligations:			
	Unpaid obligations, start of year:			
72.40	Obligated balance, start of year	709	699	758
72.95	From Federal sources: Receivables and unpaid, unfilled orders	7	7	7
72.99	Total unpaid obligations, start of year	716	706	765
73.10	Total new obligations	1,901	1,506	1,596
73.20	Total outlays (gross)	−1,829	−1,447	−1,384
73.40	Adjustments in expired accounts (net)	−14		
73.45	Adjustments in unexpired accounts	−69		
	Unpaid obligations, end of year:			
74.40	Obligated balance, end of year	699	758	970
74.95	From Federal sources: Receivables and unpaid, unfilled orders	7	7	7
74.99	Total unpaid obligations, end of year	706	765	977
	Outlays (gross), detail:			
86.90	Outlays from new discretionary authority	1,248	1,059	1,121
86.93	Outlays from discretionary balances	581	388	263
87.00	Total outlays (gross)	1,829	1,447	1,384
	Offsets:			
	Against gross budget authority and outlays:			
88.00	Offsetting collections (cash) from: Federal sources	−12	−12	−12
	Net budget authority and outlays:			
89.00	Budget authority	1,812	1,495	1,584
90.00	Outlays	1,816	1,435	1,372

Summary of Budget Authority and Outlays

(in millions of dollars)

	1999 actual	*2000 est.*	*2001 est.*
Enacted/requested:			
Budget Authority	1,812	1,495	1,584
Outlays	1,817	1,435	1,372
Supplemental proposal:			
Budget Authority		13	
Outlays		9	2
Total:			
Budget Authority	1,812	1,508	1,584
Outlays	1,817	1,444	1,374

This appropriation provides for Servicewide information systems operations and maintenance, ensuring Year 2000 (Y2K) compliance, and investments to enhance current operating systems. The appropriation includes staffing, telecommunications, hardware and software (including commercial-off-the-shelf), and contractual services.

Operations and Maintenance.—This activity provides the salaries, benefits, and related costs to manage, maintain, and operate the information systems that support tax administration. The Service's business activities rely on these information systems to process tax and information returns, account for tax revenues collected, send bills for taxes owed, issue refunds, assist in the selection of tax returns for audit, and provide telecommunications services for all business activities including the public's toll free access to tax information. These systems are located in a variety of sites including the Martinsburg, Tennessee and Detroit Computing Centers; Service Centers; and in other field office operations. The staffing in this activity is used to maintain the millions of lines of programming code running the systems and to operate and administer the Service's hardware infrastructure of mainframes, minicomputers, personal computers, and networks. Other responsibilities include development and maintenance of the applications supporting all aspects of the tax processing pipeline, corporate masterfile of the entire taxpayer spectrum, and a variety of management information systems.

Year 2000.—This activity provides the salaries, benefits, and related costs associated with the Y2K conversion of the Service's Information Systems, which also includes funding for Mainframe Consolidation and the Integrated Submission and Remittance Processing System. (This applies to 1999 and 2000 only.)

Business Line Investments.—This activity provides for funding of Business Line Investments. Business Line Investments denotes those projects that respond to specific requirements, unique to one or more of the new business lines. Business Line Investments work will include high-payoff needs for small-targeted systems for customers not immediately impacted by modernization. This includes support for the Taxpayer Advocate, Integrated Compliance System, Electronic Transcript Delivery, issue tracking/secure e-mail for Large and Mid-Size Business, determination support for Tax Exempt and Government Entities, and secure dial-in for Small Business/Self Employed field employees.

Object Classification (in millions of dollars)

Identification code 20–0919–0–1–803		1999 actual	2000 est.	2001 est.
	Direct obligations:			
	Personnel compensation:			
11.1	Full-time permanent	462	422	450
11.3	Other than full-time permanent	19	6	6
11.5	Other personnel compensation	24	20	16
11.9	Total personnel compensation	505	448	472
12.1	Civilian personnel benefits	114	95	98
21.0	Travel and transportation of persons	25	25	21
22.0	Transportation of things	1	3	3
23.3	Communications, utilities, and miscellaneous charges	215	239	252
24.0	Printing and reproduction	2	1	1
25.1	Advisory and assistance services	40	14	7
25.2	Other services	463	329	335
25.4	Operation and maintenance of facilities	9	3	8
25.7	Operation and maintenance of equipment	115	122	127
26.0	Supplies and materials	13	14	16
31.0	Equipment	387	201	244
99.0	Subtotal, direct obligations	1,889	1,494	1,584
99.0	Reimbursable obligations	12	12	12
99.9	Total new obligations	1,901	1,506	1,596

Personnel Summary

Identification code 20–0919–0–1–803		1999 actual	2000 est.	2001 est.
	Direct:			
1001	Total compensable workyears: Full-time equivalent employment	9,917	7,531	7,531
	Reimbursable:			
2001	Total compensable workyears: Full-time equivalent employment	15	16	16

INFORMATION TECHNOLOGY INVESTMENTS

For necessary expenses of the Internal Revenue Service, $119,000,000, to remain available until September 30, 2003, and $375,000,000 to become available on October 1, 2001, and to remain available until September 30, 2005, for the capital asset acquisition of information technology systems, including management and related contractual costs of such acquisition, and including contractual costs associated with operations authorized by 5 U.S.C. 3109: Provided, That none of these funds shall be obligated until 15 days after the Internal Revenue Service submits to Congress a plan for expenditure that (1) meets the capital planning and investment control requirements established by the Office of Management and Budget in OMB Circular A–11, part 3; (2) is approved by the Department of the Treasury and by the Office of Management and Budget; and (3) has been submitted to the General Accounting Office for review.

Program and Financing (in millions of dollars)

Identification code 20–0921–0–1–803		1999 actual	2000 est.	2001 est.
	Obligations by program activity:			
00.01	Information technology investments	26	274	320
10.00	Total new obligations	26	274	320
	Budgetary resources available for obligation:			
21.40	Unobligated balance available, start of year	295	480	206
22.00	New budget authority (gross)	211		119
23.90	Total budgetary resources available for obligation	506	480	325
23.95	Total new obligations	−26	−274	−320
24.40	Unobligated balance available, end of year	480	206	5
	New budget authority (gross), detail:			
	Discretionary:			
40.00	Appropriation	211		119
	Change in unpaid obligations:			
72.40	Unpaid obligations, start of year: Obligated balance, start of year		25	114
73.10	Total new obligations	26	274	320
73.20	Total outlays (gross)	−1	−185	−239
74.40	Unpaid obligations, end of year: Obligated balance, end of year	25	114	195
	Outlays (gross), detail:			
86.90	Outlays from new discretionary authority			54
86.93	Outlays from discretionary balances	1	185	185
87.00	Total outlays (gross)	1	185	239
	Net budget authority and outlays:			
89.00	Budget authority	211		119
90.00	Outlays	1	185	239

This appropriation provides for revamping business practices and acquiring new technology. The agency is using a formal methodology to prioritize, approve, fund, and evaluate its portfolio of business systems modernization investments. This methodology enforces a documented, repeatable, and measurable process for managing investments throughout their life cycle. Investment decisions are approved by the IRS Core Business System Executive Steering Committee, chaired by the Commissioner.

Object Classification (in millions of dollars)

Identification code 20–0921–0–1–803		1999 actual	2000 est.	2001 est.
25.1	Advisory and assistance services	10	170	320
31.0	Equipment	16	104	
99.9	Total new obligations	26	274	320

PAYMENT WHERE EARNED INCOME CREDIT EXCEEDS LIABILITY FOR TAX

Program and Financing (in millions of dollars)

Identification code 20–0906–0–1–609		1999 actual	2000 est.	2001 est.
	Obligations by program activity:			
10.00	Total new obligations (object class 44.0)	25,632	25,676	25,799

General and special funds—Continued

Payment Where Earned Income Credit Exceeds Liability for Tax—Continued

Program and Financing (in millions of dollars)—Continued

Identification code 20–0906–0–1–609	1999 actual	2000 est.	2001 est.
Budgetary resources available for obligation:			
22.00 New budget authority (gross)	25,632	25,676	25,799
23.95 Total new obligations	–25,632	–25,676	–25,799
New budget authority (gross), detail:			
Mandatory:			
60.05 Appropriation (indefinite)	25,632	25,676	25,799
Change in unpaid obligations:			
73.10 Total new obligations	25,632	25,676	25,799
73.20 Total outlays (gross)	–25,632	–25,676	–25,799
Outlays (gross), detail:			
86.97 Outlays from new mandatory authority	25,632	25,676	25,799
Net budget authority and outlays:			
89.00 Budget authority	25,632	25,676	25,799
90.00 Outlays	25,632	25,676	25,799

Summary of Budget Authority and Outlays

(in millions of dollars)

Enacted/requested:	*1999 actual*	*2000 est.*	*2001 est.*
Budget Authority	25,632	25,676	25,799
Outlays	25,632	25,676	25,799
Legislative proposal, subject to PAYGO:			
Budget Authority			15
Outlays			15
Total:			
Budget Authority	25,632	25,676	25,814
Outlays	25,632	25,676	25,814

As provided by law, there will be instances wherein the earned income tax credit will exceed the amount of tax liability owed through the individual income tax system, resulting in an additional payment to the tax filer. The Earned Income Credit was originally authorized by the Tax Reduction Act of 1975 (Public Law 94–12) and made permanent by the Revenue Adjustment Act of 1978 (Public Law 95–600). The Tax Reform Act of 1986 and the Omnibus Budget Reconciliation Acts of 1990 and 1993 have increased the credit amount and expanded the eligibility for earned income credit.

Payment Where Earned Income Credit Exceeds Liability for Tax

(Legislative proposal, subject to PAYGO)

Program and Financing (in millions of dollars)

Identification code 20–0906–4–1–609	1999 actual	2000 est.	2001 est.
Obligations by program activity:			
10.00 Total new obligations (object class 44.0)			15
Budgetary resources available for obligation:			
22.00 New budget authority (gross)			15
23.95 Total new obligations			–15
New budget authority (gross), detail:			
Mandatory:			
60.05 Appropriation (indefinite)			15
Change in unpaid obligations:			
73.10 Total new obligations			15
73.20 Total outlays (gross)			–15
Outlays (gross), detail:			
86.97 Outlays from new mandatory authority			15
Net budget authority and outlays:			
89.00 Budget authority			15
90.00 Outlays			15

This legislative proposal will increase the credit for families with three or more children, phase out the credit more slowly for families with two or more children, provide marriage penalty relief for two-earner couples, and simplify the earned income calculation.

Payment Where Child Credit Exceeds Liability for Tax

Program and Financing (in millions of dollars)

Identification code 20–0922–0–1–999	1999 actual	2000 est.	2001 est.
Obligations by program activity:			
10.00 Total new obligations (object class 41.0)	445	550	520
Budgetary resources available for obligation:			
22.00 New budget authority (gross)	445	550	520
23.95 Total new obligations	–445	–550	–520
New budget authority (gross), detail:			
Mandatory:			
60.05 Appropriation (indefinite)	445	550	520
Change in unpaid obligations:			
73.10 Total new obligations	445	550	520
73.20 Total outlays (gross)	–445	–550	–520
Outlays (gross), detail:			
86.97 Outlays from new mandatory authority	445	550	520
Net budget authority and outlays:			
89.00 Budget authority	445	550	520
90.00 Outlays	446	550	520

As provided by law, there will be instances wherein the child credit will exceed the amount of tax liability owed through the individual income tax system, resulting in an additional payment to the tax filer. The child credit was originally authorized by the Taxpayer Relief Act of 1997 (Public Law 105–34).

Payment Where Child and Dependent Care Tax Credit Exceeds Liability for Tax

(Legislative proposal, subject to PAYGO)

This legislative proposal will make the child and dependent care tax credit refundable beginning in 2003. As a result, there will be instances wherein the child and dependent care tax credit will exceed the amount of tax liability owed through the individual income tax system, resulting in an additional payment to the tax filer. Beginning in 2001 the proposal will also simplify and gradually increase the child and dependent care tax credit.

Payment Where Long-Term Care or Disability Tax Credit Exceeds Liability for Tax

(Legislative proposal, subject to PAYGO)

Program and Financing (in millions of dollars)

Identification code 20–0923–4–1–551	1999 actual	2000 est.	2001 est.
Obligations by program activity:			
10.00 Total new obligations (object class 41.0)			8
Budgetary resources available for obligation:			
22.00 New budget authority (gross)			8
23.95 Total new obligations			–8

New budget authority (gross), detail:				
	Mandatory:			
60.05	Appropriation (indefinite)			8
Change in unpaid obligations:				
73.10	Total new obligations			8
73.20	Total outlays (gross)			−8
Outlays (gross), detail:				
86.97	Outlays from new mandatory authority			8
Net budget authority and outlays:				
89.00	Budget authority			8
90.00	Outlays			8

This schedule reflects the effects of the proposed long-term care tax credit. The Administration proposes to provide a new long-term care tax credit. The credit could be claimed by a taxpayer for himself or herself or for a spouse or dependent with long-term care needs. There would be instances wherein the long-term care tax credit would exceed the amount of tax liability owed through the individual income tax system, resulting in an additional payment to the tax filer. This schedule also reflects the effects of the proposed disability tax credit.

Refundable Tax Credit for Electronic Tax Return Filers

(Legislative proposal, subject to PAYGO)

Outlays beginning in 2002 result from a new legislative proposal to provide a refundable tax credit to individual taxpayers who file their returns electronically. This $10, refundable credit will provide an incentive for filing on-line and reward individual taxpayers who transact their business with the IRS in a way that helps improve the accuracy and efficiency of IRS processing. Taxpayers using Telefile, filing returns using their telephone, will receive a $5 refundable credit under this proposal.

Refunding Internal Revenue Collections, Interest

Program and Financing (in millions of dollars)

Identification code 20–0904–0–1–908		1999 actual	2000 est.	2001 est.
Obligations by program activity:				
10.00	Total new obligations (object class 43.0)	2,724	3,157	3,307
Budgetary resources available for obligation:				
22.00	New budget authority (gross)	2,724	3,157	3,307
23.95	Total new obligations	−2,724	−3,157	−3,307
New budget authority (gross), detail:				
	Mandatory:			
60.05	Appropriation (indefinite)	2,724	3,157	3,307
Change in unpaid obligations:				
73.10	Total new obligations	2,724	3,157	3,307
73.20	Total outlays (gross)	−2,724	−3,157	−3,307
Outlays (gross), detail:				
86.97	Outlays from new mandatory authority	2,724	3,157	3,307
Net budget authority and outlays:				
89.00	Budget authority	2,724	3,157	3,307
90.00	Outlays	2,724	3,157	3,307

Under certain circumstances, as provided in 26 U.S.C. 6611, interest is paid on Internal Revenue collections that must be refunded. The Tax Equity and Fiscal Responsibility Act of 1982 (Public Law 97–248) provides for daily compounding of interest. Under the Tax Reform Act of 1986 (Public Law 99–514), interest paid on Internal Revenue collections will equal the Federal short-term rate plus two percentage points, such rate to be adjusted quarterly.

Informant Payments

Unavailable Collections (in millions of dollars)

Identification code 20–5433–0–2–803		1999 actual	2000 est.	2001 est.
	Balance, start of year:			
01.99	Balance, start of year			
	Receipts:			
02.01	Underpayment and fraud collection	8	8	8
	Appropriation:			
05.01	Informant payments	−8	−8	−8
07.99	Total balance, end of year			

Program and Financing (in millions of dollars)

Identification code 20–5433–0–2–803		1999 actual	2000 est.	2001 est.
Obligations by program activity:				
10.00	Total new obligations (object class 91.0)	8	8	8
Budgetary resources available for obligation:				
22.00	New budget authority (gross)	8	8	8
23.95	Total new obligations	−8	−8	−8
New budget authority (gross), detail:				
	Mandatory:			
60.25	Appropriation (special fund, indefinite)	8	8	8
Change in unpaid obligations:				
73.10	Total new obligations	8	8	8
73.20	Total outlays (gross)	−8	−8	−8
Outlays (gross), detail:				
86.97	Outlays from new mandatory authority	8	8	8
Net budget authority and outlays:				
89.00	Budget authority	8	8	8
90.00	Outlays	7	8	8

As provided by law (26 U.S.C. 7623), the Treasury Secretary may make payments to individuals resulting from information given that leads to the collection of Internal Revenue taxes. The Taxpayer Bill of Rights of 1996 (Public Law 104–168) provides for payments of such sums to individuals from the proceeds of amounts (other than interest) collected by reason of the information provided, and any amount collected shall be available for such payments. This information must lead to the detection of underpayments of taxes, or detection and bringing to trial and punishment persons guilty of violating the internal revenue laws (in cases where such expenses are not otherwise provided for by law).

Public enterprise funds:

Federal Tax Lien Revolving Fund

Program and Financing (in millions of dollars)

Identification code 20–4413–0–3–803		1999 actual	2000 est.	2001 est.
Obligations by program activity:				
10.00	Total new obligations (object class 32.0)	6	6	6
Budgetary resources available for obligation:				
21.40	Unobligated balance available, start of year	3	3	3
22.00	New budget authority (gross)	6	6	6
23.90	Total budgetary resources available for obligation	9	9	9
23.95	Total new obligations	−6	−6	−6
24.40	Unobligated balance available, end of year	3	3	3
New budget authority (gross), detail:				
	Mandatory:			
69.00	Offsetting collections (cash)	6	6	6
Change in unpaid obligations:				
72.40	Unpaid obligations, start of year: Obligated balance, start of year	3	3	3

Public enterprise funds—Continued

FEDERAL TAX LIEN REVOLVING FUND—Continued

Program and Financing (in millions of dollars)—Continued

Identification code 20–4413–0–3–803	1999 actual	2000 est.	2001 est.
73.10 Total new obligations	6	6	6
73.20 Total outlays (gross)	−6	−6	−6
74.40 Unpaid obligations, end of year: Obligated balance, end of year	3	3	3
Outlays (gross), detail:			
86.97 Outlays from new mandatory authority	6	6	6
Offsets:			
Against gross budget authority and outlays:			
88.40 Offsetting collections (cash) from: Non-Federal sources	−6	−6	−6
Net budget authority and outlays:			
89.00 Budget authority	....	....	....
90.00 Outlays	....	....	....

This revolving fund was established pursuant to section 112(a) of the Federal Tax Lien Act of 1966, to serve as the source of financing the redemption of real property by the United States. During the process of collecting unpaid taxes, the government places a tax lien on real estate in order to protect the government's interest. Situations arise where property of this nature is collateral for other indebtedness and the tax lien is subordinate to the original indebtedness. In this circumstance, it is often to the government's interest to purchase the property during the foreclosure sale. The advantage arises when the property is worth substantially more than the first lienholder's equity but is being sold for an amount that barely covers that equity, thereby leaving no proceeds to apply against delinquent taxes. Under these circumstances, if the Government buys the property and subsequently puts it up for sale under more advantageous conditions, it is possible to realize sufficient profit on the transaction to fully or partially collect the amount of taxes due. The revolving fund is reimbursed from the proceeds of the sale in an amount equal to the amount expended from the fund for the redemption. The balance of the proceeds are applied against the amount of the tax, interest, penalties, and additions thereto, and for the costs of sale. The remainder, if any, would revert to the parties legally entitled to it.

ADMINISTRATIVE PROVISIONS—INTERNAL REVENUE SERVICE

SEC. 101. Not to exceed 5 percent of any appropriation made available in this Act to the Internal Revenue Service may be transferred to any other Internal Revenue Service appropriation upon [the] advance [approval of the] *notification to the House and Senate* Committees on Appropriations.

SEC. 102. The Internal Revenue Service shall maintain a training program to ensure that Internal Revenue Service employees are trained in taxpayers' rights, in dealing courteously with the taxpayers, and in cross-cultural relations.

SEC. 103. The Internal Revenue Service shall institute and enforce policies and procedures that will safeguard the confidentiality of taxpayer information.

[SEC. 104. Funds made available by this or any other Act to the Internal Revenue Service shall be available for improved facilities and increased manpower to provide sufficient and effective 1–800 help line service for taxpayers. The Commissioner shall continue to make the improvement of the Internal Revenue Service 1–800 help line service a priority and allocate resources necessary to increase phone lines and staff to improve the Internal Revenue Service 1–800 help line service.]

[SEC. 105. Notwithstanding any other provision of law, no reorganization of the field office structure of the Internal Revenue Service Criminal Investigation Division will result in a reduction of criminal investigators in Wisconsin and South Dakota from the 1996 level.] *(Treasury Department Appropriations Act, 2000.)*

UNITED STATES SECRET SERVICE

Federal Funds

General and special funds:

SALARIES AND EXPENSES

For necessary expenses of the United States Secret Service, including purchase of not to exceed [777] *844* vehicles for police-type use, of which [739] *541* shall be for replacement only, and hire of passenger motor vehicles; hire of aircraft; training and assistance requested by State and local governments, which may be provided without reimbursement; services of expert witnesses at such rates as may be determined by the Director; rental of buildings in the District of Columbia, and fencing, lighting, guard booths, and other facilities on private or other property not in Government ownership or control, as may be necessary to perform protective functions; for payment of per diem and/or subsistence allowances to employees where a protective assignment during the actual day or days of the visit of a protectee require an employee to work 16 hours per day or to remain overnight at his or her post of duty; the conducting of and participating in firearms matches; presentation of awards; for travel of Secret Service employees on protective missions without regard to the limitations on such expenditures in this or any other Act [if approval is obtained in advance from the Committees on Appropriations]; for research and development; for making grants to conduct behavioral research in support of protective research and operations; not to exceed $20,000 for official reception and representation expenses; not to exceed $50,000 to provide technical assistance and equipment to foreign law enforcement organizations in counterfeit investigations; for payment in advance for commercial accommodations as may be necessary to perform protective functions; and for uniforms without regard to the general purchase price limitation for the current fiscal year, [$667,312,000] *$821,596,000*: *Provided*, That up to $18,000,000 provided for protective travel shall remain available until September 30, [2001] *2002*. *(Treasury Department Appropriations Act, 2000.)*

[SEC. 240. For necessary expenses of the United States Secret Service, an additional $10,000,000 is appropriated for "Salaries and Expenses". In addition, for the purposes of meeting additional requirements of the United States Secret Service for fiscal year 2000, the Secretary of the Treasury is authorized and directed to transfer $21,000,000 to the United States Secret Service out of all the funds available to the Department of the Treasury no later than 120 days after enactment of this Act: *Provided*, That the transfer authority provided in this section is in addition to any other transfer authority contained elsewhere in this or any other Act: *Provided further*, That such transfers pursuant to this section be taken from programs, projects, and activities as determined by the Secretary of the Treasury and subject to the advance approval of the Committee on Appropriations.] *(Miscellaneous Appropriations, 2000, as enacted by section 1000(a)(5) of the Consolidated Appropriations Act, 2000 (P.L. 106–113).)*

Program and Financing (in millions of dollars)

Identification code 20–1408–0–1–751	1999 actual	2000 est.	2001 est.
Obligations by program activity:			
Direct program:			
00.01 Protection, investigations, and uniformed activities	582	677	822
00.02 Other security programs	84	21	....
09.01 Reimbursable program	17	79	4
10.00 Total new obligations	683	777	826
Budgetary resources available for obligation:			
21.40 Unobligated balance available, start of year	3	21	....
22.00 New budget authority (gross)	701	756	826
23.90 Total budgetary resources available for obligation	704	777	826
23.95 Total new obligations	−683	−777	−826
23.98 Unobligated balance expiring or withdrawn	−1	....	....
24.40 Unobligated balance available, end of year	21	....	....
New budget authority (gross), detail:			
Discretionary:			
40.00 Appropriation	681	677	822

40.75	Reduction pursuant to P.L. 106–51	–1		
42.00	Transferred from other accounts	4		
43.00	Appropriation (total discretionary)	684	677	822
	Spending authority from offsetting collections:			
68.00	Offsetting collections (cash)	3	79	4
68.10	From Federal sources: Change in receivables and unpaid, unfilled orders	14		
68.90	Spending authority from offsetting collections (total discretionary)	17	79	4
70.00	Total new budget authority (gross)	701	756	826
	Change in unpaid obligations:			
	Unpaid obligations, start of year:			
72.40	Obligated balance, start of year	70	114	184
72.95	From Federal sources: Receivables and unpaid, unfilled orders		14	14
72.99	Total unpaid obligations, start of year	70	128	198
73.10	Total new obligations	683	777	826
73.20	Total outlays (gross)	–622	–707	–812
73.40	Adjustments in expired accounts (net)	–3		
	Unpaid obligations, end of year:			
74.40	Obligated balance, end of year	114	184	198
74.95	From Federal sources: Receivables and unpaid, unfilled orders	14	14	14
74.99	Total unpaid obligations, end of year	128	198	212
	Outlays (gross), detail:			
86.90	Outlays from new discretionary authority	573	688	744
86.93	Outlays from discretionary balances	49	19	68
87.00	Total outlays (gross)	622	707	812
	Offsets:			
	Against gross budget authority and outlays:			
88.00	Offsetting collections (cash) from: Federal sources	–3	–79	–4
	Against gross budget authority only:			
88.95	From Federal sources: Change in receivables and unpaid, unfilled orders	–14		
	Net budget authority and outlays:			
89.00	Budget authority	684	677	822
90.00	Outlays	619	628	808

The Secret Service is responsible for the security of the President, the Vice President and other dignitaries and designated individuals; for enforcement of laws relating to obligations and securities of the United States and financial crimes such as financial institution fraud and other fraud; and for protection of the White House and other buildings within Washington, DC.

Investigations, protection, and uniformed activities.—The Service must provide for the protection of the President of the United States, immediate family members, the President-elect, the Vice President, or other officer next in the order of succession to the Office of the President, and the Vice President-elect, and the members of their immediate families unless the members decline such protection; protection of the person of a visiting head and accompanying spouse of a foreign state or foreign government and, at the direction of the President, other distinguished foreign visitors to the United States and official representatives of the United States performing special missions abroad; the protection of former Presidents, their spouses and minor children, unless such protection is declined. The Service is also responsible for investigation of counterfeiting of currency, and securities; forgery and altering of Government checks and bonds; thefts and frauds relating to Treasury electronic funds transfers; financial access device fraud, telecommunications fraud, computer and telemarketing fraud; fraud relative to federally insured financial institutions; and other criminal and noncriminal cases.

The Secret Service Uniformed Division protects the Executive Residence and grounds in the District of Columbia; any building in which White House offices are located; the President and members of his immediate family; the official residence and grounds of the Vice-President in the District of Columbia; the Vice President and members of his immediate family; foreign diplomatic missions located in the Washington metropolitan area; the Treasury Building, its Annex and grounds, and such other areas as the President may direct on a case-by-case basis.

Presidential candidate protective activities.—The Secret Service is authorized to protect major Presidential and Vice-Presidential candidates, as determined by the Secretary of the Treasury after consultation with an advisory committee. In addition, the Service is authorized to protect the spouses of major Presidential and Vice-Presidential candidates; however, such protection may not commence more than 120 days prior to the general Presidential election.

PERFORMANCE INDICATORS

	1999 actual	*2000 est.*	*2001 est.*
Cases Closed—The total number of cases worked and closed, excluding protective intelligence, protective surveys, and administratively closed cases	22,558	21,000	22,000
Counterfeit Notes Passed—Value of counterfeit notes passed expressed in dollars	$40,606,200	$55,000,000	$55,000,000
Permanent Protection (Protection is measured in numbers of protectee stops. A stop is generally considered a city visited by a protectee.)	3,987	3,500	3,500
Foreign Dignitaries Protection	1,736	1,400	1,400
Candidate/Nominee Protection	0	1,000	300

Object Classification (in millions of dollars)

Identification code 20–1408–0–1–751		1999 actual	2000 est.	2001 est.
	Direct obligations:			
	Personnel compensation:			
11.1	Full-time permanent	221	249	280
11.3	Other than full-time permanent	34	24	28
11.5	Other personnel compensation	83	84	90
11.9	Total personnel compensation	338	357	398
12.1	Civilian personnel benefits	102	108	134
21.0	Travel and transportation of persons	56	53	70
22.0	Transportation of things	4	6	8
23.1	Rental payments to GSA	39	52	56
23.2	Rental payments to others	3	7	1
23.3	Communications, utilities, and miscellaneous charges	13	15	24
24.0	Printing and reproduction	1	3	2
25.2	Other services	43	48	57
26.0	Supplies and materials	8	10	13
31.0	Equipment	51	36	54
32.0	Land and structures	8	3	4
41.0	Grants, subsidies, and contributions			1
99.0	Subtotal, direct obligations	666	698	822
99.0	Reimbursable obligations	17	79	4
99.9	Total new obligations	683	777	826

Personnel Summary

Identification code 20–1408–0–1–751		1999 actual	2000 est.	2001 est.
1001	Total compensable workyears: Full-time equivalent employment	4,893	5,103	5,543

ACQUISITION, CONSTRUCTION, IMPROVEMENTS, AND RELATED EXPENSES

For necessary expenses of construction, repair, alteration, and improvement of facilities, [$4,923,000] *$5,021,000*, to remain available until expended. *(Department of the Treasury Appropriations Act, 2000.)*

Program and Financing (in millions of dollars)

Identification code 20–1409–0–1–751		1999 actual	2000 est.	2001 est.
	Obligations by program activity:			
10.00	Total new obligations	17	4	15

General and special funds—Continued

ACQUISITION, CONSTRUCTION, IMPROVEMENTS, AND RELATED EXPENSES—Continued

Program and Financing (in millions of dollars)—Continued

Identification code 20–1409–0–1–751	1999 actual	2000 est.	2001 est.
Budgetary resources available for obligation:			
21.40 Unobligated balance available, start of year	17	9	10
22.00 New budget authority (gross)	8	4	5
23.90 Total budgetary resources available for obligation	25	13	15
23.95 Total new obligations	–17	–4	–15
24.40 Unobligated balance available, end of year	9	10	
New budget authority (gross), detail:			
Discretionary:			
40.00 Appropriation	8	5	5
40.76 Reduction pursuant to P.L. 106–113		–1	
43.00 Appropriation (total discretionary)	8	4	5
Change in unpaid obligations:			
72.40 Unpaid obligations, start of year: Obligated balance, start of year	26	7	7
73.10 Total new obligations	17	4	15
73.20 Total outlays (gross)	–36	–4	–3
74.40 Unpaid obligations, end of year: Obligated balance, end of year	7	7	19
Outlays (gross), detail:			
86.90 Outlays from new discretionary authority	8		1
86.93 Outlays from discretionary balances	28	3	2
87.00 Total outlays (gross)	36	4	3
Net budget authority and outlays:			
89.00 Budget authority	8	4	5
90.00 Outlays	36	4	3

This account provides funding for security upgrades of existing facilities and the James J. Rowley Training Center to continue development of the current Master Plan and to maintain and renovate existing facilities to ensure efficient and full utilization of the center. In 2001, the Treasury Forfeiture Fund will provide $3.9 million for Vice Presidential residence security upgrades.

Object Classification (in millions of dollars)

Identification code 20–1409–0–1–751	1999 actual	2000 est.	2001 est.
23.3 Communications, utilities, and miscellaneous charges	3	2	2
25.2 Other services	4	1	3
31.0 Equipment	7		2
32.0 Land and structures	3	1	8
99.9 Total new obligations	17	4	15

CONTRIBUTION FOR ANNUITY BENEFITS

Program and Financing (in millions of dollars)

Identification code 20–1407–0–1–751	1999 actual	2000 est.	2001 est.
Obligations by program activity:			
10.00 Total new obligations (object class 12.1)	80	100	110
Budgetary resources available for obligation:			
22.00 New budget authority (gross)	80	100	110
23.95 Total new obligations	–80	–100	–110
New budget authority (gross), detail:			
Mandatory:			
60.05 Appropriation (indefinite)	80	100	110
Change in unpaid obligations:			
72.40 Unpaid obligations, start of year: Obligated balance, start of year	2	5	15
73.10 Total new obligations	80	100	110
73.20 Total outlays (gross)	–77	–90	–100
74.40 Unpaid obligations, end of year: Obligated balance, end of year	5	15	25
Outlays (gross), detail:			
86.97 Outlays from new mandatory authority	77	89	99
86.98 Outlays from mandatory balances		1	1
87.00 Total outlays (gross)	77	90	100
Net budget authority and outlays:			
89.00 Budget authority	80	100	110
90.00 Outlays	77	89	99

The District of Columbia is reimbursed for benefit payments made from the revenue of the District of Columbia to or for members of the Secret Service Uniformed Division and such members of the U.S. Secret Service entitled to benefits under the Policemen and Firemen's Retirement and Disability Act (4 D.C. Code 521).

COMPTROLLER OF THE CURRENCY

Trust Funds

ASSESSMENT FUNDS

Program and Financing (in millions of dollars)

Identification code 20–8413–0–8–373	1999 actual	2000 est.	2001 est.
Obligations by program activity:			
10.00 Total new obligations	403	384	391
Budgetary resources available for obligation:			
21.40 Unobligated balance available, start of year	73	64	69
22.00 New budget authority (gross)	394	389	397
23.90 Total budgetary resources available for obligation	467	453	466
23.95 Total new obligations	–403	–384	–391
24.40 Unobligated balance available, end of year	64	69	75
New budget authority (gross), detail:			
Mandatory:			
69.00 Offsetting collections (cash)	394	389	397
Change in unpaid obligations:			
72.40 Unpaid obligations, start of year: Obligated balance, start of year	240	240	240
73.10 Total new obligations	403	384	391
73.20 Total outlays (gross)	–403	–384	–391
74.40 Unpaid obligations, end of year: Obligated balance, end of year	240	240	240
Outlays (gross), detail:			
86.97 Outlays from new mandatory authority	394	384	391
86.98 Outlays from mandatory balances	8		
87.00 Total outlays (gross)	403	384	391
Offsets:			
Against gross budget authority and outlays:			
Offsetting collections (cash) from:			
88.00 Federal sources	–14	–13	–13
88.40 Non-Federal sources: Assessments	–380	–376	–384
88.90 Total, offsetting collections (cash)	–394	–389	–397
Net budget authority and outlays:			
89.00 Budget authority			
90.00 Outlays	8	–5	–6
Memorandum (non-add) entries:			
92.01 Total investments, start of year: U.S. securities: Par value	309	309	309
92.02 Total investments, end of year: U.S. securities: Par value	309	309	309

The Office of the Comptroller of the Currency was created for the purpose of establishing and regulating a national banking system. The National Currency Act of 1863 (12 U.S.C. 1 et seq., 12 Stat. 665) provided for the chartering and supervising functions in this connection. The income of the bureau is derived principally from assessments paid by national banks and interest on investments in U.S. Government obligations.

As the Administrator of National Banks, the Office of the Comptroller of the Currency charters new banking institutions only after investigation and due consideration of charter applications. Supervision of existing national banks is aided by the required submission of periodic reports and detailed onsite examinations, which are conducted by a staff of approximately 1,903 national bank examiners. At present, there are approximately 2,383 national banks with total assets of more than $3.2 trillion.

In addition, the Comptroller considers applications for mergers in which the resulting bank will be a national bank and applications from banks to establish branches. The Comptroller of the Currency also promulgates rules and regulations for the guidance of national banks and bank directors.

Object Classification (in millions of dollars)

Identification code 20–8413–0–8–373		1999 actual	2000 est.	2001 est.
	Personnel compensation:			
11.1	Full-time permanent	209	214	218
11.3	Other than full-time permanent	6	5	5
11.5	Other personnel compensation	2	4	4
11.9	Total personnel compensation	217	223	227
12.1	Civilian personnel benefits	51	53	54
21.0	Travel and transportation of persons	31	27	27
22.0	Transportation of things	1	1	1
23.2	Rental payments to others	28	24	25
23.3	Communications, utilities, and miscellaneous charges	9	11	10
24.0	Printing and reproduction	1	1	1
25.1	Advisory and assistance services	40	26	27
26.0	Supplies and materials	7	6	6
31.0	Equipment	17	10	11
32.0	Land and structures	1	2	2
99.9	Total new obligations	403	384	391

Personnel Summary

Identification code 20–8413–0–8–373		1999 actual	2000 est.	2001 est.
2001	Total compensable workyears: Full-time equivalent employment	2,946	3,047	3,047

OFFICE OF THRIFT SUPERVISION

Federal Funds

Public enterprise funds:

OFFICE OF THRIFT SUPERVISION

Program and Financing (in millions of dollars)

Identification code 20–4108–0–3–373		1999 actual	2000 est.	2001 est.
	Obligations by program activity:			
10.00	Total new obligations	155	156	160
	Budgetary resources available for obligation:			
21.40	Unobligated balance available, start of year	154	142	142
22.00	New budget authority (gross)	143	156	160
23.90	Total budgetary resources available for obligation	297	298	302
23.95	Total new obligations	−155	−156	−160
24.40	Unobligated balance available, end of year	142	142	142
	New budget authority (gross), detail:			
	Mandatory:			
69.00	Offsetting collections (cash)	143	156	160
	Change in unpaid obligations:			
72.40	Unpaid obligations, start of year: Obligated balance, start of year	1	14	14
73.10	Total new obligations	155	156	160
73.20	Total outlays (gross)	−142	−156	−160
74.40	Unpaid obligations, end of year: Obligated balance, end of year	14	14	14
	Outlays (gross), detail:			
86.97	Outlays from new mandatory authority	142	156	160
	Offsets:			
	Against gross budget authority and outlays:			
	Offsetting collections (cash) from:			
88.20	Interest on U.S. securities	−6	−6	−6
88.40	Non-Federal sources	−137	−150	−154
88.90	Total, offsetting collections (cash)	−143	−156	−160
	Net budget authority and outlays:			
89.00	Budget authority	....	....	....
90.00	Outlays	−1	....	....
	Memorandum (non-add) entries:			
92.01	Total investments, start of year: U.S. securities: Par value	160	156	157
92.02	Total investments, end of year: U.S. securities: Par value	156	157	158

The Office of Thrift Supervision (OTS) was created by the Financial Institutions Reform, Recovery, and Enforcement Act of 1989 (12 U.S.C. 1811 note). The OTS assumed the regulatory functions of the Federal Home Loan Bank Board dissolved by the same act.

The OTS charters, regulates and examines Federal thrifts, all of which are insured by the Savings Association Insurance Fund. In addition, the OTS cooperates in the examination and supervision of State-chartered thrifts insured by the Savings Association Insurance Fund. The OTS sets capital standards for Federal and State thrifts and reviews applications of State-chartered thrifts for conversion to Federal thrifts. It also reviews applications for establishment of branch offices.

Income of the bureau is derived principally from assessments on thrifts, examination fees and interest on investments in U.S. Government obligations. At present, the OTS oversees more than 1,100 thrifts with more than 10,000 operating branches and total assets of more than $800 billion.

Object Classification (in millions of dollars)

Identification code 20–4108–0–3–373		1999 actual	2000 est.	2001 est.
	Personnel compensation:			
11.1	Full-time permanent	87	91	94
11.5	Other personnel compensation	1	1	1
11.8	Special personal services payments	1	1	1
11.9	Total personnel compensation	89	93	96
12.1	Civilian personnel benefits	27	24	25
21.0	Travel and transportation of persons	11	11	11
22.0	Transportation of things	1	1	1
23.2	Rental payments to others	6	6	6
23.3	Communications, utilities, and miscellaneous charges	2	2	2
25.2	Other services	16	16	16
26.0	Supplies and materials	1	1	1
31.0	Equipment	2	2	2
99.9	Total new obligations	155	156	160

Personnel Summary

Identification code 20–4108–0–3–373		1999 actual	2000 est.	2001 est.
2001	Total compensable workyears: Full-time equivalent employment	1,266	1,291	1,291

INTEREST ON THE PUBLIC DEBT

Federal Funds

General and special funds:

INTEREST ON THE PUBLIC DEBT

Program and Financing (in millions of dollars)

Identification code 20–0550–0–1–901	1999 actual	2000 est.	2001 est.
Obligations by program activity:			
10.00 Total new obligations (object class 43.0)	353,511	358,980	359,536
Budgetary resources available for obligation:			
22.00 New budget authority (gross)	353,511	358,980	359,536
23.95 Total new obligations	−353,511	−358,980	−359,536
New budget authority (gross), detail:			
Mandatory:			
60.05 Appropriation (indefinite)	353,511	358,980	359,536
Change in unpaid obligations:			
73.10 Total new obligations	353,511	358,980	359,536
73.20 Total outlays (gross)	−353,511	−358,980	−359,536
Outlays (gross), detail:			
86.97 Outlays from new mandatory authority	353,511	358,980	359,536
Net budget authority and outlays:			
89.00 Budget authority	353,511	358,980	359,536
90.00 Outlays	353,511	358,980	359,536

Summary of Budget Authority and Outlays

(in millions of dollars)

Enacted/requested:	*1999 actual*	*2000 est.*	*2001 est.*
Budget Authority	353,511	358,980	359,536
Outlays	353,511	358,980	359,536
Legislative proposal, not subject to PAYGO:			
Budget Authority		65	446
Outlays		65	446
Total:			
Budget Authority	353,511	359,045	359,982
Outlays	353,511	359,045	359,982

Such amounts are appropriated as may be necessary to pay the interest each year on the public debt (31 U.S.C. 1305, 3123). Interest on Government account series securities is generally computed on a cash basis. Interest is generally computed on an accrual basis on all other types of securities.

INTEREST ON THE PUBLIC DEBT
(Legislative proposal, not subject to PAYGO)

Program and Financing (in millions of dollars)

Identification code 20–0550–2–1–901	1999 actual	2000 est.	2001 est.
Obligations by program activity:			
10.00 Total new obligations (object class 43.0)		65	446
Budgetary resources available for obligation:			
22.00 New budget authority (gross)		65	446
23.95 Total new obligations		−65	−446
New budget authority (gross), detail:			
Mandatory:			
60.05 Appropriation (indefinite)		65	446
Change in unpaid obligations:			
73.10 Total new obligations		65	446
73.20 Total outlays (gross)		−65	−446
Outlays (gross), detail:			
86.97 Outlays from new mandatory authority		65	446
Net budget authority and outlays:			
89.00 Budget authority		65	446
90.00 Outlays		65	446

A portion of interest on the public debt is paid to funds that have invested in Treasury securities. In the schedules for legislative proposals for such funds, the effect of proposals on interest receipts are shown. In this schedule, the amounts shown are the corresponding interest payments to those funds.

GENERAL FUND RECEIPT ACCOUNTS

(in millions of dollars)

	1999 actual	2000 est.	2001 est.
Governmental receipts:			
20–015800 Transportation fuels tax	849	787	808
20–019900 Miscellaneous taxes, not otherwise classified	−4		
20–065000 Deposit of earnings, Federal Reserve System	25,917	32,452	25,664
20–085000 Registration, filing, and transaction fees	6	5	5
20–086100 Charges for expenses, settlement of international claims		1	1
20–086900 Fees for legal and judicial services, not otherwise classified	61	61	61
20–089100 Miscellaneous fees for regulatory and judicial services, not otherwise classified	7	7	7
20–101000 Fines, penalties, and forfeitures, agricultural laws	2	2	2
20–102000 Fines, penalties, and forfeitures, economic stabilization laws	1		206
20–103000 Fines, penalties and forfeitures, immigration and labor laws	74	74	74
20–104000 Fines, penalties, and forfeitures, customs, commerce, and antitrust laws	95	96	96
20–105000 Fines, penalties, and forfeitures, narcotic prohibition and alcohol laws	1	1	1
20–106000 Forfeitures of unclaimed money and property	24	24	24
20–108000 Fines, penalties, and forfeitures, Federal coalmine health and safety laws	19	19	19
20–109900 Fines, penalties and forfeitures, not otherwise classified	397	397	397
20–129900 Gifts to the United States, not otherwise classified	1	1	1
20–241100 User fees for IRS, Treasury	39	40	41
Legislative proposal, subject to PAYGO			−2
20–309200 Recovery from Highway Trust Fund for refunds of taxes	1,134	942	975
20–309400 Recovery from Airport and Airway Trust Fund for refunds of taxes	4	49	50
20–309500 Recovery from Leaking underground storage tank trust fund for refunds of taxes, EPA	4	5	5
20–309990 Refunds of moneys erroneously received and recovered (20X1807)	−740	−200	−200
95–085015 Registration, filing, and transaction fees, SEC	1,174	1,179	1,302
99–011050 Individual income taxes	879,419	951,884	978,188
Legislative proposal, subject to PAYGO		−359	−5,634
99–011100 Corporation income and excess profits taxes	184,670	192,285	189,594
Legislative proposal, subject to PAYGO		110	3,942
99–015250 Other Federal fund excise taxes	−1,217	704	608
Legislative proposal, subject to PAYGO		6	−42
99–015300 Estate and gift taxes	27,782	30,482	31,975
Legislative proposal, subject to PAYGO		4	329
99–015500 Tobacco excise tax	5,400	6,742	7,158
Legislative proposal, subject to PAYGO		594	5,446
99–015600 Alcohol excise tax	7,386	7,267	7,150
Legislative proposal, subject to PAYGO		−32	32
99–015700 Telephone excise tax	5,185	5,500	5,821
99–031050 Other Federal fund customs duties	12,007	13,866	14,727
Legislative proposal, subject to PAYGO		−13	−569
99–089400 Ozone depleting chemicals tax	105	73	73
General Fund Governmental receipts	1,149,802	1,245,055	1,268,335
Offsetting receipts from the public:			
20–143500 General fund proprietary interest receipts,not otherwise classified,Treasury	173	173	173
20–145000 Interest payments from States, Cash management improvement	67	49	48
20–146310 Interest on quota in International Monetary Fund	686	686	686
20–146320 Interest on loans to International Monetary Fund	21	21	21
20–146400 Interest received on loans and credits to foreign nations	50	46	42
20–148400 Interest on deposits in tax and loan accounts	935	1,152	1,104

20–149900 Net interest received from direct loan financing accounts	7,278	8,626	9,945
20–168200 Gain by exchange on foreign currency denominated public debt securities	7	....	....
20–286800 Dollar conversion of foreign currency loan repayments, Treasury	11	11	11
20–286900 Repayment of loans and credits to foreign nations	175	253	254
20–322000 All other general fund proprietary receipts, Treasury	1,127	1,000	999
20–387500 Budget clearing account (suspense)	−186	....	....
General Fund Offsetting receipts from the public	10,344	12,017	13,283
Intragovernmental payments:			
13–141000 Interest on investment, economic development revolving fund	3	3	3
14–142400 Interest on investment, Colorado River projects	153	42	43
14–142700 Interest on advances to Colorado River Dam Fund, Boulder Canyon project	13	13	13
20–133800 Interest on loans to the Presidio	....	2	3
20–135100 Interest on loans to BPA	354	379	406
20–135400 Interest on loans for housing for the elderly or handicapped	379	274	232
20–136100 Interest on loans to the Secretary of Transportation, Railroad rehabilitation and improvement fund	3	....	....
20–136300 Interest on loans for college housing and academic facilities loans, Education	12	11	10
20–140100 Interest on loans to Commodity Credit Corporation	280	665	754
20–140500 Interest on loans to H.U.D., college housing loans, ED.	8	5	4
20–141700 Interest on loans to Tennessee Valley Authority	4	4	4
20–141800 Interest on loans to Federal Financing Bank	2,503	2,412	2,159
20–142500 Interest on loans to Rural Development Insurance Fund	107	95	67
20–143300 Interest on loans to National flood insurance fund, FEMA	28	30	24
20–149500 Interest payments on repayable advances to the Black Lung Disability Trust Fund	515	533	566
Legislative proposal, not subject to PAYGO			1,468
20–149700 Payment of interest on advances to the Railroad Retirement Board	239	218	243
20–241600 Charges for administrative expenses of Social Security Act as amended	328	269	267
20–320000 Receivables from cancelled accounts, Treasury	103	100	100
20–388500 Undistributed intragovernmental payments, Treasury	−73	....	....
72–138000 Interest on loans to A.I.D. Housing Guaranty Program	6	6	6
73–142800 Interest on advances to Small Business Administration	121	103	63
91–142200 Interest on loans, Higher Education Facilities Loan Fund	2	2	1
General Fund Intragovernmental payments	5,088	5,166	6,436

OTHER CONSOLIDATED RECEIPT ACCOUNTS

(in millions of dollars)

	1999 actual	2000 est.	2001 est.
20–977920 Interest, miscellaneous trust funds, government-wide	1	1	1

GENERAL PROVISIONS—DEPARTMENT OF THE TREASURY

[SEC. 110. Any obligation or expenditure by the Secretary of the Treasury in connection with law enforcement activities of a Federal agency or a Department of the Treasury law enforcement organization in accordance with 31 U.S.C. 9703(g)(4)(B) from unobligated balances remaining in the Fund on September 30, 2000, shall be made in compliance with reprogramming guidelines.]

SEC. [111] *110.* Appropriations to the Department of the Treasury in this Act shall be available for uniforms or allowances therefor, as authorized by law (5 U.S.C. 5901), including maintenance, repairs, and cleaning; purchase of insurance for official motor vehicles operated in foreign countries; purchase of motor vehicles without regard to the general purchase price limitations for vehicles purchased and used overseas for the current fiscal year; entering into contracts with the Department of State for the furnishing of health and medical services to employees and their dependents serving in foreign countries; and services authorized by 5 U.S.C. 3109.

SEC. [112] *111.* The funds provided to the Bureau of Alcohol, Tobacco and Firearms for fiscal year [2000] *2001* in this Act for the enforcement of the Federal Alcohol Administration Act shall be expended in a manner so as not to diminish enforcement efforts with respect to section 105 of the Federal Alcohol Administration Act.

SEC. [113] *112.* Not to exceed 2 percent of any appropriations in this Act made available to the Federal Law Enforcement Training Center, Financial Crimes Enforcement Network, Bureau of Alcohol, Tobacco and Firearms, United States Customs Service, and United States Secret Service may be transferred between such appropriations upon [the] advance [approval of] *notification to* the Committees on Appropriations. No transfer may increase or decrease any such appropriation by more than 2 percent.

SEC. [114] *113.* Not to exceed 2 percent of any appropriations in this Act made available to the Departmental Offices, Office of Inspector General, Treasury Inspector General for Tax Administration, Financial Management Service, and Bureau of the Public Debt, may be transferred between such appropriations upon [the] advance [approval of] *notification to* the Committees on Appropriations. No transfer may increase or decrease any such appropriation by more than 2 percent.

SEC. 114. Not to exceed 3 percent of any appropriation made available in this Act to the Internal Revenue Service may be transferred to the Treasury Inspector General for Tax Administration's appropriation upon the advance notice to the Committees on Appropriations. No transfer may increase or decrease any such appropriation by more than 3 percent.

SEC. 115. Of the funds available for the purchase of law enforcement vehicles, no funds may be obligated until the Secretary of the Treasury certifies that the purchase by the respective Treasury bureau is consistent with Departmental vehicle management principles: *Provided*, That the Secretary may delegate this authority to the Assistant Secretary for Management.

[SEC. 116. (a) VOLUNTARY SEPARATION INCENTIVE PAYMENTS FOR EMPLOYEES OF THE OFFICE OF THE TREASURY INSPECTOR GENERAL FOR TAX ADMINISTRATION.—During the period from October 1, 1999 through January 1, 2003, the Treasury Inspector General for Tax Administration is authorized to offer voluntary separation incentives in order to provide the necessary flexibility to carry out the plan to establish and reorganize the Office of the Treasury Inspector General for Tax Administration (referred to in this section as the "Office").]

[(b) DEFINITION.—In this section, the term "employee" means an employee (as defined by 5 U.S.C. 2105) who is employed by the Office serving under an appointment without time limitation, and has been currently employed by the Office or the Internal Revenue Service or the Office of Inspector General of the Department of the Treasury for a continuous period of at least 3 years, but does not include—

(1) a reemployed annuitant under subchapter III of chapter 83 or chapter 84 of title 5, United States Code, or another retirement system;

(2) an employee having a disability on the basis of which such employee is or would be eligible for disability retirement under the applicable retirement system referred to in paragraph (1);

(3) an employee who is in receipt of a specific notice of involuntary separation for misconduct or unacceptable performance;

(4) an employee who has previously received any voluntary separation incentive payment by the Federal Government under this section or any other authority and has not repaid such payment;

(5) an employee covered by statutory reemployment rights who is on transfer to another organization; or

(6) any employee who, during the 24-month period preceding the date of separation, has received a recruitment or relocation bonus under 5 U.S.C. 5753 or who, within the 12-month period preceding the date of separation, received a retention allowance under 5 U.S.C. 5754.]

[(c) AUTHORITY TO PROVIDE VOLUNTARY SEPARATION INCENTIVE PAYMENTS.—

(1) IN GENERAL.—The Treasury Inspector General for Tax Administration may pay voluntary separation incentive payments under

this section to any employee to the extent necessary to organize the Office so as to perform the duties specified in the Internal Revenue Service Restructuring and Reform Act of 1998 (Public Law 105–206).

(2) AMOUNT AND TREATMENT OF PAYMENTS.—A voluntary separation incentive payment—

(A) shall be paid in a lump sum after the employee's separation;

(B) shall be paid from appropriations available for the payment of the basic pay of the employees of the Office;

(C) shall be equal to the lesser of—

(i) an amount equal to the amount the employee would be entitled to receive under 5 U.S.C. 5595(c); or

(ii) an amount determined by the Treasury Inspector General for Tax Administration, not to exceed $25,000;

(D) may not be made except in the case of any qualifying employee who voluntarily separates (whether by retirement or resignation) before January 1, 2003;

(E) shall not be a basis for payment, and shall not be included in the computation, of any other type of Government benefit; and

(F) shall not be taken into account in determining the amount of any severance pay to which the employee may be entitled under 5 U.S.C. 5595 based on any other separation.]

[(d) ADDITIONAL OFFICE OF THE TREASURY INSPECTOR GENERAL FOR TAX ADMINISTRATION CONTRIBUTIONS TO THE RETIREMENT FUND.—

(1) IN GENERAL.—In addition to any other payments which it is required to make under subchapter III of chapter 83 or chapter 84 of title 5, United States Code, the Office shall remit to the Office of Personnel Management for deposit in the Treasury of the United States to the credit of the Civil Service Retirement and Disability Fund an amount equal to 15 percent of the final basic pay of each employee who is covered under subchapter III of chapter 83 or chapter 84 of title 5, United States Code, to whom a voluntary separation incentive has been paid under this section.

(2) DEFINITION.—In paragraph (1), the term "final basic pay", with respect to an employee, means the total amount of basic pay which would be payable for a year of service by such employee, computed using the employee's final rate of basic pay, and, if last serving on other than a full-time basis, with appropriate adjustment therefor.

(e) EFFECT OF SUBSEQUENT EMPLOYMENT WITH THE GOVERNMENT.—An individual who has received a voluntary separation incentive payment under this section and accepts any employment for compensation with the United States Government, or who works for any agency of the United States Government through a personal services contract, within 5 years after the date of the separation on which the payment is based, shall be required to pay, prior to the individual's first day of employment, the entire amount of the incentive payment to the Office.

(f) EFFECT ON OFFICE OF THE TREASURY INSPECTOR GENERAL FOR TAX ADMINISTRATION EMPLOYMENT LEVELS.—

(1) INTENDED EFFECT.—Voluntary separations under this section are not intended to necessarily reduce the total number of full-time equivalent positions in the Office.

(2) USE OF VOLUNTARY SEPARATIONS.—The Office may redeploy or use the full-time equivalent positions vacated by voluntary separations under this section to make other positions available to more critical locations or more critical occupations.]

[SEC. 117. None of the funds appropriated in this Act or otherwise available to the Department of the Treasury or the Bureau of Engraving and Printing may be used to redesign the $1 Federal Reserve note.]

[SEC. 118. Funds made available by this or any other Act may be used to pay premium pay for protective services authorized by section 3056(a) of title 18, United States Code, without regard to the limitation on the rate of pay payable during a pay period contained in section 5547(c)(2) of title 5, United States Code, except that such premium pay shall not be payable to an employee to the extent that the aggregate of the employee's basic and premium pay for the year would otherwise exceed the annual equivalent of that limitation. The term premium pay refers to the provisions of law cited in the first sentence of section 5547(a) of title 5, United States Code.]

[SEC. 119. (a) VOLUNTARY SEPARATION INCENTIVE PAYMENTS FOR EMPLOYEES OF THE CHICAGO FINANCIAL CENTER OF THE FINANCIAL MANAGEMENT SERVICE.—During the period from October 1, 1999, through January 31, 2000, the Commissioner of the Financial Management Service (FMS) of the Department of the Treasury is authorized to offer voluntary separation incentives in order to provide the necessary flexibility to carry out the closure of the Chicago Financial Center (CFC) in a manner which the Commissioner shall deem most efficient, equitable to employees, and cost effective to the Government.]

[(b) DEFINITION.—In this section, the term "employee" means an employee (as defined by 5 U.S.C. 2105) who is employed by FMS at CFC under an appointment without time limitation, and has been so employed continuously for a period of at least 3 years, but does not include—

(1) a reemployed annuitant under subchapter III of chapter 83 or chapter 84 of title 5, United States Code, or another retirement system;

(2) an employee with a disability on the basis of which such employee is or would be eligible for disability retirement under the retirement systems referred to in paragraph (1) or another retirement system for employees of the Government;

(3) an employee who is in receipt of a specific notice of involuntary separation for misconduct or unacceptable performance;

(4) an employee who has previously received any voluntary separation incentive payment from an agency or instrumentality of the Government of the United States under any authority and has not repaid such payment;

(5) an employee covered by statutory reemployment rights who is on transfer to another organization; or

(6) an employee who during the 24-month period preceding the date of separation has received and not repaid a recruitment or relocation bonus under section 5753 of title 5, United States Code, or who, within the 12-month period preceding the date of separation, has received and not repaid a retention allowance under section 5754 of that title.]

[(c) AGENCY PLAN; APPROVAL.—

(1) The Secretary, Department of the Treasury, prior to obligating any resources for voluntary separation incentive payments, shall submit to the Office of Management and Budget a strategic plan outlining the intended use of such incentive payments and a proposed organizational chart for the agency once such incentive payments have been completed.

(2) The agency's plan under paragraph (1) shall include—

(A) the specific positions and functions to be reduced or eliminated;

(B) a proposed coverage for offers of incentives;

(C) the time period during which incentives may be paid;

(D) the number and amounts of voluntary separation incentive payments to be offered; and

(E) a description of how the agency will operate without the eliminated positions and functions.

(3) The Director of the Office of Management and Budget shall review the agency's plan and approve or disapprove such plan, and may make appropriate modifications in the plan including waivers of the reduction in agency employment levels required by this Act.]

[(d) AUTHORITY TO PROVIDE VOLUNTARY SEPARATION INCENTIVE PAYMENTS.—

(1) A voluntary separation incentive payment under this Act may be paid by the agency head to an employee only in accordance with the strategic plan under subsection (c).

(2) A voluntary incentive payment—

(A) shall be offered to agency employees on the basis of organizational unit, occupational series or level, geographic location, other nonpersonal factors, or an appropriate combination of such factors;

(B) shall be paid in a lump sum after the employee's separation;

(C) shall be equal to the lesser of—

(i) an amount equal to the amount the employee would be entitled to receive under section 5595(c) of title 5, United States Code, if the employee were entitled to payment under such section (without adjustment for any previous payment made); or

(ii) an amount determined by the agency head, not to exceed $25,000;

(D) may be made only in the case of an employee who voluntarily separates (whether by retirement or resignation) under the provisions of this Act;

(E) shall not be a basis for payment, and shall not be included in the computation of any other type of Government benefit;

(F) shall not be taken into account in determining the amount of any severance pay to which the employee may be entitled under section 5595 of title 5, United States Code, based on any other separation; and

(G) shall be paid from appropriations or funds available for the payment of the basic pay of the employee.]

[(e) ELIGIBILITY FOR PAYMENTS.—Payments under this section may be made to any qualifying employee who voluntarily separates, whether by retirement or resignation, between October 1, 1999, and January 31, 2000.]

[(f) EFFECT ON SUBSEQUENT EMPLOYMENT WITH THE GOVERNMENT.—

(1) An individual who has received a voluntary separation incentive payment under this section and accepts any employment for compensation with any agency or instrumentality of the Government of the United States, or who works for an agency of the United States Government through a personal services contract, within 5 years after the date of the separation on which the payment is based shall be required to pay, prior to the individual's first day of employment, the entire amount of the incentive payment to FMS.

(2) The Director of the Office of Personnel Management may, at the request of the Secretary, Department of the Treasury, waive the repayment if the individual involved possesses unique abilities and is the only qualified applicant available for the position.]

[(g) CONTRIBUTIONS TO THE RETIREMENT FUND.—

(1) In addition to any other payments which it is required to make under subchapter III of chapter 83 or chapter 84 of title 5, United States Code, FMS shall remit to the Office of Personnel Management for deposit in the Treasury to the credit of the Civil Service Retirement and Disability Fund an amount equal to 15 percent of the final annual basic pay for each employee covered under subchapter III of chapter 83 or chapter 84 of title 5, United States Code, to whom a voluntary separation incentive has been paid under this section.

(2) For the purpose of paragraph (1), the term "final basic pay" with respect to an employee, means the total amount of basic pay which would be payable for a year of service by such employee, computed using the employee's final rate of basic pay, and, if last serving on other than a full-time basis, with appropriate adjustment therefor.]

[(h) REDUCTION OF AGENCY EMPLOYMENT LEVELS.—

(1) The total number of funded employee positions in the agency shall be reduced by one position for each vacancy created by the separation of any employee who has received, or is due to receive, a voluntary separation incentive payment under this Act. For the purposes of this subsection, positions shall be counted on a full-time equivalent basis.

(2) The President, through the Office of Management and Budget, shall monitor the agency and take any action necessary to ensure that the requirements of this subsection are met.

(3) At the request of the Secretary, Department of the Treasury, the Office of Management and Budget may waive the reduction in total number of funded employee positions required by paragraph (1) if it believes the agency plan required by subsection (c) satisfactorily demonstrates that the positions would better be used to reallocate occupations or reshape the workforce and to produce a more cost-effective result.]

SEC. 116. The Secretary of the Treasury may transfer funds from "Salaries and Expenses," Financial Management Service, to the Debt Services Account as necessary to cover the costs of debt collection: Provided, That such amounts shall be reimbursed to such Salaries and Expenses account from debt collections received in the Debt Services Account. (Treasury Department Appropriations Act, 2000.)

TITLE V—GENERAL PROVISIONS

THIS ACT

SEC. 501. No part of any appropriation contained in this Act shall remain available for obligation beyond the current fiscal year unless expressly so provided herein.

SEC. 502. The expenditure of any appropriation under this Act for any consulting service through procurement contract, pursuant to 5 U.S.C. 3109, shall be limited to those contracts where such expenditures are a matter of public record and available for public inspection, except where otherwise provided under existing law, or under existing Executive order issued pursuant to existing law.

SEC. 503. None of the funds made available by this Act shall be available for any activity or for paying the salary of any Government employee where funding an activity or paying a salary to a Government employee would result in a decision, determination, rule, regulation, or policy that would prohibit the enforcement of section 307 of the Tariff Act of 1930.

SEC. 504. None of the funds made available by this Act shall be available in fiscal year [2000] *2001* for the purpose of transferring control over the Federal Law Enforcement Training Center located at Glynco, Georgia, and Artesia, New Mexico, out of the Department of the Treasury.

SEC. 505. No part of any appropriation contained in this Act shall be available to pay the salary for any person filling a position, other than a temporary position, formerly held by an employee who has left to enter the Armed Forces of the United States and has satisfactorily completed his period of active military or naval service, and has within 90 days after his release from such service or from hospitalization continuing after discharge for a period of not more than 1 year, made application for restoration to his former position and has been certified by the Office of Personnel Management as still qualified to perform the duties of his former position and has not been restored thereto.

SEC. 506. No funds appropriated pursuant to this Act may be expended by an entity unless the entity agrees that in expending the assistance the entity will comply with sections 2 through 4 of the Act of March 3, 1933 (41 U.S.C. 10a–10c, popularly known as the "Buy American Act").

SEC. 507. (a) PURCHASE OF AMERICAN-MADE EQUIPMENT AND PRODUCTS.—In the case of any equipment or products that may be authorized to be purchased with financial assistance provided under this Act, it is the sense of the Congress that entities receiving such assistance should, in expending the assistance, purchase only American-made equipment and products.

(b) NOTICE TO RECIPIENTS OF ASSISTANCE.—In providing financial assistance under this Act, the Secretary of the Treasury shall provide to each recipient of the assistance a notice describing the statement made in subsection (a) by the Congress.

SEC. 508. If it has been finally determined by a court or Federal agency that any person intentionally affixed a label bearing a "Made in America" inscription, or any inscription with the same meaning, to any product sold in or shipped to the United States that is not made in the United States, such person shall be ineligible to receive any contract or subcontract made with funds provided pursuant to this Act, pursuant to the debarment, suspension, and ineligibility procedures described in sections 9.400 through 9.409 of title 48, Code of Federal Regulations.

[SEC. 509. No funds appropriated by this Act shall be available to pay for an abortion, or the administrative expenses in connection with any health plan under the Federal employees health benefit program which provides any benefits or coverage for abortions.] [1]

[SEC. 510. The provision of section 509 shall not apply where the life of the mother would be endangered if the fetus were carried to term, or the pregnancy is the result of an act of rape or incest.] [1]

SEC. [511] *509*. Except as otherwise specifically provided by law, not to exceed 50 percent of unobligated balances remaining available at the end of fiscal year [2000] *2001* from appropriations made available for salaries and expenses for fiscal year [2000] *2001* in this Act, shall remain available through September 30, [2001] *2002*, for each such account for the purposes authorized: *Provided*, That a [request] *notice* shall be submitted to the Committees on Appropriations [for approval] *at least 15 days* prior to the expenditure of such funds: *Provided further*, That these [requests] *notices* shall be made in compliance with reprogramming guidelines.

SEC. [512] *510*. None of the funds made available in this Act may be used by the Executive Office of the President to request from the Federal Bureau of Investigation any official background investigation report on any individual, except when—

(1) such individual has given his or her express written consent for such request not more than 6 months prior to the date of such request and during the same presidential administration; or

(2) such request is required due to extraordinary circumstances involving national security.

[SEC. 513. Notwithstanding section 515 of Public Law 104–208, 50 percent of the unobligated balances available to the White House Office, Salaries and Expenses appropriations in fiscal year 1997, shall

THIS ACT—Continued

remain available through September 30, 2000, for the purposes of satisfying the conditions of section 515 of the Treasury and General Government Appropriations Act, 1999.]

[SEC. 514. The cost accounting standards promulgated under section 26 of the Office of Federal Procurement Policy Act (Public Law 93–400; 41 U.S.C. 422) shall not apply with respect to a contract under the Federal Employees Health Benefits Program established under chapter 89 of title 5, United States Code.]

[SEC. 515. INVENTORY OF FEDERAL GRANT PROGRAMS. The Director of the Office of Management and Budget shall prepare an inventory of existing Federal grant programs after consulting each agency that administers Federal grant programs including formula funds, competitive grant funds, block grant funds, and direct payments. The inventory shall include the name of the program, a copy of relevant statutory and regulatory guidelines, the funding level in fiscal year 1999, a list of the eligibility criteria both statutory and regulatory, and a copy of the application form. The Director shall submit the inventory no later than 6 months after enactment to the Committees on Appropriations and relevant authorizing committees.] *(Treasury and General Government Appropriations Act, 2000.)*

[1] The Administration proposes to delete this provision and will work with the Congress to address this issue.

[TITLE VI—SURVIVOR BENEFITS]

[SEC. 601. PAYMENT.]

[(a) PAYMENT AUTHORIZATION.—The Secretary of the Treasury shall pay, out of funds not otherwise appropriated, $100,000 to the survivor, or collectively the survivors, of each of the 14 members of the Armed Forces and the one United States civilian Federal employee who were killed on April 14, 1994, when United States F–15 fighter aircraft mistakenly shot down two UH–60 Black Hawk helicopters over Iraq.] *(Miscellaneous Appropriations, 2000, as enacted by section 1000(a)(5) of the Consolidated Appropriations Act, 2000 (P.L. 106–113).)*

DEPARTMENT OF VETERANS AFFAIRS

The 2001 budget provides $22,363 million in discretionary funding for veterans health, benefits, and other services, including $22,971 million in gross discretionary budget authority and $608 million in anticipated medical collections.

The account by account information provided in the following budget schedules is supplemented by a department-wide strategic plan, published in September 1997, a performance plan submitted annually with the Budget, and an annual accountability report. The performance plan contains annual goals for each of the Department of Veterans Affairs' (VA) programs along with historic performance data, where available. The accountability report includes audited financial statements along with actual program performance as measured against goals.

VA published an initial strategic plan in September, 1997. The Department will publish a new strategic plan in 2000.

The 2001, performance plan highlights approximately 25 key measures determined by the VA's top executives as overall measures of departmental performance. In addition, the performance plan identifies the total budgetary resources, including FTE, associated with each of VA's major programs.

VETERANS HEALTH ADMINISTRATION

Federal Funds

General and special funds:

MEDICAL CARE

(INCLUDING TRANSFER OF FUNDS)

For necessary expenses for the maintenance and operation of hospitals, nursing homes, and domiciliary facilities; for furnishing, as authorized by law, inpatient and outpatient care and treatment to beneficiaries of the Department of Veterans Affairs, including care and treatment in facilities not under the jurisdiction of the department; and furnishing recreational facilities, supplies, and equipment; funeral, burial, and other expenses incidental thereto for beneficiaries receiving care in the department; administrative expenses in support of planning, design, project management, real property acquisition and disposition, construction and renovation of any facility under the jurisdiction or for the use of the department; oversight, engineering and architectural activities not charged to project cost; repairing, altering, improving or providing facilities in the several hospitals and homes under the jurisdiction of the department, not otherwise provided for, either by contract or by the hire of temporary employees and purchase of materials; uniforms or allowances therefor, as authorized by 5 U.S.C. 5901–5902; aid to State homes as authorized by 38 U.S.C. 1741; administrative and legal expenses of the department for collecting and recovering amounts owed the department as authorized under 38 U.S.C. chapter 17, and the Federal Medical Care Recovery Act, 42 U.S.C. 2651 et seq.; and not to exceed [$8,000,000] *$16,000,000* to fund cost comparison studies as referred to in 38 U.S.C. 8110(a)(5), [$19,006,000,000] *$20,281,587,000*, plus reimbursements: *Provided*, That of the funds made available under this heading, $900,000,000 is for the equipment and land and structures object classifications only, which amount shall not become available for obligation until August 1, [2000] *2001*, and shall remain available until September 30, [2001] *2002*: *Provided further*, That of the funds made available under this heading, not to exceed $900,000,000 shall be available until September 30, [2001: *Provided further*, That of the funds made available under this heading, not to exceed $27,907,000 may be transferred to and merged with the appropriation for "General operating expenses"] *2002*: *Provided further*, That the department shall conduct by contract a program of recovery audits for the fee basis and other medical services contracts with respect to payments for hospital care; and, notwithstanding 31 U.S.C. 3302(b), amounts collected, by setoff or otherwise, as the result of such audits shall be available, without fiscal year limitation, for the purposes for which funds are appropriated under this heading and the purposes of paying a contractor a percent of the amount collected as a result of an audit carried out by the contractor: *Provided further*, That all amounts so collected under the preceding proviso with respect to a designated health care region (as that term is defined in 38 U.S.C. 1729A(d)(2)) shall be allocated, net of payments to the contractor, to that region.

[In addition, in conformance with Public Law 105–33 establishing the Department of Veterans Affairs Medical Care Collections Fund, such sums as may be deposited to such Fund pursuant to 38 U.S.C. 1729A may be transferred to this account, to remain available until expended for the purposes of this account.] *(Departments of Veterans Affairs and Housing and Urban Development, and Independent Agencies Appropriations Act, 2000.)*

Unavailable Collections (in millions of dollars)

	Identification code 36–0160–0–1–703	1999 actual	2000 est.	2001 est.
	Balance, start of year:			
01.99	Balance, start of year	54	51	51
	Receipts:			
02.01	Medical care collections	574	600	
02.08	MCCF first party collections			203
02.09	MCCF third party collections			290
02.10	DOD tricare reimbursement			115
02.99	Total receipts	574	600	608
04.00	Total: Balances and collections	628	651	659
	Appropriation:			
05.01	Medical care	−577	−600	−608
07.99	Total balance, end of year	51	51	51

Program and Financing (in millions of dollars)

	Identification code 36–0160–0–1–703	1999 actual	2000 est.	2001 est.
	Obligations by program activity:			
	Direct program:			
	Operating expenses:			
	Provision of veterans health care:			
00.01	Acute hospital care	4,587	4,963	5,173
00.02	Rehabilitative care	359	375	392
00.03	Psychiatric care	1,129	1,124	1,134
00.04	Nursing home care	1,727	1,884	1,976
00.05	Subacute care	370	361	357
00.06	Residential care	337	375	395
00.07	Outpatient care	7,499	8,600	9,557
00.08	Miscellaneous benefits and services	908	956	966
00.09	CHAMPVA	118	128	139
00.91	Total operating expenses	17,034	18,766	20,089
	Capital investment:			
	Provision of veterans health care:			
01.01	Acute hospital care	254	217	233
01.02	Rehabilitative care	19	16	18
01.03	Psychiatric care	50	49	51
01.04	Nursing home care	52	82	89
01.05	Subacute care	15	16	16
01.06	Residential care	14	16	18
01.07	Outpatient care	310	375	431
01.08	Miscellaneous benefits and services	25	42	44
01.91	Total capital investment	739	813	900
01.92	Total direct program	17,773	19,579	20,989
09.01	Reimbursable program	103	117	126
10.00	Total new obligations	17,876	19,696	21,115
	Budgetary resources available for obligation:			
21.40	Unobligated balance available, start of year	1,039	1,082	1,005
22.00	New budget authority (gross)	17,923	19,615	21,016

General and special funds—Continued

MEDICAL CARE—Continued

(INCLUDING TRANSFER OF FUNDS)—Continued

Program and Financing (in millions of dollars)—Continued

Identification code 36–0160–0–1–703		1999 actual	2000 est.	2001 est.
22.10	Resources available from recoveries of prior year obligations		3	3
23.90	Total budgetary resources available for obligation	18,962	20,700	22,024
23.95	Total new obligations	−17,876	−19,696	−21,115
23.98	Unobligated balance expiring or withdrawn	−3		
24.40	Unobligated balance available, end of year	1,082	1,005	909
	New budget authority (gross), detail:			
	Discretionary:			
40.00	Appropriation	17,306	19,006	20,282
	Appropriation (special fund, indefinite):			
40.25	Appropriation (special fund, indefinite)	577	600	
40.25	Appropriation (special fund, indefinite)			608
40.75	Reduction pursuant to P.L. 106–51	−35		
40.76	Reduction pursuant to P.L. 106–113		−80	
41.00	Transferred to other accounts	−28	−28	
43.00	Appropriation (total discretionary)	17,820	19,498	20,890
68.00	Spending authority from offsetting collections: Offsetting collections (cash)	103	117	126
70.00	Total new budget authority (gross)	17,923	19,615	21,016
	Change in unpaid obligations:			
72.40	Unpaid obligations, start of year: Obligated balance, start of year	2,734	2,572	3,712
73.10	Total new obligations	17,876	19,696	21,115
73.20	Total outlays (gross)	−17,950	−18,553	−21,193
73.40	Adjustments in expired accounts (net)	−88		
73.45	Adjustments in unexpired accounts		−3	−3
74.40	Unpaid obligations, end of year: Obligated balance, end of year	2,572	3,712	3,631
	Outlays (gross), detail:			
86.90	Outlays from new discretionary authority	15,018	15,902	17,233
86.93	Outlays from discretionary balances	2,932	2,651	3,688
86.97	Outlays from new mandatory authority			272
87.00	Total outlays (gross)	17,950	18,553	21,193
	Offsets:			
	Against gross budget authority and outlays:			
	Offsetting collections (cash) from:			
88.00	Federal sources	−51	−58	−66
88.40	Non-Federal sources	−52	−59	−60
88.90	Total, offsetting collections (cash)	−103	−117	−126
	Net budget authority and outlays:			
89.00	Budget authority	17,820	19,498	20,890
90.00	Outlays	17,846	18,436	21,067

For 2001, the budget provides a total VA Medical Care program level of $20,890 million, an increase of $1,392 million over the 2000 level. This includes $20,282 million in appropriated budget authority and $608 million in anticipated medical collections. VA's authority to retain all collections from third party insurance companies, other copayments, and related medical fees is relatively uncommon in the federal government and critical to VA's success in providing care to veterans.

The 2001 budget includes a proposal to consolidate the Health Services Improvement Fund and the Extended Care Revolving Fund with the Medical Care Collections Fund. The Health Services Improvement Fund was established by the Veterans Millennium Health Care and Benefits Act, P.L. 106–117. This fund serves as a depository for amounts received or collected under the following areas as authorized by title 38, U.S.C. 1729B: (1) reimbursement from DoD for Tricare-eligible military retirees; (2) enhanced-use lease proceeds; and (3) receipts attributable to increases in medication copayments. Amounts in the fund are intended to be used to: (1) furnish medical care services and (2) for VA expenses for identification, billing, auditing and collections of amounts owed the Government. These funds are available without fiscal year limitation.

The Extended Care Revolving Fund was also established by the Veterans Millennium Health Care and Benefits Act, P.L. 106–117. This fund receives per diems and co-pays from certain patients receiving extended care services as authorized in title 38, U.S.C. 1710B. Amounts deposited in the fund are used to provide extended care services. The proposal would also return one half of the first $700,000,000 ($350,000,000), in collections received by the consolidated fund to the Treasury.

The 2001 budget also includes a legislative proposal to permanently extend current legal provisions due to expire in 2003. These provisions provide for the collection of third-party health insurance payments for care provided by the VA for service-connected veterans with nonservice connected conditions, copayments, and income verification provisions.

WORKLOAD

Provision of Veterans Health Care—

Acute hospital care.—Costs for 2001 are estimated to increase by $227 million for operating medical, neurological, surgical, contract and State home hospital beds, reflecting the shift to increased use of ambulatory care.

Estimated operating levels are:

	1999 actual	2000 est.	2001 est.
Patients treated	434,468	425,500	411,640
Average daily census	8,371	7,484	6,725
Average employment	52,526	49,322	46,359

Rehabilitative care.—An increase of $20 million in 2001 is estimated for the provision of rehabilitative care, including spinal cord injury care.

Estimated operating levels are:

	1999 actual	2000 est.	2001 est.
Patients treated	16,274	15,470	14,656
Average daily census	1,259	1,156	1,052
Average employment	4,848	4,700	4,465

Psychiatric care.—An increase of $12 million is estimated in 2001 for the inpatient care of veterans with problems related to mental illness, including alcohol and drug problems.

Estimated operating levels are:

	1999 actual	2000 est.	2001 est.
Patients treated	111,726	100,000	86,200
Average daily census	5,144	4,269	3,586
Average employment	16,447	15,000	13,800

Nursing home care.—In 2001, an increase of $99 million is estimated for the care of residents in VA nursing homes, contract nursing homes and State nursing homes.

Estimated operating levels are:

	1999 actual	2000 est.	2001 est.
Patients treated	89,217	93,030	98,929
Average daily census	32,204	32,552	32,769
Average employment	21,018	21,762	22,539

Noninstitutional extended care.—Included in estimates above in 2001 is an increase of $278 million estimated for noninstitutional extended care programs such as adult day care; home based primary care, skilled nursing and rehabilitation care; and home health aids.

Estimated operating levels are:

	1999 actual	2000 est.	2001 est.
Patients treated			
Average daily census	21,371	26,905	53,240
Average employment			

Subacute care.—A decrease of $4 million is estimated in 2001 for the treatment of veterans who require a level of care between acute and long-term care, as provided in VA hospital intermediate bed sections.

Estimated operating levels are:

	1999 actual	2000 est.	2001 est.
Patients treated	50,332	54,000	59,268
Average daily census	2,562	2,254	2,006
Average employment	5,697	5,298	4,953

Residential care.—An increase of $22 million is estimated in 2001 for the care of veterans in locations other than their own homes, such as residential rehabilitation and domiciliary care programs.

Estimated operating levels are:

	1999 actual	2000 est.	2001 est.
Patients treated	49,774	50,008	50,490
Average daily census	10,496	10,386	10,231
Average employment	4,696	4,784	4,890

Outpatient care.—An increase of $1,020 million is estimated in 2001 for the cost of outpatient medical and dental care provided by staff, physicians, and dentists participating under a fee basis arrangement for certain eligible veterans.

Estimated operating levels are:

NUMBER OF MEDICAL VISITS AND DENTAL WORKLOADS

Medical visits (in thousands):	1999 actual	2000 est.	2001 est.
Staff visits	35,236	37,700	39,000
Fee visits	1,692	1,861	2,010
Readjustment counseling	871	827	827
Total	37,799	40,388	41,837
Dental:			
Staff:			
Examinations	284,425	287,000	287,000
Treatments	155,336	159,000	159,000
Total	439,761	446,000	446,000
Fee: Cases completed	11,648	14,000	14,000
Average employment	69,503	71,486	73,883

Miscellaneous benefits and services.—An increase of $12 million is estimated in 2001 for the cost of this activity which includes items of nondirect medical care and treatment such as beneficiary travel, care of the dead, operation of personnel quarters at medical facilities, and the cost of furnishing supply, engineering, housekeeping, and other administrative support services to other departments on a nonreimbursable basis.

	1999 actual	2000 est.	2001 est.
Average employment	7,737	7,969	8,128

Civilian health and medical program of the Department of Veterans Affairs (CHAMPVA).—An increase of $11 million is estimated in 2001 for private hospital and outpatient care for dependents and survivors of certain veterans.

Estimated operating levels are:

	1999 actual	2000 est.	2001 est.
Average daily hospital census	140	140	140
Outpatient (in thousands)	1,076	1,178	1,290
Average employment	189	189	189

Object Classification (in millions of dollars)

Identification code 36–0160–0–1–703		1999 actual	2000 est.	2001 est.
	Direct obligations:			
	Personnel compensation:			
11.1	Full-time permanent	6,709	6,964	7,338
11.3	Other than full-time permanent	884	918	967
11.5	Other personnel compensation	798	828	873
11.9	Total personnel compensation	8,391	8,710	9,178
12.1	Civilian personnel benefits	2,043	2,183	2,235
13.0	Benefits for former personnel	9	132	10
	Travel and transportation of persons:			
21.0	Employee travel	46	55	55
21.0	Beneficiary travel	115	120	120
21.0	Interagency motor pool payments	15	16	16
21.0	All other	32	32	32
22.0	Transportation of things	20	20	20
23.1	Rental payments to GSA	11	12	13
23.2	Rental payments to others	61	65	68
23.3	Communications, utilities, and miscellaneous charges	485	533	531
24.0	Printing and reproduction	10	10	10
25.2	Other contractual services	1,476	1,771	2,160
	Medical care:			
25.6	Outpatient dental fees	11	14	14
25.6	Medical and nursing fees	319	363	380
25.6	Community nursing homes	205	229	239
25.6	Contract hospitalization	189	217	225
25.6	Civilian Health and Medical Program of the Department of Veterans Affairs	106	116	126
	Supplies and materials:			
26.0	Supplies and materials	3,123	3,733	4,196
26.0	Provisions	76	76	79
31.0	Equipment	486	550	626
32.0	Land and structures	253	263	274
	Grants, subsidies, and contributions:			
41.0	Grants, subsidies, and contributions	273	325	347
41.0	Grants to private organizations	16	32	33
43.0	Interest and dividends	2	2	2
99.0	Subtotal, direct obligations	17,773	19,579	20,989
99.0	Reimbursable obligations	103	117	126
99.9	Total new obligations	17,876	19,696	21,115

Personnel Summary

Identification code 36–0160–0–1–703		1999 actual	2000 est.	2001 est.
	Direct:			
1001	Total compensable workyears: Full-time equivalent employment	181,605	179,382	178,060
	Reimbursable:			
2001	Total compensable workyears: Full-time equivalent employment	1,056	1,128	1,146

MEDICAL AND PROSTHETIC RESEARCH

For necessary expenses in carrying out programs of medical and prosthetic research and development as authorized by 38 U.S.C. chapter 73, to remain available until September 30, [2001, $321,000,000] *2002, $321,000,000,* plus reimbursements. *(Departments of Veterans Affairs and Housing and Urban Development, and Independent Agencies Appropriations Act, 2000.)*

Program and Financing (in millions of dollars)

Identification code 36–0161–0–1–703		1999 actual	2000 est.	2001 est.
	Obligations by program activity:			
	Direct program:			
	Operating expenses:			
00.01	Medical research	167	185	175
00.02	Rehabilitation research	24	27	27
00.03	Health services research	39	43	43
00.04	Cooperative studies research	52	58	58
00.91	Total operating expenses	282	313	303
	Capital investment:			
01.01	Medical research	17	14	13
01.02	Rehabilitation research	3	2	2
01.03	Health services research	2	2	1
01.04	Cooperative studies research	3	3	2
01.91	Total capital investment	25	21	18
01.92	Total direct program	307	334	321
09.01	Reimbursable program	41	33	40
10.00	Total new obligations	348	367	361
	Budgetary resources available for obligation:			
21.40	Unobligated balance available, start of year	19	28	15
22.00	New budget authority (gross)	357	354	361
23.90	Total budgetary resources available for obligation	376	382	376
23.95	Total new obligations	–348	–367	–361
23.98	Unobligated balance expiring or withdrawn	–1		
24.40	Unobligated balance available, end of year	28	15	15

General and special funds—Continued

MEDICAL AND PROSTHETIC RESEARCH—Continued

Program and Financing (in millions of dollars)—Continued

Identification code 36–0161–0–1–703	1999 actual	2000 est.	2001 est.
New budget authority (gross), detail:			
Discretionary:			
40.00 Appropriation	316	321	321
68.00 Spending authority from offsetting collections: Offsetting collections (cash)	41	33	40
70.00 Total new budget authority (gross)	357	354	361
Change in unpaid obligations:			
72.40 Unpaid obligations, start of year: Obligated balance, start of year	122	110	132
73.10 Total new obligations	348	367	361
73.20 Total outlays (gross)	−358	−345	−366
73.40 Adjustments in expired accounts (net)	−2		
74.40 Unpaid obligations, end of year: Obligated balance, end of year	110	132	125
Outlays (gross), detail:			
86.90 Outlays from new discretionary authority	249	261	275
86.93 Outlays from discretionary balances	109	83	91
87.00 Total outlays (gross)	358	345	366
Offsets:			
Against gross budget authority and outlays:			
88.00 Offsetting collections (cash) from: Federal sources	−41	−33	−40
Net budget authority and outlays:			
89.00 Budget authority	316	321	321
90.00 Outlays	316	312	326

The Medical and Prosthetic Research account is an intramural program whose mission is to discover knowledge and create innovations that advance the health and care of veterans and the Nation. Veterans health issues are addressed comprehensively in the following four program divisions:

Medical Research.—Medical Research strives to understand the disease process so that efficient, rational interventions can be made to cure or alleviate the effects of disease. The program supports investigator-initiated research projects, the training of clinicians in basic and clinical research, and centers of excellence devoted to specific diseases. The research is done in areas particularly relevant to the veteran population—aging, chronic disease, mental illness, substance abuse, military occupations, and environmental exposures.

Rehabilitation Research.—Rehabilitation Research is dedicated to the development and application of science and engineering to improve the care and quality of life for the physically disabled. The program supports investigator-initiated research projects, the training of clinicians and engineers in rehabilitation research, centers of excellence devoted to specific disabilities, and technology transfer. The research is done in areas particularly relevant to the disabled veteran population—aging, sensory loss, and trauma related illness.

Health Services Research.—Health Services Research is directed toward improving the outcome effectiveness and cost efficiency of health care delivery for the veteran population. The program supports investigator-initiated research projects, the training of clinicians in applied clinical research, centers of excellence devoted to specific aspects of health care delivery, and service-directed projects addressing clinical management needs. The research focuses on the translation of research findings to clinical best practices for all veteran patients. Particular contributions are made in the areas of aging, substance abuse, health systems, and special populations.

Cooperative Studies.—Cooperative Studies Research has recently been separated from the Medical Research and Health Services Research programs and is directed toward large multi-site clinical trials. Cooperative Studies supports the clinical trials with its own statistical support centers and its own FDA-approved pharmacy. The research determines the efficacy and cost effectiveness of new medications and new treatment strategies of direct benefit to the veteran population in the areas of aging, chronic disease, mental illness, special populations, and military occupations and environmental exposures.

VA's Medical and Prosthetic Research programs are included in the 21st Century Research Fund.

SUMMARY OF BUDGETARY RESOURCES

[In millions of dollars]

	1999 actual	2000 est.	2001 est.
Medical and prosthetic research appropriation	316	321	321
Medical care appropriation	326	331	331
Federal grants (NIH)	337	343	348
Other grants (voluntary agencies, private proprietary)	143	145	147
Total budgetary resources	1,122	1,140	1,147

Object Classification (in millions of dollars)

Identification code 36–0161–0–1–703	1999 actual	2000 est.	2001 est.
Direct obligations:			
Personnel compensation:			
11.1 Full-time permanent	41	44	43
11.3 Other than full-time permanent	76	89	86
11.5 Other personnel compensation	4	4	4
11.9 Total personnel compensation	121	137	133
12.1 Civilian personnel benefits	29	35	34
21.0 Employee travel	3	3	2
23.3 Communications, utilities, and miscellaneous charges	1	1	1
25.5 Research and development contracts	101	104	100
26.0 Supplies and materials	32	34	31
31.0 Equipment	20	20	20
99.0 Subtotal, direct obligations	307	334	321
99.0 Reimbursable obligations	41	33	40
99.9 Total new obligations	348	367	361

Personnel Summary

Identification code 36–0161–0–1–703	1999 actual	2000 est.	2001 est.
Direct:			
1001 Total compensable workyears: Full-time equivalent employment	2,486	2,707	2,552
Reimbursable:			
2001 Total compensable workyears: Full-time equivalent employment	488	283	331

MEDICAL ADMINISTRATION AND MISCELLANEOUS OPERATING EXPENSES

For necessary expenses in the administration of the medical, hospital, nursing home, domiciliary, construction, supply, and research activities, as authorized by law; administrative expenses in support of capital policy activities, [$59,703,000] *$64,884,000* plus reimbursements: *Provided*, That [project] technical and consulting services offered by the Facilities Management [Service Delivery Office] *Field Service*, including [technical consulting services,] project management, real property administration (including leases, site acquisition and disposal activities directly supporting projects), shall be provided to Department of Veterans Affairs components only on a reimbursable basis, and such amounts will remain available until September 30, [2000] *2001. (Departments of Veterans Affairs and Housing and Urban Development, and Independent Agencies Appropriations Act, 2000.)*

Program and Financing (in millions of dollars)

Identification code 36–0152–0–1–703	1999 actual	2000 est.	2001 est.
Obligations by program activity:			
00.01 Operating expenses: Integrated health care system administration	58	59	64
00.02 Capital investment	5	1	1
01.00 Total direct program	63	60	65
09.01 Reimbursable program		7	7
10.00 Total new obligations	63	67	72
Budgetary resources available for obligation:			
22.00 New budget authority (gross)	63	67	72
23.95 Total new obligations	–63	–67	–72
New budget authority (gross), detail:			
Discretionary:			
40.00 Appropriation	63	60	65
68.00 Spending authority from offsetting collections: Offsetting collections (cash)		7	7
70.00 Total new budget authority (gross)	63	67	72
Change in unpaid obligations:			
Unpaid obligations, start of year:			
72.40 Obligated balance, start of year	12	13	14
72.95 From Federal sources: Receivables and unpaid, unfilled orders			1
72.99 Total unpaid obligations, start of year	12	13	15
73.10 Total new obligations	63	67	72
73.20 Total outlays (gross)	–61	–64	–74
Unpaid obligations, end of year:			
74.40 Obligated balance, end of year	13	14	12
74.95 From Federal sources: Receivables and unpaid, unfilled orders		1	1
74.99 Total unpaid obligations, end of year	13	15	13
Outlays (gross), detail:			
86.90 Outlays from new discretionary authority	52	58	65
86.93 Outlays from discretionary balances	9	6	9
87.00 Total outlays (gross)	61	64	74
Offsets:			
Against gross budget authority and outlays:			
88.45 Offsetting collections (cash) from: Offsetting governmental collections from the public		–7	–7
Net budget authority and outlays:			
89.00 Budget authority	63	60	65
90.00 Outlays	61	57	67

Supervision and administration of VA's comprehensive and integrated healthcare system.—Central office staff elements provide executive direction for all Departmental medical and construction programs through program development, implementation, and the administration of policies, plans, and objectives. In 2001, the Facilities Management Service Delivery Office will be directly reimbursed from organizations utilizing its services. The funding for tactical management and support activities is being aligned with organizations that directly utilize its services.

Object Classification (in millions of dollars)

Identification code 36–0152–0–1–703	1999 actual	2000 est.	2001 est.
Direct obligations:			
Personnel compensation:			
11.1 Full-time permanent	34	37	43
11.3 Other than full-time permanent	3	1	1
11.5 Other personnel compensation	2	3	3
11.9 Total personnel compensation	39	41	47
12.1 Civilian personnel benefits	7	7	8
21.0 Travel and transportation of persons: employee travel	1	1	1
23.1 Rental payments to GSA	5	5	6
23.3 Communications, utilities, and miscellaneous charges	1	1	1
25.2 Other services	4	3	1
26.0 Supplies and materials	1	1	
31.0 Equipment	5	1	1
99.0 Subtotal, direct obligations	63	60	65
99.0 Reimbursable obligations		7	7
99.9 Total new obligations	63	67	72

Personnel Summary

Identification code 36–0152–0–1–703	1999 actual	2000 est.	2001 est.
Direct:			
1001 Total compensable workyears: Full-time equivalent employment	488	484	527
Reimbursable:			
2001 Total compensable workyears: Full-time equivalent employment		57	57

HEALTH PROFESSIONAL SCHOLARSHIP PROGRAM

Program and Financing (in millions of dollars)

Identification code 36–0163–0–1–703	1999 actual	2000 est.	2001 est.
Change in unpaid obligations:			
72.40 Unpaid obligations, start of year: Obligated balance, start of year	2		
Net budget authority and outlays:			
89.00 Budget authority			
90.00 Outlays			

Health professional scholarship.—To assist in the recruitment and retention of staff, this program provided grants for tuition, stipend, and other educational expenses for eligible students in programs leading to a degree in nursing or other allied health disciplines.

No appropriation for this account was requested in 1999 through 2001.

MEDICAL CARE COST RECOVERY FUND

Program and Financing (in millions of dollars)

Identification code 36–5014–0–2–703	1999 actual	2000 est.	2001 est.
Change in unpaid obligations:			
72.40 Unpaid obligations, start of year: Obligated balance, start of year	1		
73.20 Total outlays (gross)	–1		
Outlays (gross), detail:			
86.98 Outlays from mandatory balances	1		
Net budget authority and outlays:			
89.00 Budget authority			
90.00 Outlays	1		

The Medical Care Cost Recovery (MCCR) Fund was established by the Omnibus Budget Reconciliation Act of 1990, P.L. 100–508. This Fund served as a depository for all third-party insurance collections. Of these funds, a portion was utilized to provide for FTE and other administrative costs associated with medical care cost recovery efforts. After providing the estimated cost of operations for the ensuing year, remaining funds were transferred to the Department of Treasury before January of the next year. Public Law 105–33, the Balanced Budget Act of 1997, established the Medical Care Collections Fund (MCCF) and terminated MCCR and required that amounts collected or recovered after June 30, 1997 be deposited in the new fund. The amounts collected will be available only for: (1) furnishing VA medical care

General and special funds—Continued

MEDICAL CARE COST RECOVERY FUND—Continued

and services during any fiscal year, and (2) for VA expenses for identification, billing, auditing and collections of amounts owed the government.

Public enterprise funds:

MEDICAL FACILITIES REVOLVING FUND

Program and Financing (in millions of dollars)

Identification code 36–4138–0–3–703		1999 actual	2000 est.	2001 est.
	Obligations by program activity:			
09.01	Reimbursable operating costs	1	1	1
09.02	Reimbursable capital expenses	2	3	3
10.00	Total new obligations	3	4	4
	Budgetary resources available for obligation:			
21.40	Unobligated balance available, start of year	5	5	4
22.00	New budget authority (gross)	3	3	3
23.90	Total budgetary resources available for obligation	8	8	7
23.95	Total new obligations	−3	−4	−4
24.40	Unobligated balance available, end of year	5	4	4
	New budget authority (gross), detail:			
	Mandatory:			
69.00	Offsetting collections (cash)	3	3	3
	Change in unpaid obligations:			
72.40	Unpaid obligations, start of year: Obligated balance, start of year	....	1	1
73.10	Total new obligations	3	4	4
73.20	Total outlays (gross)	−3	−3	−4
74.40	Unpaid obligations, end of year: Obligated balance, end of year	1	1	1
	Outlays (gross), detail:			
86.97	Outlays from new mandatory authority	....	3	3
86.98	Outlays from mandatory balances	3	2	2
87.00	Total outlays (gross)	3	3	4
	Offsets:			
	Against gross budget authority and outlays:			
88.40	Offsetting collections (cash) from: Non-Federal sources	−3	−3	−3
	Net budget authority and outlays:			
89.00	Budget authority	....	....	....
90.00	Outlays	....	....	1

This account provides funds for the operating expenses of VA medical facilities furnishing nursing home care to certain veterans in receipt of pensions. Title 38 provides that a veteran with no spouse or child will only receive $90 per month in pension beginning the third full month following the month of admission to VA furnished nursing home care. The difference between the $90 the veteran receives and the amount otherwise authorized is transferred to this fund from the Compensation and Pension account to assist in covering expenses at the facility furnishing the nursing care.

Object Classification (in millions of dollars)

Identification code 36–4138–0–3–703		1999 actual	2000 est.	2001 est.
25.2	Other services	....	1	1
26.0	Supplies and materials	1	1	1
31.0	Equipment	2	2	2
99.9	Total new obligations	3	4	4

CANTEEN SERVICE REVOLVING FUND

Program and Financing (in millions of dollars)

Identification code 36–4014–0–3–705		1999 actual	2000 est.	2001 est.
	Obligations by program activity:			
09.01	Reimbursable operating expenses	129	132	134
09.02	Reimbursable direct operations	85	89	88
09.10	Reimbursable capital investment: Sales program: Purchase of equipment and leasehold	5	6	6
10.00	Total new obligations	219	227	228
	Budgetary resources available for obligation:			
21.40	Unobligated balance available, start of year	15	14	17
22.00	New budget authority (gross)	218	228	229
23.90	Total budgetary resources available for obligation	233	242	246
23.95	Total new obligations	−219	−227	−228
24.40	Unobligated balance available, end of year	14	17	17
	New budget authority (gross), detail:			
	Mandatory:			
69.00	Offsetting collections (cash)	218	228	229
	Change in unpaid obligations:			
72.40	Unpaid obligations, start of year: Obligated balance, start of year	24	25	23
73.10	Total new obligations	219	227	228
73.20	Total outlays (gross)	−218	−229	−231
74.40	Unpaid obligations, end of year: Obligated balance, end of year	25	23	20
	Outlays (gross), detail:			
86.97	Outlays from new mandatory authority	215	225	226
86.98	Outlays from mandatory balances	3	3	3
87.00	Total outlays (gross)	218	229	231
	Offsets:			
	Against gross budget authority and outlays:			
	Offsetting collections (cash) from:			
88.00	Federal sources	−1	−2	−2
88.40	Non-Federal sources	−217	−226	−227
88.90	Total, offsetting collections (cash)	−218	−228	−229
	Net budget authority and outlays:			
89.00	Budget authority	....	....	....
90.00	Outlays	....	1	2
	Memorandum (non-add) entries:			
92.01	Total investments, start of year: U.S. securities: Par value	38	37	42
92.02	Total investments, end of year: U.S. securities: Par value	37	42	40

The Veterans Canteen Service was established to furnish, at reasonable prices, merchandise and services necessary for the comfort and well-being of veterans in VA medical facilities.

Financing.—Operations will be financed from current revenues.

Object Classification (in millions of dollars)

Identification code 36–4014–0–3–705		1999 actual	2000 est.	2001 est.
	Personnel compensation:			
11.1	Full-time permanent	38	37	38
11.3	Other than full-time permanent	21	25	25
11.9	Total personnel compensation	59	62	63
12.1	Civilian personnel benefits	15	15	15
21.0	Travel and transportation of persons	1	1	1
23.3	Communications, utilities, and miscellaneous charges	1	1	1
25.2	Other services	3	3	3
26.0	Supplies and materials	135	139	139
31.0	Equipment	5	6	6
99.9	Total new obligations	219	227	228

Personnel Summary

Identification code 36–4014–0–3–705	1999 actual	2000 est.	2001 est.
Total compensable workyears:			
2001 Full-time equivalent employment	....	3,025	3,025
2011 Exempt Full-time equivalent employment	3,010	....	....

SPECIAL THERAPEUTIC AND REHABILITATION ACTIVITIES FUND

Program and Financing (in millions of dollars)

Identification code 36–4048–0–3–703	1999 actual	2000 est.	2001 est.
Obligations by program activity:			
09.01 Contracts	24	25	25
09.02 Education and training	2	2	2
09.03 Operating expenses	13	13	13
10.00 Total new obligations	39	40	40
Budgetary resources available for obligation:			
21.40 Unobligated balance available, start of year	12	13	15
22.00 New budget authority (gross)	40	41	42
23.90 Total budgetary resources available for obligation	52	54	57
23.95 Total new obligations	–39	–40	–40
24.40 Unobligated balance available, end of year	13	15	17
New budget authority (gross), detail:			
Mandatory:			
69.00 Offsetting collections (cash)	40	41	42
Change in unpaid obligations:			
72.40 Unpaid obligations, start of year: Obligated balance, start of year	1	2	2
73.10 Total new obligations	39	40	40
73.20 Total outlays (gross)	–38	–39	–40
74.40 Unpaid obligations, end of year: Obligated balance, end of year	2	2	3
Outlays (gross), detail:			
86.97 Outlays from new mandatory authority	38	39	40
Offsets:			
Against gross budget authority and outlays:			
88.40 Offsetting collections (cash) from: Non-Federal sources	–40	–41	–42
Net budget authority and outlays:			
89.00 Budget authority	....	....	....
90.00 Outlays	–2	–2	–2

This revolving fund, established pursuant to the Veterans Omnibus Health Care Act of 1976, Public Law 94–581, provides a mechanism for the furnishing of rehabilitative services to certain veteran beneficiaries who are receiving medical care and treatment from the Department of Veterans Affairs.

Funds to operate the various rehabilitative activities and provide for the therapeutic work for remuneration for patients and members in VA health care facilities are derived from contractual arrangements with private industry or nonprofit entities. Public Law 102–54 authorizes VA to contract with any Federal agency, including VA, and authorizes the Fund to cover the training, education, and travel costs of employees associated with the rehabilitative programs. This is a self-sustaining fund, and therefore no appropriation is required to support these activities.

Statement of Operations (in millions of dollars)

Identification code 36–4048–0–3–703	1998 actual	1999 actual	2000 est.	2001 est.
0101 Revenue	41	40	41	42
0102 Expense	–39	–38	–39	–40
0105 Net income or loss (–)	2	2	2	2

Balance Sheet (in millions of dollars)

Identification code 36–4048–0–3–703	1998 actual	1999 actual	2000 est.	2001 est.
ASSETS:				
Federal assets:				
1101 Fund balances with Treasury	13	15	17	20
Investments in US securities:				
1106 Receivables, net	2	2	1	1
1206 Non-Federal assets: Receivables, net	1	2	2	2
1803 Other Federal assets: Property, plant and equipment, net	1	1	1	1
1999 Total assets	17	20	21	24
LIABILITIES:				
Federal liabilities:				
2101 Accounts payable	1	....	....	....
2105 Other	....	1	1	1
2999 Total liabilities	1	1	1	1
NET POSITION:				
3300 Cumulative results of operations	16	17	20	23
3999 Total net position	16	17	20	23
4999 Total liabilities and net position	17	18	21	24

Object Classification (in millions of dollars)

Identification code 36–4048–0–3–703	1999 actual	2000 est.	2001 est.
23.3 Communications, utilities, and miscellaneous charges	1	1	1
25.2 Other services	36	37	37
26.0 Supplies and materials	1	1	1
31.0 Equipment	1	1	1
99.9 Total new obligations	39	40	40

MEDICAL CENTER RESEARCH ORGANIZATIONS

Program and Financing (in millions of dollars)

Identification code 36–4026–0–3–703	1999 actual	2000 est.	2001 est.
Obligations by program activity:			
09.01 Operating expenses	94	96	99
09.02 Capital investments	11	11	12
10.00 Total new obligations	105	107	111
Budgetary resources available for obligation:			
21.40 Unobligated balance available, start of year	18	18	18
22.00 New budget authority (gross)	105	108	110
23.90 Total budgetary resources available for obligation	123	126	128
23.95 Total new obligations	–105	–107	–111
24.40 Unobligated balance available, end of year	18	18	18
New budget authority (gross), detail:			
Mandatory:			
69.00 Offsetting collections (cash)	105	108	110
Change in unpaid obligations:			
73.10 Total new obligations	105	107	111
73.20 Total outlays (gross)	–105	–108	–110
Outlays (gross), detail:			
86.97 Outlays from new mandatory authority	105	108	110
Offsets:			
Against gross budget authority and outlays:			
Offsetting collections (cash) from:			
88.00 Federal sources	–20	–21	–21
88.40 Non-Federal sources	–85	–87	–89
88.90 Total, offsetting collections (cash)	–105	–108	–110
Net budget authority and outlays:			
89.00 Budget authority	....	....	....
90.00 Outlays	....	....	....

These nonprofit corporations provide a flexible funding mechanism for the conduct of approved research at Depart-

Public enterprise funds—Continued

MEDICAL CENTER RESEARCH ORGANIZATIONS—Continued

ment of Veterans Affairs medical centers. These organizations will derive funds to operate various research activities from Federal and non-Federal sources. No appropriation is required to support these activities.

Object Classification (in millions of dollars)

Identification code 36–4026–0–3–703	1999 actual	2000 est.	2001 est.
21.0 Travel and transportation of persons	1	1	1
25.2 Other services	66	67	68
26.0 Supplies and materials	27	28	30
31.0 Equipment	11	11	12
99.9 Total new obligations	105	107	111

Trust Funds

GENERAL POST FUND, NATIONAL HOMES

(INCLUDING TRANSFER OF FUNDS)

[For the cost of direct loans, $7,000, as authorized by Public Law 102–54, section 8, which shall be transferred from the "General post fund": *Provided*, That such costs, including the cost of modifying such loans, shall be as defined in section 502 of the Congressional Budget Act of 1974, as amended: *Provided further*, That these funds are available to subsidize gross obligations for the principal amount of direct loans not to exceed $70,000.]

[In addition, for administrative expenses to carry out the direct loan programs, $54,000, which shall be transferred from the "General post fund", as authorized by Public Law 102–54, section 8.] *(Departments of Veterans Affairs and Housing and Urban Development, and Independent Agencies Appropriations Act, 2000.)*

Unavailable Collections (in millions of dollars)

Identification code 36–8180–0–7–705	1999 actual	2000 est.	2001 est.
Balance, start of year:			
01.99 Balance, start of year	2	2	1
Receipts:			
02.01 General post fund, national homes, deposits	30	30	30
02.02 General post fund, national homes, interest on investments	3	3	3
02.99 Total receipts	33	33	33
04.00 Total: Balances and collections	35	35	34
Appropriation:			
05.01 General post fund, national homes	−33	−34	−35
07.99 Total balance, end of year	2	1	−1

Program and Financing (in millions of dollars)

Identification code 36–8180–0–7–705	1999 actual	2000 est.	2001 est.
Obligations by program activity:			
00.01 Religious, recreational, and entertainment activities	28	28	29
00.02 Research activities	3	3	3
00.03 Therapeutic residence maintenance	1	1	1
10.00 Total new obligations	32	32	33
Budgetary resources available for obligation:			
21.40 Unobligated balance available, start of year	43	45	48
22.00 New budget authority (gross)	33	34	35
23.90 Total budgetary resources available for obligation	76	79	83
23.95 Total new obligations	−32	−32	−33
24.40 Unobligated balance available, end of year	45	48	48
New budget authority (gross), detail:			
Mandatory:			
60.27 Appropriation (trust fund, indefinite)	33	34	35
Change in unpaid obligations:			
72.40 Unpaid obligations, start of year: Obligated balance, start of year	4	7	10
73.10 Total new obligations	32	32	33
73.20 Total outlays (gross)	−29	−29	−29
74.40 Unpaid obligations, end of year: Obligated balance, end of year	7	10	13
Outlays (gross), detail:			
86.97 Outlays from new mandatory authority	26	27	28
86.98 Outlays from mandatory balances	3	2	3
87.00 Total outlays (gross)	29	29	29
Net budget authority and outlays:			
89.00 Budget authority	33	34	35
90.00 Outlays	29	29	29
Memorandum (non-add) entries:			
92.01 Total investments, start of year: U.S. securities: Par value	45	51	46
92.02 Total investments, end of year: U.S. securities: Par value	51	46	46

This fund consists of: gifts, bequests, and proceeds from the sale of property left in the care of the facilities by former beneficiaries; patients' fund balances; and, proceeds from the sale of effects of beneficiaries who die leaving no heirs or without having otherwise disposed of their estate. Such funds are used to promote the comfort and welfare of veterans at hospitals, nursing homes, and domiciliaries where no general appropriation is available. Public Law 102–54 authorizes compensation work therapy and therapeutic transitional housing and loan programs to be funded from the General Post Fund. In addition, donations from pharmaceutical companies, nonprofit corporations, and individuals to support VA medical research are deposited into this fund. (38 U.S.C. chs. 83 and 85.)

Also under this heading are the activities of the Transitional Housing Loan Program. This program provides loans to nonprofit organizations to assist them in leasing housing units exclusively for use as a transitional group residence for veterans who are in (or who have recently been in) a program for the treatment of substance abuse. The amount of the loan cannot exceed $4,500 for any single residential unit and each loan must be repaid within two years through monthly installments. The total amount of loans outstanding at any time may not exceed $100,000.

Legislation will be proposed to eliminate this program which has had no utilization to date, and for which new programs have filled the need.

Object Classification (in millions of dollars)

Identification code 36–8180–0–7–705	1999 actual	2000 est.	2001 est.
21.0 Travel and transportation of persons	2	2	2
25.2 Other services	13	13	14
26.0 Supplies and materials	13	13	13
31.0 Equipment	3	3	3
32.0 Land and structures	1	1	1
99.9 Total new obligations	32	32	33

VETERANS BENEFITS ADMINISTRATION

Federal Funds

General and special funds:

[COMPENSATION AND PENSIONS]

[For the payment of compensation benefits to or on behalf of veterans and a pilot program for disability examinations as authorized by law (38 U.S.C. 107, chapters 11, 13, 18, 51, 53, 55, and 61); pension benefits to or on behalf of veterans as authorized by law (38 U.S.C. chapters 15, 51, 53, 55, and 61; 92 Stat. 2508); and burial benefits, emergency and other officers' retirement pay, adjusted-service credits and certificates, payment of premiums due on commercial life insurance policies guaranteed under the provisions of Article IV of the Soldiers' and Sailors' Civil Relief Act of 1940, as amended, and for other benefits as authorized by law (38 U.S.C. 107, 1312, 1977, and 2106, chapters 23, 51, 53, 55, and 61; 50 U.S.C. App. 540–548; 43 Stat. 122, 123; 45 Stat. 735; 76 Stat. 1198), $21,568,364,000, to remain available until expended: *Provided*, That not to exceed $17,932,000 of the amount appropriated shall be reimbursed to "General operating expenses" and "Medical care" for necessary expenses in implementing those provisions authorized in the Omnibus Budget Reconciliation Act of 1990, and in the Veterans' Benefits Act of 1992 (38 U.S.C. chapters 51, 53, and 55), the funding source for which is specifically provided as the "Compensation and pensions" appropriation: *Provided further*, That such sums as may be earned on an actual qualifying patient basis, shall be reimbursed to "Medical facilities revolving fund" to augment the funding of individual medical facilities for nursing home care provided to pensioners as authorized.] *(Departments of Veterans Affairs and Housing and Urban Development, and Independent Agencies Appropriations Act, 2000.)*

Activities formerly included in this account are proposed to be financed by three separate appropriation accounts in 2001 and are presented below in the "Compensation", "Pensions", and "Burial benefits and miscellaneous assistance" accounts. Amounts for 1999, 2000, and 2001 are shown on a comparable basis. The following table shows the distribution of the amounts (dollars in millions) appropriated in 1999 and 2000 and requested in 2001.

Distribution of budget authority by account:	*1999 actual*	*2000 est.*	*2001 est.*
Compensation	18,663,234	18,375,028	19,567,055
Pensions	3,084,495	3,063,637	3,066,127
Burial benefits	109,329	129,699	133,094
Distribution of outlays by account:			
Compensation	17,962,565	18,957,135	19,672,390
Pensions	3,075,728	3,054,451	3,065,127
Burial benefits	109,329	129,699	133,094

COMPENSATION

For the payment of compensation benefits to or on behalf of veterans and a pilot program for disability examinations as authorized by law, $19,567,055,000, to remain available until expended, of which not to exceed $1,266,000 shall be reimbursed to "General operating expenses" for necessary expenses, as authorized by chapter 11, 13, 18, 51, 53, 55 and 61 of title 38, United States Code.

For the payment, after June 30 of the current fiscal year, of compensation benefits to or on behalf of veterans as authorized by law, for unanticipated costs incurred for the current fiscal year, such sums as may be necessary. (38 U.S.C. 107, and chapters 11, 13, and 61.)

Program and Financing (in millions of dollars)

Identification code 36–0153–0–1–701		1999 actual	2000 est.	2001 est.
	Obligations by program activity:			
	Compensation:			
	Veterans:			
00.02	World War I	1	1	
00.03	World War II	3,280	3,221	3,086
00.04	Korean conflict	1,231	1,261	1,267
00.05	Vietnam era	5,912	6,398	6,793
00.06	Peacetime service	3,036	3,250	3,430
00.07	Persian Gulf conflict	1,081	1,291	1,434
00.91	Total veterans	14,541	15,422	16,010
	Survivors:			
01.04	World War I	40	34	29
01.05	World War II	1,332	1,379	1,414
01.06	Korean conflict	412	424	433
01.07	Vietnam era	1,103	1,149	1,187
01.08	Peacetime service	450	453	449
01.09	Persian Gulf conflict	75	83	88
01.91	Total survivors	3,412	3,522	3,600
02.01	Clothing allowance	41	40	40
02.93	Total compensation	17,994	18,984	19,650
	Children:			
03.02	Vietnam era	13	9	10
	Other expenses:			
07.01	Payment to general operating expense	1	1	1
07.02	Medical exam pilot program	17	26	28
07.91	Total other expenses	18	27	29
10.00	Total new obligations (object class 42.0)	18,025	19,020	19,689
	Budgetary resources available for obligation:			
21.40	Unobligated balance available, start of year	274	769	122
22.00	New budget authority (gross)	18,663	18,375	19,567
22.21	Unobligated balance transferred to other accounts	−143		
23.90	Total budgetary resources available for obligation	18,794	19,144	19,689
23.95	Total new obligations	−18,025	−19,020	−19,689
24.40	Unobligated balance available, end of year	769	122	
	New budget authority (gross), detail:			
	Mandatory:			
60.00	Appropriation	18,663	18,375	19,567
	Change in unpaid obligations:			
72.40	Unpaid obligations, start of year: Obligated balance, start of year	1,347	1,410	1,474
73.10	Total new obligations	18,025	19,020	19,689
73.20	Total outlays (gross)	−17,963	−18,957	−19,672
74.40	Unpaid obligations, end of year: Obligated balance, end of year	1,410	1,474	1,491
	Outlays (gross), detail:			
86.97	Outlays from new mandatory authority	16,616	17,547	18,198
86.98	Outlays from mandatory balances	1,347	1,410	1,474
87.00	Total outlays (gross)	17,963	18,957	19,672
	Net budget authority and outlays:			
89.00	Budget authority	18,663	18,375	19,567
90.00	Outlays	17,963	18,957	19,672

Summary of Budget Authority and Outlays

(in millions of dollars)

Enacted/requested:	*1999 actual*	*2000 est.*	*2001 est.*
Budget Authority	18,663	18,375	19,567
Outlays	17,963	18,957	19,672
Legislative proposal, not subject to PAYGO:			
Budget Authority			345
Outlays			311
Legislative proposal, subject to PAYGO:			
Budget Authority		1,800	–1,795
Outlays		1,800	–1,795
Total:			
Budget Authority	18,663	20,175	18,117
Outlays	17,963	20,757	18,188

This appropriation provides for the payment of compensation benefits to veterans and survivors. Compensation is paid to veterans for disabilities incurred in or aggravated during active military service. Dependency and Indemnity Compensation is paid to survivors of servicepersons or veterans whose death occurred while on active duty or as a result of service-connected disabilities. Compensation and vocational rehabilitation is provided to the children of Vietnam veterans who were born with the birth defect spina bifida.

The Secretary may pay a clothing allowance to each veteran who uses a prescribed medication for a service-connected skin condition or wears a prosthetic or orthopedic appliance (including a wheelchair) which, in the judgment of the Secretary, tends to damage or tear the clothing of such veteran.

Caseload and cost tables shown below do not include proposed legislation.

AVERAGE NUMBER OF COMPENSATION CASES AND PAYMENTS

Veterans:	*1999 actual*	*2000 est.*	*2001 est.*
Mexican border period	8	7	6
World War I	109	70	40
World War II	558,252	522,560	485,762
Korean conflict	176,605	172,900	169,100
Vietnam era	732,590	739,113	747,305
Peacetime service	555,502	567,860	582,462
Persian Gulf conflict	262,057	288,200	300,400
Total	2,285,123	2,290,710	2,285,075
Average payment per case, per year	$6,382	$6,750	$7,024
Total obligations (in millions)	$14,541	$15,421	$16,010
Children of Vietnam era veterans:			
Children	844	864	864

General and special funds—Continued

COMPENSATION—Continued

AVERAGE NUMBER OF COMPENSATION CASES AND PAYMENTS—Continued

	1999 actual	*2000 est.*	*2001 est.*
Average payment per case, per year	$15	$11	$11
Total obligations (in millions)	$13	$9	$10
Chapter 18 Vocational rehabilitations:			
Rehabilitations	18	29	29
Average payment per case, per year	$628	$225	$225
Total obligations (in millions) [1]	$0	$0	$0

[1] Amounts round to less than $1 million.

Survivors:			
Prior to Spanish-American War	1	1	1
Spanish-American War	17	17	16
Mexican border period	3	1	1
World War I	3,694	3,079	2,565
World War II	116,979	115,258	113,426
Korean conflict	36,601	36,563	36,549
Vietnam era	99,117	100,497	101,895
Peacetime service	41,565	40,697	39,698
Persian Gulf conflict	5,979	6,461	6,721
Total	303,956	302,574	300,872
Average payment per case, per year	$11,227	$11,641	$11,965
Total obligations (in millions)	$3,412	$3,522	$3,600
Clothing allowance:			
Number of veterans	75,604	75,785	75,598
Average payment per case, per year	$543	$528	$528
Total obligations (in millions)	$41	$40	$40

COMPENSATION

(Legislative proposal, not subject to PAYGO)

Program and Financing (in millions of dollars)

Identification code 36–0153–2–1–701		1999 actual	2000 est.	2001 est.
	Obligations by program activity:			
	Compensation:			
	Veterans:			
00.03	World War II			51
00.04	Korean conflict			21
00.05	Vietnam era			111
00.06	Peacetime service			57
00.07	Persian Gulf conflict			24
00.91	Total veterans			264
	Survivors:			
01.04	World War I			1
01.05	World War II			31
01.06	Korean conflict			10
01.07	Vietnam era			26
01.08	Peacetime service			10
01.09	Persian Gulf conflict			2
01.91	Total survivors			80
02.01	Clothing allowance			1
02.93	Total compensation			345
10.00	Total new obligations (object class 42.0)			345
	Budgetary resources available for obligation:			
22.00	New budget authority (gross)			345
23.95	Total new obligations			−345
	New budget authority (gross), detail:			
	Mandatory:			
60.00	Appropriation			345
	Change in unpaid obligations:			
73.10	Total new obligations			345
73.20	Total outlays (gross)			−311
74.40	Unpaid obligations, end of year: Obligated balance, end of year			34
	Outlays (gross), detail:			
86.97	Outlays from new mandatory authority			311
	Net budget authority and outlays:			
89.00	Budget authority			345
90.00	Outlays			311

Legislation will be proposed to provide a cost-of-living adjustment (COLA) to all compensation beneficiaries including spouses and children. This increase, effective December 1, 2000, is expected to be 2.5 percent and cost $345 million in 2001.

Program and Financing (in millions of dollars)

Identification code 36–0153–4–1–701		1999 actual	2000 est.	2001 est.
	Obligations by program activity:			
	Compensation:			
	Veterans:			
00.03	Benefits for Fillipino veterans			5
00.04	Repeal delay of compensation benefits		1,800	−1,800
02.93	Total compensation		1,800	−1,795
10.00	Total new obligations (object class 42.0)		1,800	−1,795
	Budgetary resources available for obligation:			
22.00	New budget authority (gross)		1,800	−1,795
23.95	Total new obligations		−1,800	1,795
	New budget authority (gross), detail:			
	Mandatory:			
60.00	Appropriation		1,800	−1,795
	Change in unpaid obligations:			
73.10	Total new obligations		1,800	−1,795
73.20	Total outlays (gross)		−1,800	1,795
	Outlays (gross), detail:			
86.97	Outlays from new mandatory authority		1,800	−1,795
	Net budget authority and outlays:			
89.00	Budget authority		1,800	−1,795
90.00	Outlays		1,800	−1,795

COMPENSATION

(Legislative proposal, subject to PAYGO)

The Balanced Budget Act of 1997 requires VA to delay the issuing of October 2000 benefit payment from September 29, 2000 to October 2, 2000. Legislation will be proposed to repeal this delay.

Legislation will also be proposed to pay full disability compensation benefits to Filipino veterans and their survivors residing in the U.S. and currently receiving benefits at half the level that U.S. counterparts receive.

The Administration is proposing legislation that will extend a current legal provision due to expire in 2002 which rounds down the annual COLA increase.

PENSIONS

For the payment of pension benefits to or on behalf of veterans as authorized by law, $3,066,127,000, to remain available until expended; of which not to exceed $16,153,000 shall be reimbursed to "General operating expenses" and "Medical care" for necessary expenses as authorized by chapters 51, 53, 55, and 61 of title 38, United States Code; and of which such sums as may be earned on an actual qualifying patient basis, shall be reimbursed to "Medical facilities revolving fund" to augment the funding of individual medical facilities for nursing home care provided to pensioners as authorized by chapter 55 of such title.

For the payment, after June 30 of the current fiscal year of pension benefits to or on behalf of veterans as authorized by law, for unanticipated costs incurred for the current fiscal year, such sums as may be necessary. (38 U.S.C. chapters 15 and 61.)

Program and Financing (in millions of dollars)

Identification code 36–0154–0–1–701	1999 actual	2000 est.	2001 est.
Obligations by program activity:			
Direct program:			
Pensions:			
Veterans:			
04.01 Improved law	2,282	2,299	2,330
04.02 Prior law	50	43	37
04.91 Total veterans	2,332	2,342	2,367
Survivors:			
05.01 Improved law	645	623	608
05.02 Prior law	92	83	74
05.03 Old law	1	1	1
05.91 Total survivors	738	707	683
06.93 Total pensions	3,070	3,049	3,050
Other expenses:			
07.02 Reimbursement to GOE and VHA	15	14	16
08.00 Total direct program	3,085	3,063	3,066
Reimbursable program:			
09.01 Minimum income for widows program		4	4
10.00 Total new obligations	3,085	3,067	3,070
Budgetary resources available for obligation:			
22.00 New budget authority (gross)	3,085	3,067	3,070
23.95 Total new obligations	−3,085	−3,067	−3,070
New budget authority (gross), detail:			
Mandatory:			
60.00 Appropriation	3,085	3,063	3,066
69.00 Offsetting collections (cash)		4	4
70.00 Total new budget authority (gross)	3,085	3,067	3,070
Change in unpaid obligations:			
72.40 Unpaid obligations, start of year: Obligated balance, start of year	278	287	297
73.10 Total new obligations	3,085	3,067	3,070
73.20 Total outlays (gross)	−3,076	−3,057	−3,065
74.40 Unpaid obligations, end of year: Obligated balance, end of year	287	297	302
Outlays (gross), detail:			
86.97 Outlays from new mandatory authority	2,798	2,770	2,769
86.98 Outlays from mandatory balances	278	287	296
87.00 Total outlays (gross)	3,076	3,057	3,065
Offsets:			
Against gross budget authority and outlays:			
88.00 Offsetting collections (cash) from: Federal sources		−4	−4
Net budget authority and outlays:			
89.00 Budget authority	3,085	3,063	3,066
90.00 Outlays	3,076	3,053	3,061

Pension benefits may be paid to veterans or their survivors. A veteran's entitlement is based on active duty service of a specific length (normally 90 days or more) during a designated war period, disabilities considered permanent and total, and countable income below established levels. There is no disability requirement for survivor cases. Income support is provided at established benefit levels.

Veterans who are under the age of 45 and are in receipt of a disability pension will be evaluated to determine whether a vocational goal is reasonably feasible. Those for whom a vocational goal is feasible are eligible for a program of vocational training.

An automatic annual cost-of-living increase comparable to the annual social security increase is provided for those pensioners in the improved program and to parents receiving dependency and indemnity compensation. The increase, effective with payments made on January 1, 2001, is expected to be 2.5 percent.

AVERAGE NUMBER OF PENSION CASES AND PAYMENTS

	1999 actual	2000 est.	2001 est.
Veterans:			
Improved law	352,233	346,349	340,553
Prior law	30,353	25,968	22,236
Old law and service	372	318	271
Total	382,958	372,635	363,060
Average payment per case, per year (in dollars)	$6,088	$6,286	$6,519
Total obligations (in millions)	$2,332	$2,342	$2,367
Survivors:			
Improved law	189,921	184,550	180,094
Prior law	89,577	79,930	71,457
Old law and service	1,952	1,621	1,347
Total	281,450	266,101	252,898
Average payment per case, per year	$2,622	$2,657	$2,701
Total obligations (in millions)	$738	$707	$683
Minimum Income for Widows Program:			
Widows		594	562
Average benefit per case, per year		$6,224	$6,372
Total obligations (in millions)		$4	$4
Vocational training:			
Trainees	8	7	5
Average benefit per year	$4,625	$2,857	$3,000
Total obligations (in millions) [1]			

[1] Amounts round to less than $1 million.

Object Classification (in millions of dollars)

Identification code 36–0154–0–1–701	1999 actual	2000 est.	2001 est.
42.0 Direct obligations: Insurance claims and indemnities	3,085	3,063	3,066
99.0 Reimbursable obligations: Subtotal, reimbursable obligations		4	4
99.9 Total new obligations	3,085	3,067	3,070

The Administration is proposing legislation which will extend a current legal provision due to expire in 2002 which authorizes VA access to certain Internal Revenue Service data for determining eligibility for veterans pension benefits.

BURIAL BENEFITS AND MISCELLANEOUS ASSISTANCE

For the payment of burial benefits, emergency and other officers' retirement pay, adjusted-service credits and certificates, payment of premiums due on commercial life insurance policies guaranteed under Article IV of the Soldiers' and Sailors' Civil Relief Act of 1940, as amended, and for other benefits as authorized by law, $133,094,000, to remain available until expended. (38 U.S.C. 107, 1312, 1977, and 2106, chapters 23, 51, 53, 55, and 61; 50 U.S.C. App. 540–548; 43 Stat. 122, 123; 45 Stat. 735; 76 Stat. 1198.)

Program and Financing (in millions of dollars)

Identification code 36–0155–0–1–701	1999 actual	2000 est.	2001 est.
Obligations by program activity:			
Burial benefits:			
07.01 Burial allowances	35	35	35
07.02 Burial plots	11	11	12
07.03 Service-connected deaths	13	13	13
07.04 Burial flags	12	12	13
07.05 Headstones and markers	24	34	34
07.06 Graveliners	8	9	9
07.07 Pre-placed crypts	3	13	14
07.91 Total burial benefits	106	127	130
08.04 Equal access to justice	3	3	3
10.00 Total new obligations (object class 42.0)	109	130	133
Budgetary resources available for obligation:			
22.00 New budget authority (gross)	109	130	133

General and special funds—Continued

BURIAL BENEFITS AND MISCELLANEOUS ASSISTANCE—Continued

Program and Financing (in millions of dollars)—Continued

Identification code 36–0155–0–1–701	1999 actual	2000 est.	2001 est.
23.95 Total new obligations	–109	–130	–133
New budget authority (gross), detail:			
Mandatory:			
60.00 Appropriation	109	130	133
Change in unpaid obligations:			
73.10 Total new obligations	109	130	133
73.20 Total outlays (gross)	–109	–130	–133
Outlays (gross), detail:			
86.97 Outlays from new mandatory authority	109	130	133
Net budget authority and outlays:			
89.00 Budget authority	109	130	133
90.00 Outlays	109	130	133

Burial benefits.—Provides for: (a) the payment of an allowance of $300 (plus transportation charges where death occurs under VA care) to reimburse, in part, the burial and funeral expense of an eligible deceased veteran; (b) the payment of $150 for a plot allowance where an eligible veteran is not buried in a national cemetery or other cemetery under the jurisdiction of the United States; (c) the payment of a burial allowance up to $1,500 when a veteran dies as the result of service-connected disability; (d) furnishing a flag to drape the casket of each deceased veteran entitled thereto; (e) furnishing a headstone or marker for the grave of a veteran and, in certain cases, eligible dependents; and (f) authority to provide outer burial receptacles in the National Cemetery System.

NUMBER OF BURIAL BENEFITS

	1999 actual	*2000 est.*	*2001 est.*
Burial allowance	86,405	85,300	84,200
Burial plot	75,061	76,800	78,600
Service-connected death	9,901	9,880	9,850
Burial flags	549,018	519,400	526,200
Headstone markers	345,389	342,960	348,840
Headstone allowance	3		
Graveliners	49,738	49,583	50,362
Preplaced crypts	11,571	42,000	46,500

Miscellaneous assistance.—Provides for: (a) payments to emergency officers of World War I and certain officers of the Regular Establishment who have retired because of service-connected disability; (b) payments for claims made pursuant to the provision of the World War Adjusted Compensation Act of 1924, as amended; (c) a special allowance (38 U.S.C. 1312) to dependents of certain veterans who died after December 31, 1956, but who were not fully and currently insured under the Social Security Act; and (d) payments authorized by the Equal Access to Justice Act.

MISCELLANEOUS ASSISTANCE CASELOAD

	1999 actual	*2000 est.*	*2001 est.*
Retired Officers	2	1	1
Special allowance dependents	138	138	138
Equal Access to Justice payments	716	716	716

READJUSTMENT BENEFITS

For the payment of readjustment and rehabilitation benefits to or on behalf of veterans as authorized by 38 U.S.C. chapters 21, 30, 31, 34, 35, 36, 39, 51, 53, 55, and 61, [$1,469,000,000] *$1,634,000,000*, to remain available until expended: *Provided*, That *expenses for rehabilitation program services and assistance which the Secretary is authorized to provide under section 3104(a) of title 38, United States Code, other than under subsection (a)(1), (2), (5) and (11) of that section, shall be charged to the account: Provided further, That* funds shall be available to pay any court order, court award or any compromise settlement arising from litigation involving the vocational training program authorized by section 18 of Public Law 98–77, as amended. *(Departments of Veterans Affairs and Housing and Urban Development, and Independent Agencies Appropriations Act, 2000.)*

Program and Financing (in millions of dollars)

Identification code 36–0137–0–1–702	1999 actual	2000 est.	2001 est.
Obligations by program activity:			
Direct program:			
Education and training:			
00.01 Sons and daughters	121	126	131
00.02 Spouses	14	15	17
00.91 Total education and training	135	141	148
Special assistance to disabled veterans:			
01.01 Vocational rehabilitation	412	417	392
01.02 Housing grants	20	21	21
01.03 Automobiles, adaptive equipment, maintenance and repair	31	31	31
01.91 Total special assistance to disabled veterans	463	469	444
02.01 Work study	34	33	35
02.02 Payments to states	13	13	13
02.03 All-volunteer assistance: Veterans' basic benefits	803	806	1,025
02.04 Reporting fees		4	4
02.91 All-volunteer assistance and other	850	856	1,077
02.93 Total direct program	1,448	1,466	1,669
09.01 Veterans' basic benefits	9	7	4
09.01 Veterans' supplementary benefits	75	76	89
09.01 Reservists benefits	103	102	106
09.02 Reservist supplementary benefits	1	1	1
10.00 Total new obligations	1,636	1,652	1,869
Budgetary resources available for obligation:			
21.40 Unobligated balance available, start of year	165	35	35
22.00 New budget authority (gross)	1,362	1,654	1,834
22.10 Resources available from recoveries of prior year obligations		2	
22.22 Unobligated balance transferred from other accounts	143		
23.90 Total budgetary resources available for obligation	1,670	1,691	1,869
23.95 Total new obligations	–1,636	–1,652	–1,869
23.98 Unobligated balance expiring or withdrawn		–4	
24.40 Unobligated balance available, end of year	35	35	
New budget authority (gross), detail:			
Discretionary:			
40.00 Change for certain vocational rehabilitation activities			–30
Mandatory:			
60.00 Appropriation	1,175	1,469	1,664
69.00 Offsetting collections (cash)	187	185	200
70.00 Total new budget authority (gross)	1,362	1,654	1,834
Change in unpaid obligations:			
72.40 Unpaid obligations, start of year: Obligated balance, start of year	55	59	34
73.10 Total new obligations	1,636	1,652	1,869
73.20 Total outlays (gross)	–1,632	–1,675	–1,889
73.45 Adjustments in unexpired accounts		–2	
74.40 Unpaid obligations, end of year: Obligated balance, end of year	59	34	14
Outlays (gross), detail:			
86.90 Outlays from new discretionary authority			–30
86.97 Outlays from new mandatory authority	1,270	1,582	1,850
86.98 Outlays from mandatory balances	362	94	69
87.00 Total outlays (gross)	1,632	1,675	1,889
Offsets:			
Against gross budget authority and outlays:			
88.00 Offsetting collections (cash) from: Federal sources	–187	–185	–200
Net budget authority and outlays:			
89.00 Budget authority	1,175	1,469	1,634
90.00 Outlays	1,445	1,490	1,689

This appropriation finances educational assistance allowances for certain peacetime veterans and for eligible dependents of those veterans: (a) who died from service-connected causes or have a total and permanent rated service-connected disability; and (b) servicepersons who were captured or missing in action. In addition, certain disabled veterans are provided with vocational rehabilitation, specially adapted housing grants, and automobile grants with the associated approved adaptive equipment. The funding level in 2001 will consist of appropriated funds of $1,634 million.

The following table provides a comparison of trainees and costs for the Dependents Educational Assistance program.

NUMBER OF TRAINEES AND COST

	1999 actual	*2000 est.*	*2001 est.*
Sons and daughters:			
Number of trainees	38,700	40,300	41,900
Average cost per trainee (in dollars)	$3,135	$3,135	$3,135
Total cost (in millions)	$121	$126	$131
Spouses and widow(ers):			
Number of trainees	5,723	6,120	6,630
Average cost per trainee (in dollars)	$2,526	$2,526	$2,526
Total cost (in millions)	$14	$15	$17

Special assistance to disabled veterans.—Service-disabled veterans requiring vocational rehabilitation receive assistance to cover the costs of subsistence, tuition, books, supplies, and equipment.

Specially adapted housing grants, up to a maximum of $43,000, are provided to certain severely disabled veterans. Veterans who suffer service-connected blindness or who have lost the use of both upper extremities can receive up to $8,250.

An allowance, up to a maximum of $8,000, is provided to certain service-disabled veterans and servicepersons toward the purchase price of an automobile. Adaptive equipment and the maintenance and replacement of such equipment is also provided.

The following table shows caseload for this program. Specific performance goals are contained in VA's annual performance plan.

CASELOAD AND AVERAGE COST DATA

	1999 actual	*2000 est.*	*2001 est.*
Total number of trainees	52,284	51,630	50,985
Average cost per trainee	$7,872	$8,071	$7,686
Total cost (in millions)	$412	$417	$392
Housing grants:			
Number of housing grants	770	800	800
Average cost per grant	$26,331	$26,331	$26,331
Total cost (in millions)	$20	$21	$21
Automobiles or other conveyances:			
Number of conveyances	1,023	1,030	1,030
Average cost per conveyance	$7,368	$7,368	$7,368
Total cost (in millions)	$8	$8	$8
Adaptive equipment (including maintenance, repair and installation for automobiles):			
Number of items	8,593	8,344	8,102
Average cost	$2,775	$2,842	$2,910
Total cost (in millions)	$24	$24	$24

Work-Study.—Certain veterans pursuing a program of rehabilitation, education, or training, who are enrolled as a full-time student, can work up to 250 hours per semester, receiving the Federal ($5.15 on 9/1/97) or State minimum wage rate, whichever is higher.

	1999 actual	*2000 est.*	*2001 est.*
Number of contracts	26,543	26,500	27,400
Total cost (in millions)	$34	$33	$35

Payments to States.—State approving agencies are reimbursed for the costs of inspecting, approving, and supervising programs of education and training offered by educational institutions and training establishments in which veterans, dependents, and reservists are enrolled or are about to enter.

All Volunteer Force educational assistance (Montgomery GI Bill).—Public Law 98–525, enacted October 19, 1984, established two new peacetime educational programs: an assistance program for veterans who enter active duty during the period beginning July 1, 1985; and an assistance program for certain members of the Selected Reserve. The Readjustment benefits appropriation pays the basic benefit allowance for the peacetime veterans, except for certain Post-Vietnam Era Veterans Education participants who transferred to the Montgomery GI Bill program. Supplementary educational assistance and the basic benefit allowance for peacetime veterans, Post-Vietnam Era Veterans Education converters, and reservists are financed by payments from the Department of Defense and the Department of Transportation.

The following table shows a caseload and cost comparison for these beneficiaries under existing legislation.

CASELOAD AND AVERAGE COST DATA

	1999 actual	*2000 est.*	*2001 est.*
Veterans:			
Number of trainees	288,052	279,100	309,300
Average cost per trainee	$3,079	$3,192	$3,618
Total cost (in millions)	$887	$891	$1,119
Reservists:			
Number of trainees	73,580	71,300	70,900
Average cost per trainee	$1,395	$1,415	$1,493
Total cost (in millions)	$103	$101	$106

Object Classification (in millions of dollars)

Identification code 36–0137–0–1–702		1999 actual	2000 est.	2001 est.
41.0	Direct obligations: Grants, subsidies, and contributions	1,449	1,467	1,669
99.0	Reimbursable obligations: Subtotal, reimbursable obligations	187	185	200
99.9	Total new obligations	1,636	1,652	1,869

Reinstated Entitlement Program for Survivors Under Public Law 97–377

Program and Financing (in millions of dollars)

Identification code 36–0200–0–1–701		1999 actual	2000 est.	2001 est.
	Obligations by program activity:			
00.01	Return of overpayment	2		
01.00	Total Direct Program	2		
09.01	Reimbursables	18	16	13
09.99	Total reimbursable program	18	16	13
10.00	Total new obligations (object class 42.0)	20	16	13
	Budgetary resources available for obligation:			
21.40	Unobligated balance available, start of year	5	2	
22.00	New budget authority (gross)	19	15	13
23.90	Total budgetary resources available for obligation	24	17	13
23.95	Total new obligations	−20	−16	−13
23.98	Unobligated balance expiring or withdrawn	−2		
24.40	Unobligated balance available, end of year	2		

General and special funds—Continued

REINSTATED ENTITLEMENT PROGRAM FOR SURVIVORS UNDER PUBLIC LAW 97–377—Continued

Program and Financing (in millions of dollars)—Continued

Identification code 36–0200–0–1–701	1999 actual	2000 est.	2001 est.
New budget authority (gross), detail:			
Mandatory:			
69.00 Offsetting collections (cash)	19	15	13
Change in unpaid obligations:			
72.40 Unpaid obligations, start of year: Obligated balance, start of year	2	1	
73.10 Total new obligations	20	16	13
73.20 Total outlays (gross)	−19	−16	−13
73.40 Adjustments in expired accounts (net)	−4		
74.40 Unpaid obligations, end of year: Obligated balance, end of year	1		
Outlays (gross), detail:			
86.97 Outlays from new mandatory authority	19	15	13
86.98 Outlays from mandatory balances		1	
87.00 Total outlays (gross)	19	16	13
Offsets:			
Against gross budget authority and outlays:			
88.00 Offsetting collections (cash) from: Federal sources	−19	−15	−13
Net budget authority and outlays:			
89.00 Budget authority			
90.00 Outlays	1	1	

In accordance with Public Law 97–377, this program restores social security benefits to certain surviving spouses or children of veterans who died of service-connected causes. Financing is provided in the form of offsetting collections from the Department of Defense.

CASELOAD AND AVERAGE COST DATA

	1999 actual	*2000 est.*	*2001 est.*
Spouses	259	225	190
Average benefit	$11,838	$12,844	$13,158
Obligations (in millions)	$3	$3	$2
Children	1,098	970	840
Average benefit	$11,062	$11,969	$12,381
Obligations (in millions)	$12	$12	$10

VETERANS INSURANCE AND INDEMNITIES

For military and naval insurance, national service life insurance, servicemen's indemnities, service-disabled veterans insurance, and veterans mortgage life insurance as authorized by 38 U.S.C. chapter 19; 70 Stat. 887; 72 Stat. 487, **[**$28,670,000**]** *$19,850,000*, to remain available until expended. *(Departments of Veterans Affairs and Housing and Urban Development, and Independent Agencies Appropriations Act, 2000.)*

Program and Financing (in millions of dollars)

Identification code 36–0120–0–1–701	1999 actual	2000 est.	2001 est.
Obligations by program activity:			
Operating expenses:			
00.04 Payment to national service life insurance fund	6	2	1
00.05 Payment to service-disabled veterans insurance fund	34	22	12
00.06 Total operating expenses	9	9	9
10.00 Total new obligations	49	33	22
Budgetary resources available for obligation:			
21.40 Unobligated balance available, start of year	2	2	
22.00 New budget authority (gross)	49	31	22
23.90 Total budgetary resources available for obligation	51	33	22
23.95 Total new obligations	−49	−33	−22
24.40 Unobligated balance available, end of year	2		
New budget authority (gross), detail:			
Mandatory:			
60.00 Appropriation	46	29	20
69.00 Offsetting collections (cash)	2	2	2
70.00 Total new budget authority (gross)	48	31	22
Change in unpaid obligations:			
73.10 Total new obligations	49	33	22
73.20 Total outlays (gross)	−47	−31	−22
Outlays (gross), detail:			
86.97 Outlays from new mandatory authority	47	31	22
Offsets:			
Against gross budget authority and outlays:			
88.40 Offsetting collections (cash) from: VMLI premiums	−2	−2	−2
Net budget authority and outlays:			
89.00 Budget authority	46	29	20
90.00 Outlays	47	31	20

Note.—The Department of Veterans Affairs insurance policy loans are not an extension of Federal credit. Credit schedules previously shown for this account have been discontinued.

Military and naval insurance.—Payments are made to the U.S. Government life insurance fund for certain World War I veterans for extra hazards of military service and for claims on war risk insurance issued to servicemen and veterans of World War I.

National service life insurance.—Payments are made to the national service life insurance fund for certain World War II veterans for: (a) the extra hazards of service; (b) gratuitous insurance granted to certain persons unable to apply for national service life insurance; and (c) death claims on policies under the waiver of a premium while the insured was on active duty.

Payments are also made to policyholders and beneficiaries on nonparticipating national service life insurance policies issued to World War II veterans with service-connected disabilities.

Veterans mortgage life insurance (VMLI).—Payments are made to mortgage holders under this program which provides mortgage protection life insurance to veterans who have received a grant for specially adapted housing due to severe disabilities.

The general decline in the number of policies and the amount of insurance in force is expected to continue in 2001 as indicated in the following table.

POLICIES AND INSURANCE IN FORCE

	1999 actual	*2000 est.*	*2001 est.*
National service life insurance policies: [1]			
Number of policies	0	0	0
Amount of insurance (dollars in millions)	0	0	0
VMLI policies:			
Number of policies	3,518	3,430	3,310
Amount of insurance (dollars in millions)	201	209	207

[1] All of the National Service Life Insurance (NSLI) policies issued to veterans with service-connected disabilities were merged with the National Service Life Insurance Program.

Payment to service-disabled veterans insurance fund.—Payments are made to the service-disabled veterans insurance fund to supplement the premiums and other receipts of the fund in amounts necessary to pay claims on insurance policies issued to veterans with service-connected disabilities.

Object Classification (in millions of dollars)

Identification code 36–0120–0–1–701	1999 actual	2000 est.	2001 est.
41.0 Grants, subsidies, and contributions	40	24	13
42.0 Insurance claims and indemnities	9	9	9
99.9 Total new obligations	49	33	22

Public enterprise funds:

SERVICE-DISABLED VETERANS INSURANCE FUND

Unavailable Collections (in millions of dollars)

Identification code 36–4012–0–3–701	1999 actual	2000 est.	2001 est.
Balance, start of year:			
01.99 Balance, start of year	24	34	22
03.00 Offsetting Collections	10		
04.00 Total: Balances and collections	34	34	22
Appropriation:			
05.01 Service-disabled veterans insurance fund		−12	−18
07.99 Total balance, end of year	34	22	4

Program and Financing (in millions of dollars)

Identification code 36–4012–0–3–701	1999 actual	2000 est.	2001 est.
Obligations by program activity:			
09.01 Capital investment	12	13	12
09.01 Death claims	41	48	47
09.01 All other	8	10	9
10.00 Total new obligations	61	71	68
Budgetary resources available for obligation:			
22.00 New budget authority (gross)	61	71	68
23.95 Total new obligations	−61	−71	−68
New budget authority (gross), detail:			
Mandatory:			
69.00 Offsetting collections (cash)	71	59	50
69.26 Offsetting collections (unavailable balances)	−10	12	18
69.90 Spending authority from offsetting collections (total mandatory)	61	71	68
Change in unpaid obligations:			
72.40 Unpaid obligations, start of year: Obligated balance, start of year	7	7	6
73.10 Total new obligations	61	71	68
73.20 Total outlays (gross)	−61	−72	−68
74.40 Unpaid obligations, end of year: Obligated balance, end of year	7	6	5
Outlays (gross), detail:			
86.97 Outlays from new mandatory authority	54	65	62
86.98 Outlays from mandatory balances	7	7	6
87.00 Total outlays (gross)	61	72	68
Offsets:			
Against gross budget authority and outlays:			
Offsetting collections (cash) from:			
88.00 Federal sources: Payments from VI and I	−34	−22	−12
Non-Federal sources:			
88.40 Interest on loans	−3	−3	−4
88.40 Insurance premiums earned	−23	−24	−24
88.40 Repayments of loans	−11	−10	−10
88.90 Total, offsetting collections (cash)	−71	−59	−50
Net budget authority and outlays:			
89.00 Budget authority	−10	12	18
90.00 Outlays	−11	13	18

This fund finances the payment of claims on nonparticipating life insurance policies issued and currently is open for new issues to veterans having service-connected disabilities. The program provides insurance coverage for service-disabled veterans at standard rates. Administrative expenses are paid from the General operating expenses appropriation.

Operating costs—

Death claims.—Represents payments to designated beneficiaries.

All other.—Represents payments to policyholders who surrender their policies for their cash value and hold endowment policies which have matured.

Capital investment.—A policyholder may borrow up to 94 percent of the value of his policy.

The trend in the number and amount of policies in force is indicated in the following table.

POLICIES AND INSURANCE IN FORCE

	1999 actual	*2000 est.*	*2001 est.*
Number of policies	154,410	151,250	147,870
Insurance in force (dollars in millions)	1,440	1,406	1,372

Financing.—Operations are financed from premiums and other receipts. Additional funds are received by transfer from the veterans' insurance and indemnities appropriation, instead of direct appropriations to this fund.

Operating results and financial condition.—Since premium and other receipts are insufficient to cover operations, the fund continues to project liabilities in excess of assets. The deficit is expected to reach an estimated $454 million by September 30, 2001.

Object Classification (in millions of dollars)

Identification code 36–4012–0–3–701	1999 actual	2000 est.	2001 est.
33.0 Investments and loans	12	13	12
42.0 Insurance claims and indemnities	49	58	56
99.9 Total new obligations	61	71	68

VETERANS REOPENED INSURANCE FUND

Unavailable Collections (in millions of dollars)

Identification code 36–4010–0–3–701	1999 actual	2000 est.	2001 est.
Balance, start of year:			
01.99 Balance, start of year	476	466	452
Appropriation:			
05.01 Veterans reopened insurance fund	−10	−14	−16
07.99 Total balance, end of year	466	452	436

Program and Financing (in millions of dollars)

Identification code 36–4010–0–3–701	1999 actual	2000 est.	2001 est.
Obligations by program activity:			
09.01 Death claims	35	37	38
09.01 Dividends	24	23	22
09.01 All other	8	8	7
09.01 Capital investment: policy loans	5	5	5
10.00 Total new obligations	72	73	72
Budgetary resources available for obligation:			
22.00 New budget authority (gross)	72	73	72
23.95 Total new obligations	−72	−73	−72
New budget authority (gross), detail:			
Mandatory:			
69.00 Offsetting collections (cash)	62	59	56
69.26 Offsetting collections (unavailable balances)	10	14	16
69.90 Spending authority from offsetting collections (total mandatory)	72	73	72
Change in unpaid obligations:			
72.40 Unpaid obligations, start of year: Obligated balance, start of year	41	44	46
73.10 Total new obligations	72	73	72
73.20 Total outlays (gross)	−68	−72	−72
74.40 Unpaid obligations, end of year: Obligated balance, end of year	44	46	46
Outlays (gross), detail:			
86.97 Outlays from new mandatory authority	27	59	56
86.98 Outlays from mandatory balances	41	13	16
87.00 Total outlays (gross)	68	72	72

Public enterprise funds—Continued

VETERANS REOPENED INSURANCE FUND—Continued

Program and Financing (in millions of dollars)—Continued

Identification code 36–4010–0–3–701	1999 actual	2000 est.	2001 est.
Offsets:			
Against gross budget authority and outlays:			
Offsetting collections (cash) from:			
88.00 Federal sources: interest on U.S. securities	–40	–39	–36
Non-Federal sources:			
88.40 Interest on loans	–1	–1	–2
88.40 Insurance premiums earned	–14	–13	–12
88.40 Repayments of loans	–7	–6	–6
88.90 Total, offsetting collections (cash)	–62	–59	–56
Net budget authority and outlays:			
89.00 Budget authority	10	14	16
90.00 Outlays	7	13	16
Memorandum (non-add) entries:			
92.01 Total investments, start of year: U.S. securities: Par value	516	509	496
92.02 Total investments, end of year: U.S. securities: Par value	509	496	481

Note.—The Department of Veterans Affairs insurance policy loans are not an extension of Federal credit. Credit schedules previously shown for this account have been discontinued.

This fund pays claims and administrative costs on participating life insurance policies issued during the period May 1, 1965, through May 2, 1966, under three life insurance programs: (1) service-disabled standard insurance; (2) service-disabled rated insurance; and (3) nonservice disabled insurance availing disabled World War II and Korean conflict veterans an opportunity to acquire life insurance coverage who were no longer eligible for other Government insurance.

Budget program—

Death claims.—Represents payments to designated beneficiaries.

Dividends.—Policyholders participate in the distribution of annual dividends.

All other.—This represents payments to the General operating expenses account for the administrative costs of processing claims and maintaining the accounts, and to those policyholders who: (a) surrender their policies for cash value; (b) hold endowment policies which have matured; and (c) have purchased total disability income coverage and subsequently become disabled.

Policy loans made.—A policyholder may borrow up to 94 percent of the cash value of his policy at an interest rate adjusted to reflect private sector borrowing costs.

The following table reflects the decrease in the number of policies and the amount of insurance in force:

POLICIES AND INSURANCE IN FORCE

	1999 actual	*2000 est.*	*2001 est.*
Number of policies	82,545	77,335	71,944
Insurance in force (dollars in millions)	675	645	614

Financing.—Operations are financed from premiums collected from policyholders and interest on investments. Excess earnings of the fund are now distributed to the policyholders in the form of an annual dividend.

Object Classification (in millions of dollars)

Identification code 36–4010–0–3–701	1999 actual	2000 est.	2001 est.
33.0 Investments and loans	5	5	5
42.0 Insurance claims and indemnities	39	41	42
43.0 Interest and dividends	28	27	25
99.9 Total new obligations	72	73	72

SERVICEMEMBERS' GROUP LIFE INSURANCE FUND

Program and Financing (in millions of dollars)

Identification code 36–4009–0–3–701	1999 actual	2000 est.	2001 est.
Obligations by program activity:			
09.01 Premium payments	401	398	396
09.01 Payment to GOE account	1	1	1
10.00 Total new obligations (object class 41.0)	402	399	397
Budgetary resources available for obligation:			
21.40 Unobligated balance available, start of year	1	1	1
22.00 New budget authority (gross)	402	399	397
23.90 Total budgetary resources available for obligation	403	400	398
23.95 Total new obligations	–402	–399	–397
24.40 Unobligated balance available, end of year	1	1	1
New budget authority (gross), detail:			
Mandatory:			
69.00 Offsetting collections (cash)	402	399	397
Change in unpaid obligations:			
72.40 Unpaid obligations, start of year: Obligated balance, start of year	4	4	4
73.10 Total new obligations	402	399	397
73.20 Total outlays (gross)	–402	–399	–397
74.40 Unpaid obligations, end of year: Obligated balance, end of year	4	4	4
Outlays (gross), detail:			
86.97 Outlays from new mandatory authority	400	395	393
86.98 Outlays from mandatory balances	2	4	4
87.00 Total outlays (gross)	402	399	397
Offsets:			
Against gross budget authority and outlays:			
88.40 Offsetting collections (cash) from: Non-Federal sources: Withholdings from serviceman's pay	–402	–399	–397
Net budget authority and outlays:			
89.00 Budget authority	....	....	....
90.00 Outlays	....	....	....
Memorandum (non-add) entries:			
92.01 Total investments, start of year: U.S. securities: Par value	4	4	4
92.02 Total investments, end of year: U.S. securities: Par value	4	4	4

Budget program.—This fund finances the payment of group life insurance premiums to private insurance companies under the Servicemembers' Group Life Insurance Act of 1965, as amended.

Credit accounts:

VETERANS HOUSING BENEFIT PROGRAM FUND PROGRAM ACCOUNT

(INCLUDING TRANSFER OF FUNDS)

For the cost of direct and guaranteed loans, such sums as may be necessary to carry out the program, as authorized by 38 U.S.C. chapter 37, as amended: *Provided*, That such costs, including the cost of modifying such loans, shall be as defined in section 502 of the Congressional Budget Act of 1974, as amended: *Provided further*, That during fiscal year [2000] *2001*, within the resources available, not to exceed $300,000 in gross obligations for direct loans are authorized for specially adapted housing loans.

In addition, for administrative expenses to carry out the direct and guaranteed loan programs, [$156,958,000] *$166,484,000*, which may be transferred to and merged with the appropriation for "General operating expenses". *(Departments of Veterans Affairs and Housing and Urban Development, and Independent Agencies Appropriations Act, 2000.)*

General Fund Credit Receipt Accounts (in millions of dollars)

Identification code 36–1119–0–1–704	1999 actual	2000 est.	2001 est.
0101 GIF direct loans, downward reestimate of subsidies	619	730	....

Program and Financing (in millions of dollars)

Identification code 36–1119–0–1–704	1999 actual	2000 est.	2001 est.
Obligations by program activity:			
00.01 Direct loan subsidy	127	56	12
00.02 Guaranteed loan subsidy	250	324	154
00.05 Reestimates of direct loan subsidy	107	67	....
00.06 Interest on reestimates of the direct loan subsidy	41	39	....
00.07 Reestimates of guaranteed loan subsidy	691	658	....
00.08 Interest on reestimates of the guaranteed loan subsidy	173	165	....
00.11 Administrative expenses	159	157	166
10.00 Total new obligations	1,548	1,466	332
Budgetary resources available for obligation:			
22.00 New budget authority (gross)	1,548	1,467	332
23.95 Total new obligations	–1,548	–1,466	–332
New budget authority (gross), detail:			
Discretionary:			
40.00 Appropriation (definite)	159	157	166
Mandatory:			
60.05 Appropriation (indefinite)	1,389	1,310	166
70.00 Total new budget authority (gross)	1,548	1,467	332
Change in unpaid obligations:			
72.40 Unpaid obligations, start of year: Obligated balance, start of year	1	....	....
73.10 Total new obligations	1,548	1,466	332
73.20 Total outlays (gross)	–1,549	–1,467	–332
Outlays (gross), detail:			
86.90 Outlays from new discretionary authority	159	157	166
86.97 Outlays from new mandatory authority	1,389	1,310	166
87.00 Total outlays (gross)	1,549	1,467	332
Net budget authority and outlays:			
89.00 Budget authority	1,548	1,467	332
90.00 Outlays	1,549	1,467	332

Summary of Loan Levels, Subsidy Budget Authority and Outlays by Program (in millions of dollars)

Identification code 36–1119–0–1–704	1999 actual	2000 est.	2001 est.
Direct loan levels supportable by subsidy budget authority:			
1150 Direct loan levels	1,648	1,992	649
1159 Total direct loan levels	1,648	1,992	649
Direct loan subsidy (in percent):			
1320 Subsidy rate	7.71	2.79	1.82
1329 Weighted average subsidy rate	7.71	2.79	1.82
Direct loan subsidy budget authority:			
1330 Subsidy budget authority	127	56	12
1339 Total subsidy budget authority	127	56	12
Direct loan subsidy outlays:			
1340 Subsidy outlays	275	162	12
1349 Total subsidy outlays	275	162	12
Guaranteed loan levels supportable by subsidy budget authority:			
2150 Guaranteed loan	43,091	32,116	29,535
2150 Guaranteed loan sales	970	1,988	799
2159 Total loan guarantee levels	44,061	34,104	30,334
Guaranteed loan subsidy (in percent):			
2320 Guaranteed loan subsidy rate	0.46	0.68	0.38
2320 Guaranteed loan sales subsidy rate	5.36	5.34	5.22
2329 Weighted average subsidy rate	0.57	0.95	0.51
Guaranteed loan subsidy budget authority:			
2330 Guaranteed loan budget authority	198	218	112
2330 Guaranteed loan sale budget authority	52	106	42
2339 Total subsidy budget authority	250	324	154
Guaranteed loan subsidy outlays:			
2340 Guaranteed loan subsidy outlay	556	999	112
2340 Guaranteed loan sale subsidy outlay	558	149	42
2349 Total subsidy outlays	1,114	1,148	154
Administrative expense data:			
3510 Budget authority	159	157	166
3590 Outlays from new authority	159	157	166

As required by the Federal Credit Reform Act of 1990, this account records, for this program, the subsidy costs associated with the direct loans obligated and loan guarantees committed in 1992 and beyond, (including modifications of direct loans or loan guarantees that resulted from obligations or commitments in any year) as well as for the administrative expenses of this program. The subsidy amounts are estimated on a net present value basis.

The Federal guaranty for this program protects lenders against the following types of losses: (a) for loans of $45,000, or less, 50 percent of the loan is guaranteed; (b) for loans greater than $45,000, but not more than $56,250, $22,500; (c) for loans more than $56,250 but less than $144,000, the lesser of $36,000 or 40 percent of the loan; or (d) for loans greater than $144,000, the lesser of $50,750 or 25 percent of the loan.

As part of a continuing effort to reduce administrative costs, in addition to restructuring and consolidations, VA is conducting a study of the property management function to determine whether it would be more cost effective to contract out this activity. The study will be complete at the end of 2000.

Object Classification (in millions of dollars)

Identification code 36–1119–0–1–704	1999 actual	2000 est.	2001 est.
25.3 Purchases of goods and services from Government accounts	159	157	166
41.0 Grants, subsidies, and contributions	1,389	1,309	166
99.9 Total new obligations	1,548	1,466	332

Veterans Housing Benefit Program Fund Direct Loan Financing Account

Program and Financing (in millions of dollars)

Identification code 36–4127–0–3–704	1999 actual	2000 est.	2001 est.
Obligations by program activity:			
00.01 Direct loans	1,648	1,992	649
00.02 Interest on Treasury borrowing	234	117	109
00.03 Property sales expense	1	1	2
00.04 Property management/other expense	105	1	1
00.05 Property improvement expense	1	1	1
00.07 Reimburse LSSA for loan sale premium	....	54	....
08.02 Payment of downward reestimate to receipt account	218	80	....
08.04 Payment of excess interest earned to receipt account	76	21	....
10.00 Total new obligations	2,283	2,267	762
Budgetary resources available for obligation:			
21.40 Unobligated balance available, start of year	885	908	....
22.00 New financing authority (gross)	2,307	1,359	762
22.60 Portion applied to repay debt	....	....	....
23.90 Total budgetary resources available for obligation	3,192	2,267	762
23.95 Total new obligations	–2,283	–2,267	–762
24.40 Unobligated balance available, end of year	908	....	....
New financing authority (gross), detail:			
Mandatory:			
67.15 Authority to borrow (indefinite)	1,944	117	109
69.00 Offsetting collections (cash)	1,599	2,376	1,000
69.10 From Federal sources: Change in receivables and unpaid, unfilled orders	1	....	....

Credit accounts—Continued

VETERANS HOUSING BENEFIT PROGRAM FUND DIRECT LOAN FINANCING ACCOUNT—Continued

Program and Financing (in millions of dollars)—Continued

Identification code 36–4127–0–3–704		1999 actual	2000 est.	2001 est.
69.47	Portion applied to repay debt	–1,237	–1,134	–347
69.90	Spending authority from offsetting collections (total mandatory)	363	1,242	653
70.00	Total new financing authority (gross)	2,307	1,359	762
	Change in unpaid obligations:			
	Unpaid obligations, start of year:			
72.40	Obligated balance, start of year	–7	–1	
72.95	Receivables from federal sources		1	1
72.99	Total unpaid obligations, start of year	–7		1
73.10	Total new obligations	2,283	2,267	762
73.20	Total financing disbursements (gross)	–2,277	–2,266	–762
	Unpaid obligations, end of year:			
74.40	Obligated balance, end of year	–1		
74.95	Receivables from federal sources	1	1	1
74.99	Total unpaid obligations, end of year		1	1
87.00	Total financing disbursements (gross)	2,277	2,266	762
	Offsets:			
	Against gross financing authority and financing disbursements:			
	Offsetting collections (cash) from:			
	Federal sources:			
88.00	Federal sources:Payments from program account	–275	–162	–12
88.00	Transfer of loan sales from LSSA		–1,883	–731
88.00	Reimbursement and prepayments from LSSA sales for trustee reserve	–54		
	Non-Federal sources:			
	Non-Federal sources:			
88.40	Repayments of principal	–69	–52	–55
88.40	Proceeds from sale of loans	–949		
88.40	Interest received on loans	–99	–155	–142
88.40	Fees	–27	–42	–11
88.40	Downpayment on Vendee loan/other	–19	–57	–16
88.40	Cash sale of properties	–4	–25	–33
88.40	Other revenue	–103		
88.90	Total, offsetting collections (cash)	–1,599	–2,376	–1,000
	Against gross budget authority only:			
88.95	Change in receivables from program accounts	–1		
	Net financing authority and financing disbursements:			
89.00	Financing authority	707	–1,017	–238
90.00	Financing disbursements	678	–110	–238

Status of Direct Loans (in millions of dollars)

Identification code 36–4127–0–3–704		1999 actual	2000 est.	2001 est.
	Position with respect to appropriations act limitation on obligations:			
1111	Limitation on direct loans			
1131	Direct loan obligations exempt from limitation	1,648	1,992	649
1150	Total direct loan obligations	1,648	1,992	649
	Cumulative balance of direct loans outstanding:			
1210	Outstanding, start of year	1,104	1,588	1,459
1231	Disbursements: Direct loan disbursements	1,648	1,992	649
	Repayments:			
1251	Repayments and prepayments	–69	–52	–55
1253	Proceeds from loan asset sales to the public with recourse		–1,883	–731
	Adjustments:			
1261	Capitalized interest	57		
1262	Discount on loan asset sales to the public or discounted	–979	–105	–67
	Write-offs for default:			
1263	Direct loans	–73	–81	–86
1264	Other adjustments, net	–100		
1290	Outstanding, end of year	1,588	1,459	1,169

As required by the Federal Credit Reform Act of 1990, this non-budgetary account records all cash flows to and from the Government resulting from direct loans obligated in 1992 and beyond (including modifications of direct loans that resulted from obligations in any year). The amounts in this account are a means of financing and are not included in the budget totals.

Balance Sheet (in millions of dollars)

Identification code 36–4127–0–3–704		1998 actual	1999 actual	2000 est.	2001 est.
	ASSETS:				
	Federal assets:				
1101	Fund balances with Treasury	878	1,014	686	760
	Investments in US securities:				
1106	Receivables, net	93			
1206	Non-Federal assets: Receivables, net	26			
	Net value of assets related to post-1991 direct loans receivable:				
1401	Direct loans receivable, net	874	1,588	1,459	1,168
1499	Net present value of assets related to direct loans	874	1,588	1,459	1,168
1901	Other Federal assets: Other assets	5			
1999	Total assets	1,876	2,602	2,145	1,928
	LIABILITIES:				
2104	Federal liabilities: Resources payable to Treasury	1,870	1,944	1,588	1,758
	Non-Federal liabilities:				
2201	Accounts payable	1	103	84	92
2204	Liabilities for loan guarantees	5	555	474	78
2999	Total liabilities	1,876	2,602	2,146	1,928
4999	Total liabilities and net position	1,876	2,602	2,146	1,928

VETERANS HOUSING BENEFIT PROGRAM FUND GUARANTEED LOAN FINANCING ACCOUNT

Program and Financing (in millions of dollars)

Identification code 36–4129–0–3–704		1999 actual	2000 est.	2001 est.
	Obligations by program activity:			
00.01	Acquisition of homes	1,348	2,120	2,429
00.02	Losses on defaulted loans	842	508	530
00.03	Interest on Treasury borrowing	4		
00.04	Reimburse DLFA for loan sales	54	1,883	731
00.05	Payment to trustee reserve	68	19	7
00.06	Reimburse Liquidating for subordination certificate	232	39	37
00.07	Loan Sale Closing Costs	27	28	24
00.09	Property sales expense	86	102	127
00.10	Property management expense	62	46	67
00.11	Property improvement expense	53	41	47
00.12	Loans acquired	239	102	102
08.02	Payment of downward reestimate to receipt account	199	416	
08.04	Payment of excess interest to receipt account	126	213	
10.00	Total new obligations	3,340	5,517	4,101
	Budgetary resources available for obligation:			
21.40	Unobligated balance available, start of year	3,480	4,438	5,011
22.00	New financing authority (gross)	4,299	6,090	3,798
22.60	Portion applied to repay debt			
23.90	Total budgetary resources available for obligation	7,779	10,528	8,809
23.95	Total new obligations	–3,340	–5,517	–4,101
24.40	Unobligated balance available, end of year	4,438	5,011	4,709
	New financing authority (gross), detail:			
	Mandatory:			
67.15	Authority to borrow (indefinite)	57	19	7
	Spending authority from offsetting collections:			
	Discretionary:			
68.00	Offsetting collections (cash)	4,242	6,077	3,799
68.47	Portion applied to repay debt		–6	–8
68.90	Spending authority from offsetting collections (total discretionary)	4,242	6,071	3,791
70.00	Total new financing authority (gross)	4,299	6,090	3,798

	Change in unpaid obligations:			
72.40	Unpaid obligations, start of year: Obligated balance, start of year	139	166	384
73.10	Total new obligations	3,340	5,517	4,101
73.20	Total financing disbursements (gross)	−3,313	−5,299	−4,284
74.40	Unpaid obligations, end of year: Obligated balance, end of year	166	384	201
87.00	Total financing disbursements (gross)	3,313	5,299	4,284
	Offsets:			
	Against gross financing authority and financing disbursements:			
	Offsetting collections (cash) from:			
	Federal sources:			
	Federal sources:			
88.00	Payments from program account	−1,114	−1,148	−154
88.00	Recoveries from DLFA	−1,351	−1,716	−556
88.00	Recoveries from Liquidating acct.	−232	−39	−36
88.25	Interest on uninvested funds	−257	−247	−255
	Non-Federal sources:			
	Non-Federal sources:			
88.40	Funding fees	−613	−625	−577
88.40	Cash sale of properties	−491	−340	−1,460
88.40	Redemption of properties and other	−10	−19	−22
88.40	Refunds from Trust		−6	−7
88.40	Reimburse for prior loan sale premiums	−166	−54	
88.45	Loan sale proceeds	−8	−1,883	−732
88.90	Total, offsetting collections (cash)	−4,242	−6,077	−3,799
	Net financing authority and financing disbursements:			
89.00	Financing authority	57	13	−1
90.00	Financing disbursements	−928	−778	485

Status of Guaranteed Loans (in millions of dollars)

Identification code 36–4129–0–3–704		1999 actual	2000 est.	2001 est.
	Position with respect to appropriations act limitation on commitments:			
2111	Limitation on guaranteed loans made by private lenders			
2131	Guaranteed loan commitments exempt from limitation	43,091	32,116	29,535
2132	Guaranteed loan commitments for loan asset sales with recourse	970	1,988	799
2150	Total guaranteed loan commitments	44,061	34,104	30,334
2199	Guaranteed amount of guaranteed loan commitments	20,361	16,440	14,089
	Cumulative balance of guaranteed loans outstanding:			
2210	Outstanding, start of year	187,388	203,651	206,298
2231	Disbursements of new guaranteed loans	43,091	32,116	29,535
2232	Guarantees of loans sold to the public with recourse	970	1,988	799
2251	Repayments and prepayments	−10,586	−12,220	−13,712
	Adjustments:			
2261	Terminations for default that result in loans receivable	−114	−121	−136
2262	Terminations for default that result in acquisition of property	−1,348	−2,120	−2,429
2263	Terminations for default that result in claim payments	−555	−465	−506
2264	Other adjustments, net	−15,195	−16,531	−16,636
2290	Outstanding, end of year	203,651	206,298	203,213
	Memorandum:			
2299	Guaranteed amount of guaranteed loans outstanding, end of year	71,968	73,775	72,871
	Addendum:			
	Cumulative balance of defaulted guaranteed loans that result in loans receivable:			
2310	Outstanding, start of year	103	197	286
2331	Disbursements for guaranteed loan claims	114	121	136
2351	Repayments of loans receivable	−8	−15	−22
2361	Write-offs of loans receivable	−12	−17	−23
2390	Outstanding, end of year	197	286	377

As required by the Federal Credit Reform Act of 1990, this non-budgetary account records all cash flows to and from the Government resulting from loan guarantees committed in 1992 and beyond, including modifications of guaranteed loans that resulted from commitments in any year, and from the guarantee of loans sold through the securitization programs. The amounts in this account are a means of financing and are not included in the budget totals.

Balance Sheet (in millions of dollars)

Identification code 36–4129–0–3–704		1998 actual	1999 actual	2000 est.	2001 est.
	ASSETS:				
	Federal assets:				
1101	Fund balances with Treasury	3,618	4,603	5,301	4,814
	Investments in US securities:				
1106	Receivables, net	358	823		
	Non-Federal assets:				
1206	Receivables, net		38	41	24
1207	Advances and prepayments	38			
	Net value of assets related to post-1991 acquired defaulted guaranteed loans receivable:				
1501	Defaulted guaranteed loans receivable, gross	1,154	197	286	377
1504	Foreclosed property		966	846	776
1599	Net present value of assets related to defaulted guaranteed loans	1,154	1,163	1,132	1,153
1999	Total assets	5,168	6,627	6,474	5,991
	LIABILITIES:				
	Federal liabilities:				
2101	Accounts payable	24	166	384	201
2105	Other	324	403	413	405
2204	Non-Federal liabilities: Non-federal liabilities	4,820	6,058	5,677	5,385
2999	Total liabilities	5,168	6,627	6,474	5,991
4999	Total liabilities and net position	5,168	6,627	6,474	5,991

VETERANS HOUSING BENEFIT PROGRAM FUND LIQUIDATING ACCOUNT

Program and Financing (in millions of dollars)

Identification code 36–4025–0–3–704		1999 actual	2000 est.	2001 est.
	Obligations by program activity:			
	Capital investments:			
00.01	Acquisition of homes	200	184	175
00.02	Property improvements	17	16	16
00.03	Cash advances	−43	−32	−24
00.04	Acquisition of defaulted guaranteed loans	47	38	36
00.91	Total capital investments	221	206	203
01.00	Total capital investments	221	206	203
	Operating expenses:			
01.02	Property management expense	27	23	22
01.03	Sales expense	24	21	19
01.04	Claims processed	117	102	88
01.05	Other expenses	13	12	12
01.91	Total operating expenses	181	158	141
10.00	Total new obligations (object class 33.0)	402	364	344
	Budgetary resources available for obligation:			
21.40	Unobligated balance available, start of year	41	114	
22.00	New budget authority (gross)	938	514	440
22.40	Capital transfer to general fund	−463	−265	−96
23.90	Total budgetary resources available for obligation	516	363	344
23.95	Total new obligations	−402	−364	−344
24.40	Unobligated balance available, end of year	114		
	New budget authority (gross), detail:			
	Mandatory:			
60.00	Appropriation	154		
69.00	Offsetting collections (cash)	700	514	440
69.10	From Federal sources: Change in receivables and unpaid, unfilled orders	84		
69.90	Spending authority from offsetting collections (total mandatory)	784	514	440
70.00	Total new budget authority (gross)	938	514	440

Credit accounts—Continued

VETERANS HOUSING BENEFIT PROGRAM FUND LIQUIDATING ACCOUNT—Continued

Program and Financing (in millions of dollars)—Continued

Identification code 36–4025–0–3–704		1999 actual	2000 est.	2001 est.
	Change in unpaid obligations:			
	Unpaid obligations, start of year:			
72.40	Obligated balance, start of year	57	45	33
72.95	From Federal sources: Receivables and unpaid, unfilled orders		84	84
72.99	Total unpaid obligations, start of year	57	129	117
73.10	Total new obligations	402	364	344
73.20	Total outlays (gross)	−330	−376	−350
	Unpaid obligations, end of year:			
74.40	Obligated balance, end of year	45	33	27
74.95	From Federal sources: Receivables and unpaid, unfilled orders	84	84	84
74.99	Total unpaid obligations, end of year	129	117	111
	Outlays (gross), detail:			
86.97	Outlays from new mandatory authority	273	376	350
86.98	Outlays from mandatory balances	57		
87.00	Total outlays (gross)	330	376	350
	Offsets:			
	Against gross budget authority and outlays:			
	Offsetting collections (cash) from:			
88.00	Federal sources: Payments from direct loan financing account	−283	−276	−93
	Non-Federal sources:			
	Non-Federal sources:			
88.40	Loan and other repayments	−66	−53	−42
88.40	Sale of homes, cash	−101	−73	−209
88.40	Interest on loans	−59	−47	−38
88.40	Collection of claims (veteran indebtedness)	−49	−40	−33
88.40	Interest—Subordinate Certificates	−204	−38	−36
88.40	Other revenue	62	13	11
88.90	Total, offsetting collections (cash)	−700	−514	−440
	Against gross budget authority only:			
88.95	From Federal sources: Change in receivables and unpaid, unfilled orders	−84		
	Net budget authority and outlays:			
89.00	Budget authority	154		
90.00	Outlays	−371	−138	−90

Status of Direct Loans (in millions of dollars)

Identification code 36–4025–0–3–704		1999 actual	2000 est.	2001 est.
	Cumulative balance of direct loans outstanding:			
1210	Outstanding, start of year	327	317	289
	Disbursements:			
1231	Direct loan disbursements			
1232	Purchase of loans assets from the public	10	9	9
	Repayments:			
1251	Repayments and prepayments	−37	−36	−33
1253	Proceeds from loan asset sales to the public with recourse	−38		
	Write-offs for default:			
1263	Direct loans	−1	−1	−1
1264	Other adjustments, net	56		
1290	Outstanding, end of year	317	289	264

Status of Guaranteed Loans (in millions of dollars)

Identification code 36–4025–0–3–704		1999 actual	2000 est.	2001 est.
	Cumulative balance of guaranteed loans outstanding:			
2210	Outstanding, start of year	23,408	17,638	13,213
2232	Guarantees of loans sold to the public with recourse	38		
2251	Repayments and prepayments	−5,444	−4,101	−3,073
	Adjustments:			
2261	Terminations for default that result in loans receivable	−47	−38	−36
2262	Terminations for default that result in acquisition of property	−200	−184	−175
2263	Terminations for default that result in claim payments	−117	−102	−88
2290	Outstanding, end of year	17,638	13,213	9,841
	Memorandum:			
2299	Guaranteed amount of guaranteed loans outstanding, end of year	7,709	5,775	4,301
	Addendum:			
	Cumulative balance of defaulted guaranteed loans that result in loans receivable:			
2310	Outstanding, start of year	620	574	555
2331	Disbursements for guaranteed loan claims	103	87	75
2351	Repayments of loans receivable	−48	−40	−33
2361	Write-offs of loans receivable	−101	−66	−56
2390	Outstanding, end of year	574	555	541

Statement of Operations (in millions of dollars)

Identification code 36–4025–0–3–704		1998 actual	1999 actual	2000 est.	2001 est.
0101	Revenue	469	393	−6	45
0102	Expense	−552	−168	−146	−129
0105	Net income or loss (−)	−83	225	−152	−84

Balance Sheet (in millions of dollars)

Identification code 36–4025–0–3–704		1998 actual	1999 actual	2000 est.	2001 est.
	ASSETS:				
	Federal assets:				
1101	Fund balances with Treasury	98	160	144	130
	Investments in US securities:				
1106	Investments	9	93	84	75
	Non-Federal assets:				
1201	Investments in non-Federal securities, net	239	239	201	164
1206	Accounts Receivable, net	1	1		
	Net value of assets related to post-1991 direct loans receivable:				
1401	Direct loans receivable, gross	529	377	289	265
1499	Net present value of assets related to direct loans	529	377	289	265
1999	Total assets	876	870	718	634
	LIABILITIES:				
2105	Federal liabilities: Federal liabilities: Other	811	731	548	408
	Non-Federal liabilities:				
2201	Accounts payable	67	149	179	233
2207	Other	−2	−10	−9	−7
2999	Total liabilities	876	870	718	634
4999	Total liabilities and net position	876	870	718	634

As required by the Federal Credit Reform Act of 1990, this account records all cash flows to and from the Government resulting from direct loans obligated and loan guarantees committed prior to 1992. All new activity in this program in 1992 and beyond is recorded in the corresponding program and financing accounts.

MISCELLANEOUS VETERANS HOUSING LOANS PROGRAM ACCOUNT

NATIVE AMERICAN VETERAN HOUSING LOAN PROGRAM ACCOUNT

(INCLUDING TRANSFER OF FUNDS)

For administrative expenses to carry out the direct loan program authorized by 38 U.S.C. chapter 37, subchapter V, as amended, [$520,000] *$532,000*, which may be transferred to and merged with the appropriation for "General operating expenses". *(Departments of Veterans Affairs and Housing and Urban Development, and Independent Agencies Appropriations Act, 2000.)*

GUARANTEED TRANSITIONAL HOUSING LOANS FOR HOMELESS VETERANS PROGRAM ACCOUNT

(INCLUDING TRANSFER OF FUNDS)

[For the cost, as defined in section 13201 of the Budget Enforcement Act of 1990, including the cost of modifying loans, of guaranteed loans as authorized by 38 U.S.C. chapter 37 subchapter VI, $48,250,000, to remain available until expended: *Provided*, That no more than five loans may be guaranteed under this program prior to November 11, 2001: *Provided further*, That no more than 15 loans may be guaranteed under this program: *Provided further*, That the total principal amount of loans guaranteed under this program may not exceed $100,000,000: *Provided further*, That not] *Not* to exceed $750,000 of the amounts appropriated by this Act for "General operating expenses" and "Medical care" may be expended for the administrative expenses to carry out the guaranteed loan program authorized by 38 U.S.C. chapter 37, subchapter VI. *(Departments of Veterans Affairs and Housing and Urban Development, and Independent Agencies Appropriations Act, 2000.)*

Program and Financing (in millions of dollars)

Identification code 36–0128–0–1–704	1999 actual	2000 est.	2001 est.
Obligations by program activity:			
00.02 Guaranteed loan subsidy		10	6
00.09 Administrative expenses	1	1	1
10.00 Total new obligations	1	11	7
Budgetary resources available for obligation:			
21.40 Unobligated balance available, start of year	3	6	41
22.00 New budget authority (gross)	4	46	1
23.90 Total budgetary resources available for obligation	7	52	42
23.95 Total new obligations	−1	−11	−7
24.40 Unobligated balance available, end of year	6	41	35
New budget authority (gross), detail:			
Discretionary:			
40.00 Appropriation	1	1	1
Mandatory:			
60.00 Appropriation	3	45	
70.00 Total new budget authority (gross)	4	46	1
Change in unpaid obligations:			
73.10 Total new obligations	1	11	7
73.20 Total outlays (gross)	−1	−11	−7
Outlays (gross), detail:			
86.90 Outlays from new discretionary authority	1	1	1
86.97 Outlays from new mandatory authority		7	
86.98 Outlays from mandatory balances		3	6
87.00 Total outlays (gross)	1	11	7
Net budget authority and outlays:			
89.00 Budget authority	4	46	1
90.00 Outlays	1	11	7

Summary of Loan Levels, Subsidy Budget Authority and Outlays by Program (in millions of dollars)

Identification code 36–0128–0–1–704	1999 actual	2000 est.	2001 est.
Direct loan levels supportable by subsidy budget authority:			
1150 Direct loan levels	2	2	2
1159 Total direct loan levels	2	2	2
Direct loan subsidy (in percent):			
1320 Subsidy rate	7.72	7.72	7.72
1329 Weighted average subsidy rate	7.72	7.72	7.72
Guaranteed loan levels supportable by subsidy budget authority:			
2150 Loan guarantee levels		20	13
2159 Total loan guarantee levels		20	13
Guaranteed loan subsidy (in percent):			
2320 Subsidy rate	48.25	48.25	48.25
2329 Weighted average subsidy rate	48.25	48.25	48.25
Guaranteed loan subsidy budget authority:			
2330 Subsidy budget authority	3	10	6
2339 Total subsidy budget authority	3	10	6
Guaranteed loan subsidy outlays:			
2340 Subsidy outlays		10	6
2349 Total subsidy outlays		10	6
Administrative expense data:			
3510 Budget authority	1	1	1
3590 Outlays from new authority	1	1	1

All information from the Native American Veterans Housing Loan Program and the Guaranteed Transitional Housing Loans for Homeless Veterans Program is consolidated in a single housing fund called the Miscellaneous Veterans Housing Loans Fund.

The Native American Veterans Housing Loan Program provides direct loans to veterans living on trust lands under 38 U.S.C. chapter 37, section 3761. These loans are available to purchase, construct or improve homes to be occupied as the veteran's residence. The principal amount of a loan under this authority is generally limited to $80,000, except in areas where housing costs are significantly higher than average costs nationwide. This is a pilot program that began in 1993 and is authorized through December 31, 2001.

Public Law 105–368, the "Veterans Benefits Improvement Act of 1998," established a pilot project designed to expand the supply of transitional housing for homeless veterans and to guarantee up to 15 investment loans with a maximum aggregate value of $100 million. Not more than five loans may be guaranteed in the first three years of the program. The project must enforce sobriety standards and provide a wide range of supportive services such as counseling for substance abuse and job readiness skills. Residents will be required to pay a reasonable fee.

As required by the Federal Credit Reform Act of 1990, this account records, for these programs, the subsidy costs associated with the direct loans obligated and the guaranteed loans committed in 1992 and beyond, as well as the administrative expenses of these programs. The subsidy amounts are estimated on a present value basis; the administrative expenses are estimated on a cash basis.

Object Classification (in millions of dollars)

Identification code 36–0128–0–1–704	1999 actual	2000 est.	2001 est.
25.3 Purchases of goods and services from Government accounts	1	1	1
41.0 Grants, subsidies, and contributions		10	6
99.9 Total new obligations	1	11	7

MISCELLANEOUS VETERANS HOUSING LOANS DIRECT LOAN FINANCING ACCOUNT

Program and Financing (in millions of dollars)

Identification code 36–4130–0–3–704	1999 actual	2000 est.	2001 est.
Obligations by program activity:			
00.01 Direct loans	2	2	2
00.02 Interest on Treasury borrowing	2	1	1
10.00 Total new obligations	4	3	3
Budgetary resources available for obligation:			
21.40 Unobligated balance available, start of year	1	1	1
22.00 New financing authority (gross)	4	3	3
23.90 Total budgetary resources available for obligation	5	4	4
23.95 Total new obligations	−4	−3	−3
24.40 Unobligated balance available, end of year	1	1	1

Credit accounts—Continued

MISCELLANEOUS VETERANS HOUSING LOANS DIRECT LOAN FINANCING ACCOUNT—Continued

Program and Financing (in millions of dollars)—Continued

Identification code 36–4130–0–3–704		1999 actual	2000 est.	2001 est.
	New financing authority (gross), detail:			
	Mandatory:			
67.15	Authority to borrow (indefinite)	10	2	2
	Spending authority from offsetting collections:			
	Discretionary:			
68.00	Offsetting collections (cash)	3	2	2
68.47	Portion applied to repay debt	−9	−1	−1
68.90	Spending authority from offsetting collections (total discretionary)	−6	1	1
70.00	Total new financing authority (gross)	4	3	3
	Change in unpaid obligations:			
72.40	Unpaid obligations, start of year: Obligated balance, start of year			−3
73.10	Total new obligations	4	3	3
73.20	Total financing disbursements (gross)	−4	−6	−3
74.40	Unpaid obligations, end of year: Obligated balance, end of year		−3	−3
87.00	Total financing disbursements (gross)	4	6	3
	Offsets:			
	Against gross financing authority and financing disbursements:			
	Offsetting collections (cash) from:			
	Non-Federal sources:			
88.40	Repayment of principal	−2		
88.40	Interest received on loans	−1	−1	−1
88.40	Other revenue		−1	−1
88.90	Total, offsetting collections (cash)	−3	−2	−2
	Net financing authority and financing disbursements:			
89.00	Financing authority	1	1	1
90.00	Financing disbursements	1	4	1

Status of Direct Loans (in millions of dollars)

Identification code 36–4130–0–3–704		1999 actual	2000 est.	2001 est.
	Position with respect to appropriations act limitation on obligations:			
1111	Limitation on direct loans			
1131	Direct loan obligations exempt from limitation	2	2	2
1150	Total direct loan obligations	2	2	2
	Cumulative balance of direct loans outstanding:			
1210	Outstanding, start of year	16	17	19
1231	Disbursements: Direct loan disbursements	2	2	1
1264	Write-offs for default: Other adjustments, net	−1		
1290	Outstanding, end of year	17	19	20

Balance Sheet (in millions of dollars)

Identification code 36–4130–0–3–704		1998 actual	1999 actual	2000 est.	2001 est.
	ASSETS:				
1101	Federal assets: Fund balances with Treasury	1	1	1	1
1206	Non-Federal assets: Receivables, net				1
	Net value of assets related to post-1991 direct loans receivable:				
1401	Direct loans receivable, gross	14	17	19	20
1499	Net present value of assets related to direct loans	14	17	19	20
1999	Total assets	15	18	20	22
	LIABILITIES:				
2104	Federal liabilities: Resources payable to Treasury	15	18	20	22
2999	Total liabilities	15	18	20	22
4999	Total liabilities and net position	15	18	20	22

This account contains information on the Native American Veterans Housing Loan program.

As required by the Federal Credit Reform Act of 1990, this non-budgetary account records all cash flows to and from the Government resulting from direct loans obligation in 1992 and beyond. The amounts in the account are means of financing and are not included in the budget totals.

MISCELLANEOUS VETERANS HOUSING LOANS GUARANTEED LOAN FINANCING ACCOUNT

Program and Financing (in millions of dollars)

Identification code 36–4258–0–3–704		1999 actual	2000 est.	2001 est.
	Budgetary resources available for obligation:			
21.40	Unobligated balance available, start of year			10
22.00	New financing authority (gross)		10	7
23.90	Total budgetary resources available for obligation		10	17
24.40	Unobligated balance available, end of year		10	16
	New financing authority (gross), detail:			
	Discretionary:			
68.00	Spending authority from offsetting collections (gross): Offsetting collections (cash)		10	7
	Offsets:			
	Against gross financing authority and financing disbursements:			
	Offsetting collections (cash) from:			
88.00	Federal Sources: Payments from Program Account		−10	−6
88.25	Interest on uninvested funds			−1
88.90	Total, offsetting collections (cash)		−10	−7
	Net financing authority and financing disbursements:			
89.00	Financing authority			
90.00	Financing disbursements		−10	−7

Status of Guaranteed Loans (in millions of dollars)

Identification code 36–4258–0–3–704		1999 actual	2000 est.	2001 est.
	Position with respect to appropriations act limitation on commitments:			
2111	Limitation on guaranteed loans made by private lenders			
2131	Guaranteed loan commitments exempt from limitation		20	13
2150	Total guaranteed loan commitments		20	13
	Cumulative balance of guaranteed loans outstanding:			
2210	Outstanding, start of year			20
2231	Disbursements of new guaranteed loans		20	13
2251	Repayments and prepayments			−2
2263	Adjustments: Terminations for default that result in claim payments			
2290	Outstanding, end of year		20	31
	Memorandum:			
2299	Guaranteed amount of guaranteed loans outstanding, end of year		18	25

This account contains information on the Guaranteed Transitional Housing Loans for Homeless Veterans program.

As required by the Federal Credit Reform Act of 1990, this non-budgetary account records all cash flows to and from the Government resulting from loan guarantees committed in 1992 and beyond (including modifications of guaranteed loans that resulted from commitments in any year). The amounts in this account are a means of financing and are not included in the budget totals.

Miscellaneous Veterans Programs Loan Fund Program Account

Vocational Rehabilitation Loans Program Account

(INCLUDING TRANSFER OF FUNDS)

For the cost of direct loans, [$57,000] *$52,000*, as authorized by 38 U.S.C. chapter 31, as amended: *Provided*, That such costs, including the cost of modifying such loans, shall be as defined in section 502 of the Congressional Budget Act of 1974, as amended: *Provided further*, That these funds are available to subsidize gross obligations for the principal amount of direct loans not to exceed [$2,531,000] *$2,726,000*.

In addition, for administrative expenses necessary to carry out the direct loan program, [$415,000] *$432,000*, which may be transferred to and merged with the appropriation for "General operating expenses". *(Departments of Veterans Affairs and Housing and Urban Development, and Independent Agencies Appropriations Act, 2000.)*

Education Loan Fund Program Account

(INCLUDING TRANSFER OF FUNDS)

For the cost of direct loans, $1,000, as authorized by 38 U.S.C. 3698, as amended: *Provided*, That such costs, including the cost of modifying such loans, shall be as defined in section 502 of the Congressional Budget Act of 1974, as amended: *Provided further*, That these funds are available to subsidize gross obligations for the principal amount of direct loans not to exceed [$3,000] *$3,400*.

In addition, for administrative expenses necessary to carry out the direct loan program, [$214,000] *$220,000*, which may be transferred to and merged with the appropriation for "General operating expenses". *(Departments of Veterans Affairs and Housing and Urban Development, and Independent Agencies Appropriations Act, 2000.)*

Program and Financing (in millions of dollars)

Identification code 36–0140–0–1–702	1999 actual	2000 est.	2001 est.
Obligations by program activity:			
00.09 Administrative expenses	1	1	1
10.00 Total new obligations (object class 25.3)	1	1	1
Budgetary resources available for obligation:			
21.40 Unobligated balance available, start of year	1	....	....
22.00 New budget authority (gross)	1	1	1
22.40 Capital transfer to general fund	–1	....	....
23.90 Total budgetary resources available for obligation	1	1	1
23.95 Total new obligations	–1	–1	–1
New budget authority (gross), detail:			
Discretionary:			
40.00 Appropriation	1	1	1
Change in unpaid obligations:			
73.10 Total new obligations	1	1	1
73.20 Total outlays (gross)	–1	–1	–1
Outlays (gross), detail:			
86.90 Outlays from new discretionary authority	1	1	1
Net budget authority and outlays:			
89.00 Budget authority	1	1	1
90.00 Outlays	1	1	1

Summary of Loan Levels, Subsidy Budget Authority and Outlays by Program (in millions of dollars)

Identification code 36–0140–0–1–702	1999 actual	2000 est.	2001 est.
Direct loan levels supportable by subsidy budget authority:			
1150 Direct loan levels, vocational rehabilitation	2	3	3
1150 Direct loan levels, education loan	....	....	....
1159 Total direct loan levels	2	3	3
Direct loan subsidy (in percent):			
1320 Voc. Rehab. Loan subsidy rate	2.27	2.23	1.88
1320 Education Loan subsidy rate	32.75	29.68	18.89
1329 Weighted average subsidy rate	36.05	35.02	35.02
Administrative expense data:			
3510 Budget authority	1	1	1
3590 Outlays	1	1	1

All information from the Vocational Rehabilitation Loan Program and Education Loan Fund is consolidated in a single housing fund called the Miscellaneous Veterans Programs Loan Fund.

The Vocational Rehabilitation Loan Fund provides loans of up to $840 (based on indexed Chapter 31 Subsistence allowance rate) to veterans enrolled in a program of vocational rehabilitation who are temporarily in need of additional funds to meet their expenses.

The Education Loan program provides loans of up to $2,500 to dependents of veterans who are eligible for training benefits under chapter 35, title 38, U.S.C. and who are without sufficient funds to meet their education related expenses.

As required by the Federal Credit Reform Act of 1990, this account records, for these programs, the subsidy costs associated with the direct loans obligated in 1992 and beyond, as well as the administrative expenses of these programs. The subsidy amounts are estimated on a present value basis; the administrative expenses are estimated on a cash basis.

Miscellaneous Veterans Programs Loan Fund Direct Loan Financing Account

Program and Financing (in millions of dollars)

Identification code 36–4259–0–3–702	1999 actual	2000 est.	2001 est.
Obligations by program activity:			
00.01 Direct loans	2	2	2
10.00 Total new obligations	2	2	2
Budgetary resources available for obligation:			
22.00 New financing authority (gross)	2	2	2
22.60 Portion applied to repay debt	–2	–2	–2
23.90 Total budgetary resources available for obligation	....	....	....
23.95 Total new obligations	–2	–2	–2
24.40 Unobligated balance available, end of year	....	....	....
New financing authority (gross), detail:			
Mandatory:			
67.15 Authority to borrow (indefinite)	2	2	2
Spending authority from offsetting collections:			
Discretionary:			
68.00 Offsetting collections (cash)	2	2	2
68.47 Portion applied to repay debt	–2	–2	–2
70.00 Total new financing authority (gross)	2	2	2
Change in unpaid obligations:			
73.10 Total new obligations	2	2	2
73.20 Total financing disbursements (gross)	–2	–2	–2
87.00 Total financing disbursements (gross)	2	2	2
Offsets:			
Against gross financing authority and financing disbursements:			
88.40 Offsetting collections (cash) from: Interest on loans	–2	–2	–2
Net financing authority and financing disbursements:			
89.00 Financing authority	....	....	....
90.00 Financing disbursements	....	....	....

Status of Direct Loans (in millions of dollars)

Identification code 36–4259–0–3–702	1999 actual	2000 est.	2001 est.
Position with respect to appropriations act limitation on obligations:			
1111 Limitation on direct loans	....	....	....
1131 Direct loan obligations exempt from limitation	2	3	3
1150 Total direct loan obligations	2	3	3

Credit accounts—Continued

MISCELLANEOUS VETERANS PROGRAMS LOAN FUND DIRECT LOAN FINANCING ACCOUNT—Continued

Status of Direct Loans (in millions of dollars)—Continued

Identification code 36–4259–0–3–702	1999 actual	2000 est.	2001 est.
Cumulative balance of direct loans outstanding:			
1210 Outstanding, start of year	1	1	1
1251 Repayments: Repayments and prepayments	–2	–2	–2
1264 Write-offs for default: Other adjustments, net	2	2	2
1290 Outstanding, end of year	1	1	1

Balance Sheet (in millions of dollars)

Identification code 36–4259–0–3–702	1998 actual	1999 actual	2000 est.	2001 est.
ASSETS:				
Investments in US securities:				
1106 Federal assets: Receivables, net	–1	–1	–1	–1
1401 Net value of assets related to post-1991 direct loans receivable: Direct loans receivable, gross	1	1	1	1

This account contains information on the Vocational Rehabilitation Loan Program and Education Loan Fund.

As required by the Federal Credit Reform Act of 1990, this non-budgetary account records all cash flows to and from the Government resulting from direct loans obligated in 1992 and beyond. The amounts in the account are means of financing and are not included in the budget totals.

Trust Funds

POST-VIETNAM ERA VETERANS EDUCATION ACCOUNT

Unavailable Collections (in millions of dollars)

Identification code 36–8133–0–7–702	1999 actual	2000 est.	2001 est.
Balance, start of year:			
01.99 Balance, start of year	65	66	66
Receipts:			
02.01 Deductions from military pay	3	2	1
02.02 Contributions	3	....	....
02.99 Total receipts	6	2	1
04.00 Total: Balances and collections	71	68	67
Appropriation:			
05.01 Post-Vietnam era veterans education account	–5	–2	–1
05.99 Subtotal appropriation	–5	–2	–1
07.99 Total balance, end of year	66	66	66

Program and Financing (in millions of dollars)

Identification code 36–8133–0–7–702	1999 actual	2000 est.	2001 est.
Obligations by program activity:			
00.01 Payment to post-Vietnam era trainees	4	4	3
00.03 Participant disenrollments	15	15	15
10.00 Total new obligations	19	19	18
Budgetary resources available for obligation:			
21.40 Unobligated balance available, start of year	120	106	88
22.00 New budget authority (gross)	5	2	1
23.90 Total budgetary resources available for obligation	125	108	89
23.95 Total new obligations	–19	–19	–18
24.40 Unobligated balance available, end of year	106	88	72
New budget authority (gross), detail:			
Mandatory:			
60.27 Appropriation (trust fund, indefinite)	20	17	16
60.45 Portion precluded from obligation	–15	–15	–15
62.50 Appropriation (total mandatory)	5	2	1
Change in unpaid obligations:			
72.40 Unpaid obligations, start of year: Obligated balance, start of year	3	2	1
73.10 Total new obligations	19	19	18
73.20 Total outlays (gross)	–20	–20	–18
74.40 Unpaid obligations, end of year: Obligated balance, end of year	2	1	1
Outlays (gross), detail:			
86.97 Outlays from new mandatory authority	5	2	1
86.98 Outlays from mandatory balances	15	18	17
87.00 Total outlays (gross)	20	20	18
Net budget authority and outlays:			
89.00 Budget authority	5	2	1
90.00 Outlays	20	20	18

This account consists of voluntary contributions by eligible servicepersons and matching contributions provided by the Department of Defense. The fund provides educational assistance payments to participants who entered the service after December 31, 1976, and are pursuing training under chapter 32, title 38, U.S.C. Section 901 is a non-contributory program with educational assistance provided by the Department of Defense. Public Law 99–576, enacted October 28, 1986, closed the program permanently for new enrollments effective March 31, 1987. The estimated activity in the fund follows:

CONTRIBUTIONS, PARTICIPANTS, DISENROLLMENTS, REFUNDS AND TRAINEES

[In millions of dollars]

	1999 actual	*2000 est.*	*2001 est.*
Total budget authority	5	2	1
Servicepersons	3	2	1
Transferred from Department of Defense (matching)	2	....	....
Total participants (end of year)	231,785	209,785	189,185
Total contributors (end of year)	2,528	1,800	900
Average contribution per contributor (actual dollars)	1,011	1,011	1,011
Number of disenrollments	22,553	22,000	21,500
Total refunds	15	15	15
Total trainees	3,939	2,800	1,900
Total trainee cost	5	5	4
Average cost per trainee (actual dollars)	928	1,359	1,576
Section 901 trainees	36	40	30

Object Classification (in millions of dollars)

Identification code 36–8133–0–7–702	1999 actual	2000 est.	2001 est.
41.0 Grants, subsidies, and contributions	4	4	3
44.0 Refunds	15	15	15
99.9 Total new obligations	19	19	18

NATIONAL SERVICE LIFE INSURANCE FUND

Unavailable Collections (in millions of dollars)

Identification code 36–8132–0–7–701	1999 actual	2000 est.	2001 est.
Balance, start of year:			
01.99 Balance, start of year	10,675	10,572	10,369
Receipts:			
02.01 Premium and other receipts	204	189	179
02.02 Interest	936	907	879
02.03 Payments from general and special funds	6	2	1
02.99 Total receipts	1,146	1,098	1,059
04.00 Total: Balances and collections	11,821	11,670	11,428
Appropriation:			
05.01 National Service Life Insurance fund	–1,249	–1,301	–1,292
05.99 Subtotal appropriation	–1,249	–1,301	–1,292
07.99 Total balance, end of year	10,572	10,369	10,136

Program and Financing (in millions of dollars)

Identification code 36–8132–0–7–701	1999 actual	2000 est.	2001 est.
Obligations by program activity:			
Direct:			
Operating expenses:			
00.01 Death claims	581	608	623
00.02 Disability claims	16	16	14
00.03 Matured endowments	12	11	7
00.04 Cash surrenders	25	25	26
00.05 Dividends	432	422	395
00.06 Interest paid on dividend credits and deposits	54	56	57
00.07 Payment to general operating expenses	21	22	21
00.91 Total operating expenses	1,141	1,160	1,143
02.01 Capital investment: Policy loans	111	113	110
02.93 Total direct obligations	1,252	1,273	1,253
Reimbursable program:			
09.01 Death claims	269	276	290
09.01 Disability claims	7	7	7
09.01 Matured endowments	5	5	3
09.01 Cash surrenders	11	12	12
09.01 Dividends	200	191	183
09.01 Interest paid on dividend credits and deposits	25	25	26
09.01 Payment to general operating expenses	10	10	10
09.09 Reimbursable program	527	526	531
10.00 Total new obligations	1,779	1,799	1,784
Budgetary resources available for obligation:			
22.00 New budget authority (gross)	1,780	1,798	1,784
23.95 Total new obligations	–1,779	–1,799	–1,784
New budget authority (gross), detail:			
Mandatory:			
60.27 Appropriation (trust fund, indefinite)	1,146	1,098	1,059
69.00 Offsetting collections (cash)	531	497	492
69.26 Offsetting collections (unavailable balances)	103	203	233
69.90 Spending authority from offsetting collections (total mandatory)	634	700	725
70.00 Total new budget authority (gross)	1,780	1,798	1,784
Change in unpaid obligations:			
72.40 Unpaid obligations, start of year: Obligated balance, start of year	1,343	1,390	1,432
73.10 Total new obligations	1,779	1,799	1,784
73.20 Total outlays (gross)	–1,732	–1,756	–1,759
74.40 Unpaid obligations, end of year: Obligated balance, end of year	1,390	1,432	1,459
Outlays (gross), detail:			
86.97 Outlays from new mandatory authority	531	497	491
86.98 Outlays from mandatory balances	1,201	1,259	1,268
87.00 Total outlays (gross)	1,732	1,756	1,759
Offsets:			
Against gross budget authority and outlays:			
Offsetting collections (cash) from:			
Non-Federal sources:			
88.40 Repayments of loans	–127	–125	–123
88.40 Optional settlements	–3	–3	–3
88.40 Net income offsets adjustments	–401	–369	–366
88.90 Total, offsetting collections (cash)	–531	–497	–492
Net budget authority and outlays:			
89.00 Budget authority	1,249	1,301	1,292
90.00 Outlays	1,201	1,259	1,267
Memorandum (non-add) entries:			
92.01 Total investments, start of year: U.S. securities: Par value	12,008	11,954	11,793
92.02 Total investments, end of year: U.S. securities: Par value	11,954	11,793	11,584

Note.—The Department of Veterans Affairs insurance policy loans are not an extension of Federal credit. Credit schedules previously shown for this account have been discontinued.

This fund was established in 1940 for the World War II servicemen's and veterans' insurance program. Over 22 million policies have been issued under this program. Activity of the fund reflects a rising claim workload. The trend in the number and amount of policies in force is shown as follows:

POLICIES AND INSURANCE IN FORCE

	1999 actual	*2000 est.*	*2001 est.*
Number of policies	1,802,101	1,694,591	1,586,821
Insurance in force (dollars in millions)	17,662	16,921	16,177

This fund is operated on a commercial basis to the extent possible. The income of the fund is derived from premium receipts, interest on investments, and payments which are made to the fund from the Veterans insurance and indemnities appropriation.

Assets of the fund, which are largely invested in special interest-bearing Treasury securities and in policy loans, are expected to decrease from $12,825 million as of September 30, 2000 to $12,609 million as of September 30, 2001. The actuarial estimate of policy obligations as of September 30, 2001, total $12,205 million, leaving a balance of $404 million for contingency reserves.

The status of the fund, excluding noncash transactions, is as follows:

Status of Funds (in millions of dollars)

Identification code 36–8132–0–7–701	1999 actual	2000 est.	2001 est.
Unexpended balance, start of year:			
0100 Uninvested balance [unavailable collections]	10	9	9
0101 U.S. Securities: Par value	12,008	11,954	11,793
0199 Total balance, start of year	12,018	11,962	11,801
Cash income during the year:			
Proprietary receipts:			
0220 NSLI fund, premium and other receipts	204	189	179
Intragovernmental transactions:			
0240 NSLI fund,interest	936	907	879
0241 NSLI fund, payments from general and special funds	6	2	1
Offsetting collections:			
0280 NSLI fund, offsetting collections	531	497	492
0299 Total cash income	1,677	1,595	1,551
Cash outgo during year:			
0500 National service life insurance fund	–1,732	–1,756	–1,759
Unexpended balance, end of year:			
0700 Uninvested balance	9	9	9
0701 U.S. Securities: Par value	11,954	11,793	11,584
0799 Total balance, end of year	11,962	11,801	11,595

Object Classification (in millions of dollars)

Identification code 36–8132–0–7–701	1999 actual	2000 est.	2001 est.
Direct obligations:			
33.0 Investments and loans	111	113	110
42.0 Insurance claims and indemnities	634	661	669
43.0 Interest and dividends	507	500	473
99.0 Subtotal, direct obligations	1,252	1,274	1,252
99.0 Reimbursable obligations	527	525	532
99.9 Total new obligations	1,779	1,799	1,784

UNITED STATES GOVERNMENT LIFE INSURANCE FUND

Unavailable Collections (in millions of dollars)

Identification code 36–8150–0–7–701	1999 actual	2000 est.	2001 est.
Balance, start of year:			
01.99 Balance, start of year	66	61	56
Receipts:			
02.01 Interest and profits on investments in public debt securities	6	5	5
04.00 Total: Balances and collections	72	66	61

UNITED STATES GOVERNMENT LIFE INSURANCE FUND—Continued

Unavailable Collections (in millions of dollars)—Continued

Identification code 36–8150–0–7–701	1999 actual	2000 est.	2001 est.
Appropriation:			
05.01 United States government life insurance fund	–11	–10	–10
05.99 Subtotal appropriation	–11	–10	–10
07.99 Total balance, end of year	61	56	51

Program and Financing (in millions of dollars)

Identification code 36–8150–0–7–701	1999 actual	2000 est.	2001 est.
Obligations by program activity:			
Operating expenses:			
00.01 Death claims	4	3	3
00.05 Dividends	2	1	1
00.06 Interest paid on dividend credits and deposits	1	1	1
00.07 Other costs	1	1	1
09.01 Death Claims	2	3	3
09.02 Dividends	2	2	2
09.09 Reimbursable program	4	5	5
10.00 Total new obligations	12	11	11
Budgetary resources available for obligation:			
22.00 New budget authority (gross)	12	11	11
23.95 Total new obligations	–12	–11	–11
New budget authority (gross), detail:			
Mandatory:			
60.27 Appropriation (trust fund, indefinite)	6	5	5
69.00 Offsetting collections (cash)	1	1	1
69.26 Offsetting collections (unavailable balances)	5	5	5
69.90 Spending authority from offsetting collections (total mandatory)	6	6	6
70.00 Total new budget authority (gross)	12	11	11
Change in unpaid obligations:			
72.40 Unpaid obligations, start of year: Obligated balance, start of year	19	19	18
73.10 Total new obligations	12	11	11
73.20 Total outlays (gross)	–12	–13	–13
74.40 Unpaid obligations, end of year: Obligated balance, end of year	19	18	17
Outlays (gross), detail:			
86.97 Outlays from new mandatory authority	2	1	1
86.98 Outlays from mandatory balances	10	11	11
87.00 Total outlays (gross)	12	13	13
Offsets:			
Against gross budget authority and outlays:			
88.40 Offsetting collections (cash) from: Repayments of loans	–1	–1	–1
Net budget authority and outlays:			
89.00 Budget authority	11	10	10
90.00 Outlays	12	12	12
Memorandum (non-add) entries:			
92.01 Total investments, start of year: U.S. securities: Par value	86	80	74
92.02 Total investments, end of year: U.S. securities: Par value	80	74	69

Note.—The Department of Veterans Affairs insurance policy loans are not an extension of Federal credit. Credit schedules previously shown for this account have been discontinued.

This fund was established in 1919 to receive premiums and pay claims on insurance issued under the provisions of the War Risk Insurance Act. The general decline in the activity of the fund is indicated in the following table:

POLICIES AND INSURANCE IN FORCE

	1999 actual	2000 est.	2001 est.
Number of policies	17,973	16,263	14,583
Insurance in force (dollars in millions)	59	53	48

The fund is operated on a commercial basis to the extent possible. The income of the fund is derived from interest on investments and payments from the Veterans insurance and indemnities appropriation. Effective January 1, 1983, premiums were discontinued because reserves held in the fund were adequate to meet future liabilities of the program.

Assets of the fund, which are largely invested in interest-bearing securities and policy loans, are estimated to decrease from $78 million as of September 30, 2000, to $72 million as of September 30, 2001, as an increasing number of policies mature through death or disability. The actuarial evaluation of policy obligations as of September 30, 2001, totals $69 million, leaving a balance of $3 million for contingency reserves.

The status of the fund, excluding noncash transactions, is as follows:

Status of Funds (in millions of dollars)

Identification code 36–8150–0–7–701	1999 actual	2000 est.	2001 est.
Unexpended balance, start of year:			
0101 U.S. Securities: Par value	86	80	74
0199 Total balance, start of year	85	80	74
Cash income during the year:			
Intragovernmental transactions:			
0240 Interest and profits on investments in public debt securities, USGLI, VA	6	5	5
Offsetting collections:			
0280 Offsetting collections, USGLI	1	1	1
0299 Total cash income	7	6	6
Cash outgo during year:			
0500 United States government life insurance fund	–12	–13	–13
Unexpended balance, end of year:			
0701 U.S. Securities: Par value	80	74	69
0799 Total balance, end of year	80	74	68

Object Classification (in millions of dollars)

Identification code 36–8150–0–7–701	1999 actual	2000 est.	2001 est.
Direct obligations:			
42.0 Insurance claims and indemnities	4	4	4
43.0 Interest and dividends	3	2	2
99.0 Subtotal, direct obligations	7	6	6
99.0 Reimbursable obligations	5	5	5
99.9 Total new obligations	12	11	11

VETERANS SPECIAL LIFE INSURANCE FUND

Unavailable Collections (in millions of dollars)

Identification code 36–8455–0–8–701	1999 actual	2000 est.	2001 est.
Balance, start of year:			
01.99 Balance, start of year	1,420	1,439	1,454
03.00 Offsetting Collections	19	....	....
04.00 Total: Balances and collections	1,439	1,439	1,454
Appropriation:			
05.01 Veterans special life insurance fund	....	15	22
07.99 Total balance, end of year	1,439	1,454	1,476

Program and Financing (in millions of dollars)

Identification code 36–8455–0–8–701	1999 actual	2000 est.	2001 est.
Obligations by program activity:			
09.01 Death claims	50	57	58

		1999	2000	2001
09.01	Cash surrenders	5	5	5
09.01	Dividends	101	100	96
09.01	All other	41	36	30
09.01	Payment to general operating expenses account	5	5	5
09.02	Capital investment	18	20	20
10.00	Total new obligations	220	223	214
	Budgetary resources available for obligation:			
22.00	New budget authority (gross)	220	223	214
23.95	Total new obligations	−220	−223	−214
	New budget authority (gross), detail:			
	Mandatory:			
69.00	Offsetting collections (cash)	239	238	236
69.26	Offsetting collections (unavailable balances)		−15	−22
69.90	Spending authority from offsetting collections (total mandatory)	220	223	214
	Change in unpaid obligations:			
72.40	Unpaid obligations, start of year: Obligated balance, start of year	210	229	244
73.10	Total new obligations	220	223	214
73.20	Total outlays (gross)	−201	−207	−199
74.40	Unpaid obligations, end of year: Obligated balance, end of year	229	244	259
	Outlays (gross), detail:			
86.97	Outlays from new mandatory authority	17	17	19
86.98	Outlays from mandatory balances	184	190	180
87.00	Total outlays (gross)	201	207	199
	Offsets:			
	Against gross budget authority and outlays:			
	Offsetting collections (cash) from:			
	Non-Federal sources:			
88.40	Interest on loans	−6	−6	−7
88.40	Insurance premiums earned	−70	−68	−66
88.40	Optional settlements	−1	−1	−1
88.40	Repayments of loans	−17	−18	−19
88.45	Offsetting governmental collections from the public	−145	−145	−143
88.90	Total, offsetting collections (cash)	−239	−238	−236
	Net budget authority and outlays:			
89.00	Budget authority	−19	−15	−22
90.00	Outlays	−37	−31	−37
	Memorandum (non-add) entries:			
92.01	Total investments, start of year: U.S. securities: Par value	1,628	1,666	1,696
92.02	Total investments, end of year: U.S. securities: Par value	1,666	1,696	1,733

Note.—The Department of Veterans Affairs insurance policy loans are not an extension of Federal credit. Credit schedules previously shown for this account have been discontinued.

This fund finances the payment of claims on life insurance policies issued before January 3, 1957, to veterans who served in the Armed Forces subsequent to April 1, 1951. No new policies can be issued. Policyholders may elect to purchase total disability income coverage with the payment of additional premiums.

Budget program—

Death claims.—Represents payments to designated beneficiaries.

Cash surrenders.—A policyholder may terminate his or her insurance by cashing in the policy for its cash value.

Dividends.—Policyholders participate in the distribution of annual dividends.

All other.—Classified in this category are payments to policyholders who: (a) hold endowment policies which have matured; (b) have purchased total disability income coverage and subsequently become disabled; and (c) are paid interest on dividend credits and deposits.

The following table reflects the decrease in the number of policies and the amounts of insurance in force:

POLICIES AND INSURANCE IN FORCE

	1999 actual	*2000 est.*	*2001 est.*
Number of policies	233,893	228,143	222,393
Insurance in force (dollars in millions)	2,699	2,668	2,630

Financing.—Payments from this fund are financed primarily from premium receipts and interest on investments.

Operating results and financial condition.—Favorable mortality experience on insurance written against this fund has kept death claim payments well below the amount of premium and interest receipts, thereby producing an annual increase in the total revenue of the fund. Excess earnings of the fund are now distributed to the policyholders in the form of an annual dividend.

Object Classification (in millions of dollars)

Identification code 36–8455–0–8–701		1999 actual	2000 est.	2001 est.
33.0	Investments and loans	19	20	20
42.0	Insurance claims and indemnities	82	84	79
43.0	Interest and dividends	119	119	115
99.9	Total new obligations	220	223	214

CONSTRUCTION

Federal Funds

General and special funds:

CONSTRUCTION, MAJOR PROJECTS

For constructing, altering, extending and improving any of the facilities under the jurisdiction or for the use of the Department of Veterans Affairs, or for any of the purposes set forth in sections 316, 2404, 2406, 8102, 8103, 8106, 8108, 8109, 8110, and 8122 of title 38, United States Code, including planning, architectural and engineering services, maintenance or guarantee period services costs associated with equipment guarantees provided under the project, services of claims analysts, offsite utility and storm drainage system construction costs, and site acquisition, where the estimated cost of a project is $4,000,000 or more or where funds for a project were made available in a previous major project appropriation, **[**$65,140,000**]** ***$62,140,000***, to remain available until expended: *Provided*, That except for advance planning of projects (including market-based assessments of health care needs which may or may not lead to capital investments) funded through the advance planning fund and the design of projects funded through the design fund, none of these funds shall be used for any project which has not been considered and approved by the Congress in the budgetary process: *Provided further*, That funds provided in this appropriation for fiscal year **[**2000**]** *2001*, for each approved project, shall be obligated: (1) by the awarding of a construction documents contract by September 30, **[**2000**]** *2001*; and (2) by the awarding of a construction contract by September 30, **[**2001**]** *2002*: *Provided further*, That the Secretary shall promptly report in writing to the Committees on Appropriations any approved major construction project in which obligations are not incurred within the time limitations established above: *Provided further*, That no funds from any other account except the "Parking revolving fund", may be obligated for constructing, altering, extending, or improving a project which was approved in the budget process and funded in this account until **[**1**]** *one* year after substantial completion and beneficial occupancy by the Department of Veterans Affairs of the project or any part thereof with respect to that part only. *(Departments of Veterans Affairs and Housing and Urban Development, and Independent Agencies Appropriations Act, 2000.)*

Program and Financing (in millions of dollars)

Identification code 36–0110–0–1–703		1999 actual	2000 est.	2001 est.
	Obligations by program activity:			
00.01	Replacement and modernization	30	32	27
00.02	Nursing home care	1	1	1
00.06	Other improvements	136	130	140
00.07	National cemeteries	3	21	27
00.08	Replacement or renovation of regional offices		1	3
10.00	Total new obligations	170	185	198

General and special funds—Continued

CONSTRUCTION, MAJOR PROJECTS—Continued

Program and Financing (in millions of dollars)—Continued

Identification code 36–0110–0–1–703	1999 actual	2000 est.	2001 est.
Budgetary resources available for obligation:			
21.40 Unobligated balance available, start of year	592	565	445
22.00 New budget authority (gross)	142	65	62
23.90 Total budgetary resources available for obligation	734	630	507
23.95 Total new obligations	–170	–185	–198
24.40 Unobligated balance available, end of year	565	445	309
New budget authority (gross), detail:			
Discretionary:			
40.00 Appropriation	142	65	62
Change in unpaid obligations:			
72.40 Unpaid obligations, start of year: Obligated balance, start of year	378	258	259
73.10 Total new obligations	170	185	198
73.20 Total outlays (gross)	–290	–184	–142
74.40 Unpaid obligations, end of year: Obligated balance, end of year	258	259	315
Outlays (gross), detail:			
86.90 Outlays from new discretionary authority	8	3	3
86.93 Outlays from discretionary balances	282	181	139
87.00 Total outlays (gross)	290	184	142
Net budget authority and outlays:			
89.00 Budget authority	142	65	62
90.00 Outlays	290	184	142

Funds are requested for a seismic corrections project at Palo Alto, CA and a gravesite development project at Ft. Logan National Cemetery.

Additional funds are provided to remove asbestos from Department-owned buildings and to support advanced planning (including market based assessments of health care needs) and design activities.

Budget Authority by Program Activity

[In millions of dollars]

	1999 actual	*2000 est.*	*2001 est.*
Clinical improvements		30,500	
Ambulatory care	46,000		
Seismic corrections	73,200		26,600
Patient environment		12,700	
Other departments	42,560	29,685	37,675
Design fund offset	(1,760)	(1,245)	(2,135)
Less rescission	(13)		
Reprogramming	(17,700)	(6,500)	
Total budget authority	142,287	65,140	62,140

Object Classification (in millions of dollars)

Identification code 36–0110–0–1–703	1999 actual	2000 est.	2001 est.
11.3 Personnel compensation: Other than full-time permanent	2	2	2
25.2 Other services	42	45	43
26.0 Supplies and materials	2	2	3
31.0 Equipment	1	2	2
32.0 Land and structures	123	134	148
99.9 Total new obligations	170	185	198

Personnel Summary

Identification code 36–0110–0–1–703	1999 actual	2000 est.	2001 est.
1001 Total compensable workyears: Full-time equivalent employment	34	50	50

CONSTRUCTION, MINOR PROJECTS

For constructing, altering, extending, and improving any of the facilities under the jurisdiction or for the use of the Department of Veterans Affairs, including planning, architectural and engineering services, maintenance or guarantee period services costs associated with equipment guarantees provided under the project, services of claims analysts, offsite utility and storm drainage system construction costs, and site acquisition, or for any of the purposes set forth in sections 316, 2404, 2406, 8102, 8103, 8106, 8108, 8109, 8110, [and] 8122, *and 8162* of title 38, United States Code, where the estimated cost of a project is less than $4,000,000, [$160,000,000] *$162,000,000*, to remain available until expended, along with unobligated balances of previous "Construction, minor projects" appropriations which are hereby made available for any project where the estimated cost is less than $4,000,000: *Provided*, That funds in this account shall be available for: (1) repairs to any of the nonmedical facilities under the jurisdiction or for the use of the department which are necessary because of loss or damage caused by any natural disaster or catastrophe; and (2) temporary measures necessary to prevent or to minimize further loss by such causes. *(Departments of Veterans Affairs and Housing and Urban Development, and Independent Agencies Appropriations Act, 2000.)*

Program and Financing (in millions of dollars)

Identification code 36–0111–0–1–703	1999 actual	2000 est.	2001 est.
Obligations by program activity:			
00.01 Medical programs	159	144	132
00.06 National cemeteries	18	22	18
00.07 Staff Offices	3	5	5
00.08 Replacement or renovation of regional offices	4	5	8
10.00 Total new obligations	184	176	163
Budgetary resources available for obligation:			
21.40 Unobligated balance available, start of year	53	44	28
22.00 New budget authority (gross)	175	160	162
23.90 Total budgetary resources available for obligation	228	204	190
23.95 Total new obligations	–184	–176	–163
24.40 Unobligated balance available, end of year	44	28	27
New budget authority (gross), detail:			
Discretionary:			
40.00 Appropriation	175	160	162
Change in unpaid obligations:			
72.40 Unpaid obligations, start of year: Obligated balance, start of year	223	231	236
73.10 Total new obligations	184	176	163
73.20 Total outlays (gross)	–176	–171	–166
74.40 Unpaid obligations, end of year: Obligated balance, end of year	231	236	233
Outlays (gross), detail:			
86.90 Outlays from new discretionary authority	46	42	42
86.93 Outlays from discretionary balances	130	129	124
87.00 Total outlays (gross)	176	171	166
Net budget authority and outlays:			
89.00 Budget authority	175	160	162
90.00 Outlays	176	171	166

The Construction, Minor Projects appropriation, which funds construction projects costing less than $4 million, is used to reduce risks to patient life and safety, correct code deficiencies, improve ambulatory care settings, and improve national cemeteries.

Object Classification (in millions of dollars)

Identification code 36–0111–0–1–703	1999 actual	2000 est.	2001 est.
11.3 Personnel compensation: Other than full-time permanent	2	2	2
25.2 Other services	19	17	14
26.0 Supplies and materials	1	1	1
32.0 Land and structures	162	156	146

99.9	Total new obligations	184	176	163

Personnel Summary

Identification code 36–0111–0–1–703		1999 actual	2000 est.	2001 est.
1001	Total compensable workyears: Full-time equivalent employment	45	80	80

GRANTS FOR CONSTRUCTION OF STATE EXTENDED CARE FACILITIES

For grants to assist States to acquire or construct State nursing home and domiciliary facilities and to remodel, modify or alter existing hospital, nursing home and domiciliary facilities in State homes, for furnishing care to veterans as authorized by 38 U.S.C. 8131–8137, [$90,000,000] *$60,000,000*, to remain available until expended. *(Departments of Veterans Affairs and Housing and Urban Development, and Independent Agencies Appropriations Act, 2000.)*

Program and Financing (in millions of dollars)

Identification code 36–0181–0–1–703		1999 actual	2000 est.	2001 est.
	Obligations by program activity:			
00.01	Grants to States	37	143	60
10.00	Total new obligations (object class 41.0)	37	143	60
	Budgetary resources available for obligation:			
21.40	Unobligated balance available, start of year		53	
22.00	New budget authority (gross)	90	90	60
23.90	Total budgetary resources available for obligation	90	143	60
23.95	Total new obligations	−37	−143	−60
24.40	Unobligated balance available, end of year	53		
	New budget authority (gross), detail:			
	Discretionary:			
40.00	Appropriation	90	90	60
	Change in unpaid obligations:			
72.40	Unpaid obligations, start of year: Obligated balance, start of year	155	150	229
73.10	Total new obligations	37	143	60
73.20	Total outlays (gross)	−40	−64	−85
73.40	Adjustments in expired accounts (net)	−2		
74.40	Unpaid obligations, end of year: Obligated balance, end of year	150	229	204
	Outlays (gross), detail:			
86.93	Outlays from discretionary balances	40	64	85
	Net budget authority and outlays:			
89.00	Budget authority	90	90	60
90.00	Outlays	40	64	85

In 2000, the Department plans to obligate $143 million to acquire or construct State home facilities for furnishing domiciliary or nursing home care to veterans and expand, remodel, or alter existing buildings for furnishing domiciliary, nursing home, or hospital care to veterans.

GRANTS FOR THE CONSTRUCTION OF STATE VETERANS CEMETERIES

For grants to aid States in establishing, expanding, or improving State veteran cemeteries as authorized by 38 U.S.C. 2408, $25,000,000, to remain available until expended. *(Departments of Veterans Affairs and Housing and Urban Development, and Independent Agencies Appropriations Act, 2000.)*

Program and Financing (in millions of dollars)

Identification code 36–0183–0–1–705		1999 actual	2000 est.	2001 est.
	Obligations by program activity:			
00.01	Grants to States	5	34	25
10.00	Total new obligations (object class 41.0)	5	34	25
	Budgetary resources available for obligation:			
21.40	Unobligated balance available, start of year	4	9	
22.00	New budget authority (gross)	10	25	25
23.90	Total budgetary resources available for obligation	14	34	25
23.95	Total new obligations	−5	−34	−25
24.40	Unobligated balance available, end of year	9		
	New budget authority (gross), detail:			
	Discretionary:			
40.00	Appropriation	10	25	25
	Change in unpaid obligations:			
72.40	Unpaid obligations, start of year: Obligated balance, start of year	16	15	43
73.10	Total new obligations	5	34	25
73.20	Total outlays (gross)	−4	−8	−17
73.40	Adjustments in expired accounts (net)	−2		
74.40	Unpaid obligations, end of year: Obligated balance, end of year	15	43	51
	Outlays (gross), detail:			
86.93	Outlays from discretionary balances	4	8	17
	Net budget authority and outlays:			
89.00	Budget authority	10	25	25
90.00	Outlays	4	8	17

This program enables the Department to assist States in establishing, expanding, or improving State-operated veterans cemeteries.

Public enterprise funds:

PARKING REVOLVING FUND

For the parking revolving fund as authorized by 38 U.S.C. 8109, income from fees collected, to remain available until expended, which shall be available for all authorized expenses except operations and maintenance costs, which will be funded from "Medical care". *(Departments of Veterans Affairs and Housing and Urban Development, and Independent Agencies Appropriations Act, 2000.)*

Program and Financing (in millions of dollars)

Identification code 36–4538–0–3–703		1999 actual	2000 est.	2001 est.
	Obligations by program activity:			
00.01	Operating expenses: parking leases	2	2	2
09.01	Capital Investment: parking construction program	16	3	6
10.00	Total new obligations	18	5	8
	Budgetary resources available for obligation:			
21.40	Unobligated balance available, start of year	30	14	12
22.00	New budget authority (gross)	3	3	3
23.90	Total budgetary resources available for obligation	33	17	15
23.95	Total new obligations	−18	−5	−8
24.40	Unobligated balance available, end of year	14	12	7
	New budget authority (gross), detail:			
	Discretionary:			
68.00	Spending authority from offsetting collections (gross): Offsetting collections (cash)	3	3	3
	Change in unpaid obligations:			
72.40	Unpaid obligations, start of year: Obligated balance, start of year	12	16	14
73.10	Total new obligations	18	5	8
73.20	Total outlays (gross)	−15	−7	−7
74.40	Unpaid obligations, end of year: Obligated balance, end of year	16	14	15
	Outlays (gross), detail:			
86.90	Outlays from new discretionary authority	3	3	3
86.93	Outlays from discretionary balances	12	4	4
87.00	Total outlays (gross)	15	7	7

Public enterprise funds—Continued

PARKING REVOLVING FUND—Continued

Program and Financing (in millions of dollars)—Continued

Identification code 36–4538–0–3–703	1999 actual	2000 est.	2001 est.
Offsets:			
Against gross budget authority and outlays:			
88.40 Offsetting collections (cash) from: Non-Federal sources	–3	–3	–3
Net budget authority and outlays:			
89.00 Budget authority			
90.00 Outlays	12	4	4

The Parking Revolving Fund provides funding for the construction and lease of parking facilities at various medical centers.

Object Classification (in millions of dollars)

Identification code 36–4538–0–3–703	1999 actual	2000 est.	2001 est.
23.2 Direct obligations: Rental payments to others	2	2	2
32.0 Reimbursable obligations: Land and structures	16	3	6
99.9 Total new obligations	18	5	8

PERSHING HALL REVOLVING FUND

Program and Financing (in millions of dollars)

Identification code 36–4018–0–3–705	1999 actual	2000 est.	2001 est.
Budgetary resources available for obligation:			
21.40 Unobligated balance available, start of year	1	1	1
23.95 Total new obligations			
24.40 Unobligated balance available, end of year	1	1	1
Net budget authority and outlays:			
89.00 Budget authority			
90.00 Outlays			

The Pershing Hall Revolving Fund was created to operate and manage Pershing Hall, an asset of the United States, located in Paris, France. All operating expenses for Pershing Hall are borne by the Revolving Fund and all receipts generated by the operation of Pershing Hall are deposited in the Revolving Fund.

To facilitate account restructuring and consolidation, the Pershing Hall Revolving Fund also reflects budget information for the Nursing Home Revolving Fund. The Nursing Home Revolving Fund provides for the construction, alteration, and acquisition (including site acquisition) of nursing home facilities and is available only as provided in appropriations acts.

DEPARTMENTAL ADMINISTRATION

GENERAL OPERATING EXPENSES

For necessary operating expenses of the Department of Veterans Affairs, not otherwise provided for, including uniforms or allowances therefor; not to exceed [$25,000] *$35,000* for official reception and representation expenses; hire of passenger motor vehicles; and reimbursement of the General Services Administration for security guard services, and the Department of Defense for the cost of overseas employee mail, [$912,594,000] *$1,061,854,000*: *Provided*, That *expenses for services and assistance authorized under 38 U.S.C. 3104(a)(1), (2), (5) and (11) that the Secretary determines are necessary to enable entitled veterans (1) to the maximum extent feasible, to become employable and to obtain and maintain suitable employment; or (2) to achieve maximum independence in daily living, shall be charged to this account: Provided further, That* of the funds made available under this heading, not to exceed [$45,600,000] *$53,093,000* shall be available until September 30, [2001] *2002*: *Provided further*, That funds under this heading shall be available to administer the Service Members Occupational Conversion and Training Act. *(Departments of Veterans Affairs and Housing and Urban Development, and Independent Agencies Appropriations Act, 2000.)*

Program and Financing (in millions of dollars)

Identification code 36–0151–0–1–705	1999 actual	2000 est.	2001 est.
Obligations by program activity:			
Direct program:			
Veterans benefits:			
00.04 Compensation and pensions	510	555	645
00.05 Education	68	65	69
00.06 Vocational rehabilitation and counseling	72	82	118
00.09 Insurance[1]	3	3	3
00.11 General administration	227	236	227
01.00 Total Direct Program	880	941	1,062
Reimbursable program:			
09.01 Administration of housing credit programs	160	157	167
09.02 Administration of other credit programs	1	1	1
09.03 Administration of insurance programs	35	37	37
09.04 Other reimbursable programs	99	120	91
09.99 Total reimbursable program	295	315	296
10.00 Total new obligations	1,175	1,256	1,358
Budgetary resources available for obligation:			
22.00 New budget authority (gross)	1,177	1,256	1,358
23.95 Total new obligations	–1,175	–1,256	–1,358
23.98 Unobligated balance expiring or withdrawn	–2		
New budget authority (gross), detail:			
Discretionary:			
Appropriation:			
40.00 Appropriation	856	913	1,032
40.00 Discretionary appropriation for certain vocational rehabilitation and employment activities			30
40.75 Reduction pursuant to P.L. 106–51	–2		
42.00 Transferred from other accounts	28	28	
43.00 Appropriation (total discretionary)	882	941	1,062
68.00 Spending authority from offsetting collections: Offsetting collections (cash)	295	315	296
70.00 Total new budget authority (gross)	1,177	1,256	1,358
Change in unpaid obligations:			
72.40 Unpaid obligations, start of year: Obligated balance, start of year	136	142	139
73.10 Total new obligations	1,175	1,256	1,358
73.20 Total outlays (gross)	–1,161	–1,261	–1,369
73.40 Adjustments in expired accounts (net)	–8		
74.40 Unpaid obligations, end of year: Obligated balance, end of year	142	139	127
Outlays (gross), detail:			
86.90 Outlays from new discretionary authority	1,034	1,118	1,231
86.93 Outlays from discretionary balances	128	142	138
87.00 Total outlays (gross)	1,161	1,261	1,369
Offsets:			
Against gross budget authority and outlays:			
88.00 Offsetting collections (cash) from: Federal sources	–295	–315	–296
Net budget authority and outlays:			
89.00 Budget authority	882	941	1,062
90.00 Outlays	867	946	1,073

[1] The total cost of administering veterans insurance programs is funded through direct appropriations to this account, and through reimbursements from the insurance trust fund.

This appropriation provides for the administration of non-medical veterans benefits through the Veterans Benefits Administration (VBA) and the Department's top management direction and administrative support, including data processing, fiscal, personnel, and legal services.

Veterans benefits.—Determines eligibility and adjudicates all claims for compensation, pensions, educational assistance, housing loan assistance, and insurance awards. A summary of VBA's program objectives and anticipated workload is included in the following paragraphs. Workload data for this program is shown below. Specific performance goals relating to the processing of veterans benefits are contained in VA's annual performance plan.

Compensation and pensions.—Provides timely and efficient processing of claims for veterans and dependents relating to compensation and pension benefits under the various laws enacted by Congress.

WORKLOAD

[Claims completed in thousands]

	1999 actual	2000 est.	2001 est.
Compensation:			
Rating-Related Actions [1]	520	515	510
Non Rating Actions [2]	234	233	232
Pension:			
Rating-Related Actions [1]	110	109	107
Non Rating Actions [2]	599	596	593

[1] Rating related actions include original compensation claims (EP 010/110), original DIC claims (EP 140), original pensions claims (EP 180), reopened compensation claims (EP 020), reopened pension claims (EP 120), routine examinations (EP 310), and reviews due to hospitalizations (EP 320).

[2] Non Rating actions include dependency issues (EP 130), income issues (EP 150), IVM (EP 154), EVR (EP 155, burial/plot claims (EP 160), claims for accrued benefits (EP 165), original death pension claims (EP 190), and special eligibility determinations (EP 290).

Education.—Provides timely and efficient processing of claims for veterans and dependents relating to education benefits under the various laws enacted by Congress.

WORKLOAD

[In thousands]

	1999 actual	2000 est.	2001 est.
Education:			
Original claims	140	137	149
Adjustments/supplemental claims	872	851	937

Loan guaranty.—Facilitates the extension of private capital, on more liberal terms than generally available to non-veterans, to: assist veterans and servicepersons in obtaining housing credits; provide grants to aid permanently and totally disabled veterans in acquiring specially adapted housing; and assist veterans in retaining their homes during periods of temporary economic difficulty through intensive supplemental mortgage loan servicing.

WORKLOAD

[In thousands]

	1999 actual	2000 est.	2001 est.
Loan guaranty:			
Construction and valuation	334	315	290
Loan processing	1,039	821	790
Loan service and claims	265	275	290
Property management	62	64	65

Vocational rehabilitation and counseling.—Provides counseling and assistance to enable veterans with service-connected disabilities to achieve maximum independence in daily living and, to the maximum extent feasible, obtain and maintain suitable employment.

WORKLOAD

[In thousands]

	1999 actual	2000 est.	2001 est.
Vocational rehabilitation and counseling:			
Evaluation and planning	50	50	49
Rehabilitation services	52	52	51
Employment services status	11	12	12
Vocational/educational counseling	12	12	12

Insurance.—Provides life insurance protection for servicepersons and veterans. The VA administers six life insurance programs and supervises two others through a contractual agreement with a commercial company.

WORKLOAD

[In thousands]

	1999 actual	2000 est.	2001 est.
Insurance:			
Policy service actions	1,080	1,084	1,013
Collections	3,217	3,085	2,911
Disability claims	12	11	11
Insurance awards	930	1,201	558

General administration.—Includes Departmental executive direction and supporting offices, the General Counsel, the Board of Veterans Appeals, and the Board of Contract Appeals.

Object Classification (in millions of dollars)

Identification code 36–0151–0–1–705		1999 actual	2000 est.	2001 est.
	Direct obligations:			
	Personnel compensation:			
11.1	Full-time permanent	494	543	580
11.5	Other personnel compensation	12	12	12
11.9	Total personnel compensation	506	555	592
12.1	Civilian personnel benefits	110	122	136
13.0	Benefits for former personnel	1	1	2
	Travel and transportation of persons:			
21.0	Employee travel	10	15	14
21.0	Interagency motor pool payments	2	2	2
22.0	Transportation of things	2	2	2
23.1	Rental payments to GSA	69	77	79
23.2	Rental payments to others	14	7	6
23.3	Communications, utilities, and miscellaneous charges	23	37	47
24.0	Printing and reproduction	2	2	3
25.2	Other services	101	97	140
26.0	Supplies and materials	11	11	10
31.0	Equipment	29	13	29
99.0	Subtotal, direct obligations	880	941	1,062
99.0	Reimbursable obligations	295	315	296
99.9	Total new obligations	1,175	1,256	1,358

Personnel Summary

Identification code 36–0151–0–1–705		1999 actual	2000 est.	2001 est.
	Direct:			
1001	Total compensable workyears: Full-time equivalent employment[1]	10,510	10,907	11,317
	Reimbursable:			
2001	Total compensable workyears: Full-time equivalent employment	3,125	3,157	2,941

[1] Reflects FTE treated as reimbursements in all years and the effects of Credit Reform, per P.L. 101–508.

Office of Inspector General

[(including transfer of funds)]

For necessary expenses of the Office of Inspector General in carrying out the Inspector General Act of 1978, as amended, [$43,200,000: *Provided*, That of the amount made available under this heading, not to exceed $30,000 may be transferred to and merged with the appropriation for "General operating expenses"] *$46,464,000. (Departments of Veterans Affairs and Housing and Urban Development, and Independent Agencies Appropriations Act, 2000.)*

Program and Financing (in millions of dollars)

Identification code 36–0170–0–1–705		1999 actual	2000 est.	2001 est.
	Obligations by program activity:			
00.10	Direct program	36	43	46
09.00	Reimbursable program	2	3	3
10.00	Total new obligations	38	46	49
	Budgetary resources available for obligation:			
22.00	New budget authority (gross)	38	46	49
23.95	Total new obligations	–38	–46	–49

OFFICE OF INSPECTOR GENERAL—Continued

[(INCLUDING TRANSFER OF FUNDS)]—Continued

Program and Financing (in millions of dollars)—Continued

Identification code 36–0170–0–1–705	1999 actual	2000 est.	2001 est.
New budget authority (gross), detail:			
Discretionary:			
40.00 Appropriation	36	43	46
68.00 Spending authority from offsetting collections: Offsetting collections (cash)	2	3	3
70.00 Total new budget authority (gross)	38	46	49
Change in unpaid obligations:			
72.40 Unpaid obligations, start of year: Obligated balance, start of year	7	8	8
73.10 Total new obligations	38	46	49
73.20 Total outlays (gross)	−37	−46	−50
74.40 Unpaid obligations, end of year: Obligated balance, end of year	8	8	7
Outlays (gross), detail:			
86.90 Outlays from new discretionary authority	34	43	47
86.93 Outlays from discretionary balances	3	2	3
87.00 Total outlays (gross)	37	46	50
Offsets:			
Against gross budget authority and outlays:			
88.00 Offsetting collections (cash) from: Federal sources	−2	−3	−3
Net budget authority and outlays:			
89.00 Budget authority	36	43	46
90.00 Outlays	35	43	47

This appropriation provides Department-wide audit, investigation, and essential inspection and support functions to identify and report weaknesses and deficiencies in VA programs and operations that create conditions for existing or potential instances of fraud, waste, and mismanagement. The audit function plans and conducts internal programmatic audits of all facets of VA operations as well as contract audit services for all applicable Department contracts. The investigative function conducts proactive and reactive criminal and administrative investigations of improper and illegal activities involving VA programs, personnel, beneficiaries, and other third parties. The healthcare inspection function performs legislatively mandated medical care quality assurance reviews and oversight. The support function provides normal office administrative support.

Object Classification (in millions of dollars)

Identification code 36–0170–0–1–705	1999 actual	2000 est.	2001 est.
Direct obligations:			
11.1 Personnel compensation: Full-time permanent	23	27	29
12.1 Civilian personnel benefits	5	6	7
21.0 Travel and transportation of persons	2	2	2
23.1 Rental payments to GSA	2	2	2
25.2 Other services	2	6	6
31.0 Equipment	2		
99.0 Subtotal, direct obligations	36	43	46
99.0 Reimbursable obligations	2	3	3
99.9 Total new obligations	38	46	49

Personnel Summary

Identification code 36–0170–0–1–705	1999 actual	2000 est.	2001 est.
Direct:			
1001 Total compensable workyears: Full-time equivalent employment	319	360	369
Reimbursable:			
2001 Total compensable workyears: Full-time equivalent employment	23	24	24

NATIONAL CEMETERY ADMINISTRATION

[(INCLUDING TRANSFER OF FUNDS)]

For necessary expenses for the maintenance and operation of the National Cemetery Administration, not otherwise provided for, including uniforms or allowances therefor; cemeterial expenses as authorized by law; purchase of two passenger motor vehicles for use in cemeterial operations; and hire of passenger motor vehicles, [$97,256,000: *Provided*, That of the amount made available under this heading, not to exceed $117,000 may be transferred to and merged with the appropriation for "General operating expenses"] *$109,889,000. (Departments of Veterans Affairs and Housing and Urban Development, and Independent Agencies Appropriations Act, 2000.)*

Program and Financing (in millions of dollars)

Identification code 36–0129–0–1–705	1999 actual	2000 est.	2001 est.
Obligations by program activity:			
00.10 Direct obligations	92	97	110
10.00 Total new obligations	92	97	110
Budgetary resources available for obligation:			
22.00 New budget authority (gross)	92	97	110
23.95 Total new obligations	−92	−97	−110
New budget authority (gross), detail:			
Discretionary:			
40.00 Appropriation	92	97	110
Change in unpaid obligations:			
72.40 Unpaid obligations, start of year: Obligated balance, start of year	13	15	17
73.10 Total new obligations	92	97	110
73.20 Total outlays (gross)	−89	−94	−111
74.40 Unpaid obligations, end of year: Obligated balance, end of year	15	17	17
Outlays (gross), detail:			
86.90 Outlays from new discretionary authority	79	83	97
86.93 Outlays from discretionary balances	10	11	14
87.00 Total outlays (gross)	89	94	111
Net budget authority and outlays:			
89.00 Budget authority	92	97	110
90.00 Outlays	89	94	111

Specific performance goals relating to the National Cemetery Administration are contained in VA's annual performance plan.

The mission of the National Cemetery Administration is to honor veterans with a final resting place and lasting memorials that commemorate their service to our Nation. The National Cemetery Administration's vision is to provide a lasting tribute to our Nation's veterans by being mission-driven, results-oriented, and customer-focused. There are four related programs managed by the National Cemetery Administration including: (1) burying eligible veterans and family members in national cemeteries and maintaining the graves and their environs as national shrines; (2) providing aid to States in establishing, expanding, or improving State veteran cemeteries; (3) providing headstones and markers for the graves of eligible persons in national, State, and private cemeteries; and (4) providing presidential memorial certificates to family and friends of deceased veterans, recognizing the veteran's contribution and service to the Nation.

The National Cemetery Administration also reflects budget information for the National Cemetery Gift Fund. Through this Trust Fund, the Secretary is authorized to accept gifts and bequests which are made for the purpose of beautifying national cemeteries or are determined to be beneficial to such cemeteries, or are made for the purpose of the operation, maintenance, or improvement of the National Memorial Cemetery of Arizona.

Object Classification (in millions of dollars)

Identification code 36–0129–0–1–705	1999 actual	2000 est.	2001 est.
Personnel compensation:			
11.1 Full-time permanent	41	44	47
11.3 Other than full-time permanent	7	8	9
11.9 Total personnel compensation	48	52	56
12.1 Civilian personnel benefits	13	14	15
21.0 Travel and transportation of persons	1	1	1
23.1 Rental payments to GSA	1	1	1
23.3 Communications, utilities, and miscellaneous charges	5	6	5
25.2 Other services	9	12	19
26.0 Supplies and materials	7	7	8
31.0 Equipment	8	4	5
99.9 Total new obligations	92	97	110

Personnel Summary

Identification code 36–0129–0–1–705	1999 actual	2000 est.	2001 est.
1001 Total compensable workyears: Full-time equivalent employment	1,357	1,406	1,453

Intragovernmental funds:

SUPPLY FUND

Program and Financing (in millions of dollars)

Identification code 36–4537–0–4–705	1999 actual	2000 est.	2001 est.
Obligations by program activity:			
09.01 Reimbursable program-COGS-Merchandizing	425	603	627
09.02 Reimbursable program-Other-Operations	40	48	48
09.03 Reimbursable program-COGS-Printing and Publications	6	10	10
09.04 Reimbursable program-Other	1	1	1
09.05 Reimbursable program-Equipment-Procurement Services and Distribution	5	2	2
10.00 Total new obligations	477	664	688
Budgetary resources available for obligation:			
21.40 Unobligated balance available, start of year	132	152	152
22.00 New budget authority (gross)	495	664	688
23.90 Total budgetary resources available for obligation	627	816	840
23.95 Total new obligations	–477	–664	–688
24.40 Unobligated balance available, end of year	152	152	152
New budget authority (gross), detail:			
Mandatory:			
69.00 Offsetting collections (cash)	573	664	688
69.10 From Federal sources: Change in receivables and unpaid, unfilled orders	–78		
69.90 Spending authority from offsetting collections (total mandatory)	495	664	688
Change in unpaid obligations:			
Unpaid obligations, start of year:			
72.40 Obligated balance, start of year	–32	–23	–23
72.95 From Federal sources: Receivables and unpaid, unfilled orders	366	288	288
72.99 Total unpaid obligations, start of year	334	265	265
73.10 Total new obligations	477	664	688
73.20 Total outlays (gross)	–546	–664	–688
Unpaid obligations, end of year:			
74.40 Obligated balance, end of year	–23	–23	–23
74.95 From Federal sources: Receivables and unpaid, unfilled orders	288	288	288
74.99 Total unpaid obligations, end of year	265	265	265
Outlays (gross), detail:			
86.97 Outlays from new mandatory authority	495	664	688
86.98 Outlays from mandatory balances	51		
87.00 Total outlays (gross)	546	664	688
Offsets:			
Against gross budget authority and outlays:			
88.00 Offsetting collections (cash) from: Federal sources	–573	–664	–688
Against gross budget authority only:			
88.95 From Federal sources: Change in receivables and unpaid, unfilled orders	78		
Net budget authority and outlays:			
89.00 Budget authority			
90.00 Outlays	–28		

Under the provisions of 38 U.S.C. 8121, the Supply Fund is responsible for the operation and maintenance of a supply system for VA. The Supply Fund is an intragovernmental revolving fund without fiscal year limitations.

Budget program.—The fund provides financial support for: (1) a National Acquisition Center or central contracting office; (2) the maintenance of field station inventories; (3) a service and distribution center; (4) a service and reclamation program; (5) a national prosthetics distribution center; and (6) an asset management service.

Costs for the administration of supply activities at VA field stations are not financed by the Supply Fund. These costs are charged directly to applicable appropriations accounts.

Financing.—Costs of supplies, equipment, and services acquired through the Supply Fund and Supply Fund operating costs are recovered through reimbursements from the VA appropriations and other Government agencies receiving goods and services. For 2001, Supply Fund sales are estimated to reach $650 million. Average inventory needed to support those sales will be $30 million.

Operating results.—The Fund operated at a loss of $4 million in 1999. The new total of retained earnings is $67 million. Operating expense as related to sales was 9 percent.

Object Classification (in millions of dollars)

Identification code 36–4537–0–4–705	1999 actual	2000 est.	2001 est.
Personnel compensation:			
11.1 Full-time permanent	19	22	22
11.5 Other personnel compensation	1	1	1
11.9 Total personnel compensation	20	23	23
12.1 Civilian personnel benefits	4	4	5
21.0 Travel and transportation of persons	3	3	3
22.0 Transportation of things	1	1	2
23.1 Rental payments to GSA	1	1	1
23.3 Communications, utilities, and miscellaneous charges	3	3	3
24.0 Printing and reproduction	6	10	10
25.1 Advisory and assistance services	10	12	11
26.0 Supplies and materials	277	327	340
31.0 Equipment	152	280	290
99.9 Total new obligations	477	664	688

Personnel Summary

Identification code 36–4537–0–4–705	1999 actual	2000 est.	2001 est.
2001 Total compensable workyears: Full-time equivalent employment	357	385	385

FRANCHISE FUND

Program and Financing (in millions of dollars)

Identification code 36–4539–0–4–705	1999 actual	2000 est.	2001 est.
Obligations by program activity:			
09.01 Reimbursable program	102	135	150
10.00 Total new obligations	102	135	150
Budgetary resources available for obligation:			
21.40 Unobligated balance available, start of year	7	18	18
22.00 New budget authority (gross)	113	135	150

Intragovernmental funds—Continued

FRANCHISE FUND—Continued

Program and Financing (in millions of dollars)—Continued

Identification code 36–4539–0–4–705	1999 actual	2000 est.	2001 est.
23.90 Total budgetary resources available for obligation	120	153	168
23.95 Total new obligations	–102	–135	–150
24.40 Unobligated balance available, end of year	18	18	18
New budget authority (gross), detail:			
Mandatory:			
69.00 Offsetting collections (cash)	113	135	150
Change in unpaid obligations:			
72.40 Unpaid obligations, start of year: Obligated balance, start of year	26	16	16
73.10 Total new obligations	102	135	150
73.20 Total outlays (gross)	–111	–135	–150
74.40 Unpaid obligations, end of year: Obligated balance, end of year	16	16	16
Outlays (gross), detail:			
86.97 Outlays from new mandatory authority	111	135	150
Offsets:			
Against gross budget authority and outlays:			
88.00 Offsetting collections (cash) from: Federal sources	–113	–135	–150
Net budget authority and outlays:			
89.00 Budget authority			
90.00 Outlays	–1		

VA was chosen as a pilot Franchise Fund agency under the Government Management and Reform Act, P.L. 103–356, of 1994. Established in 1997, administrative services included in the Franchise Fund are financed on a fee-for-service basis rather than through VA's General Operating Expenses Appropriation. VA's Franchise Fund is a revolving fund used to supply common administrative services on the basis of services supplied. Enterprise Centers are the lines of business within the VA Franchise Fund and are expected to have net billings of about $150 million and employ 1,034 people, who were transferred from their parent organizations.

The Franchise Fund concept is intended to increase competition for government administrative services resulting in lower costs and higher quality.

Object Classification (in millions of dollars)

Identification code 36–4539–0–4–705	1999 actual	2000 est.	2001 est.
11.1 Personnel compensation: Full-time permanent	31	41	46
12.1 Civilian personnel benefits	6	8	9
21.0 Travel and transportation of persons	1	1	1
22.0 Transportation of things		1	1
23.1 Rental payments to GSA	3	4	4
23.3 Communications, utilities, and miscellaneous charges	21	27	30
25.2 Other services	34	45	50
26.0 Supplies and materials	1	2	2
31.0 Equipment	5	6	7
99.9 Total new obligations	102	135	150

Personnel Summary

Identification code 36–4539–0–4–705	1999 actual	2000 est.	2001 est.
2001 Total compensable workyears: Full-time equivalent employment	644	679	1,034

GENERAL FUND RECEIPT ACCOUNTS

(in millions of dollars)

	1999 actual	2000 est.	2001 est.
Offsetting receipts from the public:			
36–246800 Pharmaceutical copayments			167
36–247300 Contributions from military personnel, Veteran's Educational Assistance Act of 1984	168	186	189
36–273330 GIF direct loans, downward reestimate of subsidies	619	730	
36–310400 Medical care collections			116
General Fund Offsetting receipts from the public	787	916	472
Intragovernmental payments:			
36–246400 DOD tricare reimbursement			67
General Fund Intragovernmental payments			67

ADMINISTRATIVE PROVISIONS

(INCLUDING TRANSFER OF FUNDS)

SEC. 101. Any appropriation for fiscal year [2000] *2001* for ["Compensation and pensions",] *"Compensation", "Pension",* "Readjustment benefits", and "Veterans insurance and indemnities" may be transferred to any other of the mentioned appropriations.

SEC. 102. Appropriations available to the Department of Veterans Affairs for fiscal year [2000] *2001* for salaries and expenses shall be available for services authorized by 5 U.S.C. 3109.

SEC. 103. No appropriations in this Act for the Department of Veterans Affairs (except the appropriations for "Construction, major projects", "Construction, minor projects", and the "Parking revolving fund") shall be available for the purchase of any site for or toward the construction of any new hospital or home.

SEC. 104. No appropriations in this Act for the Department of Veterans Affairs shall be available for hospitalization or examination of any persons (except beneficiaries entitled under the laws bestowing such benefits to veterans, and persons receiving such treatment under 5 U.S.C. 7901–7904 or 42 U.S.C. 5141–5204), unless reimbursement of cost is made to the "Medical care" account at such rates as may be fixed by the Secretary of Veterans Affairs.

SEC. 105. Appropriations available to the Department of Veterans Affairs for fiscal year [2000] *2001* for ["Compensation and pensions",] *"Compensation", "Pension",* "Readjustment benefits", and "Veterans insurance and indemnities" shall be available for payment of prior year accrued obligations required to be recorded by law against the corresponding prior year accounts within the last quarter of fiscal year [1999] *2000.*

SEC. 106. Appropriations accounts available to the Department of Veterans Affairs for fiscal year [2000] *2001* shall be available to pay prior year obligations of corresponding prior year appropriations accounts resulting from title X of the Competitive Equality Banking Act, Public Law 100–86, except that if such obligations are from trust fund accounts they shall be payable from "Compensation" [and pensions"] *and "Pension".*

SEC. 107. Notwithstanding any other provision of law, during fiscal year [2000] *2001,* the Secretary of Veterans Affairs shall, from the National Service Life Insurance Fund (38 U.S.C. 1920), the Veterans' Special Life Insurance Fund (38 U.S.C. 1923), and the United States Government Life Insurance Fund (38 U.S.C. 1955), reimburse the "General operating expenses" account for the cost of administration of the insurance programs financed through those accounts: *Provided,* That reimbursement shall be made only from the surplus earnings accumulated in an insurance program in fiscal year [2000] *2001,* that are available for dividends in that program after claims have been paid and actuarially determined reserves have been set aside: *Provided further,* That if the cost of administration of an insurance program exceeds the amount of surplus earnings accumulated in that program, reimbursement shall be made only to the extent of such surplus earnings: *Provided further,* That the Secretary shall determine the cost of administration for fiscal year [2000] *2001,* which is properly allocable to the provision of each insurance program and to the provision of any total disability income insurance included in such insurance program.

SEC. 108. *Beginning in fiscal year 2001, and thereafter, funds available in any Department of Veterans Affairs appropriation or fund for salaries and other administrative expenses shall also be available to reimburse the Office of Resolution Management and the Office of Employment Discrimination Complaint Adjudication for all services provided at rates which will recover actual costs. Payments may be made in advance for services to be furnished based on estimated costs. Amounts received shall be credited to the General Operating Expenses account for use by the office that provided the service.*

[SEC. 108. (a) IN GENERAL.—The Congress supports efforts to implement improvements in health care services for veterans in rural areas.

(b) REPORT REQUIRED.—(1) Not later than 6 months after the date of the enactment of this Act, the Secretary of Veterans Affairs shall submit to the Committees on Veterans' Affairs of the Senate and the House of Representatives a report on the impact of the allocation of funds under the Veterans Equitable Resource Allocation (VERA) funding formula on the rural subregions of the health care system administered by the Veterans Health Administration.

(2) The report shall include the following:

(A) An assessment of impact of the allocation of funds under the VERA formula on—

(i) travel times to veterans health care in rural areas;

(ii) waiting periods for appointments for veterans health care in rural areas;

(iii) the cost associated with additional community-based outpatient clinics;

(iv) transportation costs; and

(v) the unique challenges that Department of Veterans Affairs medical centers in rural, low-population subregions face in attempting to increase efficiency without large economies of scale.

(B) The recommendations of the Secretary, if any, on how rural veterans' access to health care services might be enhanced.]

[SEC. 109. The Secretary of Veterans Affairs may carry out a major medical facility project to renovate and construct facilities at the Olin E. Teague Department of Veterans Affairs Medical Center, Temple, Texas, for a joint venture Cardiovascular Institute, in an amount not to exceed $11,500,000. In order to carry out that project, the amount of $11,500,000 appropriated for fiscal year 1998 and programmed for the renovation of Building 9 at the Waco, Texas, Department of Veterans Affairs Medical Center is hereby made available for that project.]

[SEC. 110. Notwithstanding any other provision of this Act, none of the funds appropriated or otherwise made available in this Act for the Medical Care appropriation of the Department of Veterans Affairs may be obligated for the realignment of the health care delivery system in VISN 12 until 60 days after the Secretary of Veterans Affairs certifies that the department has: (1) consulted with veterans organizations, medical school affiliates, employee representatives, State veterans and health associations, and other interested parties with respect to the realignment plan to be implemented; and (2) made available to the Congress and the public information from the consultations regarding possible impacts on the accessibility of veterans health care services to affected veterans.]

SEC. 109. Title 38, United States Code, is amended as follows:

(a) Section 1710B(e) is amended to read:

"(e) All amounts received by the Department under this section shall be deposited in the Department of Veterans Affairs Medical Care Collections Fund.".

(b) Section 1722A(c), as amended, is further amended by deleting the second sentence.

(c) Section 1729A is amended:

(1) in subsection (b) by:

(A) redesignating paragraphs (3), (4), (5), and (6) as (4), (5), (6), and (8) respectively:

(B) inserting a new paragraph (3) to read:

"(3) Section 1710B of this title.";

(C) inserting a new paragraph (7) after paragraph (6) (as redesignated above), to read:

"(7) Section 8165(a) of this title."; and

(D) inserting a new paragraph (9) at the end, to read:

"(9) Section 113 of Public Law 106–117, the Veterans Millennium Health Care and Benefits Act.".

(2) in subsection (c)(1) by: (a) deleting the phrase, "Subject to the provisions of appropriation Acts, amounts"; (b) inserting in lieu thereof, "Fifty percent of the first $700,000,000 received or collected each fiscal year under the provisions referred to in subsection (b), shall be transferred to the general fund of the Treasury. Remaining amounts"; and (c) inserting "and without further appropriation" after "limitation."

(3) deleting subsection (f).

(d)(1) Section 1729B is repealed.

(2) The table of sections at the beginning of chapter 17 is amended by striking out the item relating to section 1729B.

(e) Section 8165(a) is amended to read:

"(a)(1) Funds received by the Department under an enhanced-use lease and remaining after any deduction from those funds under subsection (b) shall be deposited in the Department of Veterans Affairs Medical Care Collections Fund.

"(2) Funds received by the Department from a disposal of leased property under section 8164 of this title and remaining after any deduction from such funds under the laws referred to in subsection (c) shall be deposited in the Department of Veterans Affairs Medical Care Collections Fund.".

(f) Section 113(b) of the Veterans Millennium Health Care and Benefits Act, Pub. L. No. 106–117, is amended by striking "Health Services Improvement Fund established under section 1729B of title 38, United States Code, as added by section 202" and inserting in lieu thereof, "Department of Veterans Affairs Medical Care Collections Fund".

(g) Any amounts deposited in the Department of Veterans Affairs Health Services Improvement Fund or the Extended Care Fund shall be transferred to and merged with the Medical Care Collections Fund, to be available subject to the terms and conditions of such Fund. (Departments of Veterans Affairs and Housing and Urban Development, and Independent Agencies Appropriations Act, 2000.)

TITLE IV—GENERAL PROVISIONS

SEC. 401. Where appropriations in titles I, II, and III of this Act are expendable for travel expenses and no specific limitation has been placed thereon, the expenditures for such travel expenses may not exceed the amounts set forth therefore in the budget estimates submitted for the appropriations: *Provided*, That this provision does not apply to accounts that do not contain an object classification for travel: *Provided further,* That this section shall not apply to travel performed by uncompensated officials of local boards and appeal boards of the Selective Service System; to travel performed directly in connection with care and treatment of medical beneficiaries of the Department of Veterans Affairs; to travel performed in connection with major disasters or emergencies declared or determined by the President under the provisions of the Robert T. Stafford Disaster Relief and Emergency Assistance Act; to travel performed by the Offices of Inspector General in connection with audits and investigations; or to payments to interagency motor pools where separately set forth in the budget schedules: *Provided further,* That if appropriations in titles I, II, and III exceed the amounts set forth in budget estimates initially submitted for such appropriations, the expenditures for travel may correspondingly exceed the amounts therefore set forth in the estimates in the same proportion.

SEC. 402. Appropriations and funds available for the administrative expenses of the Department of Housing and Urban Development and the Selective Service System shall be available in the current fiscal year for purchase of uniforms, or allowances therefor, as authorized by 5 U.S.C. 5901–5902; hire of passenger motor vehicles; and services as authorized by 5 U.S.C. 3109.

SEC. 403. Funds of the Department of Housing and Urban Development subject to the Government Corporation Control Act or section 402 of the Housing Act of 1950 shall be available, without regard to the limitations on administrative expenses, for legal services on a contract or fee basis, and for utilizing and making payment for services and facilities of Federal National Mortgage Association, Government National Mortgage Association, Federal Home Loan Mortgage Corporation, Federal Financing Bank, Federal Reserve banks or any member thereof, Federal Home Loan banks, and any insured bank within the meaning of the Federal Deposit Insurance Corporation Act, as amended (12 U.S.C. 1811–1831).

SEC. 404. No part of any appropriation contained in this Act shall remain available for obligation beyond the current fiscal year unless expressly so provided herein.

SEC. 405. No funds appropriated by this Act may be expended—

(1) pursuant to a certification of an officer or employee of the United States unless—

(A) such certification is accompanied by, or is part of, a voucher or abstract which describes the payee or payees and the items or services for which such expenditure is being made; or

(B) the expenditure of funds pursuant to such certification, and without such a voucher or abstract, is specifically authorized by law; and

(2) unless such expenditure is subject to audit by the General Accounting Office or is specifically exempt by law from such audit.

SEC. 406. None of the funds provided in this Act to any department or agency may be expended for the transportation of any officer or employee of such department or agency between their domicile and their place of employment, with the exception of any officer or employee authorized such transportation under 31 U.S.C. 1344 or 5 U.S.C. 7905.

SEC. 407. None of the funds provided in this Act may be used for payment, through grants or contracts, to recipients that do not share in the cost of conducting research resulting from proposals not specifically solicited by the Government: *Provided*, That the extent of cost sharing by the recipient shall reflect the mutuality of interest of the grantee or contractor and the Government in the research.

SEC. 408. None of the funds in this Act may be used, directly or through grants, to pay or to provide reimbursement for payment of the salary of a consultant (whether retained by the Federal Government or a grantee) at more than the daily equivalent of the rate paid for level IV of the Executive Schedule, unless specifically authorized by law.

SEC. 409. None of the funds provided in this Act shall be used to pay the expenses of, or otherwise compensate, non-Federal parties intervening in regulatory or adjudicatory proceedings. Nothing herein affects the authority of the Consumer Product Safety Commission pursuant to section 7 of the Consumer Product Safety Act (15 U.S.C. 2056 et seq.).

SEC. 410. Except as otherwise provided under existing law, or under an existing Executive order issued pursuant to an existing law, the obligation or expenditure of any appropriation under this Act for contracts for any consulting service shall be limited to contracts which are: (1) a matter of public record and available for public inspection; and (2) thereafter included in a publicly available list of all contracts entered into within 24 months prior to the date on which the list is made available to the public and of all contracts on which performance has not been completed by such date. The list required by the preceding sentence shall be updated quarterly and shall include a narrative description of the work to be performed under each such contract.

SEC. 411. Except as otherwise provided by law, no part of any appropriation contained in this Act shall be obligated or expended by any executive agency, as referred to in the Office of Federal Procurement Policy Act (41 U.S.C. 401 et seq.), for a contract for services unless such executive agency: (1) has awarded and entered into such contract in full compliance with such Act and the regulations promulgated thereunder; and (2) requires any report prepared pursuant to such contract, including plans, evaluations, studies, analyses and manuals, and any report prepared by the agency which is substantially derived from or substantially includes any report prepared pursuant to such contract, to contain information concerning: (A) the contract pursuant to which the report was prepared; and (B) the contractor who prepared the report pursuant to such contract.

SEC. 412. Except as otherwise provided in section 406, none of the funds provided in this Act to any department or agency shall be obligated or expended to provide a personal cook, chauffeur, or other personal servants to any officer or employee of such department or agency.

SEC. 413. None of the funds provided in this Act to any department or agency shall be obligated or expended to procure passenger automobiles as defined in 15 U.S.C. 2001 with an EPA estimated miles per gallon average of less than 22 miles per gallon.

[SEC. 414. None of the funds appropriated in title I of this Act shall be used to enter into any new lease of real property if the estimated annual rental is more than $300,000 unless the Secretary submits, in writing, a report to the Committees on Appropriations of the Congress and a period of 30 days has expired following the date on which the report is received by the Committees on Appropriations.]

SEC. [415] *414.* (a) It is the sense of the Congress that, to the greatest extent practicable, all equipment and products purchased with funds made available in this Act should be American-made.

(b) In providing financial assistance to, or entering into any contract with, any entity using funds made available in this Act, the head of each Federal agency, to the greatest extent practicable, shall provide to such entity a notice describing the statement made in subsection (a) by the Congress.

SEC. [416] *415.* None of the funds appropriated in this Act may be used to implement any cap on reimbursements to grantees for indirect costs, except as published in Office of Management and Budget Circular A–21.

SEC. [417] *416.* Such sums as may be necessary for fiscal year [2000] *2001* pay raises for programs funded by this Act shall be absorbed within the levels appropriated in this Act.

SEC. [418] *417.* None of the funds made available in this Act may be used for any program, project, or activity, when it is made known to the Federal entity or official to which the funds are made available that the program, project, or activity is not in compliance with any Federal law relating to risk assessment, the protection of private property rights, or unfunded mandates.

SEC. [419] *418.* Corporations and agencies of the Department of Housing and Urban Development which are subject to the Government Corporation Control Act, as amended, are hereby authorized to make such expenditures, within the limits of funds and borrowing authority available to each such corporation or agency and in accord with law, and to make such contracts and commitments without regard to fiscal year limitations as provided by section 104 of the Act as may be necessary in carrying out the programs set forth in the budget for [2000] *2001* for such corporation or agency except as hereinafter provided: *Provided*, That collections of these corporations and agencies may be used for new loan or mortgage purchase commitments only to the extent expressly provided for in this Act (unless such loans are in support of other forms of assistance provided for in this or prior appropriations Acts), except that this proviso shall not apply to the mortgage insurance or guaranty operations of these corporations, or where loans or mortgage purchases are necessary to protect the financial interest of the United States Government.

SEC. [420] *419.* Notwithstanding section 320(g) of the Federal Water Pollution Control Act (33 U.S.C. 1330(g)), funds made available pursuant to authorization under such section for fiscal year [2000] *2001* may be used for implementing comprehensive conservation and management plans.

SEC. [421] *420.* Notwithstanding any other provision of law, the term "qualified student loan" with respect to national service education awards shall mean any loan made directly to a student by the Alaska Commission on Postsecondary Education, in addition to other meanings under section 148(b)(7) of the National and Community Service Act.

SEC. [422] *421.* It is the sense of the Congress that, along with health care, housing, education, and other benefits, the presence of an honor guard at a veteran's funeral is a benefit that a veteran has earned, and, therefore, the executive branch should provide funeral honor details for the funerals of veterans when requested, in accordance with law.

SEC. [423] *422.* Notwithstanding any other law, funds made available by this or any other Act or previous Acts for the George E. Brown United States/Mexico Foundation for Science may be used for the endowment of such Foundation: *Provided*, That funds from the United States Government shall be matched in equal amounts with funds from Mexico: *Provided further*, That the accounts of such Foundation shall be subject to United States Government administrative and audit requirements concerning grants and requirements concerning cost principles for nonprofit organizations[: *Provided further*, That the United States/Mexico Foundation for Science is renamed the "George E. Brown United States/Mexico Foundation for Science"].

SEC. 423. NASA Full Cost Accounting. Title III of the National Aeronautics and Space Act of 1958, P.L. 85–568, is amended by adding the following new section at the end:

"Section 312. (a) Appropriations for the Administration for fiscal year 2002 and thereafter shall be made in three accounts, "Human Space Flight", "Science, Aeronautics and Technology," and an account for amounts appropriated for the necessary expenses of the Office of Inspector General. Appropriations shall remain available for two fiscal years. Each account shall include the planned full costs of the Administration's related activities.

"(b) To ensure the safe, timely, and successful accomplishment of Administration missions, the Administration may transfer amounts for Federal salaries and benefits; training, travel and awards; facility and related costs; information technology services; publishing services; science, engineering, fabricating and testing services; and other administrative services among accounts, as necessary.

"(c) The Administrator, in consultation with the Director of the Office of Management and Budget, shall determine what balances from the "Mission Support" account are to be transferred to the "Human Space Flight" and "Science, Aeronautics, and Technology" accounts. Such balances shall be transferred and merged with the

"Human Space Flight" and "Science, Aeronautics, and Technology" accounts, and remain available for the period of which originally appropriated."

[SEC. 424. None of the funds made available in this Act may be used to carry out Executive Order No. 13083.]

[SEC. 425. Unless otherwise provided for in this Act, no part of any appropriation for the Department of Housing and Urban Development shall be available for any activity in excess of amounts set forth in the budget estimates submitted for the appropriations.]

[SEC. 426. Except in the case of entities that are funded solely with Federal funds or any natural persons that are funded under this Act, none of the funds in this Act shall be used for the planning or execution of any program to pay the expenses of, or otherwise compensate, non-Federal parties to lobby or litigate in respect to adjudicatory proceedings funded in this Act. A chief executive officer of any entity receiving funds under this Act shall certify that none of these funds have been used to engage in the lobbying of the Federal Government or in litigation against the United States unless authorized under existing law.]

[SEC. 427. LAW ENFORCEMENT AGENCIES NOT INCLUDED AS OWNER OR OPERATOR. Section 101(20)(D) of the Comprehensive Environmental Response, Compensation, and Liability Act of 1980 (42 U.S.C. 9601(20)(D)) is amended by inserting "through seizure or otherwise in connection with law enforcement activity" before "involuntary" the first place it appears.]

[SEC. 428. No part of any funds appropriated in this Act shall be used by an agency of the executive branch, other than for normal and recognized executive-legislative relationships, for publicity or propaganda purposes, and for the preparation, distribution or use of any kit, pamphlet, booklet, publication, radio, television or film presentation designed to support or defeat legislation pending before the Congress, except in presentation to the Congress itself.]

[SEC. 429. The comment period on the proposed rules related to section 303(d) of the Clean Water Act published at 64 Federal Register 46012 and 46058 (August 23, 1999) shall be extended from October 22, 1999, for a period of 90 additional calendar days.]

[SEC. 430. Section 4(a) of the Act of August 9, 1950 (16 U.S.C. 777c(a)), is amended in the second sentence by striking "1999" and inserting "2000".]

[SEC. 431. PROMULGATION OF STORMWATER REGULATIONS. (a) STORMWATER REGULATIONS.—The Administrator of the Environmental Protection Agency shall not promulgate the Phase II stormwater regulations until the Administrator submits to the Committee on Environment and Public Works of the Senate and the Committee on Transportation and Infrastructure of the House of Representatives a report containing—

(1) an in-depth impact analysis on the effect the final regulations will have on urban, suburban, and rural local governments subject to the regulations, including an estimate of—

(A) the costs of complying with the six minimum control measures described in the regulations; and

(B) the costs resulting from the lowering of the construction threshold from 5 acres to 1 acre;

(2) an explanation of the rationale of the Administrator for lowering the construction site threshold from 5 acres to 1 acre, including—

(A) an explanation, in light of recent court decisions, of why a 1-acre measure is any less arbitrarily determined than a 5-acre measure; and

(B) all qualitative information used in determining an acre threshold for a construction site;

(3) documentation demonstrating that stormwater runoff is generally a problem in communities with populations of 50,000 to 100,000 (including an explanation of why the coverage of the regulation is based on a census-determined population instead of a water quality threshold); and

(4) information that supports the position of the Administrator that the Phase II stormwater program should be administered as part of the National Pollutant Discharge Elimination System under section 402 of the Federal Water Pollution Control Act (33 U.S.C. 1342).]

[(b) PHASE I REGULATIONS.—No later than 120 days after the enactment of this Act, the Environmental Protection Agency shall submit to the Environment and Public Works Committee of the Senate and the Committee on Transportation and Infrastructure of the House of Representatives a report containing a detailed explanation of the impact, if any, that the Phase I program has had in improving water quality in the United States (including a description of specific measures that have been successful and those that have been unsuccessful).

(c) FEDERAL REGISTER.—The reports described in subsections (a) and (b) shall be published in the Federal Register for public comment.

SEC. 432. PESTICIDE TOLERANCE FEES. None of the funds appropriated or otherwise made available by this Act shall be used to promulgate a final regulation to implement changes in the payment of pesticide tolerance processing fees as proposed at 64 Fed. Reg. 31040, or any similar proposals. The Environmental Protection Agency may proceed with the development of such a rule.

SEC. 433. COMMERCIAL SPACE LAUNCH INDEMNIFICATION EXTENSION. Section 70113(f) of title 49, United States Code, is amended by striking "December 31, 1999", and inserting "December 31, 2000".

SEC. 434. SPACE STATION COMMERCIAL DEVELOPMENT DEMONSTRATION PROGRAM. (a) PURPOSE.—The purpose of this section is to establish a demonstration regarding the commercial feasibility and economic viability of private sector business operations involving the International Space Station and its related infrastructure. The goal will be furthered by the early use of the International Space Station by United States commercial entities committing private capital to commercial enterprises on the International Space Station. In conjunction with this demonstration program, the National Aeronautics and Space Administration (NASA) shall establish and publish a price policy designed to eliminate price uncertainty for those planning to utilize the International Space Station and its related facilities for United States commercial use.

(b) USE OF RECEIPTS FOR COMMERCIAL USE.—Any receipts collected by NASA from the commercial use of the International Space Station shall first be used to offset any costs incurred by NASA in support of the United States commercial use of the International Space Station. Any receipts collected in excess of the costs identified pursuant to the prior sentence may be retained by NASA for use without fiscal year limitation in promoting the commercial use of the International Space Station.]

[(c) REPORT.—NASA shall submit an annual report to the Congress that identifies all receipts that are collected under this section, the use of the receipts and the status of the demonstration. NASA shall submit a final report on the status of the demonstration, including any recommendation for expansion, within 120 days of the completion of the assembly of the International Space Station or the end of fiscal year 2004, whichever is earlier.]

[(d) DEFINITIONS.—As used in this section, the term "United States commercial use" means private commercial projects that are designed to benefit the United States through the sales of goods or services or the creation of jobs, or both.]

[(e) TERMINATION.—The demonstration program established under this section shall apply to United States commercial use agreements that are entered into prior to the date of the completion of the International Space Station or the end of the fiscal year 2004, whichever is earlier.]

[SEC. 435. INSURANCE; INDEMNIFICATION; LIABILITY. (A) AMENDMENT.—The National Aeronautics and Space Act of 1958 (42 U.S.C. 2451 et seq.) is amended by inserting after section 308 the following new section:]

["*EXPERIMENTAL AEROSPACE VEHICLE*]

["(a) IN GENERAL.—The Administrator may provide liability insurance for, or indemnification to, the developer of an experimental aerospace vehicle developed or used in execution of an agreement between the Administration and the developer.]

["(b) TERMS AND CONDITIONS.—

["(1) IN GENERAL.—Except as otherwise provided in this section, the insurance and indemnification provided by the Administration under subsection (a) to a developer shall be provided on the same terms and conditions as insurance and indemnification is provided by the Administration under section 308 of this Act to the user of a space vehicle.]

["(2) INSURANCE.—

"(A) IN GENERAL.—A developer shall obtain liability insurance or demonstrate financial responsibility in amounts to compensate for the maximum probable loss from claims by—

"(i) a third party for death, bodily injury, or property damage, or loss resulting from an activity carried out in connection with the development or use of an experimental aerospace vehicle; and

"(ii) the United States Government for damage or loss to Government property resulting from such an activity.]

["(B) MAXIMUM REQUIRED.—The Administrator shall determine the amount of insurance required, but, except as provided

[“*EXPERIMENTAL AEROSPACE VEHICLE*]—Continued

in subparagraph (C), that amount shall not be greater than the amount required under section 70112(a)(3) of title 49, United States Code, for a launch. The Administrator shall publish notice of the Administrator's determination and the applicable amount or amounts in the Federal Register within 10 days after making the determination.]

[“(C) INCREASE IN DOLLAR AMOUNTS.—The Administrator may increase the dollar amounts set forth in section 70112(a)(3)(A) of title 49, United States Code, for the purpose of applying that section under this section to a developer after consultation with the Comptroller General and such experts and consultants as may be appropriate, and after publishing notice of the increase in the Federal Register not less than 180 days before the increase goes into effect. The Administrator shall make available for public inspection, not later than the date of publication of such notice, a complete record of any correspondence received by the Administration, and a transcript of any meetings in which the Administration participated, regarding the proposed increase.]

[“(D) SAFETY REVIEW REQUIRED BEFORE ADMINISTRATOR PROVIDES INSURANCE.—The Administrator may not provide liability insurance or indemnification under subsection (a) unless the developer establishes to the satisfaction of the Administrator that appropriate safety procedures and practices are being followed in the development of the experimental aerospace vehicle.]

[“(3) NO INDEMNIFICATION WITHOUT CROSS-WAIVER.—Notwithstanding subsection (a), the Administrator may not indemnify a developer of an experimental aerospace vehicle under this section unless there is an agreement between the Administration and the developer described in subsection (c).]

[“(4) APPLICATION OF CERTAIN PROCEDURES.—If the Administrator requests additional appropriations to make payments under this section, like the payments that may be made under section 308(b) of this Act, then the request for those appropriations shall be made in accordance with the procedures established by subsections (d) and (e) of section 70113 of title 49, United States Code.

“(c) CROSS-WAIVERS.—]

[“(1) ADMINISTRATOR AUTHORIZED TO WAIVE.—The Administrator, on behalf of the United States, and its departments, agencies, and related entities, may reciprocally waive claims with a developer or cooperating party and with the related entities of that developer or cooperating party under which each party to the waiver agrees to be responsible, and agrees to ensure that its own related entities are responsible, for damage or loss to its property for which it is responsible, or for losses resulting from any injury or death sustained by its own employees or agents, as a result of activities connected to the agreement or use of the experimental aerospace vehicle.]

[“(2) LIMITATIONS.—

“(A) CLAIMS.—A reciprocal waiver under paragraph (1) may not preclude a claim by any natural person (including, but not limited to, a natural person who is an employee of the United States, the developer, the cooperating party, or their respective subcontractors) or that natural person's estate, survivors, or subrogees for injury or death, except with respect to a subrogee that is a party to the waiver or has otherwise agreed to be bound by the terms of the waiver.]

[“(B) LIABILITY FOR NEGLIGENCE.—A reciprocal waiver under paragraph (1) may not absolve any party of liability to any natural person (including, but not limited to, a natural person who is an employee of the United States, the developer, the cooperating party, or their respective subcontractors) or such a natural person's estate, survivors, or subrogees for negligence, except with respect to a subrogee that is a party to the waiver or has otherwise agreed to be bound by the terms of the waiver.]

[“(C) INDEMNIFICATION FOR DAMAGES.—A reciprocal waiver under paragraph (1) may not be used as the basis of a claim by the Administration, or the developer or cooperating party, for indemnification against the other for damages paid to a natural person, or that natural person's estate, survivors, or subrogees, for injury or death sustained by that natural person as a result of activities connected to the agreement or use of the experimental aerospace vehicle.]

[“(3) EFFECT ON PREVIOUS WAIVERS.—Subsection (c) applies to any waiver of claims entered into by the Administration without regard to whether it was entered into before, on, or after the date of the enactment of this Act.]

[“(d) DEFINITIONS.—In this section:

“(1) COOPERATING PARTY.—The term ‘cooperating party’ means any person who enters into an agreement with the Administration for the performance of cooperative scientific, aeronautical, or space activities to carry out the purposes of this Act.

“(2) DEVELOPER.—The term ‘developer’ means a United States person (other than a natural person) who—]

[“(A) is a party to an agreement with the Administration for the purpose of developing new technology for an experimental aerospace vehicle;

“(B) owns or provides property to be flown or situated on that vehicle; or

“(C) employs a natural person to be flown on that vehicle.]

[“(3) EXPERIMENTAL AEROSPACE VEHICLE.—The term ‘experimental aerospace vehicle’ means an object intended to be flown in, or launched into, orbital or suborbital flight for the purpose of demonstrating technologies necessary for a reusable launch vehicle, developed under an agreement between the Administration and a developer.]

[“(4) RELATED ENTITY.—The term ‘related entity’ includes a contractor or subcontractor at any tier, a supplier, a grantee, and an investigator or detailee.]

[“(e) RELATIONSHIP TO OTHER LAWS.—

“(1) SECTION 308.—This section does not apply to any object, transaction, or operation to which section 308 of this Act applies.

“(2) CHAPTER 701 OF TITLE 49, UNITED STATES CODE.—The Administrator may not provide indemnification to a developer under this section for launches subject to license under section 70117(g)(1) of title 49, United States Code.”.]

(b) REPEAL.—Section 431 of the Departments of Veterans Affairs and Housing and Urban Development, and Independent Agencies Appropriations Act, 1999 (Public Law 105–276) is repealed. *(Departments of Veterans Affairs and Housing and Urban Development, and Independent Agencies Appropriations Act, 2000.)*

[SEC. 242. (a) The seventh paragraph under the heading “Community Development Block Grants” in title II of H.R. 2684 (Public Law 106–74) is amended by striking the figure making individual grants for targeted economic investments and inserting “$250,175,000” in lieu thereof.]

[(b) The statement of the managers of the committee of conference accompanying H.R. 2684 (Public Law 106–74; House Report No. 106–379) is deemed to be amended under the heading “Community Development Block Grants” to include in the description of targeted economic development initiatives the following:

“—$500,000 to Saint John's County, Florida for water, wastewater, and sewer system improvements;

“—$1,000,000 to the City of San Dimas, California for structural improvements, earthquake reinforcement, and compliance with the Americans with Disabilities Act, to the Walker House;

“—$2,000,000 to the City of Youngstown in Youngstown, Ohio for site acquisition, planning, architectural design, and preliminary construction activities of a convocation/community center;

“—$875,000 to Chippewa County, Wisconsin for development of the Lake Wissota Business Park;

“—$1,500,000 to Lake Marion Regional Water Agency in South Carolina, for continued development of water supply needs;

“—$650,000 to Santa Fe County, New Mexico, for the Santa Fe Regional Water Management and River Restoration Strategy (including activities of partner governments and agencies);

“—$650,000 to the Dunbar Community Center in Springfield, Massachusetts to expand its facilities”.] *(Miscellaneous Appropriations, 2000 as enacted by section 1000(a)(5) of the Consolidated Appropriations Act, 2000 (P.L. 106–113.).*

CORPS OF ENGINEERS

The following appropriations shall be expended under the direction of the Secretary of the Army and the supervision of the Chief of Engineers for authorized civil functions of the Department of the Army pertaining to rivers and harbors, flood control, beach erosion, and related purposes. *(Energy and Water Development Appropriations Act, 2000.)*

Federal Funds

General and special funds:

GENERAL INVESTIGATIONS CONSOLIDATED PROGRAM

[Budget authority in millions of dollars]

General investigations:	*1999 actual*	*2000 est.*	*2001 est.*
Direct program:			
General fund	162	162	138
Transfer to construction, general	–1		
Rescission (P.L. 106–60)		–1	
Emergency supplemental (proposed)		7	
Rivers and harbors contributed funds (cost sharing, permanent appropriation)	51	45	30
Total direct program	212	213	168
Reimbursable program	13	20	20
Total budget authority	225	233	188

GENERAL INVESTIGATIONS

For expenses necessary for the collection and study of basic information pertaining to river and harbor, flood control, shore protection, and related projects, restudy of authorized projects, miscellaneous investigations, and, when authorized by laws, surveys and detailed studies and plans and specifications of projects prior to construction, [$161,994,000] *$137,700,000*, to remain available until expended[: *Provided*, That the Secretary of the Army, acting through the Chief of Engineers, is directed to use the remaining unobligated funds appropriated in Public Law 102–377 for the Red River Waterway, Shreveport, Louisiana, to Daingerfield, Texas, project for the feasibility phase of the Red River Navigation, Southwest Arkansas, study]. *(Energy and Water Development Appropriations Act, 2000.)*

Program and Financing (in millions of dollars)

Identification code 96–3121–0–1–301		1999 actual	2000 est.	2001 est.
	Obligations by program activity:			
	Direct program:			
	Surveys and planning:			
00.01	Navigation, flood damage prevention, and shoreline protection studies	45	40	33
00.02	Comprehensive basin studies	1	1	3
00.03	Special studies	20	22	19
00.04	Review of authorized projects	16	16	11
00.05	Cooperation with other Federal agencies and non-Federal interests	6	6	6
00.07	Preconstruction engineering and design	17	18	13
	Collection and study of basic data:			
00.08	Flood plain management services	9	6	6
00.09	Other programs	20	20	18
00.10	Research and development	37	35	26
09.11	Reimbursable Program Activity	13	20	20
10.00	Total new obligations	184	184	155
	Budgetary resources available for obligation:			
21.40	Unobligated balance available, start of year	42	36	33
22.00	New budget authority (gross)	178	181	158
23.90	Total budgetary resources available for obligation	220	217	191
23.95	Total new obligations	–184	–184	–155
24.40	Unobligated balance available, end of year	36	33	36
	New budget authority (gross), detail:			
	Discretionary:			
40.00	Appropriation	162	162	138
40.35	Appropriation rescinded (P.L. 106–60)		–1	
41.00	Transferred to other accounts	–1		
43.00	Appropriation (total discretionary)	161	161	138
	Spending authority from offsetting collections:			
68.00	Offsetting collections other federal agencies	13	20	20
68.10	From Federal sources: Change in receivables and unpaid, unfilled orders	4		
68.90	Spending authority from offsetting collections (total discretionary)	17	20	20
70.00	Total new budget authority (gross)	178	181	158
	Change in unpaid obligations:			
	Unpaid obligations, start of year:			
72.40	Obligated balance, start of year	23	35	31
72.95	From Federal sources: Receivables and unpaid, unfilled orders	9	13	13
72.99	Total unpaid obligations, start of year	32	48	44
73.10	Total new obligations	184	184	155
73.20	Total outlays (gross)	–168	–188	–167
	Unpaid obligations, end of year:			
74.40	Obligated balance, end of year	35	31	19
74.95	From Federal sources: Receivables and unpaid, unfilled orders	13	13	13
74.99	Total unpaid obligations, end of year	48	44	32
	Outlays (gross), detail:			
86.90	Outlays from new discretionary authority	103	117	103
86.93	Outlays from discretionary balances	65	71	64
87.00	Total outlays (gross)	168	188	167
	Offsets:			
	Against gross budget authority and outlays:			
88.00	Offsetting collections (cash) from: Federal sources	–13	–20	–20
	Against gross budget authority only:			
88.95	From Federal sources: Change in receivables and unpaid, unfilled orders	–4		
	Net budget authority and outlays:			
89.00	Budget authority	161	161	138
90.00	Outlays	155	168	147

Summary of Budget Authority and Outlays

(in millions of dollars)

Enacted/requested:	*1999 actual*	*2000 est.*	*2001 est.*
Budget Authority	161	161	138
Outlays	155	168	147
Supplemental proposal:			
Budget Authority		7	
Outlays		7	
Total:			
Budget Authority	161	168	138
Outlays	155	175	147

Funds are included for surveys, preconstruction engineering and design, data collection, interagency coordination and research activities to determine the need, engineering feasibility, economic justification, and the environmental and social suitability of solutions to water and related land resource problems. Four comprehensive river basin surveys will be initiated with 25 percent nonfederal cost sharing.

General and special funds—Continued

GENERAL INVESTIGATIONS—Continued

Object Classification (in millions of dollars)

Identification code 96–3121–0–1–301		1999 actual	2000 est.	2001 est.
	Direct obligations:			
	Personnel compensation:			
11.1	Full-time permanent	57	61	61
11.3	Other than full-time permanent	4	4	4
11.5	Other personnel compensation	2	2	2
11.7	Military personnel	1	1	1
11.9	Total personnel compensation	64	68	68
12.1	Civilian personnel benefits	14	15	15
13.0	Benefits for former personnel	1	1	1
21.0	Travel and transportation of persons	3	3	3
23.1	Rental payments to GSA	4	4	4
23.3	Communications, utilities, and miscellaneous	2	2	2
24.0	Printing and reproduction	3	3	3
25.2	Other services	53	46	28
25.3	Purchase of goods and services from Government accounts	18	15	4
25.5	Research and development contracts	6	4	4
26.0	Supplies and materials	2	2	2
31.0	Equipment	1	1	1
99.0	Subtotal, direct obligations	171	164	135
99.0	Reimbursable obligations	13	20	20
99.9	Total new obligations	184	184	155

Personnel Summary

Identification code 96–3121–0–1–301		1999 actual	2000 est.	2001 est.
	Direct:			
1001	Total compensable workyears: Full-time equivalent employment	1,309	1,365	1,325
	Reimbursable:			
2001	Total compensable workyears: Full-time equivalent employment	31		

CONSTRUCTION, GENERAL CONSOLIDATED PROGRAM

[Budget authority in millions of dollars]

	1999 actual	2000 est.	2001 est.
Construction, general:			
Direct program:			
General fund	1,339	1,301	1,022
Transfer from General Investigations	1		
Rescissions:			
P.L. 106–60		−13	
P.L. 106–113		−16	
Supplemental (P.L. 105–277)	35		
Harbor Maintenance Trust Fund	3	9	
Harbor Services Fund			250
Inland waterway trust fund appropriation	88	75	74
Rivers and harbors contributed funds (costsharing, permanent appropriation)	173	157	165
Total direct program	1,639	1,513	1,511
Reimbursable program	515	429	424
Total budget authority	2,154	1,942	1,935

CONSTRUCTION, GENERAL

For the prosecution of river and harbor, flood control, shore protection, and related projects authorized by laws; and detailed studies, and plans and specifications, of projects (including those for development with participation or under consideration for participation by States, local governments, or private groups) authorized or made eligible for selection by law (but such studies shall not constitute a commitment of the Government to construction), [$1,400,722,000] *$1,346,000,000*, to remain available until expended, of which [such sums as are necessary for the Federal share of construction costs for facilities under the Dredged Material Disposal Facilities program shall be derived from the Harbor Maintenance Trust Fund, as authorized by Public Law 104–303] *$250,000,000 shall be derived only from the Harbor Services Fund*; and of which such sums as are necessary pursuant to Public Law 99–662 shall be derived from the Inland Waterways Trust Fund, for one-half of the costs of construction and rehabilitation of inland waterways projects, including rehabilitation costs for the Lock and Dam [25] *11*, Mississippi River, [Illinois and Missouri; Lock and Dam 14, Mississippi River,] Iowa; Lock and Dam 24, Mississippi River, Illinois and Missouri; [and] Lock and Dam 3, Mississippi River, Minnesota; London Locks and Dam; Kanawha River, West Virginia; and Lock and Dam 12, Mississippi River, Iowa projects[; and of which funds are provided for the following projects in the amounts specified:

Indianapolis Central Waterfront, Indiana, $8,000,000;

Harlan/Clover Fork including grading and landscaping of the disposal site at the Harlan floodwall, Pike County, Middlesboro, Martin County, Pike County Tug Forks Tributaries, Bell County, Harlan County, and Town of Martin elements of the Levisa and Tug Forks of the Big Sandy River and Upper Cumberland River project in Kentucky, $14,050,000;

Jackson County, Mississippi, $800,000;

Natchez Bluff, Mississippi, $2,000,000;

Passaic River Streambank Restoration, New Jersey, $6,000,000; and

Upper Mingo County (including Mingo County Tributaries), Lower Mingo County (Kermit), Wayne County, and McDowell County, elements of the Levisa and Tug Forks of the Big Sandy River and Upper Cumberland River project in West Virginia, $4,400,000]: *Provided*, That [no part of any appropriation contained in this Act shall be expended or obligated to begin Phase II on the John Day Drawdown study or to initiate a study of the drawdown of McNary Dam unless authorized by law: *Provided further*, That the Secretary of the Army, acting through the Chief of Engineers, may use $1,500,000 of funding appropriated herein to initiate construction of shoreline protection measures at Assateague Island, Maryland, subject to execution of an agreement for reimbursement by the National Park Service: *Provided further*, That] the Secretary of the Army[, acting through the Chief of Engineers, may use] *is authorized and directed to use $24,000,000 of* Construction, General funding [as directed in Public Law 105–62 and Public Law 105–245 to initiate] *provided herein for* construction of an emergency outlet from Devils Lake, North Dakota, to the Sheyenne River, *at an estimated cost of $100,000,000, which shall be cost-shared in accordance with section 103 of the Water Resources Development Act of 1986, as amended (33 U.S.C. 2213),* except that the funds shall not become available unless the Secretary of the Army determines that [an emergency (as defined in section 102 of the Robert T. Stafford Disaster Relief and Emergency Assistance Act (42 U.S.C. 5122)) exists with respect to the emergency need for the outlet and reports to Congress that] the construction is technically sound, [economically justified, and] environmentally acceptable, and in compliance with the National Environmental Policy Act of 1969 (42 U.S.C. 4321 et seq.): [*Provided further*, That the economic justification for the emergency outlet shall be prepared in accordance with the principles and guidelines for economic evaluation as required by regulations and procedures of the Army Corps of Engineers for all flood control projects, and that the economic justification be fully described, including the analysis of the benefits and costs, in the project plan documents:] *Provided further*, That the plans for the emergency outlet shall be reviewed and, to be effective, shall contain assurances provided by the Secretary of State, after consultation with the International Joint Commission, that the project will not violate the requirements or intent of the Treaty Between the United States and Great Britain Relating to Boundary Waters Between the United States and Canada, signed at Washington January 11, 1909 (36 Stat. 2448; TS 548) (commonly known as the "Boundary Waters Treaty of 1909"): *Provided further*, That the Secretary of the Army shall submit the [final] *preconstruction, engineering and design* plans [and other documents] for the emergency outlet to Congress: *Provided further*, That no funds made available under this Act or any other Act for any fiscal year may be used by the Secretary of the Army to carry out the portion of the feasibility study of the Devils Lake Basin, North Dakota, authorized under the Energy and Water Development Appropriations Act, 1993 (Public Law 102–377), that addresses the needs of the area for stabilized lake levels through inlet controls, or to otherwise study any facility or carry out any activity that would permit the transfer of water from the Missouri River Basin into Devils Lake. *(Energy and Water Development Appropriations Act, 2000.)*

Program and Financing (in millions of dollars)

Identification code 96–3122–0–1–301		1999 actual	2000 est.	2001 est.
	Obligations by program activity:			
	Direct program:			
	Navigation projects:			
	Channels and harbors:			
00.04	Projects specifically authorized by Congress	294	284	287
00.05	Projects not specifically authorized by Congress	12	9	9
00.06	Dredged Material Disposal Facilities	3	9	5
00.09	Locks and dams	101	95	95
	Beach erosion control projects:			
00.12	Projects specifically authorized by Congress	82	79	79
00.13	Projects not specifically authorized by Congress	7	8	8
	Flood control projects:			
	Local protection:			
00.16	Projects specifically authorized by Congress	449	427	427
00.17	Projects not specifically authorized by Congress	35	28	28
00.18	Emergency streambank and shoreline protection	10	11	11
00.22	Reservoirs	11	10	10
00.25	Multiple-purpose power projects	5	6	6
	Major rehabilitation and dam safety assurance projects:			
00.27	Navigation	20	17	17
00.28	Flood control	24	20	21
00.29	Multiple-purpose power projects	44	46	46
00.33	Employees' compensation	17	17	17
00.34	Environmental Projects	129	145	145
00.35	Project modification for environmental restoration	20	17	17
00.36	Aquatic plant control	3	3	3
00.37	Aquatic Ecosystems	2	4	4
00.39	Beneficial Uses of Dredged Material	4	3	3
09.00	Reimbursable Program	515	429	424
10.00	Total new obligations	1,787	1,667	1,662
	Budgetary resources available for obligation:			
21.40	Unobligated balance available, start of year	729	830	880
22.00	New budget authority (gross)	1,890	1,717	1,696
22.21	Unobligated balance transferred to other accounts	−2		
23.90	Total budgetary resources available for obligation	2,617	2,547	2,576
23.95	Total new obligations	−1,787	−1,667	−1,662
24.40	Unobligated balance available, end of year	830	880	914
	New budget authority (gross), detail:			
	Discretionary:			
	Appropriation:			
40.00	Appropriation	1,339	1,317	1,272
40.00	Appropriation (PL 105–277)	35		
40.35	Appropriation rescinded		−13	
40.76	Reduction pursuant to P.L. 106–113		−16	
42.00	Transferred from other accounts	1		
43.00	Appropriation (total discretionary)	1,375	1,288	1,272
	Spending authority from offsetting collections:			
	Offsetting collections (cash):			
68.00	Offsetting collections (cash)	364	345	345
68.00	Offsetting collections Harbor Maint. Trust	3	9	5
68.00	Offsetting collections Inland Waterways Trust	88	75	74
68.10	From Federal sources: Change in receivables and unpaid, unfilled orders	60		
68.90	Spending authority from offsetting collections (total discretionary)	515	429	424
70.00	Total new budget authority (gross)	1,890	1,717	1,696
	Change in unpaid obligations:			
	Unpaid obligations, start of year:			
72.40	Obligated balance, start of year	−132	−106	−367
72.95	From Federal sources: Receivables and unpaid, unfilled orders	735	795	795
72.99	Total unpaid obligations, start of year	603	689	428
73.10	Total new obligations	1,787	1,667	1,662
73.20	Total outlays (gross)	−1,701	−1,928	−1,702
	Unpaid obligations, end of year:			
74.40	Obligated balance, end of year	−106	−367	−407
74.95	From Federal sources: Receivables and unpaid, unfilled orders	795	795	795
74.99	Total unpaid obligations, end of year	689	428	388
	Outlays (gross), detail:			
86.90	Outlays from new discretionary authority	1,104	1,202	1,187
86.93	Outlays from discretionary balances	597	726	515
87.00	Total outlays (gross)	1,701	1,928	1,702
	Offsets:			
	Against gross budget authority and outlays:			
	Offsetting collections (cash) from:			
	Federal sources:			
88.00	Offsetting government collections	−364	−345	−345
88.00	Inland Waterways Trust	−88	−75	−74
88.00	Harbor Maint. Trust	−3	−9	−5
88.90	Total, offsetting collections (cash)	−455	−429	−424
	Against gross budget authority only:			
88.95	From Federal sources: Change in receivables and unpaid, unfilled orders	−60		
	Net budget authority and outlays:			
89.00	Budget authority	1,375	1,288	1,272
90.00	Outlays	1,246	1,499	1,278

Summary of Budget Authority and Outlays

(in millions of dollars)

	1999 actual	*2000 est.*	*2001 est.*
Enacted/requested:			
Budget Authority	1,375	1,288	1,272
Outlays	1,246	1,499	1,278
Legislative proposal, not subject to PAYGO:			
Budget Authority			
Outlays			−2
Total:			
Budget Authority	1,375	1,288	1,272
Outlays	1,246	1,499	1,276

Funds are requested for construction, rehabilitation and related activity for water resources development projects having navigation, flood control, water supply, hydroelectric, and other attendant benefits to the Nation. Funding is included for new construction projects consistent with maintaining existing infrastructure, continuing development of the Nation's ports and selected environmental and flood damage reduction projects. The major rehabilitation projects for inland and coastal waterways will derive one-half of the funding from the Inland Waterway Trust Fund. Funds to be derived from the proposed Harbor Services Fund (HSF) will be applied to cover the Federal share of Corps of Engineers port construction activities.

The Budget requests an initial appropriation for the Corps of Engineers program, Challenge 21: Riverine Ecosystem Restoration and Flood Hazard Mitigation, to encourage creation of non-structural flood control projects that protect and restore flood plain ecosystems while reducing flood hazards. This program is part of the Administration's Clean Water Action Plan.

The budget also proposes a new recreation modernization program to meet the needs of today's recreation users by improving recreation facilities and protecting the natural resources that draw people to Corps recreation areas.

Funding is also included for the restoration of the Kissimmee River in Florida and for the Poplar Island Restoration project in Maryland. The budget also includes continued funding for juvenile fish mitigation in the Columbia River Basin and funding to support Corps activities in response to the determination that certain Snake River Salmon species are threatened and endangered. The Department of the Interior's National Park Service will transfer funds to the Corps of Engineers for work it accomplishes under authority of the Everglades National Park Protection and Expansion Act. (16 U.S.C. Sect. 410–8). Funding is included for three ongoing environmental programs: Aquatic Ecosystem Restoration (Section 206), Beneficial Uses of Dredged Material (Section 204), and Everglades and South Florida Ecosystem Restoration (Section 208).

General and special funds—Continued

CONSTRUCTION, GENERAL—Continued

Funding is provided for the Continuing Authorities Program (projects which do not require specific legislation), which includes flood control (Section 205) projects, emergency streambank and shoreline protection (Section 14) projects, beach erosion control (Section 103) projects, mitigation of shore damages (Section 111) projects, navigation (Section 107) projects, and snagging and clearing (Section 208) projects.

Object Classification (in millions of dollars)

Identification code 96–3122–0–1–301		1999 actual	2000 est.	2001 est.
	Direct obligations:			
	Personnel compensation:			
11.1	Full-time permanent	133	133	134
11.3	Other than full-time permanent	10	10	10
11.5	Other personnel compensation	8	8	8
11.7	Military personnel	5	6	6
11.9	Total personnel compensation	156	157	158
12.1	Civilian personnel benefits	33	33	33
	Military personnel benefits:			
12.2	Accrued retirement	3	2	2
12.2	Other personnel	1	1	1
21.0	Travel and transportation of persons	10	10	10
23.1	Rental payments to GSA	11	11	11
23.3	Communications, utilities, and miscellaneous	5	5	5
24.0	Printing and reproduction	5	5	5
25.1	Advisory and assistance services	90	90	90
25.2	Other services	461	427	426
25.3	Purchase of goods and services from Government accounts	40	40	40
25.5	Research and development contracts	6	6	6
26.0	Supplies and materials	12	12	12
31.0	Equipment	16	16	16
32.0	Land and structures	423	423	423
99.0	Subtotal, direct obligations	1,272	1,238	1,238
99.0	Reimbursable obligations	515	429	424
99.9	Total new obligations	1,787	1,667	1,662

Personnel Summary

Identification code 96–3122–0–1–301		1999 actual	2000 est.	2001 est.
	Direct:			
1001	Total compensable workyears: Full-time equivalent employment	3,050	2,985	2,925
	Reimbursable:			
2001	Total compensable workyears: Full-time equivalent employment	1,027	1,135	1,115

(Legislative proposal, not subject to PAYGO)

Program and Financing (in millions of dollars)

Identification code 96–3122–2–1–301		1999 actual	2000 est.	2001 est.
	New budget authority (gross), detail:			
	Discretionary:			
	Appropriation:			
40.00	Appropriation (Construction, General)			–245
40.00	Appropriation (Construction, General)			–5
40.25	Appropriation (special fund, indefinite) Harbor Services Fund			250
43.00	Appropriation (total discretionary)			
	Outlays (gross), detail:			
86.90	Outlays from new discretionary authority			–2
	Net budget authority and outlays:			
89.00	Budget authority			
90.00	Outlays			–2

OPERATION AND MAINTENANCE, GENERAL CONSOLIDATED PROGRAM

[Budget authority in millions of dollars]

	1999 actual	2000 est.	2001 est.
Operation and maintenance, general:			
Direct program:			
General fund	1,617	1,116	1,120
Emergency supplemental (P.L. 105–277), HMTF	100		
Emergency supplemental (proposed)		19	
Special recreation user fees	36	33	34
Harbor Maintenance Trust Fund (HMTF)		705	
Harbor Services Fund (proposed)			700
Rivers and harbors contributed funds (cost sharing, permanent appropriation)	7	7	7
Bonneville Power Administration transfers	106	107	108
Total direct program	1,866	1,987	1,969
Reimbursable program	30	30	30
Total budget authority	1,896	2,017	1,999

OPERATION AND MAINTENANCE, GENERAL

For expenses necessary for the preservation, operation, maintenance, and care of existing river and harbor, flood control, and related works, including such sums as may be necessary for the maintenance of harbor channels provided by a State, municipality or other public agency, outside of harbor lines, and serving essential needs of general commerce and navigation; surveys and charting of northern and northwestern lakes and connecting waters; clearing and straightening channels; and removal of obstructions to navigation, **[**$1,853,618,000**]** *$1,854,000,000*, to remain available until expended, of which **[**such sums as become available in the Harbor Maintenance Trust Fund, pursuant to Public Law 99–662, may be derived from that Fund**]** *$700,000,000 shall be derived only from the Harbor Services Fund*; and of which such sums as become available from the special account established by the Land and Water Conservation Act of 1965, as amended (16 U.S.C. 460l), may be derived from that account for construction, operation, and maintenance of outdoor recreation facilities**[**: *Provided*, That no funds, whether appropriated, contributed, or otherwise provided, shall be available to the United States Army Corps of Engineers for the purpose of acquiring land in Jasper County, South Carolina, in connection with the Savannah Harbor navigation project**]**. *(Energy and Water Development Appropriations Act, 2000.)*

Unavailable Collections (in millions of dollars)

Identification code 96–3123–0–1–300		1999 actual	2000 est.	2001 est.
	Balance, start of year:			
01.99	Balance, start of year	36	33	34
	Receipts:			
02.01	Special recreation use fees	33	34	34
04.00	Total: Balances and collections	69	67	68
	Appropriation:			
05.01	Operation and maintenance, general	–36	–33	–34
07.99	Total balance, end of year	33	34	34

Note.—The receipts shown in this schedule are on deposit in Treasury account 96–5007, "Special Recreation user fees".

Program and Financing (in millions of dollars)

Identification code 96–3123–0–1–300		1999 actual	2000 est.	2001 est.
	Obligations by program activity:			
	Direct program:			
	Operation and maintenance projects:			
	Navigation projects:			
00.01	Channels and harbors	745	706	706
00.02	Locks and dams	402	371	371
	Flood control projects:			
00.05	Reservoirs	321	332	336
00.06	Channel improvements, inspections, and miscellaneous maintenance	21	20	20
00.09	Multiple-purpose power projects	387	357	357
00.91	Total operation and maintenance projects	1,876	1,786	1,790
	Miscellaneous items:			
01.01	Protection of navigation	38	40	40
01.02	National emergency preparedness	6	6	6

01.05	Special programs to improve operation and maintenance	5	4	4
01.91	Total miscellaneous items	49	50	50
01.92	Total direct program	1,925	1,836	1,840
09.00	Reimbursable Program Activity	30	30	30
10.00	Total new obligations	1,955	1,866	1,870
	Budgetary resources available for obligation:			
21.40	Unobligated balance available, start of year	100	34	159
22.00	New budget authority (gross)	1,889	1,991	1,992
23.90	Total budgetary resources available for obligation	1,989	2,025	2,151
23.95	Total new obligations	−1,955	−1,866	−1,870
24.40	Unobligated balance available, end of year	34	159	280
	New budget authority (gross), detail:			
	Discretionary:			
40.00	Appropriation	1,617	1,116	1,120
40.20	Appropriation (special fund, definite)	36	33	34
43.00	Appropriation (total discretionary)	1,653	1,149	1,154
	Spending authority from offsetting collections:			
	Offsetting collections (cash):			
68.00	Offsetting collections other Federal agencies	30	30	30
68.00	Offsetting collections (Bonneville Power)	106	107	108
68.00	Offsetting collections Harbor Maint. Trust	100	705	700
68.90	Spending authority from offsetting collections (total discretionary)	236	842	838
70.00	Total new budget authority (gross)	1,889	1,991	1,992
	Change in unpaid obligations:			
72.40	Unpaid obligations, start of year: Obligated balance, start of year	276	329	120
73.10	Total new obligations	1,955	1,866	1,870
73.20	Total outlays (gross)	−1,902	−2,075	−1,990
74.40	Unpaid obligations, end of year: Obligated balance, end of year	329	120	
	Outlays (gross), detail:			
86.90	Outlays from new discretionary authority	1,526	1,712	1,712
86.93	Outlays from discretionary balances	376	363	279
87.00	Total outlays (gross)	1,902	2,075	1,990
	Offsets:			
	Against gross budget authority and outlays:			
	Offsetting collections (cash) from:			
	Federal sources:			
88.00	Harbor Maintenance Trust Fund	−100	−705	−700
88.00	Other Federal sources (BPA)	−106	−107	−108
88.00	Other Federal sources	−30	−30	−30
88.90	Total, offsetting collections (cash)	−236	−842	−838
	Net budget authority and outlays:			
89.00	Budget authority	1,653	1,149	1,154
90.00	Outlays	1,666	1,233	1,152

Summary of Budget Authority and Outlays

(in millions of dollars)

	1999 actual	2000 est.	2001 est.
Enacted/requested:			
Budget Authority	1,653	1,149	1,154
Outlays	1,666	1,233	1,153
Supplemental proposal:			
Budget Authority		19	
Outlays		19	
Legislative proposal, not subject to PAYGO:			
Budget Authority			700
Outlays			525
Total:			
Budget Authority	1,653	1,168	1,854
Outlays	1,666	1,252	1,678

Funds are requested for operation, maintenance, and related activities of the Corps of Engineers at the navigation, flood control and multiple purpose projects for which it is responsible. Work to be accomplished consists of dredging, repair, and operation of structures and other facilities, including recreation facilities, all as authorized in the various Rivers and Harbors and Flood Control Acts. Related activities include aquatic plant control, monitoring of completed coastal projects, removal of sunken vessels, and the collection of domestic waterborne commerce statistics. This request also includes funds for National Emergency Preparedness as directed in Executive Order 11490. Funds to be derived from the proposed Harbor Services Fund (HSF) will be applied to cover 100 percent of eligible harbor maintenance costs, plus up to $1 million for payment of expenses of administration incurred by the Army Corps of Engineers related to HSF.

In accordance with Section 2406 of the National Energy Policy Act of 1992 (P.L. 102–486), the Secretary of the Army entered into an agreement with the Bonneville Power Administration (BPA) for direct funding of hydropower activities in the Pacific Northwest beginning in FY 1999.

Object Classification (in millions of dollars)

Identification code 96–3123–0–1–300		1999 actual	2000 est.	2001 est.
	Direct obligations:			
	Personnel compensation:			
11.1	Full-time permanent	561	579	598
11.3	Other than full-time permanent	67	69	71
11.5	Other personnel compensation	35	36	38
11.7	Military personnel	1	1	1
11.9	Total personnel compensation	664	685	708
12.1	Civilian personnel benefits	145	150	155
13.0	Benefits for former personnel	3	3	3
21.0	Travel and transportation of persons	22	22	22
22.0	Transportation of things	3	3	3
23.1	Rental payments to GSA	18	18	18
23.2	Rental payments to others	3	3	3
23.3	Communications, utilities, and misc. chgs.	32	27	27
24.0	Printing and reproduction	6	6	6
25.1	Advisory and assistance services	8	8	8
25.2	Other services	623	513	489
25.3	Goods and services from Government accounts	135	140	140
25.4	Operation and maintenance of facilities	9	10	10
25.5	Research and development contracts	3	3	3
26.0	Supplies and materials	96	90	90
31.0	Equipment	20	20	20
32.0	Land and structures	130	130	130
42.0	Insurance claims and indemnities	5	5	5
99.0	Subtotal, direct obligations	1,925	1,836	1,840
99.0	Reimbursable obligations	30	30	30
99.9	Total new obligations	1,955	1,866	1,870

Personnel Summary

Identification code 96–3123–0–1–300		1999 actual	2000 est.	2001 est.
	Direct:			
1001	Total compensable workyears: Full-time equivalent employment	13,634	13,719	13,810
	Reimbursable:			
2001	Total compensable workyears: Full-time equivalent employment	52		

Legislative proposal, not subject to PAYGO.

Program and Financing (in millions of dollars)

Identification code 96–3123–2–1–300		1999 actual	2000 est.	2001 est.
	New budget authority (gross), detail:			
	Discretionary:			
40.25	Appropriation (special fund, indefinite) Harbor Services Fund			700
68.00	Spending authority from offsetting collections: Offsetting collections (cash)			−700
70.00	Total new budget authority (gross)			
	Change in unpaid obligations:			
73.20	Total outlays (gross)			175

General and special funds—Continued

OPERATION AND MAINTENANCE, GENERAL—Continued

Program and Financing (in millions of dollars)—Continued

Identification code 96–3123–2–1–300	1999 actual	2000 est.	2001 est.
74.40 Unpaid obligations, end of year: Obligated balance, end of year			175
Outlays (gross), detail:			
86.90 Outlays from new discretionary authority			–175
Offsets:			
Against gross budget authority and outlays:			
88.00 Offsetting collections (cash) from: Federal sources			700
Net budget authority and outlays:			
89.00 Budget authority			700
90.00 Outlays			525

REGULATORY PROGRAM

For expenses necessary for administration of laws pertaining to regulation of navigable waters and wetlands, [$117,000,000] *$125,000,000*, to remain available until expended: *Provided*, That the Secretary [of the Army, acting through the Chief of Engineers, is directed to use $5,000,000 of funds appropriated herein to fully implement an administrative appeals process for the Corps of Engineers Regulatory Program, which administrative appeals process shall provide for a single-level appeal of jurisdictional determinations: *Provided further*, That the Secretary of the Army, acting through the Chief of Engineers, shall, using funds provided herein, prepare studies and analyses of the impacts on Regulatory Branch workload and on cost of compliance by the regulated community of proposed replacement permits for the nationwide permit 26 under section 404 of the Clean Water Act and shall submit a report based upon the aforementioned studies and analyses to the Committees on Appropriations of the House and Senate, the Transportation and Infrastructure Committee of the House, and the Committee on Environment and Public Works of the Senate] *shall establish and collect reasonable fees to provide a partial recovery of the Federal costs incurred in implementing this program, to be credited to the General Fund of the Treasury. (Energy and Water Development Appropriations Act, 2000.)*

Program and Financing (in millions of dollars)

Identification code 96–3126–0–1–301	1999 actual	2000 est.	2001 est.
Obligations by program activity:			
00.01 Permit evaluation	82	87	92
00.03 Enforcement	21	24	27
00.05 Studies	1	2	2
00.06 Administrative Appeals	1	2	2
00.07 Environmental impact statements	1	2	2
01.92 Total Direct Obligations	106	117	125
09.00 Reimbursable program	1	1	1
10.00 Total new obligations	107	118	126
Budgetary resources available for obligation:			
21.40 Unobligated balance available, start of year	4	4	4
22.00 New budget authority (gross)	107	118	126
23.90 Total budgetary resources available for obligation	111	122	130
23.95 Total new obligations	–107	–118	–126
24.40 Unobligated balance available, end of year	4	4	4
New budget authority (gross), detail:			
Discretionary:			
40.00 Appropriation	106	117	125
68.00 Spending authority from offsetting collections: Offsetting collections (cash)	1	1	1
70.00 Total new budget authority (gross)	107	118	126
Change in unpaid obligations:			
72.40 Unpaid obligations, start of year: Obligated balance, start of year	4	5	2
73.10 Total new obligations	107	118	126
73.20 Total outlays (gross)	–106	–121	–126
74.40 Unpaid obligations, end of year: Obligated balance, end of year	5	2	2
Outlays (gross), detail:			
86.90 Outlays from new discretionary authority	98	112	120
86.93 Outlays from discretionary balances	8	9	6
87.00 Total outlays (gross)	106	121	126
Offsets:			
Against gross budget authority and outlays:			
88.40 Offsetting collections (cash) from: Non-Federal sources	–1	–1	–1
Net budget authority and outlays:			
89.00 Budget authority	106	117	125
90.00 Outlays	105	120	125

This appropriation provides for costs incurred to administer laws pertaining to regulation of activities affecting U.S. waters, including wetlands, in accordance with the Rivers and Harbors Act of 1899, the Clean Water Act of 1977, and the Marine Protection, Research and Sanctuaries Act of 1972.

The requested increase is needed to maintain program performance, protect important aquatic resources, reduce the adverse impacts of permitted activities in the nation's floodplains, and broaden partnership with States and local communities through watershed planning efforts.

The Corps has not changed the regulatory program fee structure since 1977. The budget proposes to pursue reasonable changes that would reduce the fees paid by many applicants and increase recovery from commercial applicants. The amount of funding that this program requires is independent of any decisions concerning the fee structure. Revenues would reduce net Federal costs, but would not be made available to the regulatory program for its use.

Object Classification (in millions of dollars)

Identification code 96–3126–0–1–301	1999 actual	2000 est.	2001 est.
Direct obligations:			
Personnel compensation:			
11.1 Full-time permanent	61	63	65
11.3 Other than full-time permanent	4	4	4
11.5 Other personnel compensation	2	2	2
11.9 Total personnel compensation	67	69	71
12.1 Civilian personnel benefits	15	15	16
21.0 Travel and transportation of persons	3	4	4
22.0 Transportation of things	1	1	1
23.1 Rental payments to GSA	3	3	3
23.3 Communications, utilities, and miscellaneous	2	3	3
24.0 Printing and reproduction	2	2	2
25.2 Other services	9	13	18
25.3 Purchase goods & svcs. fm Government accts.	1	1	1
25.7 Operation and maintenance of equipment	1	2	2
26.0 Supplies and materials	1	2	2
31.0 Equipment	1	2	2
99.0 Subtotal, direct obligations	106	117	125
99.0 Reimbursable obligations	1	1	1
99.9 Total new obligations	107	118	126

Personnel Summary

Identification code 96–3126–0–1–301	1999 actual	2000 est.	2001 est.
1001 Total compensable workyears: Full-time equivalent employment	1,372	1,380	1,400

FLOOD CONTROL AND COASTAL EMERGENCIES

[Budget authority in millions of dollars]

Flood Control and Coastal Emergencies:	*1999 actual*	*2000 est.*	*2001 est.*
Direct program:			

General fund			
Rescission (P.L. 106–51)	–5		
Total direct program	–5		
Reimbursable program	203	215	215
Total budget authority	198	215	215

Flood Control and Coastal Emergencies

Program and Financing (in millions of dollars)

Identification code 96–3125–0–1–301		1999 actual	2000 est.	2001 est.
	Obligations by program activity:			
	Direct program:			
00.01	Disaster preparedness	16	20	20
00.02	Emergency operations	16	25	25
00.03	Rehabilitation	35	49	49
00.04	Advance Measures	17	24	24
09.00	Reimbursable Program Activity	203	215	215
10.00	Total new obligations	287	333	333
	Budgetary resources available for obligation:			
21.40	Unobligated balance available, start of year	1,104	394	161
22.00	New budget authority (gross)	–423	100	100
23.90	Total budgetary resources available for obligation	681	494	261
23.95	Total new obligations	–287	–333	–333
24.40	Unobligated balance available, end of year	394	161	–72
	New budget authority (gross), detail:			
	Discretionary:			
40.00	Appropriation			
40.75	Reduction pursuant to P.L. 106–51	–5		
43.00	Appropriation (total discretionary)	–5		
	Spending authority from offsetting collections:			
68.00	Offsetting collections other federal agencies	159	100	100
68.10	From Federal sources: Change in receivables and unpaid, unfilled orders	–577		
68.90	Spending authority from offsetting collections (total discretionary)	–418	100	100
70.00	Total new budget authority (gross)	–423	100	100
	Change in unpaid obligations:			
	Unpaid obligations, start of year:			
72.40	Obligated balance, start of year	–836	–293	–74
72.95	From Federal sources: Receivables and unpaid, unfilled orders	989	412	412
72.99	Total unpaid obligations, start of year	153	119	338
73.10	Total new obligations	287	333	333
73.20	Total outlays (gross)	–321	–114	–114
	Unpaid obligations, end of year:			
74.40	Obligated balance, end of year	–293	–74	145
74.95	From Federal sources: Receivables and unpaid, unfilled orders	412	412	412
74.99	Total unpaid obligations, end of year	119	338	557
	Outlays (gross), detail:			
86.90	Outlays from new discretionary authority	159	100	100
86.93	Outlays from discretionary balances	162	14	14
87.00	Total outlays (gross)	321	114	114
	Offsets:			
	Against gross budget authority and outlays:			
88.00	Offsetting collections (cash) from: Federal sources	–159	–100	–100
	Against gross budget authority only:			
88.95	From Federal sources: Change in receivables and unpaid, unfilled orders	577		
	Net budget authority and outlays:			
89.00	Budget authority	–5		
90.00	Outlays	162	14	14

This activity provides for preparedness activities for all natural and technological disasters, flood fighting and rescue operations, and repair of flood control and Federal hurricane or shore protection works. It also provides for emergency supplies of clean water where the source has been contaminated and, in drought distressed areas, where adequate supplies of water are needed for consumption.

No new funding is required for this account in FY 2001. The balance of available funds in the account is expected to be sufficient to meet operational requirements.

Object Classification (in millions of dollars)

Identification code 96–3125–0–1–301		1999 actual	2000 est.	2001 est.
	Direct obligations:			
	Personnel compensation:			
11.1	Full-time permanent	14	9	9
11.3	Other than full-time permanent	1	1	1
11.5	Other personnel compensation	2	1	1
11.9	Total personnel compensation	17	11	11
12.1	Civilian personnel benefits	4	2	2
21.0	Travel and transportation of persons	1	2	2
22.0	Transportation of things	2	3	3
23.1	Rental payments to GSA	2	3	3
23.2	Rental payments to others	1	3	3
23.3	Communications, utilities, and miscellaneous charges	2	3	3
24.0	Printing and reproduction	1	2	2
25.2	Other services	33	56	56
25.3	Purchases of goods and services from Government accounts	2	3	3
25.7	Operation and maintenance of equipment	2	3	3
26.0	Supplies and materials	3	4	4
31.0	Equipment	3	4	4
32.0	Land and structures	11	19	19
99.0	Subtotal, direct obligations	84	118	118
99.0	Reimbursable obligations	203	215	215
99.9	Total new obligations	287	333	333

Personnel Summary

Identification code 96–3125–0–1–301		1999 actual	2000 est.	2001 est.
	Direct:			
1001	Total compensable workyears: Full-time equivalent employment	285	180	180
	Reimbursable:			
2001	Total compensable workyears: Full-time equivalent employment	30		

Formerly Utilized Sites Remedial Action Program

For expenses necessary to clean up contamination from sites throughout the United States resulting from work performed as part of the Nation's early atomic energy program, [$150,000,000] *$140,000,000*, to remain available until expended. *(Energy and Water Development Appropriations Act, 2000.)*

Program and Financing (in millions of dollars)

Identification code 96–3130–0–1–053		1999 actual	2000 est.	2001 est.
	Obligations by program activity:			
00.01	Direct Program Activity	139	140	140
09.01	Reimbursable program	10	10	10
10.00	Total new obligations	149	150	150
	Budgetary resources available for obligation:			
21.40	Unobligated balance available, start of year	5	6	16
22.00	New budget authority (gross)	150	160	150
23.90	Total budgetary resources available for obligation	155	166	166
23.95	Total new obligations	–149	–150	–150
24.40	Unobligated balance available, end of year	6	16	16
	New budget authority (gross), detail:			
	Discretionary:			
40.00	Appropriation	140	150	140
68.00	Spending authority from offsetting collections: Offsetting collections (cash)	10	10	10
70.00	Total new budget authority (gross)	150	160	150

General and special funds—Continued

FORMERLY UTILIZED SITES REMEDIAL ACTION PROGRAM—Continued

Program and Financing (in millions of dollars)—Continued

Identification code 96–3130–0–1–053	1999 actual	2000 est.	2001 est.
Change in unpaid obligations:			
72.40 Unpaid obligations, start of year: Obligated balance, start of year	87	73	59
73.10 Total new obligations	149	150	150
73.20 Total outlays (gross)	−163	−164	−155
74.40 Unpaid obligations, end of year: Obligated balance, end of year	73	59	54
Outlays (gross), detail:			
86.90 Outlays from new discretionary authority	71	85	80
86.93 Outlays from discretionary balances	92	79	75
87.00 Total outlays (gross)	163	164	155
Offsets:			
Against gross budget authority and outlays:			
88.00 Offsetting collections (cash) from: Federal sources	−10	−10	−10
Net budget authority and outlays:			
89.00 Budget authority	140	150	140
90.00 Outlays	153	154	145

The Corps has certain responsibilities for the cleanup of certain low-level radioactive materials and mixed wastes, which are located mostly at sites contaminated as a result of the Nation's early atomic weapons development program.

Object Classification (in millions of dollars)

Identification code 96–3130–0–1–053	1999 actual	2000 est.	2001 est.
Direct obligations:			
11.1 Personnel compensation: Full-time permanent	8	9	9
12.1 Civilian personnel benefits	2	2	2
25.2 Other services	112	109	109
25.3 Purchases of goods and services from Government accounts	17	20	20
99.0 Subtotal, direct obligations	139	140	140
99.0 Reimbursable obligations	10	10	10
99.9 Total new obligations	149	150	150

Personnel Summary

Identification code 96–3130–0–1–053	1999 actual	2000 est.	2001 est.
1001 Total compensable workyears: Full-time equivalent employment	154	155	155

GENERAL EXPENSES

For expenses necessary for general administration and related functions in the Office of the Chief of Engineers and offices of the Division Engineers; activities of the Coastal Engineering Research Board, the Humphreys Engineer Center Support Activity, the Water Resources Support Center, and headquarters support functions at the USACE Finance Center, **[**$149,500,000**]** *$152,000,000*, to remain available until expended **[**: *Provided*, That no part of any other appropriation provided in title I of this Act shall be available to fund the activities of the Office of the Chief of Engineers or the executive direction and management activities of the division offices: *Provided further*, That none of these funds shall be available to support an office of congressional affairs within the executive office of the Chief of Engineers**]**. *(Energy and Water Development Appropriations Act, 2000.)*

Program and Financing (in millions of dollars)

Identification code 96–3124–0–1–301	1999 actual	2000 est.	2001 est.
Obligations by program activity:			
Executive direction and management:			
00.01 Office, Chief of Engineers	49	58	60
00.02 Division offices	71	73	74
00.09 Humphreys Engineer Center Support Activity	19	19	22
00.11 Water Resources Support Center	5	3	3
00.12 USACE Finance Center	1	1	
10.00 Total new obligations	145	154	159
Budgetary resources available for obligation:			
21.40 Unobligated balance available, start of year	13	16	9
22.00 New budget authority (gross)	148	150	152
23.90 Total budgetary resources available for obligation	161	166	161
23.95 Total new obligations	−145	−154	−159
23.98 Unobligated balance expiring or withdrawn		−3	
24.40 Unobligated balance available, end of year	16	9	2
New budget authority (gross), detail:			
Discretionary:			
40.00 Appropriation	148	150	152
Change in unpaid obligations:			
72.40 Unpaid obligations, start of year: Obligated balance, start of year	32	34	18
73.10 Total new obligations	145	154	159
73.20 Total outlays (gross)	−143	−170	−149
74.40 Unpaid obligations, end of year: Obligated balance, end of year	34	18	28
Outlays (gross), detail:			
86.90 Outlays from new discretionary authority	98	120	122
86.93 Outlays from discretionary balances	45	50	27
87.00 Total outlays (gross)	143	170	149
Net budget authority and outlays:			
89.00 Budget authority	148	150	152
90.00 Outlays	143	170	149

Executive direction and management.—The Office, Chief of Engineers, and 8 division offices supervise work in 37 district offices.

Coastal Engineering Research Board.—The Board provides policy guidance, reviews and plans requirements for conducting coastal engineering research and development, and recommends research project priorities.

Humphreys Engineer Center Support Activity.—This support center provides administrative services for the Office, Chief of Engineers and other separate field operating activities to include personnel, logistics, and finance and accounting.

Water Resources Support Center.—This support center performs studies and analyses for meeting national objectives. It develops planning techniques for comprehensive management and development of the Nation's water resources.

United States Army Corps of Engineers Finance Center.—This center was established in 1996 in Memphis, Tennessee, to begin centralization of Corps finance and accounting sites. A total of 55 Corps sites were consolidated as of August 1999. The remaining six sites, which use foreign currency applications in the financial management system, have been deferred from consolidation until 2003. The Department of Defense plans to capitalize and transfer the Finance Center to the Defense Finance and Accounting Service during FY 2000.

Object Classification (in millions of dollars)

Identification code 96–3124–0–1–301	1999 actual	2000 est.	2001 est.
Personnel compensation:			
11.1 Full-time permanent	76	79	80
11.3 Other than full-time permanent	1	1	1
11.5 Other personnel compensation	2	2	2
11.7 Military personnel	4	5	5
11.9 Total personnel compensation	83	87	88
12.1 Civilian personnel benefits	16	18	18
12.2 Accrued retirement	1	2	2
13.0 Benefits for former personnel	1	1	1
21.0 Travel and transportation of persons	5	5	6
23.1 Rental payments to GSA	7	7	6

		1999 actual	2000 est.	2001 est.
23.2	Rental payments to others	1	1	1
23.3	Communications, utilities, and miscellaneous	4	4	4
24.0	Printing and reproduction	1	1	1
25.2	Other services	13	16	20
25.3	Purchase goods & svcs. fm Government accts.	11	10	10
26.0	Supplies and materials	1	1	1
31.0	Equipment	1	1	1
99.9	Total new obligations	145	154	159

Personnel Summary

Identification code 96–3124–0–1–301		1999 actual	2000 est.	2001 est.
1001	Total compensable workyears: Full-time equivalent employment	1,119	1,111	1,081

FLOOD CONTROL, MISSISSIPPI RIVER AND TRIBUTARIES CONSOLIDATED PROGRAM

[Budget authority in millions of dollars]

Flood control, Mississippi River and tributaries:	*1999 actual*	*2000 est.*	*2001 est.*
Direct program:			
General fund	321	309	309
Emergency Supplemental	3		
Rivers and harbors contributed funds (cost sharing, permanent appropriation)	17	21	26
Total appropriation	341	330	335

FLOOD CONTROL, MISSISSIPPI RIVER AND TRIBUTARIES, ARKANSAS, ILLINOIS, KENTUCKY, LOUISIANA, MISSISSIPPI, MISSOURI, AND TENNESSEE

For expenses necessary for prosecuting work of flood control, and rescue work, repair, restoration, or maintenance of flood control projects threatened or destroyed by flood, as authorized by law (33 U.S.C. 702a and 702g–1), [$309,416,000] *$309,000,000*, to remain available until expended. *(Energy and Water Development Appropriations Act, 2000.)*

Program and Financing (in millions of dollars)

Identification code 96–3112–0–1–301		1999 actual	2000 est.	2001 est.
	Obligations by program activity:			
00.01	General investigations	5	5	5
00.03	Construction	184	174	174
00.05	Maintenance	145	130	130
09.11	Reimbursable program	16	1	1
10.00	Total new obligations	350	310	310
	Budgetary resources available for obligation:			
21.40	Unobligated balance available, start of year	13	3	3
22.00	New budget authority (gross)	340	310	310
23.90	Total budgetary resources available for obligation	353	313	313
23.95	Total new obligations	−350	−310	−310
24.40	Unobligated balance available, end of year	3	3	3
	New budget authority (gross), detail:			
	Discretionary:			
40.00	Appropriation	322	309	309
40.15	Appropriation (emergency)	2		
43.00	Appropriation (total discretionary)	324	309	309
	Spending authority from offsetting collections:			
68.00	Offsetting collections (cash)	8	1	1
68.10	From Federal sources: Change in receivables and unpaid, unfilled orders	8		
68.90	Spending authority from offsetting collections (total discretionary)	16	1	1
70.00	Total new budget authority (gross)	340	310	310
	Change in unpaid obligations:			
	Unpaid obligations, start of year:			
72.40	Obligated balance, start of year	54	51	74
72.95	From Federal sources: Receivables and unpaid, unfilled orders	2	10	10
72.99	Total unpaid obligations, start of year	56	61	84
73.10	Total new obligations	350	310	310
73.20	Total outlays (gross)	−345	−287	−310
	Unpaid obligations, end of year:			
74.40	Obligated balance, end of year	51	74	74
74.95	From Federal sources: Receivables and unpaid, unfilled orders	10	10	10
74.99	Total unpaid obligations, end of year	61	84	84
	Outlays (gross), detail:			
86.90	Outlays from new discretionary authority	278	233	233
86.93	Outlays from discretionary balances	67	54	77
87.00	Total outlays (gross)	345	287	310
	Offsets:			
	Against gross budget authority and outlays:			
88.45	Offsetting collections (cash) from: Offsetting governmental collections from the public	−8	−1	−1
	Against gross budget authority only:			
88.95	From Federal sources: Change in receivables and unpaid, unfilled orders	−8		
	Net budget authority and outlays:			
89.00	Budget authority	324	309	309
90.00	Outlays	337	286	309

Funds are requested for planning, construction, and operation and maintenance activities associated with water resources projects located in the lower Mississippi River Valley from Cape Girardeau, Missouri to the Gulf of Mexico.

Object Classification (in millions of dollars)

Identification code 96–3112–0–1–301		1999 actual	2000 est.	2001 est.
	Direct obligations:			
	Personnel compensation:			
11.1	Full-time permanent	54	55	57
11.3	Other than full-time permanent	2	2	2
11.5	Other personnel compensation	8	8	8
11.9	Total personnel compensation	64	65	67
12.1	Civilian personnel benefits	14	14	15
21.0	Travel and transportation of persons	5	5	5
23.1	Rental payments to GSA	3	3	3
23.3	Communications, utilities, and miscellaneous	3	3	3
24.0	Printing and reproduction	1	1	1
25.1	Advisory and assistance services	15	11	11
25.2	Other services	180	160	157
25.3	Purchase goods & svcs. fm Government	7	6	6
25.4	Operation and maintenance of facilities	1	1	1
26.0	Supplies and materials	5	5	5
31.0	Equipment	1	1	1
32.0	Land and structures	35	34	34
99.0	Subtotal, direct obligations	334	309	309
99.0	Reimbursable obligations	16	1	1
99.9	Total new obligations	350	310	310

Personnel Summary

Identification code 96–3112–0–1–301		1999 actual	2000 est.	2001 est.
1001	Total compensable workyears: Full-time equivalent employment	1,674	1,660	1,665

PAYMENT TO SOUTH DAKOTA TERRESTRIAL WILDLIFE HABITAT RESTORATION TRUST FUND

Program and Financing (in millions of dollars)

Identification code 96–3129–0–1–306		1999 actual	2000 est.	2001 est.
	Obligations by program activity:			
10.00	Total new obligations (object class 25.2)	10	10	10
	Budgetary resources available for obligation:			
22.00	New budget authority (gross)	10	10	10
23.95	Total new obligations	−10	−10	−10

General and special funds—Continued

PAYMENT TO SOUTH DAKOTA TERRESTRIAL WILDLIFE HABITAT RESTORATION TRUST FUND—Continued

Program and Financing (in millions of dollars)—Continued

Identification code 96–3129–0–1–306	1999 actual	2000 est.	2001 est.
New budget authority (gross), detail:			
Mandatory:			
60.00 Appropriation	10	10	10
Change in unpaid obligations:			
73.10 Total new obligations	10	10	10
73.20 Total outlays (gross)	–10	–10	–10
Outlays (gross), detail:			
86.97 Outlays from new mandatory authority	10	10	10
Net budget authority and outlays:			
89.00 Budget authority	10	10	10
90.00 Outlays	10	10	10

This fund makes payments to the South Dakota Terrestrial Wildlife Habitat Restoration Trust Fund, established by the Water Resources Act of 1999 (P.L. 106–53).

HARBOR SERVICES FUND

(Legislative Proposal, not subject to PAYGO)

Contingent upon the enactment of authorizing legislation, the Secretary shall charge a fee to commercial vessel operators for use of Federal ports and channels and such fee shall be deposited in the Harbor Services Fund, to be available for appropriation for fiscal year 2002 for the operation and maintenance and construction of Federal ports and channels, to remain available until expended: Provided, That upon enactment of such authorizing legislation, the amount appropriated from the General Fund for the Army Corps of Engineers, "Construction, General" and "Operation and Maintenance, General"; for the Saint Lawrence Seaway Development Corporation, "Operation and Maintenance"; and for Department of the Treasury, "Administration of Harbor Maintenance Trust Fund", shall be reduced by $250,000,000, $700,000,000, $13,000,000 and $3,000,000 respectively.

Unavailable Collections (in millions of dollars)

Identification code 96–5456–0–2–301	1999 actual	2000 est.	2001 est.
Balance, start of year:			
01.99 Balance, start of year			
Receipts:			
02.03 Earnings on investments, legislative proposal not subject to PAYGO			65
02.04 User fees, legislative proposal, discretionary offset			966
02.05 Transfer from Harbor maintenance trust fund, legislative proposal not subject to PAYGO			1,758
02.99 Total receipts			2,789
Appropriation:			
05.07 Army Corps of Engineers, construction, general, legislative proposal not subject to PAYGO			–250
05.08 Army Corps of Engineers, operations and maintenance, legislative proposal not subject to PAYGO			–700
05.11 Saint Lawrence Seaway Development Corporation operations and maintenance, legislative proposal subject to PAYGO			–13
05.12 Customs Service: administrative expenses, legislative proposal not subjet to PAYGO			–3
05.99 Subtotal appropriation			–966
07.99 Total balance, end of year			1,823

The March 31, 1998 decision by the Supreme Court in U.S. Shoe Corp. vs. The United States, found the Harbor Maintenance Tax (HMT) unconstitutional as applied to exports. Collection of the ad valorem tax on exports was halted on April 25, 1998. The HMT has also been the subject of questions raised by U.S. trading partners. The U.S. is currently engaged in consultations under the World Trade Organization Agreement regarding a claim by the European Union, Japan, Canada and Norway that the HMT violates the General Agreement on Tariffs and Trade.

The Administration believes an alternative mechanism is needed to replace the HMT as the funding source for maintaining Federal channel and harbor projects. Users of the network of U.S. ports served by Federal channel and harbor projects should continue to be responsible for the costs of ensuring a safe, reliable and efficient port system. The Administration also supports establishing a clear link between the amount of Federal revenue collected annually under the replacement fee mechanism and the amount annual Federal appropriations to ensure a safe and competitive system.

The Administration is proposing that the HMT be repealed and be replaced by a user fee (called the Harbor Services User Fee, or HSUF) that satisfies the Supreme Court's constitutionality test and is consistent with U.S. international obligations. It is important to note the proposed user fee will be formulated on a nationwide system basis so as to neither significantly alter the existing competitive balance among U.S. ports, nor measurably impact U.S. international and domestic trade.

The Administration believes that the HSUF should support the operation and maintenance (O&M) activities of the Corps of Engineers and the other O&M costs currently recovered from the existing Harbor Maintenance Trust Fund, and should also fund the Federal share of Corps of Engineers port construction activities, such as port deepening projects. Expanding the uses of fee revenues to include Federal port construction projects recognizes that the services provided by the U.S. port system require adequate and continual investment in new construction.

Revenue generated from the HSUF will be deposited into a new fund, the Harbor Services Fund (HSF). The Administration estimates that the annual average revenue needed to finance HSF activities during the next five years is approximately $980 million per year. This is approximately the same total amount as would have been collected under the HMT prior to the Supreme Court's declaring the HMT unconstitutional.

In fiscal year 2001, the costs will be covered by transfers from the Harbor Maintenance Trust Fund to the Harbor Services Fund. Funds collected by the HSUF are projected to be sufficient to cover O&M and construction costs to be incurred in fiscal year 2002 and thereafter.

For further discussion of the treatment of the HSUF, please see the *Analytical Perspectives* volume of the FY 2001 Budget.

PERMANENT APPROPRIATIONS

Unavailable Collections (in millions of dollars)

Identification code 96–9921–0–2–999	1999 actual	2000 est.	2001 est.
Balance, start of year:			
01.99 Balance, start of year	7	3	3
Receipts:			
02.03 Receipts from leases of lands acquired for flood control, navigation, and allied purposes	7	7	7
02.04 Licenses under Federal Power Act, improvements of navigable waters, maintenance and operation of dams, etc.	7	9	9
02.99 Total receipts	14	16	16
04.00 Total: Balances and collections	21	19	19
Appropriation:			
05.01 Permanent appropriations	–18	–16	–16
07.99 Total balance, end of year	3	3	3

Program and Financing (in millions of dollars)

Identification code 96–9921–0–2–999	1999 actual	2000 est.	2001 est.
Obligations by program activity:			
00.02 Maintenance and operation of dams and other improvements of navigable waters	23	9	9
00.03 Payments to States	7	7	7
10.00 Total new obligations	30	16	16
Budgetary resources available for obligation:			
21.40 Unobligated balance available, start of year	12		
22.00 New budget authority (gross)	18	16	16
23.90 Total budgetary resources available for obligation	30	16	16
23.95 Total new obligations	−30	−16	−16
24.40 Unobligated balance available, end of year			
New budget authority (gross), detail:			
Mandatory:			
60.25 Appropriation (special fund, indefinite)	18	16	16
Change in unpaid obligations:			
72.40 Unpaid obligations, start of year: Obligated balance, start of year		11	11
73.10 Total new obligations	30	16	16
73.20 Total outlays (gross)	−19	−16	−16
74.40 Unpaid obligations, end of year: Obligated balance, end of year	11	11	11
Outlays (gross), detail:			
86.97 Outlays from new mandatory authority	18	16	16
86.98 Outlays from mandatory balances	1		
87.00 Total outlays (gross)	19	16	16
Net budget authority and outlays:			
89.00 Budget authority	18	16	16
90.00 Outlays	19	16	16
Distribution of budget authority by account:			
Maintenance and operation of dams and other improvements of navigable waters			
Payments to States			
Total			

Use of hydraulic mining debris reservoirs in California for other purposes.—Fees paid by Pacific Gas and Electric Company for use of the Englebright Dam, Yuba River, mine debris restraining works for hydropower generation are used for maintaining the works (33 U.S.C. 683).

Maintenance and operation of dams and other improvements of navigable waters.—The Corps' share of half the fees levied by the Federal Energy Regulatory Commission (FERC) for program and administration; private use of Federal property, incuding facilities and land; private construction and operation of water management and appurtenant facilities; and private benefit from headwater improvement by others; plus appropriated excess profits (except 100 percent of fees from Indian reservations, 100 percent of program administration costs, 12.5 percent of the balance, and 100 percent of fees paid for use of public lands and national forests) are used for construction, operation, and maintenance of Federal water management facilities (16 U.S.C. 810(a)).

Payments to States.—Three-fourths of the rent received from lease of Federal lands acquired for flood control, navigation, and allied purposes is paid to States incorporating project lands to compensate for lost tax base. (33 U.S.C. 701c–3).

Object Classification (in millions of dollars)

Identification code 96–9921–0–2–999	1999 actual	2000 est.	2001 est.
11.1 Personnel compensation: Full-time permanent	2	2	2
25.2 Other services	13	5	5
41.0 Grants, subsidies, and contributions	13	7	7
99.0 Subtotal, direct obligations	28	14	14
99.5 Below reporting threshold	2	2	2
99.9 Total new obligations	30	16	16

Personnel Summary

Identification code 96–9921–0–2–999	1999 actual	2000 est.	2001 est.
1001 Total compensable workyears: Full-time equivalent employment	46	35	34

Intragovernmental funds:

Revolving Fund

Amounts in the Revolving fund are available for the costs of relocating the U.S. Army Corps of Engineers headquarters to office space in the General Accounting Office headquarters building in Washington, D.C.

Program and Financing (in millions of dollars)

Identification code 96–4902–0–4–301	1999 actual	2000 est.	2001 est.
Obligations by program activity:			
Operating Expenses:			
09.01 Plant and equipment services	14	15	15
09.02 Warehousing (GPRA)	3	3	3
09.03 Shop and facility services	1,802	1,520	1,520
09.04 General Administrative Services	1,425	1,427	1,427
09.09 Total operating expenses	3,244	2,965	2,965
Capital Investment:			
09.20 Land and structures	26	18	18
09.21 Dredges	15	10	10
09.22 Other floasting plant	16	30	30
09.23 Land-based equipment	5	6	6
09.24 Tools, office furniture, and equipment	24	21	21
09.29 Total capital investment	86	85	85
10.00 Total new obligations	3,330	3,050	3,050
Budgetary resources available for obligation:			
21.40 Unobligated balance available, start of year	519	495	495
22.00 New budget authority (gross)	3,306	3,050	3,050
23.90 Total budgetary resources available for obligation	3,825	3,545	3,545
23.95 Total new obligations	−3,330	−3,050	−3,050
24.40 Unobligated balance available, end of year	495	495	495
New budget authority (gross), detail:			
Mandatory:			
69.00 Offsetting collections (cash)	3,343	3,050	3,050
69.10 From Federal sources: Change in receivables and unpaid, unfilled orders	−37		
69.90 Spending authority from offsetting collections (total mandatory)	3,306	3,050	3,050
Change in unpaid obligations:			
Unpaid obligations, start of year:			
72.40 Obligated balance, start of year	254	357	362
72.95 From Federal sources: Receivables and unpaid, unfilled orders	180	143	143
72.99 Total unpaid obligations, start of year	434	500	505
73.10 Total new obligations	3,330	3,050	3,050
73.20 Total outlays (gross)	−3,264	−3,045	−3,045
Unpaid obligations, end of year:			
74.40 Obligated balance, end of year	357	362	367
74.95 From Federal sources: Receivables and unpaid, unfilled orders	143	143	143
74.99 Total unpaid obligations, end of year	500	505	510
Outlays (gross), detail:			
86.97 Outlays from new mandatory authority	3,264	3,045	3,045
Offsets:			
Against gross budget authority and outlays:			
Offsetting collections (cash) from:			
88.00 Federal sources	−3,327	−3,034	−3,034

Intragovernmental funds—Continued

REVOLVING FUND—Continued

Program and Financing (in millions of dollars)—Continued

Identification code 96–4902–0–4–301		1999 actual	2000 est.	2001 est.
88.40	Non-Federal sources	–16	–16	–16
88.90	Total, offsetting collections (cash)	–3,343	–3,050	–3,050
	Against gross budget authority only:			
88.95	From Federal sources: Change in receivables and unpaid, unfilled orders	37		
	Net budget authority and outlays:			
89.00	Budget authority			
90.00	Outlays	–79	–5	–5

The fund provides for the acquisition, operation, and maintenance of plant and equipment used in civil works functions; for temporary financing of services chargeable to civil appropriations; and for furnishing facilities and services for military functions of the Department of the Army, other governmental agencies and private persons, as authorized by law (33 U.S.C. 576).

Object Classification (in millions of dollars)

Identification code 96–4902–0–4–301		1999 actual	2000 est.	2001 est.
21.0	Travel and transportation of persons	23	23	23
22.0	Transportation of things	1	1	1
23.1	Rental payments to GSA	11	11	11
23.2	Rental payments to others	1	1	1
23.3	Communications, utilities, and miscellaneous charges	30	30	30
24.0	Printing and reproduction	18	18	18
25.1	Advisory and assistance services	1	1	1
25.2	Other services	2,888	2,608	2,608
25.3	Purchases of goods and services from Government accounts	143	143	143
25.7	Operation and maintenance of equipment	10	10	10
26.0	Supplies and materials	146	146	146
31.0	Equipment	39	39	39
32.0	Land and structures	17	17	17
42.0	Insurance claims and indemnities	1	1	1
44.0	Refunds	1	1	1
99.9	Total new obligations	3,330	3,050	3,050

Trust Funds

INLAND WATERWAYS TRUST FUND

Unavailable Collections (in millions of dollars)

Identification code 20–8861–0–7–301		1999 actual	2000 est.	2001 est.
	Balance, start of year:			
01.99	Balance, start of year	327	357	404
	Receipts:			
02.01	Transfer from general fund, Inland waterways revenue act taxes	104	104	107
02.02	Interest and profits on investments in public debt securities	14	18	20
02.99	Total receipts	118	122	127
04.00	Total: Balances and collections	445	479	531
	Appropriation:			
05.01	Inland waterways trust fund	–88	–75	–74
07.99	Total balance, end of year	357	404	457

Program and Financing (in millions of dollars)

Identification code 20–8861–0–7–301		1999 actual	2000 est.	2001 est.
	Obligations by program activity:			
10.00	Total new obligations (object class 25.2)	88	75	74
	Budgetary resources available for obligation:			
21.40	Unobligated balance available, start of year	–9	–9	–9
22.00	New budget authority (gross)	88	75	74
23.90	Total budgetary resources available for obligation	79	66	65
23.95	Total new obligations	–88	–75	–74
24.40	Unobligated balance available, end of year	–9	–9	–9
	New budget authority (gross), detail:			
	Discretionary:			
40.26	Appropriation (trust fund, definite)	88	75	74
	Change in unpaid obligations:			
72.40	Unpaid obligations, start of year: Obligated balance, start of year	13	13	13
73.10	Total new obligations	88	75	74
73.20	Total outlays (gross)	–88	–75	–74
74.40	Unpaid obligations, end of year: Obligated balance, end of year	13	13	13
	Outlays (gross), detail:			
86.90	Outlays from new discretionary authority	88	75	74
	Net budget authority and outlays:			
89.00	Budget authority	88	75	74
90.00	Outlays	88	75	74
	Memorandum (non-add) entries:			
92.01	Total investments, start of year: U.S. securities: Par value	346	372	372
92.02	Total investments, end of year: U.S. securities: Par value	372	372	372

The Inland Waterways Trust Fund was established in accordance with the Inland Waterways Revenue Act of 1978, Public Law 95–502, and amended by the Water Resources Development Act of 1986, Public Law 99–662. Revenue is derived from taxes imposed on fuel for vessels engaged in commercial waterway transportation and investment interest and is used to pay one half of the construction and rehabilitation costs of specified inland waterway projects. See "Construction, General" for appropriations language.

RIVERS AND HARBORS CONTRIBUTED FUNDS

Unavailable Collections (in millions of dollars)

Identification code 96–8862–0–7–301		1999 actual	2000 est.	2001 est.
	Balance, start of year:			
01.99	Balance, start of year	101	158	158
	Receipts:			
02.01	Contributions, rivers and harbors, other than port and harbor user fees, Corps of Engineers	350	258	280
04.00	Total: Balances and collections	451	416	438
	Appropriation:			
05.01	Rivers and harbors contributed funds	–293	–258	–280
07.99	Total balance, end of year	158	158	158

Program and Financing (in millions of dollars)

Identification code 96–8862–0–7–301		1999 actual	2000 est.	2001 est.
	Obligations by program activity:			
	General investigations:			
00.01	Where required for an authorized Federal study	42	40	40
00.02	Where not required for an authorized Federal study	6	4	4
	Construction:			
00.03	Where required for an authorized Federal project	107	129	129
00.04	Where not required for an authorized Federal project	14	24	24
	Flood control, Mississippi River and tributaries:			
00.05	Where required for an authorized feature	45	39	39
00.06	Where not required for an authorized Federal project	7	6	6
	Maintenance:			
00.07	Where required for an authorized Federal project	2	3	3
00.08	Where not required for an authorized Federal project	5	5	5

		1999 actual	2000 est.	2001 est.
	Coastal Wetlands:			
00.09	Coastal wetlands restoration: Where required for projects	1	1	1
10.00	Total new obligations	229	251	251
	Budgetary resources available for obligation:			
21.40	Unobligated balance available, start of year	125	189	196
22.00	New budget authority (gross)	293	258	280
23.90	Total budgetary resources available for obligation	418	447	476
23.95	Total new obligations	−229	−251	−251
24.40	Unobligated balance available, end of year	189	196	225
	New budget authority (gross), detail:			
	Mandatory:			
60.27	Appropriation (trust fund, indefinite)	293	258	280
	Change in unpaid obligations:			
72.40	Unpaid obligations, start of year: Obligated balance, start of year	70	47	40
73.10	Total new obligations	229	251	251
73.20	Total outlays (gross)	−252	−258	−280
74.40	Unpaid obligations, end of year: Obligated balance, end of year	47	40	11
	Outlays (gross), detail:			
86.97	Outlays from new mandatory authority	252	258	280
	Net budget authority and outlays:			
89.00	Budget authority	293	258	280
90.00	Outlays	252	258	280

Funds are contributed by non-Federal interests for expenditure on improvements of rivers and harbors. This includes cost-sharing contributions under terms of agreements with non-Federal interests for study, design, construction and maintenance of authorized Federal projects as well as other non-Federal contributions for 100 percent of costs of other work.

Object Classification (in millions of dollars)

Identification code 96–8862–0–7–301		1999 actual	2000 est.	2001 est.
	Personnel compensation:			
11.1	Full-time permanent	35	39	41
11.3	Other than full-time permanent	2	2	2
11.5	Other personnel compensation	1	1	1
11.9	Total personnel compensation	38	42	44
12.1	Civilian personnel benefits	8	9	10
23.1	Rental payments to GSA	1	1	1
23.3	Communications, utilities, and miscellaneous	1	1	1
25.1	Advisory and assistance services	2	2	2
25.2	Other services	75	103	100
25.3	Purchase goods & svcs. fm Government accts.	12	10	10
25.5	Research and development contracts	3	3	3
25.7	Operation and maintenance of equipment	2	2	2
26.0	Supplies and materials	1	1	1
31.0	Equipment	1	1	1
32.0	Land and structures	84	75	75
99.0	Subtotal, direct obligations	228	250	250
99.5	Below reporting threshold	1	1	1
99.9	Total new obligations	229	251	251

Personnel Summary

Identification code 96–8862–0–7–301		1999 actual	2000 est.	2001 est.
1001	Total compensable workyears: Full-time equivalent employment	918	980	1,025

Harbor Maintenance Trust Fund

Unavailable Collections (in millions of dollars)

Identification code 96–8863–0–7–301		1999 actual	2000 est.	2001 est.
	Balance, start of year:			
01.99	Balance, start of year	1,246	1,736	1,758
	Receipts:			
02.01	User fees	553	675	732
02.02	Earnings on investments	54	76	82
02.03	User fees, legislative proposal, discretionary offset			−732
02.04	Earnings on investments, legislative proposal not subject to PAYGO			−82
02.99	Total receipts	607	751	
04.00	Total: Balances and collections	1,853	2,487	1,758
	Appropriation:			
05.01	Saint Lawrence Seaway Development Corporation, operations and maintenance	−11	−12	−13
05.03	Army Corps of Engineers, operation and maintenance of commercial navigation harbors and administrative cost	−103	−714	−705
05.04	Harbor maintenance trust fund, legislative proposal not subject to PAYGO			−1,053
05.05	Harbor maintenance fee collection, Treasury	−3	−3	−3
05.05	Appropriation			3
05.08	Army Corps of Engineers, operation and maintenance, legislative proposal not subject to PAYGO			13
05.99	Subtotal appropriation	−117	−729	−1,758
07.99	Total balance, end of year	1,736	1,758	

Program and Financing (in millions of dollars)

Identification code 96–8863–0–7–301		1999 actual	2000 est.	2001 est.
	Obligations by program activity:			
10.00	Total new obligations (object class 25.3)	281	714	705
	Budgetary resources available for obligation:			
21.40	Unobligated balance available, start of year	178		
22.00	New budget authority (gross)	103	714	705
23.90	Total budgetary resources available for obligation	281	714	705
23.95	Total new obligations	−281	−714	−705
	New budget authority (gross), detail:			
	Discretionary:			
	Appropriation (trust fund, indefinite):			
40.27	Appropriation (trust fund, indefinite)—Operations and maintenance	100	705	700
40.27	Appropriation (trust fund, indefinite)—Construction	3	9	5
43.00	Appropriation (total discretionary)	103	714	705
	Change in unpaid obligations:			
73.10	Total new obligations	281	714	705
73.20	Total outlays (gross)	−281	−714	−705
	Outlays (gross), detail:			
86.90	Outlays from new discretionary authority	103	714	705
86.93	Outlays from discretionary balances	178		
87.00	Total outlays (gross)	281	714	705
	Net budget authority and outlays:			
89.00	Budget authority	103	714	705
90.00	Outlays	281	714	705
	Memorandum (non-add) entries:			
92.01	Total investments, start of year: U.S. securities: Par value	1,275	1,603	1,603
92.02	Total investments, end of year: U.S. securities: Par value	1,603	1,603	

Summary of Budget Authority and Outlays

(in millions of dollars)

Enacted/requested:	*1999 actual*	*2000 est.*	*2001 est.*
Budget Authority	103	714	705
Outlays	281	714	705

HARBOR MAINTENANCE TRUST FUND—Continued

Summary of Budget Authority and Outlays—Continued

(in millions of dollars)

	1999 actual	2000 est.	2001 est.
Legislative proposal, not subject to PAYGO:			
Budget Authority			1,053
Outlays			1,053
Total:			
Budget Authority	103	714	1,758
Outlays	281	714	1,758

The Harbor Maintenance Trust Fund is established in accordance with the Harbor Maintenance Revenue Act of 1986 (Public Law 99–662, Title XIV, as amended). Revenue is derived from receipts from a 0.125 percent *ad valorem* user fee imposed upon commercial users of specified U.S. ports; Saint Lawrence Seaway tolls; and investment interest.

The Harbor Maintenance Revenue Act also authorized expenditures from the Trust Fund to finance up to 100 percent of Corps of Engineers' harbor operation and maintenance (O&M) costs, including O&M costs associated with Great Lakes navigational projects, and fully finance the operation and maintenance of the Saint Lawrence Seaway Development Corporation.

The North American Free Trade Agreement Implementation Act, Sec. 683 (Public Law 103–182), authorized payment of administrative expenses incurred by the Department of the Treasury, the Army Corps of Engineers, and the Department of Commerce related to administration of the harbor maintenance fee, but not to exceed $5,000,000 for any fiscal year.

A summary judgment issued October 25, 1995, by the United States Court of International Trade in the case United States Shoe Corp. v. United States (Court No. 94–11–00668), found the Harbor Maintenance fee unconstitutional under the Export Clause of the Constitution (Article I, section 9, clause 5), and enjoined the Customs Service from collecting the fee.

The decision was affirmed by the Supreme Court on March 31, 1998. With the tax on exports no longer collected, revenues have been reduced by approximately 30 percent.

The Administration is proposing a Harbor Services User Fee to replace the Harbor Maintenance Tax. The legislative proposal will also establish the Harbor Services Fund into which collected fees will be deposited. The Harbor Services Fund will be funded in FY 2001 by transfer from the Harbor Maintenance Trust Fund.

HARBOR MAINTENANCE TRUST FUND

(Legislative Proposal, not subject to PAYGO)

Contingent upon the enactment of legislation to establish the Harbor Services Fund, all balances in the Harbor Maintenance Trust Fund shall be transferred to and merged with the Harbor Services Fund, to be available for the purposes of the account to which transferred.

Program and Financing (in millions of dollars)

Identification code 96–8863–2–7–301	1999 actual	2000 est.	2001 est.
Obligations by program activity:			
10.00 Total new obligations (object class 25.2)			1,053
Budgetary resources available for obligation:			
22.00 New budget authority (gross)			1,053
23.95 Total new obligations			−1,053
New budget authority (gross), detail:			
Discretionary:			
Appropriation (trust fund, indefinite):			
40.27 Appropriation (trust fund, indefinite) Harbor Maintenance Trust Fund			1,758
40.27 Appropriation (trust fund, indefinite)			−705
43.00 Appropriation (total discretionary)			1,053
Change in unpaid obligations:			
73.10 Total new obligations			1,053
73.20 Total outlays (gross)			−1,053
Outlays (gross), detail:			
86.90 Outlays from new discretionary authority			1,053
Net budget authority and outlays:			
89.00 Budget authority			1,053
90.00 Outlays			1,053

COASTAL WETLANDS RESTORATION CONSOLIDATED PROGRAM

[Budget authority in millions of dollars]

	1999 actual	2000 est.	2001 est.
Corps of Engineers	5	10	10
Environmental Protection Agency	0	10	10
Fish & Wildlife Service	3	8	8
National Marine Fisheries Service	12	13	14
Natural Resources Conservation Service	9	11	13
Total	29	52	55
Corps of Engineers	1	1	2
Environmental Protection Agency		1	2
Fish & Wildlife Service	1	1	1
National Marine Fisheries Service	1	2	2
Natural Resources Conservation Service	2	2	2
Total	5	7	9
Total appropriation	34	59	64

COASTAL WETLANDS RESTORATION TRUST FUND

Program and Financing (in millions of dollars)

Identification code 96–8333–0–7–301	1999 actual	2000 est.	2001 est.
Obligations by program activity:			
00.01 Direct Program Activity	35	30	30
10.00 Total new obligations	35	30	30
Budgetary resources available for obligation:			
21.40 Unobligated balance available, start of year	−53	−59	−36
22.00 New budget authority (gross)	29	53	51
23.90 Total budgetary resources available for obligation	−24	−6	15
23.95 Total new obligations	−35	−30	−30
24.40 Unobligated balance available, end of year	−59	−36	−15
New budget authority (gross), detail:			
Mandatory:			
62.00 Transferred from other accounts	29	53	51
Change in unpaid obligations:			
72.40 Unpaid obligations, start of year: Obligated balance, start of year	60	61	39
73.10 Total new obligations	35	30	30
73.20 Total outlays (gross)	−34	−53	−51
74.40 Unpaid obligations, end of year: Obligated balance, end of year	61	39	18
Outlays (gross), detail:			
86.97 Outlays from new mandatory authority	29	53	51
86.98 Outlays from mandatory balances	5		
87.00 Total outlays (gross)	34	53	51
Net budget authority and outlays:			
89.00 Budget authority	29	53	51
90.00 Outlays	34	53	51

The Coastal Wetlands Planning, Protection and Restoration Act (Public Law 101–646) directs the Secretary of the Interior to distribute to the Coastal Wetlands Restoration Trust Fund a portion of the amounts appropriated each fiscal year from the Sport Fish Restoration Account. The Louisiana Coastal Wetlands Conservation and Restoration Task Force, an interagency task force (including the Corps, Environmental Protection Agency, Fish and Wildlife Service, Natural Resources

Conservation Service, and the National Marine Fisheries Service) chaired by the Secretary of the Army, uses these funds to provide for the long-term conservation, protection, and restoration of coastal wetlands in the State of Louisiana. In the general provisions section for the Corps of Engineers, the budget includes proposed appropriations language to extend the authorization for spending these receipts through FY 2001.

Object Classification (in millions of dollars)

Identification code 96–8333–0–7–301	1999 actual	2000 est.	2001 est.
11.1 Personnel compensation: Full-time permanent	1	1	
25.2 Other services	34	29	30
99.9 Total new obligations	35	30	30

Personnel Summary

Identification code 96–8333–0–7–301	1999 actual	2000 est.	2001 est.
1001 Total compensable workyears: Full-time equivalent employment	24	20	10

SOUTH DAKOTA TERRESTRIAL WILDLIFE HABITAT RESTORATION TRUST FUND

Unavailable Collections (in millions of dollars)

Identification code 96–8217–0–7–306	1999 actual	2000 est.	2001 est.
Balance, start of year:			
01.99 Balance, start of year		10	21
Receipts:			
02.01 Payment from the general fund	10	10	10
02.02 Earnings on investments		1	1
02.99 Total receipts	10	11	11
04.00 Total: Balances and collections	10	21	32
07.99 Total balance, end of year	10	21	32

This fund, established by the Water Resources Development Act of 1999 (P.L. 106–53) for use by the State of South Dakota, will pay for terrestrial wildlife habitat restoration. The establishment of this fund satisfies the Federal obligation under the Fish and Wildlife Coordination Act (16 U.S.C. 1661 et. seq.) to mitigate for terrestrial habitat lost due to flooding from the Oahe and Big Bend projects, which were carried out as part of the Pick-Sloan Missouri River Basin program.

WASHINGTON AQUEDUCT

Federal Funds

General and special funds

WASHINGTON AQUEDUCT

Program and Financing (in millions of dollars)

Identification code 96–3128–0–1–301	1999 actual	2000 est.	2001 est.
Obligations by program activity:			
00.01 Direct Program Activity	26	18	
10.00 Total new obligations	26	18	
Budgetary resources available for obligation:			
21.40 Unobligated balance available, start of year	22	18	
22.00 New budget authority (gross)	22		
23.90 Total budgetary resources available for obligation	44	18	
23.95 Total new obligations	−26	−18	
24.40 Unobligated balance available, end of year	18		
New budget authority (gross), detail:			
Mandatory:			
67.10 Authority to borrow	22		
69.00 Offsetting collections (cash)	11	17	6
69.47 Portion applied to repay debt	−11	−17	−6
69.90 Spending authority from offsetting collections (total mandatory)			
70.00 Total new budget authority (gross)	22		
Change in unpaid obligations:			
72.40 Unpaid obligations, start of year: Obligated balance, start of year	19	15	
73.10 Total new obligations	26	18	
73.20 Total outlays (gross)	−30	−33	
74.40 Unpaid obligations, end of year: Obligated balance, end of year	15		
Outlays (gross), detail:			
86.98 Outlays from mandatory balances	30	33	
Offsets:			
Against gross budget authority and outlays:			
88.40 Offsetting collections (cash) from: Non-Federal sources	−11	−17	−6
Net budget authority and outlays:			
89.00 Budget authority	11	−17	−6
90.00 Outlays	19	16	−6

Section 306 of the Safe Drinking Water Act, P.L. 104–182, 110 Stat. 1613, 1985 provides borrowing authority to the Corps of Engineers for the purpose of making repairs and improvements to the Washington Aqueduct. The Aqueduct supplies drinking water to the District of Columbia, and Arlington and Falls Church, Virginia. The Safe Drinking Water Act Amendments of 1996 authorized the Corps to borrow limited amounts from Treasury to improve to the water system, to be repaid over time by the customers of the Aqueduct.

Object Classification (in millions of dollars)

Identification code 96–3128–0–1–301	1999 actual	2000 est.	2001 est.
26.0 Supplies and materials	2	1	
31.0 Equipment	12	9	
32.0 Land and structures	12	8	
99.9 Total new obligations	26	18	

ADMINISTRATIVE PROVISIONS

Appropriations in this title shall be available for official reception and representation expenses (not to exceed $5,000); and during the current fiscal year the Revolving Fund, Corps of Engineers, shall be available for purchase (not to exceed 100 for replacement only) and hire of passenger motor vehicles. *(Energy and Water Development Appropriations Act, 2000.)*

GENERAL PROVISIONS

CORPS OF ENGINEERS—CIVIL

[SEC. 101. Notwithstanding any other provisions of law, no fully allocated funding policy shall be applied to projects for which funds are identified in the Committee reports accompanying this Act under the Construction, General; Operation and Maintenance, General; and Flood Control, Mississippi River and Tributaries, appropriation accounts: *Provided*, That the Secretary of the Army, acting through the Chief of Engineers, is directed to undertake these projects using continuing contracts, as authorized in section 10 of the Rivers and Harbors Act of September 22, 1922 (33 U.S.C. 621).]

[SEC. 102. Agreements proposed for execution by the Assistant Secretary of the Army for Civil Works or the United States Army Corps of Engineers after the date of the enactment of this Act pursuant to section 4 of the Rivers and Harbor Act of 1915, Public Law

CORPS OF ENGINEERS—CIVIL—Continued

64–291; section 11 of the River and Harbor Act of 1925, Public Law 68–585; the Civil Functions Appropriations Act, 1936, Public Law 75–208; section 215 of the Flood Control Act of 1968, as amended, Public Law 90–483; sections 104, 203, and 204 of the Water Resources Development Act of 1986, as amended (Public Law 99–662); section 206 of the Water Resources Development Act of 1992, as amended, Public Law 102–580; section 211 of the Water Resources Development Act of 1996, Public Law 104–303, and any other specific project authority, shall be limited to credits and reimbursements per project not to exceed $10,000,000 in each fiscal year, and total credits and reimbursements for all applicable projects not to exceed $50,000,000 in each fiscal year.]

[SEC. 103. None of the funds made available in this Act may be used to revise the Missouri River Master Water Control Manual when it is made known to the Federal entity or official to which the funds are made available that such revision provides for an increase in the springtime water release program during the spring heavy rainfall and snow melt period in States that have rivers draining into the Missouri River below the Gavins Point Dam.]

SEC. 101. 16 U.S.C. 777c(a) is amended in the second sentence by striking "2000" and inserting "2001". (Energy and Water Development Appropriations Act, 2000.)

ALLOCATIONS RECEIVED FROM OTHER ACCOUNTS

Note.—Obligations incurred under allocations from other accounts are shown in the schedules of the parent appropriation as follows:

State and Private Forestry, Forest Service, Department of Agriculture.
Operation and Maintenance, Army, Department of the Army.
Operations, Research, and Facilities, National Oceanic and Atmospheric Administration, Department of Commerce.
Energy, Supply, Research and Development Activities, Operating Expenses, Department of Energy.
Construction, National Park Service, Department of the Interior.
Federal Buildings Fund, General Services Administration.
Acquisition and Construction of Radio Facilities, United States Information Agency.
Appalachian Regional Development Programs, Appalachian Regional Commission.
Hazardous Substance Response Trust Fund, Environmental Protection Agency.

OTHER DEFENSE—CIVIL PROGRAMS

MILITARY RETIREMENT

Federal Funds

General and special funds:

PAYMENT TO MILITARY RETIREMENT FUND

Program and Financing (in millions of dollars)

Identification code 97–0040–0–1–054	1999 actual	2000 est.	2001 est.
Obligations by program activity:			
10.00 Total new obligations (object class 13.0)	15,250	15,302	15,914
Budgetary resources available for obligation:			
22.00 New budget authority (gross)	15,250	15,302	15,914
23.95 Total new obligations	–15,250	–15,302	–15,914
New budget authority (gross), detail:			
Mandatory:			
60.05 Appropriation (indefinite)	15,250	15,302	15,914
Change in unpaid obligations:			
73.10 Total new obligations	15,250	15,302	15,914
73.20 Total outlays (gross)	–15,250	–15,302	–15,914
Outlays (gross), detail:			
86.97 Outlays from new mandatory authority	15,250	15,302	15,914
Net budget authority and outlays:			
89.00 Budget authority	15,250	15,302	15,914
90.00 Outlays	15,250	15,302	15,914

The FY 2001 payment to the military retirement fund includes funds for the amortization of the unfunded liability for all retirement benefits earned by military personnel for service prior to 1985. The amortization schedule for the unfunded liability is determined by the Department of Defense Retirement Board of Actuaries. Included in the unfunded liability are the consolidated requirements of the military departments to cover retired officers and enlisted personnel of the Army, Navy, Marine Corps, and Air Force, retainer pay of enlisted personnel of the Fleet Reserve of the Navy and Marine Corps, and survivors benefits.

Trust Funds

MILITARY RETIREMENT FUND

Unavailable Collections (in millions of dollars)

Identification code 97–8097–0–7–602	1999 actual	2000 est.	2001 est.
Balance, start of year:			
01.99 Balance, start of year	142,817	149,059	155,565
Receipts:			
02.01 Employing agency contributions	10,417	11,454	11,413
02.02 General fund payment (unfunded liability)	15,250	15,302	15,914
02.03 Earnings on investments	12,560	12,791	13,025
02.99 Total receipts	38,227	39,547	40,352
04.00 Total: Balances and collections	181,044	188,606	195,917
Appropriation:			
05.01 Military retirement fund	–31,985	–33,041	–34,016
05.99 Subtotal appropriation	–31,985	–33,041	–34,016
07.99 Total balance, end of year	149,059	155,565	161,901

Program and Financing (in millions of dollars)

Identification code 97–8097–0–7–602	1999 actual	2000 est.	2001 est.
Obligations by program activity:			
00.01 Nondisability	27,336	28,238	29,071
00.02 Temporary disability	82	85	88
00.03 Permanent disability	1,354	1,399	1,440
00.04 Fleet Reserve	1,428	1,476	1,519
00.05 Survivors' benefits	1,785	1,844	1,899
10.00 Total new obligations (object class 42.0)	31,986	33,041	34,016
Budgetary resources available for obligation:			
22.00 New budget authority (gross)	31,985	33,041	34,016
23.95 Total new obligations	–31,986	–33,041	–34,016
New budget authority (gross), detail:			
Mandatory:			
60.27 Appropriation (trust fund, indefinite)	38,227	39,547	40,352
60.45 Portion precluded from obligation	–6,242	–6,506	–6,336
62.50 Appropriation (total mandatory)	31,986	33,041	34,016
Change in unpaid obligations:			
72.40 Unpaid obligations, start of year: Obligated balance, start of year	2,698	2,794	2,894
73.10 Total new obligations	31,986	33,041	34,016
73.20 Total outlays (gross)	–31,889	–32,941	–33,914
74.40 Unpaid obligations, end of year: Obligated balance, end of year	2,794	2,894	2,997
Outlays (gross), detail:			
86.97 Outlays from new mandatory authority	31,889	32,941	33,914
Net budget authority and outlays:			
89.00 Budget authority	31,986	33,041	34,016
90.00 Outlays	31,889	32,941	33,914
Memorandum (non-add) entries:			
92.01 Total investments, start of year: U.S. securities: Par value	133,843	141,274	146,333
92.02 Total investments, end of year: U.S. securities: Par value	141,274	146,333	152,772

Public Law 98–94 provided for accrual funding of the military retirement system and for the establishment of a Department of Defense Military Retirement Fund in 1985. The fund has three sources of income. The first is payments from the Military Personnel accounts, which cover the liability for future benefits accruing to current service members. The second is a payment from the general treasury to cover the accrued unfunded liability of current members and current retirees. The third source is income from the investment of fund balances from past and current payments into the fund.

The status of the fund is as follows:

Status of Funds (in millions of dollars)

Identification code 97–8097–0–7–602	1999 actual	2000 est.	2001 est.
Unexpended balance, start of year:			
0100 Treasury balance	21	20	....
U.S. Securities:			
0101 Par value	133,843	141,274	146,333
0102 Unrealized discounts	11,651	10,559	12,126
0199 Total balance, start of year	145,515	151,853	158,459
Cash income during the year:			
Intragovernmental transactions:			
0240 Employing agency contributions, DOD military	10,413	11,450	11,409
0241 Employing agency contributions, Corps of Engineers	4	4	4
0242 Earning on investments	12,560	12,791	13,025
0243 Federal contributions	15,250	15,302	15,914

186-484 00 - 30

MILITARY RETIREMENT FUND—Continued

Status of Funds (in millions of dollars)—Continued

Identification code 97–8097–0–7–602	1999 actual	2000 est.	2001 est.
0299 Total cash income	38,227	39,547	40,352
Cash outgo during year:			
0500 Military retirement fund	–31,889	–32,941	–33,914
Unexpended balance, end of year:			
0700 Uninvested balance	20		
U.S. Securities:			
0701 Par value	141,274	146,333	152,772
0702 Unrealized discounts	10,559	12,126	12,126
0799 Total balance, end of year	151,853	158,459	164,898

EDUCATION BENEFITS

Trust Funds

EDUCATION BENEFITS FUND

Unavailable Collections (in millions of dollars)

Identification code 97–8098–0–7–702	1999 actual	2000 est.	2001 est.
Balance, start of year:			
01.99 Balance, start of year	618	676	782
Receipts:			
02.01 Employing agency contributions	197	293	300
02.02 Interest	40	38	45
02.99 Total receipts	237	331	345
04.00 Total: Balances and collections	855	1,007	1,127
Appropriation:			
05.01 Education benefits fund	–179	–225	–228
05.99 Subtotal appropriation	–179	–225	–228
07.99 Total balance, end of year	676	782	899

Program and Financing (in millions of dollars)

Identification code 97–8098–0–7–702	1999 actual	2000 est.	2001 est.
Obligations by program activity:			
00.01 Active duty program	76	124	126
00.02 Selected reserve program	103	101	103
10.00 Total new obligations (object class 25.2)	179	225	228
Budgetary resources available for obligation:			
22.00 New budget authority (gross)	179	225	228
23.95 Total new obligations	–179	–225	–228
New budget authority (gross), detail:			
Mandatory:			
60.27 Appropriation (trust fund, indefinite)	238	225	228
60.28 Appropriation (unavailable balances)	–59		
62.50 Appropriation (total mandatory)	179	225	228
Change in unpaid obligations:			
72.40 Unpaid obligations, start of year: Obligated balance, start of year	–1		
73.10 Total new obligations	179	225	228
73.20 Total outlays (gross)	–178	–225	–228
74.40 Unpaid obligations, end of year: Obligated balance, end of year			
Outlays (gross), detail:			
86.97 Outlays from new mandatory authority	179	225	228
86.98 Outlays from mandatory balances	–1		
87.00 Total outlays (gross)	178	225	228
Net budget authority and outlays:			
89.00 Budget authority	179	225	228
90.00 Outlays	178	225	228
Memorandum (non-add) entries:			
92.01 Total investments, start of year: U.S. securities: Par value	559	651	758
92.02 Total investments, end of year: U.S. securities: Par value	651	758	874

The 1985 Defense Authorization Bill, Public Law 98–525, provided for the accrual funding of certain education benefits for active duty military personnel under the authority of Chapter 30, Title 38 U.S.C., and to Selected Reserve personnel under the authority of Chapter 1606, Title 10 U.S.C. Public Law 100–48 made this program permanent. The fund is financed through actuarially-determined Government contributions from the Department of Defense military personnel appropriations and interest on investments. Funds are transferred to the Department of Veterans Affairs to make benefit payments to eligible personnel. The status of the fund is as follows:

Status of Funds (in millions of dollars)

Identification code 97–8098–0–7–702	1999 actual	2000 est.	2001 est.
Unexpended balance, start of year:			
0100 Uninvested balance	29		
U.S. Securities:			
0101 Par value	559	651	758
0102 Unrealized discounts	29	25	25
0199 Total balance, start of year	617	676	782
Cash income during the year:			
Intragovernmental transactions:			
0240 Employing agency contributions	197	293	300
0241 Interest on investments	40	38	45
0299 Total cash income	237	331	345
Cash outgo during year:			
0500 Cash outgo during the year (–)	–75	–124	–126
0501 Cash outgo during the year (–)	–103	–101	–103
0599 Total cash outgo (–)	–178	–225	–228
Unexpended balance, end of year:			
U.S. Securities:			
0701 Par value	651	758	874
0702 Unrealized discounts	25	25	25
0799 Total balance, end of year	676	782	899

AMERICAN BATTLE MONUMENTS COMMISSION

Federal Funds

General and special funds:

SALARIES AND EXPENSES

For necessary expenses, not otherwise provided for, of the American Battle Monuments Commission, including the acquisition of land or interest in land in foreign countries; purchases and repair of uniforms for caretakers of national cemeteries and monuments outside of the United States and its territories and possessions; rent of office and garage space in foreign countries; purchase (one for replacement only) and hire of passenger motor vehicles; and insurance of official motor vehicles in foreign countries, when required by law of such countries, [$28,467,000] *$26,196,000*, to remain available until expended. *(Departments of Veterans Affairs and Housing and Urban Development, and Independent Agencies Appropriations Act, 2000.)*

Program and Financing (in millions of dollars)

Identification code 74–0100–0–1–705	1999 actual	2000 est.	2001 est.
Obligations by program activity:			
00.01 Administration and U.S. memorials	3	5	5
00.02 European memorials and cemeteries	18	18	16
00.03 Mediterranean memorials and cemeteries	4	4	4
00.04 Asian memorials and cemeteries	1	1	1
10.00 Total new obligations	26	28	26

		1999 actual	2000 est.	2001 est.
	Budgetary resources available for obligation:			
22.00	New budget authority (gross)	26	28	26
23.95	Total new obligations	−26	−28	−26
	New budget authority (gross), detail:			
	Discretionary:			
40.00	Appropriation	26	28	26
	Change in unpaid obligations:			
72.40	Unpaid obligations, start of year: Obligated balance, start of year	7	7	7
73.10	Total new obligations	26	28	26
73.20	Total outlays (gross)	−26	−26	−26
74.40	Unpaid obligations, end of year: Obligated balance, end of year	7	7	7
	Outlays (gross), detail:			
86.90	Outlays from new discretionary authority	23	24	23
86.93	Outlays from discretionary balances	4		4
87.00	Total outlays (gross)	26	26	26
	Net budget authority and outlays:			
89.00	Budget authority	26	28	26
90.00	Outlays	25	26	26

The American Battle Monuments Commission is responsible for: the maintenance and construction of U.S. monuments and memorials commemorating the achievements in battle of our Armed Forces since April 6, 1917; controlling erection of monuments and markers by U.S. citizens and organizations in foreign countries; and for the design, construction, and maintenance of permanent military cemetery memorials in foreign countries.

Object Classification (in millions of dollars)

Identification code 74–0100–0–1–705		1999 actual	2000 est.	2001 est.
	Personnel compensation:			
11.1	Full-time permanent	9	11	11
11.8	Special personal services payments	1	1	1
11.9	Total personnel compensation	10	12	12
12.1	Civilian personnel benefits	4	5	4
23.3	Communications, utilities, and miscellaneous charges	4	4	4
25.2	Other services	6	5	4
26.0	Supplies and materials	2	2	2
99.9	Total new obligations	26	28	26

Personnel Summary

Identification code 74–0100–0–1–705		1999 actual	2000 est.	2001 est.
1001	Total compensable workyears: Full-time equivalent employment	362	364	364

FOREIGN CURRENCY FLUCTUATIONS

Program and Financing (in millions of dollars)

Identification code 74–0101–0–1–705		1999 actual	2000 est.	2001 est.
	Budgetary resources available for obligation:			
21.40	Unobligated balance available, start of year	4	4	4
23.95	Total new obligations			
24.40	Unobligated balance available, end of year	4	4	4
	Net budget authority and outlays:			
89.00	Budget authority			
90.00	Outlays			

Trust Funds

CONTRIBUTIONS

Unavailable Collections (in millions of dollars)

Identification code 74–8569–0–7–705		1999 actual	2000 est.	2001 est.
	Balance, start of year:			
01.99	Balance, start of year	6	19	19
	Receipts:			
02.01	Contributions, American Battle Monuments Commission	27	90	11
04.00	Total: Balances and collections	33	109	30
	Appropriation:			
05.01	Contributions	−14	−90	−11
07.99	Total balance, end of year	19	19	19

Program and Financing (in millions of dollars)

Identification code 74–8569–0–7–705		1999 actual	2000 est.	2001 est.
	Obligations by program activity:			
00.04	World War II memorial	14	90	11
10.00	Total new obligations (object class 32.0)	14	90	11
	Budgetary resources available for obligation:			
21.40	Unobligated balance available, start of year	19	19	19
22.00	New budget authority (gross)	14	90	11
23.90	Total budgetary resources available for obligation	33	109	30
23.95	Total new obligations	−14	−90	−11
24.40	Unobligated balance available, end of year	19	19	19
	New budget authority (gross), detail:			
	Mandatory:			
60.27	Appropriation (trust fund, indefinite)	14	90	11
	Change in unpaid obligations:			
72.40	Unpaid obligations, start of year: Obligated balance, start of year	2	3	3
73.10	Total new obligations	14	90	11
73.20	Total outlays (gross)	−13	−90	−10
74.40	Unpaid obligations, end of year: Obligated balance, end of year	3	3	3
	Outlays (gross), detail:			
86.97	Outlays from new mandatory authority	14	90	10
86.98	Outlays from mandatory balances			1
87.00	Total outlays (gross)	13	90	10
	Net budget authority and outlays:			
89.00	Budget authority	14	90	11
90.00	Outlays	13	90	10
	Memorandum (non-add) entries:			
92.01	Total investments, start of year: U.S. securities: Par value	9	24	53
92.02	Total investments, end of year: U.S. securities: Par value	24	53	40

Purchase of flowers.—Private citizens contribute funds for the purchase of flowers to decorate graves and tablets of the missing at the cemeteries and memorials administered by the Commission.

Repair of non-Federal war memorials.—When requested to do so and upon receipt of the necessary funds, the Commission arranges for and oversees the repair of war memorials to U.S. Forces erected in foreign countries by American citizens, States, municipalities, or associations.

World War II Memorial.—Public Law 103–32 authorized the American Battle Monuments Commission to collect private contributions to fund construction of a memorial in the District of Columbia to honor members of the Armed Forces of the United States who served in World War II. The Commission projects that contributions to the World War II Memorial Fund will reach $134 million in 2000 and $144 million

CONTRIBUTIONS—Continued

in 2001. Public Law 106–117 provides $65 million in borrowing authority for construction of the World War II Memorial. This authority assists in meeting the Commemorative Works Act requirements whether this authority is exercised or not.

ARMED FORCES RETIREMENT HOME

Trust Funds

ARMED FORCES RETIREMENT HOME

For expenses necessary for the Armed Forces Retirement Home to operate and maintain the United States Soldiers' and Airmen's Home and the United States Naval Home, to be paid from funds available in the Armed Forces Retirement Home Trust Fund, [$68,295,000] *$69,832,000*, of which [$12,696,000] *$9,832,000* shall remain available until expended for construction and renovation of the physical plants at the United States Soldiers' and Airmen's Home and the United States Naval Home: *Provided*, That, notwithstanding any other provision of law, a single contract or related contracts for development and construction, to include construction of a long-term care facility at the United States Naval Home, may be employed which collectively include the full scope of the project: *Provided further*, That the solicitation and contract shall contain the clause "availability of funds" found at 48 CFR 52.232–18 and 252.232–7007, Limitation of Government Obligations. *In addition, for completion of the long-term care facility at the United States Naval Home, $6,228,000 to become available on October 1, 2001, and remain available until expended. (Departments of Labor, Health and Human Services, and Education, and Related Agencies Appropriations Act, 2000, as enacted by section 1000(a)(4) of the Consolidated Appropriations Act, 2000 (P.L. 106–113).)*

Unavailable Collections (in millions of dollars)

Identification code 84–8522–0–7–602	1999 actual	2000 est.	2001 est.
Balance, start of year:			
01.99 Balance, start of year	94	76	121
Receipts:			
02.01 Deductions, fines and gifts, U.S. Naval Home	19	17	18
02.02 Interest on investments, Armed Forces Retirement Home	6	6	9
02.03 Fees paid by residents, U.S. Naval Home	4	5	6
02.04 Deductions, fines and gifts, U.S. Soldiers' and Airmen's Home	16	15	16
02.05 Fees paid by residents, U.S. Soldiers' and Airmen' Home	8	10	12
02.06 Land sales, Armed Forces Retirement Home		60	
02.99 Total receipts	53	113	61
04.00 Total: Balances and collections	147	189	182
Appropriation:			
05.01 Armed Forces Retirement Home	−71	−68	−70
07.99 Total balance, end of year	76	121	112

Program and Financing (in millions of dollars)

Identification code 84–8522–0–7–602	1999 actual	2000 est.	2001 est.
Obligations by program activity:			
10.00 Total new obligations	65	68	70
Budgetary resources available for obligation:			
21.40 Unobligated balance available, start of year	101	110	110
22.00 New budget authority (gross)	71	68	70
22.10 Resources available from recoveries of prior year obligations	3		
23.90 Total budgetary resources available for obligation	175	178	180
23.95 Total new obligations	−65	−68	−70
24.40 Unobligated balance available, end of year	110	110	110
New budget authority (gross), detail:			
Discretionary:			
40.26 Appropriation (trust fund, definite)	71	68	70
Change in unpaid obligations:			
72.40 Unpaid obligations, start of year: Obligated balance, start of year	22	11	15
73.10 Total new obligations	65	68	70
73.20 Total outlays (gross)	−73	−64	−70
73.45 Adjustments in unexpired accounts	−3		
74.40 Unpaid obligations, end of year: Obligated balance, end of year	11	15	15
Outlays (gross), detail:			
86.90 Outlays from new discretionary authority	55	55	58
86.93 Outlays from discretionary balances	18	9	12
87.00 Total outlays (gross)	73	64	70
Net budget authority and outlays:			
89.00 Budget authority	71	68	70
90.00 Outlays	71	64	70
Memorandum (non-add) entries:			
92.01 Total investments, start of year: U.S. securities: Par value	125	101	121
92.02 Total investments, end of year: U.S. securities: Par value	101	121	112

The 1991 Defense Authorization Act, Public Law 101–510, created an Armed Forces Retirement Home Trust Fund to finance the United States Soldiers' and Airmen's Home and the United States Naval Home. The homes, which are currently in operation, are financed by appropriations drawn from the trust fund. The homes are administered by directors appointed by the Secretary of Defense with oversight provided by the Armed Forces Retirement Home Board.

A 110 bed long-term facility will be constructed beginning in 2001 at the United States Naval Home. This long-term health care facility will be funded with the approval of $8.2 million included in the 2001 appropriation and incremental funding authority of $6.2 million in 2002 for a fully funded project cost of $14.4 million.

The Armed Forces Retirement Home is cooperating with the Department of Defense on a Most Efficient Organization Study (MEO) to consider additional outsourcing opportunities.

Proceeds for the sale of excess land at fair market value, at the highest and best economic use of the property, are projected to add $60 million to the 2000 revenue estimates.

The Armed Forces Retirement Home provides medical and domiciliary care and other authorized benefits for the relief and support of certain retired and former military personnel of the Armed Forces.

The average number of members receiving domiciliary and hospital care are shown below:

	1999 actual	*2000 est.*	*2001 est.*
Domiciliary care	1,253	1,365	1,495
Hospital care	276	280	350
Total members	1,529	1,645	1,845

Object Classification (in millions of dollars)

Identification code 84–8522–0–7–602	1999 actual	2000 est.	2001 est.
Personnel compensation:			
11.1 Full-time permanent	27	27	29
11.3 Other than full-time permanent	1	1	1
11.5 Other personnel compensation	2	2	2
11.9 Total personnel compensation	30	30	32
12.1 Civilian personnel benefits	8	8	9
23.3 Communications, utilities, and miscellaneous charges	3	4	4
25.2 Other services	8	8	9
26.0 Supplies and materials	5	5	6
31.0 Equipment	1		
32.0 Land and structures	10	13	10
99.9 Total new obligations	65	68	70

Personnel Summary

Identification code 84–8522–0–7–602	1999 actual	2000 est.	2001 est.
1001 Total compensable workyears: Full-time equivalent employment	799	785	789

CEMETERIAL EXPENSES, ARMY

Salaries and Expenses

For necessary expenses, as authorized by law, for maintenance, operation, and improvement of Arlington National Cemetery and Soldiers' and Airmen's Home National Cemetery, including the purchase of [one] *two* passenger motor [vehicle] *vehicles* for replacement only, and not to exceed $1,000 for official reception and representation expenses, [$12,473,000] *$15,949,000*, to remain available until expended. *(Departments of Veterans Affairs and Housing and Urban Development, and Independent Agencies Appropriations Act, 2000.)*

Program and Financing (in millions of dollars)

Identification code 21–1805–0–1–705	1999 actual	2000 est.	2001 est.
Obligations by program activity:			
00.01 Operation and maintenance	9	10	12
00.02 Administration	1	1	1
00.03 Construction	2	1	3
10.00 Total new obligations	12	12	16
Budgetary resources available for obligation:			
21.40 Unobligated balance available, start of year	1		
22.00 New budget authority (gross)	12	12	16
22.10 Resources available from recoveries of prior year obligations			
23.90 Total budgetary resources available for obligation	13	12	16
23.95 Total new obligations	–12	–12	–16
24.40 Unobligated balance available, end of year			
New budget authority (gross), detail:			
Discretionary:			
40.00 Appropriation	12	12	16
Change in unpaid obligations:			
72.40 Unpaid obligations, start of year: Obligated balance, start of year	5	5	6
73.10 Total new obligations	12	12	16
73.20 Total outlays (gross)	–13	–9	–15
73.45 Adjustments in unexpired accounts			
74.40 Unpaid obligations, end of year: Obligated balance, end of year	5	6	6
Outlays (gross), detail:			
86.90 Outlays from new discretionary authority	10	9	12
86.93 Outlays from discretionary balances	3		3
87.00 Total outlays (gross)	13	9	15
Net budget authority and outlays:			
89.00 Budget authority	12	12	16
90.00 Outlays	13	9	15

Operation and maintenance.—Funds requested will provide for contractual services, necessary operating supplies and equipment, and personnel.

Administration.—Provision is made for determining eligibility for burial; management of Arlington and Soldiers' and Airmen's Home National Cemeteries; and administrative support.

Construction.—Arlington National Cemetery is developing a capital investment plan for all construction projects including using contiguous land sites that will be vacated by the Services, such as the Navy Annex and portions of Ft. Myer.

Object Classification (in millions of dollars)

Identification code 21–1805–0–1–705	1999 actual	2000 est.	2001 est.
11.1 Personnel compensation: Full-time permanent	4	4	4
12.1 Civilian personnel benefits	1	1	1
25.2 Other services	5	5	8
32.0 Land and structures	1	1	1
99.0 Subtotal, direct obligations	11	11	14
99.5 Below reporting threshold	1	1	2
99.9 Total new obligations	12	12	16

Personnel Summary

Identification code 21–1805–0–1–705	1999 actual	2000 est.	2001 est.
1001 Total compensable workyears: Full-time equivalent employment	104	102	101

FOREST AND WILDLIFE CONSERVATION, MILITARY RESERVATIONS

Federal Funds

General and special funds:

Forest Products Program

Program and Financing (in millions of dollars)

Identification code 21–5285–0–2–302	1999 actual	2000 est.	2001 est.
Budgetary resources available for obligation:			
21.40 Unobligated balance available, start of year	5	3	3
22.00 New budget authority (gross)	–2		
23.90 Total budgetary resources available for obligation	3	3	3
23.95 Total new obligations			
24.40 Unobligated balance available, end of year	3	3	3
New budget authority (gross), detail:			
Mandatory:			
60.25 Appropriation (special fund, indefinite)	–2		
Net budget authority and outlays:			
89.00 Budget authority	–2		
90.00 Outlays			

Section 2665 of United States Code Title 10 authorizes the Department of Defense to retain a portion of its annual surplus forest products income. The funds may be used to reimburse unplanned expenses in forest management and forest improvement projects.

Wildlife Conservation

Unavailable Collections (in millions of dollars)

Identification code 97–5095–0–2–303	1999 actual	2000 est.	2001 est.
Balance, start of year:			
01.99 Balance, start of year			
Receipts:			
02.01 Sales of hunting and fishing permits, military reservations	–1	2	2
Appropriation:			
05.01 Wildlife conservation	–2	–2	–2
05.02 Forest products program	2		
05.99 Subtotal appropriation		–2	–2
07.99 Total balance, end of year			

Program and Financing (in millions of dollars)

Identification code 97–5095–0–2–303	1999 actual	2000 est.	2001 est.
Obligations by program activity:			
10.00 Total new obligations	2	2	2
Budgetary resources available for obligation:			
21.40 Unobligated balance available, start of year	3	3	3

General and special funds—Continued

WILDLIFE CONSERVATION—Continued

Program and Financing (in millions of dollars)—Continued

Identification code 97–5095–0–2–303	1999 actual	2000 est.	2001 est.
22.00 New budget authority (gross)	2	2	2
23.90 Total budgetary resources available for obligation	5	5	5
23.95 Total new obligations	−2	−2	−2
24.40 Unobligated balance available, end of year	3	3	3
New budget authority (gross), detail:			
Mandatory:			
60.25 Appropriation (special fund, indefinite)	2	2	2
Change in unpaid obligations:			
72.40 Unpaid obligations, start of year: Obligated balance, start of year	1	1	1
73.10 Total new obligations	2	2	2
73.20 Total outlays (gross)	−2	−2	−2
74.40 Unpaid obligations, end of year: Obligated balance, end of year	1	1	1
Outlays (gross), detail:			
86.98 Outlays from mandatory balances	2	2	2
Net budget authority and outlays:			
89.00 Budget authority	2	2	2
90.00 Outlays	2	2	2

These appropriations provide for development and conservation of fish and wildlife and recreational facilities on military installations. Proceeds from the sale of fishing and hunting permits are used for these programs at Army, Navy, Marine Corps, and Air Force installations charging such user fees. These programs are carried out through cooperative plans agreed upon by the local representatives of the Secretary of Defense, the Secretary of the Interior, and the appropriate agency of the State in which the installation is located.

Object Classification (in millions of dollars)

Identification code 97–5095–0–2–303	1999 actual	2000 est.	2001 est.
26.0 Direct obligations: Supplies and materials	1	1	1
99.5 Below reporting threshold	1	1	1
99.9 Total new obligations	2	2	2

SELECTIVE SERVICE SYSTEM

Federal Funds

General and special funds:

SALARIES AND EXPENSES

For necessary expenses of the Selective Service System, including expenses of attendance at meetings and of training for uniformed personnel assigned to the Selective Service System, as authorized by 5 U.S.C. 4101–4118 for civilian employees; and not to exceed $1,000 for official reception and representation expenses; **[**$24,000,000**]** *$24,480,000*: *Provided*, That during the current fiscal year, the President may exempt this appropriation from the provisions of 31 U.S.C. 1341, whenever he deems such action to be necessary in the interest of national defense: *Provided further*, That none of the funds appropriated by this Act may be expended for or in connection with the induction of any person into the Armed Forces of the United States. *(Departments of Veterans Affairs and Housing and Urban Development, and Independent Agencies Appropriations Act, 2000.)*

Program and Financing (in millions of dollars)

Identification code 90–0400–0–1–054	1999 actual	2000 est.	2001 est.
Obligations by program activity:			
00.01 Direct program	24	24	24
10.00 Total new obligations	24	24	24
Budgetary resources available for obligation:			
22.00 New budget authority (gross)	26	24	24
23.95 Total new obligations	−24	−24	−24
New budget authority (gross), detail:			
Discretionary:			
40.00 Appropriation	26	24	24
Change in unpaid obligations:			
72.40 Unpaid obligations, start of year: Obligated balance, start of year	10	10	10
73.10 Total new obligations	24	24	24
73.20 Total outlays (gross)	−26	−24	−24
74.40 Unpaid obligations, end of year: Obligated balance, end of year	10	10	10
Outlays (gross), detail:			
86.90 Outlays from new discretionary authority	21	17	17
86.93 Outlays from discretionary balances	5	6	6
87.00 Total outlays (gross)	26	24	24
Net budget authority and outlays:			
89.00 Budget authority	26	24	24
90.00 Outlays	26	24	24

The Selective Service System continues to register men as they reach age 18, as required by law, and maintain a data base of registrant records. Should the Nation return to conscription for a national emergency, the agency would respond to a revised requirement to have the first draftees at military processing centers 193 days after a mobilization. In cooperation with the Department of Defense, Active Duty and Reserve Officers are being reduced to reflect the reduced readiness requirements.

The SSS will continue to strengthen its partnership with the Armed Services. The agency will expand its national initiative to offer every young man that receives an acknowledgment, almost two million annually, the opportunity to volunteer for the military services.

In addition to improving its business processes and national registration compliance statistics, while helping to sustain recruiting efforts, the Agency is moving to an advanced information technology architecture to ensure faster, more accurate registrations and better customer services via the Internet, telephone, and other means.

Object Classification (in millions of dollars)

Identification code 90–0400–0–1–054	1999 actual	2000 est.	2001 est.
Personnel compensation:			
11.1 Full-time permanent	8	8	8
11.8 Special personal services payments	6	6	6
11.9 Total personnel compensation	14	14	14
12.1 Civilian personnel benefits	2	2	2
23.1 Rental payments to GSA	1	1	1
23.3 Communications, utilities, and miscellaneous charges	2	2	2
24.0 Printing and reproduction	1	1	1
25.2 Other services	4	4	4
99.9 Total new obligations	24	24	24

Personnel Summary

Identification code 90–0400–0–1–054	1999 actual	2000 est.	2001 est.
1001 Total compensable workyears: Full-time equivalent employment	165	165	165

ENVIRONMENTAL PROTECTION AGENCY

Federal Funds

General and special funds:

PROGRAM AND RESEARCH OPERATIONS

Program and Financing (in millions of dollars)

Identification code 68–0200–0–1–304	1999 actual	2000 est.	2001 est.
Change in unpaid obligations:			
72.40 Unpaid obligations, start of year: Obligated balance, start of year	2		
73.40 Adjustments in expired accounts (net)	–2		
Net budget authority and outlays:			
89.00 Budget authority			
90.00 Outlays			

Congress restructured EPA's accounts beginning in 1996. The Program and Research Operations account was eliminated and its resources moved to the new Environmental Programs and Management and Science and Technology accounts.

OFFICE OF INSPECTOR GENERAL

For necessary expenses of the Office of Inspector General in carrying out the provisions of the Inspector General Act of 1978, as amended, and for construction, alteration, repair, rehabilitation, and renovation of facilities, not to exceed $75,000 per project, [$32,409,000] *$34,094,400*, to remain available until September 30, [2001] *2002*: *Provided*, That the sums available in this account shall remain available through September 30, [2008] *2009* for liquidating obligations made in fiscal years [2000] *2001* and [2001: *Provided further*, That the obligated balance of funds transferred to this account in Public Law 105–276 shall remain available through September 30, 2007 for liquidating obligations made in fiscal years 1999 and 2000] *2002*. *(Departments of Veterans Affairs and Housing and Urban Development, and Independent Agencies Appropriations Act, 2000.)*

Program and Financing (in millions of dollars)

Identification code 68–0112–0–1–304	1999 actual	2000 est.	2001 est.
Obligations by program activity:			
00.01 Direct program: Effective Management	30	36	34
09.01 Reimbursements from Superfund Trust Fund	11	11	12
10.00 Total new obligations	41	47	46
Budgetary resources available for obligation:			
21.40 Unobligated balance available, start of year	2	4	
22.00 New budget authority (gross)	43	43	46
23.90 Total budgetary resources available for obligation	45	47	46
23.95 Total new obligations	–41	–47	–46
24.40 Unobligated balance available, end of year	4		
New budget authority (gross), detail:			
Discretionary:			
40.00 Appropriation	31	32	34
68.00 Spending authority from offsetting collections: Offsetting collections (cash)	12	11	12
70.00 Total new budget authority (gross)	43	43	46
Change in unpaid obligations:			
Unpaid obligations, start of year:			
72.40 Obligated balance, start of year	–7	–4	
72.95 From Federal sources: Receivables and unpaid, unfilled orders	13	10	10
72.99 Total unpaid obligations, start of year	6	6	10
73.10 Total new obligations	41	47	46
73.20 Total outlays (gross)	–41	–43	–46
73.40 Adjustments in expired accounts (net)	–1		
Unpaid obligations, end of year:			
74.40 Obligated balance, end of year	–4		
74.95 From Federal sources: Receivables and unpaid, unfilled orders	10	10	10
74.99 Total unpaid obligations, end of year	6	10	10
Outlays (gross), detail:			
86.90 Outlays from new discretionary authority	40	33	36
86.93 Outlays from discretionary balances	2	10	10
87.00 Total outlays (gross)	41	43	46
Offsets:			
Against gross budget authority and outlays:			
88.00 Offsetting collections (cash) from: Federal sources	–12	–11	–12
Net budget authority and outlays:			
89.00 Budget authority	31	32	34
90.00 Outlays	30	32	34

This appropriation supports EPA's core programs, and the Agency's effective management goal to establish a management infrastructure that will set and implement the highest quality standards for effective internal management and fiscal responsibility. To assist the Agency in accomplishing this goal, the Office of Inspector General (OIG) will provide audit and investigative services to improve the performance and integrity of its programs and operation, and to reduce the risk of loss from fraud, waste and mismanagement. These services will identify and recommend corrective actions on management and administrative deficiencies. The Inspector General also provides professional review and recommendations concerning Agency contracting practices, administration and changes through all phases of the procurement process. Among the audit functions, contract audits review propriety and allowability of cost claimed or charged to EPA by prime or subcontractors. Through internal audits and performance evaluations, the OIG reviews and evaluates all facets of Agency programs and operations, including the adequacy of management systems and controls. Financial audits review the soundness and accuracy of the financial accounting and reporting systems. Grant audits focus on the effectiveness and propriety of costs of individual projects. Additional funds for audit and investigative activities associated with the Superfund Trust Fund are appropriated under that account and transferred to the Inspector General account to allow for proper accounting. This appropriation also supports activities under the Working Capital Fund.

Object Classification (in millions of dollars)

Identification code 68–0112–0–1–304	1999 actual	2000 est.	2001 est.
Direct obligations:			
Personnel compensation:			
11.1 Full-time permanent	17	19	21
11.5 Other personnel compensation	1	1	1
11.9 Total personnel compensation	18	20	22
12.1 Civilian personnel benefits	4	4	5
21.0 Travel and transportation of persons	1	1	1
23.1 Rental payments to GSA	2		
25.2 Other services	2	8	3
25.3 Purchases of goods and services from Government accounts	2	2	2
31.0 Equipment	1	1	1

General and special funds—Continued

OFFICE OF INSPECTOR GENERAL—Continued

Object Classification (in millions of dollars)—Continued

Identification code 68–0112–0–1–304	1999 actual	2000 est.	2001 est.
99.0 Subtotal, direct obligations	30	36	34
99.0 Reimbursable obligations	11	11	12
99.9 Total new obligations	41	47	46

Personnel Summary

Identification code 68–0112–0–1–304	1999 actual	2000 est.	2001 est.
Direct:			
1001 Total compensable workyears: Full-time equivalent employment	240	274	277
Reimbursable:			
2001 Total compensable workyears: Full-time equivalent employment	100	100	95

SCIENCE AND TECHNOLOGY

(INCLUDING TRANSFER OF FUNDS)

For science and technology, including research and development activities, which shall include research and development activities under the Comprehensive Environmental Response, Compensation, and Liability Act of 1980 (CERCLA), as amended; necessary expenses for personnel and related costs and travel expenses, including uniforms, or allowances therefore, as authorized by 5 U.S.C. 5901–5902; services as authorized by 5 U.S.C. 3109, but at rates for individuals not to exceed the per diem rate equivalent to the maximum rate payable for senior level positions under 5 U.S.C. 5376; procurement of laboratory equipment and supplies; other operating expenses in support of research and development; construction, alteration, repair, rehabilitation, and renovation of facilities, not to exceed $75,000 per project, **[**$645,000,000**]** *$674,348,000*, which shall remain available until September 30, **[**2001**]** *2002, of which $9,700,000 shall be derived from the Environmental Services Fund*: *Provided*, That the obligated balance of sums available in this account shall remain available through September 30, **[**2008**]** *2009* for liquidating obligations made in fiscal years **[**2000 and**]** 2001 *and 2002***[**: *Provided further*, That the obligated balance of funds transferred to this account in Public Law 105–276 shall remain available through September 30, 2007 for liquidating obligations made in fiscal years 1999 and 2000**]**. *(Departments of Veterans Affairs and Housing and Urban Development, and Independent Agencies Appropriations Act, 2000.)*

Program and Financing (in millions of dollars)

Identification code 68–0107–0–1–304	1999 actual	2000 est.	2001 est.
Obligations by program activity:			
Direct program:			
00.01 Clean Air	160	188	157
00.02 Clean Water	80	98	91
00.03 Safe Food	7	15	14
00.04 Preventing Pollution	19	22	22
00.05 Waste Management	61	69	17
00.06 Global and Cross-Border	57	53	75
00.07 Right to Know	6	20	15
00.08 Sound Science	234	276	235
00.09 Credible Deterrent	10	9	11
00.10 Effective Management	9	8	21
09.01 Reimbursements from Superfund Trust Fund	40	38	36
09.02 Other Reimbursements	11	12	10
09.99 Total reimbursable program	51	50	46
10.00 Total new obligations	694	808	704
Budgetary resources available for obligation:			
21.40 Unobligated balance available, start of year	125	134	
22.00 New budget authority (gross)	708	673	704
22.10 Resources available from recoveries of prior year obligations			
23.90 Total budgetary resources available for obligation	833	807	704
23.95 Total new obligations	−694	−808	−704
23.98 Unobligated balance expiring or withdrawn	−6		
24.40 Unobligated balance available, end of year	134		
New budget authority (gross), detail:			
Discretionary:			
40.00 Appropriation	660	645	664
40.20 Appropriation (special fund, definite—Environmental Services Fund)			10
40.76 Reduction pursuant to P.L. 106–113		−3	
42.00 Transferred from other accounts	1	1	
43.00 Appropriation (total discretionary)	661	643	674
Spending authority from offsetting collections:			
68.00 Offsetting collections (cash)	43	30	30
68.10 From Federal sources: Change in receivables and unpaid, unfilled orders	4		
68.90 Spending authority from offsetting collections (total discretionary)	47	30	30
70.00 Total new budget authority (gross)	708	673	704
Change in unpaid obligations:			
Unpaid obligations, start of year:			
72.40 Obligated balance, start of year	480	512	631
72.95 From Federal sources: Receivables and unpaid, unfilled orders	62	66	66
72.99 Total unpaid obligations, start of year	542	578	697
73.10 Total new obligations	694	808	704
73.20 Total outlays (gross)	−650	−689	−694
73.40 Adjustments in expired accounts (net)	−8		
Unpaid obligations, end of year:			
74.40 Obligated balance, end of year	512	631	642
74.95 From Federal sources: Receivables and unpaid, unfilled orders	66	66	66
74.99 Total unpaid obligations, end of year	578	697	708
Outlays (gross), detail:			
86.90 Outlays from new discretionary authority	333	379	397
86.93 Outlays from discretionary balances	317	310	297
87.00 Total outlays (gross)	650	689	694
Offsets:			
Against gross budget authority and outlays:			
Offsetting collections (cash) from:			
88.00 Federal sources	−35	−27	−27
88.40 Non-Federal sources	−8	−3	−3
88.90 Total, offsetting collections (cash)	−43	−30	−30
Against gross budget authority only:			
88.95 From Federal sources: Change in receivables and unpaid, unfilled orders	−4		
Net budget authority and outlays:			
89.00 Budget authority	661	643	674
90.00 Outlays	607	659	664

This appropriation finances salary, travel, science, technology, research and development activities including laboratory and center supplies, certain operating expenses (including activities under the Working Capital Fund), contracts, grants, intergovernmental agreements, and purchases of scientific equipment. These activities provide the scientific and technology basis for EPA's regulatory actions. Funding for the Office of Research and Development and activities in this account under the Climate Change Technology Initiative are included in the 21st Century Research Fund.

Superfund research costs are appropriated in the Hazardous Substance Superfund appropriation and transferred to this account to allow for proper accounting. A portion of funding provided through this account to support the mobile sources program is to be derived from fees charged for motor vehicle engine certifications that are deposited in the Environmental Services special fund.

This appropriation supports core Agency programs and a number of the Agency's ten goals. Specifically in 2001, our emphasis will be placed on the following:

Clean Air.—To ensure that every American community has safe and healthy air to breathe, the EPA will conduct a range of science and technology activities. These include research on the effects to human health of toxic air pollutants, and research on criteria air pollutants (ozone, carbon monoxide, sulfur dioxide, nitrogen dioxide, lead, and particulate matter) to develop the scientific basis for the EPA's national ambient air quality standards. The EPA will also develop control measures for mobile sources, including the development of cleaner engine technologies, and cleaner burning fuels. The EPA will also support the Clean Air Status and Trends Network (CASNet), a dry deposition monitoring network.

Clean and Safe Water.—To support the goal of all Americans having drinking water that is clean and safe to drink, the EPA will conduct research to support efforts to attain good water quality and safe drinking water. The EPA will also conduct the research to strengthen the scientific basis for development of effective beach evaluation tools, and to enhance understanding of the structure and function of aquatic systems through the development of improved aquatic ecocriteria.

Safe Food.—To ensure that the foods Americans eat will be free from unsafe pesticide residues, the EPA laboratory support program provides analytical and environmental chemistry services in support of the EPA's registration, reregistration and tolerance/reassessment programs for food-use pesticides. Also, the pesticide laboratories will provide analytical chemistry capabilities to validate food tolerance enforcement methods.

Preventing Pollution and Reducing Risk in Communities, Homes, Workplaces and Ecosystems.—Pollution Prevention and risk management strategies will be aimed at cost-effectively eliminating, reducing, or minimizing risk due to emissions and contamination. Indoor environments will be improved through technical support, analysis and producing necessary information to understand indoor air effects, and identify health risks so that risk managers can make informed decisions.

Better Waste Management, Restoration of Contaminated Waste Sites, and Emergency Response.—To ensure that America's waste will be stored, treated, and disposed of in ways that prevent harm to people and the environment, the EPA will research ways to reduce uncertainties associated with groundwater/soil sampling and analysis, to develop methods and models of contaminant transport, and to reduce the time and cost associated with site characterization and the site remediation activities that it guides. Field analytical methods for characterizing soils are also intended to provide cheaper and more timely analyses and to reduce the uncertainty of site characterization.

Reduction of Global and Cross-Border Environmental Risks.—The United States will lead other nations in successful, multilateral efforts to reduce significant risks to human health and ecosystems from climate change, stratospheric ozone depletion, and other hazards of international concern. The Agency will continue to work with the U.S. automobile industry and other government agencies to develop a "clean car," a vehicle that would meet the 2004 goals of the Partnership for a New Generation of Vehicles (PNGV) to have three times the fuel efficiency of today's cars (representing a 67 percent reduction in carbon dioxide emissions), with no sacrifice of performance, size, or affordability while meeting stringent future safety and emission standards. Through its Transportation Efficiency Program, EPA will support ongoing efforts to provide public information about transportation choices and consumers' impact on air quality, traffic congestion and climate changes.

Expansion of Americans' Right to Know About Their Environment.—To assist efforts in providing the public with information about the environment, the EPA will focus on improving data collection and data quality and on deploying new technologies for real time and automated measurement, monitoring, and information delivery. As part of the environmental monitoring for public access and community tracking (EMPACT) initiative, which is being established to provide environmental information in the 86 largest U.S. metropolitan areas, the EPA will evaluate and modify existing risk assessment tools for use by local stakeholders.

Sound Science, Improved Understanding of Environmental Risk, and Greater Innovation to Address Environmental Problems.—The EPA will develop and apply the best available science for addressing current and future environmental hazards, as well as new approaches toward improving environmental protection. The Agency will continue to improve its understanding of risks to human health of the American public and the Nation's ecosystems. The EPA will address emerging environmental issues while seeking to develop innovative, cost-effective solutions to pollution prevention and risk reduction by working with stakeholders to identify and overcome barriers, such as the lack of credible and independent performance data. The Agency will continue to interpret and integrate scientific information to help make better regulatory decisions and provide national leadership in addressing emerging environmental issues. The EPA will seek to reduce uncertainties in risk assessment and help to prevent and manage risk by using cost-effective approaches.

A Credible Deterrent to Pollution and Greater Compliance with the Law.—The National Enforcement Investigations Center is the primary source of forensics expertise in the EPA. It provides technical services not available elsewhere to support the needs of the EPA Headquarters and Regional offices, other Federal Agencies, and state and local environmental enforcement organizations.

Object Classification (in millions of dollars)

Identification code 68–0107–0–1–304		1999 actual	2000 est.	2001 est.
	Direct obligations:			
	Personnel compensation:			
11.1	Full-time permanent	147	155	164
11.3	Other than full-time permanent	7	7	8
11.5	Other personnel compensation	3	3	4
11.7	Military personnel	2	2	2
11.9	Total personnel compensation	159	167	178
12.1	Civilian personnel benefits	33	35	39
21.0	Travel and transportation of persons	5	5	6
22.0	Transportation of things	1	1	1
23.3	Communications, utilities, and miscellaneous charges	4	4	4
24.0	Printing and reproduction	1	1	1
25.1	Advisory and assistance services	6	6	6
25.2	Other services	70	182	54
25.3	Purchases of goods and services from Government accounts	38	37	38
25.4	Operation and maintenance of facilities	9	9	9
25.5	Research and development contracts	64	63	64
25.7	Operation and maintenance of equipment	20	20	20
26.0	Supplies and materials	11	11	11
31.0	Equipment	34	33	34
41.0	Grants, subsidies, and contributions	188	184	193
99.0	Subtotal, direct obligations	643	758	658
99.0	Reimbursable obligations	51	50	46
99.9	Total new obligations	694	808	704

Personnel Summary

Identification code 68–0107–0–1–304		1999 actual	2000 est.	2001 est.
	Direct:			
1001	Total compensable workyears: Full-time equivalent employment	2,457	2,460	2,464
	Reimbursable:			
2001	Total compensable workyears: Full-time equivalent employment	151	137	128

General and special funds—Continued

ENVIRONMENTAL PROGRAMS AND MANAGEMENT

For environmental programs and management, including necessary expenses, not otherwise provided for, for personnel and related costs and travel expenses, including uniforms, or allowances therefore, as authorized by 5 U.S.C. 5901–5902; services as authorized by 5 U.S.C. 3109, but at rates for individuals not to exceed the per diem rate equivalent to the maximum rate payable for senior level positions under 5 U.S.C. 5376; hire of passenger motor vehicles; hire, maintenance, and operation of aircraft; purchase of reprints; library memberships in societies or associations which issue publications to members only or at a price to members lower than to subscribers who are not members; construction, alteration, repair, rehabilitation, and renovation of facilities, not to exceed $75,000 per project; and not to exceed $6,000 for official reception and representation expenses, [$1,900,000,000] *$2,099,461,000*, which shall remain available until September 30, [2001] *2002*: *Provided*, That the obligated balance of such sums shall remain available through September 30, [2008] *2009* for liquidating obligations made in fiscal years [2000] *2001* and *2002* [2001: *Provided further*, That none of the funds appropriated by this Act shall be used to propose or issue rules, regulations, decrees, or orders for the purpose of implementation, or in preparation for implementation, of the Kyoto Protocol which was adopted on December 11, 1997, in Kyoto, Japan at the Third Conference of the Parties to the United Nations Framework Convention on Climate Change, which has not been submitted to the Senate for advice and consent to ratification pursuant to article II, section 2, clause 2, of the United States Constitution, and which has not entered into force pursuant to article 25 of the Protocol:[1] *Provided further*, That none of the funds made available in this Act may be used to implement or administer the interim guidance issued on February 5, 1998, by the Environmental Protection Agency relating to title VI of the Civil Rights Act of 1964 and designated as the "Interim Guidance for Investigating Title VI Administrative Complaints Challenging Permits" with respect to complaints filed under such title after October 21, 1998, and until guidance is finalized. Nothing in this proviso may be construed to restrict the Environmental Protection Agency from developing or issuing final guidance relating to title VI of the Civil Rights Act of 1964: *Provided further*, That notwithstanding 7 U.S.C. 136r and 15 U.S.C. 2609, beginning in fiscal year 2000 and thereafter, grants awarded under section 20 of the Federal Insecticide, Fungicide, and Rodenticide Act, as amended, and section 10 of the Toxic Substances Control Act, as amended, shall be available for research, development, monitoring, public education, training, demonstrations, and studies: *Provided further*, That the unexpended funds remaining from the $2,200,000 appropriated under this heading in Public Law 105–276 for a grant to the Lake Ponchartrain Basin Foundation circuit rider initiative in Louisiana shall be transferred to the "State and tribal assistance grants" appropriation to remain available until expended for making grants for the construction of wastewater and water treatment facilities and groundwater protection infrastructure in accordance with the terms and conditions specified for such grants in the report accompanying that Act]. *(Departments of Veterans Affairs and Housing and Urban Development, and Independent Agencies Appropriations Act, 2000.)*

[1] We propose the deletion of this language for reasons that are primarily institutional and precedential in nature. Such language is unnecessary. The Administration has no intention of taking any actions that would contravene the purpose and clear meaning of this legislation.

Program and Financing (in millions of dollars)

Identification code 68–0108–0–1–304		1999 actual	2000 est.	2001 est.
	Obligations by program activity:			
	Direct program:			
00.01	Clean Air	171	191	188
00.02	Clean Water	401	480	411
00.03	Safe Food	58	82	72
00.04	Preventing Pollution	132	189	182
00.05	Waste Management	139	163	164
00.06	Global and Cross-Border	128	146	249
00.07	Right to Know	123	160	150
00.08	Sound Science	49	74	72
00.09	Credible Deterrent	242	280	303
00.10	Effective Management	380	261	308
09.01	Reimbursable program	48	45	45
10.00	Total new obligations	1,871	2,071	2,144
	Budgetary resources available for obligation:			
21.40	Unobligated balance available, start of year	134	131	
22.00	New budget authority (gross)	1,901	1,940	2,144
23.90	Total budgetary resources available for obligation	2,035	2,071	2,144
23.95	Total new obligations	−1,871	−2,071	−2,144
23.98	Unobligated balance expiring or withdrawn	−33		
24.40	Unobligated balance available, end of year	131		
	New budget authority (gross), detail:			
	Discretionary:			
40.00	Appropriation	1,847	1,900	2,099
40.76	Reduction pursuant to P.L. 106–113		−5	
42.00	Transferred from other accounts	6		
43.00	Appropriation (total discretionary)	1,853	1,895	2,099
	Spending authority from offsetting collections:			
68.00	Offsetting collections (cash)	39	45	45
68.10	From Federal sources: Change in receivables and unpaid, unfilled orders	9		
68.90	Spending authority from offsetting collections (total discretionary)	48	45	45
70.00	Total new budget authority (gross)	1,901	1,940	2,144
	Change in unpaid obligations:			
	Unpaid obligations, start of year:			
72.40	Obligated balance, start of year	874	795	925
72.95	From Federal sources: Receivables and unpaid, unfilled orders	71	80	80
72.99	Total unpaid obligations, start of year	945	875	1,005
73.10	Total new obligations	1,871	2,071	2,144
73.20	Total outlays (gross)	−1,912	−1,941	−2,062
73.40	Adjustments in expired accounts (net)	−28		
	Unpaid obligations, end of year:			
74.40	Obligated balance, end of year	795	925	1,007
74.95	From Federal sources: Receivables and unpaid, unfilled orders	80	80	80
74.99	Total unpaid obligations, end of year	875	1,005	1,087
	Outlays (gross), detail:			
86.90	Outlays from new discretionary authority	1,269	1,310	1,427
86.93	Outlays from discretionary balances	643	631	635
87.00	Total outlays (gross)	1,912	1,941	2,062
	Offsets:			
	Against gross budget authority and outlays:			
88.00	Offsetting collections (cash) from: Federal sources	−39	−45	−45
	Against gross budget authority only:			
88.95	From Federal sources: Change in receivables and unpaid, unfilled orders	−9		
	Net budget authority and outlays:			
89.00	Budget authority	1,853	1,895	2,099
90.00	Outlays	1,873	1,896	2,017

This appropriation includes funds for salaries, travel, contracts, grants, and cooperative agreements for pollution abatement, control, and compliance activities and administrative activities of the operating programs, including activities under the Working Capital Fund. In addition, activities in this account under the Climate Change Technology Initiative are included in the 21st Century Research Fund.

This appropriation supports core Agency programs and each of the Agency's ten goals. Specifically in 2001, EPA will emphasize the following:

Clean Air.—To ensure that every American community has safe and healthy air to breathe, EPA will develop and implement new strategies to attain ambient air quality standards for ozone and particulate matter, and reduce regional haze through geographic initiatives in areas where significant transport of pollutants occurs. EPA will continue to develop and issue national technology-based standards to reduce the quantity of toxic air pollutants emitted from industrial and manufacturing processes, as well as urban sources. EPA will also develop control measures for stationary and other sources that are regulated at the Federal level. The Acid Rain program will continue its market-based approach to achieving reduced emissions of sulfur dioxide and nitrogen oxides primarily from electric utilities.

Clean and Safe Water.—To provide all Americans with drinking water that is clean and safe to drink, EPA will emphasize developing new drinking water standards for microbiological contaminants, disinfectant and disinfection by-products, and other pollutants identified as posing potentially high risks. EPA will also work with its State and Tribal partners to address protection of drinking water sources. EPA will provide the tools and guidance for its partners to better protect the Nation's waters, and protect and restore wetlands. EPA and its partners will make progress toward completing Total Maximum Daily Loads (TMDLs) for impaired U.S. waters and improving implementation of TMDL programs. EPA will work with its partners to assure effective implementation of the National Pollution Discharge Elimination System, pretreatment, and biosolids program. EPA will also work with its partners to address sources of polluted runoff.

Safe Food.—To ensure that the foods Americans eat will be free from unsafe pesticide residues, EPA will continue to set terms and conditions of food/feed-use registration, marketing and use. Through the registration, reregistration, and special review programs, food/feed-use pesticides will undergo extensive review and evaluation of health data. EPA intends to decrease the use of pesticides with the highest potential to cause adverse effects and increase the number of registrations of safer pesticides.

Preventing Pollution and Reducing Risk in Communities, Homes, Workplaces and Ecosystems.—Pollution prevention and risk management strategies will be aimed at cost-effectively eliminating, reducing, or minimizing emissions and contamination. EPA intends to reduce public and ecosystem risks from non-food/feed-use pesticides through its registration and reregistration programs and public education and training activities, including worker protection, endangered species protection, environmental stewardship, and integrated pest management programs. EPA will also support development of safer chemicals by minimizing or eliminating regulatory burdens on new chemicals that replace riskier substances already in the marketplace. The toxicity of wastes will be reduced by focusing on reductions in persistent, bioaccumulative and toxic (PBTs) chemicals. The quantity of wastes will also be reduced through source reduction and recycling.

Better Waste Management, Restoration of Contaminated Waste Sites, and Emergency Response.—To ensure that America's waste will be stored, treated, and disposed of in ways that prevent harm to people and to the natural environment, EPA will continue its Hazardous Waste Minimization and Combustion Strategy, including setting new standards for hazardous waste incinerators and cement kilns that burn hazardous waste. In addition, the Agency will focus on controlling human exposures and groundwater releases at Resource Conservation and Recovery Act (RCRA) facilities designated as high priority for corrective action. EPA will also develop and promulgate standards, regulations, and guidelines to reduce exposure from radiation sources.

Reduction of Global and Cross-Border Environmental Risks.—The United States will lead other nations in successful, multilateral efforts to reduce significant risks to human health and ecosystems from climate change, stratospheric ozone depletion, and other environmental hazards of international concern. EPA will implement formal bilateral and multilateral environmental agreements with key countries, execute environmental components of key foreign policy initiatives, and engage in regional and global negotiations aimed at reducing environmental risks via formal and informal agreements. EPA will cooperate with other countries to ensure that domestic and international environmental laws, policies, and priorities are recognized and implemented and, where appropriate, promoted within the multilateral development assistance and trading system. EPA will also emphasize domestic and international efforts to limit the production and use of ozone-depleting substances and develop safe alternative compounds, and demonstrate and promote public/private partnership programs that reduce greenhouse gas emissions.

Expansion of Americans' Right to Know About Their Environment.—Easy access to a wealth of information about the state of their local environment will expand citizen involvement and give people tools to protect their families and their communities as they see fit. To achieve this goal, EPA will increase education, outreach, and data availability programs. The Agency will expand the coverage of pollutants, pollution sources, and data elements in EPA's Toxic Release Inventory, and ensure compliance with reporting requirements. The Agency will also improve electronic access to information by significantly expanding the type and amount of information available on the Internet. High quality, accurate environmental information is a strategic resource for protecting public health and the environment. To improve on and make the most effective use of this important resource, EPA has consolidated many of its information activities under a single program manager and office integrating various aspects of information management, policy and information technology stewardship at EPA.

Sound Science, Improved Understanding of Environmental Risk, and Greater Innovation to Address Environmental Problems.—EPA will maximize the potential to reduce uncertainties in risk assessment, and help to prevent and manage risk, by using cost-effective approaches such as the place- and facility-based strategies (e.g., the Community-Based Environmental Protection strategy).

A Credible Deterrent to Pollution and Greater Compliance With the Law.—To ensure full compliance with laws intended to protect human health and the environment, EPA will promote compliance by the regulated community, set risk-based enforcement and compliance priorities, and strategically plan and target activities to address environmental problems associated with industry sectors and communities. EPA will use traditional activities of compliance monitoring, civil enforcement and criminal enforcement actions as well as new and innovative approaches such as compliance assistance and compliance incentives.

Effective Management.—EPA will improve the quality of its internal management, contract administration, and fiscal responsibility efforts. The Agency will invest in its employees through training, education and implementation of automated and streamlined human resources processes. The Agency will focus its contracting efforts on performance-based service contracts instead of the traditional cost-plus, level-of-effort contracting, relying on guidance developed by the Office of Federal Procurement Policy. EPA will concentrate on resolution of material weaknesses previously identified in the area of grants closeouts, and on implementation of the best practices identified government-wide by the General Accounting Office (GAO) for information resources management and integration of information technology investments. EPA will also provide support for electronic reporting to reduce the burden to the Agency's highest-volume submitters.

Object Classification (in millions of dollars)

Identification code 68–0108–0–1–304		1999 actual	2000 est.	2001 est.
	Direct obligations:			
	Personnel compensation:			
11.1	Full-time permanent	677	720	775
11.3	Other than full-time permanent	29	31	32
11.5	Other personnel compensation	12	13	13
11.7	Military personnel	6	6	7
11.8	Special personal services payments	2	2	2

General and special funds—Continued

ENVIRONMENTAL PROGRAMS AND MANAGEMENT—Continued

Object Classification (in millions of dollars)—Continued

Identification code 68–0108–0–1–304	1999 actual	2000 est.	2001 est.
11.9 Total personnel compensation	726	772	829
12.1 Civilian personnel benefits	156	166	174
12.2 Military personnel benefits	1	1	1
21.0 Travel and transportation of persons	22	28	29
22.0 Transportation of things	1	1	1
23.1 Rental payments to GSA	117	144	162
23.2 Rental payments to others	12	12	13
23.3 Communications, utilities, and miscellaneous charges	12	12	13
24.0 Printing and reproduction	8	8	8
25.1 Advisory and assistance services	29	30	31
25.2 Other services	333	434	411
25.3 Purchases of goods and services from Government accounts	71	73	75
25.4 Operation and maintenance of facilities	16	17	17
25.5 Research and development contracts	2	2	2
25.7 Operation and maintenance of equipment	22	23	23
26.0 Supplies and materials	11	11	12
31.0 Equipment	25	26	26
41.0 Grants, subsidies, and contributions	258	266	272
99.0 Subtotal, direct obligations	1,822	2,026	2,099
99.0 Reimbursable obligations	48	45	45
99.5 Below reporting threshold	1	....	....
99.9 Total new obligations	1,871	2,071	2,144

Personnel Summary

Identification code 68–0108–0–1–304	1999 actual	2000 est.	2001 est.
Direct:			
1001 Total compensable workyears: Full-time equivalent employment	11,205	11,232	11,224
Reimbursable:			
2001 Total compensable workyears: Full-time equivalent employment	36	2	2

BUILDINGS AND FACILITIES

For construction, repair, improvement, extension, alteration, and purchase of fixed equipment or facilities of, or for use by, the Environmental Protection Agency, [$62,600,000] *$23,931,000*, to remain available until expended. *(Departments of Veterans Affairs and Housing and Urban Development, and Independent Agencies Appropriations Act, 2000.)*

Program and Financing (in millions of dollars)

Identification code 68–0110–0–1–304	1999 actual	2000 est.	2001 est.
Obligations by program activity:			
00.01 Effective Management	70	71	24
10.00 Total new obligations	70	71	24
Budgetary resources available for obligation:			
21.40 Unobligated balance available, start of year	20	9	....
22.00 New budget authority (gross)	57	62	24
22.10 Resources available from recoveries of prior year obligations	2	....	....
23.90 Total budgetary resources available for obligation	79	71	24
23.95 Total new obligations	–70	–71	–24
24.40 Unobligated balance available, end of year	9	....	....
New budget authority (gross), detail:			
Discretionary:			
40.00 Appropriation	57	62	24
Change in unpaid obligations:			
72.40 Unpaid obligations, start of year: Obligated balance, start of year	214	130	89
73.10 Total new obligations	70	71	24
73.20 Total outlays (gross)	–151	–112	–68
73.45 Adjustments in unexpired accounts	–2	....	....
74.40 Unpaid obligations, end of year: Obligated balance, end of year	130	89	45
Outlays (gross), detail:			
86.90 Outlays from new discretionary authority	5	11	4
86.93 Outlays from discretionary balances	146	101	64
87.00 Total outlays (gross)	151	112	68
Net budget authority and outlays:			
89.00 Budget authority	57	62	24
90.00 Outlays	151	112	68

This appropriation provides for the construction, repair, improvement, extension, alteration, and purchase of fixed equipment or facilities that are owned or used by the Environmental Protection Agency. This appropriation supports the Agency-wide goal of effective management. EPA's management infrastructure will set and implement the highest quality standards for effective internal management and fiscal responsibility. The facilities funded by this account will provide quality work environments and state-of-the-art laboratories that consider employee safety and security and pollution prevention.

Object Classification (in millions of dollars)

Identification code 68–0110–0–1–304	1999 actual	2000 est.	2001 est.
25.4 Operation and maintenance of facilities	11	11	10
32.0 Land and structures	59	60	14
99.9 Total new obligations	70	71	24

STATE AND TRIBAL ASSISTANCE GRANTS

For environmental programs and infrastructure assistance, including capitalization grants for State revolving funds and performance partnership grants, [$3,466,650,000] *$2,906,957,000*, to remain available until expended, of which [$1,350,000,000] *$800,000,000* shall be for making capitalization grants for the Clean Water State Revolving Funds under title VI of the Federal Water Pollution Control Act, as amended; [$820,000,000] *$825,000,000* shall be for capitalization grants for the Drinking Water State Revolving Funds under section 1452 of the Safe Drinking Water Act, as amended, except that, notwithstanding section 1452(n) of the Safe Drinking Water Act, as amended, none of the funds made available under this heading in this Act, or in previous appropriations Acts, shall be reserved by the Administrator for health effects studies on drinking water contaminants; [$50,000,000] *$85,000,000 shall be for a clean air partnership fund demonstration program under section 103 of the Clean Air Act to support programs to achieve early, integrated reductions in emissions of air pollutants, including local revolving funds and other mechanisms for leveraging non-federal resources;* $100,000,000 shall be for architectural, engineering, planning, design, construction and related activities in connection with the construction of high priority water and wastewater facilities in the area of the United States-Mexico Border, after consultation with the appropriate border commission; [$30,000,000] *$15,000,000* shall be for grants to the State of Alaska to address drinking water and wastewater infrastructure needs of [rural and] Alaska Native Villages; [$331,650,000 shall be for making grants for the construction of wastewater and water treatment facilities and groundwater protection infrastructure in accordance with the terms and conditions specified for such grants in the conference report and joint explanatory statement of the committee of conference accompanying this Act (H.R. 2684);] *$10,000,000 shall be for a grant to the city of New Orleans, Louisiana, to support planning, design, construction and other activities related to storm water problems in the city's sewer system; $3,000,000 shall be for grants for water infrastructure improvements in Bristol County, Massachusetts;* and [$885,000,000] *$1,068,957,000* shall be for grants, including associated program support costs, to States, federally recognized tribes, interstate agencies, tribal consortia, and air pollution control agencies for multi-media or single media pollution prevention, control and abatement and related activities, including activities pursuant to the provisions set forth under this heading in Public Law 104–134, and for making grants under section 103 of the Clean Air Act for particulate matter monitoring and data collection activities[: *Provided*, That notwithstanding section 603(d)(7) of the Federal Water Pollution Control Act, as amended, the limitation on the amounts in a State water pollution control revolving fund that may be used by a State to administer the fund shall not apply to amounts included as principal in loans made by such fund in fiscal year 2000 and prior years where such amounts represent costs of administering the fund, or by the State of New York for fiscal year 2000 and prior years, costs of capitalizing the fund, to the extent that such amounts are or were deemed reasonable by the Administrator, accounted for separately from other assets in the fund, and used for eligible purposes of the fund, including administration, or, by the State of New York for fiscal year 2000 and prior years, for capitalization of the fund], *of which $50,000,000 shall be for grants to be awarded to the aforementioned entities and local governments by EPA on a competitive basis, for improving water quality at Great Lakes "areas of concern," with the Federal share of the cost of projects funded with Federal assistance under this provision not to exceed 60 percent of the cost of the project and made on the condition that the non-Federal share is provided from non-Federal sources, and $45,000,000 shall be for Federal Water Pollution Control Act section 106 grants to States for a program to develop Total Maximum Daily Load allocations and implementation plans ("TMDL program") under section 303(d) of such Act: Provided, That notwithstanding section 106(d) of such Act, the Federal share of this TMDL program shall not exceed 60 percent of the cost incurred by the State for such program, and shall be made on the condition that the non-Federal share is provided from non-Federal sources*: *Provided* [*further*], That *for fiscal year 2001 and thereafter, and* notwithstanding section 518(f) of the Federal Water Pollution Control Act, the Administrator is authorized to use the amounts appropriated for any fiscal year under section 319 of that Act to make grants to Indian tribes pursuant to section 319(h) and 518(e) of that Act: *Provided further*, That [notwithstanding any other provision of law, in the case of a publicly owned treatment works in the District of Columbia, the Federal share of grants awarded under title II of the Federal Water Pollution Control Act, beginning October 1, 1999 and continuing through September 30, 2001, shall be 80 percent of the cost of construction, and all grants made to such publicly owned treatment works in the District of Columbia may include an advance of allowance under section 201(l)(2): *Provided further*, That the $2,200,000 appropriated in Public Law 105–276 in accordance with House Report No. 105–769, for a grant to the Charleston, Utah Water Conservancy District, as amended by Public Law 106–31, shall be awarded to Wasatch County, Utah, for water and sewer needs: *Provided further*, That the funds appropriated under this heading in Public Law 105–276 for the City of Fairbanks, Alaska, water system improvements shall instead be for the Matanuska-Susitna Borough, Alaska, water and sewer improvements: *Provided further*, That notwithstanding any other provision of law, all claims for principal and interest registered through grant dispute AA–91–AD34 (05–90–AD09) or any other such dispute hereafter filed by the Environmental Protection Agency relative to water pollution control center and sewer system improvement grants numbers C–390996–01, C–390996–2, and C–390996–3 made in 1976 and 1977 are hereby resolved in favor of the grantee.

The Environmental Protection Agency and the New York State Department of Environmental Conservation are authorized to award, from construction grant reallotments to the State of New York of previously appropriated funds, supplemental grant assistance to Nassau County, New York, for additional odor control at the Bay Park and Cedar Creek wastewater treatment plants, notwithstanding initiation of construction or prior State Revolving Fund funding. Nassau County may elect to accept a combined lump-sum of $15,000,000, paid in advance of construction, in lieu of a 75 percent entitlement, to minimize grant and project administration] *beginning in fiscal year 2001 and thereafter, notwithstanding the limitation on amounts in section 518(c) of the Federal Water Pollution Control Act, as amended, up to a total of 1½ percent of the funds appropriated for State Revolving Funds under Title VI of that Act may be reserved by the Administrator for grants under section 518(c) of such Act: Provided further, That notwithstanding sections 601(a), 603(c) and 603(d) of that Act, for fiscal year 2001, each State may reserve from funds in its Clean Water State Revolving Fund an amount equal to no more than 19 percent of the sums allotted to such State under section 604 of that Act to provide grants of no more than 60 percent of the costs of projects eligible under section 603(c) (2) or (3) of that Act. Such grants may not be made for publicly-owned treatment works as defined in section 212 of that Act. Projects receiving grant assistance must, to the maximum extent practicable, rank highest on the State's priority list that is used to prioritize projects eligible for assistance under section 603(c) of that Act. (Departments of Veterans Affairs and Housing and Urban Development, and Independent Agencies Appropriations Act, 2000.)*

Program and Financing (in millions of dollars)

Identification code 68–0103–0–1–304		1999 actual	2000 est.	2001 est.
	Obligations by program activity:			
	Direct program:			
00.01	Clean Air	198	243	308
00.02	Clean Water	2,950	4,086	2,252
00.03	Direct Program Activity			13
00.04	Preventing Pollution	84	113	72
00.05	Waste Management	63	69	119
00.06	Global and Cross-Border	59	120	100
00.07	Direct Program Activity			16
00.09	Credible Deterrent	70	79	27
09.01	Reimbursable program	7		
10.00	Total new obligations	3,431	4,710	2,907
	Budgetary resources available for obligation:			
21.40	Unobligated balance available, start of year	1,160	1,264	
22.00	New budget authority (gross)	3,415	3,446	2,907
22.10	Resources available from recoveries of prior year obligations	121		
23.90	Total budgetary resources available for obligation	4,696	4,710	2,907
23.95	Total new obligations	−3,431	−4,710	−2,907
24.40	Unobligated balance available, end of year	1,264		
	New budget authority (gross), detail:			
	Discretionary:			
40.00	Appropriation	3,408	3,467	2,907
40.76	Reduction pursuant to P.L. 106–113		−21	
43.00	Appropriation (total discretionary)	3,408	3,446	2,907
68.00	Spending authority from offsetting collections: Offsetting collections (cash)	7		
70.00	Total new budget authority (gross)	3,415	3,446	2,907
	Change in unpaid obligations:			
72.40	Unpaid obligations, start of year: Obligated balance, start of year	7,012	7,570	9,216
73.10	Total new obligations	3,431	4,710	2,907
73.20	Total outlays (gross)	−2,752	−3,064	−3,400
73.45	Adjustments in unexpired accounts	−121		
74.40	Unpaid obligations, end of year: Obligated balance, end of year	7,570	9,216	8,723
	Outlays (gross), detail:			
86.90	Outlays from new discretionary authority	381	554	624
86.93	Outlays from discretionary balances	2,371	2,510	2,776
87.00	Total outlays (gross)	2,752	3,064	3,400
	Offsets:			
	Against gross budget authority and outlays:			
88.00	Offsetting collections (cash) from: Federal sources	−7		
	Net budget authority and outlays:			
89.00	Budget authority	3,408	3,446	2,907
90.00	Outlays	2,745	3,064	3,400

This appropriation supports core Agency programs and a number of the Agency's ten goals.

Clean and Safe Water.—This Agency goal is to ensure people are provided clean and safe water to drink, and to protect and restore America's water bodies to improve public health, enhance water quality, reduce flooding, and provide wildlife habitat. In support of this goal, EPA will provide funds for capitalization grants to States for Clean Water State Revolving Funds (SRFs), the purpose of which are to make low interest loans to communities and grants to Indian Tribes and Alaska Native Villages to construct wastewater treatment infrastructure, and fund other projects to enhance water quality. Since 1989, the Federal Government has invested approxi-

General and special funds—Continued

STATE AND TRIBAL ASSISTANCE GRANTS—Continued

mately $17 billion in grants to help capitalize the 51 SRFs. With required State match, additional State contribution, and funds from program leveraging, funds available for such loans total approximately $30 billion. The Administration's goal is for the Clean Water SRFs eventually to provide an average of $2 billion a year in loans. Appropriations language is being proposed to address the growing funding needs of States and tribes to address non-point source pollution.

Capitalization grants are also provided for the Drinking Water SRFs, which make low interest loans to public water systems and grants to Indian Tribes and Alaska Native Villages to help them comply with the Safe Drinking Water Act. The Administration's goal is for the Drinking Water SRFs eventually to provide an average of $500 million a year in loans.

Direct grants are also provided to help address the significant water and wastewater infrastructure needs of Alaska Native Villages, and for U.S. cities that are facing exceptionally high capital needs and user charges.

EPA will support its partnerships with States and Tribes through media-specific and multi-media, and/or Performance Partnership grants to: (1) increase the number of community drinking water systems that meet all existing health-based standards, (2) protect watersheds by reducing point and nonpoint source pollution, (3) decrease the net loss of wetlands, and (4) address agricultural and urban runoff and storm water.

The Budget includes $50 million for a new competitive grant program with a 40 percent non-Federal cost share to clean up the polluted Great Lakes "areas of concern" defined by the bi-national Great Lakes Water Quality Agreement. The Budget also includes $45 million for a new effort to help States implement programs to develop Total Maximum Daily Load allocations for polluted waterbodies. This new effort will also include a 40 percent non-Federal cost share.

Clean Air.—To ensure that every American Community has safe and healthy air to breathe, EPA will provide funds to states to upgrade and improve air monitoring networks to obtain better data on emissions of particulate matter, air toxics in urban areas, and ozone in rural areas. EPA will offer media-specific and multi-media, and/or Performance Partnership grants to States and Tribes, and technical assistance to aid in the development of State and Tribal Implementation Plans to support solutions that address local air needs.

The Budget includes $85 million for a new Clean Air Partnership Fund that will enable the development of smart multi-pollutant strategies to protect our health and our climate. The Fund will be used to capitalize local revolving funds and provide money for other financing mechanisms to fund projects that achieve innovative and early air pollution and greenhouse gas emission reductions.

Preventing Pollution and Reducing Risk in Communities, Homes, Workplaces and Ecosystems.—EPA will offer media-specific and multi-media, and/or Performance Partnership grants to States and Tribes, and technical assistance to foster source reduction and recycling. Best approaches for encouraging recycling of non-hazardous industrial wastes will also be identified through work with the State and Tribal partners.

Better Waste Management, Restoration of Contaminated Waste Sites, and Emergency Response.—To ensure that America's waste will be stored, treated, and disposed of in ways that prevent harm to people and to the natural environment, EPA will work with States, tribes and local governments to put environmental protection and decision making in the hands of those closest to the problems, while maintaining a Federal leadership role. There will be direct assistance through media-specific, and multi-media and/or Performance Partnership grants to enable tribes to implement hazardous waste programs.

A Credible Deterrent to Pollution and Greater Compliance With the Law.—To ensure full compliance with laws intended to protect human health and the environment, EPA will provide grant assistance to States and Tribes for both compliance monitoring and compliance assistance activities. EPA will also provide direct grant funding to States and Tribes to conduct compliance inspections and compliance assurance activities under the Toxic Substances Control Act (TSCA) and Federal Insecticide, Fungicide, and Rodenticide Act (FIFRA).

Reduction of Global and Cross-Border Environmental Risks.—The Agency will provide direct grant assistance to address the serious environmental and human health problems associated with untreated and industrial and municipal sewage on the U.S.-Mexico border. In 2001 a cumulative 600 thousand residents of the U.S.-Mexico border area will be protected from health risks because of the construction of adequate water and wastewater sanitation systems since 1994. These funds also support attainment for the Clean and Safe Water goal.

Expansion of Americans' Right to Know About Their Environment.—EPA, in partnership with States and Tribes and in close consultation with its environmental information stakeholders, will develop an integrated environmental information system and data exchange network to improve environmental decision making and results reporting, reduce reporting burden on the regulated community and the States and provide more reliable, high quality information to the public. Working together, EPA, States and Tribes will establish data standards and shared business practices that cover most of the environmental information that regulated entities report to government.

Object Classification (in millions of dollars)

Identification code 68–0103–0–1–304		1999 actual	2000 est.	2001 est.
	Direct obligations:			
25.2	Other services	7	10	6
25.3	Purchases of goods and services from Government accounts	33	45	28
41.0	Grants, subsidies, and contributions	3,384	4,655	2,873
99.0	Subtotal, direct obligations	3,424	4,710	2,907
99.0	Reimbursable obligations	7		
99.9	Total new obligations	3,431	4,710	2,907

NOTE

Obligations include anticipated recoveries of prior year obligations of $25 million for 2000 and $25 million for 2001.

PAYMENT TO THE HAZARDOUS SUBSTANCE SUPERFUND

Program and Financing (in millions of dollars)

Identification code 68–0250–0–1–304		1999 actual	2000 est.	2001 est.
	Obligations by program activity:			
10.00	Total new obligations (object class 41.0)	325	700	250
	Budgetary resources available for obligation:			
22.00	New budget authority (gross)	325	700	250
23.95	Total new obligations	−325	−700	−250
	New budget authority (gross), detail:			
	Discretionary:			
40.00	Appropriation	325	700	250
	Change in unpaid obligations:			
73.10	Total new obligations	325	700	250
73.20	Total outlays (gross)	−325	−700	−250
	Outlays (gross), detail:			
86.90	Outlays from new discretionary authority	325	700	250

		1999 actual	2000 est.	2001 est.
	Net budget authority and outlays:			
89.00	Budget authority	325	700	250
90.00	Outlays	325	700	250

The Comprehensive Environmental Response, Compensation, and Liability Act of 1980, as amended, authorizes appropriations from the general fund to finance activities conducted through the Hazardous Substance Superfund. The authorization for general fund payments to the Superfund expired in 1995. The Administration will support an extension of this authority as part of Superfund reauthorization.

Environmental Services

Contingent upon enactment of authorizing legislation, the Administration shall reinstate fees for applicants for registration and amendments to registration under section 3 and experimental use permits under section 5 of the Federal Insecticide, Fungicide, and Rodenticide Act, and shall increase fees for persons required to submit data under sections 4 and 5 of the Toxic Substances Control Act. Such fees shall be deposited in a special fund in the U.S. Treasury, which thereafter will be available subject to appropriation in advance to carry out the Agency's activities for which such fees are collected.

Unavailable Collections (in millions of dollars)

Identification code 68–5295–0–2–304		1999 actual	2000 est.	2001 est.
	Balance, start of year:			
01.99	Balance, start of year	53	63	74
	Receipts:			
02.01	Environmental Services	10	11	10
02.03	Environmental Services, proposed legislation			20
02.99	Total receipts	10	11	30
04.00	Total: Balances and collections	63	74	104
	Appropriation:			
05.03	Science and technology			–10
07.99	Total balance, end of year	63	74	94

A special fund was established for the deposit of fee receipts associated with environmental programs, including motor vehicle engine certifications. Receipts in this special fund will be appropriated to the Science and Technology account in 2001 to finance the expenses of the programs that generate the receipts. Contingent appropriations language is being proposed to impose user fees on manufacturers of pesticides to recover the costs of EPA's Pesticide Registration Program and use those fees to fund the program. The appropriations language is contingent upon the enactment of legislation that authorizes the fees. Congressional action is required to activate a user fee rule promulgated by EPA that was subsequently suspended by Congress. A similar approach is being used to put into effect a proposal to modify the cap on the allowable fee that can be charged to recover the costs of EPA's Premanufacture Notification program, for which EPA will issue a rulemaking. Enactment of this appropriations language would generate $20 million in receipts that would be discretionary under the Budget Enforcement Act.

Exxon Valdez Settlement Fund

Program and Financing (in millions of dollars)

Identification code 68–5297–0–2–304		1999 actual	2000 est.	2001 est.
	Change in unpaid obligations:			
72.40	Unpaid obligations, start of year: Obligated balance, start of year	3	2	2
74.40	Unpaid obligations, end of year: Obligated balance, end of year	2	2	2
	Net budget authority and outlays:			
89.00	Budget authority			
90.00	Outlays	1		

Funds reimbursed to EPA under the Exxon Valdez settlement as a result of the Exxon Valdez oil spill are available to carry out authorized environmental restoration activities.

Reregistration and Expedited Processing Revolving Fund

Program and Financing (in millions of dollars)

Identification code 68–4310–0–3–304		1999 actual	2000 est.	2001 est.
	Obligations by program activity:			
09.01	Reimbursable program	22	30	42
10.00	Total new obligations	22	30	42
	Budgetary resources available for obligation:			
21.40	Unobligated balance available, start of year	15	12	
22.00	New budget authority (gross)	18	18	42
23.90	Total budgetary resources available for obligation	33	30	42
23.95	Total new obligations	–22	–30	–42
24.40	Unobligated balance available, end of year	12		
	New budget authority (gross), detail:			
	Mandatory:			
69.00	Offsetting collections (cash)	18	18	42
	Change in unpaid obligations:			
72.40	Unpaid obligations, start of year: Obligated balance, start of year	–1	–1	11
73.10	Total new obligations	22	30	42
73.20	Total outlays (gross)	–22	–18	–15
74.40	Unpaid obligations, end of year: Obligated balance, end of year	–1	11	38
	Outlays (gross), detail:			
86.97	Outlays from new mandatory authority	18	18	15
86.98	Outlays from mandatory balances	4		
87.00	Total outlays (gross)	22	18	15
	Offsets:			
	Against gross budget authority and outlays:			
88.45	Offsetting collections (cash) from: Offsetting governmental collections from the public	–18	–18	–42
	Net budget authority and outlays:			
89.00	Budget authority			
90.00	Outlays	4		–27
	Memorandum (non-add) entries:			
92.01	Total investments, start of year: U.S. securities: Par value	10	3	10
92.02	Total investments, end of year: U.S. securities: Par value	3	10	10

Fees are paid by industry to offset costs of accelerated reregistration, expedited processing of pesticides, and establishing tolerances for pesticide chemicals in or on food and animal feed, as authorized in the Federal Insecticide, Fungicide, and Rodenticide Act Amendments of 1988, as amended by the Food Quality Protection Act of 1996.

Object Classification (in millions of dollars)

Identification code 68–4310–0–3–304		1999 actual	2000 est.	2001 est.
11.1	Personnel compensation: Full-time permanent	20	18	20
23.1	Rental payments to GSA	2		
25.2	Other services		12	22
99.0	Subtotal, reimbursable obligations	22	30	42
99.9	Total new obligations	22	30	42

General and special funds—Continued

Reregistration and Expedited Processing Revolving Fund—Continued

Personnel Summary

Identification code 68–4310–0–3–304	1999 actual	2000 est.	2001 est.
2001 Total compensable workyears: Full-time equivalent employment	226	222	221

Intragovernmental fund:

Working Capital Fund

Program and Financing (in millions of dollars)

Identification code 68–4565–0–4–304	1999 actual	2000 est.	2001 est.
Obligations by program activity:			
09.01 ETSD Operations	118	126	121
09.02 Postage	4	4	4
09.99 Total reimbursable program	122	130	125
10.00 Total new obligations	122	130	125
Budgetary resources available for obligation:			
21.40 Unobligated balance available, start of year	15	7	
22.00 New budget authority (gross)	109	123	125
22.10 Resources available from recoveries of prior year obligations	5		
23.90 Total budgetary resources available for obligation	129	130	125
23.95 Total new obligations	−122	−130	−125
24.40 Unobligated balance available, end of year	7		
New budget authority (gross), detail:			
Spending authority from offsetting collections:			
Discretionary:			
68.00 Offsetting collections (cash)	120	123	125
68.10 From Federal sources: Change in receivables and unpaid, unfilled orders	−11		
68.90 Spending authority from offsetting collections (total discretionary)	109	123	125
Change in unpaid obligations:			
Unpaid obligations, start of year:			
72.40 Obligated balance, start of year	26	30	37
72.95 From Federal sources: Receivables and unpaid, unfilled orders	5	−6	−6
72.99 Total unpaid obligations, start of year	31	24	31
73.10 Total new obligations	122	130	125
73.20 Total outlays (gross)	−124	−123	−125
73.45 Adjustments in unexpired accounts	−5		
Unpaid obligations, end of year:			
74.40 Obligated balance, end of year	30	37	37
74.95 From Federal sources: Receivables and unpaid, unfilled orders	−6	−6	−6
74.99 Total unpaid obligations, end of year	24	31	31
Outlays (gross), detail:			
86.90 Outlays from new discretionary authority	120	123	125
86.93 Outlays from discretionary balances	4		
87.00 Total outlays (gross)	124	123	125
Offsets:			
Against gross budget authority and outlays:			
88.00 Offsetting collections (cash) from: Federal sources	−120	−123	−125
Against gross budget authority only:			
88.95 From Federal sources: Change in receivables and unpaid, unfilled orders	11		
Net budget authority and outlays:			
89.00 Budget authority			
90.00 Outlays	4		

EPA received authority to establish a Working Capital Fund (WCF) and was designated a franchise fund pilot under Public Law 103–356, the Government Management and Reform Act of 1994. EPA's WCF became operational in 1997 and includes two activities: Enterprise Technology Services Division's computer operations and Agency postage. The 2001 amount reflects only base resources and may change during the year as programmatic needs change. The Agency received permanent authority for the WCF in P.L. 105–65, which among other things is intended to increase competition for government administrative services resulting in lower costs and higher quality.

Object Classification (in millions of dollars)

Identification code 68–4565–0–4–304	1999 actual	2000 est.	2001 est.
11.1 Personnel compensation: Full-time permanent	5	7	7
12.1 Civilian personnel benefits	1	1	1
23.3 Communications, utilities, and miscellaneous charges	23	25	24
25.2 Other services	23	24	22
25.3 Purchases of goods and services from Government accounts	1	1	1
25.7 Operation and maintenance of equipment	56	59	57
31.0 Equipment	13	13	13
99.9 Total new obligations	122	130	125

Personnel Summary

Identification code 68–4565–0–4–304	1999 actual	2000 est.	2001 est.
2001 Total compensable workyears: Full-time equivalent employment	68	94	93

Abatement, Control, and Compliance Direct Loan Financing Account

Program and Financing (in millions of dollars)

Identification code 68–4322–0–3–304	1999 actual	2000 est.	2001 est.
Budgetary resources available for obligation:			
22.00 New financing authority (gross)	5	8	8
22.60 Portion applied to repay debt	−7	−6	−6
23.90 Total budgetary resources available for obligation	−2	2	2
New financing authority (gross), detail:			
Discretionary:			
68.00 Spending authority from offsetting collections (gross): Offsetting collections (cash)	5	8	8
Change in unpaid obligations:			
72.40 Unpaid obligations, start of year: Obligated balance, start of year	2		
73.20 Total financing disbursements (gross)	−3	−2	−2
87.00 Total financing disbursements (gross)	3	2	2
Offsets:			
Against gross financing authority and financing disbursements:			
88.40 Offsetting collections (cash) from: Non-Federal sources	−5	−8	−8
Net financing authority and financing disbursements:			
89.00 Financing authority	2		
90.00 Financing disbursements	−2	−6	−6

Status of Direct Loans (in millions of dollars)

Identification code 68–4322–0–3–304	1999 actual	2000 est.	2001 est.
Position with respect to appropriations act limitation on obligations:			
1111 Limitation on direct loans			
1150 Total direct loan obligations			
Cumulative balance of direct loans outstanding:			
1210 Outstanding, start of year	56	51	46
1231 Disbursements: Direct loan disbursements			
1251 Repayments: Repayments and prepayments	−5	−5	−5

1290	Outstanding, end of year	51	46	41	

Balance Sheet (in millions of dollars)

Identification code 68–4322–0–3–304		1998 actual	1999 actual	2000 est.	2001 est.
	ASSETS:				
	Investments in US securities:				
1106	Federal assets: Receivables, net	2	2	2	2
	Net value of assets related to post-1991 direct loans receivable:				
1401	Direct loans receivable, gross	56	51	46	41
1405	Allowance for subsidy cost (–)	–2	–1	–1	–1
1499	Net present value of assets related to direct loans	54	50	45	40
1999	Total assets	56	52	47	42
	LIABILITIES:				
2103	Federal liabilities: Debt	56	51	46	41
2999	Total liabilities	56	51	46	41
	NET POSITION:				
3100	Appropriated capital	2	2	2	2
3999	Total net position	2	2	2	2
4999	Total liabilities and net position	58	53	48	43

As required by the Federal Credit Reform Act of 1990, this non-budgetary account records all cash flows to and from the Government resulting from direct loans obligated in 1992 and beyond (including credit sales of acquired property that resulted from obligations in any year). The amounts in this account are a means of financing and are not included in the budget totals.

Trust Funds

Hazardous Substance Superfund

(INCLUDING TRANSFER OF FUNDS)

For necessary expenses to carry out the Comprehensive Environmental Response, Compensation, and Liability Act of 1980 (CERCLA), as amended, including sections 111(c)(3), (c)(5), (c)(6), and (e)(4) (42 U.S.C. 9611), and for construction, alteration, repair, rehabilitation, and renovation of facilities, not to exceed $75,000 per project; [$1,400,000,000 (of which $100,000,000 shall not become available until September 1, 2000)] *$1,450,000,000*, to remain available until expended, consisting of [$700,000,000] *$1,200,000,000*, as authorized by section 517(a) of the Superfund Amendments and Reauthorization Act of 1986 (SARA), as amended by Public Law 101–508, and [$700,000,000] *$250,000,000* as a payment from general revenues to the Hazardous Substance Superfund for purposes as authorized by section 517(b) of SARA, as amended [by Public Law 101–508]: *Provided*, That funds appropriated under this heading may be allocated to other Federal agencies in accordance with section 111(a) of CERCLA: *Provided further*, That [$11,000,000] of the funds appropriated under this heading, *$11,652,300* shall be transferred to the "Office of Inspector General" appropriation to remain available until September 30, [2001: *Provided further*, That $38,000,000 of the funds appropriated under this heading] *2002, and $35,870,800* shall be transferred to the "Science and technology" appropriation to remain available until September 30, [2001: *Provided further*, That notwithstanding section 111(m) of CERCLA or any other provision of law, $70,000,000 of the funds appropriated under this heading shall be available to the Agency for Toxic Substances and Disease Registry (ATSDR) to carry out activities described in sections 104(i), 111(c)(4), and 111(c)(14) of CERCLA and section 118(f) of SARA: *Provided further*, That notwithstanding any other provision of law, in lieu of performing a health assessment under section 104(i)(6) of CERCLA, the Administrator of ATSDR may conduct other appropriate health studies, evaluations or activities, including, without limitation, biomedical testing, clinical evaluations, medical monitoring, and referral to accredited health care providers: *Provided further*, That in performing any such health assessment or health study, evaluation, or activity, the Administrator of ATSDR shall not be bound by the deadlines in section 104(i)(6)(A)] *2002*: *Provided further*, That none of the funds appropriated under this heading shall be available for ATSDR to issue in excess of 40 toxicological profiles pursuant to section 104(i) of CERCLA during fiscal year [2000] *2001. (Departments of Veterans Affairs and Housing and Urban Development, and Independent Agencies Appropriations Act, 2000.)*

Unavailable Collections (in millions of dollars)

Identification code 20–8145–0–7–304		1999 actual	2000 est.	2001 est.
	Balance, start of year:			
01.99	Balance, start of year	2,154	1,539	1,594
	Receipts:			
02.01	Excise taxes	11		
02.02	Corporation income taxes	10		
02.03	Interest and profits on investments	207	198	179
02.04	Fines and penalties	4	4	5
02.05	Recoveries	320	275	225
02.06	Interfund transactions	325	700	250
02.07	Corporation income taxes, legislative proposal subject to PAYGO			1,115
02.08	Excise taxes, legislative proposal subject to PAYGO		204	942
02.09	Interest and profits on investments, legiative proposal not subject to PAYGO		74	203
02.99	Total receipts	877	1,455	2,919
04.00	Total: Balances and collections	3,031	2,994	4,513
	Appropriation:			
05.01	Hazardous substance superfund	–1,500	–1,400	–1,450
05.02	Legislative proposal, subject to PAYGO			–150
05.99	Subtotal appropriation	–1,500	–1,400	–1,600
06.20	Reduction pursuant to Public Law 106–51	8		
07.99	Total balance, end of year	1,539	1,594	2,913

Program and Financing (in millions of dollars)

Identification code 20–8145–0–7–304		1999 actual	2000 est.	2001 est.
	Obligations by program activity:			
	Direct program:			
00.01	Waste Management	1,554	1,788	1,344
00.02	Right to Know	2	4	4
00.03	Sound Science	3	5	2
00.04	Credible Deterrent	17	17	20
00.05	Effective Management	106	81	80
01.00	Subtotal direct program	1,682	1,895	1,450
09.01	Reimbursable program	83	200	200
10.00	Total new obligations	1,765	2,095	1,650
	Budgetary resources available for obligation:			
21.40	Unobligated balance available, start of year	428	495	
22.00	New budget authority (gross)	1,631	1,600	1,650
22.10	Resources available from recoveries of prior year obligations	201		
23.90	Total budgetary resources available for obligation	2,260	2,095	1,650
23.95	Total new obligations	–1,765	–2,095	–1,650
24.40	Unobligated balance available, end of year	495		
	New budget authority (gross), detail:			
	Discretionary:			
	Appropriation (trust fund, definite):			
40.26	Appropriation (trust fund, definite)	1,448	1,351	1,402
40.26	Appropriation (transfer to Inspector General)	12	11	12
40.26	Appropriation (transfer to S&T)	40	38	36
40.75	Reduction pursuant to P.L. 106–51	–8		
43.00	Appropriation (total discretionary)	1,492	1,400	1,450
	Spending authority from offsetting collections:			
68.00	Offsetting collections (cash)	140	200	200
68.10	From Federal sources: Change in receivables and unpaid, unfilled orders	–1		
68.90	Spending authority from offsetting collections (total discretionary)	139	200	200
70.00	Total new budget authority (gross)	1,631	1,600	1,650
	Change in unpaid obligations:			
	Unpaid obligations, start of year:			
72.40	Obligated balance, start of year	2,562	2,409	2,825

HAZARDOUS SUBSTANCE SUPERFUND—Continued

(INCLUDING TRANSFER OF FUNDS)—Continued

Program and Financing (in millions of dollars)—Continued

Identification code 20–8145–0–7–304	1999 actual	2000 est.	2001 est.
72.95 From Federal sources: Receivables and unpaid, unfilled orders	80	79	79
72.99 Total unpaid obligations, start of year	2,642	2,488	2,904
73.10 Total new obligations	1,765	2,095	1,650
73.20 Total outlays (gross)	−1,715	−1,679	−1,627
73.40 Adjustments in expired accounts (net)	−1		
73.45 Adjustments in unexpired accounts	−201		
Unpaid obligations, end of year:			
74.40 Obligated balance, end of year	2,409	2,825	2,848
74.95 From Federal sources: Receivables and unpaid, unfilled orders	79	79	79
74.99 Total unpaid obligations, end of year	2,488	2,904	2,927
Outlays (gross), detail:			
86.90 Outlays from new discretionary authority	262	564	577
86.93 Outlays from discretionary balances	1,455	1,115	1,050
87.00 Total outlays (gross)	1,715	1,679	1,627
Offsets:			
Against gross budget authority and outlays:			
88.00 Offsetting collections (cash) from: Federal sources	−140	−200	−200
Against gross budget authority only:			
88.95 From Federal sources: Change in receivables and unpaid, unfilled orders	1		
Net budget authority and outlays:			
89.00 Budget authority	1,492	1,400	1,450
90.00 Outlays	1,577	1,479	1,427
Memorandum (non-add) entries:			
92.01 Total investments, start of year: U.S. securities: Par value	5,296	4,593	4,625
92.02 Total investments, end of year: U.S. securities: Par value	4,593	4,625	6,190

Summary of Budget Authority and Outlays

(in millions of dollars)

Enacted/requested:	*1999 actual*	*2000 est.*	*2001 est.*
Budget Authority	1,492	1,400	1,450
Outlays	1,577	1,479	1,427
Legislative proposal, subject to PAYGO:			
Budget Authority			150
Outlays			39
Total:			
Budget Authority	1,492	1,400	1,600
Outlays	1,577	1,479	1,466

This appropriation provides funds for the implementation of the Comprehensive Environmental Response, Compensation and Liability Act of 1980, as amended (CERCLA) including activities under the Working Capital Fund. Funding for activities in this account for the Office of Research and Development are included in the 21st Century Research Fund. This appropriation supports core Agency programs and a number of the Agency's ten goals. Specifically in 2001, emphasis will be placed on the following:

Better Waste Management, Restoration of Contaminated Waste Sites, and Emergency Response.—EPA will complete cleanups at 75 sites and conduct 275 removal actions. Through 1999, cleanups had been completed at 670 sites, and 5,929 removal actions had been taken at 4,258 sites. EPA will also work to maximize responsible parties' participation in site cleanups while promoting fairness in the enforcement process, and pursue greater recovery of EPA's cleanup costs. In addition, EPA will fund supplemental brownfields site assessments in 50 communities, resulting in a cumulative total of 2,100 sites assessed, the generation of 5,400 jobs, and the leveraging of $1.8 billion in cleanup and redevelopment funds, and will fund brownfields cleanup revolving loan funds in 70 communities. EPA will allocate funds from its appropriation to other Federal agencies to carry out the Act. Legislation will be proposed to extend the taxes supporting the trust fund.

Sound Science, Improved Understanding of Environmental Risk, and Greater Innovation to Address Environmental Problems.—EPA will develop methods to assess and control the potential health and environmental risks posed by contaminated waste sites. EPA will also conduct risk management research which focuses on the remediation of surface and subsurface contaminated soils, sludge, sediments, buildings, debris, and groundwater.

A Credible Deterrent to Pollution and Greater Compliance With the Law.—EPA will investigate and refer for prosecution criminal violations of the Comprehensive Environmental Response, Compensation, and Liability Act of 1980 (CERCLA), and increase Regional support to criminal investigations in the field.

Effective Management.—EPA will work to ensure fiscal responsibility in support of site cleanups. EPA will continue to implement performance-based service contracts instead of the traditional cost-plus, level-of-effort contracts, and will improve the quality and availability of information on the status and use of resources.

Selected Annual Site Cleanup Targets

	1999 actual	2000 est.	2001 est.
NPL Site Cleanups Completed	670	755	830
Removal Action Starts	5,929	6,204	6,479

Status of Funds (in millions of dollars)

Identification code 20–8145–0–7–304	1999 actual	2000 est.	2001 est.
Unexpended balance, start of year:			
0100 Uninvested balance	68	38	38
U.S. Securities:			
0101 Par value	5,296	4,593	4,625
0102 Unrealized discounts	−221	−188	−244
0199 Total balance, start of year	5,144	4,443	4,419
Cash income during the year:			
Governmental receipts:			
0200 Excise taxes, Hazardous substance superfund, EPA	11		
0201 Corporate Income Tax, Hazardous substance superfund, EPA	10		
0202 Fines and penalties, Hazardous substance superfund, EPA	4	4	5
0203 Excise taxes, legislative proposal		204	942
0204 Corporate Income Tax, legislative proposal			1,115
Proprietary receipts:			
0220 Recoveries, Hazardous substance superfund, EPA	320	275	225
Intragovernmental transactions:			
0240 Interest and profits on investments, Hazardous substance superfund, EPA	207	198	179
0241 Interfund transactions, Hazardous substance superfund, EPA	325	700	250
0242 Interest and profits on investments, legislative proposal		74	203
Offsetting collections:			
0280 Offsetting collections	140	200	200
0297 Income under present law	1,017	1,377	859
0298 Income under proposed legislation		278	2,260
0299 Total cash income	1,017	1,655	3,119
Cash outgo during year:			
0500 Cash outgo during the year, legislative proposal (−)	−1,715	−1,679	−1,627
0502 Legislative proposal, subject to PAYGO			−39
0597 Outgo under present law (−)	−1,715	−1,679	−1,627
0598 Outgo under proposed legislation (−)			−39
0599 Total cash outgo (−)	−1,715	−1,679	−1,666
0650 Other adjustments	−1		
Unexpended balance, end of year:			
0700 Uninvested balance	38	38	38
U.S. Securities:			
0701 Par value	4,593	4,625	6,190
0702 Unrealized discounts	−188	−244	−356
0799 Total balance, end of year	4,443	4,419	5,872

Object Classification (in millions of dollars)

Identification code 20–8145–0–7–304		1999 actual	2000 est.	2001 est.
	Direct obligations:			
	Personnel compensation:			
11.1	Full-time permanent	194	212	232
11.3	Other than full-time permanent	9	10	11
11.5	Other personnel compensation	4	4	5
11.7	Military personnel	1	1	1
11.8	Special personal services payments	1	1	1
11.9	Total personnel compensation	209	228	250
12.1	Civilian personnel benefits	47	51	56
21.0	Travel and transportation of persons	11	12	12
23.1	Rental payments to GSA	32	36	38
23.2	Rental payments to others	3	5	3
23.3	Communications, utilities, and miscellaneous charges	5	5	5
24.0	Printing and reproduction	1	1	1
25.1	Advisory and assistance services	2	2	2
25.2	Other services	601	817	333
25.3	Purchases of goods and services from Government accounts	416	375	397
25.4	Operation and maintenance of facilities	5	5	5
25.5	Research and development contracts	2	2	2
25.7	Operation and maintenance of equipment	4	4	4
26.0	Supplies and materials	4	4	4
31.0	Equipment	15	14	14
41.0	Grants, subsidies, and contributions	179	166	171
99.0	Subtotal, direct obligations	1,536	1,727	1,297
99.0	Reimbursable obligations	83	200	200
	Allocation Account:			
11.1	Personnel compensation: Full-time permanent	23	26	24
12.1	Civilian personnel benefits	6	7	6
21.0	Travel and transportation of persons	2	2	2
23.1	Rental payments to GSA	1	1	1
25.2	Other services	25	31	27
26.0	Supplies and materials	1	1	1
31.0	Equipment	2	2	2
41.0	Grants, subsidies, and contributions	86	98	90
99.0	Subtotal, allocation account	146	168	153
99.9	Total new obligations	1,765	2,095	1,650

Obligations are distributed as follows:			
Environmental Protection Agency			
Agency for Toxic Substances and Disease Registry (HHS)			
National Oceanic and Atmospheric Administration			
Department of the Interior			
Federal Emergency Management Agency			
Occupational Safety and Health Administration			

Personnel Summary

Identification code 20–8145–0–7–304		1999 actual	2000 est.	2001 est.
	Direct:			
1001	Total compensable workyears: Full-time equivalent employment	3,321	3,279	3,248
	Reimbursable:			
2001	Total compensable workyears: Full-time equivalent employment	139	115	114

Hazardous Substance Superfund

(Legislative proposal, subject to PAYGO)

Program and Financing (in millions of dollars)

Identification code 20–8145–4–7–304		1999 actual	2000 est.	2001 est.
	Obligations by program activity:			
	Direct program:			
00.05	Effective Management			150
10.00	Total new obligations (object class 25.2)			150
	Budgetary resources available for obligation:			
22.00	New budget authority (gross)			150
23.95	Total new obligations			−150
	New budget authority (gross), detail:			
	Mandatory:			
60.26	Appropriation (trust fund, definite)			150
	Change in unpaid obligations:			
72.40	Unpaid obligations, start of year: Obligated balance, start of year			
73.10	Total new obligations			150
73.20	Total outlays (gross)			−39
74.40	Unpaid obligations, end of year: Obligated balance, end of year			111
	Outlays (gross), detail:			
86.97	Outlays from new mandatory authority			39
	Net budget authority and outlays:			
89.00	Budget authority			150
90.00	Outlays			39

The Administration will support Superfund legislative reforms that allow costs allocated to identifiable, but nonviable parties at sites, and certain other categories of costs, to be paid from the Hazardous Substance Superfund as mandatory spending.

Leaking Underground Storage Tank Trust Fund

For necessary expenses to carry out leaking underground storage tank cleanup activities authorized by section 205 of the Superfund Amendments and Reauthorization Act of 1986, and for construction, alteration, repair, rehabilitation, and renovation of facilities, not to exceed $75,000 per project, [$70,000,000] *$72,096,500*, to remain available until expended. *(Departments of Veterans Affairs and Housing and Urban Development, and Independent Agencies Appropriations Act, 2000.)*

Unavailable Collections (in millions of dollars)

Identification code 20–8153–0–7–304		1999 actual	2000 est.	2001 est.
	Balance, start of year:			
01.99	Balance, start of year	1,182	1,377	1,577
	Receipts:			
02.01	Interest	52	87	96
02.02	Transfers from the general fund, amounts equivalent to taxes	216	183	189
02.99	Total receipts	268	270	285
04.00	Total: Balances and collections	1,450	1,647	1,862
	Appropriation:			
05.01	LUST trust fund	−73	−70	−72
07.99	Total balance, end of year	1,377	1,577	1,790

Program and Financing (in millions of dollars)

Identification code 20–8153–0–7–304		1999 actual	2000 est.	2001 est.
	Obligations by program activity:			
00.01	Waste Management	71	71	70
00.03	Effective Management	2	3	2
10.00	Total new obligations	73	74	72
	Budgetary resources available for obligation:			
21.40	Unobligated balance available, start of year	3	4	
22.00	New budget authority (gross)	73	70	72
22.10	Resources available from recoveries of prior year obligations	2		
23.90	Total budgetary resources available for obligation	78	74	72
23.95	Total new obligations	−73	−74	−72
24.40	Unobligated balance available, end of year	4		
	New budget authority (gross), detail:			
	Discretionary:			
40.26	Appropriation (trust fund, definite)	73	70	72
	Change in unpaid obligations:			
	Unpaid obligations, start of year:			
72.40	Obligated balance, start of year	2	8	13
72.95	From Federal sources: Receivables and unpaid, unfilled orders	73	73	73
72.99	Total unpaid obligations, start of year	75	81	86

Leaking Underground Storage Tank Trust Fund—Continued

Program and Financing (in millions of dollars)—Continued

Identification code 20–8153–0–7–304	1999 actual	2000 est.	2001 est.
73.10 Total new obligations	73	74	72
73.20 Total outlays (gross)	−65	−69	−70
73.45 Adjustments in unexpired accounts	−2	....	....
Unpaid obligations, end of year:			
74.40 Obligated balance, end of year	8	13	15
74.95 From Federal sources: Receivables and unpaid, unfilled orders	73	73	73
74.99 Total unpaid obligations, end of year	81	86	88
Outlays (gross), detail:			
86.90 Outlays from new discretionary authority	37	35	36
86.93 Outlays from discretionary balances	28	34	34
87.00 Total outlays (gross)	65	69	70
Net budget authority and outlays:			
89.00 Budget authority	73	70	72
90.00 Outlays	65	69	70
Memorandum (non-add) entries:			
92.01 Total investments, start of year: U.S. securities: Par value	1,234	1,458	1,560
92.02 Total investments, end of year: U.S. securities: Par value	1,458	1,560	1,775

The Leaking Underground Storage Tank (LUST) Trust Fund, authorized by the Superfund Amendments and Reauthorization Act of 1986, as amended by the Omnibus Budget Reconciliation Act of 1990 and the Taxpayer Relief Act of 1997, provides funds for responding to releases from leaking underground petroleum tanks, including activities under the Working Capital Fund. The Trust Fund is financed by a 0.1 cent a gallon tax on motor fuels, that will expire after March 31, 2005.

Funds are allocated to the States through cooperative agreements to clean up those sites posing the greatest threat to human health and environment. Funds are also used for grants to non-state entities, including Indian Tribes, under section 8001 of the Resource Conservation and Recovery Act. EPA supports oversight, cleanup and enforcement programs which are implemented by the States. LUST Trust Fund dollars can be used for State-lead cleanups and for State oversight of responsible party cleanups.

This appropriation supports core Agency programs and two of the Agency's ten goals. Specifically in 2001, emphasis will be placed on the following:

Better Waste Management, Restoration of Contaminated Waste Sites, and Emergency Response.—To ensure that America's waste will be stored, treated, and disposed of in ways that prevent harm to people and to the natural environment, EPA will support State and Tribal efforts to design and implement risk-based corrective action programs. These programs will help to reduce the backlog of Underground Storage Tank (USTs) sites with confirmed releases waiting to be addressed, and to enforce the 1998 UST leak detection and upgrade standards.

Effective Management.—To support the States' and EPA's efforts to regulate and oversee the cleanup of Leaking Underground Storage Tanks, EPA will establish a management infrastructure that will set and implement the highest quality standards for effective internal management and fiscal responsibility.

Status of Funds (in millions of dollars)

Identification code 20–8153–0–7–304	1999 actual	2000 est.	2001 est.
Unexpended balance, start of year:			
0100 Uninvested balance	4	....	89
U.S. Securities:			
0101 Par value	1,234	1,458	1,560
0102 Unrealized discounts	−51	−69	−59
0199 Total balance, start of year	1,187	1,389	1,590
Cash income during the year:			
Governmental receipts:			
0200 Transfer from the general fund amounts equivalent to taxes, Leaking Underground Storage Tank Trust Fund, EPA	216	183	189
Intragovernmental transactions:			
0240 Earnings on investments, Leaking Underground Storage Tank Trust Fund, EPA	52	87	96
0299 Total cash income	268	270	285
Cash outgo during year:			
0500 Leaking underground storage tank trust fund	−65	−69	−70
Unexpended balance, end of year:			
0700 Uninvested balance	....	89	89
U.S. Securities:			
0701 Par value	1,458	1,560	1,775
0702 Unrealized discounts	−69	−59	−59
0799 Total balance, end of year	1,389	1,590	1,805

Object Classification (in millions of dollars)

Identification code 20–8153–0–7–304	1999 actual	2000 est.	2001 est.
11.1 Personnel compensation: Full-time permanent	4	6	6
12.1 Civilian personnel benefits	1	1	1
21.0 Travel and transportation of persons	....	....	1
23.1 Rental payments to GSA	1	1	1
25.2 Other services	4	4	4
41.0 Grants, subsidies, and contributions	63	62	59
99.9 Total new obligations	73	74	72

Personnel Summary

Identification code 20–8153–0–7–304	1999 actual	2000 est.	2001 est.
1001 Total compensable workyears: Full-time equivalent employment	70	82	82

Oil Spill Response

(including transfer of funds)

For expenses necessary to carry out the Environmental Protection Agency's responsibilities under the Oil Pollution Act of 1990, [$15,000,000] *$15,712,000*, to be derived from the Oil Spill Liability trust fund, and to remain available until expended. *(Departments of Veterans Affairs and Housing and Urban Development, and Independent Agencies Appropriations Act, 2000.)*

Program and Financing (in millions of dollars)

Identification code 68–8221–0–7–304	1999 actual	2000 est.	2001 est.
Obligations by program activity:			
00.05 Waste Management	14	36	15
00.10 Effective Management	1	3	1
01.00 Direct Program	15	39	16
09.01 Reimbursable program	19	26	26
10.00 Total new obligations	34	65	42
Budgetary resources available for obligation:			
21.40 Unobligated balance available, start of year	16	24	....
22.00 New budget authority (gross)	42	41	42
23.90 Total budgetary resources available for obligation	58	65	42
23.95 Total new obligations	−34	−65	−42
24.40 Unobligated balance available, end of year	24	....	....
New budget authority (gross), detail:			
Discretionary:			
40.26 Appropriation (trust fund, definite)	15	15	16
Spending authority from offsetting collections:			
68.00 Offsetting collections (cash)	14	26	26
68.10 From Federal sources: Change in receivables and unpaid, unfilled orders	13	....	....
68.90 Spending authority from offsetting collections (total discretionary)	27	26	26

70.00	Total new budget authority (gross)	42	41	42
	Change in unpaid obligations:			
	Unpaid obligations, start of year:			
72.40	Obligated balance, start of year	−16	−33	−7
72.95	From Federal sources: Receivables and unpaid, unfilled orders	47	60	60
72.99	Total unpaid obligations, start of year	31	27	53
73.10	Total new obligations	34	65	42
73.20	Total outlays (gross)	−38	−41	−42
	Unpaid obligations, end of year:			
74.40	Obligated balance, end of year	−33	−7	−7
74.95	From Federal sources: Receivables and unpaid, unfilled orders	60	60	60
74.99	Total unpaid obligations, end of year	27	53	53
	Outlays (gross), detail:			
86.90	Outlays from new discretionary authority	29	33	34
86.93	Outlays from discretionary balances	9	8	8
87.00	Total outlays (gross)	38	41	42
	Offsets:			
	Against gross budget authority and outlays:			
88.00	Offsetting collections (cash) from: Federal sources	−14	−26	−26
	Against gross budget authority only:			
88.95	From Federal sources: Change in receivables and unpaid, unfilled orders	−13		
	Net budget authority and outlays:			
89.00	Budget authority	15	15	16
90.00	Outlays	24	15	16

This appropriation provides for EPA's responsibilities for direction, monitoring and technical assistance of major inland oil spill response activities authorized under the Federal Water Pollution Control Act, as amended by the Oil Pollution Act of 1990 (OPA), including activities under the Working Capital Fund. This appropriation supports core Agency programs and a number of the Agency's ten goals. Specifically in FY 2001, emphasis will be placed on the following:

Better Waste Management, Restoration of Contaminated Waste Sites, and Emergency Response.—EPA will work to ensure that 400 additional facilities per year comply with the oil spill prevention, control and countermeasure provisions of the OPA. EPA will also direct response actions when appropriate. Funding of oil spill cleanup actions is provided through the Department of Transportation under the Oil Spill Liability Trust Fund.

Object Classification (in millions of dollars)

Identification code 68–8221–0–7–304		1999 actual	2000 est.	2001 est.
	Direct obligations:			
11.1	Personnel compensation: Full-time permanent	5	7	8
12.1	Civilian personnel benefits	1	1	1
23.1	Rental payments to GSA	1	7	7
25.2	Other services	8	24	
99.0	Subtotal, direct obligations	15	39	16
99.0	Reimbursable obligations	19	26	26
99.9	Total new obligations	34	65	42

Personnel Summary

Identification code 68–8221–0–7–304		1999 actual	2000 est.	2001 est.
	Direct:			
1001	Total compensable workyears: Full-time equivalent employment	93	103	102
	Reimbursable:			
2001	Total compensable workyears: Full-time equivalent employment	4		

GENERAL FUND RECEIPT ACCOUNTS

(in millions of dollars)

	1999 actual	2000 est.	2001 est.
Governmental receipts:			
68–089500 NPDES, PMN, other services	2	3	3
General Fund Governmental receipts	2	3	3

ADMINISTRATIVE PROVISION

Beginning in fiscal year 2001 and thereafter, notwithstanding 31 U.S.C. 6303(1) and 6305(1), the Administrator of the Environmental Protection Agency, in carrying out the Agency's function to directly implement Federal environmental programs required or authorized by law in the absence of an acceptable tribal program, may award cooperative agreements to federally-recognized Indian Tribes or Intertribal consortia, if authorized by their member Tribes, to assist the Administrator in implementing Federal environmental programs for Indian Tribes required or authorized by law, except that no such cooperative agreements may be awarded from funds designated for State financial assistance agreements.

ALLOCATIONS RECEIVED FROM OTHER ACCOUNTS

Note.—Obligations incurred under allocations from other accounts are included in the schedules of the parent appropriations as follows:

Commerce: "Economic Development Assistance Programs."

General Services Administration.

Transportation: "Emergency Preparedness Grants."

U.S. Agency for International Development.

Executive Office of the President, Unanticipated Needs, Information Technology Systems and Related Expenses.

EXECUTIVE OFFICE OF THE PRESIDENT

COMPENSATION OF THE PRESIDENT AND THE WHITE HOUSE OFFICE

Federal Funds

General and special funds:

COMPENSATION OF THE PRESIDENT

For compensation of the President, including an expense allowance at the rate of $50,000 per annum as authorized by 3 U.S.C. 102; [$250,000] *$390,000*: *Provided*, That none of the funds made available for official expenses shall be expended for any other purpose and any unused amount shall revert to the Treasury pursuant to section 1552 of title 31, United States Code: *Provided further*, That none of the funds made available for official expenses shall be considered as taxable to the President. *(Executive Office Appropriations Act, 2000.)*

SALARIES AND EXPENSES

For necessary expenses for the White House as authorized by law, including not to exceed $3,850,000 for services as authorized by 5 U.S.C. 3109 and 3 U.S.C. 105; subsistence expenses as authorized by 3 U.S.C. 105, which shall be expended and accounted for as provided in that section; hire of passenger motor vehicles, newspapers, periodicals, teletype news service, and travel (not to exceed $100,000 to be expended and accounted for as provided by 3 U.S.C. 103); not to exceed $19,000 for official entertainment expenses, to be available for allocation within the Executive Office of the President, [$52,444,000: *Provided*, That $10,313,000 of the funds appropriated shall be available for reimbursements to the White House Communications Agency] *$53,288,000*. *(Executive Office Appropriations Act, 2000.)*

Program and Financing (in millions of dollars)

Identification code 11–0110–0–1–802	1999 actual	2000 est.	2001 est.
Obligations by program activity:			
Direct program:			
00.01 Salaries and expenses	52	53	54
09.01 Reimbursable program	1	1	
10.00 Total new obligations	53	54	54
Budgetary resources available for obligation:			
22.00 New budget authority (gross)	54	54	54
23.95 Total new obligations	−53	−54	−54
New budget authority (gross), detail:			
Discretionary:			
40.00 Appropriation	53	53	54
Spending authority from offsetting collections:			
68.00 Offsetting collections (cash)	2	1	
68.10 From Federal sources: Change in receivables and unpaid, unfilled orders	−1		
68.90 Spending authority from offsetting collections (total discretionary)	1	1	
70.00 Total new budget authority (gross)	54	54	54
Change in unpaid obligations:			
Unpaid obligations, start of year:			
72.40 Obligated balance, start of year	13	11	12
72.95 From Federal sources: Receivables and unpaid, unfilled orders	1		
72.99 Total unpaid obligations, start of year	14	11	12
73.10 Total new obligations	53	54	54
73.20 Total outlays (gross)	−53	−53	−54
73.40 Adjustments in expired accounts (net)	−4		
Unpaid obligations, end of year:			
74.40 Obligated balance, end of year	11	12	11
74.95 From Federal sources: Receivables and unpaid, unfilled orders			
74.99 Total unpaid obligations, end of year	11	12	11
Outlays (gross), detail:			
86.90 Outlays from new discretionary authority	44	43	44
86.93 Outlays from discretionary balances	9	10	11
87.00 Total outlays (gross)	53	53	54
Offsets:			
Against gross budget authority and outlays:			
88.00 Offsetting collections (cash) from: Federal sources	−2	−1	
Against gross budget authority only:			
88.95 From Federal sources: Change in receivables and unpaid, unfilled orders	1		
Net budget authority and outlays:			
89.00 Budget authority	53	53	54
90.00 Outlays	51	52	54

These funds provide for the compensation of the President and official expenses. These funds also provide the President with staff assistance and provide administrative services for the direct support of the President.

Expenses of this account include the following:

Object Classification (in millions of dollars)

Identification code 11–0110–0–1–802	1999 actual	2000 est.	2001 est.
Direct obligations:			
11.1 Personnel compensation: Full-time permanent	22	23	23
12.1 Civilian personnel benefits	5	6	6
13.0 Benefits for former personnel			1
21.0 Travel and transportation of persons	1	1	1
23.1 Rental payments to GSA	5	5	5
23.3 Communications, utilities, and miscellaneous charges	3	3	3
24.0 Printing and reproduction	1	1	1
25.2 Other services	12	11	12
26.0 Supplies and materials		1	
31.0 Equipment	2	2	2
99.0 Subtotal, direct obligations	51	53	54
99.0 Reimbursable obligations	1	1	
99.5 Below reporting threshold	1		
99.9 Total new obligations	53	54	54

Personnel Summary

Identification code 11–0110–0–1–802	1999 actual	2000 est.	2001 est.
1001 Total compensable workyears: Full-time equivalent employment	383	400	400

EXECUTIVE RESIDENCE AT THE WHITE HOUSE

Federal Funds

General and special funds:

OPERATING EXPENSES

For the care, maintenance, repair and alteration, refurnishing, improvement, heating, and lighting, including electric power and fixtures, of the Executive Residence at the White House and official entertainment expenses of the President, [$9,260,000] *$10,900,000* to be expended and accounted for as provided by 3 U.S.C. 105, 109, 110, and 112–114. *(Executive Office Appropriations Act, 2000.)*

REIMBURSABLE EXPENSES

For the reimbursable expenses of the Executive Residence at the White House, such sums as may be necessary: *Provided*, That all

General and special funds—Continued

REIMBURSABLE EXPENSES—Continued

reimbursable operating expenses of the Executive Residence shall be made in accordance with the provisions of this paragraph: *Provided further*, That, notwithstanding any other provision of law, such amount for reimbursable operating expenses shall be the exclusive authority of the Executive Residence to incur obligations and to receive offsetting collections, for such expenses: *Provided further*, That the Executive Residence shall require each person sponsoring a reimbursable political event to pay in advance an amount equal to the estimated cost of the event, and all such advance payments shall be credited to this account and remain available until expended: *Provided further*, That the Executive Residence shall require the national committee of the political party of the President to maintain on deposit $25,000, to be separately accounted for and available for expenses relating to reimbursable political events sponsored by such committee during such fiscal year: *Provided further*, That the Executive Residence shall ensure that a written notice of any amount owed for a reimbursable operating expense under this paragraph is submitted to the person owing such amount within 60 days after such expense is incurred, and that such amount is collected within 30 days after the submission of such notice: *Provided further*, That the Executive Residence shall charge interest and assess penalties and other charges on any such amount that is not reimbursed within such 30 days, in accordance with the interest and penalty provisions applicable to an outstanding debt on a United States Government claim under section 3717 of title 31, United States Code: *Provided further*, That each such amount that is reimbursed, and any accompanying interest and charges, shall be deposited in the Treasury as miscellaneous receipts: *Provided further*, That the Executive Residence shall prepare and submit to the Committees on Appropriations, by not later than 90 days after the end of the fiscal year covered by this Act, a report setting forth the reimbursable operating expenses of the Executive Residence during the preceding fiscal year, including the total amount of such expenses, the amount of such total that consists of reimbursable official and ceremonial events, the amount of such total that consists of reimbursable political events, and the portion of each such amount that has been reimbursed as of the date of the report: *Provided further*, That the Executive Residence shall maintain a system for the tracking of expenses related to reimbursable events within the Executive Residence that includes a standard for the classification of any such expense as political or nonpolitical: *Provided further*, That no provision of this paragraph may be construed to exempt the Executive Residence from any other applicable requirement of subchapter I or II of chapter 37 of title 31, United States Code. *(Executive Office Appropriations Act, 2000.)*

Program and Financing (in millions of dollars)

Identification code 11–0210–0–1–802		1999 actual	2000 est.	2001 est.
	Obligations by program activity:			
00.01	Direct program	9	9	11
09.00	Reimbursable program	3	4	4
10.00	Total new obligations	12	13	15
	Budgetary resources available for obligation:			
22.00	New budget authority (gross)	12	13	15
23.95	Total new obligations	−12	−13	−15
	New budget authority (gross), detail:			
	Discretionary:			
40.00	Appropriation	9	9	11
68.00	Spending authority from offsetting collections: Offsetting collections (cash)	3	4	4
70.00	Total new budget authority (gross)	12	13	15
	Change in unpaid obligations:			
72.95	Unpaid obligations, start of year: From Federal sources: Receivables and unpaid, unfilled orders	1	1	2
73.10	Total new obligations	12	13	15
73.20	Total outlays (gross)	−12	−13	−15
74.95	Unpaid obligations, end of year: From Federal sources: Receivables and unpaid, unfilled orders	1	2	2
	Outlays (gross), detail:			
86.90	Outlays from new discretionary authority	12	13	15
	Offsets:			
	Against gross budget authority and outlays:			
	Offsetting collections (cash) from:			
88.00	Federal sources	−2	−1	−1
88.40	Non-Federal sources	−1	−3	−3
88.90	Total, offsetting collections (cash)	−3	−4	−4
	Net budget authority and outlays:			
89.00	Budget authority	9	9	11
90.00	Outlays	9	9	11

These funds provide for the care, maintenance, and operation of the Executive Residence.

Object Classification (in millions of dollars)

Identification code 11–0210–0–1–802		1999 actual	2000 est.	2001 est.
	Direct obligations:			
	Personnel compensation:			
11.1	Full-time permanent	5	5	6
11.5	Other personnel compensation	1	2	2
11.9	Total personnel compensation	6	7	8
12.1	Civilian personnel benefits	1	1	1
25.2	Other services	1	....	1
26.0	Supplies and materials	1	....	1
99.0	Subtotal, direct obligations	9	8	11
99.0	Reimbursable obligations	3	3	3
99.5	Below reporting threshold	....	2	1
99.9	Total new obligations	12	13	15

Personnel Summary

Identification code 11–0210–0–1–802		1999 actual	2000 est.	2001 est.
1001	Total compensable workyears: Full-time equivalent employment	86	91	95

WHITE HOUSE REPAIR AND RESTORATION

For the repair, alteration, and improvement of the Executive Residence at the White House, [$810,000] *$5,510,000*, to remain available until expanded, for [seven] *six* projects for required maintenance, safety and health issues, *Presidential transition, telecommunications infrastructure repair,* and continued preventive maintenance. *(Executive Office Appropriations Act, 2000.)*

Program and Financing (in millions of dollars)

Identification code 11–0109–0–1–802		1999 actual	2000 est.	2001 est.
	Obligations by program activity:			
10.00	Total new obligations (object class 25.2)	....	1	6
	Budgetary resources available for obligation:			
21.40	Unobligated balance available, start of year	....	....	1
22.00	New budget authority (gross)	....	1	6
23.90	Total budgetary resources available for obligation	....	1	7
23.95	Total new obligations	....	−1	−6
24.40	Unobligated balance available, end of year	....	1	1
	New budget authority (gross), detail:			
	Discretionary:			
40.00	Appropriation	....	1	6
	Change in unpaid obligations:			
73.10	Total new obligations	....	1	6
73.20	Total outlays (gross)	....	−1	−4
	Outlays (gross), detail:			
86.90	Outlays from new discretionary authority	....	1	4
	Net budget authority and outlays:			
89.00	Budget authority	....	1	6

90.00 Outlays		1	4

SPECIAL ASSISTANCE TO THE PRESIDENT AND THE OFFICIAL RESIDENCE OF THE VICE PRESIDENT

Federal Funds

General and special funds:

SALARIES AND EXPENSES

For necessary expenses to enable the Vice President to provide assistance to the President in connection with specially assigned functions, services as authorized by 5 U.S.C. 3109 and 3 U.S.C. 106, including subsistence expenses as authorized by 3 U.S.C. 106, which shall be expended and accounted for as provided in that section; and hire of passenger motor vehicles; [$3,617,000] *$3,673,000*. *(Executive Office Appropriations Act, 2000.)*

OPERATING EXPENSES

For the care, operation, refurnishing, improvement, heating and lighting, including electric power and fixtures, of the official residence of the Vice President, the hire of passenger motor vehicles, and not to exceed $90,000 for official entertainment expenses of the Vice President, to be accounted for solely on his certificate; [$345,000] *$354,000*: *Provided*, That advances or repayments or transfers from this appropriation may be made to any department or agency for expenses of carrying out such activities. *(Executive Office Appropriations Act, 2000.)*

Program and Financing (in millions of dollars)

Identification code 11–1454–0–1–802	1999 actual	2000 est.	2001 est.
Obligations by program activity:			
10.00 Total new obligations	4	4	4
Budgetary resources available for obligation:			
22.00 New budget authority (gross)	4	4	4
23.95 Total new obligations	–4	–4	–4
New budget authority (gross), detail:			
Discretionary:			
40.00 Appropriation	4	4	4
Change in unpaid obligations:			
72.40 Unpaid obligations, start of year: Obligated balance, start of year	1	1	1
73.10 Total new obligations	4	4	4
73.20 Total outlays (gross)	–4	–4	–4
74.40 Unpaid obligations, end of year: Obligated balance, end of year	1	1	1
Outlays (gross), detail:			
86.90 Outlays from new discretionary authority	4	4	4
Net budget authority and outlays:			
89.00 Budget authority	4	4	4
90.00 Outlays	4	4	4

These funds are to be used by the Vice President to carry out responsibilities assigned him by the President and by various statutes. These funds also provide for the care and operation of the Vice President's official residence. Also included in this presentation are the operations of a gift fund for the official residence of the Vice President.

Included in this account are the operating expenses of the Vice President's official residence in the amounts of $324 thousand in 1999 and estimates of $345 thousand in 2000 and $354 thousand in 2001.

Expenses of this account include the following:

Object Classification (in millions of dollars)

Identification code 11–1454–0–1–802	1999 actual	2000 est.	2001 est.
11.1 Personnel compensation: Full-time permanent	2	2	2
23.1 Rental payments to GSA	1	1	1
99.0 Subtotal, direct obligations	3	3	3
99.5 Below reporting threshold	1	1	1
99.9 Total new obligations	4	4	4

Personnel Summary

Identification code 11–1454–0–1–802	1999 actual	2000 est.	2001 est.
1001 Total compensable workyears: Full-time equivalent employment	21	23	23

Note.—1998, 1999 and 2000 include 1 FTE for the Official Residence of the Vice President.

COUNCIL OF ECONOMIC ADVISERS

Federal Funds

General and special funds:

SALARIES AND EXPENSES

For necessary expenses of the Council of Economic Advisers in carrying out its functions under the Employment Act of 1946 (15 U.S.C. 1021), [$3,840,000] *$4,110,000*. *(Executive Office Appropriations Act, 2000.)*

Program and Financing (in millions of dollars)

Identification code 11–1900–0–1–802	1999 actual	2000 est.	2001 est.
Obligations by program activity:			
10.00 Total new obligations	4	4	4
Budgetary resources available for obligation:			
22.00 New budget authority (gross)	4	4	4
23.95 Total new obligations	–4	–4	–4
New budget authority (gross), detail:			
Discretionary:			
40.00 Appropriation	4	4	4
Change in unpaid obligations:			
72.40 Unpaid obligations, start of year: Obligated balance, start of year	1	1	1
73.10 Total new obligations	4	4	4
73.20 Total outlays (gross)	–3	–4	–4
74.40 Unpaid obligations, end of year: Obligated balance, end of year	1	1	1
Outlays (gross), detail:			
86.90 Outlays from new discretionary authority	3	3	3
86.93 Outlays from discretionary balances		1	1
87.00 Total outlays (gross)	3	4	4
Net budget authority and outlays:			
89.00 Budget authority	4	4	4
90.00 Outlays	3	4	4

The Council of Economic Advisers analyzes the national economy and its various segments, advises the President on economic developments, recommends policies for economic growth and stability, appraises economic programs and policies of the Federal Government, and assists in preparation of the annual Economic Report of the President to Congress.

Object Classification (in millions of dollars)

Identification code 11–1900–0–1–802	1999 actual	2000 est.	2001 est.
Personnel compensation:			
11.1 Full-time permanent	2	2	2
11.8 Special personal services payments	1	1	1
11.9 Total personnel compensation	3	3	3
99.5 Below reporting threshold	1	1	1
99.9 Total new obligations	4	4	4

General and special funds—Continued

SALARIES AND EXPENSES—Continued

Personnel Summary

Identification code 11–1900–0–1–802	1999 actual	2000 est.	2001 est.
1001 Total compensable workyears: Full-time equivalent employment	27	35	35

COUNCIL ON ENVIRONMENTAL QUALITY AND OFFICE OF ENVIRONMENTAL QUALITY

Federal Funds

General and special funds:

COUNCIL ON ENVIRONMENTAL QUALITY AND OFFICE OF ENVIRONMENTAL QUALITY

For necessary expenses to continue functions assigned to the Council on Environmental Quality and Office of Environmental Quality pursuant to the National Environmental Policy Act of 1969, the Environmental Quality Improvement Act of 1970, and Reorganization Plan No. 1 of 1977, [$2,827,000] *$3,020,000*: *Provided,* [That, notwithstanding any other provision of law, no funds other than those appropriated under this heading shall be used for or by the Council on Environmental Quality and Office of Environmental Quality: *Provided further,*] That notwithstanding section 202 of the National Environmental Policy Act of 1970, the Council shall consist of one member, appointed by the President, by and with the advice and consent of the Senate, serving as chairman and exercising all powers, functions, and duties of the Council. *(Departments of Veterans Affairs and Housing and Urban Development, and Independent Agencies Appropriations Act, 2000.)*

Program and Financing (in millions of dollars)

Identification code 11–1453–0–1–802	1999 actual	2000 est.	2001 est.
Obligations by program activity:			
10.00 Total new obligations	3	3	3
Budgetary resources available for obligation:			
22.00 New budget authority (gross)	3	3	3
23.95 Total new obligations	−3	−3	−3
New budget authority (gross), detail:			
Discretionary:			
40.00 Appropriation	3	3	3
Change in unpaid obligations:			
72.40 Unpaid obligations, start of year: Obligated balance, start of year	1		
73.10 Total new obligations	3	3	3
73.20 Total outlays (gross)	−3	−3	−3
Outlays (gross), detail:			
86.90 Outlays from new discretionary authority	3	3	3
Net budget authority and outlays:			
89.00 Budget authority	3	3	3
90.00 Outlays	3	3	3

This appropriation provides funds for the Council on Environmental Quality (CEQ) and the Office of Environmental Quality to serve as the focal point for environmental policy development within the Administration and conduct compliance oversight activities under the National Environmental Policy Act (NEPA).

Object Classification (in millions of dollars)

Identification code 11–1453–0–1–802	1999 actual	2000 est.	2001 est.
11.1 Direct obligations: Personnel compensation: Full-time permanent	2	2	2
99.5 Below reporting threshold	1	1	1
99.9 Total new obligations	3	3	3

Personnel Summary

Identification code 11–1453–0–1–802	1999 actual	2000 est.	2001 est.
1001 Total compensable workyears: Full-time equivalent employment	18	23	26

Intragovernmental funds:

MANAGEMENT FUND, OFFICE OF ENVIRONMENTAL QUALITY

Program and Financing (in millions of dollars)

Identification code 11–3963–0–4–802	1999 actual	2000 est.	2001 est.
Obligations by program activity:			
10.00 Total new obligations	1	1	1
Budgetary resources available for obligation:			
21.40 Unobligated balance available, start of year	1		
22.00 New budget authority (gross)	1	1	1
23.90 Total budgetary resources available for obligation	2	1	1
23.95 Total new obligations	−1	−1	−1
New budget authority (gross), detail:			
Mandatory:			
69.00 Offsetting collections (cash)	1	1	1
Change in unpaid obligations:			
73.10 Total new obligations	1	1	1
73.20 Total outlays (gross)	−1	−1	−1
Outlays (gross), detail:			
86.97 Outlays from new mandatory authority	1	1	1
Offsets:			
Against gross budget authority and outlays:			
88.00 Offsetting collections (cash) from: Federal sources	−1	−1	−1
Net budget authority and outlays:			
89.00 Budget authority			
90.00 Outlays			

This fund finances study contracts that are jointly sponsored by the Office of Environmental Quality and one or more other Federal agencies and Federal interagency environmental projects (including task forces) in which the Office participates.

OFFICE OF POLICY DEVELOPMENT

Federal Funds

General and special funds:

SALARIES AND EXPENSES

For necessary expenses of the Office of Policy Development, including services as authorized by 5 U.S.C. 3109, and 3 U.S.C. 107; $4,032,000. *(Executive Office Appropriations Act, 2000.)*

Program and Financing (in millions of dollars)

Identification code 11–2200–0–1–802	1999 actual	2000 est.	2001 est.
Obligations by program activity:			
10.00 Total new obligations	4	4	4
Budgetary resources available for obligation:			
22.00 New budget authority (gross)	4	4	4
23.95 Total new obligations	−4	−4	−4
New budget authority (gross), detail:			
Discretionary:			
40.00 Appropriation	4	4	4
Change in unpaid obligations:			
72.40 Unpaid obligations, start of year: Obligated balance, start of year	2	1	1

		1999 actual	2000 est.	2001 est.
73.10	Total new obligations	4	4	4
73.20	Total outlays (gross)	−4	−4	−4
74.40	Unpaid obligations, end of year: Obligated balance, end of year	1	1	1
	Outlays (gross), detail:			
86.90	Outlays from new discretionary authority	3	3	3
86.93	Outlays from discretionary balances	1	1	1
87.00	Total outlays (gross)	4	4	4
	Net budget authority and outlays:			
89.00	Budget authority	4	4	4
90.00	Outlays	4	4	4

The Office of Policy Development supports the National Economic Council and the Domestic Policy Council in carrying out their responsibilities to advise and assist the President in the formulation, coordination, and implementation of economic and domestic policy. The Office of Policy Development also provides support for other domestic policy development and implementation activities as directed by the President.

Object Classification (in millions of dollars)

Identification code 11–2200–0–1–802		1999 actual	2000 est.	2001 est.
11.1	Personnel compensation: Full-time permanent	2	2	2
23.1	Rental payments to GSA	1	1	1
99.0	Subtotal, direct obligations	3	3	3
99.5	Below reporting threshold	1	1	1
99.9	Total new obligations	4	4	4

Personnel Summary

Identification code 11–2200–0–1–802		1999 actual	2000 est.	2001 est.
1001	Total compensable workyears: Full-time equivalent employment	29	31	31

NATIONAL SECURITY COUNCIL

Federal Funds

General and special funds:

SALARIES AND EXPENSES

For necessary expenses of the National Security Council, including services as authorized by 5 U.S.C. 3109, [$6,997,000] *$7,165,000*. *(Executive Office Appropriations Act, 2000.)*

Program and Financing (in millions of dollars)

Identification code 11–2000–0–1–802		1999 actual	2000 est.	2001 est.
	Obligations by program activity:			
10.00	Total new obligations	7	7	7
	Budgetary resources available for obligation:			
22.00	New budget authority (gross)	7	7	7
23.95	Total new obligations	−7	−7	−7
	New budget authority (gross), detail:			
	Discretionary:			
40.00	Appropriation	7	7	7
	Change in unpaid obligations:			
72.40	Unpaid obligations, start of year: Obligated balance, start of year	1	1	1
73.10	Total new obligations	7	7	7
73.20	Total outlays (gross)	−7	−7	−7
74.40	Unpaid obligations, end of year: Obligated balance, end of year	1	1	1
	Outlays (gross), detail:			
86.90	Outlays from new discretionary authority	6	6	6
86.93	Outlays from discretionary balances	1	1	1
87.00	Total outlays (gross)	7	7	7
	Net budget authority and outlays:			
89.00	Budget authority	7	7	7
90.00	Outlays	7	7	7

The National Security Council advises the President on the integration of domestic, foreign, and military policies relating to national security.

Object Classification (in millions of dollars)

Identification code 11–2000–0–1–802		1999 actual	2000 est.	2001 est.
	Personnel compensation:			
11.1	Full-time permanent	3	3	3
11.8	Special personal services payments	1	1	1
11.9	Total personnel compensation	4	4	4
12.1	Civilian personnel benefits	1	1	1
23.1	Rental payments to GSA	1	1	1
99.0	Subtotal, direct obligations	6	6	6
99.5	Below reporting threshold	1	1	1
99.9	Total new obligations	7	7	7

Personnel Summary

Identification code 11–2000–0–1–802		1999 actual	2000 est.	2001 est.
1001	Total compensable workyears: Full-time equivalent employment	41	60	60

OFFICE OF ADMINISTRATION

Federal Funds

General and special funds:

SALARIES AND EXPENSES

For necessary expenses of the Office of Administration, including services as authorized by 5 U.S.C. 3109 and 3 U.S.C. 107, and hire of passenger motor vehicles [$39,198,000] *$43,737,000*, of which [$8,806,000] *$9,905,000* shall remain available until [expended] *September 30, 2002* for a capital investment plan which provides for the continued modernization of the information technology infrastructure. *(Executive Office Appropriations Act, 2000.)*

[SEC. 235. Title III of Public Law 106–58, under the heading "Office of Administration, Salaries and Expenses", is amended by inserting after "infrastructure" the following: ": *Provided,* That the funds for the capital investment plan shall remain available until September 30, 2001".] *(Miscellaneous Appropriations, 2000, as enacted by section 1000(a)(5) of the Consolidated Appropriations Act, 2000 (P.L. 106–113).)*

Program and Financing (in millions of dollars)

Identification code 11–0038–0–1–802		1999 actual	2000 est.	2001 est.
	Obligations by program activity:			
	Direct program:			
00.01	Office of the Director	1		
00.06	Chief Financial Officer Operations			1
00.07	Financial Management	1	2	2
00.08	Human Resource Management	3	2	2
00.09	General Services	4	4	4
00.10	Facilities Management	1	3	4
00.11	Information Systems and Technology	16	16	18
00.12	Library and Research Services	2	2	2
00.13	Capital Investment Plan	22	17	10
00.14	Below Reporting Threshold		1	
01.00	Direct Program Subtotal	50	47	43
09.00	Reimbursable program	6	6	6
10.00	Total new obligations	56	53	49
	Budgetary resources available for obligation:			
21.40	Unobligated balance available, start of year		8	
22.00	New budget authority (gross)	64	45	50
23.90	Total budgetary resources available for obligation	64	53	50
23.95	Total new obligations	−56	−53	−49

General and special funds—Continued

SALARIES AND EXPENSES—Continued

Program and Financing (in millions of dollars)—Continued

Identification code 11–0038–0–1–802	1999 actual	2000 est.	2001 est.
24.40 Unobligated balance available, end of year	8		
New budget authority (gross), detail:			
Discretionary:			
40.00 Appropriation	28	39	44
42.00 Transferred from other accounts	30		
43.00 Appropriation (total discretionary)	58	39	44
68.00 Spending authority from offsetting collections: Offsetting collections (cash)	6	6	6
70.00 Total new budget authority (gross)	64	45	50
Change in unpaid obligations:			
72.40 Unpaid obligations, start of year: Obligated balance, start of year	10	18	27
73.10 Total new obligations	56	53	49
73.20 Total outlays (gross)	−46	−44	−48
73.40 Adjustments in expired accounts (net)	−1		
74.40 Unpaid obligations, end of year: Obligated balance, end of year	18	27	28
Outlays (gross), detail:			
86.90 Outlays from new discretionary authority	40	38	42
86.93 Outlays from discretionary balances	6	6	7
87.00 Total outlays (gross)	46	44	48
Offsets:			
Against gross budget authority and outlays:			
88.00 Offsetting collections (cash) from: Federal sources	−6	−6	−6
Net budget authority and outlays:			
89.00 Budget authority	58	39	44
90.00 Outlays	40	38	42

The Office of Administration's mission is to provide high-quality, cost-effective, administrative services to the Executive Office of the President. These services, defined by Executive Order 12028 of 1977, include financial, personnel, library and records services, information management systems support, and general office services.

The Office of Administration receives reimbursements for information management support and general office services.

Object Classification (in millions of dollars)

Identification code 11–0038–0–1–802	1999 actual	2000 est.	2001 est.
Direct obligations:			
11.1 Personnel compensation: Full-time permanent	9	10	12
12.1 Civilian personnel benefits	2	2	3
23.1 Rental payments to GSA	3	3	3
23.3 Communications, utilities, and miscellaneous charges	1	2	1
25.2 Other services	24	19	16
26.0 Supplies and materials	1	2	2
31.0 Equipment	8	8	6
99.0 Subtotal, direct obligations	48	46	43
99.0 Reimbursable obligations	6	7	6
99.5 Below reporting threshold	2		
99.9 Total new obligations	56	53	49

Personnel Summary

Identification code 11–0038–0–1–802	1999 actual	2000 est.	2001 est.
1001 Total compensable workyears: Full-time equivalent employment	174	192	202

ARMSTRONG RESOLUTION

Federal Funds

General and special funds:

ARMSTRONG RESOLUTION ACCOUNT

Program and Financing (in millions of dollars)

Identification code 11–1073–0–1–802	1999 actual	2000 est.	2001 est.
Obligations by program activity:			
00.01 Armstrong Resolution	1	2	1
10.00 Total new obligations	1	2	1
Budgetary resources available for obligation:			
21.40 Unobligated balance available, start of year	3	2	
23.95 Total new obligations	−1	−2	−1
24.40 Unobligated balance available, end of year	2		
Change in unpaid obligations:			
72.40 Unpaid obligations, start of year: Obligated balance, start of year	1	1	1
73.10 Total new obligations	1	2	1
73.20 Total outlays (gross)	−1	−2	−1
74.40 Unpaid obligations, end of year: Obligated balance, end of year	1	1	
Outlays (gross), detail:			
86.93 Outlays from discretionary balances	1	2	1
Net budget authority and outlays:			
89.00 Budget authority			
90.00 Outlays	1	2	1

This account is for necessary expenses for electronic communications records management activities for compliance with and resolution of Armstrong v. the Executive Office of the President.

Object Classification (in millions of dollars)

Identification code 11–1073–0–1–802	1999 actual	2000 est.	2001 est.
25.2 Direct obligations: Other services	1	1	1
99.5 Below reporting threshold		1	
99.9 Total new obligations	1	2	1

OFFICE OF MANAGEMENT AND BUDGET

Federal Funds

General and special funds:

SALARIES AND EXPENSES

For necessary expenses of the Office of Management and Budget (OMB), including hire of passenger motor vehicles and services as authorized by 5 U.S.C. 3109, **[**$63,495,000**]** *$68,786,000*, of which not to exceed $5,000,000 shall be available to carry out the provisions of chapter 35 of title 44, United States Code**[**: *Provided*, That, as provided in 31 U.S.C. 1301(a), appropriations shall be applied only to the objects for which appropriations were made except as otherwise provided by law: *Provided further,* That none of the funds appropriated in this Act for the Office of Management and Budget may be used for the purpose of reviewing any agricultural marketing orders or any activities or regulations under the provisions of the Agricultural Marketing Agreement Act of 1937 (7 U.S.C. 601 et seq.): *Provided further,* That none of the funds made available for the Office of Management and Budget by this Act may be expended for the altering of the transcript of actual testimony of witnesses, except for testimony of officials of the Office of Management and Budget, before the Committees on Appropriations or the Committees on Veterans' Affairs or their subcommittees: *Provided further,* That the preceding shall not apply to printed hearings released by the Committees on Appropriations or the Committees on Veterans' Affairs**]**. *(Executive Office Appropriations Act, 2000.)*

Program and Financing (in millions of dollars)

Identification code 11–0300–0–1–802	1999 actual	2000 est.	2001 est.
Obligations by program activity:			
00.01 National security and international affairs	7	7	8
00.02 General government and finance	7	7	8
00.03 Natural resources, energy, and science	8	8	9
00.04 Health/Personnel	6	6	7
00.05 Education, income maintenance, and labor	4	4	4
00.06 Office of federal financial management	2	3	3
00.07 Information and regulatory affairs	5	6	6
00.08 Office of federal procurement policy	3	3	3
00.09 OMB-Wide offices	19	19	21
10.00 Total new obligations	61	63	69
Budgetary resources available for obligation:			
22.00 New budget authority (gross)	61	63	69
23.95 Total new obligations	−61	−63	−69
New budget authority (gross), detail:			
Discretionary:			
40.00 Appropriation	61	63	69
Change in unpaid obligations:			
72.40 Unpaid obligations, start of year: Obligated balance, start of year	6	7	7
73.10 Total new obligations	61	63	69
73.20 Total outlays (gross)	−60	−63	−69
73.40 Adjustments in expired accounts (net)	−1		
74.40 Unpaid obligations, end of year: Obligated balance, end of year	7	7	8
Outlays (gross), detail:			
86.90 Outlays from new discretionary authority	56	58	63
86.93 Outlays from discretionary balances	4	5	5
87.00 Total outlays (gross)	60	63	69
Net budget authority and outlays:			
89.00 Budget authority	61	63	69
90.00 Outlays	59	63	69

This Office assists the President in the discharge of budgetary, management, and other executive responsibilities.

OMB-wide offices.—Executive direction and coordination for all Office of Management and Budget activities is provided. This includes the Director's immediate office as well as staff support in the areas of Budget Review, Administration, Office of Communications, Legislative Reference, Legislative Affairs, Economic Policy, and General Counsel.

Budget instructions and procedures are developed, review of agency estimates is coordinated, budget data systems are maintained, agency financial management plans are reviewed, the budget document is prepared, and scorekeeping is accomplished.

National security and international affairs; General government and finance; Natural resources, energy, and science; Education, income maintenance, and labor; and Health/Personnel.—Agency programs, budget requests, and management activities are examined, appropriations are apportioned, proposed changes in agency functions are studied, and special studies aimed at establishing goals and objectives that would result in long- and short-range improvements in the agencies' financial, administrative, and operational management are conducted.

Financial management.—In conjunction with the Chief Financial Officers Council, prepares the Government-wide financial management status report and 5-year plan, monitors execution of the plan; provides policy guidance on preparation and audit of financial statements, financial systems requirements, management controls, and cost accounting and audit requirements for the non-Federal grantee community.

Information and regulatory affairs.—Agency proposals to implement or revise Federal regulations and information collection requirements are reviewed and coordinated. Information resources management and statistical policies and practices are analyzed and developed.

Procurement policy.—The Office of Federal Procurement Policy is responsible for promoting economy, efficiency, and effectiveness in the procurement of property and services by and for the Executive branch.

Object Classification (in millions of dollars)

Identification code 11–0300–0–1–802	1999 actual	2000 est.	2001 est.
Personnel compensation:			
11.1 Full-time permanent	36	38	41
11.3 Other than full-time permanent	1	1	1
11.5 Other personnel compensation	1	1	1
11.9 Total personnel compensation	38	40	43
12.1 Civilian personnel benefits	8	8	8
23.1 Rental payments to GSA	6	6	6
23.3 Communications, utilities, and miscellaneous charges	1	1	1
24.0 Printing and reproduction	1	1	1
25.2 Other services	5	5	6
26.0 Supplies and materials	1	1	1
31.0 Equipment	1	1	2
99.0 Subtotal, direct obligations	61	63	68
99.5 Below reporting threshold			1
99.9 Total new obligations	61	63	69

Personnel Summary

Identification code 11–0300–0–1–802	1999 actual	2000 est.	2001 est.
1001 Total compensable workyears: Full-time equivalent employment	504	518	527

OFFICE OF NATIONAL DRUG CONTROL POLICY

Federal Funds

General and special funds:

Salaries and Expenses

(including transfer of funds)

For necessary expenses of the Office of National Drug Control Policy; for research activities pursuant to the Office of National Drug Control Policy Reauthorization Act of 1998 (title VII of division C of Public Law 105–277); not to exceed [$8,000] *$20,000* for official reception and representation expenses; and for participation in joint projects or in the provision of services on matters of mutual interest with nonprofit, research, or public organizations or agencies, with or without reimbursement, [$22,951,000] *$25,400,000*, of which [$1,100,000 shall be] *$2,100,000 shall remain* available *until expended, consisting of $1,100,000* for policy research and evaluation, *and* [of which] $1,000,000 [shall be available] for the National Alliance for Model State Drug Laws[, and of which up to $600,000 shall be available for the evaluation of the Drug-Free Communities Act]: *Provided*, That the Office is authorized to accept, hold, administer, and utilize gifts, both real and personal, public and private, without fiscal year limitation, for the purpose of aiding or facilitating the work of the Office[: *Provided further*, That of the amounts appropriated for salaries and expenses, $125,000 shall be transferred to the General Accounting Office for the sole purpose of entering into a contract with the private sector for a management review of the Office of National Drug Control Policy]. *(Executive Office Appropriations Act, 2000.)*

[Sec. 237. In addition to amounts appropriated to the Office of National Drug Control Policy, $3,000,000 is appropriated: *Provided*, That this amount shall be made available by grant to the United States Olympic Committee for its anti-doping program within 30 days of the enactment of this Act.] *(Miscellaneous Appropriations, 2000, as enacted by section 1000(a)(5) of the Consolidated Appropriations Act, 2000 (P.L. 106–113).)*

General and special funds—Continued

SALARIES AND EXPENSES—Continued

(INCLUDING TRANSFER OF FUNDS)—Continued

Program and Financing (in millions of dollars)

Identification code 11–1457–0–1–999	1999 actual	2000 est.	2001 est.
Obligations by program activity:			
10.00 Total new obligations	21	23	25
Budgetary resources available for obligation:			
22.00 New budget authority (gross)	21	23	25
23.95 Total new obligations	–21	–23	–25
New budget authority (gross), detail:			
Discretionary:			
40.00 Appropriation	20	23	25
42.00 Transferred from other accounts	1		
43.00 Appropriation (total discretionary)	21	23	25
Change in unpaid obligations:			
72.40 Unpaid obligations, start of year: Obligated balance, start of year	10	7	12
73.10 Total new obligations	21	23	25
73.20 Total outlays (gross)	–23	–18	–25
74.40 Unpaid obligations, end of year: Obligated balance, end of year	7	12	12
Outlays (gross), detail:			
86.90 Outlays from new discretionary authority	15	18	20
86.93 Outlays from discretionary balances	8		5
87.00 Total outlays (gross)	23	18	25
Net budget authority and outlays:			
89.00 Budget authority	21	23	25
90.00 Outlays	23	18	25

Note.—Excludes $20 million in budget authority in 2001 for activities transferred to the Office of National Drug Control Policy, Counterdrug Technology Assessment Center.

The Office of National Drug Control Policy, established by the Anti-Drug Abuse Act of 1988, and reauthorized by P.L. 105–277, is charged with developing policies, objectives and priorities for the National Drug Control Program; as defined by the Act and Executive Order 12880.

This program also includes funding for general policy research to support the formulation of the National Drug Control Strategy.

Object Classification (in millions of dollars)

Identification code 11–1457–0–1–999	1999 actual	2000 est.	2001 est.
11.1 Personnel compensation: Full-time permanent	9	9	11
12.1 Civilian personnel benefits	1	2	2
21.0 Travel and transportation of persons	1	1	1
23.1 Rental payments to GSA	2	2	2
25.2 Other services	7	7	7
31.0 Equipment			1
99.0 Subtotal, direct obligations	20	21	24
99.5 Below reporting threshold	1	2	1
99.9 Total new obligations	21	23	25

Personnel Summary

Identification code 11–1457–0–1–999	1999 actual	2000 est.	2001 est.
Direct:			
1001 Total compensable workyears: Full-time equivalent employment	106	124	125
Reimbursable:			
2001 Total compensable workyears: Full-time equivalent employment		1	1

Note.—The Special forfeiture fund is presented with the HIDTA program, both of which will remain under ONDCP control, in the Other Independent Agencies chapter under Federal Drug Control Programs.

COUNTERDRUG TECHNOLOGY ASSESSMENT CENTER

(INCLUDING TRANSFER OF FUNDS)

For necessary expenses for the Counterdrug Technology Assessment Center for research activities pursuant to the Office of National Drug Control Policy Reauthorization Act of 1998 (title VII of Division C of Public Law 105–277), [$29,250,000] *$20,400,000*, which shall remain available until expended, consisting of $16,000,000 for counternarcotics research and development projects, [and $13,250,000] $3,700,000 for the continued operation of the technology transfer program,*and $700,000 for a grant to the United States Olympic Committee for its anti-doping program*: *Provided*, That the $16,000,000 for counternarcotics research and development projects shall be available for transfer to other Federal departments or agencies. *(Executive Office Appropriations Act, 2000.)*

Program and Financing (in millions of dollars)

Identification code 11–1461–0–1–802	1999 actual	2000 est.	2001 est.
Obligations by program activity:			
10.00 Total new obligations (object class 25.3)	29	32	20
Budgetary resources available for obligation:			
22.00 New budget authority (gross)	29	32	20
23.95 Total new obligations	–29	–32	–20
New budget authority (gross), detail:			
Discretionary:			
40.00 Appropriation	29	32	20
Change in unpaid obligations:			
72.40 Unpaid obligations, start of year: Obligated balance, start of year		1	2
73.10 Total new obligations	29	32	20
73.20 Total outlays (gross)	–28	–31	–21
74.40 Unpaid obligations, end of year: Obligated balance, end of year	1	2	1
Outlays (gross), detail:			
86.90 Outlays from new discretionary authority	28	30	19
86.93 Outlays from discretionary balances		1	2
87.00 Total outlays (gross)	28	31	21
Net budget authority and outlays:			
89.00 Budget authority	29	32	20
90.00 Outlays	28	31	21

Note.—Includes $20 million in budget authority in 2001 for activities previously funded from: Office of National Drug Control Policy.

	1999 actual	2000 est.
Salaries and Expenses	29	32

Pursuant to the Office of National Drug Control Policy Reauthorization Act of 1998 (title VII of Division C of Public Law 105–277), the Counterdrug Technology Assessment Center serves as the central counterdrug research and development organization for the United States Government.

OFFICE OF SCIENCE AND TECHNOLOGY POLICY

Federal Funds

General and special funds:

OFFICE OF SCIENCE AND TECHNOLOGY POLICY

For necessary expenses of the Office of Science and Technology Policy, in carrying out the purposes of the National Science and Technology Policy, Organization, and Priorities Act of 1976 (42 U.S.C. 6601 and 6671), hire of passenger motor vehicles, and services as authorized by 5 U.S.C. 3109, not to exceed $2,500 for official reception and representation expenses, and rental of conference rooms in the District of Columbia, [$5,108,000] *$5,201,000. (Departments of Veterans Affairs and Housing and Urban Development, and Independent Agencies Appropriations Act, 2000.)*

Program and Financing (in millions of dollars)

Identification code 11–2600–0–1–802	1999 actual	2000 est.	2001 est.
Obligations by program activity:			
10.00 Total new obligations	5	5	5
Budgetary resources available for obligation:			
22.00 New budget authority (gross)	5	5	5
23.95 Total new obligations	−5	−5	−5
New budget authority (gross), detail:			
Discretionary:			
40.00 Appropriation	5	5	5
Change in unpaid obligations:			
72.40 Unpaid obligations, start of year: Obligated balance, start of year	1	1	1
73.10 Total new obligations	5	5	5
73.20 Total outlays (gross)	−5	−5	−5
74.40 Unpaid obligations, end of year: Obligated balance, end of year	1	1	1
Outlays (gross), detail:			
86.90 Outlays from new discretionary authority	5	5	5
Net budget authority and outlays:			
89.00 Budget authority	5	5	5
90.00 Outlays	5	5	5

The Office of Science and Technology Policy (OSTP) provides advice to the President concerning policies in science and technology and on the utilization of science and technology in addressing important national problems. The OSTP operations include support to other Executive Office of the President organizations on issues with science and technology considerations; review and analysis, with the Office of Management and Budget, of research and development budgets for all Federal agencies; coordination of research and development programs of the Federal Government; coordination of the implementation of a number of important international science and technology agreements; and other activities necessary to carry out the duties, functions, and activities described in Public Law 94–282, the National Science and Technology Policy, Organization, and Priorities Act of 1976.

Object Classification (in millions of dollars)

Identification code 11–2600–0–1–802	1999 actual	2000 est.	2001 est.
11.1 Personnel compensation: Full-time permanent	3	3	3
12.1 Civilian personnel benefits	1	1	1
99.0 Subtotal, direct obligations	4	4	4
99.5 Below reporting threshold	1	1	1
99.9 Total new obligations	5	5	5

Personnel Summary

Identification code 11–2600–0–1–802	1999 actual	2000 est.	2001 est.
1001 Total compensable workyears: Full-time equivalent employment	33	40	40

OFFICE OF THE UNITED STATES TRADE REPRESENTATIVE

Federal Funds

General and special funds:

SALARIES AND EXPENSES

For necessary expenses of the Office of the United States Trade Representative, including the hire of passenger motor vehicles and the employment of experts and consultants as authorized by 5 U.S.C. 3109, [$25,635,000] *$28,300,000*, of which $1,000,000 shall remain available until expended: *Provided,* That not to exceed $98,000 shall be available for official reception and representation expenses. *(Department of Commerce and Related Agencies Appropriations Act, 2000, as enacted by section 1000(a)(1) of the Consolidated Appropriations Act, 2000 (P.L. 106–113).)*

Program and Financing (in millions of dollars)

Identification code 11–0400–0–1–802	1999 actual	2000 est.	2001 est.
Obligations by program activity:			
00.01 Trade coordination and negotiation	23	22	25
00.02 Geneva trade negotiations	3	3	3
10.00 Total new obligations	26	25	28
Budgetary resources available for obligation:			
22.00 New budget authority (gross)	26	26	28
23.95 Total new obligations	−26	−25	−28
New budget authority (gross), detail:			
Discretionary:			
40.00 Appropriation	26	26	28
Change in unpaid obligations:			
72.40 Unpaid obligations, start of year: Obligated balance, start of year	5	2	3
73.10 Total new obligations	26	25	28
73.20 Total outlays (gross)	−26	−25	−29
73.40 Adjustments in expired accounts (net)	−3		
74.40 Unpaid obligations, end of year: Obligated balance, end of year	2	3	2
Outlays (gross), detail:			
86.90 Outlays from new discretionary authority	24	23	26
86.93 Outlays from discretionary balances	2	2	3
87.00 Total outlays (gross)	26	25	29
Net budget authority and outlays:			
89.00 Budget authority	26	26	28
90.00 Outlays	26	25	29

The United States Trade Representative is responsible for developing, coordinating, and advising the President on U.S. international trade policy. The Trade Representative is responsible for the conduct of international trade negotiations, including commodity and direct investment negotiations. The Trade Representative also conducts U.S. affairs relating to the World Trade Organization, in which the United States participates.

Object Classification (in millions of dollars)

Identification code 11–0400–0–1–802	1999 actual	2000 est.	2001 est.
11.1 Personnel compensation: Full-time permanent	14	14	15
12.1 Civilian personnel benefits	3	4	4
21.0 Travel and transportation of persons	3	2	2
23.1 Rental payments to GSA	2	2	2
23.3 Communications, utilities, and miscellaneous charges	2	1	2
25.2 Other services	2	2	2
31.0 Equipment			1
99.9 Total new obligations	26	25	28

Personnel Summary

Identification code 11–0400–0–1–802	1999 actual	2000 est.	2001 est.
1001 Total compensable workyears: Full-time equivalent employment	169	178	190

UNANTICIPATED NEEDS

Federal Funds

General and special funds:

UNANTICIPATED NEEDS

For expenses necessary to enable the President to meet unanticipated needs, in furtherance of the national interest, security, or de-

General and special funds—Continued

UNANTICIPATED NEEDS—Continued

fense which may arise at home or abroad during the current fiscal year, as authorized by 3 U.S.C. 108, *$3,500,000, of which $2,500,000 is to be provided to the Elections Commission of the Commonwealth of Puerto Rico as a transfer to be used for citizens' education and a choice by voters regarding the islands' future status. (Executive Office Appropriations Act, 2000.)*

Program and Financing (in millions of dollars)

Identification code 11–0037–0–1–802	1999 actual	2000 est.	2001 est.
Obligations by program activity:			
00.01 Payment to the Red Cross	30		
00.02 Payment to Commonwealth of Puerto Rico			2
00.03 Unanticipated Needs		1	1
10.00 Total new obligations	30	1	3
Budgetary resources available for obligation:			
22.00 New budget authority (gross)	31	1	3
23.95 Total new obligations	−30	−1	−3
23.98 Unobligated balance expiring or withdrawn	−1		
New budget authority (gross), detail:			
Discretionary:			
40.00 Appropriation	1	1	4
40.15 Appropriation (emergency)	30		
43.00 Appropriation (total discretionary)	31	1	4
Change in unpaid obligations:			
73.10 Total new obligations	30	1	3
73.20 Total outlays (gross)	−30	−1	−4
Outlays (gross), detail:			
86.90 Outlays from new discretionary authority	30	1	4
Net budget authority and outlays:			
89.00 Budget authority	31	1	3
90.00 Outlays	30	1	3

These funds will enable the President to meet unanticipated needs in furtherance of the national interest, security, or defense. In 2000, $325,000 was provided for establishment of the White House Council on Youth Violence.

Object Classification (in millions of dollars)

Identification code 11–0037–0–1–802	1999 actual	2000 est.	2001 est.
41.0 Grants, subsidies, and contributions	30		2
92.0 Undistributed		1	1
99.9 Total new obligations	30	1	3

UNANTICIPATED NEEDS FOR NATURAL DISASTERS

Program and Financing (in millions of dollars)

Identification code 11–0033–0–1–453	1999 actual	2000 est.	2001 est.
Budgetary resources available for obligation:			
21.40 Unobligated balance available, start of year	16	6	6
22.00 New budget authority (gross)	−10		
23.90 Total budgetary resources available for obligation	6	6	6
23.95 Total new obligations			
24.40 Unobligated balance available, end of year	6	6	6
New budget authority (gross), detail:			
Discretionary:			
40.00 Appropriation			
40.35 Appropriation rescinded	−10		
43.00 Appropriation (total discretionary)	−10		
Net budget authority and outlays:			
89.00 Budget authority	−10		
90.00 Outlays			

This schedule includes funding provided in Public Laws 101–130 and 103–211 to respond to various natural disasters. All available funds from this account were allocated to various agencies. However, certain agencies subsequently returned excess funds to this account. In P.L. 106–31, $10 million in unobligated balances were rescinded. A balance of $6 million in emergency funding remains.

INFORMATION TECHNOLOGY SYSTEMS AND RELATED EXPENSES

(INCLUDING TRANSFER OF FUNDS)

Program and Financing (in millions of dollars)

Identification code 11–1237–0–1–808	1999 actual	2000 est.	2001 est.
Obligations by program activity:			
00.01 Expenditure transfer to FAA	123		
10.00 Total new obligations	123		
Budgetary resources available for obligation:			
22.00 New budget authority (gross)	123		
22.22 Unobligated balance transferred from other accounts		5	
23.90 Total budgetary resources available for obligation	123	5	
23.95 Total new obligations	−123		
23.98 Unobligated balance expiring or withdrawn		−5	
New budget authority (gross), detail:			
Discretionary:			
40.15 Appropriation (emergency)	2,250	289	
40.60 Contingent emergency appropriation not available for obligations	−290	−239	
41.00 Transferred to other accounts	−1,837	−50	
42.00 Transferred from other accounts			
43.00 Appropriation (total discretionary)	123		
Change in unpaid obligations:			
73.10 Total new obligations	123		
73.20 Total outlays (gross)	−123		
Outlays (gross), detail:			
86.90 Outlays from new discretionary authority	123		
Net budget authority and outlays:			
89.00 Budget authority	123		
90.00 Outlays	123		

This account was created in Public Law 105–277, the Omnibus Consolidated and Emergency Supplemental Appropriations Act, 1999, to address requirements associated with Year 2000 (Y2K) computer conversion. A total of $2,250 million in contingent emergency funding was provided, to be transferred to non-defense agencies as unforseen requirements are identified. Defense-related funding was provided in the Department of Defense, Information Technology Systems and Security Transfer Account.

The $2,023 million transferred from this account to date has been allocated as follows:

Allocation of Y2K Emergency Funding in FY 1999 and 2000

[budget authority, in thousands of dollars]

Legislative and Judicial Branches	29,917
Department of Agriculture	57,103
Department of Commerce	61,568
Department of Education	5,298
Department of Energy	37,490
Department of Health and Human Services	323,858
Department of Housing and Urban Development	14,580
Department of the Interior	127,039
Department of Justice	93,998
Department of Labor	24,336
Department of State	79,744
Department of Transportation ($87 million expenditure transfer to FAA)	198,960
Department of the Treasury	650,957

Selective Service System	250
Environmental Protection Agency	3,695
Executive Office of the President/Office of Administration	29,791
Executive Office of the President/United States Trade Representative	498
FEMA	14,661
GSA	92,603
International Assistance/Agency for International Development	11,410
International Assistance/Overseas Private Investment Corporation	2,100
International Assistance/Peace Corps	1,554
International Assistance/African Development Foundation	137
Office of Personnel Management	2,428
Small Business Administration	4,840
Access Board	60
Commodity Futures Trading Commission	356
Committee for Purchase from People Who are Blind or Severely Disabled	65
Consumer Product Safety Commission	75
Corporation for National Community Service	800
Court Services and Offender Supervision Agency for the District of Columbia	848
District of Columbia	105,264
District of Columbia Courts	2,553
Export-Import Bank	400
Federal Communications Commission	8,516
Federal Labor Relations Authority	243
Federal Maritime Commission	516
Federal Trade Commission	2,599
International Trade Commission	300
Marine Mammal Commission	38
Merit Systems Protection Board	141
National Archives and Records Administration	6,662
National Capital Planning Commission	381
National Labor Relations Board	348
Office of Special Counsel	100
Railroad Retirement Board	398
Securities and Exchange Commission	8,175
Smithsonian	4,700
National Gallery of Art	165
US Holocaust Memorial Council	900
USIA	9,562
Total, Emergency Releases	2,022,979

A total of $246.158 million remains in the contingent emergency reserve for non-defense activities. This level includes $13.650 million that was allocated to the Department of Energy on February 3, 1999, but was not transferred; $1.293 million returned to the fund by the Department of Labor; $0.529 million allocated but not transferred to the Department of the Treasury; and, $3.648 million returned to the fund by the Department of Commerce. The supplemental chapter of this volume includes a proposal to reduce the remaining authority by $225 million.

186-484 00 - 31

FEDERAL EMERGENCY MANAGEMENT AGENCY

The Federal Emergency Management Agency (FEMA) was established by the President in Reorganization Plan No. 3 of 1978. FEMA's mission is to reduce the loss of life and property and protect our institutions from all hazards by leading and supporting the Nation in a comprehensive, risk-based emergency management program of mitigation, preparedness, response, and recovery.

Under the authority of the Robert T. Stafford Act, FEMA is responsible for providing assistance to maintain and enhance the nation's all-hazards emergency management capability and coordinates Federal emergency recovery and response operations. FEMA also administers the National Flood Insurance Program, which is the primary source of flood insurance in the nation, and provides essential training for State and local fire and emergency medical services personnel through the National Fire Academy. In 1999, FEMA provided $3.7 billion in direct assistance to States, local governments, and individuals stricken by natural disasters, furnished over $504 billion in flood insurance coverage to over 4 million policy holders, and awarded $181 million in grants to support emergency management preparedness and mitigation capabilities.

The President's 2001 Budget includes $3.6 billion ($971 million in discretionary budget authority and $2.6 billion in emergency funding) to:

Provide funding for FEMA's Disaster Relief Fund, the main source of Federal disaster assistance;

Develop disaster resistant communities across the nation through Project Impact;

Provide grants to State and local governments to help support a wide variety of emergency management functions, including response plans for terrorist attacks;

Provide emergency supplementary funding for non-profit organizations that feed and shelter the nation's homeless; and

Begin major reforms in the National Flood Insurance program.

To initiate the modernization of FEMA's inventory of floodplain maps, the 2001 Budget will allow FEMA to spend up to $134 million derived from two new sources. First, $104 million will be generated from a $12 map license fee. Second, an amendment to the Stafford Act is sought to allow FEMA to obligate up to $30 million derived from the Disaster Relief Fund. To begin a program of targeted purchases of insured properties with a history of repetitive flooding, an amendment to the Stafford Act is sought to allow FEMA to obligate up to $50 million per year from the Disaster Relief Fund for repetitive loss buyouts following disaster declarations.

A more detailed description of each of FEMA's programs follows the presentation of each of the budget accounts.

Federal Funds

General and special funds:

Disaster Relief

(INCLUDING TRANSFER OF FUNDS)

For necessary expenses in carrying out the Robert T. Stafford Disaster Relief and Emergency Assistance Act (42 U.S.C. 5121 et seq.), $300,000,000, and, notwithstanding 42 U.S.C. 5203, to remain available until expended, of which not to exceed $2,900,000 may be transferred to "Emergency Management Planning and Assistance" for the consolidated emergency management performance grant program[: *Provided*, That of the funds made available under this heading in this and prior appropriations Acts and under section 404 of the Stafford Act to the State of California, $2,000,000 shall be for a pilot project of seismic retrofit technology at California State University, San Bernardino; $6,000,000 shall be for a seismic retrofit project at Loma Linda University Hospital; and $2,000,000 shall be for a seismic retrofit project at the University of Redlands, Redlands, California: *Provided further*, That of the funds made available under this heading in this and prior appropriations Acts and under section 404 of the Stafford Act to the State of Florida, $1,000,000 shall be for a hurricane protection project for the St. Petersburg campus of South Florida University, and $2,500,000 shall be for a windstorm simulation project at Florida International University, Miami: *Provided further*, That of the funds made available under this heading in this and prior appropriations Acts and under section 404 of the Stafford Act to the State of North Carolina, $1,000,000 shall be for a logistical staging area concept demonstration involving warehouse facilities at the Stanly County Airport: *Provided further*, That of the funds made available under this heading in this and prior appropriations Acts and under section 404 of the Stafford Act to the State of Louisiana, $500,000 shall be for wave monitoring buoys in the Gulf of Mexico off the Louisiana coast]*; of which up to $30,000,000 may be obligated for flood map modernization activities; and up to $50,000,000 may be obligated for repetitive loss buyouts following disaster declarations.*

For an additional amount for "Disaster relief", [$2,480,425,000] *$2,609,220,000*, to remain available until expended: *Provided*, That the entire amount is designated by the Congress as an emergency requirement pursuant to section 251(b)(2)(A) of the Balanced Budget and Emergency Deficit Control Act of 1985, as amended: *Provided further*, That the entire amount shall be available only to the extent that an official budget request for a specific dollar amount, that includes designation of the entire amount of the request as an emergency requirement as defined in the Balanced Budget and Emergency Deficit Control Act of 1985, as amended, is transmitted by the President to the Congress. *(Departments of Veterans Affairs and Housing and Urban Development, and Independent Agencies Appropriations Act, 2000.)*

[Of the unobligated balances made available under the second paragraph under the heading "Federal Emergency Management Agency, Disaster Relief" in Public Law 106–74, in addition to other amounts made available, up to $215,000,000 may be used by the Director of the Federal Emergency Management Agency for the buyout of homeowners (or the relocation of structures) for principal residences that have been made uninhabitable by flooding caused by Hurricane Floyd and surrounding events and are located in a 100-year floodplain: *Provided*, That no homeowner may receive any assistance for buyouts in excess of the fair market value of the residence on September 1, 1999 (reduced by any proceeds from insurance or any other source paid or owed as a result of the flood damage to the residence): *Provided further*, That each State shall ensure that there is a contribution from non-Federal sources of not less than 25 percent in matching funds (other than administrative costs) for any funds allocated to the State for buyout assistance: *Provided further*, That all buyouts under this section shall be subject to the terms and conditions specified under 42 U.S.C. 5170c(b)(2)(B): *Provided further*, That none of the funds made available for buyouts under this paragraph may be used in any calculation of a State's section 404 allocation: *Provided further*, That the Director shall report quarterly to the House and Senate Committees on Appropriations on the use of all funds allocated under this paragraph and certify that the use of all funds are consistent with all applicable laws and requirements: *Provided further*, That the Inspector General for the Federal Emergency Management Agency shall establish a task force to review all uses of funds allocated under this paragraph to ensure compliance with all applicable laws and requirements: *Provided further*, That no funds shall be allocated for buyouts under this paragraph except in accordance with regulations promulgated by the Director: *Provided further,* That the Director shall promulgate regulations not later than December 31, 1999, pertaining to the buyout program which shall include eligibility criteria, procedures for prioritizing projects, requirements for the submission of State

General and special funds—Continued

DISASTER RELIEF—Continued

(*INCLUDING TRANSFER OF FUNDS*)—Continued

and local buyout plans, an identification of the Federal Emergency Management Agency's oversight responsibilities, procedures for cost-benefit analysis, and the process for measuring program results: *Provided further*, That the Director shall report to Congress not later than December 31, 1999, on the feasibility and justification of reducing buyout assistance to those who fail to purchase and maintain flood insurance: *Provided further*, That the entire amount shall be available only to the extent an official budget request, that includes designation of the entire amount of the request as an emergency requirement as defined by the Balanced Budget and Emergency Deficit Control Act of 1985, as amended, is transmitted by the President to the Congress: *Provided further*, That the entire amount is designated by the Congress as an emergency requirement pursuant to section 251(b)(2)(A) of the Balanced Budget and Emergency Deficit Control Act of 1985, as amended.] *(Miscellaneous Appropriations, 2000, as enacted by section 1000(a)(5) of the Consolidated Appropriations Act, 2000 (P.L. 106–113).)*

Program and Financing (in millions of dollars)

Identification code 58–0104–0–1–453	1999 actual	2000 est.	2001 est.
Obligations by program activity:			
10.00 Total new obligations	4,403	1,334	397
Budgetary resources available for obligation:			
21.40 Unobligated balance available, start of year	2,390	938	2,469
22.00 New budget authority (gross)	2,114	2,765	2,906
22.10 Resources available from recoveries of prior year obligations	838	100	100
22.21 Unobligated balance transferred to other accounts	−1		
23.90 Total budgetary resources available for obligation	5,341	3,803	5,475
23.95 Total new obligations	−4,403	−1,334	−397
24.40 Unobligated balance available, end of year	938	2,469	5,078
New budget authority (gross), detail:			
Discretionary:			
40.00 Appropriation	2,114	300	300
40.15 Appropriation (emergency)		2,480	2,609
40.60 Contingent emergency appropriation not available for obligations			
40.76 Reduction pursuant to P.L. 106–113		−12	
41.00 Transferred to other accounts		−3	−3
43.00 Appropriation (total discretionary)	2,114	2,765	2,906
Change in unpaid obligations:			
72.40 Unpaid obligations, start of year: Obligated balance, start of year	6,557	6,376	4,858
73.10 Total new obligations	4,403	1,334	397
73.20 Total outlays (gross)	−3,746	−2,752	−1,838
73.45 Adjustments in unexpired accounts	−838	−100	−100
74.40 Unpaid obligations, end of year: Obligated balance, end of year	6,376	4,858	3,317
Outlays (gross), detail:			
86.90 Outlays from new discretionary authority	632	192	193
86.93 Outlays from discretionary balances	3,114	2,560	1,645
87.00 Total outlays (gross)	3,746	2,752	1,838
Net budget authority and outlays:			
89.00 Budget authority	2,114	2,765	2,906
90.00 Outlays	3,746	2,752	1,838

Through the Disaster Relief Fund (DRF), FEMA provides a significant portion of the total Federal response to victims in Presidentially-declared major disasters and emergencies. Major disasters are declared when a State requests Federal assistance and has proven that a given disaster is beyond the State's capacity to respond. Under the DRF, FEMA provides three main types of assistance: individual and family assistance; public assistance, which includes the repair and reconstruction of State, local, and non-profit infrastructure; and hazard mitigation.

The 2001 Budget request includes a total of $2.9 billion in both regular discretionary and emergency budget resources, $300 million and $2.6 billion respectively, which represents the five-year historical average of obligations excluding the Northridge earthquake, and disaster support costs.

Object Classification (in millions of dollars)

Identification code 58–0104–0–1–453	1999 actual	2000 est.	2001 est.
Personnel compensation:			
11.1 Full-time permanent	1	2	2
11.3 Other than full-time permanent	108	85	53
11.5 Other personnel compensation	25	21	12
11.9 Total personnel compensation	134	108	67
12.1 Civilian personnel benefits	17	15	12
21.0 Travel and transportation of persons	61	53	9
22.0 Transportation of things	7	4	1
23.1 Rental payments to GSA	7	8	7
23.2 Rental payments to others	7	5	4
23.3 Communications, utilities, and miscellaneous charges	31	21	16
24.0 Printing and reproduction	4	3	1
25.1 Advisory and assistance services	1	1	1
25.2 Other services	132	70	51
25.3 Purchases of goods and services from Government accounts	211	118	65
25.4 Operation and maintenance of facilities	7	4	3
25.5 Research and development contracts	1	1	
25.7 Operation and maintenance of equipment	1	2	2
26.0 Supplies and materials	16	16	9
31.0 Equipment	30	22	14
32.0 Land and structures	1	1	
41.0 Grants, subsidies, and contributions	3,735	882	135
99.9 Total new obligations	4,403	1,334	397

Personnel Summary

Identification code 58–0104–0–1–453	1999 actual	2000 est.	2001 est.
1001 Total compensable workyears: Full-time equivalent employment	2,968	2,400	2,400

DISASTER ASSISTANCE FOR UNMET NEEDS

Program and Financing (in millions of dollars)

Identification code 58–0107–0–1–453	1999 actual	2000 est.	2001 est.
Obligations by program activity:			
10.00 Total new obligations		230	
Budgetary resources available for obligation:			
21.40 Unobligated balance available, start of year		230	
22.00 New budget authority (gross)	230		
23.90 Total budgetary resources available for obligation	230	230	
23.95 Total new obligations		−230	
24.40 Unobligated balance available, end of year	230		
New budget authority (gross), detail:			
Discretionary:			
40.00 Appropriation	230		
Change in unpaid obligations:			
72.40 Unpaid obligations, start of year: Obligated balance, start of year			156
73.10 Total new obligations		230	
73.20 Total outlays (gross)		−74	−97
74.40 Unpaid obligations, end of year: Obligated balance, end of year		156	59
Outlays (gross), detail:			
86.93 Outlays from discretionary balances		74	97
Net budget authority and outlays:			
89.00 Budget authority	230		
90.00 Outlays		74	97

Public Law 106–31 provided funding for unmet needs related to disasters declared in 1998 and 1999 for the purposes of disaster relief, buyout assistance, long-term recovery, or mitigation in communities which have not or will not be addressed by other Federal disaster assistance programs. The Department of Housing and Urban Development previously managed the unmet needs program. Funds for disaster assistance unmet needs are available until September 30, 2001.

PRE-DISASTER MITIGATION

(INCLUDING TRANSFER OF FUNDS)

For necessary expenses in carrying out pre-disaster mitigation pursuant to 42 U.S.C. 5131(a), (b), and (c), and 42 U.S.C. 5170(c), $30,000,000, to remain available until expended, of which not to exceed $2,600,000 may be transferred to "Emergency Management Planning and Assistance" for the consolidated emergency management performance grant program.

Program and Financing (in millions of dollars)

Identification code 58–0106–0–1–453	1999 actual	2000 est.	2001 est.
Obligations by program activity:			
00.01 Direct program			27
10.00 Total new obligations			27
Budgetary resources available for obligation:			
22.00 New budget authority (gross)			27
23.95 Total new obligations			–27
New budget authority (gross), detail:			
Discretionary:			
40.00 Appropriation			30
41.00 Transferred to other accounts			–3
43.00 Appropriation (total discretionary)			27
Change in unpaid obligations:			
73.10 Total new obligations			27
73.20 Total outlays (gross)			–14
74.40 Unpaid obligations, end of year: Obligated balance, end of year			13
Outlays (gross), detail:			
86.90 Outlays from new discretionary authority			14
Net budget authority and outlays:			
89.00 Budget authority			27
90.00 Outlays			14

The Pre-Disaster Mitigation program supports FEMA's Project Impact and represents a paradigm shift in the Federal government's approach to emergency management. This unique program, which began with seven pilot communities in 1997, focuses entirely on developing self-sustaining disaster mitigation programs at the community level. The 2001 Budget includes a request of $30 million and proposes a separate account for this program. Of this amount, $1 million will be allocated to protect the nation's investment in research universities and other higher educational institutions.

Communities selected to participate must demonstrate, through the grant application process, that both State and private sector parties have committed resources to the effort and that a comprehensive mitigation strategy has been adopted. The result is a self-sustaining mitigation program at the community level that uses Federal dollars to leverage additional resources and involves all sectors of the community in preparing for and preventing future losses from natural disasters. In addition to providing one-time grant funding, FEMA provides ongoing technical support to participating communities.

SALARIES AND EXPENSES

For necessary expenses, not otherwise provided for, including hire and purchase of motor vehicles as authorized by 31 U.S.C. 1343; uniforms, or allowances therefor, as authorized by 5 U.S.C. 5901–5902; services as authorized by 5 U.S.C. 3109, but at rates for individuals not to exceed the per diem rate equivalent to the maximum rate payable for senior level positions under 5 U.S.C. 5376; expenses of attendance of cooperating officials and individuals at meetings concerned with the work of emergency preparedness; transportation in connection with the continuity of Government programs to the same extent and in the same manner as permitted the Secretary of a Military Department under 10 U.S.C. 2632; and not to exceed $2,500 for official reception and representation expenses, [$180,000,000] *$221,024,000*. *(Departments of Veterans Affairs and Housing and Urban Development, and Independent Agencies Appropriations Act, 2000.)*

Program and Financing (in millions of dollars)

Identification code 58–0100–0–1–999	1999 actual	2000 est.	2001 est.
Obligations by program activity:			
Direct program:			
00.01 Response and recovery	42	47	47
00.02 Preparedness, training and exercises	21	23	24
00.03 Fire prevention and training	7	7	9
00.04 Operations support	29	28	54
00.05 Information technology services	27	26	28
00.06 Mitigation programs	7	8	10
00.07 Policy and regional operations	12	12	12
00.08 Executive direction	29	33	37
09.01 Reimbursable program	3	6	6
10.00 Total new obligations	177	190	227
Budgetary resources available for obligation:			
21.40 Unobligated balance available, start of year	4	2	
22.00 New budget authority (gross)	177	188	227
23.90 Total budgetary resources available for obligation	181	190	227
23.95 Total new obligations	–177	–190	–227
23.98 Unobligated balance expiring or withdrawn	–2		
24.40 Unobligated balance available, end of year	2		
New budget authority (gross), detail:			
Discretionary:			
40.00 Appropriation	171	180	221
42.00 Transferred from other accounts	4	2	
43.00 Appropriation (total discretionary)	175	182	221
Spending authority from offsetting collections:			
Offsetting collections (cash):			
68.00 Spending authority from offsetting collections, defense programs	3	4	4
68.00 Spending authority from offsetting collections, non-defense programs		2	2
68.90 Spending authority from offsetting collections (total discretionary)	3	6	6
70.00 Total new budget authority (gross)	178	188	227
Change in unpaid obligations:			
72.40 Unpaid obligations, start of year: Obligated balance, start of year	29	37	38
73.10 Total new obligations	177	190	227
73.20 Total outlays (gross)	–171	–189	–221
73.40 Adjustments in expired accounts (net)	2		
74.40 Unpaid obligations, end of year: Obligated balance, end of year	37	38	44
Outlays (gross), detail:			
86.90 Outlays from new discretionary authority	148	161	194
86.93 Outlays from discretionary balances	23	28	27
87.00 Total outlays (gross)	171	189	221
Offsets:			
Against gross budget authority and outlays:			
Offsetting collections (cash) from:			
Federal sources:			
88.00 Federal sources, defense programs	–3	–4	–4
88.00 Federal sources, non-defense programs		–2	–2
88.90 Total, offsetting collections (cash)	–3	–6	–6
Net budget authority and outlays:			
89.00 Budget authority	175	182	221

General and special funds—Continued

SALARIES AND EXPENSES—Continued

Program and Financing (in millions of dollars)—Continued

Identification code 58–0100–0–1–999	1999 actual	2000 est.	2001 est.
90.00 Outlays	168	183	215

Program support.—This activity provides the necessary resources to administer the Federal Emergency Management Agency's (the Agency) various programs at headquarters and in the regions.

Executive direction.—This activity provides for the general management and administration of the Agency in legal, congressional, governmental and media affairs, and financial and personnel management, as well as the management of the Agency's national security program.

The 2001 Budget request includes funding to ensure that six Urban Search and Rescue teams are fully operational for responding to any potential incidents involving weapons of mass destruction during the 2002 Winter Olympics and one-time costs associated with relocating FEMA's headquarters. FEMA's current lease expires in August 2001, and a location is sought that will be more secure and support a state-of-the-art operations center necessitated by the Agency's role in disaster response.

For a programmatic description of FEMA's eight operational components, see the descriptions under the Emergency Management, Planning, and Assistance account.

Object Classification (in millions of dollars)

Identification code 58–0100–0–1–999		1999 actual	2000 est.	2001 est.
	Direct obligations:			
	Personnel compensation:			
11.1	Full-time permanent	99	107	114
11.3	Other than full-time permanent	2	2	2
11.5	Other personnel compensation	3	5	3
11.9	Total personnel compensation	104	114	119
12.1	Civilian personnel benefits	23	24	26
21.0	Travel and transportation of persons	4	5	4
23.1	Rental payments to GSA	10	11	16
23.3	Communications, utilities, and miscellaneous charges	4	4	4
25.2	Other services	11	7	10
25.3	Purchases of goods and services from Government accounts	13	14	20
26.0	Supplies and materials	2	2	2
31.0	Equipment	3	3	9
32.0	Land and structures			11
99.0	Subtotal, direct obligations	174	184	221
99.0	Reimbursable obligations	3	6	6
99.9	Total new obligations	177	190	227

Personnel Summary

Identification code 58–0100–0–1–999		1999 actual	2000 est.	2001 est.
	Direct:			
1001	Total compensable workyears: Full-time equivalent employment	1,687	1,763	1,783
	Reimbursable:			
2001	Total compensable workyears: Full-time equivalent employment	41	57	57

EMERGENCY MANAGEMENT PLANNING AND ASSISTANCE

(INCLUDING TRANSFER OF FUNDS)

For necessary expenses, not otherwise provided for, to carry out activities under the National Flood Insurance Act of 1968, as amended, and the Flood Disaster Protection Act of 1973, as amended (42 U.S.C. 4001 et seq.), the Robert T. Stafford Disaster Relief and Emergency Assistance Act (42 U.S.C. 5121 et seq.), the Earthquake Hazards Reduction Act of 1977, as amended (42 U.S.C. 7701 et seq.), the Federal Fire Prevention and Control Act of 1974, as amended (15 U.S.C. 2201 et seq.), the Defense Production Act of 1950, as amended (50 U.S.C. App. 2061 et seq.), sections 107 and 303 of the National Security Act of 1947, as amended (50 U.S.C. 404–405), and Reorganization Plan No. 3 of 1978, [$267,000,000: *Provided*, That for purposes of pre-disaster mitigation pursuant to 42 U.S.C. 5131(b) and (c) and 42 U.S.C. 5196(e) and (i), $25,000,000 of the funds made available under this heading shall be available until expended for project grants: *Provided further*, That beginning in fiscal year 2000 and each fiscal year thereafter, and notwithstanding any other provision of law, the Director of FEMA is authorized to provide assistance from funds appropriated under this heading, subject to terms and conditions as the Director of FEMA shall establish, to any State for multi-hazard preparedness and mitigation through consolidated emergency management performance grants: *Provided further*, That notwithstanding any other provision of law, FEMA is authorized to and shall extend its cooperative agreement for the Jones County, Mississippi Emergency Operating Center, and the funds which were obligated as Federal matching funds for that Center shall remain available for expenditure until September 30, 2001] *$269,652,000. (Departments of Veterans Affairs and Housing and Urban Development, and Independent Agencies Appropriations Act, 2000.)*

Program and Financing (in millions of dollars)

Identification code 58–0101–0–1–999		1999 actual	2000 est.	2001 est.
	Obligations by program activity:			
	Direct program:			
00.01	Response and recovery	9	12	15
00.02	Preparedness	131	11	10
00.03	Fire prevention and training	25	36	61
00.04	Operations support	4	5	4
00.05	Information technology services	17	17	17
00.06	Mitigation programs	73	44	19
00.07	Policy and Regional Operations	1	1	1
00.08	Executive Direction	10	148	149
09.01	Reimbursable program	61	89	38
10.00	Total new obligations	331	363	314
	Budgetary resources available for obligation:			
21.40	Unobligated balance available, start of year	26	4	
22.00	New budget authority (gross)	311	359	314
23.90	Total budgetary resources available for obligation	337	363	314
23.95	Total new obligations	−331	−363	−314
23.98	Unobligated balance expiring or withdrawn	−2		
24.40	Unobligated balance available, end of year	4		
	New budget authority (gross), detail:			
	Discretionary:			
40.00	Appropriation	241	267	270
42.00	Transferred from other accounts	9	3	6
43.00	Appropriation (total discretionary)	250	270	276
	Spending authority from offsetting collections:			
	Offsetting collections (cash):			
68.00	Spending authority from offsetting collections, defense program	59	86	36
68.00	Spending authority from offsetting collections, non-defense program	2	3	2
68.10	From Federal sources: Change in receivables and unpaid, unfilled orders	119		
68.15	From Federal sources: Adjustments to receivables and unpaid, unfilled orders	−119		
68.90	Spending authority from offsetting collections (total discretionary)	61	89	38
70.00	Total new budget authority (gross)	311	359	314
	Change in unpaid obligations:			
	Unpaid obligations, start of year:			
72.40	Obligated balance, start of year	120	276	293
72.95	From Federal sources: Receivables and unpaid, unfilled orders	48	167	167
72.99	Total unpaid obligations, start of year	168	443	460
73.10	Total new obligations	331	363	314
73.20	Total outlays (gross)	−165	−346	−309
73.40	Adjustments in expired accounts (net)	109		

		1999 actual	2000 est.	2001 est.
	Unpaid obligations, end of year:			
74.40	Obligated balance, end of year	276	293	298
74.95	From Federal sources: Receivables and unpaid, unfilled orders	167	167	167
74.99	Total unpaid obligations, end of year	443	460	465
	Outlays (gross), detail:			
86.90	Outlays from new discretionary authority	165	211	162
86.93	Outlays from discretionary balances		135	147
87.00	Total outlays (gross)	165	346	309
	Offsets:			
	Against gross budget authority and outlays:			
88.00	Offsetting collections (cash) from: Federal sources	−61	−89	−38
	Against gross budget authority only:			
88.95	From Federal sources: Change in receivables and unpaid, unfilled orders	−119		
88.96	From Federal sources: Adjustment to receivables and unpaid, unfilled orders	119		
	Net budget authority and outlays:			
89.00	Budget authority	249	270	276
90.00	Outlays	104	257	271

Response and recovery.—This activity provides for the development and maintenance of an integrated operational capability to respond to and recover from the consequences of a disaster, regardless of its cause, in partnership with other Federal agencies, State and local governments, volunteer organizations, and the private sector. The intended results of this activity are to: provide services to disaster stricken communities with an increase in timeliness; to refine program delivery activities to effect increased cost efficiency; and, to increase customer satisfaction with the delivery of services.

Preparedness, training and exercises.—This activity provides policy guidance, financial and technical assistance, training, and exercise support required to establish or enhance the emergency management capabilities of Federal, State, and local governments, thereby fostering a decentralized capability for state and local preparedness and response for all but the most catastrophic disasters.

Fire prevention and training.—This activity prepares Federal, State and local officials, their staffs, emergency first responders, volunteer groups, and the public to meet the responsibilities of domestic emergencies through planning, mitigation, preparedness, response, and recovery. The United States Fire Administration has responsibility for all fire and emergency medical service programs and training activities. Educational programs are provided through the National Fire Academy, at the National Emergency Training Center, and through field delivery systems. The 2001 Budget includes $25 million to develop a pilot demonstration grant program to provide equipment to improve the health and safety of firefighters in needy and distressed communities.

Operations support.—This activity provides agency-wide program support services, such as logistics management and security.

Information technology services.—This activity provides leadership and direction for management of information technology resources, automated data processing, telecommunications, and information services and systems necessary to accomplish the agency's mission.

Mitigation programs.—This activity provides for the development, coordination, and implementation of policies, plans, and programs to eliminate or reduce the long-term risk to life and property from natural and technological hazards, such as earthquakes and hurricanes. A goal of this activity is to encourage and foster mitigation strategies at the State and local levels.

Policy and Regional Operations.—This activity provides support to management in the areas of policy development, strategic planning studies, and analyses.

Executive direction.—This activity develops strategies to address public information issues; provides support for enhancements to the financial management system; builds partnerships with and among State and local governments, non-government organizations, and business and industry; and supports the Agency's national security program. This activity also includes the Agency's consolidated emergency management performance grants that are provided to State emergency management agencies.

Object Classification (in millions of dollars)

Identification code 58–0101–0–1–999		1999 actual	2000 est.	2001 est.
	Direct obligations:			
23.3	Communications, utilities, and miscellaneous charges	9	9	10
24.0	Printing and reproduction	2	2	2
25.1	Advisory and assistance services	4	5	5
25.2	Other services	39	54	48
25.3	Purchases of goods and services from Government accounts	13	11	11
25.4	Operation and maintenance of facilities	4	4	4
25.7	Operation and maintenance of equipment	1	1	1
26.0	Supplies and materials	4	3	3
31.0	Equipment	5	5	8
32.0	Land and structures		4	4
41.0	Grants, subsidies, and contributions	189	176	180
99.0	Subtotal, direct obligations	270	274	276
99.0	Reimbursable obligations	61	89	38
99.9	Total new obligations	331	363	314

OFFICE OF THE INSPECTOR GENERAL

For necessary expenses of the Office of Inspector General in carrying out the Inspector General Act of 1978, as amended, [$8,015,000] *$8,476,000. (Departments of Veterans Affairs and Housing and Urban Development, and Independent Agencies Appropriations Act, 2000.)*

Program and Financing (in millions of dollars)

Identification code 58–0300–0–1–453		1999 actual	2000 est.	2001 est.
	Obligations by program activity:			
00.01	Direct program	5	8	8
10.00	Total new obligations	5	8	8
	Budgetary resources available for obligation:			
22.00	New budget authority (gross)	5	8	8
23.95	Total new obligations	−5	−8	−8
	New budget authority (gross), detail:			
	Discretionary:			
40.00	Appropriation	5	8	8
	Change in unpaid obligations:			
72.40	Unpaid obligations, start of year: Obligated balance, start of year	1	1	1
73.10	Total new obligations	5	8	8
73.20	Total outlays (gross)	−5	−8	−8
74.40	Unpaid obligations, end of year: Obligated balance, end of year	1	1	1
	Outlays (gross), detail:			
86.90	Outlays from new discretionary authority	4	7	7
86.93	Outlays from discretionary balances	1	1	1
87.00	Total outlays (gross)	5	8	8
	Net budget authority and outlays:			
89.00	Budget authority	5	8	8
90.00	Outlays	5	8	8

This appropriation provides agency-wide audit and investigative functions to identify and correct management and administrative deficiencies which create conditions for exist-

General and special funds—Continued

OFFICE OF THE INSPECTOR GENERAL—Continued

ing or potential instances of fraud, waste, and mismanagement. The audit function provides internal audit, contract audit, and inspections services. Contract audits provide professional advice to agency contracting officials on accounting and financial matters relative to the negotiation, award, administration, repricing, and settlement of contracts. Internal audits review and evaluate all facets of agency operations.

Object Classification (in millions of dollars)

Identification code 58–0300–0–1–453	1999 actual	2000 est.	2001 est.
11.1 Personnel compensation: Full-time permanent	4	7	7
12.1 Civilian personnel benefits	1	1	1
99.9 Total new obligations	5	8	8

Personnel Summary

Identification code 58–0300–0–1–453	1999 actual	2000 est.	2001 est.
1001 Total compensable workyears: Full-time equivalent employment	46	80	81

EMERGENCY FOOD AND SHELTER PROGRAM

To carry out an emergency food and shelter program pursuant to title III of Public Law 100–77, as amended, [$110,000,000] *$140,000,000*, to remain available until expended: *Provided*, That total administrative costs shall not exceed 3½ percent of the total appropriation. *(Departments of Veterans Affairs and Housing and Urban Development, and Independent Agencies Appropriations Act, 2000.)*

Program and Financing (in millions of dollars)

Identification code 58–0103–0–1–605	1999 actual	2000 est.	2001 est.
Obligations by program activity:			
01.01 Direct program	100	110	140
10.00 Total new obligations	100	110	140
Budgetary resources available for obligation:			
22.00 New budget authority (gross)	100	110	140
23.95 Total new obligations	−100	−110	−140
New budget authority (gross), detail:			
Discretionary:			
40.00 Appropriation	100	110	140
Change in unpaid obligations:			
73.10 Total new obligations	100	110	140
73.20 Total outlays (gross)	−100	−110	−140
Outlays (gross), detail:			
86.90 Outlays from new discretionary authority	100	110	140
Net budget authority and outlays:			
89.00 Budget authority	100	110	140
90.00 Outlays	100	110	140

This program provides grants to voluntary organizations at the local level to supplement their programs for emergency food and shelter. The 2001 Budget includes $140 million, reflecting the success and importance of this program in meeting the immediate needs of the homeless.

RADIOLOGICAL EMERGENCY PREPAREDNESS FUND

The aggregate charges assessed during fiscal year [2000] *2001*, as authorized by Public Law [105–276] *106–74*, shall not be less than 100 percent of the amounts anticipated by FEMA necessary for its radiological emergency preparedness program for the next fiscal year. The methodology for assessment and collection of fees shall be fair and equitable; and shall reflect costs of providing such services, including administrative costs of collecting such fees. Fees received pursuant to this section shall be deposited in the Fund as offsetting collections and will become available for authorized purposes on October 1, [2000] *2001*, and remain available until expended. *(Departments of Veterans Affairs and Housing and Urban Development, and Independent Agencies Appropriations Act, 2000.)*

Program and Financing (in millions of dollars)

Identification code 58–5436–0–1–453	1999 actual	2000 est.	2001 est.
Obligations by program activity:			
09.00 Reimbursable program	12	14	15
10.00 Total new obligations	12	14	15
Budgetary resources available for obligation:			
21.40 Unobligated balance available, start of year	....	1	....
22.00 New budget authority (gross)	13	13	15
23.90 Total budgetary resources available for obligation	13	14	15
23.95 Total new obligations	−12	−14	−15
24.40 Unobligated balance available, end of year	1	....	....
New budget authority (gross), detail:			
Discretionary:			
40.00 Appropriation	13	....	....
Spending authority from offsetting collections:			
68.00 Offsetting collections (cash)	13	15	15
68.26 Offsetting collections (unavailable balances)	....	13	15
68.45 Portion not available for obligation (limitation on obligations)	−13	−15	−15
68.90 Spending authority from offsetting collections (total discretionary)	....	13	15
70.00 Total new budget authority (gross)	13	13	15
Change in unpaid obligations:			
72.40 Unpaid obligations, start of year: Obligated balance, start of year	....	2	3
73.10 Total new obligations	12	14	15
73.20 Total outlays (gross)	−10	−13	−15
74.40 Unpaid obligations, end of year: Obligated balance, end of year	2	3	3
Outlays (gross), detail:			
86.90 Outlays from new discretionary authority	10	10	12
86.93 Outlays from discretionary balances	....	3	3
87.00 Total outlays (gross)	10	13	15
Offsets:			
Against gross budget authority and outlays:			
88.40 Offsetting collections (cash) from: Non-Federal sources	−13	−15	−15
Net budget authority and outlays:			
89.00 Budget authority	....	−2	....
90.00 Outlays	−3	−2	....

The Radiological Emergency Preparedness (REP) program assists State and local governments in the development of off-site radiological emergency plans and in preparedness within the emergency planning zones of Nuclear Regulatory Commission (NRC) licensed commercial nuclear power facilities. The fund is financed from fees assessed and collected from the NRC licensees to cover the cost of the REP program.

Personnel Summary

Identification code 58–5436–0–1–453	1999 actual	2000 est.	2001 est.
2001 Total compensable workyears: Full-time equivalent employment	79	90	90

FLOOD MAP MODERNIZATION FUND

[For necessary expenses pursuant to section 1360 of the National Flood Insurance Act of 1968, $5,000,000, and such additional sums as may be provided by State or local governments or other political subdivisions for cost shared mapping activities under section 1360(f)(2), to remain available until expended.] *(Departments of Veterans Affairs and Housing and Urban Development, and Independent Agencies Appropriations Act, 2000.)*

Program and Financing (in millions of dollars)

Identification code 58–5464–0–2–453	1999 actual	2000 est.	2001 est.
Obligations by program activity:			
00.01 Map Modernization		5	
10.00 Total new obligations		5	
Budgetary resources available for obligation:			
22.00 New budget authority (gross)		5	
23.95 Total new obligations		–5	
New budget authority (gross), detail:			
Discretionary:			
40.00 Appropriation		5	
Change in unpaid obligations:			
72.40 Unpaid obligations, start of year: Obligated balance, start of year			3
73.10 Total new obligations		5	
73.20 Total outlays (gross)		–2	–2
74.40 Unpaid obligations, end of year: Obligated balance, end of year		3	3
Outlays (gross), detail:			
86.90 Outlays from new discretionary authority		2	
86.93 Outlays from discretionary balances			2
87.00 Total outlays (gross)		2	2
Net budget authority and outlays:			
89.00 Budget authority		5	
90.00 Outlays		2	2

Summary of Budget Authority and Outlays

(in millions of dollars)

Enacted/requested:	*1999 actual*	*2000 est.*	*2001 est.*
Budget Authority		5	
Outlays		2	2
Legislative proposal, subject to PAYGO:			
Budget Authority			–104
Outlays			–57
Total:			
Budget Authority		5	–104
Outlays		2	–55

The Flood Map Modernization Fund will support a multi-year effort to update and modernize FEMA's inventory of over 100,000 flood maps.

The maps are used to determine appropriate risk-based premium rates for the National Flood Insurance Program, complete flood hazard determinations required of the nation's lending institutions for virtually all mortgage and mortgage refinancing transactions each year, plan sustainable development, and develop appropriate disaster response plans for Federal, State, and local emergency management personnel.

In 2001, FEMA plans to spend $134 million to initiate the flood map modernization initiative using funds derived from two new sources. First, $104 million will be generated from a $12 license fee for the use of flood hazard maps. Second, an amendment to the Stafford Act is sought to allow FEMA to obligate up to $30 million derived from the Disaster Relief Fund.

Flood Map Modernization Fund

(Legislative proposal, subject to PAYGO)

Program and Financing (in millions of dollars)

Identification code 58–5464–4–2–453	1999 actual	2000 est.	2001 est.
Obligations by program activity:			
09.01 Map Modernization			104
10.00 Total new obligations (object class 25.2)			104
Budgetary resources available for obligation:			
22.00 New budget authority (gross)			104
23.95 Total new obligations			–104
New budget authority (gross), detail:			
Mandatory:			
69.00 Offsetting collections (cash)			104
Change in unpaid obligations:			
73.10 Total new obligations			104
73.20 Total outlays (gross)			–47
74.40 Unpaid obligations, end of year: Obligated balance, end of year			57
Outlays (gross), detail:			
86.97 Outlays from new mandatory authority			47
Offsets:			
Against gross budget authority and outlays:			
88.40 Offsetting collections (cash) from: Non-Federal sources			–104
Net budget authority and outlays:			
89.00 Budget authority			
90.00 Outlays			–57

Public enterprise funds:

National Insurance Development Fund

[Notwithstanding the provisions of 12 U.S.C. 1735d(b) and 12 U.S.C. 1749bbb–13(b)(6), any indebtedness of the Director of the Federal Emergency Management Agency resulting from the Director borrowing sums under such sections before the date of the enactment of this Act to carry out title XII of the National Housing Act shall be canceled, and the Director shall not be obligated to repay such sums or any interest thereon, and no further interest shall accrue on such sums.] *(Departments of Veterans Affairs and Housing and Urban Development, and Independent Agencies Appropriations Act, 2000.)*

The National Insurance Development Fund was established from the proceeds of the Riot Reinsurance Program, which was terminated in 1983. Authorization for this program expired September 30, 1995. In 2000, all indebtedness related to this fund was canceled.

National Flood Insurance Fund

(including transfer of funds)

For activities under the National Flood Insurance Act of 1968, the Flood Disaster Protection Act of 1973, as amended, not to exceed [$24,333,000] *$25,736,000* for salaries and expenses associated with flood mitigation and flood insurance operations, and not to exceed [$78,710,000] *$77,307,000* for flood mitigation, including up to $20,000,000 for expenses under section 1366 of the National Flood Insurance Act, which amount shall be available for transfer to the National Flood Mitigation Fund until September 30, [2001] *2002*. In fiscal year [2000] *2001*, no funds in excess of: (1) [$47,000,000] *55,000,000* for operating expenses; (2) [$456,427,000] *$455,627,000* for agents' commissions and taxes; and (3) [$50,000,000] *$40,000,000* for interest on Treasury borrowings shall be available from the National Flood Insurance Fund without prior notice to the Committees on Appropriations. For fiscal year [2000] *2001*, flood insurance rates shall not exceed the level authorized by the National Flood Insurance Reform Act of 1994.

Public enterprise funds—Continued

NATIONAL FLOOD INSURANCE FUND—Continued

(INCLUDING TRANSFER OF FUNDS)—Continued

Section 1309(a)(2) of the National Flood Insurance Act (42 U.S.C. 4016(a)(2)), as amended by Public Law 104–208, is further amended by striking ["1999"] *"2000"* and inserting ["2000"] *"2001"*.

The first sentence of section 1376(c) of the National Flood Insurance Act of 1968, as amended (42 U.S.C. 4127(c)), is amended by striking "September 30, [1999]" *2000* and inserting "September 30, [2000]" *2001*. *(Departments of Veterans Affairs and Housing and Urban Development, and Independent Agencies Appropriations Act, 2000.)*

Unavailable Collections (in millions of dollars)

Identification code 58–4236–0–3–453	1999 actual	2000 est.	2001 est.
Balance, start of year:			
01.99 Balance, start of year	....	7	....
Appropriation:			
05.01 National flood insurance fund	....	−7	....
06.20 Reduction pursuant to Public Law 106–51	7	....	....
07.99 Total balance, end of year	7	....	....

Program and Financing (in millions of dollars)

Identification code 58–4236–0–3–453	1999 actual	2000 est.	2001 est.
Obligations by program activity:			
09.01 Insurance underwriting expense	409	474	511
09.02 Loss and adjustment expense	775	725	742
09.03 Interest expense	30	30	24
09.04 Flood insurance and mitigation program expense	70	80	83
10.00 Total new obligations	1,284	1,309	1,360
Budgetary resources available for obligation:			
22.00 New budget authority (gross)	1,282	1,309	1,360
22.10 Resources available from recoveries of prior year obligations	2	....	....
23.90 Total budgetary resources available for obligation	1,284	1,309	1,360
23.95 Total new obligations	−1,284	−1,309	−1,360
New budget authority (gross), detail:			
Mandatory:			
Offsetting collections (cash):			
69.00 Offsetting collections (cash)	1,323	1,445	1,548
69.00 Offsetting collections (cash)	93	100	104
69.26 Offsetting collections (unavailable balances)	....	7	....
69.47 Portion applied to repay debt	−107	−223	−272
69.61 Transferred to other accounts	−20	−20	−20
69.75 Reduction pursuant to P.L. 106–51	−7	....	....
69.90 Spending authority from offsetting collections (total mandatory)	1,282	1,309	1,360
Change in unpaid obligations:			
72.40 Unpaid obligations, start of year: Obligated balance, start of year	672	604	644
73.10 Total new obligations	1,284	1,309	1,360
73.20 Total outlays (gross)	−1,350	−1,270	−1,319
73.45 Adjustments in unexpired accounts	−2	....	....
74.40 Unpaid obligations, end of year: Obligated balance, end of year	604	644	685
Outlays (gross), detail:			
86.97 Outlays from new mandatory authority	1,096	1,005	1,066
86.98 Outlays from mandatory balances	254	265	253
87.00 Total outlays (gross)	1,350	1,270	1,319
Offsets:			
Against gross budget authority and outlays:			
Offsetting collections (cash) from:			
Non-Federal sources:			
88.40 Collection of program expenses	−1,323	−1,445	−1,548
88.40 Collection of program expenses	−93	−100	−104
88.90 Total, offsetting collections (cash)	−1,416	−1,545	−1,652
Net budget authority and outlays:			
89.00 Budget authority	−134	−236	−292
90.00 Outlays	−66	−275	−333

The National Flood Insurance Act of 1968, as amended, authorizes the Federal Government to provide flood insurance on a national basis. Flood insurance may be sold or continued in force only in communities which enact and enforce appropriate flood plain management measures. Communities must participate in the program within one year of the time they are identified as flood-prone in order to be eligible for flood insurance and some forms of Federal financial assistance for acquisition or construction purposes.

In addition, Federally regulated funding institutions can not provide loans to non-participating communities with an identified flood hazard. In 2001, the budget assumes collection of all of the administrative and program costs associated with flood insurance activities from policy holders.

Under the emergency program, structures in identified flood-prone areas are eligible for limited amounts of coverage at subsidized insurance rates. Under the regular program, studies must be made of different flood risks in flood-prone areas to establish actuarial premium rates. These rates are charged for insurance on new construction. Coverage is available on virtually all types of buildings and their contents in amounts up to $350 thousand for residential and $1 million for other types.

Budget program—Insurance underwriting expense.—Cost of initiating and maintaining flood insurance policies is estimated at $511 million in 2001.

Loss and adjustment expense.—Insured flood losses and associated loss adjustment expense is estimated at $742 million in 2001.

Interest expense.—Interest expenses for Treasury borrowings are projected; a ceiling of $40 million is requested to cover charges for purchasing Treasury securities and possible unanticipated interest costs.

Flood Insurance and Mitigation Program Expenses.—This activity is estimated at $103 million. FEMA will recover the cost of the following activities from a policy surcharge of $30:

Flood studies and surveys.—These studies are estimated at $50 million in 2001.

Flood hazard reduction.—This activity, which includes grants to States, is estimated at $7 million in 2001.

Mitigation assistance.—Up to $20 million will be transferred to the National Flood Mitigation Fund in 2001.

Salaries and expenses.—This activity provides for salaries and related expenses of all Federal staff administering the National Flood Insurance Program and is estimated at $26 million in 2001.

Financing.—The Administrator is authorized to borrow up to $1 billion ($1.5 billion in 1997 through 2000 only) to carry out the program. The program is financed through premium income and appropriations to repay borrowing.

Operating results.—Program experience is reviewed annually and, as necessary, flood insurance rates will be adjusted to maintain the NFIP's self-supporting status for the historical average loss year and to maintain the soundness of rates for actuarially rated policies.

Statement of Operations (in millions of dollars)

Identification code 58–4236–0–3–453	1998 actual	1999 actual	2000 est.	2001 est.
0101 Revenue	1,279	1,416	1,545	1,652
0102 Expense	−1,265	−1,284	−1,309	−1,360
0105 Net income or loss (−)	14	132	236	292

Balance Sheet (in millions of dollars)

Identification code 58–4236–0–3–453	1998 actual	1999 actual	2000 est.	2001 est.
ASSETS:				
Federal assets:				
1101 Fund balances with Treasury	87	150	10	10
Investments in US securities:				
1106 Receivables, net	3	....	....	....
Non-Federal assets:				
1206 Receivables, net	14	11	13	15
1207 Advances and prepayments	251	260	299	343
Other Federal assets:				
1801 Cash and other monetary assets	6	13	14	17
1802 Inventories and related properties	4	4	5	6
1999 Total assets	365	438	341	391
LIABILITIES:				
Federal liabilities:				
2101 Accounts payable	38	2	2	1
2102 Interest payable	19	14	15	12
2103 Debt	522	541	441	334
2104 Resources payable to Treasury	2	2	2	1
Non-Federal liabilities:				
2201 Accounts payable	459	35	26	20
2207 Other	881	1,394	772	826
2999 Total liabilities	1,921	1,988	1,258	1,194
NET POSITION:				
3100 Appropriated capital	–1,556	–1,550	–917	–803
3999 Total net position	–1,556	–1,550	–917	–803
4999 Total liabilities and net position	365	438	341	390

Note.—This statement excludes unfunded contingent liabilities under the insurance program as follows: 1999, $510 billion; 2000, $546 billion; and 2001, $585 billion.

Object Classification (in millions of dollars)

Identification code 58–4236–0–3–453	1999 actual	2000 est.	2001 est.
11.1 Personnel compensation: Full-time permanent	14	17	18
12.1 Civilian personnel benefits	3	4	4
21.0 Travel and transportation of persons	1	1	1
23.1 Rental payments to GSA	2	2	2
23.3 Communications, utilities, and miscellaneous charges	2	....	....
24.0 Printing and reproduction	2	2	2
25.2 Other services	448	515	554
25.3 Purchases of goods and services from Government accounts	1	4	4
41.0 Grants, subsidies, and contributions	6	9	9
42.0 Insurance claims and indemnities	775	725	742
43.0 Interest and dividends	30	30	24
99.9 Total new obligations	1,284	1,309	1,360

Personnel Summary

Identification code 58–4236–0–3–453	1999 actual	2000 est.	2001 est.
2001 Total compensable workyears: Full-time equivalent employment	220	266	266

NATIONAL FLOOD MITIGATION FUND

(INCLUDING TRANSFER OF FUNDS)

Notwithstanding sections 1366(b)(3)(B)–(C) and 1366(f) of the National Flood Insurance Act of 1968, as amended, $20,000,000 to remain available until September 30, [2001] *2002*, for activities designed to reduce the risk of flood damage to structures pursuant to such Act, of which $20,000,000 shall be derived from the National Flood Insurance Fund. *(Departments of Veterans Affairs and Housing and Urban Development, and Independent Agencies Appropriations Act, 2000.)*

Program and Financing (in millions of dollars)

Identification code 58–4243–0–3–453	1999 actual	2000 est.	2001 est.
Obligations by program activity:			
00.01 Flood Mitigation Assistance	18	20	20
00.02 Repetitive Loss Program	....	11	....
10.00 Total new obligations (object class 41.0)	18	31	20
Budgetary resources available for obligation:			
21.40 Unobligated balance available, start of year	9	11	....
22.00 New budget authority (gross)	20	20	20
23.90 Total budgetary resources available for obligation	29	31	20
23.95 Total new obligations	–18	–31	–20
24.40 Unobligated balance available, end of year	11	....	....
New budget authority (gross), detail:			
Mandatory:			
69.62 Transferred from other accounts	20	20	20
Change in unpaid obligations:			
72.40 Unpaid obligations, start of year: Obligated balance, start of year	21	31	44
73.10 Total new obligations	18	31	20
73.20 Total outlays (gross)	–8	–18	–25
74.40 Unpaid obligations, end of year: Obligated balance, end of year	31	44	39
Outlays (gross), detail:			
86.97 Outlays from new mandatory authority	....	2	2
86.98 Outlays from mandatory balances	8	16	23
87.00 Total outlays (gross)	8	18	25
Net budget authority and outlays:			
89.00 Budget authority	20	20	20
90.00 Outlays	8	18	25

Through fee generated funds transferred from the National Flood Insurance Fund and up to $50 million obligated under the Disaster Relief Fund, the National Flood Mitigation Fund will provide a mechanism to reduce the financial burden of pre-existing, at-risk structures that are repetitively flooded by removing or elevating these structures out of flood hazard areas, as well as provide flood mitigation assistance planning support to States and communities.

Currently, roughly two percent of the flood insurance policy base is responsible for nearly 40 percent of claim payments made by the National Flood Insurance Fund. Through grants to States, up to $70 million will be used to remove or elevate these types of properties from the floodplain. The end result will be a lower net subsidy required to operate this insurance program, less claims on the Disaster Relief Fund, and fewer individuals living in hazardous areas.

Intragovernmental revolving funds:

WORKING CAPITAL FUND

Program and Financing (in millions of dollars)

Identification code 58–4188–0–4–803	1999 actual	2000 est.	2001 est.
Obligations by program activity:			
09.01 Reimbursable program	18	30	31
10.00 Total new obligations	18	30	31
Budgetary resources available for obligation:			
21.40 Unobligated balance available, start of year	2	7	....
22.00 New budget authority (gross)	23	23	31
23.90 Total budgetary resources available for obligation	25	30	31
23.95 Total new obligations	–18	–30	–31
24.40 Unobligated balance available, end of year	7	....	....
New budget authority (gross), detail:			
Discretionary:			
68.00 Spending authority from offsetting collections (gross): Offsetting collections (cash)	23	23	31
Change in unpaid obligations:			
72.40 Unpaid obligations, start of year: Obligated balance, start of year	9	7	13
73.10 Total new obligations	18	30	31
73.20 Total outlays (gross)	–20	–24	–31
74.40 Unpaid obligations, end of year: Obligated balance, end of year	7	13	13

Intragovernmental revolving funds—Continued

WORKING CAPITAL FUND—Continued

Program and Financing (in millions of dollars)—Continued

Identification code 58–4188–0–4–803	1999 actual	2000 est.	2001 est.
Outlays (gross), detail:			
86.90 Outlays from new discretionary authority	10	14	19
86.93 Outlays from discretionary balances	10	10	12
87.00 Total outlays (gross)	20	24	31
Offsets:			
Against gross budget authority and outlays:			
88.00 Offsetting collections (cash) from: Federal sources	−23	−23	−31
Net budget authority and outlays:			
89.00 Budget authority			
90.00 Outlays	−2	1	

The Working Capital Fund is financed from fees charged for services provided at the Mt. Weather Emergency Assistance Center, including conference, training, and office support, motor pool services, and temporary lodging. These services are available to organizations within FEMA and other Federal agencies. Beginning in 2001, information technology services associated with the operation of the Mt. Weather Emergency Assistance Center will also be financed through this fund.

Object Classification (in millions of dollars)

Identification code 58–4188–0–4–803	1999 actual	2000 est.	2001 est.
Personnel compensation:			
11.1 Full-time permanent	7	8	9
11.5 Other personnel compensation	1	1	1
11.9 Total personnel compensation	8	9	10
12.1 Civilian personnel benefits	1	2	3
Communications, utilities, and miscellaneous charges:			
23.3 Communications, utilities, and miscellaneous charges	1	1	1
23.3 Communications, utilities, and miscellaneous charges	1	1	1
25.2 Other services	2	5	2
25.3 Purchases of goods and services from Government accounts	1	1	3
25.4 Operation and maintenance of facilities	1	5	4
25.7 Operation and maintenance of equipment		1	1
26.0 Supplies and materials	2	2	3
31.0 Equipment	1	1	1
32.0 Land and structures		2	2
99.9 Total new obligations	18	30	31

Personnel Summary

Identification code 58–4188–0–4–803	1999 actual	2000 est.	2001 est.
2001 Total compensable workyears: Full-time equivalent employment	178	187	251

Credit accounts:

DISASTER ASSISTANCE DIRECT LOAN PROGRAM ACCOUNT

For the cost of direct loans, [$1,295,000] *$1,678,000*, as authorized by section 319 of the Robert T. Stafford Disaster Relief and Emergency Assistance Act: *Provided*, That such costs, including the cost of modifying such loans, shall be as defined in section 502 of the Congressional Budget Act of 1974, as amended: *Provided further*, That these funds are available to subsidize gross obligations for the principal amount of direct loans not to exceed $25,000,000.

In addition, for administrative expenses to carry out the direct loan program, [$420,000] *$427,000. (Departments of Veterans Affairs and Housing and Urban Development, and Independent Agencies Appropriations Act, 2000.)*

Program and Financing (in millions of dollars)

Identification code 58–0105–0–1–453	1999 actual	2000 est.	2001 est.
Obligations by program activity:			
00.01 State Share Program subsidy		2	2
00.02 Community Disaster Loan Program subsidy	3		
00.05 Reestimate of direct loan subsidy		47	
00.06 Interest on reestimates of direct loan subsidy		21	
10.00 Total new obligations (object class 41.0)	3	70	2
Budgetary resources available for obligation:			
21.40 Unobligated balance available, start of year	5	14	14
22.00 New budget authority (gross)	7	70	2
22.10 Resources available from recoveries of prior year obligations	6		
22.22 Unobligated balance transferred from other accounts	1		
23.90 Total budgetary resources available for obligation	19	84	16
23.95 Total new obligations	−3	−70	−2
23.98 Unobligated balance expiring or withdrawn	−2		
24.40 Unobligated balance available, end of year	14	14	14
New budget authority (gross), detail:			
Discretionary:			
40.00 Appropriation	2	2	2
40.65 Contingent emergency appropriation released	5		
43.00 Appropriation (total discretionary)	7	2	2
Mandatory:			
60.05 Appropriation (indefinite)		68	
70.00 Total new budget authority (gross)	7	70	2
Change in unpaid obligations:			
72.40 Unpaid obligations, start of year: Obligated balance, start of year		3	3
73.10 Total new obligations	3	70	2
73.20 Total outlays (gross)	14	−70	−2
73.40 Adjustments in expired accounts (net)	−8		
73.45 Adjustments in unexpired accounts	−6		
74.40 Unpaid obligations, end of year: Obligated balance, end of year	3	3	3
Outlays (gross), detail:			
86.90 Outlays from new discretionary authority		2	2
86.93 Outlays from discretionary balances	−14		
86.97 Outlays from new mandatory authority		68	
87.00 Total outlays (gross)	−14	70	2
Net budget authority and outlays:			
89.00 Budget authority	7	70	2
90.00 Outlays	−14	70	2

Disaster assistance loans authorized by the Robert T. Stafford Disaster Relief and Emergency Assistance Act 42 U.S.C. 5121 et seq. are loans to States for the non-Federal portion of cost-sharing funds and community disaster loans to local governments incurring substantial loss of tax and other revenues as a result of a major disaster. The funds requested for this program include direct loans and a subsidy based on criteria including loan amount and interest charged.

As required by the Federal Credit Reform Act of 1990, this account records, for this program, the subsidy costs associated with the direct loans obligated in 1992 and beyond (including modifications of direct loans), as well as administrative expenses of this program. The subsidy amounts are estimated on a present value basis; the administrative expenses are estimated on a cash basis.

Summary of Loan Levels, Subsidy Budget Authority and Outlays by Program (in millions of dollars)

Identification code 58–0105–0–1–453	1999 actual	2000 est.	2001 est.
Direct loan levels supportable by subsidy budget authority:			
1150 States share program	25	25	25
1150 Community Disaster Loans	5		

1159 Total direct loan levels	30	25	25
Direct loan subsidy (in percent):			
1320 States share program	5.42	3.27	6.71
1320 Community Disaster Loan	92.21	99.45	96.19
1329 Weighted average subsidy rate	5.42	3.27	6.71
Direct loan subsidy budget authority:			
1330 States share program	2	2	2
1330 Community Disaster Loans	5	68	
1339 Total subsidy budget authority	7	70	2
Direct loan subsidy outlays:			
1340 States share program		2	2
1340 Community Disaster Loans		68	
1349 Total subsidy outlays		70	2

Personnel Summary

Identification code 58–0105–0–1–453	1999 actual	2000 est.	2001 est.
1001 Total compensable workyears: Full-time equivalent employment	2	3	3

Disaster Assistance Direct Loan Financing Account

Program and Financing (in millions of dollars)

Identification code 58–4234–0–3–453	1999 actual	2000 est.	2001 est.
Obligations by program activity:			
00.01 Direct loans	3	25	25
00.02 Interest on Treasury borrowing	4	26	1
10.00 Total new obligations	7	51	26
Budgetary resources available for obligation:			
22.00 New financing authority (gross)	19	51	38
22.10 Resources available from recoveries of prior year obligations	3		
22.60 Portion applied to repay debt	−15		−12
23.90 Total budgetary resources available for obligation	7	51	26
23.95 Total new obligations	−7	−51	−26
New financing authority (gross), detail:			
Discretionary:			
47.00 Authority to borrow	24	23	23
Spending authority from offsetting collections:			
68.00 Offsetting collections (cash)	3	75	15
68.10 From Federal sources: Change in receivables and unpaid, unfilled orders	−8		
68.90 Spending authority from offsetting collections (total discretionary)	−5	75	15
Mandatory:			
69.47 Portion applied to repay debt		−47	
70.00 Total new financing authority (gross)	19	51	38
Change in unpaid obligations:			
Unpaid obligations, start of year:			
72.40 Obligated balance, start of year	10	1	1
72.95 Receivables from program account	11	3	3
72.99 Total unpaid obligations, start of year	21	4	4
73.10 Total new obligations	7	51	26
73.20 Total financing disbursements (gross)	−21	−51	−26
73.45 Adjustments in unexpired accounts	−3		
Unpaid obligations, end of year:			
74.40 Obligated balance, end of year	1	1	1
74.95 Receivables from program account	3	3	3
74.99 Total unpaid obligations, end of year	4	4	4
87.00 Total financing disbursements (gross)	21	51	26
Offsets:			
Against gross financing authority and financing disbursements:			
Offsetting collections (cash) from:			
Federal sources:			
88.00 Federal funds (payments from program account)		−2	−2
88.00 Federal sources		−68	
88.20 Interest on U.S. securities	−2	−3	
Non-Federal sources:			
88.40 Repayments of principal	−1	−1	−11
88.40 Interest received on loans		−1	−2
88.90 Total, offsetting collections (cash)	−3	−75	−15
Against gross budget authority only:			
88.95 Change in receivables from program accounts	8		
Net financing authority and financing disbursements:			
89.00 Financing authority	24	−24	23
90.00 Financing disbursements	18	−24	11

Status of Direct Loans (in millions of dollars)

Identification code 58–4234–0–3–453	1999 actual	2000 est.	2001 est.
Position with respect to appropriations act limitation on obligations:			
1111 Limitation on direct loans	30	25	25
1112 Unobligated direct loan limitation	−27		
1113 Unobligated limitation carried forward			
1150 Total direct loan obligations	3	25	25
Cumulative balance of direct loans outstanding:			
1210 Outstanding, start of year	147	148	167
1231 Disbursements: Direct loan disbursements	3	25	25
1251 Repayments: Repayments and prepayments	−1	−1	−11
Write-offs for default:			
1263 Direct loans	−1		
1264 Other adjustments, forgiveness of debt		−5	−5
1290 Outstanding, end of year	148	167	176

As required by the Federal Credit Reform Act of 1990, this nonbudgetary account records, for this program, all cash flows to and from the Government resulting from direct loans obligated in 1992 and beyond (including modifications of direct loans). The amounts in this account are a means of financing and are not included in the budget totals.

Balance Sheet (in millions of dollars)

Identification code 58–4234–0–3–453	1998 actual	1999 actual	2000 est.	2001 est.
ASSETS:				
Net value of assets related to post–1991 direct loans receivable:				
1401 Direct loans receivable, gross	147	145	164	173
1402 Interest receivable	19	26	55	42
1405 Allowance for subsidy cost (–)	–122	–105	–154	–146
1499 Net present value of assets related to direct loans	44	66	65	69
Other Federal assets:				
1801 Cash and other monetary assets	10	1	1	2
1901 Other assets	–55	–56	–9	–9
1999 Total assets	–1	11	57	62
LIABILITIES:				
Federal liabilities:				
2103 Debt	50	59	35	58
2105 Other	13	3	3	3
2999 Total liabilities	63	62	38	61
NET POSITION:				
3300 Cumulative results of operations	–64	–51	18	1
3999 Total net position	–64	–51	18	1
4999 Total liabilities and net position	–1	11	56	62

Disaster Assistance Direct Loan Liquidating Account

Program and Financing (in millions of dollars)

Identification code 58–4232–0–3–453	1999 actual	2000 est.	2001 est.
New budget authority (gross), detail:			
Mandatory:			
69.00 Offsetting collections (cash)	4		
69.47 Portion applied to repay debt	−4		

Credit accounts—Continued

DISASTER ASSISTANCE DIRECT LOAN LIQUIDATING ACCOUNT—Continued

Program and Financing (in millions of dollars)—Continued

Identification code 58–4232–0–3–453	1999 actual	2000 est.	2001 est.
Offsets:			
Against gross budget authority and outlays:			
88.40 Offsetting collections (cash) from: Non-Federal sources	–4		
Net budget authority and outlays:			
89.00 Budget authority	–4		
90.00 Outlays	–4		

Status of Direct Loans (in millions of dollars)

Identification code 58–4232–0–3–453	1999 actual	2000 est.	2001 est.
Cumulative balance of direct loans outstanding:			
1210 Outstanding, start of year	37	37	37
1290 Outstanding, end of year	37	37	37

Statement of Operations (in millions of dollars)

Identification code 58–4232–0–3–453	1998 actual	1999 actual	2000 est.	2001 est.
0101 Revenue	5	4		
0105 Net income or loss (–)	5	4		

As required by the Federal Credit Reform Act of 1990, this account records, for this program, all cash flows to and from the Government resulting from direct loans obligated prior to 1992. This account is shown on a cash basis. All new activity in this program in 1992 and beyond (including modifications of direct loans) is recorded in corresponding program and financing accounts.

Balance Sheet (in millions of dollars)

Identification code 58–4232–0–3–453	1998 actual	1999 actual	2000 est.	2001 est.
ASSETS:				
Net value of assets related to pre-1992 direct loans receivable and acquired defaulted guaranteed loans receivable:				
1601 Direct loans, gross	37	37	37	37
1602 Interest receivable	31	32	36	41
1603 Allowance for estimated uncollectible loans and interest (–)	–57	–27	–27	–27
1604 Direct loans and interest receivable, net	11	42	46	51
1699 Value of assets related to direct loans	11	42	46	51
1999 Total assets	11	42	46	51
NET POSITION:				
3300 Cumulative results of operations	11	42	46	51
3999 Total net position	11	42	46	51

Trust Funds

BEQUESTS AND GIFTS

Program and Financing (in millions of dollars)

Identification code 11–8244–0–7–453	1999 actual	2000 est.	2001 est.
Budgetary resources available for obligation:			
21.40 Unobligated balance available, start of year	2	2	2
24.40 Unobligated balance available, end of year	2	2	2
Net budget authority and outlays:			
89.00 Budget authority			
90.00 Outlays			
Memorandum (non-add) entries:			
92.01 Total investments, start of year: U.S. securities: Par value		2	2
92.02 Total investments, end of year: U.S. securities: Par value	2	2	2

This fund represents contributions primarily from the estate of Cora Brown to support the activities of the Disaster Relief Fund.

GENERAL FUND RECEIPT ACCOUNTS

(in millions of dollars)

	1999 actual	2000 est.	2001 est.
Offsetting receipts from the public:			
58–089700 Radiological emergency preparedness	2		
General Fund Offsetting receipts from the public	2		

GENERAL SERVICES ADMINISTRATION

REAL PROPERTY ACTIVITIES

Federal Funds

Intragovernmental funds:

FEDERAL BUILDINGS FUND

LIMITATIONS ON AVAILABILITY OF REVENUE

(INCLUDING TRANSFER OF FUNDS)

[To carry out the purpose of] *For an additional amount to be deposited in, and to be used for the purposes of,* the Fund established pursuant to section 210(f) of the Federal Property and Administrative Services Act of 1949, as amended (40 U.S.C. 490(f)), [the] *$681,871,000. The* revenues and collections deposited into the Fund shall be available for necessary expenses of real property management and related activities not otherwise provided for, including operation, maintenance, and protection of federally owned and leased buildings; rental of buildings in the District of Columbia; restoration of leased premises; moving governmental agencies (including space adjustments and telecommunications relocation expenses) in connection with the assignment, allocation and transfer of space; contractual services incident to cleaning or servicing buildings, and moving; repair and alteration of federally owned buildings including grounds, approaches and appurtenances; care and safeguarding of sites; maintenance, preservation, demolition, and equipment; acquisition of buildings and sites by purchase, condemnation, or as otherwise authorized by law; acquisition of options to purchase buildings and sites; conversion and extension of federally owned buildings; preliminary planning and design of projects by contract or otherwise; construction of new buildings (including equipment for such buildings); and payment of principal, interest, and any other obligations for public buildings acquired by installment purchase and purchase contract; in the aggregate amount of [$5,342,416,000] *$6,256,026,000,* of which: (1) [$74,979,000] *$779,788,000* shall remain available until expended for construction of additional projects at locations and at maximum construction improvement costs (including funds for sites and expenses and associated design and construction services) as follows:

New construction:
[Maryland:
Montgomery County, FDA Consolidation, $35,000,000
Michigan:
Sault Sainte Marie, Border Station, $8,263,000
Montana:
Roosville, Border Station, $753,000
Sweetgrass, Border Station, $11,480,000
Texas:
Fort Hancock, Border Station, $277,000
Washington:
Oroville, Border Station, $11,206,000
Nationwide:
Non-prospectus, $8,000,000:]
Arkansas:
Little Rock, U.S. Courthouse Annex (additional design), $1,820,000
California:
Los Angeles, U.S. Courthouse, $31,523,000
District of Columbia:
Bureau of Alcohol, Tobacco, and Firearms Headquarters, $83,000,000
Southeast Federal Center Site Remediation, $5,000,000
U.S. Courthouse Annex, $104,050,000
Florida:
Miami, U.S. Courthouse, $110,950,000
Maryland:
Montgomery County, FDA Consolidation, $101,239,000
Maine:
Jackman, Border Station, $619,000
Michigan:
Sault Sainte Marie, Border Station, $3,630,000
Mississippi:
Biloxi-Gulfport, U.S. Courthouse, $42,715,000
Montana:
Eureka/Roosville, Border Station, $6,892,000
Raymond, Border Station, $577,000
New York:
New York, U.S. Mission to the United Nations, $58,304,000
Texas:
Del Rio III, Border Station, $1,832,000
Eagle Pass, Border Station, $2,212,000
Fort Hancock, Border Station, $2,140,000
Houston, Federal Bureau of Investigation, $6,145,000
Virginia:
Richmond, U.S. Courthouse, $19,476,000
Washington:
Seattle, U.S. Courthouse, $177,930,000
Nationwide:
Judgment Fund Repayment, $16,734,000
Non-prospectus construction projects, $3,000,000:

Provided, That each of the immediately foregoing limits of costs on new construction projects may be exceeded to the extent that savings effected in other such projects, but not to exceed 10 percent unless advance [approval is obtained from] *notice is transmitted to* the Committees on Appropriations of a greater amount: *Provided further*, That all funds for direct construction projects shall expire on September 30, [2001] *2002*, and remain in the Federal Buildings Fund except for funds for projects as to which funds for design or other funds have been obligated in whole or in part prior to such date[: *Provided further*, That of the amount provided under this heading in Public Law 104–208, $20,782,000 are rescinded and shall remain in the Fund]; (2) [$598,674,000] *$721,193,000* shall remain available until expended for repairs and alterations which includes associated design and construction services[, of which $333,000,000 shall be available for basic repairs and alterations]: *Provided further*, That funds [made available in any previous Act] in the Federal Buildings Fund for Repairs and Alterations shall, for prospectus projects, be limited to the amount [identified for each project] *by project, as follows*, except each project [in any previous Act] may be increased by an amount not to exceed 10 percent unless advance [approval is obtained from] *notice is transmitted to* the Committees on Appropriations of a greater amount:

Repairs and alterations:
Arizona:
Phoenix, Federal Building Courthouse, $26,962,000
California:
Santa Ana, Federal Building, $27,864,000
District of Columbia:
Internal Revenue Service Headquarters (Phase 1), $31,780,000
Main State Building, (Phase 3), $28,775,000
Maryland:
Woodlawn, SSA National Computer Center, $4,285,000
Michigan:
Detroit, McNamara Federal Building, $26,999,000
Missouri:
Kansas City, Richard Bolling Federal Building, $25,882,000
Kansas City, Federal Building, 8930 Ward Parkway, $8,964,000
Nebraska:
Omaha, Zorinsky Federal Building, $45,960,000
New York:
New York City, 40 Foley Square, $5,037,000
Ohio:
Cincinnati, Potter Stewart U.S. Courthouse, $18,434,000
Pennsylvania:
Pittsburgh, U.S. Post Office—Courthouse, $54,144,000
Utah:
Salt Lake City, Bennett Federal Building, $21,199,000
Virginia:
Reston, J.W. Powell Federal Building (Phase 2), $22,993,000
Nationwide:
Chlorofluorocarbons Program, $10,000,000

Intragovernmental funds—Continued

FEDERAL BUILDINGS FUND—Continued

(INCLUDING TRANSFER OF FUNDS)—Continued

Glass Fragment Retention, $30,000,000
Design Program, $21,915,000
Energy Program, $20,000,000
Basic Repairs and Alterations, $290,000,000:
Provided further, That additional projects for which prospectuses have been fully approved may be funded under this category only if advance notice is transmitted to the Committees on Appropriations: Provided further, That the amounts provided in this or any prior Act for "Repairs and Alterations" may be used to fund costs associated with implementing security improvements to buildings necessary to meet the minimum standards for security in accordance with current law and in compliance with the reprogramming guidelines of the appropriate Committees of the House and Senate: *Provided further*, That the difference between the funds appropriated and expended on any projects in this or any prior Act, under the heading "Repairs and Alterations", may be transferred to Basic Repairs and Alterations or used to fund authorized increases in prospectus projects: *Provided further*, That all funds for repairs and alterations prospectus projects shall expire on September 30, [2001] *2002*, and remain in the Federal Buildings Fund except funds for projects as to which funds for design or other funds have been obligated in whole or in part prior to such date: *Provided further*, That the amount provided in this or any prior Act for Basic Repairs and Alterations may be used to pay claims against the Government arising from any projects under the heading "Repairs and Alterations" or used to fund authorized increases in prospectus projects[: *Provided further*, That the General Services Administration is directed to use funds available for Repairs and Alterations to undertake the first construction phase of the project to renovate the Department of the Interior Headquarters Building located in Washington, D.C.]; (3) [$205,668,000] *$185,369,000* for installment acquisition payments including payments on purchase contracts which shall remain available until expended; (4) [$2,782,186,000] *$2,944,905,000* for rental of space which shall remain available until expended; and (5) [$1,580,909,000] *$1,624,771,000* for building operations which shall remain available until expended[, of which $475,000 shall be available for the Plains States De-population Symposium and of which $1,974,000 shall be available until expended for acquisition, lease, construction, and equipping of flexiplace telecommuting centers]: *Provided further, That in addition to amounts made available herein, the following sums are to be deposited into the Fund, to become available on October 1 of the fiscal year specified, and remain available until expended: fiscal year 2002, $218,957,000 of which $34,083,000 shall be for the construction of a new facility for the National Oceanic and Atmospheric Administration at Suitland, Maryland and $184,874,000 for the construction of the Food and Drug Administration Consolidation in Montgomery County, Maryland; fiscal year 2003, $162,633,000 for the construction of the Food and Drug Administration Consolidation in Montgomery County, Maryland; and fiscal year 2004, $95,894,000 for construction of the Food and Drug Administration Consolidation in Montgomery County, Maryland: Provided further*, That funds available to the General Services Administration shall not be available for expenses of any construction, repair, alteration and acquisition project for which a prospectus, if required by the Public Buildings Act of 1959, as amended, has not been approved, except that necessary funds may be expended for each project for required expenses for the development of a proposed prospectus: *Provided further*, That funds available in the Federal Buildings Fund may be expended for emergency repairs when advance [approval is obtained from] *notice is transmitted to* the Committees on Appropriations: *Provided further*, That amounts necessary to provide reimbursable special services to other agencies under section 210(f)(6) of the Federal Property and Administrative Services Act of 1949, as amended (40 U.S.C. 490(f)(6)) and amounts to provide such reimbursable fencing, lighting, guard booths, and other facilities on private or other property not in Government ownership or control as may be appropriate to enable the United States Secret Service to perform its protective functions pursuant to 18 U.S.C. 3056, shall be available from such revenues and collections: *Provided further*, That revenues and collections and any other sums accruing to this Fund during fiscal year [2000] *2001*, excluding reimbursements under section 210(f)(6) of the Federal Property and Administrative Services Act of 1949 (40 U.S.C. 490(f)(6)) in excess of [$5,342,416,000] *$6,256,026,000* shall remain in the Fund and shall not be available for expenditure except as authorized in appropriations Acts. *(Independent Agencies Appropriations Act, 2000.)*

Unavailable Collections (in millions of dollars)

Identification code 47–4542–0–4–804		1999 actual	2000 est.	2001 est.
	Balance, start of year:			
01.99	Balance, start of year	51	195	249
03.00	Offsetting Collections	195	249	186
04.00	Total: Balances and collections	246	444	435
	Appropriation:			
05.01	Federal buildings fund	−51	−195	−249
07.99	Total balance, end of year	195	249	186

Program and Financing (in millions of dollars)

Identification code 47–4542–0–4–804		1999 actual	2000 est.	2001 est.
	Obligations by program activity:			
	Capital investment program:			
09.01	Construction and acquisition of facilities	775	398	668
09.02	Repairs and alterations	607	801	775
09.03	Design and construction services	5	2	
09.04	Installment acquisition payments	206	213	195
09.05	Construction of lease purchase facilities	29	25	24
09.07	Pennsylvania Avenue activities	6	11	11
09.08	Payment to Columbia Hospital for Women		6	
09.09	Total capital investment program	1,628	1,456	1,673
	Operating programs:			
09.10	Rental of space	2,680	3,009	2,945
09.11	Building operations	1,553	1,597	1,625
09.19	Total operating program	4,233	4,606	4,570
09.20	Special services and improvements	806	952	878
10.00	Total new obligations	6,667	7,014	7,121
	Budgetary resources available for obligation:			
21.40	Unobligated balance available, start of year	3,004	2,361	1,719
22.00	New budget authority (gross)	6,201	6,471	7,205
22.10	Resources available from recoveries of prior year obligations	134		
22.22	Unobligated balance transferred from other accounts	15		
22.60	Portion applied to repay debt	−91	−99	−71
22.70	Balance of authority to borrow withdrawn	−237		
23.90	Total budgetary resources available for obligation	9,026	8,733	8,853
23.95	Total new obligations	−6,667	−7,014	−7,121
24.40	Unobligated balance available, end of year	2,361	1,719	1,732
	New budget authority (gross), detail:			
	Discretionary:			
40.00	Appropriation	450		682
	Spending authority from offsetting collections:			
	Offsetting collections (cash):			
68.00	Offsetting collections (cash)	6,494	6,511	6,460
68.00	Offsetting collections (Columbia Hospital for Women)		14	
68.10	From Federal sources: Change in receivables and unpaid, unfilled orders	−599		
68.26	Offsetting collections (unavailable balances)	51	195	249
68.45	Portion not available for obligation (limitation on obligations)	−195	−249	−186
68.90	Spending authority from offsetting collections (total discretionary)	5,751	6,471	6,523
70.00	Total new budget authority (gross)	6,201	6,471	7,205
	Change in unpaid obligations:			
	Unpaid obligations, start of year:			
72.40	Obligated balance, start of year	211	1,090	1,401
72.95	From Federal sources: Receivables and unpaid, unfilled orders	2,198	1,599	1,599
72.99	Total unpaid obligations, start of year	2,409	2,689	3,000
73.10	Total new obligations	6,667	7,014	7,121
73.20	Total outlays (gross)	−6,274	−6,704	−6,758
73.32	Obligated balance transferred from other accounts	21		
73.45	Adjustments in unexpired accounts	−134		
	Unpaid obligations, end of year:			
74.40	Obligated balance, end of year	1,090	1,401	1,764

74.95	From Federal sources: Receivables and unpaid, unfilled orders	1,599	1,599	1,599
74.99	Total unpaid obligations, end of year	2,689	3,000	3,363
	Outlays (gross), detail:			
86.90	Outlays from new discretionary authority	5,358	5,792	5,778
86.93	Outlays from discretionary balances	916	911	980
87.00	Total outlays (gross)	6,274	6,704	6,758
	Offsets:			
	Against gross budget authority and outlays:			
	Offsetting collections (cash) from:			
88.00	Federal sources	−6,440	−6,503	−6,452
	Non-Federal sources:			
88.40	Non-Federal sources	−54	−8	−8
88.40	Columbia Hospital for Women		−14	
88.90	Total, offsetting collections (cash)	−6,494	−6,525	−6,460
	Against gross budget authority only:			
88.95	From Federal sources: Change in receivables and unpaid, unfilled orders	599		
	Net budget authority and outlays:			
89.00	Budget authority	306	−54	745
90.00	Outlays	−222	179	298

The Federal Buildings Fund finances the activities of the Public Buildings Service which provides space and services for Federal agencies in a relationship similar to that of landlord and tenant.

The Fund, established in 1975, replaces direct appropriations by using income derived from rent assessments which approximate commercial rates for comparable space and services. Rent and other income to the Fund is as follows:

[In millions of dollars]

	1999 actual	2000 est.	2001 est.
Rental charges	5,369	5,551	5,574
Collections for:			
(a) Special services and improvements	938	952	878
(b) Miscellaneous income	67	22	8
Total receipts and reimbursements	6,374	6,525	6,460

The following table details the financing for the Federal Buildings Fund in 2000 and 2001.

[In millions of dollars]

	Obligations	End-of-year unobligated balance	Obligational authority: Total	New	From prior year
2000 basic program:					
1. Construction and acquisition of facilities	398	177	575	87	488
2. Repairs and alterations	801	232	1,033	666	367
3. Design and construction services	2		2		2
4. Installment acquisition payments	213	10	223	202	21
5. Construction of lease purchase facilities	25	208	233		233
6. Rental of space	3,009		3,009	2,986	23
7. Building operations	1,597		1,597	1,574	23
8. Columbia Women's Hospital	6	8	14	14	
9. Pennsylvania Avenue activities	11	32	43		43
Total basic program	6,062	667	6,729	5,529	1,200
Other programs:					
Special services and improvements	952		952	952	
Total Federal Buildings Fund	7,014	667	7,681	6,481	1,200
2001 basic program:					
1. Construction and acquisition of facilities	668	289	957	780	177
2. Repairs and alterations	775	178	953	721	232
3. Installment acquisition payments	195		195	185	10
4. Construction of lease purchase facilities	24	184	208		208
5. Rental of space	2,945		2,945	2,945	
6. Building operations	1,625		1,625	1,625	
7. Columbia Women's Hospital		8	8		8
8. Pennsylvania Avenue activities	11	21	32		32
Total basic program	6,243	680	6,923	6,256	667
Other programs:					
Special services and improvements	878		878	878	
Total Federal Buildings Fund	7,121	680	7,801	7,134	667

The Federal Buildings Fund program consists of the following activities financed from rent charges:

Construction and acquisition of facilities.—Space is acquired through the construction or purchase of facilities and prospectus-level extensions to existing buildings. All costs directly attributable to site acquisition, construction, and the full range of design and construction services and management and inspection of construction projects are funded under this activity.

Courthouse Program.—Included is $488 million for courthouse projects. This amount will fund four new construction projects scheduled to begin within the first three quarters of 2001, fund the first two design projects on the Judiciary's priority list, and complete the design work for an existing project. All projects meet the building criteria outlined in the U.S. Courts Design Guide. In addition, the scope of these projects assumes courtroom sharing as a cost-effective means for providing the space needed by the Courts. The Administration urges the Judiciary to incorporate courtroom sharing in the U.S. Courts Design Guide. The Administration will support future year funding for the other projects on the Judiciary's priority list as those projects: (1) become ready to begin construction; (2) come into conformity with the U.S. Courts Design Guide; and (3) incorporate an appropriate measure of courtroom sharing.

Repairs and alterations.—Repairs and alterations of public buildings as well as associated design and construction services are funded under this activity. Protection of the Government's investment, health and safety of building occupants, transfer of agencies from leased space, and cost effectiveness are the principal criteria used in establishing priorities. Primary consideration is given to repairs to prevent deterioration and damage to buildings, their support systems, and operating equipment. This activity also provides for conversion of existing facilities and non-prospectus extensions.

Installment acquisition payments.—Payments are made for liabilities incurred under purchase contract authority and lease purchase arrangements. The periodic payments cover principal, interest, and other requirements.

Rental of space.—Space is acquired through the leasing of buildings including space occupied by Federal agencies in U.S. Postal Service facilities, 158 million rentable square feet in 2000, and 162 million rentable square feet in 2001.

Building operations.—Services are provided for Government-owned and leased facilities, including cleaning, utilities and fuel, protection, maintenance, miscellaneous services (such as moving, evaluation of new materials and equipment, and field supervision), and general management and administration of all real property related programs including salaries and benefits paid from the Federal Buildings Fund. The following list shows the 2000 and 2001 direct program (estimated square feet and expenses in millions):

[In millions]

	2000 Square feet	2000 Expenses	2001 Square feet	2001 Expenses
Cleaning	137	217	142	220
Utilities	140	254	145	258
Maintenance	131	231	136	241
Other building services	243	248	243	255
Protection	253	247	254	258
Other staff support		330		345

Intragovernmental funds—Continued

FEDERAL BUILDINGS FUND—Continued

(INCLUDING TRANSFER OF FUNDS)—Continued

	2000		2001	
	Square feet	*Expenses*	*Square feet*	*Expenses*
IT Support		69		48
International Trade Center		1		
Pennsylvania Avenue activities		3		2
Total		1,600		1,627

Other programs.—When requested by Federal agencies, the Public Buildings Service provides building services such as tenant alterations, cleaning and other operations, and protection services which are in excess of those services provided under the commercial rental charge. For presentation purposes, the balances of the Unconditional Gifts of Real, Personal, or Other Property trust fund have been combined with the Federal Buildings Fund.

Agency debt.—The following table reflects agency debt outstanding for the construction of federal buildings under authorities previously provided:

[In millions of dollars]

FFB Held Debt:	*1999 actual*	*2000 est.*	*2001 est.*
Outstanding agency debt, SOY	1,760	2,405	2,325
New agency borrowings	736	19	14
Repayments and prepayments	-91	-99	-70
Outstanding agency debt, EOY	2,405	2,325	2,269

Statement of Operations (in millions of dollars)

Identification code 47–4542–0–4–804		1998 actual	1999 actual	2000 est.	2001 est.
0101	Revenue	6,063	6,334	6,510	6,460
0102	Expense	–5,771	–5,902	–6,301	–6,235
0105	Net income or loss (–)	292	432	209	225

Object Classification (in millions of dollars)

Identification code 47–4542–0–4–804		1999 actual	2000 est.	2001 est.
	Personnel compensation:			
11.1	Full-time permanent	380	392	401
11.3	Other than full-time permanent	4	5	5
11.5	Other personnel compensation	7	12	13
11.9	Total personnel compensation	391	409	419
12.1	Civilian personnel benefits	85	86	88
13.0	Benefits for former personnel		2	2
	Travel and transportation of persons:			
21.0	Travel and transportation of persons	16	17	18
21.0	Motor vehicle usage	5	5	5
22.0	Transportation of things	3	4	4
23.2	Rental payments to others	2,682	3,009	2,945
23.3	Communications, utilities, and miscellaneous charges	284	243	250
24.0	Printing and reproduction	3	8	8
25.2	Other services	2,209	2,079	2,284
25.4	Operation and maintenance of facilities	608	716	667
25.7	Operation and maintenance of equipment	44	46	46
26.0	Supplies and materials	72	101	95
31.0	Equipment	36	32	32
32.0	Land and structures	45	63	84
41.0	Grants, subsidies, and contributions	2	6	
43.0	Interest and dividends	182	188	174
99.9	Total new obligations	6,667	7,014	7,121
	Obligations are distributed as follows:			
	General Services Administration	6,459	6,796	6,897
	Allocation Accounts:			
	Department of Commerce	75	75	77
	Department of Defense	109	117	119
	Environmental Protection Agency	24	26	28

Personnel Summary

Identification code 47–4542–0–4–804		1999 actual	2000 est.	2001 est.
2001	Total compensable workyears: Full-time equivalent employment	7,174	7,287	7,287

ALLOCATIONS RECEIVED FROM OTHER APPROPRIATION ACCOUNTS

Note.—Obligations incurred under allocations from other accounts are included in the schedules of the parent appropriations as follows:

Smithsonian Institution:
"Construction."

General and special funds:

REAL PROPERTY RELOCATION

Program and Financing (in millions of dollars)

Identification code 47–0535–0–1–804		1999 actual	2000 est.	2001 est.
	Obligations by program activity:			
10.00	Total new obligations		11	
	Budgetary resources available for obligation:			
21.40	Unobligated balance available, start of year	11	11	
23.95	Total new obligations		–11	
24.40	Unobligated balance available, end of year	11		
	Change in unpaid obligations:			
72.40	Unpaid obligations, start of year: Obligated balance, start of year			1
73.10	Total new obligations		11	
73.20	Total outlays (gross)		–11	
74.40	Unpaid obligations, end of year: Obligated balance, end of year		1	1
	Outlays (gross), detail:			
86.93	Outlays from discretionary balances		11	
	Net budget authority and outlays:			
89.00	Budget authority			
90.00	Outlays		11	

This appropriation covers relocation costs involved in moving agencies from valuable underutilized property, targeted for public sale, to facilities determined to be more economically suitable to their needs. Relocation and disposal is considered when the benefit/cost ratio is at least 2:1. The sale of these valuable underutilized properties would provide significant revenue to the Treasury and would far outweigh the relocation costs involved.

No appropriation is requested for this program in 2001. GSA will solicit relocation proposals from agencies.

Object Classification (in millions of dollars)

Identification code 47–0535–0–1–804		1999 actual	2000 est.	2001 est.
25.2	Other services		5	
31.0	Equipment		5	
32.0	Land and structures		1	
99.9	Total new obligations		11	

PENNSYLVANIA AVENUE ACTIVITIES

Program and Financing (in millions of dollars)

Identification code 47–0118–0–1–451		1999 actual	2000 est.	2001 est.
	Budgetary resources available for obligation:			
21.40	Unobligated balance available, start of year	15		
22.21	Unobligated balance transferred to other accounts	–15		
23.90	Total budgetary resources available for obligation			
	Change in unpaid obligations:			
72.40	Unpaid obligations, start of year: Obligated balance, start of year	21		
73.31	Obligated balance transferred to other accounts	–21		
	Net budget authority and outlays:			
89.00	Budget authority			

90.00 Outlays	1		

The remaining balances of Pennsylvania Avenue Activities were merged with the Federal Buildings Fund in 1999.

DISPOSAL OF SURPLUS REAL AND RELATED PERSONAL PROPERTY

Unavailable Collections (in millions of dollars)

Identification code 47–5254–0–2–804	1999 actual	2000 est.	2001 est.
Balance, start of year:			
01.99 Balance, start of year	81	86	93
Receipts:			
02.01 Sale of surplus property	2	5	5
02.02 Other receipts, surplus real and related personal property	15	10	52
02.03 Transfers to Land and Water Conservation Fund	−8	−2	−2
02.04 Sale of property, Lorton Correctional Complex			3
02.99 Total receipts	9	13	58
04.00 Total: Balances and collections	90	99	151
Appropriation:			
05.01 Disposal	−5	−6	−8
05.02 Policy and operations			−8
05.99 Subtotal appropriation	−5	−6	−16
06.10 Unobligated balance returned to receipts	1		
07.99 Total balance, end of year	86	93	135

Program and Financing (in millions of dollars)

Identification code 47–5254–0–2–804	1999 actual	2000 est.	2001 est.
Obligations by program activity:			
00.01 Appraisers' fees, auctioneers and broker fees and surveying	1	1	1
00.02 Advertising	1	1	1
00.03 Environmental services	2	3	5
00.05 Outleasing government-owned space: Auctioneers, brokers fees and advertising...		1	1
10.00 Total new obligations (object class 25.2)	4	6	8
Budgetary resources available for obligation:			
22.00 New budget authority (gross)	5	6	8
23.95 Total new obligations	−4	−6	−8
23.98 Unobligated balance expiring or withdrawn	−1		
New budget authority (gross), detail:			
Mandatory:			
60.25 Appropriation (special fund, indefinite)	5	6	8
Change in unpaid obligations:			
72.40 Unpaid obligations, start of year: Obligated balance, start of year	2	1	1
73.10 Total new obligations	4	6	8
73.20 Total outlays (gross)	−4	−6	−8
74.40 Unpaid obligations, end of year: Obligated balance, end of year	1	1	1
Outlays (gross), detail:			
86.97 Outlays from new mandatory authority	4	6	8
Net budget authority and outlays:			
89.00 Budget authority	5	6	8
90.00 Outlays	4	6	8

Auctioneers and brokers familiar with local markets may be used to accelerate the disposal of surplus real and related personal property, including the outleasing of Government-owned buildings and space. Fees of auctioneers, brokers, appraisers, and environmental consultants, surveying costs, costs of advertising and costs of environmental and historical preservation services are paid out of receipts from disposals within each year in accordance with 40 U.S.C.A. 485(b).

Credit accounts:

COLUMBIA HOSPITAL FOR WOMEN DIRECT LOAN FINANCING ACCOUNT

Program and Financing (in millions of dollars)

Identification code 47–4029–0–3–804	1999 actual	2000 est.	2001 est.
Obligations by program activity:			
00.01 Direct loan		14	
00.02 Interest on treasury borrowing			1
10.00 Total new obligations		14	1
Budgetary resources available for obligation:			
21.40 Unobligated balance available, start of year			6
22.00 New financing authority (gross)		20	1
23.90 Total budgetary resources available for obligation		20	7
23.95 Total new obligations		−14	−1
24.40 Unobligated balance available, end of year		6	6
New financing authority (gross), detail:			
Mandatory:			
67.15 Authority to borrow (indefinite)		14	
Discretionary:			
68.00 Spending authority from offsetting collections: Offsetting collections (cash)		6	1
70.00 Total new financing authority (gross)		20	1
Change in unpaid obligations:			
73.10 Total new obligations		14	1
73.20 Total financing disbursements (gross)		−14	−1
87.00 Total financing disbursements (gross)		14	1
Offsets:			
Against gross financing authority and financing disbursements:			
Offsetting collections (cash) from:			
88.00 Federal sources		−6	
88.40 Non-Federal sources: Interest payment			−1
88.90 Total, offsetting collections (cash)		−6	−1
Net financing authority and financing disbursements:			
89.00 Financing authority		14	
90.00 Financing disbursements		8	

Status of Direct Loans (in millions of dollars)

Identification code 47–4029–0–3–804	1999 actual	2000 est.	2001 est.
Position with respect to appropriations act limitation on obligations:			
1111 Limitation on direct loans		14	
1150 Total direct loan obligations		14	
Cumulative balance of direct loans outstanding:			
1210 Outstanding, start of year			14
1231 Disbursements: Direct loan disbursements		14	
1251 Repayments: Repayments and prepayments			
1263 Write-offs for default: Direct loans			
1290 Outstanding, end of year		14	14

Summary of Loan Levels, Subsidy Budget Authority and Outlays by Program (in millions of dollars)

Identification code 47–4029–0–3–804	1999 actual	2000 est.	2001 est.
Direct loan levels supportable by subsidy budget authority:			
1150 Direct loan levels		14	
1159 Total direct loan levels		14	
Direct loan subsidy (in percent):			
1320 Subsidy rate		42.85	
1329 Weighted average subsidy rate		42.85	
Direct loan subsidy budget authority:			
1330 Subsidy budget authority		6	
1339 Total subsidy budget authority		6	

Credit accounts—Continued

COLUMBIA HOSPITAL FOR WOMEN DIRECT LOAN FINANCING ACCOUNT—Continued

Summary of Loan Levels, Subsidy Budget Authority and Outlays by Program (in millions of dollars)—Continued

Identification code 47–4029–0–3–804	1999 actual	2000 est.	2001 est.
Direct loan subsidy outlays:			
1340 Subsidy outlays	....	6	....
1349 Total subsidy outlays	....	6	....

As required by the Federal Credit Reform Act of 1990, this non-budgetary account records all cash flows to and from the Government resulting from the credit sale of Federal property to the Columbia Hospital for Women in the District of Columbia as directed by the Treasury and General Government Appropriations Act, 2000 (P.L. 106–58). The amounts in this account are a means of financing and are not included in the budget totals.

Balance Sheet (in millions of dollars)

Identification code 47–4029–0–3–804	1998 actual	1999 actual	2000 est.	2001 est.
ASSETS:				
1101 Federal assets: Fund balances with Treasury	....	....	6	6
Net value of assets related to post-1991 direct loans receivable:				
1401 Direct loans receivable, gross	....	....	14	14
1499 Net present value of assets related to direct loans	....	....	14	14
1999 Total assets	....	....	20	20

SUPPLY AND TECHNOLOGY ACTIVITIES

Federal Funds

General and special funds:

EXPENSES OF TRANSPORTATION AUDIT CONTRACTS AND CONTRACT ADMINISTRATION

Unavailable Collections (in millions of dollars)

Identification code 47–5250–0–2–804	1999 actual	2000 est.	2001 est.
Balance, start of year:			
01.99 Balance, start of year	23	20	17
Receipts:			
02.01 Recoveries of transportation overcharges	8	9	9
04.00 Total: Balances and collections	31	29	26
Appropriation:			
05.01 Expenses of transportation audit contracts and contract administration	−12	−12	−13
06.10 Unobligated balance returned to receipts	1	....	....
07.99 Total balance, end of year	20	17	13

Program and Financing (in millions of dollars)

Identification code 47–5250–0–2–804	1999 actual	2000 est.	2001 est.
Obligations by program activity:			
00.01 Audit contracts	4	5	5
00.02 Contract administration	7	7	8
10.00 Total new obligations	11	12	13
Budgetary resources available for obligation:			
22.00 New budget authority (gross)	12	12	13
23.95 Total new obligations	−11	−12	−13
23.98 Unobligated balance expiring or withdrawn	−1	....	....
New budget authority (gross), detail:			
Mandatory:			
60.25 Appropriation (special fund, indefinite)	12	12	13
Change in unpaid obligations:			
72.40 Unpaid obligations, start of year: Obligated balance, start of year	5	5	6
73.10 Total new obligations	11	12	13
73.20 Total outlays (gross)	−9	−12	−13
74.40 Unpaid obligations, end of year: Obligated balance, end of year	5	6	6
Outlays (gross), detail:			
86.97 Outlays from new mandatory authority	5	7	8
86.98 Outlays from mandatory balances	4	5	5
87.00 Total outlays (gross)	9	12	13
Net budget authority and outlays:			
89.00 Budget authority	12	12	13
90.00 Outlays	9	12	13

The expenses of Transportation Audit Contracts and Contract Administration activities are financed from overcharges collected from carriers on transportation bills paid by the Government and from other similar types of refunds. Public Law 99–627 granted GSA authority to delegate to the Government agencies prepayment audit of their transportation bills before they pay transportation carriers, permanent authority to pay transportation audit contractors from carrier overcharges collected, and authority to transfer net overpayments collected to the Treasury. With the passage of the Travel and Transportation Act of 1998, the prepayment audit of transportation bills is mandatory. The Act's changes will be effective in April 2000.

In 1999, $17 million of carrier overpayments were collected, and $9 million were returned to the U.S. Treasury, resulting in net receipts of $8 million.

Object Classification (in millions of dollars)

Identification code 47–5250–0–2–804	1999 actual	2000 est.	2001 est.
11.1 Personnel compensation: Full-time permanent	4	4	4
12.1 Civilian personnel benefits	1	1	1
25.2 Other services	4	5	5
25.3 Purchases of goods and services from Government accounts	2	2	3
99.9 Total new obligations	11	12	13

Personnel Summary

Identification code 47–5250–0–2–804	1999 actual	2000 est.	2001 est.
1001 Total compensable workyears: Full-time equivalent employment	66	67	67

Intragovernmental funds:

GENERAL SUPPLY FUND

Program and Financing (in millions of dollars)

Identification code 47–4530–0–4–804	1999 actual	2000 est.	2001 est.
Obligations by program activity:			
Supply and procurement:			
09.01 Stores, regular	754	707	704
09.02 Stores, direct delivery	33	36	36
09.03 Special order	473	393	393
09.04 Schedules	73	82	93
09.09 Subtotal, Supply and procurement	1,333	1,218	1,226
Other business lines:			
09.10 Personal property management	15	16	16
09.11 Travel and transportation	6	8	7
09.12 Vehicle acquisition and leasing	1,435	1,430	1,447
09.19 Subtotal, Other business lines	1,456	1,454	1,470

	Capital investments:			
09.21	Stores: Purchases of equipment	11	14	14
09.22	Fleet: Purchases of equipment	609	650	652
09.29	Subtotal, Capital investments	620	664	666
10.00	Total new obligations	3,409	3,336	3,362
	Budgetary resources available for obligation:			
21.40	Unobligated balance available, start of year	388	407	398
22.00	New budget authority (gross)	3,410	3,327	3,342
22.10	Resources available from recoveries of prior year obligations	19		
23.90	Total budgetary resources available for obligation	3,817	3,734	3,740
23.95	Total new obligations	−3,409	−3,336	−3,362
24.40	Unobligated balance available, end of year	407	398	378
	New budget authority (gross), detail:			
	Mandatory:			
69.00	Offsetting collections (cash)	3,455	3,327	3,342
69.10	From Federal sources: Change in receivables and unpaid, unfilled orders	−41		
69.27	Capital transfer to general fund	−4		
69.90	Spending authority from offsetting collections (total mandatory)	3,410	3,327	3,342
	Change in unpaid obligations:			
	Unpaid obligations, start of year:			
72.40	Obligated balance, start of year	−84	−53	−44
72.95	From Federal sources: Receivables and unpaid, unfilled orders	500	459	459
72.99	Total unpaid obligations, start of year	416	406	415
73.10	Total new obligations	3,409	3,336	3,362
73.20	Total outlays (gross)	−3,400	−3,327	−3,342
73.45	Adjustments in unexpired accounts	−19		
	Unpaid obligations, end of year:			
74.40	Obligated balance, end of year	−53	−44	−24
74.95	From Federal sources: Receivables and unpaid, unfilled orders	459	459	459
74.99	Total unpaid obligations, end of year	406	415	435
	Outlays (gross), detail:			
86.97	Outlays from new mandatory authority	3,096	2,973	2,988
86.98	Outlays from mandatory balances	304	354	354
87.00	Total outlays (gross)	3,400	3,327	3,342
	Offsets:			
	Against gross budget authority and outlays:			
	Offsetting collections (cash) from:			
88.00	Federal sources	−3,247	−3,127	−3,142
88.40	Non-Federal sources	−208	−200	−200
88.90	Total, offsetting collections (cash)	−3,455	−3,327	−3,342
	Against gross budget authority only:			
88.95	From Federal sources: Change in receivables and unpaid, unfilled orders	41		
	Net budget authority and outlays:			
89.00	Budget authority	−4		
90.00	Outlays	−55		

This fund finances, on a reimbursable basis, a national supply distribution system; a system of ordering supplies for direct delivery to Federal agencies; a system providing for the management, on a worldwide basis, of the sale of surplus personal property for agencies; a system of transportation and travel management which ensures discounted rates for lodging, transportation, and small package mailings for Federal customers; a Schedules contracting function providing a Government-wide program of commercial items and services; and a system of interagency Federal Fleet Management Centers. In 1988, legislation was enacted to authorize full cost recovery for all supply management, operating, and overhead expenses related to providing goods and services to other Federal agencies through the General Supply Fund. The total value of the contracts for products and services financed by the General Supply Fund exceeded $17 billion in 1999. The technical and procurement expertise available to Federal agencies through the Federal Supply Service's (FSS) four business lines reduces these agencies' own investments in acquisition administration and in the management of Federal personal property assets. This fund provides procurement vehicles for products and services through four business lines: Supply and Procurement, Personal Property Management, Travel and Transportation, and Vehicle Acquisition and Leasing.

The General Services Administration is currently reviewing the financial condition of the Federal Supply Service's national Stock Program and the viability of operating the existing warehouses. Since this review has not been concluded, the financial and employment data for the General Supply Fund reflect the continuation of the current Stock Program.

Supply and Procurement.—FSS provides the products and services required by Federal agencies to support their respective missions. There are currently over 6,800 contracts in place to meet Federal agencies' procurement needs. FSS has realized the greatest growth in the areas of services and technology. FSS Supply and Procurement business segments, which include Federal Supply Schedules, Stock, and Special Order programs, have enabled agencies to shorten procurement schedules and decrease administrative workloads and processing. These programs delivered $12.7 billion in products and services to Federal customers in 1999, a 35 percent increase over the previous year.

Schedules.—This contracting function provides a Government-wide supply support program of commercial and information technology items required by Federal agencies and other authorized users. The program enables Federal agencies to acquire more than 4 million commercial products and services directly from 6,800 GSA-approved vendors. GSA receives income for schedule contract administration in the amount of one percent of the total Schedules program business volume. This income was $114 million in 1999, and is expected to be $130 million in 2000, and $145 million in 2001. The on-line electronic catalog system, GSA Advantage, currently offers more than 750,000 products on-line, and will continue to increase the number and variety of items available electronically.

Personal Property Management.—This program generated sales of $12 million in 1999, and is estimated to generate sales of $12 million in 2000 and 2001. Receipts generated by this program, from selling surplus Government property to the public, are returned to the agencies or applied to Government deficit reduction.

Travel and Transportation.—In recent years, Federal travel and transportation budgets have totaled approximately $18 billion annually. A Federal market of this magnitude enables the Travel and Transportation program to negotiate favorable rates and provide agencies with significant savings. Through the Contract Airline City-Pairs Program, agencies achieved savings of 68 percent over unrestricted air fares in 1999, and the same savings are projected for 2000 and 2001. The household goods and freight services areas enjoyed savings of 47 percent and 45 percent, respectively, over comparable commercial rates in 1999, and the same rates are expected in 2000 and 2001.

Vehicle Acquisition and Leasing.—In 1998, the Fleet Management Division, responsible for vehicle leasing, and the Automotive Commodity Center, responsible for new motor vehicle procurements, were merged into a single entity managing vehicle-related transactions. In 1999, vehicle purchases by FSS totaled over $1 billion for more than 56,000 vehicles, at average savings of 13 to 18 percent over dealer invoice prices. FSS continued the expansion of the GSA fleet in 1999 by consolidating nearly 7,100 vehicles from other agencies, resulting in a nearly $6.8 million cost-avoidance for taxpayers in a single year. In 1999, the GSA fleet consisted of approxi-

Intragovernmental funds—Continued

GENERAL SUPPLY FUND—Continued

mately 167,000 vehicles, a 44 percent share of the Federal Fleet, and is expected to exceed 173,000 vehicles in 2000. Both consolidated buying and competitive purchasing offer Federal agencies significant savings in vehicle acquisition.

Statement of Operations (in millions of dollars)

Identification code 47–4530–0–4–804		1998 actual	1999 actual	2000 est.	2001 est.
	Supply and procurement:				
0111	Revenue	1,373	1,385	1,248	1,220
0112	Expense	–1,347	–1,346	–1,226	–1,196
0115	Net income or loss (–)	26	39	22	24
	Personal property management:				
0121	Revenue	14	16	16	17
0122	Expense	–14	–14	–16	–17
0125	Net income or loss (–)	....	2	....	....
	Travel and transportation:				
0131	Revenue	3	5	8	7
0132	Expense	–5	–6	–8	–7
0135	Net income or loss (–)	–2	–1	....	....
	Vehicle acquisition and leasing:				
0141	Revenue	1,326	1,399	1,405	1,446
0142	Expense	–1,213	–1,261	–1,266	–1,308
0145	Net income or loss (–)	113	138	139	138
0191	Total revenues	2,716	2,805	2,677	2,690
0192	Total expenses	–2,579	–2,627	–2,516	–2,528
0195	Total income or loss (–)	137	178	161	162
0199	Total Income	137	178	161	162

Object Classification (in millions of dollars)

Identification code 47–4530–0–4–804		1999 actual	2000 est.	2001 est.
	Personnel compensation:			
11.1	Full-time permanent	152	157	162
11.3	Other than full-time permanent	5	5	5
11.5	Other personnel compensation	2	2	2
11.9	Total personnel compensation	159	164	169
12.1	Civilian personnel benefits	35	36	37
	Travel and transportation of persons:			
21.0	Travel and transportation of persons	5	6	7
21.0	Motor vehicle usage	1	1	1
22.0	Transportation of things	55	56	57
23.1	Rental payments to GSA	46	45	46
23.3	Communications, utilities, and miscellaneous charges	16	16	16
24.0	Printing and reproduction	7	8	8
25.2	Other services	125	128	135
25.3	Purchases of goods and services from Government accounts	54	54	54
26.0	Supplies and materials	2,286	2,158	2,166
31.0	Equipment	620	664	666
99.9	Total new obligations	3,409	3,336	3,362

Personnel Summary

Identification code 47–4530–0–4–804		1999 actual	2000 est.	2001 est.
2001	Total compensable workyears: Full-time equivalent employment	3,215	3,199	3,199

INFORMATION TECHNOLOGY FUND

Program and Financing (in millions of dollars)

Identification code 47–4548–0–4–804		1999 actual	2000 est.	2001 est.
	Obligations by program activity:			
	Network services:			
09.01	FTS2001 long distance	829	696	532
09.02	Regional telecommunications services	365	276	287
09.09	Subtotal, Network services	1,194	972	819
	Information technology solutions:			
09.10	Information security	140	172	184
09.11	Information technology integration	3,800	3,370	3,423
09.19	Subtotal, Information technology solutions	3,940	3,542	3,607
	Capital investments network services:			
09.21	FTS2001 long distance	4	4	4
09.22	Regional telecommunications services	21	11	7
09.29	Subtotal, Capital investments networks services	25	15	11
	Capital investments information technology solutions:			
09.31	Information technology integration	6	18	18
09.39	Subtotal, Capital investments information technology solutions	6	18	18
10.00	Total new obligations	5,165	4,547	4,455
	Budgetary resources available for obligation:			
21.40	Unobligated balance available, start of year	717	687	442
22.00	New budget authority (gross)	4,866	4,302	4,278
22.10	Resources available from recoveries of prior year obligations	269	....	....
23.90	Total budgetary resources available for obligation	5,852	4,989	4,720
23.95	Total new obligations	–5,165	–4,547	–4,455
24.40	Unobligated balance available, end of year	687	442	265
	New budget authority (gross), detail:			
	Spending authority from offsetting collections:			
	Discretionary:			
68.00	Offsetting collections (cash)	4,117	4,302	4,278
68.10	From Federal sources: Change in receivables and unpaid, unfilled orders	749	....	....
68.90	Spending authority from offsetting collections (total discretionary)	4,866	4,302	4,278
	Change in unpaid obligations:			
	Unpaid obligations, start of year:			
72.40	Obligated balance, start of year	–629	–657	–517
72.95	From Federal sources: Receivables and unpaid, unfilled orders	3,108	3,857	3,857
72.99	Total unpaid obligations, start of year	2,479	3,200	3,340
73.10	Total new obligations	5,165	4,547	4,455
73.20	Total outlays (gross)	–4,176	–4,407	–4,309
73.45	Adjustments in unexpired accounts	–269	....	....
	Unpaid obligations, end of year:			
74.40	Obligated balance, end of year	–657	–517	–371
74.95	From Federal sources: Receivables and unpaid, unfilled orders	3,857	3,857	3,857
74.99	Total unpaid obligations, end of year	3,200	3,340	3,486
	Outlays (gross), detail:			
86.90	Outlays from new discretionary authority	4,088	3,227	3,179
86.93	Outlays from discretionary balances	88	1,180	1,131
87.00	Total outlays (gross)	4,176	4,407	4,309
	Offsets:			
	Against gross budget authority and outlays:			
88.00	Offsetting collections (cash) from: Federal sources	–4,117	–4,302	–4,278
	Against gross budget authority only:			
88.95	From Federal sources: Change in receivables and unpaid, unfilled orders	–749	....	....
	Net budget authority and outlays:			
89.00	Budget authority	....	....	....
90.00	Outlays	59	105	31

The Information Technology Fund was authorized by the Paperwork Reduction Reauthorization Act of 1986, as included in Public Laws 99–500 and 99–591, section 821(a)(1). The Fund provides information technology resources to Federal agencies, promoting the use of the latest technology to deliver services and facilitating the efficient management, coordination, operation, and use of such resources.

Levels of funding for capital investments and for operating capital for the Federal Technology Service (FTS) are determined through the submission and approval process of planned cost and capital requirements to OMB by GSA pursuant to section 110(a)(1), Federal Property and Administrative Services Act of 1949, as amended by Public Law 99–591.

The Fund finances, on a reimbursable basis, Government-wide information technology services through two business lines in the FTS: Network Services and Information Technology (IT) Solutions.

Network Services.—The Network Services business line offers Federal customers end-to-end telecommunications services including global voice, data, and video services, supporting both local and long distance government telecommunications users. This business line also provides advanced telecommunications products and services through special services contracts, referred to as innovative services contracts. The innovative services contracts provide customers with a variety of fully competed services for wireless communications, technical management support services, international calling, wire and cable, satellite equipment, and internet access.

FTS2001 Long Distance.—Provides long-distance telecommunications services to more than 1.7 million users through two eight-year $5 billion contracts awarded to Sprint and MCI WorldCom. The contracts provide the Government with low-cost, state-of-the-art, integrated voice, data and video telecommunications services. FTS2001 replaces the two successful FTS2000 contracts and retains many of their key features, in particular aggressive price competition. Through GSA negotiations over the past ten years, long distance telecommunications rates for Federal agencies have decreased from a national average of 27 cents per minute in 1988 to a rate of 5 cents per minute under FTS2000. Under the FTS2001 contracts, long distance rates will begin at 4 cents per minute and will fall below 1 cent per minute by the end of the contract period. Transition from FTS2000 to FTS2001 began in June 1999 and is expected to be complete within eighteen months. Under the FTS2001 contracts, FTS will no longer be a mandatory source of long-distance telecommuncations services for Federal agencies.

Local Telecommunications Services.—Provides local voice and data telecommunications services to Federal agencies nationwide. To take advantage of the changing local telecommunications marketplace, GSA has initiated the Metropolitan Area Acquisition (MAA) Program. The MAA Program will take advantage of competition and of reforms enacted by the Telecommunications Act of 1996 to achieve substantial price reductions for local telecommunications services in metropolitan areas. Awards in three initial cities—New York, Chicago, and San Francisco—were issued in May 1999. These three competitions have yielded savings of 70 percent and 66 percent over standard business and current government rates, respectively. Due to the success of the initial competitions, FTS expects Federal agencies in metropolitan areas nationwide to benefit from competitive local telephone and data services rates in the near future.

IT Solutions.—The IT Solutions business line helps agencies acquire, manage, integrate, and use technology resources and protect the security of Federal information on-line through contracts with private sector firms. IT Solutions enables agency customers to purchase through FTS contracts, through Federal Supply Service Schedules, and through the contracting offices of other Federal agencies with which IT Solutions has developed strategic partnering arrangements. The major programs under the IT Solutions business line are Regional IT Solutions, the Federal Integration and Management Center (FEDSIM), the Federal Computer Acquisition Center (FEDCAC), the IT Acquisition Services Center, the Financial Management Systems Support Center (FMSSC), the Office of Smart Card Initiatives, and the Office of Information Security (OIS).

Regional IT Solutions.—Provides agencies with systems definition and design, business and scientific software services, computer security studies and risk analyses, facilities management, and access to all FTS products and services. The Federal Acquisition Services for Technology (FAST) program is a large part of the regional program, designed to enable Federal agencies to quickly purchase commercial off-the-shelf information technology software, equipment, and non-complex services.

FEDSIM.—Assists agencies in the acquisition and use of information systems and information technology, including hardware, software, maintenance, training and analyst support and focuses on large, complex systems integration efforts.

FEDCAC.—Delivers full service management of technology acquisitions worth more than $100 million and conducts full and open competitions for contracts required by GSA customer support centers nationwide.

IT Acquisition Services Center.—Provides information technology solutions and services to GSA itself. The Center provides GSA rapid access to all FTS contractual vehicles, to the Federal Supply Service's Schedules, and to other Government-wide acquisition vehicles.

FMSSC.—Assists Federal agencies in evaluating, designing, and implementing financial and administrative systems. FMSSC works with agencies to define systems requirements and develop procurement strategies to satisfy those requirements. FMSSC is currently implementing a new FTS Enterprise Resource Planning (ERP) initiative to encourage and increase Federal agency use of ERP systems. ERP systems provide cost-effective data storage, processing, and retrieval.

Office of Smart Card Initiatives.—Provides a full range of smart card services, including mobile computing platforms for identification and authentication. In 2000, the Office of Smart Card Initiatives will compete and award a Government-wide "Common Access Identification" Smart Card contract for use by Federal agencies.

Office of Information Security.—Provides worldwide information systems and infrastructure security solutions to all U.S. Government departments and agencies. OIS also supports the security needs of our nation's allies, in the conduct of classified, sensitive, diplomatic, or military missions.

Statement of Operations (in millions of dollars)

Identification code 47–4548–0–4–804	1998 actual	1999 actual	2000 est.	2001 est.
Network services:				
0111 Revenue	1,013	1,078	923	819
0112 Expense	–1,072	–1,094	–1,014	–845
0115 Net income or loss (–)	–59	–16	–91	–26
IT solutions:				
0121 Revenue	2,402	3,098	3,379	3,459
0122 Expense	–2,396	–3,101	–3,395	–3,463
0125 Net income or loss (–)	6	–3	–16	–4
0191 Total revenues	3,415	4,176	4,302	4,278
0192 Total expenses	–3,468	–4,195	–4,409	–4,308
0195 Total income or loss (–)	–53	–19	–107	–30
0199 Total income	–53	–19	–107	–30

Object Classification (in millions of dollars)

Identification code 47–4548–0–4–804	1999 actual	2000 est.	2001 est.
Personnel compensation:			
11.1 Full-time permanent	87	97	101
11.5 Other personnel compensation	1	2	2
11.9 Total personnel compensation	88	99	103
12.1 Civilian personnel benefits	18	22	25
21.0 Travel and transportation of persons	5	7	7

Intragovernmental funds—Continued

INFORMATION TECHNOLOGY FUND—Continued

Object Classification (in millions of dollars)—Continued

Identification code 47–4548–0–4–804		1999 actual	2000 est.	2001 est.
23.1	Rental payments to GSA	11	11	11
23.3	Communications, utilities, and miscellaneous charges	2	4	4
24.0	Printing and reproduction	1	1	1
25.2	Other services	4,638	4,074	3,981
25.3	Purchases of goods and services from Government accounts	365	307	300
26.0	Supplies and materials	6	3	3
31.0	Equipment	31	19	20
99.9	Total new obligations	5,165	4,547	4,455

Personnel Summary

Identification code 47–4548–0–4–804		1999 actual	2000 est.	2001 est.
2001	Total compensable workyears: Full-time equivalent employment	1,303	1,340	1,340

GENERAL ACTIVITIES

Federal Funds

General and special funds:

POLICY AND OPERATIONS

For expenses authorized by law, not otherwise provided for, for Government-wide policy and oversight activities associated with asset management activities; utilization and donation of surplus personal property; transportation; procurement and supply; Government-wide responsibilities relating to automated data management, telecommunications, information resources management, and related technology activities; utilization survey, deed compliance inspection, appraisal, environmental and cultural analysis, and land use planning functions pertaining to excess and surplus real property; agency-wide policy direction; Board of Contract Appeals; accounting, records management, and other support services incident to adjudication of Indian Tribal Claims by the United States Court of Federal Claims; services as authorized by 5 U.S.C. 3109; and not to exceed $5,000 for official reception and representation expenses, [$116,223,000] *$136,980,000*, of which [$12,758,000] *$27,301,000* shall remain available until expended[: *Provided*, That none of the funds appropriated from this Act shall be available to convert the Old Post Office at 1100 Pennsylvania Avenue in Northwest Washington, D.C., from office use to any other use until a comprehensive plan, which shall include street-level retail use, has been approved by the Senate Committee on Appropriations, the House Committee on Transportation and Infrastructure, and the Senate Committee on Environment and Public Works: *Provided further*, That no funds from this Act shall be available to acquire by purchase, condemnation, or otherwise the leasehold rights of the existing lease with private parties at the Old Post Office prior to the approval of the comprehensive plan by the Senate Committee on Appropriations, the House Committee on Transportation and Infrastructure, and the Senate Committee on Environment and Public Works]. *In addition, not to exceed $8,000,000 may be transferred from balances in the "Disposal of surplus real and related personal property" account for costs related to the disposal of real property that are incurred by GSA on behalf of landholding agencies before the disposal is completed: Provided, That such agencies shall reimburse such "Disposal" account for such costs from subsequent disposal proceeds, unless the disposal proceeds are not sufficient to cover these costs, in which case the agencies shall make these reimbursements from any other funds available to such agencies. (40 U.S.C. 485(b); Independent Agencies Appropriations Act, 2000.)*

Program and Financing (in millions of dollars)

Identification code 47–0110–0–1–804		1999 actual	2000 est.	2001 est.
	Obligations by program activity:			
	Direct program:			
00.01	Policy	71	57	56
00.02	Operations	80	123	89
09.01	Reimbursable program	10	17	21
10.00	Total new obligations	161	197	166
	Budgetary resources available for obligation:			
21.40	Unobligated balance available, start of year		42	
22.00	New budget authority (gross)	205	155	166
23.90	Total budgetary resources available for obligation	205	197	166
23.95	Total new obligations	−161	−197	−166
23.98	Unobligated balance expiring or withdrawn	−2		
24.40	Unobligated balance available, end of year	42		
	New budget authority (gross), detail:			
	Discretionary:			
40.00	Appropriation	109	116	137
40.20	Appropriation (special fund, definite)			8
42.00	Transferred from other accounts	85	22	
43.00	Appropriation (total discretionary)	194	138	145
	Spending authority from offsetting collections:			
68.00	Offsetting collections (cash)	4	17	21
68.10	From Federal sources: Change in receivables and unpaid, unfilled orders	7		
68.90	Spending authority from offsetting collections (total discretionary)	11	17	21
70.00	Total new budget authority (gross)	205	155	166
	Change in unpaid obligations:			
	Unpaid obligations, start of year:			
72.40	Obligated balance, start of year	29	36	19
72.95	From Federal sources: Receivables and unpaid, unfilled orders	9	16	16
72.99	Total unpaid obligations, start of year	38	52	35
73.10	Total new obligations	161	197	166
73.20	Total outlays (gross)	−146	−214	−164
73.40	Adjustments in expired accounts (net)			
	Unpaid obligations, end of year:			
74.40	Obligated balance, end of year	36	19	21
74.95	From Federal sources: Receivables and unpaid, unfilled orders	16	16	16
74.99	Total unpaid obligations, end of year	52	35	37
	Outlays (gross), detail:			
86.90	Outlays from new discretionary authority	122	137	145
86.93	Outlays from discretionary balances	24	77	18
87.00	Total outlays (gross)	146	214	164
	Offsets:			
	Against gross budget authority and outlays:			
88.00	Offsetting collections (cash) from: Federal sources	−4	−17	−21
	Against gross budget authority only:			
88.95	From Federal sources: Change in receivables and unpaid, unfilled orders	−7		
	Net budget authority and outlays:			
89.00	Budget authority	194	138	145
90.00	Outlays	140	197	143

Summary of Budget Authority and Outlays

(in millions of dollars)

	1999 actual	*2000 est.*	*2001 est.*
Enacted/requested:			
Budget Authority	194	138	145
Outlays	142	197	142
Supplemental proposal:			
Budget Authority		2	
Outlays		2	
Total:			
Budget Authority	194	140	145
Outlays	142	199	142

Policy provides for Government-wide policy, evaluation, and asset management functions associated with real and personal property, supplies, information technology, acquisition support, transportation and travel management, Federal Procurement Data Center, Regulatory Information Service Center, the Catalog of Federal Domestic Assistance, and the Committee Management Secretariat. The Office of Governmentwide Policy, working cooperatively with other agencies, provides the leadership needed to develop and evaluate the implementation of policies designed to achieve the most cost-effective solutions for the delivery of administrative services and sound workplace practices, while reducing regulations and empowering employees.

Operations provides for the personal property utilization and donation activities of the Federal Supply Service and for the real property utilization and disposal activities of the Public Buildings Service, as well as agency-wide management and administration. These programs include utilization of real and personal property by Federal agencies and the transfer among agencies of excess real and personal property; disposal of surplus real property by sale, exchange, lease, permit, assignment, or transfer, as well as the protection and maintenance of excess and surplus property pending its disposition; appraisal of excess and surplus property, necessary environmental and cultural analyses, reuse planning, and real property utilization surveys; Indian Trust Accounting, administrative support of Congressional District and Senate State offices, and Critical Infrastructure Protection.

Object Classification (in millions of dollars)

Identification code 47–0110–0–1–804		1999 actual	2000 est.	2001 est.
	Direct obligations:			
	Personnel compensation:			
11.1	Full-time permanent	43	44	43
11.3	Other than full-time permanent	1	1	
11.5	Other personnel compensation	2	4	3
11.9	Total personnel compensation	46	49	46
12.1	Civilian personnel benefits	9	9	9
21.0	Travel and transportation of persons	2	2	2
23.1	Rental payments to GSA	5	8	7
23.3	Communications, utilities, and miscellaneous charges	2	3	2
24.0	Printing and reproduction	1	2	1
25.2	Other services	60	51	36
25.3	Purchases of goods and services from Government accounts	18	35	31
26.0	Supplies and materials	1	1	1
31.0	Equipment	7	20	10
99.0	Subtotal, direct obligations	151	180	145
99.0	Reimbursable obligations	9	17	21
99.5	Below reporting threshold	1		
99.9	Total new obligations	161	197	166

Personnel Summary

Identification code 47–0110–0–1–804		1999 actual	2000 est.	2001 est.
	Direct:			
1001	Total compensable workyears: Full-time equivalent employment	663	603	612
	Reimbursable:			
2001	Total compensable workyears: Full-time equivalent employment	16	17	17

OFFICE OF INSPECTOR GENERAL

For necessary expenses of the Office of Inspector General and services authorized by 5 U.S.C. 3109, [$33,317,000] *$34,520,000*: *Provided*, That not to exceed $15,000 shall be available for payment for information and detection of fraud against the Government, including payment for recovery of stolen Government property: *Provided further*, That not to exceed $2,500 shall be available for awards to employees of other Federal agencies and private citizens in recognition of efforts and initiatives resulting in enhanced Office of Inspector General effectiveness. *(Independent Agencies Appropriations Act, 2000.)*

Program and Financing (in millions of dollars)

Identification code 47–0108–0–1–804		1999 actual	2000 est.	2001 est.
	Obligations by program activity:			
10.00	Total new obligations	32	33	35
	Budgetary resources available for obligation:			
22.00	New budget authority (gross)	32	33	35
23.95	Total new obligations	−32	−33	−35
	New budget authority (gross), detail:			
	Discretionary:			
40.00	Appropriation	32	33	35
	Change in unpaid obligations:			
72.40	Unpaid obligations, start of year: Obligated balance, start of year	4	3	3
73.10	Total new obligations	32	33	35
73.20	Total outlays (gross)	−32	−33	−34
74.40	Unpaid obligations, end of year: Obligated balance, end of year	3	3	3
	Outlays (gross), detail:			
86.90	Outlays from new discretionary authority	32	33	34
	Net budget authority and outlays:			
89.00	Budget authority	32	33	35
90.00	Outlays	32	33	34

This appropriation provides agency-wide audit and investigative functions to identify and correct management and administrative deficiencies within GSA, which create conditions for existing or potential instances of fraud, waste and mismanagement. The audit function provides internal audit and contract audit services. Contract audits provide professional advice to GSA contracting officials on accounting and financial matters relative to the negotiation, award, administration, repricing, and settlement of contracts. Internal audits review and evaluate all facets of GSA operations and programs, test internal control systems, and develop information to improve operating efficiencies and enhance customer services. The investigative function provides for the detection and investigation of improper and illegal activities involving GSA programs, personnel, and operations.

Object Classification (in millions of dollars)

Identification code 47–0108–0–1–804		1999 actual	2000 est.	2001 est.
11.1	Personnel compensation: Full-time permanent	19	21	23
12.1	Civilian personnel benefits	4	4	4
21.0	Travel and transportation of persons	1	2	2
23.1	Rental payments to GSA	3	3	3
25.2	Other services	4	3	3
99.0	Subtotal, direct obligations	31	33	35
99.5	Below reporting threshold	1		
99.9	Total new obligations	32	33	35

Personnel Summary

Identification code 47–0108–0–1–804		1999 actual	2000 est.	2001 est.
1001	Total compensable workyears: Full-time equivalent employment	275	297	297

ALLOWANCES AND OFFICE STAFF FOR FORMER PRESIDENTS

(INCLUDING TRANSFER OF FUNDS)

For carrying out the provisions of the Act of August 25, 1958, as amended (3 U.S.C. 102 note), and Public Law 95–138, [$2,241,000] *$2,517,000*: *Provided*, That the Administrator of General Services shall transfer to the Secretary of the Treasury such sums as may be necessary to carry out the provisions of such Acts. *(Independent Agencies Appropriations Act, 2000.)*

General and special funds—Continued

ALLOWANCES AND OFFICE STAFF FOR FORMER PRESIDENTS—Continued

(INCLUDING TRANSFER OF FUNDS)—Continued

Program and Financing (in millions of dollars)

Identification code 47–0105–0–1–802	1999 actual	2000 est.	2001 est.
Obligations by program activity:			
00.01 Allowances and pensions	1	1	1
00.02 Office staff	1	1	2
10.00 Total new obligations	2	2	3
Budgetary resources available for obligation:			
22.00 New budget authority (gross)	2	2	3
23.95 Total new obligations	−2	−2	−3
New budget authority (gross), detail:			
Discretionary:			
40.00 Appropriation	2	2	3
Change in unpaid obligations:			
73.10 Total new obligations	2	2	3
73.20 Total outlays (gross)	−2	−2	−3
Outlays (gross), detail:			
86.90 Outlays from new discretionary authority	2	2	3
Net budget authority and outlays:			
89.00 Budget authority	2	2	3
90.00 Outlays	2	2	3

This appropriation provides support consisting of pensions, office staffs, and related expenses for former Presidents Gerald R. Ford, Jimmy Carter, Ronald Reagan, George Bush and William Jefferson Clinton, after he leaves office, and for pension and postal franking privileges for the widow of former President Lyndon B. Johnson.

Object Classification (in millions of dollars)

Identification code 47–0105–0–1–802	1999 actual	2000 est.	2001 est.
13.0 Benefits for former personnel	1	1	1
23.1 Rental payments to GSA	1	1	1
99.0 Subtotal, direct obligations	2	2	2
99.5 Below reporting threshold			1
99.9 Total new obligations	2	2	3

EXPENSES, PRESIDENTIAL TRANSITION

For expenses necessary to carry out the Presidential Transition Act of 1963, as amended, $7,100,000. (3 U.S.C. 102, note)

Program and Financing (in millions of dollars)

Identification code 47–0107–0–1–802	1999 actual	2000 est.	2001 est.
Obligations by program activity:			
00.01 Transition expenses			7
10.00 Total new obligations (object class 91.0)			7
Budgetary resources available for obligation:			
22.00 New budget authority (gross)			7
23.95 Total new obligations			−7
New budget authority (gross), detail:			
Discretionary:			
40.00 Appropriation			7
Change in unpaid obligations:			
73.10 Total new obligations			7
73.20 Total outlays (gross)			−7
Outlays (gross), detail:			
86.90 Outlays from new discretionary authority			7
Net budget authority and outlays:			
89.00 Budget authority			7
90.00 Outlays			7

Funds are appropriated in accordance with the Presidential Transition Act of 1963, as amended, to provide for an orderly transfer of executive leadership. These expenses include costs related to briefing personnel associated with the incoming administration authorized under pending legislation. New appropriations are generally requested in Presidential election years.

In the case where the President-elect is the incumbent President or in the case where the Vice President-elect is the incumbent Vice President, there shall be no expenditure of funds for the provision of services and facilities to such incumbent under this Act, and any funds appropriated for such purposes shall be returned to the general fund of the Treasury.

Public enterprise funds:

FEDERAL CONSUMER INFORMATION CENTER FUND

For necessary expenses of the *Federal* Consumer Information Center, including services authorized by 5 U.S.C. 3109, [$2,622,000] *$6,822,000*, to be deposited into the *Federal* Consumer Information Center Fund: *Provided*, That the appropriations, revenues, and collections deposited into the fund shall be available for necessary expenses of *Federal* Consumer Information Center activities in the aggregate amount of [$7,500,000] *$12,000,000*. Appropriations, revenues, and collections accruing to this fund during fiscal year [2000] *2001* in excess of [$7,500,000] *$12,000,000* shall remain in the fund and shall not be available for expenditure except as authorized in appropriations Acts. *(Departments of Veterans Affairs and Housing and Urban Development, and Independent Agencies Appropriations Act, 2000.)*

Program and Financing (in millions of dollars)

Identification code 47–4549–0–3–376	1999 actual	2000 est.	2001 est.
Obligations by program activity:			
09.01 Direct program	3	3	7
09.02 Reimbursable program	4	4	4
10.00 Total new obligations	7	7	11
Budgetary resources available for obligation:			
21.40 Unobligated balance available, start of year	1	1	1
22.00 New budget authority (gross)	7	7	11
23.90 Total budgetary resources available for obligation	8	8	12
23.95 Total new obligations	−7	−7	−11
24.40 Unobligated balance available, end of year	1	1	1
New budget authority (gross), detail:			
Discretionary:			
40.00 Appropriation	3	3	7
68.00 Spending authority from offsetting collections: Offsetting collections (cash)	4	4	4
70.00 Total new budget authority (gross)	7	7	11
Change in unpaid obligations:			
72.40 Unpaid obligations, start of year: Obligated balance, start of year	1	2	2
73.10 Total new obligations	7	7	11
73.20 Total outlays (gross)	−6	−7	−11
74.40 Unpaid obligations, end of year: Obligated balance, end of year	2	2	2
Outlays (gross), detail:			
86.90 Outlays from new discretionary authority	6	7	11
Offsets:			
Against gross budget authority and outlays:			
Offsetting collections (cash) from:			
88.00 Federal sources	−3	−3	−3

88.40	Non-Federal sources	–1	–1	–1
88.90	Total, offsetting collections (cash)	–4	–4	–4
	Net budget authority and outlays:			
89.00	Budget authority	3	3	7
90.00	Outlays	2	3	7

The Federal Consumer Information Center (FCIC) Fund provides for the efficient operation of the FCIC's activities. Under the revolving fund, the FCIC's activities are financed from moneys deposited to the fund, consisting of annual appropriations from the general funds of the Treasury, reimbursements from agencies, fees collected from the public, gifts for undertaking consumer information activities, and other income incident to FCIC activities.

Administrative expenses.—The FCIC helps Federal departments and agencies release consumer information collected as a by-product of the Government's program activities. The FCIC maintains close working relationships with more than 40 Federal agencies in order to identify, develop, promote, and make accessible to the public Federal consumer information. In addition, the FCIC promotes public awareness of this information through publication of the quarterly *Consumer Information Catalog,* through special projects promoting the Catalog, and through various media services including an Internet website located at http://www.pueblo.gsa.gov. The FCIC also produces and distributes the *Consumer's Resource Handbook*, which provides information to citizens in resolving consumer problems, and it operates a nationwide toll-free telephone system for responding to consumer inquiries about the Federal Government. Administrative expenses are funded by the direct appropriation and by fees collected from the public when ordering publications listed in the catalog.

Publications distribution.—The FCIC bills agencies and in turn reimburses the Government Printing Office for the costs of distributing free publications to the public.

Statement of Operations (in millions of dollars)

Identification code 47–4549–0–3–376		1998 actual	1999 actual	2000 est.	2001 est.
0101	Revenue	5	6	6	11
0102	Expense	–5	–6	–6	–11
0105	Net income or loss (–)				

Object Classification (in millions of dollars)

Identification code 47–4549–0–3–376		1999 actual	2000 est.	2001 est.
11.1	Personnel compensation: Full-time permanent	2	2	2
25.2	Other services	5	5	9
99.9	Total new obligations	7	7	11

Personnel Summary

Identification code 47–4549–0–3–376		1999 actual	2000 est.	2001 est.
2001	Total compensable workyears: Full-time equivalent employment	21	22	24

Intragovernmental funds:

WORKING CAPITAL FUND

Program and Financing (in millions of dollars)

Identification code 47–4540–0–4–804		1999 actual	2000 est.	2001 est.
	Obligations by program activity:			
10.00	Total new obligations	224	279	297
	Budgetary resources available for obligation:			
21.40	Unobligated balance available, start of year	36	36	36
22.00	New budget authority (gross)	217	279	297
22.10	Resources available from recoveries of prior year obligations	7		
23.90	Total budgetary resources available for obligation	260	315	333
23.95	Total new obligations	–224	–279	–297
24.40	Unobligated balance available, end of year	36	36	36
	New budget authority (gross), detail:			
	Discretionary:			
50.00	Reappropriation	4		
	Spending authority from offsetting collections:			
68.00	Offsetting collections (cash)	210	279	297
68.10	From Federal sources: Change in receivables and unpaid, unfilled orders	3		
68.90	Spending authority from offsetting collections (total discretionary)	213	279	297
70.00	Total new budget authority (gross)	217	279	297
	Change in unpaid obligations:			
	Unpaid obligations, start of year:			
72.40	Obligated balance, start of year	42	42	42
72.95	From Federal sources: Receivables and unpaid, unfilled orders	2	5	5
72.99	Total unpaid obligations, start of year	44	47	47
73.10	Total new obligations	224	279	297
73.20	Total outlays (gross)	–214	–279	–297
73.45	Adjustments in unexpired accounts	–7		
	Unpaid obligations, end of year:			
74.40	Obligated balance, end of year	42	42	42
74.95	From Federal sources: Receivables and unpaid, unfilled orders	5	5	5
74.99	Total unpaid obligations, end of year	47	47	47
	Outlays (gross), detail:			
86.90	Outlays from new discretionary authority	214	279	297
	Offsets:			
	Against gross budget authority and outlays:			
88.00	Offsetting collections (cash) from: Federal sources	–210	–279	–297
	Against gross budget authority only:			
88.95	From Federal sources: Change in receivables and unpaid, unfilled orders	–3		
	Net budget authority and outlays:			
89.00	Budget authority	4		
90.00	Outlays	4		

This fund provides for management and administration, and centralized internal and external reimbursable administrative support functions.

Centralized administration.—Centralized administrative support services are funded through reimbursable funding from GSA's benefiting accounts and from external sources including small agencies and commissions for services provided. Reimbursable services include administrative, information resources management, financial and management support, legal advice and services, and equal employment opportunity; budgetary policy and liaison activities with Congress and OMB; and management review and oversight of financial management systems. This funding provides liaison with the Small Business Administration on national minority business proposals and contracts to ensure that minority and small businesses receive a fair share of the agency's business. This activity is also responsible for implementation and execution of the functions and duties under sections 8 and 15 of the Small Business Act (P.L. 95–507).

Statement of Operations (in millions of dollars)

Identification code 47–4540–0–4–804		1998 actual	1999 actual	2000 est.	2001 est.
0101	Revenue	203	211	279	297
0102	Expense	–201	–219	–279	–297
0105	Net income or loss (–)	2	–8		

Intragovernmental funds—Continued

WORKING CAPITAL FUND—Continued

Object Classification (in millions of dollars)

Identification code 47–4540–0–4–804		1999 actual	2000 est.	2001 est.
	Personnel compensation:			
11.1	Full-time permanent	67	71	74
11.3	Other than full-time permanent	1	1	1
11.5	Other personnel compensation	9	10	11
11.9	Total personnel compensation	77	82	86
12.1	Civilian personnel benefits	32	38	40
13.0	Benefits for former personnel	1	2	2
21.0	Travel and transportation of persons	3	4	4
22.0	Transportation of things	1	2	2
23.1	Rental payments to GSA	12	14	15
23.3	Communications, utilities, and miscellaneous charges	20	24	24
24.0	Printing and reproduction	3	5	5
25.2	Other services	39	61	69
25.3	Purchases of goods and services from Government accounts	28	35	38
26.0	Supplies and materials	2	4	4
31.0	Equipment	6	8	8
99.9	Total new obligations	224	279	297

Personnel Summary

Identification code 47–4540–0–4–804		1999 actual	2000 est.	2001 est.
2001	Total compensable workyears: Full-time equivalent employment	1,330	1,368	1,373

GENERAL SERVICES ADMINISTRATION—GENERAL PROVISIONS

SEC. 401. The appropriate appropriation or fund available to the General Services Administration shall be credited with the cost of operation, protection, maintenance, upkeep, repair, and improvement, included as part of rentals received from Government corporations pursuant to law (40 U.S.C. 129).

SEC. 402. Funds available to the General Services Administration shall be available for the hire of passenger motor vehicles.

SEC. 403. Funds in the Federal Buildings Fund made available for fiscal year [2000] *2001* for Federal Buildings Fund activities may be transferred between such activities only to the extent necessary to meet program requirements: *Provided*, That *notice of* any proposed transfers shall be [approved] *transmitted* in advance [by] *to* the Committees on Appropriations.

SEC. 404. No funds made available by this Act shall be used to transmit a fiscal year [2001] *2002* request for United States Courthouse construction that: (1) does not meet the design guide standards for construction as established and approved by the General Services Administration, the Judicial Conference of the United States, and the Office of Management and Budget; and (2) does not reflect the priorities of the Judicial Conference of the United States as set out in its approved 5-year construction plan: *Provided*, That the fiscal year [2001] *2002* request must be accompanied by a standardized courtroom utilization study of each facility to be constructed, replaced, or expanded.

SEC. 405. None of the funds provided in this Act may be used to increase the amount of occupiable square feet, provide cleaning services, security enhancements, or any other service usually provided through the Federal Buildings Fund, to any agency that does not pay the rate per square foot assessment for space and services as determined by the General Services Administration in compliance with the Public Buildings Amendments Act of 1972 (Public Law 92–313).

SEC. 406. Funds provided to other Government agencies by the Information Technology Fund, General Services Administration, under 40 U.S.C. 757 and sections 5124(b) and 5128 of Public Law 104–106, Information Technology Management Reform Act of 1996, for performance of pilot information technology projects which have potential for Government-wide benefits and savings, may be repaid to this Fund from any savings actually incurred by these projects or other funding, to the extent feasible.

SEC. 407. From funds made available under the heading "Federal Buildings Fund, Limitations on Availability of Revenue", claims against the Government of less than $250,000 arising from direct construction projects and acquisition of buildings may be liquidated from savings effected in other construction projects with prior notification to the Committees on Appropriations.

[SEC. 408. Funds made available for new construction projects under the heading "Federal Buildings Fund, Limitations on Availability of Revenue" in Public Law 104–208 shall remain available until expended so long as funds for design or other funds have been obligated in whole or in part prior to September 30, 1999.]

[SEC. 409. The Federal building located at 220 East Rosser Avenue in Bismarck, North Dakota, is hereby designated as the "William L. Guy Federal Building, Post Office and United States Courthouse". Any reference in a law, map, regulation, document, paper or other record of the United States to the Federal building herein referred to shall be deemed to be a reference to the "William L. Guy Federal Building, Post Office and United States Courthouse".]

[SEC. 410. CONVEYANCE OF LAND TO THE COLUMBIA HOSPITAL FOR WOMEN. (a) ADMINISTRATOR OF GENERAL SERVICES.—Upon receipt of written notice and the consideration specified herein from the Columbia Hospital for Women (formerly Columbia Hospital for Women and Lying-In Asylum, located in Washington, District of Columbia; in this section referred to as "Columbia Hospital"), subject to subsection (f) and such other terms and conditions as the Administrator of General Services (in this section referred to as the "Administrator") shall require, the Administrator shall convey to Columbia Hospital, all right, title, and interest of the United States in and to those pieces or parcels of land in the District of Columbia, described in subsection (b), together with all improvements thereon and appurtenances thereto (in this section referred to as "the Property"). The purchase price for the Property shall be $14,000,000 (not including any accrued interest) to be paid in accordance with the terms set forth in subsection (d). The purpose of this conveyance is to provide hospital, medical and healthcare services and related uses, including but not limited to the expansion by Columbia Hospital of its Ambulatory Care Center, Betty Ford Breast Center, and the Columbia Hospital Center for Teen Health and Reproductive Toxicology Center.]

[(b) PROPERTY DESCRIPTION.—

(1) IN GENERAL.—The land referred to in subsection (a) was conveyed to the United States of America by deed dated May 2, 1888, from David Fergusson, widower, recorded in liber 1314, folio 102, of the land records of the District of Columbia, and is that portion of square numbered 25 in the city of Washington in the District of Columbia which was not previously conveyed to such hospital by the Act of June 28, 1952 (66 Stat. 287; chapter 486).

(2) PARTICULAR DESCRIPTION.—The Property is more particularly described as square 25, lot 803, or as follows: all that piece or parcel of land situated and lying in the city of Washington in the District of Columbia and known as part of square numbered 25, as laid down and distinguished on the plat or plan of said city as follows: beginning for the same at the northeast corner of the square being the corner formed by the intersection of the west line of Twenty-fourth Street Northwest, with the south line of north M Street Northwest and running thence south with the line of said Twenty-fourth Street Northwest for the distance of two hundred and thirty-one feet ten inches, thence running west and parallel with said M Street Northwest for the distance of two hundred and thirty feet six inches and running thence north and parallel with the line of said Twenty-fourth Street Northwest for the distance of two hundred and thirty-one feet ten inches to the line of said M Street Northwest and running thence east with the line of said M Street Northwest to the place of beginning two hundred and thirty feet and six inches together with all the improvements, ways, easements, rights, privileges, and appurtenances to the same belonging or in anywise appertaining.]

[(c) DATE OF CONVEYANCE.—

(1) DATE.—The date of the conveyance of the Property shall be no later than 90 days from the date upon which the Administrator receives from Columbia Hospital written notice of its intent to purchase the Property during which time the parties shall execute all necessary purchase and sale documents, and shall pay the initial cash consideration in an amount at minimum equal to the first of 30 equal annual installment payments of the purchase price as contemplated in subsection (d)(2) hereinbelow.

(2) DEADLINE FOR CONVEYANCE OF THE PROPERTY.—Written notification and payment of the consideration set forth under subsection

(c)(1) from Columbia Hospital shall be ineffective, and all rights granted Columbia Hospital under this section to purchase the Property shall lapse, and become void and of no further force and effect, if that written notification and installment payment are not received by the Administrator before the date which is one (1) year after the date of the enactment of this section.

(3) QUITCLAIM DEED.—Any conveyance of the Property to Columbia Hospital under this section shall be by quitclaim deed.]

[(d) CONVEYANCE TERMS.—

(1) IN GENERAL.—The conveyance of the Property shall be consistent with the terms and conditions set forth in this section and such other terms and conditions as the Administrator deems to be in the interest of the United States, including but not limited to—

(A) credit and payment provisions, including the provision for the prepayment of the full purchase price if mutually acceptable to the parties;

(B) restrictions on the use of the Property for the purposes set forth in subsection (a);

(C) conditions under which the Property or interests therein may be sold, mortgaged, assigned, or otherwise conveyed in order to facilitate financing to fulfill its intended use; and

(D) consequences in the event of default by Columbia Hospital for failing to pay all installments payments toward the total purchase price when due, including reversion of the described property to the United States.

(2) PAYMENT OF PURCHASE PRICE.—Columbia Hospital shall pay the total purchase price of $14,000,000.00 for the Property. The terms and conditions of the sale shall be as deemed by the Administrator to be in the best interests of the United States. Such terms may include financing the payment of the purchase price in annual installments for a term not to exceed 30 years with interest on the unpaid balance not to exceed four and five-tenths percent (4.5%) per annum (except during periods of default or upon entry of a final judgment amount).

(3) The Administrator shall have full authority to administer the credit granted to Columbia Hospital in accordance with this section including, without limitation, the authority to adjust, settle, or compromise the amounts specified in this section or in the documents of conveyance.

(4) EXECUTION OF DOCUMENTS.—The Columbia Hospital shall execute and provide to the Administrator such written instruments including but not limited to contracts for purchase and sale, notes, mortgages, deeds of trust, restrictive covenants, indenture deeds, and assurances as the Administrator may reasonably request to effect this transaction and to protect the interests of the United States under this section.]

[(e) TREATMENT OF AMOUNTS RECEIVED.—Amounts received by the United States as payments under this section shall be paid into the fund established by section 210(f) of the Federal Property and Administrative Services Act of 1949 (40 U.S.C. 490(f)), and may be expended by the Administrator for real property management and related activities not otherwise provided for, without further authorization.]

[(f) REVERSIONARY INTEREST.—

(1) IN GENERAL.—The Property, once conveyed as authorized under subsection (a), shall revert to the United States, together with any improvements thereon—

(A) One (1) year from the date on which Columbia Hospital defaults in paying to the United States any amount when due; or

(B) immediately, upon any attempt by Columbia Hospital to assign, sell, mortgage, or convey the Property without the Administrator's prior written consent before the United States has received full purchase price, plus accrued interest.

(2) RELEASE OF REVERSIONARY INTEREST.—The Administrator may release, upon request, any restriction imposed on the use of the Property authorized in subsection (d)(1)(B) for the purposes set forth in subsection (a), and release any reversionary interest of the United States in the Property upon receipt by the United States of full payment of the purchase price, including any accrued interest, specified under subsection (d)(2), or such other terms and conditions as may be determined by the Administrator to be in the best interests of the United States as set forth in subsection (d).

(3) PROPERTY RETURNED TO THE GENERAL SERVICES ADMINISTRATION.—Any portion of the Property that reverts to the United States under this subsection shall be under the jurisdiction, custody and control of the General Services Administration and shall be available for use or disposition by the Administrator in accordance with applicable Federal law.]

[SEC. 411. VOLUNTARY SEPARATION INCENTIVE PAYMENT FOR EMPLOYEES OF THE GENERAL SERVICES ADMINISTRATION. (a) AUTHORITY.—During the period October 1, 1999, through April 30, 2001, the Administrator of General Services is authorized to offer a voluntary separation incentive in order to provide the necessary flexibility to carry out the closing of the Federal Supply Service distribution centers, forward supply points, and associated programs in a manner which the Administrator shall deem most efficient, equitable to all employees, and cost effective for the Government.]

[(b) DEFINITION.—In this section, the term "employee" means an employee (as defined by 5 U.S.C. 2105) who is employed by GSA under an appointment without time limitation, and has been so employed continuously for a period of at least 3 years, but does not include—

(1) a reemployed annuitant under subchapter III of chapter 83 or chapter 84 of title 5, United States Code, or another retirement system;

(2) an employee having a disability on the basis of which such employee is or would be eligible for disability retirement under the retirement systems referred to in paragraph (1) or another retirement system for employees of the Government;

(3) an employee who is in receipt of a specific notice of involuntary separation for misconduct or unacceptable performance;

(4) an employee who has previously received any voluntary separation incentive payment from an agency or instrumentality of the Government of the United States under any authority;

(5) an employee covered by statutory reemployment rights who is on transfer to another organization; or

(6) an employee who during the 24 month period preceding the date of separation, has received a recruitment or relocation bonus under section 5753 of title 5, United States Code, or who, within the 12 month period preceding the date of separation, has received and not repaid a retention allowance under section 5754 of that title.]

[(c) AGENCY STRATEGIC PLAN.—The Administrator of General Services, prior to obligating any resources for voluntary separation incentive payments, shall submit to the Office of Management and Budget a strategic plan outlining the intended use of such incentive payments and a proposed organizational chart for the agency once such incentive payments have been completed.

(1) The agency's plan shall include:

(A) the specific positions and functions to be reduced or eliminated;

(B) a proposed coverage for offers of incentives;

(C) the time period during which incentives may be paid;

(D) the number and amounts of voluntary separation incentive payments to be offered; and

(E) a description of how the agency will operate without the eliminated positions and functions.

(2) The Director of the Office of Management and Budget shall review the agency's plan and approve or disapprove such plan, and may make any appropriate modifications in the plan.]

[(d) AUTHORITY TO PROVIDE VOLUNTARY SEPARATION INCENTIVE PAYMENTS.—

(1) The agency head may pay a voluntary separation incentive payment under this section to an employee only in accordance with the strategic plan under subsection (c).

(2) A voluntary separation incentive payment—

(A) shall be offered to agency employees on the basis of organizational unit, occupational series or level, geographic location, other nonpersonal factors, or an appropriate combination of such factors;

(B) shall be paid in a lump sum after the employee's separation;

(C) shall be equal to the lesser of—

(i) an amount equal to the amount the employee would be entitled to receive under section 5595(c) of title 5, United States Code; if the employee were entitled to payment under such section (without adjustment for any previous payment made); or

(ii) an amount determined by the agency head, not to exceed $25,000.

(D) may be made only in the case of an employee who voluntarily separates (whether by retirement or resignation) under the provisions of this section;

(E) shall not be a basis for payment, and shall not be included in the computation of any other type of Government benefit;

(F) shall not be taken into account in determining the amount of any severance pay to which the employee may be entitled under section 5595 of title 5, United States Code, based on any other separation; and

(G) shall be paid from appropriations or funds available for the payment of the basic pay of the employee.]

[(e) ELIGIBILITY FOR PAYMENTS.—Payments under this section may be made to any qualifying employee who voluntarily separates, whether by retirement or resignation, between October 1, 1999 through April 30, 2001.]

[(f) EFFECT OF SUBSEQUENT EMPLOYMENT WITH THE GOVERNMENT.—

(1) An individual who has received a voluntary separation incentive payment under this section and accepts any employment for compensation with the Government of the United States within 5 years after the date of the separation on which the payment is based shall be required to pay, prior to the individual's first day of employment, the entire amount of the incentive payment to the agency that paid the incentive payment.

(2)(A) If the employment under this subsection is with an Executive agency (as defined by section 105 of title 5, United States Code, but excluding the General Accounting Office), the United States Postal Service, or the Postal Rate Commission, the Director of the Office of Personnel Management may, at the request of the head of the agency, waive the repayment if the individual involved possesses unique abilities and is the only qualified applicant available for the position.

(B) If the employment under this subsection is with an entity in the Legislative Branch, the head of the entity or the appointing official may waive the repayment if the individual involved possesses unique abilities and is the only qualified applicant available for the position.

(C) If the employment under this subsection is with the Judicial Branch, the Director of the Administrative Office of the United States Courts may waive the repayment if the individual involved possesses unique abilities and is the only qualified applicant available for the position.

(D) Employment under a personal services contract with the Government of the United States shall be included in the term "employment" with respect to paragraph (1), but shall be excluded with respect to paragraph (2).]

[(g) CONTRIBUTIONS TO THE RETIREMENT FUND.—

(1) In addition to any other payments which it is required to make under subchapter III of chapter 83 or chapter 84 of title 5, United States Code, the General Services Administration shall remit to the Office of Personnel Management for deposit in the Treasury to the credit of the Civil Service Retirement and Disability Fund an amount equal to 15 percent of the final annual basic pay for each employee covered under subchapter III of chapter 83 or chapter 84 of title 5, United States Code, to whom a voluntary separation incentive has been paid under this section.

(2) For the purpose of paragraph (1), the term "final basic pay" with respect to an employee, means the total amount of basic pay which would be payable for a year of service by such employee, computed using the employee's final rate of basic pay, and, if last serving on other than a full-time basis, with appropriate adjustment therefor.]

[(h) REDUCTION OF AGENCY EMPLOYMENT LEVELS.—

(1) The total number of funded employee positions in the agency shall be reduced by one position for each vacancy created by the separation of any employee who has received, or is due to receive, a voluntary separation incentive payment under this section. For the purposes of this subsection positions shall be counted on a full-time equivalent basis.

(2) The Director of the Office of Management and Budget shall monitor the agency and take any action necessary to ensure that the requirement of this subsection is met.

(3) At the request of the Administrator of General Services, the Office of Management and Budget may waive the application of paragraph (1) if he or she determines that the plan required by subsection (c) satisfactorily demonstrates downsizing or other restructuring within GSA that would produce a cost-effective result.]

SEC. 408. Section 411 of Public Law 106–58 is amended to change "April 30, 2001" to "April 30, 2002". (Independent Agencies Appropriations Act, 2000.)

INTERNATIONAL ASSISTANCE PROGRAMS

INTERNATIONAL SECURITY ASSISTANCE

Federal Funds

General and special funds:

Economic Support Fund

For necessary expenses to carry out the provisions of chapter 4 of part II, [$2,345,500,000] *$2,313,000,000*, to remain available until [September 30, 2001: *Provided*, That of the funds appropriated under this heading, not less than $960,000,000 shall be available only for Israel, which sum shall be available on a grant basis as a cash transfer and shall be disbursed within 30 days of the enactment of this Act or by October 31, 1999, whichever is later: *Provided further*, That not less than $735,000,000 shall be available only for Egypt, which sum shall be provided on a grant basis, and of which sum cash transfer assistance shall be provided with the understanding that Egypt will undertake significant economic reforms which are additional to those which were undertaken in previous fiscal years, and of which not less than $200,000,000 shall be provided as Commodity Import Program assistance: *Provided further*, That in exercising the authority to provide cash transfer assistance for Israel, the President shall ensure that the level of such assistance does not cause an adverse impact on the total level of nonmilitary exports from the United States to such country and that Israel enters into a side letter agreement at least equivalent to the fiscal year 1999 agreement: *Provided further*, That of the funds appropriated under this heading, not less than $150,000,000 should be made available for assistance for Jordan: *Provided further*, That of the funds appropriated under this heading, not less than $25,000,000 should be made available for assistance for East Timor: *Provided further*, That notwithstanding any other provision of law, not to exceed $11,000,000 may be used to support victims of and programs related to the Holocaust] *expended*: *Provided* [*further*], That notwithstanding any other provision of law, [of the] funds appropriated under this heading[, $1,000,000 shall] *may* be made available to nongovernmental organizations located outside of the People's Republic of China to support activities which preserve cultural traditions and promote sustainable development and environmental conservation in Tibetan communities in that country*: Provided further, That funds appropriated under this heading may be made available, notwithstanding any other provision of law, to provide payment to the government of the People's Republic of China for property loss and damage arising out of the May 7, 1999 incident in Belgrade, Yugoslavia*.

[For an additional amount for "Economic Support Fund" for assistance for Jordan and for the West Bank and Gaza, $450,000,000, to remain available until September 30, 2002, of which $100,000,000 of the funds made available for the West Bank and Gaza shall become available for obligation on September 30, 2000: *Provided*, That the entire amount is designated by the Congress as an emergency requirement pursuant to section 251(b)(2)(A) of the Balanced Budget and Emergency Deficit Control Act of 1985, as amended: *Provided further*, That the entire amount provided shall be available only to the extent that an official budget request that includes designation of the entire amount as an emergency requirement pursuant to section 251(b)(2)(A) of the Balanced Budget and Emergency Deficit Control Act of 1985, as amended, is transmitted by the President to the Congress.] *(Foreign Operations, Export Financing, and Related Programs Appropriation Act, 2000, as enacted by section 1000(a)(2) of the Consolidated Appropriations Act, 2000 (P.L. 106–113).)*

[International Fund for Ireland]

[For necessary expenses to carry out the provisions of chapter 4 of part II of the Foreign Assistance Act of 1961, $19,600,000, which shall be available for the United States contribution to the International Fund for Ireland and shall be made available in accordance with the provisions of the Anglo-Irish Agreement Support Act of 1986 (Public Law 99–415): *Provided*, That such amount shall be expended at the minimum rate necessary to make timely payment for projects and activities: *Provided further*, That funds made available under this heading shall remain available until September 30, 2001.] *(Foreign Operations, Export Financing, and Related Programs Appropriation Act, 2000, as enacted by section 1000(a)(2) of the Consolidated Appropriations Act, 2000 (P.L. 106–113).)*

Program and Financing (in millions of dollars)

Identification code 72–1037–0–1–152		1999 actual	2000 est.	2001 est.
	Obligations by program activity:			
10.00	Total new obligations	2,637	2,993	2,313
	Budgetary resources available for obligation:			
21.40	Unobligated balance available, start of year	251	201	
22.00	New budget authority (gross)	2,609	2,792	2,313
22.10	Resources available from recoveries of prior year obligations	18		
22.21	Unobligated balance transferred to other accounts	−38		
23.90	Total budgetary resources available for obligation	2,840	2,993	2,313
23.95	Total new obligations	−2,637	−2,993	−2,313
23.98	Unobligated balance expiring or withdrawn	−1		
24.40	Unobligated balance available, end of year	201		
	New budget authority (gross), detail:			
	Discretionary:			
40.00	Appropriation	2,598	2,815	2,313
40.35	Appropriation rescinded	−5		
40.76	Reduction pursuant to P.L. 106–113		−23	
41.00	Transferred to other accounts	−43		
42.00	Transferred from other accounts	59		
43.00	Appropriation (total discretionary)	2,608	2,792	2,313
	Change in unpaid obligations:			
	Unpaid obligations, start of year:			
72.40	Obligated balance, start of year	2,958	3,227	3,863
72.95	From Federal sources: Receivables and unpaid, unfilled orders	1	1	
72.99	Total unpaid obligations, start of year	2,959	3,228	3,863
73.10	Total new obligations	2,637	2,993	2,313
73.20	Total outlays (gross)	−2,349	−2,358	−2,329
73.40	Adjustments in expired accounts (net)	−2		
73.45	Adjustments in unexpired accounts	−18		
	Unpaid obligations, end of year:			
74.40	Obligated balance, end of year	3,227	3,863	3,847
74.95	From Federal sources: Receivables and unpaid, unfilled orders	1		
74.99	Total unpaid obligations, end of year	3,228	3,863	3,847
	Outlays (gross), detail:			
86.90	Outlays from new discretionary authority	1,363	1,078	943
86.93	Outlays from discretionary balances	986	1,280	1,386
87.00	Total outlays (gross)	2,349	2,358	2,329
	Net budget authority and outlays:			
89.00	Budget authority	2,609	2,792	2,313
90.00	Outlays	2,349	2,358	2,329

This account supports U.S. foreign policy objectives by providing economic assistance to allies and countries in transition to democracy, supporting the Middle East peace process, and financing economic stabilization programs, frequently in a multi-donor context. Key objectives include:

(1) Supporting strategically significant friends and allies through assistance designed to increase the role of the private sector in the economy, reduce government controls over markets, enhance job creation, and improve economic growth.

(2) Developing and strengthening institutions necessary for sustainable democracy. Typical areas of assistance include technical assistance to administer and monitor elections, capacity-building for non-governmental organizations, judicial

General and special funds—Continued

[INTERNATIONAL FUND FOR IRELAND]—Continued

training, and women's participation in politics. Assistance is also provided to support the transformation of the public sector to encourage democratic development, including training to improve public administration, promote decentralization, strengthen local governments, parliaments, independent media and non-governmental organizations.

(3) Strengthening the capacity to manage the human dimension of the transition to democracy and a market economy, and to help sustain the neediest sectors of the population during the transition period.

Object Classification (in millions of dollars)

Identification code 72–1037–0–1–152	1999 actual	2000 est.	2001 est.
25.2 Other services	32	30	30
41.0 Grants, subsidies, and contributions	2,605	2,963	2,283
99.9 Total new obligations	2,637	2,993	2,313

CENTRAL AMERICA AND THE CARIBBEAN EMERGENCY DISASTER RECOVERY FUND

Program and Financing (in millions of dollars)

Identification code 72–1096–0–1–151	1999 actual	2000 est.	2001 est.
Obligations by program activity:			
00.01 Direct Program	479	105	
10.00 Total new obligations	479	105	
Budgetary resources available for obligation:			
21.40 Unobligated balance available, start of year		115	
22.00 New budget authority (gross)	592	–10	
23.90 Total budgetary resources available for obligation	592	105	
23.95 Total new obligations	–479	–105	
24.40 Unobligated balance available, end of year	115		
New budget authority (gross), detail:			
Discretionary:			
40.00 Appropriation	621		
41.00 Transferred to other accounts	–39	–10	
42.00 Transferred from other accounts	10		
43.00 Appropriation (total discretionary)	592	–10	
Change in unpaid obligations:			
72.40 Unpaid obligations, start of year: Obligated balance, start of year		470	343
73.10 Total new obligations	479	105	
73.20 Total outlays (gross)	–10	–232	–228
74.40 Unpaid obligations, end of year: Obligated balance, end of year	470	343	115
Outlays (gross), detail:			
86.90 Outlays from new discretionary authority	10		
86.93 Outlays from discretionary balances		232	228
87.00 Total outlays (gross)	10	232	228
Net budget authority and outlays:			
89.00 Budget authority	592	–10	
90.00 Outlays	10	232	228

Object Classification (in millions of dollars)

Identification code 72–1096–0–1–151	1999 actual	2000 est.	2001 est.
25.2 Other services	35	13	
41.0 Grants, subsidies, and contributions	444	92	
99.9 Total new obligations	479	105	

FOREIGN MILITARY FINANCING PROGRAM

For expenses necessary for grants to enable the President to carry out the provisions of section 23 of the Arms Export Control Act, [$3,420,000,000] *$3,538,200,000*: *Provided*, That [of the funds appropriated under this heading, not less than $1,920,000,000 shall be available for grants only for Israel, and not less than $1,300,000,000 shall be made available for grants only for Egypt: *Provided further*, That the] funds appropriated by this paragraph for Israel shall be disbursed within 30 days of the enactment of this Act or by October 31, [1999] *2000*, whichever is later: [*Provided further*, That to the extent that the Government of Israel requests that funds be used for such purposes, grants made available for Israel by this paragraph shall, as agreed by Israel and the United States, be available for advanced weapons systems, of which not less than 26.3 percent shall be available for the procurement in Israel of defense articles and defense services, including research and development: *Provided further*, That of the funds appropriated by this paragraph, not less than $75,000,000 should be available for assistance for Jordan: *Provided further*, That of the funds appropriated by this paragraph, not less than $7,000,000 shall be made available for assistance for Tunisia: *Provided further*, That during fiscal year 2000, the President is authorized to, and shall, direct the draw-downs of defense articles from the stocks of the Department of Defense, defense services of the Department of Defense, and military education and training of an aggregate value of not less than $4,000,000 under the authority of this proviso for Tunisia for the purposes of part II of the Foreign Assistance Act of 1961 and any amount so directed shall count toward meeting the earmark in the preceding proviso: *Provided further*, That of the funds appropriated by this paragraph up to $1,000,000 should be made available for assistance for Ecuador and shall be subject to the regular notification procedures of the Committees on Appropriations:] *Provided further*, That funds appropriated by this paragraph shall be nonrepayable notwithstanding any requirement in section 23 of the Arms Export Control Act: [*Provided further*, That funds made available under this paragraph shall be obligated upon apportionment in accordance with paragraph (5)(C) of title 31, United States Code, section 1501(a)].

None of the funds made available under this heading shall be available to finance the procurement of defense articles, defense services, or design and construction services that are not sold by the United States Government under the Arms Export Control Act unless the foreign country proposing to make such procurements has first signed an agreement with the United States Government specifying the conditions under which such procurements may be financed with such funds: *Provided*, [That all country and funding level increases in allocations shall be submitted through the regular notification procedures of section 515 of this Act: *Provided further*, That none of the funds appropriated under this heading shall be available for assistance for Sudan and Liberia: *Provided further*,] That funds made available under this heading may be used, notwithstanding any other provision of law, for demining, the clearance of unexploded ordnance, and related activities, and may include activities implemented through nongovernmental and international organizations: *Provided further*, [That none of the funds appropriated under this heading shall be available for assistance for Guatemala: *Provided further*], That only those countries for which assistance was justified for the "Foreign Military Sales Financing Program" in the fiscal year 1989 congressional presentation for security assistance programs may utilize funds made available under this heading for procurement of defense articles, defense services or design and construction services that are not sold by the United States Government under the Arms Export Control Act: *Provided further*, That funds appropriated under this heading shall be expended at the minimum rate necessary to make timely payment for defense articles and services: *Provided further*, That not more than [$30,495,000] *$33,000,000* of the funds appropriated under this heading may be obligated for necessary expenses, including the purchase of passenger motor vehicles for replacement only for use outside of the United States, for the general costs of administering military assistance and sales: *Provided further*, That not more than [$330,000,000] *$335,000,000* of funds realized pursuant to section 21(e)(1)(A) of the Arms Export Control Act may be obligated for expenses incurred by the Department of Defense during fiscal year [2000] *2001* pursuant to section 43(b) of the Arms Export Control Act, except that this limitation may be exceeded only through the regular notification procedures of the Committees on Appropriations [: *Provided further*, That not later than 45 days after the date of the enactment of this Act, the Secretary of Defense shall report to the Committees on Appropriations regarding the appropriate host institution to support and advance the efforts of the Defense Institute for International and Legal Studies in both legal and political education: *Provided further*, That none of the funds made available under this heading shall be available for any non-NATO country participating in the Partnership for Peace Program except through the regular notification procedures of the Committees on Appropriations.]

[For an additional amount for "Foreign Military Financing Program", $1,375,000,000, to remain available until September 30, 2002, of which $1,200,000,000 shall be for grants only for Israel, $25,000,000 shall be for grants only for Egypt, and $150,000,000 shall be for grants only for Jordan: *Provided*, That $300,000,000 of the funds made available for Israel and $100,000,000 of the funds made available for Jordan shall become available for obligation on September 30, 2000: *Provided further*, That funds appropriated under this heading shall be nonrepayable, notwithstanding section 23 of the Arms Export Control Act: *Provided further*, That funds appropriated under this heading shall be expended at the minimum rate necessary to make timely payment for defense articles and services: *Provided further*, That to the extent that the Government of Israel requests that funds be used for such purposes, grants made available for Israel by this paragraph shall, as agreed by Israel and the United States, be available for advanced weapons systems, of which not to exceed 26.3 percent shall be available for the procurement in Israel of defense articles and defense services, including research and development: *Provided further*, That the entire amount is designated by the Congress as an emergency requirement pursuant to section 251(b)(2)(A) of the Balanced Budget and Emergency Deficit Control Act of 1985, as amended: *Provided further*, That the entire amount provided shall be available only to the extent that an official budget request that includes designation of the entire amount as an emergency requirement pursuant to section 251(b)(2)(A) of the Balanced Budget and Emergency Deficit Control Act of 1985, as amended, is transmitted by the President to the Congress: *Provided further*, That notwithstanding any other provision of this Act, not to exceed $1,370,000,000 of the funds appropriated for Israel under this heading in title III shall be disbursed within 30 days of the enactment of this Act.] *(Foreign Operations, Export Financing, and Related Programs Appropriation Act, 2000, as enacted by section 1000(a)(2) of the Consolidated Appropriations Act, 2000 (P.L. 106–113).)*

Program and Financing (in millions of dollars)

Identification code 11–1082–0–1–152		1999 actual	2000 est.	2001 est.
	Obligations by program activity:			
	Direct program:			
00.01	Israel FMF grant	1,860	1,920	1,980
00.02	Israel Wye River grant		1,200	
00.03	Egypt FMF grant	1,300	1,300	1,300
00.04	Egypt Wye River grant		25	
00.05	Jordan FMF grant	45	75	75
00.06	Jordan Wye River grant	50	150	
00.07	Other FMF grants	115	89	150
00.08	Administrative Expenses	30	30	33
01.92	Total Direct Obligations	3,400	4,789	3,538
09.01	Reimbursable program	1		
09.99	Total reimbursable program	1		
10.00	Total new obligations	3,401	4,789	3,538
	Budgetary resources available for obligation:			
22.00	New budget authority (gross)	3,401	4,789	3,538
23.95	Total new obligations	−3,401	−4,789	−3,538
	New budget authority (gross), detail:			
	Discretionary:			
40.00	Appropriation	3,380	4,795	3,538
40.76	Reduction pursuant to P.L. 106–113		−6	
42.00	Transferred from other accounts	20		
43.00	Appropriation (total discretionary)	3,400	4,789	3,538
68.00	Spending authority from offsetting collections: Offsetting collections (cash)	1		
70.00	Total new budget authority (gross)	3,401	4,789	3,538
	Change in unpaid obligations:			
72.40	Unpaid obligations, start of year: Obligated balance, start of year	2,339	2,383	4,225
73.10	Total new obligations	3,401	4,789	3,538
73.20	Total outlays (gross)	−3,357	−2,947	−4,296
74.40	Unpaid obligations, end of year: Obligated balance, end of year	2,383	4,225	3,467
	Outlays (gross), detail:			
86.90	Outlays from new discretionary authority	1,901	1,696	2,028
86.93	Outlays from discretionary balances	1,456	1,251	2,268
87.00	Total outlays (gross)	3,357	2,947	4,296
	Offsets:			
	Against gross budget authority and outlays:			
88.45	Offsetting collections (cash) from: Offsetting governmental collections from the public	−1		
	Net budget authority and outlays:			
89.00	Budget authority	3,400	4,789	3,538
90.00	Outlays	3,356	2,947	4,296

Summary of Budget Authority and Outlays

(in millions of dollars)

	1999 actual	2000 est.	2001 est.
Enacted/requested:			
Budget Authority	3,400	4,789	3,538
Outlays	3,356	2,947	4,296
Supplemental proposal:			
Budget Authority		31	
Outlays		2	9
Total:			
Budget Authority	3,400	4,820	3,538
Outlays	3,356	2,949	4,305

The foreign military financing (FMF) program enables selected friendly and allied countries to improve their ability to defend themselves by financing their acquisition of U.S. military articles, services, and training. This account provides the grant financing portion of the FMF program. Credit financing, in the form of direct loans, is provided in the FMF loan program account.

Object Classification (in millions of dollars)

Identification code 11–1082–0–1–152		1999 actual	2000 est.	2001 est.
	Direct obligations:			
25.2	Other services	30	30	33
	Grants, subsidies, and contributions:			
41.0	Grants—Israel FMF	1,860	1,920	1,980
41.0	Grants—Israel Wye River		1,200	
41.0	Grants—Egypt FMF	1,300	1,300	1,300
41.0	Grants—Egypt Wye River		25	
41.0	Grants—Jordan FMF	45	75	75
41.0	Grants—Jordan Wye River	50	150	
41.0	Grant—Other FMF grants	115	89	150
99.0	Subtotal, direct obligations	3,400	4,789	3,538
99.0	Reimbursable obligations	1		
99.9	Total new obligations	3,401	4,789	3,538

INTERNATIONAL MILITARY EDUCATION AND TRAINING

For necessary expenses to carry out the provisions of section 541 of the Foreign Assistance Act of 1961, [$50,000,000] *$55,000,000*, of which up to $1,000,000 may remain available until expended: *Provided*, That the civilian personnel for whom military education and training may be provided under this heading may include civilians who are not members of a government whose participation would contribute to improved civil-military relations, civilian control of the military, or respect for human rights[: Provided further, That funds appropriated under this heading for grant financed military education and training for Indonesia and Guatemala may only be available for expanded international military education and training and funds made available for Guatemala may only be provided through the regular notification procedures of the Committees on Appropriations: *Provided further*, That none of the funds appropriated under this heading may be made available to support grant financed military education and training at the School of the Americas unless the Secretary of Defense certifies that the instruction and training provided by the School of the Americas is fully consistent with training

General and special funds—Continued

INTERNATIONAL MILITARY EDUCATION AND TRAINING—Continued

and doctrine, particularly with respect to the observance of human rights, provided by the Department of Defense to United States military students at Department of Defense institutions whose primary purpose is to train United States military personnel: *Provided further*, That the Secretary of Defense shall submit to the Committees on Appropriations, no later than January 15, 2000, a report detailing the training activities of the School of the Americas and a general assessment regarding the performance of its graduates during 1997 and 1998]. *(Foreign Operations, Export Financing, and Related Programs Appropriation Act, 2000, as enacted by section 1000(a)(2) of the Consolidated Appropriations Act, 2000 (P.L. 106–113).)*

Program and Financing (in millions of dollars)

Identification code 11–1081–0–1–152	1999 actual	2000 est.	2001 est.
Obligations by program activity:			
10.00 Total new obligations	50	50	55
Budgetary resources available for obligation:			
22.00 New budget authority (gross)	50	50	55
23.95 Total new obligations	−50	−50	−55
New budget authority (gross), detail:			
Discretionary:			
40.00 Appropriation	50	50	55
Change in unpaid obligations:			
72.40 Unpaid obligations, start of year: Obligated balance, start of year	41	44	41
73.10 Total new obligations	50	50	55
73.20 Total outlays (gross)	−43	−53	−54
73.40 Adjustments in expired accounts (net)	−4		
74.40 Unpaid obligations, end of year: Obligated balance, end of year	44	41	42
Outlays (gross), detail:			
86.90 Outlays from new discretionary authority	22	25	28
86.93 Outlays from discretionary balances	20	28	27
87.00 Total outlays (gross)	43	53	54
Net budget authority and outlays:			
89.00 Budget authority	50	50	55
90.00 Outlays	43	53	54

Summary of Budget Authority and Outlays

(in millions of dollars)

Enacted/requested:	*1999 actual*	*2000 est.*	*2001 est.*
Budget Authority	50	50	55
Outlays	42	53	55
Supplemental proposal:			
Budget Authority		3	
Outlays		2	1
Total:			
Budget Authority	50	53	55
Outlays	42	55	56

This assistance provides grants for military education and training to military and civilian students from foreign countries. In addition to helping these countries move toward self-sufficiency in defending themselves, this program also exposes foreign students to American democratic values, particularly military respect for civilian rule and for internationally recognized standards of individual and human rights.

Object Classification (in millions of dollars)

Identification code 11–1081–0–1–152	1999 actual	2000 est.	2001 est.
26.0 Supplies and materials	5	5	5
41.0 Grants, subsidies, and contributions	45	45	50
99.9 Total new obligations	50	50	55

MILITARY-TO-MILITARY CONTACT PROGRAM

Program and Financing (in millions of dollars)

Identification code 11–1084–0–1–152	1999 actual	2000 est.	2001 est.
Change in unpaid obligations:			
72.40 Unpaid obligations, start of year: Obligated balance, start of year	1	1	
73.20 Total outlays (gross)		−1	
74.40 Unpaid obligations, end of year: Obligated balance, end of year	1		
Outlays (gross), detail:			
86.93 Outlays from discretionary balances		1	
Net budget authority and outlays:			
89.00 Budget authority			
90.00 Outlays		1	

This program financed expenses associated with direct contacts between U.S. military and the military establishments of Eastern Europe and the Baltic and Pacific regions.

PEACEKEEPING OPERATIONS

For necessary expenses to carry out the provisions of section 551 of the Foreign Assistance Act of 1961, [$153,000,000: *Provided*, That none of the funds appropriated under this heading shall be obligated or expended except as provided through the regular notification procedures of the Committees on Appropriations] *$134,000,000. (Foreign Operations, Export Financing, and Related Programs Appropriation Act, 2000, as enacted by section 1000(a)(2) of the Consolidated Appropriations Act, 2000 (P.L. 106–113).)*

Program and Financing (in millions of dollars)

Identification code 72–1032–0–1–152	1999 actual	2000 est.	2001 est.
Obligations by program activity:			
00.01 Direct Program Activity	137	152	134
09.01 Reimbursable program	5		
10.00 Total new obligations	142	152	134
Budgetary resources available for obligation:			
21.40 Unobligated balance available, start of year		1	
22.00 New budget authority (gross)	125	152	134
22.22 Unobligated balance transferred from other accounts	18		
23.90 Total budgetary resources available for obligation	143	153	134
23.95 Total new obligations	−142	−152	−134
23.98 Unobligated balance expiring or withdrawn	−2		
24.40 Unobligated balance available, end of year	1		
New budget authority (gross), detail:			
Discretionary:			
40.00 Appropriation	77	153	134
40.76 Reduction pursuant to P.L. 106–113		−1	
42.00 Transferred from other accounts	43		
43.00 Appropriation (total discretionary)	120	152	134
68.00 Spending authority from offsetting collections: Offsetting collections (cash)	5		
70.00 Total new budget authority (gross)	125	152	134
Change in unpaid obligations:			
72.40 Unpaid obligations, start of year: Obligated balance, start of year	36	80	89
73.10 Total new obligations	142	152	134
73.20 Total outlays (gross)	−98	−143	−140
74.40 Unpaid obligations, end of year: Obligated balance, end of year	80	89	83
Outlays (gross), detail:			
86.90 Outlays from new discretionary authority	74	105	92
86.93 Outlays from discretionary balances	24	38	48
87.00 Total outlays (gross)	98	143	140

		1999 actual	2000 est.	2001 est.
	Offsets:			
	Against gross budget authority and outlays:			
88.40	Offsetting collections (cash) from: Non-Federal sources	–5		
	Net budget authority and outlays:			
89.00	Budget authority	120	152	134
90.00	Outlays	93	143	140

This account funds U.S. assistance to international efforts to monitor and maintain the peace in areas of special concern to the United States, and provides funds to other related programs carried out in furtherance of the national security interests of the United States. In 2001, contributions are planned for the Multinational Force and Observers in the Sinai, Europe, Africa, OSCE activities in Bosnia, Croatia, and Kosovo and other regional programs, and other activities.

Object Classification (in millions of dollars)

Identification code 72–1032–0–1–152		1999 actual	2000 est.	2001 est.
41.0	Direct obligations: Grants, subsidies, and contributions	137	152	134
99.0	Reimbursable obligations: Subtotal, reimbursable obligations	5		
99.9	Total new obligations	142	152	134

Nonproliferation, Anti-Terrorism, Demining and Related Programs

For necessary expenses for nonproliferation, anti-terrorism and related programs and activities, [$216,600,000] *$311,500,000*, to carry out the provisions of chapter 8 of part II of the Foreign Assistance Act of 1961 for anti-terrorism assistance, section 504 of the FREEDOM Support Act for the Nonproliferation and Disarmament Fund, section 23 of the Arms Export Control Act or the Foreign Assistance Act of 1961 for demining activities, the clearance of unexploded ordnance, *the destruction of small arms,* and related activities, notwithstanding any other provision of law, including activities implemented through nongovernmental and international organizations, section 301 of the Foreign Assistance Act of 1961 for a voluntary contribution to the International Atomic Energy Agency (IAEA) and a voluntary contribution to the Korean Peninsula Energy Development Organization (KEDO), *for design and construction of a training facility to support security and anti-terrorism programs,* and for a United States contribution to the Comprehensive Nuclear Test Ban Treaty Preparatory Commission: *Provided,* [That the Secretary of State shall inform the Committees on Appropriations at least 20 days prior to the obligation of funds for the Comprehensive Nuclear Test Ban Treaty Preparatory Commission: *Provided further,*] That of this amount not to exceed $15,000,000, to remain available until expended, may be made available for the Nonproliferation and Disarmament Fund, notwithstanding any other provision of law, to promote bilateral and multilateral activities relating to nonproliferation and disarmament: *Provided further,* That such funds may also be used for such countries other than the Independent States of the former Soviet Union and international organizations when it is in the national security interest of the United States to do so: [*Provided further,* That such funds shall be subject to the regular notification procedures of the Committees on Appropriations: *Provided further,* That funds appropriated under this heading may be made available for the International Atomic Energy Agency only if the Secretary of State determines (and so reports to the Congress) that Israel is not being denied its right to participate in the activities of that Agency: *Provided further,* That of the funds appropriated under this heading, $40,000,000 should be made available for demining, clearance of unexploded ordnance, and related activities:] *Provided further,* That of the funds made available for demining and related activities, not to exceed $500,000, in addition to funds otherwise available for such purposes, may be used for administrative expenses related to the operation and management of the demining program. *(Foreign Operations, Export Financing, and Related Programs Appropriation Act, 2000, as enacted by section 1000(a)(2) of the Consolidated Appropriations Act, 2000 (P.L. 106–113).)*

Program and Financing (in millions of dollars)

Identification code 11–1075–0–1–152		1999 actual	2000 est.	2001 est.
	Obligations by program activity:			
00.01	Comprehensive test ban treaty prepcom	29	14	22
00.02	Demining	43	40	40
00.03	Export control	9	11	14
00.04	Nonproliferation and disarmament assistance	9	15	15
00.05	Anti-terrorism assistance	34	33	68
00.06	IAEA voluntary contribution	40	43	47
00.07	KEDO payment	70	35	55
00.08	Science centers in NIS	17		45
00.09	Unallocated		20	
00.10	Small arms destruction			2
00.11	Terrorist interdiction		5	4
09.01	Reimbursable program	6		
10.00	Total new obligations	257	216	312
	Budgetary resources available for obligation:			
21.40	Unobligated balance available, start of year	26	35	38
22.00	New budget authority (gross)	245	218	312
22.22	Unobligated balance transferred from other accounts	21		
23.90	Total budgetary resources available for obligation	292	253	350
23.95	Total new obligations	–257	–216	–312
24.40	Unobligated balance available, end of year	35	38	38
	New budget authority (gross), detail:			
	Discretionary:			
40.00	Appropriation	198	217	312
40.15	Appropriation (emergency)	20		
40.76	Reduction pursuant to P.L. 106–113		–1	
42.00	Transferred from other accounts	21	2	
43.00	Appropriation (total discretionary)	239	218	312
68.00	Spending authority from offsetting collections: Offsetting collections (cash)	6		
70.00	Total new budget authority (gross)	245	218	312
	Change in unpaid obligations:			
72.40	Unpaid obligations, start of year: Obligated balance, start of year	72	109	121
73.10	Total new obligations	257	216	312
73.20	Total outlays (gross)	–222	–204	–283
74.40	Unpaid obligations, end of year: Obligated balance, end of year	109	121	150
	Outlays (gross), detail:			
86.90	Outlays from new discretionary authority	179	142	203
86.93	Outlays from discretionary balances	43	62	80
87.00	Total outlays (gross)	222	204	283
	Offsets:			
	Against gross budget authority and outlays:			
88.00	Offsetting collections (cash) from: Federal sources	–6		
	Net budget authority and outlays:			
89.00	Budget authority	239	218	312
90.00	Outlays	215	204	283

This account funds contributions to certain organizations supporting nonproliferation, and provides assistance for nonproliferation, demining, antiterrorism, and export control activities.

Object Classification (in millions of dollars)

Identification code 11–1075–0–1–152		1999 actual	2000 est.	2001 est.
	Direct obligations:			
21.0	Travel and transportation of persons	1	1	1
25.2	Other services	126	112	151
31.0	Equipment	4	4	5
41.0	Grants, subsidies, and contributions	120	99	155
99.0	Subtotal, direct obligations	251	216	312
99.0	Reimbursable obligations	6		
99.9	Total new obligations	257	216	312

General and special funds—Continued

Assistance for Relocation of Facilities in Israel

Program and Financing (in millions of dollars)

Identification code 11–1088–0–1–152	1999 actual	2000 est.	2001 est.
Budgetary resources available for obligation:			
21.40 Unobligated balance available, start of year	2		
Change in unpaid obligations:			
72.49 Unpaid obligations, start of year: Obligated balance, start of year: Contract authority	3		
73.40 Adjustments in expired accounts (net)	–3		
Net budget authority and outlays:			
89.00 Budget authority			
90.00 Outlays			

Status of Contract Authority (in millions of dollars)

Identification code 11–1088–0–1–152	1999 actual	2000 est.	2001 est.
0100 Balance, start of year	3		
0360 Adjustments in expired accounts	–3		

This account shows financial transactions related to the construction of two airfields in Israel that were part of the Camp David agreement. The 1999 transactions are the last ones in this account.

Non-Proliferation and Disarmament Fund

Program and Financing (in millions of dollars)

Identification code 11–1071–0–1–152	1999 actual	2000 est.	2001 est.
Budgetary resources available for obligation:			
21.40 Unobligated balance available, start of year	2	1	1
24.40 Unobligated balance available, end of year	1	1	
Change in unpaid obligations:			
72.40 Unpaid obligations, start of year: Obligated balance, start of year	11	8	3
73.20 Total outlays (gross)	–3	–5	–3
74.40 Unpaid obligations, end of year: Obligated balance, end of year	8	3	
Outlays (gross), detail:			
86.93 Outlays from discretionary balances	3	5	3
Net budget authority and outlays:			
89.00 Budget authority			
90.00 Outlays	3	5	3

This account provided financial and technical assistance to support nonproliferation and disarmament efforts in foreign countries, including education and training, elimination of weapons of mass destruction, and development of export control capabilities. Starting in 1997, these activities have been funded from the Non-Proliferation, Anti-Terrorism, Demining and Related Programs account. This schedule reflects the spend-out of prior-year obligations.

Credit accounts:

Foreign Military Financing Loan Program Account

General Fund Credit Receipt Accounts (in millions of dollars)

Identification code 11–1085–0–1–152	1999 actual	2000 est.	2001 est.
0101 Foreign military financing, downward reestimates of subsidies	3		

Program and Financing (in millions of dollars)

Identification code 11–1085–0–1–152	1999 actual	2000 est.	2001 est.
Obligations by program activity:			
00.05 Direct program—upward reestimates	4	152	
00.06 Direct program—interest on upward reestimates	1	37	
10.00 Total new obligations	5	189	
Budgetary resources available for obligation:			
22.00 New budget authority (gross)	5	189	
23.95 Total new obligations	–5	–189	
New budget authority (gross), detail:			
Discretionary:			
40.00 Appropriation	20		
41.00 Transferred to other accounts	–20		
Mandatory:			
60.05 Appropriation (indefinite)	5	189	
70.00 Total new budget authority (gross)	5	189	
Change in unpaid obligations:			
72.40 Unpaid obligations, start of year: Obligated balance, start of year	181	162	124
73.10 Total new obligations	5	189	
73.20 Total outlays (gross)	–24	–227	–66
74.40 Unpaid obligations, end of year: Obligated balance, end of year	162	124	58
Outlays (gross), detail:			
86.93 Outlays from discretionary balances	19	38	66
86.97 Outlays from new mandatory authority	5	189	
87.00 Total outlays (gross)	24	227	66
Net budget authority and outlays:			
89.00 Budget authority	5	189	
90.00 Outlays	24	227	66

As required by the Federal Credit Reform Act of 1990, this account records the subsidy costs associated with the direct loans obligated for foreign military financing committed in 1992 and beyond, as well as the administrative expenses of this program. The foreign military financing credit program provides loans that finance sales of defense articles, defense services, and design and construction services to foreign countries and international organizations. The subsidy amounts are estimated on a present value basis; the administrative expenses are estimated on a cash basis.

Summary of Loan Levels, Subsidy Budget Authority and Outlays by Program (in millions of dollars)

Identification code 11–1085–0–1–152	1999 actual	2000 est.	2001 est.
Direct loan subsidy (in percent):			
1320 Subsidy rate	0.00	0.00	0.00
1329 Weighted average subsidy rate	0.00	0.00	0.00
Direct loan subsidy budget authority:			
1330 Subsidy budget authority	5	189	
1339 Total subsidy budget authority	5	189	
Direct loan subsidy outlays:			
1340 Subsidy outlays	24	227	66
1349 Total subsidy outlays	24	227	66

Foreign Military Financing Direct Loan Financing Account

Program and Financing (in millions of dollars)

Identification code 11–4122–0–3–152	1999 actual	2000 est.	2001 est.
Obligations by program activity:			
00.01 Interest on debt owed to the Treasury	114	102	103
08.02 Downward reestimate paid to receipt accounts	3		
10.00 Total new obligations	117	102	103

	Budgetary resources available for obligation:			
22.00	New financing authority (gross)	117	102	102
23.95	Total new obligations	–117	–102	–103
	New financing authority (gross), detail:			
	Mandatory:			
67.15	Authority to borrow (indefinite)	3	–189	....
	Spending authority from offsetting collections:			
	Discretionary:			
68.00	Offsetting collections (cash)	407	733	609
68.10	Change in receivables from program account	–19	–38	–66
68.47	Portion applied to repay debt	–274	–404	–441
68.90	Spending authority from offsetting collections (total discretionary)	114	291	102
70.00	Total new financing authority (gross)	117	102	102
	Change in unpaid obligations:			
	Unpaid obligations, start of year:			
72.40	Obligated balance, start of year	1,541	1,214	786
72.95	Receivables from program account	181	162	124
72.99	Total unpaid obligations, start of year	1,722	1,376	910
73.10	Total new obligations	117	102	103
73.20	Total financing disbursements (gross)	–463	–568	–696
	Unpaid obligations, end of year:			
74.40	Obligated balance, end of year	1,214	786	258
74.95	Receivables from program account	162	124	58
74.99	Total unpaid obligations, end of year	1,376	910	316
87.00	Total financing disbursements (gross)	463	568	696
	Offsets:			
	Against gross financing authority and financing disbursements:			
	Offsetting collections (cash) from:			
88.00	Federal sources-subsidy	–24	–227	–66
88.25	Interest on uninvested funds	–25	....	....
	Non-Federal sources:			
88.40	Non-Federal sources—principal	–263	–313	–373
88.40	Non-Federal sources—interest	–95	–193	–170
88.90	Total, offsetting collections (cash)	–407	–733	–609
	Against gross budget authority only:			
88.95	Change in receivables from program accounts	19	38	66
	Net financing authority and financing disbursements:			
89.00	Financing authority	–271	–593	–441
90.00	Financing disbursements	56	–165	87

Status of Direct Loans (in millions of dollars)

Identification code 11–4122–0–3–152		1999 actual	2000 est.	2001 est.
	Cumulative balance of direct loans outstanding:			
1210	Outstanding, start of year	1,582	1,665	1,818
1231	Disbursements: Direct loan disbursements	345	466	594
1251	Repayments: Repayments and prepayments	–262	–313	–373
1290	Outstanding, end of year	1,665	1,818	2,039

As required by the Federal Credit Reform Act of 1990, this non-budgetary account records all cash flows to and from the Government resulting from direct loans for foreign military financing obligated in 1992 and beyond. The foreign military financing credit program provides loans that finance sales of defense articles, defense services, and design and construction services to foreign countries and international organizations. The amounts in this account are a means of financing and are not included in budget totals.

Balance Sheet (in millions of dollars)

Identification code 11–4122–0–3–152		1998 actual	1999 actual	2000 est.	2001 est.
	ASSETS:				
	Federal assets:				
1101	Fund balances with Treasury	169	79	....	....
	Investments in US securities:				
1106	Receivables, net	181	162	124	58
	Net value of assets related to post-1991 direct loans receivable:				
1401	Direct loans receivable, gross	1,582	1,665	1,818	2,039
1402	Interest receivable	17	16	17	19
1405	Allowance for subsidy cost (–)	–227	–252	–303	–438
1499	Net present value of assets related to direct loans	1,372	1,429	1,532	1,620
1901	Other Federal assets: Other assets	1,372	1,135	707	178
1999	Total assets	3,094	2,805	2,363	1,856
	LIABILITIES:				
	Federal liabilities:				
2103	Debt	1,541	1,508	1,532	1,620
2105	Other	1,553	1,297	831	236
2999	Total liabilities	3,094	2,805	2,363	1,856
4999	Total liabilities and net position	3,094	2,805	2,363	1,856

Foreign Military Loan Liquidating Account

Program and Financing (in millions of dollars)

Identification code 11–4121–0–3–152		1999 actual	2000 est.	2001 est.
	Obligations by program activity:			
00.01	Direct program-Defaults Guaranteed Commercial Bank Loans	25	14	21
00.02	Direct program-Defaults FFB Loans	18	31	21
10.00	Total new obligations	43	45	42
	Budgetary resources available for obligation:			
22.00	New budget authority (gross)	43	45	42
23.95	Total new obligations	–43	–45	–42
	New budget authority (gross), detail:			
	Mandatory:			
60.05	Appropriation (indefinite)	38	38	31
	Offsetting collections (cash):			
69.00	Offsetting collections (cash)	228	624	548
69.00	Offsetting collections (cash) debt reduction	1	11	....
69.27	Capital transfer to general fund	–6	–408	–303
69.47	Portion applied to repay debt	–218	–220	–234
69.90	Spending authority from offsetting collections (total mandatory)	5	7	11
70.00	Total new budget authority (gross)	43	45	42
	Change in unpaid obligations:			
73.10	Total new obligations	43	45	42
73.20	Total outlays (gross)	–43	–45	–42
	Outlays (gross), detail:			
86.97	Outlays from new mandatory authority	43	45	42
	Offsets:			
	Against gross budget authority and outlays:			
	Offsetting collections (cash) from:			
88.00	Federal sources—debt reduction	–1	–11	....
	Non-Federal sources:			
88.40	Non-Federal sources—loans other than FFB	–10	–404	–315
88.40	Non-Federal sources—FFB loan principal	–218	–220	–233
88.90	Total, offsetting collections (cash)	–229	–635	–548
	Net budget authority and outlays:			
89.00	Budget authority	–186	–590	–506
90.00	Outlays	–186	–590	–506

Status of Direct Loans (in millions of dollars)

Identification code 11–4121–0–3–152		1999 actual	2000 est.	2001 est.
	Cumulative balance of direct loans outstanding:			
1210	Outstanding, start of year	5,387	4,805	4,270
1231	Disbursements: Direct loan disbursements	7	7	7
1251	Repayments: Repayments and prepayments	–595	–522	–451
1261	Adjustments: Capitalized interest	12	....	....
1264	Write-offs for default: Other adjustments, net Loss on Sale of Assets	–6	–20	....
1290	Outstanding, end of year	4,805	4,270	3,826

Credit accounts—Continued

FOREIGN MILITARY LOAN LIQUIDATING ACCOUNT—Continued

Status of Guaranteed Loans (in millions of dollars)

Identification code 11–4121–0–3–152	1999 actual	2000 est.	2001 est.
Cumulative balance of guaranteed loans outstanding:			
2210 Outstanding, start of year	5,304	4,924	4,553
2251 Repayments and prepayments	−379	−366	−349
2261 Adjustments: Terminations for default that result in loans receivable	−1	−5	−8
2290 Outstanding, end of year	4,924	4,553	4,196
Memorandum:			
2299 Guaranteed amount of guaranteed loans outstanding, end of year	4,432	4,098	3,779
Addendum:			
Cumulative balance of defaulted guaranteed loans that result in loans receivable:			
2310 Outstanding, start of year	1	14	25
2331 Disbursements for guaranteed loan claims	24	14	21
2364 Other adjustments, net	−11	−3	
2390 Outstanding, end of year	14	25	46

As required by the Federal Credit Reform Act of 1990, this account records all cash flows to and from the Government resulting from direct loans obligated and loan guarantees for foreign military financing committed prior to 1992. This account is shown on a cash basis and reflects the transactions resulting from loans provided to finance sales of defense articles, defense services, and design and construction services to foreign countries and international organizations. All new foreign military financing credit activity in 1992 and beyond (including modifications of direct loans or loan guarantees that resulted from obligations or commitments in any year) is recorded in corresponding program and financing accounts.

Statement of Operations (in millions of dollars)

Identification code 11–4121–0–3–152	1998 actual	1999 actual	2000 est.	2001 est.
0111 Revenue	302	237	212	190
0112 Expense	−307	−238	−212	−190
0115 Net income or loss (−)	−5	−1		
0195 Total income or loss (−)	−5	−1		
0199 Total comprehensive income	−5	−1		

Balance Sheet (in millions of dollars)

Identification code 11–4121–0–3–152	1998 actual	1999 actual	2000 est.	2001 est.
ASSETS:				
Net value of assets related to pre–1992 direct loans receivable and acquired defaulted guaranteed loans receivable:				
1601 Direct loans, gross	5,386	4,805	4,270	3,826
1602 Interest receivable	1,104	917	821	735
1604 Direct loans and interest receivable, net	6,490	5,722	5,091	4,561
1699 Value of assets related to direct loans	6,490	5,722	5,091	4,561
1701 Defaulted guaranteed loans, gross	1	2	5	15
1702 Interest receivable		12	20	33
1799 Value of assets related to loan guarantees	1	14	25	48
1999 Total assets	6,491	5,736	5,116	4,609
LIABILITIES:				
Federal liabilities:				
2102 Accrued Interest Payable to FFB	44	41	37	33
2103 Debt—Principal owed to FFB	2,829	2,611	2,390	2,157
2104 Resources payable to Treasury	2,558	3,084	2,689	2,419
2999 Total liabilities	5,431	5,736	5,116	4,609
NET POSITION:				
3300 Cumulative results of operations	1,060			
3999 Total net position	1,060			
4999 Total liabilities and net position	6,491	5,736	5,116	4,609

MILITARY DEBT REDUCTION FINANCING ACCOUNT

Program and Financing (in millions of dollars)

Identification code 11–4174–0–3–152	1999 actual	2000 est.	2001 est.
Obligations by program activity:			
09.01 Reimbursable program—Payment to Liquidating Account	1	11	
09.02 Reimbursable program—Interest to Treasury	1	1	1
10.00 Total new obligations	2	12	1
Budgetary resources available for obligation:			
22.00 New financing authority (gross)	2	12	1
23.95 Total new obligations	−2	−12	−1
New financing authority (gross), detail:			
Mandatory:			
67.15 Authority to borrow (indefinite)	1	8	
Spending authority from offsetting collections:			
Discretionary:			
68.00 Offsetting collections (cash)	1	8	4
68.47 Portion applied to repay debt		−4	−3
68.90 Spending authority from offsetting collections (total discretionary)	1	4	1
Mandatory:			
69.00 Offsetting collections (cash)		4	1
69.47 Portion applied to repay debt		−4	−1
70.00 Total new financing authority (gross)	2	12	1
Change in unpaid obligations:			
73.10 Total new obligations	2	12	1
73.20 Total financing disbursements (gross)	−1	−12	−1
87.00 Total financing disbursements (gross)	1	12	1
Offsets:			
Against gross financing authority and financing disbursements:			
Offsetting collections (cash) from:			
88.00 Federal sources		−12	−5
88.40 Non-Federal sources—interest	−1		
88.90 Total, offsetting collections (cash)	−1	−12	−5
Net financing authority and financing disbursements:			
89.00 Financing authority	1		−4
90.00 Financing disbursements			−4

Status of Direct Loans (in millions of dollars)

Identification code 11–4174–0–3–152	1999 actual	2000 est.	2001 est.
Position with respect to appropriations act limitation on obligations:			
1111 Limitation on direct loans	1	11	
1150 Total direct loan obligations	1	11	
Cumulative balance of direct loans outstanding:			
1210 Outstanding, start of year	9	10	10
1233 Disbursements: Purchase of loans assets from a liquidating account	1	11	
1263 Write-offs for default: Direct loans		−11	−8
1290 Outstanding, end of year	10	10	2

As required by the Federal Credit Reform Act of 1990, this non-budgetary account records all cash flows to and from the Government resulting from restructuring foreign military loans. The amounts in this account are a means of financing and are not included in budget totals.

Balance Sheet (in millions of dollars)

Identification code 11–4174–0–3–152	1998 actual	1999 actual	2000 est.	2001 est.
ASSETS:				
Net value of assets related to post–1991 direct loans receivable:				
1401 Direct loans receivable, gross	9	10	10	2
1405 Allowance for subsidy cost (–)	–2	–3	–3	
1499 Net present value of assets related to direct loans	7	7	7	2
1999 Total assets	7	7	7	2
LIABILITIES:				
2103 Federal liabilities: Debt	7	7	7	7
2999 Total liabilities	7	7	7	7
4999 Total liabilities and net position	7	7	7	7

Object Classification (in millions of dollars)

Identification code 11–4174–0–3–152	1999 actual	2000 est.	2001 est.
33.0 Investments and loans	1	11	
43.0 Interest and dividends	1	1	1
99.9 Total new obligations	2	12	1

INTERNATIONAL DEVELOPMENT ASSISTANCE

MULTILATERAL ASSISTANCE

Federal Funds

General and special funds:

INTERNATIONAL FINANCIAL INSTITUTIONS

GLOBAL ENVIRONMENT FACILITY

For the United States contribution for the Global Environment Facility, [$35,800,000], *$175,566,667*, to the International Bank for Reconstruction and Development as trustee for the Global Environment Facility, by the Secretary of the Treasury, to remain available until expended. *(Foreign Operations, Export Financing, and Related Programs Appropriation Act, 2000, as enacted by section 1000(a)(2) of the Consolidated Appropriations Act, 2000 (P.L. 106–113).)*

Program and Financing (in millions of dollars)

Identification code 11–0077–0–1–151	1999 actual	2000 est.	2001 est.
Obligations by program activity:			
10.00 Total new obligations (object class 33.0)	168	36	176
Budgetary resources available for obligation:			
21.40 Unobligated balance available, start of year	7,663	7,663	7,663
22.00 New budget authority (gross)	168	36	176
23.90 Total budgetary resources available for obligation	7,831	7,699	7,839
23.95 Total new obligations	–168	–36	–176
24.40 Unobligated balance available, end of year	7,663	7,663	7,663
New budget authority (gross), detail:			
Discretionary:			
40.00 Appropriation	193	36	176
40.35 Reduction pursuant to P.L. 106–31	–25		
43.00 Appropriation (total discretionary)	168	36	176
Change in unpaid obligations:			
72.40 Unpaid obligations, start of year: Obligated balance, start of year	147	261	245
73.10 Total new obligations	168	36	176
73.20 Total outlays (gross)	–54	–52	–54
74.40 Unpaid obligations, end of year: Obligated balance, end of year	261	245	367
Outlays (gross), detail:			
86.90 Outlays from new discretionary authority	15		
86.93 Outlays from discretionary balances	39	52	54
87.00 Total outlays (gross)	54	52	54
Net budget authority and outlays:			
89.00 Budget authority	168	36	176
90.00 Outlays	54	52	54

The International Bank for Reconstruction and Development (IBRD or World Bank) provides market-rate financing and technical assistance to support infrastructure investment and policy reform. IBRD operations are designed to increase borrowing countries' capacity to attain equitable, sustainable economic growth, including through targeted investments in basic human needs, private-sector development, and core policy reforms.

The IBRD made new commitments of $22.2 billion during 1999, IBRD gross disbursements were $18.2 billion. Since its establishment in 1945, the IBRD has made loans totaling $339 billion—$170 for every $1 of U.S. paid in capital. No request is being made for IBRD capital in 2001.

The IBRD acts as trustee for the Global Environment Facility (GEF) Trust Fund. The GEF provides technical assistance and partial funding for developing country investments designed to provide global environmental benefits by reducing international water pollution and ozone depletion, and by promoting biodiversity and energy conservation. With its highly specific focus on global environmental issues—where both costs and benefits are shared across international borders—the GEF occupies an important niche in the system of international financial institutions. Its basic mission is to support innovative and cost-effective pilot investments whose design and environmental benefits can be duplicated (and financed) elsewhere. Under strong U.S. leadership, the GEF has been making substantial progress in leveraging its limited resources. The World Bank, the UN Development Program, the UN Environment Program and, increasingly, private investors, provide substantial co-financing for GEF projects. Since its inception in 1994, total GEF commitments amount to about $2.6 billion, with associated co-financing of about $7.8 billion.

The initial U.S. commitment to the GEF in 1995 amounted to $430 million. In March 1998, the Administration concluded negotiation of a $2.75 billion second GEF replenishment (GEF–2) covering 1999 to 2002. We limited our GEF–2 pledge to GEF–1 levels of $430 million over four years. The 2000 appropriation allowed us to clear all GEF–1 arrears and make a $10.8 million payment towards GEF–2. However, over the past two years, we accrued arrears to GEF–2 of $204.2 million. The 2001 request of $175.6 million would clear one-third of these arrears and would cover one year of annual contributions to GEF.

CONTRIBUTION TO THE INTERNATIONAL DEVELOPMENT ASSOCIATION

For payment to the International Development Association by the Secretary of the Treasury, [$775,000,000] *$835,570,000*, to remain available until expended. *(Foreign Operations, Export Financing, and Related Programs Appropriation Act, 2000, as enacted by section 1000(a)(2) of the Consolidated Appropriations Act, 2000 (P.L. 106–113).)*

Program and Financing (in millions of dollars)

Identification code 11–0073–0–1–151	1999 actual	2000 est.	2001 est.
Obligations by program activity:			
10.00 Total new obligations (object class 33.0)	800	771	836
Budgetary resources available for obligation:			
22.00 New budget authority (gross)	800	771	836
23.95 Total new obligations	–800	–771	–836
New budget authority (gross), detail:			
Discretionary:			
40.00 Appropriation	800	775	836

General and special funds—Continued

INTERNATIONAL FINANCIAL INSTITUTIONS—Continued

CONTRIBUTION TO THE INTERNATIONAL DEVELOPMENT ASSOCIATION—Continued

Program and Financing (in millions of dollars)—Continued

Identification code 11–0073–0–1–151	1999 actual	2000 est.	2001 est.
40.76 Reduction pursuant to P.L. 106–113	....	–4	....
43.00 Appropriation (total discretionary)	800	771	836
Change in unpaid obligations:			
72.40 Unpaid obligations, start of year: Obligated balance, start of year	2,761	2,567	2,346
73.10 Total new obligations	800	771	836
73.20 Total outlays (gross)	–994	–992	–1,077
74.40 Unpaid obligations, end of year: Obligated balance, end of year	2,567	2,346	2,105
Outlays (gross), detail:			
86.90 Outlays from new discretionary authority	147	56	60
86.93 Outlays from discretionary balances	847	936	1,017
87.00 Total outlays (gross)	994	992	1,077
Net budget authority and outlays:			
89.00 Budget authority	800	771	836
90.00 Outlays	994	992	1,077

The International Development Association (IDA) is a member of the World Bank Group and provides development financing on highly concessional terms to the world's poorest nations. These countries are primarily in Sub-Saharan Africa and South Asia, but also in Latin America, Eastern Europe, and the former Soviet Union. IDA places special emphasis on poverty alleviation, environmental protection, and economic reform and growth. IDA is the single largest source of multilateral lending extended on concessional terms to developing countries. Projects have to meet the same economic, financial, and environmental standards as other World Bank projects. IDA resources for new lending are increasingly provided by earnings and repayments of existing loans and are augmented by new donor contributions through periodic "replenishments."

During 1999, IDA made new commitments of $6.8 billion, and IDA's gross disbursements were $6 billion. Since its establishment, IDA has made commitments totalling $115.9 billion (as of June 30, 1999).

Under the twelfth replenishment (IDA–12), IDA will provide total resources for prospective new loan commitments of about $20 billion over the 2000–2002 period. The United States pledged $2,410.29 million over three years (20.86 percent of total donor contributions). The 2001 request would clear IDA–12 new arrears and cover the second year of our commitment under the replenishment.

CONTRIBUTION TO MULTILATERAL INVESTMENT GUARANTEE AGENCY

For payment to the Multilateral Investment Guarantee Agency by the Secretary of the Treasury, [$4,000,000] *$16,000,000,* for the United States paid-in share of the increase in capital stock, to remain available until expended.

LIMITATION ON CALLABLE CAPITAL *SUBSCRIPTIONS*

The United States Governor of the Multilateral Investment Guarantee Agency may subscribe without fiscal year limitation for the callable capital portion of the United States share of such capital stock in an amount not to exceed [$20,000,000] *$80,000,000. (Foreign Operations, Export Financing, and Related Programs Appropriation Act, 2000, as enacted by section 1000(a)(2) of the Consolidated Appropriations Act, 2000 (P.L. 106–113).)*

Program and Financing (in millions of dollars)

Identification code 11–0084–0–1–151	1999 actual	2000 est.	2001 est.
Obligations by program activity:			
00.01 Direct Program Activity	....	4	16
10.00 Total new obligations	....	4	16
Budgetary resources available for obligation:			
22.00 New budget authority (gross)	....	4	16
23.95 Total new obligations	....	–4	–16
New budget authority (gross), detail:			
Discretionary:			
40.00 Appropriation	....	4	16
Change in unpaid obligations:			
72.40 Unpaid obligations, start of year: Obligated balance, start of year	22	22	25
73.10 Total new obligations	....	4	16
73.20 Total outlays (gross)	....	–1	–6
74.40 Unpaid obligations, end of year: Obligated balance, end of year	22	25	35
Outlays (gross), detail:			
86.90 Outlays from new discretionary authority	....	1	3
86.93 Outlays from discretionary balances	....	....	3
87.00 Total outlays (gross)	....	1	6
Net budget authority and outlays:			
89.00 Budget authority	....	4	16
90.00 Outlays	....	1	6

The Multilateral Investment Guarantee Agency (MIGA) is a member of the World Bank Group. MIGA is designed to encourage the flow of foreign private investment to and among developing countries by: (1) issuing guarantees against noncommercial risks and (2) carrying out investment promotion activities.

During World Bank fiscal year 1999, the MIGA issued 72 guarantees, with a maximum aggregate contingent liability of $1.3 billion. Aggregate direct investment facilitated is $30.4 billion. There are no claims pending against MIGA.

Negotiations of MIGA's first General Capital Increase (GCI) were completed in 1998. The United States committed to contribute a total of $30 million in paid-in capital and $150 million in callable capital over three years. The agreement included MIGA commitments on a range of policy issues of substantial importance to the U.S., including environment, labor, and institutional governance. In 2000, the Administration sought and received Congressional authorization for $180 million to participate in the MIGA GCI.

The 2001 request includes budget authority of $16 million for paid-in capital subscriptions, including $6 million in arrears, and $80 million in program limitations for callable capital subscriptions, including $30 million in arrears.

[CONTRIBUTION TO THE INTER-AMERICAN DEVELOPMENT BANK]

[For payment to the Inter-American Development Bank by the Secretary of the Treasury, for the United States share of the paid-in share portion of the increase in capital stock, $25,610,667.]

CONTRIBUTION TO THE INTER-AMERICAN INVESTMENT CORPORATION

For payment to the Inter-American Investment Corporation, by the Secretary of the Treasury, [$16,000,000] *$34,000,000,* for the United States share of the increase in subscriptions to capital stock, to remain available until expended.

[LIMITATION ON CALLABLE CAPITAL SUBSCRIPTIONS]

[The United States Governor of the Inter-American Development Bank may subscribe without fiscal year limitation to the callable capital portion of the United States share of such capital stock in an amount not to exceed $1,503,718,910.] *(Foreign Operations, Export Financing, and Related Programs Appropriation Act, 2000, as enacted by section 1000(a)(2) of the Consolidated Appropriations Act, 2000 (P.L. 106–113).)*

Program and Financing (in millions of dollars)

Identification code 11–0072–0–1–151	1999 actual	2000 est.	2001 est.
Obligations by program activity:			
00.01 Paid-in capital	26	26	
00.02 Fund for special operations	21		
00.03 International Investment Corp.		16	34
10.00 Total new obligations	47	42	34
Budgetary resources available for obligation:			
21.40 Unobligated balance available, start of year	3,797	3,797	3,797
22.00 New budget authority (gross)	47	42	34
23.90 Total budgetary resources available for obligation	3,844	3,839	3,831
23.95 Total new obligations	−47	−42	−34
24.40 Unobligated balance available, end of year	3,797	3,797	3,797
New budget authority (gross), detail:			
Discretionary:			
40.00 Appropriation	47	42	34
Change in unpaid obligations:			
72.40 Unpaid obligations, start of year: Obligated balance, start of year	79	84	80
73.10 Total new obligations	47	42	34
73.20 Total outlays (gross)	−42	−46	−48
74.40 Unpaid obligations, end of year: Obligated balance, end of year	84	80	67
Outlays (gross), detail:			
86.90 Outlays from new discretionary authority	6	8	7
86.93 Outlays from discretionary balances	36	37	41
87.00 Total outlays (gross)	42	46	48
Net budget authority and outlays:			
89.00 Budget authority	47	42	34
90.00 Outlays	42	46	48

The Inter-American Development Bank (IDB) promotes sustainable economic growth and development, poverty reduction, private sector development, and good governance in Latin America and the Caribbean through loans and technical assistance.

In 1999, the IDB made new lending commitments of $9.5 billion; gross disbursements were $8.2 billion. Since its inception in 1960, the Bank has lent over $100 billion.

The Bank provides financing through: (1) the Ordinary Capital window that lends at market-based rates; and, (2) the Fund for Special Operations (FSO), which provides financing on concessional terms to the region's poorest nations.

In 2000, the U.S. made the final payment on its contribution to the IDB's eighth general capital increase. No request is being made for the IDB or FSO in 2001.

The Inter-American Investment Corporation (IIC), established in 1984, is a member of the Inter-American Development Bank, whose purpose is to promote development of private small and medium sized enterprises (SMEs) in Latin America and the Caribbean. It is a legally autonomous entity whose resources and management are separate from those of the Inter-American Development Bank itself. Through direct loans and equity investments in SMEs as well as through lending to private financial intermediaries, the IIC helps SMEs in the region to access the medium/long-term capital necessary to start-up, expand, or modernize their operations.

During 1999, the Corporation approved 22 projects totaling $190 million. Since its inception, the IIC has approved 223 projects for a total amount of $1.2 billion. Of these, 106 projects representing $860 million remain active.

The 2001 request includes budget authority of $25 million for paid-in capital subscription for the second payment on the $125.18 million United States' share of the IIC's first general capital increase, as well as $9 million for arrears.

[CONTRIBUTION TO THE ASIAN DEVELOPMENT BANK]

[For payment to the Asian Development Bank by the Secretary of the Treasury for the United States share of the paid-in portion of the increase in capital stock, $13,728,263, to remain available until expended.]

[LIMITATION ON CALLABLE CAPITAL SUBSCRIPTIONS]

[The United States Governor of the Asian Development Bank may subscribe without fiscal year limitation to the callable capital portion of the United States share of such capital stock in an amount not to exceed $672,745,205.]

CONTRIBUTION TO THE ASIAN DEVELOPMENT FUND

For the United States contribution by the Secretary of the Treasury to the increase in resources of the Asian Development Fund, as authorized by the [Asia] *Asian* Development Bank Act, as amended, [$77,000,000] *$125,000,000*, to remain available until expended[, for contributions previously due]. *(Foreign Operations, Export Financing, and Related Programs Appropriation Act, 2000, as enacted by section 1000(a)(2) of the Consolidated Appropriations Act, 2000 (P.L. 106–113).)*

Program and Financing (in millions of dollars)

Identification code 11–0076–0–1–151	1999 actual	2000 est.	2001 est.
Obligations by program activity:			
00.01 Paid-in capital	13	14	
00.02 Asian development fund	210	77	125
10.00 Total new obligations	223	91	125
Budgetary resources available for obligation:			
21.40 Unobligated balance available, start of year	748	748	748
22.00 New budget authority (gross)	223	91	125
23.90 Total budgetary resources available for obligation	971	839	873
23.95 Total new obligations	−223	−91	−125
24.40 Unobligated balance available, end of year	748	748	748
New budget authority (gross), detail:			
Discretionary:			
40.00 Appropriation	223	91	125
Change in unpaid obligations:			
72.40 Unpaid obligations, start of year: Obligated balance, start of year	641	609	510
73.10 Total new obligations	223	91	125
73.20 Total outlays (gross)	−255	−190	−177
74.40 Unpaid obligations, end of year: Obligated balance, end of year	609	510	458
Outlays (gross), detail:			
86.90 Outlays from new discretionary authority	38	15	21
86.93 Outlays from discretionary balances	217	175	156
87.00 Total outlays (gross)	255	190	177
Net budget authority and outlays:			
89.00 Budget authority	223	91	125
90.00 Outlays	255	190	177

The Asian Development Bank (ADB) fosters broad-based sustainable economic development, poverty alleviation, and cooperation in the Asia/Pacific region. The ADB has two main financing windows: (i) the ordinary capital window which lends at market-based rates; and (ii) the Asian Development Fund (ADF) which lends at concessional rates to the region's poorest nations.

ADF resources are derived in part from donor contributions through periodic "replenishments." In the most recent replenishment, ADF–7, the United States successfully negotiated a 41 percent reduction in the total U.S. pledge, lowering our total 4-year commitment from $680 million to $400 million.

In 1999, the Bank lent $3.9 billion of its ordinary capital resources and extended loans and grants of $1.1 billion from ADF resources for development projects. Since its founding in 1966, the ADB has committed over $50 billion, and the ADF has committed $22 billion. In addition the ADB has

General and special funds—Continued

INTERNATIONAL FINANCIAL INSTITUTIONS—Continued

CONTRIBUTION TO THE ASIAN DEVELOPMENT FUND—Continued

made cumulative private sector loans and equity investments of over $2 billion.

In 2000, the U.S. made the final payment to the ADB's fourth general capital increase. No request is being made for ADB in 2001.

The 2001 request for the ADF is for $125 million in budget authority which includes $100 million for our final scheduled payment to ADF–7 and $25 million for arrears.

CONTRIBUTION TO THE AFRICAN DEVELOPMENT BANK

For payment to the African Development Bank by the Secretary of the Treasury, [$4,100,000] *$6,100,000*, for the United States paid-in share of the increase in capital stock, to remain available until expended.

LIMITATION ON CALLABLE CAPITAL SUBSCRIPTIONS

The United States Governor of the African Development Bank may subscribe without fiscal year limitation for the callable capital portion of the United States share of such capital stock in an amount not to exceed [$64,000,000] *$95,983,122*.

CONTRIBUTION TO THE AFRICAN DEVELOPMENT FUND

For the United States contribution by the Secretary of the Treasury to the increase in resources of the African Development Fund, [$128,000,000] *$100,000,000*, to remain available until expended. *(Foreign Operations, Export Financing, and Related Programs Appropriation Act, 2000, as enacted by section 1000(a)(2) of the Consolidated Appropriations Act, 2000 (P.L. 106–113).)*

Program and Financing (in millions of dollars)

Identification code 11–0079–0–1–151	1999 actual	2000 est.	2001 est.
Obligations by program activity:			
00.01 Fund	128	127	100
00.02 Ordinary Capital		4	6
10.00 Total new obligations	128	131	106
Budgetary resources available for obligation:			
22.00 New budget authority (gross)	128	131	106
23.95 Total new obligations	−128	−131	−106
New budget authority (gross), detail:			
Discretionary:			
40.00 Appropriation	128	132	106
40.76 Reduction pursuant to P.L. 106–113		−1	
43.00 Appropriation (total discretionary)	128	131	106
Change in unpaid obligations:			
72.40 Unpaid obligations, start of year: Obligated balance, start of year	287	319	351
73.10 Total new obligations	128	131	106
73.20 Total outlays (gross)	−95	−99	−100
74.40 Unpaid obligations, end of year: Obligated balance, end of year	319	351	357
Outlays (gross), detail:			
86.90 Outlays from new discretionary authority		3	3
86.93 Outlays from discretionary balances	95	97	97
87.00 Total outlays (gross)	95	99	100
Net budget authority and outlays:			
89.00 Budget authority	128	131	106
90.00 Outlays	95	99	100

The African Development Bank group is composed of (i) the African Development Bank (AFDB), which lends at market-based rates, and (ii) the African Development Fund (AFDF), which lends at concessional rates to the poorest African countries. In 1998, the AFDB approved 18 new projects amounting to about $932 million. Since its inception in 1963, the AFDB has financed 772 projects amounting to about $21.9 billion.

The African Development Fund (AFDF) approved around $810 million for 115 projects in 1999. Since its inception in 1974, cumulative AFDF lending totals over $12.4 billion for 1,404 development projects.

The 2001 request for the African Development Bank Group includes $106.1 million in budget authority and $96 million in program limitations for callable capital subscriptions. The budget authority request consists of $5.1 million in paid-in capital for the second installment on the U.S. share of the AFDB's fifth capital increase; $1 million for paid-in capital arrears; $79.99 million in program limitations on callable capital; $15.99 million in arrears on program limitations on callable capital; and $100 million for the second installment on the U.S. share of AFDF–8.

CONTRIBUTION TO THE EUROPEAN BANK FOR RECONSTRUCTION AND DEVELOPMENT

For payment to the European Bank for Reconstruction and Development by the Secretary of the Treasury, $35,778,717, for the United States share of the paid-in portion of the increase in capital stock, to remain available until expended.

LIMITATION ON CALLABLE CAPITAL SUBSCRIPTIONS

The United States Governor of the European Bank for Reconstruction and Development may subscribe without fiscal year limitation to the callable capital portion of the United States share of such capital stock in an amount not to exceed $123,237,803. *(Foreign Operations, Export Financing, and Related Programs Appropriation Act, 2000, as enacted by section 1000(a)(2) of the Consolidated Appropriations Act, 2000 (P.L. 106–113).)*

Program and Financing (in millions of dollars)

Identification code 11–0088–0–1–151	1999 actual	2000 est.	2001 est.
Obligations by program activity:			
10.00 Total new obligations (object class 33.0)	36	36	36
Budgetary resources available for obligation:			
22.00 New budget authority (gross)	36	36	36
23.95 Total new obligations	−36	−36	−36
New budget authority (gross), detail:			
Discretionary:			
40.00 Appropriation	36	36	36
Change in unpaid obligations:			
72.40 Unpaid obligations, start of year: Obligated balance, start of year	19	30	39
73.10 Total new obligations	36	36	36
73.20 Total outlays (gross)	−25	−27	−31
74.40 Unpaid obligations, end of year: Obligated balance, end of year	30	39	44
Outlays (gross), detail:			
86.90 Outlays from new discretionary authority	14	19	19
86.93 Outlays from discretionary balances	11	9	12
87.00 Total outlays (gross)	25	27	31
Net budget authority and outlays:			
89.00 Budget authority	36	36	36
90.00 Outlays	25	27	31

The European Bank for Reconstruction and Development (EBRD) supports market-oriented economic reform and democratic pluralism through predominately private sector lending and investments in the nations of Central and Eastern Europe and the former Soviet Union. Over eighty percent of projects approved in 1998 were in the private sector. The United States and other shareholders signed the articles of agreement of the EBRD on May 29, 1990, and the Bank officially began operating on April 15, 1991.

In April 1996, shareholders approved a doubling of EBRD's capital base from ECU 10 billion to ECU 20 billion (approximately $24 billion) which went into effect in April 1997. The annual payment for the U.S.'s ten percent share is $35.8 million payable over a period of 8 years. At the end of 1998, the EBRD had a portfolio of over 550 projects with a total net value of $10 billion.

The 2001 request consists of $35.8 million in budget authority for paid-in capital and $123.2 million in program limitations for callable capital for the fourth of eight installments on the U.S. subscription to the general capital increase.

NORTH AMERICAN DEVELOPMENT BANK

Program and Financing (in millions of dollars)

Identification code 11–1008–0–1–151	1999 actual	2000 est.	2001 est.
Change in unpaid obligations:			
72.40 Unpaid obligations, start of year: Obligated balance, start of year	51	51	51
73.20 Total outlays (gross)	....	....	-11
74.40 Unpaid obligations, end of year: Obligated balance, end of year	51	51	40
Outlays (gross), detail:			
86.93 Outlays from discretionary balances	....	....	11
Net budget authority and outlays:			
89.00 Budget authority	....	....	....
90.00 Outlays	....	....	11

The North American Development Bank (NADBank) provides financing for environmental infrastructure projects in the border region and, more broadly in the United States and Mexico for NAFTA-related community adjustment and investment. The NADBank's capital ($450 million in paid-in and $2.55 billion in callable capital) was contributed equally by the United States and Mexico over a four-year period. The final U.S. installment was appropriated in 1998, and there is no paid-in capital request for 2001.

The NADBank finances environmental infrastructure projects that have been certified by the U.S.-Mexican Border Environment Cooperation Commission (BECC), an institution designed to assist border states and local communities in coordinating border clean-up. As of December 1999, the NADBank has authorized a total of $182 million in loans, guarantees and grants to help finance 22 environmental projects, representing a total investment of over $600 million and benefitting over four-and-a-half million residents on both sides of the border.

In 2001, the Administration proposes that $10 million be appropriated for the Community Adjustment and Investment Program (CAIP). This appropriation is sought in the Treasury chapter as a domestic assistance program. The CAIP offers financing directly and through existing federal credit programs, such as those run by the Small Business Administration, to both new and existing businesses within communities that suffered job losses as a result of changing trade patterns with Canada and Mexico. The program launched its lending operations during 1997. An Advisory Committee, which includes low income community representatives and non-governmental organizations, helps ensure broad public participation in the community adjustment window of the NADBank.

CONTRIBUTION TO ENTERPRISE FOR THE AMERICAS MULTILATERAL INVESTMENT FUND

For payment to the Enterprise for the Americas Multilateral Investment Fund by the Secretary of the Treasury, for the United States contribution to the fund, $25,900,000, to remain available until expended.

Program and Financing (in millions of dollars)

Identification code 11–0089–0–1–151	1999 actual	2000 est.	2001 est.
Obligations by program activity:			
10.00 Total new obligations (object class 33.0)	50	....	26
Budgetary resources available for obligation:			
22.00 New budget authority (gross)	50	....	26
23.95 Total new obligations	-50	....	-26
New budget authority (gross), detail:			
Discretionary:			
40.00 Appropriation	50	....	26
Change in unpaid obligations:			
72.40 Unpaid obligations, start of year: Obligated balance, start of year	275	296	254
73.10 Total new obligations	50	....	26
73.20 Total outlays (gross)	-30	-42	-46
74.40 Unpaid obligations, end of year: Obligated balance, end of year	296	254	234
Outlays (gross), detail:			
86.90 Outlays from new discretionary authority	1	....	1
86.93 Outlays from discretionary balances	29	42	45
87.00 Total outlays (gross)	30	42	46
Net budget authority and outlays:			
89.00 Budget authority	50	....	26
90.00 Outlays	30	42	46

The Multilateral Investment Fund (MIF), administered by the Inter-American Development Bank, provides grants and loans to support private-sector development and finance and labor sector reforms in Latin America and the Caribbean. Special consideration is given to reforms that encourage private foreign direct investment and promote privatization. Grants and loans are used for technical assistance to identify and resolve investment constraints, for investment in human capital, and for business infrastructure and development.

The U.S. made a commitment to the MIF in 1992 amounting to $500 million, of which we have paid $401.25 million. The 2001 request for the MIF is $25.9 million for partial payment of outstanding U.S. commitments to the U.S. share of MIF resources.

INTERNATIONAL AFFAIRS TECHNICAL ASSISTANCE

For necessary expenses to carry out the provisions of section 129 of the Foreign Assistance Act of 1961 (relating to international affairs technical assistance activities), [$1,500,000] *$7,000,000*, to remain available until expended, which shall be available nowithstanding [and] *any* other provision of law. *(Foreign Operations, Export Financing, and Related Programs Appropriation Act, 2000, as enacted by section 1000(a)(2) of the Consolidated Appropriations Act, 2000 (P.L. 106–113).)*

Program and Financing (in millions of dollars)

Identification code 11–1045–0–1–151	1999 actual	2000 est.	2001 est.
Obligations by program activity:			
00.01 New Obligations	....	4	4
10.00 Total new obligations	....	4	4
Budgetary resources available for obligation:			
21.40 Unobligated balance available, start of year	....	3	1
22.00 New budget authority (gross)	3	2	7
23.90 Total budgetary resources available for obligation	3	5	8
23.95 Total new obligations	....	-4	-4
24.40 Unobligated balance available, end of year	3	1	4
New budget authority (gross), detail:			
Discretionary:			
40.00 Appropriation	3	2	7

General and special funds—Continued

INTERNATIONAL AFFAIRS TECHNICAL ASSISTANCE—Continued

Program and Financing (in millions of dollars)—Continued

Identification code 11–1045–0–1–151	1999 actual	2000 est.	2001 est.
40.75 Reduction pursuant to P.L. 106–51			
43.00 Appropriation (total discretionary)	3	2	7
Change in unpaid obligations:			
72.40 Unpaid obligations, start of year: Obligated balance, start of year			1
73.10 Total new obligations		4	4
73.20 Total outlays (gross)		–2	–2
74.40 Unpaid obligations, end of year: Obligated balance, end of year		1	3
Outlays (gross), detail:			
86.93 Outlays from discretionary balances		2	2
Net budget authority and outlays:			
89.00 Budget authority	3	2	7
90.00 Outlays		2	2

This account will provide technical assistance to other countries in support of the responsibilities of the U.S. Treasury Department to formulate, conduct and coordinate the international financial policies of the United States. In addition to overseeing U.S. interests in the work of international financial institutions, including the International Monetary Fund, the World Bank and the various regional development banks, the Treasury Department frequently has the lead responsibility for implementing fiscal and financial policy aspects of U.S. foreign policy toward individual countries. Technical assistance provided through this account will facilitate key short- and medium-term reforms in the policy and management areas of budget, tax, government debt, financial institutions and financial crimes enforcement.

Using funding provided under the SEED and FREEDOM Support Acts, U.S. Treasury Department advisors have provided policy and management advice in the areas described above to countries in Eastern Europe and the former Soviet Union in their transition to market economies and democratic fiscal structures. Beginning in 1997, advisors have also provided assistance, using funding from USAID Development Assistance and the Economic Support Fund, to the governments of South Africa and Haiti. The flexibility provided by direct funding permits the Department to be responsive when governments make decisions to implement key fiscal and financial reforms, and allows it to act quickly to help select governments strengthen governmental fiscal and financial institutions during crucial transition periods toward market-oriented economies.

The proposed $7 million appropriation will fully fund approximately 13 resident advisors, including program related administrative costs and intermittent expert visits in support of the advisors. This appropriation will permit expansion of the program to countries outside Central and Eastern Europe and the Former Soviet Union, including implementation of programs in Asia, Africa, and Central and Latin America. The Treasury Department will closely coordinate with international financial institutions and with USAID, the Department of State and other relevant U.S. Government agencies when determining where its technical assistance program can have the greatest positive impact.

Object Classification (in millions of dollars)

Identification code 11–1045–0–1–151	1999 actual	2000 est.	2001 est.
11.1 Personnel compensation: Full-time permanent			1
21.0 Travel and transportation of persons			1
25.1 Advisory and assistance services		4	2
99.9 Total new obligations		4	4

Personnel Summary

Identification code 11–1045–0–1–151	1999 actual	2000 est.	2001 est.
1001 Total compensable workyears: Full-time equivalent employment			10

INTERNATIONAL ORGANIZATIONS AND PROGRAMS

For necessary expenses to carry out the provisions of section 301 of the Foreign Assistance Act of 1961, and of section 2 of the United Nations Environment Program Participation Act of 1973, [$183,000,000: *Provided*, That none of the funds appropriated under this heading shall be made available for the United Nations Fund for Science and Technology: *Provided further*, That not less than $5,000,000 should be made available to the World Food Program: *Provided further*, That none of the funds appropriated under this heading may be made available to the Korean Peninsula Energy Development Organization (KEDO) or the International Atomic Energy Agency (IAEA)] *$356,000,000. (Foreign Operations, Export Financing, and Related Programs Appropriation Act, 2000, as enacted by section 1000(a)(2) of the Consolidated Appropriations Act, 2000 (P.L. 106–113).)*

Program and Financing (in millions of dollars)

Identification code 72–1005–0–1–151	1999 actual	2000 est.	2001 est.
Obligations by program activity:			
01.01 UN Children's Fund	105	110	110
01.02 UN Development Program	100	80	90
01.03 UN Population Fund		25	25
01.04 Global Alliance for Vaccines and Immunization			50
01.05 World Food Program	5	5	5
01.08 Various other organizations	98	74	74
10.00 Total new obligations	308	294	354
Budgetary resources available for obligation:			
22.00 New budget authority (gross)	308	294	356
23.95 Total new obligations	–308	–294	–354
New budget authority (gross), detail:			
Discretionary:			
40.00 Appropriation	187	183	354
40.76 Reduction pursuant to P.L. 106–113		–1	
42.00 Transferred from other accounts	121	112	2
43.00 Appropriation (total discretionary)	308	294	356
Change in unpaid obligations:			
72.40 Unpaid obligations, start of year: Obligated balance, start of year	58	25	24
73.10 Total new obligations	308	294	354
73.20 Total outlays (gross)	–338	–295	–350
73.40 Adjustments in expired accounts (net)	–3		
74.40 Unpaid obligations, end of year: Obligated balance, end of year	25	24	28
Outlays (gross), detail:			
86.90 Outlays from new discretionary authority	295	273	331
86.93 Outlays from discretionary balances	43	22	19
87.00 Total outlays (gross)	338	295	350
Net budget authority and outlays:			
89.00 Budget authority	308	294	356
90.00 Outlays	338	295	350

In addition to its assessed payments, the United States contributes to voluntary funds of many international organizations and programs involved in a wide range of sustainable development, humanitarian, and scientific activities. Any funds made available for United Nations Population Fund will not be used for activities in the People's Republic of China and will be maintained in a separate account and not commingled with any other funds.

Credit accounts:

DEBT RESTRUCTURING

For the cost, as defined in section 502 of the Congressional Budget Act of 1974, of modifying loans and loan guarantees, as the President may determine, for which funds have been appropriated or otherwise made available for programs within the International Affairs Budget Function 150, including the cost of selling, reducing, or canceling amounts owed to the United States as a result of concessional loans made to eligible countries, pursuant to parts IV and V of the Foreign Assistance Act of 1961 [(including up to $1,000,000 for necessary expenses for the administration of activities carried out under these parts),] and of modifying concessional credit agreements with least developed countries, as authorized under section 411 of the Agricultural Trade Development and Assistance Act of 1954, as amended, and concessional loans, guarantees and credit agreements, as authorized under section 572 of the Foreign Operations, Export Financing, and Related Programs Appropriations Act, 1989 (Public Law 100–461), [$123,000,000, to remain available until expended: *Provided*, That of this amount, not less than $13,000,000 *$25,000,000* shall be made available to carry out the provisions of part V of the Foreign Assistance Act of 1961] *to become available on October 1 of the year specified and to remain available until expended, as follows: for 2001, $262,000,000, of which $37,000,000 shall be to carry out part V of the Act; for 2002, $240,000,000; and for 2003, $135,000,000: Provided, That of this entire amount, up to $390,000,000 shall be available for a contribution to the Heavily Indebted Poor Countries Trust Fund of the International Bank for Reconstruction and Development*: *Provided further*, That any limitation of subsection (e) of section 411 of the Agricultural Trade Development and Assistance Act of 1954 shall not apply to funds appropriated [hereunder or previously appropriated] under this heading: *Provided further*, That the authority provided by section 572 of Public Law 100–461 may be exercised only with respect to countries that are eligible to borrow from the International Development Association, but not from the International Bank for Reconstruction and Development, commonly referred to as "IDA-only" countries. *(Foreign Operations, Export Financing, and Related Programs Appropriation Act, 2000, as enacted by section 1000(a)(2) of the Consolidated Appropriations Act, 2000 (P.L. 106–113).)*

Program and Financing (in millions of dollars)

Identification code 11–0091–0–1–151	1999 actual	2000 est.	2001 est.
Obligations by program activity:			
00.05 Reestimates of Direct Loan Subsidy		5	
01.01 Paris club/HIPC debt reduction	43	189	75
01.02 HIPC Trust Fund			150
01.03 Tropical Forest Conservation Initiative		13	37
10.00 Total new obligations (object class 41.0)	43	207	262
Budgetary resources available for obligation:			
21.40 Unobligated balance available, start of year	48	79	
22.00 New budget authority (gross)	74	128	262
23.90 Total budgetary resources available for obligation	122	207	262
23.95 Total new obligations	−43	−207	−262
24.40 Unobligated balance available, end of year	79		
New budget authority (gross), detail:			
Discretionary:			
40.00 Appropriation	74	123	262
Mandatory:			
60.05 Appropriation (indefinite)		5	
70.00 Total new budget authority (gross)	74	128	262
Change in unpaid obligations:			
72.40 Unpaid obligations, start of year: Obligated balance, start of year		20	107
73.10 Total new obligations	43	207	262
73.20 Total outlays (gross)	−23	−120	−136
74.40 Unpaid obligations, end of year: Obligated balance, end of year	20	107	233
Outlays (gross), detail:			
86.90 Outlays from new discretionary authority	13	31	66
86.93 Outlays from discretionary balances	10	84	70
86.97 Outlays from new mandatory authority		5	
87.00 Total outlays (gross)	23	120	136
Net budget authority and outlays:			
89.00 Budget authority	74	128	262
90.00 Outlays	23	120	136

Summary of Budget Authority and Outlays

(in millions of dollars)

	1999 actual	*2000 est.*	*2001 est.*
Enacted/requested:			
Budget Authority	74	128	262
Outlays	23	120	136
Supplemental proposal:			
Budget Authority		210	
Outlays		53	105
Total:			
Budget Authority	74	338	262
Outlays	23	173	241

Debt Reduction for the Poorest. For the poorest countries, debt reduction provides an incentive to implement macroeconomic and structural reforms necessary to improve economic performance and creditworthiness. Debt relief, economic reform and poverty reduction contribute to economic growth and social development, which can mean expanded opportunities for trade and investment for the United States. For the poorest and most heavily indebted countries, the United States will continue support for the Paris Club of official creditors and provide additional relief complementary to the enhanced Heavily Indebted Poor Country (HIPC) Initiative.

To support this initiative, the Administration requests a total of $810 million, of which $210 million will be made available in 2000 through the Administration's supplemental budget request to meet the United States commitment to contribute its share to the HIPC Trust Fund administered by the World Bank. The HIPC Trust Fund helps regional development banks and other multilateral institutions meet their costs of debt relief. The Department of the Treasury is submitting the necessary authorizing legislation. Our request for support for the HIPC Trust Fund is $600 million, of which $210 million is requested in the 2000 supplemental, $150 million is for 2001, and $240 million is for 2002. The Administration expects that a U.S. contribution to the HIPC Trust Fund will leverage contributions from other creditors.

For the cost of bilateral debt reduction under this initiative, we are requesting $210 million, of which $75 million is for 2001 and $135 million is to be made available on October 1, 2002. The $210 million in bilateral debt reduction will reduce approximately $2.1 billion in face value of debt. In total, our participation in the enhanced HIPC initiative can leverage up to $90 billion in debt relief.

Debt Buyback/Swap Program. For Latin America and the Caribbean, the Administration proposes that debt reduction be effected at zero cost through buybacks and swaps of eligible concessional debt, linked to commitment of local currency payments to support environment or child survival projects. The Administration will be seeking new authority for no-cost buybacks and swaps of P.L. 480 concessional debt and the approval of the Appropriations Committee for this program.

Tropical Forest Debt Relief. This authorizing legislation received strong bipartisan support and was signed into law by the President in July 1998. Modeled after the very successful Enterprise for the Americas Initiative (EAI), P.L. 105–214 will allow the Administration to reduce outstanding concessional USAID and PL–480 debt stocks to support conservation of the endangered tropical forests and promote economic reforms in eligible countries. Debt relief or buybacks in eligible countries will leverage payment of local currency resources into funds to support programs to conserve their tropical forests. The Administration anticipates that $37 mil-

Credit accounts—Continued

DEBT RESTRUCTURING—Continued

lion in appropriations could provide as much as $100 million in face value forgiveness of debt owed to the United States by eligible countries.

AGENCY FOR INTERNATIONAL DEVELOPMENT

Federal Funds

General and special funds:

SUSTAINABLE DEVELOPMENT ASSISTANCE

(INCLUDING TRANSFER OF FUNDS)

For necessary expenses to carry out the provisions of sections 103 through 106, [and] *but excluding* chapter 10 of part I of the Foreign Assistance Act of 1961, [title V of the International Security and Development Cooperation Act of 1980 (Public Law 96–533) and the provisions of section 401 of the Foreign Assistance Act of 1969, $1,228,000,000] *$948,822,000*, to remain available until September 30, [2001] *2002*: *Provided*, That [of the amount appropriated under this heading, up to $5,000,000 may be made available for and apportioned directly to the Inter-American Foundation: *Provided further*, That of the amount appropriated under this heading, up to $14,400,000 may be made available for the African Development Foundation and shall be apportioned directly to that agency: *Provided further*, That] none of the funds made available in this Act nor any unobligated balances from prior appropriations may be made available to any organization or program which, as determined by the President of the United States, supports or participates in the management of a program of coercive abortion or involuntary sterilization: *Provided further*, That none of the funds made available under this heading may be used to pay for the performance of abortion as a method of family planning or to motivate or coerce any person to practice abortions; and that in order to reduce reliance on abortion in developing nations, funds shall be available only to voluntary family planning projects which offer, either directly or through referral to, or information about access to, a broad range of family planning methods and services, and that any such voluntary family planning project shall meet the following requirements: (1) service providers or referral agents in the project shall not implement or be subject to quotas, or other numerical targets, of total number of births, number of family planning acceptors, or acceptors of a particular method of family planning (this provision shall not be construed to include the use of quantitative estimates or indicators for budgeting and planning purposes); (2) the project shall not include payment of incentives, bribes, gratuities, or financial reward to: (A) an individual in exchange for becoming a family planning acceptor; or (B) program personnel for achieving a numerical target or quota of total number of births, number of family planning acceptors, or acceptors of a particular method of family planning; (3) the project shall not deny any right or benefit, including the right of access to participate in any program of general welfare or the right of access to health care, as a consequence of any individual's decision not to accept family planning services; (4) the project shall provide family planning acceptors comprehensible information on the health benefits and risks of the method chosen, including those conditions that might render the use of the method inadvisable and those adverse side effects known to be consequent to the use of the method; and (5) the project shall ensure that experimental contraceptive drugs and devices and medical procedures are provided only in the context of a scientific study in which participants are advised of potential risks and benefits; and, not less than 60 days after the date on which the Administrator of the United States Agency for International Development determines that there has been a violation of the requirements contained in paragraph (1), (2), (3), or (5) of this proviso, or a pattern or practice of violations of the requirements contained in paragraph (4) of this proviso, the Administrator shall submit to the Committee on International Relations and the Committee on Appropriations of the House of Representatives and to the Committee on Foreign Relations and the Committee on Appropriations of the Senate, a report containing a description of such violation and the corrective action taken by the Agency: *Provided further*, That in awarding grants for natural family planning under section 104 of the Foreign Assistance Act of 1961 no applicant shall be discriminated against because of such applicant's religious or conscientious commitment to offer only natural family planning; and, additionally, all such applicants shall comply with the requirements of the previous proviso: *Provided further*, That for purposes of this or any other Act authorizing or appropriating funds for foreign operations, export financing, and related programs, the term "motivate", as it relates to family planning assistance, shall not be construed to prohibit the provision, consistent with local law, of information or counseling about all pregnancy options: *Provided further*, That nothing in this paragraph shall be construed to alter any existing statutory prohibitions against abortion under section 104 of the Foreign Assistance Act of 1961: *Provided further*, That, notwithstanding section 109 of the Foreign Assistance Act of 1961, of the funds appropriated under this heading in this Act, and of the unobligated balances of funds previously appropriated under this heading, $2,500,000 may be transferred to "International Organizations and Programs" for a contribution to the International Fund for Agricultural Development (IFAD): *Provided further*, That none of the funds appropriated under this heading may be made available for any activity which is in contravention to the Convention on International Trade in Endangered Species of Flora and Fauna (CITES): *Provided further*, That of the funds appropriated under this heading that are made available for assistance programs for displaced and orphaned children and victims of war, not to exceed $25,000, in addition to funds otherwise available for such purposes, may be used to monitor and provide oversight of such programs[: *Provided further*, That of the funds appropriated under this heading not less than $500,000 should be made available for support of the United States Telecommunications Training Institute: *Provided further*, That, of the funds appropriated by this Act for the Microenterprise Initiative (including any local currencies made available for the purposes of the Initiative), not less than one-half should be made available for programs providing loans of less than $300 to very poor people, particularly women, or for institutional support of organizations primarily engaged in making such loans].

[CYPRUS]

[Of the funds appropriated under the headings "Development Assistance" and "Economic Support Fund", not less than $15,000,000 shall be made available for Cyprus to be used only for scholarships, administrative support of the scholarship program, bicommunal projects, and measures aimed at reunification of the island and designed to reduce tensions and promote peace and cooperation between the two communities on Cyprus.]

[LEBANON]

[Of the funds appropriated under the headings "Development Assistance" and "Economic Support Fund", not less than $15,000,000 should be made available for Lebanon to be used, among other programs, for scholarships and direct support of the American educational institutions in Lebanon.]

[BURMA]

[Of the funds appropriated under the headings "Economic Support Fund", "Child Survival and Disease Programs Fund" and "Development Assistance", not less than $6,500,000 shall be made available to support democracy activities in Burma, democracy and humanitarian activities along the Burma-Thailand border, and for Burmese student groups and other organizations located outside Burma: *Provided*, That funds made available for Burma-related activities under this heading may be made available notwithstanding any other provision of law: *Provided further*, That the provision of such funds shall be made available subject to the regular notification procedures of the Committees on Appropriations.]

[PRIVATE AND VOLUNTARY ORGANIZATIONS]

[None of the funds appropriated or otherwise made available by this Act for development assistance may be made available to any United States private and voluntary organization, except any cooperative development organization, which obtains less than 20 percent of its total annual funding for international activities from sources other than the United States Government: *Provided*, That the Administrator of the Agency for International Development may, on a case-by-case basis, waive the restriction contained in this paragraph, after taking into account the effectiveness of the overseas development activities of the organization, its level of volunteer support, its financial viability and stability, and the degree of its dependence for its financial support on the agency.]

[Funds appropriated or otherwise made available under title II of this Act should be made available to private and voluntary organizations at a level which is at least equivalent to the level provided in fiscal year 1995.] *(Foreign Operations, Export Financing, and Related Programs Appropriation Act, 2000, as enacted by section 1000(a)(2) of the Consolidated Appropriations Act, 2000 (P.L. 106–113).)*

Program and Financing (in millions of dollars)

Identification code 72–1021–0–1–151	1999 actual	2000 est.	2001 est.
Obligations by program activity:			
00.01 Functional development assistance	1,207	1,334	919
09.01 Reimbursable program	5		
10.00 Total new obligations	1,212	1,334	919
Budgetary resources available for obligation:			
21.40 Unobligated balance available, start of year	127	133	
22.00 New budget authority (gross)	1,194	1,199	932
22.10 Resources available from recoveries of prior year obligations	37		
22.21 Unobligated balance transferred to other accounts	−5		
23.90 Total budgetary resources available for obligation	1,353	1,332	932
23.95 Total new obligations	−1,212	−1,334	−919
23.98 Unobligated balance expiring or withdrawn	−7		
24.40 Unobligated balance available, end of year	133		15
New budget authority (gross), detail:			
Discretionary:			
40.00 Appropriation	1,225	1,228	949
40.76 Reduction pursuant to P.L. 106–113		−5	
41.00 Transferred to other accounts	−36	−24	−17
43.00 Appropriation (total discretionary)	1,189	1,199	932
68.00 Spending authority from offsetting collections: Offsetting collections (cash)	5		
70.00 Total new budget authority (gross)	1,194	1,199	932
Change in unpaid obligations:			
72.40 Unpaid obligations, start of year: Obligated balance, start of year	1,570	1,974	2,139
73.10 Total new obligations	1,212	1,334	919
73.20 Total outlays (gross)	−771	−1,169	−1,136
73.45 Adjustments in unexpired accounts	−37		
74.40 Unpaid obligations, end of year: Obligated balance, end of year	1,974	2,139	1,922
Outlays (gross), detail:			
86.90 Outlays from new discretionary authority	89	85	66
86.93 Outlays from discretionary balances	682	1,084	1,068
87.00 Total outlays (gross)	771	1,169	1,136
Offsets:			
Against gross budget authority and outlays:			
88.45 Offsetting collections (cash) from: Offsetting governmental collections from the public	−5		
Net budget authority and outlays:			
89.00 Budget authority	1,189	1,199	932
90.00 Outlays	766	1,169	1,136

Sustainable Development Assistance Program.—The Sustainable Development Assistance account funds sustainable development assistance activities that are not related to funds requested under the separate Development Fund for Africa account or to child survival, disease prevention and basic education. While these latter activities are funded in the Child Survival and Disease Programs account, the Sustainable Development Assistance account funds programs in the areas of economic growth, democracy, family planning, human capacity development and global environment.

However, activities funded through these three accounts are key components of USAID's principal mission of supporting the people of developing and transitional countries in their efforts to achieve sustainable economic and social progress. These activities support five key USAID strategic goals:

(1) *Encouraging broad-based economic growth and agricultural development,* with the objectives of expanding and strengthening critical private markets, achieving more rapid and enhanced agricultural development and food security, and, expanding access to economic opportunity for the rural and urban poor.

(2) *Strengthening democracy and good governance,* with the objectives of strengthening the rule of law and respect for human rights of both men and women, encouraging credible and competitive political processes, promoting the development of a politically active civil society, and encouraging more transparent and accountable government institutions.

(3) *Building human capacity through education and training,* with the objectives of expanding access to quality basic education, especially for girls and women, and, increasing the contributions of institutions of higher education to sustainable development.

(4) *Stabilizing the world population and protecting human health,* with the objectives of reducing unintended pregnancies, improving infant and child health and nutrition and reducing infant and child mortality, reducing deaths, nutrition insecurity and adverse health outcomes to women as a result of pregnancy and child birth, reducing HIV transmission and the impact of the HIV/AIDS pandemic in developing countries, and, reducing the threat of infectious diseases of major public health importance.

(5) *Protecting the world's environment,* with the objectives of preparing national environmental management strategies, improving conservation of biologically significant habitats, reducing the rate of growth of net emissions of greenhouse gases, increasing the access of urban populations to adequate environmental services, conserving energy through increased efficiency and reliance on renewable sources, and reducing the loss of forest area.

Development Assistance Programs

(Funded through Sustainable Development Assistance, Development Fund for Africa and Child Survival and Disease Program accounts). The following regional and strategic goal area allocations are preliminary, and changes may be reflected in the USAID 2001 Congressional Presentation.

[In thousands of dollars]

Regional Allocations:	
Africa	836,997
Asia/Near East	369,097
Latin America/Caribbean	350,121
Global	497,838
Other	84,947
Total	2,139,000
Strategic Goal Allocations:	
Economic Growth	443,953
Human Capacity Development	145,882
Population, Health, & Nutrition	1,049,000
Environment	333,000
Democracy	167,165
Total	2,139,000

The above figures include the amounts for which permissive transfers for the Development Credit Account and the International Fund for Agricultural Development were requested.

Object Classification (in millions of dollars)

Identification code 72–1021–0–1–151	1999 actual	2000 est.	2001 est.
Direct obligations:			
11.8 Personnel compensation: Special personal services payments	2	2	1
21.0 Travel and transportation of persons	2	2	1
22.0 Transportation of things	3	3	2
25.1 Advisory and assistance services	25	25	15
25.2 Other services	79	80	60
26.0 Supplies and materials	8	8	5

General and special funds—Continued

SUSTAINABLE DEVELOPMENT ASSISTANCE—Continued

[PRIVATE AND VOLUNTARY ORGANIZATIONS]—Continued

Object Classification (in millions of dollars)—Continued

Identification code 72–1021–0–1–151		1999 actual	2000 est.	2001 est.
41.0	Grants, subsidies, and contributions	1,085	1,214	835
99.0	Subtotal, direct obligations	1,204	1,334	919
99.0	Reimbursable obligations	5		
41.0	Allocation Account: Grants, subsidies, and contributions	3		
99.9	Total new obligations	1,212	1,334	919

CHILD SURVIVAL AND DISEASE PROGRAMS FUND

For necessary expenses to carry out the provisions of [chapters 1 and 10 of part I] *sections 103 through 106* of the Foreign Assistance Act of 1961, for child survival, basic education, assistance to combat tropical and other diseases, and related activities, in addition to funds otherwise available for such purposes, [$715,000,000] *$659,250,000*, to remain available until expended: *Provided*, That this amount shall be made available for such activities as: (1) immunization programs; (2) oral rehydration programs; (3) health and nutrition programs, and related education programs, which address the needs of mothers and children; (4) water and sanitation programs; (5) assistance for displaced and orphaned children; (6) programs for the prevention, treatment, and control of, and research on, tuberculosis, HIV/AIDS, polio, malaria and other diseases; and (7) [up to $98,000,000 for] basic education programs for children: *Provided further*, That none of the funds appropriated under this heading may be made available for nonproject assistance for health and child survival programs, except that funds may be made available for such assistance for ongoing health programs[: *Provided further*, That $35,000,000 shall be available only for the HIV/AIDS programs requested under this heading in House Document 106–101]. *(Foreign Operations, Export Financing, and Related Programs Appropriation Act, 2000, as enacted by section 1000(a)(2) of the Consolidated Appropriations Act, 2000 (P.L. 106–113).)*

Program and Financing (in millions of dollars)

Identification code 72–1095–0–1–151		1999 actual	2000 est.	2001 est.
	Obligations by program activity:			
00.01	Direct program	629	630	659
10.00	Total new obligations	629	630	659
	Budgetary resources available for obligation:			
21.40	Unobligated balance available, start of year	58	28	
22.00	New budget authority (gross)	595	602	659
22.10	Resources available from recoveries of prior year obligations	3		
23.90	Total budgetary resources available for obligation	656	630	659
23.95	Total new obligations	−629	−630	−659
24.40	Unobligated balance available, end of year	28		
	New budget authority (gross), detail:			
	Discretionary:			
40.00	Appropriation	700	715	659
40.76	Reduction pursuant to P.L. 106–113		−3	
41.00	Transferred to other accounts	−105	−110	
43.00	Appropriation (total discretionary)	595	602	659
	Change in unpaid obligations:			
72.40	Unpaid obligations, start of year: Obligated balance, start of year	835	1,030	1,155
73.10	Total new obligations	629	630	659
73.20	Total outlays (gross)	−430	−505	−546
73.45	Adjustments in unexpired accounts	−3		
74.40	Unpaid obligations, end of year: Obligated balance, end of year	1,030	1,155	1,266
	Outlays (gross), detail:			
86.90	Outlays from new discretionary authority	42	43	47
86.93	Outlays from discretionary balances	388	462	499
87.00	Total outlays (gross)	430	505	546
	Net budget authority and outlays:			
89.00	Budget authority	595	602	659
90.00	Outlays	430	505	546

This program provides economic resources to developing countries including those in sub-Saharan Africa to support programs to: (1) improve infant and child health and nutrition with the aim of reducing infant and child mortality rates; (2) reduce HIV transmission and the impact of the HIV/AIDS pandemic in developing countries; (3) reduce the threat of infectious diseases of major public health importance such as polio and malaria; and (4) expand access to quality basic education, especially for girls and women.

Object Classification (in millions of dollars)

Identification code 72–1095–0–1–151		1999 actual	2000 est.	2001 est.
21.0	Travel and transportation of persons	2	2	2
25.2	Other services	46	50	55
41.0	Grants, subsidies, and contributions	581	578	602
99.9	Total new obligations	629	630	659

DEVELOPMENT FUND FOR AFRICA

For necessary expenses to carry out the provisions of chapter 10 of part I of the Foreign Assistance Act of 1961, in addition to amounts otherwise available for such purposes, $532,928,000, to remain available until September 30, 2002.

Program and Financing (in millions of dollars)

Identification code 72–1014–0–1–151		1999 actual	2000 est.	2001 est.
	Obligations by program activity:			
00.01	Direct program	39	39	533
10.00	Total new obligations	39	39	533
	Budgetary resources available for obligation:			
21.40	Unobligated balance available, start of year	58	39	
22.00	New budget authority (gross)			533
22.10	Resources available from recoveries of prior year obligations	20		
23.90	Total budgetary resources available for obligation	78	39	533
23.95	Total new obligations	−39	−39	−533
24.40	Unobligated balance available, end of year	39		
	New budget authority (gross), detail:			
	Discretionary:			
40.00	Appropriation			533
	Change in unpaid obligations:			
72.40	Unpaid obligations, start of year: Obligated balance, start of year	511	336	255
73.10	Total new obligations	39	39	533
73.20	Total outlays (gross)	−194	−120	−133
73.45	Adjustments in unexpired accounts	−20		
74.40	Unpaid obligations, end of year: Obligated balance, end of year	336	255	655
	Outlays (gross), detail:			
86.90	Outlays from new discretionary authority			38
86.93	Outlays from discretionary balances	194	120	95
87.00	Total outlays (gross)	194	120	133
	Net budget authority and outlays:			
89.00	Budget authority			533
90.00	Outlays	193	120	133

For 2001, the Administration is requesting reinstatement of a separate appropriation for this account to highlight the United States' commitment to tackling Africa's complex development challenges. The fund, while modest in scope, will provide resources for improving millions of lives in sub-Saharan Africa and will enable the United States to meet the challenges and opportunities for sustainable development in that region. As with the Sustainable Development Assistance account, the Development Fund for Africa will program resources in five USAID strategic goal areas: promoting broad-based and sustainable economic growth and agricultural development, strengthening democracy and good governance, building human capacity through education and training, stabilizing the world population and protecting human health, and protecting the world's environment. Funding in this region for child survival, infectious diseases and basic education will be separately funded out of the Child Survival and Disease Program Fund.

Object Classification (in millions of dollars)

Identification code 72–1014–0–1–151	1999 actual	2000 est.	2001 est.
25.2 Other services	2	2	45
41.0 Grants, subsidies, and contributions	37	37	488
99.9 Total new obligations	39	39	533

Assistance for Eastern Europe and the Baltic States

(a) For necessary expenses to carry out the provisions of the Foreign Assistance Act of 1961 and the Support for East European Democracy (SEED) Act of 1989, [$535,000,000] *$610,000,000*, to remain available until September 30, [2001] *2002*, which shall be available, notwithstanding any other provision of law, for assistance and for related programs for Eastern Europe and the Baltic States[: *Provided*, That of the funds appropriated under this heading not less than $150,000,000 should be made available for assistance for Kosova: *Provided further*, That of the funds made available under this heading and the headings "International Narcotics Control and Law Enforcement" and "Economic Support Fund", not to exceed $130,000,000 shall be made available for Bosnia and Herzegovina: *Provided further*, That none of the funds made available under this heading for Kosova shall be made available until the Secretary of State certifies that the resources pledged by the United States at the upcoming Kosova donors conference shall not exceed 15 percent of the total resources pledged by all donors: *Provided further*, That none of the funds made available under this heading for Kosova shall be made available for large scale physical infrastructure reconstruction].

(b) Funds appropriated under this heading or in prior appropriations Acts that are or have been made available for an Enterprise Fund may be deposited by such Fund in interest-bearing accounts prior to the Fund's disbursement of such funds for program purposes. The Fund may retain for such program purposes any interest earned on such deposits without returning such interest to the Treasury of the United States and without further appropriation by the Congress. Funds made available for Enterprise Funds shall be expended at the minimum rate necessary to make timely payment for projects and activities.

(c) Funds appropriated under this heading shall be considered to be economic assistance under the Foreign Assistance Act of 1961 for purposes of making available the administrative authorities contained in that Act for the use of economic assistance.

[(d) None of the funds appropriated under this heading may be made available for new housing construction or repair or reconstruction of existing housing in Bosnia and Herzegovina unless directly related to the efforts of United States troops to promote peace in said country.]

[(e) With regard to funds appropriated under this heading for the economic revitalization program in Bosnia and Herzegovina, and local currencies generated by such funds (including the conversion of funds appropriated under this heading into currency used by Bosnia and Herzegovina as local currency and local currency returned or repaid under such program) the Administrator of the Agency for International Development shall provide written approval for grants and loans prior to the obligation and expenditure of funds for such purposes, and prior to the use of funds that have been returned or repaid to any lending facility or grantee.]

[(f) The provisions of section 532 of this Act shall apply to funds made available under subsection (e) and to funds appropriated under this heading.]

[(g) The President is authorized to withhold funds appropriated under this heading made available for economic revitalization programs in Bosnia and Herzegovina, if he determines and certifies to the Committees on Appropriations that the Federation of Bosnia and Herzegovina has not complied with article III of annex 1–A of the General Framework Agreement for Peace in Bosnia and Herzegovina concerning the withdrawal of foreign forces, and that intelligence cooperation on training, investigations, and related activities between Iranian officials and Bosnian officials has not been terminated.] *(Foreign Operations, Export Financing, and Related Programs Appropriation Act, 2000, as enacted by section 1000(a)(2) of the Consolidated Appropriations Act, 2000 (P.L. 106–113).)*

Program and Financing (in millions of dollars)

Identification code 72–1010–0–1–151	1999 actual	2000 est.	2001 est.
Obligations by program activity:			
10.00 Total new obligations	420	683	610
Budgetary resources available for obligation:			
21.40 Unobligated balance available, start of year	134	150	
22.00 New budget authority (gross)	436	533	610
22.10 Resources available from recoveries of prior year obligations	8		
22.21 Unobligated balance transferred to other accounts	−5		
23.90 Total budgetary resources available for obligation	574	683	610
23.95 Total new obligations	−420	−683	−610
23.98 Unobligated balance expiring or withdrawn	−2		
24.40 Unobligated balance available, end of year	150		
New budget authority (gross), detail:			
Discretionary:			
40.00 Appropriation	550	535	610
40.76 Reduction pursuant to P.L. 106–113		−2	
41.00 Transferred to other accounts	−114		
43.00 Appropriation (total discretionary)	436	533	610
Change in unpaid obligations:			
Unpaid obligations, start of year:			
72.40 Obligated balance, start of year	625	513	663
72.95 From Federal sources: Receivables and unpaid, unfilled orders	2	2	
72.99 Total unpaid obligations, start of year	627	515	663
73.10 Total new obligations	420	683	610
73.20 Total outlays (gross)	−523	−535	−327
73.45 Adjustments in unexpired accounts	−8		
Unpaid obligations, end of year:			
74.40 Obligated balance, end of year	513	663	946
74.95 From Federal sources: Receivables and unpaid, unfilled orders	2		
74.99 Total unpaid obligations, end of year	515	663	946
Outlays (gross), detail:			
86.90 Outlays from new discretionary authority	172	74	31
86.93 Outlays from discretionary balances	351	461	297
87.00 Total outlays (gross)	523	535	327
Net budget authority and outlays:			
89.00 Budget authority	436	533	610
90.00 Outlays	523	535	327

Summary of Budget Authority and Outlays

(in millions of dollars)

	1999 actual	2000 est.	2001 est.
Enacted/requested:			
Budget Authority	436	533	610
Outlays	523	535	328
Supplemental proposal:			
Budget Authority		195	
Outlays		20	64
Total:			
Budget Authority	436	728	610
Outlays	523	555	392

General and special funds—Continued

ASSISTANCE FOR EASTERN EUROPE AND THE BALTIC STATES—Continued

This account provides funds to promote country-specific strategies that build on common, region-wide strategic goals; including economic restructuring, democratic transition, and social stabilization. Authorized Support for Eastern European Democracy (SEED) programs concentrate on (a) the development and strengthening of institutions and civic action necessary for sustainable democracy; (b) the development of market economies and a strong private sector; and the improvement of the basic quality of life in selected areas. This interagency program is managed by the SEED coordinator, who is located in the State Department's Bureau of European Affairs.

SEED assistance is now focused on Southeast Europe, with the single largest program designed for Kosovo. The U.S. is contributing to international efforts toward recovery from the conflict with Milosevic and to building effective governance and a functioning economy in Kosovo. While implementation of the Dayton Accords still requires significant, albeit reducing support in Bosnia, additional resources are needed in Serbia and Montenegro. Two wars in the region in recent years demonstrated the need for a special effort to provide for peaceful cooperation among neighbors. The Southeast Europe Initiative builds on the country programs in the Balkans to help stabilize the region as a whole and prepare for integration into the European and international mainstream.

Object Classification (in millions of dollars)

Identification code 72–1010–0–1–151		1999 actual	2000 est.	2001 est.
	Direct obligations:			
11.8	Personnel compensation: Special personal services payments	2	2	2
21.0	Travel and transportation of persons	1	1	1
25.1	Advisory and assistance services	35	50	42
25.2	Other services	50	85	70
41.0	Grants, subsidies, and contributions	330	545	495
99.0	Subtotal, direct obligations	418	683	610
41.0	Allocation Account: Grants, subsidies, and contributions	2		
99.9	Total new obligations	420	683	610

ASSISTANCE FOR THE INDEPENDENT STATES OF THE FORMER SOVIET UNION

(a) For necessary expenses to carry out the provisions of [chapter 11] *chapters 11 and 12* of part I of the Foreign Assistance Act of 1961 and the FREEDOM Support Act, for assistance for the Independent States of the former Soviet Union and for related programs, [$839,000,000] *$830,000,000,* to remain available until September 30, [2001] *2002*: *Provided*, That the provisions of such [chapter] *chapters* shall apply to funds appropriated by this paragraph: *Provided further*, That such sums as may be necessary may be transferred to the Export-Import Bank of the United States for the cost of any financing under the Export-Import Bank Act of 1945 for activities for the Independent States[: *Provided further*, That of the funds made available for the Southern Caucasus region, 15 percent should be used for confidence-building measures and other activities in furtherance of the peaceful resolution of the regional conflicts, especially those in the vicinity of Abkhazia and Nagorno-Karabagh: *Provided further*, That of the amounts appropriated under this heading not less than $20,000,000 shall be made available solely for the Russian Far East: *Provided further*, That of the funds made available under this heading $10,000,000 shall be made available for salaries and expenses to carry out the Russian Leadership Program enacted on May 21, 1999 (113 Stat. 93 et seq.)].

[(b) Of the funds appropriated under this heading, not less than $180,000,000 should be made available for assistance for Ukraine.]

[(c) Of the funds appropriated under this heading, not less than 12.92 percent shall be made available for assistance for Georgia.]

[(d) Of the funds appropriated under this heading, not less than 12.2 percent shall be made available for assistance for Armenia.]

[(e)] *(b)* Section 907 of the FREEDOM Support Act [shall not apply to—

(1) activities to support democracy or assistance under title V of the FREEDOM Support Act and section 1424 of Public Law 104–201;

(2) any assistance provided by the Trade and Development Agency under section 661 of the Foreign Assistance Act of 1961 (22 U.S.C. 2421);

(3) any activity carried out by a member of the United States and Foreign Commercial Service while acting within his or her official capacity;

(4) any insurance, reinsurance, guarantee, or other assistance provided by the Overseas Private Investment Corporation under title IV of chapter 2 of part I of the Foreign Assistance Act of 1961 (22 U.S.C. 2191 et seq.);

(5) any financing provided under the Export-Import Bank Act of 1945; or

(6) humanitarian assistance] *is hereby repealed.*

[(f) Of the funds made available under this heading for nuclear safety activities, not to exceed 9 percent of the funds provided for any single project may be used to pay for management costs incurred by a United States national lab in administering said project.]

[(g) Not more than 25 percent of the funds appropriated under this heading may be made available for assistance for any country in the region. Activities authorized under title V (nonproliferation and disarmament programs and activities) of the FREEDOM Support Act shall not be counted against the 25 percent limitation.]

[(h) Of the funds] *(c) Funds* appropriated under title II of this Act [not less than $12,000,000 should], *including funds appropriated under this heading, may* be made available for assistance for Mongolia [of which not less than $6,000,000 should be made available from funds appropriated under this heading]: *Provided*, That funds made available for assistance for Mongolia may be made available in accordance with the purposes and utilizing the authorities provided in chapter 11 of part I of the Foreign Assistance Act of 1961.

[(i)(1) Of the funds appropriated under this heading that are allocated for assistance for the Government of the Russian Federation, 50 percent shall be withheld from obligation until the President determines and certifies in writing to the Committees on Appropriations that the Government of the Russian Federation has terminated implementation of arrangements to provide Iran with technical expertise, training, technology, or equipment necessary to develop a nuclear reactor, related nuclear research facilities or programs, or ballistic missile capability.

(2) Paragraph (1) shall not apply to—

(A) assistance to combat infectious diseases and child survival activities; and

(B) activities authorized under title V (Nonproliferation and Disarmament Programs and Activities) of the FREEDOM Support Act.]

[(j) None of the funds appropriated under this heading may be made available for the Government of the Russian Federation, until the Secretary of State certifies to the Committees on Appropriations that: (1) Russian armed and peacekeeping forces deployed in Kosova have not established a separate sector of operational control; and (2) any Russian armed forces deployed in Kosova are operating under NATO unified command and control arrangements.]

[(k) Of the funds appropriated under this title, not less than $14,700,000 shall be made available for maternal and neo-natal health activities in the independent states of the former Soviet Union, of which at least 60 percent should be made available for the preventive care and treatment of mothers and infants in Russia.] *(Foreign Operations, Export Financing, and Related Programs Appropriation Act, 2000, as enacted by section 1000(a)(2) of the Consolidated Appropriations Act, 2000 (P.L. 106–113).)*

Program and Financing (in millions of dollars)

Identification code 72–1093–0–1–151		1999 actual	2000 est.	2001 est.
	Obligations by program activity:			
10.00	Total new obligations	555	1,074	830
	Budgetary resources available for obligation:			
21.40	Unobligated balance available, start of year	219	238	
22.00	New budget authority (gross)	587	836	830
22.10	Resources available from recoveries of prior year obligations	6		

		1999 actual	2000 est.	2001 est.
22.21	Unobligated balance transferred to other accounts	−17		
23.90	Total budgetary resources available for obligation	795	1,074	830
23.95	Total new obligations	−555	−1,074	−830
23.98	Unobligated balance expiring or withdrawn	−1		
24.40	Unobligated balance available, end of year	238		
	New budget authority (gross), detail:			
	Discretionary:			
40.00	Appropriation	847	839	830
40.76	Reduction pursuant to P.L. 106–113		−3	
41.00	Transferred to other accounts	−262		
42.00	Transferred from other accounts	2		
43.00	Appropriation (total discretionary)	587	836	830
	Change in unpaid obligations:			
72.40	Unpaid obligations, start of year: Obligated balance, start of year	881	778	1,262
73.10	Total new obligations	555	1,074	830
73.20	Total outlays (gross)	−652	−590	−682
73.45	Adjustments in unexpired accounts	−6		
74.40	Unpaid obligations, end of year: Obligated balance, end of year	778	1,262	1,409
	Outlays (gross), detail:			
86.90	Outlays from new discretionary authority	43	72	72
86.93	Outlays from discretionary balances	609	518	610
87.00	Total outlays (gross)	652	590	682
	Net budget authority and outlays:			
89.00	Budget authority	587	836	830
90.00	Outlays	652	590	682

This account provides funds for a program of assistance to the independent states that emerged from the former Soviet Union. The request for the Independent States totals $830 million. This request will fund continuing programs of USAID and other agencies in support of economic and democratic transitions. It also includes a new emphasis on programs to address the security implications of the economic transition.

Funding is requested for the Expanded Threat Reduction Initiative, which was begun in 2000, for programs such as the Civilian Research and Development Foundation and export control and border security enhancements. These efforts contribute to economic and infrastructure reforms as well as to reducing risks of proliferation of weapons of mass destruction, weapons delivery systems, materials, technology and scientific and technical expertise and reduce regional tensions.

Collectively, these programs for the Independent States are designed to consolidate the process of political and economic transition to market democracies, and to help address major socioeconomic dislocations where they occur during these transitions. Funds will support economic restructuring by helping to create conditions that encourage: trade and investment and private sector growth; improved government fiscal policy, revenue collection, and financial management; a market-oriented financial sector; and a more efficient energy sector and a cleaner environment. Funds will support democratic transitions by promoting citizen participation, establishing the rule of law, and strengthening local governments.

Program resources requested in 2001 will be increasingly aimed at: (1) enhancing local public and private institutional capacity as part of the comprehensive strategy to expand trade and investment, develop and strengthen small and medium enterprises, mobilize capital, reduce crime and corruption, and build viable civil societies; and (2) mitigating social impact of transitions, which will initially broaden public support for needed reforms.

Object Classification (in millions of dollars)

Identification code 72–1093–0–1–151		1999 actual	2000 est.	2001 est.
	Direct obligations:			
11.8	Personnel compensation: Special personal services payments	2	4	3
21.0	Travel and transportation of persons	1	2	1
25.1	Advisory and assistance services	15	30	20
25.2	Other services	45	90	60
41.0	Grants, subsidies, and contributions	462	948	746
99.0	Subtotal, direct obligations	525	1,074	830
41.0	Allocation Account: Grants, subsidies, and contributions	30		
99.9	Total new obligations	555	1,074	830

Sub-Saharan Africa Disaster Assistance

Program and Financing (in millions of dollars)

Identification code 72–1040–0–1–151		1999 actual	2000 est.	2001 est.
	Budgetary resources available for obligation:			
21.40	Unobligated balance available, start of year	3	7	7
22.10	Resources available from recoveries of prior year obligations	4		
23.90	Total budgetary resources available for obligation	7	7	7
24.40	Unobligated balance available, end of year	7	7	7
	Change in unpaid obligations:			
72.40	Unpaid obligations, start of year: Obligated balance, start of year	6	2	
73.20	Total outlays (gross)		−2	
73.45	Adjustments in unexpired accounts	−4		
74.40	Unpaid obligations, end of year: Obligated balance, end of year	2		
	Outlays (gross), detail:			
86.93	Outlays from discretionary balances		2	
	Net budget authority and outlays:			
89.00	Budget authority			
90.00	Outlays		2	

In 1993, this account provided funding for timely relief, rehabilitation and reconstruction for disasters in Africa. Since 1994, these activities have been funded under the International Disaster Assistance Program.

International Disaster Assistance

For necessary expenses for international disaster relief, rehabilitation, and reconstruction assistance pursuant to section 491 of the Foreign Assistance Act of 1961, as amended, [$202,880,000] *$220,000,000*, to remain available until expended[: *Provided*, That the Agency for International Development shall submit a report to the Committees on Appropriations at least 5 days prior to providing assistance through the Office of Transition Initiatives for a country that did not receive such assistance in fiscal year 1999.] *(Foreign Operations, Export Financing, and Related Programs Appropriation Act, 2000, as enacted by section 1000(a)(2) of the Consolidated Appropriations Act, 2000 (P.L. 106–113).)*

Program and Financing (in millions of dollars)

Identification code 72–1035–0–1–151		1999 actual	2000 est.	2001 est.
	Obligations by program activity:			
10.00	Total new obligations	341	274	220
	Budgetary resources available for obligation:			
21.40	Unobligated balance available, start of year	8	72	
22.00	New budget authority (gross)	388	202	220
22.10	Resources available from recoveries of prior year obligations	17		
23.90	Total budgetary resources available for obligation	413	274	220

General and special funds—Continued

INTERNATIONAL DISASTER ASSISTANCE—Continued

Program and Financing (in millions of dollars)—Continued

Identification code 72–1035–0–1–151	1999 actual	2000 est.	2001 est.
23.95 Total new obligations	–341	–274	–220
24.40 Unobligated balance available, end of year	72		
New budget authority (gross), detail:			
Discretionary:			
40.00 Appropriation	388	203	220
40.76 Reduction pursuant to P.L. 106–113		–1	
43.00 Appropriation (total discretionary)	388	202	220
Change in unpaid obligations:			
72.40 Unpaid obligations, start of year: Obligated balance, start of year	309	338	376
73.10 Total new obligations	341	274	220
73.20 Total outlays (gross)	–295	–236	–261
73.45 Adjustments in unexpired accounts	–17		
74.40 Unpaid obligations, end of year: Obligated balance, end of year	338	376	335
Outlays (gross), detail:			
86.90 Outlays from new discretionary authority	74	51	55
86.93 Outlays from discretionary balances	221	185	206
87.00 Total outlays (gross)	295	236	261
Net budget authority and outlays:			
89.00 Budget authority	388	202	220
90.00 Outlays	295	236	261

The International Disaster Assistance (IDA) account provides funds for two separate offices. The Office of U.S. Foreign Disaster Assistance (OFDA) manages relief, rehabilitation, and reconstruction assistance to foreign countries struck by natural and man-made disasters and supports disaster prevention, mitigation and preparedness. OFDA's program has been placing increasing emphasis on complex emergencies, a product of ethnic and national tensions leading to civil strife and the displacement of large numbers of people. The $165 million request for OFDA for 2001 will be used to provide temporary shelter, blankets, supplementary food, potable water, medical supplies and agricultural rehabilitation aid, including seeds and hand tools.

The Office of Transition Initiatives (OTI) addresses the opportunties amd challenges facing conflict-prone countries and those making the transition from the initial crisis stage of a complex emergency (frequently addressed by OFDA) to the path of sustainable development. OTI collaborates closely with the Department of State, the National Security Council, the Department of Defense and USAID's regional bureaus in the selection of high foreign policy priority countries for OTI's emergency assistance and in the design and monitoring of OTI programs. OIT's efforts to advance peace and stability include support for: demobilization and re-integration of ex-combatants; community self-help programs that reduce tensions and promote grass-roots democratic media; and conflict resolution measures. The 2001 request for OTI is $55 million.

Object Classification (in millions of dollars)

Identification code 72–1035–0–1–151	1999 actual	2000 est.	2001 est.
Direct obligations:			
11.8 Personnel compensation: Special personal services payments	6	5	4
21.0 Travel and transportation of persons	4	2	2
25.2 Other services	38	25	22
26.0 Supplies and materials	13	10	8
31.0 Equipment	1		
41.0 Grants, subsidies, and contributions	278	232	184
99.0 Subtotal, direct obligations	340	274	220
41.0 Allocation Account: Grants, subsidies, and contributions	1		
99.9 Total new obligations	341	274	220

OPERATING EXPENSES OF THE AGENCY FOR INTERNATIONAL DEVELOPMENT

For necessary expenses to carry out the provisions of section 667, [$520,000,000: *Provided*, That, none of the funds appropriated under this heading may be made available to finance the construction (including architect and engineering services), purchase, or long term lease of offices for use by the Agency for International Development, unless the Administrator has identified such proposed construction (including architect and engineering services), purchase, or long term lease of offices in a report submitted to the Committees on Appropriations at least 15 days prior to the obligation of these funds for such purposes: *Provided further*, That the previous proviso shall not apply where the total cost of construction (including architect and engineering services), purchase, or long term lease of offices does not exceed $1,000,000] *$520,000,000, to remain available until September 30, 2002. (Foreign Operations, Export Financing, and Related Programs Appropriation Act, 2000, as enacted by section 1000(a)(2) of the Consolidated Appropriations Act, 2000 (P.L. 106–113).)*

Program and Financing (in millions of dollars)

Identification code 72–1000–0–1–151	1999 actual	2000 est.	2001 est.
Obligations by program activity:			
Direct program:			
00.01 Direct program	508	538	539
00.02 Foreign national separation fund	3	5	2
09.00 Reimbursable program	4	4	4
10.00 Total new obligations	515	547	545
Budgetary resources available for obligation:			
21.40 Unobligated balance available, start of year	20	31	21
22.00 New budget authority (gross)	505	523	524
22.10 Resources available from recoveries of prior year obligations	22	14	12
23.90 Total budgetary resources available for obligation	547	568	557
23.95 Total new obligations	–515	–547	–545
24.40 Unobligated balance available, end of year	31	21	12
New budget authority (gross), detail:			
Discretionary:			
40.00 Appropriation	480	520	520
40.75 Reduction pursuant to P.L. 106–51	–2		
40.76 Reduction pursuant to P.L. 106–113		–1	
42.00 Transferred from other accounts	23		
43.00 Appropriation (total discretionary)	501	519	520
68.00 Spending authority from offsetting collections: Offsetting collections (cash)	4	4	4
70.00 Total new budget authority (gross)	505	523	524
Change in unpaid obligations:			
72.40 Unpaid obligations, start of year: Obligated balance, start of year	206	211	212
73.10 Total new obligations	515	547	545
73.20 Total outlays (gross)	–488	–532	–529
73.45 Adjustments in unexpired accounts	–22	–14	–12
74.40 Unpaid obligations, end of year: Obligated balance, end of year	211	212	216
Outlays (gross), detail:			
86.90 Outlays from new discretionary authority	359	388	389
86.93 Outlays from discretionary balances	129	144	140
87.00 Total outlays (gross)	488	532	529
Offsets:			
Against gross budget authority and outlays:			
88.00 Offsetting collections (cash) from: Federal sources	–4	–4	–4
Net budget authority and outlays:			
89.00 Budget authority	501	519	520
90.00 Outlays	484	528	525

Summary of Budget Authority and Outlays

(in millions of dollars)

Enacted/requested:	*1999 actual*	*2000 est.*	*2001 est.*
Budget Authority	501	519	520
Outlays	484	528	525
Supplemental proposal:			
Budget Authority		22	
Outlays		14	4
Total:			
Budget Authority	501	541	520
Outlays	484	542	529

These funds cover the appropriated dollar costs of managing U.S. Agency for International Development (USAID) programs, including salaries and other expenses of direct hire personnel as well as costs associated with physical security of Agency personnel. USAID currently maintains resident staff in more than 70 foreign countries as well as a headquarters in Washington, which supports field programs and manages regional and worldwide activities as well as costs associated with physical security of agency personnel.

Object Classification (in millions of dollars)

Identification code 72–1000–0–1–151		1999 actual	2000 est.	2001 est.
	Direct obligations:			
	Personnel compensation:			
11.1	Full-time permanent	154	159	163
11.3	Other than full-time permanent	4	5	3
11.5	Other personnel compensation	10	11	11
11.8	Special personal services payments	42	45	47
11.9	Total personnel compensation	210	220	224
12.1	Civilian personnel benefits	54	61	65
13.0	Benefits for former personnel	1	2	
21.0	Travel and transportation of persons	21	22	23
22.0	Transportation of things	9	9	9
23.1	Rental payments to GSA	26	25	26
23.2	Rental payments to others	23	25	27
23.3	Communications, utilities, and miscellaneous charges	10	13	14
24.0	Printing and reproduction	1	1	1
25.1	Advisory and assistance services	3	3	3
25.2	Other services	57	63	64
25.3	Purchases of goods and services from Government accounts	26	27	30
25.4	Operation and maintenance of facilities	4	6	6
25.6	Medical care		1	
25.7	Operation and maintenance of equipment	15	17	19
26.0	Supplies and materials	8	8	7
31.0	Equipment	25	21	20
32.0	Land and structures	14	18	2
42.0	Insurance claims and indemnities	2	1	1
99.0	Subtotal, direct obligations	509	543	541
99.0	Reimbursable obligations	4	4	4
99.5	Below reporting threshold	2		
99.9	Total new obligations	515	547	545

Personnel Summary

Identification code 72–1000–0–1–151		1999 actual	2000 est.	2001 est.
	Direct:			
	Total compensable workyears:			
1001	Full-time equivalent employment	2,313	2,270	2,265
1011	Exempt Full-time equivalent employment	10		
	Reimbursable:			
2001	Total compensable workyears: Full-time equivalent employment	4	4	4

PAYMENT TO THE FOREIGN SERVICE RETIREMENT AND DISABILITY FUND

For payment to the "Foreign Service Retirement and Disability Fund", as authorized by the Foreign Service Act of 1980, [$43,837,000] *$44,489,000*. *(Foreign Operations, Export Financing, and Related Programs Appropriation Act, 2000, as enacted by section 1000(a)(2) of the Consolidated Appropriations Act, 2000 (P.L. 106–113).)*

Program and Financing (in millions of dollars)

Identification code 72–1036–0–1–153		1999 actual	2000 est.	2001 est.
	Obligations by program activity:			
10.00	Total new obligations (object class 13.0)	45	44	44
	Budgetary resources available for obligation:			
22.00	New budget authority (gross)	45	44	44
23.95	Total new obligations	–45	–44	–44
	New budget authority (gross), detail:			
	Mandatory:			
60.00	Appropriation	45	44	44
	Change in unpaid obligations:			
73.10	Total new obligations	45	44	44
73.20	Total outlays (gross)	–45	–44	–44
	Outlays (gross), detail:			
86.97	Outlays from new mandatory authority	45	44	44
	Net budget authority and outlays:			
89.00	Budget authority	45	44	44
90.00	Outlays	45	44	44

The 2001 request will finance the 2001 installment of the unfunded liability created by the addition of U.S. Agency for International Development (USAID) Foreign Service personnel to the foreign service retirement system and by subsequent salary increases and changes in legislation affecting benefits.

OPERATING EXPENSES OF THE AGENCY FOR INTERNATIONAL DEVELOPMENT OFFICE OF INSPECTOR GENERAL

For necessary expenses to carry out the provisions of section 667, [$25,000,000] *$27,000,000*, to remain available until September 30, [2001] *2002*, which sum shall be available for the Office of the Inspector General of the Agency for International Development. *(Foreign Operations, Export Financing, and Related Programs Appropriation Act, 2000, as enacted by section 1000(a)(2) of the Consolidated Appropriations Act, 2000 (P.L. 106–113).)*

Program and Financing (in millions of dollars)

Identification code 72–1007–0–1–151		1999 actual	2000 est.	2001 est.
	Obligations by program activity:			
00.01	Direct program	29	28	30
10.00	Total new obligations	29	28	30
	Budgetary resources available for obligation:			
21.40	Unobligated balance available, start of year	7	7	4
22.00	New budget authority (gross)	29	25	27
23.90	Total budgetary resources available for obligation	36	32	31
23.95	Total new obligations	–29	–28	–30
24.40	Unobligated balance available, end of year	7	4	1
	New budget authority (gross), detail:			
	Discretionary:			
40.00	Appropriation	31	25	27
41.00	Transferred to other accounts	–4		
42.00	Transferred from other accounts	2		
43.00	Appropriation (total discretionary)	29	25	27
	Change in unpaid obligations:			
72.40	Unpaid obligations, start of year: Obligated balance, start of year	11	11	13
73.10	Total new obligations	29	28	30
73.20	Total outlays (gross)	–29	–24	–27
74.40	Unpaid obligations, end of year: Obligated balance, end of year	11	13	15
	Outlays (gross), detail:			
86.90	Outlays from new discretionary authority	23	18	19
86.93	Outlays from discretionary balances	6	6	8

General and special funds—Continued

OPERATING EXPENSES OF THE AGENCY FOR INTERNATIONAL DEVELOPMENT OFFICE OF INSPECTOR GENERAL—Continued

Program and Financing (in millions of dollars)—Continued

Identification code 72–1007–0–1–151	1999 actual	2000 est.	2001 est.
87.00 Total outlays (gross)	29	24	27
Net budget authority and outlays:			
89.00 Budget authority	29	25	27
90.00 Outlays	29	24	27

The funds cover the costs of operations of the Office of the Inspector General, Agency for International Development, and include salaries, expenses, and support costs of the Inspector General's personnel.

Object Classification (in millions of dollars)

Identification code 72–1007–0–1–151	1999 actual	2000 est.	2001 est.
Personnel compensation:			
11.1 Full-time permanent	12	12	13
11.5 Other personnel compensation	1		1
11.8 Special personal services payments		1	1
11.9 Total personnel compensation	13	13	15
12.1 Civilian personnel benefits	3	4	4
21.0 Travel and transportation of persons	2	2	2
22.0 Transportation of things	1	1	
23.1 Rental payments to GSA	2	2	2
23.2 Rental payments to others	1	2	2
25.2 Other services	2	1	2
25.3 Purchases of goods and services from Government accounts	4	3	3
31.0 Equipment	1		
99.9 Total new obligations	29	28	30

Personnel Summary

Identification code 72–1007–0–1–151	1999 actual	2000 est.	2001 est.
1001 Total compensable workyears: Full-time equivalent employment	167	165	170

Public enterprise funds:

PROPERTY MANAGEMENT FUND

Program and Financing (in millions of dollars)

Identification code 72–4175–0–3–151	1999 actual	2000 est.	2001 est.
Obligations by program activity:			
09.01 Reimbursable program		2	1
10.00 Total new obligations		2	1
Budgetary resources available for obligation:			
21.40 Unobligated balance available, start of year	3	3	2
22.00 New budget authority (gross)		1	
23.90 Total budgetary resources available for obligation	3	4	2
23.95 Total new obligations		−2	−1
24.40 Unobligated balance available, end of year	3	2	
New budget authority (gross), detail:			
Mandatory:			
69.00 Offsetting collections (cash)		1	
Change in unpaid obligations:			
73.10 Total new obligations		2	1
73.20 Total outlays (gross)		−1	
Outlays (gross), detail:			
86.97 Outlays from new mandatory authority		1	
86.98 Outlays from mandatory balances		1	
87.00 Total outlays (gross)		1	
Offsets:			
Against gross budget authority and outlays:			
88.40 Offsetting collections (cash) from: Non-Federal sources		−1	
Net budget authority and outlays:			
89.00 Budget authority			
90.00 Outlays			

This Fund, as authorized by Public Law 101–513, is maintained for the deposit of proceeds from the sale of overseas property acquired by the U.S. Agency for International Development (USAID). The proceeds are available to construct or otherwise acquire outside the United States: (1) essential living quarters, office space, and necessary supporting facilities for use of USAID personnel; and, (2) schools (including dormitories and boarding facilities) and hospitals for use of USAID personnel, U.S. Government personnel, and their dependents. In addition, the proceeds may be used to equip, staff, operate, and maintain such schools and hospitals.

Intragovernmental funds:

ADVANCE ACQUISITION OF PROPERTY—REVOLVING FUND

Program and Financing (in millions of dollars)

Identification code 72–4590–0–4–151	1999 actual	2000 est.	2001 est.
Budgetary resources available for obligation:			
21.40 Unobligated balance available, start of year	1	1	1
23.95 Total new obligations			
24.40 Unobligated balance available, end of year	1	1	1
Net budget authority and outlays:			
89.00 Budget authority			
90.00 Outlays			

This revolving fund finances the acquisition and rehabilitation of U.S. Government-owned excess property, at minimal cost, for purchase by friendly countries and eligible organizations, for use in conjunction with economic development programs. Excess property, most of it obtained from the Department of Defense, includes heavy construction equipment, vehicles, heavy machinery, electrical generating equipment, and medical equipment and supplies. The program is self-financed from service fees and reimbursements by equipment purchasers ultimately funded from development assistance appropriations to the U.S. Agency for International Development.

ASSISTANCE FOR THE INDEPENDENT STATES OF THE FORMER SOVIET UNION: UKRAINE EXPORT CREDIT INSURANCE FINANCING ACCOUNT

Program and Financing (in millions of dollars)

Identification code 72–4345–0–3–151	1999 actual	2000 est.	2001 est.
Obligations by program activity:			
08.02 Downward Re-estimate paid to reciept account		30	
10.00 Total new obligations		30	
Budgetary resources available for obligation:			
21.40 Unobligated balance available, start of year	28	30	
22.00 New financing authority (gross)	2		
23.90 Total budgetary resources available for obligation	30	30	
23.95 Total new obligations		−30	
24.40 Unobligated balance available, end of year	30		
New financing authority (gross), detail:			
Discretionary:			
68.00 Spending authority from offsetting collections (gross): Offsetting collections (cash)	2		
Change in unpaid obligations:			
73.10 Total new obligations		30	

	1999 actual	2000 est.	2001 est.
73.20 Total financing disbursements (gross)		–30	
87.00 Total financing disbursements (gross)		30	
Offsets:			
Against gross financing authority and financing disbursements:			
88.25 Offsetting collections (cash) from: Interest on uninvested funds	–2		
Net financing authority and financing disbursements:			
89.00 Financing authority			
90.00 Financing disbursements	–2	30	

Status of Guaranteed Loans (in millions of dollars)

Identification code 72–4345–0–3–151	1999 actual	2000 est.	2001 est.
Cumulative balance of guaranteed loans outstanding:			
2210 Outstanding, start of year	61		
2251 Repayments and prepayments	–61		
2290 Outstanding, end of year			

As required by the Federal Credit Reform Act of 1990, this non-budgetary account records all cash flows to and from the Government resulting from direct loans obligated in 1992 and beyond (including modifications of direct loans that resulted from obligations in any year). The amounts in this account are a means of financing and are not included in the budget totals.

Balance Sheet (in millions of dollars)

Identification code 72–4345–0–3–151	1998 actual	1999 actual	2000 est.	2001 est.
ASSETS:				
1101 Federal assets: Fund balances with Treasury	28	30		
1999 Total assets	28	30		
LIABILITIES:				
2204 Non-Federal liabilities: Liabilities for loan guarantees	28	30		
2999 Total liabilities	28	30		
4999 Total liabilities and net position	28	30		

Debt Reduction, Financing Account

Program and Financing (in millions of dollars)

Identification code 72–4137–0–3–151	1999 actual	2000 est.	2001 est.
Obligations by program activity:			
00.01 Payment to liquidating accounts		56	
00.02 Interest		1	
00.03 Subsidy for Modifications		12	14
00.04 Interest on Treasury borrowing-EAI debt	31	9	8
10.00 Total new obligations	31	78	22
Budgetary resources available for obligation:			
21.40 Unobligated balance available, start of year	109	66	5
22.00 New financing authority (gross)	31	83	26
22.60 Portion applied to repay debt	–43	–66	
23.90 Total budgetary resources available for obligation	97	83	31
23.95 Total new obligations	–31	–78	–22
24.40 Unobligated balance available, end of year	66	5	9
New financing authority (gross), detail:			
Mandatory:			
67.15 Authority to borrow (indefinite)		39	1
Spending authority from offsetting collections:			
Discretionary:			
68.00 Offsetting collections (cash)	74	82	80
68.47 Portion applied to repay debt	–43	–38	–55
68.90 Spending authority from offsetting collections (total discretionary)	31	44	25
70.00 Total new financing authority (gross)	31	83	26
Change in unpaid obligations:			
72.40 Unpaid obligations, start of year: Obligated balance, start of year			–5
73.10 Total new obligations	31	78	22
73.20 Total financing disbursements (gross)	–31	–83	–26
74.40 Unpaid obligations, end of year: Obligated balance, end of year		–5	–9
87.00 Total financing disbursements (gross)	31	83	26
Offsets:			
Against gross financing authority and financing disbursements:			
Offsetting collections (cash) from:			
88.00 Federal sources—Paris club debt reduction	–9	–22	–20
88.25 Interest on uninvested funds		–3	–3
88.40 Repayment of principal—EAI debt	–65	–57	–57
88.90 Total, offsetting collections (cash)	–74	–82	–80
Net financing authority and financing disbursements:			
89.00 Financing authority	–43	1	–54
90.00 Financing disbursements	–43	1	–54

Status of Direct Loans (in millions of dollars)

Identification code 72–4137–0–3–151	1999 actual	2000 est.	2001 est.
Position with respect to appropriations act limitation on obligations:			
1111 Limitation on direct loans			
Cumulative balance of direct loans outstanding:			
1210 Outstanding, start of year	282	217	232
1233 Disbursements: Purchase of loans assets from a liquidating account		72	3
1251 Repayments: Repayments and prepayments	–65	–57	–57
1290 Outstanding, end of year	217	232	178

As required by the Federal Credit Reform Act of 1990, this non-budgetary account records all cash flows to and from the Government resulting from restructuring loans administered by the U.S. Agency for International Development.

Balance Sheet (in millions of dollars)

Identification code 72–4137–0–3–151	1998 actual	1999 actual	2000 est.	2001 est.
ASSETS:				
1101 Federal assets: Fund balances with Treasury	109	66		
Net value of assets related to post–1991 direct loans receivable:				
1401 Direct loans receivable, gross	282	217	232	174
1405 Allowance for subsidy cost (–)	–142	–126	–137	–141
1499 Net present value of assets related to direct loans	140	91	95	33
1999 Total assets	249	157	95	33
LIABILITIES:				
Federal liabilities:				
Debt:				
2103 Debt (EAI)	249	148	81	–31
2103 Debt (Paris Club debt reduction)		9	–15	–2
2999 Total liabilities	249	157	66	–33
4999 Total liabilities and net position	249	157	66	–33

Loan Guarantees to Israel Financing Account

Program and Financing (in millions of dollars)

Identification code 72–4119–0–3–151	1999 actual	2000 est.	2001 est.
Budgetary resources available for obligation:			
21.40 Unobligated balance available, start of year	515	550	581
22.00 New financing authority (gross)	35	31	31
23.90 Total budgetary resources available for obligation	550	581	612
23.95 Total new obligations			
24.40 Unobligated balance available, end of year	550	581	612

Intragovernmental funds—Continued

Loan Guarantees to Israel Financing Account—Continued

Program and Financing (in millions of dollars)—Continued

Identification code 72–4119–0–3–151	1999 actual	2000 est.	2001 est.
New financing authority (gross), detail:			
Discretionary:			
68.00 Spending authority from offsetting collections (gross): Offsetting collections (cash)	35	31	31
Offsets:			
Against gross financing authority and financing disbursements:			
88.25 Offsetting collections (cash) from: Interest on uninvested funds	−35	−31	−31
Net financing authority and financing disbursements:			
89.00 Financing authority			
90.00 Financing disbursements	−35	−31	−31

Status of Guaranteed Loans (in millions of dollars)

Identification code 72–4119–0–3–151	1999 actual	2000 est.	2001 est.
Cumulative balance of guaranteed loans outstanding:			
2210 Outstanding, start of year	9,226	9,226	9,226
2251 Repayments and prepayments			
2290 Outstanding, end of year	9,226	9,226	9,226
Memorandum:			
2299 Guaranteed amount of guaranteed loans outstanding, end of year	9,226	9,226	9,226

As required by the Federal Credit Reform Act of 1990, this non-budgetary account records all cash flows to and from the Government resulting from direct loans obligated in 1992 and beyond (including modifications of direct loans that resulted from obligations in any year). The amounts in this account are a means of financing and are not included in the budget totals.

Balance Sheet (in millions of dollars)

Identification code 72–4119–0–3–151	1998 actual	1999 actual	2000 est.	2001 est.
ASSETS:				
1101 Federal assets: Fund balances with Treasury	515	550	581	612
1999 Total assets	515	550	581	612
LIABILITIES:				
2204 Non-Federal liabilities: Liabilities for loan guarantees	515	550	581	612
2999 Total liabilities	515	550	581	612

[Urban and Environmental Credit Program Account]

[For the cost, as defined in section 502 of the Congressional Budget Act of 1974, of guaranteed loans authorized by sections 221 and 222 of the Foreign Assistance Act of 1961, $1,500,000, to remain available until expended: *Provided*, That these funds are available to subsidize loan principal, 100 percent of which shall be guaranteed, pursuant to the authority of such sections. In addition, for administrative expenses to carry out guaranteed loan programs, $5,000,000, all of which may be transferred to and merged with the appropriation for Operating Expenses of the Agency for International Development: *Provided further*, That commitments to guarantee loans under this heading may be entered into notwithstanding the second and third sentences of section 222(a) of the Foreign Assistance Act of 1961.] *(Foreign Operations, Export Financing, and Related Programs Appropriation Act, 2000, as enacted by section 1000(a)(2) of the Consolidated Appropriations Act, 2000 (P.L. 106–113).)*

Program and Financing (in millions of dollars)

Identification code 72–0401–0–1–151	1999 actual	2000 est.	2001 est.
Obligations by program activity:			
00.02 Direct program	2	2	
00.09 Direct program	5	5	
10.00 Total new obligations	7	7	
Budgetary resources available for obligation:			
22.00 New budget authority (gross)	7	7	
23.95 Total new obligations	−7	−7	
New budget authority (gross), detail:			
Discretionary:			
40.00 Appropriation	7	7	
Change in unpaid obligations:			
72.40 Unpaid obligations, start of year: Obligated balance, start of year	19	8	5
73.10 Total new obligations	7	7	
73.20 Total outlays (gross)	−18	−10	−5
74.40 Unpaid obligations, end of year: Obligated balance, end of year	8	5	
Outlays (gross), detail:			
86.90 Outlays from new discretionary authority	3	3	
86.93 Outlays from discretionary balances	15	7	5
87.00 Total outlays (gross)	18	10	5
Net budget authority and outlays:			
89.00 Budget authority	7	7	
90.00 Outlays	17	10	5

Summary of Loan Levels, Subsidy Budget Authority and Outlays by Program (in millions of dollars)

Identification code 72–0401–0–1–151	1999 actual	2000 est.	2001 est.
Guaranteed loan levels supportable by subsidy budget authority:			
2150 Loan guarantee levels	12	11	
2159 Total loan guarantee levels	12	11	
Guaranteed loan subsidy (in percent):			
2320 Subsidy rate	1.30	1.38	0.00
2329 Weighted average subsidy rate	1.07	1.38	0.00
Guaranteed loan subsidy budget authority:			
2330 Subsidy budget authority	2	2	
2339 Total subsidy budget authority	2	2	
Guaranteed loan subsidy outlays:			
2340 Subsidy outlays	11	5	2
2349 Total subsidy outlays	11	5	2
Administrative expense data:			
3510 Budget authority	5	5	
3580 Outlays from balances	4	2	2
3590 Outlays from new authority	3	3	1

Beginning in 2001, this program will be subsumed under the new development credit account.

Object Classification (in millions of dollars)

Identification code 72–0401–0–1–151	1999 actual	2000 est.	2001 est.
11.1 Personnel compensation: Full-time permanent	2	2	
21.0 Travel and transportation of persons	1	1	
23.2 Rental payments to others	1	1	
25.3 Purchases of goods and services from Government accounts	1	1	
41.0 Grants, subsidies, and contributions	2	2	
99.9 Total new obligations	7	7	

Personnel Summary

Identification code 72–0401–0–1–151	1999 actual	2000 est.	2001 est.
1001 Total compensable workyears: Full-time equivalent employment	19	21	....

URBAN AND ENVIRONMENTAL CREDIT PROGRAM GUARANTEED LOAN FINANCING ACCOUNT

Program and Financing (in millions of dollars)

Identification code 72–4344–0–3–151	1999 actual	2000 est.	2001 est.
Budgetary resources available for obligation:			
21.40 Unobligated balance available, start of year	49	67	80
22.00 New financing authority (gross)	18	13	10
23.90 Total budgetary resources available for obligation	67	80	90
23.95 Total new obligations	....	....	....
24.40 Unobligated balance available, end of year	67	80	90
New financing authority (gross), detail:			
Discretionary:			
68.00 Spending authority from offsetting collections (gross): (cash)	18	13	10
Offsets:			
Against gross financing authority and financing disbursements:			
Offsetting collections (cash) from:			
88.00 Federal sources	–11	–5	–2
88.25 Interest on uninvested funds	–4	–5	–5
88.40 Non-Federal sources	–3	–3	–3
88.90 Total, offsetting collections (cash)	–18	–13	–10
Net financing authority and financing disbursements:			
89.00 Financing authority	....	....	....
90.00 Financing disbursements	–18	–13	–10

Status of Guaranteed Loans (in millions of dollars)

Identification code 72–4344–0–3–151	1999 actual	2000 est.	2001 est.
Position with respect to appropriations act limitation on commitments:			
2131 Guaranteed loan commitments exempt from limitation	12	11	....
2150 Total guaranteed loan commitments	12	11	....
Cumulative balance of guaranteed loans outstanding:			
2210 Outstanding, start of year	407	534	545
2231 Disbursements of new guaranteed loans	147	37	11
2251 Repayments and prepayments	–20	–26	–27
2290 Outstanding, end of year	534	545	529
Memorandum:			
2299 Guaranteed amount of guaranteed loans outstanding, end of year	534	545	529

As required by the Federal Credit Reform Act of 1990, this non-budgetary account records all cash flows to and from the Government resulting from loan guarantees under the United States Agency for International Development (USAID) Urban and Environmental Credit Program committed in 1992 and beyond. The amounts in this account are a means of financing and are not included in the budget totals.

Balance Sheet (in millions of dollars)

Identification code 72–4344–0–3–151	1998 actual	1999 actual	2000 est.	2001 est.
ASSETS:				
Federal assets:				
1101 Fund balances with Treasury	49	67	80	90
Investments in US securities:				
1106 Receivables, net	....	8	5	....
1999 Total assets	49	75	85	90
LIABILITIES:				
2204 Non-Federal liabilities: Liabilities for loan guarantees	49	75	85	90
2999 Total liabilities	49	75	85	90
4999 Total liabilities and net position	49	75	85	90

HOUSING AND OTHER CREDIT GUARANTY PROGRAMS LIQUIDATING ACCOUNT

Program and Financing (in millions of dollars)

Identification code 72–4340–0–3–151	1999 actual	2000 est.	2001 est.
Obligations by program activity:			
00.01 Claims payments	64	24	40
00.02 Interest on borrowing	6	6	....
10.00 Total new obligations	70	30	40
Budgetary resources available for obligation:			
21.40 Unobligated balance available, start of year	69	6	....
22.00 New budget authority (gross)	101	159	74
Capital transfer to general fund:			
22.40 Capital transfer to general fund	–70	–81	–34
22.40 Capital transfer to general fund	....	–6	....
22.60 Portion applied to repay debt	–24	–48	....
23.90 Total budgetary resources available for obligation	76	30	40
23.95 Total new obligations	–70	–30	–40
24.40 Unobligated balance available, end of year	6	....	....
New budget authority (gross), detail:			
Mandatory:			
60.05 Appropriation (indefinite)	17	35	17
69.00 Offsetting collections (cash)	84	124	57
70.00 Total new budget authority (gross)	101	159	74
Change in unpaid obligations:			
72.40 Unpaid obligations, start of year: Obligated balance, start of year	....	8	....
73.10 Total new obligations	70	30	40
73.20 Total outlays (gross)	–62	–38	–40
74.40 Unpaid obligations, end of year: Obligated balance, end of year	8	....	....
Outlays (gross), detail:			
86.97 Outlays from new mandatory authority	62	38	40
Offsets:			
Against gross budget authority and outlays:			
Offsetting collections (cash) from:			
88.00 Federal sources (debt reduction)	....	–56	....
Non-Federal sources:			
88.40 Receipts of principal resulting from rescheduled claims	–19	–17	–16
88.40 Recoveries of claims receivable	–35	–32	–28
88.40 Fees	–6	–6	–6
88.40 Interest & late pmt. collection	–15	–6	–5
88.40 Non-Federal sources	–9	–7	–2
88.90 Total, offsetting collections (cash)	–84	–124	–57
Net budget authority and outlays:			
89.00 Budget authority	17	35	17
90.00 Outlays	–21	–86	–17

Status of Guaranteed Loans (in millions of dollars)

Identification code 72–4340–0–3–151	1999 actual	2000 est.	2001 est.
Cumulative balance of guaranteed loans outstanding:			
2210 Outstanding, start of year	1,834	1,760	1,684
2251 Repayments and prepayments	–18	–44	–44
2261 Adjustments: Terminations for default that result in loans receivable	–56	–32	–40
2290 Outstanding, end of year	1,760	1,684	1,600
Memorandum:			
2299 Guaranteed amount of guaranteed loans outstanding, end of year	1,760	1,684	1,600

Intragovernmental funds—Continued

Housing and Other Credit Guaranty Programs Liquidating Account—Continued

Status of Guaranteed Loans (in millions of dollars)—Continued

Identification code 72–4340–0–3–151	1999 actual	2000 est.	2001 est.
Addendum:			
Cumulative balance of defaulted guaranteed loans that result in loans receivable:			
2310 Outstanding, start of year	485	500	508
2331 Disbursements for guaranteed loan claims	56	32	40
Repayments of loans receivable:			
2351 Repayments of loans receivable	–19	–16	–24
2351 Repayments of loans receivable (debt reduction)		–8	–2
2364 Other adjustments, net	–22		
2390 Outstanding, end of year	500	508	522

As required by the Federal Credit Reform Act of 1990, this account records, for the Urban and Environmental Credit Program, all cash flows to and from the Government resulting from direct loans obligated and loan guarantees committed prior to 1992. This account is shown on a cash basis. All new activity in this program in 1992 and beyond is recorded in corresponding program and financing accounts.

Statement of Operations (in millions of dollars)

Identification code 72–4340–0–3–151	1998 actual	1999 actual	2000 est.	2001 est.
0111 Revenue	26	38	36	34
0112 Expense	–42	–6	–6	
0115 Net income or loss (–)	–16	32	30	34
0195 Total income or loss (–)	–16	32	30	34
0199 Total comprehensive income	–16	32	30	34

Balance Sheet (in millions of dollars)

Identification code 72–4340–0–3–151	1998 actual	1999 actual	2000 est.	2001 est.
ASSETS:				
1101 Federal assets: Fund balances with Treasury	69	14		
1206 Non-Federal assets: Receivables, net		2	2	2
Net value of assets related to pre-1992 direct loans receivable and acquired defaulted guaranteed loans receivable:				
1701 Defaulted guaranteed loans, gross	525	500	508	522
1702 Interest receivable		31	30	29
1703 Allowance for estimated uncollectible loans and interest (–)	–333	–238	–226	–215
1704 Defaulted guaranteed loans and interest receivable, net	192	293	312	336
1799 Value of assets related to loan guarantees	192	293	312	336
1999 Total assets	261	309	314	338
LIABILITIES:				
Federal liabilities:				
2103 Debt	72	48		
2104 Resources payable to Treasury		–89	–20	17
2105 Other	3	2		
Non-Federal liabilities:				
2201 Accounts payable	2			
2204 Liabilities for loan guarantees	376	348	334	321
2999 Total liabilities	453	309	314	338
NET POSITION:				
3100 Appropriated capital	234			
Cumulative results of operations:				
3300 Cumulative results of operations	–50			
3300 Cumulative results of operations	–376			
3999 Total net position	–192			
4999 Total liabilities and net position	261	309	314	338

Object Classification (in millions of dollars)

Identification code 72–4340–0–3–151	1999 actual	2000 est.	2001 est.
42.0 Insurance claims and indemnities	64	24	40
43.0 Interest and dividends	6	6	
99.9 Total new obligations	70	30	40

[Micro and Small Enterprise Development Program Account]

[For the cost of direct loans and loan guarantees, $1,500,000, as authorized by section 108 of the Foreign Assistance Act of 1961, as amended: *Provided*, That such costs shall be as defined in section 502 of the Congressional Budget Act of 1974: *Provided further*, That guarantees of loans made under this heading in support of microenterprise activities may guarantee up to 70 percent of the principal amount of any such loans notwithstanding section 108 of the Foreign Assistance Act of 1961. In addition, for administrative expenses to carry out programs under this heading, $500,000, all of which may be transferred to and merged with the appropriation for Operating Expenses of the Agency for International Development: *Provided further*, That funds made available under this heading shall remain available until September 30, 2001.] *(Foreign Operations, Export Financing, and Related Programs Appropriation Act, 2000, as enacted by section 1000(a)(2) of the Consolidated Appropriations Act, 2000 (P.L. 106–113).)*

Program and Financing (in millions of dollars)

Identification code 72–0400–0–1–151	1999 actual	2000 est.	2001 est.
Obligations by program activity:			
00.02 Guaranty loan subsidy—Microenterprise credits	2	2	
00.09 Administrative expenses	1	1	
10.00 Total new obligations	3	3	
Budgetary resources available for obligation:			
21.40 Unobligated balance available, start of year	2	1	
22.00 New budget authority (gross)	2	2	
23.90 Total budgetary resources available for obligation	4	3	
23.95 Total new obligations	–3	–3	
24.40 Unobligated balance available, end of year	1		
New budget authority (gross), detail:			
Discretionary:			
40.00 Appropriation	2	2	
Change in unpaid obligations:			
72.40 Unpaid obligations, start of year: Obligated balance, start of year	4	6	6
73.10 Total new obligations	3	3	
73.20 Total outlays (gross)	–1	–3	–2
74.40 Unpaid obligations, end of year: Obligated balance, end of year	6	6	4
Outlays (gross), detail:			
86.90 Outlays from new discretionary authority	1	2	
86.93 Outlays from discretionary balances		1	2
87.00 Total outlays (gross)	1	3	2
Net budget authority and outlays:			
89.00 Budget authority	2	2	
90.00 Outlays	1	3	2

Beginning with 2001, this program will be subsumed under the new development credit account.

Summary of Loan Levels, Subsidy Budget Authority and Outlays by Program (in millions of dollars)

Identification code 72–0400–0–1–151	1999 actual	2000 est.	2001 est.
Guaranteed loan levels supportable by subsidy budget authority:			
2150 Loan guarantee levels	50	56	
2159 Total loan guarantee levels	50	56	

Guaranteed loan subsidy (in percent):			
2320 Subsidy rate	4.16	4.94	0.00
2329 Weighted average subsidy rate	4.16	4.94	0.00
Guaranteed loan subsidy budget authority:			
2330 Subsidy budget authority	2	2	
2339 Total subsidy budget authority	2	2	
Guaranteed loan subsidy outlays:			
2340 Subsidy outlays		2	2
2349 Total subsidy outlays		2	2
Administrative expense data:			
3510 Budget authority	1	1	

Object Classification (in millions of dollars)

Identification code 72–0400–0–1–151	1999 actual	2000 est.	2001 est.
41.0 Direct obligations: Grants, subsidies, and contributions	2	2	
99.5 Below reporting threshold	1	1	
99.9 Total new obligations	3	3	

Microenterprise and Small Enterprise Development Credit Direct Loan Financing Account

Program and Financing (in millions of dollars)

Identification code 72–4342–0–3–151	1999 actual	2000 est.	2001 est.
Obligations by program activity:			
00.01 Obligations of Direct Loan Activity	2	2	2
10.00 Total new obligations	2	2	2
Budgetary resources available for obligation:			
22.00 New financing authority (gross)	2	2	2
23.95 Total new obligations	−2	−2	−2
New financing authority (gross), detail:			
Mandatory:			
67.15 Authority to borrow (indefinite)	1	1	1
Discretionary:			
68.00 Spending authority from offsetting collections: Offsetting collections (cash)	1	1	1
70.00 Total new financing authority (gross)	2	2	2
Change in unpaid obligations:			
73.10 Total new obligations	2	2	2
87.00 Total financing disbursements (gross)	1	1	1
Offsets:			
Against gross financing authority and financing disbursements:			
88.40 Offsetting collections (cash) from: Non-Federal sources	−1	−1	−1
Net financing authority and financing disbursements:			
89.00 Financing authority	1	1	1
90.00 Financing disbursements			

Status of Direct Loans (in millions of dollars)

Identification code 72–4342–0–3–151	1999 actual	2000 est.	2001 est.
Position with respect to appropriations act limitation on obligations:			
1111 Limitation on direct loans			
1131 Direct loan obligations exempt from limitation	2		
1150 Total direct loan obligations	2		
Cumulative balance of direct loans outstanding:			
1210 Outstanding, start of year	3	3	3
1231 Disbursements: Direct loan disbursements	1	1	1
1251 Repayments: Repayments and prepayments	−1	−1	−1
1290 Outstanding, end of year	3	3	3

As required by the Federal Credit Reform Act of 1990, this non-budgetary account records all cash flows to and from the Government resulting from direct loans obligated under the United States Agency for International Development (USAID) Microenterprise and Small Enterprise Development Credit Direct Loan program in 1992 and beyond (including modifications of direct loans that resulted from obligations in any year). The amounts in this account are a means of financing and are not included in the budget totals.

Balance Sheet (in millions of dollars)

Identification code 72–4342–0–3–151	1998 actual	1999 actual	2000 est.	2001 est.
ASSETS:				
1101 Federal assets: Fund balances with Treasury	1			
Net value of assets related to post–1991 direct loans receivable:				
1401 Direct loans receivable, gross	1	3	3	2
1499 Net present value of assets related to direct loans	1	3	3	2
1999 Total assets	2	3	3	2
LIABILITIES:				
2201 Non-Federal liabilities: Accounts payable	2	3	3	2
2999 Total liabilities	2	3	3	2

Microenterprise and Small Enterprise Development Guaranteed Loan Financing Account

Program and Financing (in millions of dollars)

Identification code 72–4343–0–3–151	1999 actual	2000 est.	2001 est.
Obligations by program activity:			
00.01 Default claims	2	1	1
10.00 Total new obligations	2	1	1
Budgetary resources available for obligation:			
21.40 Unobligated balance available, start of year	3	2	6
22.00 New financing authority (gross)	1	3	3
23.90 Total budgetary resources available for obligation	4	5	9
23.95 Total new obligations	−2	−1	−1
24.40 Unobligated balance available, end of year	2	6	7
New financing authority (gross), detail:			
Discretionary:			
68.00 Spending authority from offsetting collections (gross): Offsetting collections (cash)	1	3	3
Change in unpaid obligations:			
73.10 Total new obligations	2	1	1
73.20 Total financing disbursements (gross)	−2	−1	−1
87.00 Total financing disbursements (gross)	2	1	1
Offsets:			
Against gross financing authority and financing disbursements:			
Offsetting collections (cash) from:			
88.00 Federal sources		−2	−2
88.40 Non-Federal sources	−1	−1	−1
88.90 Total, offsetting collections (cash)	−1	−3	−3
Net financing authority and financing disbursements:			
89.00 Financing authority			
90.00 Financing disbursements	1	−2	−2

Status of Guaranteed Loans (in millions of dollars)

Identification code 72–4343–0–3–151	1999 actual	2000 est.	2001 est.
Position with respect to appropriations act limitation on commitments:			
2131 Guaranteed loan commitments exempt from limitation	50	56	

Intragovernmental funds—Continued

MICROENTERPRISE AND SMALL ENTERPRISE DEVELOPMENT GUARANTEED LOAN FINANCING ACCOUNT—Continued

Status of Guaranteed Loans (in millions of dollars)—Continued

Identification code 72–4343–0–3–151	1999 actual	2000 est.	2001 est.
2150 Total guaranteed loan commitments	50	56	
Cumulative balance of guaranteed loans outstanding:			
2210 Outstanding, start of year	31	42	64
2231 Disbursements of new guaranteed loans	39	44	30
2251 Repayments and prepayments	−26	−21	−19
2261 Adjustments: Terminations for default that result in loans receivable	−2	−1	−1
2290 Outstanding, end of year	42	64	74
Memorandum:			
2299 Guaranteed amount of guaranteed loans outstanding, end of year	20	32	38
Addendum:			
Cumulative balance of defaulted guaranteed loans that result in loans receivable:			
2310 Outstanding, start of year	1	3	4
2331 Disbursements for guaranteed loan claims	2	1	1
2390 Outstanding, end of year	3	4	5

As required by the Federal Credit Reform Act of 1990, this non-budgetary account records all cash flows to and from the Government resulting from loan guarantees under the United States Agency for International Development (USAID) Microenterprise and Small Enterprise Development Guarantee program committed in 1992 and beyond (including modifications of loan guarantees that resulted from commitments in any year). The amounts in this account are a means of financing and are not included in the budget totals.

Balance Sheet (in millions of dollars)

Identification code 72–4343–0–3–151	1998 actual	1999 actual	2000 est.	2001 est.
ASSETS:				
1101 Federal assets: Fund balances with Treasury	3	4	4	5
1999 Total assets	3	4	4	5
LIABILITIES:				
2204 Non-Federal liabilities: Liabilities for loan guarantees	3	4	4	5
2999 Total liabilities	3	4	4	5
4999 Total liabilities and net position	3	4	4	5

PRIVATE SECTOR REVOLVING FUND LIQUIDATING ACCOUNT

Status of Guaranteed Loans (in millions of dollars)

Identification code 72–4341–0–3–151	1999 actual	2000 est.	2001 est.
Cumulative balance of guaranteed loans outstanding:			
2210 Outstanding, start of year	1	1	1
2290 Outstanding, end of year	1	1	1

As required by the Federal Credit Reform Act of 1990, this account records all cash flows to and from the Government resulting from direct loans obligated and loan guarantees committed under the Private Sector Loan Fund prior to 1992. This account is shown on a cash basis. All new activity in this program in 1992 and beyond is recorded in corresponding program and financing accounts.

DEVELOPMENT CREDIT [AUTHORITY] PROGRAM ACCOUNT

For the cost of direct loans and loan guarantees, up to [$3,000,000] *$15,000,000,* to be derived by transfer from funds appropriated by this Act to carry out part I of the Foreign Assistance Act of 1961, as amended, and funds appropriated by this Act under the heading, "ASSISTANCE FOR EASTERN EUROPE AND THE BALTIC STATES", to remain available until expended, as authorized by section 635 of the Foreign Assistance Act of 1961, *to be available for the purposes of part I of such Act: Provided,* That such costs, including the cost of modifying such loans, shall be as defined in section 502 of the Congressional Budget Act of 1974: *Provided further,* [That for administrative expenses to carry out the direct and guaranteed loan programs, up to $500,000 of this amount may be transferred to and merged with the appropriation for "Operating Expenses of the Agency for International Development": *Provided further,*]That the provisions of section 107A(d) (relating to general provisions applicable to the Development Credit Authority) of the Foreign Assistance Act of 1961, as contained in section 306 of H.R. 1486 as reported by the House Committee on International Relations on May 9, 1997, shall be applicable to direct loans and loan guarantees provided under this heading.

In addition, for administrative expenses to carry out the direct and loan guarantee program, $8,000,000, which may be transferred to and merged with the appropriaton for "Operating Expenses," Agency for International Development. (Foreign Operations, Export Financing, and Related Programs Appropriation Act, 2000, as enacted by section 1000(a)(2) of the Consolidated Appropriations Act, 2000 (P.L. 106–113).)

Program and Financing (in millions of dollars)

Identification code 72–1264–0–1–151	1999 actual	2000 est.	2001 est.
Obligations by program activity:			
00.02 Guaranteed loan subsidy	4	4	15
00.09 Administrative Expenses			8
10.00 Total new obligations	4	4	23
Budgetary resources available for obligation:			
21.40 Unobligated balance available, start of year		1	
22.00 New budget authority (gross)		3	23
22.22 Unobligated balance transferred from other accounts	5		
23.90 Total budgetary resources available for obligation	5	4	23
23.95 Total new obligations	−4	−4	−23
24.40 Unobligated balance available, end of year	1		
New budget authority (gross), detail:			
Discretionary:			
40.00 Appropriation			8
42.00 Transferred from other accounts		3	15
43.00 Appropriation (total discretionary)		3	23
Change in unpaid obligations:			
72.40 Unpaid obligations, start of year: Obligated balance, start of year		4	5
73.10 Total new obligations	4	4	23
73.20 Total outlays (gross)		−3	−13
74.40 Unpaid obligations, end of year: Obligated balance, end of year	4	5	13
Outlays (gross), detail:			
86.90 Outlays from new discretionary authority		1	10
86.93 Outlays from discretionary balances		2	3
87.00 Total outlays (gross)		3	13
Net budget authority and outlays:			
89.00 Budget authority		3	23
90.00 Outlays		3	13

Summary of Loan Levels, Subsidy Budget Authority and Outlays by Program (in millions of dollars)

Identification code 72–1264–0–1–151	1999 actual	2000 est.	2001 est.
Guaranteed loan levels supportable by subsidy budget authority:			
2150 Loan guarantee levels	93	69	213

		1999 actual	2000 est.	2001 est.
2159	Total loan guarantee levels	93	69	213
	Guaranteed loan subsidy (in percent):			
2320	Subsidy rate	3.78	6.40	7.04
2329	Weighted average subsidy rate	3.78	6.40	7.04
	Guaranteed loan subsidy budget authority:			
2330	Subsidy budget authority	4	4	15
2339	Total subsidy budget authority	4	4	15
	Guaranteed loan subsidy outlays:			
2340	Subsidy outlays		3	7
2349	Total subsidy outlays		3	7
	Administrative expense data:			
3510	Budget authority			23
3580	Outlays from balances			3

For 2001, the Administration proposes merging USAID's three credit programs as one consolidated Development Credit account. This single program, which includes a consolidated credit administrative budget, allows USAID to use credit as a flexible development tool for a wide range of development purposes. Rather than requesting a direct appropriation, USAID requests transfer authority from the Development Assistance and other grant accounts to cover the subsidy cost of DCA credits. This allows USAID to choose between credit or grant mechanisms for any given development objective. However, because there is a cap on total credit subsidy transfers, credit will continue to be used only in those cases where it is a particularly appropriate or effective mechanism for achieving a specific objective.

The new Development Credit Account (DCA) permits the Agency to substitute credit assistance (loans and loan guarantees) for grant assistance to achieve any of the economic development purposes authorized by the Congress in Part I of the Foreign Assistance Act of 1961, as amended. Subject to limits in annual appropriations acts and the normal congressional notification processes, disciplined credit assistance under DCA is principally intended for use where a development activity is financially viable, where borrowers are creditworthy, and where there is true risk sharing with private lenders. DCA augments grant assistance by mobilizing private capital in developing countries for sustainable development projects. It is intended that all future Agency credit assistance will be offered under DCA and the strict disciplines of the Federal Credit Reform Act of 1990.

Object Classification (in millions of dollars)

Identification code 72–1264–0–1–151		1999 actual	2000 est.	2001 est.
11.1	Personnel compensation: Full-time permanent			3
21.0	Travel and transportation of persons			1
25.1	Advisory and assistance services			3
25.3	Purchases of goods and services from Government accounts			1
41.0	Grants, subsidies, and contributions	4	4	15
99.9	Total new obligations	4	4	23

Personnel Summary

Identification code 72–1264–0–1–151		1999 actual	2000 est.	2001 est.
1001	Total compensable workyears: Full-time equivalent employment			29

Development Credit Authority Guaranteed Loan Financing Account

Program and Financing (in millions of dollars)

Identification code 72–4266–0–3–151		1999 actual	2000 est.	2001 est.
	Budgetary resources available for obligation:			
21.40	Unobligated balance available, start of year			4
22.00	New financing authority (gross)		4	8
23.90	Total budgetary resources available for obligation		4	12
23.95	Total new obligations			
24.40	Unobligated balance available, end of year		4	12
	New financing authority (gross), detail:			
	Discretionary:			
68.00	Spending authority from offsetting collections (gross): Offsetting collections (cash)		4	8
	Offsets:			
	Against gross financing authority and financing disbursements:			
	Offsetting collections (cash) from:			
88.00	Federal sources: Subsidy payments from program account		−3	−7
88.40	Non-Federal sources: Fees		−1	−1
88.90	Total, offsetting collections (cash)		−4	−8
	Net financing authority and financing disbursements:			
89.00	Financing authority			
90.00	Financing disbursements		−4	−8

Status of Guaranteed Loans (in millions of dollars)

Identification code 72–4266–0–3–151		1999 actual	2000 est.	2001 est.
	Position with respect to appropriations act limitation on commitments:			
2131	Guaranteed loan commitments exempt from limitation	93	69	213
2150	Total guaranteed loan commitments	93	69	213
	Cumulative balance of guaranteed loans outstanding:			
2210	Outstanding, start of year			75
2231	Disbursements of new guaranteed loans		75	114
2261	Adjustments: Terminations for default that result in loans receivable			
2290	Outstanding, end of year		75	189
	Memorandum:			
2299	Guaranteed amount of guaranteed loans outstanding, end of year		38	95
	Addendum:			
	Cumulative balance of defaulted guaranteed loans that result in loans receivable:			
2310	Outstanding, start of year			
2331	Disbursements for guaranteed loan claims			
2390	Outstanding, end of year			

As required by the Federal Credit Reform Act of 1990, this non-budgetary account records all cash flows to and from the Government resulting from direct loans obligated in 1992 and beyond (including modifications of direct loans that resulted from obligations in any year). The amounts in this account are a means of financing and are not included in the budget totals.

Balance Sheet (in millions of dollars)

Identification code 72–4266–0–3–151		1998 actual	1999 actual	2000 est.	2001 est.
	ASSETS:				
1101	Federal assets: Fund balances with Treasury			4	12
1999	Total assets			4	12
	LIABILITIES:				
2204	Non-Federal liabilities: Liabilities for loan guarantees			4	12
2999	Total liabilities			4	12
4999	Total liabilities and net position			4	12

Intragovernmental funds—Continued

ECONOMIC ASSISTANCE LOANS—LIQUIDATING ACCOUNT

Program and Financing (in millions of dollars)

Identification code 72–4103–0–3–151	1999 actual	2000 est.	2001 est.
Budgetary resources available for obligation:			
21.40 Unobligated balance available, start of year	114	67	....
22.00 New budget authority (gross)	1,075	782	700
Capital transfer to general fund:			
22.40 Capital transfer to general fund	–1,121	–770	–696
22.40 Capital transfer to Debt Red. Fin. Acct	....	–67	....
22.40 Capital transfer to Debt Red. Fin. Acct	–1	–12	–4
23.90 Total budgetary resources available for obligation	67	....	....
24.40 Unobligated balance available, end of year	67	....	....
New budget authority (gross), detail:			
Mandatory:			
Offsetting collections (cash):			
69.00 Offsetting collections (cash)	1,075	770	696
69.00 Offsetting collections (cash)	....	12	4
69.90 Spending authority from offsetting collections (total mandatory)	1,075	782	700
Offsets:			
Against gross budget authority and outlays:			
Offsetting collections (cash) from:			
88.00 Federal sources	–1	–12	–4
Non-Federal sources:			
88.40 Non-Federal sources-Principal	–734	–563	–512
88.40 Non-Federal sources-Interest	–340	–207	–184
88.90 Total, offsetting collections (cash)	–1,075	–782	–700
Net budget authority and outlays:			
89.00 Budget authority	....	....	....
90.00 Outlays	–1,075	–782	–700

Status of Direct Loans (in millions of dollars)

Identification code 72–4103–0–3–151	1999 actual	2000 est.	2001 est.
Cumulative balance of direct loans outstanding:			
1210 Outstanding, start of year	11,435	10,660	10,064
Repayments:			
Repayments and prepayments:			
1251 Repayments and prepayments	–734	–563	–512
1251 Repayments and prepayments	–1	–12	–4
1264 Write-offs for default: Other adjustments, net	–40	–21	–14
1290 Outstanding, end of year	10,660	10,064	9,534

Balance Sheet (in millions of dollars)

Identification code 72–4103–0–3–151	1998 actual	1999 actual	2000 est.	2001 est.
ASSETS:				
1101 Federal assets: Fund balances with Treasury	114	....	....	....
Net value of assets related to pre-1992 direct loans receivable and acquired defaulted guaranteed loans receivable:				
1601 Direct loans, gross	11,435	10,660	10,064	9,534
1602 Interest receivable	379	310	294	279
1603 Allowance for estimated uncollectible loans and interest (–)	–5,235	–5,856	–5,547	–5,265
1699 Value of assets related to direct loans	6,579	5,114	4,811	4,548
1999 Total assets	6,693	5,114	4,811	4,548
LIABILITIES:				
2104 Federal liabilities: Resources payable to Treasury	6,693	5,114	4,844	4,599
2999 Total liabilities	6,693	5,114	4,844	4,599
NET POSITION:				
3300 Cumulative results of operations	....	....	–33	–51
3999 Total net position	....	....	–33	–51
4999 Total liabilities and net position	6,693	5,114	4,811	4,548

The Economic Assistance Loans liquidating account consolidates liquidating credit activity from three previous accounts: Economic Support Fund, Functional Development Assistance Program, and the Development Loans Revolving Fund. This was done to simplify presentation. As required by the Federal Credit Reform Act of 1990, this account records all cash flows to and from the Government resulting from direct loans prior to 1992. This account is shown on a cash basis.

Trust Funds

FOREIGN SERVICE NATIONAL SEPARATION LIABILITY TRUST FUND

Program and Financing (in millions of dollars)

Identification code 72–8342–0–7–602	1999 actual	2000 est.	2001 est.
Obligations by program activity:			
10.00 Total new obligations (object class 12.1)	3	5	2
Budgetary resources available for obligation:			
22.00 New budget authority (gross)	3	3	3
23.95 Total new obligations	–3	–5	–2
New budget authority (gross), detail:			
Mandatory:			
60.27 Appropriation (trust fund, indefinite)	3	3	3
Change in unpaid obligations:			
72.40 Unpaid obligations, start of year: Obligated balance, start of year	10	12	16
73.10 Total new obligations	3	5	2
73.20 Total outlays (gross)	–1	–1	–1
74.40 Unpaid obligations, end of year: Obligated balance, end of year	12	16	17
Outlays (gross), detail:			
86.97 Outlays from new mandatory authority	1	1	1
Net budget authority and outlays:			
89.00 Budget authority	3	3	3
90.00 Outlays	....	1	1

This Fund is maintained to pay separation costs for Foreign Service National employees of the U.S. Agency for International Development in those countries in which such pay is legally required. The Fund, as authorized by Public Law 102–138, is maintained by annual Government contributions which are appropriated in several Agency accounts.

MISCELLANEOUS TRUST FUNDS, AID

Program and Financing (in millions of dollars)

Identification code 72–9971–0–7–151	1999 actual	2000 est.	2001 est.
Budgetary resources available for obligation:			
21.40 Unobligated balance available, start of year	1	1	....
24.40 Unobligated balance available, end of year	1	....	....
Change in unpaid obligations:			
72.40 Unpaid obligations, start of year: Obligated balance, start of year	1	1	....
74.40 Unpaid obligations, end of year: Obligated balance, end of year	1	....	....
Net budget authority and outlays:			
89.00 Budget authority	....	....	....
90.00 Outlays	....	....	....

The Miscellaneous Trust Funds account includes gifts and donations that AID receives from other governments, nongovernmental organizations, or private citizens. AID has authority to spend these gifts and donations for development purposes under Section 635(d) of the Foreign Assistance Act. In 1997, this account received $50 million from Israel that was used to finance part of the Mideast Peace and Stability Fund.

OVERSEAS PRIVATE INVESTMENT CORPORATION

Federal Funds

Public enterprise funds:

OVERSEAS PRIVATE INVESTMENT CORPORATION

NONCREDIT ACCOUNT

The Overseas Private Investment Corporation is authorized to make, without regard to fiscal year limitations, as provided by 31 U.S.C. 9104, such expenditures and commitments within the limits of funds available to it and in accordance with law as may be necessary: *Provided*, That the amount available for administrative expenses to carry out the credit and insurance programs (including an amount for official reception and representation expenses which shall not exceed $35,000) shall not exceed [$35,000,000] *$39,000,000*: *Provided further*, That project-specific transaction costs, including direct and indirect costs incurred in claims settlements, and other direct costs associated with services provided to specific investors or potential investors pursuant to section 234 of the Foreign Assistance Act of 1961, shall not be considered administrative expenses for the purposes of this heading. *(Foreign Operations, Expert Financing, and Related Programs Appropriations Act, 2000, as enacted by section 1000(a)(2) of the Consolidated Appropriations Act, 2000 (P.L. 106–113).)*

Unavailable Collections (in millions of dollars)

Identification code 71–4184–0–3–151	1999 actual	2000 est.	2001 est.
Balance, start of year:			
01.99 Balance, start of year	2,579	2,757	2,961
03.00 Offsetting collections	178	204	220
04.00 Total: Balances and collections	2,757	2,961	3,181
07.99 Total balance, end of year	2,757	2,961	3,181

These balances are reserves held for potential claims and are not expected to be obligated.

Program and Financing (in millions of dollars)

Identification code 71–4184–0–3–151	1999 actual	2000 est.	2001 est.
Obligations by program activity:			
09.01 Noncredit administrative expenses	14	14	16
09.02 Insurance claim payments/provisions	50	60	40
09.03 Credit administrative expenses	20	21	23
09.04 Reimbursable agreements	1	....	....
10.00 Total new obligations	85	95	79
Budgetary resources available for obligation:			
21.40 Unobligated balance available, start of year	104	147	166
22.00 New budget authority (gross)	85	98	85
22.10 Resources available from recoveries of prior year obligations	1	1	1
22.22 Unobligated balance transferred from other accounts	42	15	....
23.90 Total budgetary resources available for obligation	232	261	252
23.95 Total new obligations	−85	−95	−79
24.40 Unobligated balance available, end of year	147	166	173
New budget authority (gross), detail:			
Discretionary:			
41.00 Transferred to other accounts	−70	−45	−47
42.00 Transferred from other accounts	1	....	....
43.00 Appropriation (total discretionary)	−69	−45	−47
Spending authority from offsetting collections:			
68.00 Offsetting collections (cash)	328	339	346
68.10 From Federal sources: Change in receivables and unpaid, unfilled orders	4	8	6
68.45 Portion not expected to be obligated	−178	−204	−220
68.90 Spending authority from offsetting collections (total discretionary)	154	143	132
70.00 Total new budget authority (gross)	85	98	85
Change in unpaid obligations:			
Unpaid obligations, start of year:			
72.40 Obligated balance, start of year	109	134	67
72.95 From Federal sources: Receivables and unpaid, unfilled orders	51	55	63
72.99 Total unpaid obligations, start of year	160	189	130
73.10 Total new obligations	85	95	79
73.20 Total outlays (gross)	−55	−153	−55
73.45 Adjustments in unexpired accounts	−1	−1	−1
Unpaid obligations, end of year:			
74.40 Obligated balance, end of year	134	67	84
74.95 From Federal sources: Receivables and unpaid, unfilled orders	55	63	69
74.99 Total unpaid obligations, end of year	189	130	153
Outlays (gross), detail:			
86.90 Outlays from new discretionary authority	33	32	35
86.93 Outlays from discretionary balances	22	121	20
87.00 Total outlays (gross)	55	153	55
Offsets:			
Against gross budget authority and outlays:			
Offsetting collections (cash) from:			
88.00 Federal sources	−23	−22	−23
88.20 Interest on U.S. securities	−215	−234	−243
88.40 Non-Federal sources	−90	−83	−80
88.90 Total, offsetting collections (cash)	−328	−339	−346
Against gross budget authority only:			
88.95 From Federal sources: Change in receivables and unpaid, unfilled orders	−4	−8	−6
Net budget authority and outlays:			
89.00 Budget authority	−247	−249	−267
90.00 Outlays	−271	−186	−291
Memorandum (non-add) entries:			
92.01 Total investments, start of year: U.S. securities: Par value	2,807	3,084	3,202
92.02 Total investments, end of year: U.S. securities: Par value	3,084	3,202	3,220

The Overseas Private Investment Corporation encourages the participation of United States private sector capital and skills in the economic and social development of developing countries and emerging market economies. Its primary noncredit program is political risk insurance against losses due to expropriation, inconvertibility, and damage due to political violence.

Status of Funds (in millions of dollars)

Identification code 71–4184–0–3–151	1999 actual	2000 est.	2001 est.
Unexpended balance, start of year:			
0100 Treasury balance	6	−22	18
U.S. Securities:			
0101 Par value	2,807	3,084	3,202
0102 Unrealized discounts	−21	−23	−25
0199 Total balance, start of year	2,792	3,038	3,194
Cash income during the year:			
Offsetting collections:			
0280 Offsetting collections	328	339	346
Cash outgo during year:			
0500 Overseas private investment corporation noncredit account	−55	−153	−55
0645 Balance transferred, net	−27	−30	−47
Unexpended balance, end of year:			
0700 Treasury balance	−22	18	244
U.S. Securities:			
0701 Par value	3,084	3,202	3,220
0702 Unrealized discounts	−23	−25	−25
0799 Total balance, end of year	3,038	3,194	3,438

Public enterprise funds—Continued

OVERSEAS PRIVATE INVESTMENT CORPORATION—Continued

NONCREDIT ACCOUNT—Continued

INSURANCE PROGRAM ACTIVITY

[In millions of dollars]

	1998 actual	1999 actual	2000 est.	2001 est.
Aggregate insurance outstanding, start of year	26,579	26,234	26,469	26,733
Aggregate insurance issued during year	4,842	4,638	5,500	5,700
Aggregate insurance reductions and cancellations	−5,187	−4,403	−5,236	−5,288
Aggregate insurance outstanding, end of year	26,234	26,469	26,733	27,145
Net growth/(decline) of portfolio	−345	235	264	412
Net growth rate of insurance portfolio (in percent)	−1.30	0.90	1.00	1.54

STATUS OF INSURANCE AUTHORITY

[In millions of dollars]

	1998 actual	1999 actual	2000 est.	2001 est.
Statutory authority limitation [1]	29,000	29,000	29,000	29,000
Maximum contingent liability, end of year	11,852	12,778	12,905	13,104
Estimated potential exposure to claims, end of year	6,876	7,557	7,632	7,750

[1] This is a combined insurance and finance limitation. OPIC will monitor issuance and runoff to stay within the limitation.

Object Classification (in millions of dollars)

Identification code 71–4184–0–3–151	1999 actual	2000 est.	2001 est.
11.1 Personnel compensation: Full-time permanent	14	17	17
12.1 Civilian personnel benefits	4	2	3
21.0 Travel and transportation of persons	....	1	1
23.2 Rental payments to others	6	2	3
25.1 Advisory and assistance services	8	10	12
25.2 Other services	1	3	3
26.0 Supplies and materials	2	....	....
42.0 Insurance claims and indemnities	50	60	40
99.9 Total new obligations	85	95	79

Personnel Summary

Identification code 71–4184–0–3–151	1999 actual	2000 est.	2001 est.
2001 Total compensable workyears: Full-time equivalent employment	190	202	209

Credit accounts:

OVERSEAS PRIVATE INVESTMENT CORPORATION

PROGRAM ACCOUNT

For the cost of direct and guaranteed loans, $24,000,000, as authorized by section 234 of the Foreign Assistance Act of 1961 to be derived by transfer from the Overseas Private Investment Corporation noncredit account: *Provided*, That such costs, including the cost of modifying such loans, shall be as defined in section 502 of the Congressional Budget Act of 1974: *Provided further*, That such sums shall be available for direct loan obligations and loan guaranty commitments incurred or made during fiscal years **[**2000 and 2001**]** *2001, 2002, 2003 and 2004*: *Provided further*, That such sums shall remain available through fiscal year **[**2008**]** *2012* for the disbursement of direct and guaranteed loans obligated in fiscal year **[**2000, and through fiscal year 2009 for the disbursement of direct and guaranteed loans obligated in fiscal year 2001**]** *years 2001 through 2004*: *Provided further*, That in addition, such sums as may be necessary for administrative expenses to carry out the credit program may be derived from amounts available for administrative expenses to carry out the credit and insurance programs in the Overseas Private Investment Corporation Noncredit Account and merged with said account**[**: *Provided further*, That funds made available under this heading or in prior appropriations Acts that are available for the cost of financing under section 234 of the Foreign Assistance Act of 1961, shall be available for purposes of section 234(g) of such Act, to remain available until expended**]**. *(Foreign Operations, Export Financing, and Related Programs Appropriation Act, 2000, as enacted by section 1000(a)(2) of the Consolidated Appropriations Act, 2000 (P.L. 106–113).)*

Program and Financing (in millions of dollars)

Identification code 71–0100–0–1–151	1999 actual	2000 est.	2001 est.
Obligations by program activity:			
00.01 Direct loan subsidy	7	15	14
00.02 Guaranteed loan subsidy	11	35	10
00.09 Credit administrative expenses	22	22	23
10.00 Total new obligations	40	72	47
Budgetary resources available for obligation:			
21.40 Unobligated balance available, start of year	63	68	42
22.00 New budget authority (gross)	72	45	47
22.10 Resources available from recoveries of prior year obligations	16	....	....
23.90 Total budgetary resources available for obligation	151	113	89
23.95 Total new obligations	−40	−72	−47
23.98 Unobligated balance expiring or withdrawn	−41	....	....
24.40 Unobligated balance available, end of year	68	42	42
New budget authority (gross), detail:			
Discretionary:			
42.00 Transferred from other accounts	72	45	47
43.00 Appropriation (total discretionary)	72	45	47
Change in unpaid obligations:			
72.40 Unpaid obligations, start of year: Obligated balance, start of year	106	89	109
73.10 Total new obligations	40	72	47
73.20 Total outlays (gross)	−42	−50	−56
73.45 Adjustments in unexpired accounts	−16	....	....
74.40 Unpaid obligations, end of year: Obligated balance, end of year	89	109	100
Outlays (gross), detail:			
86.90 Outlays from new discretionary authority	22	21	23
86.93 Outlays from discretionary balances	20	29	33
87.00 Total outlays (gross)	42	50	56
Net budget authority and outlays:			
89.00 Budget authority	72	45	47
90.00 Outlays	42	50	56

Summary of Loan Levels, Subsidy Budget Authority and Outlays by Program (in millions of dollars)

Identification code 71–0100–0–1–151	1999 actual	2000 est.	2001 est.
Direct loan levels supportable by subsidy budget authority:			
1150 Direct loan levels	136	136	127
1159 Total direct loan levels	136	136	127
Direct loan subsidy (in percent):			
1320 Subsidy rate	11.00	11.00	11.00
1329 Weighted average subsidy rate	11.00	11.00	11.00
Direct loan subsidy budget authority:			
1330 Subsidy budget authority	15	15	14
1339 Total subsidy budget authority	15	15	14
Direct loan subsidy outlays:			
1340 Subsidy outlays	1	10	10
1349 Total subsidy outlays	1	10	10
Guaranteed loan levels supportable by subsidy budget authority:			
2150 Loan guarantee levels	2,333	2,333	1,000
2159 Total loan guarantee levels	2,333	2,333	1,000
Guaranteed loan subsidy (in percent):			
2320 Subsidy rate	1.50	1.50	1.00
2329 Weighted average subsidy rate	1.50	1.50	1.00
Guaranteed loan subsidy budget authority:			
2330 Subsidy budget authority	35	35	10

2339	Total subsidy budget authority	35	35	10
	Guaranteed loan subsidy outlays:			
2340	Subsidy outlays	19	19	19
2349	Total subsidy outlays	19	19	19
	Administrative expense data:			
3510	Budget authority	20	22	23
3590	Outlays from new authority	20	21	23

The Overseas Private Investment Corporation encourages the participation of United States private sector capital and skills in the economic and social development of developing countries and emerging market economies. Its primary credit program is investment financing through loans and guaranteed loans.

As required by the Federal Credit Reform Act of 1990, the Program Account records the subsidy costs associated with the direct loans obligated and loan guarantees committed in 1992 and beyond (including modifications of direct loans or loan guarantees that resulted from obligations or commitments in any year), as well as administrative expenses of this program. The subsidy amounts are estimated on a present value basis; the administrative expenses are estimated on a cash basis.

Object Classification (in millions of dollars)

Identification code 71–0100–0–1–151		1999 actual	2000 est.	2001 est.
25.2	Other services (contracts)	22	22	23
41.0	Grants, subsidies, and contributions	18	50	24
99.9	Total new obligations	40	72	47

Overseas Private Investment Corporation Direct Loan Financing Account

Program and Financing (in millions of dollars)

Identification code 71–4074–0–3–151		1999 actual	2000 est.	2001 est.
	Obligations by program activity:			
00.01	Direct loan obligations	154	169	173
00.02	Interest on borrowings	4	9	9
10.00	Total new obligations	158	178	182
	Budgetary resources available for obligation:			
21.40	Unobligated balance available, start of year	28	34	
22.00	New financing authority (gross)	155	175	193
22.10	Resources available from recoveries of prior year obligations	18		
22.60	Portion applied to repay debt	−9	−31	−11
23.90	Total budgetary resources available for obligation	192	178	182
23.95	Total new obligations	−158	−178	−182
24.40	Unobligated balance available, end of year	34		
	New financing authority (gross), detail:			
	Mandatory:			
67.15	Authority to borrow (indefinite)	134	136	127
	Spending authority from offsetting collections:			
	Discretionary:			
68.00	Offsetting collections (cash)	16	34	62
68.10	From Federal sources: Change in receivables and unpaid, unfilled orders	5	5	4
68.90	Spending authority from offsetting collections (total discretionary)	21	39	66
70.00	Total new financing authority (gross)	155	175	193
	Change in unpaid obligations:			
	Unpaid obligations, start of year:			
72.40	Obligated balance, start of year	84	205	358
72.95	Receivables from program account	12	17	22
72.99	Total unpaid obligations, start of year	96	222	380
73.10	Total new obligations	158	178	182
73.20	Total financing disbursements (gross)	−13	−20	−23
73.45	Adjustments in unexpired accounts	−18		
	Unpaid obligations, end of year:			
74.40	Obligated balance, end of year	205	358	513
74.95	Receivables from program account	17	22	26
74.99	Total unpaid obligations, end of year	222	380	539
87.00	Total financing disbursements (gross)	13	20	23
	Offsets:			
	Against gross financing authority and financing disbursements:			
	Offsetting collections (cash) from:			
88.00	Federal sources	−1	−10	−10
88.25	Interest on uninvested funds	−2	−1	−2
	Non-Federal sources:			
88.40	Repayments of Principal	−6	−14	−27
88.40	Interest received on loans	−5	−8	−16
88.40	Fees	−2	−1	−7
88.90	Total, offsetting collections (cash)	−16	−34	−62
	Against gross budget authority only:			
88.95	Change in receivables from program accounts	−5	−5	−4
	Net financing authority and financing disbursements:			
89.00	Financing authority	134	136	127
90.00	Financing disbursements	−3	−14	−41

Status of Direct Loans (in millions of dollars)

Identification code 71–4074–0–3–151		1999 actual	2000 est.	2001 est.
	Position with respect to appropriations act limitation on obligations:			
1111	Limitation on direct loans			
1131	Direct loan obligations exempt from limitation	136	136	127
1150	Total direct loan obligations	136	136	127
	Cumulative balance of direct loans outstanding:			
1210	Outstanding, start of year	63	64	70
1231	Disbursements: Direct loan disbursements	7	20	23
1251	Repayments: Repayments and prepayments	−5	−13	−12
1263	Write-offs for default: Direct loans	−1	−1	−1
1290	Outstanding, end of year	64	70	80

As required by the Federal Credit Reform Act of 1990, this non-budgetary account records all cash flows to and from the Government resulting from direct loans obligated in 1992 and beyond (including modifications of direct loans that resulted from obligations in any year). The amounts in this account are a means of financing and are not included in the budget totals.

Balance Sheet (in millions of dollars)

Identification code 71–4074–0–3–151		1998 actual	1999 actual	2000 est.	2001 est.
	ASSETS:				
	Federal assets:				
1101	Fund balances with Treasury	29	23	3	3
	Investments in US securities:				
1106	Receivables, net	8	17	8	8
1206	Non-Federal assets: Receivables, net	2		2	2
	Net value of assets related to post-1991 direct loans receivable:				
1401	Direct loans receivable, gross	63	64	70	78
1402	Interest receivable	1		1	1
1405	Allowance for subsidy cost (–)	–20	–23	–20	–20
1499	Net present value of assets related to direct loans	44	41	51	59
1999	Total assets	83	81	64	72
	LIABILITIES:				
	Federal liabilities:				
2101	Accounts payable	4		4	4
2103	Debt	74	63	55	63
2105	Other Federal liabilities	4	17	4	4
2207	Non-Federal liabilities: Other	1	1	1	1
2999	Total liabilities	83	81	64	72
4999	Total liabilities and net position	83	81	64	72

Credit accounts—Continued

Overseas Private Investment Corporation Guaranteed Loan Financing Account

Program and Financing (in millions of dollars)

Identification code 71–4075–0–3–151	1999 actual	2000 est.	2001 est.
Obligations by program activity:			
00.01 Default claims	17	50	50
00.02 Capitalized costs	4	6	6
10.00 Total new obligations	21	56	56
Budgetary resources available for obligation:			
21.40 Unobligated balance available, start of year	282	372	447
22.00 New financing authority (gross)	115	131	140
22.60 Portion applied to repay debt	−4		
23.90 Total budgetary resources available for obligation	393	503	587
23.95 Total new obligations	−21	−56	−56
24.40 Unobligated balance available, end of year	372	447	531
New financing authority (gross), detail:			
Discretionary:			
68.00 Spending authority from offsetting collections (gross): Offsetting collections (cash)	115	131	140
Change in unpaid obligations:			
72.40 Unpaid obligations, start of year: Obligated balance, start of year	17	4	3
73.10 Total new obligations	21	56	56
73.20 Total financing disbursements (gross)	−19	−56	−56
74.40 Unpaid obligations, end of year: Obligated balance, end of year	4	3	3
87.00 Total financing disbursements (gross)	19	56	56
Offsets:			
Against gross financing authority and financing disbursements:			
Offsetting collections (cash) from:			
88.00 Federal sources: Payments from program account	−19	−19	−19
88.25 Interest on uninvested funds	−20	−15	−20
Non-Federal sources:			
88.40 Claim recoveries	−3	−5	−5
88.40 Fees	−73	−92	−96
88.90 Total, offsetting collections (cash)	−115	−131	−140
Net financing authority and financing disbursements:			
89.00 Financing authority			
90.00 Financing disbursements	−96	−75	−84

Status of Guaranteed Loans (in millions of dollars)

Identification code 71–4075–0–3–151	1999 actual	2000 est.	2001 est.
Position with respect to appropriations act limitation on commitments:			
2111 Limitation on guaranteed loans made by private lenders	2,333	2,333	1,000
2150 Total guaranteed loan commitments	2,333	2,333	1,000
Cumulative balance of guaranteed loans outstanding:			
2210 Outstanding, start of year	2,613	2,904	3,004
2231 Disbursements of new guaranteed loans	426	600	800
2251 Repayments and prepayments	−130	−450	−500
2261 Adjustments: Terminations for default that result in loans receivable	−5	−50	−50
2290 Outstanding, end of year	2,904	3,004	3,254
Memorandum:			
2299 Guaranteed amount of guaranteed loans outstanding, end of year	2,904	3,004	3,254
Addendum:			
Cumulative balance of defaulted guaranteed loans that result in loans receivable:			
2310 Outstanding, start of year	15	17	62
2331 Disbursements for guaranteed loan claims	5	50	50
2351 Repayments of loans receivable	−3	−5	−17
2390 Outstanding, end of year	17	62	95

As required by the Federal Credit Reform Act of 1990, this non-budgetary account records all cash flows to and from the Government resulting from loan guarantees committed in 1992 and beyond (including modifications of loan guarantees that resulted from commitments in any year). The amounts in this account are a means of financing and are not included in the budget totals.

Balance Sheet (in millions of dollars)

Identification code 71–4075–0–3–151	1998 actual	1999 actual	2000 est.	2001 est.
ASSETS:				
1101 Federal assets: Fund balances with Treasury	279	369	413	435
1206 Non-Federal assets: Receivables, net	31	13	17	17
Net value of assets related to post-1991 acquired defaulted guaranteed loans receivable:				
1501 Defaulted guaranteed loans receivable, gross	21	17	62	95
1599 Net present value of assets related to defaulted guaranteed loans	21	17	62	95
1999 Total assets	331	399	492	547
LIABILITIES:				
Non-Federal liabilities:				
2204 Liabilities for loan guarantees	298	353	379	418
2207 Other non-fed	21	27	71	86
2999 Total liabilities	319	380	450	504
NET POSITION:				
3300 Cumulative results of operations	12	19	42	43
3999 Total net position	12	19	42	43
4999 Total liabilities and net position	331	399	492	547

Overseas Private Investment Corporation Liquidating Account

Program and Financing (in millions of dollars)

Identification code 71–4030–0–3–151	1999 actual	2000 est.	2001 est.
Obligations by program activity:			
00.01 Anticipated claim payment	1	14	
10.00 Total new obligations	1	14	
Budgetary resources available for obligation:			
21.40 Unobligated balance available, start of year	58	26	
22.00 New budget authority (gross)	11	3	
22.21 Unobligated balance transferred to other accounts	−42	−15	
23.90 Total budgetary resources available for obligation	27	14	
23.95 Total new obligations	−1	−14	
24.40 Unobligated balance available, end of year	26		
New budget authority (gross), detail:			
Mandatory:			
69.00 Offsetting collections (cash)	11	3	
Change in unpaid obligations:			
73.10 Total new obligations	1	14	
73.20 Total outlays (gross)	−1	−14	
Outlays (gross), detail:			
86.97 Outlays from new mandatory authority	1	3	
86.98 Outlays from mandatory balances		11	
87.00 Total outlays (gross)	1	14	
Offsets:			
Against gross budget authority and outlays:			
Offsetting collections (cash) from:			
88.20 Interest on U.S. securities	−1		
88.40 Non-Federal sources	−10	−3	
88.90 Total, offsetting collections (cash)	−11	−3	

		1999 actual	2000 est.	2001 est.
	Net budget authority and outlays:			
89.00	Budget authority			
90.00	Outlays	–10	11	
	Memorandum (non-add) entries:			
92.01	Total investments, start of year: U.S. securities: Par value	35		

Status of Direct Loans (in millions of dollars)

Identification code 71–4030–0–3–151		1999 actual	2000 est.	2001 est.
	Cumulative balance of direct loans outstanding:			
1210	Outstanding, start of year	24	14	9
1251	Repayments: Repayments and prepayments	–7	–3	
1264	Write-offs for default: Other adjustments, net	–3	–2	–6
1290	Outstanding, end of year	14	9	3

Status of Guaranteed Loans (in millions of dollars)

Identification code 71–4030–0–3–151		1999 actual	2000 est.	2001 est.
	Cumulative balance of guaranteed loans outstanding:			
2210	Outstanding, start of year	81	69	55
2251	Repayments and prepayments	–11		–55
2263	Adjustments: Terminations for default that result in claim payments	–1	–14	
2290	Outstanding, end of year	69	55	
	Memorandum:			
2299	Guaranteed amount of guaranteed loans outstanding, end of year	69	55	

As required by the Federal Credit Reform Act of 1990, this account records, for this program, all cash flows to and from the Government resulting from direct loans obligated and loan guarantees committed prior to 1992. This account is shown on a cash basis. All new activity in this program in 1992 and beyond (including modifications of direct loans or loan guarantees that resulted from obligations or commitments in any year) is recorded in corresponding program, financing, and noncredit accounts.

Statement of Operations (in millions of dollars)

Identification code 71–4030–0–3–151		1998 actual	1999 actual	2000 est.	2001 est.
0101	Revenue	13	11	3	
0102	Expense	–2	–1	–14	
0105	Net income or loss (–)	11	10	–11	

Balance Sheet (in millions of dollars)

Identification code 71–4030–0–3–151		1998 actual	1999 actual	2000 est.	2001 est.
	ASSETS:				
1101	Federal assets: Fund balances with Treasury	27	26		
	Net value of assets related to pre–1992 direct loans receivable and acquired defaulted guaranteed loans receivable:				
1601	Direct loans, gross	22	14	9	3
1603	Allowance for estimated uncollectible loans and interest (–)	–16	–9	–7	–3
1604	Direct loans and interest receivable, net	6	5	2	
1699	Value of assets related to direct loans	6	5	2	
1706	Defaulted guaranty acquired	2	2		
1799	Value of assets related to loan guarantees	2	2		
1999	Total assets	35	33	2	
	LIABILITIES:				
2207	Non-Federal liabilities: Other	10	5	2	
2999	Total liabilities	10	5	2	
	NET POSITION:				
3300	Cumulative results of operations	25	26		
3999	Total net position	25	26		
4999	Total liabilities and net position	35	31	2	

Object Classification (in millions of dollars)

Identification code 71–4030–0–3–151		1999 actual	2000 est.	2001 est.
33.0	Investments and loans		14	
43.0	Interest and dividends	1		
99.9	Total new obligations	1	14	

TRADE AND DEVELOPMENT AGENCY

Federal Funds

General and special funds:

TRADE AND DEVELOPMENT AGENCY

For necessary expenses to carry out the provisions of section 661 of the Foreign Assistance Act of 1961, [$44,000,000] *$54,000,000*, to remain available until September 30, [2001: *Provided*, That the Trade and Development Agency may receive reimbursements from corporations and other entities for the costs of grants for feasibility studies and other project planning services, to be deposited as an offsetting collection to this account and to be available for obligation until September 30, 2001, for necessary expenses under this paragraph: *Provided further*, That such reimbursements shall not cover, or be allocated against, direct or indirect administrative costs of the agency] *2002*. *(Foreign Operations, Export Financing, and Related Programs Appropriation Act, 2000, as enacted by section 1000(a)(2) of the Consolidated Appropriations Act, 2000 (P.L. 106–113).)*

Program and Financing (in millions of dollars)

Identification code 11–1001–0–1–151		1999 actual	2000 est.	2001 est.
	Obligations by program activity:			
00.01	Feasibility studies, and other activities	57	57	47
00.02	Operating expenses	6	7	7
10.00	Total new obligations	63	64	54
	Budgetary resources available for obligation:			
21.40	Unobligated balance available, start of year	17	18	
22.00	New budget authority (gross)	59	44	54
22.10	Resources available from recoveries of prior year obligations	3	2	2
22.22	Unobligated balance transferred from other accounts	2		
23.90	Total budgetary resources available for obligation	81	64	56
23.95	Total new obligations	–63	–64	–54
24.40	Unobligated balance available, end of year	18		1
	New budget authority (gross), detail:			
	Discretionary:			
40.00	Appropriation	44	44	54
42.00	Transferred from other accounts	15		
43.00	Appropriation (total discretionary)	59	44	54
	Change in unpaid obligations:			
72.40	Unpaid obligations, start of year: Obligated balance, start of year	86	93	98
73.10	Total new obligations	63	64	54
73.20	Total outlays (gross)	–49	–57	–57
73.40	Adjustments in expired accounts (net)	–4		
73.45	Adjustments in unexpired accounts	–3	–2	–2
74.40	Unpaid obligations, end of year: Obligated balance, end of year	93	98	93
	Outlays (gross), detail:			
86.90	Outlays from new discretionary authority	13	12	14
86.93	Outlays from discretionary balances	36	45	42
87.00	Total outlays (gross)	49	57	57
	Net budget authority and outlays:			
89.00	Budget authority	59	44	54

General and special funds—Continued

TRADE AND DEVELOPMENT AGENCY—Continued

Program and Financing (in millions of dollars)—Continued

Identification code 11–1001–0–1–151	1999 actual	2000 est.	2001 est.
90.00 Outlays	49	57	57

Appropriated funds provide for the costs of the U.S. Trade and Development Agency (TDA), which include: program costs of grants for feasibility studies and other project planning activities; and, the cost of managing the TDA programs such as salaries and expenses of direct hire personnel, and obtaining the services of consultants. TDA finances these activities for major projects in the developing world to foster economic development and to encourage the use of U.S. technology, goods, and services in project implementation.

Object Classification (in millions of dollars)

Identification code 11–1001–0–1–151	1999 actual	2000 est.	2001 est.
11.1 Personnel compensation: Full-time permanent	2	3	3
12.1 Civilian personnel benefits	1	1	1
25.1 Advisory and assistance services	3	3	3
41.0 Grants, subsidies, and contributions	57	57	47
99.9 Total new obligations	63	64	54

Personnel Summary

Identification code 11–1001–0–1–151	1999 actual	2000 est.	2001 est.
1001 Total compensable workyears: Full-time equivalent employment	39	43	45

PEACE CORPS

Federal Funds

General and special funds:

PEACE CORPS

For necessary expenses to carry out the provisions of the Peace Corps Act (75 Stat. 612), [$245,000,000] *$275,000,000*, including the purchase of not to exceed five passenger motor vehicles for administrative purposes for use outside of the United States: *Provided*, That [none of the funds appropriated under this heading shall be used to pay for abortions: *Provided further*, That] [1] funds appropriated under this heading shall remain available until September 30, [2001] *2002*. *(Foreign Operations, Export Financing, and Related Programs Appropriation Act, 2000, as enacted by section 1000(a)(2) of the Consolidated Appropriations Act, 2000 (P.L. 106–113).)*

[1] The Administration proposes to delete this provision and will work with Congress to address this issue.

Program and Financing (in millions of dollars)

Identification code 11–0100–0–1–151	1999 actual	2000 est.	2001 est.
Obligations by program activity:			
Direct program:			
00.01 Growth in Volunteer corps			4
00.02 Africa region	56	53	55
00.03 Europe, Mediterranean & Asia region	39	42	43
00.04 Inter-America & Pacific region	42	44	45
00.05 Other volunteer support	112	118	128
09.01 Reimbursable program	7	7	7
10.00 Total new obligations	256	264	282
Budgetary resources available for obligation:			
21.40 Unobligated balance available, start of year	7	13	
22.00 New budget authority (gross)	264	252	283
23.90 Total budgetary resources available for obligation	271	265	283
23.95 Total new obligations	−256	−264	−282
23.98 Unobligated balance expiring or withdrawn	−1	−1	−1
24.40 Unobligated balance available, end of year	13		
New budget authority (gross), detail:			
Discretionary:			
40.00 Appropriation	240	245	275
40.75 Reduction pursuant to P.L. 106–51	−1		
40.76 Reduction pursuant to P.L. 106–113		−1	
42.00 Transferred from other accounts	17		
43.00 Appropriation (total discretionary)	256	244	275
68.00 Spending authority from offsetting collections: Offsetting collections (cash)	8	8	8
70.00 Total new budget authority (gross)	264	252	283
Change in unpaid obligations:			
72.40 Unpaid obligations, start of year: Obligated balance, start of year	60	68	60
73.10 Total new obligations	256	264	282
73.20 Total outlays (gross)	−245	−272	−277
73.40 Adjustments in expired accounts (net)	−2		
74.40 Unpaid obligations, end of year: Obligated balance, end of year	68	60	65
Outlays (gross), detail:			
86.90 Outlays from new discretionary authority	202	203	228
86.93 Outlays from discretionary balances	42	69	49
87.00 Total outlays (gross)	245	272	277
Offsets:			
Against gross budget authority and outlays:			
Offsetting collections (cash) from:			
88.00 Federal sources	−7	−7	−7
88.40 Non-Federal sources	−1	−1	−1
88.90 Total, offsetting collections (cash)	−8	−8	−8
Net budget authority and outlays:			
89.00 Budget authority	256	244	275
90.00 Outlays	238	264	269

Peace Corps' operating expenses will provide direct and indirect support for an average of 6,176 Americans engaged in voluntary services in 78 countries worldwide in 2000. The Volunteers help fill the trained manpower needs of developing countries and encourage self-sustaining development of skilled manpower. The Peace Corps promotes mutual understanding between the peoples of the developing world and the United States and focuses the attention of the American people on the benefits of volunteerism. Peace Corps Volunteers work primarily in the areas of agriculture, education, economic development, health, and environment.

Growth in the Volunteer Corps.—This 2000 presidential initiative will support the Peace Corps' efforts to place a total of 4,216 new trainees in the field in 2001 and will put the Peace Corps on a path to a Volunteer corps of 10,000 in the new century.

Africa Region.—The Africa Region will support 1,404 new trainees and an average of 2,126 Volunteers during 2000. These Volunteers and trainees will work in 24 sub-Saharan countries.

Europe, Mediterranean, and Asia Region.—In 2000 an average of 1,968 Volunteers will work in 24 countries in Eastern and Central Europe, the former Soviet Union, North Africa, and Asia. The region will support 1,359 new trainees.

Inter-America and Pacific Region.—An average of 2,003 Volunteers will work in 30 countries in the Caribbean, Central America, South America, and the Pacific. This office will also fund 1,240 new trainees in 2000.

Other Volunteer Support.—These activities fund a wide range of volunteer- and program-related costs, including medical support for Volunteers, recruitment and placement, technical resources, domestic programs, policy and direction, and related administration and oversight.

Object Classification (in millions of dollars)

Identification code 11–0100–0–1–151	1999 actual	2000 est.	2001 est.
Direct obligations:			
Personnel compensation:			
11.1 Full-time permanent	46	47	50
11.3 Other than full-time permanent	2	2	2
11.5 Other personnel compensation	1	2	2
Special personal services payments:			
11.8 Special personal services payments	....	1	1
11.8 Trainees and volunteers	26	22	24
11.9 Total personnel compensation	75	74	79
12.1 Civilian personnel benefits	41	43	45
21.0 Travel and transportation of persons	28	29	31
22.0 Transportation of things	1	5	5
23.1 Rental payments to GSA	7	7	8
23.2 Rental payments to others	8	8	8
23.3 Communications, utilities, and miscellaneous charges	6	7	8
24.0 Printing and reproduction	1	1	1
25.2 Other services	38	42	45
25.3 Purchases of goods and services from Government accounts	5	6	8
25.4 Operation and maintenance of facilities	1	1	1
25.6 Medical care	14	12	13
25.7 Operation and maintenance of equipment	1	1	1
26.0 Supplies and materials	11	9	9
31.0 Equipment	11	11	12
99.0 Subtotal, direct obligations	248	256	274
99.0 Reimbursable obligations	6	6	6
99.5 Below reporting threshold	2	2	2
99.9 Total new obligations	256	264	282

Personnel Summary

Identification code 11–0100–0–1–151	1999 actual	2000 est.	2001 est.
Direct:			
1001 Total compensable workyears: Full-time equivalent employment	1,048	1,155	1,162
Reimbursable:			
2001 Total compensable workyears: Full-time equivalent employment	4	4	4

Peace Corps Miscellaneous Trust Funds

Unavailable Collections (in millions of dollars)

Identification code 11–9972–0–7–151	1999 actual	2000 est.	2001 est.
Balance, start of year:			
01.99 Balance, start of year	....	....	....
Receipts:			
02.01 Miscellaneous trust funds, Peace Corps	1	1	1
Appropriation:			
05.01 Peace Corps miscellaneous trust fund	–1	–1	–1
07.99 Total balance, end of year	....	....	....

Program and Financing (in millions of dollars)

Identification code 11–9972–0–7–151	1999 actual	2000 est.	2001 est.
Obligations by program activity:			
10.00 Total new obligations (object class 26.0)	1	2	1
Budgetary resources available for obligation:			
21.40 Unobligated balance available, start of year	1	2	1
22.00 New budget authority (gross)	1	1	1
23.90 Total budgetary resources available for obligation	2	2	2
23.95 Total new obligations	–1	–2	–1
24.40 Unobligated balance available, end of year	2	1	1
New budget authority (gross), detail:			
Mandatory:			
60.27 Appropriation (trust fund, indefinite)	1	1	1
Change in unpaid obligations:			
73.10 Total new obligations	1	2	1
73.20 Total outlays (gross)	–1	–1	–1
Outlays (gross), detail:			
86.98 Outlays from mandatory balances	1	1	1
Net budget authority and outlays:			
89.00 Budget authority	1	1	1
90.00 Outlays	1	1	1

Miscellaneous contributions received by gift, devise, bequest, or from foreign governments are used for the furtherance of the program, as authorized by 22 U.S.C. 2509(a)(3) (75 Stat. 612, as amended). Trust funds also include a fund to pay separation costs for Foreign Service National employees of the Peace Corps in those countries in which such pay is legally authorized. The fund, as authorized by Public Law 102–138, is maintained by annual Government contributions which are appropriated in the Peace Corps salaries and expenses account.

Personnel Summary

Identification code 11–9972–0–7–151	1999 actual	2000 est.	2001 est.
1001 Total compensable workyears: Full-time equivalent employment	3	3	3

INTER-AMERICAN FOUNDATION

Federal Funds

General and special funds:

Inter-American Foundation

For expenses necessary to carry out the functions of the Inter-American Foundation in accordance with the provisions of section 401 of the Foreign Assistance Act of 1969, $20,000,000, to remain available until September 30, 2002.

Program and Financing (in millions of dollars)

Identification code 11–3100–0–1–151	1999 actual	2000 est.	2001 est.
Obligations by program activity:			
00.01 Development grants	23	15	21
00.02 Evaluations and other activities	3	1	1
00.04 Program management and operations	7	6	5
10.00 Total new obligations	33	22	27
Budgetary resources available for obligation:			
21.40 Unobligated balance available, start of year	25	21	9
22.00 New budget authority (gross)	28	10	20
23.90 Total budgetary resources available for obligation	53	31	29
23.95 Total new obligations	–33	–22	–27
24.40 Unobligated balance available, end of year	21	9	2
New budget authority (gross), detail:			
Discretionary:			
40.00 Appropriation	....	....	20
42.00 Transferred from other accounts	20	5	....
43.00 Appropriation (total discretionary)	20	5	20
68.00 Spending authority from offsetting collections: Offsetting collections (cash)	8	5	....
70.00 Total new budget authority (gross)	28	10	20
Change in unpaid obligations:			
72.40 Unpaid obligations, start of year: Obligated balance, start of year	29	40	41
73.10 Total new obligations	33	22	27
73.20 Total outlays (gross)	–21	–21	–28
74.40 Unpaid obligations, end of year: Obligated balance, end of year	40	41	40
Outlays (gross), detail:			
86.90 Outlays from new discretionary authority	9	6	9
86.93 Outlays from discretionary balances	12	15	19

General and special funds—Continued

INTER-AMERICAN FOUNDATION—Continued

Program and Financing (in millions of dollars)—Continued

Identification code 11–3100–0–1–151	1999 actual	2000 est.	2001 est.
87.00 Total outlays (gross)	21	21	28
Offsets:			
Against gross budget authority and outlays:			
88.00 Offsetting collections (cash) from: Federal sources	−8	−5	
Net budget authority and outlays:			
89.00 Budget authority	20	5	20
90.00 Outlays	13	16	28

Established by the 1969 Foreign Assistance Act, the Inter-American Foundation (IAF) supports grassroots development initiatives in Latin America and the Caribbean with a direct impact on the lives and the capacity for self reliance of people at the lowest economic levels. In 2001, the IAF will continue its new strategic programming approaches that focus on: (1) building partnerships among grassroots organizations, non-governmental organizations, local governments, and private enterprises to foster social and economic development at the local level; and, (2) increasing the participation of U.S. corporate and national private business sector resources in grassroots development initiatives. This strategy entails the promotion of corporate and business social investment in Latin America and the Caribbean among the U.S. private business sector to address a host of social and economic issues that will improve the quality of life of the poor in the region. The IAF will continue to apply its system of measuring the results of its grants to improve Foundation decision-making and identify and disseminate good practice and lessons to new private sector contributors and development practitioners. Using results and evaluation information, the IAF will incorporate lessons learned into the IAF's strategic planning and grant decision-making processes. It will also disseminate the results assessment system and development information to new private sector contributors, to donors, and to grassroots practitioners. The IAF will also implement an integrated program management information system which will increase efficiency in its operations and facilitate grant monitoring and results reporting.

Development Grants.—This activity includes the cost of all grants made directly to local private, non-profit organizations working in partnerships with businesses and local authorities to carry out development projects in Latin America and the Caribbean. In 2001, the IAF plans to award approximately 50 grants and 5 grant supplements in 10 countries.

Evaluations and Other Activities.—This activity funds grant results assessments by in-country specialists and evaluations from a sample of the grants supported by the IAF. This activity also funds the publications that convey the IAF's partnership, corporate social responsibility experiences, and lessons to businesses, development practitioners, members of partnerships, and other donors.

Program Management and Operation.—This activity includes Foundation expenses for salaries and benefits, travel, rent, service contracts, and other support costs.

Object Classification (in millions of dollars)

Identification code 11–3100–0–1–151	1999 actual	2000 est.	2001 est.
11.1 Personnel compensation: Full-time permanent	4	3	3
12.1 Civilian personnel benefits	1	1	1
23.2 Rental payments to others	1	1	1
25.1 Advisory and assistance services	2	1	1
41.0 Grants, subsidies, and contributions	24	15	21
99.0 Subtotal, direct obligations	32	21	27
99.5 Below reporting threshold	1	1	
99.9 Total new obligations	33	22	27

Personnel Summary

Identification code 11–3100–0–1–151	1999 actual	2000 est.	2001 est.
1001 Total compensable workyears: Full-time equivalent employment	59	54	50

AFRICAN DEVELOPMENT FOUNDATION

Federal Funds

General and special funds:

AFRICAN DEVELOPMENT FOUNDATION

To carry out Title V of the International Security and Development Cooperation Act of 1980, Public Law 96–533, $16,000,000 to remain available until September 30, 2002: Provided, That funds made available to grantees may be invested pending expenditure for project purposes when authorized by the President of the Foundation: Provided further, That interest earned shall be used only for the purposes for which the grant was made: Provided further, That this authority applies to interest earned both prior to and following enactment of this provision: Provided further, That notwithstanding section 505(a)(2) of the African Development Foundation Act, in exceptional circumstances the board of directors of the Foundation may waive the $250,000 limitation contained in that section with respect to a project: Provided further, That the Foundation shall provide a report to the Committees on Appropriations after such waiver authority is exercised: Provided further, That amounts obligated hereunder and any appropriations heretofore are, if deobligated, available for reobligation for the same period as the respective appropriations or until September 30, 2001, whichever is later and for the same general purpose as originally obligated: Provided, That the Committees on Appropriations are notified 15 days in advance of the reobligation of such funds in accordance with the regular notification procedures of such Committees.

Program and Financing (in millions of dollars)

Identification code 11–0700–0–1–151	1999 actual	2000 est.	2001 est.
Obligations by program activity:			
00.01 Advance sustainable development and empowerment of the poor in Africa	8	10	12
00.02 Enhance US assistance and relations with Africa	1	1	1
00.03 Expand use of participatory development policies and practices	1	2	2
00.04 Internal agency objectives	1	1	1
10.00 Total new obligations	11	14	16
Budgetary resources available for obligation:			
21.40 Unobligated balance available, start of year			
22.00 New budget authority (gross)	12	15	17
23.90 Total budgetary resources available for obligation	12	15	17
23.95 Total new obligations	−11	−14	−16
New budget authority (gross), detail:			
Discretionary:			
40.00 Appropriation			16
42.00 Transferred from other accounts	11	14	
43.00 Appropriation (total discretionary)	11	14	16
68.00 Spending authority from offsetting collections: Offsetting collections (cash)	1	1	1
70.00 Total new budget authority (gross)	12	15	17
Change in unpaid obligations:			
72.40 Unpaid obligations, start of year: Obligated balance, start of year	17	17	17
73.10 Total new obligations	11	14	16
73.20 Total outlays (gross)	−12	−14	−17
74.40 Unpaid obligations, end of year: Obligated balance, end of year	17	17	18
Outlays (gross), detail:			
86.90 Outlays from new discretionary authority	6	7	8

86.93	Outlays from discretionary balances	6	7	9
87.00	Total outlays (gross)	12	14	17
	Offsets:			
	Against gross budget authority and outlays:			
88.00	Offsetting collections (cash) from: Federal sources	−1	−1	−1
	Net budget authority and outlays:			
89.00	Budget authority	11	14	16
90.00	Outlays	11	13	16

The African Development Foundation (ADF), a public corporation, is a unique agency of the U.S. Government that supports community-based, self-help initiatives to alleviate poverty and to promote sustainable development in Africa. Through its grant program, ADF has pioneered participatory development in Africa. Foundation grants are made directly to grassroots African groups and foster self-reliance through the promotion of African leadership and ownership of the development process.

In 2001, ADF will provide assistance to fifteen countries in Africa. This budget request will fund the Foundation's operating costs and almost 100 small grants to African non-governmental organizations, community-based groups and researchers. ADF has three strategic goals.

Program Components:

(1) Advance sustainable development and empowerment of the poor in Africa.—ADF will promote micro and small enterprise development which will generate employment and enhance income. ADF will also seek to improve community-based natural resource management for sustainable rural development. Increasing participation of African grassroots enterprises and producer groups in trade and investment relationships with the U.S. and within Africa is another primary focus of ADF. Finally, ADF will work to strengthen civil society and local governance and to encourage African governments to expand grassroots participation in policy-making and resource allocation processes. Examples of projects which will be funded are: micro-finance capital; business development services, training and technical assistance; soil and water reclamation; civic education; and advocacy training.

(2) Enhance U.S. assistance and relations with Africa.—ADF will share its experience and encourage expanded U.S. funding for participatory grassroots development, improve program and policy coordination on grassroots development among U.S. foreign assistance and foreign policy agencies, and leverage public and private resources through strategic partnerships.

(3) Expand use of participatory development policies and practices.—ADF will intensify its efforts to develop, evaluate and disseminate new interventions and methodologies for participatory development, and encourage African governments to increase utilization of participatory development "best practices."

Object Classification (in millions of dollars)

Identification code 11–0700–0–1–151		1999 actual	2000 est.	2001 est.
11.1	Personnel compensation: Full-time permanent	2	2	2
41.0	Grants, subsidies, and contributions	8	10	12
99.0	Subtotal, direct obligations	10	12	14
99.5	Below reporting threshold	1	2	2
99.9	Total new obligations	11	14	16

Personnel Summary

Identification code 11–0700–0–1–151		1999 actual	2000 est.	2001 est.
1001	Total compensable workyears: Full-time equivalent employment	26	28	29

INTERNATIONAL MONETARY PROGRAMS

Federal Funds

General and special funds:

UNITED STATES QUOTA IN THE INTERNATIONAL MONETARY FUND

Program and Financing (in millions of dollars)

Identification code 11–0003–0–1–155		1999 actual	2000 est.	2001 est.
	Obligations by program activity:			
00.01	Quota Increase	14,763		
00.02	Direct program	562		
10.00	Total new obligations	15,325		
	Budgetary resources available for obligation:			
21.40	Unobligated balance available, start of year	20,902	19,166	19,166
22.00	New budget authority (gross)	14,763		
22.10	Resources available from recoveries of prior year obligations	−820		
23.90	Total budgetary resources available for obligation	34,845	19,166	19,166
23.95	Total new obligations	−15,325		
23.98	Unobligated balance expiring or withdrawn	−353		
24.40	Unobligated balance available, end of year	19,166	19,166	19,166
	New budget authority (gross), detail:			
	Discretionary:			
40.00	Appropriation	14,763		
	Change in unpaid obligations:			
72.40	Unpaid obligations, start of year: Obligated balance, start of year	15,137	31,449	31,449
73.10	Total new obligations	15,325		
73.20	Total outlays (gross)	167		
73.45	Adjustments in unexpired accounts	820		
74.40	Unpaid obligations, end of year: Obligated balance, end of year	31,449	31,449	31,449
	Outlays (gross), detail:			
86.98	Outlays from mandatory balances	−167		
	Net budget authority and outlays:			
89.00	Budget authority	14,763		
90.00	Outlays	−167		

As part of a general increase in IMF quota resources, on November 17, 1998, the United States consented to an increase in its quota to SDR 37,149.3 million (about $52 billion). The increase in the U.S. quota involves no net budget outlays. Similarly, use by the IMF of the quota commitment does not result in net budget outlays because the United States receives an increase in its international monetary reserves corresponding to any transfer of dollars under the U.S. quota subscription. The United States can use these interest-bearing reserves to meet a balance of payments financing need.

FOR LOANS TO THE INTERNATIONAL MONETARY FUND—NEW ARRANGEMENTS TO BORROW

Program and Financing (in millions of dollars)

Identification code 11–0074–0–1–155		1999 actual	2000 est.	2001 est.
	Obligations by program activity:			
00.01	Direct Program Activity	458		
10.00	Total new obligations	458		
	Budgetary resources available for obligation:			
21.40	Unobligated balance available, start of year	5,319	9,710	9,710
22.00	New budget authority (gross)	3,450		
22.10	Resources available from recoveries of prior year obligations	1,399		
23.90	Total budgetary resources available for obligation	10,168	9,710	9,710
23.95	Total new obligations	−458		
24.40	Unobligated balance available, end of year	9,710	9,710	9,710

General and special funds—Continued

FOR LOANS TO THE INTERNATIONAL MONETARY FUND—NEW ARRANGEMENTS TO BORROW—Continued

Program and Financing (in millions of dollars)—Continued

Identification code 11–0074–0–1–155	1999 actual	2000 est.	2001 est.
New budget authority (gross), detail:			
Discretionary:			
40.00 Appropriation	3,450		
Change in unpaid obligations:			
72.40 Unpaid obligations, start of year: Obligated balance, start of year	941		
73.10 Total new obligations	458		
73.45 Adjustments in unexpired accounts	−1,399		
Net budget authority and outlays:			
89.00 Budget authority	3,450		
90.00 Outlays			

The General Arrangements to Borrow (GAB) were established in 1962 by 10 industrial countries, including the United States, as a means of supplementing the IMF's resources when needed to forestall or cope with an impairment of the international monetary system. GAB members agreed in early 1983 to increase their financial commitments to the GAB from approximately SDR 6.3 billion to SDR 17 billion, with the U.S. share rising from $2.0 billion to approximately $6.4 billion.

In January 1997, the Executive Board of the IMF approved the creation of the New Arrangements to Borrow (NAB) to further supplement resources available to the IMF to forestall or cope with an impairment of the international monetary system or to deal with an exceptional situation that poses a threat to the stability of the system. The NAB became effective on November 17, 1998. Twenty-five countries and institutions participate in the NAB through a set of credit arrangements with the IMF totaling SDR 34 billion (about $48 billion on the date of establishment), of which the U.S. share is approximately SDR 6.7 billion (about $9.4 billion). Although the GAB continues to exist, the sum of loans advanced under the NAB and GAB cannot exceed SDR 34 billion. The sum of U.S. loans advanced under both arrangements cannot exceed the U.S. share of the NAB.

Financing extended by the United States under the GAB and NAB does not result in any net budget outlays because such financing results in an equivalent increase in U.S. international reserve assets in the form of a claim on the IMF.

During 1998 (July), the IMF made one call on GAB participants in support of an assistance program for Russia, of which the U.S. share was approximately $483 million. On December 15, 1998, the IMF made a call on NAB participants in support of an assistance program for Brazil, of which the U.S. share was approximately $860 million. The GAB and NAB loans were paid back in full on March 11, 1999. In 1999, no calls were made on GAB or NAB participants, and no loans were outstanding at the end of the fiscal year.

CONTRIBUTION TO THE ENHANCED STRUCTURAL ADJUSTMENT FACILITY OF THE INTERNATIONAL MONETARY FUND

Program and Financing (in millions of dollars)

Identification code 11–0005–0–1–155	1999 actual	2000 est.	2001 est.
Change in unpaid obligations:			
72.40 Unpaid obligations, start of year: Obligated balance, start of year	48	26	10
73.20 Total outlays (gross)	−22	−16	−10
74.40 Unpaid obligations, end of year: Obligated balance, end of year	26	10	
Outlays (gross), detail:			
86.93 Outlays from discretionary balances	22	16	10
Net budget authority and outlays:			
89.00 Budget authority			
90.00 Outlays	22	16	10

On November 22, 1999, the Enhanced Structural Adjustment Facility (ESAF) was replaced by Poverty Reduction and Growth Facility (PRGF). Like the ESAF, the PRGF will provide financing on concessional terms to poor countries with protracted balance of payments problems. As its name suggests, however, the PRGF aims to make poverty reduction efforts among low-income member countries of the IMF a key and more explicit element of a growth-oriented economic strategy. Other defining features of the new PRGF approach include: (1) reliance on a comprehensive poverty reduction strategy to be prepared by the national authorities of the borrowing country in consultation with the public and civil society groups (this strategy will serve as a point of reference and guide for both IMF and World Bank concessional lending activities in a particular country); (2) closer cooperation between staffs of the IMF and World Bank; (3) stronger linkage between macroeconomics policies, on the one hand, and poverty reduction and growth objectives on the other; and (4) greater emphasis on good governance.

Certain terms and conditions that applied to ESAF will continue to apply to the PRGF. For example, the same set of countries that were eligible for ESAF will also be eligible for the new facility. Commitments of IMF resources will continue to be based on a three-year program incorporating performance criteria and periodic reviews of progress. Disbursement of financing will be semiannual (or quarterly in select cases), the interest rate will be 0.5 percent, and loans will mature in 5½–10 years.

Like the ESAF, the PRGF will advance critical U.S. interests by promoting economic and financial conditions which foster growth, stability, and the development of more open and accountable democratic institutions.

Financing for the PRGF, as for the ESAF, is provided by members of the IMF through loans to a trust account (formerly the ESAF Trust, now the PRGF Trust), or through contributions to an interest subsidy account.

MILITARY SALES PROGRAMS

Federal Funds

Public enterprise funds:

SPECIAL DEFENSE ACQUISITION FUND

Program and Financing (in millions of dollars)

Identification code 11–4116–0–3–155	1999 actual	2000 est.	2001 est.
Obligations by program activity:			
09.00 Reimbursable program		18	
10.00 Total new obligations (object class 25.2)		18	
Budgetary resources available for obligation:			
21.40 Unobligated balance available, start of year	110	63	63
22.00 New budget authority (gross)		18	
22.10 Resources available from recoveries of prior year obligations	1		
22.40 Capital transfer to general fund	−48		
23.90 Total budgetary resources available for obligation	63	81	63
23.95 Total new obligations		−18	
24.40 Unobligated balance available, end of year	63	63	63
New budget authority (gross), detail:			
Discretionary:			
40.29 Appropriation available in prior year		18	
Spending authority from offsetting collections:			
68.00 Offsetting collections (cash)	8	10	

68.27	Capital transfer to general fund	−8	−10	
70.00	Total new budget authority (gross)		18	
	Change in unpaid obligations:			
72.40	Unpaid obligations, start of year: Obligated balance, start of year	28	20	20
73.10	Total new obligations		18	
73.20	Total outlays (gross)	−6	−18	−6
73.45	Adjustments in unexpired accounts	−1		
74.40	Unpaid obligations, end of year: Obligated balance, end of year	20	20	15
	Outlays (gross), detail:			
86.90	Outlays from new discretionary authority		17	
86.93	Outlays from discretionary balances	6	1	6
87.00	Total outlays (gross)	6	18	6
	Offsets:			
	Against gross budget authority and outlays:			
88.40	Offsetting collections (cash) from: Non-Federal sources	−8	−10	
	Net budget authority and outlays:			
89.00	Budget authority	−8	8	
90.00	Outlays	−2	8	6

This fund shows the financing transactions related to the procurement of defense articles prior to orders being placed by foreign countries and international organizations. This program is being phased out.

Trust Funds

FOREIGN MILITARY SALES TRUST FUND

Unavailable Collections (in millions of dollars)

Identification code 11–8242–0–7–155		1999 actual	2000 est.	2001 est.
	Balance, start of year:			
01.99	Encumbered future receipts, start of year	−14,652	−11,740	−10,250
	Receipts:			
02.01	Deposits, advances, foreign military sales	11,624	10,560	10,760
04.00	Total: Balances and collections	−3,028	−1,180	510
	Appropriation:			
05.01	Foreign military sales trust fund	−8,712	−9,070	−10,730
07.99	Total balance, end of year	−11,740	−10,250	−10,220

Program and Financing (in millions of dollars)

Identification code 11–8242–0–7–155		1999 actual	2000 est.	2001 est.
	Obligations by program activity:			
09.01	Military personnel	82	57	67
09.02	Operations and maintenance	260	173	205
09.03	Procurement	7,286	7,616	9,162
09.04	Research, development, test and evaluation	37	13	16
09.05	Special defense acquisition fund	6	10	
09.06	Revolving and management funds	624	712	842
09.07	Construction	79	83	98
09.08	Other	338	406	340
10.00	Total new obligations (object class 25.3)	8,712	9,070	10,730
	Budgetary resources available for obligation:			
22.00	New budget authority (gross)	8,712	9,070	10,730
23.95	Total new obligations	−8,712	−9,070	−10,730
	New budget authority (gross), detail:			
	Mandatory:			
60.27	Appropriation (trust fund, indefinite)	11,624	10,560	10,760
60.49	Portion applied to liquidate contract authority	−11,624	−10,560	−10,760
66.15	Contract authority (indefinite)	8,712	9,070	10,730
70.00	Total new budget authority (gross)	8,712	9,070	10,730
	Change in unpaid obligations:			
	Unpaid obligations, start of year:			
72.40	Obligated balance, start of year	6,044	5,509	5,509
72.49	Obligated balance, start of year: Contract authority	14,652	11,740	10,250
72.99	Total unpaid obligations, start of year	20,696	17,249	15,759
73.10	Total new obligations	8,712	9,070	10,730
73.20	Total outlays (gross)	−12,159	−10,560	−10,760
	Unpaid obligations, end of year:			
74.40	Obligated balance, end of year	5,509	5,509	5,509
74.49	Obligated balance, end of year: Contract authority	11,740	10,250	10,220
74.99	Total unpaid obligations, end of year	17,249	15,759	15,729
	Outlays (gross), detail:			
86.97	Outlays from new mandatory authority	1,398	1,214	1,237
86.98	Outlays from mandatory balances	10,761	9,346	9,523
87.00	Total outlays (gross)	12,159	10,560	10,760
	Net budget authority and outlays:			
89.00	Budget authority	8,712	9,070	10,730
90.00	Outlays	12,159	10,560	10,760

Status of Contract Authority (in millions of dollars)

Identification code 11–8242–0–7–155		1999 actual	2000 est.	2001 est.
0100	Balance, start of year	14,652	11,740	10,250
	Contract authority:			
0200	Contract authority	8,712	9,070	10,730
0400	Appropriation to liquidate contract authority	−11,624	−10,560	−10,760
0700	Balance, end of year	11,740	10,250	10,220

This trust fund facilitates government-to-government sales of defense articles, defense services, and design and construction services. Estimates of sales used in this budget are (in millions of dollars):

ESTIMATES OF NEW SALES

	1999 actual	*2000 est.*	*2001 est.*
Estimates of new orders (sales)	12,207	12,713	14,912

Orders placed through this trust fund can be combined with procurement for U.S. military departments. The savings are shared by the United States and foreign governments. The net impact of foreign military sales on the budget is (in millions of dollars):

FMS TRUST FUND TRANSACTIONS

	1999 actual	*2000 est.*	*2001 est.*
Obligations of the fund	8,712	9,070	10,730
Receipts from foreign governments (appropriation)	–11,624	–10,560	–10,760
Net budget authority	–2,912	–1,490	–30
Payments from the fund (outlays)	12,159	10,560	10,760
Receipts from foreign governments (appropriation)	11,624	–10,560	–10,760
Net outlays	535	0	0

KUWAIT CIVIL RECONSTRUCTION TRUST FUND

Program and Financing (in millions of dollars)

Identification code 11–8238–0–7–155		1999 actual	2000 est.	2001 est.
	Budgetary resources available for obligation:			
21.40	Unobligated balance available, start of year	2	2	2
23.98	Unobligated balance expiring or withdrawn			
24.40	Unobligated balance available, end of year	2	2	2
	Net budget authority and outlays:			
89.00	Budget authority			
90.00	Outlays			

This trust fund was established to show the U.S. costs in helping the Government of Kuwait survey and assess the

KUWAIT CIVIL RECONSTRUCTION TRUST FUND—Continued

cost of repairing its civil infrastructure. This program is being phased out.

SPECIAL ASSISTANCE FOR CENTRAL AMERICA

Federal Funds

General and special funds:

DEMOBILIZATION AND TRANSITION FUND

Program and Financing (in millions of dollars)

Identification code 72–1500–0–1–152	1999 actual	2000 est.	2001 est.
Change in unpaid obligations:			
72.40 Unpaid obligations, start of year: Obligated balance, start of year	3	3	3
74.40 Unpaid obligations, end of year: Obligated balance, end of year	3	3	3
Outlays (gross), detail:			
86.93 Outlays from discretionary balances	1		
Net budget authority and outlays:			
89.00 Budget authority			
90.00 Outlays	1		

Funds for this account were transferred from Foreign Military Financing pursuant to P.L. 101–513 to support costs of demobilization, retraining, relocation, and reemployment in civilian pursuits of former combatants in the conflict in El Salvador.

CENTRAL AMERICAN RECONCILIATION ASSISTANCE

Program and Financing (in millions of dollars)

Identification code 72–1038–0–1–152	1999 actual	2000 est.	2001 est.
Change in unpaid obligations:			
72.40 Unpaid obligations, start of year: Obligated balance, start of year	1	1	1
74.40 Unpaid obligations, end of year: Obligated balance, end of year	1	1	1
Net budget authority and outlays:			
89.00 Budget authority			
90.00 Outlays			

Funds for this account were transferred from the Department of Defense in accordance with Public Law 101–14 in order to provide humanitarian assistance to the Nicaraguan democratic resistance. Adjustments to the account were made in Public Law 101–119 and Public Law 101–215.

GENERAL FUND RECEIPT ACCOUNTS

(in millions of dollars)

	1999 actual	2000 est.	2001 est.
Offsetting receipts from the public:			
11–146800 Interest on foreign military credit sales	131		
11–272430 Foreign military financing, downward reestimates of subsidies	3		
11–296800 Repayment of loans, foreign military credit sales	367		
11–310800 Return of contribution to international buffer stocks		80	
72–273130 Assistance for the New Independent States of the Former Soviet Union: Ukraine export credit insurance, downward reestimates		30	
72–304200 Recoveries from the Polish American enterprise fund		80	40
General Fund Offsetting receipts from the public	501	190	40

TITLE V—GENERAL PROVISIONS

OBLIGATIONS DURING LAST MONTH OF AVAILABILITY

SEC. 501. Except for the appropriations entitled "International Disaster Assistance", and "United States Emergency Refugee and Migration Assistance Fund", not more than 15 percent of any appropriation item made available by this Act shall be obligated during the last month of availability.

PROHIBITION OF BILATERAL FUNDING FOR INTERNATIONAL FINANCIAL INSTITUTIONS

SEC. 502. Notwithstanding section 614 of the Foreign Assistance Act of 1961, none of the funds contained in title II of this Act may be used to carry out the provisions of section 209(d) of the Foreign Assistance Act of 1961[: *Provided*, That none of the funds appropriated by title II of this Act may be transferred by the Agency for International Development directly to an international financial institution (as defined in section 533 of this Act) for the purpose of repaying a foreign country's loan obligations to such institution].

LIMITATION ON RESIDENCE EXPENSES

SEC. 503. Of the funds appropriated or made available pursuant to this Act, not to exceed $126,500 shall be for official residence expenses of the Agency for International Development during the current fiscal year: *Provided*, That appropriate steps shall be taken to assure that, to the maximum extent possible, United States-owned foreign currencies are utilized in lieu of dollars.

LIMITATION ON EXPENSES

SEC. 504. Of the funds appropriated or made available pursuant to this Act, not to exceed $5,000 shall be for entertainment expenses of the Agency for International Development during the current fiscal year.

LIMITATION ON REPRESENTATIONAL ALLOWANCES

SEC. 505. Of the funds appropriated or made available pursuant to this Act, not to exceed $95,000 shall be available for representation allowances for the Agency for International Development during the current fiscal year: *Provided*, That appropriate steps shall be taken to assure that, to the maximum extent possible, United States-owned foreign currencies are utilized in lieu of dollars: *Provided further*, That of the funds made available by this Act for general costs of administering military assistance and sales under the heading "Foreign Military Financing Program", not to exceed $2,000 shall be available for entertainment expenses and not to exceed $50,000 shall be available for representation allowances: *Provided further*, That of the funds made available by this Act under the heading "International Military Education and Training", not to exceed $50,000 shall be available for entertainment allowances: *Provided further*, That of the funds made available by this Act for the Inter-American Foundation, not to exceed $2,000 shall be available for entertainment and representation allowances: *Provided further*, That of the funds made available by this Act for the Peace Corps, not to exceed a total of $4,000 shall be available for entertainment expenses: *Provided further*, That of the funds made available by this Act under the heading "Trade and Development Agency", not to exceed $2,000 shall be available for representation and entertainment allowances.

PROHIBITION ON FINANCING NUCLEAR GOODS

SEC. 506. None of the funds appropriated or made available (other than funds for "Nonproliferation, Anti-terrorism, Demining and Related Programs") pursuant to this Act, for carrying out the Foreign Assistance Act of 1961, may be used, except for purposes of nuclear safety, to finance the export of nuclear equipment, fuel, or technology.

PROHIBITION AGAINST DIRECT FUNDING FOR CERTAIN COUNTRIES

SEC. 507. None of the funds appropriated or otherwise made available pursuant to this Act shall be obligated or expended to finance directly any assistance or reparations to Cuba, Iraq, Libya, North Korea, Iran, Sudan, or Syria *unless the President determines that to do so is in the national interest of the United States*: *Provided*, That for purposes of this section, the prohibition on obligations or expenditures shall include direct loans, credits, insurance and guarantees of the Export-Import Bank or its agents.

MILITARY COUPS

SEC. 508. None of the funds appropriated or otherwise made available pursuant to this Act shall be obligated or expended to finance directly any assistance to any country whose duly elected head of government is deposed by military coup or decree: *Provided*, That assistance may be resumed to such country if the President determines and reports to the Committees on Appropriations that subsequent to the termination of assistance a democratically elected government has taken office: *Provided further, That this section shall not apply to assistance to promote democracy and the rule of law for the purpose of supporting a country's transition to democratic government.*

TRANSFERS BETWEEN ACCOUNTS

SEC. 509. None of the funds made available by this Act may be obligated under an appropriation account to which they were not appropriated, except for transfers specifically provided for in this Act, unless the President, prior to the exercise of any authority contained in the Foreign Assistance Act of 1961 to transfer funds, consults with and provides a written policy justification to the Committees on Appropriations of the House of Representatives and the Senate.

DEOBLIGATION/REOBLIGATION AUTHORITY

SEC. 510. (a) Amounts certified pursuant to section 1311 of the Supplemental Appropriations Act, 1955, as having been obligated against appropriations heretofore made under the authority of the Foreign Assistance Act of 1961 for the same general purpose as any of the headings under title II of this Act are, if deobligated, hereby continued available for the same period as the respective appropriations under such headings or until September 30, [2000] *2001*, whichever is later, and for the same general purpose, and for countries within the same region as originally obligated: *Provided*, That the Appropriations Committees of both Houses of the Congress are notified 15 days in advance of the reobligation of such funds in accordance with regular notification procedures of the Committees on Appropriations.

(b) Obligated balances of funds appropriated to carry out section 23 of the Arms Export Control Act as of the end of the fiscal year immediately preceding the current fiscal year are, if deobligated, hereby continued available during the current fiscal year for the same purpose under any authority applicable to such appropriations under this Act: *Provided*, That the authority of this subsection may not be used in fiscal year [2000] *2001*.

AVAILABILITY OF FUNDS

SEC. 511. No part of any appropriation contained in this Act shall remain available for obligation after the expiration of the current fiscal year unless expressly so provided in this Act: *Provided*, That funds appropriated for the purposes of chapters 1, 8, [and 11] *11, and 12* of part I, section 667, and chapter 4 of part II of the Foreign Assistance Act of 1961, as amended, and funds provided under the heading "Assistance for Eastern Europe and the Baltic States", shall remain available until expended if such funds are initially obligated before the expiration of their respective periods of availability contained in this Act: *Provided further*, That, notwithstanding any other provision of this Act, any funds made available for the purposes of chapter 1 of part I and chapter 4 of part II of the Foreign Assistance Act of 1961 which are allocated or obligated for cash disbursements in order to address balance of payments or economic policy reform objectives, shall remain available until expended: *Provided further*, That the report required by section 653(a) of the Foreign Assistance Act of 1961 shall designate for each country, to the extent known at the time of submission of such report, those funds allocated for cash disbursement for balance of payment and economic policy reform purposes.

LIMITATION ON ASSISTANCE TO COUNTRIES IN DEFAULT

SEC. 512. No part of any appropriation contained in this Act shall be used to furnish assistance to *the government of* any country which is in default during a period in excess of one calendar year in payment to the United States of principal or interest on any loan made to such [country] *government* by the United States pursuant to a program for which funds are appropriated under this Act, *unless the President determines that to do so is in the national interest of the United States*: *Provided*, That this section and section 620(q) of the Foreign Assistance Act of 1961 shall not apply to funds [made] available *during the current fiscal year for Liberia, the Democratic Republic of Congo, and* for any narcotics-related assistance for Colombia, Bolivia, and Peru authorized by the Foreign Assistance Act of 1961 or the Arms Export Control Act.

[COMMERCE AND TRADE]

[SEC. 513. (a) None of the funds appropriated or made available pursuant to this Act for direct assistance and none of the funds otherwise made available pursuant to this Act to the Export-Import Bank and the Overseas Private Investment Corporation shall be obligated or expended to finance any loan, any assistance or any other financial commitments for establishing or expanding production of any commodity for export by any country other than the United States, if the commodity is likely to be in surplus on world markets at the time the resulting productive capacity is expected to become operative and if the assistance will cause substantial injury to United States producers of the same, similar, or competing commodity: *Provided*, That such prohibition shall not apply to the Export-Import Bank if in the judgment of its Board of Directors the benefits to industry and employment in the United States are likely to outweigh the injury to United States producers of the same, similar, or competing commodity, and the Chairman of the Board so notifies the Committees on Appropriations.]

[(b) None of the funds appropriated by this or any other Act to carry out chapter 1 of part I of the Foreign Assistance Act of 1961 shall be available for any testing or breeding feasibility study, variety improvement or introduction, consultancy, publication, conference, or training in connection with the growth or production in a foreign country of an agricultural commodity for export which would compete with a similar commodity grown or produced in the United States: *Provided*, That this subsection shall not prohibit—

(1) activities designed to increase food security in developing countries where such activities will not have a significant impact in the export of agricultural commodities of the United States; or

(2) research activities intended primarily to benefit American producers.]

[SURPLUS COMMODITIES]

[SEC. 514. The Secretary of the Treasury shall instruct the United States Executive Directors of the International Bank for Reconstruction and Development, the International Development Association, the International Finance Corporation, the Inter-American Development Bank, the International Monetary Fund, the Asian Development Bank, the Inter-American Investment Corporation, the North American Development Bank, the European Bank for Reconstruction and Development, the African Development Bank, and the African Development Fund to use the voice and vote of the United States to oppose any assistance by these institutions, using funds appropriated or made available pursuant to this Act, for the production or extraction of any commodity or mineral for export, if it is in surplus on world markets and if the assistance will cause substantial injury to United States producers of the same, similar, or competing commodity.]

NOTIFICATION REQUIREMENTS

SEC. [515] *513*. (a) For the purposes of providing the executive branch with the necessary administrative flexibility, none of the funds made available under this Act for "Child Survival and Disease Programs Fund", "Development Assistance", *"Development Fund for Africa"*, "International Organizations and Programs", "Trade and Development Agency", "International Narcotics Control and Law Enforcement", "Assistance for Eastern Europe and the Baltic States", "Assistance for the Independent States of the Former Soviet Union", "Economic Support Fund", "Peacekeeping Operations", "Operating Expenses of the Agency for International Development", "Operating Expenses of the Agency for International Development Office of Inspector General", "Nonproliferation, Anti-terrorism, Demining and Related Programs", "Foreign Military Financing Program", "International Military Education and Training", "Peace Corps", and "Migration and Refugee Assistance", shall be available for obligation for activities, programs, projects, type of materiel assistance, countries, or other operations not justified or in excess of the amount justified to the Appropriations Committees for obligation under any of these specific headings unless the Appropriations Committees of both Houses of Congress are previously notified 15 days in advance: *Provided*, That the President shall not enter into any commitment of funds appropriated for the purposes of section 23 of the Arms Export Control Act for the provision of major defense equipment, other than conventional ammunition, or other major defense items defined to be air-

NOTIFICATION REQUIREMENTS—Continued

craft, ships, missiles, or combat vehicles, not previously justified to Congress or 20 percent in excess of the quantities justified to Congress unless the Committees on Appropriations are notified 15 days in advance of such commitment: *Provided further*, That this section shall not apply to any reprogramming for an activity, program, or project under chapter 1 of part I of the Foreign Assistance Act of 1961 of less than 10 percent of the amount previously justified to the Congress for obligation for such activity, program, or project for the current fiscal year: *Provided further*, That the requirements of this section or any similar provision of this Act or any other Act, including any prior Act requiring notification in accordance with the regular notification procedures of the Committees on Appropriations, may be waived if failure to do so would pose a substantial risk to human health or welfare *or if waiving such requirement is in the national interest of the United States*: *Provided further*, That in case of any such waiver, notification to the Congress, or the appropriate congressional committees, shall be provided as early as practicable, but in no event later than 3 days after taking the action to which such notification requirement was applicable, in the context of the circumstances necessitating such waiver: *Provided further*, That any notification provided pursuant to such a waiver shall contain an explanation of the emergency circumstances.

(b) Drawdowns made pursuant to section 506(a)(2) of the Foreign Assistance Act of 1961 shall be subject to the regular notification procedures of the Committees on Appropriations.

LIMITATION ON AVAILABILITY OF FUNDS FOR INTERNATIONAL ORGANIZATIONS AND PROGRAMS

SEC. [516] *514*. Subject to the regular notification procedures of the Committees on Appropriations, funds appropriated under this Act or any previously enacted Act making appropriations for foreign operations, export financing, and related programs, which are returned or not made available for organizations and programs because of the implementation of section 307(a) of the Foreign Assistance Act of 1961, shall remain available for obligation until September 30, [2001] *2002*.

INDEPENDENT STATES OF THE FORMER SOVIET UNION

SEC. [517] *515*. [(a) None of the funds appropriated under the heading "Assistance for the Independent States of the Former Soviet Union" shall be made available for assistance for a government of an Independent State of the former Soviet Union—

(1) unless that government is making progress in implementing comprehensive economic reforms based on market principles, private ownership, respect for commercial contracts, and equitable treatment of foreign private investment; and

(2) if that government applies or transfers United States assistance to any entity for the purpose of expropriating or seizing ownership or control of assets, investments, or ventures.

Assistance may be furnished without regard to this subsection if the President determines that to do so is in the national interest.]

[(b) None of the funds appropriated under the heading "Assistance for the Independent States of the Former Soviet Union" shall be made available for assistance for a government of an Independent State of the former Soviet Union if that government directs any action in violation of the territorial integrity or national sovereignty of any other Independent State of the former Soviet Union, such as those violations included in the Helsinki Final Act: *Provided*, That such funds may be made available without regard to the restriction in this subsection if the President determines that to do so is in the national security interest of the United States.]

[(c) None of the funds appropriated under the heading "Assistance for the Independent States of the Former Soviet Union" shall be made available for any state to enhance its military capability: *Provided*, That this restriction does not apply to demilitarization, demining or nonproliferation programs.]

[(d) Funds appropriated under the heading "Assistance for the Independent States of the Former Soviet Union" shall be subject to the regular notification procedures of the Committees on Appropriations.]

[(e) Funds made available in this Act for assistance for the Independent States of the former Soviet Union shall be subject to the provisions of section 117 (relating to environment and natural resources) of the Foreign Assistance Act of 1961.]

[(f)] Funds appropriated in this or prior appropriations Acts that are or have been made available for an Enterprise Fund in the Independent States of the Former Soviet Union may be deposited by such Fund in interest-bearing accounts prior to the disbursement of such funds by the Fund for program purposes. The Fund may retain for such program purposes any interest earned on such deposits without returning such interest to the Treasury of the United States and without further appropriation by the Congress. Funds made available for Enterprise Funds shall be expended at the minimum rate necessary to make timely payment for projects and activities.

[(g) In issuing new task orders, entering into contracts, or making grants, with funds appropriated in this Act or prior appropriations Acts under the headings "Assistance for the New Independent States of the Former Soviet Union" and "Assistance for the Independent States of the Former Soviet Union", for projects or activities that have as one of their primary purposes the fostering of private sector development, the Coordinator for United States Assistance to the New Independent States and the implementing agency shall encourage the participation of and give significant weight to contractors and grantees who propose investing a significant amount of their own resources (including volunteer services and in-kind contributions) in such projects and activities.]

PROHIBITION ON FUNDING FOR ABORTIONS AND INVOLUNTARY STERILIZATION

SEC. [518] *516*. None of the funds made available to carry out part I of the Foreign Assistance Act of 1961, as amended, may be used to pay for the performance of abortions as a method of family planning or to motivate or coerce any person to practice abortions. None of the funds made available to carry out part I of the Foreign Assistance Act of 1961, as amended, may be used to pay for the performance of involuntary sterilization as a method of family planning or to coerce or provide any financial incentive to any person to undergo sterilizations. None of the funds made available to carry out part I of the Foreign Assistance Act of 1961, as amended, may be used to pay for any biomedical research which relates in whole or in part, to methods of, or the performance of, abortions or involuntary sterilization as a means of family planning. None of the funds made available to carry out part I of the Foreign Assistance Act of 1961, as amended, may be obligated or expended for any country or organization if the President certifies that the use of these funds by any such country or organization would violate any of the above provisions related to abortions and involuntary sterilizations: *Provided*, That none of the funds made available under this Act may be used to lobby for or against abortion.

EXPORT FINANCING TRANSFER AUTHORITIES

SEC. [519] *517*. Not to exceed 5 percent of any appropriation other than for administrative expenses made available for fiscal year [2000] *2001*, for programs under title I of this Act may be transferred between such appropriations for use for any of the purposes, programs, and activities for which the funds in such receiving account may be used, but no such appropriation, except as otherwise specifically provided, shall be increased by more than 25 percent by any such transfer: *Provided*, That the exercise of such authority shall be subject to the regular notification procedures of the Committees on Appropriations.

[SPECIAL NOTIFICATION REQUIREMENTS]

[SEC. 520. None of the funds appropriated by this Act shall be obligated or expended for Colombia, Haiti, Liberia, Pakistan, Panama, Serbia, Sudan, or the Democratic Republic of Congo except as provided through the regular notification procedures of the Committees on Appropriations.]

DEFINITION OF PROGRAM, PROJECT, AND ACTIVITY

SEC. [521] *518*. For the purpose of this Act, "program, project, and activity" shall be defined at the appropriations Act account level and shall include all appropriations and authorizations Acts earmarks, ceilings, and limitations with the exception that for the following accounts: Economic Support Fund and Foreign Military Financing Program, "program, project, and activity" shall also be considered to include country, regional, and central program level funding within each such account; for the development assistance accounts of the Agency for International Development "program, project, and activity" shall also be considered to include central program level funding, either as: (1) justified to the Congress; or (2) allocated by the executive branch in accordance with a report, to be provided to the Committees on Appropriations within 30 days of the enactment of this Act, as required by section 653(a) of the Foreign Assistance Act of 1961.

CHILD SURVIVAL AND DISEASE PREVENTION ACTIVITIES

SEC. [522] *519.* Up to [$10,000,000] *$12,000,000* of the funds made available by this Act for assistance under the heading "Child Survival and Disease Programs Fund", may be used to reimburse United States Government agencies, agencies of State governments, institutions of higher learning, and private and voluntary organizations for the full cost of individuals (including for the personal services of such individuals) detailed or assigned to, or contracted by, as the case may be, the Agency for International Development for the purpose of carrying out child survival, basic education, and infectious disease activities: *Provided*, That up to $1,500,000 of the funds made available by this Act for assistance under the heading "Development Assistance" may be used to reimburse such agencies, institutions, and organizations for such costs of such individuals carrying out other development assistance activities: *Provided further*, That funds appropriated by this Act that are made available for child survival activities or disease programs including activities relating to research on, and the prevention, treatment and control of, Acquired Immune Deficiency Syndrome may be made available notwithstanding any provision of law that restricts assistance to foreign countries: [*Provided further*, That funds appropriated under title II of this Act may be made available pursuant to section 301 of the Foreign Assistance Act of 1961 if a primary purpose of the assistance is for child survival and related programs:] *Provided further*, That funds appropriated by this Act that are made available for family planning activities may be made available notwithstanding section 512 of this Act and section 620(q) of the Foreign Assistance Act of 1961.

PROHIBITION AGAINST INDIRECT FUNDING TO CERTAIN COUNTRIES

SEC. [523] *520.* None of the funds appropriated or otherwise made available pursuant to this Act shall be obligated to finance indirectly any assistance or reparations to Cuba, Iraq, Libya, Iran, Syria, North Korea, or the People's Republic of China, unless the President of the United States certifies that the withholding of these funds is contrary to the national interest of the United States.

[NOTIFICATION ON EXCESS DEFENSE EQUIPMENT]

[SEC. 524. Prior to providing excess Department of Defense articles in accordance with section 516(a) of the Foreign Assistance Act of 1961, the Department of Defense shall notify the Committees on Appropriations to the same extent and under the same conditions as are other committees pursuant to subsection (f) of that section: *Provided*, That before issuing a letter of offer to sell excess defense articles under the Arms Export Control Act, the Department of Defense shall notify the Committees on Appropriations in accordance with the regular notification procedures of such Committees: *Provided further*, That such Committees shall also be informed of the original acquisition cost of such defense articles.]

[AUTHORIZATION REQUIREMENT]

[SEC. 525. Funds appropriated by this Act may be obligated and expended notwithstanding section 10 of Public Law 91–672 and section 15 of the State Department Basic Authorities Act of 1956.]

DEMOCRACY IN CHINA

SEC. [526] *521.* Notwithstanding any other provision of law that restricts assistance to foreign countries, funds appropriated by this Act for "Economic Support Fund" may be made available to provide general support and grants for nongovernmental organizations located outside the People's Republic of China that have as their primary purpose fostering democracy in that country, and for activities of nongovernmental organizations located outside the People's Republic of China to foster democracy in that country: *Provided*, That none of the funds made available for activities to foster democracy in the People's Republic of China may be made available for assistance to the government of that country, except that funds appropriated by this Act under the heading "Economic Support Fund" that are made available for the National Endowment for Democracy or its grantees may be made available for activities to foster democracy in that country notwithstanding this proviso and any other provision of law: *Provided further*, That funds made available pursuant to the authority of this section shall be subject to the regular notification procedures of the Committees on Appropriations[: *Provided further*, That notwithstanding any other provision of law that restricts assistance to foreign countries, of the funds appropriated by this Act under the heading "Economic Support Fund", $1,000,000 shall be made available to the Robert F. Kennedy Memorial Center for Human Rights for a project to disseminate information and support research about the People's Republic of China, and related activities].

PROHIBITION ON BILATERAL ASSISTANCE TO TERRORIST COUNTRIES

SEC. [527] *522.* (a) [Notwithstanding any other provision of law, funds] *Funds* appropriated for bilateral assistance under any heading of this Act and funds appropriated under any such heading in a provision of law enacted prior to the enactment of this Act, shall not be made available to any country which the President determines—

(1) grants sanctuary from prosecution to any individual or group which has committed an act of international terrorism; or

(2) otherwise supports international terrorism.

(b) The President may waive the application of subsection (a) to a country if the President determines that national security or humanitarian reasons justify such waiver. The President shall publish each waiver in the Federal Register and, at least 15 days before the waiver takes effect, shall notify the Committees on Appropriations of the waiver (including the justification for the waiver) in accordance with the regular notification procedures of the Committees on Appropriations.

(c) This section shall not apply to the provision of assistance from funds appropriated under the headings, "Migration and Refugee Assistance" and "United States Emergency Refugee and Migration and Assistance Fund", and assistance for relief and rehabilitation from funds appropriated under the heading, "International Disaster Assistance".

COMMERCIAL LEASING OF DEFENSE ARTICLES

SEC. [528] *523.* Notwithstanding any other provision of law, and subject to the regular notification procedures of the Committees on Appropriations, the authority of section 23(a) of the Arms Export Control Act may be used to provide financing to Israel, Egypt and NATO and major non-NATO allies for the procurement by leasing (including leasing with an option to purchase) of defense articles from United States commercial suppliers, not including Major Defense Equipment (other than helicopters and other types of aircraft having possible civilian application), if the President determines that there are compelling foreign policy or national security reasons for those defense articles being provided by commercial lease rather than by government-to-government sale under such Act.

[COMPETITIVE INSURANCE]

[SEC. 529. All Agency for International Development contracts and solicitations, and subcontracts entered into under such contracts, shall include a clause requiring that United States insurance companies have a fair opportunity to bid for insurance when such insurance is necessary or appropriate.]

[STINGERS IN THE PERSIAN GULF REGION]

[SEC. 530. Except as provided in section 581 of the Foreign Operations, Export Financing, and Related Programs Appropriations Act, 1990, the United States may not sell or otherwise make available any Stingers to any country bordering the Persian Gulf under the Arms Export Control Act or chapter 2 of part II of the Foreign Assistance Act of 1961.]

DEBT-FOR-DEVELOPMENT

SEC. [531] *524.* In order to enhance the continued participation of nongovernmental organizations in economic assistance activities under the Foreign Assistance Act of 1961, including endowments, debt-for-development and debt-for-nature exchanges, a nongovernmental organization which is a grantee or contractor of the Agency for International Development may place in interest bearing accounts funds made available under this Act or prior Acts or local currencies which accrue to that organization as a result of economic assistance provided under title II of this Act and any interest earned on such investment shall be used for the purpose for which the assistance was provided to that organization.

[SEPARATE ACCOUNTS]

[SEC. 532. (a) SEPARATE ACCOUNTS FOR LOCAL CURRENCIES.—(1) If assistance is furnished to the government of a foreign country under chapters 1 and 10 of part I or chapter 4 of part II of the Foreign Assistance Act of 1961 under agreements which result in the generation of local currencies of that country, the Administrator of the Agency for International Development shall—

(A) require that local currencies be deposited in a separate account established by that government;

[SEPARATE ACCOUNTS]—Continued

(B) enter into an agreement with that government which sets forth—

(i) the amount of the local currencies to be generated; and

(ii) the terms and conditions under which the currencies so deposited may be utilized, consistent with this section; and

(C) establish by agreement with that government the responsibilities of the Agency for International Development and that government to monitor and account for deposits into and disbursements from the separate account.

(2) USES OF LOCAL CURRENCIES.—As may be agreed upon with the foreign government, local currencies deposited in a separate account pursuant to subsection (a), or an equivalent amount of local currencies, shall be used only—

(A) to carry out chapters 1 or 10 of part I or chapter 4 of part II (as the case may be), for such purposes as—

(i) project and sector assistance activities; or

(ii) debt and deficit financing; or

(B) for the administrative requirements of the United States Government.

(3) PROGRAMMING ACCOUNTABILITY.—The Agency for International Development shall take all necessary steps to ensure that the equivalent of the local currencies disbursed pursuant to subsection (a)(2)(A) from the separate account established pursuant to subsection (a)(1) are used for the purposes agreed upon pursuant to subsection (a)(2).

(4) TERMINATION OF ASSISTANCE PROGRAMS.—Upon termination of assistance to a country under chapters 1 or 10 of part I or chapter 4 of part II (as the case may be), any unencumbered balances of funds which remain in a separate account established pursuant to subsection (a) shall be disposed of for such purposes as may be agreed to by the government of that country and the United States Government.

(5) REPORTING REQUIREMENT.—The Administrator of the Agency for International Development shall report on an annual basis as part of the justification documents submitted to the Committees on Appropriations on the use of local currencies for the administrative requirements of the United States Government as authorized in subsection (a)(2)(B), and such report shall include the amount of local currency (and United States dollar equivalent) used and/or to be used for such purpose in each applicable country.]

[(b) SEPARATE ACCOUNTS FOR CASH TRANSFERS.—(1) If assistance is made available to the government of a foreign country, under chapters 1 or 10 of part I or chapter 4 of part II of the Foreign Assistance Act of 1961, as cash transfer assistance or as nonproject sector assistance, that country shall be required to maintain such funds in a separate account and not commingle them with any other funds.

(2) APPLICABILITY OF OTHER PROVISIONS OF LAW.—Such funds may be obligated and expended notwithstanding provisions of law which are inconsistent with the nature of this assistance including provisions which are referenced in the Joint Explanatory Statement of the Committee of Conference accompanying House Joint Resolution 648 (House Report No. 98–1159).

(3) NOTIFICATION.—At least 15 days prior to obligating any such cash transfer or nonproject sector assistance, the President shall submit a notification through the regular notification procedures of the Committees on Appropriations, which shall include a detailed description of how the funds proposed to be made available will be used, with a discussion of the United States interests that will be served by the assistance (including, as appropriate, a description of the economic policy reforms that will be promoted by such assistance).

(4) EXEMPTION.—Nonproject sector assistance funds may be exempt from the requirements of subsection (b)(1) only through the notification procedures of the Committees on Appropriations.]

COMPENSATION FOR UNITED STATES EXECUTIVE DIRECTORS TO INTERNATIONAL FINANCIAL INSTITUTIONS

SEC. [533] *525.* (a) No funds appropriated by this Act may be made as payment to any international financial institution while the United States Executive Director to such institution is compensated by the institution at a rate which, together with whatever compensation such Director receives from the United States, is in excess of the rate provided for an individual occupying a position at level IV of the Executive Schedule under section 5315 of title 5, United States Code, or while any alternate United States Director to such institution is compensated by the institution at a rate in excess of the rate provided for an individual occupying a position at level V of the Executive Schedule under section 5316 of title 5, United States Code.

(b) For purposes of this section, "international financial institutions" are: the International Bank for Reconstruction and Development, the Inter-American Development Bank, the Asian Development Bank, the Asian Development Fund, the African Development Bank, the African Development Fund, the International Monetary Fund, the North American Development Bank, and the European Bank for Reconstruction and Development.

COMPLIANCE WITH UNITED NATIONS SANCTIONS AGAINST IRAQ

SEC. [534] *526.* None of the funds appropriated or otherwise made available pursuant to this Act to carry out the Foreign Assistance Act of 1961 (including title IV of chapter 2 of part I, relating to the Overseas Private Investment Corporation) or the Arms Export Control Act may be used to provide assistance to any country that is not in compliance with the United Nations Security Council sanctions against Iraq unless the President determines and so certifies to the Congress that—

(1) such assistance is in the national interest of the United States;

(2) such assistance will directly benefit the needy people in that country; or

(3) the assistance to be provided will be humanitarian assistance for foreign nationals who have fled Iraq and Kuwait.

AUTHORITIES FOR THE PEACE CORPS, INTERNATIONAL FUND FOR AGRICULTURAL DEVELOPMENT, INTER-AMERICAN FOUNDATION AND AFRICAN DEVELOPMENT FOUNDATION

SEC. [535] *527.* (a) Unless expressly provided to the contrary, provisions of this or any other Act, including provisions contained in prior Acts authorizing or making appropriations for foreign operations, export financing, and related programs, shall not be construed to prohibit activities authorized by or conducted under the Peace Corps Act, the Inter-American Foundation Act or the African Development Foundation Act. The agency shall promptly report to the Committees on Appropriations whenever it is conducting activities or is proposing to conduct activities in a country for which assistance is prohibited.

(b) Unless expressly provided to the contrary, limitations on the availability of funds for "International Organizations and Programs" in this or any other Act, including prior appropriations Acts, shall not be construed to be applicable to the International Fund for Agricultural Development.

IMPACT ON JOBS IN THE UNITED STATES

SEC. [536] *528.* None of the funds appropriated by this Act may be obligated or expended to provide—

(a) any financial incentive to a business enterprise currently located in the United States for the purpose of inducing such an enterprise to relocate outside the United States if such incentive or inducement is likely to reduce the number of employees of such business enterprise in the United States because United States production is being replaced by such enterprise outside the United States;

(b) assistance for the purpose of establishing or developing in a foreign country any export processing zone or designated area in which the tax, tariff, labor, environment, and safety laws of that country do not apply, in part or in whole, to activities carried out within that zone or area, unless the President determines and certifies that such assistance is not likely to cause a loss of jobs within the United States; or

(c) assistance for any project or activity that contributes to the violation of internationally recognized workers rights, as defined in section 502(a)(4) of the Trade Act of 1974, of workers in the recipient country, including any designated zone or area in that country: *Provided*, That in recognition that the application of this subsection should be commensurate with the level of development of the recipient country and sector, the provisions of this subsection shall not preclude assistance for the informal sector in such country, micro and small-scale enterprise, and smallholder agriculture.

FUNDING [PROHIBITION] FOR [SERBIA] *KOSOVA AND MONTENEGRO*

SEC. [537] *529.* [None of the funds appropriated by this Act may be made available for assistance for the Republic of Serbia: *Provided*, That this restriction shall not apply to assistance for Kosova or Montenegro, or to assistance to promote democratization: *Provided further*, That section] *Section* 620(t) of the Foreign Assistance Act of 1961, as amended, shall not apply to Kosova or Montenegro.

SPECIAL AUTHORITIES

SEC. [538] *530.* (a) Funds appropriated in titles I and II of this Act that are made available for Afghanistan, Lebanon, Montenegro, and for victims of war, displaced children, displaced Burmese, humanitarian assistance for Romania, and humanitarian assistance for the peoples of Kosova, may be made available notwithstanding any other provision of law: *Provided*, That any such funds that are made available for Cambodia shall be subject to the provisions of section 531(e) of the Foreign Assistance Act of 1961 and section 906 of the International Security and Development Cooperation Act of 1985.

(b) Funds appropriated by this Act to carry out the provisions of sections 103 through 106 of the Foreign Assistance Act of 1961 may be used, notwithstanding any other provision of law, for the purpose of supporting tropical forestry and biodiversity conservation activities and, subject to the regular notification procedures of the Committees on Appropriations, energy programs aimed at reducing greenhouse gas emissions: *Provided*, That such assistance shall be subject to sections 116, 502B, and 620A of the Foreign Assistance Act of 1961.

(c) The Agency for International Development may employ personal services contractors, notwithstanding any other provision of law, for the purpose of administering programs for the West Bank and Gaza.

(d)[(1) WAIVER.—The President may waive the provisions of section 1003 of Public Law 100–204 if the President determines and certifies in writing to the Speaker of the House of Representatives and the President pro tempore of the Senate that it is important to the national security interests of the United States.

(2) PERIOD OF APPLICATION OF WAIVER.—Any waiver pursuant to paragraph (1) shall be effective for no more than a period of 6 months at a time and shall not apply beyond 12 months after the enactment of this Act.] *Title X of P.L. 100–204 and the second sentence of section 212(a)(3)(B)(i) of the Immigration and Nationality Act of 1952, as amended, are repealed.*

(e) During fiscal year 2001, the President may use up to $50,000,000 under the authority of section 451 of the Foreign Assistance Act of 1961, notwithstanding the funding ceiling in section 451(a).

[POLICY ON TERMINATING THE ARAB LEAGUE BOYCOTT OF ISRAEL]

[SEC. 539. It is the sense of the Congress that—

(1) the Arab League countries should immediately and publicly renounce the primary boycott of Israel and the secondary and tertiary boycott of American firms that have commercial ties with Israel;

(2) the decision by the Arab League in 1997 to reinstate the boycott against Israel was deeply troubling and disappointing;

(3) the Arab League should immediately rescind its decision on the boycott and its members should develop normal relations with their neighbor Israel; and

(4) the President should—

(A) take more concrete steps to encourage vigorously Arab League countries to renounce publicly the primary boycotts of Israel and the secondary and tertiary boycotts of American firms that have commercial relations with Israel as a confidence-building measure;

(B) take into consideration the participation of any recipient country in the primary boycott of Israel and the secondary and tertiary boycotts of American firms that have commercial relations with Israel when determining whether to sell weapons to said country;

(C) report to Congress on the specific steps being taken by the President to bring about a public renunciation of the Arab primary boycott of Israel and the secondary and tertiary boycotts of American firms that have commercial relations with Israel and to expand the process of normalizing ties between Arab League countries and Israel; and

(D) encourage the allies and trading partners of the United States to enact laws prohibiting businesses from complying with the boycott and penalizing businesses that do comply.]

ANTI-NARCOTICS ACTIVITIES

SEC. [540] *531.* Of the funds appropriated or otherwise made available by this Act for "Economic Support Fund", assistance may be provided to strengthen the administration of justice in countries in Latin America and the Caribbean and in other regions consistent with the provisions of section 534(b) of the Foreign Assistance Act of 1961, except that programs to enhance protection of participants in judicial cases may be conducted notwithstanding section 660 of that Act. [Funds made available pursuant to this section may be made available notwithstanding section] *Section* 534(c) and the second and third sentences of section 534(e) of the Foreign Assistance Act of 1961 *are repealed*.

ELIGIBILITY FOR ASSISTANCE

SEC. [541] *532.* (a) ASSISTANCE THROUGH NONGOVERNMENTAL ORGANIZATIONS.—Restrictions contained in this or any other Act with respect to assistance for a country shall not be construed to restrict assistance in support of programs of nongovernmental organizations from funds appropriated by this Act to carry out the provisions of chapters 1, 10, [and 11] *11, and 12* of part I and chapter 4 of part II of the Foreign Assistance Act of 1961, and from funds appropriated under the heading "Assistance for Eastern Europe and the Baltic States": *Provided*, That the President shall take into consideration, in any case in which a restriction on assistance would be applicable but for this subsection, whether assistance in support of programs of nongovernmental organizations is in the national interest of the United States: *Provided further*, That before using the authority of this subsection to furnish assistance in support of programs of nongovernmental organizations, the President shall notify the Committees on Appropriations under the regular notification procedures of those committees, including a description of the program to be assisted, the assistance to be provided, and the reasons for furnishing such assistance: *Provided further*, That nothing in this subsection shall be construed to alter any existing statutory prohibitions against abortion or involuntary sterilizations contained in this or any other Act.

(b) PUBLIC LAW 480.—During fiscal year [2000] *2001*, restrictions contained in this or any other Act with respect to assistance for a country shall not be construed to restrict assistance under the Agricultural Trade Development and Assistance Act of 1954: *Provided*, That none of the funds appropriated to carry out title I of such Act and made available pursuant to this subsection may be obligated or expended except as provided through the regular notification procedures of the Committees on Appropriations.

(c) EXCEPTION.—This section shall not apply—

(1) with respect to section 620A of the Foreign Assistance Act of 1961 or any comparable provision of law prohibiting assistance to countries that support international terrorism; or

(2) with respect to section 116 of the Foreign Assistance Act of 1961 or any comparable provision of law prohibiting assistance to [countries that violate] *the government of a country that violates* internationally recognized human rights.

EARMARKS

SEC. [542] *533.* (a) Funds appropriated by this Act which are earmarked may be reprogrammed for other programs within the same account notwithstanding the earmark if compliance with the earmark is made impossible by operation of any provision of this or any other Act or, with respect to a country with which the United States has an agreement providing the United States with base rights or base access in that country, if the President determines that the recipient for which funds are earmarked has significantly reduced its military or economic cooperation with the United States since the enactment of the Foreign Operations, Export Financing, and Related Programs Appropriations Act, 1991; however, before exercising the authority of this subsection with regard to a base rights or base access country which has significantly reduced its military or economic cooperation with the United States, the President shall consult with, and shall provide a written policy justification to the Committees on Appropriations: *Provided*, That any such reprogramming shall be subject to the regular notification procedures of the Committees on Appropriations: *Provided further*, That assistance that is reprogrammed pursuant to this subsection shall be made available under the same terms and conditions as originally provided.

(b) In addition to the authority contained in subsection (a), the original period of availability of funds appropriated by this Act and administered by the Agency for International Development that are earmarked for particular programs or activities by this or any other Act shall be extended for an additional fiscal year if the Administrator of such agency determines and reports promptly to the Committees on Appropriations that the termination of assistance to a country or a significant change in circumstances makes it unlikely that such earmarked funds can be obligated during the original period of availability: *Provided*, That such earmarked funds that are continued available for an additional fiscal year shall be obligated only for the purpose of such earmark.

CEILINGS AND EARMARKS

SEC. [543] *534.* Ceilings and earmarks contained in this Act shall not be applicable to funds or authorities appropriated or otherwise made available by any subsequent Act unless such Act specifically so directs. Earmarks or minimum funding requirements contained in any other Act shall not be applicable to funds appropriated by this Act.

PROHIBITION ON PUBLICITY OR PROPAGANDA

SEC. [544] *535.* No part of any appropriation contained in this Act shall be used for publicity or propaganda purposes within the United States not authorized before the date of the enactment of this Act by the Congress[: *Provided*, That not to exceed $750,000 may be made available to carry out the provisions of section 316 of Public Law 96–533].

PURCHASE OF AMERICAN-MADE EQUIPMENT AND PRODUCTS

SEC. [545. (a)] *536.* To the maximum extent possible, assistance provided under this Act should make full use of American resources, including commodities, products, and services.

[(b) It is the sense of the Congress that, to the greatest extent practicable, all agriculture commodities, equipment and products purchased with funds made available in this Act should be American-made.]

[(c) In providing financial assistance to, or entering into any contract with, any entity using funds made available in this Act, the head of each Federal agency, to the greatest extent practicable, shall provide to such entity a notice describing the statement made in subsection (b) by the Congress.]

[(d) The Secretary of the Treasury shall report to Congress annually on the efforts of the heads of each Federal agency and the United States directors of international financial institutions (as referenced in section 514) in complying with this sense of the Congress.]

[PROHIBITION OF PAYMENTS TO UNITED NATIONS MEMBERS]

[SEC. 546. None of the funds appropriated or made available pursuant to this Act for carrying out the Foreign Assistance Act of 1961, may be used to pay in whole or in part any assessments, arrearages, or dues of any member of the United Nations or, from funds appropriated by this Act to carry out chapter 1 of part I of the Foreign Assistance Act of 1961, the costs for participation of another country's delegation at international conferences held under the auspices of multilateral or international organizations.]

[CONSULTING SERVICES]

[SEC. 547. The expenditure of any appropriation under this Act for any consulting service through procurement contract, pursuant to section 3109 of title 5, United States Code, shall be limited to those contracts where such expenditures are a matter of public record and available for public inspection, except where otherwise provided under existing law, or under existing Executive order pursuant to existing law.]

[PRIVATE VOLUNTARY ORGANIZATIONS—DOCUMENTATION]

[SEC. 548. None of the funds appropriated or made available pursuant to this Act shall be available to a private voluntary organization which fails to provide upon timely request any document, file, or record necessary to the auditing requirements of the Agency for International Development.]

[PROHIBITION ON ASSISTANCE TO FOREIGN GOVERNMENTS THAT EXPORT LETHAL MILITARY EQUIPMENT TO COUNTRIES SUPPORTING INTERNATIONAL TERRORISM]

[SEC. 549. (a) None of the funds appropriated or otherwise made available by this Act may be available to any foreign government which provides lethal military equipment to a country the government of which the Secretary of State has determined is a terrorist government for purposes of section 40(d) of the Arms Export Control Act. The prohibition under this section with respect to a foreign government shall terminate 12 months after that government ceases to provide such military equipment. This section applies with respect to lethal military equipment provided under a contract entered into after October 1, 1997.]

[(b) Assistance restricted by subsection (a) or any other similar provision of law, may be furnished if the President determines that furnishing such assistance is important to the national interests of the United States.]

[(c) Whenever the waiver of subsection (b) is exercised, the President shall submit to the appropriate congressional committees a report with respect to the furnishing of such assistance. Any such report shall include a detailed explanation of the assistance to be provided, including the estimated dollar amount of such assistance, and an explanation of how the assistance furthers United States national interests.]

[WITHHOLDING OF ASSISTANCE FOR PARKING FINES OWED BY FOREIGN COUNTRIES]

[SEC. 550. (a) IN GENERAL.—Of the funds made available for a foreign country under part I of the Foreign Assistance Act of 1961, an amount equivalent to 110 percent of the total unpaid fully adjudicated parking fines and penalties owed to the District of Columbia by such country as of the date of the enactment of this Act shall be withheld from obligation for such country until the Secretary of State certifies and reports in writing to the appropriate congressional committees that such fines and penalties are fully paid to the government of the District of Columbia.]

[(b) DEFINITION.—For purposes of this section, the term "appropriate congressional committees" means the Committee on Foreign Relations and the Committee on Appropriations of the Senate and the Committee on International Relations and the Committee on Appropriations of the House of Representatives.]

[LIMITATION ON ASSISTANCE FOR THE PLO FOR THE WEST BANK AND GAZA]

[SEC. 551. None of the funds appropriated by this Act may be obligated for assistance for the Palestine Liberation Organization for the West Bank and Gaza unless the President has exercised the authority under section 604(a) of the Middle East Peace Facilitation Act of 1995 (title VI of Public Law 104–107) or any other legislation to suspend or make inapplicable section 307 of the Foreign Assistance Act of 1961 and that suspension is still in effect: *Provided*, That if the President fails to make the certification under section 604(b)(2) of the Middle East Peace Facilitation Act of 1995 or to suspend the prohibition under other legislation, funds appropriated by this Act may not be obligated for assistance for the Palestine Liberation Organization for the West Bank and Gaza.]

WAR CRIMES TRIBUNALS DRAWDOWN

SEC. [552] *537.* If the President determines that doing so will contribute to a just resolution of charges regarding genocide or other violations of international humanitarian law, the President may direct a drawdown pursuant to section 552(c) of the Foreign Assistance Act of 1961, as amended, of up to $30,000,000 of commodities and services for the United Nations War Crimes Tribunal established with regard to the former Yugoslavia by the United Nations Security Council or such other tribunals or commissions as the Council may establish to deal with such violations, without regard to the ceiling limitation contained in paragraph (2) thereof: *Provided*, That the determination required under this section shall be in lieu of any determinations otherwise required under section 552(c): *Provided further*, That 60 days after the date of the enactment of this Act, and every 180 days thereafter, the Secretary of State shall submit a report to the Committees on Appropriations describing the steps the United States Government is taking to collect information regarding allegations of genocide or other violations of international law in the former Yugoslavia and to furnish that information to the United Nations War Crimes Tribunal for the former Yugoslavia[: *Provided further*, That the drawdown made under this section for any tribunal shall not be construed as an endorsement or precedent for the establishment of any standing or permanent international criminal tribunal or court: *Provided further*, That funds made available for tribunals other than Yugoslavia or Rwanda shall be made available subject to the regular notification procedures of the Committees on Appropriations.]

LANDMINES

SEC. [553] *538.* Notwithstanding any other provision of law, demining equipment available to the Agency for International Development and the Department of State and used in support of the clearance of landmines and unexploded ordnance for humanitarian purposes may be disposed of on a grant basis in foreign countries, subject to such terms and conditions as the President may prescribe[: *Provided*, That section 1365(c) of the National Defense Authorization Act for Fiscal Year 1993 (Public Law 102–484; 22 U.S.C., 2778 note) is amended by striking "During the five-year period beginning on October 23, 1992" and inserting "During the 11-year period beginning on October 23, 1992"].

[RESTRICTIONS CONCERNING THE PALESTINIAN AUTHORITY]

[SEC. 554. None of the funds appropriated by this Act may be obligated or expended to create in any part of Jerusalem a new office of any department or agency of the United States Government for the purpose of conducting official United States Government business with the Palestinian Authority over Gaza and Jericho or any successor Palestinian governing entity provided for in the Israel-PLO Declaration of Principles: *Provided*, That this restriction shall not apply to the acquisition of additional space for the existing Consulate General in Jerusalem: *Provided further*, That meetings between officers and employees of the United States and officials of the Palestinian Authority, or any successor Palestinian governing entity provided for in the Israel-PLO Declaration of Principles, for the purpose of conducting official United States Government business with such authority should continue to take place in locations other than Jerusalem. As has been true in the past, officers and employees of the United States Government may continue to meet in Jerusalem on other subjects with Palestinians (including those who now occupy positions in the Palestinian Authority), have social contacts, and have incidental discussions.]

PROHIBITION OF PAYMENT OF CERTAIN EXPENSES

SEC. [555] *539*. None of the funds appropriated or otherwise made available by this Act under the headings "International Military Education and Training" or "Foreign Military Financing Program" for Informational Program activities or under the headings "Child Survival and Disease Programs Fund", "Development Assistance", and "Economic Support Fund" may be obligated or expended to pay for—

(1) alcoholic beverages; or

(2) entertainment expenses for activities that are substantially of a recreational character, including entrance fees at sporting events and amusement parks.

[COMPETITIVE PRICING FOR SALES OF DEFENSE ARTICLES]

[SEC. 556. Direct costs associated with meeting a foreign customer's additional or unique requirements will continue to be allowable under contracts under section 22(d) of the Arms Export Control Act. Loadings applicable to such direct costs shall be permitted at the same rates applicable to procurement of like items purchased by the Department of Defense for its own use.]

SPECIAL DEBT RELIEF FOR THE POOREST

SEC. [557] *540*. (a) AUTHORITY TO REDUCE DEBT.—The President may reduce amounts owed to the United States (or any agency of the United States) by an eligible country as a result of—

(1) guarantees issued under sections 221 and 222 of the Foreign Assistance Act of 1961;

(2) credits extended or guarantees issued under the Arms Export Control Act; or

(3) any obligation or portion of such obligation, to pay for purchases of United States agricultural commodities guaranteed by the Commodity Credit Corporation under export credit guarantee programs authorized pursuant to section 5(f) of the Commodity Credit Corporation Charter Act of June 29, 1948, as amended, section 4(b) of the Food for Peace Act of 1966, as amended (Public Law 89–808), or section 202 of the Agricultural Trade Act of 1978, as amended (Public Law 95–501).

(b) LIMITATIONS.—

(1) The authority provided by subsection (a) may be exercised only to implement multilateral official debt relief and referendum agreements, commonly referred to as "Paris Club Agreed Minutes".

(2) The authority provided by subsection (a) may be exercised only in such amounts or to such extent as is provided in advance by appropriations Acts.

(3) The authority provided by subsection (a) may be exercised only with respect to countries with heavy debt burdens that are eligible to borrow from the International Development Association, but not from the International Bank for Reconstruction and Development, commonly referred to as "IDA-only" countries.

(c) CONDITIONS.—The authority provided by subsection (a) may be exercised only with respect to a country whose government—

(1) does not have an excessive level of military expenditures;

(2) has not repeatedly provided support for acts of international terrorism;

(3) is not failing to cooperate on international narcotics control matters;

(4) (including its military or other security forces) does not engage in a consistent pattern of gross violations of internationally recognized human rights; and

(5) is not ineligible for assistance because of the application of section 527 of the Foreign Relations Authorization Act, Fiscal Years 1994 and 1995.

(d) AVAILABILITY OF FUNDS.—The authority provided by subsection (a) may be used only with regard to funds appropriated by this Act under the heading "Debt Restructuring".

(e) CERTAIN PROHIBITIONS INAPPLICABLE.—A reduction of debt pursuant to subsection (a) shall not be considered assistance for purposes of any provision of law limiting assistance to a country. The authority provided by subsection (a) may be exercised notwithstanding section 620(r) of the Foreign Assistance Act of 1961 or section 321 of the International Development and Food Assistance Act of 1975.

AUTHORITY TO ENGAGE IN DEBT BUYBACKS OR SALES

SEC. [558] *541*. (a) LOANS ELIGIBLE FOR SALE, REDUCTION, OR CANCELLATION.—

(1) AUTHORITY TO SELL, REDUCE, OR CANCEL CERTAIN LOANS.—Notwithstanding any other provision of law, the President may, in accordance with this section, sell to any eligible purchaser any concessional loan or portion thereof made before January 1, 1995, pursuant to the Foreign Assistance Act of 1961, to the government of any eligible country as defined in section 702(6) of that Act or on receipt of payment from an eligible purchaser, reduce or cancel such loan or portion thereof, only for the purpose of facilitating—

(A) debt-for-equity swaps, debt-for-development swaps, or debt-for-nature swaps; or

(B) a debt buyback by an eligible country of its own qualified debt, only if the eligible country uses an additional amount of the local currency of the eligible country, equal to not less than 40 percent of the price paid for such debt by such eligible country, or the difference between the price paid for such debt and the face value of such debt, to support activities that link conservation and sustainable use of natural resources with local community development, and child survival and other child development, in a manner consistent with sections 707 through 710 of the Foreign Assistance Act of 1961, if the sale, reduction, or cancellation would not contravene any term or condition of any prior agreement relating to such loan.

(2) TERMS AND CONDITIONS.—Notwithstanding any other provision of law, the President shall, in accordance with this section, establish the terms and conditions under which loans may be sold, reduced, or canceled pursuant to this section.

(3) ADMINISTRATION.—The Facility, as defined in section 702(8) of the Foreign Assistance Act of 1961, shall notify the administrator of the agency primarily responsible for administering part I of the Foreign Assistance Act of 1961 of purchasers that the President has determined to be eligible, and shall direct such agency to carry out the sale, reduction, or cancellation of a loan pursuant to this section. Such agency shall make an adjustment in its accounts to reflect the sale, reduction, or cancellation.

(4) LIMITATION.—The authorities of this subsection shall be available only to the extent that appropriations for the cost of the modification, as defined in section 502 of the Congressional Budget Act of 1974, are made in advance.

(b) DEPOSIT OF PROCEEDS.—The proceeds from the sale, reduction, or cancellation of any loan sold, reduced, or canceled pursuant to this section shall be deposited in the United States Government account or accounts established for the repayment of such loan.

(c) ELIGIBLE PURCHASERS.—A loan may be sold pursuant to subsection (a)(1)(A) only to a purchaser who presents plans satisfactory to the President for using the loan for the purpose of engaging in debt-for-equity swaps, debt-for-development swaps, or debt-for-nature swaps.

(d) DEBTOR CONSULTATIONS.—Before the sale to any eligible purchaser, or any reduction or cancellation pursuant to this section, of any loan made to an eligible country, the President should consult with the country concerning the amount of loans to be sold, reduced, or canceled and their uses for debt-for-equity swaps, debt-for-development swaps, or debt-for-nature swaps.

(e) AVAILABILITY OF FUNDS.—The authority provided by subsection (a) may be used only with regard to funds appropriated by this Act under the heading "Debt Restructuring".

[ASSISTANCE FOR HAITI]

[SEC. 559. (a) POLICY.—In providing assistance to Haiti, the President should place a priority on the following areas:

(1) aggressive action to support the Haitian National Police, including support for efforts by the Inspector General to purge corrupt and politicized elements from the Haitian National Police;

(2) steps to ensure that any elections undertaken in Haiti with United States assistance are full, free, fair, transparent, and democratic;

(3) support for a program designed to develop an indigenous human rights monitoring capacity;

(4) steps to facilitate the continued privatization of state-owned enterprises;

(5) a sustainable agricultural development program; and

(6) establishment of an economic development fund for Haiti to provide long-term, low interest loans to United States investors and businesses that have a demonstrated commitment to, and expertise in, doing business in Haiti, in particular those businesses present in Haiti prior to the 1994 United Nations embargo.]

[(b) REPORT.—Beginning 6 months after the date of the enactment of this Act, and 6 months thereafter until September 30, 2001, the President shall submit a report to the Committee on Appropriations and the Committee on Foreign Relations of the Senate and the Committee on Appropriations and the Committee on International Relations of the House of Representatives with regard to—

(1) the status of each of the governmental institutions envisioned in the 1987 Haitian Constitution, including an assessment of the extent to which officials in such institutions hold their positions on the basis of a regular, constitutional process;

(2) the status of the privatization (or placement under long-term private management or concession) of the major public entities, including a detailed assessment of the extent to which the Government of Haiti has completed all required incorporating documents, the transfer of assets, and the eviction of unauthorized occupants from such facilities;

(3) the status of efforts to re-sign and implement the lapsed bilateral Repatriation Agreement and an assessment of the extent to which the Government of Haiti has been cooperating with the United States in halting illegal emigration from Haiti;

(4) the status of the Government of Haiti's efforts to conduct thorough investigations of extrajudicial and political killings and—

(A) an assessment of the progress that has been made in bringing to justice the persons responsible for these extrajudicial or political killings in Haiti; and

(B) an assessment of the extent to which the Government of Haiti is cooperating with United States authorities and with United States-funded technical advisors to the Haitian National Police in such investigations;

(5) an assessment of actions taken by the Government of Haiti to remove and maintain the separation from the Haitian National Police, national palace and residential guard, ministerial guard, and any other public security entity or unit of Haiti those individuals who are credibly alleged to have engaged in or conspired to conceal gross violations of internationally recognized human rights;

(6) the status of steps being taken to secure the ratification of the maritime counter-narcotics agreements signed October 1997;

(7) an assessment of the extent to which domestic capacity to conduct free, fair, democratic, and administratively sound elections has been developed in Haiti; and

(8) an assessment of the extent to which Haiti's Minister of Justice has demonstrated a commitment to the professionalism of judicial personnel by consistently placing students graduated by the Judicial School in appropriate judicial positions and has made a commitment to share program costs associated with the Judicial School, and is achieving progress in making the judicial branch in Haiti independent from the executive branch.]

[(c) EQUITABLE ALLOCATION OF FUNDS.—Not more than 17 percent of the funds appropriated by this Act to carry out the provisions of sections 103 through 106 and chapter 4 of part II of the Foreign Assistance Act of 1961, that are made available for Latin America and the Caribbean region may be made available, through bilateral and Latin America and the Caribbean regional programs, to provide assistance for any country in such region.]

[REQUIREMENT FOR DISCLOSURE OF FOREIGN AID IN REPORT OF SECRETARY OF STATE]

[SEC. 560. (a) FOREIGN AID REPORTING REQUIREMENT.—In addition to the voting practices of a foreign country, the report required to be submitted to Congress under section 406(a) of the Foreign Relations Authorization Act, fiscal years 1990 and 1991 (22 U.S.C. 2414a), shall include a side-by-side comparison of individual countries' overall support for the United States at the United Nations and the amount of United States assistance provided to such country in fiscal year 1999.]

[(b) UNITED STATES ASSISTANCE.—For purposes of this section, the term "United States assistance" has the meaning given the term in section 481(e)(4) of the Foreign Assistance Act of 1961 (22 U.S.C. 2291(e)(4)).]

[RESTRICTIONS ON VOLUNTARY CONTRIBUTIONS TO UNITED NATIONS AGENCIES]

[SEC. 561. (a) PROHIBITION ON VOLUNTARY CONTRIBUTIONS FOR THE UNITED NATIONS.—None of the funds appropriated by this Act may be made available to pay any voluntary contribution of the United States to the United Nations (including the United Nations Development Program) if the United Nations implements or imposes any taxation on any United States persons.]

[(b) CERTIFICATION REQUIRED FOR DISBURSEMENT OF FUNDS.—None of the funds appropriated by this Act may be made available to pay any voluntary contribution of the United States to the United Nations (including the United Nations Development Program) unless the President certifies to the Congress 15 days in advance of such payment that the United Nations is not engaged in any effort to implement or impose any taxation on United States persons in order to raise revenue for the United Nations or any of its specialized agencies.]

[(c) DEFINITIONS.—As used in this section the term "United States person" refers to—

(1) a natural person who is a citizen or national of the United States; or

(2) a corporation, partnership, or other legal entity organized under the United States or any State, territory, possession, or district of the United States.]

HAITI

SEC. [562] *542*. The Government of Haiti shall be eligible to purchase defense articles and services under the Arms Export Control Act (22 U.S.C. 2751 et seq.), for the civilian-led Haitian National Police and Coast Guard[: *Provided*, That the authority provided by this section shall be subject to the regular notification procedures of the Committees on Appropriations].

[LIMITATION ON ASSISTANCE TO THE PALESTINIAN AUTHORITY]

[SEC. 563. (a) PROHIBITION OF FUNDS.—None of the funds appropriated by this Act to carry out the provisions of chapter 4 of part II of the Foreign Assistance Act of 1961 may be obligated or expended with respect to providing funds to the Palestinian Authority.]

[(b) WAIVER.—The prohibition included in subsection (a) shall not apply if the President certifies in writing to the Speaker of the House of Representatives and the President pro tempore of the Senate that waiving such prohibition is important to the national security interests of the United States.]

[(c) PERIOD OF APPLICATION OF WAIVER.—Any waiver pursuant to subsection (b) shall be effective for no more than a period of 6 months at a time and shall not apply beyond 12 months after the enactment of this Act.]

[LIMITATION ON ASSISTANCE TO SECURITY FORCES]

[SEC. 564. None of the funds made available by this Act may be provided to any unit of the security forces of a foreign country if the Secretary of State has credible evidence that such unit has committed gross violations of human rights, unless the Secretary determines and reports to the Committees on Appropriations that the government of such country is taking effective measures to bring the responsible members of the security forces unit to justice: *Provided*, That nothing in this section shall be construed to withhold funds made available by this Act from any unit of the security forces of a foreign country not credibly alleged to be involved in gross violations of human rights: *Provided further*, That in the event that funds are withheld from any unit pursuant to this section, the Secretary of State shall promptly inform the foreign government of the basis for such action and shall, to the maximum extent practicable, assist the foreign government in taking effective measures to bring the responsible members of the security forces to justice.]

[LIMITATIONS ON TRANSFER OF MILITARY EQUIPMENT TO EAST TIMOR]

[SEC. 565. In any agreement for the sale, transfer, or licensing of any lethal equipment or helicopter for Indonesia entered into by the United States pursuant to the authority of this Act or any other Act, the agreement shall state that the items will not be used in East Timor.]

[RESTRICTIONS ON ASSISTANCE TO COUNTRIES PROVIDING SANCTUARY TO INDICTED WAR CRIMINALS]

[SEC. 566. (a) BILATERAL ASSISTANCE.—None of the funds made available by this or any prior Act making appropriations for foreign operations, export financing and related programs, may be provided for any country, entity or municipality described in subsection (e).]

[(b) MULTILATERAL ASSISTANCE.—

(1) PROHIBITION.—The Secretary of the Treasury shall instruct the United States executive directors of the international financial institutions to work in opposition to, and vote against, any extension by such institutions of any financial or technical assistance or grants of any kind to any country or entity described in subsection (e).

(2) NOTIFICATION.—Not less than 15 days before any vote in an international financial institution regarding the extension of financial or technical assistance or grants to any country or entity described in subsection (e), the Secretary of the Treasury, in consultation with the Secretary of State, shall provide to the Committee on Appropriations and the Committee on Foreign Relations of the Senate and the Committee on Appropriations and the Committee on Banking and Financial Services of the House of Representatives a written justification for the proposed assistance, including an explanation of the United States position regarding any such vote, as well as a description of the location of the proposed assistance by municipality, its purpose, and its intended beneficiaries.

(3) DEFINITION.—The term "international financial institution" includes the International Monetary Fund, the International Bank for Reconstruction and Development, the International Development Association, the International Finance Corporation, the Multilateral Investment Guaranty Agency, and the European Bank for Reconstruction and Development.]

[(c) EXCEPTIONS.—

(1) IN GENERAL.—Subject to paragraph (2), subsections (a) and (b) shall not apply to the provision of—

(A) humanitarian assistance;

(B) democratization assistance;

(C) assistance for cross border physical infrastructure projects involving activities in both a sanctioned country, entity, or municipality and a nonsanctioned contiguous country, entity, or municipality, if the project is primarily located in and primarily benefits the nonsanctioned country, entity, or municipality and if the portion of the project located in the sanctioned country, entity, or municipality is necessary only to complete the project;

(D) small-scale assistance projects or activities requested by United States Armed Forces that promote good relations between such forces and the officials and citizens of the areas in the United States SFOR sector of Bosnia;

(E) implementation of the Brcko Arbitral Decision;

(F) lending by the international financial institutions to a country or entity to support common monetary and fiscal policies at the national level as contemplated by the Dayton Agreement;

(G) direct lending to a non-sanctioned entity, or lending passed on by the national government to a non-sanctioned entity; or

(H) assistance to the International Police Task Force for the training of a civilian police force.

(2) NOTIFICATION.—Every 60 days the Secretary of State, in consultation with the Administrator of the Agency for International Development, shall publish in the Federal Register and/or in a comparable publicly accessible document or Internet site, a listing and justification of any assistance that is obligated within that period of time for any country, entity, or municipality described in subsection (e), including a description of the purpose of the assistance, project and its location, by municipality.]

[(d) FURTHER LIMITATIONS.—Notwithstanding subsection (c)—

(1) no assistance may be made available by this Act, or any prior Act making appropriations for foreign operations, export financing and related programs, in any country, entity, or municipality described in subsection (e), for a program, project, or activity in which a publicly indicted war criminal is known to have any financial or material interest; and

(2) no assistance (other than emergency foods or medical assistance or demining assistance) may be made available by this Act, or any prior Act making appropriations for foreign operations, export financing and related programs for any program, project, or activity in a community within any country, entity or municipality described in subsection (e) if competent authorities within that community are not complying with the provisions of Article IX and Annex 4, Article II, paragraph 8 of the Dayton Agreement relating to war crimes and the Tribunal.]

[(e) SANCTIONED COUNTRY, ENTITY, OR MUNICIPALITY.—A sanctioned country, entity, or municipality described in this section is one whose competent authorities have failed, as determined by the Secretary of State, to take necessary and significant steps to apprehend and transfer to the Tribunal all persons who have been publicly indicted by the Tribunal.]

[(f) SPECIAL RULE.—Subject to subsection (d), subsections (a) and (b) shall not apply to the provision of assistance to an entity that is not a sanctioned entity, notwithstanding that such entity may be within a sanctioned country, if the Secretary of State determines and so reports to the appropriate congressional committees that providing assistance to that entity would promote peace and internationally recognized human rights by encouraging that entity to cooperate fully with the Tribunal.]

[(g) CURRENT RECORD OF WAR CRIMINALS AND SANCTIONED COUNTRIES, ENTITIES, AND MUNICIPALITIES.—

(1) IN GENERAL.—The Secretary of State shall establish and maintain a current record of the location, including the municipality, if known, of publicly indicted war criminals and a current record of sanctioned countries, entities, and municipalities.

(2) INFORMATION OF THE DCI AND THE SECRETARY OF DEFENSE.—The Director of Central Intelligence and the Secretary of Defense should collect and provide to the Secretary of State information concerning the location, including the municipality, of publicly indicted war criminals.

(3) INFORMATION OF THE TRIBUNAL.—The Secretary of State shall request that the Tribunal and other international organizations and governments provide the Secretary of State information concerning the location, including the municipality, of publicly indicted war criminals and concerning country, entity and municipality authorities known to have obstructed the work of the Tribunal.

(4) REPORT.—Beginning 30 days after the date of the enactment of this Act, and not later than September 1 each year thereafter, the Secretary of State shall submit a report in classified and unclassified form to the appropriate congressional committees on the location, including the municipality, if known, of publicly indicted war criminals, on country, entity and municipality authorities known to have obstructed the work of the Tribunal, and on sanctioned countries, entities, and municipalities.

(5) INFORMATION TO CONGRESS.—Upon the request of the chairman or ranking minority member of any of the appropriate congressional committees, the Secretary of State shall make available to that committee the information recorded under paragraph (1) in a report submitted to the committee in classified and unclassified form.]

[(h) WAIVER.—

(1) IN GENERAL.—The Secretary of State may waive the application of subsection (a) or subsection (b) with respect to specified bilateral programs or international financial institution projects or programs in a sanctioned country, entity, or municipality upon providing a written determination to the Committee on Appropriations and the Committee on Foreign Relations of the Senate and the Committee on Appropriations and the Committee on International Relations of the House of Representatives that such assistance directly supports the implementation of the Dayton Agreement and its Annexes, which include the obligation to apprehend and transfer indicted war criminals to the Tribunal.

(2) REPORT.—Not later than 15 days after the date of any written determination under paragraph (1) the Secretary of State shall submit a report to the Committee on Appropriations and the Committee on Foreign Relations of the Senate and the Committee on Appropriations and the Committee on International Relations of

[RESTRICTIONS ON ASSISTANCE TO COUNTRIES PROVIDING SANCTUARY TO INDICTED WAR CRIMINALS]—Continued

the House of Representatives regarding the status of efforts to secure the voluntary surrender or apprehension and transfer of persons indicted by the Tribunal, in accordance with the Dayton Agreement, and outlining obstacles to achieving this goal.

(3) ASSISTANCE PROGRAMS AND PROJECTS AFFECTED.—Any waiver made pursuant to this subsection shall be effective only with respect to a specified bilateral program or multilateral assistance project or program identified in the determination of the Secretary of State to Congress.]

[(i) TERMINATION OF SANCTIONS.—The sanctions imposed pursuant to subsections (a) and (b) with respect to a country or entity shall cease to apply only if the Secretary of State determines and certifies to Congress that the authorities of that country, entity, or municipality have apprehended and transferred to the Tribunal all persons who have been publicly indicted by the Tribunal.]

[(j) DEFINITIONS.—As used in this section—

(1) COUNTRY.—The term "country" means Bosnia-Herzegovina, Croatia, and Serbia.

(2) ENTITY.—The term "entity" refers to the Federation of Bosnia and Herzegovina, Kosova, Montenegro, and the Republika Srpska.

(3) DAYTON AGREEMENT.—The term "Dayton Agreement" means the General Framework Agreement for Peace in Bosnia and Herzegovina, together with annexes relating thereto, done at Dayton, November 10 through 16, 1995.

(4) TRIBUNAL.—The term "Tribunal" means the International Criminal Tribunal for the Former Yugoslavia.]

[(k) ROLE OF HUMAN RIGHTS ORGANIZATIONS AND GOVERNMENT AGENCIES.—In carrying out this section, the Secretary of State, the Administrator of the Agency for International Development, and the executive directors of the international financial institutions shall consult with representatives of human rights organizations and all government agencies with relevant information to help prevent publicly indicted war criminals from benefiting from any financial or technical assistance or grants provided to any country or entity described in subsection (e).]

[TO PROHIBIT FOREIGN ASSISTANCE TO THE GOVERNMENT OF THE RUSSIAN FEDERATION SHOULD IT ENACT LAWS WHICH WOULD DISCRIMINATE AGAINST MINORITY RELIGIOUS FAITHS IN THE RUSSIAN FEDERATION]

[SEC. 567. None of the funds appropriated under this Act may be made available for the Government of the Russian Federation, after 180 days from the date of the enactment of this Act, unless the President determines and certifies in writing to the Committees on Appropriations and the Committee on Foreign Relations of the Senate that the Government of the Russian Federation has implemented no statute, executive order, regulation or similar government action that would discriminate, or would have as its principal effect discrimination, against religious groups or religious communities in the Russian Federation in violation of accepted international agreements on human rights and religious freedoms to which the Russian Federation is a party.]

[GREENHOUSE GAS EMISSIONS]

[SEC. 568. (a) Funds made available in this Act to support programs or activities the primary purpose of which is promoting or assisting country participation in the Kyoto Protocol to the Framework Convention on Climate Change (FCCC) shall only be made available subject to the regular notification procedures of the Committees on Appropriations.]

[(b) The President shall provide a detailed account of all Federal agency obligations and expenditures for climate change programs and activities, domestic and international obligations for such activities in fiscal year 2000, and any plan for programs thereafter related to the implementation or the furtherance of protocols pursuant to, or related to negotiations to amend the FCCC in conjunction with the President's submission of the Budget of the United States Government for Fiscal Year 2001: *Provided*, That such report shall include an accounting of expenditures by agency with each agency identifying climate change activities and associated costs by line item as presented in the President's Budget Appendix: *Provided further*, That such report shall identify with regard to the Agency for International Development, obligations and expenditures by country or central program and activity.]

[EXCESS DEFENSE ARTICLES FOR CERTAIN EUROPEAN COUNTRIES]

[SEC. 569. Section 105 of Public Law 104–164 (110 Stat. 1427) is amended by striking "1996 and 1997" and inserting "1999 and 2000".]

AID TO THE GOVERNMENT OF THE DEMOCRATIC REPUBLIC OF CONGO

SEC. [570] *543.* None of the funds appropriated or otherwise made available by this Act may be provided to the Central Government of the Democratic Republic of Congo*: Provided, That this section shall not apply to assistance to promote democracy and the rule of law for the purpose of supporting the country's transition to democratic government.*

[ASSISTANCE FOR THE MIDDLE EAST]

[SEC. 571. Of the funds appropriated in titles II and III of this Act under the headings "Economic Support Fund", "Foreign Military Financing Program", "International Military Education and Training", "Peacekeeping Operations", for refugees resettling in Israel under the heading "Migration and Refugee Assistance", and for assistance for Israel to carry out provisions of chapter 8 of part II of the Foreign Assistance Act of 1961 under the heading "Nonproliferation, Anti-Terrorism, Demining and Related Programs", not more than a total of $5,321,150,000 may be made available for Israel, Egypt, Jordan, Lebanon, the West Bank and Gaza, the Israel-Lebanon Monitoring Group, the Multinational Force and Observers, the Middle East Regional Democracy Fund, Middle East Regional Cooperation, and Middle East Multilateral Working Groups: *Provided*, That any funds that were appropriated under such headings in prior fiscal years and that were at the time of the enactment of this Act obligated or allocated for other recipients may not during fiscal year 2000 be made available for activities that, if funded under this Act, would be required to count against this ceiling: *Provided further*, That funds may be made available notwithstanding the requirements of this section if the President determines and certifies to the Committees on Appropriations that it is important to the national security interest of the United States to do so and any such additional funds shall only be provided through the regular notification procedures of the Committees on Appropriations.]

[ENTERPRISE FUND RESTRICTIONS]

[SEC. 572. Prior to the distribution of any assets resulting from any liquidation, dissolution, or winding up of an Enterprise Fund, in whole or in part, the President shall submit to the Committees on Appropriations, in accordance with the regular notification procedures of the Committees on Appropriations, a plan for the distribution of the assets of the Enterprise Fund.]

CAMBODIA

SEC. [573. (a)] *544.* The Secretary of the Treasury should instruct the United States executive directors of the international financial institutions to use the voice and vote of the United States to oppose loans to the Central Government of Cambodia, except loans to support basic human needs.

(b) None of the funds appropriated by this Act may be made available for assistance for the Central Government of Cambodia*: Provided, That this paragraph shall not apply to assistance to promote democracy and the rule of law for the purpose of supporting the country's transition to democratic government.*

[CUSTOMS] *LAW ENFORCEMENT* ASSISTANCE

SEC. [574] *545.* Section 660[(b)] of the Foreign Assistance Act of 1961 is [amended by—

(1) striking the period at the end of paragraph (6) and inserting a semicolon; and

(2) adding the following new paragraph:

"(7) with respect to assistance provided to customs authorities and personnel, including training, technical assistance and equipment, for customs law enforcement and the improvement of customs laws, systems and procedures."] *hereby repealed.*

[FOREIGN MILITARY TRAINING REPORT]

[SEC. 575. (a) The Secretary of Defense and the Secretary of State shall jointly provide to the Congress by March 1, 2000, a report on all military training provided to foreign military personnel (excluding sales, and excluding training provided to the military personnel of countries belonging to the North Atlantic Treaty Organization) under programs administered by the Department of Defense and the Department of State during fiscal years 1999 and 2000, including those proposed for fiscal year 2000. This report shall include, for each such military training activity, the foreign policy justification and purpose for the training activity, the cost of the training activity, the number of foreign students trained and their units of operation, and the location of the training. In addition, this report shall also include, with respect to United States personnel, the operational benefits to United States forces derived from each such training activity and the United States military units involved in each such training activity. This report may include a classified annex if deemed necessary and appropriate.]

[(b) For purposes of this section a report to Congress shall be deemed to mean a report to the Appropriations and Foreign Relations Committees of the Senate and the Appropriations and International Relations Committees of the House of Representatives.]

KOREAN PENINSULA ENERGY DEVELOPMENT ORGANIZATION

SEC. [576. (a) Of the funds] *546. Funds* made available under the heading "Nonproliferation, Anti-terrorism, Demining and Related Programs"[, not to exceed $35,000,000] may be made available for the Korean Peninsula Energy Development Organization [(hereafter referred to in this section as "KEDO")], notwithstanding any other provision of law, only for the administrative expenses and heavy fuel oil costs associated with the Agreed Framework.

[(b) Of the funds made available for KEDO, up to $15,000,000 may be made available prior to June 1, 2000, if, 30 days prior to such obligation of funds, the President certifies and so reports to Congress that—

(1) the parties to the Agreed Framework have taken and continue to take demonstrable steps to implement the Joint Declaration on Denuclearization of the Korean Peninsula in which the Government of North Korea has committed not to test, manufacture, produce, receive, possess, store, deploy, or use nuclear weapons, and not to possess nuclear reprocessing or uranium enrichment facilities;

(2) the parties to the Agreed Framework have taken and continue to take demonstrable steps to pursue the North-South dialogue;

(3) North Korea is complying with all provisions of the Agreed Framework;

(4) North Korea has not diverted assistance provided by the United States for purposes for which it was not intended; and

(5) North Korea is not seeking to develop or acquire the capability to enrich uranium, or any additional capability to reprocess spent nuclear fuel.]

[(c) Of the funds made available for KEDO, up to $20,000,000 may be made available on or after June 1, 2000, if, 30 days prior to such obligation of funds, the President certifies and so reports to Congress that—

(1) the effort to can and safely store all spent fuel from North Korea's graphite-moderated nuclear reactors has been successfully concluded;

(2) North Korea is complying with its obligations under the agreement regarding access to suspect underground construction;

(3) North Korea has terminated its nuclear weapons program, including all efforts to acquire, develop, test, produce, or deploy such weapons; and

(4) the United States has made and is continuing to make significant progress on eliminating the North Korean ballistic missile threat, including further missile tests and its ballistic missile exports.]

[(d) The President may waive the certification requirements of subsections (b) and (c) if the President determines that it is vital to the national security interests of the United States and provides written policy justifications to the appropriate congressional committees prior to his exercise of such waiver. No funds may be obligated for KEDO until 30 days after submission to Congress of such waiver.]

[(e) The Secretary of State shall submit to the appropriate congressional committees a report (to be submitted with the annual presentation for appropriations) providing a full and detailed accounting of the fiscal year 2001 request for the United States contribution to KEDO, the expected operating budget of the KEDO, to include unpaid debt, proposed annual costs associated with heavy fuel oil purchases, and the amount of funds pledged by other donor nations and organizations to support KEDO activities on a per country basis, and other related activities.]

AFRICAN DEVELOPMENT FOUNDATION

SEC. [577] *547.* Funds made available to grantees of the African Development Foundation may be invested pending expenditure for project purposes when authorized by the President of the Foundation: *Provided*, That interest earned shall be used only for the purposes for which the grant was made: *Provided further*, That this authority applies to interest earned both prior to and following the enactment of this provision: *Provided further*, That notwithstanding section 505(a)(2) of the African Development Foundation Act, in exceptional circumstances the board of directors of the Foundation may waive the $250,000 limitation contained in that section with respect to a project: *Provided further*, That the Foundation shall provide a report to the Committees on Appropriations in advance of exercising such waiver authority.

[PROHIBITION ON ASSISTANCE TO THE PALESTINIAN BROADCASTING CORPORATION]

[SEC. 578. None of the funds appropriated or otherwise made available by this Act may be used to provide equipment, technical support, consulting services, or any other form of assistance to the Palestinian Broadcasting Corporation.]

VOLUNTARY SEPARATION INCENTIVES FOR EMPLOYEES OF THE UNITED STATES AGENCY FOR INTERNATIONAL DEVELOPMENT

SEC. [579] *548.* [(a) DEFINITIONS.—For the purposes of this section—

(1) the term "agency" means the United States Agency for International Development;

(2) the term "Administrator" means the Administrator, United States Agency for International Development; and

(3) the term "employee" means an employee (as defined by section 2105 of title 5, United States Code) who is employed by the agency, is serving under an appointment without time limitation, and has been currently employed for a continuous period of at least 3 years, but does not include—

(A) a reemployed annuitant under subchapter III of chapter 83 or chapter 84 of title 5, United States Code, or another retirement system for employees of the agency;

(B) an employee having a disability on the basis of which such employee is or would be eligible for disability retirement under the applicable retirement system referred to in subparagraph (A);

(C) an employee who is to be separated involuntarily for misconduct or unacceptable performance, and to whom specific notice has been given with respect to that separation;

(D) an employee who has previously received any voluntary separation incentive payment by the Government of the United States under this section or any other authority and has not repaid such payment;

(E) an employee covered by statutory reemployment rights who is on transfer to another organization; or

(F) any employee who, during the 24-month period preceding the date of separation, received a recruitment or relocation bonus under section 5753 of title 5, United States Code, or who, within the 12-month period preceding the date of separation, received a retention allowance under section 5754 of such title 5, United States Code.]

[(b) AGENCY STRATEGIC PLAN.—

(1) IN GENERAL.—The Administrator, before obligating any resources for voluntary separation incentive payments under this section, shall submit to the Committees on Appropriations and the Office of Management and Budget a strategic plan outlining the intended use of such incentive payments and a proposed organizational chart for the agency once such incentive payments have been completed.

(2) CONTENTS.—The agency's plan shall include—

(A) the positions and functions to be reduced or eliminated, identified by organizational unit, geographic location, occupational category and grade level;

(B) the number and amounts of voluntary separation incentive payments to be offered;

(C) a description of how the agency will operate without the eliminated positions and functions; and

(D) the time period during which incentives may be paid.

(3) APPROVAL.—The Director of the Office of Management and Budget shall review the agency's plan and approve or disapprove the plan and may make appropriate modifications in the plan with respect to the coverage of incentives as described under paragraph (2)(A), and with respect to the matters described in paragraphs (2)(B) through (D).]

[(c) AUTHORITY TO PROVIDE VOLUNTARY SEPARATION INCENTIVE PAYMENTS.—

VOLUNTARY SEPARATION INCENTIVES FOR EMPLOYEES OF THE UNITED STATES AGENCY FOR INTERNATIONAL DEVELOPMENT—Continued

(1) IN GENERAL.—A voluntary separation incentive payment under this section may be paid by the agency to employees of such agency and only to the extent necessary to eliminate the positions and functions identified by the strategic plan.

(2) AMOUNT AND TREATMENT OF PAYMENTS.—A voluntary separation incentive payment under this section—

(A) shall be paid in a lump sum after the employee's separation;

(B) shall be paid from appropriations or funds available for the payment of the basic pay of the employees;

(C) shall be equal to the lesser of—

(i) an amount equal to the amount the employee would be entitled to receive under section 5595(c) of title 5, United States Code, if the employee were entitled to payment under such section; or

(ii) an amount determined by the agency head not to exceed $25,000;

(D) may not be made except in the case of any employee who voluntarily separates (whether by retirement or resignation) on or before December 31, 2000;

(E) shall not be a basis for payment, and shall not be included in the computation, of any other type of Government benefit; and

(F) shall not be taken into account in determining the amount of any severance pay to which the employee may be entitled under section 5595 of title 5, United States Code, based on any other separation.]

[(d) ADDITIONAL AGENCY CONTRIBUTIONS TO THE RETIREMENT FUND.—

(1) IN GENERAL.—In addition to any other payments which it is required to make under subchapter III of chapter 83 or chapter 84 of title 5, United States Code, the agency shall remit to the Office of Personnel Management for deposit in the Treasury of the United States to the credit of the Civil Service Retirement and Disability Fund an amount equal to 15 percent of the final basic pay of each employee of the agency who is covered under subchapter III of chapter 83 or chapter 84 of title 5, United States Code, to whom a voluntary separation incentive has been paid under this section.

(2) DEFINITION.—For the purpose of paragraph (1), the term "final basic pay", with respect to an employee, means the total amount of basic pay which would be payable for a year of service by such employee, computed using the employee's final rate of basic pay, and, if last serving on other than a full-time basis, with appropriate adjustment therefor.]

[(e) EFFECT OF SUBSEQUENT EMPLOYMENT WITH THE GOVERNMENT.—

(1) An individual who has received a voluntary separation incentive payment under this section and accepts any employment for compensation with the Government of the United States, or who works for any agency of the Government of the United States through a personal services contract, within 5 years after the date of the separation on which the payment is based shall be required to pay, prior to the individual's first day of employment, the entire amount of the incentive payment to the agency that paid the incentive payment.

(2) If the employment under paragraph (1) is with an Executive agency (as defined by section 105 of title 5, United States Code), the United States Postal Service, or the Postal Rate Commission, the Director of the Office of Personnel Management may, at the request of the head of the agency, waive the repayment if the individual involved possesses unique abilities and is the only qualified applicant available for the position.

(3) If the employment under paragraph (1) is with an entity in the legislative branch, the head of the entity or the appointing official may waive the repayment if the individual involved possesses unique abilities and is the only qualified applicant available for the position.

(4) If the employment under paragraph (1) is with the judicial branch, the Director of the Administrative Office of the United States Courts may waive the repayment if the individual involved possesses unique abilities and is the only qualified applicant for the position.]

[(f) REDUCTION OF AGENCY EMPLOYMENT LEVELS.—

(1) IN GENERAL.—The total number of funded employee positions in the agency shall be reduced by one position for each vacancy created by the separation of any employee who has received, or is due to receive, a voluntary separation incentive payment under this section. For the purposes of this subsection, positions shall be counted on a full-time-equivalent basis.

(2) ENFORCEMENT.—The President, through the Office of Management and Budget, shall monitor the agency and take any action necessary to ensure that the requirements of this subsection are met.]

[(g) REGULATIONS.—The Office of Personnel Management may prescribe such regulations as may be necessary to implement this section.]

Section 579(c)(2)(D) of the Foreign Operations, Export Financing, and Related Programs Appropriations Act, 2000, as enacted by section 1000(a)(2) of the Consolidated Appropriations Act, 2000 (P.L. 106–113), is amended by striking "December 31, 2000" and inserting in lieu thereof "December 31, 2001".

IRAQ OPPOSITION

SEC. [580] *549.* Notwithstanding any other provision of law, [of the] funds appropriated under the heading "Economic Support Fund"[, $10,000,000 shall] *may* be made available to support efforts to bring about political transition in Iraq, [of which not less than $8,000,000 shall be made available only to Iraqi opposition groups designated under the Iraq Liberation Act (Public Law 105–338) for political, economic, humanitarian, and other activities of such groups, and not more than $2,000,000 may be made available for groups and activities seeking the prosecution of Saddam Hussein and other Iraqi government officials for war crimes] *including assistance to: (1) the Iraqi democratic opposition for such activities as organization, training, communication and dissemination of information, and developing and implementing agreements among opposition groups, and (2) non-governmental organizations for such activities as establishing and publicizing an international record of Iraqi war crimes, crimes against humanity, genocide, and other violations of international law and encouraging the formation of an international commission and an ad hoc international criminal tribunal to investigate and prosecute these crimes.*

[AGENCY FOR INTERNATIONAL DEVELOPMENT BUDGET SUBMISSION]

[SEC. 581. Beginning with the fiscal year 2001 budget, the Agency for International Development shall submit to the Committees on Appropriations a detailed budget for each fiscal year. The Agency shall submit to the Committees on Appropriations a proposed budget format no later than October 31, 1999, or 30 days after the enactment of this Act, whichever occurs later. The proposed format shall include how the Agency's budget submission will address: (1) estimated levels of obligations for the current fiscal year and actual levels for the two previous fiscal years; (2) the President's request for new budget authority and estimated carryover obligational authority for the budget year; (3) the disaggregation of budget data by program and activity for each bureau, field mission, and central office; and (4) staff levels identified by program.]

[AMERICAN CHURCHWOMEN IN EL SALVADOR]

[SEC. 582. (a) Information relevant to the December 2, 1980 murders of four American churchwomen in El Salvador shall be made public to the fullest extent possible.]

[(b) The Secretary of State and the Department of State are to be commended for fully releasing information regarding the murders.]

[(c) The President shall order all Federal agencies and departments that possess relevant information to make every effort to declassify and release to the victims' families relevant information as expeditiously as possible.]

[(d) In making determinations concerning the declassification and release of relevant information, the Federal agencies and departments shall presume in favor of releasing, rather than of withholding, such information.]

[(e) Not later than 45 days after the date of the enactment of this Act, the Attorney General shall provide a report to the Committees on Appropriations describing in detail the circumstances under which individuals involved in the murders or the cover-up of the murders obtained residence in the United States.]

[KYOTO PROTOCOL]

[SEC. 583. None of the funds appropriated by this Act shall be used to propose or issue rules, regulations, decrees, or orders for the purpose of implementation, or in preparation for implementation, of the Kyoto Protocol, which was adopted on December 11, 1997, in Kyoto, Japan, at the Third Conference of the Parties to the United States Framework Convention on Climate Change, which has not been submitted to the Senate for advice and consent to ratification pursuant to article II, section 2, clause 2, of the United States Constitution, and which has not entered into force pursuant to article 25 of the Protocol.]

ADDITIONAL REQUIREMENTS RELATING TO STOCKPILING OF DEFENSE ARTICLES FOR FOREIGN COUNTRIES

SEC. [584] *550.* (a) VALUE OF ADDITIONS TO STOCKPILES.—Section 514(b)(2)(A) of the Foreign Assistance Act of 1961 (22 U.S.C. 2321h(b)(2)(A)) is amended by striking ["$50,000,000 for each of the fiscal years 1996 and 1997, $60,000,000 for fiscal year 1998, and" and inserting before the period at the end, the following: "and $60,000,000 for fiscal year 2000"] *"$60,000,000 for fiscal year 2000, and", and inserting before the period at the end, the following: "and $50,000,000 for fiscal year 2001".*

WORKING CAPITAL FUND

SEC. 551. (a) Section 635 of the Foreign Assistance Act of 1961 (22 U.S.C. 2395) is amended by adding a new subsection (l) as follows:

"(l) There is hereby established a working capital fund for the Agency for International Development which shall be available without fiscal year limitation for the expenses of personal and nonpersonal services, equipment and supplies for International Cooperative Administrative Support Services.

"(2) The capital of the fund shall consist of the fair and reasonable value of such supplies, equipment and other assets pertaining to the functions of the fund as the Administrator determines, rebates from the use of United States Government credit cards, and any appropriations made available for the purpose of providing capital, less related liabilities and unpaid obligations.

"(3) The fund shall be reimbursed or credited with advance payments for services, equipment or supplies provided from the fund from applicable appropriations and funds of the agency, other Federal agencies and other sources authorized by section 607 of this Act at rates that will recover total expenses of operation, including accrual of annual leave and depreciation. Receipts from the disposal of, or payments for the loss or damage to, property held in the fund, rebates, reimbursements, refunds and other credits applicable to the operation of the fund may be deposited in the fund.

"(4) The agency shall transfer to the Treasury as miscellaneous receipts as of the close of the fiscal year such amounts which the Administrator determines to be in excess of the needs of the fund.

"(5) The fund may be charged with the current value of supplies and equipment returned to the working capital of the fund by a post, activity or agency and the proceeds shall, if otherwise authorized, be credited to current applicable appropriations.".

(b) REQUIREMENTS RELATING TO THE REPUBLIC OF KOREA AND THAILAND.—Section 514(b)(2)(B) of such Act (22 U.S.C. 2321h(b)(2)(B)) is amended by [striking "Of the amount specified in subparagraph (A) for each of the fiscal years 1996 and 1997, not more than $40,000,000 may be made available for stockpiles in the Republic of Korea and not more than $10,000,000 may be made available for stockpiles in Thailand. Of the amount specified in subparagraph (A) for fiscal year 1998, not more than $40,000,000 may be made available for stockpiles in the Republic of Korea and not more than $20,000,000 may be made available for stockpiles in Thailand."; and at the end inserting the following sentence: "Of the amount specified in subparagraph (A) for fiscal year 2000, not more than $40,000,000 may be made available for stockpiles in the Republic of Korea and not more than $20,000,000 may be made available for stockpiles in Thailand."] *inserting at the end thereof the following sentence: "Of the amount specified in subparagraph (A) for fiscal year 2001, not more than $50,000,000 may be made available for stockpiles in the Republic of Korea".*

[RUSSIAN LEADERSHIP PROGRAM]

[SEC. 585. Section 3011 of the 1999 Emergency Supplemental Appropriations Act (Public Law 106–31; 113 Stat. 93) is amended—

(1) by striking "fiscal year 1999" in subsections (a)(1), (b)(4)(B), (d)(3), and (h)(1)(A) and inserting "fiscal years 1999 and 2000"; and

(2) by striking "2000" in subsection (a)(2), (e)(1), and (h)(1)(B) and inserting "2001".]

[ABOLITION OF THE INTER-AMERICAN FOUNDATION]

[SEC. 586. (a) DEFINITIONS.—In this section:

(1) DIRECTOR.—The term "Director" means the Director of the Office of Management and Budget.

(2) FOUNDATION.—The term "Foundation" means the Inter-American Foundation.

(3) FUNCTION.—The term "function" means any duty, obligation, power, authority, responsibility, right, privilege, activity, or program.]

[(b) ABOLITION OF INTER-AMERICAN FOUNDATION.—During fiscal year 2000, the President is authorized to abolish the Inter-American Foundation. The provisions of this section shall only be effective upon the effective date of the abolition of the Inter-American Foundation.]

[(c) TERMINATION OF FUNCTIONS.—

(1) Except as provided in subsection (d)(2), there are terminated upon the abolition of the Foundation all functions vested in, or exercised by, the Foundation or any official thereof, under any statute, reorganization plan, Executive order, or other provisions of law, as of the day before the effective date of this section.

(2) REPEAL.—Section 401 of the Foreign Assistance Act of 1969 (22 U.S.C. 6290f) is repealed upon the effective date specified in subsection (j).

(3) FINAL DISPOSITION OF FUNDS.—Upon the date of transmittal to Congress of the certification described in subsection (d)(4), all unexpended balances of appropriations of the Foundation shall be deposited in the miscellaneous receipts account of the Treasury of the United States.]

[(d) RESPONSIBILITIES OF THE DIRECTOR OF THE OFFICE OF MANAGEMENT AND BUDGET.—

(1) IN GENERAL.—The Director of the Office of Management and Budget shall be responsible for—

(A) the administration and wind-up of any outstanding obligation of the Federal Government under any contract or agreement entered into by the Foundation before the date of the enactment of the Foreign Operations, Export Financing, and Related Programs Appropriations Act, 2000, except that the authority of this subparagraph does not include the renewal or extension of any such contract or agreement; and

(B) taking such other actions as may be necessary to wind-up any outstanding affairs of the Foundation.

(2) TRANSFER OF FUNCTIONS TO THE DIRECTOR.—There are transferred to the Director such functions of the Foundation under any statute, reorganization plan, Executive order, or other provision of law, as of the day before the date of the enactment of this section, as may be necessary to carry out the responsibilities of the Director under paragraph (1).

(3) AUTHORITIES OF THE DIRECTOR.—For purposes of performing the functions of the Director under paragraph (1) and subject to the availability of appropriations, the Director may—

(A) enter into contracts;

(B) employ experts and consultants in accordance with section 3109 of title 5, United States Code, at rates for individuals not to exceed the per diem rate equivalent to the rate for level IV of the Executive Schedule; and

(C) utilize, on a reimbursable basis, the services, facilities, and personnel of other Federal agencies.

(4) CERTIFICATION REQUIRED.—Whenever the Director determines that the responsibilities described in paragraph (1) have been fully discharged, the Director shall so certify to the appropriate congressional committees.]

[(e) REPORT TO CONGRESS.—The Director of the Office of Management and Budget shall submit to the appropriate congressional committees a detailed report in writing regarding all matters relating to the abolition and termination of the Foundation. The report shall be submitted not later than 90 days after the termination of the Foundation.]

[(f) TRANSFER AND ALLOCATION OF APPROPRIATIONS.—Except as otherwise provided in this section, the assets, liabilities (including contingent liabilities arising from suits continued with a substitution or addition of parties under subsection (g)(3)), contracts, property, records, and unexpended balance of appropriations, authorizations, allocations, and other funds employed, held, used, arising from, available to, or to be made available in connection with the functions, terminated by subsection (c)(1) or transferred by subsection (d)(2) shall be transferred to the Director for purposes of carrying out the responsibilities described in subsection (d)(1).]

[(g) SAVINGS PROVISIONS.—

(1) CONTINUING LEGAL FORCE AND EFFECT.—All orders, determinations, rules, regulations, permits, agreements, grants, con-

[ABOLITION OF THE INTER-AMERICAN FOUNDATION]—Continued

tracts, certificates, licenses, registrations, privileges, and other administrative actions—

(A) that have been issued, made, granted, or allowed to become effective by the Foundation in the performance of functions that are terminated or transferred under this section; and

(B) that are in effect as of the date of the abolition of the Foundation, or were final before such date and are to become effective on or after such date,

shall continue in effect according to their terms until modified, terminated, superseded, set aside, or revoked in accordance with law by the President, the Director, or other authorized official, a court of competent jurisdiction, or by operation of law.

(2) NO EFFECT ON JUDICIAL OR ADMINISTRATIVE PROCEEDINGS.—Except as otherwise provided in this section—

(A) the provisions of this section shall not affect suits commenced prior to the date of the abolition of the Foundation; and

(B) in all such suits, proceedings shall be had, appeals taken, and judgments rendered in the same manner and effect as if this section had not been enacted.

(3) NONABATEMENT OF PROCEEDINGS.—No suit, action, or other proceeding commenced by or against any officer in the official capacity of such individual as an officer of the Foundation shall abate by reason of the enactment of this section. No cause of action by or against the Foundation, or by or against any officer thereof in the official capacity of such officer, shall abate by reason of the enactment of this section.

(4) CONTINUATION OF PROCEEDING WITH SUBSTITUTION OF PARTIES.—If, before the date of the abolition of the Foundation, the Foundation, or officer thereof in the official capacity of such officer, is a party to a suit, then effective on such date such suit shall be continued with the Director substituted or added as a party.

(5) REVIEWABILITY OF ORDERS AND ACTIONS UNDER TRANSFERRED FUNCTIONS.—Orders and actions of the Director in the exercise of functions terminated or transferred under this section shall be subject to judicial review to the same extent and in the same manner as if such orders and actions had been taken by the Foundation immediately preceding their termination or transfer. Any statutory requirements relating to notice, hearings, action upon the record, or administrative review that apply to any function transferred by this section shall apply to the exercise of such function by the Director.]

[(h) CONFORMING AMENDMENTS.—

(1) AFRICAN DEVELOPMENT FOUNDATION.—Section 502 of the International Security and Development Cooperation Act of 1980 (22 U.S.C. 290h) is amended—

(A) by inserting "and" at the end of paragraph (2);

(B) by striking the semicolon at the end of paragraph (3) and inserting a period; and

(C) by striking paragraphs (4) and (5).

(2) SOCIAL PROGRESS TRUST FUND AGREEMENT.—Section 36 of the Foreign Assistance Act of 1973 is amended—

(A) in subsection (a)—

(i) by striking "provide for" and all that follows through "(2) utilization" and inserting "provide for the utilization"; and

(ii) by striking "member countries;" and all that follows through "paragraph (2)" and inserting "member countries.";

(B) in subsection (b), by striking "transfer or";

(C) by striking subsection (c);

(D) by redesignating subsection (d) as subsection (c); and

(E) in subsection (c) (as so redesignated), by striking "transfer or".

(3) FOREIGN ASSISTANCE ACT OF 1961.—Section 222A(d) of the Foreign Assistance Act of 1961 (22 U.S.C. 2182a(d)) is repealed.]

[(i) DEFINITION.—In this section, the term "appropriate congressional committees" means the Committee on Appropriations and the Committee on Foreign Relations of the Senate and the Committee on Appropriations and the Committee on International Relations of the House of Representatives.]

[(j) EFFECTIVE DATES.—The repeal made by subsection (c)(2) and the amendments made by subsection (h) shall take effect upon the date of transmittal to Congress of the certification described in subsection (d)(4).]

[WEST BANK AND GAZA PROGRAM]

[SEC. 587. For fiscal year 2000, 30 days prior to the initial obligation of funds for the bilateral West Bank and Gaza Program, the Secretary of State shall certify to the appropriate committees of Congress that procedures have been established to assure the Comptroller General of the United States will have access to appropriate United States financial information in order to review the uses of United States assistance for the Program funded under the heading "Economic Support Fund" for the West Bank and Gaza.]

[HUMAN RIGHTS ASSISTANCE]

[SEC. 588. Of the funds made available under the heading "International Narcotics Control and Law Enforcement", not less than $500,000 should be provided to the Colombia Attorney General's Human Rights Unit, not less than $500,000 should be made available to support the activities of Colombian nongovernmental organizations involved in human rights monitoring, not less than $250,000 should be provided to the United Nations High Commissioner for Human Rights to assist the Government of Colombia in strengthening its human rights policies and programs, not less than $1,000,000 should be made available for personnel and other resources to enhance United States Embassy monitoring of assistance to the Colombian security forces and responding to reports of human rights violations, and not less than $5,000,000 should be made available for administration of justice programs including support for the Colombia Attorney General's Technical Investigations Unit.]

[INDONESIA]

[SEC. 589. (a) Funds appropriated by this Act under the headings "International Military Education and Training" and "Foreign Military Financing Program" may be made available for Indonesia if the President determines and submits a report to the appropriate congressional committees that the Indonesian government and the Indonesian armed forces are—

(1) taking effective measures to bring to justice members of the armed forces and militia groups against whom there is credible evidence of human rights violations;

(2) taking effective measures to bring to justice members of the armed forces against whom there is credible evidence of aiding or abetting militia groups;

(3) allowing displaced persons and refugees to return home to East Timor, including providing safe passage for refugees returning from West Timor;

(4) not impeding the activities of the International Force in East Timor (INTERFET) or its successor, the United Nations Transitional Authority in East Timor (UNTAET);

(5) demonstrating a commitment to preventing incursions into East Timor by members of militia groups in West Timor; and

(6) demonstrating a commitment to accountability by cooperating with investigations and prosecutions of members of the Indonesian armed forces and militia groups responsible for human rights violations in Indonesia and East Timor.]

[MAN AND THE BIOSPHERE]

[SEC. 590. None of the funds appropriated or otherwise made available by this Act may be provided for the United Nations Man and the Biosphere Program or the United Nations World Heritage Fund for programs in the United States.]

[IMMUNITY OF FEDERAL REPUBLIC OF YUGOSLAVIA]

[SEC. 591. (a) Subject to subsection (b), the Federal Republic of Yugoslavia shall be deemed to be a state sponsor of terrorism for the purposes of 28 U.S.C. 1605(a)(7).]

[(b) This section shall not apply to Montenegro or Kosova.]

[(c) This section shall become null and void when the President certifies in writing to the Congress that the Federal Republic of Yugoslavia (other than Montenegro and Kosova) has completed a democratic reform process that results in a newly elected government that respects the rights of ethnic minorities, is committed to the rule of law and respects the sovereignty of its neighbor states.]

[(d) The certification provided for in subsection (c) shall not affect the continuation of litigation commenced against the Federal Republic of Yugoslavia prior to its fulfillment of the conditions in subsection (c).]

[UNITED STATES ASSISTANCE POLICY FOR OPPOSITION-CONTROLLED AREAS OF SUDAN]

[SEC. 592. (a) Notwithstanding any other provision of law, the President, acting through appropriate Federal agencies, may provide food assistance to groups engaged in the protection of civilian populations from attacks by regular government of Sudan forces, associated militias, or other paramilitary groups supported by the Government of Sudan. Such assistance may only be provided in a way that: (1) does not endanger, compromise or otherwise reduce the United States' support for unilateral, multilateral or private humanitarian operations or the beneficiaries of those operations; or (2) compromise any ongoing or future people-to-people reconciliation efforts. Any such assistance shall be provided separate from and not in proximity to current humanitarian efforts, both within Operation Lifeline Sudan or outside of Operation Lifeline Sudan, or any other current or future humanitarian operations which serve noncombatants. In considering eligibility of potential recipients, the President shall determine that the group respects human rights, democratic principles, and the integrity of ongoing humanitarian operations, and cease such assistance if the determination can no longer be made.]

[(b) Not later than February 1, 2000, the President shall submit to the Committees on Appropriations a report on United States bilateral assistance to opposition-controlled areas of Sudan. Such report shall include—

(1) an accounting of United States bilateral assistance to opposition-controlled areas of Sudan, provided in fiscal years 1997, 1998, 1999, and proposed for fiscal year 2000, and the goals and objectives of such assistance;

(2) the policy implications and costs, including logistics and administrative costs, associated with providing humanitarian assistance, including food, directly to National Democratic Alliance participants and the Sudanese People's Liberation Movement operating outside of the United Nations' Operation Lifeline Sudan structure, and the United States agencies best suited to administer these activities; and

(3) the policy implications of increasing substantially the amount of development assistance for democracy promotion, civil administration, judiciary, and infrastructure support in opposition-controlled areas of Sudan and the obstacles to administering a development assistance program in this region.]

[CONSULTATIONS ON ARMS SALES TO TAIWAN]

[SEC. 593. Consistent with the intent of Congress expressed in the enactment of section 3(b) of the Taiwan Relations Act, the Secretary of State shall consult with the appropriate committees and leadership of Congress to devise a mechanism to provide for congressional input prior to making any determination on the nature or quantity of defense articles and services to be made available to Taiwan.]

[AUTHORIZATIONS]

[SEC. 594. The Secretary of the Treasury may, to fulfill commitments of the United States: (1) effect the United States participation in the fifth general capital increase of the African Development Bank, the first general capital increase of the Multilateral Investment Guarantee Agency, and the first general capital increase of the Inter-American Investment Corporation; and (2) contribute on behalf of the United States to the eighth replenishment of the resources of the African Development Fund and the twelfth replenishment of the International Development Association. The following amounts are authorized to be appropriated without fiscal year limitation for payment by the Secretary of the Treasury: $40,847,011 for paid-in capital, and $639,932,485 for callable capital, of the African Development Bank; $29,870,087 for paid-in capital, and $139,365,533 for callable capital, of the Multilateral Investment Guarantee Agency; $125,180,000 for paid-in capital of the Inter-American Investment Corporation; $300,000,000 for the African Development Fund; and $2,410,000,000 for the International Development Association.]

[ASSISTANCE FOR COSTA RICA]

[SEC. 595. Of the funds appropriated by Public Law 106–31, under the heading "Central America and the Caribbean Emergency Disaster Recovery Fund", $8,000,000 shall be made available only for Costa Rica.]

[SILK ROAD STRATEGY ACT OF 1999]

[SEC. 596. (a) SHORT TITLE.—This section may be cited as the "Silk Road Strategy Act of 1999".]

[(b) AMENDMENT TO THE FOREIGN ASSISTANCE ACT OF 1961.—Part I of the Foreign Assistance Act of 1961 (22 U.S.C. 2151 et seq.) is amended by adding at the end the following new chapter:

"CHAPTER 12—SUPPORT FOR THE ECONOMIC AND POLITICAL INDEPENDENCE OF THE COUNTRIES OF THE SOUTH CAUCASUS AND CENTRAL ASIA

"SEC. 499. UNITED STATES ASSISTANCE TO PROMOTE RECONCILIATION AND RECOVERY FROM REGIONAL CONFLICTS.

"(a) PURPOSE OF ASSISTANCE.—The purposes of assistance under this section include—

"(1) the creation of the basis for reconciliation between belligerents;

"(2) the promotion of economic development in areas of the countries of the South Caucasus and Central Asia impacted by civil conflict and war; and

"(3) the encouragement of broad regional cooperation among countries of the South Caucasus and Central Asia that have been destabilized by internal conflicts.

"(b) AUTHORIZATION FOR ASSISTANCE.—

"(1) IN GENERAL.—To carry out the purposes of subsection (a), the President is authorized to provide humanitarian assistance and economic reconstruction assistance for the countries of the South Caucasus and Central Asia to support the activities described in subsection (c).

"(2) DEFINITION OF HUMANITARIAN ASSISTANCE.—In this subsection, the term 'humanitarian assistance' means assistance to meet humanitarian needs, including needs for food, medicine, medical supplies and equipment, education, and clothing.

"(c) ACTIVITIES SUPPORTED.—Activities that may be supported by assistance under subsection (b) include—

"(1) providing for the humanitarian needs of victims of the conflicts;

"(2) facilitating the return of refugees and internally displaced persons to their homes; and

"(3) assisting in the reconstruction of residential and economic infrastructure destroyed by war.

"SEC. 499A. ECONOMIC ASSISTANCE.

"(a) PURPOSE OF ASSISTANCE.—The purpose of assistance under this section is to foster economic growth and development, including the conditions necessary for regional economic cooperation, in the South Caucasus and Central Asia.

"(b) AUTHORIZATION FOR ASSISTANCE.—To carry out the purpose of subsection (a), the President is authorized to provide assistance for the countries of the South Caucasus and Central Asia to support the activities described in subsection (c).

"(c) ACTIVITIES SUPPORTED.—In addition to the activities described in section 498, activities supported by assistance under subsection (b) should support the development of the structures and means necessary for the growth of private sector economies based upon market principles.

"SEC. 499B. DEVELOPMENT OF INFRASTRUCTURE.

"(a) PURPOSE OF PROGRAMS.—The purposes of programs under this section include—

"(1) to develop the physical infrastructure necessary for regional cooperation among the countries of the South Caucasus and Central Asia; and

"(2) to encourage closer economic relations and to facilitate the removal of impediments to cross-border commerce among those countries and the United States and other developed nations.

"(b) AUTHORIZATION FOR PROGRAMS.—To carry out the purposes of subsection (a), the following types of programs for the countries of the South Caucasus and Central Asia may be used to support the activities described in subsection (c):

"(1) Activities by the Export-Import Bank to complete the review process for eligibility for financing under the Export-Import Bank Act of 1945.

"(2) The provision of insurance, reinsurance, financing, or other assistance by the Overseas Private Investment Corporation.

"(3) Assistance under section 661 of this Act (relating to the Trade and Development Agency).

"(c) ACTIVITIES SUPPORTED.—Activities that may be supported by programs under subsection (b) include promoting actively the participation of United States companies and investors in the planning, financing, and construction of infrastructure for communications, transportation, including air transportation, and energy and trade including highways, railroads, port facilities, shipping, banking, insurance, telecommunications networks, and gas and oil pipelines.

"SEC. 499C. BORDER CONTROL ASSISTANCE.

"(a) PURPOSE OF ASSISTANCE.—The purpose of assistance under this section includes the assistance of the countries of the South Caucasus and Central Asia to secure their borders and implement effective controls necessary to prevent the trafficking of illegal narcotics and the proliferation of technology and materials related to weapons of mass destruction (as defined in section 2332a(c)(2) of title 18, United States Code), and to contain and inhibit transnational organized criminal activities.

"(b) AUTHORIZATION FOR ASSISTANCE.—To carry out the purpose of subsection (a), the President is authorized to provide assistance to the countries of the South Caucasus and Central Asia to support the activities described in subsection (c).

"(c) ACTIVITIES SUPPORTED.—Activities that may be supported by assistance under subsection (b) include assisting those countries of the South Caucasus and Central Asia in developing capabilities to maintain national border guards, coast guard, and customs controls.

"SEC. 499D. STRENGTHENING DEMOCRACY, TOLERANCE, AND THE DEVELOPMENT OF CIVIL SOCIETY.

"(a) PURPOSE OF ASSISTANCE.—The purpose of assistance under this section is to promote institutions of democratic government and to create the conditions for the growth of pluralistic societies, including religious tolerance and respect for internationally recognized human rights.

"(b) AUTHORIZATION FOR ASSISTANCE.—To carry out the purpose of subsection (a), the President is authorized to provide the following types of assistance to the countries of the South Caucasus and Central Asia:

"(1) Assistance for democracy building, including programs to strengthen parliamentary institutions and practices.

"(2) Assistance for the development of nongovernmental organizations.

"(3) Assistance for development of independent media.

"(4) Assistance for the development of the rule of law, a strong independent judiciary, and transparency in political practice and commercial transactions.

"(5) International exchanges and advanced professional training programs in skill areas central to the development of civil society.

"(6) Assistance to promote increased adherence to civil and political rights under section 116(e) of this Act.

"(c) ACTIVITIES SUPPORTED.—Activities that may be supported by assistance under subsection (b) include activities that are designed to advance progress toward the development of democracy.

"SEC. 499E. ADMINISTRATIVE AUTHORITIES.

"(a) ASSISTANCE THROUGH GOVERNMENTS AND NONGOVERNMENTAL ORGANIZATIONS.—Assistance under this chapter may be provided to governments or through nongovernmental organizations.

"(b) USE OF ECONOMIC SUPPORT FUNDS.—Except as otherwise provided, any funds that have been allocated under chapter 4 of part II for assistance for the independent states of the former Soviet Union may be used in accordance with the provisions of this chapter.

"(c) TERMS AND CONDITIONS.—Assistance under this chapter shall be provided on such terms and conditions as the President may determine.

"(d) AVAILABLE AUTHORITIES.—The authority in this chapter to provide assistance for the countries of the South Caucasus and Central Asia is in addition to the authority to provide such assistance under the FREEDOM Support Act (22 U.S.C. 5801 et seq.) or any other Act, and the authorities applicable to the provision of assistance under chapter 11 may be used to provide assistance under this chapter.

"SEC. 499F. DEFINITIONS.

"In this chapter:

"(1) APPROPRIATE CONGRESSIONAL COMMITTEES.—The term 'appropriate congressional committees' means the Committee on Foreign Relations of the Senate and the Committee on International Relations of the House of Representatives.

"(2) COUNTRIES OF THE SOUTH CAUCASUS AND CENTRAL ASIA.—The term 'countries of the South Caucasus and Central Asia' means Armenia, Azerbaijan, Georgia, Kazakstan, Kyrgyzstan, Tajikistan, Turkmenistan, and Uzbekistan.".]

[(c) CONFORMING AMENDMENTS.—Section 102(a) of the FREEDOM Support Act (Public Law 102–511) is amended in paragraphs (2) and (4) by striking each place it appears "this Act)" and inserting "this Act and chapter 12 of part I of the Foreign Assistance Act of 1961)".]

[(d) ANNUAL REPORT.—Section 104 of the FREEDOM Support Act (22 U.S.C. 5814) is amended—

(1) by striking "and" at the end of paragraph (3);

(2) by striking the period at the end of paragraph (4) and inserting "; and"; and

(3) by adding at the end the following new paragraph:

"(5) with respect to the countries of the South Caucasus and Central Asia—

"(A) an identification of the progress made by the United States in accomplishing the policy described in section 3 of the Silk Road Strategy Act of 1999;

"(B) an evaluation of the degree to which the assistance authorized by chapter 12 of part I of the Foreign Assistance Act of 1961 has accomplished the purposes identified in that chapter;

"(C) a description of the progress being made by the United States to resolve trade disputes registered with and raised by the United States embassies in each country, and to negotiate a bilateral agreement relating to the protection of United States direct investment in, and other business interests with, each country; and

"(D) recommendations of any additional initiatives that should be undertaken by the United States to implement the policy and purposes contained in the Silk Road Strategy Act of 1999.".]

[COUNTRY REPORTS ON HUMAN RIGHTS PRACTICES]

[SEC. 597. Section 116 of the Foreign Assistance Act of 1961 is amended by adding the following new subsection:

"(f)(1) The report required by subsection (d) shall include—

"(A) a list of foreign states where trafficking in persons, especially women and children, originates, passes through, or is a destination; and

"(B) an assessment of the efforts by the governments of the states described in paragraph (A) to combat trafficking. Such an assessment shall address—

"(i) whether government authorities in each such state tolerate or are involved in trafficking activities;

"(ii) which government authorities in each such state are involved in anti-trafficking activities;

"(iii) what steps the government of each such state has taken to prohibit government officials and other individuals from participating in trafficking, including the investigation, prosecution, and conviction of individuals involved in trafficking;

"(iv) what steps the government of each such state has taken to assist trafficking victims;

"(v) whether the government of each such state is cooperating with governments of other countries to extradite traffickers when requested;

"(vi) whether the government of each such state is assisting in international investigations of transnational trafficking networks; and

"(vii) whether the government of each such state refrains from prosecuting trafficking victims or refrains from other discriminatory treatment towards victims.

"(2) In compiling data and assessing trafficking for the purposes of paragraph (1), United States Diplomatic Mission personnel shall consult with human rights and other appropriate nongovernmental organizations.

"(3) For purposes of this subsection—

"(A) the term 'trafficking' means the use of deception, coercion, debt bondage, the threat of force, or the abuse of authority to recruit, transport within or across borders, purchase, sell, transfer, receive, or harbor a person for the purposes of placing or holding such person, whether for pay or not, in involuntary servitude, slavery or slavery-like conditions, or in forced, bonded, or coerced labor;

"(B) the term 'victim of trafficking' means any person subjected to the treatment described in subparagraph (A).".]

[OPIC MARITIME FUND]

[SEC. 598. It is the sense of the Congress that the Overseas Private Investment Corporation shall within 1 year from the date of the enactment of this Act select a fund manager for the purpose of creating a maritime fund with total capitalization of up to $200,000,000. This fund shall leverage United States commercial maritime expertise to support international maritime projects.]

[SANCTIONS AGAINST SERBIA]

[SEC. 599. (a) CONTINUATION OF EXECUTIVE BRANCH SANCTIONS.—The sanctions listed in subsection (b) shall remain in effect for fiscal year 2000, unless the President submits to the Committees on Appropriations and Foreign Relations in the Senate and the Committees on Appropriations and International Relations of the House of Representatives a certification described in subsection (c).]

[(b) APPLICABLE SANCTIONS.—

(1) The Secretary of the Treasury shall instruct the United States executive directors of the international financial institutions to work in opposition to, and vote against, any extension by such institutions of any financial or technical assistance or grants of any kind to the government of Serbia.

(2) The Secretary of State should instruct the United States Ambassador to the Organization for Security and Cooperation in Europe (OSCE) to block any consensus to allow the participation of Serbia in the OSCE or any organization affiliated with the OSCE.

(3) The Secretary of State should instruct the United States Representative to the United Nations to vote against any resolution in the United Nations Security Council to admit Serbia to the United Nations or any organization affiliated with the United Nations, to veto any resolution to allow Serbia to assume the United Nations' membership of the former Socialist Federal Republic of Yugoslavia, and to take action to prevent Serbia from assuming the seat formerly occupied by the Socialist Federal Republic of Yugoslavia.

(4) The Secretary of State should instruct the United States Permanent Representative on the Council of the North Atlantic Treaty Organization to oppose the extension of the Partnership for Peace program or any other organization affiliated with NATO to Serbia.

(5) The Secretary of State should instruct the United States Representatives to the Southeast European Cooperative Initiative (SECI) to oppose and to work to prevent the extension of SECI membership to Serbia.]

[(c) CERTIFICATION.—A certification described in this subsection is a certification that—

(1) the representatives of the successor states to the Socialist Federal Republic of Yugoslavia have successfully negotiated the division of assets and liabilities and all other succession issues following the dissolution of the Socialist Federal Republic of Yugoslavia;

(2) the Government of Serbia is fully complying with its obligations as a signatory to the General Framework Agreement for Peace in Bosnia and Herzegovina;

(3) the Government of Serbia is fully cooperating with and providing unrestricted access to the International Criminal Tribunal for the former Yugoslavia, including surrendering persons indicted for war crimes who are within the jurisdiction of the territory of Serbia, and with the investigations concerning the commission of war crimes and crimes against humanity in Kosova;

(4) the Government of Serbia is implementing internal democratic reforms; and

(5) Serbian federal governmental officials, and representatives of the ethnic Albanian community in Kosova have agreed on, signed, and begun implementation of a negotiated settlement on the future status of Kosova.]

[(d) STATEMENT OF POLICY.—It is the sense of the Congress that the United States should not restore full diplomatic relations with Serbia until the President submits to the Committees on Appropriations and Foreign Relations in the Senate and the Committees on Appropriations and International Relations in the House of Representatives the certification described in subsection (c).]

[(e) EXEMPTION OF MONTENEGRO AND KOSOVA.—The sanctions described in subsection (b) shall not apply to Montenegro or Kosova.]

[(f) DEFINITION.—The term "international financial institution" includes the International Monetary Fund, the International Bank for Reconstruction and Development, the International Development Association, the International Finance Corporation, the Multilateral Investment Guaranty Agency, and the European Bank for Reconstruction and Development.]

[(g) WAIVER AUTHORITY.—The President may waive the application in whole or in part, of any sanction described in subsection (b) if the President certifies to the Congress that the President has determined that the waiver is necessary to meet emergency humanitarian needs.]

[CLEAN COAL TECHNOLOGY]

[SEC. 599A. (a) FINDINGS.—The Congress finds as follows:

(1) The United States is the world leader in the development of environmental technologies, particularly clean coal technology.

(2) Severe pollution problems affecting people in developing countries, and the serious health problems that result from such pollution, can be effectively addressed through the application of United States technology.

(3) During the next century, developing countries, particularly countries in Asia such as China and India, will dramatically increase their consumption of electricity, and low quality coal will be a major source of fuel for power generation.

(4) Without the use of modern clean coal technology, the resultant pollution will cause enormous health and environmental problems leading to diminished economic growth in developing countries and, thus, diminished United States exports to those growing markets.]

[(b) STATEMENT OF POLICY.—It is the policy of the United States to promote the export of United States clean coal technology. In furtherance of that policy, the Secretary of State, the Secretary of the Treasury (acting through the United States executive directors to international financial institutions), the Secretary of Energy, and the Administrator of the United States Agency for International Development (USAID) should, as appropriate, vigorously promote the use of United States clean coal technology in environmental and energy infrastructure programs, projects and activities. Programs, projects and activities for which the use of such technology should be considered include reconstruction assistance for the Balkans, activities carried out by the Global Environment Facility, and activities funded from USAID's Development Credit Authority.]

[RESTRICTION ON UNITED STATES ASSISTANCE FOR CERTAIN RECONSTRUCTION EFFORTS IN THE BALKANS REGION]

[SEC. 599B. (a) Funds appropriated or otherwise made available by this Act for United States assistance for reconstruction efforts in the Federal Republic of Yugoslavia or any contiguous country should to the maximum extent practicable be used for the procurement of articles and services of United States origin.]

[(b) DEFINITIONS.—In this section:

(1) ARTICLE.—The term "article" means any agricultural commodity, steel, communications equipment, farm machinery or petrochemical refinery equipment.

(2) FEDERAL REPUBLIC OF YUGOSLAVIA.—The term "Federal Republic of Yugoslavia" includes Serbia, Montenegro and Kosova.]

[CONTRIBUTIONS TO UNITED NATIONS POPULATION FUND]

[SEC. 599C. (1) LIMITATIONS ON AMOUNT OF CONTRIBUTION.—Of the amounts made available under "International Organizations and Programs", not more than $25,000,000 for fiscal year 2000 shall be available for the United Nations Population Fund (hereafter in this subsection referred to as the "UNFPA").

(2) PROHIBITION ON USE OF FUNDS IN CHINA.—None of the funds made available under "International Organizations and Programs" may be made available for the UNFPA for a country program in the People's Republic of China.

(3) CONDITIONS ON AVAILABILITY OF FUNDS.—Amounts made available under "International Organizations and Programs" for fiscal year 2000 for the UNFPA may not be made available to UNFPA unless—

(A) the UNFPA maintains amounts made available to the UNFPA under this section in an account separate from other accounts of the UNFPA;

(B) the UNFPA does not commingle amounts made available to the UNFPA under this section with other sums; and

(C) the UNFPA does not fund abortions.

(4) REPORT TO THE CONGRESS AND WITHHOLDING OF FUNDS.—

(A) Not later than February 15, 2000, the Secretary of State shall submit a report to the appropriate congressional committees indicating the amount of funds that the United Nations Population Fund is budgeting for the year in which the report is submitted for a country program in the People's Republic of China.

(B) If a report under subparagraph (A) indicates that the United Nations Population Fund plans to spend funds for a country program in the People's Republic of China in the year covered by the report, then the amount of such funds that the UNFPA plans to spend in the People's Republic of China shall be deducted from the funds made available to the UNFPA after March 1 for obligation for the remainder of the fiscal year in which the report is submitted.]

"SEC. 499F. DEFINITIONS.—Continued

[AUTHORIZATION FOR POPULATION PLANNING]

[SEC. 599D. (a) AUTHORIZATION.—Not to exceed $385,000,000 of the funds appropriated in title II of this Act may be available for population planning activities or other population assistance.]

[(b) RESTRICTION ON ASSISTANCE TO FOREIGN ORGANIZATIONS THAT PERFORM OR ACTIVELY PROMOTE ABORTIONS.—

(1) PERFORMANCE OF ABORTIONS.—(A) Notwithstanding section 614 of the Foreign Assistance Act of 1961, or any other provision of law, no funds appropriated by title II of this Act for population planning activities or other population assistance may be made available for any foreign private, nongovernmental, or multilateral organization until the organization certifies that it will not, during the period for which the funds are made available, perform abortions in any foreign country, except where the life of the mother would be endangered if the pregnancy were carried to term or in cases of forcible rape or incest.

(B) Subparagraph (A) may not be construed to apply to the treatment of injuries or illnesses caused by legal or illegal abortions or to assistance provided directly to the government of a country.

(2) LOBBYING ACTIVITIES.—(A) Notwithstanding section 614 of the Foreign Assistance Act of 1961, or any other provision of law, no funds appropriated by title II of this Act for population planning activities or other population assistance may be made available for any foreign private, nongovernmental, or multilateral organization until the organization certifies that it will not, during the period for which the funds are made available, violate the laws of any foreign country concerning the circumstances under which abortion is permitted, regulated, or prohibited, or engage in activities or efforts to alter the laws or governmental policies of any foreign country concerning the circumstances under which abortion is permitted, regulated, or prohibited.

(B) Subparagraph (A) shall not apply to activities in opposition to coercive abortion or involuntary sterilization.

(3) APPLICATION TO FOREIGN ORGANIZATIONS.—The prohibitions and certifications of this subsection apply to funds made available to a foreign organization either directly or as a subcontractor or subgrantee.]

[(c) WAIVER AUTHORITY.—

(1) AUTHORITY.—The President may waive the restrictions contained in subsection (b) that require certifications from foreign private, nongovernmental, or multilateral organizations.

(2) REDUCTION OF ASSISTANCE.—In the event the President exercises the authority contained in paragraph (1) to waive either or both subsections (b)(1) and (b)(2), then—

(A) assistance authorized by subsection (a) and allocated for population planning activities or other population assistance shall be reduced by a total of $12,500,000, and that amount shall be transferred from funds appropriated by this Act under the heading "Development Assistance" and consolidated and merged with funds appropriated by this Act under the heading "Child Survival and Disease Programs Fund"; and

(B) Notwithstanding any other provision of law, such transferred funds that would have been made available for population planning activities or other population assistance shall be made available for infant and child health programs that have a direct, measurable, and high impact on reducing the incidence of illness and death among children.

(3) LIMITATION.—The authority provided in paragraph (1) may be exercised to allow the provision of not more than $15,000,000, in the aggregate, to all foreign private, nongovernmental, or multilateral organizations with respect to which such authority is exercised.

(4) ADDITIONAL REQUIREMENTS.—Upon exercising the authority provided in paragraph (1), the President shall report in writing to the Committee on Appropriations and the Committee on Foreign Relations of the Senate and the Committee on Appropriations and the Committee on International Relations of the House of Representatives.]

[OPIC AUTHORIZATION]

[SEC. 599E. Section 235(a)(2) of the Foreign Assistance Act of 1961 (22 U.S.C. 2195(a)(2)) is amended by striking "1999" and inserting "November 1, 2000".] *(Foreign Operations, Export Financing, and Related Programs Appropriation Act, 2000, as enacted by section 1000(a)(2) of the Consolidated Appropriations Act, 2000 (P.L. 106–113).)*

NATIONAL AERONAUTICS AND SPACE ADMINISTRATION

Federal Funds

General and special funds:

Human Space Flight

For necessary expenses, not otherwise provided for, in the conduct and support of human space flight research and development activities, including research, development, operations, and services; maintenance; construction of facilities including [repair, rehabilitation,] *revitalization* and modification of [real and personal property,] *facilities, construction of new facilities and additions to existing facilities, facility planning and design,* and acquisition or condemnation of real property, as authorized by law; space flight, spacecraft control and communications activities including operations, production, and services; and purchase, lease, charter, maintenance and operation of mission and administrative aircraft, [$5,510,900,000] *$5,499,900,000*, to remain available until September 30, [2001: *Provided*, That $40,000,000 of the amount provided in this paragraph shall be available to the space shuttle program only for preparations necessary to carry out a life and micro-gravity science mission, to be flown between STS–107 and December 2001] *2002. For necessary expenses of the International Space Station, to become available on October 1 of the fiscal year specified and remain available for that and the following fiscal year, as follows: for fiscal year 2002, $1,858,500,000; for fiscal year 2003, $1,452,500,000; for fiscal year 2004, $1,327,000,000; and for fiscal year 2005, $1,275,000,000. (Departments of Veterans Affairs and Housing and Urban Development, and Independent Agencies Appropriations Act, 2000.)*

Program and Financing (in millions of dollars)

Identification code 80–0111–0–1–252		1999 actual	2000 est.	2001 est.
	Obligations by program activity:			
	Direct program:			
00.01	Space station	2,252	2,464	2,125
00.02	Payload and ELV support			86
00.03	Investments and support			123
00.04	Space shuttle	2,956	2,858	3,156
00.05	Payload and utilization operations	199	261	8
09.01	Reimbursable program	183	204	195
10.00	Total new obligations	5,590	5,787	5,693
	Budgetary resources available for obligation:			
21.40	Unobligated balance available, start of year	271	368	274
22.00	New budget authority (gross)	5,663	5,692	5,695
22.10	Resources available from recoveries of prior year obligations	24		
23.90	Total budgetary resources available for obligation	5,958	6,060	5,969
23.95	Total new obligations	−5,590	−5,787	−5,693
24.40	Unobligated balance available, end of year	368	274	276
	New budget authority (gross), detail:			
	Discretionary:			
40.00	Appropriation	5,480	5,511	5,500
40.76	Reduction pursuant to P.L. 106–113		−23	
43.00	Appropriation (total discretionary)	5,480	5,488	5,500
	Spending authority from offsetting collections:			
68.00	Offsetting collections (cash)	174	204	195
68.10	From Federal sources: Change in receivables and unpaid, unfilled orders	9		
68.90	Spending authority from offsetting collections (total discretionary)	183	204	195
70.00	Total new budget authority (gross)	5,663	5,692	5,695
	Change in unpaid obligations:			
	Unpaid obligations, start of year:			
72.40	Obligated balance, start of year	1,662	1,627	1,740
72.95	From Federal sources: Receivables and unpaid, unfilled orders	23	32	32
72.99	Total unpaid obligations, start of year	1,685	1,659	1,772
73.10	Total new obligations	5,590	5,787	5,693
73.20	Total outlays (gross)	−5,591	−5,674	−5,655
73.40	Adjustments in expired accounts (net)	1		
73.45	Adjustments in unexpired accounts	−24		
	Unpaid obligations, end of year:			
74.40	Obligated balance, end of year	1,627	1,740	1,778
74.95	From Federal sources: Receivables and unpaid, unfilled orders	32	32	32
74.99	Total unpaid obligations, end of year	1,659	1,772	1,810
	Outlays (gross), detail:			
86.90	Outlays from new discretionary authority	3,753	3,864	3,864
86.93	Outlays from discretionary balances	1,838	1,810	1,791
87.00	Total outlays (gross)	5,591	5,674	5,655
	Offsets:			
	Against gross budget authority and outlays:			
	Offsetting collections (cash) from:			
88.40	Non-Federal sources	−29	−44	−40
88.45	Offsetting governmental collections from the public	−145	−160	−155
88.90	Total, offsetting collections (cash)	−174	−204	−195
	Against gross budget authority only:			
88.95	From Federal sources: Change in receivables and unpaid, unfilled orders	−9		
	Net budget authority and outlays:			
89.00	Budget authority	5,480	5,488	5,500
90.00	Outlays	5,417	5,470	5,460

Summary of Budget Authority and Outlays

(in millions of dollars)

Enacted/requested:	*1999 actual*	*2000 est.*	*2001 est.*
Budget Authority	5,480	5,488	5,500
Outlays	5,417	5,470	5,460
Supplemental proposal:			
Budget Authority		−20	
Outlays		−13	−6
Total:			
Budget Authority	5,480	5,468	5,500
Outlays	5,417	5,457	5,454

This appropriation provides funding for human space flight activities, including development and operations of the Space Station, the Space Station research program, and operation of the Space Shuttle. This includes development of contingency capabilities for the Space Station, high priority investments to improve the safety of the Space Shuttle, and required construction projects in direct support of Space Station and Space Shuttle programs.

Performance Objectives

Space station.—The International Space Station (ISS) is an international laboratory in low Earth orbit on which American, Russian, Canadian, European, and Japanese astronauts will conduct unique scientific and technological investigations in a microgravity environment. The goal of the Station is to support activities requiring the unique attributes of humans in space and establish a permanent human presence in Earth orbit. The proposed budget provides multi-year funding through an advance appropriation for the continued development of the vehicle and its research components and for current operations, assembly and utilization of the station. With the first launches successfully completed, the budget includes funding to keep subsequent assembly missions on schedule for completion in 2004–2005 and continue work to-

General and special funds—Continued

HUMAN SPACE FLIGHT—Continued

wards a long-term solution to the safe return of the full complement of station crewmembers in the event of an emergency.

In FY 1999, successful launches of the first two components of the Station—the FGB control module and the first node—were completed in November and December respectively, and the elements were assembled in orbit and activated. A third flight delivering supplies to support the first crews was successfully performed in May 1999. Flight hardware elements for the next six U.S. assembly launches—the Z1 and S0 trusses, the control moment gyros, the first photo-voltaic array and battery sets, initial thermal radiators, communication equipment, the U.S. Laboratory, the mobile servicing system and the Multi-Purpose Logistics Carrier—were delivered to the launch site, and the first phases of multi-element integrated testing (MEIT) were completed. Crew training, payload processing, hardware element processing, and mission operations were supported. In 2000, fabrication of flight hardware, qualification testing, assembly, integration and mission operations will all continue. Difficulties with completion of U.S. MEIT testing, coupled with delays to the Russian Service Module, caused by recent failures of the Proton launch system, have delayed planned assembly and expedition flights. The Service Module will be launched in mid- to late-2000, and assembly and expedition flights will follow. The Russian launch of a Soyuz vehicle will enable permanent occupation of the station with rotating crews of three. In 2001 plans are to launch seven U.S. missions to station, including the lab module. Phase 2 of the station assembly will be completed with the launch of the airlock, and preparations will continue for the start of Phase 3 and the first shuttle mission dedicated to research utilization in late 2001/early 2002.

As part of the FY 1999 operating plan, Russian Program Assurance (RPA) was re-established within the Space Station budget line. The RPA funding provides contingency activities to address ISS program requirements resulting from delays or shortfalls on the part of Russia in meeting its commitments to the ISS program. The first step in the contingency plan is to protect against a potential further delay in the Russian Service Module (SM) and its capabilities. The ISS program is purchasing, from the U.S. Naval Research Laboratory (NRL), an interim control module (ICM) to provide backup attitude control and reboost functions for the ISS. Additionally, the Shuttle fleet is being configured for reaction control system (RCS) interconnectivity modifications to enable greater Shuttle reboost capability to the ISS. A permanent U.S. propulsion capability is being developed for implementation in the 2002 timeframe. This includes a propulsion module, carriers, and activities to support propulsion logistics. An agreement negotiated with the Russians in 1999 will provide needed hardware and services to the U.S., including services to provide additional crew return capability when the station attains the ability to support a permanent crew of six.

Phase I development of a crew return vehicle (CRV), to provide the U.S. capability to return up to seven crew members, is initiated in 2000. Design and operational technologies tested and demonstrated in Phase I will reduce CRV development risk. The X–38, including the space test flight in 2002, is being transitioned to merge with the ISS CRV funding in 2000 because of the overlap of CRV and X–38 technology developments. Pending a final decision on CRV development, which will be part of broader future launch decisions, Phase 2 development funding will be included in the Aero-Space Technology budget estimates beginning in FY 2002.

Payload and Expendable Launch Vehicle (ELV) support.—Activities funded by the payload processing budget support the required technical expertise and facilities to perform the payload buildup, test and checkout, integration, servicing, transportation and installation in the launch vehicle. In FY 1999, launch and landing payload support activities were provided for four Space Shuttle missions, including the first American segment of the ISS, and payload processing support activities and facilities for six manifested major payloads. In FY 2000, launch and landing payload support activities will be provided for six Space Shuttle missions including the Hubble Space Telescope (HST–03A) launch, the Shuttle Radar Topography Mission (SRTM) launch, and three assembly flights for the ISS. In FY 2001, launch and landing payload support activities will be provided for nine Space Shuttle missions, including seven ISS assembly and utilization flights. During this period, five pallets will be used in Space Shuttle missions, including the fourth HST servicing mission and three of the ISS assembly flights. In FY 2000 and 2001, over 20 major and secondary payloads will be supported, including major hardware for ISS assembly.

The ELV Mission Support budget provides funds for acquiring requisite launch services to meet all NASA requirements and for technical insight of commercially provided launch services. Advanced mission design/analysis and leading edge integration services are provided for the full range of NASA missions under consideration for launch on ELVs. During FY 1999, 10 ELV launches and 1 secondary ELV mission were successfully launched. Support for 13 missions, including Tracking and Data Relay Satellite–H (TDRS–H), Terra and Geostationary Operational Environmental Satellite–L (GOES–L), and four planetary missions are planned for launch in FY 2000, and integration and technical management of 28 payloads are planned for launch in FY 2000 and FY 2001. Support for 11 missions and 1 secondary payload is planned for FY 2001.

Investments and support.—Beginning in FY 2001, the Human Exploration and Development of Space (HEDS) Commercialization and Technology Initiative will include human space exploration and development activities emphasizing highly innovative technologies, advances in science, and enabling synergistic commercial space development efforts.

A new project activity will begin in FY 2001 to ensure NASA's rocket propulsion test capabilities are properly managed and maintained in world class condition. The project will significantly enhance our ability to properly manage NASA's rocket testing activities and infrastructure across all four participating NASA centers.

Engineering and technical base (ETB) activity will continue to support the institutional capability in the operation of space flight laboratories, technical facilities, and testbeds; to conduct independent safety, and reliability assessments; and to stimulate science and technical competence in the United States.

Space shuttle.—The Space Shuttle is a partially reusable space vehicle that provides several unique capabilities to the United States space program. These include retrieving payloads from orbit for reuse, servicing and repairing satellites in space, safely transporting humans to and from space, launching ISS components and providing an assembly platform in space, and operating and returning space laboratories. In FY 1999, the Space Shuttle launched four flights successfully including the first ISS assembly mission, one resupply flight to the ISS, one microgravity research mission which included the return to space of Senator John Glenn, and the successful deployment of the Chandra—Advanced X-Ray Astrophysics Facility (AXAF).

The six flights manifested in FY 2000 include the emergency HST Servicing Mission 3A which will replace failing gyros on the HST and the Shuttle Radar Topography Mission (SRTM), a joint DOD/NASA payload to study the earth. The Space Shuttle will also visit the ISS four more times, for both assembly and maintenance. Finally, the first crew will begin the permanent occupation and presence aboard the ISS in FY 2000.

Nine flights are planned during FY 2001, including seven ISS assembly and servicing missions. In addition, a dedicated microgravity research flight and another HST Servicing Mission (3B) will be flown.

The 2002 budget estimate for this account is $5.5 billion, including advance appropriations.

Object Classification (in millions of dollars)

Identification code 80–0111–0–1–252		1999 actual	2000 est.	2001 est.
	Direct obligations:			
22.0	Transportation of things	4	4	4
23.3	Communications, utilities, and miscellaneous charges	55	57	56
24.0	Printing and reproduction	2	2	2
25.1	Advisory and assistance services	5	5	5
25.2	Other services	132	136	134
25.3	Purchases of goods and services from Government accounts	125	129	127
25.4	Operation and maintenance of facilities	1,389	1,429	1,412
25.5	Research and development contracts	3,220	3,333	3,274
25.7	Operation and maintenance of equipment	43	44	44
26.0	Supplies and materials	148	152	151
31.0	Equipment	95	98	97
32.0	Land and structures	146	150	148
41.0	Grants, subsidies, and contributions	43	44	44
99.0	Subtotal, direct obligations	5,407	5,583	5,498
99.0	Reimbursable obligations	183	204	195
99.9	Total new obligations	5,590	5,787	5,693

SCIENCE, AERONAUTICS AND TECHNOLOGY

For necessary expenses, not otherwise provided for, in the conduct and support of science, aeronautics and technology research and development activities, including research, development, operations, and services; maintenance; construction of facilities including [repair, rehabilitation] *revitalization*, and modification of [real and personal property] *facilities, construction of new facilities and additions to existing facilities, facility planning and design*, and acquisition or condemnation of real property, as authorized by law; space flight, spacecraft control and communications activities including operations, production, and services; and purchase, lease, charter, maintenance and operation of mission and administrative aircraft, [$5,606,700,000] *$5,929,400,000*, to remain available until September 30, [2001] *2002*. *(Departments of Veterans Affairs and Housing and Urban Development, and Independent Agencies Appropriations Act, 2000.)*

Program and Financing (in millions of dollars)

Identification code 80–0110–0–1–999		1999 actual	2000 est.	2001 est.
	Obligations by program activity:			
	Direct program:			
00.01	Space science	2,211	2,224	2,389
00.02	Life and microgravity science	246	294	301
00.03	Earth science	1,478	1,427	1,408
00.04	Aero-space technology	1,342	1,093	1,190
00.05	Space operations			503
00.06	Academic programs	146	152	102
00.07	Mission communication services	375	394	20
09.01	Reimbursable program	574	606	548
10.00	Total new obligations	6,372	6,190	6,461
	Budgetary resources available for obligation:			
21.40	Unobligated balance available, start of year	401	281	278
22.00	New budget authority (gross)	6,228	6,187	6,477
22.10	Resources available from recoveries of prior year obligations	25		
23.90	Total budgetary resources available for obligation	6,654	6,468	6,755
23.95	Total new obligations	−6,372	−6,190	−6,461
23.98	Unobligated balance expiring or withdrawn	−1		
24.40	Unobligated balance available, end of year	281	278	294
	New budget authority (gross), detail:			
	Discretionary:			
40.00	Appropriation	5,654	5,607	5,929
40.76	Reduction pursuant to P.L. 106–113		−26	
43.00	Appropriation (total discretionary)	5,654	5,581	5,929
	Spending authority from offsetting collections:			
68.00	Offsetting collections (cash)	542	606	548
68.10	From Federal sources: Change in receivables and unpaid, unfilled orders	32		
68.90	Spending authority from offsetting collections (total discretionary)	574	606	548
70.00	Total new budget authority (gross)	6,228	6,187	6,477
	Change in unpaid obligations:			
	Unpaid obligations, start of year:			
72.40	Obligated balance, start of year	2,997	2,977	3,195
72.95	From Federal sources: Receivables and unpaid, unfilled orders	318	350	350
72.99	Total unpaid obligations, start of year	3,315	3,327	3,545
73.10	Total new obligations	6,372	6,190	6,461
73.20	Total outlays (gross)	−6,327	−5,972	−6,183
73.40	Adjustments in expired accounts (net)	−9		
73.45	Adjustments in unexpired accounts	−25		
	Unpaid obligations, end of year:			
74.40	Obligated balance, end of year	2,977	3,195	3,473
74.95	From Federal sources: Receivables and unpaid, unfilled orders	350	350	350
74.99	Total unpaid obligations, end of year	3,327	3,545	3,823
	Outlays (gross), detail:			
86.90	Outlays from new discretionary authority	3,209	3,123	3,222
86.93	Outlays from discretionary balances	3,118	2,849	2,962
87.00	Total outlays (gross)	6,327	5,972	6,183
	Offsets:			
	Against gross budget authority and outlays:			
	Offsetting collections (cash) from:			
88.40	Non-Federal sources	−24	−42	−37
88.45	Offsetting governmental collections from the public	−518	−564	−511
88.90	Total, offsetting collections (cash)	−542	−606	−548
	Against gross budget authority only:			
88.95	From Federal sources: Change in receivables and unpaid, unfilled orders	−32		
	Net budget authority and outlays:			
89.00	Budget authority	5,654	5,581	5,929
90.00	Outlays	5,785	5,366	5,635

This appropriation provides for the research and development activities of the National Aeronautics and Space Administration. Funds are included for the construction, maintenance, and operation of programmatic facilities. Space science, earth science, life and microgravity science, and aero-space technology programs are included in the 21st Century Research Fund.

Performance Objectives

Space science.—The Space Science program seeks to answer fundamental questions concerning: the galaxy and the universe; the connection between the Sun, Earth and heliosphere; the origin and evolution of planetary systems; and the origin and distribution of life in the universe. The Space Science program is comprised of a base program of research and development activities, including research and flight mission activities, and major space-based facilities.

In 1999, the Space Science program produced many notable scientific accomplishments. The Hubble Space Telescope fulfilled one of its most important objectives in May 1999, when the Hubble Space Telescope Key Project Team announced the results of their studies, which yielded an estimate of the Hubble constant to within 10% accuracy. The Hubble constant indicates the rate at which the universe is expanding

General and special funds—Continued

SCIENCE, AERONAUTICS AND TECHNOLOGY—Continued

from the primordial "Big Bang" and is one of the most important numbers in cosmology because it is needed to estimate the age and size of the universe. Combining the Hubble constant measurement with estimates of the density of the universe, the team estimated that the universe is approximately 12 billion years old. The Chandra X-ray Observatory (CXO), the third of the four "great observatories," was successfully launched and activated. As soon as science operations began, images showing astonishing detail of X-ray sources were obtained. With its unprecedented capabilities in energy coverage, spatial resolution, spectral resolution and sensitivity, CXO has just begun to investigate some of the most important topics in space science, including the age and size of the universe, dark matter, and X-ray background radiation. Other scientific discoveries related to the structure and evolution of the universe include the detection of "middleweight" black holes that are 100 to 10,000 times as massive as the Sun but occupy less space that the Moon, and the first-ever optical image of a gamma ray burst. Gamma ray bursts are the most powerful explosions in the universe, and for a very short period produce more energy than the rest of the universe combined. Also in 1999, several teams of researchers supported by NASA discovered many new planets orbiting nearby stars, including evidence of the first known planet orbiting a pair of stars. Within our own solar system, the Mars Global Surveyor (MGS) generated the first global three-dimensional view of Mars. These images revealed an impact basin deep enough to swallow Mount Everest, as well as pathways for water flow. Scientists using MGS' magnetometer discovered surprising evidence of past movement of the Martian crust, further evidence that ancient Mars was a more dynamic, Earth-like planet than it is today. A dramatic time-lapse movie by the Hubble Space Telescope showed, for the first time, seasonal changes on Uranus. The Galileo spacecraft produced new images showing volcanic activity on Jupiter's moon Io, similar to that which occurred on Earth eons ago. Analysis of data from the Lunar Prospector spacecraft confirmed that the Moon has a small core, supporting the theory that the bulk of the Moon was ripped away from the Earth when an object the size of Mars collided with the Earth. In the field of solar science, NASA sponsored scientists using the Japanese Yokoh spacecraft discovered that an S-shaped structure often appears on the Sun in advance of a coronal mass ejection (CME), a violent eruption that is as powerful as billions of nuclear explosions. The Solar and Heliospheric Observatory (SOHO) spacecraft discovered the source of high-speed solar wind, a stream of electrified gas that affects the Earth's space environment.

To capitalize on these enormous successes during the past year, the NASA budget request for FY 2001 once again highlights Space Science. The President's request includes an enhanced Solar System Exploration program to establish a sustained presence at multiple locations on and around Mars and other potential research targets. Using outposts of numerous, networked spacecraft, NASA will greatly enhance the science return and overall success of future missions. Eventually, such outposts will bring continuous access to live data and video so that researchers and the public can explore and experience other worlds first-hand. Space Science continues to focus on the Origins program and fundamental questions regarding the creation of the universe and planetary systems and the possibility of life on places other than planet Earth. Planning and technology development continues for the deployment of powerful telescopes to detect Earth-like planets beyond our solar system, for the launch of a mission to directly observe subsurface oceans on Europa, and for future missions to seek evidence of past or present life on Mars.

The Administration's request also includes a "Living With a Star" Initiative to develop better solar weather forecasting capabilities and to better protect high-tech infrastructure from dangerous solar phenomena. The Space Science program is responsible for agency-wide core technology development, and funding is provided in this program to enhance and enable future missions through the administration's information technology (IT) initiative and other high-leverage technologies. These technologies will increase the return of the Space Science program and other NASA programs many fold through revolutionary capabilities in the areas of networking, intelligent systems, nanotechnology, communications, lightweight structures, miniaturization, mobility, and propulsion for robotic spacecraft and rovers.

Development activities continue on the Relativity (Gravity Probe-B) mission, which is now scheduled for launch in 2001. The Space Infrared Telescope Facility (SIRTF) initiated development in April 1998, with launch planned for December 2001. Development activities on the Thermosphere, Ionosphere, Mesosphere Energetics and Dynamics (TIMED) mission continued in 1999, with launch planned in 2000. Development activities on the Stratospheric Observatory for Infrared Astronomy (SOFIA) continue. The upgraded Hubble Space Telescope (HST) is providing new insights into our universe. Funding for HST continues to support operations, as well as preparation for servicing mission 3B in 2001 and servicing mission 4 in 2003.

In Explorer missions, development activities continue for the Microwave Anisotropy Probe (MAP) and Imager for Magnetosphere-to-Aurora Global Exploration (IMAGE). MAP will be launched in November 2000, IMAGE in February 2000. Two new MIDEX missions were selected in 1999: Full-sky Astrometric Mapping Explorer (FAME) scheduled for launch in 2004, and Swift, a multi-wavelength observatory for gamma-ray burst astronomy, to be launched in 2003. Three Small (SMEX) missions continued development in FY 1999: the High Energy Spectroscopic Imager (HESSI) is to launch in 2000; the Galaxy Evolution Explorer (GALEX) will launch in 2001; and the Two Wide-Angle Neutral Atom Spectrometers (TWINS) has been selected as a mission of opportunity, to be launched in 2002 and 2004. These missions emphasize reduced mission costs and accelerated launch schedules.

The Mars Global Surveyor entered Mars orbit in September 1997, the Mars Climate Orbiter was launched in December 1998 and the Mars Polar Lander was launched in January 1999. Unfortunately, the Orbiter was lost while attempting to enter Mars orbit in September 1999, and the Lander was lost during entry, descent and landing in December 1999. Funds are requested for the development of future Mars missions to establish a sustained presence at Mars that will increase the science return and overall success of the Mars program. A review to be accomplished in 2000 will provide the plan for future launches.

In the Discovery program, the fourth mission, Stardust, was launched on schedule in February 1999, and is operating normally during its cruise to comet Wild-2, with the encounter scheduled for 2004. Two Discovery missions selected in 1997 are proceeding on schedule: the Comet Nucleus Tour (CONTOUR) will begin development in CY 2000 and will be launched in 2002; the Genesis solar wind sample return mission has begun development and will be launched in 2001. Two new missions were selected for implementation during 1999: The MErcury Surface, Space ENvironment, GEochemistry and Ranging (MESSENGER) mission to orbit Mercury; and the Deep Impact mission to fly by and fire an impactor into a comet. Both MESSENGER and Deep Impact are planned for launch in 2004. The President's request supports a new class of Discovery micromissions that will also be undertaken in 2001 to complement solar system exploration efforts with more frequent and varied research opportunities.

The Flight Validation program is providing flight demonstrations of critical new technologies which will reduce the mass and cost of future science and spacecraft subsystems, while maintaining or improving mission capabilities. The Deep Space-1 mission was launched in October 1998, and has validated its technologies and completed its primary mission, and is now in an extended mission. The Deep Space-2 mission which was launched with the Mars Polar Lander in January 1999, and was lost, along with the Lander, during entry, descent and landing on Mars in December 1999. The Space Technology 4 mission was terminated during 1999 due to the need to fund higher priority programs within the Space Science Enterprise. Also in 1999, NASA selected the Nanosat Constellation Trailblazer as the Space Technology-5 Flight Validation mission. This mission will feature three very small satellites (each about the size of a large birthday cake), that will fly in formation and test eight technologies in the harsh space environment near the boundary of Earth's protective magnetic field. The Flight Validation program has been restructured to enhance openness and competition as well as to increase the number of opportunities for technologies to be flight-validated. Funding for the restructured program has been increased.

Life and microgravity science.—This program uses the microgravity environment of space to conduct basic and applied research to understand the effect of gravity on living systems and to conduct research in the areas of fluid physics, combustion science, fundamental physics, materials science and biotechnology. In FY 1999, the program flew one science mission (STS–95) on a Spacehab carrier with ISS precursor science experiments. STS–95 included commercially sponsored research as well as research on the effects of aging conducted in collaboration with the National Institutes of Health's National Institute on Aging. FY 1999 has also seen the beginning of ISS assembly. In FY 2000, the Russian Service Module will be launched, enabling permanent human presence aboard the ISS. In FY 2001, the U.S. laboratory module for the ISS will be launched, which will enable initial life and microgravity hardware and experiments to be established aboard the ISS. This will begin a new era of research. In FY 2001, the Administration introduces a Bioastronautics Initiative to accelerate research and develop countermeasures that will improve the health and safety of astronauts aboard the International Space Station. Devices and countermeasures developed through this initiative may also have many health benefits on Earth. As assembly of the ISS continues to advance, ISS Crew Health Care System (CHECS) components will be utilized to provide on-orbit medical, environmental, and countermeasure capabilities for all ISS crew members. In early FY 2001, prior to full research capabilities aboard the ISS, the program will fly a dedicated Space Shuttle research mission which will extend previous Space Shuttle research results and help the program as well as the community prepare for increasing research operations on the ISS.

Earth science.—The purpose of NASA's Earth Science Enterprise (ESE) is to understand the total Earth system and the effects of natural and human-induced changes on the global environment. ESE is pioneering the new interdisciplinary field of research called Earth system science, which recognizes that the Earth's land surface, oceans, atmosphere, ice sheets and *biota* are both dynamic and highly interactive. Earth system science is an area of research with the potential for immense benefit to the nation, yielding new knowledge and tools for weather forecasting, agriculture, urban and land use planning, and other areas of economic and environmental importance. In concert with other agencies and the global research community, ESE is providing the scientific foundation needed for the complex policy choices that lie ahead on the road to sustainable development. ESE has established three broad goals to fulfill its purpose: (1) expand scientific knowledge of the Earth system using NASA's unique capabilities from the vantage points of space, aircraft and *in situ* platforms; (2) disseminate information about the Earth system; and, (3) enable productive use of Earth science and technology in the public and private sectors.

FY 1999 was a year of substantial scientific accomplishment in our understanding of the major elements that comprise the Earth system. Over the oceans, ESE had several accomplishments. ESE reduced the uncertainty in global rainfall over the tropics by one half, helping improve predictions for short-term weather and availability of fresh water globally; produced near-daily ocean color maps that help us understand the role of oceans in removing carbon dioxide from the atmosphere; documented the waxing and waning of El Niño, enabling seasonal climate prediction; and resumed global measurement of winds at the ocean surface to improve short-term weather prediction and tracking of major hurricanes and tropical storms globally. Over the ice caps, researchers determined the thinning and thickening rates for the Greenland ice sheet; provided the first detailed radar mosaic for Antarctica; and provided the daily observations of the Polar Regions from space.

Over the land, ESE produced the first satellite-derived assessments of global forest cover, began refreshing the global archive of 30-meter land cover data, and conducted an international field experiment in the Amazonia to help understand the role of vegetation on Earth in removing carbon dioxide from the atmosphere. In the solid Earth, ESE and the United States Geological Survey (USGS) measured surface displacement, which is a precursor to earthquakes. In the atmosphere, ESE continued to measure concentrations of both ozone and ozone-depleting substances and assess the recovery of upper ozone correlation and implemented a 17-year data record of aerosols and cloud properties toward predicting annual to decadal climate variations.

The Earth Observing System (EOS), the centerpiece of Earth Science, is a program of multiple spacecraft, supporting technology and interdisciplinary science investigations to provide a long-term data set of key parameters needed to understand global climate change. The first EOS satellite launches began in 1999 with the launches of Landsat-7, Terra (formerly AM–1), and QuikSCAT. EOS PM–1 and Chemistry are on schedule to launch in 2000 and 2002 respectively. Preceding the EOS are a number of individual satellite and Shuttle-based missions which are helping to reveal basic processes.

Complementing EOS, under the Earth Probes Program, will be a series of small, rapid development Earth System Science Pathfinder (ESSP) missions to study emerging science questions and to use innovative measurement techniques in support of EOS. The first two ESSP missions, Vegetation Canopy Lidar (VCL) and Gravity Recovery and Climate Experiment (GRACE), are scheduled for launch in 2000 and 2001, respectively. The second pair of ESSP missions, the Pathfinder Instruments for Cloud and Aerosol Spaceborne Observations—Climatologie Etendue des Nuages et des Aerosols (PICASSO–CENA) mission, and Cloudsat, will be launched together in 2003.

Data from Earth Science missions, both current and future, will be captured, processed into useful information, and broadly distributed by the EOS Data Information System (EOSDIS). EOSDIS will ensure that data from these diverse missions remain available in active archives for use by current and future scientists. These data are expected to find uses well beyond the Earth Science research community. Therefore, ESE is engaging in a variety of public/private partnerships to extend the utility of Earth science data to environmental decision-makers, resource managers, commercial

General and special funds—Continued

SCIENCE, AERONAUTICS AND TECHNOLOGY—Continued

firms, social scientists and the general academic community, educators, state and local governments and others.

The ESE research and analysis program is essential to the discovery of new concepts and to the design of future missions. ESE research is coordinated through the U.S. Global Change Research Program (USGCRP), the Committee on the Environment and Natural Resources (CENR) and its Subcommittee on Global Change Research, and the various boards and committees at the National Academy of Sciences.

Aero-space technology.—The mission of this Enterprise is to pioneer the identification, development, verification, transfer, application, and commercialization of high-payoff aerospace technologies. Through its research and technology accomplishments, Aero-space technology promotes economic growth and national security through a safe, efficient national aviation system and affordable, reliable space transportation. To meet this challenge, the Enterprise has established three pillar goals. Within these three pillar goals, a set of ten objectives, each with its own roadmap, has been defined to address current and future National needs. The technologies associated with these objectives are pre-competitive, long-term, high-risk research endeavors with high-payoff in terms of market growth, safety, low acquisition cost, consumer affordability and a cleaner environment. The goals of this Enterprise directly support National policy in Aero-Space, documented in the 1999 National R&D Plan for Aviation Safety, Security, Efficiency, and Environmental Compatibility and the 1994 National Space Transportation Policy.

The first pillar, Global Civil Aviation, addresses the fundamental, systemic issues in the aviation system to ensure continued growth and development appropriate to the needs of the national and global economies. These systemic issues—safety, capacity, environmental compatibility, and affordability—cut across markets including large subsonic civil transports, air cargo, commuter and general aviation, and rotorcraft. The second pillar, Revolutionary Technology Leaps, will revolutionize air travel and the way in which aircraft are designed, built, and operated, and addresses the challenges in small aircraft, short-haul transportation; supersonic, transoceanic transportation; design tools, and experimental planes. The third pillar, Access to Space, will enable greater commercial potential of space and the expansion of space research and exploration by significantly reducing the cost of space transportation systems while improving reliability, operability, responsiveness, and safety.

A major restructuring and replanning of the Aero-Space Enterprise's base R&T program was accomplished during 1999 to integrate the Enterprise's existing space transportation and aeronautics base R&T development programs into a single entity. There were several benefits that accrued from this effort. First, the restructuring better aligned the required technology development efforts with our core competencies and brought the expertise resident in the Aeronautics Research Centers to bear on the technological challenges associated with space transportation. Second, the integration of space and aeronautics development needs resulted in a synergistic technology development plan that better utilized our resources, eliminated overlaps, and allowed dual use, between the space transportation and aeronautics users, to be planned up front rather than relying on serendipitous events.

The President's request for NASA increases investments in technology development activities that will address the challenges (safety, environmental impact, capacity, and space transportation costs) that face the aero-space community.

The Administration's request supports the development of Smart Air Transport System (SATS) technologies that could enable a revolution in accessibility and mobility in America. The product of the SATS (Phase I) Program will demonstrate the technological potential for transportation-driven economic development throughout the nation.

The Administration's request also supports a Quiet Airplane Technology program that will build upon the highly successful noise reduction efforts that were begun in the Aero-Space Technology (AST) enterprise and maintain progress toward meeting the enterprise's noise reduction goal. The achievement of these goals will lead to an air transportation system that contains objectionable aircraft noise within airport boundaries.

By the end of the decade, NASA will conduct a competitive launch services procurement to support the launch requirements of human spaceflight operations—the 2nd Generation RLV Focused Program. The objectives will be to dramatically improve safety while significantly reducing the cost of such launch services, and to eliminate the current need for the Government to own and operate the full system. The President's request includes new funding through the Space Launch Initiative to support this competition and fulfills a 1994 National Space Transportation Policy guideline calling for government and private sector decisions by 2000 on development of an operational, next-generation reusable launch system.

As part of NASA's response to the national goal of reducing aircraft accidents by a factor of 5 by 2001, NASA increased its safety base R&T efforts in order to provide a foundation for a focused safety program beginning in FY 2000. In 1999, the base R&T programs matured these required safety related technologies to the point where they were successfully transferred to the focused Aviation Safety Program (AvSP) which begins in FY 2000. These technologies will provide the foundation for focused safety development efforts in the future. They also will result in some near term achievements. For example, in FY 1999, the causes of controlled flight into terrain (responsible for 30% of fatal accidents) were identified and 13 contracts issued via a NASA research announcement (NRA) to develop and demonstrate approaches for fully operational and certifiable synthetic vision and health management systems. Also in FY 1999, the preparations for flight evaluation of a crew-centered synthetic vision display were completed and a study initiated to understand the applicability of synthetic vision to General Aviation (GA) type aircraft was begun. In FY 2000, the AvSP program will produce an icing training program for GA and commuter pilots, complete a flight evaluation of an initial national capability for digital data link and graphical display of weather information, and demonstrate a concept for the integration of air traffic control runway incursion information onto aircraft flight deck displays. In FY 2001, the AvSP will complete a laboratory demonstration of a fuel system modification to reduce flammability, define the architecture for an integrated onboard health management system, and down-select synthetic vision concepts suitable for retrofit in commercial, business, and general aviation aircraft. The base R&T will continue to develop the technologies that will contribute to the FY 2007 goal. For example, in FY 2001, NASA will downselect ground-based remote sensor technologies for a prototype ground-system to sense icing conditions and continue work on a related computer.

NASA also continued its efforts to reduce the environmental impact associated with aviation systems. In FY 1999, in partnership with industry, a demonstration in an engine test rig of a low emission combustor that produced a 50% reduction in oxides of nitrogen (NO_X) emissions was successfully demonstrated. The Ultra Efficient Engine Technology (UEET) program will carry this effort forward and demonstrate a system that achieves significant reductions in NO_X and carbon dioxide (CO_X) emissions in FY 2001. The UEET is a new focused program that begins in FY 2000 and is planned and designed to develop high-payoff, high-risk technologies to enable the next breakthroughs in propulsion systems to spawn a new generation of high performance, operationally efficient and economical, reliable and environmentally compatible U.S. aircraft.

Similarly with noise, in FY 1999, NASA validated an Aircraft Noise Impact model and demonstrated that improved high-lift systems in combination with advanced operational procedures have the potential to reduce community impact by the equivalent of 2-4 db source noise reduction. In 2000, NASA will validate the technologies required to reduce community noise impact by up to 10 dB relative to 1992 technology.

In 1999, the Aviation System Capacity program conducted field evaluation of an initial demonstration of Aircraft Vortex Spacing System (AVOSS) technologies with transport of vortices and class-wise spacing features that have the potential to reduce approach spacing standards. In FY 2000, NASA will demonstrate all technologies in a realistic Terminal Area environment achieving a 12–15% increase in single runway throughput and proving the ability to space aircraft closer than 3,400 feet on parallel runways while meeting all Federal Aviation Administration (FAA) safety criteria. In FY 2001, NASA will demonstrate transition airspace decision support tools for: (1) Air Traffic Control (ATC)/airline operations center and ATC/cockpit information exchange, and (2) conflict resolution.

Building on its world record setting performances, the Environmental Research Aircraft and Sensor technology (ERAST) project in FY 1999 demonstrated a multistage turbocharged RPA to 60,000 feet for an 8 hour duration. The Centurion solar-powered airplane, a vehicle with a wingspan greater than 200 ft., completed initial low altitude evaluation under battery power. The Centurion solar-powered RPA was modified to a wingspan configuration of greater than 245 ft., named Helios and will continue flight testing in FY 2000. This configuration will be more suitable for extreme endurance as well as short flights to the 100,000 ft. altitude. In FY01, the Flight Research program will demonstrate a solar powered RPA at 100,000 ft and complete development of a heavyweight energy storage system under the ERAST project. Both achievements will demonstrate technologies that will provide atmospheric satellites for commercial use, disaster relief efforts such as communication relays and real time sensing, and increase the Nation's capability to make scientific sampling high in the atmosphere.

Also in FY 2000, NASA initiated a new project entitled Revolutionary Concepts (REVCON) to accelerate the exploration of high-risk, breakthrough technologies in order to enable revolutionary departures from traditional approaches to air vehicle design. At the end of FY 1999, three concepts were accepted for inclusion in the REVCON program. Flights of these vehicles will begin in FY 2001 or 2002. Also in FY 2001, NASA will issue the first NRA under REVCON to select the next set of REVCON concepts.

Low-cost space transportation remains the key enabler for a more aggressive civil space program. NASA's Integrated Space Transportation Planning activities have identified a strategy based upon competition, safety, industry leadership and a comprehensive systems approach to NASA requirements. Funding supports aggressive technical risk reduction and advanced development for multiple reusable launch vehicle concepts. Identification and preliminary development of NASA unique systems and near-term pursuit of alternative access for key space station needs are also both critical elements of the Integrated Space Transportation Plan (ISTP). All of these efforts combined will move NASA closer to a full and open Reusable Launch Vehicle (RLV) competition in the 2005 timeframe to meet NASA's human space flight needs by the end of the decade.

Under ISTP, the 2nd Generation RLV Focused Program continues to develop, apply and demonstrate new technologies that significantly advance the ability of the launch vehicle industry to initiate commercially viable reusable launch systems.

The X–33 and X–34 have completed several major hardware fabrication and test milestones. However, technical difficulties and program replanning have delayed the flight testing of these advanced technology demonstrators. The X–34 is now expected to fly in 2000. The X–33 flight schedule is under review, following the failure of the composite liquid hydrogen tanks during testing. The X–37 complements the X–33 and X–34 vehicles by investigating the orbit-to-Earth and orbital operations regimes of the flight spectrum, and will begin flight tests in 2002.

The Commercial Technology Program's focus in FY 1999 was continued investment of 10–20 percent of the NASA R&D budget in commercial partnerships with industry. Based on experience to date, these commercial partnerships are expected to increase the return on the government's R&D investment, allowing NASA to do more with limited funds, and strengthening the international competitiveness of key industry sectors. In FY 2000 and 2001, the program will continue to emphasize increasing commercial partnerships with industry and continue to refine and expand a technology and partnership database.

Space operations.—The primary goal of space operations is to provide highly reliable, cost-effective space operations services in support of NASA's science and aeronautics programs. In addition, support is provided to interagency, international, and commercial space-faring enterprises on a reimbursable basis. The Space Communications Mission and Data Services program is composed of Operations, Mission and Data Service Upgrades, Tracking and Data Relay Satellite Replenishment, and Technology Projects, as well as spectrum management and data standards coordination. Services are provided to a large number of NASA Missions including planetary, and interplanetary missions; human space flight missions; near-earth and earth orbiting missions; and sub-orbital and aeronautical flight tests. A Consolidated Space Operations (CSOC) was successfully implemented by the Space Operations Management Office at Johnson Space Center and Lockheed Martin Space Operations Company. The CSOC provides end-to-end mission and data services to both NASA and non-NASA customers. A total of nine contracts were consolidated at inception, and four more have been consolidated in FY 2000 to date, with two additional contracts to be consolidated in FY 2001. Management responsibility for all Wide Area Network data distribution services for all human space flight, earth orbiting and deep space missions and NASA administrative communications was outsourced by CSOC in FY 2000. Development of the TDRS Replenishment Spacecraft is ongoing, with the first satellite scheduled for launch in FY 2000.

Academic programs.—The goal of this program is to promote excellence in America's education system through enhancing and expanding scientific and technological competence. NASA's education programs span the elementary through graduate levels and are directed at both students and faculty. The goal of the Minority University Research Program is to expand opportunities for talented students from underrepresented groups who are pursuing degrees in science and engineering and to strengthen the research capabilities of minority universities and colleges. The range of activities conducted under this program will continue to capture the interest of all students in science and technology, develop talented students at the undergraduate and graduate levels, provide research opportunities for students and faculty members at NASA centers, and strengthen and enhance the research capabilities of the Nation's colleges and universities.

General and special funds—Continued

SCIENCE, AERONAUTICS AND TECHNOLOGY—Continued

The 2002 budget estimates for this account is $5.9 billion.

Object Classification (in millions of dollars)

Identification code 80–0110–0–1–999		1999 actual	2000 est.	2001 est.
	Direct obligations:			
22.0	Transportation of things	5	5	5
23.3	Communications, utilities, and miscellaneous charges	54	52	55
24.0	Printing and reproduction	5	5	5
25.1	Advisory and assistance services	109	105	111
25.2	Other services	772	743	787
25.3	Purchases of goods and services from Government accounts	223	215	227
25.4	Operation and maintenance of facilities	264	254	269
25.5	Research and development contracts	3,132	3,016	3,194
25.7	Operation and maintenance of equipment	82	79	84
26.0	Supplies and materials	210	202	214
31.0	Equipment	101	97	103
32.0	Land and structures	24	23	24
41.0	Grants, subsidies, and contributions	817	788	834
99.0	Subtotal, direct obligations	5,798	5,584	5,912
99.0	Reimbursable obligations	574	606	549
99.9	Total new obligations	6,372	6,190	6,461

MISSION SUPPORT

For necessary expenses, not otherwise provided for, in carrying out mission support for human space flight programs and science, aeronautical, and technology programs, including research operations and support; [space communications activities including operations, production and services;] maintenance; construction of facilities including [repair, rehabilitation,] *revitalization* and modification of facilities, [minor] construction of new facilities and additions to existing facilities, facility planning and design, environmental compliance and restoration, and acquisition or condemnation of real property, as authorized by law; program management; personnel and related costs, including uniforms or allowances therefor, as authorized by 5 U.S.C. 5901–5902; travel expenses; purchase, lease, charter, maintenance, and operation of mission and administrative aircraft; not to exceed [$35,000] *$40,000* for official reception and representation expenses; and purchase (not to exceed 33 for replacement only) and hire of passenger motor vehicles, [$2,515,100,000] *$2,584,000,000* to remain available until September 30, [2001] *2002*. *(Departments of Veterans Affairs and Housing and Urban Development, and Independent Agencies Appropriations Act, 2000.)*

Program and Financing (in millions of dollars)

Identification code 80–0112–0–1–999		1999 actual	2000 est.	2001 est.
	Obligations by program activity:			
	Direct program:			
00.01	Safety, mission assurance, engineering, and advanced concepts	39	43	47
00.02	Research and program management	2,110	2,202	2,292
00.03	Construction of facilities	173	193	233
00.04	Space communication services	184	91	5
01.00	Total direct program	2,506	2,529	2,577
09.01	Reimbursable program	97	127	132
10.00	Total new obligations	2,603	2,656	2,709
	Budgetary resources available for obligation:			
21.40	Unobligated balance available, start of year	85	86	69
22.00	New budget authority (gross)	2,597	2,639	2,716
22.10	Resources available from recoveries of prior year obligations	7		
23.90	Total budgetary resources available for obligation	2,689	2,725	2,785
23.95	Total new obligations	–2,603	–2,656	–2,709
24.40	Unobligated balance available, end of year	86	69	76
	New budget authority (gross), detail:			
	Discretionary:			
40.00	Appropriation	2,511	2,515	2,584
40.75	Reduction pursuant to P.L. 106–51	–11		
40.76	Reduction pursuant to P.L. 106–113		–3	
43.00	Appropriation (total discretionary)	2,500	2,512	2,584
	Spending authority from offsetting collections:			
68.00	Offsetting collections (cash)	122	127	132
68.10	From Federal sources: Change in receivables and unpaid, unfilled orders	–25		
68.90	Spending authority from offsetting collections (total discretionary)	97	127	132
70.00	Total new budget authority (gross)	2,597	2,639	2,716
	Change in unpaid obligations:			
	Unpaid obligations, start of year:			
72.40	Obligated balance, start of year	487	586	594
72.95	From Federal sources: Receivables and unpaid, unfilled orders	66	41	41
72.99	Total unpaid obligations, start of year	553	627	635
73.10	Total new obligations	2,603	2,656	2,709
73.20	Total outlays (gross)	–2,517	–2,648	–2,685
73.40	Adjustments in expired accounts (net)	–5		
73.45	Adjustments in unexpired accounts	–7		
	Unpaid obligations, end of year:			
74.40	Obligated balance, end of year	586	594	618
74.95	From Federal sources: Receivables and unpaid, unfilled orders	41	41	41
74.99	Total unpaid obligations, end of year	627	635	659
	Outlays (gross), detail:			
86.90	Outlays from new discretionary authority	2,011	2,134	2,197
86.93	Outlays from discretionary balances	506	514	488
87.00	Total outlays (gross)	2,517	2,648	2,685
	Offsets:			
	Against gross budget authority and outlays:			
	Offsetting collections (cash) from:			
88.40	Non-Federal sources	–21	–14	–24
88.45	Offsetting governmental collections from the public	–101	–113	–108
88.90	Total, offsetting collections (cash)	–122	–127	–132
	Against gross budget authority only:			
88.95	From Federal sources: Change in receivables and unpaid, unfilled orders	25		
	Net budget authority and outlays:			
89.00	Budget authority	2,500	2,512	2,584
90.00	Outlays	2,395	2,521	2,553

Summary of Budget Authority and Outlays

(in millions of dollars)

	1999 actual	2000 est.	2001 est.
Enacted/requested:			
Budget Authority	2,500	2,512	2,584
Outlays	2,395	2,521	2,553
Supplemental proposal:			
Budget Authority		20	
Outlays		16	3
Total:			
Budget Authority	2,500	2,532	2,584
Outlays	2,395	2,537	2,556

This appropriation provides funding for mission support and includes: safety, mission assurance, engineering and advanced concepts activities supporting agency programs; salaries and related expenses in support of research in NASA field installations; design, repair, rehabilitation and modification of institutional facilities and construction of new institutional facilities; and other operations activities supporting conduct of agency programs.

Performance Objectives

Safety, mission assurance, engineering, and advanced concepts.—The goal of this program is to invest in the safety and success of NASA missions by assuring that sound and robust policies, processes, and tools for safety, reliability, quality assurance, and engineering disciplines are in place and applied throughout NASA. The program also examines long-term technology requirements for NASA's strategic objectives.

Research and program management.—This activity provides for the salaries, travel support, other personnel expenses of the entire NASA civil service workforce, and includes vital support to the physical plant at the Centers and at NASA Headquarters.

Construction of facilities.—This activity provides for facility construction activities to preserve NASA's infrastructure; environmental compliance and restoration activities, design of facilities projects, and advanced planning related to future facilities needs. In 1999–2001, activities in support of construction projects to repair and modernize the basic infrastructure and institutional facilities at NASA centers will continue, as well as activities in support of environmental compliance and restoration requirements.

The 2002 budget estimate for this account is $2.6 billion.

Object Classification (in millions of dollars)

Identification code 80–0112–0–1–999		1999 actual	2000 est.	2001 est.
	Direct obligations:			
	Personnel compensation:			
11.1	Full-time permanent	1,201	1,264	1,343
11.3	Other than full-time permanent	28	21	25
11.5	Other personnel compensation	28	27	37
11.8	Special personal services payments	11	12	14
11.9	Total personnel compensation	1,268	1,324	1,419
12.1	Civilian personnel benefits	270	276	314
13.0	Benefits for former personnel	11	10	
21.0	Travel and transportation of persons	48	52	53
22.0	Transportation of things	5	5	5
23.1	Rental payments to GSA	15	14	13
23.3	Communications, utilities, and miscellaneous charges	33	31	29
24.0	Printing and reproduction	6	6	5
25.1	Advisory and assistance services	6	6	5
25.2	Other services	224	214	195
25.3	Purchases of goods and services from Government accounts	26	25	23
25.4	Operation and maintenance of facilities	139	133	121
25.5	Research and development contracts	129	123	112
25.6	Medical care	6	6	5
25.7	Operation and maintenance of equipment	90	86	78
26.0	Supplies and materials	36	34	31
31.0	Equipment	46	43	40
32.0	Land and structures	144	137	125
41.0	Grants, subsidies, and contributions	4	4	4
99.0	Subtotal, direct obligations	2,506	2,529	2,577
99.0	Reimbursable obligations	97	127	132
99.9	Total new obligations	2,603	2,656	2,709

Personnel Summary

Identification code 80–0112–0–1–999		1999 actual	2000 est.	2001 est.
	Direct:			
1001	Total compensable workyears: Full-time equivalent employment	18,178	18,031	18,641
	Reimbursable:			
2001	Total compensable workyears: Full-time equivalent employment	100	100	100

Research and Development

Program and Financing (in millions of dollars)

Identification code 80–0108–0–1–999		1999 actual	2000 est.	2001 est.
	New budget authority (gross), detail:			
	Spending authority from offsetting collections:			
	Discretionary:			
68.00	Offsetting collections (cash)	10	19	
68.10	From Federal sources: Change in receivables and unpaid, unfilled orders	–10	–19	
68.90	Spending authority from offsetting collections (total discretionary)			
	Change in unpaid obligations:			
	Unpaid obligations, start of year:			
72.40	Obligated balance, start of year	51	29	
72.95	From Federal sources: Receivables and unpaid, unfilled orders	29	19	
72.99	Total unpaid obligations, start of year	80	48	
73.20	Total outlays (gross)	–28	–48	
73.40	Adjustments in expired accounts (net)	–4		
	Unpaid obligations, end of year:			
74.40	Obligated balance, end of year	29		
74.95	From Federal sources: Receivables and unpaid, unfilled orders	19		
74.99	Total unpaid obligations, end of year	48		
	Outlays (gross), detail:			
86.93	Outlays from discretionary balances	28	48	
	Offsets:			
	Against gross budget authority and outlays:			
88.45	Offsetting collections (cash) from: Offsetting governmental collections from the public	–10	–19	
	Against gross budget authority only:			
88.95	From Federal sources: Change in receivables and unpaid, unfilled orders	10	19	
	Net budget authority and outlays:			
89.00	Budget authority			
90.00	Outlays	18	29	

Since FY 1995 NASA's Research and Development activities have been performed in Human Space Flight; Science, Aeronautics and Technology; and Mission Support. This account shows spending from balances prior to the account restructuring.

Space Flight, Control and Data Communications

Program and Financing (in millions of dollars)

Identification code 80–0105–0–1–252		1999 actual	2000 est.	2001 est.
	Change in unpaid obligations:			
72.40	Unpaid obligations, start of year: Obligated balance, start of year	20	14	2
73.20	Total outlays (gross)	–2	–12	–2
73.40	Adjustments in expired accounts (net)	–4		
74.40	Unpaid obligations, end of year: Obligated balance, end of year	14	2	
	Outlays (gross), detail:			
86.93	Outlays from discretionary balances	2	12	2
	Net budget authority and outlays:			
89.00	Budget authority			
90.00	Outlays	2	12	2

Since FY 1995 NASA's Space Flight, Control and Data Communications activities have been performed in Human Space Flight; Science, Aeronautics and Technology; and Mission Support. This account shows spending from balances prior to the account restructuring.

Construction of Facilities

Program and Financing (in millions of dollars)

Identification code 80–0107–0–1–999		1999 actual	2000 est.	2001 est.
	Obligations by program activity:			
00.01	Supporting activity	7	13	
00.02	Space transportation	5		
00.04	Aeronautical research and technology	4		
10.00	Total new obligations	16	13	

General and special funds—Continued

CONSTRUCTION OF FACILITIES—Continued

Program and Financing (in millions of dollars)—Continued

Identification code 80–0107–0–1–999	1999 actual	2000 est.	2001 est.
Budgetary resources available for obligation:			
21.40 Unobligated balance available, start of year	29	13	
23.95 Total new obligations	−16	−13	
24.40 Unobligated balance available, end of year	13		
Change in unpaid obligations:			
72.40 Unpaid obligations, start of year: Obligated balance, start of year	30	18	6
73.10 Total new obligations	16	13	
73.20 Total outlays (gross)	−27	−25	−6
73.40 Adjustments in expired accounts (net)	−1		
74.40 Unpaid obligations, end of year: Obligated balance, end of year	18	6	
Outlays (gross), detail:			
86.93 Outlays from discretionary balances	27	25	6
Net budget authority and outlays:			
89.00 Budget authority			
90.00 Outlays	26	25	6

Since FY 1995 NASA's Construction of Facilities activities have been performed in Human Space Flight; Science, Aeronautics and Technology; and Mission Support. This account shows spending from balances prior to the account restructuring.

Object Classification (in millions of dollars)

Identification code 80–0107–0–1–999	1999 actual	2000 est.	2001 est.
25.2 Other services	1	1	
32.0 Land and structures	15	12	
99.9 Total new obligations	16	13	

RESEARCH AND PROGRAM MANAGEMENT

Program and Financing (in millions of dollars)

Identification code 80–0103–0–1–999	1999 actual	2000 est.	2001 est.
Change in unpaid obligations:			
72.40 Unpaid obligations, start of year: Obligated balance, start of year	1		
73.40 Adjustments in expired accounts (net)	−1		
Net budget authority and outlays:			
89.00 Budget authority			
90.00 Outlays			

Since FY 1995 NASA's Research and Program Management activities have been performed in Mission Support. This account shows spending from balances prior to the account restructuring.

OFFICE OF INSPECTOR GENERAL

For necessary expenses of the Office of Inspector General in carrying out the Inspector General Act of 1978, as amended, [$20,000,000] *$22,000,000*. *(Departments of Veterans Affairs and Housing and Urban Development, and Independent Agencies Appropriations Act, 2000.)*

Program and Financing (in millions of dollars)

Identification code 80–0109–0–1–252	1999 actual	2000 est.	2001 est.
Obligations by program activity:			
10.00 Total new obligations	20	20	22
Budgetary resources available for obligation:			
22.00 New budget authority (gross)	20	20	22
23.95 Total new obligations	−20	−20	−22
New budget authority (gross), detail:			
Discretionary:			
40.00 Appropriation	20	20	22
Change in unpaid obligations:			
72.40 Unpaid obligations, start of year: Obligated balance, start of year	2	3	5
73.10 Total new obligations	20	20	22
73.20 Total outlays (gross)	−19	−20	−21
74.40 Unpaid obligations, end of year: Obligated balance, end of year	3	5	5
Outlays (gross), detail:			
86.90 Outlays from new discretionary authority	18	18	19
86.93 Outlays from discretionary balances	1	2	2
87.00 Total outlays (gross)	19	20	21
Net budget authority and outlays:			
89.00 Budget authority	20	20	22
90.00 Outlays	19	20	21

The mission of the Office of Inspector General is to conduct audits and investigations of agency activities. The Inspector General keeps the Administrator informed of problems and deficiencies in agency programs and operations.

The 2002 budget estimate for this account is $22 million.

Object Classification (in millions of dollars)

Identification code 80–0109–0–1–252	1999 actual	2000 est.	2001 est.
11.1 Personnel compensation: Full-time permanent	15	16	17
12.1 Civilian personnel benefits	3	3	3
21.0 Travel and transportation of persons	1	1	2
25.2 Other services	1		
99.9 Total new obligations	20	20	22

Personnel Summary

Identification code 80–0109–0–1–252	1999 actual	2000 est.	2001 est.
1001 Total compensable workyears: Full-time equivalent employment	191	210	213

Trust Funds

SCIENCE, SPACE, AND TECHNOLOGY EDUCATION TRUST FUND

Unavailable Collections (in millions of dollars)

Identification code 80–8978–0–7–503	1999 actual	2000 est.	2001 est.
Balance, start of year:			
01.99 Balance, start of year	18	15	15
Receipts:			
02.01 Earnings on investments; Science, Space and Technology Education, Trust Fund	−2	1	1
04.00 Total: Balances and collections	16	16	16
Appropriation:			
05.01 Science, space, and technology education trust fund	−1	−1	−1
07.99 Total balance, end of year	15	15	15

Program and Financing (in millions of dollars)

Identification code 80–8978–0–7–503	1999 actual	2000 est.	2001 est.
Obligations by program activity:			
10.00 Total new obligations (object class 41.0)	1		
Budgetary resources available for obligation:			
22.00 New budget authority (gross)	1	1	1
23.95 Total new obligations	−1		

	New budget authority (gross), detail:			
	Mandatory:			
60.27	Appropriation (trust fund, indefinite)	1	1	1
	Change in unpaid obligations:			
73.10	Total new obligations	1		
73.20	Total outlays (gross)	−1	−1	−1
	Outlays (gross), detail:			
86.97	Outlays from new mandatory authority	1	1	1
	Net budget authority and outlays:			
89.00	Budget authority	1	1	1
90.00	Outlays	1	1	1
	Memorandum (non-add) entries:			
92.01	Total investments, start of year: U.S. securities: Par value	17	13	17
92.02	Total investments, end of year: U.S. securities: Par value	13	17	17

Administrative Provisions

Notwithstanding the limitation on the availability of funds appropriated for "Human space flight", "Science, aeronautics and technology", or "Mission support" by this appropriations Act, when any activity has been initiated by the incurrence of obligations for construction of facilities as authorized by law, such amount available for such activity shall remain available until expended. This provision does not apply to the amounts appropriated in "Mission support" pursuant to the authorization for [repair, rehabilitation and modification of facilities,] minor *revitalization and* construction of [new facilities and additions to existing] facilities, and facility planning and design.

Notwithstanding the limitation on the availability of funds appropriated for "Human space flight", "Science, aeronautics and technology", or "Mission support" by this appropriations Act, the amounts appropriated for construction of facilities shall remain available until September 30, [2002] *2003*.

Notwithstanding the limitation on the availability of funds appropriated for "Mission support" and "Office of Inspector General", amounts made available by this Act for personnel and related costs and travel expenses of the National Aeronautics and Space Administration shall remain available until September 30, [2000] *2001* and may be used to enter into contracts for training, investigations, costs associated with personnel relocation, and for other services, to be provided during the next fiscal year. *Funds for announced prizes otherwise authorized shall remain available, without fiscal year limitation, until the prize is claimed or the offer is withdrawn.*

[Unless otherwise provided for in this Act or in the joint explanatory statement of the committee of conference accompanying this Act, no part of the funds appropriated for "Human space flight" may be used for the development of the International Space Station in excess of the amounts set forth in the budget estimates submitted as part of the budget request for fiscal year 2000.] *(Departments of Veterans Affairs and Housing and Urban Development, and Independent Agencies Appropriations Act, 2000.)*

NATIONAL SCIENCE FOUNDATION

NATIONAL SCIENCE FOUNDATION

Federal Funds

General and special funds:

RESEARCH AND RELATED ACTIVITIES

For necessary expenses in carrying out the National Science Foundation Act of 1950, as amended (42 U.S.C. 1861–1875), and the Act to establish a National Medal of Science (42 U.S.C. 1880–1881); services as authorized by 5 U.S.C. 3109; *authorized travel;* maintenance and operation of aircraft and purchase of flight services for research support; acquisition of aircraft; [$2,966,000,000] *$3,540,680,000*, of which not to exceed [$253,000,000] *$285,410,000* shall remain available until expended for Polar research and operations support, and for reimbursement to other Federal agencies for operational and science support and logistical and other related activities for the United States Antarctic program; the balance to remain available until September 30, [2001] *2002*: *Provided*, That receipts for scientific support services and materials furnished by the National Research Centers and other National Science Foundation supported research facilities may be credited to this appropriation: *Provided further*, That to the extent that the amount appropriated is less than the total amount authorized to be appropriated for included program activities, all amounts, including floors and ceilings, specified in the authorizing Act for those program activities or their subactivities shall be reduced proportionally[: *Provided further*, That $60,000,000 of the funds available under this heading shall be made available for a comprehensive research initiative on plant genomes for economically significant crop: *Provided further*, That none of the funds appropriated or otherwise made available to the National Science Foundation in this or any prior Act may be obligated or expended by the National Science Foundation to enter into or extend a grant, contract, or cooperative agreement for the support of administering the domain name and numbering system of the Internet after September 30, 1998: *Provided further*, That no funds in this or any other Act shall be used to acquire or lease a research vessel with ice-breaking capability built or retrofitted by a shipyard located in a foreign country if such a vessel of United States origin can be obtained at a cost no more than 50 per centum above that of the least expensive technically acceptable foreign vessel bid: *Provided further*, That, in determining the cost of such a vessel, such cost be increased by the amount of any subsidies or financing provided by a foreign government (or instrumentality thereof) to such vessel's construction: *Provided further*, That if the vessel contracted for pursuant to the foregoing is not available for the 2002–2003 austral summer Antarctic season, a vessel of any origin may be leased for a period of not to exceed 120 days for that season and each season thereafter until delivery of the new vessel]. *(Departments of Veterans Affairs and Housing and Urban Development, and Independent Agencies Appropriations Act, 2000.)*

Program and Financing (in millions of dollars)

Identification code 49–0100–0–1–999		1999 actual	2000 est.	2001 est.
	Obligations by program activity:			
	Direct program:			
00.01	Biological sciences	392	414	511
00.02	Computer and information science and engineering	299	388	529
00.03	Engineering	370	382	457
00.05	Geosciences	478	488	583
00.06	Mathematical and physical sciences	734	758	881
00.07	Social, behavioral and economic sciences	142	146	175
00.09	U.S. Polar research programs	183	190	223
00.10	U.S. Antarctic logistical support activities	63	63	63
00.11	Integrative activities	161	129	119
09.01	Reimbursable programs	84	100	100
10.00	Total new obligations	2,906	3,058	3,641
	Budgetary resources available for obligation:			
21.40	Unobligated balance available, start of year	41	2	
22.00	New budget authority (gross)	2,853	3,058	3,641
22.10	Resources available from recoveries of prior year obligations	16		
23.90	Total budgetary resources available for obligation	2,910	3,060	3,641
23.95	Total new obligations	−2,906	−3,058	−3,641
23.98	Unobligated balance expiring or withdrawn	−2		
24.40	Unobligated balance available, end of year	2		
	New budget authority (gross), detail:			
	Discretionary:			
40.00	Appropriation	2,770	2,966	3,541
40.75	Reduction pursuant to P.L. 106–51	−1		
40.76	Reduction pursuant to P.L. 106–113		−8	
42.00	Transferred from other accounts	5		
43.00	Appropriation (total discretionary)	2,774	2,958	3,541
	Spending authority from offsetting collections:			
68.00	Offsetting collections (cash)	68	100	100
68.10	From Federal sources: Change in receivables and unpaid, unfilled orders	11		
68.90	Spending authority from offsetting collections (total discretionary)	79	100	100
70.00	Total new budget authority (gross)	2,853	3,058	3,641
	Change in unpaid obligations:			
	Unpaid obligations, start of year:			
72.40	Obligated balance, start of year	2,770	3,174	3,527
72.95	From Federal sources: Receivables and unpaid, unfilled orders	7	18	18
72.99	Total unpaid obligations, start of year	2,777	3,192	3,545
73.10	Total new obligations	2,906	3,058	3,641
73.20	Total outlays (gross)	−2,461	−2,705	−3,063
73.40	Adjustments in expired accounts (net)	−15		
73.45	Adjustments in unexpired accounts	−16		
	Unpaid obligations, end of year:			
74.40	Obligated balance, end of year	3,174	3,527	4,105
74.95	From Federal sources: Receivables and unpaid, unfilled orders	18	18	18
74.99	Total unpaid obligations, end of year	3,192	3,545	4,123
	Outlays (gross), detail:			
86.90	Outlays from new discretionary authority	674	768	902
86.93	Outlays from discretionary balances	1,785	1,937	2,161
87.00	Total outlays (gross)	2,461	2,705	3,063
	Offsets:			
	Against gross budget authority and outlays:			
88.00	Offsetting collections (cash) from: Federal sources	−68	−100	−100
	Against gross budget authority only:			
88.95	From Federal sources: Change in receivables and unpaid, unfilled orders	−11		
	Net budget authority and outlays:			
89.00	Budget authority	2,774	2,958	3,541
90.00	Outlays	2,393	2,605	2,963

The research and related activities appropriation enables the United States to uphold world leadership in all aspects of science and engineering. This appropriation provides resources for NSF to achieve the following outcome goals: discoveries at and across the frontier of science and engineering, and connections to its use in the service of society; a diverse, internationally competitive and globally-engaged workforce of scientists, engineers and well-prepared citizens; and broadly accessible, state-of-the-art information bases and shared research and education tools. Research activities will contribute to the achievement of these goals through development of intellectual capital, integration of research and education, and

General and special funds—Continued

RESEARCH AND RELATED ACTIVITIES—Continued

promotion of partnerships. This appropriation supports NSF's active development of performance indicators.

Program activities in the research and related activities appropriation are included in the 21st Century research fund.

The major research program activities of the Foundation are:

Biological sciences.—This activity promotes scientific progress in biology through support of research ranging from the study of molecules, through cells and organisms, to studies of ecosystems. This activity also supports a comprehensive research initiative on plant genomes, including research on economically significant crops.

Computer and information sciences and engineering.—Research is directed at "information technology" in the broadest sense of the term, ranging from fundamental theory to systems engineering.

Engineering.—Research supported by this activity aims to increase U.S. engineering capability and strength, and focus that capability and strength on areas which are relevant to national problems and long-term needs. This activity also includes small business innovation research.

Geosciences.—This research advances knowledge of the properties and dynamics of the planet Earth.

Mathematical and physical sciences.—Research in this activity is directed at increasing understanding of natural laws and phenomena. It includes research in mathematical sciences, astronomy, physics, chemistry, and materials science.

Social, behavioral and economic sciences.—This activity supports research in social, behavioral and economic sciences, facilitates international scientific cooperation, and funds science resources studies.

U.S. polar research programs.—This activity supports Arctic and Antarctic research and operational science support and other related activities for the United States polar research programs. This activity includes funding for the expenses of the Arctic Research Commission.

U.S. Antarctic logistical support activities.—This activity provides funding for reimbursing Federal agencies for logistical and other related activities for the United States Antarctic program.

Integrative activities.—This activity supports emerging cross-disciplinary research efforts and major research instrumentation. This activity also provides support for the Science and Technology Policy Institute.

Object Classification (in millions of dollars)

Identification code 49–0100–0–1–999		1999 actual	2000 est.	2001 est.
	Direct obligations:			
21.0	Travel and transportation of persons	5	7	10
25.1	Advisory and assistance services	15	16	23
25.2	Other services	3	3	3
25.3	Purchases of goods and services from Government accounts	2	2	2
25.4	Operation and maintenance of facilities	125	125	125
25.5	Research and development contracts	25	25	25
31.0	Equipment	1	1	1
41.0	Grants, subsidies, and contributions	2,646	2,779	3,352
99.0	Subtotal, direct obligations	2,822	2,958	3,541
99.0	Reimbursable obligations	83	100	100
99.5	Below reporting threshold	1		
99.9	Total new obligations	2,906	3,058	3,641

Personnel Summary

Identification code 49–0100–0–1–999		1999 actual	2000 est.	2001 est.
1001	Total compensable workyears: Full-time equivalent employment	3	3	4

ACADEMIC RESEARCH INFRASTRUCTURE

Program and Financing (in millions of dollars)

Identification code 49–0150–0–1–251		1999 actual	2000 est.	2001 est.
	Budgetary resources available for obligation:			
22.10	Resources available from recoveries of prior year obligations	2		
	Change in unpaid obligations:			
72.40	Unpaid obligations, start of year: Obligated balance, start of year	74	35	16
73.20	Total outlays (gross)	−37	−19	−11
73.40	Adjustments in expired accounts (net)	−1		
73.45	Adjustments in unexpired accounts	−2		
74.40	Unpaid obligations, end of year: Obligated balance, end of year	35	16	5
	Outlays (gross), detail:			
86.93	Outlays from discretionary balances	37	19	11
	Net budget authority and outlays:			
89.00	Budget authority			
90.00	Outlays	37	19	11

The academic research infrastructure facilities activity has been terminated. A program to support the acquisition of major research instrumentation has been funded through the research and related activities appropriation since 1997. This account shows spending from balances prior to the account restructuring.

MAJOR RESEARCH EQUIPMENT

For necessary expenses of major construction projects pursuant to the National Science Foundation Act of 1950, as amended, [including award-related travel, $95,000,000] *including authorized travel, $138,540,000,* to remain available until expended. *For necessary expenses of the Large Hadron Collider, to become available on October 1 of the fiscal year specified and remain available until expended, as follows: fiscal year 2002, $16,900,000; and fiscal year 2003, $9,700,000. For necessary expenses of the Network for Earthquake Engineering Simulation, to become available on October 1 of the fiscal year specified and remain available until expended, as follows: fiscal year 2002, $24,400,000; fiscal year 2003, $4,500,000; and fiscal year 2004, $17,000,000. For necessary expenses of the Terascale Computing System, to become available on October 1, 2001 and remain available until expended, $55,000,000. For necessary expenses of EarthScope: U.S. Array and San Andreas Fault Observatory at Depth, to become available on October 1 of the fiscal year specified and remain available until expended, as follows: fiscal year 2002, $28,460,000; fiscal year 2003, $15,740,000; and fiscal year 2004, $13,170,000. For necessary expenses of the National Ecological Observatory Network, to become available on October 1 of the fiscal year specified and remain available until expended, as follows: fiscal year 2002, $20,000,000; fiscal year 2003, $27,000,000; fiscal year 2004, $20,000,000; and fiscal year 2005, $14,000,000.* (Departments of Veterans Affairs and Housing and Urban Development, and Independent Agencies Appropriations Act, 2000.)

Program and Financing (in millions of dollars)

Identification code 49–0551–0–1–251		1999 actual	2000 est.	2001 est.
	Obligations by program activity:			
10.00	Total new obligations	57	161	139
	Budgetary resources available for obligation:			
21.40	Unobligated balance available, start of year	35	68	
22.00	New budget authority (gross)	90	93	139
23.90	Total budgetary resources available for obligation	125	161	139
23.95	Total new obligations	−57	−161	−139
24.40	Unobligated balance available, end of year	68		
	New budget authority (gross), detail:			
	Discretionary:			
40.00	Appropriation	90	95	139

Identification code		1999 actual	2000 est.	2001 est.
40.76	Reduction pursuant to P.L. 106–113	....	−2	....
43.00	Appropriation (total discretionary)	90	93	139
	Change in unpaid obligations:			
72.40	Unpaid obligations, start of year: Obligated balance, start of year	72	29	117
73.10	Total new obligations	57	161	139
73.20	Total outlays (gross)	−99	−73	−90
74.40	Unpaid obligations, end of year: Obligated balance, end of year	29	117	166
	Outlays (gross), detail:			
86.90	Outlays from new discretionary authority	40	10	15
86.93	Outlays from discretionary balances	59	63	75
87.00	Total outlays (gross)	99	73	90
	Net budget authority and outlays:			
89.00	Budget authority	90	93	139
90.00	Outlays	99	73	90

Object Classification (in millions of dollars)

Identification code 49–0551–0–1–251		1999 actual	2000 est.	2001 est.
25.5	Research and development contracts	26	85	14
41.0	Grants, subsidies, and contributions	31	76	125
99.9	Total new obligations	57	161	139

The major research equipment activity supports the construction and procurement of unique national research platforms and major research equipment. Performance is measured against established construction schedules, costs and milestones.

Funding for major research equipment is included in the 21st Century research fund.

SALARIES AND EXPENSES

For salaries and expenses necessary in carrying out the National Science Foundation Act of 1950, as amended (42 U.S.C. 1861–1875); services authorized by 5 U.S.C. 3109; hire of passenger motor vehicles; not to exceed $9,000 for official reception and representation expenses; uniforms or allowances therefor, as authorized by 5 U.S.C. 5901–5902; rental of conference rooms in the District of Columbia; reimbursement of the General Services Administration for security guard services; [$149,000,000] *$157,890,000*: *Provided*, That contracts may be entered into under "Salaries and expenses" in fiscal year [2000] *2001* for maintenance and operation of facilities, and for other services, to be provided during the next fiscal year. *(Departments of Veterans Affairs and Housing and Urban Development, and Independent Agencies Appropriations Act, 2000.)*

Program and Financing (in millions of dollars)

Identification code 49–0180–0–1–251		1999 actual	2000 est.	2001 est.
	Obligations by program activity:			
00.01	Administration and management	144	149	158
09.01	Reimbursable programs	5	5	5
10.00	Total new obligations	149	154	163
	Budgetary resources available for obligation:			
22.00	New budget authority (gross)	149	154	163
23.95	Total new obligations	−149	−154	−163
	New budget authority (gross), detail:			
	Discretionary:			
40.00	Appropriation	144	149	158
	Spending authority from offsetting collections:			
68.00	Offsetting collections (cash)	4	5	5
68.10	From Federal sources: Change in receivables and unpaid, unfilled orders	1	....	....
68.90	Spending authority from offsetting collections (total discretionary)	5	5	5
70.00	Total new budget authority (gross)	149	154	163
	Change in unpaid obligations:			
	Unpaid obligations, start of year:			
72.40	Obligated balance, start of year	19	24	17
72.95	From Federal sources: Receivables and unpaid, unfilled orders	....	1	1
72.99	Total unpaid obligations, start of year	19	25	18
73.10	Total new obligations	149	154	163
73.20	Total outlays (gross)	−142	−162	−162
73.40	Adjustments in expired accounts (net)	−1	....	....
	Unpaid obligations, end of year:			
74.40	Obligated balance, end of year	24	17	18
74.95	From Federal sources: Receivables and unpaid, unfilled orders	1	1	1
74.99	Total unpaid obligations, end of year	25	18	19
	Outlays (gross), detail:			
86.90	Outlays from new discretionary authority	129	138	146
86.93	Outlays from discretionary balances	13	24	16
87.00	Total outlays (gross)	142	162	162
	Offsets:			
	Against gross budget authority and outlays:			
88.00	Offsetting collections (cash) from: Federal sources	−4	−5	−5
	Against gross budget authority only:			
88.95	From Federal sources: Change in receivables and unpaid, unfilled orders	−1	....	....
	Net budget authority and outlays:			
89.00	Budget authority	144	149	158
90.00	Outlays	138	157	157

This account provides funds to administer and manage NSF programs. NSF continually devises and refines performance measures for development and monitoring of programs.

Salaries and expenses is included in the 21st Century research fund.

Object Classification (in millions of dollars)

Identification code 49–0180–0–1–251		1999 actual	2000 est.	2001 est.
	Direct obligations:			
	Personnel compensation:			
11.1	Full-time permanent	69	72	77
11.3	Other than full-time permanent	11	12	13
11.5	Other personnel compensation	2	2	2
11.8	Special personal services payments	1	1	1
11.9	Total personnel compensation	83	87	93
12.1	Civilian personnel benefits	16	17	18
21.0	Travel and transportation of persons	4	4	1
23.1	Rental payments to GSA	16	17	18
23.3	Communications, utilities, and miscellaneous charges	4	3	4
25.1	Advisory and assistance services	1	1	1
25.2	Other services	4	4	4
25.3	Purchases of goods and services from Government accounts	1	1	1
25.7	Operation and maintenance of equipment	5	5	6
26.0	Supplies and materials	2	2	2
31.0	Equipment	8	8	10
99.0	Subtotal, direct obligations	144	149	158
99.0	Reimbursable obligations	4	5	5
99.5	Below reporting threshold	1	....	....
99.9	Total new obligations	149	154	163

Personnel Summary

Identification code 49–0180–0–1–251		1999 actual	2000 est.	2001 est.
1001	Total compensable workyears: Full-time equivalent employment	1,142	1,150	1,150

OFFICE OF INSPECTOR GENERAL

For necessary expenses of the Office of Inspector General as authorized by the Inspector General Act of 1978, as amended, [$5,450,000] *$6,280,000*, to remain available until September 30, [2001] *2002*.

General and special funds—Continued

OFFICE OF INSPECTOR GENERAL—Continued

(Departments of Veterans Affairs and Housing and Urban Development, and Independent Agencies Appropriations Act, 2000.)

Program and Financing (in millions of dollars)

Identification code 49–0300–0–1–251	1999 actual	2000 est.	2001 est.
Obligations by program activity:			
10.00 Total new obligations	5	5	6
Budgetary resources available for obligation:			
22.00 New budget authority (gross)	5	5	6
23.95 Total new obligations	−5	−5	−6
New budget authority (gross), detail:			
Discretionary:			
40.00 Appropriation	5	5	6
Change in unpaid obligations:			
72.40 Unpaid obligations, start of year: Obligated balance, start of year	1	2	1
73.10 Total new obligations	5	5	6
73.20 Total outlays (gross)	−5	−6	−6
74.40 Unpaid obligations, end of year: Obligated balance, end of year	2	1	1
Outlays (gross), detail:			
86.90 Outlays from new discretionary authority	4	4	5
86.93 Outlays from discretionary balances	1	1	1
87.00 Total outlays (gross)	5	6	6
Net budget authority and outlays:			
89.00 Budget authority	5	5	6
90.00 Outlays	5	6	6

This appropriation provides agency-wide audit and investigative functions to identify and correct management and administrative deficiencies which create conditions for existing or potential instances of fraud, waste, and mismanagement consistent with the Inspector General Act of 1978, as amended (5 U.S.C. App. 3).

The Office of Inspector General is included in the 21st Century research fund.

Object Classification (in millions of dollars)

Identification code 49–0300–0–1–251	1999 actual	2000 est.	2001 est.
11.1 Personnel compensation: Full-time permanent	3	3	4
12.1 Civilian personnel benefits	1	1	1
25.1 Advisory and assistance services	1	1	1
99.9 Total new obligations	5	5	6

Personnel Summary

Identification code 49–0300–0–1–251	1999 actual	2000 est.	2001 est.
1001 Total compensable workyears: Full-time equivalent employment	44	46	50

EDUCATION AND HUMAN RESOURCES

For necessary expenses in carrying out science and engineering education and human resources programs and activities pursuant to the National Science Foundation Act of 1950, as amended (42 U.S.C. 1861–1875), including services as authorized by 5 U.S.C. 3109, [award-related travel,] *authorized travel,* and rental of conference rooms in the District of Columbia, [$696,600,000] *$729,010,000*, to remain available until September 30, [2001] *2002*: *Provided*, That to the extent that the amount of this appropriation is less than the total amount authorized to be appropriated for included program activities, all amounts, including floors and ceilings, specified in the authorizing Act for those program activities or their subactivities shall be reduced proportionally[: *Provided further*, That $10,000,000 shall be available for the purpose of establishing an office of innovation partnerships]. *(Departments of Veterans Affairs and Housing and Urban Development, and Independent Agencies Appropriations Act, 2000.)*

Program and Financing (in millions of dollars)

Identification code 49–0106–0–1–251	1999 actual	2000 est.	2001 est.
Obligations by program activity:			
Obligations by program activity:			
Direct program:			
Appropriated activities:			
00.01 Educational system reform	116	114	110
00.02 Office of innovation partnerships	49	60	48
00.03 Elementary, secondary and informal education	194	184	191
00.04 Undergraduate education	101	116	141
00.05 Graduate education	74	78	89
00.06 Human resource development	73	77	82
00.07 Research, evaluation and communication	55	62	68
00.91 Subtotal appropriated activities	662	691	729
H–1B non-immigrant petitioner fee activities:			
01.01 Scholarships for individuals (low-income students)	1	45	23
01.02 Grants for enrichment courses		7	4
01.03 Systemic reform activities		7	4
01.91 Subtotal H–1B non-immigrant petitioner fee activities	1	59	31
02.00 Total direct obligations	663	750	760
09.01 Reimbursable programs	14	15	15
10.00 Total new obligations	677	765	775
Budgetary resources available for obligation:			
21.40 Unobligated balance available, start of year		26	
22.00 New budget authority (gross)	703	739	775
23.90 Total budgetary resources available for obligation	703	765	775
23.95 Total new obligations	−677	−765	−775
24.40 Unobligated balance available, end of year	26		
New budget authority (gross), detail:			
Discretionary:			
40.00 Appropriation	662	697	729
40.76 Reduction pursuant to P.L. 106–113		−6	
43.00 Appropriation (total discretionary)	662	691	729
Mandatory:			
60.25 Appropriation (special fund, indefinite)	27	33	31
Discretionary:			
68.00 Spending authority from offsetting collections: Offsetting collections (cash)	14	15	15
70.00 Total new budget authority (gross)	703	739	775
Change in unpaid obligations:			
72.40 Unpaid obligations, start of year: Obligated balance, start of year	860	941	996
73.10 Total new obligations	677	765	775
73.20 Total outlays (gross)	−585	−710	−724
73.40 Adjustments in expired accounts (net)	−10		
74.40 Unpaid obligations, end of year: Obligated balance, end of year	941	996	1,047
Outlays (gross), detail:			
86.90 Outlays from new discretionary authority	91	105	110
86.93 Outlays from discretionary balances	494	545	584
86.97 Outlays from new mandatory authority		33	31
86.98 Outlays from mandatory balances		27	
87.00 Total outlays (gross)	585	710	724
Offsets:			
Against gross budget authority and outlays:			
88.00 Offsetting collections (cash) from: Federal sources	−14	−15	−15
Net budget authority and outlays:			
89.00 Budget authority	689	724	760
90.00 Outlays	571	695	709

Summary of Budget Authority and Outlays

(in millions of dollars)

	1999 actual	2000 est.	2001 est.
Enacted/requested:			
Budget Authority	689	724	760
Outlays	571	695	710
Supplemental proposal:			
Budget Authority	....	1	....
Outlays	....	....	....
Total:			
Budget Authority	689	725	760
Outlays	571	695	710

Education and human resources (EHR) activities provide a comprehensive set of programs that further NSF's goal of ensuring a diverse, internationally competitive and globally-engaged workforce of scientists, engineers and well-prepared citizens. At the pre-kindergarten through grade 12 (pre K–12) level, EHR catalyzes systemic reform of science, mathematics, engineering and technology (SMET) education in States, cities, school districts, and rural areas. Its pre K–12 programs provide new instructional materials and pedagogical techniques that incorporate the latest advances in teaching, learning, and educational technologies. They also provide enrichment activities for teachers and students. Undergraduate initiatives improve curricula in all SMET fields and lead reform efforts in mathematics, chemistry, and other disciplines. EHR programs strengthen laboratory course offerings and enhance faculty. Programs for advanced technological education strengthen education for students preparing to enter the high-technology workforce. Graduate level support is directed primarily to research and education fellowships and traineeships to guarantee the U.S. world leadership in science and technology. All EHR programming focuses on broadening participation of groups underrepresented in SMET fields including activities focused on the improvement of infrastructure and academic programs at minority-serving institutions. The Office of Innovation Partnerships was initiated in FY 2000 to examine means of helping institutions expand their research capacity and competitiveness so as to develop a truly national scientific research community. Included is the Experimental program to stimulate competitive research (EPSCoR) that broadens participation of States and regions in science and engineering. EHR supports research that advances SMET education, as well as development and effective implementation of learning technologies. Evaluation and communications activities ensure accountability by developing indicators that measure program impact and inform the education community of best practices and relevant information. Also included within EHR are funds resulting from the collection and use of H–1B non-immigrant fees, for scholarships, enrichment courses, and systemic reform activities. This appropriation also supports NSF's active development of performance indicators.

Education and human resources programs are included in the 21st Century research fund.

Object Classification (in millions of dollars)

Identification code 49–0106–0–1–251	1999 actual	2000 est.	2001 est.
Direct obligations:			
21.0 Travel and transportation of persons	2	2	3
25.1 Advisory and assistance services	18	19	21
41.0 Grants, subsidies, and contributions	642	729	736
99.0 Subtotal, direct obligations	662	750	760
99.0 Reimbursable obligations	14	15	15
99.5 Below reporting threshold	1	....	....
99.9 Total new obligations	677	765	775

Trust Funds

Donations

Unavailable Collections (in millions of dollars)

Identification code 49–8960–0–7–251	1999 actual	2000 est.	2001 est.
Balance, start of year:			
01.99 Balance, start of year	....	....	3
Receipts:			
02.01 Donations to the National Science Foundation	37	45	37
04.00 Total: Balances and collections	37	45	40
Appropriation:			
05.01 Donations	−37	−42	−35
07.99 Total balance, end of year	....	3	5

Program and Financing (in millions of dollars)

Identification code 49–8960–0–7–251	1999 actual	2000 est.	2001 est.
Obligations by program activity:			
00.01 Ocean drilling programs	18	20	20
00.02 Gemini telescope	13	20	13
00.03 Other	2	2	2
10.00 Total new obligations	33	42	35
Budgetary resources available for obligation:			
21.40 Unobligated balance available, start of year	10	14	14
22.00 New budget authority (gross)	37	42	35
23.90 Total budgetary resources available for obligation	47	56	49
23.95 Total new obligations	−33	−42	−35
24.40 Unobligated balance available, end of year	14	14	14
New budget authority (gross), detail:			
Mandatory:			
60.27 Appropriation (trust fund, indefinite)	37	42	35
Change in unpaid obligations:			
72.40 Unpaid obligations, start of year: Obligated balance, start of year	22	13	13
73.10 Total new obligations	33	42	35
73.20 Total outlays (gross)	−42	−42	−35
74.40 Unpaid obligations, end of year: Obligated balance, end of year	13	13	13
Outlays (gross), detail:			
86.97 Outlays from new mandatory authority	31	42	35
86.98 Outlays from mandatory balances	11	....	....
87.00 Total outlays (gross)	42	42	35
Net budget authority and outlays:			
89.00 Budget authority	37	42	35
90.00 Outlays	42	42	35

This account consists of contributions from foreign governments, organizations and individuals to fund various cooperative efforts in science, research and education. These efforts include major international projects, such as operation and construction of the GEMINI telescope, and the NSF Ocean drilling program. Other smaller activities supported include cooperative research, joint seminars, exchange of senior scientists, short-term research development visits, international conferences, and support for certain special functions of NSF and the National Science Board. These funds are not otherwise available.

Object Classification (in millions of dollars)

Identification code 49–8960–0–7–251	1999 actual	2000 est.	2001 est.
25.4 Operation and maintenance of facilities	16	20	20
41.0 Grants, subsidies, and contributions	17	22	15
99.9 Total new obligations	33	42	35

OFFICE OF PERSONNEL MANAGEMENT

Federal Funds

General and special funds:

SALARIES AND EXPENSES

(INCLUDING TRANSFER OF TRUST FUNDS)

For necessary expenses to carry out functions of the Office of Personnel Management pursuant to Reorganization Plan Numbered 2 of 1978 and the Civil Service Reform Act of 1978, including services as authorized by 5 U.S.C. 3109; medical examinations performed for veterans by private physicians on a fee basis; rental of conference rooms in the District of Columbia and elsewhere; hire of passenger motor vehicles; not to exceed $2,500 for official reception and representation expenses; advances for reimbursements to applicable funds of the Office of Personnel Management and the Federal Bureau of Investigation for expenses incurred under Executive Order No. 10422 of January 9, 1953, as amended; and payment of per diem and/or subsistence allowances to employees where Voting Rights Act activities require an employee to remain overnight at his or her post of duty, [$90,584,000] *$100,558,000*; and in addition [$95,486,000] *$101,986,000* for administrative expenses, to be transferred from the appropriate trust funds of the Office of Personnel Management without regard to other statutes, including direct procurement of printed materials, for the retirement and insurance programs, of which [$4,000,000] *$10,500,000* shall remain available until expended for the cost of automating the retirement recordkeeping systems: *Provided*, That the provisions of this appropriation shall not affect the authority to use applicable trust funds as provided by sections 8348(a)(1)(B) and 8909(g) of title 5, United States Code: *Provided further*, That no part of this appropriation shall be available for salaries and expenses of the Legal Examining Unit of the Office of Personnel Management established pursuant to Executive Order No. 9358 of July 1, 1943, or any successor unit of like purpose: *Provided further*, That the President's Commission on White House Fellows, established by Executive Order No. 11183 of October 3, 1964, may, during fiscal year [2000] *2001*, accept donations of money, property, and personal services in connection with the development of a publicity brochure to provide information about the White House Fellows, except that no such donations shall be accepted for travel or reimbursement of travel expenses, or for the salaries of employees of such Commission. *(Independent Agencies Appropriations Act, 2000.)*

Program and Financing (in millions of dollars)

Identification code 24–0100–0–1–805	1999 actual	2000 est.	2001 est.
Obligations by program activity:			
Direct program:			
00.01 Merit systems oversight and effectiveness	19	21	21
00.02 Employment service	26	29	36
00.03 Retirement and insurance service	107	111	115
00.04 Workforce compensation and performance service	8	8	8
00.05 Investigations service	3	3	3
00.06 Workforce relations	4	4	4
00.07 Executive resources	2	2	2
00.08 Administrative services	14	18	19
00.09 Executive and other services	14	12	14
09.01 Reimbursable program	9	10	10
10.00 Total new obligations	206	218	232
Budgetary resources available for obligation:			
21.40 Unobligated balance available, start of year	−3	8	
22.00 New budget authority (gross)	219	219	232
23.90 Total budgetary resources available for obligation	216	227	232
23.95 Total new obligations	−206	−218	−232
23.98 Unobligated balance expiring or withdrawn	−2	−8	
24.40 Unobligated balance available, end of year	8		
New budget authority (gross), detail:			
Discretionary:			
40.00 Appropriation	85	91	101
40.76 Reduction pursuant to P.L. 106–113			
42.00 Transferred from other accounts	2		
43.00 Appropriation (total discretionary)	87	90	101
Spending authority from offsetting collections:			
68.00 Offsetting collections (cash)	105	128	131
68.10 From Federal sources: Change in receivables and unpaid, unfilled orders	27		
68.90 Spending authority from offsetting collections (total discretionary)	132	128	131
70.00 Total new budget authority (gross)	219	219	232
Change in unpaid obligations:			
Unpaid obligations, start of year:			
72.40 Obligated balance, start of year	37	−7	−6
72.95 From Federal sources: Receivables and unpaid, unfilled orders	32	59	59
72.99 Total unpaid obligations, start of year	69	52	53
73.10 Total new obligations	206	218	232
73.20 Total outlays (gross)	−206	−217	−227
73.40 Adjustments in expired accounts (net)	−17		
Unpaid obligations, end of year:			
74.40 Obligated balance, end of year	−7	−6	−1
74.95 From Federal sources: Receivables and unpaid, unfilled orders	59	59	59
74.99 Total unpaid obligations, end of year	52	53	58
Outlays (gross), detail:			
86.90 Outlays from new discretionary authority	181	206	219
86.93 Outlays from discretionary balances	25	11	8
87.00 Total outlays (gross)	206	217	227
Offsets:			
Against gross budget authority and outlays:			
88.00 Offsetting collections (cash) from: Federal sources	−105	−128	−131
Against gross budget authority only:			
88.95 From Federal sources: Change in receivables and unpaid, unfilled orders	−27		
Net budget authority and outlays:			
89.00 Budget authority	87	91	101
90.00 Outlays	101	89	96

Summary of Budget Authority and Outlays

(in millions of dollars)

	1999 actual	*2000 est.*	*2001 est.*
Enacted/requested:			
Budget Authority	87	90	101
Outlays	101	89	96
Supplemental proposal:			
Budget Authority		1	
Outlays		1	
Total:			
Budget Authority	87	91	101
Outlays	101	90	96

The Office of Personnel Management (OPM) is responsible for personnel management functions which include the following activities:

Merit systems oversight and effectiveness.—This activity includes: (a) evaluating human resources management (HRM) in Federal agencies through various methods, including onsite reviews and special studies; (b) administering classification appeals, Fair Labor Standards Act, and Intergovernmental Personnel programs to ensure that agencies adhere to the statutory requirements; (c) helping agencies develop merit-based HRM accountability systems to support mission accomplishment; (d) assessing the effectiveness of Governmentwide HRM policies and programs and serving as a clear-

General and special funds—Continued

SALARIES AND EXPENSES—Continued

(INCLUDING TRANSFER OF TRUST FUNDS)—Continued

inghouse for best practices; (e) testing and evaluating innovative HRM practices and systems, including demonstration projects under 5 U.S.C. Chapter 47; (f) providing readily accessible statistics on the Federal workforce; and (g) administering parts of the Voting Rights Act of 1965.

Program performance.—The activity's performance measures are designed to assess the value-added outcomes which oversight reviews, accountability and demonstration projects, and workforce information have on the Federal HRM community and employees. Client feedback is solicited on each review, product, and service. For example, clients rate the overall value of the oversight work as 4 on a 5-point scale. The quality of data that is provided to clients is regularly assessed, and is used in reviews, studies, and projects. Of each agency's records entered into the Central Personnel Data File, at least 97 percent are correct on all core elements. The *Merit System Principles Questionnaire,* used to collect employee perceptions of the merit system principles, is content valid and reliable. The questionnaire was streamlined for 2000 and beyond. In 2000 and 2001 OPM will conduct 15 to 16 nationwide agency oversight reviews to ensure compliance with Federal Civil Service merit principles.

Employment service.—The Employment Service provides leadership and manages the merit-based employment system for the Federal government. In partnership with agencies, the Service provides a high-quality, diverse workforce through a mix of policy direction, technical assistance, and reimbursable services in the following areas: employment information; assessment; merit-based staffing services; veterans' preference; workforce diversity; automated human resources management systems; workforce restructuring and placement, and organizational analysis and improvement. These operations are carried out through a network of Service Centers throughout the country. Special emphasis in 2000 and 2001 will continue to be given to improving Federal employment opportunities for adults with disabilities and Hispanic Americans, and to enhancing the Government's ability to recruit, develop, and retain computer security professionals.

Program performance.—The Employment Service establishes annual performance goals and objectives designed to accomplish long-term goals identified in OPM's Strategic Plan. Progress is monitored through a mix of outcome and output measures, including results of oversight reviews, qualitative feedback on the usefulness of policies and information processes, customer satisfaction with services, cost-comparison analyses, workload accomplishment data, and quality and timeliness of information.

The Employment Service provided employment information to over 14.8 million people in 1999 through a nationwide system available 24 hours a day, 7 days a week, by telephone, fax, internet, and touch screen kiosks. USAJOBS averages more than 40,000 visits daily. This is a seventy percent increase from the previous year and is expected to continue to grow.

The Employment Service conducts a recertification and training program for all agency Delegated Examining Units to ensure that agencies are carrying out their delegated responsibilities in accordance with law and regulation, and accomplished all scheduled recertifications. In 1999, they revised the delegation handbook and developed a new training program.

In 1999, the Employment Service promptly issued regulations implementing new laws, such as the Veterans Employment Opportunity Act, and changes in voluntary early retirement authority. It also implemented Presidential initiatives, such as hiring persons with disabilities and eliminated approximately 46 redundant excepted appointment authorities. In 1999 the Employment Service began a competency-based study of the information technology (IT) occupation. When completed in 2000, this study will form the foundation of a Federal Cyber Services (FCS) initiative, designed to strengthen the information security (IS) occupation in the workforce. In 2000 and 2001, Centers of IT Excellence, sources of IT training for Federal employees, will be identified; a scholarship-for-service program will be developed (with the National Science Foundation) to provide undergraduate and graduate support in exchange for government service; and a high school outreach program will be designed and tested.

In 1999, the Employment Service assisted over 9,500 employees with outplacement assistance and selection priority for other Federal jobs. Nearly 4,300 of these individuals were placed in other positions within the same agency. Another 183 were rehired through the Reemployment Priority List.

Retirement and Insurance.— This Activity encompasses administration of Earned Employee Benefits—the retirement and insurance programs—for Federal employees, retired Federal employees, and their families. These programs include the Civil Service Retirement System, the Federal Employees' Retirement System, the Federal Employees Group Life Insurance Program, and the Federal Employees and Retired Employees Health Benefits Programs. In 2000, the Administration proposed a new program to offer group long term care insurance for Federal employees and retirees, their spouses, parents and parents-in-law. In addition, this Activity includes OPM's efforts designed to stay abreast of, and respond to, developments in non-Federal fringe benefits practices.

Program performance.—During 2001, modernization of the Federal Employee Retirement Systems will continue. The Retirement Systems Modernization Project (RSM) will shift from blueprint planning to initiation of the core applications that will transform the provision of Retirement services. The RSM effort will result in changes to current processes and systems so that claims processing, record keeping, benefits counseling and financial management functions are performed more efficiently and effectively.

Customer satisfaction with the delivery of retirement program services to annuitants continued, as 96 percent of customers reported they were generally to very satisfied with OPM's overall retirement services.

OPM continued efforts to expand and improve its telecommunications services. Toll-free telephone access is provided to all call centers, and the number of customer service representatives provided to answer incoming customer calls during 2000 increased 20 percent over 1999. Customers are also better served by the extended hours of operations at the Pittsburgh center where calls can now be received until 8:00 PM. In addition, interactive features were added to the OPM web site so that annuitants can make the same changes to their payment accounts as they can through the Agency's toll-free interactive telephone system. The increase in these interactive self-service technologies and the increased capacity for handling telephone inquiries resulted in a 26 percent increase in the volume of telephone calls both received and handled compared to 1998 volumes. Customer satisfaction levels regarding the courtesy, clarity, and timeliness of telephone services remains high at 90 percent.

The volume of new annuity claims remained steady. OPM received and processed an average of 86,600 Civil Service and Federal Employee Retirement Systems annuity claims annually over the past five years. The processing times for interim annuity payments were reduced significantly, from 7 days in 1995 to 3.4 days today, with 40 percent of these payments being authorized within one day of receiving retirement applications at OPM. During the same time frame, the time needed to calculate and begin paying retirees their final annuity has steadily decreased.

OPM also maintained its leadership in the direct deposit program to ensure that customers receive their annuity payment on time each month. During 1998, a direct mail campaign was implemented by OPM to inform annuitants and survivors of the convenience and desirability of direct deposit. At the start of 1998, 79 percent of annuity payments were made by electronic funds transfer. Spurred by OPM's campaign, participation continues to grow and today, nearly 92 percent of annuitants receive their payments this way.

In the health insurance program, during 2000, OPM fully implemented the Patients' Bill of Rights across the entire Federal Employees Health Benefits (FEHBP) Program. This included publishing final regulations that prohibit health plans from limiting the disclosures physicians may make to patients regarding treatment options.

To strengthen its leadership role in the health insurance industry, OPM continued to build and maintain strong relationships with the National Committee for Quality Assurance (NCQA), the Joint Commission on Accreditation of Healthcare Organizations (JCAHO), the Health Care Financing Administration and other components of the Department of Health and Human Services, and the Foundation for Accountability (FAACT). These partnerships have been instrumental in promoting the use of health care quality outcome measures by the Federal Government and health care purchasers and providers throughout the Nation. During 2000, OPM also gathered Health Employees Data Information Sets (HEDIS) data from FEHBP participating Health Maintenance Organizations and selected Preferred Provider Organizations. During 2001, congruent with activities of the Federal Quality Interagency Coordination (QuIC) Task Force, OPM will provide guidance to the FEHBP participating carriers on instituting initiatives to improve health care quality through the prevention of medical errors and enhancements in patient safety. In addition, in 2001, the FEHB Program's benefit structure will, for the first time, provide for parity in the provision of mental health and substance abuse benefits with medical benefits.

Workforce compensation and performance.—This activity includes; (a) developing and implementing pay and leave administration policy and evaluating the effectiveness of alternative compensation systems; (b) developing classification policies and systems and designing flexible alternatives to current systems; and (c) developing Governmentwide policy concerning employee performance management.

Program performance.—The workforce compensation and performance program area uses a variety of measures to identify its level of success. Overall customer service is measured through OPM's Customer Satisfaction Survey. The 1999 survey showed that at least 68 percent of human resources specialists were satisfied with information sharing in each program area, and at least 66 percent were satisfied with technical assistance in each program area. Ninety-two percent of specialists were satisfied with guidance materials dealing with Federal salary tables, the highest single rating on the entire survey. In 1999 the Workforce Compensation and Performance Service staged the first Strategic Compensation Conference. Eighty-seven percent of attendees rated it good to excellent overall. The latest editions of the Human Resources HRCD-ROM have been expanded to include additional information on salary tables and performance-related documents, and the human resources specialists increased their satisfaction rating with the materials from 76 percent in 1998 to 78 percent.

Investigations.—This activity focuses on assuring applicant and appointee fitness and suitability, and oversight of the investigative contract company.

Workforce relations.—This activity includes: (a) developing and administering policies, regulations and guidelines on employee relations, including adverse and performance-based actions and violence in the workplace; (b) facilitating and supporting Federal work and family programs; (c) providing leadership and policy guidance in support of agency human resource development programs and training technology initiatives; and (d) providing guidance and assistance to Federal agencies on labor-management relations and partnership, including managing the activities of the national Partnership Council on behalf of the Council Chair.

Program performance.—OPM's workforce relations performance measures are designed to determine the value added by OPM's policy leadership and guidance on employee and labor-management relations issues, work and family programs, and human resource development programs. The Office of Workforce Relations (OWR) uses a variety of measures to identify its level of success. For instance, surveys at regular intervals assess the extent to which our customers feel that their needs are met by OWR products and services such as printed and electronic materials, and conferences, seminars, and workshops, as well as by legislative and regulatory proposals coming from OWR.

Executive resources.—This activity provides Governmentwide program leadership, policy direction and technical assistance on all aspects of the Senior Executive Service personnel system and comparable executive systems.

Administrative services.—This activity includes: OPM personnel and equal employment opportunity, security, facilities, telecommunications, publishing, acquisitions, and information resources management to support all OPM programs.

Executive and other services.—This activity includes: executive direction, policy development, legal advice and representation, public affairs, legislative activities, financial management, and the operating expenses of the President's Commission on White House Fellows.

Reimbursable programs.—OPM performs reimbursable work at the request of other agencies. OPM also provides administrative, information resources management, and executive services to other OPM accounts on a reimbursable basis.

Object Classification (in millions of dollars)

Identification code 24–0100–0–1–805		1999 actual	2000 est.	2001 est.
	Direct obligations:			
	Personnel compensation:			
11.1	Full-time permanent	95	95	99
11.3	Other than full-time permanent	5	5	5
11.5	Other personnel compensation	4	4	4
11.9	Total personnel compensation	104	104	108
12.1	Civilian personnel benefits	21	24	25
21.0	Travel and transportation of persons	2	2	2
23.1	Rental payments to GSA	17	18	17
23.3	Communications, utilities, and miscellaneous charges	10	11	11
24.0	Printing and reproduction	3	3	3
25.2	Other services	30	35	45
26.0	Supplies and materials	2	3	3
31.0	Equipment	8	8	8
99.0	Subtotal, direct obligations	197	208	222
99.0	Reimbursable obligations	9	10	10
99.9	Total new obligations	206	218	232

Personnel Summary

Identification code 24–0100–0–1–805		1999 actual	2000 est.	2001 est.
	Direct:			
1001	Total compensable workyears: Full-time equivalent employment	1,975	2,082	2,097
	Reimbursable:			
2001	Total compensable workyears: Full-time equivalent employment	80	98	98

General and special funds—Continued

OFFICE OF INSPECTOR GENERAL

SALARIES AND EXPENSES

(INCLUDING TRANSFER OF TRUST FUNDS)

For necessary expenses of the Office of Inspector General in carrying out the provisions of the Inspector General Act, as amended, including services as authorized by 5 U.S.C. 3109, hire of passenger motor vehicles, [$960,000] *$1,360,000*; and in addition, not to exceed [$9,645,000] *$9,745,000* for administrative expenses to audit, investigate, and provide other oversight of the Office of Personnel Management's retirement and insurance programs, to be transferred from the appropriate trust funds of the Office of Personnel Management, as determined by the Inspector General: *Provided*, That the Inspector General is authorized to rent conference rooms in the District of Columbia and elsewhere. *(Independent Agencies Appropriations Act, 2000.)*

Program and Financing (in millions of dollars)

Identification code 24–0400–0–1–805	1999 actual	2000 est.	2001 est.
Obligations by program activity:			
10.00 Total new obligations	10	11	11
Budgetary resources available for obligation:			
22.00 New budget authority (gross)	10	11	11
23.95 Total new obligations	−10	−11	−11
New budget authority (gross), detail:			
Discretionary:			
40.00 Appropriation	1	1	1
68.00 Spending authority from offsetting collections: Offsetting collections (cash)	9	10	10
70.00 Total new budget authority (gross)	10	11	11
Change in unpaid obligations:			
72.40 Unpaid obligations, start of year: Obligated balance, start of year	....	−2	....
73.10 Total new obligations	10	11	11
73.20 Total outlays (gross)	−10	−11	−11
74.40 Unpaid obligations, end of year: Obligated balance, end of year	−2	....	
Outlays (gross), detail:			
86.90 Outlays from new discretionary authority	10	11	11
86.93 Outlays from discretionary balances	....	−2	....
87.00 Total outlays (gross)	10	11	11
Offsets:			
Against gross budget authority and outlays:			
88.00 Offsetting collections (cash) from: Federal sources	−9	−10	−10
Net budget authority and outlays:			
89.00 Budget authority	1	1	1
90.00 Outlays	1	1	1

This appropriation provides agency-wide audit, investigative, evaluation, inspection, and administrative sanction functions to identify management and administrative deficiencies that may create conditions for fraud, waste, and mismanagement. The audits function provides internal agency audit, insurance audit, and contract audit services. Contract audits provide professional advice to agency contracting officials on accounting and financial matters regarding the negotiation, award, administration, repricing, and settlement of contracts. Internal agency audits review and evaluate all facets of agency operations, including financial statements. Evaluation and inspection services provide detailed technical evaluations of agency operations. Insurance audits review the operations of health and life insurance carriers, health care providers, and insurance subscribers. The investigative function provides for the detection and investigation of improper and illegal activities involving programs, personnel, and operations. Administrative sanctions debar from participation in the health insurance program those health care providers whose conduct may pose a threat to the financial integrity of the program itself or to the well-being of insurance program enrollees. These Inspector General activities resulted in positive financial impact approximately $52 million in 1999. This request includes an additional $0.5 million above the approved 2000 resource level to implement P.L. 105–266, The Health Care Protection Act of 1998, and conduct performance audits of agency programs. These additional resources will enhance the Inspector General's ability to protect the integrity of the Federal Employees' Health Benefits Program, assist OPM in recovering funds improperly paid to health care providers, and improve the economy and efficiency of program operations.

Object Classification (in millions of dollars)

Identification code 24–0400–0–1–805	1999 actual	2000 est.	2001 est.
11.1 Personnel compensation: Full-time permanent	6	6	6
12.1 Civilian personnel benefits	1	2	2
23.1 Rental payments to GSA	1	1	1
25.2 Other services	1	1	1
99.0 Subtotal, direct obligations	9	10	10
99.5 Below reporting threshold	1	1	1
99.9 Total new obligations	10	11	11

Personnel Summary

Identification code 24–0400–0–1–805	1999 actual	2000 est.	2001 est.
Direct:			
1001 Total compensable workyears: Full-time equivalent employment	93	106	111
Reimbursable:			
2001 Total compensable workyears: Full-time equivalent employment	....	1	1

GOVERNMENT PAYMENT FOR ANNUITANTS, EMPLOYEES HEALTH BENEFITS

For payment of Government contributions with respect to retired employees, as authorized by chapter 89 of title 5, United States Code, and the Retired Federal Employees Health Benefits Act (74 Stat. 849), as amended, such sums as may be necessary. *(Independent Agencies Appropriations Act, 2000.)*

Program and Financing (in millions of dollars)

Identification code 24–0206–0–1–551	1999 actual	2000 est.	2001 est.
Obligations by program activity:			
00.01 Government contribution for annuitants benefits (1959 Act)	4,607	4,992	5,425
00.02 Government contribution for annuitants benefits (1960 Act)	3	3	2
10.00 Total new obligations (object class 13.0)	4,610	4,995	5,427
Budgetary resources available for obligation:			
22.00 New budget authority (gross)	4,611	4,995	5,427
23.95 Total new obligations	−4,610	−4,995	−5,427
New budget authority (gross), detail:			
Mandatory:			
60.05 Appropriation (indefinite)	4,611	4,995	5,427
Change in unpaid obligations:			
72.40 Unpaid obligations, start of year: Obligated balance, start of year	228	391	407
73.10 Total new obligations	4,610	4,995	5,427
73.20 Total outlays (gross)	−4,448	−4,979	−5,407
74.40 Unpaid obligations, end of year: Obligated balance, end of year	391	407	427
Outlays (gross), detail:			
86.97 Outlays from new mandatory authority	4,219	4,588	5,000
86.98 Outlays from mandatory balances	228	391	407
87.00 Total outlays (gross)	4,448	4,979	5,407

		1999 actual	2000 est.	2001 est.
	Net budget authority and outlays:			
89.00	Budget authority	4,611	4,995	5,427
90.00	Outlays	4,448	4,979	5,407

Summary of Budget Authority and Outlays

(in millions of dollars)

	1999 actual	2000 est.	2001 est.
Enacted/requested:			
Budget Authority	4,611	4,995	5,427
Outlays	4,447	4,979	5,407
Legislative proposal, not subject to PAYGO:			
Budget Authority			–73
Outlays			–73
Total:			
Budget Authority	4,611	4,995	5,354
Outlays	4,447	4,979	5,334

This appropriation covers: (1) the Government's share of the cost of health insurance for 1,851,000 annuitants as defined in sections 8901 and 8906 of title 5, United States Code; (2) the Government's share of the cost of health insurance for about 5,500 annuitants (who were retired when the Federal employees health benefits law became effective), as defined in the Retired Federal Employees Health Benefits Act of 1960; and (3) the Government's contribution for payment of administrative expenses incurred by the Office of Personnel Management in administration of the Act.

The budget authority for this account recognizes the amounts being remitted by the U.S. Postal Service (USPS) to finance a portion of its post-1971 annuitants' health benefit costs. As of the end of 1999, this group of USPS annuitants totalled 419,000 persons.

Government Payment for Annuitants, Employees Health Benefits

(Legislative proposal, not subject to PAYGO)

Program and Financing (in millions of dollars)

Identification code 24–0206–2–1–551		1999 actual	2000 est.	2001 est.
	Obligations by program activity:			
00.01	Government contribution for annuitants benefits (1959 Act)			–73
10.00	Total new obligations (object class 13.0)			–73
	Budgetary resources available for obligation:			
22.00	New budget authority (gross)			–73
23.95	Total new obligations			73
	New budget authority (gross), detail:			
	Mandatory:			
60.05	Appropriation (indefinite)			–73
	Change in unpaid obligations:			
73.10	Total new obligations			–73
73.20	Total outlays (gross)			73
	Outlays (gross), detail:			
86.97	Outlays from new mandatory authority			–73
	Net budget authority and outlays:			
89.00	Budget authority			–73
90.00	Outlays			–73

The Administration will propose legislation that will help control the future rate of growth of FEHB premiums by leveraging the purchasing power of the Federal Government. If enacted, this initiative will enable OPM to develop a comprehensive dental insurance benefit that would be available to Federal employees, annuitants, and their families.

Government Payment for Annuitants, Employee Life Insurance

For payment of Government contributions with respect to employees retiring after December 31, 1989, as required by chapter 87 of title 5, United States Code, such sums as may be necessary. *(Independent Agencies Appropriations Act, 2000.)*

Program and Financing (in millions of dollars)

Identification code 24–0500–0–1–602		1999 actual	2000 est.	2001 est.
	Obligations by program activity:			
10.00	Total new obligations (object class 25.2)	31	33	35
	Budgetary resources available for obligation:			
22.00	New budget authority (gross)	31	33	35
23.95	Total new obligations	–31	–33	–35
	New budget authority (gross), detail:			
	Mandatory:			
60.00	Appropriation	31	33	35
	Change in unpaid obligations:			
72.40	Unpaid obligations, start of year: Obligated balance, start of year	3	3	3
73.10	Total new obligations	31	33	35
73.20	Total outlays (gross)	–31	–33	–35
74.40	Unpaid obligations, end of year: Obligated balance, end of year	3	3	3
	Outlays (gross), detail:			
86.97	Outlays from new mandatory authority	28	30	32
86.98	Outlays from mandatory balances	3	3	3
87.00	Total outlays (gross)	31	33	35
	Net budget authority and outlays:			
89.00	Budget authority	31	33	35
90.00	Outlays	31	33	35

This appropriation finances the Government's share of premiums, which is one-third the cost, for Basic life insurance for annuitants retiring after December 31, 1989, and who are less than 65 years old.

Payment to Civil Service Retirement and Disability Fund

For financing the unfunded liability of new and increased annuity benefits becoming effective on or after October 20, 1969, as authorized by 5 U.S.C. 8348, and annuities under special Acts to be credited to the Civil Service Retirement and Disability Fund, such sums as may be necessary: *Provided*, That annuities authorized by the Act of May 29, 1944, as amended, and the Act of August 19, 1950, as amended (33 U.S.C. 771–775), may hereafter be paid out of the Civil Service Retirement and Disability Fund. *(Independent Agencies Appropriations Act, 2000.)*

Program and Financing (in millions of dollars)

Identification code 24–0200–0–1–805		1999 actual	2000 est.	2001 est.
	Obligations by program activity:			
00.02	Payment of Government share of retirement costs	8,759	8,838	8,940
00.03	Transfers for interest on unfunded liability and payment of military service annuities	12,581	12,346	12,508
00.05	Spouse equity payment	61	61	61
10.00	Total new obligations	21,401	21,245	21,509
	Budgetary resources available for obligation:			
22.00	New budget authority (gross)	21,401	21,245	21,509
23.95	Total new obligations	–21,401	–21,245	–21,509
	New budget authority (gross), detail:			
	Mandatory:			
	Appropriation (indefinite):			
60.05	Appropriation (indefinite)	12,642	12,407	12,569
60.05	Appropriation (indefinite)	8,759	8,838	8,940
62.50	Appropriation (total mandatory)	21,401	21,245	21,509

General and special funds—Continued

PAYMENT TO CIVIL SERVICE RETIREMENT AND DISABILITY FUND—Continued

Program and Financing (in millions of dollars)—Continued

Identification code 24–0200–0–1–805	1999 actual	2000 est.	2001 est.
Change in unpaid obligations:			
73.10 Total new obligations	21,401	21,245	21,509
73.20 Total outlays (gross)	−21,401	−21,245	−21,509
Outlays (gross), detail:			
86.97 Outlays from new mandatory authority	21,401	21,245	21,509
Net budget authority and outlays:			
89.00 Budget authority	21,401	21,245	21,509
90.00 Outlays	21,401	21,245	21,509

Summary of Budget Authority and Outlays

(in millions of dollars)

Enacted/requested:	1999 actual	2000 est.	2001 est.
Budget Authority	21,401	21,245	21,509
Outlays	21,401	21,245	21,509
Legislative proposal, not subject to PAYGO:			
Budget Authority			1
Outlays			1
Total:			
Budget Authority	21,401	21,245	21,510
Outlays	21,401	21,245	21,510

Payment of Government share of retirement costs.—This payment amortizes increases in the static unfunded liability created since October 20, 1969 by any statute which authorizes new or liberalized benefits, an extension of retirement coverage, or pay increases.

Transfers for interest on static unfunded liability and payment of military service annuities.—This transfer covers interest on the static unfunded liability and annuity disbursements attributable to military service.

Payments for spouse equity.—This payment provides survivor annuities to eligible former spouses of annuitants who died between September 1978 and May 1986 and who did not elect survivor coverage.

Object Classification (in millions of dollars)

Identification code 24–0200–0–1–805	1999 actual	2000 est.	2001 est.
12.1 Civilian personnel benefits	8,759	8,838	8,940
13.0 Benefits for former personnel	12,642	12,407	12,569
99.9 Total new obligations	21,401	21,245	21,509

PAYMENT TO CIVIL SERVICE RETIREMENT AND DISABILITY FUND

(Legislative proposal, not subject to PAYGO)

Program and Financing (in millions of dollars)

Identification code 24–0200–2–1–805	1999 actual	2000 est.	2001 est.
Obligations by program activity:			
00.02 Payment of Government share of retirement costs			−1
00.03 Transfers for interest on unfunded liability and payment of military service annuities			2
10.00 Total new obligations			1
Budgetary resources available for obligation:			
22.00 New budget authority (gross)			1
23.95 Total new obligations			−1
New budget authority (gross), detail:			
Mandatory:			
Appropriation (indefinite):			
60.05 Appropriation (indefinite)			−1
60.05 Appropriation (indefinite)			2
62.50 Appropriation (total mandatory)			1
Change in unpaid obligations:			
73.10 Total new obligations			1
73.20 Total outlays (gross)			−1
Outlays (gross), detail:			
86.97 Outlays from new mandatory authority			1
Net budget authority and outlays:			
89.00 Budget authority			1
90.00 Outlays			1

The Administration will propose legislation that would restore Federal employment retirement contributions to pre-1999 levels and provide Government-wide buyout authority.

Object Classification (in millions of dollars)

Identification code 24–0200–2–1–805	1999 actual	2000 est.	2001 est.
12.1 Civilian personnel benefits			−1
13.0 Benefits for former personnel			2
99.9 Total new obligations			1

Intragovernmental funds:

REVOLVING FUND

Program and Financing (in millions of dollars)

Identification code 24–4571–0–4–805	1999 actual	2000 est.	2001 est.
Obligations by program activity:			
09.01 DOD testing	7	8	8
09.02 Employment service	31	34	37
09.03 Investigations	94	131	150
09.04 Workforce relations	43	45	46
09.05 Executive resources	21	25	26
10.00 Total new obligations	196	243	267
Budgetary resources available for obligation:			
21.40 Unobligated balance available, start of year	31	20	20
22.00 New budget authority (gross)	185	243	267
23.90 Total budgetary resources available for obligation	216	263	287
23.95 Total new obligations	−196	−243	−267
24.40 Unobligated balance available, end of year	20	20	20
New budget authority (gross), detail:			
Spending authority from offsetting collections:			
Discretionary:			
68.00 Offsetting collections (cash)	203	243	267
68.10 From Federal sources: Change in receivables and unpaid, unfilled orders	−18		
68.90 Spending authority from offsetting collections (total discretionary)	185	243	267
Change in unpaid obligations:			
Unpaid obligations, start of year:			
72.40 Obligated balance, start of year	29	51	51
72.95 From Federal sources: Receivables and unpaid, unfilled orders	160	142	142
72.99 Total unpaid obligations, start of year	189	193	193
73.10 Total new obligations	196	243	267
73.20 Total outlays (gross)	−192	−243	−267
Unpaid obligations, end of year:			
74.40 Obligated balance, end of year	51	51	51
74.95 From Federal sources: Receivables and unpaid, unfilled orders	142	142	142
74.99 Total unpaid obligations, end of year	193	193	193
Outlays (gross), detail:			
86.90 Outlays from new discretionary authority	185	243	267
86.93 Outlays from discretionary balances	7		

		1999	2000	2001
87.00	Total outlays (gross)	192	243	267
	Offsets:			
	Against gross budget authority and outlays:			
	Offsetting collections (cash) from:			
88.00	Federal sources	−202	−242	−266
88.40	Non-Federal sources	−1	−1	−1
88.90	Total, offsetting collections (cash)	−203	−243	−267
	Against gross budget authority only:			
88.95	From Federal sources: Change in receivables and unpaid, unfilled orders	18		
	Net budget authority and outlays:			
89.00	Budget authority			
90.00	Outlays	−11		

DOD testing.—OPM conducts military entrance exams for the Department of Defense (DOD) as a cost-effective and reliable provider. The Employment Service continued to provide testing for the Department of Defense, conducting approximately 14,789 student test sessions and 22,033 enlistment sessions.

Employment service.—OPM delivers employment information, examining services, automated staffing, and related human resource management services to Federal agencies nationwide. In 1999, 51 Executive Branch, five Legislative Branch, one Judicial Branch, and one-non-appropriated fund, and 9 State and municipal agencies contracted with the Employment Service for a wide array of products and services.

Investigations.—Through a contract with an employee-owned private company, OPM conducts National Agency Check and Inquiry cases and background security investigations for Federal agencies on a reimbursable basis. To the extent that OPM is required to pay a fee to the Federal Bureau of Investigation for name and fingerprint checks, agencies are required to reimburse OPM for such fees through the revolving fund.

Workforce relations.—OPM provides training and management assistance (TMA) to Federal agencies in support of their producing training products, services, humans resource management systems and other human resource development interventions through partnership with Federal agencies and private sector firms specializing in instructional systems.

Program performance.—The TMA program performance measures are designed to determine the value added to Federal agencies through human resource management assistance utilizing an instructional systems design approach. They include workload business well-being indicators such as maintaining a positive retained earnings contribution to OPM's revolving fund; and customer satisfaction measures to better define the benefit to TMA services.

Executive resources.—OPM conducts residential and non-residential programs for Federal executives and managers to improve the effectiveness and efficiency of Federal programs, and manages the President's quality awards program.

WORKLOAD COUNT

	1999 actual	*2000 est.*	*2001 est.*
Participant training days	78,456	80,754	83,260
Background security investigations processed	44,005	56,000	66,000
National and special agency check and inquiry cases	325,652	365,000	380,000

Object Classification (in millions of dollars)

Identification code 24–4571–0–4–805		1999 actual	2000 est.	2001 est.
	Personnel compensation:			
11.1	Full-time permanent	19	22	23
11.3	Other than full-time permanent	6	6	6
11.5	Other personnel compensation	1	2	2
11.9	Total personnel compensation	26	30	31
12.1	Civilian personnel benefits	6	7	8
21.0	Travel and transportation of persons	3	4	4
23.1	Rental payments to GSA	7	7	7
23.3	Communications, utilities, and miscellaneous charges	5	6	6
24.0	Printing and reproduction	1	1	1
25.2	Other services	143	183	204
26.0	Supplies and materials	2	2	2
31.0	Equipment	3	3	4
99.9	Total new obligations	196	243	267

Personnel Summary

Identification code 24–4571–0–4–805		1999 actual	2000 est.	2001 est.
2001	Total compensable workyears: Full-time equivalent employment	620	697	677

Trust Funds

Civil Service Retirement and Disability Fund

Unavailable Collections (in millions of dollars)

Identification code 24–8135–0–7–602		1999 actual	2000 est.	2001 est.
	Balance, start of year:			
01.99	Balance, start of year	446,957	477,477	507,804
	Receipts:			
02.01	Employee contributions	4,213	4,034	4,078
02.02	Agency contributions	9,094	8,879	9,335
02.03	District of Columbia contributions	73	74	68
02.04	Postal Service agency contributions	2,589	2,897	2,980
02.05	Postal Service supplemental contributions	3,412	3,540	3,644
02.06	Federal Financing Bank interest	2,600	1,377	1,372
02.07	Employee deposits, redeposits and other contributions	135	136	138
02.08	Treasury interest	30,979	33,791	34,418
02.09	General fund payment to the Civil Service Retirement and Disability fund	21,401	21,245	21,509
02.10	Re-employed annuitants salary offset	26	27	26
02.15	Employee contributions, legislative proposal not subject to PAYGO			−9
02.16	Agency contributions, legislative proposal not subject to PAYGO			−34
02.18	Treasury interest, legislative proposal not subject to PAYGO			−8
02.19	General fund payment, legislative proposal not subject to PAYGO			1
02.20	Employee contributions, legislative proposal subject to PAYGO			−427
02.99	Total receipts	74,522	76,000	77,091
04.00	Total: Balances and collections	521,479	553,477	584,895
	Appropriation:			
05.01	Civil service retirement and disability fund	−44,002	−45,673	−47,770
05.02	Proposed legislation, subject to PAYGO			2
05.03	Proposed legislation, not subject to PAYGO			−27
05.99	Subtotal appropriation	−44,002	−45,673	−47,795
07.99	Total balance, end of year	477,477	507,804	537,100

Program and Financing (in millions of dollars)

Identification code 24–8135–0–7–602		1999 actual	2000 est.	2001 est.
	Obligations by program activity:			
00.01	Annuities	43,538	45,242	47,326
00.02	Refunds and death claims	354	325	335
00.03	OPM Administration	108	104	107
00.04	Transfer to MSPB	2	2	2
10.00	Total new obligations	44,002	45,673	47,770
	Budgetary resources available for obligation:			
22.00	New budget authority (gross)	44,002	45,673	47,770
23.95	Total new obligations	−44,002	−45,673	−47,770
	New budget authority (gross), detail:			
	Discretionary:			
40.26	Appropriation (trust fund, definite)	78	83	90
	Mandatory:			
60.27	Appropriation (trust fund, indefinite)	74,354	75,666	76,702
60.45	Portion precluded from obligation	−30,430	−30,076	−29,022

CIVIL SERVICE RETIREMENT AND DISABILITY FUND—Continued

Program and Financing (in millions of dollars)—Continued

Identification code 24–8135–0–7–602	1999 actual	2000 est.	2001 est.
62.50 Appropriation (total mandatory)	43,924	45,590	47,680
70.00 Total new budget authority (gross)	44,002	45,673	47,770
Change in unpaid obligations:			
72.40 Unpaid obligations, start of year: Obligated balance, start of year	3,726	3,796	4,014
73.10 Total new obligations	44,002	45,673	47,770
73.20 Total outlays (gross)	–43,932	–45,455	–47,540
74.40 Unpaid obligations, end of year: Obligated balance, end of year	3,796	4,014	4,244
Outlays (gross), detail:			
86.90 Outlays from new discretionary authority	78	83	90
86.97 Outlays from new mandatory authority	40,128	41,576	43,436
86.98 Outlays from mandatory balances	3,726	3,796	4,014
87.00 Total outlays (gross)	43,932	45,455	47,540
Net budget authority and outlays:			
89.00 Budget authority	44,002	45,673	47,770
90.00 Outlays	43,932	45,455	47,540
Memorandum (non-add) entries:			
92.01 Total investments, start of year: U.S. securities: Par value	450,674	481,274	511,814
92.02 Total investments, end of year: U.S. securities: Par value	481,274	511,814	541,340

Summary of Budget Authority and Outlays

(in millions of dollars)

	1999 actual	*2000 est.*	*2001 est.*
Enacted/requested:			
Budget Authority	44,002	45,673	47,770
Outlays	43,932	45,455	47,540
Legislative proposal, not subject to PAYGO:			
Budget Authority			27
Outlays			27
Legislative proposal, subject to PAYGO:			
Budget Authority			–2
Outlays			–2
Total:			
Budget Authority	44,002	45,673	47,795
Outlays	43,932	45,455	47,565

This fund: (1) pays annuities to retired employees or their survivors; (2) makes refunds to separated employees for amounts withheld and to beneficiaries of employees who died before retirement or before annuities equaled the amount withheld; and (3) pays expenses of the Office of Personnel Management and the Merit Systems Protection Board for administering the program. The fund covers two Federal civilian retirement systems: the Civil Service Retirement System (CSRS) and the Federal Employees' Retirement System (FERS).

CSRS is basically a defined benefit plan, covering Federal employees hired prior to 1984. CSRS participants do not participate in the Social Security system. FERS is a three-tiered pension program that uses Social Security as a base, provides an additional basic benefit, and includes a thrift savings plan. FERS covers employees hired after 1983 and formerly CSRS-covered employees who elected to join FERS.

	1999 actual	*2000 est.*	*2001 est.*
Active employees	2,667,800	2,655,900	2,654,800
Annuitants:			
Employees	1,736,964	1,742,200	1,749,700
Survivors	631,153	634,400	638,400
Total, annuitants	2,368,117	2,376,600	2,388,100

Status of Funds (in millions of dollars)

Identification code 24–8135–0–7–602	1999 actual	2000 est.	2001 est.
Unexpended balance, start of year:			
0100 Treasury balance	15	3	8
U.S. Securities:			
0101 Par value	450,674	481,274	511,814
0102 Unrealized discounts	–6	–4	–4
0199 Total balance, start of year	450,683	481,273	511,818
Cash income during the year:			
Governmental receipts:			
0200 Employee contributions, Civil Service Retirement and Disability Fund	4,213	4,034	4,078
0201 Employee contributions, legislative proposal not subject to PAYGO			–9
0202 District of Columbia contributions	73	74	68
0203 Employee deposits, redeposits, and voluntary contributions	135	136	138
0206 Employee contributions, legislative proposal subject to PAYGO			–427
Intragovernmental transactions:			
0240 Agency contributions, Civil Service Retirement and Disability Fund	9,094	8,879	9,335
0241 Agency contributions, legislative proposal not subject to PAYGO			–34
0242 Postal Service agency contributions, Civil Service Retirement and Disability Fund	2,589	2,897	2,980
0243 Postal Service supplemental contributions, Civil Service Retirement and Disability Fund	3,412	3,540	3,644
0244 Federal Financing Bank interest, Civil Service Retirement and Disability Fund	2,600	1,377	1,372
0245 Treasury interest, Civil Service Retirement and Disability Fund	30,979	33,791	34,418
0246 Treasury interest, legislative proposal not subject to PAYGO			–8
0247 General fund payment to the Civil Service Retirement and Disability Fund	21,401	21,245	21,509
0248 General fund payment, legislative proposal not subject to PAYGO			1
0250 Re-employed annuitant salary offset, Civil Service Retirement and Disability Fund	26	27	26
0297 Income under present law	74,522	76,000	77,568
0298 Income under proposed legislation			–477
0299 Total cash income	74,522	76,000	77,091
Cash outgo during year:			
0501 Payment of claims to retired employees	–36,507	–37,671	–39,211
0502 Payment of alternative annuity refunds	–6	–4	–4
0505 Payment of claims to survivor annuitants	–6,975	–7,346	–7,881
0506 Lump sum payments to estates or beneficiaries of deceased annuitants and employees	–127	–136	–161
0507 Refunds to living separated employees	–207	–189	–174
0508 Administration	–110	–109	–109
0509 Proposed legislation, not subject to PAYGO			–27
0510 Proposed legislation, subject to PAYGO			2
0597 Outgo under present law (–)	–43,932	–45,455	–47,540
0598 Outgo under proposed legislation (–)			–25
0599 Total cash outgo (–)	–43,932	–45,455	–47,565
Unexpended balance, end of year:			
0700 Uninvested balance	3	8	8
U.S. Securities:			
0701 Par value	481,274	511,814	541,340
0702 Unrealized discounts	–4	–4	–4
0799 Total balance, end of year	481,273	511,818	541,344

Object Classification (in millions of dollars)

Identification code 24–8135–0–7–602	1999 actual	2000 est.	2001 est.
25.2 Other services	110	106	109
42.0 Insurance claims and indemnities	43,538	45,242	47,326
44.0 Refunds and death claims	354	325	335
99.9 Total new obligations	44,002	45,673	47,770

CIVIL SERVICE RETIREMENT AND DISABILITY FUND
(Legislative proposal, not subject to PAYGO)

Program and Financing (in millions of dollars)

Identification code 24–8135–2–7–602	1999 actual	2000 est.	2001 est.
Obligations by program activity:			
00.01 Annuities			27
10.00 Total new obligations (object class 42.0)			27
Budgetary resources available for obligation:			
22.00 New budget authority (gross)			27
23.95 Total new obligations			–27
New budget authority (gross), detail:			
Mandatory:			
60.27 Appropriation (trust fund, indefinite)			–50
60.45 Portion precluded from obligation			77
62.50 Appropriation (total mandatory)			27
Change in unpaid obligations:			
73.10 Total new obligations			27
73.20 Total outlays (gross)			–27
Outlays (gross), detail:			
86.97 Outlays from new mandatory authority			27
Net budget authority and outlays:			
89.00 Budget authority			27
90.00 Outlays			27

The Administration will propose legislation that would restore Federal employee retirement contributions to pre-1999 levels, provide Government-wide buyout authority, correct retirement coverage errors, and make various human resources management improvements.

CIVIL SERVICE RETIREMENT AND DISABILITY FUND
(Legislative proposal, subject to PAYGO)

Program and Financing (in millions of dollars)

Identification code 24–8135–4–7–602	1999 actual	2000 est.	2001 est.
Obligations by program activity:			
00.01 Annuities			–2
10.00 Total new obligations (object class 42.0)			–2
Budgetary resources available for obligation:			
22.00 New budget authority (gross)			–2
23.95 Total new obligations			2
New budget authority (gross), detail:			
Mandatory:			
60.27 Appropriation (trust fund, indefinite)			–427
60.45 Portion precluded from obligation			425
62.50 Appropriation (total mandatory)			–2
Change in unpaid obligations:			
73.10 Total new obligations			–2
73.20 Total outlays (gross)			2
Outlays (gross), detail:			
86.97 Outlays from new mandatory authority			–2
Net budget authority and outlays:			
89.00 Budget authority			–2
90.00 Outlays			–2

The Administration will propose legislation that would restore Federal employee retirement contributions to pre-1999 levels, correct retirement coverage errors, eliminate certain retirement inequities, and make various human resources management improvements.

EMPLOYEES LIFE INSURANCE FUND

Program and Financing (in millions of dollars)

Identification code 24–8424–0–8–602	1999 actual	2000 est.	2001 est.
Obligations by program activity:			
09.01 Regular program premiums	1,113	1,075	1,170
09.02 Optional program premiums	717	713	849
09.03 Beneficial program premiums	2	2	2
09.04 Administration	2	2	2
10.00 Total new obligations (object class 25.2)	1,834	1,792	2,023
Budgetary resources available for obligation:			
21.40 Unobligated balance available, start of year	19,682	20,446	21,843
22.00 New budget authority (gross)	2,598	3,189	3,282
23.90 Total budgetary resources available for obligation	22,280	23,635	25,125
23.95 Total new obligations	–1,834	–1,792	–2,023
24.40 Unobligated balance available, end of year	20,446	21,843	23,102
New budget authority (gross), detail:			
Discretionary:			
68.00 Spending authority from offsetting collections: Offsetting collections (cash)	2	2	2
Mandatory:			
69.00 Offsetting collections (cash)	2,943	3,149	3,286
69.10 From Federal sources: Change in receivables and unpaid, unfilled orders	–347	39	–6
69.90 Spending authority from offsetting collections (total mandatory)	2,596	3,188	3,280
70.00 Total new budget authority (gross)	2,598	3,190	3,282
Change in unpaid obligations:			
Unpaid obligations, start of year:			
72.40 Obligated balance, start of year	–580	40	41
72.95 From Federal sources: Receivables and unpaid, unfilled orders	715	368	407
72.99 Total unpaid obligations, start of year	135	408	448
73.10 Total new obligations	1,834	1,792	2,023
73.20 Total outlays (gross)	–1,560	–1,752	–1,966
Unpaid obligations, end of year:			
74.40 Obligated balance, end of year	40	41	104
74.95 From Federal sources: Receivables and unpaid, unfilled orders	368	407	401
74.99 Total unpaid obligations, end of year	408	448	505
Outlays (gross), detail:			
86.90 Outlays from new discretionary authority	2	2	2
86.97 Outlays from new mandatory authority	1,559	1,750	1,964
87.00 Total outlays (gross)	1,560	1,752	1,966
Offsets:			
Against gross budget authority and outlays:			
Offsetting collections (cash) from:			
88.00 Agency contributions	–394	–408	–436
88.20 Interest on U.S. securities	–1,311	–1,371	–1,334
Non-Federal sources:			
88.40 Regular program	–581	–612	–658
88.40 Optional program	–659	–760	–860
88.90 Total, offsetting collections (cash)	–2,945	–3,151	–3,288
Against gross budget authority only:			
88.95 From Federal sources: Change in receivables and unpaid, unfilled orders	347	–39	6
Net budget authority and outlays:			
89.00 Budget authority			
90.00 Outlays	–1,384	–1,399	–1,322
Memorandum (non-add) entries:			
92.01 Total investments, start of year: U.S. securities: Par value	19,377	20,755	21,734
92.02 Total investments, end of year: U.S. securities: Par value	20,755	21,734	23,055

This fund finances payments to private insurance companies for Federal employees' group life insurance and expenses of the Office of Personnel Management in administering the program.

Employees Life Insurance Fund—Continued

Budget program.—The status of the basic (regular and optional) life insurance program on September 30 is as follows:

Life insurance in force (in billions of dollars):	1999 actual	2000 est.	2001 est.
On active employees	452	462	472
On retired employees	48	50	52
Total	500	512	524
Number of participants (in thousands):			
Active employees	2,360	2,470	2,456
Annuitants	1,593	1,597	1,601
Total	3,853	4,067	4,057

Financing.—Non-Postal Service employees and all retirees under 65 pay two-thirds of the premium costs for Basic coverage; agencies pay the remaining third. Optional and certain post-retirement Basic coverages are paid entirely by enrollees. The status of the reserves at the end of the year is as follows:

Status of Reserves	1999 actual	2000 est.	2001 est.
Held in reserve (in millions of dollars):			
Contingency reserve	65	65	65
Beneficial association program reserve	1	1	1
U.S. Treasury reserve	20,755	21,734	23,055
Total reserves	20,821	21,800	23,121

Employees and Retired Employees Health Benefits Funds

Program and Financing (in millions of dollars)

Identification code 24–9981–0–8–551		1999 actual	2000 est.	2001 est.
	Obligations by program activity:			
09.01	Benefit payments	18,451	19,892	21,205
09.02	Payments from OPM contingency reserve	180	220	230
09.03	Government payment for annuitants (1960 Act)	3	3	2
09.04	Administration	20	23	23
10.00	Total new obligations (object class 25.6)	18,654	20,138	21,460
	Budgetary resources available for obligation:			
21.40	Unobligated balance available, start of year	4,548	4,142	3,875
22.00	New budget authority (gross)	18,247	19,871	21,339
23.90	Total budgetary resources available for obligation	22,795	24,013	25,214
23.95	Total new obligations	−18,654	−20,138	−21,460
24.40	Unobligated balance available, end of year	4,142	3,875	3,753
	New budget authority (gross), detail:			
	Discretionary:			
68.00	Spending authority from offsetting collections: Offsetting collections (cash)	20	23	23
	Mandatory:			
69.00	Offsetting collections (cash)	18,019	19,761	21,242
69.10	From Federal sources: Change in receivables and unpaid, unfilled orders	208	87	74
69.90	Spending authority from offsetting collections (total mandatory)	18,227	19,848	21,316
70.00	Total new budget authority (gross)	18,247	19,871	21,339
	Change in unpaid obligations:			
	Unpaid obligations, start of year:			
72.40	Obligated balance, start of year	1,688	1,671	1,716
72.95	From Federal sources: Receivables and unpaid, unfilled orders	688	896	983
72.99	Total unpaid obligations, start of year	2,376	2,567	2,699
73.10	Total new obligations	18,654	20,138	21,460
73.20	Total outlays (gross)	−18,463	−20,005	−21,411
	Unpaid obligations, end of year:			
74.40	Obligated balance, end of year	1,671	1,716	1,692
74.95	From Federal sources: Receivables and unpaid, unfilled orders	896	983	1,057
74.99	Total unpaid obligations, end of year	2,567	2,699	2,749
	Outlays (gross), detail:			
86.90	Outlays from new discretionary authority	20	23	23
86.97	Outlays from new mandatory authority	17,755	19,087	20,405
86.98	Outlays from mandatory balances	688	896	983
87.00	Total outlays (gross)	18,463	20,005	21,411
	Offsets:			
	Against gross budget authority and outlays:			
	Offsetting collections (cash) from:			
	Federal sources:			
88.00	Agency contributions	−7,662	−8,509	−9,035
88.00	Government contributions for annuitants	−5,097	−5,683	−6,178
88.20	Interest on U.S. securities	−360	−285	−295
	Non-Federal sources:			
88.40	Employee salary withholdings	−2,573	−2,797	−2,990
88.40	Annuity withholdings	−2,280	−2,452	−2,710
88.40	Contributions from D.C. Government	−67	−58	−57
88.90	Total, offsetting collections (cash)	−18,039	−19,784	−21,265
	Against gross budget authority only:			
88.95	From Federal sources: Change in receivables and unpaid, unfilled orders	−208	−87	−74
	Net budget authority and outlays:			
89.00	Budget authority			
90.00	Outlays	424	221	146
	Memorandum (non-add) entries:			
92.01	Total investments, start of year: U.S. securities: Par value	6,265	5,835	5,609
92.02	Total investments, end of year: U.S. securities: Par value	5,835	5,609	5,463

Summary of Budget Authority and Outlays

(in millions of dollars)

Enacted/requested:	1999 actual	2000 est.	2001 est.
Budget Authority			
Outlays	424	222	146
Legislative proposal, not subject to PAYGO:			
Budget Authority			
Outlays			194
Legislative proposal, subject to PAYGO:			
Budget Authority			
Outlays			−194
Total:			
Budget Authority			
Outlays	424	222	146

Status of Funds (in millions of dollars)

Identification code 24–9981–0–8–551		1999 actual	2000 est.	2001 est.
	Unexpended balance, start of year:			
0100	Treasury balance	6	1	5
	U.S. Securities:			
0101	Par value	6,265	5,835	5,609
0102	Unrealized discounts	−34	−23	−23
0199	Total balance, start of year	6,236	5,813	5,591
	Cash income during the year:			
	Offsetting collections:			
0280	Contributions from Employing Agencies	4,864	5,316	5,689
0281	Contributions from Postal Service for Active Employees	2,798	3,194	3,346
0282	Contributions from Postal Service for Annuitants	649	704	771
0283	Government Payment for Annuitant Health Benefits	4,448	4,979	5,407
0284	Interest Earned	360	285	295
0285	Contributions from DC Government	67	58	57
0286	Contributions from Active Employees	2,573	2,797	2,990
0287	Contributions from Annuitants	2,280	2,452	2,710
0288	Offsetting collections			−78
0289	Offsetting collections, legislative proposal not subject to PAYGO			−194
0297	Income under present law	18,039	19,785	21,265
0298	Income under proposed legislation			−272
0299	Total cash income	18,039	19,784	20,993
	Cash outgo during year:			
0501	Benefit Payments (−)	−18,264	−19,763	−21,158
0502	Payments to Carriers from OPM Contingency Reserves (−)	−180	−220	−230
0503	Administration (−)	−20	−23	−23
0504	Cash outgo during the year (−)			272

		1999 actual	2000 est.	2001 est.
0597	Outgo under present law (−)	−18,464	−20,006	−21,411
0598	Outgo under proposed legislation (−)			272
0599	Total cash outgo (−)	−18,463	−20,005	−21,139
	Unexpended balance, end of year:			
0700	Uninvested balance	1	5	5
	U.S. Securities:			
0701	Par value	5,835	5,609	5,463
0702	Unrealized discounts	−23	−23	−23
0799	Total balance, end of year	5,813	5,591	5,445

This display combines the Federal Employees Health Benefits (FEHB) fund and the Retired Employees Health Benefit (REHB) fund.

The FEHB fund provides for the cost of health benefits for: (1) active employees; (2) employees who retired after June 1960, or their survivors; (3) those annuitants transferred from the REHB program as authorized by Public Law 93–246; and (4) the related expenses of the Office of Personnel Management (OPM) in administering the program.

The REHB fund, created by the Retired Employees Health Benefits Act of 1960, provides for: (1) the cost of health benefits for retired employees and survivors who enroll in a Government-sponsored uniform health benefits plan; (2) the contribution to retired employees and survivors who retain or purchase private health insurance; and (3) expenses of OPM in administering the program.

Budget program.—The balance of the FEHB fund is available for payments without fiscal year limitation. Numbers of participants at the end of each fiscal year are as follows:

	1999 actual	2000 est.	2001 est.
Active employees	2,272	2,262	2,262
Annuitants	1,851	1,859	1,869
Total	4,123	4,121	4,131

In determining a biweekly subscription rate to cover program costs, one percent is added for administrative expenses and three percent is added for a contingency reserve held by OPM for each carrier. OPM is authorized to transfer unused administrative reserve funds to the contingency reserve.

The REHB fund is available without fiscal year limitation. The amounts contributed by the Government are paid into the fund from annual appropriations. The number of participants at the end of each fiscal year are as follows:

	1999 actual	2000 est.	2001 est.
Uniform plan	1,300	1,100	900
Private plans	4,200	3,500	2,900
Total	5,500	4,600	3,800

Financing.—The funds are financed by: (1) withholdings from active employees and annuitants; (2) agency contributions for active employees; (3) Government contributions for annuitants appropriated to OPM; and (4) contributions made by the United States Postal Service in accordance with the provisions of Public Law 101–508 and Public Law 103–66.

Operating results.—Funds made available to carriers but not used to pay claims in the current period are carried forward as special reserves for use in subsequent periods.

OPM maintains a contingency reserve, funded by employee and Government contributions, that may be used to defray future cost increases or provide increased benefits. OPM makes payments to carriers from this reserve whenever carrier-held reserves fall below levels prescribed by OPM regulations or when carriers can demonstrate good cause such as unexpected claims experience or variations from expected community rates.

Employees and Retired Employees Health Benefits Funds

(Legislative proposal, not subject to PAYGO)

Program and Financing (in millions of dollars)

Identification code 24–9981–2–8–551		1999 actual	2000 est.	2001 est.
	Obligations by program activity:			
09.01	Benefit payments			−194
10.00	Total new obligations (object class 25.6)			−194
	Budgetary resources available for obligation:			
22.00	New budget authority (gross)			−194
23.95	Total new obligations			194
	New budget authority (gross), detail:			
	Mandatory:			
69.00	Offsetting collections (cash)			−194
	Change in unpaid obligations:			
73.10	Total new obligations			−194
74.95	Unpaid obligations, end of year: From Federal sources: Receivables and unpaid, unfilled orders			−194
	Offsets:			
	Against gross budget authority and outlays:			
	Offsetting collections (cash) from:			
	Federal sources:			
88.00	Agency contributions			121
88.00	Government contributions for annuitants			73
88.90	Total, offsetting collections (cash)			194
	Net budget authority and outlays:			
89.00	Budget authority			
90.00	Outlays			

The Administration will propose legislation that will help control the future rate of growth of FEHB premiums by leveraging the purchasing power of the Federal Government. If enacted, this initiative will enable OPM to develop a comprehensive dental insurance benefit that would be available to Federal employees, annuitants, and their families. This schedule also reflects an Administration proposal to authorize OPM to effect FEHBP enrollments necessary to comply with State court orders.

Employees and Retired Employees Health Benefits Funds

(Legislative proposal, subject to PAYGO)

Program and Financing (in millions of dollars)

Identification code 24–9981–4–8–551		1999 actual	2000 est.	2001 est.
	Obligations by program activity:			
09.01	Benefit payments			−78
10.00	Total new obligations (object class 25.6)			−78
	Budgetary resources available for obligation:			
22.00	New budget authority (gross)			−78
23.95	Total new obligations			78
	New budget authority (gross), detail:			
	Mandatory:			
69.00	Offsetting collections (cash)			−78
	Change in unpaid obligations:			
72.95	Unpaid obligations, start of year: From Federal sources: Receivables and unpaid, unfilled orders			
73.10	Total new obligations			−78
73.20	Total outlays (gross)			272
74.95	Unpaid obligations, end of year: From Federal sources: Receivables and unpaid, unfilled orders			194
	Outlays (gross), detail:			
86.97	Outlays from new mandatory authority			−272

Employees and Retired Employees Health Benefits Funds—Continued

Program and Financing (in millions of dollars)—Continued

Identification code 24–9981–4–8–551		1999 actual	2000 est.	2001 est.
	Offsets:			
	Against gross budget authority and outlays:			
	Offsetting collections (cash) from:			
	Non-Federal sources:			
88.40	Employee salary withholdings			40
88.40	Annuity withholdings			37
88.40	Contributions from D.C. Government			1
88.90	Total, offsetting collections (cash)			78
	Net budget authority and outlays:			
89.00	Budget authority			
90.00	Outlays			–194

The Administration will propose legislation that will help control the future rate of growth of FEHB premiums by leveraging the purchasing power of the Federal Government. If enacted, this initiative will enable OPM to develop a comprehensive dental insurance benefit that would be available to Federal employees, annuitants, and their families. This schedule also reflects an Administration proposal to authorize OPM to effect FEHBP enrollments necessary to comply with State court orders.

SMALL BUSINESS ADMINISTRATION

The budget requests $1,062 million in new budget authority for the Small Business Administration (SBA). This funding request represents a very strategic investment of the Federal budget dollar. Therefore, we characterized the theme of our 2001 budget as "Managing for Results." The Administration's spending plans for 2000 and 2001 have been developed in conjunction with the Government Performance and Results Act (GPRA) and provide better service and more assistance to small businesses as we enter the 21st century.

SBA has identified two broad goals: helping small businesses succeed and modernization. The first goal reflects an emphasis on increasing assistance and access to individuals and firms in new market areas and involves providing a wide range of services and programs including capital, credit, technical assistance, training, education, and procurement assistance. The second goal emphasizes improvements in the delivery of services to customers by upgrading the systems that support programs, by investing in training to enhance skill levels of employees, and by improving the overall operation of the Agency.

This budget includes a comprehensive new markets agenda to better serve small businesses in these areas including: an expanded new markets venture capital program of $150 million in debentures with $30 million in related technical assistance; $15 million for PRIME technical assistance; an expanded microloan loan program of $60 million with $45 million in related technical assistance; $6.6 million for an expanded BusinessLINC mentor-protege program; and $3 million to establish reservation-based Native American Small Business Development Centers.

Federal Funds

General and special funds:

SALARIES AND EXPENSES

For necessary expenses, not otherwise provided for, of the Small Business Administration as authorized by Public Law 105–135, including hire of passenger motor vehicles as authorized by 31 U.S.C. 1343 and 1344, and not to exceed $3,500 for official reception and representation expenses, [$282,300,000] *$163,000,000*: *Provided*, That the Administrator is authorized to charge fees to cover the cost of publications developed by the Small Business Administration, and certain loan servicing activities: *Provided further*, That, notwithstanding 31 U.S.C. 3302, revenues received from all such activities shall be credited to this account, to be available for carrying out these purposes without further appropriations[: *Provided further*, That $84,500,000 shall be available to fund grants for performance in fiscal year 2000 or fiscal year 2001 as authorized by section 21 of the Small Business Act, as amended.]

[In addition, for the costs of programs related to the New Markets Venture Capitol program, $10,500,000, of which $1,500,000 shall be for BusinessLINC, and of which $9,000,000 shall be for technical assistance: *Provided*, That the funds appropriated under this paragraph shall not be available for obligation until the New Markets Venture Capitol program is authorized by subsequent legislation.] *In addition, to reimburse the Small Business Administration for qualified expenses of delinquent non-tax debt collection, to be derived from increased agency collections of delinquent debt, 5 percent of such collections but not to exceed $3,000,000. (Departments of Commerce, Justice, and State, the Judiciary, and Related Agencies Appropriations Act, 2000, as enacted by section 1000(a)(1) of the Consolidated Appropriations Act, 2000 (P.L. 106–113).)*

Program and Financing (in millions of dollars)

Identification code 73–0100–0–1–376		1999 actual	2000 est.	2001 est.
	Obligations by program activity:			
00.01	Government contracting and minority enterprise development	26	30	20
00.02	Disaster assistance	116	118	124
00.04	Management and administration	74	71	96
00.05	Executive direction	11	12	10
00.06	General counsel	7	7	7
00.07	Congressional and legislative affairs	1	1	1
00.08	Hearings and appeals	1	1	1
00.09	Communications and publications	3	3	3
00.11	Advocacy	5	6	5
00.12	Field operations	2	2	1
00.13	Equal employment opportunity and civil rights compliance	2	2	2
00.14	Regional and district offices	134	137	142
00.15	Chief financial officer	11	11	7
00.16	Capital Access	43	59	28
00.17	Entrepreneurial development	137	134	6
00.18	Small disadvantaged businesses	8	12	....
10.00	Total new obligations	581	606	453
	Budgetary resources available for obligation:			
21.40	Unobligated balance available, start of year	17	3	....
22.00	New budget authority (gross)	568	601	453
22.10	Resources available from recoveries of prior year obligations	3	2	....
22.21	Unobligated balance transferred to other accounts	....	....	....
22.22	Unobligated balance transferred from other accounts	....	....	....
23.90	Total budgetary resources available for obligation	588	606	453
23.95	Total new obligations	–581	–606	–453
23.98	Unobligated balance expiring or withdrawn	–4	....	....
24.40	Unobligated balance available, end of year	3	....	....
	New budget authority (gross), detail:			
	Discretionary:			
40.00	Appropriation	288	323	163
40.76	Reduction pursuant to P.L. 106–113	....	–3	....
42.00	Transferred from other accounts	5	....	....
43.00	Appropriation (total discretionary)	293	320	163
68.00	Spending authority from offsetting collections: Offsetting collections (cash)	275	281	290
70.00	Total new budget authority (gross)	568	601	453
	Change in unpaid obligations:			
72.40	Unpaid obligations, start of year: Obligated balance, start of year	182	217	224
73.10	Total new obligations	581	606	453
73.20	Total outlays (gross)	–538	–585	–521
73.40	Adjustments in expired accounts (net)	–5	–12	....
73.45	Adjustments in unexpired accounts	–3	–2	....
74.40	Unpaid obligations, end of year: Obligated balance, end of year	217	224	156
	Outlays (gross), detail:			
86.90	Outlays from new discretionary authority	436	457	380
86.93	Outlays from discretionary balances	102	128	141
87.00	Total outlays (gross)	538	585	521
	Offsets:			
	Against gross budget authority and outlays:			
	Offsetting collections (cash) from:			
	Federal sources:			
88.00	Payments from business loan program account	–114	–129	–133
88.00	Payments from disaster loan program account	–147	–136	–154
88.00	Federal sources	–11	–13	....
88.40	Non-Federal sources	–3	–3	–3

General and special funds—Continued

SALARIES AND EXPENSES—Continued

Program and Financing (in millions of dollars)—Continued

Identification code 73–0100–0–1–376		1999 actual	2000 est.	2001 est.
88.90	Total, offsetting collections (cash)	–275	–281	–290
	Net budget authority and outlays:			
89.00	Budget authority	293	320	163
90.00	Outlays	263	304	231

The Administration proposes to separate the Salaries and Expenses account into the following two accounts: (1) Salaries and Expenses—includes compensation and benefits, technological investments, supplies, contracts, and the general administrative costs of operating SBA's various programs, etc; (2) Non-Credit Business Assistance Programs—includes a variety of programs in Entrepreneurial Development, Government Contracting and Minority and Enterprise Development, and Capital Access, as well as the offices of Advocacy and the National Ombudsman. The following components of the Salaries and Expenses Account are detailed below.

Executive Direction.—Executive Direction includes the Office of the Administrator, Equal Employment Opportunity and Civil Rights Compliance (EEO&CRC), Congressional and Legislative Affairs (CLA), Hearings and Appeals (HA), General Counsel, Field Operations, Communications and Public Liaison (CPL), and the Office of the Chief Financial Officer (CFO). The Office of the Administrator provides general management to the SBA organization. The Office of EEO & CRC ensures SBA and its programs comply with all applicable equal opportunity laws and regulations. The Office of CLA provides agency wide support and coordination for all congressional activities. The Office of HA decides size, Small Disadvantaged Business, FOIA and other administrative appeals and processes SBREFA complaints for the Agency. The Office of the General Counsel provides agency wide legal support and advice. The Office of Field Operations oversees and provides management and operational support to SBA's regional and district offices. SBA's field offices are an important delivery mechanism of SBA services to small businesses. The Office of CPL coordinates SBA's marketing, public outreach, and public information programs. The Office of the CFO administers SBA's budget and financial management activities, including financial systems, subsidy rates, financial reporting, and internal control activities. SBA also has a Policy unit that directs and coordinates the Agency's planning and oversight of management processes under the Government Performance and Results Act (GPRA).

Management and Administration.—The Associate Deputy Administrator for Management and Administration (ADA) directs the Office of the Chief Information Officer (OCIO), Office of Administration (OA), and Office of Human Resources (OHR). The OCIO has lead responsibility for SBA's systems modernization initiatives and its Y2K resolution. The Office of Administration administers SBA's space management, printing, and procurement and grants management programs. The Office of Human Resources administers SBA's workforce planning and management efforts, including workforce training programs.

Program Performance

Management and Administration:

Workforce Transition.—In order to effectively transition SBA's workforce to the new roles and responsibilities facing the Agency today and into the 21st Century, we request $4 million (included in the operating expenses) to support increased training and to transition our staff to a more customer-focused and community-based structure.

SBA Modernization.—The funding request of $13 million (included in the operating expenses) provides the next annual installment of $8 million toward this multi-year systems effort, plus $5 million toward the disaster loan systems project. This systems modernization project will result in more modern and efficient delivery of SBA's programs and services and increases efficiencies. The upgrading and/or replacement of our financial management systems for loan programs and budgeting transactions will have a positive impact on our internal risk management, planning, control processes, financial reporting and compliance with law in areas such as systems security, standard general ledger, etc. Also, we anticipate that the deployment of a paperless disaster home loan application process may result in as much as $20–$25 million annually in reduced administrative expenses, making this extra systems investment very cost effective. We have in place a five-year plan to modernize all of our major systems and processes. Significant progress was made on Phase I (Loan Monitoring and Oversight) in 1998 and 1999. We anticipate hardware acquisition and software development in 2000 and 2001, leading to full modernization implementation in 2002–2003.

Other Information Technology Investments.—The budget includes $7.0 million (in the operating expenses) to contract for on-going computer upgrades, maintenance, and acquisition of the latest operating system. SBA's technology infrastructure is two generations behind current standards and may not be supported in the near future. This investment will improve our extensive interaction with the public and external resource partners and will support our systems modernization efforts, which require increased computer capability.

Administrative Operating Expenses.—For 2001, the funding request for general and administrative operating expenses is $328.5 million ($163 from the Salaries and Expenses account, $132.5 million from the Business Loans program account, and $30 million from the Disaster Loan Program account, and $3 million in fees). This funding level maintains the current workforce. The increased funds in 2001 will allow us to maintain a current services level of operations, provide an employee pay raise in January of 2001, and cover anticipated inflationary increases in areas such as telephones and rents.

Performance Goals

Program and Policy Goals under the GPRA.—Small business success remains a primary policy of this Administration. The SBA's mission is to maintain and strengthen the nation's economy by aiding, counseling, assisting, and protecting the interests of small businesses and by helping families and businesses recover from disasters. The following three program and policy goals form the basis of the programs for which we are requesting funding: (1) help small businesses succeed, particularly in new market segments, through fair and equitable access to capital, government contracts, business development, and policy representation and advocacy support; (2) modernize the SBA through a trained and motivated workforce, expanded use of electronic tools, upgraded information systems, and improved lender oversight; and (3) help families and businesses recover from natural disasters through access to needed capital and credit.

SBA's Strategic Plan.—SBA's five-year strategic plan developed in 1998 includes the specific goals and strategies to be employed in 1998–2003 to accomplish this mission. This plan is updated annually based on current actual performance against measurable goals, the impact of actual appropriations, and their impact on Agency goals and objectives for future years. Monthly reviews are completed to determine actual performance against goals; recommendations are made on the review process for any unfavorable variances.

Object Classification (in millions of dollars)

Identification code 73–0100–0–1–376	1999 actual	2000 est.	2001 est.
Personnel compensation:			
11.1 Full-time permanent	167	169	169
11.3 Other than full-time permanent	10	11	10
11.5 Other personnel compensation	5	5	5
11.9 Total personnel compensation	182	185	184
12.1 Civilian personnel benefits	42	42	43
21.0 Travel and transportation of persons	6	5	5
23.1 Rental payments to GSA	28	29	29
23.3 Communications, utilities, and miscellaneous charges	9	10	10
24.0 Printing and reproduction	1		
25.2 Other services	46	45	56
26.0 Supplies and materials		1	1
31.0 Equipment	2	1	1
41.0 Grants, subsidies, and contributions	143	160	
Undistributed:			
92.0 Undistributed (disaster loan making)	86	87	90
92.0 Undistributed (disaster loan servicing)	28	29	34
92.0 Undistributed (SDB)	8	12	
99.9 Total new obligations	581	606	453

Personnel Summary

Identification code 73–0100–0–1–376	1999 actual	2000 est.	2001 est.
1001 Total compensable workyears: Full-time equivalent employment	4,567	4,509	4,288

Note.—The personnel summary includes regular (non-disaster) full-time equivalents (FTEs) of 2,979, 3,242, and 3,279 in 1998, 1999, and 2000 respectively.

NON-CREDIT BUSINESS ASSISTANCE PROGRAMS

For non-credit programs authorized under the Small Business Act, as amended, $256,050,000, of which $89,500,000 shall be for grants for performance in fiscal year 2001 or fiscal year 2002: Provided, That (1) $85,000,000 shall be for grants for the purposes authorized by section 21 of such Act, (2) $3,000,000 to establish a reservation-based Native American Small Business Development Center network, including subcenters, to serve Native Americans on a national basis subject to section 21 of such Act but without the necessity for matching funds, and (3) $1,500,000 to support the Tribal Business Information Centers: Provided further, That any balances of FY2000 funds appropriated for these non-credit programs under the heading, "Salaries and Expenses", may be transferred to this heading, to be available to carry out these programs and to be available for the time period originally provided.

Program and Financing (in millions of dollars)

Identification code 73–1155–0–1–376	1999 actual	2000 est.	2001 est.
Obligations by program activity:			
00.01 Non-Credit Business Assistance Programs (Gross)			256
09.02 Reimbursable program			9
10.00 Total new obligations			265
Budgetary resources available for obligation:			
22.00 New budget authority (gross)			265
23.95 Total new obligations			−265
24.40 Unobligated balance available, end of year			
New budget authority (gross), detail:			
Discretionary:			
40.00 Appropriation			256
68.00 Spending authority from offsetting collections: Offsetting collections (cash)			9
70.00 Total new budget authority (gross)			265
Change in unpaid obligations:			
73.10 Total new obligations			265
73.20 Total outlays (gross)			−150
74.40 Unpaid obligations, end of year: Obligated balance, end of year			115
Outlays (gross), detail:			
86.90 Outlays from new discretionary authority			150
Offsets:			
Against gross budget authority and outlays:			
88.00 Offsetting collections (cash) from: Federal sources			−9
Net budget authority and outlays:			
89.00 Budget authority			256
90.00 Outlays			141

This appropriation funds the non-credit business assistance programs administered by SBA, including Small Business Development Centers (SBDCs), Women's Business Centers, HUBZone Empowerment Contracting, Electronic Commerce, New Markets Technical Assistance, and PRIME. The administrative funding for most of these programs is provided in the Salaries and Expenses account. The following program areas are responsible for the direction of the non-credit business assistance programs:

Entrepreneurial Development.—The Associate Deputy Administrator (ADA) for this function directs the following SBA programs: Women's Business Ownership; Small Business Development Centers; Veteran's Affairs; Office of Native American Affairs; and Business Initiatives, which includes the Service Corps of Retired Executives. These programs provide outreach and technical assistance to small business communities, especially women, Veterans, and minorities. Through special initiatives such as the One Stop Capital Shops, Distance Learning, Welfare to Work and Entrepreneurship for Adults with Disabilities, SBA will increase its access to entrepreneurs, particularly in "new markets."

Government Contracting and Minority Enterprise Development.—The Associate Deputy Administrator for this function directs the following SBA programs: Government Contracting; Section 8(a) Business Development; Technology; HUBZone Empowerment Contracting; and Size Standards. These offices are responsible for effectively advocating for small businesses in the area of government contracting and Federal research and development. Government contracting activities are aimed at ensuring that small businesses receive a fair share of Federal procurement awards. The Section 8(a) Business Development program provides assistance to socially and economically disadvantaged small business concerns, primarily in the areas of business development and Federal procurement. Through this office, SBA assists firms that are owned by disadvantaged persons to help them develop into viable competitive businesses in a reasonable period of time. This office also administers the government-wide Small Disadvantaged Business (SDB) program, certifying firms as SDB to facilitate their active participation in Federal procurement. The HUBZone Empowerment Contracting program promotes economic development, community empowerment, and job growth in underutilized urban and rural communities.

Capital Access.—The Associate Deputy Administrator (ADA) for this function directs the following SBA programs: Financial Assistance; Surety Bond Guarantees; Investment; and International Trade. These offices are responsible for the administration of all SBA credit and international trade and lending programs. The capital and credit programs administered through these offices and delivered in SBA's field offices provide small businesses access to the financing needs they have to start and grow their businesses, especially those businesses and individuals located in new market areas. SBA offers many lending programs, such as 7(a) and SBIC, and tools, such as LowDoc and SBA Express to enhance small business access to these programs.

General and special funds—Continued

NON-CREDIT BUSINESS ASSISTANCE PROGRAMS—Continued

Program Performance

Entrepreneurial Development:

Small Business Development Centers (SBDCs).—The SBDCs provide long term counseling to small businesses at about 1,000 locations in 50 states and Puerto Rico, Guam, and the District of Columbia. In 1999, more than 595,000 customers were served, of which 42 percent were women and 23 percent were minorities. For 2001, the budget process proposes federal funding of $85 million.

Native American Small Business Development Centers (NASBDs).—The budget proposes $3 million to establish a reservation-based Native American Small Business Development Center network to serve Native American entrepreneurs.

Women's Business Centers.—Through this program, the SBA awards grants to nonprofit organizations to deliver entrepreneurial training programs to women business owners or those interested in starting businesses. In 1999, 59 funded and 22 graduated women's business centers were operating in 47 states, the District of Columbia, Puerto Rico, and the Virgin Islands. Each offers financial, management, marketing and technical assistance to current and potential women business owners. In 2000, with the $9 million appropriation we will fund approximately 12 recompeted centers, approximately 6–8 new centers, and the continuation of funding for 45 centers. With the 2001 funding request of $12 million, we will expand coverage in all 50 states. We propose that in 2001, there will be 46 centers with current funding cycles, 12 centers with ongoing second funding cycles, 13 additional recompeted centers, and approximately 15 new centers. In addition, we will continue two initiatives begun in 1996: OWBOZone, an intranet that links all of the Women's Business Centers; and the Online Women's Business Center on the Internet, which allows women nationwide to have access to the same services offered by the centers.

One Stop Capital Shops (OSCS).—OSCSs are located in Empowerment Zones and Enterprise Communities. This program's objective is to stimulate and sustain economic revitalization in distressed areas. An OSCS is a partnership between SBA and a local community designed to offer small business assistance under one roof from an easy to access, retail location. Each is unique, is located in a distressed area, and targets new urban and rural markets. For 2001, we propose funding of $10.0 million for the OSCS program to support the existing network of One-Stop locations and to open new OSCS centers in the new Empowerment Zones.

Native American Outreach Through Tribal Business Information Centers (TBICs).—With $1.5 million SBA will provide reservation and non-reservation-based entrepreneurs access to state-of-the-art computer hardware and software, one-on-one business counseling services, and business development workshops. The facilitators of these centers have received extensive technical training in SBA's lending, business development and entrepreneurial development programs. In 1999, these centers served approximately 3,926 clients, provided 4,757 hours of business counseling, held approximately 200 workshops, assisted in the completion of approximately 192 business plans and 123 loan packages, and were instrumental in the startup of approximately 171 new businesses.

Veteran's Outreach.—The budget proposes $4 million in 2001 to implement the Veteran's Entrepreneurship and Small Business Development Act of 1999. With this funding, SBA will be able to assist the authorized corporation in its operation and provide enhanced training and technical assistance to America's veterans.

Service Corps of Retired Executives (SCORE).—For 2001, the budget proposes a funding level of $5.0 million for this program. The additional funding will provide upgrades to the SCORE computer network. Using one-on-one counseling and workshops, SCORE reaches approximately 383,000 business owners annually using approximately 12,500 counselors through 389 chapters located across the country. Counseling costs to the Government are less than $3 per hour.

Business Information Centers (BIC).—These centers offer self-help hardware, software and reference materials, and on-site counseling provided by SCORE volunteers. Individuals who are in business or are interested in starting a business will find many resources specifically targeted at helping businesses grow or find new market niches. For 2001, the budget includes $700 thousand to support these locations.

Government Contracting and Minority Enterprise Development:

Section 8(a) Business Development.—SBA administers a number of programs and initiatives to support the business development and contracting goals of socially and economically disadvantaged businesses. These include the Section 8(a) program and the Section 7(j) technical assistance programs. The Section 8(a) program certifies firms for participation in sole-source federal contracts and access to targeted business development, executive development, and technical assistance through the Section 7(j) program. For 2001, the budget proposes $5 million in Section 7(j) technical assistance funding to support the expanding executive development and business assistance needs of these entrepreneurs.

Small Disadvantaged Business (SDB) Certification and Eligibility.—Since 1998, SBA was designated as the lead agency in the certification of SDB firms. This certification process enables firms to receive federal contract preferences. Funding for this program is provided through reimbursements from the 20 largest Federal procuring agencies. The program's funding level for 2001 is proposed to be $9 million.

HUBZones.—The budget proposes $5 million for this program. Legislation passed in 1998 created a national program to support economic development and job growth in "historically underutilized zones". SBA certifies small firms in HUBZone areas that hire residents of such areas as eligible for federal contract preferences.

Pro-Net.—The budget proposes $750 thousand for 2001 for this program. The Procurement Marketing Network (PRO-Net) program helps ensure that small businesses can be competitive in a changing procurement environment. By providing an interface with other electronic procurement applications such as the Electronic Posting System and the Commerce Business Daily, the more than 188,000 small businesses that are currently registered will be aware of procurement opportunities.

Electronic Commerce.—With the $5 million proposed in the budget, SBA will work with the Departments of Commerce and Agriculture to implement an education, training, and outreach program to ensure small businesses remain competitive by participating in electronic commerce.

BusinessLINC.—With the $6.6 million proposed in the budget, SBA will assist in the support of BusinessLINC, an initiative to link large businesses with small businesses in order to expand their access to markets, enhance management development, obtain technical assistance and leverage core strategies; promote best practices; and help grow small businesses in distressed urban, Native American, and isolated communities.

Small Business Innovation and Research (SBIR) Program Awards.—The budget proposes $14 million to implement a three-year new matching grant pilot program to support Phase III commercialization of the technology developed under SBIR grants. Federal contributions would match contributions from non-Federal sources in a 1:2 ratio, to an average award of $250,000. SBA would award approximately 56 grants each year. In addition, $1 million is proposed to develop multi-agency SBIR solicitation topics, solicite white papers and hold workshops for small businesses

Capital Access:

U.S. Export Assistance Centers.—The 2001 budget includes a request for $3.5 million to continue these services. As nearly 97 percent of U.S. export firms are small businesses, they account for 31 percent of the total U.S. export sales. The SBA is a partner with the Department of Commerce and the Export-Import Bank in the U.S. Export Assistance Center (USEAC) Program. Through a network of 19 USEACs located across the nation, SBA delivers financial and technical assistance and business development counseling to small businesses that sell their products globally.

Microloan Technical Assistance.—The 2001 budget requests $45 million for this program, which is needed to support the current portfolio of microloans and the anticipated lending to be done in 2000 and 2001. The Microloan Program technical assistance component helps small businesses gain access to private sector financing and assists SBA's Microloan program through grants to microloan intermediaries for on-going management advice and counseling to microborrowers. The program also supports the Administration's initiative to help individuals receiving welfare assistance move to work by providing opportunities to start up small businesses. Currently, there are 128 intermediaries and 19 non-lending technical assistance intermediaries versus a statutory limit of 200. We are proposing changes in the legislation that will provide flexibility in lending and technical assistance, which will result in greater access to capital. We anticipate that the Microloan program will play a major role in the new markets initiative.

PRIME.—The budget proposes funding this program at the authorized level of $15 million. The PRIME program provides grants to non-profit organizations for: 1) training and technical assistance for low/very low-income entrepreneurs, 2) training and capacity building services to the non-profit providers, and 3) research and development in best practices for low income entrepreneurs.

New Markets Venture Capital Technical Assistance.—In support of the President's New Markets initiative, SBA is proposing legislation that authorizes $150 million in venture capital ($150 million in face value and approximately $100 million in cash value) for small businesses in distressed rural and urban Areas. These are the areas that are underserved by traditional financial institutions. SBA proposes to provide business development, managerial and technical assistance support through New Market Venture Capital companies. The 2001 budget includes $30 million to provide the necessary level of technical assistance supporting the $150 million program level.

Other Programs and Initiatives.—In addition to the above, SBA proposes to fund the Women's Council for 2001 at $1 million and the Survey of Women Owned Businesses as part of the Census for $1 million. This account also includes $1.5 million for the Office of Advocacy and $500,000 for the Office of the National Ombudsman. The Office of Advocacy is the principal voice for small business within the government. The Office of the National Ombudsman facilitates the examination of ideas, interests, and concerns of small business to create a fair regulatory environment.

Object Classification (in millions of dollars)

Identification code 73–1155–0–1–376		1999 actual	2000 est.	2001 est.
	Direct obligations:			
11.1	Personnel compensation: Full-time permanent			12
12.1	Civilian personnel benefits			4
92.0	Undistributed			240
99.0	Subtotal, direct obligations			256
99.0	Reimbursable obligations			9
99.9	Total new obligations			265

Personnel Summary

Identification code 73–1155–0–1–376		1999 actual	2000 est.	2001 est.
1001	Total compensable workyears: Full-time equivalent employment			190

OFFICE OF INSPECTOR GENERAL

For necessary expenses of the Office of Inspector General in carrying out the provisions of the Inspector General Act of 1978, as amended (5 U.S.C. App.), [$11,000,000] *$14,315,000. (Departments of Commerce, Justice, and State, the Judiciary, and Related Agencies Appropriations Act, 2000, as enacted by section 1000(a)(1) of the Consolidated Appropriations Act, 2000 (P.L. 106–113).)*

Program and Financing (in millions of dollars)

Identification code 73–0200–0–1–376		1999 actual	2000 est.	2001 est.
	Obligations by program activity:			
00.01	General Office	1	1	2
00.02	Audit	4	4	5
00.03	Investigations	5	5	6
00.04	Management / Legal Counsel / Inspection and Evaluation	1	1	1
10.00	Total new obligations	11	11	14
	Budgetary resources available for obligation:			
21.40	Unobligated balance available, start of year		1	
22.00	New budget authority (gross)	11	11	14
23.90	Total budgetary resources available for obligation	11	12	14
23.95	Total new obligations	–11	–11	–14
23.98	Unobligated balance expiring or withdrawn	–1		
24.40	Unobligated balance available, end of year	1		
	New budget authority (gross), detail:			
	Discretionary:			
40.00	Appropriation	11	11	14
68.00	Spending authority from offsetting collections: Offsetting collections (cash)			
70.00	Total new budget authority (gross)	11	11	14
	Change in unpaid obligations:			
72.40	Unpaid obligations, start of year: Obligated balance, start of year	1		1
73.10	Total new obligations	11	11	14
73.20	Total outlays (gross)	–11	–11	–14
74.40	Unpaid obligations, end of year: Obligated balance, end of year		1	
	Outlays (gross), detail:			
86.90	Outlays from new discretionary authority	10	10	13
86.93	Outlays from discretionary balances	1		1
87.00	Total outlays (gross)	11	11	14
	Offsets:			
	Against gross budget authority and outlays:			
88.00	Offsetting collections (cash) from: Federal sources			
	Net budget authority and outlays:			
89.00	Budget authority	11	11	14
90.00	Outlays	10	11	14

The budget proposes $14.3 million for the Office of the Inspector General for 2001. The increased funding will enable the OIG to support an expanded monitoring role of the Agency's Government Performance and Results Act in reviewing the Agency's programs, performance measures, and regulations to conserve resources and increase program efficiency and effectiveness.

General and special funds—Continued

Office of Inspector General—Continued

This appropriation provides funds for agency-wide audit, investigative, and inspection/evaluation functions to promote economy and efficiency in agency operations and to prevent and detect fraud, waste, and abuse. The audit function provides internal and external audits and other oversight activities. Internal audits assess the general management and efficiency of SBA program operations. External audits review program participants and their compliance with SBA regulations and procedural requirements. Inspections/evaluations address specific issues related to program management and effectiveness. The investigative function detects and investigates allegations of illegal and improper activities involving agency personnel and program participants.

Object Classification (in millions of dollars)

Identification code 73–0200–0–1–376	1999 actual	2000 est.	2001 est.
11.1 Personnel compensation: Full-time permanent	9	9	11
12.1 Civilian personnel benefits	2	2	3
99.9 Total new obligations	11	11	14

Personnel Summary

Identification code 73–0200–0–1–376	1999 actual	2000 est.	2001 est.
1001 Total compensable workyears: Full-time equivalent employment	109	117	142

Public enterprise funds:

Surety Bond Guarantees Revolving Fund

Program and Financing (in millions of dollars)

Identification code 73–4156–0–3–376	1999 actual	2000 est.	2001 est.
Obligations by program activity:			
09.01 Reimbursable obligations	8	5	5
10.00 Total new obligations	8	5	5
Budgetary resources available for obligation:			
21.40 Unobligated balance available, start of year	4	4	3
22.00 New budget authority (gross)	7	4	4
23.90 Total budgetary resources available for obligation	11	8	7
23.95 Total new obligations	−8	−5	−5
24.40 Unobligated balance available, end of year	4	3	3
New budget authority (gross), detail:			
Discretionary:			
40.00 Appropriation	3		
68.00 Spending authority from offsetting collections: Offsetting collections (cash)	4	4	4
70.00 Total new budget authority (gross)	7	4	4
Change in unpaid obligations:			
72.40 Unpaid obligations, start of year: Obligated balance, start of year	38	37	37
73.10 Total new obligations	8	5	5
73.20 Total outlays (gross)	−8	−5	−5
74.40 Unpaid obligations, end of year: Obligated balance, end of year	37	37	37
Outlays (gross), detail:			
86.90 Outlays from new discretionary authority	7	4	4
86.93 Outlays from discretionary balances	1	1	
87.00 Total outlays (gross)	8	5	5
Offsets:			
Against gross budget authority and outlays:			
88.40 Offsetting collections (cash) from: Non-Federal sources	−4	−4	−4
Net budget authority and outlays:			
89.00 Budget authority	3		
90.00 Outlays	5	1	1

The SBA is authorized to issue bond guarantees to surety companies for construction, service, and supply contracts that do not exceed $1,250,000 and to reimburse these sureties up to 90 percent of the losses sustained if the contractor defaults. Under the Preferred Surety Bond (PSP) Program, participating sureties are authorized to issue, monitor, and service bonds without SBA's prior approval. Guarantees for this program are limited to 70 percent. Currently, there are 15 participating sureties in the program. SBA's guarantees provide the incentive necessary for sureties to issue bonds to small contractors who could not otherwise compete in the contracting industry.

In 2001, the budget proposes a $1.7 billion program level that is anticipated to be sufficient to accommodate demand from prior-approval and preferred sureties. This program does not require a subsidy appropriation.

Statement of Operations (in millions of dollars)

Identification code 73–4156–0–3–376	1998 actual	1999 actual	2000 est.	2001 est.
0101 Revenue	12	9	7	7
0102 Expense	−10	−7	−6	−6
0105 Net income or loss (−)	2	2	1	1

Balance Sheet (in millions of dollars)

Identification code 73–4156–0–3–376	1998 actual	1999 actual	2000 est.	2001 est.
ASSETS:				
1101 Federal assets: Fund balances with Treasury	42	41	39	42
1206 Non-Federal assets: Receivables, net				
1999 Total assets	42	41	39	42
LIABILITIES:				
2201 Non-Federal liabilities: Accounts payable	38	37	35	36
2999 Total liabilities	38	37	35	36
NET POSITION:				
3100 Appropriated capital	329	332	333	332
3300 Cumulative results of operations	−325	−326	−328	−326
3999 Total net position	4	6	5	6
4999 Total liabilities and net position	42	43	40	42

Credit accounts:

Business Loans Program Account

For the cost of *direct loans, $5,370,000, to be available until expended; and for the cost of* guaranteed loans, [$137,800,000] *$194,360,000*, as authorized by 15 U.S.C. 631 note or subsequently authorized for the New Markets Venture Capital program, of which $45,000,000 shall remain available until September 30, [2001] *2002*: *Provided*, [That of the total provided, $6,000,000 shall be available only for the cost of guaranteed loans under the New Markets Venture Capitol program and shall become available for obligation only upon authorization of such program by the enactment of subsequent legislation in fiscal year 2000: *Provided further*,] That such costs, including the cost of modifying such loans, shall be as defined in section 502 of the Congressional Budget Act of 1974, as amended: *Provided further*, That during fiscal year [2000] *2001*, commitments to guarantee loans under section 503 of the Small Business Investment Act of 1958, as amended, shall not exceed [the amount of financings authorized under section 20(e)(1)(B)(ii) of the Small Business Act, as amended: *Provided further*, That during fiscal year 2000, commitments for general business loans authorized under section 7(a) of the Small Business Act, as amended, shall not exceed $10,000,000,000 without prior notification of the Committees on Appropriations of the House of Representatives and Senate in accordance with section 605 of this Act] *$3,750,000,000*: *Provided further*, That during fiscal year [2000] *2001*, commitments to guarantee loans under section

303(b) of the Small Business Investment Act of 1958, as amended, shall not exceed [the amount of guarantees of debentures authorized under section 20(e)(1)(C)(ii) of the Small Business Act, as amended] *$500,000,000*.

In addition, for administrative expenses to carry out the direct and guaranteed loan programs, [$129,000,000] *$132,525,000*, which may be transferred to and merged with the appropriations for Salaries and Expenses. *(Departments of Commerce, Justice, and State, the Judiciary, and Related Agencies Appropriations Act, 2000, as enacted by section 1000(a)(1) of the Consolidated Appropriations Act, 2000 (P.L. 106–113).)*

(RESCISSION)

[Of the unobligated balances available under this heading, $13,100,000 are rescinded.] *(Departments of Commerce, Justice, and State, the Judiciary, and Related Agencies Appropriations Act, 2000, as enacted by section 1000(a)(1) of the Consolidated Appropriations Act, 2000 (P.L. 106–113).)*

General Fund Credit Receipt Accounts (in millions of dollars)

Identification code 73–1154–0–1–376	1999 actual	2000 est.	2001 est.
0101 Business loan program, downward reestimates of subsidies	695	301	

Program and Financing (in millions of dollars)

Identification code 73–1154–0–1–376	1999 actual	2000 est.	2001 est.
Obligations by program activity:			
00.01 Direct loan subsidy	2	3	5
00.02 Guaranteed loan subsidy	216	146	194
00.07 Reestimate of loan guarantee subsidy	28	3	
00.08 Interest on reestimates of loan guarantee subsidy	7	2	
00.09 Administrative expenses	114	129	133
10.00 Total new obligations	367	283	332
Budgetary resources available for obligation:			
21.40 Unobligated balance available, start of year	104	76	53
22.00 New budget authority (gross)	311	259	332
22.10 Resources available from recoveries of prior year obligations	36		
22.22 Transferred from other accounts	7		
23.90 Total budgetary resources available for obligation	458	335	385
23.95 Total new obligations	−367	−283	−332
23.98 Unobligated balance expiring or withdrawn	−15		
24.40 Unobligated balance available, end of year	76	53	53
New budget authority (gross), detail:			
Discretionary:			
40.00 Appropriation	224	267	332
40.36 Unobligated balance rescinded		−13	
42.00 Transferred from other accounts	1		
43.00 Appropriation (total discretionary)	225	254	332
Mandatory:			
60.05 Appropriation (indefinite)	35	5	
Discretionary:			
68.00 Spending authority from offsetting collections: Offsetting collections (cash)	51		
70.00 Total new budget authority (gross)	311	259	332
Change in unpaid obligations:			
72.40 Unpaid obligations, start of year: Obligated balance, start of year	136	109	110
73.10 Total new obligations	367	283	332
73.20 Total outlays (gross)	−358	−282	−314
73.45 Adjustments in unexpired accounts	−36		
74.40 Unpaid obligations, end of year: Obligated balance, end of year	109	110	128
Outlays (gross), detail:			
86.90 Outlays from new discretionary authority	192	160	209
86.93 Outlays from discretionary balances	131	117	105
86.97 Outlays from new mandatory authority	35	5	
87.00 Total outlays (gross)	358	282	314
Offsets:			
Against gross budget authority and outlays:			
88.00 Offsetting collections (cash) from: Federal sources	−51		
Net budget authority and outlays:			
89.00 Budget authority	260	259	332
90.00 Outlays	307	282	314

Summary of Loan Levels, Subsidy Budget Authority and Outlays by Program (in millions of dollars)

Identification code 73–1154–0–1–376	1999 actual	2000 est.	2001 est.
Direct loan levels supportable by subsidy budget authority:			
1150 Micro loans	23		60
1159 Total direct loan levels	23		60
Direct loan subsidy (in percent):			
1320 Micro loans	9.54	8.54	8.95
1329 Weighted average subsidy rate	9.54	8.54	8.95
Direct loan subsidy budget authority:			
1330 Micro loans	2		5
1339 Total subsidy budget authority	2		5
Direct loan subsidy outlays:			
1340 Micro loans	1	2	3
1349 Total subsidy outlays	1	2	3
Guaranteed loan levels supportable by subsidy budget authority:			
2150 Microloan guarantees	1	16	
2150 General business—7(a)	9,471	9,827	11,500
2150 General business—7(a) DELTA	37	50	50
2150 Section 504	1,979	3,500	3,750
2150 Section 504 DELTA	3	5	5
2150 SBIC debentures	352	800	500
2150 SBIC participating securities	1,015	1,350	2,000
2150 New Market Venture Capital		40	150
2150 Y2K	4		
2159 Total loan guarantee levels	12,862	15,588	17,955
Guaranteed loan subsidy (in percent):			
2320 Microloan guarantees	7.97	8.32	8.37
2320 General business—7(a)	1.39	1.16	1.24
2320 General business—7(a) DELTA	2.08	1.83	1.92
2320 Section 504	0.00	0.00	0.00
2320 Section 504 DELTA	1.29	1.13	0.89
2320 SBIC debentures	1.38	0.00	0.78
2320 SBIC participating securities	2.19	1.80	1.31
2320 New Market Venture Capital	0.00	15.00	14.44
2320 Y2K	4.04	4.07	4.04
2329 Weighted average subsidy rate	1.11	1.20	1.08
Guaranteed loan subsidy budget authority:			
2330 Microloan guarantees			
2330 General business—7(a)	159	108	143
2330 General business—7(a) DELTA			
2330 Section 504	34	5	
2330 Section 504 DELTA			
2330 SBIC Debentures	6		4
2330 SBIC participating securities	22	24	26
2330 New Market Venture Capital		6	21
2330 Y2K	1		
2339 Total subsidy budget authority	222	143	194
Guaranteed loan subsidy outlays:			
2340 Micorloan guarantees	1	1	
2340 General business—7(a)	136	113	130
2340 General business—7(a) DELTA	1	2	2
2340 Section 504	26	5	
2340 Section 504 DELTA			
2340 SBIC debentures	5		4
2340 SBIC participating securities	22	24	24
2340 New Market Venture Capital		5	18
2340 Y2K	1	1	
2349 Total subsidy outlays	192	151	178
Administrative expense data:			
3510 Budget authority	94	129	133
3580 Outlays from balances			
3590 Outlays from new authority	114	129	133

Credit accounts—Continued

BUSINESS LOANS PROGRAM ACCOUNT—Continued

(RESCISSION)—Continued

As required by the Federal Credit Reform Act of 1990, as amended, this account records, for this program, the subsidy costs associated with the direct loans obligated and loan guarantees committed in 1992 and beyond (including modifications of direct loans or loan guarantees that resulted from obligations or commitments in any year), as well as administrative expenses of this program. The subsidy amounts are estimated on a present value basis; the administrative expenses are estimated on a cash basis. For 2001, the allocation of funding for administrative expenses has been adjusted based on a completed cost allocation study undertaken to allow SBA to more accurately reflect the portion of SBA's Salaries and Expenses operating budget that supports these programs.

Section 7(a) Program.—The Section 7(a) program is SBA's largest credit assistance program to serve the financial needs of small businesses. Under this program, SBA developed the SBA LowDoc and SBA Express programs aimed at increasing small business access to credit, especially in "new markets". SBA has experienced record levels of demand for these loans with approvals increasing $1 billion from 1998 to 1999. A similar increase is expected in 2000. Therefore, we request a program level of $11.5 billion in 2001 to continue to meet the needs of small businesses to start and grow their businesses. In addition, to encourage more small loans and to reduce the cost of loans to small businesses, we propose a simplification of the current fee and guaranty structure.

Small Business Investment Companies (SBIC).—This program provides the debt and equity capital needed by small businesses to start and grow. The Small Business Investment Act, as amended, authorizes the SBA to guarantee the timely payment of all principal and interest, as scheduled, on debentures issued by such companies. In addition, the SBA may guarantee the performance of participating securities issued by these companies. A program level of $2.0 billion in participating securities and $500 million in debentures is requested.

New Markets Venture Capital.—During 2000, SBA will begin to administer the newly created "New Markets Venture Capital Program": This program would require investment groups to have a minimum of $5 million of investment capital and $1.5 million of technical assistance funding available over 5 years to participate in the program. For 2001, a total of $150 million of leverage in face value (approximately $100 million in cash) will be available to fund New Market Venture Capital organizations. There would also be a significant technical assistance component, which would be in the form of a grant equal to 30 percent of the amount of investment capital disbursed over 5 years also on a matching basis.

Low and Moderate Income (LMI) Initiative.—Using SBA's SBIC debenture program, SBA will encourage SBIC investments in businesses located in inner cities and rural areas, or who draw at least 35 percent of their employees from those areas by refining program regulations for participating SBICs. The LMI initiative differs from New Market Venture Capital (NMVC) initiative in the investment criteria and the size of the loan. Loans made under LMI meet the same criteria as SBIC investments, but are made to smaller enterprises. Also, NMVC loans are smaller than LMI.

Microloans.—For 2001, SBA proposes to expand the Microloan direct program to $60 million from $30 million in 2000. In addition, we are proposing legislative changes that will provide flexibility in the lending and technical assistance, which will result in greater access to capital. The Microloan program will be a key component of Agency's pursuit of its new markets initiative. At present, small business capital needs of less than $25,000 are met through SBA's microloan direct and guarantee programs. We propose to raise that limit to $35,000 in 2001. SBA loans money to financial intermediaries which in turn make loans to these businesses to start and grow. A key component of this program is SBA's provision of technical assistance grants to microlending intermediaries, enabling firms to obtain the necessary managerial and business development assistance in order to be successful.

Program Performance

Program performance and policy goals.—SBA has the following program performance and policy objectives to support its first GPRA goal of increasing small business opportunities to succeed: (1) emphasizing lending to "new markets" small businesses; (2) offering specialized financing, such as venture capital, export financing, and bonding opportunities; (3) improving methods of providing credit assistance through an expanded range of lending partners, electronic transmission of data, and high volume lending technologies; (4) reducing costs by maintaining a high quality portfolio through innovative oversight procedures and an improved liquidation process; and, (5) effectively implementing a loan asset sales program.

Performance Indicators.—Appropriate finance program effectiveness assessment involves the consideration of a number of indicators. First, effectiveness can be assessed by loan-making activity levels, the number and dollar amount of loans guaranteed by SBA. Second, effectiveness can be measured by the health of the loan portfolio, its currency and default figures, and the agency's ultimate record on loan recovery. Beyond these very tangible indicators of success are the more difficult-to-measure indicators. These include such things as the economic benefits that accrue to the small business, its employees, and the community in which it is located.

During the past three years SBA has focused on quantitative, measureable lending goals with particular emphasis on underserved segments of the small business market in each of SBA's districts, e.g., minorities, women, and small exporters. The SBA began this process in 1994 when it established internal performance agreements that contained two-year lending goals. Using goal monitoring, the agency is able to track, on a regular basis, the status of each district office's progress in meeting these goals.

The number and dollar volume of loans made under the Section 7(a) loan program has increased dramatically in recent years. In 1992, SBA made or guaranteed approximately 24,000 loans totaling about $5.9 billion. In 1999, the SBA approved over 43,000 loans totaling $10.1 billion. For 2001, we are requesting $142.6 million in budget authority to support a program level of $11.5 billion. The section 504 program has also shown impressive growth. In 1992, the SBA provided about 2,000 financings totaling nearly $560 million. By 1999, those figures had increased to 4,700 financing for $1.8 billion.

Section 7(a).—The performance of the 7(a) loan program continues to improve. However, the Treasury discount rate increased this year causing a slight increase in the loan subsidy rate to 1.24 percent.

Section 504.—The performance of this program continues to improve. As a result, the fee to borrowers will again be reduced in 2001 from the 2000 level of .60 percent to .472 percent.

Loan asset sales.—SBA conducted its first asset sale during August, 1999, which was highly successful bringing $95 million in additional revenues to the government above what would have been realized if SBA was to hold the loans and service them. The sale included direct and purchased 7(a) and 504 loans. It was especially important to SBA to establish a foothold in the financial market from which to conduct future asset sales of the remaining $9 billion loan portfolio. Future sales will include disaster home and business loans. Two sales are planned for 2000. SBA is requesting authorization to take advantage of "gainsharing" provisions extended to federal agencies. These sales also greatly impact SBA in its workforce transition efforts. The Business Loan program's administrative expenses includes $1.525 million to cover the cost of the program financial advisor for the asset sales program.

Microloan Program.—The performance of the microloan program continues to improve. However, the Treasury discount rate increased this year, causing a slight increase in the loan subsidy rate to 8.95 percent.

Small Business Investment Companies (SBICs).—For the participating securities program, the subsidy rate will be lowered to 1.31 percent from 1.8 percent in 2000. For the debentures program, the subsidy rate will be 0.78 percent due to technical adjustments.

As the engine for continued economic growth, small business success remains a primary policy concern of the Clinton Administration. Small firms represent a significant portion of the Nation's productive capacity, produce constant innovations, offer opportunities for the under-served, and create jobs. Although it is difficult to attribute a causal relationship between SBA assistance and economic growth, factors that may contribute to continued economic growth include: increased numbers and growth of small businesses, increased jobs, increased revenues, and taxes paid.

SBA measures job creation and increased sales from Census/SBA longitudinal databases, client or trade association reporting, contracted surveys/evaluations, and derivative statistics. Using an updated Census/SBA database on firms, SBA will be able to measure more effectively job creation and growth by firm size. For instance, between 1990 and 1995, this database indicated that 76.5 percent of new jobs came from small firms with less than 500 employees, and about 49 percent came from firms with less than 20 employees. Startups provided about a third of the new jobs.

For the 503/504 program, the calculation for jobs created/retained every year is based on the dollar amount of debentures sold and job data. A ratio of one job per $12,855 debenture sold has been calculated. For the SBIC program, surveys conducted by the National Venture Capital Association and the Investment Advisory Council estimate that each $32,500 invested results in one job. For the microloan program, a database maintained on jobs created/maintained by microloan recipients reflects that the overall performance since the inception of the program is 1.6 jobs created or retained per average $10,000 loan.

Object Classification (in millions of dollars)

Identification code 73–1154–0–1–376		1999 actual	2000 est.	2001 est.
25.2	Other services	114	129	133
41.0	Grants, subsidies, and contributions	253	154	199
99.9	Total new obligations	367	283	332

Business Direct Loan Financing Account

Program and Financing (in millions of dollars)

Identification code 73–4148–0–3–376		1999 actual	2000 est.	2001 est.
	Obligations by program activity:			
00.01	Direct loans	15	30	60
00.02	Interest on Treasury borrowing	26	24	14
	Other expenses:			
00.03	Other expenses	30		
00.91	Direct Program by Activities—Subtotal (1 level)	71	54	74
08.01	Negative subsidy from loan asset sales			1
08.02	Payment of downward reestimate to receipt account	2		
08.06	Payment to liquidating account to purchase loan assets(73–4154)		15	
08.91	Direct Program by Activities—Subtotal (1 level)	2	15	1
10.00	Total new obligations	73	69	75
	Budgetary resources available for obligation:			
21.40	Unobligated balance available, start of year	271	311	
22.00	New financing authority (gross)	127	93	116
22.10	Resources available from recoveries of prior year obligations	1		
22.40	Capital transfer to general fund		−297	−5
22.60	Portion applied to repay debt	−15	−36	−36
23.90	Total budgetary resources available for obligation	384	71	75
23.95	Total new obligations	−73	−69	−75
24.40	Unobligated balance available, end of year	311		
	New financing authority (gross), detail:			
	Mandatory:			
67.15	Authority to borrow (indefinite)	37		54
	Spending authority from offsetting collections:			
	Discretionary:			
68.00	Offsetting collections (cash)	73	79	61
68.10	Change in receivables from program account	17	14	1
68.90	Spending authority from offsetting collections (total discretionary)	90	93	62
70.00	Total new financing authority (gross)	127	93	116
	Change in unpaid obligations:			
	Unpaid obligations, start of year:			
72.40	Obligated balance, start of year	38	26	28
72.95	Receivables from program account	2	19	33
72.99	Total unpaid obligations, start of year	40	45	61
73.10	Total new obligations	73	69	75
73.20	Total financing disbursements (gross)	−68	−55	−75
73.45	Adjustments in unexpired accounts	−1		
	Unpaid obligations, end of year:			
74.40	Obligated balance, end of year	26	28	27
74.95	Receivables from program account	19	33	34
74.99	Total unpaid obligations, end of year	45	61	61
87.00	Total financing disbursements (gross)	68	55	75
	Offsets:			
	Against gross financing authority and financing disbursements:			
	Offsetting collections (cash) from:			
88.00	Federal sources: Payments from program account	−1	−2	−3
	Non-Federal sources:			
88.40	Repayments of principal, net	−15	−10	−19
88.40	Interest received on loans	−18	−16	−22
88.40	Gross proceeds from loan asset sales	−34	−51	
88.40	Other income	−5		−17
88.90	Total, offsetting collections (cash)	−73	−79	−61
	Against gross budget authority only:			
88.95	Change in receivables from program accounts	−17	−14	−1
	Net financing authority and financing disbursements:			
89.00	Financing authority	37		54
90.00	Financing disbursements	−5	−24	14

Status of Direct Loans (in millions of dollars)

Identification code 73–4148–0–3–376		1999 actual	2000 est.	2001 est.
	Position with respect to appropriations act limitation on obligations:			
1111	Limitation on direct loans			
1131	Direct loan obligations exempt from limitation	15	30	60
1150	Total direct loan obligations	15	30	60
	Cumulative balance of direct loans outstanding:			
1210	Outstanding, start of year	99	93	109
1231	Disbursements: Direct loan disbursements	15	30	60
1251	Repayments: Repayments and prepayments	−16	−8	−8
1263	Write-offs for default: Direct loans	−5	−6	−7
1290	Outstanding, end of year	93	109	154

As required by the Federal Credit Reform Act of 1990, as amended, this non-budgetary account records all cash flows

Credit accounts—Continued

BUSINESS DIRECT LOAN FINANCING ACCOUNT—Continued

to and from the Government resulting from direct loans obligated in 1992 and beyond (including modifications of direct loans that resulted from obligations in any year). The amounts in this account are a means of financing and are not included in the budget totals.

Balance Sheet (in millions of dollars)

Identification code 73–4148–0–3–376	1998 actual	1999 actual	2000 est.	2001 est.
ASSETS:				
Investments in US securities:				
1106 Federal assets: Receivables, net	328	355	362	367
Net value of assets related to post-1991 direct loans receivable:				
1401 Direct loans receivable, gross	99	83	81	84
1405 Allowance for subsidy cost (–)	–6	–46	–56	–56
1499 Net present value of assets related to direct loans	93	37	25	27
1504 Net value of assets related to post-1991 acquired defaulted guaranteed loans receivable: Foreclosed property		9		
1999 Total assets	421	401	387	395
LIABILITIES:				
Federal liabilities:				
2101 Accounts payable		24	26	28
2104 Resources payable to Treasury	421	377	361	367
2999 Total liabilities	421	401	387	395
NET POSITION:				
3100 Appropriated capital				
3999 Total net position				
4999 Total liabilities and net position	421	401	387	395

BUSINESS GUARANTEED LOAN FINANCING ACCOUNT

Program and Financing (in millions of dollars)

Identification code 73–4149–0–3–376	1999 actual	2000 est.	2001 est.
Obligations by program activity:			
00.01 Default claims	501	511	532
00.05 Other Expenses	37	13	40
00.91 Direct Program by Activities—Subtotal (1 level)	538	524	572
08.02 Payment of downward reestimate to receipt account	310	239	
08.04 Payment of interest on downward reestimate to receipt account	515	47	
08.06 Payment to liqudating account to purchase loan assets(73–4154)		220	150
08.91 Direct Program by Activities—Subtotal (1 level)	825	506	150
10.00 Total new obligations	1,363	1,030	722
Budgetary resources available for obligation:			
21.40 Unobligated balance available, start of year	1,367	815	663
22.00 New financing authority (gross)	811	878	645
23.90 Total budgetary resources available for obligation	2,178	1,693	1,308
23.95 Total new obligations	–1,363	–1,030	–722
24.40 Unobligated balance available, end of year	815	663	586
New financing authority (gross), detail:			
Discretionary:			
68.00 Spending authority from offsetting collections (gross): Offsetting collections (cash)	811	878	645
Change in unpaid obligations:			
72.40 Unpaid obligations, start of year: Obligated balance, start of year	–157	7	437
73.10 Total new obligations	1,363	1,030	722
73.20 Total financing disbursements (gross)	–1,198	–600	–575
74.40 Unpaid obligations, end of year: Obligated balance, end of year	7	437	584
87.00 Total financing disbursements (gross)	1,198	600	575
Offsets:			
Against gross financing authority and financing disbursements:			
Offsetting collections (cash) from:			
Federal sources:			
88.00 Payments from program account	–192	–151	–179
88.00 Upward restimate	–28	–3	
88.00 Interest on reestimate	–7	–2	
88.25 Interest on uninvested funds	–22	–65	–45
Non-Federal sources:			
88.40 Fees	–105	–154	–92
88.40 Proceeds from loan asset sales	–34	–439	–300
88.40 other	–423	–64	–29
88.90 Total, offsetting collections (cash)	–811	–878	–645
Net financing authority and financing disbursements:			
89.00 Financing authority			
90.00 Financing disbursements	387	–278	–70

Status of Guaranteed Loans (in millions of dollars)

Identification code 73–4149–0–3–376	1999 actual	2000 est.	2001 est.
Position with respect to appropriations act limitation on commitments:			
2111 Limitation on guaranteed loans made by private lenders	13,500	16,500	18,213
2112 Uncommitted loan guarantee limitation	–2,050	–247	
2131 Guaranteed loan commitments exempt from limitation	1,202	1,507	1,571
2150 Total guaranteed loan commitments	12,652	17,760	19,784
Cumulative balance of guaranteed loans outstanding:			
2210 Outstanding, start of year	33,695	36,767	40,917
2231 Disbursements of new guaranteed loans	10,785	7,534	7,738
2251 Repayments and prepayments	–7,036	–2,741	–2,821
Adjustments:			
2261 Terminations for default that result in loans receivable	–630	–643	–656
2264 Other adjustments, net	–47		
2290 Outstanding, end of year	36,767	40,917	45,178
Memorandum:			
2299 Guaranteed amount of guaranteed loans outstanding, end of year	29,266	33,058	36,495
Addendum:			
Cumulative balance of defaulted guaranteed loans that result in loans receivable:			
2310 Outstanding, start of year	834	753	738
2331 Disbursements for guaranteed loan claims	630	643	656
2351 Repayments of loans receivable	–137	–82	–50
2361 Write-offs of loans receivable	–285	–164	–65
2364 Other adjustments, net	–289	–412	–300
2390 Outstanding, end of year	753	738	979

As required by the Federal Credit Reform Act of 1990, as amended, this non-budgetary account records all cash flows to and from the Government resulting from loan guarantees committed in 1992 and beyond (including modifications of loan guarantees that resulted from commitments in any year). The amounts in this account are a means of financing and are not included in the budget totals.

Balance Sheet (in millions of dollars)

Identification code 73–4149–0–3–376	1998 actual	1999 actual	2000 est.	2001 est.
ASSETS:				
Federal assets:				
1101 Fund balances with Treasury	1,209	822	838	855
Investments in US securities:				
1106 Receivables, net	221	66	176	176
Net value of assets related to post-1991 acquired defaulted guaranteed loans receivable:				
1501 Defaulted guaranteed loans receivable, gross	834	753	738	979
1502 Interest receivable	38	17	37	41
1505 Allowance for subsidy cost (–)	–215		–78	–78

1599 Net present value of assets related to defaulted guaranteed loans	657	770	697	942
1901 Other Federal assets: Other assets	245	128	238	238
1999 Total assets	2,332	1,786	1,949	2,211
LIABILITIES:				
2204 Non-Federal liabilities: Liabilities for loan guarantees	2,332	1,786	1,949	2,211
2999 Total liabilities	2,332	1,786	1,949	2,211
NET POSITION:				
3100 Appropriated capital				
3999 Total net position				
4999 Total liabilities and net position	2,332	1,786	1,949	2,211

Business Loan Fund Liquidating Account

Program and Financing (in millions of dollars)

Identification code 73–4154–0–3–376	1999 actual	2000 est.	2001 est.
Obligations by program activity:			
00.01 Interest Expense to Treasury	51	30	10
00.03 Msc. program expenses	–35	115	77
00.05 Guaranteed loan default claims	10	40	41
10.00 Total new obligations	26	185	128
Budgetary resources available for obligation:			
21.40 Unobligated balance available, start of year	273	240	
22.00 New budget authority (gross)	313	421	419
22.21 Unobligated balance transferred to other accounts	–7		
22.40 Capital transfer to general fund	–273	–446	–262
22.60 Portion applied to repay debt	–40	–30	–29
23.90 Total budgetary resources available for obligation	266	185	128
23.95 Total new obligations	–26	–185	–128
24.40 Unobligated balance available, end of year	240		
New budget authority (gross), detail:			
Mandatory:			
69.00 Offsetting collections (cash)	313	421	419
Change in unpaid obligations:			
72.40 Unpaid obligations, start of year: Obligated balance, start of year	513	539	577
73.10 Total new obligations	26	185	128
73.20 Total outlays (gross)		–147	–159
74.40 Unpaid obligations, end of year: Obligated balance, end of year	539	577	546
Outlays (gross), detail:			
86.97 Outlays from new mandatory authority		147	159
Offsets:			
Against gross budget authority and outlays:			
Offsetting collections (cash) from:			
Loan repayments:			
Non-Federal sources:			
88.40 Financing programs-principal	–97	–70	–75
88.40 Investment programs-principal	–16	–10	–10
88.40 Interest Income-Business	–73	–30	–50
88.40 Interest income-Investment	–10	–8	–5
88.40 Net changes in Receivables from the Public Business	42	–5	–25
88.40 Net changes in Receivables from the public-Investment	16	10	–7
88.40 Sale of acquired collateral-business	–17	–15	–16
88.40 Principal collections on judgements, notes,and other receivables-Business	–48	–10	–10
88.40 Principal collections on judgements and other receivables-Investment	–15	–13	–15
88.40 Recoveries	21	–1	–30
88.40 collection on FFB loans	–40	–30	–22
88.40 Other Income-both Business and Investment	–15	–4	–4
88.40 Net asset sale proceeds	–61		
88.40 Asset sale proceeds		–235	–150
88.90 Total, offsetting collections (cash)	–313	–421	–419
Net budget authority and outlays:			
89.00 Budget authority			
90.00 Outlays	–313	–274	–260

Status of Direct Loans (in millions of dollars)

Identification code 73–4154–0–3–376	1999 actual	2000 est.	2001 est.
Business Loan Fund, Direct Loans			
Cumulative balance of direct loans outstanding:			
1210 Outstanding, start of year	757	555	451
1232 Disbursements: Purchase of loans assets from the public	34	32	22
1251 Repayments: Repayments and prepayments	–129	–22	–6
1262 Adjustments: Discount on loan asset sales to the public or discounted	–86	–94	–100
1263 Write-offs for default: Direct loans	–21	–20	–3
1290 Outstanding, end of year	555	451	364
Small Business Investment Company, Direct Loans			
Section 503 Development Company, Direct Loans			
Cumulative balance of direct loans outstanding:			
1210 Outstanding, start of year	233	193	170
Repayments:			
1251 Repayments and prepayments	–22	–13	–11
1252 Proceeds from loan asset sales to the public or discounted	–18	–10	–9
1290 Outstanding, end of year	193	170	150

Status of Guaranteed Loans (in millions of dollars)

Identification code 73–4154–0–3–376	1999 actual	2000 est.	2001 est.
Business Loan Fund, Loan Guarantees			
Cumulative balance of guaranteed loans outstanding:			
2210 Outstanding, start of year	3,804	2,652	2,073
2231 Disbursements of new guaranteed loans	2	1	1
2251 Repayments and prepayments	–1,078	–532	–399
Adjustments:			
2261 Terminations for default that result in loans receivable	–69	–41	–28
2264 Other adjustments, net	–7	–7	–6
2290 Outstanding, end of year	2,652	2,073	1,641
Memorandum:			
2299 Guaranteed amount of guaranteed loans outstanding, end of year	2,321	1,956	1,630
Addendum:			
Cumulative balance of defaulted guaranteed loans that result in loans receivable:			
2310 Outstanding, start of year	1,466	1,378	1,210
2331 Disbursements for guaranteed loan claims	69	41	28
2361 Write-offs of loans receivable	–35	–9	–6
2364 Other adjustments, net	–122	–200	–300
2390 Outstanding, end of year	1,378	1,210	932

As required by the Federal Credit Reform Act of 1990, as amended, this account records, for this program, all cash flows to and from the Government resulting from direct loans obligated and loan guarantees committed prior to 1992. This account is shown on a cash basis. All new activity in this program in 1992 and beyond (including modifications of direct loans or loan guarantees that resulted from obligations or commitments in any year) is recorded in corresponding program and financing accounts.

Statement of Operations (in millions of dollars)

Identification code 73–4154–0–3–376	1998 actual	1999 actual	2000 est.	2001 est.
0101 Revenue	102	151	107	75
0102 Expense	–99	–73	–68	–64
0105 Net income or loss (–)	3	78	39	11

Credit accounts—Continued

BUSINESS LOAN FUND LIQUIDATING ACCOUNT—Continued

Balance Sheet (in millions of dollars)

Identification code 73–4154–0–3–376		1998 actual	1999 actual	2000 est.	2001 est.
	ASSETS:				
	Federal assets:				
1101	Fund balances with Treasury	787	779	466	466
	Investments in US securities:				
1104	Agency securities, par	283	245	186	186
1107	Advances and prepayments	6	6	5	4
	Non-Federal assets:				
1206	Receivables, net	480	214	269	214
1207	Advances and prepayments	8	8	7	7
	Net value of assets related to pre–1992 direct loans receivable and acquired defaulted guaranteed loans receivable:				
1601	Direct loans, gross	990	748	621	514
1603	Allowance for estimated uncollectible loans and interest (–)	–626	–303	–207	–136
1699	Value of assets related to direct loans	364	445	414	378
1901	Other Federal assets: Other assets	29	21	19	17
1999	Total assets	1,957	1,718	1,366	1,272
	LIABILITIES:				
	Federal liabilities:				
2101	Accounts payable	1,325	1,123	930	878
2102	Interest payable	69	57	96	96
2103	Debt to the FFB	233	193	156	123
	Non-Federal liabilities:				
2201	Accounts payable	14	13	15	15
2204	Liabilities for loan guarantees	31	18	73	73
2207	Other Liabilities	285	313	105	102
2999	Total liabilities	1,957	1,717	1,375	1,287
4999	Total liabilities and net position	1,957	1,717	1,375	1,287

Object Classification (in millions of dollars)

Identification code 73–4154–0–3–376		1999 actual	2000 est.	2001 est.
42.0	Insurance claims and indemnities	–25	155	118
43.0	Interest and dividends	51	30	10
99.9	Total new obligations	26	185	128

DISASTER LOANS PROGRAM ACCOUNT

For the cost of direct loans authorized by section 7(b) of the Small Business Act, as amended, **[**$140,400,000**]** *$142,100,000* to remain available until expended: *Provided*, That such costs, including the cost of modifying such loans, shall be as defined in section 502 of the Congressional Budget Act of 1974, as amended.

In addition, for administrative expenses to carry out the direct loan program, **[**$136,000,000**]** *$154,000,000*, which may be transferred to and merged with appropriations for Salaries and Expenses**[**, of which $500,000 is for the Office of Inspector General of the Small Business Administration for audits and reviews of disaster loans and the disaster loan program and shall be transferred to and merged with appropriations for the Office of Inspector General: *Provided*, That any amount in excess of $20,000,000 to be transferred to and merged with appropriations for Salaries and Expenses for indirect administrative expenses shall be treated as a reprogramming of funds under section 605 of this Act and shall not be available for obligation or expenditure except in compliance with the procedures set forth in that section**]**. *(Departments of Commerce, Justice, and State, the Judiciary, and Related Agencies Appropriations Act, 2000, as enacted by section 1000(a)(1) of the Consolidated Appropriations Act, 2000 (P.L. 106–113).)*

General Fund Credit Receipt Accounts (in millions of dollars)

Identification code 73–1152–0–1–453		1999 actual	2000 est.	2001 est.
0101	Disaster loan program, downward reestimates of subsidies	10		

Program and Financing (in millions of dollars)

Identification code 73–1152–0–1–453		1999 actual	2000 est.	2001 est.
	Obligations by program activity:			
00.01	Direct loan subsidy	170	231	152
00.03	Subsidy for Modification of Direct Loans			
00.05	Upward reestimate of direct loan subsidy	246		
00.06	Interest on reestimates of direct loan subsidy	91		
00.09	Administrative expense	146	136	154
10.00	Total new obligations	653	367	306
	Budgetary resources available for obligation:			
21.40	Unobligated balance available, start of year	81	81	
22.00	New budget authority (gross)	635	276	296
22.10	Resources available from recoveries of prior year obligations	19	10	10
23.90	Total budgetary resources available for obligation	735	367	306
23.95	Total new obligations	–653	–367	–306
24.40	Unobligated balance available, end of year	81		
	New budget authority (gross), detail:			
	Discretionary:			
40.00	Appropriation	293	276	296
42.00	Transferred from USDA	5		
43.00	Appropriation (total discretionary)	298	276	296
	Mandatory:			
60.05	Appropriation (indefinite)	337		
70.00	Total new budget authority (gross)	635	276	296
	Change in unpaid obligations:			
72.40	Unpaid obligations, start of year: Obligated balance, start of year	59	41	82
73.10	Total new obligations	653	367	306
73.20	Total outlays (gross)	–653	–316	–310
73.45	Adjustments in unexpired accounts	–19	–10	–10
74.40	Unpaid obligations, end of year: Obligated balance, end of year	41	82	66
	Outlays (gross), detail:			
86.90	Outlays from new discretionary authority	202	213	228
86.93	Outlays from discretionary balances	114	104	82
86.97	Outlays from new mandatory authority	337		
87.00	Total outlays (gross)	653	316	310
	Net budget authority and outlays:			
89.00	Budget authority	635	276	296
90.00	Outlays	653	316	310

Summary of Budget Authority and Outlays

(in millions of dollars)

	1999 actual	*2000 est.*	*2001 est.*
Enacted/requested:			
Budget Authority	635	276	296
Outlays	653	317	310
Supplemental proposal:			
Budget Authority		50	
Outlays			
Total:			
Budget Authority	635	326	296
Outlays	653	317	310

Summary of Loan Levels, Subsidy Budget Authority and Outlays by Program (in millions of dollars)

Identification code 73–1152–0–1–453		1999 actual	2000 est.	2001 est.
	Direct loan levels supportable by subsidy budget authority:			
1150	Direct Disaster Loans	762	1,041	871
1159	Total direct loan levels	762	1,041	871
	Direct loan subsidy (in percent):			
1320	Subsidy rate	13.10	22.20	17.46
1329	Weighted average subsidy rate	13.10	22.20	17.46
	Direct loan subsidy budget authority:			
1330	Disaster subsidy budget authority	100	140	142
1339	Total subsidy budget authority	100	140	142

	Direct loan subsidy outlays:			
1340	Disaster subsidy outlays	507	180	156
1349	Total subsidy outlays	507	180	156
	Administrative expense data:			
3510	Budget authority	146	136	154
3580	Outlays from balances			
3590	Outlays from new authority	146	136	154

As required by the Federal Credit Reform Act of 1990, as amended, this account records, for loans made pursuant to section 7(b) of the Small Business Act, as amended, the subsidy costs associated with the direct loans obligated in 1992 and beyond (including modifications of direct loans or loan guarantees that resulted from obligations or commitments in any year), as well as administrative expenses of this program. The subsidy amounts are estimated on a present value basis; the administrative expenses are estimated on a cash basis.

Disaster loans made pursuant to Section 7(b) of the Small Business Act are the primary form of Federal assistance for non-farm, private sector disaster losses. For this reason, the program is the only form of SBA assistance not limited to small businesses. Through this program, SBA helps homeowners, renters, businesses of all sizes, and non-profit organizations pay for the cost of rebuilding. Pursuant to the Small Business Act, the government subsidizes borrowers who have incurred uninsured losses or economic injury as the result of a natural disaster. These loans are also a critical source of economic stimulation in disaster-ravaged communities, helping to spur employment and stabilize the local tax base. Eligibility is based on financial criteria. The disaster loan programs include: physical disaster loans to individuals; physical disaster loans to businesses of any size; pre-disaster mitigation loans for small businesses; and economic injury loans to small businesses without credit available elsewhere (including the military reservist economic injury loan program).

2001 Budget Authority.—For 2001, SBA requests funding to support the 5-year average loan volume, excluding the Northridge disaster event, or $871 million in loans, within the discretionary spending budget caps.

This request also includes funding for the disaster administrative expenses within the discretionary spending budget caps. The amount requested for loan subsidy is $142 million. The amount requested for direct disaster loan making is $90 million, or 10 percent of the program level. The amount requested for direct disaster loan servicing is $34 million, reflecting the increased cost of salaries and minor inflationary increases. The transfer to Salaries and Expenses for indirect expenses supporting this program is estimated at $30 million.

Program Performance

Over the 45-year history of the program, SBA has helped more than 1.4 million disaster victims by providing more than $26.7 billion in disaster assistance. Over 90 percent has been to borrowers that otherwise would not have been able to rebuild. During 1999 alone, SBA approved over 36,000 disaster loans, exceeding $936 million to homeowners, renters, and businesses.

Program Performance and Policy Goals.—The SBA program performance and policy goals are to: 1) provide disaster assistance to victims in the most effective and cost efficient manner; 2) deliver an effective program that achieves its public policy objectives; 3) provide customer-focused assistance that satisfactorily accommodates the needs of all disaster victims; 4) simplify and streamline the loan-making process by re-engineering forms, procedures and processes; and, 5) effectively implement the proposed asset sales program.

SBA will coordinate with FEMA and other Federal, state and local officials as appropriate to ensure that SBA's field presence is established in the disaster area within 3 days of a disaster for 98 percent of declared events. SBA will recruit, employ and train sufficient staff to increase the number of disaster loan applications processed within 21 days of receipt from 65 percent in 1999 to 70 percent in 2001. In cooperation with SBA's regional/district offices, the Agency will meet with local bankers to emphasize bridge lending to businesses.

As part of our efforts to enhance the efficiency of disaster assistance, SBA has developed a standardized loan officer training curriculum, conducts quality reviews in each Disaster Area Office, began the process of automating the disaster loan making process, and reviewed the current processes for required policy, organizational, and procedural changes. SBA and FEMA will continue efforts to develop a joint loss inspection process.

Based on efforts to improve commercial and home loan servicing, a number of goals have been set, subject to the availability of staff. To ameliorate commercial loan servicing, SBA intends to improve the currency rate to 96 percent on all SBA serviced loans, increase loan receipts to 16 percent on all SBA serviced loans, review 100 percent of all delinquent accounts each week, and reduce turn around times on all servicing actions to 2 days. For disaster home servicing, SBA intends to improve the currency rate to 95 percent, reduce the delinquency rate to 2 percent, increase loan receipts to 16.2 percent, and review 100 percent of all delinquent accounts each week. To improve loan liquidation, SBA will increase the number of cases closed each month to 360 and increase average collections on loans in liquidation by 20 percent.

In addition, as mentioned above under systems modernization, the disaster program is developing a paperless home loan application and other delivery improvements that should substantially increase efficiencies and lower costs over time.

Object Classification (in millions of dollars)

Identification code 73–1152–0–1–453		1999 actual	2000 est.	2001 est.
25.2	Other services	146	136	154
41.0	Grants, subsidies, and contributions	507	231	152
99.9	Total new obligations	653	367	306

Disaster Direct Loan Financing Account

Program and Financing (in millions of dollars)

Identification code 73–4150–0–3–453		1999 actual	2000 est.	2001 est.
	Obligations by program activity:			
00.01	Direct loans	762	630	813
00.02	Interest on Treasury borrowing	579	388	388
00.91	Direct Program by Activities—Subtotal (1 level)	1,341	1,018	1,201
08.02	Payment of downward reestimate to receipt account	10		
08.04	Payment of interest on downward reestimates to receipt account	1		
08.06	Payment to liquidating account to purchase loan assets (73 4153)		226	96
08.91	Direct Program by Activities—Subtotal (1 level)	11	226	96
10.00	Total new obligations	1,352	1,244	1,297
	Budgetary resources available for obligation:			
21.40	Unobligated balance available, start of year	3,956	5,124	4,169
22.00	New financing authority (gross)	3,182	2,071	2,159
22.60	Portion applied to repay debt	−662	−1,782	−2,888
23.90	Total budgetary resources available for obligation	6,476	5,413	3,440
23.95	Total new obligations	−1,352	−1,244	−1,297
24.40	Unobligated balance available, end of year	5,124	4,169	2,143
	New financing authority (gross), detail:			
	Mandatory:			
67.15	Authority to borrow (indefinite)	936	811	717

Credit accounts—Continued

Disaster Direct Loan Financing Account—Continued

Program and Financing (in millions of dollars)—Continued

Identification code 73–4150–0–3–453	1999 actual	2000 est.	2001 est.
Spending authority from offsetting collections:			
Discretionary:			
68.00 Offsetting collections (cash)	2,244	1,297	1,442
68.10 Change in receivables from program account	2	−37	
68.90 Spending authority from offsetting collections (total discretionary)	2,246	1,260	1,442
70.00 Total new financing authority (gross)	3,182	2,071	2,159
Change in unpaid obligations:			
Unpaid obligations, start of year:			
72.40 Obligated balance, start of year	990	328	20
72.95 Receivables from program account	39	41	4
72.99 Total unpaid obligations, start of year	1,029	369	24
73.10 Total new obligations	1,352	1,244	1,297
73.20 Total financing disbursements (gross)	−2,012	−1,589	−1,208
Unpaid obligations, end of year:			
74.40 Obligated balance, end of year	328	20	109
74.95 Receivables from program account	41	4	4
74.99 Total unpaid obligations, end of year	369	24	113
87.00 Total financing disbursements (gross)	2,012	1,589	1,208
Offsets:			
Against gross financing authority and financing disbursements:			
Offsetting collections (cash) from:			
Federal sources:			
88.00 Payments from program account	−170	−270	−127
88.00 Payments from program account—reestimates	−337		
Non-Federal sources:			
88.40 Repayments of principal, net	−566	−368	−385
88.40 Collection of misc. receivables	−962	−9	
88.40 Interest received on loans	−209	−424	−407
88.40 Proceeds from loan sales		−226	−523
88.90 Total, offsetting collections (cash)	−2,244	−1,297	−1,442
Against gross budget authority only:			
88.95 Change in receivables from program accounts	−2	37	
Net financing authority and financing disbursements:			
89.00 Financing authority	936	811	717
90.00 Financing disbursements	−232	292	−234

Status of Direct Loans (in millions of dollars)

Identification code 73–4150–0–3–453	1999 actual	2000 est.	2001 est.
Position with respect to appropriations act limitation on obligations:			
1111 Limitation on direct loans			
1131 Direct loan obligations exempt from limitation	814	221	951
1150 Total direct loan obligations	814	221	951
Cumulative balance of direct loans outstanding:			
1210 Outstanding, start of year	5,605	5,658	5,827
Disbursements:			
1231 Direct loan disbursements	755	510	902
1233 Purchase of loans assets from a liquidating account		140	290
Repayments:			
1251 Repayments and prepayments	−566	−368	−385
1252 Proceeds from loan asset sales to the public or discounted			−424
1262 Adjustments: Discount on loan asset sales to the public or discounted			−1,644
1264 Write-offs for default: Other adjustments, net	−136	−113	−114
1290 Outstanding, end of year	5,658	5,827	4,452

As required by the Federal Credit Reform Act of 1990, as amended, this non-budgetary account records all cash flows to and from the Government resulting from direct loans obligated in 1992 and beyond (including modifications of direct loans that resulted from obligations in any year). The amounts in this account are a means of financing and are not included in the budget totals.

Balance Sheet (in millions of dollars)

Identification code 73–4150–0–3–453	1998 actual	1999 actual	2000 est.	2001 est.
ASSETS:				
Federal assets:				
Investments in US securities:				
Receivables, net:				
1106 Program account	39	41	4	4
1106 Interest/Accounts Receivables	5,247	5,761	5,953	5,550
Net value of assets related to post-1991 direct loans receivable:				
1401 Direct loans receivable, gross	5,605	5,658	5,687	3,756
1405 Allowance for subsidy cost (−)	−973	−1,439	−1,254	−1,254
1499 Net present value of assets related to direct loans	4,632	4,219	4,433	2,502
1999 Total assets	9,918	10,021	10,390	8,056
LIABILITIES:				
2104 Federal liabilities: Resources payable to Treasury	9,918	10,021	10,390	8,056
2999 Total liabilities	9,918	10,021	10,390	8,056
NET POSITION:				
3100 Appropriated capital				
3999 Total net position				
4999 Total liabilities and net position	9,918	10,021	10,390	8,056

Disaster Loan Fund Liquidating Account

Program and Financing (in millions of dollars)

Identification code 73–4153–0–3–453	1999 actual	2000 est.	2001 est.
Obligations by program activity:			
01.01 Interest expense to Treasury	51	51	17
01.03 Other expenses	4	10	10
10.00 Total new obligations	55	61	27
Budgetary resources available for obligation:			
21.40 Unobligated balance available, start of year	196	15	
22.00 New budget authority from offsetting collections (gross)	70	130	29
22.40 Capital transfer to general fund	−196	−84	−2
23.90 Total budgetary resources available for obligation	70	61	27
23.95 Total new obligations	−55	−61	−27
24.40 Unobligated balance available, end of year	15		
New budget authority (gross), detail:			
Mandatory:			
69.00 Offsetting collections (cash)	229	296	103
69.47 Portion applied to repay debt	−159	−166	−74
69.90 Spending authority from offsetting collections (total mandatory)	70	130	29
Change in unpaid obligations:			
72.40 Unpaid obligations, start of year: Obligated balance, start of year	60	52	52
73.10 Total new obligations	55	61	27
73.20 Total outlays (gross)	−63	−61	−27
74.40 Unpaid obligations, end of year: Obligated balance, end of year	52	52	52
Outlays (gross), detail:			
86.97 Outlays from new mandatory authority	59	61	27
86.98 Outlays from mandatory balances	4		
87.00 Total outlays (gross)	63	61	27
Offsets:			
Against gross budget authority and outlays:			
Offsetting collections (cash) from:			
Non-Federal sources:			
88.40 Asset Sale Proceeds (73–4150)		−226	−96

88.40	Loan repayments	−166	−50	−5
88.40	Interest income	−52	−10	−1
88.40	Other income	−11	−10	−1
88.90	Total, offsetting collections (cash)	−229	−296	−103
	Net budget authority and outlays:			
89.00	Budget authority	−159	−166	−74
90.00	Outlays	−165	−235	−76

Status of Direct Loans (in millions of dollars)

Identification code 73–4153–0–3–453		1999 actual	2000 est.	2001 est.
	Cumulative balance of direct loans outstanding:			
1210	Outstanding, start of year	1,254	1,067	487
	Repayments:			
1251	Repayments and prepayments	−166	−50	−5
1252	Proceeds from loan asset sales to the public or discounted		−104	−96
1262	Adjustments: Discount on loan asset sales to the public or discounted		−416	−386
1263	Write-offs for default: Direct loans	−21	−10	
1290	Outstanding, end of year	1,067	487	

As required by the Federal Credit Reform Act of 1990, as amended, this account records, for this program, all cash flows to and from the Government resulting from direct loans obligated prior to 1992. This account is shown on a cash basis. All new activity in this program in 1992 and beyond (including modifications of direct loans or loan guarantees that resulted from obligations or commitments in any year) is recorded in corresponding program and financing accounts.

Statement of Operations (in millions of dollars)

Identification code 73–4153–0–3–453		1998 actual	1999 actual	2000 est.	2001 est.
0101	Revenue	64	52	42	5
0102	Expense	−93	−53	−43	−16
0105	Net income or loss (−)	−29	−1	−1	−11

Balance Sheet (in millions of dollars)

Identification code 73–4153–0–3–453		1998 actual	1999 actual	2000 est.	2001 est.
	ASSETS:				
1101	Federal assets: Fund balances with Treasury	256	226	200	133
1206	Non-Federal assets: Receivables, net	64	59	51	5
	Net value of assets related to pre–1992 direct loans receivable and acquired defaulted guaranteed loans receivable:				
1601	Direct loans, gross	1,254	1,067	487	
1603	Allowance for estimated uncollectible loans and interest (−)	−114	−46	−30	
1699	Value of assets related to direct loans	1,140	1,021	457	
	Other Federal assets:				
1801	Cash and other monetary assets				
1803	Property, plant and equipment, net	1			
1999	Total assets	1,461	1,306	708	138
	LIABILITIES:				
2102	Federal liabilities: Interest payable	59	52	31	20
2201	Non-Federal liabilities: Accounts payable	1,402	1,254	990	586
2999	Total liabilities	1,461	1,306	1,021	606
4999	Total liabilities and net position	1,461	1,306	1,021	606

Object Classification (in millions of dollars)

Identification code 73–4153–0–3–453		1999 actual	2000 est.	2001 est.
25.2	Other services	4	10	10
43.0	Interest and dividends	51	51	17
99.9	Total new obligations	55	61	27

Pollution Control Equipment Fund Liquidating Account

Program and Financing (in millions of dollars)

Identification code 73–4147–0–3–376		1999 actual	2000 est.	2001 est.
	Obligations by program activity:			
00.01	Direct program	3	3	1
10.00	Total new obligations	3	3	1
	Budgetary resources available for obligation:			
	Unobligated balance available, start of year:			
21.40	Unobligated balance available, start of year	12	9	8
21.40	Unobligated balance available, start of year	2	−9	−8
21.99	Total unobligated balance, start of year	14		
22.00	New budget authority (gross)	4	3	1
22.40	Capital transfer to general fund	−14	−2	
23.90	Total budgetary resources available for obligation	4	1	1
23.95	Total new obligations	−3	−3	−1
	Unobligated balance available, end of year:			
24.40	Unobligated balance available, end of year	9	8	8
24.40	Unobligated balance available, end of year	−9	−8	−8
24.99	Total unobligated balance, end of year			
	New budget authority (gross), detail:			
	Mandatory:			
67.15	Authority to borrow (indefinite)	4	3	1
	Change in unpaid obligations:			
73.10	Total new obligations	3	3	1
73.20	Total outlays (gross)	−3	−3	−1
	Outlays (gross), detail:			
86.97	Outlays from new mandatory authority	2	3	1
86.98	Outlays from mandatory balances	1		
87.00	Total outlays (gross)	3	3	1
	Net budget authority and outlays:			
89.00	Budget authority	4	3	1
90.00	Outlays	2	3	1

Status of Guaranteed Loans (in millions of dollars)

Identification code 73–4147–0–3–376		1999 actual	2000 est.	2001 est.
	Cumulative balance of guaranteed loans outstanding:			
2210	Outstanding, start of year	57	46	35
	Adjustments:			
2261	Terminations for default that result in loans receivable			
2263	Terminations for default that result in claim payments	−11	−11	−11
2290	Outstanding, end of year	46	35	24
	Memorandum:			
2299	Guaranteed amount of guaranteed loans outstanding, end of year	46	35	24
	Addendum:			
	Cumulative balance of defaulted guaranteed loans that result in loans receivable:			
2310	Outstanding, start of year	45	47	46
2331	Disbursements for guaranteed loan claims	3		
2351	Repayments of loans receivable	−1	−1	−1
2390	Outstanding, end of year	47	46	45

Public Law 94–305 established this fund to alleviate the adverse impact of pollution regulations on small businesses. As a result of the elimination of tax exempt financing associated with the Pollution Control Guaranteed program, no new activity is anticipated for this program.

During 1992, the Small Business Administration started the process of redeeming a large number of outstanding bonds on which it has taken over loan payments. Most of these targeted bonds are ten years old and voluntary redemption is now viable under the bond documents. Redemption of these

Credit accounts—Continued

POLLUTION CONTROL EQUIPMENT FUND LIQUIDATING ACCOUNT—Continued

obligations would preclude the SBA from paying excessive interest over the next ten years.

Statement of Operations (in millions of dollars)

Identification code 73–4147–0–3–376	1998 actual	1999 actual	2000 est.	2001 est.
0101 Revenue	....	4	3	1
0102 Expense	3	–3	–3	–1
0105 Net income or loss (–)	3	1	....	....

Balance Sheet (in millions of dollars)

Identification code 73–4147–0–3–376	1998 actual	1999 actual	2000 est.	2001 est.
ASSETS:				
1101 Federal assets: Fund balances with Treasury	14	2	11	11
1206 Non-Federal assets: Receivables, net	9	9	9	9
1701 Net value of assets related to pre–1992 direct loans receivable and acquired defaulted guaranteed loans receivable: Defaulted guaranteed loans, gross	6	8	6	6
1999 Total assets	29	19	26	26
LIABILITIES:				
2104 Federal liabilities: Resources payable to Treasury	22	–29	21	21
2201 Non-Federal liabilities: Accounts payable	....	....	....	....
2999 Total liabilities	22	–29	21	21
NET POSITION:				
3100 Appropriated capital	....	....	....	....
3300 Cumulative results of operations	7	48	5	5
3999 Total net position	7	48	5	5
4999 Total liabilities and net position	29	19	26	26

ADMINISTRATIVE PROVISION—SMALL BUSINESS ADMINISTRATION

Not to exceed 5 percent of any appropriation made available for the current fiscal year for the Small Business Administration in this Act may be transferred between such appropriations, but no such appropriation shall be increased by more than 10 percent by any such transfers: *Provided*, That any transfer pursuant to this paragraph shall be treated as a reprogramming of funds under section 605 of this Act and shall not be available for obligation or expenditure except in compliance with the procedures set forth in that section. *(Departments of Commerce, Justice, and State, the Judiciary, and Related Agencies Appropriations Act, 2000, as enacted by section 1000(a)(1) of the Consolidated Appropriations Act, 2000 (P.L. 106–113).)*

GENERAL FUND RECEIPT ACCOUNTS

(in millions of dollars)

	1999 actual	2000 est.	2001 est.
Offsetting receipts from the public:			
73–272130 Disaster loan program, downward reestimates of subsidies	10	....	....
73–272230 Business loan program, Downward resstimates of subsidies	695	301	....
General Fund Offsetting receipts from the public	705	301	....

SOCIAL SECURITY ADMINISTRATION

Federal Funds

General and special funds:

PAYMENTS TO SOCIAL SECURITY TRUST FUNDS

For payment to the Federal Old-Age and Survivors Insurance and the Federal Disability Insurance trust funds, as provided under sections 201(m), 228(g), and 1131(b)(2) of the Social Security Act, [$20,764,000] *$20,400,000. (Departments of Labor, Health and Human Services, and Education, and Related Agencies Appropriations Act, 2000, as enacted by section 1000(a)(4) of the Consolidated Appropriations Act, 2000 (P.L. 106–113).)*

Program and Financing (in millions of dollars)

Identification code 28–0404–0–1–651		1999 actual	2000 est.	2001 est.
	Obligations by program activity:			
00.01	Taxation of benefits	10,810	11,642	10,965
01.01	Other	14	21	21
10.00	Total new obligations	10,824	11,663	10,986
	Budgetary resources available for obligation:			
21.40	Unobligated balance available, start of year	16	16	15
22.00	New budget authority (gross)	10,830	11,663	10,985
23.90	Total budgetary resources available for obligation	10,846	11,679	11,000
23.95	Total new obligations	–10,824	–11,663	–10,986
23.98	Unobligated balance expiring or withdrawn	–7		
24.40	Unobligated balance available, end of year	16	15	15
	New budget authority (gross), detail:			
	Mandatory:			
60.00	Appropriation	20	21	20
60.05	Appropriation (indefinite)	10,810	11,642	10,965
62.50	Appropriation (total mandatory)	10,830	11,663	10,985
	Change in unpaid obligations:			
72.40	Unpaid obligations, start of year: Obligated balance, start of year	2	1	2
73.10	Total new obligations	10,824	11,663	10,986
73.20	Total outlays (gross)	–10,824	–11,664	–10,986
74.40	Unpaid obligations, end of year: Obligated balance, end of year	1	2	2
	Outlays (gross), detail:			
86.97	Outlays from new mandatory authority	10,824	11,663	10,985
86.98	Outlays from mandatory balances		1	
87.00	Total outlays (gross)	10,824	11,664	10,986
	Net budget authority and outlays:			
89.00	Budget authority	10,830	11,663	10,985
90.00	Outlays	10,826	11,664	10,986

This general fund appropriation reimburses the Social Security trust funds annually for (1) special payments to certain uninsured persons, (2) pension reform, and (3) interest on unnegotiated checks. It also includes amounts from taxation of Social Security benefits.

Object Classification (in millions of dollars)

Identification code 28–0404–0–1–651		1999 actual	2000 est.	2001 est.
25.2	Other services	3	3	6
42.0	Insurance claims and indemnities	10,821	11,660	10,980
99.9	Total new obligations	10,824	11,663	10,986

SPECIAL BENEFITS FOR DISABLED COAL MINERS

For carrying out title IV of the Federal Mine Safety and Health Act of 1977, [$383,638,000] *$365,748,000*, to remain available until expended.

For making, after July 31 of the current fiscal year, benefit payments to individuals under title IV of the Federal Mine Safety and Health Act of 1977, for costs incurred in the current fiscal year, such amounts as may be necessary.

For making benefit payments under title IV of the Federal Mine Safety and Health Act of 1977 for the first quarter of fiscal year [2001, $124,000,000] *2002, $114,000,000*, to remain available until expended. *(Departments of Labor, Health and Human Services, and Education, and Related Agencies Appropriations Act, 2000, as enacted by section 1000(a)(4) of the Consolidated Appropriations Act, 2000 (P.L. 106–113).)*

Program and Financing (in millions of dollars)

Identification code 28–0409–0–1–601		1999 actual	2000 est.	2001 est.
	Obligations by program activity:			
10.00	Total new obligations	552	524	492
	Budgetary resources available for obligation:			
21.40	Unobligated balance available, start of year	10	2	2
22.00	New budget authority (gross)	543	525	490
23.90	Total budgetary resources available for obligation	553	527	492
23.95	Total new obligations	–552	–524	–492
24.40	Unobligated balance available, end of year	2	2	
	New budget authority (gross), detail:			
	Mandatory:			
60.00	Appropriation	383	384	366
65.00	Advance appropriation	160	141	124
70.00	Total new budget authority (gross)	543	525	490
	Change in unpaid obligations:			
72.40	Unpaid obligations, start of year: Obligated balance, start of year	46	44	41
73.10	Total new obligations	552	524	492
73.20	Total outlays (gross)	–554	–527	–497
74.40	Unpaid obligations, end of year: Obligated balance, end of year	44	41	36
	Outlays (gross), detail:			
86.97	Outlays from new mandatory authority	520	483	455
86.98	Outlays from mandatory balances	34	44	42
87.00	Total outlays (gross)	554	527	497
	Net budget authority and outlays:			
89.00	Budget authority	543	525	490
90.00	Outlays	554	527	497

Title IV of the Federal Mine Safety and Health Act authorizes monthly benefits to coal miners disabled from coal workers' pneumoconiosis (black lung) and to their widows and certain other dependents. SSA is responsible for processing and paying only those claims for coal miners' benefits that were filed between December 30, 1969, when the program originated, and June 30, 1973, when program administration was transferred to the Department of Labor (DOL).

Object Classification (in millions of dollars)

Identification code 28–0409–0–1–601		1999 actual	2000 est.	2001 est.
11.5	Personnel compensation: Other personnel compensation	1	2	2
25.3	Purchases of goods and services from Government accounts	3	3	3

General and special funds—Continued

SPECIAL BENEFITS FOR DISABLED COAL MINERS—Continued

Object Classification (in millions of dollars)—Continued

Identification code 28–0409–0–1–601	1999 actual	2000 est.	2001 est.
42.0 Insurance claims and indemnities	548	519	486
99.0 Subtotal, direct obligations	552	524	491
99.5 Below reporting threshold			1
99.9 Total new obligations	552	524	492

SUPPLEMENTAL SECURITY INCOME PROGRAM

For carrying out titles XI and XVI of the Social Security Act, section 401 of Public Law 92–603, section 212 of Public Law 93–66, as amended, and section 405 of Public Law 95–216, including payment to the Social Security trust funds for administrative expenses incurred pursuant to section 201(g)(1) of the Social Security Act, [$21,503,085,000] *$23,053,000,000*, to remain available until expended: *Provided*, That any portion of the funds provided to a State in the current fiscal year and not obligated by the State during that year shall be returned to the Treasury.

[From funds provided under the previous paragraph, not less than $100,000,000 shall be available for payment to the Social Security trust funds for administrative expenses for conducting continuing disability reviews.]

In addition, [$200,000,000] *$210,000,000*, to remain available until September 30, [2001] *2002*, for payment to the Social Security trust funds for administrative expenses for continuing disability reviews as authorized by section 103 of Public Law 104–121 and section 10203 of Public Law 105–33. The term "continuing disability reviews" means reviews and redeterminations as defined under section 201(g)(1)(A) of the Social Security Act, as amended.

For making, after June 15 of the current fiscal year, benefit payments to individuals under title XVI of the Social Security Act, for unanticipated costs incurred for the current fiscal year, such sums as may be necessary.

For making benefit payments under title XVI of the Social Security Act for the first quarter of fiscal year [2001, $9,890,000,000] *2002, $10,470,000,000*, to remain available until expended. *(Departments of Labor, Health and Human Services, and Education, and Related Agencies Appropriations Act, 2000, as enacted by section 1000(a)(4) of the Consolidated Appropriations Act, 2000 (P.L. 106–113).)*

Unavailable Collections (in millions of dollars)

Identification code 28–0406–0–1–609	1999 actual	2000 est.	2001 est.
Balance, start of year:			
01.99 Balance, start of year		2	2
Receipts:			
02.01 State supplemental fees	2		
04.00 Total: Balances and collections	2	2	2
07.99 Total balance, end of year	2	2	2

Program and Financing (in millions of dollars)

Identification code 28–0406–0–1–609	1999 actual	2000 est.	2001 est.
Obligations by program activity:			
00.01 Direct program	30,521	31,664	33,153
Reimbursable programs:			
09.01 State supplementation payments	3,219	3,310	3,410
09.02 Administration of State supplementation payments	75	80	91
10.00 Total new obligations	33,815	35,054	36,654
Budgetary resources available for obligation:			
21.40 Unobligated balance available, start of year	129	44	
22.00 New budget authority (gross)	33,728	35,010	36,654
22.10 Resources available from recoveries of prior year obligations	2		
23.90 Total budgetary resources available for obligation	33,859	35,054	36,654
23.95 Total new obligations	−33,815	−35,054	−36,654
24.40 Unobligated balance available, end of year	44		
New budget authority (gross), detail:			
Discretionary:			
40.00 Appropriation	2,321	2,360	2,592
Mandatory:			
60.00 Appropriation	19,408	19,343	20,671
60.05 Appropriation (indefinite)	25	367	
62.50 Appropriation (total mandatory)	19,433	19,710	20,671
65.00 Advance appropriation	8,680	9,550	9,890
Discretionary:			
68.00 Spending authority from offsetting collections: Offsetting collections (cash)	75	80	91
Mandatory:			
69.00 Offsetting collections (cash)	3,219	3,310	3,410
70.00 Total new budget authority (gross)	33,728	35,010	36,654
Change in unpaid obligations:			
72.40 Unpaid obligations, start of year: Obligated balance, start of year	695	542	543
73.10 Total new obligations	33,815	35,054	36,654
73.20 Total outlays (gross)	−33,966	−35,053	−36,652
73.45 Adjustments in unexpired accounts	−2		
74.40 Unpaid obligations, end of year: Obligated balance, end of year	542	543	545
Outlays (gross), detail:			
86.90 Outlays from new discretionary authority	2,396	2,189	2,406
86.93 Outlays from discretionary balances	176	250	275
86.97 Outlays from new mandatory authority	31,265	32,570	33,971
86.98 Outlays from mandatory balances	129	44	
87.00 Total outlays (gross)	33,966	35,053	36,652
Offsets:			
Against gross budget authority and outlays:			
Offsetting collections (cash) from:			
Non-Federal sources:			
88.40 Non-Federal sources	−3,219	−3,310	−3,410
88.40 Non-Federal sources	−75	−80	−91
88.90 Total, offsetting collections (cash)	−3,294	−3,390	−3,501
Net budget authority and outlays:			
89.00 Budget authority	30,434	31,620	33,153
90.00 Outlays	30,673	31,663	33,151

Summary of Budget Authority and Outlays

(in millions of dollars)

Enacted/requested:	*1999 actual*	*2000 est.*	*2001 est.*
Budget Authority	30,434	31,620	33,153
Outlays	30,672	31,663	33,151
Legislative proposal, subject to PAYGO:			
Budget Authority		2,190	−2,190
Outlays		2,190	−2,190
Legislative proposal, discretionary offset:			
Budget Authority			
Outlays			
Total:			
Budget Authority	30,434	33,810	30,963
Outlays	30,672	33,853	30,961

Title XVI of the Social Security Act established a supplemental security income (SSI) program to provide monthly cash benefits as a federally guaranteed minimum income for the needy aged, blind, and disabled.

Object Classification (in millions of dollars)

Identification code 28–0406–0–1–609	1999 actual	2000 est.	2001 est.
Direct obligations:			
41.0 Grants, subsidies, and contributions	28,118	29,189	30,483
92.0 Undistributed	2,403	2,475	2,670
99.0 Subtotal, direct obligations	30,521	31,664	33,153
99.0 Reimbursable obligations	3,294	3,390	3,501
99.9 Total new obligations	33,815	35,054	36,654

SUPPLEMENTAL SECURITY INCOME PROGRAM

(Legislative proposal, subject to PAYGO)

Program and Financing (in millions of dollars)

Identification code 28–0406–4–1–609	1999 actual	2000 est.	2001 est.
Obligations by program activity:			
10.00 Total new obligations	....	2,190	−2,190
Budgetary resources available for obligation:			
21.40 Unobligated balance available, start of year	....	....	....
22.00 New budget authority (gross)	....	2,190	−2,190
23.90 Total budgetary resources available for obligation	....	2,190	−2,190
23.95 Total new obligations	....	−2,190	2,190
24.40 Unobligated balance available, end of year	....	....	....
New budget authority (gross), detail:			
Mandatory:			
60.00 Appropriation	....	....	−2,190
60.05 Appropriation (indefinite)	....	2,190	....
62.50 Appropriation (total mandatory)	....	2,190	−2,190
Change in unpaid obligations:			
72.40 Unpaid obligations, start of year: Obligated balance, start of year	....	....	....
73.10 Total new obligations	....	2,190	−2,190
73.20 Total outlays (gross)	....	−2,190	2,190
74.40 Unpaid obligations, end of year: Obligated balance, end of year	....	....	....
Outlays (gross), detail:			
86.97 Outlays from new mandatory authority	....	2,190	−2,190
Net budget authority and outlays:			
89.00 Budget authority	....	2,190	−2,190
90.00 Outlays	....	2,190	−2,190

This schedule reflects the Administration's proposal to repeal the Public Law 105–33 provision that altered the timing of the October 2000 supplemental security income benefit payments.

SPECIAL BENEFITS FOR CERTAIN WORLD WAR II VETERANS

Program and Financing (in millions of dollars)

Identification code 28–0401–0–1–701	1999 actual	2000 est.	2001 est.
Obligations by program activity:			
10.00 Total new obligations	....	8	11
Budgetary resources available for obligation:			
22.00 New budget authority (gross)	....	8	11
23.95 Total new obligations	....	−8	−11
New budget authority (gross), detail:			
Discretionary:			
40.05 Appropriation (indefinite)	....	3	2
Mandatory:			
60.05 Appropriation (indefinite)	....	5	9
70.00 Total new budget authority (gross)	....	8	11
Change in unpaid obligations:			
73.10 Total new obligations	....	8	11
73.20 Total outlays (gross)	....	−8	−11
Outlays (gross), detail:			
86.90 Outlays from new discretionary authority	....	3	2
86.97 Outlays from new mandatory authority	....	5	9
87.00 Total outlays (gross)	....	8	11
Net budget authority and outlays:			
89.00 Budget authority	....	8	11
90.00 Outlays	....	8	11

Public Law 106–169 established a benefit program for certain individuals who are at least 65 years old, were in the United States military forces, including members of Fillipino units, during World War II, and who are currently eligible for supplemental security income. To receive this benefit these individuals must reside outside the United States.

Object Classification (in millions of dollars)

Identification code 28–0401–0–1–701	1999 actual	2000 est.	2001 est.
25.2 Other services	....	3	2
42.0 Insurance claims and indemnities	....	5	9
99.9 Total new obligations	....	8	11

OFFICE OF INSPECTOR GENERAL

(INCLUDING TRANSFER OF FUNDS)

For expenses necessary for the Office of Inspector General in carrying out the provisions of the Inspector General Act of 1978, as amended, **[**$15,000,000**]** *$17,000,000*, together with not to exceed **[**$51,000,000**]** *$56,000,000*, to be transferred and expended as authorized by section 201(g)(1) of the Social Security Act from the Federal Old-Age and Survivors Insurance Trust Fund and the Federal Disability Insurance Trust Fund.

In addition, an amount not to exceed 3 percent of the total provided in this appropriation may be transferred from the "Limitation on Administrative Expenses", Social Security Administration, to be merged with this account, to be available for the time and purposes for which this account is available: *Provided*, That notice of such transfers shall be transmitted promptly to the Committees on Appropriations of the House and Senate. *(Departments of Labor, Health and Human Services, and Education, and Related Agencies Appropriations Act, 2000, as enacted by section 1000(a)(4) of the Consolidated Appropriations Act, 2000 (P.L. 106–113).)*

Program and Financing (in millions of dollars)

Identification code 28–0400–0–1–651	1999 actual	2000 est.	2001 est.
Obligations by program activity:			
10.00 Total new obligations	55	66	73
Budgetary resources available for obligation:			
22.00 New budget authority (gross)	56	66	73
23.95 Total new obligations	−55	−66	−73
23.98 Unobligated balance expiring or withdrawn	−1	....	....
New budget authority (gross), detail:			
Discretionary:			
40.00 Appropriation	12	15	17
Spending authority from offsetting collections:			
68.00 Offsetting collections (cash)	46	55	55
68.10 From Federal sources: Change in receivables and unpaid, unfilled orders	−2	−4	1
68.90 Spending authority from offsetting collections (total discretionary)	44	51	56
70.00 Total new budget authority (gross)	56	66	73
Change in unpaid obligations:			
Unpaid obligations, start of year:			
72.40 Obligated balance, start of year	−10	−1	....
72.95 From Federal sources: Receivables and unpaid, unfilled orders	18	16	12
72.99 Total unpaid obligations, start of year	8	15	12
73.10 Total new obligations	55	66	73
73.20 Total outlays (gross)	−50	−69	−72
73.40 Adjustments in expired accounts (net)	2	....	....
Unpaid obligations, end of year:			
74.40 Obligated balance, end of year	−1	....	....
74.95 From Federal sources: Receivables and unpaid, unfilled orders	16	12	13
74.99 Total unpaid obligations, end of year	15	12	13
Outlays (gross), detail:			
86.90 Outlays from new discretionary authority	46	55	62

General and special funds—Continued

OFFICE OF INSPECTOR GENERAL—Continued

(INCLUDING TRANSFER OF FUNDS)—Continued

Program and Financing (in millions of dollars)—Continued

Identification code 28–0400–0–1–651		1999 actual	2000 est.	2001 est.
86.93	Outlays from discretionary balances	4	14	10
87.00	Total outlays (gross)	50	69	72
	Offsets:			
	Against gross budget authority and outlays:			
88.00	Offsetting collections (cash) from: Federal sources	−46	−55	−55
	Against gross budget authority only:			
88.95	From Federal sources: Change in receivables and unpaid, unfilled orders	2	4	−1
	Net budget authority and outlays:			
89.00	Budget authority	12	15	17
90.00	Outlays	4	14	17

The Office of Inspector General provides agency-wide audit and investigative functions to help find and correct operational and administrative deficiencies which create conditions for existing or potential instances of fraud, waste, and mismanagement.

Object Classification (in millions of dollars)

Identification code 28–0400–0–1–651		1999 actual	2000 est.	2001 est.
11.1	Personnel compensation: Full-time permanent	31	42	45
12.1	Civilian personnel benefits	9	10	13
21.0	Travel and transportation of persons	3	3	3
23.1	Rental payments to GSA	2	2	2
23.3	Communications, utilities, and miscellaneous charges		1	1
25.2	Other services	1	1	1
25.3	Purchases of goods and services from Government accounts	6	3	4
26.0	Supplies and materials	1	1	1
31.0	Equipment	1	3	2
32.0	Land and structures	1		
99.0	Subtotal, direct obligations	55	66	72
99.5	Below reporting threshold			1
99.9	Total new obligations	55	66	73

Personnel Summary

Identification code 28–0400–0–1–651		1999 actual	2000 est.	2001 est.
1001	Total compensable workyears: Full-time equivalent employment	428	536	584

Trust Funds

FEDERAL OLD-AGE AND SURVIVORS INSURANCE TRUST FUND

Unavailable Collections (in millions of dollars)

Identification code 20–8006–0–7–651		1999 actual	2000 est.	2001 est.
	Balance, start of year:			
01.99	Balance, start of year	622,960	731,054	858,752
	Receipts:			
02.01	Transfers from general fund (FICA taxes)	364,423	386,948	405,417
02.02	Transfers from general fund (SECA taxes)	20,437	23,166	23,532
02.03	Federal employer contributions (FICA taxes)	6,146	6,508	6,788
02.04	Refunds	−1,301	−1,531	−1,627
02.05	Interest received by trust funds	46,847	53,400	60,625
02.09	Federal payments to the FOASI trust fund	10,188	11,014	10,341
02.10	Payments for military service credits	228	226	231
02.11	Payments for military service credits, legislative proposal not subject to PAYGO			−231
02.12	Tax refund offset	9	10	10
02.14	Attorney fees		1	1
02.99	Total receipts	446,977	479,742	505,087
04.00	Total: Balances and collections	1,069,937	1,210,796	1,363,839
	Appropriation:			
05.01	Current law	−338,891	−352,046	−367,995
05.02	Legislative proposal not subject to PAYGO			231
05.99	Subtotal appropriation	−338,891	−352,046	−367,764
06.20	Reduction pursuant to Public Law 106–51	8	2	
07.99	Total balance, end of year	731,054	858,752	996,075

Program and Financing (in millions of dollars)

Identification code 20–8006–0–7–651		1999 actual	2000 est.	2001 est.
	Obligations by program activity:			
00.01	Direct program	341,375	354,387	370,564
09.01	Reimbursable program	20	39	39
10.00	Total new obligations	341,395	354,426	370,603
	Budgetary resources available for obligation:			
22.00	New budget authority (gross)	341,395	354,426	370,603
23.95	Total new obligations	−341,395	−354,426	−370,603
	New budget authority (gross), detail:			
	Discretionary:			
40.26	Appropriation (trust fund, definite)	1,746	1,749	1,900
40.75	Reduction pursuant to P.L. 106–51	−8		
40.76	Reduction pursuant to P.L. 106–113		−2	
43.00	Appropriation (total discretionary)	1,738	1,747	1,900
	Mandatory:			
60.27	Appropriation (trust fund, indefinite)	445,239	477,992	503,398
60.45	Portion precluded from obligation	−108,094	−127,695	−137,303
62.50	Appropriation (total mandatory)	337,145	350,297	366,095
69.00	Offsetting collections (cash)	2,512	2,382	2,608
70.00	Total new budget authority (gross)	341,395	354,426	370,603
	Change in unpaid obligations:			
72.40	Unpaid obligations, start of year: Obligated balance, start of year	30,353	31,320	32,382
73.10	Total new obligations	341,395	354,426	370,603
73.20	Total outlays (gross)	−340,428	−353,364	−369,405
74.40	Unpaid obligations, end of year: Obligated balance, end of year	31,320	32,382	33,580
	Outlays (gross), detail:			
86.90	Outlays from new discretionary authority	1,355	1,330	1,721
86.93	Outlays from discretionary balances	219	514	269
86.97	Outlays from new mandatory authority	310,866	351,520	367,415
86.98	Outlays from mandatory balances	27,987		
87.00	Total outlays (gross)	340,428	353,364	369,405
	Offsets:			
	Against gross budget authority and outlays:			
	Offsetting collections (cash) from:			
88.00	Federal sources	−2,492	−2,343	−2,569
88.40	Non-Federal sources	−3	−3	−3
88.45	Offsetting governmental collections from the public	−17	−36	−36
88.90	Total, offsetting collections (cash)	−2,512	−2,382	−2,608
	Net budget authority and outlays:			
89.00	Budget authority	338,883	352,044	367,995
90.00	Outlays	337,916	350,982	366,797
	Memorandum (non-add) entries:			
92.01	Total investments, start of year: U.S. securities: Par value	653,282	762,226	891,342
92.02	Total investments, end of year: U.S. securities: Par value	762,226	891,342	1,029,634

Summary of Budget Authority and Outlays

(in millions of dollars)

	1999 actual	2000 est.	2001 est.
Enacted/requested:			
Budget Authority	338,883	352,044	367,995
Outlays	337,915	350,982	366,797
Legislative proposal, not subject to PAYGO:			
Budget Authority			−231
Outlays			

Total:			
Budget Authority	338,883	352,044	367,764
Outlays	337,915	350,982	366,797

The old-age and survivors insurance (OASI) program provides monthly cash benefits to retired workers and their dependents and to survivors of deceased workers.

Status of Funds (in millions of dollars)

Identification code 20–8006–0–7–651		1999 actual	2000 est.	2001 est.
	Unexpended balance, start of year:			
0100	Treasury balance	32	150	−208
0101	U.S. Securities: Par value	653,282	762,226	891,342
0199	Total balance, start of year	653,313	762,374	891,134
	Cash income during the year:			
	Governmental receipts:			
0200	Transfers from general fund (FICA taxes)	364,423	386,948	405,417
0203	Transfers from general fund (SECA taxes)	20,437	23,166	23,532
0204	Refunds	−1,301	−1,531	−1,627
	Proprietary receipts:			
0221	Tax refund offset	9	10	10
0223	Attorney fees		1	1
	Intragovernmental transactions:			
0240	Federal employer contributions (FICA taxes)	6,146	6,508	6,788
0241	Interest received by trust fund	46,847	53,400	60,625
0243	Individual income taxes on OASI benefits	10,176	10,996	10,324
0244	Special benefits for certain aged persons	1		
0245	Pension reform	2	3	6
0246	Credit for unnegotiated OASI checks	9	14	11
0247	Federal payments for military service credits	228	226	231
0248	Federal payments for military service credits, legislative proposal not subject to PAYGO			−231
	Offsetting collections:			
0280	Offsetting collections	2,512	2,382	2,608
0297	Income under present law	449,489	482,124	507,926
0298	Income under proposed legislation			−231
0299	Total cash income	449,489	482,124	507,695
	Cash outgo during year:			
0500	Benefit payments (−)	−332,383	−345,359	−359,989
0501	Payments to Railroad Retirement Board (−)	−3,681	−3,613	−3,511
0502	Administrative expenses (subject to limitation (−)	−1,574	−1,844	−1,990
0503	Administrative expenses (Department of Treasury) (−)	−277	−166	−162
0504	Outlays from offsetting collections (−)	−2,512	−2,382	−2,608
0505	Pre–1957 military service credits (−)			−1,145
0599	Total cash outgo (−)	−340,428	−353,364	−369,405
	Unexpended balance, end of year:			
0700	Uninvested balance	150	−208	−210
0701	U.S. Securities: Par value	762,226	891,342	1,029,634
0799	Total balance, end of year	762,374	891,134	1,029,424

Object Classification (in millions of dollars)

Identification code 20–8006–0–7–651		1999 actual	2000 est.	2001 est.
	Direct obligations:			
25.3	Office of the Inspector General	27	32	35
42.0	Retirement and survivors insurance benefits	333,054	346,305	361,277
44.0	Refunds-Pre 1957 military service credits			1,145
	Undistributed:			
92.0	Reimbursement for administrative expenses of Department of the Treasury	277	166	162
92.0	Payment to railroad retirement account (net settlement) (45 U.S.C. 228g)	3,681	3,613	3,511
	Administrative expenses: Portion of limitation on administrative expenses, Social Security Administration:			
	Limitation on expenses:			
93.0	OASI program	1,844	1,928	1,865
93.0	SSI program	2,492	2,343	2,569
99.0	Subtotal, direct obligations	341,375	354,387	370,564
99.0	Reimbursable obligations	20	39	39
99.9	Total new obligations	341,395	354,426	370,603

Federal Old-Age and Survivor's Insurance Trust Fund

(Legislative proposal, not subject to PAYGO)

Program and Financing (in millions of dollars)

Identification code 20–8006–2–7–651		1999 actual	2000 est.	2001 est.
	Budgetary resources available for obligation:			
22.00	New budget authority (gross)			−231
24.40	Unobligated balance available, end of year			−231
	New budget authority (gross), detail:			
	Mandatory:			
60.27	Appropriation (trust fund, indefinite)			−231
	Net budget authority and outlays:			
89.00	Budget authority			−231
90.00	Outlays			

This schedule reflects the program effects of the Administration's proposal to eliminate social security wage credits for non-monetary compensation to military personnel.

Federal Disability Insurance Trust Fund

Unavailable Collections (in millions of dollars)

Identification code 20–8007–0–7–651		1999 actual	2000 est.	2001 est.
	Balance, start of year:			
01.99	Balance, start of year	70,162	85,724	105,956
	Receipts:			
02.01	Transfers from general fund (FICA taxes)	57,891	64,653	68,849
02.02	Transfers from general fund (SECA taxes)	3,224	3,787	4,000
02.03	Federal employer contributions (FICA taxes)	975	1,088	1,153
02.04	Refunds	−206	−260	−276
02.05	Interest received by trust funds	5,223	6,256	7,513
02.06	CMIA interest	1		
02.08	Federal payments to the FDI trust fund	636	649	644
02.09	Payments for military service credits	36	38	40
02.10	Payments for military service credits, legislative proposal not subject to PAYGO			−40
02.11	Tax refund offset	11	6	6
02.12	Attorney fees		12	25
02.99	Total receipts	67,791	76,229	81,914
04.00	Total: Balances and collections	137,953	161,953	187,870
	Appropriation:			
05.01	Federal disability insurance trust fund	−52,229	−56,019	−60,453
05.02	Legislative proposal not subject to PAYGO			40
05.99	Subtotal appropriation	−52,229	−56,019	−60,413
06.20	Reduction pursuant to Public Law 106–113		22	
07.99	Total balance, end of year	85,724	105,956	127,457

Program and Financing (in millions of dollars)

Identification code 20–8007–0–7–651		1999 actual	2000 est.	2001 est.
	Obligations by program activity:			
10.00	Total new obligations	52,229	55,997	60,453
	Budgetary resources available for obligation:			
22.00	New budget authority (gross)	52,229	55,997	60,453
23.95	Total new obligations	−52,229	−55,997	−60,453
	New budget authority (gross), detail:			
	Discretionary:			
40.26	Appropriation (trust fund, definite)	1,406	1,435	1,534
40.76	Reduction pursuant to P.L. 106–113		−22	
43.00	Appropriation (total discretionary)	1,406	1,413	1,534
	Mandatory:			
60.27	Appropriation (trust fund, indefinite)	66,385	74,816	80,420
60.45	Portion precluded from obligation	−15,562	−20,232	−21,501
62.50	Appropriation (total mandatory)	50,823	54,584	58,919
70.00	Total new budget authority (gross)	52,229	55,997	60,453

Federal Disability Insurance Trust Fund—Continued

Program and Financing (in millions of dollars)—Continued

Identification code 20–8007–0–7–651	1999 actual	2000 est.	2001 est.
Change in unpaid obligations:			
72.40 Unpaid obligations, start of year: Obligated balance, start of year	6,817	6,904	7,244
73.10 Total new obligations	52,229	55,997	60,453
73.20 Total outlays (gross)	−52,142	−55,657	−60,118
74.40 Unpaid obligations, end of year: Obligated balance, end of year	6,904	7,244	7,579
Outlays (gross), detail:			
86.90 Outlays from new discretionary authority	1,293	1,239	1,361
86.93 Outlays from discretionary balances	179	196	203
86.97 Outlays from new mandatory authority	50,670	54,222	58,554
87.00 Total outlays (gross)	52,142	55,657	60,118
Net budget authority and outlays:			
89.00 Budget authority	52,229	55,997	60,453
90.00 Outlays	52,142	55,657	60,118
Memorandum (non-add) entries:			
92.01 Total investments, start of year: U.S. securities: Par value	76,996	92,666	113,213
92.02 Total investments, end of year: U.S. securities: Par value	92,666	113,213	135,023

Summary of Budget Authority and Outlays

(in millions of dollars)

Enacted/requested:	*1999 actual*	*2000 est.*	*2001 est.*
Budget Authority	52,229	55,997	60,453
Outlays	52,142	55,657	60,118
Legislative proposal, not subject to PAYGO:			
Budget Authority			−40
Outlays			
Total:			
Budget Authority	52,229	55,997	60,413
Outlays	52,142	55,657	60,118

The disability insurance (DI) program provides monthly cash benefits for disabled workers under age 65 and their dependents.

Status of Funds (in millions of dollars)

Identification code 20–8007–0–7–651	1999 actual	2000 est.	2001 est.
Unexpended balance, start of year:			
0100 Treasury balance	−17	−37	−13
0101 U.S. Securities: Par value	76,996	92,666	113,213
0199 Total balance, start of year	76,979	92,628	113,200
Cash income during the year:			
Governmental receipts:			
0200 FICA taxes	57,891	64,653	68,849
0203 SECA Taxes	3,224	3,787	4,000
0204 Refunds	−206	−260	−276
Proprietary receipts:			
0222 Tax refund offset	11	6	6
0223 CMIA interest	1		
0224 Attorney user fees		12	25
Intragovernmental transactions:			
0240 Federal employer contributions	975	1,088	1,153
0241 Interest received by trust fund	5,223	6,256	7,513
0243 Individual income taxes on DI benefits	634	646	641
0244 Credit for unnegotiated DI checks	2	3	3
0245 Federal payments for military service credits	36	38	40
0246 Federal payments for military service credits, legislative proposal not subject to PAYGO			−40
0297 Income under present law	67,791	76,229	81,954
0298 Income under proposed legislation			−40
0299 Total cash income	67,791	76,229	81,914
Cash outgo during year:			
0500 Benefit payments (−)	−50,424	−53,964	−58,292
0501 Payments to Railroad Retirement Board (−)	−135	−147	−126
0502 Administrative expenses (subject to limitation) (−)	−1,472	−1,435	−1,564
0503 Administrative expenses (Department of Treasury) (−)	−48	−32	−31
0504 Beneficiary services (−)	−63	−79	−86
0505 Demonstration projects(−)			−12
0506 Pre-1957 military sevice credits (−)			−7
0599 Total cash outgo	−52,142	−55,657	−60,118
Unexpended balance, end of year:			
0700 Uninvested balance	−37	−13	−27
0701 U.S. Securities: Par value	92,666	113,213	135,023
0799 Total balance, end of year	92,628	113,200	134,996

Object Classification (in millions of dollars)

Identification code 20–8007–0–7–651	1999 actual	2000 est.	2001 est.
Purchases of goods and services from Government accounts:			
25.3 Office of the Inspector General	17	19	21
25.3 Beneficiary services	73	79	86
25.3 Demonstration projects	1		12
42.0 Disability insurance benefits	50,635	54,266	58,657
44.0 Refunds—Pre-1957 military service credits			7
Undistributed:			
92.0 Reimbursement for administrative expenses of Department of the Treasury	48	32	31
92.0 Payment to railroad retirement account (net settlement)	135	147	126
93.0 Administrative expenses: Portion of limitation on administrative expenses, Social Security Administration	1,320	1,454	1,513
99.0 Subtotal, direct obligations	52,229	55,997	60,453
99.9 Total new obligations	52,229	55,997	60,453

Disability Insurance Trust Fund

(Legislative proposal, not subject to PAYGO)

Program and Financing (in millions of dollars)

Identification code 20–8007–2–7–651	1999 actual	2000 est.	2001 est.
Budgetary resources available for obligation:			
22.00 New budget authority (gross)			−40
24.40 Unobligated balance available, end of year			−40
New budget authority (gross), detail:			
Mandatory:			
60.27 Appropriation (trust fund, indefinite)			−40
Net budget authority and outlays:			
89.00 Budget authority			−40
90.00 Outlays			

This schedule reflects the program effects of the Administration's proposal to eliminate social security wage credits for non-monetary compensation to military personnel.

Limitation on Administrative Expenses

For necessary expenses, including the hire of two passenger motor vehicles, and not to exceed $10,000 for official reception and representation expenses, not more than [$6,111,871,000] *$6,593,000,000* may be expended, as authorized by section 201(g)(1) of the Social Security Act, from any one or all of the trust funds referred to therein: *Provided*, That not less than $1,800,000 shall be for the Social Security Advisory Board: *Provided further*, That unobligated balances at the end of fiscal year [2000] *2001* not needed for fiscal year [2000] *2001* shall remain available until expended to invest in the Social Security Administration [computing network] *information technology and telecommunications hardware and software infrastructure*, including related equipment and non-payroll administrative expenses [associated solely with this network: *Provided further*, That reimbursement to the trust funds under this heading for expenditures for official time for employees of the Social Security Administration pursuant to section 7131 of title 5, United States Code, and for facilities or support services for labor organizations pursuant to policies, regulations, or procedures referred to in section 7135(b) of such title shall be made by the Secretary of the Treasury, with interest, from amounts in the general fund not otherwise appropriated, as soon as possible after such expenditures are made].

[From funds provided under the previous paragraph, notwithstanding the provision under this heading in Public Law 105–277 regarding unobligated balances at the end of fiscal year 1999 not needed for such fiscal year, an amount not to exceed $100,000,000 from such unobligated balances shall, in addition to funding already available under this heading for fiscal year 2000, be available for necessary expenses.]

From funds provided under the first paragraph, not less than $200,000,000 shall be available for conducting continuing disability reviews.

In addition to funding already available under this heading, and subject to the same terms and conditions, [$405,000,000] *$450,000,000*, to remain available until September 30, [2001] *2002*, for continuing disability reviews as authorized by section 103 of Public Law 104–121 and section 10203 of Public Law 105–33. The term "continuing disability reviews" means reviews and redeterminations as defined under section 201(g)(1)(A) of the Social Security Act, as amended.

In addition, [$80,000,000] *$91,000,000* to be derived from administration fees in excess of $5.00 per supplementary payment collected pursuant to section 1616(d) of the Social Security Act or section 212(b)(3) of Public Law 93–66, which shall remain available until expended. To the extent that the amounts collected pursuant to such section 1616(d) or 212(b)(3) in fiscal year [2000] *2001* exceed [$80,000,000] *$91,000,000*, the amounts shall be available in fiscal year [2001] *2002* only to the extent provided in advance in appropriations Acts.

[From amounts previously made available under this heading for a state-of-the-art computing network, not to exceed $100,000,000 shall be available for necessary expenses under this heading, subject to the same terms and conditions.]

From funds [provided under the first paragraph, the Commissioner of Social Security may direct up to $3,000,000, in addition to funds] previously appropriated for this purpose, *any unobligated balances at the end of fiscal year 2000 shall be available* to continue Federal-State partnerships which will evaluate means to promote Medicare buy-in programs targeted to elderly and disabled individuals under titles XVIII and XIX of the Social Security Act. *(Departments of Labor, Health and Human Services, and Education, and Related Agencies Appropriations Act, 2000, as enacted by section 1000(a)(4) of the Consolidated Appropriations Act, 2000 (P.L. 106–113).)*

Program and Financing (in millions of dollars)

	1999 actual	2000 est.	2001 est.
Obligations by program activity:			
Direct program	6,484	6,860	7,134
Reimbursable program	20	39	39
Total obligations	6,504	6,899	7,173
Budgetary resources available for obligation:			
Unobligated balance available, start of year:			
Appropriation: U.S. securities: Par value	390	288	0
New budget authority (gross)	6,451	6,611	7,173
Recovery of prior year obligations	4	0	0
Unobligated balance expiring	−33	0	0
Total budgetary resources available for obligation	6,792	6,899	7,173
New obligations	6,504	6,899	7,173
Unobligated balance available, end of year:			
Appropriation: U.S. securities: Par value	288	0	0
New budget authority (gross), detail:			
Limitation on administrative expenses (LAE):			
Appropriations	6,071	6,192	6,684
Reduction pursuant to P.L. 106–51	−8	0	0
Reduction pursuant to P.L. 106–113	0	−5	0
Distribution by funding sources:			
Old Age and Survivors Insurance Trust Fund	1,711	1,715	1,865
Disability Insurance Trust Fund	1,211	1,209	1,273
Supplemental Security Income (SSI) Appropriation:			
Payment to OASI Trust Fund	2,114	2,142	2,359
Hospital Insurance Trust Fund	531	556	581
Supplementary Medical Insurance Trust Fund	421	482	513
Increased fee for administration of State supplemental payments	75	80	91
Special Benefits for Certain World War II Veterans permanent indefinite appropriation	0	3	2
Spending authority from reimbursable agreements	33	39	39
Subtotal, LAE	6,096	6,226	6,723
Adjustments to discretionary caps:			
Continuing disability reviews	355	405	450
Reduction pursuant to P.L. 106–113	0	−20	0
Total, including adjustments to discretionary caps	6,451	6,611	7,173
Change in unpaid obligations:			
Unpaid obligations, start of year: Obligated balance:			
U.S. Securities: Par value	1,164	1,155	1,336
New obligations	6,504	6,899	7,173
Total outlays (gross)	6,513	6,718	7,316
Unpaid obligations, end of year: Obligated balance:			
U.S. Securities: Par value	1,155	1,336	1,193
Outlay (gross), detail:			
Outlays from new current authority	5,650	5,821	6,469
Outlays from current balances	863	897	847
Total outlays (gross)	6,513	6,718	7,316
Offsets:			
Against gross budget authority and outlays:			
Offsetting collections (cash) from:			
Federal sources	13	26	26
Non-Federal sources	7	13	13
Total offsetting collections (cash)	20	39	39
Net budget authority and outlays:			
Budget authority	6,418	6,572	7,134
Outlays	6,493	6,679	7,277

The Limitation on administrative expenses account provides resources for the Social Security Administration (SSA) to administer the old-age, survivors, and disability insurance programs, the supplemental security income program, the special benefits for certain World War II veterans program and certain health insurance functions for the aged, disabled, and economically disadvantaged.

Object Classification (in millions of dollars)

Identification code 20–8007–0–7–651		1999 actual	2000 est.	2001 est.
	Limitation Acct—Direct Obligations:			
	Personnel compensation:			
11.1	Full-time permanent	2,728	2,987	3,125
11.3	Other than full-time permanent	127	138	144
11.5	Other personnel compensation	194	121	60
11.8	Special personal services payments	1	1	1
11.9	Total personnel compensation	3,050	3,247	3,330
12.1	Civilian personnel benefits	620	707	762
13.0	Benefits for former personnel	3	3	3
21.0	Travel and transportation of persons	45	46	48
22.0	Transportation of things	6	7	8
23.1	Rental payments to GSA	358	364	387
23.2	Rental payments to others	2	2	2
23.3	Communications, utilities, and miscellaneous charges	261	277	263
24.0	Printing and reproduction	24	38	41
25.1	Advisory and assistance services	8	7	8
25.2	Other services	1,654	1,675	1,729
25.3	Purchases of goods and services from Government accounts	61	53	74
25.4	Operation and maintenance of facilities	60	111	137
25.7	Operation and maintenance of equipment	87	110	120
26.0	Supplies and materials	34	49	55
31.0	Equipment	165	114	126
32.0	Land and structures	29	35	28
42.0	Insurance claims and indemnities	10	8	8
43.0	Interest and dividends	7	7	5
93.0	Limitation on expenses	−6,484	−6,860	−7,134
99.0	Subtotal, limitation acct—direct obligations	....	....	....
	Limitation Acct—Reimbursable Obligations:			
	Personnel compensation:			
11.1	Full-time permanent	11	18	18

LIMITATION ON ADMINISTRATIVE EXPENSES—Continued

Object Classification (in millions of dollars)—Continued

Identification code 20–8007–0–7–651		1999 actual	2000 est.	2001 est.
11.5	Other personnel compensation	1	1	1
11.9	Total personnel compensation	12	19	19
12.1	Civilian personnel benefits	2	3	3
23.1	Rental payments to GSA	1	1	2
23.3	Communications, utilities, and miscellaneous charges	1	1	1
25.3	Purchases of goods and services from Government accounts	4	12	11
25.4	Operation and maintenance of facilities		1	1
25.7	Operation and maintenance of equipment		1	1
31.0	Equipment		1	1
93.0	Limitation on expenses	−20	−39	−39
99.0	Subtotal, limitation acct—reimbursable obligations			

Personnel Summary

Identification code 20–8007–0–7–651		1999 actual	2000 est.	2001 est.
	Limitation account—direct:			
6001	Total compensable workyears: Full-time equivalent employment	62,314	62,514	62,256
	Limitation account—reimbursable:			
7001	Total compensable workyears: Full-time equivalent employment	230	296	296

GENERAL FUND RECEIPT ACCOUNTS

(in millions of dollars)

	1999 actual	2000 est.	2001 est.
Offsetting receipts from the public:			
75–241800 Receipts from SSI administrative fee	147	148	150
75–309600 Recovery of beneficiary overpayments from SSI program	1,330	1,400	1,462
General Fund Offsetting receipts from the public	1,477	1,548	1,612
Intragovernmental payments:			
20–310510 Quinquennial adjustment for military service credits, FOASI			1,145
20–310520 Quinquennial adjustment for military service credits, Federal disability insurance			7
General Fund Intragovernmental payments			1,152

As directed by Section 104 of P.L. 103–296, the Social Security Independence and Program Improvements Act of 1994, the Commissioner of Social Security shall prepare an annual budget for the Social Security Administration (SSA), which shall be submitted by the President to the Congress without revision, together with the President's annual budget for SSA.

The Commissioner's annual budget for fiscal year 2001 includes a total administrative budget of $7,466 million. This represents $7,390 million for SSA administrative expenses (including $450 million in funds not subject to the discretionary spending caps for conducting continuing disability reviews and $40 million in no-year capital investment funds) and $76 million for the Office of Inspector General.

OTHER INDEPENDENT AGENCIES

ADVISORY COUNCIL ON HISTORIC PRESERVATION

Federal Funds

General and special funds:

Salaries and Expenses

For necessary expenses of the Advisory Council on Historic Preservation (Public Law 89–665, as amended), [$3,000,000] *$3,189,000*: *Provided*, That none of these funds shall be available for compensation of level V of the Executive Schedule or higher positions. *(Department of the Interior and Related Agencies Appropriations Act, 2000, as enacted by section 1000(a)(3) of the Consolidated Appropriations Act, 2000 (P.L. 106–113).)*

Program and Financing (in millions of dollars)

Identification code 95–2300–0–1–303		1999 actual	2000 est.	2001 est.
	Obligations by program activity:			
10.00	Total new obligations	3	3	3
	Budgetary resources available for obligation:			
22.00	New budget authority (gross)	3	3	3
23.95	Total new obligations	–3	–3	–3
	New budget authority (gross), detail:			
	Discretionary:			
40.00	Appropriation	3	3	3
	Change in unpaid obligations:			
73.10	Total new obligations	3	3	3
73.20	Total outlays (gross)	–3	–3	–3
	Outlays (gross), detail:			
86.90	Outlays from new discretionary authority	3	3	3
	Net budget authority and outlays:			
89.00	Budget authority	3	3	3
90.00	Outlays	3	3	3

The Council provides independent advice to the President and the Congress relating to the national historic preservation program.

Object Classification (in millions of dollars)

Identification code 95–2300–0–1–303		1999 actual	2000 est.	2001 est.
11.1	Direct obligations: Personnel compensation: Full-time permanent	2	2	2
99.5	Below reporting threshold	1	1	1
99.9	Total new obligations	3	3	3

Personnel Summary

Identification code 95–2300–0–1–303		1999 actual	2000 est.	2001 est.
1001	Total compensable workyears: Full-time equivalent employment	36	34	34

APPALACHIAN REGIONAL COMMISSION

Federal Funds

General and special funds:

Appalachian Regional Commission

For expenses necessary to carry out the programs authorized by the Appalachian Regional Development Act of 1965, as amended, **for necessary expenses for the Federal Co-Chairman and the alternate on the Appalachian Regional Commission, for payment of the Federal share of the administrative expenses of the Commission, including services as authorized by 5 U.S.C. 3109, and hire of passenger motor vehicles, [$66,400,000] *$71,400,000*, to remain available until expended. *(Energy and Water Development Appropriations Act, 2000.)***

Program and Financing (in millions of dollars)

Identification code 46–0200–0–1–452		1999 actual	2000 est.	2001 est.
	Obligations by program activity:			
	Direct program:			
	Appalachian regional development programs:			
01.01	Appalachian development highway system	16	8	
01.02	Area development program	89	73	61
01.03	Local development district and technical assistance program	8	6	6
01.91	Total Appalachian regional development programs	113	87	67
	Salaries and expenses:			
02.01	Federal Co-chairman and staff	1	1	1
02.02	Administrative expenses	3	3	3
02.91	Total salaries and expenses	4	4	4
10.00	Total new obligations	117	91	71
	Budgetary resources available for obligation:			
21.40	Unobligated balance available, start of year	59	20	
22.00	New budget authority (gross)	66	66	71
22.10	Resources available from recoveries of prior year obligations	10	5	
23.90	Total budgetary resources available for obligation	135	91	71
23.95	Total new obligations	–117	–91	–71
24.40	Unobligated balance available, end of year	20		
	New budget authority (gross), detail:			
	Discretionary:			
40.00	Appropriation	66	66	71
	Change in unpaid obligations:			
72.40	Unpaid obligations, start of year: Obligated balance, start of year	328	292	227
73.10	Total new obligations	117	91	71
73.20	Total outlays (gross)	–141	–151	–113
73.45	Adjustments in unexpired accounts	–10	–5	
74.40	Unpaid obligations, end of year: Obligated balance, end of year	292	227	185
	Outlays (gross), detail:			
86.90	Outlays from new discretionary authority	6	6	7
86.93	Outlays from discretionary balances	135	145	106
87.00	Total outlays (gross)	141	151	113
	Net budget authority and outlays:			
89.00	Budget authority	66	66	71
90.00	Outlays	141	151	113

This appropriation establishes a framework for joint Federal and State efforts to create opportunities for self-sustaining economic development and improved quality of life for the people of Appalachia. Program investments are made in the Appalachian Region for wide-ranging assistance including development highways and area development. The States, acting through the Appalachian Regional Commission (ARC), are responsible for recommending local and State projects within their borders for assistance under this program. Special targeting to distressed counties is a part of the State allocation formula.

General and special funds—Continued

APPALACHIAN REGIONAL COMMISSION—Continued

Appalachian development highway system.—The Appalachian development highway system (ADHS), including local access roads, is designed to improve the accessibility of Appalachia; to reduce highway transportation costs to and within Appalachia; and to provide the highway transportation facilities necessary to accelerate the overall development of Appalachia. Studies have found that the ADHS has been important to economic development in the Region.

Starting in FY 1999, funding for the ADHS is provided solely from the Highway Trust Fund. The Transportation Equity Act for the 21st Century (TEA21) authorized $2.25 billion for the construction of the Appalachian Development Highway System (ADHS) and local access road projects under Section 201 of the Appalachian Regional Development Act. TEA21 authorizes $450 million annually to be appropriated out of the Highway Trust Fund for each of fiscal years 1999 through 2003. The ARC exercises programmatic and administrative control over these funds, as it has with appropriated funds.

The cumulative status of the system of roads, including mileage prefinanced by the States, follows:

Development systems miles (Prefinanced miles included) (cumulative):	1999 actual	2000 est.*	2001 est.*
Miles contracted	2,457	2,482	2,501
Miles completed	2,321	2,340	2,350
Access Roads (cumulative):			
Miles contracted	890	887	889
Miles completed	863	864	866
Funds committed (cumulative-in millions of dollars):			
Development highway	4,757	5,055	5,406
Access roads	231	233	235
Administration and other	45	47	49
Totals	5,033	5,335	5,690
Prefinanced by States	204	157	135
Annual obligations ($ millions)	404	450	450

* Includes TEA21 funds.

Area development program.—Area development funds are provided to each of the Appalachian States by allocation. This funding is used to help the regional economy become more competitive by putting in place the building blocks for self-sustaining economic development, with assistance targeted at the Region's most distressed and underdeveloped counties.

The Appalachian Regional Development Reform Act of 1988 reflects the ARC's prior policy of targeting resources to the region's most distressed counties. By FY 1999, nearly half of all ARC program funding went to projects in the 108 counties designated as economically distressed. These counties represent about one quarter of the region's total and contain roughly 10% of the region's population

The area development program funds projects which advance the goals and objectives of ARC's strategic plan. This strategic plan commits ARC to achieving five broad goals which are undergirded by 14 objectives. These five goals are: (1) Appalachian residents will have the skills and knowledge necessary to compete in the world economy in the 21st century; (2) Appalachian communities will have the physical infrastructure necessary for self-sustaining economic development and improved quality of life; (3) the people of Appalachia will have the vision and capacity to mobilize and work together for sustained economic progress and improvement of their communities; (4) Appalachian residents will have access to financial and technical resources to help build dynamic and self-sustaining local economies; and, (5) Appalachian residents will have access to affordable, quality health care. The Commission has taken aggressive steps to ensure that the area development program will make progress on accomplishing these goals, to better target resources to those communities with the greatest needs, and to increase flexibility in project submission.

Each Governor submits for Commission approval an annual strategy statement detailing the areas of emphasis within the Region for ARC funds. All project applications submitted by the Governors describe the goals and objectives, and projected inputs, outputs, and outcomes. During the project implenentation cycle and after project completion, projected outputs and outcomes will be compared to actual results.

In addition to the regular allocation of area development funds to states, the ARC identifies regional problems and opportunities and sets aside resources for special initiatives. The ongoing entrepreneurship initiative seeks to ensure that Appalachian communities have the commitment and resources to help entrepreneurs start and expand local businesses. The budget provides $10 million for the entrepreneurship initiative to continue and build upon progress made to date. This includes assisting over 80 projects, leveraging roughly $9 million to complement ARC resources, and helping establish or expand over 1,200 businesses while creating 1,300 jobs.

The budget for 2001 provides $61 million for area development.

The approximate project workload follows:

	1999 actual	2000 est.	2001 est.
Area development projects	483	487	490

Local development districts and technical assistance programs.—The multi-county local development districts (LDDs) are the mechanism for ensuring that the local governments in Appalachia plan and work together on a regional basis. LLD funding from the ARC provides a cost-share with member governments, enabling local professional staff to help plan, initiate, and implement projects at the grass roots level. Technical assistance serves to strengthen the state and local governments, LDDs and non-profit organizations in the Region. TEA21 added seven new counties to the Region, for a total of 406. This increased the number of LDDs served from 69 to 71. The 2001 Budget provides $5 million for the LDDs and $1 million for technical assistance, with the approximate approved workload as follows:

	1999 actual	2000 est.	2001 est.
Planning districts aided	71	71	71
Technical assistance projects	20	22	24

Salaries and expenses.—The Federal Co-Chairman represents the Federal Government on the Commission and leads in the coordination of the Appalachian program with Federal agencies. Since 1989, the Office of the Federal Co-Chairman includes an Inspector General.

The Federal Government contributes half of the expenses of a professional staff which works with the States and the Federal staff in operating the program. The other half of these non-Federal employee expenses are provided by member States. The budget for 2001 provides $4 million for salaries and expenses.

Object Classification (in millions of dollars)

Identification code 46–0200–0–1–452		1999 actual	2000 est.	2001 est.
	Direct obligations:			
11.1	Personnel compensation: Full-time permanent	1	1	1
25.2	Other services	3	3	3
41.0	Grants, subsidies, and contributions	35	21	21
99.0	Subtotal, direct obligations	39	25	25
	Allocation Account:			
11.1	Personnel compensation: Full-time permanent	2	1	1
41.0	Grants, subsidies, and contributions	76	65	45
99.0	Subtotal, allocation account	78	66	46
99.9	Total new obligations	117	91	71

Obligations are distributed as follows:			
Appalachian Regional Commission	47	46	39
Department of Agriculture	24	19	19
Department of Commerce	9	3	2
Department of Defense	0	0	0
Department of Education	1	1	1
Department of Energy	0	0	0
Department of Health and Human Services	0	0	0
Department of Housing and Urban Development	14	11	8
Department of Interior	0	0	0
Department of Transportation	16	8	0
Environmental Protection Agency	2	1	1
Tennessee Valley Authority	4	2	1

Personnel Summary

Identification code 46–0200–0–1–452	1999 actual	2000 est.	2001 est.
1001 Total compensable workyears: Full-time equivalent employment	10	11	11

Trust Funds

Miscellaneous Trust Funds

Unavailable Collections (in millions of dollars)

Identification code 46–9971–0–7–452	1999 actual	2000 est.	2001 est.
Balance, start of year:			
01.99 Balance, start of year	....	....	....
Receipts:			
02.01 General fund contributions, Appalachian Regional Commission	3	3	3
02.02 Fees for services, Appalachian Regional Commission	3	3	3
02.99 Total receipts	6	6	6
Appropriation:			
05.01 Miscellaneous trust funds	−6	−6	−6
07.99 Total balance, end of year	....	....	....

Program and Financing (in millions of dollars)

Identification code 46–9971–0–7–452	1999 actual	2000 est.	2001 est.
Obligations by program activity:			
10.00 Total new obligations	6	6	6
Budgetary resources available for obligation:			
21.40 Unobligated balance available, start of year	1	1	1
22.00 New budget authority (gross)	6	6	6
23.90 Total budgetary resources available for obligation	7	7	7
23.95 Total new obligations	−6	−6	−6
24.40 Unobligated balance available, end of year	1	1	1
New budget authority (gross), detail:			
Mandatory:			
60.27 Appropriation (trust fund, indefinite)	6	6	6
Change in unpaid obligations:			
72.40 Unpaid obligations, start of year: Obligated balance, start of year	....	1	1
73.10 Total new obligations	6	6	6
73.20 Total outlays (gross)	−5	−5	−5
74.40 Unpaid obligations, end of year: Obligated balance, end of year	1	1	1
Outlays (gross), detail:			
86.97 Outlays from new mandatory authority	4	5	5
86.98 Outlays from mandatory balances	1	1	1
87.00 Total outlays (gross)	5	5	5
Net budget authority and outlays:			
89.00 Budget authority	6	6	6
90.00 Outlays	5	5	5

As authorized in the Appalachian Regional Development Act, the 13 Appalachian States share with the Federal Government the administrative expenses of the Appalachian Regional Commission.

Object Classification (in millions of dollars)

Identification code 46–9971–0–7–452	1999 actual	2000 est.	2001 est.
11.8 Personnel compensation: Special personal services payments	4	4	4
12.1 Civilian personnel benefits	1	1	1
23.2 Rental payments to others	1	1	1
99.9 Total new obligations	6	6	6

ARCHITECTURAL AND TRANSPORTATION BARRIERS COMPLIANCE BOARD

Federal Funds

General and special funds:

Salaries and Expenses

For expenses necessary for the Architectural and Transportation Barriers Compliance Board, as authorized by section 502 of the Rehabilitation Act of 1973, as amended, [$4,633,000] *$4,795,000*: *Provided*, That, notwithstanding any other provision of law, there may be credited to this appropriation funds received for publications and training expenses. *(Department of Transportation and Related Agencies Appropriations Act, 2000.)*

Program and Financing (in millions of dollars)

Identification code 95–3200–0–1–751	1999 actual	2000 est.	2001 est.
Obligations by program activity:			
10.00 Total new obligations	4	5	5
Budgetary resources available for obligation:			
22.00 New budget authority (gross)	4	5	5
23.95 Total new obligations	−4	−5	−5
New budget authority (gross), detail:			
Discretionary:			
40.00 Appropriation	4	5	5
Change in unpaid obligations:			
72.40 Unpaid obligations, start of year: Obligated balance, start of year	4	4	5
73.10 Total new obligations	4	5	5
73.20 Total outlays (gross)	−4	−5	−5
74.40 Unpaid obligations, end of year: Obligated balance, end of year	4	5	5
Outlays (gross), detail:			
86.90 Outlays from new discretionary authority	4	5	5
86.93 Outlays from discretionary balances	....	....	1
87.00 Total outlays (gross)	4	5	5
Net budget authority and outlays:			
89.00 Budget authority	4	5	5
90.00 Outlays	4	5	5

The Architectural and Transportation Barriers Compliance Board (Access Board) was established by section 502 of the Rehabilitation Act of 1973 to ensure compliance with the Architectural Barriers Act of 1968. Since that time, the Access Board has been the only independent Federal agency whose primary mission is accessibility for people with disabilities. The Access Board has responsibility under three major pieces of legislation: the Architectural Barriers Act of 1968 (ABA); the Americans with Disabilities Act of 1990 (ADA); and the Telecommunications Act of 1996.

The Access Board's first major responsibility was to enforce the ABA, ensuring accessibility in facilities built, altered, or leased using certain Federal funds. In fiscal year 2001, the Board will continue to process, investigate, and resolve complaints of noncompliance. The Access Board has a proven record of voluntary, amicable resolution of access issues.

General and special funds—Continued

SALARIES AND EXPENSES—Continued

Under the Americans with Disabilities Act (ADA), the Access Board gained responsibility for two major public roles: to develop minimum accessibility guidelines for places of public accommodation, commercial facilities, State and local government facilities, and transportation vehicles and facilities, all of which are covered under the ADA; and to offer training and technical assistance to individuals and organizations throughout the country on removing architectural, transportation and communication barriers.

In pursuing these responsibilities under the ADA, the Board uses citizens' advisory committees, negotiated rulemaking, and other communication channels to encourage the public's full participation in the Federal rulemaking process for developing its ADA Accessibility Guidelines (ADAAG). In addition, the Board is working with the building industry toward the development of a single set of minimum accessibility guidelines, using ADAAG as the basis.

Under the Telecommunications Act, the Access Board is charged with developing accessibility guidelines for telecommunications equipment and customer premises equipment, in conjunction with the Federal Communications Commission. The Telecommunications Act requires that such equipment be "designed, developed, and fabricated to be accessible to and usable by individuals with disabilities, if readily achievable."

Consistent with the Government Performance and Results Act, (GPRA) the Access Board has adopted the following mission statement to guide its programs: *The Board is the catalyst for achieving an accessible America.* This statement recognizes that achieving an accessible America requires bringing together public and private sectors. The Board has established long range goals that aim to bring together public and private sectors for achieving an accessible America. The Board's long-range goals are to:

- Take a leadership role in the development of codes and standards for accessibility
- Work in partnership with Federal agencies and others to make the Federal government a model of compliance with accessibility standards
- Be known as the leading source of information about accessibility and disseminate that information to our customers in effective ways

In FY 2001, the Board will continue to work on its major goal of taking a leadership role in the development of codes and standards for accessibility. The Board plans to complete work on a major revision to its basic ADA guidelines, and will add a section on access to recreation facilities and outdoor developed areas. Pursuant to the amendments to Section 508 of the Rehabilitation Act made by P.L. 105–220, the Board will develop accessibility standards for electronic and information technology purchased by the Federal government. Following its second goal, the Board will continue work with other Federal agencies to identify and publicize best practices in compliance with the Architectural Barriers Act. In line with its third goal, the Board will be in position to make better use of its web pages to disseminate information to the public. For example, pursuant to P.L. 105–394, which extends the Section 508 purchasing requirements to State governments and mandates that the Access Board will train and provide technical assistance to Federal and State officials on the new requirements, the Board will develop a web based training application available to both Federal and State users and sponsor a nation-wide training conference.

Object Classification (in millions of dollars)

Identification code 95–3200–0–1–751	1999 actual	2000 est.	2001 est.
11.1 Direct obligations: Personnel compensation: Full-time permanent	2	3	3
99.5 Below reporting threshold	2	2	2
99.9 Total new obligations	4	5	5

Personnel Summary

Identification code 95–3200–0–1–751	1999 actual	2000 est.	2001 est.
1001 Total compensable workyears: Full-time equivalent employment	31	30	30

BARRY GOLDWATER SCHOLARSHIP AND EXCELLENCE IN EDUCATION FOUNDATION

Trust Funds

BARRY GOLDWATER SCHOLARSHIP AND EXCELLENCE IN EDUCATION FOUNDATION FUND

Unavailable Collections (in millions of dollars)

Identification code 95–8281–0–7–502	1999 actual	2000 est.	2001 est.
Balance, start of year:			
01.99 Balance, start of year	....	....	....
Receipts:			
02.01 Interest on investments, Barry Goldwater Scholarship and Excellence in Education Foundation	3	4	4
Appropriation:			
05.01 Barry Goldwater Scholarship and Excellence in Education Foundation	−3	−4	−4
07.99 Total balance, end of year	....	....	....

Program and Financing (in millions of dollars)

Identification code 95–8281–0–7–502	1999 actual	2000 est.	2001 est.
Obligations by program activity:			
10.00 Total new obligations (object class 41.0)	3	3	3
Budgetary resources available for obligation:			
21.40 Unobligated balance available, start of year	61	61	62
22.00 New budget authority (gross)	3	4	4
23.90 Total budgetary resources available for obligation	64	65	66
23.95 Total new obligations	−3	−3	−3
24.40 Unobligated balance available, end of year	61	62	63
New budget authority (gross), detail:			
Mandatory:			
60.27 Appropriation (trust fund, indefinite)	3	4	4
Change in unpaid obligations:			
73.10 Total new obligations	3	3	3
73.20 Total outlays (gross)	−3	−3	−3
Outlays (gross), detail:			
86.97 Outlays from new mandatory authority	3	3	3
Net budget authority and outlays:			
89.00 Budget authority	3	4	4
90.00 Outlays	3	3	3
Memorandum (non-add) entries:			
92.01 Total investments, start of year: U.S. securities: Par value	61	61	62
92.02 Total investments, end of year: U.S. securities: Par value	61	62	63

Public Law 99–661 established the Barry Goldwater Scholarship and Excellence in Education Foundation to operate the scholarship program that is the sole permanent tribute to the former Senator from Arizona. The Foundation awards scholarships to outstanding undergraduate students who intend to pursue careers in mathematics, science and engineering. The Foundation awards approximately 300 scholarships each fiscal year.

Personnel Summary

Identification code 95–8281–0–7–502	1999 actual	2000 est.	2001 est.
1001 Total compensable workyears: Full-time equivalent employment	2	2	2

BROADCASTING BOARD OF GOVERNORS

Federal Funds

General and special funds:

INTERNATIONAL BROADCASTING OPERATIONS

For expenses necessary to enable the Broadcasting Board of Governors, as authorized by the United States Information and Educational Exchange Act of 1948, as amended, the United States International Broadcasting Act of 1994, as amended, Reorganization Plan No. 2 of 1977, as amended, and the Foreign Affairs Reform and Restructuring Act of 1998, to carry out international communication activities, [$388,421,000] *$405,056,000*, of which not to exceed $16,000 may be used for official receptions within the United States as authorized by section 804(3) of such Act of 1948 (22 U.S.C. 1747(3)), not to exceed $35,000 may be used for representation abroad as authorized by section 302 of such Act of 1948 (22 U.S.C. 1452) and section 905 of the Foreign Service Act of 1980 (22 U.S.C. 4085), and not to exceed $39,000 may be used for official reception and representation expenses of Radio Free Europe/Radio Liberty; and in addition, notwithstanding any other provision of law, not to exceed $2,000,000 in receipts from advertising and revenue from business ventures, not to exceed $500,000 in receipts from cooperating international organizations, and not to exceed $1,000,000 in receipts from privatization efforts of the Voice of America and the International Broadcasting Bureau, to remain available until expended for carrying out authorized purposes. *(Department of State and Related Agencies Appropriations Act, 2000, as enacted by section 1000(a)(1) of the Consolidated Appropriations Act, 2000 (P.L. 106–113).)*

Program and Financing (in millions of dollars)

Identification code 95–0206–0–1–154		1999 actual	2000 est.	2001 est.
	Obligations by program activity:			
00.01	International Broadcasting Bureau	269	302	312
00.03	Radio Free Europe/Radio Liberty	75	68	69
00.04	Radio Free Asia	24	22	24
01.00	Subtotal, direct obligations	368	392	405
09.01	Reimbursable program	1	1	1
10.00	Total new obligations	369	393	406
	Budgetary resources available for obligation:			
21.40	Unobligated balance available, start of year	6	20	
22.00	New budget authority (gross)	363	373	406
22.10	Resources available from recoveries of prior year obligations	17		
22.21	Unobligated balance transferred to other accounts	−1		
22.22	Unobligated balance transferred from other accounts	4		
23.90	Total budgetary resources available for obligation	389	393	406
23.95	Total new obligations	−369	−393	−406
24.40	Unobligated balance available, end of year	20		
	New budget authority (gross), detail:			
	Discretionary:			
40.00	Appropriation	362	388	405
40.36	Unobligated balance rescinded		−15	
40.75	Reduction pursuant to P.L. 106–51	−1		
40.76	Reduction pursuant to P.L. 106–113		−1	
42.00	Transferred from other accounts	1		
43.00	Appropriation (total discretionary)	362	372	405
68.00	Spending authority from offsetting collections: Offsetting collections (cash)	1	1	1
70.00	Total new budget authority (gross)	363	373	406
	Change in unpaid obligations:			
72.40	Unpaid obligations, start of year: Obligated balance, start of year	75	63	71
73.10	Total new obligations	369	393	406
73.20	Total outlays (gross)	−363	−385	−403
73.45	Adjustments in unexpired accounts	−17		
74.40	Unpaid obligations, end of year: Obligated balance, end of year	63	71	72
	Outlays (gross), detail:			
86.90	Outlays from new discretionary authority	317	313	341
86.93	Outlays from discretionary balances	47	72	62
87.00	Total outlays (gross)	363	385	403
	Offsets:			
	Against gross budget authority and outlays:			
88.00	Offsetting collections (cash) from: Federal sources	−1	−1	−1
	Net budget authority and outlays:			
89.00	Budget authority	362	372	405
90.00	Outlays	363	384	402

This appropriation provides operational funding for the Broadcasting Board of Governors (BBG), the Voice of America, Radio Free Europe/Radio Liberty (RFE/RL), Radio Free Asia, and the necessary engineering and technical, program and administrative support activities.

Funding for Radio and Television Broadcasting to Cuba is provided in a separate account.

The Foreign Affairs Reform and Restructuring Act of 1998, enacted as part of P.L. 105–277, abolished the U.S. Information Agency and established the BBG as an independent agency. The BBG's responsibilities remain consistent with those delineated in the International Broadcasting Act of 1994. As part of the consolidation with the State Department, USIA transferred associated support funding and personnel, where appropriate, to the BBG for various administrative functions that were provided by USIA through FY 1999. Personnel and funding associated with interactive dialogues with foreign media using Worldnet were transferred to the Department of State.

In compliance with the Government Performance and Results Act, the BBG will submit a FY 2001 performance plan.

Object Classification (in millions of dollars)

Identification code 95–0206–0–1–154		1999 actual	2000 est.	2001 est.
	Direct obligations:			
	Personnel compensation:			
11.1	Full-time permanent	115	126	133
11.3	Other than full-time permanent	5	6	6
11.5	Other personnel compensation	7	8	8
11.9	Total personnel compensation	127	140	147
12.1	Civilian personnel benefits	28	31	33
21.0	Travel and transportation of persons	6	5	5
22.0	Transportation of things	2	2	2
23.1	Rental payments to GSA		17	17
23.2	Rental payments to others	20	17	18
23.3	Communications, utilities, and miscellaneous charges	30	36	38
25.1	Advisory and assistance services	1		
	Other services:			
25.2	Other services	25	30	28
25.2	Other services			
25.4	Operation and maintenance of facilities	3	3	3
25.5	Research and development contracts	1	1	2
25.7	Operation and maintenance of equipment	2	3	3
26.0	Supplies and materials	14	12	12
31.0	Equipment	10	5	4
41.0	Grants, subsidies, and contributions	99	90	93
99.0	Subtotal, direct obligations	368	392	405
99.0	Reimbursable obligations	1	1	1
99.9	Total new obligations	369	393	406

General and special funds—Continued

INTERNATIONAL BROADCASTING OPERATIONS—Continued

Personnel Summary

Identification code 95–0206–0–1–154	1999 actual	2000 est.	2001 est.
1001 Total compensable workyears: Full-time equivalent employment	2,292	2,635	2,639

BROADCASTING CAPITAL IMPROVEMENTS

For the purchase, rent, construction, and improvement of facilities for radio transmission and reception, and purchase and installation of necessary equipment for radio and television transmission and reception as authorized by section 801 of the United States Information and Educational Exchange Act of 1948 (22 U.S.C. 1471), [$11,258,000] *$19,760,000*, to remain available until expended, as authorized by section 704(a) of such Act of 1948 (22 U.S.C. 1477b(a)). *(The Department of State and Related Agencies Appropriations Act, 2000, as enacted by section 1000(a)(1) of the Consolidated Appropriations Act, 2000 (P.L. 106–113).)*

Program and Financing (in millions of dollars)

Identification code 95–0204–0–1–154	1999 actual	2000 est.	2001 est.
Obligations by program activity:			
00.01 New construction	3	1	....
00.02 Upgrade of existing relay station capabilities	4	1	7
00.03 Maintenance, improvements, replacement and repair	18	10	11
00.04 Broadcast, facility leases and rentals	....	....	1
00.05 Satellite and terrestrial feed systems	1	2	1
10.00 Total new obligations	26	14	20
Budgetary resources available for obligation:			
21.40 Unobligated balance available, start of year	13	4	....
22.00 New budget authority (gross)	13	10	20
22.10 Resources available from recoveries of prior year obligations	3	....	....
22.22 Unobligated balance transferred from other accounts	1	....	....
23.90 Total budgetary resources available for obligation	30	14	20
23.95 Total new obligations	−26	−14	−20
24.40 Unobligated balance available, end of year	4	....	....
New budget authority (gross), detail:			
Discretionary:			
40.00 Appropriation	13	11	20
40.76 Reduction pursuant to P.L. 106–113	....	−1	....
43.00 Appropriation (total discretionary)	13	10	20
Change in unpaid obligations:			
72.40 Unpaid obligations, start of year: Obligated balance, start of year	67	49	41
73.10 Total new obligations	26	14	20
73.20 Total outlays (gross)	−41	−22	−16
73.45 Adjustments in unexpired accounts	−3	....	....
74.40 Unpaid obligations, end of year: Obligated balance, end of year	49	41	45
Outlays (gross), detail:			
86.90 Outlays from new discretionary authority	4	3	6
86.93 Outlays from discretionary balances	37	19	10
87.00 Total outlays (gross)	41	22	16
Net budget authority and outlays:			
89.00 Budget authority	13	10	20
90.00 Outlays	41	22	16

This account provides funding for maintenance and improvement of the International Broadcasting Bureau's worldwide transmission network.

Upgrade of existing relay station capabilities.—This activity funds the upgrade of our existing relay stations to improve transmission quality and avoid the need for future new construction and to relocate the Philippines medium wave transmitter to a new site.

Major improvements, replacements and repairs.—This activity funds the continuing repairs and improvements required to maintain existing global radio and television network, including the conversion of program production and operations from an analog to a digital domain and enhancing security requirements and establishing an IBB internet unit.

Broadcast leases and land rentals.—This activity primarily funds the placement of IBB products with regional affiliates.

Satellite and terrestrial feed systems.—This activity provides funding for the construction and maintenance of the Satellite Interconnect System (SIS) and Television Receive Only (TVRO) earth stations.

Object Classification (in millions of dollars)

Identification code 95–0204–0–1–154	1999 actual	2000 est.	2001 est.
23.3 Communications, utilities, and miscellaneous charges	1	....	....
25.1 Advisory and assistance services	3	2	2
25.2 Other services	1	1	1
26.0 Supplies and materials	2	1	2
31.0 Equipment	18	10	14
32.0 Land and structures	1	....	1
99.9 Total new obligations	26	14	20

BROADCASTING TO CUBA

For expenses necessary to enable the Broadcasting Board of Governors to carry out the Radio Broadcasting to Cuba Act, as amended, the Television Broadcasting to Cuba Act, and the International Broadcasting Act of 1994, and the Foreign Affairs Reform and Restructuring Act of 1998, including the purchase, rent, construction, and improvement of facilities for radio and television transmission and reception, and purchase and installation of necessary equipment for radio and television transmission and reception, [$22,095,000] *$23,456,000*, to remain available until expended: *Provided*, That funds may be used to purchase or lease, maintain, and operate such aircraft (including aerostats) as may be required to house and operate necessary television broadcasting equipment. *(The Department of State and Related Agencies Appropriations Act, 2000, as enacted by section 1000(a)(1) of the Consolidated Appropriations Act, 2000 (P.L. 106–113).)*

Program and Financing (in millions of dollars)

Identification code 95–0208–0–1–154	1999 actual	2000 est.	2001 est.
Obligations by program activity:			
10.00 Total new obligations	21	25	23
Budgetary resources available for obligation:			
21.40 Unobligated balance available, start of year	2	3	....
22.00 New budget authority (gross)	22	22	23
23.90 Total budgetary resources available for obligation	24	25	23
23.95 Total new obligations	−21	−25	−23
24.40 Unobligated balance available, end of year	3	....	....
New budget authority (gross), detail:			
Discretionary:			
40.00 Appropriation	22	22	23
Change in unpaid obligations:			
72.40 Unpaid obligations, start of year: Obligated balance, start of year	4	7	10
73.10 Total new obligations	21	25	23
73.20 Total outlays (gross)	−18	−22	−23
74.40 Unpaid obligations, end of year: Obligated balance, end of year	7	10	10
Outlays (gross), detail:			
86.90 Outlays from new discretionary authority	17	18	19
86.93 Outlays from discretionary balances	1	4	5
87.00 Total outlays (gross)	18	22	23
Net budget authority and outlays:			
89.00 Budget authority	22	22	23

90.00 Outlays	18	22	23

This account provides funding for Radio Marti and TV Marti. Radio Marti currently broadcasts 127 hours a week to provide news and information to the people of Cuba. TV Marti is currently broadcasting 17 hours per week via UHF. The request for FY 2001 includes funding to replace a 100 kw transmitter to improve the operations, reliability, and efficiency of Radio Marti broadcasts.

Object Classification (in millions of dollars)

Identification code 95–0208–0–1–154	1999 actual	2000 est.	2001 est.
Personnel compensation:			
11.1 Full-time permanent	8	10	11
11.5 Other personnel compensation	1		
11.9 Total personnel compensation	9	10	11
12.1 Civilian personnel benefits	2	3	3
21.0 Travel and transportation of persons	1	1	1
23.1 Rental payments to GSA	2	2	2
23.3 Communications, utilities, and miscellaneous charges	1	3	3
25.2 Other services	5	4	3
31.0 Equipment	1	2	
99.9 Total new obligations	21	25	23

Personnel Summary

Identification code 95–0208–0–1–154	1999 actual	2000 est.	2001 est.
1001 Total compensable workyears: Full-time equivalent employment	147	163	163

Buying Power Maintenance

Program and Financing (in millions of dollars)

Identification code 95–1147–0–1–154	1999 actual	2000 est.	2001 est.
Budgetary resources available for obligation:			
21.40 Unobligated balance available, start of year			4
22.22 Unobligated balance transferred from other accounts		4	
23.90 Total budgetary resources available for obligation		4	4
23.95 Total new obligations			
24.40 Unobligated balance available, end of year		4	4
Net budget authority and outlays:			
89.00 Budget authority			
90.00 Outlays			

This account provides funding to offset losses due to exchange rate and overseas wage and price fluctuations unanticipated in the budget. As authorized, gains due to fluctuations will be deposited into this account to be available to offset future losses.

Trust Funds

Foreign Service National Separation Liability Trust Fund

Program and Financing (in millions of dollars)

Identification code 95–8285–0–7–602	1999 actual	2000 est.	2001 est.
Budgetary resources available for obligation:			
21.40 Unobligated balance available, start of year			3
22.22 Unobligated balance transferred from other accounts		3	
23.90 Total budgetary resources available for obligation		3	3
24.40 Unobligated balance available, end of year		3	3
Change in unpaid obligations:			
73.20 Total outlays (gross)		−1	
Outlays (gross), detail:			
86.98 Outlays from mandatory balances		1	
Net budget authority and outlays:			
89.00 Budget authority			
90.00 Outlays		1	

This fund is maintained to pay separation costs for Foreign Service National employees of the Broadcasting Board of Governors in those countries in which such pay is legally authorized. The fund, as authorized by Public Law 102–138, and amended by the Foreign Affairs Reform and Restructuring Act of 1998 is maintained by annual government contributions which are appropriated in the International broadcasting operations account.

CENTRAL INTELLIGENCE AGENCY

Federal Funds

General and special funds:

Central Intelligence Agency Retirement and Disability System Fund

For payment to the Central Intelligence Agency Retirement and Disability System Fund, to maintain proper funding level for continuing the operation of the Central Intelligence Agency Retirement and Disability System, [$209,100,000] *$216,000,000. (Department of Defense Appropriations Act, 2000.)*

Program and Financing (in millions of dollars)

Identification code 56–3400–0–1–054	1999 actual	2000 est.	2001 est.
Obligations by program activity:			
10.00 Total new obligations	202	209	216
Budgetary resources available for obligation:			
22.00 New budget authority (gross)	202	209	216
23.95 Total new obligations	−202	−209	−216
New budget authority (gross), detail:			
Mandatory:			
60.00 Appropriation	202	209	216
Change in unpaid obligations:			
73.10 Total new obligations	202	209	216
73.20 Total outlays (gross)	−202	−209	−216
Outlays (gross), detail:			
86.97 Outlays from new mandatory authority	202	209	216
Net budget authority and outlays:			
89.00 Budget authority	202	209	216
90.00 Outlays	202	209	216

This appropriation provides for payment to the Fund: (a) for interest on the unfunded liability; (b) for the cost of annuity disbursements attributable to military service; (c) for the amount of normal costs not met by employee and employer contributions; and (d) for financing, in 30 equal installments, the unfunded liability created by new or liberalized benefits, new groups of beneficiaries, and salary increases. The request for 2001 includes the twenty-fourth installment for the unfunded liability created by the liberalized benefits authorized by Public Law 94–522, and the appropriate annual installments for salary increases authorized in prior years.

Object Classification (in millions of dollars)

Identification code 56–3400–0–1–054	1999 actual	2000 est.	2001 est.
12.1 Civilian personnel benefits	77	77	81
13.0 Benefits for former personnel	125	132	135
99.9 Total new obligations	202	209	216

CHEMICAL SAFETY AND HAZARD INVESTIGATION BOARD

Federal Fund

General and special funds:

CHEMICAL SAFETY AND HAZARD INVESTIGATION BOARD

SALARIES AND EXPENSES

For necessary expenses in carrying out activities pursuant to section 112(r)(6) of the Clean Air Act, including hire of passenger vehicles, and for services authorized by 5 U.S.C. 3109, but at rates for individuals not to exceed the per diem equivalent to the maximum rate payable for senior level positions under 5 U.S.C. 5376, $8,000,000[: *Provided*, That the Chemical Safety and Hazard Investigation Board shall have not more than three career Senior Executive Service positions]. *(Departments of Veterans Affairs and Housing and Urban Development, and Independent Agencies Appropriations Act, 2000.)*

Program and Financing (in millions of dollars)

Identification code 95–3850–0–1–304	1999 actual	2000 est.	2001 est.
Obligations by program activity:			
10.00 Total new obligations	6	8	8
Budgetary resources available for obligation:			
22.00 New budget authority (gross)	7	8	8
23.95 Total new obligations	−6	−8	−8
New budget authority (gross), detail:			
Discretionary:			
40.00 Appropriation	7	8	8
Change in unpaid obligations:			
72.40 Unpaid obligations, start of year: Obligated balance, start of year	2	3	
73.10 Total new obligations	6	8	8
73.20 Total outlays (gross)	−5	−11	−8
74.40 Unpaid obligations, end of year: Obligated balance, end of year	3		
Outlays (gross), detail:			
86.90 Outlays from new discretionary authority	3	8	8
86.93 Outlays from discretionary balances	2	3	
87.00 Total outlays (gross)	5	11	8
Net budget authority and outlays:			
89.00 Budget authority	7	8	8
90.00 Outlays	5	11	8

The Chemical Safety and Hazard Investigation Board, as authorized by the Clean Air Act Amendments of 1990, became operational in FY 1998. It is an independent, non-regulatory agency that promotes chemical safety and accident prevention through investigating chemical accidents; making recommendations for accident prevention; conducting special studies; and advising the President and Congress on key issues relating to chemical safety and on actions taken by the Environmental Protection Agency, the Department of Labor, and other Federal agencies to implement Board recommendations. As authorized by law, the Board will be submitting a separate request to Congress and OMB concurrently for FY 2001.

Object Classification (in millions of dollars)

Identification code 95–3850–0–1–304	1999 actual	2000 est.	2001 est.
11.1 Personnel compensation: Full-time permanent	2	4	4
25.2 Other services	1	1	1
31.0 Equipment	1		
99.0 Subtotal, direct obligations	4	5	5
99.5 Below reporting threshold	2	3	3
99.9 Total new obligations	6	8	8

Personnel Summary

Identification code 95–3850–0–1–304	1999 actual	2000 est.	2001 est.
1001 Total compensable workyears: Full-time equivalent employment	25	40	40

CHRISTOPHER COLUMBUS FELLOWSHIP FOUNDATION

Trust Funds

CHRISTOPHER COLUMBUS FELLOWSHIP FOUNDATION

Unavailable Collections (in millions of dollars)

Identification code 76–8187–0–7–502	1999 actual	2000 est.	2001 est.
Balance, start of year:			
01.99 Balance, start of year			
Receipts:			
02.03 Gifts and donations	1		
Appropriation:			
05.01 Christopher Columbus Fellowship Foundation	−1		
07.99 Total balance, end of year			

Program and Financing (in millions of dollars)

Identification code 76–8187–0–7–502	1999 actual	2000 est.	2001 est.
Obligations by program activity:			
10.00 Total new obligations (object class 41.0)	2	1	1
Budgetary resources available for obligation:			
21.40 Unobligated balance available, start of year	8	7	6
22.00 New budget authority (gross)	1		
23.90 Total budgetary resources available for obligation	9	7	6
23.95 Total new obligations	−2	−1	−1
24.40 Unobligated balance available, end of year	7	6	5
New budget authority (gross), detail:			
Mandatory:			
60.27 Appropriation (trust fund, indefinite)	1		
Change in unpaid obligations:			
73.10 Total new obligations	2	1	1
Net budget authority and outlays:			
89.00 Budget authority	1		
90.00 Outlays	2	1	1
Memorandum (non-add) entries:			
92.01 Total investments, start of year: U.S. securities: Par value	7	7	6
92.02 Total investments, end of year: U.S. securities: Par value	7	6	5

Public Law 102–281 established the Christopher Columbus Fellowship Foundation "to encourage and support research, study, and labor designed to produce new discoveries in all fields of endeavor for the benefit of mankind." Surcharges from Christopher Columbus Quincentenary coins were placed in the Foundation's trust fund. The trust fund will be used to operate the Foundation's programs.

The Foundation will support programs totaling $1 million in FY 2000 and 2001. The Foundation supports a three-tiered program encompassing *Frontiers of Discovery—Past, Present and Future.* The *Past* program supports a competition to reward an individual American whose creative thinking has led to a process, product or discovery that has made a significant impact on our society. The *Present* program supports a competition to reward an individual American who is attempting to improve the world through ingenuity and innovation, and to provide incentive and opportunity for continuing research. The *Future* program supports a community innovation competition program encouraging youth to develop creative solutions to community problems, and sponsors youth inductees into the National Gallery for America's Young Inventors recognizing their innovations.

Personnel Summary

Identification code 76–8187–0–7–502	1999 actual	2000 est.	2001 est.
1001 Total compensable workyears: Full-time equivalent employment	1	1	1

COMMISSION OF FINE ARTS

Federal Funds

General and special funds:

SALARIES AND EXPENSES

For expenses made necessary by the Act establishing a Commission of Fine Arts (40 U.S.C. 104), [$1,005,000] *$1,078,000*: *Provided*, That the Commission is authorized to charge fees to cover the full costs of its publications, and such fees shall be credited to this account as an offsetting collection, to remain available until expended without further appropriation. *(Department of the Interior and Related Agencies Appropriations Act, 2000, as enacted by section 1000(a)(3) of the Consolidated Appropriations Act, 2000 (P.L. 106–113).)*

Program and Financing (in millions of dollars)

Identification code 95–2600–0–1–451	1999 actual	2000 est.	2001 est.
Obligations by program activity:			
10.00 Total new obligations (object class 99.5)	1	1	1
Budgetary resources available for obligation:			
22.00 New budget authority (gross)	1	1	1
23.95 Total new obligations	−1	−1	−1
New budget authority (gross), detail:			
Discretionary:			
40.00 Appropriation	1	1	1
Change in unpaid obligations:			
73.10 Total new obligations	1	1	1
73.20 Total outlays (gross)	−1	−1	−1
Outlays (gross), detail:			
86.90 Outlays from new discretionary authority	1	1	1
Net budget authority and outlays:			
89.00 Budget authority	1	1	1
90.00 Outlays	1	1	1

The Commission advises the President, Congress, and department heads on matters of architecture, sculpture, painting, and other fine arts. Its primary function is to preserve and enhance the appearance of the National Capital.

Personnel Summary

Identification code 95–2600–0–1–451	1999 actual	2000 est.	2001 est.
1001 Total compensable workyears: Full-time equivalent employment	7	7	8

NATIONAL CAPITAL ARTS AND CULTURAL AFFAIRS

For necessary expenses as authorized by Public Law 99–190 (20 U.S.C. 956(a)), as amended, [$7,000,000] *$7,000,000*. *(Department of the Interior and Related Agencies Appropriations Act, 2000, as enacted by section 1000(a)(3) of the Consolidated Appropriations Act, 2000 (P.L. 106–113).)*

Program and Financing (in millions of dollars)

Identification code 95–2602–0–1–503	1999 actual	2000 est.	2001 est.
Obligations by program activity:			
10.00 Total new obligations (object class 41.0)	7	7	7
Budgetary resources available for obligation:			
22.00 New budget authority (gross)	7	7	7
23.95 Total new obligations	−7	−7	−7
New budget authority (gross), detail:			
Discretionary:			
40.00 Appropriation	7	7	7
Change in unpaid obligations:			
73.10 Total new obligations	7	7	7
73.20 Total outlays (gross)	−7	−7	−7
Outlays (gross), detail:			
86.90 Outlays from new discretionary authority	7	7	7
Net budget authority and outlays:			
89.00 Budget authority	7	7	7
90.00 Outlays	7	7	7

This program provides payments for general operating support to Washington, D.C. arts and other cultural organizations.

D.C. ARTS EDUCATION GRANTS

To carry out the "D.C. Arts Education Grants" program, $1,000,000, which shall be available to make grants to District of Columbia-based arts education organizations and individuals that provide training and exposure to artistic disciplines to disadvantaged District youth.

Program and Financing (in millions of dollars)

Identification code 95–2604–0–1–451	1999 actual	2000 est.	2001 est.
Obligations by program activity:			
10.00 Total new obligations (object class 41.0)			1
Budgetary resources available for obligation:			
22.00 New budget authority (gross)			1
23.95 Total new obligations			−1
New budget authority (gross), detail:			
Discretionary:			
40.00 Appropriation			1
Change in unpaid obligations:			
73.10 Total new obligations			1
Outlays (gross), detail:			
86.90 Outlays from new discretionary authority			1
Net budget authority and outlays:			
89.00 Budget authority			1
90.00 Outlays			1

COMMISSION ON CIVIL RIGHTS

Federal Funds

General and special funds:

SALARIES AND EXPENSES

For necessary expenses of the Commission on Civil Rights, including hire of passenger motor vehicles, [$8,900,000: *Provided*, That not to exceed $50,000 may be used to employ consultants] *$11,000,000*: *Provided* [*further*], That none of the funds appropriated in this paragraph shall be used to employ in excess of four full-time individuals under Schedule C of the Excepted Service exclusive of one special assistant for each Commissioner: *Provided further*, That none of the funds appropriated in this paragraph shall be used

General and special funds—Continued

SALARIES AND EXPENSES—Continued

to reimburse Commissioners for more than 75 billable days, with the exception of the chairperson, who is permitted 125 billable days. *(Departments of Commerce, Justice, and State, the Judiciary, and Related Agencies Appropriations Act, 2000, as enacted by section 1000(a)(1) of the Consolidated Appropriations Act, 2000 (P.L. 106–113).)*

Program and Financing (in millions of dollars)

Identification code 95–1900–0–1–751	1999 actual	2000 est.	2001 est.
Obligations by program activity:			
10.00 Total new obligations	9	9	11
Budgetary resources available for obligation:			
22.00 New budget authority (gross)	9	9	11
23.95 Total new obligations	−9	−9	−11
New budget authority (gross), detail:			
Discretionary:			
40.00 Appropriation	9	9	11
Change in unpaid obligations:			
72.40 Unpaid obligations, start of year: Obligated balance, start of year	1	1	1
73.10 Total new obligations	9	9	11
73.20 Total outlays (gross)	−9	−9	−11
74.40 Unpaid obligations, end of year: Obligated balance, end of year	1	1	1
Outlays (gross), detail:			
86.90 Outlays from new discretionary authority	8	8	10
86.93 Outlays from discretionary balances			1
87.00 Total outlays (gross)	9	9	11
Net budget authority and outlays:			
89.00 Budget authority	9	9	11
90.00 Outlays	8	9	11

Summary of Budget Authority and Outlays

(in millions of dollars)

	1999 actual	*2000 est.*	*2001 est.*
Enacted/requested:			
Budget Authority	9	9	11
Outlays	8	8	11
Supplemental proposal:			
Budget Authority		1	
Outlays			
Total:			
Budget Authority	9	10	11
Outlays	8	8	11

The Commission engages in studies concerning areas in which there may be denials of civil rights and reports on these matters to the President and the Congress. Hearings by the Commissioners are held to investigate and obtain information about denials of civil rights. Conferences and open meetings are held by staff and State Advisory Committees to gather data and issue reports providing information about civil rights problems. In addition, the Commission appraises and reports on Federal agencies enforcement of civil rights laws. Complaints alleging discrimination are referred to the proper Federal agencies.

The Commission provides liaison with private groups, public groups, and the media to provide civil rights information to Government officials, organizations, and the public. The Commission issues publications and public service announcements to discourage discrimination and denial of equal protection of the laws. The Commission also provides a library resource to support civil rights research, studies, hearings, and other Commission activities, and makes this information available to the general public.

Object Classification (in millions of dollars)

Identification code 95–1900–0–1–751	1999 actual	2000 est.	2001 est.
Personnel compensation:			
11.1 Full-time permanent	5	5	6
11.3 Other than full-time permanent	1	1	1
11.9 Total personnel compensation	6	6	7
12.1 Civilian personnel benefits	1	1	1
23.1 Rental payments to GSA	1	1	1
25.2 Other services	1	1	2
99.9 Total new obligations	9	9	11

Personnel Summary

Identification code 95–1900–0–1–751	1999 actual	2000 est.	2001 est.
1001 Total compensable workyears: Full-time equivalent employment	78	85	102

COMMITTEE FOR PURCHASE FROM PEOPLE WHO ARE BLIND OR SEVERELY DISABLED

Federal Funds

General and special funds:

SALARIES AND EXPENSES

For necessary expenses of the Committee for Purchase From People Who Are Blind or Severely Disabled established by the Act of June 23, 1971, Public Law 92–28, [$2,674,000] *$4,158,000. (Independent Agencies Appropriations Act, 2000.)*

Program and Financing (in millions of dollars)

Identification code 95–2000–0–1–505	1999 actual	2000 est.	2001 est.
Obligations by program activity:			
10.00 Total new obligations	2	3	4
Budgetary resources available for obligation:			
22.00 New budget authority (gross)	2	3	4
23.95 Total new obligations	−2	−3	−4
New budget authority (gross), detail:			
Discretionary:			
40.00 Appropriation	2	3	4
Change in unpaid obligations:			
72.40 Unpaid obligations, start of year: Obligated balance, start of year	1	1	
73.10 Total new obligations	2	3	4
73.20 Total outlays (gross)	−3	−4	−4
74.40 Unpaid obligations, end of year: Obligated balance, end of year	1		
Outlays (gross), detail:			
86.90 Outlays from new discretionary authority	2	3	4
86.93 Outlays from discretionary balances	1	1	
87.00 Total outlays (gross)	3	4	4
Net budget authority and outlays:			
89.00 Budget authority	2	3	4
90.00 Outlays	3	4	4

Summary of Budget Authority and Outlays

(in millions of dollars)

	1999 actual	*2000 est.*	*2001 est.*
Enacted/requested:			
Budget Authority	2	3	4
Outlays	3	4	4
Supplemental proposal:			
Budget Authority		1	
Outlays		1	
Total:			
Budget Authority	2	4	4

Outlays	3	5	4

The Committee for Purchase From People Who Are Blind or Severely Disabled administers the Javits-Wagner-O'Day (JWOD) Act of 1971, as amended. Its primary objective is to use the purchasing power of the Federal Government to provide people who are blind or have other severe disabilities with employment and training that will develop and improve job skills as well as prepare them for employment options outside the JWOD Program. In 2001, approximately 34,000 people who are blind or have other severe disabilities are projected to be employed in 640 producing nonprofit agencies. The Committee's duties include promoting the program; determining which products and services are suitable for Government procurement from qualified nonprofit agencies serving people who are blind or have other severe disabilities; maintaining a procurement list of such products and services; determining the fair market price for products and services on the procurement list; and making rules and regulations necessary to carry out the purposes of the Act. In 2001 the Committee expects to have sales of $950 million.

The Committee staff's responsibilities include promoting and assessing the overall programs; supervising the selection and assignment of new products and services; assisting in establishing prices; reviewing and adjusting these prices; verifying the qualifications of nonprofit agencies; and monitoring their performance. The increased resources proposed for 2001 would enable the Committee to further expand its marketing efforts, which are essential to protecting jobs for people with disabilities involved in supplying commercial-type products such as office supplies to Federal customers under the JWOD Program. The education functions to be supported by these funds would focus on informing Federal purchase card holders about JWOD products and working with private sector distributors of those products, including e-commerce vendors.

Object Classification (in millions of dollars)

Identification code 95–2000–0–1–505	1999 actual	2000 est.	2001 est.
11.1 Personnel compensation: Full-time permanent	1	1	2
24.0 Printing and reproduction			1
99.0 Subtotal, direct obligations	1	1	3
99.5 Below reporting threshold	1	2	1
99.9 Total new obligations	2	3	4

Personnel Summary

Identification code 95–2000–0–1–505	1999 actual	2000 est.	2001 est.
1001 Total compensable workyears: Full-time equivalent employment	19	24	29

COMMODITY FUTURES TRADING COMMISSION

Federal Funds

General and special funds:

COMMODITY FUTURES TRADING COMMISSION

For necessary expenses to carry out the provisions of the Commodity Exchange Act (7 U.S.C. 1 et seq.), including the purchase and hire of passenger motor vehicles; the rental of space (to include multiple year leases) in the District of Columbia and elsewhere; and not to exceed $25,000 for employment under 5 U.S.C. 3109, **[**$63,000,000**]** *$72,000,000*, including not to exceed **[**$1,000**]** *$2,000* for official reception and representation expenses: *Provided*, That for fiscal year **[**2000**]** *2001* and thereafter, the Commission is authorized to charge reasonable fees to attendees of Commission sponsored educational events and symposia to cover the Commission's costs of providing those events and symposia, and notwithstanding 31 U.S.C. 3302, said fees shall be credited to this account, to be available without further appropriation. *(Agriculture, Rural Development, Food and Drug Administration, and Related Agencies Appropriations Act, 2000.)*

Program and Financing (in millions of dollars)

Identification code 95–1400–0–1–376	1999 actual	2000 est.	2001 est.
Obligations by program activity:			
00.01 Market surveillance, analysis, and research	11	10	11
00.02 Enforcement	24	25	29
00.03 Trading and markets	18	19	22
00.04 Proceedings	3	3	3
00.05 General counsel	5	6	7
10.00 Total new obligations	61	63	72
Budgetary resources available for obligation:			
22.00 New budget authority (gross)	61	63	72
23.95 Total new obligations	−61	−63	−72
New budget authority (gross), detail:			
Discretionary:			
40.00 Appropriation	61	63	72
Change in unpaid obligations:			
72.40 Unpaid obligations, start of year: Obligated balance, start of year	8	8	8
73.10 Total new obligations	61	63	72
73.20 Total outlays (gross)	−61	−63	−71
74.40 Unpaid obligations, end of year: Obligated balance, end of year	8	8	9
Outlays (gross), detail:			
86.90 Outlays from new discretionary authority	54	57	65
86.93 Outlays from discretionary balances	6	7	6
87.00 Total outlays (gross)	61	63	71
Net budget authority and outlays:			
89.00 Budget authority	61	63	72
90.00 Outlays	61	63	71

The Commodity Futures Trading Commission (CFTC) administers the Commodity Exchange Act of 1936, as amended. The purpose of the CFTC is to further the economic utility of the futures markets by encouraging their efficiency, assuring their integrity, and protecting participants against abusive trade practices, fraud, and deceit. The object of commodity futures trading regulation is to enable the markets to better serve their designated functions of providing a price discovery mechanism and a means of offsetting price risk. By properly serving these functions, the futures markets serve the public interest by contributing toward better planning, more efficient distribution and consumption, and more economical marketing. The commodity futures and options markets represent one of America's most innovative and competitive contributions to the international financial services industry.

The Administration proposes additional resources above the fiscal year 2000 level for the Commission. These increases would enhance the Commission's ability to investigate and detect fraud and abuse and ensure the continued integrity of the commodities markets. In addition, such increases would provide the Commission with the enforcement and surveillance resources necessary to respond to the continued growth and use of complex trading and derivative instruments.

Market surveillance, analysis and research.—Responsibilities under this program include daily surveillance of the market activity of large individual traders and fundamental economic market factors to insure orderly markets. Contract terms and conditions are reviewed to insure conformity with current cash marketing conditions and adequate deliverable supplies. This program also systematically investigates the functioning of markets and market users and develops better tools to assist in detecting and preventing price distortions.

General and special funds—Continued

COMMODITY FUTURES TRADING COMMISSION—Continued

	1999 actual	2000 est.	2001 est.
Trader and broker reports analyzed (thousands)	8,100	24,050	30,050
Market surveillance reports prepared	2,567	2,800	3,000
Review of futures contract rule changes completed	143	144	145
Review of new futures contract designation applications completed	73	74	75

Enforcement.—The enforcement program is responsible for detecting, investigating, and litigating violations of the Act or regulations. These violations may include actual and attempted market manipulations, cheating and defrauding customers, and abusive trading practices such as fictitious trading, wash trading, and pre-arranged trading. This program may seek remedies through the administrative process or by injunctive actions in the Federal Courts.

	1999 actual	2000 est.	2001 est.
Investigations:			
Opened	98	97	108
Completed	145	114	118
Cases:			
Opened	45	45	47
Completed	41	41	42

Trading and markets.—This program is designed to protect customer funds, prevent and detect financial, sales practice and trading abuses, and to assure the financial integrity and fitness of firms holding customer funds. In order to assure compliance with statutory requirements, this program monitors compliance activities of designated contract markets and the National Futures Association, conducts audits and reviews of registrants, and reviews self-regulatory organizations' rules and proposed rule changes. The program also develops regulations pursuant to statutory requirements and coordinates with other domestic and international regulators relative to cross border financial services affecting futures and options products.

	1999 actual	2000 est.	2001 est.
Oversight audits of self-regulatory organizations	38	60	65
Review self-regulatory organization rules	259	440	440
Review adequacy of self-regulatory organization disciplinary actions	348	620	620
Audits of clearing organizations and firms handling customer money	25	26	30
Written requests for regulatory exemptive relief granted	266	297	315

	1999 actual	2000 est.	2001 est.
Reparations:			
Cases pending (beginning balance)	106	116	116
Cases received	195	210	210
Cases dismissed, settled, or disposed	185	210	210
Cases pending (ending balance)	116	116	116

General Counsel.—The Office of the General Counsel provides legal services and support to the Commission's program divisions, including engaging in defensive, appellate, and amicus litigation; assisting the Commission in the performance of its adjudicatory functions; drafting regulations; interpreting the Commodity Exchange Act; and providing no-action letters and opinions to the public.

Object Classification (in millions of dollars)

Identification code 95–1400–0–1–376		1999 actual	2000 est.	2001 est.
	Personnel compensation:			
11.1	Full-time permanent	33	36	39
11.3	Other than full-time permanent	3	3	3
11.5	Other personnel compensation	1	1	1
11.9	Total personnel compensation	37	40	43
12.1	Civilian personnel benefits	8	8	10
21.0	Travel and transportation of persons	1	1	1
23.2	Rental payments to others	8	8	9
23.3	Communications, utilities, and miscellaneous charges	2	1	1
25.2	Other services	3	3	5
26.0	Supplies and materials	1	1	1
31.0	Equipment	1	1	2
99.9	Total new obligations	61	63	72

Personnel Summary

Identification code 95–1400–0–1–376		1999 actual	2000 est.	2001 est.
1001	Total compensable workyears: Full-time equivalent employment	567	561	621

CONSUMER PRODUCT SAFETY COMMISSION

Federal Funds

General and special funds:

SALARIES AND EXPENSES

For necessary expenses of the Consumer Product Safety Commission, including hire of passenger motor vehicles, services as authorized by 5 U.S.C. 3109, but at rates for individuals not to exceed the per diem rate equivalent to the maximum rate payable under 5 U.S.C. 5376, purchase of nominal awards to recognize non-Federal officials' contributions to Commission activities, and not to exceed $500 for official reception and representation expenses, [$49,000,000] *$52,500,000*. *(Department of Veterans Affairs and Housing and Urban Development, and Independent Agencies Appropriations Act, 2000.)*

Program and Financing (in millions of dollars)

Identification code 61–0100–0–1–554		1999 actual	2000 est.	2001 est.
	Obligations by program activity:			
	Direct program:			
00.01	Reducing product hazards to children and families	39	40	43
00.02	Identifying and researching product hazards	8	9	9
09.01	Reimbursable program	2	2	3
10.00	Total new obligations	49	51	55
	Budgetary resources available for obligation:			
22.00	New budget authority (gross)	49	51	55
23.95	Total new obligations	−49	−51	−55
	New budget authority (gross), detail:			
	Discretionary:			
40.00	Appropriation	47	49	52
68.00	Spending authority from offsetting collections: Offsetting collections (cash)	2	2	3
70.00	Total new budget authority (gross)	49	51	55
	Change in unpaid obligations:			
72.40	Unpaid obligations, start of year: Obligated balance, start of year	7	7	7
73.10	Total new obligations	49	51	55
73.20	Total outlays (gross)	−49	−51	−55
74.40	Unpaid obligations, end of year: Obligated balance, end of year	7	7	7
	Outlays (gross), detail:			
86.90	Outlays from new discretionary authority	42	46	49
86.93	Outlays from discretionary balances	6	5	6
87.00	Total outlays (gross)	49	51	55
	Offsets:			
	Against gross budget authority and outlays:			
88.00	Offsetting collections (cash) from: Federal sources	−2	−2	−3
	Net budget authority and outlays:			
89.00	Budget authority	47	49	52
90.00	Outlays	47	49	52

The Commission addresses a number of product safety areas. These include fire and thermal burn hazards, electrical hazards, acute and chronic chemical hazards, children's and recreational product hazards, power equipment hazards, and household structural products hazards.

Object Classification (in millions of dollars)

Identification code 61–0100–0–1–554		1999 actual	2000 est.	2001 est.
	Direct obligations:			
	Personnel compensation:			
11.1	Full-time permanent	29	31	33
11.3	Other than full-time permanent	1	1	1
11.9	Total personnel compensation	30	32	34
12.1	Civilian personnel benefits	6	6	7
21.0	Travel and transportation of persons	1	1	1
23.1	Rental payments to GSA	3	3	3
23.3	Communications, utilities, and miscellaneous charges	1	1	1
25.2	Other services	4	3	4
25.3	Purchases of goods and services from Government accounts		1	1
31.0	Equipment	1		
99.0	Subtotal, direct obligations	46	47	51
99.0	Reimbursable obligations	2	2	3
99.5	Below reporting threshold	1	2	1
99.9	Total new obligations	49	51	55

Personnel Summary

Identification code 61–0100–0–1–554		1999 actual	2000 est.	2001 est.
1001	Total compensable workyears: Full-time equivalent employment	466	480	480

CORPORATION FOR NATIONAL AND COMMUNITY SERVICE

Federal Funds

General and special funds:

National and Community Service Programs

Operating Expenses

(including transfer of funds)

For necessary expenses for the Corporation for National and Community Service [(referred to in the matter under this heading as the "Corporation")] in carrying out [programs, activities, and initiatives under] the National and Community Service Act of 1990 [(referred to in the matter under this heading as the "Act") (42 U.S.C. 12501 et seq.), $434,500,000] *(Public Law 103–82), $533,700,000,* to remain available until September 30, [2000: *Provided*, That not more than $28,500,000 shall be available] *2002, of which not to exceed $35,600,000 is* for administrative expenses [authorized] under section 501(a)(4) [of the Act (42 U.S.C. 12671(a)(4)) with not less than $1,500,000 targeted to administrative needs, not including salaries and expenses, identified as urgent by the Corporation without regard to the provisions of section 501(a)(4)(B) of the Act: *Provided further*, That not more than]*; not to exceed* $2,500 [shall be] *is* for official reception and representation expenses[: *Provided further*, That not more than]*; not to exceed* [$70,000,000] *$79,600,000*, to remain available [without fiscal year limitation] *until expended*, shall be transferred to the National Service Trust [account] for educational awards authorized under subtitle D of title I of the Act [(42 U.S.C. 12601 et seq.)], of which not to exceed [$5,000,000] *$7,500,000* shall be available for national service scholarships for high school students performing community service[: *Provided further*, That not more than $234,000,000 of the amount provided under this heading shall be available for grants under the National Service Trust program authorized under subtitle C of title I of the Act (42 U.S.C. 12571 et seq.) (relating to activities including the AmeriCorps program), of which not more than $45,000,000 may be used to administer, reimburse, or support any national service program authorized under section 121(d)(2) of such Act (42 U.S.C. 12581(d)(2)): *Provided further*, That not more than $7,500,000 of the funds made available under this heading shall be made available for the Points of Light Foundation for activities authorized under title III of the Act (42 U.S.C. 12661 et seq.): *Provided further*, That no funds shall be available for national service programs run by Federal agencies authorized under section 121(b) of such Act (42 U.S.C. 12571(b)): *Provided further*, That to the maximum extent feasible, funds appropriated under subtitle C of title I of the Act shall be provided in a manner that is consistent with the recommendations of peer review panels in order to ensure that priority is given to programs that demonstrate quality, innovation, replicability, and sustainability: *Provided further*, That not more than $18,000,000 of the funds made available under this heading shall be available for the Civilian Community Corps authorized under subtitle E of title I of the Act (42 U.S.C. 12611 et seq.): *Provided further*, That not more than $43,000,000 shall be available for school-based and community-based service-learning programs authorized under subtitle B of title I of the Act (42 U.S.C. 12521 et seq.): *Provided further*, That not more than $28,500,000 shall be available for quality and innovation activities authorized under subtitle H of title I of the Act (42 U.S.C. 12853 et seq.): *Provided further*, That not more than $5,000,000 shall be available for audits and other evaluations authorized under section 179 of the Act (42 U.S.C. 12639): *Provided further*, That to the maximum extent practicable, the Corporation shall increase significantly the level of matching funds and in-kind contributions provided by the private sector, shall expand significantly the number of educational awards provided under subtitle D of title I, and shall reduce the total Federal costs per participant in all programs: *Provided further*, That of amounts available in the National Service Trust account from previous appropriations Acts, $80,000,000 shall be rescinded;] *not more than $7,500,000 shall be only for a grant to America's Promise—The Alliance for Youth, Inc., only to support efforts to mobilize individuals, groups and organizations to build and strengthen the character and competence of the Nation's youth; and not to exceed $51,000,000 shall be for school-based and community-based service learning programs under subtitle B of title I of the Act, of which not more than $8,000,000 shall be for community coaches and youth empowerment grants under 42 U.S.C. 12544 and which shall not be considered in determining the amounts available under 42 U.S.C. 12681(a): Provided, That any amount provided to a State under section 126(a) greater than the amount provided in fiscal year 2000 will not be subject to the limitations in section 126(a)(2). (Department of Veterans Affairs and Housing and Urban Development, and Independent Agencies Appropriations Act, 2000.)*

Program and Financing (in millions of dollars)

Identification code 95–2720–0–1–506		1999 actual	2000 est.	2001 est.
	Obligations by program activity:			
00.01	National Service Trust	70	69	80
00.02	AmeriCorps grants	214	282	284
00.03	Innovation assistance and other activities	37	40	42
00.04	Evaluation	7	7	5
00.05	National Civilian Community Corps	18	18	21
00.06	Learn and Serve America	44	46	51
00.07	NCSA program administration	28	32	36
00.08	Points of Light Foundation	6	7	8
00.09	America's Promise			7
10.00	Total new obligations	424	501	534
	Budgetary resources available for obligation:			
21.40	Unobligated balance available, start of year	155	168	100
22.00	New budget authority (gross)	437	434	534
23.90	Total budgetary resources available for obligation	592	602	634
23.95	Total new obligations	–424	–501	–534
24.40	Unobligated balance available, end of year	168	100	100
	New budget authority (gross), detail:			
	Discretionary:			
40.00	Appropriation	436	435	534
40.76	Reduction pursuant to P.L. 106–113		–1	
42.00	Transferred from other accounts	1		
43.00	Appropriation (total discretionary)	437	433	534
	Change in unpaid obligations:			
72.40	Unpaid obligations, start of year: Obligated balance, start of year	426	478	560
73.10	Total new obligations	424	501	534
73.20	Total outlays (gross)	–372	–419	–499
74.40	Unpaid obligations, end of year: Obligated balance, end of year	478	560	595
	Outlays (gross), detail:			
86.90	Outlays from new discretionary authority	120	118	145
86.93	Outlays from discretionary balances	252	301	353

General and special funds—Continued

OPERATING EXPENSES—Continued

(INCLUDING TRANSFER OF FUNDS)—Continued

Program and Financing (in millions of dollars)—Continued

Identification code 95–2720–0–1–506	1999 actual	2000 est.	2001 est.
87.00 Total outlays (gross)	372	419	499
Net budget authority and outlays:			
89.00 Budget authority	437	434	534
90.00 Outlays	372	419	499

The Corporation for National and Community Service engages Americans of all ages and backgrounds in community-based service which addresses the Nation's educational, human, public safety, and environmental needs to achieve meaningful results. In doing so, the Corporation fosters civic responsibility, strengthens the ties that bind us together as a people, and provides educational opportunity for those who make a substantial commitment to service.

National Service Trust.—The Trust serves as a secure repository for educational awards set aside for eligible participants in National Service programs.

AmeriCorps grants.—With funds both channelled through States and provided directly to community based organizations, AmeriCorps grants enable communities to address problems they identify by using the skills of individuals serving in National Service positions.

Innovation, assistance, and other activities.—This activity provides support to programs receiving assistance under AmeriCorps or Learn and Serve America or to organizations or States which would like to create programs or apply to the Corporation for funding.

Evaluation.—This activity supports studies of the impact and effectiveness of Corporation programs.

National Civilian Community Corps.—This residential National Service program provides unique service opportunities for members and communities.

Learn and Serve America.—Through grants to State educational agencies, colleges and consortia of colleges and nonprofit organizations, and other means, opportunities will be provided to students to participate in service learning activities.

NCSA program administration.—These funds will be provided to State Commissions to develop National Service plans and manage these activities within their States and will be used by the Corporation to administer these activities.

Points of Light Foundation.—A grant will be provided to this nongovernment, nonprofit 501(c)(3) entity to enable it to increase opportunities for Americans to participate in voluntary activities.

America's Promise.—A grant will be provided to this nongovernment, nonprofit 501(c)(3) entity to enable it to mobilize individuals, groups and organizations to build and strengthen the character and competence of the Nation's youth.

Object Classification (in millions of dollars)

Identification code 95–2720–0–1–506	1999 actual	2000 est.	2001 est.
Personnel compensation:			
11.1 Full-time permanent	14	16	17
11.3 Other than full-time permanent	8	7	8
11.9 Total personnel compensation	22	23	25
12.1 Civilian personnel benefits	4	5	5
21.0 Travel and transportation of persons	3	4	4
23.3 Communications, utilities, and miscellaneous charges	3	4	4
25.2 Other services	13	14	15
26.0 Supplies and materials	1	1	1
41.0 Grants, subsidies, and contributions	308	381	400
92.0 National Service Trust	70	69	80
99.9 Total new obligations	424	501	534

Personnel Summary

Identification code 95–2720–0–1–506	1999 actual	2000 est.	2001 est.
1001 Total compensable workyears: Full-time equivalent employment	274	304	350

DOMESTIC VOLUNTEER SERVICE PROGRAMS, OPERATING EXPENSES

For expenses necessary for the Corporation for National and Community Service to carry out the provisions of the Domestic Volunteer Service Act of 1973, as amended, [$295,645,000: *Provided*, That none of the funds made available to the Corporation for National and Community Service in this Act for activities authorized by part E of title II of the Domestic Volunteer Service Act of 1973 shall be used to provide stipends to volunteers or volunteer leaders whose incomes exceed the income guidelines established for payment of stipends under the Foster Grandparent and Senior Companion programs: *Provided further*, That the foregoing proviso shall not apply to the Seniors for Schools program] *$312,616,000. (Departments of Labor, Health and Human Services, and Education, and Related Agencies Appropriations Act, 2000, as enacted by section 1000(a)(4) of the Consolidated Appropriations Act, 2000 (P.L. 106–113).)*

Program and Financing (in millions of dollars)

Identification code 95–0103–0–1–506	1999 actual	2000 est.	2001 est.
Obligations by program activity:			
Direct program:			
00.01 Volunteers in Service to America	73	81	86
00.03 National Senior Service Corps	174	183	193
00.05 Program support	29	31	34
09.01 Reimbursable program	7	7	7
10.00 Total new obligations	283	302	320
Budgetary resources available for obligation:			
22.00 New budget authority (gross)	283	302	320
23.95 Total new obligations	−283	−302	−320
New budget authority (gross), detail:			
Discretionary:			
40.00 Appropriation	276	296	313
40.76 Reduction pursuant to P.L. 106–113	....	−1	....
43.00 Appropriation (total discretionary)	276	295	313
68.00 Spending authority from offsetting collections: Offsetting collections (cash)	7	7	7
70.00 Total new budget authority (gross)	283	302	320
Change in unpaid obligations:			
72.40 Unpaid obligations, start of year: Obligated balance, start of year	205	233	256
73.10 Total new obligations	283	302	320
73.20 Total outlays (gross)	−255	−279	−313
74.40 Unpaid obligations, end of year: Obligated balance, end of year	233	256	263
Outlays (gross), detail:			
86.90 Outlays from new discretionary authority	147	170	183
86.93 Outlays from discretionary balances	108	107	132
87.00 Total outlays (gross)	255	279	313
Offsets:			
Against gross budget authority and outlays:			
Offsetting collections (cash) from:			
88.00 Federal sources	−2	−2	−2
88.40 Non-Federal sources	−5	−5	−5
88.90 Total, offsetting collections (cash)	−7	−7	−7
Net budget authority and outlays:			
89.00 Budget authority	276	295	313
90.00 Outlays	248	272	306

Volunteers in Service to America.—The AmeriCorps*VISTA program assists communities working to resolve local poverty-related problems in areas such as illiteracy, hunger, unemployment, substance abuse, homelessness, and lack of adequate health support.

National Senior Service Corps.—These programs provide opportunities for people aged 55 and over, including those who are low-income, to volunteer their services to the community in many socially useful activities including helping children learn to read and working with the emotionally disturbed, the mentally retarded, and physically disabled, as well as the isolated and infirm elderly.

Program support.—Costs of program direction and administration are financed by this activity.

Object Classification (in millions of dollars)

Identification code 95–0103–0–1–506	1999 actual	2000 est.	2001 est.
Direct obligations:			
Personnel compensation:			
11.1 Full-time permanent	15	16	17
11.3 Other than full-time permanent	2	2	2
11.8 Special personal services payments	42	46	49
11.9 Total personnel compensation	59	64	68
12.1 Civilian personnel benefits	5	5	5
21.0 Travel and transportation of persons	4	5	5
23.1 Rental payments to GSA	3	3	3
23.3 Communications, utilities, and miscellaneous charges	4	4	5
25.2 Other services	11	13	15
41.0 Grants, subsidies, and contributions	190	201	212
99.0 Subtotal, direct obligations	276	295	313
99.0 Reimbursable obligations	7	7	7
99.9 Total new obligations	283	302	320

Personnel Summary

Identification code 95–0103–0–1–506	1999 actual	2000 est.	2001 est.
1001 Total compensable workyears: Full-time equivalent employment	295	315	331

Office of Inspector General

For necessary expenses of the Office of Inspector General in carrying out the Inspector General Act of 1978, as amended, [$4,000,000] *$5,000,000. (Departments of Veterans Affairs and Housing and Urban Development, and Independent Agencies Appropriations Act of 2000.)*

Program and Financing (in millions of dollars)

Identification code 95–2721–0–1–506	1999 actual	2000 est.	2001 est.
Obligations by program activity:			
10.00 Total new obligations	3	4	5
Budgetary resources available for obligation:			
22.00 New budget authority (gross)	3	4	5
23.95 Total new obligations	−3	−4	−5
New budget authority (gross), detail:			
Discretionary:			
40.00 Appropriation	3	4	5
Change in unpaid obligations:			
72.40 Unpaid obligations, start of year: Obligated balance, start of year	2	2	2
73.10 Total new obligations	3	4	5
73.20 Total outlays (gross)	−3	−4	−5
74.40 Unpaid obligations, end of year: Obligated balance, end of year	2	2	2
Outlays (gross), detail:			
86.90 Outlays from new discretionary authority	1	2	3
86.93 Outlays from discretionary balances	2	2	2
87.00 Total outlays (gross)	3	4	5
Net budget authority and outlays:			
89.00 Budget authority	3	4	5
90.00 Outlays	3	4	5

The Office of the Inspector General provides an independent assessment of Corporation operations, primarily through audits and investigations, with a goal of preventing fraud, waste, and abuse.

Object Classification (in millions of dollars)

Identification code 95–2721–0–1–506	1999 actual	2000 est.	2001 est.
11.1 Personnel compensation: Full-time permanent	1	1	1
25.2 Other services	1	2	3
99.0 Subtotal, direct obligations	2	3	4
99.5 Below reporting threshold	1	1	1
99.9 Total new obligations	3	4	5

Personnel Summary

Identification code 95–2721–0–1–506	1999 actual	2000 est.	2001 est.
1001 Total compensable workyears: Full-time equivalent employment	9	18	18

Trust Funds

Gifts and Contributions

Unavailable Collections (in millions of dollars)

Identification code 95–9972–0–7–506	1999 actual	2000 est.	2001 est.
Balance, start of year:			
01.99 Balance, start of year	....	....	....
Receipts:			
02.02 Interest on investment	26	19	20
02.03 Payment from the general fund	70	70	80
02.99 Total receipts	96	89	100
Appropriation:			
05.01 Gifts and contributions	−96	−89	−100
05.99 Subtotal appropriation	−96	−89	−100
07.99 Total balance, end of year	....	....	....

Program and Financing (in millions of dollars)

Identification code 95–9972–0–7–506	1999 actual	2000 est.	2001 est.
Obligations by program activity:			
10.00 Total new obligations (object class 25.2)	56	75	85
Budgetary resources available for obligation:			
21.40 Unobligated balance available, start of year	358	398	332
22.00 New budget authority (gross)	96	9	100
23.90 Total budgetary resources available for obligation	454	407	432
23.95 Total new obligations	−56	−75	−85
24.40 Unobligated balance available, end of year	398	332	347
New budget authority (gross), detail:			
Discretionary:			
40.27 Appropriation (trust fund, indefinite)	70	70	80
40.36 Unobligated balance rescinded	....	−80	....
43.00 Appropriation (total discretionary)	70	−10	80
Mandatory:			
60.27 Appropriation (trust fund, indefinite)	26	19	20
70.00 Total new budget authority (gross)	96	9	100
Change in unpaid obligations:			
72.40 Unpaid obligations, start of year: Obligated balance, start of year	1	1	1
73.10 Total new obligations	56	75	85
73.20 Total outlays (gross)	−56	−75	−84
74.40 Unpaid obligations, end of year: Obligated balance, end of year	1	1	1

General and special funds—Continued

GIFTS AND CONTRIBUTIONS—Continued

Program and Financing (in millions of dollars)—Continued

Identification code 95–9972–0–7–506	1999 actual	2000 est.	2001 est.
Outlays (gross), detail:			
86.93 Outlays from discretionary balances	56	75	84
Net budget authority and outlays:			
89.00 Budget authority	96	9	100
90.00 Outlays	56	75	84
Memorandum (non-add) entries:			
92.01 Total investments, start of year: U.S. securities: Par value	341	380	314
92.02 Total investments, end of year: U.S. securities: Par value	380	314	328

The gifts and contributions account is a consolidation of two trust accounts. In one, gifts and contributions from individuals and organizations are deposited for use in furthering program goals. In the other, funds appropriated to make educational awards to individuals who successfully complete national service are maintained until such time as the individual uses those awards.

CORPORATION FOR PUBLIC BROADCASTING

Federal Funds

General and special funds:

CORPORATION FOR PUBLIC BROADCASTING

For payment to the Corporation for Public Broadcasting, as authorized by the Communications Act of 1934, an amount which shall be available within limitations specified by that Act, for the fiscal year [2002, $350,000,000] *2003, $365,000,000*: *Provided*, That no funds made available to the Corporation for Public Broadcasting by this Act shall be used to pay for receptions, parties, or similar forms of entertainment for Government officials or employees: *Provided further*, That none of the funds contained in this paragraph shall be available or used to aid or support any program or activity from which any person is excluded, or is denied benefits, or is discriminated against, on the basis of race, color, national origin, religion, or sex: [*Provided further*, That in addition to the amounts provided above, $10,000,000 shall be for digitalization, only if specifically authorized by subsequent legislation enacted by September 30, 2000]. *In addition, for costs related to digital program production, development, and distribution associated with the transition of public broadcasters to digital broadcasting, in the fiscal year specified: fiscal year 2001, $20,000,000; fiscal year 2002, $35,000,000; fiscal year 2003, $30,000,000, to be awarded as determined by the Corporation in consultation with public radio and television licensees or permittees, or their designated representatives. (Departments of Labor, Health and Human Services, and Education, and Related Agencies Appropriations Act, 2000, as enacted by section 1000(a)(4) of the Consolidated Appropriations Act, 2000 (P.L. 106–113).)*

Program and Financing (in millions of dollars)

Identification code 20–0151–0–1–503	1999 actual	2000 est.	2001 est.
Obligations by program activity:			
00.01 General programming and system support	250	300	340
00.02 Digital transition		10	20
00.03 Satellite replacement	31	17	
10.00 Total new obligations (object class 41.0)	281	327	360
Budgetary resources available for obligation:			
22.00 New budget authority (gross)	281	326	360
23.95 Total new obligations	−281	−327	−360
New budget authority (gross), detail:			
Discretionary:			
Appropriation:			
40.00 Appropriation—Digital		10	20
40.00 Appropriation—Satellite	31		
43.00 Appropriation (total discretionary)	31	10	20
Advance appropriation:			
55.00 Advance appropriation—General Programming	250	300	340
55.00 Advance appropriation—Satellite		17	
55.76 Reduction pursuant to P.L. 106–113		−1	
55.90 Advance appropriation (total discretionary)	250	316	340
70.00 Total new budget authority (gross)	281	326	360
Change in unpaid obligations:			
72.40 Unpaid obligations, start of year: Obligated balance, start of year			9
73.10 Total new obligations	281	327	360
73.20 Total outlays (gross)	−281	−318	−345
74.40 Unpaid obligations, end of year: Obligated balance, end of year		9	24
Outlays (gross), detail:			
86.90 Outlays from new discretionary authority	281	317	342
86.93 Outlays from discretionary balances			3
87.00 Total outlays (gross)	281	318	345
Net budget authority and outlays:			
89.00 Budget authority	281	326	360
90.00 Outlays	281	318	345

The Corporation for Public Broadcasting provides grants to qualified public television and radio stations to be used at their discretion for purposes related to program production or acquisition and general operations. The Corporation also supports the production and acquisition of radio and television programs for national distribution. In addition, the Corporation assists in the financing of several system-wide activities, including national satellite interconnection services and the payment of music royalty fees, and provides limited technical assistance, research, and planning services to improve system-wide capacity and performance. The appropriation for the Corporation is enacted two years in advance. For 2002, an appropriation of $350 million was enacted in the 2000 appropriations act.

For 2003, the Administration is requesting $365 million for general programming and system support. In addition, the Corporation should be reauthorized this year, its most recent authorization having expired at the end of fiscal year 1996. Public broadcasting plays a vital role in the educational and cultural development of our Nation. The proposed funding level will allow the Corporation to carry out its role of facilitating the provision of universally available educational, noncommercial public telecommunications services that meet the needs of local communities across the country.

In April 1997, the Federal Communications Commission issued regulations requiring broadcasters to transition from analog to digital broadcasting. Public broadcasters must convert to digital by May 1, 2003. Advance appropriation is requested for a multi-year program to allow advance planning and certainty in the public broadcasting system's transition to digital. Funds made available from this program to the Corporation for Public Broadcasting (CPB) will facilitate public broadcasters' transition to digital broadcasting. CPB funding will be used in coordination with funds made available to the Commerce Department as part of a $450 million, five-year initiative now in its third year. Funding through the Commerce Department will be targeted for digital transmission equipment, while funding for CPB will support necessary investments related to digital program production, development and distribution associated with the transition of public broadcasters to digital broadcasting. The following tables illustrate the proposed funding levels.

Operations, 2001–2003 (in millions of dollars)

	2001 enacted	2002 enacted	2003 proposed
Operations	340	350	365

Digital transition, 1999–2003 (in millions of dollars)

	1999 actual	2000 enacted	2001 est.	2002 est.	2003 est.
Digital transition	0	10	20	35	30

COURT OF [VETERANS] APPEALS *FOR VETERANS CLAIMS*

Federal Funds

General and special funds:

SALARIES AND EXPENSES

For necessary expenses for the operation of the United States Court of [Veterans] Appeals *for Veterans Claims,* as authorized by 38 U.S.C. 7251–7298, [$11,450,000] *$12,500,000,* of which [$910,000] *$950,000,* shall be available for the purpose of providing financial assistance as described, and in accordance with the process and reporting procedures set forth, under this heading in Public Law 102–229. *(Departments of Veterans Affairs and Housing and Urban Development, and Independent Agencies Appropriations Act, 2000.)*

Program and Financing (in millions of dollars)

Identification code 95–0300–0–1–705	1999 actual	2000 est.	2001 est.
Obligations by program activity:			
10.00 Total new obligations	10	11	12
Budgetary resources available for obligation:			
22.00 New budget authority (gross)	10	11	12
23.95 Total new obligations	−10	−11	−12
New budget authority (gross), detail:			
Discretionary:			
40.00 Appropriation	10	11	12
Change in unpaid obligations:			
72.40 Unpaid obligations, start of year: Obligated balance, start of year	1	1	1
73.10 Total new obligations	10	11	12
73.20 Total outlays (gross)	−9	−11	−12
74.40 Unpaid obligations, end of year: Obligated balance, end of year	1	1	1
Outlays (gross), detail:			
86.90 Outlays from new discretionary authority	8	10	11
86.93 Outlays from discretionary balances	1	1	1
87.00 Total outlays (gross)	9	11	12
Net budget authority and outlays:			
89.00 Budget authority	10	11	12
90.00 Outlays	9	11	12

The Veterans Judicial Review Act, 38 U.S.C. §§7251–7292 (1988) established the United States Court of Veterans Appeals (renamed United States Court of Appeals for Veterans Claims as of March 1, 1999, Public Law 105–368) under Article I of the United States Constitution. The Court is empowered to review decisions of the Board of Veterans' Appeals and may affirm, modify, revise, or remand a decision of the Board of Veterans' Appeals as it deems appropriate. The type of review performed by the Court is similar to that which is performed in Article III courts under the Administrative Procedure Act, title 5 U.S.C. §§551 et seq. In actions before it, the Court has the authority to decide all relevant questions of law, to interpret constitutional, statutory, and regulatory provisions, and to determine the meaning or applicability of the terms of an action by the Secretary of the Department of Veterans Affairs. The Court, being created by an act of Congress, may issue all writs necessary or appropriate in aid of its jurisdiction, 28 U.S.C. §1651.

The Court is empowered to: compel actions of the Secretary that are found to have been unlawfully withheld or unreasonably delayed; and set aside decisions, findings, conclusions, rules, and regulations issued or adopted by the Secretary, the Board of Veterans' Appeals, or the Chairman of the Board that are found to be arbitrary or capricious. The Court may also set aside decisions which are abuse of discretion or otherwise not in accordance with the law, contrary to constitutional right, in excess of statutory jurisdiction or authority, or without observance of the procedures required by law. In cases involving benefits under the laws administered by the Department, the Court may hold unlawful or set aside findings of material facts if the findings are clearly erroneous.

The Court's principal office location is Washington, D.C.; however, it is a national court, empowered to sit anywhere in the United States.

Practice Registration Fees.—This fund is established under 38 U.S.C. §7285. The fund, which receives no appropriations, will be used by the U.S. Court of Appeals for Veterans Claims to employ independent counsel to pursue disciplinary matters involving practitioners and to defray costs for the implementation of the standards of practice before the Court.

Object Classification (in millions of dollars)

Identification code 95–0300–0–1–705	1999 actual	2000 est.	2001 est.
11.3 Personnel compensation: Other than full-time permanent	5	6	6
12.1 Civilian personnel benefits	1	2	2
23.1 Rental payments to GSA	2	1	2
41.0 Grants, subsidies, and contributions	1	1	1
99.0 Subtotal, direct obligations	9	10	11
99.5 Below reporting threshold	1	1	1
99.9 Total new obligations	10	11	12

Personnel Summary

Identification code 95–0300–0–1–705	1999 actual	2000 est.	2001 est.
1001 Total compensable workyears: Full-time equivalent employment	75	88	88

Trust Funds

COURT OF [VETERANS] APPEALS *FOR VETERANS CLAIMS*
RETIREMENT FUND

Unavailable Collections (in millions of dollars)

Identification code 95–8290–0–7–705	1999 actual	2000 est.	2001 est.
Balance, start of year:			
01.99 Balance, start of year	3	3	4
Receipts:			
02.03 Employing agency contributions	....	1	1
04.00 Total: Balances and collections	3	4	5
07.99 Total balance, end of year	3	4	5

This fund, established under 38 U.S.C. §7298 will be used to pay judges' retired pay and annuities, refunds, and allowances to surviving spouses and dependent children. Participating judges pay one percent of their salaries to cover creditable service for retirement annuity purposes for which payment is required and 3.5 percent of their salaries for survivor annuity purposes for which payment is required. Additional funds as are needed to cover the unfunded liability may be transferred from the annual appropriation of the U.S. Court of Appeals for Veterans Claims.

COURT SERVICES AND OFFENDER SUPERVISION AGENCY FOR THE DISTRICT OF COLUMBIA

Federal Funds

General and special funds:

FEDERAL PAYMENT TO THE COURT SERVICES AND OFFENDER SUPERVISION AGENCY FOR THE DISTRICT OF COLUMBIA

For salaries and expenses of the Court Services and Offender Supervision Agency for the District of Columbia, as authorized by the National Capital Revitalization and Self-Government Improvement Act of 1997, (Public Law 105–33; 111 Stat. 712), [$93,800,000] *$103,527,000*, of which [$58,600,000] *$61,551,000* shall be for necessary expenses of [Parole Revocation, Adult Probation, Offender Supervision,] *Community Supervision* and Sex Offender Registration, to include expenses relating to supervision of adults subject to protection orders or provision of services for or related to such persons; [$17,400,000] *$18,487,000* shall be available to the Public Defender Service; and [$17,800,000] *$23,489,000* shall be available to the Pretrial Services Agency: *Provided*, That notwithstanding any other provision of law, all amounts under this heading shall be apportioned quarterly by the Office of Management and Budget and obligated and expended in the same manner as funds appropriated for salaries and expenses of other Federal agencies[: *Provided further*, That of the amounts made available under this heading, $20,492,000 shall be used in support of universal drug screening and testing for those individuals on pretrial, probation, or parole supervision with continued testing, intermediate sanctions, and treatment for those identified in need, of which $7,000,000 shall be for treatment services]. *(District of Columbia Appropriations Act, 2000.)*

Program and Financing (in millions of dollars)

Identification code 95–1734–0–1–752		1999 actual	2000 est.	2001 est.
	Obligations by program activity:			
00.01	Community supervision program	34	57	62
00.02	Pretrial Services Agency	11	20	24
00.03	Public Defender Service	14	17	18
10.00	Total new obligations	59	94	104
	Budgetary resources available for obligation:			
22.00	New budget authority (gross)	60	94	104
23.95	Total new obligations	−59	−94	−104
	New budget authority (gross), detail:			
	Discretionary:			
40.00	Appropriation	59	94	104
42.00	Transferred from other accounts	1		
43.00	Appropriation (total discretionary)	60	94	104
	Change in unpaid obligations:			
72.40	Unpaid obligations, start of year: Obligated balance, start of year			19
73.10	Total new obligations	59	94	104
73.20	Total outlays (gross)	−57	−77	−102
74.40	Unpaid obligations, end of year: Obligated balance, end of year		19	21
	Outlays (gross), detail:			
86.90	Outlays from new discretionary authority	57	75	83
86.93	Outlays from discretionary balances			19
87.00	Total outlays (gross)	57	77	102
	Net budget authority and outlays:			
89.00	Budget authority	60	94	104
90.00	Outlays	57	77	102

The National Capital Revitalization and Self-Government Improvement Act established the Court Services and Offender Supervision Agency for the District of Columbia as an independent Federal agency, which has assumed the District of Columbia pretrial services, adult probation, and parole supervision functions. The mission of the Agency, including the D.C. Pretrial Services Agency, is to increase public safety, prevent crime, reduce recidivism and support the fair administration of justice in close collaboration with the community. The D.C. Public Defender Service provides legal representation services within the District of Columbia, and transmits its budget with that of the Agency, yet operates as an independent District of Columbia agency, as required by law.

The Agency's budget supports the Community Supervision Program, the Pretrial Services Agency, and the Public Defender Service. For 2001, $17,064,000 in additional resources is requested within the Community Oriented Policing Services grant program for treatment, graduated sanctions, and restrictive supervision contract beds.

Community Supervision Program.—This activity provides supervision of adult offenders on probation, parole or supervised release, consistent with a proven crime prevention strategy that integrates supervision, routine drug testing, treatment, and graduated sanctions. For 2001, $4,589,000 is requested to provide immediate and graduated sanctions to offenders who violate conditions of their release, improve the supervision of sex offenders, initiate DNA testing of offenders, and provide ancillary treatment services. Resources have also been included to move Community Supervision Officers out of downtown District of Columbia Court offices into the community, fully implement and evaluate the Agency's performance management strategy, provide staff to adequately support the information technology program, and improve employee training.

Pretrial Services Agency.—This activity assists the trial and appellate levels of both the Federal and local courts in determining eligibility for pretrial release by providing background information on all arrestees. The Pretrial Services Agency is further responsible for supervising conditions of release and reporting on compliance to the court. For 2001, $3,720,000 is requested to improve the level of supervision provided to defendants on pretrial release and to fund routine drug testing, treatment, graduated sanctions, and information technology improvements and support.

Public Defender Service.—This activity provides legal representation to defendants and provides support in the form of training, consultation and legal reference services to members of the local bar appointed as counsel in criminal, juvenile, and mental health cases involving indigent individuals. For 2001, $545,000 is requested to address the increase in workload related to improvements in parole processing, to provide the court with sentencing assistance, and for travel for client and witness interviews as District sentenced offenders are relocated to federal correctional institutions.

In 2001, the Court Services and Offender Supervision Agency will continue to work closely with all elements of the District of Columbia and Federal criminal justice, courts, corrections, and rehabilitation systems to improve offender supervision and court services programs, policy, and practice.

Object Classification (in millions of dollars)

Identification code 95–1734–0–1–752		1999 actual	2000 est.	2001 est.
	Personnel compensation:			
11.1	Full-time permanent			46
11.8	Special personal services payments			14
11.9	Total personnel compensation			60
12.1	Civilian personnel benefits			12
21.0	Travel and transportation of persons			2
23.2	Rental payments to others			11
23.3	Communications, utilities, and miscellaneous charges			1
25.1	Advisory and assistance services			3
25.2	Other services			8
25.3	Purchases of goods and services from Government accounts			1
26.0	Supplies and materials			1
31.0	Equipment			4
32.0	Land and structures			1
41.0	Grants, subsidies, and contributions	59	94	

99.9	Total new obligations	59	94	104

Personnel Summary

Identification code 95–1734–0–1–752		1999 actual	2000 est.	2001 est.
1001	Total compensable workyears: Full-time equivalent employment			1,094

DEFENSE NUCLEAR FACILITIES SAFETY BOARD

Federal Funds

General and special funds:

SALARIES AND EXPENSES

For necessary expenses of the Defense Nuclear Facilities Safety Board in carrying out activities authorized by the Atomic Energy Act of 1954, as amended by Public Law 100–456, section 1441, [$17,000,000] *$18,500,000*, to remain available until expended. *(Energy and Water Development Appropriations Act, 2000.)*

Program and Financing (in millions of dollars)

Identification code 95–3900–0–1–053		1999 actual	2000 est.	2001 est.
	Obligations by program activity:			
10.00	Total new obligations	18	18	19
	Budgetary resources available for obligation:			
21.40	Unobligated balance available, start of year	3	2	1
22.00	New budget authority (gross)	17	17	18
23.90	Total budgetary resources available for obligation	20	19	19
23.95	Total new obligations	–18	–18	–19
24.40	Unobligated balance available, end of year	2	1	1
	New budget authority (gross), detail:			
	Discretionary:			
40.00	Appropriation	17	17	18
	Change in unpaid obligations:			
72.40	Unpaid obligations, start of year: Obligated balance, start of year	6	7	7
73.10	Total new obligations	18	18	19
73.20	Total outlays (gross)	–17	–18	–18
74.40	Unpaid obligations, end of year: Obligated balance, end of year	7	7	8
	Outlays (gross), detail:			
86.90	Outlays from new discretionary authority	8	10	11
86.93	Outlays from discretionary balances	9	8	8
87.00	Total outlays (gross)	17	18	18
	Net budget authority and outlays:			
89.00	Budget authority	17	17	18
90.00	Outlays	17	18	18

The Defense Nuclear Facilities Safety Board, authorized by Public Law 100–456, is responsible for evaluating the content and implementation of the standards relating to the design, construction, operation, and decommissioning of defense nuclear facilities of the Department of Energy (DOE) (as defined in Public Law 100–456). The Board also reviews the design of new DOE defense nuclear facilities, and periodically reviews and monitors construction of such facilities to ensure adequate protection of public and worker health and safety. In addition, the National Defense Authorization Act for 1992 and 1993 (Public Law 102–190) expanded the Board's jurisdiction to include facilities and activities involved with the assembly, disassembly, and testing of nuclear weapons. The Board is also responsible for investigating any event or practice at a defense nuclear facility which has or may adversely affect public health and safety. The Board makes specific recommendations to the Secretary of Energy on measures that should be adopted to ensure that both public and employee health and safety are adequately protected.

Object Classification (in millions of dollars)

Identification code 95–3900–0–1–053		1999 actual	2000 est.	2001 est.
11.1	Personnel compensation: Full-time permanent	9	10	11
12.1	Civilian personnel benefits	2	2	3
21.0	Travel and transportation of persons	1	1	1
23.1	Rental payments to GSA	2	2	2
25.1	Advisory and assistance services	2	2	1
25.2	Other services	1	1	1
99.0	Subtotal, direct obligations	17	18	19
99.5	Below reporting threshold	1		
99.9	Total new obligations	18	18	19

Personnel Summary

Identification code 95–3900–0–1–053		1999 actual	2000 est.	2001 est.
1001	Total compensable workyears: Full-time equivalent employment	94	99	105

DELTA REGIONAL AUTHORITY

Federal Funds

General and special funds:

(Legislative proposal, not subject to PAYGO)

Program and Financing (in millions of dollars)

Identification code 95–0750–2–1–452		1999 actual	2000 est.	2001 est.
	Obligations by program activity:			
10.00	Total new obligations			3
	Budgetary resources available for obligation:			
22.00	New budget authority (gross)			30
23.95	Total new obligations			–3
24.40	Unobligated balance available, end of year			27
	New budget authority (gross), detail:			
	Discretionary:			
40.00	Appropriation			30
	Change in unpaid obligations:			
73.10	Total new obligations			3
73.20	Total outlays (gross)			–3
	Outlays (gross), detail:			
86.90	Outlays from new discretionary authority			3
	Net budget authority and outlays:			
89.00	Budget authority			30
90.00	Outlays			3

The Administration proposes to create the Delta Regional Authority (DRA), modeled on other regional economic development authorities. The DRA will be designed to assist the 219-county region in seven states established by P.L. 100–460. The economic distress in the Delta region is widespread and protracted—over half the Delta counties have had poverty rates over 20 percent for the past four decades. The Authority will assist in directing its resources and the resources of other federal agencies to the Delta region, with a focus on those counties with the highest levels of poverty and unemployment.

The President would appoint the Federal Co-Chairperson of the DRA. The Governors of the seven member states would serve as Authority members and would elect one of these Governors as States' Co-Chairperson.

General and special funds—Continued

Object Classification (in millions of dollars)

Identification code 95–0750–2–1–452	1999 actual	2000 est.	2001 est.
11.1 Personnel compensation: Full-time permanent			1
41.0 Grants, subsidies, and contributions			2
99.9 Total new obligations			3

Personnel Summary

Identification code 95–0750–2–1–452	1999 actual	2000 est.	2001 est.
1001 Total compensable workyears: Full-time equivalent employment			5

DENALI COMMISSION

Federal Funds

General and special funds:

DENALI COMMISSION

For expenses of the Denali Commission including the purchase, construction and acquisition of plant and capital equipment as necessary and other expenses, $20,000,000, to remain available until expended. *(Energy and Water Development Appropriations Act, 2000.)*

Program and Financing (in millions of dollars)

Identification code 95–1200–0–1–452	1999 actual	2000 est.	2001 est.
Obligations by program activity:			
01.01 Direct Program Activity	18	20	20
10.00 Total new obligations (object class 41.0)	18	20	20
Budgetary resources available for obligation:			
22.00 New budget authority (gross)	20	20	20
23.95 Total new obligations	−18	−20	−20
New budget authority (gross), detail:			
Discretionary:			
40.00 Appropriation	20	20	20
Change in unpaid obligations:			
72.40 Unpaid obligations, start of year: Obligated balance, start of year		18	18
73.10 Total new obligations	18	20	20
73.20 Total outlays (gross)	−1	−20	−20
74.40 Unpaid obligations, end of year: Obligated balance, end of year	18	18	18
Outlays (gross), detail:			
86.90 Outlays from new discretionary authority	1	1	1
86.93 Outlays from discretionary balances		18	19
87.00 Total outlays (gross)	1	20	20
Net budget authority and outlays:			
89.00 Budget authority	20	20	20
90.00 Outlays	1	20	20

Personnel Summary

Identification code 95–1200–0–1–452	1999 actual	2000 est.	2001 est.
1001 Total compensable workyears: Full-time equivalent employment	4	3	4

Trust Funds

DENALI COMMISSION TRUST FUND

Program and Financing (in millions of dollars)

Identification code 95–8056–0–7–452	1999 actual	2000 est.	2001 est.
Obligations by program activity:			
01.01 Direct Program Activity		10	10
10.00 Total new obligations (object class 41.0)		10	10
Budgetary resources available for obligation:			
22.00 New budget authority (gross)		10	10
23.95 Total new obligations		−10	−10
New budget authority (gross), detail:			
Discretionary:			
40.27 Appropriation (trust fund, indefinite)		10	10
Change in unpaid obligations:			
73.10 Total new obligations		10	10
73.20 Total outlays (gross)		−10	−10
Outlays (gross), detail:			
86.90 Outlays from new discretionary authority		10	10
Net budget authority and outlays:			
89.00 Budget authority		10	10
90.00 Outlays		10	10

DISTRICT OF COLUMBIA

DISTRICT OF COLUMBIA COURTS

Federal Funds

General and special funds:

FEDERAL PAYMENT TO THE DISTRICT OF COLUMBIA COURTS

For salaries and expenses for the District of Columbia Courts, [$99,714,000] ***$103,000,000*** to be allocated as follows: for the District of Columbia Court of Appeals, [$7,209,000] ***$7,709,000***; for the District of Columbia Superior Court, [$68,351,000] ***$72,399,000***; for the District of Columbia Court System, [$16,154,000] ***$17,892,000***; and [$8,000,000] ***$5,000,000***, to remain available until September 30, [2001] ***2002***, for capital improvements for District of Columbia courthouse facilities: [*Provided*, That of the amounts available for operations of the District of Columbia Courts, not to exceed $2,500,000 shall be for the design of an Integrated Justice Information System and that such funds shall be used in accordance with a plan and design developed by the courts and approved by the Committees on Appropriations of the House of Representatives and the Senate:] *Provided* [*further*], That notwithstanding any other provision of law, all amounts under this heading shall be apportioned quarterly by the Office of Management and Budget and obligated and expended in the same manner as funds appropriated for salaries and expenses of other Federal agencies, with payroll and financial services to be provided on a contractual basis with the General Services Administration (GSA), said services to include the preparation of monthly financial reports, copies of which shall be submitted directly by GSA to the President and to the Committees on Appropriations of the Senate and House of Representatives, the Committee on Governmental Affairs of the Senate, and the Committee on Government Reform of the House of Representatives. *(District of Columbia Appropriations Act, 2000.)*

Program and Financing (in millions of dollars)

Identification code 20–1712–0–1–806	1999 actual	2000 est.	2001 est.
Obligations by program activity:			
10.00 Total new obligations (object class 41.0)	131	100	103
Budgetary resources available for obligation:			
22.00 New budget authority (gross)	131	100	103
23.95 Total new obligations	−131	−100	−103
New budget authority (gross), detail:			
Discretionary:			
40.00 Appropriation	128	100	103

42.00	Transferred from other accounts	3		
43.00	Appropriation (total discretionary)	131	100	103
	Change in unpaid obligations:			
72.40	Unpaid obligations, start of year: Obligated balance, start of year		3	13
73.10	Total new obligations	131	100	103
73.20	Total outlays (gross)	−128	−90	−103
74.40	Unpaid obligations, end of year: Obligated balance, end of year	3	13	13
	Outlays (gross), detail:			
86.90	Outlays from new discretionary authority	128	90	93
86.93	Outlays from discretionary balances			10
87.00	Total outlays (gross)	128	90	103
	Net budget authority and outlays:			
89.00	Budget authority	131	100	103
90.00	Outlays	128	90	103

Under the National Capital Revitalization and Self-Government Improvement Act of 1997, the Federal Government is required to finance the District of Columbia Courts beginning in 1998. This Federal payment to the District of Columbia Courts funds the operations of the District of Columbia Court of Appeals, Superior Court and the Court System. Beginning in 1999, the Federal Government also provides funds for capital improvements. Beginning in 2000, funding for Defender Services in the District of Columbia Courts will be provided through a separate account.

By law, the annual budget includes estimates of the expenditures for the operations of the District of Columbia Courts prepared by the Joint Committee on Judicial Administration in the District of Columbia and the President's recommendation for funding District Courts operations. The President's recommended level of $103 million includes: $98 million for District of Columbia Court of Appeals, Superior Court of the District of Columbia and the District of Columbia Court System operations; and, $5 million for capital improvements for District courthouse facilities. In addition, the recommendation includes $38 million for Defender Services. Under a separate transmittal to Congress, the District Courts are requesting $123 million, $105 million for operations and $18 million for capital improvements, with an additional $42 million for Defender Services.

Defender Services in District of Columbia Courts

For payments authorized under section 11–2604 and section 11–2605, D.C. Code (relating to representation provided under the District of Columbia Criminal Justice Act), payments for counsel appointed in proceedings in the Family Division of the Superior Court of the District of Columbia under chapter 23 of title 16, D.C. Code, and payments for counsel authorized under section 21–2060, D.C. Code (relating to representation provided under the District of Columbia Guardianship, Protective Proceedings, and Durable Power of Attorney Act of 1986), [$33,336,000] *$38,387,000*, to remain available until expended: *Provided*, That the funds provided in this Act under the heading "Federal Payment to the District of Columbia Courts" (other than the [$8,000,000] *$5,000,000* provided under such heading for capital improvements for District of Columbia courthouse facilities) may also be used for payments under this heading: *Provided further*, That [in addition to the funds provided under this heading,] the Joint Committee on Judicial Administration in the District of Columbia shall use [the interest earned on the Federal payment made to the District of Columbia courts under the District of Columbia Appropriations Act, 1999, together with] funds provided in this Act under the heading "Federal Payment to the District of Columbia Courts" (other than the [$8,000,000] *$5,000,000* provided under such heading for capital improvements for District of Columbia courthouse facilities), to make payments described under this heading for obligations incurred during fiscal year [1999] *2000* if the Comptroller General certifies that the amount of obligations lawfully incurred for such payments during fiscal year [1999] *2000* exceeds the obligational authority otherwise available for making such payments: *Provided further*, That such funds shall be administered by the Joint Committee on Judicial Administration in the District of Columbia: *Provided further*, That notwithstanding any other provision of law, this appropriation shall be apportioned quarterly by the Office of Management and Budget and obligated and expended in the same manner as funds appropriated for expenses of other Federal agencies, with payroll and financial services to be provided on a contractual basis with the General Services Administration (GSA), said services to include the preparation of monthly financial reports, copies of which shall be submitted directly by GSA to the President and to the Committees on Appropriations of the Senate and House of Representatives, the Committee on Governmental Affairs of the Senate, and the Committee on Government Reform of the House of Representatives: *Provided further, That the District of Columbia Courts shall implement the recommendations in the General Accounting Office Report GAO/AIMD/OGC–99–226 regarding payments to court-appointed attorneys and shall report to the Office of Management and Budget and to the House and Senate Appropriations Committees quarterly on the status of these reforms. (District of Columbia Appropriations Act, 2000.)*

Program and Financing (in millions of dollars)

Identification code 95–1736–0–1–806		1999 actual	2000 est.	2001 est.
	Obligations by program activity:			
10.00	Total new obligations (object class 41.0)		33	38
	Budgetary resources available for obligation:			
22.00	New budget authority (gross)		33	38
23.95	Total new obligations		−33	−38
	New budget authority (gross), detail:			
	Discretionary:			
40.00	Appropriation		33	38
	Change in unpaid obligations:			
72.40	Unpaid obligations, start of year: Obligated balance, start of year			3
73.10	Total new obligations		33	38
73.20	Total outlays (gross)		−30	−37
74.40	Unpaid obligations, end of year: Obligated balance, end of year		3	3
	Outlays (gross), detail:			
86.90	Outlays from new discretionary authority		30	34
86.93	Outlays from discretionary balances			3
87.00	Total outlays (gross)		30	37
	Net budget authority and outlays:			
89.00	Budget authority		33	38
90.00	Outlays		30	37

Federal Payment to the District of Columbia Criminal Justice System

Program and Financing (in millions of dollars)

Identification code 20–1708–0–1–806		1999 actual	2000 est.	2001 est.
	Obligations by program activity:			
00.02	Offender supervision trustee	4		
10.00	Total new obligations (object class 41.0)	4		
	Budgetary resources available for obligation:			
22.00	New budget authority (gross)	4		
23.95	Total new obligations	−4		
	New budget authority (gross), detail:			
	Discretionary:			
40.00	Appropriation	4		
	Change in unpaid obligations:			
73.10	Total new obligations	4		
73.20	Total outlays (gross)	−4		

General and special funds—Continued

FEDERAL PAYMENT TO THE DISTRICT OF COLUMBIA CRIMINAL JUSTICE SYSTEM—Continued

Program and Financing (in millions of dollars)—Continued

Identification code 20–1708–0–1–806	1999 actual	2000 est.	2001 est.
Outlays (gross), detail:			
86.90 Outlays from new discretionary authority	4		
Net budget authority and outlays:			
89.00 Budget authority	4		
90.00 Outlays	4		

FEDERAL PAYMENT TO THE DISTRICT OF COLUMBIA JUDICIAL RETIREMENT AND SURVIVORS ANNUITY FUND

Program and Financing (in millions of dollars)

Identification code 20–1713–0–1–752	1999 actual	2000 est.	2001 est.
Obligations by program activity:			
10.00 Total new obligations (object class 13.0)	6	5	5
Budgetary resources available for obligation:			
22.00 New budget authority (gross)	6	5	5
23.95 Total new obligations	–6	–5	–5
New budget authority (gross), detail:			
Mandatory:			
60.00 Appropriation	6	5	5
Change in unpaid obligations:			
73.10 Total new obligations	6	5	5
73.20 Total outlays (gross)	–6	–5	–5
Outlays (gross), detail:			
86.97 Outlays from new mandatory authority	6	5	5
Net budget authority and outlays:			
89.00 Budget authority	6	5	5
90.00 Outlays	6	5	5

Trust Funds

DISTRICT OF COLUMBIA JUDICIAL RETIREMENT AND SURVIVORS ANNUITY FUND

Unavailable Collections (in millions of dollars)

Identification code 20–8212–0–7–602	1999 actual	2000 est.	2001 est.
Balance, start of year:			
01.99 Balance, start of year		65	69
Receipts:			
02.01 Amortization payment	6	5	5
02.02 Deductions from employees salaries	1		
02.04 Interest earnings	–2	4	4
02.05 Proceeds from the sale of pension assets	66		
02.99 Total receipts	71	9	9
04.00 Total: Balances and collections	71	74	78
Appropriation:			
05.01 District of Columbia Judicial Retirement and Survivors Annuity Fund	–6	–5	–5
07.99 Total balance, end of year	65	69	73

Program and Financing (in millions of dollars)

Identification code 20–8212–0–7–602	1999 actual	2000 est.	2001 est.
Obligations by program activity:			
00.01 Retirement Payments	2	6	6
10.00 Total new obligations (object class 13.0)	2	6	6
Budgetary resources available for obligation:			
21.40 Unobligated balance available, start of year	6	10	9
22.00 New budget authority (gross)	6	5	5
23.90 Total budgetary resources available for obligation	12	15	14
23.95 Total new obligations	–2	–6	–6
24.40 Unobligated balance available, end of year	10	9	8
New budget authority (gross), detail:			
Mandatory:			
60.27 Appropriation (trust fund, indefinite)	6	5	5
Change in unpaid obligations:			
73.10 Total new obligations	2	6	6
73.20 Total outlays (gross)	–2	–6	–6
Outlays (gross), detail:			
86.98 Outlays from mandatory balances	2	6	6
Net budget authority and outlays:			
89.00 Budget authority	6	5	5
90.00 Outlays	2	6	6
Memorandum (non-add) entries:			
92.01 Total investments, start of year: U.S. securities: Par value	5	77	82
92.02 Total investments, end of year: U.S. securities: Par value	77	82	86

The National Capital Revitalization and Self-Government Improvement Act of 1997 requires the Federal Government to assume responsibility for financing the District of Columbia retirement program for judges. The District of Columbia Judicial Retirement and Survivors Annuity Fund has been established in the Treasury to finance judges' retirement pay, annuities, and expenses associated with the administration of the Fund.

FEDERAL PAYMENT TO THE DISTRICT OF COLUMBIA CORRECTIONS TRUSTEE OPERATIONS

For salaries and expenses of the District of Columbia Corrections Trustee, [$176,000,000] *$134,300,000* for the administration and operation of correctional facilities and for the administrative operating costs of the Office of the Corrections Trustee, as authorized by section 11202 of the National Capital Revitalization and Self-Government Improvement Act of 1997 (Public Law 105–33; 111 Stat. 712) *of which $1,000,000 is to fund an initiative to improve case processing in the District of Columbia criminal justice system*: *Provided*, That notwithstanding any other provision of law, funds appropriated in this Act for the District of Columbia Corrections Trustee shall be apportioned quarterly by the Office of Management and Budget and obligated and expended in the same manner as funds appropriated for salaries and expenses of other Federal agencies: *Provided further*, That in addition to the funds provided under this heading, the District of Columbia Corrections Trustee may use [a portion of the] *any remaining* interest earned on the Federal payment made to the Trustee under the District of Columbia Appropriations Act, 1998, [(not to exceed $4,600,000)] to carry out the activities funded under this heading. *(District of Columbia Appropriations Act, 2000.)*

Program and Financing (in millions of dollars)

Identification code 95–1735–0–1–806	1999 actual	2000 est.	2001 est.
Obligations by program activity:			
10.00 Total new obligations (object class 41.0)	185	175	134
Budgetary resources available for obligation:			
22.00 New budget authority (gross)	185	175	134
23.95 Total new obligations	–185	–175	–134
New budget authority (gross), detail:			
Discretionary:			
40.00 Appropriation	185	176	134
40.76 Reduction pursuant to P.L. 106–113		–1	
43.00 Appropriation (total discretionary)	185	175	134

Change in unpaid obligations:			
72.40 Unpaid obligations, start of year: Obligated balance, start of year		33	
73.10 Total new obligations	185	175	134
73.20 Total outlays (gross)	−152	−209	−134
74.40 Unpaid obligations, end of year: Obligated balance, end of year	33		
Outlays (gross), detail:			
86.90 Outlays from new discretionary authority	152	175	134
86.93 Outlays from discretionary balances		33	
87.00 Total outlays (gross)	152	209	134
Net budget authority and outlays:			
89.00 Budget authority	185	175	134
90.00 Outlays	152	209	134

The National Capital Revitalization and Self-Government Improvement Act requires that the adult felon population of the District of Columbia be transferred to the Federal Prison System over the next several years. To assist in this transition, the Act established a Corrections Trustee to provide financial oversight of, and assistance to, the District of Columbia Department of Corrections during this period. The Corrections Trustee also provides funding to the D.C. Department of Corrections associated with the prisoner population that will eventually be transferred to the Federal Prison System. The current D.C. felon inmate population is approximately 6,000, in addition to 2,000 inmates who have already been transferred permanently to the Federal Prison System. The remaining inmates will be transferred to the Federal Prison System when the D.C. prison facilities at Lorton, Virginia, are closed or by December 31, 2001, whichever is earlier.

In 2001, the Corrections Trustee will continue to work with the D.C. Department of Corrections on the initiatives in progress to close the Lorton facilities. Four of the seven prison facilities located at the Lorton site have been closed and one additional facility will be closed in 2000. This closing initiative has been accomplished by transferring 1,250 inmates to facilities contracted by the D.C. Department of Corrections with the State of Virginia during 1999 and by transferring an additional 2,000 inmates to the Federal Prison System.

The Corrections Trustee will continue to place a high priority in 2001 on advising the D.C. Department of Corrections on the improvement of its system of internal controls; audits to enhance the quality and accountability of operations; and oversight of contract prison facilities.

In an effort to assist the District of Columbia Criminal Justice System, the Corrections Trustee, in consultation with the D.C. Criminal Justice Coordinating Council, will fund a study, not to exceed $1 million, to review improvements in inmate case processing in the District's criminal justice system.

District of Columbia General and Special Payments

Federal Funds

General and special funds:

Federal Payment for Resident Tuition Support

For a Federal payment to the District of Columbia for a program to be administered by the Mayor for District of Columbia resident tuition support, [subject to the enactment of authorizing legislation for such program by Congress,] $17,000,000, to remain available until expended: *Provided*, That such funds may be used on behalf of eligible District of Columbia residents to pay an amount based upon the difference between in-State and out-of-State tuition at public institutions of higher education, usable at both public and private institutions of higher education[: *Provided further*, That the awarding of such funds may be prioritized on the basis of a resident's academic merit and such other factors as may be authorized: *Provided further*, That if the authorized program is a nationwide program, the Mayor may expend up to $17,000,000: *Provided further*, That if the authorized program is for a limited number of States, the Mayor may expend up to $11,000,000: *Provided further*, That the District of Columbia may expend funds other than the funds provided under this heading, including local tax revenues and contributions, to support such program]. *(District of Columbia Appropriations Act, 2000.)*

Program and Financing (in millions of dollars)

Identification code 20–1736–0–1–502	1999 actual	2000 est.	2001 est.
Obligations by program activity:			
10.00 Total new obligations (object class 41.0)		17	17
Budgetary resources available for obligation:			
22.00 New budget authority (gross)		17	17
23.95 Total new obligations		−17	−17
New budget authority (gross), detail:			
Discretionary:			
40.00 Appropriation		17	17
Change in unpaid obligations:			
73.10 Total new obligations		17	17
73.20 Total outlays (gross)		−17	−17
Outlays (gross), detail:			
86.90 Outlays from new discretionary authority		17	17
Net budget authority and outlays:			
89.00 Budget authority		17	17
90.00 Outlays		17	17

Federal Support for Economic Development and Management Reforms in the District

Federal Payment for Incentives for Adoption of Children

For a Federal payment to the District of Columbia to create incentives to promote the adoption of children in the District of Columbia foster care system, $5,000,000: *Provided*, That such funds shall remain available until September 30, [2001] *2002* and shall be used in accordance with a program established by the Mayor and the Council of the District of Columbia [and approved by the Committees on Appropriations of the House of Representatives and the Senate]: *Provided further*, That funds provided under this heading may be used to cover the costs to the District of Columbia of providing tax credits to offset the costs incurred by individuals in adopting children in the District of Columbia foster care system and in providing for the health care needs of such children, in accordance with legislation enacted by the District of Columbia government.

[Federal Payment to the Citizen Complaint Review Board]

[For a Federal payment to the District of Columbia for administrative expenses of the Citizen Complaint Review Board, $500,000, to remain available until September 30, 2001].

[Federal Payment to the Department of Human Services]

[For a Federal payment to the Department of Human Services for a mentoring program and for hotline services, $250,000].

[Children's National Medical Center]

[For a Federal contribution to the Children's National Medical Center in the District of Columbia, $2,500,000 for construction, renovation, and information technology infrastructure costs associated with establishing community pediatric health clinics for high risk children in medically underserved areas of the District of Columbia].

[Federal Payment for Metropolitan Police Department]

[For payment to the Metropolitan Police Department, $1,000,000, for a program to eliminate open air drug trafficking in the District of Columbia: *Provided*, That the Chief of Police shall provide quarterly reports to the Committees on Appropriations of the Senate and House of Representatives by the 15th calendar day after the end of each quarter beginning December 31, 1999, on the status of the project financed under this heading].

[Federal Payment to the General Services Administration]

[For a Federal payment to the Administrator of General Services for activities carried out as a result of the transfer of the property

General and special funds—Continued

[FEDERAL PAYMENT TO THE GENERAL SERVICES ADMINISTRATION]—Continued

on which the Lorton Correctional Complex is located to the General Services Administration, $6,700,000, to remain available until expended.] *(District of Columbia Appropriations Act, 2000.)*

METRORAIL CONSTRUCTION

For a contribution to the Washington Metropolitan Area Transit Authority for construction of a Metrorail station located at New York and Florida Avenues, Northeast, $25,000,000, to remain available until expended.

FEDERAL PAYMENT FOR THE NATIONAL MUSEUM OF AMERICAN MUSIC

For a payment to the Federal City Council to establish a National Museum of American Music complex, $3,000,000, to remain available until expended: Provided, That such funds shall be for the staff, consultants, design, environmental assessments and preparation of Request for Proposals necessary to complete the planning phase of such museum.

FEDERAL PAYMENT FOR BROWNFIELD REMEDIATION

For a payment to the District of Columbia, $10,000,000, for brownfield remediation and site preparation at Poplar Point.

PRESIDENTIAL INAUGURATION

For a payment to the District of Columbia to reimburse the District for expenses incurred in connection with Presidential inauguration activities, $6,211,000, which shall be distributed by the Mayor within the various District agencies.

Program and Financing (in millions of dollars)

Identification code 20–1707–0–1–806	1999 actual	2000 est.	2001 est.
Obligations by program activity:			
00.01 Metro improvements	25		25
00.02 Boys Town Operations	7		
00.03 Infrastructure Fund	19		
00.05 Citizen Complaint Review Office	1	1	
00.06 Firefighters pay raise	3		
00.07 Waterfront Park Improvements		1	
00.08 City and National Museums	1	2	3
00.11 Public Education	16		
00.12 Children's Medical Center	1	3	
00.14 Capital Infrastructure improvements	50		
00.15 National Capital Revitalization Corporation		25	
00.16 Special Education	30		
00.17 Y2K	82	43	
00.18 Metropolitan Police Department		1	
00.19 Adoption incentives		5	5
00.20 Poplar Point remediation			10
00.21 Presidential Inauguration expenses			6
00.22 United States Park Police	9		
10.00 Total new obligations (object class 41.0)	244	81	49
Budgetary resources available for obligation:			
21.40 Unobligated balance available, start of year		49	
22.00 New budget authority (gross)	297	32	49
23.90 Total budgetary resources available for obligation	297	81	49
23.95 Total new obligations	−244	−81	−49
23.98 Unobligated balance expiring or withdrawn	−4		
24.40 Unobligated balance available, end of year	49		
New budget authority (gross), detail:			
Discretionary:			
40.00 Appropriation	220	18	49
41.00 Transferred to General Services Administration	−7	−7	
42.00 Transferred from Y2K emergency fund	84	21	
43.00 Appropriation (total discretionary)	297	32	49
Change in unpaid obligations:			
73.10 Total new obligations	244	81	49
73.20 Total outlays (gross)	−244	−81	−49
Outlays (gross), detail:			
86.90 Outlays from new discretionary authority	244	32	49
86.93 Outlays from discretionary balances		49	
87.00 Total outlays (gross)	244	81	49
Net budget authority and outlays:			
89.00 Budget authority	297	32	49
90.00 Outlays	243	81	49

The 2001 budget includes $38 million to support District of Columbia infrastructure and economic development initiatives, including $25 million for the Federal share of construction of a Metro station at the intersection of New York and Florida Avenues, in Northeast D.C. This $25 million will be matched by $25 million from the District and $25 million in private funds to improve an important "Gateway" into the Nation's Capital. The $38 million for economic development also includes $3 million to complete the planning phase of the National Museum of American Music and $10 million for brownfield remediation and site preparation at Poplar Point.

FEDERAL PAYMENT FOR MANAGEMENT REFORM

Program and Financing (in millions of dollars)

Identification code 20–1703–0–1–806	1999 actual	2000 est.	2001 est.
Obligations by program activity:			
10.00 Total new obligations (object class 41.0)	25		
Budgetary resources available for obligation:			
22.00 New budget authority (gross)	25		
23.95 Total new obligations	−25		
New budget authority (gross), detail:			
Discretionary:			
40.00 Appropriation	25		
Change in unpaid obligations:			
73.10 Total new obligations	25		
73.20 Total outlays (gross)	−25		
Outlays (gross), detail:			
86.90 Outlays from new discretionary authority	25		
Net budget authority and outlays:			
89.00 Budget authority	25		
90.00 Outlays	25		

The District of Columbia Management Reform Act of 1997 (Title XI of the Balanced Budget Act of 1997) requires the Financial Responsibility and Management Assistance Authority to work with the District government to develop and implement management reform plans for nine District agencies and four government-wide functions. Congress provided $8 million in 1998 to cover costs associated with hiring consultants to develop the reform plans. The 1999 District of Columbia Appropriations Act included $25 million to continue management reform projects in the District. Neither the 2000 nor the 2001 budget includes additional funding for the management reform program.

FEDERAL PAYMENT FOR MEDICARE COORDINATED CARE DEMONSTRATION PROJECT IN THE DISTRICT OF COLUMBIA

Program and Financing (in millions of dollars)

Identification code 20–1709–0–1–806	1999 actual	2000 est.	2001 est.
Obligations by program activity:			
10.00 Total new obligations (object class 41.0)	3		
Budgetary resources available for obligation:			
22.00 New budget authority (gross)	3		
23.95 Total new obligations	−3		

New budget authority (gross), detail:			
Discretionary:			
40.00 Appropriation	3		
Change in unpaid obligations:			
73.10 Total new obligations	3		
73.20 Total outlays (gross)	−3		
Outlays (gross), detail:			
86.90 Outlays from new discretionary authority	3		
Net budget authority and outlays:			
89.00 Budget authority	3		
90.00 Outlays	3		

The 1999 District of Columbia Appropriations Act (P.L. 105–100, section 101(c).) provided $3 million to fund a Medicare Coordinated Care Demonstration Project in the District, as authorized under the Balanced Budget Act of 1997.

Federal Payment for Water and Sewer Services

Program and Financing (in millions of dollars)

Identification code 20–0155–0–1–806	1999 actual	2000 est.	2001 est.
Obligations by program activity:			
09.00 Reimbursable program	23	22	22
10.00 Total new obligations (object class 23.3)	23	22	22
Budgetary resources available for obligation:			
22.00 New budget authority (gross)	23	22	22
23.95 Total new obligations	−23	−22	−22
New budget authority (gross), detail:			
Mandatory:			
69.00 Offsetting collections (cash)	23	22	22
Change in unpaid obligations:			
72.40 Unpaid obligations, start of year: Obligated balance, start of year	26	12	12
73.10 Total new obligations	23	22	22
73.20 Total outlays (gross)	−37	−22	−22
74.40 Unpaid obligations, end of year: Obligated balance, end of year	12	12	12
Outlays (gross), detail:			
86.97 Outlays from new mandatory authority	22	22	22
86.98 Outlays from mandatory balances	14		
87.00 Total outlays (gross)	37	22	22
Offsets:			
Against gross budget authority and outlays:			
88.00 Offsetting collections (cash) from: Federal sources	−23	−22	−22
Net budget authority and outlays:			
89.00 Budget authority			
90.00 Outlays	14		

Federal agencies make payments to this account for the water and sewer services provided by the District.

Federal Supplemental District of Columbia Pension Fund

Unavailable Collections (in millions of dollars)

Identification code 20–1714–0–1–601	1999 actual	2000 est.	2001 est.
Balance, start of year:			
01.99 Balance, start of year	356	651	868
03.00 Offsetting Collections	16	36	48
04.00 Total: Balances and collections	372	687	916
Appropriation:			
05.01 Federal supplemental District of Columbia Pension Fund	279	181	181
07.99 Total balance, end of year	651	868	1,097

Program and Financing (in millions of dollars)

Identification code 20–1714–0–1–601	1999 actual	2000 est.	2001 est.
New budget authority (gross), detail:			
Mandatory:			
60.05 Appropriation (indefinite)	279	181	181
60.45 Portion precluded from obligation	−279	−181	−181
69.00 Offsetting collections (cash)	−21	36	48
Offsets:			
Against gross budget authority and outlays:			
88.20 Offsetting collections (cash) from: Interest on U.S. securities	21	−36	−48
Net budget authority and outlays:			
89.00 Budget authority	21	−36	−48
90.00 Outlays	21	−36	−48
Memorandum (non-add) entries:			
92.01 Total investments, start of year: U.S. securities: Par value	356	614	868
92.02 Total investments, end of year: U.S. securities: Par value	614	868	1,097

The National Capital Revitalization and Self-Government Improvement Act of 1997 established the Federal Supplemental District of Columbia Pension Fund to pay retirement benefits for District of Columbia law enforcement officers, firefighters and teachers after the District of Columbia Federal Pension Liability Trust Fund has been depleted. This fund consists of amounts deposited into the fund, any amount appropriated to the fund, and any income earned on the investment of the assets of the fund. At the end of each fiscal year, beginning in 1998, the Secretary will pay into this fund from the General Fund of the Treasury an annual amount to amortize the unfunded liability over 30 years, the net experience gain or loss over 10 years, and any other changes in actuarial liability over 20 years, and to pay the covered administrative expenses for the year.

Trust Funds

District of Columbia Federal Pension Liability Trust Fund

Unavailable Collections (in millions of dollars)

Identification code 20–8230–0–7–601	1999 actual	2000 est.	2001 est.
Balance, start of year:			
01.99 Balance, start of year		3,185	2,906
Receipts:			
02.01 Proceeds from the sale of pension assets	3,398		
02.02 Interest earnings	−41	171	156
02.99 Total receipts	3,357	171	156
04.00 Total: Balances and collections	3,357	3,356	3,062
Appropriation:			
05.01 Federal pension liability trust fund	−172	−450	−454
07.99 Total balance, end of year	3,185	2,906	2,608

Program and Financing (in millions of dollars)

Identification code 20–8230–0–7–601	1999 actual	2000 est.	2001 est.
Obligations by program activity:			
00.01 Retirement Payments	172	450	454
10.00 Total new obligations (object class 13.0)	172	450	454
Budgetary resources available for obligation:			
22.00 New budget authority (gross)	172	450	454
23.95 Total new obligations	−172	−450	−454
New budget authority (gross), detail:			
Mandatory:			
60.27 Appropriation (trust fund, indefinite)	172	450	454

General and special funds—Continued

DISTRICT OF COLUMBIA FEDERAL PENSION LIABILITY TRUST FUND—Continued

Program and Financing (in millions of dollars)—Continued

Identification code 20–8230–0–7–601	1999 actual	2000 est.	2001 est.
Change in unpaid obligations:			
72.40 Unpaid obligations, start of year: Obligated balance, start of year	....	32	32
73.10 Total new obligations	172	450	454
73.20 Total outlays (gross)	–140	–450	–454
74.40 Unpaid obligations, end of year: Obligated balance, end of year	32	32	32
Outlays (gross), detail:			
86.97 Outlays from new mandatory authority	140	450	454
Net budget authority and outlays:			
89.00 Budget authority	172	450	454
90.00 Outlays	140	450	454
Memorandum (non-add) entries:			
92.01 Total investments, start of year: U.S. securities: Par value	3,231	3,231	3,231
92.02 Total investments, end of year: U.S. securities: Par value	3,231	3,231	3,231

Subtitle A of the National Capital Revitalization and Self-Government Improvement Act of 1997 requires the Federal Government to make benefit payments associated with the pension plans for law enforcement officers, firefighters, and teachers of the District of Columbia. This District of Columbia Federal Pension Liability Trust Fund is established and will consist of accumulated pension assets transferred from the District Retirement Fund to fund benefit payments and any necessary expenses to administer the Fund. Assets were transferred from the District Retirement Fund during 1999.

GENERAL FUND RECEIPT ACCOUNTS

(in millions of dollars)

	1999 actual	2000 est.	2001 est.
Governmental receipts:			
20–086300 District of Columbia court fees	13	....	....
General Fund Governmental receipts	13	....	....

GENERAL PROVISIONS[1]

GENERAL PROVISIONS

[SEC. 101. The expenditure of any appropriation under this Act for any consulting service through procurement contract, pursuant to 5 U.S.C. 3109, shall be limited to those contracts where such expenditures are a matter of public record and available for public inspection, except where otherwise provided under existing law, or under existing Executive order issued pursuant to existing law.]

[SEC. 102. Except as otherwise provided in this Act, all vouchers covering expenditures of appropriations contained in this Act shall be audited before payment by the designated certifying official, and the vouchers as approved shall be paid by checks issued by the designated disbursing official.]

[SEC. 103. Whenever in this Act, an amount is specified within an appropriation for particular purposes or objects of expenditure, such amount, unless otherwise specified, shall be considered as the maximum amount that may be expended for said purpose or object rather than an amount set apart exclusively therefor.]

[SEC. 104. Appropriations in this Act shall be available, when authorized by the Mayor, for allowances for privately owned automobiles and motorcycles used for the performance of official duties at rates established by the Mayor: *Provided*, That such rates shall not exceed the maximum prevailing rates for such vehicles as prescribed in the Federal Property Management Regulations 101–7 (Federal Travel Regulations).]

[SEC. 105. Appropriations in this Act shall be available for expenses of travel and for the payment of dues of organizations concerned with the work of the District of Columbia government, when authorized by the Mayor: *Provided*, That in the case of the Council of the District of Columbia, funds may be expended with the authorization of the chair of the Council.]

[SEC. 106. There are appropriated from the applicable funds of the District of Columbia such sums as may be necessary for making refunds and for the payment of judgments that have been entered against the District of Columbia government: *Provided*, That nothing contained in this section shall be construed as modifying or affecting the provisions of section 11(c)(3) of title XII of the District of Columbia Income and Franchise Tax Act of 1947 (70 Stat. 78; Public Law 84–460; D.C. Code, sec. 47–1812.11(c)(3)).]

[SEC. 107. Appropriations in this Act shall be available [for the payment of public assistance without reference to the requirement of section 544 of the District of Columbia Public Assistance Act of 1982 (D.C. Law 4–101; D.C. Code, sec. 3–205.44), and] for the payment of the non-Federal share of funds necessary to qualify for grants under subtitle A of title II of the Violent Crime Control and Law Enforcement Act of 1994.]

[SEC. 108. No part of any appropriation contained in this Act shall remain available for obligation beyond the current fiscal year unless expressly so provided herein.]

[SEC. 109. No funds appropriated in this Act for the District of Columbia government for the operation of educational institutions, the compensation of personnel, or for other educational purposes may be used to permit, encourage, facilitate, or further partisan political activities. Nothing herein is intended to prohibit the availability of school buildings for the use of any community or partisan political group during non-school hours.]

[SEC. 110. None of the funds appropriated in this Act shall be made available to pay the salary of any employee of the District of Columbia government whose name, title, grade, salary, past work experience, and salary history are not available for inspection by the House and Senate Committees on Appropriations, the Subcommittee on the District of Columbia of the House Committee on Government Reform, the Subcommittee on Oversight of Government Management, Restructuring and the District of Columbia of the Senate Committee on Governmental Affairs, and the Council of the District of Columbia, or their duly authorized representative.]

[SEC. 111. There are appropriated from the applicable funds of the District of Columbia such sums as may be necessary for making payments authorized by the District of Columbia Revenue Recovery Act of 1977 (D.C. Law 2–20; D.C. Code, sec. 47–421 et seq.).]

[SEC. 112. No part of this appropriation shall be used for publicity or propaganda purposes or implementation of any policy including boycott designed to support or defeat legislation pending before Congress or any State legislature.]

[SEC. 113. At the start of the fiscal year, the Mayor shall develop an annual plan, by quarter and by project, for capital outlay borrowings: *Provided*, That within a reasonable time after the close of each quarter, the Mayor shall report to the Council of the District of Columbia and the Congress the actual borrowings and spending progress compared with projections.]

[SEC. 114. The Mayor shall not borrow any funds for capital projects unless the Mayor has obtained prior approval from the Council of the District of Columbia, by resolution, identifying the projects and amounts to be financed with such borrowings.]

[SEC. 115. The Mayor shall not expend any moneys borrowed for capital projects for the operating expenses of the District of Columbia government.]

[SEC. 116. None of the funds provided under this Act to the agencies funded by this Act, both Federal and District government agencies, that remain available for obligation or expenditure in fiscal year 2000, or provided from any accounts in the Treasury of the United States derived by the collection of fees available to the agencies funded by this Act, shall be available for obligation or expenditure for an agency through a reprogramming of funds which: (1) creates new programs; (2) eliminates a program, project, or responsibility center; (3) establishes or changes allocations specifically denied, limited or increased by Congress in this Act; (4) increases funds or personnel by any means for any program, project,

[1] The Administration would like to work with the Congress and the District of Columbia to identify and limit the number of general provisions in a manner consistent with the principle of home rule or as otherwise necessary.

or responsibility center for which funds have been denied or restricted; (5) reestablishes through reprogramming any program or project previously deferred through reprogramming; (6) augments existing programs, projects, or responsibility centers through a reprogramming of funds in excess of $1,000,000 or 10 percent, whichever is less; or (7) increases by 20 percent or more personnel assigned to a specific program, project, or responsibility center; unless the Appropriations Committees of both the Senate and House of Representatives are notified in writing 30 days in advance of any reprogramming as set forth in this section.]

[SEC. 117. None of the Federal funds provided in this Act shall be obligated or expended to provide a personal cook, chauffeur, or other personal servants to any officer or employee of the District of Columbia government.]

[SEC. 118. None of the Federal funds provided in this Act shall be obligated or expended to procure passenger automobiles as defined in the Automobile Fuel Efficiency Act of 1980 (94 Stat. 1824; Public Law 96–425; 15 U.S.C. 2001(2)), with an Environmental Protection Agency estimated miles per gallon average of less than 22 miles per gallon: *Provided*, That this section shall not apply to security, emergency rescue, or armored vehicles.]

[SEC. 119. (a) CITY ADMINISTRATOR.—The last sentence of section 422(7) of the District of Columbia Home Rule Act (D.C. Code, sec. 1–242(7)) is amended by striking ", not to exceed" and all that follows and inserting a period.

(b) BOARD OF DIRECTORS OF REDEVELOPMENT LAND AGENCY.—Section 1108(c)(2)(F) of the District of Columbia Government Comprehensive Merit Personnel Act of 1978 (D.C. Code, sec. 1–612.8(c)(2)(F)) is amended to read as follows:

"(F) Redevelopment Land Agency board members shall be paid per diem compensation at a rate established by the Mayor, except that such rate may not exceed the daily equivalent of the annual rate of basic pay for level 15 of the District Schedule for each day (including travel time) during which they are engaged in the actual performance of their duties.".]

[SEC. 120. Notwithstanding any other provisions of law, the provisions of the District of Columbia Government Comprehensive Merit Personnel Act of 1978 (D.C. Law 2–139; D.C. Code, sec. 1–601.1 et seq.), [enacted pursuant to section 422(3) of the District of Columbia Home Rule Act (87 Stat. 790; Public Law 93–198; D.C. Code, sec. 1–242(3)),] shall apply with respect to the compensation of District of Columbia employees: *Provided*, That for pay purposes, employees of the District of Columbia government shall not be subject to the provisions of title 5, United States Code.]

[SEC. 121. No later than 30 days after the end of the first quarter of the fiscal year ending September 30, 2000, the Mayor of the District of Columbia shall submit to the Council of the District of Columbia the new fiscal year 2000 revenue estimates as of the end of the first quarter of fiscal year 2000. These estimates shall be used in the budget request for the fiscal year ending September 30, 2001. The officially revised estimates at midyear shall be used for the midyear report.]

[SEC. 122. No sole source contract with the District of Columbia government or any agency thereof may be renewed or extended without opening that contract to the competitive bidding process as set forth in section 303 of the District of Columbia Procurement Practices Act of 1985 (D.C. Law 6–85; D.C. Code, sec. 1–1183.3), except that the District of Columbia government or any agency thereof may renew or extend sole source contracts for which competition is not feasible or practical: *Provided*, That the determination as to whether to invoke the competitive bidding process has been made in accordance with duly promulgated rules and procedures and said determination has been reviewed and approved by the District of Columbia Financial Responsibility and Management Assistance Authority.]

[SEC. 123. For purposes of the Balanced Budget and Emergency Deficit Control Act of 1985 (99 Stat. 1037; Public Law 99–177), the term "program, project, and activity" shall be synonymous with and refer specifically to each account appropriating Federal funds in this Act, and any sequestration order shall be applied to each of the accounts rather than to the aggregate total of those accounts: *Provided*, That sequestration orders shall not be applied to any account that is specifically exempted from sequestration by the Balanced Budget and Emergency Deficit Control Act of 1985.]

[SEC. 124. In the event a sequestration order is issued pursuant to the Balanced Budget and Emergency Deficit Control Act of 1985 (99 Stat. 1037; Public Law 99–177), after the amounts appropriated to the District of Columbia for the fiscal year involved have been paid to the District of Columbia, the Mayor of the District of Columbia shall pay to the Secretary of the Treasury, within 15 days after receipt of a request therefor from the Secretary of the Treasury, such amounts as are sequestered by the order: *Provided*, That the sequestration percentage specified in the order shall be applied proportionately to each of the Federal appropriation accounts in this Act that are not specifically exempted from sequestration by such Act.]

[SEC. 125. (a) An entity of the District of Columbia government may accept and use a gift or donation during fiscal year 2000 if—

(1) the Mayor approves the acceptance and use of the gift or donation: *Provided*, That the Council of the District of Columbia may accept and use gifts without prior approval by the Mayor; and

(2) the entity uses the gift or donation to carry out its authorized functions or duties.

(b) Each entity of the District of Columbia government shall keep accurate and detailed records of the acceptance and use of any gift or donation under subsection (a) of this section, and shall make such records available for audit and public inspection.

(c) For the purposes of this section, the term "entity of the District of Columbia government" includes an independent agency of the District of Columbia.

(d) This section shall not apply to the District of Columbia Board of Education, which may, pursuant to the laws and regulations of the District of Columbia, accept and use gifts to the public schools without prior approval by the Mayor.]

[SEC. 126. None of the Federal funds provided in this Act may be used by the District of Columbia to provide for salaries, expenses, or other costs associated with the offices of United States Senator or United States Representative under section 4(d) of the District of Columbia Statehood Constitutional Convention Initiatives of 1979 (D.C. Law 3–171; D.C. Code, sec. 1–113(d)).]

[SEC. 127. (a) The University of the District of Columbia shall submit to the Mayor, the District of Columbia Financial Responsibility and Management Assistance Authority and the Council of the District of Columbia no later than 15 calendar days after the end of each quarter a report that sets forth—

(1) current quarter expenditures and obligations, year-to-date expenditures and obligations, and total fiscal year expenditure projections versus budget broken out on the basis of control center, responsibility center, and object class, and for all funds, non-appropriated funds, and capital financing;

(2) a list of each account for which spending is frozen and the amount of funds frozen, broken out by control center, responsibility center, detailed object, and for all funding sources;

(3) a list of all active contracts in excess of $10,000 annually, which contains the name of each contractor; the budget to which the contract is charged, broken out on the basis of control center and responsibility center, and contract identifying codes used by the University of the District of Columbia; payments made in the last quarter and year-to-date, the total amount of the contract and total payments made for the contract and any modifications, extensions, renewals; and specific modifications made to each contract in the last month;

(4) all reprogramming requests and reports that have been made by the University of the District of Columbia within the last quarter in compliance with applicable law; and

(5) changes made in the last quarter to the organizational structure of the University of the District of Columbia, displaying previous and current control centers and responsibility centers, the names of the organizational entities that have been changed, the name of the staff member supervising each entity affected, and the reasons for the structural change.

(b) The Mayor, the Authority, and the Council shall provide the Congress by February 1, 2000, a summary, analysis, and recommendations on the information provided in the quarterly reports.]

[SEC. 128. Funds authorized or previously appropriated to the government of the District of Columbia by this or any other Act to procure the necessary hardware and installation of new software, conversion, testing, and training to improve or replace its financial management system are also available for the acquisition of accounting and financial management services and the leasing of necessary hardware, software or any other related goods or services, as determined by the District of Columbia Financial Responsibility and Management Assistance Authority.]

[SEC. 129. (a) None of the funds contained in this Act may be made available to pay the fees of an attorney who represents a party who prevails in an action, including an administrative pro-

GENERAL PROVISIONS—Continued

ceeding, brought against the District of Columbia Public Schools under the Individuals with Disabilities Education Act (20 U.S.C. 1400 et seq.) if—

(1) the hourly rate of compensation of the attorney exceeds 120 percent of the hourly rate of compensation under section 11–2604(a), District of Columbia Code; or

(2) the maximum amount of compensation of the attorney exceeds 120 percent of the maximum amount of compensation under section 11–2604(b)(1), District of Columbia Code, except that compensation and reimbursement in excess of such maximum may be approved for extended or complex representation in accordance with section 11–2604(c), District of Columbia Code.

(b) Notwithstanding the preceding subsection, if the Mayor, District of Columbia Financial Responsibility and Management Assistance Authority and the Superintendent of the District of Columbia Public Schools concur in a Memorandum of Understanding setting forth a new rate and amount of compensation, then such new rates shall apply in lieu of the rates set forth in the preceding subsection.]

[SEC. 130. None of the funds appropriated under this Act shall be expended for any abortion except where the life of the mother would be endangered if the fetus were carried to term or where the pregnancy is the result of an act of rape or incest.] [2]

[SEC. 131. None of the funds made available in this Act may be used to implement or enforce the Health Care Benefits Expansion Act of 1992 (D.C. Law 9–114; D.C. Code, sec. 36–1401 et seq.) or to otherwise implement or enforce any system of registration of unmarried, cohabiting couples (whether homosexual, heterosexual, or lesbian), including but not limited to registration for the purpose of extending employment, health, or governmental benefits to such couples on the same basis that such benefits are extended to legally married couples.]

[SEC. 132. The Superintendent of the District of Columbia Public Schools shall submit to the Congress, the Mayor, the District of Columbia Financial Responsibility and Management Assistance Authority, and the Council of the District of Columbia no later than 15 calendar days after the end of each quarter a report that sets forth—

(1) current quarter expenditures and obligations, year-to-date expenditures and obligations, and total fiscal year expenditure projections versus budget, broken out on the basis of control center, responsibility center, agency reporting code, and object class, and for all funds, including capital financing;

(2) a list of each account for which spending is frozen and the amount of funds frozen, broken out by control center, responsibility center, detailed object, and agency reporting code, and for all funding sources;

(3) a list of all active contracts in excess of $10,000 annually, which contains the name of each contractor; the budget to which the contract is charged, broken out on the basis of control center, responsibility center, and agency reporting code; and contract identifying codes used by the District of Columbia Public Schools; payments made in the last quarter and year-to-date, the total amount of the contract and total payments made for the contract and any modifications, extensions, renewals; and specific modifications made to each contract in the last month;

(4) all reprogramming requests and reports that are required to be, and have been, submitted to the Board of Education; and

(5) changes made in the last quarter to the organizational structure of the District of Columbia Public Schools, displaying previous and current control centers and responsibility centers, the names of the organizational entities that have been changed, the name of the staff member supervising each entity affected, and the reasons for the structural change.]

[SEC. 133. (a) IN GENERAL.—The Superintendent of the District of Columbia Public Schools and the University of the District of Columbia shall annually compile an accurate and verifiable report on the positions and employees in the public school system and the university, respectively. The annual report shall set forth—

(1) the number of validated schedule A positions in the District of Columbia public schools and the University of the District of Columbia for fiscal year 1999, fiscal year 2000, and thereafter on full-time equivalent basis, including a compilation of all positions by control center, responsibility center, funding source, position type, position title, pay plan, grade, and annual salary; and

(2) a compilation of all employees in the District of Columbia public schools and the University of the District of Columbia as of the preceding December 31, verified as to its accuracy in accordance with the functions that each employee actually performs, by control center, responsibility center, agency reporting code, program (including funding source), activity, location for accounting purposes, job title, grade and classification, annual salary, and position control number.

(b) SUBMISSION.—The annual report required by subsection (a) of this section shall be submitted to the Congress, the Mayor, the District of Columbia Council, the Consensus Commission, and the Authority, not later than February 15 of each year.]

[SEC. 134. (a) No later than November 1, 1999, or within 30 calendar days after the date of the enactment of this Act, whichever occurs later, and each succeeding year, the Superintendent of the District of Columbia Public Schools and the University of the District of Columbia shall submit to the appropriate congressional committees, the Mayor, the District of Columbia Council, the Consensus Commission, and the District of Columbia Financial Responsibility and Management Assistance Authority, a revised appropriated funds operating budget for the public school system and the University of the District of Columbia for such fiscal year that is in the total amount of the approved appropriation and that realigns budgeted data for personal services and other-than-personal services, respectively, with anticipated actual expenditures.

(b) The revised budget required by subsection (a) of this section shall be submitted in the format of the budget that the Superintendent of the District of Columbia Public Schools and the University of the District of Columbia submit to the Mayor of the District of Columbia for inclusion in the Mayor's budget submission to the Council of the District of Columbia pursuant to section 442 of the District of Columbia Home Rule Act (Public Law 93–198; D.C. Code, sec. 47–301).]

[SEC. 135. The District of Columbia Financial Responsibility and Management Assistance Authority, acting on behalf of the District of Columbia Public Schools (DCPS) in formulating the DCPS budget, the Board of Trustees of the University of the District of Columbia, the Board of Library Trustees, and the Board of Governors of the University of the District of Columbia School of Law shall vote on and approve the respective annual or revised budgets for such entities before submission to the Mayor of the District of Columbia for inclusion in the Mayor's budget submission to the Council of the District of Columbia in accordance with section 442 of the District of Columbia Home Rule Act (Public Law 93–198; D.C. Code, sec. 47–301), or before submitting their respective budgets directly to the Council.]

[SEC. 136. (a) CEILING ON TOTAL OPERATING EXPENSES.—

(1) IN GENERAL.—Notwithstanding any other provision of law, the total amount appropriated in this Act for operating expenses for the District of Columbia for fiscal year 2000 under the heading "Division of Expenses" shall not exceed the lesser of—

(A) the sum of the total revenues of the District of Columbia for such fiscal year; or

(B) $5,515,379,000 (of which $152,753,000 shall be from intra-District funds and $3,113,854,000 shall be from local funds), which amount may be increased by the following:

(i) proceeds of one-time transactions, which are expended for emergency or unanticipated operating or capital needs approved by the District of Columbia Financial Responsibility and Management Assistance Authority; or

(ii) after notification to the Council, additional expenditures which the Chief Financial Officer of the District of Columbia certifies will produce additional revenues during such fiscal year at least equal to 200 percent of such additional expenditures, and that are approved by the Authority.

(2) ENFORCEMENT.—The Chief Financial Officer of the District of Columbia and the Authority shall take such steps as are necessary to assure that the District of Columbia meets the requirements of this section, including the apportioning by the Chief Financial Officer of the appropriations and funds made available to the District during fiscal year 2000, except that the Chief Financial Officer may not reprogram for operating expenses any funds derived from bonds, notes, or other obligations issued for capital projects.

(b) ACCEPTANCE AND USE OF GRANTS NOT INCLUDED IN CEILING.—

(1) IN GENERAL.—Notwithstanding subsection (a), the Mayor, in consultation with the Chief Financial Officer, during a control year, as defined in section 305(4) of the District of Columbia Financial Responsibility and Management Assistance Act of 1995 (Public Law

[2] The Administration proposes to delete this provison and will work with Congress to address this issue.

104–8; 109 Stat. 152), may accept, obligate, and expend Federal, private, and other grants received by the District government that are not reflected in the amounts appropriated in this Act.

(2) REQUIREMENT OF CHIEF FINANCIAL OFFICER REPORT AND AUTHORITY APPROVAL.—No such Federal, private, or other grant may be accepted, obligated, or expended pursuant to paragraph (1) until—

(A) the Chief Financial Officer of the District of Columbia submits to the Authority a report setting forth detailed information regarding such grant; and

(B) the Authority has reviewed and approved the acceptance, obligation, and expenditure of such grant in accordance with review and approval procedures consistent with the provisions of the District of Columbia Financial Responsibility and Management Assistance Act of 1995.

(3) PROHIBITION ON SPENDING IN ANTICIPATION OF APPROVAL OR RECEIPT.—No amount may be obligated or expended from the general fund or other funds of the District government in anticipation of the approval or receipt of a grant under paragraph (2)(B) of this subsection or in anticipation of the approval or receipt of a Federal, private, or other grant not subject to such paragraph.

(4) QUARTERLY REPORTS.—The Chief Financial Officer of the District of Columbia shall prepare a quarterly report setting forth detailed information regarding all Federal, private, and other grants subject to this subsection. Each such report shall be submitted to the Council of the District of Columbia, and to the Committees on Appropriations of the House of Representatives and the Senate, not later than 15 days after the end of the quarter covered by the report.

(c) REPORT ON EXPENDITURES BY FINANCIAL RESPONSIBILITY AND MANAGEMENT ASSISTANCE AUTHORITY.—Not later than 20 calendar days after the end of each fiscal quarter starting October 1, 1999, the Authority shall submit a report to the Committees on Appropriations of the House of Representatives and the Senate, the Committee on Government Reform of the House, and the Committee on Governmental Affairs of the Senate providing an itemized accounting of all non-appropriated funds obligated or expended by the Authority for the quarter. The report shall include information on the date, amount, purpose, and vendor name, and a description of the services or goods provided with respect to the expenditures of such funds.]

[SEC. 137. If a department or agency of the government of the District of Columbia is under the administration of a court-appointed receiver or other court-appointed official during fiscal year 2000 or any succeeding fiscal year, the receiver or official shall prepare and submit to the Mayor, for inclusion in the annual budget of the District of Columbia for the year, annual estimates of the expenditures and appropriations necessary for the maintenance and operation of the department or agency. All such estimates shall be forwarded by the Mayor to the Council, for its action pursuant to sections 446 and 603(c) of the District of Columbia Home Rule Act, without revision but subject to the Mayor's recommendations. Notwithstanding any provision of the District of Columbia Home Rule Act (87 Stat. 774; Public Law 93–198) the Council may comment or make recommendations concerning such annual estimates but shall have no authority under such Act to revise such estimates.]

[SEC. 138. (a) Notwithstanding any other provision of law, rule, or regulation, an employee of the District of Columbia public schools shall be—

(1) classified as an Educational Service employee;

(2) placed under the personnel authority of the Board of Education; and

(3) subject to all Board of Education rules.

(b) School-based personnel shall constitute a separate competitive area from nonschool-based personnel who shall not compete with school-based personnel for retention purposes.]

[SEC. 139. (a) RESTRICTIONS ON USE OF OFFICIAL VEHICLES.—Except as otherwise provided in this section, none of the funds made available by this Act or by any other Act may be used to provide any officer or employee of the District of Columbia with an official vehicle unless the officer or employee uses the vehicle only in the performance of the officer's or employee's official duties. For purposes of this paragraph, the term "official duties" does not include travel between the officer's or employee's residence and workplace (except: (1) in the case of an officer or employee of the Metropolitan Police Department who resides in the District of Columbia or is otherwise designated by the Chief of the Department; (2) at the discretion of the Fire Chief, an officer or employee of the District of Columbia Fire and Emergency Medical Services Department who resides in the District of Columbia and is on call 24 hours a day; (3) the Mayor of the District of Columbia; and (4) the Chairman of the Council of the District of Columbia).

(b) INVENTORY OF VEHICLES.—The Chief Financial Officer of the District of Columbia shall submit, by November 15, 1999, an inventory, as of September 30, 1999, of all vehicles owned, leased or operated by the District of Columbia government. The inventory shall include, but not be limited to, the department to which the vehicle is assigned; the year and make of the vehicle; the acquisition date and cost; the general condition of the vehicle; annual operating and maintenance costs; current mileage; and whether the vehicle is allowed to be taken home by a District officer or employee and if so, the officer or employee's title and resident location.]

[SEC. 140. (a) SOURCE OF PAYMENT FOR EMPLOYEES DETAILED WITHIN GOVERNMENT.—For purposes of determining the amount of funds expended by any entity within the District of Columbia government during fiscal year 2000 and each succeeding fiscal year, any expenditures of the District government attributable to any officer or employee of the District government who provides services which are within the authority and jurisdiction of the entity (including any portion of the compensation paid to the officer or employee attributable to the time spent in providing such services) shall be treated as expenditures made from the entity's budget, without regard to whether the officer or employee is assigned to the entity or otherwise treated as an officer or employee of the entity.

(b) MODIFICATION OF REDUCTION IN FORCE PROCEDURES.—The District of Columbia Government Comprehensive Merit Personnel Act of 1978 (D.C. Code, sec. 1–601.1 et seq.), is further amended in section 2408(a) by striking "1999" and inserting "2000"; in subsection (b), by striking "1999" and inserting "2000"; in subsection (i), by striking "1999" and inserting "2000"; and in subsection (k), by striking "1999" and inserting "2000".]

[SEC. 141. Notwithstanding any other provision of law, not later than 120 days after the date that a District of Columbia Public Schools (DCPS) student is referred for evaluation or assessment—

(1) the District of Columbia Board of Education, or its successor, and DCPS shall assess or evaluate a student who may have a disability and who may require special education services; and

(2) if a student is classified as having a disability, as defined in section 101(a)(1) of the Individuals with Disabilities Education Act (84 Stat. 175; 20 U.S.C. 1401(a)(1)) or in section 7(8) of the Rehabilitation Act of 1973 (87 Stat. 359; 29 U.S.C. 706(8)), the Board and DCPS shall place that student in an appropriate program of special education services.]

[SEC. 142. (a) COMPLIANCE WITH BUY AMERICAN ACT.—None of the funds made available in this Act may be expended by an entity unless the entity agrees that in expending the funds the entity will comply with the Buy American Act (41 U.S.C. 10a–10c).

(b) SENSE OF THE CONGRESS; REQUIREMENT REGARDING NOTICE.—

(1) PURCHASE OF AMERICAN-MADE EQUIPMENT AND PRODUCTS.—In the case of any equipment or product that may be authorized to be purchased with financial assistance provided using funds made available in this Act, it is the sense of the Congress that entities receiving the assistance should, in expending the assistance, purchase only American-made equipment and products to the greatest extent practicable.

(2) NOTICE TO RECIPIENTS OF ASSISTANCE.—In providing financial assistance using funds made available in this Act, the head of each agency of the Federal or District of Columbia government shall provide to each recipient of the assistance a notice describing the statement made in paragraph (1) by the Congress.

(c) PROHIBITION OF CONTRACTS WITH PERSONS FALSELY LABELING PRODUCTS AS MADE IN AMERICA.—If it has been finally determined by a court or Federal agency that any person intentionally affixed a label bearing a "Made in America" inscription, or any inscription with the same meaning, to any product sold in or shipped to the United States that is not made in the United States, the person shall be ineligible to receive any contract or subcontract made with funds made available in this Act, pursuant to the debarment, suspension, and ineligibility procedures described in sections 9.400 through 9.409 of title 48, Code of Federal Regulations.]

[SEC. 143. None of the funds contained in this Act may be used for purposes of the annual independent audit of the District of Columbia government (including the District of Columbia Financial Responsibility and Management Assistance Authority) for fiscal year 2000 unless—

(1) the audit is conducted by the Inspector General of the District of Columbia pursuant to section 208(a)(4) of the District of Colum-

GENERAL PROVISIONS—Continued

bia Procurement Practices Act of 1985 (D.C. Code, sec. 1–1182.8(a)(4)); and

(2) the audit includes a comparison of audited actual year-end results with the revenues submitted in the budget document for such year and the appropriations enacted into law for such year.

[SEC. 144. Nothing in this Act shall be construed to authorize any office, agency or entity to expend funds for programs or functions for which a reorganization plan is required but has not been approved by the District of Columbia Financial Responsibility and Management Assistance Authority. Appropriations made by this Act for such programs or functions are conditioned only on the approval by the Authority of the required reorganization plans.]

[SEC. 145. Notwithstanding any other provision of law, rule, or regulation, the evaluation process and instruments for evaluating District of Columbia Public School employees shall be a non-negotiable item for collective bargaining purposes.]

[SEC. 146. None of the funds contained in this Act may be used by the District of Columbia Corporation Counsel or any other officer or entity of the District government to provide assistance for any petition drive or civil action which seeks to require Congress to provide for voting representation in Congress for the District of Columbia.]

[SEC. 147. None of the funds contained in this Act may be used to transfer or confine inmates classified above the medium security level, as defined by the Federal Bureau of Prisons classification instrument, to the Northeast Ohio Correctional Center located in Youngstown, Ohio.]

[SEC. 148. (a) Section 202(i) of the District of Columbia Financial Responsibility and Management Assistance Act of 1995 (Public Law 104–8), as added by section 155 of the District of Columbia Appropriations Act, 1999, is amended to read as follows:

"(j) RESERVE.—

"(1) IN GENERAL.—Beginning with fiscal year 2000, the plan or budget submitted pursuant to this Act shall contain $150,000,000 for a reserve to be established by the Mayor, Council of the District of Columbia, Chief Financial Officer for the District of Columbia, and the District of Columbia Financial Responsibility and Management Assistance Authority.

"(2) CONDITIONS ON USE.—The reserve funds—

"(A) shall only be expended according to criteria established by the Chief Financial Officer and approved by the Mayor, Council of the District of Columbia, and District of Columbia Financial Responsibility and Management Assistance Authority, but, in no case may any of the reserve funds be expended until any other surplus funds have been used;

"(B) shall not be used to fund the agencies of the District of Columbia government under court ordered receivership; and

"(C) shall not be used to fund shortfalls in the projected reductions budgeted in the budget proposed by the District of Columbia government for general supply schedule savings and management reform savings.

"(3) REPORT REQUIREMENT.—The Authority shall notify the Appropriations Committees of both the Senate and House of Representatives in writing 30 days in advance of any expenditure of the reserve funds.".

(b) Section 202 of such Act (Public Law 104–8), as amended by subsection (a), is further amended by adding at the end the following:

"(k) POSITIVE FUND BALANCE.—

"(1) IN GENERAL.—The District of Columbia shall maintain at the end of a fiscal year an annual positive fund balance in the general fund of not less than 4 percent of the projected general fund expenditures for the following fiscal year.

"(2) EXCESS FUNDS.—Of funds remaining in excess of the amounts required by paragraph (1)—

"(A) not more than 50 percent may be used for authorized non-recurring expenses; and

"(B) not less than 50 percent shall be used to reduce the debt of the District of Columbia.".]

[SEC. 149. (a) No later than November 1, 1999, or within 30 calendar days after the date of the enactment of this Act, whichever occurs later, the Chief Financial Officer of the District of Columbia shall submit to the appropriate committees of Congress, the Mayor, and the District of Columbia Financial Responsibility and Management Assistance Authority a revised appropriated funds operating budget for all agencies of the District of Columbia government for such fiscal year that is in the total amount of the approved appropriation and that realigns budgeted data for personal services and other-than-personal-services, respectively, with anticipated actual expenditures.

(b) The revised budget required by subsection (a) of this section shall be submitted in the format of the budget that the District of Columbia government submitted pursuant to section 442 of the District of Columbia Home Rule Act (Public Law 93–198; D.C. Code, sec. 47–301).

[SEC. 150. (a) None of the funds contained in this Act may be used for any program of distributing sterile needles or syringes for the hypodermic injection of any illegal drug.

(b) Any individual or entity who receives any funds contained in this Act and who carries out any program described in subsection (a) shall account for all funds used for such program separately from any funds contained in this Act.]

[SEC. 151. (a) RESTRICTIONS ON LEASES.—Upon the expiration of the 60-day period that begins on the date of the enactment of this Act, none of the funds contained in this Act may be used to make rental payments under a lease for the use of real property by the District of Columbia government (including any independent agency of the District) unless the lease and an abstract of the lease have been filed (by the District of Columbia or any other party to the lease) with the central office of the Deputy Mayor for Economic Development, in an indexed registry available for public inspection.

(b) ADDITIONAL RESTRICTIONS ON CURRENT LEASES.—

(1) IN GENERAL.—Upon the expiration of the 60-day period that begins on the date of the enactment of this Act, in the case of a lease described in paragraph (3), none of the funds contained in this Act may be used to make rental payments under the lease unless the lease is included in periodic reports submitted by the Mayor and Council of the District of Columbia to the Committees on Appropriations of the House of Representatives and Senate describing for each such lease the following information:

(A) The location of the property involved, the name of the owners of record according to the land records of the District of Columbia, the name of the lessors according to the lease, the rate of payment under the lease, the period of time covered by the lease, and the conditions under which the lease may be terminated.

(B) The extent to which the property is or is not occupied by the District of Columbia government as of the end of the reporting period involved.

(C) If the property is not occupied and utilized by the District government as of the end of the reporting period involved, a plan for occupying and utilizing the property (including construction or renovation work) or a status statement regarding any efforts by the District to terminate or renegotiate the lease.

(2) TIMING OF REPORTS.—The reports described in paragraph (1) shall be submitted for each calendar quarter (beginning with the quarter ending December 31, [1999] *2000*) not later than 20 days after the end of the quarter involved, plus an initial report submitted not later than 60 days after the date of the enactment of this Act, which shall provide information as of the date of the enactment of this Act.

(3) LEASES DESCRIBED.—A lease described in this paragraph is a lease in effect as of the date of the enactment of this Act for the use of real property by the District of Columbia government (including any independent agency of the District) which is not being occupied by the District government (including any independent agency of the District) as of such date or during the 60-day period which begins on the date of the enactment of this Act.]

[SEC. 152. (a) MANAGEMENT OF EXISTING DISTRICT GOVERNMENT PROPERTY.—Upon the expiration of the 60-day period that begins on the date of the enactment of this Act, none of the funds contained in this Act may be used to enter into a lease (or to make rental payments under such a lease) for the use of real property by the District of Columbia government (including any independent agency of the District) or to purchase real property for the use of the District of Columbia government (including any independent agency of the District) or to manage real property for the use of the District of Columbia (including any independent agency of the District) unless the following conditions are met:

(1) The Mayor and Council of the District of Columbia certify to the Committees on Appropriations of the House of Representatives and Senate that existing real property available to the District (whether leased or owned by the District government) is not suitable for the purposes intended.

(2) Notwithstanding any other provisions of law, there is made available for sale or lease all real property of the District of Columbia that the Mayor from time-to-time determines is surplus to the needs of the District of Columbia, unless a majority of the members of the Council override the Mayor's determination during the 30-day period which begins on the date the determination is published.

(3) The Mayor and Council implement a program for the periodic survey of all District property to determine if it is surplus to the needs of the District.

(4) The Mayor and Council within 60 days of the date of the enactment of this Act have filed with the Committees on Appropriations of the House of Representatives and Senate, the Committee on Government Reform and Oversight of the House of Representatives, and the Committee on Governmental Affairs of the Senate a report which provides a comprehensive plan for the management of District of Columbia real property assets, and are proceeding with the implementation of the plan.

(b) TERMINATION OF PROVISIONS.—If the District of Columbia enacts legislation to reform the practices and procedures governing the entering into of leases for the use of real property by the District of Columbia government and the disposition of surplus real property of the District government, the provisions of subsection (a) shall cease to be effective upon the effective date of the legislation.]

[SEC. 153. Section 603(e)(2)(B) of the Student Loan Marketing Association Reorganization Act of 1996 (Public Law 104–208; 110 Stat. 3009–293) is amended—

(1) by inserting "and public charter" after "public"; and

(2) by adding at the end the following: "Of such amounts and proceeds, $5,000,000 shall be set aside for use as a credit enhancement fund for public charter schools in the District of Columbia, with the administration of the fund (including the making of loans) to be carried out by the Mayor through a committee consisting of three individuals appointed by the Mayor of the District of Columbia and two individuals appointed by the Public Charter School Board established under section 2214 of the District of Columbia School Reform Act of 1995.".]

[SEC. 154. The Mayor, District of Columbia Financial Responsibility and Management Assistance Authority, and the Superintendent of Schools shall implement a process to dispose of excess public school real property within 90 days of the enactment of this Act.]

[SEC. 155. Section 2003 of the District of Columbia School Reform Act of 1995 (Public Law 104–134; D.C. Code, sec. 31–2851) is amended by striking "during the period" and "and ending 5 years after such date.".]

[SEC. 156. Section 2206(c) of the District of Columbia School Reform Act of 1995 (Public Law 104–134; D.C. Code, sec. 31–2853.16(c)) is amended by adding at the end the following: ", except that a preference in admission may be given to an applicant who is a sibling of a student already attending or selected for admission to the public charter school in which the applicant is seeking enrollment.".]

[SEC. 157. (a) TRANSFER OF FUNDS.—There is hereby transferred from the District of Columbia Financial Responsibility and Management Assistance Authority (hereafter referred to as the "Authority") to the District of Columbia the sum of $18,000,000 for severance payments to individuals separated from employment during fiscal year 2000 (under such terms and conditions as the Mayor considers appropriate), expanded contracting authority of the Mayor, and the implementation of a system of managed competition among public and private providers of goods and services by and on behalf of the District of Columbia: *Provided*, That such funds shall be used only in accordance with a plan agreed to by the Council and the Mayor and approved by the Committees on Appropriations of the House of Representatives and the Senate: *Provided further*, That the Authority and the Mayor shall coordinate the spending of funds for this program so that continuous progress is made. The Authority shall release said funds, on a quarterly basis, to reimburse such expenses, so long as the Authority certifies that the expenses reduce re-occurring future costs at an annual ratio of at least 2 to 1 relative to the funds provided, and that the program is in accordance with the best practices of municipal government.

(b) SOURCE OF FUNDS.—The amount transferred under subsection (a) shall be derived from interest earned on accounts held by the Authority on behalf of the District of Columbia.]

[SEC. 158. (a) IN GENERAL.—The District of Columbia Financial Responsibility and Management Assistance Authority (hereafter referred to as the "Authority"), working with the Commonwealth of Virginia and the Director of the National Park Service, shall carry out a project to complete all design requirements and all requirements for compliance with the National Environmental Policy Act for the construction of expanded lane capacity for the Fourteenth Street Bridge.

(b) SOURCE OF FUNDS; TRANSFER.—For purposes of carrying out the project under subsection (a), there is hereby transferred to the Authority from the District of Columbia dedicated highway fund established pursuant to section 3(a) of the District of Columbia Emergency Highway Relief Act (Public Law 104–21; D.C. Code, sec. 7–134.2(a)) an amount not to exceed $5,000,000.]

[SEC. 159. (a) IN GENERAL.—The Mayor of the District of Columbia shall carry out through the Army Corps of Engineers, an Anacostia River environmental cleanup program.

(b) SOURCE OF FUNDS.—There are hereby transferred to the Mayor from the escrow account held by the District of Columbia Financial Responsibility and Management Assistance Authority pursuant to section 134 of division A of the Omnibus Consolidated and Emergency Supplemental Appropriations Act, 1999 (Public Law 105–277; 112 Stat. 2681–552), for infrastructure needs of the District of Columbia, $5,000,000.]

[SEC. 160. (a) PROHIBITING PAYMENT OF ADMINISTRATIVE COSTS FROM FUND.—Section 16(e) of the Victims of Violent Crime Compensation Act of 1996 (D.C. Code, sec. 3–435(e)) is amended—

(1) by striking "and administrative costs necessary to carry out this chapter"; and

(2) by striking the period at the end and inserting the following: ", and no monies in the Fund may be used for any other purpose.".

(b) MAINTENANCE OF FUND IN TREASURY OF THE UNITED STATES.—

(1) IN GENERAL.—Section 16(a) of such Act (D.C. Code, sec. 3–435(a)) is amended by striking the second sentence and inserting the following: "The Fund shall be maintained as a separate fund in the Treasury of the United States. All amounts deposited to the credit of the Fund are appropriated without fiscal year limitation to make payments as authorized under subsection (e).".

(2) CONFORMING AMENDMENT.—Section 16 of such Act (D.C. Code, sec. 3–435) is amended by striking subsection (d).

(c) DEPOSIT OF OTHER FEES AND RECEIPTS INTO FUND.—Section 16(c) of such Act (D.C. Code, sec. 3–435(c)) is amended by inserting after "1997," the second place it appears the following: "any other fines, fees, penalties, or assessments that the Court determines necessary to carry out the purposes of the Fund,".

(d) ANNUAL TRANSFER OF UNOBLIGATED BALANCES TO MISCELLANEOUS RECEIPTS OF TREASURY.—Section 16 of such Act (D.C. Code, sec. 3–435), as amended by subsection (b)(2), is further amended by inserting after subsection (c) the following new subsection:

"(d) Any unobligated balance existing in the Fund in excess of $250,000 as of the end of each fiscal year (beginning with fiscal year 2000) shall be transferred to miscellaneous receipts of the Treasury of the United States not later than 30 days after the end of the fiscal year.".

(e) RATIFICATION OF PAYMENTS AND DEPOSITS.—Any payments made from or deposits made to the Crime Victims Compensation Fund on or after April 9, 1997 are hereby ratified, to the extent such payments and deposits are authorized under the Victims of Violent Crime Compensation Act of 1996 (D.C. Code, sec. 3–421 et seq.), as amended by this section.]

[SEC. 161. CERTIFICATION.—None of the funds contained in this Act may be used after the expiration of the 60-day period that begins on the date of the enactment of this Act to pay the salary of any chief financial officer of any office of the District of Columbia government (including any independent agency of the District) who has not filed a certification with the Mayor and the Chief Financial Officer of the District of Columbia that the officer understands the duties and restrictions applicable to the officer and their agency as a result of this Act.]

[SEC. 162. The proposed budget of the government of the District of Columbia for fiscal year 2001 that is submitted by the District to Congress shall specify potential adjustments that might become necessary in the event that the management savings achieved by the District during the year do not meet the level of management savings projected by the District under the proposed budget.]

[SEC. 163. In submitting any document showing the budget for an office of the District of Columbia government (including an independent agency of the District) that contains a category of activities labeled as "other", "miscellaneous", or a similar general, nondescriptive term, the document shall include a description of the types of activities covered in the category and a detailed breakdown of the amount allocated for each such activity.]

GENERAL PROVISIONS—Continued

[SEC. 164. (a) AUTHORIZING CORPS OF ENGINEERS TO PERFORM REPAIRS AND IMPROVEMENTS.—In using the funds made available under this Act for carrying out improvements to the Southwest Waterfront in the District of Columbia (including upgrading marina dock pilings and paving and restoring walkways in the marina and fish market areas) for the portions of Federal property in the Southwest quadrant of the District of Columbia within Lots 847 and 848, a portion of Lot 846, and the unassessed Federal real property adjacent to Lot 848 in Square 473, any entity of the District of Columbia government (including the District of Columbia Financial Responsibility and Management Assistance Authority or its designee) may place orders for engineering and construction and related services with the Chief of Engineers of the United States Army Corps of Engineers. The Chief of Engineers may accept such orders on a reimbursable basis and may provide any part of such services by contract. In providing such services, the Chief of Engineers shall follow the Federal Acquisition Regulations and the implementing Department of Defense regulations.

(b) TIMING FOR AVAILABILITY OF FUNDS UNDER 1999 ACT.—

(1) IN GENERAL.—The District of Columbia Appropriations Act, 1999 (Public Law 105–277; 112 Stat. 2681–124) is amended in the item relating to "FEDERAL FUNDS—FEDERAL PAYMENT FOR WATERFRONT IMPROVEMENTS"—

(A) by striking "existing lessees" the first place it appears and inserting "existing lessees of the Marina"; and

(B) by striking "the existing lessees" the second place it appears and inserting "such lessees".

(2) EFFECTIVE DATE.—This subsection shall take effect as if included in the District of Columbia Appropriations Act, 1999.

(c) ADDITIONAL FUNDING FOR IMPROVEMENTS CARRIED OUT THROUGH CORPS OF ENGINEERS.—

(1) IN GENERAL.—There is hereby transferred from the District of Columbia Financial Responsibility and Management Assistance Authority to the Mayor the sum of $3,000,000 for carrying out the improvements described in subsection (a) through the Chief of Engineers of the United States Army Corps of Engineers.

(2) SOURCE OF FUNDS.—The funds transferred under paragraph (1) shall be derived from the escrow account held by the District of Columbia Financial Responsibility and Management Assistance Authority pursuant to section 134 of division A of the Omnibus Consolidated and Emergency Supplemental Appropriations Act, 1999 (Public Law 105–277; 112 Stat. 2681–552), for infrastructure needs of the District of Columbia.

(d) QUARTERLY REPORTS ON PROJECT.—The Mayor shall submit reports to the Committee on Appropriations of the House of Representatives and the Committee on Appropriations of the Senate on the status of the improvements described in subsection (a) for each calendar quarter occurring until the improvements are completed.]

[SEC. 165. It is the sense of the Congress that the District of Columbia should not impose or take into consideration any height, square footage, set-back, or other construction or zoning requirements in authorizing the issuance of industrial revenue bonds for a project of the American National Red Cross at 2025 E Street Northwest, Washington, D.C., in as much as this project is subject to approval of the National Capital Planning Commission and the Commission of Fine Arts pursuant to section 11 of the joint resolution entitled "Joint Resolution to grant authority for the erection of a permanent building for the American National Red Cross, District of Columbia Chapter, Washington, District of Columbia", approved July 1, 1947 (Public Law 100–637; 36 U.S.C. 300108 note).]

[SEC. 166. (a) PERMITTING COURT SERVICES AND OFFENDER SUPERVISION AGENCY TO CARRY OUT SEX OFFENDER REGISTRATION.—Section 11233(c) of the National Capital Revitalization and Self-Government Improvement Act of 1997 (D.C. Code, sec. 24–1233(c)) is amended by adding at the end the following new paragraph:

"(5) SEX OFFENDER REGISTRATION.—The Agency shall carry out sex offender registration functions in the District of Columbia, and shall have the authority to exercise all powers and functions relating to sex offender registration that are granted to the Agency under any District of Columbia law.".

(b) AUTHORITY DURING TRANSITION TO FULL OPERATION OF AGENCY.—

(1) AUTHORITY OF PRETRIAL SERVICES, PAROLE, ADULT PROBATION AND OFFENDER SUPERVISION TRUSTEE.—Notwithstanding section 11232(b)(1) of the National Capital Revitalization and Self-Government Improvement Act of 1997 (D.C. Code, sec. 24–1232(b)(1)), the Pretrial Services, Parole, Adult Probation and Offender Supervision Trustee appointed under section 11232(a) of such Act (hereafter referred to as the "Trustee") shall, in accordance with section 11232 of such Act, exercise the powers and functions of the Court Services and Offender Supervision Agency for the District of Columbia (hereafter referred to as the "Agency") relating to sex offender registration (as granted to the Agency under any District of Columbia law) only upon the Trustee's certification that the Trustee is able to assume such powers and functions.

(2) AUTHORITY OF METROPOLITAN POLICE DEPARTMENT.—During the period that begins on the date of the enactment of the Sex Offender Registration Emergency Act of 1999 and ends on the date the Trustee makes the certification described in paragraph (1), the Metropolitan Police Department of the District of Columbia shall have the authority to carry out any powers and functions relating to sex offender registration that are granted to the Agency or to the Trustee under any District of Columbia law.]

[SEC. 167. (a) None of the funds contained in this Act may be used to enact or carry out any law, rule, or regulation to legalize or otherwise reduce penalties associated with the possession, use, or distribution of any schedule I substance under the Controlled Substances Act (21 U.S.C. 802) or any tetrahydrocannabinols derivative.

(b) The Legalization of Marijuana for Medical Treatment Initiative of 1998, also known as Initiative 59, approved by the electors of the District of Columbia on November 3, 1998, shall not take effect.]

[SEC. 168. (a) IN GENERAL.—There is hereby transferred from the District of Columbia Financial Responsibility and Management Assistance Authority (hereinafter referred to as the "Authority") to the District of Columbia the sum of $5,000,000 for the Mayor, in consultation with the Council of the District of Columbia, to provide offsets against local taxes for a commercial revitalization program, such program to be available in enterprise zones and low and moderate income areas in the District of Columbia: *Provided*, That in carrying out such a program, the Mayor shall use Federal commercial revitalization proposals introduced in Congress as a guideline.

(b) SOURCE OF FUNDS.—The amount transferred under subsection (a) shall be derived from interest earned on accounts held by the Authority on behalf of the District of Columbia.

(c) REPORT.—Not later than 180 days after the date of the enactment of this Act, the Mayor shall report to the Committees on Appropriations of the Senate and House of Representatives on the progress made in carrying out the commercial revitalization program.]

[SEC. 169. Section 456 of the District of Columbia Home Rule Act (section 47–231 et seq. of the D.C. Code, as added by the Federal Payment Reauthorization Act of 1994 (Public Law 103–373)) is amended—

(1) in subsection (a)(1), by striking "District of Columbia Financial Responsibility and Management Assistance Authority" and inserting "Mayor"; and

(2) in subsection (b)(1), by striking "Authority" and inserting "Mayor".]

[SEC. 170. (a) FINDINGS.—The Congress finds the following:

(1) The District of Columbia has recently witnessed a spate of senseless killings of innocent citizens caught in the crossfire of shootings. A Justice Department crime victimization survey found that while the city saw a decline in the homicide rate between 1996 and 1997, the rate was the highest among a dozen cities and more than double the second highest city.

(2) The District of Columbia has not made adequate funding available to fight drug abuse in recent years, and the city has not deployed its resources as effectively as possible. In fiscal year 1998, $20,900,000 was spent on publicly funded drug treatment in the District compared to $29,000,000 in fiscal year 1993. The District's Addiction and Prevention and Recovery Agency currently has only 2,200 treatment slots, a 50 percent drop from 1994, with more than 1,100 people on waiting lists.

(3) The District of Columbia has seen a rash of inmate escapes from halfway houses. According to Department of Corrections records, between October 21, 1998 and January 19, 1999, 376 of the 1,125 inmates assigned to halfway houses walked away. Nearly 280 of the 376 escapees were awaiting trial including two charged with murder.

(4) The District of Columbia public schools system faces serious challenges in correcting chronic problems, particularly long-standing deficiencies in providing special education services to the 1 in 10 District students needing program benefits, including backlogged assessments, and repeated failure to meet a compliance

agreement on special education reached with the Department of Education.

(5) Deficiencies in the delivery of basic public services from cleaning streets to waiting time at Department of Motor Vehicles to a rat population estimated earlier this year to exceed the human population have generated considerable public frustration.

(6) Last year, the District of Columbia forfeited millions of dollars in Federal grants after Federal auditors determined that several agencies exceeded grant restrictions and in other instances, failed to spend funds before the grants expired.

(7) Findings of a 1999 report by the Annie E. Casey Foundation that measured the well-being of children reflected that, with one exception, the District ranked worst in the United States in every category from infant mortality to the rate of teenage births to statistics chronicling child poverty.

(b) SENSE OF THE CONGRESS.—It is the sense of the Congress that in considering the District of Columbia's fiscal year 2001 budget, the Congress will take into consideration progress or lack of progress in addressing the following issues:

(1) Crime, including the homicide rate, implementation of community policing, the number of police officers on local beats, and the closing down of open-air drug markets.

(2) Access to drug abuse treatment, including the number of treatment slots, the number of people served, the number of people on waiting lists, and the effectiveness of treatment programs.

(3) Management of parolees and pretrial violent offenders, including the number of halfway house escapes and steps taken to improve monitoring and supervision of halfway house residents to reduce the number of escapes.

(4) Education, including access to special education services and student achievement.

(5) Improvement in basic city services, including rat control and abatement.

(6) Application for and management of Federal grants.

(7) Indicators of child well-being.]

[SEC. 171. The Mayor, prior to using Federal Medicaid payments to Disproportionate Share Hospitals to serve a small number of childless adults, should consider the recommendations of the Health Care Development Commission that has been appointed by the Council of the District of Columbia to review this program, and consult and report to Congress on the use of these funds.]

[SEC. 172. GAO STUDY OF DISTRICT OF COLUMBIA CRIMINAL JUSTICE SYSTEM. Not later than 1 year after the date of the enactment of this Act, the Comptroller General of the United States shall—

(1) conduct a study of the law enforcement, court, prison, probation, parole, and other components of the criminal justice system of the District of Columbia, in order to identify the components most in need of additional resources, including financial, personnel, and management resources; and

(2) submit to Congress a report on the results of the study under paragraph (1).]

[SEC. 173. Nothing in this Act bars the District of Columbia Corporation Counsel from reviewing or commenting on briefs in private lawsuits, or from consulting with officials of the District government regarding such lawsuits.]

[SEC. 174. WIRELESS COMMUNICATIONS.—(a) IN GENERAL.—Not later than 7 days after the date of the enactment of this Act, the Secretary of the Interior, acting through the Director of the National Park Service, shall—

(1) implement the notice of decision approved by the National Capital Regional Director, dated April 7, 1999, including the provisions of the notice of decision concerning the issuance of right-of-way permits at market rates; and

(2) expend such sums as are necessary to carry out paragraph (1).

(b) ANTENNA APPLICATIONS.—

(1) IN GENERAL.—Not later than 120 days after the receipt of an application, a Federal agency that receives an application submitted after the enactment of this Act to locate a wireless communications antenna on Federal property in the District of Columbia or surrounding area over which the Federal agency exercises control shall take final action on the application, including action on the issuance of right-of-way permits at market rates.

(2) EXISTING LAW.—Nothing in this subsection shall be construed to affect the applicability of existing laws regarding—

(A) judicial review under chapter 7 of title 5, United States Code (the Administrative Procedure Act), and the Communications Act of 1934;

(B) the National Environmental Policy Act, the National Historic Preservation Act and other applicable Federal statutes; and

(C) the authority of a State or local government or instrumentality thereof, including the District of Columbia, in the placement, construction, and modification of personal wireless service facilities.]

[SEC. 175. (a)(1) The first paragraph under the heading "Community Development Block Grants" in title II of H.R. 2684 (Public Law 106–74) is amended by inserting after "National American Indian Housing Council," the following: "$4,000,000 shall be available as a grant for the Special Olympics in Anchorage, Alaska to develop the Ben Boeke Arena and Hilltop Ski Area,"; and

(2) The paragraph that includes the words "Economic Development Initiative (EDI)" under the heading "Community Development Block Grants" in title II of H.R. 2684 (Public Law 106–74) is amended by striking "$240,000,000" and inserting "$243,500,000".

(b) The statement of the managers of the committee of conference accompanying H.R. 2684 is deemed to be amended under the heading "Community Development Block Grants" to include in the description of targeted economic development initiatives the following:

"—$1,000,000 for the New Jersey Community Development Corporation for the construction of the New Jersey Community Development Corporation's Transportation Opportunity Center;

"—$750,000 for South Dakota State University in Brookings, South Dakota for the development of a performing arts center;

"—$925,000 for the Florida Association of Counties for a Rural Capacity Building Pilot Project in Tallahassee, Florida;

"—$500,000 for the Osceola County Agriculture Center for construction of a new and expanded agriculture center in Osceola County, Florida;

"—$1,000,000 for the University of Syracuse in Syracuse, New York for electrical infrastructure improvements."; and the current descriptions are amended as follows:

"—$1,700,000 to the City of Miami, Florida for the development of a Homeownership Zone to assist residents displaced by the demolition of public housing in the Model City area;" is amended to read as follows:

"—$1,700,000 to Miami-Dade County, Florida for an economic development project at the Opa-locka Neighborhood Center;";

"—$250,000 to the Arizona Science Center in Yuma, Arizona for its after-school program for inner-city youth;" is amended to read as follows:

"—$250,000 to the Arizona Science Center in Phoenix, Arizona for its after-school program for inner-city youth;";

"—$200,000 to the Schuylkill County Fire Fighters Association for a smoke-maze building on the grounds of the firefighters facility in Morea, Pennsylvania;" is amended to read as follows:

"—$200,000 to the Schuylkill County Fire Fighters Association for a smoke-maze building and other facilities and improvements on the grounds of the firefighters facility in Morea, Pennsylvania;".

(c) Notwithstanding any other provision of law, the $2,000,000 made available pursuant to Public Law 105–276 for Pittsburgh, Pennsylvania to redevelop the Sun Co./LTV Steel Site in Hazelwood, Pennsylvania is available to the Department of Economic Development in Allegheny County, Pennsylvania for the development of a technology based project in the county.

(d) Insert the following new sections at the end of the administrative provisions in title II of H.R. 2684 (Public Law 106–74):

"FHA MULTIFAMILY MORTGAGE CREDIT DEMONSTRATION

"SEC. 226. Section 542 of the Housing and Community Development Act of 1992 is amended—

"(1) in subsection (b)(5) by striking 'during fiscal year 1999' and inserting 'in each of the fiscal years 1999 and 2000'; and

"(2) in the first sentence of subsection (c)(4) by striking 'during fiscal year 1999' and inserting 'in each of fiscal years 1999 and 2000'.

"DRUG ELIMINATION PROGRAM

"SEC. 227. (a) Section 5126(4) of the Public and Assisted Housing Drug Elimination Act of 1990 is amended—

"(1) in subparagraph (B), by inserting after '1965;' the following: 'or';

"(2) in subparagraph (C), by striking '1937: or' and inserting '1937.'; and

"(3) by striking subparagraph (D).

"(b) The amendments made by subsection (a) shall be construed to have taken effect on October 21, 1998.".

GENERAL PROVISIONS—Continued

(e) The current description in the statement of the managers of the committee of conference accompanying H.R. 2684 (Public Law 106–74; House Report No. 106–379) under the heading "Community Development Block Grants" in title II is amended as follows:

"—$500,000 to the City of Citrus Heights, California for the revitalization of the Sunrise Mall;" is amended to read as follows:

"—$500,000 to the City of Citrus Heights, California for the revitalization of the Sunrise Marketplace;".

(f) The Departments of Veterans Affairs and Housing and Urban Development, and Independent Agencies Appropriations Act, 2000 (Public Law 106–74) is amended under the heading "Corporation for National and Community Service, National and Community Service Programs Operating Expenses" in title III by striking "to remain available until September 30, 2000" and inserting "to remain available until September 30, 2001".

(g) The statement of the managers of the committee of conference accompanying H.R. 2684 (Public Law 106–74; House Report No. 106–379) is deemed to be amended in the matter related to targeted economic development initiatives under the heading "Community Development Block Grants" by reducing by $100,000 the amount available to the University of Maryland in College Park, Maryland for the renovation of the James McGregor Burn Academy of Leadership, and by adding the following item:

"—$100,000 to St. Mary's College in Maryland for the St. Mary's River Project;".]

[SEC. 176. GEORGETOWN WATERFRONT PARK FUND. (a) IN GENERAL.—The District of Columbia Appropriations Act, 1999 (Public Law 105–277; 112 Stat. 2681–123) is amended in the item relating to "FEDERAL FUNDS—Federal Payment to the Georgetown Waterfront Park Fund" by striking the colon and inserting ", to remain available until expended:".

(b) EFFECTIVE DATE.—This section shall take effect as if included in the District of Columbia Appropriations Act, 1999.] *(District of Columbia Appropriations Act, 2000.)*

EQUAL EMPLOYMENT OPPORTUNITY

Federal Funds

General and special funds:

SALARIES AND EXPENSES

For necessary expenses of the Equal Employment Opportunity Commission as authorized by title VII of the Civil Rights Act of 1964, as amended (29 U.S.C. 206(d) and 621–634), the Americans with Disabilities Act of 1990, and the Civil Rights Act of 1991, including services as authorized by 5 U.S.C. 3109; hire of passenger motor vehicles as authorized by 31 U.S.C. 1343(b); non-monetary awards to private citizens; and not to exceed $29,000,000 for payments to State and local enforcement agencies for services to the Commission pursuant to title VII of the Civil Rights Act of 1964, as amended, sections 6 and 14 of the Age Discrimination in Employment Act, the Americans with Disabilities Act of 1990, and the Civil Rights Act of 1991, [$282,000,000] *$322,000,000*: *Provided*, That the Commission is authorized to make available for official reception and representation expenses not to exceed $2,500 from available funds. *(Departments of Commerce, Justice, and State, the Judiciary, and Related Agencies Appropriations Act, 2000, as enacted by section 1000(a)(1) of the Consolidated Appropriations Act, 2000 (P.L. 106–113).)*

Program and Financing (in millions of dollars)

Identification code 45–0100–0–1–751	1999 actual	2000 est.	2001 est.
Obligations by program activity:			
00.01 Executive direction and program support	37	35	46
00.02 Enforcement	213	217	247
00.03 State and local grants	29	29	29
10.00 Total new obligations	279	281	322
Budgetary resources available for obligation:			
22.00 New budget authority (gross)	279	281	322
23.95 Total new obligations	−279	−281	−322
New budget authority (gross), detail:			
Discretionary:			
40.00 Appropriation	279	282	322
40.76 Reduction pursuant to P.L. 106–113		−1	
43.00 Appropriation (total discretionary)	279	281	322
Change in unpaid obligations:			
72.40 Unpaid obligations, start of year: Obligated balance, start of year	36	58	79
73.10 Total new obligations	279	281	322
73.20 Total outlays (gross)	−256	−262	−321
74.40 Unpaid obligations, end of year: Obligated balance, end of year	58	79	80
Outlays (gross), detail:			
86.90 Outlays from new discretionary authority	256	261	301
86.93 Outlays from discretionary balances			20
87.00 Total outlays (gross)	256	262	321
Net budget authority and outlays:			
89.00 Budget authority	279	281	322
90.00 Outlays	256	262	321

The Equal Employment Opportunity Commission (EEOC) is the Federal agency responsible for enforcement of: the Age Discrimination in Employment Act of 1967; title VII of the Civil Rights Act of 1964, as amended; the Equal Pay Act of 1963; in the Federal sector only, section 501 of the Rehabilitation Act of 1963; the Americans with Disabilities Act of 1990; and the Civil Rights Act of 1991. These acts prohibit employment discrimination based on race, sex, religion, national origin, age, or handicap status. The EEOC is also responsible for carrying out Executive Order 12067, which promotes coordination and minimizes conflict and duplication among Federal agencies that administer statutes or regulations involving employment discrimination.

WORKFLOW ANALYSIS

	1999 actual	2000 est.	2001 est.
Title VII:			
Only:			
Charges filed	47,892	48,854	48,854
Charges resolved	58,973	58,192	54,189
With concurrents:			
Charges filed	57,582	58,739	58,739
Charges resolved	71,571	70,624	65,765
Age Discrimination in Employment Act:			
Only:			
Charges filed	6,899	7,038	7,038
Charges resolved	9,423	9,298	8,659
With concurrents:			
Charges filed	14,141	14,425	14,425
Charges resolved	18,908	18,658	17,374
Equal Pay Act:			
Only:			
Charges filed	64	65	65
Charges resolved	48	47	44
With concurrents:			
Charges filed	1,044	1,065	1,065
Charges resolved	1,251	1,234	1,150
Americans with Disabilities Act:			
Only:			
Charges filed	11,091	11,314	11,314
Charges resolved	14,452	14,261	13,280
With concurrents:			
Charges filed	17,007	17,349	17,349
Charges resolved	22,120	21,827	20,326
Total:			
Charges filed	77,444	79,000	79,000
Charges resolved	97,846	96,551	89,909

Totals for all charges do not equal the sum of all statutes because many charge filings allege issues/bases under more than one statute.

The EEOC's budget supports three activities:

Executive direction and support.—This activity provides for the direction and coordination of the Commission's programs. It also provides administrative and management support services for the agency. Increased funds for technology will enable EEOC to continue modernization of antiquated information systems, enhance support to end-users, and implement enhancements to communication systems used for staff interaction throughout the organization during fiscal year 2001.

Enforcement.—This activity resolves charges of employment discrimination filed with the Commission and pursues litigation to enforce compliance with Title VII, the Equal Pay Act, the Age Discrimination in Employment Act, the Americans with Disabilities Act, and the Civil Rights Act of 1991. In 2001, EEOC will continue its commitment to reduce charge inventories through a Comprehensive Enforcement Program that will increase collaboration between investigatory and legal staff in all phases of the Commission's work, including outreach, intake, and investigation, to expedite charge resolution; and, when cases are not settled through mediation, to ensure that these, and other older and more complex cases, are addressed in a fair and efficient manner. The increase for 2001 also includes funds for the Commission to provide training and technical assistance to about 3,000 employers on how to comply with equal pay requirements and to launch a public service announcement campaign on wage issues as part of the President's Equal Pay Initiative for 2001. Funding increases will also be targeted at reducing excessive backlogs in hearings and appeals in the Federal Sector Program. Increased funds will enable the Commission to mount effective education, outreach, and voluntary compliance initiatives in the private and federal sectors.

State and local grants.—This activity provides funds to State and local fair employment practice agencies to assist in the resolution of employment discrimination complaints. For 2001, the agency will continue working with State and Local Fair Employment Practices Agencies and Tribal Employment Rights Organizations to improve employment discrimination charge processing and other approaches for addressing workplace discrimination.

Object Classification (in millions of dollars)

Identification code 45–0100–0–1–751		1999 actual	2000 est.	2001 est.
	Personnel compensation:			
11.1	Full-time permanent	134	150	166
11.3	Other than full-time permanent	2	2	2
11.5	Other personnel compensation	13	13	14
11.9	Total personnel compensation	149	165	182
12.1	Civilian personnel benefits	31	35	39
21.0	Travel and transportation of persons	4	4	5
23.1	Rental payments to GSA	23	23	25
23.3	Communications, utilities, and miscellaneous charges	5	5	5
25.2	Other services	23	10	23
26.0	Supplies and materials	3	3	6
31.0	Equipment	12	7	8
41.0	Grants, subsidies, and contributions	29	29	29
99.9	Total new obligations	279	281	322

Personnel Summary

Identification code 45–0100–0–1–751		1999 actual	2000 est.	2001 est.
1001	Total compensable workyears: Full-time equivalent employment	2,593	2,839	3,055

Public enterprise funds:

EEOC Education, Technical Assistance, and Training Revolving Fund

Program and Financing (in millions of dollars)

Identification code 45–4019–0–4–751		1999 actual	2000 est.	2001 est.
	Obligations by program activity:			
10.00	Total new obligations (object class 99.5)	2	3	3
	Budgetary resources available for obligation:			
21.40	Unobligated balance available, start of year	2	2	2
22.00	New budget authority (gross)	2	3	3
23.90	Total budgetary resources available for obligation	4	5	5
23.95	Total new obligations	−2	−3	−3
24.40	Unobligated balance available, end of year	2	2	3
	New budget authority (gross), detail:			
	Mandatory:			
69.00	Offsetting collections (cash)	2	3	4
	Change in unpaid obligations:			
72.40	Unpaid obligations, start of year: Obligated balance, start of year	1	1	2
73.10	Total new obligations	2	3	3
73.20	Total outlays (gross)	−1	−2	−2
74.40	Unpaid obligations, end of year: Obligated balance, end of year	1	2	3
	Outlays (gross), detail:			
86.98	Outlays from mandatory balances	1	2	2
	Offsets:			
	Against gross budget authority and outlays:			
88.40	Offsetting collections (cash) from: Non-Federal sources	−2	−3	−4
	Net budget authority and outlays:			
89.00	Budget authority			−1
90.00	Outlays	−1	−2	−2

The EEOC Education, Technical Assistance, and Training Revolving Fund Act of 1992 created a revolving fund to pay for the cost of providing education, technical assistance and training relating to the laws administered by the Commission.

EXPORT-IMPORT BANK OF THE UNITED STATES

Federal Funds

Credit accounts:

Export-Import Bank Loans Program Account

The Export-Import Bank of the United States is authorized to make such expenditures within the limits of funds and borrowing authority available to such corporation, and in accordance with law, and to make such contracts and commitments without regard to fiscal year limitations, as provided by section 104 of the Government Corporation Control Act, as may be necessary in carrying out the program for the current fiscal year for such corporation: *Provided*, That none of the funds available during the current fiscal year may be used to make expenditures, contracts, or commitments for the export of nuclear equipment, fuel, or technology to any country other than a nuclear-weapon state as defined in Article IX of the Treaty on the Non-Proliferation of Nuclear Weapons eligible to receive economic or military assistance under this Act that has detonated a nuclear explosive after the date of the enactment of this Act.

SUBSIDY APPROPRIATION

For the cost of direct loans, loan guarantees, insurance, and tied-aid grants as authorized by section 10 of the Export-Import Bank Act of 1945, as amended, [$759,000,000] *$963,000,000,* to remain available until September 30, [2003] *2004*: *Provided*, That such costs, including the cost of modifying such loans, shall be as defined in section 502 of the Congressional Budget Act of 1974: *Provided further*, That such sums shall remain available until September 30, [2018] *2019* for the disbursement of direct loans, loan guarantees, insurance and tied-aid grants obligated in fiscal years [2000,] 2001, 2002, [and] 2003, *and 2004*: *Provided further*, That none of the funds appropriated by this Act or any prior Act appropriating funds for foreign operations, export financing, or related programs for tied-aid credits or grants may be used for any other purpose except through the regular notification procedures of the Committees on Appropriations: *Provided further*, That funds appropriated by this paragraph are made available notwithstanding section 2(b)(2) of the Export Import Bank Act of 1945, in connection with the purchase or lease of any product by any East European country, any Baltic State or any agency or national thereof.

Credit accounts—Continued

EXPORT-IMPORT BANK LOANS PROGRAM ACCOUNT—Continued

ADMINISTRATIVE EXPENSES

For administrative expenses to carry out the direct and guaranteed loan and insurance programs [to be computed on an accrual basis], including hire of passenger motor vehicles and services as authorized by 5 U.S.C. 3109, and not to exceed [$25,000] *$35,000* for official reception and representation expenses for members of the Board of Directors, [$55,000,000] *$63,000,000*: *Provided*, That necessary expenses (including special services performed on a contract or fee basis, but not including other personal services) in connection with the collection of moneys owed the Export-Import Bank, repossession or sale of pledged collateral or other assets acquired by the Export-Import Bank in satisfaction of moneys owed the Export-Import Bank, or the investigation or appraisal of any property, or the evaluation of the legal or technical aspects of any transaction for which an application for a loan, guarantee or insurance commitment has been made, shall be considered nonadministrative expenses for the purposes of this heading: *Provided further*, That, notwithstanding subsection (b) of section 117 of the Export Enhancement Act of 1992, subsection (a) thereof shall remain in effect until October 1, [2000] *2001. (Foreign Operations, Export Financing, and Related Programs Appropriation Act, 2000, as enacted by section 1000(a)(2) of the Consolidated Appropriations Act, 2000 (P.L. 106–113).)*

General Fund Credit Receipt Accounts (in millions of dollars)

Identification code 83–0100–0–1–155	1999 actual	2000 est.	2001 est.
0101 Export-Import Bank loans, negative subsidies	13	15	15
0102 Export-Import Bank loans, downward reestimates of subsidies	....	2,236	....

Program and Financing (in millions of dollars)

Identification code 83–0100–0–1–155	1999 actual	2000 est.	2001 est.
Obligations by program activity:			
00.01 Direct loan subsidy and grants	53	59	97
00.02 Guaranteed loan subsidy	603	916	967
00.03 Guaranteed loan modifications	21	13	14
00.04 Direct loan modifications	....	1	1
00.05 Reestimate of direct loan subsidy	....	505	....
00.06 Interest on reestimates of direct loan subsidy	....	328	....
00.07 Reestimates of loan guarantee subsidy	....	682	....
00.08 Interest on reestimates of loan guarantee subsidy	....	148	....
00.09 Administrative expenses	50	55	63
10.00 Total new obligations	727	2,707	1,142
Budgetary resources available for obligation:			
21.40 Unobligated balance available, start of year	334	480	292
22.00 New budget authority (gross)	825	2,474	1,026
22.10 Resources available from recoveries of prior year obligations	48	45	90
23.90 Total budgetary resources available for obligation	1,207	2,999	1,408
23.95 Total new obligations	−727	−2,707	−1,142
24.40 Unobligated balance available, end of year	480	292	266
New budget authority (gross), detail:			
Discretionary:			
Appropriation:			
40.00 Appropriation	765	759	963
40.00 Appropriation	50	55	63
40.76 Reduction pursuant to P.L. 106–113	....	−3	....
42.00 Transferred from other accounts	10	....	....
43.00 Appropriation (total discretionary)	825	811	1,026
Mandatory:			
60.05 Appropriation (indefinite)	....	1,663	....
70.00 Total new budget authority (gross)	825	2,474	1,026
Change in unpaid obligations:			
72.40 Unpaid obligations, start of year: Obligated balance, start of year	1,372	1,265	1,652
73.10 Total new obligations	727	2,707	1,142
73.20 Total outlays (gross)	−746	−2,275	−664
73.40 Adjustments in expired accounts (net)	−40	....	....
73.45 Adjustments in unexpired accounts	−48	−45	−90
74.40 Unpaid obligations, end of year: Obligated balance, end of year	1,265	1,652	2,040
Outlays (gross), detail:			
86.90 Outlays from new discretionary authority	213	274	307
86.93 Outlays from discretionary balances	533	339	358
86.97 Outlays from new mandatory authority	....	1,663	....
87.00 Total outlays (gross)	746	2,275	664
Net budget authority and outlays:			
89.00 Budget authority	825	2,474	1,026
90.00 Outlays	746	2,275	664

Summary of Loan Levels, Subsidy Budget Authority and Outlays by Program (in millions of dollars)

Identification code 83–0100–0–1–155	1999 actual	2000 est.	2001 est.
Direct loan levels supportable by subsidy budget authority:			
1150 Direct loans	848	771	890
1150 Direct Loans: Tied Aid War Chest	55	65	70
1159 Total direct loan levels	903	836	960
Direct loan subsidy (in percent):			
1320 Direct loans	4.36	4.67	5.17
1320 Direct Loans: Tied Aid War Chest	29.09	36.92	37.14
1329 Weighted average subsidy rate	5.87	7.18	7.50
Direct loan subsidy budget authority:			
1330 Direct loans	37	36	46
1330 Direct Loans: Tied Aid War Chest	16	24	26
1339 Total subsidy budget authority	53	60	72
Direct loan subsidy outlays:			
1340 Direct loans	93	39	29
1340 Direct Loans: Tied Aid War Chest	7	6	10
1349 Total subsidy outlays	100	45	39
Guaranteed loan levels supportable by subsidy budget authority:			
2150 Loan guarantees	12,165	14,664	15,040
2159 Total loan guarantee levels	12,165	14,664	15,040
Guaranteed loan subsidy (in percent):			
2320 Guaranteed Loans	5.13	6.34	6.70
2329 Weighted average subsidy rate	5.13	6.34	6.70
Guaranteed loan subsidy budget authority:			
2330 Subsidy budget authority	624	929	1,007
2339 Total subsidy budget authority	624	929	1,007
Guaranteed loan subsidy outlays:			
2340 Subsidy outlays	607	520	555
2349 Total subsidy outlays	607	520	555
Administrative expense data:			
3510 Budget authority	50	55	63
3580 Outlays from balances	....	7	8
3590 Outlays	39	40	53

The purpose of the Export-Import Bank (Eximbank) is to aid in the financing and promotion of U.S. exports. To accomplish its objectives, the bank's authority and resources are used to: assume commercial and political risks that exporters or private institutions are unwilling or unable to undertake; overcome maturity and other limitations in private sector export financing; assist U.S. exporters to meet officially sponsored foreign export credit competition; and, provide leadership and guidance in export financing to the U.S. exporting and banking communities and to foreign borrowers. The bank provides its export credit support through direct loan, loan guarantee and insurance programs. The bank is actively assisting small- and medium-sized businesses.

The bank's request for administrative expenses for 2001 is $63 million.

As required by the Federal Credit Reform Act of 1990, this account records, for Eximbank, the subsidy costs associated with direct loans and direct grants obligated, and loan guarantees and insurance committed in 1992 and beyond, as well as administrative expenses. The subsidy amounts are estimated on a present value basis; administrative expenses are estimated on a cash basis.

Object Classification (in millions of dollars)

Identification code 83–0100–0–1–155		1999 actual	2000 est.	2001 est.
11.1	Personnel compensation: Full-time permanent	26	29	32
12.1	Civilian personnel benefits	7	7	8
21.0	Travel and transportation of persons	1	1	2
23.1	Rental payments to GSA	3	4	4
23.3	Communications, utilities, and miscellaneous charges	1	1	1
25.2	Other services	8	10	12
26.0	Supplies and materials	2	2	2
31.0	Equipment	2	1	2
41.0	Grants, subsidies, and contributions	677	2,652	1,079
99.9	Total new obligations	727	2,707	1,142

Personnel Summary

Identification code 83–0100–0–1–155		1999 actual	2000 est.	2001 est.
1001	Total compensable workyears: Full-time equivalent employment	414	427	434

Debt Reduction Financing Account

Program and Financing (in millions of dollars)

Identification code 83–4028–0–3–155		1999 actual	2000 est.	2001 est.
	Obligations by program activity:			
00.01	Payment to liquidating account	2	7	
00.02	Interest on Treasury borrowing	4	2	
00.03	Subsidy for modifications		20	36
00.05	Reestimates of direct loan subsidy		5	
10.00	Total new obligations	6	34	36
	Budgetary resources available for obligation:			
22.00	New financing authority (gross)	6	34	36
23.95	Total new obligations	−6	−34	−36
	New financing authority (gross), detail:			
	Mandatory:			
67.15	Authority to borrow (indefinite)	4	26	35
	Discretionary:			
68.00	Spending authority from offsetting collections: Offsetting collections (cash)	2	8	1
70.00	Total new financing authority (gross)	6	34	36
	Change in unpaid obligations:			
73.10	Total new obligations	6	34	36
73.20	Total financing disbursements (gross)	−6	−34	−36
87.00	Total financing disbursements (gross)	6	34	36
	Offsets:			
	Against gross financing authority and financing disbursements:			
	Offsetting collections (cash) from:			
88.00	Federal sources	−2	−5	3
88.40	Non-Federal sources		−3	−4
88.90	Total, offsetting collections (cash)	−2	−8	−1
	Net financing authority and financing disbursements:			
89.00	Financing authority	4	26	35
90.00	Financing disbursements		26	35

Status of Direct Loans (in millions of dollars)

Identification code 83–4028–0–3–155		1999 actual	2000 est.	2001 est.
	Cumulative balance of direct loans outstanding:			
1210	Outstanding, start of year	64	108	226
1233	Disbursements: Purchase of loans assets from a liquidating account	44	118	
1290	Outstanding, end of year	108	226	226

Balance Sheet (in millions of dollars)

Identification code 83–4028–0–3–155		1998 actual	1999 actual	2000 est.	2001 est.
	ASSETS:				
	Net value of assets related to post-1991 direct loans receivable:				
1401	Direct loans receivable, gross	514	108	226	226
1405	Allowance for subsidy cost (−)	−360	−97	−203	−203
1499	Net present value of assets related to direct loans	154	11	23	23
1999	Total assets	154	11	23	23
	LIABILITIES:				
2103	Federal liabilities: Debt	154	11	23	23
2999	Total liabilities	154	11	23	23
4999	Total liabilities and net position	154	11	23	23

As required by the Federal Credit Reform Act of 1990, this account records all cash flows to and from the Government resulting from restructuring either loans or claims against guarantees made by the Export-Import Bank of the U.S.

Export-Import Bank Direct Loan Financing Account

Program and Financing (in millions of dollars)

Identification code 83–4161–0–3–155		1999 actual	2000 est.	2001 est.
	Obligations by program activity:			
00.01	Direct loans	903	836	960
00.02	Interest on Treasury borrowing	425	516	602
00.91	Direct Program by Activities—Subtotal (1 level)	1,328	1,352	1,562
08.01	Payment to negative subsidy receipt account	13	14	15
08.02	Downward reestimates paid to receipt accounts		682	
08.04	Interest on downward reeestimates paid to receipt accounts		271	
08.91	Direct Program by Activities—Subtotal (1 level)	13	967	15
10.00	Total new obligations	1,341	2,319	1,577
	Budgetary resources available for obligation:			
21.40	Unobligated balance available, start of year	586	1,550	
22.00	New financing authority (gross)	3,215	2,274	1,487
22.10	Resources available from recoveries of prior year obligations	−680	45	90
22.60	Portion applied to repay debt	−230	−1,550	
23.90	Total budgetary resources available for obligation	2,891	2,319	1,577
23.95	Total new obligations	−1,341	−2,319	−1,577
24.40	Unobligated balance available, end of year	1,550		
	New financing authority (gross), detail:			
	Mandatory:			
67.15	Authority to borrow (indefinite)	2,418	156	68
	Spending authority from offsetting collections:			
	Discretionary:			
68.00	Offsetting collections (cash)	972	2,110	1,388
68.10	Change in receivables from program account	−175	8	31
68.90	Spending authority from offsetting collections (total discretionary)	797	2,118	1,419
70.00	Total new financing authority (gross)	3,215	2,274	1,487
	Change in unpaid obligations:			
	Unpaid obligations, start of year:			
72.40	Obligated balance, start of year	3,614	3,159	2,825
72.95	Receivables from program account	389	214	222
72.99	Total unpaid obligations, start of year	4,003	3,373	3,047
73.10	Total new obligations	1,341	2,319	1,577
73.20	Total financing disbursements (gross)	−2,651	−2,600	−1,406
73.45	Adjustments in unexpired accounts	680	−45	−90
	Unpaid obligations, end of year:			
74.40	Obligated balance, end of year	3,159	2,825	2,874
74.95	Receivables from program account	214	222	253
74.99	Total unpaid obligations, end of year	3,373	3,047	3,127

Credit accounts—Continued

EXPORT-IMPORT BANK DIRECT LOAN FINANCING ACCOUNT—Continued

Program and Financing (in millions of dollars)—Continued

Identification code 83–4161–0–3–155	1999 actual	2000 est.	2001 est.
87.00 Total financing disbursements (gross)	2,651	2,600	1,406
Offsets:			
Against gross financing authority and financing disbursements:			
Offsetting collections (cash) from:			
Federal sources:			
88.00 Federal sources: upward reestimate		−833	
88.00 Federal sources: payment from program account	−100	−45	−39
88.25 Interest on uninvested funds	−150		
Non-Federal sources:			
88.40 Repayments and prepayments	−367	−667	−786
88.40 Fees and interest on loans	−355	−565	−563
88.90 Total, offsetting collections (cash)	−972	−2,110	−1,388
Against gross financing authority only:			
88.95 Change in receivables from program accounts	175	−8	−31
Net financing authority and financing disbursements:			
89.00 Financing authority	2,418	156	68
90.00 Financing disbursements	1,679	490	18

Status of Direct Loans (in millions of dollars)

Identification code 83–4161–0–3–155	1999 actual	2000 est.	2001 est.
Position with respect to appropriations act limitation on obligations:			
1131 Direct loan obligations exempt from limitation	903	836	960
1150 Total direct loan obligations	903	836	960
Cumulative balance of direct loans outstanding:			
1210 Outstanding, start of year	5,027	7,054	7,478
1231 Disbursements: Direct loan disbursements	2,375	1,117	790
1251 Repayments: Repayments and prepayments	−348	−693	−817
1290 Outstanding, end of year	7,054	7,478	7,451

Balance Sheet (in millions of dollars)

Identification code 83–4161–0–3–155	1998 actual	1999 actual	2000 est.	2001 est.
ASSETS:				
1101 Federal assets: Fund balances with Treasury	586	5,050	5,302	5,568
Net value of assets related to post-1991 direct loans receivable:				
1401 Direct loans receivable, gross	5,027	7,054	7,406	7,451
1402 Interest receivable	78	103	107	112
1405 Allowance for subsidy cost (−)	−1,306	−2,091	−2,194	−2,305
1499 Net present value of assets related to direct loans	3,799	5,066	5,319	5,258
1803 Other Federal assets: Property, plant and equipment, net	3	7	8	8
1999 Total assets	4,388	10,123	10,629	10,834
LIABILITIES:				
Federal liabilities:				
2102 Interest payable	264	425	446	468
2103 Debt	3,956	6,603	6,933	7,280
2104 Resources payable to Treasury		253	266	279
Non-Federal liabilities:				
2201 Accounts payable	2	6	6	6
2207 Other	6	246	258	271
2999 Total liabilities	4,228	7,533	7,909	8,304
NET POSITION:				
3300 Cumulative results of operations	160	2,590	2,720	2,530
3999 Total net position	160	2,590	2,720	2,530
4999 Total liabilities and net position	4,388	10,123	10,629	10,834

As required by the Federal Credit Reform Act of 1990, this non-budgetary account records all cash flows to and from the Government resulting from direct loans obligated in 1992 and beyond. The amounts in this account are a means of financing and are not included in the budget totals.

This account reflects direct loan activity through 2001.

EXPORT-IMPORT BANK GUARANTEED LOAN FINANCING ACCOUNT

Program and Financing (in millions of dollars)

Identification code 83–4162–0–3–155	1999 actual	2000 est.	2001 est.
Obligations by program activity:			
00.01 Guarantee claims	1,391	424	656
08.01 Payment to negative subsidy receipt account		1	1
08.02 Downward reestimates paid to receipt accounts		867	
08.04 Interest on downward reestimates paid to receipt accounts		417	
08.91 Direct Program by Activities—Subtotal (1 level)		1,285	1
10.00 Total new obligations	1,391	1,709	657
Budgetary resources available for obligation:			
21.40 Unobligated balance available, start of year	3,872	4,312	4,931
22.00 New financing authority (gross)	1,831	2,328	1,533
23.90 Total budgetary resources available for obligation	5,703	6,640	6,464
23.95 Total new obligations	−1,391	−1,709	−657
24.40 Unobligated balance available, end of year	4,312	4,931	5,807
New financing authority (gross), detail:			
Discretionary:			
47.00 Authority to borrow	4		
68.00 Spending authority from offsetting collections: Offsetting collections (cash)	1,827	2,328	1,533
70.00 Total new financing authority (gross)	1,831	2,328	1,533
Change in unpaid obligations:			
73.10 Total new obligations	1,391	1,709	657
73.20 Total financing disbursements (gross)	−1,391	−1,709	−657
87.00 Total financing disbursements (gross)	1,391	1,709	657
Offsets:			
Against gross financing authority and financing disbursements:			
Offsetting collections (cash) from:			
Federal sources:			
88.00 Payments from program account	−607	−520	−555
88.00 Federal sources: upward reestimate		−830	
88.25 Interest on uninvested funds	−212	−284	−284
88.40 Fees and premiums	−1,008	−694	−694
88.90 Total, offsetting collections (cash)	−1,827	−2,328	−1,533
Net financing authority and financing disbursements:			
89.00 Financing authority	4		
90.00 Financing disbursements	−436	−619	−876

Status of Guaranteed Loans (in millions of dollars)

Identification code 83–4162–0–3–155	1999 actual	2000 est.	2001 est.
Position with respect to appropriations act limitation on commitments:			
2111 Limitation on guaranteed loans made by private lenders			
2131 Guaranteed loan commitments exempt from limitation	12,165	14,664	15,040
2150 Total guaranteed loan commitments	12,165	14,664	15,040
Cumulative balance of guaranteed loans outstanding:			
2210 Outstanding, start of year	22,714	24,151	30,166
2231 Disbursements of new guaranteed loans	8,901	11,998	11,512
2251 Repayments and prepayments	−6,464	−5,699	−11,641
2263 Adjustments: Terminations for default that result in claim payments	−1,000	−284	−425
2290 Outstanding, end of year	24,151	30,166	29,612
Memorandum:			
2299 Guaranteed amount of guaranteed loans outstanding, end of year	24,151	30,166	29,612

As required by the Federal Credit Reform Act of 1990, this non-budgetary account records all cash flows to and from the Government resulting from loan guarantees committed in 1992 and beyond. The amounts in this account are a means of financing and are not included in the budget totals.

This account reflects actual and expected loan guarantee activity through 2001.

Balance Sheet (in millions of dollars)

Identification code 83–4162–0–3–155	1998 actual	1999 actual	2000 est.	2001 est.
ASSETS:				
1101 Federal assets: Fund balances with Treasury	3,872	3,263	3,426	3,597
1206 Non-Federal assets: Receivables, net	920	698	733	770
1999 Total assets	4,792	3,961	4,159	4,367
LIABILITIES:				
2104 Federal liabilities: Resources payable to Treasury	....	740	777	816
Non-Federal liabilities:				
2201 Accounts payable	4	31	33	34
2204 Liabilities for loan guarantees	503	1,007	1,058	1,111
2207 Other	633	6,096	6,400	6,720
2999 Total liabilities	1,140	7,874	8,268	8,681
NET POSITION:				
3300 Cumulative results of operations	3,652	–3,913	–4,109	–4,314
3999 Total net position	3,652	–3,913	–4,109	–4,314
4999 Total liabilities and net position	4,792	3,961	4,159	4,367

Public enterprise funds:

EXPORT-IMPORT BANK OF THE UNITED STATES LIQUIDATING ACCOUNT

Program and Financing (in millions of dollars)

Identification code 83–4027–0–3–155	1999 actual	2000 est.	2001 est.
Obligations by program activity:			
00.06 Claim payments, gross	258	17	22
10.00 Total new obligations (object class 33.0)	258	17	22
Budgetary resources available for obligation:			
21.40 Unobligated balance available, start of year	561	1,053	908
22.00 New budget authority (gross)	1,150	617	597
Capital transfer to general fund:			
22.40 Capital transfer to general fund	– 400	– 743	– 868
22.40 Capital transfer to general fund (Debt Reduction)	....	– 2	....
23.90 Total budgetary resources available for obligation	1,311	925	637
23.95 Total new obligations	– 258	– 17	– 22
24.40 Unobligated balance available, end of year	1,053	908	615
New budget authority (gross), detail:			
Mandatory:			
Offsetting collections (cash):			
69.00 Offsetting collections (cash)	1,140	615	597
69.00 Offsetting collections (cash)	10	2	....
69.90 Spending authority from offsetting collections (total mandatory)	1,150	617	597
Change in unpaid obligations:			
72.40 Unpaid obligations, start of year: Obligated balance, start of year	161	255	272
73.10 Total new obligations	258	17	22
73.20 Total outlays (gross)	– 164	....	....
74.40 Unpaid obligations, end of year: Obligated balance, end of year	255	272	294
Outlays (gross), detail:			
86.98 Outlays from mandatory balances	258	17	22
Offsets:			
Against gross budget authority and outlays:			
Offsetting collections (cash) from:			
88.00 Federal sources: Debt Reduction	– 10	– 2	....
88.20 Interest on U.S. securities	– 47	– 54	– 46
Non-Federal sources:			
88.40 Loans repaid	– 731	– 349	– 353
88.40 Interest and fee revenue from loans	– 349	– 202	– 188
88.40 Guarantee fees	– 13	– 10	– 10
88.90 Total, offsetting collections (cash)	– 1,150	– 617	– 597
Net budget authority and outlays:			
89.00 Budget authority	....	....	....
90.00 Outlays	– 892	– 600	– 575
Memorandum (non-add) entries:			
92.01 Total investments, start of year: U.S. securities: Par value	528	1,017	865
92.02 Total investments, end of year: U.S. securities: Par value	1,017	865	550

Status of Direct Loans (in millions of dollars)

Identification code 83–4027–0–3–155	1999 actual	2000 est.	2001 est.
Cumulative balance of direct loans outstanding:			
1210 Outstanding, start of year	5,721	5,169	4,820
Repayments:			
Repayments and prepayments:			
1251 Repayments and prepayments	– 542	– 342	– 353
1251 Repayments and prepayments: Debt Reduction	– 10	– 2	....
1264 Write-offs for default: Other adjustments, net	....	– 5	....
1290 Outstanding, end of year	5,169	4,820	4,467

Status of Guaranteed Loans (in millions of dollars)

Identification code 83–4027–0–3–155	1999 actual	2000 est.	2001 est.
Cumulative balance of guaranteed loans outstanding:			
2210 Outstanding, start of year	1,707	1,214	864
2251 Repayments and prepayments	– 493	– 350	– 317
2290 Outstanding, end of year	1,214	864	547
Memorandum:			
2299 Guaranteed amount of guaranteed loans outstanding, end of year	1,214	864	547

DATA ON DIRECT LOANS

[In millions of dollars]

	1999 actual	*2000 est.*	*2001 est.*
Undisbursed loan authorizations, end of year	2,902	2,470	2,582
Credit authorizations	1,326	836	990
Credit cancellations	277	151	80
Loan disbursements	1,759	1,117	798
Capitalized interest	623	72	75
Loan principal repayments	814	1,109	1,139
Loan write-offs	9	26	31
Loans outstanding, end of year	10,126	10,180	9,883

DATA ON GUARANTEES

[In millions of dollars]

	1999 actual	*2000 est.*	*2001 est.*
Undisbursed balance, end of year	10,084	10,978	14,504
Authorizations	8,299	11,343	12,145
Cancellations	1,586	2,171	440
Shipments	7,147	8,279	8,179
Repayments	6,003	4,265	8,354
Outstanding balance, end of year	23,979	27,993	27,817

DATA ON INSURANCE

[In millions of dollars]

	1999 actual	*2000 est.*	*2001 est.*
Undisbursed balance, end of year	5,430	4,285	4,248
Authorizations	3,866	3,550	3,835
Cancellations	1,312	975	198
Shipments	1,895	3,719	3,675
Repayments	2,093	1,767	3.620
Outstanding balance, end of year	1,386	3,339	3,393

DATA ON GRANT PORTION OF TIED-AID CREDIT

[In millions of dollars]

	1999 actual	*2000 est.*	*2001 est.*
Grant portion of tied-aid credit	16	10	12
Estimated outlays	4	6	7

Public enterprise funds—Continued

EXPORT-IMPORT BANK OF THE UNITED STATES LIQUIDATING ACCOUNT—Continued

POSITION WITH RESPECT TO LENDING, GUARANTEE AND INSURANCE AUTHORITY

[In millions of dollars]

	1998 actual	1999 actual	2000 est.	2001 est.
Statutory authority	75,000	75,000	75,000	75,000
Charges against authority:				
Loan Program:				
Loans Outstanding	8,566	10,126	10,180	9,883
Loans Undisbursed	3,612	2,902	2,470	2,582
Outstanding Claims	3,342	4,511	5,188	5,966
Subtotal	15,520	17,539	17,838	18,431
Export guarantees and insurance program:				
Export Credit Insurance	6,355	6,816	7,624	7,641
Export Credit Guarantees	33,353	34,063	38,970	42,321
Subtotal	39,708	40,879	46,594	49,962
Total Charges against authority	55,228	58,418	64,432	68,393
Unused Authority	19,772	16,582	10,568	6,607

Operating results and financial condition.—The bank is a wholly owned Government corporation. Capital stock of $1 billion was purchased by the U.S. Treasury, and the bank is authorized to borrow up to $6 billion from the Treasury. The bank pays interest on such borrowings.

The bank has a reserve for possible credit losses, which provides for the risk of loss inherent in the lending process. This reserve is a general reserve, available to absorb credit losses related to the total loan portfolio. The reserve is increased by provisions charged to expenses and decreased by charge-offs, net of recoveries.

The provision for possible credit losses is based on the bank's evaluation of the adequacy of the reserve, taking into consideration a variety of factors, including repayment status of loans, future risk factors, the relationship of the reserve to the portfolio, and worldwide economic conditions. Providing for such possible losses does not imply that any loans will be written off. It simply recognizes the fact that the prospects for collection of some of the bank's loans are impaired. It does not provide for losses on a country-by-country basis and is intended only to provide an overall revaluation of the loan portfolio.

The bank's net operating income was $214 million in 1999. Total Government equity in the corporation was $184 million on September 30, 1999.

Statement of Operations (in millions of dollars)

Identification code 83–4027–0–3–155	1998 actual	1999 actual	2000 est.	2001 est.
0101 Revenue	444	546	212	198
0102 Expense	–93	....	....	....
0105 Net income or loss (–)	351	546	212	198

Balance Sheet (in millions of dollars)

Identification code 83–4027–0–3–155	1998 actual	1999 actual	2000 est.	2001 est.
ASSETS:				
Federal assets:				
1101 Fund balances with Treasury	36	55	30	30
Investments in US securities:				
1102 Treasury securities, par	528	1,017	865	550
1206 Non-Federal assets: Receivables, net	5	5	5	5
Net value of assets related to pre-1992 direct loans receivable and acquired defaulted guaranteed loans receivable:				
Direct loans, gross:				
1601 Direct loans, gross	5,721	5,169	4,827	4,474
1601 Direct loans, gross [Debt Reduction]	–1,000	....	–7	–7
1602 Interest receivable	38	45	40	30
1603 Allowance for estimated uncollectible loans and interest (–)	–1,475	–3,514	–3,272	–3,033
1699 Value of assets related to direct loans	3,284	1,700	1,588	1,464
1701 Defaulted guaranteed loans, gross	609	765	750	735
1702 Interest receivable	5	6	6	6
1703 Allowance for estimated uncollectible loans and interest (–)	–261	–300	–295	–290
1704 Defaulted guaranteed loans and interest receivable, net	353	471	461	451
1799 Value of assets related to loan guarantees	353	471	461	451
1999 Total assets	4,206	3,248	2,949	2,500
LIABILITIES:				
Non-Federal liabilities:				
2202 Interest payable	1	1	1	1
2203 Debt	10	215	175	125
2204 Liabilities for loan guarantees	130	43	35	25
2207 Other	500	448	350	300
2999 Total liabilities	641	707	561	451
NET POSITION:				
3100 Appropriated capital	20	54	55	55
Cumulative results of operations:				
3300 Cumulative results of operations	3,551	3,502	3,275	2,867
3300 Cumulative results of operations [Debt Reduction]	–6	–1,015	–942	–873
3999 Total net position	3,565	2,541	2,388	2,049
4999 Total liabilities and net position	4,206	3,248	2,949	2,500

As required by the Federal Credit Reform Act of 1990, this account records, for Eximbank, all cash flows to and from the Government resulting from direct loans obligated and loan guarantees and insurance committed prior to 1992. This account is shown on a cash basis. All new activity in this program in 1992 and beyond is recorded in corresponding program and financing accounts.

GENERAL FUND RECEIPT ACCOUNTS

(in millions of dollars)

	1999 actual	2000 est.	2001 est.
Offsetting receipts from the public:			
83–272710 Export-Import Bank Loans, negative subsidies	13	15	16
83–272730 Export-Import Bank Loans, downward reestimates of subsidies	....	2,236	....
General Fund Offsetting receipts from the public	13	2,251	16

FARM CREDIT ADMINISTRATION

Federal Funds

Public enterprise funds:

[LIMITATION OF ADMINISTRATIVE EXPENSES]

[Not to exceed $35,800,000 (from assessments collected from farm credit institutions and from the Federal Agricultural Mortgage Corporation) shall be obligated during the current fiscal year for administrative expenses as authorized under 12 U.S.C. 2249: *Provided*, That this limitation shall not apply to expenses associated with receiverships.] *(Agriculture, Rural Development, Food and Drug Administration, and Related Agencies Appropriations Act, 2000.)*

Program and Financing (in millions of dollars)

Identification code 78–4131–0–3–351	1999 actual	2000 est.	2001 est.
Obligations by program activity:			
09.00 Reimbursable program	33	37	38
10.00 Total new obligations	33	37	38
Budgetary resources available for obligation:			
21.40 Unobligated balance available, start of year	11	10	9
22.00 New budget authority (gross)	33	37	37

23.90	Total budgetary resources available for obligation	44	47	46
23.95	Total new obligations	−33	−37	−38
24.40	Unobligated balance available, end of year	10	9	9
	New budget authority (gross), detail:			
	Mandatory:			
69.00	Offsetting collections (cash)	34	36	37
	Change in unpaid obligations:			
72.40	Unpaid obligations, start of year: Obligated balance, start of year	5	5	5
73.10	Total new obligations	33	37	38
73.20	Total outlays (gross)	−34	−36	−37
74.40	Unpaid obligations, end of year: Obligated balance, end of year	5	5	5
	Outlays (gross), detail:			
86.97	Outlays from new mandatory authority	34	36	37
	Offsets:			
	Against gross budget authority and outlays:			
88.40	Offsetting collections (cash) from: Non-Federal sources	−34	−36	−37
	Net budget authority and outlays:			
89.00	Budget authority	−1	1	
90.00	Outlays	2		
	Memorandum (non-add) entries:			
92.01	Total investments, start of year: U.S. securities: Par value	17	14	14
92.02	Total investments, end of year: U.S. securities: Par value	14	14	14

The Farm Credit Administration (FCA) is an independent Federal agency that examines and regulates the Farm Credit System (System) for safety and soundness. The System is a cooperative agricultural credit system of farm credit banks and associations that lends to farmers, ranchers, and their cooperatives. Since 1990, the FCA also performs annual examinations of the Federal Agricultural Mortgage Corporation. In addition, FCA annually examines The National Consumer Cooperative Bank and its affiliate, The NCCB Development Corporation.

As of October 1, 1999, the System was comprised of six Farm Credit Banks, one Agricultural Credit Bank, 178 associations, four service corporations, the Federal Farm Credit Bank Funding Corporation, the Farm Credit System Financial Assistance Corporation, and the Federal Agricultural Mortgage Corporation. The Agricultural Credit Bank makes loans to agricultural, aquatic, and public utility cooperatives and other persons or organizations owned by or having transactions with such cooperatives.

Assessments based upon estimated administrative expenses are collected from institutions in the System and the Federal Agricultural Mortgage Corporation and are available for administrative expenses. Obligations are incurred within fiscal year budgets approved by the Farm Credit Administration Board.

Object Classification (in millions of dollars)

Identification code 78–4131–0–3–351		1999 actual	2000 est.	2001 est.
	Personnel compensation:			
11.1	Full-time permanent	21	23	23
11.5	Other personnel compensation	2	2	3
11.9	Total personnel compensation	23	25	26
12.1	Civilian personnel benefits	5	6	6
21.0	Travel and transportation of persons	2	2	3
25.2	Other services	2	3	2
31.0	Equipment	1	1	1
99.9	Total new obligations	33	37	38

Personnel Summary

Identification code 78–4131–0–3–351		1999 actual	2000 est.	2001 est.
2001	Total compensable workyears: Full-time equivalent employment	295	310	309

FARM CREDIT SYSTEM FINANCIAL ASSISTANCE CORPORATION

FINANCIAL ASSISTANCE CORPORATION ASSISTANCE FUND, LIQUIDATING ACCOUNT

Program and Financing (in millions of dollars)

Identification code 78–4134–0–3–351		1999 actual	2000 est.	2001 est.
	Obligations by program activity:			
00.02	Interest expenses	105	79	71
10.00	Total new obligations (object class 43.0)	105	79	71
	Budgetary resources available for obligation:			
21.40	Unobligated balance available, start of year	1,868	1,562	1,546
22.00	New budget authority (gross)	194	151	137
22.60	Portion applied to repay debt	−397	−89	
23.90	Total budgetary resources available for obligation	1,665	1,624	1,683
23.95	Total new obligations	−105	−79	−71
24.40	Unobligated balance available, end of year	1,562	1,546	1,612
	New budget authority (gross), detail:			
	Mandatory:			
69.00	Offsetting collections (cash)	194	151	137
	Change in unpaid obligations:			
73.10	Total new obligations	105	79	71
73.20	Total outlays (gross)	−105	−79	−71
	Outlays (gross), detail:			
86.97	Outlays from new mandatory authority	194	79	71
86.98	Outlays from mandatory balances	305		
87.00	Total outlays (gross)	105	79	71
	Offsets:			
	Against gross budget authority and outlays:			
	Offsetting collections (cash) from:			
88.00	Federal sources	−3		
88.20	Interest on U.S. securities	−58	−57	−53
88.40	Non-Federal sources	−133	−94	−84
88.90	Total, offsetting collections (cash)	−194	−151	−137
	Net budget authority and outlays:			
89.00	Budget authority			
90.00	Outlays	305	−72	−66
	Memorandum (non-add) entries:			
92.01	Total investments, start of year: U.S. securities: Par value	1,004	659	659
92.02	Total investments, end of year: U.S. securities: Par value	659	659	659

Status of Direct Loans (in millions of dollars)

Identification code 78–4134–0–3–351		1999 actual	2000 est.	2001 est.
	Cumulative balance of direct loans outstanding:			
1210	Outstanding, start of year	933	900	883
1251	Repayments: Repayments and prepayments	−33	−17	−15
1290	Outstanding, end of year	900	883	868

Statement of Operations (in millions of dollars)

Identification code 78–4134–0–3–351		1998 actual	1999 actual	2000 est.	2001 est.
0101	Revenue		70	70	70
0102	Expense		−70	−70	−70
0105	Net income or loss (−)				

FINANCIAL ASSISTANCE CORPORATION ASSISTANCE FUND, LIQUIDATING ACCOUNT—Continued

Statement of Operations (in millions of dollars)—Continued

Identification code 78–4134–0–3–351	1998 actual	1999 actual	2000 est.	2001 est.
0191 Total revenues	....	70	70	70
0192 Total expenses	....	–70	–70	–70
0195 Total income or loss (–)	....	....	....	....

Balance Sheet (in millions of dollars)

Identification code 78–4134–0–3–351	1998 actual	1999 actual	2000 est.	2001 est.
ASSETS:				
Federal assets:				
Investments in US securities:				
1102 Treasury securities, par	....	619	530	530
1106 Receivables, net	....	259	259	259
1201 Non-Federal assets: Investments in non-Federal securities, net	....	268	268	268
1901 Other Federal assets: Other assets	....	22	22	22
1999 Total assets	....	1,168	1,079	1,079
LIABILITIES:				
Non-Federal liabilities:				
2201 Accounts payable	....	285	285	285
2202 Interest payable	....	17	17	17
2203 Debt	....	863	774	774
2207 Other	....	3	3	3
2999 Total liabilities	....	1,168	1,079	1,079
4999 Total liabilities and net position	....	1,168	1,079	1,079

The Farm Credit System Financial Assistance Corporation (FAC) was created by the Agricultural Credit Act of 1987 to provide funds to System institutions experiencing financial difficulties. Authority for FAC to issue obligations and provide assistance expired in 1992, after $1.26 billion in FAC debt had been issued. Proceeds of FAC debt issuances were paid into, and amounts for assistance and other expenses were paid from, the FAC Assistance Fund. The FAC was re-classified from a Government-sponsored enterprise to a Federal entity beginning in 1993, when most of the private capital in FAC, provided by the System, was rebated from the FAC Trust Fund pursuant to the Reconciliation and Agriculture Appropriations Acts of 1989.

Except for debt issued for Capital Preservation cash-outs, the U.S. Treasury pays all the interest on 15-year, uncollateralized FAC obligations in the first five years, and up to half the interest in the second five years. The system is responsible for a greater share of the interest payment in the second five years if retained earnings exceed five percent of assets. FAC estimates that the system will pay 100 percent of the 1999 expense and 100 percent of the 2000 expense. The System is required to eventually reimburse Treasury for these payments and will redeem FAC debt upon maturity or call. Under the terms of the Act, no interest payments will be made by Treasury after the year 2000.

The FAC Trust Fund holds and rebates the private capital contributed by the System. Remaining amounts in the Trust Fund are available to cover System defaults on FAC principal and interest payments.

Trust Funds

FINANCIAL ASSISTANCE CORPORATION TRUST FUND

Unavailable Collections (in millions of dollars)

Identification code 78–8202–0–7–351	1999 actual	2000 est.	2001 est.
Balance, start of year:			
01.99 Balance, start of year	....	....	....
Receipts:			
02.02 Interest on investments	7	5	6
Appropriation:			
05.01 Financial assistance corporation trust fund	–7	–5	–6
07.99 Total balance, end of year	....	....	....

Program and Financing (in millions of dollars)

Identification code 78–8202–0–7–351	1999 actual	2000 est.	2001 est.
Budgetary resources available for obligation:			
21.40 Unobligated balance available, start of year	99	106	113
22.00 New budget authority (gross)	7	5	6
23.90 Total budgetary resources available for obligation	106	111	119
24.40 Unobligated balance available, end of year	106	113	119
New budget authority (gross), detail:			
Mandatory:			
60.27 Appropriation (trust fund, indefinite)	7	5	6
Net budget authority and outlays:			
89.00 Budget authority	7	5	6
90.00 Outlays	....	....	....
Memorandum (non-add) entries:			
92.01 Total investments, start of year: U.S. securities: Par value	109	109	109
92.02 Total investments, end of year: U.S. securities: Par value	109	109	109

FARM CREDIT SYSTEM INSURANCE CORPORATION

Federal Funds

Public enterprise funds:

FARM CREDIT SYSTEM INSURANCE FUND

Program and Financing (in millions of dollars)

Identification code 78–4171–0–3–351	1999 actual	2000 est.	2001 est.
Obligations by program activity:			
09.00 Reimbursable program	2	2	2
10.00 Total new obligations	2	2	2
Budgetary resources available for obligation:			
21.40 Unobligated balance available, start of year	1,382	1,502	1,611
22.00 New budget authority (gross)	122	111	118
23.90 Total budgetary resources available for obligation	1,504	1,613	1,729
23.95 Total new obligations	–2	–2	–2
24.40 Unobligated balance available, end of year	1,502	1,611	1,727
New budget authority (gross), detail:			
Mandatory:			
69.00 Offsetting collections (cash)	122	111	118
Change in unpaid obligations:			
72.40 Unpaid obligations, start of year: Obligated balance, start of year	–75	–132	–132
73.10 Total new obligations	2	2	2
73.20 Total outlays (gross)	–59	–2	–2
74.40 Unpaid obligations, end of year: Obligated balance, end of year	–132	–132	–132
Outlays (gross), detail:			
86.97 Outlays from new mandatory authority	59	2	2
Offsets:			
Against gross budget authority and outlays:			
Offsetting collections (cash) from:			
88.20 Interest on U.S. securities	–102	–89	–89
88.40 Non-Federal sources	–20	–22	–29
88.90 Total, offsetting collections (cash)	–122	–111	–118
Net budget authority and outlays:			
89.00 Budget authority	....	....	....
90.00 Outlays	–63	–109	–116

Memorandum (non-add) entries:				
92.01	Total investments, start of year: U.S. securities: Par value	1,316	1,415	1,415
92.02	Total investments, end of year: U.S. securities: Par value	1,376	1,519	1,519

The Farm Credit System Insurance Corporation (Corporation) was established to ensure the timely payment of principal and interest on System debt obligations purchased by investors. The Corporation is managed by a three member Board of Directors that consists of the same members as the Farm Credit Administration Board of Directors. The Corporation derives its revenues from insurance premiums collected from insured System banks and from the investment income earned on its investment portfolio. Insurance premiums are assessed on System banks based on the level of accruing and non-accruing loans outstanding in each bank and its affiliated associations' loan portfolio. Congress established a secure base amount of 2 percent of outstanding System obligations, or such other amounts determined by its Board of Directors to be actuarially sound to maintain the Insurance Fund. The Insurance Fund was at the secure base amount at September 30, 1999. Also in September, the Corporation's Board reduced premiums beginning in January 2000 to zero for all loan categories except non-accrual loans.

The Insurance Fund is available for payment on System obligations if an insured System bank defaults on its primary liability. The Insurance Fund is also available to ensure the timely retirement of certain eligible borrower stock, pay the operating costs of the Corporation, and satisfy defaults by System institutions on obligations issued by the FAC after amounts in the FAC Trust Fund are exhausted. The Corporation can exercise its authority to make loans, purchase System bank assets or obligations, provide other financial assistance and otherwise act to reduce its exposure to losses.

The Corporation has the authority to make refunds of excess Insurance Fund balances. No refunds are anticipated before 2006.

Statement of Operations (in millions of dollars)

Identification code 78–4171–0–3–351		1998 actual	1999 actual	2000 est.	2001 est.
0101	Revenue	112	121	88	93
0102	Expense	–11	–12	–13	–14
0105	Net income or loss (–)	101	109	75	79

Balance Sheet (in millions of dollars)

Identification code 78–4171–0–3–351		1998 actual	1999 actual	2000 est.	2001 est.
	ASSETS:				
	Investments in US securities:				
1102	Federal assets: Treasury securities, par	1,315	1,376	1,493	1,578
	Non-Federal assets:				
	Receivables, net:				
1206	Accrued interest receivable	21	24	21	23
1206	Premium receivable	15	35	2	2
1901	Other Federal assets: Other assets	31	67	72	76
1999	Total assets	1,382	1,502	1,588	1,679
	LIABILITIES:				
2207	Non-Federal liabilities: Other	146	157	167	179
2999	Total liabilities	146	157	167	179
	NET POSITION:				
3100	Appropriated capital	1,236	1,345	1,421	1,500
3999	Total net position	1,236	1,345	1,421	1,500
4999	Total liabilities and net position	1,382	1,502	1,588	1,679

Object Classification (in millions of dollars)

Identification code 78–4171–0–3–351		1999 actual	2000 est.	2001 est.
11.1	Reimbursable obligations: Personnel compensation: Full-time permanent	1	1	1
99.5	Below reporting threshold	1	1	1
99.9	Total new obligations	2	2	2

Personnel Summary

Identification code 78–4171–0–3–351		1999 actual	2000 est.	2001 est.
2001	Total compensable workyears: Full-time equivalent employment	10	10	10

FEDERAL COMMUNICATIONS COMMISSION

Federal Funds

General and special funds:

Salaries and Expenses

For necessary expenses of the Federal Communications Commission, as authorized by law, including uniforms and allowances therefor, as authorized by 5 U.S.C. 5901–5902; not to exceed $600,000 for land and structure; not to exceed $500,000 for improvement and care of grounds and repair to buildings; not to exceed $4,000 for official reception and representation expenses; purchase (not to exceed 16) and hire of motor vehicles; special counsel fees; and services as authorized by 5 U.S.C. 3109, **[**$210,000,000**]** *$237,188,000*, of which not to exceed $300,000 shall remain available until September 30, **[**2001**]** *2002*, for research and policy studies: *Provided*, That **[**$185,754,000**]** *$200,146,000* of offsetting collections shall be assessed and collected pursuant to section 9 of title I of the Communications Act of 1934, as amended, and shall be retained and used for necessary expenses in this appropriation, and shall remain available until expended: *Provided further*, That the sum herein appropriated shall be reduced as such offsetting collections are received during fiscal year **[**2000**]** *2001* so as to result in a final fiscal year **[**2000**]** *2001* appropriation estimated at **[**$24,246,000**]** *$37,042,000*: *Provided further*, That any offsetting collections received in excess of **[**$185,754,000**]** *$200,146,000* in fiscal year **[**2000**]** *2001* shall remain available until expended, but shall not be available for obligation until October 1, **[**2000**]** *2001*. *(Departments of Commerce, Justice, and State, the Judiciary, and Related Agencies Appropriations Act, 2000, as enacted by section 1000(a)(1) of the Consolidated Appropriations Act, 2000 (P.L. 106–113).)*

Program and Financing (in millions of dollars)

Identification code 27–0100–0–1–376		1999 actual	2000 est.	2001 est.
	Obligations by program activity:			
	Direct program:			
00.01	Licensing	19	24	37
00.05	Year 2000 Compliance	4	4	
01.00	Total direct program	23	28	37
09.00	Reimbursable program	217	246	243
10.00	Total new obligations	240	274	280
	Budgetary resources available for obligation:			
21.40	Unobligated balance available, start of year	6	19	2
22.00	New budget authority (gross)	253	257	279
23.90	Total budgetary resources available for obligation	259	276	281
23.95	Total new obligations	–240	–274	–280
24.40	Unobligated balance available, end of year	19	2	1
	New budget authority (gross), detail:			
	Discretionary:			
40.00	Appropriation	19	24	37
42.00	Transferred from other accts	9		
43.00	Appropriation (total discretionary)	28	24	37
	Spending authority from offsetting collections:			
	Offsetting collections (cash):			
68.00	Offsetting collections (reimbursable Federal)	2	1	1
68.00	Cost of conducting spectrum auctions	50	41	41
68.00	Spending authority from offsetting collections (regulatory fees)	173	191	200
68.90	Spending authority from offsetting collections (total discretionary)	225	233	242

General and special funds—Continued

SALARIES AND EXPENSES—Continued

Program and Financing (in millions of dollars)—Continued

Identification code 27–0100–0–1–376	1999 actual	2000 est.	2001 est.
70.00 Total new budget authority (gross)	253	257	279
Change in unpaid obligations:			
72.40 Unpaid obligations, start of year: Obligated balance, start of year	43	52	47
73.10 New Obligations	240	274	280
73.20 Total outlays (gross)	–231	–279	–280
74.40 Unpaid obligations, end of year: Obligated balance, end of year	52	47	47
Outlays (gross), detail:			
86.90 Outlays from new discretionary authority	214	256	277
86.93 Outlays from discretionary balances	17	23	1
87.00 Total outlays (gross)	231	279	280
Offsets:			
Against gross budget authority and outlays:			
Offsetting collections (cash) from:			
88.00 Federal sources	–2	–1	–1
88.40 Cost of conducting spectrum auctions	–50	–41	–41
88.45 Regulatory Fees	–173	–191	–200
88.90 Total, offsetting collections (cash)	–225	–233	–242
Net budget authority and outlays:			
89.00 Budget authority	28	24	37
90.00 Outlays	6	46	38

Summary of Budget Authority and Outlays

(in millions of dollars)

	1999 actual	2000 est.	2001 est.
Enacted/requested:			
Budget Authority	28	24	37
Outlays	6	46	36
Legislative proposal, not subject to PAYGO:			
Budget Authority			2
Outlays			2
Total:			
Budget Authority	28	24	39
Outlays	6	46	38

Licensing.—This activity includes the authorization or licensing of radio stations, telecommunications equipment, radio operators, as well as the authorization of common carrier and other services and facilities. It also includes policy direction, program development, legal services, and executive direction, as well as support services associated with licensing activities.

Competition.—This activity includes formal inquiries, rule making proceedings to establish or amend the Commission's rules and regulations, action on petitions for rule making and requests for rule interpretations or waivers, economic studies and analyses, and development of equipment standards. It also includes policy direction, program development, legal services, and executive direction, as well as support services associated with activities to promote competition in the public interest.

Enforcement.—This activity includes enforcement of the Commission's rules, regulations and authorizations—including investigations, inspections, compliance monitoring and sanctions of all types. It also includes the receipt and disposition of formal complaints regarding common carrier rates and services; the review and acceptance/rejection of carrier tariffs; and the review, prescription and audit of carrier accounting practices. Additionally, it also includes policy direction, program development, legal services, and executive direction, as well as support services associated with enforcement activities.

Consumer Information Services.—This activity includes the publication and dissemination of Commission decisions and actions, and related activities; public reference and library services; the duplication and dissemination of Commission records and databases; the receipt and disposition of public inquiries and informal consumer complaints; consumer, small business and public assistance; and public affairs and media relations. It also includes policy direction, program development, legal services, and executive direction, as well as support services associated with consumer information activities.

Spectrum Management.—This activity includes management of the electromagnetic spectrum as mandated by the Communications Act of 1934 as amended. Spectrum management includes the structure and processes for allocating, assigning, licensing, and regulating the use of this scarce resource to the private sector and state and local governments in a way that promotes competition while ensuring that the public interest is best served. In order to manage spectrum in both an efficient and equitable manner, the Commission evaluates needs; prepares economic, technical and engineering studies; coordinates with Federal agencies; develops cross-border sharing arrangements; and represents U.S. interests in international fora. It also includes policy direction, program development, legal services, and executive direction, as well as support services associated with spectrum management activities.

Object Classification (in millions of dollars)

Identification code 27–0100–0–1–376	1999 actual	2000 est.	2001 est.
Direct obligations:			
Personnel compensation:			
11.1 Full-time permanent	10	13	17
11.3 Other than full-time permanent	2	2	3
11.9 Total personnel compensation	12	15	20
12.1 Civilian personnel benefits	3	3	5
23.1 Rental payments to GSA	2	3	8
23.3 Communications, utilities, and miscellaneous charges	1	1	1
25.2 Other services	3	2	1
25.3 Purchases of goods and services from Government accounts		1	
25.7 Operation and maintenance of equipment	1	3	2
31.0 Equipment	1		
99.0 Subtotal, direct obligations	23	28	37
99.0 Reimbursable obligations	217	246	243
99.9 Total new obligations	240	274	280

Personnel Summary

Identification code 27–0100–0–1–376	1999 actual	2000 est.	2001 est.
Direct:			
1001 Total compensable workyears: Full-time equivalent employment	179	203	272
Reimbursable:			
2001 Total compensable workyears: Full-time equivalent employment	1,738	1,764	1,695

Program and Financing (in millions of dollars)

Identification code 27–0100–2–1–376	1999 actual	2000 est.	2001 est.
Obligations by program activity:			
Direct program:			
00.01 Analog Spectrum Lease Fee Implementation			2
01.00 Total direct program			2
10.00 Total new obligations (object class 25.2)			2
Budgetary resources available for obligation:			
22.00 New budget authority (gross)			2
23.95 Total new obligations			–2

	New budget authority (gross), detail:			
	Discretionary:			
42.00	Transferred from other accounts			2
	Change in unpaid obligations:			
73.10	Total new obligations			2
	Outlays (gross), detail:			
86.90	Outlays from new discretionary authority			2
	Net budget authority and outlays:			
89.00	Budget authority			2
90.00	Outlays			2

The Commission will receive $2 million transferred from the proposed Analog Spectrum Lease Fee to cover the cost of developing and implementing the program in 2001.

UNIVERSAL SERVICE FUND

Unavailable Collections (in millions of dollars)

Identification code 27–5183–0–2–376		1999 actual	2000 est.	2001 est.
	Balance, start of year:			
01.99	Balance, start of year			
	Receipts:			
02.01	Universal service fund	3,752	4,616	4,897
	Appropriation:			
05.01	Universal service fund	−3,752	−4,616	−4,897
07.99	Total balance, end of year			

Program and Financing (in millions of dollars)

Identification code 27–5183–0–2–376		1999 actual	2000 est.	2001 est.
	Obligations by program activity:			
10.00	Total new obligations (object class 41.0)	4,772	4,278	4,913
	Budgetary resources available for obligation:			
21.40	Unobligated balance available, start of year	1,020		337
22.00	New budget authority (gross)	3,752	4,616	4,897
23.90	Total budgetary resources available for obligation	4,772	4,616	5,234
23.95	Total new obligations	−4,772	−4,278	−4,913
24.40	Unobligated balance available, end of year		337	321
	New budget authority (gross), detail:			
	Mandatory:			
60.25	Appropriation (special fund, indefinite)	3,752	4,616	4,897
	Change in unpaid obligations:			
72.40	Unpaid obligations, start of year: Obligated balance, start of year		1,479	
73.10	Total new obligations	4,772	4,278	4,913
73.20	Total outlays (gross)	−3,293	−5,758	−4,913
74.40	Unpaid obligations, end of year: Obligated balance, end of year	1,479		
	Outlays (gross), detail:			
86.97	Outlays from new mandatory authority	3,293	4,278	4,897
86.98	Outlays from mandatory balances		1,479	16
87.00	Total outlays (gross)	3,293	5,758	4,913
	Net budget authority and outlays:			
89.00	Budget authority	3,752	4,616	4,897
90.00	Outlays	3,293	5,758	4,913

The Telecommunications Act of 1996 provides for a major restructuring of the Nation's communications laws, promotes universal service and open access to information networks, and provides for flexible government regulations. Under the Act, telecommunications carriers that provide interstate telecommunications services are required to contribute funds for the preservation and advancement of universal service. The contributions are used to provide services eligible for universal service support as prescribed by the FCC. Telecommunications carriers receive a credit towards their contribution by providing discount service to schools, libraries, and health care providers. Support will also be provided to carriers offering services in high cost areas of the United States and to carriers offering services to low income consumers.

ANALOG SPECTRUM LEASE FEE

(Legislative proposal, not subject to PAYGO)

Contingent upon the enactment of authorizing legislation, the Commission shall assess fees totaling not less than $200,000,000 for use of analog spectrum by commercial television broadcasters, and collect the fees by no later than September 30, 2001. Such fees shall be deposited as offsetting receipts to this account, to be available for transfer as follows, subject to the terms and conditions of the receiving account: "Salaries and Expenses", Federal Communications Commission, not to exceed $2,000,000, to remain available until expended, for the costs of developing and implementing the program required by this section; and for upgrading Federal public safety wireless communications equipment and facilities, to "Narrowband Communications", Department of Justice, $138,000,000; to "Department-wide Systems and Capital Investment Programs", Department of the Treasury, $55,000,000; and to "Operation of Indian Programs", Bureau of Indian Affairs, Department of the Interior, $5,000,000: Provided further, That upon enactment of authorizing legislation for such fee, the amounts appropriated from the General Fund to the above-named accounts shall be reduced by the respective amounts specified above.

Unavailable Collections (in millions of dollars)

Identification code 27–5444–0–2–376		1999 actual	2000 est.	2001 est.
	Balance, start of year:			
01.99	Balance, start of year			
	Receipts:			
02.02	Legislative proposal not subject to PAYGO			200
	Appropriation:			
05.02	Analog spectrum lease program, legislative proposal not subject to PAYGO			−200
07.99	Total balance, end of year			

Program and Financing (in millions of dollars)

Identification code 27–5444–2–2–376		1999 actual	2000 est.	2001 est.
	New budget authority (gross), detail:			
	Discretionary:			
40.25	Appropriation (special fund, indefinite)			200
41.00	Transferred to other accounts			−200
43.00	Appropriation (total discretionary)			
	Net budget authority and outlays:			
89.00	Budget authority			
90.00	Outlays			

The Administration will propose legislation authorizing the FCC to establish a lease fee on the use of analog spectrum by commercial television broadcasters, subject to appropriations as indicated in the language proposed above. The FCC will promulgate a rulemaking to apportion the aggregate fee amount among broadcasters. Upon return of its analog channel to the FCC, an individual broadcaster is exempt from the fee. As indicated in the appropriations language, the amounts collected, less Commission expenses to develop and implement the program, will be transferred to the Department of Justice, the Department of the Treasury, and the Bureau of Indian Affairs to be used for the purposes of promoting and upgrading Federal public safety wireless communications equipment and facilities.

Credit accounts:

SPECTRUM AUCTION PROGRAM ACCOUNT

Unavailable Collections (in millions of dollars)

Identification code 27–0300–0–1–376	1999 actual	2000 est.	2001 est.
Balance, start of year:			
01.99 Balance, start of year	....	....	....
Receipts:			
02.01 Spectrum auction subsidy fund	248	....	....
Appropriation:			
05.02 Spectrum auction program account	–248	....	....
07.99 Total balance, end of year	....	....	....

Program and Financing (in millions of dollars)

Identification code 27–0300–0–1–376	1999 actual	2000 est.	2001 est.
Obligations by program activity:			
00.01 Administrative Expenses	6	6	6
00.02 Direct Loan Subsidy	248	....	....
00.05 Reestimates of direct loan subsidy	980	22	....
00.06 Interest on reestimates of direct loan subsidy	176	5	....
10.00 Total new obligations	1,410	33	6
Budgetary resources available for obligation:			
21.40 Unobligated balance available, start of year	....	....	1,779
22.00 New budget authority (gross)	1,451	1,812	....
22.40 Capital transfer to general fund	–42	....	....
23.90 Total budgetary resources available for obligation	1,409	1,812	1,779
23.95 Total new obligations	–1,410	–33	–6
24.40 Unobligated balance available, end of year	....	1,779	1,773
New budget authority (gross), detail:			
Mandatory:			
60.05 Appropriation (indefinite)	1,161	....	....
60.25 Appropriation (special fund, indefinite)	248	....	....
62.50 Appropriation (total mandatory)	1,409	....	....
69.00 Offsetting collections (cash)	42	1,812	....
70.00 Total new budget authority (gross)	1,451	1,812	....
Change in unpaid obligations:			
73.10 Total new obligations	1,410	33	6
73.20 Total outlays (gross)	–1,411	–33	–6
Outlays (gross), detail:			
86.97 Outlays from new mandatory authority	1,411	33	....
86.98 Outlays from mandatory balances	....	....	6
87.00 Total outlays (gross)	1,411	33	6
Offsets:			
Against gross budget authority and outlays:			
88.00 Offsetting collections (cash) from: Federal sources	–42	–1,812	....
Net budget authority and outlays:			
89.00 Budget authority	1,409	....	....
90.00 Outlays	1,369	–1,779	6

This program provides for direct loans for the purpose of purchasing spectrum licenses at the Federal Communications Commission's auctions. The licenses are being purchased on an installment basis, which constitutes an extension of credit. The first year of activity for this program was 1996.

As required by the Federal Credit Reform Act of 1990, this account records, for this program, the subsidy costs associated with the direct loans obligated in 1992 and beyond (including modifications of direct loans or loan guarantees that resulted from obligations or commitments in any year), as well as administrative expenses of this program. The subsidy amounts are estimated on a present value basis and administrative expenses are estimated on a cash basis.

Summary of Loan Levels, Subsidy Budget Authority and Outlays by Program (in millions of dollars)

Identification code 27–0300–0–1–376	1999 actual	2000 est.	2001 est.
Direct loan levels supportable by subsidy budget authority:			
1150 Direct loan levels	733	2	....
1159 Total direct loan levels	733	2	....
Direct loan subsidy (in percent):			
1320 Subsidy rate	35.74	8.25	....
1329 Weighted average subsidy rate	0.36	0.08	....
Direct loan subsidy budget authority:			
1330 Subsidy budget authority	1,404	–1,812	....
1339 Total subsidy budget authority	1,404	–1,812	....
Direct loan subsidy outlays:			
1340 Subsidy outlays	1,363	–1,785	....
1349 Total subsidy outlays	1,363	–1,785	....
Administrative expense data:			
3510 Budget authority	6	6	....
3580 Outlays from balances	....	6	....
3590 Outlays from new authority	6	....	....

Object Classification (in millions of dollars)

Identification code 27–0300–0–1–376	1999 actual	2000 est.	2001 est.
11.1 Personnel compensation: Full-time permanent	1	1	1
25.2 Other services	5	5	5
41.0 Grants, subsidies, and contributions	1,404	27	....
99.9 Total new obligations	1,410	33	6

Personnel Summary

Identification code 27–0300–0–1–376	1999 actual	2000 est.	2001 est.
1001 Total compensable workyears: Full-time equivalent employment	8	8	8

SPECTRUM AUCTION DIRECT LOAN FINANCING ACCOUNT

Program and Financing (in millions of dollars)

Identification code 27–4133–0–3–376	1999 actual	2000 est.	2001 est.
Obligations by program activity:			
Operating expenses:			
00.01 Direct loans	733	2	....
00.03 Interest Paid to Treasury	529	512	713
00.05 Repayment of inter-account transfer	42	....	....
00.91 Direct Program by Activities—Subtotal (1 level)	1,304	514	713
08.02 Downward subsidy reestimate	....	1,523	....
08.04 Interest on downward reestimate	....	289	....
08.91 Direct Program by Activities—Subtotal (1 level)	....	1,812	....
10.00 Total new obligations	1,304	2,326	713
Budgetary resources available for obligation:			
21.40 Unobligated balance available, start of year	56	40	....
22.00 New financing authority (gross)	1,287	2,285	713
23.90 Total budgetary resources available for obligation	1,343	2,325	713
23.95 Total new obligations	–1,304	–2,326	–713
24.40 Unobligated balance available, end of year	40	....	....
New financing authority (gross), detail:			
Mandatory:			
67.10 Authority to borrow	774	1,706	224
Offsetting collections (cash):			
69.00 Offsetting collections (New Subsidy)	248	....	....
69.00 Offsetting collections (Re-estimate)	979	22	....
69.00 Offsetting collections (Int- reestimate)	176	5	....
69.00 Offsetting collections (Payment on loans)	246	296	133
69.00 Offsetting collections (Int-Treasury)	258	256	356
69.47 Portion applied to repay debt	–1,394	....	....

69.90	Spending authority from offsetting collections (total mandatory)	513	579	489
70.00	Total new financing authority (gross)	1,287	2,285	713
	Change in unpaid obligations:			
73.10	Total new obligations	1,304	2,326	713
73.20	Total financing disbursements (gross)	−1,303	−2,326	−713
87.00	Total financing disbursements (gross)	1,303	2,326	713
	Offsets:			
	Against gross financing authority and financing disbursements:			
	Offsetting collections (cash) from:			
88.00	Program account: original subsidy	−248		
88.00	Program account: total revised subsidy	−1,155	−27	
88.25	Interest on uninvested funds	−258	−256	−356
	Non-Federal sources:			
	Non-Federal sources:			
88.40	Interest received on loans	−84	−98	−95
88.40	Principal received on loans	−14	−10	−38
88.40	Recoveries	−148	−188	
88.90	Total, offsetting collections (cash)	−1907	−579	−489
	Net financing authority and financing disbursements:			
89.00	Financing authority	−620	1,706	224
90.00	Financing disbursements	−604	1,747	224

As required by the Federal Credit Reform Act of 1990, this non-budgetary account records all cash flows to and from the Government resulting from direct loans obligated in 1992 and beyond (including modifications of direct loans that resulted from obligations in any year). The amounts in this account are a means of financing and are not included in the budget totals.

Status of Direct Loans (in millions of dollars)

Identification code 27–4133–0–3–376		1999 actual	2000 est.	2001 est.
	Position with respect to appropriations act limitation on obligations:			
1111	Limitation on direct loans			
1131	Direct loan obligations exempt from limitation	733	2	2
1150	Total direct loan obligations	733	2	2
	Cumulative balance of direct loans outstanding:			
1210	Outstanding, start of year	6,789	8,287	8,279
1231	Disbursements: Direct loan disbursements	733	2	2
1251	Repayments: Repayments and prepayments	−14	−10	−38
1264	Write-offs for default: Other adjustments—correction	779		
1290	Outstanding, end of year	8,287	8,279	8,243

Balance Sheet (in millions of dollars)

Identification code 27–4133–0–3–376		1998 actual	1999 actual	2000 est.	2001 est.
	ASSETS:				
	Net value of assets related to post-1991 direct loans receivable:				
1401	Direct loans receivable, gross	6,788	8,287	8,279	8,243
1402	Interest receivable		372	350	350
1405	Allowance for subsidy cost (-)	−2,230	−4,761	−3,238	−3,200
1499	Net present value of assets related to direct loans	4,558	3,898	5,391	5,393
1901	Other Federal assets: Other assets		41		
1999	Total assets	4,558	3,939	5,391	5,393
	LIABILITIES:				
2103	Federal liabilities: Resources payable to Treasury	4,558	3,939	5,391	5,393
2999	Total liabilities	4,558	3,939	5,391	5,393
4999	Total liabilities and net position	4,558	3,939	5,391	5,393

GENERAL FUND RECEIPT ACCOUNTS

(in millions of dollars)

		1999 actual	2000 est.	2001 est.
Offsetting receipts from the public:				
27–242900	Fees for services	26	26	26
27–247400	Auction receipts	1,505	2,076	3,559
General Fund Offsetting receipts from the public		1,531	2,102	3,585

[SEC. 213. (a) REVISED SCHEDULE FOR COMPETITIVE BIDDING OF SPECTRUM.—(1) Section 337(b) of the Communications Act of 1934 (47 U.S.C. 337(b)) is amended by striking "shall—" and all that follows and inserting "shall commence assignment of licenses for public safety services created pursuant to subsection (a) no later than September 30, 1998.".

(2) Commencing on the date of the enactment of this Act, the Federal Communications Commission shall initiate the competitive bidding process previously required under section 337(b)(2) of the Communications Act of 1934 (as repealed by the amendment made by paragraph (1)).

(3) The Federal Communications Commission shall conduct the competitive bidding process described in paragraph (2) in a manner that ensures that all proceeds of such bidding are deposited in accordance with section 309(j)(8) of the Communications Act of 1934 (47 U.S.C. 309(j)(8)) not later than September 30, 2000.

(4)(A) To expedite the assignment by competitive bidding of the frequencies identified in section 337(a)(2) of the Communications Act of 1934 (47 U.S.C. 337(a)(2)), the rules governing such frequencies shall be effective immediately upon publication in the Federal Register without regard to sections 553(d), 801(a)(3), 804(2), and 806(a) of title 5, United States Code.

(B) Chapter 6 of title 5, United States Code, section 3 of the Small Business Act (15 U.S.C. 632), and sections 3507 and 3512 of title 44, United States Code, shall not apply to the rules and competitive bidding procedures governing the frequencies described in subparagraph (A).

(5) Notwithstanding section 309(b) of the Communications Act of 1934 (47 U.S.C. 309(b)), no application for an instrument of authorization for the frequencies described in paragraph (4) may be granted by the Federal Communications Commission earlier than 7 days following issuance of public notice by the Commission of the acceptance for filing of such application or of any substantial amendment thereto.

(6) Notwithstanding section 309(d)(1) of the Communications Act of 1934 (47 U.S.C. 309(d)(1)), the Federal Communications Commission may specify a period (which shall be not less than 5 days following issuance of the public notice described in paragraph (5)) for the filing of petitions to deny any application for an instrument of authorization for the frequencies described in paragraph (4).]

[(b) REPORTS.—(1) Not later than 30 days after the date of the enactment of this Act, the Director of the Office of Management and Budget and the Federal Communications Commission shall each submit to the appropriate congressional committees a report which shall—

(A) set forth the anticipated schedule (including specific dates) for—

(i) preparing and conducting the competitive bidding process required by subsection (a); and

(ii) depositing the receipts of the competitive bidding process;

(B) set forth each significant milestone in the rulemaking process with respect to the competitive bidding process; and

(C) include an explanation of the effect of each requirement in subsection (a) on the schedule for the competitive bidding process and any post-bidding activities (including the deposit of receipts) when compared with the schedule for the competitive bidding and any post-bidding activities (including the deposit of receipts) that would otherwise have occurred under section 337(b)(2) of the Communications Act of 1934 (47 U.S.C. 337(b)(2)) if not for the enactment of subsection (a).

(2) Not later than 60 days after the date of the enactment of this Act, the Federal Communications Commission shall submit to the appropriate congressional committees a report which shall set forth for each spectrum auction held by the Commission since January 1, 1998, information on—

(A) the time required for each stage of preparation for the auction;

Credit accounts—Continued

GENERAL FUND RECEIPT ACCOUNTS—Continued

(B) the date of the commencement and of the completion of the auction;

(C) the time which elapsed between the date of the completion of the auction and the date of the first deposit of receipts from the auction in the Treasury; and

(D) the amounts, summarized by month, of all subsequent deposits in a Treasury receipt account from the auction.

(3) Not later than October 31, 2000, the Federal Communications Commission shall submit to the appropriate congressional committees a report which shall—

(A) describe the course of the competitive bidding process required by subsection (a) through September 30, 2000, including the amount of any receipts from the competitive bidding process deposited in the Treasury as of September 30, 2000; and

(B) if the course of the competitive bidding process has included any deviations from the schedule set forth under paragraph (1)(A), an explanation for such deviations from the schedule.

(4) Each report required by this subsection shall be prepared by the agency concerned without influence of any other Federal department or agency.

(5) In this subsection, the term "appropriate congressional committees" means the following:

(A) The Committees on Appropriations, the Budget, and Commerce, Science, and Transportation of the Senate.

(B) The Committees on Appropriations, the Budget, and Commerce of the House of Representatives.]

[(c) CONSTRUCTION.—Nothing in this section shall be construed to supersede the requirements placed on the Federal Communications Commission by section 337(d)(4) of the Communications Act of 1934 (47 U.S.C. 337(d)(4)).]

[(d) REPEAL OF SUPERSEDED PROVISIONS.—Section 8124 of the Department of Defense Appropriations Act, 2000 is repealed.] *(Miscellaneous Appropriations Act, 2000, as enacted by section 1000(a)(5) of the Consolidated Appropriations Act, 2000 (P.L. 106–113).)*

FEDERAL DEPOSIT INSURANCE CORPORATION

The Federal Deposit Insurance Corporation (FDIC or Corporation) was created by the Banking Act of 1933 to provide protection for bank depositors and to foster sound banking practices. The Financial Institutions Reform Recovery and Enforcement Act of 1989 established the Bank Insurance Fund (BIF), the Savings Association Insurance Fund (SAIF), and the Federal Savings and Loan Insurance Corporation (FSLIC) Resolution Fund (FRF). The Federal Deposit Insurance Corporation Improvement Act of 1991 generally requires the Corporation to use the least costly method to resolve failed banks, and mandates that the Corporation take prompt corrective action against under-capitalized financial institutions.

The deposit insurance ceiling protection has been $100,000 since March 31, 1980. In order to accomplish its varied functions to protect depositors, the Corporation is authorized to promulgate and enforce rules and regulations relating to the supervision of insured institutions and to perform other regulatory and supervisory duties consistent with its responsibilities as an insurer. The Corporation is required to set assessment rates for insured financial institutions semi-annually to maintain the reserves of the BIF and SAIF at 1.25 percent of total insured deposits.

Federal Funds

Public enterprise funds:

BANK INSURANCE FUND

Unavailable Collections (in millions of dollars)

Identification code 51–4064–0–3–373	1999 actual	2000 est.	2001 est.
Balance, start of year:			
01.99 Balance, start of year		1	
Appropriation:			
05.01 Bank Insurance Fund		−1	
05.02 Legislative proposal not subject to PAYGO			4
05.03 Legislative proposal, discretionary offset			92
05.99 Subtotal appropriation		−1	96
06.20 Reduction pursuant to Public Law xx-xxx	1		
07.99 Total balance, end of year	1		96

Program and Financing (in millions of dollars)

Identification code 51–4064–0–3–373	1999 actual	2000 est.	2001 est.
Obligations by program activity:			
Administrative expenses:			
00.02 Insurance	109	106	62
00.03 Supervision	492	509	487
00.04 Receivership Management	149	149	108
00.05 General and Administrative	113	114	116
00.91 Total Administrative Expenses	863	878	773
Capital investment:			
01.01 Working Capital Outlays	322	753	532
01.02 Case resolution losses	390	546	98
01.03 Premiums on investments	216	55	55
01.04 OPM transfer for retirement benefits	186		
01.05 Other resolution obligation (unpaid)	599		
01.91 Total Capital Investment	1,713	1,354	685
10.00 Total new obligations	2,576	2,232	1,458
Budgetary resources available for obligation:			
21.40 Unobligated balance available, start of year	27,000	27,436	27,271
22.00 New budget authority (gross)	3,010	2,068	2,297
23.90 Total budgetary resources available for obligation	30,010	29,504	29,568
23.95 Total new obligations	−2,576	−2,232	−1,458
24.40 Unobligated balance available, end of year	27,436	27,271	28,110
New budget authority (gross), detail:			
Mandatory:			
69.00 Offsetting collections (cash)	3,022	2,093	2,323
69.26 Offsetting collections (unavailable balances)		1	
69.61 Transferred to other accounts	−11	−26	−26
69.75 Reduction pursuant to P.L. 106–51	−1		
69.90 Spending authority from offsetting collections (total mandatory)	3,010	2,068	2,297
Change in unpaid obligations:			
72.40 Unpaid obligations, start of year: Obligated balance, start of year	84	674	648
73.10 Total new obligations	2,576	2,232	1,458
73.20 Total outlays (gross)	−1,987	−2,258	−1,484
74.40 Unpaid obligations, end of year: Obligated balance, end of year	674	648	622
Outlays (gross), detail:			
86.97 Outlays from new mandatory authority	1,987	2,067	1,484
86.98 Outlays from mandatory balances		191	
87.00 Total outlays (gross)	1,987	2,258	1,484
Offsets:			
Against gross budget authority and outlays:			
Offsetting collections (cash) from:			
88.20 Interest on U.S. securities	−2,177	−1,737	−1,845
Non-Federal sources:			
88.40 Asset recoveries	−811	−320	−442
88.40 Premium assessments	−34	−36	−36
88.90 Total, offsetting collections (cash)	−3,022	−2,093	−2,323
Net budget authority and outlays:			
89.00 Budget authority	−12	−25	−26
90.00 Outlays	−1,035	165	−839
Memorandum (non-add) entries:			
92.01 Total investments, start of year: U.S. securities: Par value	27,445	28,359	29,024
92.02 Total investments, end of year: U.S. securities: Par value	28,359	29,024	29,024

Summary of Budget Authority and Outlays

(in millions of dollars)

Enacted/requested:	1999 actual	2000 est.	2001 est.
Budget Authority	–12	–25	–26
Outlays	–1,035	165	–839
Legislative proposal, not subject to PAYGO:			
Budget Authority			–4
Outlays			–4
Legislative proposal, discretionary offset:			
Budget Authority			–92
Outlays			–92
Total:			
Budget Authority	–12	–25	–122
Outlays	–1,035	165	–935

Status of Direct Loans (in millions of dollars)

Identification code 51–4064–0–3–373		1999 actual	2000 est.	2001 est.
	Cumulative balance of direct loans outstanding:			
1210	Outstanding, start of year	144	100	
1251	Repayments: Repayments and prepayments	–6	–100	
1263	Write-offs for default: Direct loans	–38		
1290	Outstanding, end of year	100		

The BIF, a public enterprise revolving fund, derives its income principally from insurance assessments paid by insured banks. The revolving fund represents the accumulated net income of the BIF and is reserved for the protection of depositors in insured banks, as well as for the payment of administrative and insurance expenses. As of September 1999, BIF's fund balance totaled $29 billion, excluding reserves for future failed bank resolutions. The net worth of the BIF reached 1.25 percent of total insured deposits in May 1995.

The Federal Deposit Insurance Corporation Improvement Act of 1991 authorizes the FDIC to borrow up to $30 billion from the Treasury to cover deposit insurance losses and provide additional loans from the Federal Financing Bank for working capital purposes. The BIF is not expected to borrow any of the $30 billion line of credit from the Treasury or from the Federal Financing Bank to finance working capital needs.

Object Classification (in millions of dollars)

Identification code 51–4064–0–3–373		1999 actual	2000 est.	2001 est.
11.1	Personnel compensation: Full-time permanent	388	416	388
12.1	Civilian personnel benefits	103	128	124
13.0	Benefits for former personnel	2		
21.0	Travel and transportation of persons	57	43	43
22.0	Transportation of things	2		
23.2	Rental payments to others	47	42	42
23.3	Communications, utilities, and miscellaneous charges	20	34	31
24.0	Printing and reproduction	2	3	3
25.2	Other services	135	118	94
26.0	Supplies and materials	6	7	6
31.0	Equipment	67	72	35
32.0	Land and structures	7	14	7
43.0	Interest and dividends	27	1	
	Undistributed:			
92.0	Working Capital Outlays	322	753	532
92.0	Net case resolution—losses	390	546	98
92.0	Premiums on investments	216	55	55
92.0	OPM transfer for post retirement	186		
92.0	Other resolution obligation (unpaid)	599		
99.9	Total new obligations	2,576	2,232	1,458

[1] Total obligations include expenses incurred on behalf of receiverships. Corporate operating expenses net of expenses charged to receiverships are shown separately in the program and financing schedule.

Personnel Summary

Identification code 51–4064–0–3–373		1999 actual	2000 est.	2001 est.
1001	Total compensable workyears: Full-time equivalent employment	5,772	5,660	5,118

BANK INSURANCE FUND

(Legislative proposal, not subject to PAYGO)

Program and Financing (in millions of dollars)

Identification code 51–4064–2–3–373		1999 actual	2000 est.	2001 est.
	New budget authority (gross), detail:			
	Mandatory:			
69.00	Offsetting collections (cash)			4
69.26	Offsetting collections (unavailable balances)			–4
69.90	Spending authority from offsetting collections (total mandatory)			
	Offsets:			
	Against gross budget authority and outlays:			
88.20	Offsetting collections (cash) from: Interest on U.S. securities			–4
	Net budget authority and outlays:			
89.00	Budget authority			–4
90.00	Outlays			–4

BANK INSURANCE FUND

(Legislative proposal, subject to PAYGO)

Program and Financing (in millions of dollars)

Identification code 51–4064–6–3–373		1999 actual	2000 est.	2001 est.
	New budget authority (gross), detail:			
	Mandatory:			
69.00	Offsetting collections (cash)			92
69.26	Offsetting collections (unavailable balances)			–92
69.90	Spending authority from offsetting collections (total mandatory)			
	Offsets:			
	Against gross budget authority and outlays:			
88.40	Offsetting collections (cash) from: Non-Federal sources			–92
	Net budget authority and outlays:			
89.00	Budget authority			–92
90.00	Outlays			–92

The Administration proposes to require the FDIC and the Federal Reserve to recover their respective costs for supervision and regulation of state-chartered banks and bank holding companies. In establishing the amount of the proposed collections, the appropriate Federal banking agency shall allow an appropriate credit for fees paid to state bank supervisory agencies. Additionally, the appropriate Federal regulators will not recover supervision and regulation costs from banks with less than $100 million in assets. This proposal will increase interest income and premium income collected by the Bank Insurance Fund for 2001–2005; these two effects are shown separately above.

SAVINGS ASSOCIATION INSURANCE FUND

Program and Financing (in millions of dollars)

Identification code 51–4066–0–3–373		1999 actual	2000 est.	2001 est.
	Obligations by program activity:			
	Operating Expenses:			
09.01	Insurance	11	20	15
09.02	Supervision	61	70	65
09.03	Receivership management	15	21	19
09.04	General and administrative	6	12	11
	Capital investment:			
09.10	Working capital outlays	59	135	180
09.11	Net case resolutions (losses)	4	27	33
09.13	Premium on Treasury Investments	100	48	26

Public enterprise funds—Continued

SAVINGS ASSOCIATION INSURANCE FUND—Continued

Program and Financing (in millions of dollars)—Continued

Identification code 51–4066–0–3–373		1999 actual	2000 est.	2001 est.
09.14	Other Corporate Insurance Expenses	1	1	1
10.00	Total new obligations	257	334	350
	Budgetary resources available for obligation:			
21.40	Unobligated balance available, start of year	9,782	10,217	10,556
22.00	New budget authority (gross)	692	673	695
23.90	Total budgetary resources available for obligation	10,474	10,890	11,251
23.95	Total new obligations	−257	−334	−350
24.40	Unobligated balance available, end of year	10,217	10,556	10,901
	New budget authority (gross), detail:			
	Mandatory:			
69.00	Offsetting collections (cash)	693	677	699
69.61	Transferred to other accounts	−1	−4	−4
69.90	Spending authority from offsetting collections (total mandatory)	692	673	695
	Change in unpaid obligations:			
72.40	Unpaid obligations, start of year: Obligated balance, start of year	7	7	4
73.10	Total new obligations	257	334	350
73.20	Total outlays (gross)	−257	−337	−353
74.40	Unpaid obligations, end of year: Obligated balance, end of year	7	4	1
	Outlays (gross), detail:			
86.98	Outlays from mandatory balances	257	337	353
	Offsets:			
	Against gross budget authority and outlays:			
	Offsetting collections (cash) from:			
88.20	Interest on U.S. securities	−672	−587	−598
	Non-Federal sources:			
88.40	Asset recoveries	−5	−72	−81
88.40	Premium assessments	−15	−18	−20
88.40	Reimbursement by receiverships	−1		
88.90	Total, offsetting collections (cash)	−693	−677	−699
	Net budget authority and outlays:			
89.00	Budget authority	−1	−4	−4
90.00	Outlays	−435	−340	−346
	Memorandum (non-add) entries:			
92.01	Total investments, start of year: U.S. securities: Par value	9,602	10,144	10,535
92.02	Total investments, end of year: U.S. securities: Par value	10,144	10,535	10,909

The SAIF insures depository institutions formerly insured by the Federal Savings and Loan Insurance Corporation. In July 1995, SAIF assumed responsibility for resolving failed thrifts from the Resolution Trust Corporation (RTC).

The Deposit Insurance Funds Act of 1996 imposed a special assessment to bring SAIF's reserves up to 1.25 percent of insured deposits. By the end of 1998, SAIF's reserve ratio reached 1.39 percent. However, on January 1, 1999, FDIC was required by law to transfer all funds in the SAIF above 1.25 percent to a Special Reserve. Approximately $1 billion was transferred. The Gramm Leach Bliley Act of 1999 eliminated the Special Reserve. Approximately $1 billion was transferred to the SAIF on November 12, 1999. The transfer increased the reserve ratio to 1.45 percent.

Object Classification (in millions of dollars)

Identification code 51–4066–0–3–373		1999 actual	2000 est.	2001 est.
11.1	Personnel compensation: Full-time permanent	46	59	57
12.1	Civilian personnel benefits	16	18	18
21.0	Travel and transportation of persons	5	6	6
23.2	Rental payments to others	6	6	6
23.3	Communications, utilities, and miscellaneous charges	2	5	4
25.2	Other services	16	17	13
26.0	Supplies and materials	1	1	1
31.0	Equipment	1	10	5
32.0	Land and structures	1	2	1
	Undistributed:			
92.0	Net case resolutions	4	27	33
92.0	Working Capital Outlays (net of estimated losses)	59	135	180
92.0	Premium on US Treasury Investments	100	48	26
99.9	Total new obligations	257	334	350

[1] Total obligations include expenses incurred on behalf of receiverships.

Personnel Summary

Identification code 51–4066–0–3–373		1999 actual	2000 est.	2001 est.
2001	Total compensable workyears: Full-time equivalent employment	677	798	722

FSLIC RESOLUTION FUND

Program and Financing (in millions of dollars)

Identification code 51–4065–0–3–373		1999 actual	2000 est.	2001 est.
	Obligations by program activity:			
09.02	Receivership management	135	108	94
09.03	General and administrative	15	15	15
09.04	Litigation expenses	61	80	80
	Capital investment:			
09.11	Liquidity advances	44	35	35
09.14	Interest expense—RTC debt		1,156	503
09.16	Miscellaneous	74	8	7
09.17	Other Obligations (unpaid)	21	10	10
10.00	Total new obligations	350	1,412	744
	Budgetary resources available for obligation:			
21.40	Unobligated balance available, start of year	3,030	2,841	2,926
22.00	New budget authority (gross)	3,906	2,308	733
22.40	Capital transfer to general fund	−3,745	−811	
23.90	Total budgetary resources available for obligation	3,191	4,338	3,659
23.95	Total new obligations	−350	−1,412	−744
24.40	Unobligated balance available, end of year	2,841	2,926	2,915
	New budget authority (gross), detail:			
	Mandatory:			
69.00	Offsetting collections (cash)	3,922	2,312	737
69.61	Transferred to other accounts	−16	−4	−4
69.90	Spending authority from offsetting collections (total mandatory)	3,906	2,308	733
	Change in unpaid obligations:			
72.40	Unpaid obligations, start of year: Obligated balance, start of year	18	29	35
73.10	Total new obligations	350	1,412	744
73.20	Total outlays (gross)	−339	−1,406	−738
74.40	Unpaid obligations, end of year: Obligated balance, end of year	29	35	41
	Outlays (gross), detail:			
86.98	Outlays from mandatory balances	339	1,406	738
	Offsets:			
	Against gross budget authority and outlays:			
	Offsetting collections (cash) from:			
88.20	Interest on U.S. securities	−104	−113	−113
	Non-Federal sources:			
88.40	Asset recoveries (FRF-FSLIC)	−86	−13	−3
88.40	Asset recoveries (FRF-RTC)	−360	−416	−200
88.40	Reimbursement of operating expenses by receiverships	−2		
88.40	Corporate-owned assets	−109	−36	−1
88.40	Securitization releases	−3,088	−1,685	−370
88.40	Equity partnerships	−173	−49	−50
88.90	Total, offsetting collections (cash)	−3,922	−2,312	−737
	Net budget authority and outlays:			
89.00	Budget authority	−16	−4	−4

		1999 actual	2000 est.	2001 est.
90.00	Outlays	–3,583	–906	1
	Memorandum (non-add) entries:			
92.01	Total investments, start of year: U.S. securities: Par value	2,087	2,304	2,835
92.02	Total investments, end of year: U.S. securities: Par value	2,304	2,835	2,750

Status of Direct Loans (in millions of dollars)

Identification code 51–4065–0–3–373		1999 actual	2000 est.	2001 est.
	Cumulative balance of direct loans outstanding:			
1210	Outstanding, start of year	109	75	64
1251	Repayments: Repayments and prepayments	–34	–11	
1290	Outstanding, end of year	75	64	64

The FSLIC Resolution Fund (FRF) is the successor to FSLIC assets and liabilities from thrift resolutions prior to August 1989. Beginning in August 1989, the RTC assumed responsibility for the FSLIC's unresolved cases. On December 31, 1995, the RTC was terminated and its assets and liabilities were transferred to FRF.

Funds for FRF operations have come from: income earned on its assets; liquidation proceeds from receiverships; the proceeds of the sale of bonds by the Financing Corporation; and, a portion of insurance premiums paid by SAIF members prior to 1993. The Financial Institutions Reform, Recovery, and Enforcement Act authorizes appropriations to make up for any shortfall. The FRF will terminate upon the disposition of all its assets, and any net proceeds will be paid to the Treasury. Net proceeds from the former RTC will be paid to the Resolution Funding Corporation.

Object Classification (in millions of dollars)

Identification code 51–4065–0–3–373		1999 actual	2000 est.	2001 est.
11.1	Personnel compensation: Full-time permanent	48	59	55
12.1	Civilian personnel benefits	8	18	18
13.0	Benefits for former personnel	1		
21.0	Travel and transportation of persons	3	6	6
23.2	Rental payments to others	7	6	6
23.3	Communications, utilities, and miscellaneous charges	7	5	4
24.0	Printing and reproduction	1		
25.2	Other services	71	17	13
26.0	Supplies and materials	2	1	1
31.0	Equipment	3	10	5
32.0	Land and structures	1	2	1
	Undistributed:			
92.0	Liquidation and insurance	43	35	35
92.0	Litigation settlements, Due Receivers & Trustees	67	7	7
92.0	Misc.	67	80	80
92.0	REFCORP Interest Expense		1,156	503
92.0	Undistributed	21	10	10
99.9	Total new obligations	350	1,412	744

[1] Total obligations include expenses incurred on behalf of receiverships.

Personnel Summary

Identification code 51–4065–0–3–373		1999 actual	2000 est.	2001 est.
2001	Total compensable workyears: Full-time equivalent employment	713	798	722

FDIC—Office of Inspector General

(including transfer of funds)

For necessary expenses of the Office of Inspector General in carrying out the provisions of the Inspector General Act of 1978, as amended, **[**$33,666,000**]** *$33,660,527*, to be derived from the Bank Insurance Fund, the Savings Association Insurance Fund, and the FSLIC Resolution Fund. *(Department of Veterans Affairs and Housing and Urban Development, and Independent Agencies Appropriations Act, 2000.)*

Program and Financing (in millions of dollars)

Identification code 51–4595–0–4–373		1999 actual	2000 est.	2001 est.
	Obligations by program activity:			
09.00	Reimbursable program	28	34	34
10.00	Total new obligations	28	34	34
	Budgetary resources available for obligation:			
22.00	New budget authority (gross)	28	34	34
23.95	Total new obligations	–28	–34	–34
	New budget authority (gross), detail:			
	Mandatory:			
69.62	Transferred from other accounts	28	34	34
69.90	Spending authority from offsetting collections (total mandatory)	28	34	34
	Change in unpaid obligations:			
73.10	Total new obligations	28	34	34
73.20	Total outlays (gross)	–28	–34	–34
	Outlays (gross), detail:			
86.97	Outlays from new mandatory authority	28	34	34
	Net budget authority and outlays:			
89.00	Budget authority	28	34	34
90.00	Outlays	28	34	34

FDIC's Office of Inspector General (OIG) is an independent unit within the Corporation that conducts audits and investigations of corporate activities and assists the Corporation in preventing and detecting fraud, waste, abuse, and mismanagement. The OIG was established by the FDIC Board of Directors pursuant to the Inspector General Act amendments of 1988 (Public Law 100–504). The Resolution Trust Corporation Completion Act, enacted December 17, 1993, provided that the FDIC Inspector General be appointed by the President and confirmed by the Senate. The Completion Act, thus, added FDIC to the establishments whose OIGs have separate appropriation accounts under Section 1105(a) of Title 31, United States Code. The OIG's first appropriation was for its fiscal year 1998 expenses. The OIG's appropriations are derived from the Bank Insurance Fund, the Savings Association Insurance Fund, and the FSLIC Resolution Fund.

Object Classification (in millions of dollars)

Identification code 51–4595–0–4–373		1999 actual	2000 est.	2001 est.
11.1	Personnel compensation: Full-time permanent	19	21	21
12.1	Civilian personnel benefits	6	8	7
21.0	Travel and transportation of persons	1	1	1
25.2	Other services	2	3	4
31.0	Equipment		1	1
99.9	Total new obligations	28	34	34

[1] Includes obligations that are recoverable from receiverships.

Personnel Summary

Identification code 51–4595–0–4–373		1999 actual	2000 est.	2001 est.
2001	Total compensable workyears: Full-time equivalent employment	218	231	226

Affordable Housing Program

Program and Financing (in millions of dollars)

Identification code 51–1500–0–1–604		1999 actual	2000 est.	2001 est.
	Change in unpaid obligations:			
72.40	Unpaid obligations, start of year: Obligated balance, start of year	1		

Public enterprise funds—Continued

AFFORDABLE HOUSING PROGRAM—Continued

Program and Financing (in millions of dollars)—Continued

Identification code 51–1500–0–1–604	1999 actual	2000 est.	2001 est.
Net budget authority and outlays:			
89.00 Budget authority	....	....	....
90.00 Outlays	....	....	....

From 1993 to 1996, funds were appropriated to the FDIC to carry out an affordable housing program. Under the program, certain single and multifamily properties were held off the general market for 180 days during which time low-income individuals, public agencies, and nonprofit organizations that agreed to low-income rent restrictions were allowed to bid on the properties.

FEDERAL DRUG CONTROL PROGRAMS

Federal Funds

General and special funds:

HIGH INTENSITY DRUG TRAFFICKING AREAS PROGRAM

(INCLUDING TRANSFER OF FUNDS)

For necessary expenses of the Office of National Drug Control Policy's High Intensity Drug Trafficking Areas Program, $192,000,000 for drug control activities consistent with the approved strategy for each of the designated High Intensity Drug Trafficking Areas, of which no less than 51 percent shall be transferred to State and local entities for drug control activities, which shall be obligated within 120 days of the date of the enactment of this Act: *Provided*, That up to 49 percent, *to remain available until September 30, 2002* may be transferred to Federal agencies and departments at a rate to be determined by the Director: *Provided further*, That, of this latter amount, $1,800,000 shall be used for auditing services[: *Provided further*, That, hereafter, of the amount appropriated for fiscal year 2000 or any succeeding fiscal year for the High Intensity Drug Trafficking Areas Program, the funds to be obligated or expended during such fiscal year for programs addressing the treatment or prevention of drug use as part of the approved strategy for a designated High Intensity Drug Trafficking Area (HIDTA) shall not be less than the funds obligated or expended for such programs during fiscal year 1999 for each designated HIDTA without the prior approval of the Committees on Appropriations: *Provided further*, That funds shall be provided for existing High Intensity Drug Trafficking Areas at no less than the total fiscal year 1999 level]. (*Executive Office Appropriations Act, 2000.*)

Program and Financing (in millions of dollars)

Identification code 11–1070–0–1–802	1999 actual	2000 est.	2001 est.
Obligations by program activity:			
00.02 Grants to State and local law enforcement agencies	150	154	192
10.00 Total new obligations	150	154	192
Budgetary resources available for obligation:			
22.00 New budget authority (gross)	152	154	192
23.95 Total new obligations	−150	−154	−192
New budget authority (gross), detail:			
Discretionary:			
40.00 Appropriation	185	192	192
40.76 Reduction pursuant to P.L. 106–113	....	−1	....
41.00 Transferred to other accounts	−35	−37	....
42.00 Transferred from other accounts	2	....	....
43.00 Appropriation (total discretionary)	150	154	192
Change in unpaid obligations:			
72.40 Unpaid obligations, start of year: Obligated balance, start of year	118	132	134
73.10 Total new obligations	150	154	192
73.20 Total outlays (gross)	−130	−152	−166
73.40 Adjustments in expired accounts (net)	−6	....	....
74.40 Unpaid obligations, end of year: Obligated balance, end of year	132	134	160
Outlays (gross), detail:			
86.90 Outlays from new discretionary authority	48	49	61
86.93 Outlays from discretionary balances	82	103	105
87.00 Total outlays (gross)	130	152	166
Net budget authority and outlays:			
89.00 Budget authority	152	154	192
90.00 Outlays	130	152	166

The High Intensity Drug Trafficking Areas (HIDTA) program was established by the Anti-Drug Abuse Act of 1988 to provide assistance to Federal, State and local law enforcement entities operating in those areas most adversely affected by drug trafficking. Since January, 1990, counties in 31 areas have been designated as HIDTAs: New York; Los Angeles; Miami; Houston; Baltimore/Washington, DC; Puerto Rico/Virgin Islands; Southwest Border, which includes South Texas, West Texas, New Mexico, Arizona and Southern California; Chicago; Atlanta; Philadelphia/Camden; Gulf Coast (Alabama, Louisiana, and Mississippi); Lake County (Indiana); Midwest (Iowa, Kansas, Missouri, Nebraska, North Dakota, and South Dakota); Pacific Northwest (Washington); Rocky Mountain (Colorado, Utah, and Wyoming); Northern California (San Francisco Bay area); South Eastern Michigan; Appalachia (Kentucky, Tennessee, and West Virginia); Central Florida; Milwaukee; North Texas; Central Valley California; Hawaii; New England (Connecticut, Maine, Massachusetts, New Hampshire, Rhode Island, and Vermont); Ohio; and Oregon.

Funds made available under the HIDTA program are disbursed at the discretion of the Director of the Office of National Drug Control Policy for joint local, State, and Federal initiatives.

Object Classification (in millions of dollars)

Identification code 11–1070–0–1–802	1999 actual	2000 est.	2001 est.
25.2 Other services	....	2	2
41.0 Grants, subsidies, and contributions	150	152	190
99.9 Total new obligations	150	154	192

SPECIAL FORFEITURE FUND

(INCLUDING TRANSFER OF FUNDS)

For activities to support a national anti-drug campaign for youth, and other purposes, authorized by Public Law 105–277, [$216,000,000] *$259,000,000*, to remain available until expended: *Provided*, That such funds may be transferred to other Federal departments and agencies to carry out such activities: *Provided further*, That of the funds provided, [$185,000,000] *$195,000,000* shall be to support a national media campaign, as authorized in the Drug-Free Media Campaign Act of 1998[: *Provided further*, That of the amounts provided for the Drug-Free Media Campaign, 10 percent shall not be available for obligation until ONDCP submits a corporate sponsorship plan to the Committees on Appropriations: *Provided further*, That of the funds provided, $30,000,000]*; $35,000,000* shall be to continue a program of matching grants to drug-free communities, as authorized in the Drug-Free Communities Act of 1997[: *Provided further*, That of the funds provided,]*;* $1,000,000 shall be available to the Director for transfer as [grants] *a grant* to [State and local agencies or non-profit organizations for] the National Drug Court Institute*; $3,000,000 shall be for Intelligence Architecture; and $25,000,000 shall be for a Drug Abuse Treatment Demonstration project in State and local criminal justice systems*. (*Executive Office Appropriations Act, 2000.*)

Program and Financing (in millions of dollars)

Identification code 11–1460–0–1–802	1999 actual	2000 est.	2001 est.
Obligations by program activity:			
10.00 Total new obligations	207	215	259
Budgetary resources available for obligation:			
21.40 Unobligated balance available, start of year	25	20	20
22.00 New budget authority (gross)	203	215	259
23.90 Total budgetary resources available for obligation	228	235	279
23.95 Total new obligations	−207	−215	−259
24.40 Unobligated balance available, end of year	20	20	20
New budget authority (gross), detail:			
Discretionary:			
40.00 Appropriation	217	216	259
40.76 Reduction pursuant to P.L. 106–113		−1	
41.00 Transferred to other accounts	−15		
43.00 Appropriation (total discretionary)	203	215	259
Change in unpaid obligations:			
72.40 Unpaid obligations, start of year: Obligated balance, start of year	134	164	249
73.10 Total new obligations	207	215	259
73.20 Total outlays (gross)	−178	−130	−220
74.40 Unpaid obligations, end of year: Obligated balance, end of year	164	249	288
Outlays (gross), detail:			
86.90 Outlays from new discretionary authority	178	129	155
86.93 Outlays from discretionary balances			65
87.00 Total outlays (gross)	178	130	220
Net budget authority and outlays:			
89.00 Budget authority	203	215	259
90.00 Outlays	178	130	220

The Anti-Drug Abuse Act of 1988, as amended, and the Office of National Drug Control Policy's reauthorization, P.L. 105–277, established the Special Forfeiture Fund to be administered by the Director of the Office of National Drug Control Policy. The monies deposited in the Fund support high-priority drug control programs and may be transferred to drug control agencies, or may be directly obligated by the Director of ONDCP.

Object Classification (in millions of dollars)

Identification code 11–1460–0–1–802	1999 actual	2000 est.	2001 est.
25.2 Other services	188	186	225
41.0 Grants, subsidies, and contributions	19	29	34
99.9 Total new obligations	207	215	259

FEDERAL ELECTION COMMISSION

Federal Funds

General and special funds:

SALARIES AND EXPENSES

For necessary expenses to carry out the provisions of the Federal Election Campaign Act of 1971, as amended, **[**$38,152,000**]** *$40,500,000*, of which no less than **[**$4,866,500**]** *$4,689,500* shall be available for internal automated data processing systems, and of which not to exceed $5,000 shall be available for reception and representation expenses. *(Independent Agencies Appropriations Act, 2000.)*

Program and Financing (in millions of dollars)

Identification code 95–1600–0–1–808	1999 actual	2000 est.	2001 est.
Obligations by program activity:			
10.00 Total new obligations	36	38	40
Budgetary resources available for obligation:			
22.00 New budget authority (gross)	37	38	40
23.95 Total new obligations	−36	−38	−40
23.98 Unobligated balance expiring or withdrawn	−1		
New budget authority (gross), detail:			
Discretionary:			
40.00 Appropriation	37	38	40
Change in unpaid obligations:			
72.40 Unpaid obligations, start of year: Obligated balance, start of year	5	8	5
73.10 Total new obligations	36	38	40
73.20 Total outlays (gross)	−33	−39	−39
74.40 Unpaid obligations, end of year: Obligated balance, end of year	8	5	5
Outlays (gross), detail:			
86.90 Outlays from new discretionary authority	29	34	36
86.93 Outlays from discretionary balances	4	4	4
87.00 Total outlays (gross)	33	39	39
Net budget authority and outlays:			
89.00 Budget authority	37	38	40
90.00 Outlays	33	39	39

The Federal Election Commission (the Commission) administers the disclosure of campaign finance information, enforces limitations on contributions and expenditures, supervises the public funding of Presidential elections, and performs other tasks related to Federal elections.

The Commission is authorized to submit, concurrently, budget estimates to the President and Congress.

Object Classification (in millions of dollars)

Identification code 95–1600–0–1–808	1999 actual	2000 est.	2001 est.
11.1 Personnel compensation: Full-time permanent	18	21	22
12.1 Civilian personnel benefits	4	5	5
23.1 Rental payments to GSA	3	3	4
23.3 Communications, utilities, and miscellaneous charges	1	1	1
25.2 Other services	3	3	2
25.3 Purchases of goods and services from Government accounts	1	1	1
25.7 Operation and maintenance of equipment	2	3	3
26.0 Supplies and materials	1	1	1
31.0 Equipment	1		
99.0 Subtotal, direct obligations	34	38	39
99.5 Below reporting threshold	2		1
99.9 Total new obligations	36	38	40

Personnel Summary

Identification code 95–1600–0–1–808	1999 actual	2000 est.	2001 est.
1001 Total compensable workyears: Full-time equivalent employment	323	352	352

FEDERAL FINANCIAL INSTITUTIONS EXAMINATION COUNCIL APPRAISAL SUBCOMMITTEE

Federal Funds

General and special funds:

REGISTRY FEES

Unavailable Collections (in millions of dollars)

Identification code 95–5026–0–2–376	1999 actual	2000 est.	2001 est.
Balance, start of year:			
01.99 Balance, start of year			
Receipts:			
02.01 Registry fees, Appraisal subcommittee	2	2	2
Appropriation:			
05.01 Registry fees	−2	−2	−2

General and special funds—Continued

REGISTRY FEES—Continued

Unavailable Collections (in millions of dollars)—Continued

Identification code 95–5026–0–2–376	1999 actual	2000 est.	2001 est.
07.99 Total balance, end of year	....	....	....

Program and Financing (in millions of dollars)

Identification code 95–5026–0–2–376	1999 actual	2000 est.	2001 est.
Obligations by program activity:			
00.01 Administrative expenses	1	1	1
00.02 Grants, subsidies and contributions	1	1	1
10.00 Total new obligations	2	2	2
Budgetary resources available for obligation:			
21.40 Unobligated balance available, start of year	3	3	3
22.00 New budget authority (gross)	2	2	2
23.90 Total budgetary resources available for obligation	5	5	5
23.95 Total new obligations	−2	−2	−2
24.40 Unobligated balance available, end of year	3	3	3
New budget authority (gross), detail:			
Mandatory:			
60.25 Appropriation (special fund, indefinite)	2	2	2
Change in unpaid obligations:			
72.40 Unpaid obligations, start of year: Obligated balance, start of year	....	1	....
73.10 Total new obligations	2	2	2
73.20 Total outlays (gross)	−1	−3	−2
74.40 Unpaid obligations, end of year: Obligated balance, end of year	1	....	....
Outlays (gross), detail:			
86.97 Outlays from new mandatory authority	1	2	2
86.98 Outlays from mandatory balances	....	1	....
87.00 Total outlays (gross)	1	3	2
Net budget authority and outlays:			
89.00 Budget authority	2	2	2
90.00 Outlays	2	3	2

The Financial Institutions Reform, Recovery, and Enforcement Act of 1989 (Public Law 101–73, August 9, 1989) established the Appraisal Subcommittee of the Federal Financial Institutions Examination Council. Subsequent legislation (Public Law 101–235) authorized the Secretary of the Department of Housing and Urban Development to designate a member of the Appraisal Subcommittee.

The Subcommittee is charged with ensuring that real estate appraisals used in federally-related transactions are performed in accordance with uniform standards by appraisers certified and licensed by the States. Its responsibilities include: (1) monitoring the requirements established by the States for the certification and licensing of appraisers; (2) monitoring the requirements established by the Federal financial institutions' regulatory agencies regarding appraisal standards; (3) monitoring and reviewing the practices, procedures, activities, and organization of the Appraisal Foundation; and, (4) maintaining a national registry of licensed and certified appraisers.

Subcommittee activities, including grants awarded to the Appraisal Foundation, were initially funded from a one-time appropriation of $5 million. These funds were repaid to Treasury at the end of 1998 in accordance with the Economic Growth and Regulatory Paperwork Reduction Act of 1996. The Subcommittee is now operating on fee income from state-licensed and certified real estate appraisers in the national registry.

Object Classification (in millions of dollars)

Identification code 95–5026–0–2–376	1999 actual	2000 est.	2001 est.
11.1 Personnel compensation: Full-time permanent	1	1	1
41.0 Grants, subsidies, and contributions	1	1	1
99.9 Total new obligations	2	2	2

Personnel Summary

Identification code 95–5026–0–2–376	1999 actual	2000 est.	2001 est.
1001 Total compensable workyears: Full-time equivalent employment	7	7	7

FEDERAL HOUSING FINANCE BOARD

Federal Funds

Public enterprise funds:

FEDERAL HOUSING FINANCE BOARD

Program and Financing (in millions of dollars)

Identification code 95–4039–0–3–371	1999 actual	2000 est.	2001 est.
Obligations by program activity:			
09.01 Operating Expenses	18	21	21
10.00 Total new obligations	18	21	21
Budgetary resources available for obligation:			
21.40 Unobligated balance available, start of year	2	1	1
22.00 New budget authority (gross)	18	21	21
23.90 Total budgetary resources available for obligation	20	22	22
23.95 Total new obligations	−18	−21	−21
24.40 Unobligated balance available, end of year	1	1	1
New budget authority (gross), detail:			
Mandatory:			
69.00 Offsetting collections (cash)	18	21	21
Change in unpaid obligations:			
72.40 Unpaid obligations, start of year: Obligated balance, start of year	3	4	4
73.10 Total new obligations	18	21	21
73.20 Total outlays (gross)	−18	−21	−22
74.40 Unpaid obligations, end of year: Obligated balance, end of year	4	4	3
Outlays (gross), detail:			
86.97 Outlays from new mandatory authority	14	17	17
86.98 Outlays from mandatory balances	4	4	5
87.00 Total outlays (gross)	18	21	22
Offsets:			
Against gross budget authority and outlays:			
88.40 Offsetting collections (cash) from: Non-Federal sources	−18	−21	−21
Net budget authority and outlays:			
89.00 Budget authority	....	....	....
90.00 Outlays	....	....	1

The Federal Housing Finance Board (Finance Board), an independent executive agency, was established by the Financial Institutions Reform, Recovery, and Enforcement Act of 1989 which amended the Federal Home Loan Bank Act. The duties of the Finance Board are: (1) to ensure that the twelve Federal Home Loan Banks (Banks) operate in a safe and sound manner; (2) to supervise the Banks; (3) to ensure that the Banks carry out their housing finance mission; and, (4) to ensure the Banks remain adequately capitalized and able to raise funds in the capital markets. The Finance Board succeeded the former Federal Home Loan Bank Board with respect to the Banks.

The management of the Finance Board is vested in a five-member board of directors. The board of directors is composed of the Secretary of Housing and Urban Development and four other individuals appointed by the President, with the advice and consent of the Senate. The term of a Director is seven years.

The Finance Board has the power to: (1) supervise the Banks and promulgate and enforce such regulations and orders as are necessary; (2) suspend or remove for cause a director, officer, employee, or agent of any Bank or joint office; (3) determine necessary expenditures of the Finance Board and the manner in which such expenditures shall be incurred, allowed, and paid; and, (4) use the United States mail in the same manner and under the same conditions as a department or agency of the United States.

Object Classification (in millions of dollars)

Identification code 95–4039–0–3–371		1999 actual	2000 est.	2001 est.
	Personnel compensation:			
11.1	Full-time permanent	9	9	9
11.3	Other than full-time permanent	1	1	1
11.9	Total personnel compensation	10	10	10
12.1	Civilian personnel benefits	2	3	3
21.0	Travel and transportation of persons		1	1
23.2	Rental payments to others	2	2	2
25.1	Advisory and assistance services	1	1	1
31.0	Equipment	1	1	1
99.0	Subtotal, reimbursable obligations	16	18	18
99.5	Below reporting threshold	2	3	3
99.9	Total new obligations	18	21	21

Personnel Summary

Identification code 95–4039–0–3–371		1999 actual	2000 est.	2001 est.
2001	Total compensable workyears: Full-time equivalent employment	117	107	112

FEDERAL LABOR RELATIONS AUTHORITY

Federal Funds

General and special funds:

Salaries and Expenses

For necessary expenses to carry out functions of the Federal Labor Relations Authority, pursuant to Reorganization Plan Numbered 2 of 1978, and the Civil Service Reform Act of 1978, including services authorized by 5 U.S.C. 3109, including hire of experts and consultants, hire of passenger motor vehicles, and rental of conference rooms in the District of Columbia and elsewhere, **[**$23,828,000**]** *$25,058,000*: *Provided*, That public members of the Federal Service Impasses Panel may be paid travel expenses and per diem in lieu of subsistence as authorized by law (5 U.S.C. 5703) for persons employed intermittently in the Government service, and compensation as authorized by 5 U.S.C. 3109: *Provided further*, That notwithstanding 31 U.S.C. 3302, funds received from fees charged to non-Federal participants at labor-management relations conferences shall be credited to and merged with this account, to be available without further appropriation for the costs of carrying out these conferences. *(Independent Agencies Appropriations Act, 2000.)*

Program and Financing (in millions of dollars)

Identification code 54–0100–0–1–805		1999 actual	2000 est.	2001 est.
	Obligations by program activity:			
00.01	Federal labor relations authority	12	12	13
00.02	Office of the general counsel	10	11	11
00.03	Federal service impasses panel	1	1	1
10.00	Total new obligations	23	24	25
	Budgetary resources available for obligation:			
22.00	New budget authority (gross)	23	24	25
23.95	Total new obligations	–23	–24	–25
	New budget authority (gross), detail:			
	Discretionary:			
40.00	Appropriation	23	24	25
	Change in unpaid obligations:			
72.40	Unpaid obligations, start of year: Obligated balance, start of year	3	3	3
73.10	Total new obligations	23	24	25
73.20	Total outlays (gross)	–23	–24	–25
74.40	Unpaid obligations, end of year: Obligated balance, end of year	3	3	2
	Outlays (gross), detail:			
86.90	Outlays from new discretionary authority	21	22	23
86.93	Outlays from discretionary balances	2		2
87.00	Total outlays (gross)	23	24	25
	Net budget authority and outlays:			
89.00	Budget authority	23	24	25
90.00	Outlays	22	24	25

The Federal Labor Relations Authority (FLRA): (1) serves as a neutral party in the settlement of disputes that arise between unions, employees, and agencies on matters outlined in the Federal Service Labor Management Relations Statute; (2) decides major policy issues; (3) prescribes regulations; and, (4) disseminates information appropriate to the needs of agencies, labor organizations, and the public. Establishment of the FLRA gives full recognition to the role of the Federal Government as an employer.

In addition, the FLRA is engaged in case-related interventions and training and facilitation of labor-management partnerships in its unified Collaboration and Alternative Dispute Resolution Program. Approximately 1400 case-related intervention services were conducted in 1999. Training and facilitation workload is reflected in the following manner: the FLRA promotes labor-management cooperation by providing training and assistance to labor organizations and agencies on resolving disputes; facilitates the creation of partnerships as called for in Executive Order 12871; and trains the parties on rights and responsibilities under the Federal Labor Relations Management Statute. In 1999, the FLRA conducted over 270 programs involving over 14,000 employees, union representatives, arbitrators, and other practitioners.

Components.—The FLRA is composed of the Authority, the Office of the General Counsel, and the Federal Service Impasses Panel.

Authority.—The Authority adjudicates labor-management disputes in the Federal sector including: appeals on negotiability issues; exceptions to arbitration awards; appropriate units for the purposes of exclusive recognition; eligibility of labor organizations for national consultation rights; and unfair labor practice complaints.

Within the Authority, administrative law judges hold hearings on unfair labor practice complaints, issue reports, and make recommendations to the Authority to allow timely settlement of disputes arising between agencies and unions. The Authority also provides all components with administrative services.

The Office of the Inspector General is responsible for conducting and supervising audits and investigations related to the functions of the FLRA, pursuant to the provisions of the Inspector General Act of 1978, as amended in 1988.

Case dispositions are reflected in the following table:

CASE DISPOSITIONS

	1999 actual	*2000 est.*	*2001 est.*
Arbitration appeals	141	121	138
Negotiability appeals	81	76	61

General and special funds—Continued

SALARIES AND EXPENSES—Continued

CASE DISPOSITIONS—Continued

	1999 actual	2000 est.	2001 est.
Representation appeals/requests for review	15	14	20
Unfair labor practice appeals	59	57	49

Office of the General Counsel.—The functions of this office include: (1) investigating all allegations of unfair labor practices filed and the processing of all representation petitions received; (2) exercising final authority over the issuance and prosecution of all complaints; (3) supervising and conducting elections concerning the exclusive recognition of labor organizations and the certification of the results of elections; (4) conducting all hearings to resolve disputed issues in representation cases; (5) preparing final decisions and orders in these cases; and, (6) directing and supervising all employees of the regional offices. Case dispositions are reflected in the following table:

CASE DISPOSITIONS

	1999 actual	2000 est.	2001 est.
Unfair labor practice cases:			
Investigations	5,913	5,724	5,700
Complaints prosecuted	31	40	40
Complaints voluntarily settled	216	225	225
Appeals	560	500	500
Representation cases:			
Investigations	491	506	506
Elections/hearings	180	194	194

Federal Service Impasses Panel.—The functions of the panel involve the resolution of labor negotiation impasses between Federal agencies and labor organizations which arise under the Civil Service Reform Act of 1978 and other statutes. The Panel uses a variety of procedures including factfinding and arbitration.

CASE DISPOSITIONS

	1999 actual	2000 est.	2001 est.
Impasse resolutions	159	170	170

Object Classification (in millions of dollars)

Identification code 54–0100–0–1–805		1999 actual	2000 est.	2001 est.
	Personnel compensation:			
11.1	Full-time permanent	14	15	16
11.3	Other than full-time permanent	1	1	1
11.9	Total personnel compensation	15	16	17
12.1	Civilian personnel benefits	3	3	3
21.0	Travel and transportation of persons	1	1	1
23.1	Rental payments to GSA	2	2	2
23.3	Communications, utilities, and miscellaneous charges	1	1	1
25.2	Other services	1	1	1
99.0	Subtotal, direct obligations	22	23	25
99.5	Below reporting threshold	1	1	1
99.9	Total new obligations	23	24	25

Personnel Summary

Identification code 54–0100–0–1–805		1999 actual	2000 est.	2001 est.
1001	Total compensable workyears: Full-time equivalent employment	213	216	215

FEDERAL MARITIME COMMISSION

Federal Funds

General and special funds:

SALARIES AND EXPENSES

For necessary expenses of the Federal Maritime Commission as authorized by section 201(d) of the Merchant Marine Act, 1936, as amended (46 U.S.C. App. 1111), including services as authorized by 5 U.S.C. 3109; hire of passenger motor vehicles as authorized by 31 U.S.C. 1343(b); and uniforms or allowances therefor, as authorized by 5 U.S.C. 5901–5902, [$14,150,000] *$16,222,000*: *Provided*, That not to exceed $2,000 shall be available for official reception and representation expenses. *(Departments of Commerce, Justice, and State, the Judiciary, and Related Agencies Appropriations Act, 2000, as enacted by section 1000(a)(1) of the Consolidated Appropriations Act, 2000 (P.L. 106–113).)*

Program and Financing (in millions of dollars)

Identification code 65–0100–0–1–403		1999 actual	2000 est.	2001 est.
	Obligations by program activity:			
00.01	Formal proceedings	4	4	5
00.04	Operational and administrative	2	1	1
00.06	Economics and agreement analysis	2	2	2
00.07	Tariffs, certification and licensing	2	3	3
00.08	Enforcement	2	2	3
00.10	Administration	2	2	2
10.00	Total new obligations	14	14	16
	Budgetary resources available for obligation:			
22.00	New budget authority (gross)	14	15	16
23.95	Total new obligations	−14	−14	−16
	New budget authority (gross), detail:			
	Discretionary:			
40.00	Appropriation	14	14	16
42.00	Transferred from other accounts	....	1	....
43.00	Appropriation (total discretionary)	14	15	16
	Change in unpaid obligations:			
72.40	Unpaid obligations, start of year: Obligated balance, start of year	2	1	1
73.10	Total new obligations	14	14	16
73.20	Total outlays (gross)	−14	−14	−15
74.40	Unpaid obligations, end of year: Obligated balance, end of year	1	1	1
	Outlays (gross), detail:			
86.90	Outlays from new discretionary authority	13	14	15
86.93	Outlays from discretionary balances	2	....	1
87.00	Total outlays (gross)	14	14	15
	Net budget authority and outlays:			
89.00	Budget authority	14	15	16
90.00	Outlays	15	14	15

The Federal Maritime Commission (the Commission) regulates the international waterborne commerce of the United States. In addition, the Commission has responsibility for: licensing and bonding of ocean transportation intermediaries; assuring that vessel owners or operators establish financial responsibility for death or injury to passengers or other persons on voyages to and from U.S. ports; and, indemnifying passengers for the nonperformance of transportation. Major program areas for 2001 are: carrying out investigations of foreign trade practices under the Foreign Shipping Practices Act; pursuing an active enforcement program designed to identify and prosecute violators of the shipping statutes; maintaining equitable trading conditions in U.S. ocean commerce; and, ensuring compliance with applicable shipping statutes.

Object Classification (in millions of dollars)

Identification code 65–0100–0–1–403		1999 actual	2000 est.	2001 est.
11.1	Personnel compensation: Full-time permanent	9	9	10
12.1	Civilian personnel benefits	2	2	2
23.1	Rental payments to GSA	2	2	2
25.2	Other services	1	1	1
99.0	Subtotal, direct obligations	14	14	15
99.5	Below reporting threshold	....	....	1
99.9	Total new obligations	14	14	16

Personnel Summary

Identification code 65–0100–0–1–403	1999 actual	2000 est.	2001 est.
1001 Total compensable workyears: Full-time equivalent employment	139	134	144

FEDERAL MEDIATION AND CONCILIATION SERVICE

Federal Funds

General and special funds:

SALARIES AND EXPENSES

For expenses necessary for the Federal Mediation and Conciliation Service to carry out the functions vested in it by the Labor Management Relations Act, 1947 (29 U.S.C. 171–180, 182–183), including hire of passenger motor vehicles; for expenses necessary for the Labor-Management Cooperation Act of 1978 (29 U.S.C. 175a); and for expenses necessary for the Service to carry out the functions vested in it by the Civil Service Reform Act, Public Law 95–454 (5 U.S.C. ch. 71), [$36,834,000] *$39,001,000*, including $1,500,000, to remain available through September 30, [2001] *2002*, for activities authorized by the Labor-Management Cooperation Act of 1978 (29 U.S.C. 175a): *Provided*, That notwithstanding 31 U.S.C. 3302, fees charged, up to full-cost recovery, for special training activities and other conflict resolution services and technical assistance, including those provided to foreign governments and international organizations, and for arbitration services shall be credited to and merged with this account, and shall remain available until expended: *Provided further*, That fees for arbitration services shall be available only for education, training, and professional development of the agency workforce: *Provided further*, That the Director of the Service is authorized to accept and use on behalf of the United States gifts of services and real, personal, or other property in the aid of any projects or functions within the Director's jurisdiction. *(Departments of Labor, Health and Human Services, and Education, and Related Agencies Appropriations Act, 2000, as enacted by section 1000(a)(4) of the Consolidated Appropriations Act, 2000 (P.L. 106–113).)*

Program and Financing (in millions of dollars)

Identification code 93–0100–0–1–505	1999 actual	2000 est.	2001 est.
Obligations by program activity:			
Direct program:			
00.01 Dispute mediation and preventive mediation, public information	25	27	29
00.02 Arbitration services	1	1	1
00.03 Management and administrative support	6	7	7
00.04 Labor-management cooperation project	2	2	2
00.91 Total direct program	34	37	39
01.01 Reimbursable program	2	2	2
10.00 Total new obligations	36	39	41
Budgetary resources available for obligation:			
21.40 Unobligated balance available, start of year	1	1	1
22.00 New budget authority (gross)	37	39	41
23.90 Total budgetary resources available for obligation	38	40	42
23.95 Total new obligations	−36	−39	−41
24.40 Unobligated balance available, end of year	1	1	1
New budget authority (gross), detail:			
Discretionary:			
40.00 Appropriation	35	37	39
68.00 Spending authority from offsetting collections: Offsetting governmental collections	2	2	2
70.00 Total new budget authority (gross)	37	39	41
Change in unpaid obligations:			
72.40 Unpaid obligations, start of year: Obligated balance, start of year	5	6	6
73.10 Total new obligations	36	39	41
73.20 Total outlays (gross)	−33	−37	−39
74.40 Unpaid obligations, end of year: Obligated balance, end of year	6	6	6
Outlays (gross), detail:			
86.90 Outlays from new discretionary authority	34	35	37
86.93 Outlays from discretionary balances	1		3
87.00 Total outlays (gross)	33	37	39
Offsets:			
Against gross budget authority and outlays:			
88.45 Offsetting collections (cash) from: Offsetting governmental collections from the public	−2	−2	−2
Net budget authority and outlays:			
89.00 Budget authority	35	37	39
90.00 Outlays	33	35	37

The Federal Mediation and Conciliation Service (FMCS or the Service) provides assistance to parties in labor disputes in industries affecting commerce through conciliation and mediation.

Dispute mediation.—The Service assists labor and management in the mediation and prevention of disputes, other than those involving rail and air transportation, whenever such disputes threaten to cause a substantial interruption of interstate commerce or a major impairment to the national defense. The Service also makes mediation and conciliation services available to Federal agencies and organizations representing Federal employees in the resolution of negotiation disputes. The Service provides mandatory mediation and, where necessary, impartial boards of inquiry to assist in resolving labor disputes involving private nonprofit health care institutions. The workload shown below includes assignments closed in both the private and public sectors.

MEDIATION WORKLOAD DATA

	1997 actual	1998 actual	1999 actual	2000 estimate	2001 estimate
Cases in process at beginning of year	7,183	7,771	8,267	8,172	8,178
Mediation assignments	20,844	20,263	19,200	20,400	20,400
Mediation assignments closed	20,256	19,767	19,295	20,394	20,400
Cases in process at end of year	7,771	8,267	8,172	8,178	8,178
Total mediation conferences conducted	5,643	5,784	6,188	6,000	6,000

Preventive mediation, public information, and educational activities.—Through its preventive mediation program, the Service initiates and develops labor-management committees, training programs, conferences, and specialized workshops dealing with issues in collective bargaining. Mediators also participate in public information and educational activities such as lectures, seminars, and conferences.

Arbitration services.—The Service assists parties in disputes by utilizing the arbitration process for the resolution of disputes arising under or in the negotiation of collective bargaining agreements in the private and public sectors.

ARBITRATION SERVICES WORKLOAD DATA

	1997 actual	1998 actual	1999 actual	2000 estimate	2001 estimate
Number of panels issued	31,295	19,062	17,521	20,015	20,415
Number of arbitrators appointed	10,391	8,984	9,572	10,416	10,624

Management and administrative support.—This activity provides for overall management and administration, policy planning, research and evaluation, and employee development.

Labor-management cooperation project.—The Labor Management Cooperation Act of 1978 (29 U.S.C. 175a) authorizes the Service to carry out this program of contracts and grants to support the establishment and operation of plant, area, and industry labor-management committees.

Alternative Dispute Resolution (ADR) Projects.—The Service assists other Federal agencies by providing mediation and technical assistance in the area of ADR. The ADR cases reduce litigation costs and speed federal processes. The FMCS is funded for this work through interagency reimbursable agreements.

General and special funds—Continued

SALARIES AND EXPENSES—Continued

ALTERNATIVE DISPUTE RESOLUTION (ADR) WORKLOAD DATA

	1997 actual	1998 actual	1999 actual	2000 estimate	2001 estimate
Number of ADR Cases	51	863	590	900	900

Object Classification (in millions of dollars)

Identification code 93–0100–0–1–505	1999 actual	2000 est.	2001 est.
11.1 Personnel compensation: Full-time permanent	20	22	24
12.1 Civilian personnel benefits	5	5	5
21.0 Travel and transportation of persons	2	3	3
23.1 Rental payments to GSA	4	4	4
23.3 Communications, utilities, and miscellaneous charges	1	1	1
25.2 Other services	1	1	1
31.0 Equipment	1	1	1
41.0 Grants, subsidies, and contributions	1	1	1
99.0 Subtotal, direct obligations	35	38	40
99.5 Below reporting threshold	1	1	1
99.9 Total new obligations	36	39	41

Personnel Summary

Identification code 93–0100–0–1–505	1999 actual	2000 est.	2001 est.
Direct:			
1001 Total compensable workyears: Full-time equivalent employment	277	286	286
Reimbursable:			
2001 Total compensable workyears: Full-time equivalent employment	4	6	6

FEDERAL MINE SAFETY AND HEALTH REVIEW COMMISSION

Federal Funds

General and special funds:

SALARIES AND EXPENSES

For expenses necessary for the Federal Mine Safety and Health Review Commission (30 U.S.C. 801 et seq.), [$6,159,000] *$6,320,000*. *(Departments of Labor, Health and Human Services, and Education, and Related Agencies Appropriations Act, 2000, as enacted by section 1000(a)(4) of the Consolidated Appropriations Act, 2000 (P.L. 106–113).)*

Program and Financing (in millions of dollars)

Identification code 95–2800–0–1–554	1999 actual	2000 est.	2001 est.
Obligations by program activity:			
00.01 Commission review	3	4	4
00.02 Administrative law judge determinations	3	3	3
10.00 Total new obligations	6	7	7
Budgetary resources available for obligation:			
22.00 New budget authority (gross)	6	6	6
23.95 Total new obligations	−6	−7	−7
New budget authority (gross), detail:			
Discretionary:			
40.00 Appropriation	6	6	6
Change in unpaid obligations:			
72.40 Unpaid obligations, start of year: Obligated balance, start of year	1	1	1
73.10 Total new obligations	6	7	7
73.20 Total outlays (gross)	−5	−6	−6
74.40 Unpaid obligations, end of year: Obligated balance, end of year	1	1	1
Outlays (gross), detail:			
86.90 Outlays from new discretionary authority	5	5	5
86.93 Outlays from discretionary balances	1	1	1
87.00 Total outlays (gross)	5	6	6
Net budget authority and outlays:			
89.00 Budget authority	6	6	6
90.00 Outlays	5	6	6

The Federal Mine Safety and Health Review Commission reviews and decides contested enforcement actions of the Secretary of Labor on mine safety legislation. The Commission also adjudicates claims by miners and miners' representatives concerning their rights under law. The Commission holds fact-finding hearings and issues orders affirming, modifying, or vacating the Secretary's enforcement actions.

SELECTED WORKLOAD DATA

	1999 actual	2000 est.	2001 est.
Commission review activities:			
Cases pending beginning of year	43	22	18
Cases called for review	52	54	59
Cases decided	73	58	66
Administrative law judge activities:			
Cases pending beginning of year	5,341	1,516	1,416
New cases received	2,335	2,400	2,450
Cases decided	6,160	2,500	2,550

Object Classification (in millions of dollars)

Identification code 95–2800–0–1–554	1999 actual	2000 est.	2001 est.
11.1 Personnel compensation: Full-time permanent	4	4	4
12.1 Civilian personnel benefits	1	1	1
23.1 Rental payments to GSA	1	1	1
99.0 Subtotal, direct obligations	6	6	6
99.5 Below reporting threshold		1	1
99.9 Total new obligations	6	7	7

Personnel Summary

Identification code 95–2800–0–1–554	1999 actual	2000 est.	2001 est.
1001 Total compensable workyears: Full-time equivalent employment	45	51	50

FEDERAL RETIREMENT THRIFT INVESTMENT BOARD

Federal Funds

General and special funds:

PROGRAM EXPENSES

Unavailable Collections (in millions of dollars)

Identification code 26–5290–0–2–602	1999 actual	2000 est.	2001 est.
Balance, start of year:			
01.99 Balance, start of year			
Receipts:			
02.01 Reimbursement for program expenses	75	101	80
Appropriation:			
05.01 Program expenses	−75	−101	−80
07.99 Total balance, end of year			

Program and Financing (in millions of dollars)

Identification code 26–5290–0–2–602	1999 actual	2000 est.	2001 est.
Obligations by program activity:			
00.01 Administrative expenses	75	101	80
10.00 Total new obligations	75	101	80
Budgetary resources available for obligation:			
22.00 New budget authority (gross)	75	101	80
23.95 Total new obligations	−75	−101	−80

	New budget authority (gross), detail:			
	Mandatory:			
60.25	Appropriation (special fund, indefinite)	75	101	80
	Change in unpaid obligations:			
72.40	Unpaid obligations, start of year: Obligated balance, start of year	23	39	23
73.10	Total new obligations	75	101	80
73.20	Total outlays (gross)	−59	−117	−80
74.40	Unpaid obligations, end of year: Obligated balance, end of year	39	23	23
	Outlays (gross), detail:			
86.97	Outlays from new mandatory authority	37	78	57
86.98	Outlays from mandatory balances	22	39	23
87.00	Total outlays (gross)	59	117	80
	Net budget authority and outlays:			
89.00	Budget authority	75	101	80
90.00	Outlays	59	117	80

The Federal Retirement Thrift Investment Board is responsible for managing the Thrift Savings Fund (Fund). The Fund is a special tax-deferred savings fund established by the Federal Employees' Retirement System Act of 1986. Due to the fiduciary nature of the Fund, it is not included in the totals of the Federal budget. Information on the financial status and activities of the Fund follows this account.

Program administration for the Fund is financed from the Fund. Program expenses are derived first from Fund forfeitures of agency one percent automatic contributions for employees who separate from the Federal government prior to vesting and then from earnings on all participant and agency contributions to the Fund.

Object Classification (in millions of dollars)

Identification code 26–5290–0–2–602		1999 actual	2000 est.	2001 est.
11.1	Personnel compensation: Full-time permanent	6	7	7
12.1	Civilian personnel benefits	1	2	2
23.2	Rental payments to others	2	2	2
24.0	Printing and reproduction	2	7	3
25.2	Other services	4	7	10
25.3	Purchases of goods and services from Government accounts	41	51	50
31.0	Equipment	18	25	4
99.0	Subtotal, direct obligations	74	101	78
99.5	Below reporting threshold	1		2
99.9	Total new obligations	75	101	80

Personnel Summary

Identification code 26–5290–0–2–602		1999 actual	2000 est.	2001 est.
1001	Total compensable workyears: Full-time equivalent employment	97	109	112

INFORMATION SCHEDULES FOR THE THRIFT SAVINGS FUND

The Fund is composed of individual accounts maintained by the Federal Retirement Thrift Investment Board on behalf of the individual Federal employee participants in the Fund. All Federal employees are eligible to contribute to the Fund. However, only those employees covered by the Federal Employees' Retirement System have their contributions matched by employing agencies in accordance with the formulas prescribed by law. Employees are currently entitled to select how contributions are distributed among three investment funds: a U.S. Government securities investment fund; a common stock index investment fund; and, a fixed income index investment fund. A small capitalization stock index investment fund and an international stock index fund are planned for implementation during 2000.

Employee participation in the Fund is entirely voluntary, so actual results could vary significantly from these estimates. The estimated status of the Fund is shown below:

STATUS OF THRIFT SAVINGS FUND

[In millions of dollars]

	1999 actual	2000 est.	2001 est.
Thrift Savings Fund investment balance, start of year	65,078	82,016	99,525
Income for the year:			
Employee contributions	5,650	6,304	7,018
Contributions on behalf of employees[1]	2,651	2,966	3,302
Earnings[2]	11,403	10,959	13,053
Total cash income	19,704	20,229	23,373
Outgo during the year:			
Withdrawals	2,195	2,214	2,460
Loans to employees	511	405	450
Administrative expenses	60	101	80
Total cash outgo	2,766	2,720	2,990
Thrift Savings Fund investment balance, end of year[3]	82,016	99,525	119,908

[1] 1999 Employer contributions include $605 million in automatic contributions for FERS employees and $2,046 million in matching contributions for FERS employees.

[2] 1999 Earnings include: return on investments in Government securities—$1,566 million; return on investments in non-government instruments—$9,673 million; earnings on loans—$162 million; and agency payments for lost earnings—$3 million.

[3] Investment fund balances at 9/30/99 were: Government Securities Investment Fund—$29,376 million; Barclays Equity Index Fund—$48,717 million; and Barclays U.S. Debt Index Fund—$3,923 million.

FEDERAL TRADE COMMISSION

Federal Funds

General and special funds:

SALARIES AND EXPENSES

For necessary expenses of the Federal Trade Commission, including uniforms or allowances therefor, as authorized by 5 U.S.C. 5901–5902; services as authorized by 5 U.S.C. 3109; hire of passenger motor vehicles; [and] not to exceed $2,000 for official reception and representation expenses; *and not to exceed an additional $75,000 for official reception and representation expenses related to hosting two International Marketing Supervision Network (IMSN) conferences*, [$104,024,000] *$157,600,000*: *Provided*, That not to exceed $300,000 shall be available for use to contract with a person or persons for collection services in accordance with the terms of 31 U.S.C. 3718, as amended: *Provided further*, That, notwithstanding section 3302(b) of title 31, United States Code, not to exceed [$104,024,000] *$157,600,000* of offsetting collections derived from fees collected for premerger notification filings under the Hart-Scott-Rodino Antitrust Improvements Act of 1976 (15 U.S.C. 18(a)) shall be retained and used for necessary expenses in this appropriation, and shall remain available until expended: *Provided further*, That the sum herein appropriated from the general fund shall be reduced as such offsetting collections are received during fiscal year [2000] *2001*, so as to result in a final fiscal year [2000] *2001* appropriation from the general fund estimated at not more than $0, to remain available until expended: *Provided further, That section 605 of Public Law 101–162 (15 U.S.C. § 18a note), as amended, is further amended (1) by striking "$45,000 which" and inserting: "(a) $45,000, if as a result of the acquisition, the acquiring person would hold an aggregate total amount of the voting securities and assets of the acquired person in excess of $35,000,000 but not exceeding $99,999,999; (b) $100,000, if as a result of the acquisition, the acquiring person would hold an aggregate total amount of the voting securities and assets of the acquired person equal to or in excess of $100,000,000 but not exceeding $199,999,999; or (c) $200,000, if as a result of the acquisition, the acquiring person would hold an aggregate total amount of the voting securities and assets of the acquired person equal to or in excess of $200,000,000. Such fees"; and (2) by adding the following sentence: "Any misrepresentation of the aggregate total amount of the voting securities and assets to be held as a result of the acquisition would subject the acquiring person to civil penalties and any other appropriate remedy as provided for under 15 U.S.C. § 18a(g).", immediately after the words "no notification shall be considered filed until payment*

General and special funds—Continued

SALARIES AND EXPENSES—Continued

of the fee required by this section.": Provided further, That none of the funds made available to the Federal Trade Commission shall be available for obligation for expenses authorized by section 151 of the Federal Deposit Insurance Corporation Improvement Act of 1991 (Public Law 102–242; 105 Stat. 2282–2285). *(Departments of Commerce, Justice, and State, the Judiciary, and Related Agencies Appropriations Act, 2000, as enacted by section 1000(a)(1) of the Consolidated Appropriations Act, 2000 (P.L. 106–113).)*

Unavailable Collections (in millions of dollars)

Identification code 29–0100–0–1–376		1999 actual	2000 est.	2001 est.
	Balance, start of year:			
01.99	Balance, start of year	31	22	8
03.00	Offsetting collections	22	7	7
04.00	Total: Balances and collections	53	29	15
	Appropriation:			
05.01	Salaries and expenses	−31	−21	−7
07.99	Total balance, end of year	22	8	8

Program and Financing (in millions of dollars)

Identification code 29–0100–0–1–376		1999 actual	2000 est.	2001 est.
	Obligations by program activity:			
	Direct program:			
01.01	Maintaining competition	5		
01.02	Consumer protection	5		
01.03	Y2K	2		
01.92	Subtotal, direct program	12		
	Reimbursable program:			
09.01	Maintaining competition	50	59	76
09.02	Consumer protection	57	66	89
09.03	Reimbursable program	1	1	1
09.99	Total reimbursable program	108	126	166
10.00	Total new obligations	120	126	166
	Budgetary resources available for obligation:			
21.40	Unobligated balance available, start of year	2	3	3
22.00	New budget authority (gross)	119	126	166
22.10	Resources available from recoveries of prior year obligations	2		
23.90	Total budgetary resources available for obligation	123	129	169
23.95	Total new obligations	−120	−126	−166
24.40	Unobligated balance available, end of year	3	3	3
	New budget authority (gross), detail:			
	Discretionary:			
40.00	Appropriation	10		
42.00	Transferred from other accounts	3		
43.00	Appropriation (total discretionary)	13		
	Spending authority from offsetting collections:			
68.00	Offsetting collections (cash)	98	112	166
68.26	Offsetting collections (unavailable balances)	31	21	7
68.45	Portion not available for obligation (limitation on obligations)	−22	−7	−7
68.90	Spending authority from offsetting collections (total discretionary)	107	126	166
70.00	Total new budget authority (gross)	119	126	166
	Change in unpaid obligations:			
72.40	Unpaid obligations, start of year: Obligated balance, start of year	12	17	17
73.10	Total new obligations	120	126	166
73.20	Total outlays (gross)	−113	−126	−163
73.45	Adjustments in unexpired accounts	−2		
74.40	Unpaid obligations, end of year: Obligated balance, end of year	17	17	20
	Outlays (gross), detail:			
86.90	Outlays from new discretionary authority	113	116	153
86.93	Outlays from discretionary balances		10	10
87.00	Total outlays (gross)	113	126	163
	Offsets:			
	Against gross budget authority and outlays:			
	Offsetting collections (cash) from:			
88.00	Federal sources	−1	−1	−1
88.40	Non-Federal sources	−97	−111	−165
88.90	Total, offsetting collections (cash)	−98	−112	−166
	Net budget authority and outlays:			
89.00	Budget authority	21	14	
90.00	Outlays	15	14	−3

The Federal Trade Commission (Commission) is charged by law with ensuring that competition in the marketplace is vigorous, free, and fair. This is accomplished by eliminating threats to fair and honest competition from all sources, both public and private.

Consumer protection.—The Commission is charged with eliminating unfair or deceptive acts or practices affecting commerce. The goal of the consumer protection mission is to prevent fraud, deception, and unfair business practices in the marketplace. The mission works to accomplish this goal through three objectives: (1) identify fraud, deception, and unfair practices that cause the greatest consumer injury; (2) stop fraud, deception, and unfair practices through law enforcement; and, (3) prevent consumer injury through education.

Maintaining competition.—The Commission's efforts are aimed at fostering and preserving our competitive system with the goal of maximizing consumer welfare. In addition to enforcing the antitrust laws against private sector restraints on competition, the Commission also scrutinizes regulatory policies that unduly restrain competition, and encourages policymakers to harness the benefits of competition in the development of such policies.

The President's 2001 request will fund a total of 1,139 FTE, which includes 6 reimbursable FTE. The program level for the Commission would increase from $125.0 million in 2000 to $164.6 million in 2001, allowing the Commission to enhance the performance of its missions. The 2001 requested level includes $7.0 million derived from estimated 2000 carryover fee balances and an anticipated $157.6 million from premerger notification filing fees collected in 2001.

The appropriation language provision regarding the FTC's reception and representation allowance has been modified in 2001 to cover one-time costs related to the hosting of two conferences of the International Marketing Supervision Network (IMSN). The IMSN is an organization consisting of consumer protection agencies from more than two dozen countries. The IMSN's mandate is to share information about cross-border commercial activities that could affect consumer interests and to encourage international cooperation among law enforcement agencies. The costs arise from the FTC's assuming the presidency of the IMSN for one year.

The 2001 programs administered by the FTC will be fully funded by fees assessed on Hart-Scott-Rodino Act premerger notification filings by section 605 of Public Law 101–162, as amended, and based on an amendment proposed in this request. This proposed amendment would create a three-tiered schedule of premerger notification filing fees based on the size of the transaction. The proposed schedule would impose a fee of: (1) $45,000 on mergers having a total aggregate transaction value in excess of $35,000,000 but not exceeding $99,999,999; (2) $100,000 on mergers having a total aggregate transaction value equal to or in excess of $100,000,000 but not exceeding $199,999,999; and, (3) $200,000 on mergers having a total aggregate transaction value equal to or in excess of $200,000,000. The proposed schedule would provide relief to small business by raising from $15,000,000 to $35,000,000 the threshold of the size of the transaction requiring a filing fee of $45,000. In 1999, this schedule would have eliminated filing fees for approximately 40 percent of the filers and would have maintained the existing $45,000 fee for approximately one-half of the remaining filers. Consistent with 15 U.S.C. § 18a(g), the proposed amendment would permit the Federal antitrust agencies to seek appropriate relief for a misrepresentation of the size of the transaction in a premerger notification filing.

Object Classification (in millions of dollars)

Identification code 29–0100–0–1–376	1999 actual	2000 est.	2001 est.
Direct obligations:			
Personnel compensation:			
11.1 Full-time permanent	5		
11.3 Other than full-time permanent	1		
11.9 Total personnel compensation	6		
12.1 Civilian personnel benefits	1		
23.1 Rental payments to GSA	1		
25.2 Other services	1		
31.0 Equipment	3		
99.0 Subtotal, direct obligations	12		
99.0 Reimbursable obligations	108	126	166
99.9 Total new obligations	120	126	166

Personnel Summary

Identification code 29–0100–0–1–376	1999 actual	2000 est.	2001 est.
Direct:			
1001 Total compensable workyears: Full-time equivalent employment	83		
Reimbursable:			
2001 Total compensable workyears: Full-time equivalent employment	884	985	1,139

HARRY S. TRUMAN SCHOLARSHIP FOUNDATION

Trust Funds

Harry S. Truman Memorial Scholarship Trust Fund

Unavailable Collections (in millions of dollars)

Identification code 95–8296–0–7–502	1999 actual	2000 est.	2001 est.
Balance, start of year:			
01.99 Balance, start of year			
Receipts:			
02.01 Interest on investments	4	4	4
Appropriation:			
05.01 Harry S. Truman memorial scholarship trust fund	–4	–4	–4
07.99 Total balance, end of year			

Program and Financing (in millions of dollars)

Identification code 95–8296–0–7–502	1999 actual	2000 est.	2001 est.
Obligations by program activity:			
00.01 Scholarship awards	2	2	2
00.02 Program administration	1	1	1
10.00 Total new obligations	3	3	3
Budgetary resources available for obligation:			
21.40 Unobligated balance available, start of year	54	55	56
22.00 New budget authority (gross)	4	4	4
23.90 Total budgetary resources available for obligation	58	59	60
23.95 Total new obligations	–3	–3	–3
24.40 Unobligated balance available, end of year	55	56	57
New budget authority (gross), detail:			
Mandatory:			
60.27 Appropriation (trust fund, indefinite)	4	4	4
Change in unpaid obligations:			
72.40 Unpaid obligations, start of year: Obligated balance, start of year	2	2	2
73.10 Total new obligations	3	3	3
73.20 Total outlays (gross)	–3	–3	–3
74.40 Unpaid obligations, end of year: Obligated balance, end of year	2	2	2
Outlays (gross), detail:			
86.97 Outlays from new mandatory authority	3	1	1
86.98 Outlays from mandatory balances	2	2	2
87.00 Total outlays (gross)	3	3	3
Net budget authority and outlays:			
89.00 Budget authority	4	4	4
90.00 Outlays	3	3	3
Memorandum (non-add) entries:			
92.01 Total investments, start of year: U.S. securities: Par value	55	57	58
92.02 Total investments, end of year: U.S. securities: Par value	57	58	59

Public Law 93–642 established the Harry S. Truman Scholarship Foundation to operate the scholarship program that is the permanent Federal memorial to the 33rd President of the United States. The Foundation awards scholarships for up to four years to qualified students who demonstrate outstanding potential for and interest in careers in public service at the local, State, or Federal level or in the nonprofit sector.

In its annual competition, the Foundation selects up to 80 new Truman Scholars. The maximum award is $30,000 for four years.

Scholarship awards.—This activity is comprised of scholarships awarded to cover eligible educational expenses.

Program administration.—This activity covers all costs of operating the program, including annual program announcement, interview and selection of Truman Scholars, calculation and disbursement of scholarship awards, monitoring of student progress, and special services and activities for scholars, including an orientation week for new scholars, a summer education and internship program, and workshops and conferences.

Object Classification (in millions of dollars)

Identification code 95–8296–0–7–502	1999 actual	2000 est.	2001 est.
41.0 Direct obligations: Grants, subsidies, and contributions	2	2	2
99.5 Below reporting threshold	1	1	1
99.9 Total new obligations	3	3	3

Personnel Summary

Identification code 95–8296–0–7–502	1999 actual	2000 est.	2001 est.
1001 Total compensable workyears: Full-time equivalent employment	4	4	4

INSTITUTE OF AMERICAN INDIAN AND ALASKA NATIVE CULTURE AND ARTS DEVELOPMENT

Federal Funds

General and special funds:

Payment to the Institute

For payment to the Institute of American Indian and Alaska Native Culture and Arts Development, as authorized by title XV of Public Law 99–498, as amended (20 U.S.C. 56 part A), [$2,125,000] *$4,250,000. (Department of the Interior and Related Agencies Appro-*

General and special funds—Continued

PAYMENT TO THE INSTITUTE—Continued

priations Act, 2000, as enacted by section 1000(a)(3) of the Consolidated Appropriations Act, 2000 (P.L. 106–113).)

Program and Financing (in millions of dollars)

Identification code 95–2900–0–1–502	1999 actual	2000 est.	2001 est.
Obligations by program activity:			
00.01 Payment to the Institute	4	2	4
10.00 Total new obligations (object class 41.0)	4	2	4
Budgetary resources available for obligation:			
22.00 New budget authority (gross)	4	2	4
23.95 Total new obligations	−4	−2	−4
New budget authority (gross), detail:			
Discretionary:			
40.00 Appropriation	4	2	4
Change in unpaid obligations:			
73.10 Total new obligations	4	2	4
73.20 Total outlays (gross)	−4	−2	−4
Outlays (gross), detail:			
86.90 Outlays from new discretionary authority	4	2	4
Net budget authority and outlays:			
89.00 Budget authority	4	2	4
90.00 Outlays	4	2	4

Title XV of Public Law 99–498 established the Institute of American Indian and Alaska Native Culture and Arts Development as an independent non-profit educational institution. The mission of the Institute is to serve as a multitribal center of higher education for Native Americans and is dedicated to the study, creative application, preservation and care of Indian arts and culture. The Institute is federally chartered and under the direction and control of a Board of Trustees appointed by the President of the United States.

Payment to the Institute.—This activity supports the operations of the Institute.

INTELLIGENCE COMMUNITY MANAGEMENT ACCOUNT

Federal Funds

General and special funds:

INTELLIGENCE COMMUNITY MANAGEMENT ACCOUNT

(INCLUDING TRANSFER OF FUNDS)

For necessary expenses of the Intelligence Community Management Account, [$158,015,000] *$137,631,000*, of which [$34,923,000] *$22,577,000* for the Advanced Research and Development Committee shall remain available until September 30, [2001] *2002*: *Provided*, That of the funds appropriated under this heading, $27,000,000 shall be transferred to the Department of Justice for the National Drug Intelligence Center to support the Department of Defense's counterdrug intelligence responsibilities, and of the said amount, $1,500,000 for Procurement shall remain available until September 30, [2002] *2003*, and $1,000,000 for Research, development, test and evaluation shall remain available until September 30, [2001] *2002*. *(Department of Defense Appropriations Act, 2000.)*

Program and Financing (in millions of dollars)

Identification code 95–0401–0–1–054	1999 actual	2000 est.	2001 est.
Obligations by program activity:			
10.00 Total new obligations	100	131	112
Budgetary resources available for obligation:			
21.40 Unobligated balance available, start of year	4	6	5
22.00 New budget authority (gross)	102	130	111
23.90 Total budgetary resources available for obligation	106	136	116
23.95 Total new obligations	−100	−131	−112
24.40 Unobligated balance available, end of year	6	5	4
New budget authority (gross), detail:			
Discretionary:			
40.00 Appropriation	129	157	138
41.00 Transferred to other accounts	−27	−27	−27
43.00 Appropriation (total discretionary)	102	130	111
Change in unpaid obligations:			
72.40 Unpaid obligations, start of year: Obligated balance, start of year	55	52	75
73.10 Total new obligations	100	131	112
73.20 Total outlays (gross)	−103	−108	−108
74.40 Unpaid obligations, end of year: Obligated balance, end of year	52	75	79
Outlays (gross), detail:			
86.90 Outlays from new discretionary authority	67	81	69
86.93 Outlays from discretionary balances	36	27	39
87.00 Total outlays (gross)	103	108	108
Net budget authority and outlays:			
89.00 Budget authority	102	130	111
90.00 Outlays	105	108	108

The Intelligence Community Management Account (ICMA) was established by Congressional direction to provide resources that directly support the Director of Central Intelligence (DCI) and the Intelligence Community as a whole in coordinating cross-program activities, improving budget oversight, and strengthening Community Management. The ICMA includes the Community Management Staff, the National Intelligence Council, the Center for Security Evaluations, the office of the Intelligence Community Chief Information Officer (CIO), the Advanced Research and Development program, the National Counterintelligence Center, and the National Drug Intelligence Center.

The Community Management Staff is the DCI's principal source of advice and assistance in planning and executing his intelligence community management responsibilities. These include: developing the National Foreign Intelligence Program budget; developing intelligence plans and requirements; and overseeing research and development activities. The Advanced Research and Development program is responsible for coordination of advanced technology within the Intelligence Community and for encouragement of investment in high risk/high return technologies. The National Intelligence Council provides analytical support to the DCI and national policy makers. The Center for Security Evaluation is responsible for evaluating and improving security capabilities at United States embassies. The office of the CIO supports technical activities and services of common Community concern regarding interoperability between national intelligence systems and consumers. The National Counterintelligence Center was established as the primary mechanism to coordinate U.S. government national-level counterintelligence policy and activities. The National Drug Intelligence Center was established to coordinate strategic organizational drug intelligence from national security and law enforcement agencies.

Object Classification (in millions of dollars)

Identification code 95–0401–0–1–054	1999 actual	2000 est.	2001 est.
11.3 Personnel compensation: Other than full-time permanent	23	27	27
12.1 Civilian personnel benefits	6	7	6
21.0 Travel and transportation of persons	2	2	2
25.2 Other services	64	90	72
26.0 Supplies and materials	1	1	1
31.0 Equipment	4	4	4

99.9 Total new obligations	100	131	112

Personnel Summary

Identification code 95–0401–0–1–054	1999 actual	2000 est.	2001 est.
1001 Total compensable workyears: Full-time equivalent employment	260	288	288

INTERNATIONAL TRADE COMMISSION

Federal Funds

General and special funds:

Salaries and Expenses

For necessary expenses of the International Trade Commission, including hire of passenger motor vehicles, and services as authorized by 5 U.S.C. 3109, and not to exceed $2,500 for official reception and representation expenses, **[**$44,495,000**]** *$49,100,000*, to remain available until expended. *(Department of Commerce and Related Agencies Appropriations Act, 2000, as enacted by section 1000(a)(1) of the Consolidated Appropriations Act, 2000 (P.L. 106–113).)*

Program and Financing (in millions of dollars)

Identification code 34–0100–0–1–153	1999 actual	2000 est.	2001 est.
Obligations by program activity:			
00.01 Research, investigations, and reports	44	47	49
10.00 Total new obligations	44	47	49
Budgetary resources available for obligation:			
21.40 Unobligated balance available, start of year	1	3	
22.00 New budget authority (gross)	45	44	49
22.10 Resources available from recoveries of prior year obligations	1		
23.90 Total budgetary resources available for obligation	47	47	49
23.95 Total new obligations	−44	−47	−49
24.40 Unobligated balance available, end of year	3		
New budget authority (gross), detail:			
Discretionary:			
40.05 Appropriation (indefinite)	44	44	49
Change in unpaid obligations:			
72.40 Unpaid obligations, start of year: Obligated balance, start of year	6	7	8
73.10 Total new obligations	44	47	49
73.20 Total outlays (gross)	−44	−44	−49
73.45 Adjustments in unexpired accounts	−1		
74.40 Unpaid obligations, end of year: Obligated balance, end of year	7	8	8
Outlays (gross), detail:			
86.90 Outlays from new discretionary authority	40	40	45
86.93 Outlays from discretionary balances	4	4	4
87.00 Total outlays (gross)	44	44	49
Net budget authority and outlays:			
89.00 Budget authority	45	44	49
90.00 Outlays	44	44	49

The U.S. International Trade Commission is an independent agency created by an act of Congress. The sources of the Commission's principal powers and duties are the Tariff Act of 1930; the Trade Act of 1974; the Agricultural Adjustment Act; the Trade and Tariff Act of 1984; the Omnibus Trade and Competitiveness Act of 1988; the North American Free Trade Agreement Implementation Act; and the Uruguay Round Agreements Act.

The Commission investigates and makes findings concerning *inter alia,* whether: (1) increased imports are a substantial cause of serious injury, or threat of serious injury, to a domestic industry; (2) a U.S. industry is being materially injured, or threatened with material injury, or the establishment of such an industry is being materially retarded, by reason of imported goods that are subsidized or are being sold at less than fair value; and (3) there are unfair import practices in import trade.

The Commission advises the President as to the probable economic effect on domestic industry and consumers of modification of duties and other barriers to trade which may be considered for inclusion in any proposed trade agreement with foreign countries. Further, the Commission, at the request of the U.S. Trade Representative, the House Committee on Ways and Means, the Senate Committee on Finance, or on the Commission's own motion, undertakes comprehensive studies and provides reports on issues relating to international trade and economic policy matters, and upon request provides other information and advice to the Congress and President on tariff and trade matters.

The Commission, in cooperation with the Secretary of the Treasury and the Secretary of Commerce, establishes for statistical purposes an enumeration of articles imported into the United States and exported from the United States, and seeks to establish comparability of such statistics with statistical programs for domestic production.

The Commission also issues a publication containing the U.S. tariff schedule and related matters and considers questions concerning the arrangements of such schedules and the classification of articles.

Pursuant to section 175 of the Trade Act of 1974, the budget estimates for the Commission are transmitted to Congress without revision by the President.

Object Classification (in millions of dollars)

Identification code 34–0100–0–1–153	1999 actual	2000 est.	2001 est.
Personnel compensation:			
11.1 Full-time permanent	27	26	27
11.3 Other than full-time permanent	1	1	1
11.5 Other personnel compensation	1	1	1
11.9 Total personnel compensation	29	28	29
12.1 Civilian personnel benefits	5	6	6
21.0 Travel and transportation of persons		1	1
23.1 Rental payments to GSA	5	5	5
23.3 Communications, utilities, and miscellaneous charges		1	1
25.2 Other services	2	2	3
25.3 Purchases of goods and services from Government accounts	1	2	2
26.0 Supplies and materials	1	1	1
31.0 Equipment	1	1	1
99.9 Total new obligations	44	47	49

Personnel Summary

Identification code 34–0100–0–1–153	1999 actual	2000 est.	2001 est.
1001 Total compensable workyears: Full-time equivalent employment	394	404	404

JAMES MADISON MEMORIAL FELLOWSHIP FOUNDATION

Trust Funds

James Madison Memorial Fellowship Trust Fund

Unavailable Collections (in millions of dollars)

Identification code 95–8282–0–7–502	1999 actual	2000 est.	2001 est.
Balance, start of year:			
01.99 Balance, start of year			
Receipts:			
02.02 Earnings on investments	3	3	3
Appropriation:			
05.01 James Madison Memorial Fellowship Trust Fund	−3	−3	−3
07.99 Total balance, end of year			

JAMES MADISON MEMORIAL FELLOWSHIP TRUST FUND—Continued

Program and Financing (in millions of dollars)

Identification code 95–8282–0–7–502	1999 actual	2000 est.	2001 est.
Obligations by program activity:			
00.01 Fellowship awards	1	1	1
00.02 Program administration	1	1	1
10.00 Total new obligations	2	2	2
Budgetary resources available for obligation:			
21.40 Unobligated balance available, start of year	42	43	44
22.00 New budget authority (gross)	3	3	3
23.90 Total budgetary resources available for obligation	45	46	47
23.95 Total new obligations	−2	−2	−2
24.40 Unobligated balance available, end of year	43	44	45
New budget authority (gross), detail:			
Mandatory:			
60.27 Appropriation (trust fund, indefinite)	3	3	3
Change in unpaid obligations:			
73.10 Total new obligations	2	2	2
73.20 Total outlays (gross)	−2	−2	−2
Outlays (gross), detail:			
86.97 Outlays from new mandatory authority	2	2	2
Net budget authority and outlays:			
89.00 Budget authority	3	3	3
90.00 Outlays	2	2	2
Memorandum (non-add) entries:			
92.01 Total investments, start of year: U.S. securities: Par value	42	43	44
92.02 Total investments, end of year: U.S. securities: Par value	43	44	45

Public Laws 99–500, 101–208, and 102–221 established the James Madison Memorial Fellowship Foundation to operate a fellowship program to encourage graduate study of the framing, principles, and history of the American Constitution. Appropriations of $10 million in 1988 and 1989 established the foundation's trust fund. The funds have been invested by the Secretary of the Treasury in U.S. Treasury securities, and the interest earned on these funds is available for carrying out the activities of the foundation. Funds raised from private sources and the surcharges from commemorative coin sales are also placed in the trust fund.

The foundation is authorized to award graduate fellowships of up to $24,000 to high school teachers of American history, American government, and social studies. College seniors and recent college graduates who want to become secondary school teachers of these subjects are also eligible.

Fellowship awards.—This activity is comprised of fellowship awards to cover educational expenses. It also supports the foundation's annual Summer Institute on the U.S. Constitution, which all current fellows are required to attend. The Institute is an intensive educational experience that will ensure that all fellows know the history of the framing, ratification, and implementation of the U.S. Constitution and the Bill of Rights. The foundation awarded 65 fellowships in 1999 and plans to award at least 60 in both 2000 and 2001.

Program administration.—This activity covers the costs of planning, fund-raising, and the operation of the fellowship program.

Object Classification (in millions of dollars)

Identification code 95–8282–0–7–502	1999 actual	2000 est.	2001 est.
41.0 Direct obligations: Grants, subsidies, and contributions	1	1	1
99.5 Below reporting threshold	1	1	1
99.9 Total new obligations	2	2	2

Personnel Summary

Identification code 95–8282–0–7–502	1999 actual	2000 est.	2001 est.
1001 Total compensable workyears: Full-time equivalent employment	6	6	6

JAPAN-UNITED STATES FRIENDSHIP COMMISSION

Trust Funds

JAPAN-UNITED STATES FRIENDSHIP TRUST FUND

Unavailable Collections (in millions of dollars)

Identification code 95–8025–0–7–154	1999 actual	2000 est.	2001 est.
Balance, start of year:			
01.99 Balance, start of year	16	41	41
Receipts:			
02.01 Interest on investment in public debt securities	28	3	3
04.00 Total: Balances and collections	44	44	44
Appropriation:			
05.01 Japan-United States friendship trust fund	−3	−3	−3
07.99 Total balance, end of year	41	41	41

Program and Financing (in millions of dollars)

Identification code 95–8025–0–7–154	1999 actual	2000 est.	2001 est.
Obligations by program activity:			
00.01 Grants	2	2	2
00.02 Administration	1	1	1
10.00 Total new obligations	3	3	3
Budgetary resources available for obligation:			
22.00 New budget authority (gross)	3	3	3
23.95 Total new obligations	−3	−3	−3
New budget authority (gross), detail:			
Mandatory:			
60.27 Appropriation (trust fund, indefinite)	3	3	3
Change in unpaid obligations:			
72.40 Unpaid obligations, start of year: Obligated balance, start of year		1	
73.10 Total new obligations	3	3	3
73.20 Total outlays (gross)	−2	−4	−3
74.40 Unpaid obligations, end of year: Obligated balance, end of year	1		
Outlays (gross), detail:			
86.97 Outlays from new mandatory authority	2	3	3
86.98 Outlays from mandatory balances		1	
87.00 Total outlays (gross)	2	4	3
Net budget authority and outlays:			
89.00 Budget authority	3	3	3
90.00 Outlays	2	4	3
Memorandum (non-add) entries:			
92.01 Total investments, start of year: U.S. securities: Par value	16	42	41
92.02 Total investments, end of year: U.S. securities: Par value	42	41	41

The Japan-United States Friendship Act of 1975 established the Japan-United States Friendship Trust Fund and created the Japan-United States Friendship Commission to make grants for the promotion of scholarly, cultural, and artistic activities between Japan and the United States. The Commission is authorized to make expenditures from the fund in an amount not to exceed 5 percent annually of the fund's original principal to pay Commission expenses and make grants to support Japanese studies in American universities, policy oriented research, faculty and other professional exchanges, public affairs programs, and other cultural and educational activities primarily in the United States.

Object Classification (in millions of dollars)

Identification code 95–8025–0–7–154	1999 actual	2000 est.	2001 est.
41.0 Direct obligations: Grants, subsidies, and contributions	2	2	2
99.5 Below reporting threshold	1	1	1
99.9 Total new obligations	3	3	3

Personnel Summary

Identification code 95–8025–0–7–154	1999 actual	2000 est.	2001 est.
1001 Total compensable workyears: Full-time equivalent employment	4	4	4

LEGAL SERVICES CORPORATION

Federal Funds

General and special funds:

PAYMENT TO THE LEGAL SERVICES CORPORATION

For payment to the Legal Services Corporation to carry out the purposes of the Legal Services Corporation Act of 1974, as amended, [$305,000,000] *$340,000,000*, of which [$289,000,000] *$313,000,000* is for basic field programs and required independent audits; [$2,100,000] *$2,400,000* is for the Office of Inspector General, of which such amounts as may be necessary may be used to conduct additional audits of recipients; [$8,900,000] *$12,500,000* is for management and administration, *of which $1,540,000 is for additional Compliance and Enforcement funding*; [and $5,000,000] *$10,000,000* is for client self-help and information technology; *and $2,100,000 is for a Legal Needs Assessment*. *(Departments of Commerce, Justice, and State, the Judiciary and Related Agencies Appropriations Act, 2000, as enacted by section 1000(a)(1) of the Consolidated Appropriations Act, 2000 (P.L. 106–113).)*

Program and Financing (in millions of dollars)

Identification code 20–0501–0–1–752	1999 actual	2000 est.	2001 est.
Obligations by program activity:			
10.00 Total new obligations (object class 41.0)	300	304	340
Budgetary resources available for obligation:			
22.00 New budget authority (gross)	300	304	340
23.95 Total new obligations	–300	–304	–340
New budget authority (gross), detail:			
Discretionary:			
40.00 Appropriation	300	305	340
40.76 Reduction pursuant to P.L. 106–113		–1	
43.00 Appropriation (total discretionary)	300	304	340
Change in unpaid obligations:			
72.40 Unpaid obligations, start of year: Obligated balance, start of year	23	25	26
73.10 Total new obligations	300	304	340
73.20 Total outlays (gross)	–298	–303	–337
74.40 Unpaid obligations, end of year: Obligated balance, end of year	25	26	29
Outlays (gross), detail:			
86.90 Outlays from new discretionary authority	275	278	311
86.93 Outlays from discretionary balances	23	25	26
87.00 Total outlays (gross)	298	303	337
Net budget authority and outlays:			
89.00 Budget authority	300	304	340
90.00 Outlays	298	303	337

The Legal Services Corporation distributes appropriated funds to local non-profit organizations that provide free civil legal assistance, according to locally-determined priorities, to people living in poverty. The Congress chartered the corporation as a private, non-profit entity outside of the Federal government.

ADMINISTRATIVE PROVISION—LEGAL SERVICES CORPORATION

None of the funds appropriated in this Act to the Legal Services Corporation shall be expended for any purpose prohibited or limited by, or contrary to any of the provisions of, sections 501, 502, 503, 504, 505, and 506 of Public Law 105–119, and all funds appropriated in this Act to the Legal Services Corporation shall be subject to the same terms and conditions set forth in such sections, except that all references in sections 502 and 503 to 1997 and 1998 shall be deemed to refer instead to [1999] *2000* and [2000] *2001*, respectively. *(Departments of Commerce, Justice, and State, the Judiciary and Related Agencies Appropriations Act, 2000, as enacted by section 1000(a)(3) of the Consolidated Appropriations Act, 2000 (P.L. 106–113).)*

MARINE MAMMAL COMMISSION

Federal Funds

General and special funds:

SALARIES AND EXPENSES

For necessary expenses of the Marine Mammal Commission as authorized by title II of Public Law 92–522, as amended, [$1,270,000] *$1,400,000*. *(Departments of Commerce, Justice, and State, the Judiciary and Related Agencies Appropriations Act, 2000, as enacted by section 1000(a)(1) of the Consolidated Appropriations Act, 2000 (P.L. 106–113).)*

Program and Financing (in millions of dollars)

Identification code 95–2200–0–1–302	1999 actual	2000 est.	2001 est.
Obligations by program activity:			
10.00 Total new obligations (object class 11.1)	1	1	1
Budgetary resources available for obligation:			
22.00 New budget authority (gross)	1	1	1
23.95 Total new obligations	–1	–1	–1
New budget authority (gross), detail:			
Discretionary:			
40.00 Appropriation	1	1	1
Change in unpaid obligations:			
73.10 Total new obligations	1	1	1
73.20 Total outlays (gross)	–1	–1	–1
Outlays (gross), detail:			
86.90 Outlays from new discretionary authority	1	1	1
Net budget authority and outlays:			
89.00 Budget authority	1	1	1
90.00 Outlays	1	1	1

The Commission recommends national and international marine mammal policies; develops scientific and management programs; reviews the status of marine mammal populations; recommends to the Secretaries of Commerce, Interior, and State steps to conserve marine mammals domestically and internationally; and, manages a research program.

Personnel Summary

Identification code 95–2200–0–1–302	1999 actual	2000 est.	2001 est.
1001 Total compensable workyears: Full-time equivalent employment	9	11	11

MERIT SYSTEMS PROTECTION BOARD

Federal Funds

General and special funds:

SALARIES AND EXPENSES

(INCLUDING TRANSFER OF FUNDS)

For necessary expenses to carry out functions of the Merit Systems Protection Board pursuant to Reorganization Plan Numbered 2 of 1978 and the Civil Service Reform Act of 1978, including services as authorized by 5 U.S.C. 3109, rental of conference rooms in the District of Columbia and elsewhere, hire of passenger motor vehicles, and direct procurement of survey printing, [$27,586,000] *$28,857,000*, together with not to exceed $2,430,000 for administrative expenses to adjudicate retirement appeals to be transferred from the Civil Service Retirement and Disability Fund in amounts determined by the Merit Systems Protection Board. *(Independent Agencies Appropriations Act, 2000.)*

Program and Financing (in millions of dollars)

Identification code 41–0100–0–1–805		1999 actual	2000 est.	2001 est.
	Obligations by program activity:			
	Direct program:			
00.01	Adjudication	22	24	25
00.02	Merit system studies	1	1	1
00.03	Management support	3	3	3
09.00	Reimbursable program	2	2	2
10.00	Total new obligations	28	30	31
	Budgetary resources available for obligation:			
22.00	New budget authority (gross)	28	29	31
23.95	Total new obligations	−28	−30	−31
	New budget authority (gross), detail:			
	Discretionary:			
40.00	Appropriation	26	27	29
68.00	Spending authority from offsetting collections: Offsetting collections (cash)	2	2	2
70.00	Total new budget authority (gross)	28	29	31
	Change in unpaid obligations:			
72.40	Unpaid obligations, start of year: Obligated balance, start of year	4	5	5
73.10	Total new obligations	28	30	31
73.20	Total outlays (gross)	−28	−29	−31
74.40	Unpaid obligations, end of year: Obligated balance, end of year	5	5	6
	Outlays (gross), detail:			
86.90	Outlays from new discretionary authority	25	27	29
86.93	Outlays from discretionary balances	2	2	2
87.00	Total outlays (gross)	28	29	31
	Offsets:			
	Against gross budget authority and outlays:			
88.00	Offsetting collections (cash) from: Federal sources	−2	−2	−2
	Net budget authority and outlays:			
89.00	Budget authority	26	27	29
90.00	Outlays	25	27	29

The mission of the Merit Systems Protection Board (MSPB) is to assist Federal agencies in running a merit-based civil service system. The MSPB accomplishes its mission on a case-by-case basis through hearing and deciding employee appeals, and on a systematic basis by reviewing significant actions and regulations of the Office of Personnel Management (OPM) and conducting studies of the civil service and other merit systems. The intended results (outcomes) of MSPB's efforts are to assure that (1) personnel actions taken against employees are processed within the law, and (2) actions taken by OPM and other agencies support and enhance Federal merit principles.

The number of decisions issued by the Board is shown in the following table:

DECISIONS ISSUED

	1999 actual	*2000 est.*	*2001 est.*
Retirement (legal-disability)	1,931	2,000	2,000
Adverse action appeals	3,897	4,000	4,000
Reduction-in-force appeals	564	700	700
Other	3,414	3,500	3,500

Object Classification (in millions of dollars)

Identification code 41–0100–0–1–805		1999 actual	2000 est.	2001 est.
	Direct obligations:			
	Personnel compensation:			
11.1	Full-time permanent	15	16	16
11.3	Other than full-time permanent	1	1	1
11.9	Total personnel compensation	16	17	17
12.1	Civilian personnel benefits	3	3	3
23.1	Rental payments to GSA	2	2	2
23.3	Communications, utilities, and miscellaneous charges	1	1	1
25.2	Other services	3	3	3
31.0	Equipment	....	1	1
99.0	Subtotal, direct obligations	25	27	27
99.0	Reimbursable obligations	2	2	2
99.5	Below reporting threshold	1	1	2
99.9	Total new obligations	28	30	31

Personnel Summary

Identification code 41–0100–0–1–805		1999 actual	2000 est.	2001 est.
	Direct:			
1001	Total compensable workyears: Full-time equivalent employment	208	216	216
	Reimbursable:			
2001	Total compensable workyears: Full-time equivalent employment	29	29	29

MORRIS K. UDALL SCHOLARSHIP AND EXCELLENCE IN NATIONAL ENVIRONMENTAL POLICY FOUNDATION

Federal Funds

General and special funds:

FEDERAL PAYMENT TO MORRIS K. UDALL SCHOLARSHIP AND EXCELLENCE IN NATIONAL ENVIRONMENTAL POLICY FOUNDATION

For payment to the Morris K. Udall Scholarship and Excellence in National Environmental *Policy* Trust Fund, to be available for the purposes of Public Law 102–252, [$2,000,000] *$3,000,000*, to remain available until expended. *(Independent Agencies Appropriations Act, 2000.)*

Program and Financing (in millions of dollars)

Identification code 95–0900–0–1–502		1999 actual	2000 est.	2001 est.
	Obligations by program activity:			
10.00	Total new obligations (object class 25.3)	....	2	3
	Budgetary resources available for obligation:			
22.00	New budget authority (gross)	....	2	3
23.95	Total new obligations	....	−2	−3
	New budget authority (gross), detail:			
	Discretionary:			
40.00	Appropriation	....	2	3
	Change in unpaid obligations:			
73.10	Total new obligations	....	2	3
73.20	Total outlays (gross)	....	−2	−3
	Outlays (gross), detail:			
86.90	Outlays from new discretionary authority	....	2	3
	Net budget authority and outlays:			
89.00	Budget authority	....	2	3

90.00 Outlays		2	3

Summary of Budget Authority and Outlays

(in millions of dollars)

	1999 actual	2000 est.	2001 est.
Enacted/requested:			
Budget Authority		2	3
Outlays		2	3
Legislative proposal, not subject to PAYGO:			
Budget Authority			–1
Outlays			–1
Total:			
Budget Authority		2	2
Outlays		2	2

The General Fund payment to the Morris K. Udall Fund is being used to invest in Treasury securities with maturities suitable to the needs of the Fund. Interest earnings from the investments will be used to carry out the activities of the Morris K. Udall Foundation. The Foundation will award scholarships, fellowships and grants, and will fund activities of the Udall Center.

Federal Payment to the Morris K. Udall Scholarship and Excellence in National Environmental Policy Foundation

(Legislative proposal, not subject to PAYGO)

Program and Financing (in millions of dollars)

Identification code 95–0900–2–1–502	1999 actual	2000 est.	2001 est.
Obligations by program activity:			
10.00 Total new obligations (object class 25.3)			–1
Budgetary resources available for obligation:			
22.00 New budget authority (gross)			–1
23.95 Total new obligations			1
New budget authority (gross), detail:			
Discretionary:			
40.00 Appropriation			–1
Change in unpaid obligations:			
73.10 Total new obligations			–1
73.20 Total outlays (gross)			1
Outlays (gross), detail:			
86.90 Outlays from new discretionary authority			–1
Net budget authority and outlays:			
89.00 Budget authority			–1
90.00 Outlays			–1

Proposed legislation amending the Morris K. Udall Scholarship and Excellence in National Environmental and Native American Public Policy Act of 1992 would establish a Native Nations Institute (NNI) to provide Native Americans with leadership and management training. Upon enactment of needed authorizing legislation, the Administration will submit appropriations language proposing to fund the new Native Nations Institute at $1.5 million, offset by a reduction of the same amount to the Administration's request for the general fund payment to the Morris K. Udall Trust Fund.

Environmental Dispute Resolution Fund

For payment to the Environmental Dispute Resolution Fund to carry out activities authorized in the Environmental Policy and Conflict Resolution Act of 1998, $1,250,000, to remain available until expended. *(Independent Agencies Appropriations Act, 2000.)*

Unavailable Collections (in millions of dollars)

Identification code 95–5415–0–2–306	1999 actual	2000 est.	2001 est.
Balance, start of year:			
01.99 Balance, start of year			
Receipts:			
02.01 Fees for services		1	1
Appropriation:			
05.01 Environmental dispute resolution fund			–1
07.99 Total balance, end of year			

Program and Financing (in millions of dollars)

Identification code 95–5415–0–2–306	1999 actual	2000 est.	2001 est.
Obligations by program activity:			
10.00 Total new obligations	1	2	3
Budgetary resources available for obligation:			
21.40 Unobligated balance available, start of year		3	2
22.00 New budget authority (gross)	4	1	2
23.90 Total budgetary resources available for obligation	4	4	4
23.95 Total new obligations	–1	–2	–3
24.40 Unobligated balance available, end of year	3	2	1
New budget authority (gross), detail:			
Discretionary:			
40.00 Appropriation	4	1	1
Mandatory:			
60.25 Appropriation (special fund, indefinite)			1
70.00 Total new budget authority (gross)	4	1	2
Change in unpaid obligations:			
73.10 Total new obligations	1	2	3
73.20 Total outlays (gross)	–1	–2	–3
Outlays (gross), detail:			
86.90 Outlays from new discretionary authority	3	1	1
86.93 Outlays from discretionary balances		1	
86.97 Outlays from new mandatory authority			1
87.00 Total outlays (gross)	1	2	3
Net budget authority and outlays:			
89.00 Budget authority	4	1	2
90.00 Outlays	1	2	3
Memorandum (non-add) entries:			
92.01 Total investments, start of year: U.S. securities: Par value		3	3
92.02 Total investments, end of year: U.S. securities: Par value	3	3	3

In 1998, Public Law 105–156 established the U.S. Institute for Environmental Conflict Resolution as part of the Morris K. Udall Foundation. The Institute is designed to conduct environmental conflict resolution (ECR) and training, and provides mainly Federal agencies with assessment, mediation, and other related services in connection with a dispute or conflict related to the environment, public lands, or natural resources. Contracting sponsors or parties pay fees into the Environmental Dispute Resolution Fund for environmental dispute resolution services. In 1999, its initial year of operation, the Institute began a project with the Ninth Circuit Court of Appeals to demonstrate ECR processes in Federal trial courts. In 2000, the Institute will expand its activities through a Federal partnership program, and through demonstration projects with private sector stakeholders.

Object Classification (in millions of dollars)

Identification code 95–5415–0–2–306	1999 actual	2000 est.	2001 est.
11.1 Direct obligations: Personnel compensation: Full-time permanent		1	2
99.5 Below reporting threshold	1	1	1
99.9 Total new obligations	1	2	3

General and special funds—Continued

ENVIRONMENTAL DISPUTE RESOLUTION FUND—Continued

Personnel Summary

Identification code 95–5415–0–2–306	1999 actual	2000 est.	2001 est.
1001 Total compensable workyears: Full-time equivalent employment	7	16	16

NATIVE NATIONS INSTITUTE

(Legislative proposal, not subject to PAYGO)

Program and Financing (in millions of dollars)

Identification code 95–5467–2–2–502	1999 actual	2000 est.	2001 est.
Obligations by program activity:			
10.00 Total new obligations			2
Budgetary resources available for obligation:			
22.00 New budget authority (gross)			2
23.95 Total new obligations			−2
New budget authority (gross), detail:			
Discretionary:			
40.00 Appropriation			2
Change in unpaid obligations:			
73.10 Total new obligations			2
73.20 Total outlays (gross)			−1
Outlays (gross), detail:			
86.90 Outlays from new discretionary authority			1
Net budget authority and outlays:			
89.00 Budget authority			2
90.00 Outlays			1

Proposed legislation amending the Morris K. Udall Scholarship and Excellence in National Environmental and Native American Public Policy Act of 1992 would establish the Native Nations Institute (NNI). NNI will provide Native Americans with leadership and management training and policy analysis. The budget proposes $1.5 million to create the new Native Nations Institute.

Object Classification (in millions of dollars)

Identification code 95–5467–2–2–502	1999 actual	2000 est.	2001 est.
11.1 Personnel compensation: Full-time permanent			1
41.0 Grants, subsidies, and contributions			1
99.9 Total new obligations			2

Personnel Summary

Identification code 95–5467–2–2–502	1999 actual	2000 est.	2001 est.
1001 Total compensable workyears: Full-time equivalent employment			10

Trust Funds

MORRIS K. UDALL SCHOLARSHIP AND EXCELLENCE IN NATIONAL ENVIRONMENTAL POLICY FOUNDATION

Unavailable Collections (in millions of dollars)

Identification code 95–8615–0–7–502	1999 actual	2000 est.	2001 est.
Balance, start of year:			
01.99 Balance, start of year	20	20	22
Receipts:			
02.01 General fund payments		2	3
02.02 Interest on investments	1	1	2
02.03 General fund payments, legislative proposal not subject to PAYGO			−1
02.99 Total receipts	1	3	4
04.00 Total: Balances and collections	21	23	26
Appropriation:			
05.01 Morris K. Udall Scholarship fund	−1	−1	−2
07.99 Total balance, end of year	20	22	24

Program and Financing (in millions of dollars)

Identification code 95–8615–0–7–502	1999 actual	2000 est.	2001 est.
Obligations by program activity:			
10.00 Total new obligations (object class 41.0)	1	1	2
Budgetary resources available for obligation:			
21.40 Unobligated balance available, start of year	3	3	3
22.00 New budget authority (gross)	1	1	2
23.90 Total budgetary resources available for obligation	4	4	5
23.95 Total new obligations	−1	−1	−2
24.40 Unobligated balance available, end of year	3	3	3
New budget authority (gross), detail:			
Mandatory:			
60.27 Appropriation (trust fund, indefinite)	1	1	2
Change in unpaid obligations:			
73.10 Total new obligations	1	1	2
73.20 Total outlays (gross)	−1	−1	−2
Outlays (gross), detail:			
86.97 Outlays from new mandatory authority	1	1	2
Net budget authority and outlays:			
89.00 Budget authority	1	1	2
90.00 Outlays	1	1	2
Memorandum (non-add) entries:			
92.01 Total investments, start of year: U.S. securities: Par value	24	24	26
92.02 Total investments, end of year: U.S. securities: Par value	24	26	29

Public Law 102–259 established the Morris K. Udall Scholarship and Excellence in National Environmental Policy Foundation to provide educational resources to promote studies in the natural environment and Native American public health and tribal policy. In addition, the Foundation is authorized to fund the Udall Center for Studies in Public Policy at the University of Arizona to carry out and manage programs established by the Foundation relating especially to a program of environmental conflict resolution.

In 1999, the Foundation awarded 75 undergraduate scholarships. Twelve Native American Congressional Summer Internship Program recipients spent ten weeks in Congressional offices and the White House participating in a program created by the Udall Foundation. For the third year, the Foundation awarded two Graduate Fellowships to Ph.D. candidates whose dissertation topics were in the area of environmental public policy and conflict resolution and whose work contributed to the mission of the Foundation. The Foundation, in conjunction with the Udall Center for Studies in Public Policy at the University of Arizona, sponsored a national conference on economic development on Indian reservations titled "Building American Indian Nations for the 21st Century."

In 2000 and 2001, the Foundation will maintain its current level of scholarships, fellowships and internships.

Personnel Summary

Identification code 95–8615–0–7–502	1999 actual	2000 est.	2001 est.
1001 Total compensable workyears: Full-time equivalent employment	4	6	4

NATIONAL ARCHIVES AND RECORDS ADMINISTRATION

Federal Funds

General and special funds:

OPERATING EXPENSES

For necessary expenses in connection with the administration of the National Archives (including the Information Security Oversight Office) and archived Federal records and related activities, as provided by law, and for expenses necessary for the review and declassification of documents, and for the hire of passenger motor vehicles, [$180,398,000] *$209,393,000*: *Provided*, That the Archivist of the United States is authorized to use any excess funds available from the amount borrowed for construction of the National Archives facility, for expenses necessary to provide adequate storage for holdings. *(1 U.S.C. 106a, 106b, 112, 113, 201; 3 U.S.C. 6, 11–13; 4 U.S.C. 141–146; 5 U.S.C. App. 1; 25 U.S.C. 199a; 44 U.S.C. 710, 711, 729, Chapters 15, 21, 22, 25, 29, 31, 33; Public Law 98–497, Public Law 93–526, Executive Orders 11440, 10530, 11030, 12656, 12829, 12958, 13142; Independent Agencies Appropriations Act, 2000.)*

Program and Financing (in millions of dollars)

Identification code 88–0300–0–1–804		1999 actual	2000 est.	2001 est.
	Obligations by program activity:			
	Direct program:			
00.01	Records services	191	142	171
00.02	Archives related services	10	8	9
00.04	Archives II facility	25	24	23
09.88	Reimbursable program	34	3	3
10.00	Total new obligations	260	177	206
	Budgetary resources available for obligation:			
21.40	Unobligated balance available, start of year	13	14	14
22.00	New budget authority (gross)	262	177	206
23.90	Total budgetary resources available for obligation	275	191	220
23.95	Total new obligations	−260	−177	−206
23.98	Unobligated balance expiring or withdrawn	−1		
24.40	Unobligated balance available, end of year	14	14	14
	New budget authority (gross), detail:			
	Discretionary:			
40.00	Appropriation	224	181	209
40.47	Portion applied to repay debt	−5	−6	−6
40.76	Reduction pursuant to P.L. 106–113		−1	
42.00	Transferred from other accounts	7		
43.00	Appropriation (total discretionary)	226	174	203
68.00	Spending authority from offsetting collections: Offsetting collections (cash)	36	3	3
70.00	Total new budget authority (gross)	262	177	206
	Change in unpaid obligations:			
72.40	Unpaid obligations, start of year: Obligated balance, start of year	27	36	38
73.10	Total new obligations	260	177	206
73.20	Total outlays (gross)	−248	−175	−204
73.40	Adjustments in expired accounts (net)	−3		
74.40	Unpaid obligations, end of year: Obligated balance, end of year	36	38	40
	Outlays (gross), detail:			
86.90	Outlays from new discretionary authority	235	167	194
86.93	Outlays from discretionary balances	14	9	9
87.00	Total outlays (gross)	248	175	204
	Offsets:			
	Against gross budget authority and outlays:			
	Offsetting collections (cash) from:			
88.00	Federal sources	−34	−3	−3
88.40	Non-Federal sources	−2		
88.90	Total, offsetting collections (cash)	−36	−3	−3
	Net budget authority and outlays:			
89.00	Budget authority	226	174	203
90.00	Outlays	212	172	201
	Memorandum (non-add) entries:			
92.01	Total investments, start of year: U.S. securities: Par value	14	14	14
92.02	Total investments, end of year: U.S. securities: Par value	14	14	14

The National Archives and Records Administration provides for basic operations dealing with management of the Government's archives and records, operation of Presidential Libraries, and for the review for declassification of classified security information.

Records services.—This activity provides for selecting, preserving, describing, and making available to the general public, scholars, and Federal agencies the permanently valuable historical records of the Federal Government; the historical materials and Presidential records in Presidential Libraries; for preparing related publications and exhibit programs; and for conducting the appraisal of all Federal records.

Through the records declassification program, historically valuable information in the records of the Federal Government and in donated historical materials are made available to the public by declassifying as much information as possible without endangering the national security.

This activity also provides oversight for the information security program established by Executive Order 12958 and reports annually to the President on the status of that program. It is also responsible for policy oversight for the National Industrial Security Program established under Executive Order 12829.

Archives related services.—This activity provides for the publication of the *Federal Register* the *Code of Federal Regulations,* the *U.S. Statutes-at-Large,* and Presidential documents, and for a program to improve the quality of regulations and the public's access to them.

This activity also includes the administration and reference services portion for the National Historical Publications and Records Commission. This Commission makes grants nationwide to preserve and publish records that document American history.

Archives II Facility.—Provides for construction and related services of the new archival facility which was opened to the public in 1993. Costs of construction are financed by $302 million of federally guaranteed debt issued in 1989. Since 1994 and continuing in 2001, the Archives seeks appropriations for the annual payments for interest and redemption of debt to be made under the contract for construction and related services.

Object Classification (in millions of dollars)

Identification code 88–0300–0–1–804		1999 actual	2000 est.	2001 est.
	Direct obligations:			
	Personnel compensation:			
11.1	Full-time permanent	75	58	65
11.3	Other than full-time permanent	3	2	3
11.5	Other personnel compensation	1	1	1
11.9	Total personnel compensation	79	61	69
12.1	Civilian personnel benefits	18	17	20
21.0	Travel and transportation of persons	1	2	2
22.0	Transportation of things			2
23.1	Rental payments to GSA	30	5	6
23.3	Communications, utilities, and miscellaneous charges	9	11	11
24.0	Printing and reproduction	3	2	2
25.1	Advisory and assistance services	2	1	1
25.2	Other services	10	4	15
25.3	Purchases of goods and services from Government accounts	4	4	4
25.4	Operation and maintenance of facilities	27	28	29
25.7	Operation and maintenance of equipment	5	4	4
26.0	Supplies and materials	3	5	5
31.0	Equipment	8	6	10
32.0	Land and structures	2		
43.0	Interest and dividends	25	24	23
99.0	Subtotal, direct obligations	226	174	203

General and special funds—Continued

OPERATING EXPENSES—Continued

Object Classification (in millions of dollars)—Continued

Identification code 88–0300–0–1–804	1999 actual	2000 est.	2001 est.
99.0 Reimbursable obligations	34	3	3
99.9 Total new obligations	260	177	206

Personnel Summary

Identification code 88–0300–0–1–804	1999 actual	2000 est.	2001 est.
Direct:			
1001 Total compensable workyears: Full-time equivalent employment	1,840	1,297	1,362
Reimbursable:			
2001 Total compensable workyears: Full-time equivalent employment	467	76	76

REPAIRS AND RESTORATION

For the repair, alteration, and improvement of archives facilities, and to provide adequate storage for holdings, [$22,418,000] *$92,950,000*, to remain available until expended*, of which $88,000,000 is to complete the renovation of the National Archives Building*. *(Independent Agencies Appropriations Act, 2000.)*

Program and Financing (in millions of dollars)

Identification code 88–0302–0–1–804	1999 actual	2000 est.	2001 est.
Obligations by program activity:			
10.00 Total new obligations (object class 25.2)	9	22	93
Budgetary resources available for obligation:			
21.40 Unobligated balance available, start of year	18	21	20
22.00 New budget authority (gross)	11	22	93
23.90 Total budgetary resources available for obligation	29	43	113
23.95 Total new obligations	−9	−22	−93
24.40 Unobligated balance available, end of year	21	20	20
New budget authority (gross), detail:			
Discretionary:			
40.00 Appropriation	11	22	93
Change in unpaid obligations:			
72.40 Unpaid obligations, start of year: Obligated balance, start of year	7	10	21
73.10 Total new obligations	9	22	93
73.20 Total outlays (gross)	−6	−11	−65
74.40 Unpaid obligations, end of year: Obligated balance, end of year	10	21	49
Outlays (gross), detail:			
86.90 Outlays from new discretionary authority	6	11	47
86.93 Outlays from discretionary balances			18
87.00 Total outlays (gross)	6	11	65
Net budget authority and outlays:			
89.00 Budget authority	11	22	93
90.00 Outlays	6	11	65

This account provides for the repair, alteration, and improvement of Archives facilities and Presidential Libraries nationwide, and provides adequate storage for holdings. It will better enable the National Archives to maintain its facilities in proper condition for public visitors, researchers, and employees in NARA facilities, and also maintain the structural integrity of the buildings.

NATIONAL HISTORICAL PUBLICATIONS AND RECORDS COMMISSION

GRANTS PROGRAM

[(INCLUDING RESCISSION OF FUNDS)]

For necessary expenses for allocations and grants for historical publications and records as authorized by 44 U.S.C. 2504, as amended, [$6,250,000] *$6,000,000*, to remain available until expended[: *Provided*, That of the funds appropriated under this heading in Public Law 105–277, $2,000,000 are rescinded: *Provided further*, That the Treasury and General Government Appropriations Act, 1999 (as contained in division A, section 101(h), of the Omnibus Consolidated and Emergency Supplemental Appropriations Act, 1999 (Public Law 105–277)) is amended in title IV, under the heading "National Historical Publications and Records Commission, Grants Program" by striking the proviso]. *(Independent Agencies Appropriations Act, 2000.)*

Program and Financing (in millions of dollars)

Identification code 88–0301–0–1–804	1999 actual	2000 est.	2001 est.
Obligations by program activity:			
10.00 Total new obligations (object class 41.0)	6	6	6
Budgetary resources available for obligation:			
21.40 Unobligated balance available, start of year		4	
22.00 New budget authority (gross)	10	4	6
23.90 Total budgetary resources available for obligation	10	8	6
23.95 Total new obligations	−6	−6	−6
24.40 Unobligated balance available, end of year	4		
New budget authority (gross), detail:			
Discretionary:			
40.00 Appropriation	10	6	6
40.36 Unobligated balance rescinded		−2	
43.00 Appropriation (total discretionary)	10	4	6
Change in unpaid obligations:			
72.40 Unpaid obligations, start of year: Obligated balance, start of year	6	8	8
73.10 Total new obligations	6	6	6
73.20 Total outlays (gross)	−5	−6	−6
74.40 Unpaid obligations, end of year: Obligated balance, end of year	8	8	8
Outlays (gross), detail:			
86.90 Outlays from new discretionary authority	5	4	6
86.93 Outlays from discretionary balances		2	
87.00 Total outlays (gross)	5	6	6
Net budget authority and outlays:			
89.00 Budget authority	10	4	6
90.00 Outlays	5	6	6

National Historical Publications and Records Commission Grants.—This program provides for grants funding that the Commission makes, nationwide, to preserve and publish records that document American history. Administered within the National Archives, which preserves Federal records, the NHPRC helps state, local, and private institutions preserve non-Federal records, helps publish the papers of major figures in American history, and helps archivists and records managers improve their techniques, training, and ability to serve a range of information users.

Intragovernmental fund:

RECORDS CENTER REVOLVING FUND

[(a) ESTABLISHMENT OF FUND.—There is hereby established in the Treasury a revolving fund to be available for expenses and equipment necessary to provide for storage and related services for all temporary and pre-archival Federal records, which are to be stored or stored at Federal National and Regional Records Centers by agencies and other instrumentalities of the Federal Government. The Fund shall be available without fiscal year limitation for expenses necessary for operation of these activities.]

[(b) START-UP CAPITAL.—

(1) There is appropriated $22,000,000 as initial capitalization of the Fund.

(2) In addition, the initial capital of the Fund shall include the fair and reasonable value at the Fund's inception of the inventories, equipment, receivables, and other assets, less the liabilities, transferred to the Fund. The Archivist of the United States is authorized to accept inventories, equipment, receivables and other assets from other Federal entities that were used to provide for storage and related services for temporary and pre-archival Federal records.]

[(c) USER CHARGES.—The Fund shall be credited with user charges received from other Federal Government accounts as payment for providing personnel, storage, materials, supplies, equipment, and services as authorized by subsection (a). Such payments may be made in advance or by way of reimbursement. The rates charged will return in full the expenses of operation, including reserves for accrued annual leave, worker's compensation, depreciation of capitalized equipment and shelving, and amortization of information technology software and systems.]

[(d) FUNDS RETURNED TO MISCELLANEOUS RECEIPTS OF THE DEPARTMENT OF THE TREASURY.—

(1) In addition to funds appropriated to and assets transferred to the Fund in subsection (b), an amount not to exceed 4 percent of the total annual income may be retained in the Fund as an operating reserve or for the replacement or acquisition of capital equipment, including shelving, and the improvement and implementation of the financial management, information technology, and other support systems of the National Archives and Records Administration.

(2) Funds in excess of the 4 percent at the close of each fiscal year shall be returned to the Treasury of the United States as miscellaneous receipts.]

[(e) REPORTING REQUIREMENT.—The National Archives and Records Administration shall provide quarterly reports to the Committees on Appropriations and Governmental Affairs of the Senate, and the Committees on Appropriations and Government Reform of the House of Representatives on the operation of the Records Center Revolving Fund.] *(Independent Agencies Appropriations Act, 2000.)*

Program and Financing (in millions of dollars)

Identification code 88–4578–0–4–804	1999 actual	2000 est.	2001 est.
Obligations by program activity:			
10.00 Total new obligations		99	98
Budgetary resources available for obligation:			
21.40 Unobligated balance available, start of year			17
22.00 New budget authority (gross)		116	98
23.90 Total budgetary resources available for obligation		116	115
23.95 Total new obligations		−99	−98
24.40 Unobligated balance available, end of year		17	17
New budget authority (gross), detail:			
Discretionary:			
40.00 Appropriation		22	
68.00 Spending authority from offsetting collections: Offsetting collections (cash)		94	98
70.00 Total new budget authority (gross)		116	98
Change in unpaid obligations:			
72.40 Unpaid obligations, start of year: Obligated balance, start of year			6
73.10 Total new obligations		99	98
73.20 Total outlays (gross)		−93	−98
74.40 Unpaid obligations, end of year: Obligated balance, end of year		6	6
Outlays (gross), detail:			
86.90 Outlays from new discretionary authority		93	92
86.93 Outlays from discretionary balances			5
87.00 Total outlays (gross)		93	98
Offsets:			
Against gross budget authority and outlays:			
88.00 Offsetting collections (cash) from: Federal sources		−94	−98
Net budget authority and outlays:			
89.00 Budget authority		22	
90.00 Outlays		−1	

The NARA Records Center Revolving Fund utilizes operations effectively by providing services on a standard price basis to Federal agency customers by maintaining low cost, quality storage and accession, reference, refile, and disposal services for records stored in service centers.

Object Classification (in millions of dollars)

Identification code 88–4578–0–4–804	1999 actual	2000 est.	2001 est.
Personnel compensation:			
11.1 Full-time permanent		30	31
11.3 Other than full-time permanent		5	5
11.5 Other personnel compensation		1	1
11.9 Total personnel compensation		36	37
12.1 Civilian personnel benefits		8	9
23.1 Rental payments to GSA		36	37
23.3 Communications, utilities, and miscellaneous charges		2	3
25.2 Other services		15	10
26.0 Supplies and materials		1	1
32.0 Land and structures		1	1
99.9 Total new obligations		99	98

Personnel Summary

Identification code 88–4578–0–4–804	1999 actual	2000 est.	2001 est.
2001 Total compensable workyears: Full-time equivalent employment		1,165	1,165

Trust Funds

NATIONAL ARCHIVES GIFT FUND

Unavailable Collections (in millions of dollars)

Identification code 88–8127–0–7–804	1999 actual	2000 est.	2001 est.
Balance, start of year:			
01.99 Balance, start of year			
Receipts:			
02.01 National Archives gift fund	1	1	1
Appropriation:			
05.01 National Archives gift fund	−1	−1	−1
07.99 Total balance, end of year			

Program and Financing (in millions of dollars)

Identification code 88–8127–0–7–804	1999 actual	2000 est.	2001 est.
Obligations by program activity:			
10.00 Total new obligations (object class 25.2)	1	1	1
Budgetary resources available for obligation:			
21.40 Unobligated balance available, start of year	7	7	7
22.00 New budget authority (gross)	1	1	1
23.90 Total budgetary resources available for obligation	8	8	8
23.95 Total new obligations	−1	−1	−1
24.40 Unobligated balance available, end of year	7	7	7
New budget authority (gross), detail:			
Mandatory:			
60.27 Appropriation (trust fund, indefinite)	1	1	1
Change in unpaid obligations:			
72.40 Unpaid obligations, start of year: Obligated balance, start of year	1		
73.10 Total new obligations	1	1	1
Outlays (gross), detail:			
86.97 Outlays from new mandatory authority	1	1	1
Net budget authority and outlays:			
89.00 Budget authority	1	1	1
90.00 Outlays	1	1	1

Intragovernmental fund—Continued

NATIONAL ARCHIVES GIFT FUND—Continued

Program and Financing (in millions of dollars)—Continued

Identification code 88–8127–0–7–804	1999 actual	2000 est.	2001 est.
Memorandum (non-add) entries:			
92.01 Total investments, start of year: U.S. securities: Par value	3	2	2
92.02 Total investments, end of year: U.S. securities: Par value	2	2	2

The National Archives Trust Fund Board may solicit and accept gifts or bequests of money, securities, or other personal property, for the benefit of or in connection with the national archival and records activities administered by the National Archives and Records Administration (44 U.S.C. 2305).

In accordance with 44 U.S.C. 2112, the Bush Presidential Library received a $4 million endowment from the Bush Library Foundation. The money was deposited in the gift fund and invested in accordance with established National Archives Trust and Gift Fund procedures. Income earned on the investment will be used to offset a portion of the Library's operation and maintenance costs.

NATIONAL ARCHIVES TRUST FUND

Program and Financing (in millions of dollars)

Identification code 88–8436–0–8–804	1999 actual	2000 est.	2001 est.
Obligations by program activity:			
09.01 Sales	11	8	9
09.02 Presidential libraries	6	6	6
10.00 Total new obligations	17	14	15
Budgetary resources available for obligation:			
21.40 Unobligated balance available, start of year	13	12	11
22.00 New budget authority (gross)	15	14	14
23.90 Total budgetary resources available for obligation	28	26	25
23.95 Total new obligations	−17	−14	−15
24.40 Unobligated balance available, end of year	12	11	10
New budget authority (gross), detail:			
Mandatory:			
69.00 Offsetting collections (cash)	15	14	14
Change in unpaid obligations:			
72.40 Unpaid obligations, start of year: Obligated balance, start of year	3	3	3
73.10 Total new obligations	17	14	15
73.20 Total outlays (gross)	−16	−14	−15
74.40 Unpaid obligations, end of year: Obligated balance, end of year	3	3	3
Outlays (gross), detail:			
86.97 Outlays from new mandatory authority	15	14	14
86.98 Outlays from mandatory balances	....	−1	1
87.00 Total outlays (gross)	16	14	15
Offsets:			
Against gross budget authority and outlays:			
Offsetting collections (cash) from:			
88.00 Federal sources	−1	−1	−1
88.40 Non-Federal sources	−14	−13	−13
88.90 Total, offsetting collections (cash)	−15	−14	−14
Net budget authority and outlays:			
89.00 Budget authority	....	....	....
90.00 Outlays	1	....	1
Memorandum (non-add) entries:			
92.01 Total investments, start of year: U.S. securities: Par value	14	15	15
92.02 Total investments, end of year: U.S. securities: Par value	15	15	15

The Archivist of the United States furnishes, for a fee, copies of unrestricted records in the custody of the National Archives (44 U.S.C. 2116).

Proceeds from the sale of copies of microfilm publications, reproductions, special works, and other publications, and admission fees to Presidential Library museum rooms are deposited in this fund (44 U.S.C. 2112, 2307).

Object Classification (in millions of dollars)

Identification code 88–8436–0–8–804	1999 actual	2000 est.	2001 est.
Personnel compensation:			
11.1 Full-time permanent	3	3	3
11.3 Other than full-time permanent	1	1	1
11.9 Total personnel compensation	4	4	4
12.1 Civilian personnel benefits	1	1	1
24.0 Printing and reproduction	1	....	1
25.1 Advisory and assistance services	1	....	....
25.2 Other services	3	3	3
25.3 Purchases of goods and services from Government accounts	4	4	4
26.0 Supplies and materials	3	2	2
99.9 Total new obligations	17	14	15

Personnel Summary

Identification code 88–8436–0–8–804	1999 actual	2000 est.	2001 est.
2001 Total compensable workyears: Full-time equivalent employment	115	111	111

NATIONAL CAPITAL PLANNING COMMISSION

Federal Funds

General and special funds:

SALARIES AND EXPENSES

For necessary expenses, as authorized by the National Capital Planning Act of 1952 (40 U.S.C. 71–71i), including services as authorized by 5 U.S.C. 3109, [$6,312,000] *$6,197,895*: *Provided*, That *hereafter* all appointed members *of the Commission* will be compensated at [a rate not to exceed the rate for] *the daily equivalent of the annual rate of basic pay positions at* level IV of the Executive Schedule *under 5 U.S.C. 5315, for each day such member is engaged in the actual performance of duties. (Department of the Interior and Related Agencies Appropriations Act, 2000, as enacted by section 1000(a)(3) of the Consolidated Appropriations Act, 2000 (P.L. 106–113).)*

Program and Financing (in millions of dollars)

Identification code 95–2500–0–1–451	1999 actual	2000 est.	2001 est.
Obligations by program activity:			
10.00 Total new obligations	8	6	7
Budgetary resources available for obligation:			
22.00 New budget authority (gross)	8	6	7
23.95 Total new obligations	−8	−6	−7
New budget authority (gross), detail:			
Discretionary:			
40.00 Appropriation	6	6	6
68.00 Spending authority from offsetting collections: Offsetting collections (cash)	2	....	1
70.00 Total new budget authority (gross)	8	6	7
Change in unpaid obligations:			
72.40 Unpaid obligations, start of year: Obligated balance, start of year	1	3	1
73.10 Total new obligations	8	6	7
73.20 Total outlays (gross)	−8	−6	−6

74.40	Unpaid obligations, end of year: Obligated balance, end of year	3	1	1
	Outlays (gross), detail:			
86.90	Outlays from new discretionary authority	8	6	6
	Offsets:			
	Against gross budget authority and outlays:			
88.00	Offsetting collections (cash) from: Federal sources	−2		−1
	Net budget authority and outlays:			
89.00	Budget authority	6	6	6
90.00	Outlays	4	6	5

The National Capital Planning Commission (NCPC) is the central planning agency for the Federal government in the National Capital Region. It develops long-range plans and conducts project reviews in order to ensure the orderly development of the National Capital Region. During 2001, NCPC will in cooperation with the District of Columbia, publish the comprehensive Plan for the National Capital. This principal planning document will guide future physical development in the region. NCPC will also work with the District of Columbia in 2001 to complete planning for the development of the Washington waterfront and with the Washington Geographic Information System (WGIS) consortium members to formalize its structure.

Object Classification (in millions of dollars)

Identification code 95–2500–0–1–451		1999 actual	2000 est.	2001 est.
11.1	Personnel compensation: Full-time permanent	3	3	4
23.1	Rental payments to GSA	1	1	1
25.1	Advisory and assistance services	3	1	1
99.0	Subtotal, direct obligations	7	5	6
99.5	Below reporting threshold	1	1	1
99.9	Total new obligations	8	6	7

Personnel Summary

Identification code 95–2500–0–1–451		1999 actual	2000 est.	2001 est.
	Direct:			
1001	Total compensable workyears: Full-time equivalent employment	45	49	49
	Reimbursable:			
2001	Total compensable workyears: Full-time equivalent employment	2	2	2

NATIONAL COMMISSION ON LIBRARIES AND INFORMATION SCIENCE

Federal Funds

General and special funds:

SALARIES AND EXPENSES

For necessary expenses for the National Commission on Libraries and Information Science, established by the Act of July 20, 1970 (Public Law 91–345, as amended), [$1,300,000] *$1,495,000. (Departments of Labor, Health and Human Services, and Education, and Related Agencies Appropriations Act, 2000, as enacted by section 1000(a)(4) of the Consolidated Appropriations Act, 2000 (P.L. 106–113).)*

Program and Financing (in millions of dollars)

Identification code 95–2700–0–1–503		1999 actual	2000 est.	2001 est.
	Obligations by program activity:			
10.00	Total new obligations (object class 99.5)	1	1	1
	Budgetary resources available for obligation:			
22.00	New budget authority (gross)	1	1	1
23.95	Total new obligations	−1	−1	−1
	New budget authority (gross), detail:			
	Discretionary:			
40.00	Appropriation	1	1	1
	Change in unpaid obligations:			
72.40	Unpaid obligations, start of year: Obligated balance, start of year	1	1	1
73.10	Total new obligations	1	1	1
73.20	Total outlays (gross)	−1	−1	−1
74.40	Unpaid obligations, end of year: Obligated balance, end of year	1	1	1
	Outlays (gross), detail:			
86.90	Outlays from new discretionary authority	1	1	1
	Net budget authority and outlays:			
89.00	Budget authority	1	1	1
90.00	Outlays	1	1	1

The Commission is responsible for developing plans and recommendations for meeting the library and information needs of the Nation, for coordinating Federal, State, and local activities to meet these needs, for advising the President and the Congress on implementation of national and international library and information services policies, and for providing advice on general policies about library services under the Museum and Library Services Act.

Personnel Summary

Identification code 95–2700–0–1–503		1999 actual	2000 est.	2001 est.
1001	Total compensable workyears: Full-time equivalent employment	6	9	12

NATIONAL COUNCIL ON DISABILITY

Federal Funds

General and special funds:

SALARIES AND EXPENSES

For expenses necessary for the National Council on Disability as authorized by title IV of the Rehabilitation Act of 1973, as amended, [$2,400,000] *$2,615,000. (Departments of Labor, Health and Human Services, and Education, and Related Agencies Appropriations Act, 2000, as enacted by section 1000(a)(4) of the Consolidated Appropriations Act, 2000 (P.L. 106–113).)*

Program and Financing (in millions of dollars)

Identification code 95–3500–0–1–506		1999 actual	2000 est.	2001 est.
	Obligations by program activity:			
10.00	Total new obligations	2	2	3
	Budgetary resources available for obligation:			
22.00	New budget authority (gross)	2	2	3
23.95	Total new obligations	−2	−2	−3
	New budget authority (gross), detail:			
	Discretionary:			
40.00	Appropriation	2	2	3
	Change in unpaid obligations:			
72.40	Unpaid obligations, start of year: Obligated balance, start of year		1	
73.10	Total new obligations	2	2	3
73.20	Total outlays (gross)	−2	−3	−3
74.40	Unpaid obligations, end of year: Obligated balance, end of year	1		
	Outlays (gross), detail:			
86.90	Outlays from new discretionary authority	2	2	3
86.93	Outlays from discretionary balances		1	
87.00	Total outlays (gross)	2	3	3
	Net budget authority and outlays:			
89.00	Budget authority	2	2	3

General and special funds—Continued

SALARIES AND EXPENSES—Continued

Program and Financing (in millions of dollars)—Continued

Identification code 95–3500–0–1–506	1999 actual	2000 est.	2001 est.
90.00 Outlays	2	3	3

The National Council on Disability (NCD) is composed of 15 members appointed by the President and confirmed by the U.S. Senate. Established under the Rehabilitation Act of 1973, as amended. The NCD is responsible for reviewing laws, programs, and policies of the Federal Government affecting people with disabilities. The NCD also makes recommendations on issues affecting Americans with disabilities and their families to the President, the Congress, the Rehabilitation Services Administration, the National Institute on Disability and Rehabilitation Research, and other Federal Departments and agencies, as may be appropriate.

Object Classification (in millions of dollars)

Identification code 95–3500–0–1–506	1999 actual	2000 est.	2001 est.
11.1 Direct obligations: Personnel compensation: Full-time permanent	1	1	1
99.5 Below reporting threshold	1	1	2
99.9 Total new obligations	2	2	3

Personnel Summary

Identification code 95–3500–0–1–506	1999 actual	2000 est.	2001 est.
1001 Total compensable workyears: Full-time equivalent employment	10	13	14

NATIONAL CREDIT UNION ADMINISTRATION

Federal Funds

Public enterprise funds:

OPERATING FUND

Program and Financing (in millions of dollars)

Identification code 25–4056–0–3–373	1999 actual	2000 est.	2001 est.
Obligations by program activity:			
09.01 Examination and supervision	67	85	90
09.03 Administration	40	47	50
09.99 Total reimbursable program	107	132	140
10.00 Total new obligations	107	132	140
Budgetary resources available for obligation:			
21.40 Unobligated balance available, start of year	3	2	2
22.00 New budget authority (gross)	106	132	140
23.90 Total budgetary resources available for obligation	109	134	142
23.95 Total new obligations	−107	−132	−140
24.40 Unobligated balance available, end of year	2	2	2
New budget authority (gross), detail:			
Mandatory:			
69.00 Offsetting collections (cash)	106	132	140
Change in unpaid obligations:			
72.40 Unpaid obligations, start of year: Obligated balance, start of year	23	26	26
73.10 Total new obligations	107	132	140
73.20 Total outlays (gross)	−104	−132	−140
74.40 Unpaid obligations, end of year: Obligated balance, end of year	26	26	26
Outlays (gross), detail:			
86.97 Outlays from new mandatory authority	104	132	140
Offsets:			
Against gross budget authority and outlays:			
Offsetting collections (cash) from:			
88.00 Federal sources	−50	−66	−70
88.40 Non-Federal sources	−56	−66	−70
88.90 Total, offsetting collections (cash)	−106	−132	−140
Net budget authority and outlays:			
89.00 Budget authority			
90.00 Outlays	−2		
Memorandum (non-add) entries:			
92.01 Total investments, start of year: U.S. securities: Par value	26	28	28
92.02 Total investments, end of year: U.S. securities: Par value	28	28	28

Federal credit unions are privately owned, cooperative associations organized for the purpose of promoting thrift among their members and creating a source of credit for provident or productive purposes, authorized by the Federal Credit Union Act of 1934, as amended.

The Administration's activities consist of: (a) chartering new Federal credit unions, (b) supervising established Federal credit unions, (c) making periodic examinations of their financial condition and operating practices, and (d) providing administrative services. The operating fund is reimbursed for the insurance fund's share of the agency's administrative expenses by the insurance fund. The reimbursement percentage, which is reviewed and adjusted periodically, is currently at 50 percent. Data relating to activities are shown below:

Item:	*1999 actual*	*2000 est.*	*2001 est.*
Number of new Federal credit unions chartered	9	3	3
Number of operating Federal credit unions	6,707	6,512	6,324
Assets of Federal credit unions as of June 30 (in millions)	$240,075	$254,960	$270,767

Object Classification (in millions of dollars)

Identification code 25–4056–0–3–373	1999 actual	2000 est.	2001 est.
Personnel compensation:			
11.1 Full-time permanent	62	76	80
11.3 Other than full-time permanent	3	3	3
11.9 Total personnel compensation	65	79	83
12.1 Civilian personnel benefits	17	19	20
21.0 Travel and transportation of persons	10	13	14
23.3 Communications, utilities, and miscellaneous charges	4	4	5
24.0 Printing and reproduction	1	1	1
25.2 Other services	9	14	16
31.0 Equipment	1	2	1
99.9 Total new obligations	107	132	140

Personnel Summary

Identification code 25–4056–0–3–373	1999 actual	2000 est.	2001 est.
2001 Total compensable workyears: Full-time equivalent employment	933	1,049	1,049

CREDIT UNION SHARE INSURANCE FUND

Program and Financing (in millions of dollars)

Identification code 25–4468–0–3–373	1999 actual	2000 est.	2001 est.
Obligations by program activity:			
Operating expenses:			
00.01 Payments to the operating fund for services and facilities	59	69	74
00.03 Other	1	1	1
00.91 Total operating expenses	60	70	75
01.01 Insurance Premium Rebate	118	88	97
01.02 Liquidation Expenses	5	5	5
01.91 Direct Program	123	93	102

10.00	Total new obligations	183	163	177
	Budgetary resources available for obligation:			
21.40	Unobligated balance available, start of year	3,818	4,162	4,491
22.00	New budget authority (gross)	527	492	516
23.90	Total budgetary resources available for obligation	4,345	4,654	5,007
23.95	Total new obligations	−183	−163	−177
24.40	Unobligated balance available, end of year	4,162	4,491	4,830
	New budget authority (gross), detail:			
	Mandatory:			
69.00	Offsetting collections (cash)	527	492	516
	Change in unpaid obligations:			
72.40	Unpaid obligations, start of year: Obligated balance, start of year	44	−41	−41
73.10	Total new obligations	183	163	177
73.20	Total outlays (gross)	−268	−163	−177
74.40	Unpaid obligations, end of year: Obligated balance, end of year	−41	−41	−41
	Outlays (gross), detail:			
86.97	Outlays from new mandatory authority	268	163	177
	Offsets:			
	Against gross budget authority and outlays:			
	Offsetting collections (cash) from:			
88.20	Interest on U.S. securities	−219	−238	−249
	Non-Federal sources:			
88.40	Deposit from members	−294	−242	−256
88.40	Recoveries on assets acquired	−12	−8	−5
88.40	Other interest income	−2	−4	−6
88.90	Total, offsetting collections (cash)	−527	−492	−516
	Net budget authority and outlays:			
89.00	Budget authority			
90.00	Outlays	−259	−329	−339
	Memorandum (non-add) entries:			
92.01	Total investments, start of year: U.S. securities: Par value	3,878	4,128	4,618
92.02	Total investments, end of year: U.S. securities: Par value	4,128	4,618	5,068

Status of Guaranteed Loans (in millions of dollars)

Identification code 25–4468–0–3–373		1999 actual	2000 est.	2001 est.
	Position with respect to appropriations act limitation on commitments:			
2111	Limitation on guaranteed loans made by private lenders			
2131	Guaranteed loan commitments exempt from limitation	1	1	1
2150	Total guaranteed loan commitments	1	1	1
	Cumulative balance of guaranteed loans outstanding:			
2210	Outstanding, start of year	1	1	1
2231	Disbursements of new guaranteed loans	1	1	1
2251	Repayments and prepayments	−1	−1	−1
2290	Outstanding, end of year	1	1	1
	Memorandum:			
2299	Guaranteed amount of guaranteed loans outstanding, end of year	1	1	1

The insurance fund is used to carry out a program of insurance for member accounts in Federal credit unions and State-chartered credit unions which apply and qualify for insurance, authorized by Public Law 91–468, enacted October 19, 1970.

Budget program.—The activities consist of: (a) providing member account insurance, (b) formulating standards and requirements for insured credit unions, and (c) providing for liquidation or other disposition of the assets and liabilities of solvent and insolvent insured credit unions. The fund also reimburses the operating fund for its share of the Agency's administrative costs. The reimbursement percentage, which is reviewed and adjusted periodically, is currently at 50 percent.

The extent of the program is estimated as follows:

	1999 actual	2000 est.	2001 est.
Item:			
Number of insured credit unions	10,841	10,527	10,221
Insured shares of member institutions as of June 30 (in millions of dollars)	$336,176	$357,691	$380,584

It is estimated that approximately 4,014 State-chartered credit unions will be enrolled in the program by the end of 2000.

Financing.—For insurance year 1999 the credit union's required annual insurance premium of one-twelfth of 1 percent of its total member share accounts has been waived. As a result of Public Law 98–369 (July 18, 1984), each insured credit union is also required to deposit and maintain in the insurance fund 1 percent of its member share accounts. The fund is structured to be entirely self supporting through the monies paid by member credit unions. The monies received plus the income generated from their investment are expected to cover all administrative and financial costs, as well as increase the fund balance proportionate to insured share growth. In 1999 the income generated from the 1 percent deposit eliminated the need to assess the annual premium. In addition, the fund paid a $118 million dividend to federally insured credit unions in 2000 due to an excess in the 1.3 percent reserve requirement. The fund has $100 million in borrowing authority from the Treasury for use in unforeseen emergencies.

Operating results.—Anticipated net income of $174 million will be retained in the fund, raising the balance for unforeseen emergencies to $5 billion by the end of 2001.

Object Classification (in millions of dollars)

Identification code 25–4468–0–3–373		1999 actual	2000 est.	2001 est.
25.2	Other services	60	70	75
42.0	Insurance claims and indemnities	5	5	5
44.0	Refunds	118	88	97
99.9	Total new obligations	183	163	177

CENTRAL LIQUIDITY FACILITY

During fiscal year [2000] *2001, gross obligations of the Central Liquidity Facility for the principal amount of new direct loans to member credit unions, as authorized by the National Credit Union Central Liquidity Facility Act (12 U.S.C. 1795), shall not exceed $600,000,000: Provided, That,* administrative expenses of the Central Liquidity Facility shall not exceed [$257,000: *Provided,* That, $1,000,000, together with amounts of principal and interest on loans repaid, to be available until expended, is available for loans to community development credit unions] *$296,303. (Departments of Veterans Affairs and Housing and Urban Development, and Independent Agencies Appropriations Act, 2000.)*

Program and Financing (in millions of dollars)

Identification code 25–4470–0–3–373		1999 actual	2000 est.	2001 est.
	Obligations by program activity:			
09.03	Dividends on capital stock	39	40	42
09.09	Operating Expenses—subtotal	39	40	42
	Capital Investment:			
09.11	Net loans to credit unions, total Capital investment, funded	114	120	126
09.19	Total capital investment—subtotal	114	120	126
10.00	Total new obligations	153	160	168
	Budgetary resources available for obligation:			
22.00	New budget authority (gross)	155	161	168
23.95	Total new obligations	−153	−160	−168

Public enterprise funds—Continued

CENTRAL LIQUIDITY FACILITY—Continued

Program and Financing (in millions of dollars)—Continued

Identification code 25–4470–0–3–373	1999 actual	2000 est.	2001 est.
New budget authority (gross), detail:			
Discretionary:			
40.00 Appropriation	2	1	....
68.00 Spending authority from offsetting collections: Offsetting collections (cash)	153	160	168
70.00 Total new budget authority (gross)	155	161	168
Change in unpaid obligations:			
73.10 Total new obligations	153	160	168
73.20 Total outlays (gross)	−155	−161	−168
Outlays (gross), detail:			
86.90 Outlays from new discretionary authority	155	161	168
Offsets:			
Against gross budget authority and outlays:			
Offsetting collections (cash) from:			
Non-Federal sources:			
88.40 Non-Federal Capital Stock Purchases	−102	−111	−121
88.40 Non-Federal sources	−51	−49	−47
88.90 Total, offsetting collections (cash)	−153	−160	−168
Net budget authority and outlays:			
89.00 Budget authority	2	1	....
90.00 Outlays	2	1	....

Status of Direct Loans (in millions of dollars)

Identification code 25–4470–0–3–373	1999 actual	2000 est.	2001 est.
Position with respect to appropriations act limitation on obligations:			
1111 Limitation on direct loans	600	20,700	600
1112 Unobligated direct loan limitation	−600	−20,700	−600
1150 Total direct loan obligations	....	....	....

The National Credit Union Central Liquidity Facility was established under Public Law 95–630. It began operations on October 1, 1979. The Central Liquidity Facility provides loans to member credit unions for seasonal and emergency needs.

The two primary sources of funds for the Facility are stock subscriptions from credit unions and borrowings from the Federal Financing Bank. Credit unions, which choose to become members of the Facility, are required to purchase stock equal to one-half of 1 percent of their assets. One-half of the subscription in stock is forwarded to the Facility and deposited in the fund. The remaining half of the subscription remains on call in the credit union in investments as approved by the NCUA Board.

Object Classification (in millions of dollars)

Identification code 25–4470–0–3–373	1999 actual	2000 est.	2001 est.
33.0 Investments and loans	114	120	126
43.0 Interest and dividends	39	40	42
99.9 Total new obligations	153	160	168

Personnel Summary

Identification code 25–4470–0–3–373	1999 actual	2000 est.	2001 est.
1001 Total compensable workyears: Full-time equivalent employment	2	2	2

COMMUNITY DEVELOPMENT CREDIT UNION REVOLVING LOAN FUND

For technical assistance grants to community development credit unions, $1,000,000, to remain available until September 30, 2002.

Program and Financing (in millions of dollars)

Identification code 25–4472–0–3–373	1999 actual	2000 est.	2001 est.
Obligations by program activity:			
10.00 Total new obligations (object class 33.0)	2	6	5
Budgetary resources available for obligation:			
21.40 Unobligated balance available, start of year	1	3	1
22.00 New budget authority (gross)	4	4	4
23.90 Total budgetary resources available for obligation	5	7	5
23.95 Total new obligations	−2	−6	−5
24.40 Unobligated balance available, end of year	3	1	....
New budget authority (gross), detail:			
Discretionary:			
40.00 Appropriation	....	....	1
68.00 Spending authority from offsetting collections: Offsetting collections (cash)	2	1	....
Mandatory:			
69.00 Offsetting collections (cash)	2	3	3
70.00 Total new budget authority (gross)	4	4	4
Change in unpaid obligations:			
73.10 Total new obligations	2	6	5
73.20 Total outlays (gross)	−2	−6	−5
Outlays (gross), detail:			
86.90 Outlays from new discretionary authority	2	1	1
86.97 Outlays from new mandatory authority	....	3	3
86.98 Outlays from mandatory balances	....	2	1
87.00 Total outlays (gross)	2	6	5
Offsets:			
Against gross budget authority and outlays:			
Offsetting collections (cash) from:			
88.00 Federal sources	−2	−1	....
88.40 Non-Federal sources	−2	−3	−3
88.90 Total, offsetting collections (cash)	−4	−4	−3
Net budget authority and outlays:			
89.00 Budget authority	....	....	1
90.00 Outlays	−2	2	2
Memorandum (non-add) entries:			
92.01 Total investments, start of year: U.S. securities: Par value	1	3	1
92.02 Total investments, end of year: U.S. securities: Par value	3	1	....

Status of Direct Loans (in millions of dollars)

Identification code 25–4472–0–3–373	1999 actual	2000 est.	2001 est.
Position with respect to appropriations act limitation on obligations:			
1111 Limitation on direct loans	....	....	....
1131 Direct loan obligations exempt from limitation	2	6	4
1150 Total direct loan obligations	2	6	4
Cumulative balance of direct loans outstanding:			
1210 Outstanding, start of year	7	7	10
1231 Disbursements: Direct loan disbursements	2	6	4
1251 Repayments: Repayments and prepayments	−2	−3	−3
1290 Outstanding, end of year	7	10	11

Public Law 99–609, enacted on November 6, 1986, transferred the Community Development Credit Union Revolving Loan Fund from the Department of Health and Human Services to the National Credit Union Administration. The NCUA disbursed loans of $2 million in 1999 and plans to disburse $6 million in 2000. The NCUA will conduct a study of the impact of loans and technical assistance provided to community development credit unions by the CDCURLF.

AMERICA'S EDUCATION GOALS PANEL

Federal Funds

General and special funds:

[NATIONAL EDUCATION GOALS PANEL]

[For expenses necessary for the National Education Goals Panel, as authorized by title II, part A of the Goals 2000: Educate America Act, $2,250,000.] *(Departments of Labor, Health and Human Services, and Education, and Related Agencies Appropriations Act, 2000, as enacted by section 1000(a)(4) of the Consolidated Appropriations Act, 2000 (P.L. 106–113).)*

Program and Financing (in millions of dollars)

Identification code 95–2650–0–1–503	1999 actual	2000 est.	2001 est.
Obligations by program activity:			
10.00 Total new obligations	2	2	....
Budgetary resources available for obligation:			
22.00 New budget authority (gross)	2	2	....
23.95 Total new obligations	−2	−2	....
New budget authority (gross), detail:			
Discretionary:			
40.00 Appropriation	2	2	....
Change in unpaid obligations:			
72.40 Unpaid obligations, start of year: Obligated balance, start of year	1	2	1
73.10 Total new obligations	2	2	....
73.20 Total outlays (gross)	−2	−2	−1
74.40 Unpaid obligations, end of year: Obligated balance, end of year	2	1	1
Outlays (gross), detail:			
86.90 Outlays from new discretionary authority	1	1	....
86.93 Outlays from discretionary balances	1	1	1
87.00 Total outlays (gross)	2	2	1
Net budget authority and outlays:			
89.00 Budget authority	2	2	....
90.00 Outlays	2	2	1

Summary of Budget Authority and Outlays

(in millions of dollars)

	1999 actual	*2000 est.*	*2001 est.*
Enacted/requested:			
Budget Authority	2	2	....
Outlays	2	2	1
Legislative proposal, not subject to PAYGO:			
Budget Authority	....	....	2
Outlays	....	....	1
Total:			
Budget Authority	2	2	2
Outlays	2	2	2

America's Education Goals Panel.—The Administration has proposed legislation to reauthorize the National Education Goals Panel as America's Education Goals Panel in the Elementary and Secondary Education Act. When new legislation is enacted, resources will be requested for this agency. See the "Legislative proposal, not subject to PAYGO" schedule for additional details.

Object Classification (in millions of dollars)

Identification code 95–2650–0–1–503	1999 actual	2000 est.	2001 est.
25.2 Direct obligations: Other services	1	....	....
99.5 Below reporting threshold	1	2	....
99.9 Total new obligations	2	2	....

Personnel Summary

Identification code 95–2650–0–1–503	1999 actual	2000 est.	2001 est.
1001 Total compensable workyears: Full-time equivalent employment	8	9	....

AMERICA'S EDUCATION GOALS PANEL

(Legislative proposal, not subject to PAYGO)

Program and Financing (in millions of dollars)

Identification code 95–2650–2–1–503	1999 actual	2000 est.	2001 est.
Obligations by program activity:			
10.00 Total new obligations	....	....	2
Budgetary resources available for obligation:			
22.00 New budget authority (gross)	....	....	2
23.95 Total new obligations	....	....	−2
New budget authority (gross), detail:			
Discretionary:			
40.00 Appropriation	....	....	2
Change in unpaid obligations:			
72.40 Unpaid obligations, start of year: Obligated balance, start of year	....	....	....
73.10 Total new obligations	....	....	2
73.20 Total outlays (gross)	....	....	−1
74.40 Unpaid obligations, end of year: Obligated balance, end of year	....	....	1
Outlays (gross), detail:			
86.90 Outlays from new discretionary authority	....	....	1
Net budget authority and outlays:			
89.00 Budget authority	....	....	2
90.00 Outlays	....	....	1

The resources in this schedule are proposed for later transmittal under proposed legislation to revise and reauthorize the Elementary and Secondary Education Act.

America's Education Goals Panel.—The bipartisan America's Education Goals Panel is an independent agency responsible for overseeing the development and implementation of a reporting system for America's Education Goals; monitoring and reporting annual progress toward goal achievement at national and State levels; building a national consensus for the reforms necessary to achieve education improvement; reporting on promising and effective actions; and working with State to develop high academic standards.

Object Classification (in millions of dollars)

Identification code 95–2650–2–1–503	1999 actual	2000 est.	2001 est.
25.2 Direct obligations: Other services	....	....	1
99.5 Below reporting threshold	....	....	1
99.9 Total new obligations	....	....	2

Personnel Summary

Identification code 95–2650–2–1–503	1999 actual	2000 est.	2001 est.
1001 Total compensable workyears: Full-time equivalent employment	....	....	9

NATIONAL FOUNDATION ON THE ARTS AND THE HUMANITIES

Federal Funds

General and special funds:

NATIONAL ENDOWMENT FOR THE ARTS

GRANTS AND ADMINISTRATION

For necessary expenses to carry out the National Foundation on the Arts and the Humanities Act of 1965, as amended, [$85,000,000] *$150,000,000* shall be available to the National Endowment for the Arts for the support of projects and productions in the arts through assistance to organizations and individuals pursuant to sections 5(c) and 5(g) of the Act, for program support, and for administering the functions of the Act, to remain available until expended.

[MATCHING GRANTS]

[To carry out the provisions of section 10(a)(2) of the National Foundation on the Arts and the Humanities Act of 1965, as amended, $13,000,000, to remain available until expended, to the National Endowment for the Arts: *Provided*, That this appropriation shall be available for obligation only in such amounts as may be equal to the total amounts of gifts, bequests, and devises of money, and other property accepted by the chairman or by grantees of the Endowment under the provisions of section 10(a)(2), subsections 11(a)(2)(A) and 11(a)(3)(A) during the current and preceding fiscal years for which equal amounts have not previously been appropriated.] *(Department of the Interior and Related Agencies Appropriations Act, 2000, as enacted by section 1000(a)(3) of the Consolidated Appropriations Act, 2000 (P.L. 106–113).)*

Unavailable Collections (in millions of dollars)

Identification code 59–0100–0–1–503	1999 actual	2000 est.	2001 est.
Balance, start of year:			
01.99 Balance, start of year			
Receipts:			
02.01 Gifts and donations	1	1	1
Appropriation:			
05.01 Gifts fund	–1	–1	–1
07.99 Total balance, end of year			

Program and Financing (in millions of dollars)

Identification code 59–0100–0–1–503	1999 actual	2000 est.	2001 est.
Obligations by program activity:			
Direct program:			
00.01 Promotion of the arts	83	79	80
00.02 Challenge America			49
00.03 Program Support	1	1	1
00.04 Salaries and Expenses	17	18	20
00.91 Direct Program	101	98	150
01.01 Reimbursable program	1	1	1
01.02 Permanent Authority	1	1	1
01.91 Total permanent authority program	2	2	2
10.00 Total new obligations	103	100	152
Budgetary resources available for obligation:			
21.40 Unobligated balance available, start of year	5	3	3
22.00 New budget authority (gross)	100	100	152
23.90 Total budgetary resources available for obligation	105	103	155
23.95 Total new obligations	–103	–100	–152
24.40 Unobligated balance available, end of year	3	3	3
New budget authority (gross), detail:			
Discretionary:			
40.00 Appropriation	98	98	150
Mandatory:			
60.27 Appropriation (trust fund, indefinite)	1	1	1
Discretionary:			
68.00 Spending authority from offsetting collections: Offsetting collections (cash)	1	1	1
70.00 Total new budget authority (gross)	100	100	152
Change in unpaid obligations:			
72.40 Unpaid obligations, start of year: Obligated balance, start of year	111	107	95
73.10 Total new obligations	103	100	152
73.20 Total outlays (gross)	–105	–111	–122
74.40 Unpaid obligations, end of year: Obligated balance, end of year	107	95	123
Outlays (gross), detail:			
86.90 Outlays from new discretionary authority	30	33	51
86.93 Outlays from discretionary balances	74	79	72
86.97 Outlays from new mandatory authority		1	1
87.00 Total outlays (gross)	105	111	122
Offsets:			
Against gross budget authority and outlays:			
88.00 Offsetting collections (cash) from: Federal sources	–1	–1	–1
Net budget authority and outlays:			
89.00 Budget authority	99	99	150
90.00 Outlays	104	111	122

The National Endowment for the Arts provides grants to, or contracts with, groups, individuals of exceptional talent in specified fields, and State or regional organizations engaged in or concerned with the arts in service to the American public. Programs encourage individual and institutional development of the arts, education in the arts, preservation of the American artistic heritage, wider availability and appreciation of the arts, leadership in the arts, and the stimulation of non-Federal sources of support for the Nation's artistic activities.

This presentation includes Gifts and Donations and the Arts and Artifacts Indemnity Fund which previously had been shown separately.

The National Foundation on the Arts and the Humanities Act of 1965, as amended, authorizes the Arts Endowment to receive money and other donated property. Such gifts may be used, sold, or otherwise disposed of to support arts projects and activities. Budget authority in this schedule reflects cash received each year by the Arts Endowment.

The Arts and Artifacts Indemnity Act of 1975, as amended authorizes the Federal Council on the Arts and Humanities to enter into indemnity agreements to cover certain eligible works of art while on traveling exhibition in the United States or abroad. Loss or damage claims certified by the Council are paid from this fund.

Object Classification (in millions of dollars)

Identification code 59–0100–0–1–503	1999 actual	2000 est.	2001 est.
Personnel compensation:			
11.1 Full-time permanent	8	9	10
11.3 Other than full-time permanent	2	2	2
11.9 Total personnel compensation	10	11	12
12.1 Civilian personnel benefits	2	2	2
21.0 Travel and transportation of persons	1	1	1
23.1 Rental payments to GSA	2	2	3
23.3 Communications, utilities, and miscellaneous charges	1	1	1
25.2 Other services	3	3	3
31.0 Equipment	1	1	1
41.0 Grants, subsidies, and contributions	83	79	129
99.9 Total new obligations	103	100	152

Personnel Summary

Identification code 59–0100–0–1–503	1999 actual	2000 est.	2001 est.
1001 Total compensable workyears: Full-time equivalent employment	149	162	167

Federal Funds

General and special funds:

NATIONAL ENDOWMENT FOR THE HUMANITIES

GRANTS AND ADMINISTRATION

For necessary expenses to carry out the National Foundation on the Arts and the Humanities Act of 1965, as amended, [$101,000,000] *$129,470,000*, shall be available to the National Endowment for the Humanities for support of activities in the humanities, pursuant to section 7(c) of the Act, and for administering the functions of the Act, to remain available until expended.

MATCHING GRANTS

To carry out the provisions of section 10(a)(2) of the National Foundation on the Arts and the Humanities Act of 1965, as amended, [$14,700,000] *$20,530,000*, to remain available until expended, of which [$10,700,000] *$16,530,000* shall be available to the National Endowment for the Humanities for the purposes of section 7(h): *Provided*, That this appropriation shall be available for obligation only in such amounts as may be equal to the total amounts of gifts, bequests, and devises of money, and other property accepted by the chairman or by grantees of the Endowment under the provisions of subsections 11(a)(2)(B) and 11(a)(3)(B) during the current and preceding fiscal years for which equal amounts have not previously been appropriated. *(Department of the Interior and Related Agencies Appropriations Act, 2000, as enacted by section 1000(a)(3) of the Consolidated Appropriations Act, 2000 (P.L. 106–113).)*

Unavailable Collections (in millions of dollars)

Identification code 59–0200–0–1–503	1999 actual	2000 est.	2001 est.
Balance, start of year:			
01.99 Balance, start of year			
Receipts:			
02.01 Gifts and donations	1		
Appropriation:			
05.01 Grants and administration	−1		
07.99 Total balance, end of year			

Program and Financing (in millions of dollars)

Identification code 59–0200–0–1–503	1999 actual	2000 est.	2001 est.
Obligations by program activity:			
00.01 Promotion of the humanities	92	98	128
00.02 Administration	18	18	22
09.00 Reimbursable program		1	
10.00 Total new obligations	110	117	150
Budgetary resources available for obligation:			
21.40 Unobligated balance available, start of year	3	5	5
22.00 New budget authority (gross)	112	117	150
23.90 Total budgetary resources available for obligation	115	122	155
23.95 Total new obligations	−110	−117	−150
24.40 Unobligated balance available, end of year	5	5	5
New budget authority (gross), detail:			
Discretionary:			
40.00 Appropriation	111	116	150
40.27 Appropriation (trust fund, indefinite)	1		
43.00 Appropriation (total discretionary)	112	116	150
68.00 Spending authority from offsetting collections: Offsetting collections (cash)		1	
70.00 Total new budget authority (gross)	112	117	150
Change in unpaid obligations:			
72.40 Unpaid obligations, start of year: Obligated balance, start of year	94	90	104
73.10 Total new obligations	110	117	150
73.20 Total outlays (gross)	−113	−104	−123
74.40 Unpaid obligations, end of year: Obligated balance, end of year	90	104	131
Outlays (gross), detail:			
86.90 Outlays from new discretionary authority	105	79	90
86.93 Outlays from discretionary balances	8	25	33
87.00 Total outlays (gross)	113	104	123
Offsets:			
Against gross budget authority and outlays:			
88.00 Offsetting collections (cash) from: Federal sources		−1	
Net budget authority and outlays:			
89.00 Budget authority	112	116	150
90.00 Outlays	113	103	123
Memorandum (non-add) entries:			
92.01 Total investments, start of year: U.S. securities: Par value		1	1
92.02 Total investments, end of year: U.S. securities: Par value	1	1	1

The National Endowment for the Humanities funds activities to improve the quality of education and teaching in the humanities, to strengthen the scholarly foundation for humanities study and research, to preserve cultural and intellectual resources, and to advance understanding of the humanities among general audiences.

Support is provided through outright grants, matching grants, and a combination of the two. Eligible applicants include state humanities councils, schools, higher education institutions, libraries, museums, historical organizations, professional associations, other cultural institutions, and individuals.

This presentation includes the Gifts and Donations account, which previously had been presented separately. The National Foundation on the Arts and the Humanities Act of 1965, as amended, authorizes the Humanities Endowment to receive money and other donated property. Such gifts may be used, sold, or otherwise disposed of to support humanities projects and activities. Budget authority in this schedule reflects cash received each year by the Endowment.

Object Classification (in millions of dollars)

Identification code 59–0200–0–1–503	1999 actual	2000 est.	2001 est.
Direct obligations:			
11.1 Personnel compensation: Full-time permanent	11	11	12
12.1 Civilian personnel benefits	2	2	2
23.1 Rental payments to GSA	2	2	3
25.2 Other services	2	1	2
41.0 Grants, subsidies, and contributions	91	98	128
99.0 Subtotal, direct obligations	108	114	147
99.0 Reimbursable obligations		1	
99.5 Below reporting threshold	2	2	3
99.9 Total new obligations	110	117	150

Personnel Summary

Identification code 59–0200–0–1–503	1999 actual	2000 est.	2001 est.
Direct:			
1001 Total compensable workyears: Full-time equivalent employment	165	170	175
Reimbursable:			
2001 Total compensable workyears: Full-time equivalent employment	2	2	2

ADMINISTRATIVE PROVISION

An administrative provision affecting this agency follows the Institute of Museum and Library Services.

INSTITUTE OF MUSEUM AND LIBRARY SERVICES

Federal Funds

General and special funds:

OFFICE OF MUSEUM SERVICES: GRANTS AND ADMINISTRATION

For carrying out subtitle C of the Museum and Library Services Act of 1996, as amended, [$24,400,000] *$33,378,000*, to remain avail-

General and special funds—Continued

OFFICE OF MUSEUM SERVICES: GRANTS AND ADMINISTRATION—Continued

able until expended. *(Department of the Interior and Related Agencies Appropriations Act, 2000, as enacted by section 1000(a)(3) of the Consolidated Appropriations Act, 2000 (P.L. 106–113).)*

Program and Financing (in millions of dollars)

Identification code 59–0300–0–1–503	1999 actual	2000 est.	2001 est.
Obligations by program activity:			
00.01 Assistance for museums	22	22	31
00.02 Administration	2	2	2
09.00 Reimbursable program		1	
10.00 Total new obligations	24	25	33
Budgetary resources available for obligation:			
21.40 Unobligated balance available, start of year	1	1	1
22.00 New budget authority (gross)	24	25	33
23.90 Total budgetary resources available for obligation	25	26	34
23.95 Total new obligations	−24	−25	−33
24.40 Unobligated balance available, end of year	1	1	1
New budget authority (gross), detail:			
Discretionary:			
40.00 Appropriation	24	24	33
68.00 Spending authority from offsetting collections: Offsetting collections (cash)		1	
70.00 Total new budget authority (gross)	24	25	33
Change in unpaid obligations:			
72.40 Unpaid obligations, start of year: Obligated balance, start of year	31	33	33
73.10 Total new obligations	24	25	33
73.20 Total outlays (gross)	−22	−25	−25
74.40 Unpaid obligations, end of year: Obligated balance, end of year	33	33	41
Outlays (gross), detail:			
86.90 Outlays from new discretionary authority	21	23	25
86.93 Outlays from discretionary balances	1	1	1
87.00 Total outlays (gross)	22	25	25
Offsets:			
Against gross budget authority and outlays:			
88.00 Offsetting collections (cash) from: Federal sources		−1	
Net budget authority and outlays:			
89.00 Budget authority	24	24	33
90.00 Outlays	22	24	25

The Office of Museum Services, within the Institute of Museum and Library Services, provides competitive grants to a broad range of museums which exhibit both living and non-living collections and to support collaborative activities between museums and libraries. Its programs help museums improve the quality of their programs and operations to better exhibit, preserve, and teach about our cultural, historic, and scientific heritage. This presentation includes the Gifts and Donations Account.

Object Classification (in millions of dollars)

Identification code 59–0300–0–1–503	1999 actual	2000 est.	2001 est.
Direct obligations:			
11.1 Personnel compensation: Full-time permanent	1	1	1
41.0 Grants, subsidies, and contributions	22	22	31
99.0 Subtotal, direct obligations	23	23	32
99.0 Reimbursable obligations		1	
99.5 Below reporting threshold	1	1	1
99.9 Total new obligations	24	25	33

Personnel Summary

Identification code 59–0300–0–1–503	1999 actual	2000 est.	2001 est.
1001 Total compensable workyears: Full-time equivalent employment	15	21	21

INSTITUTE OF MUSEUM AND LIBRARY SERVICES

OFFICE OF LIBRARY SERVICES: GRANTS AND ADMINISTRATION

For carrying out subtitle B of the Museum and Library Services Act, [$166,175,000] *$173,000,000*, of which [$25,000,000] *$13,000,000* shall be for [national leadership] projects *authorized by section 262*, notwithstanding section 221(a)(1)(B)[: *Provided*, That of the amount provided, $10,000,000, to remain available until expended, shall be awarded to the National Constitution Center, established by Public Law 100–433, for exhibition design, program planning, and operation of the Center to serve as a model between museums and libraries; $750,000 shall be for a Digital Geospatial and Numerical Data Library at the University of Idaho; $1,250,000 shall be awarded to the Franklin Institute, Philadelphia, Pennsylvania; $2,000,000 shall be to enhance digitization at the New York Public Library; $35,000 shall be for the Children's Museum of Manhattan; $300,000 shall be for the State Historical Society of Iowa; and $1,100,000 shall be for the Museum of Science and Industry in Chicago], to remain available until expended. *(Departments of Labor, Health and Human Services, and Education, and Related Agencies Appropriations Act, 2000, as enacted by section 1000(a)(4) of the Consolidated Appropriations Act, 2000 (P.L. 106–113).)*

Program and Financing (in millions of dollars)

Identification code 59–0301–0–1–503	1999 actual	2000 est.	2001 est.
Obligations by program activity:			
00.01 Assistance for libraries	164	163	168
00.02 Administration	3	3	5
10.00 Total new obligations	167	166	173
Budgetary resources available for obligation:			
21.40 Unobligated balance available, start of year	6	5	6
22.00 New budget authority (gross)	166	165	173
23.90 Total budgetary resources available for obligation	172	170	179
23.95 Total new obligations	−167	−166	−173
24.40 Unobligated balance available, end of year	5	6	6
New budget authority (gross), detail:			
Discretionary:			
40.00 Appropriation	166	166	173
40.76 Reduction pursuant to P.L. 106–113		−1	
43.00 Appropriation (total discretionary)	166	165	173
Change in unpaid obligations:			
72.40 Unpaid obligations, start of year: Obligated balance, start of year	166	191	184
73.10 Total new obligations	167	166	173
73.20 Total outlays (gross)	−142	−173	−173
74.40 Unpaid obligations, end of year: Obligated balance, end of year	191	184	184
Outlays (gross), detail:			
86.90 Outlays from new discretionary authority	39	41	43
86.93 Outlays from discretionary balances	103	131	129
87.00 Total outlays (gross)	142	173	173
Net budget authority and outlays:			
89.00 Budget authority	166	165	173
90.00 Outlays	142	173	173

State formula grants are made to assist public libraries in improving library services, promoting access to learning and information resources to users of all ages, to promote wider access to information through technology, and to support collaborative activities between museums and libraries. The account for the Office of Library programs was formerly shown under the Department of Education, Office of Educational Research and Improvement.

Object Classification (in millions of dollars)

Identification code 59–0301–0–1–503	1999 actual	2000 est.	2001 est.
11.1 Personnel compensation: Full-time permanent	1	1	1
23.1 Rental payments to GSA			1
25.2 Other services	1	1	2
41.0 Grants, subsidies, and contributions	164	163	168
99.0 Subtotal, direct obligations	166	165	172
99.5 Below reporting threshold	1	1	1
99.9 Total new obligations	167	166	173

Personnel Summary

Identification code 59–0301–0–1–503	1999 actual	2000 est.	2001 est.
1001 Total compensable workyears: Full-time equivalent employment	18	22	23

ADMINISTRATIVE PROVISIONS

None of the funds appropriated to the National Foundation on the Arts and the Humanities may be used to process any grant or contract documents which do not include the text of 18 U.S.C. 1913: *Provided*, That none of the funds appropriated to the National Foundation on the Arts and the Humanities may be used for official reception and representation expenses: *Provided further*, That funds from nonappropriated sources may be used as necessary for official reception and representation expenses. *(Department of the Interior and Related Agencies Appropriations Act, 2000, as enacted by section 1000(a)(3) of the Consolidated Appropriations Act, 2000 (P.L. 106–113).)*

NATIONAL LABOR RELATIONS BOARD

Federal Funds

General and special funds:

SALARIES AND EXPENSES

For expenses necessary for the National Labor Relations Board to carry out the functions vested in it by the Labor-Management Relations Act, 1947, as amended (29 U.S.C. 141–167), and other laws, [$206,500,000] *$216,438,000*: *Provided*, That no part of this appropriation shall be available to organize or assist in organizing agricultural laborers or used in connection with investigations, hearings, directives, or orders concerning bargaining units composed of agricultural laborers as referred to in section 2(3) of the Act of July 5, 1935 (29 U.S.C. 152), and as amended by the Labor-Management Relations Act, 1947, as amended, and as defined in section 3(f) of the Act of June 25, 1938 (29 U.S.C. 203), and including in said definition employees engaged in the maintenance and operation of ditches, canals, reservoirs, and waterways when maintained or operated on a mutual, nonprofit basis and at least 95 percent of the water stored or supplied thereby is used for farming purposes. *(Departments of Labor, Health and Human Services, and Education, and Related Agencies Appropriations Act, 2000, as enacted by section 1000(a)(4) of the Consolidated Appropriations Act, 2000 (P.L. 106–113).)*

Program and Financing (in millions of dollars)

Identification code 63–0100–0–1–505	1999 actual	2000 est.	2001 est.
Obligations by program activity:			
00.01 Field investigation	145	162	170
00.02 Administrative law judge hearing	12	14	15
00.03 Board adjudication	17	19	20
00.04 Securing compliance with Board orders	9	10	10
00.05 Internal Review	1	1	1
10.00 Total new obligations	184	206	216
Budgetary resources available for obligation:			
22.00 New budget authority (gross)	184	206	216
23.95 Total new obligations	–184	–206	–216
New budget authority (gross), detail:			
Discretionary:			
40.00 Appropriation	184	207	216
40.76 Reduction pursuant to P.L. 106–113		–1	
43.00 Appropriation (total discretionary)	184	206	216
Change in unpaid obligations:			
72.40 Unpaid obligations, start of year: Obligated balance, start of year	12	13	21
73.10 Total new obligations	184	206	216
73.20 Total outlays (gross)	–182	–198	–221
74.40 Unpaid obligations, end of year: Obligated balance, end of year	13	21	16
Outlays (gross), detail:			
86.90 Outlays from new discretionary authority	171	186	201
86.93 Outlays from discretionary balances	11	12	21
87.00 Total outlays (gross)	182	198	221
Net budget authority and outlays:			
89.00 Budget authority	184	206	216
90.00 Outlays	182	198	221

The Board resolves representation disputes in industry, and remedies and prevents specified unfair labor practices by employers or labor organizations. Case intake and additional program statistics appear in the table below.

PROGRAM STATISTICS

	1999 actual	*2000 est.*	*2001 est.*
Case intake:			
Unfair labor practice cases	27,051	30,000	30,000
Representation cases	6,306	6,005	6,200
Administrative law judges:			
Hearings closed	431	534	600
Adjustments after hearings closed	0	1	1
Decisions issued	474	569	611
Board adjudication:			
Contested Board decisions issued	422	478	635
Regional director decisions	704	725	905
Representation election cases:			
Decisions issued	216	167	177
Objection rulings	160	176	218
Board decisions requiring court enforcement	103	112	114

Field investigation.—Charges of unfair labor practices and petitions for elections to resolve representation disputes are investigated by regional office personnel. Ninety percent of the unfair labor practice cases and 85 percent of the representation cases are closed by settlement, dismissal, or withdrawal. The remainder are prepared for public hearing. The agency strives to maximize the voluntary settlement of all cases and to avoid litigation.

Administrative law judge hearing.—Administrative law judges conduct public hearings in unfair labor practice cases. Their findings and recommendations are set forth in their decisions.

Board adjudication.—In an unfair labor practice case, a judge's decision becomes a Board order if no exceptions are filed. About 30 percent of these decisions become automatic Board orders or are complied with voluntarily. The remainder, with exceptions filed, requires contested Board decision. In representation cases, regional directors initially decide the issues by Board delegation. The Board itself decides representation issues on referral from regional directors or by granting a request for review of a regional director's decision. The Board also rules on objection and challenge questions in election cases.

Securing compliance with Board orders.—If the parties do not voluntarily comply with the Board's order involving unfair labor practices, the Board must request that the appellate courts enforce its decisions.

Object Classification (in millions of dollars)

Identification code 63–0100–0–1–505	1999 actual	2000 est.	2001 est.
Personnel compensation:			
11.1 Full-time permanent	116	124	131

General and special funds—Continued

SALARIES AND EXPENSES—Continued

Object Classification (in millions of dollars)—Continued

Identification code 63–0100–0–1–505		1999 actual	2000 est.	2001 est.
11.3	Other than full-time permanent	4	5	4
11.5	Other personnel compensation	2	2	2
11.9	Total personnel compensation	122	131	137
12.1	Civilian personnel benefits	23	27	30
21.0	Travel and transportation of persons	3	5	6
23.1	Rental payments to GSA	21	22	22
23.3	Communications, utilities, and miscellaneous charges	2	3	3
25.2	Other services	9	14	13
26.0	Supplies and materials	1	1	1
31.0	Equipment	3	3	4
99.9	Total new obligations	184	206	216

Personnel Summary

Identification code 63–0100–0–1–505		1999 actual	2000 est.	2001 est.
1001	Total compensable workyears: Full-time equivalent employment	1,823	1,947	2,002

NATIONAL MEDIATION BOARD

Federal Funds

General and special funds:

SALARIES AND EXPENSES

For expenses necessary to carry out the provisions of the Railway Labor Act, as amended (45 U.S.C. 151–188), including emergency boards appointed by the President, [$9,600,000: *Provided*, That unobligated balances at the end of fiscal year 2000 not needed for emergency boards shall remain available for other statutory purposes through September 30, 2001] *$10,400,000*. *(Departments of Labor, Health and Human Services, and Education, and Related Agencies Appropriations Act, 2000, as enacted by section 1000(a)(4) of the Consolidated Appropriations Act, 2000 (P.L. 106–113).)*

Program and Financing (in millions of dollars)

Identification code 95–2400–0–1–505		1999 actual	2000 est.	2001 est.
	Obligations by program activity:			
00.01	Mediatory services	6	7	7
00.03	Arbitration services	2	3	3
10.00	Total new obligations	8	10	10
	Budgetary resources available for obligation:			
22.00	New budget authority (gross)	8	10	10
23.95	Total new obligations	−8	−10	−10
	New budget authority (gross), detail:			
	Discretionary:			
40.00	Appropriation	8	10	10
	Change in unpaid obligations:			
72.40	Unpaid obligations, start of year: Obligated balance, start of year	2	1	1
73.10	Total new obligations	8	10	10
73.20	Total outlays (gross)	−9	−10	−10
74.40	Unpaid obligations, end of year: Obligated balance, end of year	1	1	1
	Outlays (gross), detail:			
86.90	Outlays from new discretionary authority	7	9	9
86.93	Outlays from discretionary balances	2	1	2
87.00	Total outlays (gross)	9	10	10
	Net budget authority and outlays:			
89.00	Budget authority	8	10	10
90.00	Outlays	9	10	10

Mediatory services.—The Board mediates disputes over wages, hours, and working conditions for some 746 rail and air carriers and approximately 795,000 employees in the two industries.

The Board also provides technical assistance to enable labor and industry representatives to explore informally the relevant economic and noneconomic problems that condition collective bargaining in the railroad and airline industries.

Mediation cases:	1999 actual	2000 est.	2001 est.
Pending, start of year	159	112	130
Received during year	114	120	130
Closed during year	161	102	102
Pending, end of year	112	130	158

Employee Representation.—The Board investigates representation disputes involving the various crafts or classes of railroad and airline employees to determine their choice of representatives for the purpose of collective bargaining.

Representation cases:	1999 actual	2000 est.	2001 est.
Pending, start of year	11	14	14
Received during year	75	80	85
Closed during year	72	80	85
Pending, end of year	14	14	14
Freedom of Information Act (FOIA) requests received	44	60	60
Investigation cases closed	26	32	32

Emergency disputes.—When the parties fail to resolve their disputes through mediation, they are urged to submit their differences to arbitration. If neither mediation nor voluntary arbitration is successful, the President, when notified of disputes which substantially threaten to interrupt essential service, may appoint emergency boards to investigate and report on the dispute. Such reports usually serve as a basis for resolving the disputes.

The Northeast Rail Service Act of 1981 (P.L. 102–29) amended the Railway Labor Act (RLA) by adding a new emergency dispute procedure covering disputes between a publicly funded and operated commuter carrier and its employees. The 1981 Act requires the Board to appoint the public members of factfinding panels on Conrail.

Boards/panels created:	1999 actual	2000 est.	2001 est.
Emergency (sec. 160)	0	2	2
Emergency (sec. 159a)	0	2	2
Arbitration Boards	5	8	10
Arbitration Panels (PL 102–29)	0	0	0
Airline SBA Panels	97	120	125
ICC–LPP Panels	6	10	12

Arbitration under sections 3 and 7 of the RLA.—Railroad employee grievances resulting from disputes over the interpretation or application of collective bargaining contracts may be brought for settlement to the National Railroad Adjustment Board (NRAB). The divisions of the Board are composed of an equal number of carrier and union representatives compensated by the party or parties they represent. Public Law 89–456 provides for the adjustment of disputes involving grievances resulting from interpretation or application of bargaining agreements in the railroad industry otherwise referable to the NRAB.

Administrative direction and support for the public law boards, special boards of adjustment, and the NRAB are provided by Federal employees who are compensated by the National Mediation Board.

Arbitration cases:	1999 actual	2000 est.	2001 est.
Pending, start of year	11,010	11,237	11,115
Received during year	5,880	5,536	5,536
Closed during year	[1] 5,653	5,658	5,658
Pending, end of year	11,237	11,115	10,993

[1] Includes 951 cases withdrawn or decided by the parties.

Object Classification (in millions of dollars)

Identification code 95–2400–0–1–505		1999 actual	2000 est.	2001 est.
	Personnel compensation:			
11.1	Full-time permanent	3	5	5

11.8	Special personal services payments	2	2	2
11.9	Total personnel compensation	5	7	7
12.1	Civilian personnel benefits	1	1	1
21.0	Travel and transportation of persons	1	1	1
23.1	Rental payments to GSA	1	1	1
99.9	Total new obligations	8	10	10

Personnel Summary

Identification code 95–2400–0–1–505		1999 actual	2000 est.	2001 est.
1001	Total compensable workyears: Full-time equivalent employment	43	48	52

NATIONAL TRANSPORTATION SAFETY BOARD

Federal Funds

General and special funds:

Salaries and Expenses

For necessary expenses of the National Transportation Safety Board, including hire of passenger motor vehicles and aircraft; services as authorized by 5 U.S.C. 3109, but at rates for individuals not to exceed the per diem rate equivalent to the rate for a GS–15; uniforms, or allowances therefor, as authorized by law (5 U.S.C. 5901–5902) [$57,000,000] *$62,942,000*, of which not to exceed $2,000 may be used for official reception and representation expenses*: Provided, That contingent upon the enactment of authorizing legislation, the Chairman of the Board shall charge a fee to be levied on all air, motor, ocean, rail, and pipeline carriers for accident investigations, and such fee shall be deposited as an offsetting collection to this appropriation, to remain available until expended for the purpose of such accident investigations: Provided further, That upon enactment of such authorizing legislation, the amount appropriated above from the General Fund shall be reduced by $10,000,000. (Department of Transportation and Related Agencies Appropriations Act, 2000.)*

Program and Financing (in millions of dollars)

Identification code 95–0310–0–1–407		1999 actual	2000 est.	2001 est.
	Obligations by program activity:			
00.01	Policy and direction	13	13	14
00.02	Safety Recommendations	2	2	2
00.03	Aviation safety	18	18	20
00.04	Surface transportation safety	13	13	15
00.05	Research and engineering	10	10	10
00.06	Administrative law judges	1	1	2
10.00	Total new obligations	57	57	63
	Budgetary resources available for obligation:			
21.40	Unobligated balance available, start of year	3	2	
22.00	New budget authority (gross)	55	57	63
23.90	Total budgetary resources available for obligation	58	59	63
23.95	Total new obligations	–57	–57	–63
24.40	Unobligated balance available, end of year	2		
	New budget authority (gross), detail:			
	Discretionary:			
	Appropriation:			
40.00	Appropriation	53	57	63
40.00	Appropriation	2		
43.00	Appropriation (total discretionary)	55	57	63
	Change in unpaid obligations:			
72.40	Unpaid obligations, start of year: Obligated balance, start of year	28	25	8
73.10	Total new obligations	57	57	63
73.20	Total outlays (gross)	–60	–76	–63
74.40	Unpaid obligations, end of year: Obligated balance, end of year	25	8	8
	Outlays (gross), detail:			
86.90	Outlays from new discretionary authority	48	51	57
86.93	Outlays from discretionary balances	12	24	6
87.00	Total outlays (gross)	60	76	63
	Net budget authority and outlays:			
89.00	Budget authority	55	57	63
90.00	Outlays	60	76	63

Summary of Budget Authority and Outlays

(in millions of dollars)

Enacted/requested:	1999 actual	2000 est.	2001 est.
Budget Authority	55	57	63
Outlays	60	75	63
Supplemental proposal:			
Budget Authority		18	
Outlays		16	2
Legislative proposal, not subject to PAYGO:			
Budget Authority			–10
Outlays			–10
Total:			
Budget Authority	55	75	53
Outlays	60	91	55

The National Transportation Safety Board (NTSB), as an independent nonregulatory agency, is charged with promoting transportation safety through the investigation of accidents, the conduct of special studies, the development of recommendations to prevent accidents, the evaluation of the effectiveness of other Government agencies in preventing transportation accidents, and the review of appeals of adverse certificate and civil penalty actions taken by the Administrators of agencies of the Department of Transportation involving airman and seaman certificates and licenses.

In 2001, the Administration requests a total funding level of $63 million for NTSB Salaries and Expenses, including $10 million to be derived from a proposed commercial accident investigation fee. This funding level represents a 10.4 percent increase above the 2000 enacted level of $57 million, and will allow the NTSB to fulfill its role in improving safety on the Nation's transportation system.

Object Classification (in millions of dollars)

Identification code 95–0310–0–1–407		1999 actual	2000 est.	2001 est.
	Personnel compensation:			
11.1	Full-time permanent	29	30	33
11.3	Other than full-time permanent	1	1	2
11.5	Other personnel compensation	1	1	1
11.9	Total personnel compensation	31	32	36
12.1	Civilian personnel benefits	7	8	9
21.0	Travel and transportation of persons	3	4	4
23.1	Rental payments to GSA	6	6	6
23.3	Communications, utilities, and miscellaneous charges	2	2	2
25.2	Other services	5	3	4
26.0	Supplies and materials	1	1	1
31.0	Equipment	1	1	1
99.0	Subtotal, direct obligations	56	57	63
99.5	Below reporting threshold	1		
99.9	Total new obligations	57	57	63

Personnel Summary

Identification code 95–0310–0–1–407		1999 actual	2000 est.	2001 est.
1001	Total compensable workyears: Full-time equivalent employment	439	439	458

National Transportation Safety Board

(Legislative proposal, not subject to PAYGO)

Program and Financing (in millions of dollars)

Identification code 95–0310–2–1–407		1999 actual	2000 est.	2001 est.
	Obligations by program activity:			
00.01	Aviation safety			–6

General and special funds—Continued

NATIONAL TRANSPORTATION SAFETY BOARD—Continued

Program and Financing (in millions of dollars)—Continued

Identification code 95–0310–2–1–407	1999 actual	2000 est.	2001 est.
00.02 Surface transportation safety			−4
09.01 Aviation Safety			6
09.02 Surface Transportation			4
10.00 Total new obligations			
New budget authority (gross), detail:			
Discretionary:			
40.00 Appropriation			−10
68.00 Spending authority from offsetting collections: Offsetting collections (cash)			10
70.00 Total new budget authority (gross)			
Change in unpaid obligations:			
73.10 Total new obligations			
73.20 Total outlays (gross)			
Offsets:			
Against gross budget authority and outlays:			
88.40 Offsetting collections (cash) from: Non-Federal sources			−10
Net budget authority and outlays:			
89.00 Budget authority			−10
90.00 Outlays			−10

To offset a portion of the NTSB's growing cost of commercial accident investigations, a new aviation accident recovery and investigation fee is proposed. This fee, which would be paid by commercial air, motor, ocean, rail, and pipeline carriers based on a proxy for risk, would collect an estimated $10 million in 2001.

Object Classification (in millions of dollars)

Identification code 95–0310–2–1–407	1999 actual	2000 est.	2001 est.
Direct obligations:			
11.1 Personnel compensation: Full-time permanent			−5
12.1 Civilian personnel benefits			−2
23.1 Rental payments to GSA			−1
25.2 Other services			−1
26.0 Supplies and materials			−1
99.0 Subtotal, direct obligations			−10
99.0 Reimbursable obligations			10
99.9 Total new obligations			

Personnel Summary

Identification code 95–0310–2–1–407	1999 actual	2000 est.	2001 est.
Direct:			
1001 Total compensable workyears: Full-time equivalent employment			−75
Reimbursable:			
2001 Total compensable workyears: Full-time equivalent employment			75

EMERGENCY FUND

Program and Financing (in millions of dollars)

Identification code 95–0311–0–1–407	1999 actual	2000 est.	2001 est.
Budgetary resources available for obligation:			
21.40 Unobligated balance available, start of year	1	2	2
22.00 New budget authority (gross)	1		
23.90 Total budgetary resources available for obligation	2	2	2
23.95 Total new obligations			
24.40 Unobligated balance available, end of year	2	2	2
New budget authority (gross), detail:			
Discretionary:			
40.00 Appropriation	1		
Net budget authority and outlays:			
89.00 Budget authority	1		
90.00 Outlays			

The National Transportation Safety Board is mandated by Congress to investigate all catastrophic transportation accidents and, therefore, has no control over the frequency of costly accident investigations. The emergency fund provides a funding mechanism by which periodic accident investigation cost fluctuations can be met without delaying critical phases of the investigations. The current balance of $2 million is sufficient to cover unanticipated costs associated with an increased number of accidents, and thus the Administration does not propose new funding in 2001.

NEIGHBORHOOD REINVESTMENT CORPORATION

Federal Funds

General and special funds:

PAYMENT TO THE NEIGHBORHOOD REINVESTMENT CORPORATION

For payment to the Neighborhood Reinvestment Corporation for use in neighborhood reinvestment activities, as authorized by the Neighborhood Reinvestment Corporation Act (42 U.S.C. 8101–8107), [$75,000,000] *$90,000,000. (Departments of Veterans Affairs and Housing and Urban Development, and Independent Agencies Appropriations Act, 2000.)*

Program and Financing (in millions of dollars)

Identification code 82–1300–0–1–451	1999 actual	2000 est.	2001 est.
Obligations by program activity:			
10.00 Total new obligations (object class 41.0)	90	75	90
Budgetary resources available for obligation:			
22.00 New budget authority (gross)	90	75	90
23.95 Total new obligations	−90	−75	−90
New budget authority (gross), detail:			
Discretionary:			
40.00 Appropriation	90	75	90
Change in unpaid obligations:			
73.10 Total new obligations	90	75	90
73.20 Total outlays (gross)	−90	−75	−90
Outlays (gross), detail:			
86.90 Outlays from new discretionary authority	90	75	90
Net budget authority and outlays:			
89.00 Budget authority	90	75	90
90.00 Outlays	90	75	90

The major activities of the Corporation include: establishing neighborhood partnership programs known as NeighborWorks Organizations (NWOs); assisting in the expansion of NeighborWorks organizations to additional neighborhoods; providing training and technical assistance; identifying, evaluating, supporting and replicating successful neighborhood preservation projects that show promise for reversing neighborhood decline; promoting a national secondary market and other financing mechanisms for NWOs; and granting lending and equity capital to promote homeownership and other affordable housing.

The Corporation receives both Federal and non-Federal funding to finance its program activities. For 2001, a program level of $90,000,000 is requested. The following tables reflect the total program activity of the Corporation and include all sources of financing, both Federal and non-Federal.

BUDGET ACTIVITY

[In millions of dollars]

	1999 actual	2000 est.	2001 est.
Neighborworks Programs:			
1. Creation of new programs	2	2	2
2. Capacity building	31	28	30
3. Preserving affordable housing/equity capital	34	23	32
4. Program reviews	3	3	4
5. Training and informing	12	12	13
6. Secondary market activities	8	8	8
7. General administration	7	8	8
Total corporate obligations	97	84	97
Sources of financing:			
1. Federal appropriation	90	75	90
2. Reimbursements for services provided	4	4	3
3. Other sources	4	3	4
Unused balance, start of year	1	2	0
Net obligations incurred	97	84	97
Unused balance, end of year	2	0	0
Obligated balances, start of year	5	8	8
Obligated balances, end of year	8	8	8
Net corporate outlay	94	84	97

Statement of Operations (in millions of dollars)

Identification code 82–1300–0–1–451		1998 actual	1999 actual	2000 est.	2001 est.
0101	Revenue	57	96	82	96
0102	Expense	–57	–97	–82	–96
0105	Net income or loss (–)		–1		

Balance Sheet (in millions of dollars)

Identification code 82–1300–0–1–451		1998 actual	1999 actual	2000 est.	2001 est.
	ASSETS:				
1601	Net value of assets related to pre–1992 direct loans receivable and acquired defaulted guaranteed loans receivable: Direct loans, gross	1			
	Other Federal assets:				
1801	Cash and other monetary assets	6	8	7	7
1803	Property, plant and equipment, net	1	1	2	2
1999	Total assets	8	9	9	9
	LIABILITIES:				
	Non-Federal liabilities:				
2201	Accounts payable	3	3	3	3
2207	Other	2	5	3	3
2999	Total liabilities	5	8	6	6
	NET POSITION:				
3300	Cumulative results of operations	3	1	3	3
3999	Total net position	3	1	3	3
4999	Total liabilities and net position	8	9	9	9

Object Classification of Corporation Obligations (in millions of dollars)

	1999 actual	2000 est.	2001 est.
Salaries and benefits	19	19	20
Occupancy	2	2	3
Professional services	4	6	5
Travel and transportation of persons	2	2	2
Conferences and workshops	1	1	1
Grants and grant commitments	64	50	61
Other operating costs	5	4	5
Total obligations	97	84	97

Personnel Summary

	1999 actual	2000 est.	2001 est.
Non-Federal employees: Total compensable workyears:			
Full-time equivalent employment	262	245	255
Full-time equivalent of overtime and holiday hours	7	7	7

NUCLEAR REGULATORY COMMISSION

Federal Funds

General and special funds:

SALARIES AND EXPENSES

For necessary expenses of the Commission in carrying out the purposes of the Energy Reorganization Act of 1974, as amended, and the Atomic Energy Act of 1954, as amended, including official representation expenses (not to exceed $15,000), [$465,000,000] *$481,900,000*, to remain available until expended: *Provided*, That of the amount appropriated herein, [$19,150,000] *$21,600,000* shall be derived from the Nuclear Waste Fund: *Provided further*, That revenues from licensing fees, inspection services, and other services and collections estimated at [$442,000,000] *$447,958,000* in fiscal year [2000] *2001* shall be retained and used for necessary salaries and expenses in this account, notwithstanding 31 U.S.C. 3302, and shall remain available until expended: *Provided further*, That [$3,850,000] *$3,200,000* of the funds herein appropriated for regulatory reviews and [other] assistance [provided to the Department of Energy and] *to* other Federal agencies *and States* shall be excluded from license fee revenues, notwithstanding 42 U.S.C. 2214: *Provided further*, That the sum herein appropriated shall be reduced by the amount of revenues received during fiscal year [2000] *2001* so as to result in a final fiscal year [2000] *2001* appropriation estimated at not more than [$23,000,000] *$33,942,000*. *(Energy and Water Development Appropriations Act, 2000.)*

Unavailable Collections (in millions of dollars)

Identification code 31–0200–0–1–276		1999 actual	2000 est.	2001 est.
	Balance, start of year:			
01.99	Balance, start of year			
	Receipts:			
02.01	Nuclear facility fees, Nuclear Regulatory Commission	442	447	454
	Appropriation:			
05.01	Salaries and expenses	–442	–441	–448
05.03	Office of Inspector General		–6	–6
05.99	Subtotal appropriation	–442	–447	–454
07.99	Total balance, end of year			

Program and Financing (in millions of dollars)

Identification code 31–0200–0–1–276		1999 actual	2000 est.	2001 est.
	Obligations by program activity:			
	Direct program:			
00.01	Nuclear Reactor Safety	211	223	217
00.02	Nuclear Materials Safety	53	59	57
00.03	Nuclear Waste Safety	48	55	58
00.04	International Nuclear Safety Support	4	5	5
00.06	Management and Support	155	147	145
09.01	Reimbursable program	5	5	6
10.00	Total new obligations	476	494	488
	Budgetary resources available for obligation:			
21.40	Unobligated balance available, start of year	29	29	
22.00	New budget authority (gross)	467	468	486
22.10	Resources available from recoveries of prior year obligations	8		
22.21	Unobligated balance transferred to other accounts		–4	
23.90	Total budgetary resources available for obligation	504	493	486
23.95	Total new obligations	–476	–494	–488
24.40	Unobligated balance available, end of year	29		
	New budget authority (gross), detail:			
	Discretionary:			
40.00	Appropriation	5	4	12
	Appropriation (special fund, definite):			
40.20	Appropriation (special fund, definite)	442	441	448
40.20	Appropriation (special fund, definite)	17	19	22
40.75	Reduction pursuant to P.L. 106–51	–1		
43.00	Appropriation (total discretionary)	463	464	482
68.00	Spending authority from offsetting collections: Offsetting collections (cash)	4	4	4
70.00	Total new budget authority (gross)	467	468	486

General and special funds—Continued

SALARIES AND EXPENSES—Continued

Program and Financing (in millions of dollars)—Continued

Identification code 31–0200–0–1–276	1999 actual	2000 est.	2001 est.
Change in unpaid obligations:			
72.40 Unpaid obligations, start of year: Obligated balance, start of year	122	111	136
73.10 Total new obligations	476	494	488
73.20 Total outlays (gross)	–478	–469	–482
73.40 Adjustments in expired accounts (net)	–1		
73.45 Adjustments in unexpired accounts	–8		
74.40 Unpaid obligations, end of year: Obligated balance, end of year	111	136	142
Outlays (gross), detail:			
86.90 Outlays from new discretionary authority	356	352	366
86.93 Outlays from discretionary balances	122	116	116
87.00 Total outlays (gross)	478	469	482
Offsets:			
Against gross budget authority and outlays:			
88.00 Offsetting collections (cash) from: Federal sources	–4	–4	–4
Net budget authority and outlays:			
89.00 Budget authority	463	464	482
Outlays:			
90.00 Outlays	457	447	457
90.00 Outlays	17	18	21

Nuclear Reactor Safety.—A major part of the NRC's mission is to ensure that its licensees design, construct, and operate civilian reactor facilities safely. The Atomic Energy Act and the Energy Reorganization Act provide the foundation for regulating the Nation's civilian nuclear power industry. Nuclear reactor safety encompasses all NRC efforts to ensure that civilian nuclear reactor facilities and non-power reactors are operated in a manner that provides adequate protection of public health and safety and the environment, and protects against radiological sabotage and theft or diversion of special nuclear materials. These efforts include reactor licensing; reactor license renewal; operator licensing; financial assurance; inspection; performance assessment; identification and resolution of safety issues; reactor regulatory research; regulation development; operating experience evaluation; incident investigation; threat assessment; emergency response; investigation of alleged wrong doing by licensees, applicants, contractors, or vendors; imposition of enforcement sanctions for violations of NRC requirements; and reactor technical and regulatory training.

Nuclear Materials Safety.—Nuclear materials safety encompasses all NRC efforts to ensure that NRC-regulation aspects of nuclear fuel cycle facilities and nuclear materials activities are handled in a manner that provides adequate protection of public health and safety. These efforts include regulation and guidance development; nuclear materials research; licensing/certification, inspection, and enforcement activities; identification and resolution of safety and safeguard issues; operating experience evaluation; incident investigation; threat assessment; emergency response; technical training; and investigation of alleged wrongdoing by licensees, applicants, certificate holders, contractors and vendors. This arena provides regulatory assistance to the Department of Energy, including activities related to the anticipated commercial vitrification of high-level waste in Hanford tanks.

Nuclear Waste Safety.—Nuclear waste safety encompasses the NRC's high-level waste regulatory activities associated with high-level waste disposal at Yucca Mountain as mandated by the Nuclear Waste Policy Act, the Nuclear Waste Policy Amendments Act; the Energy Policy Act; NRC regulatory and oversight activities for decommissioning, which involves safely removing a facility from service and reducing residual radiation to a level that permits the property to be released; the safe and secure storage and transportation of radioactive materials through the certification of spent fuel storage containers and transportation packages; and assistance to Agreement States to complete activities associated with the closure of formerly licensed NRC sites when the original owner or successor cannot be found. Low-level radioactive waste activities associated with the disposal of waste are addressed in accordance with the Low-Level Radioactive Waste Policy Act.

International Nuclear Safety Support.—International Nuclear Safety Support encompasses NRC international activities, some of which support the agency's domestic mission and many of which support broader U.S. national interests. These activities include international policy formulation, export-import licensing of nuclear materials and equipment, treaty implementation, international information exchange activities, and international safety and safeguards assistance, and deterring nuclear proliferation.

Management and Support.—Management and support encompasses NRC central policy direction, legal advice for the Commission, analysis of long-term policy issues, administrative proceedings review and advice, liaison with outside constituents and other government agencies, financial management, all administrative and logistical support, information resources management, executive management services for the Commission, personnel and training, and matters involving small and disadvantaged businesses and civil rights.

Object Classification (in millions of dollars)

Identification code 31–0200–0–1–276	1999 actual	2000 est.	2001 est.
Direct obligations:			
Personnel compensation:			
11.1 Full-time permanent	216	212	221
11.3 Other than full-time permanent	4	4	4
11.5 Other personnel compensation	7	7	7
11.8 Special personal services payments	1	30	1
11.9 Total personnel compensation	228	253	233
12.1 Civilian personnel benefits	47	45	48
21.0 Travel and transportation of persons	12	13	14
22.0 Transportation of things	1	1	1
23.1 Rental payments to GSA	19	18	19
23.3 Communications, utilities, and miscellaneous charges	7	8	9
24.0 Printing and reproduction	2	2	2
25.1 Advisory and assistance services	2	2	2
25.2 Other services	55	54	56
25.3 Purchases of goods and services from Government accounts	72	70	73
25.4 Operation and maintenance of facilities	3	2	3
25.7 Operation and maintenance of equipment	3	2	3
26.0 Supplies and materials	2	2	1
31.0 Equipment	17	16	17
41.0 Grants, subsidies, and contributions	1	1	1
99.0 Subtotal, direct obligations	471	489	482
99.0 Reimbursable obligations	5	5	6
99.9 Total new obligations	476	494	488

Personnel Summary

Identification code 31–0200–0–1–276	1999 actual	2000 est.	2001 est.
1001 Total compensable workyears: Full-time equivalent employment	2,796	2,801	2,776

OFFICE OF INSPECTOR GENERAL

(INCLUDING TRANSFER OF FUNDS)

For necessary expenses of the Office of Inspector General in carrying out the provisions of the Inspector General Act of 1978, as amended, [$5,000,000] *$6,200,000*, to remain available until expended: *Provided, That revenues from licensing fees, inspection services, and other services and collections estimated at $6,076,000 in* *fiscal year 2001 shall be retained and be available until expended, for necessary salaries and expenses in this account: Provided further,* That the sum herein appropriated shall be reduced by the amount of revenues received during fiscal year [2000] *2001* so as to result in a final fiscal year [2000] *2001* appropriation estimated at not more than [$0] *$124,000. (Energy and Water Development Appropriations Act, 2000.)*

Program and Financing (in millions of dollars)

Identification code 31–0300–0–1–276		1999 actual	2000 est.	2001 est.
	Obligations by program activity:			
00.01	Inspector General	5	6	6
10.00	Total new obligations	5	6	6
	Budgetary resources available for obligation:			
21.40	Unobligated balance available, start of year	1	1	
22.00	New budget authority (gross)	5	6	6
23.90	Total budgetary resources available for obligation	6	7	6
23.95	Total new obligations	−5	−6	−6
24.40	Unobligated balance available, end of year	1		
	New budget authority (gross), detail:			
	Discretionary:			
40.00	Appropriation	5		
40.20	Appropriation (special fund, definite)		6	6
43.00	Appropriation (total discretionary)	5	6	6
	Change in unpaid obligations:			
72.40	Unpaid obligations, start of year: Obligated balance, start of year	1	2	2
73.10	Total new obligations	5	6	6
73.20	Total outlays (gross)	−5	−6	−6
74.40	Unpaid obligations, end of year: Obligated balance, end of year	2	2	2
	Outlays (gross), detail:			
86.90	Outlays from new discretionary authority	5	5	5
86.93	Outlays from discretionary balances			1
87.00	Total outlays (gross)	5	6	6
	Net budget authority and outlays:			
89.00	Budget authority	5	6	6
90.00	Outlays	5	6	6

The Inspector General Act Amendments of 1988 established a statutory Office of the Inspector General within the NRC that provides the Commission and Congress with an independent review and appraisal of the integrity of NRC programs and operations. The function of the Office of the Inspector General is to conduct and supervise audits and investigations relating to all facets of agency programs and operations.

Object Classification (in millions of dollars)

Identification code 31–0300–0–1–276		1999 actual	2000 est.	2001 est.
11.1	Personnel compensation: Full-time permanent	3	4	4
12.1	Civilian personnel benefits	1	1	1
25.2	Other services	1	1	1
99.9	Total new obligations	5	6	6

Personnel Summary

Identification code 31–0300–0–1–276		1999 actual	2000 est.	2001 est.
1001	Total compensable workyears: Full-time equivalent employment	40	44	44

NUCLEAR WASTE TECHNICAL REVIEW BOARD

Federal Funds

General and special funds:

SALARIES AND EXPENSES

(INCLUDING TRANSFER OF FUNDS)

For necessary expenses of the Nuclear Waste Technical Review Board, as authorized by Public Law 100–203, section 5051, [$2,600,000] *$3,200,000*, to be derived from the Nuclear Waste Fund, and to remain available until expended. *(Energy and Water Development Appropriations Act, 2000.)*

Program and Financing (in millions of dollars)

Identification code 48–0500–0–1–271		1999 actual	2000 est.	2001 est.
	Obligations by program activity:			
10.00	Total new obligations	3	3	3
	Budgetary resources available for obligation:			
22.00	New budget authority (gross)	3	3	3
23.95	Total new obligations	−3	−3	−3
	New budget authority (gross), detail:			
	Discretionary:			
40.20	Appropriation (special fund, definite)	3	3	3
	Change in unpaid obligations:			
73.10	Total new obligations	3	3	3
73.20	Total outlays (gross)	−2	−3	−3
	Outlays (gross), detail:			
86.90	Outlays from new discretionary authority	2	3	3
	Net budget authority and outlays:			
89.00	Budget authority	3	3	3
90.00	Outlays	2	3	3

The Nuclear Waste Technical Review Board is directed to evaluate the technical and scientific validity of the activities of the Department of Energy's nuclear waste disposal program undertaken after the enactment of the Nuclear Waste Policy Amendments Act of 1987. The Board must report its findings not less than two times a year to the Congress and the Secretary of Energy.

Object Classification (in millions of dollars)

Identification code 48–0500–0–1–271		1999 actual	2000 est.	2001 est.
11.1	Direct obligations: Personnel compensation: Full-time permanent	1	1	1
99.5	Below reporting threshold	2	2	2
99.9	Total new obligations	3	3	3

Personnel Summary

Identification code 48–0500–0–1–271		1999 actual	2000 est.	2001 est.
1001	Total compensable workyears: Full-time equivalent employment	16	19	19

OCCUPATIONAL SAFETY AND HEALTH REVIEW COMMISSION

Federal Funds

General and special funds:

SALARIES AND EXPENSES

For expenses necessary for the Occupational Safety and Health Review Commission (29 U.S.C. 661), [8,500,000] *$8,720,000. (Departments of Labor, Health and Human Services, and Education, and Related Agencies Appropriations Act, 2000, as enacted by section*

General and special funds—Continued

SALARIES AND EXPENSES—Continued

1000(a)(4) of the Consolidated Appropriations Act, 2000 (P.L. 106–113).)

Program and Financing (in millions of dollars)

Identification code 95–2100–0–1–554	1999 actual	2000 est.	2001 est.
Obligations by program activity:			
00.01 Commission review	3	3	4
00.02 Administrative law judge determinations	3	3	3
00.03 Executive direction	2	2	2
10.00 Total new obligations	8	8	9
Budgetary resources available for obligation:			
22.00 New budget authority (gross)	8	8	9
23.95 Total new obligations	−8	−8	−9
New budget authority (gross), detail:			
Discretionary:			
40.00 Appropriation	8	8	9
Change in unpaid obligations:			
72.40 Unpaid obligations, start of year: Obligated balance, start of year	2	2	2
73.10 Total new obligations	8	8	9
73.20 Total outlays (gross)	−8	−8	−9
74.40 Unpaid obligations, end of year: Obligated balance, end of year	2	2	2
Outlays (gross), detail:			
86.90 Outlays from new discretionary authority	7	7	8
86.93 Outlays from discretionary balances	1	1	2
87.00 Total outlays (gross)	8	8	9
Net budget authority and outlays:			
89.00 Budget authority	8	8	9
90.00 Outlays	8	8	9

The Review Commission, established by the Occupational Safety and Health Act of 1970, adjudicates contested enforcement actions of the Secretary of Labor. The Commission holds factfinding hearings and issues orders affirming, modifying, or vacating the Secretary's enforcement actions.

SELECTED WORKLOAD DATA

	1999 actual	*2000 est.*	*2001 est.*
Commission review activities:			
Cases pending beginning of year	72	65	54
New cases received	36	49	55
Cases decided	43	60	60
Administrative law judge activities:			
Cases pending beginning of year	842	985	1,060
New cases received	2,324	2,450	2,550
Cases disposition:			
After assignment but without hearing	2,025	2,205	2,280
Heard and decided by judge	156	170	170

Object Classification (in millions of dollars)

Identification code 95–2100–0–1–554	1999 actual	2000 est.	2001 est.
11.1 Personnel compensation: Full-time permanent	5	6	6
12.1 Civilian personnel benefits	1	1	1
23.1 Rental payments to GSA	1	1	1
99.0 Subtotal, direct obligations	7	8	8
99.5 Below reporting threshold	1		1
99.9 Total new obligations	8	8	9

Personnel Summary

Identification code 95–2100–0–1–554	1999 actual	2000 est.	2001 est.
1001 Total compensable workyears: Full-time equivalent employment	65	70	70

OFFICE OF GOVERNMENT ETHICS

Federal Funds

General and special funds:

SALARIES AND EXPENSES

For necessary expenses to carry out functions of the Office of Government Ethics pursuant to the Ethics in Government Act of 1978, as amended and the Ethics Reform Act of 1989, including services as authorized by 5 U.S.C. 3109, rental of conference rooms in the District of Columbia and elsewhere, hire of passenger motor vehicles, and not to exceed $1,500 for official reception and representation expenses, [$9,114,000] *$9,684,000*. *(Independent Agencies Appropriations Act, 2000.)*

Program and Financing (in millions of dollars)

Identification code 95–1100–0–1–805	1999 actual	2000 est.	2001 est.
Obligations by program activity:			
10.00 Total new obligations	8	9	10
Budgetary resources available for obligation:			
22.00 New budget authority (gross)	9	9	10
23.95 Total new obligations	−8	−9	−10
New budget authority (gross), detail:			
Discretionary:			
40.00 Appropriation	8	9	10
Change in unpaid obligations:			
72.40 Unpaid obligations, start of year: Obligated balance, start of year	1	1	1
73.10 Total new obligations	8	9	10
73.20 Total outlays (gross)	−8	−9	−10
74.40 Unpaid obligations, end of year: Obligated balance, end of year	1	1	1
Outlays (gross), detail:			
86.90 Outlays from new discretionary authority	7	8	9
86.93 Outlays from discretionary balances	1	1	1
87.00 Total outlays (gross)	8	9	10
Net budget authority and outlays:			
89.00 Budget authority	8	9	9
90.00 Outlays	8	9	10

The Office of Government Ethics (OGE) is charged by law to provide overall direction of executive branch policies designed to prevent conflicts of interest and insure high ethical standards. The OGE discharges its responsibilities to preserve and promote public confidence in the integrity of executive branch officials by developing rules and regulations pertaining to conflicts of interest, post employment restrictions, standards of conduct, and public and confidential financial disclosure in the executive branch; by monitoring compliance with the public and confidential financial disclosure requirements of the Ethics in Government Act of 1978 and the Ethics Reform Act of 1989, to determine possible violations of applicable laws or regulations and recommending appropriate corrective action; by consulting with and assisting various officials in evaluating the effectiveness of applicable laws and the resolution of individual problems; and by preparing formal advisory opinions, informal letter opinions, policy memoranda, and Federal Register entries on how to interpret and comply with the requirements on conflicts of interest, post employment, standards of conduct, and financial disclosure.

Object Classification (in millions of dollars)

Identification code 95–1100–0–1–805	1999 actual	2000 est.	2001 est.
11.1 Personnel compensation: Full-time permanent	5	6	6
12.1 Civilian personnel benefits	1	1	2
23.1 Rental payments to GSA	1	1	1
99.0 Subtotal, direct obligations	7	8	9
99.5 Below reporting threshold	1	1	1

99.9	Total new obligations	8	9	10

Personnel Summary

Identification code 95–1100–0–1–805		1999 actual	2000 est.	2001 est.
1001	Total compensable workyears: Full-time equivalent employment	80	84	84

OFFICE OF NAVAJO AND HOPI INDIAN RELOCATION

Federal Funds

General and special funds:

SALARIES AND EXPENSES

For necessary expenses of the Office of Navajo and Hopi Indian Relocation as authorized by Public Law 93–531, [$8,000,000] *$15,000,000*, to remain available until expended: *Provided,* That funds provided in this or any other appropriations Act are to be used to relocate eligible individuals and groups including evictees from District 6, Hopi-partitioned lands residents, those in significantly substandard housing, and all others certified as eligible and not included in the preceding categories: *Provided further,* That none of the funds contained in this or any other Act may be used by the Office of Navajo and Hopi Indian Relocation to evict any single Navajo or Navajo family who, as of November 30, 1985, was physically domiciled on the lands partitioned to the Hopi Tribe unless a new or replacement home is provided for such household: *Provided further,* That no relocatee will be provided with more than one new or replacement home: *Provided further,* That the Office shall relocate any certified eligible relocatees who have selected and received an approved homesite on the Navajo reservation or selected a replacement residence off the Navajo reservation or on the land acquired pursuant to 25 U.S.C. 640d–10. *(Department of the Interior and Related Agencies Appropriations Act, 2000, as enacted by section 1000(a)(3) of the Consolidated Appropriations Act, 2000 (P.L. 106–113).)*

Program and Financing (in millions of dollars)

Identification code 48–1100–0–1–808		1999 actual	2000 est.	2001 est.
	Obligations by program activity:			
00.01	Operation of relocation office	6	6	5
00.03	Relocation payments (housing)	14	8	9
00.04	Discretionary fund payments	3	1	1
10.00	Total new obligations	23	15	15
	Budgetary resources available for obligation:			
21.40	Unobligated balance available, start of year	17	7	1
22.00	New budget authority (gross)	13	8	15
22.10	Resources available from recoveries of prior year obligations	....	1	....
23.90	Total budgetary resources available for obligation	30	16	16
23.95	Total new obligations	−23	−15	−15
24.40	Unobligated balance available, end of year	7	1	1
	New budget authority (gross), detail:			
	Discretionary:			
40.00	Appropriation	13	8	15
	Change in unpaid obligations:			
72.40	Unpaid obligations, start of year: Obligated balance, start of year	6	8	8
73.10	Total new obligations	23	15	15
73.20	Total outlays (gross)	−21	−15	−18
73.45	Adjustments in unexpired accounts	....	−1	....
74.40	Unpaid obligations, end of year: Obligated balance, end of year	8	8	5
	Outlays (gross), detail:			
86.90	Outlays from new discretionary authority	10	6	10
86.93	Outlays from discretionary balances	11	8	9
87.00	Total outlays (gross)	21	15	18
	Net budget authority and outlays:			
89.00	Budget authority	13	8	15
90.00	Outlays	21	15	18

The Office of Navajo and Hopi Indian Relocation was established by Public Law 93–531 to plan and conduct relocation activities associated with the settlement of a land dispute in northern Arizona between the two tribes.

Bonuses are paid to clients who volunteered for relocation prior to July 7, 1985. Relocation of clients includes such activities as certification, housing acquisition and construction, and land acquisition. Discretionary funds will be used for activities which will facilitate and expedite the overall relocation effort.

Object Classification (in millions of dollars)

Identification code 48–1100–0–1–808		1999 actual	2000 est.	2001 est.
11.1	Personnel compensation: Full-time permanent	4	4	3
12.1	Civilian personnel benefits	1	1	1
25.2	Other services	1	1	1
32.0	Land and structures	14	8	9
41.0	Grants, subsidies, and contributions	3	1	1
99.9	Total new obligations	23	15	15

Personnel Summary

Identification code 48–1100–0–1–808		1999 actual	2000 est.	2001 est.
1001	Total compensable workyears: Full-time equivalent employment	70	71	61

OFFICE OF SPECIAL COUNSEL

Federal Funds

General and special funds:

SALARIES AND EXPENSES

For necessary expenses to carry out functions of the Office of Special Counsel pursuant to Reorganization Plan Numbered 2 of 1978, the Civil Service Reform Act of 1978 (Public Law 95–454), the Whistleblower Protection Act of 1989 (Public Law 101–12), Public Law 103–424, and the Uniformed Services Employment and Reemployment Act of 1994 (Public Law 103–353), including services as authorized by 5 U.S.C. 3109, payment of fees and expenses for witnesses, rental of conference rooms in the District of Columbia and elsewhere, and hire of passenger motor vehicles; [$9,740,000] *$11,147,000. (Independent Agencies Appropriations Act, 2000.)*

Program and Financing (in millions of dollars)

Identification code 62–0100–0–1–805		1999 actual	2000 est.	2001 est.
	Obligations by program activity:			
00.01	Investigation and prosecution of reprisals for whistle blowing	9	10	11
10.00	Total new obligations	9	10	11
	Budgetary resources available for obligation:			
22.00	New budget authority (gross)	9	10	11
23.95	Total new obligations	−9	−10	−11
	New budget authority (gross), detail:			
	Discretionary:			
40.00	Appropriation	9	10	11
	Change in unpaid obligations:			
72.40	Unpaid obligations, start of year: Obligated balance, start of year	1	1	1
73.10	Total new obligations	9	10	11
73.20	Total outlays (gross)	−9	−10	−11
74.40	Unpaid obligations, end of year: Obligated balance, end of year	1	1	1
	Outlays (gross), detail:			
86.90	Outlays from new discretionary authority	8	9	10
86.93	Outlays from discretionary balances	1	1	1

General and special funds—Continued

SALARIES AND EXPENSES—Continued

Program and Financing (in millions of dollars)—Continued

Identification code 62–0100–0–1–805	1999 actual	2000 est.	2001 est.
87.00 Total outlays (gross)	9	10	11
Net budget authority and outlays:			
89.00 Budget authority	9	10	11
90.00 Outlays	9	10	11

The Office of Special Counsel (OSC) (1) investigates Federal employee allegations of prohibited personnel practices (including reprisal for whistleblowing) and when appropriate prosecutes before the Merit Systems Protection Board (MSPB); (2) provides a channel for whistleblowing by Federal employees; and (3) enforces the Hatch Act. The OSC may transmit whistleblower allegations to the agency head concerned and require an agency investigation and a report to the Congress and the President when appropriate.

Overall in 1999, there were more than 6,482 instances in which the assistance or action of the OSC was sought by Federal employees and other persons. Many prohibited personnel practice and Hatch Act cases investigated by the OSC are resolved without recourse to formal proceedings before the MSPB. In 1999, the OSC obtained 52 corrective or other favorable actions, and efforts to obtain such negotiated resolutions will continue. In 1999, the OSC also filed six enforcement actions before the MSPB in prohibited personnel practice and Hatch Act matters. The OSC also issued 2,063 Hatch Act advisory opinions (both written and oral) to people who sought advice. During 1999, the OSC's Disclosure Unit received 369 new disclosure matters for possible referral and completed 413. Fifteen Disclosure Unit matters were referred to agency heads for their review.

In 2001, the OSC will continue to review its operations and procedures. The aim of these efforts will be to make the OSC more resposive to those individuals who seek the agency's assistance, to improve the productivity of the OSC's employees, and to ensure that the OSC is an easily accessible source of information about the rights of government employees.

The request will enable OSC to reduce its long-standing case-processing backlogs, and will ensure that OSC's customers receive prompt and timely service in accordance with the time frames laid out in 5 U.S.C. § 1214(b)(2)(A)(ii) (240 days to process prohibited practice complaints) and 5 U.S.C. § 1213(b) (15 days to make initial determination on whistleblower disclosure). Already during 1999, in part due to newly-implemented investigative streamlining techniques, and in part due to reallocation of existing resources, OSC has made significant progress in two areas: (1) in the whistleblower disclosure unit, for the first time in recent years, OSC processed more cases (413) than it received (369); and (2) in the Investigation Division, OSC achieved a 10 percent increase in the number of prohibited personnel practice cases investigated (303 cases completed in 1999, versus 277 in 1998). OSC's goal is to eliminate its case-processing backlogs by the end of 2004.

In furtherance of its responsibilities, and the goals and objectives set forth in the agency's strategic plan, the OSC performance goals in 2001 will be to: (1) reduce the backlog of overage matters within each OSC program; (2) bring before the MSPB more cases in which OSC believes that a prohibited personnel practice (especially reprisal based on whistle blowing) has occurred; (3) informally seek more stays, corrective actions, and disciplinary actions in cases in which an impartial investigation reveals reasonable grounds to believe that a prohibited personnel practice has been committed; (4) identify and enter appearances in cases in which OSC's expertise could favorably influence the development of whistleblower protection law; (5) raise Federal employees' awareness of their rights and responsibilities under the statutes enforced by OSC; and (6) develop and maintain OSC's processes, human resources, and systems to support a continually improving, highly effective organization with vigor to meet demanding program needs.

The following tables display the anticipated workloads:

ALLEGATIONS RECEIVED

	1999 actual	*2000 est.*	*2001 est.*
Reprisal for whistleblowing	749	740	740
Other personnel practices	3,623	3,580	3,580
Hatch Act	47	50	50

ALLEGATIONS CLOSED

	1999 actual	*2000 est.*	*2001 est.*
Reprisal for whistleblowing	778	820	905
Other personnel practices	3,971	4,189	4,625
Hatch Act	105	105	105

Object Classification (in millions of dollars)

Identification code 62–0100–0–1–805	1999 actual	2000 est.	2001 est.
11.1 Personnel compensation: Full-time permanent	6	7	8
12.1 Civilian personnel benefits	1	1	2
23.1 Rental payments to GSA	1	1	1
99.0 Subtotal, direct obligations	8	9	11
99.5 Below reporting threshold	1	1	
99.9 Total new obligations	9	10	11

Personnel Summary

Identification code 62–0100–0–1–805	1999 actual	2000 est.	2001 est.
1001 Total compensable workyears: Full-time equivalent employment	88	96	106

OKLAHOMA CITY NATIONAL MEMORIAL TRUST

Program and Financing (in millions of dollars)

Identification code 95–4333–0–3–303	1999 actual	2000 est.	2001 est.
Obligations by program activity:			
10.00 Total new obligations (object class 32.0)	5		
Budgetary resources available for obligation:			
22.22 Unobligated balance transferred from other accounts	5		
23.95 Total new obligations	−5		
Change in unpaid obligations:			
72.40 Unpaid obligations, start of year: Obligated balance, start of year		3	
73.10 Total new obligations	5		
73.20 Total outlays (gross)	−2	−3	
74.40 Unpaid obligations, end of year: Obligated balance, end of year	3		
Outlays (gross), detail:			
86.93 Outlays from discretionary balances	2	3	
Net budget authority and outlays:			
89.00 Budget authority			
90.00 Outlays	2	3	
Memorandum (non-add) entries:			
92.01 Total investments, start of year: U.S. securities: Par value		3	3
92.02 Total investments, end of year: U.S. securities: Par value	3	3	3

The Oklahoma City National Memorial Act of 1997 (P.L. 105–58), established the Oklahoma City National Memorial Trust, a wholly owned government corporation, to operate the memorial to commemorate the victims of the April 19, 1995 bombing of the Alfred P. Murrah Federal Building. The Act authorized $5 million in appropriations, subject to a non-Federal match, for the activities of the Trust, managed by the Oklahoma City Memorial Foundation.

OTHER COMMISSIONS AND BOARDS

Federal Funds

General and special funds:

COMMISSION FOR THE PRESERVATION OF AMERICA'S HERITAGE ABROAD

SALARIES AND EXPENSES

For expenses for the Commission for the Preservation of America's Heritage Abroad, [$490,000] *$390,000*, as authorized by Public Law 99–83, section 1303. *(Departments of Commerce, Justice, and State, the Judiciary, and Related Agencies Appropriations Act, 2000, as enacted by section 1000(a)(1) of the Consolidated Appropriations Act, 2000 (P.L. 106–113).)*

Unavailable Collections (in millions of dollars)

Identification code 95–9911–0–1–808	1999 actual	2000 est.	2001 est.
Balance, start of year:			
01.99 Balance, start of year	3	3	5
Receipts:			
02.01 Miscellaneous deposits, Miscellaneous trust funds, Independent agencies		1	1
02.02 Interest, Miscellaneous trust funds, Independent agencies		1	1
02.99 Total receipts		2	2
04.00 Total: Balances and collections	3	5	7
07.99 Total balance, end of year	3	5	7

Program and Financing (in millions of dollars)

Identification code 95–9911–0–1–808	1999 actual	2000 est.	2001 est.
Obligations by program activity:			
10.00 Total new obligations (object class 25.2)	1	3	2
Budgetary resources available for obligation:			
21.40 Unobligated balance available, start of year	2	2	2
22.00 New budget authority (gross)	1	3	
23.90 Total budgetary resources available for obligation	3	5	2
23.95 Total new obligations	−1	−3	−2
24.40 Unobligated balance available, end of year	2	2	
New budget authority (gross), detail:			
Discretionary:			
42.00 Transferred from other accounts	1	3	
43.00 Appropriation (total discretionary)	1	3	
Change in unpaid obligations:			
73.10 Total new obligations	1	3	2
73.20 Total outlays (gross)	−1	−3	−2
Outlays (gross), detail:			
86.90 Outlays from new discretionary authority	1	2	
86.93 Outlays from discretionary balances		1	2
87.00 Total outlays (gross)	1	3	2
Net budget authority and outlays:			
89.00 Budget authority	1	3	
90.00 Outlays	1	3	2

The "Other commissions and boards" account presents data on small independent commissions and other entities on a consolidated basis.

This consolidated account includes the $390 thousand request for the Commission for the Preservation of America's Heritage Abroad, which works to encourage the preservation of cemeteries, monuments, and historic buildings associated with the foreign heritage of the United States. It also reflects transfers to the Presidential Advisory Commission on Holocaust assets in the United States, which conducts and reviews research on the collection and disposition of Holocaust-era assets that came under the control of the United States Government.

PANAMA CANAL COMMISSION

Federal Funds

Public enterprise funds:

PANAMA CANAL REVOLVING FUND

Program and Financing (in millions of dollars)

Identification code 95–4061–0–3–403	1999 actual	2000 est.	2001 est.
Obligations by program activity:			
09.01 Reimbursable program	600	208	26
09.09 Total operating expenses	600	208	26
Capital investment:			
09.10 Reimbursable program	92	92	
09.19 Total capital investment	92	92	
10.00 Total new obligations	692	300	26
Budgetary resources available for obligation:			
21.40 Unobligated balance available, start of year	86	150	26
22.00 New budget authority (gross)	756	176	
23.90 Total budgetary resources available for obligation	842	326	26
23.95 Total new obligations	−692	−300	−26
24.40 Unobligated balance available, end of year	150	26	
New budget authority (gross), detail:			
Discretionary:			
68.00 Spending authority from offsetting collections (gross): Offsetting collections (cash)	756	176	
Change in unpaid obligations:			
72.40 Unpaid obligations, start of year: Obligated balance, start of year	215	224	
73.10 Total new obligations	692	300	26
73.20 Total outlays (gross)	−683	−524	−26
74.40 Unpaid obligations, end of year: Obligated balance, end of year	224		
Outlays (gross), detail:			
86.90 Outlays from new discretionary authority	556	176	
86.93 Outlays from discretionary balances	127	47	
86.98 Outlays from mandatory balances		301	26
87.00 Total outlays (gross)	683	524	26
Offsets:			
Against gross budget authority and outlays:			
88.40 Offsetting collections (cash) from: Non-Federal sources	−756	−176	
Net budget authority and outlays:			
89.00 Budget authority			
90.00 Outlays	−73	348	26

Note.—Authority to borrow is available to the Panama Canal Commission on a permanent indefinite basis. This authority is limited only in that the amount of borrowing outstanding at any time cannot exceed $100 million.

The Panama Canal Act of 1979 established the Panama Canal Commission to operate and maintain the interoceanic waterway. Pursuant to Public Law 104–106, the Commission is a wholly-owned government corporation and is funded by a revolving fund. In accordance with the Panama Canal Treaty, the United States transferred ownership of the Canal to the Republic of Panama on December 31, 1999. Fiscal year 2000 data in the following tables cover first quarter operations and transfer-related obligations, including severance

Public enterprise funds—Continued

PANAMA CANAL REVOLVING FUND—Continued

pay and accumulated leave. Fiscal year 2001 expenses are for the settlement of remaining accident and contract claims against the Commission.

Object Classification (in millions of dollars)

Identification code 95–4061–0–3–403		1999 actual	2000 est.	2001 est.
	Personnel compensation:			
11.1	Full-time permanent	234	66	
11.3	Other than full-time permanent	33	4	
11.5	Other personnel compensation	66	67	
11.9	Total personnel compensation	333	137	
12.1	Civilian personnel benefits	42	10	
13.0	Benefits for former personnel	15		
21.0	Travel and transportation of persons	4	2	
22.0	Transportation of things	2		
23.3	Communications, utilities, and miscellaneous charges	3	1	
25.1	Advisory and assistance services	2	1	
25.2	Other services	21	−3	
26.0	Supplies and materials	63	24	
31.0	Equipment	62	43	
32.0	Land and structures	37	51	
41.0	Grants, subsidies, and contributions	99	25	
42.0	Insurance claims and indemnities	9	9	26
99.9	Total new obligations	692	300	26

Personnel Summary

Identification code 95–4061–0–3–403		1999 actual	2000 est.	2001 est.
2001	Total compensable workyears: Full-time equivalent employment	9,188	2,343	

PANAMA CANAL COMMISSION DISSOLUTION FUND

Unavailable Collections (in millions of dollars)

Identification code 95–4073–0–3–403		1999 actual	2000 est.	2001 est.
	Balance, start of year:			
01.99	Balance, start of year	6		
	Appropriation:			
05.01	Panama Canal Commission dissolution fund	−6		
07.99	Total balance, end of year			

Program and Financing (in millions of dollars)

Identification code 95–4073–0–3–403		1999 actual	2000 est.	2001 est.
	Obligations by program activity:			
09.01	Office of Transition Administration		5	2
10.00	Total new obligations (object class 11.1)		5	2
	Budgetary resources available for obligation:			
21.40	Unobligated balance available, start of year		7	2
22.00	New budget authority (gross)	7		
23.90	Total budgetary resources available for obligation	7	7	2
23.95	Total new obligations		−5	−2
24.40	Unobligated balance available, end of year	7	2	
	New budget authority (gross), detail:			
	Mandatory:			
69.00	Offsetting collections (cash)	1		
69.26	Offsetting collections (unavailable balances)	6		
69.90	Spending authority from offsetting collections (total mandatory)	7		
	Change in unpaid obligations:			
72.40	Unpaid obligations, start of year: Obligated balance, start of year			
73.10	Total new obligations		5	2
73.20	Total outlays (gross)		−5	−2
74.40	Unpaid obligations, end of year: Obligated balance, end of year			
	Outlays (gross), detail:			
86.98	Outlays from mandatory balances		5	2
	Offsets:			
	Against gross budget authority and outlays:			
88.00	Offsetting collections (cash) from: Federal sources	−1		
	Net budget authority and outlays:			
89.00	Budget authority	6		
90.00	Outlays	−1	5	2
	Memorandum (non-add) entries:			
92.01	Total investments, start of year: U.S. securities: Par value	6	7	7
92.02	Total investments, end of year: U.S. securities: Par value	7	7	7

Pursuant to 22 USC 3714a., Sec. 1305., there is established in the Treasury of the United States a fund known as the "Panama Canal Commission Dissolution Fund". The Fund, which became available on October 1, 1998, is being used by the Commission to operate an Office of Transition Administration. This office will manage the Commission's transfer-related obligations, such as severance pay and accident and contract claims.

Personnel Summary

Identification code 95–4073–0–3–403		1999 actual	2000 est.	2001 est.
2001	Total compensable workyears: Full-time equivalent employment		50	20

POSTAL SERVICE

Federal Funds

General and special funds:

PAYMENT TO THE POSTAL SERVICE FUND

For payment to the Postal Service Fund for revenue forgone on free and reduced rate mail, pursuant to subsections (c) and (d) of section 2401 of title 39, United States Code, [$93,436,000] *$96,093,000*, of which [$64,436,000] *$67,093,000*, shall not be available for obligation until October 1, [2000] *2001*: *Provided*, That mail for overseas voting and mail for the blind shall continue to be free: *Provided further*, That 6-day delivery and rural delivery of mail shall continue at not less than the 1983 level: *Provided further*, That none of the funds made available to the Postal Service by this Act shall be used to implement any rule, regulation, or policy of charging any officer or employee of any State or local child support enforcement agency, or any individual participating in a State or local program of child support enforcement, a fee for information requested or provided concerning an address of a postal customer: *Provided further*, That none of the funds provided in this Act shall be used to consolidate or close small rural and other small post offices in fiscal year [2000] *2001*. *(Postal Service Appropriations Act, 2000.)*

Program and Financing (in millions of dollars)

Identification code 18–1001–0–1–372		1999 actual	2000 est.	2001 est.
	Obligations by program activity:			
00.01	Current year			
00.02	Reconciliation adjustment			
00.03	Prior years' liabilities	29	29	29
00.04	Advanced Appropriation from the previous year		69	[1] 64
00.05	Advanced Appropriation—Reconciliation Adjustment from previous year		2	
10.00	Total new obligations (object class 41.0)	29	100	93
	Budgetary resources available for obligation:			
22.00	New budget authority (gross)	29	100	93
23.95	Total new obligations	−29	−100	−93

	New budget authority (gross), detail:			
	Discretionary:			
40.00	Appropriation	29	29	29
	Advance appropriation:			
55.00	Advance appropriation		69	64
55.00	Advance appropriation		2	
55.00	Advance appropriation			
55.90	Advance appropriation (total discretionary)		71	64
70.00	Total new budget authority (gross)	29	100	93
	Change in unpaid obligations:			
73.10	Total new obligations	29	100	93
73.20	Total outlays (gross)	–29	–100	–93
	Outlays (gross), detail:			
86.90	Outlays from new discretionary authority	29	100	93
	Net budget authority and outlays:			
89.00	Budget authority	29	100	93
90.00	Outlays	29	100	93

[1] Represents a $70,880,000 current year estimate and a –$6,444,000 reconciliation adjustment.

Pursuant to Public Law 93–328, the 2001 appropriation request of the U.S. Postal Service for Payment to the Postal Service Fund is $96,093,000. This amount includes: $66,473,000 requested for free mail for the blind and overseas voting; $620,000 as a reconciliation adjustment for 1998 actual mail volume of free mail for the blind and overseas voting; and $29,000,000 for prior years' liability under the Revenue Forgone Reform Act of 1993. The U.S. Postal Service requests that all of these funds be appropriated and made available for obligation in 2001. In addition to these funds, $64,436,000 (an advance appropriation from 2000 for the 2000 costs and the 1997 reconciliation adjustment for free mail for the blind and overseas voting) will become available to the U.S. Postal Service in 2001.

Public enterprise funds:

POSTAL SERVICE FUND

Program and Financing (in millions of dollars)

Identification code 18–4020–0–3–372		1999 actual	2000 est.	2001 est.
	Obligations by program activity:			
	Reimbursable Program:			
09.01	Postal field operations	43,778	44,968	47,333
09.02	Transportation	4,363	4,592	4,835
09.03	Building occupancy	1,668	1,789	1,747
09.04	Supplies and services	4,399	4,234	4,551
09.05	Research and development	67	45	45
09.06	Administration and area operations	4,983	5,311	5,490
09.07	Interest	1,812	1,837	2,032
09.08	Servicewide expenses	67	71	76
09.09	Subtotal	61,137	62,847	66,109
09.10	Capital Investment	3,780	4,000	3,300
10.00	Total new obligations	64,917	66,847	69,409
	Budgetary resources available for obligation:			
22.00	New budget authority (gross)	68,550	70,526	70,060
22.60	Portion applied to repay debt	–3,633	–3,679	–651
23.90	Total budgetary resources available for obligation	64,917	66,847	69,409
23.95	Total new obligations	–64,917	–66,847	–69,409
	New budget authority (gross), detail:			
	Mandatory:			
67.15	Authority to borrow (indefinite)	5,607	5,516	1,575
69.00	Offsetting collections (cash)	62,943	65,010	68,485
70.00	Total new budget authority (gross)	68,550	70,526	70,060
	Change in unpaid obligations:			
72.40	Unpaid obligations, start of year: Obligated balance, start of year	21,154	22,107	22,446
73.10	Total new obligations	64,917	66,847	69,409
73.20	Total outlays (gross)	–63,964	–66,508	–68,932
74.40	Unpaid obligations, end of year: Obligated balance, end of year	22,107	22,446	22,923
	Outlays (gross), detail:			
86.97	Outlays from new mandatory authority	63,964	66,508	68,932
	Offsets:			
	Against gross budget authority and outlays:			
	Offsetting collections (cash) from:			
88.00	Federal sources	–957	–985	–1,037
88.20	Interest on U.S. securities	–29	–27	–27
88.40	Non-Federal sources	–61,957	–63,998	–67,421
88.90	Total, offsetting collections (cash)	–62,943	–65,010	–68,485
	Net budget authority and outlays:			
89.00	Budget authority	5,607	5,516	1,575
90.00	Outlays	1,021	1,498	447
	Memorandum (non-add) entries:			
92.01	Total investments, start of year: U.S. securities: Par value	1,000	809	809
92.02	Total investments, end of year: U.S. securities: Par value	809	809	809

The Postal Reorganization Act of 1970, Public Law 91–375, converted the Post Office Department into the U.S. Postal Service, an independent establishment within the executive branch. The Postal Service commenced operations July 1, 1971. This agency is charged with providing patrons with reliable mail service at reasonable rates and fees.

The U.S. Postal Service is governed by an 11-member Board of Governors, including 9 Governors appointed by the President, a Postmaster General who is selected by the Governors, and a Deputy Postmaster General who is selected by the Governors and the Postmaster General.

Decisions on changes in domestic rates of postage and fees for postal services are recommended to the Governors of the Postal Service by the independent Postal Rate Commission after a hearing on the record under the Administrative Procedure Act. The Commission also recommends decisions on changes in the domestic mail classification schedule to the Governors. Decisions of the Governors on rates of postage, fees for postal services, and mail classification are final, subject to judicial review.

Effective in 1986, the Postal Service Fund (Fund) was included in the congressional and executive budget process and taken into account in making calculations under the Balanced Budget and Emergency Deficit Control Act of 1985 (Gramm-Rudman-Hollings). The Omnibus Budget Reconciliation Act of 1989 amended title 39 of the U.S. Code by adding a new section, 2009a, which provides that, beginning in 1990, the receipts and disbursements of the Fund shall not be considered as part of the congressional and executive budget process and shall not be taken into account in making calculations under Gramm-Rudman-Hollings.

Programs.—Included are all postal activities providing window services; processing, delivery, and transportation of mail; research and development; administration of postal field activities; and associated expenses of providing facilities and financing.

The rapid development of electronic messaging systems promises to increase the effectiveness of the Nation's communications infrastructure and United States competitiveness in the future. As the provider of a universally available hard copy delivery system, the United States Postal Service is encouraged to examine these emerging communications technologies and to cooperate with the private sector on issues of integration, directory service, and strategic alliances that will facilitate the development of secure and reliable electronic messaging networks.

The transition from hard copy to electronic messaging already has begun. The Postal Service should assist in devel-

Public enterprise funds—Continued

POSTAL SERVICE FUND—Continued

oping future messaging systems. The Postal Service's participation should recognize the changing needs of its business, governmental, and individual customers; should focus on determining an appropriate means for public and private sector cooperation; and should be consistent with the agency's vision of evolving into a premier provider of 21st century postal communications. The Postal Service should seek to leverage its comprehensive delivery, messaging security, and addressing directory management capabilities in a manner that promotes universal access to the benefits of these new technologies for all citizens who desire them.

Financing.—The activities of the U.S. Postal Service are financed from the following sources: (1) mail and services revenue; (2) reimbursements from Federal and non-Federal sources; (3) proceeds from borrowing; (4) interest from U.S. securities and other investments; and (5) appropriations by the Congress. All receipts and deposits are made to the Postal Service Fund and are available without fiscal year limitation for payment of all expenses incurred, retirement of obligations, investment in capital assets, and investment in obligations and securities.

Separate legislation also increased the Postal Service's statutory borrowing authority beginning in 1991. Section 2005 of title 39, United States Code, as amended, increased the Postal Service's borrowing authority by $2.5 billion in 1991 for a revised ceiling of $12.5 billion and an additional $2.5 billion in 1992 for a revised total ceiling of $15 billion. The total net increase in amounts outstanding in any one fiscal year were also increased and now may not exceed $2.0 billion in obligations issued for the purpose of capital improvements and $1.0 billion for the purpose of paying operating expenses. As of September 30, 2001, it is expected that the total debt instruments issued and outstanding pursuant to this authority will amount to $9.151 billion.

Operating.—Estimated revenue will total $68.285 billion in 2001. This includes $68.191 billion from mail and services revenue, $27 million from investment income, and $67 million accrued for revenue foregone appropriations in 2001. Total expenses are estimated at $67.785 billion in 2001.

The Postal Reorganization Act of 1970 established the Postal Service as a fully self-sufficient, independent entity. Postal revenues were to cover the full costs of postal operations. When the Act was passed, the Postal Service received substantial taxpayer subsidies, both appropriated and unappropriated. Consistent with the intent of the 1970 Act, Congress has taken steps over time to reduce these subsidies. Under the 1974 Civil Service Retirement Fund—Postal Employee Benefits Act, the Postal Service assumed responsibility for paying unfunded retirement costs from wage schedule increases under postal labor contracts. These costs are not covered by normal employee/employer contributions to the retirement fund. The 1985 Reconciliation Act shifted responsibility for paying health benefit costs of Postal annuitants retiring after 1986 from OPM to the Postal Service. The 1987 Reconciliation Act had the Postal Service make one-time payments to defray annuitant health benefit costs in 1988 and 1989 and retirement COLA costs in 1988. (Retirement COLAs, like wage schedule increases, result in retirement liabilities not covered by normal retirement fund contributions.) Under the 1989 Reconciliation Act, the Postal Service assumed responsibility for paying health benefits of survivors of post-86 annuitants and unfunded retirement COLA liabilities for post-86 annuitants.

The Omnibus Budget Reconciliation Act of 1990 superseded certain existing legislation and expanded the Postal Service's responsibility for benefit costs of postal annuitants. Effective October 1, 1990, the Postal Service is required to fund Civil Service Retirement System (CSRS) COLAs and the employer's share of Federal Employee Health Benefit Program (FEHBP) premiums for postal annuitants who retired after June 30, 1971, and their survivors. In addition, the Postal Service is required to fund the retroactive CSRS COLA and FEHBP premium costs for which the Postal Service would have been liable if the provisions of this new legislation had been in effect as of July 1, 1971.

Under the Omnibus Reconciliation Act of 1993, the Postal Service was required to make certain payments for past COLAs and health benefits, over and above any other payments required by law, of $693 million to the Civil Service Retirement and Disability Fund, and $348 million to the Employees Health Benefits Fund. These two payments were made in three equal annual installments, beginning in fiscal year 1996.

The Balanced Budget Act of 1997 repealed the authorization for transitional appropriations to the Postal Service which had funded the liabilities of the former Post Office Department to the Employees' Compensation Fund. Effective October 1, 1997, these liabilities became liabilities of the Postal Service payable out of the Postal Service Fund.

Statement of Operations (in millions of dollars)

Identification code 18–4020–0–3–372		1998 actual	1999 actual	2000 est.	2001 est.
0101	Revenue	60,116	62,755	64,817	68,286
0102	Expense	–59,566	–62,392	–64,717	–67,786
0105	Net income or loss (–)	550	363	100	500

Object Classification (in millions of dollars)

Identification code 18–4020–0–3–372		1999 actual	2000 est.	2001 est.
	Personnel compensation:			
11.1	Full-time permanent	26,150	26,705	27,605
11.3	Other than full-time permanent	4,849	5,209	5,402
11.5	Other personnel compensation	4,887	4,757	4,765
11.9	Total personnel compensation	35,886	36,671	37,772
12.1	Civilian personnel benefits	10,177	10,761	12,011
13.0	Benefits for former personnel	1,272	1,512	1,704
21.0	Travel and transportation of persons	262	274	279
22.0	Transportation of things	4,769	5,027	5,287
23.1	Rental payments to GSA	36	37	37
23.2	Rental payments to others	826	874	812
23.3	Communications, utilities, and miscellaneous charges	724	798	812
24.0	Printing and reproduction	101	95	98
25.2	Other services	3,297	3,224	3,496
26.0	Supplies and materials	1,986	1,601	1,626
31.0	Equipment	2,118	2,557	2,182
32.0	Land and structures	1,523	1,443	1,122
42.0	Insurance claims and indemnities	128	136	139
	Interest and dividends:			
43.0	Interest and dividends	220	248	430
43.0	Interest and dividends	1,592	1,589	1,602
99.9	Total new obligations	64,917	66,847	69,409

Personnel Summary

Identification code 18–4020–0–3–372		1999 actual	2000 est.	2001 est.
2011	Total compensable workyears: Exempt Full-time equivalent employment	851,461	848,187	843,425

PRESIDIO TRUST

Federal Funds

General and special funds:

PRESIDIO TRUST

For necessary expenses to carry out title I of the Omnibus Parks and Public Lands Management Act of 1996, [$24,400,000] *$23,400,000* shall be available to the Presidio Trust, to remain available until expended[, of which up to $1,040,000 may be for the cost of guaranteed loans, as authorized by section 104(d) of the Act: *Provided*, That such costs, including the cost of modifying such loans, shall be as defined in section 502 of the Congressional Budget Act of 1974: *Provided further*, That these funds are available to subsidize total loan principal, any part of which is to be guaranteed, not to exceed $200,000,000]. The Trust is authorized to issue obligations to the Secretary of the Treasury pursuant to section 104(d)(3) of the Act, in an amount not to exceed [$20,000,000] *$10,000,000. (Department of the Interior and Related Agencies Appropriations Act, 2000, as enacted by section 1000(a)(3) of the Consolidated Appropriations Act, 2000 (P.L. 106–113).)*

Program and Financing (in millions of dollars)

Identification code 95–4331–0–4–303		1999 actual	2000 est.	2001 est.
	Obligations by program activity:			
00.01	Operations	15	24	23
00.02	Loan Guarantee Subsidy	....	1	....
01.00	Operations	15	25	23
09.00	Reimbursable program	25	49	80
10.00	Total new obligations	40	74	103
	Budgetary resources available for obligation:			
21.40	Unobligated balance available, start of year	1	37	47
22.00	New budget authority (gross)	75	82	73
23.90	Total budgetary resources available for obligation	76	119	120
23.95	Total new obligations	−40	−74	−103
24.40	Unobligated balance available, end of year	37	47	17
	New budget authority (gross), detail:			
	Discretionary:			
40.00	Appropriation	14	24	23
47.00	Authority to borrow	20	20	10
	Spending authority from offsetting collections:			
	Offsetting collections (cash):			
68.00	Offsetting collections (cash)	25	25	25
68.00	Offsetting collections (cash)	15	12	14
68.10	From Federal sources: Change in receivables and unpaid, unfilled orders	1	1	1
68.90	Spending authority from offsetting collections (total discretionary)	41	38	40
70.00	Total new budget authority (gross)	75	82	73
	Change in unpaid obligations:			
	Unpaid obligations, start of year:			
72.40	Obligated balance, start of year	1	6	31
72.95	From Federal sources: Receivables and unpaid, unfilled orders	....	1	1
72.99	Total unpaid obligations, start of year	1	7	32
73.10	Total new obligations	40	74	103
73.20	Total outlays (gross)	−35	−49	−66
	Unpaid obligations, end of year:			
74.40	Obligated balance, end of year	6	31	69
74.95	From Federal sources: Receivables and unpaid, unfilled orders	1	1	1
74.99	Total unpaid obligations, end of year	7	32	70
	Outlays (gross), detail:			
86.90	Outlays from new discretionary authority	35	28	24
86.93	Outlays from discretionary balances	....	21	42
87.00	Total outlays (gross)	35	49	66
	Offsets:			
	Against gross budget authority and outlays:			
	Offsetting collections (cash) from:			
88.00	Federal sources	−30	−30	−30
88.40	Non-Federal sources	−10	−7	−9
88.90	Total, offsetting collections (cash)	−40	−37	−39
	Against gross budget authority only:			
88.95	From Federal sources: Change in receivables and unpaid, unfilled orders	−1	−1	−1
	Net budget authority and outlays:			
89.00	Budget authority	34	44	33
90.00	Outlays	−7	12	27

		1999 actual	2000 est.	2001 est.
	Memorandum (non-add) entries:			
92.01	Total investments, start of year: U.S. securities: Par value	....	45	55
92.02	Total investments, end of year: U.S. securities: Par value	45	55	48

Summary of Loan Levels, Subsidy Budget Authority and Outlays by Program (in millions of dollars)

Identification code 95–4331–0–4–303		1999 actual	2000 est.	2001 est.
	Guaranteed loan levels supportable by subsidy budget authority:			
2150	Loan guarantee levels	....	....	200
2159	Total loan guarantee levels	....	....	200
	Guaranteed loan subsidy (in percent):			
2320	Subsidy rate	....	....	0.46
2329	Weighted average subsidy rate	....	....	0.46
	Guaranteed loan subsidy budget authority:			
2330	Subsidy budget authority	....	....	1
2339	Total subsidy budget authority	....	....	1
	Guaranteed loan subsidy outlays:			
2340	Subsidy outlays	....	....	1
2349	Total subsidy outlays	....	....	1

The Presidio Trust is a wholly owned government corporation established by the Omnibus Parks and Public Lands Management Act of 1996 (Public Law 104–333) to manage, improve, maintain and lease property in the Presidio of San Francisco. After this former military base was transferred to the National Park Service (NPS), the Trust was created to take over responsibility for managing the hundreds of houses, office buildings, and other facilities in an innovative manner that uses private-sector resources, but is consistent with surrounding NPS lands. This appropriation funds the operation of the Trust. It also authorizes the Trust to borrow up to $10 million from the U.S. Treasury in 2001 to rehabilitate and prepare facilities for leasing. No additional borrowing from the U.S. Treasury is planned.

The Trust repays the funds borrowed from Treasury with amounts collected from the rental of buildings and facilities as follows:

(In thousands of dollars)

	1999 actual	*2000 est.*	*2001 est.*
New Borrowing Authority	20,000	20,000	10,000
Beginning	....	20,000	40,000
Loan Payment	....	....	....
Principal Payment (non-add)	....	....	....
Interest Payment (non-add)	221	2,000	2,500
Ending Period Balance	20,000	40,000	50,000

Object Classification (in millions of dollars)

Identification code 95–4331–0–4–303		1999 actual	2000 est.	2001 est.
	Direct obligations:			
11.1	Personnel compensation: Full-time permanent	6	10	9
12.1	Civilian personnel benefits	2	3	3
23.3	Communications, utilities, and miscellaneous charges	3	5	6
25.2	Other services	2	3	2
26.0	Supplies and materials	....	3	2
32.0	Land and structures	2	1	1
99.0	Subtotal, direct obligations	15	25	23
	Reimbursable obligations:			
11.1	Personnel compensation: Full-time permanent	5	9	11
12.1	Civilian personnel benefits	2	3	3
22.0	Transportation of things	....	1	2
24.0	Printing and reproduction	....	1	2
25.1	Advisory and assistance services	1	1	3
25.2	Other services	2	6	20
25.3	Purchases of goods and services from Government accounts	4	4	4
26.0	Supplies and materials	4	4	7
31.0	Equipment	1	4	6
32.0	Land and structures	6	16	22

General and special funds—Continued

PRESIDIO TRUST—Continued

Object Classification (in millions of dollars)—Continued

Identification code 95–4331–0–4–303	1999 actual	2000 est.	2001 est.
99.0 Subtotal, reimbursable obligations	25	49	80
99.9 Total new obligations	40	74	103

Personnel Summary

Identification code 95–4331–0–4–303	1999 actual	2000 est.	2001 est.
Direct:			
1001 Total compensable workyears: Full-time equivalent employment	180	189	162
Reimbursable:			
2001 Total compensable workyears: Full-time equivalent employment	147	168	198

PRESIDIO TRUST GUARANTEED LOAN FINANCING ACCOUNT

Program and Financing (in millions of dollars)

Identification code 95–4332–0–3–303	1999 actual	2000 est.	2001 est.
Obligations by program activity:			
10.00 Total new obligations			1
Budgetary resources available for obligation:			
22.00 New financing authority (gross)			1
23.95 Total new obligations			−1
New financing authority (gross), detail:			
Discretionary:			
68.00 Spending authority from offsetting collections (gross): Offsetting collections (cash)			1
Change in unpaid obligations:			
73.10 Total new obligations			1
74.40 Unpaid obligations, end of year: Obligated balance, end of year			1
Offsets:			
Against gross financing authority and financing disbursements:			
88.00 Offsetting collections (cash) from: Payment from program account *			−1
Net financing authority and financing disbursements:			
89.00 Financing authority			
90.00 Financing disbursements			−1

Status of Guaranteed Loans (in millions of dollars)

Identification code 95–4332–0–3–303	1999 actual	2000 est.	2001 est.
Position with respect to appropriations act limitation on commitments:			
2111 Limitation on guaranteed loans made by private lenders		200	200
2112 Uncommitted loan guarantee limitation		−200	−100
2150 Total guaranteed loan commitments			100
2199 Guaranteed amount of guaranteed loan commitments			100
Cumulative balance of guaranteed loans outstanding:			
2210 Outstanding, start of year			
2231 Disbursements of new guaranteed loans			100
2251 Repayments and prepayments			
2290 Outstanding, end of year			100
Memorandum:			
2299 Guaranteed amount of guaranteed loans outstanding, end of year			100

Balance Sheet (in millions of dollars)

Identification code 95–4332–0–3 303	1998 actual	1999 actual	2000 est.	2001 est.
ASSETS:				
1101 Federal assets: Fund balances with Treasury				1
Net value of assets related to post-1991 acquired defaulted guaranteed loans receivable:				
1505 Allowance for subsidy cost (−)				−1
1599 Net present value of assets related to defaulted guaranteed loans				−1
1999 Total assets				

RAILROAD RETIREMENT BOARD

Federal Funds

General and special funds:

[DUAL BENEFITS PAYMENTS ACCOUNT] *FEDERAL WINDFALL SUBSIDY*

For payment to the [Dual Benefits Payments] *Federal Windfall Subsidy* Account, authorized under section 15(d) of the Railroad Retirement Act of 1974, [$174,000,000] *$160,000,000*, which shall include amounts becoming available in fiscal year [2000] *2001* pursuant to section 224(c)(1)(B) of Public Law 98–76; and in addition, an amount, not to exceed 2 percent of the amount provided herein, shall be available proportional to the amount by which the product of recipients and the average benefit received exceeds [$174,000,000] *$160,000,000*: *Provided,* That the total amount provided herein shall be credited in 12 approximately equal amounts on the first day of each month in the fiscal year. *(Departments of Labor, Health and Human Services, and Education, and Related Agencies Appropriations Act, 2000, as enacted by section 1000(a)(4) of the Consolidated Appropriations Act, 2000 (P.L. 106–113).)*

Program and Financing (in millions of dollars)

Identification code 60–0111–0–1–601	1999 actual	2000 est.	2001 est.
Obligations by program activity:			
10.00 Total new obligations (object class 41.0)	188	173	160
Budgetary resources available for obligation:			
22.00 New budget authority (gross)	189	173	160
23.95 Total new obligations	−188	−173	−160
23.98 Unobligated balance expiring or withdrawn	−1		
New budget authority (gross), detail:			
Discretionary:			
40.00 Appropriation	189	174	160
40.76 Reduction pursuant to P.L. 106–113		−1	
43.00 Appropriation (total discretionary)	189	173	160
Change in unpaid obligations:			
73.10 Total new obligations	188	173	160
73.20 Total outlays (gross)	−188	−173	−160
Outlays (gross), detail:			
86.90 Outlays from new discretionary authority	188	173	160
Net budget authority and outlays:			
89.00 Budget authority	189	173	160
90.00 Outlays	188	173	160

This appropriation is a Federal subsidy to the rail industry pension for costs not financed by the railroad sector.

FEDERAL PAYMENTS TO THE RAILROAD RETIREMENT ACCOUNTS

For payment to the accounts established in the Treasury for the payment of benefits under the Railroad Retirement Act for interest earned on unnegotiated checks, $150,000, to remain available through September 30, [2001] *2002*, which shall be the maximum amount available for payment pursuant to section 417 of Public Law 98–76. *(Departments of Labor, Health and Human Services, and Edu-*

cation, and Related Agencies Appropriations Act, 2000, as enacted by section 1000(a)(4) of the Consolidated Appropriations Act, 2000 (P.L. 106–113).)

Program and Financing (in millions of dollars)

Identification code 60–0113–0–1–601	1999 actual	2000 est.	2001 est.
Obligations by program activity:			
10.00 Total new obligations (object class 42.0)	493	370	326
Budgetary resources available for obligation:			
22.00 New budget authority (gross)	493	370	326
23.95 Total new obligations	–493	–370	–326
New budget authority (gross), detail:			
Mandatory:			
60.05 Appropriation (indefinite)	493	370	326
Change in unpaid obligations:			
73.10 Total new obligations	493	370	326
73.20 Total outlays (gross)	–493	–370	–326
Outlays (gross), detail:			
86.97 Outlays from new mandatory authority	493	370	326
Net budget authority and outlays:			
89.00 Budget authority	493	370	326
90.00 Outlays	493	370	326

This account funds interest on uncashed checks and income taxes on Tier I and Tier II railroad retirement benefits.

Trust Funds

RAILROAD UNEMPLOYMENT INSURANCE TRUST FUND

Program and Financing (in millions of dollars)

Identification code 60–8051–0–7–603	1999 actual	2000 est.	2001 est.
Obligations by program activity:			
00.01 Benefit payments	95	101	107
10.00 Total new obligations (object class 42.0)	95	101	107
Budgetary resources available for obligation:			
22.00 New budget authority (gross)	95	101	107
23.95 Total new obligations	–95	–101	–107
New budget authority (gross), detail:			
Mandatory:			
60.27 Appropriation (trust fund, indefinite)	110	117	123
61.00 Transferred to other accounts	–15	–16	–16
62.50 Appropriation (total mandatory)	95	101	107
Change in unpaid obligations:			
72.40 Unpaid obligations, start of year: Obligated balance, start of year	–25	2	2
73.10 Total new obligations	95	101	107
73.20 Total outlays (gross)	–68	–101	–107
74.40 Unpaid obligations, end of year: Obligated balance, end of year	2	2	2
Outlays (gross), detail:			
86.97 Outlays from new mandatory authority	93	99	105
86.98 Outlays from mandatory balances	–25	2	2
87.00 Total outlays (gross)	68	101	107
Net budget authority and outlays:			
89.00 Budget authority	95	101	107
90.00 Outlays	68	101	107

Note.—Appropriations language for the 2001 request for administrative expenses is included with the limitation on administration of the Rail Industry Pension Fund.

The Board administers a separate fund for unemployment and sickness insurance payments. Administrative expenses are financed from employer unemployment taxes.

WORKLOAD

	1983 actual	1990 actual	1999 actual	2000 est.	2001 est.
Unemployment claims	1,919,160	300,351	99,870	104,000	106,000
Cumulative workload decline (%)		–84%	–95%	–95%	–94%
Sickness claims	411,877	269,926	170,305	176,000	179,000
Cumulative workload decline (%)		–34%	–59%	–57%	–57%

RAIL INDUSTRY PENSION FUND

Unavailable Collections (in millions of dollars)

Identification code 60–8011–0–7–601	1999 actual	2000 est.	2001 est.
Balance, start of year:			
01.99 Balance, start of year	14,773	15,018	15,786
Receipts:			
02.01 Interest and profits on investments in public debt securities	257	996	1,038
02.02 Refunds	–4	–5	–5
02.03 Taxes	2,542	2,555	2,609
02.05 Federal payments to railroad retirement trust funds	394	265	238
02.99 Total receipts	3,189	3,811	3,880
04.00 Total: Balances and collections	17,962	18,829	19,666
Appropriation:			
05.01 Rail industry pension fund	–2,944	–3,043	–3,101
05.99 Subtotal appropriation	–2,944	–3,043	–3,101
07.99 Total balance, end of year	15,018	15,786	16,565

Program and Financing (in millions of dollars)

Identification code 60–8011–0–7–601	1999 actual	2000 est.	2001 est.
Obligations by program activity:			
00.01 Direct program	3,016	3,087	3,146
09.01 RRA-administrative reimbursement	4	4	4
10.00 Total new obligations	3,020	3,091	3,150
Budgetary resources available for obligation:			
22.00 New budget authority (gross)	3,020	3,091	3,149
23.95 Total new obligations	–3,020	–3,091	–3,150
New budget authority (gross), detail:			
Discretionary:			
40.26 Appropriation (trust fund, definite)	96	96	98
Mandatory:			
60.27 Appropriation (trust fund, indefinite)	3,228	3,759	3,825
60.45 Portion precluded from obligation	–380	–812	–822
62.00 Transferred from other accounts	72	44	44
62.50 Appropriation (total mandatory)	2,920	2,991	3,047
Discretionary:			
68.00 Spending authority from offsetting collections: Offsetting collections (cash)	4	4	4
70.00 Total new budget authority (gross)	3,020	3,091	3,149
Change in unpaid obligations:			
72.40 Unpaid obligations, start of year: Obligated balance, start of year	216	237	243
73.10 Total new obligations	3,020	3,091	3,150
73.20 Total outlays (gross)	–3,000	–3,085	–3,149
74.40 Unpaid obligations, end of year: Obligated balance, end of year	237	243	244
Outlays (gross), detail:			
86.90 Outlays from new discretionary authority	97	97	102
86.93 Outlays from discretionary balances			3
86.97 Outlays from new mandatory authority	2,903	2,988	3,044
87.00 Total outlays (gross)	3,000	3,085	3,149
Offsets:			
Against gross budget authority and outlays:			
88.00 Offsetting collections (cash) from: Federal sources	–4	–4	–4
Net budget authority and outlays:			
89.00 Budget authority	3,016	3,087	3,145
90.00 Outlays	2,996	3,081	3,145

General and special funds—Continued

RAIL INDUSTRY PENSION FUND—Continued

Program and Financing (in millions of dollars)—Continued

Identification code 60–8011–0–7–601	1999 actual	2000 est.	2001 est.
Memorandum (non-add) entries:			
92.01 Total investments, start of year: U.S. securities: Par value	19,764	22,347	16,036
92.02 Total investments, end of year: U.S. securities: Par value	22,347	16,036	16,815

Railroad retirees generally receive the equivalent to a social security benefit and a rail industry pension collectively bargained like other private pension plans but embedded in Federal law. About 107,000 individuals also receive a "windfall" benefit.

Status of Funds (in millions of dollars)

Identification code 60–8011–0–7–601	1999 actual	2000 est.	2001 est.
Unexpended balance, start of year:			
0100 Uninvested balance	–55	–13	–7
U.S. Securities:			
0101 Par value	19,764	22,347	16,036
0102 Unrealized discounts	–4,720	–7,079	....
0199 Total balance, start of year	14,989	15,255	16,029
Cash income during the year:			
Governmental receipts:			
0200 Refunds, Rail Industry Pension Fund	–4	–5	–5
0201 Taxes, Rail Industry Pension Fund	2,542	2,555	2,609
Intragovernmental transactions:			
0240 Interest and profits on investments in public debt securities, Rail Industry Pension Fund	257	996	1,038
0242 Federal payments to railroad retirement trust funds, Rail Industry Pension Fund	394	265	238
Offsetting collections:			
0280 Offsetting collections, Rail Industry Pension Fund	4	4	4
0299 Total cash income	3,193	3,815	3,884
Cash outgo during year:			
0500 Rail Industry Pension Fund	–3,000	–3,085	–3,149
0645 Balance transferred, net	72	44	44
Unexpended balance, end of year:			
0700 Uninvested balance	–13	–7	–7
U.S. Securities:			
0701 Par value	22,347	16,036	16,815
0702 Unrealized discounts	–7,079	....	....
0799 Total balance, end of year	15,255	16,029	16,809

Object Classification (in millions of dollars)

Identification code 60–8011–0–7–601	1999 actual	2000 est.	2001 est.
Direct obligations:			
42.0 Benefit payments	2,920	2,990	3,046
43.0 Interest and dividends	1	1	1
93.0 Administrative expenses (see separate schedule)	95	96	99
99.0 Subtotal, direct obligations	3,016	3,087	3,146
99.0 Reimbursable obligations	4	4	4
99.9 Total new obligations	3,020	3,091	3,150

LIMITATION ON ADMINISTRATION

For necessary expenses for the Railroad Retirement Board for administration of the Railroad Retirement Act and the Railroad Unemployment Insurance Act, **[**$91,000,000**]** *$92,500,000,* to be derived in such amounts as determined by the Board from the railroad retirement accounts and from moneys credited to the railroad unemployment insurance administration fund. *(Departments of Labor, Health and Human Services, and Education, and Related Agencies Appropriations Act, 2000, as enacted by section 1000(a)(4) of the Consolidated Appropriations Act, 2000 (P.L. 106–113).)*

Program and Financing (In millions of dollars)

	1999 actual	2000 est.	2001 est.
Obligations by program activity:			
Direct program:			
Rail Industry Pension Fund:			
Subtotal, Rail Industry Pension Fund	50	50	51
Railroad Social Security Equivalent Benefit:			
Subtotal, Railroad Social Security Equivalent Benefit	24	24	25
Supplemental Annuity Pension Fund:			
Subtotal, Supplemental Annuity Pension Fund	2	2	2
Railroad Unemployment Insurance Trust Fund:			
Subtotal, Railroad Unemployment Insurance Trust Fund	14	15	15
Total, direct program	90	91	93
Reimbursable program	4	4	4
Total new obligations	94	95	97
Budgetary resources available for obligation:			
Offsetting collections from: Trust funds	–4	–4	–4
Unobligated balance expiring	....	....	....
Limitation	90	91	93
Change in unpaid obligations:			
Obligations incurred, net	90	91	93
Obligated balance, start of year	....	9	9
Obligated balance, end of year	–9	–9	–9
Outlays from limitation	81	91	93

The table below shows anticipated workloads.

	1997 actual	1998 actual	1999 actual	2000 est.	2001 est.
Pending, start of year	8,767	8,038	7,562	6,497	5,497
New Railroad Retirement applications	48,068	46,047	45,132	46,000	45,000
New Social Security certifications	5,980	5,995	6,108	6,000	6,000
Total dispositions (excluding partial awards)	54,777	52,518	52,305	53,000	52,000
Pending, end of year	8,038	7,562	6,497	5,497	4,497

As shown below, the Board projects this workload will continue to decline as the number of beneficiaries declines.

	1980 actual	1990 actual	1998 actual	1999 actual	2000 est.	2001 est.
Total beneficiaries	1,009,500	894,196	727,603	704,159	684,100	662,800

In recognition of the continuing decline in virtually all its major workloads, the Board will explore and adopt new approaches to improve service to beneficiaries.

Object Classification (in millions of dollars)

Identification code 60–8011–0–7–601	1999 actual	2000 est.	2001 est.
Limitation Acct—Direct Obligations:			
Personnel compensation:			
11.1 Full-time permanent	57	58	60
11.3 Other than full-time permanent	1	1	1
11.5 Other personnel compensation	1	1	1
11.9 Total personnel compensation	59	60	62
12.1 Civilian personnel benefits	12	12	13
13.0 Benefits for former personnel	....	2	....
21.0 Travel and transportation of persons	1	1	1
23.1 Rental payments to GSA	3	3	3
23.3 Communications, utilities, and miscellaneous charges	3	3	3
25.2 Other services	8	7	8
26.0 Supplies and materials	1	1	1
31.0 Equipment	2	1	1
93.0 Limitation on expenses	–89	–90	–92
99.0 Subtotal, limitation acct—direct obligations	....	....	....
Limitation Acct—Reimbursable Obligations:			
11.1 Personnel compensation: Full-time permanent	3	3	3
12.1 Civilian personnel benefits	1	1	1
93.0 Limitation on expenses	–4	–4	–4
99.0 Subtotal, limitation acct—reimbursable obligations	....	....	....

Personnel Summary

Identification code 60–8011–0–7–601	1999 actual	2000 est.	2001 est.
Limitation account—direct:			
6001 Total compensable workyears: Full-time equivalent employment	1,152	1,092	1,068
Limitation account—reimbursable:			
7001 Total compensable workyears: Full-time equivalent employment	44	44	44

Limitation on the Office of Inspector General

For expenses necessary for the Office of Inspector General for audit, investigatory and review activities, as authorized by the Inspector General Act of 1978, as amended, not more than [$5,400,000] *$5,700,000*, to be derived from the railroad retirement accounts and railroad unemployment insurance account: *Provided*, That none of the funds made available in any other paragraph of this Act may be transferred to the Office; used to carry out any such transfer; used to provide any office space, equipment, office supplies, communications facilities or services, maintenance services, or administrative services for the Office; used to pay any salary, benefit, or award for any personnel of the Office; used to pay any other operating expense of the Office; or used to reimburse the Office for any service provided, or expense incurred, by the Office. *(Departments of Labor, Health and Human Services, and Education, and Related Agencies Appropriations Act, 2000, as enacted by section 1000(a)(4) of the Consolidated Appropriations Act, 2000 (P.L. 106–113).)*

Program and Financing (in millions of dollars)

	1999 actual	2000 est.	2001 est.
Obligations by program activity:			
Operations (total new obligations)	6	5	6
Budgetary resources available for obligation:			
Offsetting collections from trust funds	....	....	....
Unobligated balance expiring	....	....	....
Limitation	6	5	6
Change in unpaid obligations:			
Obligations incurred, net	6	5	6
Obligated balance, start of year	....	....	....
Obligated balance, end of year	....	....	....
Outlays from limitation	6	5	6

Object Classification (in millions of dollars)

Identification code 60–8011–0–7–601	1999 actual	2000 est.	2001 est.
11.1 Personnel compensation: Full-time permanent	4	4	5
12.1 Civilian personnel benefits	1	1	1
93.0 Limitation on expenses	−5	−5	−6
99.0 Subtotal, limitation account—allocation	....	....	....

Personnel Summary

Identification code 60–8011–0–7–601	1999 actual	2000 est.	2001 est.
8001 Total compensable workyears: Full-time equivalent employment	56	58	57

Supplemental Annuity Pension Fund

Unavailable Collections (in millions of dollars)

Identification code 60–8012–0–7–601	1999 actual	2000 est.	2001 est.
Balance, start of year:			
01.99 Balance, start of year	35	49	49
Receipts:			
02.01 Interest and profits on investments in public debt securities	3	3	3
02.03 Supplemental annuity taxes	91	71	57
02.99 Total receipts	94	74	60
04.00 Total: Balances and collections	129	123	109
Appropriation:			
05.01 Supplemental Annuity Pension Fund	−78	−74	−71
05.99 Subtotal appropriation	−78	−74	−71
07.99 Total balance, end of year	49	49	38

Program and Financing (in millions of dollars)

Identification code 60–8012–0–7–601	1999 actual	2000 est.	2001 est.
Obligations by program activity:			
10.00 Total new obligations (object class 42.0)	76	72	69
Budgetary resources available for obligation:			
22.00 New budget authority (gross)	76	72	69
23.95 Total new obligations	−76	−72	−69
New budget authority (gross), detail:			
Mandatory:			
60.27 Appropriation (trust fund, indefinite)	82	74	71
60.45 Portion precluded from obligation	−4	....	....
61.00 Transferred to other accounts	−2	−2	−2
62.50 Appropriation (total mandatory)	76	72	69
Change in unpaid obligations:			
72.40 Unpaid obligations, start of year: Obligated balance, start of year	6	7	7
73.10 Total new obligations	76	72	69
73.20 Total outlays (gross)	−75	−72	−69
74.40 Unpaid obligations, end of year: Obligated balance, end of year	7	7	7
Outlays (gross), detail:			
86.97 Outlays from new mandatory authority	69	65	62
86.98 Outlays from mandatory balances	6	7	7
87.00 Total outlays (gross)	75	72	69
Net budget authority and outlays:			
89.00 Budget authority	76	72	69
90.00 Outlays	75	72	69
Memorandum (non-add) entries:			
92.01 Total investments, start of year: U.S. securities: Par value	43	57	57
92.02 Total investments, end of year: U.S. securities: Par value	57	57	46

In addition to rail social security, rail industry pensions, and special windfalls, the Railroad Retirement Board pays supplemental annuities to rail workers retiring at age 60 with 30 years of creditable rail service or at age 65 with 25–29 years of creditable service. Monthly benefit amounts are calculated from a base of $23, adding $4 for every year of service over 25, up to a maximum monthly benefit of $43. Employers finance benefits on a pay-as-you-go basis by a cents-per-hour tax, currently established at 26.5 cents per hour.

Status of Funds (in millions of dollars)

Identification code 60–8012–0–7–601	1999 actual	2000 est.	2001 est.
Unexpended balance, start of year:			
0100 Treasury balance	−2	....	....
0101 U.S. Securities: Par value	43	57	57
0199 Total balance, start of year	41	56	56
Cash income during the year:			
Governmental receipts:			
0200 Supplemental annuity taxes, Supplemental Annuity Pension Fund, RRB	91	71	57
Intragovernmental transactions:			
0240 Interest and profits on investments in public debt securities, Supplemental Annuity Pension Fund, RRB	3	3	3
0299 Total cash income	94	74	60

General and special funds—Continued

SUPPLEMENTAL ANNUITY PENSION FUND—Continued

Status of Funds (in millions of dollars)—Continued

Identification code 60–8012–0–7–601	1999 actual	2000 est.	2001 est.
Cash outgo during year:			
0500 Supplemental Annuity Pension Fund	–75	–72	–69
0645 Balance transferred, net	–2	–2	–2
Unexpended balance, end of year:			
0701 U.S. Securities: Par value	57	57	46
0799 Total balance, end of year	56	56	45

RAILROAD SOCIAL SECURITY EQUIVALENT BENEFIT ACCOUNT

Unavailable Collections (in millions of dollars)

Identification code 60–8010–0–7–601	1999 actual	2000 est.	2001 est.
Balance, start of year:			
01.99 Balance, start of year	1,434	1,415	1,728
Receipts:			
02.01 Interest and profits on investments in public debt securities	95	114	130
02.02 Income tax credits	98	105	88
02.03 Interest transferred to Federal hospital insurance trust fund	–42	–36	–38
02.04 Taxes	1,906	2,031	2,071
02.05 Receipts transferred to Federal hospital insurance trust fund	–388	–388	–393
02.06 Receipts from Federal old-age survivors insurance trust fund	3,681	3,613	3,511
02.07 Receipts from Federal disability insurance trust fund	135	147	126
02.10 Refunds, railroad social security equivalent benefit account	–3	–4	–4
02.99 Total receipts	5,482	5,582	5,491
04.00 Total: Balances and collections	6,916	6,997	7,219
Appropriation:			
05.01 Rail industry social security equivalent benefit account	–5,501	–5,269	–5,382
05.99 Subtotal appropriation	–5,501	–5,269	–5,382
07.99 Total balance, end of year	1,415	1,728	1,837

Program and Financing (in millions of dollars)

Identification code 60–8010–0–7–601	1999 actual	2000 est.	2001 est.
Obligations by program activity:			
10.00 Total new obligations	5,306	5,325	5,376
Budgetary resources available for obligation:			
22.00 New budget authority (gross)	5,306	5,325	5,376
23.95 Total new obligations	–5,306	–5,325	–5,376
New budget authority (gross), detail:			
Mandatory:			
60.27 Appropriation (trust fund, indefinite)	5,501	5,557	5,466
60.45 Portion precluded from obligation	....	–288	–84
60.47 Portion applied to repay debt	–3,132	–2,992	–3,074
61.00 Transferred to other accounts	–55	–26	–26
62.50 Appropriation (total mandatory)	2,314	2,251	2,282
67.15 Authority to borrow (indefinite)	2,992	3,074	3,094
70.00 Total new budget authority (gross)	5,306	5,325	5,376
Change in unpaid obligations:			
72.40 Unpaid obligations, start of year: Obligated balance, start of year	531	519	534
73.10 Total new obligations	5,306	5,325	5,376
73.20 Total outlays (gross)	–5,318	–5,310	–5,370
74.40 Unpaid obligations, end of year: Obligated balance, end of year	519	534	540
Outlays (gross), detail:			
86.97 Outlays from new mandatory authority	4,787	4,791	4,836
86.98 Outlays from mandatory balances	531	519	534
87.00 Total outlays (gross)	5,318	5,310	5,370
Net budget authority and outlays:			
89.00 Budget authority	5,306	5,325	5,376
90.00 Outlays	5,318	5,310	5,370
Memorandum (non-add) entries:			
92.01 Total investments, start of year: U.S. securities: Par value	2,003	1,942	2,263
92.02 Total investments, end of year: U.S. securities: Par value	1,942	2,263	2,378

All railroad retirees receive the equivalent of a social security benefit, and they may also receive other add-ons including rail industry pension payments, windfall payments, and supplemental annuities. Social security benefits for former railroad employees are funded by the social security trust funds, and rail industry pension payments are the responsibility of the rail sector.

Under current law, a financial interchange occurs once each year between the social security trust funds and the social security equivalent benefit (SSEB) account. The SSEB receives monthly advances from the general fund equal to an estimate of the transfer the SSEB would have received for the previous month if the financial interchange transfers were on a monthly basis. Advances from the previous year are repaid annually to the general fund immediately after the financial interchange is received. In 1999, $2,992 million was advanced and $3,132 million was repaid.

Status of Funds (in millions of dollars)

Identification code 60–8010–0–7–601	1999 actual	2000 est.	2001 est.
Unexpended balance, start of year:			
0100 Treasury balance	–38	–7	....
0101 U.S. Securities: Par value	2,003	1,942	2,263
0105 Outstanding debt to Treasury	–3,132	–2,992	–3,074
0199 Total balance, start of year	–1,167	–1,058	–812
Cash income during the year:			
Governmental receipts:			
0200 Railroad Soc. Sec. equivalent ben. acct., Taxes	1,906	2,031	2,071
0201 Railroad Soc. Sec. equivalent ben. acct., Receipts transferred to Federal hospital insurance trust fund	–388	–388	–393
0202 Railroad Soc. Sec. Equivalent Ben. Acct., Refunds	–3	–4	–4
Intragovernmental transactions:			
0240 Railroad Soc. Sec. equivalent ben. acct., Interest and profits on investments in public debt securities	95	114	130
0241 Railroad Soc. Sec. equivalent ben. acct., Income tax credits	98	105	88
0242 Railroad Soc. Sec. equivalent ben. acct., Interest transferred to Federal hospital insurance trust fund	–42	–36	–38
0243 Railroad Soc. Sec. equivalent ben. acct., Receipts from Federal old-age survivors ins. trust fund	3,681	3,613	3,511
0244 Railroad Soc. Sec. equivalent ben. acct., Receipts from Federal disability ins. trust fund	135	147	126
0299 Total cash income	5,482	5,582	5,491
Cash outgo during year:			
0500 Railroad social security equivalent benefit account	–5,318	–5,310	–5,370
0645 Balance transferred, net	–55	–26	–26
Unexpended balance, end of year:			
0700 Uninvested balance	–7	....	....
0701 U.S. Securities: Par value	1,942	2,263	2,378
0705 Outstanding debt to Treasury	–2,992	–3,074	–3,094
0799 Total balance, end of year	–1,058	–812	–717

Object Classification (in millions of dollars)

Identification code 60–8010–0–7–601	1999 actual	2000 est.	2001 est.
42.0 Benefit payments	5,075	5,095	5,131
43.0 Interest and dividends	1	1	1
92.0 Repayment of interest on benefit advances	230	229	244
99.9 Total new obligations	5,306	5,325	5,376

RESOLUTION TRUST CORPORATION

Federal Funds

Public enterprise funds:

RTC REVOLVING FUND

Program and Financing (in millions of dollars)

Identification code 22–4055–0–3–373	1999 actual	2000 est.	2001 est.
Budgetary resources available for obligation:			
21.40 Unobligated balance available, start of year	4	4	
23.95 Total new obligations			
23.98 Unobligated balance expiring or withdrawn		−4	
24.40 Unobligated balance available, end of year	4		
Net budget authority and outlays:			
89.00 Budget authority			
90.00 Outlays			

The Financial Institutions Reform, Recovery, and Enforcement Act (FIRREA) of 1989 established the Resolution Trust Corporation (RTC) as a temporary agency to dispose of insolvent thrift institutions. The Savings Association Insurance Fund took over responsibility for resolving failed thrifts on July 1, 1995, and the RTC's assets and liabilities were transferred to the FSLIC Resolution Fund on December 31, 1995.

Of $18.3 billion appropriated to RTC in 1994 by the RTC Completion Act, the Thrift Depositor Protection Oversight Board determined that only $4.6 billion was required and the excess was returned to Treasury on December 31, 1997. When the RTC terminated, the Oversight Board's primary function ceased. On October 29, 1998, the Board was abolished and its remaining responsibility to oversee the Resolution Funding Corporation (REFCORP), which provided financing for the RTC, was transferred to the Secretary of the Treasury.

SECURITIES AND EXCHANGE COMMISSION

Federal Funds

General and special funds:

SALARIES AND EXPENSES

For necessary expenses for the Securities and Exchange Commission, including services as authorized by 5 U.S.C. 3109, the rental of space (to include multiple year leases) in the District of Columbia and elsewhere, and not to exceed $3,000 for official reception and representation expenses, [$173,800,000] ***$282,800,000*** from fees collected in fiscal year [2000] ***2001*** to remain available until expended, and from fees collected in fiscal year [1998, $194,000,000] ***1999, $140,000,000,*** to remain available until expended; of which not to exceed $10,000 may be used toward funding a permanent secretariat for the International Organization of Securities Commissions; and of which not to exceed $100,000 shall be available for expenses for consultations and meetings hosted by the Commission with foreign governmental and other regulatory officials, members of their delegations, appropriate representatives and staff to exchange views concerning developments relating to securities matters, development and implementation of cooperation agreements concerning securities matters and provision of technical assistance for the development of foreign securities markets, such expenses to include necessary logistic and administrative expenses and the expenses of Commission staff and foreign invitees in attendance at such consultations and meetings including: (1) such incidental expenses as meals taken in the course of such attendance; (2) any travel and transportation to or from such meetings; and (3) any other related lodging or subsistence: *Provided*, That fees and charges authorized by sections 6(b)(4) of the Securities Act of 1933 (15 U.S.C. 77f(b)(4)) and 31(d) of the Securities Exchange Act of 1934 (15 U.S.C. 78ee(d)) shall be credited to this account as offsetting collections. *(Departments of Commerce, Justice, and State, the Judiciary, and Related Agencies Appropriations Act, 2000, as enacted by section 1000(a)(1) of the Consolidated Appropriations Act, 2000 (P.L. 106–113).)*

Unavailable Collections (in millions of dollars)

Identification code 50–0100–0–1–376	1999 actual	2000 est.	2001 est.
Balance, start of year:			
01.99 Balance, start of year	344	614	866
03.00 Offsetting Collections	377	460	375
04.00 Total: Balances and collections	721	1,074	1,241
Appropriation:			
05.01 Salaries and expenses	−107	−208	−148
07.99 Total balance, end of year	614	866	1,093

Program and Financing (in millions of dollars)

Identification code 50–0100–0–1–376	1999 actual	2000 est.	2001 est.
Obligations by program activity:			
Direct program:			
00.01 Full disclosure	55	57	65
00.02 Prevention and suppression of fraud	116	135	150
00.03 Supervision and regulation of securities markets	49	53	59
00.04 Investment management regulation	66	70	78
00.05 Legal and economic services	23	24	27
00.07 Program direction	42	43	44
09.01 Reimbursable program	1	1	1
10.00 Total new obligations	352	383	424
Budgetary resources available for obligation:			
21.40 Unobligated balance available, start of year	31	36	36
22.00 New budget authority (gross)	353	383	424
22.10 Resources available from recoveries of prior year obligations	4		
23.90 Total budgetary resources available for obligation	388	419	460
23.95 Total new obligations	−352	−383	−424
24.40 Unobligated balance available, end of year	36	36	36
New budget authority (gross), detail:			
Discretionary:			
40.00 Appropriation	23		
42.00 Transferred from other accounts	8		
43.00 Appropriation (total discretionary)	31		
Spending authority from offsetting collections:			
68.00 Offsetting governmental collections (cash)	592	635	651
68.26 Offsetting collections (unavailable balances)	107	208	148
68.45 Portion not available for obligation (limitation on obligations)	−377	−460	−375
68.90 Spending authority from offsetting collections (total discretionary)	322	383	424
70.00 Total new budget authority (gross)	353	383	424
Change in unpaid obligations:			
72.40 Unpaid obligations, start of year: Obligated balance, start of year	75	84	96
73.10 Total new obligations	352	383	424
73.20 Total outlays (gross)	−339	−371	−415
73.45 Adjustments in unexpired accounts	−4		
74.40 Unpaid obligations, end of year: Obligated balance, end of year	84	96	105
Outlays (gross), detail:			
86.90 Outlays from new discretionary authority	306	329	365
86.93 Outlays from discretionary balances	33	42	50
87.00 Total outlays (gross)	339	371	415
Offsets:			
Against gross budget authority and outlays:			
Offsetting collections (cash) from:			
88.00 Federal sources	−1	−1	−1
88.40 Non-Federal sources	−591	−634	−650
88.90 Total, offsetting collections (cash)	−592	−635	−651
Net budget authority and outlays:			
89.00 Budget authority	−239	−252	−227
90.00 Outlays	−255	−264	−236

The primary mission of the Securities and Exchange Commission (the Commission) is to administer and enforce the

General and special funds—Continued

SALARIES AND EXPENSES—Continued

Federal securities laws in order to protect investors, and to maintain fair, honest, and efficient markets.

Full disclosure.—This program ensures that investors will be provided with material information in the public offering, trading, voting and tendering of securities. Standards of financial reporting are established and enforced to enhance the transparency, relevance, and reliability of financial reporting so that financial statements used by investors in making investment decisions are presented fairly and have credibility. Issuers that have conducted public offerings, have securities traded in the public markets, or have total assets and security holder populations of specified sizes, are required to furnish management, financial, and business information to investors and the Commission on a continuing basis in proxy materials and in annual and other periodic reports. The staff reviews these documents on a selected basis for compliance with the disclosure requirements. In addition, all registration statements of issuers that are making their initial public offerings of securities and all third party tender offer filings are reviewed by the staff. As a result of the review process, the staff may issue comments to issuers to elicit better compliance or, where appropriate, refer matters for enforcement action.

Electronic filing (EDGAR).—The Commission's EDGAR system provides the agency with the capability for electronic receipt, analysis, and dissemination of virtually all of its full disclosure filings. Since becoming operational in 1993, EDGAR has received and successfully processed over 2.8 million documents submitted in approximately 1.1 million separate submissions from over 28,000 companies and funds registered with the SEC.

In order to take advantage of changes in technology and respond to the demands of filers and investors, the SEC awarded a three year contract for EDGAR modernization on July 1, 1998. This multi-year modernization effort will improve the presentation quality and data structure of SEC filings.

The first major modernization milestone, a newly privatized dissemination subsystem, was delivered on time and within budget on November 1, 1998. This modernized dissemination subsystem is now faster, more reliable, and has resulted in a further reduction of subscriber costs from $79,000 to $44,571 per year, a savings of approximately $233,000 when compared to the cost prior to privatization.

The second major milestone, the inclusion of Hypertext Mark-up Language (HTML) and unofficial PDF filings, was delivered on time and within budget on May 24, 1999. The third milestone, allowing filings over the Internet, is scheduled for delivery in May 2000 and is anticipated to be within budget.

SELECTED WORKLOAD DATA

	1999 actual	2000 est.	2001 est.
Filings of initial 1933 Act registration statements—other than investment companies	1,086	1,085	1,085
Filings of repeat 1933 Act registration statements and post-effective amendments—other than investment companies	5,690	5,690	5,690
Filings of definitive proxy and information statements (uncontested)—other than investment companies	9,935	9,935	9,935
Filings of annual and periodic reports—other than investment companies	84,170	84,170	84,170
Filings of Director and Officer ownership and transaction reports	302,350	302,350	302,350

Prevention and suppression of fraud.—This program evaluates information indicating possible violations of the Federal securities laws. Possible violations include, among other things, the illegal distribution of unregistered securities; fraud in the offer, purchase, and sale of securities; insider trading, market manipulation; and, illegal conduct by broker-dealers, investment advisers, and other regulated entities. Investigations of possible violations are conducted and, if appropriate, enforcement actions are initiated. Actions include civil proceedings, seeking injunctive and other relief, and administrative proceedings. The Commission is authorized to seek court orders imposing civil monetary penalties for any securities law violation as well as to seek such penalties against regulated entities in administrative proceedings. Under appropriate circumstances matters are referred for criminal prosecution.

SELECTED WORKLOAD DATA

	1999 actual	2000 est.	2001 est.
Investigations opened	520	540	560
Administrative proceedings opened	298	298	298
Civil actions opened	227	227	227

Supervision and regulation of securities markets.—Trading in the securities markets is regulated to protect investors against fraud and manipulation and to ensure the maintenance of fair, orderly, efficient, and competitive markets. The Commission oversees the work of self-regulatory organizations, monitors securities markets and broker-dealer operations, and develops regulatory strategies for coping with market stress, promoting compliance, and meeting changing domestic and international conditions. The Commission also conducts examinations of broker-dealers and inspections of transfer agents, clearing agencies, and self-regulatory organizations.

SELECTED WORKLOAD DATA

	1999 actual	2000 est.	2001 est.
Review of changes in the rules and procedures of self-regulatory organizations	534	525	525
Inspections of self-regulatory organizations	30	34	34
Broker-dealer registration applications	756	800	800
Broker-dealer oversight and cause examinations	681	650	650
Transfer agent and clearing agency examinations	225	177	177

Investment management regulation.—This program administers the Investment Company Act of 1940 and the Investment Advisers Act of 1940. Mutual funds and other investment companies manage over $6 trillion for more than 48 million households. The staff reviews disclosure documents filed by investment companies and investment advisers and regulates and inspects investment companies and investment advisers to protect investors against fraud, self-dealing, inadequate disclosure, and other abuse. The staff refers serious violations for enforcement action. This program also is responsible for administering the Public Utility Holding Company Act of 1935.

SELECTED WORKLOAD DATA

	1999 actual	2000 est.	2001 est.
Investment company assets inspected ($ trillions)	1.5	1.5	1.7
Investment company portfolios and amendments filed	26,600	23,550	24,900
Investment company proxy statements filed	780	785	790
Investment advisers inspected	1,508	1,550	1,540
Investment adviser registration statements filed	1,110	1,100	1,100
Exemptive applications closed	400	425	435
Public utility filings processed	118	140	175
Public utility annual and periodic reports examined	1,400	1,500	1,700

Legal and economic services.—This program provides a range of legal services and economic analyses to the Commission concerning its law enforcement, regulatory, and legislative activities, including: (i) prosecution of enforcement actions in appellate courts; (ii) representation of the Commission in all other appellate litigation, in private litigation where the Commission appears as *amicus curiae,* and in corporate reorganizations; (iii) representation of the Commission in actions brought against the Commission and its employees; (iv) preparation of Congressional testimony and comments and advice concerning proposed securities legislation; (v) advice to the Commission concerning issues arising from its law enforcement and regulatory activities; (vi) preparation of draft opinions of adjudicatory decisions and advice to the Commission regarding its adjudicatory decisions; (vii) advice to the Commission regarding compliance with Government-wide statutes and the statutes and rules applicable to the agency's activities; and (viii) economic analyses of proposed regulations and legislation, litigation support in enforcement cases, and independent studies of issues affecting the securities markets. In addition, the administrative law judges conduct hearings and issue initial decisions in formal administrative proceedings where the Commission has determined that hearings are appropriate in the public interest and for the protection of public investors.

SELECTED WORKLOAD DATA

	1999 actual	2000 est.	2001 est.
Litigation matters opened	263	265	275
Adjudicatory matters received	73	75	80
Adjudicatory matters completed	69	80	80
Legislative matters	291	250	250
Chapter 11 disclosure statements commented on	116	120	120
Administrative proceedings disposed by Administrative Law Judges	62	61	61

Program direction.—This program assists the Commission in fulfilling its statutory requirements and in responding to changes in the securities industry by carefully evaluating priorities, formulating and implementing policies, and managing agency resources. The staff provides management direction and analysis, internal control, financial management, personnel management, data processing, public affairs, records management, information dissemination, general administrative services, and processing of equal employment opportunity complaints.

The Commission continues to follow the fee reduction schedule established in the "National Securities Markets Improvement Act of 1996" (P.L. 104–290). Title IV of this law amends fee language found in Section 6(b) of the Securities Act of 1933 and Section 31 of the Securities and Exchange Act of 1934. Under this law, the Section 6(b) fee rate paid by corporations to register securities with the Commission was reduced from $278 per $1,000,000 of the aggregate price of securities offered in 1999 to $264 per $1,000,000 in 2000, and will be further reduced in 2001 to $250 per $1,000,000 of the offering amount. The first $200 per $1,000,000 of this fee shall be deposited in the general fund of the U.S. Treasury, and the remaining increment will be made available for use by the Commission. In addition, to promote equity across securities markets, the "National Securities Markets Improvement Act of 1996" extended Section 31 transaction fees to the over-the-counter market at a rate of 1/300 of one percent of the aggregate dollar amount of securities transacted, the rate currently paid by all national and regional exchanges. These transaction fees are also made available for use by the Commission.

Object Classification (in millions of dollars)

Identification code 50–0100–0–1–376	1999 actual	2000 est.	2001 est.
Personnel compensation:			
11.1 Full-time permanent	181	205	237
11.3 Other than full-time permanent	2	2	2
11.5 Other personnel compensation	3	3	4
11.8 Special personal services payments	1	1	1
11.9 Total personnel compensation	187	211	244
12.1 Civilian personnel benefits	43	50	57
21.0 Travel and transportation of persons	8	9	9
23.2 Rental payments to others	25	26	27
23.3 Communications, utilities, and miscellaneous charges	7	13	14
24.0 Printing and reproduction	2	2	3
25.1 Advisory and assistance services	2	3	3
25.2 Other services	15	22	19
25.4 Operation and maintenance of facilities	2	2	2
25.7 Operation and maintenance of equipment	41	34	36
26.0 Supplies and materials	6	4	4
31.0 Equipment	8	5	5
32.0 Land and structures	3	1	1
42.0 Insurance claims and indemnities	1		
99.0 Subtotal, direct obligations	350	382	424
99.5 Below reporting threshold	2	1	
99.9 Total new obligations	352	383	424

Personnel Summary

Identification code 50–0100–0–1–376	1999 actual	2000 est.	2001 est.
Direct:			
1001 Total compensable workyears: Full-time equivalent employment	2,776	2,960	3,037
Reimbursable:			
2001 Total compensable workyears: Full-time equivalent employment	1	1	1

Public enterprise funds:

INVESTMENT IN SECURITIES INVESTOR PROTECTION CORPORATION

Program and Financing (in millions of dollars)

Identification code 50–4068–0–3–376	1999 actual	2000 est.	2001 est.
Budgetary resources available for obligation:			
21.40 Unobligated balance available, start of year	1,000	1,000	1,000
23.95 Total new obligations			
24.40 Unobligated balance available, end of year	1,000	1,000	1,000
Net budget authority and outlays:			
89.00 Budget authority			
90.00 Outlays			

The Securities Investor Protection Corporation (SIPC) may borrow up to $1 billion from the U.S. Department of the Treasury, through the Commission, in the event that the fund maintained by SIPC is insufficient to satisfy the claims of customers of failing brokerage firms. To date, SIPC has not needed these loans.

SMITHSONIAN INSTITUTION

Federal Funds

General and special funds:

SALARIES AND EXPENSES

For necessary expenses of the Smithsonian Institution, as authorized by law, including research in the fields of art, science, and history; development, preservation, and documentation of the National Collections; presentation of public exhibits and performances; collection, preparation, dissemination, and exchange of information and publications; conduct of education, training, and museum assistance programs; maintenance, alteration, operation, lease (for terms not to exceed 30 years), and protection of buildings, facilities, and approaches; not to exceed $100,000 for services as authorized by 5 U.S.C. 3109; up to five replacement passenger vehicles; purchase, rental, repair, and cleaning of uniforms for employees, [$372,901,000] *$396,800,000*, of which not to exceed [$43,318,000] *$55,133,000* for the instrumentation program, collections acquisition, Museum Support Center equipment and move, exhibition reinstallation, the National Museum of the American Indian, the repatriation of skeletal remains program, research equipment, information management, and Latino programming shall remain available until expended [and of which $2,500,000 shall remain available until expended for the National Museum of Natural History's Arctic Studies Center to include assistance to other museums for the planning and development of institutions and facilities that enhance the display of collections], and including such funds as may be necessary to support American overseas research centers and a total of $125,000 for the Council of American Overseas Research Centers: *Provided*, That funds appropriated herein are available for advance payments to independent contractors performing research services or participating in official Smithsonian presentations: *Provided further*, That the Smithsonian Institution may expend Federal appropriations des-

General and special funds—Continued

SALARIES AND EXPENSES—Continued

ignated in this Act for lease or rent payments for long term and swing space, as rent payable to the Smithsonian Institution, and such rent payments may be deposited into the general trust funds of the Institution to the extent that federally supported activities are housed in the 900 H Street, N.W. building in the District of Columbia: *Provided further*, That this use of Federal appropriations shall not be construed as debt service, a Federal guarantee of, a transfer of risk to, or an obligation of, the Federal Government: *Provided further*, That no appropriated funds may be used to service debt which is incurred to finance the costs of acquiring the 900 H Street building or of planning, designing, and constructing improvements to such building. *(Department of the Interior and Related Agencies Appropriations Act, 2000, as enacted by section 1000(a)(3) of the Consolidated Appropriations Act, 2000 (P.L. 106–113).)*

Program and Financing (in millions of dollars)

Identification code 33–0100–0–1–503	1999 actual	2000 est.	2001 est.
Obligations by program activity:			
00.01 Research and collections management	196	201	214
00.02 Education, public programs, and exhibitions	17	17	20
00.03 Administration	42	51	56
00.04 Facilities and security	86	101	107
09.11 Reimbursable program—Transportation	1	1	
09.12 Reimbursable program—Millennium	3		
10.00 Total new obligations	345	371	397
Budgetary resources available for obligation:			
21.40 Unobligated balance available, start of year	7	14	14
22.00 New budget authority (gross)	352	371	397
23.90 Total budgetary resources available for obligation	359	385	411
23.95 Total new obligations	−345	−371	−397
23.98 Unobligated balance expiring or withdrawn			
24.40 Unobligated balance available, end of year	14	14	12
New budget authority (gross), detail:			
Discretionary:			
40.00 Appropriation	348	373	397
40.75 Reduction pursuant to P.L. 106–51	−1		
40.76 Reduction pursuant to P.L. 106–113		−2	
42.00 Transferred from other accounts	5		
43.00 Appropriation (total discretionary)	352	371	397
Change in unpaid obligations:			
72.40 Unpaid obligations, start of year: Obligated balance, start of year	45	58	58
73.10 Total new obligations	345	371	397
73.20 Total outlays (gross)	−329	−371	−394
73.40 Adjustments in expired accounts (net)	−3		
74.40 Unpaid obligations, end of year: Obligated balance, end of year	58	58	59
Outlays (gross), detail:			
86.90 Outlays from new discretionary authority	313	352	373
86.93 Outlays from discretionary balances	16	19	19
87.00 Total outlays (gross)	329	371	394
Net budget authority and outlays:			
89.00 Budget authority	352	371	397
90.00 Outlays	329	371	394

The Smithsonian Institution conducts research in the natural and physical sciences and in the history of cultures, technology, and the arts. The Institution acquires and preserves for reference and study purposes over one hundred and forty million items of scientific, cultural, and historic importance. It maintains public exhibits in a variety of fields.

The Institution operates and maintains 16 museums; a zoological park and animal conservation and research center; research facilities; and supporting facilities.

Included in the presentation of the Salaries and Expenses account are data for the Canal Zone biological area fund. Donations, subscriptions, and fees are appropriated and used to defray part of the expenses of maintaining and operating the Canal Zone biological area (60 Stat. 1101; 20 U.S.C. 79, 79a).

Object Classification (in millions of dollars)

Identification code 33–0100–0–1–503	1999 actual	2000 est.	2001 est.
Direct obligations:			
Personnel compensation:			
11.1 Full-time permanent	186	196	205
11.3 Other than full-time permanent	4	4	4
11.5 Other personnel compensation	6	7	7
11.9 Total personnel compensation	196	207	216
12.1 Civilian personnel benefits	46	48	52
21.0 Travel and transportation of persons	3	4	4
22.0 Transportation of things	1	1	1
23.2 Rental payments to others	9	11	11
23.3 Communications, utilities, and miscellaneous charges	29	30	30
24.0 Printing and reproduction	2	4	4
25.2 Other services	21	25	34
25.3 Purchases of goods and services from Government accounts	1	1	1
26.0 Supplies and materials	16	19	19
31.0 Equipment	16	19	24
32.0 Land and structures	1	1	1
99.0 Subtotal, direct obligations	341	370	397
99.0 Reimbursable obligations	4	1	
99.9 Total new obligations	345	371	397

Personnel Summary

Identification code 33–0100–0–1–503	1999 actual	2000 est.	2001 est.
1001 Total compensable workyears: Full-time equivalent employment	4,200	4,300	4,329

MUSEUM PROGRAMS AND RELATED RESEARCH (SPECIAL FOREIGN CURRENCY PROGRAM)

Program and Financing (in millions of dollars)

Identification code 33–0102–0–1–503	1999 actual	2000 est.	2001 est.
Budgetary resources available for obligation:			
21.40 Unobligated balance available, start of year	1	1	1
23.95 Total new obligations			
24.40 Unobligated balance available, end of year	1	1	1
Change in unpaid obligations:			
72.40 Unpaid obligations, start of year: Obligated balance, start of year	2	1	
73.20 Total outlays (gross)	−1		
73.40 Adjustments in expired accounts (net)			
74.40 Unpaid obligations, end of year: Obligated balance, end of year	1		
Outlays (gross), detail:			
86.93 Outlays from discretionary balances	1		
Net budget authority and outlays:			
89.00 Budget authority			
90.00 Outlays	1		

This account supports a program of grants to U.S. universities, museums, and other institutions of higher learning, paid for by excess U.S.-owned foreign currencies. Areas of research include archeology and related disciplines, systematic and environmental biology, astrophysics and Earth sciences, and museum programs.

REPAIR, [REHABILITATION] *RESTORATION* AND ALTERATION OF FACILITIES

[(INCLUDING TRANSFERS OF FUNDS)]

For necessary expenses of repair, [rehabilitation] *restoration,* and alteration of facilities owned or occupied by the Smithsonian Institution, by contract or otherwise, as authorized by section 2 of the Act of August 22, 1949 (63 Stat. 623), including not to exceed $10,000 for services as authorized by 5 U.S.C. 3109, [$47,900,000] *$62,200,000,* to remain available until expended[, of which $6,000,000 is provided for repair, rehabilitation and alteration of facilities at the National Zoological Park]: *Provided,* That contracts awarded for environmental systems, protection systems, and repair or [rehabilitation] *restoration* of facilities of the Smithsonian Institution may be negotiated with selected contractors and awarded on the basis of contractor qualifications as well as price[: *Provided further,* That funds previously appropriated to the "Construction and Improvements, National Zoological Park" account and the "Repair and Restoration of Buildings" account may be transferred to and merged with this "Repair, Rehabilitation and Alteration of Facilities" account]. *For necessary expenses of the major capital renewal of the Patent Office Building, to become available on October 1 of the fiscal year specified and remain available until expended, as follows: for fiscal year 2002, $17,000,000; for fiscal year 2003, $18,000,000. (Department of the Interior and Related Agencies Appropriations Act, 2000, as enacted by section 1000(a)(3) of the Consolidated Appropriations Act, 2000 (P.L. 106–113).)*

Program and Financing (in millions of dollars)

Identification code 33–0132–0–1–503	1999 actual	2000 est.	2001 est.
Obligations by program activity:			
10.00 Total new obligations	55	48	62
Budgetary resources available for obligation:			
21.40 Unobligated balance available, start of year	17	6	6
22.00 New budget authority (gross)	44	48	62
23.90 Total budgetary resources available for obligation	61	54	68
23.95 Total new obligations	−55	−48	−62
24.40 Unobligated balance available, end of year	6	6	6
New budget authority (gross), detail:			
Discretionary:			
40.00 Appropriation	44	48	62
Change in unpaid obligations:			
72.40 Unpaid obligations, start of year: Obligated balance, start of year	54	65	51
73.10 Total new obligations	55	48	62
73.20 Total outlays (gross)	−44	−62	−35
74.40 Unpaid obligations, end of year: Obligated balance, end of year	65	51	78
Outlays (gross), detail:			
86.90 Outlays from new discretionary authority	9	10	12
86.93 Outlays from discretionary balances	35	52	23
87.00 Total outlays (gross)	44	62	35
Net budget authority and outlays:			
89.00 Budget authority	44	48	62
90.00 Outlays	44	62	35

This account encompasses repairs, restorations, code compliance changes, minor construction, alterations and modifications, and building system renewals of Smithsonian museum buildings and facilities for storage and conservation of collections, research, and support.

Object Classification (in millions of dollars)

Identification code 33–0132–0–1–503	1999 actual	2000 est.	2001 est.
25.2 Other services	54	47	61
26.0 Supplies and materials	1	1	1
99.9 Total new obligations	55	48	62

CONSTRUCTION

For necessary expenses for construction, [$19,000,000] *$4,000,000,* to remain available until expended. *For necessary expenses for construction, $2,500,000, to become available on October 1, 2001 and remain available until expended. (Department of the Interior and Related Agencies Appropriations Act, 2000, as enacted by section 1000(a)(3) of the Consolidated Appropriations Act, 2000 (P.L. 106–113).)*

Program and Financing (in millions of dollars)

Identification code 33–0133–0–1–503	1999 actual	2000 est.	2001 est.
Obligations by program activity:			
00.06 National Museum of the American Indian	9	19	
00.07 Natural History East Court building	4		
00.08 Air and Space Museum Extention	2		
00.09 National Zoological Park Water Exhibit			1
00.10 Smithsonian Environmental Research Center			1
00.11 Smithsonian Astrophysical Observ.—Hilo Building			2
10.00 Total new obligations (object class 25.2)	15	19	4
Budgetary resources available for obligation:			
21.40 Unobligated balance available, start of year	37	38	38
22.00 New budget authority (gross)	16	19	4
23.90 Total budgetary resources available for obligation	53	57	42
23.95 Total new obligations	−15	−19	−4
24.40 Unobligated balance available, end of year	38	38	38
New budget authority (gross), detail:			
Discretionary:			
40.00 Appropriation	16	19	4
Change in unpaid obligations:			
72.40 Unpaid obligations, start of year: Obligated balance, start of year	9	7	17
73.10 Total new obligations	15	19	4
73.20 Total outlays (gross)	−17	−10	−16
73.40 Adjustments in expired accounts (net)			
74.40 Unpaid obligations, end of year: Obligated balance, end of year	7	17	5
Outlays (gross), detail:			
86.90 Outlays from new discretionary authority	8	10	2
86.93 Outlays from discretionary balances	9		14
87.00 Total outlays (gross)	17	10	16
Net budget authority and outlays:			
89.00 Budget authority	16	19	4
90.00 Outlays	17	10	16

This account provides funding for major new construction projects to support the Smithsonian's existing and future programs in research, collections management, public exhibitions and education. The 2001 budget request provides funds for the construction of the National Zoological Park water exhibit, infrastructure at the Smithsonian Environmental Research center, and the Smithsonian Astrophysical Observatory's base building at Hilo, Hawaii.

JOHN F. KENNEDY CENTER FOR THE PERFORMING ARTS

OPERATIONS AND MAINTENANCE

For necessary expenses for the operation, maintenance and security of the John F. Kennedy Center for the Performing Arts, $14,000,000. *(Department of the Interior and Related Agencies Appropriations Act, 2000, as enacted by section 1000(a)(3) of the Consolidated Appropriations Act, 2000 (P.L. 106–113).)*

Program and Financing (in millions of dollars)

Identification code 33–0302–0–1–503	1999 actual	2000 est.	2001 est.
Obligations by program activity:			
10.00 Total new obligations	12	14	14
Budgetary resources available for obligation:			
22.00 New budget authority (gross)	12	14	14

General and special funds—Continued

JOHN F. KENNEDY CENTER FOR THE PERFORMING ARTS—Continued

OPERATIONS AND MAINTENANCE—Continued

Program and Financing (in millions of dollars)—Continued

Identification code 33–0302–0–1–503	1999 actual	2000 est.	2001 est.
23.95 Total new obligations	–12	–14	–14
New budget authority (gross), detail:			
Discretionary:			
40.00 Appropriation	12	14	14
Change in unpaid obligations:			
72.40 Unpaid obligations, start of year: Obligated balance, start of year	2	3	3
73.10 Total new obligations	12	14	14
73.20 Total outlays (gross)	–11	–14	–14
74.40 Unpaid obligations, end of year: Obligated balance, end of year	3	3	3
Outlays (gross), detail:			
86.90 Outlays from new discretionary authority	10	11	11
86.93 Outlays from discretionary balances	1	2	3
87.00 Total outlays (gross)	11	14	14
Net budget authority and outlays:			
89.00 Budget authority	12	14	14
90.00 Outlays	11	14	14

This appropriation provides for the operating and maintenance expenses of the John F. Kennedy Center for the Performing Arts, including maintenance, security, memorial interpretation, janitorial, short-term repair, and other services.

Object Classification (in millions of dollars)

Identification code 33–0302–0–1–503	1999 actual	2000 est.	2001 est.
11.1 Personnel compensation: Full-time permanent	3	3	3
23.3 Communications, utilities, and miscellaneous charges	3	3	3
25.2 Other services	6	7	7
99.0 Subtotal, direct obligations	12	13	13
99.5 Below reporting threshold	....	1	1
99.9 Total new obligations	12	14	14

Personnel Summary

Identification code 33–0302–0–1–503	1999 actual	2000 est.	2001 est.
1001 Total compensable workyears: Full-time equivalent employment	46	55	55

JOHN F. KENNEDY CENTER FOR THE PERFORMING ARTS

CONSTRUCTION

For necessary expenses for capital repair and [rehabilitation] *restoration* of the existing features of the building and site of the John F. Kennedy Center for the Performing Arts, $20,000,000, to remain available until expended. *(Department of the Interior and Related Agencies Appropriations Act, 2000, as enacted by section 1000(a)(3) of the Consolidated Appropriations Act, 2000 (P.L. 106–113).)*

Program and Financing (in millions of dollars)

Identification code 33–0303–0–1–503	1999 actual	2000 est.	2001 est.
Obligations by program activity:			
10.00 Total new obligations (object class 25.2)	17	20	20
Budgetary resources available for obligation:			
21.40 Unobligated balance available, start of year	13	16	16
22.00 New budget authority (gross)	20	20	20
23.90 Total budgetary resources available for obligation	33	36	36
23.95 Total new obligations	–17	–20	–20
24.40 Unobligated balance available, end of year	16	16	16
New budget authority (gross), detail:			
Discretionary:			
40.00 Appropriation	20	20	20
Change in unpaid obligations:			
72.40 Unpaid obligations, start of year: Obligated balance, start of year	6	11	9
73.10 Total new obligations	17	20	20
73.20 Total outlays (gross)	–12	–22	–18
74.40 Unpaid obligations, end of year: Obligated balance, end of year	11	9	11
Outlays (gross), detail:			
86.93 Outlays from discretionary balances	12	22	18
Net budget authority and outlays:			
89.00 Budget authority	20	20	20
90.00 Outlays	12	22	18

This appropriation provides for the repair, restoration and renovation of the Kennedy Center building, including major projects related to plumbing and electrical systems, air handling systems, and major repair of interior spaces, including access for persons with disabilities. The Kennedy Center plans to continue Phase II of the renovation of the interior of the presidential memorial.

NATIONAL GALLERY OF ART

SALARIES AND EXPENSES

For the upkeep and operations of the National Gallery of Art, the protection and care of the works of art therein, and administrative expenses incident thereto, as authorized by the Act of March 24, 1937 (50 Stat. 51), as amended by the public resolution of April 13, 1939 (Public Resolution 9, Seventy-sixth Congress), including services as authorized by 5 U.S.C. 3109; payment in advance when authorized by the treasurer of the Gallery for membership in library, museum, and art associations or societies whose publications or services are available to members only, or to members at a price lower than to the general public; purchase, repair, and cleaning of uniforms for guards, and uniforms, or allowances therefor, for other employees as authorized by law (5 U.S.C. 5901–5902); purchase or rental of devices and services for protecting buildings and contents thereof, and maintenance, alteration, improvement, and repair of buildings, approaches, and grounds; and purchase of services for restoration and repair of works of art for the National Gallery of Art by contracts made, without advertising, with individuals, firms, or organizations at such rates or prices and under such terms and conditions as the Gallery may deem proper, [$61,538,000] *$64,848,000*, of which not to exceed [$3,026,000] *$2,349,000* for the special exhibition program shall remain available until expended. *(Department of the Interior and Related Agencies Appropriations Act, 2000, as enacted by section 1000(a)(3) of the Consolidated Appropriations Act, 2000 (P.L. 106–113).)*

Program and Financing (in millions of dollars)

Identification code 33–0200–0–1–503	1999 actual	2000 est.	2001 est.
Obligations by program activity:			
10.00 Total new obligations	58	62	65
Budgetary resources available for obligation:			
21.40 Unobligated balance available, start of year	1	1	....
22.00 New budget authority (gross)	58	61	65
23.90 Total budgetary resources available for obligation	59	62	65
23.95 Total new obligations	–58	–62	–65
24.40 Unobligated balance available, end of year	1	....	....
New budget authority (gross), detail:			
Discretionary:			
40.00 Appropriation	58	61	65
Change in unpaid obligations:			
72.40 Unpaid obligations, start of year: Obligated balance, start of year	4	4	5

73.10	Total new obligations	58	62	65
73.20	Total outlays (gross)	−58	−62	−65
74.40	Unpaid obligations, end of year: Obligated balance, end of year	4	5	5
	Outlays (gross), detail:			
86.90	Outlays from new discretionary authority	53	56	59
86.93	Outlays from discretionary balances	5	4	5
87.00	Total outlays (gross)	58	62	65
	Net budget authority and outlays:			
89.00	Budget authority	58	61	65
90.00	Outlays	58	62	65

The National Gallery of Art receives, holds, and administers works of art acquired for the Nation by the Gallery's board of trustees. It also maintains the Gallery buildings to give maximum care and protection to art treasures and to enable these works of art to be exhibited.

Object Classification (in millions of dollars)

Identification code 33–0200–0–1–503		1999 actual	2000 est.	2001 est.
	Personnel compensation:			
11.1	Full-time permanent	30	33	35
11.3	Other than full-time permanent	1	1	1
11.5	Other personnel compensation	3	3	3
11.9	Total personnel compensation	34	37	39
12.1	Civilian personnel benefits	8	9	9
22.0	Transportation of things	1	1	1
23.3	Communications, utilities, and miscellaneous charges	5	5	6
25.2	Other services	7	6	6
26.0	Supplies and materials	2	2	2
31.0	Equipment	1	1	2
99.0	Subtotal, direct obligations	58	61	65
99.5	Below reporting threshold		1	
99.9	Total new obligations	58	62	65

Personnel Summary

Identification code 33–0200–0–1–503		1999 actual	2000 est.	2001 est.
1001	Total compensable workyears: Full-time equivalent employment	792	838	845

NATIONAL GALLERY OF ART

REPAIR, RESTORATION AND RENOVATION OF BUILDINGS

For necessary expenses of repair, restoration and renovation of buildings, grounds and facilities owned or occupied by the National Gallery of Art, by contract or otherwise, as authorized, [$6,311,000] *$14,101,000*, to remain available until expended: *Provided,* That contracts awarded for environmental systems, protection systems, and exterior repair or renovation of buildings of the National Gallery of Art may be negotiated with selected contractors and awarded on the basis of contractor qualifications as well as price. *(Department of the Interior and Related Agencies Appropriations Act, 2000, as enacted by section 1000(a)(3) of the Consolidated Appropriations Act, 2000 (P.L. 106–113).)*

Program and Financing (in millions of dollars)

Identification code 33–0201–0–1–503		1999 actual	2000 est.	2001 est.
	Obligations by program activity:			
10.00	Total new obligations	5	9	14
	Budgetary resources available for obligation:			
21.40	Unobligated balance available, start of year	2	4	1
22.00	New budget authority (gross)	6	6	14
23.90	Total budgetary resources available for obligation	8	10	15
23.95	Total new obligations	−5	−9	−14
24.40	Unobligated balance available, end of year	4	1	1
	New budget authority (gross), detail:			
	Discretionary:			
40.00	Appropriation	6	6	14
	Change in unpaid obligations:			
72.40	Unpaid obligations, start of year: Obligated balance, start of year	5	3	4
73.10	Total new obligations	5	9	14
73.20	Total outlays (gross)	−7	−8	−7
74.40	Unpaid obligations, end of year: Obligated balance, end of year	3	4	12
	Outlays (gross), detail:			
86.90	Outlays from new discretionary authority		1	1
86.93	Outlays from discretionary balances	7	7	5
87.00	Total outlays (gross)	7	8	7
	Net budget authority and outlays:			
89.00	Budget authority	6	6	14
90.00	Outlays	6	8	7

This account encompasses repairs, alterations, and improvements; additions, renovations, and restorations of a long-term nature and utility; and facilities planning and design. The funds are used to keep National Gallery of Art facilities in good repair and efficient operating condition.

Object Classification (in millions of dollars)

Identification code 33–0201–0–1–503		1999 actual	2000 est.	2001 est.
25.2	Other services	1	1	1
32.0	Land and structures	4	8	13
99.9	Total new obligations	5	9	14

Personnel Summary

Identification code 33–0201–0–1–503		1999 actual	2000 est.	2001 est.
1001	Total compensable workyears: Full-time equivalent employment	2	3	3

WOODROW WILSON INTERNATIONAL CENTER FOR SCHOLARS

SALARIES AND EXPENSES

For expenses necessary in carrying out the provisions of the Woodrow Wilson Memorial Act of 1968 (82 Stat. 1356) including hire of passenger vehicles and services as authorized by 5 U.S.C. 3109, [$6,790,000] *$6,763,000*. *(Department of the Interior and Related Agencies Appropriations Act, 2000, as enacted by section 1000(a)(3) of the Consolidated Appropriations Act, 2000 (P.L. 106–113).)*

Program and Financing (in millions of dollars)

Identification code 33–0400–0–1–503		1999 actual	2000 est.	2001 est.
	Obligations by program activity:			
10.00	Total new obligations	6	7	7
	Budgetary resources available for obligation:			
22.00	New budget authority (gross)	6	7	7
23.95	Total new obligations	−6	−7	−7
	New budget authority (gross), detail:			
	Discretionary:			
40.00	Appropriation	6	7	7
	Change in unpaid obligations:			
72.40	Unpaid obligations, start of year: Obligated balance, start of year	4	3	3
73.10	Total new obligations	6	7	7
73.20	Total outlays (gross)	−6	−7	−7
74.40	Unpaid obligations, end of year: Obligated balance, end of year	3	3	3
	Outlays (gross), detail:			
86.90	Outlays from new discretionary authority	4	5	5
86.93	Outlays from discretionary balances	2	2	2

General and special funds—Continued

WOODROW WILSON INTERNATIONAL CENTER FOR SCHOLARS—Continued

SALARIES AND EXPENSES—Continued

Program and Financing (in millions of dollars)—Continued

Identification code 33–0400–0–1–503	1999 actual	2000 est.	2001 est.
87.00 Total outlays (gross)	6	7	7
Net budget authority and outlays:			
89.00 Budget authority	6	7	7
90.00 Outlays	7	7	7

The Woodrow Wilson Center facilitates scholarship of the highest quality in the social sciences and humanities and communicates that scholarship to a wide audience within and beyond Washington. This is accomplished through a resident body of fellowship awardees, conferences, publication, and dialogue.

Object Classification (in millions of dollars)

Identification code 33–0400–0–1–503	1999 actual	2000 est.	2001 est.
11.1 Personnel compensation: Full-time permanent	2	3	3
12.1 Civilian personnel benefits	1	1	1
25.2 Other services	2	2	2
41.0 Grants, subsidies, and contributions	1	1	1
99.9 Total new obligations	6	7	7

Personnel Summary

Identification code 33–0400–0–1–503	1999 actual	2000 est.	2001 est.
1001 Total compensable workyears: Full-time equivalent employment	39	46	50

[ADMINISTRATIVE PROVISIONS, SMITHSONIAN INSTITUTION]

[None of the funds in this or any other Act may be used to initiate the design for any proposed expansion of current space or new facility without consultation with the House and Senate Appropriations Committees.]

[The Smithsonian Institution shall not use Federal funds in excess of the amount specified in Public Law 101–185 for the construction of the National Museum of the American Indian.]

[None of the funds in this or any other Act may be used for the Holt House located at the National Zoological Park in Washington, D.C., unless identified as repairs to minimize water damage, monitor structure movement, or provide interim structural support.] *(Department of the Interior and Related Agencies Appropriations Act, 2000, as enacted by section 1000(a)(3) of the Consolidated Appropriations Act, 2000 (P.L. 106–113).)*

STATE JUSTICE INSTITUTE

Federal Funds

General and special funds:

SALARIES AND EXPENSES

For necessary expenses of the State Justice Institute, as authorized by the State Justice Institute Authorization Act of 1992 (Public Law 102–572 (106 Stat. 4515–4516)), $6,850,000, to remain available until expended: *Provided,* That not to exceed $2,500 shall be available for official reception and representation expenses. *(Departments of Commerce, Justice, and State, the Judiciary, and Related Agencies Appropriations Act, 2000, as enacted by section 1000(a)(4) of the Consolidated Appropriations Act, 2000 (P.L. 106–113).)*

Program and Financing (in millions of dollars)

Identification code 48–0052–0–1–752	1999 actual	2000 est.	2001 est.
Obligations by program activity:			
10.00 Total new obligations (object class 41.0)	8	9	7
Budgetary resources available for obligation:			
21.40 Unobligated balance available, start of year	3	2	
22.00 New budget authority (gross)	7	7	7
23.90 Total budgetary resources available for obligation	10	9	7
23.95 Total new obligations	−8	−9	−7
24.40 Unobligated balance available, end of year	2		
New budget authority (gross), detail:			
Discretionary:			
40.00 Appropriation	7	7	7
Change in unpaid obligations:			
72.40 Unpaid obligations, start of year: Obligated balance, start of year	8	7	2
73.10 Total new obligations	8	9	7
73.20 Total outlays (gross)	−8	−14	−8
74.40 Unpaid obligations, end of year: Obligated balance, end of year	7	2	1
Outlays (gross), detail:			
86.90 Outlays from new discretionary authority	1	5	6
86.93 Outlays from discretionary balances	7	9	2
87.00 Total outlays (gross)	8	14	8
Net budget authority and outlays:			
89.00 Budget authority	7	7	7
90.00 Outlays	8	14	8

The State Justice Institute was established by the Congress in 1984 as a private, non-profit corporation to make grants and undertake other activities designed to improve the administration of justice in the United States. Appropriations in 2001 are intended to provide for continuation of Institute operations at a reduced level.

TENNESSEE VALLEY AUTHORITY

Federal Funds

Public enterprise funds:

TENNESSEE VALLEY AUTHORITY FUND

Program and Financing (in millions of dollars)

Identification code 64–4110–0–3–999	1999 actual	2000 est.	2001 est.
Obligations by program activity:			
Power program:			
09.01 Power program: Operating expenses	5,511	5,090	5,058
09.02 Power program: Capital expenditures	1,294	1,195	1,003
09.09 Total power program	6,805	6,285	6,061
Operating Expenses:			
09.10 Water and Land Stewardship	51	9	3
09.11 Land Between The Lakes	11		
09.12 Land Between The Lakes-Transition	10		
09.19 Total Operating Expenses	72	9	3
Capital Investment:			
09.21 Water and Land Stewardship	−5	1	
09.22 Land Between The Lakes	1		
09.29 Total Capital Investments	−4	1	
10.00 Total new obligations	6,874	6,295	6,064
Budgetary resources available for obligation:			
21.40 Unobligated balance available, start of year	545	259	277
22.00 New budget authority (gross)	6,588	6,313	5,990
23.90 Total budgetary resources available for obligation	7,133	6,572	6,267
23.95 Total new obligations	−6,874	−6,295	−6,064
24.40 Unobligated balance available, end of year	259	277	203

	New budget authority (gross), detail:			
	Discretionary:			
40.00	Appropriation	50		
68.00	Spending authority from offsetting collections: Offsetting collections (cash)	9	3	3
	Mandatory:			
69.00	Offsetting collections (cash)	6,895	6,669	6,800
69.27	Capital transfer to general fund	–57	–56	–55
69.47	Portion applied to repay debt	–309	–303	–758
69.90	Spending authority from offsetting collections (total mandatory)	6,529	6,310	5,987
70.00	Total new budget authority (gross)	6,588	6,313	5,990
	Change in unpaid obligations:			
72.40	Unpaid obligations, start of year: Obligated balance, start of year	417	385	314
73.10	Total new obligations	6,874	6,295	6,064
73.20	Total outlays (gross)	–6,906	–6,366	–5,990
74.40	Unpaid obligations, end of year: Obligated balance, end of year	385	314	388
	Outlays (gross), detail:			
86.90	Outlays from new discretionary authority	54	3	3
86.93	Outlays from discretionary balances	6	53	
86.97	Outlays from new mandatory authority	6,529	6,310	5,987
86.98	Outlays from mandatory balances	317		
87.00	Total outlays (gross)	6,906	6,366	5,990
	Offsets:			
	Against gross budget authority and outlays:			
	Offsetting collections (cash) from:			
88.00	Federal sources	–77	–79	–82
88.40	Non-Federal sources	–6,827	–6,593	–6,721
88.90	Total, offsetting collections (cash)	–6,904	–6,672	–6,803
	Net budget authority and outlays:			
89.00	Budget authority	–316	–359	–813
90.00	Outlays	2	–306	–813

Note.—Authority to borrow available to the Tennessee Valley Authority continues to be available on a permanent, indefinite basis. This authority is limited only in that the amount of borrowing outstanding at any time cannot exceed $30 billion.

Status of Direct Loans (in millions of dollars)

Identification code 64–4110–0–3–999		1999 actual	2000 est.	2001 est.
	Position with respect to appropriations act limitation on obligations:			
1111	Limitation on direct loans			
1131	Direct loan obligations exempt from limitation	16	22	22
1150	Total direct loan obligations	16	22	22
	Cumulative balance of direct loans outstanding:			
1210	Outstanding, start of year	43	47	55
1231	Disbursements: Direct loan disbursements	16	22	22
1251	Repayments: Repayments and prepayments	–11	–13	–13
1263	Write-offs for default: Direct loans	–1	–1	–1
1290	Outstanding, end of year	47	55	63

The Tennessee Valley Authority (TVA) was created in 1933 as a Government-owned corporation for the unified development of a river basin comprised of parts of seven States. The President's Budget proposes that the agency's program in 2001 be financed from two sources: (1) proceeds available from current power operations and borrowings against future power revenues; and (2) proceeds available from nonpower activities.

The following tables provide detailed information on programs financed by power proceeds and borrowings and programs financed by appropriations and nonpower proceeds.

POWER PROGRAM (in millions of dollars)

	Power proceeds and borrowings		
	1999 actual	2000 est.	2001 est.
Obligations by program activity:			
Operating expenses:			
Power program: Power supply and use (total operating expenses)	5,511	5,090	5,058
Capital investment:			
Power program: Power supply and use (total capital investment)	1,294	1,195	1,003
Total new obligations	6,805	6,285	6,061
Budget authority (gross)	7,057	6,562	6,264
Budgetary resources available for obligation:			
Mandatory:			
Spending authority from offsetting collections (new)	6,895	6,669	6,800
Capital transfer to general fund	–57	–56	–55
Portion applied to debt reduction	–309	–303	–758
Spending authority from offsetting collections (total)	6,529	6,310	5,987
Change in unpaid obligations:			
Total obligations	6,805	6,285	6,061
Obligated balance, start of year:			
Authority to borrow	380	339	314
Obligated balance, end of year	339	314	388
Total outlays (gross)	6,846	6,310	5,987
Offsets:			
Against gross offsetting collections:			
Spending authority from offsetting collections:			
Federal funds	–77	–79	–82
Non-federal sources	–6,818	–6,590	–6,718
Total, offsetting collections	–6,895	–6,669	–6,800
Net budget authority and outlays:			
Budget Authority	–366	–359	–813
Outlays	–49	–359	–813

TVA's nonpower programs.—As a Federal corporation, TVA serves national interests by operating infrastructure services for the production of electricity, economic development and the stewardship of natural resources in 201 counties in seven States.

Prior to 2000, appropriations provided for public services to maintain and operate public resources—navigable channels, flood control, recreation, and non-regulatory, community-based programs that protect the water quality of the Tennessee River system. Federal appropriations do not support TVA's power program. The Budget proposes that in 2001, these services be funded entirely by TVA's power revenues, user fees and sources other than appropriations.

Effective October 1, 1999, administrative jurisdiction over the Land Between the Lakes National Recreation Area (LBL) was transferred to the Department of Agriculture, Forest Service, pursuant to the LBL Protection Act of 1998. TVA's 1999 nonpower expenses include an obligation of approximately $9.8 million for certain transition costs, in accordance with that Act.

TVA has a statutory obligation to operate 54 dams and reservoirs to regulate stream-flow for the multi-purpose objectives of navigation, flood control, recreation and aquatic habitat conservation; perform cyclic maintenance and repair of 14 navigation locks, maintain dam machinery and spillway gates; perform channel, lock and mooring modifications to maintain safety and passability for increasingly larger cargo vessels; conserve and improve water quality and supply in 12 watersheds and dam tailwaters for fisheries and potable supply for 4 million people; control mosquitoes and plant pests; prevent shoreline erosion and manage residential development in riparian zones; plan for and manage 550,000 hectares (1.4 million acres) of land; provide services and edu-

Public enterprise funds—Continued

TENNESSEE VALLEY AUTHORITY FUND—Continued

cation to watershed communities; operate public recreation areas; and, meet Federal regulatory law requirements.

TVA's Power Program.—TVA's role as the sole supplier of electric power to an area of 80,000 square miles in the seven Tennessee Valley States is being reviewed as the Nation considers ways to restructure the electric power industry. Income from power operations, net of interest charges and depreciation, and other operating expenses is estimated at $100,000,000 in 2001. Power generating facilities are financed from power proceeds and borrowings. The Budget reflects specific cost-cutting measures the agency is taking to implement its 10-Year Business plan and improve its ability to supply power at competitive prices.

APPROPRIATIONS AND NONPOWER PROCEEDS (in millions of dollars)

	1999 actual	2000 est.	2001 est.
Obligations by program activity:			
Operating expenses:			
1. Water and land stewardship	51	9	3
2. Land Between The Lakes	11		
3. Land Between The Lakes—Transition	10		
Total operating expenses	72	9	3
Capital investment:			
1. Water and land stewardship	–4	1	
2. Land Between The Lakes	1		
Total capital investment	–3	1	
Total obligations	69	10	3
Unobligated balance available, start of year: Fund balance	17	7	
Unobligated balance available, end of year: Fund balance	7		
Budget authority (gross)	59	3	3
Budgetary resources available for obligation:			
:Discretionary appropriation	50		
Discretionary:			
Spending authority from offsetting collections (new)	9	3	3
Change in unpaid obligations:			
Total obligations	69	10	3
Obligated balance, start of year: Fund balance	37	46	
Obligated balance, end of year: Fund balance	46		
Outlays (gross)	60	56	3
Offsets:			
Against gross budget authority and outlays:			
Deductions for offsetting collections:			
Non-Federal sources	9	3	3
Total, offsetting collections	9	3	3
Net budget authority and outlays:			
Budget authority	50		
Outlays	51	53	

Financing.—Amounts estimated to become available in 2001 are to be derived from (1) nonpower revenues and receipts of $2,790,000; and (2) power revenues and receipts of $6,800,000,000.

Operating results and financial conditions.—Payments to the Treasury from power proceeds in 2001 are estimated at $55,000,000–$35,000,000 as a dividend (return on the appropriation investment in the power program) and $20,000,000 as a reduction in the appropriation investment in the power program. Outstanding borrowings for the power program are expected to decrease by $758,000,000 during 2001.

Total assets are estimated to decrease by $703,000,000 during 2001 as depreciation of existing assets exceeds expenditures for new assets. The estimate of liabilities at September 30, 2001, is $738,000,000 less than the estimate at September 30, 2000. Total Government equity at September 30, 2001, is estimated to be $35,000,000 greater than that at September 2000. This change includes the net income from power operations, less payments to the Treasury.

Statement of Operations (in millions of dollars)

Identification code 64–4110–0–3–999	1998 actual	1999 actual	2000 est.	2001 est.
0101 Revenue	6,729	6,583	6,669	6,800
0102 Expense	–6,496	–6,464	–6,462	–6,700
0105 Net income or loss (–)	233	119	207	100

Balance Sheet (in millions of dollars)

Identification code 64–4110–0–3–999	1998 actual	1999 actual	2000 est.	2001 est.
ASSETS:				
Federal assets:				
1101 Fund balances with Treasury	241	219	5	2
Investments in US securities:				
1106 Receivables, net	15	4	11	7
Non-Federal assets:				
1201 Investments in non-Federal securities, net	578	731	797	877
1206 Receivables, net	779	724	748	704
1207 Advances and prepayments	2	2	2	2
Net value of assets related to pre–1992 direct loans receivable and acquired defaulted guaranteed loans receivable:				
1601 Direct loans, gross	155	166	190	212
1603 Allowance for estimated uncollectible loans and interest (–)	–4	–13	–12	–5
1604 Direct loans and interest receivable, net	151	153	178	207
1699 Value of assets related to direct loans	151	153	178	207
Other Federal assets:				
1801 Cash and other monetary assets	2,601	2,745	2,734	2,173
1802 Inventories and related properties	464	479	464	505
1803 Property, plant and equipment, net	29,715	29,221	29,167	28,926
1999 Total assets	34,546	34,278	34,106	33,403
LIABILITIES:				
Federal liabilities:				
2101 Accounts payable	6	93	65	60
2102 Interest payable	70	1	1	1
2104 Resources payable to Treasury	3,200			
Non-Federal liabilities:				
2201 Accounts payable	532	427	450	463
2202 Interest payable	418	463	449	438
2203 Debt	23,484	26,376	26,073	25,315
2207 Other	1,780	1,847	1,863	1,886
2999 Total liabilities	29,490	29,207	28,901	28,163
NET POSITION:				
3300 Cumulative results of operations	5,056	5,071	5,205	5,240
3999 Total net position	5,056	5,071	5,205	5,240
4999 Total liabilities and net position	34,546	34,278	34,106	33,403

Object Classification (in millions of dollars)

Identification code 64–4110–0–3–999	1999 actual	2000 est.	2001 est.
Personnel compensation:			
11.1 Full-time permanent	793	661	632
11.5 Other personnel compensation	74	60	58
11.9 Total personnel compensation	867	721	690
12.1 Civilian personnel benefits	279	237	227
21.0 Travel and transportation of persons	29	26	26
22.0 Transportation of things	286	267	257
23.2 Rental payments to others	79	73	71
24.0 Printing and reproduction	2	2	2
25.1 Advisory and assistance services	22	21	20
25.2 Other services	821	767	740
25.7 Operation and maintenance of equipment	323	303	292
26.0 Supplies and materials	1,563	1,425	1,354
31.0 Equipment	12	89	91
32.0 Land and structures	7	7	7
33.0 Investments and loans	205	192	186
41.0 Grants, subsidies, and contributions	303	306	314
43.0 Interest and dividends	2,076	1,859	1,787

99.9	Total new obligations	6,874	6,295	6,064

Personnel Summary

Identification code 64–4110–0–3–999		1999 actual	2000 est.	2001 est.
2001	Total compensable workyears: Full-time equivalent employment	13,465	13,300	13,200

UNITED MINE WORKERS OF AMERICA BENEFIT FUNDS

Federal Funds

FEDERAL PAYMENT TO UNITED MINE WORKERS OF AMERICA COMBINED BENEFIT FUND

(Legislative proposal, not subject to PAYGO)

Program and Financing (in millions of dollars)

Identification code 95–2850–2–1–551		1999 actual	2000 est.	2001 est.
	Obligations by program activity:			
10.00	Total new obligations (object class 42.0)			38
	Budgetary resources available for obligation:			
22.00	New budget authority (gross)			38
23.95	Total new obligations			−38
	New budget authority (gross), detail:			
	Mandatory:			
60.00	Appropriation			38
	Change in unpaid obligations:			
73.10	Total new obligations			38
73.20	Total outlays (gross)			−38
	Outlays (gross), detail:			
86.97	Outlays from new mandatory authority			38
	Net budget authority and outlays:			
89.00	Budget authority			38
90.00	Outlays			38

The Administration will propose legislation to maintain health benefits under the Coal Act for retired miners and their families as well as to secure the long-term solvency of the UMWA Combined Benefit Fund. The legislation has three parts. (See both here and below.) First, the legislation will provide for a specified annual transfer of general Federal funds to the Combined Benefit Fund. This schedule reflects the transfer of those general Federal funds. Second, the legislation will reverse the effects of the court decision in "National Coal v. Chater" regarding the calculation of the premiums charged coal companies that had contractually agreed to pay for their miner employees' retirement health benefits. This will support medical cost containment. Third, the legislation will clarify a provision of the Coal Act regarding the timing of the Social Security Administration's assignment of retired miners to the companies that had employed them and had agreed to pay for their retirement health benefits. That clarifying provision has no effects that may be scored.

Trust Funds

UNITED MINE WORKERS OF AMERICA COMBINED BENEFIT FUND

Unavailable Collections (in millions of dollars)

Identification code 95–8295–0–7–551		1999 actual	2000 est.	2001 est.
	Balance, start of year:			
01.99	Balance, start of year			
	Receipts:			
02.01	Premiums, combined benefit fund & 1992 pension plan, UMWA	148	142	138
02.02	Premiums, combined benefit fund & 1992 pension plan, legislative proposal subject to PAYGO			11
02.03	Transfers from abandoned mine reclamation fund	82	109	67
02.05	Federal payment, legislative proposal not subject to PAYGO			38
02.99	Total receipts	230	251	254
	Appropriation:			
05.01	United mine workers of America 1992 benefit plan	−28	−28	−29
05.02	United mine workers of America combined benefit fund	−202	−223	−176
05.03	United mine workers of America combined benefit fund, legislative proposal subject to PAYGO			−49
05.99	Subtotal appropriation	−230	−251	−254
07.99	Total balance, end of year			

Note.—The unavailable collections table (above) includes entries that pertain both to the combined benefit fund and the 1992 benefit plan.

Program and Financing (in millions of dollars)

Identification code 95–8295–0–7–551		1999 actual	2000 est.	2001 est.
	Obligations by program activity:			
10.00	Total new obligations (object class 42.0)	202	223	176
	Budgetary resources available for obligation:			
22.00	New budget authority (gross)	202	223	176
23.95	Total new obligations	−202	−223	−176
	New budget authority (gross), detail:			
	Mandatory:			
60.27	Appropriation (trust fund, indefinite)	202	223	176
	Change in unpaid obligations:			
73.10	Total new obligations	202	223	176
73.20	Total outlays (gross)	−202	−223	−176
	Outlays (gross), detail:			
86.97	Outlays from new mandatory authority	202	223	176
	Net budget authority and outlays:			
89.00	Budget authority	202	223	176
90.00	Outlays	202	223	176

Summary of Budget Authority and Outlays

(in millions of dollars)

Enacted/requested:	*1999 actual*	*2000 est.*	*2001 est.*
Budget Authority	202	223	176
Outlays	202	223	176
Legislative proposal, subject to PAYGO:			
Budget Authority			49
Outlays			49
Total:			
Budget Authority	202	223	225
Outlays	202	223	225

The Combined Benefit Fund was established by the Coal Industry Retiree Health Benefit Act of 1992 to take over paying for medical care of retired miners and their dependents who were eligible for health care from the private 1950 and 1974 United Mine Workers of America Benefit Plans. The Fund's trustees represent the United Mine Workers of America and coal companies. The Fund is financed by assessments on current and former signatories to labor agreements with the United Mine Workers; past transfers from an overfunded United Mine Workers pension fund; and transfers from the Abandoned Mine Land Reclamation fund.

UNITED MINE WORKERS OF AMERICA COMBINED BENEFIT FUND

(Legislative proposal, subject to PAYGO)

Program and Financing (in millions of dollars)

Identification code 95–8295–4–7–551	1999 actual	2000 est.	2001 est.
Obligations by program activity:			
10.00 Total new obligations (object class 42.0)			49
Budgetary resources available for obligation:			
22.00 New budget authority (gross)			49
23.95 Total new obligations			−49
New budget authority (gross), detail:			
Mandatory:			
60.27 Appropriation (trust fund, indefinite)			49
Change in unpaid obligations:			
73.10 Total new obligations			49
73.20 Total outlays (gross)			−49
Outlays (gross), detail:			
86.97 Outlays from new mandatory authority			49
Net budget authority and outlays:			
89.00 Budget authority			49
90.00 Outlays			49

The Administration will propose legislation to maintain health benefits under the Coal Act for retired miners and their families as well as to secure the long-term solvency of the UMWA Combined Benefit Fund. This schedule reflects the effects on the Combined Benefit Fund of the transfer of Federal funds and also of the restored calculation of premiums.

UNITED MINE WORKERS OF AMERICA 1992 BENEFIT PLAN

Program and Financing (in millions of dollars)

Identification code 95–8260–0–7–551	1999 actual	2000 est.	2001 est.
Obligations by program activity:			
10.00 Total new obligations (object class 42.0)	28	28	29
Budgetary resources available for obligation:			
22.00 New budget authority (gross)	28	28	29
23.95 Total new obligations	−28	−28	−29
New budget authority (gross), detail:			
Mandatory:			
60.27 Appropriation (trust fund, indefinite)	28	28	29
Change in unpaid obligations:			
73.10 Total new obligations	28	28	29
73.20 Total outlays (gross)	−28	−28	−29
Outlays (gross), detail:			
86.97 Outlays from new mandatory authority	28	28	29
Net budget authority and outlays:			
89.00 Budget authority	28	28	29
90.00 Outlays	28	28	29

The 1992 Benefit Plan was established by the Coal Industry Retiree Health Benefit Act of 1992. It pays for health care of those miners who retired between July 21, 1992 and September 30, 1994, and their dependents, who are eligible for benefits under an employer plan and cease to be covered, usually because an employer is out of business. Plan trustees are appointed by the United Mine Workers of America and the Bituminous Coal Operators Association, a coal industry bargaining group. The Plan is supported by signers of the 1988 labor agreement with the United Mine Workers of America.

UNITED STATES ENRICHMENT CORPORATION

Federal Funds

Public enterprise funds:

UNITED STATES ENRICHMENT CORPORATION FUND

Program and Financing (in millions of dollars)

Identification code 95–4054–0–3–271	1999 actual	2000 est.	2001 est.
Budgetary resources available for obligation:			
21.40 Unobligated balance available, start of year	482	482	477
22.00 New budget authority (gross)		−5	−12
22.10 Resources available from recoveries of prior year obligations			
22.21 Unobligated balance transferred to other accounts			
22.40 Capital transfer to general fund			
23.90 Total budgetary resources available for obligation	482	477	465
23.95 Total new obligations			
24.40 Unobligated balance available, end of year	482	477	465
New budget authority (gross), detail:			
Discretionary:			
41.00 Transferred to other accounts		−5	−12
68.00 Spending authority from offsetting collections: Offsetting collections (cash)			
70.00 Total new budget authority (gross)		−5	−12
Change in unpaid obligations:			
72.40 Unpaid obligations, start of year: Obligated balance, start of year	1	−4	−4
73.10 Total new obligations			
73.20 Total outlays (gross)	−5		
73.45 Adjustments in unexpired accounts			
74.40 Unpaid obligations, end of year: Obligated balance, end of year	−4	−4	−4
Outlays (gross), detail:			
86.98 Outlays from mandatory balances	5		
Offsets:			
Against gross budget authority and outlays:			
88.40 Offsetting collections (cash) from: Non-Federal sources			
Net budget authority and outlays:			
89.00 Budget authority		−5	−12
90.00 Outlays	5		

On July 28, 1998, the Federal Government transferred its entire ownership interest in the United States Enrichment Corporation (USEC) to the private sector. The Government received $1.9 billion from the sale of USEC, which included the proceeds from the sale of equity securities, plus $500 million in cash from a USEC borrowing in the bank market. Most of USEC's assets and liabilities were transferred to the private sector. Other assets and liabilities were transferred to the Department of Energy.

UNITED STATES HOLOCAUST MEMORIAL COUNCIL

Federal Funds

General and special funds:

HOLOCAUST MEMORIAL COUNCIL

For expenses of the Holocaust Memorial Council, as authorized by Public Law 96–388 (36 U.S.C. 1401), as amended, [$33,286,000] *$34,564,000*, of which [$1,575,000] *$1,900,000* for the museum's repair and rehabilitation program and $1,264,000 for the museum's exhibitions program shall remain available until expended. *(Department of the Interior and Related Agencies Appropriations Act, 2000, as enacted by section 1000(a)(3) of the Consolidated Appropriations Act, 2000 (P.L. 106–113).)*

Program and Financing (in millions of dollars)

Identification code 95–3300–0–1–808	1999 actual	2000 est.	2001 est.
Obligations by program activity:			
10.00 Total new obligations	36	35	34
Budgetary resources available for obligation:			
21.40 Unobligated balance available, start of year	3	2	
22.00 New budget authority (gross)	35	33	35
23.90 Total budgetary resources available for obligation	38	35	35
23.95 Total new obligations	−36	−35	−34
24.40 Unobligated balance available, end of year	2		
New budget authority (gross), detail:			
Discretionary:			
40.00 Appropriation	32	33	35
40.15 Appropriation (emergency)	2		
42.00 Transferred from other accounts	1		
43.00 Appropriation (total discretionary)	35	33	35
Change in unpaid obligations:			
72.40 Unpaid obligations, start of year: Obligated balance, start of year	13	12	14
73.10 Total new obligations	36	35	34
73.20 Total outlays (gross)	−36	−33	−34
73.40 Adjustments in expired accounts (net)	−1		
74.40 Unpaid obligations, end of year: Obligated balance, end of year	12	14	15
Outlays (gross), detail:			
86.90 Outlays from new discretionary authority	25	24	25
86.93 Outlays from discretionary balances	11	9	9
87.00 Total outlays (gross)	36	33	34
Net budget authority and outlays:			
89.00 Budget authority	35	33	35
90.00 Outlays	36	33	34

The Council operates a permanent living memorial museum to the victims of the Holocaust. The memorial, which opened in April 1993, also provides for appropriate ways for the Nation to commemorate the Days of Remembrance.

Object Classification (in millions of dollars)

Identification code 95–3300–0–1–808	1999 actual	2000 est.	2001 est.
Personnel compensation:			
11.1 Full-time permanent	10	11	12
11.3 Other than full-time permanent	1	1	1
11.9 Total personnel compensation	11	12	13
12.1 Civilian personnel benefits	3	3	3
21.0 Travel and transportation of persons	1	1	1
23.1 Rental payments to GSA	1	1	1
23.3 Communications, utilities, and miscellaneous charges	2	2	2
25.2 Other services	9	4	4
25.3 Purchases of goods and services from Government accounts	1	1	
25.4 Operation and maintenance of facilities	4	8	8
25.7 Operation and maintenance of equipment	1		
26.0 Supplies and materials	1	1	1
31.0 Equipment	2	1	1
99.0 Subtotal, direct obligations	36	34	34
99.5 Below reporting threshold		1	
99.9 Total new obligations	36	35	34

Personnel Summary

Identification code 95–3300–0–1–808	1999 actual	2000 est.	2001 est.
1001 Total compensable workyears: Full-time equivalent employment	221	246	246

UNITED STATES INSTITUTE OF PEACE

Federal Funds

General and special funds:

Operating Expenses

For necessary expenses of the United States Institute of Peace as authorized in the United States Institute of Peace Act, [$13,000,000] *$14,450,000. (Departments of Labor, Health and Human Services, and Education, and Related Agencies Appropriations Act, 2000, as enacted by section 1000(a)(4) of the Consolidated Appropriations Act, 2000 (P.L. 106–113).)*

Program and Financing (in millions of dollars)

Identification code 95–1300–0–1–153	1999 actual	2000 est.	2001 est.
Obligations by program activity:			
10.00 Total new obligations	12	13	14
Budgetary resources available for obligation:			
22.00 New budget authority (gross)	12	13	14
23.95 Total new obligations	−12	−13	−14
New budget authority (gross), detail:			
Discretionary:			
40.00 Appropriation	12	13	14
Change in unpaid obligations:			
72.40 Unpaid obligations, start of year: Obligated balance, start of year	1	1	1
73.10 Total new obligations	12	13	14
73.20 Total outlays (gross)	−12	−13	−14
74.40 Unpaid obligations, end of year: Obligated balance, end of year	1	1	1
Outlays (gross), detail:			
86.90 Outlays from new discretionary authority	11	12	13
86.93 Outlays from discretionary balances	1	1	1
87.00 Total outlays (gross)	12	13	14
Net budget authority and outlays:			
89.00 Budget authority	12	13	14
90.00 Outlays	12	13	14

The United States Institute of Peace was established by Congress to help strengthen the Nation's capacity to promote peaceful resolution of international conflicts. Program activity includes policy assessments for the Executive and Legislative Branches; conflict resolution training for foreign affairs professionals; facilitation of dialogue among parties to conflicts; summer institutes and educational materials for teachers at high school and undergraduate levels; grants and fellowships; publications; a research library; a national student essay contest; and, other programs to increase public understanding about the nature of international conflicts.

Object Classification (in millions of dollars)

Identification code 95–1300–0–1–153	1999 actual	2000 est.	2001 est.
11.1 Personnel compensation: Full-time permanent	4	4	5
12.1 Civilian personnel benefits	1	1	1
21.0 Travel and transportation of persons	1	1	1
25.2 Other services	1	1	1
41.0 Grants, subsidies, and contributions	5	6	6
99.9 Total new obligations	12	13	14

Personnel Summary

Identification code 95–1300–0–1–153	1999 actual	2000 est.	2001 est.
1001 Total compensable workyears: Full-time equivalent employment	59	64	68

OTHER MATERIALS

PROPOSED CHANGES TO 2000 ESTIMATES

This Budget contains $3,986 million in proposals for emergency appropriations, $35 million in proposals for mandatory appropriations, and proposals for $444 million in non-emergency appropriations. All of the non-emergency proposals are offset.

SUMMARY OF SUPPLEMENTAL PROGRAMS

(In millions of dollars)

	2000 Budget Authority	Outlays		
		2000	2001	2002
Supplemental Proposals:				
Department of Commerce	$56	$25	$24	$9
Department of Defense—Military	2,269	1,589	494	....
Department of Energy	49	59	27	4
Department of Health and Human Services	35	5	21	7
Department of Housing and Urban Development	*43	32	16	1
Department of the Interior	111	4	4	2
Department of State	1,192	451	372	238
Department of Transportation	18	18	–24	–13
Department of the Treasury	36	34	4	1
Corps of Engineers Civil	26	26	....	....
Executive Office of the President (non-add)	(–225)	....	....	....
General Services Administration	2	2	....	....
International Security Assistance	461	91	183	94
National Aeronautics and Space Administration	....	3	–3	....
Small Business Administration	50	....	....	....
National Transportation Safety Board	18	16	2	....
Other	3	2	....	....
General Provisions	....	6,046	–6,046	....
Total, Supplemental Proposals	4,370	8,403	–4,926	342
Rescission Proposals:				
Department of Energy	–25	–9	–3	–1
Department of Housing and Urban Development	–103	....	....	....
Total, Rescission Proposals	–128	–9	–3	–1
Total, Supplementals and Rescissions	4,242	8,394	–4,929	341

* An estimated $6 million is reappropriated in 2001.

SUPPLEMENTAL PROPOSALS

The following information concerns supplemental appropriations requests for 2000 proposed for congressional consideration.

Department of Commerce

ECONOMIC DEVELOPMENT ADMINISTRATION

Salaries and Expenses

(Supplemental now requested, existing legislation)

For an additional amount for "Salaries and expenses," $1,250,000, to remain available until expended, for expenses resulting from Hurricane Floyd and other recent natural disasters: Provided, That the entire amount is designated by the Congress as an emergency requirement pursuant to section 251(b)(2)(A) of the Balanced Budget and Emergency Deficit Control Act of 1985, as amended.

Program and Financing (in millions of dollars)

Identification code 13–0125–1–1–452	1999 actual	2000 est.	2001 est.
Obligations by program activity:			
10.00 Total new obligations (object class 99.5)		1	
Budgetary resources available for obligation:			
22.00 New budget authority (gross)		1	
23.95 Total new obligations		−1	
New budget authority (gross), detail:			
Discretionary:			
40.15 Appropriation (emergency)		1	
Change in unpaid obligations:			
73.10 Total new obligations		1	
73.20 Total outlays (gross)		−1	
Outlays (gross), detail:			
86.90 Outlays from new discretionary authority		1	
Net budget authority and outlays:			
89.00 Budget authority		1	
90.00 Outlays		1	

This supplemental request would fund expenses associated with administering post-disaster planning grants and related assistance to East Coast communities impacted by Hurricane Floyd and other recent natural disasters.

The entire amount requested has been designated by the President as an emergency requirement pursuant to the Balanced Budget and Emergency Deficit Control Act of 1985, as amended.

Economic Development Assistance Programs

(Supplemental now requested, existing legislation)

For an additional amount for "Economic development assistance programs," $23,750,000, to remain available until expended, for expenses resulting from Hurricane Floyd and other recent natural disasters: Provided, That the entire amount is designated by the Congress as an emergency requirement pursuant to section 251(b)(2)(A) of the Balanced Budget and Emergency Deficit Control Act of 1985, as amended.

Program and Financing (in millions of dollars)

Identification code 13–2050–1–1–452	1999 actual	2000 est.	2001 est.
Obligations by program activity:			
Direct program:			
00.02 Hurricane Floyd		24	
10.00 Total new obligations (object class 41.0)		24	
Budgetary resources available for obligation:			
22.00 New budget authority (gross)		24	
23.95 Total new obligations		−24	
New budget authority (gross), detail:			
Discretionary:			
40.15 Appropriation (emergency)		24	
Change in unpaid obligations:			
72.40 Unpaid obligations, start of year: Obligated balance, start of year			21
73.10 Total new obligations		24	
73.20 Total outlays (gross)		−3	−13
74.40 Unpaid obligations, end of year: Obligated balance, end of year		21	8
Outlays (gross), detail:			
86.90 Outlays from new discretionary authority		3	
86.93 Outlays from discretionary balances			13
87.00 Total outlays (gross)		3	13
Net budget authority and outlays:			
89.00 Budget authority		24	
90.00 Outlays		3	13

This supplemental request would fund post-disaster planning grants and related assistance to East Coast communities impacted by Hurricane Floyd and other recent natural disasters. Planning grants would be targeted at economic recovery and disaster mitigation projects designed to help communities re-emerge from disaster situations as vibrant economic centers. Public works grants will assist with capital projects including, water, sewer, and public access type projects.

The entire amount requested has been designated by the President as an emergency requirement pursuant to the Balanced Budget and Emergency Deficit Control Act of 1985, as amended.

NATIONAL OCEANIC AND ATMOSPHERIC ADMINISTRATION

Operations, Research, and Facilities

(Supplemental now requested, existing legislation)

For an additional amount for "Operations, research and facilities," $25,800,000, to remain available until expended, for expenses related to losses and equipment damages incurred by fishermen and charter boat operators and other expenses resulting from Hurricanes Floyd and Dennis: Provided, That the entire amount is designated by the Congress as an emergency requirement pursuant to section 251(b)(2)(A) of the Balanced Budget and Emergency Deficit Control Act of 1985, as amended.

Program and Financing (in millions of dollars)

Identification code 13–1450–1–1–306	1999 actual	2000 est.	2001 est.
Obligations by program activity:			
Direct program:			
00.02 Hurricanes Floyd and Dennis		26	

OPERATIONS, RESEARCH, AND FACILITIES—Continued

Program and Financing (in millions of dollars)—Continued

Identification code 13–1450–1–1–306	1999 actual	2000 est.	2001 est.
10.00 Total new obligations (object class 25.2)		26	
Budgetary resources available for obligation:			
22.00 New budget authority (gross)		26	
23.95 Total new obligations		–26	
New budget authority (gross), detail:			
Discretionary:			
40.15 Appropriation (emergency)		26	
Change in unpaid obligations:			
72.40 Unpaid obligations, start of year: Obligated balance, start of year			10
73.10 Total new obligations		26	
73.20 Total outlays (gross)		–16	–10
74.40 Unpaid obligations, end of year: Obligated balance, end of year		10	
Outlays (gross), detail:			
86.90 Outlays from new discretionary authority		16	
86.93 Outlays from discretionary balances			10
87.00 Total outlays (gross)		16	10
Net budget authority and outlays:			
89.00 Budget authority		26	
90.00 Outlays		16	10

This supplemental request would fund losses sustained by North Carolina and Florida fishermen and charter boat operators due to the loss of traps, death and displacement of fish, and lost days-at-sea during Hurricanes Floyd and Dennis. In addition, the supplemental request would fund roof repairs and the rewiring of corroded lines to the Beaufort laboratory in North Carolina damaged as a result of wind and rain during Hurricane Floyd.

The entire amount requested has been designated by the President as an emergency requirement pursuant to the Balanced Budget and Emergency Deficit Control Act of 1985, as amended.

NATIONAL TECHNICAL INFORMATION SERVICE

NTIS REVOLVING FUND

(Supplemental now requested, existing legislation)

Program and Financing (in millions of dollars)

Identification code 13–4295–1–3–376	1999 actual	2000 est.	2001 est.
Obligations by program activity:			
10.00 Total new obligations (object class 13.0)		4	
Budgetary resources available for obligation:			
22.00 New budget authority (gross)		4	
23.95 Total new obligations		–4	
New budget authority (gross), detail:			
Discretionary:			
42.00 Transferred from other accounts		4	
Change in unpaid obligations:			
73.10 Total new obligations		4	
73.20 Total outlays (gross)		–4	
Outlays (gross), detail:			
86.90 Outlays from new discretionary authority		4	
Net budget authority and outlays:			
89.00 Budget authority		4	
90.00 Outlays		4	

This supplemental request would provide $4 million to the NTIS revolving fund for the one-time costs of the shutdown of the NTIS. The Department of Commerce has proposed legislation to close NTIS.

NATIONAL INSTITUTE OF STANDARDS AND TECHNOLOGY

SCIENTIFIC AND TECHNICAL RESEARCH AND SERVICES

(Supplemental now requested, existing legislation)

For an additional amount for "Scientific and technical research and services," $1,000,000.

Program and Financing (in millions of dollars)

Identification code 13–0500–1–1–376	1999 actual	2000 est.	2001 est.
Obligations by program activity:			
Operating expenses:			
Measurement and engineering research and standards:			
00.10 Computer science and applied mathematics		1	
10.00 Total new obligations (object class 25.2)		1	
Budgetary resources available for obligation:			
22.00 New budget authority (gross)		1	
23.95 Total new obligations		–1	
New budget authority (gross), detail:			
Discretionary:			
40.00 Appropriation		1	
Change in unpaid obligations:			
73.10 Total new obligations		1	
73.20 Total outlays (gross)		–1	
Outlays (gross), detail:			
86.90 Outlays from new discretionary authority		1	
Net budget authority and outlays:			
89.00 Budget authority		1	
90.00 Outlays		1	

This supplemental request would provide additional funds to accelerate the design and development of the President's Critical infrastructure protection initiative, the Expert review team. The Expert review team would help agencies identify vulnerabilities, plan secure systems, and implement Critical infrastructure protection plans.

Personnel Summary

Identification code 13–0500–1–1–376	1999 actual	2000 est.	2001 est.
1001 Total compensable workyears: Full-time equivalent employment		1	

INDUSTRIAL TECHNOLOGY SERVICES

(Supplemental now requested, existing legislation)

For an additional amount for "Industrial technology services," $4,000,000. In addition, $4,500,000 shall be transferred from any balances available under this heading to the "NTIS revolving fund."

Program and Financing (in millions of dollars)

Identification code 13–0525–1–1–376	1999 actual	2000 est.	2001 est.
Obligations by program activity:			
Extramural programs:			
00.03 Institute for Information Infrastructure Protection		4	
10.00 Total new obligations		4	
Budgetary resources available for obligation:			
21.40 Unobligated balance available, start of year			–4

		1999 actual	2000 est.	2001 est.
23.95	Total new obligations		−4	
24.40	Unobligated balance available, end of year		−4	−4
	New budget authority (gross), detail:			
	Discretionary:			
40.00	Appropriation		4	
41.00	Transferred to other accounts		−4	
43.00	Appropriation (total discretionary)			
	Change in unpaid obligations:			
72.40	Unpaid obligations, start of year: Obligated balance, start of year			4
73.10	Total new obligations		4	
73.20	Total outlays (gross)			−1
74.40	Unpaid obligations, end of year: Obligated balance, end of year		4	3
	Outlays (gross), detail:			
86.93	Outlays from discretionary balances			1
	Net budget authority and outlays:			
89.00	Budget authority			
90.00	Outlays			1

This supplemental request would provide additional funds to accelerate the design and development of a key component of the President's Critical infrastructure protection initiative, the Institute for Information Infrastructure Protection. The Institute, which would be housed at the National Institute of Standards and Technology, would coordinate, fund, and integrate research to develop key infrastructure protection technologies, beginning in 2000.

In addition, the supplemental request would transfer $4 million from available balances to the NTIS revolving fund.

Object Classification (in millions of dollars)

Identification code 13–0525–1–1–376		1999 actual	2000 est.	2001 est.
25.2	Other services		1	
25.3	Purchases of goods and services from Government accounts		1	
41.0	Grants, subsidies, and contributions		2	
99.9	Total new obligations		4	

Personnel Summary

Identification code 13–0525–1–1–376		1999 actual	2000 est.	2001 est.
1001	Total compensable workyears: Full-time equivalent employment		3	

Department of Defense—Military

OPERATIONS AND MAINTENANCE

Operation and Maintenance, Defense-wide

(Supplemental now requested, existing legislation)

For an additional amount for "Operation and maintenance, Defense-wide," $27,400,000: Provided, That such amount is for emergency expenses incurred at United States military facilities or installations in the United States directly resulting from storm damage or other natural disasters: Provided further, That the entire amount is designated by the Congress as an emergency requirement pursuant to section 251(b)(2)(A) of the Balanced Budget and Emergency Deficit Control Act of 1985, as amended: Provided further, That the Secretary of Defense may transfer the funds provided herein only to appropriations for operation and maintenance; the Defense Health Program; military construction; family housing; and the working capital funds: Provided further, That such funds may be used to execute projects or programs that were deferred in order to carry out emergency repairs resulting from such storm damage or other natural disasters: Provided further, That the funds transferred shall be merged with and shall be available for the same purposes and for the same time period, as the appropriation to which transferred: Provided further, That the transfer authority provided in this paragraph is in addition to any other transfer authority available to the Department of Defense.

Program and Financing (in millions of dollars)

Identification code 97–0100–1–1–051		1999 actual	2000 est.	2001 est.
	Obligations by program activity:			
00.01	Coast Guard		−3	
00.02	Hurricane Floyd		27	
10.00	Total new obligations		24	
	Budgetary resources available for obligation:			
22.00	New budget authority (gross)		24	
23.95	Total new obligations		−24	
	New budget authority (gross), detail:			
	Discretionary:			
40.15	Appropriation (emergency)		27	
41.00	Transferred to Coast Guard		−3	
43.00	Appropriation (total discretionary)		24	
	Change in unpaid obligations:			
72.40	Unpaid obligations, start of year: Obligated balance, start of year			6
73.10	Total new obligations		24	
73.20	Total outlays (gross)		−18	−5
74.40	Unpaid obligations, end of year: Obligated balance, end of year		6	
	Outlays (gross), detail:			
86.90	Outlays from new discretionary authority		18	
86.93	Outlays from discretionary balances			5
87.00	Total outlays (gross)		18	5
	Net budget authority and outlays:			
89.00	Budget authority		24	
90.00	Outlays		18	5

This supplemental request would fund repair costs associated with Hurricane Floyd. Due to the severity of the storm, all the Services and the Defense Health Program suffered damage to buildings, roads, and other base infrastructure. Unfortunately, final review and approval of the requirements could not be completed in time for detailed inclusion in the budget. Therefore, the budget requests this funding centrally in order to provide for maximum visibility and control over the eventual allocation of funding.

The entire amount requested has been designated by the President as an emergency requirement pursuant to the Balanced Budget and Emergency Deficit Control Act of 1985, as amended.

A general provision would permit the transfer of funding from the Department of Defense to the Coast Guard to ensure that the Coast Guard has the ability to finance the health care that their beneficiaries obtain through the Department of Defense TRICARE system. The costs of medical care provided through the TRICARE system and military treatment facilities have increased significantly in the past few years. The Coast Guard did not have sufficient information to budget for these increased costs in their 2000 Budget.

Object Classification (in millions of dollars)

Identification code 97–0100–1–1–051		1999 actual	2000 est.	2001 est.
25.1	Advisory and assistance services		−3	
26.0	Supplies and materials		27	
99.9	Total new obligations		24	

Overseas Contingency Operations Transfer Fund

(Supplemental now requested, existing legislation)

For an additional amount for the "Overseas contingency operations transfer fund," $2,050,400,000, to remain available until expended: Provided, That the entire amount is designated by the Congress as an emergency requirement pursuant to section 251(b)(2)(A) of the Bal-

OVERSEAS CONTINGENCY OPERATIONS TRANSFER FUND—Continued

anced Budget and Emergency Deficit Control Act of 1985, as amended: Provided further, That the Secretary of Defense may transfer the funds provided herein only to appropriations for military personnel; operation and maintenance, including Overseas humanitarian, disaster assistance, and civic aid; procurement; research, development, test and evaluation; the Defense Health Program; and working capital funds: Provided further, That the funds transferred shall be merged with and shall be available for the same purposes and for the same time period, as the appropriation to which transferred: Provided further, That the transfer authority provided in this paragraph is in addition to any other transfer authority available to the Department of Defense: Provided further, That upon a determination that all or part of the funds transferred from this appropriation are not necessary for the purposes provided herein, such amounts may be transferred back to this appropriation.

Program and Financing (in millions of dollars)

Identification code 97–0118–1–1–051	1999 actual	2000 est.	2001 est.
Obligations by program activity:			
10.00 Total new obligations		2,050	
Budgetary resources available for obligation:			
22.00 New budget authority (gross)		2,050	
23.95 Total new obligations		−2,050	
New budget authority (gross), detail:			
Discretionary:			
40.15 Appropriation (emergency)		2,050	
Change in unpaid obligations:			
72.40 Unpaid obligations, start of year: Obligated balance, start of year			523
73.10 Total new obligations		2,050	
73.20 Total outlays (gross)		−1,527	−408
74.40 Unpaid obligations, end of year: Obligated balance, end of year		523	115
Outlays (gross), detail:			
86.90 Outlays from new discretionary authority		1,527	
86.93 Outlays from discretionary balances			408
87.00 Total outlays (gross)		1,527	408
Net budget authority and outlays:			
89.00 Budget authority		2,050	
90.00 Outlays		1,527	408

This supplemental would fund the operation and maintenance and personnel costs associated with the sustainment of approximately 6,200 U.S. personnel in Kosovo as part of the NATO-led Kosovo Force (KFOR) and up to 1,000 personnel providing support in surrounding countries, as well as enforcement of the international sanctions regime on the Former Republic of Yugoslavia. The funds would also cover continued naval support to KFOR. Such additional costs include equipment preparation; airlift and sealift; other transportation within theater; in-theater support for all deployed forces, including logistics; consumables and spare parts; incremental air and ground OPTEMPO (flying hours and tank miles); additional steaming days; equipment maintenance; per diem of deployed personnel; rotational travel; leased communications; intelligence activities and support; and equipment reconstitution. Also included are funds for additional military personnel costs associated with Kosovo operations. These costs include Imminent Danger Pay, Family Separation Allowance, Foreign Duty Pay, Basic Allowance for Subsistence for enlisted personnel, mobilized reserve component pay and allowances, and subsistence in kind.

Of this amount, $25 million funds U.S. military support to the International Force in East Timor. This support consists primarily of logistics, transportation, and communications.

The entire amount requested has been designated by the President as an emergency requirement pursuant to the Balanced Budget and Emergency Deficit Control Act of 1985, as amended.

DRUG INTERDICTION AND COUNTER-DRUG ACTIVITIES, DEFENSE

(Supplemental now requested, existing legislation)

For an additional amount for "Drug interdiction and counter-drug activities, Defense," $98,400,000, to remain available until expended: Provided, That the entire amount is designated by the Congress as an emergency requirement pursuant to section 251(b)(2)(A) of the Balanced Budget and Emergency Deficit Control Act of 1985, as amended: Provided further, That the Secretary of Defense may transfer the funds provided herein only to appropriations for military personnel; operation and maintenance; procurement; research, development, test and evaluation; the Defense Health Program; and working capital funds: Provided further, That the funds transferred shall be merged with and shall be available for the same purposes and for the same time period, as the appropriation to which transferred: Provided further, That the transfer authority provided in this paragraph is in addition to any other transfer authority available to the Department of Defense.

Program and Financing (in millions of dollars)

Identification code 97–0105–1–1–051	1999 actual	2000 est.	2001 est.
Obligations by program activity:			
10.00 Total new obligations (object class 26.0)		98	
Budgetary resources available for obligation:			
22.00 New budget authority (gross)		98	
23.95 Total new obligations		−98	
New budget authority (gross), detail:			
Discretionary:			
40.15 Appropriation (emergency)		98	
Change in unpaid obligations:			
72.40 Unpaid obligations, start of year: Obligated balance, start of year			65
73.10 Total new obligations		98	
73.20 Total outlays (gross)		−34	−43
74.40 Unpaid obligations, end of year: Obligated balance, end of year		65	22
Outlays (gross), detail:			
86.90 Outlays from new discretionary authority		34	
86.93 Outlays from discretionary balances			43
87.00 Total outlays (gross)		34	43
Net budget authority and outlays:			
89.00 Budget authority		98	
90.00 Outlays		34	43

This additional funding is requested for the support of Plan Colombia which would greatly boost counter-drug efforts, strengthen the capacity of Colombia's national and local governments, encourage economic recovery and assist in the peace process. The funds would train two additional counter-drug battalions; enhance Army air bases to accommodate additional helicopters; assist an on-going program to eliminate corruption and human rights violations; enhance various reconnaissance operations; and aid in the enhancement of ground interdiction operations.

The entire amount requested has been designated by the President as an emergency requirement pursuant to the Balanced Budget and Emergency Deficit Control Act of 1985, as amended.

PROCUREMENT

AIRCRAFT PROCUREMENT, AIR FORCE

(Supplemental now requested, existing legislation)

For an additional amount for "Aircraft procurement, Air Force," $73,000,000, to remain available until September 30, 2001: Provided, That the entire amount is designated by the Congress as an emergency *requirement pursuant to section 251(b)(2)(A) of the Balanced Budget and Emergency Deficit Control Act of 1985, as amended.*

Program and Financing (in millions of dollars)

Identification code 57–3010–1–1–051	1999 actual	2000 est.	2001 est.
Obligations by program activity:			
10.00 Total new obligations		61	6
Budgetary resources available for obligation:			
21.40 For completion of prior year budget plans			12
22.00 New budget authority (gross)		73	
23.90 Total budgetary resources available for obligation		73	12
23.95 Total new obligations		−61	−6
24.40 For completion of prior year budget plans		12	6
New budget authority (gross), detail:			
Discretionary:			
40.15 Appropriation (emergency)		73	
Change in unpaid obligations:			
72.40 Unpaid obligations, start of year: Obligated balance, start of year			48
73.10 Total new obligations		61	6
73.20 Total outlays (gross)		−13	−29
74.40 Unpaid obligations, end of year: Obligated balance, end of year		48	25
Outlays (gross), detail:			
86.90 Outlays from new discretionary authority		13	
86.93 Outlays from discretionary balances			29
87.00 Total outlays (gross)		13	29
Net budget authority and outlays:			
89.00 Budget authority		73	
90.00 Outlays		13	29

Budget Plan (in millions of dollars)
(amount for procurement actions programmed)

Identification code 57–3010–1–1–051	1999 actual	2000 est.	2001 est.
Direct:			
0704 Other aircraft		73	
0893 Total budget plan		73	

This supplemental would provide $73 million to procure and modify a dedicated aircraft to support the Foreign Emergency Support Team (FEST) and to be operated and maintained by DOD. The FEST is an interagency team that assists the ambassador and host government to manage a terrorist incident in a foreign country. DoD provides airlift for the FEST in order to ensure rapid response to a crisis. In addition to reliability concerns, the current 36-year old FEST aircraft no longer meets mission requirements. The Administration believes that a replacement aircraft should be procured as soon as possible in order to ensure effective and reliable support to this high-priority counterterrorism mission.The entire amount requested has been designated by the President as an emergency requirement pursuant to the Balanced Budget and Emergency Deficit Control Act of 1985, as amended.

RESEARCH, DEVELOPMENT, TEST, AND EVALUATION

Research, Development, Test, and evaluation, Defense-wide

(Supplemental now requested, existing legislation)

Program and Financing (in millions of dollars)

Identification code 97–0400–1–1–051	1999 actual	2000 est.	2001 est.
Obligations by program activity:			
Direct program:			
00.02 Applied research		−3	
00.03 Advanced technology development		−4	−1
00.04 Demonstration/validation		−2	
00.07 Operational system development		−4	−1
10.00 Total new obligations (object class 25.5)		−13	−2
Budgetary resources available for obligation:			
21.40 Unobligated balance available, start of year			−2
22.00 New budget authority (gross)		−15	
23.90 Total budgetary resources available for obligation		−15	−2
23.95 Total new obligations		13	2
24.40 Unobligated balance available, end of year		−2	
New budget authority (gross), detail:			
Discretionary:			
41.00 Transferred to Coast Guard		−15	
Change in unpaid obligations:			
72.40 Unpaid obligations, start of year: Obligated balance, start of year			−6
73.10 Total new obligations		−13	−2
73.20 Total outlays (gross)		7	6
74.40 Unpaid obligations, end of year: Obligated balance, end of year		−6	−2
Outlays (gross), detail:			
86.90 Outlays from new discretionary authority		−7	
86.93 Outlays from discretionary balances			−6
87.00 Total outlays (gross)		−7	−6
Net budget authority and outlays:			
89.00 Budget authority		−15	
90.00 Outlays		−7	−6

Budget Plan (in millions of dollars)
(amount for procurement actions programmed)

Identification code 97–0400–1–1–051	1999 actual	2000 est.	2001 est.
Direct:			
0702 Applied research		−3	
0703 Advanced technology development		−5	
0704 Demonstration/validation		−2	
0705 Engineering and manufacturing development		−1	
0707 Operation system develoipment		−4	
0893 Total budget plan		−15	

A general provision would permit the transfer of funding from the Department of Defense to the Coast Guard to ensure that the Coast Guard has the ability to finance the health care that their beneficiaries obtain through the Department of Defense TRICARE system. The costs of medical care provided through the TRICARE system and military treatment facilities have increased significantly in the past few years. The Coast Guard did not have sufficient information to budget for these increased costs in their 2000 Budget.

MILITARY CONSTRUCTION

Military Construction, Defense-wide

(Supplemental now requested, existing legislation)

For an additional amount for "Military construction, Defense-Wide," $38,600,000, to remain available until expended: Provided, That the entire amount is designated by the Congress as an emergency requirement pursuant to section 251(b)(2)(A) of the Balanced Budget and Emergency Deficit Control Act of 1985, as amended.

Program and Financing (in millions of dollars)

Identification code 97–0500–1–1–051	1999 actual	2000 est.	2001 est.
Obligations by program activity:			
00.01 Major construction		20	12
10.00 Total new obligations		20	12
Budgetary resources available for obligation:			
21.40 For completion of prior year budget plans			19

MILITARY CONSTRUCTION, DEFENSE-WIDE—Continued

Program and Financing (in millions of dollars)—Continued

Identification code 97–0500–1–1–051	1999 actual	2000 est.	2001 est.
22.00 New budget authority (gross)	....	39	....
23.90 Total budgetary resources available for obligation	....	39	19
23.95 Total new obligations	....	−20	−12
24.40 For completion of prior year budget plans	....	19	7
New budget authority (gross), detail:			
Discretionary:			
40.15 Appropriation (emergency)	....	39	....
Change in unpaid obligations:			
72.40 Unpaid obligations, start of year: Obligated balance, start of year	....	....	16
73.10 Total new obligations	....	20	12
73.20 Total outlays (gross)	....	−4	−15
73.40 Adjustments in expired accounts (net)	....	....	....
74.40 Unpaid obligations, end of year: Obligated balance, end of year	....	16	13
Outlays (gross), detail:			
86.90 Outlays from new discretionary authority	....	4	....
86.93 Outlays from discretionary balances	....	....	15
87.00 Total outlays (gross)	....	4	15
Net budget authority and outlays:			
89.00 Budget authority	....	39	....
90.00 Outlays	....	4	15

Budget Plan (in millions of dollars)
(amount for procurement actions programmed)

Identification code 97–0500–1–1–051	1999 actual	2000 est.	2001 est.
0701 Major construction	....	39	....

This supplemental would fund construction of a forward operating location in Manta, Ecuador. This funding will allow the Department of Defense to continue regional drug interdiction activities with minimal disruption following the DoD departure from Panama.

Department of Energy

ATOMIC ENERGY DEFENSE ACTIVITIES

WEAPONS ACTIVITIES

(Supplemental now requested, existing legislation)

For an additional amount for "Weapons activities," $55,000,000, to remain available until expended.

Program and Financing (in millions of dollars)

Identification code 89–0240–1–1–053	1999 actual	2000 est.	2001 est.
Obligations by program activity:			
10.00 Total new obligations (object class 25.4)	....	55	....
Budgetary resources available for obligation:			
22.00 New budget authority (gross)	....	55	....
23.95 Total new obligations	....	−55	....
New budget authority (gross), detail:			
Discretionary:			
40.00 Appropriation	....	55	....
Change in unpaid obligations:			
72.40 Unpaid obligations, start of year: Obligated balance, start of year	....	....	19
73.10 Total new obligations	....	55	....
73.20 Total outlays (gross)	....	−36	−17
74.40 Unpaid obligations, end of year: Obligated balance, end of year	....	19	2
Outlays (gross), detail:			
86.90 Outlays from new discretionary authority	....	36	....
86.93 Outlays from discretionary balances	....	....	17
87.00 Total outlays (gross)	....	36	17
Net budget authority and outlays:			
89.00 Budget authority	....	55	....
90.00 Outlays	....	36	17

This supplemental request would fund the additional costs to support personnel and other resources at Department of Energy weapons production facilities that are needed to meet milestones in the weapons refurbishment schedule developed jointly by the Departments of Energy and Defense. The requested funds would continue activities necessary to restart enriched uranium operations at the Y–12 Plant, complete critical facility projects at the Kansas City Plant, and address critical skills retention and other concerns at the Y–12, Kansas City, and Pantex Plants.

OTHER DEFENSE ACTIVITIES

(Supplemental now requested, existing legislation)

Of the funds made available under this heading for fiscal year 1999 to implement a United States/Russian accord for the disposition of excess weapons plutonium, $40,000,000 shall be transferred to "Other nuclear security activities" as authorized by the Fiscal Year 2000 National Defense Authorization Act (P.L. 106–65), and shall become available on October 1, 2002.

Program and Financing (in millions of dollars)

Identification code 89–0309–1–1–053	1999 actual	2000 est.	2001 est.
Budgetary resources available for obligation:			
21.40 Unobligated balance available, start of year	....	....	−40
22.00 New budget authority (gross)	....	−40	....
23.90 Total budgetary resources available for obligation	....	−40	−40
23.95 Total new obligations	....	....	....
24.40 Unobligated balance available, end of year	....	−40	−40
New budget authority (gross), detail:			
Discretionary:			
40.36 Unobligated balance deferred	....	−40	....
Net budget authority and outlays:			
89.00 Budget authority	....	−40	....
90.00 Outlays	....	....	....

This supplemental request would defer the availability of $40 million appropriated in 1999 for U.S.-Russian plutonium disposition activities (as an emergency appropriation) to 2003. These funds were originally appropriated in the Other Defense Activities account. However, the Department of Energy reorganization, mandated in Public Law 106–65, requires the transfer of the balances for plutonium disposition to this new account.

ENVIRONMENTAL AND OTHER DEFENSE ACTIVITIES

OTHER DEFENSE ACTIVITIES

(Supplemental now requested, existing legislation)

For an additional amount for "Other defense activities," $18,000,000, to remain available until expended, of which $4,000,000 shall be derived by transfer from unobligated balances in the "Biomass energy development" account.

Program and Financing (in millions of dollars)

Identification code 89–0243–1–1–053	1999 actual	2000 est.	2001 est.
Obligations by program activity:			
10.00 Total new obligations (object class 25.2)	....	18	....
Budgetary resources available for obligation:			
22.00 New budget authority (gross)	....	18	....

	1999 actual	2000 est.	2001 est.
23.95 Total new obligations		−18	
New budget authority (gross), detail:			
Discretionary:			
40.00 Appropriation		14	
42.00 Transferred from other accounts		4	
43.00 Appropriation (total discretionary)		18	
Change in unpaid obligations:			
72.40 Unpaid obligations, start of year: Obligated balance, start of year			5
73.10 Total new obligations		18	
73.20 Total outlays (gross)		−12	−5
74.40 Unpaid obligations, end of year: Obligated balance, end of year		5	
Outlays (gross), detail:			
86.90 Outlays from new discretionary authority		12	
86.93 Outlays from discretionary balances			5
87.00 Total outlays (gross)		12	5
Net budget authority and outlays:			
89.00 Budget authority		18	
90.00 Outlays		12	5

This supplemental request would provide $10 million to continue the Department of Energy's full and independent investigation of environment, safety, and health issues associated with operation of the gaseous diffusion plants at Paducah, Portsmouth, and the East Tennessee Technology Park, past and present, and support additional medical monitoring for workers, who may have been exposed to plutonium and possibly other radioactive materials, and other activities. This supplemental request would also provide $8 million to support additional physical and cyber-security activities at Department of Energy facilities.

ENERGY PROGRAMS

Uranium Enrichment Decontamination and Decommissioning Fund

(Supplemental now requested, existing legislation)

For an additional amount for "Uranium enrichment decontamination and decommissioning fund," $16,000,000, to be derived from the Fund, to remain available until expended.

Program and Financing (in millions of dollars)

Identification code 89–5231–1–2–271	1999 actual	2000 est.	2001 est.
Obligations by program activity:			
10.00 Total new obligations		16	
Budgetary resources available for obligation:			
22.00 New budget authority (gross)		16	
23.95 Total new obligations		−16	
New budget authority (gross), detail:			
Discretionary:			
40.20 Appropriation (special fund, definite)		16	
Change in unpaid obligations:			
72.40 Unpaid obligations, start of year: Obligated balance, start of year			5
73.10 Total new obligations		16	
73.20 Total outlays (gross)		−11	−5
74.40 Unpaid obligations, end of year: Obligated balance, end of year		5	
Outlays (gross), detail:			
86.90 Outlays from new discretionary authority		11	
86.93 Outlays from discretionary balances			5
87.00 Total outlays (gross)		11	5
Net budget authority and outlays:			
89.00 Budget authority		16	
90.00 Outlays		11	5

This supplemental request would provide funds to accelerate environmental cleanup of the Paducah, Kentucky and Portsmouth, Ohio gaseous diffusion plants, which are sites leased and operated by the United State Enrichment Corporation. The activities to be performed include environmental assessment, characterization, remediation, and decontamination and decommissioning of contaminated facilities. These cleanup activities will be specifically directed toward protecting the health and safety of workers, the public, and the environment.

Object Classification (in millions of dollars)

Identification code 89–5231–1–2–271	1999 actual	2000 est.	2001 est.
25.1 Advisory and assistance services		10	
25.2 Other services		2	
25.4 Operation and maintenance of facilities		4	
99.9 Total new obligations		16	

Department of Health and Human Services

ADMINISTRATION FOR CHILDREN AND FAMILIES

Payments to States for Foster Care and Adoption Assistance

(Supplemental now requested, existing legislation)

For an additional amount for "Payments to States for foster care and adoption assistance," $35,000,000.

Program and Financing (in millions of dollars)

Identification code 75–1545–1–1–506	1999 actual	2000 est.	2001 est.
Obligations by program activity:			
00.02 Independent living		35	
10.00 Total new obligations (object class 41.0)		35	
Budgetary resources available for obligation:			
22.00 New budget authority (gross)		35	
23.95 Total new obligations		−35	
New budget authority (gross), detail:			
Mandatory:			
60.00 Appropriation		35	
Change in unpaid obligations:			
72.40 Unpaid obligations, start of year: Obligated balance, start of year			30
73.10 Total new obligations		35	
73.20 Total outlays (gross)		−5	−21
74.40 Unpaid obligations, end of year: Obligated balance, end of year		30	9
Outlays (gross), detail:			
86.97 Outlays from new mandatory authority		5	
86.98 Outlays from mandatory balances			21
87.00 Total outlays (gross)		5	21
Net budget authority and outlays:			
89.00 Budget authority		35	
90.00 Outlays		5	21

This supplemental request would, together with the $105 million already appropriated for 2000, ensure that the foster care and adoption assistance program is fully funded. The Foster Care Independence Act of 1999 (P.L. 106–169) amended the Independent Living Program to expand and improve the services provided to older youth in foster care, and young people who have aged out of foster care without the emotional or financial support of a family. The program helps people leaving foster care to complete their education, find employment, secure housing, and otherwise prepare for life as re-

PAYMENTS TO STATES FOR FOSTER CARE AND ADOPTION ASSISTANCE—Continued

sponsible, self-sufficient adults. In order to strengthen services provided to this vulnerable population, the law increased funding for the program to $140 million. Since the authorized level was fully offset in P.L. 106–169, there are no additional costs associated with this request.

Department Housing and Urban Development

HOUSING PROGRAMS

FHA-GENERAL AND SPECIAL RISK PROGRAM ACCOUNT

(Supplemental now requested, existing legislation)

For an additional amount for "FHA General and special risk program account" for the cost of guaranteed loans, as authorized by sections 238 and 519 of the National Housing Act (12 U.S.C. 1715z-3 and 1735c), including the cost of loan modifications (as that term is defined in section 502 of the Congressional Budget Act of 1974, as amended), $49, 000,000, to remain available until expended.

Program and Financing (in millions of dollars)

Identification code 86–0200–1–1–371		1999 actual	2000 est.	2001 est.
	Obligations by program activity:			
00.04	Guaranteed loan subsidy		49	
10.00	Total new obligations (object class 41.0)		49	
	Budgetary resources available for obligation:			
22.00	New budget authority (gross)		49	
23.95	Total new obligations		−49	
	New budget authority (gross), detail:			
	Discretionary:			
40.00	Appropriation		49	
	Change in unpaid obligations:			
72.40	Unpaid obligations, start of year: Obligated balance, start of year			12
73.10	Total new obligations		49	
73.20	Total outlays (gross)		−37	−12
74.40	Unpaid obligations, end of year: Obligated balance, end of year		12	
	Outlays (gross), detail:			
86.90	Outlays from new discretionary authority		37	
86.93	Outlays from discretionary balances			12
87.00	Total outlays (gross)		37	12
	Net budget authority and outlays:			
89.00	Budget authority		49	
90.00	Outlays		37	12

Summary of Loan Levels, Subsidy Budget Authority and Outlays by Program (in millions of dollars)

Identification code 86–0200–1–1–371		1999 actual	2000 est.	2001 est.
	Guaranteed loan levels supportable by subsidy budget authority:			
2150	Apartments NC/SC		462	
2150	221d3 NP/Coop owned apartments		11	
2150	Mixed income (Hope d4)		1	
2150	241a supplemental loans for apartments		12	
2150	Section 234: condominiums		1,916	
2150	Section 203(k): rehabilitation mortgages		315	
2150	Section 221(d)(2): low income housing		6	
2150	Property improvements		110	
2150	Manufactured housing		2	
2159	Total loan guarantee levels		2,835	
	Guaranteed loan subsidy budget authority:			
2330	Subsidy budget authority		49	
	Guaranteed loan subsidy outlays:			
2340	Subsidy outlays		37	12

This supplemental request would provide sufficient positive credit subsidy to enter into previously estimated levels of mortgage loan commitments. The subsidy rates projected in the 2000 President's Budget for single family risk categories have been revised in light of a lower premium structure than used in preparation of that budget. This increase is necessary to avoid potential delays or disruptions in the processing and endorsement of mortgage guarantees.

FHA GENERAL AND SPECIAL RISK GUARANTEED LOAN FINANCING ACCOUNT

(Supplemental now requested, existing legislation)

Program and Financing (in millions of dollars)

Identification code 86–4077–1–3–371		1999 actual	2000 est.	2001 est.
	Obligations by program activity:			
	Capital investment, claims and other:			
00.01	Default claims and other		1	5
10.00	Total new obligations		1	5
	Budgetary resources available for obligation:			
21.40	Unobligated balance available, start of year			61
22.00	New financing authority (gross)		62	17
23.90	Total budgetary resources available for obligation		62	78
23.95	Total new obligations		−1	−5
24.40	Unobligated balance available, end of year		61	73
	New financing authority (gross), detail:			
	Discretionary:			
68.00	Spending authority from offsetting collections (gross): Offsetting collections (cash)		62	17
	Change in unpaid obligations:			
72.40	Unpaid obligations, start of year: Obligated balance, start of year			1
73.10	Total new obligations		1	5
74.40	Unpaid obligations, end of year: Obligated balance, end of year		1	6
87.00	Total financing disbursements (gross)			
	Offsets:			
	Against gross financing authority and financing disbursements:			
	Offsetting collections (cash) from:			
88.00	Payments from program account		−49	
	Non-Federal sources:			
88.40	Fees and premiums		−13	−16
88.40	Single family property recoveries			−1
88.90	Total, offsetting collections (cash)		−62	−17
	Net financing authority and financing disbursements:			
89.00	Financing authority			
90.00	Financing disbursements		−62	−17

Status of Guaranteed Loans (in millions of dollars)

Identification code 86–4077–1–3–371		1999 actual	2000 est.	2001 est.
	Position with respect to appropriations act limitation on commitments:			
2111	Limitation on guaranteed loans made by private lenders			
2112	Uncommitted loan guarantee limitation		2,835	
2150	Total guaranteed loan commitments		2,835	
	Cumulative balance of guaranteed loans outstanding:			
2210	Outstanding, start of year			2,260
2231	Disbursements of new guaranteed loans		2,260	122
	Adjustments:			
2261	Terminations for default that result in loans receivable			−2
2262	Terminations for default that result in acquisition of property			−4
2290	Outstanding, end of year		2,260	2,376

	Memorandum:			
2299	Guaranteed amount of guaranteed loans outstanding, end of year		2,260	2,376
	Addendum:			
	Cumulative balance of defaulted guaranteed loans that result in loans receivable:			
2310	Outstanding, start of year			
2331	Disbursements for guaranteed loan claims			2
2390	Outstanding, end of year			2

As required by the Federal Credit Reform Act of 1990, this non-budgetary account records all cash flows to and from the Government resulting from loan guarantees committed in 1992 and beyond (including modifications of loan guarantees that resulted from commitments in any year). The amounts in this account are a means of financing and are not included in the budget totals.

MANAGEMENT AND ADMINISTRATION

Office of Inspector General

(Supplemental now requested, existing legislation)

Under this heading in P.L. 106–74, add the words, "to remain available until September 30, 2001," after "$83,000,000,".

Program and Financing (in millions of dollars)

Identification code 86–0189–1–1–451		1999 actual	2000 est.	2001 est.
	Obligations by program activity:			
10.00	Total new obligations		−6	6
	Budgetary resources available for obligation:			
22.00	New budget authority (gross)		−6	6
23.95	Total new obligations		6	−6
	New budget authority (gross), detail:			
	Discretionary:			
40.00	Appropriation		−6	
50.00	Reappropriation			6
70.00	Total new budget authority (gross)		−6	6
	Change in unpaid obligations:			
73.10	Total new obligations		−6	6
73.20	Total outlays (gross)		5	−4
74.40	Unpaid obligations, end of year: Obligated balance, end of year			1
	Outlays (gross), detail:			
86.90	Outlays from new discretionary authority		−5	5
86.93	Outlays from discretionary balances			−1
87.00	Total outlays (gross)		−5	4
	Net budget authority and outlays:			
89.00	Budget authority		−6	6
90.00	Outlays		−5	4

This supplemental request would extend the time period for expenditure of funds from one year to two years. This will facilitate judicious completion of the implementation of the Anti-fraud initiative, including the hiring of the remaining new staff needed and coordination, where applicable, with local enforcement officials. The Administration urges quick action by the Congress on this supplemental request in order to achieve the full benefits of this proposal.

Object Classification (in millions of dollars)

Identification code 86–0189–1–1–451		1999 actual	2000 est.	2001 est.
11.1	Personnel compensation: Full-time permanent		−3	3
12.1	Civilian personnel benefits		−1	1
21.0	Travel and transportation of persons		−1	1
25.1	Advisory and assistance services		−1	1
99.9	Total new obligations		−6	6

Personnel Summary

Identification code 86–0189–1–1–451		1999 actual	2000 est.	2001 est.
1001	Total compensable workyears: Full-time equivalent employment		−45	45

Department of the Interior

BUREAU OF LAND MANAGEMENT

Wildland Fire Management

(Supplemental now requested, existing legislation)

For an additional amount for "Wildland fire management," $100,000,000, to remain available until expended, for emergency rehabilitation and wildfire suppression activities: Provided, That the entire amount is designated by Congress as an emergency requirement pursuant to section 251(b)(2)(A) of the Balanced Budget and Emergency Deficit Control Act of 1985, as amended; Provided further, That this amount shall be available only to the extent that an official budget request for a specific dollar amount, that includes designation of the entire amount of the request as an emergency requirement as defined by such Act, is transmitted by the President to the Congress.

Program and Financing (in millions of dollars)

Identification code 14–1125–1–1–302		1999 actual	2000 est.	2001 est.
	Budgetary resources available for obligation:			
21.40	Unobligated balance available, start of year			100
22.00	New budget authority (gross)		100	
23.90	Total budgetary resources available for obligation		100	100
23.95	Total new obligations			
24.40	Unobligated balance available, end of year		100	100
	New budget authority (gross), detail:			
	Discretionary:			
40.15	Appropriation (emergency)		100	
	Net budget authority and outlays:			
89.00	Budget authority		100	
90.00	Outlays			

This supplemental request would allow the Interior Department to quickly meet any unusually severe wildland firefighting needs. Currently, Interior has no remaining contingency funds to draw upon. During the summer of 1999, major fires in western States resulted in costs that greatly exceeded those of the average firefighting season. In September, the President released the remaining $50 million in contingent emergency funding of the $100 million appropriated by P.L. 104–208, the Omnibus Consolidated Appropriations Act, 1997.

UNITED STATES GEOLOGICAL SURVEY

Surveys, Investigations and Research

(Supplemental now requested, existing legislation)

For an additional amount for "Surveys, investigations and research," $1,800,000, to remain available until expended, to repair or replace stream monitoring equipment and associated facilities damaged by natural disasters: Provided, That the entire amount is designated by Congress as an emergency requirement pursuant to section 251(b)(2)(A) of the Balanced Budget and Emergency Deficit Control Act of 1985, as amended.

Program and Financing (in millions of dollars)

Identification code 14–0804–1–1–300		1999 actual	2000 est.	2001 est.
	Obligations by program activity:			
	Direct program:			
00.03	Water resources investigations		2	
10.00	Total new obligations (object class 31.0)		2	

SURVEYS, INVESTIGATIONS AND RESEARCH—Continued

Program and Financing (in millions of dollars)—Continued

Identification code 14–0804–1–1–300	1999 actual	2000 est.	2001 est.
Budgetary resources available for obligation:			
22.00 New budget authority (gross)		2	
23.95 Total new obligations		−2	
New budget authority (gross), detail:			
Discretionary:			
40.15 Appropriation (emergency)		2	
Change in unpaid obligations:			
73.10 Total new obligations		2	
73.20 Total outlays (gross)		−2	
Outlays (gross), detail:			
86.90 Outlays from new discretionary authority		2	
Net budget authority and outlays:			
89.00 Budget authority		2	
90.00 Outlays		2	

This supplemental request would provide funds to repair or to replace stream monitoring equipment and structures damaged by rain, winds, floods and other acts of nature, including Hurricanes Dennis, Floyd, and Irene. These stations and associated equipment provide critical information on stream flow to the National Weather Service (NWS) in disaster situations.

A supplemental is needed at this time to replace damaged stream gauges before potential spring flooding. Stream monitoring is necessary to predict areas of potential flooding and to assist the National Weather Service in issuing flood warnings to local communities.

The entire amount requested for 2000 has been designated by the President as an emergency requirement pursuant to the Balanced Budget and Emergency Deficit Control Act of 1985, as amended.

UNITED STATES FISH AND WILDLIFE SERVICE

CONSTRUCTION

(Supplemental now requested, existing legislation)

For an additional amount for "Construction," $5,000,000, to remain available until expended, to repair or replace buildings, equipment, roads, and water control structure's damaged by natural disasters: Provided, That the entire amount is designated by Congress as an emergency requirement pursuant to section 251(b)(2)(A) of the Balanced Budget and Emergency Deficit Control Act of 1985, as amended.

Program and Financing (in millions of dollars)

Identification code 14–1612–1–1–303	1999 actual	2000 est.	2001 est.
Obligations by program activity:			
Direct program:			
Construction and rehabilitation:			
00.01 Refuges		5	
10.00 Total new obligations (object class 32.0)		5	
Budgetary resources available for obligation:			
22.00 New budget authority (gross)		5	
23.95 Total new obligations		−5	
New budget authority (gross), detail:			
Discretionary:			
40.15 Appropriation (emergency)		5	
Change in unpaid obligations:			
72.40 Unpaid obligations, start of year: Obligated balance, start of year			4
73.10 Total new obligations		5	
73.20 Total outlays (gross)		−1	−3
74.40 Unpaid obligations, end of year: Obligated balance, end of year		4	1
Outlays (gross), detail:			
86.90 Outlays from new discretionary authority		1	
86.93 Outlays from discretionary balances			3
87.00 Total outlays (gross)		1	3
Net budget authority and outlays:			
89.00 Budget authority		5	
90.00 Outlays		1	3

This supplemental request would provide funds to repair damaged or destroyed property and structures including buildings, equipment, roads, and water control structures on FWS-owned lands and facilities damaged by rain, winds, floods and other acts of nature, including Hurricanes Dennis, Floyd, and Irene.

A supplemental is needed at this time to ensure the safety of employees and visitors to National Wildlife Refuges is not compromised and to protect Federal investments in endangered species recovery programs.

The entire amount requested has been designated by the President as an emergency requirement pursuant to the Balanced Budget and Emergency Deficit Control Act of 1985, as amended.

NATIONAL PARK SERVICE

CONSTRUCTION

(Supplemental now requested, existing legislation)

For an additional amount for "Construction," $4,000,000, to remain available until expended, to repair or replace visitor facilities, equipment, roads and trails, and cultural sites and artifacts at national park units damaged by natural disasters: Provided, That the entire amount is designated by Congress as an emergency requirement pursuant to section 251(b)(2)(A) of the Balanced Budget and Emergency Deficit Control Act of 1985, as amended.

Program and Financing (in millions of dollars)

Identification code 14–1039–1–1–303	1999 actual	2000 est.	2001 est.
Obligations by program activity:			
Direct program:			
00.01 Line item construction and maintenance		4	
10.00 Total new obligations (object class 25.2)		4	
Budgetary resources available for obligation:			
22.00 New budget authority (gross)		4	
23.95 Total new obligations		−4	
New budget authority (gross), detail:			
Discretionary:			
40.15 Appropriation (emergency)		4	
Change in unpaid obligations:			
72.40 Unpaid obligations, start of year: Obligated balance, start of year			3
73.10 Total new obligations		4	
73.20 Total outlays (gross)		−1	−1
74.40 Unpaid obligations, end of year: Obligated balance, end of year		3	1
Outlays (gross), detail:			
86.90 Outlays from new discretionary authority		1	
86.93 Outlays from discretionary balances			1
87.00 Total outlays (gross)		1	1
Net budget authority and outlays:			
89.00 Budget authority		4	
90.00 Outlays		1	1

This supplemental request would provide funds to repair destroyed or damaged property and structures including visitor facilities, equipment, roads and trails, and cultural sites and artifacts at national park units damaged by rain, winds, floods and other acts of nature, including Hurricanes Dennis, Floyd, and Irene.

A supplemental is needed at this time to begin the repair of NPS cultural sites and artifacts before further deterioration occurs and to repair NPS visitor facilities for the peak summer visitor season. Repairs will focus on those needed to ensure visitor safety.

The entire amount requested has been designated by the President as an emergency requirement pursuant to the Balanced Budget and Emergency Deficit Control Act of 1985, as amended.

Department of State

ADMINISTRATION OF FOREIGN AFFAIRS

Diplomatic and Consular Programs

(Supplemental now requested, existing legislation)

Notwithstanding section 15 of the State Department Basic Authorities Act of 1956, for an additional amount for "Diplomatic and Consular Programs," $24,000,000, to remain available until expended: Provided, That the entire amount is designated by the Congress as an emergency requirement pursuant to section 251(b)(2)(A) of the Balanced Budget and EmergencyDeficit Control Act of 1985, as amended.

Program and Financing (in millions of dollars)

Identification code 19–0113–1–1–153	1999 actual	2000 est.	2001 est.
Obligations by program activity:			
10.00 Total new obligations		24	
Budgetary resources available for obligation:			
22.00 New budget authority (gross)		24	
23.95 Total new obligations		−24	
New budget authority (gross), detail:			
Discretionary:			
40.15 Appropriation (emergency)		24	
Change in unpaid obligations:			
72.40 Unpaid obligations, start of year: Obligated balance, start of year			3
73.10 Total new obligations		24	
73.20 Total outlays (gross)		−21	−2
74.40 Unpaid obligations, end of year: Obligated balance, end of year		3	1
Outlays (gross), detail:			
86.90 Outlays from new discretionary authority		21	
86.93 Outlays from discretionary balances			2
87.00 Total outlays (gross)		21	2
Net budget authority and outlays:			
89.00 Budget authority		24	
90.00 Outlays		21	2

This supplemental request would fund the increased needs of the Department of State resulting from the enhanced diplomatic, public diplomacy, and security activity relating to activities in Kosovo and the surrounding region.

The entire amount requested for has been designated by the President as an emergency requirement pursuant to the Balanced Budget and Emergency Deficit Control Act of 1985, as amended.

Object Classification (in millions of dollars)

Identification code 19–0113–1–1–153	1999 actual	2000 est.	2001 est.
21.0 Travel and transportation of persons		2	
22.0 Transportation of things		1	
23.3 Communications, utilities, and miscellaneous charges		4	
25.2 Other services		12	
25.4 Operation and maintenance of facilities		1	
26.0 Supplies and materials		1	
31.0 Equipment		3	
99.9 Total new obligations		24	

Security and Maintenance of United States Missions

(Supplemental now requested, existing legislation)

Notwithstanding section 15 of the State Department Basic Authorities Act of 1956, for an additional amount for "Security and maintenance of United States missions," $239,000,000, to remain available until expended: Provided, That the entire amount is designated by the Congress as an emergency requirement pursuant to section 251(b)(2)(A) of the Balanced Budget and Emergency Deficit Control Act of 1985, as amended.

Program and Financing (in millions of dollars)

Identification code 19–0535–1–1–153	1999 actual	2000 est.	2001 est.
Obligations by program activity:			
Direct program:			
00.01 State Department		239	
10.00 Total new obligations (object class 32.0)		239	
Budgetary resources available for obligation:			
22.00 New budget authority (gross)		239	
23.95 Total new obligations		−239	
New budget authority (gross), detail:			
Discretionary:			
40.15 Appropriation (emergency)		239	
Change in unpaid obligations:			
72.40 Unpaid obligations, start of year: Obligated balance, start of year			167
73.10 Total new obligations		239	
73.20 Total outlays (gross)		−72	−65
74.40 Unpaid obligations, end of year: Obligated balance, end of year		167	102
Outlays (gross), detail:			
86.90 Outlays from new discretionary authority		72	
86.93 Outlays from discretionary balances			65
87.00 Total outlays (gross)		72	65
Net budget authority and outlays:			
89.00 Budget authority		239	
90.00 Outlays		72	65

This supplemental request would fund secure facility and other construction in Kosovo and the surrounding region, as well as other security construction needs as appropriate.

The entire amount requested for has been designated by the President as an emergency requirement pursuant to the Balanced Budget and Emergency Deficit Control Act of 1985, as amended.

INTERNATIONAL ORGANIZATIONS AND CONFERENCES

Contributions for International Peacekeeping Activities

(Supplemental now requested, existing legislation)

Notwithstanding section 15 of the State Department Basic Authorities Act of 1956, for an additional amount for "Contributions for international peacekeeping activities," $107,000,000, to remain available until September 30, 2001: Provided, That the entire amount is designated by the Congress as an emergency requirement pursuant to section 251(b)(2)(A) of the Balanced Budget and Emergency Deficit Control Act of 1985, as amended.

CONTRIBUTIONS FOR INTERNATIONAL PEACEKEEPING ACTIVITIES—Continued

Program and Financing (in millions of dollars)

Identification code 19–1124–1–1–153	1999 actual	2000 est.	2001 est.
Obligations by program activity:			
00.11 U.N. mission in East Timor		16	
00.19 U.N. mission in Kosovo		91	
10.00 Total new obligations (object class 41.0)		107	
Budgetary resources available for obligation:			
22.00 New budget authority (gross)		107	
23.95 Total new obligations		–107	
New budget authority (gross), detail:			
Discretionary:			
40.00 Appropriation		107	
Change in unpaid obligations:			
73.10 Total new obligations		107	
73.20 Total outlays (gross)		–107	
Outlays (gross), detail:			
86.90 Outlays from new discretionary authority		107	
Net budget authority and outlays:			
89.00 Budget authority		107	
90.00 Outlays		107	

This supplemental request would fund anticipated United Nations peacekeeping operations, particularly those in Kosovo and East Timor.

The entire amount requested for has been designated by the President as an emergency requirement pursuant to the Balanced Budget and Emergency Deficit Control Act of 1985, as amended.

OTHER

ASSISTANCE TO PLAN COLOMBIA

(Supplemental now requested, existing legislation)

For necessary expenses to carry out section 481 of the Foreign Assistance Act of 1961 to support Plan Colombia, $818,000,000, to remain available until expended: Provided, That such funds shall be in addition to amounts otherwise available for such purposes: Provided further, That section 482(b) of the Act shall not apply to such funds: Provided further, That, for purposes of supporting Plan Colombia, any agency of the United States Government to which funds are transferred or allocated under any authority of the Act may utilize, in addition to any authorities available for carrying out section 481, any authorities available to that agency for carrying out related activities, including utilization of such funds for administrative expenses: Provided further, That funds obligated prior to the date of enactment of this Act for administrative expenses in support of Plan Colombia may be finally charged to funds made available for such purposes by this Act: Provided further, That any limitations on amounts that an agency may use for a particular purpose or activity shall not apply to funds made available under this supplemental Act to support Plan Colombia: Provided further, That the entire amount is designated by the Congress as an emergency requirement pursuant to section 251(b)(2)(A) of the Balanced Budget and Emergency Deficit Control Act of 1985, as amended.

Program and Financing (in millions of dollars)

Identification code 19–1154–1–1–151	1999 actual	2000 est.	2001 est.
Obligations by program activity:			
01.01 Push into southern Colombia		481	
01.02 Drug trafficking interdiction		132	
01.03 Colombian National Police support		68	
01.04 Economic development		92	
01.05 Boost governing capacity		45	
10.00 Total new obligations		818	
Budgetary resources available for obligation:			
22.00 New budget authority (gross)		818	
23.95 Total new obligations		–818	
New budget authority (gross), detail:			
Discretionary:			
40.15 Appropriation (emergency)		818	
Change in unpaid obligations:			
72.40 Unpaid obligations, start of year: Obligated balance, start of year			569
73.10 Total new obligations		818	
73.20 Total outlays (gross)		–249	–303
74.40 Unpaid obligations, end of year: Obligated balance, end of year		569	266
Outlays (gross), detail:			
86.90 Outlays from new discretionary authority		249	
86.93 Outlays from discretionary balances			303
87.00 Total outlays (gross)		249	303
Net budget authority and outlays:			
89.00 Budget authority		818	
90.00 Outlays		249	303

This supplemental request would fund United States assistance to Plan Colombia to reduce the supply of narcotics to the United States from the Andean region and aid Colombia in overcoming its current economic and societal problems. The funds would support the Colombian Army's push into southern Colombia in support of the Colombian National Police, enhance drug interdiction in Colombia and the region, increase support to the Colombian National Police, provide for economic development in Colombia and the Andean region, and boost Colombia's local and national governing capacity.

The entire amount requested has been designated by the President as an emergency requirement pursuant to the Balanced Budget and Emergency Deficit Control Act of 1985, as amended.

Object Classification (in millions of dollars)

Identification code 19–1154–1–1–151	1999 actual	2000 est.	2001 est.
11.1 Personnel compensation: Full-time permanent		1	
25.2 Other services		1	
25.8 Subsistence and support of persons		174	
26.0 Supplies and materials		2	
31.0 Equipment		535	
41.0 Grants, subsidies, and contributions		104	
99.0 Subtotal, direct obligations		817	
99.5 Below reporting threshold		1	
99.9 Total new obligations		818	

Personnel Summary

Identification code 19–1154–1–1–151	1999 actual	2000 est.	2001 est.
1001 Total compensable workyears: Full-time equivalent employment		9	

EDUCATIONAL AND CULTURAL EXCHANGE PROGRAMS

(Supplemental now requested, existing legislation)

Notwithstanding section 15 of the State Department Basic Authorities Act of 1956 and section 701 of the United States Information and Educational Exchange Act of 1948, for an additional amount for "Educational and cultural exchange programs," $3,622,000, to remain available until expended: Provided, That the entire amount is designated by the Congress as an emergency requirement pursuant to section 251(b)(2)(A) of the Balanced Budget and Emergency Deficit Control Act of 1985, as amended.

Program and Financing (in millions of dollars)

Identification code 19–0209–1–1–154	1999 actual	2000 est.	2001 est.
Obligations by program activity:			
10.00 Total new obligations (object class 41.0)		4	
Budgetary resources available for obligation:			
22.00 New budget authority (gross)		4	
23.95 Total new obligations		−4	
New budget authority (gross), detail:			
Discretionary:			
40.15 Appropriation (emergency)		4	
Change in unpaid obligations:			
72.40 Unpaid obligations, start of year: Obligated balance, start of year			2
73.10 Total new obligations		4	
73.20 Total outlays (gross)		−2	−2
74.40 Unpaid obligations, end of year: Obligated balance, end of year		2	
Outlays (gross), detail:			
86.90 Outlays from new discretionary authority		2	
86.93 Outlays from discretionary balances			2
87.00 Total outlays (gross)		2	2
Net budget authority and outlays:			
89.00 Budget authority		4	
90.00 Outlays		2	2

This supplemental request would fund the establishment of a Fulbright exchange program for Kosovo and expansion of student exchange, international visitor, and citizen exchange programs in Kosovo and the region.

The entire amount requested for has been designated by the President as an emergency requirement pursuant to the Balanced Budget and Emergency Deficit Control Act of 1985, as amended.

Department of Transportation

COAST GUARD

Operating Expenses

Program and Financing (in millions of dollars)

Identification code 69–0201–1–1–999	1999 actual	2000 est.	2001 est.
Obligations by program activity:			
Direct program:			
00.01 Search and rescue		2	
00.02 Aids to navigation		3	
00.03 Marine safety		2	
00.04 Marine environmental protection		2	
00.05 Enforcement of laws and treaties		8	
00.06 Ice operations		1	
10.00 Total new obligations (object class 25.6)		18	
Budgetary resources available for obligation:			
22.00 New budget authority (gross)		18	
23.95 Total new obligations		−18	
New budget authority (gross), detail:			
Discretionary:			
42.00 Transferred from other accounts		18	
43.00 Appropriation (total discretionary)		18	
Change in unpaid obligations:			
73.10 Total new obligations		18	
73.20 Total outlays (gross)		−18	
Outlays (gross), detail:			
86.90 Outlays from new discretionary authority		18	
Net budget authority and outlays:			
89.00 Budget authority		18	
90.00 Outlays		18	

The supplemental request includes a general provision in the Department of Defense that would transfer funding from the Department of Defense to the Coast Guard to ensure that the Coast Guard has the ability to finance the health care that their beneficiaries obtain through the Department of Defense TRICARE system. The costs of medical care provided through the TRICARE system and military treatment facilities have increased significantly in the past few years. The Coast Guard did not have sufficient information to budget for these increased costs in their 2000 Budget.

FEDERAL AVIATION ADMINISTRATION

Grants-in-Aid for Airports

(LIQUIDATION OF CONTRACT AUTHORIZATION)

(AIRPORT AND AIRWAY TRUST FUND)

(Supplemental now requested, existing legislation)

Public Law 106–69 is amended under this heading as follows:

(1) by reducing the obligation limitation to $1,845,638,000;

(2) by inserting before the current final proviso: "Provided further, That any funds thus obligated for administration may, after reauthorization, be reimbursed from funds limited under this heading:"; and

(3) by inserting before the period at the end thereof: ": Provided further, That not more than $12,858,000 of funds limited under this heading shall be available for obligation and expenditure for the Essential Air Service program under subchapter II of chapter 417 of title 49, United States Code, in satisfaction of section 41742(a) of such subchapter.".

Program and Financing (in millions of dollars)

Identification code 69–8106–1–7–402	1999 actual	2000 est.	2001 est.
Obligations by program activity:			
00.01 Grants-in-aid for airports		−63	
00.02 Essential air service		13	
10.00 Total new obligations (object class 41.0)		−50	
Budgetary resources available for obligation:			
21.40 Unobligated balance available, start of year			50
23.95 Total new obligations		50	
24.40 Unobligated balance available, end of year		50	50
Change in unpaid obligations:			
72.40 Unpaid obligations, start of year: Obligated balance, start of year			−50
73.10 Total new obligations		−50	
73.20 Total outlays (gross)		−2	26
74.40 Unpaid obligations, end of year: Obligated balance, end of year		−50	−24
Outlays (gross), detail:			
86.90 Outlays from new discretionary authority		2	−7
86.93 Outlays from discretionary balances			−19
87.00 Total outlays (gross)		2	−26
Net budget authority and outlays:			
89.00 Budget authority			
90.00 Outlays		2	−26

This supplemental request would permit the FAA to meet better the current demands of air traffic, address increasing delays, and continue high levels of safety and security. Specifically, these funds will be used for critical activities such as contracted service programs, operational contracts, telecommunications, and support of the national airspace system modernization.

Operations

(AIRPORT AND AIRWAY TRUST FUND)

(INCLUDING TRANSFER OF FUNDS)

(Supplemental now requested, existing legislation)

In fiscal year 2000, the Secretary of Transportation may transfer to "Operations" any unobligated balances available to the Department of Transportation: Provided, That such transfers shall not be made until fifteen days after written notification to the House and Senate Committees on Appropriations: Provided further, That such transfers may be derived only from those accounts for which the outlay rate equals or exceeds that of "Operations."

Program and Financing (in millions of dollars)

Identification code 69–8104–1–7–402	1999 actual	2000 est.	2001 est.
Obligations by program activity:			
00.01 Air traffic services		13	
00.02 Essential air service		–13	
10.00 Total new obligations			
Change in unpaid obligations:			
73.10 Total new obligations			
73.20 Total outlays (gross)		2	–2
Outlays (gross), detail:			
86.90 Outlays from new discretionary authority		–2	2
Net budget authority and outlays:			
89.00 Budget authority			
90.00 Outlays		–2	2

This supplemental request would permit the FAA to meet better the current demands of air traffic, address increasing delays, and continue high levels of safety and security. Specifically, these funds will be used for critical activities such as contracted service programs, operational contracts, telecommunications, and support of the national airspace system modernization.

Object Classification (in millions of dollars)

Identification code 69–8104–1–7–402	1999 actual	2000 est.	2001 est.
21.0 Travel and transportation of persons		4	
25.2 Other services		9	
41.0 Grants, subsidies, and contributions		–13	
99.9 Total new obligations			

Department of the Treasury

FINANCIAL MANAGEMENT SERVICE

Biomass Energy Development

(Supplemental now requested, existing legislation)

Program and Financing (in millions of dollars)

Identification code 20–0114–1–1–271	1999 actual	2000 est.	2001 est.
Budgetary resources available for obligation:			
21.40 Unobligated balance available, start of year			–4
22.00 New budget authority (gross)		–4	
23.90 Total budgetary resources available for obligation		–4	–4
23.95 Total new obligations			
24.40 Unobligated balance available, end of year		–4	–4
New budget authority (gross), detail:			
Discretionary:			
41.00 Transferred to other accounts		–4	
Net budget authority and outlays:			
89.00 Budget authority		–4	
90.00 Outlays			

This supplemental request would transfer $4 million of balances to "Other defense activities" in the Department of Energy.

INTERNAL REVENUE SERVICE,

Processing, Assistance and Management

(Supplemental now requested, existing legislation)

For an additional amount for "Processing, assistance and management," $19,796,000.

Program and Financing (in millions of dollars)

Identification code 20–0912–1–1–803	1999 actual	2000 est.	2001 est.
Obligations by program activity:			
Direct program:			
00.01 Submission processing		5	
00.02 Telephone and correspondence		12	
00.03 Document matching		3	
10.00 Total new obligations		20	
Budgetary resources available for obligation:			
22.00 New budget authority (gross)		20	
23.95 Total new obligations		–20	
New budget authority (gross), detail:			
Discretionary:			
40.00 Appropriation		20	
Change in unpaid obligations:			
72.40 Unpaid obligations, start of year: Obligated balance, start of year			2
73.10 Total new obligations		20	
73.20 Total outlays (gross)		–18	
74.40 Unpaid obligations, end of year: Obligated balance, end of year		2	
Outlays (gross), detail:			
86.90 Outlays from new discretionary authority		18	
86.93 Outlays from discretionary balances			2
87.00 Total outlays (gross)		18	
Net budget authority and outlays:			
89.00 Budget authority		20	
90.00 Outlays		18	

This supplemental request would provide increased staffing to address falling compliance enforcement and customer service activities. This request is part of a $40 million proposal by the Internal Revenue Service to begin immediate implementation of the Staffing Tax Administration for Balance and Equity (STABLE) initiative proposed for 2001. Early implementation is needed to permit improvements in customer service and compliance performance as soon as possible.

Object Classification (in millions of dollars)

Identification code 20–0912–1–1–803	1999 actual	2000 est.	2001 est.
Personnel compensation:			
11.1 Full-time permanent		6	
11.3 Other than full-time permanent		3	
11.9 Total personnel compensation		9	
12.1 Civilian personnel benefits		3	
21.0 Travel and transportation of persons		1	
25.1 Advisory and assistance services		2	
26.0 Supplies and materials		1	
31.0 Equipment		4	
99.9 Total new obligations		20	

Personnel Summary

Identification code 20–0912–1–1–803	1999 actual	2000 est.	2001 est.
1001 Total compensable workyears: Full-time equivalent employment		238	

TAX LAW ENFORCEMENT

(Supplemental now requested, existing legislation)

For an additional amount for "Tax law enforcement," $6,807,000.

Program and Financing (in millions of dollars)

Identification code 20–0913–1–1–999	1999 actual	2000 est.	2001 est.
Obligations by program activity:			
Direct program:			
00.02 Examination		1	
00.03 Collection		5	
00.04 Tax exempt and government entities		1	
10.00 Total new obligations		7	
Budgetary resources available for obligation:			
22.00 New budget authority (gross)		7	
23.95 Total new obligations		−7	
New budget authority (gross), detail:			
Discretionary:			
40.00 Appropriation		7	
Change in unpaid obligations:			
73.10 Total new obligations		7	
73.20 Total outlays (gross)		−7	
Outlays (gross), detail:			
86.90 Outlays from new discretionary authority		7	
Net budget authority and outlays:			
89.00 Budget authority		7	
90.00 Outlays		7	

This supplemental request would provide increased staffing to address falling compliance enforcement and customer service activities. This request is part of a $40 million proposal by the Internal Revenue Service to begin immediate implementation of the Staffing Tax Administration for Balance and Equity (STABLE) initiative proposed for 2001. Early implementation is needed to permit improvements in customer service and compliance performance as soon as possible.

Object Classification (in millions of dollars)

Identification code 20–0913–1–1–999	1999 actual	2000 est.	2001 est.
11.1 Personnel compensation: Full-time permanent		2	
12.1 Civilian personnel benefits		1	
21.0 Travel and transportation of persons		1	
25.2 Other services		2	
31.0 Equipment		1	
99.9 Total new obligations		7	

Personnel Summary

Identification code 20–0913–1–1–999	1999 actual	2000 est.	2001 est.
1001 Total compensable workyears: Full-time equivalent employment		63	

INFORMATION SYSTEMS

(Supplemental now requested, existing legislation)

For an additional amount for "Information systems," $13,180,000, to remain available until September 30, 2002.

Program and Financing (in millions of dollars)

Identification code 20–0919–1–1–803	1999 actual	2000 est.	2001 est.
Obligations by program activity:			
Direct program:			
00.01 Operational information systems		13	
10.00 Total new obligations		13	
Budgetary resources available for obligation:			
22.00 New budget authority (gross)		13	
23.95 Total new obligations		−13	
New budget authority (gross), detail:			
Discretionary:			
40.00 Appropriation		13	
Change in unpaid obligations:			
72.40 Unpaid obligations, start of year: Obligated balance, start of year			4
73.10 Total new obligations		13	
73.20 Total outlays (gross)		−9	
74.40 Unpaid obligations, end of year: Obligated balance, end of year		4	2
Outlays (gross), detail:			
86.90 Outlays from new discretionary authority		9	
86.93 Outlays from discretionary balances			2
87.00 Total outlays (gross)		9	
Net budget authority and outlays:			
89.00 Budget authority		13	
90.00 Outlays		9	

This supplemental request would provide increased staffing to address falling compliance enforcement and customer service activities. This request is part of a $40 million proposal by the Internal Revenue Service to begin immediate implementation of the Staffing Tax Administration for Balance and Equity (STABLE) initiative proposed for 2001. Early implementation is needed to permit improvements in customer service and compliance performance as soon as possible.

Object Classification (in millions of dollars)

Identification code 20–0919–1–1–803	1999 actual	2000 est.	2001 est.
23.3 Communications, utilities, and miscellaneous charges		8	
31.0 Equipment		5	
99.9 Total new obligations		13	

Department of Defense—Civil

Department of the Army

CORPS OF ENGINEERS—CIVIL

GENERAL INVESTIGATIONS

(Supplemental now requested, existing legislation)

For an additional amount for "General investigations" to complete preconstruction engineering and design of an emergency outlet from Devils Lake, North Dakota, to the Sheyenne River, $6,600,000, to remain available until expended: Provided, That the work shall include an Environmental Impact Statement and the international coordination required to comply with the Boundary Waters Treaty of 1909: Provided further, That the funds may be used to restore funding to studies from which funds were reprogrammed to respond to the urgent requirements at Devils Lake: Provided further, That the entire amount is designated by the Congress as an emergency requirement pursuant to section 251(b)(2)(A) of the Balanced Budget and Emergency Deficit Control Act of 1985, as amended.

Program and Financing (in millions of dollars)

Identification code 96–3121–1–1–301	1999 actual	2000 est.	2001 est.
Obligations by program activity:			
Direct program:			
Surveys and planning:			
00.01 Navigation, flood damage prevention, and shoreline protection studies		7	
10.00 Total new obligations (object class 25.3)		7	
Budgetary resources available for obligation:			
22.00 New budget authority (gross)		7	
23.95 Total new obligations		−7	

GENERAL INVESTIGATIONS—Continued

Program and Financing (in millions of dollars)—Continued

Identification code 96–3121–1–1–301	1999 actual	2000 est.	2001 est.
New budget authority (gross), detail:			
Discretionary:			
40.15 Appropriation (emergency)		7	
Change in unpaid obligations:			
73.10 Total new obligations		7	
73.20 Total outlays (gross)		–7	
Outlays (gross), detail:			
86.90 Outlays from new discretionary authority		7	
Net budget authority and outlays:			
89.00 Budget authority		7	
90.00 Outlays		7	

This supplemental request would provide funding to complete preconstruction engineering and design, including the associated Environmental Impact Statement and international coordination to ensure compliance with the Boundary Waters Treaty of 1909, for an emergency outlet from Devils Lake, North Dakota, to the Sheyenne River. It will also permit restoration of funding to studies that were used as sources for reprogramming funds to continue the Devils Lake planning on an expedited basis.

The entire amount requested has been designated by the President as an emergency requirement pursuant to the Balanced Budget and Emergency Deficit Control Act of 1985, as amended.

OPERATION AND MAINTENANCE, GENERAL

(Supplemental now requested, existing legislation)

For an additional amount for emergency repairs and dredging due to hurricane damages, $19,175,000, to remain available until expended, of which such amounts for eligible navigation projects which may be derived from the Harbor Maintenance Trust Fund pursuant to Public Law 99–662, shall be derived from that Fund: Provided, That the entire amount is designated by the Congress as an emergency requirement pursuant to section 251(b)(2)(A) of the Balanced Budget and Emergency Deficit Control Act of 1985, as amended.

Program and Financing (in millions of dollars)

Identification code 96–3123–1–1–300	1999 actual	2000 est.	2001 est.
Obligations by program activity:			
10.00 Total new obligations (object class 25.3)		19	
Budgetary resources available for obligation:			
22.00 New budget authority (gross)		19	
23.95 Total new obligations		–19	
New budget authority (gross), detail:			
Discretionary:			
40.15 Appropriation (emergency)		19	
Change in unpaid obligations:			
73.10 Total new obligations		19	
73.20 Total outlays (gross)		–19	
Outlays (gross), detail:			
86.90 Outlays from new discretionary authority		19	
Net budget authority and outlays:			
89.00 Budget authority		19	
90.00 Outlays		19	

This supplemental request would provide funds to complete repairs of damages caused primarily by the high seas and flooding during Hurricane Floyd in Atlantic Seaboard states including Delaware, Maryland, North Carolina, South Carolina, and Virginia, to navigation channels and harbors, including dredging, disposal areas, snagging, drift and debris removal and scour protection.

The entire amount requested has been designated by the President as an emergency requirement pursuant to the Balanced Budget and Emergency Deficit Control Act of 1985, as amended.

Executive Office of the President

UNANTICIPATED NEEDS

INFORMATION TECHNOLOGY SYSTEMS AND RELATED EXPENSES

(Supplemental now requested, existing legislation)

Under this heading in division B, title III, chapter 5 of Public Law 105–277 strike "$2,250,000,000" and insert "$2,025,000,000."

Program and Financing (in millions of dollars)

Identification code 11–1237–1–1–808	1999 actual	2000 est.	2001 est.
Budgetary resources available for obligation:			
23.95 Total new obligations			
New budget authority (gross), detail:			
Discretionary:			
40.15 Appropriation (emergency)		–225	
40.60 Contingent emergency appropriation not available for obligations		225	
43.00 Appropriation (total discretionary)			
Net budget authority and outlays:			
89.00 Budget authority			
90.00 Outlays			

This supplemental request would reduce funding made available by the Omnibus Consolidated and Emergency Supplemental Appropriations Act to address requirements associated with year 2000 (Y2K) computer conversion. Unused funds are no longer needed.

For more information on this account, see the Executive Office of the President chapter of this volume.

Federal Emergency Management Agency

DISASTER RELIEF

(Supplemental now requested, existing legislation)

Under this heading in the Miscellaneous Appropriations Act, 2000, as enacted by section 1000(a)(5) of the Consolidated Appropriations Act, 2000 (P.L. 106–113), delete "$215,000,000" and insert, "$292,400,000".

This supplemental request would permit an additional $77.4 million in contingent emergency funds appropriated to the Federal Emergency Management Agency to be used for home buyouts and relocation assistance for flood victims of Hurricane Floyd in North Carolina and other affected states. There would be no increase in outlays.

The entire amount requested for 2000 has been designated by the President as an emergency requirement pursuant to the Balanced Budget and Emergency Deficit Control Act of 1985, as amended.

General Services Administration

POLICY AND OPERATIONS

(Supplemental now requested, existing legislation)

For an additional amount for "Policy and operations", $2,000,000, to remain available until expended.

Program and Financing (in millions of dollars)

Identification code 47–0110–1–1–804	1999 actual	2000 est.	2001 est.
Obligations by program activity:			
10.00 Total new obligations (object class 25.2)		2	
Budgetary resources available for obligation:			
22.00 New budget authority (gross)		2	
23.95 Total new obligations		−2	
New budget authority (gross), detail:			
Discretionary:			
40.00 Appropriation		2	
Change in unpaid obligations:			
73.10 Total new obligations		2	
73.20 Total outlays (gross)		−2	
Outlays (gross), detail:			
86.90 Outlays from new discretionary authority		2	
Net budget authority and outlays:			
89.00 Budget authority		2	
90.00 Outlays		2	

This supplemental request would provide funds to accelerate and expand the design and development of a key component of the President's Critical Infrastructure Protection initiative, the Federal Computer Incident Response Capability (FedCIRC) Program. These funds will provide computer security incident identification, containment and recovery services to all civilian agencies and departments. The FedCIRC Program serves as a central point to Federal civilian agencies to respond to incidents and to share information system vulnerability data.

International Assistance Programs

INTERNATIONAL SECURITY ASSISTANCE

Foreign Military Financing Program

(Supplemental now requested, existing legislation.)

For an additional amount for "Foreign military financing program" to enable the President to carry out section 23 of the Arms Export Control Act, $31,000,000, to remain available until September 30, 2001, for grants to countries of the Balkans and southeast Europe: Provided, That these funds shall be nonrepayable, notwithstanding sections 23(b) and 23(c) of the Act: Provided further, That the entire amount is designated by Congress as an emergency requirement pursuant to section 251(b)(2)(A) of the Balanced Budget and Emergency Deficit Control Act of 1985, as amended.

Program and Financing (in millions of dollars)

Identification code 11–1082–1–1–152	1999 actual	2000 est.	2001 est.
Obligations by program activity:			
10.00 Total new obligations (object class 41.0)		31	
Budgetary resources available for obligation:			
22.00 New budget authority (gross)		31	
23.95 Total new obligations		−31	
New budget authority (gross), detail:			
Discretionary:			
40.15 Appropriation (emergency)		31	
Change in unpaid obligations:			
72.40 Unpaid obligations, start of year: Obligated balance, start of year			29
73.10 Total new obligations		31	
73.20 Total outlays (gross)		−2	−9
74.40 Unpaid obligations, end of year: Obligated balance, end of year		29	20
Outlays (gross), detail:			
86.90 Outlays from new discretionary authority		2	
86.93 Outlays from discretionary balances			9
87.00 Total outlays (gross)		2	9
Net budget authority and outlays:			
89.00 Budget authority		31	
90.00 Outlays		2	9

These funds are being requested in conjunction with the implementation of the Kosovo settlement accords and for strengthening NATO ties with Balkan countries and countries of southeast Europe.

The entire amount requested has been designated by the President as an emergency requirement pursuant to the Balanced Budget and Emergency Deficit Control Act of 1985, as amended.

International Military Education and Training

(Supplemental now requested, existing legislation)

For an additional amount for "International military education and training," $2,875,000, to remain available until September 30, 2001, for grants to countries of the Balkans and southeast Europe: Provided, That the entire amount is designated by Congress as an emergency requirement pursuant to section 251(b)(2)(A) of the Balanced Budget and Emergency Deficit Control Act of 1985, as amended.

Program and Financing (in millions of dollars)

Identification code 11–1081–1–1–152	1999 actual	2000 est.	2001 est.
Obligations by program activity:			
10.00 Total new obligations (object class 41.0)		3	
Budgetary resources available for obligation:			
22.00 New budget authority (gross)		3	
23.95 Total new obligations		−3	
New budget authority (gross), detail:			
Discretionary:			
40.15 Appropriation (emergency)		3	
Change in unpaid obligations:			
72.40 Unpaid obligations, start of year: Obligated balance, start of year			1
73.10 Total new obligations		3	
73.20 Total outlays (gross)		−2	−1
74.40 Unpaid obligations, end of year: Obligated balance, end of year		1	
Outlays (gross), detail:			
86.90 Outlays from new discretionary authority		2	
86.93 Outlays from discretionary balances			1
87.00 Total outlays (gross)		2	1
Net budget authority and outlays:			
89.00 Budget authority		3	
90.00 Outlays		2	1

These funds are being requested to increase assistance to southeast European countries to promote professionalization of the military, including enhancement of self-defense capabilities, inter-operability, and improved civilian-military relationships to solidify democratic reform efforts.

The entire amount requested has been designated by the President as an emergency requirement pursuant to the Balanced Budget and Emergency Deficit Control Act of 1985, as amended.

MULTILATERAL ASSISTANCE

Debt Restructuring

(Supplemental now requested, existing legislation)

For an additional amount for "Debt restructuring," $210,000,000 for a contribution to the "Heavily Indebted Poor Countries Trust

186-484 00 - 40

DEBT RESTRUCTURING—Continued

Fund" of the International Bank for Reconstruction and Development (HIPC Trust Fund). There are authorized to be appropriated to the President in fiscal years 2000 through 2003, $600,000,000 for contributions to the HIPC Trust Fund, to remain available until expended.

Section 62 of the Bretton Woods Agreements Act (22 U.S.C. 286 et seq.) is amended:

(1) by inserting "and" at the end of paragraph (1)(B); and

(2) by striking paragraph (1)(D).

Program and Financing (in millions of dollars)

Identification code 11–0091–1–1–151	1999 actual	2000 est.	2001 est.
Obligations by program activity:			
01.02 Heavily Indebted Poor Countries trust fund		210	
10.00 Total new obligations (object class 41.0)		210	
Budgetary resources available for obligation:			
22.00 New budget authority (gross)		210	
23.95 Total new obligations		−210	
New budget authority (gross), detail:			
Discretionary:			
40.00 Appropriation		210	
Change in unpaid obligations:			
72.40 Unpaid obligations, start of year: Obligated balance, start of year			157
73.10 Total new obligations		210	
73.20 Total outlays (gross)		−53	−105
74.40 Unpaid obligations, end of year: Obligated balance, end of year		157	52
Outlays (gross), detail:			
86.90 Outlays from new discretionary authority		53	
86.93 Outlays from discretionary balances			105
87.00 Total outlays (gross)		53	105
Net budget authority and outlays:			
89.00 Budget authority		210	
90.00 Outlays		53	105

This proposed supplemental would provide funds for a U.S. contribution to the Heavily Indebted Poor Countries Trust Fund of the International Bank for Reconstruction and Development (HIPC Trust Fund) to support the participation of the International Financial Institutions in the enhanced HIPC initiative. The 2000 appropriation includes $110 million for bilateral debt forgiveness, but fails to provide authorization or appropriation for the U.S. contribution to the HIPC trust fund. This supplemental would also authorize the appropriation of $600,000,000 for U.S. contributions to the HIPC Trust Fund in 2000 through 2003, and, by removing the limitation provided for in paragraph (1)(D) of section 62 of the Bretton Woods Agreements Act, would authorize the Secretary of the Treasury to instruct the United States Executive Director of the International Monetary Fund to vote to approve the use of the full amount of the earnings on the investment of the profits of gold sales by the International Monetary Fund for the purpose of providing debt relief under the modified HIPC Initiative.

AGENCY FOR INTERNATIONAL DEVELOPMENT

ASSISTANCE FOR EASTERN EUROPE AND THE BALTIC STATES

(Supplemental now requested, existing legislation)

For an additional amount for "Assistance for Eastern Europe and the Baltic States," $195,000,000, to remain available until September 30, 2001: Provided, That the entire amount is designated by the Congress as an emergency requirement pursuant to section 251(b)(2)(A) of the Balanced Budget and Emergency Deficit Control Act of 1985, as amended.

Program and Financing (in millions of dollars)

Identification code 72–1010–1–1–151	1999 actual	2000 est.	2001 est.
Obligations by program activity:			
10.00 Total new obligations (object class 41.0)		145	50
Budgetary resources available for obligation:			
21.40 Unobligated balance available, start of year			50
22.00 New budget authority (gross)		195	
23.90 Total budgetary resources available for obligation		195	50
23.95 Total new obligations		−145	−50
24.40 Unobligated balance available, end of year		50	
New budget authority (gross), detail:			
Discretionary:			
40.15 Appropriation (emergency)		195	
Change in unpaid obligations:			
72.40 Unpaid obligations, start of year: Obligated balance, start of year			125
73.10 Total new obligations		145	50
73.20 Total outlays (gross)		−20	−64
74.40 Unpaid obligations, end of year: Obligated balance, end of year		125	111
Outlays (gross), detail:			
86.90 Outlays from new discretionary authority		20	
86.93 Outlays from discretionary balances			64
87.00 Total outlays (gross)		20	64
Net budget authority and outlays:			
89.00 Budget authority		195	
90.00 Outlays		20	64

These funds are necessary to continue fostering a peaceful transition in the Balkans toward a market-oriented, democratic future. Supplemental funds are intended for a still-fragile Kosovo, where unforeseen problems with UNMIK's operations have arisen, and to address unforseen circumstances elsewhere in the region—the electoral defeat of the Nationalist government opens the prospect of a new pro-reform government in Croatia, new pressures on the democratic forces within Montenegro, and new opportunities for U.S. and EU support to the anti-Milosevic opposition in Serbia.

The entire amount requested has been designated by the President as an emergency requirement pursuant to the Balanced Budget and Emergency Deficit Control Act of 1985, as amended.

OPERATING EXPENSES OF THE AGENCY FOR INTERNATIONAL DEVELOPMENT

(Supplemental now requested, existing legislation)

For an additional amount for "Operating expenses of the Agency for International Development," $22,000,000, to remain available until September 30, 2001: Provided, That the entire amount is designated by Congress as an emergency requirement pursuant to section 251(b)(2)(A) of the Balanced budget and Emergency Deficit Control Act of 1985, as amended.

Program and Financing (in millions of dollars)

Identification code 72–1000–1–1–151	1999 actual	2000 est.	2001 est.
Obligations by program activity:			
10.00 Total new obligations		17	5
Budgetary resources available for obligation:			
21.40 Unobligated balance available, start of year			5
22.00 New budget authority (gross)		22	
23.90 Total budgetary resources available for obligation		22	5
23.95 Total new obligations		−17	−5
24.40 Unobligated balance available, end of year		5	

	1999 actual	2000 est.	2001 est.
New budget authority (gross), detail:			
Discretionary:			
40.15 Appropriation (emergency)		22	
Change in unpaid obligations:			
72.40 Unpaid obligations, start of year: Obligated balance, start of year			3
73.10 Total new obligations		17	5
73.20 Total outlays (gross)		−14	−4
74.40 Unpaid obligations, end of year: Obligated balance, end of year		3	4
Outlays (gross), detail:			
86.90 Outlays from new discretionary authority		14	
86.93 Outlays from discretionary balances			4
87.00 Total outlays (gross)		14	4
Net budget authority and outlays:			
89.00 Budget authority		22	
90.00 Outlays		14	4

These funds are requested in order to insure safe, secure facilities and adequate support, oversight, and management, for unforseen program requirements in the Balkans as part of an overall package of assistance for that region. Funding will cover costs of additional personnel and expanded facilities and the associated security costs to insure maximum accountability for USAID programs in a region beset by multiple crises.

The entire amount requested for 2000 has been designated by the President as an emergency requirement pursuant to the Balanced Budget and Emergency Deficit Control Act of 1985, as amended.

Object Classification (in millions of dollars)

Identification code 72–1000–1–1–151	1999 actual	2000 est.	2001 est.
11.8 Personnel compensation: Special personal services payments		1	1
12.1 Civilian personnel benefits		1	1
22.0 Transportation of things		1	
23.2 Rental payments to others		3	1
25.3 Purchases of goods and services from Government accounts		1	1
31.0 Equipment		3	
32.0 Land and structures		6	1
99.0 Subtotal, direct obligations		16	5
99.5 Below reporting threshold		1	
99.9 Total new obligations		17	5

National Aeronautics and Space Administration

Human Space Flight

(Supplemental now requested, existing legislation)

The last proviso under this heading in Public Law 106–74 is repealed: Provided, That from amounts provided in such Act, $20,200,000 shall be transferred to "Mission support."

Program and Financing (in millions of dollars)

Identification code 80–0111–1–1–252	1999 actual	2000 est.	2001 est.
Obligations by program activity:			
10.00 Total new obligations (object class 25.5)		−20	
Budgetary resources available for obligation:			
22.00 New budget authority (gross)		−20	
23.95 Total new obligations		20	
New budget authority (gross), detail:			
Discretionary:			
41.00 Transferred to other accounts		−20	
Change in unpaid obligations:			
72.40 Unpaid obligations, start of year: Obligated balance, start of year			−7
73.10 Total new obligations		−20	
73.20 Total outlays (gross)		13	6
74.40 Unpaid obligations, end of year: Obligated balance, end of year		−7	−1
Outlays (gross), detail:			
86.90 Outlays from new discretionary authority		−13	
86.93 Outlays from discretionary balances			−6
87.00 Total outlays (gross)		−13	−6
Net budget authority and outlays:			
89.00 Budget authority		−20	
90.00 Outlays		−13	−6

This supplemental request would repeal a requirement for an additional unfunded space shuttle research mission in 2001 and the partial funding provided for the mission. The funds would then be used for space shuttle safety investments. These investments include $20 million for safety upgrades and $20 million for personnel needs in Mission support.

Mission Support

(Supplemental now requested, existing legislation)

Program and Financing (in millions of dollars)

Identification code 80–0112–1–1–999	1999 actual	2000 est.	2001 est.
Obligations by program activity:			
10.00 Total new obligations		20	
Budgetary resources available for obligation:			
22.00 New budget authority (gross)		20	
23.95 Total new obligations		−20	
New budget authority (gross), detail:			
Discretionary:			
42.00 Transferred from other accounts		20	
Change in unpaid obligations:			
72.40 Unpaid obligations, start of year: Obligated balance, start of year			4
73.10 Total new obligations		20	
73.20 Total outlays (gross)		−16	−4
74.40 Unpaid obligations, end of year: Obligated balance, end of year		4	
Outlays (gross), detail:			
86.90 Outlays from new discretionary authority		16	
86.93 Outlays from discretionary balances			3
87.00 Total outlays (gross)		16	4
Net budget authority and outlays:			
89.00 Budget authority		20	
90.00 Outlays		16	4

This supplemental request would fund additional personnel at Human Space Flight field centers who will address capacity and safety concerns for space shuttle operations.

Object Classification (in millions of dollars)

Identification code 80–0112–1–1–999	1999 actual	2000 est.	2001 est.
11.1 Personnel compensation: Full-time permanent		15	
12.1 Civilian personnel benefits		5	
99.9 Total new obligations		20	

Personnel Summary

Identification code 80–0112–1–1–999	1999 actual	2000 est.	2001 est.
1001 Total compensable workyears: Full-time equivalent employment		282	

ASSISTANCE FOR EASTERN EUROPE AND THE BALTIC STATES—Continued

National Science Foundation

EDUCATION AND HUMAN RESOURCES

(Supplemental now requested, existing legislation)

For an additional amount for "Education and human resources," $1,000,000.

Program and Financing (in millions of dollars)

Identification code 49–0106–1–1–251	1999 actual	2000 est.	2001 est.
Obligations by program activity:			
Obligations by progam activity:			
Direct program:			
Appropriated activities:			
00.01 Federal cyber service [scholarships for service]	....	1	....
10.00 Total new obligations (object class 41.0)	....	1	....
Budgetary resources available for obligation:			
22.00 New budget authority (gross)	....	1	....
23.95 Total new obligations	....	−1	....
New budget authority (gross), detail:			
Discretionary:			
40.00 Appropriation	....	1	....
Change in unpaid obligations:			
73.10 Total new obligations	....	1	....
73.20 Total outlays (gross)	....	....	....
Net budget authority and outlays:			
89.00 Budget authority	....	1	....
90.00 Outlays	....	....	....

This supplemental request would provide additional funds to accelerate and expand the design and development of a key component of the President's Critical Infrastructure Protection initiative, the Federal Cyber Services Program. The additional funding will help agencies meet a critical need for highly trained information security personnel.

Office of Personnel Management

SALARIES AND EXPENSES

(Supplemental now requested, existing legislation)

For an additional amount for "Salaries and expenses," $1,000,000.

Program and Financing (in millions of dollars)

Identification code 24–0100–1–1–805	1999 actual	2000 est.	2001 est.
Obligations by program activity:			
Direct program:			
00.01 Employment service—Federal cyber service	....	1	....
10.00 Total new obligations (object class 25.2)	....	1	....
Budgetary resources available for obligation:			
22.00 New budget authority (gross)	....	1	....
23.95 Total new obligations	....	−1	....
New budget authority (gross), detail:			
Discretionary:			
40.00 Appropriation	....	1	....
Change in unpaid obligations:			
73.10 Total new obligations	....	1	....
73.20 Total outlays (gross)	....	−1	....
Outlays (gross), detail:			
86.90 Outlays from new discretionary authority	....	1	....
Net budget authority and outlays:			
89.00 Budget authority	....	1	....
90.00 Outlays	....	1	....

This supplemental request would provide additional funds to accelerate and expand the design and development of a key component of the President's Critical Infrastructure Protection initiative, the Federal Cyber Services Program. The additional funding will help agencies meet a critical need for highly trained information security personnel.

Small Business Administration

DISASTER LOANS PROGRAM ACCOUNT

(Supplemental now requested, existing legislation)

For an additional amount for "Disaster loans program account" for the cost of direct loans, $31,000,000, to remain available until expended: Provided, That such costs, including the cost of modifying such loans, shall be as defined in section 502 of the Congressional Budget Act of 1974; and for administrative expenses to carry out the disaster loans program, an additional $19,500,000, to remain available until expended, which may be transferred to and merged with "Salaries and expenses": Provided, That the entire amount is designated by the Congress as an emergency requirement pursuant to section 251(b)(2)(A) of the Balanced Budget and Emergency Deficit Control Act of 1985, as amended: Provided further, That the entire amount shall be available only to the extent that an official budget request, that includes designation of the entire amount of the request as an emergency requirement as defined in the Balanced Budget and Emergency Deficit Control Act of 1985, as amended, is transmitted by the President to the Congress.

Program and Financing (in millions of dollars)

Identification code 73–1152–1–1–453	1999 actual	2000 est.	2001 est.
Budgetary resources available for obligation:			
21.40 Unobligated balance available, start of year	....	....	50
22.00 New budget authority (gross)	....	50	....
23.90 Total budgetary resources available for obligation	....	50	50
23.95 Total new obligations	....	....	....
24.40 Unobligated balance available, end of year	....	50	50
New budget authority (gross), detail:			
Discretionary:			
40.15 Appropriation (emergency)	....	50	....
Net budget authority and outlays:			
89.00 Budget authority	....	50	....
90.00 Outlays	....	....	....

This supplemental request would allow this program to continue to provide assistance to victims of Hurricane Floyd in Delaware, Florida, Maryland, Connecticut, New Hampshire, Vermont, Maine, South Carolina, North Carolina, Virginia, Pennsylvania, New York, and New Jersey. Funds would also be used for requirements resulting from previously declared disasters and from anticipated disaster activity for the remainder of the year. Funding is required for both administrative and loan subsidy expenses.

Other Independent Agencies

COMMISSION ON CIVIL RIGHTS

SALARIES AND EXPENSES

(Supplemental now requested, existing legislation)

For an additional amount for "Salaries and expenses," $800,000.

Program and Financing (in millions of dollars)

Identification code 95–1900–1–1–751	1999 actual	2000 est.	2001 est.
Obligations by program activity:			
10.00 Total new obligations (object class 25.2)	....	1	....

		1999 actual	2000 est.	2001 est.
	Budgetary resources available for obligation:			
22.00	New budget authority (gross)		1	
23.95	Total new obligations		−1	
	New budget authority (gross), detail:			
	Discretionary:			
40.00	Appropriation		1	
	Change in unpaid obligations:			
73.10	Total new obligations		1	
73.20	Total outlays (gross)			
	Net budget authority and outlays:			
89.00	Budget authority		1	
90.00	Outlays			

This supplemental request would fund completion of a number of civil rights research projects scheduled for completion in 2000, including fact-finding, completing, printing, and distributing reports on: racial tensions, enforcement of the Americans with Disabilities Act, crisis of African-American men in inner cities, and fair employment law.

COMMITTEE FOR THE PURCHASE FROM PEOPLE WHO ARE BLIND OR SEVERELY DISABLED

Salaries and Expenses

(Supplemental now requested, existing legislation)

For an additional amount for "Salaries and expenses," $687,000.

Program and Financing (in millions of dollars)

Identification code 95–2000–1–1–505		1999 actual	2000 est.	2001 est.
	Obligations by program activity:			
10.00	Total new obligations (object class 99.5)		1	
	Budgetary resources available for obligation:			
22.00	New budget authority (gross)		1	
23.95	Total new obligations		−1	
	New budget authority (gross), detail:			
	Discretionary:			
40.00	Appropriation		1	
	Change in unpaid obligations:			
73.10	Total new obligations		1	
73.20	Total outlays (gross)		−1	
	Outlays (gross), detail:			
86.90	Outlays from new discretionary authority		1	
	Net budget authority and outlays:			
89.00	Budget authority		1	
90.00	Outlays		1	

This supplemental request would finance substantially expanded marketing of Javits-Wagner-O'Day (JWOD) products to Federal employees as a result of fundamental shifts in Federal acquisition of commercial-type products, such as office supplies, cleaning materials, and medical items. Such products are increasingly bought by Federal purchase cardholders who have not been sufficiently informed about the JWOD program to realize that they are required by law to buy JWOD products. The primary objective of the JWOD Act is to use the purchasing power of the Federal Government to provide employment and training to approximately 34,000 people with severe disabilities. The need to better educate Federal customers about JWOD products and where to buy them has increased as a result of confusion about the status of the General Services Administration's stock program, which has historically distributed JWOD products.

FEDERAL MARITIME COMMISSION

Salaries and Expenses

(Supplemental now requested, existing legislation)

For an additional amount for "Salaries and Expenses," $490,000.

This supplemental request would provide funding for a Presidentially-appointed fifth Commissioner and staff. It would also provide funding to complete the Congressionally mandated implementation of the Ocean Shipping Reform Act of 1998, which amends the Shipping Act of 1984, and allow the Federal Maritime Commission to identify and initiate necessary rule changes.

NATIONAL TRANSPORTATION SAFETY BOARD

Salaries and Expenses

(Supplemental now requested, existing legislation)

For an additional amount for "Salaries and expenses," $17,596,000, for emergency expenses associated with the investigation of the Egypt Air 990 accident: Provided: That such funds shall be available for wreckage location and recovery, facilities, technical support, testing, wreckage mock-up and local assistance: Provided further, That these funds shall be available only to the extent an official budget request, for a specific dollar amount, that includes designation of the entire amount as an emergency requirement as defined in the Balanced Budget and Emergency Deficit Control Act of 1985, as amended, is transmitted by the President to the Congress: Provided further, That the entire amount is designated by Congress as an emergency requirement pursuant to section 251(b)(2)(A) of the Balanced Budget and Emergency Deficit Control Act of 1985, as amended.

Program and Financing (in millions of dollars)

Identification code 95–0310–1–1–407		1999 actual	2000 est.	2001 est.
	Obligations by program activity:			
00.01	Egypt Air 990 investigation		18	
10.00	Total new obligations		18	
	Budgetary resources available for obligation:			
22.00	New budget authority (gross)		18	
23.95	Total new obligations		−18	
	New budget authority (gross), detail:			
	Discretionary:			
40.15	Appropriation (emergency)		18	
	Change in unpaid obligations:			
72.40	Unpaid obligations, start of year: Obligated balance, start of year			2
73.10	Total new obligations		18	
73.20	Total outlays (gross)		−16	
74.40	Unpaid obligations, end of year: Obligated balance, end of year		2	
	Outlays (gross), detail:			
86.90	Outlays from new discretionary authority		16	
86.93	Outlays from discretionary balances			2
87.00	Total outlays (gross)		16	
	Net budget authority and outlays:			
89.00	Budget authority		18	
90.00	Outlays		16	

This supplemental request provide funds to reimburse the Navy for wreckage location and recovery of Egypt Air 990, as well as for facilities, technical assistance, testing, and local assistance associated with the investigation. The National Transportation Safety Board is an independent, non-regulatory agency charged with promoting transportation safety through the investigation of accidents.

The entire amount requested for 2000 has been designated by the President as an emergency requirement pursuant to

SALARIES AND EXPENSES—Continued

the Balanced Budget and Emergency Deficit Control Act of 1985, as amended.

Object Classification (in millions of dollars)

Identification code 95–0310–1–1–407	1999 actual	2000 est.	2001 est.
21.0 Travel and transportation of persons	....	1	....
25.2 Other services	....	17	....
99.9 Total new obligations	....	18	....

GENERAL PROVISIONS

(Supplemental now requested, existing legislation)

SEC. 101. *Funds appropriated by this supplemental Act, or made available by the transfer of funds herein, for intelligence activities are deemed to be specifically authorized by the Congress for purposes of section 504 of the National Security Act of 1947 (50 U.S.C. 414).*

This provision would provide the authorization required by the National Security Act of 1947 to obligate funds provided in proposed supplemental appropriations for intelligence activities.

SEC. 102. *Notwithstanding 10 U.S.C. 2215, from amounts appropriated in the Department of Defense Appropriations Act, 2000, not to exceed $18,000,000 may be transferred to the Coast Guard to cover costs related to the delivery of health care to Coast Guard personnel and retirees, and their dependents, to be derived as follows: not to exceed $15,000,000 from "Research, development, test and evaluation, Defense-wide", and not to exceed $3,000,000 from "Operation and maintenance, Defense-wide."*

This provision would permit the transfer of funding from the Department of Defense to the Coast Guard to ensure that the Coast Guard has the ability to finance the health care that their beneficiaries obtain through the Department of Defense TRICARE system. The costs of medical care provided through the TRICARE system and military treatment facilities have increased significantly in the past few years. The Coast Guard did not have sufficient information to budget for these increased costs in their 2000 Budget.

SEC. 103. *Authority for the Department of Defense to Provide Additional Support for Counter-drug Activities of Colombia*

(a) Authority to Provide Support—

Using amounts appropriated in this supplemental Act, the Secretary of Defense may provide the support described in subsection (b) for counter-drug activities of the government of Colombia. In addition, using unobligated balances from the Department of Defense Appropriations Act, 1999, the Secretary of Defense may transfer one light observation aircraft to Colombia for counter-drug activities. In providing support to Colombia under this section, the Secretary of Defense shall consult with the Secretary of State. The support provided under this section shall be in addition to support provided to Colombia under any other provision of law.

(b) Types of Support—

The authority under subsection (a) is limited to the following types of support to Colombia:

(1) The types of support specified in paragraphs (1), (2), and (3) of section 1031(b) of the National Defense Authorization Act for Fiscal Year 1997 (Public Law 104-201).

(2) The maintenance, repair, or upgrading of equipment of the government of Colombia that is used for counter-drug activities.

(3) The transfer of nonlethal individual and organizational equipment for two additional Colombian Army air mobile counter-drug battalions, one air mobile counter-drug brigade headquarters, and one Colombian Army counter-drug aviation battalion.

(4) The operating costs of equipment of the government of Colombia that is used for counter-drug activities.

(c) Funding limitation on obligations—

Of the amount authorized to be appropriated under this supplemental Act, an amount not to exceed $30,000,000 shall be available for the provision of support under this section.

(d) Conditions on provision of support—

(1) The Secretary of Defense may not obligate or expend funds appropriated pursuant to this supplemental Act to provide support under this section to Colombia until the end of the 15-day period beginning on the date on which the Secretary submits the written certification for fiscal year 2000, pursuant to section 1033(f)(1) of the National Defense Authorization Act for Fiscal Year 1998 (Public Law 105–85).

(2) The elements of the written certification submitted for fiscal year 2000, described in section 1033(g) of such Act, shall apply to, and the written certification will address, the support provided under this section to Colombia.

This section provides specific authority for the funds appropriated in the supplemental request by reference to existing DoD counterdrug authorities and through specific expansion of authorities consistent with the requirements of Plan Colombia.

SEC. 104. *Section 216 of title II, Department of Health and Human Services Appropriations Act, 2000, as enacted by section 1000(a)(4), division B, of the Consolidated Appropriations Act, 2000 (P.L. 106–113), is repealed.*

This supplemental language would repeal a provision enacted in the Department of Health and Human Services (HHS) Appropriations Act, 2000, that delayed the availability of certain funds provided in the Act until September 29, 2000. The delay would have affected the following HHS programs: the National Institutes of Health; the Health Resources and Services Administration; the Centers for Disease Control and Prevention; the Social Services Block Grant; the Substance Abuse and Mental Health Services Administration; and, Children and Families Services Programs.

SEC. 105. *Sections 8175 and 8176 of title VIII, Department of Defense Appropriations Act, 2000, as amended by section 215, title II, Miscellaneous Appropriations Act, 2000, as enacted by section 1000(a)(5), division B, of the Consolidated Appropriations Act, 2000 (P.L. 106–113), are repealed.*

This supplemental language would repeal provisions in the Department of Defense Appropriations Act, 2000, that would have: (1) extended the payment dates for progress payments made to contractors by five days; and, (2) changed existing prompt payment procedures, in the last month of the fiscal year, to require that payments be made no earlier than one day before the date on which the payment is due.

SEC. 106. *Sections 305 and 306 of title III, Miscellaneous Appropriations Act, 2000, as enacted by section 1000(a)(5), division B, of the Consolidated Appropriations Act, 2000 (P.L. 106–113), are repealed.*

This supplemental language would repeal two provisions enacted in the Miscellaneous Appropriations Act, 2000, that shifted the last pay date in fiscal year 2000 to October 1, 2000, for the military and certain civilian employees.

RESCISSION PROPOSALS

This budget contains proposals to reduce 2000 spending by $168 million. These proposed reductions include $128 million in proposed rescissions detailed below and a proposal to defer $40 million from 2000 to 2003 detailed in the Supplemental Proposals chapter of the Budget.

Under the provisions of the Impoundment Control Act of 1974 (Public Law 93–344), whenever the President proposes a rescission of enacted appropriations, a special message must be sent to the Congress giving details of the proposals. Included below are related budget schedules and narrative explanations of proposals submitted in a special message at the time this budget was transmitted.

Department of Energy

ATOMIC ENERGY DEFENSE ACTIVITIES

Defense Environmental Restoration and Waste Management

(Rescission proposal)

Program and Financing (in millions of dollars)

Identification code 89–0242–5–1–053	1999 actual	2000 est.	2001 est.
Obligations by program activity:			
10.00 Total new obligations (object class 25.4)	....	–13	....
Budgetary resources available for obligation:			
22.00 New budget authority (gross)	....	–13	....
23.95 Total new obligations	....	13	....
New budget authority (gross), detail:			
Discretionary:			
40.36 Unobligated balance rescission proposal (R00–01)	....	–13	....
Change in unpaid obligations:			
72.40 Unpaid obligations, start of year: Obligated balance, start of year	....	....	–4
73.10 Total new obligations	....	–13	....
73.20 Total outlays (gross)	....	9	3
74.40 Unpaid obligations, end of year: Obligated balance, end of year	....	–4	–1
Outlays (gross), detail:			
86.90 Outlays from new discretionary authority	....	–9	....
86.93 Outlays from discretionary balances	....	....	–3
87.00 Total outlays (gross)	....	–9	–3
Net budget authority and outlays:			
89.00 Budget authority	....	–13	....
90.00 Outlays	....	–9	–3

This recission proposal would rescind $13 million appropriated in 2000 for overhead activities supporting research and development at environmental management laboratories that is in excess of current requirements.

ENERGY PROGRAMS

SPR Petroleum Account

(Rescission proposal)

Program and Financing (in millions of dollars)

Identification code 89–0233–5–1–274	1999 actual	2000 est.	2001 est.
Budgetary resources available for obligation:			
21.40 Unobligated balance available, start of year	....	....	–12
22.00 New budget authority (gross)	....	–12	....
23.90 Total budgetary resources available for obligation	....	–12	–12
23.95 Total new obligations	....	....	....
24.40 Unobligated balance available, end of year	....	–12	–12
New budget authority (gross), detail:			
Discretionary:			
40.36 Unobligated balance rescission proposal (R00–02)	....	–12	....
Net budget authority and outlays:			
89.00 Budget authority	....	–12	....
90.00 Outlays	....	....	....

This rescission proposal would rescind $12 million in prior year balances originally appropriated to fund acquisition, transportation, and injection of petroleum into the Strategic Petroleum Reserve and for draw down and distribution of the Reserve. These balances are no longer needed because only de minimus oil acquisition, transportation, and injection is occurring. In the event that draw down and distribution of the Reserve is necessary, authority has been provided to the Department of Energy to transfer balances from other departmental accounts.

Department of Housing and Urban Development

PUBLIC AND INDIAN HOUSING

Housing Certificate Fund

(Rescission proposal)

Program and Financing (in millions of dollars)

Identification code 86–0319–5–1–604	1999 actual	2000 est.	2001 est.
Budgetary resources available for obligation:			
22.00 New budget authority (gross)	....	–103	....
23.95 Total new obligations	....	....	....
New budget authority (gross), detail:			
Discretionary:			
40.36 Unobligated balance rescission proposal (R00–03)	....	–103	....
Net budget authority and outlays:			
89.00 Budget authority	....	–103	....
90.00 Outlays	....	....	....

This rescission proposal would rescind $103 million of obligated balances estimated to be recaptured during 2000. These recaptures will result from the elimination of excess funds available on some long-term section 8 contracts.

AMENDMENTS TO AND REVISIONS IN BUDGET AUTHORITY FOR 2000

(Between the Transmittal of the 2000 and 2001 Budgets)

A statement of all amendments to or revisions in budget authority requested between transmittal of the 2000 Budget and the 2001 Budget is presented below. This statement is being included in the budget in accordance with the Congressional Budget Act of 1974 (31 U.S.C. 1105(d)).

The modifications to requests for 2000 budget authority that were made through the course of the past year took several forms:

- If the Congress had not yet acted on a pending request, the President sent amendments to the budget requests transmitted on February 1, 1999.
- If appropriations had been enacted, the President proposed either supplemental budget authority or rescission of enacted appropriations.
- Finally, the President made available certain emergency appropriations. The availability of these funds was made contingent upon the President submitting a budget request to the Congress and designating the amounts requested as an emergency requirement.

Amendments, requests for supplemental appropriations, and releases of contingent emergency funds are printed in the documents of the House of Representatives that are identified on the following listing. The President's proposals for rescissions are included in special messages to the Congress under the Impoundment Control Act of 1974 (Public Law 93–344). Both the special messages and monthly cumulative reports on the items covered by special messages are printed in the *Federal Register*.

AMENDED AND SUPPLEMENTAL REQUESTS RELATING TO 2000 BUDGET AUTHORITY

Transmitted to Congress on	Agencies affected	Printed as
February 19, 1999	International Assistance Programs	H. Doc. No. 106–24
May 14, 1999	Department of Energy	H. Doc. No. 106–66
	Department of Transportation	
	Legislative Branch	
June 8, 1999	Department of Commerce	H. Doc. No. 106–81
	Department of Defense	
	Department of Justice	
	Department of State	
	Department of Transportation	
July 14, 1999	Department of Energy	H. Doc. No. 106–95
	Department of Labor	
	Corps of Engineers	
July 19, 1999	Department of Defense	H. Doc. No. 106–101
	Department of Health and Human Services	
	Department of Justice	
	Agency for International Development	
September 21, 1999	Department of Commerce	H. Doc. No. 106–129
	Department of Defense	
	Department of Energy	
	Department of State	
	Department of the Treasury	
	General Services Administration	
	International Assistance Programs	
	National Science Foundation	
	Office of Personnel Management	
October 4, 1999	Department of Defense	H. Doc. No. 106–140
October 12, 1999	Department of Agriculture	H. Doc. No. 106–143
	Department of the Interior	
	Department of Labor	
	Department of State	
	Federal Emergency Management Agency	
	General Services Administration	
	International Trade Commission	
	Merit Systems Protection Board	
October 18, 1999	Department of Health and Human Services	H. Doc. No. 106–144
October 29, 1999	Department of Agriculture	H. Doc. No. 106–152
November 24, 1999	Department of Labor	Not available
	General Services Administration	
	District of Columbia	
	Federal Maritime Commission	
December 6, 1999	Department of Agriculture	Not available
	Department of Commerce	
	Department of Education	
	Department of Health and Human Services	
	International Assistance Programs	
December 6, 1999	Department of Defense	Not available
January 18, 2000	Department of Defense	Not available

ADVANCE APPROPRIATIONS, ADVANCE FUNDING, AND FORWARD FUNDING

I. An *advance appropriation* is one made to become available one fiscal year or more beyond the fiscal year for which the appropriation act is passed. Advance appropriations in fiscal year 2001 appropriations acts will become available for programs in 2002 or beyond. Since these appropriations are not available until after fiscal year 2001, the amounts will not be included in fiscal year 2001 budget totals, but will be reflected in the budget totals for the fiscal year for which they are requested.

The Congressional Budget Act of 1974 (31 U.S.C. 1105(a)(17)) requires inclusion in the budget of "information on estimates of appropriations for the fiscal year following the fiscal year for which the budget is submitted for grants, contracts, and other payments under each program for which there is an authorization of appropriations for that following fiscal year when the appropriations are authorized to be included in an appropriation law for the fiscal year before the fiscal year in which the appropriation is to be available for obligation." In fulfillment of this requirement, the table below lists those accounts authorized to receive, in fiscal year 2001, advance appropriations for fiscal year 2002 and beyond and cites the authorizing statute. The listing is in two parts: Part A shows the amounts of advance appropriations included in the 2001 budget. Part B is a listing of accounts for which advance appropriations are authorized but not requested in the 2001 budget.

The Administration proposes to work with the Congress to replace certain advance appropriations with up-front budget authority for the full amount of the program. This proposal is discussed further in Chapter 13, "Preview Report," of the *Analytical Perspectives* volume of the budget.

A. Accounts for which advance appropriations are included in the 2001 budget:
- Department of Agriculture:
  - National forest system (16 U.S.C. 4601–6a(i)): $15 million for 2002.
- Department of Commerce:
  - National Oceanic and Atmospheric Administration; Procurement, acquisition and construction: $732 million for 2002; $705 million for 2003; $706 million for 2004; $657 million for 2005.
  - Public telecommunications facilities, planning, and construction (47 U.S.C. 305, 91, 392, 606, 721): $110 million for 2002; $88 million for 2003.
- Department of Defense:
  - Military construction, Army: $210 million for 2002; $83 million for 2003; $11 million for 2004.
  - Military construction, Navy: $69 million for 2002.
  - Military construction, Defense-wide: $231 million for 2002; $147 million for 2003; $50 million for 2004; $19 million for 2005.
- Department of Education:
  - Special education (20 U.S.C. 1411): $3,742 million for 2002.[1]
  - Vocational and adult education (20 U.S.C. 2301): $791 million for 2002.[1]
- Department of Energy:
  - Other nuclear security activities: $40 million for 2003; $49 million for 2004.
  - Science: $300 million for 2002; $232 million for 2003; $150 million for 2004; $115 million for 2005.
  - Clean coal technology: $236 million for 2002.
  - Elk Hills school land funds: $36 million for 2002; $36 million for 2003; $36 million for 2004; $60 million for 2005; $60 million for 2006.
- Department of Health and Human Services:
  - Food and Drug Administration, Salaries and expenses (21 U.S.C. 393, P.L. 100–607): $23 million for 2002.
  - Indian health facilities (25 U.S.C. 13, P.L. 83–568, the Snyder Act; Section 301 of P.L. 94–437, the Indian Health Care Improvement Act): $18 million for 2002.
  - Disease control, research and training (Section 321(a) of the Public Health Service Act): $21 million for 2002; $21 million for 2003.
  - National Institutes of Health: $26 million for 2002.
  - Grants to States for Medicaid (42 U.S.C. 1396): $36,208 million for 2002.
  - Payments to states for child support enforcement and family support programs (24 U.S.C. Ch. 9): $1,000 million for 2002.
  - Low income home energy assistance (P.L 97–35): $1,100 million for 2002.
  - Payments to States for the child care and development block grant (42 U.S.C. 9858): $2,000 million for 2002.
  - Children and families services programs (42 U.S.C. 9834): $1,400 million for 2002.[1]
  - Payments to states for foster care and adoption assistance (P.L 96–272): $1,736 million for 2002.
- Department of Housing and Urban Development:
  - Housing certificate fund: $4,200 million for 2002.[1]
- Department of the Interior:
  - National Park Service, Construction and major maintenance (16 U.S.C. 1–1c, 7a–7e, 461–467): $21 million for 2002; $17 million for 2003; $11 million for 2004.
  - Assistance to territories (P.L. 94–241, 90 Stat. 272): $10 million for 2002.
- Department of Justice:
  - Federal Prison System, Buildings and facilities (18 U.S.C. 4003, 4009, 4010, 4013(a)(4), 4042, 4125; Department of Justice Appropriations Act, 2000): $791 million for 2002; $535 million for 2003.
- Department of Labor:
  - Training and employment services (29 U.S.C. 2801 et seq.): $2,463 million for 2002.[1]
- Department of State:
  - Embassy security, construction, and maintenance: $650 million for 2002; $800 million for 2003; $950 million for 2004; $950 million for 2005.
- Department of Transportation:
  - Federal Aviation Administration, Facilities and equipment (49 U.S.C. 48101): $638 million for 2002; $590 million for 2003; $565 million for 2004; $537 million for 2005; $325 million for 2006; $169 million for 2007; $120 million for 2008.
- Department of the Treasury:
  - Internal Revenue Service, Information technology investments (5 U.S.C. 3109): $375 million for 2002.
- Other Defense Civil Programs:
  - Armed forces retirement home (P.L. 101–510, 1991 Defense Authorization Act): $6 million for 2002.
- General Services Administration:
  - Federal buildings fund (40 U.S.C. 490(f)): $219 million for 2002; $163 million for 2003; $96 million for 2004.
- International Assistance Programs:
  - Debt restructuring: $240 million for 2002; $135 million for 2003.
- National Aeronautics and Space Administration:
  - Human space flight (42 U.S.C. 2451, et seq.): $1,858 million for 2002; $1,452 million for 2003; $1,327 million for 2004; $1,275 million for 2005.
- National Science Foundation:
  - Major research equipment (42 U.S.C. 1862(a)(1)): $144 million for 2002; $58 million for 2003; $50 million for 2004; $14 million for 2005.
- Social Security Administration:
  - Special benefits for disabled coal miners (30 U.S.C. 921): $114 million for 2002.

Supplemental security income program (42 U.S.C. 1381): $10,470 million for 2002.
Corporation for Public Broadcasting:
Corporation for public broadcasting (47 U.S.C. 396): $35 million for 2002; $395 million for 2003.
Postal Service:
Payment to the Postal Service fund (39 U.S.C. 2401): $67 million for 2002.[1]
Smithsonian Institution:
Repair, restoration, and alteration of facilities (20 U.S.C. 53a): $17 million for 2002; $18 million for 2003.
Construction (20 U.S.C. 53a): $2 million for 2002.

B. Accounts authorized to receive advance appropriations but for which none are requested in the 2001 budget:
Department of Agriculture:
Food program administration (42 U.S.C. 1752).
Child nutrition programs (42 U.S.C. 1752).
Department of Education (20 U.S.C. 1223 and 29 U.S.C. 703):[2]
Education reform.
Education for the disadvantaged.
Impact aid.
School improvement programs.
Reading excellence.
Indian education.
Bilingual and immigrant education.
American Printing House for the Blind.
National Technical Institute for the Deaf.
Gallaudet University.
Rehabilitation services and disability research.
Student financial assistance.
Federal family education loans.
Federal direct student loan program.
Higher education.
Higher education facilities loans.
College housing and academic facilities loans.
Howard University.
Historically black college and university capital financing program.
Education research, statistics, and improvement.
Libraries.
Department of Justice:
Working capital fund (28 U.S.C. 527 note).

[1] Potential candidate for replacement with up-front budget authority for the full amount of the program. See Chapter 13, "Preview Report," of the *Analytical Perspectives* volume of the Budget.

[2] These statutes erroneously refer to "advance funding". Since these statutes describe and clearly intend to provide advance appropriations, the affected accounts are listed here.

II. Advance funding is budget authority that is to be charged to the appropriation in the succeeding year but which authorizes obligations to be incurred in the last quarter of the fiscal year if necessary to meet higher than anticipated benefit payments in excess of the specific amount appropriated for the year. When such budget authority is used, an adjustment is made to increase the budget authority for the fiscal year in which it is used and to reduce the budget authority of the succeeding fiscal year. Essentially, this is a device for avoiding supplemental requests late in the fiscal year for certain programs, should the appropriations for the current year prove to be low. The table below lists those accounts for which advance funding authority is requested in the 2001 budget.

Department of Labor:
Special benefits.
Federal unemployment benefits and allowances.
Department of Veterans Affairs:
Veterans insurance and indemnities.
Burial benefits and miscellaneous assistance.
Readjustment benefits.

III. Forward funding is budget authority that is made available for obligation beginning in the last quarter of the fiscal year for the financing of ongoing grant programs during the next succeeding fiscal year. The budget authority for such programs is included in the budget totals for the year in which it is appropriated. This device is often used for education programs, so that grants can be made on a school year basis. The language providing forward funding for education programs will specify that amounts appropriated, in most but not all cases, will not be available until some time into the year of the appropriation (e.g., July 1, 2001) and in most cases will specify that such amounts will remain available until the end of the succeeding fiscal year. In other cases (e.g., Federal Pell grants), the funds become available on October 1st but are not normally obligated until July 1st or later and are available for obligation for an additional year. The table below lists those accounts for which forward funding exists or is requested in whole or in part in the 2001 budget.

Department of Education:
Education reform.
Education for the disadvantaged.
School improvement programs.
Education reform.
Reading excellence.
Special education.
Vocational and adult education.
Student financial assistance.
Educational research, statistics, and improvement.
Department of the Interior:
Operation of Indian programs.

In the training and employment area, forward funding for youth training grant programs provides appropriations for a program year that starts on April 1st of the fiscal year of the appropriation. Financing extends through June 30th of the following fiscal year. For most other training and employment programs, forward funding provides appropriations for a program year that starts on July 1st of the fiscal year of the appropriation. Financing extends through June 30th of the following fiscal year. Program years are authorized for training programs under the Workforce Investment Act and operation of the State Employment Service under section 6 of the Wagner-Peyser Act. The table below lists accounts for which forward funding is requested in the 2001 budget.

Department of Labor:
Training and employment services.
State unemployment insurance and employment service operations.

FINANCING VEHICLES AND THE BOARD OF GOVERNORS OF THE FEDERAL RESERVE

This chapter contains descriptions of and data on financing vehicles and the Board of Governors of the Federal Reserve listed below.

—The Financing Corporation functions as a financing vehicle for the FSLIC Resolution Fund. It operates under the supervision and control of the Federal Housing Finance Board.

—The Resolution Funding Corporation provided financing for the Resolution Trust Corporation (RTC) and is subject to the general oversight and direction of the Secretary of the Treasury.

The Board of Governors of the Federal Reserve System's transactions are not included in the budget because of its unique status in the conduct of monetary policy. The Board provides data on its administrative budget on a calendar year basis, which is included here for information. Its budget schedules and statements are not subject to review by the President.

FINANCING VEHICLES

Financing Corporation

The Financing Corporation (FICO) is a mixed-ownership government corporation, chartered by the Federal Home Loan Bank Board pursuant to the Federal Savings and Loan Insurance Corporation Recapitalization Act of 1987, as amended (the "Act"). FICO's sole purpose was to function as a financing vehicle for the FSLIC Resolution Fund, formerly the Federal Savings and Loan Insurance Corporation (FSLIC). FICO operates under the supervision and control of the Federal Housing Finance Board (the "Finance Board"). Pursuant to the Act, FICO was authorized to issue debentures, bonds and other obligations subject to limitations contained in the Act, the net proceeds of which were to be used solely to purchase capital certificates issued by the FSLIC Resolution Fund, or to refund any previously issued obligations. The Resolution Trust Corporation Refinancing, Restructuring, and Improvement Act of 1991 terminated the FICO's borrowing authority.

The Act provided formulas pursuant to which the Federal Home Loan Banks made capital contributions to FICO at the direction of the Finance Board for the purchase of FICO capital stock. FICO used the proceeds received from the sales of such capital stock to purchase non-interest bearing securities for deposit in a segregated account as required by the Act. The non-interest bearing securities held in the segregated account will be the primary source of repayment of the principal of the FICO obligations. Securities in the segregated account are kept separate from other FICO accounts and funds but are not specifically pledged as collateral for the payment of obligations. The primary source of payment of interest on the obligations is the receipt of assessments imposed on and collected from institutions' accounts which are insured by the Bank Insurance Fund (the "BIF") and the Savings Association Insurance Fund (the "SAIF").

Statement of Operations (in millions of dollars)

99–4033		1998 actual	1999 actual	2000 est.	2001 est.
0101	Revenue	926	938	951	965
0102	Expense	–795	–795	–795	–796
0105	Net income or loss (–)	131	143	156	169

Balance Sheet (in millions of dollars)

99–4033		1998 actual	1999 actual	2000 est.	2001 est.
	ASSETS:				
	Investments in US securities:				
1102	Segregated accounts investment, net	1,606	1,749	1,905	2,074
1801	Cash, cash equivalents, and interest receivable	266	266	269	269
1901	Other assets	11	11	10	10
1999	Total assets	1,884	2,026	2,184	2,353
	LIABILITIES:				
2202	Interest payable	236	236	236	236
2203	Debt	8,145	8,146	8,147	8,149
2207	Other	67	65	67	65
2999	Total liabilities	8,447	8,447	8,450	8,449
	NET POSITION:				
3100	FICO capital stock purchased by FHLBanks	680	680	680	680
	Cumulative results of operations:				
3300	Cumulative results of operations	927	1,069	1,225	1,394
3300	FSLIC capital certificates	–8,170	–8,170	–8,170	–8,170
3999	Total net position	–6,563	–6,421	–6,265	–6,096
4999	Total liabilities and net position	1,884	2,026	2,185	2,353

Resolution Funding Corporation

The Resolution Funding Corporation (the "REFCORP") is a mixed-ownership government corporation established by Title V of the Financial Institutions Reform, Recovery, and Enforcement Act of 1989 (FIRREA). The sole purpose of REFCORP was to provide financing for the Resolution Trust Corporation (the "RTC"). Pursuant to FIRREA, REFCORP was authorized to issue debentures, bonds, and other obligations, subject to limitations contained in the Act and regulations established by the Thrift Depositor Protection Oversight Board. The proceeds of the debt (less any discount, plus any premium, net of issuance cost) were used solely to purchase nonredeemable capital certificates of the RTC or to refund any previously issued obligations.

Until October 29, 1998, REFCORP was subject to the general oversight and direction of the Thrift Depositor Protection Oversight Board. At that time, the Oversight Board was abolished and its authority and duties were transferred to the Secretary of the Treasury. The day-to-day operations of REFCORP are under the management of a three-member Directorate comprised of the Director of the Office of Finance of the Federal Home Loan Banks and two members selected from among the presidents of the twelve Federal Home Loan Banks ("the FHLBanks"). Members of the Directorate serve without compensation, and REFCORP is not permitted to have any paid employees.

FIRREA and the regulations adopted by the Thrift Depositor Protection Oversight Board and the Secretary of the Treasury provide formulas pursuant to which the Federal Home Loan Banks made capital contributions to REFCORP's Principal Fund and continue to make interest payments on outstanding REFCORP obligations. FIRREA also provides that the U.S. Treasury cover any interest shortfall. Funds designated for the Principal Funds were used to purchase zero-coupon bonds. The zero-coupon bonds will be held in the Principal Fund and are the primary source of repayment of the principal of the obligations at maturity.

RESOLUTION FUNDING CORPORATION—Continued

Statement of Operations (in millions of dollars)

99–4029		1998 actual	1999 actual	2000 est.	2001 est.
0101	Revenue	2,965	2,995	3,023	3,054
0102	Expense	–2,626	–2,626	–2,626	–2,626
0105	Net income or loss (–)	339	369	397	428

Balance Sheet (in millions of dollars)

99–4029		1998 actual	1999 actual	2000 est.	2001 est.
	ASSETS:				
	Investments in US securities:				
1102	Principal fund account investment, net	4,504	4,868	5,263	5,689
1206	Assessments receivable for interest expense	888	881	881	881
1999	Total assets	5,393	5,750	6,144	6,570
	LIABILITIES:				
2202	Accrued interest payable on long-term obligations	888	881	881	881
2203	Debt	30,069	30,067	30,064	30,062
2999	Total liabilities	30,957	30,948	30,945	30,943
	NET POSITION:				
3100	Nonvoting capital stock issued to FHLBanks	2,513	2,513	2,513	2,513
	Cumulative results of operations:				
3300	Cumulative results of operations	2,153	2,519	2,916	3,344
3300	RTC nonredeemable capital certificates	–31,286	–31,286	–31,286	–31,286
3300	Contributed capital—principal fund assessments	1,056	1,056	1,056	1,056
3999	Total net position	–25,564	–25,198	–24,801	–24,373
4999	Total liabilities and net position	5,393	5,750	6,144	6,570

BOARD OF GOVERNORS OF THE FEDERAL RESERVE SYSTEM

Program and Financing (in millions of dollars)

99–4450		1998 actual	1999 est.	2000 est.
	Obligations by program activity:			
09.01	Monetary and economic policy	81	80	85
09.02	Services to financial institutions and the public	3	4	4
09.03	Supervision and regulation of financial institutions	67	71	78
09.04	System policy direction and oversight	35	36	35
09.09	Subtotal: Board operating expenses	186	191	202
09.10	Office of Inspector General operating expenses	3	3	3
10.00	Total new obligations	189	194	205
	Budgetary resources available for obligation:			
22.00	New budget authority (gross)	189	194	205
23.95	Total new obligations	– 189	– 194	– 205
	New budget authority (gross), detail:			
	Mandatory:			
69.00	Offsetting collections (cash)	189	194	205
	Change in unpaid obligations:			
72.40	Unpaid obligations, start of year: Obligated balance, start of year	....	....	....
73.10	Total new obligations	189	194	205
73.20	Total outlays (gross)	– 189	– 194	– 205
74.40	Unpaid obligations, end of year: Obligated balance, end of year	....	....	....
	Outlays (gross), detail:			
86.97	Outlays from new mandatory authority	189	194	205
	Offsets:			
	Against gross budget authority and outlays:			
88.40	Offsetting collections (cash) from: Non-Federal sources	– 189	– 194	– 205
	Net budget authority and outlays:			
89.00	Budget authority	....	....	....
90.00	Outlays	....	....	....

The figures presented may differ from other Board financial material because they are prepared in accordance with OMB guidelines which vary from the Board's budget and accounting procedures.

The Federal Reserve System operates under the provisions of the Federal Reserve Act of 1913, as amended, and other acts of Congress.

Program.—To carry out its responsibilities under the Act, the Board determines general monetary, credit, and operating policies for the System as a whole and formulates the rules and regulations necessary to carry out the purposes of the Federal Reserve Act. The Board's principal duties consist of exerting an influence over credit conditions and supervising the Federal Reserve banks and member banks.

Financing.—Under the provisions of section 10 of the Federal Reserve Act, the Board of Governors levies upon the Federal Reserve banks, in proportion to their capital and surplus, an assessment sufficient to pay its estimated expenses. The Board, under the Act, determines and prescribes the manner in which its obligations are incurred and its expenses paid. Funds derived from assessments are deposited in the Federal Reserve Bank of Richmond, and the Act provides that such funds "shall not be construed to be Government funds or appropriated moneys." No Government appropriation is required to support operations of the Board.

The information presented pertains to Board operations only. Expenditures made on behalf of the Federal Reserve banks for production, issuance, retirement, and shipment of Federal Reserve notes are not included, since they are reimbursed in full by the Federal Reserve banks.

Object Classification (in millions of dollars)

99–4450		1998 actual	1999 est.	2000 est.
	Reimbursable obligations:			
	Personnel compensation:			
11.1	Full-time permanent	104	110	114
11.3	Other than full-time permanent	2	2	2
11.5	Other personnel compensation	2	2	2
11.9	Total personnel compensation	108	114	118
12.1	Civilian personnel benefits	19	17	18
21.0	Travel and transportation of persons	5	5	5
23.3	Communications, utilities, and miscellaneous charges	10	10	11
24.0	Printing and reproduction	2	3	2
25.1	Advisory and assistance services	4	4	4
25.2	Other services	21	20	21
26.0	Supplies and materials	6	8	7
31.0	Equipment	11	10	16
99.0	Subtotal, reimbursable obligations	186	191	202
25.2	Allocation Account: Other services	3	3	3
99.9	Total new obligations	189	194	205

GOVERNMENT-SPONSORED ENTERPRISES

This chapter contains descriptions of and data on the Government-sponsored enterprises listed below. These enterprises were established and chartered by the Federal Government for public policy purposes. They are not included in the Federal budget because they are private companies. However, because of their public purpose, detailed statements of financial operations and condition are presented, to the extent such information is available, on a basis that is as consistent as practicable with the basis for the budget data of Government agencies. These statements are not reviewed by the President; they are presented as submitted by the enterprises.

—The Student Loan Marketing Association is a for-profit financial corporation chartered by Congress in 1972 under the Higher Education Act (HEA) to help increase the availability of student loans. Sallie Mae carries out secondary market and other functions.

—The Federal National Mortgage Association and the Federal Home Loan Mortgage Corporation provide assistance to the secondary market for residential mortgages. Both are supervised by the Department of Housing and Urban Development for their roles in helping to finance low-, moderate-, and middle-income housing; both are regulated for financial safety and soundness by the Office of Federal Housing Enterprise Oversight.

—Institutions of the Farm Credit System the Agricultural Credit Bank and Farm Credit Banks—provide financial assistance to agriculture. They are supervised by the Farm Credit Administration.

—The Federal Agricultural Mortgage Corporation, under the supervision of the Farm Credit Administration, provides a secondary mortgage market for agricultural real estate and certain rural housing loans as well as for farm and business loans guaranteed by the U.S. Department of Agriculture.

—The Federal Home Loan Banks assist thrift institutions, banks, insurance companies, and credit unions in providing financing for housing and community development and are supervised by the Federal Housing Finance Board.

STUDENT LOAN MARKETING ASSOCIATION

STUDENT LOAN MARKETING ASSOCIATION

Status of Direct Loans (in millions of dollars)

99–1500		1999 actual	2000 est.	2001 est.
1131	Direct loan obligations	14,023	5,989	9,146
1150	Total direct loan obligations	14,023	5,989	9,146
	Cumulative balance of direct loans outstanding:			
1210	Outstanding, start of year	29,468	37,797	33,870
1231	Disbursements: Direct loan disbursements	14,023	8,989	9,146
	Repayments:			
1251	Repayments and prepayments	−3,986	−4,125	−3,364
1252	Proceeds from loan asset sales or discounted	−1,971	−9,000	−12,000
1264	Write-offs for default: Other adjustments, net	263	209	188
1290	Outstanding, end of year	37,797	33,870	27,840

The Student Loan Marketing Association (Sallie Mae) was created as a shareholder-owned government sponsored enterprise (GSE) by the Education Amendments of 1972 to expand funds available for student loans by providing liquidity to lenders engaged in the Federal Family Education Loan Program (FFELP), formerly the guaranteed student loan program (GSLP). Sallie Mae was privatized in 1997 pursuant to the authority granted by the Student Loan Marketing Association Reorganization Act of 1996. The GSE is a wholly owned subsidiary of SLM Holding Corporation and must wind down and be liquidated by September 30, 2008. Under legislation passed in 1998, if SLM Holding Corporation affiliates with a depository institution, the GSE must wind down within two years (unless such period is extended by the Department of the Treasury).

The GSE provides liquidity through direct purchase of insured student loans from eligible lenders and through warehousing advances, which are loans to lenders secured by insured student loans, Government or agency securities, or other acceptable collateral. In capital shortage areas, the GSE is authorized, at the request of Federal officials, to make insured loans directly to students. The GSE is authorized to advance funds to State agencies that will provide loans to students. The GSE is also authorized to provide a secondary market for noninsured loans; to serve as a guarantee agency in support of loan availability at the request of the Secretary of Education; to purchase and underwrite student loan revenue bonds; to provide certain additional services as determined by its board of directors to be supportive of the credit needs of students generally; and to provide financing for academic facilities and equipment.

The GSE is authorized by the Health Professions Educational Assistance Act of 1976 to provide a secondary market for federally insured loans to graduate health professions students.

Generally, under the privatization legislation, the GSE cannot engage in any new business activities or acquire any additional program assets other than purchasing student loans and serving, at the request of the Secretary of Education, as a lender-of-last-resort. The GSE can continue to make warehousing advances under contractual commitments existing on August 7, 1997.

Operations.—The forecast data with respect to operations are based on certain general economic and specific FFELP loan volume assumptions and should not be relied upon as an official forecast of the corporation's future business. The 1999 loan volume amounts reflect the purchase of the Nellie Mae Corporation, including its $2.6 billion student loan portfolio.

ANNUAL LOAN ACTIVITY

[In millions of dollars]

	1999 actual	2000 est.	2001 est.
Guaranteed student loans:			
Stafford:			
Purchased	10,716	7,043	7,292
Warehoused	713	300	150
PLUS/SLS: Purchased	1,121	732	758
Consolidations	909	594	614
Health professions loans: Purchased	69		
Subtotal, Guaranteed student loans	13,528	8,669	8,814
Other	495	320	332
Total	14,023	8,989	9,146

Financing.—The GSE is financed by borrowing in the private debt markets and securitizing its assets. The GSE must wind down and be liquidated by September 30, 2008. All obligations of the GSE remaining upon liquidation must be placed into a defeasance trust. The GSE's outstanding adjust-

STUDENT LOAN MARKETING ASSOCIATION—Continued

able rate cumulative preferred stock is required to be redeemed prior to such date.

The financial data contained in this material relating to future periods represents estimates that have been prepared specifically for inclusion in the President's Budget. These data should not be viewed as official forecasts of the corporation's future position, nor should they be used as a basis for making financial or investment decisions relating to the corporation. The data have been developed on the basis of certain economic assumptions that are subject to periodic review and revision. Consequently, the estimates are subject to forecast error and actual results from future business operations are likely to differ from these data.

Statement of Operations (in millions of dollars)

99–1500		1998 actual	1999 actual	2000 est.	2001 est.
0101	Revenue	3,116	2,854	....	....
0102	Expense	–2,595	–2,391	....	....
0105	Net income or loss (–)	521	463	....	....

Balance Sheet (in millions of dollars)

99–1500		1998 actual	1999 actual	2000 est.	2001 est.
	ASSETS:				
	Investments in US securities:				
1102	Treasury securities, par	1,404	1,401	1,429	1,458
1104	Agency securities, par	....	....	....	....
1106	Receivables, net	669	942	848	678
1201	Investments in other securities, net	2,728	2,009	1,543	864
1206	Receivables, net	706	684	616	431
1207	Advances and prepayments	15	16	17	18
	Net value of assets related to direct loans receivable and acquired defaulted guaranteed loans receivable:				
1601	Direct loans, gross	29,586	37,947	34,005	27,951
1603	Allowance for estimated uncollectible loans and interest (–)	–118	–150	–135	–111
1699	Value of assets related to direct loans	29,468	37,797	33,870	27,840
1801	Cash and other monetary assets	50	38	40	42
1803	Property, plant and equipment, net	182	172	180	189
1901	Other assets	358	435	457	480
1999	Total assets	35,580	43,494	39,000	32,000
	LIABILITIES:				
2202	Interest payable	300	293	264	238
2203	Debt	33,517	41,591	37,125	30,215
2207	Other	883	677	711	747
2999	Total liabilities	34,700	42,561	38,100	31,200
	NET POSITION:				
3300	Invested Capital	880	933	900	800
3999	Total net position	880	933	900	800
4999	Total liabilities and net position	35,580	43,494	39,000	32,000

FEDERAL NATIONAL MORTGAGE ASSOCIATION

PORTFOLIO PROGRAMS

Status of Direct Loans (in millions of dollars)

99–2500		1999 actual	2000 est.	2001 est.
1131	Direct loan obligations	201,660	133,917	152,021
1150	Total direct loan obligations	201,660	133,917	152,021
	Cumulative balance of direct loans outstanding:			
1210	Outstanding, start of year	393,210	518,629	599,719
	Disbursements:			
1231	Direct loan disbursements	208,542	132,281	151,144
1232	Purchase of loans assets	19,258	335	362
1251	Repayments: Repayments and prepayments	–100,348	–51,525	–59,117
1264	Write-offs for default: Other adjustments, net	–2,033	....	....
1290	Outstanding, end of year	518,629	599,719	692,108

The Federal National Mortgage Association (Fannie Mae) is a federally-chartered, privately-owned company with a public mission to provide stability and to increase the liquidity of the residential mortgage market and to help increase the availability of mortgage credit to low- and moderate-income families and in underserved areas. In carrying out its mission, Fannie Mae engages primarily in two forms of business: investing in portfolios of residential mortgages and guaranteeing residential mortgage securities. As of September 30, 1999, Fannie Mae held a net mortgage portfolio totaling $504 billion and had net outstanding guaranteed mortgage-backed securities of over $670 billion.

Through a federal charter, Congress has equipped Fannie Mae with certain attributes to help it carry out its public mission. These include an exemption from state and local taxes (except real property taxes), an exemption of its debt and mortgage securities from Securities and Exchange Commission registration requirements, and conditional access to a $2.25 billion line of credit from the U.S. Treasury. Securities guaranteed by Fannie Mae and debt issued by the company are solely the corporation's obligations and are not backed by the full faith and credit of the U.S. Government. The common stock of the corporation is owned by the public, is fully transferable, and trades on the New York, Midwest, and Pacific stock exchanges.

Fannie Mae was established in 1938 to assist private markets in providing a steady supply of funds for housing. Fannie Mae was originally a subsidiary of the Reconstruction Finance Corporation and was permitted to purchase only loans insured by the Federal Housing Administration (FHA). In 1954, Fannie Mae was restructured as a mixed ownership (part government, part private) corporation. Congress sold the government's remaining interest in Fannie Mae in 1968 and completed the transformation to private shareholder ownership in 1970. Using the proceeds from the sale of subordinated debentures, Fannie Mae paid the Treasury $216 million for the government's preferred stock, which was retired, and for the Treasury's interest in the corporation's earned surplus. As a result, the corporation was taken off the federal budget.

In 1992, Congress reaffirmed and clarified Fannie Mae's role in the housing finance system through charter act amendments included in the Federal Housing Enterprises Financial Safety and Soundness Act of 1992 ("The Act"). Fannie Mae's charter purposes, as amended by the Act, are: "to provide stability in the secondary market for residential mortgages; respond appropriately to the private capital market; provide ongoing assistance to the secondary market for residential mortgages (including activities relating to mortgages on housing for low- and moderate-income families involving a reasonable economic return that may be less than the return earned on other activities); and promote access to mortgage credit throughout the Nation (including central cities, rural areas, and underserved areas) by increasing the liquidity of mortgage investments and improving the distribution of investment capital for residential mortgage financing."

In December 1995, the U.S. Department of Housing and Urban Development (HUD) set affordable housing goals for 1996–1999 and established the requirements for counting mortgage purchases to low- and moderate-income families and families living in underserved areas with specific census tract and minority concentration requirements. Under the regulations, the low- and moderate-income goal is 42 percent; the geographically targeted goal is 24 percent and the special affordable housing goal is 14 percent. Fannie Mae exceeded all of the housing goals in 1998 with low- and moderate-income purchases at 44.1 percent, geographically targeted purchases at 27 percent, and special affordable housing purchases at 14.3 percent.

HUD is publishing a proposed rule for public comment that would set new affordable housing goals for the period covering 2000 to 2003. After a transition period, the goals would be 50 percent for the low- and moderate-income goal, 31 percent for the geographically targeted goal, and 20 percent for the special affordable housing goal.

The Act also established the Office of Federal Housing Enterprise Oversight (OFHEO), an independent office within HUD, headed by a Director who reports directly to the Congress. OFHEO has statutory responsibility for ensuring that Fannie Mae is adequately capitalized and operating in a safe and sound manner. Included among the express statutory authorities of the Director is the authority to conduct examinations of the financial health of the company and to issue minimum and risk-based capital standards. The minimum capital requirements are computed from statutorily established ratios that are applied to the assets and off-balance sheet risks of Fannie Mae. The risk-based capital standard determines the amount of capital that Fannie Mae must hold to withstand the impact of simultaneous adverse credit and interest rate stresses over a 10-year period, plus an additional amount to cover management and operations risk. Total capital (shareholder's equity plus allowance for loan losses) at the end of September 1999 was $17.9 billion. The company has continued to remain in compliance with applicable capital standards and has been deemed adequately capitalized by OFHEO since its first classification in June 1993.

Through the third quarter of 1999, Fannie Mae earned $2.87 billion.

Income and retained earnings for the years ended September 30, 1998 and 1999 follow (in thousands of dollars):

	1998 actual	*1999 actual*
Gross revenue	30,510,100	35,255,700
Gross expenses	25,885,200	30,289,400
Income before Federal income tax	4,624,900	4,966,300
Federal income tax	1,365,800	1,280,300
Net income	3,259,100	3,686,000
Retained earnings, beginning of year	12,766,100	15,064,600
Dividends on common stock	(960,600)	(1,076,500)
Retained earnings, end of year	15,064,600	17,674,100

The financial data contained in this material relating to future periods represent estimates that have been prepared specifically for inclusion in the President's Budget. These data should not be viewed as an official forecast of the corporation's future position, nor should they be used as a basis for making financial or investment decisions relating to the corporation. The data have been developed on the basis of certain economic assumptions that are subject to periodic review and revision. Consequently, the estimates are subject to forecast error and actual results from future business operations are likely to differ from these data.

Balance Sheet (in millions of dollars)

99–2500		1998 actual	1999 actual	2000 est.	2001 est.
	ASSETS:				
1101	Fund balances	19	4		
	Investments in US securities:				
1102	Treasury securities, par	123	34		
1104	Other	68,714	36,498	44,772	48,800
	Net value of assets related to direct loans receivable and acquired defaulted guaranteed loans receivable:				
1601	Direct loans (net of discount)	362,478	477,130	580,250	670,984
1602	Federal Agencies	13,854	27,367	4,164	4,081
1603	Allowance for estimated uncollectible loans and interest (–)	–254	–194	–188	–190
1699	Value of assets related to direct loans	376,078	504,303	584,226	674,875
1801	Cash and other monetary assets	9,974	10,513	10,622	12,029
1803	Property, plant and equipment, net	191	180		
1999	Total assets	455,099	551,532	639,620	735,704
	LIABILITIES:				
2101	Accounts payable	400	254		
2102	Accrued interest payable	5,544	6,574	7,198	8,341
2105	Other	8	11		
2203	Debt	430,582	524,879	609,566	702,060
2204	Estimated liability for loan guarantees	3,135	2,311	3,035	2,863
2206	Pension and other actuarial liabilities	225	288		
2207	Subtotal, Federal taxes payable	353	160		
2999	Total liabilities	440,247	534,477	619,799	713,264
	NET POSITION:				
	Cumulative results of operations:				
3300	Cumulative results of operations	15,065	17,674	20,730	24,170
3300	Change in Stockholder Equity	–213	–619	–909	–1,730
3999	Total net position	14,852	17,055	19,821	22,440
4999	Total liabilities and net position	455,099	551,532	639,620	735,704

MORTGAGE-BACKED SECURITIES

Status of Direct Loans (in millions of dollars)

99–2501		1999 actual	2000 est.	2001 est.
1131	Direct loan obligations	297,503	208,781	228,595
1150	Total direct loan obligations	297,503	208,781	228,595
	Cumulative balance of direct loans outstanding:			
1210	Outstanding, start of year	798,460	938,484	1,033,975
1231	Disbursements: Direct loan disbursements	348,792	208,781	228,595
1251	Repayments: Repayments and prepayments	– 208,768	– 113,290	– 122,309
1290	Outstanding, end of year	938,484	1,033,975	1,140,261

According to accounting practices for private corporations, the mortgages in the pools of loans supporting the mortgage-backed securities are considered to be owned by the holders of these securities. Consequently, on the books of the Federal National Mortgage Association (Fannie Mae), these mortgages are not considered assets and the securities outstanding are not considered liabilities. However, the concepts of the budget of the U.S. Government consider these mortgages and mortgage-backed securities to be assets and liabilities, respectively, of Fannie Mae. For the purposes of this document, therefore, they are presented as assets and liabilities in the accompanying schedules. On the schedule of Status of direct loans for mortgage-backed securities, the items labeled "New loans" and "Recoveries: Repayments and prepayments" are budgetary terms. However, from the Corporation's perspective, these items are "Amounts issued" and "Amounts passed through to the holders of securities", respectively.

The financial data contained in this material relating to future periods represent estimates that have been prepared specifically for inclusion in the President's Budget. These data should not be viewed as an official forecast of the corporation's future position, nor should they be used as a basis for making financial or investment decisions relating to the corporation. The data have been developed on the basis of certain economic assumptions that are subject to periodic review and revision. Consequently, the estimates are subject to forecast error and actual results from future business operations are likely to differ from these data.

PORTFOLIO PROGRAMS—Continued

MORTGAGE-BACKED SECURITIES—Continued

Balance Sheet (in millions of dollars)

99–2501	1998 actual	1999 actual	2000 est.	2001 est.
ASSETS:				
Net value of assets related to direct loans receivable and acquired defaulted guaranteed loans receivable:				
1601 Direct loans, gross	799,006	939,092	1,034,576	1,140,862
1603 Allowance for estimated uncollectible loans and interest (–)	–546	–608	–601	–600
1699 Value of assets related to direct loans	798,460	938,484	1,033,975	1,140,261
1999 Total assets	798,460	938,484	1,033,975	1,140,261
LIABILITIES:				
2104 Resources payable	798,460	938,484	1,033,975	1,140,261
2999 Total liabilities	798,460	938,484	1,033,975	1,140,261

FEDERAL HOME LOAN MORTGAGE CORPORATION

PORTFOLIO PROGRAMS

Status of Direct Loans (in millions of dollars)

99–4420	1999 actual	2000 est.	2001 est.
1131 Direct loan obligations	156,862	69,700	77,500
1150 Total direct loan obligations	156,862	69,700	77,500
Cumulative balance of direct loans outstanding:			
1210 Outstanding, start of year	216,522	315,968	355,811
1231 Disbursements: Direct loan disbursements	156,862	69,700	77,500
1251 Repayments: Repayments and prepayments	–57,416	–29,857	–37,492
1290 Outstanding, end of year	315,968	355,811	395,819

The Federal Home Loan Mortgage Corporation (Freddie Mac), is a federally-charted, private shareholder-owned company with a public mission to provide stability and increase the liquidity of the residential mortgage market, and to help increase the availability of mortgage credit to low- and moderate-income families and in underserved areas. In carrying out its mission, Freddie Mac engages primarily in two forms of business: investing in portfolios of residential mortgages and guaranteeing residential mortgage securities. As of September 30, 1999, Freddie Mac held a mortgage portfolio totaling $315 billion and had outstanding guaranteed mortgage-backed securities of $739 billion.

Through a federal charter, Congress has equipped Freddie Mac with certain advantages over wholly private firms in carrying out these activities. These advantages include an exemption from state and local taxes (except real property taxes), an exemption for their debt and mortgage securities from SEC filing registration requirements, and conditional access to a $2.25 billion line of credit from the U.S. Treasury. Securities guaranteed by Freddie Mac and debt issued by the company are explicitly not backed by the full faith and credit of the U.S. Government. The common stock of the corporation is owned by the public, is fully transferable, and trades on the New York and Pacific stock exchanges.

Freddie Mac was established in 1970 under the Emergency Home Finance Act. Congress chartered Freddie Mac to provide mortgage lenders with an organized national secondary market enabling them to manage their conventional mortgage portfolio more effectively and gain indirect access to a ready source of additional funds to meet new demands for mortgages. Freddie Mac served as a conduit facilitating the flow of investment dollars from the capital markets to mortgage lenders, and ultimately, to homebuyers, increasing the amount of mortgage credit available and making it more affordable.

The Financial Institutions Reform, Recovery, and Enforcement Act of 1989 (FIRREA) significantly changed the corporate governance of Freddie Mac. The company's three member Board of Directors, which had corresponded with the Federal Home Loan Bank Board, was replaced with an eighteen member Board of Directors. Thirteen board members are elected annually by shareholders and five are annually appointed by the President of the United States. In addition, FIRREA converted Freddie Mac's 60 million shares of non-voting, senior participating preferred stock into voting common stock. As a result, the corporation was taken off the federal budget.

FIRREA also clarified Freddie Mac's role in the housing finance delivery system through amendments to its charter act. Specifically, FIRREA established Freddie Mac's public mission: "to provide stability in the secondary market for residential mortgages; respond appropriately to the private capital market; and provide ongoing assistance to the secondary market for residential mortgages (including activities relating to mortgages on housing for low- and moderate-income families involving a reasonable economic return that may be less than the return earned on other activities. The Federal Housing Enterprise Financial Safety and Soundness Act of 1992 ("The Act") added to Freddie Mac's public mission the promotion of "access to mortgage credit throughout the Nation (including central cities, rural areas, and underserved areas) by increasing the liquidity of mortgage investments and improving the distribution of investment capital for residential mortgage financing."

The Act also established affordable housing goals that are designed to improve the flow of mortgage funds to low- and moderate-income families in central cities, rural areas, and other underserved areas. In December 1995, the U.S. Department of Housing and Urban Development (HUD) affordable housing goals for 1996–1999 and established the requirements for counting mortgage purchases for meeting these goals. The goals provide that, of the total number of dwelling units financed by Freddie Mac's mortgage purchases, 42 percent meet the low- and moderate-income goal, 24 percent meet the geographically targeted goal, and 14 percent meet the special affordable goal.

Freddie Mac exceeded all of the housing goals in 1998 with low- and moderate-income purchases of 42.9 percent, geographically targeted purchases of 26.1 percent, special affordable purchases of 15.9 percent, and the multifamily portion of the special affordable purchases of $2.7 billion in qualifying multifamily mortgages.

HUD is publishing a proposed rule for public comment that would set new affordable housing goals for the period covering 2000 to 2003. After a transition period, the goals would be 50 percent for the low- and moderate-income goal, 31 percent for the geographically targeted goal, and 20 percent for the special affordable housing goal.

The Act also enhanced the regulatory oversight of Freddie Mac by establishing the Office of Federal Housing Enterprise Oversight (OFHEO), an independent office within HUD, headed by a Director appointed by the President. OFHEO is responsible for ensuring that Freddie Mac is adequately capitalized and operating in a safe and sound manner. Included among the express statutory authorities of the Director is the authority to conduct examinations of the financial health of the company and to issue minimum and risk-based capital standards. The minimum capital requirements are computed from statutorily established ratios that are applied to the assets and off-balance sheet risks of Freddie Mac. The risk-based capital standard determines the amount of capital that Freddie Mac must hold to withstand the impact of simultaneous adverse credit and interest rate stresses over a 10-year period, plus an additional amount to cover management and operations risk.

Through the third quarter of 1999, Freddie Mac recorded net income of $1.63 billion.

The financial data contained in this material relating to future periods represent estimates that have been prepared specifically for inclusion in the President's budget. These data should not be viewed as an official forecast of the corporation's future position, nor should they be used as a basis for making financial or investment decisions relating to the corporation. The data have been developed on the basis of certain economic assumptions that are subject to periodic review and revision. Consequently, the estimates are subject to forecast error and actual results from future business operations are likely to differ from these data.

According to generally accepted accounting principles utilized by private corporations, the mortgages in the pools of loans supporting PCs are considered to be owned by the holder of these securities. Therefore, Freddie Mac does not show these mortgages as assets. However, the budget philosophy of the United States Government includes these mortgages and mortgages pass-through securities as assets and liabilities, respectively, of Freddie Mac. For the purpose of this document, therefore, they are presented as assets and liabilities in the accompanying schedules. On the Status of Direct Loans schedule for mortgage pass-through securities, the items labeled "Disbursements" and "Repayments" are budgetary terms. However, from Freddie Mac's perspective, these amounts represent "Sales of PCs" and "Amounts passed through to PC holders," respectively.

Balance Sheet (in millions of dollars)

99–4420		1998 actual	1999 actual	2000 est.	2001 est.
	ASSETS:				
1201	Investments in other securities, net	30,825	26,515	48,265	49,965
1206	Receivables, net	12,271	18,643	18,532	18,413
1207	Advances and prepayments	255	487	507	507
	Net value of assets related to direct loans receivable and acquired defaulted guaranteed loans receivable:				
1601	Retained mortgage inventory	216,522	315,968	355,811	395,819
1603	Allowances (–)	–294	–467	–742	–1,179
1699	Value of assets related to direct loans	216,228	315,501	355,069	394,640
1801	Cash and other monetary assets	1,286	1,992	2,000	2,000
1803	Property, plant and equipment, net	1,153	1,251	1,384	1,571
1901	Other assets	1,238	496	1,351	1,856
1999	Total assets	263,256	364,885	427,108	468,952
	LIABILITIES:				
2101	Accounts payable	1	115		
2201	Accounts payable	804	2,146	3,002	2,951
2202	Interest payable	1,543	2,311	3,373	4,366
2203	Debt	236,387	341,014	403,441	442,529
2206	Pension and other actuarial liabilities	13	19	28	41
	Other:				
2207	Accrued payroll and benefits	62	82	108	142
2207	Accrued annual leave (funded or unfunded)	1	2	4	8
2207	Other Liabilities	15,157	8,056	4,117	4,266
2999	Total liabilities	253,968	353,745	414,073	454,303
	NET POSITION:				
3100	Invested capital	9,288	11,140	13,035	14,649
3999	Total net position	9,288	11,140	13,035	14,649
4999	Total liabilities and net position	263,256	364,885	427,108	468,952

Mortgage-Backed Securities

Status of Direct Loans (in millions of dollars)

99–4440		1999 actual	2000 est.	2001 est.
1131	Direct loan obligations	270,798	162,000	188,900
1150	Total direct loan obligations	270,798	162,000	188,900
	Cumulative balance of direct loans outstanding:			
1210	Outstanding, start of year	490,687	529,213	616,832
1231	Disbursements: Direct loan disbursements	270,798	162,000	188,900
1251	Repayments: Repayments and prepayments	–232,272	–74,381	–87,360
1290	Outstanding, end of year	529,213	616,832	718,372

Balance Sheet (in millions of dollars)

99–4440		1998 actual	1999 actual	2000 est.	2001 est.
	ASSETS:				
1901	Underlying Mortgages	490,687	529,231	616,832	718,372
1999	Total assets	490,687	529,231	616,832	718,372
	LIABILITIES:				
2104	Resources payable	490,687	529,213	616,832	718,372
2999	Total liabilities	490,687	529,213	616,832	718,372

FARM CREDIT SYSTEM

The Farm Credit System is a government sponsored enterprise that provides privately financed credit to agricultural and rural communities. The major functional entities of the system are: (1) Agricultural Credit Bank (ACB), (2) Farm Credit Banks (FCB), and (3) direct lender associations. The history and specific functions of the bank entities are discussed after the presentation of financial schedules for each bank entity. As part of the Farm Credit System (FCS), these entities are regulated and examined by the Farm Credit Administration (FCA), an independent Federal agency. The administrative costs of FCA are currently financed by assessments of system institutions. System banks finance loans primarily from sales of bonds to the public and their own capital funds. The system bonds issued by the banks are not guaranteed by the U.S. Government either as to principal or interest. The bonds are backed by an insurance fund, administered by the Farm Credit System Insurance Corporation (FCSIC), an independent Federal agency that collects insurance premiums from member banks to pay its administrative expenses and fund insurance reserves. All of the banks' current operating expenses are paid from their own income and do not require budgetary resources from the Federal Government. Limited Federal assistance is provided to support interest payments on special FCS Financial Assistance Corporation (FAC) debt obligations (see discussion of FAC elsewhere in this document).

Agricultural Credit Bank

On July 1, 1999, the remaining cooperative entity, the St. Paul Bank for Cooperatives, merged into CoBank ACB. This bank is headquartered in Denver, Colorado and serves eligible cooperatives nationwide, and provides funding to Agricultural Credit Associations (ACAs) in one of its regions. An ACB operates under statutory authority that combines the authorities of a FCB and a Bank for Cooperatives (BC). In exercising its FCB authority, CoBank ACB's charter limits its lending to ACAs located in the region previously served by the Farm Credit Bank of Springfield. As an entity lending to Cooperatives, CoBank is independently chartered to provide credit and related services nationwide to eligible cooperatives primarily engaged in farm supply, grain, marketing and proc-

AGRICULTURAL CREDIT BANK—Continued

essing (including sugar and dairy). CoBank also makes loans to rural utilities, including telecommunications companies and it provides international loans for the financing of agricultural exports.

Status of Direct Loans (in millions of dollars)

99–4130	1999 actual	2000 est.	2001 est.
1131 Direct loan obligations	49,522	50,000	50,000
1150 Total direct loan obligations	49,522	50,000	50,000
Cumulative balance of direct loans outstanding:			
1210 Outstanding, start of year	16,612	18,093	18,545
1231 Disbursements: Direct loan disbursements	49,503	50,000	50,000
1251 Repayments: Repayments and prepayments	−47,884	−49,532	−48,808
1263 Write-offs for default: Direct loans	−138	−16	−16
1290 Outstanding, end of year	18,093	18,545	19,721

Statement of Operations (in millions of dollars)

99–4130	1998 actual	1999 actual	2000 est.	2001 est.
0101 Total interest income	1,460	1,424	1,493	1,592
0102 Total interest expense	−1,103	−1,063	−1,116	−1,191
0105 Net income or loss (−)	357	361	377	401
0111 Other income	35	46	49	52
0112 Other expense	−201	−323	−246	−249
0115 Net income or loss (−)	−166	−277	−197	−197
0191 Total revenues	1,495	1,470	1,542	1,644
0192 Total expenses	−1,304	−1,386	−1,362	−1,440
0195 Total income or loss (−)	191	84	180	204
0199 Total comprehensive income	191	84	180	204

Balance Sheet (in millions of dollars)

99–4130	1998 actual	1999 actual	2000 est.	2001 est.
ASSETS:				
1201 Cash and investment securities	3,892	3,755	3,848	4,093
1206 Accrued interest receivable on loans	190	182	187	198
Net value of assets related to direct loans receivable and acquired defaulted guaranteed loans receivable:				
1601 Direct loans, gross	16,612	18,093	18,545	19,721
1603 Allowance for estimated uncollectible loans and interest (−)	−294	−314	−322	−342
1699 Value of assets related to direct loans	16,318	17,779	18,223	19,379
1803 Property, plant and equipment, net	204	159	178	178
1999 Total assets	20,604	21,875	22,436	23,848
LIABILITIES:				
2104 Resources payable	206	167	174	178
Accounts payable:				
2201 Consolidated systemwide and other bank bonds	18,079	19,468	19,954	21,220
2201 Notes payable and other interest-bearing liabilities	437	351	360	383
2202 Accrued interest payable	186	228	234	248
2999 Total liabilities	18,908	20,214	20,722	22,029
NET POSITION:				
3300 Cumulative results of operations	1,697	1,660	1,714	1,818
3999 Total net position	1,697	1,660	1,714	1,818
4999 Total liabilities and net position	20,605	21,874	22,436	23,847

Statement of Changes in Net Worth (in millions of dollars)

99–4130	1998 actual	1999 actual	2000 est.	2001 est.
Beginning balance of net worth	1,582	1,697	1,660	1,714
Capital stock and participations issued	7	5	5	5
Capital stock and participations retired	40	80	90	65
Net income	191	84	179	204
Cash/Dividends/Patronage Distributions	−48	−27	−40	−40
Other, net	5	(19)	0	0
Ending balance of net worth	1,697	1,660	1,714	1,818

Financing Activities (in millions of dollars)

99–4130	1998 actual	1999 actual	2000 est.	2001 est.
Beginning balance of outstanding system obligations	**18,573**	**18,079**	**19,468**	**19,954**
Consolidated systemwide and other bank bonds issued	9,686	11,875	12,000	12,000
Consolidated systemwide and other bank bonds retired	11,073	9,657	11,913	11,235
Consolidated systemwide notes, net	893	−829	400	500
Ending balance of outstanding system obligations	18,079	19,468	19,954	21,220

FARM CREDIT BANKS

Status of Direct Loans (in millions of dollars)

99–4160	1999 actual	2000 est.	2001 est.
1131 Direct loan obligations	38,051	40,530	39,957
1150 Total direct loan obligations	38,051	40,530	39,957
Cumulative balance of direct loans outstanding:			
1210 Outstanding, start of year	44,061	45,823	46,966
1231 Disbursements: Direct loan disbursements	38,015	40,483	39,402
1251 Repayments: Repayments and prepayments	−36,182	−39,340	−37,429
1264 Write-offs for default: Other adjustments, net	−71		
1290 Outstanding, end of year	45,823	46,966	48,939

Note.—Loans outstanding at end of year do not include nonaccrual loans and sales contracts.

The Agricultural Credit Act of 1987 (1987 Act) required the Federal Land Banks (FLBs) and Federal Intermediate Credit Banks (FICBs) to merge into a Farm Credit Bank (FCB) in each of the 12 Farm Credit districts. The FCBs operate under statutory authority that combines the prior authorities of the FLB and the FICB. No merger occurred in the Jackson district in 1988 because the FLB was in receivership. Pursuant to section 410(e) of the 1987 Act, as amended by the Farm Credit Banks Safety and Soundness Act of 1992, the FICB of Jackson merged with the FCB of Columbia on October 1, 1993. Mergers and consolidations of FCBs across district lines, that began in 1992 continued through mid-1995. As a result of this restructuring activity, 6 FCBs headquartered in the following cities, remain: AgFirst FCB, Columbia, South Carolina; AgAmerica FCB, Sacramento, California; AgriBank FCB, St. Paul, Minnesota; FCB of Wichita, Wichita, Kansas; FCB of Texas, Austin, Texas; and Western FCB, Sacramento, California.

The FCBs serve as discount banks and as of October 1, 1999 provided funds to 50 Federal Land Credit Associations (FLCA), 60 Production Credit Associations (PCAs), and 49 Agricultural Credit Associations (ACAs). These direct lender associations, in turn, make short-term production loans (PCAs and ACAs) and long-term real estate loans (FLCAs and ACAs) to eligible farmers and ranchers. Also, as of October 1, 1999, 18 Federal Land Bank Associations originated and serviced long-term real estate loans for 2 of the 6 FCBs. FCBs can also lend to local financing institutions, including commercial banks, as authorized by the Farm Credit Act of 1971, as amended.

All the capital stock of the FICB's, from organization in 1923 to December 31, 1956, was held by the U.S. Government. The 1956 Act provided a long-range plan for the eventual ownership of the credit banks by the production credit associations and the gradual retirement of the Government's investment in the banks. This retirement was accomplished in full on December 31, 1968. The last of the Government capital that had been invested in the FLB's was repaid in 1947.

Statement of Operations (in millions of dollars)

99–4160		1998 actual	1999 actual	2000 est.	2001 est.
0101	Total interest income	3,348	3,317	3,413	3,562
0102	Total interest expense	–2,652	–2,662	–2,885	–3,085
0105	Net income or loss (–)	696	655	528	477
0111	Other income	55	59	41	43
0112	Other expenses	–279	–325	–251	–244
0115	Net income or loss (–)	–224	–266	–210	–201
0191	Total revenues	3,403	3,376	3,454	3,605
0192	Total expenses	–2,931	–2,987	–3,136	–3,329
0195	Total income or loss (–)	472	389	318	276
0199	Total comprehensive income	472	389	318	276

Balance Sheet (in millions of dollars)

99–4160		1998 actual	1999 actual	2000 est.	2001 est.
	ASSETS:				
1201	Cash and investment securities	8,727	9,590	9,554	9,636
1206	Accrued Interest Receivable	809	790	698	703
	Net value of assets related to direct loans receivable and acquired defaulted guaranteed loans receivable:				
1601	Direct loans, gross	44,061	45,823	46,967	48,984
1603	Allowance for estimated uncollectible loans and interest (–)	–446	–358	–254	–244
1699	Value of assets related to direct loans	43,615	45,465	46,713	48,740
1803	Property, plant and equipment, net	629	336	332	334
1999	Total assets	53,780	56,181	57,297	59,413
	LIABILITIES:				
2104	Resources payable	196	222	248	249
	Accounts payable:				
2201	Consolidated systemwide and other bank bonds	47,714	50,087	51,905	54,074
2201	Notes payable and other interest-bearing liabilities	901	902	324	192
2202	Accrued interest payable	502	547	534	548
2999	Total liabilities	49,313	51,758	53,011	55,063
	NET POSITION:				
3300	Cumulative results of operations	4,467	4,423	4,285	4,350
3999	Total net position	4,467	4,423	4,285	4,350
4999	Total liabilities and net position	53,780	56,181	57,296	59,413

Statement of Changes in Net Worth (in millions of dollars)

99–4160	1998 actual	1999 actual	2000 est.	2001 est.
Beginning balance of net worth	4,404	4,467	4,423	4,285
Capital stock and participations issued	67	68	92	36
Capital stock and participations retired	87	124	184	18
Surplus Retired			85	
Net income	472	389	318	276
Cash/Dividends/Patronage Distributions	(383)	(342)	(267)	(230)
Other, net	–7	–35	–12	
Ending balance of net worth	4,467	4,423	4,285	4,350

Financing Activities (in millions of dollars)

99–4160	1998 actual	1999 actual	2000 est.	2001 est.
Beginning balance of outstanding system obligations	43,588	47,714	50,087	53,646
Consolidated systemwide and other bank bonds issued	51,216	43,119	44,444	45,020
Consolidated systemwide and other bank bonds retired	48,689	39,878	38,882	41,175
Consolidated systemwide notes, net	1,599	–868	–2,003	34
Ending balance of outstanding system obligations	47,714	50,087	53,646	57,524

Federal Agricultural Mortgage Corporation

Farmer Mac is authorized under the Farm Credit Act of 1971 (the Act), as amended by the Agricultural Credit Act of 1987, to create a secondary market for agricultural real estate and rural home mortgages that meet minimum credit standards. The Farmer Mac title of the Act was amended by the 1990 farm bill to authorize Farmer Mac to purchase, pool, and securitize the guaranteed portions of farmer program, rural business and community development loans guaranteed by the USDA. The Farmer Mac title was further amended in 1991 to clarify Farmer Mac's authority to issue debt obligations, provide for the establishment of minimum capital standards, and establish the Office of Secondary Market Oversight at the Farm Credit Administration (FCA) and expand the agency's rulemaking authority. Most recently, the Farm Credit System Reform Act of 1996 amended the Farmer Mac title to allow Farmer Mac to purchase loans directly from lenders and to issue and guarantee mortgage-backed securities without requiring that a minimum cash reserve or subordinated (first loss) interest be maintained by the lenders, poolers or investors as had been required under its original authority. The 1996 Act also increased Farmer Mac's capital requirements over time and expanded the regulatory authorities of the FCA.

Farmer Mac operates through two programs, "Farmer Mac I," which involves mortgage loans secured by first liens on agricultural real estate or rural housing (qualified loans), and "Farmer Mac II," which involves guaranteed portions of USDA guaranteed loans. Farmer Mac operates by: (i) purchasing, or committing to purchase, newly originated or existing qualified loans or guaranteed portions from lenders; (ii) purchasing "AgVantage" bonds backed by qualified loans or guaranteed portions from lenders; and (iii) exchanging qualified loans or guaranteed portions for guaranteed securities. Loans purchased by Farmer Mac are aggregated into pools that back Farmer Mac guaranteed securities which are held by Farmer Mac or sold into the capital markets. Farmer Mac is intended to attract new capital for financing qualified loans and guaranteed portions, foster increased long-term, fixed-rate lending, and provide greater liquidity to agricultural and rural lenders.

Farmer Mac is governed by a 15 member Board of Directors. Ten Board members are elected by stockholders, including five by the Farm Credit System and five by commercial lenders. Five are appointed by the President, subject to Senate confirmation.

Financing

Financial support and funding for Farmer Mac's operations come from several sources: sale of common and preferred stock; issuance of debt obligations; gain on sale of guaranteed loan-backed securities; guarantee fees; and income from investments. Under procedures specified in the Act, Farmer Mac may issue obligations to the U.S. Treasury in a cumulative amount not to exceed $1.5 billion to fulfill its guarantee obligations.

Farmer Mac must maintain core and risk based capital as provided in the Act and FCA regulations.

Available funds of Farmer Mac are invested in U.S. agency securities or other high-grade commercial investments. No stock dividends are allowed under the Act until the Board

FEDERAL AGRICULTURAL MORTGAGE CORPORATION—Continued

determines that an adequate loss reserve has been funded to back Farmer Mac guarantees.

GUARANTEES

Farmer Mac provides a guarantee of timely payment of principal and interest on securities backed by qualified loans or pools of qualified loans. These securities are not guaranteed by the United States, and are not "government securities". The 1996 Act removed requirements that loan originators or other third parties maintain cash reserves or subordinated securities in connection with the issuance of Farmer Mac's guaranteed securities.

Farmer Mac is subject to reporting requirements under securities laws and its guaranteed mortgage-backed securities are subject to registration with the Securities and Exchange Commission under the 1933 and 1934 Securities Acts.

REGULATION

Farmer Mac is federally regulated by the FCA's Office of Secondary Market Oversight (OSMO). OSMO is responsible for examination of and rulemaking for Farmer Mac, including the establishment of risk-based capital requirements by regulation. On November 12, 1999, FCA published a notice of proposed rulemaking, stress test, and a request for public comments. Following the comment period, a final risk-based capital rule and stress test will be developed by FCA and published in the *Federal Register.* The 1996 amendments to the Farmer Mac title expanded FCA's regulatory authority to include provisions for establishing a conservatorship or receivership, if necessary, and provided for increased levels of core capital phased in over three years. As of September 30, 1999, Farmer Mac's total capital exceeds regulatory and statutory requirements. Lastly, in connection with the enactment of the 1996 Act, Congress requested, during Farmer Mac's transition to the expanded capital requirements thereunder, that FCA, in a cooperative effort with the U.S. Treasury, monitor Farmer Mac's financial condition and report to Congress semiannually.

Status of Guaranteed Loans (in millions of dollars)

99–4180		1999 actual	2000 est.	2001 est.
2111	Limitation on guaranteed loans	1,662	2,077	2,597
2131	Guaranteed loan commitments	1,662	2,077	2,597
2150	Total guaranteed loan commitments	3,324	4,154	5,194
	Cumulative balance of guaranteed loans outstanding:			
2210	Outstanding, start of year	1,048	2,057	3,318
2231	Disbursements of new guaranteed loans	1,662	2,077	2,597
2251	Repayments and prepayments	−653	−816	−1,021
2290	Outstanding, end of year	2,057	3,318	4,894
	Memorandum:			
2299	Guaranteed amount of guaranteed loans outstanding, end of year	2,057	3,318	4,894

Statement of Operations (in millions of dollars)

99–4180		1998 actual	1999 actual	2000 est.	2001 est.
	Revenue:				
0101	Net Interest Income	6	14	18	22
0101	Guarantee Fee Income	2	6	8	10
0101	Gain on Security Issuance	2			
0102	Expense	−7	−14	−18	−23
0105	Net income or loss (−)	3	6	8	9
0199	Total comprehensive income	3	7	9	9

Balance Sheet (in millions of dollars)

99–4180		1998 actual	1999 actual	2000 est.	2001 est.
	ASSETS:				
1201	Investment in securities	622	853	853	853
1206	Receivables, net	2	3	3	4
1207	Advances and prepayments	5	12	15	18
	Net value of assets related to direct loans receivable:				
1401	Direct loans receivable, gross	614	1,278	1,598	1,998
1402	Interest receivable	17	30	37	46
1499	Net present value of assets related to direct loans	631	1,308	1,635	2,044
1801	Cash and other monetary assets	435	506	476	89
1999	Total assets	1,695	2,682	2,982	3,008
	LIABILITIES:				
2201	Accounts payable	8	4	4	6
2202	Interest payable	7	12	15	18
2203	Debt	1,598	2,573	2,861	2,870
2204	Liabilities for loan guarantees	3	6	7	9
2999	Total liabilities	1,616	2,595	2,887	2,903
	NET POSITION:				
3300	Invested capital	79	87	95	105
3999	Total net position	79	87	95	105
4999	Total liabilities and net position	1,695	2,682	2,982	3,008

FEDERAL HOME LOAN BANK SYSTEM

FEDERAL HOME LOAN BANKS

Status of Direct Loans (in millions of dollars)

99–4200		1999 actual	2000 est.	2001 est.
1111	Limitation on direct loans			
1131	Direct loan obligations	2,181,262	2,181,262	2,181,262
1150	Total direct loan obligations	2,181,262	2,181,262	2,181,262
	Cumulative balance of direct loans outstanding:			
1210	Outstanding, start of year	245,647	366,842	368,885
1231	Disbursements: Direct loan disbursements	2,181,262	2,181,262	2,181,262
1251	Repayments: Repayments and prepayments	2,060,067	2,179,219	2,179,219
1290	Outstanding, end of year	366,842	368,885	370,928

The 12 Federal Home Loan Banks were chartered by the Federal Home Loan Bank Board under the authority of the Federal Home Loan Bank Act of 1932 (the Act). The FHLBanks are under the supervision of the Federal Housing Finance Board. The common mission of the FHLBanks is to facilitate the extension of credit through their members. To accomplish this mission, the FHLBanks make loans, called advances, and provide other credit products and services to their 7,226 member commercial banks, savings associations, insurance companies, and credit unions. Advances and letters of credit must be fully secured by eligible collateral and long-term advances may be made only for the purpose of providing funds for residential housing finance. However, "community financial institutions" may also use long-term advances to finance small businesses, small farms, and small agri-businesses. Additionally, specialized advance programs provide funds for community reinvestment and affordable housing programs. All regulated financial depositories, "community financial institutions," and insurance companies engaged in residential housing finance are eligible for membership. Each FHLBank operates in a geographic district designated by the Board and together the FHLBanks cover all of the United States as well as the District of Columbia, Puerto Rico, the Virgin Islands, Guam, American Samoa, and the Northern Mariana Islands.

Advances outstanding on September 30, 1999 totaled approximately $367 billion, a net increase of approximately $120 billion from the September 30, 1998 level of $246 billion.

The principal source of funds for the lending operation is the sale of consolidated obligations to the public. On September 30, 1999, $477 billion of these obligations were outstanding. The consolidated obligations are not guaranteed by the U.S. Government as to principal or interest. Other sources of lendable funds include members' deposits and capital. Deposits totaled $16 billion and total capital amounted to $27 billion as of September 30, 1999. Funds not immediately needed for advances to members are invested.

The capital stock of the Federal Home Loan Banks is owned entirely by the members. Initially the U.S. Government purchased stock of the banks in the amount of $125 million. The banks had repurchased the Government's investment in full by mid-1951.

The operating expenses of the FHLBanks are paid from their own income and are not included in the budget of the United States. Included in these expenses are the assessments by the Finance Board to cover its administrative and other costs. The Finance Board's budget and expenditures, however, are included in the budget of the United States.

The Act, as amended in 1989, requires each FHLBank to operate an Affordable Housing Program (AHP). Each FHLBank provides subsidies in the form of direct grants or below-market rate advances for members that use the funds for qualifying affordable housing projects. The FHLBank System sets aside for its AHPs the greater of $100 million annually or 10 percent of the preceding year's net income. The Act also requires that the FHLBanks contribute 20 percent of net earnings annually to assist in the payment of interest on bonds issued by the Resolution Funding Corporation.

The forecast data for 2000 and 2001 contained in this material represents estimates and should not be construed as an official forecast of the FHLBanks System's future position.

Statement of Operations (in millions of dollars)

99–4200		1998 actual	1999 actual	2000 est.	2001 est.
0101	Revenue	20,408	24,596	24,596	24,596
0102	Expense (excludes payments to REFCORP)	−18,810	−22,553	−22,553	−22,553
0105	Net income or loss (−)	1,598	2,043	2,043	2,043

Balance Sheet (in millions of dollars)

99–4200		1998 actual	1999 actual	2000 est.	2001 est.
	ASSETS:				
	Investments in US securities:				
1102	Treasury securities, net	433	233	233	233
1201	Investments in other securities, net	135,167	155,471	155,471	155,471
1206	Accounts receivable	5,944	8,057	8,057	8,057
1401	Net value of assets related to direct loans receivable: Direct loans receivable, gross	246,107	366,842	368,885	370,928
1801	Cash and other monetary assets	422	399	399	399
1803	Property, plant and equipment, net	146	88	88	88
1901	Other assets	175	261	261	261
1999	Total assets	388,394	531,351	533,394	535,437
	LIABILITIES:				
2101	REFCORP and Affordable Housing Program	510	580	580	580
2201	Accounts payable	165	59	59	59
2202	Interest payable	6,427	8,709	8,709	8,709
2203	Debt	336,262	477,472	477,472	477,472
	Other:				
2207	Deposit funds and other borrowings	23,550	16,147	16,147	16,147
2207	Other	354	1,452	1,452	1,452
2999	Total liabilities	367,268	504,419	504,419	504,419
	NET POSITION:				
3100	Invested capital	21,126	26,932	28,975	31,018
3999	Total net position	21,126	26,932	28,975	31,018
4999	Total liabilities and net position	388,394	531,351	533,394	535,437

INDEX

Y

Z

Need Additional Copies ???

Copies of the Budget and related Office of Management and Budget documents may be purchased at any of the GPO bookstores listed below. (Paper copies only.)

GPO BOOKSTORES

ALABAMA
O'Neill Building
2021 Third Ave., North
Birmingham, Alabama 35203
(205) 731-1056
FAX (205) 731-3444

CALIFORNIA
ARCO Plaza, C-Level
505 South Flower Street
Los Angeles, California 90071
(213) 239-9844
FAX (213) 239-9848

Marathon Plaza, Room 141-S
3C3 Second Street
San Francisco, California 94107
(415) 512-2770
FAX (415) 512-2776

COLORADO
Suite 130
1660 Wynkoop Street
Denver, Colorado 80202
(303) 844-3964
FAX (303) 844-4000

Norwest Banks Building
201 West 8th Street
Pueblo, Colorado 81003
(719) 544-3142
FAX (719) 544-6719

DISTRICT OF COLUMBIA
U.S. Government Printing Office
710 North Capitol Street, NW
Washington, DC 20401
(202) 512-0132
FAX (202) 512-1355

1510 H Street, NW
Washington, DC 20005
(202) 653-5075
FAX (202) 376-5055

FLORIDA
100 W. Bay Street
Suite 100
Jacksonville, Florida 32202
(904) 353-0569
FAX (904) 353-1280

GEORGIA
First Union Plaza
999 Peachtree Street, NE
Suite 120
Atlanta, Georgia 30309
(404) 347-1900
FAX (404) 347-1897

ILLINOIS
One Congress Center, Suite 124
401 South State Street
Chicago, Illinois 60605
(312) 353-5133
FAX (313) 353-1590

MARYLAND
Retail Sales Outlet
8660 Cherry Lane
Laurel, Maryland 20707
(301) 953-7974
FAX (301) 498-8995

MASSACHUSETTS
Thomas P. O'Neill Fed. Bldg.
10 Causeway Street, Rm. 169
Boston, Massachusetts 02222
(619) 720-4180
FAX (617) 720-5753

MICHIGAN
Suite 160, Federal Building
477 Michigan Avenue
Detroit, Michigan 48226
(313) 226-7816
FAX (313) 226-4698

MISSOURI
120 Bannister Mall
5600 E. Bannister Road
Kansas City, Missouri 64137
(816) 765-2256
FAX (816) 767-8233

NEW YORK
Federal Building, Room 2-120
26 Federal Plaza
New York, New York 10278
(212) 264-3825/2922
FAX (212) 264-9318

OHIO
Room 1653, Federal Building
1240 East 9th Street
Cleveland, Ohio 44199
(216) 522-4922
FAX (216) 522-4714

Room 207, Federal Building
200 North High Street
Columbus, Ohio 43215
(614) 469-6956
FAX (614) 469-5374

OREGON
1305 SW. First Avenue
Portland, Oregon 97201
(503) 221-6127
FAX (503) 225-0563

PENNSYLVANIA
Robert Morris Building
100 North 17th Street
Philadelphia, Pennsylvania 19103
(215) 636-1900
FAX (215) 636-1903

Room 118, Federal Building
1000 Liberty Avenue
Pittsburgh, Pennsylvania 15222
(412) 395-5021
FAX (412) 395-4547

TEXAS
Room 1C50, Federal Building
1100 Commerce Street
Dallas, Texas 75242
(214) 767-0076
FAX (214) 767-3239

Texas Crude Building
801 Travis Street, Ste 120
Houston, Texas 77002
(713) 228-1187
FAX (713) 228-1186

WASHINGTON
Room 194, Federal Building
915 Second Avenue
Seattle, Washington 98174
(206) 553-4270
FAX (206) 553-6717

WISCONSIN
The Reuss Federal Plaza
310 West Wisconsin
Avenue, Ste 150W
Milwaukee, Wisconsin 53203
(414) 297-1304
FAX (414) 297-1300

There is a 25% discount on all orders for 100 or more copies of a single title mailed to a single address. No discount is allowed if such orders are mailed to multiple addresses.

Superintendent of Documents Publications Order Form

Order Processing Code: *8163

All prices include regular domestic postage and handling and are good through July 2000. After this date, please call the Order and Information Desk at (202) 512–1800 to verify prices. To fax your orders and inquiries—(202) 512–2250.

Qty.	Stock Number	Title	Price Each	Total Price
	041-001-00533-1	Budget of the United States Government, Fiscal Year 2001	$38.00	
	041-001-00534-0	Budget of the United States Government, Fiscal Year 2001—Appendix	$72.00	
	041-001-00535-8	Analytical Perspectives, Fiscal Year 2001	$54.00	
	041-001-00536-6	Historical Tables, Fiscal Year 2001	$28.00	
	041-001-00537-4	A Citizen's Guide to the Federal Budget, Fiscal Year 2001	$3.75	
	041-001-00538-2	The Budget System and Concepts, Fiscal Year 2001	$3.25	
	041-001-00539-1	The Budget on CD-ROM, Fiscal Year 2001	$17.00	

(International customers—please add an additional 25%.) Total for Publications

Please Print or Type

(Company or personal name)

(Additional address/attention line)

(Street address)

(City, State, ZIP Code)

(Daytime phone—including area code)

Mail To: Superintendent of Documents
Government Printing Office,
Washington, DC 20402–9325

Please choose method of payment:

☐ Check payable to the Superintendent of Documents

☐ GPO Deposit Account ☐☐☐☐☐☐☐ - ☐

☐ VISA or MasterCard Account

(Credit card expiration date)

Thank you for your order!

(Signature)

ISBN 0-16-050236-5
90000
9 780160 502361